THE
CONCISE OXFORD
FRENCH DICTIONARY

FRENCH—ENGLISH

COMPILED BY

A. CHEVALLEY AND M. CHEVALLEY

ENGLISH—FRENCH

COMPILED BY

G. W. F. R. GOODRIDGE

OXFORD
AT THE CLARENDON PRESS

Oxford University Press, Walton Street, Oxford OX2 6DP

OXFORD LONDON GLASGOW NEW YORK
TORONTO MELBOURNE WELLINGTON CAPE TOWN
IBADAN NAIROBI DAR ES SALAAM LUSAKA ADDIS ABABA
KUALA LUMPUR SINGAPORE JAKARTA HONG KONG TOKYO
DELHI BOMBAY CALCUTTA MADRAS KARACHI

ISBN 0 19 864103 6

First published 1940
Reprinted (with corrections) 1942, 1947, 1950
1952, 1954, 1957, 1958, 1961, 1963, 1964, 1968,
1970, 1974, and 1977

Printed in Great Britain
at the University Press, Oxford
by Vivian Ridler
Printer to the University

THE CONCISE OXFORD FRENCH–ENGLISH DICTIONARY

COMPILED BY

ABEL CHEVALLEY

AND

MARGUERITE CHEVALLEY

OXFORD

AT THE CLARENDON PRESS

INTRODUCTION

THIS CONCISE FRENCH–ENGLISH DICTIONARY aims at being a worthy companion to the *Concise Oxford Dictionary of Current English*, and it is in this respect a rather audacious enterprise.

Its main and special purpose, comparatively unambitious, is to prove more integrally helpful to students and translators than some existing works of the same class. Each generation requires new 'current use' dictionaries, not only of its own language[1] but still more definitely of other languages comparable with its own. New words appear on both sides. Old words take on in each tongue a new and unforeseeable colour, and the equivalents of yesterday are no longer equivalent to-day. The cumulative effect of this metabolism on two generations and two languages necessitates a frequent revision of bilingual dictionaries. When new principles are involved, when fresh material is introduced and original devices adopted, a new dictionary needs no justification.

VOCABULARY

In accordance with our wish to emulate in the French–English field the work of the brothers Fowler on current English, the principles governing the selection of vocabulary in the *Concise Oxford Dictionary* have been adopted.

This book is not meant to give information about the things represented by French words, but only about the nearest equivalence between French and English of the words and phrases which represent these things. We do not agree that a French–English Dictionary consists 'of French words with English explanations' as stated in the *Concise Oxford Dictionary*, art. 'Dictionary'. We aim at *translations*, not *explanations*. In very infrequent cases no complete equivalence can be found, no satisfactory translation evolved, except by a periphrase. Then we risk a definition (see *brader*, *braderie*, *crépinette*, *salpicon*, *rouflaquette*, *chinoiserie*, *foutaise*, *fichaise*, *foucade*, (*faire des*) *cuirs*, *schlitte*, *schlitter*, *riz-pain-sel*, *ferrade*, *bouillabaisse*, *bouilleur de cru*, *questeur*, *boîtier*, *rombière*, *vadrouille*, &c.). But we avoid all English renderings in several words of French terms that

[1] Cf. Delacroix, quoting Sweet, Zaharoff Lecture, Oxford, 1925.

can be rendered in one. The more common the word, the more space is given to it, the more care bestowed upon its different uses and meanings and the selection of its English equivalents.

We subscribe to the notion of 'currency' adopted in the *Concise English Dictionary*, and it has guided our admission or rejection of different sorts of French words. Old technical terms are excluded as being of small or no use. We have regretfully sacrificed about a hundred words describing the operations of an artisan era now defunct, that occur in our edition of *La Maison Rustique* (1760). We have preserved those still in use concerning whatever is still 'made at home'. Archaisms that are mere curiosities are avoided, except those that are embedded in proverbs or well-known quotations. We have not treated as archaisms words, expressions, or senses now no longer used, that occur with their original freshness in the classic literature of the last three centuries. They are marked 'obs.' (obsolete).

We have stretched our notion of currency to include many terms indicating recent developments of practical science or industry which have already passed into universal recognition and which are yet often unrecorded in French–English dictionaries. Thus, for example, among terms relating to motoring, aeroplanes, &c., *carlingue*, for which most dictionaries give only the nautical sense 'keelson', means also, in aeronautics, 'car, carlingue'. Technical words omitted in some or most dictionaries include *grippage*, *gripper*, *gicleur*, *pointeau*, *démarreur*, *pont-arrière*, *soupape d'admission*, *d'échappement*, *spider* (in the French sense of 'dickey'), (*palier de*) *butée*, *came d'allumage*, *de distribution*, *arbre à cames*, *levier de commande* (or *des vitesses*), *de frein à main*, *levier démonte-pneu*, and *manche à balai* (joystick). English tourists, nonplussed by the terms in use in French garages to describe repairs or spare parts, need no longer despair. The utility and importance of our full-page illustrations in these and similar connexions will be realized. The same remarks apply to recent additions to the vocabulary of trades, especially luxury trades (e.g. *ensemble* in dressmaking, *table gigogne*, *pendentif* in jewellery), modern psychiatry (e.g. *schizophrène*, *schizophrénie*), housekeeping, dressing, cookery, gastronomy, wine-tasting—terms sadly deficient in works of this kind; see, for example, *faire revenir de la viande*, *bavaroise*, *essoreuse*, *aspirateur*, *cireuse*, *extrafort*, *gros-grain*. Mere scholastic and scholiastic words are excluded; we fight shy of the penny-a-line logomachy represented in dictionaries of all languages. A kind of game of forfeits, which might usefully be played by all lexicographers wishing to reduce their vocabulary to current French and current English, is to extract in a given time, from the small *Larousse* for instance, the greatest number of words which none but specialists can explain.

The colloquial portion of a language being the most alive and fertile, we need not justify the admission of a good many familiar, even slangy expressions, but they are labelled as such. The difficulty was to find English equivalents. We do not consider it sufficient to give in a more or less abstract form the intellectual sense in English of a familiar French word or phrase. What is wanted is an equi-valent, not an equi-distant English rendering. Now the value of an English translation lies in the similarity of its impact on the English mind with the impact of the original on the French mind. What is only intellectual, logical, not affective, has no momentum. It misses both colour and warmth. This is what makes so many translations, although scrupulously faithful to the sense of the text, so unbearably nauseous to the reader's senses.

Within a comparatively small space this dictionary contains nearly 40,000 words (proper names included), out of which 37,200 are distributed as follows:

	words		*words*		*words*		*words*
A	3,538	G	1,325	M	2,614	S	2,539
B	1,770	H	766	N	670	T	2,255
C	4,538	I	1,610	O	712	U	208
D	2,000	J	258	P	3,355	V	1,165
E	3,280	K	132	Q	210	W.X.Y.	72
F	1,380	L	1,310	R	2,401	Z	92

From the above, C emerges an easy first. A, P, E come far behind, but none the less make up between them one-third of the entries. Six letters out of 24, viz. C, A, P, E, M, S, supply more than half the total.

These figures are not meant to countenance 'word-counting' as a test of the expressive power in the vocabulary of a language, a person, or a book. Speaking in terms of life, there is no such thing as a 'separate' word. When you speak or write, none of your words stands alone; they derive their form, colour, function, special meaning, or strength from the context, and there are as many words in a living word as there are different meanings. A dictionary is like an herbarium. It can only present words in a dried state, and must, for the sake of reference, give them in the alphabetical order

But it can:

Give the different senses of a word with more or less exactness, and, in any case, avoid glaring blunders.

Discriminate more or less efficiently between them by means of appropriate devices—figures, for instance, and abbreviations.

Enumerate and exemplify them in an order more or less consonant with their actuality, their 'common use'.

It can also, by means of numerous examples, reflect more or less strikingly in English the force and colour of French words, especially when used in their figurative sense. It can, for example, at the cost of much time and research, always translate an idiom by an idiom, a gallicism by the corresponding anglicism, a popular or slang term by a term of the same order and tint, a metaphor by a metaphor of approximately the same power.

And although this has not previously been attempted, it can warn students and translators against innumerable pitfalls by the use of printed indications and short cautions.

RENDERINGS

It is not sufficient to be a Frenchman, even highly educated, if you want to succeed as a French–English lexicographer. Nor can an Englishman, even with first-class honours in French, be guaranteed to find the best English equivalents for French words or idioms. Every living language gets stratified as it grows. Very few people are at home in its different strata. Mrs. Malaprop's language was probably free of malapropisms when she spoke to her cook, and the most purist *précieuse* would perpetrate malapropisms of another sort if she had to deal with the butcher and the grocer. Languages are like houses: they must be *lived in*—from attic to basement—before they can be called ours. The number of people who have become familiar, in this intimate manner, not only with one but with several houses is, of course, limited.

Culture and knowledge are not sufficient. A taste for words as words; an instinct of divination leading *in abstracto* to the 'mot juste', and an insight into the risks and difficulties of others, less gifted; the sporting spirit that sustains, year in year out, a lifelong word-hunt; an acute sense of the correspondences and discrepancies between words of apparently the same sort and sound in two languages that are now *frères ennemis* and then 'heavenly twins', these are also not enough.

A great thing, perhaps the greatest, is to have *lived* both French and English, meeting on their own ground all conditions of men, and transacting with them all kinds of business; to have travelled, under the sting of necessity, up and down the social order, always in a spirit of comprehensive sympathy but with that touch of amusement that goes to the making of humour. You must have run a hundred times, half angry, half smiling, from loft to cellar before you can flatter yourself that you know every turning, nook, and corner in your own house; and even then you knock your shins against unsuspected obstacles.

What if the house were a double affair, more than half built in the air, of metaphors, shadows and shades, and visions, ever changing, ever moving, without perhaps one single exact counterpart in the two enchanted fabrics? I am not sure that the King's English does in this sense belong to the King rather than to the bricklayer, and the French of France to the *Académie* rather than to the nearest pub. But I am sure that the lexicographer who has frequented both is also the best prepared for the task. These conditions must be sadly missing in the world of dictionaries. Ours grew quite inadvertently—as is often said, with equal approximation, of the British Empire. It was only in the course of its completion that we realized, on the strength of experience, that the field of French–English lexicography was strewn with wild weeds and rubbish-heaps. So that the first part (quite unsuspected) of our labours was to clear the ground in many places, and sweep away the refuse.

The least that can be expected of French–English dictionaries is that they be kept free of the 'howlers' which are a godsend to comic papers. It is not our intention to pose as censors of our predecessors, though the French critics of French–English dictionaries published in France are less squeamish. Let it suffice that we have tried to avoid making such obvious blunders as 'lavatory carriage' for *voiture d'occasion* (second-hand carriage), or giving any excuse for such ingenuities as that of the schoolboy who, finding the word *primat* in his dictionary translated simply by 'primate', rendered *le primat des Gaules* by 'the great Gallic monkey'.

As we have previously remarked, we have also endeavoured to improve the rendering of everyday metaphors or idioms by finding the exact English equivalent, in status as well as in meaning, for the French phrase. Thus *chacun fait comme il l'entend* certainly *means* 'everybody does as he thinks proper' or 'as he likes'; but these renderings are nevertheless not satisfactory. *Entend* in the French is synonymous with *comprend* and implies not so much morality or will as enlightenment. Besides, the French is a common saying, almost a proverb, and should be translated as such; for these reasons the translation we prefer is 'every one according to his lights'.

Special care has been given to the translation of very familiar or even slangy words, metaphors, and idioms. Everybody now reads French books (for example those of Carco, Daudet, Céline, &c.) which are full of them. Technical or school jargon is frequent. Readers of Jules Romains want to know what is a *turne*, a *canular*, a *tala*, a *tapir*. Dictionaries frequently omit to tell their readers that *le receveur* is usually the 'tram-conductor', that *rasant* often means 'boring, tedious', that an *éteignoir* (extinguisher) also has the figurative sense 'wet blanket', or that *tétine*, besides 'udder', means also 'teat' (for a baby's bottle). Sometimes they are misleading or mistaken, as when *paterne* ('rather benignant, affecting benevolence') is translated by 'paternal' or by 'patronizing' or 'heavy-father'; or *populo* (which means 'crowd' and (adj.) 'vulgar') by 'chubby child'; or *saut-de-lit* ('dressing-gown, morning wrap') by 'bed-side carpet' (= *descente de lit*); or *être dans les petits papiers de quelqu'un* by 'to be in some one's bad books'—the exact reverse of its true meaning, which is 'to be in favour with some one, to be in his confidence'; or *eau de vaisselle* by 'thin broth'.

Although we have given room to a good many slangy terms, we have thought that some discrimination was necessary. Certain catchwords are singularly void of sense, and deemed to be short-lived (e.g. *en voulez-vous des z'homards ?*). There is no place for them here. Similarly, we think that it is necessary to discriminate between the popular expression, alive, well coined, picturesque, and what is simply a faulty way of speaking, a grammatical howler, heard sometimes, but not to be encouraged. We have refused to countenance by inclusion such expressions as *c'est une dame que son mari est mort*, or *où que vous allez ?*, or *causer à quelqu'un*, or *où restez-vous ?* (for *où habitez-vous ?*), or *j'ai resté trois mois à Paris sans sortir de ma chambre*, or *ne pas durer à un travail*. All these are simply incorrect and very vulgar ways of speaking, and no more worthy of a place in such a dictionary as this than *ous'que* (as in *c'est là ous'que je suis né*) or *cintième* (for *cinquième*), *mécredi* (*mercredi*), *pasque* (*parce que*); to include these would be equivalent to printing all the words beginning with an H a second time as special entries without H in an English dictionary, because some people in England drop their aitches.

FALSE FRIENDS

The borrowings from French that began with the Norman Conquest, coming on top of a common stock of Latin words, and the long predominance in England of French culture and literature, followed in recent times by reciprocal exchanges of vocabulary, have created in both languages a sort of neutral zone in which all words that are sounded or spelt alike are liable to be taken as having the same sense. At first sight only; for though, in many cases, they do mean the same in at least one of their acceptations, usually the oldest, they differ widely in all the others.

Such couples of words have been called *False Friends.* If we must have slogans, they might just as well have been nicknamed the 'Tricky Twins', or the 'Slovenly Twins'. Whatever name you care to call them by, they are responsible for an enormous proportion of those mistranslations which, merely amusing in most cases, are positively harmful in legal or international documents, and are the despair of whoever cares for mutual comprehension between the English and the French. Need we give instances of these poisonous errors? We might cull them from official translations or documents, where they are less numerous but far more dangerous than in school tasks. For instance, 'to control' means in English not merely to check, to verify (this is the old sense, now smothered or outgrown by the new one), but to dominate, to command, to direct. *Contrôler*, in French (from *contre-rôle*, revised copy), means only to exercise supervision (i.e. to verify), at the utmost to have means of restraint. Imagine what happens if, in a contract, an official letter, an international document, '*contrôler*' is literally translated by 'to control', or if 'to control' is rendered by '*contrôler*'. And it *has* happened. '*Nous nous réservons le droit de contrôler l'emploi de ces sommes*', said the French. 'We reserve to ourselves the control of this expenditure', read the English. . . . What a source of misunderstandings, private and public, are coupled words! These 'spurious spawn of counterfeit counters', so much alike in form, and so widely different in value, tone, colour, sense, and sentiment, are the arch-enemies of the translator: for instance, *affronter* and 'to affront', *assumer* and 'to assume', *dérider* and 'to deride', *attirer* and 'to attire', *abuser* and 'to abuse', *achever* and 'to achieve', &c. No wonder that the Federation of Intellectual Unions has directed one of its very first efforts towards their signalization. 'For political reasons that are evident, we have decided', says M. Émile Borel, the well-known mathematician, member of Parliament, former Director of the École Normale Supérieure, 'to devote ourselves to the task of preparing, before any other, a Franco–German and German–French list and commentary of the several hundred words especially liable to be mistranslated on account of their apparent resemblance' (letter to Messrs. Koessler and Derocquigny). Except that 'several hundred' should be replaced by a much larger number, the case for a similar French–English and English–French dictionary is the same. Messrs. Koessler and Derocquigny have compiled a list of 'several hundred' of these 'False Friends' and commented on them most judiciously and felicitously. M. Félix Boillot at once capped their learned but restricted discovery by denouncing *currente calamo* several hundred more, and we have a store more ample than their common stock. It is all very well to prepare special dictionaries of these caltrops or *chausse-trapes*. But special dictionaries are only for specialists. How much better if *general* dictionaries could in one way or another at least signalize in their hundreds the words that lend themselves to grievous or comical mistranslations. This we have attempted in this dictionary. Considerations of space have compelled us to a mere signalization with a brief remark, a short commentary. We do not claim to have exhausted the subject. We have only paved the way, because we believe that no modern dictionary is complete and really useful if it does not warn readers and translators of the dangers and pitfalls offered by apparently too easy translations. Koessler–Derocquigny have criticized in the following terms one of the most renowned of French–English and English–French dictionaries published in France for falling into some of these pitfalls:

> 'X translates "bier" by *bière*, instead of *brancard, civière*.'

In the English–French part, this same work

> 'gives "deception": *déception*, and "liable to deception": *sujet à être trompé*; his interpretation of the word "deception" is so completely wrong that he takes good care not to adopt his own rendering in the translation of the example quoted. Is it possible to contradict oneself more flagrantly? And how can we avoid being scared when we read: "dainty" = *délicat, difficile, fastidieux*? . . . *Fastidieux*, why *fastidieux*? It is such an obvious intrusion! Merely because some English dictionary has been consulted, in which "fastidious" is given as a synonym of "dainty". Hence the French *fastidieux* ("boring", "tedious", "dull") as a translation of "dainty".'

Without citing further examples, let us say that more than 600 signs of 'danger' (△) are to be found in these pages, and that, aiming at usefulness and the avoiding of an excessive number of danger signals, we have not signalized words like '*narre*' (1st and 3rd pers. of v. *narrer*), and 'narre' adj., old form of 'nearer', to be found in Spenser; or '*car*' conj., which nobody will confuse with '(motor-)car'; or *lac* and '(to) lack'; or *rêve* and 'reve' (obsolete form of 'to reave', which is not itself very current). We do not consider such pairs, which are superabundant in Boillot's list, as very treacherous, and for the sake of space leave them out. But we certainly object to 'exquisite' as the only translation of *exquis*, 'idiom' of *idiome*, or 'petrol' of *pétrole*, &c., &c.

ETYMOLOGY

Etymology is both historical and scientific. Its enormous importance in these respects should not blind us to its comparative unimportance for practical purposes. 'It conveys a false idea of the nature of a vocabulary; its interest is merely to help us to understand how it was formed' (Vendryes, *Le Langage*, p. 206). Even that limited object can only be attained if one enters into the detail of a word's filiation. Very few etymologies are simple and self-sufficient. An etymological dictionary cannot be abridged. The fallacy of one fundamental sense for each word, from which all others are derived, has already been mentioned. We must beware too of the related fallacy, however pleasant to the lay mind, of one single origin for each single word. Does there exist such a thing in reality as a single word? Words are not used according to their historical, but according to their immediate and practical, value. Their meaning is different according to the moment when they are used, and the use to which they are put. Outside their moment and their object they fall into nothingness. Let us again quote Delacroix:

> 'A word is primarily a tissue of associations; it is swathed in associative relations. To borrow an instance from Saussure, the word *enseignement* is related by its sense to *éducation*, by its origin to *enseigner*, by its process of formation to *armement*, by its rhythm and sound to *justement*. . . .'

The only excuse for introducing etymology in a concise practical and bilingual dictionary is to prevent false etymologies from intruding themselves upon the mind of the half-learned and so adding to the numberless causes of error in translation, which it is our business to restrict. Hence the frequency of the words '(etym. dubious)', to be found in these pages, even when it implies sacrificing picturesque traditions, as in the case of *isabelle* (colour). As often as possible we give the remotest origin known. But often this is dubious, at least in its form, and we give the word of the language from which French received it. For instance many nautical terms, probably originating in Old Norse, have come to us either through Dutch or from English or even German. As regards words of Arabic or oriental origin, we have as a rule printed the original word in the form accepted in England, but transliteration from languages which have not the same alphabet as ours is apt to vary in different countries.

GRAMMATICAL FORMS

Adjectives which were originally formed with the past or present participle of a verb are labelled 'p. adj.'; these words, used as adjectives, take the *s* of the plural as well as the feminine termination, but used as participles, follow the rules of participles (cf. *ignorant*, *décidé*, &c.).

Our grammatical nomenclature needs no special comment. When the feminine of a substantive or adjective is very different from the masculine, in form or in sense, it is either given in full or accorded a special entry (cf. *loup*, *louve*, *coadjuteur*, *coadjutrice*, *gouverneur*, *gouvernante*, *blanc*, *blanche*, &c.). Though a dictionary is not a grammar, we take care, when giving illustrative examples of the use of defective or irregular verbs, to include idiomatic combinations of words in which the most irregular forms are used: *chaloir*: *peu m'en chaut*; *gésir*: *je gis*, *nous gisons*, *ci-gît*, &c.

PRONUNCIATION

The pronunciation of French words is indicated according to the Passy–Michaelis system, adopted by the *Association Internationale de Phonétique*. The notation has been slightly simplified in order to make it accessible to every reader without previous study of phonetics. A glance at the key at the foot of each pair of facing pages will be enough to enable him to master the phonetic notation. Though the Passy–Michaelis notation has been adopted, it will be noticed that all words are not given here with the pronunciation indicated by Passy, who is sometimes misleading, especially in the words beginning with '*ex*'. No educated French person would pronounce *exclusion* ɛsklyzjɔ̃, *excuse* ɛskyz, *expert* ɛspɛr, *extraordinaire* ɛstrɔrdinɛr. It would bring him at once to the social level of the kitchen-maid who left '*une casterole dans le colidor*'.

ABBREVIATIONS

With a view to making this dictionary really useful to the unspecialized reader, the list of abbreviations has been made as short as possible. A few abridged words may be found in the text which are not included in the list; but in these cases the sense of the abridged word is unmistakable, and they are not of frequent recurrence.

ILLUSTRATIONS

In the choice of illustrations we have borne in mind that this is a dictionary of words, not an encyclopaedia of things; and, further, that the ordinary user of this dictionary, who knows what a cat or a peacock is, is not really helped by the addition of an illustration to the English equivalent of *chat*, *paon*. But certain terms of architecture are hard to define without a diagram. The reader of an early voyage may need help in identifying the parts of a sailing-ship; the traveller on a steam-ship or aeroplane, the owner of a motor-car or camera may wish to find quickly the French and English equivalent of technical terms, and a diagram affords an easy way.

. . . . . .

It is not for us to decide whether all the peculiarities in this French–English dictionary as compared with others can be considered as improvements. But we trust that, under the several heads mentioned above, something new and useful has been achieved.

Before saying good-bye to a work which has been a daily companion for several years, and submitting it to the public, the authors wish to express their thanks to the staff of the Clarendon Press, and to Mrs. Jessie Coulson, who has read the proofs concurrently with them and has proved a most valuable help in many respects.

A. C.
M. C.

PARIS.

IRREGULAR

NOTE: (*a*) Where not given the FUTURE is regular. (*b*) 1st person PRES. COND. in all cases is

Pres. Inf. Fut. Participles	*Pres. Indicative*
FIRST CONJUGATION (Verbs in ER)	
aller, to go; FUT. irai; PRES. P. allant; P.P. allé	*je* vais *tu* vas *il* va *nous* all-ons *vous* all-ez *ils* vont
envoyer, to send; FUT. enverrai; COND. enverrais; otherwise regular	
SECOND CONJUGATION (Verbs in IR)	
acquérir, to acquire; FUT. acquerrai; PRES. P. acquérant; P.P. acquis	acqu-iers ~iers ~iert acqu-érons ~érez ~ièrent
bouillir, to boil (intrans.); PRES. P. bouillant; P.P. bouilli	bous bous bout bouill-ons ~ez ~ent
courir, to run; PRES. P. courant; P.P. couru; FUT. courrai	cours cours court cour-ons ~ez ~ent
fuir, to flee; PRES. P. fuyant; P.P. fui	fuis fuis fuit fuy-ons ~ez fuient
mentir, to lie; PRES. P. mentant; P.P. menti	mens mens ment ment-ons ~ez ~ent
dormir, partir, servir, sentir, se repentir, sortir, like **mentir**	
mourir, to die; FUT. mourrai; PRES. P. mourant; P.P. mort	meurs meurs meurt mour-ons ~ez meurent
ouvrir, to open; PRES. P. ouvrant; P.P. ouvert	ouvre ouvres ouvre ouvr-ons ~ez ~ent
couvrir, offrir, souffrir, like **ouvrir**	
tressaillir, to shudder; PRES. P. tressaillant; P.P. tressailli; so **assaillir,** to assault; **défaillir,** to fail, faint; **cueillir,** to gather; but FUT. cueillerai	tressaill-e ~es ~e tressaill-ons ~ez ~ent
venir, to come; FUT. viendrai; PRES. P. venant; P.P. venu	viens viens vient ven-ons ~ez viennent
tenir, to hold, like **venir**	
vêtir, to clothe; PRES. P. vêtant; P.P. vêtu	vêts vêts vêt vêt-ons ~ez ~ent
DEFECTIVE	
faillir, to fail, miss; FUT. faillirai (rare); P.P. failli	NONE
gésir, to lie; PRES. P. gisant; IMPF. gisais (throughout)	NONE NONE gît gis-ons ~ez ~ent
ouïr, to hear; P.P. ouï; and comp. tenses	NONE
THIRD CONJUGATION (Verbs in OIR)	
s'asseoir, to sit; PRES. P. s'asseyant; P.P. assis; FUT. m'assiérai (m'assoirai)	m'assieds t'assieds s'assied n. assey-ons v. ~ez s'~ent
falloir, to be necessary; no PRES. P.; P.P. fallu; FUT. il faudra	il faut
mouvoir, to move; P.P. mû, *f.* mue, so **émouvoir,** but P.P. ému	meus meus meut mouv-ons ~ez meuvent
pleuvoir, to rain; P.P. plu	il pleut
pouvoir, to be able; PRES. P. pouvant; P.P. pu; FUT. pourrai	peux (OR puis) peux peut pouv-ons ~ez peuvent
savoir, to know; PRES. P. sachant; P.P. su; FUT. saurai	sais sais sait sav-ons ~ez ~ent
surseoir, to postpone; PRES. P. sursoyant; P.P. sursis; FUT. surseoirai	sursois sursois sursoit sursoy-ons ~ez sursoient

the Future + s. (*c*) Abbreviations: Present Participle, PRES. P.; Past Participle, P.P.

Imperative	*Pres. Subjunctive*	*Pret. & Impf. Subj.*
va (vas + y) allons allez	*que j'*aille *que tu* ailles *qu'il* aille *que nous* all-ions *que vous* all-iez *qu'ils* aillent	j'allai *que j'*allasse
acquiers acquérons acquérez	acqu-ière ~ières ~ière acqu-érions ~ériez ~ièrent	acquis acquisse
bous bouillons bouillez	bouill-e ~es ~e bouill-ions ~iez ~ent	bouillis bouillisse
cours courons courez	coure coures coure cour-ions ~iez ~ent	courus courusse
fuis fuyons fuyez	fuie fuies fuie fuy-ions ~iez fuient	fuis fuisse
mens mentons mentez	mente mentes mente ment-ions ~iez ~ent	mentis mentisse
meurs mourons mourez	meure meures meure mour-ions ~iez meurent	mourus mourusse
ouvre ouvrons ouvrez	ouvre ouvres ouvre ouvr-ions ~iez ~ent	ouvris ouvrisse
tressaille tressaillons tressaillez	tressaill-e ~es ~e tressaill-ions ~iez ~ent	tressaillis tressaillisse
viens venons venez	vienne viennes vienne ven-ions ~iez viennent	vins vinsse
vêts vêtons vêtez	vête vête vête vêt-ions ~iez ~ent	vêtis vêtisse
NONE	NONE	faillis . . . NONE
NONE	NONE	NONE NONE
NONE	NONE	j'ouïs . . . (rare) NONE
assieds-toi asseyons-nous asseyez-vous	m'assey-e t'~es s'~e n. assey-ions v. ~iez s'~ent	m'assis m'assisse
NONE	il faille	il fallut il fallût
meus mouvons mouvez	meuve meuves meuve mouv-ions ~iez meuvent	mus musse
NONE	il pleuve	il plut il plût
NONE	puisse puisses puisse puiss-ions ~iez ~ent	pus pusse
sache sachons sachez	sache saches sache sach-ions ~iez ~ent	sus susse
sursois sursoyons sursoyez	sursoie sursoies sursoie sursoy-ions ~iez sursoient	sursis sursisse

Pres. Inf. Fut. Participles	*Pres. Indicative*
valoir, to be worth; PRES. P. valant; P.P. valu; FUT. vaudrai	vaux vaux vaut val-ons ~ez ~ent
voir, to see; PRES. P. voyant; P.P. vu; FUT. verrai; so **pourvoir,** exc. FUT. pourvoirai; PRET. pourvus	vois vois voit voy-ons ~ez voient
vouloir, to wish; PRES. P. voulant; P.P. voulu; FUT. voudrai	veux veux veut voul-ons ~ez veulent
DEFECTIVE	
échoir, to fall due; PRES. P. échéant; P.P. échu; FUT. il écherra	il échoit OR il échet
seoir, to be becoming; PRES. P. seyant OR séant; FUT. il siéra, ils siéront; IMPF. il seyait, ils seyaient	il sied ils siéent
FOURTH CONJUGATION (Verbs in RE)	
boire, to drink; PRES. P. buvant; P.P. bu	bois bois boit buv-ons ~ez boivent
conclure, to conclude; PRES. P. concluant; P.P. conclu; so **exclure**	conclus conclus conclut conclu-ons ~ez ~ent
conduire, to lead; PRES. P. conduisant; P.P. conduit; so all verbs in **-uire** exc. **luire, nuire**; P.P.'s lui, nui; and **luire** has no Pret. or Impf. Subj.	conduis conduis conduit conduis-ons ~ez ~ent
confire, to preserve fruit; PRES. P. confisant; P.P. confit; so **suffire**; exc. P.P. suffi	confis confis confit confis-ons ~ez ~ent
coudre, to sew; PRES. P. cousant; P.P. cousu	couds couds coud cous-ons ~ez ~ent
craindre, to fear; PRES. P. craignant; P.P. craint; so all verbs in **-aindre, -eindre, -oindre**	crains crains craint craign-ons ~ez ~ent
croire, to believe; PRES. P. croyant; P.P. cru	crois crois croit croy-ons ~ez croient
croître, to grow; PRES. P. croissant; P.P. crû; so **accroître, décroître, recroître,** but these have circumflex only on **i+t**	croîs croîs croît croiss-ons ~ez ~ent
dire, to say; PRES. P. disant; P.P. dit; so **redire,** other comps. 2nd pers. pl. pres. ind. ~isez exc. **maudire** below	dis dis dit disons dites disent
écrire, to write; PRES. P. écrivant; P.P. écrit	écris écris écrit écriv-ons ~ez ~ent
faire, to make; PRES. P. faisant; P.P. fait; FUT. ferai	fais fais fait faisons faites font
lire, to read; PRES. P. lisant; P.P. lu	lis lis lit lis-ons ~ez ~ent
maudire, to curse; PRES. P. maudissant; P.P. maudit	maudis maudis maudit maudiss-ons ~ez ~ent
mettre, to put; PRES. P. mettant; P.P. mis	mets mets met mett-ons ~ez ~ent
moudre, to grind; PRES. P. moulant; P.P. moulu	mouds mouds moud moul-ons ~ez ~ent
naître, to be born, PRES. P. naissant; P.P. né; so **connaître** exc. Pret. connus; IMPF. SUBJ. connusse; P.P. connu; **paraître** as **connaître**	nais nais naît naiss-ons ~ez ~ent
paître, to graze; PRES. P. paissant; P.P. NONE; **repaître** has P.P. repu; Pret. repus	pais pais paît paiss-ons ~ez ~ent
plaire, to please; PRES. P. plaisant; P.P. plu	plais plais plaît plais-ons ~ez ~ent
prendre, to take; PRES. P. prenant; P.P. pris	prends prends prend prenons prenez prennent
résoudre, to resolve; PRES. P. résolvant; P.P. résolu (resolved), résous (invar. chem. dissolved); so **absoudre, dissoudre,** exc. P.P.'s absous, dissous and no Prets. or Impfs. Subj.	résous résous résout résolv-ons ~ez ~ent

Imperative	*Pres. Subjunctive*	*Pret. & Impf. Subj.*
NOT USED	vaille vailles vaille	valus
	val-ions ~iez vaillent	valusse
vois	voie voies voie	vis
voyons voyez	voy-ions ~iez voient	visse
veux	veuille veuilles veuille	voulus
voulons voulez OR veuillez	voul-ions ~iez veuillent	voulusse
NONE	NONE	il échut
		NONE
NONE	il siée ils siéent	NONE
		NONE
bois	boive boives boive	bus
buvons buvez	buv-ions ~iez boivent	busse
conclus	conclu-e ~es ~e	conclus
concluons concluez	conclu-ions ~iez ~ent	conclusse
conduis	conduis-e ~es ~e	conduisis
conduisons conduisez	conduis-ions ~iez ~ent	conduisisse
confis	confis-e ~es ~e	confis
confisons confisez	confis-ions ~iez ~ent	confisse
couds	couse couses couse	cousis
cousons cousez	cous-ions ~iez ~ent	cousisse
crains	craign-e ~es ~e	craignis
craignons craignez	craign-ions ~iez ~ent	craignisse
crois	croie croies croie	crus
croyons croyez	croy-ions ~iez croient	crusse
croîs	croiss-e ~es ~e	crûs
croissons croissez	croiss-ions ~iez ~ent	crûsse
dis	dise dises dise	dis
disons dites	dis-ions ~iez ~ent	disse
écris	écriv-e ~es ~e	écrivis
écrivons écrivez	écriv-ions ~iez ~ent	écrivisse
fais	fasse fasses fasse	fis
faisons faites	fass-ions ~iez ~ent	fisse
lis	lise lises lise	lus
lisons lisez	lis-ions ~iez ~ent	lusse
maudis	maudiss-e ~es ~e	maudis
maudiss-ons ~ez	maudiss-ions ~iez ~ent	maudisse
mets	mett-e ~es ~e	mis
mettons mettez	mett-ions ~iez ~ent	misse
mouds	moul-e ~es ~e	moulus
moulons moulez	moul-ions ~iez ~ent	moulusse
nais	naiss-e ~es ~e	naquis
naissons naissez	naiss-ions ~iez ~ent	naquisse
pais	paiss-e ~es ~e	NONE
paissons paissez	paiss-ions ~iez ~ent	NONE
plais	plais-e ~es ~e	plus
plaisons plaisez	plais-ions ~iez ~ent	plusse
prends	prenn-e ~es ~e	pris
prenons prenez	pren-ions ~iez prennent	prisse
résous	résolv-e ~es ~e	résolus
résolvons résolvez	résolv-ions ~iez ~ent	résolusse

Pres. Inf. Fut. Participles	*Pres. Indicative*
rire, to laugh; PRES. P. riant; P.P. ri	ris ris rit rions riez rient
suivre, to follow; PRES. P. suivant; P.P. suivi	suis suis suit suiv-ons ~ez ~ent
traire, to milk; PRES. P. trayant; P.P. trait	trais trais trait tray-ons ~ez traient
vaincre, to conquer; PRES. P. vainquant; P.P. vaincu	vaincs vaincs vainc vainqu-ons ~ez ~ent
vivre, to live, PRES. P. vivant; P.P. vécu	vis vis vit viv-ons ~ez ~ent
DEFECTIVE	
braire, to bray; PRES. P. brayant; P.P. brait; FUT. braira and brairont; IMPF. brayait and brayaient	il brait ils braient
bruire, to rustle, PRES. P. bruissant; IMPF. bruissai-t ~ent	il bruit
clore, to shut; PRES. P. closant; P.P. clos; FUT. clorai	clos clos clôt - - closent
frire, to fry; P.P. frit. **faire frire** takes its place.	fris fris frit NO PL.

WEIGHTS AND MEASURES

WEIGHT:

1 milligramme (1/1,000 gm.)	= 0·015 gr.
1 centigramme (1/1,000 gm.)	= 0·154 gr.
1 décigramme (1/10 gm.)	= 1·543 gr.
1 GRAMME	= 15·432 gr.

(A gramme is the weight of 1 cubic centimètre of water at 4° centigrade)

1 décagramme (10 gm.)	= 5·644 dr.
1 hectogramme (100 gm.)	= 3·527 oz.
1 KILOGRAMME (1,000 gm.)	= 2·205 lb.
1 quintal métrique (100 kg.)	= 1·968 cwt.
1 tonne (1,000 kg.)	= 19 cwt. 2 qr. 21 lb.

LINEAR MEASURE:

1 millimètre (1/1,000 m.)	= 0·039 in.
1 centimètre (1/100 m.)	= 0·394 in.
1 décimètre (1/10 m.)	= 3·937 in.
1 MÈTRE	= 39·370 in. or 1·094 yds.
1 décamètre (10 m.)	= 10·937 yds.
1 hectomètre (100 m.)	= 109·361 yds.
1 KILOMÈTRE (1,000 m.)	= 1093·614 yds. (about 5/8 mile)

Imperative	*Pres. Subjunctive*	*Pret. & Impf. Subj.*
ris	rie ries rie	ris
rions riez	ri-ions ∼iez ∼ent	risse
suis	suiv-e ∼es ∼e	suivis
suivons suivez	suiv-ions ∼iez ∼ent	suivisse
trais	traie traies traie	NONE
trayons trayez	tray-ions ∼iez traient	NONE
vaincs	vainqu-e ∼es ∼e	vainquis
vainquons vainquez	vainqu-ions ∼iez ∼ent	vainquisse
vis	vive vives vive	vécus
vivons vivez	viv-ions ∼iez ∼ent	vécusse
NONE	NONE	NONE
		NONE
NONE	NONE	NONE
		NONE
NONE	close closes close	NONE
	clos-ions ∼iez ∼ent	NONE
NONE	NONE	NONE
		NONE

WEIGHTS AND MEASURES

SQUARE MEASURE:

1 are (100 sq. mètres)	= 119·599 sq. yds.
1 HECTARE (100 ares or 10,000 sq. mètres)	= 2·471 acres.

CUBIC MEASURE:

1 STÈRE (1 cubic mètre)	= {35·315 cubic ft. 1·308 cubic yds.

MEASURE OF CAPACITY:

1 millilitre (1/1,000 litre)	= 0·007 gill
1 centilitre (1/100 litre)	= 0·070 gill
1 décilitre (1/10 litre)	= 0·176 pint
1 LITRE	= 1·760 pint
1 décalitre (10 litres)	= 2·200 gallons
1 hectolitre (100 litres)	= 2·750 bushels
1 kilolitre (1,000 litres)	= 3·437 quarters

PRINCIPAL ABBREVIATIONS

⍏ = pitfall! beware of apparent analogy!

a., active (verb)
abs., absolute
adj., adjective, adjectival(ly)
admin., administration
adv., adverb(ial)
aeron., aeronautics
agric., agriculture
alg., algebra
anat., anatomy
anc., ancient
ant., antiquities
arch., architecture
arith., arithmetic
art., article
astr., astronomy
astrol., astrology
bibl., biblical
biol., biology
book-keep., book-keeping
bot., botany
Braz., Brazilian
Bret., Breton
build., building
butch., butchery
c., century
carp., carpentry
Cath., Catholic
cf., compare
chem., chemistry
child., children's or childish
class., classical
colloq., colloquial(ly)
comb., combination
comm., commerce
comp., compound
conch., conchology
conj., conjunction
contr., contraction
crust., crustacea
danc., dancing
def., defective
dem., demonstrative
deriv., derivative
dim., diminutive
dressm., dressmaking
dub., dubious
eccles., ecclesiastical
eng., engineering
engr., engraving
ent., entomology
etym., etymology
euphem., euphemism
ex., example
exc., except
excl., exclamation
expl., expletive
ext., extension
f. and fem., feminine
f. (in etymologies), from
falc., falconry
fam., familiar(ly)
fenc., fencing
feud., feudal
fig., figurative(ly)
fin., finance
fish., fishing
fort., fortification
Fr. French
gard., gardening
geog., geography, geographical
geol., geology
geom., geometry
Germ., German (but OLG for Old Low German)
Goth., Gothic
gram., grammar
Gr., Greek
gymn., gymnastics
Hebr., Hebrew
hist., history
horol., horology
hort., horticulture
hunt., hunting
hydr., hydraulics
ichth., ichthyology
ill., illustration
imit., imitative
impers., impersonal
ind., indefinite
Ind., Indian
indic., indicative
inf., infinitive
int., interrogative(ly)
interj., interjection
invar., invariable
iron., ironically
irreg., irregular(ly)
It., Italian
join., joinery
kg., kilogram
kilom., kilometre
L, Latin
LL, late Latin
land surv., land surveying
lit., literal(ly)
Lit., literature or literary
liturg., liturgy, liturgical
loc., locution (=phrase)
log., logic
m. and masc., masculine
mach., machinery
mason., masonry
math., mathematics
mech., mechanics
med., medicine
meteor., meteorology
mil., military
min., mineralogy
moll., mollusca
motor., motoring
mus., music
myth., mythology
n., name
n., neuter (verb)
nat.hist., natural history
naut., nautical
nav., naval
neg., negative
neol., neologism
Norw., Norwegian
num., numeral
obs., obsolete
OF, Old French
OHG, Old High German
onom., onomatopoeic
opt., optics
ord., ordinal
orig., origin
ornith., ornithology
p., participial
p.p., past participle
parl., parliament
part., participle
pathol., pathology
pej., pejorative
perh., perhaps
Pers., Persian
pers., personal
pharm., pharmacy
phil., philosophy
phon., phonetics
photo., photography
phr., phrase
phys., physics
plur. or pl., plural
Pol., Polish
polit., politics
pop., popular(ly)
Port., Portuguese
poss., possessive
pr., pronominal
pref., prefix
prep., preposition
pres., present
prob., probably
pron., pronoun
prop. n., proper name
pros., prosody
prov., proverb
rad., radical
rail., railways
rel., relative
rhet., rhetoric
rid., riding
Rom., Roman
s., substantive, noun
Sansk., Sanskrit
Scand., Scandinavian
scient., scientific
Script., scriptural
sculpt., sculpture
sing., singular
Span., Spanish
sport., sporting
subj., subjunctive,
subst., substantival(ly)
surg., surgery
syn., synonym
techn., technical
teleph., telephony
Teut., Teutonic
theatr., theatrical
theol., theology
therap., therapeutics
Turk., Turkish
unkn., unknown
v., verb
var., variant
vet., veterinary (surgery)
vulg., vulgar
wd, word
zool., zoology

FRENCH DICTIONARY

A, a (a and ɑ), s.m. [1st letter of alphabet, derived from the Phoenician alphabet] A, a; *un a majuscule*, a capital a; *l'a.b.c.*, (fig.) the first notions, the rudiments; *l'a.b.c. de l'archéologie*, the elements of archaeology; *ne savoir ni ~ ni b*, to be a perfect ignoramus; *prouver par ~ +b*, to demonstrate mathematically, to prove up to the hilt, or in black and white.

a (a), 3rd pers. sing. pres. ind. of *avoir*. Has. See AVOIR.

à (a), **au** (contraction of *à le*) (o), prep. [L *ad*] **1.** To, into; *je vais ~ Paris*, I am going to Paris; *il entra au grenier*, he got into the loft; *prêt ~ jouer*, ready to play; *vous n'avez rien ~ craindre*, you have nothing to fear; *elle est ~ plaindre*, she is to be pitied; *~ louer*, to let; **2.** at, in, within; *habiter ~ Orléans*, to live at Orleans; *habiter ~ Paris*, to live in Paris; *il jeta une pierre au chien*, he threw a stone at the dog; *parler au hasard*, to talk at random; *descendre au Grand Hôtel*, to put up at the Grand Hotel; *nous sommes ~ la campagne*, we are in the country; *la mer est ~ cinq minutes*, the sea is within five minutes' walk; **3.** on, upon, about; *~ bord*, on board; *~ cheval*, on horseback; *tournez ~ droite*, turn to the right; *une girouette au toit*, a weathercock on the roof; *des fleurs aux champs*, flowers in the fields; **4.** by, with; *au clair de la lune*, by moonlight; *~ la fourchette*, with a fork; *~ toute vitesse*, with all speed; *fait ~ la machine*, machine-made; *sauce ~ la menthe*, mint-sauce; *~ côté*, by the side; *~ midi le vent augmenta*, by noon the wind increased; **5.** for; *~ vendre*, for sale; *table ~ thé*, tea-table; *cartes ~ jouer*, playing-cards; *machine ~ écrire*, typewriter; **6.** after; *~ la française*, after the French fashion; *filer ~ l'anglaise*, to take French leave; **7.** from; *boire au robinet*, to drink from the tap; *ôtez ce fusil ~ l'enfant*, take that gun from the child; **8.** as to, according to; *quant ~ lui*, as for him; *~ son avis*, according to him; **9.** deserving to, calculated to, capable of, likely to; *il est ~ gifler*, he deserves to be kicked out; *elle est ~ faire peur*, she is a fright; **10.** as far as, sold for, worth; *l'eau monta ~ dix pieds*, the water rose up to ten feet; *le pain était ~ deux sous*, bread was a penny a pound; **11.** something, anything, enough to, sufficient; *donnez-lui ~ manger, ~ boire*, give him something to eat, to drink; *il a ~ faire*, he has work to do; *avoir affaire (à faire) avec*, to have business (to transact) with; **12.** in the act of; *ils sont ~ jouer*, they are playing; **13.** (indicating possession); *ceci est ~ moi, ~ vous*, this is mine, yours; **14.** (indicating rotation periodicity); *~ lui de jouer*, his turn to play; **15.** peculiar to; *une méthode, un tour de main ~ eux*, a method, a trick peculiar to them; **16.** under; *être ~ l'abri*, to be in shelter or under cover; **17.** till, until; *~ demain, ~ l'an prochain*, good-bye till to-morrow, until next year; **18.** under the sign of, trade-marked; *cognac aux trois étoiles*, three-star brandy; **19.** against; *appuyez l'échelle au mur*, prop the ladder against the wall; **20.** various locutions, *gare ~ vous!*, look out!; *~ lui seul*, by himself, unassisted; *~ nous deux*, let's have a go; *~ votre aise*, as you prefer; *~ qui mieux mieux*, as best who can; *c'est ~ qui fera le plus de bruit*, each tries to be the noisiest; *~ vous de voir*, that is your look-out; *~ vous de choisir*, you must choose; *~ vous de l'aider*, it is your business (or your duty) to help him; *~ tout prendre*, taking all in all; *~ vrai dire*, properly speaking; *~ vous lire*, expecting a prompt answer.

abaissable (abɛsabl), adj. That can be lowered.

abaissant, -e (abɛsɑ̃), adj. Lowering; (fig.) degrading.

abaisse (abɛs), s.f. Rolled-out pie-crust, undercrust.

abaissement (abɛsmɑ̃), s.m. Lowering, letting or pulling down; (fig.) fall, decline, disgrace, abasement, humiliation, humility, humbleness, stooping; decrease, abatement; (geog.) sloping, sinking, dipping, dip; (surg.) couching (of cataract).

abaisser (abɛse), v.a. [*à +baisser*] To lower, to let or pull or bring down; to lessen, to abate, to reduce; to shorten, to flatten, to lop off; (math.) to reduce; to bring down; (geom.) to let fall; to cast down (one's eyes); (cook.) to roll out (paste); (fig.) to humble, to disgrace, to depreciate; **s'~**, v.pr. to stoop, to humble oneself, to lower oneself, to cringe, to fall into vulgarity, to cheapen oneself; to condescend; to be lowered, to sink, to subside, to decrease, to abate, to slope, to slant; *qui s'élève s'abaisse*, self-praise is no recommendation; *je ne m'abaisserai pas à me venger*, I will not stoop to make reprisals.

abaisseur (abɛsœr), adj.m. s.m. (anat.) Depressor.

abajoue (abaʒu), s.f. [f. *bajoue*] Cheek-pouch; chop.

abalourdir (abalurdir), v.a. [f. *lourd*] to render dull or stupid, to stupefy.

abandon (abɑ̃dɔ̃), s.m. [OF *bandon* = power] Desertion, forsaking; surrender, relinquishment, renunciation; abandonment, carelessness, neglect, forlornness, destitution; spontaneousness, freshness; open-heartedness; *dans un instant d'~*, in an unguarded moment; *faire ~ de*, to give up, to relinquish; *laisser à l'~*, to neglect; syn. RENONCIATION, DÉSISTEMENT, ABANDONNEMENT.

abandonnataire (abɑ̃dɔnatɛr), s.m.f. (law) Abandonee, releasee.

abandonnat-eur, -rice (abɑ̃dɔnatœr), s.m.f. (law) Abandoner, releasor.

abandonné, -e (abɑ̃dɔne), p. adj. **1.** Forsaken, abandoned, forlorn, deserted; untenanted; **2.** shameless, careless, neglected. ~, s.m.f. Forsaken person. ⚠ In French *une femme abandonnée* usually means a deserted woman, not an abandoned woman, which = *une femme de mauvaises mœurs.*

abandonnement (abɑ̃dɔnmɑ̃), s.m. **1.** Desertion; **2.** relinquishment, surrender giving-up, abandonment. ⚠ 'Abandonment' in English means also careless freedom of manner, impulsiveness = French *abandon*, not *abandonnement.*

abandonner (abɑ̃dɔne), v.a. To forsake, to desert, to leave, to quit; to give up, to forgo, to relinquish, to resign, to give over, to renounce, to surrender, to hand over, to raise (a siege); (med.) to give up (as lost); syn. DÉLAISSER, RENONCER À; **s'~**, v.pr. to give up one's own cause; to neglect oneself, to give up cleanliness and orderliness; ~ *à*, to give oneself up to, to addict oneself to, to give way to.

abaque (abak), s.m. [L *abacus*] (arch.) Abacus; (math.) abacus.

abas. See ABAT.

abasourdir (abazurdir), v.a. [f. *sourd*] To stun, to deafen; to astound, to dumbfound, to flabbergast.

abasourdissant, -e (abazurdisɑ̃), adj. Astounding, stunning, overwhelming.

abasourdissement (abazurdismɑ̃), s.m. Astonishment, stupefaction, amazement.

abat[1], **abas** (aba), s.m. Sudden shower.

abat[2] (aba), s.m. Killing (of animals); ~*s* (pl.) offal, liver, lights. See ABATIS.

abatage (abataʒ), s.m. [f. *abattre*] Felling (of trees), cutting-down; lopping (of branches); slaughtering (of animals); (mech.) power, purchase; (naut.) heaving down (for careening); (pop.) a good blowing-up, wigging, slating; *il m'a flanqué un ~*, he gave it me hot, he gave me a rare dressing-down.

abâtardi, -e (abɑtardi), adj. [f. *bâtard*] Degenerate, corrupt.

abâtardir (abɑtardir), v.a. To debase, to render degenerate, to corrupt; **s'~**, v.pr. to degenerate.

abâtardissement (abɑtardismɑ̃), s.m. Degeneracy, debasement, decay.

abatée (abate), s.f. (naut.) Falling-off; *faire une ~, faire son ~*, to fall off.

abat-faim (abafɛ̃), s.m. Substantial dish, solid joint.

abatis (abati), s.m. **1.** Giblets (of fowl, &c.); (fig. pop.) legs, hands, feet, ankles; *avoir l'~ peuple*, to be thick-jointed (like working people); *avoir les ~ canailles*, to have beetle-crushers and mutton fists; **2.** felling (of trees, &c.); felled trees, material thrown down.

abat-jour (abaʒur), s.m. Reflector; shade, lamp-shade; (arch.) skylight.

abat-son (abasɔ̃), s.m. Louvre-board, luffer board.

abattage. See ABATAGE.

abattant (abatɑ̃), s.m. Flap; shutter, lid.

abattement (abatmɑ̃), s.m. [f. *abattre*] **1.** Despondency; prostration; faintness; dejection; syn. DÉPRESSION, DÉCOURAGEMENT, TORPEUR; **2.** (fin.) ~ *à la base*, preliminary deduction.

abatteur (abatœr), s.m. Cutter; feller; slaughterer; ~ *de besogne, bourreau de travail*, a glutton for work.

abattoir (abatwar), s.m. Slaughter-house.

abattre (abatr), v.a. [*à* + *battre*] To beat, knock, bring, throw, strike, pull, cut, blow, hew or break down; to fell (trees); to clear; to slaughter (animals), to kill, to destroy; (fig.) to depress, to cast down, to deject, to dispirit, to damp, to dishearten; to allay; to abate; (naut.) to fall off; ~ *de la besogne*, to get through a lot of work; ~ *son jeu*, ~ *ses cartes*, to lay one's cards on the table; *petite pluie abat grand vent*, a little rain lays much wind; *en ~*, to sweat, to get through a great deal of work; **s'~**, v.pr. to fall down, to come down; to abate, to subside; to alight, to swoop down; to come down (*sur*, upon), to pounce; to be cast down, to despond; (of storms) to burst; *un cyclone s'est abattu sur la ville*, a cyclone burst on the town.

abattu, -e (abaty), adj. [p.p. of *abattre*] Dejected, depressed, cast down, despondent, crestfallen, downcast; *à bride ~e*, at full speed, at breakneck speed.

abatture (abatyr), s.f. Knocking-down (fruit, nuts, &c.); ~*s* (pl.) foil or traces (left by a stag).

abat-vent (abavɑ̃), s.m. Louvre-window, windscreen; penthouse; lean-to.

abat-voix (abavwɑ), s.m. Sounding-board (of a pulpit).

abbatial, -e, (aux) (abasjal), adj. Abbatial, pertaining to an abbey.

abbaye (abɛi), s.f. [f. LL *abbatia*] Abbey, monastery.

abbé (abe), s.m. [L *abbas*] **1.** Abbot, head of abbey; **2.** abbé, any ecclesiastic, priest; *oui monsieur l'~*, yes, sir; yes,

reverend sir; ~ *Durand*, Father Durand; the Rev. Mr. Durand.
abbesse (abɛs) s.f. Abbess.
A.B.C. (abese) s.m. Spelling-book; rudiments; *l'~*, the very beginning.
abcéder (absede), v.n. [f. *abcès*] To form into an abscess; to come to a head.
abcès (absɛ), s.m. [L *abscessus*] Abscess, gathering; *former ~*, to gather.
abdicataire (abdikatɛr), s.m.f. One who is abdicating.
abdication (abdika'sjɔ̃), s.f. Abdication.
abdiquer (abdike), v.n. [L *abdicare*] To abdicate; ~, v.a. to renounce, to forswear, to lay aside; syn. SE DÉMETTRE.
abdomen (abdɔmɛn), s.m. Abdomen, belly.
abdominal, -e, (aux) (abdɔminal), adj. Abdominal.
abduct-eur, -rice (abdyktœr), adj. Abducent. ~, s.m. (anat.) Abductor.
abduction (abdyksjɔ̃), s.f. [L *abductio*] Abduction.
abécédaire (abesedɛr), s.m. [f. *A.B.C.*] Spelling-book. ~, adj. Alphabetical.
abecquer (abeke), v.a. [f. *bec*] To feed (a bird).
abée (abe), s.f. [OF *bée* = *baie*] Penstock, mill-leat.
abeille (abɛj), s.f. [L *apicula*] Bee, honey-bee, hive-bee, *la reine des ~s*, the queen bee; *~ ouvrière*, worker bee.
aberrant, -e (abɛrɑ̃), adj. Aberrant.
aberration (abɛrra'sjɔ̃), s.f. [L *aberratio*] Aberration; syn. TROUBLE, ÉGAREMENT.
aberrer (abɛrre), v.n. To err, to make mistakes.
abêtir (abɛtir), v.a. [f. *bête*] To render stupid; to dull, to blunt; **s'~**, v.pr. to grow dull or stupid, to become besotted.
abêtissement (abɛtismɑ̃), s.m. Dullness, stupidity, besotting process.
abhorrer (abɔrre), v.a. [f. L *ab.* + *horror*] To abhor, to detest, to loathe, to hate; syn. DÉTESTER, EXÉCRER.
abîme (abɪm), s.m. [Gr. *abussos*] Abyss; (poet.) abysm; chasm, gulf; the deep; hell, the bottomless pit; perdition; mystery, enigma; mine, unending supply; utmost degree, unfathomable depth; *courir à l'~*, or *aux ~s*, to run to perdition, or destruction; *sur le bord de l'~*, on the brink of the abyss; on the brink of ruin.
abîmer (abime), v.a. To damage, to spoil; to undo, to destroy, to sink, to swallow up; *abîmé de dettes*, over head and ears in debt; *abîmé de douleur*, overwhelmed with grief; **s'~**, v.pr. to sink, to be swallowed up; to get spoiled, to rust, to decay, to get damaged; *l'appareil vint s'~ dans la mer*; *sur les rochers*, the machine was swallowed up in the sea; came crashing on the rocks; *s'~ la santé*, to injure one's health.
ab intestat (abɛ̃tɛsta), adj. loc. [L wds] (law) From an intestate; *héritier ~*, heir-at-law, next of kin; *succession ~*, intestate estate.
abject, -e (abʒɛkt), adj. [L *abjectus*] Abject, base, vile, despicable.
abjectement (abʒɛktəmɑ̃), adv. Abjectly, basely, vilely.
abjection (abʒɛksjɔ̃), s.f. Abjection, abjectness, meanness; syn. BASSESSE.
abjuration (abʒyra'sjɔ̃), s.f. [L *abjuratio*] Abjuration.
abjurer (abʒyre), v.a.n. To abjure, to recant; to give up, to renounce.
ablati-f, -ve (ablatif), adj. s.m. [L *ablativus*] Ablative; *à l'~*, in the ablative.
ablation (abla'sjɔ̃), s.f. [L *ablatio*] (surg.) Ablation, removal, cutting-off.
able (abl), s.m. (ichth.) Any small fresh-water fish resembling bleak.
ablégat (ablega), s.m. [L *ab+legatus*] Sub-legate, ablegate.
ableret, ablier (ablərɛ, ablje), s.m. (fish.) Net for small fish; bleak-net.
ablette (ablɛt), s.f. [f. L *albula*] (ichth.) Bleak, ablet.
ablier. See ABLERET.
abluant, -e (ablɥɑ̃), adj. (med.) Abluent, cleansing.
abluer (ablɥe), v.a. [L *abluere*] To cleanse, to revive (old manuscripts).
ablution (ablysjɔ̃), s.f. [L *ablutio*] Ablution; *faire ses ~s*, to wash oneself.
abnégation (abnega'sjɔ̃), s.f. [L *abnegatio*] Abnegation, self-denial; *faire ~ de soi*, to sacrifice oneself.
aboi, aboiement (abwa, abwamɑ̃), s.m. [f. *aboyer*] Bark, barking, baying; *être aux ~s*, to be at bay; to be reduced to the last extremity, to be in a fix, to be on one's beam-ends; to be at one's last shift.
abolir (abɔlir), v.a. [L *abolere*] To abolish, to repeal, to do away with.
abolissement (abɔlismɑ̃), s.m. **abolition** (abɔlisjɔ̃), s.f. Abolition, abolishment, repeal, suppression.
abolitionnisme (abɔlisjɔnism), s.m. Abolitionism.
abolitionniste (abɔlisjɔnist), adj. s.m.f. Abolitionist.
abomasum (abɔmazɔm), s.m. See syn. CAILLETTE.
abominable (abɔminabl), adj. [L *abominabilis*] Abominable, detestable, loathsome; *c'est ~ !*, it 's a downright shame !
abominablement (abɔminabləmɑ̃), adv. Abominably.
abomination (abɔminasjɔ̃), s.f. Abomination; *être en ~ à X*, to be abominated by X, to be loathsome to X; *avoir (quelque chose) en ~*, to hold (something) in detestation; to abominate (something).
abominer (abɔmine), v.a. To abominate, to loathe.

abondamment (abɔ̃damɑ̃), adv. Abundantly, plentifully, plenteously.
abondance (abɔ̃dɑ̃s), s.f. [L *abundantia*] Plenty, abundance; affluence, fullness; fluency, diffuseness; (school slang) weak wine and water, slops; *parler d'~*, to speak extempore, with a natural eloquence; *parler avec ~*, to speak fluently; *~ de biens ne nuit pas*, store is no sore; you can't have too much of a good thing; *corne d'~*, cornucopia, horn of plenty.
abondant, -e (abɔ̃dɑ̃), adj. Abundant, plentiful; (Lit.) diffuse, prolix, verbose.
abonder (abɔ̃de), v.n. [L *abundare*] To abound, to overflow; *il abonda dans mon sens*, he entirely agreed with me.
abonné, -e (abɔne), s.m.f. adj. (that is a) Subscriber; season- or yearly ticket-holder.
abonnement (abɔnmɑ̃), s.m. Subscription; season- or yearly ticket; retainer; *fonds d'~*, fixed allowance for expenses; *prendre un ~ à*, to subscribe to; to take a season-ticket for.
abonner (abɔne), v.a. [*à* +*bonne*, corrupt. of *borne*] To subscribe (for somebody else); **s'~** (*à*) v.pr. to subscribe (to), to take in; (law) to compound (with).
abonnir (abɔnir), v.a.n. [f. *bon*] To improve; **s'~**, v.pr. to get better, to improve.
abord (abɔr), s.m. [*à* +*bord*] Access, approach; air, manner, address; *~s* (pl.) vicinity, surroundings, outskirts; *au premier ~, tout d'~, de prime ~, dès l'~*, at first, at first sight, from the very first; *d'un ~ facile*, of easy access.
abordable (abɔrdabl), adj. Accessible, easy of approach.
abordage (abɔrdaʒ), s.m. Boarding; fouling, running foul, collision; *monter à l'~ (de)*, to board (an enemy's ship); to grapple (a ship).
aborder (abɔrde), v.n. To land, to arrive; ~, v.a. to accost, to reach; to address; to charge, to attack; to board; to collide with, to grapple; *il m'a abordé poliment*, he addressed (or accosted) me politely; **s'~**, v.pr. to accost each other; to collide, to run foul of each other.
abordeur (abɔrdœr), adj. m. (of a ship) Boarding; causing a collision.
aborigène (abɔriʒɛn), adj. [L *ab* +*origo*] Aboriginal, native. ~, s.m.f. Native; (pl. only) aborigines.
abornement (abɔrnmɑ̃), s.m. Marking-out, delimitation (of field, &c.).
aborner (abɔrne), v.a. [f. *borne*] To mark out, to delimit, to set boundary-stones to (fields, &c.).
aborti-f, -ve (abɔrtif), adj. Abortive.
abouchement (abuʃmɑ̃), s.m. Interview, parley, meeting.
aboucher (abuʃe), v.a. [f. *bouche*] To bring together; **s'~**, v.pr. to meet, to get in touch (*avec*, with), to confer, to parley.
abouler (abule), v.a. (pop.) To fork out, to give, to shell out; to bring; **s'~**, v.pr. to come along, to pop in, to turn up.
aboulie (abuli), s.f. [Gr. *a* +*boulē*] Mental disease resulting in loss of will-power.
about (abu), s.m. [*à* +*bout*] Butt-end of a plank; eking-piece.
aboutage (abutaʒ), s.m. (naut. &c.) Splicing (of ropes).
aboutement (abutmɑ̃), s.m. Joining end to end.
abouter (abute), v.a. [f. *bout*] To join end to end; (naut.) to splice (ropes).
aboutir (abutir), v.n. [f. *bout*] To tend (*à*, to), to lead; to join, to converge; to terminate (in), to run (into); to abut (upon); to end, to come (to); (med.) to come to a head, to burst; *cela n'aboutira à rien*, that will come to nothing; that will end in nothing.
aboutissant, -e (abutisɑ̃), p. adj. Running into, ending in. **~s**, s.m. pl. Circumstances, influences, particulars; *les tenants et ~s*, the ins and outs; the long and short; the influences at work.
aboutissement (abutismɑ̃), s.m. Result, issue; (med.) gathering, suppuration; (nav.) endings.
aboyer (abwaje), v.n. [f. OF *bayer*] To bark, to bay, to yelp; (fig.) to cry out (against); *chien qui aboie ne mord pas*, barking dogs seldom bite.
aboyeu-r, -se (abwajœr), adj. Barking, baying. ~, s.m. (fig.) Snarler; street newsvendor, hawker, snarling critic; (slang) revolver, 'barker'.
abracadabra (abrakadabra), s.m. Abracadabra (magic word arranged thus:)

a b r a c a d a b r a
b r a c a d a b r
r a c a d a b
a c a d a
c a d
a

abracadabrant, -e (abrakadabrɑ̃), adj. Stupendous, disconcerting, incoherent, amazing, stunning.
abrasi-f, -ve (abrazif), adj. (techn.) Abrasive.
abrasion (abra'zjɔ̃), s.f. [L *ab* +*radere, rasum*] Abrasion.
abrégé, -e (abreʒe), adj. Abridged, short. ~, s.m. Abridgement, summary, abstract epitome, compendium, digest; *en ~*, briefly, in short.
abrègement (abrɛʒmɑ̃), s.m. Abridging shortening, abridgement, curtailment.
abréger (abreʒe), v.a. [L *abbreviare*] To abridge, to shorten, to abbreviate, to curtail; *pour ~*, in short; to be brief; *cela abrège le chemin d'un mille*, it shortens

the way by a mile; *abrégez !*, be brief !; (fam.) cut it short !

abreuvage, abreuvement (abrœvaʒ, abrœvmɑ̃), s.m. Watering (of cattle, &c.).

abreuver (abrœve), v.a. [L *ab* + *bibere*] To water, to give drink or water to; to soak, to steep, to imbue; to overwhelm, to load (*de*, with); ~ *d'injures*, to overwhelm with abuse; *abreuvé de larmes*, steeped in tears; **s'~**, v.pr. to drink, to quench one's thirst; (fig.) to satiate oneself (with); to wallow (in); *le tyran s'abreuvait de sang*, the tyrant wallowed in blood.

abreuvoir (abrœvwar), s.m. Watering-place, horse-pond, trough.

abréviat-eur, -rice (abrevjatœr), s.m.f. Abridger, abbreviator.

abréviati-f, -ve (abrevjatif), adj. Abbreviatory.

abréviation (abrevja'sjɔ̃), s.f. Abbreviation, abridgement, shortening.

A few French abbreviations:

A.I. *Altesse Impériale*, Imperial Highness; **A.R.** *Altesse Royale*, Royal Highness; **LL.AA.** *Leurs Altesses*, Their Highnesses; **LL.Ém.** *Leurs Éminences*, Their Eminences; **S.M.**; **LL. MM.** *Sa Majesté*. His or Her Majesty; *Leurs Majestés*, Their Majesties; **S.E.** *Son Excellence*, His or Her Excellency; **S. Ém.** *Son Éminence*, His Eminence; **S.H.** *Sa Hautesse*, (Sultan) Sa Hautesse; **S.G.** *Sa Grandeur*, (Cathol. Bishop) Sa Grandeur, or *Sa Grâce*, His or Her Grace; **S.P.** *Saint Père*, (the Pope); **S.S.** *Sa Sainteté*, His Holiness; **B^{on}, B^{onne}.** *Baron, Baronne*, Baron, Baroness; **B.P.F.** *Bon pour Francs*; **et Cie.** *Et Compagnie*, and Co; **C.c.** *Compte courant*, current account; **Cte, Ctesse.** *Comte, Comtesse*, Count, Countess; **Cf.** *Conférer*, Cf.; **C.V.** *Chevaux-Vapeur*, H.P. horse power; **D^{o}.** or **d^{o}.** *ditto*, d^{o}. ditto; **D^{r}.** *Docteur*, Dr. Doctor; **E.V.** *en ville*, in town; **F^{co}.** *franco*, free on delivery; **F., Fr.** *frère*, Brother; **F.·.** *frère trois points*, Masonic Brother; **G.C.** *Grand Croix*, **G.O.** *Grand officier*, **O.** *Officier*, **C.** *Chevalier*; **L.H.** *Légion d'Honneur*; **M.** *Monsieur*, Mr.; **Mme.** *Madame*, Mrs.; **Mlle.** *Mademoiselle*, Miss; **MM.** *Messieurs*, Messrs.; **Mgr.** *Monseigneur*, Mgr.; **N.B.** nota bene, N.B.; **P.P.** *port payé*, carriage paid; **P.p.c.** *pour prendre congé*, to take leave; **P.T.T.** *Postes, Télégraphes, Téléphones*, P.O.; **S.V.P.** *S'il vous plaît*, please; **S.$^{t(e)}$** *Saint(e)*, S., Saint; **T. s.v.p.** *tournez s'il vous plaît*, turn over; **T.S.F.** *télégraphie sans fil*, wireless.

abréviativement (abrevjativmɑ̃), adv. Briefly, by abbreviation.

abri (abri), s.m. [f. L *apricare*] Shelter, dug-out, cover, refuge; screen, shade, concealment, defence, protection; *à l'~ d'un arbre*, under a tree; *à l'~ de la pluie, du danger*, sheltered from the rain, from danger; *mettre à l'~*, *donner ~ à*, to shelter; *se mettre à l'~*, to take shelter; *sans ~*, shelterless, homeless.

abricot (abriko), s.m. [L *praecox*] Apricot.

abricotier (abrikɔtje), s.m. (bot.) Apricot-tree.

abriter (abrite), v.a. [f. *abri*] To shelter, to screen, to shield, to cover, to shade, to protect; ~ *contre*, to shelter from; **s'~**, v.pr. to take shelter; to get under cover; to take refuge.

abrivent (abrivɑ̃), s.m. [*abri* + *vent*] Shed; shelter; sentry-box; (hort.) matting.

abrogati-f, -ve (abrɔgatif), adj. Intended to abrogate.

abrogation (abrɔga'sjɔ̃), s.f. [L *abrogatio*] Abrogation, repeal.

abrogatoire (abrɔgatwar), adj. Abrogatory.

abroger (abrɔʒe), v.a. [L *abrogare*] To abrogate, to repeal, to cancel.

abrouti, -e (abruti), adj. [f. *brouter*] Browsed, cropped.

abrupt, -e (abrypt), adj. [L *abruptus*] Abrupt, rugged, steep, craggy; (fig.) blunt, rough, sharp.

abruptement (abryptəmɑ̃), adv. Abruptly.

abruti, -e (abryti), adj. [f. *abrutir*] Besotted, rendered stupid, addle-headed, stunned. ~, s.m.f. Dunce, blockhead, stupid brutish person; *un ~ de Chaillot*, a blockhead, a cabbage-head.

abrutir (abrytir), v.a. [f. *brute*] To brutify, to besot, to hebetate, to render stupid or brutish; to tire out; ~ *de fatigue*, to tire to death; **s'~**, v.pr. to become stupid, to become brutish, to make a beast of oneself.

abrutissant, -e (abrytisɑ̃), adj. Stupefying, besotting, rendering stupid.

abrutissement (abrytismɑ̃), s.m. Brutishness, sottishness; stupefying, besotting.

abscisse (absis), s.f. [f. L *abscissa*] (geom.) Abscissa.

abscons, -e (abskɔ̃s), adj. Abstruse, hidden; syn. ABSTRUS.

absence (absɑ̃s), s.f. [L *absentia*] Absence, non-attendance; lack, want; abstraction, absence of mind, wandering; *en mon ~*, while I am (or was) away; *il a des ~s*, he has moments of inattention, fits of absent-mindedness.

absent, -e (absɑ̃), adj. Absent, missing, out, away, away from home; abstracted in mind, absent-minded. ~, s.m. Absent one, absentee; *les ~s ont toujours tort*, the absent are always in the wrong; when absent, one is never in the right.

absentéisme (absɑ̃teism), s.m. Absenteeism.
absentéiste (absɑ̃teist), adj. s.m.f. Absentee.
(s')absenter (sabsɑ̃te), v.pr. To absent oneself, to leave home.
absidal, -e, (aux) (absidal), adj. Apsidal.
abside (absid), s.f. [Gr. *apsis*] Apse.
absidiole (absidjɔl), s.f. Small apse.
absinthe (absɛ̃t), s.f. [Gr. *apsinthion*] **1.** (bot.) Absinth, wormwood; **2.** the liqueur made from wormwood; (fig.) bitterness.
absinther (absɛ̃te), v.a. To mix with absinthe; **s'~**, v.pr. to intoxicate oneself with absinth.
absolu, -e (absɔly), adj. [L *absolutus*] Absolute, complete, perfect, pure, unrestricted; peremptory, despotic, imperious, utter, downright; (gram.) absolute; *ablatif ~*, ablative absolute. **~**, s.m., Absolute; absoluteness.
absolument (absɔlymɑ̃), adv. Absolutely; by all means, altogether; strictly; arbitrarily, despotically; *refuser ~*, to refuse flatly; (gram.) absolutely.
absolution (absɔlysjɔ̃), s.f. [f. L *absolutio*] Absolution; forgiveness of sin, remission of penance, pardon; syn. PARDON, RÉMISSION DES PÉCHÉS.
absolutisme (absɔlytism), s.m. Absolutism.
absolutiste (absɔlytist), adj. s.m.f. Absolutist.
absolutoire (absɔlytwar), adj. Absolving, absolvatory.
absorbable (absɔrbabl), adj. Absorbable.
absorbant, -e (absɔrbɑ̃), p. adj. Absorbent, absorptive; engrossing, absorbing; *occupations ~es*, unremitting labour; engrossing work. **~**, s.m. Absorbent.
absorber (absɔrbe), v.a. [L *absorbere*] To absorb, to imbibe, to drink, to suck up; to consume, to eat, to drink; to engross the attention of; **s'~**, v.pr. to be absorbed.
absorption (absɔrbsjɔ̃), s.f. [L *absorptio*] Absorption; ingestion; sucking-in; mental engrossment.
absorptivité (absɔrbtivite), s.f. Absorptiveness.
absoudre (absudr), v.a. [L *absolvere*] To absolve; to acquit, to discharge, to pardon, to remit (sins), to forgive; *~ X*, to absolve X, to discharge or acquit X.
absoute (absut), s.f. General absolution.
abstème (abstɛm), adj. [L *abstemius*] Abstemious.
(s')abstenir (sabstənir), v.pr. To abstain, to refrain, to forbear; to abstain (from voting); *s'~ d'alcool*, to abstain from alcohol; to refrain from alcohol; *dans le doute, abstiens-toi*, when in doubt, do nothing.
abstention (abstɑ̃sjɔ̃), s.f. Abstention (*de*, from), keeping-off.
abstentionniste (abstɑ̃sjɔnist, s.m.f. Nonvoter; abstainer. **~**, adj. That abstains.
abstergent, -e (abstɛrʒɑ̃), adj. (med.) Abstergent.
absterger (abstɛrʒe), v.a. [L *abstergere*] To absterge, to cleanse.
abstinence (abstinɑ̃s), s.f. [L *abstinentia*] Abstinence, fasting.
abstinent, -e (abstinɑ̃), adj. Abstinent.
abstracteur (abstraktœr), s.m. One given to abstractions; *~ de quintessence*, subtle reasoner; abstraction-monger.
abstracti-f, -ve (abstraktif), adj. Abstractive.
abstraction (abstraksjɔ̃), s.f. [L *abstractio*] Abstraction; abstract, abstract term; abstractedness; fit of absence of mind; *~ faite de*, setting aside; after deducting; exclusive of; *faire ~ de*, to set aside, to exclude; *par ~*, abstractedly.
abstraire (abstrɛr), v.a. [f. L *abs* + *trahere*] To abstract, to set aside, to separate, to exclude; **s'~**, v.pr. to be engrossed, to abstract oneself, to isolate oneself, to concentrate.
abstrait, -e (abstrɛ), adj. [L *abstractus*] Abstract; abstruse; abstracted, absentminded, withdrawn in thought. **~**, s.m. Abstract; *dans l'~*, in the abstract.
abstraitement (abstrɛtmɑ̃), adv. Abstractly.
abstrus, -e (abstry), adj. [L *abstrusus*] Abstruse.
absurde (absyrd), adj. [L *absurdus*] Absurd, incongruous, silly, preposterous. **~**, s.m. Absurdity; *démontrer par l'~*, to demonstrate by a 'reductio ad absurdum.'
absurdement (absyrdəmɑ̃), adv. Absurdly.
absurdité (absyrdite), s.f. Absurdity, folly, unreasonableness, nonsense, absurd statement or act.
abus (aby), s.m. [f. L *ab* + *usus*] Abuse, misuse, corrupt practice, grievance; excessive use or ingestion (of drink, food, tobacco, &c, &c.); embezzlement, misappropriation; *~ de confiance*, breach of trust; *appel comme d'~*, appeal by writ of error or for excess of power.
abuser (abyze), v.a.n. To abuse, to deceive, to mislead; to seduce, to lead astray; *~ de*, to force; to take (unfair) advantage of; to overwork; to use too freely, to misuse; *j'abuse de votre bonté*, I am trespassing on your kindness; *si ce n'était ~ de votre obligeance*, if it was not troubling you too much; **s'~**, v.pr. to deceive oneself, to be deceived, to be mistaken. ⚠ *Abuser* in French has never the sense of to 'abuse', 'to revile', 'to insult' = *injurier*.

abusi-f, -ve (abyzif), adj. Abusive; excessive.
abusivement (abyzivmɑ̃), adv. Abusively; excessively.
abuter (abyte), v.a.n. [f. *but*] To aim at, to abut.
abyssal, -e, (aux) (abisal), adj. Abyssal; abysmal, unfathomable.
abysse (abis), s.m. [Gr. *abussos*] Abyss (below sea surface); abyssal zone.
abyssin, -e, abyssinien, -ne (abisɛ̃, abisinjɛ̃), adj. s.m.f. Abyssinian.
acabit (akabi), s.m. [f. Arab. *al-qâlib*] Quality, nature, stamp; (slightly pej.) *des gens du même* ~, birds of a feather; people tarred with the same brush; fellows of the same kidney; *un gaillard de cet* ~, a fellow of that stamp.
acacia (akasja), s.m. (bot.) Acacia.
académicien, -ne (akademisjɛ̃), s.m.f. Academician.
académie (akademi), s.f. [f. Gr. *Akademos, akademeia*] Academy; French regional school-administration; (paint.) nude figure.
académique (akademik), adj. Academic; belonging to an academy; academical.
académiquement (akademikmɑ̃), adv. Academically.
académiste (akademist), s.m.f. Conductor of an academy; pupil of an academy.
(s')acagnarder (sakaɲarde), v.pr. [f. *cagnard*] To grow lazy; to lead an idle, easy life; to linger in a comfortable place; to take it easy in pleasant surroundings.
acajou (akaʒu), s.m. [Braz. *acajoba*] (bot.) Mahogany; *noix d'*~, cashew nut.
acanthe (akɑ̃t), s.f. [f. Gr. *akantha*] (bot.) Acanthus, bear's breech.
acanthoptérygiens (akɑ̃tɔpteriʒjɛ̃), s.m. pl. (ichth.) Acanthopterygians.
acariâtre (akarjɑtr), adj. [f. St. *Acaire*] Peevish, contrary, cross, cross-grained, crabbed, sour-tempered, shrewish, quarrelsome.
acarides, acariens (akarid, akarjɛ̃), s.m. pl. (ent.) Acaridae.
acarpe (akarp), adj. [f. Gr. *a* +*karpos*] (bot.) Acarpous.
acarus (akarys), s.m. (ent.) Acarus, itch-mite, tick.
acatalectique (akatalɛktik), adj. [Gr. *akatalektos*] (pros.) Acatalectic.
acatalepsie (akatalɛpsi), s.f. [Gr. *akatalepsia*] (philos.) Acatalepsy.
acatène (akatɛn), adj. [L *a* +*catena*] Chainless (bicycle).
acaule (akol), adj. [L *a* +*caulis*] (bot.) Acaulous.
accablant, -e (akɑblɑ̃), p.adj. Overwhelming, overpowering, crushing, oppressive, sultry, sweltering.
accablement (akɑbləmɑ̃), s.m. Despondency, prostration, dejection, heaviness; syn. ABATTEMENT, DÉCOURAGEMENT.
accabler (akɑble), v.a. [f. Gr. *a* +*katabolē*] To crush, to overwhelm, to overburden, to weigh down; to overpower, to overcome; to stifle, to depress, to dishearten; *accablé d'affaires*, overbusy, overburdened; ~ *de bienfaits*, to overwhelm with kindness; ~ *de reproches*, to load with reproaches; *ne l'accablez pas*, don't be too hard on him.
accalmie (akalmi), s.f. [f. *calme*] Lull, breathing-space, period of quiet.
accaparement (akaparmɑ̃), s.m. Monopolizing, cornering, forestalling, speculative purchase.
accaparer (akapare), v.a. [It. *accaparrare*] To buy up, to monopolize, to forestall, to corner, to secure, to keep all to oneself; *il accapare les grains*, he buys up all cereals; he corners the cereals; *ne vous laissez pas* ~ *par lui*, don't let him monopolize you.
accapareu-r, -se (akaparœr), s.m.f. Monopolizer; cornerer, forestaller.
accastillage (akastijaʒ), s.m. (naut.) Upper works (of a ship).
accéder (aksede), v.n. [L *accedere*] **1.** To have access, to accede, to reach; **2.** to comply, to agree, to consent; ~ *au trône*, to succeed to the throne; to succeed; *il accède à ma demande*, he agrees to my request; he complies with my wish.
accélérat-eur, -rice (akseleratœr), adj. Accelerating. ~, s.m. (motor.) Accelerator.
accélération (akselera'sjɔ̃), s.f. [L *acceleratio*] Acceleration; increase of speed.
accélérer (akselere), v.a. To accelerate, to quicken; ~ *le pas*, to put on speed; *pas accéléré*, quick step, quick march.
accent (aksɑ̃), s.m. [f. L *ad* +*cantus*] Accent; ~ *aigu*, acute accent; ~ *circonflexe*, circumflex accent; ~ *grave*, grave accent; (fig.) accent, stress, pitch, tone, intensity, emphasis; sound, tune, song; *cela manque d'*~, this is expressionless; this lacks accent or tone.
accenteur (aksɑ̃tœr), s.m. (ornith.) Accentor.
accentuation (aksɑ̃tɥa'sjɔ̃), s.f. Accentuation; accenting.
accentué, -e (aksɑ̃tɥe), p. adj. Accented; accentuated; (fig.) stressed, forcible, loud, intense; emphasized; *des traits* ~*s*, strongly marked features.
accentuer (aksɑ̃tɥe), v.a. To accent; to accentuate, to emphasize, to stress, to heighten, to set off, to make evident or conspicuous, to lay emphasis upon; *accentuez cette partie de votre discours*, emphasize this part of your speech; **s'**~, v.pr. to be accented; to grow more marked, to become evident.

acceptabilité (aksɛptabilite), s.f. Acceptableness, acceptability.
acceptable (aksɛptabl), adj. [L *acceptabilis*] Acceptable, welcome, worth taking.
acceptant, -e (aksɛptɑ̃), p. adj. Accepting. ~, s.m.f. Acceptor.
acceptation (aksɛpta'sjɔ̃), s.f. Acceptance; (obs.) acceptation. ⚠ In English nowadays the word 'acceptation' means a particular sense given to a word or phrase = French *acception*.
accepter (aksɛpte), v.a. [L *acceptare*] To accept, to receive; to admit, to agree to; to submit to, to bear; **s'~**, v.pr. to be accepted, to be acceptable.
accepteur (aksɛptœr), s.m. Acceptor.
acception (aksɛpsjɔ̃), s.f. [L *acceptio*] Acceptation; regard, respect, preference; *sans faire ~ de personnes*, without acceptance of persons, without showing personal preferences; without taking persons into consideration; *dans toute l'~ du mot*, in the full acceptation (or sense) of the word.
accès (aksɛ), s.m. [L *accessus*] **1.** Access, approach, admittance, entrance, passage, channel; *d'~ facile*, easy of access; **2.** fit, access, outburst, attack, bout; *~ de fièvre*, attack of fever, access or bout of fever; *~ de mauvaise humeur*, fit of peevishness; *par ~*, by fits and starts.
accessibilité (aksɛsibilite), s.f. Accessibility.
accessible (aksɛsibl), adj. Accessible, approachable, open to influence.
accession (aksɛsjɔ̃), s.f. [f. L *accessio*] **1.** Accession; *~ au trône*, accession to the throne; **2.** accession, addition, thing added; **3.** assent, adhesion.
accessit (aksɛsit), s.m. [L wd] Honourable mention, accessit.
accessoire (aksɛswar), adj. [LL *accessorius*] Accessory, additional, unessential, adventitious, subordinate. ~, s.m. Accessory; *~s* (pl.) fittings; (theatr.) stage-property, property; *chef-d'~s*, property-man.
accessoirement (aksɛswarmɑ̃), adv. Accessorily.
accident (aksidɑ̃), s.m. [L *accidens*] Accident, chance, occurrence, incident; mishap, misfortune, casualty; unevenness, irregularity in structure, varied aspect, undulation; (med.) unexpected symptom, sudden complication; (mus. paint.) accidental; (gram.) accidence; *par ~*, by accident, accidentally; *~s de terrain*, inequalities of ground, broken ground.
accidentaliser (aksidɑ̃talize), v.a. To make accidental.
accidentalité (aksidɑ̃talite), s.f. Accidentality, accidentalness.
accidenté, -e (aksidɑ̃te), adj. Unequal, uneven, broken; hilly; picturesque, eventful, chequered; (pop.) damaged through an accident; *terrain ~*, broken ground; *vie ~e*, chequered life, eventful life.
accidentel, -le (aksidɑ̃tɛl), adj. Accidental, occasional, not essential, unexpected; (mus.) accidental; syn. FORTUIT.
accidentellement (aksidɑ̃tɛlmɑ̃), adv. Accidentally, by chance.
accidenter (aksidɑ̃te), v.a. To variegate, to make picturesque.
accise (aksiz), s.f. Excise.
acclamati-f, -ve (aklamatif), adj. Acclamatory, cheering.
acclamation (aklama'sjɔ̃), s.f. [L *acclamatio*] Acclamation, cheer, acclaim, shout, applause; *voté par ~*, carried by acclamation.
acclamer (aklame), v.a. [L *ad* + *clamare*] To acclaim, to hail, to salute; to cheer.
acclimatable (aklimatabl), adj. That may be acclimatized; acclimatizable.
acclimatation (aklimata'sjɔ̃), s.f. Acclimatization; *jardin d'~*, Zoo (colloq.).
acclimater (aklimate), v.a. [f. *climat*] To acclimatize; **s'~**, v.pr. to become acclimatized, or adapted.
acclimateur (aklimatœr), s.m. Acclimatizer.
accoinçon (akwɛ̃sɔ̃), s.m. (carp.) Furring; piece of timber used in roofing.
accointance (akwɛ̃tas), s.f. (pej.) Acquaintance, familiarity; access, admittance; connexion.
(s')accointer (sakwɛ̃te), v.pr. [f. L *accognoscere*] (pej.) To become intimate and familiar (*avec*, with).
accolade (akɔlad), s.f. [f. It. *accollata*] **1.** Embrace, accolade, hug; *donner l'~ à*, to dub a knight; *recevoir l'~*, to be made a knight; **2.** brace, bracket, {; (mus.) accolade.
accolader (akɔlade), v.a. To join by a brace, to brace together; **s'~**, v.pr. to hug each other.
accolage (akɔlaʒ), s.m. (agric.) Tying-up (branches, &c., an operation of vine-growing).
accolement (akɔlmɑ̃), s.m. Joining.
accoler (akɔle), v.a. [f. L *ad* + *collum*] To hug, to embrace; to join; (vine-growing) to tie up (branches, shoots); *je n'aime pas voir mon nom accolé au sien*, I do not like my name to be coupled with his.
accombant, -e (akɔ̃bɑ̃), adj. (bot.) Accumbent, lying on another part (of plant).
accommodable (akɔmɔdabl), adj. That may be arranged or accommodated.
accommodage (akɔmɔdaʒ), s.m. Cooking, dressing (of food).
accommodant, -e (akɔmɔdɑ̃), p. adj. Accommodating, obliging, compliant,

easy to deal with; *il n'est guère* ~, he is hard to deal with.

accommodation (akɔmɔda'sjɔ̃), s.f. Accommodation, adjustment, arrangement.

accommodement (akɔmɔdmɑ̃), s.m. Accommodation, settlement, compromise; *en venir à un* ~, to come to terms, to compromise.

accommoder (akɔmɔde), v.a. [f. L *accommodare*] To accommodate, to fit up, to adapt, to adjust, to suit; to cook, to prepare, to dress (food); to conciliate; to let one have; (colloq.) ~ *X*, (*a*) to slander X; (*b*) to 'sit upon' X; **s'**~, v.pr. to put up (*de*, with); to come to terms.

accompagnat-eur, -rice (akɔ̃paɲatœr), s.m.f. Accompanist.

accompagnement (akɔ̃paɲmɑ̃), s.m. Appendage; attendance; (mus.) accompaniment.

accompagner (akɔ̃paɲe), v.a. To accompany, to go with, to escort, to attend on; to suit, to match; to add to; (mus.) to accompany; *bagages non accompagnés*, luggage forwarded as goods; ~ *ses conseils de remontrances*, to add rebuke to advice; **s'**~, v.pr. to be accompanied; (mus.) to accompany oneself.

accompli, -e (akɔ̃pli), p. adj. **1.** Completed, finished; *il a vingt ans* ~*s*, he is nearing (or approaching) twenty-one; **2.** perfect, accomplished, thorough; *un cavalier* ~ a perfect rider; syn. PARFAIT, ACHEVÉ.

accomplir (akɔ̃plir), v.a. [f. L *ad*+*complere*] To achieve, to accomplish, to complete, to carry out; to fulfil; to obey; **s'**~, v.pr. impers. to happen, to be fulfilled.

accomplissement (akɔ̃plismɑ̃), s.m. Achievement, execution, fulfilment, completion, accomplishment. ⚠ French *accomplissements* has not like English 'accomplishments' the sense of 'superficial acquirements', 'talents', 'perfections' = *talents de société, perfections, arts d'agrément.*

accon. See ACON.

accorage (akɔraʒ), s.m. (naut.) Propping-up, shoring-up.

accord (akɔr), s.m. [f. *accorder*] Agreement, accord, concurrence, harmony, concord; settlement, bargain, convention, treaty; (gram.) concordance; (mus.) chord; tuning; ~*s* (pl.) (fig.) strains; *d'*~*!*, granted!, agreed!; *d'un commun* ~, by common consent; *nous sommes d'*~, that is agreed upon; *tomber d'*~, to come to an agreement, to agree; *demeurer d'*~, to agree; *mettre d'*~, to reconcile, to conciliate; *ces meubles ne sont pas d'*~ *avec le style de la pièce*, these pieces of furniture are not in harmony with the style of the room; (mus.) *les violons ne sont pas d'*~, the violins are not in tune; ~ *de dominante*, dominant chord; ~ *de septième*, chord of the seventh.

accordable (akɔrdabl), adj. Reconcilable, that may be accorded; that may be tuned.

accordage, accordement (akɔrdaʒ, akɔrdəmɑ̃), s.m. Tuning.

accordailles (akɔrdɑj), s.f. pl. Betrothal.

accordé, -e (akɔrde), s.m.f. Betrothed.

accordéon (akɔrdeɔ̃), s.m. (mus.) Accordion.

accordéoniste (akɔrdeɔnist), s.m.f. Accordionist.

accorder (akɔrde), v.a. [f. L *ad*+*cor, cordis*] To grant, to confer, to give, to allow; to reconcile, to conciliate, to make agree, to bring into accord; to adjust, to harmonize, to match; (mus.) to tune; *je vous l'accorde*, I grant you that; *il m'a été accordé de*, it has been my privilege to; *accordez vos flûtes*, you should first agree with each other; **s'**~, v.pr. to agree, to concur; to harmonize, to match, to suit; to become betrothed; (gram.) to agree (*avec*, with), to be in concord (with); (mus.) to tune one's instrument.

accordeur (akɔrdœr), s.m. Tuner.

accordoir (akɔrdwar), s.m. Tuning-key.

accore (akɔr), s.m. (naut.) Prop, shore. ~, adj. Abrupt, sheer, steep.

accorer (akɔre), v.a. (naut.) To prop up, to shore up.

accort, -e (akɔr), adj. [It. *accorto*] Gracious, pleasant, engaging, alert, sprightly.

accortement (akɔrtəmɑ̃), adv. Graciously engagingly, alertly.

accortise (akɔrtiz), s.f. Grace, complaisance, affability, sprightliness.

accostable (akɔstabl), adj. Easy of access, approachable.

accostage (akɔstaʒ), s.m. (naut.) Boarding, drawing alongside.

accoster (akɔste), v.a. [f. L *ad*+*costa*] To accost, to address, to speak to; (naut.) to come alongside, to board.

accotement (akɔtmɑ̃), s.m. (road-making) Space between highway and ditch; sideway, driftway.

accoter (akɔte), v.a. To prop up, to support, to stay; **s'**~, v.pr. to lean (*contre*, against).

accotoir (akɔtwar), s.m. Arm-rest, railing, prop.

accouardir (akuardir), v.a. To make a coward; **s'**~, v.pr. to become a coward.

accouchée (akuʃe), s.f. Woman in childbed, lying-in woman; *l'*~, the mother.

accouchement (akuʃmɑ̃), s.m. Confinement, delivery, accouchement, childbed, labour; *faire un* ~, to deliver a woman; *maison d'*~, maternity home, lying-in home.

accoucher (akuʃe), v.n. To give birth (*de*, to), to lie in, to be brought to bed, to be delivered; ~, v.a. to deliver; (fig.) to speak out, to bring to light; *accouchez donc!*, out with it!

accoucheu-r, -se (akuʃœr), s.m.f. Accoucheur, maternity doctor; *~se*, midwife, accoucheuse.

accoudement (akudmɑ̃), s.m. **1.** Leaning (on); **2.** (mil.) close rank.

(s')accouder (sakude), v.pr. To rest one's elbow (*sur*, on), to lean on one's elbow.

accoudoir (akudwar), s.m. Elbow-rest, rail.

accouer (akue), v.a. [f. *queue*] To tie horses head to tail for marching in file.

accouple (akupl), s.f. Leash.

accouplement (akupləmɑ̃), s.m. Pairing, coupling; copulation; (mech.) coupling; *barre d'~*, coupling-rod.

accoupler (akuple), v.a. [f. *couple*] To couple, to pair; to yoke, to cause to copulate; (techn.) to couple; **s'~**, v.pr. to couple, to copulate, to mate.

accourci (akursi), s.m. Abridgement.

accourcir (akursir), v.a. To shorten; see RACCOURCIR.

accourcissement (akursismɑ̃), s.m. Shortening.

accourir (akurir), v.n. [f. L *ad* + *currere*] To rush up, to run up, to hurry, to hasten; to flock.

accourse (akurs), s.f. Outside passage between rooms.

accoutrement (akutrəmɑ̃), s.m. (often pej.) Garb, rig, rig-out, costume, trappings.

accoutrer (akutre), v.a. [etym. dub.] To rig out, to disguise, (pej.) to dress, to accoutre; **s' ~**, v.pr. to rig oneself out.

accoutumance (akutymɑ̃s), s.f. Habit, custom, use; usage, wont.

accoutumé, -e (akutyme), p.adj. **1.** Usual, customary, wonted; **2.** accustomed, used, habituated, inured; *avoir ~ de*, to be in the habit of; *à l'~e*, usually, as usual, customarily; *chose ~e n'est pas fort prisée*, familiarity breeds contempt.

accoutumer (akutyme), v.a. [*à* + *coutume*] To accustom, to habituate, to inure, to train (*à*, to); **s'~**, v.pr. to get used, accustomed, &c. (*à*, to).

accouvage (akuvaʒ), s.m. Hatching (by artificial means), incubation.

accouver (akuve), v.a. To set (a hen); **s'~**, v.pr. (colloq.) to squat, to crouch.

accréditer (akredite), v.a. [f. *crédit*] To accredit; to give credit to, to authorize, to countenance, to obtain credit for; to spread; to give vogue to; *être accrédité auprès de X*, to be sent to X with credentials, to be accredited to X; *~ une légende*, to spread a fiction; **s'~**, v.pr. to gain credit; to be spread, to gain favour, or vogue; *il s'accréditait au palais*, he was making himself trusted among barristers.

accréditeur (akreditœr), s.m. Guarantor, surety.

accrescent, -e (akrɛssɑ̃), adj. [L *accrescens*] (bot.) Accrescent.

accroc (akro), s.m. [f. *accrocher*] Rent, tear; (fig.) hitch, hindrance, impediment; stain, blemish; blow; *faire un ~ à sa robe*, to tear one's dress; *avoir un ~ à sa robe*, to have a tear in one's dress; *avoir un ~ à sa réputation*, to have a stain on one's character.

accrochage (akrɔʃaʒ), s.m. Hooking, grappling; (motor.) collision; (mil.) engagement; (fig.) hitch, hindrance, difficulty.

accroche-cœur (akrɔʃkœr), s.m. Kiss-curl, spit-curl.

accrochement (akrɔʃmɑ̃), s.m. Hooking; hitch, catching, stop; see ACCROCHAGE.

accroche-plat (akrɔʃpla), s.m. Plate-hanger.

accrocher (akrɔʃe), v.a. [f. *croc*] To hang up, to hook; to catch, to run against, to hitch, to catch and tear; to keep back; (pop.) to pawn; to get hold of; **s'~**, v.pr., to catch, to get hold of; to hang on; to fasten oneself on; to be caught, to be hooked on; (colloq.) to come to blows; to collide; to stick (to), to cling, to be importunate; *le tablier s'accroche à la capote*, the rug fastens inside the hood; *un homme qui se noie s'accroche à tout*, a drowning man catches at a straw; *il s'accroche désespérément*, he sticks like a limpet.

accrocheu-r, -se (akrɔʃœr), s.m.f. One who hooks, hangs up, &c.; one who cunningly gets some advantage.

accroire (akrwɑr), v.a.n. (Only used with *faire* in the inf.) [*à* + *croire*] To believe; *en faire ~ à X*, to impose upon X; *s'en faire ~*, to overrate oneself, to be self-conceited, to 'kid' oneself.

accroissement (akrwasmɑ̃), s.m. Increase, extension, enlargement, development, growth.

accroître (akrwɑtr), v.a. [L *accrescere*] To augment, to enlarge, to increase, to amplify, to heap up; **s'~**, v.pr. to increase, to grow, to rise, to improve, to accrue.

accroupi, -e (akrupi), adj. Squatting, squat, crouching, crouched, cowering.

(s')accroupir (sakrupir), v.pr. [f. *croupe*] To squat, to crouch, to sit down upon the hams.

accroupissement (akrupismɑ̃), s.m. Squatting, crouching, cowering.

accru (akry), s.m. (agric.) Sucker, scion.

accrue (akry), s.f. [f. *accroître*] Increase (of land through retreat of waters); encroachment (of a forest on adjoining ground).

accu (aky), s.m. [abbrev. of *accumulateur*] (motor. electr.) Accumulator.

accueil (akœj), s.m. Reception; welcome; *faire ~ à X*, to greet X; to make much of X; *faire bon ~ à X*, to welcome X; *faire bon ~ à une traite*, to meet a bill; *faire mauvais ~ à X*, to give X an ungracious reception; to receive X ungraciously.

accueillant, -e (akœjɑ̃), p.adj. Welcoming, affable, engaging.

accueillir (akœjir), v.a. [*ad* + *cueillir*] To receive, to welcome; to accept, to believe; to meet, to honour (a bill).

accul (akyl), s.m. [f. *acculer*] **1.** Cornering, bringing or driving to bay; **2.** blind alley, hole.

acculement (akylmɑ̃), s.m. Cornering, being cornered, bringing or driving to bay; being at bay.

acculer (akyle), v.a.n. [*à* + *cul*] To drive into a corner, to corner, to bring to bay, to cut off all ways of retreat; (naut.) to be down at the stern; **s'~**, v.pr. to set one's back (*à*, against).

accumulat-eur, -rice (akymylatœr), adj. Accumulating, storing, heaping-up. ~, s.m. Accumulator; see ACCU.

accumulation (akymyla'sjɔ̃), s.f. Accumulation; pile, heap, mass.

accumuler (akymyle), v.a. [L *accumulare*] To accumulate, to amass, to heap up, to store, to hoard up; **s'~**, v.pr. to accumulate.

accusable (akyzabl), adj. Accusable, chargeable, impeachable.

accusat-eur, -rice (akyzatœr), adj. Accusing, accusatory. ~, s.m. Accuser, indicter; ~ *public*, public prosecutor.

accusati-f, -ve (akyzatif), s.m. (gram.) adj. Accusative; *à l'~*, in the accusative.

accusation (akyza'sjɔ̃), s.f. [f. L *accusatio*] Accusation, charge, accusing, indictment; prosecution; *acte d'~* bill of indictment; *mise en ~*, arraignment; *prononcer la mise en ~ de*, to find a true bill against; *chef d'~*, count of indictment; *intenter une ~ contre X*, to prosecute X; to prefer an indictment against X.

accusatoire (akyzatwar), adj. Accusatory.

accusé, -e (akyze), s.m.f. The accused, prisoner, culprit, defendant; ~ *de réception*, acknowledgement (of a letter, receipt, &c). ~, adj. Marked; *des traits peu ~s*, indistinct features.

accuser (akyze), v.a. [L *accusare*] To accuse, to complain of; to indict, to charge (*de* with), to tax (with), to prosecute; to blame, to reproach; to declare, to state, to tell; *le thermomètre accuse 35°*, the thermometer stands at 35°; *elle accuse son âge*, she looks her age; *n'accusez pas nos différends*, do not emphasize our differences; ~ *réception de*, to acknowledge the receipt of; **s'~** v.pr. to accuse oneself (*de*, of), to own (to); to accuse each other.

acéphale (asefal), adj. [Gr. *akephalos*] Acephalous.

acérage (aseraʒ), s.m. Steeling (of tools).

acérain, -e (aserɛ̃), adj. [f. *acier*] Steely, of steel.

acerbe (asɛrb), adj. [L *acerbus*] Sour, sharp, harsh, rough, bitter, acerb.

acerbité (asɛrbite), s.f. Acerbity, harshness, sourness.

acère (asɛr), adj. [f. Gr. *a* + *keras*] (ent.) Hornless, without feelers.

acéré, -e (asere), p. adj. **1.** Steeled; **2.** sharp, acute, stinging, cutting.

acérer (asere), v.a. [f. *acier*] To steel; to sharpen.

acérure (aseryr), s.f. Piece of steel welded on the edge of tools.

acescence (asɛssɑ̃s), s.f. Acescence.

acescent, -e (asɛssɑ̃)), adj. [L *acescens*] Acescent, turning sour or acid.

acétabule (asetabyl), s.m. [L *acetabulum*] (anat. zool.) Acetabulum.

acétate (asetat), s.m. (chem.) Acetate.

acéteu-x, -se (asetø), adj. Acetous, tasting like vinegar.

acétification (asetifika'sjɔ̃), s.f. Acetification.

acétifier (asetifje), v.a. [f. L *acetum*] (chem.) To acetify.

acétique (asetik), adj. [f. L *acetum*] (chem.) Acetic.

acétol (asetɔl), s.m. Pharmaceutical vinegar.

acétomel (asetɔmɛl), s.m. Syrup of vinegar and honey.

acétone (asetɔn), s.f. (chem.) Acetone.

acétoselle (asetozɛl), s.f. (bot.) Wood-sorrel.

acétylène (asetilɛn), s.f. Acetylene; *lampe à ~*, acetylene lamp.

achalandage (aʃalɑ̃daʒ), s.m. Custom, customers, goodwill.

achalandé, -e (aʃalɑ̃de), p. adj. Having customers; *bien ~*, well frequented, doing good business.

achalander (aʃalɑ̃de), v.a. To draw customers to, to bring custom to.

acharné, -e (aʃarne), adj. Relentless, unremitting, eager (after); furious, desperate, ruthless, intent (on); (obs. hunt.) fleshed.

acharnement (aʃarnəmɑ̃), s.m. Fierceness, animosity, furious obstinacy; *mettre de l'~ à*, to do (something) with a furious obstinacy; to go at (a thing) like mad; *avec ~*, desperately.

acharner (aʃarne), v.a. [*à* + *chair*] To excite, to set on, to flesh (dogs, &c.) **s'~**, v.pr. (*sur*, *à*) to pursue furiously, to set about (a thing) furiously, to go at (a thing) furiously, to go at (a thing) like mad; *s'~ au travail*, to work unremittingly; *la malchance s'acharne sur lui*, ill luck pursues him relentlessly.

achat (aʃa), s.m. Purchase; *faire des ~s*, to go shopping; to buy.

ache (aʃ), s.f. [L *apium*] (bot.) Wild celery, smallage.

acheminement (aʃminmɑ̃), s.m. Forwarding; way, progress.

acheminer (aʃmine), v.a. [*à*+*cheminer*] To forward, to send on, to put in the way; **s'~**, v.pr. to make one's way (*vers*, towards); to proceed (towards).

achetable (aʃtabl), adj. Purchasable.

acheter (aʃte), v.a. [f. LL *accaptare*] To purchase, to buy; to bribe; (fig.) to pay for; *~ à vil prix*, to buy dirt-cheap; *~ chat en poche*, to buy a pig in a poke; *une expérience chèrement achetée*, a dearly bought experience; *~ un espion*, to bribe a spy; (slang) *~ X*, to make fun of X; to pull X's leg; **s'~**, v.pr. to be bought.

acheteu-r, -se (aʃtœr), s.m.f. Buyer, purchaser.

achevage. See syn. ACHÈVEMENT.

achevé, -e (aʃve), adj. Finished, complete, thorough, perfect; arrant, downright.

achèvement (aʃɛvmɑ̃), s.m. Completion, finishing; conclusion; syn. ACHEVAGE.

achever (aʃve), v.a. [f. L *ad*+*caput*] To complete, to end, to finish, to conclude, to put the finishing touch to; to achieve, to consummate; to kill, to do for, to dispatch; *n'achevez pas!*, say no more!; *achevez!*, have done with it!; *voilà qui va l'~*, that will do for him; *~ de lire*, to go on reading to the end (of); **s'~**, v.pr. to come to an end, to end, to be completed, to draw to its close; syn. FINIR, TERMINER, SE TERMINER.

achillée (akille), s.f. (bot.) Milfoil, yarrow.

achoppement (aʃɔpmɑ̃), s.m. Obstacle, hindrance, impediment, hitch; *pierre d'~*, stumbling-block.

achopper (aʃɔpe), v.n., and **s'~**, v.pr. To stumble; (fig.) to fail, to come to grief.

achromatique (akrɔmatik), adj. [f. Gr. *a*+*khrōma*] Achromatic.

aciculaire (asikylɛr), adj. [f. L *acus*] Acicular, needle-shaped.

acide (asid), adj. [L *acidus*] Acid, sour. ~, s.m. Acid.

acidifiable (asidifjabl), adj. Acidifiable.

acidifiant, -e (asidifjɑ̃), adj. Acidifying.

acidification (asidifika'sjɔ̃), s.f. Acidification.

acidifier (asidifje), v.a. To acidify; **s'~**, v.pr. to become acid.

acidimètre (asidimɛtr), s.m. Acidimeter.

acidimétrie (asidimetri), s.f. Acidimetry.

acidité (asidite), s.f. Acidity; (fig.) sourness, acidity.

acidulé, -e (asidyle), adj. Acidulous, acidulated, sourish.

aciduler (asidyle), v.a. To acidulate.

acier (asje), s.m. [f. L *acies*] Steel; *~ de cémentation*, blister steel; *~ doux*, mild steel; *~ fondu*, cast steel; *~ laminé*, rolled steel; *tôle d'~*, sheet steel; *~ chromé*, chrome steel; (fig.) *des muscles d'~*, muscles of steel.

aciérage (asjeraʒ), s.m. Acierage, steeling, plating with steel.

aciération (asjera'sjɔ̃), s.f. Steeling, converting into steel.

aciérer (asjere), v.a. To steel, to turn into steel.

aciéreu-x, -se (asjerø), adj. Steely; pertaining to steel.

aciérie (asjeri), s.f. Steel-works.

aclinique (aklinik), adj. [Gr. *aklines*] Aclinic.

acmé (akme), s.m. [Gr. wd] Acme.

acné (akne), s.m. [etym. dub.] (med.) Acne.

acolytat (akɔlita), s.m. Acolytate, order of acolytes.

acolyte (akɔlit), s.m. [Gr. *akolouthos*] Acolyte; attendant, second, assistant; (pej.) accomplice.

acompte (akɔ̃t), s.m. [*à*+*compte*] Partial payment in advance; instalment, payment on account.

acon, accon, (akɔ̃), s.m. (naut.) Flat-bottomed boat; punt.

aconit (akɔnit), s.m. [Gr. *akoniton*] (bot.) Aconite, wolf's-bane, monk's-hood.

aconitine (akɔnitin), s.f. (chem.) Aconitine.

acoquiner (akɔkine), v.a. [f. *coquin*] To entice, to allure, to captivate; **s'~**, v.pr. (pej.) to get fond of, to be bewitched, to grow accustomed, to cotton (with), to cotton up (to).

acotylédone (akɔtiledɔn), adj. [f. Gr. *a*+*kotulē*] (bot.) Acotyledonous. ~, s.f. Acotyledon.

à-coup (aku), s.m. Jerk; *par ~s*, by fits and starts; syn. SACCADE.

acoustique (akustik), s.f. [Gr. *akoustikos*] Acoustics. ~, adj. Acoustic; *cornet ~*, ear-trumpet.

acquéreur (akerœr), s.m. Buyer, purchaser; syn. ACHETEUR.

acquérir (akerir), v.a. [L *acquirere*] To acquire, to purchase, to buy; to get; ~, v.n. to improve; *il m'est tout acquis*, he is quite devoted to me; *il est acquis à la bonne cause*, he has been won over to the good cause; *bien mal acquis ne profite pas*, ill-gotten gains benefit no one; **s'~**, v.pr. to be got, to be acquired or won.

acquêt (akɛ), s.m. (law) Acquest, acquisition; *communauté réduite aux ~s*, marriage settlement in which future acquisitions or future property only are to be held in common.

acquiescement (akjɛsmɑ̃), s.m. Acquiescence, consent.

acquiescer (akjɛse), v.n. [L *acquiescere*] To acquiesce (*à*, in), to consent, to assent (*à*, to), to comply (with).

acquis, -e (aki), p. adj. Acquired; secured; *vitesse ~e*, acquired speed; *droits ~*, unquestionable rights.

acquis (aki), s.m. Experience, acquirements, previous knowledge.

acquisiti-f, -ve (akizitif), adj. Acquisitive.

acquisition (akizisjɔ̃), s.f. [L *acquisitio*] Acquisition; purchase.

acquisivité (akizivite), s.f. Acquisitiveness.

acquit (aki), s.m. Discharge, acquittance, receipt; *pour ~*, received; acquittal; *sentence d'~*, acquittal; *pour l'~ de sa conscience*, for conscience' sake; *par manière d'~*, for form's sake; *~ à caution*, (customs) transit tax.

acquittable (akitabl), adj. Acquittable, payable.

acquittement (akitmɑ̃), s.m. **1.** Payment; **2.** discharge, acquittal.

acquitter (akite), v.a. [*à* + *quitter*] **1.** To acquit, to discharge, to clear, to free; **2.** to perform, to fulfil; **3.** to pay, to pay off; **4.** to receipt; **s'~** (**de**), v.pr. **1.** to discharge (a debt); **2.** to perform, to execute; **3.** to deliver (a message); **4.** to be quits.

acre (akr), s.m. [L *ager*] Acre. (The old French *acre* was 52 ares. The English acre is 40½ ares.)

âcre (ɑkr), adj. [L *acer*] Acrid, sour, sharp.

âcrement (ɑkrəmɑ̃), adv. Sourly, bitterly, with acridity.

âcreté (ɑkrəte), s.f. Acridity, sourness.

acridie (akridi), s.f. (ent.) Cricket.

acrimonie (akrimɔni), s.f. [L *acrimonia*] Acrimony.

acrimonieusement (akrimɔnjøzmɑ̃), adv. Acrimoniously.

acrimonieu-x, -se (akrimɔnjø), adj. Acrimonious.

acrobate (akrɔbat), s.m.f. [f. Gr. *akros* + *batein*] Acrobat; rope-dancer; syn. JONGLEUR, ÉQUILIBRISTE, TRAPÉZISTE, &c.

acrobatie (akrɔbasi), s.f. Acrobatics, difficult performance; acrobatism; (aeron.) stunt.

acrobatique (akrɔbatik), adj. Acrobatic.

acrobatisme (akrɔbatism), s.m. Acrobatism.

acrocéphale (akrɔsefal), adj. (anat.) Acrocephalic.

acromion (akrɔmjɔ̃), s.m. (anat.) Acromion.

acropole (akrɔpɔl), s.f. [Gr. *akros* + *polis*] Acropolis.

acrostiche (akrɔstiʃ), s.m. [Gr. *akros* + *stichos*] Acrostic.

acrotère (akrɔtɛr), s.m. (arch.) Acroterium.

acte (akt), s.m. [L *actum*] **1.** Action, deed, act; **2.** transaction; document, instrument, title-deed, agreement, contract; certificate; acknowledgement; writ, resolution, bill, decree; *~s*, (pl.) registers, rolls, proceedings, transactions; *faire ~ de présence*, to make only a short appearance; to put in an appearance; to be present at (but not to participate in); *faire ~ de*, to declare, to show oneself; *~ de naissance*, birth-certificate; *prendre ~ de*, to note down; to require an acknowledgement of; *faire prendre ~ de*, to obtain registration of; to have a minute taken of; *donner ~*, to acknowledge, to deliver an official certificate.

act-eur, -rice (aktœr), s.m.f. Actor, actress, player.

acti-f, -ve (aktif), adj. Active; brisk, energetic, active, busy; able-bodied; *service ~*, active service; *dettes ~ves*, assets. **~**, s.m. (gram.) Active voice; (comm.) assets, credit account; *mettre à l'~ de X*, to credit X with; *avoir à son ~*, to have to one's credit.

actinie (aktini), s.f. (zool.) Sea-anemone, actinia.

actinique (aktinik), adj. [f. Gr. *aktis*] Actinic.

actinisme (aktinism), s.m. Actinism.

actinium (aktinjɔm), s.m. (chem.) Actinium.

actinomètre (aktinɔmɛtr), s.m. Actinometer.

action (aksjɔ̃), s.f. [L *actio*] **1.** Act, deed; **2.** movement, operation, influence, effect; **3.** gesture; **4.** lawsuit; **5.** engagement, encounter, battle; **6.** (Lit.) thread, 'story' in a novel or drama; **7.** step, action (of a horse); **8.** share (in a joint-stock company); *mauvaise ~*, evil deed; *~s de grâce*, thanksgiving; *être en ~*, *hors d'~*, to be in gear, out of gear; *~ de capital*, preference share; *~ de jouissance*, bonus share.

actionnable (aksjɔnabl), adj. (law) Actionable.

actionnaire (aksjɔnɛr), s.m.f. Shareholder, stock-holder.

actionner (aksjɔne), v.a. **1.** (law) To bring an action against, to action, to sue; **2.** to put in motion, to set going, to drive, to work, to operate.

activant, -e (aktivɑ̃), adj. Stimulating.

activation (aktivaˈsjɔ̃), s.f. Activation, rendering active.

activement (aktivmɑ̃), adv. Actively, energetically, briskly; (gram.) in an active sense.

ɔ, note, glotte; **ɔ̃**, monter, ronde; **ø**, feu, creux; **œ**, peur, sœur; **œ̃**, un; **ʃ**, chez, schisme; **u**, tout; **w**, oui, doit, douaire; **y**, mur, pu; **ɥ**, huile, muette; **z**, zèle, rose; **ʒ**, déjà, gentil.

activer (aktive), v.a. To quicken, to accelerate, to urge on, to press, to expedite; to spur on, to stir up; to poke (*le feu*, the fire); **s'~**, v.pr. to bustle, to bestir oneself, to hasten; (of things) to be quickened; *allons, activez !*, or *activez-vous !*, get a move on !, put some vim into it !
activité (aktivite), s.f. [f. L *activitas*] Activity, exertion of energy, diligence, nimbleness, briskness; spirit, vigour; bustle; active employment, active service; active forces.
actuaire (aktɥɛr), s.m.f. [L *actuarius*] Actuary.
actualisation (aktɥaliza'sjɔ̃), s.f. Actualization.
actualiser (aktɥalize), v.a. To actualize.
actualité (aktɥalite), s.f. Actuality, thing or event of present interest, topic of the hour; *ceci n'est pas d'~*, this is not of topical interest.
actuel, -le (aktɥɛl), adj. [LL *actualis*] Actual, of the present time, for the time being; of present interest; effective. ⚠ In English 'actual' has also, and generally, the sense of 'existing in fact', 'real' = *réel*.
actuellement (aktɥɛlmɑ̃), adv. Now, at present, for the time being; actually. ⚠ The most usual translation of English 'actually' is: *en fait, en réalité, réellement*.
acuité (akɥite), s.f. [f. L *acutus*] Acuteness, sharpness, keenness, pointedness.
aculé, -e (akyle), adj. [f. L *aculeus*] (ent.) Aculeate.
aculéiforme (akyleiform), adj. (bot.) Aculeiform, spine-shaped.
acuminé, -e (akymine), adj. [f. L *acumen*] (bot.) Acuminate.
acutangle (akytɑ̃gl), adj. (geom.) Acute-angled.
acutangulaire, acutangulé, -e (akytɑ̃gylɛr, acytɑ̃gyle), adj. Acute-angled.
acutesse (akytɛs), s.f. [f. L *acutus*] Acuteness.
adage (adaʒ), s.m. [L *adagium*] Adage, saying, proverb.
adagio (adaʒjo), s.m. [It. wd] Adagio.
adamantin, -e (adamɑ̃tɛ̃), adj. [f. Gr. *adamas, adamantos*] Adamantine.
adamique (adamik), adj. [f. *Adam*] Adamic.
adamite (adamit), s.m.f. Adamite.
adaptable (adaptabl), adj. Adaptable.
adaptation (adapta'sjɔ̃), s.f. Adaptation, fitting.
adapter (adapte), v.a. [f. L *ad* + *aptare*] To adapt, to fit, to adjust, to suit; **s'~**, v.pr. to adapt oneself (*à*, to); to fit, to apply (to), to suit.
additi-f, -ve (aditif), adj. Additive.
addition (adisjɔ̃), s.f. [L. *additio*] Addition, adding-up, sum; addition, thing added; bill, reckoning; (print.) side note.
additionnel, -le (adisjɔnɛl), adj. Additional.
additionner (adisjɔne), v.a. To add up; to add in; to cast up; to increase; *additionné d'eau*, diluted with water.
adducteur (addyktœr), adj. [f. L *ad* + *ducere*] Adducent. **~**, s.m. (anat.) Adductor.
adducti-f, -ve (addyktif), adj. Adducent.
adduction (addyksjɔ̃), s.f. [f. L *adductio*] Adduction.
adénite (adenit), s.f. [f. Gr. *adēn*] (path.) Adenitis.
adénoïde (adenɔid), adj. [f. Gr. *adēn*] Adenoid; *végétations ~s*, adenoids.
adent (adɑ̃), s.m. [f. *dent*] (join.) Dovetail, tenon.
adenter (adɑ̃te), v.a. To join with mortise and tenon.
adepte (adɛpt), s.m.f. [L *adeptus*] Adept.
adéquat, -e (adekwa), adj. [f. L *ad* + *aequare*] Adequate (*à*, to).
adhérence (aderɑ̃s), s.f. Adherence.
adhérent, -e (aderɑ̃), adj. Adherent. **~**, s.m.f. Adherent, supporter, follower, partisan.
adhérer (adere), v.n. [f. L *ad* + *haerere*] To adhere (*à*, to); to stick, to cling; to cleave.
adhési-f, -ve (adezif), adj. Adhesive, sticky.
adhésion (adezjɔ̃), s.f. Adhesion, adhering, concurrence, consent.
adhésivité (adezivite), s.f. Adhesivity.
adiabatique (adjabatik), adj. (phys.) Adiabatic.
adiante (adjɑ̃t), s.m. (bot.) Adiantum, maiden-hair (fern).
adieu (pl. x) (adjø), s.m. [*à* + *Dieu*] Adieu, farewell, good-bye; leave-taking; *faire ses ~x*, to take one's leave; *faire ses ~x à X*, to bid farewell to X; to take leave of X; *sans ~ !*, see you later !, good-bye for the present, so long !; *dire ~ à*, to renounce (a thing); to say good-bye to; *~ les plaisirs !*, good-bye to fun and good times !
adipeu-x, -se (adipø), adj. [f. L *adeps*] Adipose.
adiposité (adipozite), s.f. Adiposity.
adjacence (adʒasɑ̃s), s.f. Adjacency.
adjacent, -e (adʒasɑ̃), adj. [f. L *ad* + *jacere*] Adjacent, contiguous.
adjecti-f, -ve (adʒɛktif), adj. [L *adjectivus*] Adjective. **~**, s.m. (gram.) Adjective.
adjectivement (adʒɛktivmɑ̃), adv. Adjectively.
adjoindre (adʒwɛ̃dr), v.a. [L *ad* + *jungere*] To join, to join to, to adjoin, to add to, to associate; to assign as an assistant; **s'~**, v.pr. to take as an assistant, to associate (with).
adjoint, -e (adʒwɛ̃), adj. s.m.f. Assistant, deputy, associate; *~ au maire*, deputy-

mayor; *institutrice-~e*, assistant mistress; *commissaire ~*, joint commissioner.
adjonction (adʒɔ̃ksjɔ̃), s.f. Adjunction, addition.
adjudant (adʒydɑ̃), s.m. [f. L *adjuvare*] (mil.) Non-commissioned officer in the French army, above sergeant-major; *~ major*, adjutant (of a battalion); colloq. syn. (slang) ADJUPÈTE. ⚠ One must not confuse English 'adjutant' (who is always an officer) with French *adjudant* (=English N.C.O.).
adjudicataire (adʒydikatɛr), s.m.f. Highest bidder; contractor.
adjudicat-eur, -rice (adʒydikatœr), s.m.f. Awarder (of contracts), adjudicator.
adjudication (adʒydika'sjɔ̃), s.f. Adjudication; award of contract; auction sale, syn. VENTE AUX ENCHÈRES.
adjuger (adʒyʒe), v.a. [f. L *ad+judicare*] To adjuge, to adjudicate; to grant; to award; to knock down (at auction sale); *adjugé!*, gone!; (fig.) agreed! **s'~**, v.pr. to award to oneself.
adjupète. See ADJUDANT.
adjuration (adʒyra'sjɔ̃), s.f. Adjuration.
adjurer (adʒyre), v.a. [L *adjurare*] To adjure, to beseech, to call upon, to pray, to entreat.
adjuvant, -e (adʒyvɑ̃), adj. [f. L *ad+juvare*] Adjuvant, auxiliary.
admettre (admɛtr), v.a. [L *ad+mittere*] To admit, to admit of, to allow, to acknowledge, to recognize; to let in, to include; to accept, to concede; *faire ~ quelqu'un*, to obtain admittance or recognition for somebody; *faire ~ une idée*, to get an idea adopted, to obtain acceptance for an opinion; *j'admets que*, (in a discussion) I concede that; let it be granted that.
adminicule (adminikyl), s.m. [L *adminiculum*] Adminicle; subsidiary means.
administrat-eur, -rice (administratœr), s.m.f. Administrator, manager, manageress, director, governor, trustee; guardian, overseer, executor.
administrat-if, -ve (administratif), adj. Administrative.
administration (administra'sjɔ̃), s.f. **1.** Administration, management, direction, government, conduct; **2.** ministration, ministering; **3.** committee, council, directorate, managers; **4.** offices, office; **5.** trusteeship, guardianship; **6.** (of legal evidence), production; *conseil d'~*, governing body, directors; *~ des sacrements*, administration of the sacraments.
administrativement (administrativmɑ̃), adv. Administratively.
administrer (administre), v.a. [L *ad+ministrare*] **1.** To administer, to manage, to direct, to rule; **2.** to dispense, to confer, to distribute, to minister; **3.** to apply; **4.** to administer the last sacrament to; **5.** to produce (legal evidence). **s'~**, v.pr. **1.** To be administered; **2.** to give oneself, to take, to offer oneself, to inflict upon oneself; to give each other.
admirable (admirabl), adj. Admirable, wonderful.
admirablement (admirabləmɑ̃), adv. Admirably, wonderfully.
admirat-eur, -rice (admiratœr), s.m.f. Admirer.
admirati-f, -ve (admiratif), adj. Admiring.
admiration (admira'sjɔ̃), s.f. [f. L *admiratio*] Admiration, wonder; *faire l'~ de*, to elicit the admiration of; *saisi d'~*, struck with wonder.
admirativement (admirativmɑ̃), adv. Admiringly, with admiration.
admirer (admire), v.a. [f. L *ad+mirari*] To admire, to wonder at; **s'~**, v.pr. to admire oneself; to admire each other; to be admired.
admissibility (admisibilite), s.f. [f. *admettre*] Admissibility.
admissible (admisibl), adj. Admissible; allowable; receivable; plausible.
admission (admisjɔ̃), s.f. [L *admissio*] Admission; admittance; acknowledgement.
admixtion (admikstjɔ̃), s.f. [f. L *ad+miscere*] Admixture.
admonestation (admɔnɛsta'sjɔ̃), s.f. Admonition, reproof, admonishment.
admonester (admɔnɛste), v.a. [f. L *admonere*] To admonish, to reprimand, to lecture.
admonition (admɔnisjɔ̃), s.f. Admonition, warning.
adné, -e (adne), adj. (bot.) Adnate.
adolescence (adɔlɛssɑ̃s), s.f. [f. L *adolescere*] Adolescence, youth.
adolescent, -e (adɔlɛssɑ̃), adj. Adolescent. **~**, s.m. Youth, lad, stripling. **~e**, s.f. Girl, maiden, lass.
adonc, adoncques (adɔ̃k), adv. Then; well, then.
adonide (adɔnid), s.f. (bot.) Adonis, pheasant's eye.
adonien, adonique (adɔnjɛ̃, adɔnik), adj. (pros.) Adonic (metre; i.e. dactyl + spondee).
adonis (adɔnis), s.m. [f. *Adonis*] Adonis, beau; (bot.) adonis.
adoniser (adɔnize), v.a. [f. *Adonis*] To bedizen, to deck out, to adonize; **s'~**, v.pr. to bedizen oneself.
adonné, -e (adɔne), adj. Addicted (*à*, to).
(s')adonner (sadɔne), v.pr. To addict oneself (*à*, to), to devote oneself, to apply oneself.
adoptable (adɔptabl), adj. Adoptable.
adoptant, -e (adɔptɑ̃), s.m.f. Adopter.
adopter (adɔpte), v.a. [f. L *ad+optare*] To adopt; to take (as), to choose, to

admit, to approve, to sanction; to pass, to carry; to embrace, to espouse.

adopti-f, -ve (adɔptif), adj. Adoptive.

adoption (adɔpsjɔ̃), s.f. Adoption; admission, carrying.

adorable (adɔrabl), adj. Adorable; charming, divine.

adorablement (adɔrabləmɑ̃), adv. Adorably, divinely.

adorat-eur, -rice (adɔratœr), s.m.f. Adorer, worshipper, admirer, lover.

adoration (adɔra'sjɔ̃), s.f. Worship, adoration.

adorer (adɔre), v.a.n. [L *adorare*] To adore, to worship, to idolize, to be extremely fond of; **s'~**, v.pr. to idolize oneself; to adore each other, to dote upon each other.

ados (ado), s.m. (hort.) Sloping bed.

adosser (adose), v.a. [f. *dos*] To place or fix the back of (*à*, *contre*, against), to lean (against); to put back to back; **s'~**, v.pr. to lean one's back (against).

adouber (adube), v.a. [f. OHG *dubban*] To repair, to armour; (at chess) to touch a piece without moving it.

adoucir (adusir), v.a. [f. *doux*] To soften, to soothe, to smooth; to sweeten, to allay, to assuage, to alleviate, to make easier; **s'~**, v.pr. to grow mild; to soften; (of weather) to grow milder.

adoucissant, -e (adusisɑ̃), p. adj. Softening, soothing, lenitive. ~, s.m. Emollient.

adoucissement (adusismɑ̃), s.m. Softening, soothing, smoothing, sweetening; mitigation, assuagement; abatement; consolation.

adoué, -e (adwe), adj. (hunt.) Paired.

adragante (adragɑ̃t), adj.f. [corrupt. of *tragacanthe*] Tragacanth.

adrénaline (adrenalin), s.f. (therap.) Adrenalin.

adresse (adrɛs), s.f. [*à* + *droit*, *dresser*] **1.** Dexterity, skill, adroitness, address, handiness; **2.** shrewdness, cunning, adroitness, tact; **3.** direction, address (of a letter, of a person), superscription; **4.** address, petition, motion, vote of thanks; *à l'~ de*, directed to; intended for, pointed at; *ce sarcasme est allé à son ~*, this sarcasm struck home; *tour d'~*, legerdemain, sleight-of-hand trick; *avec ~*, adroitly, cleverly.

adresser (adrɛse), v.a. To address, to direct; to send, to forward; to offer up (a prayer); to aim, to hit; **s'~** (*à*), v.pr. to address oneself (to), to apply (to), to have recourse (to), to look (to), to apply (to); to speak; to be addressed, directed aimed (at); *s'~ ici*, inquire or apply within; *c'est à vous que je m'adresse*, I am speaking to you; *s'~ mal*, to get into the wrong bus; *ah! vous vous adressez bien!*, (iron.) you have, indeed, well chosen your man, (or your place, or your moment); you have mistaken your man.

adroit, -e (adrwa), adj. Dexterous, skilful, handy, adroit; clever; shrewd, sharp; crafty, cunning, artful.

adroitement (adrwatmɑ̃), adv. Dexterously, skilfully; adroitly, cunningly.

adulat-eur, -rice (adylatœr), s.m.f. Adulator, flatterer, sycophant. ~, adj. Adulatory, sycophantic.

adulation (adyla'sjɔ̃), s.f. Adulation, flattery, sycophancy.

adulatoire (adylatwar), adj. Adulatory.

aduler (adyle), v.a. [f. L *adulari*] To adulate, to fawn on, to flatter, to cringe to; syn. ENCENSER.

adulte (adylt), adj. s.m.f. [L *adultus*] Adult, grown up.

adultérateur (adylteratœr), s.m. Adulterator.

adultération (adyltera'sjɔ̃), s.f. Adulteration, falsification.

adultère (adyltɛr), adj. [f. L *adulter*] Adulterous. ~, s.m.f. Adulterer, adulteress. ~, s.m. Adultery.

adultérer (adyltere), v.a. To adulterate, to falsify.

adultérin, -e (adylterɛ̃), adj. Adulterine.

aduste (adyst), adj. [L *adustus*] Sunburnt, scorched, adust, parched.

advenir (advənir), v.n. impers. [L *ad*+*venire*] To happen, to occur, to come to pass; to befall, to fall; to become (of), to come (of), to fare; *advienne que pourra*, come what may; *il advint que*, it chanced that; *il m'advint une telle aventure*, such an adventure (experience) befell me; *que lui est-il advenu?*, what has happened to him?; *qu'est-il advenu de lui?*, what has become of him?; *qu'en est-il advenu?*, what has come of it?

adventice (advɑ̃tis), adj. [L *adventicius*] Adventitious.

adventi-f, -ve (advɑ̃tif), adj. (bot.) Adventitious; (law) casual.

adverbe (advɛrb), s.m. [f. L *ad*+*verbum*] Adverb.

adverbial, -e, (aux) (advɛrbjal), adj. Adverbial.

adverbialement (advɛrbjalmɑ̃), adv. Adverbially.

adversaire (advɛrsɛr), s.m. [f. L *adversus*] Adversary, antagonist, opponent, enemy, foe; rival.

adversati-f, -ve (advɛrsatif), adj. (gram.) Adversative.

adverse (advɛrs), adj. [L *adversus*] Adverse, contrary, opposite, opposing; hostile, inimical; calamitous; *la partie ~*, the opposite side; *la fortune ~*, adversity.

adversité (advɛrsite), s.f. Adversity, misfortune, adverse fortune.

adynamie (adinami), s.f. Adynamia, want of vital force.

aède (aɛd), s.m. [Gr. *aoidos*] Epic poet, bard (in Gr. antiquity).

aérage (aeraʒ), s.m., **aération** (aera'sjɔ̃), s.f. Airing, ventilation, ventilating; *puits d'*~, air-shaft.

aérer (aere), v.a. [f. Gr. *aēr*] To air, to ventilate; **s'**~, v.pr. to be ventilated.

aérien, -ne (aerjɛ̃), adj. Aerial; airy; ethereal, elfish.

aérifère (aerifɛr), adj. Conducting air.

aériforme (aerifɔrm), adj. Aeriform.

aérodrome (aerɔdrom), s.m. Aerodrome.

aérodynamique (aerodinamik), s.f. Aerodynamics.

aerolithe (aerɔlit), s.m. [f. Gr. *aēr*+*lithos*] Aerolite, aerolith.

aéromètre (aerɔmɛtr), s.m. [f. Gr. *aēr*+ *metron*] Aerometer.

aérométrie (aerɔmetr), s.f. Aerometry.

aéronaute (aerɔnot), s.m. [f. Gr. *aēr*+ *nautēs*] Aeronaut.

aéronautique (aerɔnotik), adj. Aeronautic(al). ~, s.f. Aeronautics, aerial navigation.

aéronef (aerɔnɛf), s.m. Airship, aircraft.

aérophagie (aerofaʒi), s.f. (pathol.) Aerophagy.

aérophobie (aerofɔbi), s.f. (pathol.) Aerophobia.

aéroplane (aerɔplan), s.m. Aeroplane, flying-machine, plane, airplane.

aérostat (aerɔsta), s.m. [f. Gr. *aēr*+*statos*] Aerostat, balloon, airship.

aérostation (aerɔsta'sjɔ̃), s.f. Aerostation, air-navigation.

aérostatique (aerɔstatik), adj. Aerostatic. ~, s.f. Aerostatics.

aérostier (aerɔstje), s.m. Aeronaut, air navigator, balloonist.

aérotechnique (aerotɛknik), adj. s.f. Aerotechnic, aeronautics.

aétite (aetit), s.f. (min.) Eagle-stone, aetites.

affabilité (afabilite), s.f. Affability, courteousness.

affable (afabl), adj. [L *affabilis*] Affable, courteous, benign.

affablement (afabləmɑ̃), adv. Affably, courteously.

affabulation (afabyla'sjɔ̃), s.f. [L *affabulatio*] Plot; moral (of a fable).

affadir (afadir), v.a. [f. *fade*] To make insipid; to deaden, to flatten; to cloy, to pall, to satiate.

affadissant, -e (afadisɑ̃), adj. Sickening, mawkish, insipid.

affadissement (afadismɑ̃), s.m. Growing insipid or dull; sickening.

affaiblir (afɛblir), v.a. [f. *faible*] To weaken, to enfeeble; to debilitate; to impair; to lessen, to alleviate, to abate, to soften; to unman; to damp; **s'**~, v.pr. to grow weaker, to decline, to flag; to abate.

affaiblissant, -e (afɛblisɑ̃), adj. Weakening, debilitating.

affaiblissement (afɛblismɑ̃), s.m. Weakening, decline, debilitation, enfeebling, decay; (of coins) debasement.

affaire (afɛr), s.f. [*à*+*faire*] **1.** Affair, business, matter; ~ *de cœur*, matter of feeling; love affair; ~ *d'argent*, money matter; *être à son* ~, to be interested, to be on one's own subject; *être tout à son* ~, to be engrossed in one's pursuit, or business, or occupation; *être en* ~*s*, to be engaged or busy; ~ *de rien*, trifle; trifling business; *en voilà une* ~*!*, what a to-do!, what a fuss!; *assoupir une* ~, to hush up a scandal; *chacun son* ~, let the cobbler stick to his last; *le meilleur de l'*~, the cream of the matter or of the joke; *il ne se tient pas à son* ~, he does not stick to his trade (or occupation); **2.** transaction, speculation, deal, job, bargain; *a-t-il trouvé* ~*?*, has he found a job? ; *c'est un faiseur d'*~*s*, he is a stock-jobber, a company-promoter; *être en* ~*s avec X*, to have business with X, to do business with X; *c'est une* ~ *d'or*, this is a real bargain; *pour* ~*s*, on business; *être bien* (*mal*) *dans ses* ~*s*, to be well (badly) off, to be in good (poor) circumstances; *être au-dessus de ses* ~*s*, to have money to spare; *être dans les* ~*s*, to be in business; *avez-vous fait* ~*?*, have you done business? ; *on ne fait plus d'*~*s*, business is at a standstill; *faire de bonnes* ~*s*, to drive a good trade; to succeed in business; *faire de mauvaises* ~*s*, to sell at a loss, to be on the road to bankruptcy; *avoir* ~ *à forte partie*, to have to deal with a tough customer; *homme d'*~*s*, business man; *cabinet d'*~*s*, general agency; *les* ~*s sont les* ~*s*, business is business; **3.** question, concern, duty; *cela, c'est mon* ~, that is my business, or my look-out, or my own concern; *j'en fais mon* ~, I take all responsibility for the matter; I will see to it; I will take it in hand; *cela ne fait rien à l'*~, that has nothing to do with the question; *je ne raconte pas mes* ~*s*, I keep my concerns to myself; *mêlez-vous de vos* ~*s* (or *de ce qui vous regarde*), mind your own business; *ce serait bien son* ~, that would suit him perfectly; that would be exactly in his line; *ceci fera l'*~, this will do, this will do well enough; **4.** law-suit; ~ *civile*, cause; ~ *criminelle*, criminal case, prosecution, trial; quarrel, scrape; *faire une* ~ *à X*, to pick a quarrel with X; to draw X into a quarrel, a scrape; **5.** action, engagement; *ce n'est pas sa première* ~, it is not his first duel; he has been in other rows before; *l'*~ *fut chaude*, it was warm work; it was a keen fight, a hard battle;

difficulty, trouble; *se tirer d'~*, to shift for oneself, to get out of a difficulty, to escape scot free; to get on; **6.** belongings, luggage, movables; *emportez vos ~s*, take your things away; *il a laissé toutes ses ~s dans sa chambre*, he has left all his luggage in his room; **7.** situation, state of things; *dites-moi l'état des ~s*, tell me how things stand; point, object, aim; *vous n'êtes pas à l'~*, you do not follow, you do not see the point; *mon ~ est de gagner du temps*, my object is to gain time; **8.** need, want; *voilà mon ~*, this is what I was looking for, that suits me to a T; *ça ne fait pas mon ~*, this is not what I want; that's a nuisance; I don't like that; **9.** end, finishing blow; *il lui a fait son ~*, he did for him, he dealt him a death-blow; *régler son ~ à X*, to 'do for' X; *son ~ est faite*, he is ruined; he is past recovery; it is all over with him; *il est hors d'~*, he is out of danger; **10.** (pl.) public affairs, office; *reviendra-t-il aux ~s?*, will he return to power?; *son passage aux ~s fut court*, he was not long in office, in the cabinet, in politics, in Parliament; **11.** (fam. loc.) *la belle ~!*, stuff and nonsense!; it's not worth speaking of; *l'~ est dans le sac*, the matter is (satisfactorily) settled; it's getting on swimmingly; (U.S.) it's a cinch!

affairé, -e (afɛre), adj. Busy, in a bustle, bustling; *il fait l'~*, he pretends to be busy.

affairement (afɛrmɑ̃), s.m. Press of business, bustle.

affaissé, -e (afɛse), adj. Depressed; sunk; bent or bowed down; weighed down; in low spirits.

affaissement (afɛsmɑ̃), s.m. Subsidence, collapse, depression, weakness.

affaisser (afɛse), v.a. [f. *faix*] To weigh down, to depress; **s'~**, v.pr. to sink, to subside, to collapse, to fall in, to sag, to crumple up.

affaiter (afɛte), v.a. [f. L *affectare*] **1.** To train (hawks); **2.** to dress (leather).

affalé, -e (affale), adj. (naut.) Adrift on a lee shore; (often used fig.) sprawling; *il était ~ sur un divan*, he was lolling on a sofa.

affaler (afale), v.a. [Dutch *afhalen*] (naut.) To haul down (rope, &c.); to drive ashore; **s'~**, v.pr. (naut.) to be driven ashore; (colloq.) to let oneself fall into an armchair, to crumple up, to collapse in a heap.

affamé, -e (afame), adj. Hungry, famished, starving, starved; *ventre ~ n'a pas d'oreilles*, hungry man, angry man; (fig.) greedy (*de*, for), eager (for), hungering (after) or thirsting (for). **~**, s.m.f. Starveling.

affamer (afame), v.a. [f. *à*+(L) *fames*] To famish, to starve, to reduce (an enemy) by blockade.

affameu-r, -se (afamœr), s.m.f. One who causes others to starve.

affectation (afɛktaˈsjɔ̃), s.f. [L *affectatio*] **1.** Destination, appropriation, attribution; **2.** affectation, mannerism, pretension, airs, preciosity, gush; see syn. AFFÉTERIE.

affecté, -e (afɛkte), p. adj. Affected, mincing, lackadaisical; *elle est terriblement ~e*, she is a mass of affectation.

affecter (afɛkte), v.a. [L *affectare*] **1.** To allot; to destine, to appropriate; **2.** to feign, to sham; **3.** to move, to influence, to touch; **4.** to be in or take the form of; *~ une forme pyramidale*, to be in the form of a pyramid; **s'~**, v.pr. to be affected; to grieve.

affecti-f, -ve (afɛktif), adj. Affective.

affection (afɛksjɔ̃), s.f. [L *affectio*] Affection, fondness, attachment, liking; (med.) affection, disease; *prendre X en ~*, to take a liking (or a fancy) to X; *marques d'~*, tokens of affection.

affectionné, -e (afɛksjɔne), adj. Affectionate, loving.

affectionnément (afɛksjɔnemɑ̃), adv. Affectionately.

affectionner (afɛksjɔne), v.a. To like, to have a liking for, to be partial to, to take kindly to.

affectivité (afɛktivite), s.f. Affectivity.

affectueusement (afɛktɥøzmɑ̃), adv. Affectionately, kindly.

affectueu-x, -se (afɛktɥø), adj. Affectionate, kind, warm-hearted.

affenage (afnaʒ), s.m. [f. L *faenum*] The act of foddering.

afférent, -e (aferɑ̃), adj. [L *afferre*] Belonging, appertaining, pertaining, accruing (*à*, to); (anat.) afferent.

affermable (afɛrmabl), adj. Rentable, farmable.

affermage (afɛrmaʒ), s.m. Renting, farming.

affermer (afɛrme), v.a. [f. *ferme*] **1.** To let out on lease; **2.** to farm, to rent; syn. LOUER.

affermir (afɛrmir), v.a. [f. *ferme*] To strengthen, to fix, to make firm; (fig.) to confirm, to consolidate, to fortify; **s'~**, v.pr. to grow stronger, to establish oneself, to confirm oneself; to encourage or fortify each other.

affermissement (afɛrmismɑ̃), s.m. Strengthening, hardening, confirmation.

affété, -e (afete), adj. [f. L *affectare*] Affected, finical.

afféterie (afetri), s.f. Affectation, mannerism, affectedness, primness, finicalness.

affichage (afiʃaʒ), s.m. Placarding, bill-sticking, bill-posting.

affiche (afiʃ), s.f. [*à+fiche*] Poster, bill, placard; ~ *électorale*, election poster; ~ *de théâtre*, play-bill; *poser une* ~, to post a bill; *homme* ~, sandwich-man; *petites* ~*s*, advertising sheet; *notre pièce tient l'*~ *depuis deux mois*, our play has been running two months.

afficher (afiʃe), v.a. **1.** To placard, to stick up, to post up; *défense d'*~, stick no bills; **2.** to affect, to make a show of, to parade; *il affiche ses préférences*, he shows partiality; **3.** to publish, to proclaim; **s'**~, v.pr. to expose oneself; to attract notice; to set up (for); *s'*~ *avec X*, to parade one's relations with X, to make oneself conspicuous with X.

afficheur (afiʃœr), s.m. Bill-sticker, bill-poster.

affidé, -e (afide), adj. [It. *affidato*] Trusty. ~, s.m.f. Member of a secret society, secret agent; gangster.

affilage (afilaʒ), s.m. [f. *fil*] Sharpening, setting, whetting.

affilé, -e (afile), adj. Sharp, cutting; *avoir la langue bien* ~*e*, to have a glib, sharp or caustic tongue; *d'*~*e*, adv. loc. running; uninterruptedly, at a stretch; right off the reel.

affiler (afile), v.a. [f. *fil*] To sharpen, to whet, to put an edge on.

affileur (afilœr), s.m. Sharpener, knife-grinder.

affiliation (afilja'sjɔ̃), s.f. Affiliation.

affilié, -e (afilje), adj. Affiliated. ~, s.m.f. Affiliated member.

affilier (afilje), v.a. [L *affiliare*] To affiliate; **s'**~, v.pr. to affiliate oneself, to become affiliated (*à*, to, with), to join.

affiloir (afilwar), s.m. [f. *affiler*] Sharpener, whetstone, hone, steel, strop, sharpening-machine.

affinage, affinement (afinaʒ, afinmɑ̃), s.m. Refining, fining, finishing.

affiner (afine), v.a. [*à+fin*] **1.** To refine, to purify; to extract the best of or from; ~ *le plomb*, to extract silver from lead ore; **2.** to heckle (flax); **3.** to finish, to give a finishing touch to; (fig.) to improve, to make finer, more delicate, more expressive.

affinerie (afinri), s.f. Refinery; refining-hearth.

affineu-r, -se (afinœr), s.m.f. Refiner.

affinité (afinite), s.f. [L *affinitas*] Affinity; similarity, liking, attraction; (chem.) affinity.

affiquet (afikɛ), s.m. [OF *affique*] **1.** Knitting-sheath; **2.** trinket, bauble, frills, dress accessories.

affirmati-f, -ve (afirmatif), adj. Affirmative. ~**ve**, s.f. Affirmative; *répondre par l'*~, to answer in the affirmative.

affirmation (afirma'sjɔ̃), s.f. [f. L *affirmatio*] Affirmation; assertion, asseveration.

affirmativement (afirmativmɑ̃), adv. Affirmatively, in the affirmative.

affirmer (afirme), v.a. [L *affirmare*] **1.** To affirm; to assert, to aver; **2.** to declare on oath; ~ *sa créance*, to prove one's claim.

affistoler (afistɔle), v.a. (colloq.) To deck, to dress.

affixe (afiks), s.m. [L *affixus*] (gram.) Affix.

affleurage (aflœraʒ), s.m. Dilution of the pulp in paper-making.

affleurement (aflœrmɑ̃), s.m. Levelling; (geol.) outcrop; cropping-out.

affleurer (aflœre), v.a. [f. *à+fleur*]. To level, to make flush; ~, v.n. to be level or flush; to crop out.

afflicti-f, -ve (afliktif), adj. Afflictive, affecting the person; corporal.

affliction (afliksjɔ̃), s.f. [L *afflictio*] Affliction, distress, pain, sorrow, calamity; syn. CHAGRIN, PEINE.

affligé, -e (afliʒe), p. adj. Afflicted, distressed, grieved, sorrowful; ~ *de*, affected by; distressed with. ~, s.m.f. Sufferer.

affligeant, -e (afliʒɑ̃), p. adj. Distressing, saddening, sad.

affliger (afliʒe), v.a. [L *affligere*] To afflict, to distress, to grieve; to mortify; **s'**~, v.pr. to grieve, to mourn, to fret.

afflouer (aflue), v.a. [f. *à+flot*] (naut.) To set afloat, to refloat.

affluence (aflɥɑ̃s), s.f. [L *affluentia*] Affluence, crowd, throng; influx, flow, abundance; concourse.

affluent, -e (aflɥɑ̃), adj. Affluent, tributary. ~, s.m. Affluent, tributary stream.

affluer (aflɥe), v.n. [L *affluere*] To flow, to run; to abound, to arrive in abundance; to flock, to crowd, to rush.

afflux (afly), s.m. Afflux; rush.

affolant, -e (afɔlɑ̃), p. adj. Maddening, bewildering; infatuating, exciting.

affolé, -e (afɔle), p. adj. Maddened, bewildered; infatuated (*par*, with); (of magnetic needle), defective, deranged.

affolement (afɔlmɑ̃), s.m. Distraction, panic, terror, excessive excitement; infatuation, fascination.

affoler (afɔle), v.a. To madden, to disturb, to make dizzy; to infatuate; to excite; to strike with panic, or terror; **s'**~, v.pr. to lose control; to get excited; to become unable to think logically or consequently; *ne nous affolons pas*, let us keep cool (or take things quietly).

affouage (afuaʒ), s.m. [OF *affouer*, to heat, f. *feu*] **1.** Estovers, firebote = right of cutting firewood; **2.** supply of fuel; **3.** (feudal) hearth-tax.

affouillement (afujmɑ̃), s.m. Undermining (by water).

affouiller (afuje), v.a. To undermine, to wash away.

affourrager (afuraʒe), v.a. To fodder, to give fodder to.
affourche (afurʃ), s.f. (naut.) Small bower anchor; two anchors and cable.
affourcher (afurʃe), v.a. (naut.) To moor with two anchors.
affranchi, -e (afrɑ̃ʃi), p. adj. **1.** Freed; emancipated; **2.** postage-paid, stamped, prepaid. **~**, s.m.f. Freedman, freedwoman; (slang) member of a criminal gang.
affranchir (afrɑ̃ʃir), v.a. [f. *franc*] **1.** To free; to enfranchise; to emancipate; to liberate; to deliver, to relieve, to discharge, to set free; to absolve (from blame); **2.** to frank, to stamp (letters); to prepay (carriage, postage); **3.** to fire (new casks); **4.** to castrate; **s'~**, v.pr. to free or rid oneself (*de*, of) (or get free, get rid of); to shake off; (abs.) to purchase one's freedom, to become independent.
affranchissement (afrɑ̃ʃismɑ̃), s.m. **1.** Enfranchisement, setting-free, liberation, releasing; emancipation; exemption, discharge; **2.** prepayment, postage; **~** *insuffisant*, insufficiently stamped.
affres (afr), s.f.pl. [OHG *eivar*] Terrors, pangs, dread.
affrètement (afrɛtmɑ̃), s.m. Chartering, freighting.
affréter (afrete), v.a. [f. *fret*] To charter, to freight.
affréteur (afretœr), s.m. Charterer, freighter.
affreusement (afrøzmɑ̃), adv. Frightfully, dreadfully, shockingly, horribly.
affreu-x, -se (afrø), adj. Frightful, dreadful, horrible; shocking; syn. HORRIBLE.
affriander (afriɑ̃de), v.a. [f. *friand*] To entice, to lure, to tempt.
affricher (afriʃe), v.a. [f. *friche*] (agric.) To leave fallow.
affriolant, -e (afriɔlɑ̃), p. adj. Alluring, tempting.
affrioler (afriɔle), v.a. To allure, to tempt, to entice.
affront (afrɔ̃), s.m. [*à*+*front*] **1.** Affront, insult, wrong, outrage; *essuyer* (*subir*, *dévorer*, *boire*) *un* **~**, to receive (put up with, pocket) an affront; *faire* **~** *à X*, to disgrace X, to shame X; syn. INSULTE, OUTRAGE, AVANIE.
affronté, -e (afrɔ̃te), p. adj. (herald.) Affrontée, placed face to face.
affronter (afrɔ̃te), v.a. **1.** To put face to face and level; **2.** to face; to brave, to confront. ⚠ Not to be translated by 'to affront', which means 'to insult openly' = *insulter*.
affruiter (afrɥite), v.a. [f. *fruit*] To plant with fruit-trees.
affublement (afybləmɑ̃), s.m. Rig-out, 'get-up', grotesque garb.
affubler (afyble), v.a. [LL *affibulare*] To rig out; to dress up, to wrap up, to muffle up; **s'~**, v.pr. to rig oneself out, to dress grotesquely.
affusion (affyzjɔ̃), s.f. [f. L *affundere*] Affusion, pouring-on.
affût (afy), s.m. [*à* + OF *fust* or *fût*; L *fustis*] **1.** Gun-carriage; **2.** hiding-place; *chasser à l'~*, to shoot from cover; *être à l'~*, to be on the watch, (*de*, for) to lie in wait; **3.** look-out; *vivre à l'~ des bonnes occasions*, to live with an eye on the main chance; to be continually on the look-out.
affûtage (afytaʒ), s.m. Sharpening; set or chest of tools.
affûter (afyte), v.a. [f. *affût*] To sharpen, to whet, to grind; syn. AIGUISER.
affûteur (afytœr), s.m. **1.** Sharpener, knife-grinder; **2.** one who fires from cover.
affutiau (pl. -x) (afytjo), s.m. Trinket, frills, knick-knack.
afghan, -e (afgɑ̃), adj. s.m.f. Afghan.
afin (afɛ̃), conj. [*à*+*fin*] **~** *de*, in order to, so as to; **~** *que*, in order that, so that, that.
afistoler. See AFFISTOLER.
africain, -e (afrikɛ̃), adj. s.m.f. African.
aga, agha (aga), s.m. [Turk. wd] Aga.
agaçant, -e (agasɑ̃), adj. Teasing, annoying, aggravating, irritating, provoking; exciting; enticing.
agacement (agasmɑ̃), s.m. Irritation, setting on edge.
agacer (agase), v.a. [etym. dub.] **1.** To set (the teeth) on edge; to irritate; to plague; to torment; (fam.) *ça l'agace*, it gets his goat; **2.** to incite, to excite, to allure, to entice; (fig.) to set one's cap at; **s'~**, v.pr. to be irritated; to tease each other.
agacerie (agasri), s.f. Allurement, flirtation, advance, provocation; *elle lui fait des ~s*, she is setting her cap at him.
agame (agam), adj. [f. Gr. *a*+*gamos*] (bot.) Agamous.
agami (agami), s.m. [native wd, Guiana] (ornith.) Agami, trumpeter-bird.
agape (agap), s.f. [Gr. wd] **1.** Agape, love-feast (of primitive Christians); **2.** banquet, feast, brotherly meal.
agar-agar (agaragar), s.m. (bot., pharm.) Agar-agar.
agaric (agarik), s.m. (bot.) [L *agaricum*] Agaric, mushroom.
agasse, ajasse (agas, aʒas), s.f. [OHG *agalstra*] Magpie; syn. PIE.
agate (agat), s.f. [L *achates*] (min.) Agate.
agave (agav), s.m. [f. Gr. *agauē*] (bot.) Agave, American aloe.
age (aʒ), s.m. [Germ. *haga*] Plough-beam.
âge (aʒ), s.m. [OF *aage, edage, eage*; f. L *aevum*] **1.** Age, duration of life; **2.** age, period of life; *bas* **~**, infancy, childhood; *fleur de l'~*, prime of life; **~** *viril*, **~**

d'homme, manhood, man's estate; ~ *de raison*, years of discretion; *entre deux ~s*, middle-aged; *porter son ~*, to look one's age; *être d'~ à*, to be old enough to; *l'~ n'est que pour les chevaux*, nothing's old but the devil; *on apprend à tout ~*, it is never too late to learn; *elle ne porte pas son ~*, she carries her years well; **3.** old age; *prendre de l'~*, to grow old; *c'est un homme d'~*, he is an old man; *le poids de l'~*, the weight of years; **4.** number of years; *quel ~ a-t-il ?*, how old is he?; *il est de mon ~*, he is of my age (as old as I); *hors d'~*, (of horses) more than seven years old; **5.** period, epoch, time, century; *le Moyen Âge*, the Middle Ages; *l'~ de Victoria*, the Victorian era; *d'~ en ~*, from generation to generation.

âgé, -e (aʒe), adj. Aged, old; ~ *de 10 ans*, ten years old.

agence (aʒɑ̃s), s.f. [f. *agent*] Agency, office, bureau; ~ *de placement*, employment bureau.

agencement (aʒɑ̃smɑ̃), s.m. Arrangement, disposition, order; fitting-up, fixtures; (Lit.) composition.

agencer (aʒɑ̃se), v.a. To arrange, to dispose, to fit up; to combine, to order.

agenda (aʒɛ̃da), s.m. [L wd] Note-book, diary. ⚠ Not to be translated by English 'agenda', which means: 'things to be done', 'items to be considered', 'programme of the day's work' = *ordre du jour*; *programme de travail*.

agénésie (aʒenezi), s.f. [f. Gr. *a+genesis*] Sterility, impotence.

agenouillement (aʒnujmɑ̃), s.m. Kneeling.

(s')agenouiller (saʒnuje), v.pr. [f. *genou*] To kneel down.

agenouilloir (aʒnujwar), s.m. Kneeling-stool, hassock; syn. PRIE-DIEU.

agent (aʒɑ̃), s.m. [LL *agens*, It. *agente*] Agent; intermediary; middleman; policeman; medium; ~ *d'affaires*, agent, business man; ~ *de change*, stock-broker; ~ *de circulation*, circulating medium, currency; ~ *comptable*, accountant; ~ *de police*, policeman.

agglomérat (aglɔmera), s.m. (geol., min.) Conglomerate, agglomerate.

agglomération (aglɔmera'sjɔ̃), s.f. Agglomeration; village, town.

agglomérés (aglɔmere), s.m.pl. Compressed or patent fuel, briquettes.

agglomérer (aglɔmere), v.a. and **s'~**, v.pr. [L *agglomerare*] To agglomerate, to assemble, to collect into a mass.

agglutinant, -e (aglytinɑ̃), adj. Agglutinative; *langue ~e*, agglutinative language.

agglutinati-f, -ve (aglytinatif), adj. Agglutinative, adhesive.

agglutination (aglytina'sjɔ̃), s.f. Agglutination.

agglutiner (aglytine), v.a. [f. L *agglutinare*] To agglutinate; **s'~**, v.pr. to agglutinate.

aggravant, -e (agravɑ̃), adj. Aggravating, increasing the gravity of (offence, burden, &c.); *circonstance ~e*, aggravating circumstance. ⚠ 'Aggravating' means also 'exasperating' = *exaspérant*: Oh! you are aggravating! = *Ah! vous êtes exaspérant.*

aggravation (agrava'sjɔ̃), s.f. Aggravation, increase, getting worse.

aggraver (agrave), v.a. [L *aggravare*] To aggravate, to increase, to make worse; **s'~**, v.pr. to augment, to get worse. ⚠ 'To aggravate' means also 'to exasperate' = *exaspérer*; ex.: threats only served to aggravate people (Thackeray) = *les menaces n'ont servi qu'à exaspérer ces gens*; in French *aggraver* cannot be applied to persons.

agha. See AGA.

agile (aʒil), adj. [L *agilis*] Agile, active, nimble, quick; syn. PRESTE.

agilement (aʒilmɑ̃), adv. Nimbly, agilely, quickly.

agilité (aʒilite), s.f. Agility, nimbleness; syn. PRESTESSE.

agio (aʒjo), s.m. [It. *aggio*] Agio, premium, stock-jobbing.

agiotage (aʒjɔtaʒ), s.m. Stock-jobbing, speculation, gambling, agiotage.

agioteu-r, -se (aʒjɔtœr), s.m.f. Stock-jobber, gambler.

agir (aʒir), v.n. [L *agere*] **1.** To act; to operate, to take effect, to behave; *moment d'~*, time for action; *bien ~*, *mal ~*, to do right, to do wrong; *il en a mal agi avec moi*, he did me wrong, he did not behave (act) as a friend (a gentleman) towards me; he dealt crookedly with me; *le remède agit sur*, the remedy is taking effect (operating) on; *faire ~*, to set going, to employ, to bring to bear (upon), to use the influence of; **2.** to proceed against, to prosecute, to sue; **s'~**, v.pr. impers. **1.** to be in question; *de quoi s'agit-il ?*, what is the matter? what is in question?; *il s'agit de vous*, you are concerned; *il ne s'agit point de cela*, that is not the question; *l'affaire dont il s'agit*, the business in hand, or in point, or at issue; **2.** to be at stake; *il s'agit* (or *il y va*) *de votre honneur*, your honour is involved; **3.** *il ne s'agit point que*, this is no case for.

agissant, -e (aʒisɑ̃), adj. Busy, stirring, efficient, active.

agissement (aʒismɑ̃), s.m. Doing, dealing, deed; (pej.) *~s*, carryings-on, intrigues.

agitat-eur, -rice (aʒitatœr), s.m.f. **1.** Agitator; **2.** glass rod, agitator.

agitation (aʒitaˊsjɔ̃), s.f. **1.** Agitation; act of shaking; being shaken; tossing, jolting, stirring; **2.** agitation, trouble, tumult, emotion, flutter, restlessness, uneasiness; ~ *des nerfs, des muscles, des lèvres*, quivering, tingling of the nerves, muscles, lips.

agiter (aʒite), v.a. [L *agitare*] To agitate, to stir, to shake; to wag, to wave, to move; to disturb, to disquiet, to excite, to make restless; to revolve mentally, to discuss (plans, &c.); **s'~**, v.pr. to bestir oneself, to stir about, to be agitated, restless, uneasy; to fret, to fidget; *la mer s'agite*, the sea is getting rough.

agnat (aɲa), s.m. [L *agnatus*] Agnate.

agneau (aɲo) (pl. **-x**), s.m. [L *agnus*] Lamb; (fig.) lamb-like person.

agnel (aɲɛl), s.m. (obs.) A French gold coin of the 13th century.

agnelage (aɲəlaʒ), s.m. Lambing, lambing-time.

agneler (aɲəle), v.n.a. To lamb, to yean.

agnelet (aɲəlɛ), s.m. Lambkin.

agnelin (aɲəlɛ̃), s.m. Lambskin (with the wool on).

agneline (aɲəlin), adj.f. Lamb's; *laine* ~, lamb's-wool.

agnelle (aɲɛl), s.f. Ewe lamb; (fig.) innocent, naïve girl.

agnès (aɲɛs), s.f. [f. character in Moliere's *L'École des Femmes*] Naïve, bashful girl; *faire l'~*, to play the innocent.

agnosticisme (agnɔstisism), s.m. [f. Gr. *a+gnōsis*] Agnosticism.

agnostique (agnɔstik), adj. s.m.f. Agnostic.

agonie (agɔni), s.f. [Gr. *agōnia*] Agony, death-struggle, pangs of death; *être à l'~*, to be at death's door; to be dying; to be at the point of death; (fig.) anguish, anxiety, torture, pangs.

agonir (agɔnir), v.a. [f. OF *ahonnir*] To blackguard, to slang, to load with abuse, to abuse, to insult grossly; ~ *X de sottises*, to call X all sorts of names, to slang X.

agonisant, -e (agɔnizɑ̃), p. adj. Dying, in a dying condition. ~, s.m.f. Dying person.

agoniser (agɔnize), v.n. [f. *agonie*] To be dying.

agonistique (agɔnistik), adj. [f. Gr. *agonistēs*] Agonistic, pertaining to athletic contests.

agora (agɔra), s.f. [Gr. wd] Agora.

agoraphobie (agɔrafɔbi), s.f. (pathol.) Agoraphobia.

agouti (aguti), s.m. [native wd, W. Indies] (zool.) Agouti, agouty.

agrafage (agrafaʒ), s.m. Hooking.

agrafe (agraf), s.f. [etym. dub., perh. Germ. *greifen*] Hook, clasp; (arch.) cramp-iron; ~ *et porte*, hook and eye.

agrafer (agrafe), v.a. To hook, to clasp, to fasten; **s'~**, v.pr. to be fastened.

agraire (agrɛr), adj. [L *agrarius*] Agrarian.

agrandir (agrɑ̃dir), v.a. [*à+grandir*] To enlarge, to extend; to aggrandize, to promote, to exalt, to dignify; to lengthen, to widen, to increase, to augment, to raise; **s'~**, v.pr. to grow larger; to extend one's estate or territory; syn. AUGMENTER.

agrandissement (agrɑ̃dismɑ̃), s.m. Enlargement; extension, aggrandizement.

agrarianisme (agrarjanism), s.m. Agrarianism.

agrarien, -ne (agrarjɛ̃), adj. [f. L *agrarius*] Agrarian.

agréable (agreabl), adj. Agreeable, pleasant, graceful; comfortable; *une sensation* ~, a pleasurable sensation; ~ *au goût*, palatable; *nouvelles ~s*, welcome news; *une soirée* ~, a pleasant evening; *avoir* or *tenir pour* ~, to allow, to permit; *faire l'~*, to make advances; syn. DÉLECTABLE. ⚠ *Agréable* has not like 'agreeable' the sense of 'conformable', 'willing', 'assenting' = *d'accord, conforme.*

agréablement (agreabləmɑ̃), adv. Pleasantly, agreeably; see ⚠ AGRÉABLE.

agréé (agree), s.m. Lawyer, solicitor (at the *Tribunal de Commerce*).

agréer (agree), v.a. [f. *gré*] To accept, to receive favourably; to approve, to sanction; to like, to allow, to permit; ~ (*à*), v.n. to please; *vous agréerait-il de?*, would you like to?

agrégat (agrega), s.m. Aggregate.

agrégation (agregaˊsjɔ̃), s.f. Aggregation; fellowship; admission; *concours d'~*, competitive examination for a fellowship.

agrégé, -e (agreʒe), s.m.f. Fellow; *professeur* ~, professor.

agréger (agreʒe), v.a. [L *aggregare*] To admit; to receive, to incorporate; to aggregate.

agrément (agremɑ̃), s.m. [f. *agréer*] **1.** Consent, approbation, approval; **2.** favour; **3.** pleasure, pleasantness; *arts, talents d'~*, accomplishments; **4.** (mus.) grace-notes. ⚠ The English 'agreement' cannot translate *agrément*; it means 'mutual understanding', 'covenant', 'treaty' = *arrangement, convention, traité*, &c.; but *agrément* is never used in that sense.

agrémenter (agremɑ̃te), v.a. To ornament, to adorn, to trim, to set off.

agrès (agrɛ), s.m.pl. [f. *gréer*] (naut.) Rigging, tackle; ~ *de gymnastique*, ropes, gymnastic appliances.

agresseur (agrɛsœr), s.m. Aggressor.

agressi-f, -ve (agrɛsif), adj. Aggressive.

agression (agrɛsjɔ̃), s.f. [L *aggressio*] Aggression, attack.

agressivement (agrɛsivmɑ̃), adv. Aggressively.

agressivité (agrɛsivite), s.f. Aggressiveness.
agreste (agrɛst), adj. [f. L *ager*] Agrestic, rural, rustic.
agrestement (agrɛstəmɑ̃), adv. Rustically.
agricole (agrikɔl), adj. [L *agricola*] Agricultural.
agriculteur (agrikyltœr), s.m. Agriculturist, farmer, husbandman.
agricultural, -e,(aux) (agrikyltyral), adj. Agricultural.
agriculture (agrikyltyr), s.f. [L *agricultura*] Agriculture, husbandry, farming.
agriffer (agrife), v.a. [f. *griffe*] To catch hold of, to clutch; **s'~**, v.pr. to catch hold, to cling.
agrion (agriɔ̃), s.m. (ent.) Dragon-fly; syn. DEMOISELLE, LIBELLULE.
agripaume (agripom), s.f. (bot.) Motherwort, *Leonurus cardiaca*.
agripper (agripe), v.a. To clutch, to seize eagerly, to grab, to snatch.
agronome (agrɔnom), s.m. [f. Gr. *agros*+*nomos*] Agronomist, agriculturist.
agronomie (agrɔnomi), s.f. Agronomy.
agronomique (agrɔnomik), adj. Agronomic(al).
agrostemme (agrɔstɛm), s.f. (bot.) Corn-cockle, rose-campion, *Agrostemma coronaria*.
agrostide (agrɔstid), s.f. (bot.) Bent-grass, agrostis.
agrouper (agrupe), v.a. To group, to place in groups.
aguerrir (agɛrir), v.a. [f. *guerre*] To inure to war; to season, to harden; **s'~**, v.pr. to become inured to war, to hardships, &c., to harden oneself, to become hardened or seasoned.
aguerrissement (agɛrismɑ̃), s.m. Inuring to war, hardships, &c., hardening, seasoning.
aguets (agɛ), s.m.pl. [*à*+*guet*] Watch; *être* or *se tenir aux ~*, to be lying in wait, to be on the watch, in ambush, on the look-out.
aguicher (agiʃe), v.a. (pop.) To entice, to allure, to decoy, to tempt, to lead on.
ah ! (ɑ), interj. Ah !, ha !, aha !; *~ çà !*, well now !, now then !, I say !, why !, oh !
ahan (aɑ̃), s.m. [onom.] Groan, great exertion, panting; *suer d'~*, to toil and moil.
ahaner (aane), v.n. [f. *ahan*] To groan, to pant, to toil.
aheurtement (aœrtəmɑ̃), s.m. Stubbornness.
(s')aheurter (saœrte) v.pr. [*à*+*heurter*] To remain obdurate, to stick (to), to persist (in).
ahuri, -e (ayri), adj. [f. *hure*] Bewildered, flurried, confused. ~, s.m.f. Giddy-head.
ahurir (ayrir), v.a. To confuse, to bewilder, to astound, to fluster, to flurry, to strike all of a heap.
ahurissement (ayrismɑ̃), s.m. Bewilderment, confusion, flurry, perplexity.
aï (ai), s.m. [onom.] (zool.) Three-toed sloth.
aiche (ɛʃ), s.f. [L *esca*] (fish.) Bait.
aide[1] (ɛd), s.f. [f. *aider*] Help, relief, assistance, succour, aid; *à l'~ !*, help !; *à l'~ de*, with, by means of, with the help of; *venir en ~*, to lend assistance; *Dieu lui soit en ~*, God help him; *un peu d'~ fait grand bien*, every little helps.
aide[2] (ɛd), s.m. Aide, assistant; help; under-; (nav.) mate; *~ chirurgien*, *~ pharmacien*, assistant surgeon, assistant druggist; *~-maçon*, mason's labourer.
aides (ɛd) s.f.pl. (obs.) Taxes.
aider (ɛde), v.a. [L *adjutare*] To help, to aid, to assist; to relieve, to succour; to promote, to contribute to (a success); (pej.) to abet; **s'~**, v.pr. to help oneself, or each other; to make use (*de*, of); to exert oneself; *aide-toi, le ciel t'aidera*, heaven helps those who help themselves.
aïe ! (ai), interj. Oh dear ! ow !, ouch ! (expressing pain, suffering).
aïeul, -e (pl. s) (ajœl), s.m.f. [f. L *aviolus*] Grandfather, grandmother; **aïeux**, s.m. pl. forefathers, ancestors, ancestry.
aigle (ɛgl), s.m. [L *aquila*] **1.** (ornith.) Eagle; *l'~ ne chasse point aux mouches*, eagles do not catch flies; (fig.) genius, star; *ce n'est pas un ~*, he is not a genius; **2.** eagle-lectern, reading-desk (in churches only); **3.** (herald.) eagle; *~ royal*, golden eagle; **4.** *papier grand ~*, double-elephant paper; ~, s.f. eagle (the hen bird); standard; *les ~s romaines*, the Roman eagles.
aiglefin, aigrefin (ɛgləfɛ̃, ɛgrəfɛ̃), s.m. (ichth.) Haddock.
aiglette (ɛglɛt), s.f. (herald.) Eaglet.
aiglon, -ne (ɛglɔ̃), s.m.f. Eaglet; *l'~*, Napoleon's son, *le Roi de Rome*.
aigre (ɛgr) adj. [L *acer*] Sour, acid; harsh; bitter; shrill, crisp; (fig.) acrimonious, tart, sharp, severe. ~, s.m. sourness, acidity, keenness; *sentir l'~*, to smell sour or stale.
aigre-dou-x, -ce (ɛgrədu), adj. Sourish, bitter-sweet.
aigrefin (ɛgrəfɛ̃), s.m. Sharper; see also AIGLEFIN.
aigrelet, -te (ɛgrəlɛ), adj. Sourish, acid.
aigrement (ɛgrəmɑ̃), adv. Bitterly, sourly, acidly, sharply.
aigremoine (ɛgrəmwan), s.f. (bot.) Agrimony.
aigremore (ɛgrəmɔr), s.m. Powdered charcoal (for fireworks).
aigrette (ɛgrɛt), s.f. [f. Provenç. *aigron* = *héron*] **1.** (ornith.) Egret; **2.** tuft, crest; horn (of the owl).
aigretté, -e (ɛgrɛte), adj. Tufted.

aigreur (ɛgrœr), s.f. Sourness, acidity; sharpness, bitterness, spite; *il y a de l'~ entre eux*, there is some acrimony in their relations; *~s*, acidities, acidity of the stomach.

aigrir (ɛgrir), v.a.n. **1.** To sour, to turn sour; **2.** to irritate, to exasperate (persons); **3.** to embitter, to envenom, to aggravate (quarrels); **s'~**, v.pr. to turn sour; to grow angry.

aigrissement (ɛgrismɑ̃), s.m. Souring, turning sour; irritation, aggravation, bitterness.

aigu, -ë (ɛgy), adj. [L *acutus*] Sharp, acute, pointed; shrill; *voix ~ë, cri ~*, shrill voice, cry; *maladie ~ë*, acute disease; *accent ~*, acute accent; *angle ~*, acute angle.

aiguade (ɛgɥad), s.f. [f. OF *aigue* = *eau*] Fresh water supply, watering-place; *faire ~*, to take in fresh water.

aiguail, aigail (ɛgaj), s.m. Dew; syn. ROSÉE.

aiguayer (ɛgɥɛje), v.a. (obs.) To wash, to rinse out.

aigue-marine (ɛgmarin), s.f. Aquamarine.

aiguière (ɛgjɛr), s.f. [f. OF *aigue* = *eau*] Ewer, water-jug.

aiguillade (ɛgɥijad), s.f. Goad.

aiguillage (ɛgɥijaʒ), s.m. (rail.) Switching, shifting of points.

aiguillat (ɛgɥija), s.m. (ichth.) Dog-fish; syn. CHIEN DE MER.

aiguille (ɛgɥij), s.f. [L *acicula*] **1.** Needle; **2.** hand; index; cock; **3.** spindle; spire; peak; obelisk; **4.** (rail.) point, switch; **5.** (ichth.) garfish, pipe-fish; *~ à coudre*, sewing-needle; *~ à repriser*, darning-needle; *~ à tricoter*, knitting-needle; *~ d'emballeur*, packing-needle; *disputer sur des pointes d'~*, to quibble; to dispute about trifles; *petite ~*, hour-hand; *grande ~*, minute-hand; *~ marine*, mariner's compass or needle; *de fil en ~*, bit by bit; one thing leading to another; *c'est chercher une ~ dans une botte de foin*, it 's like looking for a needle in a bottle of hay; *ouvrage à l'~*, or *d'~*, needlework; *~ aimantée*, magnetic needle; (rail.) *~ mobile*, tongue-rail.

aiguillée (ɛgɥije), s.f. Needleful.

aiguiller (ɛgɥije), v.a.n. (rail.) To switch, to set the points, to shunt (a train, carriage, &c.).

aiguilleter (ɛgɥijte), v.a. To tag; (naut.) to lash, to tie; to seize.

aiguillette (ɛgɥijɛt), s.f. Tag; shoulder-knot; (cook.) slice (of fowl, &c.); (naut.) lanyard.

aiguilleur (ɛgɥijœr), s.m. (rail.) Points-man, switchman.

aiguillier (ɛgɥijie), s.m. **1.** Needle-case; **2.** needle-maker.

aiguillon (ɛgɥijɔ̃), s.m. Goad; sting (of bees, &c.); prickle; (fig.) spur, incentive, stimulus; lust; thorn (in the flesh).

aiguillonnant, -e (ɛgɥijɔnɑ̃), p. adj. Goading, stimulating.

aiguillonnement (ɛgɥijɔnmɑ̃), s.m. Goading.

aiguillonner (ɛgɥijɔne), v.a. To goad, to prick, to sting; (fig.) to stimulate, to spur on, to goad.

aiguillot (ɛgɥijo), s.m. (naut.) Pintle.

aiguisage (ɛgɥizaʒ), s.m. Sharpening, grinding, whetting.

aiguiser (ɛgɥize), v.a. [f. *aigu*] To sharpen, to whet, to grind; (fig.) to stimulate, to make keen or piquant.

aiguiseu-r, -se (ɛgɥizœr), s.m.f. Sharpener, grinder.

aiguisoir (ɛgɥizwar), s.m. Sharpening-tool, sharpener, whetstone.

ail (aj), (pl. **aulx**) s.m. [L *allium*] (bot.) Garlic; *~ d'ascalon*, or *échalote*, shallot; *gousse d'~*, clove of garlic.

ailante (ɛlɑ̃t), s.m. (bot.) Ailanthus; tree of heaven.

aile (ɛl), s.f. [L *ala*] Wing; sweep, sail; flank; aisle; mudguard; (fig.) protection; *bouts d'~s*, pinions, firsts, best quills; *à tire d'~*, swiftly; *tirer de l'~*, to take wing; *il ne bat plus que d'une ~*, he is on his last legs; he is a lame duck; *il en a dans l'~*, he is done for, he cannot go far; *tirer pied ou ~ de*, to get something or other out of; *voler de ses propres ~s*, to stand on one's own legs; to shift for oneself; *c'est la plus belle plume de son ~*, it is the finest gem of his crown; *on va lui rogner les ~s*, they are going to clip his wings; *~ d'hélice*, blade of screw propeller; *~ de moulin*, windmill sail; (motor.) *~ d'avant*, front mudguard; *~ d'arrière*, rear mudguard; (aeron.) wing, plane, aerofoil.

ailé, -e (ɛle), adj. Winged.

aileron (ɛlrɔ̃), s.m. Pinion; (of fishes, &c.) fin; float board; (aeron.) aileron.

ailette (ɛlɛt), s.f. [f. *aile*] Winglet; (motor.) flange; vane, fan-blade; wing, gill, fin; *~s de refroidissement*, radiating gills; *radiateur à ~s*, winged radiator.

aillade (ajad), s.f. Garlic sauce.

ailleurs (ajœr), adv. [L *aliorsum*] Elsewhere, somewhere else, anywhere else; *nulle part ~*, nowhere else; *partout ~*, everywhere else; *par ~*, besides, otherwise; *d'~*, besides, moreover; also; in other respects; on the other hand; nevertheless, however, after all, furthermore, for the matter of that; in addition to which.

ailloli (ajɔli), s.m. [f. *ail*] Garlic sauce; a dish strongly flavoured with garlic.

aimable (ɛmabl), adj. [f. *aimer*] Amiable, pleasant, lovable, lovely, engaging, civil, courteous, kind.

aimablement (ɛmabləmɑ̃), adv. Amiably, kindly, courteously, pleasantly.

aimant, -e (ɛmɑ̃), adj. Loving, affectionate.

aimant (ɛmɑ̃), s.m. [contr. of Gr. *adamas*] Magnet, loadstone.

aimantation (ɛmɑ̃ta'sjɔ̃), s.f. Magnetization.

aimanté, -e (ɛmɑ̃te), adj. Magnetic.

aimanter (ɛmɑ̃te), v.a. To make magnetic, to magnetize; **s'~**, v.pr. to become magnetic.

aimantin, -e (ɛmɑ̃tɛ̃), adj. Magnetic.

aimé, -e (ɛme), adj. Loved, beloved, darling; *le bien ~*, the well-beloved.

aimer (ɛme), v.a.n. [L *amare*] To love; to like, to be fond of, to be partial to, to delight in; to be in love; *~ d'amour*, to love; *~ mieux*, to prefer, to like better; *j'aime à croire que*, I trust, I would rather think that; *j'aime autant, j'aimerais autant*, I had rather; *j'aimerais mieux n'y pas aller*, I had rather not go there; *qui m'aime, aime mon chien*, love me, love my dog; *qui aime bien châtie bien*, spare the rod, and spoil the child; *qui m'aime me suive*, let whoso loves me follow me; *se faire ~ de X*, to endear oneself to X; **s'~**, v.pr. to love oneself; to love each other.

aine (ɛn), s.f. [L *inguen*] Groin. ⚠ *Groin*, Fr. word, means 'snout' = *museau de cochon*, or *de sanglier*.

aîné, -e (ɛne), adj. s.m.f. [OF *ains+né*] Eldest, elder, senior; *Dupont ~*, Dupont senior.

aînesse (ɛnɛs), s.f. Primogeniture, seniority; *droit d'~*, birthright.

ainsi (ɛ̃si), adv. conj. [L *in sic*] So, thus, in this (that) way, like this (that); likewise; for instance; therefore; *~ dit, ~ fait*, no sooner said than done; *~ du reste*; *~ de suite*, and so forth ; and so on; *~ donc*, so then; *~ soit-il*, so be it; *~ fut fait*, and done it was; *il a décidé, ainsi agissons*, he has decided, therefore let us act; *~ que*, as well as, even as, just as, so as, along with, as; *~ que je vous l'ai dit*, as I told you; *lui ~ que moi, nous . . .*, he as well as I, we . . .; *quand ~ serait*, even were it so.

air (ɛr), s.m. [L *aer*] **1.** Air, atmosphere, wind, breeze; *coup d'~*, chill, cold, swelled face (from a draught); *courant d'~*, draught; (aeron.) *appel d'~*, indraught; *prendre l'~ du bureau*, to look in at the office; to see how matters stand at headquarters; *donner de l'~ (à un tableau)*, to bring out, to give an impression of space; *prendre l'~*, to take an airing, a walk; *faire prendre l'~ à*, to give an airing to; to take (one) for a walk; *prendre un ~ de feu*, just to warm oneself a little; *en plein ~*, in the open air; *fortune en l'~*, imaginary wealth; *vivre de l'~ du temps*, to live upon nothing; to live on nothing a year; *propos en l'~*, idle stories; empty words; *être en l'~*, to be in a flutter; *mettre en l'~*, to excite, to set agog; *tout est en l'~ chez nous*, everything is upside down at home; *il y a quelque chose dans l'~*, there is something brewing; **2.** look, appearance, mien, countenance, bearing, expression, manner, way; *~ de famille*, family likeness; *avoir l'~*, to look, to appear; *avoir l'~ de*, to look as if, to seem to; *il a grand ~*, he looks every inch a gentleman; *cette maison a grand ~*, that house looks fine (grand, opulent); *avoir l'~ bon*, to look good-natured; *cela en a tout l'~*, it looks like it; *votre fils a votre ~*, your son takes after you; *avoir l'~ comme il faut*, to look respectable, to have good manners; *il a un faux ~ de curé*, he looks something like a priest; (slang) *jouer la fille de l'~*, to leg it; **3.** (mus.) air, aria, song, tune, melody.

airage (ɛraʒ), s.m. **1.** Angle of mill-sails; **2.** (mining) ventilation shaft.

airain (ɛrɛ̃), s.m. [L *aeramen*] Bronze; brass; (fig.) cannon; bells; vessel; steel, iron; *statue d'~*, bronze statue; *ciel d'~*, burning sky; *cœur d'~*, heart of stone; ruthless, inflexible heart or will; *front d'~*, (*a*) bold front; (*b*) (pej.) brazen face, impudent attitude.

aire (ɛr), s.f. [L *area*] **1.** Area, space, threshing-floor; **2.** superficies, area, surface; **3.** aerie, eyrie; **4.** (naut.) *~ de vent*, direction of the wind, point of the compass.

airelle (ɛrɛl), s.f. [L L *atrella*] (bot.) Whortleberry, bilberry.

ais (ɛ), s.m. [L *axis*] Board, plank.

aisance (ɛzɑ̃s), s.f. [f. *aise*] Ease; facility; freedom; comfort; easy circumstances, competency; *il est dans l'~*, he is well off; *cabinet d'~s* or *lieux d'~s*, water-closet; *fosse d'~s*, cesspool; *honnête ~*, small fortune.

aise (ɛz), s.f. [etym. dub.] **1.** Ease, comfort, convenience; *être à l'~, être à son ~*, to be at ease, comfortable, at home; free; unembarrassed; to be in easy circumstances, well off; *mal à l'~, mal à son ~*, ill at ease, uneasy, uncomfortable; badly off; *il en prend à son ~*, he does just as he likes; he takes things easy; *il en parle à son ~ !*, easy for him to talk !; *mettez-vous à votre ~*, make yourself comfortable or at home; *mettre quelqu'un à son ~*, to set a person at ease, to make a person feel welcome; *aimer ses ~s*, to be self-indulgent; **2.** gladness, joy, enjoyment, gratification; *ne pas se sentir d'~*, to be beside oneself (with joy); *sauter d'~*, to jump for joy. **~**, adj.

Glad; *j'en suis bien* ~, I am glad of that.
aisé, -e (ɛze), adj. Easy; well off; *plus* ~ *à dire qu'à faire*, easier said than done; *une famille* ~*e*, a well-to-do family.
aisément (ɛzemɑ̃), adv. Easily.
aisseau (pl. **-x**) (ɛso), s.m. [f. *ais*] Shingle, wooden roofing-tile.
aisselle (ɛsɛl), s.f. [L *axilla*] **1.** Armpit; **2.** (bot.) axil.
aissette (ɛsɛt), s.f. (techn.) Adze, hooked hammer.
aîtres (ɛtr), s.m.pl. [etym. dub.] Whereabouts, ins and outs.
ajasse. See AGASSE.
ajointer (aʒwɛ̃te), v.a. To join end to end.
ajonc (aʒɔ̃), s.m. [LL *adjotum*] (bot.) Furze, gorse, whin.
ajoupa (ɑʒupa), s.f. [native wd, Guadeloupe] Hut.
ajour (aʒur), s.m. (arch., sculpt.) Hole, aperture, open-work.
ajouré, -e (aʒure), p. adj. Pierced, perforated.
ajourer (aʒure), v.a. [f. *jour*] To pierce, to perforate, to adorn with open work.
ajournement (aʒurnəmɑ̃), s.m. Adjournment, postponement.
ajourner (aʒurne), v.a. [f. *jour*] To adjourn, to put off, to postpone; **s'**~, v.pr. to adjourn, to be adjourned.
ajoutage (aʒutaʒ), s.m. Addition, joining; eking-piece.
ajouter (aʒute), v.a. [f. L *ad+juxta*] To add, to join, to interpolate; ~ *foi à*, to believe; **s'**~, v.pr. to be added.
ajust (aʒyt), s.m. (naut.) *Nœud d'*~, granny knot; fisherman's knot.
ajustage (aʒystaʒ), s.m. Adjustment, fitting.
ajustement (aʒystəmɑ̃), s.m. **1.** Adjustment, fitting, arranging, fitting-up; conciliation, settlement; **2.** dress, dressing, attire.
ajuster (aʒyste), v.a. [f. *juste*] **1.** To adjust, to adapt, to conciliate, to settle, to reconcile; **2.** to fit, to fit up (a house); to lay out (a garden); **3.** to attire, to dress, to bedizen, to deck out; **4.** to tune; **5.** to aim, to aim at, to take aim at; (fig.) *ajustez-vous*, be consistent, all say the same thing; **s'**~, v.pr. to fit, to agree; to dress oneself; to adapt oneself, to get ready.
ajusteur (aʒystœr), s.m. Fitter, sizer; weigher at the mint.
ajustoir (aʒystwar), s.m. Assay-scale.
ajut. See AJUST.
ajutage (aʒytaʒ), s.m. (mech.) Nozzle, jet, adjutage.
akène (akɛn), s.m. (bot.) Achene.
alabastrite (alabastrit), s.f. (min.) Alabaster.
alacrité (alakrite), s.f. [L *alacritas*] Alacrity.
alambic (alɑ̃bik), s.m. [Arab. wd] Alembic, still.
alambiqué, -e (alɑ̃bike), adj. Fine-spun, fine-drawn, over-refined, strained, far-fetched.
alambiquer (alɑ̃bike), v.a.n. To subtilize, to strain; to puzzle; *s'*~ *l'esprit*, to puzzle one's head, to over-refine.
alangui, -e (alɑ̃gi), adj. Languid, drooping.
alanguir (alɑ̃gir), v.a. [*à+languir*] To render languid, to enfeeble, to weaken; **s'**~, v.pr. to droop, to flag, to slacken, to become languid.
alanguissement (alɑ̃gismɑ̃), s.m. Languor, languidness, slackness.
alarmant, -e (alarmɑ̃), adj. Alarming.
alarme (alarm), s.f. [f. It. *all'arme!*] Alarm, fright, fear, disquiet, uneasiness; *donner l'*~ *à*, to alarm, to startle, to sound the alarm, to arouse to a sense of danger.
alarmer (alarme), v.a. [f. *alarme*] To alarm, to startle, to make uneasy, to disturb; **s'**~, v.pr. to take alarm, to be uneasy, to be alarmed; *ne vous alarmez pas*, do not worry.
alarmiste (alarmist), adj. s.m.f. Alarmist, panic-monger.
alaterne (alatɛrn), s.m. (bot.) Alaternus, privet, buckthorn, *Rhamnus alaternus*.
albanais, -e (albanɛ), adj. s.m.f. Albanian.
albarelle (albarɛl), s.f. (bot.) Mushroom.
albâtre (albɑtr), s.m. [Gr. *alabastron*] Alabaster.
albatros (albatros), s.m. [Span. *alcatraz*] (ornith.) Albatross.
alberge (albɛrʒ), s.f. Clingstone peach.
albergier (albɛrʒje), s.m. (bot.) Alberge-tree.
albide (albid), adj. Whitish.
albigeois, -e (albiʒwɑ), adj. s.m.f. Albigensian; (hist.) s.m.pl. Albigenses.
albinisme (albinism), s.m. Albinism.
albinos (albinos), adj. s.m.f. Albino.
albite (albit), s.f. (min.) Albite, white feldspar.
album (albɔm), s.m. [f. L *albus*] Album, sketch-book; autograph-book, photograph-album.
albumen (albymɛn), s.m. [L wd] Albumen, white of egg.
albumine (albymin), s.f. Albumin; *avoir de l'*~, to suffer from albuminuria.
albuminé, -e (albymine), adj. Albuminous.
albumineu-x, -se (albyminø), adj. Albuminose, albuminous.
albuminoïde (albyminɔid), adj. s.m. Albuminoid.
albuminose (albyminoz), s.f. Albuminose.
albuminurie (albyminyri), s.f. (pathol.) Albuminuria.

albuminurique (albyminyrik), adj. Suffering from albuminuria.
alcade (alkad), s.m. [Arab. *al+qaid*] Alcade, alcalde.
alcaïque (alkaik), adj. s.m. [f. Gr. *alkaikos*] (pros.) Alcaic.
alcalescence (alkalɛssɑ̃s), s.f. Alkalescence.
alcali (alkali), s.m. [Arab. *al+ḳaliy*] (chem.) Alkali; ~ *volatil*, ammonia.
alcalin, -e (alkalɛ̃), adj. Alkaline.
alcalinité (alkalinite), s.f. Alkalinity.
alcaloïde (alkalɔid), s.m. adj. (chem.) Alkaloid.
alcarazas (alkarazɑs), s.m. [Span. wd] Alcarraza; porous jug.
alcée (alse), s.f. (bot.) Hollyhock; syn. ROSE TRÉMIÈRE.
alchimie (alʃimi), s.f. [Arab. *al+kimia*] Alchemy.
alchimique (alʃimik), adj. Alchemic, alchemical.
alchimiste (alʃimist), s.m.f. Alchemist.
alcool (alkɔ'l), s.m. [Arab. *al+kohl*] Alcohol; ~ *à brûler*, methylated spirit.
alcoolat (alkɔɔla), s.m. (pharm.) Alcoholate.
alcoolique (alkɔɔlik), adj. Alcoholic. ~, s.m.f. Inebriate, drunkard.
alcoolisation (alkɔɔliza'sjɔ̃), s.f. Alcoholization.
alcooliser (alkɔɔlize), v.a. To alcoholize; **s'~**, v.pr. to become alcoholized, to become inebriate, to drink alcohol regularly.
alcoolisme (alkɔɔlism), s.m. Alcoholism.
alcoolomètre (alkɔɔlɔmɛtr), s.m. Alcoholometer.
alcôve (alkov), s.f. [f. Span. *alcoba*] Alcove, recess; (fig.) conjugal privacy.
alcyon (alsjɔ̃), s.m. [f. Gr. *alkuōn*] Halcyon.
alcyonien, -ne (alsjɔnjɛ̃), adj. Halcyon, peaceful.
aldéhyde (aldeid), s.f. (chem.) Aldehyde.
aléa (alea), s.m. [L wd] Risk, chance.
aléatoire (aleatwar), adj. Aleatory, risky, hazardous.
alêne (alɛn), s.f. [f. Span. *alesna*] Awl.
alénois (alenwɑ), adj. [for *orlénois*, f. *Orléans*] *Cresson* ~, cress.
alentissement. See RALENTISSEMENT.
alentour (alɑ̃tur), adv. [*à+l'entour*] Around, about; *d'~*, surrounding, neighbouring; *ne confondez pas autour avec* ~, mind the difference; it's as different as chalk is from cheese.
alentours (alɑ̃tur), s.m.pl. Surroundings, neighbourhood, vicinity, connexions.
alépine (alepin), s.f. [f. *Alep*, Syria] Bombazine.
alérion (alerjɔ̃), s.m. (herald.) Eaglet (without beak or feet).
alerte (alɛrt), s.f. [It. *all'erta*] Alert, alarm; *en* ~, on the look-out, ready, watchful. ~, adj. Alert, quick, active, nimble; sharp, smart, shrewd, quick-witted; vigilant, watchful, wide awake; *peu* ~, slow. *~!*, interj. Up!, look out!
alerter (alɛrte), v.a. To give the alarm to, to give warning (of danger) to.
alésage (alezaʒ), s.m. (motor. mech.) Bore, boring; ~ *du cylindre*, bore of cylinder; ~ *de 80*, 80-bore.
alèse, alèze (alez), s.f. Draw-sheet.
aléser (aleze), v.a. (mech.) To bore.
alésoir (alezwar), s.m. Boring-tool.
alester (alɛste), v.a. (naut.) To lighten (a ship).
alésure (alezyr), s.f. Metal turnings or filings.
aleurone (alørɔn), s.f. (chem.) Aleuron.
alevin (alvɛ̃), s.m. [f. L *allevare*] (ichth.) Fry.
alevinage (alvinaʒ), s.m. Breeding young fish; stocking with fry.
aleviner (alvine), v.a. To stock with fry.
alexandrin[1], **-e** (alɛksɑ̃drɛ̃), adj. s.m.f. Alexandrine.
alexandrin[2] (alɛksɑ̃drɛ̃), s.m. (pros.) Alexandrine.
alexipharmaque (alɛksifarmak), adj. (obs.) Alexipharmic.
alezan, -e (alzɑ̃), adj. [Span. *alazan* f. Arab. orig.] Chestnut (horse).
alèze. See ALÈSE.
alfa (alfa), s.m. [North Afric. wd.] (bot.) Alfa, alfa grass.
alfange (alfɑ̃ʒ), [Span. wd.] s.m. Moorish scimitar.
alfénide (alfenid), s.m. [f. *Halphen*, inventor] Britannia metal; a whitish alloy.
algalie (algali), s.f. (surg.) Catheter.
algarade (algarad), s.f. [Span. *algarrada*] Sudden attack, upbraiding, blowing-up, rating.
algaroth (algarɔt), s.m. [f. *Algarotti*, discoveror] (chem.) Oxy-chloride of antimony, powder of algaroth.
algazelle (algazɛl), s.f. (zool.) White antelope.
algèbre (alʒɛbr), s.f. [Arab. *al+jebr*] Algebra; *c'est de l'~ pour moi*, it's Greek to me.
algébrique (alʒebrik), adj. Algebraic, algebraical.
algébriquement (alʒebrikmɑ̃), adv. Algebraically.
algébriste (alʒebrist), s.m.f. Algebraist.
algérien, -ne (alʒerjɛ̃), adj. s.m.f. Algerian (from *Algérie*).
algérois, -e (alʒerwɑ), adj. s.m.f. (Native) of the town of Algiers. See ALGÉRIEN.
algide (alʒid), adj. [L *algidus*] (pathol.) Cold, algid.
algidité (alʒidite), s.f. (pathol.) Algidity, coldness.
algorithme (algɔritm), s.m. [f. Arab. *al+Khowarazmi*] Algorism (the Arabic or decimal system of numeration).

---

o, n**o**te, gl**o**tte; ɔ̃, m**on**ter, r**on**de; ø, f**eu**, cr**eu**x; œ, p**eu**r, s**œu**r; œ̃, **un**; ʃ, **ch**ez, s**ch**isme; u, t**ou**t; w, **ou**i, d**o**it, d**ou**aire; y, m**u**r, p**u**; ɥ, h**u**ile, m**u**ette; z, **z**èle, ro**s**e; ʒ, dé**j**à, **g**entil.

alguazil (alguazil), s.m. [Span. wd] Alguazil.
algue (alg), s.f. [L *alga*] (bot.) Sea-weed, alga.
alibi (alibi), s.m. [L *alius*+*ibi*] Alibi.
alibiforain (alibifɔrɛ̃), s.m. Irrelevant speech; evasive answer.
alibile (alibil), adj. [L *alibilis*] Nutritive.
alibilité (alibilite), s.f. Nutritiveness.
aliboron (alibɔrɔ̃), s.m. [etym. dub. perh. f. *helleborum*] Donkey; jack-ass; (fig.) blockhead, ass; *maître*~, master long-ears.
aliboufier (alibufje), s.m. (bot.) Styrax; syn. STYRAX.
alicante (alikɑ̃t), s.m. [f. *Alicante*, Spain] Alicante (wine).
alidade (alidad), s.f. [Arab. *al*+*'idad*] Alidad, index of astrolabe or quadrant.
aliénabilité (aljenabilite), s.f. Alienability.
aliénable (aljenabl), adj. Alienable, transferable.
aliénataire (aljenatɛr), s.m.f. Alienee.
aliénat-eur, -rice (aljenatœr), s.m.f. Alienator.
aliénation (aljena'sjɔ̃), s.f. **1.** Alienation, transfer, conveyance of property to another person; **2.** estrangement, loss; **3.** madness, lunacy, insanity; ~ *mentale*, lunacy, mental derangement.
aliéné, -e (aljene), p. adj. s.m.f. Lunatic, insane (person); *hospice d'*~*s*, lunatic asylum.
aliéner (aljene), v.a. [L *alienare*] To alienate, to sell, to transfer; to estrange, to lose; **s'**~, v.pr. to lose, to alienate from oneself; *s'*~*l'affection de X*, to lose X's love.
aliénisme (aljenism), s.m. Alienism, science of mental diseases; psychopathy.
aliéniste (aljenist), s.m.f. adj. Specialist in mental diseases, alienist.
alifère (alifɛr), adj. (ent.) Wing-bearing.
aliforme (alifɔrm), adj. Wing-shaped.
alignée (aliɲe), s.f. Line, range.
alignement (aliɲmɑ̃), s.m. Setting, standing, or laying out in a straight line; falling into line; straight line, row, line; (mil.) alignment, dressing, line; (command) *à droite*~*!*, by the right, dress!; *perdre l'*~, to get out of line; *rentrer dans l'*~, to fall into line; *prendre un* ~, to stake out a line; *faire mettre X à l'*~, to make X toe the line.
aligner (aliɲe), v.a. [f. *ligne*] To arrange, dispose or set in a line, to set, form, put, in one or several lines; to square; (mil.) to dress, to draw up in a line; (print.) to range; **s'**~, v.pr. to fall into line, to keep the line, to toe the line; (pop.) to start a fight, to have a set-to, to scuffle.
aliment (alimɑ̃), s.m. [L *alimentum*] Aliment, food, nutriment, sustenance, nourishment; supply; *les* ~*s*, the food; (law) alimony, maintenance.
alimentaire (alimɑ̃tɛr), adj. Alimentary, dietetic; *régime* ~, dietary; *pension* ~, maintenance, alimony.
alimentation (alimɑ̃ta'sjɔ̃), s.f. Alimentation; nutrition, food; supplying, supply; feeding (of a fire, an engine); *tuyau d'*~, feed-pipe.
alimenter (alimɑ̃te), v.a. To feed, to support, to maintain; to supply; to keep up; **s'**~, v.pr. to feed (on); to take food; to be fed, to be kept alive.
alinéa (alinea), s.m. [L *ad*+*lineam*] Paragraph; break.
alinéaire (alineɛr), adj. Marking a new paragraph.
alios (aljos), s.m. (min). Brown freestone.
aliquante (alikɑ̃t), adj.f. (math.) Aliquant, contained in another number, but not an exact number of times: *deux est une partie* ~ *de neuf*.
aliquote (alikɔt), adj.f. (math.) Aliquot.
alise (aliz), s.f. (bot.) Sorb-apple, beam-tree berry.
alisé. See ALIZÉ.
alisier (alizje), s.m. (bot.) Whitebeam.
alisme (alism), s.m. (bot.) Water-plantain.
alitement (alitmɑ̃), s.m. Confinement to bed.
aliter (alite), v.a. To confine to bed; *être alité*, to be laid up; to be in bed; to be bed-ridden; **s'**~, v.pr. to keep one's bed, to take to one's bed.
alizarine (alizarin), s.f. Alizarin, madder extract.
alizé (alize), adj. s.m. [OF *alis*, smooth, regular] ~*s*, *vents* ~*s*, trade-winds.
alkékenge (alkekɑ̃ʒ), s.f. (bot.) Winter-cherry, *Physalis alkekengi*.
alkermès (alkɛrmɛs), s.m. [Arab. wd.] Alkermes (liqueur).
allaise (alɛz), s.f. Sandbank (in a river).
allaitement (allɛtmɑ̃), s.m. Suckling, nursing.
allaiter (allɛte), v.a. [f. *lait*] To suckle, to nurse, to give suck to.
allant, -e (alɑ̃), adj. Active, brisk, stirring, bustling.
allant (alɑ̃), s.m. Go, spirit, heartiness; *avoir de l'*~, to be full of go or of beans; (U.S.A.) to be full of pep; ~*s*, s.m.pl. goers; *les* ~*s et venants*, passers-by, comers and goers.
alléchant, -e (alleʃɑ̃), adj. Attractive, alluring, enticing, tempting.
allèchement (allɛʃmɑ̃), s.m. Allurement, lure, temptation, enticement.
allécher (alleʃe), v.a. [L *allicere*] To attract, to lure, to tempt, to entice.
allée (ale), s.f. **1.** Garden path, lane, walk; alley. ⚠ In English 'alley' is mostly used for a town passage or small street =*ruelle*, *passage*; **2.** going; ~*s et venues*, going to and fro; running about.
allégation (allega'sjɔ̃), s.f. [f. *alléguer*] Allegation, assertion.

---

allège (allɛʒ), s.f. (naut.) Lighter; tender; (arch.) sill.
allégeance (alleʒɑ̃s), s.f. Allegiance.
allègement (allɛʒmɑ̃), s.m. Lightening, relief, alleviation.
alléger (alleʒe), v.a. [L *alleviare*] To lighten, to unload; to alleviate, to relieve, to ease; **s'~**, v.pr. to ease oneself, to get lighter, to be relieved.
allégir (alleʒir), v.a. To reduce the size of (timber, &c.).
allégorie (allegɔri), s.f. [L *allegoria*] Allegory.
allégorique (allegɔrik), adj. Allegorical.
allégoriquement (allegɔrikmɑ̃), adv. Allegorically.
allégoriser (allegɔrize), v.a.n. To allegorize.
allégoriste (allegɔrist), s.m.f. Allegorist.
allègre (allɛgr), adj. [L *alacer*] Sprightly, lively, brisk, cheerful, jolly.
allégrement (allɛgrəmɑ̃), adv. Briskly, cheerfully.
allégresse (allegrɛs), s.f. Cheerfulness, alacrity, mirth, glee, gaiety, joy.
alléguer (allege), v.a. [L *allegare*] To allege, to plead, to state, to urge, to adduce; to quote.
alléluia (allelyja), s.m. [Hebr. wd] **1.** Hallelujah, alleluia; **2.** (bot.) wood-sorrel.
allemand, -e (almɑ̃), adj. s.m.f. German. **~e**, s.f. Allemande (dance).
aller (ale), v.n. irreg. [etym. dub., perh. L *adire*] **1.** To go, to proceed; *~ à pied, à cheval, en voiture, en auto, en avion* (*à*); to walk, to ride, to drive, to motor, to fly (to); *~ à la chasse, à la pêche*, to go shooting, fishing; *~ en justice*, to go to law; *~ aux renseignements*, to make inquiries; (parl.) *~ aux voix*, to divide; *~ à l'eau*, to fetch water; *~ au marché*, to go to market; *~ son chemin*, to keep one's way, to mind one's own business; *la route va tout droit à*, the road leads straight to; *~ au plus pressé*, to do the most urgent thing; *les premiers vont devant*, first come, first served; **2.** to advance, to get on, to progress, to move; to reach, to amount; to last, to keep on; *son travail va vite*, he is getting on fast; *ces arbres vont lentement*, these trees grow slowly; *les réparations iront à deux ans*; the reconstruction will take (last) two years; *le prix ira à 10,000 livres*, the cost will reach £10,000; *sa colère va jusqu'à la folie*, his anger amounts to madness; **3.** to be, to do; *comment allez-vous?*, (pop.) *comment ça va?*, how are you?; *ça va*, all right; *ça ne va pas fort*, only middling; *ça ne va pas mal*, not so bad; **4.** to grow, to get; *je vais mieux*, I am better; *il va de pire en pire*, he gets worse and worse; **5.** to be going to, on the point of, about to; *je vais sortir*, I am going out; *je vais aller à*, I am about to go to; *je vais dîner à Versailles*, I shall dine at Versailles; *on va dîner*, dinner is ready; **6.** (imperative) *vous allez finir!*, stop that! *n'allez pas l'irriter!*, beware of annoying him; **7.** to fit, to be becoming; *ce chapeau vous va bien*, that hat suits you; **8.** to aim, to lead, to tend; to attain, to obtain; *tous chemins vont à Rome*, all roads lead to Rome; *il va à l'argent*, he aims at money; *il est allé au succès par des voies faciles*, he obtained success without effort; **9.** to act; *il va droit devant lui*, he acts honorably, uprightly, he is straightforward; *il n'y va pas de main morte*, he hits hard, he goes at it in dead earnest; **10.** *~ à*, to stand, to bear; *cette robe va à la lessive*, this dress will wash; *ces assiettes vont au feu*, these plates stand heat; **11.** other gallicisms: *allons!*, come on!, now then; *allons donc!*, pooh!, never!, nonsense!; indeed!, you don't mean that!; *allons, bon!*, now!, I say!, what!; *allez!, va!* (*a*) go!, begone!; (*b*) depend upon it!, I assure you!; *va pour*, let it be, let us have; *eh! va donc*, get along with you; *cela va de soi, cela va sans dire*, it goes without saying, it stands to reason; *faire ~*, to purge; *~ à la selle*, to go to stool; *~ ensemble*, to match, to make a pair; *~ de pair avec*, to rank with; *~ sur*, to be about; *elle va sur quarante ans*, she is about forty; *se laisser ~*, (*a*) to indulge (*à*, in); (*b*) to get shabby, dowdy; *vous y allez un peu fort*, you are coming it rather strong; *en ~*, to happen, to turn out; *il n'en ira pas ainsi*, it shall not happen; *il en va de cette affaire comme des autres*, this business is turning out like the others; *vas-y, allez-y!*, now then!, go it!; *allez-y doucement*, go gently; *j'y vais de cent francs*, I stake one hundred francs; *il y va de votre vie*, your life is at stake; *il n'y va pas par quatre chemins*, he does not beat about the bush; *on y va!*, coming!; **s'en ~**, v.pr. **1.** To be off, to leave; *va-t'en!, allez-vous-en!*, off with you!; **2.** to be dying, to fade; *mon malade s'en va*, my patient is dying; **3.** to leak, to evaporate; *ce tonneau s'en va*, this cask leaks; **s'~**, (archaic) *s'~ promener*, to go for a walk.
aller (ale), s.m. Going; *billet d'~ et retour*, return ticket; *un pis ~*, a last shift; *au pis ~*, at the worst.
alleu (allø), s.m. [LL *alodium*] (feud.) Allodium, allodial tenure; *franc ~*, freehold.
alliacé, -e (aljase), adj. [f. L *allium*] (bot.) Alliaceous, smelling of garlic.
alliage (aljaʒ), s.m. [f. *allier*] Alloy, mixture; (math.) alligation.
alliaire (aljɛr), s.f. (bot.) Alliaria, Jack-by-the-hedge, hedge-garlic.

alliance (aljɑ̃s), s.f. **1.** Alliance, union, community, combination, confederation; marrying; **2.** wedding-ring.
allié, -e (alje), s.m.f. Ally. **~,** adj. Allied, united, combined.
allier (alje), v.a. [L *alligare*] **1.** To alloy; **2.** To match, to marry; **3.** to unite, to confederate; **s'~,** v. pr. to unite; to alloy; to intermarry.
allier. See HALLIER.
alligator (alligatɔr), s.m. (zool.) Alligator.
allitération (allitera'sjɔ̃), s.f. [f. L *ad*+ *litera*] Alliteration.
allobroge (allɔbrɔʒ), s.m. [L *Allobrox*] **1.** Allobroge; **2.** (fig.) lout, country bumpkin.
allocation (allɔka'sjɔ̃), s.f. [f. LL *allocare*] Allocation, allowing, allowance, allotment, subsidy.
allocution (allɔkysjɔ̃), s.f. [f. L *ad*+ *loqui*] Allocution, speech, address.
allodial, -e, (aux) (allɔdjal), adj. Allodial.
allonge (alɔ̃ʒ), s.f. Eking-piece; leaf (of a table); meat-hook; (naut.) futtock.
allongé, -e (alɔ̃ʒe), p. adj. Elongated, lengthened, slim; stretched; laid up, confined to bed or sofa.
allongement (alɔ̃ʒmɑ̃), s.m. Elongation, lengthening, protraction, eking-out; stretching; delay.
allonger (alɔ̃ʒe), v.a. [f. *long*] To lengthen, to eke out, to elongate, to stretch out, to extend, to protract; to delay; to fetch, to deal (a blow); **~** *le pas*, to step out; (slang) **~** *sa monnaie*, to fork out; **s'~,** v.pr. to get longer, to become lengthened; to stretch oneself; to lie down; to fall down at full length; *il s'est allongé sur le bitume*, he came a cropper on the asphalt.
allonyme (allɔnim), adj. [f. Gr. *allos*+ *onuma*] Published under the name of another.
allopathe (allɔpat), s.m.f. adj. Allopathist.
allopathie (allɔpati), s.f. [f. Gr. *allos*+ *pathos*] Allopathy.
allopathique (allɔpatik), adj. Allopathic.
allotropie (allɔtrɔpi), s.f. [f. Gr. *allos*+ *tropos*] Allotropy.
allotropique (allɔtrɔpik), adj. Allotropic, allotropical.
allouable (alluabl), adj. Allowable; grantable.
allouer (allue), v.a. [L *adlocare*] To allow, to grant.
allumage (alymaʒ), s.m. Lighting, kindling; (motor.) ignition, sparking, firing; *avance à l'~*, advance sparking; *distributeur d'~*, spark-timer; *mettre de l'avance à l'~*, to advance the ignition; *point d'~*, point of ignition; *raté d'~*, misfire.
allume-feu (alymfø), s.m. Fire-lighter, firewood, tinder.
allumer (alyme), v.a. [f. L *ad*+*lumen*] To light, to light up, to kindle; (fig.) to excite, to allure, to fire; (motor.) to ignite, to light; **s'~,** v.pr. to light up; to kindle.
allumette (alymet), s.f. Match; **~** *bougie*, vesta; **~** *amorphe*, safety match; **~** *de papier*, **~** *de copeau*, spill, pipe-light; *frotter une* **~**, to strike a match.
allumettier (alymɛtje), s.m. Maker of matches.
allumeu-r, -se (alymœr), s.m.f. Lamp-lighter; (motor.) igniter.
allumière (alymjɛr), s.f. Match-factory.
allumoir (alymwar), s.m. Gas-lighter for cigars, any apparatus used to kindle a light or a fire.
allure (alyr), s.f. [f. *aller*] Gait, walk, carriage, pace, tread; looks, appearance; manner, way, ways, behaviour, demeanour; direction, turn, bent; *son* **~** *l'a trahi*; his gait betrayed him; *cela a beaucoup d'~*, that looks smart or (vulg.) classy.
allusi-f, -ve (allyzif), adj. Allusive.
allusion (allyzjɔ̃), s.f. [L *allusio*] Allusion; hint; reference; *faire* **~** *à*, to allude to; to hint at; to refer to; **~** *malicieuse*, innuendo.
alluvial, -e, (aux) (allyvjal), adj. Alluvial.
alluvion (allyvjɔ̃), s.f. [L *alluvio*] Alluvium.
alluvionnaire (allyvjɔnɛr), adj. Alluvial.
almageste (almaʒɛst), s.m. [Arab. *al*+ *majesti*] Almagest.
almanach (almanak), s.m. [etym. dub.] Almanac, annual calendar, directory; (iron.) *c'est un* **~** *de l'an passé*, he is a back number.
almée (alme), s.f. [f. Arab. *almah*] Dancing-girl.
aloès (alɔɛs), s.m. [Gr. *aloē*] (bot.) Aloe, aloes.
aloi (alwɑ), s.m. [f. *aloyer*] Degree, purity, quality, standard, condition; *une célébrité de mauvais* **~**, an unenviable celebrity; *style de mauvais* **~**, debased style; *argument de bon* **~**, sound argument, cogent reason.
alopécie (alɔpesi), s.f. [Gr. *alopekia*] Baldness; syn. CALVITIE.
alors (alɔr), adv. [*à*+*lors*] Then; at that time; in that case; *c'était le prix d'~*, it was then the price; **~** *que*, then, when; **~** *même que*, even when; **~** *comme* **~**, time enough when that comes; *ah non* **~** *!*, I should think not!
alose (aloz), s.f. [L *alausa*] (ichth.) Shad, allice-shad.
alouette (aluɛt), s.f. [L *alauda*] Lark, skylark; **~** *de mer*, sandpiper; *pied d'~*, (bot.) larkspur; *attendre que les* **~***s vous tombent toutes rôties*, to expect fortune to come wooing.

aloudir (alurdir), v.a. [f. *lourd*] To make heavy, to increase the weight of; to render dull; **s'~**, v.pr. to grow heavy, fat, or dull.
alourdissement (alurdismɑ̃), s.m. Increase of weight, heaviness, dullness.
aloyage (alwajaʒ), s.m. Alloying.
aloyau (pl. **-x**) (alwajo), s.m. [etym. dub.] Sirloin.
aloyer (alwaje), v.a. [f. *à* + *loi*] To alloy, to reduce (gold or silver) to the legal standard of purity.
alpaca, alpaga (alpaga), s.m. **1.** (zool.) Alpaca, llama; **2.** alpaca (fabric).
alpage (alpaʒ), s.m. Pasturage in the Alps.
alpestre (alpɛstr), adj. [f. *Alpes*] Alpine.
alpha (alfa), s.m. [Gr. wd] Alpha; (fig.) the rudiments or beginning; *connaître l'~ et l'oméga de*, to know all there is to know about.
alphabet (alfabɛ), s.m. [f. Gr. *alpha*+ *bēta*] Alphabet; spelling-book.
alphabétique (alfabetik), adj. Alphabetical.
alphabétiquement (alfabetikmɑ̃), adv. Alphabetically.
alphabétiser (alfabetize), v.a. To classify in alphabetical order.
alpicole (alpikɔl), adj. (bot.) Alpine.
alpin, -e (alpɛ̃), adj. [f. *Alpes*] Alpine.
alpinisme (alpinism), s.m. Mountaineering.
alpiniste (alpinist), s.m.f. Alpinist, mountaineer.
alpique (alpik), adj. [f. *Alpes*] Alpine.
alpiste (alpist), s.m. (bot.) Canary-grass, *Phalaris canariensis*.
alsacien, -ne (alzasjɛ̃), adj. s.m.f. Alsatian.
alsine. See syn. MOURON.
altaïque (altaik), adj. (geog.) Altaic; *ouralo-~*, Ural-Altaic.
altérabilité (alterabilite), s.f. Alterability.
altérable (alterabl), adj. Alterable.
altérant, -e (alterɑ̃), adj. Causing thirst.
altérati-f, -ve (alteratif), adj. Alterative.
altération (altera'sjɔ̃), s.f. [f. *altérer*] **1.** Alteration, change, modification; **2.** debasing (of money), deterioration, corruption, falsification; **3.** weakening (of health), discomposure, change of countenance; **4.** thirst.
altercation (altɛrka'sjɔ̃), s.f. [L *altercatio*] Altercation, wrangling, wrangle, dispute, quarrel; (fam.) row.
altéré, -e (altere), p. adj. **1.** Distorted, altered; **2.** thirsty.
altérer (altere), v.a. [f. L *alter*] **1.** To alter, to change; to spoil, to deteriorate, to damage, to injure, to impair; to debase, to weaken, to mar; to falsify, to distort, to misrepresent; **2.** to make thirsty; **s'~**, v.pr. to alter, to degenerate, to be corrupted, to get spoiled; *cette couleur s'altère rapidement*, that colour soon fades.
alternance (altɛrnɑ̃s), s.f. Alternation, succession, rotation.
alternant, -e (altɛrnɑ̃), adj. Alternating; rotating.
alternat (altɛrna), s.m. Alternation.
alternateur (altɛrnatœr), s.m. (electr.) Alternator.
alternati-f, -ve (altɛrnatif), adj. Alternate, alternative; *courant ~*, alternating current; *mouvement ~*, alternate motion; *culture ~ve*, rotation of crops.
alternation (altɛrna'sjɔ̃), s.f. Alternation, rotation.
alternative (altɛrnativ), s.f. Alternative; choice, option, possibility; dilemma.
alternativement (altɛrnativmɑ̃), adv. Alternatively, by turns.
alterne (altɛrn), adj. (geom.) Alternate; (bot.) alternate.
alterner (altɛrne), v.n.a. [L *alternare*] To alternate; to succeed each other by turns; (agric.) to grow in rotation; to alternate (crops).
altesse (altɛs), s.f. [It. *altezza*] Highness; *son ~*, his or her Highness.
althaea (altea), s.m. (bot.) Marsh mallow; althaea.
alti-er, -ère (altje), adj. [f. L *altus*] Haughty, lordly, proud, lofty, arrogant.
altièrement (altjɛrmɑ̃), adv. Haughtily.
altimètre (altimɛtr), s.m. Altimeter.
altise (altiz), s.f. (ent.) Flea-beetle.
altitude (altityd), s.f. [L *altitudo*] Altitude.
alto (alto), s.m. [It. wd] **1.** Alto-viola; **2.** contralto; **3.** alto, highest male voice.
altruisme (altrɥism), s.m. [f. L *alter*] Altruism, unselfishness.
altruiste (altrɥist), adj. Altruistic. **~**, s.m.f. Altruist.
alude. See ALUTE.
alumelle (alymɛl), s.f. Blade of a plane; sword-blade.
aluminate (alyminat), s.m. (chem.) Alum, aluminate.
alumine (alymin), s.f. (chem.) Alumina.
alumineu-x, -se (alyminø), adj. Aluminous.
aluminium (alyminjɔm), s.m. (chem.) Aluminium.
alun (alœ̃), s.m. [L *alumen*] Alum.
alute, alude (alyt, alyd), s.f. [f. L. *aluta*] Basil, coloured sheepskin (used for book-binding).
alvéolaire (alveolɛr), adj. Alveolar, alveolate.
alvéole (alveɔl), s.m. [L *alveolus*] Cell (of honeycomb); alveolus; socket (of tooth).
alvéolé, -e (alveɔle), adj. Alveolate.
alvin, -e (alvɛ̃), adj. (anat.) Alvine, pertaining to the belly.

alysse (alis), s.m. (bot.) Alyssum; madwort.
amabilité (amabilite), s.f. Amiableness, kindness; favour; *ayez l'~ de*, will you be kind enough to; do me the favour of.
amadou (amadu), s.m. [etym. dub.] Amadou, German tinder, touchwood.
amadouer (amadue), v.a. To coax, to wheedle, to cajole, to flatter, to pacify, to calm, to get round.
amaigrir (amɛgrir), v.a. [f. *maigre*] **1.** To make thin, lean, lank, to emaciate, to waste; **2.** (agric.) to impoverish (soil); **3.** (paint.) to tone down, to attenuate; **s'~**, v.pr. to grow thin, to lose flesh, to waste away.
amaigrissant, -e (amɛgrisɑ̃), adj. Emaciating, reducing, thinning; *régime ~*, reducing diet; *sels ~s*, reducing salts.
amaigrissement (amɛgrismɑ̃), s.m. Emaciation, growing thin; reducing; wasting away.
amalgamation (amalgama'sjɔ̃), s.f. Amalgamation.
amalgame (amalgam), s.m. [L *amalgama*] Amalgam; (fig.) medley, strange mixture.
amalgamer (amalgame), v.a. To amalgamate; **s'~**, v.pr. to mix, to unite; to be amalgamated.
aman (amɑ̃), s.m. [Arab. wd] Submission; *demander l'~*, to surrender.
amande (amɑ̃d), s.f. [L *amygdala*] Almond, kernel; *~ amère*, bitter almond; *~ mondée*, shelled almond; *des yeux en ~*, almond eyes.
amandé, -e (amɑ̃de), adj. Containing almond-oil. ~, s.m. Milk of almonds.
amandier (amɑ̃dje), s.m. (bot.) Almond-tree.
amanite (amanit), s.f. (bot.) Amanite, mushroom.
amant, -e (amɑ̃), s.m.f. Lover, suitor, sweetheart; paramour; votary; lady-love, mistress; *~ de cœur*, fancy man.
amarante (amarɑ̃t), s.f. [Gr. *amarantos*] (bot.) Amaranth; coxcomb; prince's feather. ~, adj. Amaranth-coloured, amaranthine.
amarinage (amarinaʒ), s.m. (naut.) Manning.
amariner (amarine), v.a. [f. *mer, marine*] (naut.) To man (a prize); to inure (a crew) to the sea.
amarrage (amaraʒ), s.m. (naut.) Mooring, lashing, anchoring, fastening.
amarre (amar), s.f. Rope, cable, hawser, line; *~ de touée*, towline; *~ d'arrière*, stern-fast; *~ de bout*, headfast; *~ de travers*, breastfast.
amarrer (amare), v.a. [f. Dutch *marren*] (naut.) To moor, to fasten, to lash, to hitch, to make fast, to belay.
amaryllis (amarillis), s.f. (bot.) Amaryllis, lily, asphodel.
amas (amɑ), s.m. [f. *amasser*] Heap, mass, pile, accumulation; agglomeration.
amasser (amɑse), v.a. [f. *masse*] To amass, to collect, to accumulate; to pile, to hoard up; **s'~**, v.pr. to gather, to collect, to crowd, to assemble; syn. ACCUMULER, ENTASSER.
amassette (amɑsɛt), s.f. Palette-knife.
amateloter (amatlɔte), v.a. (naut.) To class (a crew) by twos.
amateur (amatœr), s.m. Amateur, lover, connoisseur, fancier; smatterer, amateur, non-professional.
amatir (amatir), v.a. [f. *mat*] To deaden, to dull (gold, silver, &c.).
amaurose (amoroz), s.f. [Gr. *amaurōsis*] (pathol.) Amaurosis.
amazone (amazɔn), s.f. [Gr. *amazon*] **1.** Amazon; **2.** riding-habit; **3.** horsewoman, female equestrian.
ambages (ɑ̃baʒ), s.f.pl. [L wd] Ambiguity; circumlocutions; *parlez sans ~*, speak straight out; *je vous dirai sans ~*, I will tell you in plain English, or without beating about the bush.
ambassade (ɑ̃basad), s.f. [f. LL *ambactia*] Embassy; mission, diplomatic mission.
ambassad-eur, -rice (ɑ̃basadœr), s.m.f. Ambassador, ambassadress; (fig.) envoy, messenger.
ambe (ɑ̃b), s.m. [f. L *ambo*] A combination of two (numbers, letters, words, &c.).
ambiance (ɑ̃bjɑ̃s), s.f. Surroundings, atmosphere.
ambiant, -e (ɑ̃bjɑ̃), adj. [L *ambiens*] Ambient, environing, surrounding.
ambidextre (ɑ̃bidɛkstr), adj. [f. L *ambo+dextra*] Ambidextrous.
ambigu, -ë (ɑ̃bigy), adj. [L *ambiguus*] Ambiguous.
ambigu (ɑ̃bigy), s.m. Cold collation; (fig.) odd mixture.
ambiguïté (ɑ̃bigɥite), s.f. Ambiguity.
ambigument (ɑ̃bigymɑ̃), adv. Ambiguously, equivocally.
ambitieusement (ɑ̃bisjøzmɑ̃), adv. Ambitiously.
ambitieu-x, -se (ɑ̃bisjø), adj. Ambitious; aspiring, pretentious.
ambition (ɑ̃bisjɔ̃), s.f. [f. L *ambire*] Ambition.
ambitionner (ɑ̃bisjɔne), v.a. To be ambitious of; to aspire to; to aim at, to hope for.
amble (ɑ̃bl), s.m. [f. L *ambulare*] Amble, ambling; *aller l'~*, to amble.
ambler (ɑ̃ble), v.n. To amble.
ambleu-r, -se (ɑ̃blœr), adj. Ambling.
amblyopie (ɑ̃bliɔpi), s.f. (pathol.) Amblyopia, impaired vision.
ambon (ɑ̃bɔ̃), s.m. [Gr. wd] (arch.) Ambo.
ambre (ɑ̃br), s.m. [Arab. *anbar*] Amber; *~ gris*, ambergris; *il est fin comme l'~*, he is as sharp as a needle.

ambré, -e (ɑ̃bre), p. adj. Ambered, amber-scented; amber-coloured.
ambrer (ɑ̃bre), v.a. To perfume with ambergris; to make amber-coloured.
ambrette (ɑ̃brɛt), s.f. (bot.) Amber-seed, musk-seed.
ambroisie (ɑ̃brwazi), s.f. [Gr. *ambrosios*] Ambrosia.
ambrosiaque (ɑ̃brozjak), adj. Ambrosial.
ambroisien, -ne (ɑ̃brwazjɛ̃), adj. [f. *St Ambroise*] Ambrosian.
ambulance (ɑ̃bylɑ̃s), s.f. [f. L *ambulare*] Ambulance, field hospital; *voiture d'~*, ambulance-wagon or -car.
ambulanci-er, -ère (ɑ̃bylɑ̃sje), s.m.f. Ambulance-man; nurse; stretcher-bearer.
ambulant, -e (ɑ̃bylɑ̃), adj. [f. L *ambulare*] Ambulant; itinerant; strolling; movable; *marchand ~*, pedlar, hawker.
ambulation (ɑ̃byla'sjɔ̃), s.f. Ambulation.
ambulatoire (ɑ̃bylatwar), adj. Ambulatory.
âme (ɑm), s.f. [L *anima*] **1.** Soul; mind, spirit, heart; feeling; essence; *avoir la mort dans l'~*, to be grieved to death; *~ en peine*, tormented spirit, forlorn vagrant; *une ~ basse, une ~ de boue, une ~ de laquais*, a low, base, or grovelling mind (or soul); *il n'y avait ~ qui vive*, there was not a living soul; *rendre l'~* to give up the ghost; *~ damnée*, (pej.) tool, instrument; inspirer, evil spirit; *force d'~*, fortitude; *grandeur d'~*, magnanimity; *égalité d'~*, equanimity; *dans l'~*, at heart; every inch; **2.** *~s*, (pl.) people; **3.** motto (of a device); bore (of a gun); sound-post (of a violin); core (of a cast); small wood (of a faggot).
améliorable (ameljɔrabl), adj. Improvable.
amélioration (ameljɔra'sjɔ̃), s.f. Amelioration, improvement, betterment; *~s* (pl.) repairs, embellishments, improvements.
améliorer (ameljɔre), v.a. [f. L *melior*] To ameliorate, to improve, to better; **s'~**, v.pr. to improve.
amen (amɛn), s.m. [Hebr. wd] Amen; so be it; *dire oui et ~ à tout*, to agree to everything.
aménagement (amenaʒmɑ̃), s.m. [f. *ménage, aménager*] Fitting-up, disposition, arrangement, choice (of furniture); parcelling-out.
aménager (amenaʒe), v.a. To fit up; to dispose; to parcel out; *une maison bien aménagée* a well fitted and furnished house.
amendable (amɑ̃dabl), adj. Amendable, improvable.
amende (amɑ̃d), s.f. [f. *amender*] Fine, penalty, costs, forfeit, mulct; *mettre à l'~*, to fine; *faire ~ honorable*, to apologize; *les battus paient l'~*, woe to the weak!, the loser pays.
amendement (amɑ̃dmɑ̃), s.m. Amendment; improvement; (agric.) fertilizer, fertilizing; (Parl.) amendment.
amender (amɑ̃de), v.a. [f. L *emendare*] To amend, to improve; (agric.) to fertilize, to manure; **s'~**, v.pr. to mend, to amend.
amener (amne), v.a. [f. *mener*] **1.** To bring, to draw, to pull; to bring in, to bring out, up, down; to bring over, to introduce; **2.** to cause, to induce, to lead; **3.** to throw (at dice); **4.** (nav.) to lower, to strike; **s'~**, v.pr. (slang) to come along, to turn up, to blow along.
aménité (amenite), s.f. [L *amoenitas*] Amenity, kindness.
amentacé, -e (amɑ̃tase), adj. (bot.) Amentaceous.
amenuiser (amənɥize), v.a. [f. *menu*] To thin, to make thinner, to thin down, to reduce.
am-er, -ère (amɛr), adj. [L *amarus*] Bitter, biting, acrid, sharp, galling, sarcastic; briny, acrid. ~, s.m. Bitter, gall.
amer (amɛr), s.m. (usually in the pl.) [f. *mer*] (naut.) Seamark.
amèrement (amɛrmɑ̃), adv. Bitterly.
américain, -e (amerikɛ̃), adj. s.m.f. American; *à l'~e*, in the American style; *vol à l'~e*, confidence trick. **~e,** s.f. Trap, light vehicle.
américaniser (amerikanize), v.a. To Americanize.
américanisme (amerikanism), s.m. Americanism.
amérissage, amerrissage (amɛrisaʒ), s.m. (aeron.) Amerrissage.
amerrir (amɛrir) v.n. (aeron.) To alight on the water.
amertume (amɛrtym), s.f. Bitterness.
améthyste (ametist), s.f. [Gr. *amethustos*] Amethyst.
ameublement (amœbləmɑ̃), s.m. Furniture, set of furniture, suite.
ameublir (amœblir), v.a. [f. *meuble*] (agric.) To mellow (land), to loosen, to pulverize, to break (ground).
ameublissement (amœblismɑ̃), s.m. Breaking ground, mellowing, loosening (of soil).
ameulonner (amølɔne), v.a. (agric.) To shock, to stook, to heap, to stack, to cock.
ameutement (amøtmɑ̃), s.m. Collecting together (a crowd); exciting.
ameuter (amøte), v.a. [f. *meute*] **1.** To stir up, to set (*contre*, against), to raise, to excite; to collect, to bring together; to train (hounds) to hunt together; *~ la foule*, to cause, to get up a riot; **s'~**, v.pr. to rebel.
ami, -e (ami), s.m.f. [L *amicus*] **1.** Friend; lover, dear, sweetheart; *chambre d'~*, spare bedroom; *~ de cœur*,

bosom friend; *hé l'~!*, I say, man!; *les bons comptes font les bons ~s*, short reckonings make long friends; *on connaît l'~ au besoin*, a friend in need is a friend indeed; *bon ~, bonne ~e*, lover, sweetheart; (archaic) *m'amie*, my dear girl; **2.** favourer, supporter, ally.
ami, -e (ami), adj. Fond (*de*, of), friendly (to); kind, propitious; *~ lecteur*, gentle reader.
amiable (amjabl), adj. Amicable; *vente à l'~*, private sale, sale by private contract; *régler une affaire à l'~*, to settle a business (a difference) amicably, privately.
amiablement (amjabləmɑ̃), adv. Amicably.
amiante (amjɑ̃t), s.m. [Gr. *amiantos*] Amianthus, asbestos.
amibe (amib), s.f. (zool.) Amoeba.
amical, -e, (aux) (amikal), adj. Friendly, kind, amicable; *peu ~*, unfriendly.
amicalement (amikalmɑ̃), adv. In a friendly way, kindly, amicably.
amict (ami), s.m. [L *amictus*] Amice.
amide (amid), s.f. (chem.) Amide.
amidon (amidɔ̃), s.m. [Gr. *amulon*] Starch.
amidonnage (amidɔnaʒ), s.m. Starching.
amidonner (amidɔne), v.a. To starch.
amidonnerie (amidɔnri), s.f. Starch-works.
amidonnier (amidɔnje), s.m. Starch-maker.
aminche (amɛ̃ʃ), s.m. (slang, vulg.) Chum, pal.
amincir (amɛ̃sir), v.a.n. [f. *mince*] To make thinner, to make (a person) look slim, slender; *cette rayure amincit*, these stripes give slenderness to the figure; **s'~**, v.pr. to become thin or thinner.
amincissement (amɛ̃sismɑ̃), s.m. Thinning, growing thin.
amiral, (aux) (amiral), s.m. [f. Arab. *amir*] Admiral; *grand ~*, Admiral of the Fleet; *vice-~*, vice-admiral; *contre ~*, rear admiral; *vaisseau ~*, flagship.
amiralat (amirala), s.m. Admiralship; admiralty.
amirale (amiral), s.f. Admiral's wife.
amirauté (amirote), s.f. Admiralty.
amissible (amisibl), adj. (law) That may be lost.
amission (amisjɔ̃), s.f. [L *amissio*] (law) Loss.
amitié (amitje), s.f. [L *amicitat-*] Friendship; liking; affection, fondness; *prendre X en ~*, to take a liking to X; favour, kindness, pleasure; *faites-moi l'~ de*, do me the favour of; amity (between states, nations); regards, compliments, attentions; *meilleures ~s, mille ~s*, (at the end of a letter) kindest regards.
ammonia-c, -que (amɔnjak), adj. [Gr. *ammoniakon*] Ammoniac; *gaz ~*, ammonia; *sel ~*, sal ammoniac; *gomme ~que*, gum ammoniac; see AMMONIAQUE.
ammoniacal, -e, (aux) (amɔnjakal), adj. Ammoniacal.
ammoniaque (amɔnjak), s.f. (Liquid) ammonia; syn. ALCALI VOLATIL.
ammonite (ammɔnit), s.f. (zool.) Ammonite (fossil shell).
ammonium (ammɔnjɔm), s.m. (chem.) Ammonium.
amnésie (amnezi), s.f. [f. Gr. *a+mnēsis*] Amnesia, loss of memory.
amnicole (amnikɔl), adj. [f. L *amnis+colere*] (bot.) Growing near rivers.
amnios, amnion (amnjos, amnjɔ̃), s.m. [Gr. *amnion*] Amnion.
amniotique (amnjɔtik), adj. Amniotic, of the amnion.
amnistie (amnisti), s.f. [Gr. *amnēstia*] Amnesty.
amnistié, -e (amnistje), s.m.f. Amnestied person.
amnistier (amnistje), v.a. To amnesty.
amocher (amɔʃe), v.a. (colloq.) To knock about, to bruise, to wound, to ill-treat; to damage, to make a mess of.
amodiataire (amɔdjatɛr), s.m.f. Lessee.
amodiat-eur, -rice (amɔdjatœr), s.m.f. Lessor.
amodiation (amɔdja'sjɔ̃), s.f. Leasing, letting out on contract.
amodier (amɔdje), v.a. [f. L *ad+modium*] To lease out, to farm out.
amoindrir (amwɛ̃drir), v.a. [f. *moindre*] To lessen, to decrease, to diminish; **s'~**, v.pr. to fall off, to diminish; (fig.) to cheapen oneself.
amoindrissement (amwɛ̃drismɑ̃), s.m. Lessening, decrease, diminution; loss of reputation or prestige.
amollir (amɔlir), v.a. [f. *mol, mou*] To soften, to mollify, to unnerve, to unman; to damp (ardour); **s'~**, v.pr. to soften, to be mollified; (of wind) to abate; to become weak, inefficient.
amollissant, -e (amɔlisɑ̃), p. adj. Softening; enervating, unmanning, weakening.
amollissement (amɔlismɑ̃), s.m. Softening, mollification, weakening, effeminacy.
amonceler (amɔ̃sle), v.a. [f. *monceau*] To heap up, to pile up, to accumulate; to hoard; to drift; **s'~**, v.pr. to gather, to accumulate, to be driven into heaps; *les nuages s'amoncellent*, the clouds are gathering.
amoncellement (amɔ̃sɛlmɑ̃), s.m. Heap, accumulation, gathering, drift.
amont (amɔ̃), s.m. [f. *mont*] Upper part; *en ~*, up-stream, above; *vent d'~*, easterly wind.
amorçage (amɔrsaʒ), s.m. Priming; baiting.
amorce (amɔrs), s.f. [f. L *ad+morsus*] Bait; priming; percussion cap.

amorcer (amɔrse), v.a. **1.** To bait; ~ *une souricière,* to bait a mouse-trap; (fig.) to lure, to allure, to decoy; ~ *par des louanges,* to lure with flattery; **2.** to prime (fire-arms, &c.); **3.** to exhaust (a syphon); **4.** to cut into, to open, to begin; **s'~,** v.pr. *ces fusils s'amorcent seuls,* these guns are self-priming.

amorceu-r, -se (amɔrsœr), s.m.f. Tempter: one who allures, baits, or tries to catch; starter.

amorçoir (amɔrswar), s.m. (techn.) Wimble; instrument for beginning holes; gouge or centre-bit of an auger, prick-punch of a drill.

amoroso (amɔrozo), adv. [It. wd] Tenderly; *chanter* ~, to sing tenderly, with feeling.

amorphe (amɔrf), adj. [Gr. *a*+*morphē*] Amorphous, shapeless; *phosphore* ~, amorphous (or red) phosphorus; *allumettes* ~*s,* safety matches.

amorphie (amɔrfi), s.f. Amorphy, shapelessness.

amortir (amɔrtir), v.a. [f. *mort*] **1.** To deaden, to break, to lessen; ~ *une chute,* to break a fall; ~ *un coup,* to deaden a blow; to calm down, to assuage, to subdue; to reduce (inflammation, &c.); to blunt; ~ *les sens,* to blunt the senses; to slacken (a fire); to tone down; *une lumière amortie,* a subdued light; to slow down; ~ *l'aire d'un bâtiment,* to deaden a ship's way; *une balle amortie,* a spent ball; **2.** to pay, to liquidate; ~ *une hypothèque,* to pay off a mortgage; **3.** (cook.) to keep (meat) to make it tender; **s'~,** v.pr. to be deadened, weakened.

amortissable (amɔrtisabl), adj. Redeemable (annuities, &c.).

amortissement (amɔrtismɑ̃), s.m. **1.** Deadening, *l'~ d'un choc,* the deadening of a shock; **2.** depreciation; **3.** liquidation, redemption; *l'~ d'une rente,* the redemption of an annuity; *fond d'~,* fund for paying off a debt; depreciation fund; **4.** (arch.) any ornament completing the upper part of a building.

amortisseur (amɔrtisœr), s.m. (motor. aeron.) Shock-absorber.

amouillante (amujɑ̃t), adj.f. [f. *à*+*mouiller*] Calving (cow).

amour (amur), s.m. (and poet. or iron. s.f. pl.) [L *amor*] **1.** Love, passion, flame; (pl.) amours; *faire l'~,* to court, to woo, to make love (to); to copulate; *languir d'~,* to be love-sick; *les premières ~s,* first love, (iron.) calf-love; *vivre d'~ et d'eau fraîche,* to live on bread and cheese and kisses; *il n'y a point de laides ~s,* all your geese are swans; *un remède d'~,* an ugly woman; strong affection (for persons or ideas); *l'~ de la patrie,* true patriotism; *l'~ filial,* filial affection; *faites-le pour l'~ de moi,* do it for my sake; *il l'a fait comme pour l'~ de Dieu,* he did it with an ill grace; **2.** the person beloved; *mon* ~, my darling; *il est l'~ de sa mère,* he is his mother's darling; any pretty thing or person; *ce vase est un* ~, this vase is a joy, a beauty; *quel ~ d'enfant!,* what a lovely child!; **3.** (myth.) Love, Cupid.

amouracher (amuraʃe), v.a. [f. *amour*] (iron.) To enamour, to inflame with love; **s'~,** v.pr. to be enamoured, to fall in love, to be smitten; *il s'est ~ d'une danseuse,* he has gone crazy about a dancer.

amourette (amurɛt), s.f. [dim. of *amour*] **1.** Intrigue, love-affair, amourette; **2.** (pl.) (cook.) calf's or sheep's marrow; **3.** (bot.) (pop.) lily-of-the-valley; ~ *des prés,* quaking grass; *bois d'~,* mimosa-wood.

amoureusement (amurøzmɑ̃), adv. **1.** Lovingly; **2.** amorously; **3.** con amore.

amoureu-x, -se (amurø), adj. In love (*de,* with), enamoured (*de,* of); (pej.) amorous, amatory; *devenir ~ de,* to fall in love with; *éperdument* ~, desperately or head-over-ears in love. **~,** s.m.f. Lover, sweetheart.

amour-propre (amurprɔpr), s.m. Self-respect, self-esteem; pride.

amovibilité (amɔvibilite), s.f. [f. L *amovere*] **1.** Removability (of officials); **2.** uncertain tenure (of an office).

amovible (amɔvibl), adj. Removable; liable to dismissal, not permanent or for life (of appointments).

ampélidées (ɑ̃pelide), s.f. pl. [Gr. *ampelos*] Ampelideae or vine family.

ampélographie (ɑ̃pelɔgrafi), s.f. [Gr. *ampelos*+*graphein*] Ampelography.

ampère (ɑ̃pɛr), s.m. [f. *Ampère,* French mathematician and physicist, d. 1836] Ampere, unit of current; ~ *heure,* ampere-hour; ~ *mètre,* ampere-meter.

amphibie (ɑ̃fibi), adj. [Gr. *amphi*+*bios*] Amphibious; (fig.) double. **~,** s.m. Amphibian (pl. amphibia or amphibians).

amphibiens (ɑ̃fibjɛ̃), s.m. pl. Amphibia, amphibians.

amphibole (ɑ̃fibɔl), adj. [Gr. *amphi*+*bolos*] (min.) Amphibole, hornblende.

amphibologie (ɑ̃fibɔlɔʒi), s.f. Amphibology.

amphibologique (ɑ̃fibɔlɔʒik), adj. Amphibological.

amphibologiquement (ɑ̃fibɔlɔʒikmɑ̃), adv. Amphibologically.

amphibraque (ɑ̃fibrak), s.m. (pros.) Amphibrach.

amphictyon (ɑ̃fiktjɔ̃), s.m. [Gr. hist.] Amphictyon, deputy belonging to an assembly or council.

amphictyonide (ãfiktjɔnid), adj. Entitled to be represented in the amphictyonic council.
amphictyonie (ãfiktjɔni), s.f. [Gr. hist.] Amphictyony.
amphictyonique (ãfiktjɔnik), adj. Amphictyome.
amphigame (ãfigam), adj. [Gr. *amphi*+ *gamos*] (bot.) Amphigamous.
amphigène (ãfiʒɛn), adj. (bot.) Amphigenous.
amphigouri (ãfiguri), s.m. [Gr. *amphi*+ *guros*] Amphigouri or amphigory, burlesque composition, rigmarole.
amphigourique (ãfigurik), adj. Unintelligible, ludicrous, nonsensical.
amphigouriquement (ãfigurikmã), adv. Unintelligibly, nonsensically.
amphioxus (ãfiɔksys), s.m. [Gr. *amphi*+ *oxus*] (ichth.) Amphioxus, lancelet.
amphipode (ãfipɔd), s.m. [Gr. *amphi*+ *pous, podos*] Amphipod.
amphiptère (ãfitɛr), s.m. [Gr. *amphi* + *pteron*] (herald.) Winged dragon.
amphisbène (ãfisbɛn), s.m. [Gr. *amphi*+ *baino*] Amphisbaena.
amphiscien (ãfisjɛ̃), s.m. [Gr. *amphi*+ *skia*] (geog.) Amphiscian, inhabitant of the torrid zone.
amphithéâtre (ãfiteɑtr), s.m. [Gr. *amphi* +*theatron*] **1.** Amphitheatre; lecture-room; *terrain en* ~, ground rising in the form of an amphitheatre; ~ *anatomique*, dissecting theatre; **2.** the higher seats in a modern theatre.
amphitryon (ãfitriɔ̃), s.m. [proper n. myth.] Amphitryon, host, entertainer, giver of a feast.
amphore (ãfɔr), s.f. [L *amphora*] Amphora.
ample (ãpl), adj. [L *amplus*] Ample, spacious, large, wide, full, abundant, copious, liberal; *un plus* ~ *théâtre*, a wider stage; *un* ~ *discours*, a lengthy speech; *une* ~ *moisson*, an abundant harvest; *une* ~ *récompense*, a liberal reward.
amplecti-f, -ve (ãplektif), adj. [L *amplecti*] (bot.) Amplective.
amplement (ãpləmã), adv. Amply, largely, widely, abundantly, fully.
ampleur (ãplœr), s.f. **1.** Ampleness, breadth; abundance; (fig.) wide range; *l'*~ *de son front*, the breadth of his forehead; *l'*~ *de son style*, the dignity of his style; *ce commerce a pris une certaine* ~, this business has become of considerable importance; *elle prend de l'*~, she is filling out, she is putting on flesh; **2.** (dress.) fullness; *cette cape manque de l'*~, this cloak lacks fullness.
amplexicaule (ãplɛksikol), adj. [L *amplexus*+*caulis*] (bot.) Amplexicaul.
ampliateur (ãpliatœr), s.m. [f. *ampliation*] Duplicator.
ampliati-f, -ve (ãpliatif), adj. Ampliative, duplicating.
ampliation (ãplia'sjɔ̃), s.f. [L *ampliatio*] **1.** Office copy, duplicate; *pour* ~, this is a true copy; **2.** expansion; *l'*~ *des poumons*, the expansion of the lungs.
amplifiant, -e (ãplifjã), p. adj. Magnifying; *verre* ~, magnifying glass.
amplificat-eur -rice (ãplifikatœr), adj. Amplifying. ~, s.m.f. **1.** Amplifier; **2.** (pej.) exaggerator; **3.** (photo.) amplifier, enlarger.
amplificati-f, -ve (ãplifikatif), adj. (opt.) Magnifying.
amplification (ãplifika'sjɔ̃), s.f. **1.** Amplification, development; **2.** (pej.) exaggeration; **3.** magnification.
amplifier (ãplifje), v.a. [L *amplificare*] **1.** To amplify, to enlarge upon, to develop; **2.** to exaggerate; *les voyageurs ont l'habitude d'*~, travellers are apt to exaggerate; **3.** to magnify (with a lens).
amplissime (ãplisim), adj. [L *amplissimus*] Very considerable, (of persons) worthy of consideration; (obs.) honorary title of the Rector of the University of Paris.
amplitude (ãplityd), s.f. [f. *ample*] Amplitude, largeness, extent.
ampoule (ãpul), s.f. [L *ampulla*] **1.** Ampulla, bellied phial; *la Sainte* ~, *Ampulla Remensis*, the phial containing the sacred oil used formerly for anointing the kings of France; **2.** blister; *il ne se fait pas d'*~*s aux mains*, he'll not die of overwork; **3.** (bot.) ampulla, spongiole; **4.** (electr.) bulb, lamp.
ampoulé, -e (ãpule), adj. Turgid, bombastic, inflated; *discours* ~, fustian, bombast; *style* ~, pompous style; syn. EMPHATIQUE, BOURSOUFLÉ.
amputation (ãpyta'sjɔ̃), s.f. Amputation; *faire l'*~ *de*, to amputate; ~ *à lambeaux*, flap amputation.
amputé, -e (ãpyte), p. adj. Amputated.
amputer (ãpyte), v.a.n. [L *amputare*] (surg.) To amputate, to cut off.
amulette (amylɛt), s.f. [L *amuletum*] Amulet, charm, talisman.
amunitionnement (amynisjɔnmã), s.m. Provisionment, (archaic) munition.
amunitionner (amynisjɔne), v.a. To provide with stores, to provision.
amure (amyr), s.f. [L *ad*+*murum*] (naut.) Tack, clew-line; *point d'*~, weather-tack; ~ *à tribord*, starboard tacks aboard.
amurer (amyre), v.a. (naut.) To tack, to haul aboard a tack.
amusable (amyzabl), adj. Amusable, capable of being amused.
amusant, -e (amyzã), p. adj. Amusing, entertaining, diverting, pleasing; *un récit* ~, an amusing tale, a diverting story.
amusement (amyzmã), s.m. Amuse-

ment, diversion, pastime; deception, pretext; *tout ce que vous me dites là n'est qu'un* ~, all this that you are telling me is mere deception.

amuser (amyze), v.a. [*à+muser*] **1.** To amuse, to entertain, to divert; *cette aventure a amusé toute la ville,* this adventure was the talk of the town; **2.** to deceive, to mislead; (fig.) to beguile; *il s'aperçut qu'on l'amusait,* he saw that he was being trifled with; ~ *l'ennemi,* to mislead the enemy; **s'**~, v.pr. **1.** to be amused, to enjoy, to amuse or to divert oneself; *amusez-vous bien,* have a good time; **2.** to make fun of; *il s'est amusé de lui,* he made sport of him; **3.** to waste, to idle away time; *s'*~ *à la moutarde,* to waste one's time on trifles; *il s'est beaucoup amusé étant jeune,* he led a very fast life in his youth.

amusette (amyzɛt), s.f. **1.** Toy, petty amusement, child's-play; *ce n'est pour lui qu'une* ~, it is mere child's-play to him; *elle ne lui a été qu'une* ~, she was a mere plaything to him; **2.** (mil.) amusette, a light field-cannon.

amuseu-r, -se (amyzœr), s.m.f. Amuser.

amusoire (amyzwar), s.f. (rare) The means or instrument of amusement.

amygdale (amigdal), s.f. [Gr. *amugdalē*] (anat.) Tonsil.

amygdalées (amigdale), s.f. pl. (bot.) Amygdalaceae.

amygdalin, -e (amigdalɛ̃), adj. (chem.) Amygdaline.

amygdalite (amigdalit), s.f. (pathol.) Amygdalitis, tonsillitis.

amygdaloïde (amigdalɔid), adj. (min.) Amygdaloid.

amylacé, -e (amilase), adj. [Gr. *amulon*] Amylaceous, starchy.

amyle (amil), s.m. [Gr. *amulon*] (chem.) Amyl.

amylène (amilɛn), s.m. (chem.) Amylene.

amylique (amilik), adj. (chem.) Amylic.

an (ɑ̃), s.m. [L *annus*] **1.** Year, twelvemonth; *il y a un* ~, a year ago; *dans un* ~, a year hence; *elle n'a pas encore vingt* ~*s,* she is still in her teens; *âgé d'un* ~, one year old; (of horses) yearling; *tous les deux* ~*s,* every other year, biennially; *de trois en trois* ~*s,* every third year, triennially; *le jour de l'*~, New Year's Day; *bon* ~, *mal* ~, one year with another, on an average; *bout de l'*~, year's-mind, anniversary mass (in memory of a person's death); *avoir tant par* ~, to have so much a year; *elle va sur ses trente* ~*s,* she is not far off thirty; *je m'en moque comme de l'*~ *quarante,* I don't care a rap (a straw, a pin) for it (him, her); **2.** ~*s,* (pl.) years, days, old age; *la fleur des* ~*s,* the prime of youth; *dès ses jeunes* ~*s,* from his early youth; *le poids, le fardeau, des* ~*s,* the weight (burden) of years (age); *l'injure des* ~*s,* the ravages of time; see ANNÉE.

ana (ana), s.m. invar. [Gr. wd] Ana, (pl.) anas, collection of thoughts, sayings, &c.

anabaptisme (anabatism), s.m. [Gr. *ana* +*baptismos*] Anabaptism.

anabaptiste (anabatist), s.m.f. Anabaptist. ~, adj. Anabaptistical, anabaptist.

anacarde (anakard), s.m. [Gr. *ana+cardion*] (bot.) Cashew-nut.

anacardier (anakardje), s.m. (bot.) Cashew-nut tree, *Anacardium occidentale.*

anachorète (anakɔrɛt), s.m. [Gr. *ana+khōreo*] Anchoret, anchorite, recluse.

anachorétisme (anakɔretism), s.m. Anchoretical existence; the desire for such an existence.

anachronique (anakrɔnik), adj. Anachronic.

anachronisme (anakrɔnism), s.m. [Gr. *ana+khronos*] Anachronism.

anacoluthe (anakɔlyt), s.f. [Gr. *ana+kolouthos*] (gram.) Anacoluthon.

anaconda (anakɔ̃da), s.m. (zool.) Anaconda; syn. EUNECTE.

anacoste (anakɔst), s.f. Anacosta, a kind of serge.

anacréontique (anakreɔ̃tik), adj. Anacreontic.

anacréontisme (anakreɔ̃tism), s.m. Imitation of Anacreontic lyrics or philosophy.

anacrouse (anakruz), s.f. [Gr. *anakrousis*] (pros., mus.) Anacrusis.

anadrome (anadrom), adj. [Gr. *ana+dromos*] (ichth.) Anadromous.

anadyomène (anadjɔmɛn), adj. [Gr. *anaduomai*] Anadyomene.

anaglyphe (anaglif), s.m. [Gr. *ana+glupho*] Anaglyph.

anagogie (anagɔʒi), s.f. [Gr. *anagōgē*] Anagoge, spiritual interpretation.

anagramme (anagram), s.f. Anagram.

anagyre (anaʒir), s.m. [Gr. *ana+guros*] (bot.) Bean-trefoil.

anal, -e, (aux) (anal), adj. [L *anus*] Anal; *nageoire* ~*e,* anal fin.

analectes (analekt), s.m. pl. [Gr. *analekta*] Analecta, analects.

analepsie (analepsi), s.f. [Gr. *analēpsis*] (med.) Convalescence.

analeptique (analeptik), adj. (med.) Analeptic.

analgésie, analgie (analʒezi, analʒi), s.f. [Gr. *an+algos*] (med.) Analgesia.

analgésine (analʒezin), s.f. (pharm.) Antipyrine; syn. ANTIPYRINE.

analgie. See ANALGÉSIE.

analogie (analɔʒi), s.f. [Gr. *analogia*] Analogy; ~ *frappante,* striking analogy; *raisonner par* ~, to analogize.

analogique (analɔʒik), adj. Analogical.

analogiquement (analɔʒikmɑ̃), adv. Analogically.
analogisme (analɔʒism), s.m. Analogy.
analogue (analɔg), adj. Analogous, similar. ~, s.m. Analogue; *ce mot n'a point d'~ en anglais,* this word has no English equivalent.
analysable (analizabl), adj. Analysable.
analyse (analiz), s.f. [Gr. *analusis*] **1.** Analysis; *en dernière* ~, after careful examination, in conclusion, after all; the upshot is; **2.** (gram.) parsing; *faire l'~ grammaticale de,* to parse; *faire l'~ logique de,* to analyse (logically).
analyser (analize), v.a. **1.** To analyse, to make an analysis of; **2.** (gram.) to parse; to analyse; ~ *grammaticalement une phrase,* to parse a sentence; ~ *logiquement une phrase,* to analyse (logically) a sentence; **3.** to review; ~ *un livre,* to review a book.
analyste (analist), s.m.f. Analyser, analyst.
analytique (analitik), adj. Analytical, analytic. ~, s.f. Analytics.
analytiquement (analitikmɑ̃), adv. Analytically.
anamorphose (anamɔrfoz), s.f. [Gr. *ana +morphē*] Anamorphosis; a distorted projection or drawing; abnormal transformation of a fungus, &c.
ananas (anana), s.m. [Peruvian orig.] Pine-apple, ananas.
anapeste (anapɛst), s.m. [f. Gr. *anapaistos*] (pros.) Anapaest.
anaphore (anafɔr), s.f. [Gr. *ana+phero*] (rhet.) Anaphora, repetition.
anaplastie (anaplasti), s.f. [f. Gr. *ana+plassein*] (surg.) Anaplasty.
anarchie (anarʃi), s.f. [f. Gr. *anarkhia*] Anarchy, confusion.
anarchique (anarʃik), adj. Anarchic, anarchical.
anarchiquement (anarʃikmɑ̃), adv. Anarchically.
anarchiser (anarʃize), v.a. To anarchize, to disorganize.
anarchisme (anarʃism), s.m. Anarchism.
anarchiste (anarʃist), adj. s.m.f. Anarchist.
anastigmate, anastigmatique (anastigmat, anastigmatik), adj. (photo.) Anastigmatic.
anastomose (anastɔmoz), s.f. [Gr. *anastomōsis*] (anat.) Anastomosis, inosculation.
anastrophe (anastrɔf), s.f. [f. Gr. *ana+strepho*] (gram.) Anastrophe.
anathématique (anatematik), adj. Offered in expiation, against the effects of anathema.
anathématisation (anatematiza'sjɔ̃), s.f. Anathematization.
anathématiser (anatematize), v.a. To anathematize, to declare accursed; to reprobate, to blame severely.
anathème (anatɛm), s.m. [f. Gr. *anathema*] **1.** Anathema, curse; reprobation, blame; *frapper d'~,* to declare accursed, to anathematize; *lancer un ~ contre,* to launch an anathema against; **2.** ~, s.m.f. anathematized person. ~, adj. Accursed, anathematized.
anatife (anatif), s.m. (zool.) Barnacle, bernacle.
anatomie (anatɔmi), s.f. [f. Gr. *anatomia*] **1.** The science of anatomy, the art of dissecting; **2.** anatomy, skeleton, bodily structure.
anatomique (anatɔmik), adj. Anatomical.
anatomiquement (anatɔmikmɑ̃), adv. Anatomically.
anatomiser (anatɔmize), v.a. To anatomize, to dissect (a body), to examine minutely, to analyse (a book, &c.).
anatomiste (anatɔmist), s.m.f. Anatomist.
anatrope (anatrɔp), adj. [f. Gr. *ana+trepein*] (bot.) Anatropous.
ancestral, -e, (aux) (ɑ̃sɛstral), adj. Ancestral; *la demeure ~e,* the ancestral home.
ancêtre (ɑ̃sɛtr), s.m.f. [f. L *antecessor*] (masc.) Ancestor, (fem.) ancestress; (m. pl.) ancestors, forefathers; syn. (pl.) AÏEUX, PÈRES.
anche (ɑ̃ʃ), s.f. [f. OHG *ancha*] Reed (of a clarinet, &c.), reed-pipe (of an organ); *jeu d' ~s,* reed-stop (of an organ)
anchilops (ɑ̃kilɔps), s.m. [f. Gr. *agkhi+ops*] (med.) Anchilops.
anchois (ɑ̃ʃwa), s.m. [f. Span. *anchoa*] Anchovy; *beurre d'~,* anchovy paste.
ancien, -ne (ɑ̃sjɛ̃), adj. [L *ante*] **1.** Old, ancient, antique, early; *mœurs ~nes,* ancient customs; *meubles ~s,* antique furniture; (mil.) *plus ~,* senior; *moins ~,* junior; *cette statue est de date plus ~ne,* this statue is of earlier date; **2.** old-fashioned; *cette maison est d'un genre ~,* this house has an old-fashioned appearance; **3.** former, late, retired; *c'est un ~ officier,* he is a retired officer; *l'~ ministre de la guerre,* the ex-minister for war. ~, s.m. Old man; *les ~s,* the Ancients.
anciennement (ɑ̃sjɛnmɑ̃), adv. Formerly, of old, anciently, in the days of yore; syn. JADIS, AUTREFOIS.
ancienneté (ɑ̃sjɛnte), s.f. **1.** Ancientness, ancientry, antiquity; **2.** seniority; *par ~,* or *à l'~,* by, in order of, seniority.
ancile (ɑ̃sil), s.m. [L wd] (anc. Rome) Ancile.
ancipité, -e (ɑ̃sipite), adj. [L *anceps, ancipitis*] (bot.) Ancipital, ancipitous.
ancolie (ɑ̃kɔli), s.f. [L *aquilegia*] (bot.) Columbine.

ancrage (ãkraʒ), s.m. (naut.) Anchorage.
ancre (ãkr), s.f. [LL *ancora*] Anchor; *maîtresse* ~, ~ *de salut*, sheet-anchor; ~ *à jet*, kedge-anchor; *mouiller l'*~, to cast anchor; *lever l'*~, to weigh anchor; *brider l'*~, to shoe anchor; *chasser sur ses* ~*s*, to drag one's anchors; (fig.) *c'était mon* ~ *de salut*, it was my sheet-anchor, my last resource.
ancrer (ãkre), v.a. To anchor; (build.) to brace; (fig.) to establish, to secure, to settle; **s'**~, to settle oneself, to get a footing.
ancrure (ãkryr), s.f. (techn.) S-iron, T-iron, tie-rod.
andain (ãdɛ̃), s.m. [f. root of It. *andare*] Swath (in mowing).
andalou, -se (ãdalu), adj. s.m.f. Andalusian.
andouille (ãduj), s.f. [LL *inductilis*] Chitterling stuffed with meat; (slang) muff; *faire l'*~, to play the fool.
andouiller (ãduje), s.m. [L *ante*+Fr. *œil*] Antler; *maître* ~, brow antler.
andouillette (ãdujɛt), s.f. Small chitterling.
andrinople (ãdrinɔpl), s.f. [f. *Andrinople*, Thrace] Turkey twill; *rouge d'*~, Turkey red.
androgénie (ãdrɔʒeni), s.f. Androgenesis.
androgyne (ãdrɔʒin), adj. s.m.f. [Gr. *androgunos*] Androgynous; androgyne, hermaphrodite.
androïde (ãdrɔid), s.m. [Gr. *andros*+*eidos*] Android, automaton.
androphobe (ãdrɔfɔb), s.m. adj. [Gr. *andros*+*phobos*] Misanthrope, misanthropist.
androphobie (ãdrɔfɔbi), s.f. Aversion to men, misanthropy.
andropogon (ãdrɔpɔgɔ̃), s.m. [Gr. *andros* +*pogon*] (bot.) Andropogon, lemon-grass.
âne (ɑn), s.m. [L *asinus*; OF *asne*] Ass, donkey, jack-ass; (fig.) jack-ass, fool, dolt; *bonnet d'*~, dunce's cap; *pont aux* ~*s*, pons asinorum; *c'est un* ~ *bâté*, he is a downright ass; *sérieux comme un* ~ *qu'on étrille*, as solemn as a judge; *brider son* ~ *par la queue*, to put the cart before the horse, to get hold of the wrong end of the stick; *un* ~ *ne trébuche pas deux fois sur la même pierre*, once bitten, twice shy; *faute d'un point, Martin perdit son* ~, a miss is as good as a mile; *comme l'*~ *de Buridan*, like a donkey between two haystacks; *donner le coup de pied de l'*~, to kick a man when he is down; *l'*~ *revêtu de la peau du lion*, the ass in a lion's skin; the daw in peacock's feathers; *il fait l'*~ *pour avoir du son*, there is method in his madness; *il y a plus d'un* ~ *à la foire qui s'appelle Martin*, there's more than one Jack at the fair; *on ne peut faire boire un* ~ *s'il n'a pas soif*, you may lead a horse to the water, but you cannot make him drink; *à laver la tête d'un* ~ *on perd sa lessive*, there is no washing a blackamoor white.
anéantir (aneãtir), v.a. [*à*+*néant*] **1.** To annihilate, to destroy, to suppress (privileges, &c.), to annul (documents), to crush; **2.** (fig.) to paralyse, to dumbfound; *anéanti par la crainte*, prostrated by fear; **s'**~, v.pr. to come to nothing; to prostrate oneself, to humble oneself; syn. DÉTRUIRE.
anéantissement (aneãtismã), s.m. **1.** Annihilation, destruction, ruin, abolition; **2.** self-abasement; **3.** prostration (of body or mind).
anecdote (anɛkdɔt), s.f. [Gr. *anekdotos*] Anecdote.
anecdotier (anɛkdɔtje), s.m. Anecdotist.
anecdotique (anɛkdɔtik), adj. Anecdotic.
anecdotiser (anɛkdɔtize), v.n. To collect anecdotes; to relate anecdotes.
ânée (ɑne), s.f. Donkey-load.
anémie (anemi), s.f. [Gr. *an*+*haima*] (med.) Anaemia.
anémier (anemje), v.a. To render anaemic.
anémique (anemik), adj. Anaemic. ~, s.m.f. Person affected with anaemia.
anémographe (anemɔgraf), s.m. (meteor.) Anemograph.
anémographie (anemɔgrafi), s.f. [Gr. *anemos*+*graphein*] Anemography.
anémomètre (anemɔmɛtr), s.m. [Gr. *anemos*+*metron*] Anemometer.
anémone (anemɔn), s.f. [Gr. *anemos*] (bot.) Anemone, wind-flower; *greffe* or *patte d'*~, anemone-bulb or root.
anémoscope (anemɔskɔp), s.m. Anemoscope, weather-cock, wind-vane.
anencéphale (anãsefal), adj. s.m.f. [Gr. *an*+*encephalon*] Anencephalous.
ânerie (ɑnri), s.f. **1.** Stupidity, gross ignorance; **2.** blunder; *dire des* ~*s*, to make an ass of oneself.
anéroïde (anerɔid), adj. [Gr. *a*+*nêros*] Aneroid.
ânesse (ɑnɛs), s.f. She-ass, she-donkey.
anesthésie (anɛstezi), s.f. [Gr. *an*+*aisthēsis*] (med.) Anaesthesia, anaesthesis.
anesthésier (anɛstezje), v.a. To anaesthetize.
anesthésique (anɛstezik), adj. s.m. (med.) Anaesthetic.
anévrismatique (anevrismatik), adj. (med.) Aneurismal.
anévrisme (anevrism), s.m. [Gr. *aneurusma*] (med.) Aneurism.
anfractueu-x, -se (ãfraktɥø), adj. Anfractuous.
anfractuosité (ãfraktɥozite), s.f. [L *anfractuosus*] Anfractuosity.
ange (ãʒ), s.m. [Gr. *aggelos*] **1.** Angel; ~ *gardien*, guardian angel; *être aux* ~*s*, to

be in raptures; *rire aux ~s*, to smile unconsciously, to smile in one's sleep; **2.** angel, gold coin; **3.** (ichth.) angel-fish.
angelet (ɑ̃ʒlɛ), s.m. Little angel, cherub.
angélique (ɑ̃ʒelik), adj. Angelic; *le docteur ~*, the angelical doctor, St. Thomas Aquinas. **~**, s.f. (bot.) Angelica.
angéliquement (ɑ̃ʒelikmɑ̃), adv. Angelically.
angéliser (ɑ̃ʒelize), v.a. To angelize.
angelot (ɑ̃ʒlo), s.m. **1.** Cherub, angel; **2.** angel, a gold coin issued by Louis IX; **3.** angelot cheese; **4.** (ichth.) angel-fish.
angélus (ɑ̃ʒelys), s.m. Angelus; *sonner l'~*, to ring the angelus.
angevin, -e (ɑ̃ʒvɛ̃), adj. s.m.f. Angevin.
angine (ɑ̃ʒin), s.f. [L *angina*] (med.) Angina; *~ tonsilaire*, tonsillitis, quinsy; *~ couenneuse, pseudo-membraneuse*, croup; *~ de poitrine*, angina pectoris.
angineu-x, -se (ɑ̃ʒinø), adj. (med.) Anginous, anginal.
angiosperme (ɑ̃ʒjospɛrm), adj. (bot.) Angiospermous. **~**, s.f. Angiosperm.
anglais, -e (ɑ̃glɛ), adj. English; *à l'~e*, after the English fashion, in the English style; *filer à l'~e*, to slip off, to take French leave; (dressm.) *couture ~e*, French seam. **~**, s.m.f. Englishman, Englishwoman.
anglaiser (ɑ̃glɛze), v.a. To nick (a horse).
angle (ɑ̃gl), s.m. [L *angulus*] (geom.) Angle; corner, bend, turn; *à l'~ de la rue*, at the corner of the street; *~ aigu, obtus, droit*, acute, obtuse, right angle; *à ~ droit avec*, perpendicular to, at right angles with.
anglet (ɑ̃glɛ), s.m. (mason.) Channel, splay.
angleu-x, -se (ɑ̃glø), adj. Lobed, wrinkled (of fruits), many-cornered.
anglican, -e (ɑ̃glikɑ̃), adj. Anglican; *l'Église ~e*, the Church of England.
anglicanisme (ɑ̃glikanism), s.m. Anglicanism.
angliciser (ɑ̃glisize), v.a. To anglicize.
anglicisme (ɑ̃glisism), s.m. Anglicism.
anglomane (ɑ̃glɔman), adj. s.m.f. Anglomaniac.
anglomanie (ɑ̃glɔmani), s.f. Anglomania.
anglophile (ɑ̃glɔfil), s.m.f. adj. Anglophile.
anglophobe (ɑ̃glɔfɔb), s.m.f. adj. Anglophobe.
anglophobie (ɑ̃glɔfɔbi), s.f. [*anglo*+Gr. *phobos*] Anglophobia.
anglo-saxon, -ne (ɑ̃glosaksɔ̃), adj. s.m.f. Anglo-Saxon.
angoissant, -e (ɑ̃gwasɑ̃), adj. Causing extreme anxiety, agonizing (of suffering); *douleur ~e*, agonizing pain.
angoisse (ɑ̃gwas), s.f. [L *angustia*] Anguish, agony, violent pain; pang, spasm; *poire d'~*, choke-pear.
angoisser (ɑ̃gwase), v.a. To anguish, to agonize (with pain); to cause anxiety.
angon (ɑ̃gɔ̃), s.m. [Frank. wd] **1.** Combined javelin and short pike; **2.** (fish.) lobster-hook.
angora (ɑ̃gɔra), s.m. adj. [f. *Angora*, Asia Minor] Angora; *chèvre ~*, angora goat.
angosture (ɑ̃gɔstyr), s.f. See ANGUSTURE.
angrois (ɑ̃grwɑ), s.m. Wedge (for hammer-head).
anguiforme (ɑ̃gifɔrm), adj. [L *anguis*+*forme*] Anguilliform, eel-shaped.
anguille (ɑ̃gij), s.f. [L *anguilla*] (ichth.) Eel; *~ plat-bec*, grig; *~ de mer*, conger-eel; *~ de Surinam* or *torpille*, electric eel; *comme une ~*, as slippery as an eel; *il y a ~ sous roche*, there is a snake in the grass; there is a nigger in the wood-pile; I smell a rat; *nœud d'~*, slip-knot.
anguillère (ɑ̃gijɛr), s.f. Eel-pond.
angulaire (ɑ̃gylɛr), adj. [L *angulus*] Angular; (lit. and fig.) *pierre ~*, cornerstone; *dent ~*, canine tooth; *figure ~*, angular face.
angulairement (ɑ̃gylɛrmɑ̃), adv. Angularly.
angulé, -e (ɑ̃gyle), adj. Provided with angles.
anguleu-x, -se (ɑ̃gylø) Angular, rough, rugged; *figure ~se*, angular face; *traits ~*, rugged features.
angusticlave (ɑ̃gystiklav), s.m. [L *angustus*+*clavus*] Angusticlave.
angustifolié, -e (ɑ̃gystifɔlje), adj. [L *angustus*+*folium*] (bot.) Angustifoliate, angustifolious.
angusture, angosture (ɑ̃gystyr, ɑ̃gɔstyr), s.f. [f. *Angustura*, S. America] (med.) Angustura bark.
anhélation (anela'sjɔ̃), s.f. (med.) Anhelation.
anhéler (anele), v.n. [L *anhelare*] (med.) To breathe with difficulty.
anhéleu-x, -se (anelø), adj. (med.) Anhelose, panting.
anhydre (anidr), adj. [Gr. *an*+*hudōr*] (chem.) Anhydrous; *chaux ~*, quick-lime.
anicroche (anikrɔʃ), s.f. Small hindrance, hitch, snag.
âni-er, -ère (ɑnje), s.m.f. Donkey-driver.
aniline (anilin), s.f. (chem.) Aniline.
animadversion (animadvɛrsjɔ̃), s.f. [L *animadversio*] Animadversion.
animal (pl. **aux**) (animal), s.m. [L *animalis*] **1.** Animal; **2.** (abuse) beast, brute; *va-t-en ~ !*, get out, you beast !; (playfully) *il en a une chance, l'~ !*, what a lucky blighter he is !
animal, -e, (aux) (animal), adj. Animal; *noir ~*, animal charcoal, bone black.
animalcule (animalkyl), s.m. [L *animalculum*] Animalcule, (pl.) animalcules or animalcula.
animalesque (animalɛsk), adj. Animal.

animalier (animalje), adj. s.m. Animalist, painter or sculptor of animals.
animalisation (animaliza'sjɔ̃), s.f. Animalization.
animaliser (animalize), v.a. To animalize; **s'~**, v. pr. to be animalized; (fig.) to be bestialized.
animalité (animalite), s.f. Animality.
animat-eur, -rice (animatœr), adj. Animating, animative. ~, s.m.f. Animator.
animation (anima'sjɔ̃), s.f. Animation, sprightliness, liveliness; (med.) quickening (of the foetus).
animé, -e (anime), adj. Animated; excited; lively; bright, high, heightened; *teint* ~, heightened colour; (herald.) animé.
animer (anime) v.a. [L *animare*] **1.** To animate, to impel, to stimulate, to quicken; ~ *la conversation*, to enliven the conversation; ~ *quelqu'un par un bel exemple*, to inspire a person by a fine example; *la force qui anime le boulet*, the force which impels the cannon-ball; **2.** to incense, to excite, to exasperate; *il anima le peuple contre le roi*, he incited the people against the king; **3.** to brighten, to give colour to; ~ *les yeux*, to give brightness to the eyes; **s'~**, v.pr. **1.** to become animated, to cheer up, to brighten, to take courage; **2.** to grow excited; *il s'est animé contre moi*, he became much incensed against me.
animique (animik), adj. Animistic.
animisme (animism), s.m. [L *anima*] Animism.
animiste (animist), adj. Animistic. ~, s.m. Animist.
animosité (animozite), s.f. Animosity.
anis (ani), s.m. [Gr. *anison*] (bot.) Anise.
aniser (anize), v.a. To flavour with aniseed.
anisé, -e (anize), p. adj. Anisated.
anisette (anizɛt), s.f. Anisette.
anisosthémone (anizɔstemɔn), adj. [Gr. *anisos+stēmōn*] Anisostemonous.
ankylose (ɑ̃kiloz), s.f. [Gr. *agkulosis*] (pathol.) Ankylosis.
ankyloser (ɑ̃kiloze), v.a. (pathol.) To ankylose, to stiffen; **s'~**, v.pr. to grow ankylosed; to grow stiff.
annal, -e, (aux) (anal), adj. (rare) [L *annalis*] Annual, yearly.
annales (anal), s.f. pl. [L *annales (libri)*] Annals.
annaliste (analist), s.m. Annalist.
annamite (anamit), adj. s.m.f. Annamite.
annate (anat), s.f. [LL *annata*] Annates (pl.).
anneau (pl. **x**) (ano), s.m. [L *annellus*] Ring; ~ *brisé*, split ring; link (of a chain); curl, ringlet (of hair); coil (of a serpent).
année (ane), s.f. [L *annus*] Year; ~ *bissextile*, leap-year; ~ *scolaire*, school year, academic year; *d'~ en ~*, from year to year; *bonne ~!*, a happy New Year to you!; syn. AN.
annelé, -e (anle), adj. Annulated, ringed, annelid; curled. **~s**, s.m. pl. (zool.) Annelida, earthworms.
anneler (anle), v.a. To curl (hair); (agric.) to ring (pigs).
annelet (anlɛ), s.m. Annulet; (arch.) fillet.
annélides (anelid), s.m. pl. (zool.) Annelida, annelides.
annelure (anlyr), s.f. Curling (of hair); annulation.
annexe (anɛks), adj. [L *annexus*] Annexed; auxiliary. ~, s.f. Annex, dependency; appendix, voucher (annexed to a report, &c.).
annexer (anɛkse), v.a. To annex; **s'~**, v.pr. (*a*) to be annexed (to); (*b*) to attach to one's service, to acquire the services of.
annexion (anɛksjɔ̃), s.f. Annexation, annexing.
annexionisme, annexionnisme (anɛksjɔnism), s.m. Theory of the annexationists.
annexioniste, annexionniste (anɛksjɔnist), s.m. adj. Annexationist, annexionist.
annihilable (aniilabl), adj. Annihilable.
annihilation (aniila'sjɔ̃), s.f. Annihilation, annulment.
annihiler (aniile), v.a. [L *ad+nihil*] To annihilate, to annul, to blot out of existence.
anniversaire (anivɛrsɛr), s.m. adj. Anniversary.
annonaire (anɔnɛr), adj. [L *annona*] Of provisions.
annonce (anɔ̃s), s.f. **1.** Announcement, notice, notification; **2.** banns (of marriage); **3.** advertisement; *faire* or *mettre une ~ dans les journaux*, to put an advertisement in the newspapers.
annoncer (anɔ̃se), v.a. [L *annuntiare*] **1.** To announce, to give notice or information of, to declare; *il se présenta sans se faire ~*, he entered without sending in his name; **2.** to predict, to foretell; *ce vent annonce la tempête*, this wind is the precursor of a storm; **3.** to publish (banns); **4.** to advertise; **5.** to preach; ~ *l'Évangile*, to preach the Gospel; **s'~**, v.pr. to announce oneself, to make oneself known; to manifest oneself.
annonceur (anɔ̃sœr), s.m. Announcer.
annonciade (anɔ̃sjad), s.f. Annunciade-nun.
annonciat-eur, -rice (anɔ̃sjatœr), adj. Premonitory, forewarning.
annonciation (anɔ̃sja'sjɔ̃), s.f. Annunciation, announcement; (feast of) Annunciation.
annoncier (anɔ̃sje), s.m. Advertisement manager.

annone (anɔn), s.f. [L *annona*] Year's supply of provisions (anc. Rome).
annotat-eur, -rice (anɔtatœr), s.m.f. Annotator.
annotati-f, -ve (anɔtatif), adj. Annotative.
annotation (anɔta'sjɔ̃), s.f. Annotation.
annoter (anɔte), v.a. [L *annotare*] To annotate.
annuaire (anɥɛr), s.m. Year-book, annual, annuary, directory, almanac; ~ *militaire*, Army List; ~ *du téléphone*, telephone directory.
annualité (anɥalite), s.f. Annual quality.
annuel, -le (anɥɛl), adj. Annual, yearly; *plantes ~les*, annuals.
annuellement (anɥɛlmɑ̃), adv. Annually, yearly; per year, per annum (of income).
annuitaire (anɥitɛr), adj. Paid by annuities.
annuité (anɥite), s.f. Annuity.
annulabilité (anylabilite), s.f. State of being annullable.
annulable (anylabl), adj. Annullable, voidable.
annulaire (anylɛr), adj. [L *annularius*] Annular. ~, s.m. Ring-finger, third finger.
annulati-f, -ve (anylatif), adj. Annulling, cancelling.
annulation (anyla'sjɔ̃), s.f. Annulment; voidance (of a contract); reversal (of a judgement).
annulement (anylmɑ̃), s.m. (naut.) Annulling, annulment (of a signal).
annuler (anyle), v.a. [LL *annullare*] To annul, to render null and void; to cancel (a contract); to reverse (a judgement).
anobli, -e (anɔbli), adj. Ennobled. ~, s.m.f. Ennobled person.
anoblir (anɔblir), v.a. [*à+noble*] To ennoble (by conferring rank, title, and privileges). See ENNOBLIR.
anoblissement (anɔblismɑ̃), s.m. Ennoblement; *lettres d'~*, letters of nobility.
anode (anɔd), s.f. [Gr. *anodos*] (phys.) Anode.
anodin, -e (anɔdɛ̃), adj. Anodyne, palliative, tame, spiritless; *critique ~e*, tame criticism. ~, s.m. Anodyne.
anodonte (anɔdɔ̃t), s.m. [Gr. *anodons*] (zool.) Anodont.
anolis (anɔlis), s.m. [f. native name in Antilles, *anoalli, anoli*] (zool.) Anoli, anolis, or anole.
anomal, -e, (aux) (anɔmal), adj. [Gr. *anōmalos*] Anomalous; (gram.) irregular.
anomalie (anɔmali), s.f. Anomaly, irregularity.
anomalistique (anɔmalistik), adj. (astr.) Anomalistic.
ânon (ɑnɔ̃), s.m. Young ass, foal of an ass.
anone (anɔn), s.f. (bot.) Anona, custard-apple.
ânonnement (ɑnɔnmɑ̃), s.m. Faltering, stammering, hemming and hawing.
ânonner (ɑnɔne), v.a. To hesitate, to falter, to hem and haw.
ânonneu-r, -se (ɑnɔnœr), adj. Stammering, faltering, hesitating. ~, s.m.f. Stammerer.
anonymat (anɔnima), s.m. Anonymity, anonymousness; syn. ANONYMIE.
anonyme (anɔnim), adj. [Gr. *an+onoma*] Anonymous; *société ~*, incorporated joint-stock company, limited liability company.
anonymement (anɔnimmɑ̃), adv. Anonymously.
anonymie (anɔnimi), s.f. Anonymity; syn. ANONYMAT.
anoplothérium (anɔplɔteriɔm), s.m. [Gr. *anoplos+thērion*] (zool.) Anoplotherium.
anordir (anɔrdir), v.n. [*à+nord*] (naut.) To veer to the north.
anorexie (anɔrɛksi), s.f. [Gr. *an+orexis*] (med.) Anorexy, anorexia, loss of appetite.
anormal, -e, (aux) (anɔrmal), adj. [*a+normal*] Abnormal.
anormalement (anɔrmalmɑ̃), adv. Abnormally.
anosmie (anɔsmi), s.f. [f. Gr. *a+osmē*] (med.) Anosmia, loss of sense of smell.
anoure (anur), adj. [f. Gr. *a+oura*] Anourous, tailless. ~, s.m. pl. Order of tailless amphibia.
anoxémie (anɔksemi), s.f. [f. Gr. *a+oxus +haima*] (med.) Anoxyemia, anoxaemia.
anse (ɑ̃s), s.f. [L *ansa*] **1.** Handle (of basket, pot, bomb, &c.); *faire danser l'~ du panier*, to get more than the market penny; to get pickings; **2.** (geog.) cove, creek, inlet; **3.** (geom.) ~ *de panier*, three-centred curve.
anse, s.f., **anséatique**, adj. See HANSE and HANSÉATIQUE.
anser (ɑ̃sɛr), s.m. [L wd] Wild goose, barnacle goose.
ansérine (ɑ̃serin), s.f. (bot.) Goose-foot, wild spinach.
ansette (ɑ̃sɛt), s.f. Loop (terminating a rope, laces, &c.).
ansière (ansjɛr), s.f. Fishing-net (made specially for use in small bays).
anspect (ɑ̃spɛk), s.m. [Engl. *handspike*] (naut.) Handspike.
anspessade (ɑ̃spɛsad), s.m. [It. *lancia spezzata*] Lance-corporal (in French army, sixteenth and seventeenth centuries).
antagonique (ɑ̃tagɔnik), adj. Antagonistic.
antagonisme (ɑ̃tagɔnism), s.m. [Gr. *anti+agōnizomai*] Antagonism.
antagoniste (ɑ̃tagɔnist), s.m.f. Antagonist. ~, adj. Antagonistic.
antalgique (ɑ̃talʒik), adj. [Gr. *anti+algos*] Antalgic.

antan (ɑ̃tɑ̃), s.m. [L *ante annum*] (archaic) Olden days; *où sont les neiges d'~?*, 'Where are the snows of yesteryear?'; here to-day and gone to-morrow.
antanaclase (ɑ̃tanaklɑz), s.f. [Gr. *anti*+ *anaklasis*] (rhet.) Antanaclasis.
antarctique (ɑ̃tarktik), adj. [Gr. *ant-*+ *arktikos*] Antarctic.
ante[1] (ɑ̃t), s.f. [L *anta*] **1.** Wooden support for wing of windmill; **2.** (arch.) **~s,** (pl.) facings, pilasters.
ante[2] (ɑ̃t), s.f. [L *hasta*] Handle (of painter's brush).
antébois, antibois (ɑ̃tebwɑ, ɑ̃tibwɑ), s.m. Chair-rail (to avoid scratched wall-papers).
antécédemment (ɑ̃tesedamɑ̃), adv. Antecedently, previously.
antécédence (ɑ̃tesedɑ̃s), s.f. Antecedence; precedence.
antécédent, -e (ɑ̃tesedɑ̃), adj. s.m. [L *antecedere*] Antecedent.
antéchrist (ɑ̃tekrist), s.m. Antichrist.
antédiluvien, -ne (ɑ̃tedilyvjɛ̃), adj. [L *ante*+*diluvium*] Antediluvian.
antéfixe (ɑ̃tefiks), s.f. [L *antefixus*] (arch.) Antefix, Greek tile.
antenne (ɑ̃tɛn), s.f. [L *antenna*] **1.** (zool.) Antenna (pl. antennae); feeler; **2.** (naut.) lateen-yard; **3.** (naut.) cross-row (of casks); **4.** (wireless) aerial.
anténuptial, -e, (aux) (ɑ̃tenypsjal), adj. Antenuptial.
antéoccupation (ɑ̃teɔkypa'sjɔ̃), s.f. (rhet.) Prolepsis.
antépénultième (ɑ̃tepenyltjɛm), adj. Antipenultimate. **~,** s.f. Antipenultima, antipenult.
antérieur, -e (ɑ̃terjœr), adj. [L *anterior*] Anterior, previous; fore, foremost, front.
antérieurement (ɑ̃terjœrmɑ̃), adv. Anteriorly, previously.
antériorité (ɑ̃terjɔrite), s.f. Anteriority, priority.
anthelmintique (ɑ̃tɛlmɛ̃tik), adj. s.m. [Gr. *anti*+*helminthos*] (med.) Anthelmintic, vermifuge.
anthémis (ɑ̃temis), s.m. [Gr. *anthemis*] (bot.) Anthemis.
anthère (ɑ̃tɛr), s.f. [Gr. *anthēros*] (bot.) Anther, tip.
anthéridie (ɑ̃teridi), s.f. (bot.) Antheridium (pl. antheridia).
anthérozoïde (ɑ̃terɔzɔid), s.m. [Gr. *anthēros*+*zōon*+*eidos*] Antherozooid.
anthèse (ɑ̃tɛz), s.f. [Gr. *anthesis*] (bot.) Anthesis, full bloom.
anthologie (ɑ̃tɔlɔʒi), s.f. [Gr. *anthos*+ *legein*] Anthology.
anthozoaires (ɑ̃tɔzɔɛr), s.m. pl. See syn. CORALLIAIRES.
anthracène (ɑ̃trasɛn), s.m. [Gr. *anthrax*] Anthracene.
anthracite (ɑ̃trasit), s.m. [Gr. *anthrax*] Anthracite.
anthrax (ɑ̃traks), s.m. [Gr. wd.] (pathol.) Anthrax.
anthropoïde (ɑ̃trɔpɔid), adj. s.m. [Gr. *anthropos*+*eidos*] Anthropoid.
anthropologie (ɑ̃trɔpɔlɔʒi), s.f. [Gr. *anthropos*+*logos*] Anthropology.
anthropologique (ɑ̃trɔpɔlɔʒik), adj. Anthropological.
anthropologiste, anthropologue (ɑ̃trɔpɔlɔʒist, ɑ̃trɔpɔlɔg), s.m.f. Anthropologist.
anthropométrie (ɑ̃trɔpɔmetri), s.f. [Gr. *anthropos*+*metron*] Anthropometry.
anthropométrique (ɑ̃trɔpɔmetrik), adj. Anthropometric.
anthropomorphe (ɑ̃trɔpɔmɔrf), adj. [Gr. *anthropos*+*morphē*] Anthropomorphous.
anthropomorphisme (ɑ̃trɔpɔmɔrfism), s.m. Anthropomorphism.
anthropophage (ɑ̃trɔpɔfaʒ), adj. Anthropophagous. **~,** s.m.f. Cannibal.
anthropophagie (ɑ̃trɔpɔfaʒi), s.f. [Gr. *anthropos*+*phagein*] Anthropophagy, cannibalism.
anthyllide (ɑ̃tilid), s.f. (bot.) Kidney-vetch, *Vulneraria.*
antialcoolique (ɑ̃tialkɔ'lik), adj. Anti-alcoholic.
antiapoplectique (ɑ̃tiapɔplɛktik), adj. Anti-apoplectic.
antiar (ɑ̃tjar), s.m. (bot.) Antiar, upas-tree.
antiarthritique (ɑ̃tiartritik), adj. Anti-arthritic.
antiartistique (ɑ̃tiartistik), adj. Anti-artistic.
antiasthmatique (ɑ̃tiasmatik), adj. Anti-asthmatic.
antibois. See ANTÉBOIS.
anticatarrhal, -e, (aux) (ɑ̃tikataral), adj. Anticatarrhal.
antichambre (ɑ̃tiʃɑ̃br), s.f. Antechamber, waiting-room; *faire* **~,** to dance attendance; *propos d'~*, idle gossip, servant's gossip.
anticholérique (ɑ̃tikɔlerik), adj. Anticholera.
antichrèse (ɑ̃tikrɛz), s.f. [Gr. *anti*+ *khresis*] Assignment of revenues of real estate (for payment of debt).
antichrétien, -ne (ɑ̃tikretjɛ̃), adj. Antichristian.
anticipant, -e (ɑ̃tisipɑ̃), adj. (med.) Anticipant, anticipating.
anticipation (ɑ̃tisipa'sjɔ̃), s.f. Anticipation; *par* ~, in advance.
anticipé, -e (ɑ̃tisipe), adj. Anticipatory; immature.
anticiper (ɑ̃tisipe), v.a.n. [L *anticipare*] To anticipate, to forestall; to encroach; ~ *sur les droits d'autrui*, to encroach on (to usurp) the rights of others.
anticlérical, -e, (aux) (ɑ̃tiklerikal), adj. Anticlerical.

anticléricalisme (ɑ̃tiklerikalism), s.m. Anticlericalism.
anticomanie (ɑ̃tikomani), s.f. Mania for antiques.
anticombustible (ɑ̃tikɔ̃bystibl), adj. Anticombustible.
anticonstitutionnel, -le (ɑ̃tikɔ̃stitysjɔnɛl), adj. Anticonstitutional.
anticonstitutionnellement (ɑ̃tikɔ̃stitysjɔnɛlmɑ̃), adv. Anticonstitutionally.
antidate (ɑ̃tidat), s.f. Antedate.
antidater (ɑ̃tidate), v.a. To antedate.
antidérapant (ɑ̃tiderapɑ̃), adj. s.m. Non-skid.
antidote (ɑ̃tidɔt), s.m. [Gr. *anti+dotos*] Antidote.
antienne (ɑ̃tjɛn), s.f. [L *antiphona*] Anthem; *chanter toujours la même* ~, to be always harping on the same string.
antiesclavagiste (ɑ̃tiɛsklavaʒist), s.m.f. adj. Abolitionist.
antiévangélique (ɑ̃tievɑ̃ʒelik), adj. Anti-evangelical.
antifébrile (ɑ̃tifebril), adj. (med.) Anti-febrile.
antiferment (ɑ̃tifɛrmɑ̃), s.m. Antifermentative.
antifermentescible (ɑ̃tifɛrmɑ̃tɛsibl), adj. Unfermentable.
antifriction (ɑ̃tifriksjɔ̃), s.f. Antifriction.
antigouvernemental, -e, (aux) (ɑ̃tiguvɛrnəmɑ̃tal), adj. Antigovernment.
antihumain, -e (ɑ̃tiymɛ̃), adj. Inhuman.
antihygiénique (ɑ̃tiiʒjenik), adj. Unhygienic.
anti-jui-f, -ve (ɑ̃tiʒɥif), adj. Antisemitic; syn. ANTISÉMITIQUE.
antilégal, -e, (aux) (ɑ̃tilegal), adj. Antilegal.
antilibéral, -e, (aux) (ɑ̃tiliberal), adj. Antiliberal.
antilibéralisme (ɑ̃tiliberalism), s.m. Antiliberalism.
antilogie (ɑ̃tilɔʒi), s.f. [Gr. *anti+logos*] Antilogy, contradiction.
antilogique (ɑ̃tilɔʒik), adj. Antilogical.
antilope (ɑ̃tilɔp), s.f. (zool.) Antelope.
antiméphitique (ɑ̃timefitik), adj. Antimephitic.
antimigraineu-x, -se (ɑ̃timigrɛnø), adj. Headache-curing.
antimilitarisme (ɑ̃timilitarism), s.m. Antimilitarism.
antimilitariste (ɑ̃timilitarist), adj. Antimilitary.
antiministériel, -le (ɑ̃tiministerjɛl), adj. Antiministerial.
antimoine (ɑ̃timwan), s.m. [L *antimonium*] (min. chem.) Antimony.
antimonarchique (ɑ̃timɔnarʃik), adj. Antimonarchical.
antimonarchiste (ɑ̃timɔnarʃist), adj. s.m.f. Antimonarchist.
antimonial, -e, (aux) (ɑ̃timɔnjal), adj. Antimonial.
antimoniate (ɑ̃timɔnjat), s.m. (chem.) Antimoniate.
antinational, -e, (aux) (ɑ̃tinasjɔnal), adj. Antinational.
antinéphrétique (ɑ̃tinefretik), adj. Antinephritic.
antinévralgique (ɑ̃tinevralʒik), adj. Antineuralgic.
antinomie (ɑ̃tinɔmi), s.f. [Gr. *anti+nomos*] Antinomy.
antinomique (ɑ̃tinɔmik), adj. Antinomic.
antipape (ɑ̃tipap), s.m. Antipope.
antiparlementaire (ɑ̃tiparləmɑ̃tɛr), adj. Antiparliamentary.
antipathie (ɑ̃tipati), s.f. [Gr. *anti+pathos*] Antipathy.
antipathique (ɑ̃tipatik), adj. Antipathetic, antipathetical; antipathic; distasteful.
antipatriote (ɑ̃tipatriɔt), s.m.f. Bad patriot, unpatriotic person.
antipatriotique (ɑ̃tipatriɔtik), adj. Unpatriotic.
antipériodique (ɑ̃tiperiɔdik), adj. (med.) Antiperiodic.
antipéristaltique (ɑ̃tiperistaltik), adj. [Gr. *anti+peristallein*] (med.) Antiperistaltic.
antipéristase (ɑ̃tiperistɑz), s.f. [Gr. *anti+peristasis*] Antiperistasis.
antipesteu-x, -se (ɑ̃tipɛstø), adj. Antipestilential.
antiphernal, -e, (aux) (ɑ̃tifɛrnal), adj. (law) *Biens antiphernaux*, Property given to wife by husband in marriage settlement.
antiphilosophique (ɑ̃tifilɔzɔfik), adj. Antiphilosophical.
antiphlogistique (ɑ̃tiflɔʒistik), adj. s.m. (med.) Antiphlogistic.
antiphonaire, antiphonier (ɑ̃tifɔnɛr, ɑ̃tifɔnje), s.m. [L *antiphona*] Antiphonary.
antiphrase (ɑ̃tifrɑz), s.f. [Gr. *antiphrasis*] Antiphrasis.
antipode (ɑ̃tipɔd), s.m. [Gr. *anti+pous, podos*] Antipode, antipodes.
antipoétique (ɑ̃tipɔetik), adj. Antipoetical.
antiprogressiste (ɑ̃tiprɔgrɛsist), s.m.f. adj. Antiprogressive.
antiprohibitionniste (ɑ̃tiprɔibisjɔnist), adj. s.m.f. Antiprohibitionist.
antiprotectionniste (ɑ̃tiprɔtɛksjɔnist), adj. s.m.f. Antiprotectionist, free-trader.
antiputride (ɑ̃tipytrid), adj. s.m. Antiputrefactive, antiseptic.
antipyrine (ɑ̃tipirin), s.f. [Gr. *anti+pyr*] (pharm.) Antipyrine.
antiquaille (ɑ̃tikɑj), s.f. [It. *anticaglia*] (pej.) Old curiosity, worthless antique, lumber.

antiquaire (ɑ̃tikɛr), s.m. Antiquarian, antiquary.
antique (ɑ̃tik), adj. [L *antiquus*] Antique, ancient, past, former; *usage* ~, ancient custom; old-fashioned, antiquated, quaint. ~, s.m. The antique (in speaking of art), ancient art; ~, (obs.) s.f. (nowadays s.m.) an antique (an individual work of art). ⚠ Never 'antic' which = *gambade, bouffonnerie*; and adj. *grotesque, bouffon.*
antiquement (ɑ̃tikmɑ̃), adv. **1.** Quaintly, antiquely; **2.** formerly, in ancient times.
antiquité (ɑ̃tikite), s.f. [L *antiquitas*] Antiquity.
antirabique (ɑ̃tirabik), adj. s.m. [Gr. *anti*+L *rabere*] Antirabietic.
antiréglementaire (ɑ̃tireglәmɑ̃tɛr), adj. Irregular, against the regulations.
antireligieu-x, -se (ɑ̃tirәliʒjø), adj. Antireligious.
antirépublicain, -e (ɑ̃tirepyblikɛ̃), adj. s.m.f. Antirepublican.
antirépublicanisme (ɑ̃tirepyblikanism), s.m. Antirepublicanism.
antirévolutionnaire (ɑ̃tirevɔlysjɔnɛr), adj. s.m.f. Antirevolutionary.
antirouille (ɑ̃tiruj), s.f. Rust-preventive.
antiscien, -ne (ɑ̃tisjɛ̃), adj. [Gr. *anti*+*skia*] Antiscian. ~**s**, s.m. pl. Antiscii (people living on the same meridian, but on opposite sides of the equator).
antiscorbutique (ɑ̃tiskɔrbytik), adj. s.m. (med.) Antiscorbutic.
antiscrofuleu-x, -se (ɑ̃tiskrɔfylø), adj. Antiscrofulous.
antisémite (ɑ̃tisemit), s.m.f. Anti-Semite.
antisémitique (ɑ̃tisemitik), adj. Antisemitic.
antisémitisme (ɑ̃tisemitism), s.m. Antisemitism.
antisepsie (ɑ̃tisɛpsi), s.f. [Gr. *anti*+*sepsis*] Antisepsis.
antiseptique (ɑ̃tisɛptik), adj. s.m. Antiseptic.
antisociable (ɑ̃tisɔsjabl), adj. Unsociable.
antisocial, -e, (aux) (ɑ̃tisɔsjal), adj. Antisocial.
antispasmodique (ɑ̃tispasmɔdik), adj. Antispasmodic.
antistrophe (ɑ̃tistrɔf), s.f. [Gr. *anti*+*strepho*] Antistrophe.
antitétanique (ɑ̃titetanik), adj. [Gr. *anti*+*tetanos*] (med.) Antitetanus, antitetanic.
antithèse (ɑ̃titɛz), s.f. [Gr. *antithesis*] Antithesis.
antithétique (ɑ̃titetik), adj. Antithetic, antithetical.
antitoxine (ɑ̃titɔksin), s.f. [Gr. *anti*+*toxikon*] Antitoxin.
antivénéneu-x, -se (ɑ̃tivenenø), adj. Antivenomous.
antivermineu-x, -se (ɑ̃tivɛrminø), adj. Anthelmintic, vermifuge.
antivivisectionniste (ɑ̃tiviviseksjɔ̃nist), adj. s.m.f. Antivivisectionist.
antoit (ɑ̃twa), s.m. Bent-lever.
antonomase (ɑ̃tɔnɔmɑz), s.f. [Gr. *antonomazo*] Antonomasia.
antonyme (ɑ̃tɔnim), s.m. [Gr. *anti*+*onuma*] Antonym.
antre (ɑ̃tr), s.m. [L *antrum*] Cave, cavern; den (of wild beasts, thieves, &c.); syn. CAVERNE, GROTTE.
(s')anuiter (sanɥite), v.pr. To be benighted, to let oneself be overtaken by the night.
anurie, anurèse (anyri, anyrɛz), s.f. [Gr. *an*+*ouron*] (pathol.) Anuria.
anus (anys), s.m. [L *anus*] Anus.
anxiété (ɑ̃ksjete), s.f. [L *anxietas*] Anxiety, uneasiness; (med.) restlessness.
anxieusement (ɑ̃ksjøzmɑ̃), adv. Anxiously.
anxieu-x, -se (ɑ̃ksjø), adj. Anxious.
aoriste (aɔrist), s.m. [Gr. *aoristos*] (gram.) Aorist.
aorte (aɔrt), s.f. [Gr. *aortē*] (anat.) Aorta.
aortique (aɔrtik), adj. (anat.) Aortic, aortal.
aortite (aortit), s.f. (pathol.) Aortitis.
août (au or u), s.m. [L *augustus*] August; harvest-time; *faire l'*~, to harvest.
aoûtage (autaʒ), s.m. Harvest-work, harvesting.
aoûtat (auta), s.m. (ent.) Harvest bug.
aoûté, -e (aute), adj. Ripened.
aoûteron (autrɔ̃), s.m. Harvest-hand, month's-man.
apache (apaʃ), s.m. [name given to Red Indians in Western States and Mexico] Apache; (colloq.) apache, hooligan, bandit, ruffian.
apaisement (apɛzmɑ̃), s.m. Appeasement.
apaiser (apɛze), v.a. [L *ad*+*pacem*] To appease, to pacify, to stay (hunger), to allay, slake, quench (thirst); to make up (a quarrel, &c.); to quell, to suppress (a rebellion, &c.); **s'**~, v.pr. to calm oneself, to be appeased; to subside, to abate (as a fever, &c.), to lull, to moderate, to abate (as a wind); syn. SE CALMER.
apalachine (apalaʃin), s.f. [f. *Apalaches* or *Alleghany* mountains] (bot.) Appalachian tea, emetic holly.
apanage (apanaʒ), s.m. [LL *apanare*] Apanage or appanage; attribute, prerogative; lot, portion.
apanager (apanaʒe), v.a. To endow with an apanage.
apanagiste (apanaʒist), s.m. adj. Apanagist, holder of an apanage.
(s')apapelardir (sapaplardir), v.pr. [f. *papelard*] To become hypocritical (in matters of religion).

aparté (aparte), s.m. [L wd] (theatr.) Aside.
apathie (apati), s.f. [Gr. *a+pathos*] Apathy.
apathique (apatik), adj. s.m.f. Apathetic, apathetical.
apathiquement (apatikmɑ̃), adv. Apathetically.
apatite (apatit), s.f. (min.) Apatite.
apepsie (apɛpsi), s.f. [Gr. *a+peptō*] Apepsy.
aperceptibilité (apɛrsɛptibilite), s.f. (phil.) Perceptibility.
aperceptible (apɛrsɛptibl), adj. (phil.) Perceptible.
apercepti-f, -ve (apɛrsɛptif), adj. (phil.) Perceptive.
aperception (apɛrsɛpsjɔ̃), s.f. [f. L *ad+percipere*] (phil.) Apperception.
aperceptivité (apɛrsɛptivite), s.f. (phil.) Perceptivity.
apercevable (apɛrsəvabl), adj. Perceivable, perceptible.
apercevance (apɛrsəvɑ̃s), s.f. Perception, perspicacity.
apercevoir (apɛrsəvwar), v.a. [L *ad+percipere*] **1.** To perceive, to discover, to descry (an object at a certain distance); **2.** to remark, to notice, to observe; **3.** to perceive (intellectually), to discern; **s'~**, v.pr. to perceive, to observe, to remark; *il s'aperçut que le temps passait,* he noticed that time was passing; *il s'aperçut de son erreur,* he perceived his mistake.
aperçu (apɛrsy), s.m. **1.** Cursory view, glimpse, idea; *je n'en ai qu'un ~,* I have only a general idea of it; **2.** brief account, statement, estimate; *un ~ de la dépense,* a rough estimate of the outlay; **3.** (naut.) made-out flag (to show that signal has been read).
apériti-f, -ve (aperitif), adj. [L *aperio*] Appetizing. **~**, s.m. Appetiser, bitters, drink before a meal; (colloq. abbrev.) APÉRO. ⚠ Not to be translated by 'aperitive' or 'aperient' which means 'laxative' = *laxatif.*
apertement (apɛrtəmɑ̃), adv. [L *apertus*] Openly, overtly, manifestly.
apertise (apɛrtiz), (obs.) s.f. Feat.
apétale (apetal), adj. [Gr. *a+petalon*] (bot.) Apetalous.
apétalie (apetali), s.f. (bot.) Apetalousness.
apetissement (apətismɑ̃), s.m. [f. *à+petit*] Lessening, diminution.
apetisser (apətise), v.a. To lessen; **s'~**, v.pr. to shrink, to contract (see RAPETISSER).
à peu près (apøprɛ), adv. loc. Nearly, about, more or less, thereabouts, much in the same way; *j'ai à peu près fini,* I have about finished. **~**, s.m. Approximation; *ne vous contentez pas d'à peu près,* do not be satisfied with something just more or less.
apeuré, -e (apœre), adj. Frightened.
apex (apɛks), s.m. [L wd] Apex, summit.
aphaniptères (afaniptɛr), s.m. pl. [Gr. *aphanēs+pteron*] (ent.) Aphaniptera.
aphasie (afɑzi), s.f. [Gr. *a+phasis*] (pathol.) Aphasia.
aphasique (afɑzik), adj. Aphasic.
aphélie (afeli), s.m. [Gr. *apo+hēlios*] (astr.) Aphelion.
aphérèse (aferɛz), s.f. [Gr. *aphairesis*] (rhet.) Aphaeresis.
aphidiens (afidjɛ̃), s.m. pl. [Gr. *aphis+idos*] (ent.) Aphides.
aphlogistique (aflɔʒistik), adj. [Gr. *a+phlox*] Aphlogistic, flameless.
aphone (afɔn), adj. [Gr. *a+phōnē*] Aphonous, voiceless.
aphonie (afɔni), s.f. (med.) Aphony.
aphorisme (afɔrism), s.m. [Gr. *aphorismos*] Aphorism.
aphoristique (afɔristik), adj. Aphoristic, aphoristical.
aphrodisiaque (afrɔdizjak), adj. s.m. [Gr. *Aphroditē,* Venus] (med.) Aphrodisiac.
aphte (aft), s.m. [Gr. *aphtha*] **1.** (med.) Aphtha; **2.** (pl.) aphthae, (pop.) thrush.
aphteu-x, -se (aftø), adj. (med.) Aphthous.
aphylle (afil), adj. [Gr. *a+phullon*] (bot.) Aphyllous.
api (api), s.m. [f. *Appius,* a Roman who obtained that kind of apple by grafting] (hort.) Api, *malum Appianum,* small red apple.
apiaires (apjɛr), s.m. pl. [L *apis*] (zool.) The bee tribe.
apicole (apikɔl), adj. [L *apis+colere*] Apicultural.
apiculteur (apikyltœr), s.m. Apiarist, bee-keeper.
apiculture (apikyltyr), s.f. Apiculture.
apion (apjɔ̃), s.m. (zool.) Apion, clover-weevil.
apiquage (apikaʒ), s.m. (naut.) Peaking.
apiquer (apike), v.a. [f. *à+pic*] (naut.) To top, to peak.
apitoiement (apitwa'mɑ̃), s.m. Compassion, pity.
apitoyer (apitwaje), v.a. [f. *pitié*] To move to compassion, to move, to soften; **s'~**, v.pr. to be moved to compassion, to feel pity (for); *s'~ sur,* to pity, to compassionate.
apivore (apivɔr), adj. [L *apis+vorare*] Apivorous, bee-eating.
aplaigner, aplaner (aplɛɲe, aplane), v.a. [L *ad+planus*] To lay the nap (of cloth).
aplaigneu-r, -se (aplɛɲœr), adj. Nap-laying. **~**, s.m.f. Nap-layer.
aplaner (aplane), v.a. To polish (wood) with spoke-shave or turning-chisel; see APLAIGNER.

aplanétique (aplanetik), adj. Aplanetic (surface, lens, &c.).
aplanir (aplanir), v.a. To smooth, to render even, to level; (fig.) to smooth down, to remove (difficulties); **s'~**, v.pr. **1.** to become level, smooth, to become flat; **2.** to be removed, to disappear.
aplanissement (aplanismɑ̃), s.m. Smoothing, levelling; smoothness, levelness; (fig.) removal, disappearance.
aplatir (aplatir), v.a. [f. *plat*] To flatten, to make, or beat flat; to lower, to debase; to hush up; **s'~**, v.pr. **1.** to be flattened, to grow, to get, to become flat; to lower; to fall; **2.** (fig.) (fam.) to humble oneself; *il s'est aplati devant eux*, he grovelled before them.
aplatissement (aplatismɑ̃), s.m. **1.** Flattening, flatness; **2.** (fig.) depression; setting down; grovelling.
aplatissoir (aplatiswar), s.m. **aplatissoire**, s.f. (techn.) Flatter, flatting-mill, rolling-mill.
aplomb (aplɔ̃), s.m. [*à+plomb*] **1.** Perpendicular, perpendicularity; (techn.) plumb; **2.** equilibrium, balance; (fig.) assurance, self-possession, coolness; cheek, nerve; *il répondit avec* ~, he replied with assurance; (fam.) *il ne manque pas d'~*, he has no lack of cheek. *d'~*, adv. loc. Perpendicular(ly), plumb, upright; *ce mur est hors d'~*, this wall is out of plumb, is out of the straight; *cette table n'est pas d'~*, this table wobbles, is unsteady; (colloq.) *il est bien d'~*, he is game, or strong; he is all there.
apocalypse (apɔkalips), s.f. [Gr. *apokalupsis*] Apocalypse; *l'~*, the Revelation of St. John the Divine; *style d'~*, cryptic, obscure style; *le cheval de l'~*, the pale horse of the Apocalypse, (fig.) a sorry jade, a wretched hack.
apocalyptique (apɔkaliptik), adj. Apocalyptic; *style* ~, obscure, cryptic style.
apocope (apɔkɔp), s.f. [Gr. *apokopto*] (gram.) Apocope.
apocopé, -e (apɔkɔpe), adj. (gram.) Apocopated.
apocrisiaire (apɔkrizjɛr), s.m. [Gr. *apokrisis*] Apocrisiary, chancellor; (eccles.) envoy, nuncio.
apocryphe (apɔkrif), adj. [Gr. *apokruphos*] Apocryphal; *les livres ~s*, the Apocrypha. ~, s.m. An apocryphon, a non-canonical writing.
apocyn, apocin (apɔsɛ̃), s.m. [Gr. *apo+kuon*] (bot.) Apocynum; ~ *gobemouches*, dog-bane.
apocynacées, apocynées (apɔsinase, apɔsine), s.f. pl. (bot.) Apocynaceae, dog-bane family.
apode (apɔd), adj. [Gr. *apous*] Apod, apode.
apodictique (apɔdiktik), adj. [Gr. *apodeiknumai*] Apodictic, apodictical, incontrovertibly established.
apodose (apɔdoz), s.m. [Gr. *apodosis*] (rhet.) Apodosis.
apogée (apɔʒe), s.m. [Gr. *apogaion*] **1.** (astr.) Apogee; **2.** (fig.) zenith, height, climax, culmination, acme; *à l'~ de sa gloire*, in the zenith of his glory; *l'art grec a atteint son ~ quand . . .*, Greek art attained its climax when . . .
apographe (apɔgraf), s.m. [Gr. *apo+graphein*] Apograph, transcript. ~, adj. Apographal.
apologétique, apologique (apɔlɔʒetik, apɔlɔʒik), adj. s.f. Apologetic.
apologie (apɔlɔʒi), s.f. [Gr. *apologia*] Apology, defence, excuse, vindication; *faire l'~ de*, to vindicate.
apologique (apɔlɔʒik), adj. See syn. APOLOGÉTIQUE.
apologiste (apɔlɔʒist), s.m.f. Apologist.
apologue (apɔlɔg), s.m. [Gr. *apo+logos*] Apologue.
apomorphine (apɔmɔrfin), s.f. [Gr. *apo+morphia*] Apomorphia, apomorphine.
aponévrose (apɔnevroz), s.f. [Gr. *apo+neuron*] (anat.) Aponeurosis.
aponévrotique (apɔnevrɔtik), adj. (anat.) Aponeurotic.
apophtegme (apɔftɛgm), s.m. [Gr. *apophthegma*] Apophthegm.
apophyse (apɔfiz), s.f. [Gr. *apo+phuomai*] (anat.) Apophysis.
apoplectique (apɔplɛktik), adj. Apoplectic.
apoplexie (apɔplɛksi), s.f. [Gr. *apoplexia*] Apoplexy; ~ *foudroyante*, apoplexia fortissima, thundering apoplexy; *être frappé d'~*, to have a stroke; *tomber en ~*, to have an apoplectic fit.
apostasie (apɔstazi), s.f. [Gr. *apostasia*] Apostasy.
apostasier (apɔstazje), v.n. To apostatize.
apostat (apɔsta), adj. s.m. [Gr. *apostatês*] Apostate.
apostème (apɔstem), s.m. See APOSTUME.
aposter (apɔste), v.a. [*à+poster*] (pej.) To post, to set on the watch.
apostille (apɔstij), s.f. [*a*+LL *postilla*] Apostil, marginal note; postscript.
apostiller (apɔstije), v.a. To add a rider or a recommendatory note; to add a postscript.
apostolat (apɔstɔla), s.m. [L *apostolatus*] Apostleship, apostolate.
apostolicité (apɔstɔlisite), s.f. (theol.) Apostolicity, apostolicism.
apostolique (apɔstɔlik), adj. Apostolic, apostolical.
apostoliquement (apɔstɔlikmɑ̃), adv. Apostolically.
apostrophe (apɔstrɔf), s.f. [Gr. *apostrophos*] **1.** (rhet. gram.) Apostrophe; (pej.)

apostrophe, reproach, exclamatory address; **2.** apostrophe, sign of omission of letter.
apostropher (apɔstrɔfe), v.a. To apostrophize.
apostume, apostème (apɔstym, apɔstem), s.m. [Gr. *apostema*] (pathol.) Imposthume, abscess.
apostumer (apɔstyme), v.n. (med.) To gather, to form an abscess.
apothème (apɔtem), s.m. [Gr. *apotithenai*] **1.** (geom.) Apothem; **2.** (chem.) apothema.
apothéose (apɔteoz), s.f. [Gr. *apo+theos*] Apotheosis; *on lui décerna l'~*, his apotheosis was decreed.
apothèse (apɔtɛz), s.f. [Gr. *apothesis*] (surg.) Apothesis, setting of a limb.
apothicaire (apɔtikɛr), s.m. [Gr. *apothēkē*] Apothecary; (colloq.) *compte* or *mémoire d'~*, a stiff bill, an exorbitant bill; *~ sans sucre*, a cobbler without an awl.
apôtre (apotr), s.m. [Gr. *apostolos*] Apostle; *le Symbole des ~s*, the Apostles' Creed; *faire le bon ~*, to play the saint.
apozème (apɔzɛm), s.m. [Gr. *apozema*] (pharm.) Apozem, decoction, infusion.
apparaître (aparɛtr), v.a. [f. L *apparere*] To appear, to become visible; to start up; *une voile apparut à l'horizon*, a sail appeared on the horizon; *Dieu apparut à Moïse*, God appeared to Moses.
apparat (apara), s.m. Pomp, state, solemnity; *discours d'~*, a formal speech; (pej.) parade, display, ostentation; *il fait tout avec ~*, he does everything with display.
apparaux (aparo), s.m. pl. (naut.) Furniture, tackle.
appareil (aparɛj), s.m. [L *apparatus*] **1.** Display preparations, preparatives (for ceremonies); *l'~ de guerre*, the pomp and circumstance of war; *l'~ d'une fête*, the preparations for a festival; *on fait de grands ~s*, great preparations are being made; **2.** train, equipage, equipment; **3.** (scient. anat.) apparatus; **4.** (photo.) camera; **5.** (arch.) dressing; course; **6.** (surg.) dressing; *lever l'~*, to remove the dressing; *faire un premier ~*, to apply a first dressing; **7.** (mason.) bond work; **8.** (naut.) gear, tackle; **9.** (cook.) mixture; **10.** (mech.) appliance, apparatus, machinery.
appareillage (aparɛjaʒ), s.m. (naut.) Getting into sailing trim; getting under sail, getting up steam.
appareillement (aparɛjmɑ̃), s.m. (agric.) Matching, pairing.
appareiller (aparɛje), v.a. **1.** To match; **2.** (naut.) to get into sailing trim; to get up steam.
appareilleur (aparɛjœr), s.m. (arch.) Stone-dresser.
apparemment (aparamɑ̃), adv. Apparently; evidently.
apparence (aparɑ̃s), s.f. [L *apparentia*] **1.** Appearance, look; *en ~*, apparently; *juger sur l'~*, to judge by appearances; *toutes les ~s sont contre vous*, all (the) appearances are against you; *sauver les ~s*, to save appearances; **2.** handsome look, presence; *avoir belle ~*, to look well; to appear to be of good quality; to have a fine presence, bearing; **3.** probability, likelihood; *il y a ~*, so it seems; *je n'y vois que trop d'~*, I am afraid it is only too probable.
apparent, -e (aparɑ̃), adj. **1.** Apparent, evident; *son droit est ~*, his right is apparent; **2.** apparent, seeming; *le mouvement ~ du soleil*, the apparent movement of the sun; *prétexte ~*, ostensible reason, plausible pretext; **3.** noticeable, conspicuous.
apparentage (aparɑ̃taʒ), s.m. Connexion by marriage (abstract sense).
apparenter (aparɑ̃te), v.a. To marry, to connect by a matrimonial alliance; *bien ~ ses enfants*, to make good marriages for one's children; **s'~**, v.pr. to marry (*à*, into); *s'~ à la noblesse*, to marry into the aristocracy.
appariement (aparimɑ̃), s.m. Matching, pairing.
apparier (aparje), v.a. To pair, to match in pairs; **s'~** v.pr. to pair, to couple.
appariteur (aparitœr), s.m. [L *apparitor*] **1.** Apparitor (of an ecclesiastical court); **2.** beadle (of a university), usher.
apparition (aparisjɔ̃), s.f. [L *apparitio*] **1.** Sudden appearing, appearance; *l'~ d'une comète*, the appearance of a comet; **2.** brief visit; *il n'a fait qu'une ~*, he paid a flying visit, he only looked in for a moment; **3.** apparition, spectre.
apparoir (aparwar), v. impers. defect. (used only in the inf. and *il appert*) (law) To appear, to be apparent, evident.
appartement (apartəmɑ̃), s.m. [It. *appartamento*; L *appartimentum*] **1.** Flat; **2.** apartment, suite of apartments; *d'~*, indoor; *jeux d'~*, indoor games.
appartenance (apartənɑ̃s) (obs.) s.f. Appurtenance.
appartenant, -e (apartənɑ̃), adj. Appertaining, belonging (to).
appartenir (apartənir), v.n. [L *ad+pertinere*] **1.** To appertain, to belong (*à*, to), to be the property (of); **2.** to beseem, to become; *la gaîté appartient à l'enfance*, gaiety is becoming to childhood; **3.** to belong to, to form part of; *le pin appartient à la famille des conifères*, the fir belongs to the conifer family; **s'~**, v.pr. to be free, independent; *je m'appartiens*, I am my own master.

appas (apɑ), s.m. pl. **1.** Attractions, charms; **2.** physical charms; breasts.
appât (apɑ), s.m. [L *ad+pastus*] **1.** Bait; *mettre l'~ à un piège*, to bait a trap; **2.** (fig.) bait, lure, enticement.
appâter (apɑte), v.a. **1.** To bait, to lay bait for; **2.** to cram; *~ des oies*, to fatten geese; **3.** (fig.) to lure, to attract, to draw on.
appauvrir (apovrir), v.a. [f. *pauvre*] To impoverish, to exhaust (soil); **s'~**, v.pr. to become impoverished, to grow poor.
appauvrissement (apovrismɑ̃), s.m. **1.** Impoverishment; **2.** degeneration, deterioration (of a breed).
appeau (pl.-**x**) (apo), s.m. [form of *appel*] Bird-call, quail-pipe.
appel (apɛl), s.m. [f. *appeler*] **1.** Call; *un ~ au secours*, a cry for help; **2.** roll-call; *faire l'~*, to call over, to call the roll; **3.** (law) appeal; *cour d'~*, court of appeal; **4.** (obs.) challenge (to duel); **5.** (comm.) call; *~ de fonds*, call for funds; **6.** (mil.) *passer l'~*, to pass muster; *battre l'~*, to sound the fall-in; *faire l'~*, to call the roll; **7.** (aeron.) *~ d'air*, indraught; **8.** appeal; *~ aux passions*, appeal to passions.
appelant, -e (aplɑ̃), p. adj. Appealing. **~**, s.m.f. (law) Appellant. **~**, s.m. Decoy-bird.
appelé (aple), s.m. adj. (mil.) Called-up reservist; (fig.) *beaucoup d'appelés et peu d'élus*, many are called but few are chosen.
appeler (aple), v.a. [L *appellare*] **1.** To call in, out, up, or down, to summon; *~ un médecin*, to call in a doctor; *~ les pompiers*, to call out the fire-brigade; **2.** to name (persons), to call, to term; *~ les choses par leur nom*, to call a spade a spade; **3.** (mil.) to call up (reserves), to call over (the roll); **4.** to challenge; *~ en duel*, to call out; **5.** *en ~*, to appeal; *en ~ à César*, to appeal unto Caesar; *en ~ de Philippe ivre à Philippe sobre*, to appeal from Philip drunk to Philip sober; **6.** *faire ~*, to send for; **s'~** v.pr. to be called, to be named; to call oneself; to call each other.
appellati-f, -ve (apɛllatif), adj. Appellative.
appellation (apɛlla'sjɔ̃), s.f. Naming, appellation.
appendice (apɛ̃dis), s.m. [f. L *appendere*] Appendix; appendage.
appendicite (apɛ̃disit), s.f. (pathol.) Appendicitis.
appendiculaire (apɛ̃dikylɛr), adj. Appendicular.
appendre (apɑ̃dr), v.a. To hang up, to suspend.
appentis (apɑ̃ti), s.m. [f. L *ad+pendere*] Penthouse, lean-to.
appert (apɛr), v. (see APPAROIR). *Il ~*, it appears, it is evident.
appesantir (apəzɑ̃tir), v.a. [f. *pesant*] **1.** To make heavy, to weigh down; *~ le joug*, to increase the burden (of tyranny); **2.** (fig.) to make dull; **s'~**, v.pr. to become heavier, to be weighed down; (fig.) to grow heavy, to grow dull; *s'~ sur un sujet*, to dwell upon a subject.
appesantissement (apəzɑ̃tismɑ̃), s.m. Heaviness; (fig.) heaviness, dullness.
appétence (apetɑ̃s), s.f. [L *appetentia*] Appetence, appetency.
appéter (apete), v.a. [L *appetere*] To desire, to covet.
appétissant, -e (apetisɑ̃), adj. Appetizing, inviting, tempting; (fig.) desirable.
appétit (apeti), s.m. [L *appetitus*] **1.** Appetite, hunger; *aiguiser l'~* to whet the appetite; *~ de cheval*, ravenous appetite; *bon ~ !*, make a good meal; *il n'est chère que d'~*, hunger is the best sauce; (fig.) *l'~ vient en mangeant*, much would have more; *pain dérobé réveille l'~*, stolen fruits are sweet; **2.** (pl.) desires, cravings, fleshly appetites.
appétiti-f, -ve (apetitif), adj. Appetitive.
appétition (apetisjɔ̃), s.f. Craving, keen desire.
applaudir (aplodir), v.a. [L *applaudere*] To applaud, to cheer; to praise, to commend; **s'~**, v.pr. to boast, to glory (*de*, in); to rejoice (at); to congratulate oneself (on).
applaudissement (aplodismɑ̃), s.m. Applause; cheering, cheer; praise, commendation.
applaudisseu-r, -se (aplodisœr), s.m.f. Noisy applauder.
applicabilité (aplikabilite), s.f. Applicability, appositeness.
applicable (aplikabl), adj. Applicable, apposite.
applicage (aplikaʒ), s.m. Applying, application.
application (aplika'sjɔ̃), s.f. [f. L *applicare*] **1.** Application; *~ d'Angleterre*, Honiton lace; inlaying; appliqué work; **2.** infliction (of penalty); **3.** diligence, care, attention; *il travaille avec ~*, he works diligently; ⚠ *Application* cannot be used like English 'application' in the sense of request = *demande, requête.*
applique (aplik), s.f. **1.** Bracket-fittings, wall-candelabrum; **2.** trimming; inlaying.
appliquer (aplike), v.a. [L *applicare*] To apply, to fix, to affix, (fig.) to bestow; (surg.) *~ des ventouses*, to cup; *~ mal à propos*, to misapply; *~ un soufflet*, to give a slap, to box a person's ears; **s'~**, v.pr. **1.** to apply oneself, to study, to endeavour; **2.** to attribute to oneself, to

appropriate to oneself; *il s'applique toutes les louanges*, he takes all the praise.

appliqueuse (aplikøz), s.f. Appliqué-lace maker.

appogiature (apɔʒjatyr), s.f. [It. *appoggiatura*] (mus.) Appoggiatura.

appoint (apwɛ̃), s.m. **1.** Odd money, difference, balance; *faire l'~*, to pay the difference; *d'~*, odd; **2.** (comm.) after-payment.

appointage (apwɛ̃taʒ), s.m. Pointing, making pointed.

appointements (apwɛ̃tmɑ̃), s.m. pl. Salary, pay, stipend, emoluments; *être aux ~s de*, to receive a salary from.

appointer[1] (apwɛ̃te), v.a. **1.** To salary, to put upon a stipend. ⚠ *Appointer* cannot be translated by 'to appoint', which means: *nommer* (*un délégué*), *fixer* (*une heure, un rendez-vous, &c.*).

appointer[2] (apwɛ̃te), v.a. [*pointe*] To sharpen to a point, to point.

appointeu-r, -se (apwɛ̃tœr), s.m.f. adj. Person paying a salary or stipend.

appointir (apwɛ̃tir), v.a. To sharpen, to point.

appontement (apɔ̃tmɑ̃), s.m. [f. *pont*] Gangway, landing-gangway.

apport (apɔr), s.m. Contribution; material brought; supply, share of capital; (marriage) share contributed to joint estate; (law) deposit.

apporter (apɔrte), v.a. [L *ad+portare*] To bring, to furnish, to supply; *~ tant en mariage*, to furnish so much towards the joint estate; *~ des raisons*, to adduce reasons; *~ des difficultés*, to raise difficulties; *~ des soins*, to bestow care (*à*, upon); *~ de la précaution*, to use precaution.

apposer (apoze), v.a. **1.** To put up, to affix; *~ une affiche*, to stick up a poster; *~ les scellés*, to seal up (a house, room, &c.); syn. APPLIQUER; **2.** to insert (a clause); *~ sa signature*, to sign.

appositi-f, -ve (apɔzitif), adj. s.m (gram.) Appositive, apposition.

apposition (apɔzisjɔ̃), s.f. [L *appositio*] Affixing, insertion, (gram.) apposition.

appréciabilité (apresjabilite), s.f. Appreciability.

appréciable (apresjabl), adj. Appreciable, valuable.

appréciat-eur, -rice (apresjatœr), s.m.f. Appraiser, valuer, one who appreciates. ~, adj. Appreciative.

appréciati-f, -ve (apresjatif), adj. Appreciative.

appréciation (apresja'sjɔ̃), s.f. Appreciation, estimation; *~ de marchandises*, valuation of goods.

apprécier (apresje), v.a. [L *appretiare*] **1.** To value, to estimate, to judge; **2.** to appreciate, to esteem, to approve of; syn. ESTIMER, PRISER; **s'~**, v.pr. to value oneself, to value, appreciate each other; to be estimated.

appréhender (apreɑ̃de), v.a. [L *apprehendere*] **1.** To take up, to arrest, to seize; *~ au corps*, to arrest; **2.** to fear, to apprehend; *j'appréhende qu'il ne soit trop tard*, I fear it will be too late; **3.** (phil.) to perceive (by senses or intellect), to apprehend.

appréhensible (apreɑ̃sibl), adj. Apprehensible.

appréhensi-f, -ve (apreɑ̃sif), adj. Apprehensive, anxious, timid.

appréhension (apreɑ̃sjɔ̃), s.f. Apprehension, fear.

apprendre (aprɑ̃dr), v.a. [L *apprehendere*] **1.** To learn, to acquire, to study; *~ à se taire*, to learn to hold one's tongue; **2.** to hear of, to be informed of; *~ une nouvelle*, to hear a piece of news; **3.** to teach, to train; *~ un métier à un enfant*, to put a child to a trade; *~ le calcul à X*, to teach X arithmetic; **4.** to apprise, to inform; *~ une nouvelle à X*, to announce a piece of news to X.

apprenti, -e (aprɑ̃ti), s.m.f. [f. *apprendre*] **1.** Apprentice; articled pupil; **2.** (fig.) novice, tyro.

apprentissage (aprɑ̃tisaʒ), s.m. **1.** Apprenticeship, articles; *faire son ~*, to serve one's apprenticeship; *brevet d'~*, apprentice's indentures; *mettre en ~*, to apprentice, to article; *sortir d'~*, to finish one's time, one's apprenticeship; **2.** (fig.) trial, experiment.

apprêt (aprɛ), s.m. [f. L *ad+praestus*] **1.** Preparation, dressing, trimming (of food); *l'~ des viandes*, the cooking of meat; **2.** dressing, stiffening (for cloth, leather, &c.); (paint.) priming; **3.** (fig.) affectation; *style plein d'~*, affected style; **4.** (pl.) preparatives; *faire de grands ~s*, to make great preparations.

apprêtage (aprɛtaʒ), s.m. Dressing, stiffening (of textiles).

apprêté, -e (aprɛte), p. adj. [f. *apprêt*] Studied, affected, stiff, unnatural; *des manières ~es*, affected manners.

apprêter (aprɛte), v.a. **1.** To prepare, to season (meat, &c.); **2.** to dress, to starch, to finish (cloth, &c.); *~ une robe*, to get up a dress; *~ un chapeau*, to trim a hat; **3.** (fig.) *~ à rire*, to afford food for laughter; **s'~**, v.pr. to prepare oneself, to get ready; *s'~ de grands embarras*, to bring trouble on oneself.

apprêteu-r, -se (aprɛtœr), s.m.f. Preparer; painter on glass; (fem.) hat-trimmer; cutter-out, dresser.

apprivoisable (aprivwazabl), adj. Tameable.

apprivoisement (aprivwazmɑ̃), s.m. Taming.

apprivoiser (aprivwaze), v.a. [f. L *ad+privus*] To tame; to make (persons) tractable, sociable; **s'~**, v.pr. to grow tame, to grow accustomed (*à*, to); (fam. of persons) to thaw; *s'~ avec le danger*, to become familiar with danger.

apprivoiseu-r, -se (aprivwazœr), s.m.f. Tamer.

approbat-eur, -rice (aprɔbatœr), s.m.f. Approver, applauder. **~**, adj. Approving, applauding.

approbati-f, -ve (aprɔbatif), adj. Approbatory.

approbation (aprɔba'sjɔ̃), s.f. [L *approbatio*] Approbation, sanction, approval; *incliner la tête en signe d'~*, to nod assent.

approbativement (aprɔbativmɑ̃), adv. Approvingly, with approbation.

approbativité (aprɔbativite), s.f. Approbativeness.

approchable (aprɔʃabl), adj. Approachable, easy of access.

approchant, -e (aprɔʃɑ̃), p. adj. Similar, approximate, bordering on. **~**, adv. About, thereabouts, approximately.

approche (aprɔʃ), s.f. Approach, advance, coming; *lunette d'~*, spy-glass; *travaux d'~*, advance works; *~s*, pl. approaches, access, proximity, nearness; *aux ~s de la cinquantaine*, nearing fifty.

approcher (aprɔʃe), v.a. [OF *aprochier*, f. LL *ad+propiare*] To bring forward, to advance, to draw near; *~ la table du feu*, to draw the table up to the fire; **~**, v.n. **1.** *~ de*, to approach to, to be something like; **2.** to approach; to draw near; *l'heure approche*, the hour approaches; *il me fit ~ de lui*, he made me draw near him; **s'~**, v.pr. to approach, to draw near (*de*, to), to advance.

approfondir (aprɔfɔ̃dir), v.a. [L *ad+pro+fundus*] **1.** To deepen, to make deeper; **2.** to investigate, to examine, to fathom; *~ une question*, to examine, to sift, to probe a question; **s'~**, v.pr. to become deeper.

approfondissement (aprɔfɔ̃dismɑ̃), s.m. **1.** Deepening; **2.** fathoming, investigation, careful study.

appropriable (aprɔprijabl), adj. Assimilable, that may be rendered appropriate; that may be taken possession of.

appropriation (aprɔprija'sjɔ̃), s.f. Appropriation; adaptation, assimilation; taking possession; (law) conversion.

approprier (aprɔprije), v.a. [L *appropriare*] **1.** To accommodate, to suit, to adapt; *~ sa voix aux circonstances*, to suit one's tone to the circumstances; **2.** to clean, to tidy up; **s'~**, v.pr. **1.** to conform, to adapt oneself; **2.** to appropriate, to usurp.

approuvable (apruvabl), adj. That may be approved.

approuver (apruve), v.a. [L *approbare*] To sanction, to ratify, to authorize; to approve, to approve of; to pass (accounts); *approuvé l'écriture ci-dessus*, examined and found correct.

approvisionnement (aprɔvizjɔnmɑ̃), s.m. Provisions, stock; victualling; *vaisseau d'~*, victualling-ship.

approvisionner (aprɔvizjɔne), v.a. [L *ad+provisionem*] To stock, to provision, to victual; **s'~**, v.pr. to lay in supplies, to buy food.

approvisionneu-r, -se (aprɔvizjɔnœr), s.m.f. Caterer, purveyor, victualler.

approximati-f, -ve (aprɔksimatif), adj. Approximate.

approximation (aprɔksima'sjɔ̃), s.f. [L *approximare*] Approximation; conjecture, rough estimate.

approximativement (aprɔksimativmɑ̃), adv. Approximately, roughly, approximatively.

appui (apɥi), s.m. **1.** Support, prop, stay; *à hauteur d'~*, breast-high; *hauteur d'~*, breast-height; *point d'~*, basis, base; **2.** (mech.) fulcrum; **3.** (gram.) stress; **4.** (fig.) support, corroboration, help, succour; *être l'~ des faibles*, to be the support of the helpless; *à l'~ de*, in support of; *sans ~*, helpless, friendless; *ce cheval a l'~ bon*, this horse is soft-mouthed.

appui-main (apɥimɛ̃), s.m. (pl. *appuis-main*) Hand-rest; (painter's) maulstick.

appui-tête (apɥitɛt), s.m. (pl. *appuis-tête*) (photo.) Head-rest.

appuyer (apɥije), v.a. [LL *appodiare*] **1.** To prop, to stay, to support; **2.** to lean; *~ une échelle contre un mur*, to lean a ladder against a wall; **3.** (fig.) to second, to uphold, to back up; *~ une demande*, to second a petition; *être appuyé sur de bons titres*, to be founded on just grounds; *~ les chiens*, to urge on the hounds; v.n. **~**, to weigh (*sur*, upon), to press (on); to lay stress (upon); *~ sur un mot*, to stress a word; to insist; *~ sur un passage*, to dwell upon a passage; *~ sur un incident*, to harp upon an incident; **s'~**, v.pr. to lean (*sur*, upon), to rest (upon); (fig.) to rely (upon); *s'~ sur un roseau*, to lean on a broken reed; (colloq.) to treat oneself (to); *s'~ un bon dîner*, to treat oneself to a good dinner.

âpre (ɑpr), adj. [L *asper*] **1.** Hard, harsh, rough; sharp, tart; *goût ~*, bitter flavour; bleak, raw; *vent ~*, biting wind; grating (sound); **2.** (fig.) avid, eager, violent; *~ à la curée*, eager for the prey; *~ au gain*, greedy of gain; *~ à se venger*, eager for revenge; **3.** (fig.) austere, rigid; peevish; *un caractère ~*, a crabbed nature.

âprement (aprəmɑ̃), adv. **1.** Harshly, roughly, sharply, bitterly; **2.** eagerly, greedily, violently; **3.** peevishly, crabbedly.

après (aprɛ), prep. adv. [*à*+*près*] After, behind; next to; *et*~?, well?, what then?, what if I did?; *ci*-~, hereafter; ~ *coup*, too late, when the thing is done; ~ *tout*, after all, after all said and done; in pursuit of; *tout le monde crie* ~ *lui*, every one is against him; (pop.) *être toujours* ~ *quelqu'un*, to be always after a person; *d'*~, after, from, according to; *peindre d'*~ *nature*, to paint from nature; *d'*~ *Botticelli*, after Botticelli; *d'*~ *vous cela signifie que*, according to you it would mean that; *l'instant d'*~, the moment after.

après-demain (aprɛdəmɛ̃), adv. s.m. The day after to-morrow.

après-dîner (aprɛdine), s.m (pl. *après-dîners*) Evening; after-dinner hour.

après-midi (aprɛmidi), s.m. or f. (pl. invar.). Afternoon.

après-souper (aprɛsupe), s.m. (pl. *après-soupers*) After-supper hour.

âpreté (ɑprəte), s.f. **1.** Harshness, roughness; sharpness, bitterness; **2.** (fig.) eagerness, violence; *l'*~ *à l'argent*, the lust of gold; **3.** acrimony, asperity.

à-propos (aprɔpo), adv. In good time. ~, s.m. **1.** Timely word, act, or event; timeliness, pertinency; *l'*~ *donne du prix à tout*, nothing is worthless in its proper place; **2.** play or poem written for special event.

apside (apsid), s.f. [L f. Gr. *apsis, -idos*] (astr.) Apsis; (arch.) apse.

apte (apt), adj. [L *aptus*] Apt, suitable, fit, qualified; ~ *à apprendre*, quick to learn; *peu* ~, unfit.

aptère (aptɛr), adj. [Gr. *a*+*pteron*] Wingless, (bot.) apterous.

aptéryx (apteriks), s.m. (ornith.) Apteryx.

aptitude (aptityd), s.f. [f. *apte*] **1.** Aptitude, ability, natural disposition; *avoir de l'*~ *pour*, to have a talent for, a turn for; *certificat d'*~, teacher's certificate; **2.** (law) capacity (to receive legacy, &c.).

apurement (apyrmɑ̃), s.m. [f. *à*+*pur*] Audit, verification.

apurer (apyre), v.a. To audit, to verify.

apyre (apir), adj. [Gr. *a*+*pur*] Incombustible, infusible, fireproof.

apyrétique (apiretik), adj. (med.) Apyretic, without fever.

apyrexie (apirɛksi), s.f. Apyrexy.

aqua-fortiste (akwafɔrtist), s.m.f. [It. *acqua-forte*] Aquafortist, etcher.

aquamanile (akwamanil), s.m. [L *aqua* +*manus*] Washhand basin (medieval).

aquapuncture (akwapɔ̃ktyr), s.f. [L *aqua*+*punctura*] (med.) Aquapuncture.

aquarelle (akwarɛl), s.f. [It. *acquerella*] Aquarelle, water-colour.

aquarelliste (akwarɛlist), s.m.f. Water-colour painter.

aquarium (akwarjɔm), s.m. [f. L *aqua*] Aquarium.

aquatile (akwatil), adj. [f. L *aqua*] (bot.) Aquatic (of plants only).

aqua-tinta (akwatinta), s.f. [It. *aqua*+*tinta*] Aquatint.

aquatintiste (akwatɛ̃tist), s.m.f. Engraver in aquatint, aquatinter.

aquatique (akwatik), adj. Aquatic.

aquatiquement (akwatikmɑ̃), adv. Aquatically.

aqueduc (akədyk), s.m. [L *aquae ductus*] Aqueduct, conduit; (anat.) duct.

aqueu-x, -se (akwø), adj. [L *aquosus*] Aqueous, watery.

aquicole (akwikɔl), adj. [L *aqua*+*colere*] Aquatic.

aquiculteur (akwikyltœr), s.m. Water-plant grower.

aquiculture (akwikyltyr), s.f. [L *aqua*+*cultura*] Aquiculture.

aquifère (akwifɛr), adj. [L *aqua*+*fero, ferre*] (geol.) Aquiferous.

aquifoliacées (akwifɔljase), s.f. pl. (bot.) Aquifoliaceae.

aquilin, -e (akilɛ̃), adj. [L *aquilinus*] Aquiline.

aquilon (akilɔ̃), s.m. [L *aquilo, -onis*] North wind, cold blast, tempest.

aquitanien, -e (akitanjɛ̃), adj. s.m.f. Aquitanian.

aquosité (akɔzite), s.f. [f. L *aqua*] Aquosity, wateriness.

ara (ara), s.m. [abbrev. of *araraca*] (ornith.) Macaw.

araba (araba), s.m. [Turk. wd] Araba, a Turkish carriage.

arabe (arab), adj. s.m.f. **1.** Arab, Arabian; Arabic (language); **2.** (fam.) screw, miser, usurer. ⚠ Not used in the sense of 'street Arab', which = *petit vagabond, gavroche, petit voyou, petit va-nu-pieds, 'Poulbot'*.

arabesque (arabɛsk), adj. Arabesque, Arabian. ~, s.f. Arabesque.

arabique (arabik), adj. Arabic, Arabian; *gomme* ~, gum Arabic.

arabisant, -e, arabiste (arabizɑ̃, arabist), s.m.f. Arabic scholar, arabist.

arabisme (arabism), s.m. Arabicism.

arable (arabl), adj. [L *arabilis*] Arable, fit for tillage.

arachide (araʃid), s.f. [Gr. *arachidna*] (bot.) Earth-nut, pea-nut, arachis; *huile d'*~, arachis oil.

arachnéen, -ne (arakneɛ̃), adj. [Gr. *arakhnē*] Arachnidean, cobweb-like.

arachnides (araknid), s.m. pl. (zool.) Arachnida.

arachnoïde (araknɔid), s.f. Arachnoid.

arachnoïdien, -ne (araknɔidjɛ̃), adj. Arachnoid; (bot.) cobweb-like, filamentous.
arack (arak), s.m. [Arab. wd] Arrack.
aragne (araɲ), s.f. (archaic); Spider.
aragonite (aragɔnit), s.f. [f. Span. province *Aragon*] (geol.) Aragonite.
araignée (arɛɲe), s.f. [L *aranea*] **1.** Spider; ~ *de mer*, spider-crab; (colloq.) *pattes d'*~, hieroglyphics, sprawling handwriting; (jest.) *il a une* ~ *dans le plafond*, he has a bee in his bonnet; he is off his chump; *ôter les* ~*s*, to sweep away the cobwebs; *toile d'*~, spider's web, cobweb; **2.** (naut.) crowfoot; **3.** (mil.) series of galleries in a mine; **4.** any spider-like object or part.
araire (arɛr), s.m. [f. L *arare*] Swing-plough.
aranéïdes (araneid), s.f. pl. (zool.) Araneidans, araneida; weavers.
arantèle, arantelle (arɑ̃tɛl), s.f. (obs.) [L *aranea*+*tela*] **1.** Spider's web; **2.** fine linen.
arasement (arɑzmɑ̃), s.m. Levelling.
araser (arɑze), v.a. [*à*+*ras*] To level, to make even; to saw off; *scie à* ~, tenon saw.
arases (arɑz), s.f. pl. (mason.) Levelling course; also called *pierres d'arase*.
aratoire (aratwar), adj. [L *aratorius*] Agricultural, farming; *instruments* ~*s*, agricultural implements.
araucaria (arokarja), s.m. (bot.) Araucaria, monkey-puzzle.
arbalète (arbalɛt), s.f. [L *arcus*+*balista*] **1.** Arbalest, cross-bow; (naut.) Jacob's staff; *attelage en* ~, unicorn team; *cheval en* ~, leader in unicorn team; **2.** dormouse-trap.
arbalétée (arbalete), s.f. Cross-bow-shot (obs. measure of distance).
arbalétrier (arbaletrie), s.m. **1.** Crossbowman; **2.** (build.) principal rafters; **3.** (ornith.) swift (*Cypselus apus*).
arbalétrière, arbalétière (arbaletrijɛr, arbaletjɛr), s.f. Loophole.
arbitrage (arbitraʒ), s.m. Arbitration; arbitrament; arbitrage. ⚠ In English 'arbitrage' means usually: traffic in bills of exchange or stocks, to take advantage of different prices in other markets = *spéculation sur les différences de valeurs des titres sur diverses places*.
arbitraire (arbitrɛr), adj. Arbitrary, absolute; despotic; (law) discretionary. ~, s.m. Arbitrariness.
arbitrairement (arbitrɛrmɑ̃), adv. Arbitrarily; despotically.
arbitral, -e, (aux) (arbitral), adj. Arbitral, by arbitration.
arbitralement (arbitralmɑ̃), adv. By arbitration.
arbitration (arbitra'sjɔ̃), s.f. Arbitration.
arbitre (arbitr), s.m.f. [L *arbiter*] **1.** Arbiter, arbitrator; judge, (fem.) arbitress; disposer, umpire, referee; *tiers* ~, umpire; **2.** (phil.) will; *libre* ~, free-will.
arbitrer (arbitre), v.a. [f. *arbitre*] To arbitrate, to determine, to settle; to decree; to umpire (in games).
arborer (arbɔre), v.a. [f. L *arbor*] **1.** To hoist, to unfurl, to put up; ~ *un pavillon*, to hoist a flag; ~ *l'étendard de la révolte*, to raise the standard of rebellion; **2.** (fig.) to put on.
arborescence (arbɔrɛssɑ̃s), s.f. [f. L *arborescere*] Arborescence.
arborescent, -e (arbɔrɛssɑ̃), adj. Arborescent.
arboricole (arbɔrikɔl), adj. [L *arbor*+*colere*] (zool. bot.) Tree-living, arboricole.
arboriculteur (arbɔrikyltœr), s.m. Arboriculturist.
arboriculture (arbɔrikyltyr), s.f. Arboriculture.
arborisation (arbɔriza'sjɔ̃), s.f. Arborization.
arborisé, -e (arbɔrize), adj. Arborized.
arboriser (arbɔrize), v.n. [L *arbor*] To cultivate trees.
arboriste (arbɔrist), s.m. (rare) Arboriculturist; syn. PÉPINIÉRISTE.
arbouse (arbuz), s.f. [L *arbutus*] (bot.) Arbutus-berry.
arbousier (arbuzje), s.m. (bot.) Arbutus, strawberry-tree.
arbre (arbr), s.m. [L *arbor*] **1.** Tree; ~ *de haute futaie*, forest-tree; ~ *en buisson*, bush; ~ *vert*, evergreen; ~ *nain*, dwarf-tree; (fig.) tree; ~ *généalogique*, genealogical tree, family tree; ~ *de la Croix*, the Cross of Christ; *tel* ~, *tel fruit*, by their fruits ye shall know them; *l'*~ *ne tombe pas du premier coup*, Rome was not built in a day; *couper l'*~ *pour avoir le fruit*, to kill the goose that lays the golden eggs; *entre l'*~ *et l'écorce il ne faut pas mettre le doigt*, no good comes of meddling with other folks' feuds; *se tenir au gros de l'*~, to be on the safe side; *faire l'*~ *fourchu*, to walk on one's hands; *faire monter à l'*~, to kid, to pull the leg of; **2.** (mech.) arbor; shaft; spindle; axle-tree; ~ *de couche*, horizontal shaft, driving-shaft; ~ *coudé*, crank shaft; ~ *moteur*, main-shaft; ~ *vertical*, upright shaft; *grand* ~, shaft; ~ *de tour*, mandrel; **3.** (naut.) mast; ~ *de mestre*, mainmast; ~ *de plein vent* standard; ~ *de trinquet*, foremast; **4.** (chem.) ~ *de diane* or *philosophique*, arbor Dianae, amalgam of silver.
arbrisseau (pl. -x) (arbriso), s.m. Shrub.
arbuste (arbyst), s.m. Bush, shrub.
arbusti-f, -ve (arbystif), adj. Pertaining to bushes; *plantations* ~*ves*, plantations of bushes.
arc (ark), s.m. [L *arcus*] **1.** Bow, longbow; *à portée d'*~, within bow-shot; *tirer de l'*~, or *bander un* ~, to draw the bow;

tir à l'~, archery; *corde de l'~*, bow-string; *débander l'~ ne guérit pas la plaie*, it's shutting the stable door after the horse is stolen; *avoir plusieurs cordes à son ~*, to have more than one string to one's bow; **2.** (geom. phys., &c.) arc; *en ~ de cercle*, semicircular; *lampe à ~*, arc light; **3.** (arch.) arch; *~ de triomphe*, triumphal arch; *~ en plein cintre*, semicircular arch; *~ en ogive*, pointed arch.

arcade (arkad), s.f. [It. *arcata*] Arcade.

arcane (arkan), s.m. [L *arcanus*] (alchemy) Arcanum; (fig.) secret, mystery.

arcanne (arkan), s.f. Red ochre, ruddle.

arcanson (arkɑ̃sɔ̃), s.m. Colophony; syn. COLOPHANE.

arcasse (arkas), s.f. [L *arca*] (naut.) Stern frame.

arcature (arkatyr), s.f. (arch.) Ornamental arcading, blind arcade, arcade work.

arc-boutant (arkbutɑ̃), s.m. (pl. *arcs-boutants*). Flying buttress.

arc-bouter (arkbute), v.a. To strengthen with flying buttresses; (fig.) to strengthen, to buttress up; **s'~**, v.pr. to lean oneself (against); to stiffen oneself.

arc-doubleau (arkdublo), s.m. (pl. *arcs-doubleaux*) (arch.) Groin (of vault).

arceau (pl. **-x**) (arso), s.m. **1.** Arch (curved portion only); **2.** hoop (croquet).

arc-en-ciel (arkɑ̃sjɛl) s.m. (pl. *arcs-en-ciel*) Rainbow.

archaïque (arkaik), adj. [Gr. *arkhaikos*] Archaic.

archaïsme (arkaism), s.m. Archaism.

archal (arkal), s.m. [L *aurichalcum*] *Fil d'~*, brass wire.

archange (arkɑ̃ʒ), s.m. [Gr. *arkhaggelos*] Archangel.

archangélique (arkɑ̃ʒelik), adj. Archangelic.

arche[1] (arʃ), s.f. [L *arcus*] Arch, vault.

arche[2] (arʃ), s.f. [L *arca*] Ark; *l'~ sainte* or *l'~ d'alliance*, the Ark of the Covenant; *~ de Noé*, Noah's ark; *l'~ du Seigneur*, the ark of the Lord; (fig.) *c'est l'~ sainte*, it is forbidden ground.

archée[1] (arʃe), s.f. [Gr. *archē*] **1.** (anc. physiol.) Principle of life; **2.** (alchemy) central fire.

archée[2] (arʃe) s.f. [f. *arc*] Bow-shot.

archégone (arkegɔn), s.m. (bot.) Sporangium.

archelet (arʃlɛ), s.m. [L *arcus*] Drill-bow.

archéologie (arkeɔlɔʒi), s.f. [Gr. *arkhaiologia*] Archaeology.

archéologique (arkeɔlɔʒik), adj. Archaeological.

archéologue (arkeɔlɔg), s.m.f. Archaeologist.

archer (arʃe), s.m. [f. L *arcus*] **1.** Archer, bowman; *le petit ~*, Cupid; **2.** (obs.) bailiff, constable.

archerot (arʃəro), s.m. Little archer; Cupid.

archet (arʃɛ), s.m. [f. L *arcus*] **1.** Bow, fiddle-stick; **2.** drill-bow; **3.** top, hood (of cradle).

archétype (arketyp), s.m. [Gr. *arkhē*+ *tupos*] Archetype, prototype, model.

archevêché (arʃəvɛʃe), s.m. **1.** Archiepiscopal diocese; **2.** archbishop's residence or palace.

archevêque (arʃəvɛk), s.m. [Gr. *arkhē*+ *episcopos*] Archbishop.

archi- (arʃi *or* arki), pref. [Gr. *arkhē*] Arch-, archi-, chief; principal, first; original (can be used before many adj.; see ex. ARCHICOMBLE.

archichancelier (arʃiʃɑ̃səlje), s.m. Grand chancellor.

archichapelain (arʃiʃaplɛ̃), s.m. (Fr. hist.) Principal Chaplain, chief of French clergy; head of the Chapel Royal.

archicomble (arʃikɔ̃bl), adj. Full to overflowing; syn. ARCHIBONDÉ, ARCHIPLEIN.

archiconfrérie (arʃikɔ̃freri), s.f. Title given to certain religious societies.

archidiaconat (arʃidjakɔna), s.m. [f. Gr. *arkhidiakonos*] Archdeaconry (office).

archidiaconé (arʃidjakɔne), s.m. Archdeaconry (part of diocese).

archidiacre (arʃidjakr), s.m. Archdeacon.

archidiocésain, -e (arʃidjɔsezɛ̃), adj. Archdiocesan.

archiduc (arʃidyk), s.m. [OF *archeduc*] Archduke.

archiducal, -e, (aux) (arʃidykal), adj. Archducal.

archiduché (arʃidyʃe), s.m. Archduchy, archdukedom.

archiduchesse (arʃidyʃɛs), s.f. Archduchess.

archiépiscopal, -e, (aux) (arʃiepiskɔpal), adj. Archiepiscopal.

archiépiscopat (arʃiepiskɔpa), s.m. Archiepiscopate.

archière, archère (arʃjɛr, arʃɛr), s.f. [f. L *arcus*] Loop-hole.

archi-fou, -folle (arʃifu), adj. Stark-mad.

archimandrite (arʃimɑ̃drit), s.m. [Gr. *arkhimandrites*] Archimandrite.

archipel (arʃipɛl), s.m. [It. *arcipelago*] Archipelago.

archipompe (arʃipɔ̃p), s.f. (naut.) Pump-well.

archiprêtre (arʃiprɛtr), s.m. [Gr. *arkhē*+ *presbuteros*] Archpriest.

architecte (arʃitɛkt), s.m. [Gr. *arkhitekton*] Architect.

architectonique (arʃitɛktɔnik), adj. Architectonic. **~**, s.f. Architectonics.

architectural, -e, (aux) (arʃitɛktyral), adj. Architectural.

architecture (arʃitɛktyr), s.f. Architecture.

architrave (arʃitrav), s.f. Architrave.

archives (arʃiv), s.f. pl. [f. Gr. *arkheion*] Archives, records.

archiviste (arʃivist), s.m.f. Archivist, keeper of the records; registrar.

archivolte (arʃivɔlt), s.f. [It. *archivolto*] (arch.) Archivolt.

archontat (arkɔ̃ta), s.m. [f. Gr. *archon*] Archonship.

archonte (arkɔ̃t), s.m. Archon.

arçon (arsɔ̃), s.m. [L *arcus*] **1.** Saddle-bow; *être ferme sur les ~s*, to have a good seat; (fig.) to be true to one's principles; *perdre* or *vider les ~s*, to be unhorsed; (fig.) to lose countenance; to be disconcerted; *pistolet d'~*, horse-pistol; **2.** (vitic.) vine-twig; **3.** (techn.) bow.

arçonner (arsɔne), v.a. To card, to dress (wool, &c.).

arçonneur (arsɔnœr), s.m. Carder, dresser (of wool, &c.).

arcot (arko), s.m. (metall.) Scoria, dross.

arctique (arktik), adj. [Gr. *arktikos*] Arctic.

arcure (arkyr), s.f. [L *arcus*] (hort.) Arching (of vines, &c.).

ardélion (ardeljɔ̃), s.m. (obs.) [L *ardelio*] Ardelion (obs.), busybody.

ardemment (ardamɑ̃), adv. Ardently.

ardent, -e (ardɑ̃), adj. [L *ardere*] Burning, ardent, fiery; corrosive, scorching; (Fr. hist.) *Chambre ~e*, a court for trying heinous crimes for which the penalty was the stake; *mal des ~s*, St. Anthony's fire; *verre-~*, burning-glass; *chapelle ~e*, funeral decorations and candles at a lying-in-state; **2.** (fig.) violent, ardent, intense, vehement; **3.** red, reddish (of hair).

arder, ardre (arde, ardr), v.a. (obs.) [L *ardere*] To burn.

ardeur (ardœr), s.f. [f. L *ardere*] **1.** Intense heat, ardency; **2.** (fig.) ardour, fervour, earnestness; *avec ~*, spiritedly; *cheval plein d'~*, high-mettled horse.

ardillon (ardijɔ̃), s.m. Tongue (of a buckle); barb (of a hook).

ardoise (ardwaz), s.f. [etym. unkn.] **1.** Slate; *couvreur en ~s*, slater; *crayon d'~*, slate-pencil; **2.** (colloq.) score, account (of drinks).

ardoisé, -e (ardwaze), adj. Slate-coloured.

ardoisi-er, -ère (ardwazje), **ardoiseu-x, -se** (ardwazø), adj. Slaty.

ardoisier (ardwazje), s.m. Slate-quarry-man, slate-worker.

ardoisière (ardwazjɛr), s.f. Slate-quarry.

ardu, -e (ardy), adj. [L *arduus*] Steep, abrupt; (fig.) arduous.

are (ar), s.m. [L *area*] One hundred square metres.

aréage (areaʒ), s.m. Surveying, measuring in square metres.

arec, aréquier (arɛk, arɛkje), s.m. (bot.) Areca, areca-nut.

arénacé, -e (arenase), adj. [f. L *arena*] Arenaceous, sandy.

arénation (arena'sjɔ̃), s.f. Arenation.

arène (arɛn), s.f. [L *arena*] **1.** Arena; **2.** (fig.) cockpit, battleground, theatre, scene; **3.** *~s*, pl. (poet.) river-sands, desert-sands.

aréner (arene), v.n. and **s'aréner,** v.pr. To sink, to subside (of a building).

aréneu-x, -se (arenø), adj. Sandy, arenose.

arénicole (arenikɔl), adj. [L *arena*+*colere*] (zool.) Living in sandy places. ~, s.f. Sand-worm.

arénifère (arenifɛr), adj. [L *arena*+*ferre*] (geol.) Areniferous.

arénuleu-x, -se (arenylø), adj. Finely sandy, like grains of sand.

aréolaire (areɔlɛr), adj. Areolar.

aréolation (areɔla'sjɔ̃), s.f. Areolation.

aréole (areɔl), s.f. [L *areola*] Areola.

aréomètre (areɔmɛtr), s.m. [Gr. *araios*+*metron*] Araeometer, areometer, hydrometer.

aréométrie (areɔmetri), s.f. Araeometry.

aréométrique (areɔmetrik), adj. Araeometrical.

aréopage (areɔpɑʒ), s.m. [f. Gr. *Areios pagos*] Areopagus.

aréopagite (areɔpaʒit), s.m. Areopagite.

aréopagitique (areɔpaʒitik), adj. Areopagitic.

aréostyle (areɔstil), s.m. [Gr. *araios*+*stylos*] Araeostyle.

aréotectonique (ɑreɔtɛktɔnik), s.f. [Gr. *areios*+*tektonikē*] Areotectonics, military architecture.

arête (arɛt), s.f. [L *arista*] **1.** Fish-bone; skeleton of a fish; **2.** awn or beard of wheat, &c.; **3.** (arch.) arris; edge; *~ de poisson*, herring-bone work; *à vive ~*, sharp edged; **4.** (geom.) line of intersection of two surfaces, corner; **5.** (geog.) ridge.

arêtier (arɛtje), s.m. (carp.) Hip, hip-rafter.

argent (arʒɑ̃), s.m. [L *argentum*] **1.** Silver; *à pomme d'~*, silver-headed; *~ doré*, silver-gilt; *vaisselle d'~*, silver plate; *vif-~*, quicksilver; **2.** silver money; **3.** money, cash; *~ comptant*, ready money; *~ dormant*, money lying idle; *~ en caisse*, cash in hand; *~ mignon*, pin-money; *~ monnayé*, coined money; *~ mort*, money paying no interest; *placer de l'~*, to invest money; *rapporter de l'~*, to bring in money; *toucher de l'~*, to receive money; *~ comptant porte médecine*, money cures all ills; *c'est de l'~ en barre*, it is as safe as the Bank of England; *en avoir pour son ~*, to get one's money's worth; *faire ~ de tout*, to turn everything to account, to gold; *faire rentrer de l'~*, to call in money, funds; *pas d'~ pas de Suisse*, no pay, no piper; show me first your penny;

(fig.) *prendre quelque chose pour ~ comptant,* to take a thing as gospel truth; *y aller bon jeu, bon ~,* to play a square game, to be above-board; *avoir le temps et l'~,* to have all a man can desire; *jeter son ~ par les fenêtres,* to play ducks and drakes with one's money; *plaie d'~ n'est pas mortelle,* there are worse things than poverty; *bourreau d'~,* spendthrift; *avoir un ~ fou,* to have pots of money, to be rolling (in money); **4.** (herald.) argent; (poet.) *au croissant d' ~,* argent-horned.

argentage (arʒɑ̃taʒ), s.m. See syn. ARGENTURE.

argentan (arʒɑ̃tɑ̃), s.m. German silver.

argenté, -e (arʒɑ̃te), p. adj. Plated, silver-plated; (fig.) silvered, silvery.

argenter (arʒɑ̃te), v.a. To plate, to silver over; (fig.) to silver.

argenterie (arʒɑ̃tri), s.f. Plate (silver understood unless otherwise stated).

argenteur (arʒɑ̃tœr), s.m. Plater, silverer.

argenteu-x, -se (arʒɑ̃tø), adj. (pop.) Moneyed.

argentier (arʒɑ̃tje), s.m. **1.** (Fr. hist.) Treasurer; **2.** silversmith; **3.** silver-chest, silver-cupboard.

argentifère (arʒɑ̃tifɛr), adj. [L *argentum* +*ferre*] Argentiferous.

argentin[1], **-e** (arʒɑ̃tɛ̃), adj. (of sounds) Silvery, silver-toned.

argentin[2], **-e** (arʒɑ̃tɛ̃), adj. s.m.f. Argentine, from the Argentine Republic.

argentine (arʒɑ̃tin), s.f. **1.** (bot.) Silverweed, wild tansy; **2.** (zool.) argentine.

argenture (arʒɑ̃tyr), s.f. Silvering; silver-plating.

argien, -ne (arʒjɛ̃), adj. s.m.f. (Native) of Argos.

argilacé, -e (arʒilase), adj. Clayey, argillaceous.

argile (arʒil), s.f. [L *argilla*] **1.** Clay; potter's clay, argil; *~ à porcelaine,* china-clay; *~ réfractaire,* fire-clay; **2.** (fig.) vase, &c., made of clay.

argileu-x, -se (arʒilø), adj. Clayey, argillaceous.

argilifère (arʒilifɛr), adj. [L *argilla*+ *ferre*] Argilliferous, yielding clay.

argon (argɔ̃), s.m. (chem.) Argon.

argonaute (argɔnot), s.m. [Gr. *argonautēs*] Argonaut; (zool.) nautilus.

argot[1] (argo), s.m. [etym. unkn.] Slang; apache slang; professional slang, jargon.

argot[2] (argo), s.m. See ERGOT.

argoter (argɔte), v.a. [etym. dub.] (forestry) To cut the stub of.

argotique (argɔtik), adj. Slangy.

argoulet (argule), s.m. (Fr. hist.) Mounted archer.

argousin (arguzɛ̃), s.m. [f. Span. *alguazil*] **1.** Convict-warder; **2.** (slang) bobby, copper.

argue (arg), s.f. (mech.) Drawplate; wire-drawing machine.

arguer (argɥe), v.a. [L *arguere*] To infer, to argue.

argueu-x, -se (argɥø), adj. Reproachful, offensive; *paroles ~ses,* offensive remarks.

argument (argymɑ̃), s.m. [L *argumentum*] **1.** Argument; *~ dans les règles,* argument in due form; **2.** proof, evidence; **3.** summary, theme, argument (of book, &c.).

argumentant, -e (argymɑ̃tɑ̃), s.m.f. (law) Arguer, wrangler; disputant.

argumentat-eur, -rice (argymɑ̃tatœr), s.m.f. Arguer, wrangler. *~,* adj. Argumentative.

argumentation (argymɑ̃ta'sjɔ̃), s.f. Argumentation.

argumenter (argymɑ̃te), v.n. To argue.

argus (argys), s.m. [f. prop. n. *Argus* (myth.)] Argus, watchful guardian; (ent. ornith.) argus.

argutie (argysi), s.f. [L *argutia*] Quibble, subtlety, cavil.

aria (arja), s.m. [OF *harier,* to worry], (pop.) Nuisance, fuss, bother; *que d'~s!* what a fuss!

arianisme (arjanism), s.m. [f. *Arius*] Arianism.

aride (arid), adj. [f. L *arere*] Arid, dry; *terre ~,* barren ground; (fig.) uninteresting, dry.

aridité (aridite), s.f. Aridness, aridity, barrenness; (fig.) dryness.

arien (arjɛ̃), adj. s.m.f. [f. *Arius*] Arian.

ariette (arjet), s.f. [It. *arietta*] (mus.) Arietta.

arille (arij), s.m. [L *arillus*] (bot.) Aril.

arillé, -e (arije), adj. Arillate, arilled.

aristocrate (aristɔkrat), s.m.f. (colloq. abbr. *aristo*). Aristocrat~, adj. Aristocratic.

aristocratie (aristɔkrasi), s.f. [Gr. *aristos* +*kratos*] Aristocracy.

aristocratique (aristɔkratik), adj. Aristocratic.

aristocratiquement (aristɔkratikmɑ̃), adv. Aristocratically.

aristoloche (aristolɔʃ), s.f. [Gr. *aristos*+ *lokheia*] (bot.) Aristolochia, birthwort.

aristophanesque (aristɔfanɛsk), adj. [f. *Aristophanes*] Aristophanic, in the style of Aristophanes.

aristotélicien, -ne (aristɔtelisjɛ̃), adj. [f. *Aristoteles*] Aristotelian. *~,* s.m.f. Disciple of Aristotle.

aristotélique (aristɔtelik), adj. Aristotelian.

aristotélisme (aristɔtelism), s.m. Aristotelianism, Aristotelian philosophy.

arithméticien, -ne (aritmetisjɛ̃), s.m.f. Arithmetician.

arithmétique (aritmetik), s.f. [Gr. *arith-*

mos] Arithmetic. ~, adj. Arithmetical; *rapport* ~, arithmetical ratio.

arithmétiquement (aritmetikmɑ̃), adv. Arithmetically.

arithmographie (aritmɔgrafi), s.f. [Gr. *arithmos*+*graphein*] Arithmography, representation of a number by letters.

arithmologie (aritmɔlɔʒi), s.f. [Gr. *arithmos*+*logos*] Arithmology.

arithmomancie (aritmɔmɑ̃si), s.f. [Gr. *arithmos*+*manteia*] Arithmomancy, divination by numbers.

arithmomètre (aritmɔmɛtr),) s.m. [Gr. *arithmos*+*metron*] Arithmometer, calculating-machine.

arlequin (arləkɛ̃), s.m. [It. *arlecchino*] **1.** Harlequin; *habit d'*~, motley; (fig.) medley, miscellany; **2.** leavings, hodgepodge, broken food; **3.** (ornith.) spotted red-shank; **4.** (fig.) turn-coat, weathercock.

arlequinade (arləkinad) s.f. Harlequinade; (fig.) buffoonery.

armadille (armadij), s.f. [Span. *armadillo* dim. of *armado*] **1.** (nav.) Fleet of small ships of war, Armadilla; **2.** (zool.) armadillo.

armagnac (armaɲak), s.m. [geog. Fr. orig.] Armagnac brandy.

armateur (armatœr), s.m. [L *armator*] **1.** Ship-owner; **2.** captain of a privateer; privateer.

armature (armatyr), s.f. [L *armatura*] **1.** Armature, iron braces, stays, &c.; (of a dynamo) armature; **2.** (mus.) key-signature.

arme (arm), s.f. [L *arma*] **1.** Arm, weapon; ~*s à feu*, fire-arms; ~*s blanches*, side-arms; cold steel; *en venir aux* ~*s*, to come to blows, to start a war; *faire* or *tirer des* ~*s*, to fence; *passer par les* ~*s*, to shoot, or to put to the sword; *faire ses premières* ~*s*, to make one's first campaign; (fig.) to make one's début; *faire des* ~*s*, to fence; *fournir des* ~*s contre soi*, to provide a rod for one's own back; (pop.) to be asking for it; *jaque d'*~*s*, coat of mail; *pas d'*~*s*, passage of arms; (mil. slang) *passer l'*~ *à gauche*, to kick the bucket, to go west; *rendre les* ~*s*, to lay down one's arms, to surrender; *salle d'*~*s*, fencing-school; armoury; *fait d'*~*s*, feat of arms; *maître d'*~*s*, fencing-master; *être sous les* ~*s*, to serve, to be under the colours; (colloq.) *se mettre sous les* ~*s*, to attire oneself in all one's finery, to be in full feather or in full fig; **2.** branch or arm of the service, troops, forces; *l'*~ *offensive, défensive*, offensive, defensive forces; **3.** (herald.) arms, armorial bearings.

armé, -e (arme), p. adj. **1.** Armed, equipped; *à main* ~*e*, by force of arms; ~ *de toutes pièces*, armed from top to toe; **2.** (herald.) armed (with claws, horns, teeth, &c.); **3.** reinforced; *ciment* ~, reinforced concrete.

armée (arme), s.f. Army; forces, troops, host; fleet; (fig.) body or organization; ~ *permanente*, standing army; *corps d'*~, army corps; *fournisseur de l'*~, army contractor; *la Grande* ~, Napoleon's forces in the 1812 campaign.

armeline (armәlin), s.f. Ermine(skin).

armement (armәmɑ̃), s.f. [f. L *arma*] Armament; accoutrements; (naut.) equipment, arming, fitting-out.

arménien, -ne (armenjɛ̃), adj. s.m.f. Armenian.

armenteu-x, -se (armɑ̃tø), adj. (rare) [L *armentum*] Rich in flocks and herds.

armer (arme), v.a. [L *armare*] **1.** To arm, to equip, to furnish with an armament; **2.** (artill.) to load, to mount (guns, &c.); **3.** to strengthen; ~ *une poutre de bandes de fer*, to strengthen a beam with iron bands; **4.** (mus.) to give a key-signature to; **5.** (fig.) to fortify, to strengthen; **s'**~, v.pr. to arm oneself, to take arms; to fortify oneself; *s'*~ *de tout son courage*, to summon up all one's courage.

armet (armɛ), s.m. (medieval) Head-piece, helmet.

armillaire (armillɛr), adj. [L *armilla*] (astr.) Armillary.

armille (armij), s.f. [L *armilla*] **1.** (ant.) Bracelet, armlet; **2.** (astr.) armilla; **3.** (arch.) annulet (of the Doric capital).

arminien (arminjɛ̃), or **remontrant** (rәmɔ̃trɑ̃), s.m. [f. prop. n. *Arminius*] Arminian.

armistice (armistis), s.m. [L *arma*+*sistere*] Armistice, short truce.

armoire (armwar), s.f. [L *armarium*] Cupboard, clothes-press, wardrobe.

armoiries (armwari), s.f. pl. [L *arma*] Arms, armorial bearings.

armoise (armwaz), s.f. [L *artemisia*] **1.** (bot.) Artemisia, wormwood; ~ *commune*, mugwort; **2.** (techn.) syn. of ARMOISIN.

armoisin (armwazɛ̃), s.m. Sarsenet, a silken material.

armon (armɔ̃), s.m. [orig. dub,] Futchel (of a coach).

armorial (armɔrjal), s.m. Armorial.

armoricain, -e (armɔrikɛ̃), adj. s.m.f. Armorican (of Brittany).

armorier (armɔrje), v.a. To blazon, to paint a coat of arms (upon); *bouclier armorié*, emblazoned shield.

armoriste (armɔrist), s.m. Armorist, heraldic engraver.

armure (armyr), s.f. [L *armatura*] **1.** Armour; *revêtir son* ~, to buckle on one's armour; **2.** armature (of magnet,

&c.); **3.** (agric.) tree-guard; cradle (of a scythe); **4.** (mus.) key-signature; **5.** (fig.) defence, protection.

armurerie (armyrri), s.f. Armoury; arms-factory; arms-trade.

armurier (armyrje), s.m. Armourer, gunsmith, sword-cutler.

arnica (arnika), s.f. and m., **arnique** (arnik), s.f. (bot.) Arnica.

arobe, arrobe (arɔb), s.f. Arroba, Spanish liquid measure (10/16 litres) and weight (12/15 kilos).

aromate (arɔmat), s.m. [Gr. *arōma*] An aromatic.

aromatique (arɔmatik), adj. Aromatic.

aromatisation (arɔmatiza′sjɔ), s.f. Aromatization.

aromatiser (arɔmatize), v.a. To aromatize.

arome (arom), s.m. [Gr. *arōma*] Aroma.

aronde (arɔ̃d), s.f. (obs.) Swallow; (carp.) *en queue d'*~, dovetailed.

arondelle (arɔ̃dɛl), s.f. **1.** Fishing-tackle with line of hooks; **2.** ~ *de mer*, any small vessel.

arpège (arpɛʒ), s.m. [It. *arpeggio*] Arpeggio.

arpéger (arpeʒe), v.a. To play arpeggios.

arpent (arpɑ̃), s.m. [L *arepennis*] French acre, or about one and a quarter English acres.

arpentage (arpɑ̃taʒ), s.m. Land-surveying.

arpenter (arpɑ̃te), v.a. To survey, to measure; (fig.) to stride along at a great pace.

arpenteur (arpɑ̃tœr), s.m. Land-surveyor.

arpenteuse (arpɑ̃tøz), s.f. (ent.) Spanworm, larva of the geometer moth.

arpète (arpɛt), s.f. (slang) Apprentice or errand-girl employed by a dressmaker or milliner.

arpion (arpjɔ̃), s.m. (slang) Beetle-crusher, foot.

arqué, -e (arke), adj. [f. L *arcus*] Bent, curved, bowed.

arquebusade (arkəbyzad), s.f. Arquebusade, harquebusade.

arquebuse (arkəbyz), s.f. [It. *archibuso*] Arquebus, harquebus.

arquebuser (arkəbyze), v.a. To shoot, to kill with an arquebus.

arquebuserie (arkəbyzri), s.f. **1.** Musketry, arquebus-firing; **2.** gunsmithery, arquebus-factory.

arquebusier (arkəbyzje), s.m. **1.** Arquebusier, harquebusier; **2.** (obs.) syn. of ARMURIER.

arquer (arke), v.a. [f. L *arcus*] To bend, to curve, to arch; ~, v.n. to bend, to curve, to be arched; **s'**~, v.pr. to bow down, to bend.

arrachage (araʃaʒ), s.m. Pulling-up, digging-up of vegetables or roots.

arrache-clous (araʃklu), s.m. (invar. pl.) Nail-extractor.

arrachement (araʃmɑ̃), s.m. Rooting-up, pulling; drawing, extraction; (build.) toothing.

(d')arrache-pied (daraʃpje), adv. loc. With a will, like a horse, without interruption; *travailler six heures* ~, to work for six hours at a stretch.

arracher (araʃe), v.a. [L *eradicare*] **1.** To pull or tear up, out or away; to extract, to uproot, to grub up; ~ *de mauvaises herbes*, to pull up weeds, to weed; **2.** (fig.) to wring, to wrest, to extract, to extort; *lui* ~ *son secret*, to get his secret out of him; **3.** (fig.) to remove from, to tear away; ~ *quelqu'un au jeu*, to tear a person away from the tables; **s'**~, v.pr. to tear oneself away, to get away; to break away; (colloq.) *on se l'arrache*, he (or she) is all the rage; *s'*~ *au sommeil*, to shake off sleep; *s'*~ *les cheveux*, to tear one's hair; (fig.) *s'*~ *les yeux*, to tear each other's eyes out.

arracheur (araʃœr), s.m. Extractor; *mentir comme un* ~ *de dents*, to lie unblushingly.

arrachis (araʃi), s.m. **1.** Rooting-up of young trees; forest clearing; **2.** a plant pulled up by the roots.

arrachoir (araʃwar), s.m. **arracheu-r, -se** (araʃœr), s.m.f. (agric.) Scuffle, extirpator, digger.

arraisonnement (arɛzɔnmɑ̃), s.m. [f. *raison*] (naut.) Sanitary inspection.

arraisonner (arɛzɔne), v.a. (naut.) To hail, to speak, to inspect, to examine the papers of (a ship).

arrangeable (arɑ̃ʒabl), adj. That can be arranged.

arrangeant, -e (arɑ̃ʒɑ̃), p.adj. Accommodating, easy to deal with, tractable, amenable.

arrangement (arɑ̃ʒmɑ̃), s.m. **1.** Arrangement, disposition; **2.** agreement, settlement; ~*s*, terms; *entrer en* ~, to compound; *prendre des* ~*s avec X*, to come to terms with X; ~ *à l'amiable*, friendly agreement.

arranger (arɑ̃ʒe), v.a. [*à*+*ranger*] **1.** To arrange, to put in order; ~ *quelque chose*, to contrive something; *cela m'arrange*, that suits me; **2.** to fit up, to do up; ~ *une robe*, to alter a dress; *comme vous voilà arrangé!*, what a sight you look!; **3.** to ill-treat; ~ *quelqu'un de la bonne manière*, to give it a person straight from the shoulder; **s'**~, v.pr. **1.** to prepare oneself, to make arrangements (*pour*, for); **2.** to come to an agreement (*avec*, with); **3.** to make shift, to put up (*de*, with); *arrangez-vous*, do as best you can; (unsympathetic) that is your look-out; *cela s'arrangera*, it will come right

in the end; *qu'il s'arrange comme il voudra*, let him do as he likes.
arrangeur (arɑ̃ʒœr), s.m. One who arranges, adapter.
arrentement (arɑ̃tmɑ̃), s.m. [f. *rente*] Renting; *tenir par* ~, to rent.
arrenter (arɑ̃te), v.a. To rent, to let.
arrérager (areraʒe), v.n. To let arrears of payment accumulate.
arrérages (areraʒ), s.m. pl. [L *ad+retro*] Arrears; *laisser courir ses* ~*s*, to let one's arrears mount up.
arrestation (arɛsta'sjɔ̃), s.f. [f. L *ad+restare*] Arrest; custody; *être en état d'*~, to be in custody.
arrêt (arɛ), s.m. [OF *arester*, f. L *ad+restare*] **1.** Stop, pause, stoppage, halt, interruption; *robinet d'*~, stop-cock; *chien d'*~, setter, pointer; **2.** sentence; decree; ~ *de mort*, death-sentence; ~ *par défaut*, judgement by default; *prononcer un* ~, to pass sentence; **3.** arrest, apprehension; *faire* ~ *sur des marchandises*, to seize goods; *maison d'*~, lock-up, jail; *mandat d'*~, warrant; **4.** (mil.) *aux* ~*s*, under arrest; (school) kept in; (mil.) *mettre aux* ~*s simples*, to place under open arrest; (mil.) *lever les* ~*s*, to release from arrest; (mil.) ~*s de rigueur*, close arrest.
arrêté, -e (arɛte), p. adj. **1.** Stopped; arrested; **2.** agreed upon, resolved; *avoir des idées arrêtées*, to have fixed or preconceived notions (about). ~, s.m. Agreement, resolution; decree; ~ *ministériel*, order in council.
arrête-bœuf (arɛtbœf), s.m. (invar. pl.) (bot.) Cammock, rest-harrow.
arrêter (arɛte), v.a. [L *ad+restare*] **1.** To check, to stop; to delay, to detain; ~ *ses yeux sur*, to fix one's eyes upon; *rien ne l'arrête*, he sticks at nothing; **2.** to arrest; *on l'a fait* ~, they have had him arrested; **3.** to engage, to book; ~ *une chambre, un domestique*, to engage a room, a servant; **4.** to decide, to decree; *qu'a-t-on arrêté?*, what has been decided?; **5.** to settle, to conclude; ~ *un marché*, to conclude a bargain; ~, v.n. to stop, to cease, to leave off (doing, speaking, &c.); *il arrêta de parler*, he ceased speaking; s'~, v.pr. **1.** to stop, to pause; to leave off; **2.** to be decided, to be concluded.
arrêtiste (arɛtist), s.m. [f. *arrêt*] Compiler of decrees.
arrêtoir (arɛtwar), s.m. (mech.) Stop, catch.
arrher (are), v.a. [f. *arrhes*] To give earnest-money to.
arrhes (ar), s.f. pl. [Gr. *arrhabōn*] Deposit, earnest money; *donner des* ~, to pay an instalment confirming contract.
arrière (arjɛr), adv. [L *ad retro*] Behind (of time or place); backward; (naut.) aft, abaft, astern; *avoir vent* ~, to run before the wind. ~, interj. Away! avaunt! ~, s.m. Back part, rear; (naut.) stern; *voyager en* ~, to travel with one's back to the engine, horses, &c.; *faire machine en* ~, to reverse the engines; *marche* ~, reverse (motion).
arriéré, -e (arjere), adj. In arrears, overdue, behind the times; backward, behindhand, undeveloped; *enfant* ~, backward child. ~, s.m. Arrears; *liquider l'*~, to pay up arrears; *il a beaucoup d'*~ *dans sa correspondance*, he is very much behindhand with his correspondence.
arrière-ban (arjɛrbɑ̃), s.m. (pl. *arrière-bans*) General levy.
arrière-bec (arjɛrbɛk), s.m. (pl. *arrière-becs*) (of a bridge) Downstream cutwater.
arrière-bouche (arjɛrbuʃ), s.f. (pl. *arrière-bouches*) Pharynx, back of mouth.
arrière-boutique (arjɛrbutik), s.f. (pl. *arrière-boutiques*) Back-room (behind a shop).
arrière-corps (arjɛrkor), s.m. (invar. pl.) (naut.) Stern, stern-sheets; back (of building).
arrière-cour (arjɛrkur), s.f. (pl. *arrière-cours*) Back yard; back court.
arrière-fief (arjɛrfjɛf), s.m. (pl. *arrière-fiefs*) Sub-fief.
arrière-garde (arjɛrgard), s.f. (pl. *arrière-gardes*) Rear-guard.
arrière-gorge (arjɛrgorʒ), s.f. (pl. *arrière-gorges*) Back of the throat.
arrière-goût (arjɛrgu), s.m. (pl. *arrière-goûts*) After-taste.
arrière-grand'mère (arjɛrgrɑ̃mɛr), s.f. (pl. *arrière-grand'mères*) Great-grandmother.
arrière-grand-oncle (arjɛrgrɑ̃tɔ̃kl), s.m. (pl. *arrière-grands-oncles*) Great-great-uncle.
arrière-grand-père (arjɛrgrɑ̃pɛr), s.m. (pl. *arrière-grands-pères*) Great-grandfather.
arrière-grand'tante (arjɛrgrɑ̃tɑ̃t), s.f. Great-great-aunt.
arrière-main (arjɛrmɛ̃), s.m. (pl. *arrière-mains*) **1.** Back of the hand; **2.** (tennis) back-hander; **3.** hindquarters (of a horse).
arrière-neveu (arjɛrnəvø), s.m. (pl. *arrière-neveux*) Great-nephew.
arrière-nièce (arjɛrnjɛs), s.f. (pl. *arrière-nièces*) Great-niece.
arrière-pensée (arjɛrpɑ̃se), s.f. (pl. *arrière-pensées*) Mental reservation, ulterior motive.
arrière-petit-fils (arjɛrpətifis), s.m. (pl. *arrière-petits-fils*) Great-grandson.
arrière-petite-fille (arjɛrpətitfij), s.f. (pl. *arrière-petites-filles*) Great-granddaughter.

arrière-petits-enfants (arjɛrpətizɑ̃fɑ̃), s.m. pl. Great-grandchildren.

arrière-plan (arjɛrplɑ̃), s.m. (pl. *arrière-plans*) (paint. theatr.) Background.

arrière-point (arjɛrpwɛ̃), s.m. (pl. *arrière-points*) Back-stitch.

arrière-port (arjɛrpɔr), s.m. (pl. *arrière-ports*) Inner harbour.

arriérer (arjere), v.a. To defer, to put off, to leave in arrears; **s'~**, v.pr. to stay behind, to fall in arrears.

arrière-saison (arjɛrsɛzɔ̃), s.f. **1.** Late autumn; **2.** (fig.) the last part of a period; *l'~ de la vie,* the autumn, the evening of life; syn. AUTOMNE.

arrière-train (arjɛrtrɛ̃), s.m. **1.** Hind-carriage, back portion (of a vehicle); **2.** hindquarters (of an animal).

arrimage (arimaʒ), s.m. (naut.) Stowage, stowing; trimming (of the hold); *planches, nattes d'~,* dunnage planks, mats; *changer l'~,* to break bulk.

arrimer (arime), v.a. [etym. dub.] (naut.) To stow (cargo); to trim (the hold); *~ en breton,* to stow (casks, &c.) a-burton (or athwart-ships).

arrimeur (arimœr), s.m. (naut.) Stevedore.

arriser, ariser (arize), v.a. (naut.) To lower (the yards); to reef (sails).

arrivage (arivaʒ), s.m. **1.** Arrival (of ships or cargo); **2.** goods arriving at a port, &c.; *de beaux ~s,* a fine consignment.

arrivée (arive), s.f. Arrival; *à l'~,* on arrival; (motor.) *~ d'air,* air-intake.

arriver (arive), v.n. [*à*+*rive*; f. L *ripa*] **1.** To arrive, to come; *~ bien à propos,* to come at the right moment; *les idées lui arrivent plus vite que les paroles,* his mind works faster than his tongue; *~ comme mars en Carême,* to come round like Christmas, to be as regular as clockwork; *quoi qu'il arrive,* come what may; *~ à grands pas,* to come striding along; *un malheur n'arrive jamais seul,* troubles never come singly; *un accident lui est arrivé,* he has met with an accident; **2.** *~ à,* to attain, to arrive at, to reach; *~ à ses fins* or *à son but,* to compass one's ends; *~ jusqu'à X,* to gain access to X; **3.** (naut.) to bear up, to fall off; *sans ~*; nothing off! *arrivez!,* bear up!; *~*, v. impers. to happen; *il m'est arrivé un accident,* an accident has happened to me; (colloq.) *croire que c'est arrivé,* to be too credulous or enthusiastic; to take things too seriously.

arriviste (arivist), s.m.f. Time-server, unscrupulous man, man on the make, hustler, pushful 'get-rich-quick' fellow or woman, careerist.

arroche (arɔʃ), s.f. (bot.) Orach; *~ cultivée,* garden spinach or mountain spinach; *~ puante,* stinking goosefoot.

arrogamment (arɔgamɑ̃), adv. Arrogantly.

arrogance (arɔgɑ̃s), s.f. [L *arrogantia*] Arrogance, haughtiness; *c'est le comble de l'~,* it is the height of arrogance.

arrogant, -e (arɔgɑ̃), adj. Arrogant, haughty.

(s')arroger (sarɔʒe), v.pr. [L *arrogare*] To arrogate to oneself, to claim.

arroi (arwa), s.m. [L *ad*+Germ. *rät*] Array, equipage (rare); *être en mauvais ~,* to be in a sad pickle.

arrondir (arɔ̃dir), v.a. [f. *rond*] **1.** To give a circular shape to; to round off; (fig.) *~ les angles,* to smooth things down, to pour oil on the waters; **2.** (rhet.) to round (a period); *une phrase bien arrondie,* a well-turned sentence; **3.** (naut.) to double; **4.** (fam.) to round off, to increase; *il a bien arrondi sa pelote,* he has feathered his nest well; **s'~**, v.pr. to grow round, to get fat; (fig.) *sa fortune s'arrondit,* his wealth increases.

arrondissement (arɔ̃dismɑ̃), s.m. **1.** Rounding-off; **2.** roundness; **3.** (in France) a civil district, a division of a department.

arrosage (arozaʒ), s.m. Watering, sprinkling.

arroser (aroze), v.a. [LL *arrosare*] **1.** To water, to sprinkle, to irrigate; to bathe (with tears); (fig.) *~ un repas de vin,* to wash down a meal with wine; **2.** (cook.) to baste; **3.** (colloq.) to distribute gratuities, bribes to; *~ ses créditeurs,* to pay one's creditors a trifle; *~ ses galons,* to stand drinks; **4.** to water, to flow through (of rivers).

arroseu-r, -se (arozœr), s.m.f. A person who waters. **~se**, s.f. Watering-machine.

arrosoir (arozwar), s.m. Watering-can, watering-pot.

arrugie (aryʒi), s.f. [L *arrugia*] (mining) Drain, sough.

ars (ar or ars), s.m. [L *artus*] **1.** (vet.) The fold at the junction of the breast and foreleg of a horse; **2.** plat-vein.

arsenal (pl. **aux**) (arsənal), s.m. [It. *arsenale*] Arsenal, yard, dockyard.

arséniate (arsenjat), s.m. (chem). Arseniate.

arsenic (arsənik), s.m. [L *arsenicum*] (chem.) Arsenic.

arsenical, -e, (aux), arsénié, -e (arsənikal, arsenje), adj. (chem.) Arsenical; treated with arsenic.

arsénieux (arsenjø), adj.m. (chem.) Arsenious.

arsénique (arsenik), adj. (chem.) Arsenical.

arsénite (arsenit), s.m. (chem.) Arsenite.

arséniure (arsenjyr), s.m. (chem.) Arseniuret, arsenide.

arsin (arsɛ̃), s.m. [f. L *ardere, arsum*] Wood damaged by fire.
arsis (arsis), s.m. (pros.) Arsis.
arsouille (arsuj), s.m. Debauchee, low cad. ~, adj. Blackguardly, caddish.
art (ar), s.m. [L *ars*] Art; *~s d'agrément*, accomplishments; *il a l'~ de réussir*, he has the secret of success, the knack of succeeding; *les beaux ~s*, the fine arts; *maître ès ~s*, master of arts.
artère (artɛr), s.f. [Gr. *artēria*] **1.** Artery; **2.** thoroughfare.
artérialisation (arterjaliza'sjɔ̃), s.f. Arterialization.
artérialiser (arterjalize), v.a. To arterialize.
artériel, -le (arterjɛl), adj. Arterial.
artériole (arterjɔl), s.f. Arteriole.
artériologie (arterjɔlɔʒi), s.f. Arteriology.
artériologique (arterjɔlɔʒik), adj. Arteriological.
artériosclérose (arterjoskleroz), s.f. [Gr. *artēria+sklēros*] Arterio-sclerosis.
artériotomie (arterjotɔmi), s.f. [Gr. *artēria+tome*] Arteriotomy.
artérite (arterit), s.f. (pathol.) Arteritis.
artésien, -ne (artezjɛ̃), adj. [f. *Artois*] Artesian; *puits ~*, artesian well.
arthralgie (artralʒi), s.f. [Gr. *arthron+algos*] (med.) Arthralgia, articular neuralgia.
arthrite (artrit), s.f. [Gr. *arthritis*] Arthritis.
arthritique (artritik), adj. s.m.f. Arthritic.
arthritisme (artritism), s.m. Arthritism.
arthropodes (artrɔpɔd), s.m. pl. [Gr. *arthron+pous, podos*] Arthropoda.
artichaut (artiʃo), s.m. [It. *articiocco*] Artichoke.
artichautière (artiʃotjɛr), s.f. Artichoke-bed.
article (artikl), s.m. [L *articulus*] **1.** Article (in all English senses except 'apprenticeship', *apprentissage*); *~ de fond*, leading article; *à l'~ de la mort*, at the point of death; *~ de Paris*, novelty, speciality of Parisian manufacture; (comm.) *rayon ~s de Paris*, fancy department; *ce n'est pas un ~ de foi*, it is not Gospel truth; *faire l'~*, to puff one's goods (lit. and fig.); **2.** (ent. bot.) part between two joints or articulations.
articulaire (artikylɛr), adj. Articular.
articulation (artikyla'sjɔ̃), s.f. Articulation, joint.
articulé, -e (artikyle), p. adj. Articulate, clear, distinct, jointed, articulated; *d'une manière ~e*, articulately, distinctly. **~s**, s.m. pl. (zool.) Articulata.
articuler (artikyle), v.a. To articulate; to pronounce distinctly; (law) to enumerate (facts); **s'~**, v.pr. to be articulated.
artifice (artifis), s.m. [L *artificium*] Artifice, contrivance; skill, dexterity; trick, cunning, stratagem; *tirer un feu d'~*, to let off fireworks; (fig.) to show off; *un feu d'~*, fireworks; (fig.) a flash in the pan.
artificiel, -le (artifisjɛl), adj. Artificial.
artificiellement (artifisjɛlmɑ̃), adv. Artificially.
artificier (artifisje), s.m. Pyrotechnist, fireworks maker. ⚠ Not 'artificer', which = *artisan, inventeur, constructeur, mécanicien militaire.*
artificieusement (artifisjøzmɑ̃), adv. Artfully, craftily, cunningly.
artificieu-x, -se (artifisjø), adj. Artful, crafty, cunning.
artillerie (artijri), s.f. [LL *articularius*] Artillery; *~ de campagne*, field artillery; *piece d'~*, (piece of) ordnance.
artilleur (artijœr), s.m. Artilleryman, gunner.
artimon (artimɔ̃), s.m. [L *artemo*] (naut.) Storm trysail; mizen; *hune d'~*, mizen-top; *mât d'~*, mizen-mast; *étai d'~*, mizen-stay.
artiodactyles (artjɔdaktil), s.m. pl. [Gr. *artios+daktulos*] (zool.) Artiodactyls.
artisan (artizɑ̃), s.m. [It. *artigiano*] Artisan, handicraftsman, (social hist.) artificer.
artison (artizɔ̃), s.m. (ent.) Woodfretter moth, destructive moth; (pop.) woodworm.
artiste (artist), s.m. [L *ars, artis*] Artist; player, performer.
artistement (artistəmɑ̃), adv. Artistically, skilfully.
artistique (artistik), adj. Artistic.
artistiquement (artistikmɑ̃), adv. Artistically, with taste.
artocarpe (artokarp), s.m. [Gr. *artos+karpos*] (bot.) Bread-fruit tree, *Artocarpus incisa.*
arum (arɔm), s.m. (bot.) Arum, cuckoo-pint.
aruspice (aryspis), s.m. [L *aruspex*] (anc. Rom.) Haruspex.
arvicole (arvikɔl), adj. [L *arvum+colere*] Living in fields.
aryen, -ne (arjɛ̃), adj. [Sansk. *arya*] Aryan.
aryténoïde (aritenɔid), s.m. adj. [Gr. *arutaina+eidēs*] (anat.) Arytenoid.
arythmique (aritmik), adj. [Gr. *a+rhuthmos*] Rhythmless.
arzel (arzɛl), s.m. [Arab. *arjal*] Whitefoot, (horse having one or both the hind-feet white).
as (ɑs), s.m. [L *as*, Gr. *eis*] Ace; *~ de pique, de carreau, de cœur, de trèfle*, ace of spades, diamonds, hearts, clubs; *il est fichu comme l'~ de pique*, he looks a scarecrow; (colloq.) *c'est un ~*, he is a clipper, a oner, an A1 man; *plein aux ~*, flush, having plenty of money.
asaret (azarɛ), s.m. [L *asarum*] (bot.) *Asara-bacca*, hazel-wort.

asbeste (asbɛst), s.m. [Gr. *asbestos*] Asbestos.
ascaride, ascaris (askarid, askaris), s.m. [f. Gr. *askarizein*] Ascaride, intestinal worm.
ascendance (asɑ̃dɑ̃s), s.f. **1.** Rising (of a star, &c.); **2.** ascending line (of kindred), forefathers.
ascendant, -e (asɑ̃dɑ̃), p. adj. [f. L *ascendere*] Ascending, ascendant.
ascendant (asɑ̃dɑ̃), s.m. **1.** (astr.) Ascendant; **2.** ascendancy; *avoir de l'~ sur*, to have influence over; **3.** *~s et descendants*, ancestry and descendants.
ascenseur (asɑ̃sœr), s.m. Lift, elevator.
ascension (asɑ̃sjɔ̃), s.f. **1.** (astr.) Ascension; **2.** Ascension Day; **3.** ascent.
ascensionnel, -le (asɑ̃sjɔnɛl), adj. Ascensional.
ascensionniste (asɑ̃sjɔnist), s.m.f. Climber; balloonist.
ascète (asɛt), s.m.f. [Gr. *askētēs*] Ascetic.
ascétique (asetik), adj. Ascetic.
ascétiser (asetize), v.a. To make ascetic; **s'~**, v.pr. to become ascetic.
ascétisme (asetism), s.m. Asceticism.
ascidie (asidi), s.f. (bot.) Ascidian.
ascien (asjɛ̃), s.m. [Gr. *a+skia*] (geog.) Inhabitant of the torrid zone.
ascite (asit), s.f. [Gr. *askos*] (pathol.) Common dropsy.
asclépiade (asklepjad), s.m. [f. n. of Gr. poet *Asklēpiadēs*] (pros.) Asclepiad. **~**, adj. Asclepiadean.
asclépiade (asklepjad), s.f. (bot.) Asclepiad, swallow-wort.
asepsie (asɛpsi), s.f. [Gr. *a+sēpsis*] (med.) Asepsis; aseptic principles, methods, treatment, &c.
aseptique (asɛptik), adj. s.m. Aseptic.
asexué, -e, asexuel, -le (asɛksɥe, asɛksɥɛl), adj. Asexual.
asiarcat (azjarka), s.m. (anc. hist.) Asiarchate.
asiarque (azjark,) s.m. [Gr. *asiarches*] (anc. hist.) Asiarch.
asiatique (azjatik), adj. s.m.f. Asiatic.
asile (azil), s.m. [L *asylum*] Asylum, place of refuge, sanctuary; home (for the aged, &c.); *salle d'~*, infant school; *droit d'~*, right of sanctuary; *sans ~*, shelterless, homeless; *servir d'~ à*, to shelter; (fig.) protection, refuge; syn. REFUGE.
asine (azin), adj. f. [L *asinus*] Asinine.
asparagine (asparaʒin), s.f. [f. L *asparagus*] (chem.) Asparagine.
aspe, asple (asp, aspl), s.m. Winder for silk.
aspect (aspɛ, aspɛk before a vowel), s.m. [L *aspectus*] Aspect.
asperge (aspɛrʒ), s.f. [L *asparagus*] Asparagus; *une botte d'~*, a bundle of asparagus; (fig.) tall thin person, 'lamp-post', 'long string of misery'.
aspergement (aspɛrʒmɑ̃), s.m. Aspersion.
asperger (aspɛrʒe), v.a. [L *aspergere*] To sprinkle (*de*, with).
aspergerie, aspergière (aspɛrʒri, aspɛrʒjɛr), s.f. Asparagus-bed.
aspergès (aspɛrgɛs), s.m. [L wd] Aspergillum; asperges.
aspérité (asperite), s.f. [f. L *asper*] Asperity; roughness.
asperme (aspɛrm), adj. [Gr. *a+sperma*] (bot.) Aspermous, seedless.
aspersion (aspɛrsjɔ̃), s.f. Aspersion, sprinkling. ⚠ Not as in Engl. 'slander'.
aspersoir (aspɛrswar), s.m. **1.** Holy-water sprinkler; **2.** nozzle (of watering-pot.)
aspérule (asperyl), s.f. [f. L *asper*] (bot.) Asperula, woodruff.
asphaltage (asfaltaʒ), s.m. Asphalting, asphalt.
asphalte (asfalt), s.m. [Gr. *asphaltos*] Asphalt, bitumen.
asphalter (asfalte), v.a. To asphalt.
asphodèle (asfɔdɛl), s.m. [Gr. *asphodelos*] (bot.) Asphodel.
asphyxiant, -e (asfiksjɑ̃), p. adj. Asphyxiating.
asphyxie (asfiksi), s.f. [Gr. *asphuxia*] (med.) Asphyxia, asphyxy.
asphyxié, -e (asfiksje), adj. Asphyxiated.
asphyxier (asfiksje), v.a. To asphyxiate; **s'~**, v.pr. to asphyxiate oneself.
aspic[1] (aspik), s.m. [Gr. *aspis*] (zool.) Asp, viper; (fig.) *langue d'~*, backbiter.
aspic[2] (aspik), s.m. [etym. dub.] (bot.) Spike-lavender.
aspic[3] (aspik), s.m. (cook.) aspic, cold dish in jelly.
aspidistra (aspidistra), s.m. (bot.) Aspidistra.
aspirail (pl. **aux**) (aspiraj), s.m. [L *ad+spirare*] (techn.) Air-hole, draught-hole.
aspirant, -e (aspirɑ̃), p. adj. (techn.) Sucking, suction; *pompe ~e*, suction-pump, exhauster.
aspirant, -e (aspirɑ̃), s.m.f. Aspirant, candidate, suitor; (naut.) midshipman.
aspirat-eur, -rice (aspiratœr), adj. Inhaling, aspiring. **~**, s.m. Vacuum cleaner; ventilator; exhauster, aspirator; *~ électrique*, electric vacuum cleaner.
aspirati-f, -ve (aspiratif), adj. Aspirated.
aspiration (aspira'sjɔ̃), s.f. [L *aspiratio*] **1.** (gram.) Aspiration; **2.** (physiol.) inhaling, inspiration; **3.** (techn.) exhaustion; suction; **4.** (fig.) aspiration, yearning.
aspiratoire (aspiratwar), adj. Aspiratory.
aspiré, -e (aspire), p. adj. s.f. (gram.) Aspirated, aspirate.
aspirer (aspire), v.a. [L *ad+spirare*] **1.** (gram.) To aspirate; **2.** (physiol.) to inspire, to inhale; **3.** (techn.) to suck in; to exhaust; **4.** (fig.) to drink in; *~ à*, v.n. to aspire (to or after), to aim (at).

aspre (aspr), s.m. Asper (small Turkish coin).
assa fœtida (asafetida), s.f. (pharm.) Asafoetida.
assagir (asaʒir), v.a. [f. *sage*] To impart wisdom to; to calm, to moderate; **s'~**, v.pr. to become wise.
assaillant, -e (asajɑ̃), p. adj. Attacking, aggressive, assailing. **~**, s.m.f. Aggressor, assailant.
assaillir (asajir), v.a. [L *ad+salire*] To assault, to assail; (fig.) to worry, to beset.
assainir (asɛnir), v.a. [f. *sain*] To cleanse, to make healthy; (fig.) to cleanse, to purify; **s'~**, v.pr. to become healthy.
assainissement (asɛnismɑ̃), s.m. Cleansing, purification; salubrity, improved sanitary condition (of a place).
assaisonnant, -e (asɛzɔnɑ̃), p. adj. Seasoning, savoury.
assaisonnement (asɛzɔnmɑ̃), s.m. Condiment, seasoning, dressing.
assaisonner (asɛzɔne), v.a. [f. *saison*] To season, to flavour, to dress (salads, &c.); (fig.) to give a zest to.
assarmenter (asarmɑ̃te), v.a. [f. *sarment*] To prune (vines).
assassin, -e (asasɛ̃), adj. [Arab. *ḥashshāshīn*, f. *hashish*] Murderous, murdering. **~**, s.m. Assassin, murderer.
assassinant, -e (asasinɑ̃), adj. (fam.) Wearisome, boring.
assassinat (asasina), s.m. Assassination, murder.
assassiner (asasine), v.a. To assassinate, to murder; (fig., fam.) to annoy, to bore (a person) to death.
assation (asa'sjɔ̃), s.f. [L *assatio*] (med.) Assation, baking.
assaut (aso), s.m. [L *assaltus*] Assault, onset; *colonne d'~*, storming-party; *emporter une ville d'~*, to carry a town by storm; (mil.) *char d'~*, tank; *~ d'armes*, fencing match; (fig.) *faire ~ d'esprit*, to vie in wit. ⚠ *Assaut* has not like 'assault' the sense of unlawful personal attack (including menacing words) = *voies de fait, violences*.
assavoir (asavwar), v.a. (only used in the loc: *faire ~*) (obs.) See SAVOIR.
asseau (pl.-**x**)(aso), s.m. Slater's hammer.
assèchement (asɛʃmɑ̃), s.m. [f. *sécher*] Drying-up, drainage.
assécher (aseʃe), v.a. To drain; **~**, v.n. (naut.) to be left high and dry.
assemblage (asɑ̃blaʒ), s.m. **1.** Assemblage, gathering, coupling, holding together; **2.** (print.) gathering; **3.** (carp.) bond, scarf, joint.
assemblé (asɑ̃ble), s.m. (dancing) Third position.
assemblée (asɑ̃ble), s.f. Assembly, meeting, party; congregation (in churches); (hunt.) meet; *~ de jeu*, card-party; (mil.) *quartier d'~*, parade-ground.
assemblement (asɑ̃blmɑ̃), s.m. Gathering, assembling.
assembler (asɑ̃ble), v.a. [L *assimulare*] To assemble, to gather together; to put together; (print.) to gather; (carp.) to trim, to scarf; to join; **s'~**, v.pr. to assemble, to meet, to congregate; *qui se ressemble s'assemble*, birds of a feather flock together; syn. JOINDRE, UNIR, RASSEMBLER.
assembleu-r, -se (asɑ̃blœr), s.m.f. Assembler; (print.) gatherer.
asséner (asene), v.a. [L *assignare*] To strike, to deal (a blow).
assentiment (asɑ̃timɑ̃), s.m. Assent, agreement.
assentir (asɑ̃tir), v.n. **1.** To assent, to agree (to); **2.** (hunt.) to scent.
asseoir (aswar), v.a. [L *assidere*] **1.** To seat, to set, to place; *faire ~ X*, to offer X a seat; (colloq.) *cela m'a assis*, I was absolutely crushed; **2.** (mil.) to pitch (a camp); **3.** (fig.) to establish; *~ un gouvernement*, to establish a government; *~ l'impôt*, to assess taxes; **s'~**, v.pr. to sit, to take a seat, to settle; to perch.
assermenté, -e (asɛrmɑ̃te), p. adj. Sworn in; attested.
assermenter (asɛrmɑ̃te), v.a. [f. *serment*] To swear in, to attest, to administer the oath to.
asserti-f, -ve (asɛrtif), adj. Assertive.
assertion (asɛrsjɔ̃), s.f. [L *assertio*] Assertion.
asservir (asɛrvir), v.a. [f. L *servus*] To enslave; to master, to subdue, to conquer; **s'~**, v.pr. to be the slave (*à*, of), to submit (to).
asservissant, -e (asɛrvisɑ̃), p. adj. Enslaving; slavish, servile.
asservissement (asɛrvismɑ̃), s.m. Bondage, subjection, servitude, enslavement.
asservisseur (asɛrvisœr), s.m. Enslaver, subduer, conqueror.
assesseur (asɛsœr), s.m. [L *assessor*] Assessor.
assessoral, assessorial, -e, (aux) (asɛsoral, asɛsorjal), adj. Assessorial.
assessorat, assessoriat (asɛsora, asɛsorja), s.m. Assessorship.
assette (asɛt), s.f. See syn. ASSEAU, s.m.
asseuler (asœle), v.a. See ESSEULER.
assez (ase), adv. [L *ad+satis*] **1.** Enough; *d'~ bon cœur*, readily enough; *en voilà ~*, that will do; *j'en ai ~*, I've had enough of it; I am fed up with it; **2.** tolerably, passably; *c'est ~ joli*, it is rather pretty; *il est ~ sage*, he is tolerably good.
assibilation (asibila'sjɔ̃), s.f. (phon.) Assibilation.
assibiler (asibile), v.a. [L *assibilare*] To assibilate.

assidu, -e (assidy), adj. [L *assiduus*] Assiduous.
assiduité (asidɥite), s.f. Assiduity.
assidûment (asidymɑ̃), adv. Assiduously.
assiégé, -e (asjeʒe), p. adj. s.m.f. Besieged; (fig.) besieged, importuned.
assiégeant, -e (asjeʒɑ̃), p. adj. Besieging. ~, s.m.f. Besieger.
assiéger (asjeʒe), v.a. [L *ad+sedere*] To besiege, to lay siege to; (fig.) to beset, to dun (of creditors), to importune.
assiette (asjət), s.f. [f. *asseoir*] **1.** Posture, attitude, firm position; seat (in the saddle); *perdre son ~*, to lose one's seat; **2.** position, site; *l'~ d'un camp*, the site of a camp; **3.** (naut.) trim; **4.** assessment; *l'~ de l'impôt*, the basis of taxation; **5.** tone, state, disposition; *il n'est pas dans son ~*, he is out of sorts or off colour; **6.** plate, plateful; (pop.) *avoir l'~ au beurre*, to have the loaves and fishes, to be in clover; *casseur d'~s*, swashbuckler; *un pique-~*, a sponger; *manger une ~ de soupe*, to eat a plate (or plateful) of soup; *~ à potage*, soup-plate.
assiettée (asjɛte), s.f. Plateful.
assignable (asiɲabl), adj. Assignable.
assignat (asiɲa), s.m. Assignat (French paper money, 1789-97).
assignation (asiɲa'sjɔ̃), s.f. **1.** Assignment (of a fund, &c. in payment); order to pay such a sum; **2.** summons, writ; *signifier une ~ à X*, to serve a writ upon X.
assigner (asiɲe), v.a. [f. L *ad+signum*] **1.** To assign (property in payment of debts, &c.); **2.** to cite, to summon; *obtenir permission d'~ X*, to take out a writ against X; **3.** to appoint, to fix (a rendezvous, &c.).
assimilabilité (asimilabilite), s.f. Assimilability.
assimilable (asimilabl), adj. Assimilable.
assimilat-eur, -rice (asimilatœr), adj. Assimilatory.
assimilati-f, -ve (asimilatif), adj. Assimilative.
assimilation (asimila'sjɔ̃), s.f. Assimilation.
assimilé (asimile), s.m. (mil.) A member of the non-combatant services attached to the army.
assimiler (asimile), v.a. [L *assimilare*] To assimilate (*à*, to), to liken (to); to cause to resemble, to make like; **s'~**, v.pr. **1.** to compare oneself; *s'~ aux poètes*, to liken oneself to the poets; **2.** (lit. and fig.) to assimilate; *s'~ des aliments*, to assimilate one's food.
assis, -e (asi), p. adj. **1.** Seated; *rester ~*, to keep one's seat, to remain seated; **2.** situated; *une ville ~e sur une colline*, a city situated on a hill; **3.** imposed (of taxes); *des impôts mal ~*, injudiciously imposed taxation; **4.** (fig.) established; *une réputation bien ~e*, a well-established reputation.
assise (asiz), s.f. [f. *asseoir*] (mason.) Course. ⚠ Not 'assize' in the sense of statutory price (of bread and ale) = *taxation du pain et de l'ale*. **~s**, s.f. pl. Assizes, court of assize; *être renvoyé devant la cour d'~s*, to be committed for trial at the Assizes.
assistance (asistɑ̃s), s.f. **1.** Presence, attendance; *droit d'~*, attendance-fee; **2.** audience, company; congregation; *une ~ nombreuse*, a large audience; **3.** assistance, help, relief; *~ publique*, poor-law relief or administration.
assistant, -e (asistɑ̃), adj. s.m.f. Assistant, help; *~s*, s.m. pl. those present; bystanders, onlookers; *parmi les ~s* among those present.
assisté, -e (asiste), p. adj. s.m.f. Pauper; *enfants ~s*, pauper children.
assister (asiste), v.n. [L *ad+sistere*] To attend, to be present; *~ à*, to be present at; to witness; ~, v.a. to assist, to help, to succour; *~ les pauvres*, to relieve the poor.
association (asɔsja'sjɔ̃), s.f. **1.** Association; **2.** (comm.) partnership; *contrat d'~* deed of partnership; **3.** society; *~ de secours mutuel*, mutual benefit society, friendly society; **4.** association (football) (abbrev.) soccer.
associé, -e (asɔsje), s.m.f. **1.** Associate, member; **2.** partner; *~ bailleur de fonds*, or *~ commanditaire*, sleeping partner; *~ gérant*, managing partner.
associer (asɔsje), v.a. [L *associare*] **1.** To associate, to link up, to connect; *~ des idées*, to associate ideas; **2.** to take into partnership; **3.** to divide, to share interests with (a person); *~ un ami à une entreprise*, to give a friend an interest (a share) in an undertaking; **s'~**, v.pr. to associate oneself (*à*, *avec*, with); to enter into partnership (with); to take part (*à*, in).
assoiffé, -e (aswafe), p. adj. Thirsty, athirst; (fig.) athirst (*de*, for), eager (for).
assolement (asɔlmɑ̃), s.m. (agric.) Rotation (of crops).
assoler (asɔle), v.a. [f. *sole*] (agric.) To vary, to rotate (crops).
assombrir (asɔ̃brir), v.a. [f. *sombre*] To darken, to make gloomy, to cloud, to throw a gloom over; (fig.) *son front s'assombrit*, his brow clouded over; **s'~**, v.pr. to darken, to become dark or gloomy.
assommant, -e (asɔmɑ̃), p. adj. **1.** (fam.) Boring; *c'est ~*, it is the limit; **2.** oppressive (of heat.)
assommer (asɔme), v.a. [f. *somme*] **1.** To knock on the head, to kill; to

slaughter (cattle); ~ *à coups de bâton*, to beat to death; **2.** to overwhelm, to confound; **3.** (fam.) to bore to death; ~ *de questions*, to deluge with questions.

assommeur (asɔmœr), s.m. **1.** Slaughterer, feller (of cattle); **2.** (fam.) bore.

assommoir (asɔmwar), s.m. **1.** Pole-axe; loaded bludgeon; *coup d'~*, a knock-down blow; **2.** low tavern, drinking-den, low dram-shop.

assomption (asɔ̃psjɔ̃), s.f. [L *assumptio*] **1.** (eccles.) Assumption; **2.** assumption.

assonance (asɔnɑ̃s), s.f. [L *assonare*] Assonance.

assonant, -e (asɔnɑ̃), adj. Assonant.

assorti, -e (asɔrti), p. adj. Assorted, mixed; stocked; matched, to match, well matched; suitable; *un mariage bien ~*, a very suitable match.

assortiment (asɔrtimɑ̃), s.m. Assortment, set, stock, collection; matching; harmony (of colour, &c.).

assortir (asɔrtir), v.a. [f. *sorte*] **1.** To match, to assort, to pair; ~ *des couleurs*, to match colours; *mal ~*, to mismatch; **2.** to stock, to furnish; ~ *une boutique*, to stock a shop; **s'~**, v.pr. to match, to be suitable, to go well together.

assortissant, -e (asɔrtisɑ̃), p. adj. Suitable, matching, that goes well (with something else).

assouchement (asuʃmɑ̃), s.m. [f. *souche*] (arch.) Base (of the triangle in a pediment).

assoupir (asupir), v.a. [L *ad+sopire*] To make drowsy, sleepy, heavy; (fig.) to assuage, to allay, to deaden; ~ *la douleur*, to deaden pain; **s'~**, v.pr. to grow drowsy, sleepy, heavy; to doze; (fig.) to be assuaged, appeased, stilled.

assoupissant, -e (asupisɑ̃), p. adj. Soporific.

assoupissement (asupismɑ̃), s.m. Drowsiness, sleepiness, heaviness; *un court ~*, forty winks; (fig.) supineness, sloth.

assouplir (asuplir), v.a. [f. *souple*] To make supple, to make flexible; to break in (a horse); to soften; **s'~**, v.pr. to become supple; (fig.) to become manageable, tractable.

assouplissement (asuplismɑ̃), s.m. Making supple, docile, tractable; softening.

assourdir (asurdir), v.a. [f. *sourd*] To deafen, to stun; to muffle (a bell, oar, &c.); (paint.) to subdue (colours, &c.); to darken; to deaden (noises.)

assourdissant, -e (asurdisɑ̃), p. adj. Deafening.

assourdissement (asurdismɑ̃), s.m. Deafening, muffling, deadening; a deafening noise; temporary deafness.

assouvir (asuvir), v.a. [var. of *assoupir*] To satiate, to satisfy, to glut; ~ *sa faim*, to satisfy one's hunger; ~ *ses passions*, to gratify one's passions; **s'~**, v.pr. to satiate oneself, to be satiated, satisfied, glutted.

assouvissement (asuvismɑ̃), s.m. Glutting, satiating; gratification, glut, satiation.

assujettir, assujétir (asyʒɛtir), v.a. [f. *sujet*] To bring under subjection, to subdue, to subjugate; to compel, to force; to fix, to fasten; ~ *un rayon*, to fix a shelf; **s'~**, v.pr. to subject oneself, to submit.

assujettissant, assujétissant, -e (asyʒɛtisɑ̃), p. adj. Subjecting, binding, constraining.

assujettissement, assujétissement (asyʒɛtismɑ̃), s.m. Subjugation, subjection, enthralment; (fig.) obligation, compulsion, constraint; *la grandeur a ses ~s*, greatness carries its own obligations.

assumer (asyme), v.a. [L *assumere*] To assume, to take upon oneself.

assurable (asyrabl), adj. Insurable.

assurance (asyrɑ̃s), s.f. **1.** Assurance; *agréez l'~ de mes sentiments distingués*, believe me yours very sincerely (truly); **2.** (fig.) conviction; boldness, hardihood; *il parle avec ~*, he speaks boldly; **3.** insurance, underwriting; ~ *sur la vie*, life-insurance; *courtier d'~*, insurance broker; *prime d'~*, premium; **4.** security; *donnez-moi une ~*, give me a security.

assuré, -e (asyre), p. adj. **1.** Assured, confident; certain; *sa perte est ~e*, his ruin is inevitable; **2.** bold, firm; **3.** trusty; *une retraite ~e*, a safe retreat; **4.** insured; *il est ~ sur la vie*, his life is insured. **~**, s.m.f. Insured person.

assurément (asyremɑ̃), adv. Assuredly, confidently; boldly; undoubtedly; ~ *non*, certainly not.

assurer (asyre), v.a. [f. *sûr*] **1.** To assure, to vouch for, to assert; ~ *un fait à X*, to vouch for a fact to X; ~ *X d'une chose*, to assure X of a thing; **2.** to secure; ~ *le bonheur de X*, to secure X's happiness; **3.** to steady, to fix securely; ~ *un meuble*, to steady a piece of furniture; **4.** to insure; ~ *contre l'incendie*, to insure against fire; **s'~**, v.pr. **1.** to make sure of, to ascertain; *nous nous sommes assurés que*, we have ascertained that; **2.** to arrest; **3.** to insure oneself, to be insured.

assureur (asyrœr), s.m. Underwriter, insurer, assurer.

assyrien, -ne (asirjɛ̃), adj. s.m.f. Assyrian.

assyriologie (asirjɔlɔʒi), s.f. Assyriology.

assyriologue (asirjɔlɔg), s.m. Assyriologist.

astatique (astatik), adj. [Gr. *astatos*] Astatic.

aster (astɛr), s.m. [Gr. wd] (bot.) Aster, starwort.

astérie (asteri), s.f. [f. Gr. *astēr*] **1.** (zool.) Asterias, star-fish; **2.** (min.) asteria; ~ *fossile*, asterialite.

astérisme (asterism), s.m. [Gr. *astēr*] (astr.) Asterism, constellation.
astérisque (asterisk), s.m. [f. Gr. *astēr*] Asterisk.
astéroïde (asterɔid), s.m. [f. Gr. *astēr*+*eidēs*] **1.** (astr.) Asteroid; **2.** (meteor.) aerolith.
asthénie (asteni), s.f. [Gr. *a*+*sthenos*] (med.) Asthenia, debility.
asthénique (astenik), adj. (med.) Asthenic.
asthmatique (asmatik), adj. Asthmatical. **~**, s.m.f. Person suffering from asthma; asthmatic.
asthme (asm), s.m. [Gr. *asthma*] Asthma.
astic (astik), s.m. (cobbling) Longstick.
asticot (astiko), s.m. [etym. dub.] (ent.) Worm, gentle, maggot.
asticoter (astikɔte), v.a. (colloq.) To plague, to rag, to nag, to worry; *il est toujours à m'* **~**, he is always nagging at me.
astigmate (astigmat), adj. Astigmatic.
astigmatisme (astigmatism), s.m. [Gr. *a*+*stigma*] Astigmatism.
astiquage (astikaʒ), s.m. Polishing; brass-polishing.
astiquer (astike), v.a. To polish; (colloq.) *un homme bien astiqué*, a well-groomed man; **s'~**, v.pr. to smarten one's appearance.
astragale (astragal), s.m. [Gr. *astragalos*] **1.** (arch.) Astragal; **2.** (anat.) astragalus, ankle-bone; **3.** (bot.) astragalus, milk-vetch.
astrakan (astrakɑ̃), s.m. [geog. orig.] Astrakhan.
astral, -e, (aux), (astral), adj. [f. Gr. *astēr*] Astral, stellar.
astre (astr), s.m. [Gr. *astēr*] Star, heavenly body; *l'~ de la nuit*, the orb of night, the moon; (fig.) star, luminary.
astreindre (astrɛ̃dr), v.a. [L *astringere*] To compel (*à*, to), to constrain, to force; **s'~**, v.pr. to confine oneself, to tie oneself down (*à*, to).
astreinte (astrɛ̃t), s.f. Compulsion; syn. CONTRAINTE.
astricti-f, -ve (astriktif), adj. [L *astringere*] (med.) Astrictive, astringent.
astriction (astriksjɔ̃), s.f. (med.) Astriction.
astringence (astrɛ̃ʒɑ̃s), s.f. Astringency.
astringent, -e (astrɛ̃ʒɑ̃), adj. [L *astringere*] Astringent. **~**, s.m. Astringent.
astrolabe (astrɔlab), s.m. [Gr. *astron*+*lambanein*] (astr.) Astrolabe.
astrolâtre (astrɔlɑtr), s.m. [Gr. *astron*+*latreuein*] Star-worshipper.
astrolâtrie (astrɔlɑtri), s.f. Astrolatry, star-worship.
astrologie (astrɔlɔʒi), s.f. [Gr. *astron*+*logos*] Astrology.
astrologique (astrɔlɔʒik), adj. Astrological.
astrologiquement (astrɔlɔʒikmɑ̃), adv. Astrologically.
astrologue (astrɔlɔg), s.m. Astrologist.
astronome (astrɔnɔm), s.m. [Gr. *astron*+*nomos*] Astronomer.
astronomie (astrɔnɔmi), s.f. Astronomy.
astronomique (astrɔnɔmik), adj. Astronomical.
astronomiquement (astrɔnɔmikmɑ̃), adv. Astronomically.
astuce (astys), s.f. [L *astutia*] Astuteness, craft, guile, cunning.
astucieusement (astysjøzmɑ̃), adv. Astutely, cunningly, craftily.
astucieu-x, -se (astysjø), adj. **1.** (pej.) Astute, crafty, cunning, guileful; **2.** (not pej.) cleverly contrived (this sense is new, derived from school slang).
asymétrie (asimetri), s.f. [Gr. *a*+*sun*+*metron*] Asymmetry.
asymétrique (asimetrik), adj. Asymmetrical.
asymptote (asɛ̃ptɔt), s.f. [Gr. *asumptōtos*] (geom.) Asymptote.
asymptotique (asɛ̃ptɔtik), adj. Asymptotic.
asynartète (asinartɛt), s.m. adj. [Gr. *asunartētos*] (pros.) Asynartete.
asyndète (asɛ̃dɛt), s.f. [Gr. *a*+*sundein*] (rhet.) Asyndeton.
asystolie (asistɔli), s.f. [Gr. *a*+*sustolē*] (med.) Asystole.
ataraxie (ataraksi), s.f. [Gr. *ataraxia*] (pathol.) Ataraxia.
atavique (atavik), adj. Atavistic.
atavisme (atavism), s.m. [f. L *atavus*] Atavism.
ataxie (ataksi), s.f. [Gr. *ataxia*] (pathol.) Ataxy, ataxia.
ataxique (ataksik), adj. s.m.f. (pathol.) Ataxic.
atèle (atɛl), s.m. (zool.) Spider-monkey.
atelier (atəlje), s.m. [f. L *assula*; OF *astele*] **1.** Workshop (of artisans); *chef d'~*, foreman, overseer; **2.** studio, atelier (of artists); **3.** (fig.) followers or pupils of an artist.
atermoiement (atɛrmwamɑ̃), s.m. Delay, time, composition (with creditors); (fig.) delay, evasion, hesitation, shift.
atermoyer (atɛrmwaje), [*à*+OF *termoyer*; f. *terme*] To procrastinate.
athée (ate), adj. s.m.f. [Gr. *a*+*theos*] Atheist.
athéisme (ateism), s.m. Atheism.
athéistique (ateistik), adj. Atheistic, atheistical.
athénée (atene), s.m. [f. Gr. *Athēnē*], Athenaeum.
athénien, -ne (atenjɛ̃), adj. s.m.f. Athenian.
athermal, -e, (aux) (atɛrmal), adj. [Gr. *a*+*thermos*] (of mineral springs) Cold.
athermane, athermique (atɛrman,

atɛrmik), adj. [Gr. *a+thermainein*] Athermanous, impermeable to radiant heat.
athlète (atlɛt), s.m. [Gr. *athlētēs*] Athlete.
athlétique (atletik), adj. Athletic.
athlétisme (atletism), s.m. Athleticism.
atlante (atlɑ̃t), s.m. [f. *Atlas*, myth. n.] Atlas (pl. Atlantes).
Atlantique (atlɑ̃tik), adj. s.m. [f. *Atlas*] Atlantic.
atlas (atlɑs), s.m. [f. *Atlas*] **1.** (anat.) Atlas, uppermost cervical vertebra; **2.** atlas, volume of maps.
atmosphère (atmɔsfɛr), s.f. [Gr. *atmos +sphaira*] Atmosphere; weather.
atmosphérique (atmɔsferik), adj. Atmospheric.
atoll, attoll (atɔl), s.m. [Native n. of Maldive Islands, *atollon*] Atoll.
atome (atom), s.m. [Gr. *atomos*] Atom; (fig.) minute portion, atom, grain; *il n'a pas un ~ de vanité*, he is without a grain of vanity.
atomicité (atɔmisite), s.f. (chem.) Atomicity.
atomique (atɔmik), adj. Atomic; *poids ~*, atomic weight.
atomisme (atɔmism), s.m. Atomism.
atomistique (atɔmistik), adj. Atomistic. ~, s.f. Atomistic theory.
atone (atɔn), adj. [Gr. *a+tonos*] Atonic, dull; lack-lustre, expressionless (of the eye).
atonie (atɔni), s.f. Atony, debility.
atonique (atɔnik), adj. Atonic.
atour (atur), s.m. (chiefly in pl.) [f. *atourner*] Woman's attire, dress, ornament; *être parée de ses plus beaux ~s*, to be dressed in one's best; (iron.) to be decked out in all one's finery; *dame d'~*, lady of the bedchamber.
atourner (aturne), v.a. (obs.) [*à+tourner*] To attire, to dress up; to deck out.
atout (atu), s.m. [*à+tout*] **1.** Trump, trump-card; *jouer ~*, to play trumps, to lead trumps; *couper avec l'~*, to trump; (fig.) *avoir tous les ~s en main*, to have every chance, to have great advantages, to have all the trump cards; **2.** (colloq.) blow; *il a reçu un fameux ~*, he has had a nasty blow.
atoxique (atɔksik), adj. [Gr. *a+toxikon*] Non-poisonous.
atrabilaire (atrabilɛr), adj. Atrabilious. ~, s.m.f. Atrabilarian.
atrabile (atrabil), s.f. [L *atra bilis*] (anc. med.) Black bile, hypochondria.
âtre (ɑtr), s.m. [OHG *astrih*] Hearth; *au coin de l'~*, in the chimney-corner.
atrium (atriɔm), s.m. [L wd] Atrium.
atroce (atrɔs), adj. [L *atrox, -ocis*] Atrocious, dreadful; (of pain) excruciating.
atrocement (atrɔsmɑ̃), adv. Atrociously; excruciatingly.
atrocité (atrɔsite), s.f. Atrocity.
atrophie (atrɔfi), s.f. [Gr. *a+trophē*] (med.) Atrophy.
atrophié, -e (atrɔfje), p. adj. (med.) Atrophied, withered; stunted.
atrophier (atrɔfje), v.a. (med.) To cause atrophy; **s'~**, v.pr. to become atrophied, to waste away, to wither away.
atropine (atrɔpin), s.f. [L *atropa*] (chem.) Atropine, atropia.
(s)'attabler, v.pr. [f. *à+table*] To sit down to table.
attachant, -e (ataʃɑ̃), p. adj. Interesting, engaging, winning.
attache (ataʃ), s.f. Tie, fastening; bond, cord, strap; (anat.) wrist or ankle; *avoir les ~s fines*, to have delicate wrists and ankles; *mettre un chien à l'~*, to tie a dog up; *être toujours à l'~*, to be always slaving; (naut.) *port d'~*, home-port; (fig.) attachment, strong affection; *vivre sans ~s*, to live without ties.
attaché (ataʃe), s.m. Attaché (of an embassy).
attachement (ataʃmɑ̃), s.m. **1.** Attachment; affection, liaison; eagerness, zeal; *~ à l'étude*, fondness for study; **2.** **~s**, (pl.) architect's memoranda.
attacher (ataʃe), v.a. [OF *atachier*] **1.** To fasten, to attach, to secure; *~ avec de la colle*, to paste, to stick; *~ avec une épingle*, to pin; *~ avec une courroie*, to strap, to fix; *~ les yeux sur quelque chose*, to fix one's eyes on a thing; **2.** (fig.) to apply, to attribute; *~ de la valeur à quelque chose*, to set value upon a thing; *~ du prix à*, to set store on; **3.** to associate; to engage, to bind, to endear; *tout ce qui nous attache à la vie*, all that binds us to life; to interest; *ce livre n'attache point le lecteur*, this book does not compel the reader's attention; **s'~**, v.pr. **1.** to take hold, to attach oneself; *la vigne s'attache à tout*, the vine clings to everything; *s'~ aux pas de X*, to dog X's steps; **2.** to attach (to); *une grande gloire s'attache à cette action*, great fame attaches to this action; **3.** to become attached to; *le chien s'attache à son maître*, the dog becomes attached to his master; **4.** to strive; *s'~ à faire son devoir*, to strive to do one's duty.
attaquable (atakabl), adj. Assailable; of doubtful validity.
attaquant, -e (atakɑ̃), s.m.f. Attacker, assailant.
attaque (atak), s.f. **1.** Attack; (pop.) *être d'~*, to be fit, game; **2.** fit, stroke.
attaquer (atake), v.a. [It. *attaccare*] **1.** To attack, to assault; to take hold of, to seize; *~ le taureau par les cornes*, to take the bull by the horns; (fig.) to attack, to begin; *le sujet que j'attaquerai*, the subject which I shall attack; (mus.)

~ *bien la note*, to have a good attack; **2.** to contest; ~ *la validité d'un document*, to contest the validity of a document; ~ *X en justice*, to enter an action against X; **3.** to corrode; **s'~ à**, v.pr. to attack, to fall upon, to defy; *il s'est attaqué à forte partie*, he has met his match.

attarder (atarde), v.a. [f. *tard*] To delay; *être attardé*, to be delayed; **s'~**, v.pr. to be belated; to loiter, to linger.

atteindre (atɛ̃dr), v.a. [L *attingere*] **1.** To attain, to reach; ~ *le but*, to reach the goal; **2.** to hit, to strike; *une balle l'atteignit au front*, a bullet struck him in the forehead; **3.** to overtake; *je l'atteindrai sur la route*, I shall overtake him on the way; ~ **(à)**, v.n. to reach with difficulty, to attain; ~ *à la perfection*, to attain perfection; ~ *au plafond*, to reach up to the ceiling.

atteint, -e (atɛ̃), p. adj. **1.** Hit, struck; **2.** seized, affected; ~ *d'une grave maladie*, affected with a serious disease; ~ *d'un crime*, arraigned for a crime; **3.** reached.

atteinte (atɛ̃t), s.f. **1.** Blow, stroke; *être hors des ~s de X*, to be out of X's reach; **2.** (med.) fit, seizure; *une légère ~ de goutte*, a touch of the gout; **3.** injury, damage; *les ~s du feu*, damage by fire; *porter ~ à*, to injure, to impair, (fig.) to cast a slur on.

attelable (atlabl), adj. Fit for harness.

attelage (atlaʒ), s.m. **1.** Harnessing, yoking; **2.** team, yoke, pair (of cattle, horses, &c.); carriage, horses; (colonial) span; **3.** (rail.) coupling; *chaîne d'~*, coupling-chain.

atteler (atle), v.a.n. [L *ad+telum*] To harness, to yoke; to put horses, &c. (*à*, to); (fig.) *c'est une charrette mal attelée*, they are an ill-assorted couple; (fig.) to subjugate, to drag at one's heels; **s'~**, v.pr. to be harnessed (*à*, to), to be yoked (*avec*, with); to put one's shoulder to the wheel, to undertake a work, task, &c.

attelle (atɛl), s.f. [L *hasta*] **1.** Hame (of a horse's collar); **2.** (surg.) splint.

attellement (atɛlmɑ̃), s.m. Harnessing, yoking; coupling; syn. ATTELAGE.

atteloire (atlwar), s.f. Draught-peg, draught-staple.

attenant, -e (atnɑ̃), adj. [f. *à+tenir*] Adjoining, contiguous.

(en) attendant (ɑ̃atɑ̃dɑ̃), loc. adv. conj. prep. ~, for the time being, meanwhile; in the meantime; ~ *que*, till, until; ~ *mieux*, till something better turns up.

attendre (atɑ̃dr), v.a.n. [L *attendere*] To wait for, to stay for, to await; ~ *le train*, to wait for the train; *se faire ~*, to keep people waiting; *attendez-moi sous l'orme*, you may wait till doomsday; to expect, to look forward to; *je l'attends ce soir*, I am expecting him this evening; *il l'attend avec impatience*, he is looking forward to it very much; **~**, v.n. to wait, to delay; *qu'il attende*, let him wait; *attendons encore un peu*, let us wait a little longer; *tout vient à point à qui sait ~*, everything comes to him who waits; *attendez !*, wait a moment !; *vous ne perdez rien pour ~*, you will lose nothing by waiting; **s'~ (à)**, v.pr. to hope for, to expect, to count on; *je m'y attendais*, I was prepared for that; *après cela on peut s'~ à tout*, after that we may fear the worst; *attendez-vous y*, depend upon it !

attendrir (atɑ̃drir), v.a. [f. *tendre*] **1.** To soften, to make tender; ~ *de la viande*, to make meat tender; **2.** (fig.) to move, to touch, to affect, to mollify; *il faut l'~*, he must be mollified; **s'~**, v.pr. to be moved to pity, to relent; (pej.) to become maudlin; *s'~ sur le sort de X*, to pity X's fate.

attendrissant, -e (atɑ̃drisɑ̃), p. adj. Moving, affecting, touching.

attendrissement (atɑ̃drismɑ̃), s.m. Relenting, being moved, compassion, pity; tenderness; tears.

attendu (atɑ̃dy), p.p., prep., s.m. Considering, on account of, in consideration of; ~ *que* (loc. conj.), as, whereas, since, seeing that.

attentat (atɑ̃ta), s.m. [f. L *attentare*] Outrage, attempt, attempted murder, criminal attempt; ~ *à la pudeur*, assault, outrage.

attentatoire (atɑ̃tatwar), adj. Prejudicial (*à*, to), damaging.

attente (atɑ̃t), s.f. Waiting; hope, expectation; (comm.) *dans l'~ de vous lire*, awaiting the favour of a reply; *être dans l'~ de*, to be expecting; *salle d'~*, waiting-room; *d'~*, temporary; (surg.) *ligature d'~*, temporary ligature; (mason.) *pierre d'~*, toothing; *contre toute ~*, contrary to all expectations.

attenter (atɑ̃te), v.n. [L *attentare*] To make a criminal attempt; ~ *à la vie de X*, to make an attempt upon X's life; ~ *à ses jours*, to attempt suicide.

attenti-f, -ve (atɑ̃tif), adj. Attentive, heedful, considerate; *être ~ à*, to observe, to be mindful of, to be intent on.

attention (atɑ̃sjɔ̃), s.f. [f. L *ad+tendere*] **1.** Attention, notice; *faire ~*, to be careful; *attention !*, look out ! stand by !; (mil.) ~ *au commandement !*, attention !; *cela mérite ~*, that deserves notice; *faites donc ~*, mind what you are doing; *faire une chose avec grande ~*, to do a thing very carefully; *manque d'~*, heedlessness; *n'y faites pas ~*, never mind; *s'attirer l'~ du public*, to attract public notice; **2.** regard, respect, consideration, (pl.) attentions; *il a eu l'~ de me prévenir*, he was good enough to warn me; *il a de grandes ~s pour moi*, he is full of delicate attentions for me.

attentionné, -e (atɑ̃sjɔne), adj. Considerate.
attentivement (atɑ̃tivmɑ̃), adv. Attentively, carefully.
atténuant, -e (atenɥɑ̃), p. adj. Extenuating, attenuant, mitigating; (law) extenuatory. See CIRCONSTANCE.
atténuer (atenɥe), v.a. [L *ad+tenuis*] To extenuate, to attenuate; to make smaller, thinner, feebler; to weaken; to palliate, to underrate; ~ *un crime*, to extenuate a crime.
atterrage (atɛraʒ), s.m. [f. *à+terre*] (naut.) Landing; landfall.
atterrer (atɛre), v.a. [f. *à+terre*] To strike down, to overthrow, to destroy; (fig.) to crush, to cast down; to overwhelm; (fam.) to strike all of a heap; ~, v.n. (naut.) to make for shore, to draw near land.
atterrir (atɛrir), v.n. (naut., aeron.) To land, to make land; to alight; to go ashore.
atterrissage (atɛrisaʒ), s.m. (naut., aeron.) Landing; alighting; making land; *train d'*~, landing-gear.
atterrissement (atɛrismɑ̃), s.m. Alluvion, alluvium, accretion.
attestation (atɛsta'sjɔ̃), s.f. [L *attestatio*] Attestation, testimony; warrant, affidavit; testimonial.
attester (atɛste), v.a. [L *attestari*] **1.** To attest, to avouch, to witness; **2.** to call to witness; *j'en atteste le ciel*, I call heaven to witness; *j'en atteste les dieux*, witness, ye gods!
atticisme (atisism), s.m. [Gr. *attikismos*] Atticism.
atticiste (atisist), s.m.f. Atticist.
attiédir (atjedir), v.a. [f. *tiède*] **1.** To cool, to make lukewarm; (fig.) to abate, to cool down; *le temps attiédira leur zèle*, time will abate their zeal; **2.** to warm slightly; **s'**~, v.pr. to grow cool or lukewarm; to grow slightly warmer; (fig.) to cool off.
attiédissement (atjedismɑ̃), s.m. Abatement, cooling-off, lukewarmness.
attifage, attifement (atifaʒ, atifmɑ̃), s.m. Decking out, get-up, rig-out.
attifer (atife), v.a. [OF *à+tiffer*] To bedizen, (fam.) to rig out; **s'**~, v.pr. to deck oneself, to dress up, to rig oneself out.
attifet (atifɛ), s.m. (obs.) Small bonnet worn in the sixteenth century; woman's head-ornament.
attiger (atiʒe), v.n.a. (slang) To exaggerate, to come it strong.
attique (atik), adj. [Gr. *attikos*] **1.** Attic; (fig.) witty, urbane; **2.** (arch.) attic.
attiquement (atikmɑ̃), adv. After the Attic style.
attirable (atirabl), adj. Attractable (by the magnet, &c.).
attirail (atiraj), s.m. [f. *attirer*] **1.** Paraphernalia (of war); baggage-train; **2.** apparatus, utensils, gear, tackle; **3.** (fam.) paraphernalia, superfluous baggage; pomp; implements, tackle.
attirant, -e (atirɑ̃), p. adj. Alluring, enticing, prepossessing, attractive, engaging.
attirer (atire), v.a. [f. *à+tirer*] To attract, to draw; ~ *l'ennemi dans une embuscade*, to draw the enemy into an ambush; *un malheur en attire un autre*, troubles never come singly; (fig.) to lure, to wheedle, to attract; ~ *par des caresses*, to wheedle; ~ *les regards de tout le monde*, to attract all eyes; **s'**~, v.pr. to attract each other; to incur, to bring upon oneself; *s'~ des affaires*, to get into scrapes.
attisage, attisement (atizaʒ, atizmɑ̃), s.m. Poking-up, stirring-up, fanning (of a flame).
attiser (atize), v.a. [f. L *ad+titio*] To stir up, to poke; (fig.) to stir up; (fig.) ~ *le feu*, to fan the flame.
attiseu-r, -se (atizœr), s.m.f. One who stirs the fire.
attisoir (atizwar), s.m. Poker (usually a furnace-poker).
attitré, -e (atitre), p. adj. **1.** Recognized, appointed; *juges* ~*s*, appointed judges; **2.** regular; *marchands* ~*s*, accredited tradespeople; **3.** mercenary, hired; *assassin* ~, hired assassin.
attitrer (atitre), v.a. [*à+titre*] **1.** To appoint, to recognize; **2.** (shooting) to station (dogs) to look out for game.
attitude (atityd), s.f. [It. *attitudine*; f. L *attitudo*] Attitude.
attoll. See ATOLL.
attouchement (atuʃmɑ̃), s.m. [f. *à+toucher*] Touch, feeling, contact.
attract-eur, -rice (atraktœr), adj. Attracting, attractile.
attracti-f, -ve (atraktif), adj. Attractive (⚠ not used figuratively in French).
attraction (atraksjɔ̃), s.f. **1.** Attraction; (pl.) distractions; **2.** (theatr.) music-hall turn, feature.
attractivement (atraktivmɑ̃), adv. Attractively.
attraire (atrɛr), v.a. [L *attrahere*] To attract, to draw; to allure, to entice.
attrait (atrɛ), s.m. [L *ad+tractus*, f. *trahere*] **1.** Attraction, charm; *l'~ des plaisirs*, the lure of pleasure; **2.** inclination, taste; *suivre son* ~, to follow one's own bent; **3.** (pl.) charms (of a woman); syn. (pl.) APPAS, CHARMES.
attrapade (atrapad), s.f. (colloq.) Bickering, squabble, quarrel.
attrapage (atrapaʒ), s.m. (fam.) Severe scolding, telling-off.
attrape (atrap), s.f. [f. *attraper*] **1.** Trap, gin; **2.** (fig.) ruse; catch, booby-trap, hoax; **3.** (naut.) hawser.
attrape-lourdaud (atraplurdo), s.m. (pl. *attrape-lourdauds*) Have-on, take-in; syn. ATTRAPE-NIAIS, ATTRAPE-NIGAUD.

attrape-mouches (atrapmuʃ), s.m. invar. Fly-trap; (bot.) fly-trap, Venus's fly-trap; (ornith.) fly-catcher.

attrape-niais, attrape-nigaud (atrapniɛ, atrapnigo) s.m. (pl. *attrape-nigauds*), Booby-trap; clap-trap, catchpenny, take-in; syn. ATTRAPE-LOURDAUD.

attraper (atrape), v.a. [f. *trappe*] **1.** To trap (animals, &c.); **2.** to catch, to seize; to take; *tiens, attrape!*, here, take that! (often accompanied by a blow, &c.); ~ *X sur le fait*, to catch X red-handed; *le coup l'a attrapé à la tempe*, the blow caught him on the temple; to overtake, to catch up; *je pourrai encore l'*~ *en route*, I shall still be able to catch him up on the way; to get, to catch (unintentionally); ~ *un rhume*, to catch cold; ~ *un coup de pied*, to get kicked; (fig.) to hit off, to imitate; ~ *une ressemblance*, to hit off, to catch a likeness; **3.** (fig.) to take in, to cheat, to bamboozle; *il en a attrapé de plus fins que vous*, he has swindled shrewder men than you; **4.** (fam.) to scold, to rate; *tu vas te faire* ~, you'll catch it; **s'**~, v.pr. (colloq.) to quarrel (*avec*, with).

attrapeu-r, -se (atrapœr), s.m.f. Deceiver, trickster, cheat.

attrapoire (atrapwar), s.f. Trap, pitfall, snare; (fig.) pitfall, wile, snare.

attrayant, -e (atrɛjɑ̃), adj. Attractive, winning, charming.

attremper (atrɑ̃pe), v.a. [*à*+*tremper*] To anneal (glass); to temper (steel).

attribuable (atribɥabl), adj. Attributable, referable, ascribable (*à*, to).

attribuer (atribɥe), v.a. [L *ad*+*tribuere*] To assign, to confer, to allot; ~ *des privilèges à une charge*, to attach privileges to an office; (fig.) to attribute, to ascribe; *on lui attribua les poèmes*, the poems were attributed to him; **s'**~, v.pr. to assume, to claim; *il s'attribue de grandes richesses*, he lays claim to great wealth.

attribut (atriby), s.m. Attribute; symbol, emblem; (logic) that which may be predicated; (gram.) attribute.

attributaire (atribytɛr), s.m.f. (law) Person on whom an inheritance (&c.) has been conferred.

attributi-f, -ve (atribytif), adj. (gram.) Attributive.

attribution (atribysjɔ̃), s.f. **1.** Attribution, conferment; grant; **2.** prerogative; **3.** province, department; *cela sort de mes* ~*s*, that is outside my province; **4.** (law) cognizance, competence.

attristant, -e (atristɑ̃), p. adj. [f. *triste*] Saddening, grievous.

attrister (atriste), v.a. [f. *triste*] To sadden, to grieve, to cast down; **s'**~, v.pr. to grieve (*sur*, over), to become sad, to become sorrowful.

attrition (atrisjɔ̃), s.f. [L *attritio*] Attrition.

attroupement (atrupmɑ̃), s.m. Crowd, gathering, mob, rabble; *loi contre les* ~*s*, Riot Act.

attrouper (atrupe), v.a. [f. *troupe*] To gather, to assemble; *il attroupa toute la canaille*, he gathered all the rabble together; **s'**~, v.pr. to flock together, to gather in crowds, to collect (of a crowd).

au (pl. **aux**) (o), art. [Contraction of *à le*, *à les*], to the.

aubade (obad), s.f. [f. *aube*] Aubade, morning complimentary music; (iron.) row, hot reception.

aubain (obɛ̃), s.m. [f. L *alibi*] Alien, foreigner.

aubaine (obɛn), s.f. [f. *aubain*] Godsend, piece of luck, windfall, good job; (law) escheat, escheatage.

aube[1] (ob), s.f. [L *alba*] **1.** Dawn; *à la pointe de l'*~, at daybreak; **2.** (eccles.) alb.

aube[2] (ob) s.f. (of a mill) Water-wheel; (of a ship) paddle-wheel, paddle-board.

aubépine (obepin), s.f. [L *alba*+Fr. *épine*] Hawthorn, whitethorn, may.

aubère (obɛr), adj. [Span. *hobero*] Flea-bitten grey; *cheval* ~, flea-bitten grey horse.

auberge (obɛrʒ), s.f. [Germ. *Herberge*] Inn; public-house, tavern; *descendre à l'*~, to put up at an inn; *vivre à l'*~, to live at an inn; *tenir une* ~, to keep an inn; *une* ~ *sur la route*, a wayside inn.

aubergine (obɛrʒin), s.f. [Span. *alberenjena*] (bot.) Aubergine, egg-plant, *Solanum esculentum.*

aubergiste (obɛrʒist), s.m.f. Innkeeper, landlord, publican, host.

aubier (obje), s.m. [f. L *albus*] (bot.) Sap-wood, alburnum.

aubifoin (obifwɛ̃), s.m. [L *albus*+*foenum*] (bot.) (pop.) Blue centaury, cornflower.

aubin (obɛ̃), s.m. [Engl. *hobby*] Canter, hand-gallop, Canterbury gallop.

aubiner (obine), v.n. [f. *aubin*] To canter.

aucun, -e (okœ̃), adj. ind. pron. [L *aliquis*+*unus*] No, none, no one, not any; ~ *homme*, no man; ~ *ne le dira*, no one will say so; *il n'a fait* ~*es dispositions*, he has made no arrangements; *je ne connais* ~ *de vos juges*, I know none of your judges; *d'*~*s le disent*, some (people) say so.

aucunement (okynmɑ̃), adv. Not at all, not in the least, in nowise, by no means; *je ne le connais* ~, I do not know him at all; *est-il* ~ *question de?*, is there the least chance for? ; do they consider in the least (doing, giving, &c.)?

audace (odas), s.f. [L *audax*] Audacity, daring, boldness; (pej.) impudence, insolence; *avec* ~, audaciously; *payer d'*~, to brazen it out, to put on a bold face.

audacieusement (odasjøzmã), adv. Audaciously, boldly, rashly; (pej.) impudently.
audacieu-x, -se (odasjø), adj. Audacious, daring, bold; (pej.) impudent, insolent. ~, s.m. Bold man; (pej.) impudent fellow.
au deçà, au dedans, au dehors, au delà, see DEÇÀ, DEDANS, DEHORS, DELÀ.
au-dessous (odsu), adv. Below.
au-dessus (odsy), adv. Above.
au-devant (odvã), adv. Towards; *aller ~ de X*, to go to meet X.
audience (odjãs), s.f. [L *audire*] **1.** Audience, hearing, reception; levee (of a sovereign); *donner ~*, to give audience (to) to hold a levee; **2.** sitting, session; court; (law.) *~ à huis clos*, a case heard in camera; *~ publique*, open court; *en pleine ~*, in open court; *se faire mettre hors de l'~*, to be turned out of court; *l'~ est levée*, the sitting is over; *l'~ est reprise*, the case is resumed; *tenir l'~*, (of a judge) to sit, to preside.
audiencier (odjãsje), adj. m. *Huissier ~*, court crier. ~, s.m. Crier, usher (of a court).
audiomètre (odjɔmɛtr), s.m. [L *audire*+ Gr. *metron*] Audiometer.
audiophone (odjɔfɔn), s.m. [L *audire*+ Gr. *phōnē*] Audiphone.
audit-eur, -rice (oditœr), s.m.f. [f. L *audire*] **1.** Hearer, listener; **2.** (comm.) auditor. ~, adj. Acting as auditor.
auditi-f, -ve (oditif), adj. Auditory.
audition (odisjɔ̃), s.f. [L *auditio*] **1.** Hearing; *l'~ des témoins*, the hearing of witnesses; **2.** auditing (of accounts); **3.** private performance, concert; trial, audition (of a musician or other performer).
auditoire (oditwar), s.m. Audience (in theatre, &c.); congregation (in church).
auge (oʒ), s.f. [L *alveus*] **1.** Trough; pig-trough, drinking-trough, &c.; *~ d'écurie*, manger; **2.** (mason.) hod; **3.** bucket (of a water-wheel, &c.); **4.** (electr.) cell; **5.** cavity between the branches of a horse's lower jaw; **6.** (naut.) *~ à goudron*, tar-bucket.
augée (oʒɛ), s.f. **1.** Troughful; mangerful; **2.** hodful; **3.** bucketful.
auget (oʒe), s.m. **1.** Little trough; seed-trough (of a bird-cage); **2.** bucket (of water-wheel); *roue à ~s*, overshot water-wheel.
augment (ɔgmã), s.m. [L *augmentum*] **1.** (Gr. gram.) Augment; **2.** (OF law) increase (of jointure).
augmentable (ɔgmãtabl), adj. Augmentable.
augmentati-f, -ve (ɔgmãtatif), adj. s.m. Augmentative.
augmentation (ɔgmãta'sjɔ̃), s.f. Augmentation, increase; rise (in salary).
augmenter (ɔgmãte), v.a. [L *augmentare*] To augment, to increase; to increase the salary of; *je vais ~ mon commis*, I am going to give my clerk a rise; ~, v.n. to augment, to increase; to rise (of prices); s'~, v.pr. to increase, to multiply; *leur nombre s'augmente*, their numbers multiply.
augural, -e, (aux) (ogyral), adj. Augural.
augure (ogyr), s.m. [L *augur*] **1.** Augur, soothsayer; **2.** augury, omen; *de bon ~*, auspicious; *de mauvais ~*, ominous, portentous, ill-boding.
augurer (ogyre), v.a. To augur; (fig.) to conjecture, to surmise; *je n'en augure rien de bon*, no good will come of it.
auguste (ogyst), adj. [L *augustus*] August.
augustin, -e (ogystɛ̃), s.m.f. [f. *St Augustin*] Augustinian or Austin friar or nun.
aujourd'hui (oʒurdɥi), adv. [*au jour de hui*; *hui* f. L *hodie*] **1.** To-day; *dès ~*, from henceforth; *il y a huit, quinze, jours ~*, a week, a fortnight, ago to-day; *d'~ en huit, en quinze*, this day week, fortnight; *ce n'est pas d'~ que nous nous connaissons*, we are old acquaintances; **2.** nowadays, the present day; *la mode d'~*, the present fashion.
aulique (olik), adj. [f. L *aula*] Aulic; *conseiller ~*, member of the Aulic Council.
aulne (on), s.m. See AUNE[2].
aulx (o), s.m.pl. Usual pl. form of AIL.
aumaille (omaj), s.f. [L *animalia*] Cattle. ~, adj. Horned; *bêtes ~s*, horned cattle.
aumône (omon), s.f. [Gr. *eleēmosunē*] **1.** alms, almsgiving; *demander l'~*, to beg; *être réduit à l'~*, to be reduced to beggary; *faire l'~*, to give alms; **2.** (fig.) favour, charity, dole; *faites-moi l'~ d'un regard*, bestow on me the favour of a glance.
aumônerie (omonri), s.f. Almonry; chaplaincy.
aumônier (omonje), s.m. (anc.) Almoner, ordinary; (mod. and mil.) chaplain; (Fr. hist.) *Grand ~ du roi*, Chief Almoner to the king.
aumonière (omonjɛr), s.f. Alms-purse; hanging-pocket.
aumusse, aumuce (omys), s.f. [Germ. *Mütze*] Cowl, hood; fur badge worn by canons (in France) on the left arm.
aunage (onaʒ), s.m. [f. *aune*] **1.** Measuring; **2.** length in ells of a piece of cloth.
aunaie, aulnaie (onɛ), s.f. Alder-plot, alder-grove.
aune[1] (on), s.f. [OHG *elina*] Ell; *acheter à l'~*, to buy by the ell; (fig.) measure, standard; *en avoir tout du long de l'~*, to get it in the neck, to get it with a vengeance; *il sait ce qu'en vaut l'~*, he knows it to his cost; *les hommes ne se mesurent pas à l'~*, it is not growing like a tree, in

bulk, that makes men better be; *mesurer les autres à son* ~, to judge others by oneself.

aune,[2] **aulne** (on), s.m. [L *alnus*] (bot.) Alder-tree.

aunée[1] (one), s.f. Ell, ell-length.

aunée,[2] **aulnée** (one) s.f. (bot.) Elecampane, *Inula helenium.*

auner (one), v.a. [f. *aune*] To measure by the ell; ~ *l'habit de X*, to measure one's stick across X's back.

auparavant (oparavɑ̃), adv. [*au+par+avant*] Previously, earlier.

auprès (oprɛ), adv. [*au+près*] Near, by, close by; *auprès de,* near to, close to; in comparison with; *être bien* ~ *de quelqu'un,* to be in a person's good books; *il cherche à me nuire* ~ *de vous,* he is trying to lower me in your esteem; *votre mal n'est rien* ~ *du sien,* your distress is nothing to his.

auquel (okɛl), rel. pron. m. (fem. *à laquelle*) [contr. of *à lequel*] To whom, to which.

auréolaire (oreɔlɛr), adj. Aureole-like.

auréole (oreɔl), s.f. [L *aureolus*] Aureole, halo.

auréolé, -e (oreɔle), adj. Aureoled, haloed.

auréoler (oreɔle), v.a. [f. *auréole*] To crown with a halo.

auriculaire (orikylɛr), adj. [f. L *auricula*] Auricular; *témoin* ~, ear-witness. ~, s.m. Little finger.

auricule (orikyl), s.f. [L *auricula*] (anat.) Lobe, auricle; auricula.

auriculé, -e (orikyle), adj. (bot.) Auriculate, eared.

auriculiste, auriste (orikylist, orist), adj. (med.) Dealing with the diseases of the ear. ~, s.m. Aurist.

aurifère (orifɛr), adj. [f. L *aurum+ferre*] Auriferous.

aurification (orifika'sjɔ̃), s.f. (dental surg.) Gold stopping.

aurifier (orifje), v.a. [f. L *aurum*] (dental surg.) To stop with gold.

aurifique (orifik), adj. Aurific, producing gold.

aurique (orik), adj. s.f. [f. L *auris*] (naut.) Lug; *voile* ~, shoulder-of-mutton sail.

auriste (orist), s.m. adj. [f. L *auris*] Aurist.

aurochs (orɔks), s.m. [Germ. *Auerochs*] Aurochs, wild ox.

aurore (ɔrɔr), s.f. [L *aurora*] **1.** Dawn, daybreak; east; *du couchant à l'*~, from west to east; (prov.) *travail d'*~ *amène l'or,* early to bed and early to rise makes a man healthy, wealthy, and wise; **2.** (fig.) dawn, beginning; *l'*~ *de la vie,* the morn of life; **3.** (astr.) aurora; ~ *boréale,* aurora borealis. ~, adj. Golden yellow.

auscultation (oskylta'sjɔ̃), s.f. (med.) Ausculation.

ausculter (oskylte), v.a. [L *auscultare*] To auscultate, to sound (with a stethoscope).

auspice (ospis), s.m. [f. L *auspicium*] Auspice, omen; ~*s*, (pl.) (fig.) auspices, patronage.

aussi (osi), adv. [L *aliud sic,* LL *alsi*] **1.** Also, too, likewise; *et les enfants* ~, and the children too; moreover, as well; *prenez cela* ~, take that as well; **2.** ~, comp. adv. as; *il est* ~ *sage que vaillant,* he is as wise as he is brave; **3.** ~, conj. and so, therefore, consequently; but then; *les fruits ont augmenté,* ~ *je n'en ai pris que peu,* fruit has gone up in price, consequently I have only bought a little; **4.** conj. loc. ~ *bien que,* as well as; ~ *peu que,* no more than, as little as; ~ *bien,* in fact, indeed, for; *je ne veux pas aller au spectacle* ~ *bien est-il trop tard,* I won't go to the theatre, for indeed it is too late.

aussière (osiɛr), s.f. See HAUSSIÈRE.

aussitôt (osito), adv. [*aussi+tôt*] At once, forthwith; immediately; directly; *dites-lui de venir* ~, tell him to come at once; ~ *après son départ,* immediately after his departure; ~ *dit* ~ *fait,* no sooner said than done; conj. loc. ~ *que,* as soon as.

auster (ostɛr), s.m. [f. Gr. *auō*] Auster, south wind.

austère (ostɛr), adj. [Gr. *austēros*] **1.** Austere, stern; **2.** (rare) sharp, astringent (of flavour); syn. SÉVÈRE, RUDE, RIGIDE.

austèrement (ostɛrmɑ̃), adv. Austerely, sternly.

austérité (osterite), s.f. Austerity, sternness.

austral, -e (pl. **als** or **aux**) (ostral), adj. [L *australis*] Austral, southern.

australasien, -ne (ostralazjɛ̃), adj. s.m.f. Australasian.

australien, -ne (ostraljɛ̃), adj. s.m.f. Australian.

austrasien, -ne (ostrazjɛ̃), adj. s.m.f. (Native) of Austrasia (eastern kingdom of the Franks).

autan (otɑ̃), s.m. [Prov. *autan,* L *altanus*] Stormy south wind; (poet.) Auster, southern blast.

autant (otɑ̃), adv. [L *aliud tantum*] **1.** As much, as many, as far, as long, &c.; ~ *de têtes,* ~ *d'avis,* so many men, so many minds; ~ *dire,* you might as well say; *cela est fini, ou* ~ *vaut,* that is as good as done; *une fois* ~, as much again; ~ *en emporte le vent,* that 's all moonshine; there is nothing in that; **2.** conj. loc. ~ *que,* as much as, as far as, in the same way as; ~ *que possible,* as far as possible; *d'*~ *que,* inasmuch as, forasmuch as; *d'*~ *que je sache,* for aught I know; *d'*~ *qu'il m'a semblé nécessaire,* forasmuch as it seemed expedient to me; **3.** adv. loc. *d'*~, by so much, in the same proportion; *cela vous diminuera la dette d'*~, that will lessen your debt by so much; *tout* ~, just as much, just the same; *d'~ plus*, all the more; *d'~ moins*, all the less; *d'~ mieux*, all the better.

autel (otɛl), s.m. [L *altare*] Altar; *maître* ~, high altar; *il en prendrait sur l'~*, he would rob a church; *nappe d'~*, altar-cloth; *tableau d'~*, altar-piece; *qui sert à l'~ doit vivre de l'~*, the labourer is worthy of his hire; **2.** (fig.) religion, Church; *le trône et l'~*, the mitre and the crown; ~ *contre* ~, creed against creed; *destiné aux ~s*, destined for the Church; (fig.) pl. altars; *élever des ~ à X*, to raise altars to X.

auteur (otœr), s.m. [L *auctor*] Author; *droits d'~*, copyright; royalty; *nommez votre ~*, quote your authority; *se faire ~*, to turn author. ~, adj. *Femme ~*, authoress.

authenticité (otɑ̃tisite), s.f. Authenticity.

authentifier (otɑ̃tifje), v.a. See syn. AUTHENTIQUER.

authentique (otɑ̃tik), adj. [Gr. *authentikos*] Authentic, authenticated.

authentiquement (otɑ̃tikmɑ̃), adv. Authentically.

authentiquer (otɑ̃tike), v.a. **1.** To authenticate; **2.** (law) to make legal and binding.

auto- (otɔ), pref. [Gr. *auto*] Auto-, self-.

auto (oto), s.m.f. (usually f. nowadays) [abbrev. of *automobile*] Car.

autobiographie (otɔbiɔgrafi), s.f. [Gr. *auto+bios+graphein*] Autobiography.

autobiographique (otɔbiɔgrafik), adj. Autobiographical.

autobus (otɔbys), s.m. [*auto+bus*, abbrev. of *omnibus*] Motor omnibus, (fam.) bus.

autocar (otɔkar), s.m. (Motor-)charabanc.

autochenille (otoʃənij), s.f. [*auto+chenille*] Car with caterpillar wheels.

autochtone (otɔktɔn), adj. [Gr. *auto+khthōn*] Autochthonous, autochthonal. ~, s.m.f. Autochthon.

autoclave (otɔklav), adj. [*auto-*+L *clavis*] Self-regulating. ~, s.m. (surg.) Sterilizer; (cook.) autoclave (pan with steam-tight lid).

autocopie (otokɔpi), s.f. [*auto-*+*copie*] Method of obtaining duplicate copies.

autocopier (otokɔpje), v.a. To duplicate by the method of *autocopie*.

autocopiste (otokɔpist), s.m. Duplicating machine; person who works this.

autocrate (otɔkrat), s.m. [Gr. *auto-+kratos*] Autocrat.

autocratie (otɔkrasi), s.f. Autocracy.

autocratique (otɔkratik), adj. Autocratic.

autocratiquement (otɔkratikmɑ̃), adv. Autocratically.

autodafé (otodafe), s.m. (pl. *autodafés*) [Port. *auto da fé*] Auto-da-fé (pl. autos-da-fé).

autodidacte (otodidakt), adj. [*auto-*+ Gr. *didaskein*] Self-taught. ~, s.m.f. Self-taught person.

autofécondation (otofekɔ̃da'sjɔ̃), s.f. [*auto-*+*fécondation*] (bot., zool.) Autogamy, self-fertilization.

autogène (otɔʒɛn), adj. [*auto-*+Gr. *genesis*] Autogenous; *soudure ~*, autogenous welding.

autographe (otɔgraf), adj. [*auto-*+Gr. *graphein*] Autographic. ~, s.m. Autograph.

autographie (otɔgrafi), s.f. Autography.

autographier (otɔgrafje), v.a. To autograph.

autographique (otɔgrafik), adj. Autographic.

automate (otɔmat), s.m. [Gr. *automatos*] Automaton, robot.

automatique (otɔmatik), adj. Automatic, self-acting; *distributeur ~*, penny-in-the-slot machine.

automatiquement (otɔmatikmɑ̃), adv. Automatically.

automatiser (otɔmatize), v.a. To automatize.

automatisme (otɔmatism), s.m. Automatism.

automédon (otɔmedɔ̃), s.m. [Gr. prop. n. *Automedon*] Driver; (iron.) Jehu.

automitrailleuse (otomitrɑjøz), s.f. Motor machine-gun.

automnal, -e, (aux) (otɔnal), adj. [f. *automne*] Autumnal.

automne (otɔn), s.m. and f. [L *autumnus*] Autumn; (U.S.A.) fall.

automobile (otɔmɔbil), adj. [*auto-*+L *mobilis*] Self-moving, self-propelling. ~, s.m.f. (usually f. nowadays) Motor-car, automobile; *aller en ~*, to motor; *faire de l'~*, to go in for motoring.

automobilisme (otɔmɔbilism), s.m. Automobilism, motoring.

automobiliste (otɔmɔbilist), s.m.f. Automobilist, motorist.

automot-eur, -rice (otɔmɔtœr), adj. Self-propelling, self-acting.

autonome (otɔnom), adj. [Gr. *autonomos*] Autonomous.

autonomie (otɔnɔmi), s.f. Autonomy, self-government.

autoplastie (otɔplasti), s.f. (surg.) Autoplasty.

autoplastique (otɔplastik), adj. (surg.) Autoplastic.

autopsie (otɔpsi), s.f. [Gr. *autopsia*] Autopsy, post-mortem examination.

autopsier (otɔpsje), v.a. To perform an autopsy on or conduct a post-mortem examination of.

autorisable (otɔrizabl), adj. Authorizable.

autorisation (otɔriza'sjɔ̃), s.f. Authorization, consent, warrant, permission; *donner son ~*, to give one's consent.
autoriser (otɔrize), v.a. [L *auctor, auctorizare*] To authorize, to empower; to allow, to permit, to sanction; **s'~**, v.pr. to have, get or assume authority; to act on the authority (*de*, of); to be authorized (*de*, by).
autoritaire (otɔritɛr), adj. Domineering, tyrannical, authoritative, commanding. ~, s.m.f. Authoritative person, (fam.) martinet.
autoritairement (otɔritɛrmɑ̃), adv. Authoritatively.
autoritarisme (otɔritarism), s.m. Authoritativeness.
autorité (otɔrite), s.f. [L *auctoritas*] **1.** Authority, legal power; *être en ~, avoir ~*, to be invested with authority; **2.** authority, important functionary; *aller saluer les ~s*, to pay one's respects to the authorities; **3.** authority, influence; *faire ~*, to be an authority; *invoquer Platon comme ~*, to quote Plato as one's authority; *d'~*, on one's own initiative, making use of one's rights to the full; *de son ~ privée*, on one's own initiative.
autosuggestion (otosygʒɛstjɔ̃), s.f. Autosuggestion.
autour (otur), adv. [*au+tour*] **1.** About, round, around; *tourner ~, rôder ~*, to hang about; *tout ~*, all round; *regarder tout ~*, to look all round; *il ne faut pas confondre ~ avec alentour*, don't mistake one thing for another; be careful; **2.** prep. loc. *~ de*, round; *~ de la cité*, round about the city; (fig. colloq.) *tourner ~ du pot*, to beat about the bush; *~ d'un million*, about a million.
autour (otur), s.m. [L *astur*] (ornith.) Goshawk.
autourserie (otursəri), s.f. Falconry, goshawk-training.
autoursier (otursje), s.m. Falconer.
autre (otr, otrə), adj. [L *alter*] **1.** Different, distinct, other, another; *d'~ part*, on the other hand; *~ part*, elsewhere; *~s temps, ~s mœurs*, manners change with the times; *c'est ~ chose*, it is another thing, another story; *c'est une ~ paire de manches*, that is quite another pair of shoes; that's quite a different proposition; *nous ~s Français*, we Frenchmen; *de temps à ~*, from time to time; *l'~ jour*, the other day; **2.** another, similar; *c'est un ~ moi-même*, he is my second self. ~, ind. pron. Another person, some one or something else; *causer de choses et d'~s*, to talk of one thing and another, to talk of cabbages and kings; *de part et d'~*, on both sides, on all sides; *il dit d'une façon et il fait d'une ~*, he says one thing and does another; *il en sait bien d'autres*, he knows a trick worth two of that; *j'en ai vu bien d'~s*, I have seen worse things in my time; *l'un dans l'~*, on an average; *l'un et l'~*, both; *l'un l'~*, each other, one another; *les uns et les ~s*, all of them, the whole lot; *l'un vaut l'~*, it is six of one and half a dozen of the other, they are as bad as each other; *ni l'un ni l'~*, neither; *nul ~*, no one else; *tout ~*, any one else, anybody else; *un ~ le fera*, somebody else will do it; (iron.) *à d'~s!*, take your tale elsewhere!; tell that to the marines! don't tell *me* that!; *en voici bien d'une ~!*, and now what's more; now, that's really a bit too stiff!, *il n'en fait jamais d'~s*, that's just like him; he is at it again; he is always doing that kind of thing.
autrefois (otrəfwɑ), adv. Formerly, in former times; of old; *d'~*, bygone; of yore.
autrement (otrəmɑ̃), adv. **1.** Otherwise, after another fashion; *faisons ~*, let us go to work in another way; *pas ~*, not so very; *pas ~ à plaindre*, not so very much to be pitied; *il est ~ plus riche que moi*, he is infinitely wealthier than I; **2.** otherwise, else, or else, or; *obéissez, ~ vous serez puni*, obey or you will be punished.
autrichien, -ne (otriʃjɛ̃), adj. s.m.f. Austrian.
autruche (otryʃ), s.f. [L *avis struthio*] Ostrich; *avoir un estomac d'~*, to have the digestion of an ostrich.
autrucherie (otryʃri), s.f. Ostrich-farm.
autruchon (otryʃɔ̃), s.m. Young ostrich.
autrui (otrɥi), ind. pron. [L *alteri*] Others, other people; *dépendre d'~*, to be dependent on others; *faire à ~ ce que nous voudrions qu'on nous fît*, to do as we would be done by.
auvent (ovɑ̃), s.m. [etym. dub.] Penthouse roof, lean-to.
auvergnat, -e (ovɛrɲa), adj. s.m.f. From, belonging to, of Auvergne; inhabitant of Auvergne.
auvergne (ovɛrɲ), s.f. Tan-liquor; process in which it is employed.
auvernat (ovɛrna), s.m. **1.** Species of vine cultivated in Loiret; **2.** red wine made from this.
auxiliaire (oksiljɛr), adj. s.m.f. [L *auxilium*] Auxiliary; *verbe ~*, auxiliary verb.
auxiliairement (oksiljɛrmɑ̃), adv. In an auxiliary manner.
avachi, -e (avaʃi), adj. Out of shape, worn out; (fam.) dead beat. ~, s.m.f. Flabby, useless person; (slang) dud.
avachir (avaʃir), v.a. [*à*+Germ. *weich*] To make limp or flabby; (fig.) to enervate; **s'~**, v.pr. (fam.) to get flabby, to get slipshod; to flag; to get out of shape.

avachissement (avaʃismɑ̃), s.m. Flabbiness, limpness.
aval[1] (aval), s.m. (pl. *avals*) [f. *à*+*valoir*] (comm.) Guarantee, endorsement.
aval[2] (aval), [f. *à*+*val*] s.m. Down-stream; *le vent vient d'~*, the wind is blowing upstream; adv. loc. *en ~ de*, down-stream from, below; *Rouen est en ~ de Paris*, Rouen is below Paris.
avalage (avalaʒ), s.m. [f. *aval*] **1.** Passage down-stream; **2.** cellaring (of wine, &c.).
avalaison, avalasse (avalɛzɔ̃, avalas), s.f. [f. *aval*] Torrential stream, stream in flood, in spate.
avalanche (avalɑ̃ʃ), s.f. [L *ad*+*vallis*] Avalanche.
avalant, -e (avalɑ̃), p. adj. [f. *aval*] Descending, passing down-stream.
avalement (avalmɑ̃), s.m. [f. *avaler*] Swallowing.
avaler (avale), v.a. [f. *aval*] **1.** To swallow, to swallow down; to drink, to toss off, to gulp down; **2.** to engulf; to let down, to lower (goods, &c.); **3.** (fig.) to endure, to pocket; to believe; *~ des couleuvres*, to pocket many affronts; *~ des yeux*, to devour with one's eyes; *~ un affront*, to pocket an insult; *~ la pilule*, to swallow a bitter pill; *~ sa langue*, to be dumb, taciturn, shy; to have lost one's tongue; ~, v.n. to go, or to glide down-stream.
avaleu-r, -se (avalœr), s.m.f. (fam.) Glutton.
avalies (avali), s.f.pl. Pelt-wool.
avaliser (avalize), v.a. [*à*+*valoir*] To guarantee.
avaliste (avalist), s.m.f. [f. *avaliser*] Guarantor. ~, adj. Guaranteeing.
avaloire (avalwar), s.f. [f. *avaler*] **1.** Breeching (of horse's harness); **2.** (pop.) throat, mug (in this sense also *avaloir*, s.m.)
avalure (avalyr), s.f. (vet.) Sloughing of the hoof.
avançage (avɑ̃saʒ), s.m. (obs.) [f. *avancer*] Privilege granted to certain cabs of being stationed beyond usual rank; privileged place in cabstand.
avance (avɑ̃s), s.f. [f. *avancer*] **1.** Projection (on a building, &c.); **2.** start, advance; *avoir une ~ d'une lieue*, to be a league in advance, to have a start of one league; **3.** advance, payment in advance; *faire une ~ à un employé*, to make an employee an advance; **4.** (motor.) *~ à l'allumage*, advanced ignition; **5.** (fig.) advances; attentions; *faire les premières ~s*, to make the first advances; **6.** advantage; *la belle ~!*, what good is that to me (or to you, to him, &c.); adv. loc. *d'~*, *par ~*, in advance; *payer par ~*, to pay in advance; *en ~*, beforehand, early (of time); *arriver en ~*, to arrive too soon.
avancé, -e (avɑ̃se), p. adj. [f. *avancer*] Advanced, forward, early; *je n'en suis pas plus ~*, I'm none the wiser or I'm no better off than I was before; *me voilà bien avancé!*; that's all I get for my pains!; *~ en âge*, elderly; *le travail est bien ~*, the work is well forward; (mil.) *poste ~*, advanced post, outpost; *les arbres sont ~s*, the trees are early; *avoir des opinions ~es*, to have advanced opinions; *une heure ~e*, an advanced hour (of the night); **2.** put forward, announced; *prouver les faits ~s*, to prove the alleged facts; **3.** overripe (of fruit), high (of game), tainted (of meat). **~e**, s.f. (mil.) Outpost; (mining) forward part of a gallery.
avancement (avɑ̃smɑ̃), s.m. **1.** Advance, progress; projection; *l'~ d'un pied devant l'autre*, putting one foot before the other; **2.** (fig.) advancement; preferment, promotion, rise; *obtenir de l'~* to get advancement; **3.** (law) sum paid in advance (to an heir); advance (on a legacy); **4.** (motor.) ~ or *avance à l'allumage*, advanced ignition; *donner de l'~*, to advance the ignition.
avancer (avɑ̃se), v.a. [f. *avant*] **1.** To advance, to bring, push, put forward; *~ une chaise*, to bring forward a chair; *~ la main*, to put out one's hand; (fig.) *~ une théorie*, to put forward a theory; (iron.) *cela m'avance bien!*, well, that's useful!; **2.** to advance, to pay in advance; *~ de l'argent comptant*, to advance ready money; **3.** to hasten, to put forward; *~ le dîner d'une heure*, to put dinner forward an hour; *~ la pendule*, to put on the clock; ~, v.n. to advance, to proceed, to make progress, to gain ground; *la pendule avance*, the clock is fast; *avancez donc!*, come along!; (in traffic) move on please!; *l'ouvrage avance*, the work is getting on; s'~, v.pr. to advance, to move forward; (fig.) to commit onself.
avanie (avani), s.f. [late Gr. *avania*] Insult, affront; *essuyer une ~*, to swallow an affront; (fam.) to get it in the neck.
avant (avɑ̃), s.m. [f. L *ab*+*ante*] **1.** Front, front part, head, prow, bow (of a ship); *aller de l'~*, to go ahead; *de l'~ à l'arrière*, from stem to stern; (motor.) *roue ~*, front wheel; **2.** (football) forward.
avant (avɑ̃), prep. and adv. [f. L *ab*+*ante*] Before, in front (of), in advance (of) (of time place or order); *~ tout*, first of all, before everything; *bien ~ dans la nuit*, far into the night; *bien ~ dans la terre*, deep into the earth; *40 ~ J.-C.*, 40 B.C.; *~ de partir*, before leaving; *mettre en ~*, to bring forward; to propound, to allege, to put forth; *la nuit d'~*, the previous night, the night before;

n'allez pas trop ~, don't go too far; *~ qu'il soit un an,* before a year has passed; *~ que de parler,* before speaking; *~ qu'il vînt,* before he came; adv. loc. *en ~!* forward!; (fam.) go ahead!; *en ~,* to the front.

avantage (avɑ̃taʒ), s.m. [f. *avant*] Advantage, benefit; success; privilege, profit; (tennis) vantage; *avoir l'~* to win, to prevail; *avoir l'~ sur,* to have the advantage over; *à son ~,* to his advantage, in his favour; *quel ~ vous en revient-il?,* what benefit do you reap by it?; *s'habiller à son ~,* to dress to the best advantage; *tirer ~ de tout,* to turn everything to account; *~s,* (colloq. jest.) woman's breasts; (very low slang) 'charlies'.

avantager (avɑ̃taʒe), v.a. To advantage, to give the advantage to, to favour.

avantageusement (avɑ̃taʒøzmɑ̃), adv. Advantageously, to advantage; favourably; *parler ~ de X,* to speak highly of X.

avantageu-x, -se (avɑ̃taʒø), adj. Advantageous, profitable; becoming (of dress); cheap (of bargains); commanding; priggish, conceited; *prendre un ton ~,* to assume a priggish tone, to attitudinize, to put on side, to swagger.

avant-bassin (avɑ̃basɛ̃), s.m. (pl. *avant-bassins*) (naut.) Outer dock.

avant-bec (avɑ̃bɛk), s.m. (pl. *avant-becs*) Starling, ice-breaker (on a bridge).

avant-bras (avɑ̃bra), s.m. (pl. invar.) Forearm.

avant-cale (avɑ̃kal), s.f. (pl. *avant-cales*) (naut.) Launch-ways.

avant-clou (avɑ̃klu), s.m. (pl. *avant-clous*) Gimlet.

avant-corps (avɑ̃kɔr), s.m. (pl. invar.) (arch.) Forepart, front (of a building).

avant-cour (avɑ̃kur), s.f. (pl. *avant-cours*) Outer court.

avant-coureur (avɑ̃kurœr), s.m. (pl. *avant-coureurs*) (fig.) Forerunner, harbinger, precursor. ~, adj. Preceding, premonitory, presaging, forewarning.

avant-courri-er, -ère (avɑ̃kurje), s.m.f. (pl. *avant-courriers*) Harbinger, forerunner.

avant-derni-er, -ère (avɑ̃dɛrnje), adj. s.m.f. (pl. *avant-derniers*) Last but one; (gram.) penultimate.

avant-fossé (avɑ̃fose), s.m. (pl. *avant-fossés*) (fort.) Advance fosse.

avant-garde (avɑ̃gard), s.f. (pl. *avant-gardes*) Vanguard; advance guard; (naut.) guard-ship; (fig.) *à l'~ du progrès,* ahead of all, in the van of social progress; favouring the newest reforms.

avant-goût (avɑ̃gu), s.m. (pl. *avant-goûts*) Foretaste; earnest, anticipation.

avant-hier (avɑ̃tjɛr), adv. loc. The day before yesterday.

avant-main (avɑ̃mɛ̃), s.m. (pl. *avant-mains*) **1.** Flat of the hand; **2.** forehand (of a horse); **3.** (tennis) forehand stroke; **4.** (cards) lead.

avant-mur (avɑ̃myr), s.m. (pl. *avant-murs*) (arch.) Screen-wall; (fort.) outer wall.

avant-port (avɑ̃pɔr), s.m. (pl. *avant-ports*) Outer harbour, tide-dock.

avant-poste (avɑ̃pɔst), s.m. (pl. *avant-postes*) (mil.) Outpost, advanced post; (fig.) outer defence.

avant-première (avɑ̃prəmjɛr), s.f. (pl. *avant-premières*) Private view (of pictures, exhibitions, &c.); private first performance (of plays, &c.)

avant-projet (avɑ̃prɔʒe), s.m. (pl. *avant-projets*) Rough draft.

avant-propos (avɑ̃prɔpo), s.m. (pl. invar.) Preface (to a book); preamble, introduction.

avant-scène (avɑ̃sɛn), s.f. (pl. *avant-scènes*) **1.** Proscenium; **2.** stage-box.

avant-toit (avɑ̃twɑ), s.m. (pl. *avant-toits*) Projecting roof; eaves.

avant-train (avɑ̃trɛ̃), s.m. (pl. *avant-trains*) Fore-carriage, limber; forequarters (of an animal).

avant-veille (avɑ̃vɛj), s.f. (pl. *avant-veilles*) The second day before, two days before.

avare (avar), s.m.f. [L *avarus*] Miser, niggard. ~, adj. Avaricious, miserly, niggardly; (fig.) *être ~ de ses louanges,* to be sparing of praise; (prov.) *à père ~, enfant prodigue,* a sparing sire makes a spendthrift son; syn. AVARICIEUX.

avarement (avarmɑ̃), adv. Avariciously.

avariable (avarjabl), adj. [f. *avarier*] Perishable (of goods).

avarice (avaris), s.f. [L *avaritia*] Avarice, greed, covetousness; niggardliness, stinginess.

avaricieusement (avarisjøzmɑ̃), adv. Avariciously, meanly, stingily.

avaricieu-x, -se (avarisjø), adj. Avaricious, mean, stingy.

avarie (avari), s.f. [It. *avaria*] **1.** Damage (to a ship or cargo); damage, deterioration; *~s simples,* ordinary damage; *causer une ~,* to damage; *sans ~,* without mishap; *par suite d'~s de machine,* owing to a disabled engine; **2.** (euphem.) syphilis.

avarié, -e (avarje), p. adj. **1.** Damaged; **2.** ~, adj. s.m.f. (euphem.) syphilitic.

avarier (avarje), v.a. To damage, to spoil, to injure; *s'~,* v.pr. to become damaged, to get damaged.

avatar (avatar), s.m. [f. Sansk. *avatāra*] Avatar.

à vau-de-route (avodrut), adv. loc. In disorder, helter-skelter.

à-vau-l'eau (avolo), adv. loc. Downstream; (fig.) *toutes ses entreprises sont* *allées* ~, all his undertakings have gone to rack and ruin.

avé, avé Maria (avemarja), s.m. [L wds] Ave, Ave Maria.

avec (avɛk), prep. [L *ab hoc*] **1.** With; at the same time as; (colloq.) ~ *ça!* nonsense!, what next!; *que le diable l'emporte, et toi ~!*, devil take him, and you too!; ~ *ça que*, just as if, you can't pretend that; nonsense!, I dare say!, tell that to the marines! **2.** in spite of; ~ *tout cela*, for all that; *d'~*, from; *distinguer l'ami d'~ le flatteur*, to distinguish friends from flatterers.

avecque, avecques (avɛk), prep. Archaic var. of AVEC.

aveindre (avɛ̃dr), v.a. (obs.) [L *ad+venire*] To take, to reach.

aveine (avɛn), s.f. [Archaic var. of AVOINE], Oats.

aveinière, avénière (avɛnjɛr, avenjɛr), s.f. Oat-field.

avelanède (avlanɛd), s.f. Vallonia, acorn-cup.

aveline (avlin), s.f. [L *avellana*] Filbert.

avelinier (avlinje), s.m. (bot.) Filbert-tree.

aven (avɛn), s.m. [Celt. *avon*] Pot-hole, gulf (in limestone districts).

avénacées (avenase), s.f.pl. [L *avena*] (bot.) Avenaceae.

avenage (avnaʒ), s.m. [L *avena*] (feud. law) Avenage (payment in oats made to a feudal superior).

avenant (avnɑ̃), s.m. (insurance) Rider, endorsement; addition or change to a policy of insurance or other deed.

avenant, -e (avnɑ̃), adj. [f. *avenir*] Prepossessing, comely; *manières ~es*, engaging manners. ~, s.m. What is in keeping; *tout à l'~*, all in keeping (*de*, with).

avènement (avɛnmɑ̃), s.m. [f. *advenir*] Advent, coming; accession, succession (to a throne, &c).

avèneron (avɛnrɔ̃), s.m. [L *avena*] Wild oats.

avénière. See AVEINIÈRE.

avenir (avnir), s.m. [L *advenire*] Future, future existence, futurity; posterity; *à l'~*, in the future, henceforth; *cet homme a de l'~*, that man has a future; *l'~ nous jugera*, posterity will judge us.

à-venir (avnir), s.m. (law.) Summons to appear. ~, adj. Coming, impending.

avent (avɑ̃), s.m. [L *adventus*] Advent.

aventure (avɑ̃tyr), s.f. [f. L *adventurus*] **1.** Adventure; **2.** chance, luck, venture; (comm.) *contrat à la grosse ~*, bottomry bond; *prime à la grosse ~*, bottomry premium; *à l'~*, at random; *d'~* or *par ~*, by chance, perchance; *si par ~*, if peradventure; *tenter l'~*, to try one's luck; *une diseuse de bonne ~*, a fortune-teller; *dire la bonne ~ à X*, to tell X's fortune; **3.** intrigue, love-affair.

aventurer (avɑ̃tyre), v.a. To venture, to hazard, to risk; **s'~**, v.pr. to take one's chance, to venture, to hazard oneself.

aventureusement (avɑ̃tyrøzmɑ̃), adv. Adventurously.

aventureu-x, -se (avɑ̃tyrø), adj. Venturesome, adventurous; risky, left to chance.

aventuri-er, -ère (avɑ̃tyrje), s.m.f. (usually pej.) Adventurer, impostor, (fem.) adventuress.

aventurine (avɑ̃tyrin), s.f. (min.) Aventurine.

avenu, -e (avny), p. adj. [f. *advenir*] Happened, occurred, having come to pass; (law) *nul et non ~*, null and void.

avenue (avny), s.f. [f. *venir*] Avenue, approach, drive.

avéré, -e (avere), p. adj. Authenticated, ascertained, proved.

avérer (avere), v.a. [f. L *ad+verus*] To verify, to confirm, to establish the truth of; **s'~**, v.pr. to be confirmed.

avers (aver), s.m. [L *adversus*] Obverse (of coins, &c.).

averse (avɛrs), s.f. [f. *verser*] Short sudden shower, downpour; *essuyer une ~*, to get a drenching; (fig.) flood, deluge.

aversion (avɛrsjɔ̃), s.f. [L *aversio*] Aversion, distaste, dislike; *avoir X en ~*, to have a dislike for X; *prendre X en ~*, to take a dislike to X.

averti, -e (avɛrti), p. adj. Warned, informed; *se tenir pour ~*, to take it as a warning, to be on one's guard; *un homme ~ en vaut deux*, forewarned is forearmed.

avertin (avɛrtɛ̃), s.m. [L *vertex*] **1.** (archaic) Vertigo; **2.** (vet. surg.) sturdy, turn-sick.

avertir (avɛrtir), v.a. [L *advertere*] To inform, to warn; *faire ~ de*, to give notice of; syn. INFORMER, DONNER AVIS.

avertissement (avɛrtismɑ̃), s.m. Information, notification, advice; warning, caution; admonition; preface (of a book, &c.).

avertisseur (avɛrtisœr), s.m. **1.** Informer, monitor; **2.** (theatr.) call-boy; **3.** alarm; ~ *d'incendie*, fire-alarm.

aveu (avø), s.m. (pl. -x) [f. *avouer*] **1.** Admission, avowal, confession; *faire l'~ de*, to admit, to confess; **2.** approbation, consent; *sans votre ~*, without your consent; *homme sans ~*, vagrant, vagabond.

aveuglant, -e (avœglɑ̃), p. adj. Blinding, dazzling; (fig.) (*a*) obvious; (*b*) misleading.

aveugle (avœgl), adj. [f. L *alboculus, aboculus*] Blind, sightless; *à l'~*, blindly, at random; *obéissance ~*, implicit obedience; *changer son cheval borgne contre un ~*, to jump out of the frying-pan into the fire; to change from bad to worse. ~, s.m.f. Blind person; *c'est un ~ qui en conduit un autre*, it's a case of the blind leading

the blind; *un ~ y mordrait*, a blind man couldn't miss it.
aveuglement (avœgləmɑ̃), s.m. Blindness; (fig.) infatuation, delusion.
aveuglément (avœglemɑ̃), adv. Blindly, rashly; syn. À L'AVEUGLE, À L'AVEUGLETTE.
aveugle-né, -e (avœgləne), adj. (pl. *aveugles-nés*) Born blind; blind from birth. ~, s.m.f. A person born blind, one blind from birth.
aveugler (avœgle), v.a. **1.** To blind, to make blind, to dazzle; (fig.) to blind, to dazzle, to delude; **2.** (naut.) to fother (a leak); **s'~**, v.pr. to blind oneself, to delude oneself; to shut one's eyes to.
aveuglette (avœglɛt), s.f. adv. loc. *A l'~*, in the dark, blindly, rashly.
aveulir (avølir), v.a. [f. *veule*] To render weak, to enervate, to enfeeble.
aveulissement (avølismɑ̃), s.m. Enfeeblement, enervation, weakening, depriving of energy.
aviat-eur, -rice (avjatœr), s.m.f. Aviator, pilot. ~, adj. Flying.
aviation (avja'sjɔ̃), s.f. [f. L *avis*] Aviation.
aviceptologie (avisɛptɔlɔʒi), s.f. [f. L *avis*+*capere*+Gr. *logos*] Treatise on fowling.
avicule (avikyl), s.f. [L *avicula*] (zool.) Avicula.
aviculteur (avikyltœr), s.m. [L *avis*+*cultor*] Aviarist; poultry-breeder.
aviculture (avikyltyr), s.f. Aviculture, bird-raising; poultry-farming.
avide (avid), adj. [L *avidus*] Greedy, eager (*de*, for), thirsting (for), avid (of); *~ de gain*, greedy for gain; *un homme ~*, a covetous man.
avidement (avidmɑ̃), adv. Greedily, voraciously; eagerly.
avidité (avidite), s.f. [f. *avide*] Avidity, greediness; eagerness.
avilir (avilir), v.a. [f. *vil*] To debase, to disparage; to lower; to degrade, to disgrace; **s'~**, v.pr. to degrade oneself, to disgrace oneself.
avilissant, -e (avilisɑ̃), p. adj. Degrading, debasing.
avilissement (avilismɑ̃), s.m. Debasement, degradation; disparagement.
avinage (avinaʒ), s.m. [f. *vin*] Filling or soaking with wine.
aviné, -e (avine), p. adj. Drunk; (of a cask) wine-soaked.
aviner (avine), v.a. [f. *vin*] To soak or fill with wine; **s'~**, v.pr. to get drunk, (fam.) to soak.
avion (avjɔ̃), s.m. [f. L *avis*] Aeroplane, plane; syn. AÉROPLANE.
aviron (avirɔ̃), s.m. [f. *virer*] Oar; *~ de couple*, scull; *~ de galère*, sweep; *aller à l'~*, to row.
avis (avi), s.m. [f. L *ad*+*visum*] **1.** Opinion, way of thinking, judgement; advice, counsel; *deux ~ valent mieux qu'un*, two heads are better than one; *dire son ~*, to speak one's mind; *à mon ~*, in my opinion; (pop.) *m'est ~ que*, methinks; it strikes me that; *faute d'~*, for want of advice; *être d'~ que*, to be of opinion that; *changer d'~*, to change one's mind; *autant de têtes, autant d'~*, so many men, so many minds; **2.** information, notice, warning; *~ au lecteur*, note to the reader; (comm.) *lettre d'~*, letter of advice; **3.** hint; *donner un ~ assez clair à X*, to give X a pretty broad hint; *sauf ~ contraire*, unless (or until) advised to the contrary.
avisé, -e (avize), p. adj. [f. *aviser*] **1.** Shrewd, wary, clear-sighted, circumspect; wise; *il est fort ~*, he is very discreet; **2.** thought of, imagined; *ce fut à lui bien ~*, that was a clever find on his part.
aviser (avize), v.a. [f. *avis*] **1.** To perceive, to espy; **2.** to inform, to apprise; (comm.) to advise by letter; ~, v.n. to think (*à*, about) to consider, to look (to); *avisons à sortir d'ici*, let us consider how to get out of here; **s'~**, v.pr. to think (*de*, of), to find; to bethink oneself; to dare, to presume; *il s'avisa de*, he took it into his head to; *il ne s'avise jamais de rien*, he is so feckless, he never thinks of anything; *ne vous avisez pas de dire*, mind, you had better not say, do not take it into your head to say.
aviso (avizo), s.m. [Span. wd] (naut.) Aviso, dispatch-boat.
avitaillement (avitɑjmɑ̃), s.m. (mil., nav.) Victualling, stores.
avitailler (avitɑje), v.a. [f. OF *vitaille*] To victual, to supply with stores.
avivage (avivaʒ), s.m. Polishing, brightening; reviving, sharpening.
aviver (avive), v.a. [f. *vif*] **1.** To revive, to brighten; *~ le feu*, to revive, to stir up the fire; to polish, to burnish; **2.** (carp.) to sharpen the edges of; **3.** (fig.) to irritate, to exacerbate; **4.** (surg.) to clean up (a wound).
avocasser (avɔkase), v.n. [f. *avocat*] (pej.) To pettifog, to drudge at the bar.
avocasserie (avɔkasri), s.f. (pej.) Pettifoggery, chicanery, quibbling.
avocassi-er, -ère (avɔkasje), adj. Pettifogging. ~, s.m.f. Pettifogger.
avocat,[1] -e (avɔka), s.m.f. [L *advocatus*] Barrister, advocate, counsel; *plaider par ~*, to be represented by counsel; *~ consultant*, consulting barrister, consultant; *~ général*, Solicitor-General; *~ de Ponce Pilate*, *~ sous l'orme*, *~ de causes perdues*, briefless barrister; (fig.) pleader, advocate, champion, intercessor.
avocat[2] (avɔka), s.m. (bot.) Avocado, alligator pear.

avocatier (avɔkatje), s.m. (bot.) Avocado-tree.
avocatoire (avɔkatwar), adj. Recalling (of letters, &c.).
avocette (avɔset), s.f. (ornith.) Avocet, avoset.
avoine (avwan), s.f. [L *avena*] Oats; *d'~*, oaten; *farine d'~*, oatmeal; *gruau d'~*, groats; *folle ~*, wild oats.
avoir (avwar), v.a. [L *habere*] **1.** To have, to possess, to get; *~ la parole*, (parl.) to have the ear of the House; *~ pour patron* to have as master; *~ une chose à bon compte*, to get a thing cheap; *~ tort*, to be wrong; *~ raison*, to be right; *~ raison de X*, to get the better of X; *faire ~ une chose à X*, to procure a thing for X; *~ de quoi vivre*, to have enough to live on; *il aura le prix*, he will get the prize; **2.** to have on, to wear; *il avait un pardessus gris*, he was wearing a grey overcoat (when referring to one particular occasion); **3.** to feel; *~ faim, soif, peur, honte*, to be hungry, thirsty, afraid, ashamed; *qu'avez-vous?*, what is the matter with you? **4.** to consider, to deem; *~ pour agréable*, to appreciate, to like; **5.** to measure (in size, age, &c.); *la Tour Eiffel a 300 mètres de haut*, the Eiffel Tower is 300 metres high; *~ quarante ans*, to be forty (years old); **6.** *~ de*, to take after; *~ de son père*, to take after one's father; **7.** *~ à*, to have to: *~ à parler à X* to have something to say to X; *~ à payer*, to have to pay; *j'ai à travailler*, I have work to do; *il n'en a pas pour longtemps*, he won't live long; *j'en ai pour deux heures*, I shall be two hours over it; **8.** *en ~ assez*, to be irritated; *j'en ai assez*, I have had enough of this (of it); I am fed up with it; *en ~ contre X*, to bear a grudge against X; **9.** (various loc.) *malgré qu'on en ait*, willy nilly; in spite of oneself; *il l'a eu*, he has had him, he scored off him; *on les aura!*, we will down them!; *c'est là que vous m'avez*, that's where you have me; *~*, v. impers. *il y a*, there is, there exists; *il y a deux mois de cela*, that was two months ago; *il y a un an qu'il est mort*, he has been dead a year; *il n'y en a pas deux comme lui*, there is no one like him; *il y en a encore*, there is (or are) still some left; *il y a plus*, moreover; nay, more; *il y a de quoi s'impatienter*, there's good reason for getting impatient; *il n'y a pas de quoi*, don't mention it, not at all, *il n'y a pas de quoi manger*, there is nothing to eat.
avoir (avwar), s.m. Possessions, property; *voilà tout mon ~*, this is all I have; (comm.) credit, credit-side.
avoisinant, -e (avwazinɑ̃), p. adj. Neighbouring, adjoining.
avoisiner (avwazine), v.a. [f. *voisin*] To border upon, to be contiguous to; to neighbour.
avortement (avɔrtəmɑ̃), s.m. [L *ab + ortus*] Abortion, miscarriage; (fig.) failure, miscarriage.
avorter (avɔrte), v.n. To miscarry, to have a miscarriage; (fig.) to prove abortive, to fail; *faire ~*, to cause, to procure abortion.
avorton (avɔrtɔ̃), s.m. Abortion; abortive child; (fig.) abortion, miserable specimen, wretch.
avouable (avwabl), adj. Avowable.
avoué (avwe), s.m. [L *advocatus*] Attorney, solicitor; *une étude d'~*, an attorney's office.
avouer (avwe), v.a.n. [L *advocare*] **1.** To admit, to confess, to avow; *il a avoué le fait*, he has confessed the deed; **s'~**, v.pr. *s'~ vaincu*, to admit oneself beaten; **2.** to acknowledge, to own; *il l'avoue comme sien*, he acknowledges it as his; **3.** to approve; *j'avoue tout ce que vous avez fait*, I approve all that you have done.
avoyer (avwaje), s.m. [f. *avoué*] Chief magistrate in some Swiss cantons.
avril (avril), s.m. [L *aprilis*] April; *recevoir un poisson d'~*, to be made an April fool of; *donner un poisson d'~ à X*, to make an April fool of a X.
avrillé, -e (avrije), adj. Sown or planted in April.
avrillet (avrijɛ), s.m. Wheat sown in April.
avulsi-f, -ve (avylsif), adj. Avulsive.
avulsion (avylsjɔ̃), s.f. [f. L *avulsum*] (surg.) Avulsion.
avunculaire (avɔ̃kylɛr), adj. [f. L *avunculus*] Avuncular.
axe (aks), s.m. [L *axis*] Axis; (mech.) axle, axle-tree; *~ coudé*, crank-axle, crank-shaft; *~ moteur*, driving-shaft; (fig.) central support, pivot.
axial, -e, axuel, -le (aksjal, aksɥɛl), adj. Axial.
axile (aksil), adj. Axile, axial.
axillaire (aksillɛr), adj. [f. L *axilla*] (anat.) Axillary.
axiome (aksjom), s.m. [Gr. *axiōma*] Axiom; (fig.) axiom, truism; syn. MAXIME, SENTENCE, APOPHTEGME, APHORISME.
axiomètre (aksjomɛtr), s.m. [Gr. *axios + metron*] (naut.) Tell-tale (of the tiller).
axis (aksis), s.m. (anat.) Axis.
axolotl (aksɔlɔtl), s.m. [Aztec wd] (zool.) Axolotl.
axonge (aksɔ̃ʒ), s.f. [L *axungia*] (pharm.) Axunge, hog's lard.
axonométrique (aksɔnɔmetrik), s.f. [Gr. *axon+metron*] Axonometry, measurement of axes. ~, adj. Axonometric.
ay, aï (ai), s.m. [f. *Ay*, a commune in Champagne] Ay wine.

ayant cause (ɛjɑ̃koz), s.m. (pl. *ayants cause*) (law) Assign, representative.
ayant droit (ɛjɑ̃drwa), s.m. (pl. *ayants droit*) (law) Party entitled; party to whom another's rights have been transferred.
aye-aye (aiai), s.m. (zool.) Aye-aye.
azalée (azale), s.f. [Gr. *azaleos*] (bot.) Azalea.
azédarac (azedarak), s.m. (bot.) Bead-tree, *Melia azedarach*.
azerole (azrɔl), s.f. (bot.) Azarole, Neapolitan medlar.
azerolier (azrɔlje), s.m. (bot.) Azarole-tree.
azimut (azimyt), s.m. [Arab. *al-samt*] (astr.) Azimuth.
azimutal, -e, (aux) (azimytal), adj. Azimuthal. ~, s.m. A form of mariner's compass.
azotate (azɔtat), s.m. (chem.) Nitrate.
azote (azɔt), s.m. [Gr. *a+zōē*] (chem.) Nitrogen, azote.
azoté, -e, azoteu-x, -se (azɔte, azɔtø), adj. Azotized, nitrogenized.
azotique (azɔtik), adj. Azotic, nitric.
azotite (azɔtit), s.m. Salt of nitrous acid.
azoture (azɔtyr), s.m. (chem.) Nitride.
aztèque (aztɛk), adj. s.m.f. Aztec; (jest. colloq.) puny creature, guy.
azur (azyr), s.m. [Arab. orig.] Azure ,sky-blue; *pierre d'~*, lapis-lazuli; (herald.) azure.
azuré, -e (azyre), adj. Azure, azure-coloured, sky-blue; *la voûte ~e*, the azure dome, the sky; *la plaine ~e*, the azure floor, the sea.
azurer (azyre), v.a. To stain azure-coloured, to blue.
azurescent, -e (azyrɛsɑ̃), adj. Bluish, faintly azured.
azurine (azyrin), s.f. Azurine, pale blue.
azygos (azygɔs), s.f. [Gr. *a+zugon*] (anat.) Azygos.
azyme (azim), adj. [Gr. *a+zumē*] Azymous, unleavened. ~, s.m. Azyme, unleavened bread; *la fête des ~s*, the feast of unleavened bread.
azymique (azimik), adj. [f. *azyme*] Unsuitable for fermentation.

B

B, b (be), s.m. 2nd letter of the alphabet.
baba (baba), s.m. [f. Pol. *baba*] Bun, French tipsy-cake; (colloq.) *en rester ~*, to be struck all of a heap.
babel (babɛl), s.f. [geog. orig.] Babel, scene of confusion and uproar.
babeurre (babœr), s.m. [f. *battre+beurre*] Buttermilk.
babi (babi), s.m. Babi, adept of babism (see BABISME).
babil (babi), s.m. [onom.] Prattle, chatter, twaddle.
babillage (babijaʒ), s.m. Prattling, chattering, babbling, twaddle.
babillard, -e (babijar), adj. Twaddling, prating, chattering, talkative; *fauvette ~e*, (ornith.) white throat. ~, s.m.f. Twaddler, prater, &c.; *tais-toi ~!*, shut up, you chatter-box!
babiller (babije), v.n. To prattle, to chatter, to babble, to gossip.
babine, babouine (babin, babwin), s.f. [f. L *labia*] Pendent lip, chops, gills; *il s'en lèche les ~s*, he is smacking his lips over it; (mockingly pej.) *essuie tes ~s!*, wipe your thick lips.
babiole (babjɔl), s.f. [f. It. *babbola*] Plaything, bauble, gew-gaw, gimcrack, trifle, trinket; (fig.) *~s!*, nonsense!, mere talk!
babiroussa (babirusa), s.m. [Malay wd] (zool.) Babiroussa, horned hog (of Java).
babisme (babism), s.m. Babism, doctrine of Bab (Persian religious reformer, 1820–50).
bâbord (babɔr), s.m. [f. Scand. *bagbord*] (naut.) Larboard, port. ~, adv. Port, a-port; *~ tout!*, hard a-port.
babouche (babuʃ), s.f. [f. Arab. *bābūj*] Babouche, Turkish slipper.
babouin (babwɛ̃), s.m. [etym. dub.] **1.** Baboon; **2.** (med.) pimple on the lip; **3.** (fam.) tiresome child, brat, monkey, horrid little monkey.
babouvisme (babuvism), s.m. [f. *Gracchus Babeuf*, Fr. revolutionary, 1760–97] Babouvism, revolutionary doctrine of communist tendency.
babouviste (babuvist), s.m.f. adj. Babouvist.
babylonièn, -ne (babilɔnjɛ̃), adj. s.m.f. Babylonian.
bac (bak), s.m. [f. Germ. *back*] **1.** Ferry-boat; **2.** tank, vat, trough; *~ d'accumulateur*, accumulator-case; **3.** abbrev. of *baccara*; **4.** abbrev. of *baccalauréat*.
baccalauréat (bakalɔrea), s.m. [f. L *baccalarius*] Baccalaureate, bachelor's degree.
baccara (bakara), s.m. [unkn. orig.] Baccara (game).
baccarat (bakara), s.m. [f. *Baccarat*, French town] Crystal from Baccarat.
bacchanal (bakanal), s.m. [f. *Bacchus*] Uproar, shindy; *~e*, s.f. Bacchanal, Bacchanalia, wild dance.
bacchante (bakɑ̃t), s.f. [f. *Bacchus*] Bacchante, termagant.
bacchius (bakjys), s.m. [Gr. wd] (pros.) Bacchius (a foot composed of one short and two long syllables).
baccifère (baksifɛr), adj. [f. L *bacca* + *ferre*] (bot.) Bacciferous, berry-bearing.
bacciforme (baksifɔrm), adj. Berry-shaped.

bacha, bach-aga (baʃa, baʃaga), s.m. See PACHA.
bâche (bɑʃ), s.f. **1.** Tarpaulin, wagon-cloth, rick-cloth, awning; **2.** (gard.) forcing-frame; **3.** (fish.) net, drag-net.
bachelette (baʃlɛt), s.f. (obs.) [fem. of *bachelier*] Young girl, lass, damsel.
bachelier (baʃlje), s.m. [etym. dub.] **1.** (feud. obs.) Aspirant to knighthood; **2.** (approx.) bachelor (of arts, science, &c.). ⚠ 'Bachelor' has also the sense of unmarried man = *célibataire*, but *bachelier* cannot be used in that sense.
bachelière (baʃljɛr), s.f. Woman with degree of bachelor.
bâcher (bɑʃe), v.a. To cover, to tilt, to furnish with a tilt.
bachi-bouzouk (baʃibuzuk), s.m. [Turk. wd] Bashi-bazouk, Turkish irregular.
bachelick (baʃlik), s.m. Woollen scarf for the head.
bachique (baʃik), adj. [f. *Bacchus*] Bacchic, convivial.
bachot (baʃo), s.m. [f. *bac*] **1.** Wherry, small flat-bottomed boat; **2.** (fam.) baccalaureate; *boîte à* ~, cramming school for intensive preparation for baccalaureate; *passer son* ~, to go up for the baccalaureate.
bachotage (baʃɔtaʒ), s.m. **1.** Ferryman's business; **2.** intensive preparation for baccalaureate.
bachotte (baʃɔt), s.f. Fish-vat.
bacillaire (basillɛr), adj. Bacillary. ~, s.f. (bot.) An alga (of the diatomaceae).
bacille (basil), s.m. [L *bacillus*] Bacillus, (pl. bacilli).
bacilliforme (basilifɔrm), adj. Bacilliform.
bacillose (basilloz). s.f. See syn. TUBERCULOSE.
bâclage (bɑklaʒ), s.m. **1.** Closing of a port; stockade; line of boats in a port; **2.** hasty work, hasty conclusion of an affair.
bâcle (bɑkl), s.f. [f. L *baculus*] Wooden bar for a door.
bâcler (bɑkle), v.a. **1.** To bar up (a door or window); **2.** to moor (a boat) near a quay; **3.** to stockade (a river); **4.** to botch (a work), to conclude (an affair) hastily; *c'est une affaire bâclée,* it is a patched-up affair.)
baconien, -ne, baconiste (bakɔnjɛ̃, bakɔnist), adj. s.m.f. [f. *Francis Bacon*] Baconian.
Bactériacées (bakterjase), s.f.pl. (bot.) Bacteriaceae.
bactéricide (bakterisid), adj. [f. Fr. *bactérie* + L *caedere*] Bactericide.
bactéridie (bakteridi), s.f. Bacteridium.
bactérie (bakteri), s.f. [f. Gr. *baktron*] Bacterium (pl. bacteria); syn. MICROBE.
bactérien, -ne (bakterjɛ̃), adj. Bacterial.
bactériologie (bakterjɔlɔʒi), s.f. Bacteriology; syn. MICROBIOLOGIE.
bactrien, -ne (baktrjɛ̃), adj. s.m.f. Bactrian.
bacul (baky), s.m. [*bat*+*cul*] Crupper.
baculite (bakylit), s.f. [f. L *baculum*] Baculite (fossil shell).
badaud, -e (bado), s.m.f. [f. L *badare*] Idler, lounger, gaping booby. ~, adj. Lounging, idling, silly.
badauder (badode), v.n. To go sauntering about, to gape idly, to lounge, to loiter.
badauderie (badodri), s.f. Sauntering, idling, loitering.
badelaire (badlɛr), s.m. [L *badarellus*] Short scimitar.
baderne (badɛrn), s.f. [f. Bret. *badern*] **1.** (naut.) Fender; **2.** (fig.) worn-out person or thing, rubbish, old fogy.
badiane (badjan), s.f. [f. Pers. *badian*] (bot.) Aniseed-tree, *Illicium anisatum.*
badigeon (badiʒɔ̃), s.m. [unkn. orig.] Whitewash, limewash, badigeon, paint.
badigeonnage (badiʒɔnaʒ), s.m. Whitewashing, quick painting, daubing.
badigeonner (badiʒɔne), v.a. To wash walls with a solution of lime, whiting, or colour, to paint quickly, to daub; to anoint with tincture of iodine, &c., to badigeon. ⚠ 'To badigeon' = *remplir les creux d'un morceau de sculpture ou de muraille avec du badigeon,* but *badigeonner* has this particular sense as well as the others.
badigeonneur (badiʒɔnœr), s.m. Whitewasher, colour-washer; (fam.) dauber, sorry painter.
badigoinces (badigwɛ̃s), s.f.pl. [OF; cf. Rabelais] Cheeks, chops; (slang) *se caler les* ~*s,* to have a good fill, to eat greedily.
badin, -e (badɛ̃), adj. Playful, merry, jocular, humorous. ~, s.m. Joker.
badinage (badinaʒ), s.m. Playfulness, jesting, banter, chaff, fooling.
badine (badin), s.f. Switch, flexible stick, wand.
badiner (badine), v.n. **1.** To play, to trifle, to frolic, to jest; **2.** to play freely; *faire* ~ *une dentelle,* to make a lace edging wave or flounce slightly.
badinerie (badinri), s.f. Jest, trifling, idle talk.
badoche (badɔʃ), s.f. Salt cod, stockfish.
badois, -e (badwɑ), adj. s.m.f. Badener, (native) of grand duchy of Baden.
bafouer (bafue), v.a. To scout, to flout, to make game of.
bafouillage (bafujaʒ), s.m. Incoherent jabbering, sputtering.
bafouiller (bafuje), v.a.n. To jabber, to sputter; syn. BREDOUILLER.

bâfre, bâfrée (bɑfr, bɑfre), s.f. (pop.) Blow-out, guttling, guzzling.

bâfrer (bɑfre), v.a.n. [etym. dub.] To eat greedily, to guzzle, to guttle, to gobble up, to bolt; to have a blow-out.

bagage (bagaʒ), s.m. [f. LL *baga*] Luggage, baggage (of an army); *plier* ~, to pack off; (fig.) to die, to make one's exit; ~ *littéraire*, literary knowledge. ⚠ *Bagage*: not English 'baggage', 'impudent young hussy'=*effrontée.*

bagarre (bagar), s.f. [unkn. orig.] Row, hubbub, brawl, tumult, squabble, confusion, scuffle.

bagasse (bagas), s.f. **1.** Bagasse, canetrash; **2.** (Provenç.) ~ *!*, confound it!

bagatelle (bagatɛl), s.f. [It. *bagatella*] Bagatelle, trifle, trinket, nonsense, knickknack; petty love-affair, sexual indulgence, un-Platonic love-making, amours.

bagne (baɲ), s.m. [f. It. *bagno*] Convict prison; penal servitude.

bagnole (baɲɔl), s.f. **1.** Horse-box (on the railway); **2.** wretched car or carriage; **3.** wretched dwelling; **4.** (jest.) any car.

bagout (bagu), s.m. Gab, gabble; *quel* ~*!*, what a gab!; *avoir du* ~, to have the gift of the gab.

baguage (bagaʒ), s.m. (arboriculture) Girdling, ringing.

bague (bag), s.f. [f. L *bacca*] Finger-ring, ring; *jeu de* ~, running at the ring; ~ *de piston*, piston-ring; ~ *de lubrification*, splash-ring.

baguenaude (bagnod), s.f. (bot.) Bladder-nut.

baguenauder (bagnode), v.n. To trifle away one's time, to dawdle, to potter or loiter about.

baguenaudier (bagnodje), s.m. (bot.) Bladder-nut tree; bastard-senna-tree.

baguer (bage), v.a. **1.** To tack in (the lining of a coat); **2.** (arboriculture) to girdle, to ring.

baguette (bagɛt), s.f. [f. L *baculus*] **1.** Switch, rod, wand; (fig.) *mener à la* ~, to rule despotically; ~ *divinatoire*, dowser's wand or rod, divining-rod. **2.** ramrod (of a fire-arm); **3.** stick (of a rocket); **4.** (arch.) baguette, fillet; **5.** ~ *de tambour*, drum-stick.

baguier (bagje), s.m. Ring-box, ring-stand.

bah! (bɑ), interj. Bah!, pshaw!, pooh!; *ah* ~ *!*, indeed!, you don't say so!

bahut (bay), s.m. [unkn. orig.] **1.** Chest, trunk, press; **2.** (slang) school.

bahutier (baytje), s.m. Maker of chests, wardrobes, presses, and trunks.

bai, -e (bɛ), adj. [f. L *badius*] Bay; ~ *châtain*, chestnut.

baie[1] (bɛ), s.f. [f. L *baia*] **1.** (geog.) Bay, bight; **2.** (arch.) bay, bay-window, opening.

baie[2] (bɛ), s.f. [f. L *bacca*] (bot.) Berry.

baignade (bɛɲad), s.f. Bathing, bath; (fam.) dousing, ducking.

baigner (bɛɲe), v.a. [f. L *balneare*] To bath(e), to wash; *les pleurs baignaient son visage*, tears bedewed his (or her) face; *la rivière baigne les remparts de la ville*, the river washes the walls of the town; ~, v.n. to be immersed, soaked; *il faut que ces prunes baignent dans l'alcool*, these prunes must be soaked in alcohol; ~ *dans son sang*, to welter in one's blood; **se** ~, v.pr. to bathe.

baigneu-r, -se (bɛɲœr), s.m.f. **1.** Bath-keeper, bath-man, bath-woman; **2.** bather, summer visitor.

baignoire (bɛɲwar), s.f. Bath, bath-tub; (theatr.) pit-box.

bail (pl. **baux**) (baj), s.m. [f. *bailler*] Lease; *passer un* ~, to draw up a lease; *résilier un* ~, to cancel a lease; *à* ~, on lease. ⚠ *Bail* must not be translated by English 'bail', which usually=*caution.*

baille (bɑj), s.f. [f. It. *baglia*] Bucket, tub.

bâillement (bɑjmɑ̃), s.m. **1.** Yawning, gaping; a yawn, a gape; **2.** gap, hiatus.

bailler (bɑje), v.a. [f. LL *bajulare*] To give; *vous nous la baillez belle!*, you are trying to humbug us!, a pretty story you are telling us!, tell that to the marines!

bâiller (bɑje), v.n. [f. LL *batare*] **1.** To yawn, to gape; **2.** to be ajar, to show a chink.

baillet (bajɛ), adj. m. Sorrel (speaking of the colour of a horse).

baill-eur, -eresse (bɑjœr), s.m.f. Lessor; *le* ~ *et le preneur*, lessor and lessee; ~ *de fonds*, sleeping partner, money-lender.

bâilleu-r, -se (bɑjœr), s.m.f. Yawner.

bailli (baji), s.m. [f. LL *bajulus*] Bailiff; ~**ve**, s.f. (obs.) bailiff's wife.

bailliage (bajaʒ), s.m. (obs.) Bailiwick.

bâillon (bɑjɔ̃), s.m. [f. *bâiller*] Gag.

bâillonnement (bɑjɔnmɑ̃), s.m. Gagging.

bâillonner (bɑjɔne), v.a. To gag; (fig.) to silence.

bain (bɛ̃), s.m. [f. L *balneum*] Bath(e), bathing-place, bathing-establishment, bathing-room; ~ *de siège*, hip-bath; ~ *de pieds*, foot-bath; (cook.) ~ *Marie*, bain-Marie; (chem.) water-bath; (photo.) ~ *de fixage*, fixing bath or solution; (motor.) ~ *d'huile*, oil bath.

baïonnette (bajɔnɛt), s.f. [f. *Bayonne*, French town] Bayonet; *mettre* ~ *au canon*, to fix bayonets.

baïoque (bajɔk), s.f. [It. *baiocco*] Bajocco (old papal coin).

baïram, beïram (bɛiram), s.m. [Turk. wd] Bairam.

baisemain (bɛzmɛ̃), s.m. [*baise*+*main*] Kissing of hands, homage.

---

baisement (bɛzmɑ̃), s.m. [f. *baiser*] Kissing; espec. kissing of the Pope's slipper.
baiser (bɛze), v.a. [f. L *basiare*] To kiss; (slang) *se faire* ~, to get found out, to be caught. ⚠ *Baiser* is often used in the sense of 'to have sexual intercourse with'; great care is required in the use of this verb.
baiser (bɛze), s.m. Kiss; ~ *de Judas*, traitor's kiss.
baiseu-r, -se (bɛzœr), s.m.f. Kisser.
baisoter (bɛzɔte), v.a. To kiss frequently; **se** ~, v. pr. to be always kissing one another, to bill and coo.
baisse (bɛs), s.f. Fall, decline, subsidence, going down (of the waters of a river); *jouer à la* ~, to speculate for a fall; *joueur à la* ~, bear (on the Stock Exch.); *en* ~, falling.
baissement (bɛsmɑ̃), s.m. Lowering, drooping, stooping.
baisser (bɛse), v.a. [f. LL *bassiare*] To lower, to let down, to bring down, to droop, to lower (the voice); (mus.) to flatten the pitch of; to bow (the head), to hang down (the head); ~ *les yeux*, to cast down one's eyes; (naut.) ~ *pavillon*, to haul down one's colours; (fig.) to surrender, to give way; ~, v.n. to decline, to fall, to get low, to ebb (of the tide); to sink; to set (of the sun); **se** ~, v.pr. to stoop, to bow down.
baissier (bɛsje), s.m. Bear (on the Stock Exch.).
baissière (bɛsjɛr), s.f. Bottom of a cask; (agric.) hollow, rain-pool.
baisure (bɛzyr), s.f. Kissing-crust (of bread).
bajoue (baʒu), s.f. [*bas* + *joue*] Chap, chop, cheek (of a pig); jowl.
bajoyer (baʒwaje), s.m. [etym. dub.] Chamber wall (of a canal lock).
bal (bal), s.m. [f. LL *ballare*] Ball; dancing-hall, dancing-room; ~ *costumé* (or *travesti*), fancy-dress ball; *ouvrir le* ~, to open the ball.
balade (balad), s.f. (pop.) Stroll, ramble.
balader (balade), v.a. (pop.) To take somebody or something with one, to carry; *je l'ai baladé toute la matinée*, I walked him round all morning; *envoyer* ~ *X*, to send X to the right-about; **se** ~, v.pr. to take a stroll, to stroll about, to mike, to gad about, to gallivant.
baladeur (baladœr), adj. (motor.) Shifting; *train* ~, sliding double-change speed wheels, change-speed gear.
baladeuse (baladøz), s.f. **1.** Trailer; **2.** street hand-barrow; **3.** (motor.) portable electric lamp.
baladin, -e (baladɛ̃), s.m.f. [f. *bal, baller*] Dancer, buffoon, popular singer, mountebank, baladine.
baladinage (baladinaʒ), s.m. Coarse jesting, buffoonery.
balafre (balafr), s.f. [prob. Germ. orig.] Gash, slash, scar.
balafrer (balafre), v.a. To gash, to wound on the face.
balai (balɛ), s.m. [f. Bret. *balan*] **1.** Broom, house-brush; besom (when made of twigs); *donner un coup de* ~, (*a*) to sweep; (*b*) (fig.) to clear the place; *manche à* ~, broom-stick; *rôtir le* ~, to lead the devil of a life; **2.** (falc.) tail of a hawk; **3.** (hunt.) brush (tip of a fox's or dog's tail); **4.** (aeron.) *manche à* ~, gear, control column, joy-stick.
balais (balɛ), adj. m. [f. L *balascius*] Balas; *rubis* ~, balas-ruby.
balance (balɑ̃s), s.f. [f. L *bilanx*] **1.** Balance, scales (pl.); ~ *de précision*, precision balance; ~ *d'essai*, assay-balance; ~ *romaine*, steelyard; ~ *à bascule*, weighing-machine; *faire pencher la* ~, to turn the scale; **2.** balance, equilibrium, suspense; *tenir la* ~ *égale entre deux parties*, to hold the balance even between two parties; *entrer en* ~, to be comparable; *la* ~ *d'un compte*, the balance of an account; *la victoire fut longtemps en* ~, victory was long in suspense (or doubtful); **3.** (astr.) Balance; Libra.
balancé (balɑ̃se), s.m. (danc.) Balancing. ~, **e**, adj. (colloq.) *Un garçon bien* ~, a fine, well-built fellow.
balancelle (balɑ̃sɛl), s.f. (naut.) Felucca.
balancement (balɑ̃smɑ̃), s.m. **1.** Balancing, hesitation; **2.** swaying, rocking, waving (of branches); **3.** (astr.) libration (of the moon).
balancer (balɑ̃se), v.a.n. **1.** To balance, to put in equilibrium, to poise, to weigh, to counterbalance, to compensate; *ses vertus balancent ses vices*, his virtues counterbalance his vices; **2.** to sway, to swing, to wave, to rock; **3.** to hesitate; *il accepta sans* ~, he agreed without hesitation; **4.** (slang) to dismiss, to give the sack, to get rid of; **se** ~, v.pr. (*a*) to swing, to sway, to have a swing, to rock, to wave, to oscillate, to swing (on a swing); (*b*) to balance, to be counterbalanced; *les comptes se balancent*, the accounts balance.
balancier (balɑ̃sje), s.m. **1.** Pendulum (of a clock), balance-wheel (of a watch); **2.** coining-press; **3.** (danc.) balancing pole; **4.** (naut.) gimbals; **5.** (mech.) fly, side-lever, beam; **6.** scale-and-weight maker.
balancine (balɑ̃sin), s.f. (naut.) Lift (of a sail).
balançoire (balɑ̃swar), s.f. **1.** Swing, see-saw, sway; **2.** (pop.) flam, chaff, fib, plant, rubbish, nonsense.

balandre, bélandre (balɑ̃dr, belɑ̃dr), s.m. [f. L *palandaria*, Dutch *bijlander*] (naut.) Bilander, a kind of flat-bottomed boat or tender, used on rivers, canals, &c.
balane (balan), s.m. (conch.) Sea-acorn, balanus, acorn-shell.
balanifère (balanifɛr), adj. (bot.) Acorn-bearing.
balayage (balɛjaʒ), s.m. Sweeping.
balayer (balɛje), v.a. [f. *balai*] To sweep, to sweep out, to sweep up, to clear, to clear away, to scour.
balayette (balɛjɛt), s.f. Small broom, hand-broom, carpet-brush.
balayeu-r, -se (balɛjœr), s.m.f. Sweeper, street-sweeper.
balayeuse (balɛjøz), s.f. **1.** Road-sweeper; **2.** flounce.
balayures (balɛjyr), s.f.pl. Sweepings.
balbutie (balbysi), s.f. Stammering.
balbutiement (balbysimɑ̃), s.m. Stammering, stuttering.
balbutier (balbysje), v.n. [f. L *balbutire*] To stammer, to stutter; ~, v.a. to stammer out.
balbuzard (balbyzar), s.m. [f. Engl. *bald buzzard*] (ornith.) Osprey, bald-buzzard.
balcon (balkɔ̃), s.m. [f. It. *balcone*] Balcony; (theatr.) dress circle.
baldaquin (baldakɛ̃), s.m. [f. It. *baldacchino*] Baldachin, tester, canopy.
bale, balle (bal), s.f. (bot.) Glume, husk, chaff.
baleine (balɛn), s.f. [f. L *balaena*] **1.** (zool.) Whale; *blanc de* ~, spermaceti; **2.** whalebone, rib; **3.** (astr.) Cetus.
baleiné, -e (balɛne), adj. Whale-boned.
baleineau (pl. **-x**) (balɛno), s.m. (zool.) Whale-calf.
baleinier (balɛnje), s.m. **1.** Whaler; **2.** whale-bone dealer. ~, adj. Whaling.
baleinière (balɛnjɛr), s.f. Whale-boat, launch.
baleinoptère (balɛnɔptɛr), s.m. (zool.) Balaenopter, rorqual.
balèvre (balɛvr), s.f. [pej. pref. *ba*+*lèvre*] **1.** Underlip; the two lips; **2.** (arch.) jutting of one stone beyond another.
balisage (balizaʒ), s.m. (naut.) Erecting of beacons, buoying; syn. BALISEMENT.
balise[1] (baliz), s.f. [etym. dub.] (naut.) Beacon, buoy, tow-path.
balise[2] (baliz), s.f. (bot.) Canna-seed.
baliser (balize), v.a. (naut.) To put up beacons in; to lay down buoys in, to mark with beacons, to buoy (a channel, &c.).
baliseur (balizœr), s.m. Overseer of towing-paths, beacons, buoys.
balisier (balizje), s.m. (bot.) Canna; syn. CANNA.
baliste (balist), s.f. [f. Gr. *ballein*] Ballista.
balistique (balistik), s.f. Ballistics.
balivage (balivaʒ), s.m. (forestry) Staddling, marking of staddles.
baliveau (pl. **-x**) (balivo), s.m. [f. LL *bayvellus*] Staddle, young tree, scaffold-pole.
baliverne (balivɛrn), s.f. [unkn. orig.] Nonsense, bosh; ~*s que tout cela!*, that 's all stuff.
baliverner (balivɛrne), v.n. To fiddle-faddle, to talk idly.
balkanique (balkanik), adj. s.m.f. Balkan, of the Balkans.
ballade (balad), s.f. [f. LL *ballare*] Ballad, poem, ballade.
ballant, -e (balɑ̃), adj. Swinging, loose, dangling. ~, s.m. Want of steadiness, oscillation, vacillation; (fig.) margin, extra amount, elasticity.
ballast (balast), s.m. [Engl. wd] Ballast.
ballastage (balastaʒ), s.m. Ballasting.
balle (bal), s.f. [OHG. *balla*] **1.** Ball; (fig.) *renvoyer la* ~, to give tit for tat; *prendre la* ~ *au bond*, to take the ball on the rebound; *enfant de la* ~, (fig.) any one following his parent's profession, esp. the theatrical profession; **2.** bullet, ball; *tirer à* ~, to fire ball-cartridges; (fig., of arguments) *faire* ~, to tell, to strike home; **3.** (slang) one franc; face, head; **4.** bale, pack; **5.** chaff, glume; (see BALE.)
baller (balle), (obs.) v.n. To dance.
ballerine (balrin), s.f. Ballet-girl, dancer.
ballet (balɛ), s.m. Ballet; *maître de* ~, ballet-master; *corps de* ~, corps-de-ballet.
ballon (balɔ̃), s.m. [f. *balle*] **1.** Balloon, aerostat; ~ *captif*, captive balloon; ~ *dirigeable*, airship, dirigible; ~ *d'essai*, pilot balloon; test balloon; (fig.) feeler; ~ *sonde*, sounding balloon; **2.** ball, foot-ball; **3.** mountain with a round top; *le* ~ *d'Alsace*, the Alsace Balloon; **4.** (chem.) balloon, glass balloon.
ballonnement (balɔnmɑ̃), s.m. Distension of the abdomen, tympanites; (in cattle) heaves, hoove.
ballonner (balɔne), v.a. To swell, to distend.
ballonnet (balɔnɛ), s.m. Air-bag; small balloon.
ballonnier (balɔnje), s.m. Ball-maker, maker of toy balloons.
ballot (balo), s.m. Bale, pack, bundle. ~, s.m. adj. (slang) Thick-headed (person); idiot; moron, duffer, fathead.
ballote (balɔt), s.f. (bot.) Horehound.
ballotin (balɔtɛ̃), s.m. Small bundle. ~**e**, s.f. (cook.) Sort of meat-pie.
ballottade (balɔtad), s.f. (rid.) Ballottade, horse's leap with all four legs bent.
ballottage (balɔtaʒ), s.m. Balloting, ballot, second ballot; *scrutin de* ~, second balloting. ⚠ 'Ballot', 'balloting', means

'vote', 'voting' = *mise aux voix*; *ballottage* in French implies a first indecisive election; *il y a ballottage* when the number of votes cast on one side do not sufficiently exceed those on the other side or sides; then a second ballot, *un second scrutin*, is necessary.

ballottement (balɔtmɑ̃), s.m. Tossing, shaking.

ballotter (balɔte), v.a. **1.** To toss, to toss about, to knock about; **2.** to ballot between; ~, v.n. to shake about.

balnéaire (balneɛr), adj. [f. L *balneum*] Balneal, bathing; *station* ~, watering-place; *saison* ~, bathing-season.

balnéothérapie (balnɛoterapi), s.f. [f. L *balneum*+Gr. *therapeia*] Balneotherapy.

balourd, -e (balur), adj. s.m.f. [It. *balordo*] Dull, heavy, thick-headed; dunce.

balourdise (balurdiz), s.f. Stupid blunder, doltishness.

balsamier (balzamje), s.m. See BAUMIER.

balsamifère (balzamifɛr), adj. [f. L *balsamum*+*ferre*] (bot.) Balsamiferous.

balsamine (balzamin), s.f. [f. Gr. *balsamon*] (bot.) Garden balsam, *Impatiens balsamina*.

balsamique (balzamik), adj. Balsamic.

balsamite (balzamit), s.f. (bot.) Costmary, alecost, *Pyrethrum tanacetum*.

balthazar (baltazar), s.m. [f. prop. n. in Bible] (colloq.) Regular tuck-in, blow-out.

baluchon (balyʃɔ̃), s.m. Small bundle; personal belongings.

balustrade (balystrad), s.f. Balustrade.

balustre (balystr), s.m. [It. *balaustro*] Baluster.

balustrer (balystre), v.a. To balustrade, to rail in.

balzan, -e (balzɑ̃), adj. [It. *balzano*] *Cheval* ~, white-footed horse.

balzane (balzan), s.f. White foot (of a horse).

bambin, -e (bɑ̃bɛ̃), s.m.f. [f. It. *bambino*] Little boy or girl, brat, chit, kid.

bamboche (bɑ̃bɔʃ), s.f. [f. It. *bamboccio*] **1.** Large puppet; **2.** spree; in this sense, also *bambochade*.

bambocher (bɑ̃bɔʃe), v.n. To go (or be) on the spree.

bambocheu-r, -se (bɑ̃bɔʃœr), adj. s.m.f. Fast fellow or woman, rioter, rake.

bambou (bɑ̃bu), s.m. [Malay wd] (bot.) Bamboo.

bamboula (bɑ̃bula), s.f. Bambula, a drum used by negroes; a negro dance; (fig.) uproarious dance or merry-making.

ban[1] (bɑ̃), s.m. [f. *bannir*] **1.** Ban, proclamation; ~*s de mariage*, banns (pl.); **2.** (feud.) convocation for military service, ban; (fig.) *convoquer le* ~ *et l'arrière-*~, to collect all one's supporters; **3.** ban, fine, order of exile; *être en rupture de* ~, to leave one's assigned place of abode; (fig.) to be out of bounds; *il est mis au* ~ *de l'opinion*, he is condemned by public opinion; he has become an outcast; **4.** round of applause, rhythmical clapping of hands.

ban[2] (bɑ̃), s.m. Ban; *le* ~ *de Croatie*, Ban of Croatia.

banal, -e, (aux), (banal), adj. [f. *ban*] **1.** Banal; common; trivial, commonplace, hackneyed; **2.** (feud.) banal, bannal, of compulsory feudal service; *moulin* ~, bannal mill.

banalement (banalmɑ̃), adv. Tritely, in a commonplace manner.

banaliser (banalize), v.a. To vulgarize, to hackney.

banalité (banalite), s.f. **1.** Commonplace, triviality; **2.** (feud.) compulsory use of a mill, well, bakehouse, kiln, &c. belonging to the lord.

banane (banan), s.f. Banana.

bananier (bananje), s.m. (bot.) Banana-tree.

banat, bannat (bana), s.m. Banate (province in Croatia, Transylvania, &c.).

banc (bɑ̃), s.m. [f. LL *bancus*, Germ. *Bank*] **1.** Bench, form (in schools); *être encore sur les* ~*s*, to be still at school; **2.** bank (of turf); **3.** pew; ~ *d'œuvre*, church-warden's pew; **4.** (naut.) bank, shoal (of fish); ~ *de sable*, sand-bank; ~ *de harengs*, shoal of herrings; ~ *d'huîtres*, oyster-bed; **5.** (techn.) carrier, stand, bench, frame, bed; ~ *d'essai*, test-stand or bench, brake-carrier; **6.** (law) dock, bar, box; **7.** (geol.) layer, stratum, bed.

bancable (bɑ̃kabl), adj. Bankable.

bancaire (bɑ̃kɛr), adj. Bank- . ., banking, of banks.

bancal, -e (bɑ̃kal), adj. [etym. dub.] Bandy-legged. ~, s.m.f. Bandy-legged person; syn. BANCROCHE. ~, s.m. Curved sabre.

banco (bɑ̃ko), adj. invar. [It. wd] (Exch.) Banco (applied to bank money of account, as distinguished from currency).

bancroche (bɑ̃krɔʃ), adj. s.m.f. Bandy-legged, rickety (person); see syn. BANCAL.

bandage (bɑ̃daʒ), s.m. [f. *bande*] **1.** Bandage, truss, bandaging; ~ *herniaire*, truss; **2.** (motor.) tyre, tire; ~ *plein*, solid tyre; ~ *à talons*, flanged or beaded tyre.

bandagiste (bɑ̃daʒist), s.m.f. Bandage-maker, truss-maker.

bande (bɑ̃d), s.f. [f. OHG *binda*] **1.** Band, stripe, strip, slip, streak; ~ *de toile*, band or strip of linen, bandage; ~ *de papier*, slip of paper; ~ *de cuir*, leather strap; ~ *d'un billard*, cushion of a billiard table; ~ *de journal*, newspaper wrapper; ~ *d'un livre*, (narrow) jacket of a book, (by ext.) blurb (because in France the blurb is usually printed on the paper band which is used instead of a jacket); ~ *de gazon*, strip of turf; **2.** bandage; **3.** (arch.) plain moulding; **4.** (herald.) bend; **5.** (naut.) heeling; *donner de la* ~, to heel over; *avoir de la* ~, to have a list; **6.** troop, gang, set, crew, company; ~ *de loups*, pack of wolves; *faire* ~ *à part*, to keep or hold aloof.

bandeau (pl. **-x**) (bãdo), s.m. [f. *bande*] **1.** Head-band, frontlet; **2.** bandage (over the eyes); *mettre un* ~ *à X*, to blindfold X; **3.** (arch.) band, fillet.

bandelette (bãdlɛt), s.f. Bandelet; small band or fillet

bander (bãde), v.a. **1.** To bind up, to bandage; **2.** ~ *les yeux à*, to blindfold; **3.** to bend (a bow); **4.** to tighten, to draw taut; *ressort bandé*, loaded spring.

bandereau (pl. **-x**) (bãdro), s.m. Bugle-sling.

banderille (bãdrij), s.f. [f. Span. wd] Banderilla.

banderole (bãdrɔl), s.f. **1.** Pennant, streamer, flag; **2.** shoulder-belt, sling (of a musket).

bandière (bãdjɛr), s.f. [f. *bannière*] *En front de* ~, in battle array.

bandit (bãdi), s.m. [f. It. *bandito*] Bandit, ruffian, robber.

banditisme (bãditism), s.m. Robbery, crime.

bandoulier (bãdulje), s.m. [f. Span. *bandolero*] **1.** Highwayman; **2.** Pyrenean smuggler.

bandoulière (bãduljɛr), s.f. [f. Span. *bandolera*] (mil.) Bandoleer, cross-belt, shoulder-belt; *en* ~, slung over the shoulder.

banian (banjã), s.m. [Arab. wd] **1.** Banian; **2.** (bot.) banyan.

banlieue (bãljø), s.f. [*ban*+*lieue*] Outskirts, suburbs (pl.).

banne (ban), s.f. [f. L *benna*] **1.** Hamper; **2.** coal-cart; **3.** (mining) corf, corb.

banneret (banrɛ), s.m. [f. *bannière*] Banneret; *seigneur* ~, knight-banneret.

banneton (bantɔ̃), s.m. [f. *banne*] **1.** Bread-basket; **2.** (fish.) creel.

bannette (banɛt), s.f. [f. *banne*] Small hamper or basket.

banni, -e (bani), adj. s.m.f. [f. *bannir*] Banished (person), driven away; exile, outlaw.

bannière (banjɛr), s.f. [f. LL *bandum*] Banner, flag, colours, streamer; *se ranger sous la* ~ *de X*, to take sides with X; (colloq.) *il faut la croix et la* ~ *pour lui parler*, or *pour le décider*, one has no end of trouble to get access to him; talk of a fuss to make him take a decided step, or to make him decide.

bannir (banir), v.a. [f. *ban*] To banish, to exile, to dismiss, to proscribe.

bannissement (banismã), s.m. Banishment, exile.

banque (bãk), s.f. [f. It. *banca*] Banking business, bank, banking-house; *compte en* ~, bank-account; ~ *d'émission*, bank of issue; ~ *de dépôt*, deposit-bank; *billet de* ~, banknote; (gambling) *faire sauter la* ~, to break the bank; *tenir la* ~, to bank, to be banker; *tailler une* ~, to hold and distribute the cards (at *pharaon*, *baccara* and other card-games).

banqueroute (bãkrut), s.f. [f. It. *banca rotta*] Bankruptcy; *faire* ~, to be or to become bankrupt; ~ *frauduleuse*, fraudulent bankruptcy; syn. FAILLITE.

banqueroutier (bãkrutje), s.m. Bankrupt.

banquet (bãkɛ), s.m. [f. It. *banchetto*] Banquet, feast, dinner.

banqueter (bãkte), v.n. To banquet, to feast.

banquette (bãkɛt), s.f. [f. *banc*] Bench; (theatr.) *jouer devant les* ~*s*, to play to empty benches; (fort.) banquette; turf bank.

banqui-er, -ère (bãkje), s.m.f. Banker.

banquise (bãkiz), s.f. Floating ice, ice-berg, ice-floe; ice-pack, pack.

banquiste (bãkist), s.m. Mountebank.

bantam (bãtam), adj. [f. *Bantam*, in Java] Bantam (fowl); (fig.) dwarf; *poids* ~, bantam-weight (boxing competitions).

baobab (baɔbab), s.m. (bot.) Baobab, monkey-bread tree, *Adamsonia digitata*.

baptême (batɛm), s.m. [f. Gr. *baptismos*] Baptism; christening; *nom de* ~, baptismal (or Christian) name.

baptiser (batize), v.a. **1.** To baptize, to christen; **2.** (pop.) to mix water with.

baptismal, -e, (aux) (batismal), adj. Baptismal; *fonts* ~*aux*, baptismal font.

baptistaire (batistɛr), adj. Of baptism.

baptiste (batist), s.m.f. Baptist.

baptistère (batistɛr), s.m. Baptistery.

baquet (bakɛ), s.m. [f. *bac*] Tub, trough, bucket.

baqueter (bakte), v.a. To bale (water out of a tub), to scoop.

baquetures (baktyr), s.f.pl. Drippings of wine.

bar[1] (bar), s.m. [f. Germ. *Barsch*] (ichth.) Bass; (herald.) mullet.

bar[2] (bar), s.m. [Engl. wd] Bar, public-house; set of tumblers, shakers, liqueurs, flagons, &c. for private use.

baragouin (baragwɛ̃), s.m. [etym. dub.] Gibberish, jabber; jargon, lingo, balderdash.

baragouinage (baragwinaʒ), s.m. Gibberish, jabbering.

baragouiner (baragwine), v.a.n. To jabber, to mangle (a language), to speak incorrectly and with difficulty; ~ *un mauvais anglais*, to murder the King's English.

baraque (barak), s.f. [f. LL *baraca*] Barrack hut; booth, stall (in a fair); hovel, hole, wretched house. ⚠ Not to be translated by English 'barracks' which = *caserne*.

baraquement (barakmɑ̃), s.m. **1.** Camping in huts; **2.** temporary wooden lodging or barracks.

baraquer (barake), v.a.n. To hut, to lodge soldiers in huts.

baraterie (baratri), s.f. (naut.) Barratry.

barattage (barataʒ), s.m. Churning.

baratte (barat), s.f. [f. Celt. *barax*] Churn.

baratter (barate), v.a. To churn.

barbacane (barbakan), s.f. [f. Arab. *barbak-khaneh*] (fort.) Barbican; (arch.) weeping-hole, outlet.

barbacole (barbakɔl), s.m. [f. *Barbacola*, schoolmaster in the '*Carnaval*' of Lulli] Pedagogue, pedant.

barbare (barbar), adj. [f. Gr. *barbaros*] **1.** Barbarian; **2.** barbarous, cruel, inhuman; (gram.) incorrect. ~, s.m. Barbarian.

barbarement (barbarmɑ̃), adv. Barbarously.

barbaresque (barbarɛsk), adj. Of Barbary.

barbarie (barbari), s.f. Barbarousness, cruelty, barbarity; barbarism; *les siècles de* ~, the dark ages; *les* ~ *commises par* . . ., the outrages, barbarities, committed by . . .

barbarin, -e (barbarɛ̃), adj. Of Barbary. ~, s.m. (ichth.) Surmullet, red mullet; syn. SURMULET, ROUGET.

barbarisme (barbarism), s.m. (gram.) Barbarism; ex. *il a recouvert la vue*, instead of *il a recouvré la vue*.

barbe[1] (barb), s.f. [f. L *barba*] **1.** Beard; *porter toute la* ~, to wear a full beard; *faire la* ~ *à*, to shave; (fig.) to beard; *se faire la* ~, to shave; *dire quelque chose à la* ~ *de X*, to say something to X's face; to beard X; ~ *de bouc*, or *bouc*, goatee; *du côté de la* ~ *est la toute-puissance*, man rules the roost; *vieille* ~, old fogy; **2.** barb (of feathers, &c.); awn (of barley, wheat, &c.); **3.** fin (of fish); **4.** (techn.) rough edge of castings or metal work; **5.** (slang) *la* ~ *!*, (*a*) shut up !, (*b*) what a bother !

barbe[2] (barb), adj. s.m. Barb, Barbary horse.

barbeau (pl. **-x**) (barbo), s.m. [f. L *barbellus*] **1.** (ichth.) Barbel; **2.** (bot.) bluebottle, blue centaury; *bleu* ~, light greenish-blue.

barbe-de-capucin (barb də kapysɛ̃), s.f. (bot.) Wild chicory.

barbelé, -e (barbəle), adj. Barbed; spiked.

barber (barbe), v.a. (slang) To bore; *oh c'est barbant*, what a bore !, how tedious !, how dull !

barbet, -te (barbɛ), adj. s.m. [etym dub.] Barbet (dog), water-spaniel, poodle; *être crotté comme un* ~, to be all over dirt or mud.

barbette (barbɛt), s.f. **1.** Wimple; **2.** (mil.) barbette.

barbeyer (barbɛje), v.n. (naut.) To shiver (as a sail in the wind).

barbiche (barbiʃ), s.f. [f. *barbe*] Billy-goat beard, goatee.

barbichon, barbichet (barbiʃɔ̃, barbiʃɛ), s.m. **1.** Barbet pup, water-spaniel pup; **2.** goatee.

barbier (barbje), s.m. Barber.

barbifier (barbifje), v.a. (fam.) To shave.

barbille (barbij), s.f. Burr, rough edge.

barbillon (barbijɔ̃), s.m. **1.** Young barbel; **2.** gill, wattle (of a cock); **3.** barbule, barbel (of certain fishes); **4.** barb (of an arrow or fish-hook); **5.** (vet.) barbles.

barbiton, barbitos (barbitɔ̃, barbitos), s.m. [Gr. wd] (mus.) Barbiton, lyre.

barbon (barbɔ̃), s.m. Graybeard, dotard, fogy.

barbotage (barbɔtaʒ), s.m. **1.** Paddling, dabbling; **2.** (agric.) mash; **3.** (motor.) splashing; *graissage par* ~, splash lubrication; **4.** (slang) 'pinching', scrounging.

barboter (barbɔte), v.n. [onom.] To dabble, to paddle, to wade, to splash about; to make a mess; (fig.) to mumble, to stutter, to make mistakes; ~, v.a.n. (slang) to pinch, to scrounge, to nail, to bone, to snaffle, to pouch.

barboteuse (barbɔtøz), s.f. **1.** Child's garment, 'rompers'; **2.** washing apparatus.

barbotière (barbɔtjɛr), s.f. Duck-pond.

barbotine (barbɔtin), s.f. Paste for pottery.

barbouillage, barbouilles (barbujaʒ, barbuj), s.m. **1.** Daubing, coarse painting; daub; **2.** scrawl, scribbling.

barbouiller (barbuje), v.a. **1.** To daub, to besmear; **2.** to scribble; **3.** to trouble; *avoir le cœur barbouillé*, to be sick, or seasick.

barbouilleu-r, -se (barbujœr), s.m.f. **1.** Dauber, sorry painter; **2.** scribbler, sorry author, driveller.

barbu, -e (barby), adj. Bearded; (bot.) barbate, bearded; *blé* ~, bearded wheat; *comète* ~*e*, bearded comet.

barbue (barby), s.f. (ichth.) Brill.

barcarolle (barkarɔl), s.f. [f. It. *barca*] (mus.) Barcarolle.

barcelonnette (barslɔnɛt) s.f. See BERCELONNETTE.

bard, bar (bar), s.m. [f. Germ. *Bahre*] Stretcher; syn. BAYART.

barda (barda), s.m. [f. Arab. *bardah* = luggage] (slang) **1.** Soldier's entire kit; **2.** luggage, parcels, burden.

bardane (bardan), s.f. (bot.) Burdock.

barde[1] (bard), s.m. [f. Celt. *bard*] Bard.

barde[2] (bard), s.f. [f. LL *barda*] **1.** Bard, armour for a horse; **2.** (cook.) bard (very thin slice of bacon, used to cover a fowl or a joint before roasting it).

bardé, -e (barde), p. adj. Barded, covered, protected; covered with a very thin slice of bacon, barded.

bardeau (pl. **-x**) (bardo), s.m. (roof.) Shingle; (bot.) wayfaring-tree; (print.) case for spare types.

barder (barde), v.a. **1.** To bard, to caparison; **2.** (cook.) to lard, to cover with bards; **3.** (slang) to become stormy, to rain (blows, &c.); (fig.) *ça va ~*, it's getting stormy; there's going to be a row; *oh! çà barde!*, what a set-to!; things are humming now!

bardot (bardo), s.m. Hinny (mule), drudge.

barège (barɛʒ), s.m. [f. *Barèges*, in the Pyrenees] A thin material, barège.

barême (barɛm), s.m. [f. *François Barême*, 1640–1703] Ready reckoner.

baréter, v.n. See syn. BARRIR.

barge (barʒ), s.f. [f. LL *barga*] **1.** Barge; **2.** (ornith.) godwit, *Limosa*.

barguignage (barginaʒ), s.m. Haggling; hesitating, wavering.

barguigner (bargiɲe), v.n. [f. LL *barcaniare*] To hesitate, to shilly-shally, to waver; to haggle; *il n'a pas barguigné*, he made no bones about it.

barigoule (barigul), s.f. [Provenç. wd] (cook.) *Artichauts à la ~*, artichokes stuffed and fried in oil.

baril (bari), s.m. **1.** Barrel, cask, keg; **2.** (mil.) fire-barrel.

barillage (barijaʒ), Barrel-making; barrel-filling.

barillet (barijɛ), s.m. **1.** Small barrel; **2.** (horol.) barrel; **3.** (anat.) middle-ear; **4.** cylinder of a revolver.

bariolage (barjɔlaʒ), s.m. Medley, motley.

bariolé, -e (barjɔle), p. adj. Motley, many-coloured, checkered; syn. BIGARRÉ.

barioler (barjɔle), v.a. To daub with a motley mixture of colours, to variegate.

barium (barjɔm), s.m. (chem.) Barium.

barlong, -ue (barlɔ̃), adj. [f. *bar+long*] Oblong; lopsided.

barlotière (barlɔtjɛr), s.f. Cross bar (of window-frames).

barnabite (barnabit), s.m. Barnabite.

barnache (barnaʃ) s.f. See syn. BERNACHE.

barne (barn), s.f. Salt-works.

baromètre (barɔmɛtr), s.m. [f. Gr. *baros +metron*] Barometer.

barométrique (barɔmetrik), adj. Barometric, barometrical.

barométriquement (barɔmetrikmɑ̃), adv. Barometrically.

barométrographe (barɔmetrɔgraf), s.m. Barometrograph.

baron (barɔ̃), s.m. [orig. dub.] **1.** Baron; **2.** (cook.) *~ d'agneau*, joint of mutton.

baronnage (barɔnaʒ), s.m. Baronage.

baronne (barɔn), s.f. Baroness.

baronnial, -e, (aux) (barɔnjal), adj. Baronial.

baronnie (barɔni), s.f. Barony.

baroque (barɔk), adj. [f. Span. *barrueco*] Queer-looking, whimsical, baroque.

baroscope (barɔskɔp), s.m. [f. Gr. *baros+skopein*] (phys.) Baroscope.

barque (bark), s.f. [f. It. *barca*] (naut.) Boat, barge, (fig.) bark; *bien conduire sa ~*, to manage one's affairs well; *la ~ de Caron*, Charon's bark.

barquerolle (barkrɔl), s.f. Small canal-boat, barge.

barquette (barkɛt), s.f. **1.** Small boat; **2.** boat-shaped piece of pastry.

barrage (baraʒ), s.m. [f. *barre*] Barrier, bar, barrage, dam, weir.

barre (bar), s.f. [Celt. orig.] **1.** Bar; *~ de fer*, iron bar; (fig.) inflexible person; *~ d'appui*, hand-rail; *or en ~*, bar gold; (fig.) as good as hard cash; **2.** line, stroke; **3.** (law) bar; *se présenter à la ~ du tribunal*, to appear at the bar of the court; **4.** (herald.) bar; **5.** (naut.) bar, handspike, lever; helm, tiller; *~ au vent!*, weather the helm!; *~ sous le vent!*, helm alee, down with the helm!; *homme de ~*, steersman; *~ (de la Seine* or *mascaret*), bore; *~ du Nil, du Niger*, the bar of the Nile, of the Niger; **6.** *~s*, prisoner's base (a game); *ne faire que toucher ~s*, to call at a place without stopping; **7.** *avoir ~ sur X*, to have the advantage of X; **8.** *~s*, bars (of a horse's mouth); **9.** (motor. techn.) *~ d'accouplement de la direction*, coupling-rod of steering gear; *~ des freins*, brake-shaft; **10.** (gymn.) *~s parallèles*, parallel bars.

barré, -e (bare), p. adj. **1.** Barred; **2.** struck out, crossed out; *trois mots ~s*, three words struck out; *chèque ~*, crossed cheque; (herald.) barred.

barreau (pl. **-x**) (baro), s.m. [f. *barre*] **1.** Small bar; **2.** the Bar; *se destiner au ~*, to intend to be a barrister; *l'éloquence du ~*, the eloquence of the Bar.

barréoles (bareɔl), s.f. pl. [f. *barre*] (gymn.) Parallel bars; syn. BARRES PARALLÈLES.

barrer (bare), v.a. To bar, to fasten, to thwart, to cut off, to intercept, to obstruct; to cross out, to strike out; (herald.) to add a bar to; (naut.) to steer; **se ~**, v.pr. (slang) to make off, to cut and run, to leg it.

barrette, barette (barɛt), s.f. [f. It. *berretta*] **1.** Biretta; **2.** jewelled safety-pin, or bar; fancy pin or brooch.

barreur (barœr), s.m. (naut.) Steersman, coxswain.

barricade (barikad), s.f. Barricade.

barricader (barikade), v.a. To barricade; **se** ~ v.pr. to barricade oneself.

barrière (barjɛr), s.f. [f. *barre*] Barrier, gate, town-gate, town toll-house; (fig.) hindrance, obstacle, limitation.

barrique (barik), s.f. [f. Provenç. *barrica*] Barrel, cask.

barrir (barir), v.n. To roar, to trumpet (said of the elephant); syn. BARÉTER.

barrissement, barrit (barismɑ̃, bari), s.m. [f. L *barritus*] Trumpeting, roaring of the elephant.

barroter (barɔte), v.a. To load (a vessel) up to the cross-bars, or beams.

bartavelle (bartavɛl), s.f. (ornith.) Red partridge, Guernsey partridge.

baryte (barit), s.f. [f. Gr. *barus*] (chem.) Baryta.

baryton (baritɔ̃), s.m. [f. Gr. *barutonos*] **1.** Barytone; hence (colloq. pej.) **barytoner** (v.n.), to sing or talk in a rich, mellow voice; **2.** (Gr. gram.) barytone.

baryum (barjɔm), s.m. [f. Gr. *barus*] (chem.) Barium.

bas, -se (bɑ), adj. [f. L *bassus*] **1.** Low, lower, not acute, not noisy, not high, shallow; *marée ~se*, low tide; *les ~ côtés d'une église*, the aisles of a church; *le jour est ~*, the day is drawing to a close; *au ~ mot*, at the least; *à ~se température*, at a low temperature; *~ses terres*, lowlands; *à ~ prix*, cheap; *avoir la vue ~se*, to be short-sighted; *à voix ~se*, in a whisper; **2.** (fig.) base, low, vile, mean, abject; *sentiments ~*, low thoughts; *style ~*, low style; *faire main ~se sur*, to steal, to seize violently.

bas[1] (bɑ), s.m. Bottom, lower part; *il y a des hauts et des ~ dans la vie*, there are ups and downs in life; *au ~ de la liste*, at the bottom of the list.

bas[2] (bɑ), s.m. Stocking; *~ bleu*, bluestocking, priggish lady, female pedant; (fig.) *~ de laine*, nest-egg.

bas (bɑ), adv. Low; *être bien ~*, to be very ill, very low; *parler ~*, to speak low; *couler ~*, to sink; *mettre ~ les armes*, to lay down one's arms, to yield; *mettre chapeau ~*, to take off one's hat; *je venais, chapeau ~*, I was coming hat in hand; *chapeau ~!*, hats off; *mettre ~*, to bring forth (of animals), to litter, to cub, to whelp, to foal, to calve, to kitten, to pig, to farrow, to pup, &c.; *à ~*, down, down from; off; *mettre à ~*, to pull, or throw down; *à ~!*, down with; *en ~*, below, down below; downwards; *traiter X de haut en ~*, to treat X with contemptuous arrogance; to sit upon X; *en ~ de*, at the bottom of, at the foot of; *ici-~*, here below, in this lower world; *là-~*, yonder, down yonder.

basalte (bazalt), s.m. Basalt.

basaltique (bazaltik), adj. Basaltic.

basane (bazan), s.f. [f. Span. *badana*] Basil, tanned sheep-skin.

basané, -e (bazane), p. adj. Sunburnt, tanned.

basaner (bazane), v.a. To tan.

bascule (baskyl), s.f. [f. *battre+cul*] **1.** Poise, sweep, see-saw, sway; *cheval à ~*, rocking-horse; *chaise à ~*, rocking-chair; *levier à ~*, trip lever; **2.** weighing-machine.

basculer (baskyle), v.n.a. To sway up and down, to tip up, to fall; *camion à benne basculante*, tip, tipping lorry.

bas-dessus (bɑdəsy), (obs.) s.m. Low treble voice, mezzo-soprano; syn. MEZZO-SOPRANO.

base (bɑz), s.f. [f. Gr. *basis*] Base, foundation, bottom; (fig.) basis, fundamental principle, groundwork; (chem., geom., math.) base.

baselle (bɑzɛl), s.f. (bot.) Basella, Malabar nightshade.

baser (bɑze), v.a. To base, to ground, to found; **se** ~, v.pr. **1.** to be based, grounded, or founded; **2.** to take one's stand.

bas-fond (bɑfɔ̃), s.m. Bottom, low alluvial soil; dale, dell; (naut.) shallow water.

basicité (bɑzisite), s.f. (chem.) Basicity.

basilic (bazilik), s.m. **1.** [f. Gr. *basilikos*] (bot.) Sweet-basil; **2.** [Gr. *basiliskos*] (zool.) basilisk; (fig.) *elle le regarde avec des yeux de ~*, she looks at him as if she could kill him; she looks daggers at him.

basilique (bazilik), s.f. [f. Gr. *basilikos*] Basilica. ~, adj. *Veine ~*, basilic vein.

basin (bazɛ̃), s.m. [f. *bombasin*] Dimity.

basique (bazik), adj. (chem.) Basic.

bas-latin (bɑlatɛ̃), s.m. Low Latin.

bas-mât (bɑmɑ), s.m. (naut.) Lower mast.

basoche (bazɔʃ), s.f. [f. L *basilica*] Basoche (corporation of lawyers).

basochien, -ne (bazɔʃjɛ̃), adj. s.m.f. (Member) of the basoche.

basque[1] (bask), adj. s.m.f. (Native) of the Basque country; *tambour de ~*, tambourine.

basque[2] (bask), s.f. [etym. dub.] Skirt (of a coat), tail or skirt (of a jacket), flap; *il est toujours pendu à ses ~s*, he is always at his (or her) heels; he is tied to her apron-strings.

basquine (baskın), (obs.) s.f. Basquine (a sort of outer petticoat).

bas-relief (bɑrəljɛf), s.m. (sculpt.) Low relief, bas-relief, basso-relievo.

basse (bɑs), s.f. **1.** Bass, bass-voice, bass-viol, bass-viol-player; **2.** (naut.) reef.

basse-contre (bɑskɔ̃tr), s.f. (pl. *basses-contre*) (mus.) The lowest bass voice.

basse-cour (bɑs-kur), s.f. (pl. *basses-cours*) Poultry-yard, farm-yard.

basse-couri-er, -ère (bɑskurje), s.m.f. Farm-servant.

basse-fosse (basfos), s.f. (pl. *basses-fosses*) Dungeon; *cul de* ~, deepest dungeon.
bassement (basmɑ̃), adv. Basely, meanly, sordidly, vulgarly.
bassesse (basɛs), s.f. **1.** Lowness, baseness, meanness, vulgarity; **2.** mean action, base action, servility.
basset (basɛ), s.m. **1.** Basset (dog), dachshund; (fig.) bandy-legged man; **2.** (mus.) *cor de* ~, basset-horn.
basse-taille (bastaj), s.f. Bass-voice, bass-singer.
bassette (basɛt), s.f. Basset (card-game).
bassin (basɛ̃), s.m. [f. Celt. *bac*] **1.** Basin; pool; port; collection-plate; (colloq.) *cracher au* ~, to fork out; **2.** (geog.) the land drained by a river; **3.** (anat.) pelvis; **4.** bed-pan; **5.** (naut.) dock; ~ *de radoub*, graving dock; ~ *d'échouage*, dry-dock.
bassinage (basinaʒ), s.m. **1.** Bathing, fomenting; **2.** warming (of a bed).
bassine (basin), s.f. Large pan, basin, copper pan.
bassinée (basine), s.f. Panful.
bassiner (basine), v.a. **1.** To foment, to bathe; **2.** to warm (a bed); **3.** (slang) to bore.
bassinet (basinɛ), s.m. **1.** Pan (of a flint-lock gun); **2.** (armoury) steel head-piece; **3.** (anat.) calix (of kidney); **4.** (bot.) creeping crow-foot; calyx.
bassinoire (basinwar), s.f. **1.** Warming pan; **2.** (slang) boring discourse or action.
bassiste, bassier (basist, basje), s.m. Bass-viol player.
basson (basɔ̃), s.m. [f. It. *bassone*] Bassoon, bassoon-player.
bassorine (basorin), s.f. [f. *Bassorah*] (chem.) Bassorine.
baste, bast (bast), interj. [f. It. *basta*] Pooh !, pshaw !, nonsense !, let it be so !
baste (bast), s.m. (at cards) Basto (the ace of clubs in several games); ~, s.f. **1.** vintage vat; **2.** basket of a pack-horse or donkey.
basterne (bastɛrn), s.f. (obs.) [f. L *basterna*] Bastern (cart drawn by oxen; litter carried by mules).
bastide (bastid), s.f. [Provenç. wd] **1.** Small country-house; **2.** (obs.) blockhouse.
bastille (bastij), s.f. [f. OF *bastir*] Fortress; prison; bastille.
bastillé, -e (bastije), adj. (herald.) Having inverted crenels.
bastin (bastɛ̃), s.m. (naut.) Coir-rope.
bastingage (bastɛ̃gaʒ), s.m. (naut.) Netting, hand-rail, bulwark netting, hammock nettings; ~ *de combat*, top-arming mantelet (screen protecting gunners).
bastingue (bastɛ̃g), s.f. (naut.) Waist-cloth.
bastinguer (bastɛ̃ge), v.a. (naut.) To barricade, to rig the boarding netting.
bastion (bastjɔ̃), s.m. [f. It. *bastione*] Bastion.
bastionner (bastjone), v.a. To furnish with bastions.
bastonnade (bastonad), s.f. [f. OF *baston*] Bastonade, bastinado, cudgelling.
bastringue (bastrɛ̃g), s.f. [unkn. orig.] **1.** Low-class public ball; uproar, noisy rejoicings; **2.** (mech.) spokeshave.
bas-ventre (bavɑ̃tr), s.m. Lower belly, abdomen.
bat (bat), s.m. **1.** Tail (of a fish); **2.** cricket-bat. ⚠ Not 'bat' = *chauve-souris*.
bât (bɑ), s.m. [f. Gr. *bastazein*] Pack-saddle; *cheval de* ~, pack-horse, bât-horse; *c'est là que le* ~ *le blesse*, that's where the shoe pinches.
bataclan (bataklɑ̃), s.m. [onom.] Kit, paraphernalia, any collection of things; set of tools; *tout le* ~, the whole bag of tricks, the whole caboodle.
bataille (bataj), s.f. [f. LL *battualia*] Battle, fight, engagement; *livrer* ~, to give battle; *cheval de* ~, charger; (fig.) favourite argument; *champ de* ~, battle-field; *ranger en* ~, to draw up (an army) in battle array.
batailler (bataje), v.n. To fight, to give battle, to struggle.
batailleu-r, -se (batajœr), adj. Fighting, disputatious, pugnacious, quarrelsome.
bataillon (batajɔ̃), s.m. **1.** (mil.) Battalion; ~ *carré*, hollow square; *chef de* ~, major; **2.** troop, gang, regiment, flight (of birds).
bâtard, -e (batar), adj. s.m.f. [f. OF *bastard*, of Gallic origin] **1.** Bastard; mongrel (of animals); **2.** degenerate; **3.** intermediate; *porte* ~*e*, house-door of moderate size; *écriture* ~*e*, slanting round hand.
batardeau (pl. **-x**) (batardo), s.m. Embankment, coffer-dam; (fort.) batardeau.
bâtardise (batardiz), s.f. Bastardy.
batavique (batavik), adj. *Larmes* ~*s*, Prince Rupert's drops.
batayole (batajɔl), s.f. (naut.) Stanchion.
bâté, -e (bate), part. adj. Saddled; *âne* ~, stupid donkey; stupid obstinate fellow.
bateau (pl. **-x**) (bato), s.m. [f. Celt. *bat*] **1.** Boat; **2.** any boat-shaped object; **3.** (slang) deception, trick; *monter un* ~ (*à*), to play a trick (on), to 'rag', to pull the leg (of); *être du dernier* ~, to be in the latest fashion.
batelage (batəlaʒ), s.m. **1.** Boating, boatman's fare, conveyance by boat; **2.** juggling.
batelée (batle), s.f. Boat-load.
bateler (batle), v.a. To boat; ~, v.n. to juggle.
batelet (batlɛ), s.m. Small boat.
bateleu-r, -se (batlœr), s.m.f. [f. LL *bastellus*] Juggler, conjuror, buffoon, mountebank.

bateli-er, -ère (batlje), s.m.f. Boatman, boatwoman. ~, adj. Pertaining to boating.
batellerie (batɛlri), s.f. Boating trade; inland navigation; river-boats.
bâter (bɑte), v.a. To put a pack-saddle on.
bat-flanc (baflɑ̃), s.m. invar. Horse-box partition.
bathymétrie (batimetri), s.f. [f. Gr. *bathus+metron*] Bathymetry, sounding of depths, depth-measurement.
bâti (bɑti), s.m. [f. *bâtir*] **1.** (build.) Stud-work, frame, frame-work; **2.** (sewing) basting; *fils de* ~, basting threads; **3.** (motor., aeron.) frame.
bâtière (bɑtjɛr), s.f. [f. *bât*] Pack-saddle roof.
batifolage (batifɔlaʒ), s.m. Frolicking, rollicking, romping.
batifoler (batifɔle), v.n. [f. It. *battifolle*] To frolic, to romp, to make merry, to skylark.
bâtiment (bɑtimɑ̃), s.m. **1.** Building, edifice; **2.** building trade; **3.** (naut.) ship, vessel; ~ *de commerce*, merchant ship.
bâtir (bɑtir), v.a. [f. LL *bastire*] **1.** To build, to construct, to erect, to raise; ~ *sur le sable*, to build on sand; **2.** (dressm.) to tack, to baste.
bâtisse (bɑtis), s.f. Masonry of a building; building.
bâtisseu-r, -se (bɑtisœr), s.m. Builder. ~, adj. Given to building.
batiste (batist), s.f. [f. *Baptiste*, inventor] Cambric.
bâton (bɑtɔ̃), s.m. [f. LL *basto*] Stick, staff, cane, baton, rod, wand; (herald.) baton; (fig.) *mettre des* ~*s dans les roues*, to put a spoke in the wheel; *à* ~*s rompus*, desultorily, off and on; ~ *de vieillesse*, prop of old age; *tours de* ~, sly pickings, tricks; ~ *de maréchal*, marshal's baton or truncheon; (math.) ~*s de Napier*, Napier's rods.
bâtonnat (bɑtɔna), s.m. Presidency of the corporation of barristers.
bâtonner (bɑtɔne), v.a. **1.** To cudgel, to beat with a stick; **2.** (rare) to strike out, to cross out.
bâtonnet (bɑtɔnɛ), s.m. Small stick; (pl.) cylindrial infusoria.
bâtonnier (bɑtɔnje), s.m. President of the corporation of barristers.
batracien (batrasjɛ̃), s.m. [f. Gr. *batrakhos*] (zool.) Batrachian (pl. batrachia).
battage (bataʒ), s.m. **battaison** (batɛzɔ̃), s.f. Threshing (of corn), beating (of cloth); churning (of butter); (slang) shamming, bluff, humbug.
battant (batɑ̃), s.m. [f. *battre*] **1.** Clapper (of a bell); **2.** leaf (of a door); *porte à deux* ~*s*, double door; *il nous faut du*~, we must have a reserve (of cash, of orders, of time, of stock-in-trade) to draw upon in case of emergency; **3.** (naut.) fly of a flag (breadth from staff to end). ~, part. adj. Beating, fighting; (fig.) *tambour* ~, pressing hard, without delay or hesitation; *pluie* ~*e*, pelting rain; *tout* ~ *neuf*, brand new.
batte (bat), s.f. **1.** Beater; **2.** wooden sword (of Harlequin); bat; churn-staff; mallet.
battée (bate), s.f. Part of the jamb against which the door strikes when closing.
battellement (batɛlmɑ̃), s.m. Eaves.
battement (batmɑ̃), s.m. Clapping (of hands); flapping (of wings), beating, throb, throbbing, palpitation; beating, oscillation (of a pendulum); (mus.) shake, trill; (danc.) battement; (cards) shuffling.
batterie (batri), s.f. **1.** Fight, row; **2.** (artill.) battery; *mettre les pièces en* ~, to place ordnance in battery; (fig.) *dresser ses* ~*s*, to prepare one's means of action; **3.** (mus.) the percussive instruments; **4.** (electr.) battery; **5.** (cook.) ~ *de cuisine*, kitchen utensils.
batteu-r, -se (batœr), s.m.f. Thresher, beater; ~ *d'or*, gold-beater; ~ *d'estrade*; rambler, tramp; ~ *d'œufs*, egg-whisk.
batteuse (batøz), s.f. Threshing-machine, thresher.
battitures (batityr), s.f.pl. [f. *battre*] Scales that fall from hot iron when forged; protoxide of iron.
battoir (batwar), s.m. Beater, bat, beetle; (pop.) flipper, beefy hand.
battologie (batɔlɔʒi), s.f. [f. *Battos*, King of Cyrene] Battology, tautology.
battre (batr) v.a.n. [f. L *battuere*] **1.** To beat, to strike, to hammer, to thrash, to belabour, to cane, to cudgel, to whip; ~ *les buissons*, to beat about the bush; ~ *le tambour*, to beat the drum; ~ *le rappel*, to call to arms; (fig.) to gather; to secure the services of people; to enlist; ~ *des œufs*, to beat (or beat up) eggs, to whisk eggs; ~ *le fer pendant qu'il est chaud*, to strike while the iron is hot; to make hay while the sun shines; **2.** to beat, to defeat; **3.** ~ *monnaie*, to coin money; **4.** (cards) to shuffle; **5.** (fig.) ~ *le pavé*, to run about the streets; ~ *la campagne*, to ramble over the country; (fig.) to rave; to ramble; to wander in discourse; ~ *en brèche*, to batter down, to ruin, to nonplus; ~ *à plate(s) couture(s)*, to beat hollow; ~ *en retraite*, to beat a retreat, to give way, to yield; ~ *des mains*, to clap the hands, to applaud; ~ *des ailes*, to flap the wings; *ne* ~ *que d'une aile*, to be almost done up; ~ *un record*, to beat a record; **se** ~, v.pr. to fight; to beat oneself.
battu, -e (baty), part. adj. Beaten,

thrashed, battered; *les chemins ~s*, the beaten track; *terre ~e*, hardened, beaten soil; *avoir les yeux ~s*, to look tired about the eyes; *les ~s payent l'amende*, the losers pay.

battue (baty), s.f. (sport.) Battue.

batture (batyr), s.f. **1.** Gold lacquer; **2.** (naut.) reef.

bau (pl. -x) (bo), s.m. [f. Germ. *balken*] (naut.) Beam.

baudet (bodɛ), s.m. [OF *baud*] **1.** Ass, donkey, jackass; (fig.) stupid, obstinate person; **2.** sawyer's trestle.

baudrier (bodrije), s.m. [OF *baudré*] Baldrick, cross-belt, shoulder-belt.

baudroie (bodrwɑ), s.f. (ichth.) Angler, sea-devil, *Lophius piscatorius*.

baudruche (bodryʃ), s.f. [etym. dub.] Goldbeater's skin.

bauge (boʒ), s.f. [f. LL *baugium*] **1.** Lair; (fig.) miserable, dirty bed or house; **2.** mortar of loam and chopped straw.

baugue, bauque (bog, bok), s.f. [f. LL *balcha*] Sea-weed, grass-wrack.

baume (bom), s.m. [f. Gr. *balsamon*] Balsam, balm; (fig.) balm.

baumier (bomje), s.m. (bot.) Balsam-tree, amyris.

bauquière (bokjɛr), s.f. [f. *bau*] (naut.) Clamp, sea-craft.

bauxite (boxit), s.f. [f. *Les Baux*, southern France] Bauxite, alumina and iron ore.

bavard, -e (bavar), adj. Talkative, loquacious. ~, s.m.f. Prater, gossip, chatterbox.

bavardage (bavardaʒ), s.m. Idle talk, gossip, small talk, prating.

bavarder (bavarde), v.n. [f. *bave*] To chatter, to prate, to gossip; to tell tales.

bavarois, -e (bavarwɑ), adj. s.m.f. Bavarian. ~, s.m. (cook.) bavarois (a sweet; see BAVAROISE).

bavaroise (bavarwaz), s.f. (cook.) Bavaroise, bavarois (a sweet, usually a custard, flavoured with liqueur or chocolate or coffee, to which some whipped cream has been added; the mixture is poured into a mould and allowed to set).

bave (bav), s.f. [onom.] Drivel, saliva spittle; slobber, foam, slime; (fig.) heinous, calumnious discourse.

baver (bave), v.n. To drivel, to slobber, to foam; (fig.) to beslaver; (slang) *il en bave!*, (*a*) he is completely flabbergasted!; (*b*) he is simply mad with rage, he is foaming at the mouth.

bavette (bavɛt), s.f. Bib; (fig.) *tailler une ~*, to have a chat.

baveu-x, -se (bavø), adj. Drivelling, slobbering, slavering; moist (said of an omelette); (print.) smudgy.

bavocher (bavɔʃe), v.n. To print indistinctly, to make blurred lines.

bavochure (bavɔʃyr), s.f. Blur.

bavolet (bavɔlɛ), s.m. [*bas+volet*] Cap (of peasant woman).

bavure (bavyr), s.f. [f. *baver*] (metall.) Seam; (print. drawing) blur.

bayadère (bajadɛr), s.f. [f. Port. *bailadeira*] Bayadere (Hindu dancing girl).

bayart (bajar), s.m. See syn. BARD.

bayer (bɛje), v.n. [f. OF *béer*] To gape, stand gaping; ~ *aux corneilles*, to stand gaping.

bazar (bɑzar), s.m. [Pers. wd] Bazaar; (jest.) hovel, blessed place; (slang) any collection of things; *et tout le ~!*, and the whole bally show!

bazarder (bazarde), v.a. (pop.) To sell off, to dispose of.

bdelle (bdɛl), s.f. (bot.) Bdellium.

béant, -e (beɑ̃), adj. [f. OF *béer*] Gaping, open-mouthed, open, yawning; *gouffre ~*, yawning abyss.

béarnais, -e (bearnɛ), adj. s.m.f. Bearnese; *le B~*, Henri IV, King of France.

béat, -e (bea), adj. s.m.f. [L *beatus*] Sanctimonious, blissful, saint, quiet (person).

béatement (beatmɑ̃), adv. Peacefully, blissfully, sanctimoniously.

béatification (beatifika'sjɔ̃), s.f. Beatification.

béatifier (beatifje), v.a. To beatify.

béatifique (beatifik), adj. Beatific.

béatilles (beatij), s.f.pl. [f. L *beatus*] Tit-bits, dainties.

béatitude (beatityd), s.f. [f. L *beatitudo*] Beatitude, blessedness, bliss; *les neufs ~s*, the nine beatitudes.

beau (**bel** before a vowel), fem. **belle**, pl. **beaux** (bo, bɛl), adj. [f. L *bellus*] Beautiful, handsome, fair; (poet.) beauteous; fine, noble, grand, lofty, exalted; great, considerable; *il y a ~ temps que*, it seems an age since; *il m'a fait une belle peur!*, he has frightened me out of my wits!; *les beaux-arts*, the fine arts; *les belles-lettres*, literature, belles-lettres; *une belle occasion*, a favourable opportunity; *avoir ~ jeu*, to have good cards; (fig.) to have a good chance, a good opportunity; *une belle quantité de*, a large quantity of; *me voilà dans un bel état!*, here am I in a nice mess!; *je suis dans de ~x draps!*, I am in a pretty pickle!; *il l'a échappée belle*, he had a narrow escape; *vous me la baillez belle!*, a pretty tale you are telling me!; *j'en entends de belles sur votre compte!*, I hear fine tales about you!; *mourir de sa belle mort*, to die a natural death; *il recommence de plus belle*, he begins again worse than ever; *de plus en plus ~*, better and better, worse and worse; *se montrer ~ joueur*, to be a good loser, a true sportsman; ~ *parleur*, affected talker; *tout cela est bel et bon mais*, that's all very fine, but; *un* ~ *jour*, one fine day; *une belle fortune*, a handsome fortune; *un* ~ *cadeau*, a handsome present; *le* ~ *sexe*, the fair sex; *ma belle*, my fair one; *coucher à la belle étoile*, to sleep out of doors. ~, adv. *Il va faire* ~, it's going to be fine; *a* ~ *mentir qui vient de loin*, a traveller may lie with impunity; *tout nouveau, tout* ~, everything new is nice; *il a* ~ *dire*, it's no use for him to talk; *il a* ~ *faire*, he tries in vain; *voir tout en* ~, to see everything through rose-coloured spectacles; *il ferait* ~ *voir que*, it would be a nice thing to see; *il ferait* ~ *voir*, it would be a strange thing; *tout* ~ *!* gently, softly; keep your hair on!

beau (bo), s.m. **1.** Beauty, the beautiful; the best; *le* ~ *de l'affaire*, the beauty of it; the cream of the joke; *quand on achète il faut prendre du* ~, when you buy, choose the best; *le goût du* ~, the love of (or taste for) what is beautiful (or beauty); *faire le* ~, to sit up and beg (as a dog); *le baromètre est à* ~ *fixe*, the barometer stands at set fair; **2.** fop, coxcomb, beau. ⚠ Not 'lover', 'sweetheart', as in English: 'He is her beau', = *c'est son galant*.

beauceron, -ne (bosrɔ̃), adj. s.m.f. (Native) of Beauce.

beaucoup (boku), adv. [*beau*+*coup*] A good deal, a great deal, many, a great many, a good many; much, very much; highly, considerably; *à* ~ *près*, by far, by a great deal; *de* ~, by much, by far. ~, pron. Many people; ~ *l'ont essayé mais peu ont réussi*, many have tried but only a few succeeded.

beau-fils (bofis), s.m. (pl. *beaux-fils*) **1.** Son-in-law (obs.); **2.** stepson.

beau-frère (bofrɛr), s.m. (pl. *beaux-frères*) Brother-in-law.

beau-père (bopɛr), s.m. (pl. *beaux-pères*). **1.** Father-in-law; **2.** stepfather.

beaupré (bopre), s.m. [f. Engl. *bowsprit*] (naut.) Bowsprit.

beauté (bote), s.f. Beauty, handsomeness, fineness, perfection, nobleness; (colloq.) beautiful woman, beauty, professional beauty; *être en* ~, to look one's best.

beaux-parents (boparɑ̃), s.m.pl. Parents-in-law.

bébé (bebe), s.m. [f. Engl. *baby*] Baby; (slang) *ta bouche*, ~ *!*, dry up!

bec (bɛk), s.m. [Celt. wd] Beak, bill; snout (of insects, fishes, &c.); spout (of a jug); nib (of a pen); beak, prow (of a ship); mouth-piece (of a musical instrument); (geog.) point of confluence of two rivers, as *bec d'Ambès*; ~ *de gaz*, gas-burner, gas jet; *avoir bon* ~, to have a sharp tongue; *avoir* ~ *et ongles*, to have beak and claws, to be able to defend oneself; *blanc* ~, greenhorn (see BÉJAUNE); *prise de* ~, dispute, set to, slanging-match, quarrel; *clore le* ~ *à X*, to silence X; *tenir X le* ~ *dans l'eau*, to keep X dancing attendance, to keep X in suspense, or on a string; ~ *de corbin*, hook; *canne à* ~ *de corbin*, crook-handled walking stick; ~ *de canne*, spring-lock, picklock; ~ *de lièvre*, hare-lip; (prov.) *il n'est bon* ~ *que de Paris*, for a really sharp tongue go to Paris.

bécane (bekan), s.f. (pop.) Bike, bicycle.

bécarre (bekar), s.m. adj. [It. *be quadro*] (mus.) Natural; *ré* ~, D natural.

bécasse (bekas), s.f. [f. *bec*] (ornith.) Woodcock; (fig.) goose, ninny, simpleton.

bécasseau (pl. **-x**) (bekaso), s.m. Young woodcock; sandpiper.

bécassine (bekasin), s.f. (ornith.) Snipe; jacksnipe.

becfigue (bɛkfig), s.m. (ornith.) Beccafico, figeater.

becfin (bɛkfɛ̃), s.m. (ornith.) Warbler.

bêchage (bɛʃaʒ), s.m. Digging; (fig.) sharp criticism, slating.

béchamelle (beʃamɛl), adj. s.f. [f. *M. de Béchamel*, 17th cent.] (cook.) Bechamel (sauce).

bêchard (bɛʃar), s.m. Strong double-headed hoe.

bêche (bɛʃ), s.f. [f. Celt. *bec*, *bac*] **1.** (gard.) Spade; **2.** (ent.) wine-weevil; **3.** ~*-de-mer* or *biche-de-mer* (rare), echinoderm, trepang (sea-slug eaten by the Chinese as a luxury).

bêcher (bɛʃe), v.a. [f. *bêche*] **1.** To dig; **2.** (pop.) to speak ill of (somebody), to slate, to pick to pieces.

bêcheu-r, -se (bɛʃœr), s.m.f. Digger.

béchique (beʃik), adj. s.m. [f. Gr. *bêx*] (med.) Bechic (cough-curing, cough-medicine).

bêchoir (bɛʃwar), s.m. Mattock, strong square hoe.

bécot (beko), s.m. (pop.) Little kiss, peck.

bécoter (bekɔte), v.a. To kiss; **se** ~, v.pr. to kiss.

becquée (bɛke), s.f. [f. *bec*] Beakful, billful; spoon-feeding; *donner la* ~, to give food; (fig.) to spoon-feed.

becqueter (bɛkte), v.a. To peck (as a bird); hence (slang) **becquetance**, s.f. food, grub.

bedaine (bədɛn), s.f. [OF *boudine*] (pop.) Paunch, belly, corporation.

bédane (bedan), s.f. [f. *bec*+*d'âne*] Mortise-chisel.

bedeau (pl. **-x**) (bədo), s.m. [f. LL *bedellus*] Beadle.

bédegar (bedgar), s.m. (bot.) Bedeguar, rose-gall.

bedon (bədɔ̃), s.m. Fat belly; syn. BEDAINE.

bedondaine (bədɔ̃dɛn), s.f. **1.** Paunch, belly; **2.** fat-guts.
bedonner (bədɔne), v.n. To get a corporation, to become obese.
bédouin, -e (bedwɛ̃), adj. s.m.f. [Arab. wd] Bedouin.
bée (be), adj. Open, wide-open; *rester bouche* ~, to stand gaping.
béer (bee), v.n. To stand open; see BAYER.
beffroi (bɛfrwa), s.m. [OF *berfrei*, f. MHG *bercvrit*] Belfry.
bégard (begar), s.m. [f. *Lambert le Bègue*] Beghard, lay brother (13th century).
bégayement, bégaiement (begɛmɑ̃), s.m. Stammering, stuttering, lisping.
bégayer (begɛje), v.n.a. [f. LL *bigare*] To stammer, to stutter, to lisp, to stammer out; ~ *un compliment*, to stammer out a compliment.
bégonia (begɔnja), s.m. [f. *Michel Bégon*] (bot.) Begonia.
bègue (bɛg), adj. s.m.f. Stammering, stuttering (person).
bégueule (begœl), adj. s.f. [f. *bée+gueule*] Prude, squeamish, strait-laced fool; *faire sa* ~, to play the prude.
bégueulerie (begœlri), s.f. Excessive prudery.
béguin (begɛ̃), s.m. [f. *Béguine*] **1.** Beguine cap; **2.** baby's cap; **3.** (slang) infatuation; *avoir un* ~ *pour*, to be gone on, to be keen on, to have a crush on.
béguinage (beginaʒ), s.m. A convent of beguines.
béguine (begin), s.f. [f. the *Beghard* doctrine or heresy] Beguine; (fig.) an affectedly devout woman.
beige (bɛʒ), adj. [f. It. *bigio*] Beige, natural; *serge* ~, serge of undyed wool; *une robe* ~, a beige frock.
beigne (bɛɲ), s.f. (slang) Blow, slap, cuff.
beignet (bɛɲɛ), s.m. [f. OF *bigne*] (cook.) Fritter.
béjaune (beʒon), s.m. [*bec+jaune*] (falc.) Young hawk; (fig.) young silly, ninny, beginner, simpleton; syn. BEC.
bel. See BEAU.
bélandre (belɑ̃dr). s.f. [Dutch *bijlander*] (naut.) Bilander; see syn. BALANDRE.
bêlement (bɛlmɑ̃), s.m. [f. *bêler*] Bleating.
bélemnite (belɛmnit), s.f. [f. Gr. *belemnon*] Belemnite, fossil shell.
bêler (bɛle), v.n. [f. L *balare*] To bleat, to baa.
belette (bəlɛt), s.f. [Celt. *bele*] Weasel.
belge (bɛlʒ), adj. s.m.f. Belgian.
bélier (belje), s.m. [f. Flem. *bel*, the ram bearing the bell] **1.** Ram; **2.** (mil.) battering-ram; **3.** (astr.) the Ram.
bélière, (beljɛr), s.f. Clapper-ring; sheep-bell; (mil.) belt-sling.
bélître (belitr), s.m. [f. Germ. *Bettler*] (pedantic) Cad; caitiff.
belladone (bɛladɔn), s.f. [f. It. *bella+donna*] (bot.) Belladonna, deadly nightshade.
bellâtre (bɛlatr), s.m. Vain coxcomb, fop, affected beau.
belle (bɛl), adj. f. (see BEAU), (bot.) ~*-dame*, belladonna, orach; ~*-fille*, daughter-in-law, stepdaughter; ~*-mère*, mother-in-law, stepmother; ~*-sœur*, sister-in-law, stepsister. ~, s.f. **1.** Belle, fair lady; **2.** third and decisive game; **3.** (bot.) ~ *de jour*, convolvulus tricolor; ~ *de nuit*, marvel of Peru; (fig.) gay woman; ~ *d'un jour*, day-lily, *Hemerocallis*; ~ *d'onze heures*, star of Bethlehem.
bellement (bɛlmɑ̃), adv. Gently, nicely.
belligérance (bɛlliʒerɑ̃s), s.f. Belligerence.
belligérant, -e (bɛlliʒerɑ̃), adj. s.m.f. [f. L *belligerare*] Belligerent, belligerent party or power.
belliqueu-x, -se (bɛlliko), adj. [L *bellicosus*] Bellicose, quarrelsome, warlike.
bellis (bɛllis), s.f. (bot.) Field-daisy.
bellissime (bɛllisim), adj. Most beautiful.
bellot, -te (bɛlo), adj. Pretty, good-looking.
bellotte (bɛllɔt), s.f. (bot.) Barbary oak.
belluaire (bɛllɥɛr), s.m. [f. L *bellua*] (ant.) Beast-fighter.
belote (bəlɔt), s.f. Belote (card game).
belvédère (bɛlvedɛr), s.m. [It. *belvedere*] Belvedere.
bémol (bemɔl), s.m. adj. (mus.) Flat.
bémoliser (bemɔlize), v.a. To mark with a flat.
ben (bɛn), s.m. (bot.) Ben-tree, *Moringa pterygosperma*.
benedicité (benedisite), s.m. [L wd] Grace.
bénédictin, -e (benediktɛ̃), s.m.f. Benedictine (monk or nun); (fig.) patient scholar. ~**e**, s.f. A liqueur.
bénédiction (benediksjɔ̃), s.f. [L *benedictio*] Benediction, consecration, blessing; *quelle* ~*!*, what a blessing!
bénef (benɛf), s.m. (slang) Profit, perks, pickings, benefit.
bénéfice (benefis), s.m. [L *beneficium*] **1.** Benefit, profit, advantage, gain; *sous* ~ *d'inventaire*, on condition of not being liable for debts in excess of the assets; (fig.) for what it is worth; **2.** (feud.) benefice, fief; **3.** (eccles.) benefice, living.
bénéficiaire (benefisjɛr), s.m.f. adj. Beneficiary.
bénéficial, -e, (aux) (benefisjal), adj. Belonging to a benefice.
bénéficier (benefisje), v.n. To make a profit, to profit (by), to have the advantage or profit.
bénéficier (benefisje), s.m. Beneficed clergyman, beneficiary.
benêt (bənɛ), s.m. [f. L *benedictus*] Booby, fool, simpleton; moron. ~ adj. Silly, foolish.

bénévole (benevɔl), adj. [L *benevolus*] Benevolent, gratuitous, of good-will, gentle; *représentant, secrétaire* ~, honorary representative, secretary.
bénévolement (benevɔlmɑ̃), adv. Benevolently, kindly, from pure good-will, gratuitously.
bengali (bɛ̃gali), adj. s.m.f. **1.** Bengali, Bengalee, Bengalese; **2.** ~, s.m. (ornith.) Bengal bengaly.
béni, -e (beni), part. adj. Blessed, hallowed; see BÉNIT.
bénignement (beniɲmɑ̃), adv. Benignly, kindly.
bénignité (beniɲite), s.f. [L *benignitas*] Benignity.
bénin, (fem.) **bénigne** (benɛ̃, beniɲ), adj. Benign, benignant, benevolent, mild.
bénir (benir), v.a. [f. L *benedicere*] To bless, to consecrate, to give a benediction (to); to praise, to thank; *Dieu vous bénisse!*, God bless you!
bénissage (benisaʒ), s.m. **1.** Blessing, consecrating; **2.** affected, exaggerated indulgence or praise.
bénisseu-r, -se (benisœr), s.m.f. Toady. ~, adj. Toadyish, mealy-mouthed.
bénit, -e (beni), part. adj. Blessed, hallowed, consecrated; *eau ~e*, holy water; (fig.) *eau ~e de cour*, vain promises, blarney; *c'est pain* ~, that is just as it should be; it serves you (or him, her, &c.) right.
bénitier (benitje), s.m. **1.** Holy-water basin or font; *se démener comme un diable dans un* ~, to rush about half-mad; **2.** a kind of large shell-fish.
benjamin, -e (bɛ̃ʒamɛ̃), s.m.f. Youngest son or daughter; darling, favourite.
benjoin (bɛ̃ʒwɛ̃), s.m. [f. Port. *beijoim*] (bot.) Benjamin-tree; benzoin.
benne, banne (bɛn, ban), s.f. [LL *benna* from Celtic] Hamper, basket, skip, scuttle.
benoît, -e (bənwa), adj. [L *benedictus*] Blessed, sanctimonious.
benoîte (bənwat), s.f. (bot.) Herb bennet.
benoîtement (bənwatmɑ̃), adv. Sanctimoniously.
benzine (bɛ̃zin), s.f. (chem.) Benzine; (used to remove grease stains).
benzoate (bɛ̃zɔat), s.m. (chem.) Benzoate.
benzoïque (bɛ̃zɔik), adj. (chem.) Benzoic.
benzol (bɛ̃zɔl), s.m. Benzene, benzole.
béotien, -ne (beɔsjɛ̃), adj. s.m.f. Boeotian; (fig.) dunce, ignoramus, dullard, blockhead.
béotisme (beɔtism), s.m. Dullness, stupidity, crass ignorance.
béquée. See BECQUÉE.
béquillard, -e (bekijar), adj. s.m.f. (Cripple) walking with crutches.
béquille (bekij), s.f. [f. *bec*] **1.** Crutch; *marcher avec des ~s*, to walk with crutches, or to go on crutches; (fig.) to be on one's last legs; **2.** T-handle (of a lock); **3.** (naut.) shore; **4.** (motor.) sprag, prop, tail-skid.
béquiller (bekije), v.n. To walk with crutches.
béquillon (bekijɔ̃), s.m. Crutch-handled walking-stick.
ber (bɛr), s.m. [f. *berceau*] (naut.) Cradle.
berbère (bɛrbɛr), adj. s.m.f. Berber.
berbéris (bɛrberis), s.m. (bot.) Berberis, barberry; syn. ÉPINE-VINETTE.
bercail (bɛrkaj), s.m. [f. LL *berbicale*] Sheepfold; *ramener au* ~, to bring back to the fold.
berce (bɛrs), s.f. (bot.) Cow-parsnip, *Heracleum sphondylium.*
berceau (pl. **-x**) (bɛrso), s.m. [f. LL *berciolum*] **1.** Cradle; (fig.) origin, beginning, infancy; *la Grèce fut le ~ de la civilisation*, Greece was the cradle of civilization; **2.** (naut.) cradle; **3.** (hort.) bower, arbour; **4.** (arch.) semicircular vault.
bercelonnette, barcelonnette (bɛrslɔnɛt, barslɔnɛt), s.f. [f. *berceau*] Swing-cot.
bercement (bɛrsmɑ̃), s.m. Rocking.
bercer (bɛrse), v.a. To rock, to lull (to sleep); (fig.) to delude, to lull with vain promises; (engr.) to cradle; **se** ~, v.pr. to rock oneself; to delude oneself.
berceuse (bɛrsøz), s.f. **1.** Rocker; **2.** lullaby.
béret, berret (berɛ), s.m. [f. LL *bereta*] Beret.
bergamote (bɛrgamɔt), s.f. [It. *bergamotta*] (bot.) **1.** Bergamot pear; **2.** bergamot orange, *Mella rosa.*
bergamotier (bɛrgamɔtje), s.m. (bot.) Bergamot-orange-tree.
berge (bɛrʒ), s.f. [perh. f. Germ. *Berg*] **1.** Bank (of a river or canal); **2.** flat-bottomed boat.
berger (bɛrʒe), s.m. [f. LL *berbicarius*] Shepherd; (poet.) swain; *l'étoile du* ~, the planet Venus; (fig. in the vocabulary of passion) *l'heure du* ~, the surrender, the time for surrendering.
bergère (bɛrʒɛr), s.f. **1.** Shepherdess; **2.** deep easy chair (with a feather cushion).
bergerette (bɛrʒərɛt), s.f. **1.** Young shepherdess; **2.** (ornith.) wagtail.
bergerie (bɛrʒəri), s.f. **1.** Sheepfold, sheepcot, sheep-farm; *enfermer le loup dans la* ~, to shut up the wolf with the sheep; **2.** pastoral poem; **3.** a mawkish, affectedly innocent work of art.
bergeronnette (bɛrʒrɔnɛt), s.f. (ornith.) Wagtail.
béribéri (beriberi), s.m. [Cingalese wd] Beriberi.
berle (bɛrl), s.f. [f. L *berula*] (bot.) Skirret, *Sium sisarum.*
berline (bɛrlin), s.f. [f. *Berlin*, where first made] Berlin (carriage).

berlingot (bɛrlɛ̃go), s.m. **1.** (obs.) Single-seated berlin; **2.** a caramel sweetmeat.
berlinois, -e (bɛrlinwɑ), adj. s.m.f. Of Berlin, Berliner.
berloque (bɛrlɔk) s.f. See BRELOQUE.
berlue (bɛrly), s.f. [etym. dub.; f. L *bis+lux*?] Dimness of sight; *avoir la ~*, to be dim-sighted; to have a confused notion; to see things which do not exist.
berme (bɛrm), s.f. [f. Dutch *berm*] Berm (narrow ledge).
bernache, bernacle (bɛrnaʃ, bɛrnakl), s.f. (ornith.) Barnacle goose; (moll.) barnacle.
bernardin, -e (bɛrnardɛ̃), adj. s.m.f. [f. *St. Bernard*] Bernardine or Cistercian.
bernard-l'hermite (bɛrnarlɛrmit), s.m. (crust.) Hermit-crab.
berne (bɛrn), s.f. **1.** Tossing in a blanket; **2.** waft; *pavillon en ~*, flag at half-mast.
bernement (bɛrnmɑ̃), s.m. Tossing, blanketing; bantering, ridicule.
berner (bɛrne), v.a. [f. Span. *bernia*] To toss in a blanket; (fig.) to ridicule to make a fool of.
bernicle. See BERNACHE.
bernique (bɛrnik), interj. Not a bit of it!, no go!, what a sell!
berquinade (bɛrkinad), s.f. [f. *Berquin* Fr. author d. 1791] Insipid work of fiction.
berrichon, -ne (bɛriʃɔ̃), adj. s.m.f. Of Berry, native of Berry.
berthe (bɛrt), s.f. [f. *Reine Berthe*] Berthe, bertha.
béryl, béril (beril), s.m. [L *beryllus*] Beryl.
besace (bəzas), s.f. [f. L *bisaccium*] Wallet, beggar's wallet; *être réduit à la ~*, to be reduced to beggary.
besacier (bəzasje), s.m. Wallet-bearer, tramp.
besaigre (bəzɛgr), adj. [f. *aigre*] Tart, sour; *tourner au ~*, to turn sour.
besaiguë, bisaiguë (bizɛgy), s.f. [f. *bis+aigu*] Twibill, double-bladed axe.
besant (bəzɑ̃), s.m. [f. L *byzantius*] Bezant, besant; (herald.) bezant.
besas, beset (bəzɑs, bəzɛ), s.m. Ambsace, double ace.
besi (bəzi), s.m. Kind of pear.
bési. See BÉSIGUE.
bésicles (bezikl), s.f.pl. [f. LL *beryllus*, OF *béricle*] Spectacles.
bésigue (bezig), s.m. [unkn. orig.] (cards) Bezique.
besogne (bəzɔɲ), s.f. [f. *besoin*] Work, labour, piece of work, task, business, job; *abattre beaucoup de ~*, to get through a lot of work; *aller vite en ~*, to be quick at work, to be precipitate, or hasty; *mâcher la ~ à X*, to get everything ready for X; *tailler de la ~ à X*, to cut out work for X; (sometimes pej.) dreary, low work.
besogner (bəzɔɲe), v.n. To work.
besogneu-x, -se (bəzɔɲø), adj. s.m.f. Needy, necessitous (person).
besoin (bəzwɛ̃), s.m. [LL *bisonium*] Want, need, requirement, necessity; hunger; poverty; *au ~*, in case of need, as the case may be; *avoir ~ de*, to want, to need; *il est ~ de*, there is need of; *être dans le ~*, to be poor, needy, in narrow circumstances; *faire un ~* or *ses ~s*, to go to the privy, to make water.
bessonneau (pl. -x) (bɛsɔno), s.m. (aeron. slang) Canvas hangar.
bestiaire (bɛstjɛr), s.m. [L *bestiarius*] Beast-fighter; bestiary.
bestial, -e, (aux) (bɛstjal), adj. Bestial, brutish, beastly.
bestialement (bɛstjalmɑ̃), adv. Bestially.
bestialité (bɛstjalite), s.f. Bestiality.
bestiaux (bɛstjo), s.m.pl. Cattle.
bestiole (bɛstjɔl), s.f. [f. *bête*] Little or tiny animal.
bêta, -sse (bɛta) s.m.f. Blockhead; dunce, noodle. ~ adj. Silly.
bétail (no pl., see BESTIAUX) (betaj), s.m. [f. L *bestia*] Cattle.
bête (bɛt), s.f. [L *bestia*] Beast, animal, dumb creature; animal nature; body; *~s à cornes*, cattle, horned beasts; *~s à laine*, sheep; (ent.) *~ à bon Dieu*, lady-bird; (fig.) *~ noire*, enemy, pet aversion; *faire la ~*, to play the fool; *remonter sur sa ~*, to get on one's legs again, to have one's courage and self-confidence restored; *morte la ~, mort le venin*, dead dogs don't bite; *chercher la petite ~*, to pick holes, to be over-particular.
bête (bɛt), adj. Stupid, foolish, silly, amiss; *~ comme ses pieds*, *~ à manger du foin*, a downwright ass; as stupid as a post; *c'est ~ comme chou*, it is so simple that any fool can understand it, it is self-evident, it is a 'gift'.
bétel (betɛl), s.m. (bot.) Betel.
bêtement (bɛtmɑ̃), adv. Foolishly, stupidly; *tout ~*, quite simply, without any intricacies.
bêtifier (bɛtifje), v.a. To stupefy, to make dull or stupid.
bêtise (bɛtiz), s.f. [f. *bête*] **1.** Foolishness, stupidity, absurdity; **2.** piece of folly, blunder, foolery, nonsense; **3.** trifle, trinket, thing of no value, of no importance; **4.** *~s de Cambrai*, a sort of sweet.
bétoine (betwan), s.f. (bot.) Betony.
béton (betɔ̃), s.m. [f. L *bitumen*] Concrete; *~ armé*, reinforced concrete; ferro-concrete.
bétonnage (betɔnaʒ), s.m. Concrete-work.
bétonner (betɔne), v.a. To concrete, to build with concrete.
bette (bɛt), s.f. (bot.) Beet; syn. POIRÉE.
betterave (bɛtrav), s.f. (bot.) Beetroot;

~ *fourragère*, mangold-wurzel, mangel-wurzel.
beuglant (bøglɑ̃), s.m. (slang) Low café-chantant or music-hall.
beuglement (bøgləmɑ̃), s.m. Bellowing, lowing, roaring, roar.
beugler (bøgle), v.a. [onom.] To bellow, to low, to roar; (fig.) to clamour, to vociferate, to shout, to bawl, to roar.
beurre (bœr), s.m. [L *butyrum*] Butter; *au ~ noir*, with browned butter; *avoir les yeux pochés au ~ noir*, to have a pair of black eyes; (pop., fig.) *faire son ~*, to make nice pickings, to make money; *ça entre comme dans du ~*, it is as easy as anything; *au prix où est le ~*, as prices stand; *cela mettra du ~ dans ses épinards*, that will grease the wheels of life for him; *assiéger l'assiette au ~*, to be a pot-hunter (in political life).
beurré (bœre), s.m. [f. *beurre*] Beurré, butter pear.
beurrée (bœre), s.f. Slice of buttered bread.
beurrer (bœre), v.a. To butter; *il sait de quel côté son pain est beurré*, he knows on which side his bread is buttered.
beurrerie (bœrri), s.f. Butter dairy.
beurrier (bœrje), s.m. **1.** Butter-dish, butter-cooler; **2.** dairyman, butter-dealer.
bévue (bevy), s.f. [f. *bis+vue*] Blunder, silly mistake, oversight; howler; syn. GAFFE, BÊTISE.
bey (be), s.m. [Arab. wd] Bey.
beylical, -e, (aux) (bɛlikal), adj. Concerning the bey.
bézoard (bezɔar), s.m. [Pers. *pādzahr*] Bezoar.
biais (bjɛ), s.m. [f. L *bifax*] Slope, bias, obliquity, slant; bias band; (fig.) expedient, shift; *en ~, de ~*, obliquely, slanting, aslant, askew; (when cutting material) on the cross. ~, adj. Skew, slanting.
biaisement (bjɛzmɑ̃), s.m. Sloping.
biaiser (bjɛze), v.n. To slope, to slant; (fig.) to shift, to dodge, to be dilatory. ⚠ *Biaiser* (fig.) is not 'to bias' which = *influencer, rendre partial.*
bibelot (biblo), s.m. Knick-knack, gew-gaw, trifle, trinket.
bibeloter (biblɔte), v.a. To collect, buy or sell *bibelots* or curios.
biberon (bibrɔ̃), s.m. **1.** Feeding-bottle; *élever au ~*, to bring up by hand; **2.** drunkard.
bibi (bibi), s.m. (colloq.) **1.** Woman's hat; **2.** myself, number one, this child; *c'est pour ~*, that 's for me.
bible (bibl), s.f. [Gr. *biblia*] Bible.
bibliographe (bibliɔgraf), s.m.f. Bibliographer.
bibliographie (bibliɔgrafi), s.f. [f. Gr. *biblion+graphein*] Bibliography.
bibliographique (bibliɔgrafik), adj. Bibliographical.
bibliomane (bibliɔman), s.m.f. adj. Bibliomaniac.
bibliomanie (bibliɔmani), s.f. [f. Gr. *biblion +mania*] Bibliomania.
bibliophile (bibliɔfil), s.m.f. adj. [f. Gr. *biblion+philos*] Bibliophile.
bibliothécaire (bibliɔtekɛr), s.m.f. Librarian.
bibliothèque (bibliɔtɛk), s.f. [f. Gr. *biblion+thēkē*] Library; book-case, book-shelves, book-stand; (fig.) *rat de ~*, book-worm.
biblique (biblik), adj. Biblical.
bicarbonate (bikarbɔnat), s.m. (chem.) Bicarbonate.
biceps (bisɛps), s.m. [L wd] (anat.) Biceps; (pop.) *avoir du ~*, to be strong.
biche (biʃ), s.f. [unkn. orig] (zool.) Hind; (pop.) darling, love; *pied de ~*, hind's foot; handle (of a bell-pull); (techn.) nail-claw, lever.
biche-de-mer (biʃdəmɛr), s.f. [f. Port. *bicho do mar*] (zool.) *Holothuria edulis*; bêche-de-mer. See BÊCHE **3.**
bicher (biʃe), v.n. (slang) To agree, to get along, to get on well; *alors ça ne biche pas ?*, well, nothing doing ?; *ça biche épatamment*, it 's going rippingly; *ça ne biche pas entre eux*, they don't get on well.
bichette (biʃɛt), s.f. Little darling.
bichon (biʃɔ̃), s.m. [abbrev. of *barbichon*] **1.** Maltese dog, lap-dog; **2.** dear, ducky; **3.** velvet pad.
bichonner (biʃɔne), v.a. To curl, to dress up, to smarten up; to caress, to take excessive care of.
bicoque (bikɔk), s.f. [f. It. *bicocca*] Hovel, shanty, wretched dwelling.
bicorne (bikɔrn), s.m. [*bi+corne*] Two-cornered hat. ~ adj. Bicorn, two-horned, two-cornered.
bicycle (bisikl), s.m. [*bi+cycle*] Bicycle.
bicyclette (bisiklɛt), s.f. Bicycle, bike.
bicycliste (bisiklist), s.m.f. Cyclist; syn. CYCLISTE.
bidet (bidɛ), s.m. [It. *bidetto*] **1.** Nag, cob; **2.** bidet (kind of bath).
bidon (bidɔ̃), s.m. [etym. dub.] Can, canteen, water-bottle; (naut.) mess-tub; ~ *à essence*, petrol-can.
bief (bjɛf), s.m. Mill-race: reach (of a canal); syn. BIEZ.
bielle (bjɛl), s.f. [unkn. orig.] Connecting-rod, side-rod; *tête de ~*, big end or bottom end of connecting-rod; *coussinet de ~*, connecting-rod bearing.
bien (bjɛ̃), s.m. [L *bene*] **1.** Good, welfare, benefit, good thing, boon, comfort; *en ~*, favourably; *aller à ~, venir à ~*, to prosper, to be successful; *mener à ~*, to bring to a good end; *nul ~ sans peine*, no gains without pains; *grand ~*

vous fasse!, much good may it do you!; **2.** goodness, virtue, right; *en tout ~ tout honneur*, with the most excellent intentions; **3.** property, goods, estate; *avoir du ~ au soleil*, to have landed property; *abondance de ~s ne saurait nuire*, store is no sore, one cannot have too much of a good thing.

bien (bjɛ̃), adv. [L *bene*] Well, right, rightly, duly, proper, properly, full, fully, comfortable, comfortably, abundantly, a great deal, a great many; *~ du plaisir!*, much pleasure to you!; *c'est ~ à vous de me le reprocher!*, it behoves you indeed to reproach me!; *c'est ~ de lui!*, that's just like him!; *très ~*, very well, all right; *~ avant*, long before; *~ mieux*, much better still; *~ mal*, very bad indeed; very ill; *il est malheureux, il l'a ~ voulu*, he is unhappy, but it's all his own fault!; *~ lui en a pris!*, and right he was, it was a good impulse; *~ que*, though, although; *si ~ que*, so that; *eh ~?*, well?

bien-aimé, -e (bjɛ̃nɛme), adj. s.m.f. Well-beloved, beloved one, darling, lover.

bien-dire (bjɛ̃dir), s.m. Fine speaking.

bien-disant, -e (bjɛ̃dizɑ̃), adj. Well-spoken.

bien-être (bjɛ̃nɛtr), s.m. Well-being, comfort, ease, welfare.

bienfaisance (bjɛ̃fɛzɑ̃s), s.f. Beneficence, charity; *bureau de ~*, board of charity, relief committee.

bienfaisant, -e (bjɛ̃fɛzɑ̃), adj. **1.** Charitable, bountiful, kind; **2.** salutary, healing, consoling.

bienfait (bjɛ̃fɛ), s.m. [*bien+fait*] Kindness, good office, benefaction, charity, blessing, mercy.

bienfait-eur, -rice (bjɛ̃fɛtœr), s.m.f. Benefactor, benefactress.

bien-fonds (bjɛ̃fɔ̃), s.m. Landed property, real estate.

bienheureu-x, -se (bjɛ̃nœrø), adj. Blessed, blissful, happy. ~, s.m.f. Blessed spirit, saint.

biennal, -e, (aux) (bjɛnnal), adj. [f. L *bis+annus*] Biennial.

bienséance (bjɛ̃seɑ̃s), s.f. [f. L *bene+sedere*] Propriety, decorum, fitness, decency.

bientôt (bjɛ̃to), adv. Soon, shortly, quickly, before long; *à ~!*, bye-bye!, so long!

bienveillance (bjɛ̃vɛjɑ̃s), s.f. Benevolence, goodwill, favour, kindness.

bienveillant, -e (bjɛ̃vɛjɑ̃), adj. [*bien+veuillant*] Kind, benevolent, favourable.

bienvenu, -e (bjɛ̃vəny), adj. Welcome; *soyez le ~*, welcome!

bienvenue (bjɛ̃vəny), s.f. Welcome; *souhaiter la ~ à X*, to welcome X.

bien-vivre (bjɛ̃vivr), s.m. Comfort.

bière[1] (bjɛr), s.f. [etym. dub. OHG *pior*?] Beer; *ce n'est pas de la petite ~*, that is no small matter, that's first class, that's no small beer.

bière[2] (bjɛr), s.f. [f. Germ. *Bahre*] Coffin, bier; syn. CERCUEIL.

biez (bje), s.m. See BIEF.

biffer (bife), v.a. [etym. dub.] To erase, to cross out, to scratch out, to strike out, to cancel.

biffin (bifɛ̃), s.m. (colloq.) Rag-picker.

bifide (bifid), adj. [L *bifidus*] Bifid, forked.

bifteck (biftɛk), s.m. [Engl. *beefsteak*] Beefsteak.

bifurcation (bifyrka'sjɔ̃), s.f. Bifurcation, fork, forking.

bifurquer (bifyrke), v.n. [f. L *bis+furca*] To bifurcate, to fork.

bigame (bigam), adj. [f. L *bis*+Gr. *gamos*] Bigamous. ~, s.m.f. Bigamist.

bigamie (bigami), s.f. Bigamy.

bigarade (bigarad), s.f. Bitter orange.

bigaradier (bigaradje), s.m. (bot.) Bitter-orange-tree.

bigarré, -e (bigare), p. adj. Many-hued, parti-coloured; see BARIOLÉ.

bigarreau (pl. **-x**) (bigaro), s.m. Bigaroon (cherry).

bigarreautier (bigarotje), s.m. (bot.) Bigaroon-tree.

bigarrer (bigare), v.a. To paint with contrasting colours; see BARIOLER.

bigarrure (bigaryr), s.f. Medley, motley.

bigle (bigl), adj. [f. L *bis+oculus*] Squinting.

bigle (bigl), s.m. [f. Engl. *beagle*] Beagle.

bigne (biɲ), s.f. [OF *buigne*] Bump on the head; syn. BEIGNE.

bignoniacées (biɲɔnjase), s.f.pl. (bot.) Bignoniaceae.

bigorne (bigɔrn), s.f. [f. L *bicornis*] (techn.) Bickern, two-pointed anvil.

bigorneau (pl. **-x**) (bigɔrno), s.m. **1.** Small bickern, hand-anvil; **2.** (moll.) periwinkle.

bigot, -e (bigo), adj. [LL *bigoti*] Bigoted. ~, s.m.f. Bigot.

bigoterie (bigɔtri), s.f. **bigotisme** (bigɔtism), s.m. Bigotry.

bigoudi (bigudi), s.m. Hair-curler.

bigre (bigr), interj. Bless me!, confound it!, hang it!

bigrement (bigrəmɑ̃), adv. Exceedingly, deucedly, awfully.

bigue (big), s.f. [f. LL *biga*] (build.) Sheers (pl.).

bihebdomadaire (biɛbdɔmadɛr), adj. Twice a week.

bihoreau (pl. **-x**) (biɔro), s.m. (ornith.) Night-heron, *Ardea nycticorax*.

bijou (pl. **-x**) (biʒu), s.m. [f. Low Bret. *bizou*] Jewel, trinket; (fig.) anything elegant, ornate; darling.

bijouterie (biʒutri), s.f. **1.** Jewellery; **2.** jeweller's trade; jeweller's shop.
bijouti-er, -ère (biʒutje), s.m.f. Jeweller.
bilabié, -e (bilabje), adj. (bot.) Bilabiate.
bilan (bilɑ̃), s.m. [L *bilanx*] **1.** Balance-sheet; **2.** schedule (of debts and assets); *déposer son* ~, to file one's petition in bankruptcy, to stop payment.
bilatéral, -e, (aux) (bilateral), adj. Bilateral.
bilboquet (bilbɔkɛ), s.m. [*bille+bocquet*] **1.** Cup and ball (toy); **2.** (print.) job-work.
bile (bil), s.f. [L *bilis*] Bile; *s'échauffer la* ~, (fig.) to work oneself into a passion; *se faire de la* ~, or (slang) *se biler*, to fret; *il ne se fait pas de* ~, he takes things easy.
biliaire (biljɛr), adj. Biliary.
bilieu-x, -se (biljø), adj. Bilious, choleric, ill-tempered, splenetic.
bilingue (bilɛ̃g), adj. [L *bilinguis*] Bilingual.
billard (bijar), s.m. [f. *bille*] Billiards; billiard-table, billiard-room.
bille (bij), s.f. [etym. dub.] **1.** Billiard-ball; **2.** marble (toy); **3.** log (of timber); **4.** packing stick; **5.** (techn.) ball; *roulement à* ~*s*, ball-bearings; *cuvette à* ~*s*, ball-cups, ball-race; *monté sur* ~*s*, with ball-bearings; **6.** (slang) face, mug, phiz.
billebaude (bijbod), s.f. Confusion, disorder; *à la* ~, hurly-burly, helter-skelter.
billet (bijɛ), s.m. [f. LL *bulla*] **1.** Note, short letter; ~ *doux*, love-letter, billet-doux; **2.** ticket; ~ *d'entrée*, admission ticket; ~ *d'aller et retour*, return ticket; ~ *de faveur*, free admission ticket, order; **3.** promissory note, note of hand, note; ~ *de banque*, banknote; ~ *à ordre*, bill payable to order; ~ *au porteur*, bill payable to the bearer; ~ *à courte échéance*, short-dated bill; ~ *à longue échéance*, long-dated bill, long bill; *je vous en donne mon* ~, I warrant you, I can tell you, mark my words; **4.** certificate; (Cath. liturg.) ~ *de confession*, certificate of confession; (mil.) ~ *de logement*, billet.
billette (bijɛt), s.f. **1.** Log of firewood; **2.** (herald.) billet, an oblong rectangular figure; **3.** (arch.) billet (ornamental moulding in Norman architecture).
billevesée (bijvəze), s.f. [f. OF *bille+veze*, full of wind] Nonsense, silly stuff, idle story.
billion (biljɔ̃), s.m. A thousand millions; syn. MILLIARD. ⚠ In English 'billion' = a million millions, but in U.S.A. and France *billion* = a thousand millions.
billon (bijɔ̃), s.m. [f. LL *billio*] **1.** Copper coin; **2.** (agric.) ridge.
billonnage (bijɔnaʒ), s.m. (agric.) Ridging (of ploughed soil).
billonner (bijɔne), v.n. **1.** To ridge; **2.** (obs.) to traffic in base coin.
billot (bijo) s.m. [f. *bille*] **1.** Block; **2.** yoke.
bilobé, -e (bilɔbe), adj. [f. L *bis+lobus*] Bilobed, bilobate.
biloquer (bilɔke), v.a. [f. L *bis+locare*] To plough deeply.
bimane (biman), adj. [f. L *bis+manus*] Bimanous. ~**s**, s.m.pl. Bimana.
bimbelot (bɛ̃blo), s.m. [f. *bibelot*] Plaything, knick-knack.
bimbeloterie (bɛ̃blɔtri), s.f. Manufacture of or trade in toys and knick-knacks.
bimensuel, -le (bimɑ̃sɥɛl), adj. Twice a month, fortnightly; bi-monthly.
bimétallisme (bimetalism), s.m. Bimetallism.
binage (binaʒ), s.m. (agric.) Hoeing.
binaire (binɛr), adj. [L *binarius*] Binary.
binard (binar), s.m. Lorry, truck, trolley.
biner (bine), v.a.n. [f. L *bini*] **1.** To give (the soil) a second tillage; **2.** to say mass twice in one day; **3.** to merge two offices into one.
binette (binɛt), s.f. [f. *biner*] **1.** (agric.) Hoe; **2.** (slang) face, phiz.
biniou (pl. **-s**) (binju), s.m. [Bret. wd] Bagpipe, hornpipe (in Brittany).
binocle (binɔkl), s.m. [f. L *bini+oculus*] Double eye-glass; syn. LORGNON.
binoculaire (binɔkylɛr), adj. Binocular.
binôme (binom), s.m. (alg.) Binomial.
binot (bino), s.m. [f. *biner*] Light plough.
biochimie (bjɔʃimi), s.f. [f. Gr. *bios+chimie*] Bio-chemistry, vital chemistry; syn. CHIMIE BIOLOGIQUE.
biognose (bjɔgnoz), s.f. [f. Gr. *bios+gnōsis*] Biognosis.
biographe (biɔgraf), s.m.f. Biographer.
biographie (biɔgrafi), s.f. [f. Gr. *bios+graphein*] Biography.
biographique (biɔgrafik), adj. Biographical.
biologie (biɔlɔʒi), s.f. [f. Gr. *bios+logos*] Biology.
biologique (biɔlɔʒik), adj. Biological.
biologiste (biɔlɔʒist), s.m.f. Biologist.
bion (bjɔ̃), s.m. (bot.) Shoot.
bioxyde (bjɔxid), s.m. (chem.) Dioxide.
biparti, -te (biparti), adj. Bipartite.
bipède (bipɛd), adj. [f. L *bis+pedis*] Biped, two-footed. ~, s.m.f. Biped.
biplace (biplas), s.m. (aeron.) Two-seater.
biplan (biplɑ̃), s.m. (aeron.) Biplane.
bipolaire (bipɔlɛr), adj. Bipolar.
bique (bik), s.f. [It. *becco*] She-goat, nanny-goat.
biquet (bikɛ), s.m. Kid. ⚠ *Biquet* is not used like 'kid' in the sense of 'child'.
biquette (bikɛt), s.f. She-kid.
biribi (biribi), s.m. [f. It. *biribisso*] **1.** (gambling) Biribi; **2.** (army slang) biribi (penal battalions in Algeria).
birloir (birlwar), s.m. Window-catch.

birman, -e (birmɑ̃), adj. Burmese. ~, s.m.f. Burman.
bis, -e (bi), adj. [LL *bisus*] Light greyish brown; *pain* ~, brown bread.
bis (bis), adv. [L wd] Bis; twice. ~, interj. Again!, over again!, bis!, encore! ~, s.m. (at concerts, &c.) Encore.
bisaïeul, -e (pl. **-s**), (bizajœl), s.m.f. [*bis*+*aïeul*] Great-grandfather; great-grandmother.
bisaiguë (bizɛgy), s.f. See syn. BESAIGUË.
bisannuel, -le (bizanɥɛl), adj. Biennial.
bisbille (bisbij), s.f. [f. It. *bisbiglio*] Wrangling, bickering, tiff, quarrel; *être en* ~ *avec*, to wrangle with; to be at variance with; *ils sont en* ~, they are at loggerheads.
biscaïen, -ne (biskajɛ̃), adj. s.m.f. [f. *Biscaye*] Biscayan. ~, s.m. **1.** Large musket; **2.** grape-shot.
bischof (biʃɔf), s.m. Bishop (a drink).
biscornu (biskɔrny), adj. [*bis*+*cornu*] Odd, irregular, out of shape, complicated, queer.
biscotin (biskɔtɛ̃), s.m.f. [f. It. *biscottino*] Sweet biscuit.
biscotte (biskɔt), s.f. [f. It. *biscotto*] Rusk.
biscuit (biskɥi), s.m. [*bis*+*cuit*] **1.** Biscuit, sponge-cake; ~*s à la cuiller*, finger biscuits; **2.** sea-bread, ship biscuit; *s'embarquer sans* ~, to commence an enterprise without due preparation; **3.** (porcelain) biscuit.
bise (biz), s.f. [etym. dub.] Cold wind; blast.
biseau (pl. **-x**) (bizo), s.m. [unkn. orig.] **1.** Bevel, bezel; *taillé en* ~, bevelled, bezelled; **2.** (print.) foot-stick.
biseautage (bizotaʒ), s.m. Bevelling.
biseauter (bizote), v.a. To bevel; *carte biseautée*, bevel-edged card (for cheating at cards); *glace biseautée*, bevelled looking-glass.
biser (bize), v.a. To dye again; ~, v.n. (agric.) to turn rusty.
biset (bizɛ), s.m. (ornith.) Rock-pigeon, rock-dove.
bisette (bizɛt), s.f. [f. *bis*] **1.** Ecru lace edging; **2.** (ornith.) black diver.
bismuth (bismyt), s.m. [unkn. orig.] Bismuth.
bison (bizɔ̃), s.m. [L wd] **1.** (zool.) Bison; **2.** cold wind, cold draught.
bisonne (bizɔn), s.f. **1.** Cow bison; **2.** grey cloth used for lining.
bisontin, -e (bizɔ̃tɛ̃), adj. s.m.f. [f. L *Bisontium* now *Besançon*] Of Besançon, inhabitant of Besançon.
bisquain (biskɛ̃), s.m. Sheepskin with the wool on.
bisque (bisk), s.f. **1.** Bisk, crayfish soup, or sauce; **2.** (tennis) bisque, odds.
bisquer (biske), v.n. (pop.) To be vexed, to fret; *faire* ~ *X*, to vex X, to rile X.
bissac (bisak), s.m. [*bis*+*sac*] Wallet, bag; syn. BESACE.
bissect-eur, -rice (bisɛktœr), adj. Bisecting. ~**rice**, s.f. Bisector.
bissection (bisɛksjɔ̃), s.f. [f. L *bi*+*secare*] Bisection.
bisser (bise), v.n. To cry encore; to perform a second time; ~, v.a. to encore.
bissexte (bisɛkst), s.m. [L *bissextus*] The twenty-ninth of February in leap-years.
bissextil, -e (bisɛkstil), adj. [f. *bissexte*] Bissextile; *année* ~, leap-year.
bisexué, -e (bisɛksɥe), adj. Bisexual.
bistorte (bistɔrt), s.v. [f. L *bis*+*tortus*] (bot.) Bistort, snake-weed.
bistouri (bisturi), s.m. [etym. dub.] Bistoury, scalpel; syn. SCALPEL.
bistourner (bisturne), v.a. [*bis*+*tourner*] To twist; *tout bistourné*, crooked, twisted.
bistre (bistr), adj. s.m. Bistre, bister.
bistré, -e (bistre), adj. Bistre-coloured, tanned, swarthy, tawny.
bistrer (bistre), v.a. To colour with bistre, to tan (in colour).
bistro (bistro), s.m. Pub, wine-shop; pub-keeper.
bisulfate (bisylfat), s.m. (chem.) Bisulphate.
biterrois, -e (bitɛrwɑ), adj. s.m.f. Of Béziers, native of Béziers.
bitord (bitɔr), s.m. [L *bis*+*tortus*] Spun yarn.
bitte (bit), s.f. [f. Scand. *biti*] (naut.) Bitt.
bitter (bitɛr), s.m. [Dutch and Engl. wd] Bitters (a drink).
bitume (bitym), s.m. [L *bitumen*] Bitumen, asphalt.
bitumer, bituminer (bityme, bitymine), v.a. To bituminate, to asphalt.
bitumineu-x, -se (bityminø), adj. Bituminous.
biture (bityr), s.f. (slang) Booze, drinking-bout.
bivalve (bivalv), adj. [f. L *bis*+*valva*] Bivalve, bivalved. ~, s.m. Bivalve.
bivouac (bivwak), s.m. [f. Germ. *beiwacht*] Bivouac.
bivouaquer (bivwake), v.n. To bivouac.
bizarre (bizar), adj. [f. Span. *bizarro*] Strange, odd, queer, whimsical, extraordinary. ~, s.m. Oddity, whimsicality, the whimsical, the fantastical.
bizarrement (bizarmɑ̃), adv. Oddly, whimsically, strangely, queerly.
bizarrerie (bizarri), s.f. Oddity, whimsicality, oddness, strangeness, queerness.
blackbouler (blakbule), v.a. [f. Engl. *black*+Fr. *boule*] To blackball.
blafard, -e (blafar), adj. [f. Germ. *bleich* +*Farbe*] Pale, pallid, wan, sallow, dull, leaden.
blague (blag), s.f. [f. Germ. *Balg*] **1.** Tobacco-pouch; **2.** joke, falsehood, fudge,

rot, hoax; gift of the gab; *quelle ~!*, what a joke!, I do not believe it!; *~ à part*, all joking aside; *tout ça c'était de la ~*, the whole thing was a plant, it was all eyewash.

blaguer (blage), v.n.a. To hoax, to make fun of, to jest, to banter, to draw the long bow; *~ X*, to chaff X, to pull X's leg.

blagueu-r, -se (blagœr), adj. s.m.f. Humbug, hoaxing, chaffing (person), joker, story-teller.

blaireau (pl. -x) (blɛro), s.m. [unkn. orig.] **1.** Badger; **2.** badger's-hair brush, shaving-brush; badger (paint-brush).

blâmable (blɑmabl), adj. Blamable.

blâme (blɑm), s.m. Blame, reprimand, reproof; *rejeter le ~ sur X*, to throw the blame on X.

blâmer (blɑme), v.a. [f. L *blasphemare*] To blame, to find fault with, to reprimand, to censure, to condemn.

blanc, blanche (blɑ̃, blɑ̃ʃ), adj. [f. OHG *blanch*] **1.** White; hoar, hoary; *gelée ~he*, hoar frost; *vin ~*, white wine; *sauce ~he*, white sauce; *eau ~he*, Goulard's water (a lotion of subacetate of lead); *monnaie ~he*, silver coin; *armes ~hes*, steel weapons (not firearms); **2.** blank, void; not rhymed; *avoir carte ~he*, to get full authority (to act for another person); *passer une nuit ~he*, to have a sleepless night; *vers ~s*, blank verse; **3.** clean, unsoiled; (fig.) innocent, unsullied; *linge ~*, clean linen; *sortir d'une affaire ~ comme neige*, to get out of a scrape without moral stain; *c'est bonnet ~ et ~ bonnet*, it is six of one and half a dozen of the other.

blanc (blɑ), s.m. **1.** White, whiteness; white clothes, linen; *magasin de ~*, linen warehouse; **2.** blank, blank space; *une ligne en* (or *de*) *~*, a blank line; **3.** breast (of a fowl); **4.** white (of an egg); **5.** white man; (*une blanche*, a white woman); **6.** blank, an old French coin; **7.** various white substances or things: *~ de baleine*, spermaceti; *~ d'Espagne*, whiting; *~ de champignon*, mushroom spawn; *~ de chaux*, white lime; *~ de plomb*, white lead; *le ~ de l'œil*, the white of the eye; *regarder X dans le ~ des yeux*, to look X full in the face; *de but en ~*, point-blank, bluntly; *chauffer à ~*, to raise to a white heat; *tirer à ~*, to fire with blank cartridge; *saigner à ~*, to bleed to death.

blanc-bec (blɑ̃bɛk), s.m. (pl. *blancs-becs*) Raw youngster, greenhorn.

blanchaille (blɑ̃ʃaj), s.f. [f. *blanc*] White fry, whitebait.

blanchâtre (blɑ̃ʃatr), adj. Whitish.

blanche (blɑ̃ʃ), s.f. **1.** White woman; **2.** (mus.) minim.

blanchet (blɑ̃ʃɛ), s.m. **1.** (pharm.) Strainer, filter; **2.** (print.) blanket.

blancheur (blɑ̃ʃœr), s.f. [f. *blanc*] Whiteness; (fig.) purity, innocence.

blanchiment (blɑ̃ʃimɑ̃), s.m. Bleaching; whitewashing.

blanchir (blɑ̃ʃir), v.a. To whiten, to bleach, to wash, to whitewash, to grow pale, to clear, to prove innocent; **~**, v.n. to become hoary, to turn white or grey; to whiten, to bleach, to fade; **se ~**, v.pr. to be bleached, to whiten oneself; to clear or exculpate oneself.

blanchissage (blɑ̃ʃisaʒ), s.m. Washing, wash, laundering; *~ à la chaux*, lime-washing; *~ à la colle*, whitewashing.

blanchisserie (blɑ̃ʃisri), s.f. Bleaching-works, bleaching-trade; steam-laundry; wash-house.

blanchisseu-r, -se (blɑ̃ʃisœr), s.m.f. Laundry-man, laundress, washer-woman; *~se de fin*, clear-starcher.

blanc-manger (blɑ̃mɑ̃ʒe), s.m. (pl. *blancs-mangers*) (cook.) Blancmange.

blanc-seing (blɑ̃sɛ̃), s.m. (pl. *blancs-seings*) Signature on a blank paper, blank cheque.

blanque (blɑ̃k), s.f. [f. It. *blanca*] **1.** Blanque (a card game); **2.** a kind of white grape.

blanquette (blɑ̃kɛt), s.f. [f. *blanc*] **1.** Blanquette, stew with white sauce; **2.** white wine; **3.** blanquette (pear).

blaser (blɑze), v.a. [etym. dub.] To dull, to pall, to deaden; **se ~** (*sur*), v.pr. to become indifferent (to), to become satiated (with).

blason (blɑzɔ̃), s.m. [etym. dub.] Blazon, blazonry, heraldry; coat-of-arms, armorial bearings.

blasonner (blɑzɔne), v.a. **1.** To blazon, to emblazon; **2.** to criticize.

blasphémat-eur, -rice (blasfematœr), s.m.f. Blasphemer. **~**, adj. Blaspheming.

blasphématoire (blasfematwar), adj. Blasphemous.

blasphème (blasfɛm), s.m. [f. Gr. *blasphēmia*] Blasphemy.

blasphémer (blasfeme), v.a.n. To blaspheme.

blaste (blast), s.m. [f. Gr. *blastos*] (bot.) Tigelle, radicle. ⚠ Not 'blast', which = *coup de vent violent*; *dose d'explosif*; *éclat de son* (*de trompettes*, &c.).

blatier (blatje), s.m.f. adj. [f. L *bladum*] Corn-chandler.

blatte (blat), s.f. [f. L *blatta*] (ent.) Cockroach; syn. CANCRELAT, CAFARD.

blaude (blod), s.f. Smock-frock.

blé (ble), s.m. [f. L *bladum*, OF *bled*] Corn, wheat (*Triticum*); *~ méteil*, maslin, wheat and rye mixed; *~ noir* (syn. SARRASIN), buckwheat; *~ de Turquie*, maize, Indian corn; *manger son ~ en herbe*, to anticipate one's income; to eat the calf in the cow's belly; *crier famine sur un tas de* ~, to cry famine in the midst of plenty.

bled (blɛd), s.m. Inland (North Africa), veldt (South Africa).

bleime (blɛm), s.f. (vet.) Corn (inflammation of horse's foot).

blême (blɛm), adj. [perhaps f. Germ. *bleich*] Wan, pale, ghastly, pallid.

blêmir (blɛmir), v.n. To turn pale, to blanch.

blende (blɛ̃d), s.f. [Germ. wd] (min.) Blende, black jack.

blennorrhagie (blɛnɔraʒi), s.f. (med.) Gonorrhoea.

bléser (bleze), v.n. [f. L *blaesus*] To lisp; syn. ZÉZAYER.

blessant, -e (blɛsɑ̃), adj. Offensive.

blessé, -e (blɛse), adj. s.m.f. Wounded (person); (fig.) offended.

blesser (blɛse), v.a. [etym. dub.] To wound, to injure, to hurt; to offend against; *chacun sait où le bât le blesse*, every one knows where his own shoe pinches; ~ *les convenances*, to offend against propriety; ~ *l'oreille*, to grate upon the ear; **se** ~, v.pr. to wound oneself; to wound each other; to be offended, to take offence.

blessure (blɛsyr), s.f. Wound, injury, hurt, cut, offence; (law) *coups et* ~*s*, aggravated assault; *rouvrir une* ~, to reopen a wound, to revive one's grief.

blet, -te (blɛ), adj. [etym. dub.] Over-ripe.

blettir (blɛtir), v.n. To become overripe.

bleu, -e (blø), adj. [f. Germ. *blau*] Blue; *colère* ~*e*, towering rage, awful bate; (fam.) *cordon* ~, perfect (female) cook; *bas* ~, pedantic woman, blue-stocking.

bleu (blø), s.m. **1.** Blue; ~ *de ciel*, sky-blue; ~ *d'azur*, azure blue; ~ *marine*, navy blue; *n'y voir que du* ~, to be unable to make anything of it; *poisson cuit au* ~, fish boiled in wine; *passer le linge au* ~, to blue linen; **2.** bruise; *couvert de* ~*s*, bruised all over; **3.** (pop.) young soldier, recruit, rookie; syn. CONSCRIT; **4.** *petit* ~, express correspondence; syn. PNEUMATIQUE, PNEU; **5.** (polit.) republican.

bleuâtre (bløɑtr), adj. Bluish.

bleuet (blɥɛ), s.m. See BLUET.

bleuir (bløir), v.a. To blue; ~, v.n. to turn blue.

bleuté, -e (bløte), adj. Bluish.

blindage (blɛ̃daʒ), s.m. (naut.) Armour-plating; (mil.) blindage; screen.

blinder (blɛ̃de), v.a. [f. Germ. *blind*] (mil.) To provide with screens; (naut.) to armour, to armour-plate, to iron-case; *train blindé*, armoured train; (slang) *blindé*, dead drunk, blind drunk.

bloc (blɔk), s.m. [f. Germ. *Block*] Block, log (of wood); stock; lump; stocks; *en* ~, in the lump; *à* ~, tight; *fourrer au* ~, (slang) to put in prison; (army slang) to get in clink, in choky; (political jargon) coalition of groups.

blocage (blɔkaʒ), s.m. **1.** Rubble; **2.** (techn.) locking (of wheels, brake, &c.); *écrou de* ~, lock-nut.

blockhaus (blɔkos), s.m. [Germ. wd] Blockhouse.

bloc-notes (blɔknɔt), s.m. (pl. *blocs-notes*) Writing-pad.

blocus (blɔkys), s.m. Blockade.

blond, -e (blɔ̃), adj. [etym. dub.] Fair, blond, light, flaxen, fair-haired. ~, s.m.f. **1.** Fair colour of hair or complexion; **2.** fair-haired person.

blonde (blɔ̃d), s.f. Blonde lace.

blondin, -e (blɔ̃dɛ̃), adj. s.m.f. Fair-haired (child, youth, or young girl).

blondir (blɔ̃dir), v.n. To grow yellow, to turn golden.

blondissant, -e (blɔ̃disɑ̃), adj. Turning golden or yellow.

bloquer (blɔke), v.a. [f. *bloc*] **1.** To blockade; **2.** to block up; **3.** (mason.) to fill up; **4.** (at billiards) to pocket; **5.** to tighten; ~ *les freins*, to brake hard, to jam on the brakes; (techn.) ~ *les roues*, to lock the wheels.

(se) blottir (səblɔtir), v.pr. [etym. unkn.] To squat, to crouch down; to nestle.

blouse (bluz), s.f. [etym. dub.] Smock-frock, blouse, smock, overall, bodice; pocket (of a billiard table).

blouser (bluze), v.n. **1.** (at billiards) To pocket; **2.** (dressm.) to be bloused, to have length in excess so that it may fall loose over the belt; ~, v.a. to mislead; **se** ~, v.pr. to make a mistake, to blunder, to be in the wrong box, to get on the wrong tack.

bluet, bleuet (blɥɛ), s.m. [f. *bleu*] (bot.) Cornflower.

bluette (blɥɛt), s.f. [OF *beluette*] Small spark, flash; literary trifle.

bluff (blœf), s.m. [Engl. wd] Bluff.

bluffer (blœfe), v.n.a. [f. *bluff*] To bluff.

blutage (blytaʒ), s.m. Bolting, sifting, dressing (of flour).

bluter (blyte), v.a. [OF *buleter*] To bolt, to sift (flour).

blutoir, bluteau (blytwar, blyto), s.m. Bolter.

boa (bɔa), s.m. [L wd] (zool.) **1.** Boa, boa constrictor; **2.** boa, woman's feather stole.

bobard (bɔbar), s.m. (slang) Lie, fib, humbug, tommy-rot, bosh; *ne me raconte pas de* ~*s*, come off it; come off the bird-lime; tell that to the marines.

bobèche (bɔbɛʃ), s.f. [unkn. orig.] Candle-ring, glass or metal plate on candlestick to collect wax.

bobéchon (bɔbeʃɔ̃), s.m. (slang) Head, nut; *se monter le* ~, to get enthusiastic; to kid oneself.

bobinage (bɔbinaʒ), s.m. Reeling; winding; ~ *d'induit,* armature winding.

bobine (bɔbin), s.f. [unkn. orig.] Bobbin, spool, reel, coil; ~ *d'induction,* induction coil; ~ *à trembleur,* trembler coil.

bobiner (bɔbine), v.a. To reel, to wind.

bobinette (bɔbinɛt), (obs.) s.f. Wooden latch.

bobo (bobo), s.m. (nursery word) Slight ailment, sore, bruise; *avoir du* ~, to feel a pain (somewhere); *cela fait* ~, it hurts.

boc (bɔk), s.m. Douche, glass or enamelled iron douche; india-rubber douche-bag.

bocage (bɔkaʒ), s.m. [f. LL *boscus*] Grove, thicket, woodland.

bocag-er, -ère (bɔkaʒe), adj. Of the woods, rustic.

bocal (pl. **aux**) (bɔkal), s.m. [f. It. *boccale*] Glass jar, fish-globe.

bocard (bɔkar), s.m. (metall.) Crushing-mill.

bocarder (bɔkarde), v.a. To crush (ore).

boche (bɔʃ), adj. s.m.f. [etym. dub.] (war slang) German, Hun.

bock (bɔk), s.m. [Germ. wd] Beer glass; glass of beer.

boëtte (bwɛt), s.f. (fish.). See BOITTE.

bœuf (bœf, bø in the plural), s.m. [L *bos, bovis*] Ox (pl. oxen), bullock; (butch., cook.) beef; *mettre la charrue avant les ~s,* to put the cart before the horse; *donner un œuf pour avoir un* ~, to throw a sprat to catch a herring; *un filet de* ~, a fillet of beef; (U.S.A.) a tenderloin of beef; *une langue de* ~, an ox-tongue; *avoir un ~ sur la langue,* to be bound to secrecy; not to tell tales; *ayez un ~ sur la langue,* mum is the word !; (cook.) ~ *à la mode,* à la mode beef. ~, adj. (slang) Tremendous.

bogie, boggie (bɔʒi, bɔgi), s.m. [Engl. wd] Bogie.

bogue (bɔg), s.f. [f. Provenç. *boga*] **1.** Chestnut-bur; **2.** shovel for loading rubbish-cart.

bohème (boɛm), adj. s.m.f. [f. *Bohemia*] **1.** (Person) living from hand to mouth, or living a free-and-easy sort of life; bohemian. **2.** ~, s.f. Such people collectively; *vie de* ~, bohemian life.

bohémien, -ne (boemjɛ̃), adj. Of Bohemia; Bohemian. ~, s.m.f. Gipsy, wanderer, vagrant, improvident person; Bohemian.

boire (bwar), v.a.n. [L *bibere*] **1.** To drink, to swallow a liquid; to tipple, to drink too much; to suck up; *ce n'est pas la mer à* ~, that is not such a difficult matter; ~ *la santé* (or *à la santé*) *de X,* to drink X's health; ~ *comme un trou,* to drink like a fish; *qui a bu boira,* once a drunkard always a drunkard; use is second nature; **2.** (fig.) to swallow, to pocket, to endure; ~ *un affront,* to pocket, or to endure an affront.

boire, s.m. Drink, drinking; *en perdre le ~ et le manger,* to be so excited (or distraught) that one forgets meal-times.

bois (bwɑ), s.m. [LL *boscus*] **1.** Wood, timber, firewood; *ustensiles en* ~, wooden utensils; *jambe de* ~, wooden leg; ~ *de chauffage,* firewood; ~ *de charpente,* timber; ~ *de Panama,* quillaia bark; *faire flèche de tout* ~, to make use of all the means at one's disposal; *trouver visage de* ~, to find the door shut; *il verra de quel ~ je me chauffe,* he shall see what sort of stuff I am made of; **2.** wood, grove; ~ *de chênes,* an oak-wood; ~ *taillis,* coppice, copse; *être volé comme dans un* ~, to be badly swindled; **3.** horns, antlers; **4.** bedstead; **5.** stock (of fire-arms); **6.** (naut.) hull; **7.** (slang) *avoir la gueule de* ~, to feel chippy; to have a head; to have a mouth like the bottom of a parrot's cage.

boisage (bwazaʒ), s.m. Woodwork, casing, propping (in mines).

boisé, -e (bwaze), adj. Wooded.

boisement (bwazmɑ̃), s.m. Afforestation, planting of trees.

boiser (bwaze), v.a. **1.** To furnish with woodwork, to wainscot; **2.** to afforest, to plant with trees.

boiserie (bwazri), s.f. Wainscot, wainscoting, woodwork.

boisseau (pl. **-x**) (bwaso), s.m. [LL *buscellus*] Bushel; *mettre la lumière sous le* ~, to hide one's light under a bushel.

boisselée (bwasle), s.f. Bushelful.

boisselier (bwaslje), s.m. Cooper, bushel-maker.

boissellerie (bwasɛlri), s.f. **1.** Making and selling of wooden measures; **2.** wooden ware.

boisson (bwasɔ̃), s.f. [f. *boire*] **1.** Drink, beverage; **2.** liquor; **3.** drunkenness; *être pris de* ~, to be in liquor, to be drunk; **4.** weak cider, weak drink, water with vinegar, extracts, tea, infusions, &c.

boîte (bwat), s.f. [LL *buxida*] Box, case, caddy, canister, casket, chest, can, tin; boxful, tinful; ~ *aux lettres,* letter-box, pillar-box; ~ *à outils,* tool-box, tool-chest; ~ *à chapeau,* band-box; ~ *à violon,* violin-case; ~ *de bonbons,* box of sweets; ~ *crânienne,* brain-pan, skull; (techn.) ~ *de vitesse,* change-speed gear-box; ~ *à vapeur,* steam chest; ~ *d'essieu,* axle sleeve or bush; ~ *du différentiel,* or *carter,* gear-case; case of the differential; (colloq). regular hole; cheap inefficient school; the place where one works; wretched concern; badly-organized show; ~ *de nuit,* café chantant, dance club; (mil. slang) *il l'a flanqué à la* ~, he put him in clink; (slang) *mettre en* ~, to prevent (an orator) from speaking.

boitement (bwatmɑ̃), s.m. **boiterie** (bwatri), s.f. [f. *boiter*] Halting, limping.
boiter (bwate), v.n. To be lame, to halt, to limp.
boiteu-x, -se (bwatø), adj. Lame, limping. ~, s.m.f. Lame person, cripple.
boîtier (bwatje), s.m. **1.** Box of surgical instruments; **2.** watch-case; (motor. techn.) casing; **3.** box-maker; **4.** member of Parliament who is entrusted by a few colleagues with their votes.
boitte, boëtte (bwat, bwɛt), s.f. [Bret. wd] (fish.) Bait for cod-fishing.
bol[1] (bɔl), s.m. [f. Engl. *bowl*] Bowl, basin, finger-bowl; basinful.
bol[2] (bɔl), s.m. [f. Gr. *bōlos*] **1.** (min.) Bole; ~ *d'Arménie*, Armenian bole; **2.** bolus, large pill, ball; ~ *alimentaire*, bolus of masticated food.
bolchevisme (bɔlʃəvism), s.m. [f. Russ. *bolsheviki*] Bolshevism.
bolcheviste, bolchevik (bɔlʃəvist, bɔlʃəvik), adj. s.m.f. Bolshevik, (colloq.) bolshy, bolshie.
boléro (bɔlero), s.m. [Span. wd] **1.** Spanish dance, bolero; **2.** bodice, bolero.
bolet (bɔlɛ), s.m. [f. L *boletus*] (bot.) Boletus (a genus of fungi).
bolide (bɔlid), s.m. [f. Gr. *bolis, bolidos*] (meteor.) Bolide, meteor, fire-ball; (fam.) any object arriving with excessive speed.
bolivien, -ne (bɔlivjɛ̃), adj. s.m.f. Bolivian.
bolonais, -e (bɔlɔnɛ), adj. s.m.f. Bolognese.
bombance (bɔ̃bɑ̃s), s.f. [possibly f. L *bombus*] Feasting, good cheer; *faire* ~, to make good cheer; to junket, to feast; syn. RIPAILLE.
bombarde (bɔ̃bard), s.f. [f. L *bombus*] Bombard, catapult; syn. MORTIER.
bombardement (bɔ̃bardəmɑ̃), s.m. Bombardment, shelling.
bombarder (bɔ̃barde), v.a. To bombard, to shell; (fig.) (*a*) to beset, to worry; (*b*) to appoint suddenly to a charge, or post; *il s'est fait* ~ *directeur*, he wangled himself into a directorship.
bombardier (bɔ̃bardje), s.m. (mil., obs.) Grenadier, bomber. ⚠ Not English 'bombardier' which means an artillery non-commissioned officer = (approxim.) *maréchal-des-logis d'artillerie*.
bombardon (bɔ̃bardɔ̃), s.m. (mus.) Bombardon.
bombe (bɔ̃b), s.f. [f. L *bombus*] **1.** Bomb, shell; **2.** ~ *glacée*, ice pudding; ice-cream in a mould; **3.** disorderly life; (slang) *faire la* ~, to go on the spree; to paint the town red.
bombé, -e (bɔ̃be), p. adj. Convex, bulged; (of a road) cambered.
bombement (bɔ̃bmɑ̃), s.m. Convexity, bulging out.
bomber (bɔ̃be), v.a. To make convex, to cause to bulge out, to camber (a road); ~, v.n. to be convex, to bulge.
bombeur (bɔ̃bœr), s.m. Glass-blower. ⚠ Not English 'bomber' which = *lanceur de grenades*.
bombonne (bɔ̃bɔn), s.f. See BONBONNE.
bombyx (bɔ̃biks), s.m. [Gr. *bombux*] (ent.) Bombyx, silk-worm.
bon, -ne (bɔ̃), adj., adv. [L *bonus*] Good, good-natured, kind, nice, right, valid, safe, strict, accurate, proper, advisable, well, comfortable, advantageous; *à quoi* ~*?*, what is the use (of), what is the good of it?, what for?; ~*!*, *c'est* ~*!*, right!, all right!, that 's enough; *il est* ~ *que*, it is proper (or right) that; ~ *à rien*, good (or fit) for nothing; *à* ~ *compte*, cheap; *arriver au* ~ *moment*, to arrive at the right time; *tout lui est* ~, all is fish that comes to his net; *sentir* ~, to smell nice; *il a pris la* ~*ne route*, he has taken the right road; ~ *an mal an*, taking one year with another; *trouvez* ~ *que je*, allow me to; *comme* ~ *vous semble*, as you think right, as you like; *pour de* ~, *pour tout de* ~, in earnest, for good and all; *être dans son* ~ *sens*, to be all there; *avoir* ~ *pied* ~ *œil*, to be sound of wind and limb; *un* ~ *mot*, a witty remark; a pun; *une* ~*ne fois*, once for all; *il fait* ~ *ici*, it 's pleasantly warm in here; ~*ne année!*, happy New Year!; *ceci ne présage rien de* ~, this bodes no good; *de* ~*ne foi*, bona fide, fair and square; *de* ~*ne heure*, early.
bon (bɔ̃), s.m. **1.** Good, goodness, profitableness, best (of it), cream; **2.** bond, order, draft, debenture; ticket, bill; ~ *de poste*, postal order; ~ *du Trésor*, Treasury bond.
bonace (bɔnas), s.f. [It. *bonaccia*] Calm (at sea), smooth sea, fall of wind.
bonasse (bɔnas), adj. Goody-goody, soft, silly.
bon-bec (bɔ̃bɛk), s.m. (pl. *bons-becs*), Gossip, chatterbox; see BEC.
bonbon (bɔ̃bɔ̃), s.m. [*bon+bon*] Bonbon, sweet, sweetmeat, comfit.
bonbonne, bombonne (bɔ̃bɔn), s.f. [Provenç. *boumbouno*] Carboy, jar, demijohn, large bottle, tin oil-can; syn. DAME-JEANNE.
bonbonnière (bɔ̃bɔnjɛr), s.f. [f. *bonbon*] Sweetmeat box; (fig.) elegant snug little house or flat.
bon-chrétien (bɔ̃kretjɛ̃), s.m. (bot.) Bon-chrétien pear, William.
bond (bɔ̃), s.m. [f. *bondir*] Bound, rebound, leap, spring; *prendre la balle au* ~, to strike the ball on the rebound; (fig.) to seize the opportunity; *faire faux* ~ (*à*), to give the slip (to), to forfeit, to disappoint; to fail, to let down.

bonde (bɔ̃d), s.f. [Provenç. *bonda*] Bung-hole, bung, plug, sluice.

bonder (bɔ̃de), v.a. To load, to overload, to cram, to fill completely; *salle bondée*, crowded room.

bondir (bɔ̃dir), v.n. [f. L *bombitare*] To bound, to leap, to spring, to bounce, to dash, to dart, to rush; *faire ~ le cœur*, to make one's heart leap (for joy); *~ d'indignation*, to be filled with indignation.

bondissement (bɔ̃dismɑ̃), s.m. Bounding, rebounding, bouncing, leaping.

bondon (bɔ̃dɔ̃), s.m. [f. *bonde*] **1.** Bung; **2.** small bung-shaped cheese.

bondrée (bɔ̃dre), s.f. (ornith.) Pern, honey-buzzard, *Pternis apivorus*.

bonduc (bɔ̃dyk), s.m. (bot.) Nicker-tree, Molucca bean.

bonheur (bonœr), s.m. [*bon*+*heur*] Happiness, felicity; good fortune, good luck; piece of good luck; success; *par ~*, luckily, happily; *au petit ~*, at a venture, happen what may; in a happy-go-lucky way; *porter ~*, to bring good luck; *~ du jour*, escritoire; *un ~ insolent !*, the devil's own luck !; *faire le ~ de X*, to delight X, to enchant X.

bonhomie (bonomi), s.f. Good nature, easy temper, simplicity, amiableness; bonhomie. (French *bonhomie* = not merely benevolence, but smiling equanimity and somewhat sly gentleness.)

bonhomme (bonom), s.m. [*bon*+*homme*] (pl. *bonshommes*) **1.** Good-natured man, good soul; *faux ~*, hypocritical fellow; **2.** simple, credulous man; **3.** old man, old fogy; **4.** man, fellow; *un singulier ~*, a queer fellow; **5.** mannikin, puppet, ill-drawn human figure; **6.** *Jacques ~*, a collective name for the French peasantry; **7.** (war wd) soldier, tommy; **8.** various loc.: *petit ~ vit encore*, Jack's alive: *faire son petit ~ de chemin*, to get along joggingly, slowly but surely, towards one's goal (or aim).

boni (boni), s.m. [f. L *bonus*] Bonus, profit, surplus.

boniche (boniʃ), s.f. (slang) Young maid-servant, skivvy.

bonification (bonifika'sjɔ̃), s.f. Improvement; allowance.

bonifier (bonifje), v.a. [L *bonus*+*facere*] To improve; **se ~**, v.pr. to improve.

boniment (bonimɑ̃), s.m. Mountebank's speech, showman's speech, claptrap; humbug, smooth talk, eye-wash; *avoir du ~*, to have the gift of the gab; *faire le ~*, to puff; to proclaim the excellence of one's wares; to do the talking; *faire du ~ à une femme*, to make love to a woman.

bonite (bonit), s.f. [LL *boniton*] (ichth.) Bonito.

bonjour (bɔ̃ʒur), s.m. [*bon*+*jour*] Good-morning, salutation, compliments; *bien le ~*, a good morning to you; *c'est simple comme ~*, it is as easy as anything; (slang) it 's a gift !, easy as lying !

bonne (bon), s.f. [f. *bon*] Maid-servant, servant-girl, nursemaid; *~ à tout faire*, general servant, general, maid-of-all-work; *~ d'enfant*, nursery-maid.

bonne-dame (bondam), s.f. (pl. *bonnes-dames*) (bot.) Orach, mountain-spinach; syn. ARROCHE.

bonne-maman (bonmamɑ̃), s.f. (pl. *bonnes-mamans*) Grandmamma; granny.

bonnement (bonmɑ̃), adv. Simply, frankly, sincerely, honestly.

bonnet (bonɛ), s.m. [unkn. orig.] **1.** Cap, head-covering for men, head-dress for women; *~ de nuit*, night-cap; (mil.) *~ de police*, forage-cap; *~ d'âne*, dunce's cap; *~ à poil*, grenadier's cap, bearskin; *~ phrygien*, Phrygian cap; *prendre le ~*, or *du ~*, to take a doctor's degree; *les gros ~s*, the big-wigs, the nobs, the big bugs; *avoir la tête près du ~*, to be hot-headed, passionate; *prendre une chose sous son ~*, (*a*) to do a thing on one's own responsibility; (*b*) to invent a tale, a fact, &c.; *ce sont deux têtes dans un ~*, they are hand and glove together; *c'est ~ blanc et blanc ~*, it is six of one and half a dozen of the other; *triste comme un ~ de nuit*, as dull as ditch-water; down in the dumps; *opiner du ~*, to nod assent; *jeter son ~ par dessus les moulins*, to leave one's reputation behind one; to throw off all moral restraint; to kick over the traces; **2.** (anat.) honeycomb bag, second stomach of ruminants. ⚠ Not English 'bonnet' which = *chapeau* (*de femme*).

bonneteau (pl. **-x**) (bonto), s.m. Card-sharper's game.

bonneterie (bontri, bonɛtri), s.f. Hosiery, hosiery trade or manufacture.

bonneteur (bontœr), s.m. Card-sharper.

bonneti-er, -ère (bontje), s.m.f. Hosier.

bonnette (bonɛt), s.f. **1.** (fort.) Bonnet; **2.** (naut.) studding-sail.

bon-papa (bɔ̃papa), s.m. (pl. *bons-papas*) Grandfather, grandpa.

bonsoir (bɔ̃swar), s.m. [*bon*+*soir*] Good-evening, good-night; *donner, souhaiter le ~ à X*, to bid, to wish X good-night.

bonté (bɔ̃te), s.f. [L *bonitas*] Goodness, excellence, kindness, benevolence, good quality; *~s*, favours, indulgence, kindnesses; *~ divine !*, goodness gracious !; *ayez la ~ de vous taire*, have the kindness to keep silent; *il vous a comblé de ses ~s*, he has loaded you with favours.

bonze (bɔ̃z), s.m. [Jap. *bonzô*] Bonze, buddhist priest; (slang) old fogy, old crock.

bonzerie (bɔ̃zri), s.f. Monastery of bonzes.

bookmaker (bukmakœr), s.m. [Engl. wd] Bookmaker.

boqueteau (pl. -x) (bɔkto), s.m. [f. *bosquet*] Spinney.

bora (bɔra), s.m. Bora, NE. wind on the Adriatic.

boracique (bɔrasik), adj. Boracic.

borate (bɔrat), s.m. (chem.) Borate.

borax (bɔraks), s.m. [f. Arab. *bauraq*] (chem.) Borax.

borborygme (bɔrbɔrigm), s.m. [f. Gr. *borboruzein*] Borborygmus, intestinal rumbling.

bord (bɔr), s.m. [OHG *bort*] **1.** Edge, border, brink, rim, brim; (fig.) brink, verge, eve; *chapeau à larges ~s*, broad-brimmed hat; *le ~ d'un verre*, the rim of a glass; *un rouge ~*, a brimmer; *le ~ d'un précipice*, the brink (or edge) of a precipice; *être au ~ du tombeau*, to be on the brink of the grave; **2.** side, board, shore, bank; *au ~ de la route*, by the road-side; *les ~s du fleuve*, the banks of the river; *virer de ~*, to veer, to tack about; *~ à ~*, alongside; *aller* (or *monter*) *à bord*, to go on board; *jeter par dessus ~*, to throw overboard; *vaisseau de haut ~*, ship fit to navigate the high seas; *papiers de ~*, ship's papers; *il est seul de son ~*, he is alone in his opinion; *les sombres ~s*, the gloomy shores, the infernal regions; *au ~ de la mer*, at the seaside; (aeron.) *~ d'attaque* (*de l'aile*), entering edge, front edge, of wing or aerofoil; *~ de sortie*, trailing edge, rear edge, after edge.

bordage (bɔrdaʒ), s.m. **1.** Edging, bordering; **2.** planking, planks.

borde, borderie (bɔrd, bɔrdəri), s.f. Small farm.

bordeaux (bɔrdo), s.m. [f. *Bordeaux*, French town] Bordeaux wine, claret.

bordée (bɔrde), s.f. [f. *bord*] **1.** (naut.) Broadside, volley; *lâcher une ~*, to fire a broadside; (fig.) *~ d'injures*, a volley of abuse; **2.** board; *courir une ~*, to make a board, or a tack; **3.** (slang) *tirer une ~*, to go on the spree (ashore).

bordel (bɔrdɛl), s.m. [f. *borde*] Brothel.

bordelais, -e (bɔrdəlɛ), adj. s.m.f. Of Bordeaux, native of Bordeaux. **~e, s.f. 1.** A bottle of special size and shape (about two-thirds of a litre); **2.** cask of 225 to 230 litres.

border (bɔrde), v.a. **1.** To border, to adjoin, to hem, to edge, to bind, to tuck in, to encircle, to line; **2.** (naut.) to plank (the sides of a ship); *~ la côte*, to run along the coast; *~ une écoute*, to haul a sheet taut, or to tally a sheet.

bordereau (pl. -x) (bɔrdəro), s.m. [f. *bord*] Memorandum, account, docket.

bordi-er, -ère (bɔrdje), s.m.f. Farmer who shares the produce of land with the owner; syn. MÉTAYER.

bordure (bɔrdyr), s.f. [f. *bord*] Border, edging, frame, margin, kerb, kerb-stone; skirt; (herald.) bordure; (gard.) border.

bore (bɔr), s.m. (chem.) Boron.

boréal -e, (aux) (bɔreal), adj. Boreal, northern; *aurore ~e*, aurora borealis.

borgne (bɔrɲ), fem. **borgnesse** (bɔrɲɛs), adj. s.m.f. One-eyed (person); (fig.) paltry, low, equivocal, suspicious; *au royaume des aveugles les ~s sont rois*, in the country of the blind the one-eyed man is king; the mediocre shine among the dunces; *un ~ parmi les aveugles*, a Triton among the minnows; *cabaret ~*, low pub; (Amer.) 'speakeasy'.

borin (bɔrɛ̃), s.m. Pitman, collier.

borinage (bɔrinaʒ), s.m. **1.** Coal-digging; **2.** colliers collectively.

borique (bɔrik), adj. (chem.) Boric, boracic.

bornage (bɔrnaʒ), s.m. [f. *borner*] Setting of boundaries; boundaries.

borne (bɔrn), s.f. [f. LL *bodula*] **1.** Bound, boundary, landmark; milestone, pillar; **2.** limit, bound; *cela passe toutes les ~s*, that passes all bounds; that's the limit!; *mettre des ~s à*, to set bounds to.

borné, -e (bɔrne), p. adj. Bounded, limited; (fig.) short-witted, narrow-minded, shallow, dull.

borne-fontaine (bɔrnfɔ̃tɛn), s.f. (pl. *bornes-fontaines*) Street fountain, street water supply.

borner (bɔrne), v.a. To bound, to limit, to restrict, to confine, to circumscribe; **se ~**, v.pr. to limit, restrict, confine oneself; to end (*à*, in), to stop (at).

borraginées (bɔraʒine), s.f.pl. [f. L *borrago*] (bot.) Boragineae.

bosniaque (bɔsnjak), adj. s.m.f. Bosnian, of Bosnia.

bosquet (bɔskɛ), s.m. [f. L *boscus*] Grove, thicket, spinney.

bossage (bɔsaʒ), s.m. [f. *bosse*] (arch.) Bossage; relief, embossed work.

bosse (bɔs), s.f. [etym. dub.] **1.** Bump, protuberance; *avoir la ~ de la musique*, to have a natural talent for music; hunch, hump; *le chameau a deux ~s*, the camel has two humps; *rouler sa ~*, to roam about the world, to hike; **2.** dint, dent, bruise; **3.** knoll, hillock; **4.** (sculpt., paint.) relievo, relief, plaster cast; *dessiner d'après la ~*, to draw from plaster models; **5.** (pop.) tuck-out, tuck-in; *s'en donner une ~*, to eat to one's heart's content; *se donner une ~ de rire*, to split one's sides with laughing.

bosselage (bɔslaʒ), s.m. [f. *bosseler*] Embossing (of plate).

bosseler (bɔsle), v.a. [f. *bosse*] **1.** To emboss; **2.** to dent, to bruise (any metal vessel); (slang) *machine à ~*, knuckle-duster; (by ext.) cudgel, heavy club.

bosselure, bossellement (bɔslyr, bɔsɛlmɑ̃), s.f. **1.** Embossment; **2.** bump, bruise.

bosser (bɔse), v.a. (naut.) To stopper, to stow (a cable).
bossette (bɔsɛt), s.f. [f. *bosse*] Boss, sculptured keystone; ornament of a bridle bit.
bossoir (bɔswar), s.m. (naut.) Cathead, bow.
bossu, -e (bɔsy), adj. s.m.f. [f. *bosse*] Hump-backed (person); hunch-back; *rire comme un* ~, to laugh heartily.
bossuer (bɔsɥe), v.a. To dent, to bruise.
boston (bɔstɔ̃), s.m. [f. *Boston*] **1.** Card-game; **2.** boston, a ballroom dance.
bostonner (bɔstɔne), v.n. To dance a boston.
bot, -e (bo), adj. *Pied* ~, club-foot; *main* ~*e*, deformed hand. ~, s.m. Club-foot.
botanique (bɔtanik), s.f. [Gr. *botanikē*] Botany. ~, adj. Botanical.
botaniser (bɔtanize), v.n. To botanize.
botaniste (bɔtanist), s.m.f. Botanist.
botte[1] (bɔt), s.f. [Celt. *bôtel*] Bottle, truss, bundle, bunch; ~ *de foin*, truss of hay; ~ *de carottes*, bunch of carrots.
botte[2] (bɔt), s.f. [LL *botta*] Boot, Wellington boot; ~*s de sept lieues*, seven-league boots; ~*s à revers*, top-boots; *avoir du foin dans ses* ~*s*, to have ample resources; *à propos de* ~*s*, irrelevantly, by the by.
botte[3] (bɔt), s.f. [It. *botta*] (fenc.) Lunge, thrust; *pousser une* ~ *à X*, to make a thrust at X; (fig.) to attack X with sharp words.
botté, -e (bɔte), p. adj. Booted, in boots; *Chat* ~, Puss-in-boots.
bottelage (bɔtlaʒ), s.m. Trussing, bundling.
botteler (bɔtle), v.a. [f. *botte*] To truss, to bundle, to bind.
botteleu-r, -se (bɔtlœr), s.m.f. Trusser (of hay); binder (of wheat-sheaves).
botter (bɔte), v.a. **1.** To supply with boots; **2.** to help (a person) on with his boots; **3.** (fig.) to suit, to fit; *ça me botte!*, that just suits me!; **4.** (pop.) to kick (some one or something); ~ *un but*, to kick a placed ball; ~ *le derrière à X*, to kick X; **se** ~, v.pr. to put on one's boots.
bottier (bɔtje), s.m. Bootmaker.
bottillon (bɔtijɔ̃), s.m. [f. *botte*] Small bundle, small bunch.
bottine (bɔtin), s.f. [f. *botte*] Half-boot, ankle-boot; boot (for women).
bouc (buk), s.m. [f. Germ. *Bock*] **1.** He-goat, goat-skin; ~ *émissaire*, scape-goat; **2.** goat's beard, goatee.
boucage (bukaʒ) s.m. (bot.). See syn. ANIS.
boucan (bukã), s.m. [Braz. wd] **1.** Buccan, framework for smoking meat; **2.** uproar, shindy, rumpus; *faire du* ~ or *du raffût*, to kick up a row.
boucaner (bukane), v.a.n. To smoke (meat), to buccan; to hunt the wild ox.
boucanier (bukanje), s.m. Buccaneer.
boucaut (buko), s.m. Cask; hogshead.
bouchage (buʃaʒ), s.m. [f. *boucher*] **1.** Stopping, stopping up; **2.** corking.
bouche (buʃ), s.f. [f. L *bucca*] **1.** Mouth; lips; **2.** orifice, entrance, muzzle (of a fire-arm), mouth, delta; ~ *de chaleur*, hot-air vent, hot-air hole; ~ *d'incendie*, fire-plug; ~ *close!*, silence!, not a word about it; ~ *cousue*, silent, silence, mum; *à* ~ *que veux-tu*, freely, plentifully; *de* ~, by word of mouth; *de* ~ *en* ~, from mouth to mouth; *garder pour la bonne* ~, to leave something nice for a finish; (fig.) to keep the best for the last; (slang), *ta* ~*!* or *ta* ~, *bébé!*, shut up!, dry up!; *faire venir l'eau à la* ~, to make one's mouth water; *faire la petite* ~, to be hard to please; to turn up one's nose (*à*, at); *faire la* ~ *en cœur*, to be all smirks and smiles; *avoir la* ~ *mauvaise* (or *amère*), to have a bitter taste in one's mouth; *être porté sur la* ~, to be a great eater, or a dainty eater; *n'en pas ouvrir la* ~, not to say a word about it; *avoir la menace à la* ~, to use threatening language; *la déesse aux cent* ~*s*, the hundred-mouthed goddess, Fame; ~ *de miel, cœur de fiel*, a honey tongue, a heart of gall; *les* ~*s du Nil*, the mouths of the Nile; ~ *à feu*, mortar cannon.
bouché, -e (buʃe), p. adj. **1.** Stopped, stopped up, corked; bottled; **2.** stupid; **3.** (of the weather) rainy, cloudy.
bouchée (buʃe), s.f. **1.** Mouthful; **2.** large chocolate-coated sweetmeat; **3.** patty, *bouchée à la Reine.*
boucher (buʃe), v.a. [etym. dub.] To stop, to stop up, to choke up, to obstruct; to cork, to block up; **se** ~, v.pr. to be stopped; *se* ~ *les oreilles*, to stop one's ears; *se* ~ *les yeux*, to close one's eyes, to refuse to see; *se* ~ *le nez*, to hold one's nose.
bouch-er, -ère (buʃe), s.m.f. Butcher, butcher's wife; ~ *en gros*, carcase butcher.
boucherie (buʃri), s.f. Butcher's shop; slaughter-house; butchering trade; (fig.) slaughter, massacre, butchery.
bouche-trou (buʃtru), s.m. (pl. *bouche-trous*) Substitute, stop-gap.
bouchon (buʃɔ̃), s.m. [etym. dub.] Stopper, plug, cork, bung; (fish.) cork-float; (game) chuck-farthing; (pop.) wine-shop, public house; ~ *de paille*, wisp of straw; *mettre en* ~, to bundle; ~ *de radiateur*, radiator cap.
bouchonner (buʃɔne), v.a. **1.** To crumple, to bundle; **2.** to rub down (a horse) with a wisp of straw.
bouchonnier (buʃɔnje), s.m. Cork cutter; cork dealer.

bouchot (buʃo), s.m. [OF *bousche*] Mussel bed; crawl.
bouchoteur (buʃɔtœr), s.m. Mussel farmer.
boucle (bukl), s.f. [L *buccula*] Buckle, ring, curl (of hair), ringlet; knocker, loop; *~s d'oreilles*, ear-rings; *se serrer la ~*, to stint oneself, to tighten one's belt.
boucler (bukle), v.a.n. **1.** To buckle; to buckle up; to curl; *ses cheveux bouclent*, her hair is naturally curly; **2.** to lock up (prisoners); **3.** (aeron.) *~ la boucle*, to loop the loop, to loop; **4.** *c'est une affaire bouclée*, it's a settled matter; **5.** (slang) *se faire ~*, to get run in; to be put in quod (or clink); **se ~**, v.pr. see syn. SE SERRER LA BOUCLE.
bouclette (buklɛt), s.f. Small curl; small loop.
bouclier (buklje), s.m. Buckler, shield; *levée de ~s*, rising in arms; (fig.) unanimous public protest.
bouddhique (budik), adj. Buddhist.
bouddhisme (budism), s.m. [f. Sansk. *buddha*] Buddhism.
bouddhiste (budist), s.m.f. adj. Buddhist.
bouder (bude), v.n.a. [unkn. orig.] To pout (at), to sulk, to be sulky (with), to funk; (at dominoes) to be unable to play, to knock; *je boude*, I can't go!, I am knocking; **se ~**, v.pr. to be sulky with each other.
bouderie (budri), s.f. Pouting, sulks, sulking, sulkiness.
boudeu-r, -se (budœr), adj. s.m.f. Pouting, sulky, sullen (person).
boudin (budɛ̃), s.m. [f. LL *botellus*] Black pudding; roll; (arch.) torus; flange (of a railway-carriage wheel); *ressort à ~*, spiral spring; *s'en aller en eau de ~*, to come to nothing.
boudine (budin), s.f. (in glass) Bull's-eye; knob.
boudiner (budine), v.a. (spinning) To rove, to slub; *boudiné dans ses vêtements*, dressed in ill-fitting, too tight clothes.
boudoir (budwar), s.m. [f. *bouder*] Boudoir.
boue (bu), s.f. [unkn. orig.] Mud, dirt, mire, clay, sediment; *garde-~*, mud-guard; (fig.) abjection; *une âme de ~*, a grovelling mind; *traîner X dans la ~*, to defame X.
bouée (bue), s.f. [f. L *boia*] Buoy, life-buoy.
boueur, boueux (buœr, buø), s.m. Scavenger, street-sweeper.
boueu-x, -se (buø), adj. Muddy, miry, foul.
bouffant, -e (bufɑ̃), adj. Puffy, puffed. ~, s.m. Puff.
bouffarde (bufard), s.f. [f. *bouffée*] (fam.) Tobacco-pipe.
bouffe (buf), adj. [It. *buffa*] Comic. ~, s.m. Buffo; *Les Bouffes Parisiens*, a theatre in Paris.
bouffée (bufe), s.f. Puff, gust, blast, whiff; fit, outburst, flush; *une ~ de colère*, a fit of anger.
bouffer (bufe), v.n. [onom.] To puff, to puff out, to swell out, to rise; (slang) to eat, to stuff; (slang) ~, v.a. to eat; to swallow, to gobble up; *il ne te bouffera pas*, he won't eat you, don't be afraid.
bouffette (bufɛt), s.f. [f. *bouffer*] Bow, ear-knot, rosette, tuft.
bouffi, -e (bufi), p. adj. Puffed, swelled, puffy, inflated; (fig.) bombastic, inflated; *style ~*, inflated, turgid style.
bouffir (bufir), v.a.n. To puff up, to swell, to bloat, to inflate.
bouffissure (bufisyr), s.f. Puffiness, swelling; bombast, turgidness.
bouffon (bufɔ̃), s.m. [It. *buffone*] Buffoon, jester, merry andrew, jack pudding, clown; laughing-stock, butt. ~, **-ne**, adj. Droll, comic, comical, ludicrous, farcical; syn. BURLESQUE.
bouffonner (bufɔne), v.n. To play the buffoon.
bouffonnerie (bufɔnri), s.f. Buffoonery; (colloq.) *c'est une ~!*, what a fraud!
bouge (buʒ), s.m. [f. LL *bugia*] **1.** Closet; **2.** hole, dirty lodging, hovel; low pot-house; **3.** bulge; **4.** (ship-build.) camber.
bougeoir (buʒwar), s.m. [f. *bougie*] Flat candlestick, bedroom candlestick.
bougeotte (buʒɔt), s.f. (colloq.) *Avoir la ~*, to be always wanting a change, to be always on the wing, or on the move; to have the fidgets.
bouger (buʒe), v.n. [f. LL *bullicare*] To stir, to budge, to go out, or away (from), to move; ~, v.a. to move.
bougette (buʒɛt), s.f. Budget, small bag.
bougie (buʒi), s.f. [f. town *Bougie*, Algeria] **1.** Candle, taper, wax-candle, candle-light; **2.** (motor.) plug, sparking-plug; **3.** (surg.) bougie.
bougillon (buʒijɔ̃), s.m. adj. Fidget, fidgety.
bougnat (buɲa), s.m. [abbrev. of *charbonnier*] Coal-man.
bougon, -ne (bugɔ̃), adj. Grumbling. ~, s.m.f. Grumbler, growler, grouser.
bougonner (bugɔne), v.n. [unkn. orig.] To grumble, to grouse.
bougran (bugrɑ̃), s.m. [f. *Boukhara*, Asia] Buckram.
bougre (bugr), s.m. [f. LL *Bulgarus*, OF *boulgre*] Bugger, ruffian; (fam.) fellow; *il est bon ~*, he is not a bad sort; *un pauvre ~*, a poor devil.
bougrement (bygrəmɑ̃), adv. (colloq.) Awfully, extremely, intensely.
boui-boui (buibui), s.m. (pl. *bouis-bouis*) (pop.) Low theatre; gaff, penny gaff.
bouif (buif), s.m. (slang) Cobbler; syn. GNAF.
bouillabaisse (bujabɛs), s.f. [f. Provenç.

bouiabaisso] (cook.) Bouillabaisse, a fish-soup.
bouillant, -e (bujɑ̃), p. adj. Boiling, scalding, hot; (fig.) hot-headed, fiery, impetuous; ~ *de colère*, boiling with anger; *la ~e jeunesse*, fiery youth.
bouillerie (bujri), s.f. Brandy-distillery.
bouilleur (bujœr), s.m. **1.** Boiler tube; **2.** brandy-distiller; ~ *de cru*, one who distils the products of his own growing.
bouilli (buji), s.m. Boiled beef.
bouillie (buji), s.f. Pap, hasty-pudding; rag-pulp; (fig.) ~ *pour les chats*, failure, fruitless and ill-done labour; botchy work.
bouillir (bujir), v.n.a. [L *bullire*] To boil, to ferment; ~ *à gros bouillons*, to boil fast; ~ *à petits bouillons*, or *doucement*, to simmer, to boil gently; *faire ~*, to boil, to make boil; *cela fait ~ le sang*, that makes one's blood boil.
bouilloire (bujwar), s.f. Kettle, boiler.
bouillon (bujɔ̃), s.m. [f. *bouillir*] **1.** Bubble, bubbling, ripple, ebullition, outburst; *sortir à gros ~s*, to gush out; **2.** broth, soup, stock, beef-tea; (fig.) *boire un ~*, to experience a heavy loss in business or speculation; ~ *pointu*, enema, clyster; **3.** a cheap restaurant; **4.** air-bubble (in glass); **5.** (bot.) ~ *blanc*, mullein.
bouillonnement (bujɔnmɑ̃), s.m. Ebullition, boiling, bubbling; (fig.) agitation.
bouillonner (bujɔne), v.n. **1.** To bubble up, to boil over; **2.** to gush out; ~ v.a. (dressm.) to puff, to trim with puffings, to ruche, to make full.
bouillotte (bujɔt), s.f. **1.** Kettle; **2.** foot-warmer; **3.** (card game) bouillotte.
bouillotter (bujɔte), v.n. To simmer.
boujaron (buʒarɔ̃), s.m. (naut.) Tot, a measure for grog.
boulaie (bulɛ), s.f. [f. *bouleau*] Birch grove or plantation.
boulange (bulɑ̃ʒ), s.f. Baking-trade; *bois de ~*, oven fuel.
boulang-er, -ère (bulɑ̃ʒe), s.m.f. Baker, bakeress, baker's wife; (obs.) *~ère*, a dance; (motor.) *camionnette~ère*, delivery-van.
boulanger (bulɑ̃ʒe), v.n.a. To make bread, to bake bread.
boulangerie(bulɑ̃ʒri),s.f. Bakery, baker's shop; bread-making; baker's trade; baking-business.
boule (bul), s.f. [f. L *bulla*] **1.** Ball; (fam.) head; *perdre la ~*, to lose one's presence of mind; **2.** bowl, bowls, bowling-green, bowling-alley; *le jeu de ~s*, the game of bowls; **3.** ballot-ball; **4.** (army slang) ~, ~ *de son*, ration loaf; 'tommy' or 'brown tommy'; **5.** (mech.) ~ *de régulateur*, governor, weight; *flotteur à ~*, ball float.
boule, boulle (bul), s.m. [f. *Boulle*, French cabinet-maker, d. 1732] *Meuble de ~*, Boule work, piece of buhl furniture.
bouleau (pl. **-x**) (bulo), s.m. [L *betula*] Birch-tree.
bouledogue (buldɔg), s.m. [f. Engl. *bulldog*] Bulldog.
bouler (bule), v.n.a. **1.** To send rolling like a ball; *envoyer ~*, to send away, to get rid of, to send to the right-about; **2.** to swell, to rise; **3.** to pout (as pigeons); **4.** to floor, to knock down.
boulet (bulɛ), s.m. **1.** Cannon-ball; **2.** punishment of dragging a cannon-ball chained to one's leg; *traîner son ~*, to lead a wearisome life; **3.** fetlock-joint; **4.** small block of compressed coal-dust.
boulette (bulɛt), s.f. **1.** Pellet, small ball; poison ball; **2.** (pop.) blunder, mistake, bloomer.
bouleu-x, -se (buløø), s.m.f. Cob, stout hack; plodder.
boulevard (bulvar), s.m. [f. Germ. *Bollwerk*] **1.** Bulwark; **2.** boulevard; **3.** (fig.) protection, defence.
boulevardier (bulvardje), s.m. Frequenter of the (Paris) boulevards. ~, adj. Parisian, elegant, frivolous, witty.
bouleversement (bulvɛrsəmɑ̃), s.m. Overthrow, confusion, destruction, commotion, turmoil, panic, subversion, upsetting.
bouleverser (bulvɛrse), v.a. [*boule+verser*] To overthrow, to upset, to overturn, to destroy, to disarrange, to throw into disorder; to turn upside down, or topsyturvy; to throw into confusion, to distract.
boulier (bulje), s.m. [f. *boule*] **1.** Ball-frame, abacus; **2.** earthen pot.
boulimie (bulimi), s.f. [Gr. *boulimia*] (med.) Boulimia, bulimy, morbid hunger.
bouline (bulin), s.f. (naut.) Bowline; *naviguer à la ~*, to turn to windward.
boulingrin (bulɛ̃grɛ̃), s.m. [Engl. *bowling-green*] Bowling-green, grass-plot.
boulle (bul), s.m. See BOULE.
boulon (bulɔ̃), s.m. [f. *boule*] Bolt, pin; ~ *à clavette*, cotter pin, crank pin; ~ *avec écrou*, bolt and nut; ~ *moleté*, milled-edge bolt.
boulonner (bulɔne), v.a. To bolt, to pin; ~, v.n. (slang) to toil.
boulot, -te (bulo), adj. s.m.f. Dumpy, roly-poly, stumpy, plump, squabby (person). ~, s.m. (pop.) Work, business, job.
boulotter (bulɔte), v.n. (colloq.) To get on pretty well, to jog along, to grub along; ~, v.a.n. (pop.) to eat, to grub, to devour.
bouquet (bukɛ), s.m. [var. of *bosquet*] **1.** Cluster, clump (of trees); **2.** nosegay, posy, bunch, tuft; **3.** bouquet, aroma; **4.** gerbe (firework); finish, crowning piece; **5.** (ichth.) prawn.

bouquetière (buktjɛr), s.f. [f. *bouquet*] Flower-girl, flower-woman.
bouquetin (buktɛ̃), s.m. [f. *bouc*] (zool.) Ibex, bouquetin.
bouquin (bukɛ̃), s.m. **1.** [f. *bouc*] Old he-goat; **2.** old book; any book.
bouquiner (bukine), v.n. To hunt after old books, to pore over books.
bouquiniste (bukinist), s.m.f. Second-hand bookseller.
bouracan (burakɑ̃), s.m. [f. Arab. *barra-kān*] Barracan (a coarse fabric).
bourbe (burb), s.f. [unkn. orig.] Mire, mud.
bourbeu-x, -se (burbø), adj. Miry, muddy.
bourbier (burbje), s.m. Slough, quagmire; (fig.) (*a*) sink of vice; (*b*) mess, scrape.
bourbillon (burbijɔ̃), s.m. Core of a boil.
bourcette (burset), s.f. See syn. MÂCHE.
bourdaine (burdɛn), s.f. (bot.) Alder, buckthorn, *Rhamnus frangula*; syn. BOURGÈNE.
bourdalou (burdalu), s.m. Hatband.
bourde (burd), s.f. [unkn. orig.] Fib, sham, humbug; blunder, bull, bloomer, howler.
bourdon[1] (burdɔ̃), s.m. [f. LL *bordonus*] Pilgrim's staff; (bot.) ~ *de St Jacques*, marshmallow.
bourdon[2] (burdɔ̃), s.m. [onom.] **1.** Drone, bourdon; **2.** great bell; **3.** (ent.) humble bee, drone bee, drone.
bourdonnement (burdənmɑ̃), s.m. Humming, buzzing, buzz; singing (in the ears).
bourdonner (burdəne), v.n.a. To hum, to buzz, to drone, to boom, to sing, to bore, to pester.
bourg (bur), s.m. [LL *burgus*, Germ. *Burg*] Town, market-town, borough.
bourgade (burgad), s.f. Small town; large village.
bourgène (burʒen) s.f. See BOURDAINE.
bourgeois, -e (burʒwɑ), s.m.f. [f. *bourg*] Burgher, burgess; citizen, citizeness; townsman, townswoman of middle class; commoner (not a noble); civilian (not a soldier); *en* ~, in plain clothes, in mufti; employer, master, governor, mistress, landlady, wife; *bon* ~, worthy citizen; *petit* ~, man of the lower middle class; (jest.) *ma* (or *la*) ~*e*, my missus.
bourgeois, -e, adj. Middle-class; private, plain, homely, civil; common, vulgar, narrow-minded; 'bourgeois'; *pension* ~*e*, private boarding-house; *cuisine* ~*e*, good plain cooking; *l'esprit* ~, the 'bourgeois' spirit.
bourgeoisement (burʒwazmɑ̃), adv. Privately, in a plain or homely way; *à louer* ~, to be let to private residents, (not for purposes of trade).
bourgeoisie (burʒwazi), s.f. Citizenship, commonalty, citizens, middle class; *haute* ~, upper middle class; *petite* ~, lower middle class; *droit de* ~, burghership, freedom of a city.
bourgeon (burʒɔ̃), s.m. [unkn. orig.] Bud, flower bud, burgeon, fruit-bud, leaf-bud; shoot; (surg.) healing granulation.
bourgeonnement (burʒənmɑ̃), s.m. Budding, burgeoning.
bourgeonner (burʒəne), v.n. **1.** To bud, to burgeon, to shoot; **2.** to become pimpled.
bourgeron (burʒərɔ̃), s.m. Smock-frock, workman's blouse; soldier's vest.
bourgmestre (burgmɛstr), s.m. [f. MHG *burgermeister*] Burgomaster.
bourgogne (burgɔɲ), s.m. [geog. orig.] Burgundy (wine).
bourguignon, -ne (burgiɲɔ̃), adj. s.m.f. Burgundian.
bourguignotte (burgiɲɔt), (obs.) s.f. A kind of helmet.
bourlinguer (burlɛ̃ge), v.n. (naut. and fig.) To labour, to strain as a ship in a heavy sea; (fig.) to hike, to tramp.
bourrache (buraʃ), s.f. [f. LL *borrago*] (bot.) Borage.
bourrade (burad), s.f. [f. *bourrer*] Snap, snapping; blow, buffet, thump, sly thrust, taunt, bullying.
bourrage (buraʒ), s.m. [f. *bourrer*] Tamping; stuffing; ~ *de crâne*, gulling, cramming, tosh; *on nous bourre le crâne*, or *c'est du* ~ *de crâne*, they are codding us.
bourrasque (burask), s.f. [It. *burrasca*] Squall.
bourre (bur), s.f. [LL *burra*] Hair, tag-wool, flock-wool; ~ *de soie*, floss silk, waste silk; padding; wadding; fibrous down (on buds of certain plants).
bourreau (pl. -x) (buro), s.m. [unkn. orig.] Executioner, hangman, headsman, Jack Ketch; (fig.) tormentor, brutal fellow, brute; ~ *d'argent*, spendthrift; ~ *des cœurs*, lovelace, lady-killer; ~ *de travail*, glutton for work.
bourrée (bure), s.f. [f. *bourrer*] **1.** Faggot of twigs, or brushwood; **2.** bourree, boree, a dance from Auvergne; the music for this.
bourreler (burle), v.a. [f. *bourreau*] To torment, to harrow; *conscience bourrelée de remords*, a conscience tortured with remorse.
bourrelet (burlɛ), s.m. [f. *bourre*] Pad, porter's pad, head-pad (for child); roll, cylindrical border, window padding; swell of the muzzle of a cannon; (vet.) cutidure; (motor.) flange (of tyre).
bourrelier (burəlje), s.m. Harness-maker.
bourrer (bure), v.a. [f. *bourre*] To stuff, to pad, to wad, to fill, to cram; to bully, to hustle; ~ *de coups*, to belabour; ~ *d'injures*, to load with abuse; (slang) *il nous bourre le crâne*, he is cramming us full of lies; he is stuffing or codding us.

bourriche (buriʃ), s.f. [etym. dub.] Long and narrow hamper used for game, fish, oysters, flowers.
bourricot (buriko), s.m. Ass foal; small donkey.
bourrique (burik), s.f. [L *burricus*] Jenny-ass, she-ass, donkey; (fig.) ass, donkey; (slang) nark, police informer, police spy.
bourriquet (burikɛ), s.m. **1.** Ass foal; **2.** shear-bench; **3.** windlass.
bourru, -e (bury), adj. Boorish, churlish, testy; rough, crabbed, crusty; unfermented (wine). ~, s.m. Bear, churl.
bourse (burs), s.f. [f. L *bursa*] **1.** Purse; *coupeur de* ~, cut-purse; *tenir les cordons de la* ~, to hold the purse-strings; *sans* ~ *délier*, without spending a penny; *la* ~ *ou la vie!*, your money or your life!; *selon ta* ~, *gouverne ta bouche*, cut your coat according to your cloth; **2.** exchange, Stock Exchange; *le cours de la* ~, quotation of prices; *jouer à la Bourse*, to speculate in the funds; **3.** scholarship, bursary; **4.** (zool.) pouch; (bot.) vulva; (anat.) ~*s*, scrotum.
boursicot (bursiko), s.m. Small purse, small savings.
boursicoter (bursikɔte), v.n. (colloq.) To speculate in the funds (on a small scale).
boursier (bursje), s.m. **1.** Speculator on the Stock Exchange. **2.** ~, *boursière*, s.m.f. Foundation scholar, bursar, exhibitioner.
boursouflage (bursuflaʒ), s.m. Swelling; bombast, fustian.
boursoufler (bursufle), v.a. [*bourse*+*souffler*] To swell, to puff out, to bloat; *visage boursouflé*, swollen or bloated face; *style boursouflé*, bombastic style.
boursouflure (bursuflyr), s.f. **boursouflement** (bursufləmɑ̃), s.m. Puffiness, swelling, bloatedness, turgidness; bombast.
bousculade (buskylad), s.f. Hustling, jostling, turning topsyturvy, bullying.
bousculer (buskyle), v.a. [f. OF *bouteculer*] To upset, to turn topsyturvy, to jostle, to hustle, to bully, to hasten; **se** ~, v.pr. to hustle or jostle each other.
bouse (buz), s.f. [unkn. orig.] Dung.
bousier (buzje), s.m. (ent.) Dung-beetle.
bousillage (buzijaʒ), s.m. Cob, cob-wall, (fig.) bungle, botched work.
bousiller (buzije), v.a.n. To build with cob or mud; (fig.) to botch work; (slang) to kill.
bousin (buzɛ̃), s.m. Sandvent (deposit of sand in a block of stone).
bousingot (buzɛ̃go), s.m. Sailor's hat.
boussole (busɔl), s.f. [f. It. *bussola*] Compass, mariner's compass; *perdre la* ~, (fam.) to lose one's head; to be all at sea; to be daft.
boustifaille (bustifɑj), s.f. (pop.) Tuck-in, tuck-out, grub, food.
bout (bu), s.m. End, extremity, remotest part, tip, top, nipple, button; *un* ~ *de chemin*, a short distance; ~ *de l'an*, anniversary mass for the dead; *au* ~ *du compte*, when all is said and done; *être au* ~ *de son rouleau*, to be at the end of one's tether, or at one's wit's end; (fig.) *c'est tout le* ~ *du monde*, that is the very utmost; *joindre les deux* ~*s*, to make both ends meet; *montrer le* ~ *de l'oreille*, to betray oneself; *un* ~ *d'homme*, a bit of a man; *à* ~ *portant*, point-blank; *être à* ~ *de force*, to be spent, exhausted; *être à* ~ *de patience*, to be out of patience; *être au* ~ *de ses peines*, to be out of the wood; *pousser à* ~, to drive to extremity, to exasperate; *venir à* ~ *de*, to overcome, to bring about, to succeed (in), to subdue; to get through; *savoir sur le* ~ *du doigt*, to have at one's finger-tips; *à tout* ~ *de champ*, at every turn, frequently; *de* ~ *en* ~, from beginning to end; ~ *à* ~, end to end; *haut* ~, upper end; *bas* ~, lower end. ⚠ Not English 'bout', which = *accès*; *fois*; *reprise*, *passe d'armes*, *'round'*.
boutade (butad), s.f. [f. *bouter*] Sally, whim, outburst; *par* ~*s*, by fits and starts.
boutargue (butarg), s.f. [f. Arab. *buṭarkha*] Botargo (relish made of mullet- or tunny-roe).
bout-dehors (budəɔr), s.m. (pl. *bouts-dehors*) (naut.) Boom.
boute-en-train (butɑ̃trɛ̃), s.m. (pl. invar.) Exhilarating companion, life of the party.
boutefeu (pl. -x) (butfø), s.m. [*boute*+*feu*] Linstock, firebrand.
bouteille (butɛj), s.f. [f. LL *butticula*] Bottle, flask; phial; jar; *aimer la* ~, or *la dive* ~, to be addicted to drinking; *c'est la* ~ *à l'encre!*, it's a very obscure affair; *mettre en* ~, to bottle; ~ *de Leyde*, Leyden jar.
bouter (bute), (obs.) v.a. To put.
bouterolle (butrɔl), s.f. **1.** Chape (of a scabbard); **2.** ward (of a lock or key).
bouteroue (butru), s.f. Stone at the corner of a porch to prevent damage by wheels.
boute-selle (butsɛl), s.m. (invar.) (mil.) Trumpet-call to saddle.
boutique (butik), s.f. [f. Gr. *apothēkē*] Shop, stall, booth, stand; (fig.) set, gang; *toute la* ~*!*, the whole lot!; the whole caboodle!; *arrière-*~, back-shop; *fermer* ~, to shut up shop; to retire from business.
boutiqui-er, -ère (butikje), s.m.f. Shopkeeper, tradesman, tradeswoman.
boutisse (butis), s.f. [f. *bout*] (mason.) Header.
boutoir (butwar), s.m. [f. *bouter*] **1.** Farrier's knife; **2.** snout (of a wild boar);

(fig.) *coup de ~*, angry remark, savage reply.
bouton (butɔ̃), s.m. [f. *bout*] **1.** Button, stud; **2.** bud; (bot.) *~ d'or*, buttercup; **3.** pimple, pustule; **4.** nipple, knob; **5.** handle, knob, push; *~s de manchettes*, sleeve-links; *~ d'électricité*, electric push.
boutonner (butɔne), v.a. To button; to button up; **~**, v.n. to bud; **se ~**, v.pr. to button one's clothes.
boutonnerie (butɔnri), s.f. Button-trade, button-making.
boutonnier (butɔnje), s.m. Button-maker.
boutonnière (butɔnjɛr), s.f. Buttonhole; gash, incision.
bouturage (butyraʒ), s.m. Propagation by cuttings or slips.
bouture (butyr), s.f. (hort.) Cutting, slip.
bouverie (buvri), s.f. [f. L *bos, bovis*] Ox-stable, ox-hovel.
bouvet (buvɛ), s.m. Grooving-plane, tonguing-plane.
bouvi-er, -ère (buvje), s.m.f. [f. L *bos, bovis*; Fr. *bœuf*] Ox-driver, drover, ox-keeper; (astr.) Boötes.
bouvillon (buvijɔ̃), s.m. [f. L *bos, bovis*; Fr. *bœuf*] Young bullock, steer.
bouvreuil (buvrœj), s.m. (ornith.) Bull-finch.
bovidé (bovide), adj. s.m. [f. L *bos, bovis*] (zool.) *Les ~s*, the bovidae.
bovin, -e (bɔvin), adj. Bovine; *peste ~*, cattle plague.
bow-window (bowindo), s.m. [Engl. wd] Bow-window.
boxe (bɔks), s.f. [Engl. *box*] Boxing, pugilism.
boxer (bɔkse), v.n.a. To box, to fight.
boxeur (bɔksœr), s.m. Boxer.
boyard (bɔjar), s.m. [Russ. wd] Boyar; (fig.) very rich man.
boyau (pl. **-x**) (bɔjo, bwajo), s.m. [f. LL *botellus*] **1.** Gut, bowel, catgut; **2.** narrow and long passage; zigzag trench.
boyaudier (bwajodje), s.m. Gut-worker.
boycottage (bɔikɔtaʒ), s.m. Boycotting.
boycotter (bɔikɔte), v.a. [Engl. *to boycott*] To boycott.
brabançon, -ne (brabɑ̃sɔ̃), adj. s.m.f. [f. *Brabant*] Brabantine, Brabanter. **~ne**, s.f. Brabançonne (patriotic national song of the Belgians).
brabant (brabɑ̃), s.m. [etym. dub.] A kind of plough.
bracelet (braslɛ), s.m. [f. *bras*] Bracelet, armlet, bangle.
brachial, -e, (aux) (brakjal), adj. [f. L *brachialis*] (anat.) Brachial.
bracycéphale (brakisefal), adj. [f. Gr. *brakhus+kephalē*] Brachycephalic.
braconnage (brakɔnaʒ), s.m. Poaching.
braconner (brakɔne), v.n.a. [f. *braque*] To poach, to go poaching.
braconnier (brakɔnje), s.m. Poacher.
bractée (brakte), s.f. [L *bractea*] (bot.) Bract, bractea.
bractéole (brakteɔl), s.f. (bot.) Bracteole; (techn.) gold leaf.
brader (brade), v.n.a. [neol.; local wd of Northern France] To undersell; to sell in the street any new or second-hand goods without possessing a commercial licence. (Such traffic is allowed only on certain appointed days.)
braderie (bradri), s.f. [f. *brader*] Street fair; see BRADER.
bradeur (bradœr), s.m. Cheapjack.
bradype (bradip), s.m. (zool.) Bradypus, sloth; syn. AÏ, PARESSEUX.
brague (brag), (obs.) s.f. **1.** Breeches; **2.** breeching (of cannon).
braguette (bragɛt), s.f. Fly (of trousers); syn. BRAYETTE.
brahmane, bramin, bramine (braman, bramin), s.m. Brahman, Brahmin.
brahmanique, brahminique (bramanik, braminik), adj. Brahminical.
brahmanisme (bramanism), s.m. Brahminism.
brai, (brɛ), s.m. [f. Scand. *brak*] Rosin, pitch, tar.
braie (brɛ), s.f. [f. Celt. *bracca*] Napkin; **~s**, s.f.pl. breeches.
braillard, -e, brailleu-r, -se (brɑjar, brɑjœr), adj. Bawling, brawling, noisy. **~**, s.m.f. Bawler, brawler.
braille (brɑj), s.m. [f. n. of Fr. inventor *Louis Braille*, d. 1852] Braille (type, system, writing, printing for the blind).
braillement (brɑjmɑ̃), s.m. **braillerie** (brɑjri), s.f. Bawling, squalling.
brailler (brɑje), v.n. To bawl, to squall.
braiment, braiement (brɛmɑ̃), s.m. [f. *braire*] Braying.
braire (brɛr), v.n. def. [f. LL *bragere*] To bray.
braise (brɛz), s.f. **1.** Embers; live, burning, or dead coals of wood; **2.** (slang) cash; tin, dibs, oof.
braiser (brɛze), v.a. (cook.) To braise.
braisière (brɛzjɛr), s.f. Braising-pan.
bramement (brɑməmɑ̃), s.m. (of deer, stags), Belling, troating.
bramer (brɑme), v.n. [OHG *brammon*] To troat (as stags), to bell.
bramin, bramine (bramin), s.m. See BRAHMANE.
bran (brɑ̃), s.m. [f. Celt. *bran*] Bran; sawdust; (pop.) excrement.
brancard (brɑ̃kar), s.m. [Provenç. *brancal*] **1.** Stretcher, litter; **2.** handbarrow; **3.** shaft, thill (of a carriage).
brancardier (brɑ̃kardje), s.m. Stretcher-bearer.
branchage (brɑ̃ʃaʒ), s.m. [f. *branche*] Branches, boughs.
branche (brɑ̃ʃ), s.f. [f. LL *branca*] **1.** Branch, bough; (fig.) any part or

subdivision of a main body or system; *tendre la ~ d'olivier*, to offer the olive-branch, to offer peace; *les ~s du Nil*, the branches of the Nile; *les différentes ~s des sciences*, the different branches of science; (slang) *ma vieille ~*, old chap, old bean; **2.** (arch.) rib; **3.** branch or leg (of compasses).

branchement (brɑ̃ʃmɑ̃), s.m. Branching, ramification; branch-pipe.

brancher (brɑ̃ʃe), v.n. and **se ~**, v.pr. To perch; ~, v.a. **1.** to branch, to fork; **2.** to hang on a branch.

branchette (brɑ̃ʃɛt), s.f. Branchlet, twig.

branchial, -e, (aux) (brɑ̃kjal), adj. (anat.) Branchial.

branchies (brɑ̃ʃi), s.f.pl. [f. Gr. *bragkhia*] (anat.) Branchiae, gills; syn. OUÏES.

branchiopodes (brɑ̃kjɔpɔd), s.m.pl. (zool.) Branchiopoda.

branchu, -e (brɑ̃ʃy), adj. Branchy.

brandade (brɑ̃dad), s.f. [Provenç. wd] (cook.) Brandade (a dish of cod).

brande (brɑ̃d), s.f. [unkn. orig.] **1.** Heather, heath, ling; **2.** faggot of heather dipped in inflammable material.

brandebourg (brɑ̃dbur), s.m. [geog. orig.] Braid, frog, shell, loop of lace (on a coat), gimp.

brandebourgeois, -e (brɑ̃dburʒwɑ), adj. s.m.f. Of Brandenburg, Brandenburger.

brandevin (brɑ̃dvɛ̃), s.m. [f. Dutch *brandewijn*] Brandy.

brandevinier (brɑ̃dvinje), s.m. Maker of brandy.

brandiller (brɑ̃dije), v.n.a. To swing, to dangle, to shake about.

brandir (brɑ̃dir), v.a. [f. OF *brand*] To brandish, to flourish.

brandon (brɑ̃dɔ̃), s.m. [f. Germ. *Brand*] Brand, fire-brand, wisp or bundle of burning straw; *un ~ de discorde*, a brand of discord.

branlant, -e (brɑ̃lɑ̃), adj. [f. *branler*] Tottering, shaky, loose.

branle (brɑ̃l), s.m. [f. *branler*] **1.** Swinging, swaying motion; **2.** impetus, impulse; *donner le ~, mettre en ~*, to set going, to give the first start; **3.** brawl, branle (an old dance).

branle-bas (brɑ̃lbɑ), s.m. invar. **1.** (naut.) Clearing (for action); quarters; **2.** confusion, hubbub, disarray.

branlement (brɑ̃lmɑ̃), s.m. Swinging, tottering, shaking.

branler (brɑ̃le), v.a. [f. OF *brandeler*] To shake, to swing, to wag, to totter; *~ dans le manche*, to be shaky, unsafe, to waver; *~ la tête*, to wag one's head (in derision or amusement).

braque (brak), s.m.f. [OHG *bracco*] **1.** Brach (hound); **2.** ~, s.m.f. adj. hare-brained, cracked (fellow), madcap.

braquemart (brakmar), s.m. [LL *braga-mardus*] Broadsword (obs.).

braquer (brake), v.a. [unkn. orig.] **1.** To point (a gun, or telescope); to direct, to turn (one's look); **2.** (motor.) to turn (the steering-wheel) as far as possible.

bras (brɑ), s.m. invar. [L *brachium*] Arm; branch; hand; *il est son ~ droit*, he is his right hand, his agent, his factotum; *accueillir à ~ ouverts*, to receive with open arms; to welcome gladly; *frapper à ~ raccourci*, to strike with all one's might; *demeurer les ~ croisés*, to do nothing; *cela me coupe* (or *casse*) *~ et jambes*, or *les ~ m'en tombent*, that astounds me, that disables me completely; *se donner le ~*, to go arm-in-arm; *avoir le ~ long*, to have far-reaching influence; *le ~ séculier*, the secular arm; *les ~ du fauteuil*, the arms of the easy-chair; *le ~ d'un levier*, the arm of a lever; *un ~ de mer*, an arm of the sea; *à ~*, by hand, by strength of arms; hand; *charrette à ~*, hand-barrow; *à tour de ~*, with might and main; *à ~ le corps*, by the waist, round the waist; *à ~ tendu*, with outstretched arm, at arm's length; *~ dessus ~ dessous*, arm-in-arm; *avoir sur les ~*, to have on one's hands; to have to maintain.

braser (brɑze), v.a. To braze, to weld, to solder.

brasero (brɑzero), s.m. [Span. wd] Brazier, brazero, coal-pan.

brasier (brɑzje), s.m. [f. *braise*] Clear, bright fire; brazier, furnace.

brasiller (brɑzije), v.a. To broil; ~, v.n. to sparkle.

brassage (brasaʒ), s.m. [f. *brasser*] **1.** Mixing, stirring-up; **2.** mashing; **3.** brewing.

brassard (brasar), s.m. [f. *bras*] **1.** Brassard, brace; **2.** armlet, arm-band, badge.

brasse (bras), s.f. [f. *bras*] **1.** (naut.) French fathom = 1m. 62; **2.** stroke (in swimming).

brassée (brase), s.f. [f. *bras*] **1.** Armful; **2.** stroke (in swimming); **3.** reach (in rowing).

brasser (brase), v.a. [f. *bras*] **1.** To mix, to stir up; **2.** to mash; **3.** to brew; (fig.) to concoct, to contrive; **4.** (naut.) to brace.

brasserie (brasri), s.f. **1.** Brewery, brew-house; **2.** beer-shop.

brasseur (brasœr), s.m. Brewer.

brassière (brasjɛr), s.f. **1.** Infant's bodice; **2.** *~s*, (pl.) shoulder straps (of a knapsack, rucksack, &c.).

brassin (brasɛ̃), s.m. [f. *brasser*] **1.** Mash-tub; **2.** brewing (quantity of beer brewed at once); boiling (quantity of soap boiled).

brasure (brɑzyr), s.f. Brazing, brazed joint; *sans ~*, unbrazed, weldless.

bravache (bravaʃ), s.m. [It. *bravaccio*]

Hector, bully, blusterer, swaggerer, fire-eater, swashbuckler.
bravade (bravad), s.f. [It. *bravata*] Bravado, brag, bluster.
brave (brav), adj. [LL *bravus*] **1.** Brave, courageous, gallant; *un homme* ~, a brave man; **2.** honest, worthy, good; *un* ~ *homme*, a worthy man, an honest man; *un* ~ *garcon*, a good, honest fellow; **3.** (obs.) spruce, well clad or adorned. ~, s.m. Brave man, gallant fellow, hero; *se conduire en* ~, to act gallantly; *mon* ~, my good man; *un* ~ *à trois poils*, a tough fellow, a splendid fighter.
bravement (bravmɑ̃), adv. Bravely, gallantly.
braver (brave), v.a. [f. *brave*] To brave, to dare, to defy, to face, to beard.
bravo (bravo), s.m. [It. wd] Bravo, applause, cheer.
bravoure (bravur), s.f. [It. *bravura*] Bravery, gallantry, valour, courage; (mus.) *air de* ~, bravura.
brayer (brɛje), v.a. (naut.) To pay, to cover with pitch.
brayer (brɛje), s.m. (surg.) Truss.
brayette (brɛjɛt), s.f. See BRAGUETTE.
break (brɛk), s.m. [Engl. wd] Brake, break, wagonette.
brebis (brəbi), s.f. [f. L *vervex*, *berbex*] Ewe, sheep; ~ *égarée*, stray sheep; ~ *galeuse*, scabby sheep; (fig.) black sheep; *à* ~ *tondue Dieu mesure le vent*, God tempers the wind to the shorn lamb.
brèche (brɛʃ), s.f. [f. Germ. *brechen*] Breach, gap, opening, notch, hole; *battre en* ~, to batter in, to breach; *réparer les* ~*s*, to stop the holes; *faire* ~, to encroach, to make a hole; *être toujours sur la* ~, to be always on duty, ever ready, always 'there'.
brèche-dent (brɛʃdɑ̃), adj. s.m.f. (pl. *brèche-dents*) Broken-mouthed; gap-toothed (person).
bréchet (breʃɛ), s.m. [f. Celt. orig.] (anat.) Breastbone, brisket, xiphoid cartilage.
bredi-breda (bredibreda), adv. loc. [onom.] Hurry-scurry.
bredouillage, bredouillement (brədujaʒ, brədujmɑ̃), s.m. Sputtering, jabbering.
bredouille (brəduj), s.f. Gammon. ~, adj. (fig.) Crestfallen, empty-handed; *revenir* ~, to return empty-handed.
bredouiller (brəduje), v.n.a. [etym. dub.] To sputter, to stammer, to jabber.
bref (brɛf), fem. **brève** (brɛv), adj. [f. L *brevis*] Brief, short, curt; *à* ~ *délai*, at short notice. ~, adv. Short, in short, briefly.
bref (brɛf), s.m. Brief.
bréhaigne (breɛɲ), adj. [unkn. orig.] Barren, sterile.
brelan (brəlɑ̃), s.m. [OF *brelenc*] Brelan (card-game); pair-royal; gambling-house.
breloque (brəlɔk), s.f. [etym. dub.] **1.** Trinket, pendant, amulet; **2.** (mil.) dismiss; *battre la* ~ or *berloque*, to sound the dismiss.
brème (brɛm), s.f. (ichth.) Bream.
brésil (brezil), s.m. Brazil-wood.
brésilien, -ne (breziljɛ̃), adj. s.m.f. Brazilian.
brésiller (brezije), v.a. To break small; ~, v.n. to fall into dust.
bressan, -e (brɛsɑ̃), adj. s.m.f. Bressan, of Bresse.
brétailler (bretɑje), v.n. [f. *brette*] To fight, to fence.
brétailleur (bretɑjœr), s.m. Fighter, bully, fire-eater.
bretelle (brətɛl), s.f. [etym. dub.] Brace, strap, sling, suspender.
breton, -ne (brətɔ̃), adj. s.m.f. Breton; ~ *bretonnant*, Breton to the backbone.
brette (brɛt), s.f. [etym. dub.] Rapier, long sword.
bretteur (brɛtœr), s.m. (pej.) Bully, duellist, fighter, swashbuckler.
breuvage (brœvaʒ), s.m. [f. L *bibere*] Beverage, draught, drink; (vet.) drench.
brève (brɛv), s.f. [f. *bref*] (pros., phon.) Breve; short syllable.
brevet (brəvɛ), s.m. [f. *bref*] **1.** Patent; brevet, commission; **2.** certificate, diploma.
breveter (brəvte), v.a. To grant a patent or licence to, to patent, to license; *faire* ~, to patent, to take out a patent for (an invention).
bréviaire (brevjɛr), s.m. [L *breviarium*] Breviary; (fig.) vade mecum, favourite book.
brévité (brevite), s.f. [f. *bref*] Shortness, brevity.
briard, -e (brijar), adj. s.m.f. (Native) of the Brie.
bribe (brib), s.f. [f. OF *briber*] **1.** Hunch, hunk (of bread); **2.** (pl.) scraps, odd bits; **3.** tiny bit. ⚠ Not 'bribe' which = *pot-de-vin, argent donné pour corrompre.*
bric-à-brac (brikabrak), s.m. invar. [onom.] Bric-à-brac, curios.
brick (brik), s.m. [Engl. *brig*] (naut.) Brig.
bricole (brikɔl) s.f. [It. *briccola*] **1.** Breast-band (of harness); **2.** shoulder-straps (of haversack, &c.); **3.** rebound (of ball at billiards); **4.** odd job, small work.
bricoler (brikɔle), v.n. **1.** To play the bricole; **2.** to do odd jobs, to potter about.
bricoleu-r, -se (brikɔlœr), s.m.f. One who does odd jobs; Jack-of-all-trades.
bride (brid), s.f. [f. OE *bridel*] Bridle, rein, reins; *tenir la* ~ *haute* (or *courte*), to ride with a tight rein; (fig.) to keep a tight hand (over); *lâcher la* ~, to slacken the reins (of), to let loose; *tenir en* ~, to curb, to control; *la* ~ *sur le cou*, with full liberty of action, loose; *à* ~ *abattue*, at full

speed, at full gallop; *tourner* ~, to turn back; string (of a bonnet, cap); stitches across a buttonhole, or in lace, stitch in crochet-work; (anat.) ligament; (mech.) flange.

brider (bride), v.a. **1.** To bridle, to curb, to check; **2.** to truss (a fowl for roasting).

bridge (bridʒ), s.m. [Engl. wd] **1.** Bridge (game of cards); **2.** bridge (dental appliance).

bridon (bridɔ̃), s.m. Bridoon, snaffle.

brie (bri), s.m. [geog. Fr. orig]. Brie cheese.

brief (brjɛf), s.m. (obs.). See BREF.

brièvement (briɛvmɑ̃), adv. Briefly.

brièveté (briɛvte), s.f. Brevity, shortness, conciseness.

briffer (brife), v.n.a. (slang) To eat, to feed, to grub, to scoff.

brigade (brigad), s.f. [It. *brigata*] Brigade; troop, gang, company; *général de* ~, brigadier-general.

brigadier (brigadje), s.m. (of cavalry) Corporal; (of *gendarmerie*, &c.) non-commissioned officer; (of a boat) bowman.

brigand (brigɑ̃), s.m. [f. It. *brigante*] Brigand, ruffian, armed robber; (fam.) scamp.

brigandage (brigɑ̃daʒ), s.m. Brigandage, robbery, plunder.

brigantin (brigɑ̃tɛ̃), s.m. [f. It. *brigantino*] (naut.) Brigantine.

brigantine (brigɑ̃tin), s.f. (naut.) Spanker (sail), driver; brigantine.

brignole (briɲɔl), s.f. (bot.) Prunello, brignole plum.

brigue (brig), s.f. [f. It. *briga*] Intrigue, manœuvre, soliciting of vote or favour; faction, party.

briguer (brige), v.a. To intrigue for, to solicit (honour, preferment, &c.); to seek, to aspire to.

brillamment (brijamɑ̃), adv. Brilliantly, splendidly.

brillant, -e (brijɑ̃), adj. [f. *briller*] Brilliant, shining, shiny, glittering, sparkling, bright; *de ~s espoirs*, bright hopes.

brillant (brijɑ̃), s.m. **1.** Brilliancy, lustre, shine; **2.** brilliant (diamond).

brillanté (brijɑ̃te), s.m. Dimity. ~, adj. Cut as a brilliant.

brillantine (brijɑ̃tin), s.f. Brilliantine.

briller (brije), v.n. [f. L *beryllus*] To shine, to glitter, to radiate, to sparkle, to gleam, to glow, to blaze, to be brilliant; (fig.) to distinguish oneself, to be conspicuous; *tout ce qui brille n'est pas or*, all is not gold that glitters; *la joie brille dans ses yeux*, his eyes are beaming with joy.

brimade (brimad), s.f. [f. *brimer*] Practical joke, bullying, rag.

brimbaler (brɛ̃bale), v.a.n. To sway backwards and forwards, to jingle (bells).

brimborion (brɛ̃bɔrjɔ̃), s.m. [etym. dub.] Gimcrack, knick-knack.

brimer (brime), v.a. To play tricks on, to bully, to rag, to haze, to ballyrag.

brin (brɛ̃), s.m. [unkn. orig.] Shoot, sprig, blade (of grass), stick, bit; staple (of (rope); *un beau ~ de fille*, a fine slip of a girl; *faire un ~ de causette*, to have a bit of a chat.

brindille (brɛ̃dij), s.f. [f. *brin*] Sprig, twig.

bringue (brɛ̃g), s.f. (slang) *Une grande* ~, a gawky girl, a big gawk.

brio (brio), s.m. [It. wd] Dash, brilliancy, spirit, go.

briochain, -e (briɔʃɛ̃), adj. s.m.f. [geog. orig.] (Native) of Saint-Brieuc (Brittany).

brioche (briɔʃ), s.f. [unkn. orig.] Brioche (a bun); (fig.) blunder.

brique (brik), s.f. [f. Engl. *brick*] Brick, bar (of soap); ~ *anglaise*, bath brick; *rouge* ~, brick-red.

briquer (brike), v.a. (naut.) To wash, to scour, to scrub.

briquet (brikɛ), s.m. **1.** Steel, flint and steel; *battre le* ~, to strike a light; **2.** fox-beagle; **3.** short sabre.

briquetage (briktaʒ), s.m. Bricklaying, brickwork.

briqueter (brikte), v.a. To brick, to adorn with or build of imitation brickwork.

briqueterie (briktri, brikɛtri), s.f. Brick-kiln, brick-making.

briqueteur (briktœr), s.m. Bricklayer.

briquetier (briktje), s.m. Brick-maker.

briquette (brikɛt), s.f. Briquette, cake, patent fuel.

bris (bri), s.m. [f. *briser*] **1.** Breaking (of seals, &c.); **2.** breaking open (a door, &c.); **3.** (naut.) wreckage.

brisant (brizɑ̃), s.m. [f. *briser*] Reef, rock, breaker (wave).

briscard, brisquard (briskar), s.m. Old soldier with stripes (*brisques*).

brise (briz), s.f. [etym. dub.] Breeze; *pare-*~, wind-screen.

brise (briz), [f. *briser*] In compounds: *~-glace*, s.m. ice-breaker, ice-boat; *~-jet*, s.m. stop-cock; *~-lames*, s.m. breakwater; *~-mottes*, s.m. clod-crusher; *~-vent*, s.m. screen.

brisé, -e (brize), p. adj. Shattered, broken, bent, crooked, worn out, done up (with fatigue); folding, jointed; (arch.) curbed; *anneau* ~, split ring; *porte ~e*, folding door; *ligne ~e*, bent, crooked line; *voix ~e* tremulous voice, broken voice.

brise-bise (brizbiz), s.m. invar. Short lace window-curtain, brise-bise.

brisées (brize), s.f.pl. [f. *briser*] Scattered boughs; (fig.) footsteps, tracks; *aller sur les ~s de X*, to tread in X's steps; to compete with X.

brisement (brizmɑ̃), s.m. Breaking.

briser (brize), v.a. [etym. dub.] To

break, to break to pieces, to smash, to crush, to snap, to split; (fig.) to destroy, to harass, to exhaust, to break off; (herald.) to break; *brisons là*, let us leave off here; no more of this; **~**, v.n. to break (as waves); **se ~**, v.pr. to break to pieces, to be broken to pieces, to break down; to fold up; to be refracted.

briseu-r, -se (brizœr), s.m.f. Breaker; *~ d'images*, iconoclast; *~s de grève*, strike-breakers; gang of men especially engaged to prevent violence being used by strikers against non-strikers.

brisis (brizi), s.m. Angle of a curbed roof.

briska (briska), s.f. [Pol. *bryczka*] Britzska (carriage).

brisoir (brizwar), s.m. Brake (for breaking flax and hemp).

brisque (brisk), s.f. [unkn. orig.] **1.** Brisque (certain cards in some games); **2.** (mil.) stripe, chevron.

bristol (bristɔl), s.m. [geog. orig.] Cardboard, bristol board; (by ext.) visiting-card, invitation-card.

brisure (brizyr), s.f. Break, folding joint, folded edge; (herald.) rebatement, brisure.

britannique (britanik), adj. British, Britannic.

broc (bro), s.m. [f. LL *brocchum*] Large jug, pitcher, can.

brocantage (brɔkɑ̃taʒ), s.m. Dealing in second-hand goods; bartering.

brocante (brɔkɑ̃t), s.f. (pej.) Dealing in second-hand goods, barter, swap, broker's trade; small job or bargain.

brocanter (brɔkɑ̃te), v.n.a. To buy and sell second-hand goods, to barter, to exchange.

brocanteu-r, -se (brɔkɑ̃tœr). Dealer in second-hand goods, curiosities or antiquities.

brocard (brɔkar), s.m. **1.** Taunt, lampoon, gibe; **2.** young roe-deer; **3.** shanty where ore is crushed.

brocarder (brɔkarde), v.a. To taunt, to lampoon, to gibe, to scoff.

brocart (brɔkar), s.m. [f. It. *broccato*] Brocade.

brocatelle (brɔkatɛl), s.f. Brocatelle; brocatello marble.

brochage (brɔʃaʒ), s.m. (of a book) Sewing (without back bands) and putting in a paper cover.

brochant, -e (brɔʃɑ̃), p. adj. (herald.) Passing over; (fig.) *~ sur le tout*, over all; overtopping all, surpassing all the rest.

broche (brɔʃ), s.f. [f. LL *brocca*] Brooch; broach; knitting-needle, spike, peg, rod, spindle; spit (for roasting), skewer; *mettre un gigot à la ~*, to spit a leg of mutton; (of a deer) broach; (of a wild boar) tusk.

brocher (brɔʃe), v.a. To sew (a book) and put it in paper covers; to peg, to nail; to weave in patterns, to figure; to hurry through.

brochet (brɔʃɛ), s.m. (ichth.) Pike.

brocheton (brɔʃtɔ̃), s.m. Pickerel, young pike.

brochette (brɔʃɛt), s.f. [f. *broche*] **1.** Skewer, brochette; **2.** pin, stick (for feeding birds); *élever à la ~*, to bring up daintily; **3.** (of orders) string, file, row.

brocheu-r, -se (brɔʃœr), s.m.f. Book-sewer; pattern-weaver.

brochure (brɔʃyr), s.f. [f. *brocher*] **1.** Sewing (of books); **2.** pamphlet, book not exceeding twelve sheets, sewed and put in paper cover; **3.** inwoven pattern (in textiles).

brocoli (brɔkɔli), s.m. [It. *broccolo*] Broccoli, cabbage sprout.

brodequin (brɔdkɛ̃), s.m. [f. Dutch *brosekin*] **1.** Sock of the ancients; (fig.) comedy; **2.** lace-boot, half-boot; **3.** (pl.) boots, bootikin, an instrument of torture in Middle Ages.

broder (brɔde), v.a. [f. Germ. and Celt. *brozd*] To embroider, to work, to ornament with needlework; (fig.) to embellish, to amplify.

broderie (brɔdri), s.f. Embroidery; (fig.) embellishment, exaggeration.

brodeu-r, -se (brɔdœr), s.m.f. Embroiderer, embroideress, embroidering-machine.

broie (brwɑ), s.f. See syn. BRISOIR.

broiement (brwɑmɑ̃), s.m. [f. *broyer*] Grinding, pounding, crushing.

brome (brom), s.m. (chem.) Bromine; **bromate,** s.m. bromate; **bromure,** s.m. bromide; **bromique,** adj. bromic.

bronche (brɔ̃ʃ), s.f. [f. Gr. *brogkhos*] (anat.) Bronchus (pl. -i); (fam.) chest.

broncher (brɔ̃ʃe), v.n. To stumble, to trip, to flinch, to falter, to err, to do wrong.

bronchial, -e, (aux) (brɔ̃kjal), adj. Bronchial; syn. BRONCHIQUE.

bronchite (brɔ̃ʃit), s.f. Bronchitis; **broncho-pneumonie** (brɔ̃kopnømɔni), s.f. broncho-pneumonia.

bronze (brɔ̃z), s.m. [It. *bronzo*] Bronze; bronze colour; bronze figure or medal; (fig.) *âme de ~*, intrepid soul; *cœur de ~*, heart of flint, unfeeling heart.

bronzer (brɔ̃ze), v.a. To bronze, to colour like bronze, to tan, to sunburn; **se ~**, v.pr. to become of a bronze colour, to tan; (fig.) to steel, to become hardened.

broquart (brɔkar), s.m. See BROCARD.

broquette (brɔkɛt), s.f. Tack, tacks.

brossage (brɔsaʒ), s.m. Brushing.

brosse (brɔs), s.f. [LL *brustia*] Brush; *~ à habits*, clothes-brush; *~ à barbe*, shaving-brush; *~ à dents*, tooth-brush; *~ à peindre*, paint-brush; *~ à tête*, hair-brush.

brossée (brɔse), s.f. Brushing; (fig.) beating, thrashing, drubbing; defeat.
brosser (brɔse), v.a. To brush; **se ~**, v.pr. to brush oneself; (fig.) to have to do without something one was expecting; *se ~ le ventre,* to starve.
brosserie (brɔsri), s.f. Brush-making; brush-trade.
brosseur (brɔsœr), s.m. (mil.) Officer's (soldier) servant.
brossier (brɔsje), s.m. Brush-maker.
brou (bru), s.m. [f. *brouter*] Husk, walnut-husk.
brouet (bruɛ), s.m. [LL *brodum*] Broth, thin soup, wish-wash; *~ noir,* black broth (of the Spartans).
brouette (bruɛt), s.f. [f. OF *berouette*] **1.** Wheelbarrow; **2.** (obs.) bath-chair.
brouettée (bruɛte), s.f. Barrow-load.
brouetter (bruɛte), v.a. To wheel in a barrow.
brouhaha (bruaa), s.m. [onom.] Confused murmurs, rumble of voices, uproar, hubbub, hullabaloo; cheers.
brouillamini (brujamini), s.m. [corrupt. of *Bol d'Arménie*] **1.** (vet.) Plaster of Armenian bole; **2.** confusion, muddle.
brouillard (brujar), s.m. [f. *brouiller*] **1.** Fog, mist; **2.** (comm.) waste-book; *papier ~,* blotting-paper.
brouillasser (brujase), v.n. To drizzle.
brouille (bruj), s.f. [f. *brouiller*] Discord, quarrel, variance, disagreement, falling-out; *être en ~ avec X,* to be on bad terms, to be at variance with X; *il y a eu de la ~ entre eux,* they have had a tiff.
brouiller (bruje), v.a. [unkn. orig.] To mix, to mingle, to confuse, to muddle, to throw into confusion, to embroil; to scramble (eggs); *~ les cartes,* to shuffle; (fig.) to embroil matters, to create confusion; *être brouillé avec X*; to be on bad terms or at variance with X; *un teint brouillé,* a mottled complexion; *~ les idées,* to confuse one's ideas; **se ~**, v.pr. to fall out, to disagree, to quarrel; to get confused, mixed, &c.
brouillerie (brujri), s.f. See syn. BROUILLE.
brouillon, -ne (brujɔ̃), adj. Meddlesome, meddling, disorderly, unreliable, bungling, mischief-making, unruly. ~, s.m.f. Meddler, mischief-maker.
brouillon (brujɔ̃), s.m. First draft, rough draft, foul copy.
brouir (bruir), v.a. To blight, to blast.
brouissure (bruisyr), s.f. Blight.
broussaille (brusɑj), s.f. (usually in plural) Brushwood, thicket, underwood, brambles, briars; *cheveux en ~,* disordered hair; *sourcils en ~,* shaggy eyebrows.
brousse (brus), s.f. Bush-veldt, wild underwood, brush, wilderness.
brouter (brute), v.a.n. To browse, to browse on; (prov., fig.) *là où la chèvre est attachée il faut qu'elle broute,* one must put up with the inconveniences of one's position.
broutille (brutij), s.f. Young shoot, twig; (fig.) trifle.
broyage (brwajaʒ), s.m. [f. *broyer*] Pounding, crushing, grinding.
broyer (brwaje), v.a. [etym. dub.; perhaps f. Germ. *brechen*] To pound, to crush, to grind; (fig.) *~ du noir,* to have the blues, to be in the dumps.
broyeu-r, -se (brwajœr), s.m.f. Grinder, crusher, pounder, breaker. ~, adj. Grinding, crushing, &c. **~se**, s.f. Grinding-machine.
bru (bry), s.f. [OHG *brût*] Daughter-in-law.
bruant, bréant (brɥɑ̃, breɑ̃), s.m. (ornith.) Bunting, yellow-hammer.
brucelles (brysɛl), s.f.pl. Pliers, tweezers.
brugnon (bryɲɔ̃), s.m. (bot.) Nectarine, clingstone.
bruine (brɥin), s.f. Light drizzle (of rain).
bruiner (brɥine), v.n. imp. To drizzle.
bruire (brɥir), v.n. def. To rustle, to murmur, to buzz, to produce a slight noise.
bruissement (brɥismɑ̃), s.m. Rustling, rustle, murmur, slight noise.
bruit (brɥi), s.m. [unkn. orig.] Noise, sound, din, report; (fig.) rumour, sensation, talk, report, news; *le ~ court que,* it is said (or rumoured) that; *faire du ~ dans le monde,* to acquire renown, make a noise in the world; *beaucoup de ~ pour rien,* much ado about nothing; *grand ~ petite besogne,* much cry, little wool; *cela fera du ~ dans Landerneau,* that will make a pretty stir in Little Pedlington.
brûlage (brylaʒ), s.m. Burning, destroying; roasting (of coffee).
brûlant, -e (brylɑ̃), p. adj. Burning, hot, scorching; (fig.) eager, fiery, ardent.
brûlé (bryle), s.m. Burning, burnt smell or taste; something burnt. **~, -e**, p. adj. Burnt, overbaked, inflamed; sunburnt.
brûle-gueule (brylgœl), s.m. invar. Short pipe, cutty; (in Ireland) dudeen.
(à) brûle-pourpoint (abrylpurpwɛ̃), adv. loc. Point-blank; close to one's face; in one's teeth; suddenly.
brûler (bryle), v.a.n. [LL *brustulare*] To burn, to singe, to scorch, to scald, to parch, to tan, to roast (coffee), to consume, to take fire; (fig.) *~ de,* to be on fire, to long for, to; *~ pour,* to love; *~ la cervelle à X,* to blow X's brains out; *~ le pavé,* to tear along (the road); *~ les planches,* to act with spirit, to star it; *~ la politesse à X,* to leave X abruptly, unceremoniously; *~ une étape,* to go on without stopping; (fig.) *~ les étapes,* to go post-haste.
brûleu-r, -se (brylœr), s.m.f. Burner.

brûloir (brylwar), s.m. Coffee-roaster.
brûlot (brylo), s.m. [f. *brûler*] **1.** (naut.) Fire-ship; **2.** (fig.) firebrand; **3.** burnt brandy.
brûlure (brylyr), s.f. Burn, scald.
brumaire (brymɛr), s.m. [f. *brume*] Brumaire (2nd month of the calendar of 1st French Republic, from 23 Oct. to 21 Nov.).
brumal, -e, (aux) (brymal), adj. Winterly, wintry, brumal.
brumasser (brymase), v.imp. To drizzle, to mizzle.
brume (brym), s.f. [L *bruma*] Mist, fog, haze.
brumeu-x, -se (brymø), adj. Foggy, misty, hazy.
brun, -e (brœ̃), adj. s.m.f. [OHG *brûn*] Brown, dun, dark; brown colour; dark-haired or -complexioned man.
brunâtre (brynɑtr), adj. Brownish.
brune (bryn), s.f. **1.** Dusk (of the evening); *à la* ~, towards dusk; **2.** brunette.
brunette (brynɛt), s.m. adj. (mus., poet.) Brunette.
brunir (brynir), v.a.n. To brown, to darken, to tan; to burnish (gold or silver).
brunissage (brynisaʒ), s.m. Burnishing.
brunisseu-r, -se (brynisœr), s.m.f. Burnisher.
brunissoir (bryniswar), s.m. Burnisher (a tool).
brunissure (brynisyr), s.f. Burnish.
brusque (brysk), adj. [f. It. *brusco*] Sudden, short, curt, unexpected, gruff, rough, abrupt.
brusquement (bryskəmɑ̃), adv. Bluntly, suddenly, unexpectedly, abruptly, gruffly, hastily.
brusquer (bryske), v.a. To treat roughly, to be sharp with; to hurry, to decide to run the risk of at once.
brusquerie (bryskəri), s.f. Bluntness, gruffness, abruptness, suddenness.
brut, -e (bryt), adj. [f. L *brutus*] Raw; gross, nett, gross weight; rough, coarse, brutish, unpolished.
brutal, -e, (aux) (brytal), adj. Brutal, brutish, rough, rude. ~, s.m. Brutal fellow, bully, churl.
brutalement (brytalmɑ̃), adv. Brutally, brutishly, roughly, rudely.
brutaliser (brytalize), v.a. To bully, to use roughly; to brutalize. ⚠ Note that 'to brutalize' has usually the sense of 'to make or to grow brutal' = *rendre brutal, devenir brutal*; *brutaliser* is never used in that sense.
brutalité (brytalite), s.f. Brutality, brutishness, roughness, rudeness; brutal act; *lasse de ses ~s*, unable to bear any longer his ill-treatment or brutalities.
brute (bryt), s.f. [f. L *bruta*] Brute, brutal person.
bruyamment (bryjamɑ̃), adv. Noisily, loudly, clamorously.
bruyant, -e (bryjɑ̃), adj. [f. *bruire*] Noisy, loud.
bruyère (bryjɛr), s.f. [f. Celt. *brûg*] (bot.) Heath, heather; *racine de* ~, briar-root (for pipes).
bryon, brion (brjɔ̃), s.m. (bot.) Tree-moss.
bryone (brjɔn), s.f. (bot.) Bryony.
buanderie (bɥɑ̃dri), s.f. [f. *buée*] Wash-house, laundry.
buandi-er, -ère (bɥɑ̃dje), s.m.f. See syn. BLANCHISSEUR.
bubale (bybal), s.m. (zool.) Bubal (kind of antelope).
bube (byb), s.f. Pimple.
bubon (bybɔ̃), s.m. (pathol.) Bubo.
bubonique (bybɔnik), adj. (pathol.) Bubonic.
buccal, -e, (aux) (bykkal), adj. [f. L *bucca*] Buccal, of the mouth.
buccin (byksɛ̃), s.m. [L *buccina*] **1.** Buccin; **2.** (moll.) whelk, trumpet-shell.
buccinateur (byksinatœr), s.m. **1.** (ant.) Buccin-player; **2.** (anat.) buccinator.
buccine (byksin), s.f. (Rom. ant.) Buccin (a kind of trumpet).
bucentaure (bysɑ̃tɔr), s.m. [f. Gr. *bous*+ *centaure*] Bucentaur (Venetian state barge).
bûche (byʃ), s.f. [LL *busca*] Log; (slang) fall; *ramasser une* ~, to come a cropper, or a mucker.
bûcher (byʃe), s.m. **1.** Wood-house; **2.** wood-pile, stake, pyre.
bûcher (byʃe), v.a. To hew, to dress, to trim. ~, v.n.a.; to work hard, to plod, to swot (at).
bûcheron, -ne (byʃrɔ̃), s.m.f. Wood-cutter.
bûchette (byʃɛt), s.f. Stick, small bit of wood.
bûcheu-r, -se (byʃœr), s.m.f. (pop.) Hard worker, plodder, swot.
bucolique (bykɔlik), adj. [f. Gr. *boukolikos*] Bucolic. ~, s.f. Bucolic.
bucrane (bykrɑn), s.m. [f. Gr. *bous*+ *kranion*] Bucrane (sculptured ornament like ox-skull).
budget (bydʒɛ), s.m. [Engl. wd, f. OF *boulgette*] Budget, estimates; ~ *d'un ménage*, household expenses in relation to income.
budgétaire (bydʒetɛr), adj. Budgetary.
buée (bɥe), s.f. Steam, mist, moisture.
buffet (byfɛ), s.m. [unkn. orig.] Sideboard; buffet, refreshment room; refreshment table, supper. ⚠ Note that in English 'buffet' has also a very different meaning: *coup, soufflet, brutale poussée*.
buffeti-er, -ère (byftje), s.m.f. Refreshment-room keeper.
buffle (byfl), s.m., fem. **bufflonne** (byflɔn), [It. *bufalo*] (zool.) Buffalo; buff leather.

buffleterie (byflɛtri), s.f. (mil.) A soldier's belts, straps, &c.
buffletin (byflətɛ̃), s.m. Young buffalo, buffalo calf.
buggy (bœge), s.m. [Engl. wd] Buggy.
bugle (bygl), s.m. [Engl. wd] (mus.) Bugle. ~, s.f. (bot.) Bugle.
buglosse (byglɔs), s.f. [L *buglossa*] (bot.) Bugloss.
bugrane (bygran), s.f. [LL *boveretna*] (bot.) Rest-harrow, cammock.
buire (bɥir), s.f. Ornamented jug, silver jug, flagon.
buis (bɥi), s.m. [f. L *buxus*] Box-tree, box-wood.
buissaie, buissière (bɥisɛ, bɥisjɛr), s.f. Box-plantation.
buisson (bɥisɔ̃), s.m. [f. *buis*] Bush, thicket; ~ *ardent* (syn. PYRACANTHE), evergreen thorn; (in Scripture) burning bush; *faire ~ creux*, to find the bird flown; to draw a blank; ~ *d'écrevisses*, a piled-up dish of crayfish; (lit. and fig.) *battre les ~s*, to beat about the bush.
buissonneu-x, -se (bɥisɔnø), adj. Bushy.
buissonni-er, -ère (bɥisɔnje), adj. Bush-; *lapin ~*, bush-rabbit; *faire l'école ~ère*, to play truant.
bulbe (bylb), s.m. [f. Gr. *bolbos*] (bot. anat.) Bulb.
bulbeu-x, -se (bylbø), adj. Bulbous.
bulgare (bylgar), adj. s.m.f. Bulgarian.
bulle (byl), s.f. [f. L *bulla*] Bubble; blister; (med.) bulla; (of the Pope) bull. ~, adj. s.m. *Papier ~*, coarse, yellowish paper.
bulletin (byltɛ̃), s.m. [It. *bolletino*] Bulletin, report, account, notice, ticket; voting-paper, vote; ~ *des lois*, statute-book.
bupreste (byprɛst), s.m. (ent.) Buprestis, golden beetle.
buraliste (byralist), s.m.f. [f. *bureau*] Office keeper, tobacconist; money-taker.
bure[1] (byr), s.f. [f. L *burra*] Drugget.
bure[2] (byr), s.f. [f. Germ. *bohren*] (mining) Shaft.
bureau (pl. **-x**) (byro), s.m. [OF *burel*] **1.** Writing-table, desk, bureau; **2.** bureau (President, vice-president, secretaries, treasurer, of a company, a committee, &c.); **3.** office-counter, counting-house, department; **4.** board, committee, committee-room; ~ *d'affaires*, agency office; ~ *de poste*, post-office; ~ *de placement*, registry office; ~ *de tabac*, tobacconist's shop; ~ *de bienfaisance*, board of charity; *chef de ~*, (in a ministry) head of a department; *garçon de ~*, office-boy, office-porter; *à ~x ouverts*, on demand over the counter; ~ *électoral*, president and polling clerks.
bureaucrate (byrokrat), s.m.f. Bureaucrat, red-tapist.
bureaucratie (byrokrasi), s.f. [*bureau*+ Gr. *kratein*] Bureaucracy, red-tape.
bureaucratique (byrokratik), adj. Bureaucratic.
burette (byrɛt), s.f. [f. *buire*] Cruet, jug; (eccles.) flagon; (techn.) oil-feeder, oil-can.
burgrave (byrgrav), s.m. [f. Germ. *Burg*+ *Graf*] Burgrave; (fam.) old fellow, fossilized person.
burgraviat (byrgravja), s.m. Burgraviate.
burin (byrɛ̃), s.m. [f. Germ. *bohren*] Graver, burin, graving-tool.
buriner (byrine), v.a. To engrave; (fig.) to trace, to portray, to write forcibly; (slang) to work hard.
burlesque (byrlɛsk), adj. [It. *burlesco*] Burlesque, ludicrous. ~, s.m. Burlesque.
burlesquement (byrlɛskmɑ̃), adv. In a burlesque manner, ludicrously.
burnous (byrnus), s.m. [Arab. *burnus*] Burnous.
bursal, -e, (aux) (byrsal), adj. [f. L *bursa*] Fiscal.
busard (byzar), s.m. [f. *buse*] (ornith.) Harrier.
busc (bysk), s.m. Busk (of stays).
buse[1] (byz), s.f. [f. L *buteo*] **1.** (ornith.) Buzzard; **2.** (fig.) dolt.
buse[2] (byz), s.f. [f. L *bucina*] Pipe, nozzle; tewel.
busqué, e- (byske), p. adj. Busked, arched, curved.
busquer (byske), v.a. To put a busk in; to curve, to shorten.
buste (byst), s.m. [f. It. *busto*] Bust, head and shoulders; *portrait en ~*, half-length portrait; (dressm.) dress-stand.
but (byt, by), s.m. [f. *buter*] Butt, target, mark, goal, winning-post; aim, object, end, purpose; *de ~ en blanc*, point-blank, abruptly, bluntly.
bute (byt), s.f. Farrier's knife.
butée (byte), s.f. Abutment, abutment-pier; (motor., aeron.) *palier de ~*, thrust bearing.
buter (byte), v.a. To prop, to buttress; ~, v.n. to stumble (*contre*, against); **se ~**, v.pr. to grow obstinate.
butin (bytɛ̃), s.m. [f. Germ. *Beute*] Booty, spoils, gleanings, profits.
butiner (bytine), v.a.n. To collect; to plunder, to collect booty; to pilfer, to gather (honey, as bees do).
butoir (bytwar), s.m. Catch, abutment, buffer-stop.
butor (bytɔr), s.m., fem. **butorde 1.** (ornith.) Bittern; **2.** churlish booby, dolt.
butte (byt), s.f. [f. *butter*] Mound, knoll, hillock, rise; *en ~ à*, exposed to.
butter (byte), v.a. [var. of *bouter*] To bank up, to earth up, to ridge.

buttoir (bytwar), s.m. **1.** Ridging-plough; **2.** buffer-stop.
butyreu-x, -se (bytirø), adj. [f. L *butyrum*] Butyrous.
butyrique (bytirik), adj. (chem.) Butyric.
buvable (byvabl), adj. Drinkable.
buvard (byvar), adj. Blotting. ~, s.m. Blotting-paper, blotting-case, dispatch box, writing-pad.
buveti-er, -ère (byvtje), s.m.f. Bar-keeper.
buvette (byvɛt), s.f. Refreshment-room, tap-room; drinking-fountain.
buveu-r, -se (byvœr), s.m.f. Drinker.
buvoter (byvɔte), v.n. To sip, to bib, to tipple.
byronien, -ne (bairɔnjɛ̃), adj. Byronic.
byrrh (bir), s.m. A drink composed of wine, quinquina, &c.
bysse, byssus (bis, bisys), s.m. [Gr. *bussos*] (zool.) Byssus; (ant. arch.) byssus.
byzantin, -e (bizɑ̃tɛ̃), adj. s.m.f. Byzantine; (fig.) *discussions ~es*, vain over-subtle discussions.

C

C (se), s.m. 3rd letter, c; (as Rom. numeral) 100.
c' (contr. of *ce*).
ça (sa), pron. [contr. of *cela*] That; *comme ~*, in that way; *comme ci, comme ~*, so-so, middling; (Revolutionary song) *~ ira!*, go on, go it!; *pas de ~!*, none of that!; (fam.) *~ ne doute de rien!*, he (or she) believes he can do anything!; *c'est ~*, that 's right; that 's it; *c'est toujours ~!*, that 's so much to the good.
çà (sa), adv. Here; *~ et là*, here and there; to and fro, hither and thither.
çà (sa), interj. Now then!, come now!; *ah ~!*, well now!, I say!
cab (kab), s.m. [Engl. wd] Hansom, hansom cab.
cabale (kabal), s.f. [f. Hebr. *kabbalah*] Cabal, cabala; *monter une ~*, to get up a cabal.
cabaler (kabale), v.n. To cabal, to intrigue, to plot (*pour*, in favour of; *contre*, against).
cabaleu-r, -se (kabalœr), s.m.f. Caballer, plotter, intriguer.
cabaliste (kabalist), s.m.f. Cabalist.
cabalistique (kabalistik), adj. Cabalistic, cabalistical.
caban (kabɑ̃), s.m. [f. Span. *gaban*] Hooded cloak, pilot cloak.
cabanage (kabanaʒ), s.m. Huts collectively, encampment.
cabane (kaban), s.f. [f. LL *capanna*] **1.** Cabin, shed, hut, cot, kennel, hutch; **2.** flat-bottomed boat.
cabaner (kabane), v.n. To hut, to camp; (naut.) to capsize.
cabanon (kabanɔ̃), s.m. Small hut, cell, black hole, padded dark-room (for mad people); *fou à mettre au ~*, raving mad.
cabaret (kabarɛ), s.m. [LL *cabaretus*] **1.** Wine-shop, tavern, public-house, pot-house; **2.** (recent extension) night-club, music-hall, tavern and dance-hall combined; **3.** set of liqueur glasses and decanters (in box or on a tray); tantalus; **4.** (bot.) asarabacca; **5.** (ornith.) siskin (linnet).
cabareti-er, -ère (kabartje), s.m.f. Wine-shop keeper, host, tavern-keeper, publican.
cabas (kabɑ), s.m. [f. L *capax*?] Rush basket, frail, flat straw basket, marketing-basket.
cabasset (kabasɛ), (obs.) s.m. Helmet (used in 16th century).
cabernet (kabɛrnɛ), s.m. [etym. unkn.] Kind of vine (grown in S.W. of France).
cabestan (kabɛstɑ̃), s.m. [f. Provenç. *cabestan*, Span. *cabestrante*] Capstan, windlass.
cabiai (kabjɛ), s.m. [Amer. wd] (zool.) Water-hog, capybara.
cabillaud (kabijo), s.m. [Dutch *kabeljauw*] Fresh cod, keeling.
cabillot (kabijo), s.m. [f. Provenç. *cabilho*] (naut.) Toggle; syn. CHEVILLOT.
cabine (kabin), s.f. [f. Engl. *cabin*] **1.** Cabin, berth, small room; **2.** (of a lift) cage, car; *~ téléphonique*, telephone box (or room).
cabinet (kabinɛ), s.m. [It. *gabinetto*] **1.** Closet, small room, small dark room; **2.** study, library, consulting-room; **3.** water-closet; **4.** cabinet council, ministry, the ministers, secretaryship of each minister; **5.** office, practice, business; *~ d'affaires*, business agency; general agency; *~ noir*, censorship of private correspondence (instituted for Louis XIV); *~ de lecture*, reading room, circulating library; **6.** piece of furniture, cabinet.
câble (kɑbl), s.m. [f. LL *capulum*] **1.** Cable, rope, line, wire; **2.** cable-length; *filer du ~*, to pay out more cable; (fig.) to gain time, to boggle; *~ de remorque*, hawser.
câblé, -e (kɑble), p. adj. Cabled, cable-laid; (arch.) cable-shaped; *pneu ~*, corded tyre.
câblé (kɑble), s.m. (kind of) Sewing-cotton; cable-cord.
câbleau (pl. -x), **câblot** (kɑblo), s.m. (naut.) Grapnel rope.
câbler (kɑble), v.a.n. **1.** To cable, to lay or twist a cable; **2.** to cable (to send a telegraph message overseas).
câblière (kɑbljɛr), s.f. Anchor-stone (for fishing).
câblogramme (kɑblɔgram), s.m. Cablegram.

cabochard, -e (kabɔʃar), adj. s.m.f. Obstinate, wilful (person).
caboche (kabɔʃ), s.f. [f. L *caput*] **1.** Pate, nob, brain-box, noddle; *il a la ~ dure,* he is slow of understanding and obstinate; he is thick-headed; **2.** hobnail.
cabochon (kabɔʃɔ̃), s.m. **1.** Cabochon, tallow-drop (precious stone); **2.** stud-nail, fancy brass, silver or gold nail; **3.** (moll.) pileopsis, foolscap limpet.
cabosse (kabɔs), s.f. [f. *caboche*] **1.** Bump, bruise; **2.** cacao-pod.
cabosser (kabɔse), v.a. To bump, to bruise, to batter, to misshape, to dent; *chapeau cabossé,* battered hat.
cabot (kabo), s.m. **1.** (ichth.) (also *chabot*) Bull-head, miller's thumb; **2.** (slang) dog, cur, tyke, mongrel; **3.** (slang) actor; see CABOTIN.
cabotage (kabɔtaʒ), s.m. [f. Span. *cabo*] (naut.) Coasting trade.
caboter (kabɔte), v.n. (naut.) To coast.
caboteur, cabotier (kabɔtœr, kabɔtje), s.m. adj. Coaster; coasting (ship).
cabotin, -e (kabɔtɛ̃), s.m.f. [unkn. orig.] Third-rate actor or actress, strolling player. **~**, adj. Showy, of cheap and gaudy effect; over-emotional.
cabotinage (kabɔtinaʒ), s.m. **1.** Bad acting; over-expressive, cheap, shameless acting; **2.** sham emotion, feigned feelings, gush, playing to the gallery, affectation.
cabotiner (kabɔtine), v.n. **1.** To act badly (seeking only personal success); **2.** to simulate feelings, to act a part (in life); to gush.
caboulot (kabulo), s.m. (slang) Small tavern, pot-house.
(se) cabrer (səkɑbre), v.pr. [f. Provenç. *cabra*] **1.** To rear; **2.** (fig.) to rebel, to kick, to take fright or offence, to fly into a passion; *faire ~*, to make (a horse) rear; (fig.) to provoke, to offend.
cabri (kabri), s.m. [f. L *capra*] Kid; *sauter comme un ~*, to dance lightly, gaily, and wildly.
cabriole (kabriɔl), s.f. [It. *capriola*] Caper, capriole; *faire la ~*, to cut a caper.
cabrioler (kabrjɔle), v.n. To caper.
cabriolet (kabrjɔle), s.m. [f. *cabrioler*] **1.** Cabriolet, open cab, gig, hood; **2.** lady's bonnet; **3.** handcuffs.
cabrioleu-r, -se (kabrjɔlœr), s.m.f. Caperer. **~**, adj. Capering.
cabus (kaby), adj. s.m. [f. Provenç.] (kind of) Cabbage.
caca (kaka), s.m. [f. L *cacare*] (child. wd) Cack; nasty, dirty thing; *faire ~*, to cack.
cacade (kakad), s.f. [f. It. *cacata*] Failure, mess, shameful retreat.
cacahuète, cacaouète (kakawɛt), s.f. (bot.) Ground-nut; syn. ARACHIDE.
cacao (kakao), s.m. [Span. *cacao*] (bot.) Cacao, cacao-nut; (comm.) cocoa.
cacaoyer, cacaotier (kakaoje, kakaotje), s.m. Cacao-tree.
cacaoyère (kakaojɛr), s.f. Cacao-plantation.
cacarder (kakarde), v.n. (of the goose) To cackle, to gabble.
cacatoès (kakatɔɛs), s.m. (ornith.) Cockatoo.
cacatois (kakatwɑ), s.m. [Malay wd.] **1.** Cockatoo; **2.** (naut.) royal sail, royal; *mât de ~*, royal mast.
cachalot (kaʃalo), s.m. [etym. unkn.] Cachalot, spermaceti-whale, sperm-whale, white whale.
cache (kaʃ), s.f. Hiding-place; (naut.) cairn; (hunt.) stake-net; (print.) fly-leaf; **~-~**, hide-and-seek. (In comp. *cache* is invar.) *~-corset,* s.m. under-bodice; *~-col,* s.m., scarf; *~-entrée,* s.m. scutcheon, drop (of a keyhole); *~-misère,* s.m. coat tightly buttoned to conceal poor garments; *~-nez,* s.m. muffler, wrapper; *~-peigne,* s.m. ornaments, flowers placed under the brim of a bonnet, at the back or side; *~-pot,* s.m. ornamental vase or cover to hide flower-pot; *~-poussière,* s.m. dust-coat, dust-cloak.
caché, -e (kaʃe), p. adj. **1.** Hidden, concealed, secret, lurking, underhand, dissembling, deceitful; **2.** retired, reserved, close, out-of-the-way, secluded.
cachectique (kaʃektik), adj. Cachectic.
cachemire (kaʃmir), s.m. [geog. orig.] Cashmere.
cacher (kaʃe), v.a. [f. LL *coacticare*] To hide, to conceal, to keep back or secret, to disguise; **se ~**, v.pr. **1.** to hide oneself; to keep away, to lurk, to abscond (from); **2.** to hide or conceal, (&c.) from oneself; **3.** to conceal from each other; **4.** to lie hidden or concealed; *il s'en cache,* he keeps it secret; *je ne m'en cache pas,* I make no secret of it; *pour vivre heureux, vivons cachés,* far from court, far from care.
cachet (kaʃe), s.m. **1.** Seal, signet, stamp, signet ring; *lettre de ~*, order to imprison a person without a trial (under king's seal); **2.** stamp, mark, seal; **3.** (fig.) style, characteristics, chic, stamp; *cela a beaucoup de ~*, that's quite stylish; **4.** price of a lesson; ticket used to pay in certain restaurants; *courir le ~*, to give private lessons in order to make a living.
cachetage (kaʃtaʒ), s.m. Sealing.
cacheté, -e (kaʃte), adj. Sealed, sealed up; (jest.) *il est ~*, he keeps his mouth shut; he tells no tales.
cacheter (kaʃte), v.a. **1.** To seal, to seal up; **2.** to close (an envelope).
cachette (kaʃɛt), s.f. Hiding-place; *en ~*,

secretly, on the sly, stealthily, underhand; *en ~ de*, without the knowledge of.

cachexie (kaʃɛksi), s.f. [f. Gr. *kakhexia*] (pathol.) Cachexy.

cachot (kaʃo), s.m. Dark cell, prison, dungeon; *mettre au ~*, to put in the black hole, to throw into a dungeon.

cachotter (kaʃɔte), v.a. To make a secret of, to conceal.

cachotterie (kaʃɔtri), s.f. Secrecy, mystery (about trifles), affectation of mysterious ways.

cachotti-er, -ère (kaʃɔtje), s.m.f. Person who is always making secrets about trifles. ~, adj. Sly, mysterious.

cachou (kaʃu), s.m. [Malay *kachu*] Catechu, cutch, cachou.

cachucha (kaʃyʃa), s.f. [Span. wd] Cachucha (dance, dance-tune).

cacique (kasik), s.m. [Span. wd] **1.** Cacique, cazique; **2.** (fig.) pupil taking first place in entrance-examination to the *École Normale Supérieure.*

cacochyme (kakɔʃim), adj. [f. Gr. *kakos+chumos*] **1.** Cacochymic; **2.** odd, eccentric, queer. ~, s.m.f. Peevish person.

cacochymie (kakɔʃimi), s.f. Cacochymia, cacochymy.

cacodyle (kakɔdil), s.m. (chem.) Cacodyle.

cacographie (kakɔgrafi), s.f. [f. Gr. *kakos+graphein*] Cacography.

cacolet (kakɔlɛ), s.m. [etym. unkn.] Horse-litter, mule-litter.

cacologie (kakɔlɔʒi), s.f. [Gr. *kakologia*] Cacology (bad choice of words).

cacologique (kakɔlɔʒik), adj. Cacological.

cacophonie (kakɔfɔni), s.f. [Gr. *kakophōnia*] Cacophony.

cacophonique (kakɔfɔnik), adj. Cacophonous.

cactacées, cactées (kaktase, kakte), s.f.pl. (bot.) Cactaceae, cacteae.

cactus, cactier (kaktys, kaktje), s.m. [Gr. *kaktos*] (bot.) Cactus.

c.-à-d. abbrev. of *c'est-à-dire*, i.e., *id est.*

cadastral, -e, (aux) (kadastral), adj. Cadastral.

cadastre (kadastr), s.m. [L *capitastrum*] Cadastre, land-survey; *employé au ~*, a clerk of the surveys; *dresser le ~*, to draw up the land-survey.

cadastrer (kadastre), v.a. To include in the cadastre; to draw up the land-survey of, to survey.

cadavéreu-x, -se (kadaverø), adj. Cadaverous, corpse-like, ashy pale.

cadavérique (kadaverik), adj. Cadaveric.

cadavre (kadɑvr), s.m. [L *cadaver*] Corpse, dead body, carcass.

cade[1] (kad), s.m. [etym. unkn.] (bot.) Cade, kind of juniper.

cade[2] (kad), s.m. [L *cadus*] Cask (used in salt-works).

cadeau (pl. -x), (kado), s.m. [etym. dub. L *capitalis*?] Present, gift; *faire ~ (de quelque chose à quelqu'un)* to present (somebody with something).

cadenas (kadnɑ), s.m. [L *catena*] Padlock.

cadenasser (kadnase), v.a. To padlock.

cadence (kadɑ̃s), s.f. [It. *cadenza*] **1.** Cadence, time, rhythm; *aller en ~*, to keep time; **2.** trill, musical ornament, arpeggio (also musical pause); **3.** (poetry) numbers.

cadencé, -e (kadɑ̃se), adj. Cadenced, musical, harmonious, rhythmical.

cadencer (kadɑ̃se), v.a. To cadence, to harmonize.

cadenette (kadnɛt), s.f. [f. *sire de Cadenet*] Tress of hair (worn by soldiers in 18th century).

cadet, -te (kadɛ), adj. s.m.f. **1.** Younger, junior, youngest (son, daughter, or brother, sister); **2.** (mil.) cadet; **3.** young fellow; **4.** small, smallish, unimportant; *c'est le ~ de mes soucis*, that is the least of my cares.

cadi (kadi), s.m. [Arab. *qādhī*] Cadi.

cadis (kadi), s.m. [unkn. orig.] Caddis (coarse woollen material).

cadméen, -ne (kadmeɛ̃), adj. Cadmean.

cadmie (kadmi), s.f. [L *cadmia*] (chem.) Calamine.

cadmium (kadmjɔm), s.m. (chem.) Cadmium.

cadogan (kadɔgɑ̃), s.m. [f. prop. n.] Knot of hair on the nape, worn in 18th century; syn. CATOGAN.

cadole (kadɔl), s.f. [LL *catabola, cataula*] Latch.

cadran (kadrɑ̃), s.m. [f. L *quadrans*] Dial, dial-plate; *~ solaire*, sundial; *faire le tour du ~*, to sleep the clock round, to sleep twelve hours.

cadrat (kadra), s.m. [f. L *quadratus*] (print.) Quadrat.

cadratin (kadratɛ̃), s.m. (print.) Em-quadrat; *demi-~*, en-quadrat.

cadrature (kadratyr), s.f. (mech.) Movement (of a clock); see QUADRATURE.

cadre (kɑdr) s.m. [f. It. *quadro*] **1.** Frame, stretcher; **2.** (arch.) framework; **3.** limits, compass; **4.** (fig.) surroundings; setting; **5.** (mil.) list of officers, roll, staff, cadre; **6.** (naut.) cot.

cadrer (kɑdre), v.n. To agree (*avec*, with), to tally, to square, to fit, to suit; *faire ~*, to square.

cadu-c, -que (kadyk), adj. [L *caducus*] **1.** Old, broken-down, decrepit, frail, feeble; *mal ~*, epilepsy; **2.** null, void, unclaimed, barred by limitation, lapsed; **3.** (bot.) caducous, deciduous.

caducée (kadyse), s.m. [L *caduceum*] Caduceus.

caducité (kadysite), s.f. **1.** Caducity,

decay, decrepitude, ruinous state; **2.** nullity, lapsing.
cadurcien, -ne (kadyrsjɛ̃), s.m.f. adj. [L *cadurci*] (Inhabitant, native) of Cahors.
caecal, -e, (aux) (sekal), adj. (anat.) Caecal.
caecum (sekɔm), s.m. [f. L *caecus*] (anat.) Caecum, blind gut.
caesium (sezjɔm), s.m. (chem.) Caesium.
cafard (kafar), s.m. **1.** (ent.) Cockroach; **2.** (slang) the blues; *avoir le* ~, to have the hump; to be in the dumps; to have an attack of cold feet.
cafard, -e (kafar), adj. [LL *caphardum*] Canting, blabbing; tale-bearing. ~, s.m.f. Hypocrite, tell-tale, sneak, Mawworm.
cafarder (kafarde), v.n. To tell tales, to blab, to play the hypocrite, to peach.
cafarderie, cafardise (kafardri, kafardiz), s.f. Cant, hypocrisy, sneaking, blabbing.
café (kafe), s.m. [f. Arab. *qahoua*] **1.** Coffee; **2.** coffee-house, coffee-room; refreshment rooms, tap-room; ~ *au lait*, coffee with milk; ~ *concert*, music-hall, smoking-concert; *faire boire à X un mauvais* ~, to poison X; *c'est un pilier de* ~, he is a pub loafer; *ça, c'est un peu fort de* ~ *!*, that takes the cake !, this is hard to believe; that 's coming it too strong !; that 's a bit too thick. ~, adj. Coffee-coloured.
caféier (kafeje), s.m. (bot.) Coffee-tree.
caféière (kafejɛr), s.f. Coffee-plantation.
caféine (kafein), s.f. (chem.) Caffeine.
cafetan, caftan (kaftɑ̃), s.m. [f. Turk. *qaftān*] Caftan.
cafeti-er, -ère (kaftje), s.m.f. Coffee-house keeper ; pub keeper.
cafetière (kaftjɛr), s.f. Coffee-pot.
cafre (kafr), s.m.f. adj. Kaffir, caffre.
caftan, cafetan (kaftɑ̃), s.m. Caftan.
cage (kaʒ), s.f. [L *cavea*] **1.** Cage; coop, crate; ~ *à poulets*, hen-coop; *on l'a mis en* ~, he has been put into jail; *la belle* ~ *ne nourrit pas l'oiseau*, fine clothes do not fill the stomach; **2.** case, frame, shaft (of a lift), shell, groove; ~ *d'escalier*, well, well-staircase.
cagée (kaʒe), s.f. Cageful (all the birds in a cage).
cageot (kaʒo), s.m. **cagette** (kaʒɛt), s.f. Small cage.
cagna (kaɲa), s.f. [war slang] Dug-out.
cagnard, -e (kaɲar), adj. s.m.f. [f. *cagne* or *coin, coignard*] **1.** Lazy, good-for-nothing, lazybones, loafer; **2.** ~, s.m. sheltered corner; **3.** (naut.) small rain-awning.
cagnarder (kaɲarde), v.n. To idle time away.
cagnardise (kaɲardiz), s.f. Laziness.
cagne (kaɲ), s.f. [f. It. *cagna*] **1.** (obs.) Bitch; **2.** bad woman, slut; **3.** (school slang) in *lycées*, the form in which pupils are coached for *École Normale Supérieure, Lettres*, as opposed to *taupe*, the form in which other pupils are coached for *E.N.S. Sciences.*
cagneu-x, -se (kaɲø), adj. Knock-kneed, bow-legged ; (of a horse) hen-toed. ~, s.m.f. Knock-kneed person.
cagnotte (kaɲɔt), s.f. [unkn. orig.] Money reserved out of stakes, money-box, pool.
cagot, -e (kago), adj. s.m.f. [Béarnese wd] **1.** Bigoted, hypocritical (person); bigot; **2.** (obs.) outcast, leper.
cagoterie (kagɔtri), s.f. Hypocrisy, bigotry; act of a cagot.
cagotisme (kagɔtism), s.m. Bigotry, affectation of extreme piety.
cagou (kagu), s.m. [f. Bret. *cacou*] (obs.) **1.** Gipsy trainer and chief of thieves, vagrant; **2.** leper.
cagoule (kagul), s.f. [f. L *cuculla*] Monk's cloak with hood covering the face, and holes for the eyes and mouth.
cahier (kaje), s.m. [f. L *quaternio*, LL *quaternium*] **1.** Copy-book, exercise-book; **2.** part of a book; **3.** (of writing-paper) quarter of a quire; **4.** (French hist.) memorandum, resolutions, claims; ~ *des charges*, conditions, specifications, stipulations; **5.** short book or magazine.
cahin-caha (kaɛ̃kaa), adv. [f. L *qua hinc qua hac*] So-so, poorly, middling, lamely; *rouler* ~, to jog on.
cahot (kao), s.m. [unkn. orig.] **1.** Jolt, jolting, shake; **2.** (fig.) hitch, obstacle.
cahotage, cahotement (kaɔtaʒ, kaɔtmɑ̃), s.m. Jolting.
cahoter (kaɔte), v.a.n. To jolt, to toss about.
cahute (kayt), s.f. [unkn. orig.] Hut, crib, hovel, shed, cabin.
caïd (kaid), s.m. [f. Arab. *qāïd*] Caid.
caie (kɛ), s.f. See CAYE.
caïeu, cayeu (kajø), s.m. [unkn. orig.] (hort.) Clove (secondary young bulb).
caillage (kajaʒ), s.m. Curdling.
caillasse (kajas), s.f. Stony deposit of tertiary period.
caille (kɑj), s.f. [LL *quacola*, prob. of older Germ. orig.] Quail.
caillé, -e (kaje) adj. Curdled, curdy. ~, s.m. Curd, clotted milk or cream.
caillebotis (kajbɔti), s.m. (naut.) Gratings.
caillebotte (kajbɔt), s.f. **1.** Curds, clotted milk; **2.** (naut.) bar of the gratings.
caillebotter (kajbɔte), v.a. To cause to curdle; **se** ~, v.pr. to curdle.
caille-lait (kajlɛ), s.m. (bot.) Cheese-rennet.
cailler (kaje), v.a. and **se** ~, v.pr. To curdle, to curd, to clot, to coagulate.
cailletage (kajtaʒ), s.m. [f. *caillette*] Gossiping, tittle-tattle.
cailleteau (pl. -x) (kajto), s.m. Young quail.

cailleter (kajte), v.n. To gossip.
caillette (kajɛt), s.f. **1.** Rennet; **2.** fourth stomach of ruminants; **3.** gossip, light-of-tongue person, frivolous woman.
caillot (kajo), s.m. Clot, coagulum; ~ *rosat*, rose-water pear.
caillou (pl. **-x**) (kaju), s.m. [OF *chail*] Flint, pebble, stone, gravel.
cailloutage (kajutaʒ), s.m. Gravelling, stone-work; (pottery) flint-ware.
caillouter (kajute), v.a. To stone, to ballast, to gravel, to metal (a road).
caillouteur (kajutœr), s.m. Roadman, flint-cutter.
caillouteu-x, -se (kajutø), adj. Flinty, stony, pebbly.
cailloutis (kajuti), s.m. Broken stone, gravel, road-metal.
caïmacam (kaimakɑ̃), s.m. [Turk. wd] Caimacam (grand vizier's lieutenant).
caïman (kaimɑ̃), s.m. [f. Span. *caiman*, f. Carib. *acayouman*] (zool.) Cayman, alligator; (colloq.) usher at *École Normale Supérieure*.
caïque (kaik), s.m. [f. Turk. *qāik*] (naut.) Caique.
caire (kɛr), s.m. [Malay *kāyar*] Coir, coconut fibre.
cairn (kɛrn), s.m. [f. Gael. *carn*] Cairn.
caisse (kɛs), s.f. [f. L *capsa*] **1.** Box, case, packing-case, coffer, chest, trunk, box, tank; ~ *à eau*, water-tank; **2.** cash-box, till, safe, pay-office, cashier's office, fund, treasury, cash; ~ *des retraites*, pension fund; ~ *d'Épargne*, Savings Bank; *garçon de* ~, collecting clerk; *faire la* ~, to make up the cash account; *sauver la* ~, to run away with the till; *tenir la* ~, (*a*) to keep the cash account; (*b*) to hold the purse-strings; *en* ~, in hand; **3.** (of a carriage), box, frame; **4.** big drum; *bander la* ~, to brace the drum; (fig.) *battre la grosse* ~, to advertise abundantly, to make a fuss, to muster one's partisans, tc collect money; **5.** (horol.) case; **6.** (phys.) catoptric cistula; **7.** (of the ear) drum; **8.** (of a pulley) heave.
caissette (kɛsɛt), s.f. Small case or box.
caissi-er, -ère (kɛsje), s.m.f. Cashier.
caisson (kɛsɔ̃), s.m. [f. It. *cassone*] **1.** Ammunition-wagon, cart; **2.** box; (naut.) locker; **3.** (of a carriage) boot, seat-box; **4.** (techn.) compartment, caisson, sunk panel; **5.** (slang) head; *se faire sauter le* ~, to blow one's brains out.
cajeput (kaʒpyt), s.m. [f. Malay *cayouputi*] Cajuput; cajuput-oil.
cajoler (kaʒole), v.a. [unkn. orig.] To wheedle, to coax, to cajole, to fawn upon.
cajolerie (kaʒolri), s.f. Cajolery, wheedling, coaxing, cajoling, fawning; *elle l'obtint de lui à force de* ~*s*, she coaxed it out of him.
cajoleu-r, -se (kaʒɔlœr), s.m.f. Cajoler, wheedler, coaxer. ~, adj. Cajoling, coaxing, gushing, fawning.
cal (kal), s.m. [f. L *callus*] Callosity; (surg.) callus.
calabrais, -e (kalabrɛ), adj. s.m.f. Calabrian.
calade, chalade (kalad, ʃalad), s.f. [It. *calata*] (rid.) Calade (sloping ground).
caladion, caladium (kaladjɔ̃, kaladjɔm), s.m. (bot.) Caladium.
calage (kalaʒ), s.m. Wedging-up, stopping, propping, securing.
calaisien, -ne (kalɛzjɛ̃), s.m.f. adj. (Inhabitant) of Calais, Calaisian.
calaison (kalɛzɔ̃), s.f. (naut.) Draught (of water); syn. TIRANT D'EAU.
calambac, calambour (kalɑ̃bak, kalɑ̃bur), s.m. Calambac, calambour, aloes-wood.
calame (kalam), s.m. [L *calamus*] Calamus.
calament (kalamɑ̃), s.m. (bot.) Calamint.
calamine (kalamin), s.f. Calamine.
calamite (kalamit), s.f. (min.) Calamite; (zool.) natterjack.
calamité (kalamite), s.f. [L *calamitas*] Calamity.
calamiteu-x, -se (kalamitø), adj. Calamitous, distressing.
calandrage (kalɑ̃draʒ), s.m. Mangling, (of linen), calendering.
calandre (kalɑ̃dr), s.f. **1.** Calender, mangle; **2.** (ent.) calandra, corn-weevil.
calandrelle (kalɑ̃drɛl), s.f. (ornith.) Short-toed lark.
calandrer (kalɑ̃dre), v.a. To calender, to mangle.
calandrette (kalɑ̃drɛt), s.f. (ornith.) Song-thrush.
calandreu-r, -se (kalɑ̃drœr), s.m.f. Mangler, calenderer. ~, adj. Mangling.
calanque (kalɑ̃k), s.f. [Provenç. *calanco*] Cove, small bay.
calao (kalao), s.m. (ornith.) Hornbill.
calcaire (kalkɛr), s.m. [f. L *calcarius*] Limestone, calcareous soil. ~, adj. Calcareous, chalky.
calcaneum (kalkaneɔm), s.m. [L wd] (anat.) Calcaneum, heel-bone.
calcédoine (kalsedwan), s.f. [L *chalcedonius*] (min.) Chalcedony.
calcédonieu-x, -se (kalsedɔnjø), adj. Chalcedonic.
calcéolaire (kalseɔlɛr), s.f. [f. L *calceolus*] (bot.) Calceolaria.
calcification (kalsifika'sjɔ̃), s.f. Calcification.
calcifier (kalsifje), v.a. To calcify.
calcin (kalsɛ̃), s.m. Calcined glass.
calcinable (kalsinabl), adj. Calcinable.
calcination (kalsina'sjɔ̃), s.f. Calcination.
calciner (kalsine), v.a. and **se** ~, v.pr. To calcine; to burn to ashes.
calcite (kalsit), s.f. (chem.) Calcite.

calcium (kalsjɔm), s.m. [f. L *calx*] (chem.) Calcium.
calcographie, chalcographie (kalkografi), s.f. [f. Gr. *khalkos+graphein*] Chalcography, engraving on copper.
calcul (kalkyl), s.m. [f. L *calculus*] **1.** Ciphering, arithmetic; **2.** calculation, reckoning, computation; **3.** consideration of personal interest, scheming; **4.** (med.) calculus, concretion, stone.
calculable (kalkylabl), adj. Calculable, computable, easy to estimate.
calculat-eur, -rice (kalkylatœr), adj. Calculating. ~, s.m.f. **1.** Calculator, reckoner, accountant; **2.** schemer.
calculer (kalkyle), v.a.n. **1.** To calculate, to reckon, to compute, to cipher; *machine à* ~, calculating-machine; **2.** to scheme, to combine, to determine.
calculeu-x, -se (kalkylø), adj. (med.) Calculous.
cale (kal), s.f. [f. It. *cala, calare*] **1.** Wedge; prop; slip; **2.** (naut.) hold, main hold; *à fond de* ~, down in the hold; (fig.) hard-up, at the end of one's resources; **3.** (arch.) stocks; **4.** landing-place; ~ *sèche*, dry-dock.
calé, -e (kale), p. adj. Wedged up, propped; (pop. fig.) (*a*) well off; (*b*) learned, proficient; *il est* ~ *en histoire*, he knows his history well; he is ready for all questions.
calebasse (kalbɑs), s.f. [f. Span. *calabaza*] **1.** Calabash, gourd; **2.** (pop.) pate, nob, sconce.
calebassier (kalbɑsje), s.m. (bot.) Calabash-tree.
calèche (kalɛʃ), s.f. [f. Pol. *koluska*, Germ. *Kalesche*] Barouche, calash.
caleçon (kalsɔ̃), s.m. [f. It. *calzone*] Pants, drawers, pair of drawers; ~ *de bain*, bathing-drawers.
calédonien, -ne (kaledɔnjɛ̃), adj. s.m.f. Caledonian.
caléfact-eur, -rice (kalefaktœr), s.m.f. Calefactor. ~ adj. Heating, cooking.
caléfaction (kalefaksjɔ̃), s.f. [f. L *calefacere*] Calefaction.
calembour (kalɑ̃bur), s.m. [uncert. orig.] Pun.
calembouriste (kalɑ̃burist), s.m.f. Punster.
calembredaine (kalɑ̃brədɛn), s.f. Pun, sham, quibble, foolery, nonsense.
calendaire (kalɑ̃dɛr), s.m. [f. L *calendarium*] Church register.
calender (kalɑ̃dɛr), s.m. Calender (dervish).
calendes (kalɑ̃d), s.f.pl. [f. L *calendae*] Kalends; *renvoyé aux* ~ *grecques*, put off till latter Lammas or till doomsday.
calendre (kalɑ̃dr), s.f. Suction-pump (used in coal-mines).
calendrier (kalɑ̃drje), s.m. [f. L *calendarium*] Calendar, almanac.
calepin (kalpɛ̃), s.m. [f. *Ambr. Calepin*, It. author of Latin-Italian dictionary, 15th c.] Small note-book.
caler (kale), v.a.n. **1.** To wedge up, to prop, to fix, to fasten, to secure; **2.** (naut.) to draw (so many feet of water), to house (a mast); **3.** (at game of marbles) to shoot; **4.** (motor.) to let a motor stop for want of petrol or air; **5.** (fig.) to give way, to sing small, to strike work; **6.** (slang) *se* ~ *les joues*, to eat heartily, to stuff.
calfait (kalfɛ), s.m. Caulking-iron.
calfat (kalfa), s.m. (naut.) Caulker.
calfatage (kalfataʒ), s.m. Caulking.
calfater (kalfate), v.a. To caulk, to calk.
calfatin (kalfatɛ̃), s.m. Caulker's boy.
calfeutrage (kalføtraʒ), s.m. Stopping-up of chinks (also material for this).
calfeutrer (kalføtre), v.a. To stop up the chinks of, to keep close, to pad; **se** ~, v.pr., to keep oneself warm, or comfortable (at home).
caliatour (kaljatur), s.m. (bot.) Caliatour-wood, a dye-wood.
calibrage (kalibraʒ), s.m. Gauging, calibration.
calibre (kalibr), s.m. [It. *calibro*] **1.** Calibre, diameter, size; **2.** (fig.) importance, size, capacity; *compas de* ~ callipers (pl.).
calibrer (kalibre), v.a. **1.** To calibrate; **2.** to gauge, to take the calibre of.
calice (kalis), s.m. [f. Gr. *kalux*, L *calix*] **1.** Chalice, communion cup, cup; **2.** (bot.) calyx, flower-cup; **3.** (fig.) cup of bitterness, affliction, sacrifice imposed; *il a bu le* ~ *jusqu'à la lie*, his cup was full.
calicot (kaliko), s.m. [f. *Calicut*, India] **1.** Calico; **2.** counter-jumper; shopman, draper's assistant.
calicule (kalikyl), s.m. (bot.) Calycle.
caliculé, -e (kalikyle), adj. (bot.) Calycled, calyculate.
califat (kalifa), s.m. Caliphate.
calife (kalif), s.m. [f. Arab. *khalīfa*] Caliph.
californien, -ne (kalifɔrnjɛ̃), adj. s.m.f. Californian.
califourchon (kalifurʃɔ̃), s.m. Hobby-horse, hobby; *à* ~, adv. loc. astride, astraddle; *se mettre à* ~ *sur*, to bestride.
calige (kaliʒ), s.m. [L *caliga*] Caligus, fish-louse, sea-louse.
câlin, -e (kalɛ̃), adj. Caressing, coaxing, fawning, wheedling. ~, s.m.f. Coaxer, wheedler, cajoler, lazybones.
câliner (kɑline), v.a. To caress, to fondle, to coddle, to pet, to cajole, to coax, to wheedle; **se** ~, v.pr. to take one's ease, to indulge in caresses and idleness.
câlinerie (kɑlinri), s.f. Fawning, fondling, wheedling, coaxing ways; caress, caresses, present, attentions.

calino (kalino), s.m. Booby, simpleton, fool.
calinotade (kalinotad), s.f. Silly act or speech.
caliorne (kaljorn), s.f. (naut.) Purchase-tackle or main-tackle.
calleu-x, -se (kalø), adj. [f. L *callosus*] Callous, hardened; (bot.) callose.
calligraphe (kalligraf), s.m.f. [f. Gr. *kallos*+*graphein*] Calligrapher, person skilled in penmanship.
calligraphie (kalligrafi), s.f. Calligraphy, penmanship.
calligraphier (kalligrafje), v.a.n. To write beautifully.
callipyge (kallipiʒ), adj. Callipygian.
callisthénie (kalisteni), s.f. [f. Gr. *kallos*+*sthenos*] Callisthenics.
callosité (kallozite), s.f. Callosity, callousness.
calmande (kalmɑ̃d), s.f. Calamanco.
calmant, -e (kalmɑ̃), p. adj. Sedative, soothing.
calmant (kalmɑ̃), s.m. Soothing remedy, sedative, anodyne.
calmar (kalmar), s.m. (zool.) Calamary, squid, sleeve-fish, pen-fish.
calme (kalm), adj. [etym. dub.] Quiet, calm, still, unruffled, composed, dispassionate; (comm.) quiet, dull, flat.
calme (kalm), s.m. Calm, calmness, quietness, stillness, repose, composure; dullness, flatness; ~ *plat*, dead calm; *il garde son* ~, he keeps cool; he keeps his hair on; *du* ~ *!*, be quiet!
calmer (kalme), v.a. To calm, to quiet, to still; to pacify, to soothe, to compose, to becalm; **se** ~, v.pr. to become calm or quiet; to be appeased, to be soothed, to compose oneself; to abate, to fall, to subside, to lull; see CALMIR.
calmir (kalmir), v.n. (naut.) To fall calm, to lull.
calmouck (kalmuk), adj. s.m.f. See KALMOUCK.
calomel (kalomɛl), s.m. [f. Gr. *kalos*+*melas*] (pharm.) Calomel.
calomniat-eur, -rice (kalomnjatœr), s.m.f. Calumniator, slanderer. ~, adj. Calumnious, slanderous.
calomnie (kalomni), s.f. [f. L *calumnia*] Calumny, slander; misrepresentation, false charge; *la* ~ *est l'arme des lâches*, calumny is the coward's weapon.
calomnier (kalomnje), v.a. To calumniate, to slander; *calomniez, calomniez, il en restera toujours quelque chose*, if you only throw enough mud some is sure to stick.
calomnieusement (kalomnjøzmɑ̃), adv. Slanderously.
calomnieu-x, -se (kalomnjø), adj. Calumnious, slanderous.
caloricité (kalorisite), s.f. Caloricity.
calorie (kalori), s.f. [f. L *calor*] Calorie.
calorifère (kalorifɛr), s.m. Heating apparatus; air-stove; central-heating apparatus. ~, adj. Heating, warming.
calorifiant, -e (kalorifjɑ̃), p. adj. Calorifacient, calorifiant.
calorification (kalorifika'sjɔ̃), s.f. Calorification, heating.
calorifique (kalorifik), adj. Calorific, heating.
calorimètre (kalorimɛtr), s.m. Calorimeter.
calorimétrie (kalorimetri), s.f. Calorimetry.
calorique (kalorik), s.m. [f. L *calor*] Caloric, heat.
calot (kalo), s.m. [f. *calotte*] **1.** Wedge; **2.** alley-taw; **3.** cap, skull-cap; forage cap.
calotin, calottin (kalotɛ̃), s.m. (pej.) **1.** Shaveling, sky-pilot, priest (calotte-wearer); **2.** stickler for priests' authority in politics.
calotte (kalot), s.f. [f. *cale*] **1.** Skull-cap, cap, coif, caul, crown of a hat; **2.** calotte (of priests); (by ext.) priesthood, clergy; *régime de la* ~, government by priests; *à bas la* ~ *!*, down with government by priests!; **3.** (anat.) skull-cap, calva; **4.** box on the ear; *donner des* ~*s*, to box the ears; **5.** surface of a half sphere; ~ *de cieux*, canopy of heaven; **6.** spherical jam-jar.
calotter (kalote), v.a. To box the ears of, to punch the head of; to cover with a cap.
calou (kalu), s.m. Palm-wine.
caloyer (kalwaje), s.m. Caloyer (Greek monk).
calque (kalk), s.m. **1.** Tracing, calquing; **2.** (fig.) copy, servile imitation.
calquer (kalke), v.a. [f. L *calcare*] To trace, to counterdraw, to calque; to copy, to imitate, to reproduce.
calquoir (kalkwar), s.m. Tracing-point.
calter (kalte), v.n. (slang) To leg it, to hook it, to hop it.
calumet (kalymɛ), s.m. Calumet, pipe.
calus (kaly), s.m. Callosity, callus.
calvados (kalvados), s.m. [f. *Calvados*, Normandy] Cider-brandy, apple-jack.
calvaire (kalvɛr), s.m. **1.** Calvary; **2.** life of suffering, expiation, moral agony.
calville (kalvil), s.f. Calville (apple).
calvinisme (kalvinism), s.m. [f. *Calvin*] Calvinism.
calviniste (kalvinist), s.m.f. Calvinist. ~, adj. Calvinistic.
calvitie (kalvisi), s.f. [f. L *calvities*] Baldness; (med.) calvities.
calycanthe (kalikɑ̃t), s.m. (bot.) Calycanthus; Japan or Carolina allspice.
cam (bois de) (kam), s.m. [etym. dub.] Camwood.
camaïeu (kamajø), s.m. [etym. dub.] Camaieu, camayeu (kind of painting in monochrome).

camail (kamaj), s.m. [f. OF *cap+mail*] Camail, cape; (for a horse) hood.

camaldule (kamaldyl), s.m. [f. *Camaldoli*, Tuscany] Monk (of religious order instituted in 11th century by St. Romuald); Camaldolite.

camarade (kamarad), s.m.f. [f. Span. *camarada*] Comrade, fellow, mate, associate, playmate, fellow-labourer, fellow-servant, fellow-workman, brother-soldier, messmate; ~ *d'école*, school-fellow.

camaraderie (kamaradri), s.f. Comradeship, fellowship, intimacy, party association, coterie, clique, clanship, party-spirit, favouritism, jobbery.

camard, -e (kamar), adj. [f. *camus*] Flat-nosed. ~, s.m.f. Flat-nosed person; *la camarde*, Death, grim Death.

camarilla (kamarilla), s.f. [Span. dim. of L *camera*] Camarilla, courtiers' coterie; coterie, cabal, clique.

camarin (kamarɛ̃), s.m. (ornith.) Red-throated diver.

camarine (kamarin), s.f. (bot.) Crowberry.

cambiste (kɑ̃bist), s.m. [f. L *cambium*] Cambist, dealer in bills of exchange.

cambium (kɑ̃bjɔm), s.m. [L wd] (bot.) Cambium.

cambodgien, -ne (kɑ̃bɔdʒjɛ̃), adj. s.m.f. Cambogian, Cambodian.

cambouis (kɑ̃bwi), s.m. [unkn. orig.] Coom, cart-coom, cart-grease.

cambrai (kɑ̃brɛ), s.m. [Fr. geog. orig.] Fine linen, cambric; lace.

cambré, -e (kɑ̃bre), adj. Cambered, cambering, arched, well-set.

cambrement (kɑ̃brəmɑ̃), s.m. Cambering, arching, curving, bending.

cambrer (kɑ̃bre), v.a. [f. LL *camerare*] To camber, to arch, to curve, to bend; **se** ~, v.pr. to camber.

cambrésine (kɑ̃brezin), s.f. adj. Fine cambric (formerly made at Cambrai).

cambrien, -ne (kɑ̃briɛ̃), adj. s.m.f. Cambrian.

cambriolage (kɑ̃briɔlaʒ), s.m. **cambriole** (kɑ̃briɔl), s.f. [f. *chambre*] Burglary, house-breaking.

cambrioler (kɑ̃briɔle), v.a. To burgle, to break into (a house).

cambrioleu-r, -se (kɑ̃briɔlœr), s.m.f. Burglar.

cambrique (kɑ̃brik), adj. Welsh.

cambrure (kɑ̃bryr), s.f. Camber, bend, arch, cambering, curving.

cambuse (kɑ̃byz), s.f. [Dutch *kabuis*] **1.** (naut.) Steward's room; **2.** canteen, low public-house, hovel; **3.** (pej.) wretched house, beastly hole.

cambusier (kɑ̃byzje), s.m. (naut.) Steward's mate.

came (kam), s.f. [f. Dutch *kam*] Cam; *arbre à* ~*s*, cam-shaft; ~ *d'allumage*, ignition cam; ~ *de distribution*, distributor cam; ~ *de régulation*, governing cam.

camée (kame), s.m. [It. *cameo*] Cameo.

caméléon (kameleɔ̃), s.m. [L *chamaeleon*] **1.** (zool.) Chameleon; **2.** time-server, trimmer.

camélia, camellia (kamelja), s.m. (bot.) Camellia.

camelin, -e (kamlɛ̃), adj. Cameline, of camels.

caméline (kamelin), s.f. (bot.) Camelina, gold of pleasure.

camelot (kamlo), s.m. [f. OF *chamelot*] **1.** Camlet; **2.** pedlar, hawker, cheap-jack, huckster; **3.** ~ *du roi*, active royalist in modern France.

camelote (kamlɔt), s.f. **1.** Trashy goods, rubbish, brummagem, cheap goods; **2.** ill-done piece of work. ~, adj. Cheap, trashy, ill-made.

cameloter (kamlɔte), v.a.n. **1.** To weave camlet; to make trash; **2.** to sell cheap, trashy goods.

camembert (kamɑ̃bɛr), s.m. [geog. orig.] Cheese made at Camembert (Orne) (or similar cheese).

camérier (kamerje), s.m. [f. It. *camera*] Chamberlain (to the Pope or to a Cardinal).

caméristе, camérière (kamerist, kamerjɛr), s.f. [f. It. *camera*] **1.** (obs.) Lady of the Chamber; **2.** lady's-maid, chambermaid.

camerlingat (kamɛrlɛ̃ga), s.m. Camerlingate (Roman Catholic dignity).

camerlingue (kamɛrlɛ̃g), s.m. [It. *camerlengo*] Camerlingo (cardinal administering the church during the vacancy of the Papal see).

camion (kamjɔ̃), s.m. [etym. dub.] **1.** Lorry, truck, wagon (road); **2.** paint-kettle; **3.** very small pin.

camionnage (kamjɔnaʒ), s.m. **1.** Carting, carriage, carrying trade; **2.** carriage (cost of).

camionner (kamjɔne), v.a. To cart, to carry, to convey on a truck.

camionneur (kamjɔnœr), s.m. Carrier, truckman.

camisard (kamizar), s.m. [f. French dialect *camiso*, chemise] (French hist.) Camisard (one of the Calvinists persecuted in the Cévennes).

camisole (kamizɔl), s.f. [f. L *camisa*] Loose bodice, with sleeves (worn by poor women, or at night). ⚠ Not English 'camisole' which = *cache-corset*; ~ *de force*, straitjacket.

camomille (kamɔmij), s.f. [LL *camomilla*] (bot.) Camomile.

camouflage (kamuflaʒ), s.m. Disguise, make-up, camouflage.

camoufler (kamufle), v.a. [etym. dub.]

To camouflage, to disguise, to splash with various colours in order to obscure the outline of; **se ~**, v.pr. to disguise oneself, to make up one's face.

camouflet (kamuflɛ), s.m. [etym. dub.] **1.** Whiff of smoke (in the face of some one); **2.** (mil.) camouflet, stifler; **3.** (fig.) affront, snub, rap over the knuckles.

camp (kɑ̃), s.m. [f. L *campus*] Camp; (in games) side; *~ volant*, flying camp; *être en ~ volant*, to be staying only a short time, ready to leave on the shortest notice; *lever le ~*, to break up the camp; (fig.) to decamp, to run away; *ficher le ~*, or *foutre le ~*, to decamp, to bolt, to make oneself scarce.

campagnard, -e (kɑ̃paɲar), s.m.f. Countryman, countrywoman, rustic. ~, adj. Rustic, rural, country, countrified.

campagne (kɑ̃paɲ), s.f. [f. L *campus*] **1.** Country, fields, countryside, open country, plains, flats; *maison de ~*, country-house, place, or seat; *en pleine ~*, in the open fields; *la ~ romaine*, the Roman Campagna; *aller à la ~*, to go into the country; *battre la ~*, to wander, to be delirious; to beat about the bush; **2.** (mil.) campaign, expedition; *entrer en ~*, *se mettre en ~*, to take the field; (fig.) to start working, to pursue an object or plan, to set out on an expedition or research; *mettre en ~*, to bring into the field; *faire ~*, to make war, to fight (for); *tenir la ~*, to keep the field; **3.** (naut., fish.) voyage, cruise; **4.** (theatr., Lit.) season.

campagnol (kɑ̃paɲɔl), s.m. (zool.) Vole, field-vole, field-mouse, water-rat; *~ volant*, nycteris, bristly bat of Senegal.

campane (kɑ̃pan), s.f. [f. L *campana*] **1.** (arch.) Bell, tasselled ornament; **2.** (bot.) campana, pasque-flower.

campanile (kɑ̃panil), s.m. [It. wd] Campanile, bell-tower.

campanule (kɑ̃panyl), s.f. [f. L *campana*] Campanula, bell-flower.

campanulé, -e (kɑ̃panyle), adj. Bell-shaped.

campé, -e (kɑ̃pe), p. adj. Encamped, situated; *c'est un gaillard bien ~*, the fellow stands well on his stumps, or, has a good pair of legs; *me voilà bien ~ !*, here am I in a fine plight !, or, in a pretty pickle !

campêche (bois de) (kɑ̃pɛʃ), s.m. Campeachy wood, logwood.

campement (kɑ̃pmɑ̃), s.m. Camp, encampment, camping.

camper (kɑ̃pe), v.n. To camp, to encamp, to live in a camp; ~, v.a. to place, to lay, to thrust, to clap; *~ là*, to leave brusquely, to leave in the lurch; **se ~**, v.pr. to stand bolt upright, to place or seat oneself; to posture boldly.

camphorate (kɑ̃fɔrat), s.m. (chem.) Camphorate.

camphorique (kɑ̃fɔrik), adj. Camphoric.

camphre (kɑ̃fr), s.m. [LL *camphora*] Camphor.

camphré, -e (kɑ̃fre), p. adj. Camphorated.

camphrer (kɑ̃fre), v.a. To camphorate.

camphrier (kɑ̃frje), s.m. (bot.) Camphor-tree.

campine (kɑ̃pin), s.f. [f. *Campine*, Belgium] Campine (fowl).

campos (kɑ̃pos), s.m. [f. L *campus*] Holiday, leave, rest; *donner ~*, to let (somebody) have a holiday.

camus, -e (kamy), adj. [prob. f. L *camurum*] **1.** Flat-nosed, snub-nosed, pug-nosed; **2.** (fig.) balked, disappointed, baffled; syn. CAMARD.

canada (kanada), s.f. [geog. orig] Variety of apple.

canadien, -ne (kanadjɛ̃), s.m.f. adj. **1.** Canadian; **2.** *~ne*, (s.f.) fur-lined short coat.

canaille (kanɑj), s.f. [f. L *canis*, It. *canaglia*] **1.** Rabble, mob, roughs; **2.** scoundrel, villain, rascal, blackguard. ~, adj. Coarse, rascally.

canaillerie (kanɑjri), s.f. Dirty trick; hostile and treacherous act, blackguardism.

canal (pl. **aux**) (kanal), s.m. [f. L *canalis*] Canal; channel (of a river); pipe, tube, duct, groove, water-course; (fig.) means, way, channel, medium.

canalicule (kanalikyl), s.m. Small channel.

canalisable (kanalizabl), adj. Canalizable.

canalisat-eur, -rice (kanalizatœr), adj. Canalizing.

canalisation (kanaliza'sjɔ̃), s.f. Canalization, piping.

canaliser (kanalize), v.a. To canalize.

canamelle (kanamɛl), s.f. [f. L *canna*+*mel*] Sugar-cane.

canapé (kanape), s.m. [f. L *conopeum*] **1.** Sofa, seat for two or three; *~-lit*, sofa-bedstead; **2.** (cook.) piece of fried bread.

canaque (kanak), s.m.f. adj. Kanak, kanaka.

canard (kanar), s.m. [etym. dub.] **1.** Duck, drake; **2.** false news, hoax; **3.** lump of sugar dipped in coffee or brandy; **4.** *chien ~*, water-spaniel.

canardeau (pl. **-x**) (kanardo), s.m. Duckling.

canarder (kanarde), v.a. To fire at, to shoot (from shelter); ~, v.n. **1.** (naut.) to dive, to pitch; **2.** (mus.) to quack, to sing badly; to make false or unpleasant notes on a reed instrument.

canardière (kanardjɛr), s.f. **1.** Duck-pond; **2.** duck-gun; **3.** (fort.) loophole.

canari (kanari), s.m. [geog. orig.] Canary-bird; (fig.) simpleton.

canasson (kanasõ), s.m. (pop.) Horse, nag, screw, jade, gee-gee.
cancale (kãkal), s.f. [Fr. geog. orig.] Variety of oyster.
cancan (kãkã), s.m. [f. L *quanquam*] **1.** Tale-bearing, gossip, backbiting, piece of scandal, tittle-tattle; **2.** cancan (vulgar dance).
cancaner (kãkane), v.a. To tittle-tattle, to gossip, to deal in scandal.
cancan-ier, -ière (kãkanje), adj. Gossipy, addicted to tittle-tattle or scandal. ~, s.m.f. Gossip, scandal-monger.
cancellariat (kãsɛllarja), s.m. Chancellorship.
cancer (kãsɛr), s.m. [L wd] **1.** (pathol.) Cancer; 2. (astr.) Cancer, the Crab.
cancéreu-x, -se (kãserø), adj. Cancerous.
cancériforme (kãseriform), adj. Cancriform.
canche (kãʃ), s.f. [unkn. orig.] (bot.) Hair-grass.
cancre (kãkr), s.m. [L *cancer*] **1.** Crab, crustacean; **2.** (in schools) dunce, lazy fellow, good-for-nothing, duffer.
cancrelat (kãkrəla), s.m. [f. Dutch *kakerlak*] (ent.) Cockroach, kakkerlak.
cancroïde (kãkrɔid), adj. s.m. (med.) Cancroid.
candélabre (kãdelɑbr), s.m. [f. L *candela*] Candelabrum, lamp-post, lamp-stand.
candeur (kãdœr), s.f. [f. L *candor*] Candour, ingenuousness, purity; (sometimes also) naïveté, silliness. ⚠ English 'candour' means also impartiality, open-mindedness = *impartialité, esprit non prévenu*, but *candeur* is not used in that sense.
candi, -e (kãdi), adj. s.m. [f. Arab. *qand*] Candied, candy.
candidat, -e (kãdida), s.m.f. [f. L *candidus*] Candidate, examinee.
candidature (kãdidatyr), s.f. Candidature, candidateship, candidacy; *poser sa* ~, to declare one's candidacy, to stand for election.
candide (kãdid), adj. [f. L *candidus*] Candid, frank, ingenuous, sincere, pure. ⚠ See CANDEUR.
candidement (kãdidmã), adv. Candidly, ingenuously.
candiote (kãdjɔt), adj. s.m.f. Candiot.
candir (kãdir), v.a. To candy (sugar); **se** ~, v.pr. to candy.
candisation (kãdizaˈsjõ), s.f. Candying.
cane (kan), s.f. [etym. dub.] Duck (female); *bec de* ~, spring-lock, pick-lock.
canepetière (kanpətjɛr), s.f. (ornith.) Field-duck, little bustard.
canéphore (kanefɔr), s.f. [f. Gr. *kaneon*+*phoros*] Canephora.
caner (kane), v.n. (pop.) To shirk work or danger; to funk, to show the white feather.
caneton (kantõ), s.m. Duckling, young drake.
canette (kanɛt), s.f. **1.** Duckling (female); **2.** (herald.) duckling represented in profile on a shield; **3.** bottle, jug, measure (for liquids); **4.** small cylinder in shuttle (of a sewing-machine).
caneur (kanœr), s.m. (pop.) Poltroon, shirker.
canevas (kanvɑ), s.m. [f. It. *canavaccio*] **1.** Canvas; **2.** (fig.) sketch, plan, outline, skeleton.
canezou (kanzu), (obs.) s.m. Lace jacket, canezou.
cange (kãʒ), s.f. Light boat (used on the Nile).
cangue (kãg), s.f. [Port. *cango*] Cang, cangue, kia (kind of pillory).
caniche (kaniʃ), s.m. [f. L *canis*] **1.** Poodle; **2.** (fig.) faithful and devoted person.
canicide (kanisid), s.m. adj. (jest.) Canicide.
caniculaire (kanikylɛr), adj. Canicular, sultry; *jours* ~*s*, canicular days, dog-days.
canicule (kanikyl), s.f. [f. *Canicula*, other name of the star Sirius] Canicula, dog-days.
canidés (kanide), s.m.pl. (zool.) Canidae.
canif (kanif), s.m. [f. Norse *knífr*] Pen-knife; *donner un coup de* ~ *dans le contrat*, to be unfaithful to one's marriage vows.
canillée (kanije), s.f. (bot.) Duckweed.
canin, -e (kanɛ̃), adj. [f. L *canis*] Canine. ~**e**, s.f. Canine tooth; (of animals) fang, tusk, tush.
canins (kanɛ̃), s.m.pl. Canines, canidae, dog tribe.
canitie (kanisi), s.f. [f. L *canities*] Whiteness or hoariness (of the hair).
caniveau (pl. **-x**) (kanivo), s.m. [etym. dub.] Channel-stone.
canna (kanna), s.m. (bot.) Canna, Indian shot; syn. BALISIER.
cannage (kanaʒ), s.m. **1.** Cane bottoming (of chairs), wicker-work; **2.** cane bottom, wicker-work bottom; **3.** measuring with the *canne*; see CANNE (3).
cannaie (kanɛ), s.f. Cane-field; sugar-cane plantation.
cannamelle (kanamɛl), s.f. See CANAMELLE.
canne (kan), s.f. [L *canna*] **1.** Stick, cane, rod, reed; ~ *à épée*, sword-stick; ~ *à pêche*, fishing-rod; ~ *à sucre*, sugar-cane; ~ *à vent*, air-cane; *sucre de* ~, cane sugar; *donner des coups de* ~ *à X*, to cane X; (fig.) *la* ~ *à la main*, idly, in an off-hand manner; *raide comme s'il avait avalé sa* ~, stiff and starched; **2.** tube (for blowing glass); **3.** measure (obs.) varying from 1·71 m. to 2·98 m.

canné, -e (kane), p. adj. Cane-bottomed.
canneberge (kanbɛrʒ), s.f. [unkn. orig.] Cranberry, moorberry.
cannebière, canebière (kanbjɛr), s.f. Hempfield; syn. CHÈNEVIÈRE.
cannel (kanɛl), s.m. [f. Engl. *cannel*] Cannel-coal; candle-coal.
cannelé, -e (kanle), p. adj. Ribbed, corded, fluted, grooved, channelled. ~, s.m. Ribbed silk.
canneler (kanle), v.a. To channel, to flute, to reed, to groove.
cannelier (kanlje), s.m. (bot.) Cinnamon-tree.
cannelle (kanɛl), s.f. [f. *canne*] **1.** Cinnamon; ~ *blanche*, white cinnamon; ~ *noire*, clove cinnamon; **2.** tap, wooden tap (see CANNETTE); **3.** eye-groove (of a needle).
cannelon (kanlɔ̃), s.m. Fluted mould.
cannelure (kanlyr), s.f. Fluting, channelling, reeding, groove.
canner (kane), v.a. **1.** To cane (a chair, &c.); **2.** to measure with the *canne*.
cannetille (kantij), s.f. [f. It. *cannettiglia*] **1.** Gold or silver twisted thread, for embroideries; **2.** brass wire, ribbon-wire, silk-wire.
cannette (kanɛt), s.f. **1.** Tap, tube; **2.** eye-groove (of needle); **3.** pot, jug, bottle, pint (of beer).
canneu-r, -se (kanœr), s.m.f. Caner, chair-caner, cane-worker.
cannibale (kannibal), s.m.f. adj. [f. Amer.-Ind. *caniba*] Cannibal.
cannibalisme (kannibalism), s.m. Cannibalism.
canon (kanɔ̃), s.m. [f. Gr. *kanōn*, It. *cannone*] **1.** Cannon, gun; *à portée de* ~, within cannon-range; (naut.) ~ *de retraite*, stern-chaser; (mil.) evening gun; *coup de* ~, gunshot; *à l'épreuve du* ~, cannon-proof; *tirer le* ~, to fire a gun or cannon; **2.** barrel, cylinder, tube, pipe, nozzle; *à* ~ *rayé*, rifle-barrelled; **3.** measure for liquids (= $\frac{1}{8}$ litre); **4.** (horse's) shank, cannon-bone, cannon; **5.** (of a key) pipe; **6.** (17th c.) breeches' lower trimming; **7.** (eccles.) canon; (adj.) *droit-*~, canon law; **8.** (mus.) canon; **9.** (print.) canon; **10.** (arch., sculpt., drawing) canon.
canonial, -e, (aux) (kanɔnjal), adj. **1.** Canonical; **2.** prebendal.
canonicat (kanɔnika), s.m. [f. L *canonicus*] Canonry.
canonicité (kanɔnisite), s.f. Canonicity, canonical status; inclusion in a canon.
canonique (kanɔnik), adj. Canonical.
canoniquement (kanɔnikmɑ̃), adv. Canonically.
canonisation (kanɔniza'sjɔ̃), s.f. Canonization.
canoniser (kanɔnize), v.a. To canonize; (fig.) to praise highly, to glorify.
canoniste (kanɔnist), s.m. Canonist.
canonnade (kanɔnad), s.f. Cannonade, cannonading.
canonnage (kanɔnaʒ), s.m. Gunnery.
canonner (kanɔne), v.a. To cannonade, to shell, to bombard, to attack with artillery.
canonnerie (kanɔnri), s.f. Cannon-foundry.
canonnier (kanɔnje), s.m. Gunner.
canonnière (kanɔnjɛr), s.f. **1.** Gun-boat; **2.** pop-gun; **3.** (obs.) loop-hole. ~, adj. Gun-.
canope (kanɔp), s.m. Old Egyptian vase; canopic vase.
canot (kano), s.m. [f. Span. *canoa*] Boat, canoe, punt, barge; *grand* ~, pinnace; *petit* ~, jolly-boat; ~ *automobile*, motor-boat; ~ *de sauvetage*, life-boat.
canotage (kanɔtaʒ), s.m. Boating, rowing.
canoter (kanɔte), v.n. To go boating.
canoti-er, -ère (kanɔtje), s.m.f. **1.** Rower, oarsman, boatman, boatwoman; **2.** ~, s.m. adj. (*chapeau*) ~, straw hat, boater.
cantabre (kɑ̃tabr), adj. Cantabrian.
cantal (kɑ̃tal), s.m. [geog. orig.] Cantal cheese.
cantaloup (kɑ̃talu), s.m. [f. *Cantalupo*, Italy] Cantaloup melon.
cantate (kɑ̃tat), s.f. [It. *cantata*] (mus.) Cantata.
cantatille (kɑ̃tatij), s.f. Cantatilla.
cantatrice (kɑ̃tatris), s.f. [L *cantatrix*] Cantatrice.
canter (kantɛr), s.m. [Engl. wd] (horse racing) Canter.
cantharelle, chanterelle (kɑ̃tarɛl, ʃɑ̃trɛl), s.f. Cantharellus, chanterelle (mushroom).
cantharide (kɑ̃tarid), s.f. [L *cantharis*] Cantharis, Spanish fly, blister-beetle.
cantharidine (kɑ̃taridin), s.f. Cantharidin (poison).
cantilène (kɑ̃tilɛn), s.f. [L *cantilena*] (mus.) Cantilena.
cantine (kɑ̃tin), s.f. Canteen.
cantini-er, -ère (kɑ̃tinje), s.m.f. Canteen-keeper, sutler.
cantique (kɑ̃tik), s.m. [L *canticum*] Hymn, canticle, song.
canton (kɑ̃tɔ̃), s.m. [f. It. *cantone*] **1.** Canton, administrative territorial division, sub-district; **2.** (fig.) division, part; **3.** (herald.) canton.
cantonade (kɑ̃tɔnad), s.f. [f. It. *cantonata*] (theatr.) Wings; *parler à la* ~, to speak to some one off.
cantonais, -e (kɑ̃tɔnɛ), adj. s.m.f. Cantonese.
cantonal, -e, (aux) (kɑ̃tɔnal), adj. Cantonal.
cantonnement (kɑ̃tɔnmɑ̃), s.m. Cantonment.
cantonner (kɑ̃tɔne), v.a. To canton, to isolate; ~, v.n. to be cantoned, to be in cantonments; *faire* ~, to canton; **se** ~,

v.pr. to canton or isolate oneself, to take up a position, to limit oneself (*dans*, to).

cantonnier (kɑ̃tɔnje), s.m. Road-labourer, roadman.

cantonnière (kɑ̃tɔnjɛr), s.f. Bed-drapery; valance.

canulant, -e (kanylɑ̃), p. adj. (slang) Boring, tiresome, annoying, tedious.

canule (kanyl), s.f. [f. L *cannula*] Injection pipe; (surg.) cannula.

canulé, -e (kanyle), p. adj. Cannular, pipe-shaped; (slang) annoyed, worried, plagued.

canuler (kanyle), v.a. (slang) To plague, to bore. Hence **canular(d)**, s.m. Plague.

canu-t, -se (kany), s.m.f. [f. *cannette*] Silk-weaver (espec. in Lyons).

canzone (kɑ̃nzɔn), s.f. [It. wd] (mus., poet.) Canzone.

canzonette (kɑ̃nzɔnɛt), s.f. Canzonet.

caouane (kawan), s.f. Loggerhead (turtle).

caoutchouc (kautʃu), s.m. [f. Carib *cahuchu*] **1.** Caoutchouc, india-rubber; hard vulcanized india-rubber; **2.** india-rubber band, elastic band; **3.** overshoe; **4.** waterproof, macintosh; **5.** (bot.) *ficus elastica.*

caoutchouter (kautʃute), v.a. To cover with caoutchouc.

cap (kap), s.m. [f. L *caput*] Cape, headland; (of a ship) head; (obs.) head; *doubler un ~*, to double or round a cape; *doubler le ~ de la quarantaine*, to turn forty; (naut.) *mettre le ~ sur*, to steer for; *le vent change ~ pour ~*, the wind veers right round; *~ de mouton*, dead eye; (colloq.) *de pied en ~*, from top to toe; from head to foot.

capable (kapabl), adj. [f. L *capax*] **1.** Capable, able (*de*, to), qualified (for, to); of good abilities; fit; efficient; *prendre un air ~*, to put on a knowing look; to assume a bumptious air; *il est ~ de tout*, he would stick at nothing; **2.** legally able (to); **3.** likely enough, just the man (to).

capablement (kapabləmɑ̃), adv. Ably, with ability.

capacité (kapasite), s.f. [L *capacitas*] **1.** Capacity; **2.** capaciousness, size; **3.** capability, power of mind, competency; **4.** (naut.) bulk, burden; **5.** legal capacity.

caparaçon (kaparasɔ̃), s.m. [Span. *caparazon*] Caparison.

caparaçonner (kaparasɔne), v.a. To caparison.

cape (kap), s.f. [Span. *capa*] **1.** Cape, sleeveless coat; *n'avoir que la ~ et l'épée*, to be titled but penniless; *roman de ~ et d'épée*, cloak-and-sword novel, novel full of battles and chivalrous adventures; *rire sous ~*, to laugh in one's sleeve; **2.** cloak with a hood, riding-hood; **3.** (naut.) trysail, main course; *mettre à la ~*, to close-reef, to lay to; *être à la ~*, to lie to; **4.** (of anchors) stock; **5.** bowler hat.

capelage (kaplaʒ), s.m. (naut.) Reeving, mast-head rigging.

capelan (kaplɑ̃), s.m. [Provenç. wd] **1.** Scrubby priest or parson; **2.** (fish.) capelan, caplin; **3.** (ent.) male glow-worm.

capeler (kaple), v.a. To clove-hitch; to reeve over or through.

capelet (kaplɛ), s.m. (vet. surg.) Capped hock, capelet.

capeline (kaplin), s.f. [f. OF *capel*] **1.** Hood (for women); broad-brimmed hat, picture hat; **2.** (surg.) capeline; **3.** (armour) cappeline.

capendu, court-pendu (kapɑ̃dy, kurpɑ̃dy), s.m. Excellent variety of apple.

capétien, -ne (kapesjɛ̃), adj. s.m.f. [f. *Hugues Capet*] Capetian.

capeyer (kapeje), v.n. (naut.) To lie to.

capharnaüm (kafarnaɔm), s.m. [geog. orig.] (fig.) Place of confusion, lumber-room, bear-garden, litter, chaos, *omnium gatherum*, glory-hole.

capillaire (kapillɛr), adj. [f. L *capillus*] Capillary, of hair, hair-shaped, for the hair. ~, s.m. **1.** Capillary; **2.** (bot.) maidenhair; *sirop de ~*, capillaire.

capillarité (kapillarite), s.f. Capillarity.

capilotade (kapilɔtad), s.f. [f. Span. *capirotada*] Kind of stew; hash, mince-meat; (fig.) *mettre en ~*, to reduce to pulp; (with blows) to smash to atoms, to break to pieces, to beat black and blue; to smash into smithereens.

capiston (kapistɔ̃), s.m. See CAPITAINE.

capitaine (kapitɛn), s.m. [f. L *caput*] Captain, commander, leader; master, chief, chieftain, (fig.) famous warrior; *~ d'armes*, master-at-arms; *~ de frégate*, commander; *~ de pavillon*, flag-captain; *~ de vaisseau*, captain R.N.; *~ de port*, harbour-master; *~ au long-cours*, master of a foreign-going ship; *grade de ~*, captaincy; syn. (mil. slang) CAPISTON.

capitainerie (kapitɛnri), s.f. Captaincy, captainship, ship's police.

capital, -e, (aux) (kapital), adj. [f. L *capitalis*] **1.** Capital, main, chief, principal, essential; **2.** mortal, deadly, death-; *peine ~e*, capital punishment; *péchés ~aux*, deadly sins.

capital (pl. **aux**) (kapital), s.m. **1.** Main point; **2.** capital, fund, stock, cash; *~ social*, joint-stock; *manger son ~*, to squander one's money or estate.

capitale (kapital), s.f. **1.** Capital (principal town); **2.** capital (letter); (print.) *grandes ~s*, full caps.; *petites ~s*, small caps.

capitalisable (kapitalizabl), adj. Capitalizable.

capitalisation (kapitaliza'sjɔ̃), s.f. Capitalization.

capitaliser (kapitalize), v.a. To capitalize; ~, v.n. to hoard.

capitalisme (kapitalism), s.m. Capitalism.
capitaliste (kapitalist), adj. s.m.f. Capitalist.
capitan (kapitɑ̃), s.m. [Span. wd] Swaggerer, hector, boaster; ~-*pasha*, capitan-pasha (Turkish admiral).
capitane (kapitan), adj. s.f. *Galère* ~, admiral's galley.
capitation (kapita'sjɔ̃), s.f. [f. L *caput*, *capitatio*] Capitation, capitation-tax, head-money, poll-tax.
capité, -e (kapite), adj. [f. L *caput*] (bot.) Capitate.
capiteu-x, -se (kapitø), adj. Heady, strong, inebriating.
capitole (kapitɔl), s.m. [f. L *capitolium*] Capitol; *monter au* ~, to triumph.
capitolin, -e (kapitɔlɛ̃), adj. Capitoline, capitolian.
capiton (kapitɔ̃), s.m. Cappadine (of a tufted chair, &c), cap, tufting, wadding.
capitonnage (kapitɔnaʒ), s.m. Padding, stuffing, tufting, quilting.
capitonner (kapitɔne), v.a. To tuft, to stuff, to pad, to quilt, to button; to wad.
capitoul (kapitul), s.m. (obs.) Capitoul (old name of municipal officers in Toulouse).
capitoulat (kapitula), s.m. Capitoulship.
capitulaire (kapitylɛr), adj. [f. L *capitularis*] Capitulary, capitular. ~**s**, s.m.pl. Capitularies (collection of ordinances, esp. of Frankish kings: *Les Capitulaires de Charlemagne*).
capitulairement (kapitylɛrmɑ̃), adv. Capitularly.
capitulant, -e (kapitylɑ̃), adj. Having a vote in chapter (of Swiss cantons, formerly furnishing mercenary troops). ~, s.m. Capitulant.
capitulation (kapityla'sjɔ̃), s.f. **1.** Capitulation, surrender; compromise, accommodation; **2.** ~**s**, s.f.pl. Capitulations (giving exterritoriality to foreign residents in Turkey).
capitule (kapityl), s.m. [L *capitulum*] **1.** (bot.) Capitulum, flower-head; **2.** (liturg.) capitulum.
capitulé, -e (kapityle), adj. Capitular.
capituler (kapityle), v.n. To capitulate, to surrender; to make a compromise.
capivard (kapivar), s.m. (zool.) Water-hog, capybara.
capoc, kapok (kapɔk), s.m. Kapok, Indian cotton-wool.
capon, -ne (kapɔ̃), s.m.f. [f. *chapon*] Coward, funk, hypocrite; (naut.) cat-tackle. ~, adj. Cowardly, funky.
caponner (kapɔne), v.n. (pop.) To show oneself a coward, to show the white feather; to have an attack of cold feet.
caponnière (kapɔnjɛr), s.f. [f. It. *capponiera*] (fort.) Caponier.
caporal (pl. **aux**) (kapɔral), s.m. [f. It. *caporale*] **1.** Corporal; *le Petit Caporal*, nickname given to Napoleon by his soldiers; **2.** (tobacco) shag.
capot (kapo), s.m. [f. *cape*] (motor.) Bonnet; (naut.) hood; (at cards) capot; (hort.) small hot-bed. ~, adj. (at cards, game, sport) Capot, beaten hollow; thrashed; (fig.) balked, abashed; *être* ~, to have lost all the tricks, to be nowhere, to be utterly defeated; *rester* ~, to look sheepish, foolish, discountenanced; *faire X* ~, to win all the tricks from X, to beat X out and out.
capotage (kapɔtaʒ), s.m. **1.** Hood; fitting of a hood (to a carriage); **2.** capsizing, heeling right over.
capote (kapɔt), s.f. [dim. of *cape*] **1.** Capote (long cloak with hood); great-coat, watch-coat; long coat; **2.** (woman's) small bonnet; **3.** hood (of a carriage or motor-car).
capoter (kapɔte), v.n. (naut., motor.) To capsize, to overturn, to be overturned, to heel right over, to upset, to be thrown head over heels; to tilt, to tip; ~ v.a. to hood (a carriage).
capouan, -e (kapuɑ̃), adj. s.m.f. [f. *Capua*] Capuan.
capraire (kaprɛr), s.f. [f. L *capra*] (bot.) Goat-weed.
câpre (kɑpr), s.f. [f. Gr. *kapparis*; Pers. *kabar*] (bot.) Caper; ~-*capucine*, pickled nasturtium-seed.
capricant, -e, caprisant, -e (kaprikɑ̃, kaprizɑ̃), adj. [f. L *capra*] Irregular, goat-leap, bounding; (med.) caprizant; *pouls* ~, caprizant pulse, goat-leap pulse.
caprice (kapris), s.m. [f. L *capra*] Caprice, whim, freak, fancy, liking; *avoir des* ~*s*, to be fickle, inconstant, to take sudden fancies, to be full of whims.
capricieusement (kaprisjøzmɑ̃), adv. Capriciously, whimsically.
capricieu-x, -se (kaprisjø), adj. Capricious, whimsical, freakish, fickle. ~, s.m.f. Capricious person.
capricorne (kaprikɔrn), s.m. [L *capricornus*] **1.** (astr.) Capricorn, the Goat; **2.** (ent.) capricorn beetle.
câprier (kɑprije), s.m. (bot.) Caper-bush, caper-tree.
câprière (kɑprijɛr), s.f. **1.** Caper-plantation; **2.** caper-pot or jar.
caprification (kaprifika'sjɔ̃), s.f. (agric.) Caprification.
caprifiguier (kaprifigje), s.m. [L *caprificus*] (bot.) Wild fig-tree, goat fig-tree.
caprin, -e (kaprɛ̃), adj. [f. L *capra*] Caprine.
capripède (kapripɛd), adj. Goat-footed, capriped.
capron (kaprɔ̃), s.m. (bot.) Hautboy strawberry.

capronier (kaprɔnje), s.m. (bot.) Hautboy strawberry plant.

capsulage (kapsylaʒ), s.m. Capsuling, capping.

capsulaire (kapsylɛr), adj. Capsular.

capsule (kapsyl), s.f. [f. L *capsula*] **1.** Capsule, membranous envelope; **2.** (bot.) capsule, seed-case, **3.** percussion-cap; **4.** cap (of a bottle); **5.** (med.) capsule; **6.** (chem.) shallow saucer for evaporation, capsule.

capsuler (kapsyle), v.a. To capsule, to cap.

captage (kaptaʒ), s.m. [f. L *captare*] Collecting and conveying water (of springs, &c.).

captal (kaptal), s.m. Medieval French title (in Gascony) = Captain.

captat-eur, -rice (kaptatœr), s.m.f. Inveigler, legacy-hunter.

captation (kapta'sjɔ̃), s.f. Inveigling, captation, undue influence over a testator.

captatoire (kaptatwar), adj. Inveigling, obtained by crooked means.

capter (kapte), v.a. [L *captare*] To gain over unfairly; to inveigle, to seduce, to attract, to win, to gain insidiously; *~ un héritage*, to obtain a legacy by undue influence; *~ l'âme d'un enfant*, to seduce a child's mind; *~ l'attention de X*, to attract X's attention by insidious means; *~ l'eau d'une source*, to collect and convey the water of a spring.

captieusement (kapsjøzmɑ̃), adv. Captiously, insidiously.

captieu-x, -se (kapsjø), adj. [L *captiosus*] Captious, insidious.

capti-f, -ve (kaptif), adj. s.m.f. [L *captivus*] Captive; *faire un ~*, to take a prisoner.

captivant, -e (kaptivɑ̃), p. adj. Captivating, fascinating, winning.

captiver (kaptive), v.a. [L *captivare*] To captivate, to charm, to win over; to enslave, to subdue, to master; *le roi était captivé*, the king was charmed.

captivité (kaptivite), s.f. [L *captivitas*] Captivity, bondage.

capture (kaptyr), s.f. [L *captura*] **1.** Capture, seizure; catching; *la ~ d'un vaisseau marchand*, the capture of a merchantman; **2.** prize, booty; *il ramena sa ~*, he brought back his prize.

capturer (kaptyre), v.a. To capture, to arrest, to seize, to catch.

capuce (kapys), s.m. [It. *cappuccio*] Cowl.

capuche (kapyʃ), s.f. Hood.

capuchon (kapyʃɔ̃), s.m. **1.** Reversible hood, generally attached to a garment; cowl; *prendre le ~*, to become a monk; **2.** chimney-cowl.

capucin (kapysɛ̃), s.m. [f. It. *cappuccino*] **1.** Capuchin; Franciscan friar of new rule, 1528; **2.** capuchin monkey or pigeon.

capucinade (kapysinad), s.f. Trivial sermon, canting discourse, cant.

capucine (kapysin), s.f. **1.** Capuchin nun; **2.** (bot.) nasturtium, Indian cress; **3.** (musketry) band; (mil. slang, obs.) *jusqu'à la troisième ~*, outright, head over ears. *~*, adj. Capucine (colour).

capucinière (kapysinjɛr), s.f. (jest.) Capuchin friary; hotbed of bigotry.

capulet (kapylɛ), s.m. Woman's hood.

caput-mortuum (kapytmɔrtɥɔm), s.m. [L wd] Caput mortuum, worthless residue.

caque (kak), s.f. [f. Flemish *kaken*] **1.** Keg, barrel; *la ~ sent toujours le hareng*, what is bred in the bone will come out in the flesh; cat will after kind; *nous étions serrés comme harengs en ~*, we were packed like sardines; **2.** octave-cask (13½ gallons, used for still champagne).

caquer (kake), v.a. To cure, press, and barrel (herrings); syn. ENCAQUER.

caquet (kakɛ), s.m. [onom.] Cackle, prattle, tittle-tattle, gossip, scandal; *~ bon bec*, magpie, chatterbox; *rabattre le ~ à X*, to make X lower his tone; to take X down a peg; to make X sing small.

caquetage (kaktaʒ), s.m. Cackling, prattling, tittle-tattle, gossiping.

caqueter (kakte), v.n. [onom.] To cackle, to prattle, to chatter, to gossip.

caqueteu-r, -se (kaktœr), s.m.f. Prattler, chatterer, gossip. *~*, adj. Cackling, gossiping, &c.

caqueu-r, -se (kakœr), s.m.f. Herring-curer or packer.

car (kar), conj. [L *quare*] For, because, as. *~*, s.m. *Les ~, les si et les mais*; ifs and buts; prudent reservations.

car (kar), s.m. [Engl. wd] Car (⚠ generally used in French for big motor chara-bancs).

carabas (Marquis de) (karabɑ), s.m. [f. *Marquis de Carabas* in Perrault's tales] Nabob.

carabe (karab), s.m. [L *carabus*] (ent.) Carabus, carnivorous beetle.

carabé (karabe), s.m. [f. Arab. *kahrabà*] Yellow amber.

carabin (karabɛ̃), s.m. **1.** Old name for soldiers armed with the long arquebuse or carbine; **2.** (colloq.) saw-bones, medical student.

carabine (karabin), s.f. [f. OF *carabin*] Carbine, carabine; *~ rayée*, rifle.

carabiné, -e (karabine), adj. Excessive, violent, hard to swallow; capital, first-rate, crack; (naut.) *brise ~e*, stormy gale; stiff gale.

carabinier (karabinje), s.m. Carabineer, carbineer, rifleman; *les ~s*, (in Italy) police-force; (in Spain) customs officers.

carabosse (karabɔs), s.f. See FÉE.
caracal (pl. -s), (karakal), s.m. [Span. wd] (zool.) Caracal.
caraco (karako), s.m. [etym. dub.] Woman's loose-fitting jacket (somewhat slatternly).
caracole (karakɔl), s.f. [Span. *caracol*] **1.** (arch.) Caracole, winding staircase; **2.** (rid.) caracole.
caracoler (karakɔle), v.n. **1.** To caracole, to wheel; **2.** (fam.) to gambol, to hop.
caracoli (karakɔli), s.m. Caracoli (alloy used by Caribee natives).
caracolle (karakɔl), s.m. (bot.) Snail-flower.
caractère (karaktɛr), s.m. [f. Gr. *kharaktēr*] **1.** Character, temper, disposition, humour; *avoir bon* ~, *être d'un bon* ~, *avoir le* ~ *bien fait*, to be good-tempered; *avoir mauvais* ~, *être d'un mauvais* ~, *avoir le* ~ *mal fait*, to be bad-(or ill-) tempered; *sortir de son* ~, to get (or to be put) out of temper; **2.** character, strongly marked peculiarities of a person, thing, &c.; *une œuvre de grand* ~, a highly distinctive work; **3.** hand-writing, type, print, letter, mark, sign; ~*s d'imprimerie*, printing characters; *en gros* ~*s*, in large print; *en petits* ~*s*, in small print; **4.** title, dignity, capacity, authority; *avoir le* ~ *de*, to enjoy the privileges of; **5.** (arith.) digit; **6.** energy, will-power; *il a du* ~, he is strong-willed; **7.** expression; *danse de* ~, expressive dance.
caractériser (karakterize), v.a. To characterize, to distinguish, to mark out, to be the distinguishing feature of; to describe, to define, to determine; **se** ~ (*par*), v.pr. to have for characteristics; to show oneself in one's true light.
caractéristique (karakteristik), adj. Characteristic, typical. ~, s.f. **1.** Characteristic; **2.** (math.) index of logarithm.
caracul (karakyl), s.m. Caracul (fur).
carafe (karaf), s.f. [It. *caraffa*] Water-bottle, decanter, glass jug, carafe; (slang) *rester en* ~, (*a*) to be left in the lurch, to be forgotten; (*b*) to stop short, to be stumped.
carafon (karafɔ̃), s.m. Liqueur bottle or decanter, small flagon; half-pint bottle, quarter-bottle.
caraïbe (karaib), adj. s.m.f. Carib, Caribbean; *chou* ~, Brazil cabbage.
caraïte (karait), s.m. Karaite, caraite (member of a Jewish sect in Russia, Turkey, &c.).
carambolage (karɑ̃bɔlaʒ), s.m. **1.** (at billiards) Cannon, carambole; **2.** (fig.) rebound, double stroke or hit; **3.** (colloq.) tumble, collision, general set-to.
caramboler (karɑ̃bɔle), v.n. (at billiards) To cannon, to make a cannon; (fig.) to rebound, to make a double hit, to run against, to knock and be knocked.
carambolier (karɑ̃bɔlje), s.m. (bot.) Carambola, averrhoa, East-India wood-sorrel.
carambouilleur (karɑ̃bujœr), s.m. Person who deals in stolen goods, especially motor-cars.
caramel (karamɛl), s.m. [f. Span. *caramelo*] **1.** Caramel, burnt sugar; **2.** colouring, browning; **3.** toffee, butter-scotch, caramel.
caramélisation (karameliza'sjɔ̃), s.f. Conversion into caramel; sweetening or colouring with caramel.
caraméliser (karamelize), v.a. To convert into caramel; to line (a mould), to sweeten or to colour with caramel; **se** ~, v.pr. to be converted into caramel.
carapa (karapa), s.m. (bot.) Carapa, crab-wood; *huile de* ~, carap-oil.
carapace (karapas), s.f. [f. Span. *carapacho*] Carapace (of a tortoise); (fig.) armour, thick hide.
(se) carapater (səkarapate), v.pr. (pop.) To take to one's heels, to decamp, to make tracks.
caraque (karak) s.f. [It. *caracca*] (naut.) Carrack, galleon. ~, adj. Carack (applied to the finest Dutch porcelain).
carat (kara), s.m. [f. Gr. *keration*] **1.** Carat; **2.** small diamonds; *c'est un sot à 24* ~*s*, he is an unalloyed fool.
caravane (karavan), s.f. [Pers. *karwan*] **1.** Caravan; **2.** party, company; **3.** travelling show; *les chiens aboient, la* ~ *passe*, go your way, let the dogs howl.
caravanier (karavanje), s.m. Caravaneer.
caravansérail (karavɑ̃seraj), s.m. [Pers. *karwan-seraī*] **1.** Caravansary, caravanserai; **2.** (pej.) large hotel.
caravelle (karavɛl), s.f. [It. *caravella*] (naut.) Caravel.
carbet (karbɛ), s.m. (naut.) Large cabin; [shed.
carbonaro (pl. -ari), s.m. [It. wd.] Carbonaro (pl. -ari). **carbonarisme, s.m.**
carbonate (karbɔnat), s.m. (chem.) Carbonate.
carbone (karbɔn), s.m. [f. L *carbo, carbonis*] (chem.) Carbon; *oxyde de* ~, carbonic oxide.
carboné, -e (karbɔne), adj. Carburetted; carbonaceous.
carboneu-x, -se (karbɔnø), adj. (chem.) Carbonous.
carbonifère (karbɔnifɛr), adj. Carboniferous.
carbonique (karbɔnik), adj. (chem.) Carbonic.
carbonisation (karbɔniza'sjɔ̃), s.f. Carbonization.
carboniser (karbɔnize), v.a. To carbonize, to char; *débris* ~*s*, charred

remains; se ~, v.pr. to become carbonized or charred.

carbonnade (karbɔnad), s.f. (cook.) Carbonado; syn. BŒUF BRAISÉ.

carborundum (karbɔrɑ̃dɔm) s.m. (chem.) Carborundum.

carburateur (karbyratœr), s.m. Carburettor. **carburat-eur, -rice,** adj. Carburizing.

carburation (karbyra'sjɔ̃), s.f. Carburation.

carbure (karbyr), s.m. Carbide, carburet.

carburé, -e (karbyre), adj. (chem.) Carburetted.

carburer (karbyre), v.a. To carburize.

carcajou (karkaʒu), s.m. (zool.) Carcajou (American badger).

carcan (karkɑ̃), s.m. [ODutch *querca*] **1.** Iron collar, pillory; **2.** jade, screw, nag; **3.** shrew, gawky shrew.

carcasse (karkas), s.f. [It. *carcassa*; OF *charcois*] **1.** Carcass, carcase; **2.** bones, body; **3.** framework; **4.** fish-basket.

carcel (karsɛl), s.f. [f. name of French inventor] Carcel lamp.

carcinome (karsinom), s.m. (pathol.) Carcinoma, cancer.

cardage (kardaʒ), s.m. [L *carduus*] Carding.

cardamine (kardamin), s.f. (bot.) Cardamine, meadow-cress; syn. CRESSON DES PRÉS (not *cresson de fontaine*).

cardamome (kardamom), s.m. (bot.) Cardamom.

cardan (kardɑ̃), s.m. [f. name of French inventor] Cardan joint, universal joint; *suspension à la* ~, cardan mounting.

carde (kard), s.f. **1.** Chard (midrib of the cardoon leaf); **2.** teasel (bur); **3.** carding-machine.

cardée (karde), s.f. Cardful (of wool).

carder (karde), v.a. To card; to teasel.

cardère (kardɛr), s.f. (bot.) Teasel; syn. CHARDON À FOULON.

carderie (kardəri), s.f. Carding-house.

cardeu-r, -se (kardœr), s.m.f. Carder. ~, adj. Carding.

cardialgie (kardjalʒi), s.f. [f. Gr. *kardia*+*algos*] Cardialgy, heartburn.

cardiaque (kardjak), adj. Cardiac. ~, s.m. (med.) Cardiac.

cardiff (kardif), s.m. [geog. orig.] Welsh or similar coal.

cardinal (pl. **aux**) (kardinal), s.m. [f. L *cardinalis*] **1.** Cardinal; **2.** (ornith.) cardinal-bird, red-bird. ~, **-e**, adj. **1.** Chief, fundamental, cardinal; *points ~aux*, cardinal points or winds, North, South, East and West; *nombre* ~, cardinal number; *vertus ~es*, cardinal virtues: justice, prudence, temperance, and fortitude.

cardinalat (kardinala), s.m. Cardinalate; *être promu au* ~, to be promoted to the cardinalate.

cardinalice (kardinalis), adj. Of a cardinal, attached to the cardinalate.

cardiologie (kardjɔlɔʒi), s.f. [f. Gr. *kardia*+*logos*] Cardiology.

cardite (kardit), s.f. Carditis, inflammation of the heart's tissue or membranes.

cardon (kardɔ̃), s.m. [f. L *carduus*] (bot.) Cardoon.

cardonnette (kardɔnɛt), s.f. See CHARDONNETTE.

carême (karɛm), s.m. [L *quadragesima*] **1.** Lent; **2.** fast, fasting; *faire* ~, to keep Lent; *~-prenant*, Shrovetide mummer, regular guy; *cela arrive comme mars en* ~, it happens regularly, automatically, as sure as fate; *cela arrive comme marée en* ~, that comes very seasonably; *face de* ~, thin, pale face; *faire ~ par force*, to starve, to be starved.

carénage (karenaʒ), s.m. (naut.) Careening, careenage.

carence (karɑ̃s), s.f. [LL *carentia*] Absence of securities or assets; carelessness, unconcern, disuse, neglect; *procès-verbal de* ~, legal document setting out the absence of anything upon which to levy; *la ~ des pouvoirs publics*, the unconcern of public authorities.

carène (karɛn), s.f. [L *carina*] **1.** (naut., aeron.) Keel; **2.** (bot.) carina.

caréner (karene), v.a. (naut.) To careen.

caressant, -e (karɛsɑ̃), p. adj. Caressing; fawning; fond; affectionate; soft.

caresse (karɛs), s.f. [It. *carezza*] Caress, endearment, fawning, fondness, kindness; pat, chuck, stroking; (fig.) smile, favour; *les ~s d'un chien*, a dog's fawning; *une ~ sur la joue*, a pat on the cheek; *défiez-vous des ~s intéressées*, beware of mercenary flatteries.

caresser (karɛse), v.a. To caress; to fondle, to pamper, to fawn upon; to flatter, to cajole, to make much of, to coax, to wheedle; to stroke, to pat; to indulge, to foster, to cherish; ~ *un projet*, to foster a plan; ~ *de vains espoirs*, to indulge vain hopes.

caret (karɛ), s.m. **1.** (zool.) Hawk's-bill turtle; **2.** rope-maker's reel; *fil de* ~, rope-yarn.

cargaison (kargɛzɔ̃), s.f. [Provenç. *cargazon*] Cargo, ship-load.

cargo (pl. **-s**) (kargo), s.m. Cargo-boat.

cargue (karg) s.f. (naut.) Brail.

carguer (karge), v.a. (naut.) To take in, to brail up, to haul up, to clew up.

cari, kari (kari), s.m. [Tamil wd] Curry.

cariatide, caryatide (karjatid) s.f. [f. L *caryatis*] Caryatid.

caribou (karibu), s.m. (zool.) Caribou, Canadian reindeer.

caricature (karikatyr), s.f. [It. *caricatura*] Caricature; guy, sight; (fig.) parody.

caricatural, -e, (aux) (karikatyral), adj. Caricatural, grotesque, ludicrous.
caricaturer (karikatyre), v.a. To caricature, to parody.
caricaturiste (karikatyrist), s.m. Caricaturist.
carie (kari), s.f. [L *caries*] (of teeth, bones) Caries, decay; (of trees, plants) rot, dry-rot.
carier (karje), v.a.n. To cause to decay, to make or become carious; **se ~**, v.pr. to decay, to rot. **carié**, p. adj. Carious, rotten; (fig.) corrupt.
carillon (karijɔ̃), s.m. [medieval L *quadrilio*] **1.** Carillon; chime; change-ringing, peal (of bells); **2.** jingling noise, clatter, racket; *horloge à ~*, chiming clock; *quel ~!*, what a noise!
carillonner (karijɔne), v.n.a. **1.** To chime; to ring the changes; to ring a peal; **2.** to clatter, to make a noise about; *fête carillonnée*, great festival, feast-day, holiday; *il carillonne ses succès*, he goes about trumpeting his achievements.
carlin (karlɛ̃), s.m. [It. *carlino*] **1.** Carlin (Italian silver coin); **2.** pug-dog, pug.
carlingue (karlɛ̃g), s.f. [unkn. orig.] (naut.) Keelson; (aeron.) car, carlingue.
carliste (karlist), s.m.f. adj. Carlist, Spanish legitimist (supporter of Don Carlos).
carlovingien, -ne (karlɔvɛ̃ʒjɛ̃), s.m. adj. Carlovingian (belonging to the 2nd French dynasty); syn. CAROLINGIEN.
carmagnole (karmaɲɔl), s.f. [etym. dub., perh. geog.] **1.** Carmagnole (jacket); **2.** revolutionary song and dance.
carme (karm), s.m. [f. *Mont Carmel*] White Friar, carmelite; *~ déchaux*, barefooted White Friar.
carmeline (karməlin), adj. s.f. [Span. *carmelina*] Vicuña wool.
carmélite (karmelit), s.f. Carmelite nun. ~, adj. (colour) Light brown, carmelite.
carmin (karmɛ̃), s.m. adj. [f. *kermes*] Carmine.
carminati-f, -ve (karminatif), adj. Carminative.
carmine (karmin), s.f. (chem.) Carminic acid.
carminé, -e (karmine), adj. Carminated, carmine.
carminer (karmine), v.a. To carminate, to paint in carmine, to redden.
carnage (karnaʒ), s.m. [It. *carnaggio*] **1.** Carnage, slaughter, massacre; **2.** carrion, food of wild beasts.
carnalité (karnalite), s.f. [f. L *carnem*] Carnality.
carnassi-er, -ère (karnasje), adj. Carnivorous.
carnassier (karnasje), s.m. **1.** Carnivorous animal, carnivore; **2.** *~s*, carnivora.
carnassière (karnasjɛr), s.f. Game-bag; syn. CARNIER.
carnation (karna'sjɔ̃), s.f. [f. L *caro*] Flesh-colour, flesh-tint.
carnaval (pl. **-s**) (karnaval), s.m. [It. *carnevale*] **1.** Carnival, Shrovetide; **2.** festivities usual during carnival revelry; **3.** queer-looking or queerly dressed fellow; **4.** (in the South) big dummy dressed as a mock king (central figure in the carnival revelry).
carnavalesque (karnavalɛsk), adj. Of carnival.
carne (karn) **1.** s.f. [f. L *cardinem*] Corner, edge; **2.** ~ s.f. [f. It. *carne*] (*a*) bad meat, cagmag; (*b*) (pop.) hag, bitch, screw, jade.
carné, -e (karne), adj. Flesh-coloured.
carnet (karnɛ), s.m. [f. L *quaternetum*] Small note-book, memorandum-book, booklet; *~ de chèques*, cheque-book; *~ de banque*, pass-book; *~ d'échéances*, bill-book; *~ de commandes*, order-book; *~ de bal*, dance card.
carnier (karnje), s.m. Game-bag; syn. CARNASSIÈRE.
carnification (karnifika'sjɔ̃), s.f. Carnification.
(se) carnifier (səkarnifje), v.pr. (med.) To become carnified.
carnivore (karnivɔr), adj. [f. L *caro, carnis+vorare*] Carnivorous; (syn. CARNASSIER, but *carnassier* is said only of animals, while *carnivore* may be said of man as well). ~, s.m. Flesh-eating animal, carnivore.
carogne (karɔɲ), s.f. [doublet of *charogne*] (pop.) Hag, bitch, slut; see CHAROGNE.
carolingien (karɔlɛ̃ʒjɛ̃), adj. s.m. See CARLOVINGIEN.
carolus (karɔlys), s.m. Silver and copper coin, issued by Charles (Carolus) VIII.
caronade (karɔnad), s.f. [Engl. geog. orig.] Carronade.
caroncule (karɔ̃kyl), s.f. [L *caruncula*] Caruncle, wattle.
carotide (karɔtid), s.f. [Gr. *karōtides*] Carotid.
carottage (karɔtaʒ), s.m. Diddling, swindle, chouse.
carotte (karɔt), s.f. [L *carota*] **1.** Carrot; **2.** roll, twist (of tobacco); **3.** swindle, trick; *tirer une ~ à X*, to trick X out of something; to squeeze or diddle money out of X.
carotter (karɔte), v.a. (fam.) **1.** To chouse, to wangle, to diddle; **2.** to shirk, to malinger.
carotti-er, -ère, carotteu-r, -se (karɔtje, karɔtœr), s.m.f. Speculator in a small way; trickster, cheat; shirker, malingerer.
caroube, carouge (karub, karuʒ), s.f. [f. Arab. *kharrub*] Carob-bean, locust-bean, St. John's bread.
caroubier (karubje), s.m. (bot.) Carob, carob-tree.
carpe[1] (karp), s.f. [L *carpa*] (ichth.)

Carp; *faire des sauts de* ~, to wriggle about; *muet comme une* ~, as dumb as an oyster; *bailler comme une* ~, to yawn one's head off; *elle fait des yeux de* ~ *pâmée*, or *frite*, she turns up the whites of her eyes; she looks like a dying duck in a thunderstorm.

carpe[2] (karp), s.m. [Gr. *karpos*] (anat.) Carpus, wrist-bones.

carp-eau (pl. **-x**), **-ette** (karpo), s.m.f. Young carp.

carpelle (karpɛl), s.m. [f. Gr. *karpos*] (bot.) Carpel.

carpette (karpɛt), s.f. [f. Engl. *carpet*] Centre-carpet.

carpien, -ne (karpjɛ̃), adj. (anat.) Carpal.

carpillon (karpijɔ̃), s.m. Very small carp.

carquois (karkwɑ), s.m. [Gr. *tarkasion*] Quiver; *avoir vidé son* ~, to be at one's wit's end.

carrare (karar), s.m. [f. *Carrara*, Italy] White or Carrara marble.

carré, -e (kare), adj. [f. L *quadratus*] Square; square-built, well-set; firm, decided, plain, flat, peremptory, categorical; ~ *dans ses opinions*, of clear-cut opinions; *une tête* ~*e*, an obstinate fellow; *une partie* ~*e*, a party of two women and two men; (math.) square; *la racine* ~*e de 81 est 9*, the square root of 81 is 9.

carré (kare), s.m. **1.** Square; quadrangle; square-piece; **2.** landing; stair-head; **3.** (gard.) bed; **4.** (of mutton) best end of the neck; **5.** (arch.) fillet; **6.** (mil.) square; **7.** (naut.) ward-room; **8.** (math.) square, second power of a number; *le* ~ *de 3 est 9*, the square of 3 is 9.

carreau (pl. **-x**) (karo), s.m. **1.** Square, lozenge; *étoffe à* ~*x*, checked material; **2.** paving-tile, paving-brick, tile flooring, brick floor; *rester sur le* ~, to be killed (or left for dead) on the spot; **3.** pane-glass, window-pane; **4.** cushion, hassock; **5.** (at cards) diamond; *se garder à* ~, (fig.) to keep a card up one's sleeve; **6.** (dressm.) goose, pressing-iron; **7.** (med.) *tabes mesenterica*; **8.** (fish.) square net; **9.** square file; **10.** (pop) eyeglass, monocle.

carrée (kare), s.f. **1.** Tester (of a bed); **2.** old square note (of music).

carrefour (karfur), s.m. [f. LL *quadrifurcus*] Cross-roads, crossing; *langage de* ~, Billingsgate; *orateur de* ~, stump orator.

carrelage (karlaʒ), s.m. Tile-flooring, brick paving, brick-pavement; cobbling.

carreler (karle), v.a. To floor or pave with tiles or bricks; to cobble.

carrelet (karlɛ), s.m. **1.** (ichth.) Plaice; **2.** square fishing-net; **3.** awl; packing-needle, sail-needle; **4.** square file; square ruler.

carrelette (karlɛt), s.f. Polishing-file, 'small rubber'. See CARREAU **9.**

carreleur (karlœr), s.m. **1.** Floor-tiler, tile or brick paver; **2.** itinerant cobbler.

carrelure (karlyr), s.f. New soles, new soling, cobbling.

carrément (karemɑ̃), adv. Squarely, straight, frankly, plainly, straightforwardly; firmly, peremptorily, categorically, flatly.

carrer (kare), v.a. To square; ~ *un nombre*, to multiply a number by itself; ~ *un cercle est impossible*, it is impossible to square the circle; ~ *sa mise*, to double one's stake; **se** ~, v.pr. to strut, to affect grand airs, to stalk; to loll.

carrick (karik), s.m. [f. Scotch prop. n.] Box-coat with several capes.

carrier (karje), s.m. Quarrier, quarryman.

carrière[1] (karjɛr), s.f. [f. LL *carraria*] **1.** Career; **2.** race-course, race-ground, arena, lists; **3.** race, course; **4.** (fig.) play, scope; *donner* ~ *à son imagination*, to give free scope to one's imagination.

carrière[2] (karjɛr), s.f. [f. LL *quadraria*] Quarry, pit.

carriole (karjɔl), s.f. [It. *carriuola*] Light van, jaunting-car, trap; (pej.) basket, tub.

carrossable (karɔsabl), adj. Passable for carriages; *chemin* ~, carriage-road.

carrossage (karɔsaʒ), s.m. (motor.) **1.** Set of the axle-pin; **2.** fitting of the body on a motor-car.

carrosse (karɔs), s.m. [f. It. *carrozza*] Coach, carriage; *rouler* ~, to have one's carriage and pair; to be rich.

carrosser (karɔse), v.a. To coach; to make (a body for the frame of a motor-car); to fit the body to the frame of (a motor-car).

carrosserie (karɔsri), s.f. Coach-making; (motor.) body-making; (by ext.) the body and fixtures of a motor-car.

carrossier (karɔsje), s.m. Carriage-builder; manufacturer of motor-car bodies; (obs.) carriage-horse, coach-horse. **carrossi-er, -ère,** adj. For coaches or carriages.

carrousel (karuzɛl), s.m. [f. It. *carosello*] **1.** Carrousel, tournament; **2.** roundabout.

carrure (karyr), s.f. [f. *carré*] Breadth of shoulders, back and shoulders; *un homme d'une belle* ~, a well-built fellow.

cartable (kartabl), s.m. [f. *carte*] Satchel, school-bag.

cartahu (kartay), s.m. [unkn. orig.] (naut.) Whip, girtline.

cartayer (kartɛje), v.n. [f. *charrette*] To avoid ruts in driving.

carte (kart), s.f. [f. L *charta*] **1.** Card; *jeu de* ~*s*, pack of cards; *partie de* ~*s*, game of cards; card-playing; *basses* ~*s*, low or small cards; *hautes* ~*s*, court-cards; *battre les* ~*s*, to shuffle the cards; *donner les* ~*s*, to deal; ~*s sur table*, above board, openly, (fig.) frankly; *tirer les ~s à X*, to tell X's fortune; (fig.) *connaître le dessous des ~s*, to be in the secret, to know what is on the cards; *il y a un dessous de ~s*, there is some underhand game here, there is more in this than meets the eye; (fig.) *brouiller les ~s*, to sow discord, to confuse the issue, to embroil matters; *c'est un château de ~s que cette maison*, this is a jerry-built house; (fig.) *château de ~s*, castle in the air; *donner ~ blanche*, to give carte blanche, to give full power; *faire abattre ses ~s à X*, to call X's bluff; **2.** pasteboard, card; (phot.) *~ album*, cabinet-size card; *~ lettre*, letter-card; *~ postale*, postcard; *~ de visite*, visiting-card; **3.** map, chart; *~ muette*, outline map, skeleton map; *perdre la ~*, to be disconcerted, to be put out, to lose one's presence of mind; **4.** ticket; *~ d'entrée*, admission ticket or card; **5.** bill; *la ~ à payer*, the bill, the reckoning; **6.** bill of fare; *à la ~*, from the bill of fare; à la carte.

cartel (kartɛl), s.m. [f. It. *cartello*] **1.** Challenge, cartel; **2.** convention between enemies for ransom or exchange of prisoners, &c.; **3.** manufacturers' union to keep up prices; **4.** *~ des gauches*, temporary political union of Left parties; **5.** dial case; **6.** cartel clock; **7.** (mil., naut.) cartel; **8.** *~ d'armoiries*, (herald.) shield.

carter (kartɛr), s.m. [Engl. wd] (bicyc., motor.) Case, gear-case, crank-case.

cartésianisme (kartezjanism), s.m. [f. *Cartesius*, L form of *Descartes*] Cartesianism.

cartésien, -ne (kartezjɛ̃), adj. Cartesian.

carthaginois, -e (kartaʒinwɑ), adj. s.m.f. [f. *Carthage*] Carthaginian.

carthame (kartam), s.m. [f. Arab. *qortoum*] (bot.) Carthamus, safflower.

carthamine (kartamin), s.f. (chem.) Carthamin.

cartier (kartje), s.m. Card-maker.

cartilage (kartilaʒ), s.m. [L *cartilago*] Cartilage, gristle.

cartilagineu-x, -se (kartilaʒinø), adj. Cartilaginous, gristly.

cartisane (kartisan), s.f. [f. It. *carteggiana*] Foil-card; *dentelle à ~*, vellum lace.

cartographe (kartɔgraf), s.m. [Fr. *carte*+Gr. *graphein*] Cartographer, map or chart-maker.

cartographie (kartɔgrafi), s.f. Cartography, map-making, mapping, chart-making; maps, charts.

cartographique (kartɔgrafik), adj. Cartographical.

cartomancie (kartɔmɑ̃si), s.f. [f. *carte*+ Gr. *manteia*] Cartomancy, fortune-telling by cards.

cartomancien, -ne (kartɔmɑ̃sjɛ̃), s.m.f. Cartomancer.

carton (kartɔ̃), s.m. [f. L *charta*, It. *cartone*] **1.** Pasteboard, millboard, cardboard, paper pulp; papier mâché, thick card; *~ cuir*, leather-board; *~ pâte*, pasteboard; *~ pierre*, statuary pasteboard; **2.** pasteboard box or case; pasteboard drawer; paper box, hat-box, &c.; *~ à chapeau*, bandbox, hat-box; **3.** portfolio; *rester dans les ~s*, to be pigeon-holed; **4.** cartoon, sketch, pattern for a tapestry (drawing or painting); **5.** ticket, invitation-card; **6.** (print.) four-page cancel; **7.** (pop.) playing-card.

cartonnage (kartɔnaʒ), s.m. Boarding, pasteboard work or covering, boards.

cartonné, -e (kartɔne), p. adj. In boards, boards.

cartonner (kartɔne), v.a. To put or bind in boards, to board, to put a pasteboard cover on; (print.) to cancel; *~*, v.n. (fam.) to play cards.

cartonnerie (kartɔnri), s.f. Pasteboard or cardboard manufactory.

cartonneu-r, -se (kartɔnœr), s.m.f. Binder of books in boards.

cartonnier (kartɔnje), s.m. **1.** Pasteboard-maker, millboard or cardboard maker; **2.** chest of pasteboard drawers.

cartonnière (kartɔnjɛr), s.f. adj. Bandbox maker, cardboard- or paper-box maker.

cartouche (kartuʃ), s.f. [It. *cartoccio*] **1.** Cartridge; **2.** (of fireworks) case, pot; **3.** s.m. (arch., draw.) cartouche, scroll; **4.** s.m. [f. name of 18th-century French robber and murderer] robber, ruffian, 'Jack Sheppard'; a terror.

cartoucherie (kartuʃri), s.f. Cartridge manufactory.

cartouchière (kartuʃjɛr), s.f. Ammunition-pouch; syn. GIBERNE.

cartulaire (kartylɛr), s.m. [f. L *charta*, *chartula*] Cartulary.

carvi (karvi), s.m. [f. Arab. *karawiya*] (bot.) Caraway.

carya, caryer (karja, karje), s.m. (bot.) Carya, hickory.

caryatide (karjatid), s.f. See CARIATIDE.

caryophyllé, -e (karjɔfile), adj. (bot.) Caryophyllaceous. **caryophyllées**, s.f.pl. Caryophyllaceae.

cas (kɑ), s.m. [L *casus*] **1.** Case, event, conjuncture, circumstance, occasion; **2.** instance, fact, matter, question, point, position, lawsuit; *dans le ~ de*, (*a*) in case of; (*b*) able to; in a position to; likely to; *dans le ~ où*, *au ~ que*, in case; *dans tous les ~*, *en tout ~*, in any case, at all events, however; *en ~ de besoin*, if need be, in case of need; *hors le ~ où*, unless, except; *selon le ~*, as the case may be; *le ~ échéant*, should such be the case, *en ce ~*, *en pareil ~*, in such a case; *c'est le ~ ou jamais*, it's now or never; *c'est bien le ~ de le dire*, one may indeed say so; it has never been so true; *un en-~*, (*a*) collation (light meal); (*b*) parasol-umbrella; *tout mauvais ~ est niable*, in a dubious cause it's safer to deny everything; *un ~ de conscience*, case of conscience; *un ~ de légitime défense*, an instance (or matter) of lawful self-defence; *un ~ de choléra*, a case of cholera; *un ~ embarrassant*, a difficult point, a debatable matter (or question); *se mettre dans un mauvais ~*, to put oneself in a false position; **3.** esteem, value; *faire ~ de*, to value, to set a value on; to take into account; *faire grand ~ de*, to esteem or value highly, to have a great respect for; **4.** (gram.) case; **5.** (very vulg.) excrement; *faire son ~*, to do one's jobs; (by ext.) posterior.

casani-er, -ère (kazanje), adj. [f. L *casa*] Stay-at-home, home-keeping, domestic, recluse.

casaque (kazak), s.f. [It. *casacca*] Cassock, cloak, jacket, coat, stable coat, racing-coat; (fig.) *tourner ~*, to flee; to turn cat in pan, to turn one's coat, to be a turn-coat.

casaquin (kazakɛ̃), s.m. Jacket; (slang) *tomber sur le ~ à X*, to give X a drubbing, to dust X's jacket.

casbah (kasba), s.f. [f. Arab. wd] Kasbah (palace-citadel in Barbary States).

cascade (kaskad), s.f. [It. *cascata*] Cascade, waterfall, bound, leap, tumble, tossing, chute, fall; (fig.) slip, freak; *des ~s de rires*, peals of laughter.

cascader (kaskade), v.n. **1.** To fall (said of a river, of water, &c.); **2.** to indulge in freaks, to lead an irregular or fast life, to go on the spree.

cascadeu-r, -se (kaskadœr), s.m.f. adj. Fast (man or woman).

cascarille (kaskarij), s.f. [Span. *cascarilla*] (bot., pharm.) Cascarilla, cascarilla bark.

cascatelle (kaskatɛl), s.f. [f. *cascade*] Small waterfall or cascade.

case (kɑz), s.f. [f. L *casa*] **1.** Small dwelling, cabin, hut; **2.** compartment, division, pigeon-hole, square (of the chess-board), point; box, drawer; **3.** (naut.) berth.

caséeu-x, -se (kazeø), adj. Caseous, cheesy.

caséine (kazein), s.f. [f. L *caseus*] Caseine.

casemate (kazmat), s.f. [It. *casamatta*] **1.** (fort.) Casemate; **2.** (fig.) prison, cell, vault; **3.** (hunt.) blind hole.

casemater (kazmate), v.a. (fort.) To casemate.

caser (kɑze), v.a. [f. *case*] **1.** To place, to find a place for, to fix, to put away, to lay by; **2.** to find a situation or berth for; to provide for; (fig.) to arrange a marriage for; **se ~**, v.pr. to get settled, to find a situation or place or family; **~**, v.n. (backgammon) to make a point.

caserel (kazrɛl), s.m. **caserette** (kazrɛt), s.f. [f. L *caseus*] Cheese-mould.

caserne (kazɛrn), s.f. [f. L *casa*] **1.** Barracks; *~ flottante*, receiving-ship; *~ de pompiers*, fire-brigade station; *plaisanteries de ~*, barrack-room jests; **2.** (fig.) large building of plain architecture, barracks.

casernement (kazɛrnmɑ̃), s.m. Quartering in barracks.

caserner (kazɛrne), v.a.n. To barrack.

casernet (kazɛrnɛ), s.m. (naut.) Book, log-book.

casernier (kazɛrnje), s.m. Barrack gate-keeper.

caset (kazɛ), s.m. Caddis, case-worm; cad-bait.

casier (kɑzje), s.m. [f. *case*] **1.** Set of pigeon-holes, nest of drawers, open case with divisions, compartment; *~ judiciaire*, record of number of convictions (of a man or woman); *~ à musique*, canterbury; **2.** (fish.) bow-net, hoop-net, floating lobster-pot.

casilleu-x, -se (kazijø), adj. [f. *casser*] Brittle (said only of glass).

casimir (kazimir), s.m. [f. Engl. *kerseymere*, corrupt. of *Cashmere*] Kerseymere.

casino (kazino), s.m. [It. wd] Casino.

casoar (kazɔar), s.m. [f. Malay *kasuari*] **1.** (zool.) Cassowary; **2.** plume of shako.

caspienne (kaspjɛn), adj. Caspian.

casque (kask), s.m. [f. Span. *casco*] **1.** Helmet, headpiece, casque; (fig.) helmet-shaped head-dress or chignon; **2.** (zool.) callous or bony protuberance found on the head or over the beak of certain birds; **3.** (moll.) helmet shell; **4.** (bot.) helmet-shaped spur of certain orchids, and of other flowers; **5.** (slang) drop too much; **6.** *~ à mèche*, cotton night-cap.

casqué, -e (kaske), adj. Helmeted; (fig.) having a helmet-shaped chignon or ornament.

casquer (kaske), v.n. (slang) To pay up, to fork out, to stump or cough up.

casquette (kaskɛt), s.f. [f. *casque*] Cap.

casquetti-er, -ère (kaskɛtje), s.m.f. Cap-maker.

cassable (kɑsabl), adj. [f. *casser*] Breakable.

cassage (kɑsaʒ), s.m. [f. *casser*] Breaking, breakage.

cassandre (kasɑ̃dr), **1.** s.m. [f. a part in OF popular comedies] Cassander, Pantaloon, old booby; **2.** s.f. [f. *Cassandra* daughter of Priam and Hecuba] Cassandra, person prophesying calamities.

cassant, -e (kɑsɑ̃), adj. **1.** Brittle, crisp,

breaking; **2.** (fig.) abrupt, curt, gruff, short, peremptory.

cassation (kasa'sjɔ̃), s.f. (law) Cassation, annulment; (final) appeal; (mil.) reducing to a lower grade or to the ranks; *Cour de ~*, (French) Highest Court of Appeal (concerned only with revising legal procedure); *se pourvoir en ~*, to appeal.

cassave (kasav), s.f. Cassava (flour).

casse (kɑs), s.f. [f. *casser*] **1.** Breakage, breaking, damage; (pop.) wounds, affray, casualties; *gare la ~*, look out for squalls !; *~-cœurs*, s.m. breaker of hearts, flirt; *~-cou*, s.m. (*a*) break-neck, foolhardy (person); (*b*) stumbling-block; (*c*) (interj.) look out !, mind !, danger !; *~-croûte*, s.m. (*a*) light meal, snack; (*b*) low-class eating-house or pub in which one can eat a bit; *~-mottes*, s.m. (agric.) clod-breaker; *~-museau*, s.m. (*a*) kind of hard cake (syn. TALMOUSE); (*b*) (fig.) blow in the face; *~-noisettes*, *~-noix*, s.m. nut-cracker, nut-crackers; *~-pierres*, s.m. (*a*) (surg.) stone-breaker; (*b*) (bot.) saxifrage; (*c*) stone-breaker, hammer; *~-poitrine*, s.m. strong spirits, cut-throat stuff; *~-tête*, s.m. (*a*) club, tomahawk; (*b*) head-splitting work, bewildering problem, worry, puzzle, deafening noise; (*c*) (naut.) splinter-netting, overhead netting; *qui fait la ~ la paie*, who makes the mistake must pay for it; *payer la ~*, to stand the racket; **2.** (bot.) cassia; *passe-moi la ~, je te passerai le séné*, one good turn deserves another; let me have my way, and I will let you have yours; scratch my back and I will scratch yours; **3.** (print.) case; **4.** glazier's ladle.

cassé, -e (kɑse), p. adj. Broken, broken down, old, weak, trembling; (of peas) split; (of a ship) hogged; *sucre cuit au ~*, sugar boiled until a drop of it becomes hard and brittle when dropped into cold water.

casseau (pl. **-x**), (kɑso), s.m. (print.) Half-case, fount-case.

cassement (kɑsmɑ̃), s.m. Breaking; *~ de tête*, head-splitting, weariness of the brain, worry.

casser (kɑse), v.a.n. [L *quassare*] **1.** To break, to crack, to snap, to split, to break down, to wear out; **2.** to annul, to reverse, to suppress; **3.** to reduce to a lower rank, to disrate; **4.** to dismiss, to discharge ; *~ bras et jambes*, to astound, to break down one's defences; *~ la croûte*, to eat a bit, to take a snack; *n'en ~ que d'une dent*, just to take the edge off one's appetite; *il nous cassait l'encensoir sur le nez*, he was smothering us with flatteries; *on ne fait pas d'omelette sans ~ des œufs*, you can't make an omelet without breaking eggs; nothing is done without trouble and sacrifice; *vous me cassez la tête avec votre bruit*, you are making my head split with your noise; *je me casse la tête à ce sujet*, I worry my head (or rack my brains) about that; *ce vin casse la tête*, this wine is very heady; *il casse les vitres*, he speaks without moderation; he speaks out boldly (in order) to bring matters to a crisis; (fig.) *~ du sucre*, to gossip (with malignity); *il a été cassé aux gages*, he has been dismissed; *à tout ~*, tremendous; *je me suis cassé le nez à sa porte*, I called in vain; I found nobody at home; I was wofully disappointed; *se ~ le nez*, (*a*) to fall on one's face; (*b*) to knock up against an obstacle; (*c*) to fail lamentably in an enterprise; *la corde a cassé*, or *s'est cassée*, the rope snapped; **se ~**, v.pr. to break, to get or be broken, to snap.

casserole (kasrɔl), s.f. [f. *casse*] **1.** Saucepan, stewpan, casserole; **2.** (slang) police informer, nark.

casserolée (kasrɔle), s.f. Saucepanful.

cassetin (kɑstɛ̃), s.m. [f. *casse*] (print.) Box.

cassette (kasɛt), s.f. [It. *cassetta*] **1.** Casket, cash-box, small case or box; **2.** privy purse.

casseu-r, -se (kɑsœr), s.m.f. Breaker, breaker of things; (fig.) *~ d'assiettes*, brawler.

casside (kasid), s.f. (ent.) Tortoise-beetle.

cassidoine (kasidwan), s.f. (min.) Chalcedony.

cassie (kasi), s.f. Cassie (kind of basket).

cassier (kasje), s.m. (bot.) Cassia-tree.

cassine (kasin), s.f. [It. *cassina*] Small country house, hut, hovel; (mil.) cassine.

cassis[1] (kasi), s.m. [unkn. orig.] **1.** Black currant; **2.** black-currant bush; **3.** black-currant liqueur.

cassis[2] (kasi), s.m. [f. *casser*] Shallow drain across a road.

cassolette (kasolɛt), s.f. [Span. *cazoleta*] **1.** Perfume pan or box; cresset, perfume; **2.** (pop.) stench; **3.** (bot.) dame's violet.

casson (kasɔ̃), s.m. [f. *casser*] **1.** Broken, roughly cut sugar; **2.** cocoa-nib.

cassonade (kasɔnad), s.f. [f. *casson*] Moist sugar, brown sugar.

cassure (kɑsyr), s.f. [f. *casser*] **1.** Fracture, break; **2.** broken place, crack, edge of a broken fragment.

castagnette (kastaɲɛt), s.f. [Span. *castañeta*] Castanet.

castalides (kastalid), s.f.pl. Castalides (Muses).

caste (kast), s.f. [Port. *casta*] Caste; (fig.) crew, lot, set; *esprit de ~*, exclusiveness; *perdre ~*, to lose caste.

castel (kastɛl), s.m. [f. Provenç. *castel* = *château*] Castle, pleasure-house.

castillan, -e (kastijɑ̃), adj. s.m.f. Castilian.

castille (kastij), s.f. [unkn. orig.] Bickering, quarrel, squabble.

castine (kastin), s.f. [f. Germ. *Kalkstein*] Limestone flux.
castor (kastɔr), s.m. [f. L *castor*] **1.** (zool.) Beaver, castor; **2.** (fur) beaver; **3.** beaver hat, beaver; **4.** (astr.) castor; **5.** (fig.) fellow of loose morals.
castoréum (kastɔreɔm), s.m. [L wd] Castoreum.
castorine (kastɔrin), s.f. [f. *castor*] **1.** (fur) Nutria, racoon; **2.** (cloth.) castor, castorine.
castramétation (kastrameta'sjɔ̃), s.f. [f. L *castrametari*] Castrametation (the art of laying out a camp).
castrat (kastra), s.m. [It. *castrato*] Castrate, eunuch.
castration (kastra'sjɔ̃), s.f. [f. L *castratio*] Castration.
castrer (kastre), v.a. To castrate.
castreur (kastrœr), s.m. Castrator, gelder.
casualité (kazɥalite), s.f. [LL *casualitas*] Casualness, fortuitousness. ⚠ Not 'casualty' which = *accident, désastre, liste des morts.*
casuel, -le (kazɥɛl), adj. [L *casualis*] **1.** Casual, chance, accidental, fortuitous, precarious; **2.** (pop.) brittle, easily broken; *revenu* ~, fees, perquisites.
casuel (kazɥɛl), s.m. [f. L *casualis*] **1.** Surplice-fees, extra-fees; **2.** fees, perquisites; **3.** chance profits.
casuellement (kazɥɛlmɑ̃), adv. Casually, fortuitously.
casuiste (kazɥist), s.m. [f. L *casus*] Casuist; *de* ~, casuistical.
casuistique (kazɥistik), s.f. Casuistry.
catachrèse (katakrɛz), s.f. [f. Gr. *katakhrēsis*] (rhet.) Catachresis.
cataclysme (kataklism), s.m. [f. Gr. *kataklusmos*] Cataclysm, disaster; flood, great crash, subversion, overthrow.
catacombe (katakɔ̃b), s.f. (usually in plural) [LL *catacumba*] Catacomb.
catacoustique (katakustik, s.f. [f. Gr. *katakouein*] Catacoustics (pl.), science of reflected sounds. ~, adj. Catacoustic.
catadioptrique (katadiɔptrik), s.f. [f. *catoptrique+dioptrique*] Catadioptrics (pl.). ~, adj. Catadioptric, of both the reflexion and the refraction of light.
catafalque (katafalk), s.m. [It. *catafalco*] Catafalco, catafalque.
cataire (katɛr), s.f. (bot.) Catmint. ~ adj. (med.) Of a cat.
catalan, -e (katalɑ̃), adj. s.m.f. Catalan, Catalonian. ~, s.m. Catalan (dialect).
catalaunien-s, -nes, catalauniques (katalonjɛ̃, katalonik), adj. pl. Catalaunian (applied to the plains around Châlons-s.-Marne).
catalectes (katalɛkt), s.m.pl. [Gr. *katalecta*] Catalecta, catalects (collection of poetic fragments).
catalectique (katalɛktik), adj. Catalectic.
catalepsie (katalɛpsi), s.f. [f. Gr. *katalēpsis*] Catalepsy, trance.
cataleptique (katalɛptik), adj. Cataleptic.
catalogue (katalɔg), s.m. [f. Gr. *katalogos*] Catalogue, price-list; roll; *dresser un* ~, to draw up a catalogue.
cataloguer (katalɔge), v.a. To catalogue.
catalpa (katalpa), s.m. [Caroline Indian wd] (bot.) Catalpa.
catalyse (kataliz), s.f. [Gr. *katalusis*] Catalysis.
catalytique (katalitik), adv. Catalytic.
cataplasme (kataplasm), s.m. [L *cataplasma*] Poultice.
catapulte (katapylt), s.f. [L *catapulta*] Catapult.
cataracte (katarakt), s.f. [f. Gr. *kataraktēs*] **1.** Cataract, waterfall, fall; **2.** (fig.) ~*s du ciel*, flood-gates; **3.** cataract (on the eye).
cataracté, -e (katarakte), adj. (med.) Affected with cataract.
catarrhal, -e, (aux) (kataral), adj. Catarrhal.
catarrhe (katar), s.m. [f. Gr. *katarrheo*] Catarrh.
catarrheu-x, -se (katarø), adj. Catarrhous, catarrhal.
catastrophe (katastrɔf), s.f. [f. Gr. *katastrophē*] Catastrophe, calamity.
catéchisation (kateʃiza'sjɔ̃), s.f. Catechization.
catéchiser (kateʃize), v.a. **1.** To catechize; **2.** to chapter, to reason with, to persuade, to teach, to train.
catéchisme (kateʃism), s.m. [f. Gr. *katēkhizein*] **1.** Catechism; **2.** (fig.) instructions, lecture, vade-mecum.
catéchiste (kateʃist), s.m. Catechist.
catéchuménat (katekymena), s.m. Catechumenate.
catéchumène (katekymɛn), s.m.f. [f. Gr. *katēkhoumenos*] Catechumen.
catégorie (kategɔri), s.f. [f. Gr. *katēgoria*] **1.** (log.) Category; **2.** class, division, set.
catégorique (kategɔrik), adj. Categorical, unequivocal; (colloq.) sharp.
catégoriquement (kategɔrikmɑ̃), adv. Categorically; (colloq.) *refuser* ~, to refuse flatly.
cathédrale (katedral), s.f. adj. f. [f. L *cathedra*] Cathedral.
cathéter (katetɛr), s.m. [Gr. wd] Catheter.
cathétérisme (kateterism), s.m. Catheterism, employment of a catheter.
cathode (katɔd), s.f. [f. Gr. *cathodos*] Cathode.
cathodique (katɔdik), adj. Cathodic; *rayons* ~*s*, cathodic rays.
catholicisme (katɔlisism), s.m. Catholicism.
catholicité (katɔlisite), s.f. **1.** Catholicity, catholicness, conformity to doctrine; **2.** the catholic world.

catholique (katɔlik), adj. [f. Gr. *katholikos*] **1.** Catholic, Roman Catholic; **2.** orthodox, correct, conforming to doctrine (religious, political, moral, &c.), acceptable, right; *voilà des opinions qui ne sont pas très ~s*, these views are not quite orthodox; **3.** universal. **~**, s.m.f. Catholic, Roman Catholic, Papist.

catholiquement (katɔlikmɑ̃), adv. In a catholic manner.

cati (kati), s.m. [f. *catir*] Lustre, gloss (imparted to cloth by pressing).

catilinaire (katilinɛr), s.f. **1.** Any of Cicero's orations against Catiline; **2.** violent satire, diatribe.

catillac, catillard (katijak, katijar) s.m. Catillac pear.

catimini (en) (ɑ̃katimini), adv. loc. Stealthily, secretly, privately.

catin (katɛ̃), s.f. [abbrev. of *Catherine*] **1.** (obs.) Kate, country wench; **2.** (pop. pej.) strumpet.

catir (katir), v.a. [OF *quatir*; f. L *coactus*] To lustre or gloss cloth.

catogan (katɔgɑ̃), s.m. [Engl. *cadogan*] Cadogan, club (of hair).

catoptrique (katɔptrik), adj. [f. Gr. *katoptron*] Catoptric. **~**, s.f. Catoptrics, branch of optics dealing with reflexion.

caucasien, -ne (kokɑzjɛ̃), adj. s.m.f. [f. *Caucase*] Caucasian.

cauchemar (koʃmar), s.m. [f. OF *cauquemare*] Nightmare; haunting care; bore, plague, nuisance, bugbear; *j'ai eu des ~s*, I had horrible dreams; *cette idée me donne le ~*, I am haunted by that idea; *X est mon ~*, X is a bugbear to me.

cauchemarder (koʃmarde), v.n. (pop.) To have nightmares.

cauchois, -e (koʃwɑ), adj. s.m.f. [f. *Caux*, Normandy] (Native, inhabitant) of Caux.

caudal, -e, (aux) (kodal), adj. [f. L *cauda*] Caudal.

caudataire (kodatɛr), s.m. Train-bearer; (fig.) toad-eater, lickspittle.

caudines (kodin), adj. f.pl. [f. L *caudinae*, f. *Caudium*, a Samnite town] Caudine; *fourches ~s*, Caudine forks; (fig.) *passer sous les fourches ~s*, to submit to a painful humiliation.

cauris (koris), s.m. Cowry.

causal, -e (kozal), adj. [f. *cause*] Causal.

causalité (kozalite), s.f. Causality.

causant, -e (kozɑ̃), adj. Chatty, talkative.

causati-f, -ve (kozatif), adj. (gram.) Causative, causal.

causation (koza'sjɔ̃), s.f. Causation.

causativement (kozativmɑ̃), adv. Causatively.

cause (koz), s.f. [L *causa*] Cause, motive, ground, reason; cause, side, interest; cause, case, (law-)suit; *être ~ de* (or *que*), to cause, to be the cause of, to bring on; *~ finale*, final cause; *il est ~ que j'ai échoué*, he is the cause of my failure; *la ~ de mon retard*, the cause of my being late; *à ~ de*, on account of, owing to, for the sake of; *à ~ que* (obs.), because; *en tout état de ~*, in any case; *et pour ~ !*, and for a very good reason !; *prendre fait et ~ pour*, to side with, to stand up for; *faire ~ commune avec*, to make common cause with; *avoir gain de ~*, to carry the day, to gain one's point (or cause); *donner gain de ~ à X*, to decide in X's favour; *la ~ est entendue*, the cause is heard, we have heard enough of this, it is settled; *mettre X en ~*, to bring X into the affair, to summon, to involve in a law-suit; *mettre hors de ~*, to dismiss from a suit, to free from all imputation, to set aside; *parler en connaissance de ~*, to have good grounds for what one says; to know what one is talking about; *~ célèbre*, celebrated trial; *avocat sans ~*, briefless barrister; *être en ~*, to be concerned (in a thing).

causer[1] (koze), v.a. To cause, to be the cause of, to occasion, to bring about, to give rise to.

causer[2] (koze), v.n. To talk, to converse, to chat (*avec*, with); to blab, to talk; *~ affaires*, to talk about business; to talk shop; *assez causé !*, enough of that, hold your jaw !; *on commence à ~, on en cause*, people are talking about it, people are becoming suspicious; *faites le ~*, draw him out; get it out of him.

causerie (kozri), s.f. [f. *causer*] **1.** Talk, chat; **2.** informal lecture.

causette (kosɛt), s.f. Chat; *faire un bout* (or *brin*) *de ~*, to have a bit of a chat.

causeu-r, -se (kozœr), adj. Talkative, chatty. **~**, s.m.f. Talker, conversationalist.

causeuse (kozøz), s.f. Small sofa, settee.

causse (kos), s.m. [f. L *calx*] Calcareous table-land.

causticité (kostisite), s.f. Causticity; caustic quality of acids; (fig.) caustic humour, bitterness of wit, causticity.

caustique (kostik), adj. [Gr. *kaustikos*] **1.** Caustic; **2.** biting, dryly satirical. **~**, s.m. Caustic; **~** s.f. caustic curve.

cautèle (kotɛl), s.f. [f. L *cautus, cautela*] Caution, craft, wile.

cauteleusement (kotløzmɑ̃), adv. Cunningly, wily, craftily.

cauteleu-x, -se (kotlø), adj. (pej.) Crafty, wily, cunning, cautelous, cautious, deceitful, knavish.

cautère (kotɛr), s.m. [f. Gr. *kautērion*] Cautery, issue, artificial ulcer; *c'est un ~ sur une jambe de bois*, it 's a poultice (or a plaster) on a wooden leg; it 's entirely inefficient.

cautérisation (koteriza'sjɔ̃), s.f. Cauterization.

cautériser (koterize), v.a. To cauterize, to sear, to burn.
caution (kosjɔ̃), s.f. [L *cautio*] **1.** Guarantee, bail, pledge, surety, security; **2.** the person giving surety (&c.); *sous* ~, on bail; *il est très sujet à* ~, he is not to be relied upon; *se porter* ~ *pour*, (*a*) to put in bail for; (*b*) to warrant the truth of; *mettre en liberté sous* ~, to liberate on bail. ⚠ Not English 'caution' which = *prudence*; *avertissement*; *précaution*.
cautionnement (kosjɔnmɑ̃), s.m. Security, bail.
cautionner (kosjɔne), v.a. To stand security for, to answer for, to guarantee, to go bail for. ⚠ Not 'to caution' which = *avertir*, *précautionner*, *mettre en garde* (*contre*).
cavalcade (kavalkad), s.f. [f. L *cavalcare*] Cavalcade.
cavalcader (kavalkade), v.n. To cavalcade, to ride.
cavalcadour (kavalkadur) (obs.), s.m. [f. It. *cavalcatore*] Equerry, master of the horse.
cavale (kaval), s.f. [It. *cavalla*] Mare.
cavaler (kavale), v.n. (slang) To run; **se** ~, v.pr. to bolt, to make tracks, to decamp, to leg it.
cavalerie (kavalri), s.f. [It. *cavalleria*] Cavalry, horse, mounted troops; *mille hommes de* ~, a thousand horse; *officier de* ~, cavalry officer; *grosse* ~, heavy cavalry; ~ *légère*, light cavalry; *la* ~ *de St Georges*, English money (sovereigns)
cavali-er, -ère (kavalje), adj. Flippant, free, off-hand, cavalier; *route* ~*e*, horse-road (or way), bridle-path. ~, s.m.f. Horseman, horsewoman, rider, horse-soldier, trooper; gentleman, attendant, partner, escort; (at chess) knight; (paper) royal; ~ *servant*, cicisbeo; *c'est un* ~ *accompli*, he is an accomplished gentleman; *à ce bal plusieurs dames manquaient de* ~, at this dance several ladies had no partner.
cavalièrement (kavaljɛrmɑ̃), adv. Flippantly, off-hand, freely, cavalierly, bluntly.
cavatine (kavatin), s.f. [It. *cavatina*] (mus.) Cavatina.
cave (kav), s.f. [f. L *cavus*] **1.** Cellar, wine-cellar, vault; **2.** (by ext.) the wine kept in a cellar; **3.** ice-cream mould; **4.** (game) pool; *monter sa* ~, to stock, to fill one's cellar; *rat-de-*~, wax-taper in the form of a cord; *maison élevée* (or *bâtie*) *sur* ~*s*, a house built on vaulted cellars; ~ *à liqueurs*, cellaret, spirit-stand, tantalus.
cave (kav), adj. [L *cavus*] **1.** Hollow, sunken; **2.** *veine* ~, vena cava; **3.** *année* ~, lunar year (incomplete year); *mois* ~, lunar month (of 29 days).
caveau (pl. **-x**) (kavo), s.m. [f. *cave*] **1.** Small cellar; **2.** vault (for the dead); vaulted excavation; vaulted gaol; **3.** drinking, singing, literary club.
cavecé, -e (kavse), adj. [f. Span. *cabeza*] Black-headed (horse or mare).
caveçon (kavsɔ̃), s.m. [It. *cavezzone*] Cavesson; (fig.) *donner un coup de* ~ *à X*, to curb, to stop, to humiliate X.
cavée (kave), s.f. Hollow way.
caver (kave), v.n.a. [f. L *cavare*] To hollow, to undermine; **se** ~, v.pr. to become hollow or sunken; v.n. [f. It. *cavare*] To stake.
caverne (kavɛrn), s.f. [f. L *caverna*] **1.** Cavern, cave; (fig.) den; *mais c'est une* ~ *de brigands*, but this is a den of thieves; *l'âge des* ~*s*, prehistoric times; **2.** (med.) cavity in the lungs caused by tuberculosis.
caverneu-x, -se (kavɛrnø), adj. [L *cavernosus*] Cavernous, hollow; (anat. med.) cavernous; *d'une voix caverneuse*, in a sepulchral voice.
cavet (kavɛ), s.m. [It. *cavetto*] (arch.) Cavetto.
caviar (kavjar), s.m. [It. *caviale*] Caviare, caviar.
cavillation (kavilla'sjɔ̃), s.f. [L *cavillatio*] Sophistry.
caviste (kavist), s.m. [f. *cave*] Cellarman.
cavité (kavite), s.f. [L *cavus*] Cavity, hollow.
cayenne (kajɛn), s.f. [etym. dub.] (naut.) Naval barracks; cook-house; receiving ship.
cayeu. See CAÏEU.
ce, cet, cette (pl. **ces**) (sə, sɛ, sɛt, sɛ), dem. adj. [L *ecce istum*] This, pl. these; that, pl. those; *ce livre-ci*, this book; *ce livre-là*, that book; *tiens, ce brave* or *vieux Léon !*, hallo, that 's Leon !; *ces enfants qui*, those children who; *cette nuit*, (*a*) to-night, this night; (*b*) last night; *cette question !* or *en voilà une question !*, what a question !, how preposterous !
ce, c' (sə), dem. pron. [L *ecce hoc*] This person, he, she, they, these people, it, this; *lisez Milton, c'est un grand poète*, read Milton, he is a great poet; *c'est une bonne amie*, she is a good friend; *sont-ce les soldats qui*, is it the soldiers who; *ce n'est pas qu'il ne puisse mieux faire*, not that he cannot do any better; *ce n'est pas que j'approuve*, not that I approve of it; *sur ce*, thereupon; *ce dont*, that of which; *c'est à qui le louera le plus*, every one is eager to praise him; *c'est à vous de le faire*, it 's your business (or duty) to do it; *ce qui, ce que*, what, that which; *à ce que*, according to what; as; *en ce que*, in what, so far as; *ce en quoi*, in what, in which; *pour ce qui est de*, as for; *ce que c'est que*, what . . . is, what is meant by; *ce que c'est que de*, what it is to; what is meant by; *ce que c'est que de nous !*, what poor mortals we are !

céans (seã), adv. [OF *çaiens*] (archaic) In here, at home.
ceci (səsi), dem. pron. This, these things.
cécité (sesite), s.f. [L *caecitas*] Blindness; *frapper de* ~, to strike blind.
cécropien, -ne (sekrɔpjɛ̃), adj. Cecropian.
cédant, -e (sedã), s.m.f. [f. *céder*] (law) **1.** Granter; **2.** transferrer.
céder (sede) [f. L *cedere*] **1.** v.a. ~ (*quelque chose à quelqu'un*), to give up, to resign, to yield, to cede, to let have, to part with, to make over, to transfer; **2.** v.n. to yield, to give in, to give up, to submit, to relent, to give way, to be second (to), to be surpassed (by); *l'intérêt privé doit* ~ *à l'intérêt général*, private interest must give way to public good; *il lui cède en tout*, he always gives in to her (or him); *il ne le cède à personne en savoir*, he is second to none in learning.
cédille (sedij), s.f. [Span. *cedilla*] Cedilla.
cédrat (sedra), s.m. [It. *cedrato*] (bot.) Cedrate, citron, *Citrus Medica*; (*a*) the fruit; (*b*) the tree.
cèdre (sɛdr), s.m. [L *cedrus*] (bot.) Cedar, cedar-tree.
cédule (sedyl), s.f. [L *schedula*] **1.** Schedule; **2.** scrip, memorandum, note of hand, acknowledgement of indebtedness.
ceindre (sɛ̃dr), v.a. (irreg.) [f. L *cingere*] To gird on; to gird, to bind, to wreath; ~ *le diadème*, to put on, to wear the diadem; ~ *son épée*, to gird on one's sword; **3.** to encircle, to surround, to gird; *ceignez vos reins*, gird up your loins; *ville ceinte de murailles*, town begirt with walls; *ceint de lauriers*, bound with victorious wreaths; **se** ~, v.pr. to gird oneself.
ceintrage (sɛ̃traʒ), s.m. (naut.) Frapping, swifting.
ceinture (sɛ̃tyr), s.f. [L *cinctura*] **1.** Belt, girdle, sash, waistband, waist-ribbon, strap; waist, middle; *bonne renommée vaut mieux que* ~ *dorée*, a good name is better than riches; ~ *de sauvetage*, lifebelt; *se serrer la* ~, to stint oneself, to tighten one's belt; *avoir de l'eau jusqu'à la* ~, to have water up to the waist; **2.** circle, enclosure, fence, zone; *une* ~ *de collines*, a girdle of hills.
ceinturer (sɛ̃tyre), v.a. **1.** To girdle, to surround; **2.** (wrestling) to seize across the body.
ceinturier (sɛ̃tyrje), s.m. Belt-maker.
ceinturon (sɛ̃tyrɔ̃), s.m. (mil.) Belt, sword-belt.
cela (səla), dem. pron. [*ce*+*la*] That, it, that thing, matters; (fam.) he, she, they; *c'est* ~, that 's right; *il est comme* ~, that 's just his way; *comme* ~, so; so-so; *comment* ~ *?*, how is that ?; *c'est* ~ *même*, that 's the very thing; *sans* ~, but for that; *comme* ~ *dort, ces enfants !*, how those children sleep !; see ÇA.
céladon (seladɔ̃), s.m. [Name of a character in *l'Astrée*, 1610] **1.** Sentimental lover. **2.** s.m. adj. Pale green colour; pale green, pastel green.
célation (sela'sjɔ̃), s.f. [L *celatio*] (law) Concealment.
célébrant (selebrã), s.m. [f. *célébrer*] Celebrant. ~, adj. Officiating.
célébration (selebra'sjɔ̃), s.f. [L *celebratio*] Celebration; commemoration, solemnization.
célèbre (selɛbr), adj. [L *celebris*] Celebrated, famous, illustrious, far-famed, renowned.
célébrer (selebre), v.a. [L *celebrare*] **1.** To celebrate, to solemnize, to officiate at; ~ *la messe*, to say mass; ~ *un mariage*, to celebrate a wedding; **2.** to praise, to glorify, to extol, to sing the praises of; *elle célèbre partout la beauté de sa sœur*, she is always extolling her sister's beauty.
célébrité (selebrite), s.f. [L *celebritas*] Celebrity, fame.
celer (səle), v.a. [L *celare*] To hide, to conceal, to keep secret.
céleri (selri), s.m. [f. L *selinum*] Celery; *un pied de* ~, a head of celery; ~*-rave*, turnip-celery, celeriac.
célérité (selerite), s.f. [L *celeritas*] Celerity, speed, swiftness.
céleste (selɛst) **1.** adj. [L *caelestis*] Heavenly, celestial; *bleu* ~, sky-blue; *la voûte* ~, the arch of heaven; *la colère* ~, the wrath of heaven; *Notre Père* ~, our heavenly Father; *le* ~ *Empire*, the Celestial Empire: China. **2.** ~, s.m.f. Chinaman, Chinawoman; Celestial; (usually in plural) the inhabitants of China.
célestin, -e (selɛstɛ̃), s.m.f. adj. Celestine (monk, or nun).
céliaque (seljak), adj. [f. L *coeliacus*] (anat.) Coeliac.
célibat (seliba), s.m. [L *caelibatus*] Celibacy, unmarried state, single life.
célibataire (selibatɛr), s.m.f. Unmarried man, bachelor; unmarried woman, spinster. ~, adj. Unmarried, single.
celle, celle-ci, celle-là. See CELUI.
cellérier (sɛllerje), s.m, [f. *cellier*] Cellarer, monk or nun catering for the convent.
cellier (sɛlje), s.m. [f. L *cellarium*] Still-room, wine-room. ⚠ Not 'cellar' which = *cave*, and is always underground.
cellulaire (sɛlylɛr), adj. Cellular, solitary; *voiture* ~, or (pop.) *panier à salade*, prison-van, 'Black Maria'.
cellule (sɛlyl), s.f. [L *cellula*] Cell.
celluleu-x, -se (sɛlylø), adj. Cellular.
celluloïd (sɛlylɔid), s.m. Celluloid.
cellulose (sɛlyloz), s.f. [f. *cellule*] Cellulose.
célosie (selozi), s.f. (bot.) Cock's-comb, *Celosia cristata*.

celte (sɛlt), s.m.f. Celt.
celtique (sɛltik), adj. Celtic.
celui, celle, pl. **ceux, celles** (səlɥi, sɛl, sø, sɛl), dem. pron. He, she, they, those; the one; *~-ci, celle-ci,* &c., this one, this person, the latter, these ones, this, this thing; *celui-là,* &c., that one, that person, those, &c.; *celui-là même,* the very man; *celui qui, celle qui,* &c., he that, he who, she that, she who, they who, those who; *que ceux qui sont de cet avis lèvent la main,* let such as are of this opinion put up their hands.
cément (semɑ̃), s.m. [f. L *caementum*] Cement.
cémentation (semɑ̃ta'sjɔ̃), s.f. Cementation; case-hardening.
cémenter (semɑ̃te), v.a. To cement.
cémenteu-x, -se (semɑ̃tø), adj. Cementitious.
cénacle (senakl), s.m. [L *cenaculum*] **1.** The room in which the Last Supper was eaten; **2.** (fig.) brotherhood, coterie, club.
cendre (sɑ̃dr), s.f. [L *cinis*] **1.** Ash, ashes; (of coals) cinders; **2.** remains, dust, ashes; *le mercredi des cendres,* Ash-Wednesday; *réduire en ~s,* to reduce to ashes; *réduit en ~s,* burnt to ashes; *renaître de ses ~s,* to rise from one's ashes.
cendré, -e (sɑ̃dre), p. adj. Ash-coloured.
cendrée (sɑ̃dre), s.f. **1.** Lead ashes; **2.** dust-shot; **3.** cement of coal-dust and lime.
cendrer (sɑ̃dre), v.a. **1.** To ash, to mix ashes with; **2.** to paint ash-grey.
cendreu-x, -se (sɑ̃drø), adj. Covered or mixed with ashes.
cendrier (sɑ̃drije), s.m. **1.** Ash-hole, ash-pit, ash-box; **2.** ash-tray.
cendrillon (sɑ̃drijɔ̃), s.f. [name in Perrault's *Fairy Tales*] Cinderella.
cène (sɛn), s.f. [L *cena*] Lord's Supper, Holy Communion.
cenelle (sənɛl), s.f. Haw, the fruit of the whitethorn.
cénobite (senɔbit), s.m. [L *coenobita*] Cenobite (monk); *vivre en ~,* to lead a secluded and austere life.
cénobitique (senɔbitik), adj. Cenobitic.
cénotaphe (senɔtaf), s.m. [f. Gr. *kenotaphion*] Cenotaph.
cens (sɑ̃s), s.m. [L *census*] **1.** Census; **2.** quit-rent; **3.** electoral tax.
cense (sɑ̃s), s.f. (obs.) [LL *censa*] Farm.
censé, -e (sɑ̃se), adj. Reputed, deemed, looked upon as, supposed to be; *nul n'est ~ ignorer la loi,* none is supposed to be ignorant of the law.
censément (sɑ̃semɑ̃), adv. Presumably, supposedly, virtually.
censeur (sɑ̃sœr), s.m. [L *censor*] **1.** Censor; **2.** critic, censurer, fault-finder, censor; **3.** proctor, vice-principal; **4.** (fin.) auditor, controller.
censi-er, -ère (sɑ̃sje), adj. To whom quit-rent was paid; *seigneur ~,* lord of the manor; *papier ~,* rent-roll of a manor.
censitaire (sɑ̃sitɛr), s.m. Vassal copyholder. ~, adj. Electorally qualified.
censorial, -e, (aux) (sɑ̃sɔrjal), adj. Censorial.
censuel, -le (sɑ̃syɛl), adj. Feudal, of quit-rent.
censurable (sɑ̃syrabl), adj. Censurable, open to censure.
censure (sɑ̃syr), s.f. [L *censura*] **1.** Censorship; **2.** censure, vote of censure; **3.** board of censors; **4.** censure, blame.
censurer (sɑ̃syre), v.a. **1.** To censure, to find fault with, to blame, to condemn; **2.** to pass a vote of censure on.
cent (sɑ̃), num. adj. s.m. (takes the sign of pl. when not followed by a number: *deux cents; deux cent trente*) [L *centum*] A hundred; (invar.) cent, a hundredth; *le ~ unième,* the hundred and first; *page ~,* page one hundred; the hundredth page; *je vous le donne en ~,* I give you a hundred guesses; *en un mot comme en ~,* once and for all; *~ pesant,* hundredweight; *x pour ~,* x per cent; *les Cent Jours* (French hist.), from 20 March to 28 June 1815, when Napoleon returned to France; *Cent-gardes,* Napoleon's bodyguard.
centaine (sɑ̃tɛn), s.f. A hundred, hundred, hundredth year; *plusieurs ~s,* several hundreds; *plusieurs ~s de mille francs,* several hundred thousand francs; *par ~s à la fois,* hundreds at a time.
centaure (sɑ̃tɔr), s.m. [f. Gr. *kentauros*] **1.** Centaur; **2.** (fig.) good horseman.
centauresse, s.f. good horsewoman.
centaurée (sɑ̃tɔre), s.f. [L *centaureum*] (bot.) Centaury.
centenaire (sɑ̃tnɛr), **1.** adj. A hundred years old, centenary, centenarian, centennial; **2.** s.m. centenary (100th anniversary); **3.** s.m.f. centenarian.
centenier (sɑ̃tnje), s.m. [f. L *centenarius*] Centurion.
centennal, -e, (aux) (sɑ̃tɛnnal), adj. Centennial.
centésimal, -e, (aux) (sɑ̃tezimal), adj. Centesimal.
centi- (sɑ̃ti), prefix = 100th part (in French weights and measures).
centiare (sɑ̃tjar), s.m. Centiare = 1 sq. metre or 1·1960 sq. yards.
centième (sɑ̃tjɛm), s.m. Hundredth; *les six ~s,* six-hundredths; *le six ~ de,* the six-hundredth (part) of.
centigrade (sɑ̃tigrad), adj. Centigrade.
centigramme (sɑ̃tigram), s.m. Centigram = 0·1543 grain.
centilitre (sɑ̃tilitr), s.m. Centilitre = 0·0704 gill, or 0·6102 cubic inch.
centime (sɑ̃tim), s.m. **1.** Centime; **2.** brass farthing, stiver; *~s additionnels,*

additional tax; *au* ~ *le franc*, so much in the pound; one per cent.
centimètre (sɑ̃timɛtr), s.m. Centimetre = 0·3937 inch.
centipède (sɑ̃tipɛd), adj. Centipedal. ~, s.m. Centipede.
centon (sɑ̃tɔ̃), s.m. [L *cento*] **1.** Cento, literary or musical patchwork; **2.** any one of the pieces assembled.
centrage (sɑ̃traʒ), s.m. Centering.
central, -e, (aux) (sɑ̃tral), adj. **1.** Central; **2.** chief, principal.
centralisat-eur, -rice (sɑ̃tralizatœr), adj. Centralizing.
centralisation (sɑ̃traliza'sjɔ̃), s.f. Centralization.
centraliser (sɑ̃tralize), v.a. To centralize.
centre (sɑ̃tr), s.m. [L *centrum*] **1.** Centre, central point; **2.** middle, midst, main part; **3.** seat, point of concentration or dispersion; ~*s Sociaux*, settlements; *provinces du* ~, midland provinces; *les grands* ~*s*, the large towns; (motor.) ~ *d'allumage*, point of ignition; ~*s nerveux*, nervous centres.
centrer (sɑ̃tre), v.a. To centre.
centrifuge (sɑ̃trifyʒ), adj. Centrifugal.
centripète (sɑ̃tripɛt), adj. Centripetal.
centumvir (sɑ̃tɔmvir), s.m. [L wd] Centumvir.
centumvirat (sɑ̃tɔmvira), s.m. Centumvirate.
centuple (sɑ̃typl), adj. s.m. [L *centuplex*] Centuple, hundred times, hundredfold; *au* ~, a hundredfold.
centupler (sɑ̃typle), v.a. To multiply by a hundred, to increase a hundredfold, to centuple.
centurie (sɑ̃tyri), s.f. [L *centuria*] Century.
centurion (sɑ̃tyrjɔ̃), s.m. Centurion.
cep (sɛp), s.m. [L *cippus*] Stem of a vine, vine-plant.
cépage (sepaʒ), s.m. Any variety of vine, vine plant.
cèpe (sɛp), s.m. [etym. dub.] Mushroom, *Boletus edulis*.
cépée (sepe), s.f. [f. *cep*] Cluster of shoots from the stools of copse-wood.
cependant (səpɑ̃dɑ̃), conj. [*ce*+*pendant*] **1.** However, yet, still, nevertheless; **2.** in the meantime, meanwhile; ~ *que*, while, whilst.
céphalalgie (sefalalʒi), s.f. [f. Gr. *kephalē* +*algos*] Cephalalgia, headache.
céphalée (sefale), s.f. Headache.
céphalique (sefalik), adj. Cephalic.
céphal- (sefal) (*in compounds*) = Concerning the head; *céphalopode*, cephalopod; *céphalotomie*, cephalotomy, &c.
céracé, -e (serase), adj. [L *ceraceus*] Ceraceous, waxy.
cérame (seram), s.m. [f. Gr. *keramos*] Terra-cotta vase; *grès*-~, terra-cotta pottery.
céramique (seramik), s.f. Ceramics. ~, adj. Ceramic, relating to pottery.
céramiste (seramist), s.m.f. Ceramist.
céraste (serast), s.m. (zool.) Cerastes, horned viper.
cérat (sera), s.m. [f. L *cera*] (pharm.) Cerate.
cerbère (sɛrbɛr), s.m. [L *Cerberus*] Cerberus.
cerceau (pl. -x) (sɛrso), s.m. [L *circellus*] **1.** Hoop; *jouer au* ~, to trundle a hoop; *des jambes en* ~, bow legs; **2.** pinion-feather; **3.** cradle (over an injured limb, &c.).
cerclage (sɛrklaʒ), s.m. Hooping (of barrels); *bois de* ~, hoop-wood.
cercle (sɛrkl), s.m. [L *circulus*] **1.** Circle, ring, hoop; *la quadrature du* ~, the squaring of the circle; *le* ~ *polaire*, the polar circle; **2.** rim; **3.** ring, round, sphere; limits; succession; *tourner dans le même* ~, to go on in the same old way; *un* ~ *vicieux*, a vicious circle; **4.** assembly, company, party; *briller dans un* ~ *d'amis*, to shine in a company of friends; **5.** club, club-house; **6.** ~*s*, (pl.) casks; *du vin en* ~*s*, wine in the cask, in the wood.
cercler (sɛrkle), v.a. To hoop, to encircle.
cercopithèque (sɛrkɔpitɛk), s.m. (zool.) Cercopithecus.
cercueil (sɛrkœj), s.m. [f. Gr. *sarkophagos*] Coffin, bier; (fig.) grave.
céréale (sereal), adj. [f. L *Ceres, cerealis*] Cereal. ~, s.f. **1.** Cereal, cereals; **2.** Cerealia (Roman games in honour of Ceres).
cérébelleu-x, -se (serebɛllø), adj. [f. L *cerebellum*] Of the cerebellum.
cérébral-e, (aux) (serebral), adj. [f. L *cerebrum*] Cerebral, of the brain; *fièvre* ~*e*, brain fever.
cérébro-spinal, -e, (aux) (serebro-spinal), adj. Cerebro-spinal.
cérémonial, -e, (aux) (seremɔnjal), adj. Ceremonial. ~, s.m. Ceremonial, ritual, formalities, etiquette.
cérémonie (seremɔni), s.f. [f. L *caerimonia*] Ceremony, fuss, ado; *de* ~, state, full-dress, formal; *en* ~, in state; *faire des* ~*s*, to stand upon ceremony; *sans* ~, informal(ly), unceremonious(ly); *que de* ~*s !*, what a fuss!
cérémonieusement (seremɔnjøzmɑ̃), adv. Ceremoniously.
cérémonieu-x, -se (seremɔnjø), adj. Ceremonious, formal.
cerf (sɛrf, sɛr), s.m. [L *cervus*] Stag, deer, red deer, hart; *bois de* ~, horns of a stag; *corne de* ~, hartshorn; ~*-volant*, (*a*) kite; (*b*) stag-beetle.
cerfeuil (sɛrfœj), s.m. [f. L *caerefolium*] (bot.) Chervil.

cerisaie (sərizɛ), s.f. Cherry-orchard.
cerise (səriz), s.f. [LL *ceresia*] **1.** Cherry; **2.** (pop.) face; (pop.) *croquer la* ~, to dance attendance; *avoir la* ~, to be down on one's luck. ~, adj. Cherry-red.
cerisette (sərizet), s.f. **1.** Dried cherry; **2.** (bot.) morel, nightshade.
cerisier (sərizje), s.m. (bot.) Cherry-tree, cherry-wood.
cerium (serjɔm), s.m. (chem.) Cerium.
cerne (sɛrn), s.m. [f. LL *circinum*] Circle, ring.
cerné, -e (sɛrne), adj. **1.** Surrounded; encircled; **2.** black-ringed.
cerneau (pl. **-x**) (sɛrno), s.m. Green walnut; kernel of green walnut.
cerner (sɛrne), v.a. **1.** To invest, to hem in, to beset, to surround, to encircle, to hem round; to cut round, to cut away (the bark of a tree); (fig.) to circumvent; **se** ~, v.pr. to become encircled by a dark ring.
céroplastie (seroplasti), s.f. [f. Gr. *kēros*+ *plastes*] Ceroplasty, modelling in wax.
certain, -e (sɛrtɛ̃), adj. [f. L *certus*] Certain, sure, positive, to be relied upon, settled, stated; (when placed before a noun) a certain, some, some moderate, certain; *êtes-vous bien* ~ *de cela?*, are you quite sure of that?; *tenir pour* ~, to hold for certain; *il est déjà d'un* ~ *âge*, he is rather elderly; *elle a un* ~ *mérite*, she has some little merit. ~, pron. (pl.) *~s pensent que*, some people think that.
certain (sɛrtɛ̃), s.m. The certain, certainty, that which is certain; *quitter le* ~ *pour l'incertain*, to leave the certain for the uncertain.
certainement (sɛrtɛnmɑ̃), adv. Certainly, assuredly, to a certainty.
certes (sɛrt), adv. Most assuredly; *non* ~, certainly not.
certificat (sɛrtifika), s.m. [f. L *certum*+ *facere*] **1.** Certificate, testimonial; **2.** character (for servants); **3.** (fig.) proof, certainty.
certificateur (sɛrtifikatœr), s.m. **1.** Certifier; **2.** guarantee.
certificati-f, -ve (sɛrtifikatif), adj. Certificatory.
certification (sɛrtifika'sjɔ̃), s.f. Certification.
certifier (sɛrtifje), v.a. To certify, to testify, to assure, to attest, to vouch for.
certitude (sɛrtityd), s.f. Certainty, certitude, unquestionableness; *avoir la* ~ *de*, to be certain of.
céruléen, -ne (seryleɛ̃), adj. Cerulean.
cerumen (serymɛn), s.m. [f. L *cera*] Cerumen, ear-wax.
cérumineu-x, -se (seryminø), adj. Ceruminous, waxy.
céruse (seryz), s.f. [f. L *cerussa*] Ceruse, carbonate of lead; *blanc de* ~, white-lead.
cervaison (sɛrvɛzɔ̃), s.f. Stag-hunting season.
cerveau (pl. **-x**) (sɛrvo), s.m. [L *cerebrum*] Brain, brains, intellect, mind; ~ *creux*, dreamer; ~ *brûlé*, hot-head; *se creuser le* ~, to cudgel or rack one's brains.
cervelas (sɛrvəlɑ), s.m. [f. It. *cervellata*] Saveloy, polony.
cervelet (sɛrvəlɛ), s.m. Cerebellum.
cervelle (sɛrvɛl), s.f. [f. L *cerebellum*] Brains; (fig.) brain, brains, intellect, mind, sense; *il se brûla la* ~, he blew out his brains; *faire sauter la* ~ *à X*, to knock out X's brains; *~s frites*, fried brains; ~ *de palmier*, pith of the palm; *se creuser la* ~, to cudgel one's brains; *tête sans* ~, giddy-pate, blockhead, empty head; *cela lui trotte dans la* ~, that keeps running in his head; *petite* ~ *prompte colère*, a little pot is soon hot.
cervical, -e, (aux) (sɛrvikal), adj. [f. L *cervix*] Cervical.
cervidés (sɛrvide), s.m.pl. [f. L *cervinus*] Cervidae.
cervier (sɛrvje), s.m. See LOUP-CERVIER
cervoise (sɛrvwaz), s.f. [L *cerevisia*] Cervisia, beer of the ancients.
ces (sɛ), dem. adj. [pl. of *ce*] These, those.
césar (sezar), s.m. [L *Caesar*] **1.** Emperor, Caesar; **2.** (fig.) great captain, emperor, prince.
césarien, -ne (sezarjɛ̃), adj. **1.** Of or belonging to Caesar; **2.** (surg.) caesarean.
césarisme (sezarism), s.m. Caesarism.
cessant, -e (sɛsɑ̃), p. adj. Suspending, ceasing, stopping; *toutes affaires ~es*, leaving all other business.
cessation (sɛsa'sjɔ̃), s.f. Cessation, discontinuance, stopping, giving up, retiring.
cesse (sɛs), s.f. Ceasing, respite; *sans* ~, unceasingly, incessantly, unremittingly, continually; *il n'a de* ~ *que*, he will have no rest till (or until); *sans repos ni* ~, with neither rest nor stop.
cesser (sɛse), v.a.n. [L *cessare*] To cease, to stop, to leave off, to give up, to discontinue, to abstain from; *cessez vos plaintes*, leave off complaining; *faire* ~, to put an end to, to stop; *il a cessé de parler*, he has ceased speaking; *elle cessera de fumer désormais*, henceforward she will abstain from smoking.
cessibilité (sɛsibilite), s.f. Transferability.
cessible (sɛsibl), adj. Transferable.
cession (sɛsjɔ̃), s.f. **1.** Transfer, cession; **2.** assignment, surrender (of property); *faire* ~ *de*, to transfer, to surrender.
cessionnaire (sɛsjɔnɛr), s.m.f. Transferee, assignee, grantee.
c'est-à-dire (sɛtadir), conj. loc. That is to say, to wit, namely, viz, i.e.

ceste (sɛst), s.m. [L *caestus*] Cestus (gauntlet).
césure (sezyr), s.f. [L *caesura*] (pros.) Caesura, rest, pause.
cet, -te (sɛt), dem. adj. See CE.
cétacé (setase), s.m. [f. L *cetus*] Whale, cetacean; *les ∼s*, the cetacea. ∼, adj. Cetacean, cetaceous.
cétérac (seterak), s.m. (bot.) Ceterach, spleenwort, asplenium.
cétoine (setwan), s.f. (ent.) Cetonia, rose-beetle.
ceux (sø), dem. pron. See CELUI.
chabler (ʃable), v.a. [f. LL *capulare*] **1.** To knock down; **2.** (naut.) to lash, to fasten; ∼ (or *gauler*) *les noyers*, to bring down walnuts with a pole.
chablis (ʃabli), s.m. **1.** [French geog. orig.] Chablis (wine); **2.** [f. *chabler*] wind-fallen wood.
chabot (ʃabo), s.m. [f. *chef*] (ichth.) Bull-head, miller's thumb.
chabraque (ʃabrak), s.f. See SCHABRAQUE.
chacal (pl. **-s**) (ʃakal), s.m. [Turk. *chakal*] Jackal.
chaconne (ʃakɔn), s.f. [Span. *chacona*] Chaconne (dance).
chacun, -e (ʃakœ̃), pron. [*chaque*+*un*] Each, each one, every one; everybody; *∼de nous*, each of us; *donner à ∼ sa part*, to give each his (or her) share; *nous avons pris ∼ notre chapeau*, we all took our hats; ∼ *pour soi et Dieu pour tous*, each for himself and God for us all; *tout un ∼*, each person.
chafouin, -e (ʃafwɛ̃), adj. s.m.f. [*chat*+ *fouin*] Weasel-faced, mean-looking (person).
chagrin[1] (ʃagrɛ̃), s.m. [unkn. orig.] Grief, sorrow, concern, affliction, vexation; ∼ *cuisant*, poignant grief; *noyer son ∼ dans le vin*, to drown one's grief in wine; *faire, causer du ∼ à X*, to cause or give sorrow to X.
chagrin, -e (ʃagrɛ̃), adj. **1.** Sorrowful, regretful, melancholy, gloomy; **2.** peevish, fretful, morose, surly; *il a l'humeur ∼e*, he is of a tetchy humour (or disposition); *quel esprit ∼ !*, what a peevish soul!
chagrin[2] (ʃagrɛ̃), s.m. [f. Turk. *saghri*] Shagreen; *peau de ∼*, shagreen leather.
chagrinant, -e (ʃagrinɑ̃), p. adj. Distressing, vexatious.
chagriné, -e (ʃagrine), p. adj. **1.** Distressed, tormented; **2.** shagreen-like.
chagriner (ʃagrine), v.a. **1.** To grieve, to pain, to distress, to vex; **2.** to shagreen; **se** ∼, v.pr. to grieve, to torment oneself.
chagrinier (ʃagrinje), s.m. Shagreen manufacturer.
chah (ʃa), s.m. See SCHAH.
chahut (ʃay), s.m. (pop.) [f. *chat huant*] Noisy disturbance, row, dance; *faire du ∼*, to kick up a noise; *organiser un ∼*, to organize a shindy; syn. CHAMBARD.
chahuter (ʃayte), v.n. To make a noisy disturbance, to rock, to dance, to tumble about noisily; ∼, v.a. to annoy, to express disapproval of in a violent, noisy way; ∼ *un professeur*, to rag a master; to give a professor (in a university) an uproarious and hostile reception.
chai, chais (ʃɛ), s.m. [f. LL *caveum*] Shed for storing wine or brandy.
chaînage (ʃɛnaʒ), s.m. **1.** (land surveying) Measuring with the chain; **2.** (arch.) system of tie-beams.
chaîne (ʃɛn), s.f. [L *catena*] **1.** Chain; **2.** warp; **3.** (obs.) land measure; **4.** range (of mountains); series; **5.** (fig.) *les∼s* (syn. LES FERS), bounds, imprisonment, bonds; *à la ∼*, (*a*) in bondage; (*b*) chained up; *faire la ∼*, to form a chain (for passing anything from hand to hand); *∼-sautoir*, neck-chain; ∼ *de montre*, watch-chain; ∼ *d'arpenteur*, surveyor's chain (10 metres) ∼ *de Vaucanson*, pitch chain; ∼ *de sûreté*, safety-chain; *les ∼s de l'amour*, the ties of love; *les ∼s du mariage*, the bond of marriage; ***travail à la ∼***, sliding-belt work.
chaîner (ʃɛne), v.a. To measure with the [chain.
chaînetier (ʃɛntje), s.m. Chain-maker.
chaînette (ʃɛnɛt), s.f. **1.** Small chain; **2.** (math.) catenary curve; **3.** (arch.) catenary arch; **4.** (needlework) *point de ∼*, chain-stitch.
chaînon (ʃɛnɔ̃), s.m. Link (of a chain); syn. MAILLON.
chair (ʃɛr), s.f. [L *caro, carnis*] **1.** Flesh, meat; *en ∼ et en os*, in flesh and blood, in person; *être bien en ∼*, to be well nourished, plump; ∼ *vive*, live flesh; ∼ *à canon*, cannon fodder; ∼ *blanche*, white meat; ∼ *à saucisse*, sausage-meat, minced pork; *ni ∼ ni poisson*, neither fish nor flesh, undecided in character; *donner la ∼ de poule*, to make the flesh creep, to give the creeps; *il essaie de nous donner la ∼ de poule*, he is trying to make our flesh creep; **2.** pulp (of fruit); **3.** the body, the animal part of human nature, the bodily appetites, carnality; living substance; *être de ∼*, to be of flesh and blood; *le péché de la ∼*, the sin of incontinence; *mortifier sa ∼*, to mortify one's flesh; *la résurrection de la ∼*, the resurrection of the body; *l'esprit est prompt mais la ∼ est faible*, the spirit is willing but the flesh is weak; *le Verbe s'est fait ∼*, the Word was made flesh; *le mari et la femme seront une seule ∼*, man and wife shall be made one flesh; **4.** (paint.) flesh parts, carnations; *les ∼s sont d'une belle couleur*, the carnations are beautiful.
chaire (ʃɛr), s.f. [L *cathedra*] **1.** Chair, seat, see, throne; **2.** pulpit, desk, chair; preaching, professorship; *l'éloquence de la∼*, pulpit eloquence; *la∼apostolique*, the

apostolic see; *le professeur est en* ~, the professor is in his chair; *être nommé à une* ~, to be appointed to a professorship.

chais (ʃɛ), s.m. See CHAI.

chaise (ʃɛz), s.f. [L *cathedra*; doublet of *chaire*] **1.** Chair; **2.** (obs.) chaise; ~ *à porteurs*, sedan-chair; ~ *longue*, couch; ~ *percée*, commode, close-stool; ~ *de poste*, post-chaise; **3.** (build.) curb, kerb, framework.

chaisi-er, -ère (ʃɛzje), s.m.f. Chair-maker. ~, s.f. Woman letting out chairs for hire.

chaland, chalan (ʃalɑ̃), s.m. [etym. dub.] (naut.) Barge.

chaland, -e (ʃalɑ̃), s.m.f. [f. OF *chaloir*] Customer, purchaser; (fig.) acquaintance, follower.

chalcédoine (kalsedwan), s.f. Chalcedony; see CALCÉDOINE.

chalcographie (kalkografi), s.f. [f. Gr. *khalkos*+*graphein*] Chalcography, engraving on copper.

chaldaïque (kaldaik), adj. Chaldaic. ~, s.m. Chaldaic (language), Chaldee.

chaldéen, -ne (kaldeɛ̃), adj. s.m.f. Chaldean.

châle (ʃɑl), s.m. [f. Pers. *shál*] Shawl.

chalet (ʃalɛ), s.m. [f. Swiss dialect] Chalet, Swiss cottage; cheese dairy.

chaleur (ʃalœr), s.f. [f. L *calorem*] **1.** Heat; (*a*) the sensation; (*b*) the cause of it; **2.** (phys.) caloric, principle of heat; *une* ~ *de trente degrés*, a heat (or temperature) of thirty degrees; **3.** hottest part of the day; (pl.) hottest part of the year; **4.** rut (of certain female animals); **5.** (fig.) ardour, zeal, vehemence, warmth, fire; *il embrassa avec* ~ *la cause du roi*, he embraced with zeal the king's cause; *dans la* ~ *du premier mouvement*, in the ardour of the first impulse.

chaleureusement (ʃalœrøzmɑ̃), adv. Warmly, vehemently, affectionately.

chaleureu-x, -se (ʃalœrø), adj. Warm, ardent, zealous, hot-blooded.

châlit (ʃɑli), s.m. [f. L *calelitus*] Bedstead, stretcher.

chaloir (ʃalwar), v.n. imp. (archaic) [f. L *calere*] To matter, to signify; *peu m'en chaut*, it matters not to me.

chaloupe (ʃalup), s.f. [Dutch *sloep*, Span. *chalupa*] (naut.) Launch, long-boat; shallop; ~ *canonnière*, gun-boat.

chalumeau (pl. **-x**) (ʃalymo), s.m. [f. L *calamus*] **1.** Tube, pipe (made of straw or reed); **2.** shepherd's pipe or flute; **3.** blow-pipe; nozzle.

chalut, chalon (ʃaly, ʃalɔ̃), s.m. (fish.) Drag-net.

chalutier (ʃalytje), s.m. Fishing-smack, trawler; (adj.) *pêche* ~*ère*, trawl-fishing, trawling.

chamade (ʃamad), s.f. [It. *chiamata*] Drum or trumpet signal; *battre la* ~, to sound a parley; (fig.) to be violently moved; *son cœur battait la* ~, his heart was beating wildly.

chamailler (ʃamɑje), v.n. [LL *clamaculare*] To squabble; **se** ~, v.pr. to squabble, to wrangle, to bicker.

chamaillerie (ʃamɑjri), s.f. Squabbling, bickering.

chamanisme (ʃamanism), s.m. [f. *shaman*] Shamanism.

chamarrer (ʃamare), v.a. [f. OF *chamarre, simarre*] To trim with lace, braid, &c.; to bedizen (*de*, with), to bedeck, to tinsel; *chamarré de décorations*, bedecked with orders.

chamarrure (ʃamaryr), s.f. Lace, braiding; bedizening, bedecking.

chambard (ʃɑ̃bar), s.m. (pop.) Disturbance, tumult, damage, turning upside-down; *faire du* ~, to kick up a shindy; syn. CHAHUT.

chambardement (ʃɑ̃bardəmɑ̃), s.m. (pop.) Destruction, upsetting of everything, revolution, great change, upheaval, overthrow.

chambarder (ʃɑ̃barde), v.a. (pop.) To upset, to disturb, to smash, to turn upside-down, to overthrow.

chambellan (ʃɑ̃bɛllɑ̃), s.m. [f. OHG *chamarlinc*] Chamberlain.

chambertin (ʃɑ̃bɛrtɛ̃), s.m. [French geog. orig.] Chambertin (red Burgundy wine).

chambranle (ʃɑ̃brɑ̃l), s.m. [orig. unkn.] Casing; jambs and lintel of a door, window, fireplace.

chambre (ʃɑ̃br), s.f. [L *camera*] **1.** Chamber, room, apartment, bedroom; ~ *à coucher*, bedroom; ~ *à feu*, room with a fireplace; ~ *meublée*, furnished rooms (usually in the plural in English); *faire la* ~, to do the room; *garder la* ~, to keep (or to be confined) within doors; *travailler en* ~, to work at home; *femme de* ~, lady's-maid; *fille de* ~, chambermaid; *pot de* ~, chamber-pot; *valet de* ~, valet; *musique de* ~, chamber music; *gentilhomme de la* ~, gentleman of the king's bedchamber; **2.** hall, room occupied by a deliberating assembly, parliament, court of justice, &c.; (by ext.) the deliberating assembly itself; sections of certain tribunals; ~ *des Députés*, Chamber of Deputies; ~ *Haute*, Upper House; ~ *Basse*, Lower House; ~ *des Notaires*, Chamber of Notaries; *la* ~ *siégera jusqu'en juillet*, the Chamber will be sitting until July; **3.** certain cavities shaped like a room; ~ *obscure*, camera obscura; **4.** (motor., bicyc.) tube, chamber; ~ *à air*, inner tube; ~ *d'allumage*, combustion chamber; ~ *de carburation*, mixing chamber, carburettor; ~ *de vapeur*, steam-chest.

chambré, -e (ʃɑ̃bre), p. adj. **1.** Confined

to one room or (fig.) to the company of one person; **2.** honeycombed; **3.** chambered.

chambrée (ʃɑ̃bre), s.f. **1.** Barrack-room (sleeping-room); *argot de ~*, barrack-room slang; **2.** the soldiers or workmen sleeping in the same room; **3.** (theatr.) house, houseful; the spectators; **4.** society gathering, the guests; *une ~ de notabilités*, a company or gathering of persons of distinction.

chambrer (ʃɑ̃bre), v.n. (obs.) To lodge, to lie in covert; ~, v.a. to seclude, to keep confined (by force, craft, or persuasion), to closet, to take aside (a person).

chambrette (ʃɑ̃brɛt), s.f. Small room, small bedroom.

chambrier (ʃɑ̃brje), (obs.) s.m. High officer of the Crown.

chambrière (ʃɑ̃brjɛr), s.f. **1.** Chambermaid; **2.** long whip, used in riding schools; **3.** prop for the shaft of a cart; **4.** forge-poker.

chameau (pl. **-x**) (ʃamo), s.m. [L *camelus*] **1.** Camel; **2.** (fig.) blighter, rotter; *~!*, (interj.) pig!, the beast!, the brute!

chamelier (ʃamlje), s.m. Camel-driver.

chamelle (ʃamɛl), s.f. Female camel.

chamelon (ʃamlɔ̃), s.m. Young camel.

chamois (ʃamwɑ), s.m. [f. OHG. *gamuz*] Chamois, shamoy, chamois-leather, shammy-leather. ~, adj. Buff, chamois-coloured.

chamoiser (ʃamwaze), v.a. To chamois, to dress like chamois-leather, to shamoy-dress.

chamoiserie (ʃamwazri), s.f. Chamois-leather manufactory.

chamoiseur (ʃamwazœr), s.m. Chamois-dresser.

champ (ʃɑ̃), s.m. [L *campus*] Field, country, open space, arena; (fig.) space, opportunity, scope, theme, subject; ground, background; (herald.) the whole surface of the escutcheon; edge; *(placé) de ~*, on edge; *~ de courses*, race-course; *~ de manœuvres*, exercise (or parade) ground; *~ de repos*, cemetery; *~ d'honneur*, field of honour; *~ de foire*, field (or green) on which a fair is held; *prendre la clef des ~s*, to run away; *être aux ~s*, to be distressed; *battre aux ~s*, to beat a salute or march (on the drum); *sur le ~*, at once; *à tout bout de ~*, at every turn, incessantly; *prendre du ~*, to retire a few steps (preparatory to an onset); *le ~ est libre*, the coast is clear; *~ clos*, lists, tilt-yard; *le ~ est ouvert aux soupcons*, there is ground for suspicion; *ce n'est pas dans le ~ de la lunette*, it is not in the field of the telescope.

champagne (ʃɑ̃paɲ), s.m. [French geog. orig.] **1.** Champagne (wine); **2.** (herald.) the lower third of the escutcheon.

champagniser (ʃɑ̃paɲize), v.a. To make (a wine) champagne-like.

champenois, -e (ʃɑ̃pnwɑ), adj. s.m.f. (Native) of Champagne.

champêtre (ʃɑ̃pɛtr), adj. [L *campestris*] Rural, country, rustic; *garde-~*, rural *garde* (rural police).

champi, -sse (ʃɑ̃pi), s.m.f. [Berry dialect] Foundling.

champignon (ʃɑ̃piɲɔ̃), s.m. [f. LL *campinolius*] Mushroom, mushroom-shaped object; (med.) fungoid excrescence; *couche de ~s*, mushroom-bed; *pousser comme un ~*, to shoot up like a mushroom; *~ de couche*, cultivated mushroom; *~ vénéneux*, toadstool, *~ à chapeaux*, hatstand; (motor.) *~ strié*, spraying cone.

champignonnière (ʃɑ̃piɲɔnjɛr), s.f. Cave, or underground galleries in which mushrooms are grown.

champignonniste (ʃɑ̃piɲɔnist), s.m.f. Mushroom-grower.

champion, -ne (ʃɑ̃pjɔ̃), s.m.f. [f. *champ*] Champion; (rare) championess.

championnat (ʃɑ̃pjɔna), s.m. Championship.

champleure, champlure (ʃɑ̃plœr, ʃɑ̃plyr), See CHANTEPLEURE.

champlever (ʃɑ̃ləve), v.a. [*champ+lever*] To hollow out the ground (for enamel, &c.).

chananéen, -ne (kananeɛ̃), s.m.f. Canaanite. ~, adj. Canaanitish.

chançard, -e (ʃɑ̃sar), adj. (pop.) Lucky.

chance (ʃɑ̃s), s.f. [f. L *cadentia*] Chance, fortune, risk, hazard, probability, possibility; luck, good luck; *bonne ~!*, good luck to you!; *pas de ~!*, no luck!, worse luck!; *courir sa ~*, to take one's chance, to risk it; *toutes les ~s sont contre lui*, the odds are greatly against him.

chancelant, -e (ʃɑ̃slɑ̃), p.adj. **1.** Tottering, staggering; **2.** (fig.) unsettled, irresolute, unsteady.

chanceler (ʃɑ̃sle), v.n. [LL *cancellare*] **1.** To totter, to stagger; **2.** (fig.) to waver, to hesitate, to be unsteady, crumbling.

chancelier (ʃɑ̃slje), s.m. [L *cancellarius*] Chancellor, vice-consul; *grand ~*, Chancellor.

chancelière (ʃɑ̃sljɛr), s.f. Foot-muff.

chancellement (ʃɑ̃sɛlmɑ̃), s.m. Tottering, reeling, crumbling, unsteadiness.

chancellerie (ʃɑ̃sɛlri), s.f. Chancellor's office, chancery, seal-office; *style de ~*, legal or court style.

chanceu-x, -se (ʃɑ̃sø), adj. **1.** Hazardous, risky; **2.** lucky.

chancir (ʃɑ̃sir), v.n. (rare). [f. L *canutus*] To get mouldy.

chancissure (ʃɑ̃sisyr), s.f. Mould, mouldiness.

chancre (ʃɑ̃kr), s.m. [L *cancer*] (See doublet CANCER.) **1.** Canker; **2.** (venereal) chancre; **3.** (fig.) anything that corrupts or consumes.

chancreu-x, -se (ʃɑ̃krø), adj. Cankerous; chancrous.

chancroïde (ʃɑ̃krɔid), s.m. Chancroid.

chandeleur (ʃɑ̃dlœr), s.f. [f. L *candela*] Candlemas.

chandelier (ʃɑ̃dəlje), s.m. [f. *chandelle*] **1.** Candlestick, candlestand; **2.** tallow chandler.

chandelle (ʃɑ̃dɛl), s.f. [L *candela*] **1.** Candle; **2.** candle-light; **3.** (build., naut.) shore, prop, stay; **4.** (fig.) *économies de bouts de ~s*, paltry saving; cheese-paring; penny-wise and pound-foolish; (fig.) *voir trente-six ~s*, to be stunned, to see stars; *brûler la ~ par les deux bouts*, to burn the candle at both ends; *il vous doit une fière ~!*, he ought to be extremely grateful to you; *le jeu n'en vaut pas la ~*, the game is not worth the candle; *à chaque saint sa ~*, honour to whom honour is due.

chanfrein (ʃɑ̃frɛ̃), s.m. [OF *chanfrain*] **1.** (of a horse) Forehead, chanfrin; **2.** (armour.) chamfron; **3.** (arch.) chamfer.

chanfreiner (ʃɑ̃frɛne), v.a. (arch.) To chamfer.

change (ʃɑ̃ʒ), s.m. [L *cambium*] **1.** Change, changing, succession; **2.** change, exchange, barter; *agent de ~*, stock-broker; *bureau de ~*, exchange office; *pair du ~*, par of exchange; *lettre de ~*, bill of exchange; *~ du jour*, current exchange; *perdre au ~*, to lose by the change, to lose by the exchange; **3.** (sport.) substitution of a new quarry for the one first started; *faire prendre le ~*, *donner le ~*, to put on the wrong scent; *prendre le ~ sur*, to be mistaken as to.

changeable (ʃɑ̃ʒabl), adj. To be changed, changeable, susceptible of being changed.

changeant, -e (ʃɑ̃ʒɑ̃), p. adj. Changeable, changing, variable, fickle, unsettled; *taffetas ~*, shot silk.

changement (ʃɑ̃ʒmɑ̃), s.m. Change, alteration, variation, mutation; *~ à vue*, scene-shifting, quick change.

changer (ʃɑ̃ʒe), v.a. [L *cambire*, LL *cambiare*] **1.** To change, to alter, to modify; to transform, to metamorphose (into); **2.** to exchange; v.n. to undergo change, to change; **se ~**, v.pr. (*a*) to be transformed (*en*, into); (*b*) to change one's clothes.

changeur, -se (ʃɑ̃ʒœr), s.m.f. Money-changer.

chanlatte (ʃɑ̃lat), s.f. Chantlate, eaves-board.

chanoine (ʃanwan), s.m. [f. L *canonicus*] Canon.

chanoinesse (ʃanwanɛs), s.f. Canoness.

chanson (ʃɑ̃sɔ̃), s.f. [f. L *cantio*] Song, ballad, carol; poem; satirical song or poem; (fig.) idle stuff, nonsense; *il n'a qu'une ~*, he is always harping on the same string; *toujours la même ~*, always the old story; *je lui ferai chanter une autre ~*, I will make him sing to another tune; *l'air ne fait pas la ~*, one must not mistake the appearance for the reality; *~s que tout cela!*, nonsense!

chansonner (ʃɑ̃sɔne), v.a. To lampoon, to ridicule (a person) in a song or ballad.

chansonnette (ʃɑ̃sɔnɛt), s.f. Little song, ditty, comic song.

chansonni-er, -ère (ʃɑ̃sɔnje), s.m.f. Satirical song-writer and singer.

chant (ʃɑ̃), s.m. [L *cantus*] Singing, chirping, crowing; song, tune; chant, chanting; melody; poem, division of epic poem; canto; dirge; *~s*, pl. strains; *plain ~*, Gregorian chant, plain-song; *~ du cygne*, swan-song; (fig.) last effort of a poet or musician; *~ du rossignol*, song of the nightingale; *l'harmonie étouffe le ~*, the harmony overpowers the melody; *~s sublimes*, sublime strains; *au ~ du coq*, at cock-crow.

chantage (ʃɑ̃taʒ), s.m. Blackmail, blackmailing, extortion by threats.

chantant, -e (ʃɑ̃tɑ̃), p. adj. Musical, tuneful, easy to sing; sing-song; *café ~*, music-hall.

chanteau (pl. **-x**) (ʃɑ̃to), s.m. [f. L *canthum*] **1.** Hunch or hunk of bread; **2.** gore, eking piece of material.

chantepleure, champlure (ʃɑ̃tplœr, ʃɑ̃plyr), s.f. [*chante*+*pleure*] Funnel with a rose outlet, spigot, tap.

chanter (ʃɑ̃te), v.a.n. [L *cantare*] **1.** To sing, to warble, to carol, to chirrup, to crow; *~ faux*, to sing out of tune; *~ juste*, to sing in tune; *c'est comme si je chantais*, I might as well talk to the wind; **2.** to chant, to celebrate, to praise, to compose poems; *pain à ~*, consecrated wafer; *qu'est-ce que tu chantes là?*, what are you talking about?, what do you mean?; *~ les louanges de X*, to sing the praises of X; *~ victoire*, to cry victory; *je chante ce héros*, I will celebrate (or praise) this hero; **3.** to resound, to vibrate (as a string); **4.** to be blackmailed, to pay under threat; *faire ~*, to blackmail, to extort hush-money from; **se ~**, v.pr. to be sung; to praise oneself, to sing for oneself; *si cela vous chante*, if you are in the mood for it.

chanterelle[1] (ʃɑ̃trɛl), s.f. [f. L *cantare*] **1.** The first string of a violin, &c.; **2.** decoy-bird.

chanterelle[2] (ʃɑ̃trɛl), s.f. [f. L *cantharellus*] (bot.) *Agaricus cantharellus*, chanterelle edible mushroom; syn. GIROLLE.

chanteu-r, -se (ʃɑ̃tœr), s.m.f. Singer,

vocalist, songster, songstress, singing bird. ~, adj. Singing; *maître-~*, blackmailer.

chantier (ʃɑ̃tje), s.m. [f. L *canterius*] **1.** Yard, timber-yard, coal-yard, building-yard, work-yard, stocks; **2.** cask-stand, block, keel-block; **3.** (fig.) stocks, anvil, work; *avoir un ouvrage sur le ~* (or *en ~*), to have a work in hand.

chantignole (ʃɑ̃tiɲɔl), s.f. (carp.) Bracket (to support purlins of roof).

chantonner (ʃɑ̃tɔne), v.a.n. To hum.

chantourner (ʃɑ̃turne), v.a. [*champ*+*tourner*] **1.** To saw or cut in profile, in a curve; to indent; **2.** to bring out the prominent features of (a painting).

chantre (ʃɑ̃tr), s.m. [L *cantor*] **1.** Chanter; **2.** singer, bard, poet; *les ~s des bois*, the feathered songsters; *le ~ d'Ilion*, the bard of Troy, Homer; *le ~ thébain*, Pindar.

chanvre (ʃɑ̃vr), s.m. [f. L *cannabis*] (bot.) Hemp; *cravate de ~*, hempen collar, hangman's cord.

chanvri-er, -ère (ʃɑ̃vrje), s.m.f. Hemp-dresser, hemp-seller. ~, s.f. Hemp-field.

chaos (kao), s.m. [Gr. wd] Chaos; (fig.) confusion, disorder.

chaotique (kaɔtik), adj. Chaotic.

chaparder (ʃaparde), v.a.n. (slang). To purloin, to steal, to pilfer, to pinch, to scrounge.

chape (ʃap), s.f. [L *capa*] **1.** (eccles.) Cope, pluvial; **2.** cloak, cape; **3.** (mason.) coat, or bed of mortar; **4.** chape (of a scabbard); **5.** (fig.) cover, cloak.

chapeau (pl. **-x**) (ʃapo), s.m. [f. *chape*] **1.** Hat; **2.** bonnet, hat; *~ de cardinal*, cardinal's hat, (fig.) cardinalship; *~ haute forme* or *haut-de-forme*, silk hat, top hat; (mus.) *~ chinois*, Chinese bells; *~ bas!*, *~!*, hats off!; **3.** (techn.) cap, bonnet, hood, cover, lid; *~ de valve*, valve cap.

chapelain (ʃaplɛ̃), s.m. [f. LL *capellanus*] Chaplain.

chapeler (ʃaple), v.a. [LL *capulare*] To rasp, to chip, to grate (bread); to hack, to mangle.

chapelet (ʃaplɛ), s.m. [f. *chape*] **1.** Chaplet, garland, string; *un ~ d'oignons*, a string of onions; **2.** rosary, string of beads; *dire son ~*, to tell one's beads; **3.** (med.) chaplet; (vet.) cradle.

chapelier (ʃapəlje), s.m. Hatter.

chapeli-er, -ère (ʃapəlje), adj. Pertaining to hats.

chapelière (ʃapəljɛr), s.f. **1.** Woman who makes or sells hats; **2.** convex trunk, hat-box.

chapelle (ʃapɛl), s.f. [f. *chape*] **1.** Chapel; *~ ardente*, funeral chamber; funeral trappings; **2.** (fig.) coterie, clique; **3.** crown (of an oven).

chapellenie (ʃapɛlni), s.f. Chaplaincy, chaplainship.

chapellerie (ʃapɛlri), s.f. Hatter's shop; hat-making; hat-manufactory.

chapelure (ʃaplyr), s.f. [f. *chapeler*] Grated bread.

chaperon (ʃaprɔ̃), s.m. [f. *chape*] **1.** Hood; chaperon; *le petit ~ rouge*, Little Red Riding Hood; **2.** shoulder knot; **3.** (falc.) hood, covering for the head of a hawk; **4.** elderly or responsible person accompanying a young girl, chaperon.

chaperonner (ʃaprɔne), v.a. To cope (a wall); to hood (a hawk); to chaperon (a young person).

chapiteau (pl. **-x**) (ʃapito), s.m. [f. L *capitellum*] **1.** (arch.) Capital (of a column); **2.** top, head, cap.

chapitral, -e, (aux) (ʃapitral), adj. Capitular.

chapitre (ʃapitr), s.m. [L *capitulum*] **1.** Chapter (of a book); **2.** subject, head, matter; *assez sur ce ~*, enough of that; **3.** chapter; body of canons or prebends; *avoir voix au ~*, to have a voice in the matter; **4.** chapter-house.

chapitrer (ʃapitre), v.a. To chapter, to rate, to scold, to lecture, to instruct, to reprimand.

chapon (ʃapɔ̃), s.m. [L *capo*] **1.** Capon; **2.** (in Gascony) crust of bread rubbed with garlic (for salad).

chaponner (ʃapɔne), v.a. To caponize, to capon.

chapska (ʃapska), s.f. See SCHAPSKA.

chaque (ʃak), adj. [f. L *quisque*] Each, every.

char (ʃar), s.m. [f. L *carrus*] Chariot; car; cart, wagon; hearse; *le ~ du Soleil*, the chariot of the Sun; *~ funèbre*, hearse; *~-à-bancs*, four-wheeled waggon with seats looking forward, drawn by one or several horses; ⚠ not Engl. 'char-à-banc' which = *autocar*.

charabia (ʃarabja), s.m. [f. Span. *algarabia*] Jargon, gibberish. [Charade.

charade (ʃarad), s.f. [f. Provenç. *charrado*]

charançon (ʃarɑ̃sɔ̃), s.m. [unkn. orig.] (ent.) Weevil. **charançonné, -e**, adj.

charbon (ʃarbɔ̃), s.m. [f. L *carbo*] **1.** Charcoal; **2.** embers, cinders; **3.** coal, coals; *être sur des ~s ardents*, to be on thorns, to be on tenterhooks; *seau à ~*, coal-scuttle; *~ de bois*, charcoal; **4.** (med.) anthrax, carbuncle; **5.** (agric.) smut, black rust.

charbonnage (ʃarbɔnaʒ), s.m. Coal-mining, colliery, coal-pit.

charbonné, -e (ʃarbɔne), p. adj. Charred, blacked, smutty.

charbonner (ʃarbɔne), v.a. **1.** To char, to carbonize; **2.** to blacken (with charcoal); ~ v.n. **1.** to char, to become charred; **2.** to draw badly, to daub.

charbonnerie (ʃarbɔnri), s.f. **1.** Coal-yard; **2.** political secret society.

charbonneu-x, -se (ʃarbonø), adj. Coaly, charry; (med.) carbuncular, carbuncled; *mouche charbonneuse*, fly transmitting carbuncle.

charbonni-er, -ère (ʃarbɔnje), s.m.f. 1. Charcoal-burner; ~ *est maître chez soi*, every man's house is his castle; 2. charcoal-dealer, coal-dealer; 3. coal-ship, collier; 4. (ornith.) ~*ère*, or *mésange* ~*ère*, s.f. coal-tit, tit. ~, adj. Pertaining to coal.

charcuter (ʃarkyte), v.a. [f. *charcutier*] 1. To cut (meat) in small pieces; 2. to mangle, to hack to pieces; 3. to cut and slash clumsily; to perform bad surgery on.

charcuterie (ʃarkytri), s.f. 1. Pork-butchery; pork-butcher's shop; 2. cooked, smoked, or salted pig-meat, sausages, &c. (sold by a pork-butcher).

charcuti-er, -ère (ʃarkytje), s.m.f. Pork-butcher; (fig.) mangler.

chardon (ʃardɔ̃), s.m. [L *carduus*] 1. (bot.) Thistle, teasel; 2. spike.

chardonneret (ʃardɔnrɛ), s.m. [f. *chardon*] (ornith.) Goldfinch.

chardonnette (ʃardɔnɛt), s.f. (bot.) Prickly artichoke.

charentais, -e (ʃarɑ̃tɛ), adj. s.m.f. (Native) of Charente.

charge (ʃarʒ), s.f. 1. Load, burden, weight, lading; (*navire*) *en* ~, lading (ship); 2. burden, encumbrance, expense, tax, care; *être à la* ~ (*de X*), to be a burden (on X); *la vie m'est à* ~, life is a burden to me; *un loyer de . . . plus les* ~*s*, a rent of . . . and the taxes; *à* ~ *de revanche*, on condition of reciprocity; one good turn deserves another; 3. function, public employment, post, trust, office, charge, commission, mandate; *une* ~ *de notaire*, the office and goodwill of a notary public; *se démettre de sa* ~, to resign one's functions; *femme de* ~, housekeeper; 4. (mil.) impetuous attack, charge, cavalry charge; loading, load (of a fire-arm); *sonner la* ~, to sound the charge; (fig.) *revenir à la* ~, to be at it again; 5. exaggeration, caricature; joke, farce; *peint en* ~, painted as a caricature; 6. charge, accusation, indictment; *il y a de lourdes* ~*s contre lui*, there is a serious charge against him; 7. charge (of electricity).

chargé, -e (ʃarʒe), p. adj. 1. Charged; ~ *d'affaires*, chargé d'affaires, diplomatic agent; ~ *de cours*, (university) deputy (or substitute) for a professor; assistant lecturer; 2. loaded, laden (as ships), burdened; 3. (med.) coated, furred, foul (of the tongue); 4. (print.) foul; 5. (post-off.) registered; 6. thick, turbid.

chargeant, -e (ʃarʒɑ̃), p. adj. Heavy (on the stomach).

chargement (ʃarʒəmɑ̃), s.m. 1. Loading, lading; 2. cargo, load, freight, shipment; 3. (post-off.) registration; 4. metalling (of a road).

charger (ʃarʒe), v.a.n. [LL *carricare*] 1. To load, to burden, (naut.) to lade; ~ *un cheval*, to load a horse; ~ *des pierres sur une charrette*, to load a cart with stones; ~ *sa conscience de*, to burden one's conscience with; 2. to register, to inscribe, to enter, to charge; 3. to load (fire-arms); 4. to commission, to entrust; *on l'a chargé de prendre la parole*, he was chosen as spokesman; *je vous charge de ce soin*, that care I entrust to you; 5. (mil.) to charge, to attack impetuously; 6. to charge, to accumulate (electricity); 7. to overcharge, to exaggerate, to caricature; 8. (med.) to make thick, to fur, to make foul; *un embarras gastrique charge la langue*, a disordered stomach furs the tongue; **se** ~, v.pr. 1. to load oneself, to saddle or burden oneself; 2. to undertake, to take charge (of), to make it one's business; 3. to accuse oneself; 4. to become overcast or clouded; 5. to become foul or thick or turbid; 6. to be loaded, &c.

chargeur (ʃarʒœr), s.m. Loader, shipper, freighter, stoker, gunner.

chariot (ʃarjo), s.m. [f. *char*] Wagon, truck, go-cart; (ant.) chariot; (techn.) sledge; slide rest, sliding piece in mechanisms; (astr.) *Grand* ~, Charles's Wain, the Great Bear, Ursa Major, the Wagoner; *Petit* ~, Little Bear, Ursa Minor.

charitable (ʃaritabl), adj. [f. *charité*] Charitable, kind, benevolent.

charitablement (ʃaritabləmɑ̃), adv. Charitably.

charité (ʃarite), s.f. [f. L *caritas*] Charity, charitableness, benevolence, alms-giving, alms, act of charity; *demander la* ~, to beg; *faire la* ~, to give alms; *par* ~ *!*, out of charity; in the name of charity !; ~ *bien ordonnée commence par soi-même*, charity begins at home; *Sœurs de* ~, Sisters of Mercy; *Bureau de* ~, Board of Charity.

charivari (ʃarivari), s.m. [f. LL *carivarium*] Charivari, uproar, discordant music, mock serenade, tin-kettle music.

charlatan (ʃarlatɑ̃), s.m. [f. It. *ciarlatano*] Quack, mountebank, charlatan, impostor.

charlatanerie (ʃarlatanri), s.f. Quackery, charlatan's trick.

charlatanesque (ʃarlatanɛsk), adj. Quackish, charlatanical.

charlatanisme (ʃarlatanism), s.m. Charlatanism.

charlemagne (ʃarləmaɲ), adv. loc. (cards) *Faire* ~, to leave off playing when winning.

charlotte (ʃarlɔt), s.f. 1. (cook.) Charlotte; 2. child's or woman's linen bonnet.

charmant, -e (ʃarmɑ̃), p. adj. Highly pleasing, delightful, charming, fascinating.

charme[1] (ʃarm), s.m. [L *carmen*] **1.** Charm, magic spell, incantation, charmed object, amulet; **2.** charm, pleasingness, allurement, fascination; *être sous le ~ de X*, to be spellbound by X; *le ~ est rompu*, the charm (or spell) is broken, the illusion is destroyed; **3.** *~s*, (pl.) charms, bosom, bodily attractions; *elle est fière de ses ~s*, she is vain of her bodily perfections.

charme[2] (ʃarm), s.m. [L *carpinus*] (bot.) Yoke-elm, hornbeam, *Carpinus betulus*; *se porter comme un ~*, to be hale and hearty.

charmer (ʃarme), v.a. To charm, to please, to fascinate, to delight, to subdue, to allay, to soothe, to beguile; to place under a spell; *le serpent charme le rossignol*, the snake fascinates the nightingale; *la musique charme la douleur*, music soothes pain; *charmé de vous voir*, delighted to see you.

charmeu-r, -se (ʃarmœr), s.m.f. adj. Charmer, fascinating (person).

charmeuse (ʃarmøz), s.f. Soft silk material, charmeuse.

charmille (ʃarmij), s.f. [f. *charme*] **1.** Young hornbeam plantation; **2.** arbour, bower, or live wall of clipped hornbeam.

charmoie (ʃarmwɑ), s.f. [f. *charme*] Hornbeam grove or plantation.

charnel, -le (ʃarnɛl), adj. [f. L *caro, carnis*] Carnal, sensual, carnal-minded.

charnellement (ʃarnɛlmɑ̃), adv. Carnally.

charnier (ʃarnje), s.m. [L *carnarium*] **1.** Charnel-house; **2.** (rare) larder; **3.** (naut.) water-butt.

charnière (ʃarnjɛr), s.f. [f. L *cardo, cardinis*] Hinge, joint.

charnu, -e (ʃarny), adj. Fleshy, brawny, plump; pulpy, pulpous.

charnure (ʃarnyr), (rare) s.f. Flesh; all the fleshy parts of the body.

charogne (ʃarɔɲ), s.f. [L *caro*] Carrion, carcass; (fig. insulting) lump of carrion; pest; see doublet CAROGNE.

charolais, -e (ʃarɔlɛ), adj. s.m.f. (Native) of the country near Charolles (Burgundy).

charpente (ʃarpɑ̃t), s.f. [f. L *carpentum*] **1.** Carpentry, timber-work, frame-work, (for roof); **2.** frame (of any structure), skeleton; *bois de ~*, building-timber; *la ~ osseuse du corps*, the bony frame of the body; *la ~ d'un roman*, the framework, the plan, or construction of a novel.

charpenté, -e (ʃarpɑ̃te), p. adj. Built, framed, constructed; *un gars bien ~*, a well-built fellow.

charpenter (ʃarpɑ̃te), v.a. [LL *carpentare*] To hew, to square, to build, to strengthen; to make or frame a plot or plan.

charpenterie (ʃarpɑ̃tri), s.f. Carpentry, timber-work.

charpentier (ʃarpɑ̃tje), s.m. **1.** Carpenter; (aeron. slang) wood butcher; **2.** (fish.) whale-cutter.

charpie (ʃarpi), s.f. [LL *carpia*] Lint; *viande en ~*, meat done (or boiled) to rags.

charrée (ʃare), s.f. [etym. dub.] Lye-ash, exhausted black-ash.

charretée (ʃarte), s.f. [f. *charrette*] Cart-load.

charretier (ʃartje), s.m. Carter, driver of a cart, wagoner; ploughman; *jurer comme un ~*, to swear like a trooper. **~, -ère,** adj. Cart; *chemin ~*, cart-way, cart-track; *porte-~ère*, cart-gateway.

charreton, charretin (ʃartɔ̃, ʃartɛ̃), s.m. Small wagon, truck.

charrette (ʃarɛt), s.f. [f. *char*] Cart; *~ à bras*, hand-cart; truck; (fig.) *mettre la ~ avant les bœufs*, to put the cart before the horse.

charriage (ʃarjaʒ), s.m. **1.** Carting, cartage; **2.** (slang) mystification.

charrier (ʃarje), v.a. **1.** To cart, to carry, to convey, to drag; (of a stream) to drift, to carry down (gold, ice, sand, &c.); (med.) to be loaded with; *le fleuve charrie des glaçons*, the river drifts ice; **2.** (slang) to mystify, to swindle; to kid, to fool, to humbug, to pull the leg of; to exaggerate.

charroi (ʃarwɑ), s.m. Carting, transport.

charron (ʃarɔ̃), s.m. [f. *char*] Wheelwright, cartwright.

charronnage (ʃarɔnaʒ), s.m. Wheelwright's work or art.

charronnerie (ʃarɔnri), s.f. The wheelwright industry.

charroyer (ʃarwɑje), v.a. To cart, to transport (heavy goods).

charroyeur (ʃarwɑjœr), s.m. Carter, carrier.

charrue (ʃary), s.f. [L *carruca*] **1.** Plough; *~ à avant-train*, wheel-plough; *~ sans avant-train*, swing-plough; (fig.) *mettre la ~ avant les bœufs*, to put the cart before the horse; *c'est un vrai cheval de ~*, he is a great powerful fellow; **2.** carucate (measure); **3.** (in electric tramcars) plough, contrivance for obtaining electric current from a rail on the ground.

charte (ʃart), s.f. [L *charta*] Charter, title-deeds; *la Grande ~*, Magna Charta (1215); *~-partie*, charter-party.

chartil (ʃarti), s.m. Harvest-wagon.

chartisme (ʃartism), s.m. (English hist.) Chartism.

chartiste (ʃartist), s.m.f. **1.** Chartist; **2.** (in France) pupil or professor of the *École des Chartes*.

chartre (ʃartr), s.f. [f. L *carcer*] **1.** Prison; *tenir X en ~ privée*, to sequestrate X without legal authority; **2.** [f. L *charta*] charter; **3.** (med.) tabes mesenterica.

chartreuse (ʃartrøz), s.f. **1.** Carthusian convent, Charterhouse; *Grande Chartreuse*, old Carthusian convent in celebrated scenery near Grenoble; **2.** Carthusian nun; **3.** lonely cottage; **4.** a liqueur.

chartreux (ʃartrø), s.m. Carthusian monk.

chartrier (ʃartrje), s.m. **1.** Charter-room; charter-chest; **2.** keeper of charters.

chas (ʃɑ), s.m. [L *capsum*] **1.** Eye of a needle; **2.** top of a plumb-line.

chasse (ʃas), s.f. [f. *chasser*] Chase, pursuit, hunting, shooting; game killed or pursued; shoot, country (of a hunt); hunt, the hunters; huntsmen, with their pack; shooting-season; (naut.) chase, chase-gun, chaser, space round a vessel at anchor; (plumbing) flushing; (print.) driving out; ~ *à courre*, hunting with hounds; ~ *au lévrier*, coursing; ~ *au tir*, shooting; ~ *au faucon*, hawking; ~ *au furet*, ferreting; ~ *au sanglier*, boar-hunting; ~ *au renard*, fox-hunting; ~ *aux perdrix*, partridge shooting; *rendez-vous de* ~, hunting box (or lodge); *permis de* ~, shooting licence; *garde-*~, game-keeper; *donner la* ~ *à*, to pursue, to hunt; (fig.) *donner une* ~ *à X*, to scold X, to give X a blowing-up; *qui va à la* ~ *perd sa place*, if you leave your place you lose it; *il n'est* ~ *que de vieux chiens*, grey hairs bring counsel, or, old hands know their business best; *louer une* ~, to rent a shoot or hunting ground; *la* ~ *a passé par ici*, the hunt has passed this way; *il vit de sa* ~, he lives on the game he kills; *cheval de* ~, hunter; *aller à la* ~, to go shooting; *l'ouverture de la* ~, the first day of the shooting season; *la* ~ *est fermée*, the shooting season is closed; ~ *d'eau*, flushing, flush.

chasse- (*in compounds*; in the pl. ~ is invar.) (ʃas), [f. *chasser*] ~*-clous*, s.m., ~*-pointe*, s.m., Punch, driving punch, puncher, nail-driver; ~*-neige*, s.m. snow-plough; ~*-pierres*, s.m. (*a*) catapult; (*b*) guard-iron; ~*-mouches*, s.m. fly-flap, fly-net.

châsse (ʃɑs), s.f. [f. L *capsa*] **1.** Reliquary, shrine; **2.** frame; **3.** scales.

chassé (ʃase), s.m. (danc.) Chassé.

chassé-croisé (ʃasekrwaze), s.m. (pl. *chassés-croisés*) **1.** (danc.) Chassé-croisé; **2.** (fig.) crossing, exchange of places.

chasselas (ʃaslɑ), s.m. [French geog. orig.] Chasselas, fine kind of white grapes.

chassepot (ʃaspo), s.m. [after the inventor] Chassepot; Chassepot-rifle.

chasser (ʃase), v.a.n. [L *captiare*] To chase, to pursue, to hunt, to shoot, to course, to go shooting; to drive, to drive in, to drive out, to expel, to discharge, to turn off, to discard; to propel, to drag, to swing; ~ *l'ennemi devant soi*, to drive the enemy before one; ~ *un clou*, to drive out (or in) a nail; *la faim chasse le loup du bois*, hunger drives the wolf from the forest; hunger will break through stone walls; *un clou chasse l'autre*, one idea drives away another; *ne chassez pas deux lièvres à la fois*, do not have too many irons in the fire; *il chasse de race*, true blue will never stain; he is a chip of the old block; *chassez le naturel, il revient au galop*, what is bred in the bone will come out in the flesh; *il fut chassé du Sénat*, he was expelled from the Senate; *ce valet a été chassé*, this valet has been turned off; *ce bateau chasse sur ses ancres*, this ship is dragging her anchors; *la pluie chasse du N.O.*, the rain is driving from the NW.; **se** ~, v.pr. to drive one another out, to be hunted, to be shot, coursed, or caught.

chasseresse (ʃasrɛs), s.f. adj. Huntress.

chasseur (ʃasœr), s.m. **1.** Hunter, sportsman, huntsman, shooter; **2.** chasseur; (*a*) footman, 'buttons', groom; (*b*) light-infantry man. ~, adj. Chasing, hunting; chaser (ship.).

chassie (ʃasi), s.f. [f. L *caecus*] Yellow mucus secreted by the glands of the eye; blearedness.

chassieu-x, -se (ʃasjø), adj. Bleared, blear-eyed.

châssis (ʃɑsi), s.m. [f. *châsse*] **1.** Sash, sash-frame; **2.** stretcher (frame for canvas); **3.** (print.) chase; **4.** (hort.) glass frame; **5.** (photo.) slide; **6.** (theatr.) frame of scenery; flat-scene; **7.** (motor.) chassis, frame.

chaste (ʃast) adj. [L *castus*] Chaste, pure. ⚠ While in French *chaste* only refers to bodily continence, 'chaste' in English is often said of style, speech, &c., and should be translated *châtié, sobre, de bon goût*.

chastement (ʃastəmɑ̃), adv. Chastely, purely.

chasteté (ʃastəte), s.f. **1.** Chastity, continence; **2.** purity of body or mind chasteness.

chasuble (ʃazybl), s.f. [f. LL *casubla*] Chasuble.

chasublerie (ʃazybləri), s.f. Trade of makers of church ornaments.

chat, -te (ʃa), s.m.f. [L *catus*] Cat, he-cat, she-cat, tom, tom-cat; (fam.) pussy, pussy-cat; (fig.) duck, ducky, dovey, darling; ~ *à neuf queues*, cat-o'-nine-tails; ~ *botté*, puss-in-boots; *avoir un* ~ *dans la gorge*; to have a frog in the throat, to be hoarse; *à bon* ~ *bon rat*, a Roland for an Oliver; tit for tat; *écrire comme un* ~, to write a regular scrawl; ~ *en poche*, a pig in a poke; *appeler un* ~ *un* ~, to call a spade a spade; not to mince matters; *il n'y a pas de quoi fouetter un* ~, it is a mere nothing;

il n'y a pas un ~, there is not a living soul; *donner sa langue aux* ~*s*, to give up guessing; ~ *échaudé craint l'eau froide*, a burnt child dreads the fire; once bitten twice shy; *n'éveillez pas le* ~ *qui dort*, let sleeping dogs lie; *la nuit tous les* ~*s sont gris*, when candles are away all cats are grey; *quand le* ~ *n'est pas là les souris dansent*, when the cat is away the mice will play; *j'ai bien d'autres* ~*s à fouetter*, I have other fish to fry; *jouer à* ~ *coupé*, to play at cross-tag.

châtaigne (ʃatɛɲ), s.f. [L *castanea*] Chestnut; ~ *d'eau*, water-caltrop; ~ (or *marron*) *d'Inde*, horse-chestnut.

châtaigneraie (ʃatɛɲərɛ), s.f. Chestnut-grove, or -plantation.

châtaignier (ʃatɛɲe), s.m. (bot.) Chestnut-tree; chestnut-wood.

châtain, -e (ʃatɛ̃), adj. Chestnut, auburn, nut-brown.

chataire (ʃatɛr), s.f. (bot.) Catmint.

chat-cervier (ʃasɛrvje), s.m. (zool.) Caracal.

château (pl. **-x**) (ʃato), s.m. [L *castellum*] Castle, palace, manor, hall, seat, mansion, court, lodge; ~*-fort*, stronghold; ~*-d'eau*, reservoir of water for fountains; water-tank (for locomotives); water-works; (naut.) ~ *de proue*, forecastle; ~ *d'arrière*, poop-castle; (fig.) *faire des* ~*x en Espagne*, to build castles in the air; (fig.) ~ *de cartes*, pretty but unsubstantial construction; house of cards.

chateaubriant (ʃatobrijɑ̃), s.m. (cook.) Fillet steak with fried potatoes.

châtelain, -e (ʃatlɛ̃), s.m.f. [f. *château*] Lord or lady of the manor. ~*e*, s.f. Chatelaine, key-chain hanging from a lady's waistband.

châtelet (ʃatlɛ), s.m. Small castle; name of old court of justice and prison in Paris.

châtellenie (ʃatɛlni), s.f. Castellany.

chat-huant (ʃaɥɑ̃), s.m. (pl. *chats-huants*) (ornith.) Screech-owl.

châtier (ʃatje), v.a. [L *castigare*] To chastise, to punish, to castigate; to chasten, to make correct, to polish; *qui aime bien châtie bien*, spare the rod and spoil the child.

chatière (ʃatjɛr), s.f. [f. *chat*] **1.** Cat-hole; **2.** trap for cats; **3.** outlet.

châtiment (ʃatimɑ̃), s.m. Chastisement, castigation, punishment, correction.

chatoiement (ʃatwamɑ̃), s.m. Chatoyement, play of colours, iridescence.

chaton[1] (ʃatɔ̃), s.m. **1.** Kitten; **2.** (bot.) catkin.

chaton[2] (ʃatɔ̃), s.m. [f. L *cista*] Bezel, part of a ring in which a gem is set.

chatonner (ʃatone), v.n. **1.** To kitten; **2.** (rare) v.a. to set (a gem) in a ring.

chatouillement (ʃatujmɑ̃), s.m. Tickling, titillation.

chatouiller (ʃatuje), v.a. [etym. dub.] To tickle, to titillate; (fig.) to please; ~ *la curiosité de X*, to tickle X's curiosity.

chatouilleu-x, -se (ʃatujø), adj. **1.** Ticklish, sensible to titillation; **2.** touchy, punctilious, excitable, delicate, nice; ~ *sur le point d'honneur*, excessively punctilious; *question, affaire* ~*se*, very ticklish or hazardous affair or question.

chatoyant, -e (ʃatwajɑ̃), p. adj. Chatoyant, iridescent, shot, glistening.

chatoyer (ʃatwaje), v.n. [f. *chat*] To have a shot effect, to glisten, to be iridescent.

chat-pard (ʃapar), s.m. (pl. *chats-pards*) [*chat*+*léopard*] (zool.) European lynx.

châtré, -e (ʃatre), p. adj. Castrated, gelt. ~, s.m. Eunuch, male soprano; see CASTRAT.

châtrer (ʃatre), v.a. [L *castrare*] **1.** To castrate; to geld (animals); **2.** (fig.) to expurgate, to purify (style, book, &c.), to bowdlerize.

châtreur (ʃatrœr), s.m. Castrator, gelder.

chattée (ʃate), s.f. [f. *chat*] Litter of kittens.

chattemite (ʃatmit), s.f. [*chatte* + L *mitis*] Demure-looking person, hypocrite.

chatter (ʃate), v.n. To kitten.

chatterie (ʃatri), s.f. [f. *chat*] **1.** Daintiness; **2.** sweetmeats, dainty bits; **3.** coaxing, winning ways, caress.

chatterton (ʃatɛrtɔ̃), s.m. [Engl. wd] (electr.) Chatterton's compound (used for insulating wires and cables).

chat-tigre (ʃatigr), s.m. (pl. *chats-tigres*) Tiger-cat.

chaud, -e (ʃo), adj. [L *calidus*] Hot, warm; zealous, ardent, animated; warm, prompt, quick; *climat* ~, hot climate; *serre* ~*e*, hot-house; *fièvre* ~*e*, burning fever; ~*es larmes*, scalding tears; *pleurer à* ~*es larmes*, to cry abundantly, to dissolve in tears; to weep copiously; *avoir la tête* ~*e*, to be hot-headed; *avoir le sang* ~, to be passionate, hot-headed; *être* ~*e*, to be in heat (as a bitch), to rut (as a doe) (syn. ÊTRE EN CHALEUR); *un* ~ *partisan*; a zealous partisan; ~*e alarme*, sudden alarm; *l'affaire a été* ~*e*, the encounter was hot, or sharp; *cela ne lui fait ni* ~ *ni froid*, that is all the same to him, that does not affect him in any way; *je vous apporte la nouvelle toute* ~*e*, I bring you the news quite fresh, at once; *une* ~*e éloquence*, a winning, overpowering eloquence; *un* ~ *coloris*, a warm colour; *il faut battre le fer pendant qu'il est* ~, strike while the iron is hot; *cent francs, c'est* ~ *!*, a hundred francs, that's a stiff price!

chaud (ʃo), adv. Hot, warm; *tenez* ~ *ce plat*, keep this dish warm; *ce manteau tient* ~, this cloak keeps one warm; *boire* ~, to drink hot; *tout* ~, (*a*) instantly;

(*b*) piping hot; *il fera ~ quand*, it will be a long time before.
chaud (ʃo), s.m. Heat, hottest point; *tenez-vous au ~*, keep indoors, stay in the warmth; *il ne craint ni le ~ ni le froid*, he fears neither heat nor cold; (fig.) *souffler le ~ et le froid*, to blow hot and cold; to praise and blame the same thing, or person; *le ~ du jour*, the hottest part of the day.
chaude (ʃod), s.f. Brisk fire, act of heating an iron; *il faut plusieurs ~s pour faire un fer à cheval*, several heatings are required to make a horse-shoe.
chaudeau (pl. **-x**) (ʃodo), s.m. Caudle, warm spiced drink.
chaudement (ʃodmɑ̃), adv. Hotly, warmly, briskly, effusively; *se vêtir ~*, to wear warm clothes; *poursuivre ~ l'ennemi*, to pursue the enemy hotly.
chaude-pisse (ʃodpis), s.f. (pathol.) Clap, gonorrhea.
chaudfroid (ʃofrwɑ), s.m. (cook.) Chaudfroid (dish of meat, poultry, &c. in jelly).
chaudière (ʃodjɛr), s.f. [f. L *caldaria*] Boiler, cauldron, copper; ~ *(à vapeur)*, steam-boiler.
chaudron (ʃodrɔ̃), s.m. [f. *chaudière*, *chauderon*] Boiler, cauldron, kettle.
chaudronnée (ʃodrɔne), s.f. Kettleful, boilerful.
chaudronnerie (ʃodrɔnri), s.f. **1.** Coppersmith's, tinsmith's and brazier's business; hollow-ware trade; **2.** copper goods, pots, saucepans.
chaudronni-er, -ère (ʃodrɔnje), s.m.f. Coppersmith, brazier, dealer in pots and pans, tinker.
chauffage (ʃofaʒ), s.m. **1.** Warming, heating; ~ *central*, central heating; **2.** (steam eng.) getting up steam; **3.** (slang) cramming for exams.
chauffard (ʃofar), s.m. (pej.) Motor scorcher, road-hog.
chauffe (ʃof), s.f. (metall.) Heating, furnace; *surface de ~*, heating surface.
chauffe-assiettes (ʃofasjɛt), s.m. (pl. *chauffe-assiettes*) Plate-warmer.
chauffe-bain (ʃofbɛ̃), s.m. (pl. *chauffe-bains*) Bath-heater, geyser.
chauffe-pieds (ʃofpje), s.m. invar. Foot-warmer.
chauffer (ʃofe), v.a.n. [L *calefacere*] **1.** To warm, to heat, to make warm or hot, to fuel; ~ *une chambre*, to warm a room; *faire ~ un bain*, to heat a bath; ~ *(une locomotive)*, to get up steam; **2.** to urge on, to coach, to cram (pupils); ~ *une affaire*, to push on an undertaking; **3.** (colloq.) to become heated, stormy, to fight; *cela va ~*, a storm is brewing; people are going to quarrel, or to fight; things are going to hum!, we are in for a hot time!; **4.** (slang) to pinch, to pilfer, to steal; **se ~**, v.pr. to warm oneself to get warm; *chauffez-vous les pieds*, warm your feet; *il verra de quel bois je me chauffe*, he shall see what I am made of.
chaufferette (ʃofrɛt), s.f. **1.** Foot-warmer, foot-stove; **2.** chafing-pan.
chaufferie (ʃofri), s.f. Chafery, stoke-hole.
chauffeur (ʃofœr), s.m. **1.** Stoker, fireman (of a steam engine); **2.** chauffeur, driver (of a motor-car); **3.** name given to brigands of Vendée who tortured their victims with fire.
chauffeuse (ʃoføz), s.f. **1.** Lady driver (of a motor-car); **2.** low-seated chair.
chauffoir (ʃofwar), s.m. **1.** Warming-room in a monastery; **2.** stove; **3.** special school coaching pupils for exams; cramming establishment.
chaufour (ʃofur), s.m. Lime-kiln.
chaufournier (ʃofurnje), s.m. Lime-burner, lime-merchant.
chaulage (ʃolaʒ), s.m. Liming, lime-washing.
chauler (ʃole), v.a. [f. *chaux*] To lime, to lime-wash.
chaumage (ʃomaʒ), s.m. Stubble-cutting, bagging.
chaume (ʃom), s.m. [f. L *calamus*] Stubble, stubble-field, thatch, thatched roof; (fig.) humble abode, poor cottage; *les perdrix se réfugient dans les ~s*, the partridges take to the stubble-fields; *Charles-Quint naquit sous le ~*, Charles-Quint was born in a humble abode.
chaumer (ʃome), v.a.n. To cut the stubble.
chaumière (ʃomiɛr), s.f. [f. *chaume*] Cottage, thatched cottage, cot.
chaumine (ʃomin), s.f. Hut, hovel, wretched cottage.
chaussant, -e (ʃosɑ̃), p. adj. Easy to put on, well-fitting; (fig.) tractable.
chausse (ʃos), s.f. [f. L *calceus*] **1.** (pl.) Hose, breeches (obs.); *tirer ses ~s*, to scamper away; *haut-de-~s*, breeches; **2.** shoulder-knot (of graduates); **3.** bag filter, jelly-bag; **4.** pipe.
chaussée (ʃose), s.f. [f. L *calciatus*] **1.** Causeway, road, roadway, embankment; **2.** dike; **3.** reef; *rez de ~*, ground-floor; ~ *des Géants*, Giant's Causeway.
chausse-pied (ʃospje), s.m. (pl. *chausse-pieds*) Shoe-horn, shoe-lift.
chausser (ʃose), v.a.n. [L *calceare*] **1.** To put on (boots, shoes, stockings, &c.); to wear; **2.** to supply with shoes; **3.** to fit, to suit; **4.** to take a certain size; **5.** (fig.) to adopt, to get into one's head; **se ~**, v.pr. to put on one's stockings, shoes, &c.; (fig.) to become infatuated (with an opinion); (fig.) ~ *le cothurne*, to become a tragedian; *les cordonniers sont les plus mal chaussés*, the shoemaker's children are the worst shod; *cela me chausse*, that suits me; *je chausse du 38*; I wear

shoes of size 5 (approx. Engl. equivalent); *il s'est chaussé de cette idée*, he has become infatuated with that idea.

chausse-trape (ʃos-trap), s.f. (pl. *chausse-trapes*) **1.** Trap; **2.** (bot.) star-thistle; **3.** (mil.) caltrop.

chaussette (ʃosɛt), s.f. Sock.

chausseur (ʃosœr), s.m. (High-class) shoemaker.

chausson (ʃosɔ̃), s.m. **1.** Sock, list-shoe, fencing-shoe; **2.** chausson (mode of fighting, using the feet) (syn. SAVATE); **3.** (cook.) puff; ~ *aux pommes*, apple-puff.

chaussure (ʃosyr), s.f. [f. *chausser*] **1.** Footwear, footgear, boots, shoes, &c.; **2.** shoe-making industry; **3.** (fig,) *trouver ~ à son pied*, (*a*) to find just what one wants; (*b*) to meet one's match.

chaut (ʃo), 3rd pers. of the present of v. *chaloir*. See CHALOIR.

chauve (ʃov) adj. [L *calvus*] Bald, bald-headed.

chauve-souris (ʃovsuri), s.f. (pl. *chauves-souris*) (zool.) Bat, flittermouse.

chauvin, -e (ʃovɛ̃), adj. s.m.f. [f. *Nicolas Chauvin*, a soldier and patriot of the 1st French Republic] Chauvinist, ultra-patriot, jingo.

chauvinisme (ʃovinism), s.m. [f. *chauvin*] Chauvinism, jingoism.

chauvir (ʃovir), v.n. [OF *chouir*] ~ *des oreilles*, (of a horse) to prick up the ears.

chaux (ʃo), s.f. [L *calx*] Lime, calx; ~ *vive*, quicklime; ~ *éteinte*, slack lime; *pierre à ~*, limestone; *lait de ~*, milk of lime; (fig.) *être bâti à ~ et à sable*, to be strongly built; to be as strong as a horse.

chavirer (ʃavire), v.n. [f. Provenç. *capvirar*] To capsize, to turn upside-down; (fig.) to fail, to be shipwrecked or stranded; to go to the dogs.

chavirement, chavirage (ʃavirmɑ̃, ʃaviraʒ), s.m. Capsize, capsizing, oversetting.

chébec (ʃebɛk), s.m. [f. It. *sciabecco*] (naut.) Xebec.

chef (ʃɛf), s.m. [L *caput*] **1.** Head; *le ~ de St Jean*, the head of St. John the Baptist; *branler le ~*, to nod slowly, to toss (or shake) one's head; **2.** chief, founder, leader, person in authority; *~ de file*, (mil.) first man in the rank; (fig.) ring-leader; *~ de bureau*, chief clerk; *~ d'orchestre*, conductor; *~ de cuisine*, head cook, chef; *~ de gare*, station-master; *~ de train*, railway guard; *en ~*, in chief; head, chief; **3.** authority, right; *il a eu cette terre du ~ de sa femme*, he had that estate in right of his wife; *de son ~ il ne devait rien*, he owed nothing on his own account; **4.** principal point, item, subdivision; *~ d'accusation*, count of indictment; *au premier ~*, in the highest degree; *sur ce ~*, about this matter; *les questions sont rangées sous trois ~ principaux*, the questions are classified under three main heads.

chef-d'œuvre (ʃɛdœvr), s.m. (pl. *chefs-d'œuvre*) **1.** Trial-piece, masterpiece; **2.** masterpiece, excellent work of any kind.

chefferie (ʃɛfri), s.f. [f. *chef*] District of a (mil.) engineer.

chef-lieu (ʃɛfljø), s.m. (pl. *chefs-lieux*) Seat, principal residence, chief town.

cheik, sheik (ʃɛik), s.m. [Arab. wd] Sheik.

cheiroptères (keirɔptɛr), s.m.pl. [f. Gr. *kheir+pteron*] (zool.) Cheiroptera.

chelem, schelem (ʃlɛm), s.m. [f. Engl. *slam*] (cards) Slam.

chélidoine (kelidwan), s.f. [f. Gr. *khelidonion*] (bot.) Celandine, swallow-wort.

chélone (kelɔn), s.f. [f. Gr. *khelōnē*] (bot.) Chelone, tortoise-flower.

chélonée (kelɔne), s.f. [Gr. wd] (zool.) Turtle, sea-tortoise.

chéloniens (kelɔnjɛ̃), s.m.pl. (zool.) Chelonia.

chemin (ʃəmɛ̃), s.m. [f. Celt. *camen*] **1.** Way, road, path; *se mettre en ~*, to start; *passer son ~*, to go one's way; *rebrousser ~*, to turn back; to retrace one's steps; *il n'y va pas par quatre ~s*, he does not beat about the bush over it, he does not mince matters, he makes no bones about it; *aller son petit bonhomme de ~*, to go plodding on; to jog on; (fig.) *faire la moitié du ~*, to make advances; to meet half-way; *~ faisant*, on the way, by the way; *faire du ~*, *faire beaucoup de ~*, to go a good distance; to make good progress; *faire son ~ (dans le monde)*, to get on (in the world); *prendre le ~ des écoliers*, to go the longest way round; *je lui ferai voir du ~*, I will lead him a fine dance; *~ de fer*, railway; *grand ~*, high road; highway; *~ de traverse*, cross-country road; (agric.) *~ d'exploitation*, occupation road; *~ de halage*, tow-path; (fort.) *~ de ronde*, round way; *~ de la croix*, way of Calvary; stations of the Cross; *tout ~ mène à Rome*, there are more ways than one to the wood; all roads lead to Rome; **2.** rate of sailing, driving, &c.; distance covered; *ce bateau fait beaucoup de ~*, that ship sails fast; *nous avons fait du ~ depuis lors*, (*a*) we have gone a long distance since then; (*b*) (fig.) we have been getting on fast since then.

chemineau (pl. **-x**) (ʃəmino), s.m. [f. *chemin*] Tramp; (Amer.) hobo, moocher; see CHEMINOT.

cheminée (ʃəmine), s.f. [f. L *caminus*] **1.** Chimney, chimney-flue, chimney-stack, funnel; fire-place, mantelpiece, hearth; *feu de ~*, a chimney on fire; *tuyau de ~*, chimney-flue; *au coin de la ~*,

by the fireside; (fig.) *sous la ~*, under the rose, secretly; *mariage fait sous la ~*, clandestine marriage; *il faut faire une croix à la ~*, we must chalk that up; *~ d'appel*, draught-flue; **2.** (fire-arms) nipple.
cheminement (ʃəminmɑ̃), s.m. [f. *chemin*] Walking, progress.
cheminer (ʃəmine), v.n. To go along, to walk, to crawl, to move on or about, to travel, to get on, to make one's way, to progress.
cheminot (ʃəmino), s.m. [f. *chemin-de-fer*] Railway man, railway operative; *grève de ~s*, railway strike; ⚠ see CHEMINEAU.
chemise (ʃəmiz), s.f. [f. L *camisia*] **1.** Chemise; shirt; *en bras de ~*, in one's shirt-sleeves; *il change de domestiques comme de ~*, he changes his servants as often as his shirt; *~ (or cotte) de mailles*, coat of mail; **2.** cover, covering, wrapper, envelope, tillet, jacket; **3.** casing (of a boiler); *~ du cylindre*, cylinder jacket.
chemiser (ʃəmize), v.a. To lute, to coat.
chemiserie (ʃəmizri), s.f. Shirt-shop or manufactory, shirt-making.
chemisette (ʃəmizɛt), s.f. Chemisette, shirt-front, front, tucker, dicky; blouse.
chemisi-er, -ère (ʃəmizje), s.m.f. Shirt-maker. ~, s.m. or *blouse ~*, shirt-blouse.
chênaie (ʃɛnɛ), s.f. [f. *chêne*] Oak-plantation or grove.
chenal (pl. **aux**) (ʃənal), s.m. [f. L *canalem*] (doublets: *canal, chéneau*) **1.** Channel pass, navigable channel; **2.** mill-race, watercourse.
chenapan (ʃnapɑ̃), s.m. [f. Germ. *Schnapphahn*] Scamp, worthless fellow, ruffian, scoundrel.
chêne (ʃɛn), s.m. [Gallic orig., LL *caxanum*] (bot.) Oak, oak-tree, oak-wood, oak-timber; *~ rouvre, Quercus robur*; *~ blanc*, white or Quebec oak; *~ vert*, evergreen oak; *~-liège*, cork-oak; *les petits coups font tomber les grands ~s*, little strokes fell great oaks.
chêneau (pl. **-x**) (ʃɛno), s.m. Oak sapling.
chéneau (pl. **-x**) (ʃeno), s.m. [See CHENAL] Leaden pipe, gutter.
chenet (ʃənɛ), s.m. [f. *chien*] **1.** Andiron, fire-dog; *vivre les pieds sur les ~s*, to lead an easy life; **2.** (naut.) cramp.
chènevière (ʃɛnvjɛr), s.f. Hemp-field.
chènevis (ʃɛnvi), s.m. [OF *cheneve*] (bot.) Hemp.
chènevotte (ʃɛnvɔt), s.f. Reed, boon, shove, stripped hemp-stalk.
chènevotter (ʃɛnvɔte), v.n. To put forth weak shoots (said of the vine).
chenil (ʃəni), s.m. [f. *chien*] **1.** Kennel; **2.** (fig.) hovel, dirty hole, wretched dwelling.
chenille (ʃənij), s.f. [f. *chien*] **1.** Caterpillar; **2.** chenille (silk trimming); **3.** (motor.) caterpillar.
chenillère (ʃənijɛr), s.f. Nest of caterpillars.
chénopode (ʃenɔpɔd), s.m. (bot.) Chenopodium, goose-foot.
chenu, -e (ʃəny), adj. [f. L *canutus*] **1.** Hoar, hoary, hoary-headed, bald, denuded; **2.** (fig.) antiquated, obsolete; **3.** improved by age; *vin ~*, old wine.
cheptel (ʃɛptɛl), s.m. [f. LL *capitale*] Live-stock leased to a farmer; *~ mort*, agricultural implements leased to a farmer; *~ vif*, live-stock.
chepteli-er, -ère (ʃɛptəlje), adj. s.m.f. (Lessee) of live-stock.
chéquard (ʃekar), s.m. (pej.) Bribed person.
chèque (ʃɛk), s.m. [Engl. *cheque, check*] (bank.) Cheque; *~ barré*, crossed cheque; *carnet de ~s*, cheque-book.
chéquier (ʃekje), s.m. Cheque-book.
cher, chère (ʃɛr), adj. [L *carus*] **1.** Dear, beloved, highly-prized, cherished; *c'est mon vœu le plus ~*, it is my most ardent (or cherished) wish; **2.** dear, costly, expensive; (adv.) dear, dearly; *le vin est ~ cette année*, wine is dear this year; *ce magasin est ~*, this shop is expensive; *vendre ~ sa vie*, to sell one's life dearly; *il me le paiera cher!*, he shall pay dearly for that!
cherché, -e (ʃɛrʃe), p. adj. [f. *chercher*] (fig.) Far-fetched.
chercher (ʃɛrʃe), v.a. [LL *circare*] **1.** To seek, to search for, to look for; to go or be in quest of; to fetch; *c'est ~ une aiguille dans une botte de foin*, it's like looking for a needle in a bottle of hay, or, in a haystack; *~ midi à quatorze heures*, to look for a knot in a bulrush; to seek for impossibilities; *il cherche dans sa tête* (or *dans sa mémoire*), he is ransacking his memory; *~ la petite bête*, to be over-nice about trifles, to be finical, finicky; *~ querelle à*, to pick a quarrel with; *~ sa vie*, to seek a livelihood; to be in quest of one's food; *allez ~ mon habit*, fetch my coat; *allez ~ le médecin*, go and fetch the doctor; **2.** *~ à*, to try to, to endeavour to, to strive to; *je cherche à lui plaire*, I endeavour to please him (or her); *ce chien cherche à mordre*, this dog is trying to bite; *il chercha à me consoler*, he sought (or strove) to comfort me; **se ~**, v.pr. to search one's own heart or mind; to look for each other; (pop.) to pick a quarrel.
chercheu-r, -se (ʃɛrʃœr), s.m.f. **1.** Searcher, seeker, explorer, hunter, learned inquirer; **2.** (opt.) finder, star- (or object-) finder. ~, adj. *Esprit ~*, inquiring mind.
chère (ʃɛr), s.f. (obs.) [f. Gr. *kara*] Face, countenance; welcoming, reception, fare; (by ext.) cheer, fare, eating and drinking; *faire maigre ~*, to have poor

fare; *faire bonne* (or *grande*) ~, to fare well, to enjoy good cheer, to eat abundantly; *faire* ~ *lie*, to live in clover.

chèrement (ʃɛrmɑ̃), adv. **1.** Dearly, tenderly, lovingly; **2.** dearly, at a high price.

chéri, -e (ʃeri), p.adj. [f. *chérir*] Cherished, beloved, dear. ~, s.m.f. Darling.

chérif (ʃerif), s.m. [f. Arab. *sharif*] Shereef, cherif.

chérifat (ʃerifa), s.m. Shereefate.

chérimolier (ʃerimɔlje), s.m. [Peruvian orig.] (bot.) Cherimoya; Peruvian custard-apple.

chérir (ʃerir), v.a. [f. *cher*] To cherish, to love dearly, to idolize; ~ *son erreur*, to hug, to cling to, one's error; **se** ~, v.pr. **1.** to cherish each other; **2.** to idolize oneself.

chérissable (ʃerisabl), adj. Lovable, worth cherishing.

cherrer (ʃɛre), v.n. (slang) To fall, to tread, to trample; ~ *dans les bégonias*, to put one's foot in it; to exaggerate, to tell fibs.

cherté (ʃɛrte), s.f. [f. *cher*] Expensiveness, high price.

chérubin (ʃerybɛ̃), s.m. [f. Hebr. *cherubim*] Cherub.

chervis (ʃɛrvi), s.m. [form of *carvi*] (bot.) Skirret, water-parsnip.

chester (tʃɛstɛr), s.m. [English orig.] Cheshire cheese.

chéti-f, -ve (ʃetif), adj. [f. L *captivus*] Puny, thin, sickly, undeveloped, weak, mean-looking, wretched, paltry, unimportant, scanty.

chétivement (ʃetivmɑ̃), adv. Wretchedly, meanly, sorrily, thinly, poorly.

cheval (pl. **aux**) (ʃəval), s.m. [L *caballus*] Horse, nag, steed, horse-flesh; horse, cavalry; (gymn.) wooden horse; horse-power; ~ *de bataille*, war-horse, charger; ~ *de selle*, saddle-horse; ~ *de charrue*, draught-horse; ~ *pur sang*, thorough-bred horse; ~ *entier*, stallion; ~ *hongre*, gelding; *homme de* ~, horseman, rider; *c'est un vrai* ~ *échappé*, he is a wild youth; *c'est son grand* ~ *de bataille*, that is his main argument, or his hobby-horse; *monter sur ses grands chevaux*, to ride the high horse; *fièvre de* ~, violent fever; *une médecine de* ~, very violent medicine; *il est bon* ~ *de trompette*, he is not easily frightened, he keeps in good humour; *à* ~ *donné on ne regarde pas les dents*, one must not look a gift-horse in the mouth; ~ *de retour*, an old offender; *c'est un vrai* ~ *de travail!*, he is a regular glutton for work; *il avait 10,000 hommes de pied avec 2,000 chevaux*, he had 10,000 foot and 2,000 horse; ~ *à bascule*, rocking-horse, hobby-horse; *chevaux de frise*, chevaux de frise; ~*-fondu*, saddle-my-nag (game); *un moteur de cinq chevaux* (*5 C.V.*), a five-horse-power motor (5 h.p.). *A* ~, loc. adv. on horseback, astride, astraddle; *monter à* ~, to ride on horseback; *à* ~ *Messieurs!*, to horse, gentlemen!; *être à* ~ *sur un mur*, to sit astride on a wall; (fig.) *être à* ~ *sur*, to be all agog for; *il est à* ~ *sur l'étiquette*, he is a stickler for etiquette; *je lui ai écrit une lettre à* ~, I wrote him a severe letter (or a letter couched in very strong terms).

chevalement (ʃəvalmɑ̃), s.m. (build.) Bearing up, shoring up, underpinning.

chevaler (ʃəvale), v.a. [f. *cheval*] To prop, to shore up, to underpin.

chevaleresque (ʃəvalrɛsk), adj. Chivalrous, knightly, gallant.

chevaleresquement (ʃəvalrɛskmɑ̃), adv. Chivalrously, gallantly, in knightly fashion.

chevalerie (ʃəvalri), s.f. [f. *chevalier*] Chivalry, knighthood, nobility; *romans de* ~, romances of chivalry.

chevalet (ʃəvalɛ), s.m. [f. *cheval*] **1.** Horse (bench used by artisans); **2.** wooden horse (instrument of torture); **3.** easel, book-rest; **4.** bridge (of a stringed instrument); **5.** trestle.

chevalier[1] (ʃəvalje), s.m. [f. *cheval*] **1.** (in anc. Rome) Member of the equestrian order; **2.** knight, chevalier; *armer* ~, to knight (a person); ~ *errant*, knight-errant; *se faire le* ~ *de*, to take up the cause of; ~ *de la Légion d'Honneur*, knight of the Legion of Honour; ~ *d'industrie*, sharper, swindler, crook; **3.** cavalier, defender, protector, suitor.

chevalier[2] (ʃəvalje), s.m. (ornith.) Sandpiper, gambet, redshank.

chevalière (ʃəvaljɛr), s.f. **1.** A lady invested with an order of knighthood; **2.** signet-ring.

chevalin, -e (ʃəvalɛ̃), adj. Equine, pertaining to horses, of horseflesh.

chevance (ʃəvɑ̃s), s.f. [f. OF *chevir*] Goods and chattels, belongings.

chevauchée (ʃəvoʃe), s.f. **1.** Ride (on horseback); **2.** round of inspection (of certain functionaries); **3.** distance; **4.** raid, incursion.

chevauchement (ʃəvoʃmɑ̃), s.m. Overlapping; crossing.

chevaucher (ʃəvoʃe), v.n.a. [f. *cheval*] **1.** To ride on horseback; **2.** to overlap; **3.** to sit astride.

chevau-léger (ʃɛvoleʒe), s.m. (pl. *chevau-légers*). Light cavalry.

chevêche (ʃəvɛʃ), s.f. [OF *chevèce*] (ornith.) Sparrow-owl.

chevelu, -e (ʃəvly), adj. [f. *cheveu*] Long-haired, hairy, bearded, comose; *le cuir* ~, the scalp; *comète* ~*e*, bearded comet; *racine* ~*e*, bearded root. ~ s.m. Beard (of a root).

chevelure (ʃəvəlyr), s.f. [f. *cheveu*] **1.** Head of hair, hair, scalp; **2.** hair, coma of a comet.

chevet (ʃəvɛ), s.m. [f. L *capitium*] **1.** Bed's head; (fig.) bedside; *un livre de ~*, a bedside book; a favourite book; *elle reste à son ~*, she does not leave his bedside; **2.** bolster, pillow; **3.** (arch.) apse, apsis.

chevêtre (ʃəvɛtr), s.m. [L *capistrum*] Halter, chevaster, binding joist.

cheveu (pl. **-x**) (ʃəvø), s.m. [L *capillus*] Hair; (fig. colloq.) trouble, difficulty, hitch; *couper des ~x en quatre*, to split hairs; *~x bouclés*, curly hair; *sortir en ~x*, to go out without a hat, bareheaded; *se prendre aux ~x*, to come to blows; *saisir l'occasion aux ~x*, to take time by the forelock; *à faire dresser les ~x*, horrifying; enough to make one's hair stand on end; *tiré par les ~x*, far-fetched; (slang) *se faire des ~x*, to worry; *avoir mal aux ~x*, to have one's copper hot; *il y a un ~*, there is a hitch; there is a fly in the ointment.

chevillard (ʃəvijar), s.m. [f. *cheville*] Carcase-butcher, meat salesman.

cheville (ʃəvij), s.f. [f. L *clavicula*] **1.** Peg, wooden pin; *l'argent est la ~ ouvrière de tout*, money is the sinews of war; **2.** ankle; *il ne lui vient pas à la ~*, he does not reach up to his ankle, he is not fit to hold a candle to him; **3.** antler (of a stag); **4.** expletive, useless word (in poetry).

cheviller (ʃəvije), v.a. To peg, to pin, to bolt, to rivet; (fig.) to fill with expletives; *il a l'âme chevillée au corps*, he has as many lives as a cat.

chevillette (ʃəvijɛt), s.f. Small peg or pin, draw-bore; latch-pin.

cheviote (ʃəvjɔt), s.f. [f. Engl. *Cheviot*] Cheviot wool, cheviot.

chèvre (ʃɛvr), s.f. [L *capra*] **1.** Goat, she-goat, nanny-goat; *ménager la ~ et le chou*, to run with the hare and hunt with the hounds; *là où la ~ est attachée il faut qu'elle broute*, where the goat is tethered it must browse; *barbe de ~*, goatee, billy-goat beard; *prendre la ~*, to take offence; **2.** (astr.) Capella; **3.** (techn.) gin, sheers, derrick, crane, crab, lifting-jack.

chevreau (pl. **-x**) (ʃəvro), s.m. [f. *chèvre*] Kid; kid-leather.

chèvrefeuille (ʃɛvrəfœj), s.m. [L *caprifolium*] (bot.) Honeysuckle.

chèvre-pied (ʃɛvrəpje), s.m. Goat-footed faun, satyr; syn. FAUNE, SATYRE.

chevrette (ʃəvrɛt), s.f. **1.** Small she-goat; **2.** doe, roe; **3.** small fire-dog; **4.** prawn.

chevreuil (ʃəvrœj), s.m. [L *capreolus*] (zool.) Roebuck, roe; *quartier de ~*, haunch of venison.

chevri-er, -ère (ʃəvrje), s.m.f. Goatherd.

chevrillard (ʃəvrijar), s.m. (zool.) Fawn (of the roe).

chevron (ʃəvrɔ̃), s.m. [f. *chèvre*] **1.** (build.) Rafter, batten, coping; **2.** chevron; **3.** (mil.) stripe or band of lace worn by non-commissioned officers.

chevronnage (ʃəvrɔnaʒ), s.m. Raftering.

chevronné, -e (ʃəvrɔne), p. adj. (herald.) Chevroned; (fig.) experienced.

chevronner (ʃəvrɔne), v.a. **1.** To rafter; **2.** to chevron; **3.** to stripe.

chevrotant, -e (ʃəvrɔtɑ̃), p. adj. Tremulous, quavering, faltering (as the voice).

chevrotement (ʃəvrɔtmɑ̃), s.m. Tremulousness, quavering, shaking or faltering of the voice.

chevroter (ʃəvrɔte), v.n. [f. *chèvre*] **1.** To speak or sing in a tremulous voice; **2.** to kid.

chevrotin (ʃəvrɔtɛ̃), s.m. [f. *chèvre*] **1.** (zool.) Chevrotain, mouse-deer; **2.** kid-leather; **3.** fawn of the roe.

chevrotine (ʃəvrɔtin), s.f. Buck-shot.

chez (ʃe), prep. [f. L *casa*] At, in, into or to the house of; *~ X*, at X's; in the country of, among, with, in; *j'ai dîné ~ mon frère*, I have dined at my brother's; *loin de ~ moi*, far from home; *il vous faudra passer ~ lui*, you will have to call at his place; *ce qui se passait ~ les ennemis*, what was happening in the enemy's country; *~ les Grecs*, among the Greeks; *c'est ~ lui une habitude*, it's a habit of his.

chez-soi, chez-lui (ʃeswa, ʃelɥi), loc. s.m. invar. Home; *il est bon d'avoir un chez-soi*, it is good to have a home of one's own; *il n'y a pas de petit chez-soi*, home is home, be it never so homely.

chialer (ʃjale), v.n. (slang) To cry, to weep, to blub.

chianti (kjɑ̃nti), s.m. [It. wd] Chianti wine.

chiasse (ʃjas), s.f. [f. *chier*] **1.** Fly-speck, excrement of flies or worms; **2.** (fig.) trash, rubbish; **3.** scum (of metals); **4.** (pop.) diarrhoea.

chibouk, chibouque (ʃibuk), s.m. [Turk. wd] Chibouk.

chic (ʃik), s.m. invar. [f. *chicane*] Chic, trick, knack, skill, style, elegance; *il a le ~ pour faire cela*; he has a knack for doing that kind of thing; *quel ~ !*, what style !; *cette robe a beaucoup de ~*, this gown is very stylish; *de ~*, without a model, not copying reality. *~*, adj. invar. Smart, spruce, natty, zippy; dashing; (fig.) generous, decent, disinterested; *ce chapeau est très ~*, this hat is stylish; *ce n'est pas ~ d'agir ainsi*, it is not gentlemanly to do that; *c'est un ~ type*, he is a brick.

chica (ʃika). **1.** s.f. Spanish dance, chica; **2.** s.m. chica, chicha (colour, liquor).

chicane (ʃikan), s.f. [unkn. orig.] Chicane,

chicanery, pettifogging, quibbling, cavilling, groundless quarrel; (pej. fig.) *la* ~, lawyers, solicitors, advocates, &c., collectively; *soulever une* ~, to raise a quibble; *chercher* ~ *à X*, to pick a quarrel with X.

chicaner (ʃikane), v.a.n. To chicane, to pettifog, to prolong a contest with tricks, to cavil, to go to law with; to plague, to pester, to grudge.

chicanerie (ʃikanri), s.f. Chicanery, pettifogging, wrangling.

chicaneu-r, -se, chicani-er, -ère (ʃikanœr, ʃikanje), s.m.f. Chicaner, pettifogger, trickster. ~, adj. Chicaning, fault-finding, pettifogging.

chicard (ʃikar), s.m. (obs. slang) Swell. ~, adj. Swell, tip-top, slap-up.

chiche (ʃiʃ), adj. [unkn. orig.] Scanty, stingy, niggardly, chary, sparing; *être* ~ *de ses paroles*, to be sparing of words; *pois*-~, chick-pea; ~ *que tu ne fais pas cela!*, you dare!, just try it on!, I bet you don't!

chichement (ʃiʃmɑ̃), adv. Scantily, stingily, niggardly, parsimoniously.

chichi (ʃiʃi), s.m. [unkn. orig.] (colloq.) **1.** Fuss; *faire des* ~*s*, to make a fuss; **2.** affected ways, snobbishness; **3.** superfluous ornament; **4.** short curl of false hair.

chicon (ʃikɔ̃), s.m. (bot.) Cos lettuce.

chicorée (ʃikɔre), s.f. [f. L *cichorium*] **1.** Endive; chicory, wild succory; ⚠ usually *chicorée* = 'endive', and French *endive* = 'chicory'; **2.** chicory, the roasted and powdered root of this used in coffee-making.

chicot (ʃiko), s.m. [orig. unkn.] Stump of a tree; remains of a broken tooth; an old tooth, a stump.

chicoter (ʃikɔte), v.n. To wrangle about trifles.

chicotin (ʃikɔtɛ̃), s.m. [f. *socotrin*] **1.** Powder or juice of socotrine aloes; **2.** extract of colocynth or bitter apple.

chie-en-lit (ʃiɑ̃li), loc. s.m. Shrovetide mummer; jack pudding.

chien, -ne (ʃjɛ̃), s.m.f. [L *canis*] Dog, hound (the fem. 'bitch' is only used in English in vulgar abuse or when there is a particular reason for mentioning the sex of the animal); (fig.) cur, hound; ~ *de garde*, watch-dog; ~ *de chasse*, sporting dog; ~ *de meute*, hound; ~ *courant*, *lévrier*, greyhound; ~ *couchant*, setter; *une meute de* ~*s*, a pack of hounds; *lâcher les* ~*s*, to let the dogs loose; *haler les* ~*s*, to set the dogs on; *rompre les* ~*s*, (*a*) to call the dogs off; (*b*) (fig.) to interrupt a conversation on a dangerous subject; *faire le* ~ *couchant*, to cringe, to fawn; *jeter sa langue aux* ~*s*, to give up guessing; *entre* ~ *et loup*, at dusk; *mener une vie de* ~, to lead a dog's life; *je lui garde un* ~ *de ma* ~*ne*, I owe him a grudge; *on l'a reçu comme un* ~ *dans un jeu de quilles*, he was welcomed like a dog at a wedding; ~ *qui aboie ne mord pas*, barking dogs never bite; *ils sont comme* ~ *et chat*, they agree like cat and dog; *bon* ~ *chasse de race*, like father, like son; *quand on veut noyer son* ~ *on dit qu'il a la rage*, give a dog a bad name and hang him; *se regarder en* ~*s de faïence*, to look at one another like stuck pigs; *il n'attache pas ses* ~*s avec des saucisses*, he is a regular miser; *il fait un temps de* ~ (or *un* ~ *de temps*), it is wretched weather; *un* ~ *regarde bien un évêque*, a cat may look at a king; *ce qu'il y a de meilleur dans l'homme, c'est le* ~, the best points in man's character are those he shares with his dog; ~*ne de vie!*, what a rotten life!; ~ *de métier!*, wretched business!; *dormir couché en* ~ *de fusil*, to sleep lying in a crooked position; (iron.) *il n'est pas bon à jeter aux* ~*s*, (they say that) he is utterly worthless; *cela ne vaut pas les quatre fers d'un* ~, it is not worth a fig's end; ~ *de fusil*, trigger, cock; (colloq.) *piquer un* ~, to take a nap.

chiendent (ʃjɛ̃dɑ̃), s.m. [*chien*+*dent*] (bot.) Squitch, couch-grass, *Triticum repens*; (fig.) hitch; *voilà le* ~*!*, there 's the rub.

chienne (ʃjɛn), s.f. See CHIEN.

chienner (ʃjɛne), v.n. To pup; to litter, to whelp.

chier (ʃje), v.n. [f. L *cacare*] (low word) To shit, to void excrement.

chiffe (ʃif), s.f. [OF *chipe*, rag] Old rag, thin, worthless tissue; (fig.) worm; a person without character or will; *mou comme une* ~, as limp as a rag; a worm of a man.

chiffon (ʃifɔ̃), s.m. [f. *chiffe*] **1.** Rag, scrap (of paper); *marchand de* ~*s*, rag-dealer; ~ *de papier*, a worthless scrap of paper; **2.** silk muslin, chiffon; **3.** ~*s*, chiffons (pl.), dress, toilet, fashions; *parler* ~*s*, to talk of dresses, of fashions, &c.

chiffonnage (ʃifɔnaʒ), s.m. Crumpling, rumpling, tousling.

chiffonner (ʃifɔne), v.a. **1.** To crumple, to rumple, to crumple up; **2.** to ruffle (one's temper); *cela vous chiffonne*, that ruffles you; *un minois chiffonné*, irregular but agreeable features; **se** ~, v.pr. to crumple, to rumple, to get crumpled.

chiffonni-er, -ère (ʃifɔnje), s.m.f. **1.** Rag-picker, bone-grubber; **2.** (furniture) chiffonnier, tallboy.

chiffrage (ʃifraʒ), s.m. **1.** Writing in cipher; **2.** estimating, figuring; **3.** stamping (with monogram, coronet, &c.).

chiffre (ʃifr), s.m. [f. Arab. *ṣifr*] **1.** Figure, digit; *les dix* ~*s*, the ten digits; ~*s arabes*, Arabic figures; ~*s romains*,

Roman numerals; *~s connus*, plain figures; **2.** total, number; **3.** cipher; *écrire en ~*, to write in cipher; **4.** monogram.
chiffré, -e (ʃifre), p. adj. **1.** Figured, numbered; (mus.) *basse ~e*, figured bass; **2.** written in cipher; **3.** stamped with a monogram, initials, &c.
chiffrer (ʃifre), v.n.a. **1.** To number, to mark with a number; **2.** to value or express in figures; **3.** to figure (a bass); **4.** to mark, to stamp, engrave or embroider with a monogram; **5.** to cipher; *~ une dépêche*, to cipher a dispatch; **se ~** (*par*), v.pr. to amount (to).
chiffreu-r, -se (ʃifrœr), s.m.f. Cipherer, calculator, reckoner.
chignon (ʃiɲɔ̃), s.m. [f. *chaîne*] **1.** Chignon; *se crêper le ~*, to have a set-to, to fight, to pull each other by the hair, to make the fur fly; **2.** nape of the neck.
chilien, -ne (ʃiljɛ̃), adj. s.m.f. Chilian.
chimère (ʃimɛr), s.f. [Gr. *khimaira*] **1.** Chimera; **2.** idle fancy; absurd, impossible notion; *se forger des ~s*, to entertain illusions, to build castles in the air; **3.** (ichth.) chimera.
chimérique (ʃimerik), adj. **1.** Fond of chimeras, given to wild fancies; **2.** chimerical.
chimériquement (ʃimerikmɑ̃), adv. Chimerically.
chimie (ʃimi), s.f. [Gr. *khēmeia*] Chemistry.
chimique (ʃimik), adj. Chemical.
chimiquement (ʃimikmɑ̃), adv. Chemically.
chimiste (ʃimist), s.m.f. Chemist, person versed in chemistry. ⚠ 'Chemist', in the sense of dealer in medical drugs, must be translated by *pharmacien*, not by *chimiste*.
chimpanzé (ʃɛ̃pɑ̃ze), s.m. [f. Afric. dialects] (zool.) Chimpanzee.
chinage (ʃinaʒ), s.m. [f. *chiner*] Printing or colouring the warp of textile fabrics.
chinchilla (ʃɛ̃ʃilla), s.m. [Span. wd] **1.** Chinchilla (S. Amer. rodent); **2.** chinchilla fur; **3.** chinchilla colour.
chiné, -e (ʃine), p. adj. Chiné, variegated; clouded.
chiner (ʃine), v.a.n. [f. *Chine*, China] **1.** To weave with a warp of contrasting colour, to variegate; **2.** (slang), to dispute, to quarrel with, to annoy, to run down.
chinois, -e (ʃinwɑ), adj. s.m.f. **1.** Chinese; Chinaman, Chinese woman; **2.** (s.m. only) candied green orange.
chinoiserie (ʃinwazri), s.f. **1.** Chinese knick-knacks; **2.** complication, unnecessary difficulty, piece of folly; red tape.
chiot (ʃjo), s.m. [f. *chien*] Pup, puppy, whelp.
chiote (kjɔt), adj. s.m.f. Chiote (of Chios).
chiourme (ʃjurm), s.f. [f. It. *ciurma*] Crew of galley-slaves or convicts; *garde-~*, convict-warder.
chiper (ʃipe), v.a. [f. OF *chipe*] (pop.) To steal, to bag, to pilfer, to crib, to pinch.
chipeu-r, -se (ʃipœr), s.m.f. Petty thief. ~, adj. Given to pilfering.
chipie (ʃipi), s.f. (pop.) Shrew, disagreeable woman, quarrelsome person.
chipolata (ʃipɔlata), s.f. [f. It. *cipollata*] **1.** Cipollata, small sausage; **2.** (obs.) ragout with onions.
chipoter (ʃipɔte), v.a.n. (pop.) [f. OF *chipe*] **1.** To dally, to trifle, to nibble, to fiddle-faddle; **2.** to argue about trifles.
chipoti-er, -ère, chipoteu-r, -se (ʃipɔtje, ʃipɔtœr), s.m.f. **1.** Fiddle-faddler, dawdler; **2.** higgler.
chique (ʃik), s.f. [etym. dub.] **1.** Quid (of tobacco); **2.** (ent.) chigoe, *Pulex penetrans*, jigger.
chiqué (ʃike), s.m. (pop.) Imitation, sham; not the real, genuine article; *c'est du ~*, it 's a fake; it 's put on; it 's a fraud.
chiquenaude (ʃiknod), s.f. [orig. unkn.] Fillip, slight flick given with the middle finger.
chiquer (ʃike), v.n. To chew tobacco; *tabac à ~*, pig-tail tobacco, twist.
chiquet (ʃikɛ), s.m. Driblet, bit; *~ à ~*, little by little.
chiqueter (ʃikte), v.a. See DÉCHIQUETER.
chiqueur (ʃikœr), s.m. Tobacco-chewer.
chiragre (kiragr), s.f. [Gr. *kheiragra*] **1.** Gout in the hand; **2.** person having gout in the hand.
chirographaire (kirɔgrafɛr), adj. [f. Gr. *kheir+graphein*] Chirographic; *créancier ~*, creditor by simple contract, not by bond.
chiromancie (kirɔmɑ̃si), s.f. [f. Gr. *kheir+manteia*] Chiromancy, palmistry.
chiromancien, -ne (kirɔmɑ̃sjɛ̃), s.m.f. Chiromancer, palmist.
chiroptère (kirɔptɛr), s.m. See CHEIROPTÈRES.
chirurgical, -e, (aux) (ʃiryrʒikal), adj. Surgical.
chirurgie (ʃiryrʒi), s.f. [f. Gr. *kheir+ergon*] Surgery.
chirurgien, -ne (ʃiryrʒjɛ̃), s.m.f. Surgeon.
chiure (ʃjyr), s.f. [f. *chier*] Fly-speck.
chlamyde (klamid), s.f. [f. Gr. *khlamus*] Chlamys.
chloral (klɔral), s.m. (chem.) Chloral.
chlorate (klɔrat), s.m. (chem.) Chlorate.
chlore (klɔr), s.m. [Gr. *khlōros*] (chem.) Chlorine; *~ liquide*, bleaching-liquid.
chloré, -e (klɔre), adj. Chlorinated.
chloreu-x, -se (klɔrø), adj. (chem.) Chlorous.
chlorhydrate (klɔridrat), s.m. (chem.) Chloride, hydrochlorate, muriate.
chlorhydrique (klɔridrik), adj. Hydrochloric.
chlorique (klɔrik), adj. Chloric.

chlorite (klɔrit) s.m. Chlorite.
chloroforme (klɔrɔfɔrm), s.m. Chloroform.
chloroformer, chloroformiser (klɔrɔfɔrme, klɔrɔfɔrmize), v.a. To chloroform; to anaesthetize with chloroform.
chlorophylle (klɔrɔfil), s.f. [f. Gr. *khlōros* + *phullon*] (bot.) Chlorophyll.
chlorose (klɔroz), s.f. [f. Gr. *khlōros*] (pathol.) Chlorosis, green sickness.
chlorotique (klɔrɔtik), adj. Chlorotic.
chlorure (klɔryr), s.m. (chem.) Chloride, chloruret.
chloruré, -e (klɔryre), p. adj. (chem.) Chlorinated, impregnated with chlorine.
choc (ʃɔk), s.m. [f. *choquer*] Shock, collision, blow, impact; conflict, clash, onset, brunt of an encounter; *~ en retour*, return shock; kicking back; *soutenir le premier ~*, to bear the brunt, to stand the shock; *amortisseur de ~*, shock-absorber.
chocolat (ʃɔkɔla), s.m. [Mexic. *chocolatl*] Chocolate. ~, adj. Chocolate-coloured; (slang) *être ~*, to be taken in, done brown.
chocolatier (ʃɔkɔlatje), s.m. Chocolate dealer or manufacturer. ~, **-ère**, adj. Pertaining to the chocolate industry.
chocolatière (ʃɔkɔlatjɛr), s.f. Chocolate-pot.
choéphore (kɔefɔr), s.m.f. [f. Gr. *khoē* + *phoros*] Choëphoros, bearer of offerings to the dead in ancient Greece.
chœur (kœr), s.m. [Gr. *khoros*] **1.** Chorus; *chanter en ~*, to sing in chorus; **2.** choir; **3.** choir of a church; *enfant de ~*, choir-boy, chorister.
choir (ʃwar), v.n. def. [L *cadere*] To fall; *laisser ~*, to drop; *se laisser ~*, to fall.
choisi, -e (ʃwazi), p. adj. [f. *choisir*] Chosen, selected, select, choice; *une société ~e*, a select company.
choisir (ʃwazir), v.a. [Goth. *kausjan*] To choose, to pick out, to select, to single out; *il y a de quoi ~*, there is abundant choice; **se ~**, v.pr. (*a*) to choose each other; (*b*) to choose for oneself.
choix (ʃwɑ), s.m. [f. *choisir*] Choice, act of choosing, selection; power of choosing, option; person or thing chosen; best part of anything; collection to choose from; *le ~ de cet homme*, (*a*) the choice made of that man; (*b*) that man's choosing; (*c*) the thing chosen by him; *à son ~*, at one's choice or option; *des fruits de ~*, choicest fruit; *vous n'avez pas le ~*, you have no alternative.
cholagogue (kɔlagɔg), adj. [Gr. *kholagōgos*] (med.) Cholagogue, carrying off bile.
cholédoque (kɔledɔk), adj. [Gr. *kholēdochos*] (anat.) *Canal ~*, choledoch.
choléra (kɔlera), s.m. [L *cholera*] Cholera.
cholériforme (kɔlerifɔrm), adj. Choleriform.
cholérine (kɔlerin), s.f. Cholerine.
cholérique (kɔlerik), adj. Choleric, pertaining to cholera, affected with cholera.
cholestérine (kɔlɛsterin), s.f. (chem.) Cholesterin.
choliambe (kɔljɑ̃b), s.m. [f. Gr. *khōlos* + *iambos*] Choliamb, choliambic verse.
chômage (ʃomaʒ), s.m. [f. *chômer*] Stoppage, cessation of labour, unemployment; standing idle (of mills, &c.), dead season in industry; *il y a beaucoup de ~*, there is a great deal of unemployment; *indemnité de ~*, dole.
chômer (ʃome), v.n. [LL *caumare*] To cease from work, to be out of work, to stand still (as factories, &c.); v.a. *~ les saints*, to keep Saints' days.
chômeu-r, -se (ʃomœr), s.m.f. Unemployed person.
chondrologie (kɔ̃drɔlɔʒi), s.f. [f. Gr. *khondros* + *logos*] Chondrology, knowledge of the cartilages.
chope (ʃɔp), s.f. [f. Germ. *Schoppen*] **1.** Beer-glass; **2.** glass of beer.
choper (ʃɔpe), v.a. (slang) To pilfer, to pinch, to steal, to arrest, to nab; *se faire ~*, to let oneself be caught, to get nabbed.
chopin (ʃɔpɛ̃), s.m. (slang) **1.** Bit of luck; **2.** pigeon; love conquest; catch. ⚠ Not 'chopin' which = *chopine*.
chopine (ʃɔpin), s.f. Chopin (nearly one pint).
chopper (ʃɔpe), v.n. [f. OF *chope*] **1.** To stumble; **2.** to blunder; see ACHOPPER.
choquant, -e (ʃɔkɑ̃), p. adj. Shocking, offensive, disgusting, forbidding.
choquer (ʃɔke), v.a. [uncert. orig., prob. Germ.] **1.** To strike against, to collide with; **2.** to shock, to offend, to be offensive to, to clash with; **3.** (naut.) to surge, to slack up suddenly; **se ~**, v.pr. (*a*) to come into collision with each other; (*b*) to be shocked or offended; (*c*) to clash.
choral (pl. **-s**) (kɔral), s.m. [f. L *chorus*] (mus.) Choral. ~, adj. Choral.
chorée (kɔre), s.f. [f. Gr. *khoreia*] Chorea, St. Vitus's dance. ~, s.m. (pros.) Choree, trochee.
chorège (kɔrɛʒ), s.m. [f. Gr. *khorēgos*] Choragus, leader of the chorus.
chorégraphe (kɔregraf), s.m. [f. Gr. *khoreia* + *graphein*] Choreographer.
chorégraphie (kɔregrafi), s.f. Choreography; (*a*) art of dancing; (*b*) designing of ballets or dances.
chorégraphique (kɔregrafik), adj. Choreographic.
choréique (kɔreik), adj. Choreic.
choriambe (kɔrjɑ̃b), s.m. [Gr. *khoriambos*] (pros.) Choriambus (foot composed of a choree (or trochee) and an iambus).

chorion (kɔrjɔ̃), s.m. [Gr. *khorion*] (anat.) Chorion.
choriste (kɔrist), s.m.f. [f. L *chorista*] Chorist, chorister, chorus singer.
chorographe (kɔrograf), s.m. [f. Gr. *khōra*+*graphē*] Chorographer, geographer.
chorographie (kɔrografi), s.f. Chorography, description of a country.
chorographique (kɔrografik), adj. Chorographic, chorographical.
choroïde (kɔrɔid), s.f. adj. [Gr. *khorion*+*eidos*] (anat.) Choroid.
choroïdite (kɔrɔidit), s.f. (med.) Choroiditis.
chorus (kɔrys), s.m. [L *chorus*] Chorus; *faire* ~, to chorus, to chime in; (fig.) to chime in; to chorus approval.
chose (ʃoz), s.f. [f. L *causa*] Thing, whatever exists, object, act (opposed to person); goods, property; happenings, event, business, cause; *appeler les* ~*s par leur nom*, to call things by their names, to call a spade a spade; to speak plainly; *c'est la même* ~, it 's all one, it comes to the same thing; *chaque* ~ *en son temps*, there is a proper time for everything; all in good time; *mettre les* ~*s au pis*, to suppose the worst; *faire bien les* ~*s*, to do things well, to spend freely (when entertaining); *autre* ~ *est de parler, autre* ~ *d'agir*, it is one thing to talk and another to act; *quelque* ~ *que vous fassiez pour lui*, whatever you do for him; *peu de* ~, *pas grand'*~, it 's no great matter, it 's a trifling matter; *toutes* ~*s égales d'ailleurs*, other things being equal; *l'esclave était la* ~ *du maître*, the slave was the property of his master; *la* ~ *publique*, the common weal; *c'est* ~ *jugée*, that is a settled matter; *le cours des* ~*s*, (*a*) the course of Destiny; (*b*) the natural course of events; *juste retour des* ~*s d'ici-bas!*, the wheel has come full circle; *quelque* ~, something; *quelque* ~ *de beau*, something beautiful; *il y a quelque* ~ *comme un mois qu'il est parti*; it is about a month since he left; *être porté sur la* ~, to be very keen on the matter; *un* (or *une*) *pas-grand'chose*, a good-for-nothing, a bad woman. ~, adj. adv. M. ~ . . . *machin*, Mr. what-d'you-call-him; *il est tout* ~, he is out of sorts.
chott (ʃɔt), s.m. [Arab. wd] Chott, shott, salt lake in North Africa.
chou (pl. -x) (ʃu), s.m. [L *caulis*] **1.** Cabbage, cole, kale; ~*-pommé*, headed cabbage; ~*x de Bruxelles*, Brussels sprouts; ~*-rave*, kohlrabi; ~*-navet*, rutabaga, turnip-cabbage; ~*-fleur*, cauliflower; ~*-marin*, sea-kale; ~*-palmiste*, cabbage-tree; *trognon de* ~, cabbage-stump; *aller planter ses* ~*x*, to retire into the country; *on l'a envoyé planter ses* ~*x*, he has been rusticated; *faire ses* ~*x gras de*, to feast on; to feather one's nest with; *ménager la chèvre et le* ~, to run with the hare and hunt with the hounds; to hold with the hare and run with the hounds; *faire* ~ *blanc*, to miss one's stroke, to draw a blank; to fail; to come to nothing; *être dans les* ~*x*, to be in the soup, in the cart; to come to nothing; *bête comme* ~, (of a person) as stupid as an ox; (of a thing) easy for any fool to understand; **2.** (fig.) darling, duck, dear; **3.** bow, round bow of ribbon; **4.** (pastry) puff; **5.** (slang) *je vais lui rentrer dans le* ~, I'll pitch (or slip) into him.
chouan, -ne (ʃuɑ̃) s.m.f. **1.** (French hist.) Chouan, Royalist insurgent in Vendée during the Revolution; **2.** (pop.) (ornith.) long-eared owl.
chouannerie (ʃuanri) s.f. **1.** Guerilla, Chouannerie; **2.** party of the Chouans.
choucas (ʃukɑ), s.m. [f. OHG *chouch*] (ornith.) Jackdaw, crow; *Corvus monedual.*
chouchou (ʃuʃu), s.m.f. (pop.) Darling, favourite pupil or person.
choucroute (ʃukrut), s.f. [Germ. *Sauerkraut*] Sauerkraut.
chouette (ʃuɛt), s.f. [f. *choue*] (ornith.) Owl, screech-owl; *faire la* ~, to be one against two. ~, adj. interj. (pop.) Fine!, lucky!, pretty!, ripping!
chou-pille (ʃupij), loc. s.m. invar. Shooting-dog.
chouque, chouquet (ʃuk, ʃukɛ), s.m. [f. *souche*] (naut.) Cap of a mast-head.
chouriner (ʃurine), v.a. [var. of *suriner*] (slang) To knife, to murder.
chourineur (ʃurinœr), s.m. (slang) Murderous ruffian.
choyer (ʃwaje), v.a. [etym. dub.] To fondle, to nurse, to pet, to coddle, to take great care of.
chrême (krɛm), s.m. [Gr. *khrisma*] Chrism.
chrêmeau (pl. -x) (krɛmo), s.m. Chrism, chrisom-cloth.
chrestomathie (krɛstɔmati, krɛstɔmasi), s.f. [Gr. *khrēstomatheia*] Chrestomathy.
chrétien, -ne (kretjɛ̃), adj. Christian. ~, s.m.f. Christian; *en bon* ~, like a Christian; *Sa Majesté très* ~*ne*, His Most Christian Majesty; *bon* ~, a kind of pear.
chrétiennement (kretjɛnmɑ̃), adv. In a Christian manner.
chrétienté (kretjɛ̃te), s.f. Christendom (both the countries inhabited by Christians and the whole body of Christians).
chrisme (krism), s.m. Monogram of Jesus Christ, as seen on Christian monuments.
christ (krist), s.m. **1.** Christ; **2.** crucifix, cross with the figure of Christ upon it.
christe-marine, criste-marine (kristə-

marin), s.f. (bot.) Samphire, *Crithmum maritimum*; saltwort, *Salicornia herbacea*.
christianiser (kristjanize), v.a. To christianize.
christianisme (kristjanism), s.m. Christianity.
christologie (kristɔlɔʒi), s.f. [f. Gr. *Khristos*+*logos*] Christology.
chromate (kromat), s.m. [f. *chrome*] (chem.) Chromate.
chromatique (krɔmatik), adj. Chromatic. ~, s.f. (opt.) Chromatics.
chromatiquement (krɔmatikmɑ̃), adv. Chromatically.
chromatisme (krɔmatism), s.m. Chromatism.
chrome (krom), s.m. [f. Gr. *khrōma*] (chem.) Chrome, chromium.
chromé, -e (krome), p. adj. Containing chromium; *acier* ~, chrome steel; *cuir* ~, chrome leather.
chromique (kromik), adj. (chem.) Chromic.
chromolithographie, chromo (kromolitografi, kromo), s.f. Chromolithography, coloured lithography.
chromule (krɔmyl), s.f. (bot.) Chromule.
chronicité (krɔnisite), s.f. [f. *chronique*] Chronic character (of a disease).
chronique (krɔnik), s.f. [f. Gr. *khronos*] Chronicle, reports, history, review; *la* ~ *scandaleuse*, the tittle-tattle of the day.
chronique (krɔnik), adj. Chronic.
chroniquement (krɔnikmɑ̃), adv. Chronically.
chroniqueu-r, -se (krɔnikœr), s.m.f. **1.** Chronicler, historian; **2.** reporter, journalist, reviewer, critic.
chronogramme (krɔnɔgram), s.m. [f. Gr. *khronos*+*gramma*] Chronogram.
chronologie (krɔnɔlɔʒi), s.f. [f. Gr. *khronos*+*logos*] Chronology.
chronologique (krɔnɔlɔʒik), adj. Chronological.
chronologiquement (krɔnɔlɔʒikmɑ̃), adv. Chronologically.
chronologiste, chronologue (krɔnɔlɔʒist, krɔnɔlɔg), s.m. Chronologer, chronologist.
chronomètre (krɔnɔmɛtr), s.m. [f. Gr. *khronos*+*metron*] Chronometer; timekeeper, watch of superior construction.
chronométreur (krɔnɔmetrœr), s.m. Time-keeper (in sports, &c.).
chronométrie (krɔnɔmetri), s.f. Chronometry.
chronométrique (krɔnɔmetrik), adj. Chronometrical, pertaining to a chronometer.
chrysalide (krizalid), s.f. [f. Gr. *khrusallis*] Chrysalis, nymph, pupa.
chrysanthème (krizɑ̃tɛm), s.m. [f. Gr. *khrusos*+*anthemon*] (bot.) Chrysanthemum.
chryséléphantin, -e (krizelefɑ̃tɛ̃), adj. [f. Gr. *khrusos*+*elephas*] (sculpt.) Chryselephantine.
chryside (krizid), s.f. (ent.) Golden wasp; ruby-tailed fly.
chrysobéryl (krizoberil), s.m. [Gr. *khrusobērullos*] (min.) Chrysoberyl.
chrysocale (krizokal), s.m. [f. Gr. *khrusos* +*khalkos*] Pinchbeck; alloy of copper and zinc resembling gold.
chrysographie (krizografi), s.f. [f. Gr. *khrusos*+*graphein*] Chrysography; art of writing in gold letters.
chrysolithe (krizɔlit), s.f. [f. Gr. *khrusos*+*lithos*] (min.) Chrysolite.
chrysoprase (krizɔprɑz), s.f. [f. Gr. *khrusoprasos*] (min.) Chrysoprase, a green variety of chalcedony.
chrysostome (krizɔstom), adj. [f. Gr. *khrusos*+*stoma*] Chrysostom; (fig.) eloquent.
chu, -e (ʃy), p.p. [of *choir*] Fallen.
chuchotement (ʃyʃɔtmɑ̃), s.m. [f. *chuchoter*] Whispering, whisper.
chuchoter (ʃyʃɔte), v.n.a. [onom.] To whisper.
chuchoterie (ʃyʃɔtri), s.f. [f. *chuchoter*] Whispering, whispers.
chuchoteu-r, -se (ʃyʃɔtœr), adj. s.m.f. Whispering, whisperer.
chuintant, -e (ʃɥɛ̃tɑ̃), p. adj. [f. *chuinter*] (phon.) Sounding like *j* and *ch* in French, and like *sh* in English.
chuintement (ʃɥɛ̃tmɑ̃), s.m. See CHUINTANT.
chuinter (ʃɥɛ̃te), v.n. [onom.] See CHUINTANT.
chut (ʃyt), interj. s.m. [onom.] Hush!, silence!
chute (ʃyt), s.f. [f. *choir*] **1.** Fall, downfall, falling, descent, slope, declivity, waterfall, cascade, failure, failing, fall, sin; *faire une* ~, to have a fall; *la* ~ *des feuilles*, the fall of the leaf, the fall; *la* ~ *des dents*, the falling-out of the teeth; *les* ~*s du Zambèze*, the Zambezi Falls; *la* ~ *d'un empire*, the fall of an empire; *la* ~ *d'une tragédie*, the failure of a tragedy; *la* ~ *d'Adam*, Adam's sin or fall; **2.** (rhet.) end, conclusion, cadence, point of an epigram; **3.** (naut.) drop; **4.** (tailoring) small pieces of material put aside when cutting a garment.
chuter (ʃyte), v.n. [f. *chute*] To fall; ~, v.a. [f. *chut!*] to hiss (a play, an actor, &c.).
chyle (ʃil), s.m. [f. Gr. *khulos*] (physiol.) Chyle.
chylifère (ʃilifɛr), adj. [f. L *chylus*+*ferre*] Chyliferous.
chylification (ʃilifika′sjɔ̃), s.f. (physiol.) Chylifaction.
chyme (ʃim), s.m. [f. Gr. *khumos*] (physiol.) Chyme.
chymification (ʃimifika′sjɔ̃), s.f. Chymification.

chypriote, cypriote (ʃiprjɔt, siprjɔt), adj. s.m.f. Cyprian, of Cyprus.
ci (si), adv. [abbrev. of *ici*] Here; *~-gît*, here lies; *~-joint*, annexed; *~-inclus*, enclosed; *cet enfant-~*, this child; *à cette heure-~*, at this very hour, now; *~-après*, further on, below, hereafter; *~-contre*, opposite, in the margin; *~-dessus*, above, aforesaid; *~-dessous*, below, underneath, hereafter, hereunder; *~-devant*, formerly, heretofore; formerly. *Ci-devant*, s.m.f. invar. (French hist.) a noble; *de-~*, *de-là*, *par-~*, *par-là*, hither and thither; now and then.
cible (sibl), s.f. [f. Germ. *Scheibe*] Target; *tirer à la ~*, to shoot at a target.
ciboire (sibwar), s.m. [L *ciborium*] Ciborium, pyx.
ciboule (sibul), s.f. [f. L *caepulla*] (bot.) Cibol, chibol, Welsh onion, *Allium fistulosum*.
ciboulette (sibulɛt), s.f. (bot.) Chives (pl.), *Allium schoenoprasum*; syn. CIVETTE, CIVE.
ciboulot (sibulo), s.m. (slang) Nut, head, block.
cicatrice (sikatris), s.f. [L *cicatrix*] Scar, seam, cicatrice, cicatrix.
cicatriciel, -le (sikatrisjɛl), adj. Pertaining to a cicatrix.
cicatrisable (sikatrizabl), adj. Cicatrizable.
cicatrisant, -e (sikatrizɑ̃), p. adj. Cicatrizing.
cicatrisation (sikatriza'sjɔ̃), s.f. Cicatrization, healing, closing.
cicatriser (sikatrize), v.a. To cicatrize, to heal, to skin over, to scar; **se ~**, v.pr. to cicatrize, to heal, to close, to be skinning over.
cicéro (sisero), s.m. (print.) Pica.
cicerone (siseron), s.m. [It. wd] Cicerone, guide.
cicéronien, -ne (siserɔnjɛ̃), adj. Ciceronian, resembling Cicero in style.
cicindèle (sisɛ̃dɛl), s.f. [L *cicindela*] (ent.) Cicindela, tiger-beetle.
cicutaire (sikytɛr), s.f. [f. L *cicuta*] (bot.) Water-hemlock, *Cicuta virosa*.
cicutine (sikytin), s.f. (chem.) Cicutine (poison).
cid (sid), s.m. [Span. wd f. Arab. *sayyid*] Lord.
cidre (sidr), s.m. [f. L *sicera*] Cider.
cidrerie (sidrəri), s.f. Cider-mill, cider-manufactory, cider-making.
ciel (usual pl. **cieux**) (sjɛl, sjø), s.m. [L *caelum*] **1.** Heaven, heaven, God; sky, atmosphere, weather; *ce secours tombe du ~*, this help is a real godsend; *être au septième ~*, to be in the seventh heaven; to be filled with joy; *remuer ~ et terre*, to move heaven and earth, to leave no stone unturned; *aide-toi, le ~ t'aidera*, God helps those who help themselves; *le royaume des cieux*, the kingdom of Heaven; *~ !, O ~ !, juste ~ !*, Heavens !; *que le ~ m'en préserve !*, God forbid !; *grâce au ~*, Heaven be praised; *plût au ~ que*, would to God that; *bleu de ~*, sky-blue; **2.** climate; *un ~ tempéré*, a temperate climate; *sous d'autres cieux*, in other countries; **3.** canopy, tester, top; *à ~ ouvert*, open at the top; in the open; *~ de lit*, canopy; **4.** (paint.) sky. ⚠ The plural *ciels* is only used in: *ciels de lit*, *ciels de tableau*, *ciels de carrière*, and *ciels* = climates.
cierge (sjɛrʒ), s.m. [f. L *cereus*] **1.** Wax candle, taper; **2.** (bot.) cereus, torch-thistle.
cigale (sigal), s.f. [L *cicada*] (ent.) **1.** Great grasshopper, cicada; **2.** (naut.) ring of an anchor.
cigare (sigar), s.m. [Span. *cigarro*] Cigar; *fume-~* (s.m.), cigar-holder.
cigarette (sigarɛt), s.f. Cigarette; *porte-~s* (s.m.), cigarette-case; *fume-~* (s.m.), cigarette-holder.
cigarière (sigarjɛr), s.f. Cigarette- or cigar-maker.
cigogne (sigɔɲ), s.f. [L *ciconia*] (ornith.) Stork.
cigogneau (pl. **-x**) (sigɔɲo), s.m. Young stork.
ciguë (sigy), s.f. [L *cicuta*] (bot.) Hemlock, *Conium maculatum*, poison; *boire la ~*, to drink the hemlock; *petite ~*, fool's parsley.
cil (sil), s.m. [L *cilium*] **1.** Eyelash; **2.** (bot., zool.) cilia (pl.).
ciliaire (siljɛr), adj. Ciliary.
cilice (silis), s.m. [L *cilicium*] Haircloth, haircloth belt.
cilicien, -ne (silisjɛ̃), adj. s.m.f. Native of Cilicia, Cilician.
cilié, -e (silje), adj. Ciliated.
cillement (sijmɑ̃), s.m. [f. *cil*] Winking, wink, twinkling.
ciller (sije), v.a.n. **1.** To open and close the eyes, to wink, to blink; **2.** to seel, to blindfold (a wild hawk).
cimaise, cymaise (simɛz), s.f. [L *cymatium*] Cyma, cymatium, ogee.
cimbrique (sɛ̃brik), adj. Cimbric.
cime (sim), s.f. [L *cyma*] Top, summit, peak; (fig.) height, apogee, acme.
ciment (simɑ̃), s.m. [L *caementum*] Cement; (fig.) bond of union, cement; *~ hydraulique*, water cement, hydraulic cement.
cimenter (simɑ̃te), v.a. (lit. and fig.) To cement; **se ~**, v.pr. to be strengthened.
cimentier (simɑ̃tje), adj. s.m. Cement-maker, mason.
cimeterre (simtɛr), s.m. [It. *scimitarra*] Scimitar.
cimetière (simtjɛr), s.m. [L *cœmiterium*] Cemetery, burial-ground, graveyard, churchyard.

cimicaire (simikɛr), s.f. [f. L *cimex*] (bot.) Bugwort, cimifuga.
cimier (simje), s.m. [f. *cime*] **1.** Crest; **2.** (herald.) helmet; **3.** buttock of beef, haunch of venison.
cimmérien, -ne (simmerjɛ̃), adj. s.m.f. Cimmerian (of the country between the Borysthenes and the Tanais).
cinabre (sinabr), s.m. [L *cinnabaris*] Cinnabar, vermilion, red sulphide of mercury.
cinchonine (sɛ̃konin), s.f. (chem.) Cinchonine.
cinématique (sinematik), s.f. [f. Gr. *kīnēma*] (math.) Kinematics, kinetics.
cinématographe, cinéma, ciné (sinematɔgraf, sinema, sine), s.m. [f. Gr. *kīnēma* +*graphein*] Cinematograph, kinematograph, 'pictures'; (U.S.A.) movies; ~ *parlant*, talkies.
cinématographique (sinematɔgrafik), adj. Cinematographic.
cinéraire (sinerɛr), s.f. [f. L *cinis*] (bot.) Cineraria, fleawort. ~, adj. Cinerary.
cinération (sinera'sjɔ̃), s.f. Cineration.
cingalais, -e (sɛ̃galɛ), adj. s.m.f. Cingalese, of Ceylon.
cinglage (sɛ̃glaʒ), s.m. [f. *cingler*] (naut.) Ship's course; run in twenty-four hours; (metall.) shingling.
cinglant, -e (sɛ̃glɑ̃), p. adj. Cutting, stinging, scathing.
cingler[1] (sɛ̃gle), v.n. [f. Germ. *segeln*] (naut.) To sail, to steer.
cingler[2] (sɛ̃gle), v.a. [f. L *singulum*] **1.** To lash, to scourge, to switch, to cut, to whip; **2.** (metall.) to shingle.
cinname, cinnamone (sinam, sinamɔn), s.m. [L *cinnamum*] Cinnamon.
cinq (sɛ̃k), adj. num. [L *quinque*] Five; *Henri V*, Henry the Fifth; *chapitre V*, chapter five; *en ~ sec*, in a jiffy, rapidly. ~, s.m. **1.** symbol of five: 5, V; **2.** (games) cinque, five; **3.** (date) the fifth; **4.** *deux heures moins ~*, five minutes to two; (fig.) *il était moins ~*, it was just time, it was in the nick of time, it was a near thing.
cinquantaine (sɛ̃kɑ̃tɛn), s.f. **1.** A number of fifty or about fifty; **2.** the age of fifty; **3.** fiftieth year or anniversary.
cinquante (sɛ̃kɑ̃t), adj. num. [L *quinquaginta*] Fifty; fiftieth.
cinquantenaire (sɛ̃kɑ̃tnɛr), s.m. Fiftieth anniversary.
cinquantenier (sɛ̃kɑ̃tnje), s.m. (obs.) Captain of fifty men.
cinquantième (sɛ̃kɑ̃tjɛm), adj. num. ord. s.m.f. Fiftieth, the fiftieth.
cinquième (sɛ̃kjɛm), adj. num. ord. Fifth. ~, s.m. The fifth; *loger au ~*, to live on the fifth floor.
cinquièmement (sɛ̃kjɛmmɑ̃), adv. Fifthly, in the fifth place.
cintrage (sɛ̃traʒ), s.m. [f. *ceintrer, cintrer*] Arching, curving, bending.
cintre (sɛ̃tr), s.m. **1.** Arch, semi-circle, vaulted roof; **2.** (build.) a timber framework sustaining an arch while it is building; *plein-~*, semi-circular arch; ~ *surbaissé*, surbased arch.
cintré, -e (sɛ̃tre), p. adj. Arched, curved.
cintrer (sɛ̃tre), v.a. [var. of *ceintrer*] To curve, to arch.
cipaye (sipɛj), s.m. [Urdu *sipāhī*] Sepoy.
cipolin (sipɔlɛ̃), s.m. adj. m. [It. *cipollino*] Cipolin.
cippe (sip), s.m. [L *cippus*] Cippus.
cirage (siraʒ), s.m. [f. *cire*] **1.** Waxing; **2.** blacking: (*a*) the act of blacking shoes; (*b*) the composition for blacking shoes.
circaète (sirkaɛt), s.m. (ornith.) Harrier-eagle.
circassien, -ne (sirkasjɛ̃), adj. s.m.f. Circassian.
circassienne, s.f. A kind of cloth made of wool and cotton.
circée (sirse), s.f. (bot.) Enchanter's nightshade, *Circaea*.
circompolaire, circumpolaire (sirkɔ̃pɔlɛr), adj. Circumpolar.
circoncire (sirkɔ̃sir), v.a. [L *circumcidere*] To circumcise.
circoncis (sirkɔ̃si), p. adj. s.m. Circumcised.
circonférence (sirkɔ̃ferɑ̃s), s.f. [f. L *circum*+*ferre*] Circumference.
circonflexe (sirkɔ̃flɛks), adj. [f. L *circum* +*flectere*] Circumflex, crooked; *mettre un accent ~ à*, to circumflex, to mark with a circumflex accent.
circonlocution (sirkɔ̃lɔkysjɔ̃), s.f. [f. L *circum*+*locutus*] Circumlocution, periphrase.
circonscription (sirkɔ̃skripsjɔ̃), s.f. **1.** Circumscription, limitation; **2.** department, district, constituency; **3.** (geom.) circumscribing.
circonscrire (sirkɔ̃skrir), v.a. [f. L *circum* +*scribere*] **1.** To circumscribe, to encircle; **2.** to limit.
circonspect, -e (sirkɔ̃spɛkt), adj. [L *circumspectus*] Circumspect, cautious, wary, guarded, prudent.
circonspection (sirkɔ̃spɛksjɔ̃), s.f. Circumspection, caution, cautiousness, wariness; *parler avec ~*, to speak cautiously.
circonstance (sirkɔ̃stɑ̃s), s.f. [L *circumstantia*] **1.** Circumstance, occurrence, case, occasion, conjuncture; *profiter des ~s*, to improve the occasion; **2.** (law) adjuncts of a fact, which make it more or less criminal; *de ~*, suitable; composed or adapted for the occasion, required by circumstances; *~s atténuantes*, extenuating circumstances; **3.** (law) appurtenances.
circonstancié, -e (sirkɔ̃stɑ̃sje), p. adj. Minutely detailed.
circonstanciel, -le (sirkɔ̃stɑ̃sjɛl), adj.

Circumstantial, accidental, not essential, indirect; (gram.) circumstantial.
circonstancier (sirkɔ̃stɑ̃sje), v.a. To circumstantiate, to describe minutely, to state the circumstances of.
circonvallation (sirkɔ̃valla'sjɔ̃), s.f. [f. L *circumvallare*] (fort.) Circumvallation.
circonvenir (sirkɔ̃vnir), v.a. [f. L *circum* +*venire*] To circumvent, to surround, to impose upon, to overreach, to get round.
circonvoisin, -e (sirkɔ̃vwazɛ̃), adj. [L *circumvicinus*] Circumjacent, adjacent, surrounding.
circonvolution (sirkɔ̃vɔlysjɔ̃), s.f. [L *circum*+*volvere*] Circumvolution, convolution.
circuit (sirkɥi), s.m. [L *circuitus*] **1.** Circuit, circumference, circuitous road or itinerary; compass, winding, circumlocution; **2.** (in England) periodical journey of judges for holding courts; **3.** (electr.) circuit; *coupe-~*, fuse; cut-out; *mise en ~ de l'allumage*, switching on the ignition circuit; *court ~*, short circuit; *couper le ~*, to switch off the current.
circulaire (sirkylɛr), adj. [L *circularis*] Circular, round. ~, s.f. Circular.
circulairement (sirkylɛrmɑ̃), adv. Circularly.
circulant, -e (sirkylɑ̃), p. adj. Circulating, current, in circulation; *espèces ~es*, circulating money; specie.
circularité (sirkylarite), s.f. Circularity.
circulation (sirkyla'sjɔ̃), s.f. **1.** Circulation, motion in a circle, regular flow (as of blood); **2.** currency (of money); **3.** traffic, passing, movement; *livré à la ~*, opened for traffic, open to traffic.
circulatoire (sirkylatwar), adj. Circulatory.
circuler (sirkyle), v.n. [L *circulare*] To circulate, to move round, to flow in a circuitous channel, to pass, to move on, to have currency, to be diffused, spread; *faire ~*, to circulate, to spread, to hand round, to put into circulation, to make (somebody) move on.
circumduction (sirkɔmdyksjɔ̃), s.f. [L *circumductio*] Circumgyration.
circumnavigateur (sirkɔmnavigatœr), s.m. Circumnavigator.
circumnavigation (sirkɔmnaviga'sjɔ̃), s.f. Circumnavigation.
circumpolaire (sirkɔ̃pɔlɛr), adj. Circumpolar.
cire (sir), s.f. [L *cera*] **1.** Wax, bees-wax; *~ à cacheter*, sealing-wax; (fig.) *c'est une ~ molle*, he or she is a very tractable person, a character without strength; **2.** cerumen; **3.** statue or object made of wax.
ciré, -e (sire), p. adj. Waxed, rubbed or smeared with wax or blacking; *toile ~e*, oil-cloth. ~, s.m. Sailor's oilskins.
cirer (sire), v.a. **1.** To wax, to smear or rub with wax, to polish; **2.** to black and clean shoes, boots, &c.
cireu-r, -se (sirœr), s.m. Boot-cleaner; **~se**, s.f. Machine for waxing floors.
cireu-x, -se (sirø), adj. Waxy, like wax; *pâleur ~se*, waxy or deadly paleness.
ciri-er, -ère (sirje), adj. Wax-making. ~, s.m. **1.** Wax-chandler; **2.** (bot.) wax-myrtle, *Myrica cerifera*.
ciron (sirɔ̃), s.m. [f. OHG *siuro*] (ent.) Mite, siro.
cirque (sirk), s.m. [f. L *circus*] Circus.
cirre, cirrhe (sir), s.m. (bot.) Cirrus, tendril.
cirrhose (siroz), s.f. [f. Gr. *kirrhos*] (pathol.) Cirrhosis.
cirripèdes (siripɛd), s.m.pl. [f. L *cirrus*+*pedis*] Cirripeds, bristle-footed animals (as barnacles).
cirrus (sirys), s.m. [L wd] (meteor.) Cirrus; *cirro-cumulus*, cirro-cumulus.
cirse (sirs), s.m. (bot.) Thistle, horse-thistle.
cirure (siryr), s.f. Preparation of wax.
cis (si, sis, siz), pref. [L wd] Cis, on this side of.
cisaille (sizɑj), s.f. [f. *ciseau*] **1.** Shears; **2.** parings (of metal).
cisailler (sizɑje), v.a. To clip, to cut off.
cisalpin, -e (sizalpɛ̃), adj. [see CIS] Cisalpine.
ciseau (pl. **-x**) (sizo), s.m. [LL *cisellus*] Chisel.
ciseaux (sizo), s.m.pl. Scissors; small shears.
ciseler (sizle), v.a. To chase, to chisel, to engrave, to carve.
ciselet (sizlɛ), s.m. Chasing-tool, small chisel, paring-tool.
ciseleur (sizlœr), s.m. Chaser, sculptor, carver.
ciselure (sizlyr), s.f. Chasing, chiselled work.
cisjuran, -e (sisʒyrɑ̃), adj. Cisjurane (on this side of the Jura).
cisleithan, -e (sislɛitɑ̃), adj. Cisleithan (on this side of the river Leitha).
cisoires (sizwar), s.f.pl. Bench-shears.
cispadan, -e (sispadɑ̃), adj. Cispadane.
ciste (sist), s.m. [Gr. *kistos*] (bot.) Cistus, rock-rose. ~ s.f. Cist, a basket used in the Eleusinian mysteries.
cistercien, -ne (sistɛrsjɛ̃), adj. [f. *Citeaux*, L *Cistercium*, near Dijon] Cistercian.
citadelle (sitadɛl), s.f. [f. It. *cittadella*] Citadel, fortress.
citadin, -e (sitadɛ̃), s.m.f. [f. It. *città*] Citizen, inhabitant of a town. **~e**, (obs.) s.f. Fly, hackney coach.
citat-eur, -rice (sitatœr), s.m.f. Quoter, citer.
citation (sita'sjɔ̃), s.f. [L *citatio*] **1.** (law) Summons, subpoena; *lancer une ~*, to

issue a summons; **2.** quotation; *faire une* ~ *de*, to quote from; **3.** mention.
cité (site), s.f. [L *civitas*] City, town; central and oldest part of a town; *droit de* ~, freedom of the city; *la* ~ *céleste*, the celestial city, Heaven; ~ *ouvrière*, group of working men's cottages.
citer (site), v.a. [L *citare*] **1.** To cite, to summon; ~ *à comparaître*, to summon to appear; ~ *un témoin*, to summon a witness; **2.** to quote, to mention; ~ *son auteur*, to name one's author; ~ *une phrase*, to quote a sentence; **3.** to mention as deserving attention; *cité pour sa bravoure*, mentioned for his gallant conduct.
citérieur, -e (siterjœr), adj. [L *citerior*] Hither, hithermost.
citerne (sitɛrn), s.f. [L *cisterna*] Cistern, tank; *bateau-*~, tank-vessel, tanker.
citerneau (pl. **-x**) (sitɛrno), s.m. Small cistern.
cithare (sitar), s.f. [Gr. *kithara*] Cithara, cithern, cittern, zither, zittar.
cithariste, citharède (sitarist, sitarɛd), s.m.f. Citharist.
citoyen, -ne (sitwajɛ̃), s.m.f. [f. *cité*] Citizen, citizeness, freeman, denizen, inhabitant, fellow.
citrate (sitrat), s.m. [f. L *citrus*] (chem.) Citrate.
citrin, -e (sitrɛ̃), adj. Citrine, lemon-coloured. ~, s.f. Oil of lemons.
citrique (sitrik), adj. (chem.) Citric.
citron (sitrɔ̃), s.m. [L *citrus*] Lemon; ⚠ not 'citron' which = *cédrat*; *écorce de* ~, lemon-peel; ~ *pressé*, lemon squash. ~, adj. Lemon-coloured.
citronnade (sitrɔnad), s.f. Lemon squash.
citronné, -e (sitrɔne), adj. Lemon-flavoured.
citronnelle (sitrɔnɛl), s.f. **1.** Citron-water; **2.** (bot.) southernwood, *Artemisia abrotanum*; balm, *Melissa officinalis*.
citronnier (sitrɔnje), s.m. **1.** (bot.) Citrus, citron-tree, lime-tree, lemon-tree; **2.** lemon-wood, citron-wood, &c.
citrouille (sitruj), s.f. [f. L *citrullus*] Pumpkin, *Cucurbita pepo*.
civadière (sivadjɛr), s.f. [It. *civadiera*] (naut.) Sprit-sail.
cive, civette (siv, sivɛt), s.f. [f. L *caepa*] (bot.) Chives, *Allium schoenoprasum*; syn. CIBOULETTE.
civet (sivɛ), s.m. [etym. dub.] (cook.) Jugged hare; jugged rabbit; *mettre en* ~, to jug.
civette (sivɛt), s.f. **1.** (zool.) Civet-cat; civet; **2.** see CIVE.
civière (sivjɛr), s.f. [etym. dub.] **1.** Stretcher, litter; **2.** (naut.) sling.
civil, -e (sivil), adj. [f. L *civis*] **1.** Civil, (*a*) opposed to military; (*b*) opposed to ecclesiastical; lay, civil; *liste* ~, civil list; *actes d'état-*~, authentic documents referring to one's civil condition; *Officier d'État-*~, Registrar; *Droit* ~, Civil Law; *mariage* ~, civil marriage; *en* ~, in plain clothes; in mufti; **2.** civil, courteous, polite, obliging. ~, s.m. **1.** Civilian; **2.** private life.
civilement (sivilmɑ̃), adv. Civilly, politely; ~ *responsable* (*de*), legally responsible (for).
civilisable (sivilizabl), adj. Civilizable.
civilisat-eur, -rice (sivilizatœr), adj. Civilizing. ~, s.m.f. Civilizer.
civilisation (siviliza'sjɔ̃), s.f. Civilization.
civiliser (sivilize), v.a. To civilize; **se** ~, v.pr. to become civilized; (fig.) to soften down.
civilité (sivilite), s.f. Civility, courtesy, politeness; (pl.) acts of civility, attentions, compliments, greetings; *la* ~ *puérile et honnête*, rules of good manners, the child's book of courtesy.
civique (sivik), adj. [L *civicus*] Civic.
civisme (sivism), s.m. Civism.
clabaud (klabo), s.m. [f. Germ. *klaffen*] **1.** Noisy hound, with flapping ears; **2.** babbler, bawler. ~, adj. m. Noisy, bawling.
clabaudage (klabodaʒ), s.m. **1.** Barking; **2.** backbiting, slander; **3.** brawling.
clabauder (klabode), v.n. **1.** To give tongue without cause, to bark furiously; **2.** to babble, to slander, to back-bite.
clabauderie (klabodri), s.f. See CLABAUDAGE **2.**
clabaudeu-r, -se (klabodœr), s.m.f. Brawler, clamourer; backbiter, scandal-monger.
claie (klɛ), s.f. [f. LL *cleta*] **1.** Large tray of wicker-work; **2.** hurdle; **3.** fishing-net; **4.** eel-pot; **5.** screen (for sifting sand); (fig.) *traîner sur la* ~, to vilify, to cry down.
clair, -e (klɛr), adj. [L *clarus*] Light, bright, luminous, clear, pale, whitish, polished, clear, transparent, pellucid, pure, limpid, thin, sparse; (fig.) plain, clear, obvious, manifest, available; *bleu* ~, light blue; *des armes* ~*es*, polished weapons; *sauce trop* ~*e*, too thin sauce; *œuf* ~, addled egg; *des vitres* ~*es*, transparent windows; *temps* ~, fair weather; *voix* ~*e*, sharp and clear voice; *argent* ~, available funds.
clair (klɛr), s.m. **1.** Light, shine; ~ *de lune*, moonshine; **2.** (paint.) (pl.) the lights, the illuminated parts of a picture; **3.** what is clear, evident; *le plus* ~ *de sa fortune*, the best part of his fortune; *tirer quelque chose au* ~, to unravel or clear up a matter, to find out how the matter stands, to sift (evidence, facts).
clair, clairement (klɛr, klɛrmɑ), adv. Clearly, distinctly, plainly; (fig.) *maintenant j'y vois* ~, now I understand it; (fig.)

je n'y vois pas ~, I can't make it out; *parler* ~ *et net*, to speak out plainly.
clairet, -te (klɛrɛ), adj. Light, pale-coloured, thin. ~, s.m. Light wine; (jewellery) pale stone.
claire-voie (klɛrvwɑ), s.f. Opening, lattice, sky-light (of a ship); *caisse à* ~, crate; *à* ~, open, latticed.
clairière (klɛrjɛr), s.f. [f. *clair*] Glade.
clair-obscur (klɛrɔbskyr), s.m. (pl. *clairs-obscurs*) (paint.) Clair-obscure, chiaroscuro.
clairon (klɛrɔ̃), s.m. [f. *clair*] **1.** Bugle, clarion; **2.** bugler.
claironner (klɛrɔne), v.a. To trumpet; (fig.) to trumpet, to proclaim.
clairsemé, -e (klɛrsəme), adj. Thin sown; thin, thinned, thinly-scattered, scarce.
clairvoyance (klɛrvwajɑ̃s), s.f. [f. *clair*+*voir*] **1.** Clear-sightedness, perspicacity; **2.** clairvoyance.
clairvoyant, -e (klɛrvwajɑ̃), adj. **1.** Clear-sighted; perspicacious; **2.** clairvoyant.
clamecer (klamse), v.n. (slang) To go west, to kick the bucket, to die, to peg out.
clamer (klame), v.a. [L *clamare*] To bawl out, to shout, to clamour; to trumpet.
clameur (klamœr), s.f. [L *clamor*] Outcry, clamour, vociferation.
clampin, -e (klɑ̃pɛ̃), s.m.f. Loiterer, idler, straggler.
clampiner (klɑ̃pine), v.n. To lag, to loiter, to straggle.
clan (klɑ̃), s.m. [Gael. *clann*] Clan, tribe.
clandestin, -e (klɑ̃dɛstɛ̃), adj. [L *clandestinus*] Clandestine, underhand, secret.
clandestinement (klɑ̃dɛstinmɑ̃), adv. Clandestinely, secretly.
clandestinité (klɑ̃dɛstinite), s.f. Clandestineness, clandestinity; secrecy.
clapet (klapɛ), s.m. [f. Germ. *klappen*] (hydraul.) Valve, clack-valve, valve flap.
clapier (klapje), s.m. [f. Germ. *klappen*] Rabbit-hutch, rabbit-burrow.
clapir (klapir), v.n. To squeak, to cry (as rabbits); **se** ~, v.pr. to squat (as a rabbit).
clapotage, clapotement, clapotis (klapɔtaʒ, klapɔtmɑ̃, klapɔti), s.m. [f. *clapoter*] Plash, plashing, splashing, swashing; (naut.) rippling.
clapoter (klapɔte), v.n. [f. Germ. *klappen*] To plash, to ripple; to play with water.
clapoteu-x, -se, clapotant, -e (klapɔtø, klapɔtɑ̃), adj. Rippling, chopping, choppy (sea.)
clapotis (klapɔti), s.m. See CLAPOTAGE.
clappement (klapmɑ̃), s.m. Smacking (of the tongue); chucking.
clapper (klape), v.n. [f. Germ. *klappen*] To smack, to clack, to chuck.
claque[1] (klak), s.f. **1.** Slap, smack, spank; **2.** clog, overshoe; **3.** (theatr.) claque; hired applauders; **4.** *partir avec ses cliques et ses* ~*s*, to clear out bag and baggage.
claque[2] (klak), s.m. **1.** Opera hat; **2.** (slang) low gambling-house, brothel.
claquedent, claquefaim (klakdɑ̃, klakfɛ̃), s.m. (pop.) Starveling, beggar.
claquement (klakmɑ̃), s.m. [f. *claquer*] Clap, clapping, crack, cracking (of a whip); snap, chattering (of the teeth).
claquemurer (klakmyre), v.a.n. [*claquer* +*murer*] To shut up, to confine, to immure; **se** ~, v.pr. to shut oneself up.
claquer (klake), v.n.a. [imit.] To crack, to clap, to clack, to smack; (slang) to die, to kick the bucket, to pop off, to snuff it; ~ *des dents*, to chatter; *faire* ~ *un fouet*, to crack a whip; ~ *des mains*, to clap the hands; (pop.) *il s'en fera* ~, he will kill himself (with overwork, or overfeeding, &c.); *il part en claquant les portes*, he is going in high dudgeon (slamming the door).
claquet (klakɛ), s.m. Clack (of a mill-hopper).
claquette (klakɛt), s.f. Clapper, rattle, gossip.
claqueur (klakœr), s.m. Hired applauder.
clarification (klarifika'sjɔ̃), s.f. Clarification.
clarifier (klarifje), v.a. [L *clarificare*] To clarify, to clear, to purify, to refine, to fine; **se** ~, v.pr. to clear up, to grow clear, to become pure, to settle.
clarine (klarin), s.f. [f. *clair*] Little cow-bell, sheep-bell.
clarinette (klarinɛt), s.f. [f. *clair*] **1.** Clarinet, clarionet; **2.** clarinettist.
clarisse (klaris), s.f. [f. *Ste Claire*] Clarisse (nun), Clare.
clarté (klarte), s.f. [L *claritas*] **1.** Light, brilliance, brightness; **2.** clearness, transparency, limpidity, thinness; **3.** (fig.) enlightenment, knowledge, notions, distinctness, obviousness; *avoir de la* ~ *dans les idées*, to be clear-minded; *avoir des* ~*s de tout*, to have a general education, to be well informed about every thing without being a specialist.
classe (klɑs), s.f. [f. L *classis*] **1.** Class, order, rank, division, category; **2.** (nat. hist., math., &c.) class (containing the subordinate divisions of order, genus, and species); **3.** class, form, school-room, class-room, school-time; *rentrée des* ~*s*, reopening of schools; **4.** (mil.) enrolment, recruitment (of a certain year); *il est de la* ~ *1930*; he belongs to the 1930 contingent; *il est de la* ~, he is among the next to be sent home.
classement (klɑsmɑ̃), s.m. Classing, classification, filing.
classer (klɑse), v.a. To class, to classify, to rank; to file; **se** ~, v.pr. to be classed, to be ranked.

classeur (klasœr), s.m. **1.** Portfolio with compartments, rack, sorter; **2.** chest of drawers used for classifying papers and manuscripts; letter-file; **3.** person who does classifying; classer.
classicisme (klasisism), s.m. Classicism.
classificat-eur, -rice (klasifikatœr), s.m.f. Classifier. ~, adj. Classificatory.
classification (klasifika'sjɔ̃), s.f. Classification.
classifier (klasifje), v.a. To classify.
classique (klasik), adj. [L *classicus*] Classic, classical. ~, s.m. Classic; classicism.
clastique (klastik), adj. [f. Gr. *klastos*] (geol., anat.) Clastic.
clatir (klatir), v.n. (hunt.) To blab (of dogs).
claudicant, -e (klodikɑ̃), p. adj. [f. L *claudicare*] Limping, lame.
claudication (klodika'sjɔ̃), s.f. [L *claudicatio*] Lameness, limping.
clause (kloz), s.f. [L *clausa*] Clause, stipulation, proviso.
claustral, -e, (aux) (klostral), adj. [f. L *claustrum*] Claustral, monastic, relating to a cloister.
claustration (klostra'sjɔ̃), s.f. Claustration, cloistering, confinement.
claustrer (klostre), v.a. To cloister, to confine; **se** ~, v.pr. to confine oneself.
clavaire (klavɛr), s.f. (bot.) Clavaria, club-shaped fungus.
claveau (pl. **-x**) (klavo), s.m. [L *clavus*] **1.** (arch.) Keystone; **2.** sheep-pox; see CLAVELÉE.
clavecin (klavsɛ̃), s.m. [f. LL *clavicymbalum*] Harpsichord.
claveciniste (klavsinist), s.m.f. Harpsichordist.
clavelé, -e (klavle), adj. (vet.) Infected with the sheep-pox.
clavelée (klavle), s.f. (vet.) Sheep-pox, scab-rot.
clavette (klavɛt), s.f. [f. L *clavus*] Key, peg, pin, linch-pin, cotter, forelock; *mortaise de* ~, key-way.
claviculaire (klavikylɛr), adj. Clavicular.
clavicule (klavikyl), s.f. [L *clavicula*] (anat.) Clavicle, collar-bone.
clavier (klavje), s.m. [f. L *clavis*] **1.** Keyboard, finger-board, clavier; **2.** key-chain, key-ring.
clayère (klɛjɛr), s.f. [f. *claie*] Oyster-bed, oyster-farm.
claymore (klɛmɔr), s.f. [Scotch wd] Claymore.
clayon (klɛjɔ̃), s.m. [f. *claie*] **1.** Wicker stand or tray; cheese-drainer; **2.** small hurdle; **3.** wattle.
clayonnage (klɛjɔnaʒ), s.m. Wattling, wicker-work.
clayonner (klɛjɔne), v.a. To wattle, to fence.
clé, clef (kle), s.f. [L *clavis*] Key; (fig.) clue, index; (techn.) spanner, wrench, screw-key; (naut.) chock, fid, hitch; *fermer à* ~, to lock; *prendre la* ~ *des champs*, to scamper away; *tenir sous* ~, to keep under lock and key; (mus.) *la* ~ *d'ut*, the C key-note; ~ *anglaise*, screw-wrench; ~*s de meute*, leading dogs; ~*-de-voûte*, keystone; *trousseau de* ~*s*, bunch of keys; (fig.) *mettre la* ~ *sous la porte*, to remove from a house without paying the rent.
clebs (klɛbs), s.m. (slang) Dog.
clématite (klematit), s.f. (bot.) Clematis.
clémence (klemɑ̃s), s.f. [L *clementia*] Clemency, mercy, leniency.
clément, -e (klemɑ̃), adj. Clement, merciful.
clémentines (klemɑ̃tin), s.f.pl. (hist.) Clementines (constitutions collected by Pope Clement V).
clenche, clenchette (klɑ̃ʃ, klɑ̃ʃɛt), s.f. [f. Germ. *Klinke*] Thumb-bit (of a latch), lift.
clephte (klɛft), s.m. Klepht (Greek mountaineer).
clepsydre (klɛpsidr), s.f. [Gr. *klepsudra*] Clepsydra, water-clock.
cleptomane (klɛptoman), s.m.f. Kleptomaniac.
cleptomanie (klɛptomani), s.f. [f. Gr. *kleptein*+*mania*] Kleptomania.
clerc (klɛr), s.m. [f. L *clericus*] **1.** Clerk, articled clerk; **2.** scholar; **3.** clergyman; *un pas-de-*~, a blunder.
clergé (klɛrʒe), s.m. Clergy; ~ *séculier*, secular clergy; ~ *régulier*, regular clergy.
clergie (klɛrʒi) (obs.), s.f. Scholarship, learning.
clérical, -e, (aux) (klerikal), adj. [L *clericalis*] **1.** Clerical; **2.** favouring the clergy. ~, s.m. Clerical.
cléricalement (klerikalmɑ̃), adv. Clerically.
cléricalisme (klerikalism), s.m. Clericalism; excessive influence or power of the clergy.
cléricature (klerikatyr), s.f. Holy orders, priesthood.
clic (klik), interj., s.m. Click; ~*-clac*, crack of a whip.
clichage (kliʃaʒ), s.m. [f. *clicher*] Stereotyping, casting.
cliché (kliʃe), s.m. **1.** Stereotype-plate; **2.** (phot.) negative; **3.** (fig.) stereotyped phrase, worn-out expression, tag.
clicher (kliʃe), v.a. [f. OF *cliquer*] To stereotype, to cast.
clicherie (kliʃri), s.f. Stereotypery, stereotype foundry.
clicheur (kliʃœr), s.m. Stereotyper, stereotype-founder.
client, -e (klijɑ̃), s.m.f. [f. L *cliens, clientis*] **1.** Client, person protected by a patron, dependant; **2.** customer,

patient, client; *un drôle de* ~, a queer customer.
clientèle (klijɑ̃tɛl), s.f. [L *clientela*] **1.** (ant.) Clients, clientage; **2.** clients, clientele, practice (of a lawyer or physician); **3.** business, custom, goodwill, connexion.
clifoire (klifwar), s.f. Wooden squirt (toy).
clignement (kliɲmɑ̃), s.m. [f. *cligner*] Wink, winking, blinking.
cligne-musette (kliɲmyzɛt), s.f. Hide-and-seek (game).
cligner (kliɲe), v.a.n. [f. LL *clinare*] To wink, to blink; ~ *de l'œil*, to wink.
clignotant, -e (kliɲɔtɑ̃), p. adj. **1.** Winking, twinkling, blinking; **2.** (zool.) nictitating.
clignotement (kliɲɔtmɑ̃), s.m. Winking, blinking, twinkling, nictitation, nictation.
clignoter (kliɲɔte), v.a.n. To wink, to blink, to twinkle, to nictitate, to nictate.
climat (klima), s.m. [Gr. *klima*] **1.** Climate, clime; **2.** region.
climatérique (klimaterik), adj. Climacteric.
climatique (klimatik), adj. (meteor.) Climatic.
climatologie (klimatɔlɔʒi), s.f. [f. Gr. *klima*+*logos*] Climatology.
climatologique (klimatɔlɔʒik), adj. Climatological.
clin (klɛ̃), s.m. [f. *cligner*] Wink, twinkling of an eye; *en un* ~ *d'œil*, in a trice.
clinfoc (klɛ̃fɔk), s.m. [Scand. orig.] (naut.) Flying jib.
clinicien, -ne (klinisjɛ̃), s.m.f. adj. Clinical (physician or surgeon).
clinique (klinik), adj. s.f. [f. Gr. *klinē*] Clinic, clinical.
clinomètre (klinɔmɛtr), s.m. **1.** Clinometer; **2.** batter-rule.
clinquant (klɛ̃kɑ̃), s.m. [etym. dub.] **1.** Tinsel; **2.** false glitter; anything shining with false lustre. ~, adj. Gaudy, showy, cheaply splendid.
clipper (klipœr), s.m. [Engl. wd] Clipper.
cliquart (klikar), s.m. Building-stone.
clique (klik), s.f. [f. OF *cliquer*] **1.** Clique, clan, set, coterie; **2.** clog; (fig.) *prendre ses* ~*s et ses claques*, to clear out, bag and baggage.
cliquet (klikɛ), s.m. (techn.) Click; clicket (of a mill); catch, pawl; sprag.
cliqueter (klikte), v.n. To clack, to clash, to click, to jingle.
cliquetis (klikti), s.m. [f. *cliqueter*] Clank, clang, jingle, jingling, click, clicking.
cliquette (klikɛt), s.f. Snap, snappers, clappers, bones.
clissage (klisaʒ), s.m. Covering with wicker-work.
clisse (klis), s.f. Cheese-drainer, wicker-mat.
clisser (klise), v.a. To wicker, to cover with wicker-work.
clitoris (klitɔris), s.m. [Gr. wd] (anat.) Clitoris.
clivage (klivaʒ), s.m. [f. *cliver*] Cleavage.
cliver (klive), v.a. [f. Germ. *klieben*] To cleave.
cloaque (klɔak), s.m. [L *cloaca*] **1.** Cloaca, sewer, sink; filthy hole; **2.** (anat.) cloaca.
cloche (klɔʃ), s.f. [LL *clocca*] Bell; cover, bell-glass; (chem.) receiver (for gas); (med.) blister; (naut.) rundle; bell-shaped stew-pan; *qui n'entend qu'une* ~ *n'entend qu'un son*, one tale is good till another is told; (fig.) *déménager à la* ~ *de bois*, to shoot the moon; ~ *à plongeur*, diving-bell.
clochement (klɔʃmɑ̃), s.m. [f. *clocher*] Halting, limping, limp, hobble.
cloche-pied (à) (aklɔʃpje), adv. loc. Hopping; *sauter à* ~, to hop.
clocher (klɔʃe), s.m. [f. *cloche*] Steeple, bell-tower, belfry; (fig.) parish, country, place; *course au* ~, steeple-chase; *rivalités de* ~, local feuds.
clocher[1] (klɔʃe), v.n. [f. L *claudicare*] **1.** To limp, to halt, to hobble; **2.** to hitch, to be lame, defective, imperfect; *il y a quelque chose qui cloche*, there is a hitch somewhere.
clocher[2] (klɔʃe), v.a. [f. *cloche*] (hort.) To cover with a hand-glass.
clocheton (klɔʃtɔ̃), s.m. [f. *clocher*] Bell-turret.
clochette (klɔʃɛt), s.f. [f. *cloche*] **1.** Small bell, hand-bell, bell-shaped ornament or flower; **2.** (bot.) bell-flower, bindweed, *Convolvulus arvensis*; daffodil, *Narcissus pseudo narcissus*.
cloison (klwazɔ̃), s.f. [f. L *claudere*] **1.** Partition, interior wall; **2.** separation; **3.** (bot., anat.) partition; **4.** (naut.) bulkhead; ~*s étanches*, water-tight bulkheads.
cloisonnage (klwazɔnaʒ), s.m. Partition-work, wood partition.
cloisonné, -e (klwazɔne), p. adj. Wainscotted, separated by partitions. ~, s.m. Cloisonné enamel.
cloisonner (klwazɔne), v.a. To partition.
cloître (klwatr), s.m. [f. L *claustrum*] **1.** Cloister; **2.** convent, monastery, close.
cloîtrer (klwatre), v.a. **1.** To cloister; **2.** to shut up, to immure; **se** ~, v.pr. **1.** to enter a cloister; **2.** to shut oneself up.
clopin-clopant (klɔpɛ̃klɔpɑ̃), adv. loc. [f. OF *cloper*] Limpingly, haltingly.
clopiner (klɔpine), v.n. To hobble along, to limp.
cloporte (klɔpɔrt), s.m. [etym. dub.] (ent.) Woodlouse (pl. woodlice).
cloque (klɔk), s.f. [f. OF *cloque, cloche*] **1.** Blister; **2.** (agric.) rust, blight.
cloquer (klɔke), v.n. To blister.

clore (klɔr), v.a.n. def. [L *claudere*] **1.** To shut, to shut up, to close, to enclose, to fence; **2.** to conclude, to put an end to, to end.

clos, -e (klo), p. adj. Closed, shut, shut up, enclosed, sealed; *champ* ~, lists, tilt-yard; *à huis* ~, with closed doors, in camera; ~ *et couvert*, wind- and water-tight; *à la nuit* ~*e*, at nightfall; *bouche* ~*e*, mum!, silence!; *c'est lettre* ~*e pour moi*, it 's impossible for me to understand, it is a sealed book to me.

clos (klo), s.m. Close, enclosure, croft, orchard, paddock, vineyard.

closeau (pl. **-x**) (klozo), s.m. **closerie** (klozri), s.f. Small close, farm, or garden.

closier (klozje), s.m. Tenant of a close.

clôture (klotyr), s.f. [f. L *claudere*] **1.** Enclosure, fence; **2.** seclusion, cloistering; **3.** close, closing, end, conclusion.

clôturer (klotyre), v.a. To close, to enclose, to conclude.

clou (pl. **-s**) (klu), s.m. [f. L *clavus*] **1.** Nail, stud, tack, hobnail; ~ *à crochet*, hooked nail; tenter-hook; ~ *à sabot*, hobnail; *cela ne vaut pas un* ~, it 's not worth a pin's head; *maigre comme un cent de* ~*s*, as lean as a rake; *il n'en fiche pas un* ~, he does not do a stroke of work; *un* ~ *chasse l'autre*, one idea drives out another; *je lui ai rivé son* ~, I shut his mouth; that was a poser for him; **2.** (bot.) clove; **3.** (med.) boil, furuncle; **4.** chief point or attraction; **5.** (slang) pawn-shop; uncle's; *mettre au* ~, to pawn; to put in pawn; to pop; to put up the spout.

clouage, clouement, cloutage (kluaʒ, klumɑ̃, klutaʒ), s.m. [f. *clouer*] Nailing.

clouer (klue), v.a. [f. *clou*] To nail, to nail down, to nail on, to fix, to rivet, to pin down, to attach.

clouter (klute), v.a. [f. *clou*] To nail, to stud, to adorn with studs.

clouterie (klutri), s.f. Nail-manufactory, nail-trade.

cloutier (klutje), s.m. Nailer, nail-smith, nail-dealer.

cloutière (klutjɛr), s.f. Nail-mould, nail-box.

clovisse (klɔvis), s.f. (moll.) Clam.

clown (klaun), s.m. [Engl. wd] Clown, circus jester. ⚠ In French *clown* has never the sense of *rustre, grossier paysan*, which is quite usual in English.

clownerie (klaunri), s.f. Farce, buffoonery, practical joking.

cloyère (klwajɛr), s.f. [f. OF *cloie, claie*] **1.** Oyster-basket; **2.** contents of an oyster-basket: 25 dozen oysters.

club (klœb), s.m. [Engl. wd] Club, political association.

cluniste (klynist), adj. s.m. [f. *Cluny*, near Mâcon in France] Cluniac (monk).

cluse (klyz), s.f. [f. *clore*] Break in a chain of mountains (ex.: *la Cluse de Nantua*).

clusiacées (klyzjase), s.f.pl. (bot.) Clusiacea.

clusie (klyzi), s.f. (bot.) Balsam-tree, clusia.

clysoir (klizwar), s.m. [f. Gr. *kluzein*] Injection tube.

clysopompe (klizɔpɔ̃p), s.m. [f. *clysoir*] Enema, injecting apparatus; (vet.) clyster-pump.

clystère (klistɛr), s.m. Clyster, injection, enema.

cnémide (knemid), s.f. [f. Gr. *knēmis*] Leggings of the Greek soldiers in antiquity.

co-, col-, com-, con- (ko, kɔl, kɔm, kɔ̃), pref. [L *cum*] Co-, joint-, fellow-, &c.

coaccusé, -e (koakyze), s.m.f. Fellow-prisoner, person accused with another, co-respondent.

coacquéreur (koakerœr), s.m. Joint-purchaser.

coacti-f, -ve (koaktif), adj. Coactive, coercive, compulsory.

coaction (koaksjɔ̃), s.f. [L *coactio*] Co-action, coercion, compulsion.

coadjuteur (koadʒytœr), s.m. Coadjutor.

coadjutorerie (koadʒytɔrri), s.f. Co-adjutorship.

coadjutrice (koadʒytris), s.f. Coadjutress, coadjutrix.

coadjuvant, -e (koadʒyvɑ̃), adj. Coacting, concurrent.

coagulable (koagylabl), adj. Coagulable.

coagulant, -e (koagylɑ̃), p. adj. Coagulative.

coagulat-eur, -rice (koagylatœr), adj. Coagulatory, coagulative.

coagulation (koagyla'sjɔ̃), s.f. Coagulation, curdling.

coaguler (koagyle), v.a. [f. L *coagulare*] To coagulate, to curdle; to concrete; **se** ~, v.pr. to coagulate.

coagulum (koagylɔm), s.m. [L wd] Coagulum.

coalescence (kɔalɛssɑ̃s), s.f. Coalescence.

coalescent, -e (kɔalɛssɑ̃), adj. Coalescent.

coalisé, -e (kɔalize), p. adj. Allied, united in coalition. ~**s**, s.m.pl. Allied powers, coalitionists.

(se) coaliser (səkɔalize), v.pr. [f. L *coalescere*] To form a coalition, to league, to confederate.

coalition (kɔalisjɔ̃), s.f. Coalition, alliance, combination.

coaltar (koaltar), s.m. [Engl. wd] Coal-tar.

coassement (kɔasmɑ̃), s.m. [f. *coasser*] Croaking, croak (of a frog).

coasser (kɔase), v.n. [f. L *coaxare*] To croak (as a frog).

coassocié, -e (koasɔsje), s.m.f. Co-partner, joint partner.

coati (kɔati), s.m. [Braz. wd] (zool.) Coati.
cob (kɔb), s.m. [Engl. wd] Cob (horse).
cobalt (kɔbalt), s.m. [Germ. *Kobalt*] (min.) Cobalt.
cobaye (kɔbaj), s.m. [var. of *cabiai*] (zool.) Guinea-pig, *Cavia cobaya.*
cobéa (kɔbea), s.m. **cobée** (kɔbe), s.f. (bot.) Cobaea.
cobra, cobra capello (kɔbra), s.m. [Port. wd] (zool.) Cobra, hooded snake.
coca (kɔka), s.m. or (usually) s.f. [Span. wd] (bot.) Coca.
cocagne (kɔkaɲ), s.f. [f. It. *cuccagna*] Cockaigne, feast; *pays de* ~, land of milk and honey; *mât de* ~, greasy pole.
cocaïne (kɔkain), s.f. [f. *coca*] Cocaine.
cocarde (kɔkard), s.f. [f. OF *coquard* = *vaniteux*] Cockade; *prendre la* ~, to enlist; (slang) *avoir sa* ~, to be tipsy.
cocardi-er, -ère (kɔkardje), adj. Enthusiast for the army, militarist, jingo.
cocasse (kɔkas), adj. [etym. dub.] Droll, farcical, ridiculous, funny, comical, ludicrous.
cocasserie (kɔkasri), s.f. Comicality, ludicrousness, grotesqueness, extravagance.
coccinelle (kɔksinɛl), s.f. [f. L *coccinus*] (ent.) Coccinella, lady-fly, lady-bird.
coccygien, -ne (kɔksiʒjɛ̃), adj. (anat.) Coccygeal.
coccyx (kɔksis), s.m. [f. Gr. *kokkux*] (anat.) Coccyx, *coccygis os.*
coche[1] (kɔʃ), s.m. [f. Germ. *Kutsche*] Coach; ~ *d'eau,* barge, passage boat; *manquer le* ~, to lose a good opportunity; *mouche du* ~, busybody.
coche[2], **encoche** (kɔʃ, ɑ̃kɔʃ), s.f. [etym. dub.] Notch, cut, indentation, score, nick; *faire une* ~, to notch.
coche[3] (kɔʃ), s.f. [etym. dub.] Sow.
cochelet, coquelet (kɔʃlɛ, kɔklɛ), s.m. [f. *coq*] Cockerel.
cochenillage (kɔʃnijaʒ), s.m. Cochineal dye.
cochenille (kɔʃnij), s.f. [f. Span. *cochinilla*] **1.** (ent.) Cochineal; **2.** coccinellin, cochinillin (colouring principle of cochineal).
cocheniller (kɔʃnije), v.n. **1.** To gather cochineals; **2.** v.a. to dye with cochineal.
cochenillier (kɔʃnije), s.m. (bot.) Cochineal plant, nopal.
cocher (kɔʃe), s.m. [f. *coche*] **1.** Coachman, driver; **2.** (astr.) Charioteer, Wagoner.
cocher (kɔʃe), v.a. To notch.
cochère (kɔʃɛr), adj. f. *Porte* ~, carriage-gate.
cochet (kɔʃɛ), s.m. [f. *coq*] Cockerel.
cochevis (kɔʃvi), s.m. (zool.) Crested lark.
cochinchinois, -e (kɔʃɛ̃ʃinwa), adj. s.m.f. Cochin-Chinese; (of fowls) Cochin-China.
cochlearia (kɔklearja), s.m. [f. L *cochlear*] (bot.) Cochlearia.
cochoir (kɔʃwar), s.m. [f. *coche*] (techn.) Cooper's axe, squaring tool.
cochon (kɔʃɔ̃), s.m. [f. *coche*] **1.** Swine, hog, pig, porker; pork; ~ *de lait,* sucking pig; ~ *d'Inde,* guinea-pig; *soies de* ~, hog's bristles; *amis comme* ~, hail fellow well met; *tour de* ~, dirty trick; *nous n'avons pas gardé les* ~*s ensemble!*, we have not been dragged up together; (fig.) filthy, lewd person; **2.** (metall.) sow, pig, dross.
cochon, -ne (kɔʃø), adj. Dirty, filthy, lewd, beastly.
cochonnaille (kɔʃɔnɑj), s.f. [f. *cochon*] (jest.) Dressed pork, sausage-meat, hog's pudding, &c; syn. CHARCUTERIE.
cochonnée (kɔʃɔne), s.f. Farrow, litter of pigs.
cochonner (kɔʃɔne), v.a. **1.** (pop.) To bungle, to botch, to spoil a work; **2.** v.n. to farrow.
cochonnerie (kɔʃɔnri), s.f. Dirtiness, filthiness, obscenity, nastiness, indecent, smutty action or language, dirty trick.
cochonnet (kɔʃɔnɛ), s.m. **1.** Little pig; **2.** jack (at bowls); **3.** twelve-sided die.
cochylis (kɔʃilis), s.m. (ent.) Cochylis (insect infecting vines with a disease).
coco[1] (kɔko), s.m. [Port. wd] **1.** Coco, fruit of coco-tree; *noix de* ~, coco-nut; **2.** (fig.) (*a*) queer fellow; *un joli* ~*!*, a nice one!, a rum one!; (*b*) darling; **3.** stick-liquorice water; **4.** (fam.) egg.
coco[2] (kɔko), s.f. [abbrev. of *cocaïne*] (pop.) Snow, cocaine.
cocodès (kɔkɔdɛs), (obs.) s.m. Swell, fop.
cocon (kɔkɔ̃), s.m. [f. L *concha,* Provenç. *coucoun*] Cocoon.
cocorico (kɔkɔriko), s.m. [onom.] Cock-a-doodle-doo.
cocotier (kɔkɔtje), s.m. (bot.) Coconut palm, *Cocos pucifera.*
cocotte (kɔkɔt), s.f. [f. *coq*] **1.** (child.) Hen; chickabiddy; **2.** *ma* ~, my darling; **3.** horse, gee-gee; *hue* ~*!*, pull up, my beauty; **4.** fast woman; **5.** cast-iron stewpan (with lid); **6.** eye-soreness; **7.** ~ *en papier,* toy made of a sheet of paper folded to look like a hen.
coction (kɔksjɔ̃), s.f. [L *coctio*] **1.** Boiling, cooking; **2.** (physiol.) coction.
cocu (kɔky), s.m. adj. [LL *cuculus*] Cuckold.
cocuage (kɔkɥaʒ), s.m. Cuckoldom.
cocufier (kɔkyfje), v.a. To cuckold.
coda (kɔda), s.f. [It. wd] (mus.) Coda.
code (kɔd), s.m. [f. L *codex*] Code, law; (fig.) rules, directing principles or maxims; (motor.) *phare* ~, regulation headlight.
codéine (kɔdein), s.f. [f. Gr. *kōdeia*] (pharm.) Codeine (hypnotic alkaloid).

codemand-eur, -eresse (kodəmɑ̃dœr), s.m.f. (law) Co-plaintiff, co-applicant.
codétent-eur, -rice (kodetɑ̃tœr), s.m.f. (law) Joint holder.
codétenu, -e (kodetny), s.m.f. Fellow-prisoner.
codex (kɔdɛks), s.m. [L wd] Pharmacopoeia.
codicillaire (kɔdisilɛr), adj. Codicillary.
codicille (kɔdisil), s.m. [L *codicillus*] Codicil.
codification (kɔdifika'sjɔ̃), s.f. [f. *codifier*] Codification.
codifier (kɔdifje), v.a. [f. *code*] To codify.
codirect-eur, -rice (kodirɛktœr), s.m.f. Co-director, joint manager.
codirection (kodirɛksjɔ̃), s.f. Co-direction, joint management.
codonataire (kodɔnatɛr), s.m.f. adj. Joint donee.
coefficient (koefisjɑ̃), s.m. (alg.) Coefficient.
cœlentérés (selɑ̃tere), s.m.pl. [f. Gr. *koilos*+*enteron*] (zool.) Coelenterata.
cœliaque (seljak), adj. [f. Gr. *koilia*] (anat.) Coeliac.
coemption (koɑ̃psjɔ̃), s.f. [f. L *co*+*emptio*] (law) Coemption.
coéquation (koekwa'sjɔ̃), s.f. Assessment of taxes.
coercibilité (kɔɛrsibilite), s.f. Coercibleness.
coercible (kɔɛrsibl), adj. [f. L *coercere*] Coercible.
coerciti-f, -ve (kɔɛrsitif), adj. Coercive.
coercition (kɔɛrsisjɔ̃), s.f. [L *coercitio*] Coercion, compulsion.
coéternel, -le (koetɛrnɛl), adj. Coeternal.
coéternité (koetɛrnite), s.f. Co-eternity.
cœur (kœr), s.m. [L *cor*] **1.** Heart; bosom; stomach; (fig.) mind, soul, warmth of affection, heartiness, ardour, courage, generosity, pity, nobleness, feelings; *il le pressa tendrement sur son* ~, he pressed him tenderly to his bosom; *les maladies du* ~, diseases of the heart; *le* ~ *me bat*; my hearts beats; *avoir mal au* ~, to be sick; *avoir le* ~ *brisé* (or *navré*), to be broken-hearted; *cela déchire le cœur*, or *cela fend le* ~, it is heart-rending; *je veux en avoir le* ~ *net*, I must have my mind clear about it; I will clear up that matter; *avoir le* ~ *sur la main*, to be open-hearted, frank; *se ronger le* ~, to eat out one's heart; *faire contre mauvaise fortune bon* ~, to make the best of a bad job; *être plein de* ~, to be full of generous feelings; *de tout* ~, *de tout mon* ~, most heartily, with all my heart; *un* ~ *de pierre*, a heart of stone; *un* ~ *d'or*, a kind, generous heart, a heart of gold; *mauvaise tête et bon* ~, a kind heart and a light head; *à* ~ *ouvert*; ~ *à* ~, unreservedly; *donner son* ~, to give one's love; *loin des yeux, loin du* ~, out of sight, out of mind; *son* ~ *a parlé*, she, or he, has fallen in love; *décharger son* ~, to unbosom oneself; *par* ~, by heart; *dîner par* ~, not to dine at all, to dine with Duke Humphrey; *cela lui reste* (or *pèse*) *sur le* ~, he cannot forget it; *les replis du* ~, the recesses of the heart; *cela lui soulève le* ~, it makes him feel sick; *s'en donner à* ~ *joie*, to enjoy a thing to one's heart's content; *prendre une chose fort à* ~, to take something very much to heart; *avoir du* ~ *au ventre*, to be full of courage and spirit; *un grand* ~, *un homme de* ~, a noble heart, a man of feeling; *si le* ~ *vous en dit*, if you have a mind to; *c'est un crève-*~, it's a cruel disappointment, it's heart-rending; *de gaieté de* ~, out of sheer wantonness; *à contre-*~, reluctantly, willy-nilly; *toucher le* ~ *de*, to touch the heart of; **2.** (fig.) central point or part; *au* ~ *de la ville*, in the heart (or centre) of the city; *le* ~ *d'une laitue*, the heart of a lettuce; *le* ~ *d'un fruit*, the core of a fruit; *au* ~ *de l'été*, in the height of summer; *au* ~ *de l'hiver*, in the depth of winter; ~ *d'artichaut, une feuille pour tout le monde*, everybody's friend is nobody's friend; **3.** any heart-shaped object; *un* ~ *à la crème*; a heart-shaped cream cheese; *un* ~ *en pain d'épices*, a heart-shaped gingerbread; **4.** (at cards) hearts; *jouer* ~, to play hearts.
coexistant, -e (koɛkzistɑ̃), p. adj. Co-existing, co-existent.
coexistence (koɛkzistɑ̃s), s.f. Co-existence.
coexister (koɛkziste), v.n. To co-exist.
coffin (kɔfɛ̃), s.m. [f. L *cophinus*] Box of a mower. ⚠ Not English 'coffin' which = *cercueil.*
coffre (kɔfr), s.m. [f. L *cophinus*] **1.** Chest; **2.** coffer, treasury; ~ *fort*, safe; strong-box; iron safe; **3.** seat-box (of carriages); **4.** trunk, chest (of the human body); **5.** (naut.) ~ *d'amarrage*, mooring buoy; **6.** (print.) coffin; **7.** (zool.) trunk-fish.
coffrer (kɔfre), v.a. [f. *coffre*] (colloq.) To lock up, to imprison.
coffret (kɔfrɛ), s.m. Small box, casket.
cofidéjusseur (kofideʒysœr), s.m. (law) Co-surety.
cogitation (kɔʒita'sjɔ̃), s.f. [L *cogitatio*] Cogitation, act of thinking, cogitativity.
cogiter (kɔʒite), v.n. To cogitate.
cognac (kɔɲak), s.m. [geog. French orig.] Cognac, brandy.
cognasse (kɔɲas), s.f. [f. *coing*] (bot.) Wild quince.
cognassier (kɔɲasje), s.m. (bot.) Quince-tree, *Cydonia vulgaris.*
cognat (kɔgna), s.m. [f. L *cognatus*] (law) Cognate, kinsman.

cognation (kɔgna'sjɔ̃), s.f. (law) Cognation, filiation.
cogne (kɔɲ), s.m. (slang, insulting) Constable, policeman, bobby, copper, (Amer.) cop.
cognée (kɔɲe), s.f. [LL *cuniata*] Felling axe; *jeter le manche après la* ~, to throw the helve after the hatchet, to give up in despair.
cogner (kɔɲe), v.n.a. [f. OF *coigner*] To beat, to knock, to knock in, to rap, to strike against, to thump; **se** ~, v.pr. to knock, to strike (*contre*, against), to fight.
cogniti-f, -ve (kɔgnitif), adj. [f. L *cognoscere*] Cognitive, cognoscitive.
cognition (kɔgnisjɔ̃), s.f. Cognition.
cohabitation (kɔabita'sjɔ̃), s.f. [L *cohabitatio*] (law) Cohabitation.
cohabiter (kɔabite), v.n. To cohabit.
cohérence (kɔerɑ̃s), s.f. [f. L *cum*+*haerere*] Coherence, coherency, cohesion, consistency.
cohérent, -e (kɔerɑ̃), adj. Coherent, consistent.
cohéreur (kɔerœr), s.m. (techn., electr.) Coherer.
cohériter (kɔerite), v.a.n. To inherit conjointly.
cohériti-er, -ère (kɔeritje), s.m.f. Co-heir, joint heir (or heiress).
cohési-f, -ve (kɔezif), adj. Cohesive.
cohésion (kɔezjɔ̃), s.f. [L *cohaesio*] Cohesion, cohesiveness.
cohobation (kɔɔba'sjɔ̃), s.f. (chem.) Cohobation (repeated distillation).
cohober (kɔɔbe), v.a. [mod. L *cohobare*] To cohobate.
cohorte (kɔɔrt), s.f. [L *cohors*] **1.** (ant.) Cohort, tenth part of a legion; **2.** body of soldiers, cohort, band, troop.
cohue (kɔy), s.f. [etym. dub.] Crowd, tumultuous throng, press, rout, crush.
coi, -te (kwa), adj. [f. L *quietus*] Quiet, still, snug; *se tenir* ~, to keep silent.
coiffe (kwaf), s.f. [LL *cofea*] **1.** Head-dress, coif (of peasant women); **2.** lining of hats; **3.** caul; **4.** (bot.) calyptra; **5.** (naut.) cap.
coiffé, -e (kwafe), p. adj. Having the head dressed; *être né* ~, to be born with a caul; to be born with a silver spoon in the mouth; ~ *d'une perruque*, wearing a wig; ~ *de ce charlatan*, infatuated with this mountebank.
coiffer (kwafe), v.a. [f. *coiffe*] **1.** To dress the hair of; ~ *Ste Catherine*, to be 25 and still unmarried; **2.** to put (something on one's head); **3.** to cap; to fasten upon the ears of; **4** (naut.) to back a sail; **se** ~, v.pr. **1.** to wear on one's head; **2.** to dress (or do) one's hair; **3.** to be infatuated (*de*, with).
coiffeu-r, -se (kwafœr), s.m.f. Hairdresser.
coiffeuse (kwaføz), s.f. Dressing-table.
coiffure (kwafyr), s.f. **1.** Head-dress, cap, hat, bonnet, &c.; **2.** style of arranging the hair; **3.** doing the hair.
coin (kwɛ̃), s.m. [L *cuneus*] **1.** Corner, angle; retired part, side, end; *le* ~ *de la bouche*, the corner of the mouth; *regarder du* ~ *de l'œil*, to cast a sidelong glance at; *le* ~ *de la rue*, the corner of the street; *jouer aux quatre* ~*s*, to play at puss in the corner; (slang) *ça vous en bouche un* ~ *!*, that 's a corker for you !, that licks you !; *je le connais dans les* ~*s*, I know him through and through; (Amer.) I know him all to pieces; *marqué au bon* ~, of the right stamp (or sort); *il est caché dans un* ~ *du verger*, he is hidden in a retired part of the orchard; *les quatre* ~*s du ciel*, the four corners of heaven; *il vit maintenant dans son* ~ *de province*, he is living now in a remote part of the country; *au* ~ *du feu*, by the fireside; **2.** wedge; **3.** stamp, die; **4.** (print.) quoin, coigne.
coinçage (kwɛ̃saʒ), s.m. [f. *coin*] Wedging.
coincement (kwɛ̃smɑ̃), s.m. [f. *coin*] Jamming.
coincer (kwɛ̃se) (the *c* takes the cedilla before *o* and *a*: *je coinçai*), v.a. [f. *coin*] To wedge, to drive in, to jam; to get (some one) in a corner.
coïncidence (kɔɛ̃sidɑ̃s), s.f. [f. *coïncider*] Coincidence, concurrence, simultaneousness.
coïncident, -e (kɔɛ̃sidɑ̃), adj. Coincident, simultaneous.
coïncider (kɔɛ̃side), v.n. [f. L *co*+*incidere*] To coincide; to concur. ⚠ 'To coincide' means also 'to agree (with X)' = *être du même avis (que X)*, but *coïncider* cannot be used in that sense.
coing (kwɛ̃), s.m. [f. L *cydonium*] (bot.) Quince; *jaune comme un* ~, yellow as saffron.
coïntéressé, -e (kɔɛ̃terɛse), s.m.f. Partner, sharer.
coït (kɔit), s.m. [L *coitus*] Coition, coitus.
coite, coitte, couette (kwat, kwɛt), s.f. [f. L *culcita*] Feather bed.
coittes (kwat), s.f.pl. (ship-build.) Bilgeways.
coke (kɔk), s.m. [Engl. wd] Coke.
col (kɔl), s.m. [L *collum*] **1.** Neck; **2.** collar; *faux-*~, collar, shirt-collar; ~ *rabattu*, turn-down collar; **3.** (geog.) pass, defile; *les* ~*s des Alpes*, the Alpine passes; **4.** (anat.) slender part joining others, neck; *le* ~ *de la matrice*, the neck of the womb; *le* ~ *du fémur*; the neck of the femur; (fig.) *le* ~ *d'une bouteille*, the neck of a bottle.
colature (kɔlatyr), s.f. [f. L *colare*] Colature, filtration, straining.

colback (kolbak), s.m. [f. Turk. *kalpak*] Calpack, colback, bearskin cap.
colchicine (kolʃisin), s.f. [f. *colchique*] Colchicine (alkaloid).
colchique (kolʃik), s.m. [L *colchicum*] (bot.) Colchicum, meadow-saffron.
colcotar (kolkotar), s.m. [Arab. wd] (chem.) Colcothar, red oxide of iron.
cold-cream (koldkrɛm), s.m. [Engl. wds] Cold cream.
colégataire (kolegatɛr), s.m.f. Co-legatee, joint legatee.
coléoptère (koleoptɛr), s.m. [f. Gr. *koleos* +*pteron*] (ent.) Coleopter, beetle; (pl.) coleoptera.
colère (kolɛr), s.f. [L *cholera*] Anger, wrath, ire, passion, rage, choler, fume; *se mettre en ~ contre X*, to get angry with X; *la ~ de Dieu*, the wrath of God; *la mer en ~*, the raging sea; *accès* (or *mouvement*) *de ~*, fit of anger. **~**, adj. Choleric, hot-headed, irascible.
coléreu-x, -se, colérique (kolerø, kolerik), adj. Choleric, irascible, passionate.
coleus (koleys), s.m. (bot.) Coleus.
colibri (kolibri), s.m. [Carib. wd] Colibri, humming-bird.
colichemarde (koliʃmard), s.f. [Germ. orig.] Rapier.
colicitant, -e (kolisitɑ̃), s.m.f. adj. (law) Co-vendor (of a joint property).
colifichet (kolifiʃɛ), s.m. [etym. dub.] **1.** Bauble, trinket, gewgaw, knick-knack; **2.** bird-cake.
colimaçon (kolimasɔ̃), s.m. [f. *limaçon*] Snail; *escalier en ~*, spiral staircase; see syn. LIMAÇON.
colin (kolɛ̃), s.m. **1.** (ichth.) Colin, coal-fish; **2.** (ornith.) Virginian quail; **3.** (theatr.) swain; *~ maillard*, blind-man's-buff; *je m'en moque comme de ~ tampon*, I don't care a fig.
colique (kolik), s.f. [f. *côlon*] Colic, gripes, griping; *avoir la ~* (or *des ~s*), to have (or feel) the colic, to gripe, to be griped; *~s hépatiques*, hepatalgia; *~s néphrétiques*, nephralgia.
colis (koli), s.m. [f. It. *collo*] Package, parcel, bale, case; *~ postal*, postal package; parcel sent by rail, not by post; *envoyer un ~ par la poste*, to send something by parcel-post.
côlite (kolit), s.f. [f. *côlon*] (med.) Colitis, inflammation of the colon.
collaborat-eur, -rice (kollaboratœr), s.m.f. Collaborator, assistant, contributor.
collaboration (kollabora'sjɔ̃), s.f. Collaboration.
collaborer (kollabore), v.n. [L *collaborare*] To work jointly, to collaborate.
collage (kolaʒ), s.m. [f. *coller*] **1.** Pasting, paper-hanging; **2.** clarifying (of wine); **3.** (pop.) amour, illicit amorous tie.

collant, -e (kolɑ̃), p. adj. [f. *coller*] **1.** Tight, close-fitting; **2.** (pop.) sticking, sticky; *il est ~!*, he sticks like a bur. **~e**, s.f. (school slang) Official summons to a university examination.
collapsus (kolapsys), s.m. [L wd] Collapse.
collataire (kollatɛr), s.m. [L *collatarius*] Collated priest, collatee.
collatéral, -e, (aux) (kollateral), adj. [f. L *cum*+*latus*] Collateral, side.
collatéralement (kollateralmɑ̃), adv. Collaterally.
collatéralité (kollateralite), s.f. Collateralness.
collateur (kollatœr), s.m. [f. L *collator*] Collator.
collati-f, -ve (kollatif), adj. Collative.
collation (kolla'sjɔ̃), s.f. [f. L *collatio*] **1.** Collation, conferring; **2.** collation, comparison; **3.** collation, light repast; *faire une ~*, to partake of a collation.
collationnement (kollasjonmɑ̃), s.m. Collation (comparison of writings).
collationner (kollasjone), v.a. To collate, to compare, to verify; **~** v.n. to lunch, to take a light meal.
colle (kol), s.f. [f. L *colla*] **1.** Paste, glue, gum, gum-arabic; *~ forte*, glue; *~ de pâte*, paste; *~ à bouche*, mouth-glue; *~ de poisson*, fish-glue; isinglass; *peinture à la ~*, distemper; **2.** (school slang) preparatory examination; interrogation; *pousser une ~ à X*, to ask X a poser.
collecte (kolɛkt), s.f. [f. L *collectus*] **1.** Collection (of money); **2.** collect; **3.** gathering.
collecteur (kolɛktœr), s.m. **1.** Collector (in old times, tax-gatherer); **2.** (phys.) commutator, upper plate of a condenser, employed for collecting electricity. **~**, adj. Collector, collecting; *égoût ~ de Paris*, great sewer of Paris.
collecti-f, -ve (kolɛktif), adj. Collective.
collection (kolɛksjɔ̃), s.f. **1.** Collection; **2.** gathering; **3.** set, assortment. ⚠ *Collection* has not in French as in English the sense of money collected in church, &c.; in that sense 'collection' must be translated by *collecte* or *quête*.
collectionner (kolɛksjone), v.a. To collect, to gather.
collectionneu-r, -se (kolɛksjonœr), s.m.f. Collector, collectress. **~**, adj. Collecting.
collectivement (kolɛktivmɑ̃), adv. Collectively.
collectivisme (kolɛktivism), s.m. Collectivism.
collectiviste (kolɛktivist), s.m.f. Collectivist.
collectivité (kolɛktivite), s.f. Collectivity.
collège (kolɛʒ), s.m. [L *collegium*] **1.** College; grammar school, high school;

2. assembly; *le ~ des Cardinaux,* the Sacred College.

collégial, -e, (aux) (kɔleʒjal), adj. Collegial, collegiate. **~e,** s.f. Collegiate church.

collégien, -ne (kɔleʒjɛ̃), adj. Collegian, collegiate. ~, s.m.f. Pupil of a college.

collègue (kɔllɛg), s.m.f. [L *collega*] Colleague.

coller (kɔle), v.a. [f. *colle*] **1.** To stick, to paste, to glue, to gum; **2.** to apply closely, to press; **3.** to give, to place, to throw; *colle ça n'importe où!,* shove it down anywhere; (slang) *colle-toi ça dans le fusil* (or *le cornet*), put that in your pipe and smoke it; just swallow that; **4.** to clarify (wine); **5.** to embarrass, to bewilder, to nonplus (with difficult questions); (school slang) to plough; to stump; *se faire ~ au bachot,* to get ploughed at the *bachot* exam; to keep in (a pupil); ~, v.n. (of clothes) to fit closely, or tightly, to sit close; (slang) to fit, to add up; *ça colle!,* agreed!, right ho!; *ça ne colle pas,* it does not add up; nothing doing; no go; **se ~,** v.pr. **1.** to stick, to adhere; **2.** to cling.

collerette (kɔlrɛt), s.f. [f. *col*] **1.** Collar, collarette; **2.** (bot.) involucre; **3.** flange.

collet (kɔlɛ), s.m. [f. *col*] **1.** Collar; *~ monté,* stuck up; stiff and starched; straitlaced, prudish; *mettre la main au ~ à X,* to collar X; **2.** cape; **3.** bands (of priests); **4.** (butch.) neck; **5.** (bot.) collar, neck; **6.** (anat.) neck (of teeth); **7.** snare of wire; *tendre un ~,* to set a snare; **8.** (naut.) throat (of a knee); crown (of an anchor); **9.** (techn.) flange.

colleter (kɔlte), v.a. To collar; **se ~,** v.pr. to fight, to collar each other.

colleteur (kɔltœr), s.m. Snarer.

colleur (kɔlœr), s.m. **1.** Paper-hanger; bill-sticker; **2.** (school slang) examiner.

colley (kɔlle), s.m. [Engl. wd] Collie (dog).

collier (kɔlje), s.m. [f. *col*] **1.** Necklace; **2.** collar; *cheval de ~,* draught-horse; *donner un coup de ~,* to give a good pull; (fig.) to make an effort; *franc du ~,* (of a horse) free; (of a person, fig.) brave, open, earnest and straightforward, frank, hearty; *~ de misère,* drudgery, toil, yoke; *~ de force,* training collar; *à ~,* (zool.) ringed; **3.** (techn.) ring, collar, hoop (of an eccentric), bow, belt, flange; **4.** (butch.) neck.

colliger (kɔlliʒe), v.a. [L *colligere*] To collect, to gather.

collignon (kɔliɲɔ̃), s.m. [f. prop. n.] (colloq.) Cabby, jarvey.

collimateur (kɔllimatœr), s.m. (astr.) Collimator.

collimation, collinéation (kɔllima'sjɔ̃, kɔllinea'sjɔ̃), s.f. [f. L *collineare*] (astr.) Collimation, collineation.

colline (kɔlin), s.f. [f. L *collis*] Hill, hillock; *la double ~,* Parnassus; *le penchant, le versant de la ~,* the hill-slope; *la ville aux sept ~s,* the city of the seven hills (Rome).

collision (kɔllizjɔ̃), s.f. [L *collisio*] Collision, colliding; (fig.) conflict, encounter.

collocation (kɔlloka'sjɔ̃), s.f. [f. L *collocare*] **1.** (law) Classing (of creditors); **2.** investment.

collodion (kɔllɔdjɔ̃), s.m. [f. Gr. *kollōdēs*] Collodion.

collodionner (kɔllɔdjɔne), v.a. To collodionize.

colloïdal, -e, (aux) (kɔllɔidal), adj. Colloidal.

colloïde (kɔllɔid), s.m. adj. Colloid.

colloque (kɔllɔk), s.m. [L *colloquium*] Colloquy, conference; conversation (slightly ironical).

colloquer (kɔllɔke), v.a. [f. L *col+locare*] **1.** (law) To class, to marshal; **2.** (fam.) to place, to palm off, to clap, to sell, to give; **3.** to collocate.

collotypie (kɔllɔtipi), s.f. Collotype.

collusion (kɔllyzjɔ̃), s.f. [L *collusio*] Collusion; deceitful, fraudulent agreement.

collusoire (kɔllyzwar), adj. Collusory, collusive.

collusoirement (kɔllyzwarmɑ̃), adv. Collusively.

collutoire (kɔllytwar), s.m. [f. L *col+luere*] (med.) Collutorium.

collyre (kɔlir), s.m. [f. Gr. *kollurion*] (med.) Collyrium, eye-salve, eye-wash.

colmatage (kɔlmataʒ), s.m. [f. It. *colmata*] (agric.) Warping.

colmater (kɔlmate), v.a. To warp (land).

colocase (kɔlɔkɑz), s.f. [L *colocasia*] (bot.) Colocasia.

colocataire (kɔlɔkatɛr), s.m.f. Joint tenant.

colombage (kɔlɔ̃baʒ), s.m. (build.) Studworks, uprights.

colombe (kɔlɔ̃b), s.f. [L *columba*] **1.** Dove, pigeon; **2.** (carp.) upright (of a partition); **3.** (join.) long plane, cooper's plane.

colombelle (kɔlɔ̃bɛl), s.f. [f. *colombe*] **1.** Dovelet; **2.** (print.) column-rule.

colombier (kɔlɔ̃bje), s.m. **1.** Dove-house, dove-cot, columbary, pigeon-house; **2.** (paper-mak.) columbier, 90×63 cm.; **3.** (print.) pigeon-hole, gap; **4.** (ship-build.) poppet.

colombin, -e (kɔlɔ̃bɛ̃), adj. [f. *colombe*] Columbine, dove-coloured. **~e,** s.f. **1.** Pigeon's dung; **2.** (bot.) columbine.

colombo (kɔlɔ̃bo), s.m. [f. *Colombo*, Ceylon] (bot., med.) Calumba (bitter root).

colombophile (kɔlɔ̃bofil), adj. [f. L

colomba + Gr. *philos*] Interested in pigeon-breeding.
colombophilie (kɔlɔ̃bofili), s.f. Carrier-pigeon breeding; pigeon-fancying.
colon (kɔlɔ̃), s.m. [f. L *colonus*] **1.** Planter, farmer, husbandman; colonist, settler; **2.** (slang abbrev.) colonel; **3.** familiar form of address: *ben mon ~!*, well old bean!
côlon (kolɔ̃), s.m. [Gr. *kolon*] (anat.) Colon.
colonel (kɔlɔnɛl), s.m. [It. *colonello*] Colonel; *grade de ~*, colonelcy.
colonelle (kɔlɔnɛl), s.f. Colonel's wife. ~, adj. (obs.) Said of the first company of a colonel's regiment.
colonial, -e, (aux) (kɔlɔnjal), adj. Colonial.
colonie (kɔlɔni), s.f. [L *colonia*] Colony; settlement, establishment; a body of persons transplanted from their mother country to a new land; the land colonized.
colonisable (kɔlɔnizabl), adj. Colonizable.
colonisat-eur, -rice (kɔlɔnizatœr), adj. Colonizing. ~, s.m.f. Colonizer.
colonisation (kɔlɔniza'sjɔ̃), s.f. Colonization, colonizing.
coloniser (kɔlɔnize), v.a. To colonize.
colonnade (kɔlɔnad), s.f. [f. *colonne*] Colonnade, range of columns.
colonne (kɔlɔn), s.f. [L *columna*] **1.** Column; *les ~s d'Hercule*, the Pillars of Hercules; **2.** any column-shaped object; **3.** (fig.) prop, supporter, pillar, succour, upholding; *les ~s de la foi*; the pillars of the Church; **4.** (print., writ.) column, perpendicular section of a page, perpendicular line of figures; **5.** bedpost; **6.** (mil.) troop; column; *défiler sur trois ~s*, to march in three columns.
colonnette (kɔlɔnɛt), s.f. Little column.
colophane (kɔlɔfan), s.f. [f. *Colophon*, Asia Minor] Colophony.
coloquinte (kɔlɔkɛ̃t), s.f. [L *colocynthis*] **1.** (bot.) Colocynth; **2.** (slang) head, nut, pate.
colorant, -e (kɔlɔrɑ̃), p. adj. [f. *colorer*] Colouring. ~, s.m. Colouring.
coloration (kɔlɔra'sjɔ̃), s.f. **1.** Coloration, colour; **2.** colouring.
coloré, -e (kɔlɔre), p. adj. **1.** Coloured; **2.** deeply coloured; **3.** ruddy (of the complexion); **4.** (fig.) glowing, highly coloured.
colorer (kɔlɔre), v.a. [f. L *color*] To colour, to tinge, to paint; (fig.) to palliate, to make plausible; **se ~**, v.pr. to colour.
coloriage (kɔlɔrjaʒ), s.m. Colouring, painting.
colorier (kɔlɔrje), v.a. To put colour on, to colour, to paint.
coloris (kɔlɔri), s.m. **1.** Colour, colouring; **2.** (fig.) brilliancy of style; **3.** hue (of the complexion).
colorisation (kɔlɔriza'sjɔ̃), s.f. Coloration, appearance of a colour, act of colouring.
coloriste (kɔlɔrist), s.m.f. Colourist, colourer.
colossal, -e, (aux) (kɔlɔsal), adj. [f. *colosse*] Colossal, huge, gigantic.
colossalement (kɔlɔsalmɑ̃), adv. Hugely, enormously, colossally.
colosse (kɔlɔs), s.m. [L *colossus*] Colossus.
colostrum (kɔlɔstrɔm), s.m. [L wd] (med.) Colostrum, first milk.
colportage (kɔlpɔrtaʒ), s.m. **1.** Hawking, peddling; **2.** communication, spreading, propagation (of news).
colporter (kɔlpɔrte), v.a. [f. L *col*+*portare*] **1.** To hawk, to peddle; **2.** (fig.) to hawk about, to spread (news).
colporteu-r, -se (kɔlpɔrtœr), s.m.f. Hawker, pedlar, colporteur.
coltin (kɔltɛ̃), s.m. [f. *col*] Large hat covering head and neck, worn by those who carry heavy sacks on their head and back.
coltinage (kɔltinaʒ), s.m. Carrying of heavy loads.
coltiner (kɔltine), v.a. [f. *coltin*] To carry (heavy loads on the shoulders or head).
coltineur (kɔltinœr), s.m. Porter, coal- or flour-heaver.
columbaire, columbarium (kɔlɔ̃bɛr, kɔlɔ̃barjɔm), s.m. [L wd] (ant.) Columbarium.
columelle (kɔlymɛl), s.f. [L *columella*] (conch.) Columella, upright pillar in centre of shells.
colure (kɔlyr), s.m. [L *colurus*] (astr., geog.) Colure.
colza (kɔlza), s.m. [f. Dutch *koolzaad*] (bot.) Colza, *Brassica campestris*; *huile de ~*, colza oil; rape-oil; *graine de ~*, rape-seed.
coma (kɔma), s.m. [Gr. *kōma*] Coma.
comateu-x, -se (kɔmatø), adj. Comatose.
combat (kɔ̃ba), s.m. [f. *combattre*] Fight, combat, battle, conflict, engagement; struggle, strife, contest; *~ naval*, sea-fight; *au fort du ~*, in the thick of the fight; *aller au ~*, to go to battle; *livrer un ~*, to give battle; *éviter le ~*, to avoid fighting; *être mis hors de ~*, to be disabled; *~ singulier*, single combat, duel; *le Dieu des ~s*, the God of war; *~ des éléments*, strife of the elements; *~ de générosité*, contest of generosity.
combati-f, -ve (kɔ̃batif), adj. Fond of fighting; bellicose; syn. BELLIQUEUX.
combativité (kɔ̃bativite), s.f. Combativeness.
combattant, -e (kɔ̃batɑ̃), p. adj. Fighting. ~, s.m.f. Fighter, champion, combatant; *anciens ~s*, ex-service men.
combattre (kɔ̃batr), v.a.n. [L *cum*+Fr. *battre*] To fight, to combat, to fight

against, to war against, to battle with; to combat, to strive with, to contend with or against, to oppose, to withstand; ~ *ses passions*, to struggle against one's passions; ~ *les préjugés*, to combat prejudice; **se** ~, v.pr. to fight, to contend with each other.

combe (kɔ̃b), s.f. [LL *cumba*] Coomb, combe, little valley.

combien (kɔ̃bjɛ̃), adv. [*comme+bien*] **1.** How much, how, to what extent; **2.** how many, what quantity, what number; **3.** how far; **4.** how long; **5.** what price; *le* ~ *sommes-nous?*, what day of the month is it?; (archaic) ~ *que*, although.

combinable (kɔ̃binabl), adj. Combinable.

combinaison (kɔ̃binɛzɔ̃), s.f. **1.** Combination, assemblage; **2.** variation among a certain number of objects or symbols taken in sets; **3.** (chem.) combination; **4.** contrivance, scheme, arrangement, device.

combine (kɔ̃bin), s.f. [slang abbrev. of *combinaison*] Scheme, trick, cunning device; *connaître les* ~*s*, to be up to snuff; to know a trick or two; to know the ropes.

combiné, -e (kɔ̃bine), p. adj. Combined. ~, s.m. Combine.

combiner (kɔ̃bine), v.a. [L *combinare*] **1.** To combine, to unite; **2.** to contrive, to scheme; **se** ~, v.pr. to combine, to unite, to be united.

comble (kɔ̃bl), s.m. [L *cumulus*] **1.** Heaping; **2.** roof, top; *loger sous les* ~*s*, to live at the top of the house, or, under the tiles; *de fond en* ~, from top to bottom, utterly, completely; **3.** (fig.) height, summit, acme, utmost; *le* ~ *de l'infortune*, the height of misfortune; *mettre le* ~ *à vos bienfaits*, to crown your kindnesses, to fill up the measure of your kindnesses; *ça, c'est le* ~*!*, or, *c'est un* ~, that puts the lid on it; that's the limit!, that's the finishing stroke.

comble (kɔ̃bl), adj. Heaped, full, quite full; *la mesure est* ~, the measure is quite full; that is the limit!, that puts the lid on it.

comblement (kɔ̃blmɑ̃), s.m. Filling-up.

combler (kɔ̃ble), v.a. [L *cumulare*] **1.** To heap, to pile above the top of a measure, to fill up; ~ *un puits*, to fill up a well; **2.** (fig.) to load, to overload, to fill, to crown, to complete, to gratify, to fulfil, to supply, to cover (a deficiency); ~ *de bienfaits*, to load with benefits or kindnesses; ~ *les souhaits de X*, to gratify X's wishes; *vous me comblez*, you overwhelm me.

combrière (kɔ̃brjɛr), s.f. [Provenç. *coumbriero*] (fish.) Tunny-net.

comburant, -e (kɔ̃byrɑ̃), adj. [f. L *comburens*] (chem.) Burning, comburent; ~, s.m. Comburent.

combustibilité (kɔ̃bystibilite), s.f. Combustibility, combustibleness.

combustible (kɔ̃bystibl), adj. Combustible; (fig.) ardent, hot-headed, combustive. ~, s.m. Fuel, combustible.

combustion (kɔ̃bystjɔ̃), s.f. [f. L *comburere*] Combustion, combination, burning, fire.

comédie (kɔmedi), s.f. [L *comoedia*] **1.** Comedy; ~ *de mœurs*, comedy of manners; *jouer la* ~, to act, to act a play; **2.** sham, shamming; *cessez cette* ~, stop this shamming, or acting.

comédien, -ne (kɔmedjɛ̃), s.f. [f. *comédie*] **1.** Comedian, actor; **2.** hypocrite, dissembler. ~, adj. Affected, feigned, artificial, gushing.

comestible (kɔmɛstibl), adj. [f. L *comedere*] Edible, eatable. ~, s.m. Eatables (pl.), victuals; *magasin de* ~*s*, provision warehouse.

cométaire (kɔmetɛr), adj. [f. *comète*] Cometary.

comète (kɔmɛt), s.f. [L *cometa*] Comet; *ruban* ~, narrow ribbon.

comice, comices (kɔmis), s.m., s.m.pl. [f. L *comitium*] **1.** (pl.) Comitia; **2.** (sing.) meeting; ~ *agricole*, agricultural meeting.

comique (kɔmik), adj. [L *comicus*] Comic, comical, funny. ~, s.m. **1.** Comic art; **2.** humour; **3.** comic author; **4.** comic actor.

comiquement (kɔmikmɑ̃), adv. Comically.

comitat (kɔmita), s.m. [L *comitatus*] Administrative subdivision of Hungary.

comité (kɔmite), s.m. [Engl. *committee*] **1.** Committee; **2.** party; *nous serons en petit* ~, there will be only a few intimate friends.

comitial, -e, (aux) (kɔmisjal), adj. Comitial; *mal* ~, epilepsy.

comma (kɔma), s.m. [Gr. wd] **1.** Comma; **2.** (mus.) comma; **3.** (print.) colon.

command (kɔmɑ̃), s.m. [f. *commander*] (law) Purchaser.

commandant (kɔmɑ̃dɑ̃), s.m. [f. *commander*] Commander, commandant, chief officer, major, commanding officer of a battalion or squadron. ~, p. adj. Commanding.

commande (kɔmɑ̃d), s.f. [f. *commander*] **1.** Order; *passer une* ~, to give an order; *de* ~, conventional, feigned, sham, pretended; *maladie de* ~, feigned illness; *sur* ~, to order; **2.** (mech.) rope-band, gasket; knittle, lever, drive; *à* ~ *automatique*, automatically operated; ~ *directe*, direct drive; *levier de* ~, control-lever.

commandement (kɔmɑ̃dmɑ̃), s.m. [f.

commander] **1.** Command, bidding, order, mandate; **2.** precept, commandment; **3.** right of commanding; **4.** a military or naval force under the command of a particular officer; *bâton de* ~, staff (of office); **5.** (law) summons, writ.

commander (kɔmɑ̃de), v.a. [f. L *commendare*] **1.** To command, to order, to have the command of, to govern; **2.** to order, to bid, to bespeak; **3.** to overlook; to drive, to control; *cela commande l'admiration*, this compels admiration; ~ *une belle vue*, to command a beautiful view; ~, v.n. to command, to govern, to rule; **se** ~, v.pr. to come at will, to be ordered or compelled.

commanderie (kɔmɑ̃dri), s.f. Commandery.

commandeur (kɔmɑ̃dœr), s.m. Commander (in orders of knighthood).

commanditaire (kɔmɑ̃ditɛr), s.m.f. Sleeping partner.

commandite (kɔmɑ̃dit), s.f. [f. *command*] Commandite (investment in joint-stock company with liability only for the sum invested).

commanditer (kɔmɑ̃dite), v.a. To be a sleeping partner in, to provide funds for (a firm or joint-stock company).

comme (kɔm), adv. [f. L *quomodo*] As, as . . . as, like, as well as, such as, so much as, as much as, as it were; how; *regardez la chose* ~ *faite*, consider the thing as done; *froid* ~ *le marbre*, as cold as marble; *cet auteur est regardé* ~ *classique*, this author is looked upon as classic; *tout* ~, just like; just the same as; even so; ~ *si*, as if, as though; ~ *cela*, like that; *c'est* ~ *cela*, so it is; ~ *tout*, like anything; ~ *vous me traitez!*, how you treat me!; ~ *il est changé!*, how changed he is!; ~ *quoi*, how, how that; ~ *ci*, ~ *ça*, so-so, indifferently, fairly well, middling.

comme (kɔm), conj. **1.** As; as . . . so . . .; **2.** while, as; ~ *j'entrais, il partait*, just as I was entering, he left; **3.** because, as; ~ *les raisons paraissaient bonnes, on s'y rendit*, as (or because) his reasons seemed good, we yielded to them.

commémoraison (kɔmmemɔrɛzɔ̃), s.f. (church) Commemoration.

commémorati-f, -ve (kɔmmemɔratif), adj. Commemorative.

commémoration (kɔmmemɔra'sjɔ̃), s.f. **1.** Commemoration; **2.** memory, remembrance.

commémorer (kɔmmemɔre), v.a. [L *commemorare*] To commemorate, to remember.

commençant, -e (kɔmɑ̃sɑ̃), s.m.f. Beginner, novice. ~, p. adj. Beginning.

commencement (kɔmɑ̃smɑ̃), s.m. Beginning, commencement, first part of a thing, source, origin, rudiments.

commencer (kɔmɑ̃se), v.a. [f. L *cum*+*initiare*] To begin, to commence, to start; ~, v.n. to begin, to take rise, to commence, to start; ~, v. impers. *il commence à faire nuit*, it is beginning to get dark; *il commence à pleuvoir*, it is beginning to rain.

commendataire (kɔmɑ̃datɛr), adj. Commendatory.

commende (kɔmɑ̃d), s.f. [f. L *commenda*] Commendam.

commensal, -e, (aux) (kɔmɑ̃sal), s.m.f. [f. L *cum*+*mensa*] Messmate, commensal, boarder, guest.

commensalité (kɔmmɑ̃salite), s.f. Commensality, admission to the king's table.

commensurabilité (kɔmmɑ̃syrabilite), s.f. (math.) Commensurability.

commensurable (kɔmmɑ̃syrabl), adj. [f. L *cum*+*mensurabilis*] Commensurable.

commensuration (kɔmmɑ̃syra'sjɔ̃), s.f. Commensuration.

comment (kɔmɑ̃), adv. [f. L *quomodo*] How, in what manner, why, wherefore, how; (interj.) what!, indeed!; (slang) *et* ~ *!*, not half! ~, s.m. How, why, wherefore; *savoir le pourquoi et le* ~ *d'une chose*, to know the why and wherefore of a thing.

commentaire (kɔmmɑ̃tɛr), s.m. [L *commentarius*] **1.** Comment, commentary; **2.** (fig. fam.) unfavourable remarks.

commentat-eur, -rice (kɔmmɑ̃tatœr), s.m.f. Commentator, commenter.

commenter (kɔmmɑ̃te), v.a. **1.** To comment, to comment on, to commentate; **2.** to criticize.

commérage (kɔmeraʒ), s.m. [f. *commère*] Gossiping, gossip, tittle-tattle.

commerçable (kɔmɛrsabl), adj. Negotiable.

commerçant, -e (kɔmɛrsɑ̃), s.m.f. Merchant, wholesale trader, dealer. ~, p. adj. Commercial, mercantile, trading.

commerce (kɔmɛrs), s.m. [L *commercium*] **1.** Commerce, trade, traffic, interchange of wares, goods, or productions; ~ *de gros*, wholesale trade; ~ *de détail*, retail trade; ~ *extérieur*, foreign trade; *Chambre de* ~, Chamber of Commerce; **2.** the commercial world, the merchants, commerce; **3.** commerce, intercourse; social, intellectual, sexual intercourse; *c'est un homme d'un* ~ *sûr*, he is a man to be depended on.

commercer (kɔmɛrse), v.n. To trade, to traffic.

commercial, -e, (aux) (kɔmɛrsjal), adj. Commercial.

commercialement (kɔmɛrsjalmɑ̃), adv. Commercially.

commercialisation (kɔmɛrsjaliza'sjɔ̃), s.f. Commercialization.

commercialiser (kɔmɛrsjalize), v.a. To commercialize.
commercialité (kɔmɛrsjalite), s.f. Commerciality.
commère (kɔmɛr), s.f. [f. L *cum+mater*] **1.** Gossip, tattling woman, shrewd woman; **2.** fellow-godmother; friend; **3.** (theatr.) leading female part in a review.
commettant (kɔmɛtɑ̃), s.m. [f. *commettre*] **1.** Constituent; **2.** employer, principal.
commettre (kɔmɛtr), v.a. [L *committere*] **1.** To commit, to give in trust, to commend, to confide, to appoint; *~ X à la garde d'un fort*, to put X in charge of a fortress; *reprenez le pouvoir que vous m'avez commis*, take back the power you gave me; *~ sa réputation*, to expose one's reputation; **2.** to do, to perpetrate, to commit; *~ un péché*, to commit a sin; **3.** to lay (ropes); **se ~**, v.pr. *ne vous commettez pas avec ces gens-là*, do not commit yourself with those people.
comminatoire (kɔmminatwar), adj. [f. L *comminari*] Comminatory.
commis (kɔmi), s.m. [f. *commettre*] Clerk, employee, assistant salesman; *~ voyageur*, commercial traveller.
commisération (kɔmmizera'sjɔ̃), s.f. [f. L *cum+miserari*] Commiseration, pity.
commissaire (kɔmisɛr), s.m. [f. L *commissus*] **1.** Commissary, commissioner; **2.** steward; *~ de la Marine*, commissioner of the navy; *~ de police*, superintendant of police; *~-priseur*, auctioneer; *~ d'un bal*, steward of a ball; *Haut-~*, High Commissioner.
commissariat (kɔmisarja), s.m. **1.** Commissary's office; **2.** commissaryship, commissariat; **3.** police-station.
commission (kɔmisjɔ̃), s.f. [f. L *commissio*] **1.** Commission, committing, perpetrating; **2.** charge, trust; **3.** committee, commission; *~ d'enquête*, committee of inquiry; *renvoyer à une ~*, to refer to a committee; *~ rogatoire*, rogatory commission; **4.** order by which a person buys or sells goods for another, commission; **5.** errand, message; *faire les ~s*, to run errands; **6.** percentage on a bargain, commission, discount.
commissionnaire (kɔmisjɔnɛr), s.m. **1.** Commission-merchant; **2.** agent, carrier; **3.** errand-boy; porter.
commissionner (kɔmisjɔne), v.a. To commission, to empower.
commissoire (kɔmiswar), adj. (law) Binding.
commissural, -e, (aux) (kɔmisyral), adj. (anat.) Commissural.
commissure (kɔmisyr), s.f. [L *commissura*] **1.** (anat.) Commissure; **2.** (build.) joint.
commodat (kɔmɔda), s.m. [f. L *commodare*] (law) Commodate, loan.
commode (kɔmɔd), adj. [L *commodus*] **1.** Commodious, convenient, well adapted, comfortable, easy, handy; **2.** (of persons) kind, good-natured, easy-going, accommodating; *il n'est pas ~ !*, he is not an easy customer. ⚠ 'Commodious' = *commode*, but also *spacieux*.
commode (kɔmɔd), s.f. Chest of drawers. ⚠ 'Commode' is also used in English, but frequently in the sense of close-stool = *chaise percée*; *commode* in French has never that sense.
commodément (kɔmɔdemɑ̃), adv. Commodiously, conveniently, comfortably.
commodité (kɔmɔdite), s.f. **1.** Convenience, commodiousness; **2.** easy circumstances, leisure; *nous voulons trop avoir nos ~s*, we think too much of our ease; **3.** accommodation; (pl.) water-closet. ⚠ Nowadays 'commodity' in English = *chose utile, denrée, marchandise*.
commodore (kɔmɔdɔr), s.m. [Engl. wd] Commodore.
commotion (kɔmosjɔ̃ and kɔmmɔsjɔ̃), s.f. [f. L *commotum*] **1.** Shock, concussion; **2.** (fig.) commotion, perturbation.
commuabilité (kɔmmɥabilite), s.f. Commutability.
commuable (kɔmmɥabl), adj. Commutable.
commuer (kɔmmɥe), v.a. [L *commutare*] To commute.
commun, -e (kɔmœ̃), adj. [L *communis*] Common, joint, common, usual, plentiful, ordinary; vulgar, low, common; (gram.) common; *n'avoir rien de ~ avec*, to have nothing in common with; *d'un ~ accord*, with one accord; *il est assez ~ de voir*, we frequently see; *il a l'air ~*, he is very common-looking.
commun (kɔmœ̃), s.m. **1.** Common stock; **2.** the greatest part, the bulk, the generality; **3.** common people, commonalty; *travailler en ~*, to work together; *le ~ des hommes*; the generality of mankind; the common herd; *un homme du ~*, a common man; *il est comme le ~ des mortels*, he is no better than other people; **4.** (pl.) out-offices, outhouses, stables, &c.; **5.** privy.
communal, -e, (aux) (kɔmynal), adj. Communal, pertaining to a commune or parish; *biens ~aux*, parish property, common.
communard, -e (kɔmynar), s.m.f. (French hist.) Partisan of the Paris Commune, 1871.
communauté (kɔmynote), s.f. **1.** Community, joint possession; **2.** society of people having common laws, rights, customs, faith; township, corporation; **3.** convent, the inhabitants of a convent.

commune (kɔmyn), s.f. [f. *commun*] 1. Smallest territorial district (in France) governed by a mayor; parish; *Chambre des Communes*, (England) House of Commons.

communément (kɔmynemɑ̃), adv. Commonly, usually.

communiant, -e (kɔmynjɑ̃), s.m.f. Communicant, one who receives the sacrament.

communicable (kɔmynikabl), adj. Communicable.

communicant, -e (kɔmynikɑ̃), p. adj. Communicating.

communicati-f, -ve (kɔmynikatif), adj. Communicative, ready to impart to others, talkative.

communication (kɔmynika'sjɔ̃), s.f. [L *communicatio*] 1. Communication, intercourse; 2. information, news, message; 3. passage, communication, propagation; traffic; *obtenir* ~ *d'une lettre*, to obtain the communication of a letter; *porte de* ~, communicating door; 4. (law) production (of documents).

communier (kɔmynje), v.n. [f. L *communicare*] 1. To communicate, to receive the sacrament; 2. to share in (an enthusiasm, an opinion); to feel with others.

communion (kɔmynjɔ̃), s.f. 1. Communion, sacrament; 2. communion, similarity of feeling or ideas; 3. communion-prayer; *faire sa première* ~, to take the sacrament for the first time.

communiqué (kɔmynike), s.m. Communication (from the authorities); communiqué, statement.

communiquer (kɔmynike), v.a.n. [L *communicare*] To communicate; to impart, to transmit; **se** ~, v.pr. to be communicated, to communicate.

communisme (kɔmynism), s.m. [f. *commun*] Communism.

communiste (kɔmynist), s.m.f. adj. Communist.

commutable (kɔmmytabl), adj. Commutable.

commutateur (kɔmmytatœr), s.m. (electr.) Switch, change-over, commutator, circuit-changer.

commutati-f, -ve (kɔmmytatif), adj. [f. L *commutare*] (law) Commutative.

commutation (kɔmmyta'sjɔ̃), s.f. [L *commutatio*] Commutation.

compacité (kɔ̃pasite), s.f. Compactness.

compact, -e (kɔ̃pakt), adj. [L *compactus*] Compact, solid, dense, close; *foule* ~*e*, dense crowd; *une majorité* ~*e*, a closely united majority; *une édition* ~*e*, a compact edition.

compagne (kɔ̃paɲ), s.f. [fem. of OF *compain, compagnon*] Companion, female partner or playfellow, helpmate, consort, wife; (of birds) mate.

compagnie (kɔ̃paɲi), s.f. [f. OF *compain*] 1. Company, companionship, fellowship, party, society; *en* ~ *d'un ami*, in company with a friend; *tenir* ~ *à X*, to keep X company; *il y a nombreuse* ~, it's a large party; there are many people; *sa* ~ *m'est précieuse*, I value his companionship very highly; *fréquenter de mauvaises* ~*s*, to be addicted to bad, low company; *aller de* ~, to go together; *dame* (or *demoiselle*) *de* ~, lady-companion; *fausser* ~ *à X*, to give X the slip; to take French leave; 2. company, association, business society, firm, corporation; ~ *d'Assurances*, Insurance Company; *former une* ~, to form, or to float a company; *mettre en* ~, to turn into a company; 3. covey (of partridges); 4. (mil.) company, platoon.

compagnon (kɔ̃paɲɔ̃), s.m. [f. LL *companium*] 1. Companion, fellow, associate, comrade; 2. journeyman, member (of a craft association); 3. equal, fellow; ~ *d'infortune*, companion in misfortune; ~ *de travail*, fellow worker; *joyeux* ~, jolly dog; *traiter X de pair à* ~, to treat X on a footing of equality; to be hail fellow well met with X.

compagnonnage (kɔ̃paɲɔnaʒ), s.m. 1. Time of service of a journeyman after apprenticeship (obs.); 2. craft association; 3. (pej.) comradeship.

comparable (kɔ̃parabl), adj. [f. *comparer*] Comparable.

comparaison (kɔ̃parɛzɔ̃), s.f. Comparison; *mettre en* ~, to compare; *soutenir la* ~, to bear comparison; ~ *n'est pas raison*, to compare is not to prove; *en* ~ *de*, in comparison with; *sans* ~, without any comparison, beyond comparison; *par* ~, in comparison; comparatively.

comparaître (kɔ̃parɛtr), v.n. [f. L *comparere*] To appear; ~ *en personne*, to appear in person; *faute de* ~, in case of non-appearance.

comparant, -e (kɔ̃parɑ̃), p. adj. s.m.f. Appearing, person appearing.

comparati-f, -ve (kɔ̃paratif), adj. Comparative. ~, s.m. (gram.) Comparative degree; *au* ~, in the comparative.

comparativement (kɔ̃parativmɑ̃), adv. Comparatively.

comparer (kɔ̃pare), v.a. [L *comparare*] To compare; **se** ~, v.pr. to compare oneself, to compare with, to bear comparison with, to be compared.

comparoir (kɔ̃parwar), v.n. defect. (used only in the infinitive) (law) To appear in a court of justice.

comparse (kɔ̃pars), s.m.f. [It. *comparsa*] 1. (theatr.) Dumb actor; figurant; 2. (by ext.) unimportant person or part.

compartiment (kɔ̃partimɑ̃), s.m. [LL

compartimentum] Compartment; division.

comparution (kɔ̃parysjɔ̃), s.f. [f. *comparaître*] (law) Appearance.

compas (kɔ̃pɑ), s.m. [f. *compasser*] **1.** Compass; pair of compasses; **2.** (naut.) compass, azimuth compass, mariner's compass; **3.** dividers; ~ *d'épaisseur, de calibre*, calipers, caliper compasses; ~ *de réduction*, proportional compasses; *branches de* ~, legs of a pair of compasses; ~ *de cordonnier*, size stick; *au* ~, with compasses; *avoir le* ~ *dans l'œil*, to have a sure eye (for measurements); **4.** (pop.) *il en a un* ~ *!*, what a stride!, what long legs he has.

compassé, -e (kɔ̃pase), p. adj. Formal, stiff, starched.

compassement (kɔ̃pasmɑ̃), s.m. **1.** Punctiliousness, formality, stiffness; **2.** measuring with compasses.

compasser (kɔ̃pase), v.a. To measure with compasses; to lay symmetrically; to measure.

compassion (kɔ̃pasjɔ̃), s.f. [L *compassio*] Compassion, commiseration, pity; *être touché de* ~, to be moved with compassion.

compatibilité (kɔ̃patibilite), s.f. Compatibility, compatibleness, consistency.

compatible (kɔ̃patibl), adj. Compatible.

compatir (kɔ̃patir), v.n. [f. L *cum+pati, passus*] To have compassion (*à*, for); to sympathize (with), to bear (with).

compatissant, -e (kɔ̃patisɑ̃), p. adj. Compassionate, sympathizing, tender-hearted.

compatriote (kɔ̃patrjɔt), s.m.f. [f. L *cum+patria*] Compatriot, fellow-countryman (or -woman).

compendieusement (kɔ̃pɑ̃djøzmɑ̃), adv. Compendiously, in brief.

compendieu-x, -se (kɔ̃pɑ̃djø), adj. Compendious, brief, abridged.

compendium (kɔ̃pɛ̃djɔm), s.m. [L wd] Compendium, epitome, summary.

compensable (kɔ̃pɑ̃sabl), adj. Compensatable.

compensat-eur, -rice (kɔ̃pɑ̃satœr), adj. Compensating, compensative, compensatory; *pendule* ~, compensation pendulum. ~, s.m. Compensator.

compensation (kɔ̃pɑ̃sa'sjɔ̃), s.f. Compensation, equivalent, amends, set-off, offset; *cela fait* ~, that is a compensation.

compensatoire (kɔ̃pɑ̃satwar), adj. Compensatory.

compenser (kɔ̃pɑ̃se), v.a. [L *compensare*] To compensate, to counterbalance, to make amends for, to set off, to make up for, to offset.

compérage (kɔ̃peraʒ), s.m. **1.** Relation of godfather and godmother; **2.** trickery, cheating, collusion.

compère (kɔ̃pɛr), s.m. [f. L *cum+pater*] **1.** Gossip, pal, crony, blade, fellow; *être* ~ *et compagnon*, to be intimate; to be hand and glove, to be cheek by jowl (with); **2.** godfather (in relation to the godmother); **3.** (theatr.) principal male part in a revue.

compère-loriot (kɔ̃pɛrlɔrjo), s.m. (pathol.) Stye (on the eye); syn. ORGELET.

compétence (kɔ̃petɑ̃s), s.f. [L *competentia*] **1.** (law) Competency; **2.** sphere, department; *cela n'est pas de ma* ~, I am not competent to judge of that; that's outside my province.

compétent, -e (kɔ̃petɑ̃), adj. Competent. ⚠ In English 'competent' has a wider sense than in French; for instance a housemaid may be said to be competent, but in French the word would be only used for judges, learned or experienced persons, &c.

compéter (kɔ̃pete), v.n. [L *competere*] (law) To be due; to be cognizable.

compétit-eur, -rice (kɔ̃petitœr), s.m.f. [f. L *cum+petere*] Competitor.

compétition (kɔ̃petisjɔ̃), s.f. Competition, rivalry.

compilat-eur, -rice (kɔ̃pilatœr), s.m.f. Compiler.

compilation (kɔ̃pila'sjɔ̃), s.f. Compilation.

compiler (kɔ̃pile), v.a. [L *compilare*] To compile.

complainte (kɔ̃plɛ̃t), s.f. [f. OF *complaindre*] **1.** Complaint, the act of complaining; **2.** song of sorrow, ballad, lament. ⚠ In English 'complaint' means also bodily ailment = *maladie*.

complaire (kɔ̃plɛr), v.n. [L *complacere*] To please, to humour; **se** ~ (*à*), v.pr. to delight (in), to take delight (in).

complaisamment (kɔ̃plɛzamɑ̃), adv. Complaisantly, obligingly.

complaisance (kɔ̃plɛzɑ̃s), s.f. [f. *complaire*] Complaisance, complacency, obliging compliance, kindness; state of being pleased, complacence; *par* ~, out of kindness; (pej.) *se regarder avec* ~, to be self-satisfied; *avoir des* ~*s pour X*, to be (rather unjustly) partial to X.

complaisant, -e (kɔ̃plɛzɑ̃), p. adj. Complaisant; complacent, obliging; (pej.) fawning. ~, s.m.f. Fawner, go-between, toad-eater; pimp, pander, abettor.

complant (kɔplɑ̃), s.m. [f. OF *complanter*] Plantation, vineyard.

complément (kɔ̃plemɑ̃), s.m. [L *complementum*] **1.** Complement, completion; **2.** (gram.) object.

complémentaire (kɔ̃plemɑ̃tɛr), adj. Complementary, completing, complemental; *angle* ~, complementary angle.

compl-et, -ète (kɔ̃plɛ), adj. [L *completus*] Complete, full, whole, entire, thorough, utter, perfect, consummate, arrant; *c'est* ~, *alors!*, I say, that's the limit! ~, s.m. **1.** Full complement; *nous sommes* *au* ~, we are all here; **2.** suit of clothes; *apportez mon* ~ *gris*, bring my grey suit.

complètement (kɔ̃plɛtmɑ̃), adv. Completely, wholly, fully, quite, entirely, thoroughly.

complétement (kɔ̃pletmɑ̃), s.m. Completing, completion.

compléter (kɔ̃plete), v.a. To complete, to perfect, to finish; to fill up.

compléti-f, -ve (kɔ̃pletif), adj. (gram.) Completive.

complexe (kɔ̃plɛks), adj. [f. L *complecti, complexus*] Complex, compound, complicated, intricate; *nombre* ~, complex number; *question* ~, intricate question. ~, s.m. (psychol.) Complex.

complexion (kɔ̃plɛksjɔ̃), s.f. [L *complexio*] **1.** Constitution, natural disposition of the body; **2.** humour, disposition. ⚠ *Complexion* must not be translated by (English) 'complexion' which = *teint, couleur de la peau*, and (fig.) *caractère, aspect*.

complexité (kɔ̃plɛksite), s.f. Complexity, complexness, intricacy.

complication (kɔ̃plika'sjɔ̃), s.f. [L *complicatio*] Complication, intricacy, entangled state of affairs; hitch, complicating circumstance; (med.) complication, sudden unfavourable turn taken by complaint.

complice (kɔ̃plis), adj. [f. L *complex*] Privy (to). ~, s.m.f. A party to; accomplice, abettor.

complicité (kɔ̃plisite), s.f. Complicity, participation, aid.

complies (kɔ̃pli), s.f.pl. [f. L *complere*] (Cath. liturg.) Compline.

compliment (kɔ̃plimɑ̃), s.m. [It. *complimento*] Compliment, expression of civility, flattery; congratulation, felicitation; congratulatory address; *trêve de ~s s'il vous plaît*, no compliments, I beg; *faire* ~ *à X de*, to compliment X upon; *il m'a prié de vous faire ses ~s*, he wished me to give you his compliments; *mes ~s!*, I congratulate you!

complimenter (kɔ̃plimɑ̃te), v.a. To compliment, to congratulate, to address with expressions of praise and civility, to pay compliments to.

complimenteu-r, -se (kɔ̃plimɑ̃tœr), adj. Complimentary, flattering. ~, s.m.f. Complimenter, flatterer.

compliqué, -e (kɔ̃plike), p. adj. Complicate, complicated, intricate, entangled.

compliquer (kɔ̃plike), v.a. [L *complicare*] To complicate, to entangle.

complot (kɔ̃plo), s.m. [uncert. orig.] Plot, scheme, conspiracy; *tramer un* ~, to lay a plot; *déjouer un* ~, to frustrate a plot.

comploter (kɔ̃plɔte), v.a.n. To plot, to scheme (against somebody), to devise, to contrive.

comploteur (kɔ̃plɔtœr), s.m. Plotter.

componction (kɔ̃pɔ̃ksjɔ̃), s.f. [L *compunctio*] Compunction, contrition.

componé, -e (kɔ̃pɔne), adj. (herald.) Having a bordure composed of a row of checkers of two colours, compony.

comporte (kɔ̃pɔrt), s.f. Wooden vat used for carrying grapes at vintage time.

comportement (kɔ̃pɔrtəmɑ̃), s.m. [f. *comporter*] Comportment, behaviour.

comporter (kɔ̃pɔrte), v.a. [f. L *cum+portare*] To allow, to admit of; to comport with; **se** ~, v.pr. to behave, to comport oneself or itself.

composant, -e (kɔ̃pozɑ̃), p. adj. Component, composing, constituting. ~, s.m. Component. ~e, s.f. (mech.) Component.

composé, -e (kɔ̃poze), p. adj. [f. *composer*] **1.** Compound, formed (*de*, of), composed (of); **2.** stiff, formal. ~, s.m. Compound. ~e, s.f. (bot.) Composite plant.

composer (kɔ̃poze), v.a. [f. L *componere*] To compose, to compound, to constitute, to form, to write (a paper, a poem, or a piece of music); ~, v.n. to compose, to come to terms, to compromise, to compound; ~ *avec sa conscience*, to compound with one's conscience; **se** ~ (*de*), v.pr. to be composed (of), to be compounded (of); to collect oneself; to compose one's countenance.

composite (kɔ̃pozit), adj. [L *compositus*] Composite. ~, s.m. (arch.) Composite order.

composit-eur, -rice (kɔ̃pozitœr), s.m.f. **1.** Composer (of music, &c.); **2.** (print.) compositor.

composition (kɔ̃pozisjɔ̃), s.f. [L *compositio*] **1.** Composition, act of composing; **2.** (print.) composition (setting types in a composing-stick); **3.** combination, compound, synthesis, arrangement; **4.** agreement, adjustment, settlement; *entrer en* ~ or *venir à* ~, to come to terms, to compromise; **5.** competitive written exercise (in schools).

compost (kɔ̃pɔst), s.m. [f. L *compositus*] (agric.) Compost.

composter (kɔ̃pɔste), v.a. (agric.) To compost.

composteur (kɔ̃pɔstœr), s.m. **1.** (print.) Composing-stick; **2.** stamping machine.

compote (kɔ̃pɔt), s.f. [f. L *compositus*] Stewed fruit, stew; *il lui mit la tête en* ~, he bruised his head all over, he beat him to a jelly.

compotier (kɔ̃pɔtje), s.m. [f. *compote*] Dish for stewed fruit, cakes, &c.

compound, adj. [Engl. wd] (mech.) Compound (of an engine, &c.). ~, s.f. A compound steam-engine.

compréhensibilité (kɔ̃preɑ̃sibilite), s.f. Comprehensibility, intelligibility.

compréhensible (kɔ̃preɑ̃sibl), adj. Comprehensible, conceivable, intelligible.

compréhensi-f, -ve (kɔ̃preɑ̃sif), adj. Comprehensive.
compréhension (kɔ̃preɑ̃sjɔ̃), s.f. [L *comprehensio*] Comprehension, understanding.
comprendre (kɔ̃prɑ̃dr), v.a. [L *comprehendere*] **1.** To comprehend, to include, to comprise, to take in; *le chauffage est compris*, heating is included (in the price); **2.** to understand, to make out, to contain in the mind; *à ce que je comprends*, from what I understand; **se ~**, v.pr. **1.** to understand each other; **2.** to understand oneself; **3.** to be included, to be understood.
compresse (kɔ̃prɛs), s.f. Compress.
compresseur (kɔ̃prɛsœr), s.m. Compressor. ~, adj. Compressing.
compressibilité (kɔ̃prɛsibilite), s.f. Compressibleness, compressibility.
compressible (kɔ̃prɛsibl), adj. Compressible.
compressi-f, -ve (kɔ̃prɛsif), adj. Compressive, repressive.
compression (kɔ̃prɛsjɔ̃), s.f. [L *compressio*] Compression, compressure, squeezing.
comprimable (kɔ̃primabl), adj. Compressible.
comprimant, -e (kɔ̃primɑ̃), p. adj. Compressing, restraining, repressing.
comprimé, -e (kɔ̃prime), p. adj. Compressed, squeezed together, pressed. ~, s.m. Tabloid.
comprimer (kɔ̃prime), v.a. [L *comprimere*] **1.** To compress, to press, to squeeze; **2.** to restrain, to check, to repress; **se ~**, v.pr. to be compressed.
compris, -e (kɔ̃pri), p. adj. [f. *comprendre*] **1.** Understood; **2.** comprised, included; *y ~*, including, included; *non ~*, not including, not included.
compromettant, -e (kɔ̃prɔmɛtɑ̃), p. adj. Compromising, dangerous.
compromettre (kɔ̃prɔmɛtr), v.a. [L *compromittere*] To compromise, to commit, to expose, to implicate, to endanger; *~ sa dignité*, to compromise one's dignity; *~ ses intérêts*, to endanger one's interest; ~, v.n. (law) to make a compromise; **se ~**, v.pr. to commit oneself, to compromise oneself, to get involved.
compromis (kɔ̃prɔmi), s.m. Compromise, adjustment by mutual concession, arrangement.
compromission (kɔ̃prɔmisjɔ̃), s.f. **1.** Compromising; **2.** act of compounding with one's principles.
comptabilité (kɔ̃tabilite), s.f. Bookkeeping, accounts; accountant's department; *~ en partie simple, double*, bookkeeping by single, double entry.
comptable (kɔ̃tabl), s.m.f. [f. *compter*] Accountant, book-keeper. ~, adj. Accountable, responsible; pertaining to book-keeping.
comptage (kɔ̃taʒ), s.m. [f. *compter*] Counting, numbering.
comptant (kɔ̃tɑ̃), p. adj. m. Ready, in cash. ~, s.m. Ready money, cash; *au ~*, cash. ~, adv. Cash.
compte (kɔ̃t), s.m. [L *computum*] Account, calculation, reckoning, computation; amount, quantity, sum, due; banking-account; *faire le ~ de*, to count; *~ rond*, round sum of money; *le ~ n'y est pas*, the account is wrong; *à bon ~*, cheaply; *de ~ à demi*, on joint and equal accounts; going halves (with); *pour le ~ de X*, on X's behalf; *clore un ~*, to close an account; *ouvrir un ~*, to open an account; *débiter un ~*, to debit an account; *créditer un ~*, to credit an account; *régler un ~*, to settle an account; *régler son ~ à un domestique*, to pay and discharge a servant; *son ~ est bon*, he will catch it; *je suis inquiet sur son ~*, I am uneasy about him; *à ce ~-là*, upon that score; at that rate; that being so; *je vous en tiendrai ~*, I will make it up to you; I will credit you with that; I will make allowance for that; *il ne tient aucun ~ de mes remontrances*, he takes no account of my remonstrances; *les bons ~s font les bons amis*, short reckonings make long friends; *~ rendu*, report, statement; *demander ~ de*, to ask for an account of; *avoir son ~*, (*a*) to have one's due; (*b*) to have caught it; (*c*) to be drunk; *entrer en ligne de ~*, (*a*) to enter into the computation; (*b*) to be taken into account, into consideration; *se rendre ~ (de)*, to understand; *au bout du ~*, after all, when all is said and done; *en fin de ~*, at last, in fine; *j'ai un ~ à régler avec lui*, I have a bone to pick with him; *elle y trouve son ~*, she finds it an advantage; *laisser quelque chose pour ~ à X*, to leave something on X's hands; *un laissé-pour-~* (s.m.), a returned article (a piece of clothing which has been ordered and is not bought after all); (fig.) unwanted thing or person.
compte courant (kɔ̃tkurɑ̃), s.m. (pl. *comptes courants*) Current account.
compte-gouttes (kɔ̃tgut), s.m. (pl. *compte-gouttes*) Drop-bottle, dropping tube; (fig.) *au ~*, sparingly, grudgingly.
compter (kɔ̃te), v.a.n. [f. *compte*; originally same as *conter*] To count, to reckon, to calculate, to number, to sum up; to include, to comprise; to charge, to reckon; to take into account; to account, to esteem, to rely (on), to consider, to be of importance, to be valuable; to intend; *~ les jours, les heures*, to reckon the days, the hours; *ses jours sont comptés*, his days are numbered, he has not many

days to live; *cent hommes, sans ~ les officiers*, a hundred men, not including the officers; *il compte le vin trop cher*, he charges too much for the wine; *cela ne compte pas*, it does not matter, it is of no importance, it need not be taken into account; *qui ne vote pas ne compte pas*, whoever has not got a suffrage counts for nothing; *je compte partir demain*, I intend to leave to-morrow; *vous pouvez ~ sur moi*, you may rely on me.

compte rendu (kɔ̃trɑ̃dy), s.m. (pl. *comptes rendus*) Report, account, statement; review.

compteur (kɔ̃tœr), s.m. **1.** Reckoner; **2.** indicator, meter; ~ *de vitesse*, speedometer, speed-indicator.

comptoir (kɔ̃twar), s.m. [f. *compter*] **1.** Counter; **2.** counting-house; **3.** branch establishment, factory, bank, business.

compulser (kɔ̃pylse), v.a. [L *compulsare*] To look through, or into, to examine (papers, books, &c.), to inspect.

compulsion (kɔ̃pylsjɔ̃), s.f. [L *compulsio*] Compulsion.

compulsoire (kɔ̃pylswar), s.m. (law) Inspection in virtue of a judge's order.

comput (kɔ̃pyt), s.m. [f. L *computare*] Computation.

computation (kɔ̃pyta'sjɔ̃), s.f. [f. L *computare*] Computation.

computer (kɔ̃pyte), v.a. [L *computare*] To compute, to count.

comtal, -e, (aux) (kɔ̃tal), adj. Of a count, of an earl.

comtat (kɔ̃ta), s.m. County.

comte (kɔ̃t), s.m. [L *comes*] **1.** Count; **2.** (in England) earl.

comté (kɔ̃te), s.m. (fem. in OF) Earldom, county, shire.

comtesse (kɔ̃tɛs), s.f. Countess.

comtois, -e (kɔ̃twɑ), adj. s.m.f. (Native) of Franche-Comté.

concasser (kɔ̃kɑse), v.a. To found, to crush.

concasseur (kɔ̃kɑsœr), s.m. Crushing-mill or -roller.

concave (kɔ̃kav), adj. [L *concavus*] Concave, hollow.

concavité (kɔ̃kavite), s.f. Concavity, hollowness.

concéder (kɔ̃sede), v.a. [L *concedere*] To concede, to grant, to yield.

concentration (kɔ̃sɑ̃tra'sjɔ̃), s.f. Concentration, reduction.

concentrer (kɔ̃sɑ̃tre), v.a. [f. L *cum+centrum*] To concentrate, to condense, to concentre; **se ~**, v.pr. to concentre, to be concentrated or condensed.

concentrique (kɔ̃sɑ̃trik), adj. Concentric.

concentriquement (kɔ̃sɑ̃trikmɑ̃), adv. Concentrically.

concept (kɔ̃sɛpt), s.m. [f. L *conceptus*] Conception, concept, idea.

conceptacle (kɔ̃sɛptakl), s.m. [f. L *cum+capere*] (bot.) Conceptacle, follicle.

conceptibilité (kɔ̃sɛptibilite), s.f. Conceivableness.

conceptible (kɔ̃sɛptibl), adj. Conceivable.

concepti-f, -ve (kɔ̃sɛptif), adj. Conceptive.

conception (kɔ̃sɛpsjɔ̃), s.f. [L *conceptio*] **1.** Conception; **2.** apprehension, understanding; **3.** conception, idea conceived.

conceptuel, -le (kɔ̃sɛptɥɛl), adj. Conceptual.

concernant (kɔ̃sɛrnɑ̃), part. used as prep. Concerning, relating to, with respect to, about.

concerner (kɔ̃sɛrne), v.a. [L *concernere*] To concern, to relate to, to belong to, to affect, to interest. ⚠ 'To be concerned' has also the sense of being troubled = *être péniblement affecté*; a 'concerned' air, *un air troublé, soucieux*; but *concerner* is not used in that sense.

concert (kɔ̃sɛr), s.m. [It. *concerto*] **1.** Concert; **2.** union, agreement, concert; *agir de ~*, to act in concert; to go hand in hand; **3.** chorus; *un ~ de louanges*, a chorus of praise.

concertant, -e (kɔ̃sɛrtɑ̃), p. adj. Joining or performed in concert; taking part in a concert. **~**, s.m.f. Performer (in a concert).

concerter (kɔ̃sɛrte), v.a. [f. *concert*] To concert, to contrive, to devise, to scheme; **~**, v.n. to join in concert; **se ~**, v. pr. to deliberate, to lay (their) heads together, to arrange a common plan of action.

concertiste (kɔ̃sɛrtist), s.m.f. Performer (in a concert).

concerto (kɔ̃sɛrto), s.m. [It. wd] Concerto.

concessible (kɔ̃sɛsibl), adj. Grantable, concessible.

concession (kɔ̃sɛsjɔ̃), s.f. [L *concessio*] Concession, grant; ~ *perpétuelle* (*au cimetière*), perpetual grant (in a cemetery).

concessionnaire (kɔ̃sɛsjɔnɛr), s.m.f. adj. Grantee; that holds a concession.

concetti (kɔ̃sɛtti), s.m.pl. [It. wd] Concetti, conceits.

concevable (kɔ̃svabl), adj. Conceivable.

concevoir (kɔ̃svwar), v.a.n. [L *concipere*] **1.** To conceive, to become pregnant; **2.** to form in the mind, to imagine; to apprehend, to entertain (a feeling); *conçoit-on que*, would you believe that, just imagine!; **se ~**, v.pr. to be conceived, to be imagined, to be intelligible; *cela se conçoit*, that's easy to understand.

conchite (kɔ̃kit), s.f. [f. Gr. *kogkhitēs*] Conchite, fossil shell.

conchoïdal, -e, (aux) (kɔ̃kɔidal), adj. Conchoidal.

conchoïde (kɔ̃koid), s.f. [f. Gr. *kogkhē*] (geom.) Conchoid.
conchylien, -ne (kɔ̃kiljɛ̃), adj. Conchiferous.
conchyliologie (kɔ̃kiljɔlɔʒi), s.f. [f. Gr. *kogkhulion+logos*] Conchology, science of shells.
conchyliologiste (kɔ̃kiljɔlɔʒist), s.m.f. Conchologist.
concierge (kɔ̃sjɛrʒ), s.m.f. [uncert. orig.] Door-keeper, porter.
conciergerie (kɔ̃sjɛrʒəri), s.f. **1.** Porter's lodge; **2.** prison in Paris at the time of the Revolution.
concile (kɔ̃sil), s.m. [L *concilium*] Council.
conciliable (kɔ̃siljabl), adj. Reconcilable.
conciliabule (kɔ̃siljabyl), s.m. [L *conciliabulum*] **1.** Conventicle; **2.** secret meeting or deliberation.
conciliaire (kɔ̃siljɛr), adj. Conciliar, relating to a council.
conciliant, -e (kɔ̃siljɑ̃), p. adj. [f. *concilier*] Conciliatory, conciliating, amiable.
conciliat-eur, -rice (kɔ̃siljatœr), s.m.f. Conciliator. ~ adj. Conciliatory, conciliating.
conciliation (kɔ̃silja'sjɔ̃), s.f. [L *conciliatio*] Conciliation; (law) *appeler en* ~, to summon (before a justice of the peace) for the purpose of conciliation.
conciliatoire (kɔ̃siljatwar), adj. Conciliatory.
concilier (kɔ̃silje), v.a. [L *conciliare*] To conciliate, to reconcile, to win over; **se** ~, v.pr. to gain, to be conciliated, to be reconciled; *il s'est concilié l'affection de tous*, he has won everybody's affection.
concis, -e (kɔ̃si), adj. [L *concisus*] Concise, brief, short.
concision (kɔ̃sizjɔ̃), s.f. Conciseness, brevity.
concitoyen, -ne (kɔ̃sitwajɛ̃), s.m.f. Fellow-citizen.
conclave (kɔ̃klav), s.m. [L *conclavis*] Conclave.
conclaviste (kɔ̃klavist), s.m. Conclavist.
concluant, -e (kɔ̃klyɑ̃), p. adj. Conclusive, final, decisive.
conclure (kɔ̃klyr), v.a.n. [L *concludere*] **1.** To conclude, to bring to a conclusion, to end, to close; **2.** to infer, to conclude; **se** ~, v.pr. to be concluded; to be settled.
conclusi-f, -ve (kɔ̃klyzif), adj. Conclusive.
conclusion (kɔ̃klyzjɔ̃), s.f. [L *conclusio*] **1.** Conclusion, settlement, final stage, final agreement, end; **2.** inference, conclusion; *tirer une* ~, to draw a conclusion; **3.** (law) motion, demand; *prendre des* ~*s*, to make a motion.
concoction (kɔ̃kɔksjɔ̃), s.f. [L *concoctio*] **1.** Concoction; **2.** digestion, solution in the stomach; **3.** maturation of humours.
concombre (kɔ̃kɔ̃br), s.m. [f. L *cucumis*] Cucumber.
concomitance (kɔ̃komitɑ̃s), s.f. Concomitancy.
concomitant, -e (kɔ̃komitɑ̃), adj. [f. L *con+comitans*] Concomitant, concurrent.
concordance (kɔ̃kɔrdɑ̃s), s.f. **1.** Concordance; **2.** (gram.) concord.
concordant, -e (kɔ̃kɔrdɑ̃), p. adj. Concordant.
concordat (kɔ̃kɔrda), s.m. [L *concordatum*] **1.** Concordat, agreement; **2.** (law) bankrupt's certificate, composition.
concordataire (kɔ̃kɔrdatɛ̃r), adj. Certificated, pertaining to a concordat.
concorde (kɔ̃kɔrd), s.f. [L *concordia*] Concord, union, harmony, peace.
concorder (kɔ̃kɔrde), v.n. [f. *concorde*] To agree, to concur, to accord.
concourant, -e (kɔ̃kurɑ̃), p. adj. Concurrent, concurring.
concourir (kɔ̃kurir), v.n. [L *concurrere*] **1.** To concur, to contribute, to co-operate; **2.** (geom.) to meet in one point, to concur; **3.** to compete.
concours (kɔ̃kur), s.m. [L *concursus*] **1.** Concourse, meeting; *le* ~ *des curieux était important*, there was a great concourse of curious people; **2.** help, assistance; cooperation; *demander son* ~ *à X pour*, to ask X's assistance in order to; **3.** competition; *hors* ~, beyond competition, in a class by itself.
concrescible (kɔ̃krɛsibl), adj. [f. L *concrescere*] Concrescible.
concr-et, -ète (kɔ̃krɛ), adj. [L *concretus*] Concrete; *terme* ~, concrete term; *nombre* ~, concrete number; *devenir* ~, to concrete. ⚠ French *concret* cannot be used as subst.; the Engl. subst. 'concrete'= *béton*.
concrétion (kɔ̃kresjɔ̃), s.f. Concretion, compound; (med.) calculus.
concrétiser (kɔ̃kretize), v.a. To render concrete.
concubinage (kɔ̃kybinaʒ), s.m. Concubinage.
concubinaire (kɔ̃kybinɛr), s.m. Concubinary.
concubine (kɔ̃kybin), s.f. [L *concubina*] Concubine.
concupiscence (kɔ̃kypisɑ̃s), s.f. [L *concupiscentia*] Concupiscence.
concupiscent, -e (kɔ̃kypisɑ̃), adj. Concupiscent.
concupiscible (kɔ̃kypisibl), adj. Concupiscible.
concurremment (kɔ̃kyramɑ̃), adv. **1.** Concurrently, conjointly; **2.** in competition.
concurrence (kɔ̃kyrɑ̃s), s.f. [f. L *cum+currere*] Competition, rivalry, concurrence; *être en* ~ *avec*, to compete with;

faire ~ *à*, to rival, to be in competition with; *jusqu'à* ~ *de*, to the amount of, to the extent of.
concurrencer (kõkyrãse), v.a. To compete with, to rival, to vie with.
concurrent, -e (kõkyrã), s.m.f. Competitor, rival. ~, adj. Concurrent.
concussion (kõkysjõ), s.f. [L *concussio*] Extortion, peculation, concussion. ⚠ 'Concussion' in English usually = *choc violent, choc nerveux*.
concussionnaire (kõkysjonɛr), s.m.f. Peculator, embezzler, extortioner. ~, adj. Guilty of extortion.
condamnable (kõdanabl), adj. Condemnable, blameable.
condamnation (kõdana'sjõ), s.f. [f. *condamner*] Condemnation, conviction; (fig.) blame, censure, condemnation; *passer* ~, to confess oneself to be in the wrong; *subir une* ~, to undergo one's sentence; ~ *à mort*, sentence of death.
condamné, -e (kõdane), s.m.f. Condemned person, convict. ~, p. adj. Condemned, sentenced.
condamner (kõdane), v.a. [L *condemnare*] **1.** To condemn, to sentence, to doom; **2.** to condemn, to blame, to censure; **3.** to give up hope for (a sick person); **4.** to block up (a door or window).
condensabilité (kõdãsabilite), s.f. Condensability.
condensable (kõdãsabl), adj. Condensable.
condensateur (kõdãsatœr), s.m. Condenser. ~, adj. Condensing.
condensation (kõdãsa'sjõ), s.f. Condensation; *appareil à* ~, condensing engine.
condenser (kõdãse), v.a. [L *condensare*] To condense; (fig.) to abridge, to condense; **se** ~ v.pr. to condense, to become more compact.
condenseur (kõdãsœr), s.m. Condenser.
condescendance (kõdɛsãdãs), s.f. [f. *condescendre*] Condescension.
condescendant, -e (kõdɛsãdã), p. adj. Condescending.
condescendre (kõdɛsãdr), v.n. [f. L *cum+descendere*] To condescend, to submit, to stoop.
condiment (kõdimã), s.m. [L *condimentum*] Condiment, seasoning.
condisciple (kõdisipl), s.m. [L *cum+discipulus*] Condisciple, school-fellow, fellow-scholar.
condition (kõdisjõ), s.f. [f. L *con+dicere*] **1.** Condition, state, situation, station in life, way of living, rank, quality; *un homme de basse* ~, a man of low station; *chacun doit vivre selon sa* ~, one ought to live according to one's station in life; *une personne de* ~ (*noble*), a person of rank or of high standing; **2.** service, employment of a servant; *entrer en* ~, to go into service; **3.** stipulation, clause, condition, terms; *quelles sont ses* ~*s?*, what are his terms?; *vendre à* ~, to sell upon condition; *à condition de*, on, upon, condition of; *à* ~ *que*, provided that, on condition that.
conditionné, -e (kõdisjone), p. adj. Conditioned, in condition; *bien* ~, downright; well conditioned.
conditionnel, -le (kõdisjonɛl), adj. Conditional. ~, s.m. (gram.) Conditional.
conditionnellement (kõdisjonɛlmã), adv. Conditionally.
conditionnement (kõdisjonmã), s.m. Conditioning; assaying (of silk).
conditionner (kõdisjone), v.a. **1.** To put in good condition; **2.** to assay (silk).
condoléance (kõdoleãs), s.f. (usually in the plural) [f. L *cum+dolere*] Condolence, condolement; *lettre de* ~*s*, letter of condolence; *faire ses* ~*s à X*, to condole with X, to express one's sympathy with X.
condominium (kõdominjom), s.f. [L wd] Condominium.
condor (kõdor), s.m. [Span. wd] (ornith.) Condor.
condottiere (kõdottjɛre), s.m. [It. wd] Condottiere; adventurer.
conduct-eur, -rice (kõdyktœr), s.m.f. [f. *conduire*] **1.** Conductor, leader, guide, director, manager, foreman; **2.** driver, guard; **3.** (phys.) conductor; *bon* ~, good conductor; *mauvais, non-*~, bad, non-conductor. ~, adj. Leading; (phys.) conducting.
conductibilité (kõdyktibilite), s.f. Conductibility.
conductible (kõdyktibl), adj. Conductible, conductive.
conduction (kõdyksjõ), s.f. **1.** (phys.) Conduction; **2.** (Rom. law) hiring.
conduire (kõdɥir), v.a. [L *conducere*] **1.** To conduct, to lead, to guide, to escort, to accompany, to lead the way (to), to direct, to show (to), to take (to), to bring (to); **2.** to lead as a chief, to superintend, to manage; **3.** (phys.) to convey, to conduct; **4.** to drive; **se** ~, v.pr. to behave, to conduct oneself; to find one's way; to be led, conducted.
conduit (kõdɥi), s.m. [f. *conduire*] Pipe, conduit, tube, duct, culvert.
conduite (kõdɥit), s.f. **1.** Conducting, command, leading, guidance; **2.** driving; **3.** behaviour, conduct, deportment; *changer de* ~, to turn over a new leaf; **4.** (phys.) transmission; **5.** pipe, conduit; **6.** escorting; (colloq.) *il m'a fait un bout de* ~, he saw me off, he came a little way with me; (colloq.) *s'acheter une* ~, to turn over a new leaf; ~ *intérieure*, saloon-car, closed car, (U.S.A.) sedan car.
condyle (kõdil), s.m. [Gr. *kondulos*] (anat.) Condylus. **condylien, -ne**, adj.

condylome (kɔ̃dilom), s.m. (med.) Condyloma.
cône (kon), s.m. [Gr. *kōnos*] Cone; ~ *droit*, right cone; ~ *tronqué*, truncated cone; *tronc de* ~, frustum of a cone; ~ *d'embrayage*, (motor.) clutch-cone; *en* ~, conical; ~ *femelle*, female cone; ~ *mâle*, male cone; ~ *garni cuir*, leather-faced cone; ~ *de moyeu*, hub-cone; ~ *de pin*, pine-cone; (zool.) conus, a marine shell.
confabulation (kɔ̃fabyla'sjɔ̃), s.f. Confabulation.
confabuler (kɔ̃fabyle), v.n. [f. L *cum*+ *fabulari*] To confabulate.
confarréation (kɔ̃farea'sjɔ̃), s.f. [L *confarreatio*] (Rom. ant.) Confarreation, the most solemn form of marriage in ancient Rome.
confection (kɔ̃fɛksjɔ̃), s.f. [f. L *conficere, confectio*] **1.** Execution, making; confection; **2.** ready-made clothes; ready-made-clothes trade; *magasin de* ~, ready-made-clothing shop. ⚠ In English the usual sense of 'confection', 'confectionery' is *confiserie, pâtisserie.*
confectionner (kɔ̃fɛksjɔne), v.a. [f. L *conficere*] To make, to execute; to make out, to draw up (lists, &c.); to make up (clothes).
confectionneu-r, -se (kɔ̃fɛksjɔnœr), s.m.f. Clothier, outfitter, maker (of clothes). ⚠ Never to be translated by 'confectioner' which = *confiseur, pâtissier.*
confédérati-f, -ve (kɔ̃federatif), adj. Federative.
confédération (kɔ̃federa'sjɔ̃), s.f. [L *confoederatio*] Confederation, confederacy, federal compact.
confédéré, -e (kɔ̃federe), p. adj. s.m.f. Confederate.
confédérer (kɔ̃federe), v.a. [L *confoederare*] To confederate.
conférence (kɔ̃ferɑ̃s), s.f. [f. *conférer*] **1.** Comparison, collation; **2.** conference, oral discussion, meeting; **3.** lecture, lesson; debating society; *maître de* ~*s*, lecturer, assistant professor in a university; *faire une* ~, to give or deliver a lecture.
conférenci-er, -ère (kɔ̃ferɑ̃sje), s.m.f. Lecturer.
conférer (kɔ̃fere), v.a. [L *conferre*] **1.** To confer, to bestow, to grant; **2.** to compare, to collate, to confer; ~, v.n. to converse, to take counsel, to confer.
confervacées (kɔ̃fɛrvase), s.f.pl. [f. *conferve*] (bot.) Confervaceae.
conferve (kɔ̃fɛrv), s.f. [L *conferva*] (bot.) Conferva, hair-weed.
conf-ès, -esse (kɔ̃fɛ), adj. (obs.) [L *confessus*] That has been to confession.
confesse (kɔ̃fɛs), s.f. (used only with a prep.) Confession; *aller à* ~, to go to confession.
confesser (kɔ̃fɛse), v.a. [f. L *confiteri*] **1.** To confess, to acknowledge (sins, faults); to avow, to own; **2.** to declare a belief in and adherence to; **3.** to hear the confession of (another); ~ *son erreur*, to acknowledge one's error; ~ *sa foi*, to declare one's faith; **se** ~, v.pr. to confess, to confess oneself; *aller se* ~, to go to confession.
confesseur (kɔ̃fɛsœr), s.m. Confessor.
confession (kɔ̃fɛsjɔ̃), s.f. Confession, avowal; declaration of faith; *on lui donnerait le bon Dieu sans* ~, she looks as if butter would not melt in her mouth.
confessionnal (pl. **aux**) (kɔ̃fɛsjɔnal), s.m. Confessional, confession-box.
confessionnel, -le (kɔ̃fɛsjɔnɛl), adj. Religious, pertaining to a confession of faith (*confession de foi*).
confetti (kɔ̃fɛtti), s.m.pl. [pl. of It. *confetto*] Confetti.
confiance (kɔ̃fjɑ̃s), s.f. [L *confidentia*] Confidence, trust, reliance, boldness, assurance; *mettre sa* ~ *en X*, to put one's trust in X; *gagner la* ~ *de X*, to obtain the confidence of X; *une personne de* ~, a trustworthy person; *abus de* ~, breach of trust; *être plein de* ~ *en soi*; to be full of assurance; *acheter de* ~, to buy in complete trust.
confiant, -e (kɔ̃fjɑ̃), p. adj. **1.** Confident, confiding, trusting; **2.** bold, assured.
confidemment (kɔ̃fidamɑ̃), adv. Confidentially, in confidence.
confidence (kɔ̃fidɑ̃s), s.f. [L *confidentia*] Confidence, intimacy; sharing of a secret; secret; *faire des* ~*s à X*, to trust X with one's secrets; *je ne suis pas dans la* ~, I am not in the secret; *en* ~, in confidence, between ourselves. ⚠ In French *confidence* cannot be used like English 'confidence' in the sense of firm trust, boldness, impudence = *assurance, confiance en soi, hardiesse.*
confident, -e (kɔ̃fidɑ̃), s.m.f. Confident, confidant, confidante.
confidentiel, -le (kɔ̃fidɑ̃sjɛl), adj. Confidential, private.
confidentiellement (kɔ̃fidɑ̃sjɛlmɑ̃), adv. Confidentially.
confier (kɔ̃fje), v.a. [L *confidere*] **1.** To trust, to entrust (to, with); *il m'a confié son trésor*, he has entrusted me with his treasure; **2.** to confide (to), to tell in confidence, to commit; *confiez-moi vos craintes*, confide your fears to me; *il serait dangereux de* ~ *cela au papier*, it would be dangerous to commit that to paper; **se** ~ (*à*), v.pr. to confide (in), to trust (in or to), to rely (on), to unbosom oneself, to be committed.
configuration (kɔ̃figyra'sjɔ̃), s.f. [f. *configurer*] Configuration, shape, form.
configurer (kɔ̃figyre), v.a. [f. L *con*+

figurare] To configure, to form, to dispose.

confinement (kɔ̃finmɑ̃), s.m. [f. *confiner*] Imprisonment, confinement. ⚠ 'Confinement' in English means also *accouchement*.

confiner (kɔ̃fine), v.n. [f. L *cum+finis*] To confine, to border (*à*, upon); ~, v.a. to shut up, to confine, to imprison; *air confiné*, stuffy atmosphere; **se** ~, v.pr. to confine oneself, to shut oneself up.

confins (kɔ̃fɛ̃), s.m.pl. [L *con+finis*] Confines, boundaries, borders, remote parts, limits.

confire (kɔ̃fir), v.a. [L *conficere*] To preserve (fruits), to pickle; to soak (leather).

confirmati-f, -ve (kɔ̃firmatif), adj. Confirmative, confirmatory.

confirmation (kɔ̃firma'sjɔ̃), s.f. **1.** Confirmation, ratification; **2.** corroboration of evidence; **3.** the sacrament of confirmation.

confirmatoire (kɔ̃firmatwar), adj. Confirmatory.

confirmer (kɔ̃firme), v.a. [L *confirmare*] **1.** To confirm, to ratify, to corroborate; **2.** to confirm, to administer the sacrament of confirmation; **3.** (pop.) to box a person's ears; **se** ~, v.pr. and v. impers. to be confirmed, to prove true; *il se confirme que l'ennemi a été battu*, that the enemy was beaten proves to be true; or it is confirmed that, &c.

confiscable (kɔ̃fiskabl), adj. Confiscable.

confiscation (kɔ̃fiska'sjɔ̃), s.f. [L *confiscatio*] Confiscation, forfeit.

confiserie (kɔ̃fizri), s.f. Confectionery.

confiseu-r, -se (kɔ̃fisœr), s.m.f. [f. *confire*] Confectioner.

confisquer (kɔ̃fiske), v.a. [f. L *con+fiscus, confiscare*] To confiscate, to take away (from).

confit, -e (kɔ̃fi), p. adj. [f. *confire*] **1.** Preserved; **2.** pickled; **3.** (fig.) steeped; ~ *en dévotion*, steeped in devotion. ~, s.m. Dish of goose-meat preserved in fat.

confiteor (kɔ̃fiteɔr), s.m. [L wd] Confiteor.

confiture (kɔ̃fityr), s.f. [f. *confit*] Preserve, jam.

confiturier (kɔ̃fityrje), s.m. Jam-dish.

conflagration (kɔ̃flagra'sjɔ̃), s.f. [f. L *conflagrare*] Conflagration.

conflit (kɔ̃fli), s.m. [L *conflictus*] Conflict, shock, encounter, struggle, clashing; *en* ~, at strife.

confluence (kɔ̃flyɑ̃s), s.f. (med.) Confluence.

confluent (kɔ̃flyɑ̃), s.m. [f. *confluer*] Confluent, confluence, conflux, junction of streams. ~, adj. Confluent.

confluer (kɔ̃flye), v.n. [f. L *confluere*] To join their waters, to meet, to be confluent.

confondre (kɔ̃fɔ̃dr), v.a. [L *confundere*] **1.** To confound, to blend, to confuse, to mix, to entangle, to mingle; *les océans confondent leurs eaux*, the oceans mingle their waters; *je confonds ces deux personnes*, I mistake one for the other; **2.** To put out of countenance, to abash, to confuse, to overthrow; *le meurtrier a été confondu par ce témoignage*, this evidence confounded the murderer; *cela confond la raison*, that confounds reason; *que le ciel te confonde!*, (may Heaven) confound you!; **se** ~, v.pr. (*a*) to be confounded, mingled, confused; (*b*) to be profuse (in civilities, apologies, &c.).

conformateur (kɔ̃fɔrmatœr), s.m. Stretcher for hats.

conformation (kɔ̃fɔrma'sjɔ̃), s.f. [f. *conformer*] Conformation, structure, shape, build.

conforme (kɔ̃fɔrm), adj. [L *conformis*] Conformable, similar, like, consistent; *pour copie* ~, conformable to the original; *avoir un train de vie* ~ *à sa fortune*, to lead a life conformable to one's fortune.

conformé, -e (kɔnfɔrme), p. adj. Conformed, shaped, made, built.

conformément (kɔ̃fɔrmemɑ̃), adv. According (*à*, to), conformably (to, with).

conformer (kɔ̃fɔrme), v.a. [L *conformare*] To conform, to form, to shape, to suit, to adapt; **se** ~ (*à*), v.pr. to conform oneself (to), to submit (to), to adapt oneself (to).

conformiste (kɔ̃fɔrmist), s.m.f. Conformist; *non*-~, nonconformist, dissenter.

conformité (kɔ̃fɔrmite), s.f. Conformity, similarity, consistency, suitableness; *en* ~ *de*, in conformity with, according to, in compliance with.

confort (kɔ̃fɔr), s.m. [f. Engl. *comfort*] Comfort, support, ease, well-being.

confortable (kɔ̃fɔrtabl), adj. Comfortable. ~, s.m. Comfort.

confortablement (kɔ̃fɔrtabləmɑ̃), adv. Comfortably.

confortant, -e (kɔ̃fɔrtɑ̃), p. adj. (med.) Corroborant, strengthening.

confortation (kɔ̃fɔrta'sjɔ̃), s.m. (med.) Strengthening, confortation.

conforter (kɔ̃fɔrte), v.a. (med.) To comfort, to strengthen.

confraternel, -le (kɔ̃fratɛrnɛl), adj. Brotherly, fellow-.

confraternité (kɔ̃fratɛrnite), s.f. Confraternity, fellowship.

confrère (kɔ̃frɛr), s.m. [f. L *cum+frater*] Confrere, brother, colleague, fellow-member.

confrérie (kɔ̃freri), s.f. Confraternity, brotherhood, sisterhood.

confrontation (kɔ̃frɔ̃ta'sjɔ̃), s.f. Confrontation, comparison.
confronter (kɔ̃frɔ̃te), v.a. [f. L *cum*+ *frons*] To confront, to compare; ~, v.n. (law) to border.
confus, -e (kɔ̃fy), adj. [L *confusus*] **1.** Confused, undistinguishable, indistinct, intricate; *notions vagues et ~es*, vague and confused notions; **2.** ashamed, abashed, confused; *je suis ~ de vos bontés*, I am overwhelmed with your kindness; *vous me rendez ~*, you embarrass me.
confusément (kɔ̃fyzemɑ̃), adv. Confusedly, vaguely, indistinctly, dimly.
confusion (kɔ̃fyzjɔ̃), s.f. [L *confusio*] **1.** Confusion, confusedness, mistake, disorder; *~ de pouvoirs*, confusion of powers; *mettre la ~ dans les rangs*, to put the ranks into disorder; **2.** shame, confusion, abasement; *couvrir X de ~*, to confound X, to bring X to confusion; *à ma ~*, to my shame.
congé (kɔ̃ʒe), s.m. [L *commeatus*] **1.** Leave, discharge, warning; **2.** (mil.) term of service; **3.** leave, permission, consent; *se marier sans le ~ de ses parents*, to marry without one's parents' consent; **4.** permit of transport (for wines), clearance, pass; **5.** leave, farewell; **6.** warning; (from landlord) notice to quit; (from tenant) notice to leave; **7.** (arch.) congé, apophyge.
congéable (kɔ̃ʒeabl), adj. Dismissable.
congédiable (kɔ̃ʒedjabl), adj. [f. *congédier*] That may be discharged, dismissable.
congédiement (kɔ̃ʒedimɑ̃), s.m. Discharge, dismissal, (pop.) sacking.
congédier (kɔ̃ʒedje), v.a. [f. It. *congedo*] To dismiss, to discharge, to turn off, to pay off; (colloq.) to give the sack to, to sack; to end an interview with.
congelable (kɔ̃ʒlabl), adj. Congealable.
congélateur (kɔ̃ʒelatœr), s.m. Refrigerator.
congélati-f, -ve (kɔ̃ʒelatif), adj. Congealing.
congélation (kɔ̃ʒela'sjɔ̃), s.f. Congelation, congealment, freezing, congealed matter.
congeler (kɔ̃ʒle), v.a. [L *congelare*] To congeal, to freeze; **se** ~, v.pr. to congeal, to freeze.
congénère (kɔ̃ʒenɛr), s.m.f. [f. L *cum*+ *generis*] Congener. ~, adj. Congenerous, congeneric.
congénital, -e, (aux) (kɔ̃ʒenital), adj. [f. L *congenitus*] Congenital.
congérie (kɔ̃ʒeri), s.f. [L *congeries*] Congeries, accumulation.
congesti-f, -ve (kɔ̃ʒɛstif), adj. Congested, congestive.
congestion (kɔ̃ʒɛstjɔ̃), s.f. [L *congestio*] Congestion, accumulation; *~ cérébrale*, congestion of the brain.
congestionner (kɔ̃ʒɛstjɔne), v.a. To congest.
congiaire (kɔ̃ʒjɛr), s.m. [L *congiarium*] (Rom. ant.) Congiary (gift divided among the people or soldiers).
conglobation (kɔ̃glɔba'sjɔ̃), s.f. Conglobation.
conglober (kɔ̃glɔbe), v.a. [L *conglobare*] To conglobate, to conglobe.
conglomérat (kɔ̃glɔmera), s.m. (min.) Conglomerate.
conglomération (kɔ̃glɔmera'sjɔ̃), s.f. Conglomeration, accumulation.
conglomérer (kɔ̃glɔmere), v.a. [L *conglomerare*] To conglomerate.
conglutinant, -e, conglutinati-f, -ve (kɔ̃glytinɑ̃, kɔ̃glytinatif), p. adj. Conglutinating, conglutinative.
conglutination (kɔ̃glytina'sjɔ̃), s.f. Conglutination.
conglutiner (kɔ̃glytine), v.a. [L *conglutinare*] To conglutinate; **se** ~, v.pr. to conglutinate.
conglutineu-x, -se (kɔ̃glytinø), adj. (med.) Glutinous.
congolais, -e (kɔ̃gɔlɛ), adj. s.m.f. Congolese, (inhabitant) of Congoland.
congratulant, -e (kɔ̃gratylɑ̃), p. adj. Flattering.
congratulat-eur, -rice (kɔ̃gratylatœr), s.m.f. (slightly iron.) Congratulator. ~, adj. Congratulatory.
congratulation (kɔ̃gratyla'sjɔ̃), s.f. Congratulation.
congratulatoire (kɔ̃gratylatwar), adj. Congratulory.
congratuler (kɔ̃gratyle), v.a. [L *congratulari*] To congratulate; **se** ~, v.pr. to felicitate oneself or each other.
congre (kɔ̃gr), s.m. [L *conger*] (ichth.) Conger, conger-eel.
congréage (kɔ̃greaʒ), s.m. (naut.) Worming.
congréer (kɔ̃gree), v.a. [f. OF *conréer*] (naut.) To worm, to wind spun yarn spirally round a cable or rope, between the strands.
congréganiste (kɔ̃greganist), s.m.f. [f. L *congregare*] Member of a congregation. ~, adj. Pertaining to a congregation; *l'enseignement ~*, tuition in schools directed by a religious congregation.
congrégation (kɔ̃grega'sjɔ̃), s.f. Congregation, assembly of persons; subdivision of a monastic order, assembly of ecclesiastics appointed by the pope.
congrès (kɔ̃grɛ), s.m. [L *congressus*] Congress: (*a*) a meeting of ambassadors; (*b*) meeting of representatives of sciences arts, industries, societies, political parties; (*c*) assembly of senators and deputies in France, and in U.S.A.
congressiste (kɔ̃grɛsist), s.m.f. Member of a congress.

congru, -e (kɔ̃gry), adj. [L *congruus*] **1.** Congruous, proper, fit, exact; *portion ~e*, hardly sufficient ration; **2.** (math.) congruent, congruous.

congruence (kɔ̃gryɑ̃s), s.f. (math.) Congruity.

congruent, -e (kɔ̃gryɑ̃), adj. Congruent, suitable, congruous.

congruité (kɔ̃gryite), s.f. Congruity.

congrument (kɔ̃grymɑ̃), adv. Congruously, properly.

conicine (kɔnisin), s.f. [f. L *conium*] (chem.) Conine, conia; syn. CICUTINE.

conicité (kɔnisite), s.f. [f. *conique*] Conicalness.

conifère (kɔnifɛr), s.m. [L *conifer*] Conifer; (pl.) coniferae. ~, adj. Coniferous.

coniforme (kɔnifɔrm), adj. Coniform, conic.

conine (kɔnin), s.f. See CONICINE.

conique (kɔnik), adj. [f. Gr. *kōnos*] Conic, conical; *sections ~s*, conic sections. ~, s.f. Conic.

conirostre (kɔnirɔstr), s.m. [f. L *conus*+ *rostrum*] (ornith.) Coniroster.

conjectural, -e, (aux) (kɔ̃ʒɛktyral), adj. Conjectural.

conjecturalement (kɔ̃ʒɛktyralmɑ̃), adj. Conjecturally.

conjecture (kɔ̃ʒɛktyr), s.f. Conjecture, surmise.

conjecturer (kɔ̃ʒɛktyre), v.a. [f. L *conjicere*] To conjecture, to surmise, to guess.

conjoindre (kɔ̃ʒwɛ̃dr), v.a. [L *con*+ *jungere*] To conjoin, to unite.

conjoint, -e (kɔ̃ʒwɛ̃), p. adj. Conjoined, wedded; (mus.) conjoint; (bot.) joined. ~, s.m.f. Married person (wife in relation to husband, husband in relation to wife).

conjointement (kɔ̃ʒwɛ̃tmɑ̃), adv. Jointly.

conjoncteur (kɔ̃ʒɔ̃ktœr), s.m. Circuit-closer; *~-disjoncteur*, circuit-breaker; syn. COUPLEUR.

conjoncti-f, -ve (kɔ̃ʒɔ̃ktif), adj. Conjunctive, uniting. ~, s.m. (gram.) Subjunctive; (anat.) conjunctive tissue.

conjonction (kɔ̃ʒɔ̃ksjɔ̃), s.f. Conjunction, union, connexion; (astr.) conjunction; (gram.) conjunction.

conjonctive (kɔ̃ʒɔ̃ktiv), s.f. [L *conjunctiva*] (anat.) Conjunctiva.

conjonctivement (kɔ̃ʒɔ̃ktivmɑ̃), adv. Conjunctively.

conjonctivite (kɔ̃ʒɔ̃ktivit), s.f. Conjunctivitis.

conjoncture (kɔ̃ʒɔ̃ktyr), s.f. [f. L *cum*+ *junctura*] Conjuncture; *dans des ~s difficiles*, in difficult circumstances.

conjugable (kɔ̃ʒygabl), adj. Conjugable.

conjugaison (kɔ̃ʒygɛzɔ̃), s.f. **1.** Joining together, conjugation; **2.** (gram.) conjugation.

conjugal, -e, (aux) (kɔ̃ʒygal), adj. [L *conjugalis*] Conjugal, connubial, matrimonial.

conjugalement (kɔ̃ʒygalmɑ̃), adv. Conjugally, connubially.

conjugué, -e (kɔ̃ʒyge), p. adj. (bot., mech., anat.) Conjugate, connected; (gram.) conjugate, conjugated; *feuilles ~es*, conjugate leaves; *diamètres ~s*, conjugate diameters. **~es**, s.f.pl. (bot.) Genus of algae.

conjuguer (kɔ̃ʒyge), v.a. [L *conjugare*] **1.** To unite; **2.** (gram.) to conjugate, to inflect; **se ~**, v.pr. to be conjugated, to be joined.

conjungo (kɔ̃ʒɔ̃go), s.m. [L wd] (pop.) Marriage state; *fuir le ~*, to fight shy of marriage.

conjurateur (kɔ̃ʒyratœr), s.m. **1.** Conspirator; **2.** conjurer.

conjuration (kɔ̃ʒyra'sjɔ̃), s.f. **1.** Conspiracy, plot, conjuration; **2.** incantation; entreaty, conjuration, solemn appeal.

conjuré, -e (kɔ̃ʒyre), p. adj. **1.** Confederate, leagued, sworn; **2.** begged; exorcised, avoided; *un danger ~*, a peril avoided. ~, s.m.f. Conspirator, plotter.

conjurer (kɔ̃ʒyre), v.a. [L *conjurare*] **1.** To conjure, to entreat, to adjure, to exorcise, to charm away, to avert; *dites cela, je vous en conjure*, I entreat you to say that; **2.** to plot; *ils ont conjuré sa perte*, they have plotted his ruin; ~, v.n. to conspire; **se ~**, v.pr. to conspire together.

connaissable (kɔnɛsabl), adj. Knowable, recognizable.

connaissance (kɔnɛsɑ̃s), s.f. **1.** Knowledge, notion, perception, cognition; knowledge, learning, information; *à ma ~*, to my knowledge; *je n'en ai pas ~*, I have not been informed of it; *venir à la ~ de X*, to come to the knowledge of X; *prendre ~ de*, to look into, to take cognizance of; *en ~ de cause*, with a thorough knowledge of the matter; *parler en ~ de cause*, to know what one is talking about; *~ des temps*, nautical almanac; *dans l'état actuel de nos ~s*, in the present state of learning; **2.** acquaintance; *faire ~ avec lui*, to get acquainted with him; *ce sont des personnes (gens) de ~*, they are acquaintances; *beaucoup de ~s, peu d'amis*, many acquaintances, but few friends; *être en pays de ~*, to be with old acquaintances; to feel at home; *je vous ferai faire sa ~*, I will make you acquainted with him; **3.** senses; *perdre ~*, to swoon, to lose consciousness, to become senseless; **4.** cognizance; *la ~ de ce crime appartient à tel tribunal*, the cognizance of this crime belongs to such and such a tribunal.

connaissant, -e (kɔ̃nɛsɑ̃), p. adj. Knowing, skilled.

connaissement (kɔ̃nɛsmɑ̃), s.m. Bill of lading, invoice.

connaisseu-r, -se (kɔnɛsœr), s.m.f. Connoisseur (*en*, in), good judge (of). ~ adj. Knowing, of a connoisseur.

connaître (kɔnɛtr), v.a. [L *cognoscere*] **1.** To know, to perceive, to understand; *je connais son caractère,* I understand his nature; **2.** to have knowledge of, to be informed of; *il connaît votre situation,* he is informed of your position; **3.** to feel, to experience, to be familiar with; *elle n'a pas connu le vrai bonheur,* she has never experienced real happiness; **4.** to be acquainted with; *se faire ~,* (*a*) to announce or send in one's name; (*b*) to make oneself known; (*c*) to come before the public eye; *~ son monde,* to know what people are; *je ne veux pas ~ ces gens-là,* I won't be acquainted with those people; **5.** (script. lang.) to have sexual intercourse with; **6.** to admit; *sa colère ne connut plus de bornes,* his rage knew no bounds; **se ~,** v.pr. *il ne se connaît plus,* he is beside himself with rage; *il s'y connaît,* he is a connoisseur, he knows all about that; *nous nous connaissons depuis vingt ans,* we have known each other for twenty years; *l'arbre se connaît à son fruit,* the tree is known by its fruit; ~, v.n. to take cognizance (*de*, of); (pop.) *connu!,* (*a*) that's nothing new!; (*b*) I've been had before; do you see any green in my eye?; (pop.) *il la connaît dans les coins,* he knows the ropes; he is up to snuff.

connecter (kɔnɛkte), v.a. To connect.

connecteur (kɔnɛktœr), s.m. adj. (teleph., electr.) Connector, connecting.

connecti-f, -ve (kɔnɛktif), adj. Connective.

connétable (kɔnetabl), s.m. [f. L *comes stabuli*] Commander-in-chief of the French Armies; Lord High Constable.

connétablie (kɔnetabli), s.f. **1.** Constableship; **2.** constablewick.

connexe (kɔnnɛks), adj. [L *connexus*] Connected, united, joined.

connexion (kɔnnɛksjɔ̃), s.f. Connection, connexion.

connexité (kɔnnɛksite), s.f. Connection, connexion, the quality of being connected.

connivence (kɔnnivɑ̃s), s.f. Connivance.

connivent, -e (kɔnnivɑ̃), adj. (anat.) Connivent, converging together.

conniver (kɔnnive), v.n. [L *connivere*] To connive.

connu, -e (kɔny), p. adj. Known, familiar; *chiffres ~s,* plain figures.

conoïdal, -e, (aux) (kɔnɔidal), adj. Conoidal.

conoïde (kɔnɔid), adj. s.m. [f. *cône*] Conoid.

conque (kɔ̃k), s.f. [f. Gr. *kogkhē*] **1.** Conch, shell; **2.** (anat.) concha.

conquérant, -e (kɔ̃kerɑ̃), p. adj. Conquering, victorious, fond of conquest; (fam.) killing, smart. ~, s.m. Conqueror; (fam.) lady-killer. ~, s.f. Conqueress (rarely used).

conquérir (kɔ̃kerir), v.a.n. [f. L *conquirere*] **1.** To conquer, to vanquish, to get possession of by force; **2.** to win, to win over, to obtain; *~ l'estime de X,* to gain the esteem of X; **se ~,** v.pr. to be conquered.

conquêt (kɔ̃kɛ), s.m. (used only in conjunction with *acquêt*) (law) Acquest, property acquired by husband and wife conjointly.

conquête (kɔ̃kɛt), s.f. Conquest: (*a*) act of conquering; (*b*) that which is conquered; *faire la ~ de X,* to win the favour or the heart of X.

conquis, -e (kɔ̃ki), p. adj. Conquered.

consacrant (kɔ̃sakrɑ̃), p. adj. Consecrating. ~, s.m. Consecrator.

consacrer (kɔ̃sakre), v.a. [L *consecrare*] **1.** To consecrate, to dedicate, to sanctify; **2.** to appropriate, to devote; *j'y consacre tout mon temps,* I devote the whole of my time to it; **3.** to sanction, to employ; *l'usage a consacré ce mot,* custom sanctions this expression; **se ~,** v.pr. to devote oneself.

consanguin, -e (kɔ̃sɑ̃gɛ̃), adj. [f. L *consanguineus*] Consanguineous.

consanguinité (kɔ̃sɑ̃ginite), s.f. Consanguinity.

consciemment (kɔ̃sjamɑ̃), adv. Consciously.

conscience (kɔ̃sjɑ̃s), s.f. [L *conscientia*] **1.** Consciousness, knowledge, perception; *avoir ~ de sa faiblesse,* to be conscious of one's weakness; **2.** conscience, internal judgement, scruple, morality, conscientiousness; *avec ~,* conscientiously; *en mon âme et ~,* upon my soul and honour; *homme sans ~,* unscrupulous person; *il a la ~ large comme la manche d'un cordelier,* he has a very accommodating conscience; *par acquit de ~,* for conscience sake; *avoir quelque chose sur la ~,* (*a*) to have been guilty of something; (*b*) to have something on one's mind; *en ~,* honestly, candidly.

consciencieusement (kɔ̃sjɑ̃sjøzmɑ̃), adv. Conscientiously.

consciencieu-x, -se (kɔ̃sjɑ̃sjø), adj. Conscientious.

conscient, -e (kɔ̃sjɑ̃), adj. Conscious (*de*, of).

conscription (kɔ̃skripsjɔ̃), s.f. Conscription, enrolment.

conscrit (kɔ̃skri), s.m. Conscript, recruit; (fig.) freshman, greenhorn.

consécrateur (kõsekratœr), adj. s.m. See syn. CONSACRANT.
consécration (kõsekra'sjõ), s.f. [f. L *consecrare*] Consecration, dedication, sanction.
consécuti-f, -ve (kõsekytif), adj. [f. L *consequi*] Consecutive, consequential.
consécution (kõsekysjõ), s.f. Consecution.
consécutivement (kõsekytivmã), adv. Consecutively.
conseil (kõsɛj), s.m. [L *consilium*] **1.** Counsel, advice; *il est de bon ~*, he is a wise adviser; *la nuit porte ~*, advise with your pillow; night brings counsel; *prendre ~ de X*, to advise with X; *tenir ~ avec*, to advise with, to hold a council with; **2.** adviser; *il a toujours été mon ~*, he has always been my adviser; **3.** purpose; **4.** council, board; *~ municipal*, town (or common) council; *~ d'État*, Council of State; Privy Council; *~ de revision*, recruiting board; *~ de guerre*, court martial; *~ d'administration*, board of directors.
conseiller (kõsɛje), v.a.n. To counsel, to advise, to recommend.
conseill-er, -ère (kõsɛje) s.m.f. **1.** Counsellor, adviser; *la colère est mauvaise ~ère*, anger is a bad counsellor; **2.** councillor; *~ municipal*, town councillor.
conseilleu-r, -se (kõsɛjœr), s.m.f. Officious adviser; *les ~s ne sont pas les payeurs*, advisers run no risks. ~ adj. (usually pej.) Officiously advising.
consensuel, -le (kõsãsɥɛl), adj. Consensual.
consensus (kõsãsys), s.m. [L wd] Consensus.
consentant, -e (kõsãtã), p. adj. Consenting, willing, agreeable.
consentement (kõsãtmã), s.m. Consent, assent.
consentir (kõsãtir), v.n. [L *consentire*] To consent, to agree, to assent, to allow; *qui ne dit mot consent*, silence gives consent; ~, v.a. to consent to, to grant, to authorize; *consentir un prêt*, to grant a loan.
conséquemment (kõsekamã), adv. **1.** Consistently; **2.** consequently, accordingly, therefore.
conséquence (kõsekãs), s.f. [L *consequentia*] **1.** Consequence, conclusion, deduction, result; **2.** importance, moment; *cela n'aura pas de ~s graves*, it will not have bad results; *cela ne tire pas à ~*, that proves nothing; that is unimportant; *tirer les ~s*, to draw inferences; *c'est une personne sans ~*, he (or she) is a person of no importance, a nobody; *en ~*, in consequence, accordingly.
conséquent, -e (kõsekã), adj. Consistent, rational; (pop.) important.
conséquent (kõsekã), s.m. (log., math.) Consequent; *par ~*, consequently, therefore, in consequence.
conservat-eur, -rice (kõsɛrvatœr), s.m.f. Conservator, keeper, guardian, preserver, commissioner. ~, adj. Conservative, preservative; *un journal ~*, a conservative newspaper.
conservation (kõsɛrva'sjõ), s.f. **1.** Conservation, preservation; **2.** jurisdiction, registration.
conservatoire (kõsɛrvatwar), s.m. Conservatory; school, museum, academy. ~, adj. Conservatory, conservative.
conserve (kõsɛrv), s.f. **1.** Preserve, conserve, tinned meat, vegetables, or fish; **2.** (pl.) preserves; (eye-)glasses; **3.** *aller* (or *naviguer*) *de ~*, to sail in company.
conserver (kõsɛrve), v.a. [L *conservare*] To preserve, to keep, to maintain; to keep up; to season, to pickle; **se ~**, v.pr. to keep.
considérable (kõsiderabl), adj. Considerable, eminent, distinguished, important.
considérablement (kõsiderabləmã), adv. Considerably, to a great extent.
considérant (kõsiderã), s.m. (law) Preamble, grounds (of a judgement).
considération (kõsidera'sjõ), s.f. **1.** Consideration, deliberation, mental view, motive; *en ~ de*, on account of; **2.** esteem, regard.
considérément (kõsideremã), adv. Considerately.
considérer (kõsidere), v.a. [L *considerare*] **1.** To consider, to examine, to ponder on; **2.** to esteem, to pay regard to; to deem; **se ~**, v.pr. to consider (or deem) oneself, or each other; to be considered.
consignataire (kõsiɲatɛr), s.m.f. Consignee, depositary.
consignat-eur, -rice (kõsiɲatœr), s.m.f. Consigner.
consignation (kõsiɲa'sjõ), s.f. Consignment, depositing, deposit, mention, entry, registering.
consigne (kõsiɲ), s.f. **1.** (mil.) Orders, instructions; **2.** regulations; **3.** left-luggage office, cloak-room; **4.** (school punishment) keeping-in.
consigner (kõsiɲe), v.a. [L *consignare*] **1.** To deposit, to put in consignment; **2.** to record; **3.** to keep in, to confine; **4.** *~ sa porte*, to refuse admittance.
consistance (kõsistãs), s.f. Consistence, consistency, stability, firmness; (fig.) credit, consideration.
consistant, -e (kõsistã), p. adj. Consistent, firm, solid, compact.
consister (kõsiste), v.n. [L *consistere*] To consist, to be made (of).
consistoire (kõsistwar), s.m. [L *consistorium*] Consistory.

consistorial, -e, (aux) (kɔ̃sistɔrjal), adj. Consistorial.
consolable (kɔ̃sɔlabl), adj. Consolable.
consolant, -e (kɔ̃sɔlɑ̃), p. adj. Consoling, comforting, cheering.
consolat-eur, -rice (kɔ̃sɔlatœr), s.m.f. Consoler, comforter. ~, adj. Consoling.
consolation (kɔ̃sɔlɑ'sjɔ̃), s.f. Consolation, solace, comfort.
consolatoire (kɔ̃sɔlatwar), adj. Consolatory.
console (kɔ̃sɔl), s.f. Console, corbel, bracket, console-table.
consoler (kɔ̃sɔle), v.a. [f. L *consolari*] To console, to soothe, to cheer, to alleviate the grief of; **se** ~, v.pr. to be consoled, comforted, &c., to console oneself or each other.
consolidation (kɔ̃sɔlida'sjɔ̃), s.f. Consolidation, funding.
consolidé, -e (kɔ̃sɔlide), p. adj. Consolidated; funded. **~s**, s.m.pl. Consols.
consolider (kɔ̃sɔlide), v.a. [L *consolidare*] To consolidate, to strengthen; (med.) to knit together, to heal up.
consommable (kɔ̃sɔmabl), adj. Consumable.
consommat-eur, -rice (kɔ̃sɔmatœr), s.m.f. **1.** Consumer, customer; **2.** (theol.) perfecter.
consommation (kɔ̃sɔma'sjɔ̃), s.f. [L *consummatio*] **1.** Consummation, completion, end; *la ~ du mariage*, the consummation of marriage; *la ~ des siècles*, the consummation of the ages; **2.** consumption, act of using and destroying; **3.** drink, refreshments; *payer les ~s*, to pay for the drinks.
consommé, -e (kɔ̃sɔme), p. adj. **1.** Consummated; **2.** consumed, used up; **3.** consummate, perfect; *habileté ~e*, consummate cleverness. ~ s.m. Gravy soup, rich broth.
consommer (kɔ̃sɔme), v.a. [f. L *consummare*] **1.** To consummate, to complete, to end; **2.** to consume, to use up; **se** ~, v.pr. to be consumed.
consomptible (kɔ̃sɔ̃ptibl), adj. Consumable.
consompti-f, -ve (kɔ̃sɔ̃ptif), adj. Consumptive.
consomption (kɔ̃sɔ̃psjɔ̃), s.f. [L *consumptio*] Consumption.
consonance (kɔ̃sɔnɑ̃s), s.f. [L *consonantia*] Consonance.
consonant, -e (kɔ̃sɔnɑ̃), p. adj. Consonant.
consonne (kɔ̃sɔn), s.f. Consonant.
consonner, consoner (kɔ̃sɔne), v.n. To be consonant.
consort (kɔ̃sɔr), adj. Consort, associated. ~, s.m.pl. Partners, consorts, associates.
consortium (kɔ̃sɔrsjɔm), s.m. [L wd] Consortium.
consoude (kɔ̃sud), s.f. [f. L *consolida*] (bot.) Comfrey; ~ *royale*, field larkspur, *Delphinium consolida*.
conspirat-eur, -rice (kɔ̃spiratœr), s.m.f. Conspirator. ~, adj. Plotting.
conspiration (kɔ̃spira'sjɔ̃), s.f. Conspiracy, plot.
conspirer (kɔ̃spire), v.n.a. [L *conspirare*] To conspire, to plot.
conspuer (kɔ̃spɥe), v.a. [L *conspuere*] To spurn, to scorn, to hoot, to hoot at, to howl down; *conspuez X!*, down with X!
constable (kɔ̃stabl), s.m. [Engl. wd] (Police) constable.
constamment (kɔ̃stamɑ̃), adv. **1.** Constantly; **2.** with constancy.
constance (kɔ̃stɑ̃s), s.f. [L *constantia*] Constancy, steadfastness, persistence, patience. ~, s.m. [f. *Groot Constantia*, Cape Colony] Constantia (a wine from Cape Colony).
constant, -e (kɔ̃stɑ̃), adj. Constant, steadfast, faithful, lasting, uninterrupted; (math.) *quantité ~e*, constant quantity, constant.
constante (kɔ̃stɑ̃t), s.f. (math.) Constant.
constat (kɔ̃sta), s.m. Constat, affidavit.
constatation (kɔ̃stata'sjɔ̃), s.f. Ascertaining, proving, authentication, inquiry, evidence given, statement.
constater (kɔ̃state), v.a. [f. L *constare*] To ascertain, to prove, to verify, to state, to record, to authenticate.
constellation (kɔ̃stɛlla'sjɔ̃), s.f. [L *constellatio*] Constellation.
constellé, -e (kɔ̃stɛlle), p. adj. Constellated, starry; (astrol.) made under the influence of a constellation.
consteller (kɔ̃stɛlle), v.a. [L *constellare*] To constellate, to strew, to dot.
consternation (kɔ̃stɛrna'sjɔ̃), s.f. [L *consternatio*] Consternation, dismay.
consterner (kɔ̃stɛrne), v.a. To dismay, to strike with consternation.
constipation (kɔ̃stipa'sjɔ̃), s.f. Constipation, costiveness.
constiper (kɔ̃stipe), v.a. [f. L *con*+*stipare*] To constipate, to bind.
constituant, -e (kɔ̃stitɥɑ̃), p. adj. Constituent, component, forming, instituting. ~ s.m. Member of the Constituent Assembly (French hist.). **~e**, s.f. Constituent Assembly (French hist.).
constituer (kɔ̃stitɥe), v.a. [f. L *constituere*] **1.** To constitute, to establish, to form, to compose; **2.** to raise, to commit; **se** ~, v.pr. to constitute oneself, to become; *se ~ prisonnier*, to surrender, to give oneself up.
constituti-f, -ve (kɔ̃stitytif), adj. Constitutive.
constitution (kɔ̃stitysjɔ̃), s.f. [L *constitutio*] Constitution, structure, composition, organization; (law) appointment, annuity.

constitutionnalité (kɔ̃stitysjɔnalite), s.f. Constitutionality.
constitutionnel, -le (kɔ̃stitysjɔnɛl), adj. Constitutional.
constitutionnellement (kɔ̃stitysjɔnɛlmɑ̃) adv. Constitutionally.
constricteur (kɔ̃striktœr), adj. [f. L *cum+stringere, strictum*] Constricting, constrictive.
constricti-f, -ve (kɔ̃striktif), adj. Constrictive.
constriction (kɔ̃striksjɔ̃), s.f. Constriction, contraction.
constringent, -e (kɔ̃strɛ̃ʒɑ̃), adj. Constringent.
constructeur (kɔ̃stryktœr), s.m. Builder, constructor, maker; ~ *de navires*, shipbuilder. ~, adj. Constructing, building.
construction (kɔ̃stryksjɔ̃), s.f. **1.** Construction, building, structure, erection; **2.** building (erected); **3.** arrangement, composition; *faire la ~ d'une phrase latine*, to construe a Latin sentence.
construire (kɔ̃strɥir), v.a. [f. L *construere*] To construct, to build, to erect, to make; to arrange, to dispose, to construe; ~ *un système*, to construct a system; ~ *une phrase*, to construe a sentence.
consubstantialité (kɔ̃sybstɑ̃sjalite), s.f. [f. L *consubstantialis*] (theol.) Consubstantiality.
consubstantiation (kɔ̃sybstɑ̃sja'sjɔ̃), s.f. (theol.) Consubstantiation.
consubstantiel, -le (kɔ̃sybstɑ̃sjɛl), adj. (theol.) Consubstantial.
consubstantiellement (kɔ̃sybstɑ̃sjɛlmɑ̃), adv. (theol.) Consubstantially.
consul (kɔ̃syl), s.m. [L wd] Consul; *Premier* ~, Bonaparte.
consulaire (kɔ̃sylɛr), adj. Consular.
consulairement (kɔ̃sylɛrmɑ̃), adv. Consularly, by order of the Consuls.
consulat (kɔ̃syla), s.m. **1.** Consulate; **2.** consular government; **3.** consulship.
consultant, -e (kɔ̃syltɑ̃), p. adj. Consulting. ~, s.m. Consultant, consulter.
consultati-f, -ve (kɔ̃syltatif), adj. Consultative.
consultation (kɔ̃sylta'sjɔ̃), s.f. **1.** Consultation; **2.** advice; **3.** meeting of physicians to consult together.
consulte (kɔ̃sylt), s.f. Consult, assembly.
consulter (kɔ̃sylte), v.a. [L *consultare*] To consult, to refer to; ~, v.n. to give consultations, to deliberate; **se** ~, v.pr. to consider; to consult each other; to be consulted.
consulteur (kɔ̃syltœr), s.m. Consulter. ~, adj. Consulting.
consumable (kɔ̃symabl), adj. Consumable.
consumant, -e (kɔ̃symɑ̃), p. adj. Consuming, devouring, wasting.
consumer (kɔ̃syme), v.a. [L *consumere*] To consume, to destroy, to wear out, to waste away, to squander; **se** ~, v.pr. to be consumed, to be wasted away, &c., to pine away, to wear oneself out; *se ~ de douleur*, to pine away with grief.
contact (kɔ̃takt), s.m. [f. L *con+tactus*] Contact, connexion, touch, close union; (electr.) switch; *couper le* ~, to switch off; *mettre le* ~, to switch on.
contadin, -e (kɔ̃tadɛ̃), adj. s.m.f. [f. It. *contadino*] Peasant, rustic.
contage (kɔ̃taʒ), s.m. [L *contagium*] Contagious matter, virus.
contagieu-x, -se (kɔ̃taʒjø), adj. [L *contagiosus*] Contagious, infectious, catching.
contagion (kɔ̃taʒjɔ̃), s.f. [L *contagio*] Contagion, infection, contagiousness.
contagionner (kɔ̃taʒjɔne), v.a. To infect, to communicate a contagious disease to.
contagiosité (kɔ̃taʒjozite), s.f. Contagiousness.
contaminable (kɔ̃taminabl), adj. Contaminable.
contamination (kɔ̃tamina'sjɔ̃), s.f. Contamination.
contaminer (kɔ̃tamine), v.a. [L *contaminare*] To contaminate.
conte (kɔ̃t), s.m. Tale, story, short story; fib; ~ *à dormir debout*, rigmarole, tale of a tub; ~ *de fées*, fairy-tale.
contemplat-eur, -rice (kɔ̃tɑ̃platœr), s.m.f. Contemplator. ~, adj. Contemplative.
contemplati-f, -ve (kɔ̃tɑ̃platif), adj. Contemplative. ~, s.m. Contemplator; (theol.) contemplative.
contemplation (kɔ̃tɑ̃pla'sjɔ̃), s.f. Contemplation.
contemplativement (kɔ̃tɑ̃plativmɑ̃), adv. Contemplatively.
contempler (kɔ̃tɑ̃ple), v.a. [f. L *contemplari*] To contemplate, to behold, to ponder; ~, v.n. to meditate; **se** ~, v.pr. to contemplate each other; to contemplate oneself; to be contemplated.
contemporain, -e (kɔ̃tɑ̃pɔrɛ̃), adj. [f. L *cum+tempus*] Contemporary, contemporaneous, coeval; *auteur* ~, contemporary author; *histoire ~e*, contemporary history. ~, s.m.f. Contemporary.
contemporanéité (kɔ̃tɑ̃pɔraneite), s.f. Contemporaneity, contemporaneousness.
contempt-eur, -rice (kɔ̃tɑ̃ptœr), s.m.f. [L *contemptor*] Contemner, scorner, despiser. ~, adj. Scornful.
contenance (kɔ̃tnɑ̃s), s.f. **1.** Capacity, contents, extent, area; **2.** countenance, mien, demeanour; *perdre* ~, to be put out of countenance; *faire bonne* ~, to put a good face on a bad matter; to keep one's countenance; *se donner une* ~, to put on a good countenance.
contenant (kɔ̃tnɑ̃), s.m. Container.

contendant, -e (kɔ̃tɑ̃dɑ̃), p. adj. [f. L *contendere*] Contending. ~, s.m. Contender.
contenir (kɔ̃tnir), v.a. [f. L *continere*] **1.** To contain, to hold, to include; **2.** to restrain, to check, to curb, to keep back; **se** ~, v.pr. to restrain onself.
content, -e (kɔ̃tɑ̃), adj. [L *contentus*] Content, glad, happy, satisfied. ~, s.m. (fam.) Enough of, sufficiency, one's heart's content, one's fill; *il en a son* ~, that 's enough for him; he has got his heart's content; he has his fill of it.
contentement (kɔ̃tɑ̃tmɑ̃), s.m. Content, contentedness, satisfaction; ~ *passe richesse*, content is beyond riches.
contenter (kɔ̃tɑ̃te), v.a. To content, to satisfy, to appease, to please; **se** ~, v.pr. to be contented, to content oneself, to indulge oneself.
contentieusement (kɔ̃tɑ̃sjøzmɑ̃), adv. Contentiously.
contentieu-x, -se (kɔ̃tɑ̃sjø), adj. Contentious, litigious, wrangling. ~, s.m. Affairs in litigation; disputed claims office (or department).
contenti-f, -ve (kɔ̃tɑ̃tif), adj. (surg.) Retaining, retentive.
contention (kɔ̃tɑ̃sjɔ̃), s.f. Contention, strife; eagerness, intenseness.
contenu, -e (kɔ̃tny), p. adj. Contained; moderate; sober. ~, s.m. Contents (pl.); *le contenant et le* ~, the container and the contained; *le* ~ *d'un livre*, the contents of a book.
conter (kɔ̃te), v.a.n. [f. L *computare*] To tell, to relate, to report; to romance, to tell fibs; to confide; *elle veut vous en* ~, she wants to deceive you, she tells you fibs; ~ *fleurette*, to flirt, to make love; to make pretty love-speeches.
contestable (kɔ̃tɛstabl), adj. Contestable, controvertible, questionable.
contestant, -e (kɔ̃tɛstɑ̃), p. adj. s.m.f. Contending, litigant, contending party.
contestation (kɔ̃tɛsta'sjɔ̃), s.f. Contest, contestation, dispute.
conteste (kɔ̃tɛst), s.f. Contestation, dispute; *sans* ~, indisputably.
contester (kɔ̃tɛste), v.a. [f. L *contestari*] To contest, to dispute, to oppose, to deny; ~, v.n. to wrangle; **se** ~, v.pr. to be contested.
conteu-r, -se (kɔ̃tœr), s.m.f. Story-teller, narrator, tale-writer; ~ *de sornettes*, teller of idle stories.
contexte (kɔ̃tɛkst), s.m. [L *contextus*] Context.
contexture (kɔ̃tɛkstyr), s.f. Contexture, texture.
contigu, -ë (kɔ̃tigy), adj. [L *contiguus*] Contiguous, adjoining.
contiguïté (kɔ̃tigɥite), s.f. Contiguity, contiguousness.
continence (kɔ̃tinɑ̃s), s.f. Continence, continency.
continent, -e (kɔ̃tinɑ̃), adj. [L *continens*] Continent, chaste.
continent (kɔ̃tinɑ̃), s.m. (geog.) Continent.
continental, -e, (aux) (kɔ̃tinɑ̃tal), adj. Continental.
contingence (kɔ̃tɛ̃ʒɑ̃s), s.f. Contingence, contingency.
contingent, -e (kɔ̃tɛ̃ʒɑ̃), adj. [L *contingens*] Contingent, casual. ~, s.m. Contingent, share, quota.
continu, -e (kɔ̃tiny), adj. Continuous, continued, uninterrupted. ~, s.m. Continuousness, continuum.
continuat-eur, -rice (kɔ̃tinɥatœr), s.m.f. Continuator, continuer, successor.
continuation (kɔ̃tinɥa'sjɔ̃), s.f. Continuation, continuance.
continuel, -le (kɔ̃tinɥɛl), adj. Continual, uninterrupted, unceasing.
continuellement (kɔ̃tinɥɛlmɑ̃), adv. Continually, unceasingly.
continuer (kɔ̃tinɥe), v.a. [L *continuare*] To continue, to go on with, to proceed with, to keep on, to carry on; ~, v.n. to continue, to go on, to extend, to hold on; *la pluie continue de tomber* (or *à tomber*), it keeps on raining; *continuez de manger*, go on eating; **se** ~, v.pr. to be continued; to extend.
continuité (kɔ̃tinɥite), s.f. **1.** Continuity; *solution de* ~, solution of continuity; (math.) ~ *uniforme*, uniform continuity; **2.** continuance, duration.
continûment (kɔ̃tinymɑ̃), adv. Continuously.
contondant, -e (kɔ̃tɔ̃dɑ̃), p. adj. Blunt, dull, bruising, contusing.
contondre (obs.) (kɔ̃tɔ̃dr), v.a.n. [f. L *cum*+*tundere*] To contuse, to contund, to bruise.
contorniate (kɔ̃tɔrnjat), adj. f. (techn.) Contorniate.
contorsion (kɔ̃tɔrsjɔ̃), s.f. [f. L *cum*+*torquere*] Contortion, twisting, distortion.
contour (kɔ̃tur), s.m. [f. L *cum*+*tornus*] Contour, outline; winding; circumference.
contourné, -e (kɔ̃turne), p. adj. Outlined, shaped, distorted, twisted; (herald.) contourné.
contourner (kɔ̃turne), v.a. **1.** To give contour to; **2.** to twist, to deform; **3.** to go round; to circle round, to wind round; **se** ~, v.pr. to become twisted, distorted, winding.
contractant, -e (kɔ̃traktɑ̃), p. adj. Contracting. ~, s.m. Contracting party.
contractation (kɔ̃trakta'sjɔ̃), s.f. Contracting.
contracté, -e (kɔ̃trakte), p. adj. Contracted.
contracter (kɔ̃trakte), v.a. [f. L *contrahere*, *contractum*] **1.** To contract, to

bargain for, to enter into, to acquire, to catch; ~ *des obligations envers X*, to lay oneself under obligations to X; ~ *de mauvaises habitudes*, to contract bad habits; ~ *une maladie*, to catch a disease; **2.** to contract, to shrink, to constringe, to condense; **se** ~, v.pr. to become contracted, &c., to shrink, to contract.

contracti-f, -ve (kɔ̃traktif), adj. Contractive.

contractile (kɔ̃traktil), adj. Contractile, contractible.

contractilité (kɔ̃traktilite), s.f. Contractility, contractibility.

contraction (kɔ̃traksjɔ̃), s.f. Contraction.

contractuel, -le (kɔ̃traktɥɛl), adj. Stipulated by contract, contractual.

contractuellement (kɔ̃traktɥɛlmɑ̃), adv. By contract.

contracture (kɔ̃traktyr), s.f. [L *contractura*] Contraction; (arch.) diminution.

contradicteur (kɔ̃tradiktœr), s.m. Contradicter, opponent.

contradiction (kɔ̃tradiksjɔ̃), s.f. [f. L *contra+dicere*] Contradiction; inconsistency; *être en* ~ *avec X*, to be at variance with X.

contradictoire (kɔ̃tradiktwar), adj. Contradictory, conflicting, inconsistent. **~s**, s.m.pl. Contradictories, contradictory terms.

contradictoirement (kɔ̃tradiktwarmɑ̃), adv. Contradictorily; after hearing both parties.

contraignable (kɔ̃trɛɲabl), adj. Compellable.

contraignant, -e (kɔ̃trɛɲɑ̃), p. adj. Compelling, compulsive, constraining.

contraindre (kɔ̃trɛ̃dr), v.a. [L *constringere*] To compel, to constrain, to force, to oblige, to put a restraint upon; (law) ~ *par corps*, to arrest, to attach; **se** ~, v.pr. to constrain oneself, to restrain oneself.

contraint, -e (kɔ̃trɛ̃), p. adj. **1.** Compelled, constrained, obliged; **2.** embarrassed, stiff, constrained; cramped.

contrainte (kɔ̃trɛ̃t), s.f. Constraint, compulsion, coercion, stiffness; (law) arrest.

contraire (kɔ̃trɛr), adj. [L *contrarius*] Contrary, adverse, opposite; unfavourable, hurtful.

contraire (kɔ̃trɛr), s.m. Contrary, reverse, opposite; *au* ~ *!*, on the contrary!; *bien au* ~, quite the contrary; *tout le* ~ *de*, quite the reverse of; *au* ~ *de*, contrary to.

contrairement (kɔ̃trɛrmɑ̃), adv. Contrarily; ~ *à*, contrary to, in contradiction to.

contralto, contralte (kɔ̃tralto, kɔ̃tralt), s.m. [It. wd] Contralto.

contrapontiste, contrapuntiste, contrepointiste (kɔ̃trapɔ̃tist, kɔ̃trəpwɛ̃tist), s.m. Contrapuntist.

contrariant, -e (kɔ̃trarjɑ̃), p. adj. Contradictious, annoying, provoking, contrary.

contrarier (kɔ̃trarje), v.a. To oppose, to be contrary to, to cross, to provoke; **se** ~, v.pr. to counteract, to cross each other, to be contrary.

contrariété (kɔ̃trarjete), s.f. Contrariety, opposition, obstacle, hindrance, annoyance; *éprouver des* ~*s*, to have annoyances (or troubles).

contrastant, -e (kɔ̃trastɑ̃), p. adj. Contrasting.

contraste (kɔ̃trast), s.m. [f. L *contra+stare*] Contrast.

contraster (kɔ̃traste), v.n. To contrast (*avec*, with).

contrat (kɔ̃tra), s.m. [f. L *contractus*] Contract, deed, agreement, covenant, bargain; ~ *de mariage*, marriage articles; *rédiger un* ~, to draw up a contract; ~ *synallagmatique*, reciprocal contract.

contravention (kɔ̃travɑ̃sjɔ̃), s.f. Infraction, infringement, contravention; *être en* ~, to infringe the regulations.

contre (kɔ̃tr), prep. [L *contra*] **1.** Against, contrary to; (law, sport.) versus; *dix* ~ *un*, ten to one; *exaspéré* ~ *lui*, enraged with him; *aller* ~ *vents et marées*, to sail against wind and tide. **2.** close to, close by, against. ~, adv. Against, con; *ci-*~, opposite; *là-*~, against that, to the contrary; *par* ~, on the other hand, by way of compensation; per contra; *tout* ~, close by, nigh; **3.** (in compounds) counter-; ~*-accusation*, s.f. countercharge; ~*-à-*~, loc. adv. (naut.) alongside; ~*-allée*, s.f. sidewalk, side-alley; ~*-amiral*, s.m. rear-admiral; ~*-appel*, s.m. second call; (fenc). caveating, disengaging; ~*-approches*, s.f. pl. counter-approaches; ~*-attaque*, s.f. counter-attack or-work; ~*-balancer*, v.a. to counterbalance; to counterpoise, to compensate; (herald.) ~*-bande*, s.f. counterbend; (herald.) ~*-barre*, s.f. counterbar; *en contre-bas* (*de*), loc. adv. downwards; lower than; ~*-battre*, v.a. to counterbatter, to oppose; *à* ~*-biais*, loc. adv. contrariwise, the other way; (naut.) *à* ~*-bord*, loc. adv. on the opposite tack, foul of each other; (naut.) ~*-bordée*, s.f. opposite tack; ~*-boutant*, s.m. counterfort; buttress; ~*-bouter*, v.a. to buttress, to prop; (naut.) ~*-brasser*, v.a. to counterbrace; ~*-calquer*, v.a. to reverse (a drawing); *à* ~*-cœur*, loc. adv. reluctantly, unwillingly; ~*-cœur*, s.m. reredos (of a fireplace); ~*-coup*, s.m. rebound, counter-stroke, result, repercussion; ~*-courant*, s.m. counter-current, undertow; ~*-déclaration*, s.f. counter-declaration; (fenc.) ~*-dégagement*, s.m. double disengagement; ~*-dégager*, v.n. to double disengage; ~*-digue*, s.f. second dike; (techn.) ~*-écrou*, s.m. lock-nut; ~*-enquête*, s.f. counter-inquest; ~-*épaulette*, s.f. epaulet (without fringes); ~-*épreuve*, s.f. counter-proof, counter-verification; ~-*espionnage*, s.m. special police to watch spies; (naut.) ~-*étambot*, s.m. false stern-post; ~-*expertise*, s.f. counter-examination; counter-valuation; *à* ~-*fil*, loc. adv. contrariwise; (mus.) ~-*fugue*, s.f. counter-fugue; ~-*gage*, s.m. surety; ~-*garde*, s.f. counterguard; ~-*hachure*, s.f. cross-hatching; ~-*hâtier*, s.m. kitchen fire-dog; *en* ~-*haut*, loc. adv. upward; higher up; (herald.) ~-*herminé*, adj. counter-ermined; ~-*indication*, s.f. contra-indication; ~-*indiquer*, v.a. to contra-indicate; ~-*interrogatoire*, s.m. cross-examination; ~-*jour*, s.m. counter-light, false light; *à* ~-*jour*, against the light; ~-*lettre*, s.f. defeasance; ~-*marée*, s.f. counter-tide, backwater; (mus.) *à* ~-*mesure*, loc. adv. against time; ~-*mine*, s.f. countermine; ~-*miner*, v.a. to countermine; ~-*mur*, s.m. outer wall; ~-*opération*, s.f. counter-operation; ~-*ordre*, s.m. countermand; ~-*partie*, s.f. counterpart; ~-*pas*, s.m. change-step; ~-*passer*, v.a. to pass per contra; to transfer, to re-endorse; ~-*pente*, s.f. counter-slope; ~-*pied*, s.m. reverse, contrary; (hunt.) wrong scent; (techn.) ~-*platine*, s.f. side-plate; screw-plate; ~-*poil*, s.m. wrong way of the hair; *à* ~-*poil*, loc. adv. against the nap, against the grain, in a wrong way; ~-*pointe*, s.f. back-edge (of a sword); ~-*pointer*, v.a. to quilt; ~-*porte*, s.f. screen-door; ~-*pression*, s.f. counter-pressure; ~-*projet*, s.m. counter-scheme; ~-*proposition*, s.f. counter-proposition, counter-motion; (naut.) ~-*quille*, s.f. keelson; ~-*rail*, s.m. guard-rail; ~-*révolution*, s.f. counter-revolution; *à* ~-*saison*, loc. adv. out of season; ~-*sanglon*, s.m. girth-strap; ~-*sceau* (or *scel*), s.m. counter-seal; ~-*sceller*, v.a. to counter-seal; (mus.) ~-*sujet*, s.m. counter-subject; ~-*taille*, s.f. (engr.) cross-line; (comm.) counter-tally; (engr.) ~-*tirer*, v.a. to counter-prove; ~-*torpilleur*, s.m. destroyer; (herald.) ~-*vair*, s.m. counter-vair; ~-*valeur*, s.f. value in exchange; *à* ~-*vapeur*, loc. adv. backward; ~-*vérité*, s.f. lie, irony, antiphrasis; ~-*visite*, s.f. second search or visit; (mil.) ~-*volte*, s.f. countervolt; &c.

contre (kɔ̃tr), s.m. The opposite; *le pour et le* ~, the pros and cons; (fenc.) counter, counter-parry; (billiards) rebound; *faire un* ~, to double.

contrebande (kɔ̃trəbɑ̃d), s.f. [f. It. *contrabbando*] Contraband, smuggling; *faire la* ~, to smuggle; *faire passer en* ~, to smuggle in.

contrebandi-er, -ère (kɔ̃trəbɑ̃dje), s.m.f. Smuggler, contrabandist.

contrebasse (kɔ̃trəbɑs), s.f. Double bass, contrabass, contrabassist.

contrebassiste (kɔ̃trəbɑsist), s.m. Contrabassist.

contrebasson (kɔ̃trəbɑsɔ̃), s.m. Double bassoon.

contrecarrer (kɔ̃trəkare), v.a. To oppose, to cross, to thwart, to counteract.

contredanse (kɔ̃trədɑ̃s), s.f. Quadrille, country-dance.

contredire (kɔ̃trədir), v.a. To contradict, to disprove, to gainsay.

contredit (kɔ̃trədi), s.m. Reply, contrary assertion; *sans* ~, indisputably.

contrée (kɔ̃tre), s.f. Country; land.

contrefaçon (kɔ̃trəfasɔ̃), s.f. **1.** Counterfeiting, imitation; **2.** counterfeit.

contrefacteur (kɔ̃trəfaktœr), s.m. Counterfeiter, imitator, pirate, infringer.

contrefaction (kɔ̃trəfaksjɔ̃), s.f. Counterfeiting, unauthorized imitation.

contrefaire (kɔ̃trəfɛr), v.a. **1.** To counterfeit, to imitate or copy without authorization, to pirate (a literary work); **2.** to mimic, to ape, to feign; **3.** to deform.

contrefaiseu-r, -se (kɔ̃trəfəzœr), s.m.f. Mimicker, mimic.

contrefait, -e (kɔ̃trəfɛ), p. adj. **1.** Counterfeited; **2.** deformed.

(se) contreficher (səkɔ̃trəfiʃe), v.pr. (fam.) To snap one's fingers (*de*, at).

contrefort (kɔ̃trəfɔr), s.m. **1.** Counterfort, buttress; **2.** stiffener, counter (of a shoe); **3.** (geog.) spur (of a mountain chain).

contremaître (kɔ̃trəmɛtr), s.m. Foreman, overseer; (naut.) mate.

contremaîtresse (kɔ̃trəmɛtrɛs), s.f. Overseer, forewoman, supervisor.

contremandement (kɔ̃trəmɑ̃dmɑ̃), s.m. Countermand.

contremander (kɔ̃trəmɑ̃de), v.a. To countermand.

contremarche (kɔ̃trəmarʃ), s.f. Countermarch.

contremarque (kɔ̃trəmark), s.f. **1.** Countermark; **2.** (theatr.) check.

contremarquer (kɔ̃trəmarke), v.a. To countermark.

contrepoids (kɔ̃trəpwɑ), s.m. Counterpoise, counterweight, counterbalance; fly (of a clock).

contrepoint (kɔ̃trəpwɛ̃), s.m. (mus.) Counterpoint.

contrepointiste (kɔ̃trapwɛ̃tist), s.m. See CONTRAPONTISTE.

contrepoison (kɔ̃trəpwazɔ̃), s.m. Counterpoison, antidote.

contrer (kɔ̃tre), v.n.a. (at bridge, &c.) To double, to double the stake.

contrescarpe (kɔ̃trɛskarp), s.f. (fort.) Counterscarp.

contreseing (kɔ̃trəsɛ̃), s.m. Countersignature.

contresens (kɔ̃trəsɑ̃s), s.m. **1.** Wrong

sense, mistake, misinterpretation, wrong translation; **2.** wrong side, wrong way; *à* ~, in a wrong way.

contresignataire (kɔ̃trəsiɲatɛr), s.m.f. Countersigner.

contresigner (kɔ̃trəsiɲe), v.a. To countersign.

contretemps (kɔ̃trətɑ̃), s.m. **1.** Wrong time; **2.** piece of ill luck, mischance, hitch; **3.** (mus.) syncopation; *à* ~, inopportunely, out of time.

contrevallation (kɔ̃trəvala′sjɔ̃), s.f. Contravallation.

contrevenant, -e (kɔ̃trəvənɑ̃), s.m.f. Contravener, infractor, transgressor, offender.

contrevenir (kɔ̃trəvənir), v.n. To contravene, to offend (*à*, against), to infringe.

contrevent (kɔ̃trəvɑ̃), s.m. Outside shutter.

contribuable (kɔ̃tribɥabl), adj. s.m.f. Tax-paying, tax-payer.

contribuer (kɔ̃tribɥe), v.n. [L *contribuere*] To contribute (*à*, to).

contributi-f, -ve (kɔ̃tribytif), adj. Contributive, contributory.

contribution (kɔ̃tribysjɔ̃), s.f. Contribution; tax; *~s directes*, direct taxes; assessed taxes; *~s indirectes*, indirect taxes, excise; *mettre à* ~, to lay under contribution.

contributoire (kɔ̃tribytwɑr), adj. Contributory.

contrister (kɔ̃triste), v.a. [L *contristare*] To grieve, to sadden.

contrit, -e (kɔ̃tri), adj. [L *contritus*] Contrite, penitent, grieved.

contrition (kɔ̃trisjɔ̃), s.f. Contrition.

contrôlable (kɔ̃trolabl), adj. Controllable.

contrôle (kɔ̃trol), s.m. [*contre*+*rôle*] **1.** Control, register, lists, muster-roll; **2.** controlling, surveying; **3.** stamp, hall-mark; **4.** controller's office, check-office (in a theatre); **5.** censure.

contrôlé, -e (kɔ̃trole), p. adj. Controlled, stamped, hall-marked; *argenterie ~e*, hall-marked silver.

contrôler (kɔ̃trole), v.a. To control, to check, to stamp, to mark, to censure, to verify; to clip, to nick (railway tickets).

contrôleu-r, -se (kɔ̃trolœr), s.m.f. Controller, comptroller, check-taker, ticket-collector, surveyor.

controuver (kɔ̃truve), v.a. To invent, to forge.

controversable (kɔ̃trɔvɛrsabl), adj. Controvertible, disputable.

controverse (kɔ̃trɔvɛrs), s.f. [f. L *contra* + *vertere, versus*] Controversy.

controverser (kɔ̃trɔvɛrse), v.a. To controvert, to debate.

controversiste (kɔ̃trɔvɛrsist), s.m.f. Controversialist, controvertist.

contumace (kɔ̃tymas), s.f. [L *contumax*] Contumacy; *par* ~, by default. ~, s.m.f. Contumacious person, defaulter. ~, adj. Contumacious.

contumax (kɔ̃tymaks), [L wd] adj. s.m.f. See CONTUMACE.

contus, -e (kɔ̃ty), adj. [f. L *contusus*] Contused, bruised.

contusion (kɔ̃tyzjɔ̃), s.f. Bruise, contusion.

contusionner (kɔ̃tyzjɔne), v.a. [f. L *contundere, contusum*] To bruise, to contuse.

convaincant, -e (kɔ̃vɛ̃kɑ̃), p. adj. Convincing.

convaincre (kɔ̃vɛ̃kr), v.a. [L *convincere*] **1.** To convince, to persuade; **2.** to convict, to prove guilty (of); **se** ~, v.pr. to be convinced; to convince oneself; to convince each other.

convaincu, -e (kɔ̃vɛ̃ky), p. adj. Convinced, earnest, full of conviction; convicted.

convainquant (kɔ̃vɛ̃kɑ̃), p. adj. [f. *convaincre*] Convincing.

convalescence (kɔ̃valɛsɑ̃s), s.f. Convalescence.

convalescent, -e (kɔ̃valɛsɑ̃), adj. s.m.f. [L *convalescens*] Convalescent.

convenable (kɔ̃vnabl), adj. **1.** Suitable, proper, fit, fitting, appropriate, convenient, meet, right, seemly; **2.** decent, proper.

convenablement (kɔ̃vnabləmɑ̃), adv. Suitably, properly, fittingly, decently, &c.

convenance (kɔ̃vnɑ̃s), s.f. **1.** Suitability, fitness, harmony, convenience, seemliness; **2.** conveniency; **~s**, pl. propriety, decency, accord with established principles, rules, or traditions; decorum, good manners; *les ~s exigent que*, decency and good manners require that; *blesser les ~s*, to offend against decorum.

convenant, -e (kɔ̃vnɑ̃), p. adj. Fitting, proper, becoming.

convenir (kɔ̃vnir), v.n. [L *convenire*] **1.** To suit, to fit, to be congruous, proper, right, suitable, convenient; **2.** to agree, to be of one mind, to settle, to concert; **3.** to admit, to own, to acknowledge, to avow, to agree; **se** ~, v.pr. to suit each other; to agree.

convent (kɔ̃vɑ̃), s.m. [L *conventus*] Freemasons' general assembly.

conventicule (kɔ̃vɑ̃tikyl), s.m. Conventicle, secret assembly.

convention (kɔ̃vɑ̃jsɔ̃), s.f. [L *conventio*] **1.** Convention, agreement, contract, covenant; **2.** stipulation, condition; **3.** assembly of representatives (French hist.); *de* ~, conventional.

conventionnel, -le (kɔ̃vɑ̃sjɔnɛl), adj. Conventional, stipulated. ~, s.m. (French hist.) Member of the Convention.

conventionnellement (kɔ̃vɑ̃sjɔnɛlmɑ̃), adv. Conventionally, by agreement.
conventualité (kɔ̃vɑ̃tɥalite), s.f. Conventual life.
conventuel, -le (kɔ̃vɑ̃tɥɛl), adj. Conventual.
conventuellement (kɔ̃vɑ̃tɥɛlmɑ̃), adv. Conventually.
convergence (kɔ̃vɛrʒɑ̃s), s.f. Convergence.
convergent, -e (kɔ̃vɛrʒɑ̃), adj. [L *convergens*] Converging, convergent; (math.) *séries* ~*es*, converging series.
converger (kɔ̃vɛrʒe), v.n. [f L *con*+*vergere*] To converge; (fig.) to tend.
convers, -e (kɔ̃vɛr), adj. [f. L *cum*+*versus*] **1.** Lay, serving; **2.** converse.
conversation (kɔ̃vɛrsa'sjɔ̃), s.f. Conversation, talk, chat, converse; *être en* ~ *avec*, to be in conversation with; *être à la* ~, to attend to the conversation; *reprendre une* ~, to resume a conversation; *faire la* ~, to carry on a conversation; *défrayer la* ~, to be the subject of a conversation; to be the topic of the day.
converse (kɔ̃vɛrs), adj. s.f. (log., math.) Converse.
converser (kɔ̃vɛrse), v.n. [L *conversari*] To converse, to hold intercourse, to talk; (mil.) to wheel about.
conversible (kɔ̃vɛrsibl), adj. See CONVERTIBLE.
conversion (kɔ̃vɛrsjɔ̃), s.f. [L *conversio*] Conversion, turning, change, transmutation; wheeling about; *la* ~ *du trois pour cent*, the conversion of the three per cent; (alg.) *la* ~ *des équations*, the conversion of equations.
converti, -e (kɔ̃vɛrti), p. adj. Converted. ~, s.m.f. Convert.
convertibilité (kɔ̃vɛrtibilite), s.f. Convertibility.
convertible (kɔ̃vɛrtibl), adj. Convertible.
convertir (kɔ̃vɛrtir), v.a. [L *convertere*] To convert, to change, to turn, to transmute; **se** ~, v.pr. to be converted, to become a convert, to be convertible.
convertissable (kɔ̃vɛrtisabl), adj. Convertible.
convertissement (kɔ̃vɛrtismɑ̃), s.m. Conversion, change.
convertisseur (kɔ̃vɛrtisœr), s.m. Converter.
convexe (kɔ̃vɛks), adj. [L *convexus*] Convex.
convexité (kɔ̃vɛksite), s.f. Convexity.
conviction (kɔ̃viksjɔ̃), s.f. [L *convictio*] Conviction, convincing proof; *avoir l'intime* ~ *de*, to be thoroughly convinced of.
convié, -e (kɔ̃vje), p. adj. s.m.f. Invited guest.
convier (kɔ̃vje), v.a. [LL *convitare*] To invite, to beg, to request, to incite, to ask.
convive (kɔ̃viv), s.m.f. [L *conviva*] Guest, table-companion.
convivialité (kɔ̃vivjalite), s.f. Conviviality.
convocation (kɔ̃vɔka'sjɔ̃), s.f. [L *convocatio*] Convocation, summons.
convoi (kɔ̃vwa), s.m. **1.** Convoy, escort; **2.** funeral procession; **3.** railway train.
convoiement (kɔ̃vwamɑ̃), s.m. Convoying.
convoitable (kɔ̃vwatabl), adj. Covetable.
convoiter (kɔ̃vwate), v.a. [f. L *cupere*] To covet, to lust after.
convoiteu-x, -se (kɔ̃vwatø), adj. Covetous.
convoitise (kɔ̃vwatiz), s.f. Covetousness, lust, greed.
convol (kɔ̃vɔl), s.m. Re-marriage.
convoler (kɔ̃vɔle), v.n. [L *convolare*] To marry; to re-marry.
convoluté, -e (kɔ̃vɔlyte), adj. [L *convolutus*] (bot.) Convolute, convoluted.
convolution (kɔ̃vɔlysjɔ̃), s.f. Convolution.
convolvulacées (kɔ̃vɔlvylase), s.f.pl. (bot.) Convolvulaceae.
convolvulus (kɔ̃vɔlvylys), s.m. (bot.) Convolvulus.
convoquer (kɔ̃vɔke), v.a. [L *convocare*] To convoke, to summon, to convene.
convoyer (kɔ̃vwaje), v.a. [f. L *cum*+*via*] To convoy, to escort.
convoyeur (kɔ̃vwajœr), adj. s.m. Convoy, convoy-ship, guard, escort.
convulsé, -e (kɔ̃vylse), p. adj. Convulsed.
convulser (kɔ̃vylse), v.a. [f. L *con*+*vellere, vulsum*] To convulse; **se** ~, v.pr. to be convulsed.
convulsi-f, -ve (kɔ̃vylsif), adj. Convulsive.
convulsion (kɔ̃vylsjɔ̃), s.f. [L *convulsio*] Convulsion.
convulsionnaire (kɔ̃vylsjɔnɛr), s.m.f. Convulsionary.
convulsionner (kɔ̃vylsjɔne), v.a. To convulse; **se** ~, v.pr. to be convulsed.
convulsivement (kɔ̃vylsivmɑ̃), adv. Convulsively.
cooccupant, -e (koɔkypɑ̃), s.m.f. Co-occupier, co-occupant.
coolie (kuli), s.m. [Hind. *kuli*] Coolie.
coopération (koɔpera'sjɔ̃), s.f. Co-operation, help.
coopérer (koɔpere), v.n. To co-operate, to concur, to act jointly.
cooptation (koɔpta'sjɔ̃), s.f. Co-optation.
coopter (koɔpte), v.a.n. To co-optate, to co-opt.
coordination (koɔrdina'sjɔ̃), s.f. [L *coordinatio*] Co-ordination.
coordonné, -e (koɔrdɔne), p. adj. Co-ordinate. ~, s.f. (usually in the plural) (math.) Co-ordinate; ~*s homogènes*, homogeneous co-ordinates.

coordonner (koordɔne), v.a. To co-ordinate, to arrange, to organize.
copahu (kɔpay), s.m. [Braz. wd] Copaiba, capivi.
copaïer (kɔpaie), s.m. (bot.) Copaiba-tree.
copain (kɔpɛ̃), s.m. **copine** (kɔpin), s.f. [f. OF *compain*, *compagnon*] Pal, chum; (U.S.A.) pard.
copal (pl. -s) (kɔpal), s.m. adj. [Mexic. *copalli*] Copal (resin).
copartageant, -e (kopartaʒɑ̃), s.m.f. adj. Joint-sharer; sharing (with others in possession, action, &c.); co-parcener.
copayer (kɔpaje), s.m. See COPAÏER.
copeau (pl. -x) (kɔpo), s.m. [f. *couper*] Chip, wood-shaving.
copie (kɔpi), s.f. [L *copia*] Copy; likeness, close imitation, article, paper, literary piece, written task; (comm.) ~ *de lettres*, letter-copying book.
copier (kɔpje), v.a. To copy, to copy out, to imitate, to mimic; *presse à* ~, copying-press; *encre à* ~, copying-ink.
copieusement (kɔpjøzmɑ̃), adv. Copiously.
copieu-x, -se (kɔpjø), adj. [L *copiosus*] Copious, ample, abundant.
copiste (kɔpist), s.m.f. Copier, copyist.
copossession (kopɔsɛsjɔ̃), s.f. Joint-possession.
coprah (kɔpra), s.f. (bot.) Copra.
copropriétaire (koprɔprijetɛr), s.m.f. Co-proprietor, joint owner.
copropriété (koprɔprijete), s.f. Joint ownership, joint property.
copte (kɔpt), s.m.f. Copt. ~, adj. Coptic.
copter (kɔpte), v.a. [f. OF *cop*, *coup*] To toll (a bell).
copulati-f, -ve (kɔpylatif), adj. [L *copulativus*] Copulative.
copulation (kɔpyla'sjɔ̃), s.f. Copulation.
copule (kɔpyl), s.f. [L *copula*] (log.) Copula.
coq (kɔk), s.m. [onom.] Cock, rooster, weather-cock; ship's cook; *chant du* ~, cock-crow; ~ *de combat*, game-cock; *combat de* ~*s*, cock-fight; ~ *de bruyère*, grouse; capercailzie, gorcock; ~ *d'Inde*, turkey-cock; *être comme un* ~ *en pâte*, to live in clover; *le* ~ *du village*, cock of the walk; *rouge comme un* ~, as red as a turkey-cock; *fier comme un* ~, cock-a-hoop.
coq-à-l'âne (kɔkalɑn), s.m. (invar.) Cock-and-bull story, nonsense.
coquard (kɔkar), s.m. [f. *coq*] Old cock, old fool.
coque (kɔk), s.f. [L *concha*] **1.** Shell, egg-shell, nutshell; *œufs à la* ~, boiled eggs; **2.** cocoon; **3.** *Coculus indicus*, Indian berry; **4.** cockle (shell-fish); **5.** loop (of ribbon); **6.** (naut.) hull, body of a ship; kink.
coquebin (kɔkbɛ̃), s.m. Ninny, young fool.
coquecigrue (kɔksigry), s.f. [etym. dub.] Fiddle-faddle, nonsense; an imaginary bird.
coquelicot (kɔkliko), s.m. (bot.) Field poppy.
coquelourde (kɔklurd), s.f. (bot.) **1.** Pasque-flower, *Anemone pulsatilla*; **2.** rose-campion, *Agrostemma coronaria*.
coqueluche (kɔklyʃ), s.f. **1.** Whooping-cough; **2.** great favourite (with); **3.** fashion, rage; **4.** hood (obs.).
coquemar (kɔkmar), s.m. [etym. dub.] Pipkin, kettle.
coquerelle (kɔkrɛl), s.f. (bot.) Winter-cherry, three hazel-nuts growing together.
coquerie (kɔkri), s.f. Galley, cook-house.
coqueron (kɔkrɔ̃), s.m. (naut.) Store-room.
coquet, -te (kɔkɛ), adj. [f. *coq*] Coquettish, elegant, natty. ~**te**, s.f. Flirt, jilt, coquette. ~, s.m. (naut.) Cock-boat.
coqueter (kɔkte), v.n. [f. *coq*] To coquet, to flirt, to trifle in love; (naut.) to scull.
coquetier (kɔktje), s.m. **1.** Egg-cup; **2.** egg-dealer.
coquetière (kɔktjɛr), s.f. Egg-boiler.
coquettement (kɔkɛtmɑ̃), adv. Coquettishly, prettily.
coquetterie (kɔkɛtri), s.f. Coquetry, coquettishness; ~*s*, coquettish tricks, flirtation.
coquillage (kɔkijaʒ), s.m. Shell-fish; shell; shell-work.
coquillart (kɔkijar), s.m. (min.) Shelly bed.
coquille (kɔkij), s.f. [f. *coque*] **1.** Shell; ~ *de noix*, nutshell; ~ *de beurre*, pat of butter; *rentrer dans sa* ~ (*comme un escargot*), to draw in one's horns; **2.** portable meat-roaster; **3.** basket-hilt (of a sword); **4.** misprint (altering sense of wd); **5.** spandrel (of staircase); **6.** (arch.) conch; **7.** post demy, small post (kind of paper); **8.** a dish served in shells; **9.** blister on bread.
coquiller (kɔkije), v.n.a. (of bread) To blister; (of ribbon, &c.) to flounce, to ruche.
coquilleu-x, -se (kɔkijø), adj. Shelly.
coquill-ier, -ère (kɔkije), adj. Conchiferous, shelly. ~, s.m. Cabinet of shells.
coquin, -e (kɔkɛ̃), s.m.f. [f. LL *coquinus*] **1.** Rogue, rascal, knave; slut; *un* ~ *fieffé*, an arrant rogue; **2.** (jest.) lucky dog, rogue, hussy, little rascal. ~, **-e**, adj. Roguish, rascally, good-for-nothing, villainous; naughty, saucy (air); ~ *de sort!*, what rotten luck!
coquinerie (kɔkinri), s.f. Knavish trick, piece of roguery, roguishness.
cor (kɔr), s.m. [f. L *cornu*] **1.** Corn (on the toe); **2.** French horn, bugle; *sonner du* ~, to blow the horn; *à* ~ *et à cri*, clamorously, with hue and cry; **3.** antler;

cerf dix-~s, full-grown stag (seven years old).
corail (pl. **aux**) (kɔraj), s.m. [f. L *corallum*] Coral.
corallère (kɔrajɛr), s.f. (naut.) Boat for coral-fishing.
corailleu-r, -se (kɔrajœr), adj. s.m. Coral, coral-fisher, coral-fishing.
corallien, -ne (kɔralljɛ̃), adj. Formed of coral.
coralliforme (kɔralliform), adj. Coralliform.
coralligène (kɔralliʒɛn), adj. Coralliferous, coralligenous.
corallin, -e (kɔrallɛ̃), adj. Coralline, coral-red.
coralline (kɔrallin), s.f. (bot.) Coralline.
coran (kɔrɑ̃), s.m. [f. Arab. *qoran*] Koran.
corbeau (pl. **-x**) (kɔrbo), s.m. [f. LL *corvellus*] **1.** Raven, crow; **2.** (astr.) Corvus.
corbeille (kɔrbɛj), s.f. [L *corbicula*] **1.** Basket; ~ *de mariage*, wedding-presents; **2.** flower-bed; **3.** (fort.) corbeil; **4.** reserved enclosure (in the French Stock Exchange).
corbeillée (kɔrbɛje), s.f. Basketful.
corbillard (kɔrbijar), s.m. [f. *corbeil*, formerly *coche de corbeil*] Hearse.
corbillat (kɔrbija), s.m. Young raven.
corbillon (kɔrbijɔ̃), s.m. Small basket; crambo (a game).
corbin (kɔrbɛ̃), s.m. (obs.) [var. of *corbeau*] Crow; *en bec de* ~, hooked.
corbleu (kɔrblø), interj. [f. *corps de Dieu*] Zounds!
cordage (kɔrdaʒ), s.m. [f. *corde*] **1.** Rope, cord, cordage; **2.** measuring wood by the cord.
cordat (kɔrda), s.m. Packing-cloth.
corde (kɔrd), s.f. [L *chorda*] **1.** Cord, rope, string, line, halter; ~ *à sauter*, skipping-rope; *échelle de* ~, rope-ladder; ~ *à linge*, clothes-line; (tennis) *friser la* ~, to graze the net; *danseuse de* ~, rope-dancer; *avoir plusieurs ~s à son arc*, to have several strings to one's bow, to be resourceful; *ce n'est pas dans mes ~s*, it 's not in my line; *il ne faut pas parler de ~ dans la maison d'un pendu*, one must not mention hemp in the house of one who has been hanged; *la ~ au cou*, the halter round the neck; *un homme de sac et de* ~, a downright villain; *il ne vaut pas la corde pour le pendre*, he is not worth his salt; *tenir la* ~, to lead; to be favourite, to be the rage; **2.** string, chord; *faire vibrer la ~ sensible*, to touch the sensitive chord; to strike home; *instrument à ~s*, stringed instrument; (fig.) *ne touchez pas cette* ~, do not harp upon that string; **3.** *~s vocales*, vocal cords; **4.** thread (of a stuff); *montrant la ~, usé jusqu'à la* ~, threadbare; **5.** cord, an old measure for wood.
cordé, -e (kɔrde), p. adj. Twisted; cordate, roped; heart-shaped.
cordeau (pl. **-x**) (kɔrdo), s.m. Line, tow-line; *tiré au* ~, as straight as a die.
cordeler (kɔrdəle), v.a. To twist, to twine.
cordelette (kɔrdəlɛt), s.f. Small cord, string.
cordelier (kɔrdəlje), s.m. Cordelier (monk).
cordelière (kɔrdəljɛr), s.f. **1.** Cordelier's girdle; **2.** silk or wool girdle; cord and tassels; **3.** (arch.) twisted fillet; **4.** (print.) border.
cordelle (kɔrdɛl), s.f. Tow-rope.
corder (kɔrde), v.a. **1.** To twist; **2.** to cord, to rope; **3.** to cord (wood.)
corderie (kɔrdəri), s.f. **1.** Ropery, rope-walk; **2.** rope-making; rope-trade.
cordial (pl. **aux**) (kɔrdjal), s.m. [f. L *cor*] Cordial. ~, **-e, (aux),** adj. **1.** Cordial, affectionate, hearty; **2.** invigorating, reviving.
cordialement (kɔrdjalmɑ̃), adv. Cordially, heartily; ~ *à vous*, sincerely yours.
cordialité (kɔrdjalite), s.f. Cordiality, heartiness.
cordier (kɔrdje), s.m. Rope-maker.
cordiforme (kɔrdiform), adj. Heart-shaped.
cordillères (kɔrdijɛr), s.f.pl. [Span. *cordillera*] Cordilleras.
cordite (kɔrdit), s.f. Cordite.
cordon (kɔrdɔ̃), s.m. [f. *corde*] **1.** Strand, yarn; **2.** string, cord, thread; shoe-string; **3.** ribbon, tape, band; **4.** check-string, draw-string, latch-string, string; *tenir les ~s de la bourse*, to hold the purse-strings; *le ~, s'il vous plaît!*, the door, please; **5.** bow-string; **6.** ribbon (insignia); ribbon of an order, especially *Légion d'Honneur*; ~ *bleu*, first-rate woman cook; **6.** ~ *ombilical*, navel-string; **7.** (arch.) cordon; **8.** (mil.) cordon; ~ *sanitaire*, sanitary cordon.
cordonner (kɔrdɔne), v.a. To twist, to braid.
cordonnerie (kɔrdɔnri), s.f. **1.** Shoe-making, shoe-maker's trade; **2.** shoe-manufactory; **3.** shoe-shop, shoe-room, cobbler's shop.
cordonnet (kɔrdɔnɛ), s.m. **1.** Twist, braid, small cord, lace; **2.** twisted silk; **3.** milling stamp (on edge of coin).
cordonni-er, -ère (kɔrdɔnje), s.m.f. [OF *cordouanier*, worker in Cordova leather] Shoe-maker, cordwainer, cobbler.
coréen, -ne (koreɛ̃), adj. s.m.f. Corean.
coreligionnaire (kɔrəliʒjɔnɛr), s.m.f. Co-religionist, fellow-believer.
coréopsis (kɔreɔpsis), s.m. (bot.) Coreopsis, tick-seed.

o, n**o**te, gl**o**tte; **ɔ̃**, m**on**ter, r**on**de; **ø**, f**eu**, cr**eu**x; **œ**, p**eu**r, s**œu**r; **œ̃**, **un**; **ʃ**, **ch**ez, **sch**isme; **u**, t**ou**t; **w**, **ou**i, d**o**it, d**o**uaire; **y**, m**u**r, p**u**; **ɥ**, h**u**ile, m**u**ette; **z**, **z**èle, ro**s**e; **ʒ**, dé**j**à, **g**entil.

corète, corette (kɔrɛt), s.f. (bot.) Jew's-mallow, *Corchorus olitorius*.
corfiote (kɔrfiɔt), adj. s.m.f. Corfiot, of Corfu.
coriace (kɔrjas), [f. L *corium*] Tough, hard; (fig.) miserly, close-fisted.
coriacé, -e (kɔrjase), adj. Coriaceous.
coriacité (kɔrjasite), s.f. Toughness.
coriandre (kɔrjɑ̃dr), s.f. (bot.) Coriander, *Coriandrum sativum*.
corindon (kɔrɛ̃dɔ̃), s.m. [f. Tamil *kurundam*] (min.) Corundum.
corinthien, -ne (kɔrɛ̃tjɛ̃), adj. s.m.f. Corinthian.
corlieu (kɔrljø), s.m. (ornith.) Curlew, whimbrel; syn. COURLIS.
corme (kɔrm), s.f. [LL *curma*] (bot.) Service-berry, sorb.
cormier (kɔrmje), s.m. (bot.) Service-tree, sorb-tree.
cormoran (kɔrmɔrɑ̃), s.m. [f. L *corvus*+*marinus*] (ornith.) Cormorant.
cornac (kɔrnak), s.m. [Cingh. wd] Elephant-driver; (fig.) showman, chaperon, cicerone.
cornage (kɔrnaʒ), s.m. (vet.) Roaring (a disease of horses).
cornaline (kɔrnalin), s.f. [f. *corne*] (min.) Cornelian, carnelian.
cornard (kɔrnar), adj. s.m. **1.** (vet.) Roaring (horse), roarer; **2.** (vulg.) cuckold.
corne (kɔrn), s.f. [f. L *cornu*] **1.** Horn; hooter; *bêtes à ~s*, horned cattle; *prendre le taureau par les ~s*, to take the bull by the horns; *peigne de ~*, horn comb; **2.** snail's feeler; *faire les ~s à X*, to mock X; **3.** shoe-horn; **4.** corner, angle; *chapeau à trois ~s*, three-cornered hat; *faire une ~ à un feuillet*, to dog's-ear a leaf, to turn down a leaf; **5.** hoof; **6.** (naut.) gaff; **7.** (pharm.) *~ de cerf*, hartshorn; **8.** wind-instrument, horn; syn. TROMPE; **9.** *faire porter des ~s à X*, to make X a cuckold.
corné, -e (kɔrne), p. adj. Horny, corneous, horned; (of a page) dog's-eared.
corneau (pl. **-x**) (kɔrno), s.m. **1.** Closet-pipe; **2.** cross between mastiff and hound.
cornée (kɔrne), s.f. (anat.) Cornea.
cornéenne (kɔrneɛn), s.f. (geol.) Aphanite, compact hornblende rock.
corneille (kɔrnɛj), s.f. [L *cornicula*] Crow, rook, jackdaw; *bayer aux ~s*, to stand gaping idly; *aller comme une ~ qui abat des noix*, to run like a bull at a hedge, to act rashly, recklessly.
cornélien, -ne (kɔrneljɛ̃), adj. Of or about Corneille; in the style of Corneille.
cornement (kɔrnəmɑ̃), s.m. Tingling noise (in the ears); roaring (of a pipe).
cornemuse (kɔrnəmyz), s.f. Bagpipe, hornpipe.
cornemuseur (kɔrnəmyzœr), s.m. Bagpiper, piper.
corner (kɔrne), v.n. **1.** To blow, to wind a horn; (motor.) to hoot; **2.** to tingle; *les oreilles me cornent*, my ears tingle; ~, v.a. **1.** to trumpet abroad, to din (in the ears); **2.** to turn down the corner of (a leaf), to dog's-ear; **3.** to gore.
cornet (kɔrnɛ), s.m. **1.** Horn, hornlet; **2.** *~ acoustique*, ear-trumpet; **3.** cornet à piston; cornetist; **4.** paper cap, screw-bag, rolled wafer; **5.** dice-box; **6.** ink-horn; **7.** (anat.) turbinated bones (of the nose); **8.** (butch.) windpipe; **9.** calamary, pen-fish; **10.** (colloq. vulg.) *s'enfiler dans le ~*, to put (a drink) down one's gullet.
cornette (kɔrnɛt), s.f. [f. *corne*] **1.** Cornet, head-dress; **2.** (naut.) broad pennant; (obs.) standard of a company of cavalry; **3.** (bot.) purple cow-wheat, *Melampyrum arvense*. ~, s.m. (obs.) Cavalry officer, bearer of the standard.
cornettiste (kɔrnɛtist), s.m. Cornetist.
corneur (kɔrnœr), s.m. Horn-blower. ~, adj. Wheezing, roaring, blowing.
corniche (kɔrniʃ), s.f. [It. *cornice*] Cornice; (naut.) counter-rail.
cornichon (kɔrniʃɔ̃), s.m. [f. *corne*] (bot.) Cornicle; gherkin; (fam.) greenhorn, ninny.
corni-er, -ère (kɔrnje), adj. At, or of the corner, corner-. **~ère**, s.f. Angle-iron, corner-plate. ~, s.m. See CORNOUILLER.
cornique (kɔrnik), adj. s.m. Cornish.
corniste (kɔrnist), s.m. Horn-player.
cornouille (kɔrnuj), s.f. [f. L *cornicula*] Cornel, cornelian cherry.
cornouiller (kɔrnuje), s.m. (bot.) Cornel-tree, dog-wood.
cornu, -e (kɔrny), adj. Horned, cornute; *blé ~*, spurred wheat; (fig.) preposterous, absurd.
cornue (kɔrny), s.f. [f. L *cornutus*] (chem.) Retort.
corollaire (kɔrɔllɛr), s.m. [f. L *corollarium*] Corollary. ~, adj. (bot.) Corollaceous, corolline.
corolle (kɔrɔl), s.f. [L *corolla*] (bot.) Corolla.
coron (kɔrɔ̃), s.m. Group of miners' dwellings.
coronaire (kɔrɔnɛr), adj. [L *coronarius*] (anat.) Coronary.
coronal, -e, (aux) (kɔrɔnal), adj. (anat.) Coronal.
coronille (kɔrɔnij), s.f. (bot.) Coronilla.
coronoïde (kɔrɔnɔid), adj. [f. Gr. *korōnē*+*eidos*] (anat.) Coronoid.
corossol (kɔrɔsɔl), s.m. (bot.) Soursop.
corozo (kɔrɔzo), s.m. Corozo, vegetable ivory.
corporal (kɔrpɔral), s.m. [f. L *corpus*] Corporal.
corporalité (kɔrpɔralite), s.f. Corporality.
corporati-f, -ve (kɔrpɔratif), adj. Corporative.

corporation (kɔrpɔra'sjɔ̃), s.f. Corporation, guild. ⚠ *Corporation* is not used in French in the sense of prominent abdomen, which = *gros ventre, obésité, bedaine.*

corporel, -le (kɔrpɔrɛl), adj. Corporal, corporeal, bodily, material, relating to the body; *châtiment ~*, corporal punishment.

corporellement (kɔrpɔrɛlmɑ̃), adv. Bodily, corporeally, materially.

corps (kɔr), s.m. [L *corpus*] **1.** Body; substance, matter; **2.** corpse, dead body; **3.** corporation, corps, staff, body; **4.** (fig.) consistency, strength, solidity; **5.** part of an army; *prendre du ~*, to get stout; *prendre ~*, to shape, to get organized; *il a le diable au ~*, the devil is in him; nothing can stop him; *se donner ~ et âme à*, to be entirely devoted to; *gardes du ~*, bodyguard; *aller en ~*, to go in a body; *~ liquide*, liquid body; *~ simples*, simple bodies; *~ composés*, compound bodies; *l'attraction des ~*, the attraction of bodies; *~ étranger*, foreign body; *~ de bâtiment*, body of a building; part of a building; *un ~ constitué*, a corporate body; *~ législatif*, legislative body; *les ~ de métiers*, the trades companies; *repas de ~*, corporation-dinner; *~ de ballet*, corps-de-ballet; *esprit de ~*, party spirit; esprit de corps; team spirit; *~ d'armée*, army corps; *~ de garde*, guard-house or -room; *plaisanterie de ~ de garde*, coarse jest; *~ de pompe*, barrel of a pump; (naut.) *~ du navire*, hull of the ship; (naut.) *~ mort*, moorings; *~ du délit*, corpus delicti; main proof; *à ~ perdu*, headlong, furiously; *avoir l'âme chevillée au ~*, to have as many lives as a cat; *~ et biens*, crew and cargo; person and property; *~ à ~*, grappling with one another, in close fight; *à bras le ~*, round the waist; *à son ~ défendant*, against one's will, in self-defence; *faire ~ avec*, to be joined with; *lui passer sur le ~*, to trample him, to rout him; *contrainte par ~*, arrest for debt; *un drôle de ~*, a queer customer, a queer fish; (math.) *~ de classes*, field of classes.

corpulence (kɔrpylɑ̃s), s.f. [L *corpulentia*] Corpulence, stoutness.

corpulent, -e (kɔrpylɑ̃), adj. Corpulent, stout.

corpusculaire (kɔrpyskylɛr), adj. Corpuscular.

corpuscule (kɔrpyskyl), s.m. Corpuscule.

correct, -e (kɔrɛkt), adj. [L *correctus*] Correct, accurate, right.

correctement (kɔrɛktəmɑ̃), adv. Correctly, accurately.

correct-eur, -rice (kɔ̃rɛktœr), s.m.f. Corrector, proof-reader. ~, adj. Correcting.

correcti-f, -ve (kɔrɛktif), adj. s.m. Corrective.

correction (kɔrɛksjɔ̃), s.f. **1.** Correction, correctness, accuracy; **2.** correcting; *je dis, sauf ~, que*, I say, under correction, that; **3.** corporal punishment; *maison de ~*, reformatory, bridewell.

correctionnel, -le (kɔrɛksjɔnɛl), adj. Correctional, relating to misdemeanours; *tribunal ~*, police-court.

correctionnellement (kɔrɛksjɔnɛlmɑ̃), adv. In connexion with misdemeanours, before the police-court.

corrégidor (kɔreʒidɔr), s.m. [Span. wd] Corregidor.

corrélati-f, -ve (kɔrrelatif), adj. s.m. Correlative.

corrélation (kɔrrela'sjɔ̃), s.f. Correlation.

correspondance (kɔrɛspɔ̃dɑ̃s), s.f. **1.** Correspondence, written intercourse, letters; *réexpédier*, or, *réadresser la ~ de X*, to forward X's letters; *faire sa ~*, to write one's letters; **2.** relation, harmony, adaptation, connexion, connection; **3.** communication, correspondence-ticket, cross-post; (rail.) connexion, connecting-service.

correspondant, -e (kɔrɛspɔ̃dɑ̃), p. adj. Corresponding, correspondent. ~, -e, s.m.f. Correspondent, representative (of a family, acting as a guardian of a child away from home); corresponding member; correspondent. ⚠ Not co-respondent, which = *complice (dans un procès pour adultère).*

correspondre (kɔrɛspɔ̃dr), v.n. [f. L *cum+respondere*] To correspond, to communicate, to suit, to fit, to answer.

corrida (kɔrrida), s.f. [Span. wd] Corrida.

corridor (kɔridɔr), s.m. [It. *corridore*] Corridor, passage.

corrigé (kɔriʒe), s.m. Corrected copy, key.

corriger (kɔriʒe), v.a. [L *corrigere*] To correct, to amend; to punish; to set right, to temper, to allay; (print.) to read (proofs); **se ~**, v.pr. to correct oneself, to amend; to be corrected; *se ~ d'un défaut*, to cure oneself of a fault.

corrigible (kɔriʒibl), adj. Corrigible.

corroborant, -e (kɔrɔbɔrɑ̃), p. adj. Corroborating, corroborant.

corroborati-f, -ve (kɔrɔbɔratif), adj. s.m. Corroborative (agent or measure).

corroboration (kɔrɔbɔra'sjɔ̃), s.f. Corroboration, confirmation.

corroborer (kɔrɔbɔre), v.a. [L *corroborare*] To corroborate.

corrodant, -e (kɔrɔdɑ̃), p. adj. Corroding. ~, s.m. Corrodent.

corroder (kɔrɔde), v.a. [L *corrodere*] To corrode.

corroi (kɔrwɑ), s.m. Currying (of leather).

corroirie (kɔrwɑri), s.f. Curriery; currying.

corrompre (kɔrɔ̃pr), v.a. [L *cum+ rumpere*] To corrupt, to spoil, to vitiate, to pervert; to bribe, to buy over (witnesses, &c.); **se ~**, v.pr. to become corrupted, to corrupt each other, or oneself; to taint, to become tainted; to rot.

corrompu, -e (kɔrɔ̃py), p. adj. Corrupted; rotten, tainted, putrid, putrefied; perverted, depraved, dissolute.

corrosi-f, -ve (kɔrozif), adj. s.m. Corrosive.

corrosion (kɔrozjɔ̃), s.f. [f. *corroder*] Corrosion.

corroyage (kɔrwajaʒ), s.m. Currying (of leather).

corroyer (kɔrwaje), v.a. To curry (leather); to weld (iron); to puddle; to plane (wood).

corroyeur (kɔrwajœr), s.m. Currier.

corrugation (kɔryga'sjɔ̃), s.f. [f. L *corrugare*] Corrugation.

corrupt-eur, -rice (kɔryptœr), adj. s.m.f. Corrupting, corrupter, corruptress; perverting, perverter; corruptive.

corruptibilité (kɔryptibilite), s.f. Corruptibility, corruptibleness.

corruptible (kɔryptibl), adj. Corruptible; perishable.

corruption (kɔrypsjɔ̃), s.f. [L *corruptio*] Corruption, decay, putrefaction; (fig.) depravity, corruption.

corsage (kɔrsaʒ), s.m. [f. *corps*] **1.** Bust, chest, breasts; **2.** bodice, body, corsage.

corsaire (kɔrsɛr), s.m. [f. It. *corsaro*] Corsair, pirate, rover; privateer (ship); commander of privateer; (fig., comm.) shark. **~**, adj. Privateer, corsair piratical.

corse (kɔrs), adj. s.m.f. Corsican.

corsé, -e (kɔrse), p. adj. [f. *corps*] Strong-bodied, strong; (fig.) substantial; spicy, racy, highly piquant, stiff; full-bodied (in reference to wine).

corselet (kɔrsəlɛ), s.m. [f. *corps*] Corselet; waistband.

corser (kɔrse), v.a. [f. *corps*] To give body to, to stiffen, to strengthen, to complicate, to flavour or season highly, to make spicy; **se ~**, v.pr. to become complicated, to grow serious; *ça se corse*, or, *l'affaire se corse*, the plot thickens, things are looking serious, the matter is taking a serious turn.

corset (kɔrsɛ), s.m. [f. *corps*] Pair of stays; corset, laced bodice; (surg.) chest-bandage.

corseter (kɔrsəte), v.a. To fit (a person) with stays; **se ~**, v.pr. to put on one's stays.

corseti-er, -ère (kɔrsətje), s.m.f. Corset-maker, stay-maker.

cortège (kɔrtɛʒ), s.m. [It. *corteggio*] Retinue, escort, train; procession, troop, pageant.

cortès (kɔrtɛs), s.f.pl. [Span. wd] Cortes.

cortical, -e, (aux) (kɔrtikal), adj. [f. L *cortex*] Cortical.

coruscation (kɔryska'sjɔ̃), s.f. [L *coruscatio*] Coruscation.

corvéable (kɔrveabl), adj. s.m. Liable to statute-labour.

corvée (kɔrve), s.f. [f. LL *corvada*] **1.** Statute-labour, corvée, duty-service; **2.** (mil.) fatigue-duty, fatigue-party; **3.** (fig., fam.) drudgery, unpleasant task or duty; *quelle ~!*, what a bore!, how tiresome!

corvette (kɔrvɛt), s.f. [f. L *corbita*] (naut.) Corvette, sloop of war (obs.)

corvidés (kɔrvide), s.m.pl. [L *corvus*] (ornith.) Corvidae.

corybante (kɔribɑ̃t), s.m. (ant.) Corybant.

corymbe (kɔrɛ̃b), s.m. [Gr. *korumbos*] (bot.) Corymb, corymbus.

corymbifère (kɔrɛ̃bifɛr), adj. (bot.) Corymbiferous.

coryphée (kɔrife), s.m. [Gr. *koruphaios*] Coryphaeus, chorus or ballet master, leader.

coryphène (kɔrifɛn), s.m. (ichth.) Coryphene.

coryza (kɔriza), s.m. [Gr. *koruza*] Coryza, cold in the head.

cosaque (kɔzak), s.m. [Turki *quzzaq*] Cossack; (fig.) ruffian.

cosécante (kɔsekɑ̃t), s.f. Cosecant.

cosignataire (kɔsiɲatɛr), s.m.f. adj. Co-signer, co-signatory.

cosinus (kɔsinys), s.m. [L *cum+sinus*] Cosine.

cosmétique (kɔsmetik), s.m. adj. [Gr. *kosmētikos*] Cosmetic.

cosmique (kɔsmik), adj. [f. Gr. *kosmos*] Cosmic.

cosmogonie (kɔsmɔgɔni), s.f. Cosmogony.

cosmogonique (kɔsmɔgɔnik), adj. Cosmogonic.

cosmographie (kɔsmɔgrafi), s.f. [f. Gr. *kosmos+graphein*] Cosmography.

cosmographique (kɔsmɔgrafik), adj. Cosmographical, cosmographic.

cosmologie (kɔsmɔlɔʒi), s.f. [f. Gr. *kosmos +logos*] Cosmology.

cosmologique (kɔsmɔlɔʒik), adj. Cosmological.

cosmopolite (kɔsmɔpɔlit), adj. [f. Gr. *kosmos + politēs*] Cosmopolitan. **~**, s.m.f. Cosmopolite, cosmopolitan.

cosmopolitisme (kɔsmɔpɔlitism), s.m. Cosmopolitanism.

cosmorama (kɔsmɔrama), s.m. [f. Gr. *kosmos+horama*] Cosmorama (peep-show with views of all parts of the world).

cosse (kɔs), s.f. [f. L *cassa?*] **1.** Pod, cod, shell, husk, hull; **2.** (naut.) thimble; **3.** (slang) *avoir la ~*, (*a*) to be lazy; (*b*) to be afraid, to be in a funk.

cosser (kɔse), v.n. [f. It. *cozzare*] To butt (as rams); (fig.) to fight; **~**, **v.a.** [f. *cosse*] to shell (peas); see ÉCOSSER.
cosson (kɔsɔ̃), s.m. [L *cossus*] **1.** (ent.) Weevil; **2.** new vine-shoot.
cossu, -e (kɔsy), adj. (bot.) Well-podded; (fig.) rich, wealthy, substantial, well-to-do.
costal, -e, (aux) (kɔstal), adj. [f. L *costa*] Costal.
costaud, -e (kɔsto), adj. (slang) Strong, thick-set, hefty, lusty, beefy. **~**, s.m. A strapper, a big strapping fellow.
costume (kɔstym), s.m. [It. *costume*] Dress, apparel, garb, costume, customary dress, fancy dress; *~ de bain*, bathing-costume; *en grand ~*, in full dress; in one's glad rags; in full feather; *le ~ est de rigueur*, fancy-dress imperative.
costumé, -e (kɔstyme), p. adj. Dressed; in fancy dress; *bal ~*, fancy dress ball.
costumer (kɔstyme), v.a. To dress, to dress up, to dress in fancy dress; **se ~**, v.pr. to dress oneself up, to don fancy dress, to dress (*en*, as).
costumi-er, -ère (kɔstymje), s.m.f. Costumier.
cotangente (kotɑ̃ʒɑ̃t), s.f. (geom.) Cotangent.
cote (kɔt), s.f. [f. L *quota*] Quota, share, quotation, letter or number (used in classification); *faire une ~ mal taillée*, to make a compromise, to split the difference; official quotation of exchange; altitude, elevation marked on a map or plan. ⚠ Not English 'cote' which = *abri*, *étable*, *toit*, &c.
côte (kot), s.f. [L *costa*] **1.** Rib; (bot.) midrib; *~ à ~*, side by side; *à ~s*, ribbed; (colloq.) *rire à s'en tenir les ~s*, to split one's sides laughing, to be convulsed with laughter; *on lui compterait les ~s*, he is nothing but skin and bone; **2.** slope, hill-side, declivity; *à mi-~*, half-way up; **3.** shore, sea-shore; *à la ~*, ashore, aground; (fig.) reduced to poverty, on the rocks, cleaned-out, stony-broke.
côté (kote), s.m. [f. L *costa*] Side, way, direction, part; *à ~*, by the side; quite near, beside; laterally; *de ~*, sideways, on one side; sidelong; slantingly; aside; *de ~ et d'autre*, here and there; *du ~ de*, on the side of, with respect to, among, towards; *d'un ~*, on one side; on the one hand; *d'un autre ~*, on the other side; on the other hand; *passer à ~*, to pass by, to elude, to miss; *par ~*, sideways; (fig.) *mettre de ~*, to save, to lay by, to put by.
coteau (pl. -x) (kɔto), s.m. Hill, hillock.
côtelé, -e (kotle), adj. Ribbed.
côtelette (kotlɛt), s.f. Chop (of pork or mutton), mutton chop; cutlet (of veal, &c.); (fig.) whiskers.
coter (kɔte), v.a. To quote, to letter, to mark; to tax, to esteem, to value.
coterie (kɔtri), s.f. Coterie, clique, set.
cothurne (kɔtyrn), s.m. [Gr. *kothornos*] Buskin, cothurnus; (fig.) *chausser le ~*, to act in tragedies.
cotice (kɔtis), s.f. [LL *coticium*] (herald.) Cotise.
coticé, -e (kɔtise), p. adj. Cotised.
côti-er, -ère (kotje), adj. Coastal, coast-, coasting; *bâtiment ~*, coaster, coasting vessel.
cotignac (kɔtiɲak), s.m. [f. L *cotoneum*] Cotignac, quince jelly.
cotillon (kɔtijɔ̃), s.m. [f. *cotte*] **1.** Petticoat; *courir le ~*, to run after women, to lead a dissolute life; **2.** cotillion (dance).
cotir (kɔtir), v.a. [etym. dub.] To bruise (fruit).
cotisation (kɔtiza'sjɔ̃), s.f. Contribution; clubbing; subscription.
cotiser (kɔtize), v.a. To assess, to rate; **se ~**, v.pr. to club together, to contribute, to get up a subscription.
cotissure (kɔtisyr), s.f. [f. *cotir*] Bruise, bruising (of fruit).
coton (kɔtɔ̃), s.m. [f. Arab. *qutun*] Cotton, cotton-plant, cotton wool, cloth made of cotton; *~ à repriser*, darning-cotton; *bobine de ~*, reel of cotton; *velours de ~*, cotton velvet; (fig.) *filer un mauvais ~*, to be in a bad way (of health or fortune); *élever son enfant dans du ~*, to bring up one's child in cotton wool; *mettre X dans du ~*, to pet, to fondle X; (slang) *il y aura du ~*, there will be much difficulty.
cotonnade (kɔtɔnad), s.f. Cotton fabric, cotton goods, cotton cloth; syn. INDIENNE.
cotonné, -e (kɔtɔne), p. adj. Cottoned, padded; (of hair) woolly.
(se) cotonner (səkɔtɔne), v.pr. **1.** To become downy; **2.** (fam.) to pad one's bust.
cotonnerie (kɔtɔnri), s.f. Cotton-plantation; cotton-factory.
cotonneu-x, -se (kɔtɔnø), adj. Cottony, downy.
cotonnier (kɔtɔnje), s.m. (bot.) Cotton-shrub, cotton-plant. **~, -ère**, adj. Pertaining to cotton; *l'industrie ~ère*, the cotton industry.
coton-poudre (kɔtɔ̃pudr), s.m. See FULMICOTON.
côtoyer (kotwaje), v.a. To coast, to run along the coast of, to skirt, to run along the edge of, to keep close to.
cotre (kɔtr), s.m. [Engl. *cutter*] (naut.) Cutter.
cotret (kɔtrɛ), s.m. [OF *costeret*] Short faggot; *il est sec comme un ~*, he is as thin as a lath.
cottage (kɔtedʒ, kɔtaʒ), s.m. [Engl. wd] Villa, sea-side or suburban house,

picturesque small country-house; cottage. ⚠ 'Cottage' in English is said of any labourer's or villager's dwelling; in French it is only used when an effect of rustic prettiness has been aimed at in building.

cotte (kɔt), s.f. [f. Celt. *cot*] **1.** Petticoat; **2.** tunic coat; ~ *de mailles*, coat of mail.

cottiennes (kɔtjɛn), adj. f. pl. Cottian (Alps).

cotyle (kɔtil), s.f. [f. Gr. *kotulē*] **1.** (ant.) Cup, measure of liquid; **2.** (anat.) cotyle.

cotylédon (kɔtiledɔ̃), s.m. [f. Gr. *kotulēdōn*] (bot.) Cotyledon.

cotylédoné, -e (kɔtiledɔne), adj. (bot.) Cotyledonous.

cou, col (ku, kɔl) (*col* is archaic except in anat. loc.: *col du fémur*, or fig.: *col d'une bouteille*; see COL), s.m. [L *collum*] Neck; *au long* ~, long-necked; *se jeter au* ~ *de quelqu'un*, to throw one's arms round a person's neck; (fig.) to show extravagant love or enthusiasm for a person; *prendre ses jambes à son* ~, to take to one's heels; *couper le* ~, to behead; *se casser* or *se rompre le* ~, to break one's neck, to ruin oneself; ~ *de pied*, instep; *se mettre la corde au* ~, to put the rope round one's own neck.

couac (kuak), s.m. [onom.] Quack, discordant noise.

couagga (kuaga), s.m. (zool.) Quagga.

couard, -e (kuar), adj. s.m.f. [f. OF *coe*, L *cauda*] Cowardly, coward.

couardise (kuardiz), s.f. Cowardice.

couchage (kuʃaʒ), s.m. **1.** Lodging, bed for the night, act of going to bed; **2.** bedding.

couchant, -e (kuʃɑ̃), p. adj. Setting; *chien* ~, setting dog, setter; (fig.) cringing, obsequious person. ~, s.m. Sunset, wane, decline; west.

couche (kuʃ), s.f. [f. *coucher*] **1.** Bed, couch; (⚠ ~ in French is not used in the sense of sofa); **2.** (pl.) confinement, childbed; *elle est morte en* ~*s*, she died in childbirth; *fausse* ~, miscarriage; *faire une fausse* ~, to miscarry; **3.** napkin, diaper (of an infant); **4.** (hort.) hot-bed; **5.** layer; **6.** (paint.) coat; **7.** (geol.) bed, stratum; (colloq.) *il en a une* ~ *!*, he is very dense !, what a moron he is; **8.** (techn.) *arbre de* ~, horizontal shaft.

couchée (kuʃe), s.f. Place where one stops for the night (in travelling).

coucher (kuʃe), v.a. [f. L *collocare*] To put to bed, to give a bed to; to lay, to lay down, to lay on, to lay flat, to spread on a surface, to set down; to couch (in writing); ~ *en joue*, to aim at; to cover; ~, v.n. to lie down for the night, to sleep, to stop for the night; (fig.) *envoyer* ~ *X*, to send X to the right about; **se** ~, v.pr. to go to bed, to lie down, to set; *comme on fait son lit on se couche*, as you have made your bed so you must lie on it; as you have brewed, so you must drink; *allez vous* ~*!*, go away !, do not bother me.

coucher (kuʃe), s.m. Bedtime, going to bed; bedding; setting (of the sun); supination.

coucherie (kuʃri), s.f. Carnal intercourse.

couchette (kuʃɛt), s.f. **1.** Small bedstead, berth, bunk; **2.** infant's napkin, diaper.

coucheu-r, -se (kuʃœr), s.m.f. Bedfellow; *mauvais* ~, unpleasant customer, disagreable fellow, troublesome bedfellow, bear.

couchis (kuʃi), s.m. Layer (of sand under pavement); lathwork.

couci-couci, couci-couça (kusi-kusi, kusi-kusa), adv. loc. [f. It. *cosi, cosi*] So-so, middling, indifferently.

coucou (kuku), s.m. [onom.] **1.** (ornith.) Cuckoo; **2.** cuckoo clock; **3.** cowslip; **4.** (obs.) one-horse chaise; **5.** (game) bo-peep; *faire* ~, to play bo-peep.

coude (kud), s.m. [f. L *cubitus*] **1.** Elbow; *jouer des* ~*s*, to elbow one's way; ~ *à* ~, side by side; (colloq.) *lever le* ~, to drink too much; to be always lifting one's elbow; **2.** angle, bend, turn; *là où la route fait un* ~, where the road makes a turn; *la rivière fait un* ~, the river makes a bend; **3.** (techn.) knee; ~ *d'un tuyau*, knee of a pipe.

coudée (kude), s.f. (obs. measure) Cubit, arm's length; *avoir les* ~*s franches*, to have plenty of elbow-room, to have full liberty of action, full scope.

couder (kude), v.a. To bend; **se** ~, v.pr. to form an elbow or angle, to have a bend, to bend; (techn.) *arbre coudé*, crank-shaft.

coudoiement (kudwamɑ̃), s.m. Elbowing.

coudoyer (kudwaje), v.a. To elbow, to jostle.

coudraie (kudrɛ), s.f. Hazel-copse.

coudre (kudr), v.a.n. [f. LL *cusire*] To sew, to seam, to do needlework; *machine à* ~, sewing-machine.

coudrette (kudrɛt), s.f. See syn. COUDRAIE.

coudrier (kudrje), s.m. [L *corulum*] (bot.) Hazel-nut-tree, filbert-tree.

couenne (kwɛn, kwan), s.f. [f. LL *cutena*] Rind, sward; (med.) buffy coat; scraped pigskin.

couenneu-x, -se (kwanœ), adj. (med.) Buffy.

couette (kwɛt, kwat), s.f. [f. L *culcita*] **1.** Feather bed; **2.** (naut.) see COITTES; **3.** iron socket; **4.** little tail.

couffe (kuf), s.f. [f. L *cophinus*] Bale, basket.

cougourde (kugurd), s.f. Bottle-gourd.

couguar (kugɥar), s.m. (zool.) Puma, cougar.

couille (kuj), s.f. [f. L *coleus*] (vulg.) Ball, testicle.

couillon (kujɔ̃), s.m. (very vulg. wd, to be avoided) Coward, funk, milksop, idiot; (also said in a friendly way) *eh bien mon ~!*, well, old bean!

coulage (kulaʒ), s.m. [f. *couler*] **1.** Leaking, waste; purloining (by servants, clerks, &c.); **2.** scalding (of linen); **3.** sinking (of a ship).

coulant, -e (kulɑ̃), p. adj. **1.** Flowing, smooth, easy, gliding; *nœud ~*, running knot, slip-knot; **2.** easy to deal with, accommodating.

coulant (kulɑ̃), s.m. Slider, cursor.

coule[1] (kul), s.f. (obs.) [L *cuculla*] Cowl.

coule[2] (kul), s.f. [f. *couler*] *Être à la ~*, to be up to the mark; to know the ins and outs of things; to know the ropes; to be up to snuff; to know what 's what.

coulé (kule), s.m. **1.** (mus.) Slur; **2.** slide (dancing step); **3.** a certain stroke in billiards.

coulée (kule), s.f. **1.** Running hand; **2.** (hunt.) path; **3.** (metall., geol.) casting; *~ de lave*, flow of lava.

coulemelle (kulmɛl), s.f. [L *columella*] A mushroom (kind of agaric).

couler (kule), v.n. [f. L *colare*] **1.** To flow, to run, to stream, to trickle; **2.** to leak, to run off; **3.** to sink, to founder; **4.** (fig.) to flow away, to glide away; **~**, v.a. **1.** to cast, to shape in a mould; **2.** to sink; **3.** to pass, to spend (time), (slang) *se la ~ douce*, to swing the lead; to take things easy; to slip (an object); **4.** (mus.) to slur; **5.** to scald (linen); **se ~**, v.pr. **1.** to slip, to creep, to crawl, to steal; **2.** to ruin oneself, to do for oneself.

couleur (kulœr), s.f. [L *color*] **1.** Colour, tint, hue, colouring, paint; *~ solide*, or *bon teint*, fast colour; **2.** complexion, flesh-tint, blush; *elle a pris des ~s*, she has a better complexion, she looks better; *haut en ~*, of a florid complexion; **3.** appearance, pretence; *sous ~ de*, under pretence of; **4.** political opinion; **5.** (pl.) fibs; **6.** (pl.) livery, favour, colours, flag; *arborer les ~s nationales*, to raise the national flag; (colloq.) *en faire voir de toutes les ~s à X*, to worry or plague X beyond all bearing.

couleuvre (kulœvr), s.f. [L *colubra*] (zool.) Snake, adder; (fig.) *avaler des ~s*, to put up with mortifications.

couleuvreau (pl. **-x**), (kulœvro), s.m. Young snake.

coulevrine (kuləvrin), s.f. **1.** (artill.) Culverin; **2.** (bot.) red-berried bryony, *Bryonia dioica*.

coulinage (kulinaʒ), s.m. Singeing (of fruit-trees).

coulis (kuli), s.m. [f. *couler*] (cook.) Cullis, thick gravy; *vent ~*, draught.

coulisse (kulis), s.f. [f. *couler*] **1.** Groove, furrow, sliding piece of wood, &c.; *porte à ~*, sliding door; **2.** draw-string or ribbon; the hem through which it passes; **3.** slip, side-scene, (pl.) wings; (fig.) (pl.) side-scenes, green-room; **4.** the body of unlicensed brokers; stock-jobbers; *faire des yeux en ~*, to ogle, to make sheep's eyes.

coulisseau (pl. **-x**) (kuliso), s.m. Slide, slide-block.

coulissier (kulisje), s.m. Stock-jobber.

couloir (kulwar), s.m. **1.** Passage, gangway; lobby (of the Chamber of Deputies); *bruits de ~*, lobby rumours; **2.** strainer.

coulomb (kulɔ̃), s.m. [f. *Charles Coulomb*] Coulomb (unit of electric quantity).

coulpe (kulp), s.f. [L *culpa*] Sin, fault; *battre sa ~*, to cry peccavi.

coulure (kulyr), s.f. **1.** (agric.) Dropping, falling-off; **2.** (metall.) running-out.

coup (ku), s.m. [f. L *colaphus*] **1.** Blow, stroke, knock, slap, smack, box, buffet, push, kick, cut, stab, rap, slash, gash, cudgel-blow, wound, bruise; *donner un ~*, to deal a blow; *détourner un ~*, to ward off a blow; *amortir le ~*, to deaden the blow; *une grêle de ~s*, a shower of blows; *donner des ~s de pied*, to kick; *~ de pied*, kick; *~ d'autorité*, act of authority; *~ d'aile*, flap of the wing; *~s de bâton*, cudgelling; *~ de coude*, nudge; *~ d'aviron*, stroke; *~ d'épée*, sword-cut; *~ d'épingle*, pin-prick; *~ de griffe*, scratch; *~ de poignard*, stab; *~ de couteau*, cut, stab; *~ de fouet*, lash, cut, smack; *~ de cravache*, cut with a horse-whip; *faire d'une pierre deux ~s*, to kill two birds with one stone; *donner un ~ d'épée dans l'eau*, to make a useless attempt; *faire le ~ de poing*, to box, to come to fisticuffs; *en venir aux ~s*, to come to blows, to begin to fight; *~ fourré*, underhand blow; *~ de grâce*, death-blow; *~ de Jarnac*, unfair blow; *~ du lapin*, finishing stroke; *frapper un grand ~*, to have recourse to strong measures; *~ de fion*, finishing touch; **2.** shot, report, discharge of a fire-arm; *~ de canon*, cannon-shot; *~ de fusil*, gun-shot, *~ de tonnerre, de foudre*, thunder-clap; thunderbolt; (fig.) *~ de foudre*, love at first sight; **3.** stroke, sudden calamity, turn of fate, hit, attempt, casual event, time; *~ de cloche*, ting, stroke of the bell; *~ de collier*, good pull; (fig.) *~ de feu*, bustle; *~ de filet*, haul, catch; *~ de main*, (fig.) (*a*) sudden attack; (*b*) help; *~ d'État*, sudden and decisive stroke of State policy; violent or unconstitutional change in government; *~ de tête*, rash act;

~ *d'œil*, glance: (see ŒIL); ~ *de sang*, apoplectic stroke; ~ *de soleil*, sunstroke; ~ *du sort*, chance, turn of fate; ~ *de théâtre*, sudden striking change; *à* ~ *sûr*, to a certainty; *par à-~s*, jerkily, by jerks; *au* (or *du*) *premier* ~, the very first time; *après* ~, after the event, too late; *à tous les ~s*, at every turn; *d'un seul* ~, at one stroke; *pour le* ~, this time; *encore un* ~, (fig.) once more; *sous le* ~ *de*, threatened with; *tout-à-~*, suddenly, all of a sudden; *tout d'un* ~, all at once; *faire les cents ~s*, to raise Cain; *être aux cent ~s*, to be utterly perplexed and dismayed; ~ *sur* ~, one after another, successively, running; *être sûr de son* ~, to feel quite sure of success; *faire un bon* ~, to make a good hit, to play a good trick; *faire un mauvais* ~, to commit a crime; *manquer son* ~, to miss one's aim; *se monter le* ~, to excite oneself, to delude oneself; *entrer en* ~ *de vent*, to come in like a whirlwind; *j'ai prévu le* ~, I have foreseen that; *tenir le* ~, to face the music; to stand the racket; **4.** draught, drop, drink; *boire un* ~ *de trop*, to take a drop too much; ~ *de l'étrier*, stirrup-cup; **5.** (at play) cast, throw, move (at chess), upcast; ~ *d'éclat*, masterly stroke, brilliant action; (colloq.) *en mettre un* ~, to make un effort, to put some vim into it; *manquer son* ~, to miss, to fail; *à ~s de dictionnaire*, with much turning-over of the dictionary.

coupable (kupabl), adj. [L *culpabilis*] Guilty, culpable, sinful. ~ s.m.f. Criminal, culprit.

coupage (kupaʒ), s.m. Mixing, diluting.

coupant, -e (kupɑ̃), p. adj. Sharp, cutting, keen-edged. ~, s.m. Edge.

coupe[1] (kup), s.f. [L *cuppa*] Wine-cup, champagne-glass; bowl, fruit-stand, fruit-dish; challenge cup, cup; ⚠ not as a rule to be translated by English 'cup' (which = *tasse*), except in some idiomatic fig. phrases; *il y a loin de la* ~ *aux lèvres*, there is many a slip twixt the cup and the lip; basin (of a fountain).

coupe[2] (kup), s.f. [f. *couper*] **1.** Cutting; (fig.) *mettre en* ~ *réglée*, to lay under regular contribution; ~ *des cheveux*, hair-cutting; *la* ~ *du foin*, hay-cutting; **2.** cut, shape; *la* ~ *d'un habit*, the cut of a coat; ~ *du visage*, shape of the face; **3.** vertical section; **4.** (at cards) cut, cutting; *faire sauter la* ~, to turn up the king or ace at will; *sous sa* ~, under his thumb; **5.** (swimm.) hand over hand; *tirer sa* ~, to swim hand over hand.

coupé, -e (kupe), p. adj. **1.** Cut, broken, loose; **2.** (arch.) *à pans ~s*, with blunted angles; (naut.) *pont* ~, half-deck; **3.** diluted, mixed with water; **4.** (herald.) couped.

coupé (kupe), s.m. Brougham; (⚠ 'coupé' is now used in English with the sense of a closed two-seater = *coupé, cabriolet*); **2.** (obs.) front seats of a coach; **3.** half-compartment of railway carriage; **4.** (dancing) coupee.

coupe-circuit (kupsirkɥi), s.m. (electr.) Cut-out, fuse, circuit-breaker.

coupée (kupe), s.f. (naut.) Entering-port (in a ship).

coupe-file (kupfil), s.m. invar. Pass, police authorization.

coupe-gorge (kupgɔrʒ), s.m. invar. Cut-throat place.

coupe-jarret (kupʒarɛ), s.m. (pl. *coupe-jarrets*) Ruffian, murderer.

coupellation (kupɛlla'sjɔ̃), s.f. (chem.) Cupellation.

coupelle (kupɛl) s.f. [f. *coupe*] (chem.) Cupel.

coupeller (kupɛlle), v.a. To assay by the cupel.

coupement (kupmɑ̃), s.m. Intersection.

coupe-paille (kuppɑj), s.m. invar. Chaff-cutter.

coupe-papier (kuppapje), s.m. invar. Paper-knife.

coupe-pâte (kuppɑt), s.m. invar. Dough-knife.

couper (kupe), [f. *coup*] v.a.n. **1.** To cut, to cut off, to cut up, to cut asunder, to amputate, to incise; to geld, to castrate; to intersect, to divide, to cross, to be sharp-edged, to intercept, to interrupt, to stop; (fig.) ~ *l'herbe sous le pied à X*, to take the wind out of X's sails, to supplant X; *cela me coupe bras et jambes*, that dumb-founds me; ~ *la retraite*, to cut off the retreat; ~ *les vivres à X*, to starve X, to stop X's allowance; ~ *la fièvre*, to stop the fever; ~ *l'appétit*, to take away one's appetite; ~ *la parole à X*, to cut X short; ~ *court à des bruits*, to stop rumours; (slang) *ça vous la coupe !*, that 's a stumper for you !; ~ *des cheveux en quatre*, to split hairs; **2.** to mix, to dilute with water; **3.** to take a short cut, to cut; **4.** (danc.) to make a coupee; **5.** (cards) to cut, to cut in; **6.** (slang) ~ *à*, v.n. to shirk, to cut; (mil. slang) to swing the lead; ~ *à une corvée*, to shirk a drudgery; *vous n'y couperez pas*, you won't escape it; *je ne coupe pas là-dedans*, I'm not taken in by that; tell that to the marines !; **se** ~, v.pr. **1.** to cut oneself; to cut one's (finger, hand, &c.); (fig.) to contradict oneself; to be cut, to chafe, to be chafed; **2.** to intersect, to cross.

coupe-racines (kup-rasin), s.m. invar. Root-cutter, turnip-cutter.

couperet (kuprɛ), s.m. **1.** Cleaver,

chopper, chopping-knife; guillotine-blade; **2.** enameller's file.
couperose (kuproz), s.f. [LL *cuprosa*] **1.** Copperas, vitriol; **2.** (med.) acne, grog-blossoms, carbuncled face.
couperosé, -e (kuproze), p. adj. Blotched, pimpled, carbuncled.
couperoser (kuproze), v.a. To blotch; **se ~**, v.pr. to get blotchy.
coupeu-r, -se (kupœr), s.m.f. Cutter; gelder; ~ *de bourse*, cutpurse.
couplage (kuplaʒ), s.m. (mech.) Coupling.
couple (kupl) s.f. [f. L *copula*] **1.** Coupling-leash or chain; **2.** pair of things or animals of same species, brace; *une ~ d'œufs*, two eggs; *une ~ de lièvres*, a brace of hares. ~ s.m. Pair, couple; (naut.) frame, rib, timber; (mech.) couplings; (electr.) couples.
coupler (kuple), v.a. To couple, to link (two things) together.
couplet (kuplɛ), s.m. [f. *couple*] **1.** Verse, stanza, tirade; **2.** (techn.) hinge, joint.
coupoir (kupwar), s.m. Cutter.
coupole (kupɔl), s.f. [It. *cupola*] Cupola, dome.
coupon (kupɔ̃), s.m. **1.** Remnant, short length of material; **2.** coupon, dividend; **3.** (theatr.) ticket.
coupure (kupyr), s.f. **1.** Cut, gash, incision, cutting; **2.** suppression of a passage in a literary or musical work; **3.** small banknote.
cour (kur), s.f. [f. LL *cortis*] **1.** Yard, court, courtyard; residence of a sovereign prince, his suite, his retinue; the courtiers; ~ *des miracles*, beggars' meet; *donner de l'eau bénite de ~*, to give vain promises; *manteau de ~*, court-mantle; *homme de ~*, courtier; **2.** courting, flattery, courtship; *faire sa ~*, to pay court, to pay one's respects; *faire la ~ à*, to make love to; **3.** court, law-court, tribunal; *Cour d'assise*, Assizes; *Cour des Comptes*, Audit Office.
courage (kuraʒ), s.m. [f. L *cor*] Courage, heart, spirit, ardour, boldness, gallantry, fortitude; *prendre ~*, to take courage; *perdre ~*, to lose courage; *prendre son ~ à deux mains*, to pluck up one's courage; *~ !*, (interj.) courage !, cheer up !; *bon ~ !*, be of good cheer !
courageusement (kuraʒøzmɑ̃), adv. Courageously, bravely, gallantly, boldly, stoutly.
courageu-x, -se (kuraʒø), adj. Courageous, brave, gallant, fearless, bold, daring.
couramment (kuramɑ̃), adv. Currently, fluently, ordinarily.
courant, -e (kurɑ̃), p. adj. [f. *courir*] Running, flowing, current, common; *l'année ~e*, the current year; *monnaie ~e*, current coin; *le mètre ~*, lineal metre; *tout ~*, hastily, in a great hurry, breathlessly.
courant (kurɑ̃), s.m. Current, stream, course, run; *~ d'air*, draught; *~ électrique*, electric current; *au ~ de la plume*, off-hand; 'currente calamo'; *être au ~ de*, to be acquainted with; to be well up in; to be aware of; to know all about; *tenez-moi au ~*, keep me informed; *fin ~*, at the end of the present month.
courante (kurɑ̃t), s.f. **1.** (danc.) Courante; **2.** running, or cursive, hand (in writing); **3.** (pop.) diarrhoea.
courbache (kurbaʃ), s.f. Heavy horse-whip.
courbatu, -e (kurbaty), adj. [f. *court*+ *battu*] **1.** Knocked-up, sore all over; **2.** (of a horse) foundered.
courbature (kurbatyr), s.f. **1.** (vet.) Foundering; **2.** over-fatigue, pains and stiffness in the joints.
courbaturer (kurbatyre), v.a. To over-fatigue; *être courbaturé*, to be knocked up.
courbe (kurb), s.f. [L *curvus*] Curve, bend, sweep, turn, knee. ~, adj. Curved, bent.
courbé, -e (kurbe), p. adj. Curved, in-curvated, bent, bowed, crooked.
courber (kurbe), v.a.n. [L *curvare*] To bend, to bow, to curve, to crook, to make stoop; **se ~**, v.pr. to bend, to be bent, &c.; to bow oneself down.
courbette (kurbɛt), s.f. Curvet; (fig.) cringing, cringe; *faire des ~s*, to cringe, to bow and scrape.
courbure (kurbyr), s.f. Curvature, bend, flexure, crookedness.
courcaillet (kurkajɛ), s.m. [onom.] Cry or call of the quail; quail-call.
courette (kurɛt), s.f. Small yard, small enclosure.
coureu-r, -se (kurœr), adj. Running, racing, coursing. ~ s.m.f. **1.** Runner, racer, courser, errand-boy, porter, rider (cyclist); driver (motorist); race-horse; **2.** vagabond, rambler; hobo; **3.** libertine, woman-hunter, inconstant lover.
courge (kurʒ), s.f. [L *cucurbita*] Pumpkin, gourd; *~ à la moelle*, vegetable marrow.
courir (kurir), v.n. [L *currere*] To run, to race, to hurry, to hasten, to speed, to run a race; *faire ~*, to run (race-horses); **2.** to flow, to stream, to make progress, to circulate; to be current; to last; *par le temps qui court*, as times go; *l'intérêt court depuis six mois*, the interest has been running on for half a year; **3.** to run (*après*, after), to search (for), to strive (for); **4.** to gad about, to ramble, to run about, to rove; **5.** to prevail, to be prevalent; ~ v.a. to run after, to pursue, to hunt; to incur; to wander over, to roam about; ~ (or *courre*) *le cerf*, to hunt a stag; *il ne faut pas ~ deux lièvres à la fois*, don't have too many irons in the

fire; ~ *le cachet*, to go from house to house giving private lessons; *j'ai couru le monde*, I have roamed about the world; ~ *un risque*, to incur a risk; ~ *un danger*, to be exposed to a danger; *ce bruit court les rues*, it is the talk of the town; ~ *la poste*, to ride post; (slang, very vulg.) *as-tu fini de me ~?* or *tu me cours!*, you are getting on my nerves.

courlis, courlieu (kurli, kurljø), s.m. [onom.] (ornith.) Curlew, whimbrel.

couronne (kurɔn), s.f. [L *corona*] **1.** Crown, coronet, garland, wreath, circular head-dress or ornament; (fig.) sovereignty; (bot.) corona; **2.** (fort.) crown-work; **3.** (vet.) coronet, cornet; **4.** (stationery) large foolscap.

couronné, -e (kurɔne), p. adj. **1.** Crowned, rewarded, completed, surrounded; **2.** (of a horse) broken-kneed.

couronnement (kurɔnmɑ̃), s.m. **1.** Coronation, crowning, completion, perfection, finishing; **2.** top, top-piece, crowning, coping; **3.** (naut.) taffrail.

couronner (kurɔne), v.a. To crown, to reward, to complete, to perfect, to finish, to surmount, to cap; **se ~**, v.pr. **1.** to crown oneself; **2.** to be crowned; **3.** (hort.) to decay at the top; **4.** (vet., of a horse) to break its knees.

courre (kur), v.a.n. [see COURIR] (hunt.) To hunt, to run.

courrier (kurje), s.m. [f. *courir*] **1.** Courier, messenger; **2.** mail, post, correspondence; *par retour du ~*, by return of post; *dépouiller son ~*, to read one's letters.

courriériste (kurjerist), s.m.f. Journalist, reporter, critic who writes in a newspaper.

courroie (kurwɑ), s.f. [f. L *corrigia*] Leather strap, thong; belt, strap; ~ *de transmission*, driving-belt (or -band).

courroucer (kuruse), v.a. [f. *courroux*] To incense, to anger, to provoke; **se ~**, v.pr. to grow angry, to rage.

courroux (kuru), s.m. [f. L *corruptus*] Anger, wrath, fury.

cours (kur), s.m. [L *cursus*] **1.** Flow, current, course, stream; **2.** course, class, lessons; treatise; *suivre un ~ de chimie*, to attend a course of lectures on chemistry; **3.** currency, vogue, duration; *cette monnaie n'a plus ~*, this money is no longer current; **4.** current price, market-price; *premier ~*, opening price; *dernier ~*, closing price; **5.** public walk, parade, row, promenade; syn. MAIL.

course (kurs), s.f. **1.** Course, race, run, running, errand, journey, ride, drive, career; *il est léger à la ~*, he is a swift runner; (naut.) cruise, privateering; (techn.) ~ *du piston*, piston-stroke, travel of a piston; ~ *utile* (*du piston*), working stroke.

coursier (kursje), s.m. Steed, charger, racer, courser. **cours-ier, -ière**, s.m.f. Errand-boy, -girl.

coursive (kursiv), s.f. [It. *corsiva*] (naut.) Passage, half-deck, alley.

courson, courçon (kursɔ̃), s.m. (hort.) Shoot which has been cut back, vine-shoot.

court, -e (kur), adj. [L *curtus*] Short, brief, scanty. ~, adv. Short, at once, suddenly; *couper ~*, to put an end to, to cut short; *rester ~*, to stop short, to be nonplussed; *prendre par le plus ~*, to take the shortest way; *être pris de ~*, to be nonplussed; to be caught unprepared; to be taken unawares; to have received too short a notice; *être à ~ d'argent*, to be short of money; *tout ~*, just that, that 's all.

courtage (kurtaʒ), s.m. [f. *courtier*] **1.** Brokerage; **2.** percentage paid to a broker; commission.

courtaud, -e (kurto), adj. Thick-set, short and thick, crop-eared (as dogs). ~, **-e**, s.m.f. Thick-set, dumpy person; ~ *de boutique*, shopkeeper's drudge.

courtauder (kurtode), v.a. To dock (a horse, a dog).

court-bouillon (kurbujɔ̃), s.m. (pl. *courts-bouillons*), (cook.) Court-bouillon, liquid in which fish is boiled.

court-circuit (kursirkɥi), s.m. (electr.) Short-circuit.

courtepointe (kurtəpwɛ̃t), s.f. Counterpane, quilt, quilted coverlet.

courti-er, -ère (kurtje), s.m.f. Broker, stock-jobber, agent, intermediate business agent; ~ *maritime*, ship-broker. ⚠ *Courtier* must not be translated by English 'courtier' which = *courtisan, homme de cour*.

courtil (kurti), s.m. [f. LL *curtile*] Small garden.

courtilière (kurtiljɛr), s.f. (ent.) Mole-cricket.

courtine (kurtin), s.f. [LL *cortina*] **1.** Bed-curtain; **2.** (fort.) curtain, part of a rampart between two bastions.

courtisan (kurtizɑ̃), s.m. [f. *cour*] Courtier, fawner. ~, adj. Courtly, fawning.

courtisane (kurtizan), s.f. Courtezan, courtesan, prostitute, whore.

courtisanerie (kurtizanri), s.f. Fawning, flattery.

courtiser (kurtize), v.a. To pay court to, to court, to woo, to flatter.

court-jointé, -e (kurʒwɛ̃te), adj. Short-jointed, thick-set.

courtois, -e (kurtwɑ), adj. Courteous, civil, polite; *armes ~es*, blunt arms.

courtoisement (kurtwazmɑ̃), adv. Courteously, politely.

courtoisie (kurtwazi), s.f. Courtesy, courteousness, kind service, good office.

couru, -e (kury), p. adj. [f. *courir*] Sought-after, in vogue, run, run over, overrun; (pop.) *c'est ~*, it's a cinch; it's a dead cert.; the result is easy to guess.
couscous (kuskus), s.m. [Arab. wd] Couscous.
couseuse (kuzøz), s.f. [f. *coudre*] Seamstress, sewer, stitcher; sewing-machine.
cousin[1], **-e** (kuzɛ̃), s.m.f. [f. L *consobrinus*] Cousin, coz; *~ germain*, first cousin, cousin german; *~s issus de germains*; first cousins once removed; *~s au second degré*, second cousins; *le roi n'est pas son ~!*, he would not call the king cousin!
cousin[2] (kuzɛ̃), s.m. [f. LL *culicinus*] (ent.) Gnat, midge.
cousinage (kuzinaʒ), s.m. Kindred, relationship of cousins.
cousiner (kuzine), v.a.n. **1.** To call cousin; **2.** to be on good terms, to be friends.
cousinière (kuzinjɛr), s.f. Mosquito-net; syn. MOUSTIQUAIRE.
cousoir (kuzwar), s.m. [f. *coudre*] Sewing-press.
coussin (kusɛ̃), s.m. [OF *coissin*] Cushion, pillow, pad; stuffing or padding of rubber, wool, &c.
coussinet (kusinɛ), s.m. **1.** Small cushion, pad, rubber; (arch.) coussinet; (rail.) chair (for rails); **2.** (bot.) cranberry, marsh-whortleberry, *Vaccinium oxycoccos*; **3.** (techn.) bearing; brasses; bush; *~ à billes*, ball-bearing; *~ à galets*, roller-bearing; *~ à cônes réglables*, adjustable cone-bearing.
cousu, -e (kuzy), p. adj. [f. *coudre*] Sewed, seamed, stitched; *être tout ~ d'or*, to be rolling in money; to be a nabob; *tenir bouche ~e*, to be close, discreet; *~ de fil blanc*, easily seen through, clumsy.
coût (ku), s.m. [f. *coûter*] Cost, price, expense, charge.
coûtant (kutɑ̃), p. adj. m. *Prix ~*, cost price, prime cost.
couteau (pl. -x) (kuto), s.m. [L *cultellus*] Knife, dagger; *~ à papier*, paper-knife; *porte-~*, knife-rest; *~ à découper*, carving-knife; *planche à ~x*, knife-board; *à ~x tirés*, at daggers drawn; *c'est comme le ~ de Jeannot*, that is like the Irishman's gun (something which has been mended so often that no part of the original article is left); *mettre le ~ sur la gorge à X*, to put a knife to X's throat, to force a person to act under threat.
coutelas (kutlɑ), s.m. Cutlass; hanger.
coutelier (kutəlje), s.m. Cutler.
coutellerie (kutɛlri), s.f. Cutlery, cutler's works, cutler's shop.
coûter (kute), v.n.a. [f. L *constare*] To cost, to be bought at a price; (fig.) to give trouble; to be done reluctantly, or with difficulty; to cause; *~ cher*, to be expensive; *il lui en coûtera cher*; he will pay dearly for it; *cela lui a coûté bien des larmes*, that has cost her many tears; *~ les yeux de la tête et la peau du dos*, to cost no end of money, to cost a mint of money; *coûte que coûte*, cost what it may; *rien ne lui coûte*, he sticks at nothing.
coûteusement (kutøzmɑ̃), adv. At a great cost.
coûteu-x, -se (kutø), adj. Costly, expensive, dear.
coutil (kuti), s.m. [f. L *culcita*] Ticking, tick, drill, tent-cloth.
coutre (kutr), s.m. [f. L *culter*] Coulter; wood-cleaver.
coutrier (kutrje), s.m. Plough without fore-part; subsoil plough.
coutume (kutym), s.f. [f. L *consuetudo*] Custom, habit; customary, unwritten law; *de ~*, customary; usually; *comme de ~*, as usual; *avoir ~ de*, to be in the habit of; *une fois n'est pas ~*, once does not count; one swallow does not make a summer.
coutumi-er, -ère (kutymje), adj. Customary, usual; accustomed to, in the habit of; *il est ~ du fait*, he is an old offender; *droit ~*, unwritten law; common law.
couture (kutyr), s.f. [f. *coudre*] **1.** Sewing, seam, needlework; *~ en surjet*, overcast seam; **2.** scar; *battre à plate ~*, to vanquish (or beat) completely, to rout; to beat hollow; to wipe the floor with.
couturer (kutyre), v.a. To scar, to seam.
couturier (kutyrje), s.m. **1.** Ladies' tailor, couturier, dressmaker; **2.** (anat.) sartorius (muscle).
couturière (kutyrjɛr), s.f. Seamstress, dressmaker.
couvain (kuvɛ̃), s.m. [f. *couver*] (of bees and insects) Nest of eggs; brood-cells.
couvaison (kuvɛzɔ̃), s.f. Brooding-time, brooding, sitting.
couvée (kuve), s.f. Brood, hatch, covey, offspring.
couvent (kuvɑ̃), s.m. [L *conventus*] Convent, monastery, nunnery, convent-school.
couver (kuve), v.a. [L *cubare*] **1.** To brood on, to sit on, to brood, to sit; to incubate; **2.** (fig.) to hatch, to breed, to brew; *~ des yeux*, to gloat over; *~ un complot*, to hatch a plot; *~ une maladie*, to be sickening for an illness; *~*, v.n. to smoulder; *le feu couve sous la cendre*, the fire is smouldering under the ashes.
couvercle (kuvɛrkl), s.m. [f. L *coopercculum*] Lid, cover, cap.
couvert (kuvɛr), s.m. [f. *couvrir*] **1.** Things on the table for a meal; *mettre le ~*, to lay the cloth, to set the table; *ôter le ~*, to clear the table; *mettre un ~*,

to lay knife and fork for one; **2.** set of fork and spoon; **3.** lodging; *le vivre et le* ~, board and lodging; **4.** covert, cover, envelope, shade, protection; *sous le* ~ *de*, under the cover or pretence of; *à* ~, under shelter, secure (from).
couvert, -e (kuvɛr), p. adj. **1.** Covered, clothed, clad; **2.** covert, sheltered, shady, loaded, covered; **3.** cloudy, husky; *d'une voix* ~*e*, with a husky voice; **4.** ambiguous, secret, concealed; *à mots* ~*s*, with ambiguous words; **5.** authorized, justified, excused.
couverte (kuvɛrt), s.f. **1.** (pottery) Glaze; **2.** covering.
couverture (kuvɛrtyr), s.f. **1.** Covering, rug, cloth, cover, coverlet, blanket; *tirer toute la* ~ *à soi*, to take more than one's share; **2.** roofing, roof; **3.** show, pretence; **4.** guarantee, security; (mil.) *troupes de* ~, covering troops.
couvet (kuvɛ), (obs.) s.m. Footwarmer.
couveuse (kuvøz), s.f. adj. Sitting (hen), brooding (hen); incubator.
couvi (kuvi), adj. m. *Œuf* ~, addle egg.
couvoir (kuvwar), s.m. Incubator.
couvre-chef (kuvrəʃɛf), s.m. (pl. *couvre-chefs*) (jest.) Headgear, hat.
couvre-feu (kuvrəfø), s.m. invar. Curfew, curfew-bell, retreat.
couvre-lit (kuvrəli), s.m. (pl. *couvre-lits*) Bedspread.
couvre-nuque (kuvrənyk), s.m. (pl. *couvre-nuques*) Rear-peak (of hat), puggaree.
couvrepied (kuvrəpje), s.m. Quilt, counterpane, coverlet.
couvreur (kuvrœr), s.m. Tiler, thatcher, slater, roofer.
couvrir (kuvrir), v.a. [f. L *cooperire*] **1.** To cover, to overspread, to lay over, to conceal, to clothe, to wrap up; **2.** to overwhelm, to load, to screen, to protect, to shield, to excuse; **3.** to be sufficient for, to be equivalent to, to defray; **4.** (of animals) to cover; **se** ~, v.pr. to cover oneself, to put on one's hat; *couvrez-vous, monsieur*, be covered sir; to be covered, overspread.
covenant (kɔvnɑ̃), s.m. [Engl. wd] Covenant.
covenantaire (kɔvnɑ̃tɛr), s.m. Covenanter.
co-vendeur (kovɑ̃dœr), s.m. Joint-vendor, joint-seller.
coxal, -e, (aux) (kɔksal), adj. [f. L *coxa*] Coxal.
coxalgie (kɔksalʒi), s.f. (pathol.) Coxalgia.
coyote (kɔjɔt), s.m. (zool.) Coyote, American wolf.
crabe (krab and krɑb), s.m. [f. Germ. *Krabbe*] (moll.) Crab.
crabier (krabje), s.m. (zool.) Crab-eater, *Ardea cracra.*
crac (krak), interj. [onom.] Crack!, pop!, in a trice!, before you can say Jack Robinson!
crachat (kraʃa), s.m. [f. *cracher*] Spit, spittle, expectoration; (med.) sputum; (pop. fig.) star (of an order).
craché, -e (kraʃe), p. adj. [f. *cracher*] *Tout* ~, the very image of; his picture to a T; the spit of.
crachement (kraʃmɑ̃), s.m. Spitting, expectoration.
cracher (kraʃe), v.n.a. [Germanic orig.] **1.** To spit, to expectorate; **2.** to sputter, to spirt (as a pen), to spout; **3.** (fig.) to utter; ~ *des injures*, to shower down abuse; *ne pas* ~ *sur*, not to despise; **4.** (pop.) to pay, to fork out, to cough up, to stump up.
cracheu-r, -se (kraʃœr), s.m.f. Spitter.
crachoir (kraʃwar), s.m. Spittoon; (fig.) *tenir le* ~, to monopolize the conversation, to hold the floor.
crachotement (kraʃɔtmɑ̃), s.m. Frequent feeble spitting.
crachoter (kraʃɔte), v.a.n. To keep feebly spitting.
cracovien, -ne (krakɔvjɛ̃), adj. s.m.f. Cracovian, Cracovienne (dance).
craie (krɛ), s.f. [L *creta*] Chalk, carbonate of lime; *tracer à la* ~, to chalk out.
crailler (krɑje), v.n. [onom.] To caw.
craindre (krɛ̃dr), v.a. [f. L *tremere, cremere,* OF *criembre*] To fear, to be afraid of, to dread, to stand in awe of; *à* ~, to be feared, formidable; *il est à* ~ *que*, it is to be expected (or feared) that.
crainte (krɛ̃t), s.f. Fear, dread, awe, apprehension; *de* ~ *de,* ~ *de*, for fear of; *de* ~ *que*, lest, for fear.
crainti-f, -ve (krɛ̃tif), adj. Fearful, timorous, easily afraid, apprehensive.
craintivement (krɛ̃tivmɑ̃), adv. Fearfully, timorously, timidly.
crambé, crambe (krɑ̃be), s.m. [L *crambe*] **1.** Sea-kale; **2.** (zool.) crambus.
cramoisi, -e (kramwazi), adj. [Arab. *karmesi*] Crimson-red, scarlet. ~, s.m. Crimson, scarlet colour.
crampe (krɑ̃p), s.f. [f. Germ. *Krampf*] Cramp.
crampon (krɑ̃pɔ̃), s.m. Cramp-iron, cramp, crampoon, calkin, frost-nail (of a horse-shoe); (fig. fam.) a bore, a person not easily got rid of; a fixture.
cramponner (krɑ̃pɔne), v.a. **1.** To fasten with cramps, to put calkins on; **2.** (fig.) to force one's company on (a person); to bore; **se** ~, v.pr. to cling desperately; to stick like a limpet.
cramponnet (krɑ̃pɔnɛ), s.m. Cramp, staple (of a lock).
cran (krɑ̃), s.m. [f. LL *crena*] Notch, indentation, nick; *baisser d'un* ~, to come down a peg; (fig.) courage; *avoir du* ~, to

be plucky; to have guts; to have plenty of go; to show courage and presence of mind; (techn.) ~ *d'arrêt*, catch.

crâne (krɑn), s.m. [Gr. *kranion*] Skull, cranium; (fig.) *bourrer le ~ à X*, to kid X; to cod or humbug X.

crâne (krɑn), adj. Bold, gallant, brave, daring, plucky, swanky, proud, smart.

crânement (krɑnmɑ̃), adv. Boldly, pluckily, dashingly, daringly, gallantly, smartly, proudly.

crâner (krɑne), v.n. (colloq.) To put up a brave show, to brave it out, to swagger, to come it strong, to boast, to put on side.

crânerie (krɑnri), s.f. [f. *crâne*] Smartness, daring, boldness, pluck.

crâneu-r, -se (krɑnœr), s.m.f. (pej.) Swaggerer, swank. ~, adj. Swanky. ⚠ *Crâne, crânement*, and *crânerie* are not pejorative; *crâneur* is pejorative; *crâner* is sometimes, but not always.

crânien, -ne (krɑnjɛ̃), adj. Cranial.

crâniologique (krɑnjɔlɔʒik), adj. Craniological.

crânioscopie (krɑnjɔskɔpi), s.f. [f. Gr. *kranion*+*skopein*] Cranioscopy.

crânologie, crâniologie (krɑnɔlɔʒi, krɑnjɔlɔʒi), s.f. Craniology.

crapaud (krapo), s.m. [etym. dub.] **1.** Toad, *Bufo*; **2.** (vet.) thrush; **3.** (adj.) *fauteuil* ~, low arm-chair; **4.** (pop.) urchin.

crapaudière (krapodjɛr), s.f. Toad-hole, swampy place.

crapaudine (krapodin), s.f. **1.** Toadstone; **2.** (bot.) iron-wort; **3.** grating (of a drain); **4.** (techn.) socket, collar; **5.** (cook.) *à la* ~, cut open and broiled.

crapouillot (krapujo), s.m. [war wd] Trench-mortar.

crapoussin, -e (krapusɛ̃), s.m.f. (pop.) Puny, ill-built person.

crapule (krapyl), s.f. [L *crapula*] **1.** Crapulence, debauchery; **2.** bad lot, dishonest person, low blackguard.

crapuler (krapyle), v.n. To live in gross debauchery.

crapuleusement (krapyløzmɑ̃), adv. Dissolutely, vilely.

crapuleu-x, -se (krapylø), adj. Crapulous, dissolute, crapulent, corrupt, filthy, vicious.

crapulos (krapylos), s.m. (pop. jest.) Very cheap cigar.

craque (krak), s.f. [f. *craquer*] (pop.) Fib, crack, bung.

craqueler (krakle), v.a. [f. *craquer*] To crack, to crackle (china, glass, &c.).

craquelin (kraklɛ̃), s.m. [f. *craquer*] Cracknel, cracker (biscuit).

craquelure (kraklyr), s.f. Crack, crackle.

craquement (krakmɑ̃), s.m. Creaking, creak, snapping, cracking, crackling.

craquer (krake), v.n. [f. *crac*] To crack, to crackle, to creak, to snap.

craquètement (krakɛtmɑ̃), s.m. Crackling, chattering of teeth, gabbling (of a stork).

craqueter (krakəte), v.n. To gabble (as a stork), to crackle.

craqueu-r, -se (krakœr), s.m.f. (pop.) Cracker, fib-teller, boaster; ~, adj. fibbing, boasting.

crase (krɑz), s.f. [Gr. *krasis*] **1.** (gram.) Crasis, contraction of vowels of two syllables into one long vowel or diphthong, synaeresis; **2.** (med.) crasis.

crassane (krasan), adj. s.f. Crassane (pear).

crasse (kras), adj. [f. L *crassus*] Crass, gross, thick, coarse; *ignorance* ~, gross ignorance.

crasse (kras), s.f. **1.** Dirt, filth; **2.** dross (of melting metals); **3.** (fig.) low condition, dunghill; **4.** sordid avarice; **5.** dirty trick; *faire une ~ à X*, be guilty of a mean action towards X; play a dirty trick on X.

crasser (krase), v.a. To foul; **se** ~, v.pr. to get foul.

crasseu-x, -se (krasø), adj. **1.** Dirty, filthy, foul; **2.** stingy, sordid. ~, s.m.f. Dirty person.

crassier (krɑsje), s.m. Slag-heap.

crassule (krasyl), s.f. [LL *crassula*] (bot.) Crassula.

cratère (kratɛr), s.m. [Gr. L *cratēr*] **1.** (ant.) Cup with two handles; **2.** (geol.) crater; **3.** (astron.) the Cup.

cravache (kravaʃ), s.f. [Turk. and Russ. orig.] Horse-whip, riding-whip.

cravacher (kravaʃe), v.a. To horse-whip, to whip.

cravate (kravat), s.f. [f. *Croate*] **1.** Cravat, necktie, neckcloth; ~ *de chanvre*, hempen rope, hanging-rope, halter. ~ s.m. adj. Croatian horse, Croat (a horse-soldier).

cravater (kravate), v.a. To put a necktie on, to arrange (a person's) necktie; **se** ~, v.pr. to put on one's necktie.

crayeu-x, -se (krɛjø), adj. Chalky.

crayon (krɛjɔ̃), s.m. [f. *craie*] **1.** Pencil, crayon; **2.** pencil-drawing; **3.** (fig.) sketch, outline.

crayonnage (krɛjɔnaʒ), s.m. Pencil-drawing, pencilling.

crayonner (krɛjɔne), v.a. **1.** To pencil, to crayon; **2.** (fig.) to sketch.

crayonneu-x, -se (krɛjɔnø), adj. Chalky, drawn with too soft a pencil.

cré (kre), adj. Pop. abbrev. of *sacré*, as in *cré nom!*

créance (kreɑ̃s), s.f. [f. L *credere*] **1.** Credence, belief, trust, confidence; *lettres de* ~, credentials; **2.** claim, debt.

créanci-er, -ère (kreɑ̃sje), s.m.f. Creditor.

o, note, glotte; ɔ̃, monter, ronde; ø, feu, creux; œ, peur, sœur; œ̃, un; ʃ, chez, schisme; u, tout; w, oui, doit, douaire; y, mur, pu; ɥ, huile, muette; z, zèle, rose; ʒ, déjà, gentil.

créat-eur, -rice (kreatœr), s.m.f. [L *creator*] Creator, inventor. ~, adj. Creative.
création (krea'sjɔ̃), s.f. **1.** Creation, making, foundation, production; **2.** creation, the universe.
créature (kreatyr), s.f. **1.** Creature; **2.** (in contempt) vile person; **3.** dependant, instrument, favourite.
crécelle (kresɛl), s.f. [unkn. orig.] Rattle.
crécerelle (kresrɛl), s.f. (ornith.) Kestrel; syn. ÉMOUCHET.
crèche (krɛʃ), s.f. [f. OHG *kripja*] **1.** Manger, crib; **2.** infants' home, day-nursery, crèche.
crécy (kresi), s.f. [geog. orig.] Crecy (kind of carrot); *potage* ~, carrot soup.
crédence (kredɑ̃s), s.f. [It. *credenza*] Credence, sideboard, prothesis.
crédencier (kredɑ̃sje), s.m. Person superintending the victuals in a public establishment.
crédibilité (kredibilite), s.f. [f. L *credibilis*] Credibility.
crédirenti-er, -ère (kredirɑ̃tje), s.m.f. Holder of annuities. ~, adj. That holds annuities.
crédit (kredi), s.m. [f. L *credere*] **1.** Credit, mercantile reputation, trust, influence, authority, repute; **2.** (book-keep.) credit; **3.** sums which may be spent according to the budget law; **4.** banking-establishment; ~ *municipal* or *mont-de-piété* or *clou* or *ma tante*, municipal pawnbroking establishment; *faire* ~, to give credit; *à* ~, on trust; on credit; *lettre de* ~, letter of credit; *n'avoir plus de* ~, to be unable to get credit; *accorder des* ~*s*, to grant credits.
créditer (kredite), v.a. To credit.
créditeur (kreditœr), s.m.f. Creditor. ~, adj. Credit.
credo (kredo), s.m. [L wd] Creed, belief, credo.
crédule (kredyl), adj. [L *credulus*] Credulous, easily deceived.
crédulement (kredylmɑ̃), adv. Credulously.
crédulité (kredylite), s.f. [L *credulitas*] Credulity, credulousness.
créer (kree), v.a. [f. L *creare*] To create, to make, to invent, to produce, to found, to settle (an annuity); (theatr.) to create (a part).
crémaillère (kremajɛr), s.f. [LL *cramaculus*] **1.** Pot-hanger, pot-hook; *pendre la* ~, to give (or to have) a house-warming (party); **2.** (mech.) rack, toothed bar; *cric à* ~, rack-jack; *engrenage à* ~, rack and pinion; *chemin de fer à* ~, cog-wheel railway.
crémaillon (kremajɔ̃), s.m. Small pot-hook.
crémation (krema'sjɔ̃), s.f. [f. L *cremare*] Cremation.
crématoire (krematwar), adj. Crematorial; *four* ~, crematorium.
crème (krɛm), s.f. [OF *cresme*, L *chrisma*] Cream, custard; (fig.) the best, the cream; the flower, the pink; *la* ~ *des honnêtes gens*, the most worthy of honest people; ~ *fouettée*, whipped cream; *tarte à la* ~, (fig.) omnibus answer, burden, constant refrain.
crément (kremɑ̃), [L *crementum*] (gram.) Increment.
crémer (kreme), v.n. To cream; ~, v.a. **1.** to incinerate; **2.** to dye a cream colour.
crémerie (kremri), s.f. Dairy(-shop), creamery, small restaurant.
crémeu-x, -se (kremø), adj. Creamy.
crémi-er, -ère (kremje), s.m.f. Dairyman or woman, keeper of a dairy(-shop) or creamery.
crémone (kremɔn), s.f. [f. *Cremona*, Italy] Window-fastening.
créneau (pl. **-x**) (kreno), s.m. [f. LL *crena*] (fort.) Crenel, loop-hole, pinnacle; (naut.) soil-pipe.
crénelage (krenlaʒ), s.m. Milled edge (of a coin), milling.
créneler (krenle), v.a. **1.** To indent; **2.** (fort.) to crenellate; **3.** to mill the edge of (coin).
crénelure (krenlyr), s.f. Indentation; (bot.) crenature.
créner (krene), v.a. To indent; (type-founding) to kern.
créole (kreɔl), adj. s.m.f. [f. Span. *criollo*] Creole.
créosote (kreɔzɔt), s.f. (chem.) Creosote.
créosoter (kreɔzɔte), v.a. To creosote (wood).
crêpage (krɛpaʒ), s.m. [f. *crêper*] Glossing of crape; (pop.) fight, tussle; ~ *de chignons*, tussle between women.
crêpe (krɛp), s.m. [f. L *crispus*] Crape; ~ *de Chine*, China-crape, crêpe-de-Chine; mourning hatband. ~, s.f. Pancake.
crêper (krɛpe), v.a. [f. L *crispare*] To crisp, to crape; **se** ~, v.pr. to become craped, or frizzled; *se* ~ *le chignon*, (of women) to have a set-to, to fight, to have a tussle.
crépi (krepi), s.m. (mason.) Rough-cast, rough coat, parget.
crépin (krepɛ̃), s.m. [f. *St Crépin*] Grindery-dealer, seller of shoe-maker's tools and materials; *porter tout son saint-Crépin avec soi*, to carry all one's belongings, or all one's paraphernalia, with one; ~*s*, grindery, shoe-maker's materials and tools.
crépine (krepin), s.f. [f. *crêpe*] **1.** Fringe; **2.** (butch.) kell, caul, thin fat membrane, used in cookery.
crépinette (krepinɛt), s.f. **1.** Flat sausage wrapped in kell; **2.** (bot.) knot-grass.

crépir (krepir), v.a. [f. OF *crespe*] To rough-cast, to parget; to grain (leather).
crépissage (krepisaʒ), s.m. Rough-casting, pargeting.
crépissure (krepisyr), s.f. Rough-cast, parget.
crépitant, -e (krepitɑ̃), p. adj. Crepitating.
crépitation (krepita'sjɔ̃), s.f. Crepitation, crackling; (med.) crepitus.
crépitement (krepitmɑ̃), s.m. See CRÉPITATION.
crépiter (krepite), v.n. [L *crepitare*] To crepitate, to crackle.
crépon (krepɔ̃), s.m. [f. *crêpe*] **1.** Crepon (a material); **2.** hair-pad.
crépu, -e (krepy), adj. Frizzled, curled, woolly.
crépusculaire (krepyskylɛr), adj. Crepuscular.
crépuscule (krepyskyl), s.m. [L *crepusculum*] **1.** Twilight, crepuscule; **2.** dawn, beginning; **3.** (fig.) decline.
crescendo (krɛʃɛndo), s.m. [It. wd] Crescendo.
cresson (krɛsɔ̃), s.m. [etym. dub.] (bot.) Cress, water-cress.
cressonnière (krɛsɔnjɛr), s.f. Cress-bed.
crésus (krezys), s.m. [prop. n.] Croesus, very rich man, nabob.
crétacé, -e (kretase), adj. [f. L *creta*] Cretaceous, chalky.
crête (krɛt), s.f. [f. L *crista*] **1.** Crest, comb (of a cock), tuft; *baisser la* ~, to be crestfallen; **2.** top, ridge, coping (of a wall), parapet.
crêté, -e (krɛte), p. adj. **1.** Crested, tufted; **2.** (pop.) offended, angry.
crête-de-coq (krɛtdəkok), s.f. (pl. *crêtes-de-coq*) (bot.) **1.** Coxcomb, *Celosia cristata*; **2.** yellow rattle, *Rhinanthus crista-galli*.
crêteler (krɛtle), v.n. (of hens) To cackle.
crételle (kretɛl), s.f. (bot.) Crested dog-tail grass, *Cynosurus cristatus*.
crêter (krɛte), v.a. [f. *crête*] To tack, to vandyke, to crest; **se** ~, v.pr. (pop.) to get angry.
crétin, -e (kretɛ̃), s.m.f. [f. Alpine patois *crestin*, L *christianus*] **1.** Cretin; **2.** (fig.) fool, idiot; moron.
crétiniser (kretinize), v.a. To idiotize, to make foolish; **se**~, v.pr. to become stupid.
crétinisme (kretinism), s.m. **1.** (pathol.) Cretinism; **2.** (fig.) idiocy.
crétois, -e (kretwa), adj. s.m.f. Cretan.
cretonne (krətɔn), s.f. [f. *Creton*, in Normandy] Cretonne, calico.
cretons (krətɔ̃), s.m.pl. [unkn. orig.] **1.** Graves (of tallow); **2.** scratchings (of lard).
creusage, creusement (krøzaʒ, krøzmɑ̃), s.m. Digging, deepening, sinking (of a well), hollowing, scooping.
creuser (krøze), v.a. [f. *creux*] **1.** To dig, to hollow, to excavate, to sink, to deepen; **2.** (fig.) to examine thoroughly; **3.** (colloq.) to give an appetite; to make (one) feel empty; **se** ~, v.pr. to become hollow; *se* ~ *la tête*, to rack one's brains.
creuset (krøzɛ), s.m. [LL *crucibulum*] Crucible, melting-pot; (fig.) test.
creu-x, -se (krø), adj. [prob. of Celt. orig.] **1.** Hollow, concave, sunken; **2.** empty; **3.** (fig.) light, unsubstantial, superficial, vain. ~, adv. Hollow; *un songe* ~, an idle dream; *sonner* ~, to sound hollow.
creux (krø), s.m. **1.** Hollow, cavity; **2.** cast, mould; **3.** (fig. pop.) strong bass voice.
crevaison (krəvɛzɔ̃), s.f. [f. *crever*] Puncture, bursting; (pop.) death, croaking, kicking the bucket.
crevant, -e (krəvɑ̃), p. adj. (pop.) **1.** Laughable, extremely funny, side-splitting; **2.** boring, dull.
crevasse (krəvas), s.f. [f. *crever*] Crevasse, crevice, crack, cleft, chink, chap, cranny; *avoir des* ~*s aux mains*, to have chapped hands.
crevasser (krəvase), v.a. To chap, to crack; **se** ~, v.pr. to crack, to chap.
crevé (krəve), s.m. **1.** Opening in sleeves; **2.** thin, weak, done-up person; *petit* ~, fop, dandy, a ridiculous elegant feeble-looking young man. ~, **-e**, p. adj. Burst; dead (pop., and speaking of animals).
crève (krɛv), s.f. (slang) Death, mortal illness; (iron.) *avoir la* ~, to be very ill; to be at the point of death.
crève-cœur (krɛvkœr), s.m. invar. Heart-break, heartsore.
crever (krəve), v.a.n. [f. L *crepare*] **1.** To burst, to break out, to break away, to break open, to split, to rend, to work to death; **2.** (of beasts) to die; (slang, of persons) to die, to peg out, to go west; *cela crève les yeux*, that stares you in the face; *il crève d'orgueil*, he is bursting with pride; ~ *de faim*, (*a*) to be ravenously hungry; (*b*) to be extremely poor.
crevette (krəvɛt), s.f. [f. *chevrette*] Shrimp.
cri (kri), s.m. [f. *crier*] Cry, scream, shout, squeak, yell, howl, shriek, squall; (fig.) outcry; voice; opinion; *pousser les hauts* ~*s*, to raise an outcry; to complain loudly; ~ *de guerre*, war-cry, war-whoop; *pousser des* ~*s*, to scream; *le* ~ *de la conscience*, the voice of conscience; *le* ~ *du cœur*, the spontaneous expression of one's passionate longing; *à cor et à* ~, with hue and cry, clamorously; *le dernier* ~, the latest fashion, the rage.
criage (kriaʒ), s.m. Public crying.
criailler (kriɑje), v.n. To bawl, to squall; (fig.) to complain loudly and frequently.
criaillerie (kriɑjri), s.f. Bawling, squalling, loud complaints, wrangling.

criant, -e (kriɑ̃), p. adj. **1.** Crying; **2.** glaring, revolting.
criard, -e (kriar), adj. Noisy, squalling, scolding, loudly grumbling, discordant, shrill; *dettes ~es*, debts for the payment of which the creditor becomes or would become clamorous, which therefore must be paid without delay, pressing debts; *couleurs ~es*, loud colours, gaudy colours.
criblage (kriblaʒ), s.m. Sifting, screening.
crible (kribl), s.m. [f. L *cribrum*] Sieve, cribble, screen.
cribler (krible), v.a. **1.** To sift, to cribble, to riddle, to screen; **2.** to riddle, to pierce all over, to pepper, to overwhelm; *~ de balles*, to riddle with bullets; *être criblé de dettes*, to be over head and ears in debt.
cribleu-r, -se (kriblœr), s.m.f. Sifter.
cribleu-x, -se (kriblø), adj. Cribrate, cribrose.
criblure (kriblyr), s.f. Siftings, screenings.
cric (krik), s.m. [onom.] Screw-jack, lifting-jack; *~-crac*, crick-crack.
cricket (krikɛt), s.m. [Engl. wd] Cricket.
cri-cri (krikri), s.m. [onom.] (ent. pop.) Cricket.
criée (krie), s.f. [f. *crier*] Sale by auction.
crier (krie), v.n.a. [L *quiritare*] To scream, to cry out, to cry, to shriek, to squall, to squeak, to bawl, to howl, to screech; (fig.) to protest, to proclaim, to hawk; *~ haro sur X*, to raise the hue and cry against X; *~ vengeance*, to cry for vengeance; *~ misère*, to complain of poverty; *~ famine*, to cry famine; *sans ~ gare*, without a word of warning.
crieu-r, -se (kriœr), s.m.f. Crier, town crier.
crime (krim), s.m. [L *crimen*] Crime, guilt, offence.
criminaliser (kriminalize), v.a. To remove from a civil to a criminal court.
criminaliste (kriminalist), s.m.f. Criminalist.
criminalité (kriminalite), s.f. Criminality.
criminel, -le (kriminɛl), adj. Criminal, unlawful, guilty. **~**, s.m.f. **1.** Criminal, culprit, offender; **2.** criminal proceedings, criminal matters.
criminellement (kriminɛlmɑ̃), adv. Criminally.
crin (krɛ̃), s.m. [L *crinis*] Horse-hair, mane, hair (of certain animals); *à tous ~s*, violent, spirited, thorough, out and out; *~ de Florence*, silkworm gut; *~ végétal*, alva marina, vegetable fibre. **~**, adj. (colloq.) *être ~*, or *à ~*, to be cranky, irritable, in a temper.
crincrin (krɛ̃krɛ̃), s.m. [onom.] Screeching fiddle.
crinière (krinjɛr), s.f. [f. *crin*] Mane; (jest.) shock of hair, mop.
crinoline (krinɔlin), s.f. [f. *crin*] Crinoline.
crique (krik), s.f. [f. Scand. *kriki*] Creek, cove, small bay.
criquet (krikɛ), s.m. [onom.] (ent.) Locust, cricket, *Gryllus domesticus*; (pop.) bit of a man; weak wine.
crise (kriz), s.f. [f. Gr. *krisis*] Crisis; fit; *~ de nerfs*, a fit of hysteria; *piquer une ~ de nerfs*, to have an attack of nerves.
crispant, -e (krispɑ̃), p. adj. (colloq.) Exasperating.
crispation (krispa'sjɔ̃), s.f. [f. *crisper*] Contraction, shrivelling, twitching; (fig.) fidgets, irritation.
crisper (krispe), v.a. [L *crispare*] To contract, to shrivel; (fig.) to exasperate; **se ~**, v.pr. to shrivel up, to fidget.
crispin (krispɛ̃), s.m. [f. It. *crispino*] **1.** Part of valet in old comedies, jester; **2.** short cloak; **3.** cuff of gloves.
criss, crid (kris, krid), [Malay *kris*] Kris, creese.
crissement (krismɑ̃), s.m. [f. *crisser*] Grating, grinding (of the teeth).
crisser (krise), v.n. [onom.] To grate, to grind.
cristal (pl. **aux**) (kristal), s.m. [f. Gr. *krustallos*] **1.** Crystal; *~ de roche*, rock-crystal; **2.** crystal glass, cut glass; **3.** (fig.) limpidity, anything transparent and cold. **cristaux**, s.m.pl. (Carbonate of) soda.
cristallerie (kristalri), s.f. **1.** Art of making crystal; **2.** glass-works, glass-shop.
cristallier (kristalje), s.m. Glass-cutter or -engraver.
cristallin, -e (kristalɛ̃), adj. Crystalline. **~**, s.m. (anat.) Crystalline lens.
cristallisable (kristalizabl), adj. Crystallizable.
cristallisation (kristaliza'sjɔ̃), s.f. Crystallization.
cristalliser (kristalize), v.a.n. To crystallize; *sucre cristallisé*, granulated sugar.
cristallisoir (kristalizwar), s.m. Crystallizing-pan.
cristallographe (kristallɔgraf), s.m.f. Crystallographer.
cristallographie (kristallɔgrafi), s.f. Crystallography.
cristallographique (kristallɔgrafik), adj. Crystallographic.
cristalloïde (kristallɔid), adj. Crystalloid.
criste-marine (kristəmarin), s.f. (bot.) Crest-marine, sea-samphire, *Crithmum maritimum*.
cristi (kristi), interj. Abbrev. of *sacristi!* = dash it!, confound it!
critère, critérium (kritɛr, kriterjɔm), s.m. [L *criterium*] Criterion, standard, test.
criticisme (kritisism), s.m. Criticism.
critiquable (kritikabl), adj. Open to criticism.

critique (kritik), adj. [f. Gr. *kritikos*] Critical, censorious, pertaining to a crisis, decisive; *l'instant* ~, the critical moment; the decisive turn.
critique (kritik), s.f. Criticism, critique, piece of criticism, review. ~, s.m.f. Critic, judge, censurer, reviewer.
critiquer (kritike), v.a. To criticize, to censure.
critiqueur (kritikœr), s.m. Fault-finder.
croassement (kroasmɑ̃), s.m. Croak, croaking, cawing (of crows).
croasser (kroase), v.n. To croak, to caw.
croate (kroat), adj. s.m.f. Croatian.
croc (kro), s.m. [LL *croccum*] **1.** Hook, drag-hook; **2.** tusk, fang; ~ *en jambe*, (krokɑ̃ʒɑ̃b), s.m. invar. trip, tripping-up; (fig.) dirty trick.
croche (krɔʃ), adj. Crooked. ~, s.f. Quaver; *double* ~, semiquaver; *triple* ~, demi-semiquaver; *quadruple* ~, semi-demi-semiquaver.
crochet (krɔʃɛ), s.m. **1.** Hook, gaff; **2.** crochet (-work); **3.** hook, crochet; **4.** fang (of certain animals, espec. snakes); **5.** porter's dosser (for carrying wood, &c.); **6.** swerve, sudden turn or change of direction; *il a fait un* ~ *pour m'éviter*, he turned out of his way to avoid me; **7.** (print.) brackets, crotchets; **8.** (colloq.) *il vit aux crochets de X*, he lives at X's charge; he sponges on X. ⚠ Not to be translated by 'crotchet', which = (mus.) *noire*; and *lubie, caprice*.
crochetable (krɔʃtabl), adj. Pickable; that may be hooked, or broken open.
crochetage (krɔʃtaʒ), s.m. Lock-picking.
crocheter (krɔʃte), v.a. [f. *crochet*] To pick (a lock); ~, v.n. (sport.) to run in zigzags, to swerve sharply; ~, v.a.n. to do crochet-work, to crochet.
crocheteur (krɔʃtœr), s.m. **1.** Street-porter; (fig.) ruffian; **2.** picklock, house-breaker.
crochu, -e (krɔʃy), adj. [f. *croc*] Hooked, crooked; *avoir les doigts* ~*s*, (fig.) (*a*) to be light-fingered; (*b*) to be greedy, rapacious.
crocodile (krɔkɔdil), s.m. [f. Gr. *krokodeilos*] Crocodile; (fig.) *larmes de* ~, crocodile tears.
crocus (krɔkys), s.m. [L wd] (bot.) Crocus, saffron.
croire (krwɑr, krwar), v.a.n. [L *credere*] To believe, to think to be true, to credit, to trust, to believe in; to be of opinion, to deem; *c'est à* ~, it is presumable; *à l'en* ~, if we are to trust him; *faire* ~, to make believe; to persuade; *croyez-vous que*, do you think that; *croyez bien, croyez le bien*, depend upon it; ~ *aux miracles*, to believe in miracles; ~ *en Dieu*, to believe in God; **se** ~, v.pr. to consider oneself; to be believed; *cela se croit aisément*, it's easy to believe; *s'en* ~, to think much of oneself.
croisade (krwɑzad), s.f. [f. *croix, croiser*] Crusade.
croisé (krwɑze), s.m. **1.** Crusader; **2.** twill, twilled tissue.
croisé, -e (krwɑze), p.adj. Crossed, folded; (of breeds) cross; (of rhymes) alternate; (of a coat, &c.) double-breasted; twilled (as a tissue); *rester les bras* ~*s*, to remain with folded arms = to remain idle; (danc.) *chassé* ~, chassé croisé, double chassé.
croisée (krwɑze), s.f. **1.** Window; **2.** cross-road, crossing; transept.
croisement (krwɑzmɑ̃), s.m. **1.** Crossing; **2.** cross-breeding.
croiser (krwɑze), v.a. **1.** To cross, to lay or put crossways, to intersect, to pass, to come across; **2.** to counteract; **3.** to lap over (one's coat, &c.); **4.** (weav.) to twist, to twill; **5.** to cross-breed; ~, v. n. (naut.) to cruise; **se** ~, v.pr. **1.** to cross each other, to pass each other, to go contrariwise; **2.** to take the cross, to become a crusader.
croisette (krwɑzɛt), s.f. **1.** Croslet; **2.** crosswort; **3.** (naut.) top-gallant cross-tree.
croiseur (krwɑzœr), s.m. [f. *croiser*] (naut.) Cruiser; ~ *cuirassé*, armoured cruiser, battle cruiser; (mining) cross-lode.
croisière (krwɑzjɛr), s.f. Cruise, cruising; (rail.) crossing.
croisillon (krwɑzijɔ̃), s.m. [f. *croix*] Cross-bar, sash-bar.
croissance (krwɑsɑ̃s), s.f. [f. *croître*] Growth; *arrêter la* ~, to stunt the growth.
croissant (krwɑsɑ̃), s.m. **1.** Crescent; *les cornes du* ~, the horns of the crescent; (fig.) the Turkish Empire; **2.** pruning-hook; **3.** crescent-shaped roll or cake.
croissant, -e (krwɑsɑ̃), p. adj. Growing, increasing.
croisure (krwɑzyr), s.f. Twilling (of tissues); alternation (of rhymes); lapping over (of clothes).
croît (krwɑ), s.m. Increase (of herd of cattle, or of flock of sheep).
croître (krwɑtr), v.n. To grow, to increase, to grow up, to shoot up, to advance, to thrive, to lengthen, to swell; ~, v.a. (obs.) to augment, to increase.
croix (krwɑ), s.f. [L *crux*] Cross; cross-shaped thing; (fig.) the Christian religion; (fig.) sorrow, tribulation; *porter sa* ~, to bear one's cross; badge, insignia of an order; *Grand* ~ *de la Légion d'honneur*, Grand Cross of the Legion of Honour; *en* ~, crosswise; *mettre en* ~, to crucify; *la* ~ *du Sud*, the Southern Cross; *il a fallu la* ~ *et la bannière*, there was no end of difficulties and fuss; *faire le signe de la* ~, to cross oneself.
cromlech (krɔmlɛk), s.m. [Celt. wd] **1.** Cromlech; **2.** circle of standing stones.

cromorne (krɔmɔrn), s.m. [f. Germ. *Krummhorn*] (mus.) Cromorne, krummhorn, cremona.

crône (kron), s.m. [Flemish *kran*] (mech.) Crane.

croquant (krɔkɑ̃), s.m. [etym. dub.] Peasant, boor, wretch, clown.

croquant, -e (krɔkɑ̃), p. adj. Crackling, crisp.

(à la) croque-au-sel (alakrɔkosɛl), adv. loc. (cook.) With a little salt only.

croquembouche (krɔkɑ̃buʃ), s.f. Any sort of crisp pastry.

croquemitaine (krɔkmitɛn), s.m. Bogey, bugbear, bogey-man.

croquemort (krɔkmɔr), s.m. (pop.) Undertaker's man.

croquenot (krɔkno), s.m. (slang) Shoe.

croque-notes (krɔknɔt), s.m. invar. (pop.) Sorry musician.

croquer (krɔke), v.a. [f. *croc*] To crunch, to scrunch, to craunch; to devour, to gobble up; to sketch; to slur over (a note); ~ *le marmot*, to dance attendance; *gentil à* ~, as pretty as a picture; ~, v.n. to be crisp, to crunch; *cela croque sous la dent*, it eats crisp.

croquet (krɔkɛ), s.m. [f. *croquet*] **1.** Dry biscuit; **2.** croquet (game).

croquette (krɔkɛt), s.f. (cook.) Croquette, fried ball.

croqueu-r,-se (krɔkœr), s.m.f. Devourer, gobbler.

croquignole (krɔkiɲɔl), s.f. [f. *croquer*] **1.** Cracknel; **2.** fillip.

croquis (krɔki), s.m. [f. *croquer*] Sketch, rough draft; *prendre des* ~, to sketch, to draw rough sketches.

crosne (kron), s.m. [f. *Crosnes*, village near Corbeil] Crosne, *Stachys tuberifera* (a vegetable originally grown in Japan).

crosse (krɔs), s.f. [f. *croc*] **1.** Crosier (of a bishop); **2.** hooked stick, hook of a stick; **3.** bat, crosse, lacrosse (game); **4.** butt-end (of a gun, pistol, &c.); **5.** bent part of anything; (anat.) arch (of the aorta).

crossé, -e (krɔse), p. adj. Crosiered.

crosser (krɔse), v.a.n. [f. *crosse*] **1.** To bat, to play lacrosse; **2.** to beat (with the butt-end of a gun); **3.** to rate soundly, to bully.

crossette (krɔsɛt), s.f. **1.** Vine-shoot, shoot; layer; **2.** (arch.) crossette.

crotale (krɔtal), s.m. [Gr. *krotalon*] **1.** (ant.) Crotalum, crotal; **2.** rattle-snake; syn. SERPENT À SONNETTES.

croton (krɔtɔ̃), s.m. [f. Gr. *krotōn*] (bot.) Croton.

crotonique (krɔtɔnik), adj. Crotonic.

crotte (krɔt), s.f. [uncert. orig.] **1.** Dung (of some animals); **2.** mud, dirt, mire; **3.** (pop.) chocolate sweets.

crotter (krɔte), v.a. To dirty, to bemire; **se** ~, v.pr. to get covered with mud, to become dirty all over.

crottin (krɔtɛ̃), s.m. [f. *crotte*] Dung (of certain quadrupeds).

croulant, -e (krulɑ̃), p. adj. Tumbling down, tottering, ruinous, falling.

croulement (krulmɑ̃), s.m. Falling, falling-in.

crouler (krule), v.n. [LL *crotulare*] To fall, to fall in, to crumble, to go to ruin, to collapse; *faire* ~, to bring down.

croup (krup), s.m. [Engl. wd] Croup; (pop.) rattles.

croupade (krupad), s.f. [f. *croupe*] (rid.) Croupade.

croupe (krup), s.f. [f. Germ. *Kruppe*] **1.** Croup, crupper, rump, buttocks; *monter en* ~, to ride behind; *prendre en* ~, to take up behind; **2.** (of a hill) brow, ridge.

(à) croupetons (akrupətɔ̃), adv. loc. Squatting.

croupi, -e (krupi), p. adj. Stagnant, putrid.

croupier (krupje), s.m. **1.** (at a gaming-table) Croupier; **2.** sleeping partner (of an *agent de change* (stockbroker)).

croupière (krupjɛr), s.f. [f. *croupe*] **1.** (harness) Crupper; *tailler des* ~*s à X*, to cut out work for X; **2.** (naut.) stern-fast; *mouiller en* ~, to cast an anchor by the stern.

croupion (krupjɔ̃), s.m. [f. *croupe*] Rump; (pop.) parson's nose.

croupir (krupir), v.n. [f. *croupe*] To lie (in filth), to stagnate, to rot, to corrupt; (fig.) to wallow, to remain.

croupissant, -e (krupisɑ̃), p. adj. [f. *croupir*] Stagnant, stagnating, putrid.

croupissement (krupismɑ̃), s.m. Stagnation, putrefaction.

croupon (krupɔ̃), s.m. Back of an ox-hide.

croustade (krustad), s.f. [f. *croûte*] (cook.) Croustade.

croustillant, -e (krustijɑ̃), p. adj. Crisp, crusty; (fig.) spicy, exciting, tickling, improper, smutty.

croustille (krustij), s.f. [Provenç. wd] Small crust; snack, slight repast.

croustiller (krustije), v.n. To eat crisp; to nibble small crusts.

croustilleu-x, -se (krustijø), adj. Spicy, smutty.

croûte (krut), s.f. [f. L *crusta*] **1.** Crust; *casser la* ~, to break bread, to eat a bit; **2.** (med.) scab; **3.** (paint. fam.) daub.

croûteu-x, -se (krutø), adj. Crusty; scabby, scurfy.

croûton (krutɔ̃), s.m. [f. *croûte*] Crust of bread, sippet, fried bread; piece of dry bread; (fig.) fogy.

crown-glass (kraunglas), s.m. [Engl. wd] Crown-glass.

croyable (krwajabl), adj. Credible, believable, likely.

croyance (krwajɑ̃s), s.f. [f. *croire*] Belief, faith, creed, conviction.

croyant, -e (krwajɑ̃), s.m.f. Believer, adept. ~, p. adj. Believing, faithful.
cru (kry), s.m. [f. *croître*] **1.** Growth, increase; **2.** vineyard, production of the vineyard; **3.** invention, making; *c'est de votre ~, cette histoire-là?*, have not you made up that story?
cru, -e (kry), adj. [L *crudus*] **1.** Raw; uncooked, unwrought; **2.** crude; *lumière ~e*, crude light; *eau ~e*, hard water; **3.** (fig.) rude, rough, improper, coarse. *à ~*, adv. loc. Next the skin; *monter à ~*, to ride without a saddle, bare-back.
cruauté (kryote), s.f. [L *crudelitas*] Cruelty, hardship.
cruche (kryʃ), s.f. [f. Germ. *Krug*] Jug, pitcher; (fig. pop.) blockhead, silly goose, simpleton.
cruchée (kryʃe), s.f. Pitcherful.
cruchette (kryʃɛt), s.f. Small jug.
cruchon (kryʃɔ̃), s.m. Stone bottle, earthenware jug; (hot-water) bottle; foot-warmer.
crucial, -e, (aux) (krysjal), adj. [f. L *crux, crucis*] Crucial, cross-like. ⚠ In English 'crucial' is most commonly applied to critical and deciding moment of events = *critique, décisif.*
crucifère (krysifɛr), s.f. [f. L *crux+ferre*] Cruciferous plant, crucifer. ~, adj. Cruciferous.
crucifiement, crucifîment (krysifimɑ̃), s.m. [f. L *crux*] Crucifixion; syn. CRUCIFIXION.
crucifier (krysifje), v.a. To crucify; (fig.) to mortify, to torture.
crucifix (krysifi), s.m. [L *crucifixus*] Crucifix, cross.
crucifixion (krysifiksjɔ̃), s.f. Crucifixion.
cruciforme (krysifɔrm), adj. Cruciform, cross-shaped.
crudité (krydite), s.f. [L *cruditas*] **1.** Rawness, crudeness, crudity; **2.** (fig.) coarse expression.
crue (kry), s.f. [f. *croître*] Rise, swelling, growth, increase; flood, inundation.
cruel, -le (kryɛl), adj. [L *crudelis*] Cruel, inhuman; grievous, painful, severe.
cruellement (kryɛlmɑ̃), adv. Cruelly, barbarously, painfully, extremely.
crûment (krymɑ̃), adv. Crudely, bluntly, harshly.
cruor (kryɔr), s.m. [L wd] (anat.) Cruor.
crural, -e, (aux) (kryral), adj. [L *cruralis*] (anat.) Crural.
crustacé, -e (krystase), adj. [f. L *crusta*] Crustaceous. ~, s.m. Crustacean.
cruzade (kryzad), s.f. [f. L *crux*] Cruzado, crusado (Portuguese coin).
cryolithe (kriɔlit), s.f. (min., chem.) Cryolite.
cryoscopie (kriɔskɔpi), s.f. [f. Gr. *kruos+skopein*] (med.) Cryoscopy.
crypte (kript), s.f. [f. Gr. *kruptos*] Crypt.
cryptogame (kriptɔgam), adj. [f. Gr. *kruptos+gamos*] Cryptogamous. ~, s.m. (bot.) Cryptogamous plant; (pl.) cryptogamia.
cryptogamie (kriptɔgami), s.f. Cryptogamy.
cryptogamique, (kriptɔgamik), adj. Cryptogamic.
cryptogramme (kriptɔgram), s.m. [f. Gr. *kruptos+gramma*] Cryptogram.
cryptographe (kriptɔgraf), s.m.f. Cryptographer.
cryptographie (kriptɔgrafi), s.f. Cryptography.
cryptographique (kriptɔgrafik), adj. Cryptographical.
crypton (kriptɔ̃), s.m. [f. Gr. *kruptos*] (chem.) Crypton.
cubage (kybaʒ), s.m. Cubature, cubic contents.
cubain, -e (kybɛ̃), adj. s.m.f. Cuban.
cubature (kybatyr), s.f. Cubature.
cube (kyb), s.m. [f. Gr. *kubos*] Cube. ~, adj. Cubic, cube.
cubèbe (kybɛb), s.m. [f. Arab. *kabāba*] (bot.) Cubeb, *Cubeba officinarum.*
cuber (kybe), v.a. To cube; to raise to the third power.
cubilot (kybilo), s.m. (metall.) Furnace.
cubique (kybik), adj. Cubic, cubical, cube; *racine ~*, cube root.
cubital, -e, (aux) (kybital), adj. Cubital, ulnar.
cubitière (kybitjɛr), s.f. [f. *cubitus*] In ancient armour, the part covering the elbow.
cubitus (kybitys), s.m. [L wd] (anat.) Ulna, cubit.
cubocube (kybokyb), s.m. (math.) Cube of the cube, the sixth power of a number.
cuboïde (kybɔid), adj. Cuboid. ~, s.m. (anat.) Cuboid, a bone of the foot.
cuculle (kykyl), s.f. [L *cucullus*] Scapulary of the Carthusians, hood.
cucurbitacées (kykyrbitase), s.f.pl. (bot.) Cucurbitaceae.
cucurbite (kykyrbit), s.f. [L *cucurbita*] Cucurbit.
cueillage (kœjaʒ), s.m. Gathering (of fruit, flowers); syn. CUEILLAISON, CUEILLE, CUEILLETTE.
cueillette (kœjɛt), s.f. [f. *cueillir*] Gathering, crop; (fig.) collection.
cueilleu-r, -se (kœjœr), s.m.f. Gatherer.
cueillir (kœjir), v.a. [f. L *colligere*] To gather, to pick, to pluck; (colloq.) (*a*) to nab, to arrest; (*b*) to pick up, to call for.
cueilloir (kœjwar), s.m. Fruit-gatherer; fruit-basket.
cuider (kɥide), v.n. (obs.) [f. L *cogitare*] To think, to believe.
cuiller, cuillère (kɥijɛr), s.f. [f. L *cochlear*] Spoon; *~ à pot*, ladle; *~ à bouche* (or *à soupe*), tablespoon; *~ à café*, teaspoon;

~ *à dessert*, dessert-spoon; *biscuit à la* ~, finger biscuit.
cuillerée (kɥijre), s.f. Spoonful; ~ *à café*, teaspoonful.
cuilleron (kɥijrɔ̃), s.m. Bowl (of a spoon).
cuir (kɥir), s.m. [f. L *corium*] **1.** Skin, hide, leather; ~ *chevelu*, scalp; ~ *à rasoir*, razor-strop; **2.** blunder, incorrect pronunciation; *faire des* ~*s*, to murder the King's English; to make a wrong liaison (in speaking).
cuirasse (kɥiras), s.f. [f. *cuir*] **1.** Cuirass; (fig.) *le défaut de la* ~, the chink in the armour, the weak side, the vulnerable point; **2.** (naut.) armour-plates; **3.** (zool.) carapace, shell.
cuirassé, -e (kɥirase), p. adj. Cuirassed, armed with a cuirass; (naut.) armoured, armour-plated; (fig.) protected, steeled, hardened.
cuirassé (kɥirase), s.m. Armoured cruiser, dreadnought, man-of-war, battleship.
cuirassement (kɥirasmɑ̃), s.m. Armour-plating.
cuirasser (kɥirase), v.a. To arm with a cuirass; to armour-plate; (fig.) to harden, to protect; **se** ~, v.pr. to prepare oneself, to harden oneself.
cuirassier (kɥirasje), s.m. (mil.) Cuirassier.
cuire (kɥir), v.a.n. [L *coquere*] **1.** To cook, to boil, to roast, to stew, to bake, to broil, to grill; (fig.) to swelter; **2.** to burn (brick, plaster, &c. in a kiln); **3.** ~, v.n. to smart (with pain); *trop gratter cuit, trop parler nuit*, least said, soonest mended; *il lui en cuira*, he will suffer or smart for it; *les yeux me cuisent*, my eyes smart.
cuisage (kɥizaʒ), s.m. Charring (of wood).
cuisant, -e (kɥizɑ̃), p. adj. Smarting, sharp, keen, acute; *remords* ~, bitter remorse.
cuisine (kɥizin), s.f. [f. L *coquina*] **1.** Kitchen; *batterie de* ~, kitchen utensils; **2.** cookery, cooking, cooks, fare, cheer; *la* ~ *française*, French cooking; ~ *bourgeoise*, plain cooking; **3.** (fig.) ~ *électorale*, gerrymandering, electioneering.
cuisiner (kɥizine), v.n.a. To cook, to dress food; (fig.) to work up, to concoct, to arrange; (police slang) to draw, to worm a confession or secret out of somebody; to pump.
cuisinier (kɥizinje), s.m. Cook, man cook, chef.
cuisinière (kɥizinjɛr), s.f. **1.** Cook, woman cook; **2.** kitchen range; kitchener.
cuissard (kɥisar), s.m. Thigh-guard (in armour).
cuisse (kɥis), s.f. [L *coxa*] Thigh; leg (of a fowl); ~*-madame*, a kind of long yellow pear.
cuisseau (pl. **-x**) (kɥiso), s.m. Leg (of veal).
cuisson (kɥisɔ̃), s.f. **1.** Cooking (roasting, broiling, &c.; see CUIRE); **2.** smarting, itching.
cuissot (kɥiso), s.m. Haunch (of venison).
cuistance (kɥistɑ̃s), s.f. (mil. slang) Cooking; food.
cuistot (kɥisto), s.m. (mil. slang) Cook.
cuistre (kɥistr), s.m. [f. LL *coquister*] **1.** Serving-man in a college (obs.); **2.** pedantic, vulgar fellow.
cuistrerie (kɥistrəri), s.f. Vulgar pedantry.
cuit, -e (kɥi), p. adj. [f. *cuire*] **1.** Cooked, baked, roasted, &c. (see CUIRE); *trop* ~, overdone; *pas assez* ~, underdone; *bien* ~ *ou saignant?*, well done or rare? (Amer.); **2.** (pop.) done for.
cuite (kɥit), s.f. **1.** (techn.) Baking (of porcelain), burning (of bricks, &c.); **2.** kilnful, ovenful; **3.** (pop.) drunken bout; *prendre* or *se flanquer une* ~, to get screwed, or drunk.
cuivrage (kɥivraʒ), s.m. [f. *cuivre*] Coppering.
cuivre (kɥivr), s.m. [L *cuprum*, f. Gr. *Kupros*, Cyprus] **1.** Copper, brass; *fil de* ~, copper wire; *monnaie de* ~, copper coins; ~ *rouge*, copper; ~ *jaune*, brass; **2.** (engr.) copperplate; ~*s*, pl. (mus.) brass instruments.
cuivré, -e (kɥivre), p. adj. **1.** Copper-coloured; **2.** ringing, clear-sounding, sonorous.
cuivrer (kɥivre), v.a. To copper, to give a copper-colour to.
cuivrette (kɥivrɛt), s.f. (mus.) Reed.
cuivreu-x, -se (kɥivrø), adj. Coppery, brassy, cupreous.
cul (ky), s.m. [L *culus*] **1.** Bottom, back, rump, arse; *donner du pied au* ~, to kick a person's backside; **2.** bottom, end; **3.** (naut.) poop, stern, after-part; ~ *de bouteille*, bottom of a bottle; ~ *par-dessus tête*, head over heels; ~ *de basse-fosse*, black hole under a dungeon; ~ *de four*, demi-cupola; ~*-de-jatte*, cripple, Jack in the bowl; ~*-de-lampe*, pendant, bracket; (print.) tail-piece; ~*-de-sac*, blind alley.
culasse (kylas), s.f. (arms) Breech; *se chargeant par la* ~, breech-loading.
culasser (kylase), v.a. To breech.
cul-blanc (kyblɑ̃), s.m. (pl. *culs-blancs*) (ornith.) Fallow-finch.
culbutant (kylbytɑ̃), s.m. (ornith.) Tumbler pigeon.
culbute (kylbyt), s.f. Somersault, fall, tumble; (fig.) downfall, ruin; *au bout du fossé la* ~*!*, come what may!; a short life and a merry one!; neck or nothing; *faire la* ~, to throw a somersault.
culbuter (kylbyte), v.a. [*cul*+*buter*] To throw down, to upset, to overthrow; ~, v.n. to fall head over heels, to come to ruin.

culbuteur (kylbytœr), s.m. (techn.) Trip lever; rocker.
culbutis (kylbyti), s.m. Heap of tumbled things.
culée (kyle), s.f. Abutment (of a bridge).
culer (kyle), v.n. To back; (naut.) to go aback.
culière, culeron (kyljɛr, kylrɔ̃), s.f. (harness) Crupper-dock; hind-girth.
culinaire (kylinɛr), adj. [f. L *culina*] Culinary.
culmifère (kylmifɛr), adj. [L *culmus+ferre*] (bot.) Culmiferous.
culminant, -e (kylminɑ̃), p.adj. Culminating, culminant, highest, most prominent.
culmination (kylmina'sjɔ̃), s.f. (astron.) Culmination.
culminer (kylmine), v.n. [f. L *culmen*] To culminate.
culot (kylo) s.m. [f. *cul*] **1.** Bottom (of a lamp); **2.** residue; **3.** (arch.) stem; **4.** (pop.) dilling, youngest child; **5.** (slang) cheek, impudence, nerve; *vous avez montré un certain* ~, it was pretty cool of you.
culottage (kylɔtaʒ), s.m. Blackening, seasoning (of a pipe-bowl).
culotte (kylɔt), s.f. [f. *cul*] **1.** Breeches, pair of breeches; (fig.) *vieille* ~ *de peau*, old soldier; **2.** (butch.) rump; **3.** (pop.) loss, run of losses at cards.
culotter (kylɔte), v.a. **1.** To put into breeches; **2.** to season (a tobacco-pipe); **se** ~, v.pr. to put on one's breeches; (of a pipe-bowl) to get blackened and seasoned.
culotti-er, -ère (kylɔtje), s.m.f. Breeches-maker.
culpabilité (kylpabilite), s.f. [f. L *culpabilis*] Culpability, guilt.
culte (kylt), s.m. [L *cultus*] Cult, worship, religious service, religion, creed, veneration, love; *rendre un véritable* ~ *à*, to worship.
cultivable (kyltivabl), adj. Cultivable.
cultivat-eur, -rice (kyltivatœr), s.m.f. Agriculturist, cultivator, farmer, grower. ~, s.m. Cultivator, a sort of hand-plough.
cultiver (kyltive), v.a. [L *cultivare*] **1.** To cultivate, to till, to produce from the soil; **2.** (fig.) to improve, to instruct, to cultivate, to keep up, to practise; ~ *sa mémoire*, to improve one's memory.
cultuel, -le (kyltɥɛl), adj. Pertaining to a cult.
cultural, -e, (aux) (kyltyral), adj. Cultural.
culture (kyltyr) s.f. [L *cultura*] Cultivation, culture, tillage, husbandry; *grande* ~, extensive farming; *petite* ~, small farming; **2.** culture, education, acquisition by study, cultivation, civilization.
cumin (kymɛ̃), s.m. [L *cuminum*] (bot.) Cummin, caraway.
cuminique (kyminik), adj. Cuminic.
cumul (kymyl) s.m. [f. *cumuler*] Accumulation, cumulation; plurality (of offices).
cumulard (kymylar), s.m. (pop.) Pluralist, person who holds several offices.
cumulati-f, -ve (kymylatif), adj. Cumulative.
cumulativement (kymylativmɑ̃), adv. Cumulatively, by accumulation.
cumuler (kymyle), v.a. [L *cumulare*] To accumulate, to cumulate; ~, v.n. to hold a plurality of offices.
cumulus (kymylys), s.m. [L wd] Cumulus (pl. cumuli).
cunéiforme (kyneifɔrm), adj. [f. L *cuneus*] Cuneiform, wedge-shaped; (bot.) cuneate.
cunette (kynɛt), s.f. [f. It. *cunetta*] (fort.) Cunette, ditch.
cupide (kypid), adj. [L *cupidus*] Covetous, greedy.
cupidité (kypidite), s.f. Cupidity, greed, covetousness.
cuprifère (kyprifɛr), adj. (min.) Cupriferous.
cupule (kypyl), s.f. [L *cupula*] Cupule, cupula, cup.
cupulifères (kypylifɛr), s.f.pl. (bot.) Cupuliferae.
curabilité (kyrabilite), s.f. Curability, curableness.
curable (kyrabl), adj. [L *curabilis*] Curable.
curaçao (kyraso), s.m. [geog. orig.; f. *Curaçao* island] Curaçao.
curage, curement (kyraʒ, kyrmɑ̃), s.m. [f. *curer*] Cleansing, cleaning-out (of canals, rivers, wells, pipes, &c.).
curare (kyrar), s.m. [Carib wd] Curare, wourali, arrow-poison.
curarine (kyrarin), s.f. Curarine.
curatelle (kyratɛl), s.f. [LL *curatela*] Guardianship, trusteeship.
curat-eur, -rice (kyratœr), s.m.f. [f. L *curator*] Curator, guardian, trustee.
curati-f, -ve (kyratif), adj. Curative.
curation (kyra'sjɔ̃), s.f. Cure, curing.
curculionidés (kyrkyljɔnide), s.m.pl. (ent.) Curculionidae (a family of coleopterous insects).
curcuma (kyrkyma), s.m. [f. Arab. *kurkum*] (bot.) Curcuma.
cure (kyr), s.f. [L *cura*] **1.** Care, concern; *il n'en a* ~, he cares nothing about it; **2.** cure, healing; **3.** cure, living; curacy; parsonage, vicarage.
curé (kyre), s.m. Catholic parish priest; *c'est Gros-Jean qui en remontre à son* ~, it 's teaching one's grandmother to suck eggs.
cure-dent (kyrdɑ̃), s.m. (pl. *cure-dents*) Tooth-pick.
curée (kyre), s.f. [LL *corata*] (hunt.) Quarry; (fig.) booty, scramble, eagerness to seize prey or gain.

cure-môle (kyrmol), s.m. (pl. *cure-môles*) Dredging-machine.
cure-oreille (kyrɔrɛj), s.m. (pl. *cure-oreilles*) Ear-pick.
cure-pied (kyrpje), s.m. (pl. *cure-pieds*) Horse-pick.
curer (kyre), v.a. [L *curare*] To cleanse, to clean out, to pick; to prune; *se ~ les dents*, to pick one's teeth. ⚠ Not Engl. 'to cure' which = *guérir*; *saler*, *mariner*.
curettage, curetage (kyrtaʒ), s.m. (med.) Scooping, curetting.
curette (kyrɛt), s.f. **1.** (surg.) Scoop, curette; **2.** scraper.
cureur (kyrœr), s.m. Cleanser (of wells, &c.).
curial, -e, (aux) (kyrjal), adj. Rectorial, vicarial, priestly.
curie (kyri), s.f. [L *curia*] (Rom. ant.) Curia (pl. curiae).
curieusement (kyrjøzmɑ̃), adv. Curiously, inquisitively.
curieu-x, -se (kyrjø), adj. [L *curiosus*] **1.** Curious, inquisitive; **2.** rare, curious, worthy of curiosity, unusual, piquant. ~, s.m.f. **1.** Curious, inquisitive person, prying person; **2.** connoisseur; **3.** curious part, curious fact; *le ~ de l'affaire est que*, the curious part of the matter is that.
curion (kyrjɔ̃), s.m. (Rom. ant.) Curio; ⚠ not in the sense of *curiosité*.
curiosité (kyrjozite), s.f. **1.** Curiosity, curiousness, inquisitiveness; **2.** object of curiosity, rarity, curio.
curseur (kyrsœr), s.m. [f. L *cursor*] Cursor, slider; (astr.) wire, spider-line.
cursi-f, -ve (kyrsif), adj. Cursive, running.
curule (kyryl), adj. [L *curulis*] (Rom. ant.) Curule.
curure (kyryr), s.f. [f. *curer*] Cleansings, mud.
curvati-f, -ve (kyrvatif), adj. Curvated, curvative.
curviligne (kyrviliɲ), adj. Curvilinear, curvilineal.
curvimètre (kyrvimɛtr), s.m. Curvometer.
cuscute (kyskyt), s.f. [f. Arab. *kashūth*] (bot.) Dodder, *Cuscuta*.
cuspide (kyspid), s.f. [f. L *cuspis*] (bot.) Point, cusp.
cuspidé, -e (kyspide), adj. Cuspidate.
custode (kystɔd), s.f. [f. L *custos*] **1.** Pyx, wafer-cover; *sous la ~*, secretly; **2.** non-opening window. **3.** ~, s.m. Custodian.
cutané, -e (kytane), adj. [L *cutaneus*] Cutaneous, cutaneal.
cuticule (kytikyl), s.f. [L *cuticula*] (anat., bot.) Cuticle.
cutter (kœtœr), s.m. [Engl. wd] (naut.) Cutter; syn. COTRE.
cuvage (kyvaʒ), s.m. **cuvaison** (kyvɛzɔ̃), s.f. Fermentation of wine.
cuve (kyv), s.f. [f. L *cupa*] Vat, tub, trough, copper; *~ à lessive*, wash-tub; *~ de vendange*, vintage-tub.
cuveau (pl. -x) (kyvo), s.m. Small tub.
cuvée (kyve), s.f. Tubful, vatful.
cuvelage, cuvellement (kyvlaʒ, kyvɛlmɑ̃), s.m. Tubbing, lining.
cuveler (kyvle), v.a. To tub, to line (the shaft of mine or pit).
cuver (kyve), v.n. To ferment, to work; v.a. *~ son vin*, to sleep off one's wine; to cool down, to get sober.
cuvette (kyvɛt), s.f. [f. *cuve*] Basin, wide basin, wash-hand basin; ditch, man-hole, (fort.) cuvette; (horol.) cap (of a watch).
cuvier (kyvje), s.m. [f. *cuve*] Wash-tub.
cyanate (sjanat), s.m. (chem.) Cyanate.
cyanhydrique (sjanidrik), adj. (chem.) Cyanhydric, hydrocyanic, prussic.
cyanique (sjanik), adj. (chem.) Cyanic.
cyanogène (sjanɔʒɛn), s.m. (chem.) Cyanogen.
cyanose (sjanoz), s.f. [f. Gr. *kuanos*] (med.) Cyanosis.
cyanuration (sjanyra'sjɔ̃), s.f. Cyanuration.
cyanure (sjanyr), s.m. (chem.) Cyanide, cyanuret.
cycas (sikɑs), s.m. (bot.) Cycad, cycas.
cyclamen (siklamɛn), s.m. (bot.) Cyclamen, sow-bread.
cycle (sikl), s.m. [f. Gr. *kuklos*] **1.** Cycle, series of phenomena recurring in a determined order; **2.** period, cycle; **3.** bicycle, &c.
cyclique (siklik), adj. Cyclic.
cyclisme (siklism), s.m. Cycling, cyclism.
cycliste (siklist), s.m.f. Cyclist.
cycloïdal, -e, (aux) (siklɔidal), adj. Cycloid, cycloidal.
cycloïde (siklɔid), s.f. (geom.) Cycloid.
cyclomètre (siklɔmɛtr), s.m. Cyclometer.
cyclonal, -e, (aux) (siklɔnal), adj. Cyclonic.
cyclone (siklon), s.m. [f. Gr. *kuklos*] Cyclone, tornado, violent hurricane; typhoon (espec. in China seas).
cyclopéen, -ne (siklɔpeɛ̃), adj. Cyclopean.
cyclostomes (siklɔstom), s.m.pl. (ichth.) Cyclostoma.
cygne (siɲ), s.m. [f. L *cycnus*] Swan; (astron.) Cygnus; *le ~ thébain*, Pindar; *le ~ de Mantoue*, Virgil; *le ~ de Cambrai*, Fénelon; *chant du ~*, swan-song; (fig.) last strains.
cylindrage (silɛ̃draʒ), s.m. Calendering; rolling.
cylindre (silɛ̃dr), s.m. [Gr. *kulindros*] **1.** Cylinder; roller, steam-roller; mangle, calender; *~ droit*, right cylinder; *~ oblique*, oblique cylinder; *~ à chemise d'eau*, water-jacketed cylinder; *parois du ~*, cylinder walls; *~s jumelés*, twin cylinders; *~s en V*, V cylinders.

cylindrée (silɛ̃dre), s.f. Cylinder capacity; the quantity of explosive mixture drawn into the cylinder by one stroke of the piston.
cylindrer (silɛ̃dre), v.a. To roll, to calender, to make cylindrical.
cylindrique (silɛ̃drik), adj. Cylindric, cylindrical.
cylindriquement (silɛ̃drikmɑ̃), adv. Cylindrically.
cylindroïde (silɛ̃drɔid), adj. Cylindroid.
cymaise (simɛz), s.f. See CIMAISE.
cymbalaire (sɛ̃balɛr), s.f. [L *cymbalaria*] (bot.) **1.** Ivy-leafed toad-flax; **2.** *Saxifraga cymbalaria.*
cymbale (sɛ̃bal), s.f. [f. Gr. *kumbalon*] Cymbal.
cymbalier (sɛ̃balje), s.m. Cymbal-player.
cyme (sim), s.f. [L *cyma*] (bot.) Cyme, cyma.
cymrique (simrik), adj. See KYMRIQUE.
cynégétique (sineʒetik), [f. Gr. *kunēgetikos*] s.f. Cynegetics, hunting, the chase. ~ adj. Relating to cynegetics.
cynips (sinips), s.m. (ent.) Cynips, gall-fly.
cynique (sinik), adj. [f. Gr. *kunikos*] **1.** (phil.) Cynical, cynic; **2.** cynical, shameless, impudent. ~, s.m. Cynic philosopher; cynic.
cyniquement (sinikmɑ̃), adv. Cynically.
cynisme (sinism), s.m. **1.** (phil.) Cynicism; **2.** cynicism, impudence, shamelessness, indecency.
cynocéphale (sinɔsefal), s.m. [f. Gr. *kunos* +*kephalē*] (zool.) Cynocephalus, baboon.
cynoglosse (sinɔglɔs), s.f. [f. Gr. *kunos*+ *glōssa*] (bot.) Cynoglossum, hound's-tongue.
cynorrhodon (sinɔrɔdɔ̃), s.m. **1.** (bot.) Dog-rose tree; **2.** hip, the fruit of the dog-rose tree.
cypéracées (siperase), s.f.pl. (bot). Cyperaceae.
cyprès (siprɛ), s.m. [f. Gr. *kuparissos*] (bot.) Cypress, cypress-tree.
cyprière (siprìɛr), s.f. Cypress-grove.
cyprin (siprɛ̃), s.m. (ichth.) Cyprinus; ~ *doré,* gold-fish, silver-fish.
cypriote (sipriɔt), adj. s.m.f. Cyprian, Cypriot.
cyrénéen, -ne (sireneɛ̃), adj. s.m.f. Cyrenian.
cysticerque (sistisɛrk), s.m. (zool.) Cysticercus, bladder-worm.
cystique (sistik), adj. Cystic.
cystite (sistit), s.f. [f. Gr. *kustis*] (med.) Cystitis.
cystotome (sistɔtom), s.m. [f. Gr. *kustis*+ *tomē*] Cystotome.
cystotomie (sistɔtɔmi), s.f. (surg.) Cystotomy.
cythéréen, -ne (sitereɛ̃), adj. s.m.f. Cytherean.
cytise (sitiz), s.m. [f. L *cytisus*] (bot.) Cytisus, laburnum.
czar, czarevitch, czarine (ksar). See TSAR, &c.

D

d (de). 4th letter of the alphabet. ~, s.m. *un D majuscule,* a capital D; *un d minuscule, un petit d,* a small d, minuscule d; (slang) *système D* [abbrev. for *débrouillard*], wangling, shiftiness; *d',* contraction of *de.*
da (da), adv. expl. *Oui-~,* yes, indeed.
dactyle (daktil), s.m. [f. Gr. *daktulos*] **1.** (pros.) Dactyl; **2.** (bot.) dactylis.
dactylographe, dactylo (daktilɔgraf, daktilo), s.m.f. Typist; (rare) type-writer.
dactylographie (daktilɔgrafi), s.f. [f. Gr. *daktulos+graphia*] Type-writing.
dada (dada), s.m. [onom. child. wd] Gee-gee, horse, hobby-horse; (fig.) hobby, fad, favourite subject.
dadais (dadɛ), s.m. Ninny, simpleton, booby.
dadaïsme (dadaism), s.m. [f. prop. n. *Dada*] (art) Dadaism.
dagorne (dagɔrn), s.f. [f. *corne*] One-horned cow.
dague (dag), s.f. Dagger, dirk; (of a deer) dag, first horn; (of a wild boar) tusk.
daguerréotype (dagɛreɔtip), s.m. [f. *Daguerre,* inventor] Daguerreotype.
daguet (dagɛ), s.m. (hunt., zool.) Brock, brocket, young stag.
dahlia (dalja), s.m. [f. *Dahl,* Swedish botanist] (bot.) Dahlia.
daigner (dɛɲe), v.a. [f. L *dignari*] To deign, to condescend, to vouchsafe.
dail (daj), s.m. **daille** (dɑj), s.f. Scythe.
daim (dɛ̃), s.m. [f. L *dama*] **1.** Deer, fallow-deer, buck; **2.** buck-skin, doe-skin, suède; **3.** (fig.) booby.
daine (dɛn and din), s.f. Doe, she-deer.
dais (dɛ), s.m. [f. L *discus*] Canopy. ⚠ In French *dais* has never the sense of 'raised platform' or 'terrace', the usual sense of English 'dais', which = *estrade.*
dallage (dalaʒ), s.m. Pavement of flag-stones, flagging; paving with flags.
dalle (dal), s.f. [uncert. orig.] Flagstone, slab, sink-stone; (pop.) throat; *se rincer la ~,* to wet one's whistle; *avoir la ~ en pente,* to be fond of a drink.
daller (dale), v.a. To flag, to pave with flags.
dalmate (dalmat), adj. s.m.f. Dalmatian.
dalmatique (dalmatik), s.f. Dalmatic, tunic.
dalot (dalo), s.m. [f. *dalle*] (naut.) Scupper.
daltonien, -ne (daltɔnjɛ̃), adj. Daltonian.
daltonisme (daltɔnism), s.m. [f. *J. Dalton,* 1766–1844] Daltonism, achromatopsia, colour-blindness.

dam (dam), s.m. [f. L *damnum*] Damage, injury, cost, detriment; (theol.) damnation; *au grand ~ de X*, to X's detriment.

damas (damɑ), s.m. [geog. orig.; f. *Damascus*] **1.** Damask; **2.** Damascus blade or steel.

damasquinage (damaskinaʒ), s.m. Damascening.

damasquiner (damaskine), v.a. To damascene.

damasser (damase), v.a. To damask; *linge damassé*, damask linen.

dame (dam), s.f. [f. L *domina*] **1.** Lady, dame; (⚠ 'Dame' in English is a title given to the wife of a baronet or to a lady member of the Order of the British Empire); married woman, mistress of the house; lady-love; *~ d'honneur*, maid of honour; *~ d'atours*, tire-woman; *Notre-Dame*, Our Lady; **2.** (draughts) draughtsman, king; (cards, chess, &c.) queen; *aller à ~*, to queen a pawn, to crown a draughtsman; **3.** paving-beetle; **4.** (bot.) *~ d'onze heures*, star of Bethlehem, *Ornithogalum umbellatum*; **5.** *~-jeanne*, demi-john, jar, carboy.

dame (dam), interj. [f. *Notre-Dame*] Indeed!, why, to be sure!, well, you see!

damer (dame), v.a. **1.** To crown (a man at draughts); to queen (a pawn at chess); *~ le pion à X*, to outdo X, to outwit X; **2.** to ram.

dameret (damrɛ), s.m. [f. *dame*] (obs.) Beau, spark, fop.

damier (damje), s.m. **1.** Draught-board; **2.** chequered pattern.

damnable (danabl), adj. Damnable.

damnablement (danabləmɑ̃), adv. Damnably.

damnation (dana'sjɔ̃), s.f. Damnation, condemnation.

damné, -e (dane), p. adj. s.m.f. Damned, damned soul; *souffrir comme un ~*, to suffer horribly, to suffer the torments of the damned; *il est son âme ~e*, he is his tool, his slave. ⚠ 'Damned', 'damn' have a stronger sense in English than *damné* in French and must be used with caution.

damner (dane), v.a. [L *damnare*] To damn, to condemn to the torments of hell; *c'est à faire ~ un saint!*, it's enough to try the patience of a saint. ⚠ See DAMNÉ.

damoiseau (pl. **-x**), **damoisel** (damwazo, damwazɛl), s.m. [f. LL *dominicellus*] **1.** (obs.) Young squire, not yet knighted; **2.** page, fop, young beau (used ironically).

damoiselle (damwazɛl), s.f. (obs.) Damsel.

danaïde (danaid), s.f. [f. *Danaüs*] **1.** (myth.) Danaid; **2.** (mech.) danaide; **3.** (ent.) a kind of butterfly.

dandin (dɑ̃dɛ̃), s.m. (obs.) [f. *dandiner*] Booby, ninny.

dandinement (dɑ̃dinmɑ̃), s.m. Swinging, slouching.

dandiner (dɑ̃dine), v.n. and **se ~**, v.pr. To slouch, to swing one's body about, to waddle.

dandy (dɑ̃di), s.m. [Engl. wd] Dandy; hence *dandysme*, s.m. dandyism.

danger (dɑ̃ʒe), s.m. [f. LL *dominiarium*] Danger, harm, peril, jeopardy; *être hors de ~*, to be out of danger, to be safe; *ah! il n'y a pas de ~ qu'il dise cela!*, it is not likely that he will say that, no fear of that!; he is not likely to say that; he won't say that, no fear!

dangereusement (dɑ̃ʒrøzmɑ̃), adv. Dangerously.

dangereu-x, -se (dɑ̃ʒrø), adj. Dangerous, unsafe.

danois, -e (danwɑ), adj. Danish. **~, -e**, s.m.f. Dane. **~**, s.m. Danish (language). **~**, s.m. Great Dane (dog).

dans (dɑ̃), prep. [f. L *intus*, OF *ens*] In, into, within, through, among, inside, during; *je reviendrai ~ huit jours*, I shall be back in a week; *~ la semaine*, within this week; *je ne commencerai que ~ un mois*, I shall not begin for a month; *~ le temps*, formerly; *agir ~ une bonne intention*, to act with a good intention.

dansant, -e (dɑ̃sɑ̃), p. adj. Dancing, fit for dancing.

danse (dɑ̃s), s.f. [Germ. orig.] Dance, dancing, dance-tune; *leçon de ~*, dancing-lesson; *mener la ~*, to lead the dance; *donner une ~ à X*, (fam.) to give X a good hiding, or a thrashing; (med.) *~ de St-Guy*, St. Vitus's dance.

danser (dɑ̃se), v.n.a. To dance; to dandle; *apprendre à ~*, to learn dancing; (fig.) *ne savoir sur quel pied ~*, not to know which way to turn; *faire ~ les écus*, to spend freely.

danseu-r, -se (dɑ̃sœr), s.m.f. Dancer; partner; *~se*, s.f. ballet-girl; *~ de corde*, rope-dancer.

dantesque (dɑ̃tɛsk), adj. Dantesque, of Dante.

danubien, -ne (danybjɛ̃), adj. Danubian.

daphné (dafne), s.m. [f. Gr. *Daphnē*] (bot.) Daphne.

dard (dar), s.m. [f. OHG *tart*; OF *dart*] **1.** Dart; **2.** sting; **3.** forked tongue (of a snake); **4.** (fish.) harpoon; **5.** (ichth.) dar, dart, dace.

darder (darde), v.a. To dart, to dart forth, to hurl, to harpoon, to emit; (fig.) *~ un regard*, to dart a look.

dare-dare (dardar), adv. loc. Hurry-skurry, in hot haste, in a hurry, in double-quick time, like a shot, in less than no time.

dariole (darjɔl), s.f. Cream-cake.

darne (darn), s.f. [f. Celt. *darn*] (cook.) Steak (of salmon, alose, &c.).

darse (dars), s.f. [f. It. *darsena*] (naut.) Wet-dock without gate; tidal basin.
dartre (dartr), s.f. (med.) Herpes, eczema, pityriasis.
dartreu-x, -se (dartrø), adj. Dartrous, herpetic, scurfy.
date (dat), s.f. [L *datum*] Date; *prendre* ~, to fix a day; *de longue* ~, of old date, of long standing; *de fraîche* ~, of recent date; *en* ~ *de*, under date of, dated; *mettre la* ~, to date; *être le premier en* ~, to have the priority.
dater (date), v.n.a. To date, to reckon, to count, to run from; to form an epoch; *à* ~ *de ce jour*, reckoning from that day; from to-day; ~ *de loin*, to date from a long time ago; *cela date*, this dates, this bears the mark of its date.
datif (datif), s.m. [L *dativus*] (gram.) Dative, dative case; *au* ~, in the dative.
dation (da'sjɔ̃), s.f. [L *datio*] (law) Giving, dation.
datte (dat), s.f. [f. Gr. *daktulos*] Date (fruit); (pop.) *n'en pas ficher une* ~, not to do a stroke (of work).
dattier (datje), s.m. (bot.) Date-tree, date-palm.
datura (datyra), s.m. [Hindu wd] (bot.) Datura.
daube (dob), s.f. [f. It. *dobbare*] (cook.) Daube, a dish of braised meat served cold; stew.
dauber (dobe), v.a.n. ~ (*sur*), To quiz, to jeer, to speak ill of, to slander; (rarely) to stew.
daubière (dobjɛr), s.f. Stew-pan.
(à la) daumont (aladomɔ̃), loc. adv. [f. *duc d'Aumont*] With four horses and two postilions; postilion(-carriage).
dauphin (dofɛ̃), s.m. [f. L *delphinus*] **1.** (zoöl.) Dolphin; **2.** [f. *Dauphiné*] dauphin (eldest son of King of France); *dauphine*, s.f. dauphiness (wife of the dauphin.)
dauphinois, -e (dofinwɑ), adj. s.m.f. Of Dauphiné; native of Dauphiné.
daurade (dorad), s.f. [f. Provenç. *daurada*] (ichth.) Gilt-head; see DORADE.
davantage (davɑ̃taʒ), adv. [*d'*+*avantage*] More, further, any longer, more highly; *bien* ~, much more; *pas* ~, no more, not any more, no longer.
davier (davje), s.m. [f. prop. n. *David*] (Dentist's) forceps; (techn.) cramp, davit.
daw, dauw (do), s.m. (zool.) Quagga.
de (də), prep. [L *de*] Of, from, out of, on account of, made of, about, some, with; (*de* is often expressed in English by the juxtaposition of the two words it connects in French: *mal* ~ *tête*, headache; *collier* ~ *perles*, pearl necklace; *lit* ~ *plume*, feather bed; but this is not a general rule: *un morceau* ~ *pain*, a bit of bread; *une goutte* ~ *vin*, a drop of wine, &c.); *cheval* ~ *course*, race-horse; *course* ~ *chevaux*, horse-race; *voyager* ~ *nuit*, to travel by night; *l'habitude* ~ *marcher*, the habit of walking; *il est temps* ~ *manger*, it 's time to eat; *traiter X* ~ *lâche*, to call X a coward; *plus* ~, more; *plus grand* ~ *toute la tête*, taller by a whole head; ~ *lui-même*, of his own accord.
dé[1] (de), s.m. [f. L *digitale*] Thimble.
dé[2] (de), s.m. [f. L *datum*] Die (pl. dice); (fig.) any cubic body; *tenir le* ~ *de la conversation*, to monopolize the conversation; to hold the floor; to have all the talk to oneself.
déambulation (deɑ̃byla'sjɔ̃), s.f. Deambulation, walking.
déambulatoire (deɑ̃bylatwar), s.m. Deambulatory (in a church).
déambuler (deɑ̃byle), v.n. [L *deambulare*] To stroll about, to promenade, to saunter.
débâcle (debɑkl), s.f. Breaking-up of ice; (fig.) breaking-up, ruin, collapse, downfall, crash, breakdown; (naut.) clearing of a port.
débâcler (debɑkle), v.a. [*dé*+*bâcler*] To clear, to open (a port, a harbour); ~, v.n. to break up.
débagouler (debagule), v.n.a. [f. L *gula*] To vomit, to spew; (fig.) to jaw, to blurt out, to blab.
déballage (debalaʒ), s.m. **1.** Unpacking; **2.** cheap goods offered for sale by hawkers.
déballer (debale), v.a. [*dé*+*balle*] To unpack; (fig. fam.) *être tout déballé*, to be crestfallen, to be in low spirits.
débandade (debɑ̃dad), s.f. Disbanding, stampede; rout; *à la* ~, helter-skelter, in confusion or disorder.
débander (debɑ̃de), v.a. To unbind; to unbend; to uncover (the eyes); **se** ~, v.pr. **1.** to slacken; to disperse, to leave the ranks; to disband; **2.** to unbind (one's wound), to uncover (one's eyes).
débaptiser (debatize), v.a. To change the name of.
débarbouillage (debarbujaʒ), s.m. Washing of one's face; cleaning, scouring.
débarbouiller (debarbuje), v.a. [*dé*+*barbouiller*] To wash the face of, to clean, to wash; **se** ~, v.pr. to wash one's face; (fig.) to extricate oneself.
débarcadère (debarkadɛr), s.m. [f. *débarquer*] Landing-place, wharf, arrival-platform.
débarder (debarde), v.a. [f. *bard*] To unlade.
débardeur (debardœr), s.m. Docker, wharf-porter, boat-ripper; (obs.) *débardeuse* (jest.), a woman in the fancy dress of a docker, a whore.
débarquement (debarkəmɑ̃), s.m. Landing, disembarking, disembarkation, unloading, arrival.

débarquer (debarke), v.a.n. [f. *barque*] To land, to disembark, to unship, to arrive; *au* ~, loc. adv. on arriving, on landing.

débarras (debara), s.m. [f. *débarrasser*] 1. Riddance; *bon* ~ *!*, good riddance !; 2. lumber-room.

débarrasser (debarase), v.a. To disencumber, to clear, to rid, to clear up, to clear away, to disentangle; **se** ~ v.pr. to get rid (*de*, of); to take off; to shake off.

débarrer (debare), v.a. To unbar.

débat (deba), s.m. [f. *débattre*] Debate, discussion; ~**s**, s.m.pl. debates, trial.

débâter (debate), v.a. To unsaddle.

débâtir (debatir), v.a.n. 1. To undo the basting of; 2. (rare) to demolish.

débattre (debatr) v.a.n. To debate, to argue, to bargain, to discuss, to negotiate; **se** ~, v.pr. to struggle, to writhe, to flutter; to be debated.

débauchage (deboʃaʒ), s.m. Enticing away from work.

débauche (deboʃ), s.f. [OF *dé*+*bauche*] Debauch, excess, debauchery; (fig.) riot (of imagination).

débauché, -e (deboʃe), p. adj. Debauched, dissolute. ~, s.m.f. Debauchee, rake.

débaucher (deboʃe), v.a. 1. To debauch, to corrupt; 2. to entice away from work; **se** ~, v.pr. to fall into debauchery.

débet (debɛ), s.m. [L wd] Debit, balance due.

débile (debil), adj. [L *debilis*] Debilitated, weak, feeble, sickly.

débilement (debilmɑ̃), adv. Weakly, feebly.

débilitant, -e (debilitɑ̃), p. adj. Debilitating.

débilitation (debilita'sjɔ̃), s.f. Debilitation.

débilité (debilite), s.f. Debility, weakness.

débiliter (debilite), v.a. To debilitate; **se** ~, v.pr. to become debilitated.

débinage (debinaʒ), s.m. (pop.) Slandering, disparagement.

débine (debin), s.f. (slang) Straits, need, mess; *être* or *tomber dans la* ~, to be, or become, hard up (for money).

débiner (debine), v.a. (pop.) To disparage, to slander, to run down; **se** ~, v.pr. (slang) to run away, to make off, to leg it, to make oneself scarce.

débit (debi), s.m. [f. *débiter*] 1. Sale, market, retail shop, licensed shop; ~ *de tabac*, tobacconist's shop; 2. beer-house, (cheap) wine-shop; 3. (book-keep.) debit, debit side; 4. cutting up of wood (in this sense *débitage* is more frequently used); 5. output, supply; 6. utterance (in speaking); *avoir le* ~ *facile*, to be a good talker, to have an easy elocution or delivery, to have the gift of the gab.

débitage (debitaʒ), s.m. Cutting-up (of wood, &c.).

débitant, -e (debitɑ̃), s.m.f. (Cheap) wine-retailer; retailer.

débiter (debite), v.a. [f. L *debitum*] 1. To sell, to retail; 2. to cut up, to cut out, to saw; 3. to supply; 4. (book-keep.) to debit; 5. to utter, to recite.

débiteu-r,[1] -se (debitœr), s.m.f. Spreader, reciter, teller, utterer.

débit-eur,[2] -rice (debitœr), s.m.f. adj. Debtor.

déblai (deblɛ), s.m. [f. *déblayer*] 1. Excavation, cutting, clearing-away; 2. earth (from a cutting), rubbish.

déblaiement (deblɛmɑ̃), s.m. Clearing-away, cutting.

déblatérer (deblatere), v.n.a. [L *deblaterare*] To rail (at), to rant, to speak against, to slander; ~ *des sottises*, to utter stupidities; ~ *contre X*, to slander X, to run down X, to rail at or against X.

déblayer (deblɛje), v.a. [*dé*+*blé*, f. L *bladum*, OF *desbleer*] To clear away, to clear, to smooth; ~, v.n. (theatr.) to recite swiftly and without stress the unimportant parts of a speech.

débloquer (deblɔke), v.a. To raise the blockade of; to free; (print.) to correct or replace (turned letters).

déboire (debwar), s.m. Nasty after-taste; (fig.) vexation, disappointment.

déboisement (debwazmɑ̃), s.m. [f. *bois*] Clearing of woods, disafforestation.

déboiser (debwaze), v.a. To clear of woods, to disafforest; **se** ~, v.pr. to become denuded of woods.

déboîtement (debwatmɑ̃), s.m. Luxation, dislocation.

déboîter (debwate), v.a. To luxate, to dislocate, to unsocket; to disconnect, to disjoint; **se** ~, v.pr. to be dislocated, &c.

débonder (debɔ̃de), **débondonner** (debɔ̃dɔne), v.a. [f. *bonde*] To unbung; to open the sluice of (a pond), to relax.

débonnaire (debɔnɛr), adj. [f. *bon*+*aire*] Gentle, meek, debonair, compliant, good-tempered and weak.

débonnairement (debɔnɛrmɑ̃), adv. Meekly, compliantly, weakly.

débonnaireté (debɔnɛrte), s.f. Meekness, gentleness, compliance, weakness.

débordement (debɔrdəmɑ̃), s.m. Overflow, inundation, flood; (fig.) excess, dissoluteness, lewdness.

déborder (debɔrde), v.n.a. [f. *bord*] 1. To overflow, to run over, to burst forth; 2. (naut.) to get clear; 3. to outflank; 4. to unborder, to untuck; *être débordé de travail*, to be unable to cope with all one's work, to be up to the eyes in work; *avoir une joie débordante*, to be overjoyed.

débosseler (debɔsle), v.a. To take the dents (or the bruises) out of; syn. DÉBOSSER.

débotté (debɔte), p. adj. With the boots off.

~, s.m. Taking-off of boots; *au* ~, immediately on arriving.
débotter (debɔte), v.a. To pull off the boots of; **se** ~, v.pr. to pull off one's boots.
débouché (debuʃe), s.m. **1.** Outlet, issue; **2.** market, opportunity.
débouchement, débouchage (debuʃmɑ̃, debuʃaʒ), s.m. Uncorking, opening, outlet.
déboucher (debuʃe), v.a. [f. *boucher*] To uncork, to open, to clear; ~, v.n. to run (into), to open out (on), to disembogue; (mil.) to debouch.
déboucler (debukle), v.a. To unbuckle, to unfasten; to uncurl (hair).
débouler (debule), v.n. (of hares, rabbits, &c.) To run suddenly out of cover.
déboulonner (debulɔne), v.a. [f. *boulon*] To unbolt, to unrivet; (fig.) to demolish.
débouquer (debuke), v.n. (naut.) To disembogue.
débourber (deburbe), v.a. [f. *bourbe*] To take the muddy taste out (of fish), to clean out mud from, to extricate (from the mire); to purge (fish).
débourrer (debure), v.a. [f. *bourre*] To draw the wad of; to worm (a gun); to empty (a pipe).
débours, déboursé (debur, deburse), s.m. Disbursement, outlay, money advanced or paid; (*débours* is generally used in the plural).
débourser (deburse), v.a. [f. *bourse*] To disburse, to pay out (money).
debout (dəbu), adv. [*de*+*bout*] Upright, standing, on end, up, out of bed, stirring; *avoir vent* ~, to have a head wind, to have the wind ahead; *cela ne tient pas* ~ *!*, that won't hold water!; ~, interj. up!, get up!
débouté (debute), s.m. (law) Dismissal, non-suit.
débouter (debute), v.a. [*dé*+*bouter*] To non-suit; *être débouté de sa demande*, to be non-suited.
déboutonner (debutɔne), v.a. [f. *bouton*] To unbutton; **se** ~, v.pr. to unbutton one's clothes; (fig.) to unbosom oneself.
débraillé, -e (debrɑje), p. adj. With one's breast uncovered; untidy, slovenly in one's dress.
(se) débrailler (sədebrɑje), v.pr. [f. *dé*+OF *brail*] To uncover one's breast; to become slovenly or untidy in one's dress.
débrayage (debrɛjaʒ), s.m. Declutch; *double* ~, double declutch.
débrayer, désembrayer (debrɛje, dezɑ̃brɛje), v.a.n. To disconnect; (motor.) to declutch.
débrider (debride), v.a.n. [f. *bride*] **1.** To unbridle; *sans* ~, at a stretch, in haste; **2.** to open (a wound); **3.** to untruss (a fowl).
débris (debri), s.m. [f. *briser*] Fragment, remains, remnant, ruin, wreck, wreckage.
débrouillard, -e (debrujar), adj. s.m.f. Full of resources, cute, capable of shifting for oneself, smart, spry, dodgy, up to snuff, shifty (fellow).
débrouiller (debruje), v.a. To disentangle, to unravel; **se** ~, v.pr. to get out of a difficulty, to shift for oneself, to get disentangled, to manage, to wangle; *il saura toujours se* ~, he will always fall on his feet.
débroussailler (debrusɑje), v.a. To clear away thickets from, to remove thickets, thorns, weeds, &c. from.
débrutir (debrytir), v.a. [f. *brut*] To rough-polish.
débucher (debyʃe), v.n. [f. *bûche*] (hunt.) To start. ~, s.m. Start.
débusquer (debyske), [doublet of *débucher*] v.a. To drive out, to oust, to dislodge.
début (deby), s.m. [*dé*+*but*] (cards) First play, lead, first throw, first stroke; (fig.) beginning, start, outset, first appearance or production.
débutant, -e (debytɑ̃), p. adj. s.m.f. Débutant(e), beginner, novice. ⚠ In English, but not in French, the fem. 'débutante' is usual in the sense of: *jeune fille faisant son entrée dans le monde.*
débuter (debyte), v.n. To play first, to throw or toss for the lead; (fig.) to begin, set out, to start; to come out, to make one's début.
déca (deka), pref. [Gr. *deka* = 10] Deca- (ten times the unit).
deçà (dəsa), prep. On this side; *en* ~ *de*, on this side of; ~ *delà*, here and there, to and fro; *jambe* ~, *jambe delà*, astride.
décacheter (dekaʃte), v.a. To break the seal of, to open (a letter).
décadaire (dekadɛr), adj. Decadal.
décade (dekad), s.f. [f. Gr. *dekas*] Decade.
décadence (dekadɑ̃s), s.f. [f. L *de*+*cadere*] Decadence, decay, decline.
décadent, -e (dekadɑ̃), adj. Declining, decadent. ~, s.m. (Lit.) Decadent.
décadi (dekadi), s.m. Décadi (tenth day of the decade in the French Republican Calendar).
décaèdre (dekaɛdr), s.m. [f. Gr. *deka*+*hedra*] Decahedron. ~, adj. Decahedral.
décagonal, -e, (aux) (dekagɔnal), adj. Decagonal.
décagone (dekagɔn), s.m. [f. Gr. *deka*+*gōnia*] Decagon.
décagramme (dekagram), s.m. Decagramme.
décaissement (dekɛsmɑ̃), s.m. Disbursement.
décaisser (dekɛse), v.a. [f. *caisse*] **1.** To

uncase, to unpack; (gard.) to untub; **2.** to disburse, to pay out.
décalage (dekalaʒ), s.m. Want of synchronism; displacement in space or time.
décalcomanie (dekalkɔmani), s.f. [f. *décalquer+manie*] Decalcomania (process of transferring pictures from prepared paper to glass, porcelain, &c.).
décaler (dekale), v.a. To unwedge.
décalitre (dekalitr), s.m. Decalitre.
décalogue (dekalɔg), s.m. [f. Gr. *deka+logos*] Decalogue.
décalque (dekalk), s.m. [f. *calque*] Transfer (of a tracing, &c.); syn. DÉCALQUAGE.
décalquer (dekalke), v.a. To transfer (a tracing, &c.).
décamètre (dekamɛtr), s.m. Decametre.
décamper (dekɑ̃pe), v.n. To decamp, to run away, to move off; to make oneself scarce.
décanat (dekana), s.m. [f. L *decanus*] Deanship, deanery.
décantage (dekɑ̃taʒ), s.m. **décantation** (dekɑ̃ta'sjɔ̃), s.f. Decanting, decantation.
décanter (dekɑ̃te), v.a. [*dé*+L *canthus*] To decant.
décapage, décapement (dekapaʒ, dekapmɑ̃), s.m. Cleaning (of metals), scouring, scraping.
décaper (dekape), v.a. [*dé+cape*] To clean (metals), to scour, to scrape; ~, v.n. (naut.) to double a cape. [heading.
décapitation (dekapita'sjɔ̃), s.f. Be-
décapiter (dekapite), v.a. [f. L *de+caput*] To behead, to decapitate.
décapode (dekapɔd), s.m. adj. [f. Gr. *deka+pous, podos*] (zool.) Decapod.
décapotable (dekapɔtabl), adj. All-weather (car).
décapuchonner (dekapyʃɔne), v.a. To uncowl, to uncover.
(se) décarcasser (sədekarkase), v.pr. (colloq.) To take much trouble, to strive, to try hard, to bestir oneself, to slave, to get up steam.
décastère (dekastɛr), s.m. Decastere (French measure for wood), ten steres or cubic metres.
décasyllabe, décasyllabique (dekasilab, dekasilabik), adj. Decasyllabic.
décatir (dekatir), v.a. To sponge, to ungloss (woollen cloth); *être tout décati*, (fig. fam.) to feel worn-out, seedy, disappointed, crestfallen.
décatissage (dekatisaʒ), s.m. Sponging (of woollen cloth).
décavé, -e (dekave), p. adj. Fleeced, cleaned out, ruined, stony-broke, on one's uppers.
décaver (dekave), v.a. [f. *cave*] (at play) To win the stake of (the stake originally being wine in the cellar); to ruin, to beggar.
décéder (desede), v.n. [L *decedere*] To die, to decease.
décèlement (desɛlmɑ̃), s.m. [f. *déceler*] Disclosure.
déceler (desle), v.a. [f. *dé+celer*] To disclose, to reveal, to betray.
décembre (desɑ̃br), s.m. [L *december*] December.
décemment (desamɑ̃), adv. Decently (⚠ see DÉCENT), with modesty.
décemvir (desɛmvir), s.m. [L wd] Decemvir.
décemvirat (desɛmvira), s.m. Decemvirate.
décence (desɑ̃s), s.f. [L *decentia*] Decency, propriety, modesty.
décennal, -e, (aux) (desɛnnal), adj. [L *decennalis*] Decennial.
décent, -e (desɑ̃), adj. Decent, modest, proper. ⚠ 'Decent' in English has a wider acceptation than *décent*. It means also, and quite usually: *acceptable, convenable, assez bien, tolérable, de bon goût*.
décentralisation (desɑ̃traliza'sjɔ̃), s.f. Decentralization.
décentraliser (desɑ̃tralize), v.a.n. To decentralize.
décentration (desɑ̃tra'sjɔ̃), s.f. **décentrement** (desɑ̃trəmɑ̃), s.m. The act of displacing the centres of lenses, &c.
décentrer (desɑ̃tre), v.a. To displace the centre of.
déception (desɛpsjɔ̃), s.f. [L *deceptio*] **1.** Deception; deceit; **2.** disappointment. ⚠ 'Deception' in English always means *tromperie* and cannot be used to translate the French *déception* in sense **2.**
décerner (desɛrne), v.a. [L *decernere*] To award, to decree, to bestow, to confer; ~ *un mandat d'arrêt*, to issue a warrant.
décès (desɛ), s.m. [f. L *decessus*] Death, demise, decease.
décevant, -e (desvɑ̃), p. adj. Fallacious, deceptive, deceitful, delusive.
décevoir (desvwar), v.a. [L *decipere*] **1.** To deceive (see DÉCEPTION ⚠); **2.** to disappoint.
déchaînement (deʃɛnmɑ̃), s.m. [f. *chaîne*] Unchaining, letting loose; wild outburst, fury.
déchaîner (deʃɛne), v.a. To unchain, to turn loose, to exasperate, to madden, to let loose; *le bruit des vents déchaînés*, the roaring of the raging winds; ~ *les passions*, to let loose or to exasperate the passions; **se ~**, v.pr. to break loose, to rage.
déchant (deʃɑ̃), s.m. Descant.
déchanter (deʃɑ̃te), v.n. [f. L *discantus*] To lower one's tone, to sing small, to come down a peg or two; *je le ferai ~*, I will make him change his tune.
décharge (deʃarʒ), s.f. [f. *décharger*] **1.** Discharge, unloading; **2.** shooting, shot, discharge; **3.** release (from an obligation), relief, discharge; **4.** outlet, drain, rubbish;

5. favourable evidence, exculpation; *à la ~ de l'accusé*, in favour of the prisoner, for the defence.
déchargement (deʃarʒəmɑ̃), s.m. Unloading, (naut.) unlading.
décharger (deʃarʒe), v.a. [*dé+charger*] To unload, to unburden, to unlade, to empty, to lighten, to ease, to release, to exculpate, to clear; to shoot, to discharge (a gun, an electric battery), to vent, to come off upon, to colour; **se ~**, v.pr. to unburden oneself, to relieve oneself; *se ~ de ce soin sur X*, to rely upon X to look after this matter, or to take this matter in hand.
déchargeur (deʃarʒœr), s.m. Unloader, wharf-porter, docker.
décharné, -e (deʃarne), p. adj. Fleshless, emaciated, skinny, bony, lean.
décharner (deʃarne), v.a. [f. *chair*] To strip the flesh off, to emaciate, to render meagre; **se ~**, v.pr. to lose flesh.
déchasser (deʃase), v.n. To slide to the left (in dancing).
déchaumage (deʃomaʒ), s.m. [f. *chaume*] Ploughing-up of the stubble.
déchaumer (deʃome), v.a. To plough up the stubble on; to break up (fallow land).
déchaussé, -e, (deʃose), p. adj. **déchaux** (deʃo), adj. m. Barefoot, barefooted; *carme* (or *moine*) *déchaux*, barefooted friar; *dent ~e*, gumless tooth.
déchaussement (deʃosmɑ̃), s.m. **1.** Pulling-off of shoes, boots, &c.; **2.** laying bare the foundations (of a wall, &c.); **3.** gumlessness (of teeth); **4.** baring (of the roots of a tree).
déchausser (deʃose), v.a. [*dé+chausser*] **1.** To pull off (shoes, stockings, &c.); **2.** to lay bare the foundations of (a wall, &c.); **3.** to lance the gum of; **4.** to bare (the roots of a tree); **se ~**, v.pr. **1.** to pull off one's shoes, &c.; **2.** (of teeth) to be denuded of the gums.
dèche (dɛʃ), s.f. (pop.) Want, need; *être dans une ~ noire*, to be stony-broke, hard up, in very low water.
déchéance (deʃeɑ̃s), s.f. [f. *déchoir*] Decadence, decay, falling-off; forfeiture; dethronement; loss of one's rights or authority.
déchet (deʃɛ), s.m. [f. *déchoir*] Waste, rubbish; (fig.) falling-off, decrease of value, diminution.
déchevêtrer (deʃvɛtre), v.a. [f. *chevêtre*] To take the halter off, to release.
déchiffrable (deʃifrabl), adj. Decipherable, legible.
déchiffrement (deʃifrəmɑ̃), s.m. Deciphering, reading at sight (of music).
déchiffrer (deʃifre), v.a. [*dé+chiffrer*] To decipher, to read; to read (music) at sight.
déchiqueter (deʃikte), v.a. [f. *chiquet*] To cut to pieces, to slash, to hack, to whittle; to pink (the edge of flounces, &c.).
déchirage (deʃiraʒ), s.m. Breaking-up, ripping-up (of boats, wood).
déchirant, -e (deʃirɑ̃), p. adj. Heart-rending, harrowing.
déchirement (deʃirmɑ̃), s.m. Tearing, rending; anguish, excruciating pain; (fig.) painful or heart-rending renunciation or parting; **~s**, s.m.pl. troubles, broils, discord.
déchirer (deʃire), v.a. [f. Germ. *scheren*] To tear, to rend, to lacerate; (fig.) to harrow, to torture; to slander, to defame; *~ à belles dents*, to tear to pieces.
déchirure (deʃiryr), s.f. Tear, rent, laceration; syn. ACCROC.
déchoir (deʃwar), v.n. def. [*dé+choir*] To fall off, to decline, to forfeit, to lose one's rank, right, or dignity.
déchu, -e (deʃy), p. adj. [part. of *déchoir*] Fallen.
déci (desi), pref. [f. L *decem*] Deci- (= one-tenth of the unit).
décidé, -e (deside), p. adj. **1.** Decided, settled; **2.** resolute.
décidément (desidemɑ̃), adv. Decidedly, really and truly; on second thoughts, positively.
décider (deside), v.a.n. [L *decidere*] To decide, to determine, to settle, to induce, to persuade; to give a decision; **se ~**, v.pr. to be decided, to be settled; to decide, to make up one's mind, to resolve, to declare (for).
décigramme (desigram), s.m. Decigramme.
décilitre (desilitr), s.m. Decilitre.
décimable (desimabl), adj. Tithable.
décimal, -e, (aux) (desimal), adj. Decimal. **~e**, s.f. Decimal.
décimateur (desimatœr), s.m. (obs.) Tithe-owner.
décimation (desima'sjɔ̃), s.f. Decimation; (fig.) destroying of a large proportion (of).
décime (desim), s.m. [f. L *decimus*] Decime (tenth part of the franc).
décimer (desime), v.a. To decimate; (fig.) to destroy a tenth, or a large proportion of; to plough down, to sweep off, to thin.
décimètre (desimɛtr), s.m. Decimetre.
décimo (desimo), adv. [L wd] Tenthly.
décisi-f, -ve (desizif), adj. Decisive, peremptory, final, conclusive.
décision (desizjɔ̃), s.f. [L *decisio*] **1.** Decision, decree; **2.** firmness, resolution.
décisivement (desizivmɑ̃), adv. Decisively, finally, peremptorily.
décistère (desistɛr), s.m. Decistere (French measure for wood).
déclamat-eur, -rice (deklamatœr), s.m.f. Declaimer; spouter, ranter. **~**, adj. Declamatory.
déclamation (deklama'sjɔ̃), s.f. [f.

déclamer] **1.** Declamation, elocution; **2.** bombastic speech.
déclamatoire (deklamatwar), adj. Declamatory, bombastic.
déclamer (deklame), v.a. [L *declamare*] To declaim, to recite, to deliver; ~, v.n. to declaim, to inveigh; ~ *contre le luxe*, to inveigh against luxury.
déclancher (deklɑ̃ʃe), v.a. See DÉCLENCHER.
déclarati-f, -ve, déclaratoire (deklaratif, deklaratwar), adj. (law) Declarative, declaratory.
déclaration (deklara'sjɔ̃), s.f. Declaration, statement, affidavit; ~ *d'amour*, declaration of love; ~ *de guerre*, declaration of war.
déclarer (deklare), v.a. [L *declarare*] To declare, to state, to proclaim, to assert, to publish, to denounce; **se** ~, v.pr. to declare oneself or itself; to propose; (of diseases) to break out; to take sides.
déclassé, -e (deklase), p. adj. s.m.f. (Person or thing) taken out of its class, out of one's sphere, socially fallen.
déclassement (deklasmɑ̃), s.m. Change of class or sphere, upsetting, confusion.
déclasser (deklase), v.a. [f. *classe*] To change the class of, to unclass, to throw into confusion, to undervalue; (naut.) to disrate (a ship); to strike off the rolls; **se** ~, v.pr. to get out of one's class or sphere, to lose one's social position.
déclenchement, déclanchement (deklɑ̃ʃmɑ̃), s.m. Getting out of gear; starting; (mil.) ~ *d'une attaque*, launching of an attack.
déclencher, déclancher (deklɑ̃ʃe), v.a. [f. *clenche*] To start, to disengage, to throw out of gear; to launch (an attack).
déclic (deklik), s.m. [onom.] Catch, click, trigger, pawl, detent.
déclin (deklɛ̃), s.m. [f. *décliner*] Decline, decay, ebb, wane; (obs.) (mil.) mainspring; *le* ~ *du jour*, the decline of day.
déclinable (deklinabl), adj. Declinable.
déclinaison (deklinɛzɔ̃), s.f. (astron., &c.) Declination; (gram.) declension.
déclinatoire (deklinatwar), s.m. (law) Declinatory plea. ~, adj. Declinatory.
décliner (dekline), v.n. [L *declinare*] To decline, to deviate, to be on the wane, to decay, to fall off. ~, v.a. to decline, to refuse, to avoid, to take exception to; (gram.) to inflect (words); ~ *l'honneur de*, to decline the honour of; ~ *ses nom et qualités*, to state one's name and titles.
déclive (dekliv), adj. [L *declivis*] Sloping, declivous, declivitous.
déclivité (deklivite), s.f. [L *declivitas*] Declivity, slope.
déclore (deklɔr), v.a. To unclose, to throw open, to disclose.
déclouer (deklue), v.a. To unnail, to take up, to draw the nails of; **se** ~, v.pr. to come unnailed.
décochement (dekɔʃmɑ̃), s.m. Shooting, discharge (of an arrow).
décocher (dekɔʃe), v.a. To shoot, to discharge (an arrow), to send, to dart (a look), to level, to pay (a compliment).
décoction (dekɔksjɔ̃), s.f. [L *decoctio*] Decoction.
décoiffer (dekwafe), v.a. To take off the head-dress of, to derange or undo the hair of, to uncap, to uncover; **se** ~, v.pr. to take off one's hat or head-dress; to undo one's hair.
décolérer (dekɔlere), v.n. To cease to be angry.
décollation (dekɔla'sjɔ̃), s.f. [f. L *decollare*] Beheading, decollation.
décollement (dekɔlmɑ̃), s.m. [f. *décoller*] Ungluing, unpasting, coming-off; (surg.) detachment.
décoller (dekɔle), v.a. **1.** To unglue, to unpaste, to loosen, to separate, to disengage; **2.** To behead, to decollate; ~ v.n. (aeron.) to fly up, to leave the ground; **se** ~, v.pr. to come off, to get loose.
décolletage (dekɔltaʒ), s.m. **1.** Cutting-low of a dress, low dress, uncovering the neck and shoulders; **2.** (techn.) turning, shaping (small pieces of metal, in lathe).
décolleter (dekɔlte), v.a. **1.** To cut (a dress) low; to bare the neck and shoulders of; **2.** to turn, or to shape (small pieces of metal in lathe); *tour à* ~, turning lathe; **se** ~, v.pr. to wear a low dress, to go bare-necked.
décolorant, -e (dekɔlɔrɑ̃), adj. s.m. Decolorant.
décoloration (dekɔlɔra'sjɔ̃), s.f. Decolorization, discoloration.
décoloré, -e (dekɔlɔre), p. adj. Colourless, faded; (fig.) tame, colourless, dull.
décolorer (dekɔlɔre), v.a. To discolour; **se** ~, v.pr. to lose one's or its colour, to fade.
décombres (dekɔ̃br), s.m.pl. [f. medieval L *cumbrus*] Rubbish, building-materials, fragmentary matter of ruined or crumbling buildings; ruins.
décommander (dekɔmɑ̃de), v.a. To countermand.
décomposable (dekɔ̃pozabl), adj. Decomposable, decompoundable.
décomposer (dekɔ̃poze), v.a. To decompose, to decompound, to analyse, to alter, to corrupt, to discompose; **se** ~, v.pr. to decompose, to be decomposed, to undergo dissolution; to be discomposed.
décomposition (dekɔ̃pozisjɔ̃), s.f. Decomposition, discomposure.
décompresseur (dekɔ̃prɛsœr), s.m. Compression release, decompressor.
décompression (dekɔ̃prɛsjɔ̃), s.f. (motor.)

Compression release; *robinet de* ~, compression-release cock.
décompte (dekɔ̃t), s.m. [f. *compte*] **1.** Discount, deduction; **2.** particulars, discount note.
décompter (dekɔ̃te), v.a. **1.** To deduct, to reckon off; **2.** to give particulars, or a discount note of; ~, v.n. to be disappointed.
déconcertant, -e (dekɔ̃sɛrtɑ̃), p. adj. Disconcerting, baffling.
déconcerter (dekɔ̃sɛrte), v.a. To disconcert, to baffle, to put out, to abash.
déconfire (dekɔ̃fir), v.a. To discomfit, to nonplus, to beat, to rout.
déconfit, -e (dekɔ̃fi), p. adj. Nonplussed, discomfited; *une mine* ~*e*, a long face, a crest-fallen look.
déconfiture (dekɔ̃fityr), s.f. Discomfiture, smash, crash, failure, ruin, insolvency; rout.
déconseiller (dekɔ̃sɛje), v.a. To dissuade, to dissuade from, to disapprove of, to advise against.
déconsidération (dekɔ̃sidera'sjɔ̃), s.f. Disrepute, discredit.
déconsidérer (dekɔ̃sidere), v.a. To discredit, to bring into disrepute, to disgrace; **se** ~, v.pr. to fall into disrepute, to disgrace oneself.
décontenancer (dekɔ̃tnɑ̃se), v.a. To put out of countenance, to abash, to nonplus; **se** ~, v.pr. to be put out of countenance, to be abashed.
déconvenue (dekɔ̃vny), s.f. [f. OF *desconvenir*, to disappoint] Disappointment, mishap, discomfiture.
décor (dekɔr), s.m. [f. *décorer*] **1.** Decoration; **2.** (fig.) frame, scene, environment, show; **3.** (theatr.) scenery.
décorateur (dekɔratœr), s.m. **1.** Decorator, house-decorator and furnisher; **2.** scene-painter; **3.** decorative painter.
décorati-f, -ve (dekɔratif), adj. Decorative.
décoration (dekɔra'sjɔ̃), s.f. **1.** Decoration, ornamentation; **2.** order, badge, medal, star, insignia, cross.
décorder (dekɔrde), v.a. To untwist (a rope); to uncord (a package).
décoré, -e (dekɔre), p. adj. **1.** Decorated, ornamented; **2.** knighted, wearing the insignia of an order.
décorer (dekɔre), v.a. [f. L *decorare*] **1.** To decorate, to ornament; **2.** to knight, to confer a knighthood, an order, on; to decorate, to invest with a decoration.
décorner (dekɔrne), v.a. To take off the horns of; *il fait un vent à* ~ *les bœufs*, there is wind enough to blow one's head off.
décortication (dekɔrtika'sjɔ̃), s.f. **décorticage** (dekɔrtikaʒ), s.m. Decortication, shelling, peeling, barking.
décortiquer (dekɔrtike), v.a. [f. *dé*+L *cortex*] To decorticate, to shell, to peel, to bark, to husk.
décorum (dekɔrɔm), s.m. (no pl.) [L wd] Decorum, propriety; *garder le* ~, to observe decorum; *manquer au* (or *de*) ~, to offend against decorum.
découcher (dekuʃe), v.n. (pej.) To sleep out, to stay out all night.
découdre (dekudr), v.a. To unstitch, to rip up; (naut.) to rip off; *nous allons en* ~, (fam.) we are going to fight it out; **se** ~, v.pr. to come unstitched, unsewed.
découlement (dekulmɑ̃), s.m. Trickling, flowing.
découler (dekule), v.n. To trickle, to flow in a small stream; (fig.) to proceed, to spring, to be derived, to be the consequence.
découpage (dekupaʒ), s.m. Cutting-out, carving; fretwork, stamping.
découpé, -e (dekupe), p. adj. Cut out, pinked out, cut, sharp, clear, sharply delineated.
découper (dekupe), v.a. [f. *couper*] To cut out, to cut up, to cut; to carve; to pink out, to punch; to cut out, to shape; **se** ~, v.pr. **1.** to be carved, to be cut up; **2.** to stand out clear (*sur*, against).
découple, découpler (dekupl, dekuple), s.m. (hunt.) Uncoupling.
découplé, -e (dekuple), p. adj. Well-built, strapping.
découpler (dekuple), v.a. [f. *couple*] To uncouple, to let loose (on).
découpoir (dekupwar), s.m. Cutting-punch, pinking-machine.
découpure (dekupyr), s.f. **1.** Cutting-out, pinking; **2.** thing cut out; **3.** notch.
décourageant, -e (dekuraʒɑ̃), p. adj. Discouraging, disheartening.
découragement (dekuraʒmɑ̃), s.m. [f. *courage*] Discouragement, despondency, dejection. ⚠ See DÉJECTION.
décourager (dekuraʒe), v.a. To discourage, to dishearten, to daunt, to deter (*de*, from), to dissuade (from); **se** ~, v.pr. to lose heart or courage; to be disheartened; *être découragé*, to be downhearted.
découronnement (dekurɔnmɑ̃), s.m. Discrowning.
découronner (dekurɔne), v.a. **1.** To discrown; (fig.) to run down; **2.** to lay bare the top of (a thing).
décours (dekur), s.m. [f. L *decursus*] Decrease, wane (of the moon).
décousu, -e (dekuzy), p. adj. Unsewed, unstitched; (fig.) loose, incoherent, desultory. ~, s.m. Looseness, desultoriness, incoherence, irrelevance.
décousure (dekuzyr), s.f. Rent (in a seam); rip, rent.
découvert, -e (dekuvɛr), p. adj. Uncovered,

bare, bare-headed, open, unsheltered, unguarded; discovered. ~, s.m. Deficit; *à* ~, adv. loc. in the open, openly, without any shelter, exposed, unguardedly; (comm.) without security, unprovided for, as a time-bargain; *vente à* ~, time-bargain.

découverte (dekuvɛrt), s.f. Discovery; detection, finding-out; (mil.) reconnoitring; *aller à la* ~, to scout, to reconnoitre.

découvreur (dekuvrœr), s.m. Discoverer.

découvrir (dekuvrir), v.a. [*dé*+*couvrir*] To discover, to find out, to detect, to uncover, to bare, to lay bare, to expose; **se** ~, v.pr. to uncover oneself, to uncover one's head; (fig.) to expose oneself, to disclose oneself; to be visible; to clear up; *le temps se découvre*, it is clearing up.

décrasser (dekrase), v.a. [f. *crasse*] To clean, to take the dirt off, to scour; (fig.) to rub up a bit, to polish; **se** ~, v.pr. to clean oneself; (fig.) to become polished, to become a gentleman (or a lady), to lose one's bad manners.

décrépir (dekrepir), v.a. To unplaster; **se** ~, v.pr. to lose its coat of plaster.

décrépit, -e (dekrepi), p. adj. [f. L *decrepare*] Decrepit, broken down, worn out.

décrépitation (dekrepita'sjɔ̃), s.f. Decrepitation, crackling.

décrépiter (dekrepite), v.n. To decrepitate, to crackle (as salt in the fire).

décrépitude (dekrepityd), s.f. Decrepitude.

décret (dekrɛ), s.m. [L *decretum*] Decree, order, writ, warrant.

décrétale (dekretal), s.f. [L *decretalis*] Decretal.

décréter (dekrete), v.a. To decree, to order, to issue a warrant, a writ, against.

décri (dekri), s.m. [f. *décrier*] Crying-down, decrial; (fig.) disrepute, discredit; *tomber dans le* ~ *public*, to fall into discredit.

décrier (dekrije), v.a. To cry down, to decry, to discredit, to disparage.

décrire (dekrir), v.a. [L *describere*] To describe; **se** ~, v.pr. to be described; to describe oneself.

décrocher (dekrɔʃe), v.a. To unhook, to take down; to get, to get hold of; **se** ~, v.pr. to come unhooked; *décrochez-moi-ça*, subst. loc., second-hand garments, old-clothes shop, reach-me-down.

décroiser (dekrwaze), v.a. To straighten, to uncross.

décroissance (dekrwasɑ̃s), s.f. (rare) **décroît** (dekrwɑ), s.m. Decrease, decline, wane; *en* ~, subsiding, diminishing.

décroissant, -e (dekrwasɑ̃), p. adj. Decreasing, diminishing; (math.) descending (as progressions).

décroître (dekrwɑtr), v.n. To decrease, to diminish, to wane, to shorten; *les jours décroissent*, the days are getting shorter, the days are drawing in.

décrottage (dekrɔtaʒ), s.m. [f. *crotte*] Cleaning, brushing.

décrotter (dekrɔte), v.a. To clean, to brush (or scrape) the mud off; (fig.) to teach the rudiments to.

décrotteur (dekrɔtœr), s.m. Boots; shoe-black.

décrottoir (dekrɔtwar), s.m. Door-scraper.

décrue (dekry), s.f. Decrease, fall (of waters).

déçu, -e (desy), p. adj. [part. of *décevoir*] Disappointed.

déculotter (dekylɔte), v.a. To take off the breeches of, to debag.

décuple (dekypl), adj. s.m. [L *decuplus*] Decuple, tenfold.

décupler (dekyple), v.a.n. To decuple, to increase tenfold.

décurie (dekyri), s.f. [L *decuria*] Decury, decuria.

décurion (dekyrjɔ̃), s.m. Decurion.

dédaigner (dedɛɲe), v.a. [*dé*+*daigner*] To disdain, to scorn, to reject, to turn up one's nose at.

dédaigneusement (dedɛɲøzmɑ̃), adv. Disdainfully, scornfully, contemptuously.

dédaigneu-x, -se (dedɛɲø), adj. Disdainful, scornful; *faire le* ~, to turn up one's nose.

dédain (dedɛ̃), s.m. [f. L *dedignatio*] Disdain, scorn; mark of contempt.

dédale (dedal), s.m. [f. myth. prop. n. *Daedalus*] Labyrinth, maze.

dedans (dədɑ̃), adv. Inside, within; *au* ~, within, inside, at home, internally; *de* ~, from within; *en* ~, within, inwardly; *là-*~, in, within, in there, therein; *par* ~, through; *mettre* or *fourrer* ~, to let in, to take in, to deceive; to imprison; *se mettre* ~, to blunder, to make a mistake, to miscalculate; *donner* ~, to fall into the snare. ~, s.m. Inside, interior; home, home-country.

dédicace (dedikas), s.f. [f. L *dedicatio*] **1.** Dedication, consecration; **2.** dedicatory inscription at the beginning of a book.

dédicatoire (dedikatwar), adj. Dedicatory.

dédier (dedje), v.a. [f. L *dedicare*] To dedicate.

dédire (dedir), v.a. [*dé*+*dire*] To contradict, to gainsay; **se** ~, v.pr. to unsay, to retract, to go back upon one's word; *il n'est plus possible de s'en* ~, there is no getting out of it now.

dédit (dedi), s.m. [f. *dédire*] Unsaying; forfeit.

dédommagement (dedɔmaʒmɑ̃), s.m. Indemnity, compensation, amends, damages.

dédommager (dedɔmaʒe), v.a. To indemnify, to compensate, to make up (for), to make amends (for); **se ~**, v.pr. to repay oneself.
dédorer (dedɔre), v.a. [*dé+dorer*] To ungild; **se ~**, v.pr. to lose its gilt.
dédoublement (dedubləmɑ̃), s.m. Division into two, reduction by half; *engrenage de ~*, two-to-one gear.
dédoubler (deduble), v.a. **1.** To take out the lining of; to unfold; **2.** to divide into two, to make into two, to diminish by half, to change from single to double; to change from double to single; **se ~**, v.pr. to divide oneself.
déducti-f, -ve (dedyktif), adj. Deductive.
déduction (dedyksjɔ̃), s.f. [L *deductio*] **1.** Deduction, inference; **2.** defalcation, abatement, deduction, deducing; *~ faite de*, after allowing for.
déduire (dedɥir), v.a. [L *deducere*] **1.** To deduct, to subtract, to take off; **2.** to deduce, to infer.
déduit (dedɥi), s.m. (obs.) Pastime, pleasure.
déesse (deɛs), s.f. [f. L *dea*] Goddess.
défaillance (defajɑ̃s), s.f. Failing; exhaustion, decay; fainting-fit, swoon; faintness; (law) non-accomplishment.
défaillant, -e (defajɑ̃), p. adj. **1.** (law) Failing to appear; defaulting; **2.** faint, feeble, faltering, swooning. **~**, s.m.f. Defaulter.
défaillir (defajir), v.n. def. [*dé+faillir*] **1.** To fail, to be wanting; **2.** to faint, to swoon.
défaire (defɛr), v.a. **1.** To undo, to unmake, to break, to break off, to loose, to unfasten, to unstitch; **2.** to take off (one's coat, &c.); **3.** to discompose, to disturb; **4.** to defeat, to rout; **5.** to rid (of), to free, to deliver (from); *défaites-vous de cette habitude*, get rid of that habit; **se ~**, v.pr. to come undone; to be put out of countenance; to rid oneself (*de*, of), to part (with).
défait, -e (defɛ), p. adj. Emaciated, wasted, fagged, exhausted(-looking), done-up.
défaite (defɛt), s.f. **1.** Defeat, rout, overthrow; **2.** evasion, subterfuge, put-off, pretence, sham, excuse.
défaitisme (defɛtism), s.m. Defeatism, the policy and opinion of those who during the war of 1914–18 were doubtful of victory or considered and advocated surrender.
défaitiste (defɛtist), adj. s.m.f. Defeatist.
défalcation (defalka'sjɔ̃), s.f. Defalcation, deduction.
défalquer (defalke), v.a. [L *defalcare*] To defalcate, to deduct.
défausser (defose), v.a. To straighten; **se ~** (*de*), v.pr. (cards) to play (unimportant cards).
défaut (defo), s.m. [f. *défaillir*] Defect, fault; blemish, deficiency, want, weak side; *le ~ de la cuirasse*, the chink in the armour; (fig.) the weak point; (law) default; *juger par ~*, to give judgement by default; *faire ~*, to default; *être en ~*, to be in fault; to be at a loss; *mettre en ~*, to put on the wrong scent, to foil; *à ~ de*, for want of, in the absence of; *sans ~*, faultless.
défaveur (defavœr), s.f. Disfavour, displeasure; *jeter la ~ sur X*, to discredit X.
défavorable (defavɔrabl), adj. Unfavourable, disadvantageous.
défavorablement (defavɔrabləmɑ̃), adv. Unfavourably, unkindly.
défécation (defeka'sjɔ̃), s.f. [f. L *defaecare*] **1.** Defecation; **2.** (pharm.) the act of separating the dregs of a liquid.
défecti-f, -ve (defɛktif), adj. [f. L *deficere*] (gram.) Defective.
défection (defɛksjɔ̃), s.f. [L *defectio*] Defection, disloyalty, falling-off, desertion.
défectueusement (defɛktɥøzmɑ̃), adv. Defectively, imperfectly.
défectueu-x, -se (defɛktɥø), adj. Defective, imperfect, faulty.
défectuosité (defɛktɥozite), s.f. Defect, imperfection, flaw, blemish, fault.
défendable (defɑ̃dabl), adj. Defensible, tenable, defendable.
défendant (defɑ̃dɑ̃), p. adj. *A son corps ~*, adv. loc. in self-defence; (fig.) with reluctance.
défend-eur, -eresse (defɑ̃dœr), s.m.f. (law) Defendant.
défendre (defɑ̃dr), v.a. [f. L *defendere*] **1.** To defend, to protect, to stand by, to stand up for, to screen, to shield, to shelter; **2.** to forbid, to prohibit; **~** v.n. (law) to defend, to be the defendant; **se ~**, v.pr. to defend oneself, to resist, to vindicate oneself; to refrain (*de*, from); to deny, to excuse oneself (*de*, from); *se ~ d'avoir dit*, to deny having said.
défénestration (defenɛstra'sjɔ̃), s.f. [f. *fenêtre*, L *fenestra*] Act of throwing people out of the windows (e.g. *Défénestration de Prague*, 1618).
défense (defɑ̃s), s.f. [L *defensio*] **1.** Defence, guard, protection, fortification, outworks; vindication, apology; (law) plea of justification; *prendre la ~ de X*, to stand up in defence of X; *se mettre en ~*, to stand on one's guard; *dans le cas de légitime ~*, in a case of fair self-defence; *sans ~*, defenceless; **2.** prohibition, forbiddance, interdiction; *~ d'entrer*, no admittance; **3.** tusk, fang (of elephants, &c).
défenseur (defɑ̃sœr), s.m. Defender, protector, vindicator, champion; advocate, counsel for the defence.
défensi-f, -ve (defɑ̃sif), adj. Defensive.

~ve, s.f. Defensive, safeguard; *se tenir sur la* ~, to stand or to be on the defensive.

défensivement (defɑ̃sivmɑ̃), adv. Defensively, in defence.

déférant (deferɑ̃), p. adj. See DÉFÉRENT.

déférence (deferɑ̃s), s.m. Deference, regard, respect.

déférent, -e (deferɑ̃), adj. [L *deferens*] Deferential; (anat., astron.) deferent.

déférer (defere), v.a. [L *deferre*] **1.** To confer, to bestow; **2.** to denounce, to hand over; ~ *X en justice*, to bring X before the court; ~, v.n. to yield, to defer (*à*, to). ⚠ In English 'to defer' has also the sense of 'to postpone' = *retarder*.

déferler (defɛrle), v.n. To break; ~ v.a. (naut.) to unfurl (sails).

déferrer (defɛre), v.a. To unshoe (a horse); (fig.) to abash, to put out; **se** ~, v.pr. to get unshod; (fig.) to be put out of countenance.

défet (defɛ), s.m. (usually in the pl.) (print.) Overplus sheets.

défeuillaison (defœjɛzɔ̃), s.f. [f. *feuille*] Defoliation; falling of leaves.

défeuiller (defœje), v.a. To strip off the leaves of.

défi (defi), s.m. [f. *défier*] Challenge, defiance; *lancer un* ~ *à X*, to challenge X.

défiance (defjɑ̃s), s.f. [f. L *diffidentia*] Distrust, mistrust, diffidence; *sans* ~, unsuspecting. See MÉFIANCE.

défiant, -e (defjɑ̃), p. adj. Distrustful, mistrustful, suspicious, diffident.

déficeler (defisle), v.a. [f. *ficelle*] To untie (a parcel).

déficit (defisit), s.m. [L wd] Deficit, deficiency; *être en* ~, to have a deficit.

défier (defje), v.a. To challenge, to defy, to dare, to set at defiance; **se** ~ (*de*), v.pr. to be distrustful, to be on one's guard (against); to beware (of).

défigurer (defigyre), v.a. To disfigure, to distort, to spoil.

défilade (defilad), s.f. [f. *défiler*] Defiling, filing-off, string.

défilé (defile), s.m. **1.** Defiling (⚠ see DÉFILER); filing-off; **2.** defile, strait, pass.

défilement (defilmɑ̃), s.m. (mil.) Defilading, defiling.

défiler (defile), v.a. To unstring; ~, v.n. to defile, (⚠ 'to defile' has also the sense of 'to befoul', 'to pollute' = *souiller*); to file off, to march by files or in files; **se** ~, v.pr. **1.** to come unstrung; **2.** (pop.) to slink away.

défini, -e (defini), p. adj. Definite; (gram.) *passé* ~, perfect tense.

définir (definir), v.a. [L *definire*] To define, to determine, to describe, to explain; **se** ~, v.pr. to be defined.

définissable (definisabl), adj. Definable.

définiti-f, -ve (definitif), adj. Definitive, final; *en* ~*ve*, adv. loc. after all, decidedly, in short, finally.

définition (definisjɔ̃), s.f. [L *definitio*] Definition.

définitivement (definitivmɑ̃), adv. Definitively, finally.

déflagration (deflagra'sjɔ̃), s.f. [L *deflagratio*] Deflagration.

déflagrer (deflagre), v.n. To deflagrate.

défleurir (deflœrir), v.n. To shed (or lose) its blossoms; ~, v.a. to nip the blossom of.

défloraison (deflɔrɛzɔ̃), s.f. Fall of blossom.

déflorer (deflore), v.a. [L *deflorare*] **1.** To deflower; **2.** to take off the freshness of.

défonçage, défoncement (defɔ̃saʒ, defɔ̃smɑ̃), s.m. **1.** Digging-up; **2.** staving (of a cask); **3.** breaking-up (of roads).

défoncer (defɔ̃se), v.a. [f. *fonds*] **1.** To dig up; **2.** to stave in, to break the bottom of (a cask); **3.** to break up (roads); *une route défoncée*, a worn-down road.

déformation (defɔrma'sjɔ̃), s.f. Deformation, deformity.

déformer (defɔrme), v.a. [f. *forme*] To deform, to alter, to mis-shape, to distort; **se** ~, v.pr. to get out of shape, to grow deformed.

défourner (defurne), v.a. [f. *four*] To take out of the oven.

défraîchir (defrɛʃir), v.a. [f. *frais*] To take off the freshness of; **se** ~, v.pr. to fade, to lose freshness, lustre, or colour.

défrayer (defrɛje), v.a. [f. *frais*] **1.** To defray; **2.** to be the theme or subject of.

défrichement (defriʃmɑ̃), s.m. [f. *friche*] **1.** Clearing (of land); **2.** the land cleared.

défricher (defriʃe), v.a. To clear (land); (fig.) to clear up, to unravel.

défriser (defrize), v.a. **1.** To uncurl (hair); **2.** (fig.) to put out, to disappoint; **se** ~, v.pr. to come uncurled.

défroncer (defrɔ̃se), v.a. [f. *fronce*] **1.** To undo gathers in; **2.** to unknit, to smooth (one's brow).

défroque (defrɔk), s.f. **1.** Effects of a deceased monk; **2.** (pej.) old clothes, cast-off clothes and things.

défroquer (defrɔke), v.a. [f. *froc*] To unfrock; **se** ~, v.pr. to throw off the cowl.

défunt, -e (defœ̃), adj. s.m.f. [L *defunctus*] Deceased, defunct.

dégagé, -e (degaʒe), p. adj. Easy, free, flippant, unconstrained.

dégagement (degaʒmɑ̃), s.m. Redeeming, clearing, disengagement; taking out of pawn; passage, exit-door.

dégager (degaʒe), v.a. To redeem, to clear, to release, to disengage, to take out of pawn, to extricate; (chem.) to emit, to evolve; to show off, to set off the shape of; ~, v.n. (danc.) to bring forward the foot which was behind; **se ~**, v.pr. to disengage oneself, to get rid of, to be cleared.

dégaine (degɛn), s.f. Gait, manner; (often pej.) awkward gait.

dégainer (degɛne), v.a.n. [f. *gaine*] To unsheath, to draw one's sword.

déganter (degɑ̃te), v.a. [f. *gant*] To unglove; **se ~**, v.pr. to take off one's gloves.

dégarnir (degarnir), v.a. To unfurnish, to strip, to untrim, to thin; **se ~**, v.pr. to part (with); to wear lighter clothing; to become empty; to get bald, to grow bald, to grow thin.

dégât (degɑ), s.m. [f. OF *gaster*] (usually in pl.) Damage, havoc, depredation, devastation.

dégauchir (degoʃir), v.a. To straighten, to plane, to prepare.

dégel (deʒɛl), s.m. [*dé*+*gel*] Thaw.

dégelée (deʒle), s.f. (pop.) Volley of blows, thrashing.

dégeler (deʒle), v.n.a. To thaw, to melt.

dégénération (deʒenera'sjɔ̃), s.f. Degeneration, degeneracy.

dégénéré, -e (deʒenere), p. adj. s.m.f. Degenerate.

dégénérer (deʒenere), v.n. [L *degenerare*] To degenerate.

dégénérescence (deʒenerɛsɑ̃s), s.f. Degeneracy, degeneration.

dégénérescent, -e (deʒenerɛsɑ̃), adj. Degenerating.

dégermer (deʒɛrme), v.a. To remove the germ (of potatoes, barley, &c.).

dégingandé, -e (deʒɛ̃gɑ̃de), adj. Gawky, ungainly, ill-shaped, loose, gaunt.

déglutir (deglytir), v.a. [L *deglutire*] To swallow.

déglutition (deglytisjɔ̃), s.f. Deglutition.

dégobillage (degɔbijaʒ), s.m. (fam.) Spew, spewing, vomit.

dégobiller (degɔbije), v.a.n. [f. *gober*] To spew, to vomit, to bring up.

dégoiser (degwɑze), v.a.n. [f. *gosier*] To rattle, to gas, to babble, to clatter, to blab, to rattle on, to chatter, to spout; *il en dégoise!*, he spins a long yarn, what a gas-bag!

dégommer (degɔme), v.a. [f. *gomme*] **1.** To degum, to ungum (silk); **2.** (pop.) to oust, to dismiss; *il a été dégommé*, he 's been cashiered; he 's been sacked, or he has got the sack.

dégonflement (degɔ̃fləmɑ̃), s.m. **1.** Reduction (of swellings); **2.** emptying (of a balloon), deflation.

dégonfler (degɔ̃fle), v.a. [*dé*+*gonfler*] **1.** To reduce (a swelling); **2.** to deflate (a tyre), to empty (a balloon); (fig.) to ease, to lighten, to give relief to; **se ~**, v.pr. to be reduced in volume; to let out its gas (as a balloon); (pop.) to collapse, to lose one's courage, to give up.

dégorgement (degɔrʒəmɑ̃), s.m. Outflow, outfall, disgorgement, cleansing, unstopping; (med.) overflowing (of the humours, &c.).

dégorgeoir (degɔrʒwar), s.m. Spout, pricker, priming-wire, drain.

dégorger (degɔrʒe), v.a. [f. *gorge*] To disgorge, to unstop, to clear; to cleanse, to overflow, to discharge; (fig.) to spout; ~, v.n. to discharge, to overflow, to disgorge; *faire ~*, to make disgorge, to cause to overflow, to cause to discharge.

dégoter (degɔte), v.a. (slang) To fetch down; to detect, to find, to discover, to espy; to oust; to surpass, to outclass; to outwit; *il a dégoté X*, he knocked X off his perch.

dégouliner (deguline), v.n. [f. *goule*] To trickle down, to roll down, to drip.

dégourdi, -e (degurdi), p. adj. **1.** Shrewd, knowing, alive, wide awake, up to snuff, lively, forward, sharp, adroit, cute; **2.** *eau ~e*, tepid water.

dégourdir (degurdir), v.a. [f. *gourd*] To remove the stiffness (or numbness) of, to restore to warmth, to stretch (one's legs); (fig.) to polish, to sharpen the wits of; to take the chill off (water); **se ~**, v.pr. to lose its or one's numbness, to revive, to feel more lively, to brighten up, to bestir oneself, to lose one's gaucherie, to get sharp, to wake up.

dégourdissement (degurdismɑ̃), s.m. Removal of numbness; taking the chill off (water).

dégoût (degu), s.m. [f. *dégoûter*] Disgust, loathing; *prendre en ~*, to take a dislike to.

dégoûtant, -e (degutɑ̃), p. adj. Disgusting, loathsome, filthy; disheartening.

dégoûté, -e (degute), p. adj. **1.** Disgusted, weary; **2.** fastidious, squeamish; *il n'est pas ~!*, he is not over-fastidious!; (iron.) he has got pretty good taste!, he knows what he is after!, he expects and will have only the best; *être ~ de*, to be tired, or sick of.

dégoûter (degute), v.a. [f. *goût*] To disgust, to rouse aversion, to inspire dislike in, to tire, to weary, to sicken, to take away the appetite of; **se ~**, v.pr. to take a dislike (to), to get tired (of).

dégoutter (degute), v.n. [f. *goutte*] To drip, to trickle, to dribble.

dégradant, -e (degradɑ̃), p. adj. Degrading, disgraceful.

dégradation (degrada'sjɔ̃), s.f. **1.** Degradation, debasement; **2.** damage, deterioration; **3.** (geol., paint., &c.) degradation.

dégrader (degrade), v.a. [*dé*+*grader*] **1.** To degrade, to debase, to dishonour; **2.** to damage; **3.** (paint.) to degrade, to

lessen gradually; **se ~**, v.pr. **1.** to be damaged, to crumble; **2.** to degrade oneself, to disgrace oneself.
dégrafer (degrafe), v.a. [contr. of *désagrafer*, f. *agrafer*] To unhook, to unclasp; **se ~**, v.pr. to come unhooked; to unhook oneself, to undo one's dress, to open one's bodice.
dégraissage, dégraissement (degrɛsaʒ, degrɛsmɑ̃), s.m. Cleaning, scouring; taking off the grease.
dégraisser (degrɛse), v.a. [f. *graisse*] To take off grease from, to take the fat out of, to skim (broth, &c.); to clean; to emaciate.
dégraisseur (degrɛsœr), s.m. French or dry cleaner; (techn.) scourer.
dégras (degrɑ), s.m. [f. *gras*] (techn.) Train-oil scouring.
dégravoiement (degravwamɑ̃), s.m. Laying-bare, mining (by water).
dégravoyer (degravwaje), v.a. [f. *gravois*] To lay bare, to mine, to wash the earth (or the gravel) out of.
degré (dəgre), s.m. [f. L *gradus*] **1.** Step; **2.** degree, intensity, extent, pitch, height, grade; (gram.) *~s de comparaison*, degrees of comparison; *angle de soixante ~s*, angle of sixty degrees; *équation du troisième ~*, equation of the third degree; *par ~s*, gradually.
dégréer (degree), v.a. (naut.) To unrig.
dégressi-f, -ve (degrɛsif), adj. Progressively diminishing.
dégrèvement (degrɛvmɑ̃), s.m. Abatement, reduction (of taxes).
dégrever (degrəve), v.a. [*dé*+*grever*] To reduce (a tax); to free (a property) from encumbrance; to disburden.
dégringolade (degrɛ̃gɔlad), s.f. Tumbling-down, tumble, come-down, fall; (fig.) ruin.
dégringoler (degrɛ̃gɔle), v.n.a. [etym. unkn.] To topple down, to tumble down, to fall; to come down.
dégriser (degrize), v.a. [*dé*+*griser*] To sober, to bring to one's senses; **se ~**, v.pr. to sober down.
dégrossir (degrosir), v.a. [*dé*+*grossir*] To rough-hew, to shape out, to form, to dress, to trim off, to clear up (an affair), to make a rough sketch of; (fig.) to polish, to fashion, to educate, to lick into shape.
dégrossissage (degrosisaʒ), s.m. Rough-hewing; trimming, dressing.
(se) dégrouiller (sədegruje), v.pr. (slang) To get a move on; see SE GROUILLER.
déguenillé, -e (degnije), adj. [f. *guenille*] Ragged, in rags, tattered. **~**, s.m.f. Ragged person, tatterdemalion.
déguerpir (degɛrpir), v.n. [f. OF *guerpir*] (law) To give up, to quit; to decamp, to pack off; to show a clean pair of heels, to take to one's heels; *faire ~*, to oust, to turn out of doors.
dégueuler (degœle), v.n.a. See DÉGOBILLER.
dégueulasse (degœlas), adj. (slang) Unpleasant, not amusing; repulsive, filthy, rotten.
déguignonner, désenguignonner (degiɲɔne, dezɑ̃giɲɔne), v.a. [f. *guignon*] To bring better luck to, to change or put an end to the ill-luck of.
déguisement (degizmɑ̃), s.m. Disguise; fancy dress; *prendre un ~*, to put on a disguise; *sans ~*, openly.
déguiser (degize), v.a. [f. *guise*] To disguise, to hide, to conceal; *~ sa pensée*, to dissemble one's thought; **se ~**, v.pr. to disguise oneself (*en*, as); to put on a fancy dress.
dégustat-eur, -rice (degystatœr), s.m.f. Taster.
dégustation (degysta'sjɔ̃), s.f. Tasting (of wines, &c.).
déguster (degyste), v.a. [L *degustare*] To taste (wines, &c.), to sip, to drink slowly and with pleasure.
déhanchement (deɑ̃ʃmɑ̃), s.m. [f. *hanche*] Waddling gait, contortion.
déhancher, v.a.n. and (se) déhancher (sədeɑ̃ʃe), v.pr. To waddle in walking, to assume loose airs, to walk wantonly.
déharnacher (deɑrnaʃe), v.a. [*dé*+*harnacher*] To unharness.
déhiscence (deissɑ̃s), s.f. (bot.) Dehiscence.
déhiscent, -e (deissɑ̃), adj. [f. L *dehiscere*] (bot.) Dehiscent.
dehors (dəɔr), adv. [*de*+*hors*] Outside, out, out of doors, in the open, on the outside, abroad; (naut.) in the offing; *toutes voiles ~*, all sails spread; *mettre ~*, to turn out; *au ~*, outside, abroad; *de ~*, from without; *du ~*, from the outside, from abroad; *en ~*, on the outside, outwards; frank; *en ~ de*, outside of, beyond, without; apart from; *par ~*, on the outside (of), outside (of). **~**, s.m. Outside, exterior, appearance; foreign countries; *des ~ trompeurs*, deceitful appearances.
déicide (deisid), adj. s.m.f. [f. L *deus*+*caedere*] Deicide.
déification (deifika'sjɔ̃), s.f. Deification.
déifier (deifje), v.a. [f. L *deus*+*facere*] To deify.
déisme (deism), s.m. [f. L *deus*] Deism.
déiste (deist), s.m.f. Deist. **~**, adj. Deistic, deistical.
déité (deite), s.f. [L *deitas*] Deity, divinity, goddess.
déjà (deʒa), adv. [*dès*+*jà*] Already, even now, previously, before some past time; before this; so quick; *pas ~ si bête*, not so very stupid after all.
déjection (deʒɛksjɔ̃), s.f. [L *dejectio*] Dejection ⚠; evacuation, motion; *~s*, excrements. ⚠ In English the usual

meaning of 'dejection' is 'despondency', 'low spirits' = *abattement mélancolique, idées noires.*

déjeter (deʒte), v.a. To warp, to make crooked; **se** ~, v.pr. to deviate, to warp.

déjettement (deʒɛtmɑ̃), s.m. Warping, deviation.

déjeuner (deʒøne), s.m. **1.** Breakfast; **2.** luncheon, lunch; **3.** breakfast-service; (fig.) ~ *de soleil,* fugitive colour.

déjeuner (deʒøne), v.n. [*dé+jeûner*] **1.** To breakfast; **2.** to take lunch; to lunch.

déjoindre (deʒwɛ̃dr), v.a. See DISJOINDRE.

déjouer (deʒue), v.a. [*dé+jouer*] To foil, to baffle, to counteract, to thwart.

déjuger (deʒyʒe), v.a. To annul (a judgement); **se** ~, v.pr. to recant one's opinion, to take up a contrary attitude.

delà (dəla), prep. [*de+là*] Beyond, further than, on the other side of; *au* ~, farther, beyond, more; *l'au* ~, s.m. eternity; *au* ~ *de,* beyond; *en* ~, beyond; *par* ~, beyond, farther.

délabré, -e (delɑbre), p. adj. Ruinous, dilapidated, in ruins, shattered; in rags, tattered, disordered, crumbling.

délabrement (delɑbrəmɑ̃), s.m. Dilapidated state, decay, wretched state, ruin, tattered state.

délabrer (delɑbre), v.a. [uncert. orig.] To shatter, to dilapidate, to ruin, to reduce to tatters, to tatter; **se,** ~ v.pr. to decay, to fall to pieces, to crumble.

délacer (delase), v.a. [*dé+lacer*] To unlace; **se** ~, v. pr. to unlace oneself; to come unlaced.

délai (delɛ), s.m. [f. L *delatio*] Delay, postponement, reprieve, fixed time, time allowed; *à bref* ~, at short notice; *dans le plus bref* ~, with the least possible delay; *dans un* ~ *de,* within; *user de* ~*s,* to procrastinate.

délaissé, -e (delɛse), p. adj. s.m.f. Forsaken, abandoned, forlorn (person).

délaissement (delɛsmɑ̃), s.m. Abandonment, forlornness, destitution.

délaisser (delɛse), v.a. [*dé+laisser*] To abandon, to neglect, to desert, to forsake, to quit, to relinquish.

délassement (delɑsmɑ̃), s.m. Recreation, relaxation, entertainment, pastime.

délasser (delɑse), v.a. [*dé+lasser*] To refresh, to rest, to relax; **se** ~, v.pr. to refresh oneself, to rest, to unbend one's mind, to be entertained.

délat-eur, -rice (delatœr), s.m.f. adj. (That is an) informer.

délation (dela'sjɔ̃), s.f. [L *delatio*] Information, delation, secret accusation.

délaver (delave), v.a. [*dé+laver*] To dilute, to soak, to make washy or faint in colour.

délayage, délayement, délaiement (delɛjaʒ, delɛmɑ̃), s.m. Dilution; (fig.) excessive dilution, verbosity.

délayer (delɛje), v.a. [f. L *diluere*] To dilute, to make weak, to mix with a liquid; (fig.) to spin out.

délébile (delebil), adj. [L *delebilis*] Delible, effaceable.

délectable (delɛktabl), adj. Delectable.

délectation (delɛkta'sjɔ̃), s.f. Delectation, delight.

délecter (delɛkte), v.a. [L *delectare*] To delight; **se** ~, v.pr. to delight, to take delight (*à,* in).

délégation (delega'sjɔ̃), s.f. Delegation, commission; (law) assignment.

délégué, -e (delege), p. adj. Delegated. ~, s.m.f. Delegate, deputy, proxy.

déléguer (delege), v.a. [f. L *de+legare*] To delegate, to assign, to mandate, to depute.

délestage (delɛstaʒ), s.m. Unballasting.

délester (delɛste), v.a. To unballast.

délétère (deletɛr), adj. [f. Gr. *dēlētērios*] Deleterious, pernicious.

délibérant, -e (deliberɑ̃), p. adj. Deliberative.

délibérati-f, -ve (deliberatif), adj. Deliberative.

délibération (delibera'sjɔ̃), s.f. Deliberation, resolution, decision; *mettre en* ~, to bring under deliberation; *prendre une* ~, to take a resolution.

délibéré (delibere), s.m. (law) Deliberation. ~, **-e,** p. adj. Deliberate, free, easy, bold; *de propos* ~, deliberately, on purpose.

délibérément (deliberemɑ̃), adv. Deliberately, resolutely.

délibérer (delibere), v.n. [L *deliberare*] To deliberate, to ponder, to debate, to resolve; ~, v.a. to bring under deliberation or discussion, to deliberate, to resolve on.

délicat, -e (delika), adj. [L *delicatus*] **1.** Delicate, refined, sensitive; **2.** feeble, weak, soft, easily injured; **3.** fastidious, difficult to please, dainty; *faire le* ~, to be over-nice, to be very particular.

délicatement (delikatmɑ̃), adv. Delicately, gently, daintily, tenderly.

délicatesse (delikatɛs), s.f. **1.** Delicacy, refinement, nicety; **2.** weakness, delicateness, frailty; **3.** fastidiousness, squeamishness; **4.** daintiness, softness, delicate management; **5.** *être en* ~ *avec X,* to be slightly at variance with X; **6.** (pl.) dainties, delicacies.

délice (delis), s.m. **délices** (delis), s.f.pl. [f. L *deliciae*] Delight, delights; *faire les* ~*s de,* to delight.

délicieusement (delisjøzmɑ̃), adv. Deliciously, delightfully.

délicieu-x, -se (delisjø), adj. Delicious, delightful, highly pleasing, sweet.

délicoter (delikɔte), v.a. [f. *licou*] To take off the halter of (a horse).

délictueu-x, -se (deliktɥø), [f. L *delictum*] adj. Guilty; felonious.
délié, -e (delje), p. adj. Slender, slim, fine, subtle, sharp, glib, voluble, loose; *avoir l'esprit* ~, to have a subtle mind; *avoir la langue* ~*e*, to have a glib (or loose) tongue, to be voluble, to have the gift of the gab. ~, s.m. Thin stroke, up-stroke, hair-stroke (in writing).
déliement (delimɑ̃), s.m. Untying.
délien, -ne (deljɛ̃), adj. s.m.f. Delian, of Delos.
délier (delje), v.a. [*dé*+*lier*] To untie, to unbind, to loosen, to unfasten; to free, to release, to absolve; ~ *d'un serment*, to release from an oath.
délimitation (delimita'sjɔ̃), s.f. Delimitation, settling the boundaries, marking the limits.
délimiter (delimite), v.a. [*dé*+*limiter*] To settle the boundaries of, to mark the limits of, to delimit.
délinéation (delinea'sjɔ̃), s.f. [f. L *delineare*] Delineation.
délinquant, -e (delɛ̃kɑ̃), s.m.f. [f. L *delinquere*] Offender; (law) delinquent.
déliquescence (delikɥɛsɑ̃s), s.f. [f. L *deliquescere*] Deliquescence.
déliquescent, -e (delikɥɛsɑ̃), adj. (chem.) Deliquescent.
délirant, -e (delirɑ̃), p. adj. Delirious, frantic, frenzied, rapturous.
délire (delir), s.m. [L *delirium*] Delirium; deliriousness, frenzy, towering rage; *avoir le* ~, to be delirious; *le* ~ *de la passion*, the frenzy of passion.
délirer (delire), v.n. To be delirious, to rave.
delirium tremens (delirjɔmtremɛ̃s), s.m. [L wd] Delirium tremens.
délit (deli), s.m. [L *delictum*] Offence, delinquency, misdemeanour; *en flagrant* ~, in the very act, red-handed; 'in flagrante delicto'; *le corps du* ~ the substance of the offence; *commettre un* ~, to commit an offence.
déliter (delite), v.a. [f. *lit*] (mason.) To lay (a stone) contrary to its cleaving grain; to split, to shale off.
délivrance (delivrɑ̃s), s.f. Deliverance, delivery, release; childbirth.
délivre (delivr), s.m. [f. *délivrer*] After-birth, secundine, placenta.
délivrer (delivre), v.a. [f. L *de*+*liberare*] To free, to release, to deliver, to set free, to rid.
déloger (delɔʒe), v.a. [*dé*+*loger*] To dislodge, to turn out, to oust, to expel; ~, v.n. to decamp, to move off; ~ *sans tambour ni trompette*, to steal away, to leave without beat of drum.
déloyal, -e, (aux) (delwajal), adj. Disloyal, dishonest, unfair.
déloyalement (delwajalmɑ̃), adv. Disloyally, dishonestly, unfairly, faithlessly.
déloyauté (delwajote), s.f. Disloyalty, treachery, unfairness.
delta (dɛlta), s.m. [f. Gr. letter] Delta.
deltoïde (dɛltɔid), adj. s.m. [f. Gr. *delta* +*eidos*] Deltoid.
déluge (delyʒ), s.m. [L *diluvium*] Deluge, flood; *passons au* ~, let us proceed.
déluré, -e (delyre), adj. [f. *déleurré*] Knowing, smart, sharp, wide-awake, cute, shrewd, no fool.
délustrer (dɛlystre), v.a. To take the gloss off.
démagogie (demagɔʒi), s.f. [f. Gr. *dēmagōgia*] Demagogy.
démagogique (demagɔʒik), adj. Demagogic.
démagogue (demagɔg), s.m.f. Demagogue.
démailloter (demajɔte), v.a. [f. *maillot*] To unswathe.
demain (dəmɛ̃), adv. [f. LL *demane*] To-morrow; *après*-~, the day after to-morrow; ~ *en huit*, to-morrow week; ~ *en quinze*, to-morrow fortnight; *à* ~ *les affaires sérieuses*, time enough for business to-morrow.
démancher (demɑ̃ʃe), v.a. [f. *manche*] To take off the handle of, to break up, to disjoin; **se** ~, v.pr. to come off the handle, to go wrong, to become unhinged.
demande (dəmɑ̃d), s.f. Request, application, call, inquiry, question, proposal; claim, demand. ⚠ 'Demand' has a stronger and narrower sense than *demande*; it means request made as of right, or peremptorily, and also the thing so asked = *exigence*, *requête péremptoire*; *chose exigée*.
demander (dəmɑ̃de), v.a. [f. L *de*+*mandare*] To ask, to inquire; to beg, to beg for, to demand (⚠ see DEMANDE); to request, to beseech, to claim, to require, to apply for, to sue for; to wish, to want; *ne pas* ~ *mieux*, to be willing, to do willingly, to ask nothing better; *on le demande*, he is wanted; *je vous demande un peu!*, did you ever!, fancy!; well now!; **se** ~, v.pr. to wonder; to be asked; *cela ne se demande pas*, (*a*) that is a matter of course; (*b*) that is not a thing to be asked; that is not a proper question.
demandeu-r, -se (dəmɑ̃dœr), s.m.f. Asker, applicant. **demand-eur, -eresse** s.m.f. (law) Applicant, plaintiff, demandant.
démangeaison (demɑ̃ʒɛzɔ̃), s.f. Itching; (fig.) teasing desire, longing, eagerness.
démanger (demɑ̃ʒe), v.n. To itch; (fig.) *la langue lui démange*, he is longing to speak.
démantèlement (demɑ̃tɛlmɑ̃), s.m. Dismantling.
démanteler (demɑ̃tle), v.a. [f. *manteau*] To dismantle.

démantibuler (demɑ̃tibyle), v.a. [f. *mandibule*] To dislocate, to put out of joint, to put out of order.
démarcation (demarka'sjɔ̃), s.f. Demarcation.
démarche (demarʃ), s.f. [f. *marcher*] **1.** Gait, bearing, step, walk; **2.** proceeding, step, application, overture; *faire des ~s pour avoir*, to take steps to obtain.
démarcheur (demarʃœr), s.m. Bank messenger or traveller.
démarquer (demarke), v.a. To take the mark off; to make an unauthorized imitation of; ~, v.n. to lose the mark of its age (of a horse).
démarrage (demaraʒ), s.m. Unmooring (of a ship); starting, moving-off (of a motor-car).
démarrer (demare), v.a. [f. *amarrer*] To unmoor; ~, v.n. to start; to move off.
démarreur (demarœr), s.m. (motor.) Starter.
démasquer (demaske), v.a. To unmask, to expose, to divulge; **se** ~, v.pr. to unmask, to let one's mask fall.
démâter (demɑte), v.a. [*dé* + *mât*] (naut.) To dismast.
démêlé (demɛle), s.m. Dispute, strife, quarrel, contest; *avoir des ~s avec X*, to quarrel with X.
démêler (demɛle), v.a. [*dé*+*mêler*] To disentangle, to unmingle, to comb out (hair); to unravel, to make out, to distinguish, to discover; to contest, to contend; **se** ~, v.pr. to become disentangled; to extricate oneself; to be unravelled, to clear up, to stand out.
démêloir (demɛlwar), s.m. Large-toothed comb.
démêlures (demɛlyr), s.f.pl. Combings.
démembrement (demɑ̃brəmɑ̃), s.m. Dismemberment, division.
démembrer (demɑ̃bre), v.a. [f. *membre*] To dismember, to tear limb from limb, to divide.
déménagement (demenaʒmɑ̃), s.m. Removal, removing, remove, moving, household removal; *voiture de ~*, furniture van.
déménager (demenaʒe), v.n.a. [f. *ménage*] To remove, to move, to move house, to change residence; (pop.) (*a*) to be off; (*b*) to die; (*c*) to be daft, crazy, cracked, barmy; *~ à la cloche de bois*, to shoot the moon, to remove secretly.
déménageur (demenaʒœr), s.m. Furniture remover.
démence (demɑ̃s), s.f. [L *dementia*] Insanity, madness, dementia; *tomber dans la ~*, to become insane, to go off one's head.
(se) démener (sɛdemne), v.pr. To struggle, to wriggle; (fig.) to bestir oneself, to strive hard, to make much ado.
démenti (demɑ̃ti), s.m. Lie, contradiction, denial; *en avoir le ~*, to find oneself wrong, mistaken, or disappointed; *recevoir un ~*, to be met with a flat denial.
démentir (demɑ̃tir), v.n.a. [*dé*+*mentir*] To give the lie (to), to contradict, to deny, to disown, to belie; **se** ~, v.pr. to contradict oneself or each other; (obs. and techn.) to fail, to flag, to give way.
démérite (demerit), s.m. Demerit, unworthiness.
démériter (demerite), v.n. [*dé*+*mériter*] To deserve blame, to forfeit esteem.
démesuré, -e (deməzyre), adj. Immoderate, enormous, excessive, inordinate, huge.
démesurément (deməzyremɑ̃), adv. Beyond all measure, excessively, immoderately, inordinately.
démettre (demɛtr), v.a. [*dé*+*mettre*] To put out of joint, to luxate; to dismiss; (law) to nonsuit; **se** ~, v.pr. to be put out of joint; to resign, to relinquish; *se ~ de ses fonctions*, to resign one's post; *se ~ le bras*, to put one's arm out of joint, to dislocate one's arm.
démeubler (demøble), v.a. To strip of furniture.
(au) demeurant (odəmœrɑ̃), adv. loc. Besides, however, after all, in other respects.
demeure (dəmœr), s.f. [f. *demeurer*] **1.** Delay, waiting, deferring; *mettre en ~*, to call upon (a person) to; to demand; to put in suit; *il n'y a pas péril en la ~*, there is no immediate danger; *à ~*, permanently, for good; fixed; **2.** abode, residence, dwelling.
demeurer (dəmœre), v.n. [L *demorari*] **1.** To reside, to dwell, to live; **2.** to stay, to tarry, to remain; *~ en reste*, to be behindhand; *j'en demeure d'accord*, I agree; *demeurons-en là*, no more of that, let's go no further; let us say no more about it; *~ court*, to stop short, to break down.
demi, -e (dəmi), adj. [f. L *dimidius*] Half; (in compounds) half, demi-, semi-; *à ~*, half, by half, by halves, partly, slightly; *ne pas faire les choses à ~*, not to do things by halves, not to stop half-way; to go through with the business; to be thorough; *une heure et ~e*, an hour and a half; half past one; *une ~-heure*, half an hour; *à trompeur, trompeur et ~*, set a thief to catch a thief. ~, s.m. (pop.) Glass of beer, 'a pint'. **~e**, s.f. Half-hour; *sonner les ~es*, to strike the half-hours. *~-cercle*, s.m. semicircle; *~-gros*, s.m. wholesale in small quantities; *~-jour*, s.m. twilight, subdued light; *~-monde*, s.m. demi-monde,

gay world, dissolute society; *~-mondaine*, s.f. woman of doubtful reputation; *comprendre à ~-mot*, to take a hint; *~-pensionnaire*, s.m.f. half-boarder; *~-place*, s.f. half-price; *~-sang*, s.m. half-blood, half-breed; *~-solde*, s.f. half pay; *~-solde*, s.m. officer on half pay; *~-soupir*, s.m. quaver rest; *~-ton*, s.m. semitone, half-tone; *~-tour*, s.m. half-turn; *~-tour à droite !*, right about face !; *à ~-voix*, in an undertone.

démission (demisjɔ̃), s.f. Resignation; *donner sa ~*, to resign.

démissionnaire (demisjɔnɛr), s.m.f. Resigner. ~, adj. That has resigned.

démissionner (demisjɔne), v.n. To resign.

démobiliser (demɔbilize), v.a. (mil.) To demobilize.

démocrate (demɔkrat), s.m.f. [f. Gr. *dēmos* + *kratos*] Democrat. ~, adj. Democratic.

démocratie (demɔkrasi), s.f. Democracy.

démocratique (demɔkratik), adj. Democratic.

démocratiquement (demɔkratikmɑ̃), adv. Democratically.

démocratiser (demɔkratize), v.a. To democratize.

démodé, -e (demɔde), p. adj. Out of fashion, old-fashioned, antiquated.

(se) démoder (sədemɔde), v.pr. [f. *mode*] To go out of fashion.

démographie (demɔgrafi), s.f. [f. Gr. *dēmos*+*graphē*] Demography.

démographique (demɔgrafik), adj. Demographic.

demoiselle (dəmwazɛl), s.f. [f. LL *dominicella*] **1.** Young lady, miss, girl, unmarried lady, spinster, (Lit. or jest.) damsel; *rester ~*, to remain single; **2.** (ent.) dragon-fly; **3.** (ornith.) demoiselle crane, Numidian crane; **4.** paving-beetle.

démolir (demɔlir), v.a. [f. L *demoliri*] To demolish.

démolisseur (demɔlisœr), s.m. Demolisher.

démolition (demɔlisjɔ̃), s.f. **1.** Demolition, pulling-down; **2.** old building materials, builders' rubbish, rubble.

démon (demɔ̃), s.m. [Gr. *daimōn*] Devil, demon, fiend, sprite, imp, spirit; *c'est un vrai ~ !*, he is a regular devil !; *c'est un petit ~*, he is a little imp.

démonétisation (demɔnetiza'sjɔ̃), s.f. Demonetization.

démonétiser (demɔnetize), v.a. [f. *monnaie*] To demonetize; **se ~**, v.pr. to become demonetized; to cheapen oneself.

démoniaque (demɔnjak), adj. Demoniac, demoniacal. ~, s.m.f. Demoniac, madman, madwoman.

démonologie (demɔnɔlɔʒi), s.f. Demonology.

démonstrateur (demɔ̃stratœr), s.m. Demonstrator, teacher, professor.

démonstrati-f, -ve (demɔ̃stratif), adj. **1.** Demonstrative, conclusive; (gram.) *adjectif ~*, demonstrative adjective; **2.** gushing, demonstrative.

démonstration (demɔ̃stra'sjɔ̃), s.f. [L *demonstratio*] Demonstration.

démonstrativement (demɔ̃strativmɑ̃), adv. Demonstratively, convincingly.

démontable (demɔ̃tabl), adj. That can be taken to pieces; removable; detachable; *jante ~*, detachable rim.

démontage (demɔ̃taʒ), s.m. Taking to pieces, taking down, removing.

démonté, -e (demɔ̃te), p. adj. **1.** Dismounted; **2.** abashed, nonplussed; **3.** raging (sea).

démonte-pneu (demɔ̃tpnø), s.m. (pl. *démonte-pneus*) Tyre-lever.

démonter (demɔ̃te), v.a. **1.** To dismount, to unseat, unhorse; **2.** to disjoint, to take to pieces; to unset (gems), to detach; **3.** to confound, to baffle, to abash, to nonplus; **se ~**, v.pr. to be taken to pieces; to be baffled, to be put out of countenance.

démontrable (demɔ̃trabl), adj. Demonstrable.

démontrer (demɔ̃tre), v.a. [L *demonstrare*] To demonstrate, to prove; to indicate; **se ~**, v.pr. to be demonstrated.

démoralisant, -e (demɔralizɑ̃), p. adj. Demoralizing.

démoralisat-eur, -rice (demɔralizatœr), adj. Demoralizing.

démoralisation (demɔraliza'sjɔ̃), s.f. Demoralization.

démoraliser (demɔralize), v.a. To demoralize, to dishearten, to dispirit; **se ~**, v.pr. to become demoralized, disheartened, dispirited, &c.; to be downhearted, to lose heart.

démordre (demɔrdr), v.n. [*dé*+*mordre*] To let go, to loose one's hold, to give up; *n'en pas ~*, to stick to it; not to give it up.

démotique (demɔtik), adj. (ant.) Demotic.

démoucheter (demuʃte), v.a. (fenc.) To uncap, to unbutton (a foil).

démoulage (demulaʒ), s.m. [f. *démouler*] Removing from the mould.

démouler (demule), v.a. [*dé*+*mouler*] To remove from the mould.

démultiplication (demyltiplika'sjɔ̃), s.f. Reduction-gearing.

démultiplié, -e (demyltiplije), adj. Geared down.

démunir (demynir), v.a. To deprive of, to degarnish; **se ~**, v.pr. to deprive oneself (of); to part with one's money.

démuseler (demyzle), v.a. To unmuzzle.

dénantir (denɑ̃tir), v.a. To deprive of securities; **se ~**, v.pr. to deprive oneself.

dénationaliser (denasjɔnalize), v.a. To denationalize.

dénatter (denate), v.a. [f. *natte*] To unmat, to unplait, to untress.
dénaturaliser (denatyralize), v.a. To denaturalize.
dénaturation (denatyra'sjɔ̃), s.f. Sophistication; adulteration.
dénaturé, -e (denatyre), p. adj. Unnatural, monstrous; denatured; *alcool* ~, methylated spirit.
dénaturer (denatyre), v.a. [f. *nature*] To alter the nature of, to distort; to adulterate to misrepresent, to misconstrue; **se** ~, v.pr. to be adulterated, distorted, &c.
dendrite (dɑ̃drit), s.f. [f. Gr. *dendron*] Dendrite (fossil).
dénégation (denega'sjɔ̃), s.f. [f. L *denegare*] Denial.
déni (deni), s.m. [f. *dénier*] Denial, refusal.
déniaiser (denjɛze), v.a. [f. *niais*] To sharpen the wits of, to gull, to strip of innocence or candour, to render less innocent or simple; **se** ~, v.pr. to get sharp, to become artful, cunning; to wake up, to lose one's candour.
dénicher (deniʃe), v.a. [f. *nid*] To take out of its nest; (fig.) to hunt out, to find out, to discover; ~, v.n. to fly from the nest, to be off.
dénicheu-r, -se (deniʃœr), s.m.f. Bird's-nester; (fig.) hunter, seeker.
denier (dənje), s.m. [f. L *denarius*] **1.** (ant.) Denarius; **2.** denier (old Fr. coin); **3.** (fig.) farthing, mite; *le* ~ *de la veuve*, the widow's mite; *le* ~ *de St Pierre*, Peter's pence; ~ *à Dieu*, gratuity; **4.** money, funds; *les* ~*s publics*, the public funds; *à beaux* ~*s comptants*, in ready money.
dénier (denje), v.a. [L *denegare*] To deny, to disown, to refuse to grant.
dénigrement (denigrəmɑ̃), s.m. Disparagement, depreciation.
dénigrer (denigre), v.a. [L *denigrare*] To disparage, to decry, to run down, to denigrate.
dénigreu-r, -se (denigrœr), s.m.f. Disparager.
dénivellation (denivɛla'sjɔ̃), s.f. **dénivellement** (denivɛlmɑ̃), s.m. Difference of level; unevenness of soil.
dénombrement (denɔ̃brəmɑ̃), s.m. Numbering, census, enumeration.
dénombrer (denɔ̃bre), v.a. [*dé*+*nombrer*] To number, to count, to enumerate.
dénominateur (denɔminatœr), s.m. (arith.) Denominator.
dénomination (denɔmina'sjɔ̃), s.f. [L *denominatio*] Denomination, appellation, name.
dénommer (denɔme), v.a. [L *denominare*] To denominate, to name.
dénoncer (denɔ̃se), v.a. [L *denuntiare*] **1.** To denounce, to denunciate, to inform against, (pop.) to tell on, to peach upon; **2.** to denounce, to give notice of.
dénonciat-eur, -rice (denɔ̃sjatœr), s.m.f. Denunciator, informer, accuser.
dénonciation (denɔ̃sja'sjɔ̃), s.f. **1.** Denouncement, denunciation, notice; **2.** information, denunciation, accusation.
dénoter (denɔte), v.a. [*dé*+*noter*] To denote, to indicate, to show.
dénouement (denumɑ̃), s.m. [f. *dénouer*] Dénouement, winding-up, issue, end, unravelling of plot (of novel or play).
dénouer (denue), v.a. [*dé*+*nouer*] To untie, to unknot, to loosen; (fig.) to unravel, to wind up, to bring to an end; **se** ~, v.pr. to come untied; to clear up, to be unravelled, to be wound up.
denrée (dɑ̃re), s.f. [f. LL *denariata*] Food, produce, ware, article of food, provisions.
dense (dɑ̃s), adj. [L *densus*] Dense, compact, thick. ⚠ In English 'dense' is often used in fig. and pej. sense = *bête, de compréhension lente.*
densité (dɑ̃site), s.f. [L *densitas*] Density.
dent (dɑ̃), s.f. [L *dens*] **1.** Tooth (pl. teeth), fang; ~ *de lait*, milk-tooth; ~ *de sagesse*, wisdom tooth; *faire ses* ~*s*, to cut one's teeth; *avoir mal aux* ~*s*, to have toothache; *grincer des* ~*s*, to gnash the teeth; *être armé jusqu'aux* ~*s*, to be armed to the teeth; *manger du bout des* ~*s*, to eat very little, without appetite; *avoir les* ~*s longues*, to be very hungry; *ne pas perdre un coup de* ~, to eat greedily; *il claque des* ~*s*, his teeth chatter; *n'avoir rien à se mettre sous la* ~, to have nothing to eat; *ne pas desserrer les* ~*s*, not to speak a word; to keep silent; *rire du bout des* ~*s*, to sham laughing; to laugh insincerely; (fig.) *avoir une* ~ *contre X*, to have a grudge against X; *déchirer à belles* ~*s*, to tear to pieces, to slander; *montrer les* ~*s*, to threaten; *prendre le mors aux* ~*s*, to get the bit between its teeth; to bolt; **2.** notch, cog, scallop.
dentaire (dɑ̃tɛr), adj. Dental, dentary. ~, s.f. (bot.) Dentaria.
dental, -e, (aux) (dɑ̃tal), adj. Dental. ~**e**, s.f. (phon.) Dental.
denté, -e (dɑ̃te), p. adj. Toothed, cogged; *roue* ~*e*, cog-wheel; *feuille* ~*e*, dentate leaf.
dentelé, -e (dɑ̃tle), p. adj. Notched, jagged, scalloped.
denteler (dɑ̃tle), v.a. To jag, to notch, to indent, to scallop.
dentelle (dɑ̃tɛl), s.f. [f. *dent*] Lace, lace-work.
dentelli-er, -ère (dɑ̃tɛlje), s.m.f. Lace-maker.
dentelure (dɑ̃tlyr), s.f. Denticulation, indentation, notching, scallop.

denter (dɑ̃te), v.a. To cog, to tooth.
denticule (dɑ̃tikyl), s.m.f. Denticle.
denticulé, -e (dɑ̃tikyle), adj. Denticulate.
dentier (dɑ̃tje), s.m. Set of (artificial) teeth, denture.
dentifrice (dɑ̃tifris), s.m. Dentifrice. ~, adj. Tooth-; *poudre* ~, tooth-powder.
dentiste (dɑ̃tist), s.m.f. Dentist.
dentisterie (dɑ̃tistəri), s.f. Dentistry.
dentition (dɑ̃tisjɔ̃), s.f. Dentition, teething, cutting of the teeth; teeth.
denture (dɑ̃tyr), s.f. Teeth, set of teeth, denture.
dénudation (denyda'sjɔ̃), s.f. Denudation.
dénuder (denyde), v.a. [L *denudare*] To denude, to strip, to lay bare, to bare; to bark (a tree); **se** ~, v.pr. to become denuded; to uncover oneself.
dénué, -e (denɥe), p. adj. Destitute, devoid (*de*, of); wanting (*de*, in).
dénuement (denymɑ̃), s.m. Destitution, extreme poverty.
dénuer (denɥe), v.a. [f. L *denudare*] To deprive, to leave destitute; **se** ~, v.pr. to deprive oneself.
dépailler (depɑje), v.a. To strip of straw.
dépannage (depanaʒ), s.m. (motor.) Fetching or repairing of a car left on the road after a breakdown.
dépanner (depane), v.a. (*a*) To repair a motor-car on the road; (*b*) to bring to a garage a motor-car left on the road after a breakdown.
dépaqueter (depakte), v.a. To unpack, to open.
dépareillé, -e (deparɛje), p. adj. Unmatched, odd, incomplete, imperfect.
dépareiller (deparɛje), v.a. [f. *pareil*] To unmatch, to spoil a set or a pair of.
déparer (depare), v.a. [f. *dé+parer*] To spoil, to disfigure, to mar, to spoil the look of.
déparier (deparje), v.a. To spoil the set of, to take away one of a pair of.
déparler (deparle), v.n. [*dé+parler*] To leave off speaking.
départ (depar), s.m. [f. *partir*] **1.** Departure, leaving, starting; **2.** [f. *départir*] separation, distinction, sorting; *faire le* ~ *entre*, to sort; to make a distinction between.
départager (departaʒe), v.a. To settle by a casting vote; to attribute to each one his due share of; to attribute to (each) his due share.
département (departəmɑ̃), s.m. Department, territorial and administrative subdivision; allotment of business or duty; (comm.) line.
départemental, -e, (aux) (departəmɑ̃tal), adj. Departmental.
départir (departir), v.a. [f. L *de+partiri*] To allot, to grant, to dispense, to divide, to apportion; **se** ~, v.pr. to give up, to desist, to swerve (from).
dépasser (depɑse), v.a.n. [*dé+passer*] To pass, to go beyond, to exceed, to overreach, to surpass, to excel, to project outward, to be longer than; ~ *les bornes*, to go too far; ~ *à la course*, to outstrip, to outrun; (colloq.) *voilà qui me dépasse !*, that beats me !, that's beyond me !
dépaver (depave), v.a. To unpave.
dépayser (depɛize), v.a. To send from home, to take out of one's element, environment, country, &c.; to throw off one's guard, to bewilder; **se** ~, v.pr. to leave one's home, one's country, to give up one's habits.
dépeçage, dépècement (depəsaʒ, depɛsmɑ̃), s.m. Cutting-up, carving, breaking-up (of old boats).
dépecer (depəse), v.a. [f. *pièce*] To cut up, to carve, to break up (old boats).
dépêche (depɛʃ), s.f. Dispatch, message; telegram.
(à) dépêche-compagnon (adepɛʃkɔ̃paɲɔ̃), loc. adv. Hurriedly, carelessly.
dépêcher (depɛʃe), v.a. [f. LL *dispedicare*] To dispatch, to send away in haste; to kill; ~, v.n. to make haste; *dépêchez !*, be quick !; **se** ~, v.pr. to hasten, to make haste, to hurry.
dépeigné, -e (depɛɲe), p. adj. Uncombed, unkempt, disordered (hair).
dépeindre (depɛ̃dr), v.a. [*dé+peindre*] To depict, to describe.
dépenaillé, -e (depnɑje), adj. [f. OF *penaillon*] In rags, ragged, in tatters, ill-clad, untidy in one's dress.
dépendance (depɑ̃dɑ̃s), s.f. [f. *dépendre*] Dependence, dependency, subordination; ~s, pl. appendages, outhouses, appurtenances.
dépendant, -e (depɑ̃dɑ̃), p. adj. Dependent. ~, s.m.f. Dependant, dependent, subordinate.
dépendre (depɑ̃dr), v.n. [f. L *dependere*] To depend, to be dependent, to result, to belong; *cela ne dépend pas de vous*, that does not depend upon you; *ne* ~ *que de soi*, to depend on nobody but oneself; ~, v.a. to unhang, to take down.
dépens (depɑ̃), s.m. (usually in pl.) [f. L *dispensum*] Costs, expense; *aux* ~ *de X*, at X's expense.
dépense (depɑ̃s), s.f. [f. L *dispensum*] **1.** Expense, expenditure; *se mettre en* ~, to go to expense; **2.** larder, pantry, steward's room.
dépenser (depɑ̃se), v.a.n. **1.** To spend; **2.** to consume, to waste; **se** ~, v.pr. (*a*) to be spent; (*b*) to strive, not to spare or grudge one's efforts, to exert oneself.

dépensi-er, -ère (depɑ̃sje), adj. Extravagant, prodigal, spendthrift. ~, s.m. In colleges, convents, communities, &c. domestic bursar; (naut.) purser.
déperdition (depɛrdisjɔ̃), s.f. [f. L *deperdere*] Deperdition, waste, loss, leakage.
dépérir (deperir), v.n. [L *deperire*] To decline, to pine away, to decay, to perish, to waste away.
dépérissement (deperismɑ̃), s.m. Decline, pining-away, decay, withering, perishing.
dépêtrer (depɛtre), v.a.n. To extricate; **se** ~, v.pr. to extricate oneself (*de*, from), to disentangle oneself (from), to get rid (of).
dépeuplement (depœpləmɑ̃), s.m. Depopulation; thinning (of a wood); destruction (of game).
dépeupler (depœple), v.a. To depopulate; to thin (a wood); to destroy (game); **se** ~, v.pr. to be depopulated.
dépilatoire (depilatwar), s.m. adj. [f. L *depilare*] Depilatory.
dépiquer (depike), v.a. [*dé*+*piquer*] To unstitch, to unquilt; (agric.) to shell; to tread out (corn); (gard.) to transplant; syn. REPIQUER.
dépister (depiste), v.a. [f. *piste*] **1.** To track, to ferret out, to hunt out; **2.** to put off the track.
dépit (depi), s.m. [f. L *despicere*] Spite, despite, vexation, rancour; *en* ~ *de*, in spite of.
dépiter (depite), v.a. To vex, to spite; **se** ~, v.pr. to fret (*de*, at).
déplacé, -e (deplase), p. adj. Out of one's or its place or element; in bad taste, ill-timed, inopportune, improper, amiss, uncalled for.
déplacement (deplasmɑ̃), s.m. Displacement, displacing, removal, change of place; journey, travelling; appointment to another post.
déplacer (deplase), v.a. [*dé*+*placer*] To displace, to move, to shift, to change, to appoint to another post, to take the place of (a person); *vous déplacez la question*, you change the ground of the question; **se** ~, v.pr. to change one's residence, to leave one's seat, to walk; to travel.
déplaire (deplɛr), v.n. [*dé*+*plaire*] To displease, to give offence, to incur displeasure, to be unpleasant; *ne vous déplaise*, with all due deference to you; by your leave; **se** ~, v.pr. (*a*) to displease each other; (*b*) to find no pleasure, to thrive ill.
déplaisant, -e (deplɛzɑ̃), p. adj. Unpleasant, unpleasing, displeasing.
déplaisir (deplɛzir), s.m. Displeasure, dissatisfaction, dislike, annoyance.
déplanter (deplɑ̃te), v.a. [*dé*+*planter*] To displant.
déplâtrer (deplɑtre), v.a. To unplaster.
déplèti-f, -ve (depletif), adj. (med.) Depletory, depletive.
déplétion (deplesjɔ̃), s.f. [f. L *deplere*] (med.) Depletion.
déplier (deplie), v.a. [*dé*+*plier*] To unfold, to lay out, to spread out, to show (goods); **se** ~, v.pr. to come unfolded.
déplissage (deplisaʒ), s.m. Unplaiting, unpleating.
déplisser (deplise), v.a. [*dé*+*plisser*] To unplait, to unpleat; **se** ~, v.pr. to come unpleated, or out of pleat.
déploiement (deplwamɑ̃), s.m. Unfolding, unfurling (of a flag), deploy; array, show, exhibition, display.
déplorable (deplɔrabl), adj. Deplorable; lamentable, wretched.
déplorablement (deplɔrabləmɑ̃), adv. Deplorably, lamentably, wretchedly.
déplorer (deplɔre), v.a. [L *deplorare*] To deplore, to lament, to bewail.
déployer (deplwaje), v.a. [*dé*+*ployer*] To display, to spread, to unfold, to unfurl, to unroll, to show, to exhibit; *rire à gorge déployée*, to laugh boisterously; **se** ~, v.pr. to come unfolded, unfurled, &c.; to display itself.
déplumer (deplyme), v.a. [*dé*+*plumer*] To unplume, to displume, to strip of feathers; **se** ~, v.pr. (fam.) to grow bald.
dépoli, -e (depɔli), p. adj. Without its polish, rough, ground; *verre* ~, ground glass.
dépolir (depɔlir), v.a. To take off the polish of, to rough, to grind (glass).
déponent, -e (depɔnɑ̃), adj. [L *deponens*] (gram.) Deponent.
dépopulation (depɔpyla'sjɔ̃), s.f. Depopulation.
déportation (depɔrta'sjɔ̃), s.f. Transportation, deportation.
déporté, -e (depɔrte), p. adj. Transported, deported. ~, s.m.f. Transport, convict.
déportement (depɔrtmɑ̃), s.m. (usually in the pl.) **1.** Deportment, behaviour, ways; **2.** misconduct.
déporter (depɔrte), v.a. To transport.
déposant, -e (depozɑ̃), p. adj. **1.** Deposing; **2.** bearing witness. ~, **-e**, s.m.f. **1.** Depositor; **2.** deponent.
déposer (depoze), v.a. [*dé*+*poser*] **1.** To put down, to set down, to lay down, to lay aside, to leave; **2.** to deposit; **3.** ~, v.n. to give evidence, to depose; **se** ~, v.pr. (of a liquid) to settle, to leave a deposit; *modèle déposé*, patent, patented pattern or invention; trade-mark protection.
dépositaire (depozitɛr), s.m.f. Trustee, depositary.
déposition (depozisjɔ̃), s.f. **1.** Deposition, deposal, divestiture; **2.** testimony, deposition.

déposséder (deposede), v.a. [*dé+posséder*] To dispossess.
dépossession (depɔsɛsjɔ̃), s.f. Dispossession.
dépôt (depo), s.m. [L *depositum*] **1.** Depositing; **2.** deposit; **3.** repository; **4.** (mil.) depot; **5.** temporary prison, lock-up; *mandat de* ~, detainer; **6.** store-room or -house; warehouse, depository; *en* ~, (*a*) on sale; (*b*) in safe keeping; in custody; **7.** (of liquids) settling; deposit.
dépoter (depɔte), v.a. **1.** To unpot (a plant); **2.** to decant.
dépotoir (depɔtwar), s.m. Cesspool; sewage-farm, night-soil deposit.
dépouille (depuj), s.f. [f. *dépouiller*] **1.** Skin, hide, slough (of a serpent); spoil; **2.** remains, mortal remains; **3.** (pl.) effects, wardrobe, spoil, plunder, booty; *se parer des* ~*s d'autrui*, to adorn oneself with the spoils of others.
dépouillement (depujmɑ̃), s.m. **1.** Spoliation, stripping; **2.** counting, summing-up (of votes by ballot).
dépouiller (depuje), v.a. [L *despoliare*] To skin, to strip off, to unclothe, to strip, to deprive, to spoil, to rob, to plunder; ~ *sa correspondance*, to go through one's letters; **2.** to count, to sum up (votes); **se** ~, v.pr. to shed its skin; to divest oneself (*de*, of), to renounce, to deprive oneself, to lay aside; to become lighter (as wine).
dépourvu, -e (depurvy), adj. Unprovided, destitute; *être pris au* ~, to be taken unawares.
dépravation (deprava'sjɔ̃), s.f. Depravation, corruption, depravity.
dépraver (deprave), v.a. [L *depravare*] To deprave, to corrupt; **se** ~, v.pr. to become depraved.
déprécati-f, -ve (deprekatif), adj. Deprecatory.
déprécation (depreka'sjɔ̃), s.f. Deprecation, beseeching.
dépréciat-eur, -rice (depresjatœr), s.m.f. Depreciator. ~, adj. Depreciatory.
dépréciation (depresja'sjɔ̃), s.f. Depreciation.
déprécier (depresje), v.a. [f. L *depretiare*] To depreciate, to underrate, to disparage, to belittle, to cheapen.
déprédat-eur, -rice (depredatœr), s.m.f. Depredator, plunderer. ~, adj. Depredatory, predatory.
déprédation (depreda'sjɔ̃), s.f. [L *depraedatio*] Depredation, plunder, damage; malversation.
déprendre (deprɑ̃dr), v.a. [*dé+prendre*] To part, to separate; **se** ~, v.pr. to detach oneself, to disengage oneself, to extricate oneself.
dépression (deprɛsjɔ̃), s.f. [L *depressio*] Depression.
déprimer (deprime), v.a. [L *deprimere*] To depress; **se** ~, v.pr. to become depressed.
dépuceler (depysle), v.a. [f. *pucelle*] To deflower.
depuis (dəpɥi), prep. Since, from, for, after; ago, past; ~ *longtemps*, long since, long ago, for a long while; ~ *lors*, ever since; ~ *peu*, lately, not long ago, a little while since; ~ *quand?*, since when?, since what time?, how long?; ~ *quelque temps*, for some time past, for some time. ~, adv. Since, from that time, ever since. ~ **que**, loc. conj. Since.
dépurati-f, -ve (depyratif), adj. s.m. Depurative.
dépuration (depyra'sjɔ̃), s.f. Depuration.
dépurer (depyre), v.a. [f. LL *depurare*] To depurate, to purify.
députation (depyta'sjɔ̃), s.f. [f. L *deputare*] **1.** Deputation, delegation; **2.** deputyship, seat in parliament.
député (depyte), s.m. Deputy, member of the (French) parliament.
députer (depyte), v.a.n. [f. L *deputare*] To depute, to delegate; to send a deputation.
déracinement (derasinmɑ̃), s.m. Uprooting, extirpation.
déraciner (derasine), v.a. [f. *racine*] To uproot, to root up, to extirpate; **se** ~, v.pr. to be uprooted, to be eradicated.
dérader (derade), v.n. [f. *rade*] (naut.) To leave the anchorage.
dérager (deraʒe), v.n. To cease to be furious; *il ne dérage pas*, he is always furious, or in a rage.
déraidir (derɛdir), v.a. [*dé+raidir*] To unstiffen, to make pliant; **se** ~, v.pr. to lose one's or its stiffness.
déraillement (derajmɑ̃), s.m. Derailment, running off the rails.
dérailler (deraje), v.n.a. [f. *rail*] To derail, to run off the rails; *faire* ~, to throw off the rails; (colloq.) to rave, to be off one's nut.
déraison (derɛzɔ̃), s.f. [*dé+raison*] Unreason, unreasonableness, folly.
déraisonnable (derɛzɔnabl), adj. Unreasonable, preposterous, foolish, unwise.
déraisonnablement (derɛzɔnabləmɑ̃), adv. Unreasonably, preposterously, unwisely.
déraisonnement (derɛzɔnmɑ̃), s.m. Talking nonsense, wandering.
déraisonner (derɛzɔne), v.n. To talk irrationally, to talk nonsense, to wander, to rave.
dérangé, -e (derɑ̃ʒe), p. adj. **1.** Deranged, out of order; **2.** insane; **3.** sick.
dérangement (derɑ̃ʒmɑ̃), s.m. Derangement, disorder, disturbance, trouble; misconduct, bad state of health or mind; ~ *d'entrailles*, diarrhoea.

déranger (derɑ̃ʒe), v.a. [*dé+ranger*] To derange, to throw into disorder, to disarrange, to put out of order, to disturb, to interfere with, to be in the way of; to distemper, to indispose, to put out of sorts; **se ~**, v.pr. (*a*) to be deranged, to be put out of order; (*b*) to inconvenience oneself, to take the trouble; (*c*) to be deranged, to be mad; to go astray, to lead a fast life.

dérapage (derapaʒ), s.m. Skidding, slipping.

déraper (derape), v.n. [f. LG *rapp*] To skid; (naut.) to trip the anchor.

dératé, -e (derate), p. adj. Deprived of the spleen; lively. **~, -e**, s.m.f. Sharp blade, alert and lively creature; *courir comme un ~*, to run like a greyhound; to go like a shot.

dérater (derate), v.a. [f. *rate*] To take out the spleen of (a dog).

derechef (dərəʃɛf), adv. [OF *chef* = head, top, beginning] Once more, over again, anew, afresh.

déréglé, -e (deregle), p. adj. Irregular, disordered, immoderate, ill-regulated, disorderly, out of order; dissolute; *avoir le pouls ~*, to have an irregular pulse; *conduite ~e*, disorderly conduct; *la pendule est déréglée*, the clock is out of order.

dérèglement (derɛgləmɑ̃), s.m. [f. *dérégler*] **1.** Irregularity, derangement, disturbance; **2.** disorder, dissoluteness; *vivre dans le ~*, to lead a dissolute life.

dérégler (deregle), v.a. [*dé+régler*] To derange, to put out of order; **se ~**, v.pr. to be deranged, to get out of order; to lead a disorderly life.

dérider (deride), v.a. [f. *ride*] To unwrinkle (rare), to smooth; (fig.) to cheer up; **se ~**, v. pr. (fig.) to cheer up, to brighten up. ⚠ *Dérider* cannot be translated by 'to deride', which = *tourner en dérision*.

dérision (derizjɔ̃), s.f. [L *derisio*] Derision, mockery; *objet de ~*, object of derision; *tourner en ~*, to turn into derision, to deride; *c'est une ~ que de*, it is a mockery to.

dérisoire (derizwar), adj. Derisive, derisory, mocking; *à prix ~*, ridiculously cheap, dirt cheap.

dérisoirement (derizwarmɑ̃), adv. Derisively.

dérivati-f, -ve (derivatif), adj. s.m. [f. L *derivativus*] Derivative.

dérivation (deriva'sjɔ̃), s.f. [f. *dériver*] Derivation; (electr.) shunt.

dérive (deriv), s.f. [f. *dériver*] (naut.) Leeway, drift, sliding keel; *en ~*, adrift; *aller à la ~*, (lit. and fig.) to go adrift, to drift away; to drift aimlessly; *ancre de ~*, drag-anchor.

dérivé, -e (derive), p. adj. Derivative. **~**, s.m. (gram.) Derivative. **~e**, s.f. (math.) Derivative.

dériver (derive), v.n. [L *derivare*] **1.** To leave the shore, to drift; **2.** to derive, be derived, proceed, be deduced; **~**, v.a. to divert, turn off, derive.

dermatologie (dɛrmatɔlɔʒi), s.f. [f. Gr. *derma, dermatos + logos*] Dermatology, dermology.

derme (dɛrm), s.m. [f. Gr. *derma*] (anat.) Derm, derma, dermis.

derni-er, -ère (dɛrnje), adj. s.m.f. [f. L *deretro*, OF *derrain*] Latter, last, final, latest, highest, extreme; *l'année ~e*, last year; *la ~e année*, the last year; *ces jours ~s*, within the last few days, quite lately; *traité avec le ~ mépris*, treated with the greatest scorn; *c'est du ~ ridicule!*, it's perfectly ridiculous, it's ridiculous to the highest degree or in the extreme; *ils sont du ~ bien ensemble*, they are on most intimate terms; *en ~ lieu*, last of all, lastly; *mettre la ~e main*, to give the finishing stroke, to put the finishing touches; *en ~ ressort*, as a last resort; *rendre le ~ soupir*, to breathe one's last.

dernièrement (dɛrnjɛrmɑ̃), adv. Lately, of late, recently.

dérobade (derɔbɑd), s.f. Evasion, shuffling excuse.

dérobé, -e (derɔbe), p. adj. **1.** Stolen; **2.** private, hidden, back; *escalier ~*, back-stairs, secret staircase; *à la ~e*, stealthily; *sortir à la ~e*, to steal away; **3.** shelled (as beans).

dérober (derɔbe), v.a. [f. Germ. *rauben*] **1.** To steal, to rob; **2.** to screen, to conceal; **3.** [f. *robe*] to shell, to skin; **se ~**, v.pr. to steal away, to escape, to shirk, to shun.

dérogation (derɔga'sjɔ̃), s.f. [f. *déroger*] Derogation.

déroger (derɔʒe), v.n. [L. *derogare*] **1.** To derogate (*à*, from); **2.** to stoop.

dérouiller (deruje), v.a. [*dé+rouiller*] To rub the rust off, furbish; brighten up; **se ~**, v.pr. lose its rust; (fig.) grow polished, brighten up; get supple and agile again; read up a subject again.

déroulement (derulmɑ̃), s.m. Unrolling, development.

dérouler (derule), v.a. [*dé+rouler*] To unroll, to unfold, to spread out; **se ~**, v.pr. to come unrolled; (fig.) to display itself, to develop.

déroutant, -e (derutɑ̃), p. adj. Baffling, disconcerting.

déroute (derut), s.f. [f. *dérouter*] Rout, defeat, overthrow, ruin; *être en ~*, to be routed; *mettre en ~*, to rout; (fig.) to silence, to beat, to defeat.

dérouter (derute), v.a. [f. *route*] To lead astray, to put out of one's way; (fig.) to baffle, to disconcert, to embarrass, to foil; **se ~**, v.pr. to lose the right way; *se laisser ~*, to be disconcerted, to be foiled or bewildered.

derrière (dɛrjɛr), adv., prep. [f. L *de*+*retro*] Behind, back; (naut.) astern, aft, astern of; *sens devant ~*, hind-before, the wrong side forward; *par ~*, behind; from behind.

derrière (dɛrjɛr), s.m. Hinder part, backside, back, back part, bottom; *le ~ de la tête*, the back of the head; *jambes de ~*, hind legs; *porte de ~*, backdoor; (naut.) stern, poop; (mil.) rear; *tomber sur les ~s de l'ennemi*, to fall on the enemy's rear.

derviche (dɛrviʃ), s.m. [Pers. wd] Dervish.

des (dɛ), art. [contr. of *de les*] **1.** Of the, from the; **2.** some, any.

dès (dɛ), prep. [f. L *de*+*ex*] From, as early as, since; *~ ce soir*, this very evening; *~ demain*, from to-morrow; *~ l'enfance*, from infancy; *~ lors*, from that time, ever since then; even then; therefore, consequently; *~ lors que*, loc. conj., since, as; *~ que*, loc. conj. as soon as; since, as.

(se) désabonner (sədezabɔne), v.pr. To discontinue one's subscription (to a periodical).

désabuser (dezabyze), v.a. [*dés*+*abuser*] To disabuse, to disillusion, to undeceive.

désaccord (dezakɔr), s.m. [*dés*+*accord*] **1.** Dissent, dissension, variance; *être en ~*, to be at variance, to disagree; **2.** (mus.) discord, dissonance.

désaccorder (dezakɔrde), v.a. **1.** To set at variance, to disunite; **2.** to put out of tune; **se ~**, v.pr. to get out of tune.

désaccoupler (dezakuple), v.a. To uncouple, to separate.

désaccoutumer (dezakutyme), v.a. To disaccustom, to break (somebody of doing something); **se ~**, v.pr. to break oneself (*de*, of), to get rid of the habit (of).

désaffecter (dezafɛkte), v.a. To disaffect.

désaffection (dezafɛksjɔ̃), s.f. Disaffection.

désaffectionner (dezafɛksjɔne), v.a. To disaffect; **se ~**, v.pr. to take a dislike to, to lose the affection of.

désagréable (dezagreabl), adj. Disagreeable, unpleasant, offensive.

désagréablement (dezagreabləmɑ̃), adv. Disagreeably, unpleasantly.

désagrégation (dezagrega'sjɔ̃), s.f. Disaggregation, disintegration.

désagréger (dezagreʒe), v.a. To disaggregate; **se ~**, v.pr. to disaggregate, to disintegrate.

désagrément (dezagremɑ̃), s.m. [*dés*+*agrément*] Disagreeableness, unpleasantness, annoyance, discomfort, trouble; *s'attirer des ~s*, to get into trouble. ⚠ Not English 'disagreement' which = *désaccord, différence.*

désaltérer (dezaltere), v.a. [*dés*+*altérer*] To quench the thirst of; (fig.) to refresh; **se ~**, v.pr. to quench one's thirst.

désappointement (dezapwɛ̃tmɑ̃), s.m. Disappointment, failure, miscarriage.

désappointer (dezapwɛ̃te), v.a. To disappoint, to defeat or frustrate the expectation of.

désapprendre (dezaprɑ̃dr), v.a. To forget (what has been learnt).

désapprobat-eur, -rice (dezaprobatœr), adj. Disapproving, disapprobatory. **~**, s.m.f. Disapprover.

désapprobation (dezaprɔba'sjɔ̃), s.f. Disapprobation, disapproval.

désapprobativement (dezaprɔbativmɑ̃), adv. Disapprovingly.

désapproprier (dezaprɔprje), v.a. To dispossess, to divest of property.

désapprouver (dezapruve), v.a. To disapprove of.

désarçonner (dezarsɔne), v.a. To unseat, to throw from the saddle; (fig.) to baffle, to disconcert.

désargenter (dezarʒɑ̃te), v.a. To remove the plating of, to cause to lose its plating; (fig.) to drain of cash; *être fort désargenté*, to be very hard-up; **se ~**, v.pr. to lose its plating; to empty one's purse.

désarmé, -e (dezarme), p. adj. Disarmed, defenceless.

désarmement (dezarməmɑ̃), s.m. Disarmament; (naut.) dismantling, unrigging.

désarmer (dezarme), v.a.n. [*dés*+*armer*] To disarm, to unarm; (fig.) to quell, to appease; to uncock (a gun, pistol, &c.); (naut.) to dismantle, to pay off.

désarroi (dezarwɑ), s.m. [*dés*+*arroi*] Disarray, confusion; *jeter dans le ~*, to throw into confusion.

désarticulation (dezartikyla'sjɔ̃), s.f. Disarticulation, disjointing.

désarticuler (dezartikyle), v.a. To disarticulate, to disjoint.

désassembler (dezasɑ̃ble), v.a. To take to pieces, to disjoint, to take asunder.

désassorti, -e (dezasɔrti), p. adj. Odd, unmatched, ill-sorted, unstocked.

désassortir (dezasɔrtir), v.a. [*dés*+*assortir*] To unmatch, to spoil a set, to unstock.

désastre (dezastr), s.m. [*dés*+*astre* (=*destinée*)] Disaster.

désastreusement (dezastrøzmɑ̃), adv. Disastrously.

désastreu-x, -se (dezastrø), adj. Disastrous, unfortunate, calamitous.

désavantage (dezavɑ̃taʒ), s.m. [*dés*+*avantage*] Disadvantage, detriment; *à son ~*, to one's disadvantage; at a disadvantage.

désavantager (dezavɑ̃taʒe), v.a. To disadvantage, to wrong, to prejudice.

désavantageusement (dezavɑ̃taʒøzmɑ̃), adv. Disadvantageously.

désavantageu-x, -se (dezavɑ̃taʒø), adj. Disadvantageous, detrimental.

désaveu (pl. **-x**) (dezavø), s.m. [*dés+aveu*] Disavowal, denial, disclaiming.

désavouer (dezavwe), v.a. [*dés+avouer*] To disavow, to deny, to disown, to disclaim; ~ *sa signature*, to disown one's signature; ~ *un mandataire*, to disavow an agent.

descellement (desɛlmɑ̃), s.m. Unsealing, unfastening, loosening (of masonry).

desceller (desɛle), v.a. [*de+sceller*] To unseal, to unfasten, to loosen.

descendance (desɑ̃dɑ̃s), s.f. Descent, lineage, posterity.

descendant, -e (desɑ̃dɑ̃), p. adj. Descending, sloping; *marée ~e*, ebb-tide. ~, **-e**, s.m.f. Descendant, scion, offspring.

descendre (desɑ̃dr), v.n. [L *descendere*] To descend, to go down, to come down (or downstairs), to step down or out, to alight; to stoop, to condescend; to spring, to proceed (*de*, from); ~ *de voiture*, to alight from a carriage; *la marée descend*, the tide is ebbing, or going out; *le thermomètre est descendu de trois degrés*, the thermometer has gone down three degrees; ~ *à terre*, to land, to go on shore, *la route descend beaucoup*, the road is very steep; ~, v.a. to take down, to reach down, to go down; (pop.) to kill; to land.

descente (desɑ̃t), s.f. [f. *descendre*] **1.** Descent, going-down, coming-down; **2.** slope, declivity; **3.** landing, disembarkation, alighting; ~ *en feuille morte*, falling leaf descent; ~ *en vrille*, spin, spinning dive; **4.** invasion, irruption, search; ~ *de justice*, domiciliary visit; **5.** taking-down; **6.** (hydr.) pipe; **7.** ~ *de lit*, bedside carpet, mat, or rug.

descripti-f, -ve (deskriptif), adj. Descriptive; *géométrie ~ve*, descriptive geometry.

description (deskripsjɔ̃), s.f. [L. *descriptio*] Description.

déséchouer (dezeʃwe), v.a. [*dés+échouer*] To set afloat, to buoy up.

désembrayer (dezɑ̃brɛje), v.n.a. See DÉBRAYER.

désemparer (dezɑ̃pare), v.n. To leave, to cease, to quit; ~, v.a. (naut.) to disable; *sans* ~, on the spot; at once; there and then; without leaving off.

désemplir (dezɑ̃plir), v.a.n. [*dés+emplir*] To empty in part; *ne pas* ~, to be constantly or always full.

désenchantement (dezɑ̃ʃɑ̃tmɑ̃), s.m. Disenchantment, disappointment.

désenchanter (dezɑ̃ʃɑ̃te), v.a. [*dés+enchanter*] To disenchant, to free from a charm, to disillusion.

désencombrer (dezɑ̃kɔ̃bre), v.a. To disencumber, to clear.

désenfiler (dezɑ̃file), v.a. To unthread; **se** ~, v.pr. to come unstrung.

désenfler (dezɑ̃fle), v.a.n. [*dés+enfler*] To reduce the swelling of; to become less swollen.

désengager (dezɑ̃gaʒe), v.a. [*dés+engager*] To disengage; to free.

désengorger (dezɑ̃gɔrʒe), v.a. [*dés+engorger*] To disgorge; to clear (anything stopped up).

désengrener (dezɑ̃grəne), v.a.n. To disengage, to free; (techn.) to throw out of mesh; to put or throw out of gear.

désenivrer (dezɑ̃nivre), v.a. To sober, to make sober; syn. DÉGRISER.

désenlacer (dezɑ̃lase), v.a. [*dés+enlacer*] To release, to part; **se** ~, v.pr. to come apart, to get free from an embrace.

désennuyer (dezɑ̃nɥije), v.a. To amuse, to drive away (a person's) ennui, tedium; **se** ~, v.pr. to divert oneself, to amuse oneself.

désensorceler (dezɑ̃sɔrsəle), v.a. [*dés+ensorceler*] To unbewitch, to disenchant.

déséquilibré, -e (dezekilibre), p. adj. Unbalanced, (slang) off one's nut.

déséquilibrer (dezekilibre), v.a. To throw out of balance, to disequilibrate.

désert, -e (dezɛr), adj. [L *desertum*] Uninhabited, deserted, unfrequented, desolate, empty.

désert (dezɛr), s.m. Desert, wilderness, solitude; *parler dans le* ~, to be a voice in the wilderness, to speak to deaf ears.

déserter (dezɛrte), v.n.a. To desert, to leave, to abandon, to forsake.

déserteur (dezɛrtœr), s.m. Deserter.

désertion (dezɛrsjɔ̃), s.f. Desertion.

désespérance (dezɛsperɑ̃s), s.f. Despair, hopelessness.

désespérant, -e (dezɛsperɑ̃), p. adj. Disheartening, dispiriting, distressing, provoking, discouraging, not to be emulated.

désespéré, -e (dezɛspere), p. adj. Desperate, hopeless, disconsolate, in despair; *une situation ~e*, a desperate state; *prendre un parti* ~, to take a desperate resolution. ~, **-e**, s.m.f. Desperate person, *se battre en* ~, to fight desperately; *crier comme un* ~, to shout like a madman.

désespérément (dezɛsperemɑ̃), adv. Desperately, despairingly.

désespérer (dezɛspere), v.n. [*dés+espérer*] To despair, to give up expectation or hope, to give up; ~, v.a. to drive to despair; **se** ~, v.pr. to despair, to give way to despair.

désespoir (dezɛspwar), s.m. [*dés+espoir*] Despair, grief, hopelessness, desperation; *être au ~ de*, to be very sorry to; *en ~ de cause*, as a last shift; out of despair, in despair; *tomber dans le* ~, to sink into despair; *mettre au* ~, to drive to despair; ~ *des peintres*, (bot.) London pride.

déshabillage (dezabijaʒ), s.m. Undressing;

(fig.) severe criticism, pulling to pieces.
déshabillé (dezabije), s.m. Dishabille, négligé, negligee, undress; *en* ~, undressed, in dishabille.
déshabiller (dezabije), v.a. [*dés*+*habiller*] To undress, to disrobe; ~ *St Pierre pour habiller St Paul*, to rob Peter to pay Paul; **se** ~, v.pr. to undress, to strip.
déshabituer (dezabitɥe), v.a. [*dés*+*habituer*] To break of a habit; **se** ~ (*de*), v.pr. to break oneself of, to leave off.
désharmonie (dezarmɔni), s.f. Discord, discordance.
déshérence (dezerɑ̃s), s.f. [f. *dés*+L *heres*] Escheat; *tomber en* ~, to escheat.
déshériter (dezerite), v.a. [*dés*+*hériter*] To disinherit.
déshonnête (dezɔnɛt), adj. Indecent, indelicate, dishonest.
déshonnêteté (dezɔnɛtte), s.f. Indecency, dishonesty.
déshonneur (dezɔnœr), s.m. [*dés*+*honneur*] Dishonour, disgrace, opprobrium; *tenir à* ~, to hold as a dishonour; *tomber dans le* ~, to be disgraced.
déshonorant, -e (dezɔnɔrɑ̃), p. adj. Dishonourable, disgraceful, shameful, disreputable.
déshonorer (dezɔnɔre), v.a. To dishonour, to disgrace; **se** ~, v.pr. to dishonour oneself, to disgrace oneself.
desideratum (dezideratɔm) (pl. *desiderata*) [L wd] Desideratum (pl. desiderata).
désignation (deziɲaˈsjɔ̃), s.f. [f. *désigner*] Designation, indication, choice, appointment.
désigner (deziɲe), v.a. [L *designare*] To designate, to indicate, to point out, to hold up (to); to denote; to choose, to appoint, to elect, to name, to nominate.
désillusion (dezilyzjɔ̃), s.f. [*dés*+*illusion*] Disillusion, disillusionment.
désillusionner (dezilyzjɔne), v.a. To disillusion, to disillusionize, to undeceive.
désincorporer (dezɛ̃kɔrpɔre), v.a. [*dés*+*incorporer*] To disincorporate.
désinence (dezinɑ̃s), s.f. [f. L *desinere*] Termination, ending (of a word).
désinfectant, -e (dezɛ̃fɛktɑ̃), p. adj. s.m. Disinfectant.
désinfecter (dezɛ̃fɛkte), v.a. [*dés*+*infecter*] To disinfect.
désinfection (dezɛ̃fɛksjɔ̃), s.f. Disinfection.
désintéressé, -e (dezɛ̃terɛse), p. adj. Disinterested, unselfish, unbias(s)ed, uninterested.
désintéressement (dezɛ̃terɛsmɑ̃), s.m. Disinterestedness.
désintéresser (dezɛ̃terɛse), v.a. [*dés*+*intéresser*] To disinterest (rare), to indemnify, to buy out, to buy the interest (or share) of; **se** ~, v.pr. to lose one's interest (*de*, in), to become indifferent (to).
désinvolte (dezɛ̃vɔlt), adj. [f. It. *disinvolto*] Easy, unconstrained; flippant.
désinvolture (dezɛ̃vɔltyr), s.f. Easy carriage, ease, unconcern, flippancy; *avec* ~, flippantly.
désir (dezir) (the old pronunciation, dəzir, still used, sounds affected), s.m. **1.** Desire, longing, wish; **2.** carnal appetite.
désirable (dezirabl), adj. Desirable.
désirer (dezire), v.a.n. [L *desiderare*] To desire, to wish, to wish for, to long for, to covet; *il serait à* ~ *que*, it would be desirable that; *cela laisse beaucoup à* ~, it is far from satisfactory; it is very imperfect; *se faire* ~, (*a*) to keep people waiting; (*b*) not to make oneself cheap.
désireu-x, -se (dezirø), adj. Desirous, eager, anxious; ~ *de s'instruire*, anxious to learn.
désistement (dezistəmɑ̃), s.m. Desistance; (law) nonsuit.
(se) désister (sədeziste), v.pr. [L *desistere*] To give up, to renounce, to waive, to relinquish (a right or claim). ⚠ Not usually to be translated by 'to desist' which = *cesser* (*de faire, dire*, &c.) and *renoncer* (from) *à*.
desman (dɛsmɑ̃), s.m. (zool.) Desman.
désobéir (dezɔbeir), v.n. [*dés*+*obéir*] To disobey, to refuse to obey; ~ *à son père*, to disobey one's father.
désobéissance (dezɔbeisɑ̃s), s.f. Disobedience, act of disobedience.
désobéissant, -e (dezɔbeisɑ̃), p. adj. Disobedient.
désobligeamment (dezɔbliʒamɑ̃), adv. Disobligingly.
désobligeance (dezɔbliʒɑ̃s), s.f. Disobligingness, unkindness, offensiveness.
désobligeant, -e (dezɔbliʒɑ̃), p. adj. Disobliging, unkind, ungracious.
désobliger (dezɔbliʒe), v.a. [*dés*+*obliger*] To disoblige, to displease.
désobstruer (dezɔbstrɥe), v.a. [*dés*+*obstruer*] To clear, to free from obstruction; (med.) to deobstruct.
désodoriser (dezɔdɔrize), v.a. [*dés*+*odoriser*] To deodorize.
désœuvré, -e (dezøvre), adj. Idle, unemployed, unoccupied. ~, **-e**, s.m.f. Idler.
désœuvrement (dezøvrəmɑ̃), s.m. Inactivity, idleness.
désolant, -e (dezɔlɑ̃), p. adj. Distressing, afflicting, grievous.
désolation (dezɔlaˈsjɔ̃), s.f. **1.** Devastation, ravage; **2.** desolation, grief, disconsolateness.
désoler (dezɔle), v.a. [L *desolare*] **1.** To desolate, to ravage; to ruin; **2.** to afflict, to distress, to desolate; **se** ~, v.pr. to grieve, to be disconsolate; (colloq.) *je suis désolé d'être en retard*, I am very sorry to be late.

désopilant, -e (dezɔpilɑ̃), p. adj. **1.** (obs.) Deobstruent; **2.** funny, droll, comical.
désopiler (dezɔpile), v.a. [*dés*+L *opilare*] **1.** (med.) To deobstruct; **2.** (fam.) *se* ~ *la rate*, to dispel the spleen, to laugh immoderately.
désordonné, -e (dezɔrdɔne), p. adj. Disorderly, irregular, disordered, excessive.
désordonnément (dezɔrdɔnemɑ̃), adv. Intemperately, excessively.
désordonner (dezɔrdɔne), v.a. To throw into disorder, to disturb.
désordre (dezɔrdr), s.m. [*dés*+*ordre*] Disorder, confusion, disturbance, irregularity; devastation; disorderly life, dissoluteness; *vivre dans le* ~, to lead a disorderly life.
désorganisat-eur, -rice (dezɔrganizatœr), adj. Disorganizing. ~, **-rice**, s.m.f. Disorganizer.
désorganisation (dezɔrganiza'sjɔ̃), s.f. Disorganization.
désorganiser (dezɔrganize), v.a. [*dés*+*organiser*] To disorganize; **se** ~, to become disorganized.
désorienter (dezɔrjɑ̃te), v.a. [*dés*+*orienter*] To disorient, to disorientate, to prevent from knowing where the east lies, to lead astray, to make lose one's way; (fig.) to bewilder, to disconcert, to nonplus; *être tout* ~, to be all at sea.
désormais (dezɔrmɛ), adv. [*dés*+*or* (L *hora*)+*mais*(L *magis*)] Henceforth, henceforward, hereafter, in future, from this time.
désossement (dezɔsmɑ̃), s.m. Boning.
désosser (dezɔse), v.a. [f. *os*] To bone, to take out the bones from; (fig.) to take to pieces.
despote (dɛspɔt), s.m. [f. Gr. *despotēs*] Despot. ~, adj. Despotic, tyrannical.
despotique (dɛspɔtik), adj. Despotic.
despotiquement (dɛspɔtikmɑ̃), adv. Despotically.
despotisme (dɛspɔtism), s.m. Despotism.
desquamation (dɛskwama'sjɔ̃), s.f. Desquamation, exfoliation.
desquamer (dɛskwame), v.a.n. [L *desquamare*] To desquamate; **se** ~, v.pr. to desquamate, to scale off.
desquels, desquelles (dɛkɛl), rel. pron. [contr. of *de lesquels*] Of whom, from whom; of which, from which.
dessaisir (desɛzir), v.a. [*des*+*saisir*] To dispossess (of), to disseize (of); **se** ~ (*de*), v.pr. to relinquish, to part with, to give up.
dessaisissement (desɛzismɑ̃), s.m. Relinquishment, dispossessing, giving-up.
dessaisonner (desɛzɔne), v.a. [f. *saison*] (agric.) To alter the rotation of crops on; (hort.) to grow out of season.
dessalé, -e (dɛsale), p. adj. Freshened, soaked, rendered less salt; (slang) wide awake, cute, up to snuff, sharp, crafty, cunning (with a touch of licentiousness). ~, **-e**, s.m.f. Person of this kind.
dessaler (dɛsale), v.a. [*des*+*saler*] To freshen, to soak the salt out of; **se** ~, v.pr. (colloq.) to become sharp, cunning, rather dissolute, or unscrupulous.
dessangler (dɛsɑ̃gle), v.a. [*des*+*sangler*] To ungird, to take the girth off.
desséchant, -e (dɛseʃɑ̃), p. adj. Drying, withering, parching.
dessèchement (dɛsɛʃmɑ̃), s.m. Drying-up, dryness, draining, drainage; withering (of plants), emaciation (of the body); dryness, want of sensibility.
dessécher (dɛseʃe), v.a. [*des*+*sécher*] To dry, to dry up, to parch, to desiccate, to wither, to drain; (fig.) to harden, to dry up, to dull; **se** ~, v.pr. to become dry, to wither, to dry up, to harden.
dessein (dɛsɛ̃), s.m. [f. L *designare*] Design, scheme, intent, purpose, aim; *à* ~, designedly, on purpose; *dans le* ~ *de*, with the intention of.
desseller (dɛsɛle), v.a. [*des*+*seller*] To unsaddle.
desserre (dɛsɛr), s.f. (obs. except in loc.) *Dur à la* ~, close-fisted.
desserrer (dɛsɛre), v.a. [*des*+*serrer*] To loosen, to slacken, to open; to unscrew; (print.) to unlock; ~ *les cordons de sa bourse*, to loosen one's purse-strings; *ne pas* ~ *les dents*, not to utter one word; **se** ~, v.pr. to come loose; to loosen one's clothes.
dessert (dɛsɛr), s.m. [f. *desservir*] Dessert.
desserte (dɛsɛrt), s.f. [f. *desservir*] **1.** Leavings (of a meal); **2.** parochial duties; **3.** *chemin de* ~, by-road, by-way.
dessertir (dɛsɛrtir), v.a. [*des*+*sertir*] To unset (gems, &c.).
desservant (dɛsɛrvɑ̃), s.m. Officiating priest.
desservir (dɛsɛrvir), v.a. [*des*+*servir*] **1.** To clear away, to remove dishes and plates from (a table); **2.** to disserve (rare), to harm, to do an ill office to; **3.** to officiate, to serve; **4.** (of a boat, railway, &c.) to touch at, to stop at, to call at, to ply on, to ply between; to connect.
dessiccation (dɛsika'sjɔ̃), s.f. [L *dessicatio*] Desiccation.
dessiller, déciller (desije), v.a. [*des*+*ciller*] (fig.) To open the eyes of, to undeceive.
dessin (dɛsɛ̃), s.m. [f. *dessiner*] Drawing, sketch, design, pattern, delineation; ~ *à main levée*, free-hand drawing; *un châle à* ~*s*, a figured shawl.
dessinat-eur, -rice (dɛsinatœr), s.m.f. Designer, draughtsman, draughtswoman, pattern-designer.
dessiner (dɛsine), v.a. [f. L *designare*] To draw, to delineate, to sketch; to design;

to set off; **se** ~, v.pr. to develop, to take shape, to stand out in relief, to be delineated; *les événements se dessinent*, events are taking shape, or are developing.

dessoler (dɛsole), v.a. [*des+sole*] **1.** (agric.) To alter the rotation of crops on (fields); **2.** to unsole (a horse, &c.).

dessouder (dɛsude), v.a. [*des+souder*] To unsolder; **se** ~, v.pr. to come unsoldered.

dessoûler, dessaouler (dɛsule), v.a.n. [*des +souler*] To make sober; syn. DÉGRISER.

dessous (dəsu), adv. prep. (obs. as a prep.) [*de+sous*] Under, underneath, below, beneath. **au-~** (*de*), loc. prep. Under, underneath, below, beneath, lower (than), unworthy of, less (than); *une stature au-~ de la moyenne*, a figure below the average height; *au-~ de quarante ans*, under forty; *vendre au-~ du cours*, to sell under the market price; *au-~ du vent*, to leeward; *ci-~*, below, under here; *de ~*, under-; from underneath, from below; *en ~*, underneath; underhand, slyly, in an underhanded way; *là-~*, under there, below, beneath that; *il y a quelque chose là-~*, there is more here than meets the eye; *par-~*, underneath, under. ~, s.m. **1.** Under-part, underside, wrong side; (pl.) underclothing, under-garments, hidden part; *~ de plat*, dish-stand, dish-mat; *connaître le ~ des cartes*, to be in the secret of an affair; **2.** disadvantage; *avoir le ~*, to be worsted, to have the worst of it; *être dans le troisième ~*, to be in very low water.

dessus (dəsy), adv. prep. [*de+sus*] On, upon, over, above, on top; *sens ~ dessous*, upside-down, topsy-turvy; in confusion; *au-~*, above, overhead; upwards; *au-~ de*, above, higher than, over, upwards of, beyond; *au-~ de quarante ans*, above forty; *ci-~*, above; *de ~*, from, from above; *en ~*, above, on top, uppermost; *là-~*, upon that, over that; thereupon, upon which, then; about that, in that, on that point; *par-~*, above, across, over, beyond, *par-~ tout*, above all; *par-~ le marché*, into the bargain, free; *jeter par-~ bord*, to throw overboard, to sacrifice. ~, s.m. Upper part, upper side, top, cover; (fig.) advantage, upper hand; (mus.) soprano, treble; *~ de lit*, bed-cover; (fig.) *le ~ du panier*, the best, the cream, the choicest; *le ~ du vent*, the weather side; *prendre*, or *avoir le ~*, to be uppermost, to get the best of it, to get the upper hand, to recover (from an illness).

destin (dɛstɛ̃), s.m. [f. *destiner*] Destiny, fate, career, course.

destinataire (dɛstinatɛr), s.m.f. Receiver, consignee, addressee, recipient, payee.

destinat-eur, -rice (dɛstinatœr), s.m.f. Sender; (the syn. EXPÉDITEUR is more generally used).

destination (dɛstina'sjɔ̃), s.f. Destination; *arriver à ~*, to arrive at one's destination.

destinée (dɛstine), s.f. Destiny, fate; see DESTIN.

destiner (dɛstine), v.a. [f. L *destinare*] To destine, to doom, to fate, to intend, to mean (for), to reserve (for); **se** ~, v.pr. to be destined (*à*, for), to intend to follow (a profession).

destituer (dɛstitɥe), v.a. [L *destituere*] To dismiss, to discharge, to remove.

destitution (dɛstitysjɔ̃), s.f. Dismissal, removal. ⚠ 'Destitution' in English has usually the meaning of being destitute of resources = *misère*.

destrier (dɛstrje), s.m. [f. L *dextera*] Steed.

destruct-eur, -rice (dɛstryktœr), adj. Destructive, destroying, ruinous. **~, -rice**, s.m.f. Destroyer, weeder-out.

destructi-f, -ve (dɛstryktif), adj. Destructive.

destruction (dɛstryksjɔ̃), s.f. [L *destructio*] Destruction, devastation, overthrow, ruin, killing, destroying.

désu-et, -ète (desɥɛ), adj. [L *desuetus*] Obsolete, fallen into disuse, out of fashion.

désuétude (desɥetyd), s.f. [L *desuetudo*] Desuetude, disuse; *tomber en ~*, to fall into desuetude or disuse, to grow obsolete.

désunion (dezynjɔ̃), s.f. Disunion, disjunction, discord; *mettre la ~ dans une famille*, to set a family at variance.

désunir (dezynir), v.a. [*dés+unir*] To disunite, to disjoin, to set at variance, to separate; **se** ~, v.pr. to be disjointed, to be disunited, to part, to be at variance.

détachage (detaʃaʒ), s.m. Cleaning, scouring, removal of stains.

détaché, -e (detaʃe), p. adj. Detached, separated, let loose, unconnected; *d'un air ~*, in a careless, easy manner.

détachement (detaʃmɑ̃), s.m. **1.** Disengagement, indifference, unconcern; **2.** (mil.) detachment, body of troops.

détacher[1] (detaʃe), v.a. [f. *tache*] To remove the stains from, to clean.

détacher[2] (detaʃe), v.a. [f. *attacher*] To loose, to loosen, to let loose, to untie, to unclasp, to unfasten, to separate, to slip; (mil.) to detach, to send; to take (one's eyes) off; to show off, to delineate; to give (a blow, a kick); **se** ~, v.pr. to get loose, to come undone, untied, unfastened, &c.; to wean oneself; to be separated; to stand out in relief.

détail (detaj), s.m. [f. *détailler*] **1.** Detail, particular, small part or portion; **2.** detailed account; **3.** retail; *magasin de* *gros et de* ~, wholesale and retail shop; *en* ~, (*a*) in detail, by inches, minutely; (*b*) retail, by retail; *pour entrer dans le* ~, to come down to brass tacks.

détaillant, -e (detajɑ̃), s.m.f. Retail dealer, retailer. ~, **-e**, p. adj. Retail.

détailler (detaje), v.a. [*dé+tailler*] **1.** To cut up; **2.** to retail; **3.** to detail, to relate minutely, to observe minutely; (theatr.) to bring out all the best points of (one's part).

détaler (detale), v.a.n. [*dé+étaler*] **1.** To remove (goods) from a shop window; **2.** to scamper away, to show a clean pair of heels, to take to one's heels.

détaxe (detaks), s.f. Reduction of a tax.

détaxer (detakse), v.a. [*dé+taxer*] To reduce a tax on.

détecteur (detɛktœr), s.m. [f. L *de+tegere*] Detector (of Hertzian waves).

détection (detɛksjɔ̃), s.f. Detection.

déteindre (detɛ̃dr), v.n. [*dé+teindre*] To lose its colour, to run, to fade; ~, v.a. to discolour, to fade.

dételer (detle), v.a.n. [f. *atteler*] To take out (the horses from a carriage), to unyoke; (colloq. fig.) to resign oneself to old age and a quiet life.

détendre (detɑ̃dr), v.a. [f. *dé+tendre*] To relax the tension of, to unbend, to slacken, to ease; to expand; **se** ~, v.pr. to relax, to slacken, to rest; to unbend; to expand; to become milder.

détenir (detnir), v.a. [f. L *detinere*] To detain, to withhold, to hold, to detain in prison.

détente (detɑ̃t), s.f. [f. *détendre*] **1.** Trigger; *lâcher la* ~, to pull the trigger; *dur à la* ~, stiff in the trigger; (fig.) close-fisted; **2.** expansion (of gas, steam, &c.); **3.** relaxation, reaction.

détent-eur, -rice (detɑ̃tœr), s.m.f. Holder, detainer.

détention (detɑ̃sjɔ̃), s.f. [f. *détenir*] **1.** Detention, detaining, holding; **2.** imprisonment.

détenu, -e (detny), p. adj. Detained, withheld, imprisoned. ~, **-e**, s.m.f. Prisoner.

détergent, -e (detɛrʒɑ̃), adj. Detergent; syn. DÉTERSIF.

déterger (detɛrʒe), v.a. [L *detergere*] To deterge, to cleanse.

détérioration (deterjɔra'sjɔ̃), s.f. Deterioration, wear and tear, damage.

détériorer (deterjɔre), v.a. [L *deteriorare*] To deteriorate, to mar, to damage, to spoil; **se** ~, v.pr. to deteriorate, to get spoiled.

déterminable (detɛrminabl), adj. Determinable.

déterminant, -e (detɛrminɑ̃), p. adj. Determinative, determinant, decisive. ~, s.m. (math.) Determinant.

déterminati-f, -ve (detɛrminatif), adj. (gram., log.) Determinative. ~, s.m. (gram.) Definitive, determinative.

détermination (detɛrmina'sjɔ̃), s.f. Determination, tendency, resolution, elucidation.

déterminé, -e (detɛrmine), p. adj. **1.** Precise, fixed, determinate; **2.** resolute, bold; **3.** (math.) limited, admitting a limited number of solutions.

déterminer (detɛrmine), v.a. [L *determinare*] **1.** To determine, to limit, to fix, to elucidate, to ascertain; **2.** to settle, to resolve, to cause, to bring about, to persuade; *je l'ai déterminé à faire cela*, I have persuaded him to do that; **se** ~, v.pr. to determine (*à*, to), to resolve (to).

déterminisme (detɛrminism), s.m. Determinism.

déterré, -e, (detɛre), p. adj. Exhumed. ~, **-e**, s.m.f. Disinterred corpse; *pâle comme un* ~, as pale as a corpse, or as white as a sheet, ghastly pale.

déterrer (detɛre), v.a. [f. *terre*] To unearth, to unbury, to exhume, to dig up, to disinter; (fig.) to discover, to ferret out.

détersi-f, -ve (detɛrsif), adj. Detersive, detergent; syn. DÉTERGENT.

détersion (detɛrsjɔ̃), s.f. [f. *déterger*] Detersion.

détestable (detɛstabl), adj. Detestable, hateful, execrable, wretched; *le temps est* ~, the weather is wretched.

détestablement (detɛstabləmɑ̃), adv. Detestably, wretchedly.

détestation (detɛsta'sjɔ̃), s.f. [L *detestatio*] Detestation, abhorrence.

détester (detɛste), v.a. [f. L *detestari*] To detest, to abhor, to loathe, to hate.

détirer (detire), v.a. [*dé+tirer*] To stretch.

détonant, -e (detɔnɑ̃), p. adj. Detonating, explosive.

détonateur (detɔnatœr), s.m. Detonator.

détonation (detɔna'sjɔ̃), s.f. Detonation, report.

detoner (detɔne), v.n. [L *detonare*] To detonate; *faire* ~, to detonate.

détonner (detɔne), v.n. [f. *ton*] (mus.) To sing or play out of tune; (fig.) to jar.

détordre (detɔrdr), v.a. [*dé+tordre*] To untwist; **se** ~, v.pr. to come untwisted.

détorquer (detɔrke), v.a. [L *detorquere*] To distort.

détors, -e (detɔr), adj. Untwisted; *soie* ~*e*, untwisted silk.

détorsion (detɔrsjɔ̃), s.f. Untwisting.

détortiller (detɔrtije), v.a. To untwist.

détour (detur), s.m. [f. *détourner*] Turning, winding, turn, bend; roundabout way, circuitous way; recess; (fig.) subterfuge, evasion, shift, circuitous or roundabout way, dodge; *faire un* ~, to go a roundabout way; (fig.) *être sans* ~, to be straightforward.

détourné, -e (deturne), p. adj. Retired,

unfrequented, indirect; *par des chemins ~s*, by unfrequented by-ways; (fig.) in an indirect way; *reproche ~*, indirect reproach.

détournement (deturnmɑ̃), s.m. **1.** Turning aside; **2.** embezzlement, misappropriation; **3.** abduction.

détourner (deturne), v.a. [*dé+tourner*] **1.** To turn aside, away, or off, to divert, to deviate, to avert, to ward off; *~ un coup*, to ward off a blow; **2.** to embezzle, to misappropriate; **3.** to dissuade, to lead astray; to disturb; *~ X de son travail*, to disturb X in his work, to take X from his work; *~ X du droit chemin*, to lead X astray; **4.** to abduct (a minor); **se ~**, v.pr. to go out of one's way, to swerve; to turn aside or away; to be diverted; to leave.

détracter (detrakte), v.a. [f. L *de+trahere*] To detract.

détract-eur, -rice (detraktœr), s.m.f. Detractor, slanderer. **~, -rice,** adj. Detracting.

détraction (detraksjɔ̃), s.f. (rare) Detraction.

détraqué, -e (detrake), p. adj. Out of order; crazy, barmy, daft. **~, -e,** s.m.f. Crazy person.

détraquement (detrakmɑ̃), s.m. Derangement; derangement of the mind or nerves.

détraquer (detrake), v.a. [*dé*+OF *trac*] To put out of order; to spoil the paces of (a horse); (fig.) to disturb, to derange (the mind, health, &c.); **se ~**, v.pr. to get out of order; to get unsettled.

détrempe (detrɑ̃p), s.f. [f. *détremper*] Distemper, painting in distemper.

détremper (detrɑ̃pe), v.a. [f. L *distemperare*] **1.** To soak, to dilute; **2.** to soften (steel).

détresse (detrɛs), s.f. [f. L *districtum*] Distress, affliction; adversity, danger; *signaux de ~*, signals of distress, S O S messages.

détriment (detrimɑ̃), s.m. [L *detrimentum*] Detriment; *tourner au ~ de X*, to prove detrimental to X.

détritus (detritys), s.m. [L *detritus*] Detritus, rubbish, remains, refuse.

détroit (detrwa), s.m. [f. L *districtus*] Strait, straits, pass, sound; *le ~ de Gibraltar*, the Straits of Gibraltar; *passer le ~ (du Pas de Calais)*, to cross the Channel.

détromper (detrɔ̃pe), v.a. [*dé+tromper*] To undeceive.

détrôner (detrone), v.a. [f. *trône*] To dethrone.

détrousser (detruse), v.a. [*dé+trousser*] **1.** To let down (a dress); **2.** to rob, to plunder.

détrousseur (detrusœr), s.m. Highwayman, robber.

détruire (detrɥir), v.a. [L *destruere*] To destroy, to ruin, to overthrow, to kill; to wipe away, to do away with; **se ~**, v.pr. to kill oneself, to kill each other; to get destroyed.

dette (dɛt), s.f. [f. L *debitum*] Debt; (fig.) debt, obligation; *faire des ~s*, to run into debt; *avoir des ~s*, to be in debt; *acquitter une ~*, to pay or discharge a debt; *qui paye ses ~s s'enrichit*, he who pays his debts grows rich; *~s actives*, assets; *~s passives*, liabilities; *être criblé de ~s*, to be head over ears in debt; *la ~ publique*, the national debt.

deuil (dœj), s.m. [f. L *dolere*] Mourning, sorrow, grief; mourning dress, mourning weeds; the mourners; *prendre le ~*, to go into mourning; *porter le ~ de X*, to be in mourning for X; *quitter le ~*, to leave off mourning; *conduire le ~*, to be chief mourner; *faire son ~ de quelque chose*, to give up something for lost; *petit ~*, light mourning; *demi ~*, half mourning; *grand ~*, deep mourning.

deux (dø, døz before a vowel or a silent *h*), adj. num. [L *duo*] Two; both; (fig.) a few; (at cards or dice) deuce; *le ~ de pique*, the two of spades; *Charles ~*, Charles the Second; *le tome ~*, the second volume; *soixante-~*, sixty-two; *le ~ avril*, the second of April, April 2nd; *~ fois*, twice; *~ à ~*, *~ par ~*, two by two; *de ~ en ~*, every second, every other; *de ~ jours l'un*, every other day; *lequel des ~?*, which of the two? ; *tous les ~*, both, both of them; *je voudrais vous dire ~ mots*, I should like to have just a word with you; *à nous ~!*, let 's have a go at it, I am your man; *piquer des ~*, to spur one's horse; *ne faire ni une ni ~*, to make no bones about it.

deuxième (døzjɛm), adj. num. ord. Second; *au ~*, on the second floor; syn. SECOND.

deuxièmement (døzjɛmmɑ̃), adv. Secondly, in the second place.

deux-points (døpwɛ̃), s.m. invar. (print.) Colon (:).

dévaler (devale), v.a. [f. *val*] To descend (rapidly), to come or run down.

dévaliser (devalize), v.a. [f. *valise*] To rifle, to rob, to plunder.

devancer (dəvɑ̃se), v.a. [f. *devant*] To precede, to outrun, to outwalk, to distance, to get ahead of; (fig.) to anticipate, to forestall, to outdo, to surpass; *~ l'appel*, to enlist before one's time.

devanc-ier, -ière (dəvɑ̃sje), s.m.f. Predecessor; (pl.) ancestors.

devant (dəvɑ̃), prep. adv. Before, (*a*) preceding in time, (*b*) preceding in space; in front of, opposite to, ahead, forward, foremost; in presence of; *aller droit ~ soi*, to go straight on; *~ que*, before; *au ~*, towards, to meet; before; *aller au-~ de ses désirs*, to anticipate his wishes; *ci-~*, formerly, ex-; ci-devant; *de ~*, fore, front; *par ~*, in front; before, in the presence of; *par ~ notaire*, before or in the presence of a notary. ~, s.m. Front, fore-part, foreground; *le ~ d'un édifice*, the front of a building; *~ de chemise*, shirt-front; *jambes de ~*, fore-legs; *~ d'autel*, frontal; *~ de cheminée*, chimney-board; *prendre les ~s*, to go ahead, to get the start of; to be the first to make overtures; to forestall.

devantier, devantiau (pl. **-x**) (dəvɑ̃tje, dəvɑ̃tjo), s.m. (obs.) Apron; dress-front.

devanture (dəvɑ̃tyr), s.f. [f. *devant*] Shop window, shop front.

dévastat-eur, -rice (devastatœr), adj. Devastating. ~, **-rice**, s.m.f. Devastator, destroyer, ravager.

dévastation (devasta'sjɔ̃), s.f. Devastation, ravage.

dévaster (devaste), v.a. [L *devastare*] To devastate, to lay waste, to ravage, to ruin, to desolate, to spoil.

déveine (devɛn), s.f. [f. *veine*] (fam.) Ill luck, run of bad luck; *avoir la ~*, to be down on one's luck.

développable (devlɔpabl), adj. That may be developed, or (geom.) evolved.

développante (devlɔpɑ̃t), adj. f. (geom.) Evolvent, involute.

développée (devlope), s.f. (geom.) Evolute.

développement (devlɔpmɑ̃), s.m. Development, growth, unfolding, unwrapping; display; (geom.) evolution; (bicyc.) distance covered by a bicycle-wheel during one revolution of the pedals; (photo.) development.

développer (devlɔpe), v.a. [*dé*+rad. of *envelopper*] To develop, to unfold, to unwrap, to unravel, to display, to evolve, to expand; **se ~**, v.pr. to develop, to grow, to expand, to spread out.

devenir (dəvənir), v.n. [L *devenire*] To become, to grow, to get, to turn, to turn out; *que devenez-vous?*, what have you been doing with yourself?; *que deviendrai-je?*, what will become of me?; *que ~?*, what is to be done now?; *il ne sait plus que ~*, he does not know which way to turn now; *~ à rien*, to come to nothing; *qu'est-il devenu?*, what has become of him?

devenir (dəvənir), s.m. Evolution, change, eternal transformation, becoming.

dévergondage (devɛrgɔ̃daʒ), s.m. Licentiousness, disorder, shameless profligacy, dissoluteness.

dévergondé, -e (devɛrgɔ̃de), p.adj. Shameless, licentious. ~, **-e**, s.m.f. Shameless person, profligate, rake; (fem.) harlot.

(se) dévergonder (sədevɛrgɔ̃de), v.pr. [f. *vergogne*] To become shameless, licentious, profligate; to lose all sense of shame.

devers (dəvɛr), prep. [*de*+*vers*] On the side of; towards; *par ~*, before; in the possession of; *il a de l'argent par ~ lui*, he has money by him, or, he has money.

dévers, -e (devɛr), adj. [L *deversus*] Leaning, not upright. ~, s.m. Slope, inclination, slant.

déversement (devɛrsmɑ̃), s.m. Inclination, sloping; pouring, flowing.

déverser (devɛrse), v.a. [*dé*+*verser*] **1.** To incline, to lean, to warp, to bend; **2.** to pour, to cause to flow; (fig.) to cast; **se ~**, v.pr. to fall, to flow (into), to run.

déversoir (devɛrswar), s.m. Weir, waste-weir, outlet; overflow.

dévêtir (devɛtir), v.a. [L *disvestire*] To undress, to unclothe, to strip; **se ~**, v.pr. to undress, to strip, to divest oneself, to take off one's clothes.

déviation (devja'sjɔ̃), s.f. [f. *dévier*] Deviation, deflection.

dévidage (devidaʒ), s.m. Winding, reeling.

dévider (devide), v.a. [*dé*+*vider*] To wind, to reel, to wind off, to unwind; (fig.) *~ son histoire*, or *le jars*, to spin one's yarn.

dévidoir (devidwar), s.m. Winder, reel, frame.

dévier (devje), v.a.n. [L *deviare*] To deviate, to swerve.

devin, -eresse (dəvɛ̃, dəvinrɛs), s.m.f. [L *divinus*] Diviner, divineress (rare), pythoness, soothsayer, fortune-teller. ~, s.m. Boa constrictor.

deviner (dəvine), v.a. [f. *devin*] To divine, to guess; to foretell, to understand, to find out.

devinette (dəvinɛt), s.f. Puzzle, riddle, conundrum, enigma, &c.

devis (dəvi), s.m. [f. *deviser*] Estimate; (obs.) chat, conversation.

dévisager (devizaʒe), v.a. [f. *visage*] **1.** To stare at; **2.** (obs.) to disfigure.

devise (dəviz), s.f. [f. *deviser*] **1.** Device, motto, posy; **2.** paper-money.

deviser (dəvize), v.n. [f. LL *divisare*] To chat, to talk leisurely.

dévisser (devise), v.a. [*dé*+*visser*] To unscrew.

dévoiement (devwamɑ̃), s.m. [f. *dévoyer*] Relaxation, diarrhoea; (arch.) sloping (of a pipe).

dévoiler (devwale), v.a. [*dé*+*voiler*] To unveil, to disclose, to unravel.

devoir (dəvwar), v.a. [L *debere*] **1.** To owe, to be indebted for, to be in debt for; **2.** to have to, to be bound to, ought to, must; *je dois le faire*, I must do it; I ought to do it; *fais ce que dois, advienne que* *pourra*, do your duty come what may; **3.** to be bound to (followed by an infinitive); *tout doit finir*, everything is bound to come to an end; *c'est lui qui doit avoir fait cela*, it must have been he who did it; *vous deviez m'écrire*, you were to write to me; *il doit y avoir du gibier ici*, it is likely there is game here; there ought to be game here; *dussé-je être blâmé*, were I to be blamed; even though I should be blamed; *cela se doit*, that ought to be done; *il a dû partir hier*, he was to have left yesterday, he had to leave yesterday; *je crois ~ le faire*, I think it my duty to do it; *il semblait ~ réussir*, he seemed likely to succeed; **se ~**, v.pr. (*a*) to owe each other; (*b*) to owe (it) to oneself; (*c*) to be owing, to be right.

devoir (dəvwar), s.m. **1.** Duty, moral obligation; (pl.) civilities, respects; *se mettre en ~ de*, to endeavour to; *s'acquitter d'un ~*, to discharge a duty; *il est de mon ~ de faire ceci*, it is incumbent on me to do this; *rentrer dans le ~*, to return to one's duty; *rendre ses ~s à X*, to pay one's respects to X; *rendre à X les derniers ~s*, to pay the last honours to X; **2.** task, exercise, work; **3.** (obs.) workmen's association.

dévolu, -e (devɔly), adj. [L *devolutus*] Devolved, awarded. **~**, s.m. Claim, choice; (fig.) *jeter son ~ sur*, to have designs upon; to set one's heart upon; to fix one's choice upon.

dévolution (devɔlysjɔ̃), s.f. Devolution.

dévorant, -e (devɔrɑ̃), p. adj. Devouring, ravenous, voracious; *un appétit ~*, a ravenous appetite; *une soif ~e*, a parching thirst.

dévorat-eur, -rice (devɔratœr), adj. Devouring.

dévorer (devɔre), v.a. [L *devorare*] To devour, to eat up (greedily); (fig.) to consume, to waste, to squander, to destroy; to suppress; *dévoré d'ambition*, eaten up with ambition; *~ des yeux*, to gloat over, to feast one's eyes upon, to stare at; *la fièvre le dévore*, fever preys upon him; *~ son chagrin, ses larmes*, to restrain one's grief, one's tears; *~ un affront*, to pocket an affront, an insult; *~ la route*, to tear along the road.

dévot, -e (devo), adj. [L *devotus*] Devout, pious; bigoted. **~, -e**, s.m.f. Devotee, bigot.

dévotement (devɔtmɑ̃), adv. Devoutly, piously.

dévotieusement (devɔsjøzmɑ̃), adv. Devoutly, reverently.

dévotion (devɔsjɔ̃), s.f. Devotion, devoutness, piety, attachment; *être à la ~ de X*, to be at X's disposal, to be devoted to X; *faire ses ~s*, to perform one's devotions; *il n'est ~ que de jeune prêtre*, a new broom sweeps clean.

dévoué, -e (devwe), p. adj. Devoted, strongly attached, faithful; *votre tout ~*, yours most sincerely, yours truly.

dévouement (devumɑ̃), s.m. Devotedness, devotion, attachment, zeal, faithfulness.

dévouer (devwe), v.a. [*dé+vouer*] To devote, to dedicate; to doom; **se ~**, v.pr. to devote oneself, to dedicate oneself.

dévoyé, -e (devwaje), p. adj. Misled, erring, corrupted. **~, -e**, s.m.f. Stray sheep, corrupted person.

dévoyer (devwaje), v.a. [f. *voie*] To mislead, to lead astray; **se ~**, v.pr. to go astray, to wander from the path of duty.

dextérité (dɛksterite), s.f. [L *dexteritas*] Dexterity; (fig.) adroitness.

dextre (dɛkstr), (archaic) s.f. [L *dextra*] Right hand. **~**, adj. (herald.) Dexter.

dextrement (dɛkstrəmɑ̃), adv. Dexterously, adroitly.

dextrine (dɛkstrin), s.f. (chem.) Dextrin.

dey (de), s.m. [Turk. wd] Dey.

dia (dja), interj. (to horses) Hoy, to the left!; *tirer à hue et à ~*, to pull different ways.

diabète (djabɛt), s.m. [Gr. *diabētēs*] (pathol.) Diabetes.

diabétique (djabetik), adj. Diabetic.

diable (djɑbl), s.m. [f. Gr. *diabolos*] **1.** Devil, deuce, old Nick, dickens; wretch, fellow; *le ~ s'en mêle*, the devil is in it; *c'est le ~ incarné!*, he is a very devil!; *il a le ~ au corps!*, the devil is in him, he is indomitable, he is never tired; *pauvre ~!*, poor wretch!, poor fellow!; *beauté du ~*, bloom of youth; *tirer le ~ par la queue*, to struggle hard for a living, to be as poor as a church mouse, to be in Queer street; *il est bon ~*, he is not a bad fellow; *que ~!*, after all; well now!; *cela ne vaut pas le ~*, it's not worth a button; *faire le ~ à quatre*, to play the devil, to raise Cain; *envoyer au ~, à tous les ~s*, to send to the devil; *que le ~ m'emporte*, devil take me; *c'est au ~ vauvert*, it is very far, a tremendous distance; *à la ~*, in a slipshod way, slapdash; in a haphazard way; *en ~*, devilishly; *c'est là le ~*, that is the devil of it, there is the rub; *ce n'est pas le ~!*, it is not much, it is not so difficult, after all!; *au ~ les importuns!*, confound the bores!; *faire voir le ~ à X*, to play all sorts of tricks on X, to be a plague to X; *loger le ~ dans sa bourse*, not to have a penny in one's purse; *c'est le ~ à confesser!*, there is the deuce to pay!; *tout le ~ et son train!*, the whole paraphernalia; the devil and all!; *comment ~ avez-vous fait?*, how the deuce did you manage?; *où ~ avez-vous pris cela?*, where the deuce did you get that?; *un ~ d'homme*, a devil of a fellow; *~!*, the deuce!, now then!, it's becoming serious!, we shall have to consider this!; **2.** truck, trolley, devil-carriage; **3.** jack-in-the-box. ⚠ The word *diable* is not in the least objectionable in French and can be used freely, whilst 'devil' is better left unsaid.

diablement (djɑbləmɑ̃), adv. Excessively, deucedly, very, awfully, devilishly.

diablerie (djɑbləri), s.f. Devilry, devil's trick.

diablesse (djɑblɛs), s.f. She-devil, fury, devil of a woman.

diablotin (djɑblɔtɛ̃), s.m. **1.** Devilkin, little devil, imp; **2.** (naut.) mizen, topmast staysail.

diabolique (djabɔlik), adj. Diabolical, devilish, infernal, malicious, satanic.

diaboliquement (djabɔlikmɑ̃), adv. Diabolically.

diabolo (djabɔlo), s.m. (game) Diabolo.

diacode (djakɔd), adj. [f. Gr. *dia*+*kōdeia*] (pharm.) Diacodium.

diaconal, -e, (aux) (djakɔnal), adj. Diaconal.

diaconat (djakɔna), s.m. [f. Gr. *diakonos*] Diaconate, deaconship.

diaconesse (djakɔnɛs), s.f. Deaconess.

diacre (djakr), s.m. [f. Gr. *diakonos*] Deacon.

diadème (djadɛm), s.m. [f. Gr. *diadēma*] Diadem; (fig.) *ceindre le ~*, to assume the crown.

diadoque (djadɔk), s.m. [Gr. *diadokhos*] Diadochian, one of the Diadochi (Macedonian generals who divided the empire of Alexander after his death).

diagnose (djagnoz), s.f. [Gr. *diagnōsis*] Diagnosis.

diagnostic (djagnɔstik), s.m. Diagnosis.

diagnostique (djagnɔstik), adj. Diagnostic.

diagnostiquer (djagnɔstike), v.a. To diagnose.

diagonal, -e, (aux) (djagɔnal), adj. [f. Gr. *dia*+*gōnia*] Diagonal. ~, s.f. Diagonal.

diagonalement (djagɔnalmɑ̃), adv. Diagonally.

diagramme (djagram), s.m. [Gr. *diagramma*] Diagram.

dialecte (djalɛkt), s.m. [f. Gr. *dialektos*] Dialect.

dialecticien, -ne (djalɛktisjɛ̃), s.m.f. Dialectician.

dialectique (djalɛktik), s.f. [f. Gr. *dialektikos*] Dialectic. ~, adj. Dialectical.

dialogue (djalɔg), s.m. [f. Gr. *dialogos*] Dialogue.

dialoguer (djalɔge), v.n.a. To converse, to carry on a dialogue; to put in dialogue, to write in dialogue.

dialyse (djaliz), s.f. [Gr. *dialusis*] (chem.) Dialysis.

diamant (djamɑ̃), s.m. [f. Gr. *adamas, adamantos*] Diamond; (by ext.) jewels; *~ de vitrier*, glazer's diamond. ⚠ 'Diamond' = also *carreau* (card-playing).

diamantaire (djamɑ̃tɛr), s.m. Diamond-cutter; diamond-merchant.

diamanter (djamɑ̃te), v.a. To set or to adorn with diamonds; to cause to sparkle like diamonds.

diamantifère (djamɑ̃tifɛr), adj. Diamantiferous.

diamantin, -e (djamɑ̃tɛ̃), adj. Adamantine.

diamétral, -e, (aux) (djametral), adj. Diametrical.

diamétralement (djametralmɑ̃), adv. Diametrically.

diamètre (djamɛtr), s.m. [f. Gr. *diametros*] Diameter.

diane (djan), s.f. [f. Span. *diana*] (mil.) Daylight call, reveille; *battre, sonner la ~*, to beat the reveille.

diantre (djɑ̃tr), interj. [f. *diable*] The deuce, the dickens.

diantrement (djɑ̃trmɑ̃), adv. Deucedly.

diapason (djapazɔ̃), s.m. [f. Gr. *dia pasōn (khordōn)*] **1.** Diapason, pitch, concert pitch; **2.** tuning-fork; *se mettre au ~ de X*, to adapt one's tone to X's.

diaphane (djafan), adj. [f. Gr. *dia*+*phainein*] Diaphanous.

diaphanéité (djafaneite), s.f. Diaphaneity.

diaphorétique (djafɔretik), adj. [f. Gr. *diaphorētikos*] (med.) Diaphoretic; increasing perspiration.

diaphragme (djafragm), s.m. [f. Gr. *diaphragma*] (anat., photo.) Diaphragm.

diapré, -e (djɑpre), p. adj. Diapered, variegated. ~e, s.f. Violet plum.

diaprer (djɑpre), v.a. [f. OF *diapre*, flowered stuff] To diaper, to variegate.

diaprure (djɑpryr), s.f. Diapering.

diarrhée (djare), s.f. [f. Gr. *diarrhoia*] Diarrhoea.

diarrhéique (djareik), adj. Diarrhoeal, diarrhoeic.

diastase (djastɑz), s.f. [f. Gr. *diastasis*] (surg.) Diastasis; (chem.) diastase.

diathèse (djatɛz), s.f. [Gr. *diathesis*] (med.) Diathesis.

diatomées (djatɔme), s.f.pl. (bot.) Diatomaceae; syn. BACILLARIÉES.

diatonique (djatɔnik), adj. [f. Gr. *diatonikos*] Diatonic.

diatribe (djatrib), s.f. [Gr. *diatribē*] Diatribe.

diaule (djol), s.f. [f. Gr. *diaulos*] Double flute, diaulos.

dichotomie (dikɔtɔmi), s.f. [f. Gr. *dikhotomia*] Dichotomy.
dicotylédone, dicotylédoné, -e (dikɔtiledɔn, dikɔtiledɔne), adj. Dicotyledonous. **~s,** s.f.pl. Dicotyledons.
dictame (diktam), s.m. [f. Gr. *diktamnon*] (bot.) Dittany; (fig.) balm, relief, solace.
dictamen (diktamɛn), s.m. [LL wd] Dictates.
dictateur (diktatœr), s.m. [L *dictator*] Dictator.
dictatorial, -e, (aux) (diktatɔrjal), adj. Dictatorial.
dictature (diktatyr), s.f. Dictatorship.
dictée (dikte), s.f. Dictation; *sous la ~,* from dictation.
dicter (dikte), v.a. [L *dictare*] To dictate; (fig.) to suggest, to dictate, to prescribe.
diction (diksjɔ̃), s.f. [L *dictio*] Diction, elocution, delivery.
dictionnaire (diksjɔnɛr), s.m. [f. LL *dictionarium*] Dictionary; *à coups de ~,* by constant reference to a dictionary; *c'est un ~ vivant,* he is a walking dictionary, a very learned person.
dicton (diktɔ̃ and ditɔ̃), s.m. [f. L *dictum*] Saying, maxim, by-word, proverb, saw.
dictum (diktɔm), s.m. (law) Dictum.
didactique (didaktik), adj. [f. Gr. *didaktikos*] Didactic, didactical. **~,** s.f. Didactics.
didactiquement (didaktikmɑ̃), adv. Didactically.
didactyle (didaktil), adj. [*di*+Gr. *daktulos*] (zool.) Didactylous, two-fingered, two-toed.
didelphe (didɛlf), adv. [f. Gr. *di*+*delphus*] (zool.) Didelphic. **~s,** s.m.pl. Didelphia; syn. MARSUPIAUX.
dièdre (diɛdr), s.m. [f. Gr. *di*+*hedra*] Dihedron. ~, adj. Dihedral, diedral.
diélectrique (dielɛktrik), adj. Dielectric, non-conducting.
dièse (djɛz), s.m. [f. Gr. *diesis*] (mus.) Diesis, sharp. ~, adj. Sharp.
diéser (djeze), v.a. (mus.) To sharpen.
diète[1] (djɛt), s.f. [f. Gr. *diaita*] Low diet; *mettre X à la ~,* to diet X; *être à la ~,* to be on a low diet. ⚠ In English the usual sense of 'diet' is *régime, nourriture habituelle,* whilst in French *diète* implies that food is given in small quantity, or not at all.
diète[2] (djɛt), s.f. [f. LL *dieta*] Diet, assembly.
diététique (djetetik), adj. (med.) Dietetic, dietary. ~, s.f. Dietetics.
dieu (pl. **-x**) (djø), s.m. [L *deus*] God, god; deity; idol; *le bon ~,* God, God Almighty; *s'il plaît à ~,* God willing; *~ m'est témoin,* God knows; *~ sait comme,* at random; *plaise à ~,* please God; *plût à ~ que,* would to God that; *à ~ ne plaise,* God forbid; *~ vous bénisse,* God bless you; *~ vous entende!,* God grant it!; *~ vous le rende,* may God reward you for it; *~ merci!,* thank God!; *mon ~!, ah mon ~!,* my God! good God, ! my goodness!, Heavens!; *grand ~!,* good gracious!, great God!; *~ soit loué!,* God be praised!; *oh mon ~, non,* dear me, no; *pour l'amour de ~,* for God's sake, for goodness' sake; *demi ~,* demigod; *~ marin,* sea-god; *comme un ~,* divinely, godlike; *jurer ses grands ~x,* to swear by all that is sacred; *l'argent est le ~ du jour,* money is the idol of our time; *on lui donnerait le bon Dieu sans confession,* she looks as if butter would not melt in her mouth, one would take him at his own estimation; *nom de ~!,* good God!, damn!; I say!, good gracious!
diffamat-eur, -rice (difamatœr), s.m.f. Defamer, slanderer. ~, adj. Defamatory.
diffamation (difama'sjɔ̃), s.f. [L *diffamatio*] Defamation, slander, libel, aspersion.
diffamatoire (difamatwar), adj. Defamatory, slanderous.
diffamer (difame), v.a. [L *diffamare*] To defame, to slander, to libel; (herald.) *lion diffamé,* tailless lion.
différemment (diferamɑ̃), adv. Differently.
différence (diferɑ̃s), s.f. [L *differentia*] **1.** Difference, dissimilarity; **2.** difference, remainder after subtraction; *couper en deux la ~,* to split the difference; *à la ~ de,* contrary to, differently from; *avec cette ~ que,* except that; with the difference that; whilst; whereas; in contrast with.
différenciation (diferɑ̃sja'sjɔ̃), s.f. Differentiation, discrimination.
différencier (diferɑ̃sje), v.a. To differentiate.
différend (diferɑ̃), s.m. Difference, variance, dispute; *faire naître un ~,* to give rise to a quarrel; *avoir un ~ avec X,* to be at variance with X; *régler un ~,* to make up a difference, to settle a quarrel.
différent, -e (diferɑ̃), adj. Different, distinct, dissimilar, unlike, various; several; *~s témoins l'ont dit,* several witnesses have said it; *~ de,* unlike, different from; *ah! c'est ~!,* that's another matter!
différentiel, -le (diferɑ̃sjɛl), adj. (math.) Differential. **~le,** s.f. (math.) Differential. ~, s.m. (motor.) Differential gear, differential; *engrenage ~,* differential wheel.
différentier (diferɑ̃sje), v.a. (math.) To differentiate.
différer (difere), v.a.n. [L *differre*] To defer, to delay, to put off, to postpone;

~, v.n. to differ, to be unlike, to be different.
difficile (difisil), adj. [L *difficilis*] Difficult, troublesome, uneasy, arduous, hard, hard to please, particular, fastidious; ~ *à vivre*, difficult to deal with; of a difficult temper; *faire le* ~, to be hard to please, to play the dainty, to carp, to be squeamish; *il m'est* ~ *de dire*, I can hardly say; *il est* ~ *de répondre*; it's difficult to answer; ~ *à reproduire*, not easily reproduced; difficult to reproduce; *des temps* ~*s*, hard times.
difficilement (difisilmɑ̃), adv. With difficulty; not easily.
difficulté (difikylte), s.f. [L *difficultas*] Difficulty, hindrance, trouble, rub; arduousness; difference, dispute, contention; *faire des* ~*s*, to raise objections; to make difficulties; *avoir des* ~*s avec*, to be at variance with, to have trouble with; *faire* ~ *de*, to scruple to; *trancher la* ~, to resolve or settle the difficulty.
difficultueusement (difikyltɥøzmɑ̃), adv. With difficulty.
difficultueu-x, -se (difikyltɥø), adj. Difficult; hard to please, over-particular, fussy.
difforme (difɔrm), adj. [L *difformis*] Deformed, distorted.
difformité (difɔrmite), s.f. [L *difformitas*] Deformity, distortion, ugliness.
diffracter (difrakte), v.a. [L *diffringere*] (opt.) To diffract.
diffraction (difraksjɔ̃), s.f. (opt.) Diffraction.
diffringent, -e (difrɛ̃ʒɑ̃), adj. Diffractive.
diffus, -e (dify), adj. [L *diffusus*] Diffuse; spread widely; prolix, verbose, long-winded.
diffuser (difyze), v.a. To diffuse, to spread; (wireless) to broadcast.
diffuseur (difyzœr), s.m. (motor.) Sprayer (part of the carburettor).
diffusion (difyzjɔ̃), s.f. Diffusion, diffuseness, dispersion, spreading; (wireless) broadcasting.
digérer (diʒere), v.a.n. [L *digerere*] To digest; (fig.) to stomach, to tolerate, to put up with, to pocket (an affront).
digeste (diʒɛst), s.m. [L *digesta*] Digest.
digesteur (diʒɛstœr), s.m. (chem.) Digester.
digestibilité (diʒɛstibilite), s.f. Digestibility.
digestible (diʒɛstibl), adj. Digestible; syn. DIGÉRABLE.
digesti-f, -ve (diʒɛstif), adj. Digestive.
digestion (diʒɛstjɔ̃), s.f. [L *digestio*] Digestion.
digital, -e, (aux) (diʒital), adj. [f. L *digitus*] (anat.) Digital.
digitale (diʒital), s.f. (bot.) Digitalis, foxglove.
digitaline (diʒitalin), s.f. (chem., pharm.) Digitalin.
digité, -e (diʒite), adj. Digitate; (bot.) digitated.
digitigrade (diʒitigrad), adj. [f. L *digitus*+*gradi*] Digitigrade. ~, s.m. Digitigrade (pl. digitigrada).
digne (diɲ), adj. [L *dignus*] Worthy, dignified, respectable, deserving; ~ *de pitié*, worthy of pity; ~ *de foi*, worthy of belief, deserving of credit, reliable; *vous êtes bien* ~*s l'un de l'autre!*, you are well matched; *avoir un air* ~, to look dignified.
dignement (diɲmɑ̃), adv. Worthily, deservedly, suitably, with dignity.
dignitaire (diɲitɛr), s.m. Officer (of State); dignitary (of the Church).
dignité (diɲite), s.f. [L *dignitas*] Dignity, stateliness, title, elevated rank, honour, worthiness, self-respect; *aspirer aux* ~*s*, to aspire to power and high rank.
digon (digɔ̃), s.m. (naut.) Flag-yard; (fish.) hook.
digressi-f, -ve (digrɛsif), adj. Digressive, digressional.
digression (digrɛsjɔ̃), s.f. [L *digressio*] Digression.
digue (dig), s.f. [f. Dutch *dijk*] Dike, dam; (fig.) barrier, hindrance, check, bulwark.
dilapidat-eur, -rice (dilapidatœr), s.m.f. Misappropriator; waster, squanderer. ~, adj. Dilapidating, extravagant.
dilapidation (dilapidaˈsjɔ̃), s.f. Dilapidation, waste.
dilapider (dilapide), v.a. [L *dilapidare*] To waste, to squander, to dilapidate. ⚠ 'To dilapidate' has a wider sense than *dilapider*; it means *ruiner*, *délabrer*, *se délabrer*; ex.: a dilapidated building, *un bâtiment délabré*, or *tombant en ruine*.
dilatable (dilatabl), adj. Dilatable.
dilatation (dilataˈsjɔ̃), s.f. Dilatation, expansion.
dilater (dilate), v.a. [L *dilatare*] To dilate, to expand; **se** ~, v.pr. to dilate, to expand, to swell; *se* ~ *la rate*, to get very merry, to cheer up.
dilatoire (dilatwar), adj. [L *dilatorius*] Dilatory.
dilection (dilɛksjɔ̃), s.f. [L *dilectio*] Love, affection.
dilemme (dilɛm), s.m. [Gr. *dilēmma*] Dilemma.
dilettante (dilɛttɑ̃t), s.m.f. [It. wd] Dilettante (pl. dilettanti).
dilettantisme (dilɛttɑ̃tism), s.m. Dilettantism.
diligemment (diliʒamɑ̃), adv. Diligently, expeditiously.
diligence (diliʒɑ̃s), s.f. [L *diligentia*] **1.** Diligence, speed; *faire* ~, to make all possible haste; **2.** diligence, coach, stage-coach.

diligent, -e (diliʒɑ̃), adj. Diligent, expeditious, steady, assiduous, quick.
diligenter (diliʒɑ̃te), v.a.n. (rare) To make haste, to hasten.
diluer (dilɥe), v.a. [L *diluere*] To dilute; **se ~**, v.pr. to become diluted.
dilution (dilysjɔ̃), s.f. Dilution.
diluvien, -ne (dilyvjɛ̃), adj. Diluvian; (geol.) diluvial.
diluvium (dilyvjɔm), s.m. [L wd] (geol.) Diluvium.
dimanche (dimɑ̃ʃ), s.m. [f. L *dies dominica*] Sunday; *tel qui rit vendredi, ~ pleurera*, laugh to-day and cry to-morrow.
dîme (dim), s.f. [f. L *decima*] **1.** Tithe; **2.** dime (American silver coin = one-tenth of a dollar).
dimension (dimɑ̃sjɔ̃), s.f. [L *dimensio*] Dimension, size, extent; (alg.) degree; (fig.) *prendre ses ~s*, to make one's calculations, to take necessary measures.
dîmer (dime), v.a.n. To tithe, to take tithe.
diminuer (diminɥe), v.a.n. [L *diminuere*] To diminish, to lessen, to abate, to decrease, to shorten, to reduce; *les jours diminuent*, the days are growing shorter; *la fièvre a diminué*, the fever has abated; *ses forces sont diminuées* or *ont diminué*, he is not so strong as he was.
diminuti-f, -ve (diminytif), adj. s.m. Diminutive.
diminution (diminysjɔ̃), Diminution, decrease, abatement, lessening, reduction.
dinanderie (dinɑ̃dri), s.f. [f. *Dinant*, town in Belgium] Brass wares, copper wares.
dinandier (dinɑ̃dje), s.m. Brazier, coppersmith.
dinar (dinar), s.m. [f. L *denarius*] Dinar: **1.** Arab gold money; **2.** Serbian silver money; **3.** very small Persian (imaginary) coin.
dînatoire (dinatwar), adj. [f. *dîner*] Similar to a dinner, serving as a dinner; *déjeuner ~*, lunch-dinner, midday dinner.
dinde (dɛ̃d), s.f. [f. *poule d'Inde*] Turkey-hen; (fig.) goose, ninny.
dindon (dɛ̃dɔ̃), s.m. [f. *dinde*] Turkey-cock, turkey; *colère comme un ~*, very hasty-tempered, choleric; *être le ~ de la farce*, to be the dupe, the butt, the laughing-stock.
dindonneau (pl. **-x**) (dɛ̃dono), s.m. Young turkey, turkey poult.
dînée (dine), s.f. (obs.) Dinner (eaten during a journey), dining-place.
dîner (dine), v.n. [f. L *disjejunare*] To dine; *avoir du monde à ~*, to give a dinner-party; *qui dort dîne*, he who sleeps, needs no dinner; *~ par cœur*, to dine with Duke Humphrey.
dîner (dine), s.m. Dinner, dinner-party; *~ prié*, dinner-party.
dînette (dinɛt), s.f. Play-dinner, doll's dinner; *faire la ~*, to play at dinner, to eat a light, dainty meal.
dîneu-r, -se (dinœr), s.m.f. Diner, guest.
dingo (dɛ̃go), s.m. Dingo, wild dog; (slang) *être ~*, to be cracked, to be insane, potty, daft, barmy.
dinguer (dɛ̃ge), v.n. (slang) To idle, to loiter, to dance attendance; *envoyer ~ X*, to send X packing; *envoyer ~ un objet*, to fling or throw away a thing.
dinosaurien (dinosorjɛ̃), s.m. [Gr. *deinos* +*saura*] (geol.) Dinosaur.
dinothérium (dinoterjɔm), s.m. [Gr. *deinos*+*thērion*] Dinotherium.
diocésain, -e (djosezɛ̃), adj. s.m. Diocesan.
diocèse (djɔsɛz), s.m. [f. Gr. *dioikēsis*] Diocese.
dioïque (djoik), adj. [f. Gr. *di*(=*dis*)+ *oikos*] (bot.) Dioecious.
dionée (djone), s.f. (bot.) Dionoea, Venus's fly-trap.
dionysiaque (djɔnizjak), adj. [f. Gr. *Dionūsos*] Dionysiac, Dionysian, bacchic. **~s**, s.f.pl. Dionysia.
dioptrie (diɔptri), s.f. [f. Gr. *dioptron*] (phys.) Dioptric: δ, unit of power of magnifying-glasses.
dioptrique (diɔptrik), s.f. Dioptrics. **~**, adj. Dioptric, dioptrical.
diorama (djɔrama), s.m. [Gr. *di*(=*dia*)+ *horama*] Diorama.
diphtérie (difteri), s.f. [f. Gr. *diphthera*] Diphtheria.
diphtérique (difterik), adj. Diphtheric, diphtheritic.
diphtongue (diftɔ̃g), s.f. [f. Gr. *dis*+ *phthoggos*] Diphthong.
diplomate (diplɔmat), s.m. [f. Gr. *diplōma*] Diplomat, diplomatist, envoy, minister. **~**, adj. Diplomatic; persuasive.
diplomatie (diplɔmasi), s.f. Diplomacy; (fig.) skill in negotiating, artful management, persuasiveness.
diplomatique (diplɔmatik), adj. Diplomatic, diplomatical; *le corps ~*, the diplomatic body. **~**, s.f. Diplomatics.
diplomatiquement (diplɔmatikmɑ̃), adv. Diplomatically.
diplôme (diplom), s.m. [f. Gr. *diplōma*] Diploma, college certificate of degree.
diplômé, -e (diplome), p. adj. Graduated, having a diploma; certificated. **~, -e**, s.m.f. Graduate.
dipsomane (dipsoman), s.m.f. adj. Dipsomaniac.
dipsomanie (dipsomani), s.f. [f. Gr. *dipsa*+*mania*] Dipsomania.
diptère (diptɛr), adj. [f. Gr. *dipteros*] (ent.) Dipterous; (arch.) dipteral. **~**, s.m. (arch.) Dipteral, dipteros. **~s**, s.m.pl. (ent.) Diptera.
diptyque (diptik), s.m. [f. Gr. *di*+*ptukhē*] Diptych.

dire (dir), v.a. [L *dicere*] To say, to tell, to speak, to state, to express; to recite, to repeat; *l'art de bien* ~, the art of speaking well; *faire* ~, to send word, to have it said; *dis donc! dites donc!*, I say; do tell me; look here; *aussitôt dit, aussitôt fait*, no sooner said than done; *soit dit en passant*, let it be said, by the way; *que dites-vous de cela?*, what do you think of that?; *se moquer du qu'en dira-t-on*, to laugh at what the world may say; *on dirait qu'il va pleuvoir*, it looks as if it were going to rain; *elle ne se l'est pas fait* ~ *deux fois*, she did not wait to be told twice; she took the hint at once; *vous avez beau* ~, it's no use for you to say; *vous m'en direz tant!*, (*a*) well, if it comes to that!, (*b*) well, that alters the case; *il n'y a pas à* ~, it's not to be denied; there is no denying; say what you will; *il y aurait bien à* ~, much might be said; *que veut* ~ *ce retard?*, what does this delay mean?; *qu'est-ce à dire?*, what do you mean by that?; *trouver à* ~, to find fault; *si le cœur vous en dit*, if you have a mind for it; *cela va sans* ~, of course, that is a matter of course; *c'est à* ~, that is to say; *c'est tout* ~, that is saying everything; that's saying enough; *à* ~ *vrai*, to say truth; *pour mieux* ~, or rather; *pour tout* ~, in a word; *pour ainsi* ~, so to speak; (fam.) *ce n'est pas pour* ~, without boasting, to say truth; *je ne vous dis que ça!*, I can tell you!, you mark my words; it's ripping!; *on le dit savant*, they say he is learned; *je me le suis tenu pour dit*, I took it for granted; I did not ask for more; *soit dit entre nous*, quite between ourselves; *cela vous plaît à* ~, *mais*, that is all very fine, but; *il était dit que je vous rencontrerais*, the Fates had willed that I should meet you; *à qui le dites-vous!*, don't I know it!; (Amer.) you're telling me!; *c'est dit!*, agreed!; (colloq.) *comme qui dirait*, as who should say; sort of; *et* ~ *que*, and to think that . . .; *cela ne me dit rien*, (*a*) I have no desire for it, that does not appeal to me; (*b*) I don't like the look of it; *quand je vous le disais!*, I told you so!; **se** ~, v.pr. to say to each other; to call or style oneself; to pretend to be; to be used; *cela ne se dit pas*, (*a*) that is not good French; (*b*) better not say that.

dire (dir), s.m. Saying, say, statement, account, report; *au* ~ *de X*, by what X says; according to X's account; *au* ~ *de tout le monde*, according to general opinion; *leurs* ~*s ne s'accordent pas*, their statements do not agree.

direct, -e (dirɛkt), adj. [L *directus*] Direct, straight, immediate; (rail.) through.

directement (dirɛktəmɑ̃), adv. Directly, straight, exactly, without circumlocutions, immediately.

direct-eur, -rice (dirɛktœr), s.m.f. [f. L *director*] Director, manager, governor, editor, head master, head mistress; ~ *de conscience*, spiritual director; ~ *général des Postes*, Postmaster general. See also DIRECTRICE. ~, adj. Directing, steering, managing.

direction (dirɛksjɔ̃), s.f. [L *directio*] **1.** Direction, tendency, aim; **2.** management, superintendance, government, guidance; **3.** directorship; **4.** department, jurisdiction; **5.** (motor.) steering-gear.

directive (dirɛktiv), s.f. (usually in the plural) General indications, directions, instructions.

directoire (dirɛktwar), s.m. Directory; (French hist.) supreme executive council of France from 1795 to 1799.

directorat (dirɛktɔra), s.m. Directorship, directorate.

directorial, -e, (aux) (dirɛktɔrjal), adj. Directorial.

directrice (dirɛktris), s.f. Directress, manageress; head, head mistress.

dirigeable (diriʒabl), adj. Dirigible. ~, s.m. Dirigible, balloon, airship.

dirigeant, -e (diriʒɑ̃), p. adj. Directing, leading; *les classes* ~*es*, the leading circles, the upper classes.

diriger (diriʒe), v.a. [L *dirigere*] To direct, to aim, to point; to lead, to guide; to manage, to govern, to conduct; to turn, to bend; to rule, to sway; to march (troops); ~ *les études de X*, to direct, or to superintend, X's studies; ~ *la conscience de X*, to be X's spiritual adviser; ~ *des poursuites contre X*, to take proceedings against X; ~ *son attention de ce côté*, to turn one's attention to this side of the matter; **se** ~, v.pr. to make (*vers*, for); to direct oneself; to be directed.

dirimant, -e (dirimɑ̃), p. adj. Nullifying, invalidating.

dirimer (dirime), v.a. [L *dirimere*] (law) To nullify, to stop, to settle.

discernable (dissɛrnabl), adj. Discernible.

discernement (dissɛrnəmɑ̃), s.m. Discernment: (*a*) act of discerning; (*b*) power of discerning, sagacity, discrimination; *l'âge de* ~, the age of discretion; (law) years of discretion.

discerner (dissɛrne), v.a. [L *discernere*] To discern, to perceive, to discriminate; ~ *la vérité d'avec le faux*, to distinguish between what is true and what is false; ~ *l'ami du flatteur*, to distinguish the friend from the flatterer.

disciple (disipl), s.m. [L *discipulus*] Disciple, pupil, follower.

disciplinable (disiplinabl), adj. Disciplinable, capable of being disciplined.

disciplinaire (disiplinɛr), adj. Disciplinary. ~, s.m. Disciplinarian.

discipline (disiplin), s.f. [L *disciplina*] **1.** Discipline; **2.** whip of discipline, scourge.
discipliner (disipline), v.a. To discipline.
discobole (diskəbəl), s.m. [f. Gr. *diskobolos*] Discobolus.
discontinu, -e (diskɔ̃tiny), p. adj. Discontinuous; (math.) *fonction ~e*, discontinuous function.
discontinuation (diskɔ̃tinɥa'sjɔ̃), s.f. Discontinuance.
discontinuer (diskɔ̃tinɥe), v.a.n. To discontinue, to leave off, to break off; *sans ~*, unceasingly, uninterruptedly.
discontinuité (diskɔ̃tinɥite), s.f. Discontinuity.
disconvenance (diskɔ̃vnɑ̃s), s.f. Unsuitableness, want of proportion.
disconvenir (diskɔ̃vnir), v.n. [*dis+convenir*] To deny, to disown; to be unsuitable; *je n'en disconviens pas*, I do not deny it.
discord (diskɔr), s.m. [f. *discorder*] Strife, dissension. **~**, adj. (obs.) Out of tune, discordant.
discordance (diskɔrdɑ̃s), s.f. Discordance, discord, disagreement; (mus.) discord, dissonance.
discordant, -e (diskɔrdɑ̃), p. adj. Discordant, harsh, inharmonious, out of tune, dissonant; *des opinions ~es*, discordant, or conflicting, opinions.
discorde (diskɔrd), s.f. [L *discordia*] Discord, dissension, strife; *semer la ~*, to sow discord; *entretenir la ~*, to foster discord; *c'est une pomme de ~*, it 's an apple of discord, or a bone of contention.
discorder (diskɔrde), v.n. To disagree, to be discordant.
discoureu-r, -se (diskurœr), s.m.f. Discourser, profuse or voluble talker.
discourir (diskurir), v.n. [L *discurrere*] To discourse, to descant, to expatiate.
discours (diskur), s.m. [L *discursus*] **1.** Discourse, speech, address, harangue, oration, treatise; *prononcer un ~*, to make a speech; *quels ~ tenez-vous là!*, what language!, how can you say such things!; **2.** (gram.) speech; *les neuf parties du ~*, the nine parts of speech.
discourtois, -e (diskurtwɑ), adj. [*dis+courtois*] Discourteous, uncivil.
discourtoisement (diskurtwazmɑ̃), adv. Discourteously, uncivilly.
discrédit (diskredi), s.m. [*dis+crédit*] Discredit, disrepute; *jeter le ~ sur X*, to bring or to throw discredit upon X; *tomber dans le ~*, to fall into disrepute, to be discredited.
discréditer (diskredite), v.a. To discredit, to bring into disrepute, to disgrace; **se ~**, v.pr. to bring discredit upon oneself; to cheapen oneself; to disgrace oneself.
discr-et, -ète (diskrɛ), adj. [L *discretus*] **1.** Discreet, prudent, cautious, reserved, close; **2.** discrete, discontinuous; *quantité ~ète*, discrete quantity. ⚠ 'Discreet' has a wider acceptation than *discret* and means also *judicieux, sage, réfléchi.*
discrètement (diskrɛtmɑ̃), adv. Discreetly, cautiously; reservedly, tactfully.
discrétion (diskresjɔ̃), s.f. [L *discretio*] **1.** Discretion, (⚠ see DISCRET) discreetness, tact, prudence, closeness, caution, wariness; *je laisse cela à votre ~*, I leave that to your judgement; *il faut user de cela avec ~*, one must use that with moderation; *on peut prendre du pain à ~*, we can have bread *ad libitum*, or, as much bread as we want; **2.** mercy, will; *être à la ~ de X*, to be at X's mercy; **3.** (fam.) stake, wager (at the discretion of the winner).
discrétionnaire (diskresjɔnɛr), adj. Discretionary.
discriminant, -e (diskriminɑ̃), p. adj. (alg.) Discriminative. **~**, s.m. (math.) Discriminant.
discrimination (diskrimina'sjɔ̃), s.f. [f. L *discriminare*] Discrimination.
disculpation (diskylpa'sjɔ̃), s.f. Exculpation.
disculper (diskylpe), v.a. [f. L *culpa*] To exculpate, to clear, to exonerate; **se ~**, v.pr. to exculpate oneself.
discursi-f, -ve (diskyrsif), adj. [f. L *discursus*] Discursive.
discussion (diskysjɔ̃), s.f. [L *discussio*] Discussion, debate, examination; disputation, wrangling, dispute, contest; *s'engager dans une ~*, to enter into a discussion; *mettre une question en ~*, to bring a question under discussion.
discutable (diskytabl), adj. Debatable; questionable.
discuter (diskyte), v.a. [L *discutere*] To discuss, to debate, to examine, to question, to argue, to dispute; (law) to distrain upon.
disert, -e (dizɛr), adj. [L *disertus*] Voluble, fluent, eloquent, speaking with fluency and elegance.
disertement (dizɛrtəmɑ̃), adv. In the manner of an accomplished speaker, fluently and elegantly.
disette (dizɛt), s.f. [uncert. orig.] Dearth, want, scarcity.
diseu-r, -se (dizœr), s.m.f. Teller, sayer; *~se de bonne aventure*, fortune-teller; *beau ~*, fine talker; *les grands ~s ne sont pas les faiseurs*, empty vessels make most noise; great talkers are no good doers; much cry and little wool.
disgrâce (disgrɑs), s.f. [*dis+grâce*] Disgrace, disfavour, misfortune; *encourir la ~ de*, to get into disfavour with.

disgracié, -e (disgrasje), p. adj. **1.** Disgraced, out of favour; **2.** ill-favoured, deformed.
disgracier (disgrasje), v.a. To disgrace.
disgracieusement (disgrasjøzmɑ̃), adv. Ungracefully, awkwardly, unpleasantly.
disgracieu-x, -se (disgrasjø), adj. Ungraceful, unsightly, awkward, ungainly.
disjoindre (disʒwɛ̃dr), v.a. [*dis+joindre*] To disjoint, to separate; (law) to sever; **se ~**, v.pr. to become disjointed, disunited, to fall to pieces.
disjoncteur (disʒɔ̃ktœr), s.m. (electr.) Circuit-breaker; (motor) cut-out.
disjoncti-f, -ve (disʒɔ̃ktif), adj. Disjunctive.
disjonction (disʒɔ̃ksjɔ̃), s.f. Disjunction, separation; (law) severance.
dislocation (dislɔka'sjɔ̃), s.f. [f. *disloquer*] Dislocation, taking to pieces; (mil.) breaking-up; (surg.) luxation, dislocation.
disloquer (dislɔke), v.a. [f. L *dis+locare*] To dislocate, to put out of joint, to take to pieces, to luxate; (mil.) to break up; **se ~**, v.pr. to be dislocated, &c.; to get out of order.
disparaître (disparɛtr), v.n. [*dis+paraître*] To disappear, to vanish, to withdraw, to pass away, to die.
disparate (disparat), adj. [L *disparatus*] Disparate, dissimilar, incongruous. **~**, s.f. Dissimilarity; (in the pl.) disparates.
disparité (disparite), s.f. [*dis+parité*] Disparity, inequality.
disparition (disparisjɔ̃), s.f. Disappearance; death.
dispendieusement (dispɑ̃djøzmɑ̃), adv. Expensively.
dispendieu-x, -se (dispɑ̃djø), adj. [L *dispendiosus*] Expensive.
dispensaire (dispɑ̃sɛr), s.m. [f. *dispenser*] Dispensary, dispensatory, pharmacopoeia.
dispensat-eur, -rice (dispɑ̃satœr), s.m.f. [L *dispensator*] Dispenser, dispensator, bestower.
dispensation (dispɑ̃sa'sjɔ̃), s.f. Dispensation, distribution, act of bestowing.
dispense (dispɑ̃s), s.f. Dispensation, exemption, licence.
dispenser (dispɑ̃se), v.a. [L *dispensare*] **1.** To dispense, to deal out, to bestow; **2.** to dispense with, to exempt, to excuse (*de*, from); **se ~** (*de*), v.pr. to exempt oneself from, to dispense with, to spare oneself.
dispersement (dispɛrsmɑ̃), s.m. Scattering; see syn. DISPERSION.
disperser (dispɛrse), v.a. [f. L *dispergere*] To disperse, to scatter, to drive away, to dispel; **se ~**, v.pr. to disperse, to be scattered.
dispersi-f, -ve (dispɛrsif), adj. Dispersive.
dispersion (dispɛrsjɔ̃), s.f. [L *dispersio*] Dispersion, scattering, dispelling.
disponibilité (disponibilite), s.f. Disposability, non-activity; *être en ~*, to be on the unattached list, on the reserve list; **~s**, s.f.pl. disposable funds.
disponible (disponibl), adj. [f. L *disponere*] Disposable, available, unoccupied, free, vacant.
dispos, -e (dispo), adj. [L *disposus*] Nimble, alert, cheerful; *frais et ~*, in good spirits, 'all there'; hale and hearty.
disposer (dispoze), v.a.n. [f. L *disponere*] To dispose, to lay out, to order, to prepare, to incline; *~ de*, to alienate; **se ~** (*à*), v.pr. to prepare (to), to be about (to), to make ready (to).
dispositif (dispozitif), s.m. (law) Purview; arrangement, disposition; contrivance, device; (aeron.) gadget.
disposition (dispozisjɔ̃), s.f. **1.** Disposition, arrangement; **2.** disposal, command; **3.** tendency, turn, taste, aptitude, mind, humour; **4.** (law) provision.
disproportion (disprɔpɔrsjɔ̃), s.f. [*dis+proportion*] Disproportion.
disproportionné, -e (disprɔpɔrsjɔne), p. adj. Disproportionate.
disproportionner (disprɔpɔrsjɔne), v.a. To disproportion, to render disproportionate.
disputailler (dispytaje), v.n. [f. L *disputare*] To wrangle, to squabble, to bicker.
dispute (dispyt), s.f. [f. *disputer*] Dispute, quarrel, bickering, contest; disputation; debate.
disputer (dispyte), v.n.a. [L *disputare*] To dispute, to contest, to oppose, to argue; to vie; to quarrel; **se ~**, v.pr. to quarrel, to dispute, to wrangle, to contest, to claim.
disputeu-r, -se (dispytœr), s.m.f. Disputer, wrangler. **~**, adj. Disputatious.
disqualifier (diskalifje), v.a. [*dis+qualifier*] To disqualify.
disque (disk), s.m. [L *discus*] Disc, disk, discus, quoit; gramophone record; (rail.) signal(-disk).
disquisition (diskizisjɔ̃), s.f. [L *disquisitio*] Disquisition.
disruption (disrypsjɔ̃), s.f. [f. L *dis+rumpere*] Disruption, breach.
dissection (disɛksjɔ̃), s.f. [L *dissectio*] Dissection.
dissemblable (disɑ̃blabl), adj. [f. L *dis+similis*] Dissimilar, unlike; ill-matched.
dissemblance (disɑ̃blɑ̃s), s.f. Dissimilarity, unlikeness.
dissémination (disemina'sjɔ̃), s.f. Dissemination, scattering, propagation, spreading.
disséminer (disemine), v.a. [f. L *dis+seminare*] To disseminate, to scatter, to propagate, to spread; **se ~**, v.pr. to be disseminated.

dissension (disɑ̃sjɔ̃), s.f. [L *dissensio*] Dissension, discord, strife, feud.
dissentiment (disɑ̃timɑ̃), s.m. Dissent, disagreement, quarrel.
disséquer (diseke), v.a. [L *dissecare*] To dissect.
dissertation (disɛrta'sjɔ̃), s.f. [L *dissertatio*] Dissertation, theme, paper, essay.
disserter (disɛrte), v.n. [L *dissertare*] To dissert, to dissertate, to discourse, to descant.
dissidence (disidɑ̃s), s.f. [L *dissidentia*] Dissent, dissidence.
dissident, -e (disidɑ̃), adj. Dissenting; dissident. **~**, s.m.f. Dissenter; dissentient; dissident.
dissimilaire (disimilɛr), adj. [*dis+similaire*] Dissimilar, unlike.
dissimilitude, dissimilarité (disimilityd, disimilarite) s.f. Dissimilarity, dissimilitude.
dissimulation (disimyla'sjɔ̃), s.f. [L *dissimulatio*] Dissimulation, dissembling, double dealing; *user de* **~**, to dissemble, to dissimulate, to make pretence.
dissimulé, -e (disimyle), p. adj. Dissembling, insincere, secretive; hidden.
dissimuler (disimyle), v.a.n. [L *dissimulare*] To dissemble, to conceal, to disguise, to dissimulate; **se ~**, v.pr. (*a*) to conceal oneself; (*b*) to conceal from oneself; (*c*) to conceal from each other.
dissipat-eur, -rice (disipatœr), s.m.f. Spendthrift, squanderer. **~**, adj. Extravagant, wasteful.
dissipation (disipa'sjɔ̃), s.f. [f. *dissiper*] **1.** Dissipation, scattering, dispersion; squandering; **2.** dissipation, frivolous amusement, relaxation; **3.** dissolute or intemperate living.
dissipé, -e (disipe), p. adj. Inattentive; dissipated. ⚠ 'Dissipated' also = *dissolu, débauché*, &c.
dissiper (disipe), v.a. [f. L *dissipare*] To dissipate, to dispel, to squander (money), to fritter away (energy, time, money); to engage in frivolous or dissolute pleasures; **se ~**, v.pr. **1.** to dissolve, to fade away; **2.** to be dissipated; to become inattentive, frivolous.
dissociation (disɔsja'sjɔ̃), s.f. Dissociation.
dissocier (disɔsje), v.a. [L *dissociare*] To dissociate, to disconnect; (chem.) to decompose.
dissolu, -e (disɔly), adj. [L *dissolutus*] Dissolute, lax in morals. **~**, s.m. Profligate.
dissolubilité (disɔlybilite), s.f. Dissolubility.
dissoluble (disɔlybl), adj. [L *dissolubilis*] Dissoluble, dissolvable.
dissolument (disɔlymɑ̃), (rare) adv. Dissolutely, licentiously.
dissolution (disɔlysjɔ̃), s.f. [L *dissolutio*] **1.** Dissolution, disintegration, liquefaction; **2.** (fig.) undoing, disintegration, falling to pieces; **3.** dissoluteness; **4.** (motor. bicyc.) rubber solution.
dissolvant, -e (disɔlvɑ̃), p. adj. s.m. Dissolvent.
dissonance (disɔnɑ̃s), s.f. [f. L *dis+sonare*] Dissonance.
dissonant, -e (disɔnɑ̃), p. adj. Dissonant.
dissoner (disɔne), v.n. To be dissonant.
dissoudre (disudr), v.a. [L *dissolvere*] To dissolve; (fig.) to disperse; to declare the dissolution of (Parliament), to put an end to, to annul; **se ~**, v.pr. to be dissolved, to dissolve.
dissou-s, -te (disu), p. adj. Dissolved; broken up, annulled, ended.
dissuader (disɥade), v.a. [f. L *dis+suadere*] To dissuade (*de*, from).
dissuasi-f, -ve (disɥazif), adj. Dissuasive.
dissuasion (disɥa'zjɔ̃), s.f. Dissuasion.
dissyllabe (disilab), adj. Disyllabic. **~**, s.m. Disyllable.
dissyllabique (disilabik), adj. Disyllabic.
dissymétrie (disimetri), s.f. [*dis+symétrie*] Dissymmetry.
dissymétrique (disimetrik), adj. Dissymmetrical.
distance (distɑ̃s), s.f. [L *distantia*] Distance, remoteness; interval; difference; *tenir à* **~**, to keep at a distance; *garder les* **~***s*, to avoid familiarity, to keep one's distance; *rapprocher les* **~***s*, to lessen social distinctions; *de* **~** *en* **~**, at certain intervals.
distancer (distɑ̃se), v.a. To distance, to leave far behind, to outrun.
distant, -e (distɑ̃), adj. Distant, remote, far apart; **~** *de trois kilomètres*, three kilometres distant; (fig.) reserved, distant.
distendre (distɑ̃dr), v.a. [L *distendere*] To distend; **se ~**, v.pr. to swell out, to be distended.
distension (distɑ̃sjɔ̃), s.f. [f. *distendre*] Distension.
distillateur (distilatœr), s.m. Distiller.
distillation (distila'sjɔ̃), s.f. Distillation.
distiller (distile), v.a.n. [L *distillare*] To distil; to trickle down; (fig.) to distil, to exude.
distillerie (distilri), s.f. **1.** Distillery, still-house; **2.** distilling.
distinct, -e (distɛ̃kt), adj. [f. *distinguer*] Distinct, distinguishable, clear; separate, plain.
distinctement (distɛ̃ktəmɑ̃), adv. Distinctly, clearly.
distincti-f, -ve (distɛ̃ktif), adj. Distinctive.
distinction (distɛ̃ksjɔ̃), s.f. [L *distinctio*] **1.** Distinction, discrimination; division, differentiation, separation; **2.** mark of honour; **3.** distinction, polished manners, gentility, good breeding, individuality.

distingué, -e (distɛ̃ge), adj. Of distinguished air, genteel, elegant, refined; remarkable, distinguished.
distinguer (distɛ̃ge), v.a. [L *distinguere*] **1.** To distinguish, to differentiate, to discriminate, to single out, to take notice of; **2.** to characterize; **se ~**, v.pr. to be distinct; to distinguish oneself, to be characterized (*par*, by).
distique (distik), s.m. [f. Gr. *distikhos*] Distich.
distordre (distɔrdr), v.a. [f. L *dis+ torquere*] To distort.
distors, -e (distɔr), adj. Distorted.
distorsion (distɔrsjɔ̃), s.f. Distortion.
distraction (distraksjɔ̃), s.f. [L *distractio*] **1.** Abstraction, separation, subtraction; **2.** inattention, heedlessness; **3.** diversion, recreation, distraction; relaxation; amusement; *la lecture est la meilleure des ~s*, reading is the best recreation; *par ~*, inadvertently. ⚠ In French *distraction* has never the sense of mental conflict, madness, frenzy, confusion, which is quite usual in English.
distraire (distrɛr), v.a. [f. L *distrahere*] **1.** To subtract, to separate, to divert, to distract; **2.** to amuse, to entertain; **se ~**, v.pr. to amuse oneself, to divert oneself. ⚠ See DISTRACTION.
distrait, -e (distrɛ), p. adj. Inattentive, absent-minded, heedless, vacant.
distraitement (distrɛtmɑ̃), adv. Inattentively, heedlessly, listlessly, carelessly, in an absent-minded way.
distrayant, -e (distrɛjɑ̃), p. adj. Diverting, amusing, entertaining.
distribuer (distribɥe), v.a. [L *distribuere*] To distribute, to deal out, to give a share of; to arrange, to dispose, to divide into parts, to classify.
distribut-eur, -rice (distribytœr), s.m.f. Distributor, dispenser; *~ automatique*, distributing machine; penny-in-the-slot machine; (motor.) *~ d'allumage*, spark-timer.
distributi-f, -ve (distribytif), adj. Distributive.
distribution (distribysjɔ̃), s.f. [L *distributio*] Distribution, apportionment, supply; dispersal; arrangement, classification; delivery (of letters); (theatr.) cast; (motor.) distribution.
district (distrik), s.m. [f. L *districtus*] District.
dit, -e (di), p. adj. [f. *dire*] Agreed, settled; surnamed, alias, so-called; *aussitôt ~, aussitôt fait*, no sooner said than done; *ce qui est ~ est ~*, a bargain is a bargain; *à l'heure ~e*, at the appointed time; *susdit*, above-mentioned; *autrement ~*, in other words; *entre nous soit ~*, between ourselves. **~**, s.m. (obs.) Saying, maxim, poem.
dithyrambe (ditirɑ̃b), s.m. [f. Gr. *dithurambos*] Dithyramb.
dithyrambique (ditirɑ̃bik), adj. Dithyrambic.
dito (dito), invar. wd [f. It. *detto*] Ditto, do.
diurétique (djyretik), adj. s.m. [f. Gr. *diourētikos*] Diuretic.
diurnal, -e, (aux) (djyrnal), adj. [L *diurnalis*] Diurnal.
diurne (djyrn), adj. Diurnal.
divagation (divaga'sjɔ̃), s.f. **1.** Straying, vagary, wandering; **2.** divagation, wandering (of the mind), incoherent speech.
divaguer (divage), v.n. [f. L *divagari*] To wander, to stray; to divagate, to digress; to be delirious.
divan (divɑ̃), s.m. [f. Pers. *diwan*] **1.** Divan, council of State; **2.** divan, sofa, settee.
dive (div), adj. f. (obs.) [f. L *diva*] Divine; (fig.) *la ~ bouteille*, rosy Bacchus.
divergence (divɛrʒɑ̃s), s.f. Divergence, divergency; (fig.) difference, disagreement, variance.
divergent, -e (divɛrʒɑ̃), adj. [L *divergens*] Divergent, diverging, different.
diverger (divɛrʒe), v.n. [L *divergere*] To diverge.
divers, -e (divɛr), adj. [L *diversus*] **1.** Diverse, divers, multiform, different, various; **2.** (pl.) several, various, many, sundry; *~ auteurs l'ont écrit*, several authors have written it; *en ~ lieux*, in sundry places.
diversement (divɛrsmɑ̃), adv. Variously, in various ways, diversely.
diversifier (divɛrsifje), v.a. To diversify, to vary, to variegate.
diversiforme (divɛrsifɔrm), adj. Diversiform; syn. HÉTÉROMORPHE.
diversion (divɛrsjɔ̃), s.f. [L *diversio*] Diversion; *faire ~, créer une ~*, to create a diversion.
diversité (divɛrsite), s.f. [L *diversitas*] Diversity, dissimilitude, variety, difference.
divertir (divɛrtir), v.a. [f. L *divertere*] **1.** To divert, to turn aside, to misapply; **2.** to divert, to entertain, to amuse; **se ~**, v.pr. to divert oneself, to amuse oneself, to make merry.
divertissant, -e (divɛrtisɑ̃), p. adj. Entertaining, amusing, diverting.
divertissement (divɛrtismɑ̃), s.m. **1.** Diversion, amusement, entertainment; **2.** (theatr.) divertissement, ballet.
divette (divɛt), s.f. [f. It. *diva*] Star, singer of operetta.
dividende (dividɑ̃d), s.m. [f. L *dividendum*] Dividend.
divin, -e (divɛ̃), adj. [L *divinus*] Divine, heavenly, godlike; (fig.) most excellent, charming.

divinat-eur, -rice (divinatœr), adj. Divining, divinatory.
divination (divina'sjɔ̃), s.f. [L *divinatio*] Divination.
divinatoire (divinatwar), adj. Divinatory, divining; *baguette* ~, divining rod.
divinement (divinmɑ̃), adv. Divinely; (fig.) supremely, exquisitely.
divinisation (diviniza'sjɔ̃), s.f. Deification.
diviniser (divinize), v.a. To deify, to divinize, to idolize.
divinité (divinite), s.f. [L *divinitas*] **1.** Divinity, deity; **2.** goddess, angel, lady-love. ⚠ *Divinité* has not like the English 'divinity' the sense of theology, (university) theological faculty = *théologie, faculté de théologie.*
diviser (divize), v.a. [L *dividere*] **1.** To divide, to separate, to share, to allot; **2.** (fig.) to disunite, to set at variance; **se** ~, v.pr. to divide, to be divided.
diviseur (divizœr), s.m. Divisor, divider.
divisibilité (divizibilite), s.f. Divisibility.
divisible (divizibl), adj. Divisible; dividable, separable.
division (divizjɔ̃), s.f. [L *divisio*] Division, separation, partition; department; portion of a class, of an army; section; discord; *mettre la* ~ *parmi les ennemis*, to sow discord among the enemy. ⚠ In English 'division' means also separation of House of Parliament into two groups for counting votes = *scrutin.*
divisionnaire (divizjɔnɛr), adj. Divisionary, divisional, of a division. ~, s.m. Lieutenant general; syn. GÉNÉRAL DE DIVISION.
divorce (divɔrs), s.m. [L *divortium*] Divorce; (fig.) separation; *faire* ~ *avec*, to break off from.
divorcer (divɔrse), v.n.a. To divorce, to be divorced (*d'avec*, from).
divulgat-eur, -rice (divylgatœr), s.m.f. Divulger. ~, adj. Divulging.
divulgation (divylga'sjɔ̃), s.f. Divulgation, divulgence, publishing.
divulguer (divulge), v.a. [L *divulgare*] To divulge, to reveal, to publish, to let out.
dix (dis, di), adj. num. s.m. [f. L *decem*] Ten, tenth; *chapitre* ~, chapter the tenth, or ten; *Louis* ~, Louis the Tenth; *le* ~ *janvier*, the tenth of January; *un* ~ *de carreau*, a ten of diamonds; ~*-huit*, eighteen, eighteenth; ~*-huitième*, eighteenth; ~*-neuf*, nineteen, nineteenth; ~*-neuvième*, nineteenth; ~*-sept*, seventeen, seventeenth; ~*-septième*, seventeenth; ~*-cors*, full-grown stag; hart of ten.
dixième (dizjɛm), adj. Tenth. ~, s.m. Tenth, tithe. ~, s.f. (mus.) Tenth.
dixièmement (dizjɛmmɑ̃), adv. Tenthly.
dizain (dizɛ̃), s.m. Ten-line stanza; decastich; decade (of a rosary); syn. DIXAIN.
dizaine (dizɛn), s.f. Ten, about ten, some ten, set of ten, half a score.
dizainier, dizenier (dizɛnje, diznje), s.m. Tithing-man.
djinn (dʒin), s.m. [Arab. wd] Djinn, jinnee.
do (do), s.m. [It. wd] (mus.) Do, ut, C.; syn. UT.
docile (dɔsil), adj. [L *docilis*] Docile, manageable, obedient, tractable.
docilement (dɔsilmɑ̃), adv. Docilely, obediently, unresistingly.
docilité (dɔsilite), s.f. [L *docilitas*] Docility, submissiveness.
docimasie (dɔsimazi), s.f. (metall.) Docimasy, assaying of metallic ores.
dock (dɔk), s.m. [Engl. wd] Dock.
docte (dɔkt), adj. [L *doctus*] Learned.
doctement (dɔktəmɑ̃), adv. (iron.) Learnedly, pedantically.
docteur (dɔktœr), s.m. (see fem. *doctoresse*) [f. L *doctor*] Doctor; *être reçu* ~, to take a doctor's degree; ~ *en médecine, médecin*, doctor of medicine, physician.
doctoral, -e, (aux) (dɔktɔral), adj. Doctoral.
doctoralement (dɔktɔralmɑ̃), adv. Doctorally.
doctorat (dɔktɔra), s.m. Doctorate, doctorship, doctor's degree.
doctoresse (dɔktɔrɛs), s.f. Woman doctor, doctoress; (the masculine *docteur* is now used also; ex.: Dr Marie Dupont).
doctrinaire (dɔktrinɛr), s.m. [f. *doctrine*] **1.** Doctrinaire; **2.** lay brother. ~, adj. Pedantic, schoolmasterly, illiberal.
doctrinal, -e, (aux) (dɔktrinal), adj. Doctrinal.
doctrinarisme (dɔktrinarism), s.m. Doctrinarianism; doctrinairism.
doctrine (dɔktrin), s.f. [L *doctrina*] Doctrine.
document (dɔkymɑ̃), s.m. [L *documentum*] Document; title-deed; evidence; instrument; written information.
documentaire (dɔkymɑ̃tɛr), adj. Documentary.
documenter (dɔkymɑ̃te), v.a. To document, to supply information concerning, to support by documents.
dodécaèdre (dɔdekaɛdr), s.m. [f. Gr. *dōdekahedros*] Dodecahedron.
dodécagone (dɔdekagɔn), s.m. [f. Gr. *dōdekagōnon*] Dodecagon.
dodeliner (dɔdline), v.a.n. [onom. f. *dodo*] To rock, to lull, to wag, to dandle; ~ *de la tête*, to wag one's head.
dodo (dodo), s.m. interj. [onom., f. *dors*] Bed, cradle; sleep; lullaby, hushaby; by-by; *faire* ~, to go to sleep; to go to by-by.

dodu, -e (dɔdy), adj. [f. *dos*] Plump, fat, chubby.
dogaresse (dɔgarɛs), s.f. [It. *dogaressa*] Doge's wife.
dogat (dɔga), s.m. [f. It. *dogato*] Dogate, dogeate.
doge (dɔʒ), s.m. (see fem. *dogaresse*) [f. L *dux*] Doge.
dogmatique (dɔgmatik), s.f. Dogmatics. ~, adj. Dogmatic, dogmatical.
dogmatiquement (dɔgmatikmɑ̃), adv. Dogmatically.
dogmatiser (dɔgmatize), v.n. To dogmatize.
dogmatisme (dɔgmatism), s.m. Dogmatism.
dogme (dɔgm), s.m. [Gr. *dogma*] Dogma.
dogre (dɔgr), s.m. [f. Dutch *dogger*] (naut.) Dogger (two-masted fishing-vessel).
dogue (dɔg), s.m. [f. Engl. *dog*] Mastiff, bull-dog, house dog; *être d'une humeur de ~*, to be as surly as a bear.
doguin, -e (dɔgɛ̃), s.m.f. Young mastiff, pup.
doigt (dwa), s.m. [L *digitus*] Finger, (of the hand); toe (of the foot); toe (of certain animals); *montrer X au ~*, to point at X; *s'en mordre les ~s*, to repent of it; *être à deux ~s de sa perte*, to be on the very brink of ruin, or of death; (fig.) *mettre le ~ sur la plaie*, to hit the nail on the head; *savoir sur le bout du ~*, to have at one's finger-ends, to know perfectly; *donner sur les ~s à X*, to give X a rap over the knuckles; (fig.) to reprimand; *être comme les deux ~s de la main*, to be hand in glove (with); *obéir au ~ et à l'œil*, to obey at a glance; to be at the beck and call of; (fig.) *se fourrer le ~ dans l'œil*, to be quite out, quite mistaken; *un ~ de vin*, a drop of wine; *mon petit ~ me l'a dit*, a little bird told me; *faire un ~ de cour à X*, to flirt with, to show some attention to X.
doigté, -e (dwate), p. adj. (mus.) Fingered. ~, s.m. Fingering.
doigter (dwate), v.a. (mus.) To finger.
doigtier (dwatje), s.m. Finger-stall, finger-cover.
doit (dwa), s.m. [f. *devoir*] Debit, debtor, debtor side, Dr; *~ et avoir*, debtor and creditor sides, debit and credit sides.
dol (dɔl), s.m. [L *dolus*] Fraud; deceit.
doléance (dɔleɑ̃s), s.f. [f. *dolent*] Complaint, complaining, grievance.
dolemment (dɔlamɑ̃), adv. Dolefully, mournfully.
dolent, -e (dɔlɑ̃), adj. [L *dolens*] Doleful, mournful, complaining, plaintive.
doler (dɔle), v.a. (techn.) To adze, to smooth, to plane.
dolichocéphale (dɔlikɔsefal), adj. s.m.f. [f. Gr. *dolichos*+*kephalē*] Dolichocephalous, long-headed.
dollar (dɔlar), s.m. [Early Dutch and Scand. *daler*] Dollar.
dolman (dɔlman, dɔlmɑ̃), s.m. [f. Turk. *dōlāmān*] Dolman, shell-jacket, jacket.
dolmen (dɔlmɛn), s.m. [Celt. wd] Dolmen, cromlech, cairn.
doloire (dɔlwar), s.f. [f. L *dolare*] (techn.) Paring-knife, adze, mason's axe.
dolomie, dolomite (dɔlɔmi-t), s.f. [f. *Guy de Dolomieu*, 1750-1801] (min.) Dolomite.
dolosi-f, -ve (dɔlozif), adj. [f. *dol*] Fraudulent, deceitful.
domaine (dɔmɛn), s.m. [f. L *dominicum*] Domain; demesne; estate, landed property; (fig.) department, province, speciality, sphere; *tomber dans le ~ public*, to become public property.
domanial, -e, (aux) (dɔmanjal), adj. Domanial.
dôme (dom), s.m. [L *domus*] Dome, vault, canopy.
domestication (dɔmɛstika'sjɔ̃), s.f. Domestication, taming.
domesticité (dɔmɛstisite), s.f. Domesticity; domesticated state; menial condition; (collect.) the servants. ⚠ 'Domesticity' frequently means also fondness for home life = *attachement à son intérieur*, or *à la vie de famille*.
domestique (dɔmɛstik), adj. [f. L *domus*] Domestic, pertaining to the home; tame, domesticated; menial. ~, s.m.f. Domestic, servant, menial, valet, maid, man-servant, maid-servant.
domestiquement (dɔmɛstikmɑ̃), adv. Domestically.
domestiquer (dɔmɛstike), v.a. To domesticate, to tame. ⚠ 'To domesticate' has a wider sense than *domestiquer*; it means *naturaliser, civiliser, rendre attaché à la vie de famille*; ex.: a domesticated woman = *une femme d'intérieur*; it would be impossible to say *une femme domestiquée*.
domicile (dɔmisil), s.m. [L *domicilium*] Domicile, abode, residence, dwelling; *élire ~*, to choose a domicile; *à ~*, at home; to one's house.
domiciliaire (dɔmisiljɛr), adj. Domiciliary.
(se) domicilier (sədɔmisilje), v.pr. To settle, to be domiciled, to reside; *être domicilié*, to reside, to be domiciled.
dominant, -e (dɔminɑ̃), p. adj. Dominant, predominant, ruling. ~e, s.f. (mus.) Dominant.
dominat-eur, -rice (dɔminatœr), adj. Dominative, tyrannical. ~, s.m.f. Dominator, tyrant.
domination (dɔmina'sjɔ̃), s.f. Domination, power, dominion, rule, sway. ~s, s.f.pl. (Cath. theol.) Dominations, the fourth order of Angels.

ɔ, note, glotte; ɔ̃, monter, ronde; ø, feu, creux; œ, peur, sœur; œ̃, *un*; ʃ, *chez*, *schisme*; u, *tout*; w, *oui*, *doit*, *douaire*; y, mur, *pu*; ɥ, huile, *muette*; z, zèle, rose; ʒ, dé*j*à, *g*entil.

dominer (domine), v.a.n. [f. L *dominari*] **1.** To dominate, to govern, to rule, to sway, to lord it over; **2.** to predominate, to rise above, to command, to be prevalent; to drown (sounds); **se ~**, v.pr. to master oneself, to control oneself, to have self-control.

dominicain, -e (dɔminikɛ̃), s.m.f. adj. [f. *St Dominique*] Dominican.

dominical, -e, (aux) (dɔminikal), adj. [f. L *dominicalis*] Dominical; *l'oraison ~e*, the Lord's prayer.

domino (dɔmino), s.m. [f. L *dominus*, Span. *domino*] **1.** Kind of hood, loose cloak with hood, domino; **2.** (game) domino; *jouer aux ~s*, to play dominoes.

dominoterie (dɔminɔtri), s.f. Fancy paper, coloured papers (for games, &c.).

dommage (dɔmaʒ), s.m. [f. L *damnum*, LL *dommagium*] Damage, detriment, injury, wrong, prejudice; *~s et intérêts*, damages; *c'est ~!*, it is a pity!; *quel ~!*, what a pity!

dommageable (dɔmaʒabl), adj. Detrimental, hurtful, damageable, injurious.

domptable (dɔ̃tabl), adj. Subduable, tameable, manageable.

dompter (dɔ̃te), v.a. [L *domitare*] To subdue, to master, to tame, to break, to crush.

dompteur (dɔ̃tœr), s.m. Subduer, tamer, breaker.

don (dɔ̃), s.m. [L *donum*] **1.** Gift, donation, present, grant; **2.** gift, aptitude, talent, knack.

donataire (dɔnatɛr), s.m.f. adj. (That is a) donee, beneficiary.

donat-eur, -rice (dɔnatœr), s.m.f. Donor, donator, giver. ~, adj. Giving, donating.

donation (dɔna'sjɔ̃), s.f. [L *donatio*] Donation, gift, grant, deed of gift.

donc (dɔ̃, dɔ̃k), conj. [L *dumque*] Therefore, consequently, then, indeed, so, accordingly, now, now then, come, &c.; of course, to be sure; *allons ~!*, pooh, pshaw!; *quoi ~?*, what then?; *dites ~ . . .*, I say . . . .

dondon (dɔ̃dɔ̃), s.f. (fam.) Plump, fat, bouncing woman.

donjon (dɔ̃ʒɔ̃), s.m. [f. L *dominus*, LL *domnionem*] Donjon, dungeon, keep, tower, turret.

donnant, -e (dɔnɑ̃), p. adj. Fond of giving, liberal, generous; ~ ~, give and take, tit for tat.

donne (dɔn), s.f. [f. *donner*] (cards) Deal.

donnée (done), s.f. Datum (pl. data), truth, information, statement, fact, basis; (math.) given, or known, quantity.

donner (done), v.a.n. [f. L *donare*] To give, to bestow, to grant, to present with, to give away, to confer; to bring about, to cause; to yield, to produce, to supply with; to hand, to hand over; to open into; to communicate; to face, to front; to indulge, to devote oneself; to bid (for) to offer; to perform; *~ lieu matière, sujet à*, to give ground for; *~ de la peine, du mal*, to cause, to give trouble; *~ tort, raison*, to declare or admit to be wrong, right; (fig.) *~ la main, les mains, à quelque chose*, to give one's consent to something, to have a hand in something; *~ à entendre*, to hint; *cela donne à réfléchir*, that sets one thinking; *~ la vie*, to give birth; *~ la mort*, to kill; *~ de l'inquiétude*, to cause anxiety; *~ de l'humeur*, to vex; *~ l'assaut à*, to storm; *~ un œuf pour avoir un bœuf*, to give a sprat to catch a herring; *ne restez pas si longtemps sans me ~ signe de vie*, don't be so long without letting me hear from you; *~ le bon exemple*, to set a good example; *~ des ordres*, to give orders; *~ un coup de balai*, to give a sweep; *~ un coup de pied*, to kick; *~ les cartes*, to deal; *~ passage*, to yield passage, to make way (*à*, for), to give way (to); *~ avis*, to give warning; *~ congé à*, (*a*) to give notice to; (*b*) to give a holiday to; *combien donnez-vous de cela?*, how much do you offer for that?; *on ne lui donnerait pas plus de trente ans*, no one would think he was over thirty; *~ rendez-vous*, to appoint a meeting-place; *je vous le donne en cent!*, I defy you to guess it; I give you a hundred guesses; *~ la chasse*, to give chase, to pursue; (colloq.) *~ une chasse*, to give a blowing-up; *~ dans le luxe*, to indulge in luxury; *~ dans le piège*, to fall into the snare; *~ tête baissée dans*, to rush headlong into; *~ un coup d'épaule*, to lend a hand, to help; *ne plus savoir où ~ de la tête*, not to know which way to turn; *~ sur les doigts à X*, to reprimand, to rate X; *le soleil vous donne dans les yeux*, the sun shines in your eyes; (fam.) *cela lui a donné dans l'œil*, that has hit his fancy; *il n'est pas donné à tout le monde de pouvoir*, it's not everybody who may; it's not everybody's lot (or privilege) to be able; *il m'a été donné de*, it has fallen to my lot to; *le moteur donne bien*, the motor works well; *~ et retenir ne vaut*, what is once given is given for good; *donnant donnant*, fair's fair; tit for tat; *~ sur la rue*, to open on the street; *le régiment a donné vaillamment*, the regiment fought gallantly; *~ de la bande*, to incline to one side; *le navire a donné contre un écueil*, the ship struck against a rock; **se ~**, v.pr. to give oneself, to give to oneself, to give to each other; to devote oneself; *se ~ pour*, to give oneself out for, to pass oneself off for; to profess to be; *se ~ garde*, to be upon one's guard, to beware; *s'en ~ à cœur joie*, to take one's fill of it, to indulge oneself in to one's heart's content, to enjoy thoroughly; *se ~ de la peine*, to take pains; *se ~ la peine de*, to take the trouble to; *se ~ en spectacle*, to make a spectacle of oneself, to make oneself conspicuous; *se ~ de grands airs*, to assume lofty airs; to give oneself airs; *cette pièce s'est donnée cent fois de suite*, that play has been performed a hundred times running.

donneu-r, -se (dɔnœr), s.m.f. Giver.

don-quichottisme (dõkiʃɔtism), s.m. [f. *Don Quichotte*, by Cervantes] Quixotism.

dont (dõ), pron. [f. L *de unde*] Whose, of whom, from whom, of which, from which, whereof, wherefrom, in which, on which, out of which.

donzelle (dõzɛl), s.f. [f. It. *donzella*] (iron.) Lass, wench; young woman of ill-fame.

dorade (dɔrad), s.f. [f. *dorer*] Gold-fish, silver-fish; dorado, coryphaena; see DAURADE.

dorage (dɔraʒ), s.m. [f. *dorer*] Gilding.

doré, -e (dɔre), p. adj. Gilt, gilded, golden, bright yellow; *~ sur tranche*, gilt-edged; *bonne renommée vaut mieux que ceinture ~e*, a good name is better than riches; *jeunesse ~e*, (French hist.) gilded youth, rich young men who united in 1794 in order to support the thermidorians; (today) idle rich young men; *avoir la langue ~e*, to be smooth-tongued, to be persuasive. ~, s.m. Gilding.

dorénavant (dɔrenavã), adv. [f. OF *d'ores et en avant*] Henceforward, henceforth, in future, for the future.

dorer (dɔre), v.a. [L *deaurare*] To gild, to glaze; (fig.) to give a bright golden appearance to, to soften down; (fig.) *~ la pilule*, to gild the pill, to render acceptable something unpleasant; *~ une patisserie*, to glaze a piece of pastry with yolk of egg; **se ~**, v.pr. to become golden.

doreu-r, -se (dɔrœr), s.m.f. Gilder.

dorien, -ne (dɔrjɛ̃), adj. s.m.f. Dorian, Doric.

dorique (dɔrik), adj. Doric; *l'ordre ~*, the Doric order.

doris[1] (dɔris), s.f. (conch.) Doris, sea-lemon.

doris[2] (dɔris), s.m. [f. Engl. *dory*] (naut.) Dory.

dorloter (dɔrlɔte), v.a. [f. OF *dorelot*] To coddle, to nurse, to nurse up, to pet; **se ~**, v.pr. to indulge oneself, to take one's ease.

dormant, -e (dɔrmã), p. adj. Sleeping, stagnant, dormant, fixed, fast, immovable; *eaux ~es*, stagnant water; (naut.) *manœuvres ~es*, standing rigging. ~, s.m. Sleeper, dormer, dormant; epergne.

dormeu-r, -se (dɔrmœr), s.m.f. Sleeper. **~se**, s.f. Earring.

dormir (dɔrmir), v.n. [L *dormire*] To sleep, to slumber, to be asleep, to go to sleep; (fig.) to be inactive, to lie dormant, to be unattended to, to be in abeyance; *~ profondément*, to sleep soundly; *~ comme une souche, comme un pieu, comme un sabot, à poings fermés*, to sleep like a log; *~ sur les deux oreilles*, to sleep soundly; (fig.) to have nothing to fear; to sleep in a whole skin; *~ debout*, to sleep standing, to be very tired; (fig.) *un conte à ~ debout*, a most incredible story, a cock-and-bull story; *avoir envie de ~*, to be, to feel sleepy; *n'éveillez pas le chat qui dort*, let sleeping dogs lie; *qui dort dîne*, sleep is as good as a dinner; *ils dorment de leur dernier sommeil*, theirs is the eternal sleep; *laisser ~ ses capitaux*, to let one's capital lie dormant; *le feu dort sous la cendre*, the fire is smouldering; *il n'y a pire eau que l'eau qui dort*, still waters run deep; ~, v.a. *dormez votre sommeil*, sleep your sleep; *~ la grasse matinée*, to lie late in bed. ~, s.m. Sleep.

dormiti-f, -ve (dɔrmitif), adj. Dormitive, somniferous. ~, s.m. Dormitive, sleeping-draught.

dorsal, -e, (aux) (dɔrsal), adj. [f. L *dorsum*] Dorsal.

dortoir (dɔrtwar), s.m. [f. L *dormitorium*] Dormitory.

dorure (dɔryr), s.f. [f. *dorer*] **1.** Gilding; **2.** gilt ornament; **3.** (pastry) glazing with yolk of egg.

dos (do), s.m. [L *dorsum*] Back, rear, top, ridge, verso; *faire le gros ~*, (of a cat) to set its back up; (fig.) to assume an air of importance and contentment; *se mettre X à ~*, to make an enemy of X; (fig.) *mettez cela sur mon ~*, throw the blame on me; *avoir bon ~*, to be indifferent to blame, to have a broad back; *se laisser manger la laine sur le ~*, to submit to anything; *~ à ~*, back to back; *renvoyer ~ à ~*, to discharge on equal terms, to nonsuit both; *tourner le ~ à X*, to turn one's back on X, to cut X; *dès que j'eus le ~ tourné*, as soon as my back was turned; (slang) *en avoir plein le ~*, to be fed up with it; *en ~ d'âne*, sloping both sides, with a shelving ridge, saddle-backed; (slang) *ne pas y aller avec le ~ de la cuiller*, not to do things by halves; to go it strong.

dosage (dozaʒ), s.m. [f. *doser*] Dosage.

dose (doz), s.f. [f. Gr. *dosis*] Dose, share.

doser (doze), v.a. To measure the quantity of (medicine) to be given; to determine

the proportion of elements in (a mixture); to dose. ⚠ Not in the sense of 'to give physic' = *faire prendre des médicaments à*.
dosseret (dosrɛ), s.m. [f. *dos*] **1.** Side-post (of a door); **2.** back (of a saw).
dossier (dosje), s.m. [f. *dos*] **1.** Back-piece, head-board; **2.** brief, record, bundle of papers, file.
dossière (dosjɛr), s.f. (of harness) Back-band; (of a cuirass) back plate.
dot (dɔt), s.f. [f. L *dos*] Marriage-portion, dower, dowry; *coureur de* ~, heiress-hunter, fortune-hunter.
dotal, -e, (aux) (dɔtal), adj. Dotal, pertaining to a dowry.
dotation (dɔta'sjɔ̃), s.f. [L *dotatio*] Dotation, endowment.
doter (dɔte), v.a. [L *dotare*] To endow, to give a portion to, to portion; ~ *sa fille*, to give a portion to one's daughter; ~ *un hôpital*, to endow a hospital.
douaire (dwɛr), s.m. [L *dotarium*] Dower, jointure, marriage-settlement.
douairière (dwɛrjɛr), s.f. Dowager; *reine* ~, queen dowager.
douane (dwan), s.f. [f. It. *dogana*] Customs, custom-house, duty.
douanier (dwanje), s.m. Custom-house officer. **douani-er, -ère,** adj. Of customs.
douar (dwar), s.m. [Arab. wd] Douar, dowar (Arab encampment).
doublage (dublaʒ), s.m. Lining; sheathing (of a ship).
double (dubl), s.m. [f. L *duplus*] Double; duplicate, copy, twice as much. ~ adj. Double, twofold; (fig.) double-faced, deceitful; *tenue de livres en partie* ~, book-keeping by double entry; *fermer à* ~ *tour*, to double-lock; *mot à* ~ *entente*, double entendre; ~ *croche*, (mus.) semi-quaver; *faire* ~ *emploi*, to be a useless repetition. ~, adv. *Voir* ~, to see double, to be drunk; *payer* ~, to pay double; *plier* ~, to fold in two.
doublé (duble), s.m. **1.** Plated work; **2.** (billiards, sport) doublet.
doublement (dubləmɑ̃), s.m. Doubling. ~, adv. Doubly.
doubler (duble), v.a. [f. *double*] **1.** To double, to double up; to understudy (an actor); ~ *un cap*, (naut.) to get round, to double, to round, a cape; **2.** to line (a garment); **3.** (on the road) to pass. ~, v.n. To double.
doublet (dublɛ), s.m. Doublet (in gram. sense); duplicate.
doublier (dublje), s.m. Double rack (in a sheepcote).
doublon (dublɔ̃), s.m. [Span. *doblon*] **1.** (coin) Doubloon; **2.** (print.) double, doublet.
doublure (dublyr), s.f. [f. *double*] **1.** Lining; **2.** (theatr.) understudy.
douce-amère (dusamɛr), s.f. (bot.) Bitter-sweet, *Solanum dulcamara*.
douceâtre (dusɑtr), adj. [f. *doux*] Sweetish; mawkish, affected.
doucement (dusmɑ̃), adv. Mildly, softly, gently, smoothly, slowly, leisurely, kindly; middlingly, indifferently; *comment allez-vous?*, *tout* ~, how are you?, so-so, not very well. ~, interj. Stop!, hold!, gently!, easy!
doucereusement (dusrøzmɑ̃), adv. Mawkishly, hypocritically.
doucereu-x, -se (dusrø), adj. Mawkish, sweetish, affectedly mild, sugared, honeyed; (of persons) mealy-mouthed.
doucet, -te (dusɛ), adj. Gentle, mild, demure-looking. **~te,** s.f. Corn salad, lamb's lettuce.
doucettement (dusɛtmɑ̃), adv. Gently, so-so, poorly, indifferently.
douceur (dusœr), s.f. [f. *doux*] Sweetness, smoothness, softness, gentleness, kindness, suavity, meekness; **~s,** pl. sweets, dainties; cajolery, compliments, flattery; *en* ~, and (slang), *en douce*, gently, unobtrusively, secretly.
douche (duʃ), s.f. [f. It. *doccia*] Shower-bath; douche; (fig.) damper, unpleasant shock or encounter, reprimand, disappointment.
doucher (duʃe), v.a. To give a shower-bath or a douche to; (fig.) to damp, to cool, to reprimand; to damp the ardour of.
doucine (dusin), s.f. [uncert. orig.] (arch.) Cyma, doucine, back ogee, moulding-plane.
doué, -e (due), p. adj. Gifted, endowed.
douer (due), v.a. [f. L *dotare*] To endow, to gift; see doublet DOTER.
douille (duj) s.f. [MHG *tülle*] Socket, sleeve, lug; cartridge-shell or -case.
douillet, -te (dujɛ), adj. [f. L *ductilis*] Soft; over-delicate, effeminate, cowardly. **~te,** s.f. Wadded garment.
douillettement (dujɛtmɑ̃), adv. Softly, delicately, comfortably, at ease.
douleur (dulœr), s.f. [L *dolor*] Pain, ache, aching, pang, anguish, twinge, throes (pl.), grief, sorrow, affliction; **~s,** pl. rheumatism; anguish of travail in childbirth.
douloureusement (dulurøzmɑ̃), adv. Painfully, achingly, sorrowfully, mournfully, grievously.
douloureu-x, -se (dulurø), adj. Painful, sore, tender, dolorous, grievous, woeful, sorrowful. ~, s.f. (colloq.) *La* ~*se*, bill to pay, reckoning.
douro (duro), s.m. [Span. *duro*] Duro (the Spanish dollar).
doute (dut), s.m. [f. *douter*] Doubt, doubting, indecision, scepticism, suspicion, misgiving, distrust; *mettre, révoquer*

en ~, to call in question, to doubt, to question; *dans le* ~, *abstiens-toi*, if you are in doubt, forbear; when in doubt, do nothing; *cela ne fait aucun* ~, there is no doubt about it; *sans* ~, no doubt, doubtless, undoubtedly, indubitably; probably, likely; *il est hors de* ~ *que*, beyond doubt, most certainly.

douter (dute), v.n. [L *dubitare*] To doubt, to waver, to question, to be distrustful, to suspect; *je doute qu'il accepte*, I do not believe he will accept; *je ne doute pas qu'il ne vienne*, I have no doubt but that he will come; *ne* ~ *de rien*, to be full of self-confidence, to be very bold; **se** ~ (*de*) v.pr. to surmise, to suspect, to fear, to have some notion (of), to foresee; *ne se* ~ *de rien*, not to have the slightest suspicion (or notion); *je m'en doutais*, I thought so.

douteu-x, -se (dutø), adj. Doubtful, dubious, ambiguous, uncertain, questionable, equivocal.

douve (duv), s.f. [etym. dub.] **1.** Stave (of a cask); **2.** ditch, moat; **3.** (bot.) spearwort.

dou-x, -ce (du), adj. [L *dulcis*] Sweet, mild, easy, dulcet, soft, gentle, smooth, bland, (of water) fresh; *poisson d'eau* ~*ce*, fresh-water fish; (of wine) unfermented. ~, adv. Gently, softly; *filer* ~, to obey, to be humble and submissive, to draw in one's horns; *tout* ~ *!*, stop !, hold !, gently !, wait a bit !. ~, s.m. Sweet, sweetness; (slang) *en* ~*ce*, secretly, unobtrusively, without violence; *se la couler* ~*ce*, to take it easy, to live in clover.

douzaine (duzɛn), s.f. Dozen; *une demi-*~, half a dozen; *à la* ~, by the dozen, cheap enough.

douze (duz), adj. [f. L *duodecim*] Twelve, twelfth; *le 12 juin*, the twelfth of June; *Charles XII*, Charles the Twelfth; *in-*~, *in-12*, duodecimo, 12mo.

douzième (duzjɛm), adj. Twelfth.

douzièmement (duzjɛməmɑ̃), adv. Twelfthly.

douzil (duzi), s.m. [f. L *duciculus*] Spigot, peg.

doyen, -ne (dwajɛ̃), s.m.f. [f. L *decanus*] Dean, senior, oldest member; head (of a university faculty).

doyenné (dwajɛne), s.m. Deanery; deanship; doyenné pear.

doyenneté (dwajɛnte), s.f. Seniority.

drachme (drakm), s.f. [Gr. *drakhmē*] Drachm, drachma, dram.

draconien, -ne (drakɔnjɛ̃), adj. [f. *Draco*, Athenian legislator] Draconian, rigorous, cruel.

dragage, draguage (dragaʒ), s.m. [f. *draguer*] Dredging.

dragée (draʒe), s.f. [f. Gr. *tragēma*] Sugared almond; *tenir la* ~ *haute à X*, to make X pay dearly for something; to keep X in suspense a long time.

drageoir (draʒwar), s.m. [f. *dragée*] Comfit-box.

drageon (draʒɔ̃), s.m. [OGerm. orig.] (hort.) Sucker.

dragon (dragɔ̃), s.m. [f. L *draco*] **1.** Dragon, monster; (astr.) Dragon, Draco; **2.** (mil.) dragoon; **3.** (fig.) termagant, virago; *un* ~ *de vertu*, a prude, aggressively austere woman.

dragonne (dragɔn), s.f. Sword-knot; umbrella-cord.

dragonnier (dragɔnje), s.m. (bot.) Dragon-tree, *Dracaena draco*.

drague (drag), s.f. [f. Engl. *drag*] Drag, dredge, dredging-machine, drag-net.

draguer (drage), v.a. To drag, to dredge.

dragueu-r, -se (dragœr), s.m.f. adj. Mud-dredger.

drain (drɛ̃), s.m. [Engl. wd] Drain, drain-pipe, drain-tile, drainage-tube; (surg.) drain.

drainage (drɛnaʒ), s.m. Draining, drainage.

draine, drenne (drɛn), s.f. (ornith.) Missel-thrush.

drainer (drɛne), v.a. To drain.

draisienne (drɛzjɛn), s.f. [f. *Drais*, inventor] Draisine, dandy-horse (the first form of the bicycle, about 1818).

dramatique (dramatik), adj. [f. *drame*] Dramatic; theatrical; *auteur* ~, dramatic author, playwright.

dramatiquement (dramatikmɑ̃), adv. Dramatically.

dramatiser (dramatize), v.a.n. To dramatize.

dramaturge (dramatyrʒ), s.m. [f. Gr. *drama, dramatos*+*ergon*] Dramatist, playwright.

dramaturgie (dramatyrʒi), s.f. Dramaturgy.

drame (dram), s.m. [f. Gr. *drama*] Drama; (fig.) tragedy, catastrophe.

drap (dra), s.m. [f. LL *drappus*] Cloth; (of a bed) sheet; *me voilà dans de beaux* ~*s !*, I am in a fine mess !, or, in a pretty pickle !; *il peut tailler en plein* ~, he has enough and to spare.

drapeau (pl. **-x**) (drapo), s.m. [f. *drap*] Flag, colours, ensign; *être sous les* ~*x*, to serve in the army or navy; *se ranger sous le* ~ *de X*, to embrace X's cause.

draper (drape), v.a. [f. *drap*] To drape, to hang with a drapery; (fig.) to rail at; **se** ~, v.pr. (fig.) to attitudinize.

draperie (drapri), s.f. **1.** Drapery; cloth manufactory, cloth and woollen stuff trade; **2.** drapery, material arranged in graceful folds.

drapi-er, -ère (drapje), s.m.f. Draper, clothier. ~**ère**, s.f. Bale-pin.

o, note, glotte; **ɔ̃**, monter, ronde; **ø**, feu, creux; **œ**, peur, sœur; **œ̃**, un; **ʃ**, chez, schisme; **u**, tout; **w**, oui, doit, douaire; **y**, mur, pu; **ɥ**, huile, muette; **z**, zèle, rose; **ʒ**, déjà, gentil.

drastique (drastik), adj. s.m. [f. Gr. *drastikos*] Drastic.
dravidien, -ne, dravidique (dravidjɛ̃, dravidik), adj. (geol.) Dravidian.
drayer (drɛje), v.a. [Bret. orig.] To flesh (hides).
drêche (drɛʃ), s.f. [Gallic orig.] **1.** Malt; **2.** grains (pl.), the residue of barley after having been used in brewing.
drège, dreige (drɛʒ), s.f. **1.** Ripple; **2.** drag-net.
drelin (drəlɛ̃), s.m. [onom.] Tinkle, jingle.
drenne (drɛn), s.f. See DRAINE.
dressage (drɛsaʒ), s.m. [f. *dresser*] **1.** Breaking, training (of horses, &c.); **2.** erection.
dresser (drɛse), v.a. [f. LL *directiare*] To erect, to set up, to put up, to raise, to prick up; to build, to prepare; ~ *un lit*, to prepare a bed; to fix, to plant, to pitch (a tent); to lay, to set (a snare); ~ *une embuscade*, to lay an ambush; to draw up (a plan, an account, a contract); to straighten; to train, to break in, to drill; ~ *l'oreille*, to prick up one's ears, to become attentive; *c'est à faire* ~ *les cheveux sur la tête*, it's enough to make one's hair stand on end; **se** ~, v.pr. to stand up, to get up, to start up, to be erected.
dresseur (drɛsœr), s.m. Trainer, tamer; dresser.
dressoir (drɛswar), s.m. [f. *dresser*] Dresser, sideboard.
drill (drij), s.m. (zool.) Drill (a baboon).
drille[1] (drij), s.m. [Bret. orig.] **1.** Soldier (obs.); **2.** fellow; *un bon, un joyeux* ~, a jolly fellow.
drille[2] (drij), s.f. [f. Dutch *dril*] (techn.) Drill.
drisse (dris), s.f. [f. It. *drizza*] (naut.) Halyard, halliard.
drogman (drɔgmɑ̃), s.m. [f. Arab. *tarjuman*] Dragoman.
drogue (drɔg), s.f. [uncert. orig.] **1.** Drug, stuff; **2.** (pop.) cocaine; **3.** (obs.) card-game.
droguer (drɔge), v.a. [f. *drogue*] To drug, to physic, to doctor; ~, v.n. (pop.) to be kept waiting; *il m'a fait* ~, he has kept me waiting.
droguerie (drɔgri), s.f. Drugs; drug-trade; drug-shop.
droguet (drɔgɛ), s.m. Drugget.
droguiste (drɔgist), s.m.f. Druggist.
droit (drwa), s.m. [f. L *directum*] **1.** Right, claim, title, due, justice, power, authority, prerogative, franchise; *à bon* ~, rightly, with good reason; *au* ~ *de*, opposite, in line with; *de* ~, rightfully, of law, by right; *de plein* ~, of right; *à qui de* ~, to whom it concerns; *faire* ~ *à*, to do justice to, to allow the justice of; *être en* ~ *de*, to have the right to; ~*s civils, politiques*, civil, political, rights; ~*s d'impression réservés*, copyright; ~*s d'auteur*, royalties; **2.** law; *faire son* ~, to study law, or for the bar; *bachelier en* ~, bachelor of laws, LL.B.; *docteur en* ~, doctor of laws, LL.D.; ~ *canon*, canon law; ~ *commun*, common law; ~ *des gens*, or ~ *international*, law of nations, international law; **3.** duty, tax, custom tax; ~*s d'octroi*, town dues; ~ *de péage*, toll.
droit, -e (drwa), adj. [f. L *directus*] Right, straight, direct, upright; straightforward, honest, righteous; *se tenir* ~, to stand upright; ~ *comme un I*, as straight as an arrow; bolt upright; *avoir l'esprit* ~, to be right-minded. ~, adv. Right, straight, straightly; *écrire* ~, to write straight; *aller* ~ *au but*, to go straight to the point; (fig.) *marcher* ~, to be well conducted, to behave well. ~**e**, s.f. Right-hand; line, straight line; right side; *gardez votre* ~, keep to the right; (polit.) *la* ~, the conservative or reactionary element.
droitement (drwatmɑ̃), adv. Rightly, equitably.
droiti-er, -ère (drwatje), adj. s.m.f. **1.** Right-handed (person); **2.** s.m. member of *la droite* in a political assembly.
droiture (drwatyr), s.f. Rightness, righteousness, rectitude, honesty.
drolatique (drolatik), adj. Humorous, ludicrous, funny.
drôle (drol), adj. [uncert. orig.] **1.** Droll, comic, funny, amusing; **2.** (pej.) queer, strange, odd; *un* ~ *de corps*, a queer fellow; an odd fish. ~, s.m. (see fem. **drôlesse**) Rogue, scamp, scapegrace, knave, scoundrel; (in the south of France *drôle* is frequently used for a boy, without pej. sense, *mon* ~ = *mon fils*, my son).
drôlement (drolmɑ̃), adv. Comically, funnily; queerly, oddly.
drôlerie (drolri), s.f. [f. *drôle*] Drollery, buffoonery.
drôlesse (drolɛs), s.f. [fem. of *drôle*] (always pej.) Jade, hussy, contemptible woman.
drôlet, -te (drolɛ), adj. Rather funny, amusing, quaint.
dromadaire (drɔmadɛr), s.m. [f. Gr. *dromas*] Dromedary.
drome (drom), s.f. [etym. dub.] **1.** (naut.) Spare masts, &c.; **2.** main beam (of forge hammer).
dronte (drɔ̃t), s.m. (ornith.) Dodo.
drosère, drosera (drɔzɛr, drozera), s.m. [Gr. *droseros*] (bot.) Sundew, *Drosera*.
drosse (drɔs), s.f. [f. It. *trozza*] (naut.) **1.** Tackle; **2.** truss, parrel; **3.** rope, tiller-rope.
drosser (drɔse), v.a. (naut.) To drive (a ship) from its course; to sheer.
dru, -e (dry), adj. [f. Celt. *drud*] Thick, thick-set, vigorous, sturdy, brisk, lively. ~, adv. Hard, fast, thick, thickly; *la pluie tombe* ~, it's raining fast.

druide (drɥid), s.m. **druidesse** (drɥides), s.f. [f. Celt. *druid*] Druid, druidess.
druidique (drɥidik), adj. Druidic.
druidisme (drɥidism), s.m. Druidism.
drupe (dryp), s.m. [f. L *drupa*] (bot.) Drupe.
druse (dryz), adj. s.m.f. Druze, of the Druze tribe.
dryade (drjad), s.f. [f. Gr. *druas*] Dryad; (bot.) dryas.
du (dy), art. [contr. of *de le*] Of the, from the, some, any; see DE.
dû, -e (dy), p. adj. Owed, owing, due; *elles croient que tout leur est* ~, they expect every attention to be paid to them. ~, s.m. Due; *réclamer son* ~, to ask for one's due.
dualisme (dɥalism), s.m. [f. L *dualis*] Dualism.
dualiste (dɥalist), s.m.f. Dualist.
dualité (dɥalite), s.f. [f. L *dualis*] Duality.
dubitati-f, -ve (dybitatif), adj. [f. L *dubitare*] Dubitative, implying doubt.
dubitativement (dybitativmɑ̃), adv. Dubitatively, doubtingly.
duc (dyk), s.m. (see fem. **duchesse**) [f. L *dux*] **1.** Duke; *grand-*~, grand duke; **2.** (ornith.) eagle-owl, *Bubo*, horn-owl; **3.** park phaeton.
ducal, -e, (aux) (dykal), adj. Ducal.
ducat (dyka), s.m. [f. It. *ducato*] Ducat.
ducaton (dykatɔ̃), s.m. Ducatoon.
duché (dyʃe), s.m. Dukedom, duchy.
duchesse (dyʃɛs), s.f. Duchess.
ducroire (dykrwar), s.m. [*du+croire*] (comm.) Del credere.
ductile (dyktil), adj. [L *ductilis*] Ductile.
ductilité (dyktilite), s.f. Ductility.
duègne (dɥɛɲ), s.f. [Span. *dueña*] Duenna.
duel (dɥɛl), s.m. [L *duellum*] **1.** Duel, duelling, single combat; *se battre en* ~, to fight a duel, to duel; **2.** (gram.) dual number. ~, **-le**, adj. Dual.
duelliste (dɥɛlist), s.m. Duellist.
duettiste (dɥɛtist), s.m.f. [f. *duo*] Duettist.
dugong (dygɔ̃g), s.m. (zool.) Dugong.
duite (dɥit), s.f. [f. obs. v. *duire*] (weaving) Weft-yarn.
dulcification (dylsifika'sjɔ̃), s.f. Dulcification.
dulcifier (dylsifje), v.a. [f. L *dulcis*] To dulcify.
dulcinée (dylsine), s.f. [f. *Dulcinée*, in 'Don Quixote'] (iron.) Dulcinea, sweetheart.
dulie (dyli), s.f. [f. Gr. *douleia*] (theol.) Dulia.
dûment (dymɑ̃), adv. [f. *dû*] Duly.
dune (dyn), s.f. [f. Celt. *dun*] Dune, downs, sand-hill.
dunette (dynɛt), s.f. [f. *dune*] Poop, poop-deck.
duo (dɥo), s.m. [It. wd] Duet, duetto, duo.
duodécimal, -e, (aux) (dɥodesimal), adj. [f. L *duodecim*] Duodecimal.
duodénum (dɥɔdenɔm), s.m. (anat.) Duodenum.
duodi (dɥɔdi), s.m. [f. L *duo+dies*] Duodi (second day of the decade in the Republican calendar).
dupe (dyp), s.f. adj. (That is a) dupe; *faire des* ~*s*, to cheat, to deceive many people; *il ne sera pas deux fois sa* ~, he won't be made a fool of twice by him (or her).
duper (dype), v.a. [unkn. orig.] To dupe, to cheat, to make a fool of, to impose on, to take in, to gull.
duperie (dypri), s.f. Dupery, imposition, cheat, fraud, trickery, take-in, sell.
dupeu-r, -se (dypœr), s.m.f. Duper, cheat, trickster.
duplicata (dyplikata), s.m. (invar.) [f. L *duplicare*] Duplicate, copy.
duplicateur (dyplikatœr), s.m. Duplicator.
duplication (dyplika'sjɔ̃), s.f. Duplication.
duplice (dyplis), s.f. [f. L *duplex*] Duplice, alliance of two powers.
duplicité (dyplisite), s.f. [L *duplicitas*] Duplicity, double-dealing.
duquel, de laquelle, desquels, desquelles, (dykɛl, dəlakɛl, dɛkɛl), rel. pr. [contr. of *de lequel*] Of or from whom, of or from which, &c.
dur, -e (dyr), adj. [f. L *durus*] Hard, firm, tough; hardened, hard-hearted, unfeeling, severe, harsh, rough, austere; distressful; *œuf* ~, hard-boiled egg; *du pain* ~, stale bread; *être* ~ *d'oreille, avoir l'oreille* ~*e*, to be hard of hearing; *faire* or *rendre la vie* ~*e à X*, to give X a hard time; *avoir la vie* ~*e*, (*a*) to have nine lives, to die hard; (*b*) to be hard put to it, to be in difficulties; *avoir la tête* ~*e*, (*a*) to be obstinate; (*b*) to be slow (of understanding); ~ *à la détente*, close-fisted; *avoir le cœur* ~, to be hard-hearted; ~ *comme fer*, as hard as nails; *mer* ~*e*, choppy sea; *les temps sont* ~*s*, these are hard times; *hiver* ~, hard winter. ~, adv. Hard, harshly, firmly, &c. ~*e*, s.f. (*a*) Hard lines, ascetic way of living; (*b*) bare ground, hard bed; *élevé à la* ~, brought up without indulgence, spartanly; *coucher sur la* ~, to sleep on the bare ground, or on bare boards; *en faire voir de* ~*es à X*, to lead X a dog's life; *en voir de* ~*es*, to rough it.
durabilité (dyrabilite), s.f. Durability, durableness.
durable (dyrabl), adj. [L *durabilis*] Durable, lasting.
durablement (dyrabləmɑ̃), adv. Durably, lastingly.
duralumin(e) (dyralymin), s.f. Duralumin, duraluminium.
durant (dyrɑ̃), prep. [f. *durer*] During, for; ~ *sa vie*, during his lifetime, while he is or

was alive; *sa vie* ~, as long as he lives or lived; *deux heures* ~, two whole hours.

durcir (dyrsir), v.a.n. [f. *dur*] To harden, to stiffen; to indurate, to toughen, to get hard; **se** ~, v.pr. to harden, to grow or get hard.

durcissement (dyrsismɑ̃), s.m. Hardening, induration.

durée (dyre), s.f. [f. *durer*] Duration, continuance; time; *de longue* ~, lasting, durable; *de peu de* ~, short-lived.

durement (dyrmɑ̃), adv. Hard, hardly, roughly, harshly, severely, rigorously; ~ *éprouvé*, hard hit.

dure-mère (dyrmɛr), s.f. (anat.) Duramater.

durer (dyre), v.n.a. [L *durare*] To last, to endure, to hold out, to subsist, to continue, to wear well, to seem long; to appear unbearably long; *le temps me dure*, time hangs heavy with me; I am bored to death.

dureté (dyrte), s.f. [f. *dur*] Hardness, firmness, toughness, harshness, roughness, hard-heartedness; ~**s**, pl. cutting or hard words.

durillon (dyrijɔ̃), s.m. [f. *dur*] Corn, callosity, horny induration.

duriuscule (dyrjyskyl), adj. [L *duriusculus*] (colloq.) Hardish, hard, very hard, somewhat hard.

duumvir (dyɔmvir), s.m. [L wd] Duumvir.

duumvirat (dyɔmvira), s.m. Duumvirate.

duvet (dyvɛ), s.m. [f. ONorse *dún*] Down, fine soft feathers, fine soft hair, nap.

duveté, -e, duveteu-x, -se (dyvte, dyvtø), adj. Downy, covered with down.

dynamique (dinamik), s.f. [f. Gr. *dunamis*] Dynamics. ~, adj. Dynamic.

dynamisme (dinamism), s.m. Dynamism.

dynamite (dinamit), s.f. [f. Gr. *dunamis*] Dynamite.

dynamiter (dinamite), v.a. To blow up with dynamite.

dynamo (dinamo), s.f. [short for *dynamo-électrique*] Dynamo.

dynamomètre (dinamomɛtr), s.m. Dynamometer, dynameter.

dynaste (dinast), s.m. [f. Gr. *dunastēs*] Dynast.

dynastie (dinasti), s.f. [f. *dynaste*] Dynasty.

dynastique (dinastik), adj. Dynastic, dynastical.

dyne (din), s.f. [f. Gr. *dunamis*] (phys.) Dyne, unit of force.

dyscole (diskɔl) adj. [f. Gr. *duscolos*] Difficult to live with.

dysenterie (disɑ̃tri), s.f. [f. Gr. *dusenteria*] (pathol.) Dysentery.

dysménorrhée (dismenɔre), s.f. [*dus*+ *ménorrhée*] (pathol.) Dysmenorrhoea.

dyspepsie (dispɛpsi), s.f. [f. Gr. *duspepsia*] (pathol.) Dyspepsia.

dyspeptique (dispɛptik), adj. s.m.f. Dyspeptic.

dyspnée (dispne), s.f. [f. Gr. *duspnoia*] (pathol.) Dyspnoea.

dysurie (dizyri), s.f. [f. Gr. *dusouria*] (pathol.) Dysuria.

dysurique (dizyrik), adj. Dysuric.

dytique (ditik), s.m. [Gr. *dutikos*] (ent.) Dytiscid, water-beetle.

E

E, e (ə, e, ɛ), s.m. 5th letter of the alphabet.

eau (pl. **-x**) (o), s.f. [L *aqua*] Water; *à fleur d'*~, on a level with the water; *aller à l'*~, to take to the water (of a dog); *au bord de l'*~, at the water's edge; ~ *bénite*, holy water; ~ *de mer*, salt water, sea-water; ~ *douce*, fresh water (as opposed to sea-water); *jet d'*~, fountain; *grandes* ~*x*, display of elaborate fountains; *faire* ~, or *faire une voie d'*~, (naut.) to spring a leak; to leak; *le supplice de l'*~, ordeal by water; *revenir sur l'*~, to come to the surface; *un diamant de la plus belle* ~, a diamond of the first water; *pièce d'*~, or *nappe d'*~, sheet of water, pond, lake, artificial lake; *se jeter à l'*~, (*a*) to jump into the water, to take the plunge, to dive; (*b*) to drown oneself; (fig.) *se mettre dans l'*~ *de peur de se mouiller*, to cut off one's nose to spite one's face; *faire venir l'*~ *à la bouche*, to make one's mouth water; *s'en aller en* ~ *de boudin*, to come to nought; (fam.) to be a wash-out; *d'ici là il passera bien de l'*~ *sous le pont*, a lot may happen between now and then; *c'est une goutte d'*~ *dans la mer*, it 's a drop in the bucket; *faire venir l'*~ *au moulin*, to bring grist to the mill; *porter de l'*~ *à la rivière*, to carry coals to Newcastle; (prov.) *il n'est pire* ~ *que celle qui dort*, still waters run deep; (prov.) *l'*~ *va toujours au moulin*, money goes where money is; *ils se ressemblent comme deux gouttes d'*~, they are as like as two peas; *nager entre deux* ~*x*, (*a*) to swim under water; (*b*) to run with the hare and hunt with the hounds; *pêcher en* ~ *trouble*, to fish in troubled waters; *se noyer dans un verre d'*~, to make mountains out of mole-hills; *ses projets sont tombés dans l'*~, his schemes have fizzled out; *tempête dans un verre d'*~, storm in a tea-cup; *aller à vau l'*~, to go to rack and ruin; to come to nothing; *coup d'épée dans l'*~, useless attempt; *eau bénite de cour*, blarney, empty promises, soft sawder; *rester le bec dans l'*~, to be kept in suspense, to be made to dance attendance; *à l'*~ *!, à l'*~ *!*, drown him !, duck him !; *la goutte d'*~ *qui fait déborder le vase*, the last straw that breaks the camel's back; ~*x d'égout*, sewage; ~ *de javel*, bleaching liquid; ~ *de* *pluie*, rain-water; ~ *potable*, drinking-water; ~ *de puits*, well-water, pump-water; ~ *rougie*, weak wine and water; ~ *de savon*, ~ *de savonnage*, soapsuds; ~ *de Seltz*, soda-water; ~ *de son*, bran tea; ~ *à souder*, soldering acid; ~ *de source*, spring water; ~ *de vaisselle*, dish-water; ~ *vive*, running water, hard water; *vive* ~, *marée de vive* ~, spring, spring-tide; (naut.) *voie d'*~, leak; *faire de l'*~, to water, to take in (fresh) water; *nappe d'*~, sheet of water; *colonne d'*~, head of water; *marteau d'*~, water-hammer; *château d'*~, water-tank, reservoir; *ne pas prendre l'*~, to be watertight, waterproof; *laver à grande* ~, to wash in plenty of water; (fig.) *mettre de l'*~ *dans son vin*, to sing small, to take a back seat, to come down a peg or two; *c'est le feu et l'*~, they are like oil and water (of two persons who don't agree); *il tombe de l'*~, it is raining; *le temps est à l'*~, it looks like rain; *tirant d'*~, draught of water; *cours d'*~, water-course, river; *faire une pleine* ~, to dive; perspiration, sweat; *être tout en* ~, to be drenched with perspiration; *suer sang et* ~, to toil and moil; **~x**, pl. watering-place, waters; *aller aux* ~*x*, to go to a watering-place.

eau-de-vie (odvi), s.f. (pl. *eaux-de-vie*) Brandy, spirits; *cerises à l'*~, cherries in brandy, brandy-cherries; ~ *de grain*, grain- or corn-spirit; ~ *de lie*, wine-spirit.

eau-forte (ofɔrt), s.f. (pl. *eaux-fortes*) Aqua fortis, etching.

ébahi, -e (ebai), p. adj. Dumbfounded, amazed; syn. ÉBAUBI.

(s')ébahir (sebair), v.pr. [f. interj. *bah!*] To wonder, to marvel (*de*, at), to be dumbfounded, to be amazed.

ébahissement (ebaismɑ̃), s.m. Amazement, astonishment.

ébarbage, ébarbement (ebarbaʒ, ebarbmɑ̃), s.m. Paring; (engr.) edging-off, scraping.

ébarber (ebarbe), v.a. [f. *é+barbe*] To pare, to trim; to remove burrs from; to scrape (engravings, &c.).

ébarbeu-r, -se (ebarbœr), s.m.f. Trimmer.

ébarboir (ebarbwar), s.m. Parer, scraper.

ébarbure (ebarbyr), s.f. Clipping; (techn.) burr.

ébarouir (ebaruir), v.a.n. To dry up, to desiccate; **s'~**, v.pr. to dry up, to become desiccated, parched.

ébats (eba), s.m.pl. [f. *ébattre*] Gambol, frolic; *prendre ses* ~, to disport oneself.

ébattement (ebatmɑ̃), s.m. (archaic) Diversion, frolic, pastime.

(s')ébattre (sebatr), v.pr. [f. *é+battre*] To sport, to gambol, to frolic.

ébaubi, -e (ebobi), p. adj. [*é*+L *balbus*] (fam.) Astounded, dumbfounded; syn. ÉBAHI.

ébaubir (ebobir), v.a. To astound; **s'~**, v.pr. to be astounded.

ébaubissement (ebobismɑ̃), s.m. (fam.) Astonishment.

ébauchage (eboʃaʒ), s.m. Sketching, drafting; rough-hewing.

ébauche (eboʃ), s.f. Sketch, rough draft; syn. ESQUISSE.

ébaucher (eboʃe), v.a. [etym. dub.; perhaps OF *baushe*, builder's mortar] To sketch, to rough-draft; to rough-cast, to rough-hew; to outline; (fig.) to indicate lightly; ~ *un sourire*, to give a suspicion of a smile.

ébaucheu-r, -se (eboʃœr), s.m.f. Sketcher; (sculpt.) rough-hewer; (techn.) watchmaker's assistant.

ébauchoir (eboʃwar), s.m. (sculpt.) Boaster, chisel; (carp.) mortise-chisel.

ébaudir (ebodir), v.a. [*é* +OF *baud*, gay] (archaic) To enliven, to divert; **s'~**, v.pr. to frolic, to frisk.

ébaudissement (ebodismɑ̃), s.m. (archaic) Merry-making.

ébénacé, -e (ebenase), adj. [f. *ébène*] Ebony-like.

ébénacées (ebenase), s.f.pl. (bot.) Ebenaceae.

ébène (ebɛn), s.f. [Gr. *ebenos*] Ebony.

ébénier (ebenje), s.m. (bot.) Ebony-tree.

ébéniste (ebenist), s.m. Cabinet-maker.

ébénisterie (ebenistəri), s.f. Cabinet-work.

éberluer (ebɛrlɥe), v.a. To astound, to nonplus; *être tout éberlué*, to be flabbergasted, or struck all of a heap.

ébiseler (ebizle), v.a. [f. *biseau*] To chamfer, to countersink, to bevel.

éblouir (ebluir), v.a. [*e*+OHG *blôdi*] To dazzle.

éblouissant, -e (ebluisɑ̃), p. adj. Dazzling.

éblouissement (ebluismɑ̃), s.m. Dazzle, dazzlement; (fig.) bewilderment, astonishment.

ébonite (ebɔnit), s.f. [f. Engl. *ebony*] Ebonite, vulcanite.

éborgnage (ebɔrɲaʒ), s.m. (hort.) Nipping, thinning (of buds).

éborgner (ebɔrɲe), v.a. [f. *borgne*] **1.** To blind in one eye; **2.** (hort.) to thin out, to nip off (buds).

ébouage (ebuaʒ), s.m. Scavenging.

ébouer (ebue), v.a. [f. *boue*] To scavenge.

éboueu-r, -se (ebuœr), s.m.f. Scavenger, road-sweeper; syn. BOUEUR. **~**, s.f. Scavenging-machine.

ébouillantage (ebujɑ̃taʒ), s.m. Scalding.

ébouillanter (ebujɑ̃te), v.a. [f. *bouillant*] To scald.

éboulement (ebulmɑ̃), s.m. **1.** Falling-in, fall, collapse; landslip; **2.** debris.

ébouler (ebule), v.a. [f. *bouler*] To knock down, to cause to fall; **s'~**, v.pr. to fall in, to collapse, to sink.

ébouleu-x, -se (ebulø), adj. Soft, liable to sink in, treacherous (of sand, &c.).
éboulis (ebuli), s.m. Fallen ground, rubbish, debris.
ébouqueter (ebukte), v.a. (hort.) To defoliate.
ébourgeonnement, ebourgeonnage (eburʒonmɑ̃, eburʒonaʒ), s.m. (hort.) Disbudding.
ébourgeonner (eburʒone), v.a. [f. *bourgeon*] (hort.) To disbud.
ébourgeonnoir (eburʒonwar), s.m. (hort.) Nipping-tool, tree-clipper.
ébouriffant, -e (eburifɑ̃), p. adj. (fig.) Startling, unheard of, amazing.
ébouriffer (eburife), v.a. [f. *bourre*] To disorder, to ruffle the hair of; (fig.) to startle, to amaze.
ébourrer (ebure), v.a. [f. *bourre*] To remove the hair from (hides, &c.).
ébouter (ebute), v.a. [f. *bout*] To cut off the end of.
ébraiser (ebrɛze), v.a. [f. *braise*] To clear (embers).
ébraisoir (ebrɛzwar), s.m. Fire-shovel, furnace-shovel.
ébranchement, ébranchage (ebrɑ̃ʃmɑ̃, ebrɑ̃ʃaʒ), s.m. [f. *branche*] Lopping, polling; (hort.) pruning.
ébrancher (ebrɑ̃ʃe), v.a. [f. *branche*] To lop, to poll; (hort.) to prune.
ébranchoir (ebrɑ̃ʃwar), s.m. Pruning-tool, branch-cutter.
ébranlable (ebrɑ̃labl), adj. Not unshakable, shaky.
ébranlement (ebrɑ̃lmɑ̃), s.m. Shock, concussion, shaking; (fig.) shock, disturbance.
ébranler (ebrɑ̃le), v.a. [f. *branle*] **1.** To shake, to disturb, to unsettle; (fig.) to disturb, to agitate, to move; **2.** to set in motion; **s'~**, v.pr. **1.** to shake, to be shaken, to totter; (fig.) to be shaken, to waver, to be disturbed, to be moved; **2.** to begin to move, to get under way, to be set in motion, to start.
ébrasement (ebrɑzmɑ̃), s.m. **ébrasure** (ebrɑzyr), s.f. (arch.) Splay, splaying.
ébraser (ebrɑze), v.a. [f. *bras*] (arch.) To splay.
ébrèchement (ebrɛʃmɑ̃), s.m. Notching.
ébrécher (ebreʃe), v.a. [f. *brèche*] To notch, to indent, to break a bit off; to chip, to make a gap in; (fig.) to impair; ~ *sa fortune*, to make a hole in one's fortune.
ébriété (ebrijete), s.f. [L *ebrietas*] Inebriety, ebriety.
ébrouement (ebrumɑ̃), s.m. Sneezing, snorting.
ébrouer (ebrue), v.a. [Germ. *bruhen*] (of dyers) To wash; **s'~**, v.pr. **1.** to snort, to sneeze; **2.** (of small birds) to take a bath.
ébruitement (ebrɥitmɑ̃), s.m. Publishing, spreading abroad, revealing.
ébruiter (ebrɥite), v.a. [f. *bruit*] To divulge, to noise abroad, to publish about, to report, to make known, to spread about.
ébuard (ebɥar), s.m. [etym. dub.] Wooden wedge (for splitting logs).
ébûcheter (ebyʃte), v.n. [f. *bûche*] To gather kindling.
ébulliomètre (ebyljomɛtr), s.m. [L *ebullire*+Gr. *metron*]; see syn. ÉBULLIOSCOPE.
ébullioscope (ebyljoskop), s.m. [L *ebullire* +Gr. *skopein*] Ebullioscope (instrument for ascertaining the strength of distilled liquors).
ébullition (ebylisjɔ̃), s.f. [L *ebullitio*] Ebullition, boiling; (fig.) effervescence, ebullition.
éburine (ebyrin), s.f. [L *ebur*] Eburin.
éburné, -e, éburnéen, -ne (ebyrne, ebyrneɛ̃), adj. Eburnean, ivory-like.
écacher (ekaʃe), v.a. [*é*+*cacher*] To crush, to crumple, to squash, to flatten, to shell.
écaillage (ekajaʒ), s.m. Scaling (of fish, &c.); peeling (of paint, varnish, &c.); opening (of oysters).
écaille (ekaj), s.f. [Goth. *kalja*] **1.** Scale; **2.** plates (of tortoiseshell); tortoiseshell; *peigne d'~*, tortoiseshell comb; ~ *d'huître*, oyster-shell.
écailler (ekaje), v.a. **1.** To scale (a fish); **2.** to roof with scale-like plates; **s'~**, v.pr. to peel (of paint, &c.).
écaill-er, -ère (ekaje), s.m.f. Oyster-seller.
écaillette (ekajɛt), s.f. Fine scale.
écailleu-x, -se (ekajø), adj. Scaly, squamous. [shell.
écale (ekal), s.f. [Frankish *skala*] Husk,
écaler (ekale), v.a. To shell, to husk.
écalot (ekalo), s.m. Shelled nut.
écanguer (ekɑ̃ge), v.a. [Celt. orig.] To beat (hemp, flax, &c.).
écangueur (ekɑ̃gœr), s.m. Hemp-beater, flax-beater.
écarlate (ekarlat), s.f. adj. [etym. dub.] Scarlet.
écarquillement (ekarkijmɑ̃), s.m. Opening wide, spreading-out.
écarquiller (ekarkije), v.a. [f. *equartiller*, f. *quart*] To open, to open wide, to spread apart; ~ *les yeux*, to open one's eyes wide, to stare.
écart (ekar), s.m. [f. *écarter*] **1.** Deviation, swerve, stepping aside; *à l'~*, aside, apart, in a solitary place; *le cheval fit un ~*, the horse shied; (acrob.) *faire le grand ~*, to do the splits; *se tenir à l'~*, to stand aloof; (fig.) variation, digression; *les ~s de l'imagination*, the flights of the imagination; **2.** (vet.) strain; **3.** ~*s* (usually pl.) isolated farms or hamlets.
écarté, -e (ekarte), p. adj. Remote, lonely, secluded.

écarté (ekarte), s.m. Écarté (game).
écartelé, -e (ekartəle), p. adj. (herald.) Quartered. ~, s.m. Quartering.
écartèlement (ekartɛlmɑ̃), s.m. Tearing to pieces, quartering.
écarteler (ekartəle), v.a. [*é*+L *quartus*] **1.** To tear to pieces, to quarter; **2.** (herald.) to quarter.
écartelure (ekartəlyr), s.f. (herald.) Quartering.
écartement (ekartmɑ̃), s.m. **1.** Putting aside, removal; **2.** distance apart, separation.
écarter (ekarte), v.a. [f. *é*+*quart*] **1.** To set aside, to keep off, away, or out; to dispel, to disperse, to scatter; to separate; ~ *la foule*, to hold the crowd in check; ~ *les jambes*, to straddle, to set one's legs wide apart; **2.** to avert; ~ *un coup*, to ward off a blow; **3.** (cards) to discard; **s'~**, v.pr. **1.** to turn aside, to deviate; to stray, to err; *s'~ de son chemin*, to go out of one's way; *s'~ de son devoir*, to swerve from one's duty; *s'~ de son sujet*, to stray from the subject; **2.** to make way; *la foule s'écarta*, the crowd made way; syn. ÉLOIGNER, METTRE À L'ÉCART.
ecce homo (ɛkseomo), s.m. invar. [L wd] **1.** Picture of Christ crowned with thorns; **2.** (fig.) suffering person; *c'est un véritable* ~, his face is a mask of suffering.
ecchymose (ɛkimoz), s.f. [Gr. *ek*+ *khumos*] Ecchymosis.
ecchymoser (ɛkimoze), v.a. To cause an ecchymosis in.
ecclésiastique (ɛklezjastik), adj. [f. Gr. *ekklēsia*] Ecclesiastic, ecclesiastical. ~, s.m. Ecclesiastic.
ecclésiastiquement (eklezjastikmɑ̃), adv. Ecclesiastically.
écervelé, -e (esɛrvəle), adj. [f. *cervelle*] Hare-brained, scatter-brained, giddy; *une tête ~e*, a madcap. ~, s.m.f. Madcap, scatter-brain; syn. ÉTOURDI, ÉVAPORÉ.
échafaud (eʃafo), s.m. [f. pop. L *catafalicum*] **1.** Scaffold, gallows; **2.** stage, platform.
échafaudage (eʃafodaʒ), s.m. **1.** Scaffolding; (fig.) erection, display, structure; ~ *de preuves*, piling-up of proofs, pile of proofs; **2.** building, making; *l'~ d'une fortune*, the making of a fortune.
échafauder (eʃafode), v.n. To erect a scaffolding; ~, v.a. **1.** to collect, to pile up, to erect; to display; **2.** (fig.) to plan out, to do the groundwork of, to build; ~ *un roman*, to plan out a novel.
échalas (eʃalɑ), s.m. [f. Gr. *kharax*] **1.** Vine-prop; hop-pole; **2.** (fam.) lamp-post; *c'est un véritable* ~, he is a regular lamp-post.
échalassement, échalassage (eʃalasmɑ̃, eʃalasaʒ), s.m. Propping.
échalasser (eʃalase), v.a. To prop.
échalier, échallier, échalis (eʃalje, eʃali), s.m. [L *scalarium*] Stile; fence, hurdle.
échalote (eʃalɔt), s.f. [LL *ascalonia*] Shallot.
échampir (eʃɑ̃pir), v.a. See RÉCHAMPIR.
échancrer (eʃɑ̃kre), v.a. [f. *chancre*] To hollow out.
échancrure (eʃɑ̃kryr), s.f. **1.** (geog.) Indentation; **2.** hollowing, opening.
échandole (eʃɑ̃dɔl), s.f. Shingle (for roofs).
échange (eʃɑ̃ʒ), s.m. [f. *échanger*] Exchange, barter; *libre-~*, free trade.
échangeable (eʃɑ̃ʒabl), adj. Exchangeable.
échanger (eʃɑ̃ʒe), v.a. [f. LL *excambiare*] To exchange, to barter; to interchange.
échangiste (eʃɑ̃ʒist), s.m. Exchanger; *libre-~*, free trader.
échanson (eʃɑ̃sɔ̃), s.m. [Frankish *skankjo*] Cup-bearer.
échansonnerie (eʃɑ̃sɔnri), s.f. (collect.) **1.** Royal cup-bearers; **2.** royal cellars.
échantillon (eʃɑ̃tijɔ̃), s.m. [OF *échantol*, standard measure] **1.** Sample, pattern; specimen; **2.** gauge (for weights and measures); **3.** (fig.) example, sample.
echantillonnage (eʃɑ̃tijɔnaʒ), s.m. **1.** Gauging; **2.** sampling.
échantillonner (eʃɑ̃tijɔne), v.a. **1.** To gauge (weights and measures); **2.** to sample; to cut samples of.
échanvrer (eʃɑ̃vre), v.a. [f. *chanvre*] (techn.) To hackle, to heckle.
échanvroir (eʃɑ̃vrwar), s.m. Hackle.
échappade (eʃapad), s.f. (rare) Escapade; see syn. ESCAPADE.
échappatoire (eʃapatwar), s.f. [f. *échapper*] (fig.) Way out (of a difficulty), loophole, shift.
échappé, -e (eʃape), s.m.f. [f. *échapper*] Fugitive, runaway; (fig.) ~ *des galères*, gaol-bird; (fig.) ~ *des Petites Maisons*, Bedlamite.
echappée (eʃape), s.f. **1.** View, opening, vista; **2.** (rare) escapade, prank; **3.** (rare) short time, snatch; ~ *de beau temps*, a spell of fine weather; **4.** (rare) turning-space (for carriages).
échappement (eʃapmɑ̃), s.m. Escape; (watchm.) escapement; (motor.) exhaust; eduction; *marcher avec ~ libre*, to run without the silencer; *soupape d'~*, exhaust valve.
échapper (eʃape), v.n. [LL *excappare*] **1.** To escape, to make one's escape, to get away, to flee; *laisser ~ une occasion*, to let slip an opportunity; *laisser ~ un mot*, to drop a word; ~ *au naufrage*, to escape shipwreck; ~ *du naufrage*, to escape from the wreck; *cela m'est échappé*, I let it out; it was a slip of mine; **2.** to be overlooked, forgotten; *cela m'a échappé*, it has slipped my memory; it escaped my notice; ~ *au*

danger, to avoid danger; to escape; *l'~ belle,* to have a narrow escape; (fam.) *je l'ai échappé belle,* it was a near thing, a near shave; **s'~,** v.pr. to get loose; to escape, to get away, to steal away; to vanish, to disappear; syn. S'ÉVADER, S'ENFUIR.

écharde (eʃard), s.f. [Germ. *Scharte*] Splinter, prickle (of a thistle, &c.).

échardonnage (eʃardɔnaʒ), s.m. [f. *chardon*] Clearing (of thistles).

échardonner (eʃardɔne), v.a. [f. *chardon*] To clear of thistles.

échardonnette (eʃardɔnɛt), s.f. **échardonnoir** (eʃardɔnwar), s.m. Thistle-hook.

écharnement, écharnage (eʃarnmɑ̃, eʃarnaʒ), s.m. Fleshing; paring.

écharner (eʃarne), v.a. [f. L *caro*] (techn.) To flesh, to pare, to scrape (hides).

écharnoir (eʃarnwar), s.m. Fleshing-knife.

écharnure (eʃarnyr), s.f. Scrapings, parings (of hides).

écharpe (eʃarp), s.f. [OHG *skerpa*] **1.** Scarf, sash; *~ de maire,* mayor's ribbon of office; *changer d'~,* to turn one's coat; *coup d'épée en ~,* slanting cut; **2.** sling; *porter le bras en ~,* to wear one's arm in a sling; *prendre en ~,* to enfilade.

écharper (eʃarpe), v.a. **1.** (techn.) To hackle; **2.** to slash, to cut; to cut to pieces; to pull to pieces, to lynch; *~ un régiment,* to cut a regiment to pieces; *il va se faire ~ par la foule,* he will be lynched; the crowd will tear him to pieces.

écharpiller (eʃarpije), v.a. [f. *écharper*] (techn.) To hackle.

échars, -e (eʃar), adj. [LL *excarpsus*] Light, below the legal standard (of coins).

échasse (eʃas), s.f. [Dutch *schaats*] **1.** Stilt; *marcher avec des ~s,* to walk on stilts; *~ d'échafaud,* scaffolding-pole; (fig.) *être toujours monté sur des ~s,* to be always riding the high horse; to be always on stilts; to be as stiff as a poker; **2.** (ornith.) stilt-bird; *~ à manteau noir,* long-legged plover.

échassiers (eʃasje), s.m.pl. [f. *échasse*] (ornith.) Grallatores, waders; (sing. fig., of a person) spindle-shanks.

échauboulé, -e (eʃobule), adj. (rare) Pimpled.

échauboulure (eʃobulyr), s.f. [f. *chaude+bouillure*] Pimple, blotch, rash.

échaudage[1] (eʃodaʒ), s.m. [f. *chaux*] Whitewash, whitewashing, limewash, limewashing; (the syn. CHAULAGE is more usual).

échaudage[2] (eʃodaʒ), s.m. [f. *chaud*] Scalding.

échaudé (eʃode), s.m. Simnel-cake.

échaudé, -e (eʃode), p. adj. **1.** Wrinkled, shrivelled (of wheat); **2.** scalded (fig.) the worse for wear; *chat ~ craint l'eau froide,* once bit twice shy; a burnt child dreads the fire.

échauder[1] (eʃode), v.a. [LL *excaldare*] To scald; *~ un client,* (fig.) to rook a customer; **s'~,** v.pr. to scald oneself; (fig.) *il s'est échaudé les doigts dans cette affaire,* he got his fingers burnt in that affair.

échauder[2] (eʃode), v.a. [f. *chaux*] **1.** To steep in lime-water; **2.** to limewash; (CHAULER or BLANCHIR À LA CHAUX are more usual).

échaudoir (eʃodwar), s.m. **1.** Scalding-house; **2.** scalding-vat.

échaudure (eʃodyr), s.f. [f. *chaud*] Scald.

échauffaison (eʃofɛzɔ̃), s.f. (pathol.) Eruption, rash.

échauffant, -e (eʃofɑ̃), p. adj. [f. *chauffer*] (med.) Heating, binding; irritating; (fig.) exciting.

échauffé (eʃofe), s.m. Hot smell; *sentir l'~,* to smell overheated.

échauffement (eʃofmɑ̃), s.m. **1.** Heating, fermentation; **2.** (med.) constipation; **3.** (fig.) excitement; **4.** (motor.) overheating.

échauffer (eʃofe), v.a. [f. *é+chauffer*] **1.** To heat, to overheat; to warm; **2.** (med.) to constipate; **3.** (fig.) to excite; *~ la bile à X,* to put X in a rage; **s'~,** v.pr. to get hot, to get over-heated; (fig.) to chafe, to fume, to wax hot; *le jeu s'échauffe,* the game is getting warm.

échauffourée (eʃofure), s.f. [OF *chauffourer*] **1.** Unsuccessful attack, skirmish, affray; **2.** (obs.) blundering enterprise, blunder, ineffectual attempt.

échauffure (eʃofyr), s.f. Red rash.

échauguette (eʃogɛt), s.f. [f. Frankish *skarwahta*] Watch-tower.

échauler (eʃole), v.a. See syn. CHAULER.

échéance (eʃeɑ̃s), s.f. [f. *échoir*] Expiration, falling due, maturity; term of payment; *à courte ~,* short-dated; *à longue ~,* long-dated; *jusqu'à l'~,* until due; *payer à l'~,* to pay at maturity.

échéancier (eʃeɑ̃sje), s.m. (comm.) Bill-book.

échéant, -e (eʃeɑ̃), p. adj. Falling due; *le cas ~,* in that case, should the occasion arise.

échec (eʃɛk), s.m. [f. *échecs*] Check; *éprouver un ~,* to meet with a check; *~ et mat,* checkmate; *faire ~ et mat,* to checkmate; *tenir en ~,* to keep in check.

échecs (eʃɛk), s.m.pl. [Pers. *sháh,* king, influenced by OF *eschec,* booty, of Germanic orig.] **1.** Chess; *jouer aux ~,* to play chess; *joueur d'~,* chess-player; **2.** chess-men; set of chess-men.

échelette (eʃlɛt), s.f. [f. *échelle*] Rack (for pack-saddles, &c.).

échelle (eʃɛl), s.f. [L *scala*] **1.** Ladder; *~ à incendie* or *de sauvetage,* fire-escape; *~ double,* trestle; *~ de commandement,* accommodation-ladder; ~ *de corde*, rope-ladder; ~ *de passavant*, gangway ladder; ~ *de siège*, scaling-ladder; *Échelles du Levant*, commercial ports of the East; *faire la courte ~ à X*, (lit.) to give X a lift up, to make a back for X; (fig.) to give X a helping hand; to give X a shove up; *après lui il faut tirer l'~*, he takes the cake; he has beaten all the records; (pop.) *monter à l'~*, to rise; to get worked up into a passion; *faire monter X à l'~*, to get, or take a rise out of X; **2.** scale; *à l'~*, to scale; *à l'~ de 1/1000*, on a scale of 1/1000; *sur une grande* or *petite ~*, on a large or small scale; ~ *mobile*, sliding-scale; (fig.) *sur une large ~*, on a vast scale.

échelon (eʃlɔ̃), s.m. [f. *échelle*] Rung, round, step (of a ladder); (fig.) stepping-stone; (mil.) echelon.

échelonnement (eʃlɔnmɑ̃), s.m. Echeloning, posting in different places; gradation.

échelonner (eʃlɔne), v.a. **1.** To graduate; **2.** to space out; **3.** (mil.) to draw up in echelon; to echelon; **s'~**, v.pr. **1.** to be graduated; **2.** to be spaced out; **3.** to slope; **4.** (mil.) to be drawn up in echelon.

échenau (pl. **x**), **écheno** (eʃno), s.m. [f. *chenal*] (metall.) Sand-basin.

échenillage (eʃnijaʒ), s.m. [f. *chenille*] Ridding of caterpillars.

écheniller (eʃnije), v.a. [f. *chenille*] **1.** To rid of caterpillars; **2.** (fig.) to weed out, to prune; *il fait ~ ses articles par X*, he gets X to trim his articles into shape.

échenilleur (eʃnijœr), s.m. Caterpillar-destroyer.

échenilloir (eʃnijwar), s.m. (hort.) Caterpillar-shears.

écheoir (eʃwar), v.n. See ÉCHOIR.

écheveau (pl. **-x**) (eʃvo), s.m. [L *scapus*] Skein, hank; (fig.) tangle, tangled skein.

échevelé, -e (eʃəvle), p. adj. [f. *cheveux*] Dishevelled; (fig.) wild, extravagant.

écheveler (eʃəvle), v.a. To dishevel.

échevette (eʃvɛt), s.f. [f. *écheveau*] (techn.) Unit of measure for wool, skein (of 100 metres in length).

échevin (eʃvɛ̃), s.m. [LL *scabinus*] Sheriff; alderman.

échevinage (eʃvinaʒ), s.m. Shrievalty, sheriffdom; aldermanry.

échidné (ekidne), s.m. [Gr. *ekhidna*] (zool.) Echidna.

échiffe, échiffre (eʃif, eʃifr), s.m. [LL *schiffa*] (arch.) Partition-wall (of a staircase).

échillon (eʃijɔ̃), s.m. (naut. in the Levant) Waterspout.

échine[1] (eʃin), s.f. [OHG *skina*] Spine, backbone; chine (of pork); (fig.) *avoir l'~ souple*, to be a fawning, cringing creature; *frotter l'~ à X*, to give X a good thrashing.

échine[2] (eʃin), s.f. [Gr. *ekhinos*] (arch.) Echinus; ovolo.

échinée (eʃine), s.f. [f. *échine*[1]] Chine, chine-piece.

échiner (eʃine), v.a. [f. *échine*[1]] To break the back of; to kill; (fig.) to knock up, to tire out; **s'~**, v.pr. to knock oneself up, to work oneself to death.

échinodermes (ekinɔdɛrm), s.m.pl. [f. Gr. *ekhinos*+*derma*] (zool.) Echinodermata.

échiqueté, -e (eʃikte), adj. [f. *échiquier*] (herald.) Chequered.

échiquier (eʃikje), s.m. [f. *échecs*] **1.** Chess-board; **2.** chequer-work, chequer-pattern; *en ~*, in squares, chequerwise; **3.** Exchequer; **4.** square net.

écho (eko), s.m. [Gr. *ēkhō*] Echo, (fig.) *faire ~ à*, to echo, to respond to, to approve of; *se faire l'~ d'un bruit*, to repeat a rumour, to spread a rumour.

échoir (eʃwar), v.n. [*é*+*choir*] **1.** To expire, to fall due, to lapse; *le payement doit ~ à Noël*, the payment falls due at Christmas; **2.** to happen, to fall to one's lot, to fall, to befall; *cela lui est échu en partage*, that fell to his lot; *si le cas y échoit*, or *le cas échéant*, should it befall, in that case.

échomètre (ekɔmɛtr) s.m. [Gr. *ēkhō*+*metron*] Echometer.

echométrie (ekɔmetri), s.f. Echometry.

échométrique (ekɔmetrik), adj. Echometric.

échoppe[1] (eʃɔp), s.f. [Germ. *Schoppen*] Booth, stall; wooden work-shop.

échoppe[2] (eʃɔp), s.f. [L *scalprum*] (engr.) Scorper, round or flat graver, burin.

échopper (eʃɔpe), v.a. To gouge, to work with a burin.

échoppi-er, -ère (eʃɔpje), s.m.f. (rare) Stall-keeper.

échouage (eʃwaʒ), s.m. [f. *échouer*] **1.** Stranding, running aground; **2.** beaching, stranding; *lieu d'~*, beaching or stranding place.

échouement (eʃumɑ̃), s.m. [f. *échouer*] Stranding, action of running aground; (fig.) failure, wreckage (of plans, &c.).

échouer (eʃwe), v.n. [L *excutere*] To run aground, to be stranded; (fig.) to miscarry, to fail, to be wrecked; *ses projets échouèrent*, his plans were wrecked; ~ *dans un examen*, to fail in an examination; to be ploughed; v.a. ~ *un navire*, to run aground, to strand (a vessel); **s'~**, v.pr. to run aground, to be stranded.

écimage (esimaʒ), s.m. [f. *cime*] Topping (of vegetables); polling, pollarding (of trees).

écimer (esime), v.a. [f. *cime*] To top (vegetables); to poll (trees).

éclaboussement (eklabusmɑ̃), s.m. Splashing, bespattering.

éclabousser (eklabuse), v.a. [etym. dub.; perhaps Gallic *klabbo*] To splash, to bespatter, to muddy; (fig.) to cast a slur upon, to throw mud at; (fig.) to humiliate, to leave far behind, to surpass (in luxury).

éclaboussure (eklabusyr), s.f. Splash, splash of mud; (fig.) undeserved opprobrium; *avoir les ~s*, to get all the blame.

éclair (eklɛr), s.m. [f. *éclairer*] **1.** Lightning, flash of lightning; flash; *~ de chaleur* or *de soleil*, sheet-lightning; *~ sinueux*, snake-lightning; *~ ramifié*, forked lightning; (fig.) flash; *~ de génie*, flash of genius; **2.** (pastry) éclair.

éclairage (eklɛraʒ), s.m. Lighting; illumination; *~ au gaz*, gas-lighting; *~ à l'électricité*, electric light.

éclairant, -e (eklɛrɑ̃), p. adj. Lighting, illuminating.

éclaircie (eklɛrsi), s.f. **1.** Break, rift, opening (in clouds, &c.); **2.** fine interval, clearing-up (of weather); **3.** clearing, glade, vista; **4.** (fig.) change for the better.

éclaircir (eklɛrsir), v.a. [L *ex+clarus*] **1.** To make clear or clearer, to clear up, to brighten; **2.** to clarify, to thin (liquids); **3.** (fig.) to throw light on, to elucidate, to explain; *~ quelqu'un*, to enlighten a person; *le temps éclaircit la vérité*, time brings truth to light; **s'~**, v.pr. to clear, to become clear, bright, or fine; (fig.) to be solved, cleared up, elucidated.

éclaircissage (eklɛrsisaʒ), s.m. Polishing (of metals, &c.).

éclaircissant, -e (eklɛrsisɑ̃), p. adj. Clearing, brightening; (fig.) elucidating.

éclaircissement (eklɛrsismɑ̃), s.m. Clearing-up, elucidation; *demander des ~s*, to ask for a precise explanation.

éclaire (eklɛr), s.f. (bot.) Celandine; *la grande, la petite ~*, greater, lesser, celandine.

éclairé, -e (eklɛre), p. adj. Lighted; well lighted; (fig.) well informed, intelligent.

éclairement (eklɛrmɑ̃), s.m. Lighting.

éclairer (eklɛre,) v.a. [L *exclarare*] **1.** To light, to lighten, to illuminate; (fig.) to enlighten, to instruct; *~ l'esprit*, to cultivate the mind; **2.** to lead, to guide; (mil.) to reconnoitre; **3.** to observe, to watch; ~, v.n. to emit light, to sparkle, to shine, to brighten, to glitter; *les yeux du chat éclairent la nuit*, a cat's eyes shine at night; (slang) to pay what's owing, to fork out, to stump up; ~, v.impers. *il éclaire*, it lightens.

éclaireu-r, -se (eklɛrœr), s.m. **1.** (mil.) Scout; boy scout, girl guide; **2.** (naut.) advice-ship; *aller en ~*, to scout.

éclampsie (eklɑ̃psi), s.f. [Gr. *eklampsis*] (pathol.) Eclampsia.

éclanche (eklɑ̃ʃ), s.f. [Germ. *Schenkel*] Shoulder of mutton.

éclat (ekla), s.m. [f. *éclater*] **1.** Burst; crash, clap, peal, sudden uproar; *~ de rire*, burst of laughter; *rire aux ~s*, to roar with laughter; *~ de colère*, burst of anger; *~ de voix*, sudden shout; sound of angry voices; **2.** shiver, splinter; *~ d'obus*, splinter of shell; *~ de bois*, splinter; *voler en ~s*, to be shivered to fragments; **3.** brightness, glitter, refulgence; (fig.) lustre, pomp, renown, fame; gaudiness (of colour); rumour, noise; *feu* or *phare à ~s*, flashing light (in lighthouse); *action d'~*, brilliant achievement; heroic deed; *faire un ~*, to protest violently; to cause an open rupture; to create a sensation; *des personnes d'~*, eminent persons.

éclatant, -e (eklatɑ̃), p. adj. **1.** Bright, brilliant, dazzling, gorgeous, magnificent; **2.** piercing, loud; **3.** signal, striking, remarkable.

éclatement (eklatmɑ̃), s.m. Bursting, breaking-up, explosion; *~ de pneu*, tyre-burst.

éclater (eklate), v.n. [etym. dub.; OHG *sleizen*?] **1.** To split, to shiver, to burst, to break in pieces; *faire ~*, to shatter, to smash; *un obus éclata*, a shell burst; **2.** to cry out, to break out, to blaze out; *~ en sanglots*, to burst into tears; *~ de rire*, to burst out laughing; *~ en injures*, to break into abuse; **3.** to shine out, to flash.

éclectique (eklɛktik), adj. s.m. [Gr. *eklektikos*] Eclectic.

éclectisme (eklɛktism), s.m. Eclecticism.

éclipse (eklips), s.f. [Gr. *ekleipsis*] Eclipse; (fig.) eclipse, disappearance.

éclipser (eklipse), v.a. To eclipse; (fig.) (*a*) to conceal, to hide; (*b*) to eclipse, to put in the shade; to outdo; **s'~**, v.pr. to outdo each other; to be eclipsed; to disappear, to vanish; to take French leave.

écliptique (ekliptik), s.f. adj. Ecliptic.

éclissage (eklisaʒ), s.m. (surg.) Putting in splints.

éclisse (eklis), s.f. [f. *éclisser*] **1.** (surg.) Splint; **2.** slat, split wood; **3.** cheese-vat.

éclisser (eklise), v.a. [orig. dub.] (surg.) To put into splints.

éclissette (eklisɛt), s.f. Little splint.

éclopé, -e (eklɔpe), p. adj. Lame, halt, crippled; limping. ~, s.m.f. Cripple, disabled person.

écloper (eklɔpe), v.a. [OF *clop*, lame; *cloper*, to limp] To cripple, to lame.

éclore (eklɔr), v.n. [*é+clore*] **1.** To hatch, to be hatched (of eggs); **2.** to open, to blossom (of flowers); **3.** to dawn, to break; (fig.) to come to light.

éclosion (eklozjɔ̃), s.f. **1.** Hatching (of eggs); **2.** blossoming, opening (of flowers); **3.** dawn; (fig.) coming to light.

éclusage (eklyzaʒ), s.m. Damming; construction of locks.

écluse (eklyz), s.f. [L *exclusum*, f. *excludere*] **1.** Lock; sluice; **2.** mill-dam; dam; (fig.) flood-gate.

éclusée (eklyze), s.f. Lockful, lockage.

écluser (eklyze), v.a. **1.** To construct locks on; **2.** to take (a boat) through a lock.

éclusi-er, -ère (eklyzje), adj. Pertaining to a lock. ~, s.m.f. Lock-keeper.

écobuage (ekɔbɥaʒ), s.m. Weeding, burning of weeds.

écobue (ekɔby), s.f. Hoe, turfing-iron.

écobuer (ekɔbye), v.a. [etym. unkn.] To cut and burn stubble on (a field).

écœurant, -e (ekœrɑ̃), p. adj. Sickening, nauseating; (fig.) sickening, loathsome.

écœurement (ekœrmɑ̃), s.m. Feeling of sickness, nausea; (fig.) disgust, loathing.

écœurer (ekœre), v.a. [f. *cœur*] To sicken, to nauseate; (fig.) to sicken, to disgust.

écoinçon, écoinson (ekwɛ̃sɔ̃), s.m. [f. *coin*] **1.** Diagonal, angle tie; **2.** door-jamb; **3.** corner-stone.

écolage (ekɔlaʒ), s.m. Schooling.

écolâtre (ekɔlɑtr), s.m. (obs.) Theological professor.

école (ekɔl), s.f. [L *schola*; OF *escole*] **1.** School, college; school-house; *camarade d'~*, schoolfellow; *maître d'~*, schoolmaster, *maîtresse d'~*, schoolmistress; *faire l'~ buissonnière*, to play truant; (fig.) *l'~ du malheur*, the school of suffering; *ça sent l'~*, it savours of pedantry; **2.** school, sect; *faire ~* (in art, philosophy, &c.), to form a school; (fig.) manner, doctrine, teaching; *être à bonne ~*, to have the best models; **3.** (mil.) training, course; *vaisseau ~*, training-ship; *faire ~*, to have firing-practice; *~ de peloton*, squad-drill; *haute ~*, acrobatic riding; **4.** *faire une ~* (backgammon), to blunder in pegging one's points; (fig.) to learn through one's blunders.

écoli-er, -ère (ekɔlje), s.m.f. Schoolboy, schoolgirl, pupil; student; *en ~*, boylike; *prendre le chemin des ~s*, to go a roundabout way; *tour d'~*, schoolboy trick, prank; *papier ~*, foolscap paper; (fig.) novice, greenhorn, tyro; *ce n'est qu'un ~*, he is a mere novice.

éconduire (ekɔ̃dɥir), v.a. [f. *conduire*] To show to the door, to show out, to bow out, to dismiss; (fig.) to put off, to refuse access.

économat (ekɔnɔma), s.m. Bursarship, stewardship; bursar's office, steward's office.

économe (ekɔnɔm), s.m.f. Bursar, steward, treasurer; housekeeper, manager (of colleges, hospitals, &c.). ~, adj. (of persons) Economical, sparing, thrifty; *être ~ de louanges*, to be sparing of praise.

économie (ekɔnɔmi), s.f. [Gr. *oikonomia*] **1.** Economy; *l'~ de l'univers*, the scheme of the universe; good management, husbandry; **2.** thrift, economy; (pl.) savings; *faire des ~s*, to put by money, to save; (prov.) *il n'y a pas de petites ~s*, take care of the pence and the pounds will take care of themselves; *faire des ~s de bouts de chandelle*, to be penny-wise and pound-foolish; to be cheese-paring.

économique (ekɔnɔmik), adj. **1.** Economic; *problèmes ~s*, economic problems; **2.** economical, cheap; *chauffage ~*, economical heating. ⚠ 'Economical' is also used in the sense of 'saving', 'thrifty' = *économe*.

économiquement (ekɔnɔmikmɑ̃), adv. Economically.

économiser (ekɔnɔmize), v.a.n. To economize, to save, to spare; to cut down expenses; *~ ses forces*, to husband one's strength.

économiste (ekɔnɔmist), s.m.f. Economist.

écope, escope (ekɔp, ɛskɔp), s.f. [O. Swed. *skopa*] Scoop, ladle; (naut.) skeet.

écoper (ekɔpe), v.a. To scoop, to ladle; (naut.) to bale out; ~, v.n. (slang) to catch it, to cop it, to be strafed.

écorçage, écorcement (ekɔrsaʒ, ekɔrsmɑ̃), s.m. Barking, stripping, peeling.

écorce (ekɔrs), s.f. [L *cortex*] **1.** Bark; rind, peel; shell; (prov.) *entre l'arbre et l'~ il ne faut pas mettre le doigt*, don't meddle in other folk's feuds; *juger du bois par l'~*, to judge by appearances; **2.** (geol.) surface, crust (of the earth).

écorcer (ekɔrse), v.a. To bark, to peel, to strip.

écorché (ekɔrʃe), s.m. (paint.) Écorché, anatomical figure.

écorchement (ekɔrʃmɑ̃), s.m. Skinning; flaying; excoriation.

écorcher (ekɔrʃe), v.a. [L *excorticare*] To skin; to flay; to peel off, to graze, to gall; to peel, to bark; (fig.) to strip, to fleece, to distort; *cela écorche les oreilles*, it is ear-splitting; *~ ses clients*, to fleece one's clients; *il crie avant qu'on l'écorche*, he cries out before he is hurt; *~ l'anguille par la queue*, to get hold of the wrong end of the stick; *jamais beau parler n'écorcha la langue*, civility costs nothing; *~ une langue*, to murder a language; s'~, v.pr. to be galled, to be grazed; to tear one's skin off; *s'~ les doigts*, to bark one's fingers; *s'~ le genou*, to graze one's knee.

écorcherie (ekɔrʃri), s.f. Knacker's yard; (fig.) fleecing; inn where travellers get fleeced.

écorcheur (ekɔrʃœr), s.m. Knacker; flayer; (fig.) fleecer.

écorchure (ekɔrʃyr), s.f. Scratch, graze, excoriation.

écorner (ekɔrne), v.a. [*é*+*corne*] **1.** To break the horns of; *il fait un vent à* ~ *les bœufs*, it is blowing great guns; **2.** to break the corners off; to dog's-ear (pages); **3.** (fig.) to impair, to diminish, to curtail; ~ *sa fortune*, to make a hole in one's fortune.

écornifler (ekɔrnifle), v.a. [f. *écorner*] To sponge upon.

écorniflerie (ekɔrnifləri), s.f. (fig.) Sponging.

écornifleu-r, -se (ekɔrniflœr), s.m.f. **1.** Sponger, hanger-on, parasite; **2.** plagiarist; (fam.) cribber.

écornure (ekɔrnyr), s.f. [f. *écorner*] Broken corner; chip, chipping.

écossais, -e (ekɔsɛ), adj. Scottish; Scotch; *douche* ~*e*, alternately hot and cold shower-bath. ~, s.m. Scot, Scotsman, Scotchman; (fem.) Scotswoman, Scotchwoman.

écosser (ekɔse), v.a. [f. *cosse*] To shell, to husk.

écosseu-r, -se (ekɔsœr), s.m.f. Person who shells or husks.

écot[1] (eko), s.m. [Low Germ. *skot*] Stump (of tree or branch).

écot[2] (eko), s.m. [OHG *skot*] Share (of a reckoning); bill, score; *payez votre* ~, pay your share; pay your shot.

écoté, -e (ekɔte), p. adj. (herald.) Lopped.

écoufle (ekufl), s.m. [Celt. orig.] **1.** (ornith.) Kite; **2.** (toy) kite.

écoulement (ekulmɑ̃), s.m. [f. *écouler*] **1.** Flowing, flow; **2.** drainage (of water-pipes); *voie d'*~, outlet; **3.** (comm.) sale, disposal; export.

écouler (ekule), v.a. [*é*+*couler*] To dispose of, to sell; **s'**~, v.pr. **1.** to flow, pass or glide away; to slip away, to elapse (of time); **2.** (comm.) to be disposed of.

écourter (ekurte), v.a. [f. *court*] **1.** To shorten, to dock, to crop; **2.** to curtail, to cut down; ~ *un discours*, to cut down a speech.

écoute[1] (ekut), s.f. [Dutch *schoote*] (naut.) Lower rigging (of sails).

écoute[2] (ekut), s.f. [f. *écouter*] **1.** Eavesdropper's hiding-place; *être aux* ~*s*, to be on the watch; to be eavesdropping; *être à l'*~, (wireless) to be listening; to listen in; **2.** (mil., mining) écoute; **3.** pl. (hunt.) wild boar's ears.

écouter (ekute), v.a. [L *auscultare*] To listen to, to hearken to, to give ear to; ~ *raison*, to listen to reason; *se faire* ~, (*a*) to obtain a hearing; (*b*) to enforce obedience; (wireless) to listen in; *écoutez !*, look here!; **s'**~, v.pr. **1.** to be fond of the sound of one's own voice; **2.** to indulge oneself; *il s'écoute trop*, he fusses too much about himself.

écouteu-r, -se (ekutœr), s.m.f. **1.** Listener; eavesdropper; **2.** s.m. (wireless) head-piece, head-phone, ear-phones.

écoutille (ekutij), s.f. [Span. *escotilla*] (naut.) Hatch.

écouvillon (ekuvijɔ̃), s.m. [OF *escouve*] **1.** Long-handled swab; **2.** (mil.) sponge (for cannon), swab.

écouvillonnage (ekuvijɔnaʒ), s.m. Swabbing, cleaning-out.

écouvillonner (ekuvijɔne), v.a. To swab out, to clean-out.

écrabouiller (ekrabuje), v.a. (pop.) To squash, to squeeze to pulp.

écran (ekrɑ̃), s.m. [etym. dub.; OF *escren*] Fire-screen; hand-screen, screen.

écrasant, -e (ekrɑzɑ̃), p. adj. [f. *écraser*] Crushing; (fig.) overwhelming; excessive, exorbitant.

écrasement (ekrɑzmɑ̃), s.m. Crushing, bruising; (fig.) overwhelming.

écraser (ekrɑze), v.a. [Scand. orig.] To crush, to squash, to tread down; (fig.) to weigh down, to overwhelm; *être écrasé de travail*, to be desperately over-worked; *manquer d'être écrasé par une auto*, to be nearly run over by a car; (slang) *en* ~, to sleep like a log.

écraseu-r, -se (ekrɑzœr), adj. Crushing. ~, s.m. **1.** Road-hog; **2.** (mech.) crusher; steam-roller.

écrémage (ekremaʒ), s.m. [f. *crème*] Skimming, separating.

écrémer (ekreme), v.a. [f. *crème*] To skim, to skim the cream off, to separate.

écrémeuse (ekremøz), s.f. Cream-separator.

écrémoir (ekremwar), s.m. Skimmer, milk-skimmer.

écrêter (ekrɛte), v.a. [f. *crête*] **1.** To take the crest off; **2.** to destroy the parapet of (a wall); **3.** to make lower; ~ *une côte*, to make a hill less steep.

écrevisse (ekrəvis), s.f. [OHG *krebitz*] **1.** Crayfish, river-lobster; *aller comme les* ~*s*, to go crabwise; *rouge comme une* ~, as red as a lobster; **2.** (astr.) Cancer; **3.** blacksmith's tongs.

(s')écrier (sekrije), v.pr. [f. *crier*] To cry out, to exclaim.

écrille (ekrij), s.f. Grate (of a fish-pond).

écrin (ekrɛ̃), s.m. [L *scrinium*] Casket, jewel-case, case.

écrire (ekrir), v.a. [L *scribere*] To write; to write down, to mark; *papier à* ~, writing-paper; ~ *que*, to write to say that; *vous trouverez tout ce qu'il faut pour* ~, you will find writing materials, or (fig.) all that you need; ~ *de bonne encre à X*, to write to X in strong terms; **s'**~, v.pr. to write to one another; to be written, to be spelt.

écrit (ekri), s.m. Writing; agreement; written work; *mettre en* or *par* ~, to put into writing, to set down in black and white; *faire un mot d'~*, to write a note, a line, a word; *par ~*, in writing, written.

écriteau (pl. **-x**) (ekrito), s.m. Bill (poster); board, notice, signboard.

écritoire (ekritwar), s.f. Writing-desk, escritoire.

écriture (ekrityr), s.f. [L *scriptura*] **1.** Writing, handwriting; *avoir une belle ~*, to write a good hand; *mauvaise ~*, scrawl; **2.** (fig.) style; *d'une ~ soignée*, carefully worded; **3.** scripture; *l'~ sainte, les saintes ~s* or *les Écritures*, the Holy Scriptures; **4.** (pl.) accounts, papers, documents, correspondence; *commis aux ~s*, copying-clerk.

écrivailler (ekrivɑje), v.a. (colloq.) To scribble.

écrivailleur (ekrivɑjœr), s.m. (colloq.) Scribbler, quill-driver.

écrivain (ekrivɛ̃), s.m. [pop. L *scribane*] **1.** Writer, author; **2.** scrivener; *~ public*, public scrivener; **3.** (naut.) purser.

écrivasser (ekrivase), v.a.n. [f. *écrire*] To scribble, to drive the quill.

écrivassi-er, -ère (ekrivasje), s.m.f. Scribbler, quill-driver, (colloq.) ink-spiller.

écrou[1] (pl. **-s**) (ekru), s.m. [Germ. *Schraube*] Screw-nut, nut, female screw; *contre-~*, check nut, lock-nut; *~ à oreilles*, winged nut.

écrou[2] (pl. **-s**) (ekru), s.m. [OHG *scrot*] Jail-entry; *livre* or *registre d'~*, jail-book; *levée d'~*, setting at liberty.

écrouelles (ekruɛl), s.f.pl. [L *scrofula*] King's evil, scrofula.

écrouelleu-x, -se (ekruɛlø), adj. Scrofulous. **~**, s.m.f. Scrofulous person, person affected with the king's evil.

écrouer (ekrue), v.a. [f. *écrou*[2]] To imprison, to lock up; to enter in the jail-book.

écrouir (ekruir), v.a. (metall.) To hard-hammer.

écrouissement, écrouissage (ekruismɑ̃, ekruisaʒ), s.m. (metall.) Hard-hammering.

écroulement (ekrulmɑ̃), s.m. Collapse, falling, crumbling, falling-in; (fig.) collapse, wreck, ruin.

(s')écrouler (sekrule), v.pr. To collapse, to fall, to fall in, to give way, to crumble; *la terre s'écroula*, the ground gave way; *un empire écroulé*, an empire overthrown.

écroûtage, écroûtement (ekrutaʒ, ekrutmɑ̃), s.m. [f. *croûte*] Taking off the crust.

écroûter (ekrute), v.a. [f. *croûte*] To remove the crust from.

écru, -e (ekry), adj. [*é*+*cru*] **1.** Raw, unbleached; *fil ~, soie ~e*, raw thread, raw silk; *toile ~e*, brown holland; **2.** (colour) ecru, cream.

ecthyma (ektima), s.f. [Gr. *ekthuma*] (pathol.) Ecthyma.

ectoderme (ektodɛrm), s.m. [Gr. *ektos*+*derma*] (nat. hist.) Ectoderm.

ectoplasme (ektoplasm), s.m. [Gr. *ektos*+*plasma*] Ectoplasm.

ectropion (ektropjɔ̃), s.m. [Gr. *ektropion*] (pathol.) Ectropion.

ectype (ektip), s.f. [Gr. *ectypon*] Ectype.

écu (eky), s.m. [L *scutum*] **1.** Shield; **2.** crown (an obsolete French coin worth three francs); **3.** (herald.) escutcheon, arms; **4.** (fig.) money, cash; (fam.) *c'est le père aux ~s*, he 's got a tidy pile, or lots of tin.

écubier (ekybje), s.m. [Span. *escoban*] (naut.) Hawse-hole.

écueil (ekœj), s.m. [L *scopulus*] Rock, reef; sandbank; (fig.) peril, danger, stumbling-block.

écuelle (ekɥɛl), s.f. [pop. L *scutella*] Porringer, bowl, basin; (colloq.) plate.

écuellée (ekɥɛle), s.f. [f. *écuelle*] Bowlful, basinful.

écuissage (ekɥisaʒ), s.m. Splitting (the trunk of a tree).

écuisser (ekɥise), v.a. [f. *cuisse*] (forestry) To split, to splinter (trees).

éculer (ekyle), v.a. [f. *cul*] To tread down at heel; **s'~**, v.pr. to wear down at heel.

écumage (ekymaʒ), s.m. [f. *écume*] Skimming.

écumant, -e (ekymɑ̃), p. adj. Foaming, frothing, seething; (fig.) storming, raging.

écume (ekym), s.f. [OHG *skum*] **1.** Foam, froth; *~ de mer*, foam, meerschaum; **2.** sweat, lather; *jeter de l'~*, to foam, to be in a lather (of horses); **3.** (fig.) scum; *l'~ de la société*, the dregs of humanity, the scum of the earth.

écumer (ekyme), v.a. To skim; (fig.) to scour; *~ les mers*, to scour the seas; (fam.) *~ la marmite*, to sponge; **~**, v.n. **1.** to foam, to froth, to seethe; (fig.) *~ de rage*, to foam with rage; **2.** to sweat, to lather (of horses).

écumeur (ekymœr), s.m. (always fig.) *~ de mer*, sea-rover; (fam.) *~ de marmite*, sponger.

écumeu-x, -se (ekymø), adj. Frothy, foaming, yeasty.

écumoire (ekymwar), s.f. Skimmer, scummer.

écurage (ekyraʒ), s.m. [f. *écurer*] Scouring, cleaning, cleaning-out.

écurer (ekyre), v.a. [*é*+*curer*] To scour, to clean, to clean out, to cleanse.

écureuil (ekyrœj), s.m. [pop. L *scuriolus*] Squirrel.

écureu-r, -se (ekyrœr), s.m.f. Scavenger; *~ de puits*, well-cleaner.

écurie (ekyri), s.f. [f. *écuyer*] Stable, stabling, mews; stud; *garçon* or *valet d'~*, stable-boy, groom, ostler; *c'est un* *cheval à l'~*, it's a constant expense; *nettoyer les ~s d'Augias*, to cleanse the Augean stable.

écusson (ekysɔ̃), s.m. [f. *écu*] **1.** (herald.) Escutcheon, coat-of-arms; **2.** (lock-making) escutcheon; **3.** (hort.) slip with bud for grafting.

écussonnage (ekysɔnaʒ), s.m. (hort.) Budding, grafting.

écussonner (ekysɔne), v.a. (hort.) To bud, to graft; syn. GREFFER EN ÉCUSSON.

écussonnoir (ekysɔnwar), s.m. Budding-knife.

écuyer (ekɥije), s.m. [L *scutarius*] **1.** Squire (archaic); **2.** equerry; *~ tranchant*, carver; *grand ~*, master of the horse; **3.** riding-master; professional horseman, circus-rider.

écuyère (ekɥijɛr), s.f. **1.** Horsewoman; *bottes à l'~*, riding-boots; top-boots; **2.** female circus-rider.

eczéma (egzema), s.m. [Gr. wd] (med.) Eczema.

eczémateu-x, -se (egzematø), adj. Eczematous. ~, s.m.f. Person afflicted with eczema.

edelweiss (edɛlvais), s.m. [Germ. *edel*+*weiss*] (bot.) Edelweiss, *Leontopodium alpinum*.

édénien, -ne, édénique (edenjɛ̃, edenik), adj. [f. *Eden*] Edenic.

édenté, -e (edɑ̃te), p. adj. **1.** Toothless; *un peigne ~*, a broken-toothed comb; *une vieille ~e*, a toothless hag; **2.** (zool.) edentate. ~, s.m. (zool.) Edentate.

édenter (edɑ̃te), v.a. To break the teeth of (combs, saws, &c.); to deprive of teeth, to edentate.

édicter (edikte), v.a. [f. L *edictum*] To decree, to enact.

édicule (edikyl), s.m. [L *aedicula*] Small erection, kiosk, &c. on the public highway.

édifiant, -e (edifjɑ̃), p. adj. Edifying.

édificateur (edifikatœr), s.m. Constructor, builder.

édification (edifika'sjɔ̃), s.f. Building, erection; (fig.) edifying, edification.

édifice (edifis), s.m. [L *aedificium*] Edifice, building.

édifier (edifje), v.a. [L *aedificare*] **1.** To erect, to build; **2.** (fig.) to edify; to enlighten; *il m'a édifié sur son compte*, now I know all about him.

édile (edil), s.m. [L *aedilis*] Aedile; town or city councillor.

édilité (edilite), s.f. Aedileship; city or town councillorship.

édit (edi), s.m. [L *edictum*] Edict, decree.

éditer (edite), v.a. [L *editus*] **1.** To publish; **2.** to edit. ⚠ 'To edit' means: *préparer la publication d'un ouvrage d'autrui*, whilst *éditer* means also and most usually 'to publish', 'to issue'.

éditeur (editœr), s.m. **1.** Publisher; **2.** (rarely) editor. ⚠ See ÉDITER.

édition (edisjɔ̃), s.f. [L *editio*] **1.** Publication; **2.** edition; *maison d'~*, publishing firm, publisher.

éditorial, -e, (aux) (editɔrial), adj. Editorial. ~, s.m. Leading article, leader.

édredon (edrədɔ̃), s.m. [Norw. *eider*+*dun*] Eider-down, eider-down quilt.

educabilité (edykabilite), s.f. Educability.

éducable (edykabl), adj. Educable.

éducat-eur, -rice (edykatœr), s.m.f. Educator.

éducati-f, -ve (edykatif), adj. Educative.

éducation (edyka'sjɔ̃), s.f. [L *educatio*] **1.** Education; training; rearing (of animals); **2.** breeding, manners; *il n'a point d'~*, he lacks breeding.

édulcoration (edylkɔra'sjɔ̃), s.f. Edulcoration.

édulcorer (edylkɔre), v.a. [f. *é*+L *dulcis*] To edulcorate.

éduquer (edyke), v.a. [L *educare*] To bring up, to educate (children).

éfaufiler (efofile), v.a. [*é*+*faufiler*] To pull out the basting threads from.

efendi (efɛ̃di), s.m. [Turk. wd] Effendi.

effaçable (ɛfasabl), adj. Effaceable.

effacement, effaçage (ɛfasmɑ̃, ɛfasaʒ), s.m. Erasing, striking out, effacement, obliteration; disappearance; (fig.) self-effacement.

effacer (ɛfase), v.a. **1.** To efface, to erase; to scratch, blot, or rub out; **2.** (fig.) to eclipse, to surpass, (fam.) to put in the shade; **3.** (fig.) to wipe out; *~ ses péchés*, to wipe out one's sins; **s'~**, v.pr. **1.** to wear away, to become blotted out or obliterated; **2.** (fig.) to keep in the background; to draw aside, to give way.

effaner (ɛfane), v.a. [*é*+*faner*] To strip of leaves.

effarement (ɛfarmɑ̃), s.m. Bewilderment, distraction, affright.

effarer (ɛfare), v.a. [Variant form of *effrayer*, f. L *efferus*] To frighten, to scare, to flurry; to bewilder.

effarouchant, -e (ɛfaruʃɑ̃), p. adj. Startling, disquieting; shocking, annoying.

effarouchement (ɛfaruʃmɑ̃), s.m. Scare, affright; umbrage.

effaroucher (ɛfaruʃe), v.a. [f. *farouche*] To startle, to frighten; to flurry, to amaze; to shock, to scare, to alarm.

effarvate (ɛfarvat), s.f. (ornith.) Reed-warbler.

effecti-f, -ve (efɛktif), adj. [f. *effet*] Actual, real, positive; available. ~, s.m. (mil.) Effective force.

effectivement (ɛfɛktivmɑ̃), adv. Indeed, in effect, actually, in fact; syn. EN EFFET.

effectuer (ɛfɛktɥe), v.a. [L *efficere*] To effect, to accomplish, to carry out;

s'~, v.pr. to be accomplished, to be carried out, to take place.
efféminati0n (ɛfemina'sjɔ̃), s.f. Effeminacy.
efféminé, -e (ɛfemine), p. adj. Effeminate, womanish.
efféminer (ɛfemine), v.a. [f. L *femina*] To render effeminate, to enervate; syn. AMOLLIR.
efférent, -e (ɛferɑ̃), adj. [L *efferre*] (anat.) Efferent.
effervescence (ɛfɛrvɛsɑ̃s), s.f. Effervescence; (fig.) excitement, ferment.
effervescent, -e (ɛfɛrvɛsɑ̃), adj. [L *effervescere*] Effervescent; (fig.) excited, excitable.
effet (ɛfɛ), s.m. [L *effectum*] **1.** Effect, result; *pour cet ~*, to that end, for this purpose; *mettre à l'~*, to carry into effect; *en ~*, indeed, in reality, in fact; (as a reply) quite so; *à quel ~?*, to what purpose?; *faire ~*, to take effect, to have an effect; **2.** impression; *il fait cela pour faire de l'~*, he does that for effect; *cela me fait cet ~*, it seems so to me; *cela fait un vilain ~*, it looks bad; *faire l'~ de*, to look like, to sound like; **3.** (comm.) bill, bill of exchange; *~ à échoir*, running bill; *faire honneur à un ~*, to honour a bill; *faire les fonds d'un ~*, to provide for a bill; **4.** (pl.) clothes; goods and chattels, movables; luggage; **5.** (comm.) (pl.) funds, stocks.
effeuillage (ɛfœjaʒ), s.m. Defoliation.
effeuillaison (ɛfœjɛzɔ̃), s.f. Fall of the leaves.
effeuillement (ɛfœjmɑ̃), s.m. Fall of the leaves; leaflessness.
effeuiller (ɛfœje), v.a. [f. *feuille*] To strip the leaves off (trees, &c).; to tear the petals off (flowers); **s'~**, v.pr. to shed its leaves, petals, &c.
effeuillure (ɛfœjyr), s.f. Fallen leaves.
efficace (ɛfikas), adj. Efficacious, effectual.
efficacement (ɛfikasmɑ̃), adv. Efficaciously.
efficacité (ɛfikasite), s.f. [L *efficacitas*] Efficacy, efficaciousness.
efficient, -e (ɛfisjɑ̃), adj. [L *efficiens*] Efficient.
effigie (ɛfiʒi), s.f. [L *effigies*] Effigy; syn. IMAGE, FIGURE, PORTRAIT.
effilage (ɛfilaʒ), s.m. [f. *fil*] Unravelling.
effilé, -e (ɛfile), p. adj. Slender, slim; (fig.) sharp, keen, trenchant. **~**, s.m. Fringe.
effiler (ɛfile), v.a. [f. *fil*] **1.** To unravel; **2.** (hunt.) to tire out (dogs); **s'~**, v.pr. to ravel out, to come unravelled.
effilochage (ɛfilɔʃaʒ), s.m. Ravelling-out; shoddying.
effiloche, effiloque (ɛfilɔʃ, ɛfilɔk), s.f. **1.** Refuse silk; **2.** silk-tag (or selvages).
effilochée (ɛfilɔʃe), s.f. Unravellings (pl.); shoddy.
effilochement, effiloquement (ɛfilɔʃmɑ̃, ɛfilɔkmɑ̃), s.m. Ravelling-out, shoddying.
effilocher, effiloquer (ɛfilɔʃe, ɛfilɔke), v.a. [f. *fil*] To ravel out, to shoddy.
effilocheu-r, -se, effileu-r, -se (ɛfilɔʃœr, ɛfilœr), s.m.f. Shoddy-manufacturer. **~se**, s.f. (techn.) Shoddy-mill.
effilochure, effilure (ɛfilɔʃyr, ɛfilyr), s.f. Unravellings (pl.).
efflanqué, -e (ɛflɑ̃ke), p. adj. Raw-boned (of animals); lean, lank, thin; (fig.) dry; *style ~*, bare style.
efflanquer (ɛflɑ̃ke), v.a. [f. *flanc*] To make lean, to emaciate.
effleurement, effleurage (ɛflœrmɑ̃, ɛflœraʒ), s.m. Grazing, skimming the surface; stroking.
effleurer (ɛflœre), v.a. [f. *fleur*] To graze; to skim the surface of; to stroke lightly; (fig.) to touch upon, to glide over; to dip into.
effleurir (ɛflœrir), v.n. or **s'effleurir**, v.pr. To effloresce.
effloraison (ɛflɔrɛzɔ̃), s.f. Blossoming, blooming.
efflorescence (ɛflɔrɛsɑ̃s), s.f. [f. L *efflorescere*] Efflorescence.
efflorescent, -e (ɛflɔrɛsɑ̃), adj. Efflorescent.
effluence (ɛflɥɑ̃s), s.f. Effluence, emanation.
effluent, -e (ɛflɥɑ̃), adj. [L *effluens*] Effluent.
effluve (ɛflyv), s.m. [L *effluvium*] Effluvium, emanation.
effondrement (ɛfɔ̃drəmɑ̃), s.m. **1.** Collapse, falling-in, sinking-in; giving way (of ground); (fig.) collapse; **2.** (agric.) trenching.
effondrer (ɛfɔ̃ndre), v.a. [f. *fond*] **1.** To overwhelm; to break in or open, to stave in; **2.** (agric.) to trench; **s'~**, v.pr. to collapse, to fall in; to give way.
effondrilles (ɛfɔ̃drij), s.f.pl. Grounds, dregs; sediment.
(s')efforcer (sɛfɔrse), v.pr. [*é*+*forcer*] To strive, to endeavour, to make great efforts, to force oneself.
effort (ɛfɔr), s.m. [f. *efforcer*] **1.** Effort, exertion; stress; endeavour; *faire ~ pour*, to make an effort to; *faire tous ses ~s*, to try one's best, to exert oneself to the uttermost; **2.** (pathol.) strain, rupture; *se donner un ~*, to strain oneself.
effraction (ɛfraksjɔ̃), s.f. [L *effractio*] Housebreaking; breaking open or into; *vol avec ~*, (by night) burglary; (in day-time) housebreaking.
effraie (ɛfrɛ), s.f. [f. *effrayer*] (ornith.) Screech-owl.
effranger (ɛfrɑ̃ʒe), v.a. [f. *frange*] To ravel out, to fray; **s'~**, v.pr. to become unravelled, to fray.

effrayant, -e (ɛfrɛjɑ̃), p. adj. Frightful, fearful, dreadful; hideous, appalling, frightening.
effrayer (ɛfrɛje), v.a. [f. *frayeur*] To frighten, to alarm, to terrify, to startle; **s'~**, v.pr. to be frightened, startled, or alarmed, to take fright.
effréné, -e (ɛfrene), adj. [L *effrenatus*] Unbridled, unruly, lawless; wild, frantic (of gestures).
effritement (ɛfritmɑ̃), s.m. **1.** Exhaustion (of soil, &c.); **2.** crumbling (of rocks).
effriter (ɛfrite), v.a. [corrupt. of *effruiter*] [L. *effrenatus*] **1.** To wear away, to crumble; **2.** to exhaust, to render sterile (soil); **s'~**, v.pr. **1.** to crumble into dust; **2.** to become exhausted or sterile.
effroi (ɛfrwɑ), s.m. [f. *effrayer*] Fright, terror, dread.
effronté, -e (ɛfrɔ̃te), adj. Shameless, brazen-faced, impudent, saucy. ~ s.m.f. Shameless, brazen-faced or impudent person or creature; (fem.) hussy.
effrontément (ɛfrɔ̃temɑ̃), adv. Impudently, shamelessly, saucily.
effronterie (ɛfrɔ̃tri), s.f. Effrontery, shamelessness, brazen-facedness, sauciness, impudence.
effroyable (ɛfrwɑjabl), adj. Frightful, dreadful, (fam.) awful.
effroyablement (ɛfrwɑjabləmɑ̃), adv. Frightfully, dreadfully, (fam.) awfully.
effruiter (ɛfrɥite), v.a. [f. *fruit*] To strip of fruit.
effusion (ɛfyzjɔ̃), s.f. [L *effusio*] Effusion, pouring-out, shedding; *avec ~*, effusively; *~ de sang*, bloodshed.
éfourceau (pl. **-x**) (efurso), s.m. [etym. dub.] Heavy two-wheeled cart, timber-cart.
égal, -e, (aux) (egal), adj. [L *aequalis*] Equal; like, alike; (fig.) indifferent, all the same; *cela m'est ~*, it is all the same to me; *tout lui est ~*, it is all one to him; *une humeur ~e*, an even temper; *c'est ~, si j'avais su*, all the same, or never mind, if I had only known. **~**, s.m.f. Equal; *d'~ à~*, between equals; *sans ~*, matchless; *traiter en ~*, to treat as an equal; *à l'~ de*, on an equality with.
égalable (egalabl), adj. That can be equalled; (archaic) equallable.
également (egalmɑ̃), adv. Equally, alike, uniformly; also, likewise, too.
également (egalmɑ̃), s.m. (law) Equalization.
égaler (egale), v.a. **1.** To equal, to be equal to, to come up to, to match; **2.** to make equal; to level; *la mort égale tous les hommes*, death reduces all men to the same level; *~ Racine à Euripide*, to deem Racine the equal of Euripides.
égalisation (egaliza'sjɔ̃), s.f. Equalization.
égaliser (egalize), v.a. To equalize; to level, to smooth; *~ le terrain*, to level the ground.
égalitaire (egalitɛr), adj. s.m.f. Equalitarian.
égalité (egalite), s.f. Equality; evenness, uniformity; *~ d'humeur*, equanimity, even temper.
égard (egar), s.m. [f. *garder*] Regard, account, consideration, respect; deference, (pl.) attentions; *à cet ~*, on that account; *à l'~ de*, with regard to; *en ~ à*, considering; *à tous ~s*, in every respect; *par ~ pour*, out of deference to; *par ~ pour vous*, for your sake; *témoigner de grands ~s à X*, to pay marked attentions to X, to show great deference to X.
égaré, -e (egare), p. adj. **1.** Wandering, strayed, mislaid; *un voyageur ~*, a lost traveller; misled; **2.** disordered, distracted, bewildered; *les yeux ~s*, haggard-eyed.
égarement (egarmɑ̃), s.m. Straying, losing one's way; aberration, mistake; *~ d'esprit*, mental aberration; disorder, bewilderment.
égarer (egare), v.a. [*é+garer*] **1.** To mislead, to misguide, to lead astray; to bewilder; **2.** to mislay (objects); **s'~**, v.pr. to be misled, to go astray; to be bewildered; to get lost, to stray; to err; *il s'égara dans la forêt*, he got lost in the forest; *il s'égara*, he lost his way.
égayant, -e (egɛjɑ̃), p. adj. Cheering, enlivening, exhilarating.
égayement, égaiement (egɛmɑ̃), s.m. Gladdening, enlivening, cheering up.
égayer (egɛje), v.a. [f. *gai*] **1.** To enliven, to gladden, to cheer, to cheer up; **2.** (hort.) to thin (trees); **s'~**, v.pr. to brighten up, to cheer up; to be cheerful, to make merry.
égide (eʒid), s.f. [Gr. *aigis*] Aegis.
églantier (eglɑ̃tje), s.m. [OF *aiglent*, prob. f. L *acus*] Eglantine, briar, dog-rose (bush).
églantine (eglɑ̃tin), s.f. (bot.) Wild rose, dog-rose.
églefin (egləfɛ̃), s.m. See syn. AIGLEFIN.
église (egliz), s.f. [Gr. *ekklēsia*] Church; *gueux comme un rat d'~*, as poor as a church mouse.
églogue (eglɔg), s.f. [Gr. *eklogē*] Eclogue.
égoïsme (egɔism), s.m. [f. L *ego*] Egoism.
égoïste (egɔist), s.m.f. Egoist. **~**, adj. Egoistic.
égoïstement (egɔistəmɑ̃), adv. Egoistically.
égorgement (egɔrʒəmɑ̃), s.m. Slaughtering, butchering; slaughter.
égorger (egɔrʒe), v.a. [f. *gorge*] To cut the throat of, to butcher, to slaughter, to kill.
égorgeur (egɔrʒœr), s.m. Slaughterer; murderer.

(s')égosiller (segozije), v.pr. To make oneself hoarse (with shouting, singing, &c.); to bawl.
égotisme (egɔtism), s.m. [f. L *ego*] Egotism.
égotiste (egɔtist), s.m.f. Egotist. ~, adj. Egotistical.
égout (egu), s.m. [f. *égoutter*] **1.** Drain, sewer; ~ *collecteur*, main sewer; *tout à l'*~, modern sanitation; **2.** drip, eavesdrop; eaves; *toit à un seul* ~, shed-roof, pent-house roof.
égoutier (egutje), s.m. Sewer-worker; scavenger.
égouttage, égouttement (egutaʒ, egutmɑ̃), s.m. **1.** Draining, drainage; **2.** dripping.
égoutter (egute), v.a. To drain, to drain off; **s'**~ v.pr. to drip, to trickle, to dry.
égouttoir (egutwar), s.m. Drainer; plate-rack; (photo.) draining-rack.
égoutture (egutyr), s.f. Drainings, last drops.
égrainer (egrɛne), v.a. See ÉGRENER.
égrappage (egrapaʒ), s.m. Picking, stripping (of grapes from the stalk).
égrapper (egrape), v.a. To pick, to strip (grapes from the bunch).
égratigner (egratiɲe), v.a. [f. *gratter*] To scratch.
égratigneu-r, -se (egratiɲœr), adj. (rare) Scratching.
égratignure (egratiɲyr), s.f. Scratch.
égravillonner (egravijɔne), v.a. [f. *gravier*] (forestry) To clear the roots of (a transplanted tree).
égrenage (egrənaʒ), s.m. Shelling (of grain, peas, &c.); picking (of grapes).
égrener, égrainer (egrəne, egrɛne), v.a. **1.** To shell; to pick (grapes from the bunch); **2.** to tell (a rosary); to unstring (beads); **s'**~, v.pr. to shed its seed, to fall from the stalk.
égreneuse (egrənøz), s.f. (mach.) Corn-sheller; cotton-gin.
égrillard, -e (egrijar), adj. Broad, free (of conversation); lively, improper.
égrisage (egrizaʒ), s.m. Grinding, polishing (of diamonds).
égrisée (egrize), s.f. Diamond-dust.
égriser (egrize), v.a. [f. *é*+Dutch *gruizen*] To grind, to polish (precious stones).
égrotant, -e (egrɔtɑ̃), adj. [L *aegrotans*] Sickly.
égrugeoir (egryʒwar), s.m. Mortar.
égruger (egryʒe), v.a. [f. *gruger*] To pound, to grind in a mortar.
égueuler (egœle), v.a. **1.** To break the neck of (a vase, &c.); **2.** to wear (a cannon at the mouth).
égyptien, -ne (eʒipsjɛ̃), adj. s.m.f. Egyptian.
égyptologie (eʒiptɔlɔʒi), s.f. [*Égypte*+ Gr. *logos*] Egyptology.
égyptologique (eʒiptɔlɔʒik), adj. Egyptological.
égyptologue (eʒiptɔlɔg), s.m.f. Egyptologist.
eh ! (e), interj. Ah !, oh ! I say !; *eh bien !*, well !
éhonté, -e (eɔ̃te), adj. Shameless. ~, s.m.f. Shameless creature.
eider (edɛr), s.m. [Scand. wd] (ornith.) Eider-duck.
éjaculat-eur, -rice (eʒakylatœr), adj. Ejaculatory.
éjaculation (eʒakyla'sjɔ̃), s.f. Ejaculation.
ejaculer (eʒakyle), v.a. [L *ejaculari*] To ejaculate.
éjecteur (eʒɛktœr), s.m. Ejector. ~, adj. *Tuyau* ~, discharge pipe.
ejection (eʒɛksjɔ̃), s.f. [L *ejectare*] Ejection.
(s')éjouir (seʒwir), v.pr. See SE RÉJOUIR.
élaboration (elabɔra'sjɔ̃), s.f. Elaboration.
élaborer (elabɔre), v.a. [L *elaborare*] To elaborate, to work out.
élagage (elagaʒ), s.m. (hort.) Lopping.
élaguer (elage), v.a. (hort.) To prune (trees); (fig.) to prune, to cut down; syn. ÉMONDER.
élaïomètre (elaiɔmɛtr), s.m. [Gr. *elaion*+ *metron*] Elaeometer (instrument for determining the specific weight of oils).
élan[1] (elɑ̃), s.m. [f. *élancer*] **1.** Spring, bound, dash; *n'avancer que par* ~*s*, to get on only by fits and starts; *franchir d'un seul* ~, to leap or clear at a bound; **2.** (sport.) start, run; (naut. mech.) way; *il prit son* ~ *et sauta*, he took a run and jumped; *il prit bien son* ~, he took off well; *prendre de l'*~, to gather way; **3.** (fig.) élan, flight, soaring, outburst, transports (pl.); ~*s de l'esprit*, flights of the mind; ~*s du cœur*, aspirations, impulses, yearnings of the heart; **4.** (fig.) life, spirit, glow; *il y a de l'*~ *dans son éloquence*, his eloquence is glowing, or lofty.
élan[2] (elɑ̃), s.m. [Lithuanian *elnis*] (zool.) Elk, moose-deer; (South African) eland.
élancé, -e (elɑ̃se), p. adj. Lank, slender, slim; well built.
élancement (elɑ̃smɑ̃), s.m. **1.** Twitch, twinge (of pain); **2.** darting; **3.** (fig.) transports (pl.), reaching out (towards).
élancer (elɑ̃se), v.a. [*é*+*lancer*] To launch, to shoot, to dart; to emit with force; ~, v.n. to shoot, to give twinges (of pain); **s'**~, v.pr. **1.** to bound, to rush, to dash, to dart; *s'*~ *sur l'ennemi*, to rush upon the enemy; *il s'élança sur son cheval*, he leapt upon his horse; *s'*~ *sur X*, to spring upon X; *il s'élança dans les bras de son ami*, he flung himself into his friend's arms; **2.** (fig.) to rise, to soar, to be lifted up; *l'âme s'élance vers Dieu*, the soul soars up towards God.
élargir (elarʒir), v.a. [f. *large*] **1.** To

widen, to make wider; to enlarge; ~ *un fossé*, to widen a ditch; ~ *des chaussures*, to stretch shoes; ~ *un habit*, to let out a coat; (fig.) to widen; **2.** to set at liberty; ~ *un prisonnier*, to set a prisoner at liberty; **s'~**, v.pr. to widen, to stretch.

élargissement (elarʒismɑ̃), s.m. **1.** Widening, enlarging; **2.** release, discharge (from prison).

élargissure (elarʒisyr), s.f. (rare) Piece let in; syn. (more usual) ÉLARGISSEMENT.

élasticité (elastisite), s.f. Elasticity, springiness.

élastique (elastik), adj. [f. scientific L *elasticus*] Elastic, springy; *une conscience* ~, an elastic conscience. ~, s.m. **1.** Elastic; **2.** india-rubber band; **3.** (anat.) spring-tissue.

élater, élatère (elatɛr), s.m. (ent.) Elater (archaic), skip-jack; (pl.) elateridae.

élatéromètre (elaterɔmɛtr), s.m. [f. Gr. *elatēr*+*metron*] Elaterometer (instrument for measuring air- or steam-pressure).

élavé, -e (elave), adj. [f. *laver*] Washed-out, discoloured; syn. (more usual) DÉLAVÉ.

elbeuf (ɛlbœf), s.m. [f. *Elbeuf*, French town] Elbeuf cloth.

eldorado (eldɔrado), s.m. [Span. wd] Eldorado.

éléatique (eleatik), adj. [f. *Elea*, native city of the philosophers Xenophanes, Parmenides, and Zeno] Eleatic.

éléatisme (eleatism), s.m. Eleaticism.

élect-eur, -rice (elɛktœr), s.m.f. adj. [L *elector*] Elector, electoral.

électi-f, -ve (elɛktif), adj. Elective.

élection (elɛksjɔ̃), s.f. Election.

électoral, -e, (aux) (elɛktɔral), adj. **1.** Electoral; *priver du droit* ~, to disfranchise; **2.** electionary.

électorat (elɛktɔra), s.m. Electorate.

électrice (elɛktris), s.f. **1.** (hist.) Elector's consort, Electress; **2.** elector, woman possessing electoral rights.

électricien, -ne (elɛktrisjɛ̃), s.m.f. Electrician.

électricité (elɛktrisite), s.f. [f. Gr. *ēlektron*] Electricity.

électrification (elɛktrifika'sjɔ̃), s.f. Electrification.

électrique (elɛktrik), adj. Electric.

électriquement (elɛktrikmɑ̃), adv. Electrically.

électrisable (elɛktrizabl), adj. Electrifiable.

électrisant, -e, (elɛktrizɑ̃), p. adj. (lit. and fig.) Electrifying.

électrisation (elɛktriza'sjɔ̃), s.f. Electrization.

électrisé, -e (elɛktrize), p. adj. (lit. and fig.) Electrified.

électriser (elɛktrize), v.a. (lit. and fig.) To electrify.

électriseur (elɛktrizœr), s.m. Electrifier, electrifying machine.

électro- (elɛktro), pref. [Gr. *ēlektron*] Electro-.

électro-aimant (elɛktroɛmɑ̃), s.m. Electro-magnet.

électrochimie (elɛktroʃimi), s.f. Electrochemistry.

électrochimique (elɛktroʃimik), adj. Electrochemical.

électrocuter (elɛktrɔkyte), v.a. To electrocute.

électrocution (elɛktrɔkysjɔ̃), s.f. Electrocution.

électrode (elɛktrɔd), s.f. Electrode.

électrodynamique (elɛktrodinamik), s.f. Electrodynamics. ~, adj. Electrodynamic.

électrodynamisme (elɛktrodinamism), s.m. Electrodynamism.

électrodynamomètre (elɛktrodinamɔmɛtr), s.m. Electrodynamometer.

électrogalvanique (elɛktrogalvanik), adj. Electrogalvanic.

électrolyse (elɛktrɔliz), s.f. [*électro*+Gr. *lusis*] Electrolysis.

électrolyser (elɛktrɔlize), v.a. To electrolyze.

électrolyte (elɛktrɔlit), s.m. Electrolyte.

électromagnétique (elɛktromaɲetik), adj. Electro-magnetic.

électromagnétisme (elɛktromaɲetism), s.m. Electro-magnetism.

électrométallurgie (elɛktrometalyrʒi), s.f. Electro-metallurgy.

électromètre (elɛktromɛtr), s.m. Electrometer.

électrométrie (elɛktrometri), s.f. Electrometry.

électromot-eur, -rice (elɛktromɔtœr), adj. Electromotive. ~, s.m. Electromotor.

électron (elɛktrɔ̃), s.m. [Gr. wd] Electron.

électronégati-f, -ve (elɛktronegatif), adj. Electro-negative.

électrophore (elɛktrɔfɔr), s.m. [*électro*+Gr. *phoros*] Electrophore, electrophorus.

électrophysiologie (elɛktrofizjɔlɔʒi), s.f. Electro-physiology.

électropositi-f, -ve (elɛktropozitif), adj. Electro-positive.

électroscope (elɛktrɔskɔp), s.m. Electroscope.

électrostatique (elɛktrostatik), adj. Electrostatic.

électrothérapie (elɛktroterapi), s.f. Electro-therapy.

électrotype (elɛktrotip), s.m. Electrotype.

électrum (elɛktrɔm), s.m. Electrum (alloy of silver and gold).

électuaire (elɛktɥɛr), s.m. [LL *electuarium*] Electuary.

élégamment (elegamɑ̃), adv. Elegantly, stylishly.

élégance (elegɑ̃s), s.f. [L *elegantia*] Elegance, style.
élégant, -e (elegɑ̃), adj. [L *elegans*] Elegant, stylish, fashionable. ~, s.m. Dandy; (archaic) exquisite. ~e, s.f. Lady of fashion; stylish, well-dressed woman.
élégiaque (eleʒjak), adj. Elegiac.
élégie (eleʒi), s.f. [f. Gr. *elegeia*] Elegy.
élégir (eleʒir), v.a. [f. *léger*] To reduce the thickness of (wood); to work a moulding on.
élément (elemɑ̃), s.m. [L *elementum*] Element; ~*s*, elements, rudiments; element, component part; *être dans son* ~, to be quite at home (in anything); to be in one's element; *les quatre* ~*s*, the four elements.
élémentaire (elemɑ̃tɛr), adj. Elementary.
élémi (elemi), s.m. [?Arab. orig.] Elemi.
élémosinaire (elemɔzinɛr), adj. [f. L *eleemosyna*] Eleemosinary.
éléodendron (eleɔdɛ̃drɔ̃), s.m. (bot.) Elaeodendron.
éléphant (elefɑ̃), s.m. [Gr. *elephas, -antos*] Elephant.
éléphanteau (pl. **-x**) (elefɑ̃to), s.m. Young elephant.
éléphantiaque, éléphantique (elefɑ̃tjak, elefɑ̃tik), adj. Elephantic, elephantine, monstrous.
éléphantiasique, éléphantesque (elefɑ̃tjazik, elefɑ̃tɛsk), adj. s.m.f. Elephantiac.
éléphantiasis (elefɑ̃tjazis), s.f. (pathol.) Elephantiasis.
éléphantin, -e (elefɑ̃tɛ̃), adj. Elephantine.
élevage (elvaʒ), s.m. Breeding, raising, rearing (of cattle).
élévat-eur, -rice (elevatœr), adj. Raising, lifting; *muscles* ~*s*, elevator muscles. ~, s.m. Elevator.
élévation (eleva'sjɔ̃), s.f. [L *elevatio*] **1.** Elevation, raising; **2.** eminence, rising ground, height; **3.** (fig.) loftiness, greatness; *l'~ de l'esprit*, greatness of mind; **4.** (eccles.) elevation.
élévatoire (elevatwar), adj. Elevatory.
élève (elɛv), s.m.f. [f. *élever*] **1.** Pupil, scholar; student; **2.** disciple; **3.** (naut.) midshipman; apprentice; ~, s.f. syn. of ÉLEVAGE; *se livrer à l'~ des bestiaux*, to devote oneself to cattle-breeding.
élevé, -e (elve), p. adj. **1.** Educated, brought up; *être bien* ~, to be well-bred; *être mal* ~, to be ill-bred, (of children) to be badly brought up; **2.** raised, high; *température* ~*e*, high temperature; (fig.) lofty, high, noble, exalted; eminent.
élever (elve), v.a. [L *elevare*] **1.** To raise, to lift up, to carry up; **2.** to augment, to increase; ~ *la voix*, to raise one's voice; ~ *le prix*, to raise the price; **3.** to raise up, to erect; *Napoléon Ier fit* ~ *la Colonne Vendôme*, Napoleon I erected the Colonne Vendôme; **4.** to bring up, to rear; ~ *des enfants*, to bring up children; ~ *des animaux*, to rear, to breed, animals; **5.** to educate; ~ *un jeune homme*, to educate a young man; **6.** to promote, to exalt; ~ *aux honneurs*, to exalt to high honours; ~ *jusqu'aux nues*, to exalt, to praise, to the skies; **s'~**, v.pr. **1.** to rise, to arise, to ascend, to mount up; *s'~ brusquement*, (aeron. slang) to hoick; **2.** to exalt oneself.
éleveu-r, -se (elvœr), s.m.f. Breeder, raiser, cattle-breeder.
élevure (elvyr), s.f. Pimple, blotch.
elfe (ɛlf), s.m. [Engl. *elf*, f. OE *ælf*; cf. Germ. *Alp*] Elf, leprechaun.
élider (elide), v.a. [L *elidere*] (gram.) To elide.
éligibilité (eliʒibilite), s.f. Eligibility (*à*, for).
éligible (eliʒibl), adj. [L *eligere*] Eligible.
élimer (elime), v.a. [*é*+*limer*] To wear thin, to wear out; *vêtements élimés*, worn-out clothes.
éliminat-eur, -rice (eliminatœr), adj. Eliminating.
élimination (elimina'sjɔ̃), s.f. Elimination.
éliminatoire (eliminatwar), adj. Eliminatory.
éliminer (elimine), v.a. [L *eliminare*] To eliminate.
élingue (elɛ̃g), s.f. [ONorse *slyngva*] (naut.) Sling, strap.
élinguer (elɛ̃ge), v.a. (naut.) To sling.
élire (elir), v.a. [L *eligere*] **1.** To elect, to choose; ~ *domicile*, to take up one's abode; **2.** (parl.) to elect, to return.
élisant, -e (elizɑ̃), p. adj. Electing.
élision (elizjɔ̃), s.f. [L *elisio*] Elision.
élite (elit), s.f. [f. *élire*] Élite, choice, pick, select few; *d'~*, picked, choice, select; *soldats d'~*, picked troops.
élixir (eliksir), s.m. [f. Arab. *al iksir*] Elixir.
elle (ɛl), pers. pron. 3rd p. fem. She, it, her.
ellébore (ɛlebɔr), s.m. [Gr. *helleboros*] (bot., pharm.) Hellebore; (fig.) *avoir besoin d'~*, to be out of one's mind.
elléborisé, -e (ɛlebɔrize), adj. Helleborized.
ellipse (ɛlips), s.f. [Gr. *elleipsis*] **1.** (geom.) Ellipse; **2.** (gram.) ellipsis.
ellipsoïdal, -e, (aux) (ɛlipsɔidal), adj. Ellipsoidal.
ellipsoïde (ɛlipsɔid), s.m. Ellipsoid.
ellipticité (ɛliptisite), s.f. Ellipticity.
elliptique (ɛliptik), adj. Elliptic, elliptical.
elliptiquement (ɛliptikmɑ̃), adv. Elliptically.
Elme (ɛlm), *Feu Saint-~*: see FEU.
élocution (elɔkysjɔ̃), s.f. [L *elocutio*] Elocution; syn. DICTION, PRONONCIATION.
éloge (elɔʒ), s.m. [L *elogium*] Praise,

eulogy, encomium; *faire l'~ de X*, to praise X, to commend the merits of X; *digne d'~*, praiseworthy; *~ funèbre*, funeral oration; *faire son propre ~*, to sound one's own praises; syn. LOUANGE.

élogieusement (elɔʒjøzmɑ̃), s.m. Eulogistically, praisefully.

élogieu-x, -se (elɔʒjø), adj. Laudatory, praiseful, eulogistic.

élogiste (elɔʒist), s.m.f. (rare) Eulogist.

éloigné, -e (elwaɲe), p. adj. **1.** Distant, remote; *cause ~e*, remote cause; *d'une manière ~e*, distantly; *se tenir ~*, to keep away, to stand aloof; *~ de 10 kilomètres*, 10 kilometres distant; *des parents ~s*, distant relations; **2.** removed.

éloignement (elwaɲmɑ̃), s.m. **1.** Removal, removing; **2.** distance, remoteness; **3.** (fig.) dislike, aversion; *témoigner de l'~ pour*, to manifest a dislike for, an aversion to.

éloigner (elwaɲe), v.a. [f. *loin*] **1.** To remove, to put, to push farther away; **2.** to dismiss; to set aside, to discard, to repudiate; (fig.) *~ un sujet*, to waive a subject; (fig.) *~ les soupçons*, to allay suspicion; (fig.) *~ l'idée du mal*, to dismiss the idea of evil; **s'~**, v.pr. to go away, to absent oneself; to stand aloof; to ramble, to digress; *s'~ de son sujet*, to digress; to differ (from), to be estranged (from); *son opinion s'éloigne de la mienne*, his opinion differs from mine; syn. ÉCARTER, METTRE À L'ÉCART.

élongation (elɔ̃ga'sjɔ̃), s.f. Elongation, lengthening.

élonger (elɔ̃ʒe), v.a. [f. *long*] **1.** To elongate; **2.** (naut.) to lay alongside of; to sheer off; to skirt; *~ la côte*, to hug the shore, the coast.

éloquemment (elɔkamɑ̃), adv. Eloquently.

éloquence (elɔkɑ̃s), s.f. [L *eloquentia*] Eloquence.

éloquent, -e (elɔkɑ̃), adj. Eloquent.

élu, -e, (ely), s.m.f. **1.** Elect, chosen; elected or chosen person; **2.** (theol.) one of the elect.

élucidation (elysida'sjɔ̃), s.m. Elucidation.

élucider (elyside), v.a. [L *elucidare*] To elucidate.

élucubration (elykybra'sjɔ̃), s.f. Lucubration.

élucubrer (elykybre), v.a. [L *elucubrare*] To lucubrate.

éludable (elydabl), adj. Eludible.

éluder (elyde), v.a. [L *eludere*] To elude.

élysée (elize), s.m. [Gr. *ēlusion*] **1.** Elysium, paradise; **2.** Élysée (official residence of French President); *les Champs ~s*, (*a*) (ant.) the Elysian Fields; (*b*) (mod.) the Champs Élysées.

élyséen, -ne (elizeɛ̃), adj. Elysian.

élytre (elitr), s.m. [Gr. *elutron*] (ent.) Elytron.

elzévir (ɛlzevir), s.m. [f. name of printers *Elzevier*] Elzevir (book).

elzévirien, -ne (ɛlzevirjɛ̃), adj. Elzevirian.

émaciation (emasja'sjɔ̃), s.f. [f. *émacié*] Emaciation.

émacié, -e (emasje), adj. [L *emaciare*] Emaciated.

émail (pl. **émaux**) (emaj), s.m. [LL *smaltum*, of Teut. orig.] **1.** Enamel, enamelled work; enamel (of teeth); **2.** (herald.) tincture; **3.** (fig.) gloss, lustre, brilliancy.

émaillage (emajaʒ), s.m. Enamelling.

émailler (emaje), v.a. To enamel; (fig.) to enamel, to adorn, to bedeck.

émaillerie (emajəri), s.f. Enamelling.

émailleur (emajœr), s.m. Enameller. ~, adj. Enamelling.

émaillure (emajyr), s.f. Enamelling.

émanation (emana'sjɔ̃), s.f. [f. *émaner*] Emanation.

émancipat-eur, -rice (emɑ̃sipatœr), adj. Emancipatory. ~, s.m.f. Emancipator.

émancipation (emɑ̃sipa'sjɔ̃), s.f. Emancipation.

émanciper (emɑ̃sipe), v.a. [L *emancipare*] To emancipate; **s'~**, v.pr. to emancipate oneself; (fig.) to overstep the mark, to become too free.

émaner (emane), v.n. [L *emanare*] To emanate (*de*, from), to issue, to originate (from, in).

émargement (emarʒəmɑ̃), s.m. **1.** Cutting the margins; **2.** marginal note; signature in the margin (on receiving one's salary).

émarger (emarʒe), v.a.n. [f. *marge*] **1.** To write or sign on the margin, esp. as a receipt, hence: **2.** to receive a regular salary; **3.** (techn.) to cut the margin of.

émarginé, -e (emarʒine), adj. (bot.) Emarginate.

émasculation (emaskyla'sjɔ̃), s.f. Emasculation.

émasculer (emaskyle), v.a. [L *emasculare*] To emasculate; (fig.) to mutilate, to enfeeble.

embabouiner (ɑ̃babwine), v.a. [f. *babouin*] (rare) To wheedle, to cajole.

embâcle (ɑ̃bɑkl), s.m. Ice-pack (in a river).

emballage (ɑ̃balaʒ), s.m. Packing; *toile d'~*, pack-cloth, packing-canvas.

emballement (ɑ̃balmɑ̃), s.m. (fam.) Over-excitement, temper.

emballer (ɑ̃bale), v.a. [f. *en+balle*] **1.** To pack up, to wrap up; **2.** (fig.) to pack off, to bundle off; **3.** to excite enthusiasm in; *~ la salle*, to bring down the house; ~, v.n. to accelerate wildly; **s'~**, v.pr. to bolt, to run away; *un cheval emballé*, a runaway horse; (fig.) to be carried away; to go off one's head (with rage, enthusiasm, &c.), to fly into a rage, passion, &c.; *ne vous emballez pas!*, keep your hair on!

emballeu-r, -se (ɑ̃balœr), s.m.f. **1.** Packer; **2.** (colloq.) charlatan, bragger.

emballotter (ɑ̃balɔte), v.a. [f. *en+ballot*] To pack, to embale.

embarbouiller (ɑ̃barbuje), v.a. [*en+barbouiller*] To besmear; (fam., fig.) to confuse, to muddle; **s'~**, v.pr. to get muddled; to get fogged.

embarcadère (ɑ̃barkadɛr), s.m. [Span. *embarcadero*] **1.** Wharf, pier, landing-stage; **2.** (rail.) terminus.

embarcation (ɑ̃barka'sjɔ̃), s.f. Small boat, small craft. ⚠ Not 'embarkation', which = *embarquement.*

embardée (ɑ̃barde), s.f. Lurch, swerve; (naut.) yaw; *faire une ~*, (motor.) to swerve violently; (naut.) to yaw, to lurch, to give a lurch.

embarder (ɑ̃barde), v.n. To lurch, to swerve; (naut.) to yaw.

embargo (ɑ̃bargo), s.m. [Span. wd] Embargo.

embarquement (ɑ̃barkmɑ̃), s.m. Embarking, embarkation; shipment (of goods).

embarquer (ɑ̃barke), v.a.n. [f. *en+barque*] To ship, to take on board, to embark; (fig.) to start (a person) off on, to embark (a person) on, to involve; **~**, v.n. to go on board; to step in, to entrain; **s'~**, v.pr. to embark, to go on board; (fig.) to embark (upon), to engage (upon).

embarras (ɑ̃barɑ), s.m. [f. *embarrasser*] **1.** Encumbrance, hindrance, impediment; *un ~ de voitures*, a traffic block; **2.** (fig.) difficulty, fuss, distress, straits; (pl.) embarrassing circumstances; *je suis dans l'~*, I am at a loss; *faire des ~*, to put on airs; to make a fuss; *des ~ d'argent*, financial difficulties; *avoir l'~ du choix*, to have too many alternatives; **3.** (med.) obstruction, derangement, stoppage.

embarrassant, -e (ɑ̃barasɑ̃), p. adj. **1.** Embarrassing, awkward; puzzling, perplexing; **2.** cumbersome, troublesome; *problème ~*, difficult problem; *colis ~*, cumbersome parcel.

embarrassé, -e (ɑ̃barase), p. adj. **1.** Embarrassed, perplexed; out of countenance; *être ~*, to be at a loss; **2.** obstructed; **3.** impeded, hampered.

embarrasser (ɑ̃barase), v.a. [It. *imbarazzare*] To obstruct, to encumber; *~ une rue*, to obstruct a thoroughfare; to hamper; *ce manteau m'embarrasse*, this coat hampers me; (fig.) to embarrass, to trouble, to disconcert; to puzzle, to snare; *il est embarrassé de sa personne*, he doesn't know what to do with himself; **s'~**, v.pr. to be hampered, to be encumbered; to be embarrassed, to be disconcerted; *il ne s'embarrasse de rien*, nothing can put him out of countenance; to falter, to get mixed up; *il s'embarrassa dans son discours*, his speech became confused, (fam.) he got mixed up in his speech.

(s')embarrer (sɑ̃bare), v.pr. [f. *en+barre*] (of horses) To get entangled in a fence.

embastillement (ɑ̃bastijmɑ̃), s.m. **1.** Imprisonment; **2.** surrounding with fortifications.

embastiller (ɑ̃bastije), v.a. [f. *la Bastille*] **1.** To imprison in the Bastille; to imprison; **2.** to surround with fortifications.

embâtage (ɑ̃bɑtaʒ), s.m. Saddling (of a beast of burden).

embâter (ɑ̃bɑte), v.a. [f. *bât*] To put a pack-saddle on, to saddle; (fig.) to saddle, to encumber.

embattage, embatage (ɑ̃bataʒ), s.m. (of a wheel) Hooping.

embattre, embatre (ɑ̃batr), v.a. [*en+battre*] To hoop (a wheel).

embauchage (ɑ̃boʃaʒ), s.m. **1.** Hiring, engaging, enrolling; **2.** (mil.) disaffecting, inciting to desertion.

embaucher (ɑ̃boʃe), v.a. To hire, to engage, to enrol (workmen).

embaucheu-r, -se (ɑ̃boʃœr), s.m.f. Hirer, enroller.

embauchoir (ɑ̃boʃwar), s.m. Boot-tree, shoe-tree.

embaumement (ɑ̃bommɑ̃), s.m. Embalming.

embaumer (ɑ̃bome), v.a. [f. *en+baume*] To embalm. ~ v.n. to be fragrant, to smell sweet.

embaumeur (ɑ̃bomœr), s.m. Embalmer.

embecquer (ɑ̃bɛke), v.a. [f. *en+bec*] To feed (a young bird).

embéguiner (ɑ̃begine), v.a. [f. *en+béguin*] **1.** To muffle up; **2.** (fig.) to infatuate, to bewitch.

embelle (ɑ̃bɛl), s.f. (naut.) Waist.

embellie (ɑ̃bɛli), s.f. [f. *beau*] Clearing (after storm), lull, calm spell.

embellir (ɑ̃bɛlir), v.a. [f. *beau, bel*] To embellish, to beautify; to adorn, to set off; **~**, v.n. to grow beautiful or handsome, to improve in appearance.

embellissement (ɑ̃bɛlismɑ̃), s.m. Beautifying; embellishment, adornment; improvement.

emberlificoter (ɑ̃bɛrlifikɔte), v.a. (pop.) To entangle, to wheedle, to muddle, to circumvent; **s'~**, v.pr. to get entangled, to get tied up (in).

(s')emberlucoquer (sɑ̃bɛrlukɔke), v.pr. (fam.) To get into one's head; to be crazy (*de*, about).

embesogné, -e (ɑ̃bəzɔɲe), adj. [f. *besogne*] Busy, busily engaged.

embêtant, -e (ɑ̃bɛtɑ̃), p. adj. (pop.)

Tiresome, tedious, boring; annoying, troublesome, bothering.

embêtement (ɑ̃bɛtmɑ̃), s.m. (fam.) Bore, nuisance, bother, annoyance, worry, trouble.

embêter (ɑ̃bɛte), v.a. [f. *bête*] (fam.) To bore; to annoy, to worry, to rile; **s'～**, v.pr. to be bored.

embeurrer (ɑ̃bœre), v.a. [f. *beurre*] To butter, to spread a layer of butter upon.

emblavage (ɑ̃blavaʒ), s.m. Sowing (esp. with wheat).

emblave (ɑ̃blav), s.f. Newly-sown land.

emblaver (ɑ̃blave), v.a. [f. *blé*] To sow with wheat, &c.

emblavure (ɑ̃blavyr), s.f. Land sown with wheat.

(d')emblée (dɑ̃ble), adv. loc. [f. *embler*] At once, at the first onset, there and then, right away.

emblématique (ɑ̃blematik), adj. Emblematical.

emblématiquement (ɑ̃blematikmɑ̃), adv. Emblematically.

emblème (ɑ̃blɛm), s.m. [Gr. *emblēma*] Emblem; (fig.) attribute; *les ～s de la royauté*, the attributes of royalty.

embler (ɑ̃ble), v.a. (obs.) [L *involare*] To snatch, to ravish, to take by force.

embobeliner (ɑ̃bɔbline), (fam.) **embobiner** (ɑ̃bɔbine), v.a. To wheedle, to inveigle, (fam.) to twist round one's little finger.

emboire (ɑ̃bwar), v.a. [*en*+*boire*] (sculpt.) To coat (a mould) with wax, oil, &c.; **s'～**, v.pr. (paint.) to become flat, to tone down.

emboîtement (ɑ̃bwatmɑ̃), s.m. Fitting-in, jointing; (carp.) clamping; (fig.) dovetailing.

emboîter (ɑ̃bwate), v.a. [f. *en*+*boîte*] **1.** To fit in, to encase, to put (a book) into its case; **2.** (carp.) to clamp; **3.** (mil.) ～ *le pas*, to march lock-step; (fig.) to tread in another's footsteps; **4.** (slang) to blackguard, to outbrave, to reduce to silence, to kick up a shindy against; **s'～**, v.pr. to fit into.

embolie (ɑ̃bɔli), s.f. [Gr. *embolē*] (med.) Embolism, embolus.

embolisme (ɑ̃bɔlism), s.m. Embolism.

embolismique (ɑ̃bɔlismik), adj. Embolismic.

embonpoint (ɑ̃bɔ̃pwɛ̃), s.m. [*en*+*bon*+*point*] Plumpness, embonpoint, stoutness; *prendre de l'～*, to put on flesh, to get stout.

emboquer (ɑ̃bɔke), v.a. [f. *en*+*boque*, *bouche*] To fatten, to cram (poultry, &c.).

embossage (ɑ̃bɔsaʒ), s.m. **1.** (naut.) Bringing a vessel broadside on; **2.** being broadside on.

embosser (ɑ̃bose), v.a. [f. *bosse*] (naut.) To lay broadside on, to bring the broadside to bear; to moor across; ⚠ not 'to emboss', which = *ciseler*, *repousser*; **s'～**, v.pr. to moor across.

embouche, embauche (ɑ̃buʃ, ɑ̃boʃ), s.f. *Pré d'～*, meadow, grass-land.

embouché, -e (ɑ̃buʃe), p. adj. Mouthed, spoken; *être mal ～*, to be foul-mouthed.

emboucher (ɑ̃buʃe), v.a. [f. *en*+*bouche*] To put to one's lips, to sound (wind-instruments); (fig.) ～ *la trompette*, to strike the lyre, to adopt an elevated style.

embouchoir (ɑ̃buʃwar), s.m. Mouthpiece.

embouchure (ɑ̃buʃyr), s.f. **1.** Mouthpiece (of musical instruments); **2.** bit (of harness); **3.** embouchure, mouth (of a river, &c.).

embouer (ɑ̃bue), v.a. [f. *boue*] To cover with mud; (fig.) to besmirch, to vilify.

embouquement (ɑ̃bukmɑ̃), s.m. (naut.) Entering a strait, a canal.

embouquer (ɑ̃buke), v.a. [f. *en*+*bouque*, *bouche*] (naut.) To enter (a canal, straits, &c.).

embourber (ɑ̃burbe), v.a. [f. *en*+*bourbe*] To bemire, to cast in the mire; (fig.) to implicate in a dirty business; **s'～**, v.pr. to stick in the mire, to get stuck in the mud; to be bogged; (fig.) to be involved (in trouble); to be vilified; to sink (morally).

embourrage, embourrement (ɑ̃buraʒ, ɑ̃burmɑ̃), s.m. Stuffing, padding.

embourrer (ɑ̃bure), v.a. [f. *en*+*bourre*] To stuff, to pad.

embourrure (ɑ̃buryr), s.f. **1.** Stuffing, padding; **2.** ticking, calico.

embourser (ɑ̃burse), v.a. [f. *en*+*bourse*] (usually fig.) To pocket, to receive; ～ *des injures*, to pocket insults.

embout (ɑ̃bu), s.m. [*en*+*bout*] Ferrule.

embouteillage (ɑ̃butɛjaʒ), s.m. **1.** Bottling; **2.** block (in traffic).

embouteiller (ɑ̃butɛje), v.a. **1.** To bottle; **2.** to block (traffic).

embouter (ɑ̃bute), v.a. [f. *en*+*bout*] To put a ferrule on.

emboutir (ɑ̃butir), v.a. [f. *en*+*bout*] **1.** To beat out (coppersmith's work); **2.** (arch.) to plate; **3.** (techn.) to press, to stamp (a piece of metal, or a frame); (hence slang) *se faire ～*, to get bumped into from behind.

embranchement (ɑ̃brɑ̃ʃmɑ̃), s.m. **1.** Ramification, branching-off, fork (of trees); **2.** branch-road, branch-line; junction; **3.** branch-pipe; **4.** (fig.) division, family.

embrancher (ɑ̃brɑ̃ʃe), v.a. [f. *branche*] To put together, to join up; **s'～**, v.pr. to branch off; to branch (of roads).

embraquer (ɑ̃brake), v.a. [f. *braquer*] To haul taut.

embrasement (ɑ̃brazmɑ̃), s.m. Conflagration, blaze, combustion; illumination.
embraser (ɑ̃brɑze), v.a. [f. *braise*] To fire, to set in a blaze; (fig.) to inflame, to kindle; **s'~**, v.pr. to blaze, to glow, to be inflamed; to fall in love.
embrassade (ɑ̃brasad), s.f. Embrace, kissing, kiss.
embrasse (ɑ̃bras), s.f. [f. *embrasser*] Curtain-loop, curtain-holder.
embrassement (ɑ̃brasmɑ̃), s.m. Kissing, embrace.
embrasser (ɑ̃brase), v.a. [f. *en+bras*] **1.** To embrace; to kiss; *allons, embrassez-vous!*, kiss and be friends; *ils se tenaient embrassés*, they remained locked in each other's arms; **2.** to encompass, to encircle, to comprise; *l'océan embrasse la terre*, the sea encircles the land; **3.** (fig.) to seize, to undertake; *~ une occasion*, to avail oneself of an opportunity; (prov.) *qui trop embrasse mal étreint*, seize (or grasp) all, lose all; **4.** to adopt, to embrace (fig.), to choose; *~ la religion chrétienne*, to embrace the Christian faith; *~ la querelle de X*, to espouse the cause of X.
embrasseu-r, -se (ɑ̃brasœr), s.m.f. Kisser, embracer.
embrasure (ɑ̃brɑzyr), s.f. [f. *embraser* for *ébraser*] Embrasure, window opening.
embrayage (ɑ̃brɛjaʒ), s.m. **1.** Connecting, coupling; **2.** (motor.) clutch, coupling gear; *~ à cône de friction*, conical friction clutch; *~ à disques*, disk clutch; *~ à galets*, roller clutch; *cône d'~*, clutch cone; *un ~ qui broute*, a fierce clutch.
embrayer (ɑ̃brɛje), v.a. [f. *en+braie*] **1.** To connect up; **2.** (motor.) to throw into gear, to put into gear; to clutch, to lock.
embrener (ɑ̃brəne), v.a. (pop.) To soil, to dirty.
embrèvement, embreuvement (ɑ̃brɛvmɑ̃, ɑ̃brøvmɑ̃), s.m. (carp.) Mortise-joint, mortise.
embrever (ɑ̃brəve), v.a. (carp.) To mortise.
embrigadement (ɑ̃brigadmɑ̃), s.m. Brigading, formation of a brigade; (fig.) enrolling.
embrigader (ɑ̃brigade), v.a. [f. *brigade*] To brigade, to form into brigades; (fig.) to enrol.
embrocation (ɑ̃brɔka'sjɔ̃), s.f. [f. Gr. *embrokhē*] Embrocation.
embrochement (ɑ̃brɔʃmɑ̃), s.m. Spitting (of meat).
embrocher (ɑ̃brɔʃe), v.a. [f. *broche*] To spit, to put upon the spit; (fig.) *~ X*, to run X through.
embroncher (ɑ̃brɔ̃ʃe), v.a. [f. *bronche*] To overlap, to overlay (tiles, &c.).
embrouillamini (ɑ̃brujamini), s.m. See BROUILLAMINI.
embrouillement (ɑ̃brujmɑ̃), s.m. Embroilment, entanglement, muddle; tangle.
embrouiller (ɑ̃bruje), v.a. [f. *brouiller*] To embroil, to entangle (people); to muddle, to jumble up (objects); (fig.) to perplex, to confuse, to muddle; **s'~**, v.pr. to become entangled; (fig.) to become confused, to get muddled.
embroussaillé, -e (ɑ̃brusɑje), adj. [f. *broussaille*] **1.** Covered with brushwood or undergrowth; **2.** bushy, matted; **3.** (fig.) intricate.
embruiné, -e (ɑ̃brɥine), adj. [f. *bruine*] Covered with drizzle; (agric.) blighted, spoilt by the rain.
embrumer (ɑ̃bryme), v.a. [f. *en+brume*] To overcast, to envelop in fog or mist; (fig.) to cloud, to darken; **s'~**, v.pr. to grow misty, foggy or hazy; (fig.) to grow gloomy, to be clouded over.
embrun (ɑ̃brœ̃), s.m. [f. *embrumer*] **1.** Spray, spindrift; **2.** damp haze.
embrunir (ɑ̃brynir), v.a. [f. *brun*] To darken, to make sombre, to make brown, to brown.
embryogénie (ɑ̃brijɔʒeni), s.f. [Gr. *embruon+genos*] Embryogeny.
embryogénique (ɑ̃brijɔʒenik), adj. Embryogenic.
embryologie (ɑ̃brijɔlɔʒi), s.f. [Gr. *embruon +logos*] Embryology.
embryologique (ɑ̃brijɔlɔʒik), adj. Embryological.
embryon (ɑ̃brijɔ̃), s.m. [Gr. *embruon*] **1.** Embryo; germ, origin; **2.** (fig.) dwarf, shrimp, midget.
embryonnaire (ɑ̃brijɔnɛr), adj. Embryonic, in embryo.
embryotomie (ɑ̃brijɔtɔmi), s.f. [Gr. *embruon+tomē*] Embryotomy.
embu, -e (ɑ̃by), p. adj. [f. *emboire*] Soaked in, dried in. **~**, s.m. Dullness, flatness (of paint).
embûche (ɑ̃byʃ), s.f. [f. *bûche*] Ambush; snare; *dresser des ~s*, to lay snares.
(s')embûcher (sɑ̃byʃe), v.pr. To return to covert (of a stag).
embuer (ɑ̃bɥe), v.a. To make misty; **s'~**, v.pr. to grow misty.
embuscade (ɑ̃byskad), s.f. [It. *imboscata*] Ambuscade, ambush; lurking-place, snare; *être, se tenir, se mettre en ~*, to lie in wait, in ambush; *tomber dans une ~*, to fall into an ambush.
embusqué (ɑ̃byske), s.m. Cuthbert, shirker (especially of soldiers who avoid the front line), soft-job man, slacker.
embusquer (ɑ̃byske), v.a. To ambush, to place in ambuscade; (colloq.) in war time: to get somebody a safe billet, a soft job; **s'~**, v.pr. to lie in wait, in ambush; (colloq.) to get a soft job.
émécher (emeʃe), v.a. [f. *mèche*] **1.** To dishevel, to untidy (hair); **2.** (fam.) *être*

éméché, to be the worse for drink, to be half seas over.
émendation (emɑ̃da'sjɔ̃), s.f. Emendation.
émender (emɑ̃de), v.a. [L *emendare*] To emend.
émeraude (emrod), s.f. [Gr. *smaragdos*] Emerald.
émergement (emɛrʒmɑ̃), s.m. See ÉMERSION.
émergence (emɛrʒɑ̃s), s.f. Emergence.
émergent, -e (emɛrʒɑ̃), adj. Emergent.
émerger (emɛrʒe), v.n. [L *emergere*] To emerge.
émeri (emri), s.m. [It. *smeriglio*] Emery; *papier* ~, emery-paper; *toile* ~, emery-cloth; *bouché à l'*~, with a ground-glass stopper; (fig.) dense, dull-witted.
émerillon (emrijɔ̃), s.m. [OF *esmerillon*, f. LL *smerillus*] **1.** (ornith.) Merlin; **2.** (naut.) swivel-hook.
émerillonné, -e (emrijɔne), adj. [f. *émerillon*] Gay, sprightly, lively.
émérite (emerit), adj. [L *emeritus*] **1.** Distinguished, remarkable; **2.** (obs.) emeritus, retired, pensioned; adept.
émersion (emɛrsjɔ̃), s.f. [L *emersio*] Emersion; syn. ÉMERGEMENT.
émerveillement (emɛrvɛjmɑ̃), s.m. Wonder, astonishment.
émerveiller (emɛrvɛje), v.a. [f. *merveille*] To astonish, to amaze; **s'~**, v.pr. to marvel, to wonder, to be astonished.
émétique (emetik), adj. s.m. [Gr. *emetikos*] (pharm.) Emetic.
émétiser (emetize), v.a. **1.** To put an emetic in (a mixture); **2.** to treat with emetics.
émett-eur, -rice (emɛtœr), adj. (wireless) Broadcasting; *poste* ~, *station* ~*rice*, broadcasting station.
émettre (emɛtr), v.a. [*é*+*mettre*] **1.** To emit, to issue, to give out; **2.** to express, to set forth; **3.** to put (coinage) into circulation; **4.** (wireless) to broadcast.
émeu (emø), s.m. [perh. f. Port. *ema*, crane, ostrich] (zool.) Emu.
émeulage (emølaʒ), s.m. Grinding, polishing (of mother-of-pearl).
émeute (emøt), s.f. [f. *émouvoir*] Riot, disturbance, outbreak; *chef d'*~, ringleader.
émeuti-er, -ère (emøtje), s.m.f. Rioter; revolutionary agent or agitator. ~, adj. Rioting, revolutionary.
émier (emje), v.a. See ÉMIETTER.
émiettement (emjɛtmɑ̃), s.m. Crumbling.
émietter (emjɛte), v.a. [f. *miette*] To crumble; **s'~**, v.pr. to crumble.
émigrant, -e (emigrɑ̃), p. adj. s.m.f. Emigrant.
émigration (emigra'sjɔ̃), s.f. Emigration.
émigré, -e (emigre), p. adj. Emigrant. ~, s.m.f. Refugee.
émigrer (emigre), v.n. [L *emigrare*] **1.** To emigrate; **2.** (of birds, &c.) to migrate.
émincé (emɛ̃se), s.m. (cook.) Thin slice, fillet, émincé.
émincer (emɛ̃se), v.a. [f. *mince*] To cut into thin slices, to fillet.
éminemment (eminamɑ̃), adv. Eminently.
éminence (eminɑ̃s), s.f. [f. *éminent*] **1.** Eminence, height; **2.** eminence (cardinal's title).
éminent, -e (eminɑ̃), adj. [L *eminens*] Eminent.
éminentissime (eminɑ̃tisim), adj. Most eminent (applied to cardinals).
émir (emir), s.m. [Arab. wd] Emir, ameer.
émissaire (emisɛr), s.m. [L *emissarius*] **1.** Emissary, messenger; ~, adj. *bouc* ~, scape-goat; **2.** overflow channel; overflow pipe.
émissi-f, -ve (emisif), adj. Emissive.
émission (emisjɔ̃), s.f. [L *emissio*] **1.** (scient.) Emission; **2.** issue; ~ *d'actions*, issue of shares; **3.** uttering, emission; **4.** putting into circulation (of coinage); **5.** (wireless) broadcasting; emission.
emmagasinage, emmagasinement (ɑ̃magazinaʒ, ɑ̃magazinmɑ̃), s.m. Warehousing; receiving (of stores).
emmagasiner (ɑ̃magazine), v.a. [f. *en*+*magasin*] To warehouse, to store; to take into store; (fig.) to store up, to amass.
emmaigrir (ɑ̃mɛgrir), v.a. (rare). See AMAIGRIR.
emmaillotement (ɑ̃majɔtmɑ̃), s.m. Swaddling, swathing.
emmailloter (ɑ̃majɔte), v.a. [f. *en*+*maillot*] To swaddle, to swathe; (fig.) to swathe, to bind.
emmanchement (ɑ̃mɑ̃ʃmɑ̃), s.m. Hafting, helving; joining, jointing, fitting together.
emmancher (ɑ̃mɑ̃ʃe), v.a. [f. *en*+*manche*] To put a handle to, to haft, to helve; (fig.) to manage, to set about; ~ *une affaire*, to set about a business; *une affaire mal emmanchée*, a badly started business or undertaking.
emmanchure (ɑ̃mɑ̃ʃyr), s.f. [f. *manche*] Arm-hole; syn. ENTOURNURE.
emmannequiner (ɑ̃mankine), v.a. (rare) [f. *mannequin*] To pack into baskets.
emmanteler (ɑ̃mɑ̃tle), v.a. **1.** To wrap in a cloak; **2.** (mil.) to enclose in a rampart.
emmêlement (ɑ̃mɛlmɑ̃), s.m. Tangle, entanglement; confusion.
emmêler (ɑ̃mɛle), v.a. To entangle, to tangle; to complicate (an affair); **s'~**, v.pr. to get entangled.
emménagement (ɑ̃menaʒmɑ̃), s.m. **1.** Moving into a new house, installation; **2.** (pl.) accommodation (on shipboard).
emménager (ɑ̃menaʒe), v.n.a. [f. *en*+*ménage*] **1.** To move in; **2.** to arrange (a ship, &c.).

emménagogue (ãmenagɔg), s.m. adj. [Gr. *emmēna+agōgos*] Emmenagogue.
emmener (ãmne), v.a. [*en+mener*] To take away, to lead away, to fetch away; to convey away.
emmenotter (ãmnɔte), v.a. [f. *menotte*] (rare) To handcuff, to manacle.
emmerder (ãmɛrde), v.a. [f. *merde*] (slang, very vulg.) To annoy, to bother, to worry; **s'~**, v.pr. to be bored to death.
emmiellé, -e (ãmjɛle), p. adj. [f. *miel*] Honeyed, cloying, honey-sweet.
emmieller (ãmjɛle), v.a. [f. *miel*] To sweeten with honey; (fig.) to coax; (slang) to annoy, to bore (euphem. for EMMERDER).
emmiellure (ãmjɛlyr), s.f. (vet.) Resolvent plaster.
emmitonner (ãmitɔne), v.a. To wrap up; (fig.) to wheedle, to coax.
emmitoufler (ãmitufle), v.a. [f. *mitoufle*] To muffle up.
emmortaiser (ãmortɛze), v.a. To mortise, to set in a mortise.
emmotté, -e (ãmɔte), adj. Covered with soil (of roots).
emmurer (ãmyre), v.a. [f. *en+mur*] **1.** To enclose within walls, to wall; **2.** (torture) to wall up; **3.** (fig.) to shut in, to restrict.
emmuseler (ãmyzle), v.a. To muzzle; (fig.) to muzzle, to silence.
émoi (emwa), s.m. [OF *esmoyer*] Emotion, flutter; excitement; *en ~*, in a stir, in a flutter.
émollient, -e (emɔljã), adj. [f. L *emollire*] Emollient, softening. **~**, s.m. Emollient.
émolument (emɔlymã), s.m. [L *emolumentum*] Emolument, fee, perquisite; (pl.) emoluments, salary.
émolumentaire (emɔlymãtɛr), adj. Emolumentary.
émonctoire (emɔ̃ktwar), s.m. [L *emunctorium*] Emunctory.
émondage, émondement (emɔ̃daʒ, emɔ̃dmã), s.m. Lopping, pruning, trimming.
émonder (emɔ̃de), v.a. [L *emundare*] (gard., hort.) To prune, to lop, to trim; (fig.) to prune, to cut down; syn. ÉLAGUER.
émondes (emɔ̃d), s.f.pl. Tree-trimmings, hedge-trimmings.
émondeur (emɔ̃dœr), s.m. Pruner, trimmer.
émondoir (emɔ̃dwar), s.m. Pruning-hook.
émorfiler (emɔrfile), v.a. To trim the rough edges off.
émoti-f, -ve (emotif), adj. Emotive.
émotion (emosjɔ̃), s.f. [L *emotio*] Emotion; stir, commotion.
émotionnable (emosjɔnabl), adj. Emotional.
émotionner (emosjɔne), v.a. To excite emotion in, to move, to flutter, to disturb; **s'~**, v.pr. to be moved, roused, stirred.
émotivité (emotivite), s.f. Emotivity.
émottage, émottement (emɔtaʒ, emɔtmã), s.m. Clod-crushing.
émotter (emɔte), v.a. [f. *motte*] To break up (soil, clods).
émotteu-r, -se (emɔtœr), adj. Clod-breaking. **~**, s.m. Sugar-cane crusher. **~se**, s.f. Clod-breaker, roller.
émottoir (emɔtwar), s.m. Clod-breaker.
émoucher (emuʃe), v.a. [*é+mouche*] To clear of flies, to drive the flies away from.
émouchet (emuʃe), s.m. (ornith.) Sparrow-hawk, kestrel.
émoucheter (emuʃte), v.a. See DÉMOUCHETER.
émouchette (emuʃɛt), s.f. [f. *émoucher*] Fly-net (for horses).
émoucheu-r, -se (emuʃœr), s.m.f. One who drives away flies.
émouchoir (emuʃwar), s.m. Fly-whisk, fly-flap.
émoudre (emudr), v.a. [*é+moudre*] To whet, to grind.
émoulage (emulaʒ), s.m. Whetting, grinding.
émouleur (emulœr), s.m. Knife-grinder.
émoulu, -e (emuly), p. adj. Sharpened, whetted; sharp; *combattre à fer ~*, to fight with cold steel; *être frais ~ de*, to be fresh from.
émousser (emuse), v.a. [f. *mousse*] To dull, to blunt, to take the edge off; (fig.) to blunt, to enfeeble, to deaden.
émoustiller (emustije), v.a. [f. *moustille*] To cheer up, to put spirit into; **s'~**, v.pr. to cheer up, to get excited, to look alive.
émouvant, -e (emuvã), p. adj. Touching, moving, stirring.
émouvoir (emuvwar), v.a. [L *emovere*] To move, to touch, to stir; to excite, to rouse; *~ le pouls*, to stir the pulses; *~ une sédition*, to incite sedition, to stir up revolt; *~ la bile à X*, to rouse X to anger; **s'~**, v.pr. to be touched, to be moved; to be stirred, to be roused; to be upset; *il s'émeut d'un rien*, the least thing upsets him.
empaillage, empaillement (ãpajaʒ, ãpajmã), s.m. **1.** Stuffing (of birds, &c.); **2.** caning (of chairs).
empailler (ãpaje), v.a. [f. *en+paille*] **1.** To stuff (birds, &c.); (fig.) *empaillé, -e*, adj. s.m.f. clumsy, awkward, slow person, noodle; **2.** to cane-bottom (chairs); **3.** to pack in straw;
empailleu-r, -se (ãpajœr), s.m.f. **1.** Taxidermist; **2.** chair-mender.
empalement (ãpalmã), s.m. [f. *pal*] Impalement.
empaler (ãpale), v.a. To impale.
empan (ãpã), s.m. [f. Germ. *spannen*] Span.
empanacher (ãpanaʃe), v.a. To plume, to adorn; (colloq.) to touch up.

empanner (ãpane), v.a. [f. *panne*] (naut.) To bring to; to heave to.
empaquetage (ãpaktaʒ), s.m. Packing, making into bundles.
empaqueter (ãpakte), v.a. [f. *paquet*] To pack up, to do up, to make into a bundle.
(s')emparer (*de*) (sãpare), v.pr. [L *ante* +*parare*] To seize, to secure, to grasp, to possess oneself of, to get hold of; *s'~ de la conversation*, to engross, or to monopolize the conversation; (fig.) *quelle fureur s'empare de vous?*, what possesses you?; *s'~ d'un héritage*, to seize upon an inheritance.
empâtement (ãpɑtmã), s.m. **1.** Stickiness, clamminess; **2.** thickness (of the voice); **3.** cramming (of poultry); **4.** (paint.) impasto; **5.** (med.) puffiness.
empâter (ãpɑte), v.a. [f. *pâte*] **1.** To make sticky or clammy; **2.** to thicken; *~ la langue*, to make the tongue white; **3.** to cram (poultry); **4.** (paint.) to impaste.
empattement, empattage (ãpatmã, ãpataʒ), s.m. **1.** Footing, foundation, base; **2.** platform (for cranes, &c.); **3.** (naut.) splicing; **4.** (motor.) wheel-base.
empatter (ãpate), v.a. [f. *patte*] **1.** (carp.) To mortise; **2.** (naut.) to splice; **3.** to support, to prop (cranes, &c.).
empaumer (ãpome), v.a. [f. *en+paume*] To receive and strike with the palm of the hand, or (by ext.) with a racquet; (fig.) (*a*) to get round, to wheedle, to lure, to get a subtle and powerful influence over; (*b*) (rare) *~ une affaire*, to secure a business and conduct it ably.
empaumure (ãpomyr), s.f. **1.** Palm (of a glove); **2.** top antler.
empêchant, -e (ãpɛʃã), p. adj. (obs.) Preventing.
empêchement (ãpɛʃmã), s.m. Hindrance, impediment; objection; bar.
empêcher (ãpɛʃe), v.a. [L *impedicare*] To prevent, to put a stop to; to hinder, to impede, to obstruct; *il m'empêche de travailler*, he hinders me from working; *cela n'empêche pas que*, or *n'empêche que*, it does not alter the fact that; and yet for all that; *l'un n'empêche pas l'autre*, the one does not bar the other; **s'~**, v.pr. to forbear, to refrain (*de*, from), to abstain (from), to prevent oneself (from); *je ne puis m'empêcher de rire*, I cannot help laughing.
empêcheu-r, -se (ãpɛʃœr), s.m.f. Hinderer, preventer; (fig.) *~ de danser en rond*, wet blanket, kill-joy.
empeigne (ãpɛɲ), s.f. Vamp, upper.
empellement (ãpɛlmã), s.m. [f. *en+pelle*] Sluice, dam.
empennage (ãpɛnaʒ), s.m. [f. *penne*] **1.** Feathering (of arrows); **2.** (aeron.) tail, tail-wings.
empenne (ãpɛn), s.f. [f. *penne*] Barb (of an arrow).
empenneler (ãpɛnle), v.a. (naut.) To back (an anchor).
empennelle (ãpɛnɛl), s.f. (naut.) Small anchor for backing; kedge-anchor.
empenner (ãpɛne), v.a. [f. *penne*] To barb (arrows).
empereur (ãprœr), s.m., fem. **impératrice** (ɛ̃peratris), [L *imperator*] Emperor (fem. empress).
emperler (ãpɛrle), v.a. [f. *perle*] **1.** To bead, to decorate with beads; **2.** (fig.) to bead (with moisture); *la sueur emperla son front*, his forehead was beaded with sweat.
empesage (ãpəzaʒ), s.m. Starching.
empesé, -e (ãpəze), p. adj. Starched; (fig.) stiff (of style), starchy, formal.
empeser (ãpəze), v.a. [f. *poix*] To starch; (fig.) to stiffen.
empeseu-r, -se (ãpəzœr), s.m.f. Starcher.
empester (ãpɛste), v.a. [f. *peste*] To infect, to taint; (fig.) to cause to stink; *cela empeste toute la maison*, it stinks the house out; to corrupt; *~ le monde de mauvaises doctrines*, to corrupt the world with false doctrines.
empêtrer (ãpɛtre), v.a. [LL *impastoriare*] To entangle, to hamper, to catch, to enmesh; (fig.) to embarrass, to worry; to involve; **s'~**, v.pr. to get entangled, to stumble, to become embarrassed.
emphase (ãfɑz), s.f. [Gr. *emphasis*] Magniloquence, bombast, pomposity, undue emphasis. ⚠ 'Emphasis' = *accent, intensité de sens ou d'expression*; 'to emphasize' = *mettre en relief, souligner*.
emphatique (ãfatik), adj. **1.** Bombastic; **2.** (gram.) emphatic.
emphatiquement (ãfatikmã), adv. **1.** Bombastically; **2.** emphatically.
emphysémateu-x, -se (ãfizematø), adj. s.m.f. Emphysematous (person).
emphysème (ãfizɛm), s.m. [Gr. *emphusēma*] (pathol.) Emphysema.
emphytéose (ãfiteoz), s.f. [Gr. *emphuteusis*] (law) Emphyteusis.
emphytéote (ãfiteɔt), s.m. Emphyteuta.
emphytéotique (ãfiteɔtik), adj. (law) Emphyteutic (obs.).
empiècement (ãpjɛsmã), s.m. [f. *pièce*] Yoke (of shirt, blouse, &c.).
empierrement (ãpjɛrmã), s.m. Ballasting, metalling; ballast, road-metal.
empierrer (ãpjɛre), v.a. [f. *pierre*] To ballast, to metal (roads).
empiètement (ãpjɛtmã), s.m. Encroaching, trespassing, encroachment, infringement, trespass.
empiéter (ãpjete), v.a. [f. *pied*] To encroach upon, to infringe, to trespass upon, to entrench upon; ~, v.n. to encroach; (fig.) *~ sur X*, to encroach upon X's rights.

empiffrer (ãpifre), v.a. [f. *en+piffre*] To cram, to stuff; to fatten; **s'~**, v.pr. to eat greedily, to stuff, to gorge oneself.

empilement, empilage (ãpilmã, ãpilaʒ), s.m. Piling, stacking, crowding.

empiler (ãpile), v.a. [f. *en+pile*] **1.** To pile up, to stack; **2.** (pop.) to swindle, to do, to let in; **s'~**, v.pr. to form a heap; to be piled up, to be heaped; to crowd, to force one's way (into a room, carriage, &c.).

empileu-r, -se (ãpilœr), s.m.f. **1.** Stacker; **2.** (pop.) humbug, bluffer; cheat, swindler.

empire (ãpir), s.m. [L *imperium*] Empire; dominions; (fig.) sway, rule, dominion; *avoir de l'~ sur soi*, to have oneself well under control; *se disputer l'~*, to contend for supremacy; *avoir un ~ absolu sur*, to have dominion over, to hold sway over; *style ~*, Empire style (in furniture, architecture, &c.).

empirer (ãpire), v.a. [f. *pire*] To make worse; ~, v.n. to grow worse; *la chose empira*, matters grew worse.

empirique (ãpirik), adj. [Gr. *empeirikos*] Empiric, empirical. ~, s.m.f. Empiricist.

empiriquement (ãpirikmã), adv. Empirically.

empirisme (ãpirism), s.m. Empiricism.

empiriste (ãpirist), s.m.f. Empiricist.

emplacement (ãplasmã), s.m. [*en+place*] Emplacement, site, situation.

emplanture (ãplãtyr), s.f. [f. *en+planter*] (naut.) Step (of a mast).

emplâtre (ãplɑtr), s.m. [Gr. *emplastron*] **1.** Plaster, salve, ointment; **2.** (fig. and fam.) helpless creature, muff, dud, bore; **3.** (slang) slap.

emplette (ãplɛt), s.f. [pop. L *implicita*] Purchase; *faire ~ de quelque chose*, to purchase something; *faire des ~s*, to go shopping; syn. ACHAT.

emplir (ãplir), v.a. [L *implere*] To fill (*de*, with), to fill up; (fig.) *~ de joie*, to fill with joy; **s'~**, v.pr. to be filled; to fill; syn. REMPLIR.

emploi (ãplwa), s.m. [f. *employer*] **1.** Employment, use; function; *faire un bon ~ de son temps*, to make good use of one's time; *~ d'un mot*, function of a word; *faire double ~*, to be a useless repetition, duplicate; *mode d'~*, directions for use; **2.** employment, occupation; *donner de l'~*, to give employment; *sans ~*, out of work, (fig.) at a loose end; **3.** (theatr.) line.

employable (ãplwajabl), adj. Employable.

employé, -e (ãplwaje), p. adj. Employed. ~, s.m.f. Employee, employé; *~ de banque*, bank-clerk; *~ de chemin de fer*, railway-servant; *~ de la gare*, railway-clerk.

employer (ãplwaje), v.a. [L *implicare*] To employ, to use, to make use of; *~ une expression*, to use a phrase; *~ son temps*, to employ, to make use of one's time; (fig.) *~ le vert et le sec*, to leave no stone unturned; to give employment to, to employ, to engage; to spend, to lay out, to invest; *~ ses capitaux*, to lay out one's capital; **s'~**, v.pr. to employ oneself, to busy oneself; to be used, to be employed.

employeu-r, -se (ãplwajœr), s.m.f. Employer.

emplumé, -e (ãplyme), p. adj. [f. *emplumer*] Feathered; *bête ~e*, feathered fowl.

emplumer (ãplyme), v.a. [f. *plume*] To feather; **s'~**, v.pr.: see SE REMPLUMER.

empocher (ãpɔʃe), v.a. [f. *en+poche*] To pocket; to pouch; (fig. and fam.) *~ des insultes*, to pocket affronts.

empoignant, -e (ãpwaɲã), p. adj. (fig.) Thrilling, poignant.

empoigner (ãpwaɲe), v.a. [f. *poing*] **1.** To grasp, to lay hold on or of, to grip; (fig.) to grip; to move deeply; **2.** (fam.) to take up; to lay hands on, (pop.) to cop; *~ le voleur*, to lay hands on the thief; *je vous ferai ~*, I'll have you taken up; **s'~**, v.pr. to lay hold of each other, to grapple with each other, to come to close quarters, to fight, to let fly at each other.

empointer[1] (ãpwɛ̃te), v.a. [f. *pointe*] To point (pins, needles, &c.); see syn. APPOINTIR, APPOINTER.

empointer[2] (ãpwɛ̃te), v.a. (rare) [f. *point*] **1.** (dressm.) To put a stitch in, to stitch lightly together; **2.** (pop.) to tease.

empois (ãpwɑ), s.m. [f. *empeser*] Starch.

empoisonné, -e (ãpwazɔne), p. adj. Poisoned; (fig.) poisonous, corrupt.

empoisonnement (ãpwazɔnmã), s.m. Poisoning; (fig.) corruption.

empoisonner (ãpwazɔne), v.a. [f. *poison*] To poison; (fig.) to infect; to mar, to corrupt; to embitter, to envenom; (fam.) *~ la vie à X*, to lead X a dog's life, to make X's life not worth living; (fig.) *empoisonnant*, boring, sickening; ~, v.n. to be poisonous; (fig.) to be malodorous, to stink; **s'~**, v.pr. to take poison, to poison oneself.

empoisonneu-r, -se (ãpwazɔnœr), s.m.f. **1.** Poisoner; (fig.) corrupter; **2.** (colloq.) execrable cook. ~, adj. Poisonous.

empoisser (ãpwase), v.a. To pitch; to make sticky; syn. POISSER.

empoissonnement (ãpwasɔnmã), s.m. [f. *poisson*] Stocking with fish.

empoissonner (ãpwasɔne), v.a. To stock with fish.

emporté, -e (ãpɔrte), p. adj. Fiery, hasty, hot-headed.

emportement (ãpɔrtəmã), s.m. Fit of passion, outburst; transport (usually used in pl.).

emporte-pièce (ãpɔrtəpjɛs), s.m. (pl. *emporte-pièces*) **1.** Punching machine, puncher; **2.** (fig.) *style à l'~*, trenchant style; *réponse à l'~*, cutting answer.

emporter (ãpɔrte), v.a. [*en+porter*] **1.** To carry away, to take away, to remove; to carry off; (fig.) to sweep away; *que le diable l'emporte*, devil take him; *le vent l'a emporté*, the wind has blown it away; *~ les blessés*, to remove the wounded; (fig.) *~ le prix*, to carry off the prize; (fig.) *emporté par sa colère*, carried away by his wrath; (fig.) *~ le morceau*, to strike home; *emporté en trois jours par une pneumonie*, carried off by pneumonia in three days; *un éclat d'obus lui emporta la jambe*, a splinter of shell took off his leg; (fig.) *emporté par l'enthousiasme*, carried, swept away by enthusiasm, excitement; **2.** *l'~ sur*, to preponderate over, to outweigh, to surpass, to prevail over, to get the better of; *cette considération l'emporte sur toutes les autres*, that consideration outweighs all the others; *l'~ sur ses ennemis*, to triumph over one's enemies; *l'amour l'emporte souvent sur la raison*, love often gets the better of reason; **3.** to imply; *un devoir qui emporte un droit*, a duty which implies a privilege; **s'~**, v.pr. to lose one's temper, to fly into a passion, to flare up; *s'~ contre quelqu'un*, to inveigh against a person; *s'~* or *monter comme une soupe au lait*, to flare up like gunpowder; **2.** to bolt (of a horse).

empotage, empotement (ãpɔtaʒ, ãpɔtmã), s.m. Potting.

empoté, -e (ãpɔte), p. adj. (pop. and fig.) Lumpy. ~, s.m.f. Lump, oaf.

empoter (ãpɔte), v.a. [f. *en+pot*] (hort.) To pot.

empouilles (ãpuj), s.f.pl. [f. *dépouille*] (obs.) Standing harvest; syn. RÉCOLTE SUR PIED.

empourprer (ãpurpre), v.a. [f. *pourpre*] To purple, to stain red or crimson; **s'~**, v.pr. to turn crimson; *son visage s'empourpra de colère*, his face went crimson with rage. ⚠ *Pourpre* in French = dark red, whilst 'purple' = *violet rougeâtre* (dark red mixed with blue).

empreindre (ãprɛ̃dr), v.a. (rare) [L *imprimere*] To imprint, to stamp, to mark, to impress; *~ ses pas sur la neige*, to leave one's footprints in the snow; *son image est empreinte dans ma mémoire*, his image is stamped upon my memory; syn. IMPRIMER.

empreinte (ãprɛ̃t), s.f. Stamp, print, impression; impress; *marqué à l'~ de*, bearing the stamp of; (fig.) *cet ouvrage porte l'~ du génie*, this work bears the stamp of genius.

empressé, -e (ãprɛse), p. adj. Eager, assiduous; (pej.) officious, (esp. of women) gushing; *un monsieur ~ auprès des dames*, a gentleman assiduous in his attentions to the ladies.

empressement (ãprɛsmã), s.m. Alacrity, eagerness, promptness; haste, hurry; *avec ~*, eagerly, with alacrity; *montrer trop d'~*, to be over-eager, to be in too much of a hurry; to be gushing; syn. ZÈLE.

(s')empresser (sãprɛse), v.pr. [f. *presser*] To bustle officiously, to hurry about, to be eager, to be assiduous; (pej.) to be officious; to gush; to hasten (*de*, to); *les courtisans s'empressent autour du roi*, the courtiers throng about the king.

emprise (ãpriz), s.f. **1.** Expropriation; **2.** (archaic) enterprise, emprise; **3.** (neol.) hold, influence.

emprisonnement (ãprizɔnmã), s.m. Imprisonment; *~ cellulaire*, solitary confinement.

emprisonner (ãprizɔne), v.a. [f. *en+prison*] To imprison.

emprunt (ãprœ̃), s.m. Borrowing; loan; *contracter* or *faire un ~*, to contract a loan; *une beauté d'~*, an artificial beauty.

emprunté, -e (ãprœ̃te), p. adj. **1.** Borrowed; factitious; *nom ~*, assumed name; embarrassed; *air ~*, embarrassed air or look.

emprunter (ãprœ̃te), v.a. [f. L *in+promutuum*] To borrow; (prov.) *ne choisit pas qui emprunte*, beggars can't be choosers.

emprunteu-r, -se (ãprœ̃tœr), adj. Borrowing, given to borrowing; not original. ~, s.m.f. Borrower.

empuantir (ãpɥãtir), v.a. [f. *puant*] To give an evil smell to, to infect, to make stink.

empuantissement (ãpɥãtismã), s.m. Stench.

empyème (ãpiɛm), s.m. [Gr. *empuēma*] (pathol.) Empyema.

empyrée (ãpire), s.m. [Gr. *empuros*] The empyrean. ~, adj. Empyrean.

empyreumatique (ãpirømatik), adj. Empyreumatic.

empyreume (ãpirøm), s.m. [Gr. *empureuma*] Empyreuma.

ému, -e (emy), p. adj. [p.p. of *émouvoir*] Moved, touched, affected; *fort ~*, much affected.

emulat-eur, -rice (emylatœr), s.m.f. (rare) Emulator, rival. ~, adj. Emulative.

émulation (emyla'sjɔ̃), s.f. [L *aemulatio*] Emulation.

émule (emyl), s.m.f. [L *aemulus*] Rival, competitor; emulator. ~, adj. Rival, emulous.

émulgent, -e (emylʒã), adj. [L *emulgens*] (physiol.) Emulgent.

émulsi-f, -ve (emylsif), adj. s.m. Emulsive, emulsion.

émulsine (emylsin), s.f. Emulsin.

émulsion (emylsjɔ̃), s.f. [f. L *emulsus*] Emulsion.
émulsionner (emylsjɔne), v.a. To emulsionize.
émyde (emid), s.f. [Gr. *emus*] (zool.) Marsh-tortoise, emys.
en (ɑ̃), prep. [L *in*] In; to; within; into; at; like, as, in the form of; out of, by, through, from; for; *agir ~ ami*, to act like a friend; *agir ~ témoin*, to act as a witness; *aller ~ France*, to go to France; *aller de mal ~ pis*, to go from bad to worse; *être ~ province*, to be out of town; *dîner ~ ville*, to dine out; *~ paix*, in peace, at peace; *~ passant*, by the way; *~ tout temps*, always; *~ nourrice*, out at nurse, with a foster-mother; *mettre ~ pension*, to send to boarding-school; *mettre ~ vente*, to put up for sale; *voir ~ songe*, to see in a dream; *vivre ~ Nabab*, to live like a lord; *~ guerre*, at war; *~ tête de*, at the head of; *~ avance sur*, in advance of; *~ dépit de*, in spite of; *déguisé ~ pélerin*, disguised as a pilgrim; *mettre ~ liberté*, to set at liberty; *~ vue de*, with a view to; *~ effet*, indeed, in fact; *de jour ~ jour*, from day to day.
en (ɑ̃), pers. pron. 3rd p., and ind. pron. [L *inde*] Of him, of her, of it, its, of them, their; from him, by him, about him, &c., thence, from there; some of it, any; *je n'~ ai pas*; *~ avez-vous?*, I haven't any, have you?, or I have none, have you any?; *où ~ êtes-vous?*, how far have you got?, where have you got to?; *~ êtes-vous?*, will you make one of us?, or, (fam.) are you game?; *~ avoir assez*, to have had enough of it; *~ venir aux mains*, to come to blows; *il veut ~ découdre*, he wants to have it out; *il ~ tient*, he is winged, hard hit; *qu'~ pensez-vous?*, what do you make of it?, or, what do you think of him (her)?; *c'~ est fait de lui*, it is all up with him; *s'~ aller*, to go, to leave, to take one's leave; *je m'~ moque*, (pop.) *je m'~ fiche*, I don't care; *~ coûter à quelqu'un*, to go against the grain; *il vous ~ coûtera cher*, you shall smart for this; *il n'~ peut mais*, he has no choice; *il n'~ peut plus*, he is at the end of his tether; *à l'~ croire*, according to him; *~ imposer à quelqu'un*, to impose upon some one; *j'~ appelle à vous*, I put it to you; *je n'~ reviens pas*, I can't get over it; *c'~ est trop*, the thing has gone too far; *il m'~ veut*, he bears me a grudge; *il faut ~ prendre et ~ laisser*; don't take it too literally; *j'~ passe et des meilleurs*, and I skip some of the best.
énallage (enalaʒ), s.m. [Gr. *enallagē*] (gram.) Enallage.
enamourer (ɑ̃namure), v.a. [f. *en+amour*] To enamour; **s'~**, v.pr. to fall in love (*de*, with); to be enamoured (of).
encablure (ɑ̃kɑblyr), s.f. [f. *en+câble*] Cable's length (about 220 yards).
encadrement (ɑ̃kadrəmɑ̃), s.m. Framing, frame; border, margin; (fig.) environment.
encadrer (ɑ̃kadre), v.a. [f. *en+cadre*] To frame; to encircle, to surround; (fig.) to environ; (mil.) to embody; **s'~**, v.pr. to be framed, introduced, inserted or enclosed.
encadreur (ɑ̃kadrœr), s.m. Picture-frame maker, framer.
encager (ɑ̃kaʒe), v.a. [f. *en+cage*] To cage, to encage, to put in a cage; (fig. and fam.) to lock up.
encaissage (ɑ̃kɛsaʒ), s.m. [f. *en+caisse*] Encasing; (hort.) tubbing.
encaissant, -e (ɑ̃kɛsɑ̃), p. adj. Encasing, confining, surrounding.
encaisse (ɑ̃kɛs), s.f. [*en+caisse*] Cash in hand, cash-balance; *~ métallique*, bullion.
encaissé, -e (ɑ̃kɛse), p. adj. Enclosed by steep banks, sunk, hollow.
encaissement (ɑ̃kɛsmɑ̃), s.m. **1.** Packing; **2.** paying-in, collecting; cashing; **3.** embankment.
encaisser (ɑ̃kɛse), v.a. [f. *en+caisse*] **1.** To encase, to pack; **2.** to collect, to receive (money, &c.), to cash; **3.** to embank (a river, &c.); **4.** (slang) to receive blows, rebuke, or insult, &c.; to accept; *je ne peux pas ~ ce garçon-là!*, I can't stick the fellow!
encaisseu-r, -se (ɑ̃kɛsœr), s.m.f. Cash-collector, cashier.
encalminé, -e (ɑ̃kalmine), p. adj. [f. *en+calme*] (naut.) Becalmed.
encan (ɑ̃kɑ̃), s.m. [f. L *in quantum*] Public auction; *mettre à l'~*, to put up for auction; (fig.) *mettre sa conscience à l'~*, to sell one's conscience to the highest bidder.
encanailler (ɑ̃kanɑje), v.a. [f. *canaille*] To degrade, to lower; **s'~**, v.pr. to keep low company, to lose caste.
encapuchonner (ɑ̃kapyʃɔne), v.a. [f. *en+capuchon*] To put a hood on; **s'~**, v.pr. to muffle up.
encaquement (ɑ̃kakmɑ̃), s.m. Packing, barrelling.
encaquer (ɑ̃kake), v.a. [f. *en+caque*] **1.** To barrel, to pack (herrings); **2.** (fig. and fam.) to pack like sardines.
encaqueu-r, -se (ɑ̃kakœr), s.m.f. Herring-packer.
encart (ɑ̃kar), s.m. Inset; (print.) middle leaves.
encarter, encartonner (ɑ̃karte, ɑ̃kartɔne) v.a. [f. *en+carte*] To insert as an inset; (print.) to press or glaze between paste-boards.
encas, en-cas, en cas (ɑ̃kɑ), s.m. **1.** Anything prepared for an emergency; **2.** sun-shade-umbrella.

(s')encasteler (sɑ̃kastəle), v.pr. [It. *incastellare*] To be hoof-bound (of horses).
encastelure (ɑ̃kastəlyr), s.f. Contraction of the hoof.
encastiller (ɑ̃kastije), v.a. (archaic) To encase, to enshrine; to put in safety.
encastrement (ɑ̃kastrəmɑ̃), s.m. Fitting-in; groove.
encastrer (ɑ̃kastre), v.a. [It. *incastrare*] To fit into, to insert, to fit together; to wedge in; **s'~**, v.pr. to fit in, to fit together.
encaustique (ɑ̃kɔstik), s.f. [Gr. *egkaustikos*] **1.** Encaustic; **2.** furniture-polish, floor-polish, wax polish. ⚠ 'Encaustic' also = *pyrogravure*.
encaustiquer (ɑ̃kɔstike), v.a. To coat with wax polish, to polish.
encavement (ɑ̃kavmɑ̃), s.m. Cellaring.
encaver (ɑ̃kave), v.a. [f. *en+cave*] To cellar, to store in a cellar.
encaveur (ɑ̃kavœr), s.m. Cellarer; wine-porter.
enceindre (ɑ̃sɛ̃dr), v.a. [L *incingere*] To enclose, to encircle, to encompass.
enceinte (ɑ̃sɛ̃t), s.f. **1.** Enclosure, walls, ring, fence; **2.** precincts, purlieu, premises; *dans cette ~*, within these walls; **3.** (fort.) enceinte.
enceinte (ɑ̃sɛ̃t), adj. f. [f. L *incincta*] Pregnant, enceinte, with child.
encelluler (ɑ̃sɛlyle), v.a. [f. *en+cellule*] To confine in a cell, to put in the cells.
encens (ɑ̃sɑ̃), s.m. [LL *incensum*] Incense, frankincense; (fig.) praise, flattery, eulogy.
encensement (ɑ̃sɑ̃smɑ̃), s.m. Censing; incensing. ⚠ See ENCENSER.
encenser (ɑ̃sɑ̃se), v.a. [f. *encens*] To incense; to cense; to burn incense before (or to); to perfume with incense; *~ l'autel*, to cense the altar; (fig.) to pay homage to, to burn incense to, to flatter; **~**, v.n. (of a horse) to move its head constantly up and down. ⚠ 'To incense' means also *fâcher*.
encenseur (ɑ̃sɑ̃sœr), s.m. **1.** (eccles.) Thurifer; **2.** (fig.) flatterer.
encensoir (ɑ̃sɑ̃swar), s.m. Censer; (fig.) flattery; *donner de l'~ à X*, or *lui casser l'~ sur le nez*, to choke X with flattery, (pop.) to lay it on thick, or with a trowel.
encéphale (ɑ̃sefal), s.m. [Gr. *egkephalon*] (anat.) Encephalon.
encéphalique (ɑ̃sefalik), adj. Encephalic.
encéphalite (ɑ̃sefalit), s.f. Encephalitis.
encéphalocèle (ɑ̃sefalosɛl), s.f. (pathol.) Encephalocele, hernia of the brain.
encéphalopathie (ɑ̃sefalɔpati), s.f. Encephalopathy.
encerclement (ɑ̃sɛrkləmɑ̃), s.m. Encircling.
encercler (ɑ̃sɛrkle), v.a. [f. *en+cercle*] To encircle.
enchaînement (ɑ̃ʃɛnmɑ̃), s.m. Linking-up; chain, connexion, succession; *un ~ d'idées*, a train of thought.
enchaîner (ɑ̃ʃɛne), v.a. [f. *en+chaîne*] To chain, to chain up or down, to enchain, to bind in chains; (fig.) to detain, to restrain, to tie down; to captivate; to link up, to connect; **~**, v.n. (theatr.) to take up one's cue quickly; **s'~**, v.pr. to bind oneself; to be connected or linked together.
enchaînure (ɑ̃ʃɛnyr), s.f. (mech.) Chain-work, connexion.
enchanté, -e (ɑ̃ʃɑ̃te), p. adj. Enchanted; (fig.) charmed, delighted.
enchantement (ɑ̃ʃɑ̃tmɑ̃), s.m. **1.** Enchantment, spell; **2.** (fig.) charm, delight; *il est dans l'~*, he is spell-bound (with delight); he is delighted.
enchanter (ɑ̃ʃɑ̃te), v.a. [L *incantare*] To enchant, to bewitch, to charm (also fig.); *je suis enchanté de vous voir*, I am charmed or delighted to see you; syn. CHARMER, RAVIR.
enchant-eur, -eresse (ɑ̃ʃɑ̃tœr), s.m.f. Enchanter (fem. enchantress), charmer; magician. **~**, adj. Bewitching, enchanting; *voix ~eresse*, bewitching voice.
enchaper (ɑ̃ʃape), v.a. [f. *en+chape*] To enclose (one cask within another).
enchaperonner (ɑ̃ʃaprɔne), v.a. [f. *en+chaperon*] To hood (a hawk, &c.).
encharner (ɑ̃ʃarne), v.a. [f. *en+charnière*] To hinge, to put hinges on.
enchâssement (ɑ̃ʃɑsmɑ̃), s.m. Enchasing, enshrining.
enchâsser (ɑ̃ʃɑse), v.a. [f. *en+châsse*] To enchase, to enshrine; to set; *~ un bijou*, to set a jewel; (fig.) to introduce; *~ une citation dans un discours*, to introduce a quotation into a speech.
enchausser (ɑ̃ʃose), v.a. [f. *en+chausse*] (agric.) To straw, to earth up.
enchère (ɑ̃ʃɛr), s.f. [f. *enchérir*] Bid; *vendre aux ~s*, to sell by auction; *mettre aux ~s*, to put up for auction, *se vendre aux ~s*, to come under the hammer; *folle ~*, bid for which one cannot pay; *mettre une ~*, to make a bid; (fig.) *être à l'~*, to fall to the highest bidder, to sell oneself to the highest bidder.
enchérir (ɑ̃ʃerir), v.a. [f. *cher*] **1.** To bid for; **2.** to outbid, to overbid; **3.** to raise (prices); **~**, v.n. to rise (in price), to become dearer; *~ sur*, to surpass, to go further than, to outdo.
enchérissement (ɑ̃ʃerismɑ̃), s.m. Rise, increase in price.
enchérisseu-r, -se (ɑ̃ʃerisœr), s.m.f. Bidder.
enchevalement (ɑ̃ʃvalmɑ̃), s.m. [f. *chevaler*] (build.) Propping, underpinning.
enchevaucher (ɑ̃ʃvoʃe), v.a. [*en+chevaucher*] To make (tiles, &c.) overlap.

enchevauchure (ɑ̃ʃvoʃyr), s.f. Overlapping.
enchevêtrement (ɑ̃ʃvɛtrəmɑ̃), s.m. Entanglement, confusion; tangle.
enchevêtrer (ɑ̃ʃvɛtre), v.a. [f. (OF) *chevêtre*] **1.** To halter (a horse); **2.** to bind with a joist; **3.** to entangle, to confuse; to ravel; **s'∼**, v.pr. to get entangled; (fig.) to get entangled, confused, or embarrassed.
enchifrènement (ɑ̃ʃifrɛnmɑ̃), s.m. Obstruction of the nose, snuffles.
enchifrener (ɑ̃ʃifrəne), v.a. [f. *chanfrein*] To stuff up the nose of; **s'∼**, v.pr. to get stuffed up, to get the snuffles.
enchymose (ɑ̃kimoz), s.f. [Gr. *egkhūmōsis*] Cutaneous hyperaemia.
encirement (ɑ̃sirmɑ̃), s.m. Smearing with wax.
encirer (ɑ̃sire), v.a. [f. *cire*] To wax, to smear with wax.
enclave (ɑ̃klav), s.f. [f. *enclaver*] Enclave, enclosed piece of land.
enclaver (ɑ̃klave), v.a. [LL *inclavare*] To enclose, to include; (techn.) to wedge in, to dovetail.
enclenchement (ɑ̃klɑ̃ʃmɑ̃), s.m. Clenching, locking, throwing into gear; automatic clutch, locking gear.
enclencher, enclancher (ɑ̃klɑ̃ʃe), v.a. [f. *clenche*] To clench; to throw into gear, to engage, to connect, to lock.
enclin, -e (ɑ̃klɛ̃), adj. [L *inclinis*] Inclined, prone, apt, given (*à*, to); ∼ *au mal*, inclined to evil-doing.
encliquetage (ɑ̃kliktaʒ), s.m. Catch, pawl, cog, cog-wheel.
encliqueter (ɑ̃klikte), v.a. [f. *cliquet*] To cog, to stop with a catch.
enclitique (ɑ̃klitik), s.f. [Gr. *egklitikos*] (gram.) Enclitic.
encloîtrer (ɑ̃klwɑtre), v.a. See syn. CLOÎTRER.
enclore (ɑ̃klɔr), v.a. [*en*+*clore*] To enclose, to fence in; to shut in; to take in.
enclos (ɑ̃klo), s.m. [f. *enclore*] Enclosure; paddock, orchard; close.
enclouer (ɑ̃klue), v.a. [*en*+*clouer*] **1.** To prick (animals) in shoeing; **2.** to spike (a gun).
enclume (ɑ̃klym), s.f. [f. L *incus*] Anvil; *billot d'∼*, anvil block; *être entre le marteau et l'∼*, to be crushed between two opposing forces; *remettre sur l'∼*, to remodel; *frapper toujours sur la même ∼*, to be always harping on the same string; *dur comme une ∼*, hard as iron; *il vaut mieux être marteau qu'∼*, better be hunter than hunted; *à dure ∼ marteau de plume*, a firm front disarms the enemy.
enclumeau (pl. -x), **enclumot** (ɑ̃klymo), s.m. Small anvil.
enclumette (ɑ̃klymɛt), s.f. Portable anvil.
encoche (ɑ̃kɔʃ), s.f. [*en*+*coche*] Notch, nick.
encocher (ɑ̃kɔʃe), v.a. **1.** To notch, to nick; **2.** to place; ∼ *une flèche*, to fit an arrow to the bow.
encoffrer (ɑ̃kɔfre), v.a. [f. *en*+*coffre*] To shut up in a coffer, to hoard; (fig.) to lock up, to put safely under lock and key.
encoignure, encognure (ɑ̃kwaɲyr, ɑ̃kɔɲyr), s.f. **1.** Corner, angle; **2.** (furniture) corner-piece; corner-cupboard.
encollage (ɑ̃kɔlaʒ), s.m. Sizing.
encoller (ɑ̃kɔle), v.a. [*en*+*coller*] To size, to gum.
encolure (ɑ̃kɔlyr), s.f. [f. *col*] **1.** Neck (of a horse); **2.** (dressm.) neck, neck-opening; **3.** (fig.) looks, general appearance, cast of countenance.
encombrant, -e (ɑ̃kɔ̃brɑ̃) p. adj. Cumbering, encumbering, cumbersome.
encombre (ɑ̃kɔ̃mbr), s.m. Obstacle, hindrance; *arriver sans ∼*, to arrive without accident; to arrive safely.
encombrement (ɑ̃kɔ̃brəmɑ̃), s.m. Obstruction, stoppage; crowding, crowd; ∼ *de voitures*, traffic block.
encombrer (ɑ̃kɔ̃bre), v.a. [f. *en*+LL *combrus*] To obstruct, to hamper, to encumber ⚠; to crowd, to throng; to fill, to cram, to block. ⚠ In English an estate may be 'encumbered' with debts; in French a room is *encombrée de meubles, de personnes*, &c. (concrete things only).
(à l')encontre (alɑ̃kɔ̃tr), prep. loc. Against, counter (*de*, to); *aller à l'∼ de quelque chose*, to run counter to a thing.
encorbellement (ɑ̃kɔrbɛlmɑ̃), s.m. [f. *en*+*corbeille*] (arch.) Corbelling.
encore (often, in poetry, *encor*) (ɑ̃kɔr), adv. [L *ad hanc horam*] **1.** Yet, still, as yet; ∼ *moins*, still less; *pas ∼*, not yet; *ce n'est ∼ qu'un enfant*, he is only a child still; *vous en servez-vous ∼?*, are you still using it?; **2.** anew, again, once more; *j'ai ∼ essayé hier*, I tried again yesterday; ∼ *une fois*, once again; ∼ *un*, one more; ∼*!*, what, again!; ∼ *un peu*, a little more, (of time) a little longer; ∼ *longtemps*, much longer; ∼ *vous!*, you again!; **3.** further, moreover; if only, even; *si ∼ il voulait m'écouter*, if only he would listen to me; *hier ∼*, only yesterday, but yesterday; *il ajouta ∼ que c'était inutile*, he added further that it was useless; *non seulement . . . mais ∼ . . .*, not only . . . but moreover . . .; *mais ∼?*, what more?, tell me more; what are your reasons?; **4.** ∼ *que*, conj. loc. although, in spite of the fact that; ∼ *qu'il soit jeune*, although he is young.
encorné, -e (ɑ̃kɔrne), p. adj. Horned.
encorner (ɑ̃kɔrne), v.a. **1.** To horn, to furnish with horns; **2.** to gore, to toss.
encourageant, -e (ɑ̃kuraʒɑ̃), p. adj. Encouraging, inspiriting, cheering.

encouragement (ãkuraʒmã), s.m. Encouragement; incentive; support.
encourager (ãkuraʒe), v.a. [f. *courage*] To encourage, to support; to be a promoter of; **s'~**, v.pr. to encourage each other, or oneself.
encourir (ãkurir), v.a. [*en*+*courir*] To incur.
encrage (ãkraʒ), s.m. [f. *encre*] (print.) Inking.
encrassement (ãkrasmã), s.m. Fouling (of fire-arms, &c.).
encrasser (ãkrase), v.a. [f. *crasse*] To dirty, to foul; **s'~**, v.pr. to get foul, greasy, dirty; (fig.) to lower oneself.
encre (ãkr), s.f. [Gr. *egkauston*] Ink; *~ de Chine*, Indian ink; *écrire de bonne ~ à X*, to write in strong terms to X; (fig.) *c'est la bouteille à l'~!*, it's a most confused business; *tacher d'~*, to ink, to make blots on.
encrer (ãkre), v.a. To ink.
encrier (ãkrie), s.m. Inkpot, inkstand, inkhorn; (print.) ink-trough.
encrine (ãkrin), s.f. [Gr. *en*+*krinon*] (zool.) Encrinite.
encroué, -e (ãkrue), adj. [etym. dub.] (forestry) Entangled; *arbre ~*, fallen tree, caught in the branches of another.
encroûtant, -e (ãkrutã), p. adj. Forming a crust; covered with a crust.
encroûté, -e (ãkrute), p. adj. **1.** Crusted; **2.** plastered (of walls); **3.** (fig.) hidebound.
encroûtement (ãkrutmã), s.m. Crusting over; (fig.) narrowing, narrowness.
encroûter (ãkrute), v.a. [f. *en*+*croûte*] **1.** To crust, to cover with a crust; **2.** to plaster (walls); **s'~**, v.pr. to crust, to get hard; to fur (of kettles, boilers, &c.); (fig.) to become hide-bound (intellectually).
encuirasser (ãkɥirase), v.a. [f. *en*+*cuirasse*] To cover with a cuirass; **s'~**, v.pr. to don one's cuirass; (fig.) to steel oneself.
encuvage, encuvement (ãkyvaʒ, akyvmã), s.m. Vatting, tubbing.
encuver (ãkyve), v.a. [f. *en*+*cuve*] To put into a vat, to tub.
encyclique (ãsiklik), adj. s.f. [Gr. *en*+*kuklos*] Encyclic(al).
encyclopédie (ãsiklɔpedi), s.f. [Gr. *en*+*kuklos*+*paideia*] Encyclopedia.
encyclopédique (ãsiklɔpedik), adj. Encyclopedic.
encyclopédiste (ãsiklɔpedist), s.m. Encyclopedist.
endaubage (ãdobaʒ), s.m. Stewing and preserving, corning (of meat).
endauber (ãdobe), v.a. [f. *en*+*daube*] To corn; to can, to preserve, to tin.
endécagone (ãdekagɔn), s.m. Hendecagon; see HENDÉCAGONE.
endémie (ãdemi), s.f. [Gr. *en*+*dēmos*] Endemic disease.
endémique (ãdemik), adj. Endemic.
endenté, -e (ãdãte), p. adj. Toothed, furnished with teeth; (fig.) *gens bien ~s*, good trenchermen, hearty feeders.
endenter (ãdãte), v.a. [f. *en*+*dent*] **1.** To cog, to tooth (a wheel, &c.); **2.** (carp.) to fit together, to dovetail.
endermique (ãdɛrmik), adj. [f. *derme*] Endermic.
endettement (ãdɛtmã), s.m. Running into debt.
endetter (ãdɛte), v.a. [f. *en*+*dette*] To get (a person) into debt; **s'~**, v.pr. to get into debt, to run into debt.
endeuiller (ãdœje), v.a. [f. *en*+*deuil*] To sadden, to make mournful; to put into mourning.
endêver (ãdɛve), v.n. [*en*+OF *desver*, to lose one's senses] (fam.) To rage, to fume, to be off one's chump; to see red; (fam.) *faire ~ X*, to rag X, to get a rise out of X.
endiablé, -e (ãdjɑble), p. adj. Mad, irrepressible; devilish, boisterous, impetuous, heady; (the sense 'possessed', 'diabolical', is obsolete); *une verve ~e*, witty vivaciousness.
endiabler (ãdjɑble), v.n. [f. *diable*] To be wild, to be furious; (fam.) *faire ~ X*, to make X mad.
endiamanté, -e (ãdjamãte), adj. **1.** Adorned with diamonds; **2.** trimmed with glittering ornaments.
endiguement, endigage (ãdigmã, ãdigaʒ), s.m. Damming, damming-up; diking.
endiguer (ãdige), v.a. [f. *en*+*digue*] To dam, to dike.
endimancher (ãdimãʃe), v.a. [f. *dimanche*] To dress in Sunday clothes; *des gens endimanchés*, folk decked out in their Sunday best; **s'~**, v.pr. to don one's Sunday best.
endive (ãdiv), s.f. [Gr. *entubon*] (bot.) Chicory. ⚠ French *endive* = chicory, and English 'endive' = *scarole, escarole, chicorée*.
endivisionnement (ãdivizjɔnmã), s.m. (mil.) Forming into divisions.
endivisionner (ãdivizjɔne), v.a. [f. *en*+*division*] (mil.) To form into divisions.
endocarde (ãdɔkard), s.m. [Gr. *endon*+*kardia*] (anat.) Endocardium.
endocardite (ãdɔkardit), s.f. (pathol.) Endocarditis.
endocarpe (ãdɔkarp), s.m. [Gr. *endon*+*karpos*] Endocarp.
endoctriner (ãdɔktrine), v.a. [f. *doctrine*] To indoctrinate, to teach, to give his cue to.
endoderme (ãdɔdɛrm), s.m. [Gr. *endon*+*derma*] Endoderm.
endogène (ãdɔʒɛn), adj. [Gr. *endon*+*gennan*] Endogenous.

endolorir (ɑ̃dɔlɔrir), v.a. [f. L *dolor*] To make painful, sore, or tender; (fig.) to make (the heart, &c.) ache.
endolorissement (ɑ̃dɔlɔrismɑ̃), s.m. Soreness, pain, ache.
endommagement (ɑ̃dɔmaʒmɑ̃), s.m. Injury, damage.
endommager (ɑ̃dɔmaʒe), v.a. [f. *dommage*] To damage, to injure.
endormant, -e (ɑ̃dɔrmɑ̃), p. adj. Soporific; (fig.) boring, sleep-compelling.
endormeu-r, -se (ɑ̃dɔrmœr), s.m.f. (fig.) Cajoler, wheedler; (fig.) bore, tiresome person.
endormi, -e (ɑ̃dɔrmi), p. adj. **1.** Asleep, sleeping; **2.** benumbed; **3.** (fig.) sleepy, drowsy, sluggish. **~**, s.m.f. Sleepy-head; *faire l'~*, to feign sleep.
endormir (ɑ̃dɔrmir), v.a. [f. *dormir*] To put, to rock, or to lull to sleep; (fig.) to lull, to calm; ~ *la vigilance de X*, to lull X's watchfulness; ~ *une douleur*, to soothe pain; (fig.) to send to sleep; *ses discours m'endorment*, his speeches send me to sleep; **s'~**, v.pr. to fall asleep, to drop off to sleep; (fig.) to be lulled into security; *il s'est endormi sur cette affaire*, he failed to keep his eyes open in that business; *s'~ du sommeil du juste*, to sleep the sleep of the just (of death); *s'~ sur ses lauriers*, to rest upon one's laurels.
endos, endossement (ɑ̃do, ɑ̃dosmɑ̃), s.m. [f. *endosser*] Endorsement.
endoscope (ɑ̃dɔskɔp), s.m. [Gr. *endon*+*skopein*] Endoscope.
endosmose (ɑ̃dɔsmoz), s.f. [Gr. *endon*+*ōsmos*] Endosmose, endosmosis.
endosmotique (ɑ̃dɔsmɔtik), adj. Endosmotic.
endosperme (ɑ̃dɔspɛrm), s.m. [Gr. *endon* +*sperma*] (bot.) Endosperm.
endossement (ɑ̃dosmɑ̃), s.m. See ENDOS.
endosser (ɑ̃dose), v.a. [f. *dos*] **1.** To put on one's back; ~ *la cuirasse*, to put one's harness on one's back; **2.** (fig.) to saddle oneself with, to shoulder; **3.** to endorse; ~ *un chèque*, to endorse a cheque.
endosseur (ɑ̃dosœr), s.m. Endorser.
endossure (ɑ̃dosyr), s.f. [f. *dos*] (bookbind.) Pasting, gluing.
endroit (ɑ̃drwa), s.m. [*en*+*droit*] **1.** Place, spot, locality; (fig.) *à l'~ de*, with regard to; ~ *faible*, weak point; ~ *sensible*, painful spot; (fig.) *frapper au bon ~*, to hit the nail on the head, to hit the mark; (colloq.) *aller au petit ~*, to go to the water-closet; **2.** face, right side (of material); *tourner un vêtement à l'~*, to turn a garment right side out.
enduire (ɑ̃dɥir), v.a. [L *inducere*] To coat, to smear, to do over.
enduit (ɑ̃dɥi), s.m. Coating, layer; plaster (for walls); glaze, varnish (for furniture, &c.).
endurable (ɑ̃dyrabl), adj. Endurable.
endurance (ɑ̃dyrɑ̃s), s.f. Endurance, staying-power.
endurant, -e (ɑ̃dyrɑ̃), p. adj. Enduring; meek; syn. PATIENT.
endurci, -e (ɑ̃dyrsi), p. adj. **1.** Hardened, inured; **2.** (fig.) obdurate; callous.
endurcir (ɑ̃dyrsir), v.a. [f. *dur*] To harden, to inure, to make resistant or enduring; (fig.) to harden, to render obdurate or callous; **s'~**, v.pr. to become hardened or inured; to harden; (fig.) to harden, to steel oneself, to become callous.
endurcissement (ɑ̃dyrsismɑ̃), s.m. Hardness; obduracy; hardness of heart, callousness.
endurer (ɑ̃dyre), v.a. [L *indurare*] To endure, to undergo; to brook, to put up with.
énergétique (enɛrʒetik), adj. Relating to energy. ⚠ Not 'energetic', which = *énergique*. ~ s.f. Energetics.
énergie (enɛrʒi), s.f. [Gr. *energeia*] Energy, strength, fortitude, strenuousness.
énergique (enɛrʒik), adj. Energetic, forcible; *remède ~*, powerful remedy.
énergiquement (enɛrʒikmɑ̃), adv. Energetically, strenuously.
énergumène (enɛrgymɛn), s.m.f. [Gr. *energoumenos*] Energumen, fanatic.
énervant, -e (enɛrvɑ̃), p. adj. **1.** Enervating, debilitating (of climate, heat, &c.); **2.** irritating, exasperating, nerve-racking.
énervation (enɛrva'sjɔ̃), s.f. Enervation, debilitation.
énervé, -e (enɛrve), p. adj. **1.** Enervated; **2.** (fig.) exasperated, unnerved; (fig. and fam.) on edge.
énervement (enɛrvmɑ̃), s.m. Fidgets, fidgetiness, irritation, exasperation.
énerver (enɛrve), v.a. [f. L *enervare*] **1.** To enervate, to debilitate; **2.** (fig.) to unnerve; **3.** (fam.) to get on a person's nerves; *il m'énerve cet homme*, that man gets on my nerves; **s'~**, v.pr. to get nervy, irritable, fidgety, to become exasperated, to fidget.
enfaîteau (pl. **-x**) (ɑ̃fɛto), s.m. [f. *faîte*] Ridge-tile.
enfaîtement (ɑ̃fɛtmɑ̃), s.m. [f. *faîte*] Ridge-lead.
enfaîter (ɑ̃fɛte), v.a. To ridge (a roof, &c.).
enfance (ɑ̃fɑ̃s), s.f. [f. *enfant*] **1.** Infancy, babyhood, childhood; boyhood or girlhood; (fig.) children; *l'~ est espiègle*, children are mischievous; **2.** dotage, second childhood; *tomber en ~*, to fall into dotage, to grow childish.
enfançon (ɑ̃fɑ̃sɔ̃), s.m. Babe.
enfant (ɑ̃fɑ̃), s.m.f. [L *infans*] Infant, baby; child, offspring; *petits-~s*, grandchildren; *petits ~s*, little children; *l'~ prodigue*, the prodigal son; *l'~*

prodige, the infant prodigy; ~ *trouvé,* foundling; *faire l'~,* to behave like a child; (eccles.) ~ *de chœur,* chorister; server; *en travail d'~,* in labour; *l'~ à naître,* the babe unborn; ~ *terrible,* enfant terrible; (colloq.) little terror; *être bien l'~ de sa mère,* to take after one's mother; (fig.) *être bon ~,* to be a good sort; *c'est un ~ de la balle,* he is born to the trade.

enfantement (ɑ̃fɑ̃tmɑ̃), s.m. Childbirth, accouchement; (fig.) production, bringing forth.

enfanter (ɑ̃fɑ̃te), v.a.n. To give birth to, to beget; to bring forth, to bear; (fig.) to produce, to bring to light, to give birth to.

enfantillage (ɑ̃fɑ̃tijaʒ), s.m. Child's play; childishness.

enfantin, -e (ɑ̃fɑ̃tɛ̃), adj. Infantile, childish; childlike; *questions ~es,* childish questions; *simplicité ~e,* childlike simplicity.

enfariné, -e (ɑ̃farine), p. adj. Floury; (pop.) *il est venu la gueule ~e,* he arrived full of mealy-mouthed phrases.

enfariner (ɑ̃farine), v.a. [f. *farine*] To flour, to sprinkle with flour.

enfer (ɑ̃fɛr), s.m. [L *inferni*] Hell; *les peines de l'~,* the torments of hell; *au fond de l'~,* in the depths of hell; *mener un train d'~,* (*a*) to drive hard, to tear along; (*b*) to kick up a row; *un feu d'~,* a scathing fire; *un jeu d'~,* a ruinous gamble; (pl.) *les Enfers,* Hades.

enfermé, -e (ɑ̃fɛrme), s.m. Close, confined air; (colloq.) fug; *cette pièce sent l'~,* this room smells close, (colloq.) there is a fug in this room.

enfermer (ɑ̃fɛrme), v.a. [*en*+*fermer*] **1.** To shut up, to shut in; ~ *un chien,* to shut up a dog; *enfermé par un mur,* shut in by a wall; **2.** to shut up, to lock up (persons); *c'est un homme à ~,* that man ought to be locked up; **3.** to lock away, to put under lock and key; *cet argent devrait être enfermé,* that money ought to be locked away; **4.** to contain; *passage qui enferme deux erreurs,* a passage which contains two errors; **s'~,** v.pr. to shut oneself up; (fig.) to seclude oneself.

enferrer (ɑ̃fɛre), v.a. [f. *fer*] To pierce, to transfix, to run through (with a sword, &c.); **s'~,** v.pr. to run oneself through; (fig.) to be one's own undoing.

enfieller (ɑ̃fjɛle), v.a. [f. *fiel*] To make bitter; (fig.) to embitter, to gall.

enfièvrement (ɑ̃fjɛvrəmɑ̃), s.m. Feverishness.

enfiévrer (ɑ̃fjevre), v.a. [f. *fièvre*] To fever, to make feverish; (fig.) to fever, to impassion, to inflame.

enfilade (ɑ̃filad), s.f. **1.** (arch.) Suite of apartments; **2.** string (of phrases); **3.** (mil.) enfilade; *feu d'~,* raking fire.

enfiler (ɑ̃file), v.a. [f. *fil*] **1.** To thread; ~ *une aiguille, des perles,* to thread a needle, beads; *je ne suis pas ici pour ~ des perles,* I'm not here on a rest-cure, or, to waste my time; ~ *son pardessus,* to slip on, to get into, one's overcoat; **2.** to pierce through, to run through (with a weapon); ~ *un homme,* to run a man through; **3.** (fig.) to engage in; ~ *un chemin,* to take a road; ~ *un discours*; to embark upon a speech; **4.** (mil.) to enfilade; **5.** (slang) **s'~** *un verre,* to toss off a drink.

enfin (ɑ̃fɛ̃), adv. [*en*+*fin*] **1.** At last; finally, at length; lastly, after all; *vous voilà ~ arrivé!,* there you are at last!; *il arriva ~ à une auberge,* he came at length to an inn; ~, *ce n'est pas si mal que ça,* it's not so bad after all; **2.** in short, in a word; *il était immense, large d'épaules, musclé, ~ un vrai colosse,* he was enormous, broad-shouldered, muscular, in short, a veritable giant; syn. (À LA) FIN, FINALEMENT.

enflammé, -e (ɑ̃flame), p. adj. **1.** On fire, in flames; **2.** (med.) inflamed; **3.** (fig.) kindled, excited, inflamed.

enflammer (ɑ̃flame), v.a. [f. *flamme*] To kindle, to set on fire, to set fire to; (fig.) to inflame, to incense; **s'~,** v.pr. to take fire, to be kindled, to blaze, to become inflamed; (fig.) to be incensed; to fall in love.

enflé, -e (ɑ̃fle), p. adj. Swelled, bloated; (fig.) inflated, puffed up; (of style) bombastic, high-flown; syn. GONFLÉ, BOUFFI, BOURSOUFLÉ.

enflécher (ɑ̃fleʃe), v.a. (naut.) To put ratlines to.

enfléchure (ɑ̃fleʃyr), s.f. [f. *flèche*] (naut.) Ratlines.

enfler (ɑ̃fle), v.a. [L *inflare*] To swell out, to swell up, to distend; *le vent enfla les voiles,* the wind swelled the sails; (fig.) to elate, to excite, to inflate, to exaggerate; **s'~,** v.pr. to swell, to become turgid; (fig.) *s'~ d'orgueil,* to be puffed up with pride.

enflure (ɑ̃flyr), s.f. Swelling; (fig.) turgidity, bombast (in style, &c.).

enfoncé, -e (ɑ̃fɔ̃se), p. adj. **1.** Deep, sunken, deep-set; *avoir les yeux ~s dans la tête,* to have deep-set eyes; (of patients) to have sunken eyes; **2.** driven in, sunk in; broken open; beaten, vanquished, done for.

enfoncement (ɑ̃fɔ̃smɑ̃), s.m. **1.** Driving-in, breaking-in, breaking through; **2.** sinking; **3.** hollow, cavity.

enfoncer (ɑ̃fɔ̃se), v.a. [f. *fond*] To thrust, to push in or down, to drive in; (fam.) *enfoncez-vous cela dans la tête,*

get that into your head; to break in, to burst in; ~ *une porte*, to break open a door; ~ *une porte ouverte*, to overcome imaginary difficulties; to upset, (fam.) to dish, to do; *il m'a enfoncé*, he has done me; ~, v.n. to sink, to founder; **s'~**, v.pr. to sink; (fig.) to bury oneself; (fig. and fam.) to make a mess of things.
enfonceur (ɑ̃fɔ̃sœr), s.m. (iron.) used only in the expression: ~ *de portes ouvertes*, braggart, one who takes a deal of trouble to solve a difficulty which does not exist.
enfonçure (ɑ̃fɔ̃syr), s.f. **1.** Hollow, cavity; **2.** bottom (of barrel, &c.).
enforcir (ɑ̃fɔrsir), v.a. (rare) [f. *force*] To strengthen, to reinforce.
enformer (ɑ̃fɔrme), v.a. [*en*+*former*] To block (hats).
enfouir (ɑ̃fwir), v.a. [L *infodere*] **1.** To thrust into the earth, to bury in the ground; **2.** (fig.) to bury (of secrets, &c.), to hide away; ~ *son talent*, to hide one's talent in the earth.
enfouissement (ɑ̃fwismɑ̃), s.m. Burying, hiding in the ground.
enfouisseur (ɑ̃fwisœr), s.m. Burier.
enfourchement (ɑ̃furʃəmɑ̃), s.m. (arch.) Crossing, point (of an arch).
enfourcher (ɑ̃furʃe), v.a. [f. *fourche*] **1.** To bestride, to bestraddle; (fig.) ~ *son dada*, to mount one's hobby-horse; **2.** to pierce with a pitchfork.
enfourchure (ɑ̃furʃyr), s.f. Fork (of a tree, of trousers, &c.).
enfournage, enfournement (ɑ̃furnaʒ, ɑ̃furnmɑ̃), s.m. **enfournée** (ɑ̃furne), s.f. Stacking in ovens or kilns; baking, firing.
enfourner (ɑ̃furne), v.a. [f. *en*+*four*] **1.** To put in the oven or kiln; to fire, to bake; **2.** (fig.) to get going; *affaire mal enfournée*, badly launched business.
enfourneur (ɑ̃furnœr), s.m. Oven-hand, kiln-hand.
enfreindre (ɑ̃frɛ̃dr), v.a. [L *infringere*] To infringe.
(s')enfuir (sɑ̃fɥir), v.pr. [f. *fuir*] To flee, to run away; (fig.) to race by, to pass, to fly (of time, &c.); to disappear; syn. S'ÉVADER, S'ÉCHAPPER.
enfumage (ɑ̃fymaʒ), s.m. Fumigating; smoking out, smoking.
enfumer (ɑ̃fyme), v.a. [*en*+*fumer*] To fill with smoke; to fumigate, to smoke (bees), to smoke out (badgers, &c.); to blacken with smoke; (fig.) to cloud.
enfumoir (ɑ̃fymwar), s.m. Fumigator (for bees).
enfûtage (ɑ̃fytaʒ), s.m. Casking.
enfutailler (ɑ̃fytaje), v.a. [f. *futaille*] To cask, to barrel.
engagé (ɑ̃gaʒe), s.m. Volunteer, voluntarily enlisted soldier.
engageable (ɑ̃gaʒabl), adj. Disposable, available.
engageant, -e (ɑ̃gaʒɑ̃), p. adj. Engaging, winning, taking; *des manières ~es*, pleasing manners; winning ways.
engagement (ɑ̃gaʒmɑ̃), s.m. **1.** Promise, obligation; bond, pledge, pledging; ~ *formel*, formal agreement; **2.** business engagement, assignation; (pl.) liabilities; **3.** (mil.) enlisting; **4.** (mil.) action, engagement; **5.** pawning.
engager (ɑ̃gaʒe), v.a.n. [f. *gage*] **1.** To pledge, to plight, to promise, to bind; ~ *son bien*, to pledge one's possessions; ~ *sa parole*, to pledge one's word; (poet.) to plight one's troth; *un serment nous engage*, we are bound by an oath; **2.** to pawn; **3.** to engage, to hire; (mil.) to enlist; ~ *un domestique*, to engage a servant; **4.** to invite pressingly, to induce, to urge; ~ *X à travailler*, to induce X to work; ~ *X à venir dîner*, to press X to come to dinner; **5.** to involve, to entangle; ~ *X dans une mauvaise affaire*, to involve X in a bad business; **6.** to place in, to insert, to introduce into; (naut.) to run; ~ *une clef dans la serrure*, to introduce a key into the lock; **7.** (mil.) to engage; **8.** to enter (names for races, &c.); **s'~**, v.pr. **1.** (mil.) to enlist; **2.** *s'~ dans*, to enter, to take, to begin to follow; *s'~ dans un bois*, to enter a wood.
engagiste (ɑ̃gaʒist), s.m. (obs.) **1.** Tenant (of Crown lands); **2.** contractor engaging hands.
engainant, -e (ɑ̃gɛnɑ̃), p. adj. (bot.) Sheathing.
engainer (ɑ̃gɛne), v.a. [f. *gaine*] To sheathe; to envelop, to encase.
engazonner (ɑ̃gazɔne), v.a. [f. *gazon*] **1.** To turf; **2.** to sow with grass.
engeance (ɑ̃ʒɑ̃s), s.f. [OF *enger*] Breed; (fig. of persons, pej.) race, kidney, spawn; *quelle ~!*, what a lot!, hopeless people!
engeigner (ɑ̃ʒɛɲe), v.a. [f. *engin*] To take in, to cheat, to impose on, to deceive, *tel qui cuyde ~ autrui bien souvent s'engeigne soi-même*, the biter is bit.
engelure (ɑ̃ʒlyr), s.f. [f. *geler*] Chilblain.
engendrement (ɑ̃ʒɑ̃drəmɑ̃), s.m. Engendering; production.
engendrer (ɑ̃ʒɑ̃dre), v.a. [L *ingenerare*] To engender, to beget; (fig.) to occasion, to give rise to, to beget; *la familiarité engendre le mépris*, familiarity breeds contempt.
engerbage (ɑ̃ʒɛrbaʒ), s.m. Sheaving.
engerber (ɑ̃ʒɛrbe), v.a. [f. *gerbe*] To sheaf, to bind; to heap up; ~ *des tonneaux*, to stow casks.
engin (ɑ̃ʒɛ̃), s.m. [L *ingenium*] **1.** Engine; snare, net; instrument; *les ~s de la guerre*, the engines of war; **2.** (fig. obs.) skill, address.
englober (ɑ̃glɔbe), v.a. [f. *globe*] To

unite in a whole, to comprise, to comprehend; (colloq.) to lump together.

engloutir (ãglutir), v.a. [LL *ingluttire*] **1.** To swallow up, to absorb, to devour, to engulf; **2.** to dissipate, to squander (a fortune, &c.); **s'~**, v.pr. to be swallowed up, engulfed, or absorbed.

engloutissement (ãglutismã), s.m. Engulfing, swallowing-up.

engloutisseu-r, -se (ãglutisœr), s.m.f. Devourer. **~**, adj. Devouring.

engluement, engluage (ãglymã, ãglɥaʒ), s.m. Gluing; liming.

engluer (ãglɥe), v.a. [f. *glu*] To lime, to daub with bird-lime; to snare; (fig.) to snare, to take in; **s'~**, v.pr. to be caught, to be limed; (fig.) to be taken in.

engobage (ãgɔbaʒ), s.m. Glazing (of pottery).

engobe (ãgɔb), s.m. Glaze.

engober (ãgɔbe), v.a. [*en*+*gober*] To glaze (pottery).

engommer (ãgɔme), v.a. [f. *gomme*] To gum.

engoncement (ãgɔ̃smã), s.m. Short-necked, cramped, or awkward appearance.

engoncer (ãgɔ̃se), v.a. [etym. dub.] (of clothes) To cramp, to give a huddled appearance to.

engorgement (ãgɔrʒəmã), s.m. **1.** Obstruction, choking-up; **2.** (med.) congestion.

engorger (ãgɔrʒe), v.a. [f. *gorge*] To choke up (a pipe, &c.), to obstruct.

engouement, engoûment (ãgumã), s.m. (med.) Choking, obstruction, congestion; (fig.) infatuation, craze.

engouer (ãgwe), v.a. [etym. dub.] (med.) To obstruct (the throat of); (fig.) to infatuate; **s'~**, v.pr. to half-choke oneself; (fig.) to be infatuated; *s'~ d'une femme*, to go crazy over a woman.

engouffrement (ãgufrəmã), s.m. Engulfing.

engouffrer (ãgufre), v.a. [f. *en*+*gouffre*] To engulf, to swallow up; (fig.) to engulf, to devour; **s'~**, v.pr. to be engulfed; to rush; *le vent s'engouffra dans la cheminée*, the wind rushed up (or down) the chimney.

engouler (ãgule), v.a. [f. *en*+*gueule*] (pop.) To bolt, to gulp down.

engoulevent (ãgulvã), s.m. [f. *engouler*+*vent*] (ornith.) Nightjar, goatsucker, fern-owl.

engoûment (ãgumã), s.m. See ENGOUEMENT.

engourdir (ãgurdir), v.a. [f. *gourd*] To numb, to benumb; to make torpid; to dull, to deaden, to blunt; *l'oisiveté engourdit l'esprit*, idleness dulls the mind; **s'~**, v.pr. to grow numb; to become torpid, dull, sleepy.

engourdissement (ãgurdismã), s.m. Numbness; torpor; *tirer X de son ~*, to rouse X from his torpor.

engrais (ãgrɛ), s.m. [f. *engraisser*] **1.** Manure; **2.** rich pasture.

engraissement, engraissage (ãgrɛsmã, ãgrɛsaʒ), s.m. Fattening.

engraisser (ãgrɛse), v.a. [L *incrassare*] **1.** To fatten, to cram (poultry, &c.); **2.** to manure; (fig.) to enrich; **~**, v.n. to grow fat; to thrive; **s'~**, v.pr. to grow fat, to put on weight or flesh, to become corpulent; (fig.) to thrive.

engraisseur (ãgrɛsœr), s.m. Fattener.

engrangement (ãgrãʒmã), s.m. Carrying, getting-in, housing (corn, &c.).

engranger (ãgrãʒe), v.a. [f. *en*+*grange*] To cart, to get in, to house (corn, &c.).

engravement (ãgravmã), s.m. (naut.) Stranding.

engraver (ãgrave), v.a. [f. *gravier*] (naut.) To strand.

engrêlé, -e (ãgrɛle), adj. (herald.) Engrailed.

engrêlure (ãgrɛlyr), s.f. **1.** Purl (of lace); **2.** (herald.) engrailing.

engrenage (ãgrənaʒ), s.m. **1.** Works (of a watch, &c.); gear, wheel-work; *~ conique*, bevel gear; *~ droit*, spur gear; *~ de distribution*, distributing gear, timing gear; **2.** (fig.) correlation (of circumstances); *être pris dans l'~*, to be caught in the toils.

engrener[1] (ãgrəne), v.a. [f. L *crena*] To engage (cogs); to throw into gear; (fig.) to get (a thing) going; **s'~**, v.pr. to engage (of wheels).

engrener[2] (ãgrəne), v.a. [f. *grain*] **1.** To put corn into (the mill-hopper); **2.** to fatten with corn.

engrenure (ãgrənyr), s.f. Engagement of teeth, cogs, &c.; cogging, toothing.

engrosser (ãgrɔse), v.a. [f. *grosse*] (colloq.) To make pregnant. ⚠ Not 'to engross', which = *absorber, retenir l'attention de; grossoyer*; *accaparer* (*blé, marchandises, &c.*).

(s')engrumeler (sãgrymle), v.pr. [f. *grumeau*] To clot, to coagulate.

engueulement (ãgœlmã), s.m. **engueulade** (ãgœlad), s.f. [f. *gueule*] (pop.) Abuse, jawing, rating, dressing-down, billingsgate.

engueuler (ãgœle), v.a. (pop.) To jaw at, to abuse, to blackguard, to give hell to; **s'~**, v.pr. to abuse each other, to quarrel violently.

enguignonné, -e (ãgiɲɔne), adj. [f. *guignon*] Having a run of ill luck.

enguirlander (ãgirlãde), v.a. [f. *guirlande*] To adorn with wreaths; (fig. iron.) to abuse, to revile, to blackguard, to dress down, to wipe the floor with.

enhardir (ãardir), v.a. [f. *hardi*] To embolden; **s'~** v.pr. to grow bold; to make bold (to).

enharmonique (ãnarmɔnik), adj. [Gr. *enarmonikos*] (mus.) Enharmonic.

enharnachement (ãarnaʃmã), s.m. (rare) Harnessing.

enharnacher (ãarnaʃe), v.a. [f. *harnais*] **1.** To harness; **2.** (fig.) to deck out, to rig out.

enherber (ãnɛrbe), v.a. [f. *herbe*] To turn (land) into pasture.

énigmatique (enigmatik), adj. Enigmatical, enigmatic.

énigmatiquement (enigmatikmã), adv. Enigmatically.

énigme (enigm), s.f. [Gr. *ainigma*] Enigma, riddle; (fig.) *trouver le mot de l'~*, to find the key to the mystery.

enivrant, -e (ãnivrã), p. adj. Intoxicating, inebriating; (fig.) intoxicating, maddening, enrapturing.

enivrement (ãnivrəmã), s.m. Drunkenness, intoxication; (fig.) rapture.

enivrer (ãnivre), v.a. [f. *ivre*] To intoxicate, to make drunk; (fig.) to enrapture, to elate; **s'~** v.pr. to get drunk, to become intoxicated; enraptured (*de*, with).

enjambée (ãʒãbe), s.f. Stride; *faire de grandes ~s*, to take long strides.

enjambement (ãʒãbmã), s.m. (pros.) Absence of end-stopping (of a line).

enjamber (ãʒãbe), v.a. [f. *jambe*] To stride over; to skip over; ~, v.n. **1.** to stride along; (fig.) to encroach upon; **2.** (pros.) to run on (of a line).

enjaveler (ãʒavle), v.a. [f. *javelle*] To sheaf.

enjeu (pl. **-x**) (ãʒø), s.m. [*en*+*jeu*] Stake; (fig.) *retirer son ~*, to back out.

enjoindre (ãʒwɛ̃dr), v.a. [L *injungere*] To enjoin, to order, to prescribe.

enjôlement (ãʒolmã), s.m. Coaxing, inveigling, cajolement.

enjôler (ãʒole), v.a. [f. *geôle*] To coax, to inveigle, to cajole.

enjôleu-r, -se (ãʒolœr), s.m.f. Coaxer, inveigler; cajoler. ~, adj. Coaxing, inveigling, wheedling.

enjolivement (ãʒɔlivmã), s.m. Embellishment, ornamentation.

enjoliver (ãʒɔlive), v.a. [f. *joli*] To embellish, to ornament, to adorn.

enjoliveur (ãʒɔlivœr), s.m. Adorner, embellisher.

enjolivure (ãʒɔlivyr), s.f. Trifling, minor adornment.

enjoué, -e (ãʒue), adj. [f. *jeu*] Playful, sprightly, jovial, sportive, bright, cheerful.

enjouement (ãʒumã), s.m. Playfulness, sprightliness, humour; *avec ~*, playfully.

enjuguer (ãʒyge), v.a. [f. *en*+*joug*] To yoke.

enjuponner (ãʒypɔne), v.a. [f. *en*+*jupon*] To put into petticoats.

enkysté, -e (ãkiste), adj. [f. *kyste*] (med.) Encysted.

(s')enkyster (sãkiste), v.pr. To become encysted.

enlacement (ãlasmã), s.m. **1.** Interlacing, entwining; lacing; **2.** embrace.

enlacer (ãlase), v.a. [*en*+*lacer*] **1.** To entwine, to interlace; to lace; **2.** to embrace.

enlaidir (ãlɛdir), v.a. [f. *laid*] To make ugly, to disfigure; ~, v.n. to grow ugly, to be disfigured; **s'~** v.pr. to make oneself ugly.

enlaidissement (ãlɛdismã), s.m. Disfigurement, growing ugly, ugliness.

enlevé, -e (ãlve), p. adj. Dashing, done with gusto, spirited; *portrait ~*, dashing portrait.

enlèvement (ãlɛvmã), s.m. **1.** Removal; **2.** rape, kidnapping, abduction; *l'~ des Sabines*, the rape of the Sabines; elopement (when the girl consents).

enlever (ãlve), v.a. [*en*+*lever*] To clear away; to remove, to rub out, to wipe out, off, or up; *~ le couvert*, to clear the table, to clear away; *~ des taches*, to take out stains; to lift, to raise, to pull up; to carry off; to kidnap; *les journaux ont été enlevés comme du pain*, the papers sold like hot cakes; *se faire ~ par*, to elope with; *la mort l'a enlevé*, death has carried him off; *~ le prix*, to carry off the prize; (fig.) *~ l'auditoire*, to carry away the audience; *enlevez-le*, or *sortez-le!*, chuck him out, down with him!; to take by surprise; *~ un poste*, to take an outpost unawares; to accomplish or do in a dashing way, to dash off; **s'~**, v.pr. to come off; to come out (of stains, &c.); to sell (of goods); to rise.

enleveur (ãlvœr), s.m. (rare) Kidnapper, ravisher.

enlevure (ãlvyr), s.f. **1.** Blister, vesicle; **2.** (sculpt.) relief. See ÉLEVURE.

enliasser (ãljase), v.a. [f. *en*+*liasse*] To tie up in bundles.

enlier (ãlje), v.a. [*en*+*lier*] (build.) To bind (stones).

enlignement (ãliɲmã), s.m. Alinement, alignment.

enligner (ãliɲe), v.a. [f. *en*+*ligne*] To aline, to align.

enlisement (ãlizmã), s.m. Swallowing up; miring; sinking (in quicksands, or (fig.) in vice, poverty, &c.).

enliser (ãlize), v.a. [f. *en*+*lise*] To sink in the mire; **s'~**, v.pr. to sink in quicksands or in mire; to be swallowed up; (fig.) to sink into degradation, poverty, &c.; to flounder, to be submerged; (fig. of coaches) to get mired, or bemired.

enluminer (ãlymine), v.a. [f. L *lumen*] **1.** To illuminate; **2.** (fig.) to flush; *visage enluminé*, flushed face.

enlumineu-r, -se (ãlyminœr), s.m.f. Illuminator.

enluminure (ãlyminyr), s.f. **1.** Illumination; **2.** (fig.) high colour, luminosity; **3.** tinsel (of style).

ennéacorde (ɛnneakɔrd), s.m. [Gr. *ennea* +*chordē*] Nine-stringed cither.

ennéade (ɛnnead), s.f. [f. Gr. *enneas*] Ennead.

ennéagonal, -e, (aux) (ɛnneagɔnal), adj. Enneagonal.

ennéagone (ɛnneagɔn), adj. [Gr. *ennea*+ *gōnia*] Enneagonal. ~, s.m. Enneagon.

ennemi, -e (ɛnmi), s.m.f. [L *inimicus*] Enemy, foe; *c'est autant de pris sur l'*~, that's so much to the good; *le mieux est l'*~ *du bien*, let well alone; *il n'y pas de petit* ~, don't despise the enemy; *tué à l'*~, killed in action. ~, -e, adj. *l'armée*~*e*, the enemy army; syn. ADVERSAIRE, ANTAGONISTE.

ennoblir (ãnɔblir), v.a. [f. *noble*] To ennoble; to dignify, to exalt; cf. ANOBLIR.

ennoblissement (ãnɔblismã), s.m. Ennobling, ennoblement; exaltation; cf. ANOBLISSEMENT.

ennui (ãnɥi), s.m. [f. *ennuyer*] Ennui, tedium, tediousness; spleen; boredom, wearisomeness; (fam.) *quel* ~ *!*, what a bore!; nuisance, vexation; pl. sorrows, trouble.

ennuyer (ãnɥije), v.a. [f. L *in*+*odium*] To bore, to weary; *tout l'ennuie*, he wearies of everything; to vex, to worry, to bother; *cela m'ennuie de le voir si pâle*, it worries me to see him so pale; to annoy. ⚠ The sense of English 'annoy' is usually stronger than that of *ennuyer*; **s'**~, v.pr. to be bored, to feel dull, to suffer from tedium, to weary (*de*, of); to mope; *je m'ennuie à la mort* or *je m'ennuie à mourir*, I'm bored to death; (colloq.) *je m'ennuie de vous*, I long to see you.

ennuyeusement (ãnɥijøzmã), adv. Tediously, irksomely, boringly.

ennuyeu-x, -se (ãnɥijø), adj. Boring, tedious, tiresome; dull; ~ *comme la pluie*, as dull as ditch-water; worrying, vexing, annoying. ~, s.m.f. Tiresome person, bore.

énoncé (enɔ̃se), s.m. **1.** Announcement, statement; **2.** terms, data, statement (of a problem, &c.).

énoncer (enɔ̃se), v.a. [L *enuntiare*] To state, to express, to word; to enunciate.

énonciati-f, -ve (enɔ̃sjatif), adj. Enunciative.

énonciation (enɔ̃sja'sjɔ̃), s.f. Enunciation, delivery, statement, utterance; expression, wording.

enorgueillir (ãnɔrgœjir), v.a. [f. *orgueil*] To elate, to puff up; **s'**~ v.pr. to grow proud, to become elated or puffed up; *s'*~ *de*, to pride oneself upon.

énorme (enɔrm), adj. [L *enormis*] Enormous, huge, tremendous.

énormément (enɔrmemã), adv. Enormously, tremendously.

énormité (enɔrmite), s.f. Enormousness, hugeness, vastness; (fig.) enormity, heinousness; howler, glaring blunder; *dire des* ~*s*, to say the most impossible things.

énouer (enue), v.a. [f. *nœud*] To unknot, to burl.

(s')enquérir (sãkerir), v.pr. [L *inquirere*] To inquire, to make inquiries, to ask (*de*, about); syn. S'INFORMER.

enquête (ãkɛt), s.f. **1.** Inquiry, investigation; **2.** (law) inquest.

enquêter (ãkɛte), v.n. To inquire, to conduct an inquiry.

enquêteu-r, -se (ãkɛtœr), s.m.f. Inquirer, official who conducts an inquiry; (neol.) literary reporter.

enquinauder (ãkinode), v.a. [f. *quinaud*] To intimidate, to nonplus.

enquiquiner (ãkikine), v.a. (colloq.) To vex, to worry, to plague.

enracinement (ãrasinmã), s.m. Rooting, taking root.

enraciner (ãrasine), v.a. [f. *racine*] To root; (fig.) to implant; **s'**~, v.pr. to take root, to become rooted; (fig.) to settle, to become established.

enragé, -e (ãraʒe), p. adj. **1.** Affected with rabies, rabid, mad; *manger de la vache*~*e*, to know hard times, to rough it; **2.** enraged, desperate, mad, crazy; *joueur* ~, card fiend, gambling fiend; *avoir une faim* ~*e*, to be crazy with hunger.

enrageant, -e (ãraʒã), p. adj. (fig.) Maddening.

enrager (ãraʒe), v.n. [f. *en*+*rage*] To be enraged, to fume; *faire* ~ *X*, to drive X wild, to madden X, to enrage X; (colloq.) to get a rise out of X.

enrayage (ãrɛjaʒ), s.m. (coach-build.) Spoking.

enrayement, enraiement (ãrɛmã), s.m. **1.** Spoking; **2.** locking, putting on the drag.

enrayer (ãrɛje), v.a. [f. *raie*] **1.** To spoke (a wheel); **2.** to put a drag or lock-chain on (a wheel); **3.** (fig.) to check, to keep down (an illness); **4.** (agric.) to plough the first furrow in.

enrayure (ãrɛjyr), s.f. **1.** Drag, lock-chain; **2.** (collect.) spokes; **3.** first furrow.

enrégimenter (ãreʒimãte), v.a. [f. *régiment*] To enregiment, to form into regiments; (fig.) to collect, to enlist the services of, to beat up (recruits); ~ *les mécontents*, to enlist the services of the malcontents.

enregistrable (ãrəʒistrabl), adj. Registrable.

enregistrement (ãrəʒistrəmã), s.m.

Registration, recording, entry; enrolment; *faire l'~*, to register; *Bureau de l'Enregistrement*, Registry Office, Registrar's Office.

enregistrer (ãrəʒistre), v.a. [f. *en+registre*] To register, to enter, to record.

enregistreu-r, -se (ãrəʒistrœr), s.m.f. **1.** Registrar; **2.** recording-machine. ~, adj. Self-registering, recording.

enrêner (ãrɛne), v.a. [*en+rêner*] To rein in; to bear up (with bearing-rein).

enrhumer (ãryme), v.a. [f. *rhume*] To give a cold to; *être enrhumé du cerveau*, to have a cold in the head; *être fortement enrhumé*, to have a bad cold; **s'~**, v.pr. to catch cold, to get a cold.

enrichi, -e (ãriʃi), adj. Newly enriched. s.m.f. Parvenu, nouveau-riche.

enrichir (ãriʃir), v.a. **1.** To enrich, to make rich; **2.** (fig.) to develop, to enrich, to enlarge, to embellish, to improve; ~ *son esprit*, to enrich one's mind; **s'~**, v.pr. to grow rich, to thrive.

enrichissement (ãriʃismã), s.m. Enrichment, embellishment.

enrober (ãrɔbe), v.a. [f. *en+robe*] To envelop, to wrap up.

enrochement (ãrɔʃmã), s.m. **1.** Submerged foundations; **2.** conglomeration.

enrocher (ãrɔʃe), v.a. [f. *en+roche*] To lay submerged foundations for.

enrôlé, -e (ãrole), s.m.f. Enrolled member, volunteer, person, &c.

enrôlement (ãrolmã), s.m. **1.** Enrolment; enlistment; **2.** certificate of enrolment.

enrôler (ãrole), v.a. [f. *en+rôle*] **1.** To enrol, to draft; to beat up (recruits); **s'~**, v.pr. to enlist.

enroué, -e (ãrue), adj. Hoarse, husky.

enrouement (ãrumã), s.m. Hoarseness, huskiness.

enrouer (ãrue), v.a. [L *in+raucus*] To make hoarse; **s'~**, v.pr. to grow or become hoarse or husky.

enrouiller (ãruje), v.a. [f. *rouille*] To rust, to make rusty.

enroulement, enroulage (ãrulmã, ãrulaʒ), s.m. **1.** Rolling-up; **2.** (arch.) scroll, volute.

enrouler (ãrule), v.a. [*en+rouler*] To roll, to roll up, to coil; **s'~**, v.pr. **1.** to roll up, to roll oneself up; **2.** to twine, to twist round (of plants).

enrubanner (ãrybane), v.a. [f. *ruban*] To beribbon.

enrue (ãry), s.f. Wide furrow.

ensablement (ãsɑblmã), s.m. **1.** Silting-up; **2.** sand-bank, sand-bar.

ensabler (ãsɑble), v.a. [f. *en+sable*] **1.** To block with sand; to sand over, to cover with sand; **2.** to strand, to gravel; **s'~**, v.pr. to run aground, to sink in sand; to silt up.

ensacher (ãsaʃe), v.a. [f. *en+sac*] To put into bags or sacks.

ensanglanter (ãsãglãte), v.a. [f. *sanglant*] To make bloody, to stain with blood; ~ *sa victoire*, to mar the victory with massacre.

enseignable (ãsɛɲabl), adj. Teachable.

enseignant, -e (ãsɛɲã), adj. Teaching; *corps ~*, teaching profession, professorial world.

enseigne (ãsɛɲ), s.f. [L (pl.) *insignia*] **1.** Standard, ensign, flag; **2.** (naut.) ensign, pennant; **3.** sign, sign-board; *à bon vin point d'~*, good wine needs no bush; *être logé à la même ~*, to be in the same boat; **4.** token, proof; *à telle ~ que*, or *à telles ~s que*, so much so that, the more by token that; *la sincérité est l'~ de l'honnêteté*, sincerity is the hall-mark of truth. ~, s.m. **1.** Ensign (officer), standard-bearer; **2.** (nav.) sub-lieutenant.

enseignement (ãsɛɲmã), s.m. **1.** Instruction, teaching, education; ~ *public*, state education; **2.** lesson, precept; *donner de bons ~s*, to give sound precepts; **3.** teaching professsion; *il est dans l'~*, he belongs to the teaching profession; *entrer dans l'~*, to go in for teaching.

enseigner (ãsɛɲe), v.a.n. [pop. L *insignare*] To teach; to instruct in, to inform of; *enseignez-nous le chemin*, show us the way; syn. INSTRUIRE.

ensellé, -e (ãsɛle), adj. Saddle-backed.

ensemble (ãsãbl), adv. [L *in+simul*] Together, at the same time; *être très bien ~*, to be very good friends. ~, s.m. **1.** Whole, mass, general effect; *le tout ~*, the general effect; the whole; *mouvement d'~*, concerted movement; **2.** unity, harmony; *manquer d'~*, to lack unity; **3.** (dressm.) two-piece suit, gown and coat; **4.** (house decoration) set of furniture, hangings, carpet, &c.

ensemencement (ãsmãsmã), s.m. Sowing.

ensemencer (ãsmãse), v.a. [f. *semence*] To sow with seed.

enserrer[1] (ãsɛre), v.a. [*en+serrer*] **1.** To enclose, to contain; **2.** to hem in, to hold tightly, to crush, to squeeze; ~ *comme dans un étau*, to grip as in a vice.

enserrer[2] (ãsɛre), v.a. [f. *en+serre*] To hothouse, to put in a greenhouse.

ensevelir (ãsəvlir), v.a. [*en+L sepelire*] **1.** To shroud; to lay out (a corpse); **2.** (fig. by ext.) to bury; ~ *les morts*, to bury the dead; **3.** to bury, to engulf; **s'~**, v.pr. to bury oneself.

ensevelissement (ãsəvlismã), s.m. Enshrouding, laying-out, burial.

ensevelisseu-r, -se (ãsəvlisœr), s.m.f. Layer-out.

ensiforme (ãsifɔrm), adj. [L *ensis* + Fr. *forme*] Ensiform.

ensilage, ensilotage (ãsilaʒ, ãsilɔtaʒ), s.m. Ensilage.

ensiler, ensiloter (ãsile, ãsilote), v.a. [f. *en+silo*] To ensilage, to ensilate.

ensoleillé, -e (ãsolɛje), adj. Sunny.

ensoleiller (ãsolɛje), v.a. [f. *en+soleil*] To light up; (fig.) to cast a ray of sunshine on.

ensommeillé, -e (ãsomɛje), adj. [f. *en+sommeil*] Heavy with sleep, drowsy; (fig.) torpid.

ensorcelant, -e (ãsorsəlã), p. adj. Bewitching, enchanting.

ensorceler (ãsorsəle), v.a. [f. *sorcier*] To bewitch.

ensorceleu-r, -se (ãsorsəlœr), p. adj. Bewitching. **~**, s.m.f. Enchanter, (fem.) enchantress.

ensorcellement (ãsorsɛlmã), s.m. Spell, enchantment, bewitchment.

ensoufrer (ãsufre), v.a. [f. *soufre*] To sulphur.

ensouple (ãsupl), s.f. [L *insubulum*] (weaving) Cylinder.

ensoutaner (ãsutane), v.a. [f. *en+soutane*] To send into the Church.

ensuifer (ãsɥife), v.a. [f. *en+suif*] To rub with tallow, to tallow.

ensuite (ãsɥit), adv. [*en+suite*] **1.** Then, in the next place; after, afterwards; *~ de quoi*, in consequence of which; *vous irez là ~*, you will go there afterwards; **2.** (int.) well?, what then?, what next?, what of that?; *~ de*, prep. loc. after.

ensuivant, -e (ãsɥivã), p. adj. (archaic) Following, ensuing.

(s')ensuivre (sãsɥivr), v.pr. [*en+suivre*] To follow, to result, to ensue; *cela ne s'ensuit pas nécessairement*, it does not necessarily follow.

entablement (ãtabləmã), s.m. [f. *table*] (arch.) Entablature.

entacher (ãtaʃe), v.a. [*en+tacher*] To tarnish, to blot, to soil, to taint (*de*, with); (law) *acte entaché de nullité*, voidable act.

entaillage (ãtajaʒ), s.m. Notching, slashing.

entaille (ãtaj), s.f. Notch, slash, gash; *se faire une ~ à la main*, to gash one's hand; *se faire une ~*, to get a gash.

entailler (ãtaje), v.a. [*en+tailler*] To notch, to gash.

entaillure (ãtajyr), s.f. Notch.

entame, entamure (ãtam, ãtamyr), s.f. First slice, outside (of loaf or joint); cut.

entamer (ãtame), v.a. [pop. L *intaminare*] To make an incision in; to begin, to cut (a new loaf, &c.), to broach (a cask); *~ la peau*, to break the skin; (fig.) to broach; to encroach upon; to impair, to injure; *~ une conversation*, to open a conversation; *~ un sujet délicat*, to broach a delicate matter; *~ la réputation de quelqu'un*, to damage, to injure a person's reputation.

entamure (ãtamyr), s.f. See ENTAME.

entassement (ãtasmã), s.m. Accumulation; heap, pile.

entasser (ãtase), v.a. [*en+tasser*] To heap or pile up; to amass; to heap or crowd together; to hoard up; *~ des écus*, to hoard up money.

entasseur (ãtasœr), s.m. Hoarder.

ente (ãt), s.f. [Gr. *emphuton*] Graft; branch bearing a graft.

entéléchie (ãteleʃi), s.f. [Gr. *entelecheia*] Entelechy.

entendement (ãtãdmã), s.m. Understanding; judgement, sense.

entendeur (ãtãdœr), s.m. One who understands; (prov.) *à bon ~ salut*, a word to the wise is enough; forewarned, forearmed.

entendre (ãtãdr), v.a.n. [L *intendere*] **1.** To hear; *~ dur*, to be hard of hearing; *à vous ~*, according to you; *~ la messe*, to hear mass; *~ les témoins*, to hear the witnesses; *j'ai entendu dire*, I heard that; I have heard tell; I have heard it said; (prov.) *il n'est pire sourd que celui qui ne veut pas ~*, there's none so deaf as he that will not hear; *~ une prière*, to hear a prayer; (fig.) *il n'entend pas de cette oreille-là*, he won't hear of that, or, you won't get him to do that; to listen to; *il n'a rien voulu ~*, he wouldn't hear of it, or, he would take no advice; *~ raison*, to listen to reason; *ne savoir auquel ~*, not to know whom to believe; (fig.) not to know where to turn; **2.** to understand; *~ à demi-mot*, to take a hint; (fam.) to be quick in the up-take; *faire l'entendu*, to look knowing; *il m'a donné à ~*, he gave me to understand, or, he hinted; *entendons-nous bien*, let us be quite clear on the subject; *qu'entendez-vous par là?*, what do you mean by that?; *donner à ~*, or *laisser ~ (que)*, to hint that, to let it be understood (that); *je vous ai mal entendu*, I misunderstood you; *~ le commerce*, to be a good business man; (prov.) *chacun fait comme il l'entend*, each man according to his lights; *~ la plaisanterie*, to be able to see a joke; to have a sense of humour; *~ raillerie*, to stand chaff, to take a joke well; *ne pas ~ malice*, to mean no harm; to see no harm; *bien entendu*, of course, naturally; *c'est entendu!*, that 's settled, that 's a bargain; *entendu!*, agreed!; *la cause est entendue*, the case is clear; enough said; **s'~**, v.pr. **1.** to hear each other's voices; to hear oneself; to be audible; **2.** to understand, to be proficient (*à*, in); to be understood; *cela s'entend*, that is obvious; *il s'entend à la critique*, he is a good critic; *il s'entend en musique*, he is well up in music; *ils s'entendent comme larrons en foire*, they are as thick as thieves; *il s'y entend comme à ramer des* *choux*, he can no more do it than fly; *je m'entends*, I know what I mean; *s'~ avec l'ennemi*, to be in secret intelligence with the enemy; *s'~ bien ensemble*, to get on well together.

enténébrer (ãtenebre), v.a. [f. *en+ténèbres*] To envelop in darkness.

entente (ãtãt), s.f. [LL *intenta*] **1.** Meaning; *mots à double ~*, equivocal phrases; *mot à double ~*, word with a double meaning, double-entendre; **2.** understanding; skill, judgement; *l'~ des affaires*, business ability; **3.** friendly understanding; *~ cordiale*, entente cordiale; *il n'y a guère d'~ dans cette famille*, there is no mutual understanding in this family.

enter (ãte), v.a. [f. *ente*] To graft (upon).

entéralgie (ãteralʒi), s.f. [Gr. *enteron+algos*] (med.) Enteralgia.

entérinement (ãterinmã), s.m. Ratification, confirmation.

entériner (ãterine), v.a. [f. *entier*] To ratify, to confirm.

entérique (ãterik), adj. (anat.) Enteric.

entérite (ãterit), s.f. [f. Gr. *enteron*] Enteritis.

enterrement (ãtɛrmã), s.m. Burial, interment; funeral; *aller* or *assister à l'~ de X*, to attend X's funeral.

enterrer (ãtɛre), v.a. [f. *en+terre*] To bury, to inter; to attend the funeral of; (fig.) to survive; **s'~**, v.pr. to bury oneself, *il est allé s'~ à la campagne*, he has gone and buried himself in the country.

en-tête (ãtɛt), s.m. (pl. *en-têtes*) Heading; headline (of newspaper); *~ de facture*, bill-head.

entêté, -e (ãtɛte), p. adj. **1.** Stubborn, obstinate, wayward; *~ comme une mule*, as obstinate as a mule; **2.** infatuated; syn. TÊTU, OPINIÂTRE, OBSTINÉ.

entêtement (ãtɛtmã), s.m. **1.** Stubbornness, obstinacy; **2.** infatuation.

entêter (ãtɛte), v.a. [f. *tête*] **1.** To affect the head of, to give a headache to; to make giddy; (of wine) to go to the head of; **2.** (fig.) to prepossess, to infatuate; (fam.) to turn (a person's) head; **s'~**, v.pr. to be stubborn, wayward or obstinate; (fam.) to stick to one's point.

enthousiasme (ãtuzjasm), s.m. [Gr. *enthousiasmos*] Enthusiasm.

enthousiasmer (ãtuzjasme), v.a. To render enthusiastic, to enrapture, to be in raptures (*de*, with); to transport; **s'~**, v.pr. to be enthusiastic (over); *il s'est enthousiasmé de l'art moderne*, he has gone crazy over modern art.

enthousiaste (ãtuzjast), adj. Enthusiastic. ~, s.m.f. Enthusiast (*de*, for).

enthymème (ãtimɛm), s.m. [Gr. *enthumēma*] (log.) Enthymeme.

entiché, -e (ãtiʃe), p. adj. (colloq.) Infatuated; *être ~ de ses opinions*, to set great store by one's opinions; to be wedded to one's opinions.

entichement (ãtiʃmã), s.m. Infatuation.

enticher (ãtiʃe), v.a. [etym. dub.] **1.** (fig.) To infatuate; **2.** (obs.) to taint, to infect; **s'~** (*de*), v.pr. to be infatuated (with), to be wedded (to).

enti-er, -ère (ãtje), adj. [L *integer*] **1.** Entire, whole; (arith.) integral; *cheval ~*, stallion; *en ~*, entirely; wholly; in full, all over; in its entirety; **2.** (fig.) obstinate, headstrong, self-willed, positive; *plus ~ que jamais*, more opinionated than ever. ~, s.m. **1.** (arith.) Integral number, integer; **2.** entirety; whole; *en son ~*, in its entirety; syn. COMPLET.

entièrement (ãtjɛrmã), adv. Entirely, wholly, utterly; syn. (EN) ENTIER.

entité (ãtite), s.f. [L *entitas*] Entity.

entoilage (ãtwalaʒ), s.m. **1.** Mounting (on canvas); **2.** canvas lining.

entoiler (ãtwale), v.a. [f. *toile*] To mount (on canvas).

entoir (ãtwar), s.m. [f. *enter*] Grafting-knife.

entôlage (ãtolaʒ), s.m. (colloq.) Decoying away with intent to rob.

entôler (ãtole), v.a. (colloq.) To decoy with intent to rob; to rob, to fleece.

entomologie (ãtɔmɔlɔʒi), s.f. [Gr. *entomon+logos*] Entomology.

entomologique (ãtɔmɔlɔʒik), adj. Entomological.

entomologiste (ãtɔmɔlɔʒist), s.m.f. Entomologist.

entomophage (ãtɔmɔfaʒ), adj. [Gr. *entomon+phagein*] Entomophagous.

entonnage, entonnement (ãtɔnaʒ, ãtɔnmã), s.m., **entonnaison** (ãtɔnɛzɔ̃), s.f. Tunning, barrelling, casking.

entonner[1] (ãtɔne), v.a. [f. *tonne*] To tun, to barrel; (fig.) to gulp down, (fam.) to swig; *il entonne bien*, he drinks hard.

entonner[2] (ãtɔne), v.a. [f. *ton*] **1.** (of instruments) To strike up; (of voices) to begin to sing, to intone; **2.** (poet. rare) to celebrate.

entonnoir (ãtɔnwar), s.m. [f. *entonner*] Funnel; *~ à tamis*, funnel with strainer; (fig. slang) throat, gullet.

entophyte (ãtɔfit), s.m. [Gr. *entos+phuton*] Entophyte.

entorse (ãtɔrs), s.f. [f. *tordre*] **1.** Sprain; strain, twist; *se donner une ~*, to sprain one's foot, ankle; **2.** (fig.) twist; *donner une ~ à la loi*, to get round the law.

entortillage (ãtɔrtijaʒ), s.m. Entanglement; twisting; subterfuge; complication.

entortillement (ãtɔrtijmã), s.m. Twisting; (fig.) intricacy, complication, obscurity; syn. ENTORTILLAGE.

entortiller (ãtɔrtije), v.a. [*en+tortiller*] To wrap up or round, to screw up (in paper); to coil round; to twist; (fig.) to entangle; to get round, to get the better of.

entour (ãtur), s.m. (usually pl.) [*en*+*tour*] **1.** Environs, adjacent parts; **2.** people around one; *à l'*~, around.

entourage (ãtura3), s.m. **1.** (fig.) Entourage, circle of friends; advisers; relations; servants, attendants; **2.** (rare) setting (of jewels, &c.).

entourer (ãture), v.a. [f. *entour*] To surround, to hem in, to encompass; to encircle; to gather round, to be about; (fig.) to overwhelm (with care, &c.); ~ *X de soins*, to lavish attentions upon X; **s'**~ (*de*), v.pr. to gather or summon round one; syn. ENVIRONNER, ENCEINDRE, ENCLORE.

entournure (ãturnyr), s.f. Arm-hole; (fig.) *être gêné aux* ~*s*, to feel awkward; *il était très gêné aux* ~*s*, he was like a cat on hot bricks.

en-tout-cas (ãtuka), s.m. invar. Umbrella-sunshade; see EN-CAS.

entozoaires (ãtɔzɔɛr), s.m.pl. [Gr. *entos* +*zōon*] Entozoon.

entozoologie (ãtɔ3ɔɔlɔ3i), s.f. Entozoology.

(s')entr'accorder (sãtrakɔrde), v.pr. To agree together.

(s')entr'accuser (sãtrakyse), v.pr. To accuse each other, or one another.

entr'acte (ãtrakt), s.m. [*entre*+*acte*] (theatr.) Interval; (fig.) interlude.

(s')entr'admirer (sãtradmire), v.pr. [*entre* +*admirer*] To admire each other, or one another.

(s')entr'aider (sãtrɛde), v.pr. [*entre*+ *aider*] To help each other, or one another.

entrailles (ãtrɑj), s.f.pl. [pop. L *intralia*] **1.** Intestines, entrails, bowels; **2.** (fig.) feelings, tenderness; pity; ~ *de la terre*, the bowels of the earth; *homme sans* ~, ruthless man.

(s')entr'aimer (sãtrɛme), v.pr. [*entre*+ *aimer*] To love each other, or one another.

entrain (ãtrɛ̃), s.m. [*en*+*train*] Warmth, heartiness; spirit, animation, life, go; *il a de l'*~, he has got some life (or go) in him.

entraînable (ãtrɛnabl), adj. **1.** Easily swayed; **2.** trainable.

entraînant, -e (ãtrɛnã), p.adj. Inspiriting, captivating; stirring; *éloquence* ~*e*, stirring eloquence; *air* ~, catchy tune.

entraînement (ãtrɛnmã), s.m. **1.** Enthusiasm; impulse, sway; allurement; **2.** training.

entraîner (ãtrɛne), v.a. [*en*+*traîner*] **1.** To draw or drag along; **2.** to carry away, to sweep away, to sweep (a person) off his feet; **3.** to gain over; ~ *des cœurs*, to win hearts; ~ *X dans l'erreur*, to lead X into error; **4.** to involve, to entail; *la guerre entraîne bien des maux*, war brings many evils in its train; **5.** to train (for sport, racing, &c.); to make the pace for.

entraîneu-r, -se (ãtrɛnœr), s.m.f. Trainer; pace-maker.

entrait (ãtrɛ), s.m. [pop. L *intractum*] Tie-beam; collar-beam.

entrant, -e (ãtrã), p. adj. [f. *entrer*] Ingoing, incoming, entering into office. ~, s.m.f. Incomer; *les* ~*s et les sortants*, the incomers and outgoers.

(s')entr'appeler (sãtraple), v.pr. [*entre*+ *appeler*] To call each other, or one another.

entrave (ãtrav), s.f. [L *in*+*trabes*] Clog, shackle, fetter; (fig.) hindrance, trammel, impediment.

entraver (ãtrave), v.a. To shackle, to clog, to trammel; to fetter; (fig.) to hinder, to thwart.

(s')entr'avertir (sãtravɛrtir), v.pr. To warn each other, or one another; to give each other (or one another) notice.

entre (ãtr), prep. [L *inter*] Between, betwixt; among, amongst; into, in; ~ *nous*, between ourselves; ~ *chien et loup*, between the lights (at dusk); ~ *les mains de quelqu'un*, in a person's hands; *sortir d'*~ *ses mains*, to escape from his clutches; ~ *ses bras*, in his arms; *c'est un homme* ~ *cent*, he is a man in a thousand; (colloq.) ~ *quatre-z-yeux*, between you and me and the door-post.

entre-bâillement (ãtrəbɑjmã), s.m. Aperture, chink, crack.

entre-bâiller (ãtrəbɑje), v.a. To half-open, to open (a door, &c).

(s')entre-baiser (sãtrəbɛze), v.pr. To kiss each other.

(s')entre-battre (sãtrəbatr), v.pr. To beat each other, to fight together.

entrechat (ãtrəʃa), s.m. [*entre*+*chasser*] (danc.) Caper, entrechat.

(s')entre-choquer (sãtrəʃɔke), v.pr. To clash; to knock or dash against each other; (fig.) to clash (of interests), to thwart each other.

entre-colonne (ãtrəkɔlɔn), **entre-colonnement**, **entrecolonnement** (ãtrəkɔlɔnmã), s.m. Intercolumniation.

entrecôte (ãtrəkot), s.m. (often fem.) [*entre*+*côte*] Rib-steak.

entrecoupé, -e (ãtrəkupe), p. adj. Broken, interrupted; *voix* ~*e de sanglots*, broken voice.

entrecouper (ãtrəkupe), v.a. [*entre*+ *couper*] **1.** To intersect; **2.** (fig.) to interrupt; to intersperse (with quotations, &c.).

entre-croisement (ãtrəkrwazmã), s.m. Intersection.

entre-croiser (ãtrəkrwaze), v.a. To intersect; **s'**~, v.pr. to cross each other.

(s')entre-déchirer (sãtrədeʃire), v.pr. To tear each other to pieces; (fig.) to tear each other's reputation to shreds.

(s')entre-détruire (sɑ̃trədetrɥir), v.pr. To exterminate each other.

entre-deux, entredeux (ɑ̃trədø), s.m. **1.** Insertion (of lace); **2.** intermediate space; **3.** (naut.) waist; **4.** trough (of a wave).

(s')entre-dévorer (sɑ̃trədevɔre), v.pr. To devour each other; to ruin each other.

(s')entre-donner (sɑ̃trədɔne), v.pr. To give each other, to exchange (gifts).

entrée (ɑ̃tre), s.f. **1.** Entry, entrance; entering, coming-in; **2.** beginning, début; *~ en matière*, opening; *faire son ~ dans le monde*, to make one's début; *faire son ~*, to enter, to appear, to make one's entry, or entrance; *l'~ de l'hiver*, the beginning of the winter; **3.** (cook.) entrée; **4.** (theatr. &c.) admission, entrance-money; **5.** free access; *avoir ses ~s à un théâtre*, to have free access to a theatre; **6.** (customs) duty; *payer une forte ~*, to pay a heavy duty; **7.** entrance, door, opening, aperture.

entrefaite (ɑ̃trəfɛt), s.f. (usually in pl.) [f. *entre+faire*] Meantime; *sur ces ~s*, in the meantime, meanwhile, thereupon.

entrefilet (ɑ̃trəfilɛ), s.m. (journalism) Note, short paragraph.

(s')entre-frapper (sɑ̃trəfrape), v.pr. To strike each other, or one another.

entregent (ɑ̃trəʒɑ̃), s.m. [f. *entre+gens*] Resourcefulness, social dexterity; *il a de l'~*, he is socially resourceful, he has social dexterity.

(s')entr'égorger (sɑ̃tregɔrʒe), v.pr. To cut each other's throats.

(s')entre-haïr (sɑ̃trəair), v.pr. To hate each other, or one another.

(s')entre-heurter (sɑ̃trəœrte), v.pr. To knock or clash against each other.

entrelacement (ɑ̃trəlasmɑ̃), s.m. Interlacing, interweaving.

entrelacer (ɑ̃trəlase), v.a. [*entre+lacer*] To interweave, to interlace, to wreath, to braid; to wattle.

entrelacs (ɑ̃trəlɑ), s.m.pl. (arch.) Interlacing work.

entrelardé, -e (ɑ̃trəlarde), p. adj. Interlarded; streaky.

entrelarder (ɑ̃trəlarde), v.a. [*entre+larder*] To interlard; (fig.) *discours entrelardé de citations*, speech interlarded with quotations.

entre-ligne, entreligne (ɑ̃trəliɲ), s.m. Interlineation; (print.) space-line, lead; syn. INTERLIGNE.

(s')entre-louer (sɑ̃trəlue), v.pr. To praise each other.

entre-luire (ɑ̃trəlɥir), v.n. To glimmer.

(s')entre-manger (sɑ̃trəmɑ̃ʒe), v.pr. To eat each other, or one another.

entremêlement (ɑ̃trəmɛlmɑ̃), s.m. Intermixing; intermixture.

entremêler (ɑ̃trəmɛle), v.a. [*entre+mêler*] To intermix, to intermingle; to intersperse; to mix up.

entremets (ɑ̃trəmɛ), s.m. [*entre+mets*] (cook.) Sweet.

entremetteu-r, -se (ɑ̃trəmɛtœr), s.m.f. (pej.) Go-between, procurer, (fem.) procuress; (rare) mediator, mediatrix.

(s')entremettre (sɑ̃trəmɛtr), v.pr. [*entre+mettre*] To mediate, to intervene; to interfere, to meddle.

entremise (ɑ̃trəmiz), s.f. **1.** Intervention, mediation; medium; *par l'~ de la presse*, through the medium of the press; *par son ~*, thanks to him; **2.** (naut.) carling.

entre-nœud (ɑ̃trənø), s.m. (bot.) Internode.

(s')entre-nuire (sɑ̃trənɥir), v.pr. To hurt, harm, or injure each other (or one another).

entrepas (ɑ̃trəpɑ), s.m. [*entre+pas*] Broken pace.

(s')entre-percer (sɑ̃trəpɛrse), v.pr. To run each other through, to pierce each other.

entrepont (ɑ̃trəpɔ̃), s.m. [*entre+pont*] Between-decks; *dans l'~*, between-decks.

entreposage (ɑ̃trəpozaʒ), s.m. Warehousing; bonding.

entreposer (ɑ̃trəpoze), v.a. [*entre+poser*] To store, to warehouse; to bond, to put in bond.

entreposeur (ɑ̃trəpozœr), s.m. Warehouseman; bonded warehouseman.

entrepositaire (ɑ̃trəpozitɛr), s.m. Bonder.

entrepôt (ɑ̃trəpo), s.m. [f. *entreposer*] Bonded warehouse; store; depot.

(s')entre-pousser (sɑ̃trəpuse), v.pr. To push each other.

entreprenant, -e (ɑ̃trəprənɑ̃), p. adj. Enterprising, pushing; daring; bold.

entreprendre (ɑ̃trəprɑ̃dr), v.a. [*entre+prendre*] **1.** To attempt, to undertake; to take in hand; **2.** to contract for or to; **3.** (fam.) to trouble, to worry; (colloq.) *~ X*, (*a*) to besiege X; (*b*) to take a rise out of X; *~*, v.n. to encroach, to infringe (upon).

entrepreneu-r, -se (ɑ̃trəprənœr), s.m.f. Contractor; *~ de pompes funèbres*, undertaker.

entreprise (ɑ̃trəpriz), s.f. [f. *entreprendre*] **1.** Enterprise; undertaking; *tenter l'~*, to make the attempt; **2.** contract; *à* or *par ~*, by contract; **3.** company, establishment, concern; *~ des messageries*, transport company.

(s')entre-quereller (sɑ̃trəkərɛle), v.pr. To quarrel with each other; to quarrel among our-, your-, or themselves.

entrer (ɑ̃tre), v.n. [L *intrare*] To enter, to come or go in; to get, walk, march or step in; *faire ~ quelque chose dans la tête de quelqu'un*, to get or drive something into a person's head; *cela ne m'est jamais entré dans la tête*, it never came into my head; ~ *au service de X*, to enter X's service; ~ *dans le monde*, to make one's début; ~ *bien avant dans*, to penetrate far into; (fig.) ~ *en jeu*, to come into play; ~ *en possession*, to come into possession; ~ *en condition*, to go into (domestic) service; *faire* ~, to show in, to usher in; to send in; ~ *en religion*, to take the veil (of women), to become a monk (of men); ~ *en matière*, to begin; to be contained, comprised, or included in; *cela n'entre pas dans le programme*, that is not included in the programme; *cela n'entre pour rien dans mes projets*, that has nothing to do with my plans; *vous n'entrez pas dans ma pensée*, you mistake my meaning; ~ *en ménage*, to set up house, to begin housekeeping; ~ *en concurrence*, to enter into competition (*avec*, with); ~ *en ligne de compte*, to be worth considering; ~ *dans ses fonctions*, to enter upon one's duties; *on n'entre pas*, or *défense d'*~, no admittance; ~, v.a. to introduce; ~ *du vin en ville*, to bring wine into the city.

entre-rail (ɑ̃trəraj), s.m. (rail.) Gauge.

entre-regarder (ɑ̃trərəgarde), v.a. To look at furtively; **s'**~, v.pr. to look at each other.

(s')entre-secourir (sɑ̃trəsəkurir), v.pr. To help each other, or one another.

entresol (ɑ̃trəsɔl), s.m. [*entre*+*sol*] (arch.) Entresol, mezzanine. ♤ But not 'mezzanine' in its theatrical sense.

(s')entre-suivre (sɑ̃trəsɥivr), v.pr. To follow, to succeed, each other, or one another.

entretaille (ɑ̃trətɑj), s.f. [*entre*+*tailler*] (engr.) Interline.

entre-temps (ɑ̃trətɑ̃), s.m. Interval, meantime.

entreteneu-r, -se (ɑ̃trətənœr), s.m.f. [f. *entretenir*] Keeper.

entretenir (ɑ̃trətənir), v.a. [*entre*+*tenir*] **1.** To keep up, to keep in repair; **2.** to maintain, to support, to provide for; **3.** to talk to, to entertain; ~ *X de promesses*, to keep X quiet with promises; **s'**~, v.pr. to converse with, to talk with.

entretenu, -e (ɑ̃trətəny), p. adj. Kept, supported; *femme* ~*e*, kept woman.

entretien (ɑ̃trətjɛ̃), s.m. **1.** Maintenance; upkeep, care; **2.** conversation, interview.

entretoile (ɑ̃trətwal), s.f. [*entre*+*toile*] Lace insertion.

entretoise (ɑ̃trətwaz), s.f. [*entre*+*toise*] (motor.) Stay, brace; (carp.) tie-beam, cross-beam; transom.

(s')entre-toucher (sɑ̃trətuʃe), v.pr. To touch each other, or one another.

(s')entre-tuer (sɑ̃trətɥe), v.pr. To kill each other, or one another.

entre-voie (ɑ̃trəvwɑ), s.f. (rail.) Six-foot way; space between the lines.

entrevoir (ɑ̃trəvwar), v.a. [*entre*+*voir*] To catch a glimpse of, to be just able to see; (fig.) to have an imperfect notion of; to foresee confusedly.

entrevous (ɑ̃trəvu), s.m. [*entre*+*voussoir*] Interjoist, space between two joists.

entrevoûter (ɑ̃trəvute), v.a. To plaster the interjoists of.

entrevue (ɑ̃trəvy), s.f. [f. *entrevoir*] Interview; meeting.

(s')entr'obliger (sɑ̃trɔbliʒe), v.pr. To oblige each other, or one another.

entr'ouvert, -e (ɑ̃truvɛr), p. adj. [f. *entr'ouvrir*] Ajar, a crack open; half-open.

entr'ouvrir (ɑ̃truvrir), v.a. [*entre*+*ouvrir*] To half-open, to open a little; **s'**~, v.pr. to open a little; to be ajar; to gape.

enture (ɑ̃tyr), s.f. [f. *enter*] (gard.) Incision, cut (for grafting).

énucléation (enyklea'sjɔ̃), s.f. [f. L *nucleus*] Enucleation.

énucléer (enyklee), v.a. To enucleate.

énumérat-eur, -rice (enymeratœr), s.m.f. Enumerator.

énumérati-f, -ve (enymeratif), adj. Enumerative.

énumération (enymera'sjɔ̃), s.f. Enumeration.

énumérer (enymere), v.a. [L *enumerare*] To enumerate.

envahir (ɑ̃vair), v.a. [L *invadere*] To invade; to overrun, to spread over; to overgrow; (fig.) to encroach upon, to usurp.

envahissant, -e (ɑ̃vaisɑ̃), p. adj. Invading, encroaching; free, too familiar, forward.

envahissement (ɑ̃vaismɑ̃), s.m. Invasion, encroachment.

envahisseu-r, -se (ɑ̃vaisœr), s.m.f. Invader. ~, adj. Invading, encroaching.

envasement (ɑ̃vɑzmɑ̃), s.m. Silting-up.

envaser (ɑ̃vɑze), v.a. [f. *vase*] To fill up, to choke with mud; to envelop in mud; **s'**~, v.pr. to silt up; to be choked with mud; to stick fast in the mud.

enveilloter (ɑ̃vɛjɔte), v.a. [f. *veillote*] (agric.) To cock (hay, &c.).

enveloppant, -e (ɑ̃vlɔpɑ̃), p. adj. Enveloping, surrounding; (fig.) captivating.

enveloppe (ɑ̃vlɔp), s.f. **1.** Envelope; wrapper, cover; *sous* ~, under cover; **2.** (techn.) coat, shell, jacket; casing; mould; tunic; (of balloon) envelope; (motor.) tyre; cover; ~ *antidérapante*, non-skid cover; **3.** (fig.) exterior, appearance.

enveloppement (ɑ̃vlɔpmɑ̃), s.m. Enveloping; envelopment; surrounding; (mil.) envelopment; wrapping-up; (med.) compress; ~ *humide*, wet compress round the body.

envelopper (ɑ̃vlɔpe), v.a. [OF *enveloper*] To wrap up, to cover, to enfold; to pack; (mil.) to envelop; to surround, to hem in;

(fig.) to wrap up, to envelop, to shroud; *sa pensée s'enveloppait de réticences*, his meaning was shrouded in reservations.

envenimement (ɑ̃vnimmɑ̃), s.m. Poisoning.

envenimer (ɑ̃vnime), v.a. [f. *venin*] To poison, to envenom, to irritate; **s'~**, v.pr. to fester, to be poisoned, to go septic; (fig.) to rankle; *la querelle s'envenima*, the quarrel became bitter.

enverger (ɑ̃vɛrʒe), v.a. [f. *verge*] To wattle.

enverguer (ɑ̃vɛrge) v.a. [f. *vergue*] (naut.) To bend (a sail).

envergure (ɑ̃vɛrgyr), s.f. (aeron.) Span; spread; (naut.) length (of a yard); (fig.) *il manque d'~*, he lacks breadth, or scope.

envers (ɑ̃vɛr), prep. [*en*+*vers*] Towards, to; *~ et contre tous*, in the face of the whole world.

envers (ɑ̃vɛr), s.m. [L *inversus*] **1.** Wrong side, reverse side, back; ugly or bad side; *mettre sa robe à l'~*, to put on one's dress inside out; **2.** contrary; *l'~ de la vérité*, the reverse of true, or the opposite of the truth.

(à l')envi (alɑ̃vi), adv. loc. and prep. [f. *envier*] In emulation of; *ils travaillent à l'~*, they vie with each other in their work.

enviable (ɑ̃vjabl), adj. To be envied, enviable.

envider (ɑ̃vide), v.a. To fill (bobbins) with thread.

envie (ɑ̃vi), s.f. [L *invidia*] **1.** Envy, enviousness; *digne d'~*, enviable; *il ne fait ~ à personne*, he is by no means to be envied; *il ne porte ~ à personne*, he envies no man; *l'~ le dévore*, he is eaten up with envy; **2.** wish, desire, longing, inclination; *si l'~ m'en prend*, if I feel inclined for it; *j'ai bien ~ de partir avec vous*, I've a good mind to go with you; *avoir ~ de dormir*, to be sleepy; *faire ~*, to be tempting; *il m'en a ôté toute ~*, he has put me out of conceit with it; (fam.) he has put me off it; *mourir d'~ de*, to be dying to; *sécher d'~*, to go green with envy; **3.** birthmark; **4.** agnail.

envieillir (ɑ̃vjɛjir), v.a. [*en*+*vieillir*] To make look old.

envier (ɑ̃vje), v.a. [f. *envie*] **1.** To envy, to be envious of; **2.** to desire, to wish for; **3.** (poet.) to grudge; syn. AVOIR ENVIE, PORTER ENVIE.

envieusement (ɑ̃vjøzmɑ̃), adv. Enviously.

envieu-x, -se (ɑ̃vjø), adj. Envious, grudging. **~**, s.m.f. Envious person.

enviné, -e (ɑ̃vine), adj. [f. *vin*] Smelling of wine (of bottles, kegs, &c.), winy, vinous.

environ (ɑ̃virɔ̃), adv. [f. *en*+*virer*] About, thereabouts, nearly. **~**, prep. Near, about.

environnant, -e (ɑ̃virɔnɑ̃), p. adj. Surrounding.

environner (ɑ̃virɔne), v.a. To surround, to encompass; to enclose.

environs (ɑ̃virɔ̃), s.m. pl. Environs, vicinity, neighbourhood.

envisager (ɑ̃vizaʒe), v.a. [f. *visage*] To look straight at, to stare in the face; to eye; (fig.) to face, to consider.

envoi (ɑ̃vwa), s.m. [f. *envoyer*] **1.** Sending; thing sent, parcel, package; consignment, shipment; (comm.) *compléter un ~*, to make up a parcel, a consignment; *faire un ~*, to send off a parcel, to dispatch a consignment; *lettre d'~*, letter of advice; **2.** (pros.) envoi.

(s')envoiler (sɑ̃vwale), v.pr. [f. *voiler*] (metall.) To warp, to bend.

envoisiner (ɑ̃vwazine), v.a. [f. *voisin*] To surround with neighbours.

envolée (ɑ̃vɔle), s.f. [f. *envoler*] Flight.

envolement, envol (ɑ̃vɔlmɑ̃, ɑ̃vɔl), s.m. Taking flight.

(s')envoler (sɑ̃vɔle), v.pr. To fly away, to take wing; to be carried off (by the wind, &c.); *l'oiseau s'est envolé*, the bird has flown; (fig.) to disappear, to vanish.

envoûtement (ɑ̃vutmɑ̃), s.m. Spell, magic charm.

envoûter (ɑ̃vute), v.a. [L *in*+*vultus*] To cast a spell upon.

envoyé, -e (ɑ̃vwaje), s.m.f. Envoy, delegate, messenger.

envoyer (ɑ̃vwaje), v.a. [f. *en*+*voie*] To send; (comm.) to dispatch, to forward; to transmit; to delegate; to send as envoy; (naut.) *envoie!*, 'bout ship!; *il m'a envoyé au diable*, he told me to go to the devil; *~ chercher*, to send for; *~ dire que*, to send word that; *~ X promener*, to send X about his business; *~ X paître*, to send X packing; (pop.) *bien envoyé!*, that's the stuff to give 'em!; *je ne le lui ai pas envoyé dire*, I told him that to his face; (slang, vulg.) *s'~*, to take; to drink.

envoyeu-r, -se (ɑ̃vwajœr), s.m.f. Sender.

enzootique (ɑ̃zɔɔtik), adj. (vet.) Enzootic.

enzyme (ɑ̃zim), s.f. (chem.) Enzyme.

éocène (eɔsɛn), adj. s.m. [Gr. *ēōs*+*kainos*] (geol.) Eocene.

éolien, -ne (eɔljɛ̃), adj. [L *aeolius*] Aeolic, Aeolian.

éolipile (eɔlipil), s.m. [*Éole*, god of wind +L *pila*] Aeolipile.

épacte (epakt), s.f. [Gr. *epaktos*] (astr.) Epact.

épagneul, -e (epaɲœl), s.m.f. adj. [f. *espagnol*] Spaniel.

épais, -se (epɛ), adj. [L *spissus*] Thick, dense; bulky; heavy, stout, thickset (of persons); (fig.) dull, gross, thick-witted; *~ d'un mètre*, one metre thick; *ténèbres ~ses*, thick darkness; *un homme ~*, a dullard, a blockhead; ~*se ignorance*, gross ignorance. ~, s.m. Thickness; *avoir plusieurs pieds d'*~, to be several feet thick or through. ~, adv. Thick, thickly; *semer* ~, to sow thick.

épaisseur (epɛsœr), s.f. Thickness, density; stoutness, bulkiness; coarseness, dullness.

épaissir (epɛsir), v.a.n. To thicken; **s'**~, v.pr. to grow thick, to thicken; to grow stout, coarse; to grow dull.

épaississant, -e (epɛsisɑ̃), p. adj. **1.** Thickening; **2.** giving an appearance of stoutness.

épaississement (epɛsismɑ̃), s.m. Thickening, thickness, growing stout.

épamprage, épamprement (epɑ̃praʒ, epɑ̃prəmɑ̃), s.m. Stripping-off, pruning (vines).

épamprer (epɑ̃pre), v.a. [f. *pampre*] (vitic.) To strip off leaves.

épanchement (epɑ̃ʃmɑ̃), s.m. Pouring out, shedding; (med.) overflow; (fig.) effusion; ~ *de cœur*, pouring out one's heart; syn. EFFUSION.

épancher (epɑ̃ʃe), v.a. [LL *expandicare*] To pour out, to shed; (fig.) to open, to discharge, to vent; **s'**~, v.pr. to overflow; to be discharged; (fig.) to open one's heart, to unbosom oneself.

épandage (epɑ̃daʒ), s.m. Scattering, strewing (especially of manure).

épandre (epɑ̃dr), v.a. [L *expandere*] To strew, to spread about, to scatter; (poet.) to shed (light, &c.).

épanorthose (epanɔrtoz), s.f. [Gr. *epanorthōsis*] (rhet.) Epanorthosis.

épanouir (epanwir), v.a. [Germ. *spannen*] To cause to open; to expand; (fig.) to brighten, to gladden; **s'**~, v.pr. to open (of flowers); to expand; *son visage s'épanouit*, his face brightened, his face lit up.

épanouissement (epanwismɑ̃), s.m. Opening, blossoming, blowing (of flowers); (fig.) brightness, glow, bloom.

épargne (eparɲ), s.f. [f. *épargner*] Thrift, saving; savings; *vivre de ses* ~*s*, to live upon one's savings; *avec* ~, sparingly; *caisse d'*~, savings bank.

épargner (eparɲe), v.a. [Germ. *sparen*] To save, to lay by; to spare, to husband; ~ *ses forces*, to husband one's strength; ~ *sur sa toilette*, to save on dress; *on ne lui épargne pas l'argent*, he is not stinted of money; *épargnez-moi*, spare me; *je veux vous* ~ *cette peine*, I want to spare you the trouble.

éparpillement (eparpijmɑ̃) s.m. Scattering, dispersing; dispersion.

éparpiller (eparpije), v.a. To scatter, to disperse, to strew about; (fig.) to fritter away, to squander.

épars, -e (epar), adj. **1.** Scattered, dispersed; **2.** sparse; **3.** straggling, dishevelled (of hair).

éparvin, épervin (eparvɛ̃, epɛrvɛ̃), s.m. [LL *spavenus*] (vet.) Spavin.

épatant, -e (epatɑ̃), p. adj. (colloq.) Ripping, topping, stunning.

épate (epat), s.f. (slang) Splash, swank; *faire de l'*~, to swank; to make a splash; to show off.

épaté, -e (epate), p.adj. **1.** Flat, squat, pug (of noses); **2.** footless (of wine-glasses, &c.); **3.** (slang) flabbergasted, winded.

épatement (epatmɑ̃), s.m. **1.** Flattening (of noses); **2.** (slang) stupefaction; stunner.

épater (epate), v.a. [f. *patte*] **1.** To break the foot off (glasses, &c.); **2.** (slang) to flabbergast; **s'**~, v.pr. to be flabbergasted, dumbfounded; *il ne s'épate de rien*, he is a cool hand.

épateu-r, -se (epatœr), s.m.f. (pop. slang) Swank.

épaulard (epolar), s.m. [f. *épaule*] (zool.) Grampus, orc.

épaule (epol), s.f. [L *spatula*] Shoulder; (fig.) *donner un coup d'*~, to give or lend a hand; *prêter l'*~ *à X*, to back X up; *porter sur les* ~*s*, to be saddled with; *hausser les* ~*s*, to shrug one's shoulders; *avoir la tête enfoncée dans les* ~*s*, to be very high-shouldered; *plier les* ~*s*, *toucher des* ~*s*, to be beaten, to surrender; *regarder X par-dessus l'*~, to look down one's nose at X; ~ *de mouton*, shoulder of mutton.

épaulée (epole), s.f. Push with the shoulder.

épaulement (epolmɑ̃), s.m. **1.** (fort.) Breast-work, shoulder, epaulement; **2.** (naut.) shoulder, bows; **3.** (carp.) shoulder.

épauler (epole), v.a.n. [f. *épaule*] **1.** To bring (one's gun) to the shoulder; (by ext.) to aim; **2.** to splay (a horse, &c.); **3.** (mil.) to protect with a breast-work; **4.** (fig.) to back up.

épaulette (epolɛt), s.f. Epaulet(te).

épaulière (epoljɛr), s.f. (armour) Shoulder-plate.

épave (epav), s.f. [L *expavidus*] Wreck; (fig.) waif; flotsam and jetsam.

épeautre (epotr), s.m. [LL *spelta*] Spelt.

épée (epe), s.f. [L *spatha*] Sword, (fig.) steel, (poet.) brand; *donner des coups d'*~ *dans l'eau*, to beat the air; *à la pointe de l'*~, at the point of the sword; *poursuivre l'*~ *dans les reins*, to press (some one) hard; (fig.) to stir (a person) up, to prod; *passer au fil de l'*~, to put to the sword; to kill; *roman de cape et d'*~, novel of adventure; cloak-and-sword novel; *croiser l'*~, or *croiser le fer*, to cross swords.

épeiche (epɛʃ), s.f. [OHG *specht*] (ornith.) Golden oriole.

épeire (epɛr), s.f. [Gr. *epi*+*eirein*] (ent.) Epeira, garden spider.

épéiste (epeist), s.m. (rare) Swordsman; syn. TIREUR, HOMME D'ÉPÉE,

épeler (eple), v.a. [Goth. *spillôn*] To spell.

épellation (epɛlla'sjɔ̃), s.m. Spelling.

épenthèse (epɑ̃tɛz), s.f. [Gr. *epenthesis*] (gram.) Epenthesis.

épenthétique (epɑ̃tetik), adj. Epenthetic.

éperdu, -e (epɛrdy), adj. Distraught, agitated, excited, distressed, dismayed, quivering, fluttering, flushed.

éperdument (epɛrdymɑ̃), adv. Recklessly, flutteringly, in a flutter, distractedly, desperately, tremulously.

éperlan (epɛrlɑ̃), s.m. [Germ. *Spierling*] (ichth.) Smelt, sparling.

éperon (eprɔ̃), s.m. [OHG *sporon*] **1.** Spur; *gagner ses ~s*, to win one's spurs; *chausser les ~s à X*, to knight X; *donner de l'~ à un cheval*, to clap spurs to a horse; *enfoncer l'~*, to dig in one's spurs; **2.** spur, gaffle (of game-cocks); **3.** spur, spur-shaped rock or mountain; **4.** (arch.) counterfort; starling, breakwater (of a bridge); **5.** (naut.) ram.

éperonné, -e (eprɔne), p. adj. (lit. and fig.) Spurred.

éperonner (eprɔne), v.a. To spur; to arm with spurs; (fig.) to spur on, to urge forward, to egg on.

éperonnerie (eprɔnəri), s.f. Spur-making; spur-trade.

éperonnier (eprɔnje), s.m. Spur-maker.

éperonnière (eprɔnjɛr), s.f. (bot.) Larkspur; syn. PIED D'ALOUETTE.

épervier (epɛrvje), s.m. [OHG *sparvari*] **1.** (ornith.) Hawk, sparrow-hawk; **2.** (fish.) cast-net.

épervière (epɛrvjɛr), s.f. (bot.) Hawkweed.

épervin (epɛrvɛ̃), s.m. See ÉPARVIN.

épeuré, -e (epœre), adj. [f. *peur*] Frightened; syn. APEURÉ.

éphèbe (efɛb), s.m. [Gr. *ephēbos*] Ephebe.

éphélide (efelid), s.f. [Gr. *epi+hēlios*] Freckle.

éphémère (efemɛr), adj. [Gr. *epi+hēmera*] Ephemeral. ~, s.m. (ent.) Ephemera, May-fly, ephemeron.

éphémèrement (efemɛrmɑ̃), adv. Ephemerally.

éphémérides (efemerid), s.f.pl. Ephemerides (sing. ephemeris).

éphod (efɔd), s.m. [Hebr. *ēphōd*] Ephod.

éphorat (efɔra), s.m. **éphorie** (efɔri), s.f. Office of ephor.

éphore (efɔr), s.m. [Gr. *ephoros*] Ephor.

épi (epi), s.m. [L *spica*] **1.** Ear (of corn); *~ bien garni*, well-filled ear; *~ de cheveux, de poils*, tuft of hair; **2.** spike (of flowers); **3.** (arch.) herring-boning, herring-bone work; **4.** herring-bone pattern.

épiage (epjaʒ), s.m. Earing (of corn).

épiaire (epjɛr), s.m. (bot.) Woundwort.

épicarpe (epikarp), s.m. [Gr. *epi+karpos*] (bot.) Epicarp.

épice (epis), s.f. [L *species*] Spice; *pain d'~*, gingerbread; *herbe aux ~s*, allspice.

épicéa (episea), s.m. [corrupt. of *picéa*] (bot.) Norwegian pine.

épicène (episɛn), adj. [Gr. *epikoinos*] (gram.) Epicene.

épicentre (episɑ̃tr), s.m. [Gr. *epi+kentros*] Epicentre, epicentrum.

épicer (epise), v.a. [f. *épice*] To spice; (fig.) *récit un peu épicé*, spicy yarn.

épicerie (episri), s.f. [f. *épice*] Grocery; grocery-trade; grocer's shop or stores.

épichérème (epikerɛm), s.m. [Gr. *epikheirēma*] (rhet.) Epicheirema.

épici-er, -ère (episje), s.m.f. Grocer; (fem.) grocer's wife.

épicrâne (epikrɑn), s.m. [Gr. *epi+kranion*] Epicranium.

épicurien, -ne (epikyrjɛ̃), adj. [f. Gr. *Epikoureios*] Epicurean. ~, s.m.f. Epicurean; (colloq.) epicure.

épicurisme, épicuréisme (epikyrism, epikyreism), s.m. Epicureanism, epicurism.

épicycle (episikl), s.m. [Gr. *epi+kuklos*] Epicycle.

épicycloïdal, -e, (aux) (episiklɔidal), adj. Epicycloidal.

épicycloïde (episiklɔid), s.f. (geom.) Epicycloid.

épidémie (epidemi), s.f. [Gr. *epi+dēmos*] Epidemic.

épidémique (epidemik), adj. Epidemic.

épidémiquement (epidemikmɑ̃), adv. Epidemically.

épiderme (epidɛrm), s.m. [Gr. *epi+derma*] Epidermis.

épidermique (epidɛrmik), adj. Epidermic, epidermal.

épidictique (epidiktik), adj. [Gr. *epideiktikos*] (rhet.) Epideictic.

épier[1] (epje), v.n. [f. *épi*] To ear, to form into ears.

épier[2] (epje), v.a. [OHG *spehon*] To watch, to spy upon; to be on the watch for; *~ l'occasion*, to watch for an opportunity.

épierrage, épierrement, (epjɛraʒ, epjɛrmɑ̃), s.m. Clearing land of stones.

épierrer (epjɛre), v.a. [f. *pierre*] To clear of stones.

épieu (pl. -x) (epjø), s.m. [OHG *speot*] Boar-spear, hunting-pole.

épieu-r, -se (epjœr), s.m.f. (rare) Watcher; eavesdropper.

épigastre (epigastr), s.m. [Gr. *epi+gastēr*] (anat.) Epigastrium.

épigastrique (epigastrik), adj. Epigastric.

épigénèse (epiʒenɛz), s.f. [Gr. *epi+genesis*] Epigenesis.

épiglotte (epiglɔt), s.f. [Gr. *epi+glōtta*] (anat.) Epiglottis.

épigrammatique (epigramatik), adj. Epigrammatic, epigrammatical.

épigrammatiquement (epigramatikmɑ̃), adv. Epigrammatically.

épigrammatiser (epigramatize), v.n. To epigrammatize.

épigrammatiste (epigramatist), s.m.f. Epigrammatist.

épigramme (epigram), s.f. [Gr. *epigramma*] Epigram.

épigraphe (epigraf), s.f. [Gr. *epi+graphein*] Epigraph.

épigraphie (epigrafi), s.f. Epigraphy.

épigraphique (epigrafik), adj. Epigraphic.

épigraphiste (epigrafist), s.m.f. Epigraphist.

épigyne (epiʒin), s.f. [Gr. *epi+gunē*] (bot.) Epigynous part. ~, adj. Epigynous.

épilation (epila'sjɔ̃), s.f. Depilation.

épilatoire (epilatwar), adj. s.m. Depilatory.

épilepsie (epilɛpsi), s.f. [Gr. *epilēpsia*] Epilepsy.

épileptique (epilɛptik), adj. s.m.f. Epileptic.

épiler (epile), v.a. [f. *é*+L *pilus*] To depilate.

épileu-r, -se (epilœr), s.m.f. Depilator (person).

épillet (epijɛ), s.m. [f. *épi*] Spikelet.

épilobe (epilɔb), s.m. [Gr. *epi+lobos*] (bot.) Willow-herb.

épilogue (epilɔg), s.m. [Gr. *epi+logos*] Epilogue.

épiloguer (epilɔge), v.n.a. To carp, to find fault, to split hairs; to criticize, to disapprove; to conclude, to sum up; to comment.

épiloir (epilwar), s.m. [f. *épiler*] Tweezers.

épinaie (epinɛ), s.f. [f. *épine*] Brake, thicket.

épinard (epinar), s.m. [Arab. *isfinā̆j*] Spinach; (mil.) *à graines d'~*, with large bullions.

épincer (epɛ̃se), v.a. [*é+pincer*] (hort.) To disbud.

épine (epin), s.f. [L *spina*] **1.** (bot.) Thorn, prickle; thorn-bush; ~ *blanche*, hawthorn; ~ *noire*, blackthorn; sloe; **2.** spine, backbone; ~ *dorsale*, backbone; **3.** (fig.) obstacle, cross, rub; ~ *dans le pied*, thorn in the side; *tirer une ~ du pied à X*, to remove a thorn from X's side; *être sur des ~s*, to be or sit on thorns; *marcher sur des ~s*, to tread on thorns, to skate on thin ice; *pas de rose sans ~s*, every rose has its thorn.

épinette (epinɛt), s.f. [It. *spinetta*, f. L *spina*] (mus.) Spinet.

épineu-x, -se (epinø), adj. Thorny, prickly; (fig.) ticklish, intricate.

épine-vinette (epinvinɛt), s.f. (bot.) Barberry.

épinglage (epɛ̃glaʒ), s.m. Pinning.

épingle (epɛ̃gl), s.f. [L *spinula*] Pin; ~ *anglaise* or ~ *à nourrice*, safety-pin; ~ *à cheveux*, hairpin; ~ *à chapeau*, hatpin; (fig.) *coup d'~*, pinprick; *chercher une ~ dans une botte de foin*, to look for a needle in a haystack; *tirer son ~ du jeu*; to save one's stake; to get well out of a bad job; *être tiré à quatre ~s*, to be dressed up to the nines; to be spick and span; to be faultlessly dressed; to be natty or well groomed; ~ *de bois*, peg; (fig.) ~*s*, gratuity, douceur; *virage en ~*, hairpin bend; *monter en ~* or *en ~ de cravate*, to make the most of.

épinglé, -e (epɛ̃gle), p. adj. **1.** Pinned; **2.** corded. ~, s.m. Terry velvet.

épingler (epɛ̃gle), v.a. To pin.

épinglerie (epɛ̃gləri), s.f. Pin-factory; pin-mill; pin-trade.

épinglette (epɛ̃glɛt), s.f. **1.** Priming-wire; **2.** (artill.) priming-iron; **3.** (mining) piercer.

épingli-er, -ère (epɛ̃glje), s.m.f. Pinmaker.

épinière (epinjɛr), adj. f. [f. *épine*] Spinal.

épiniers (epinje), s.m.pl. (hunt.) Covert, thicket.

épinoche (epinɔʃ), s.f. [f. *épine*] (ichth.) Stickleback.

épinochette (epinɔʃɛt), s.f. Common stickleback.

Épiphanie (epifani), s.f. [Gr. *epiphaneia*] **1.** Epiphany (feast of the Church); **2.** epiphany, manifestation.

épiphénomène (epifenɔmɛn), s.m. [Gr. *epi+phainomenon*] (med., philos.) Epiphenomenon, accessory symptom.

épiphonème (epifɔnɛm), s.m. [Gr. *epi+phōnēma*] (rhet.) Epiphonema.

épiphora (epifɔrɑ), s.m. [Gr. wd] (med.) Epiphora.

épiphylle (epifil), adj. [Gr. *epi+phullon*] (bot.) Epiphyllous.

épiphyse (epifiz), s.f. [Gr. *epi+phusis*] (anat.) Epiphysis.

épiphyte (epifit), adj. [Gr. *epi+phuton*] (bot.) Epiphytal.

épiploïque (epiplɔik), adj. Epiploic.

épiploon (epliplɔɔ̃), s.m. [Gr. wd] (anat.) Epiploon.

épique (epik), adj. [Gr. *epikos*] Epic.

épirote (epirɔt), adj. s.m.f. Epirot.

épiscopal, -e, (aux) (episkɔpal), adj. Episcopal.

épiscopalement (episkɔpalmɑ̃), adv. Episcopally.

épiscopat (episkɔpa), s.m. [L *episcopus*] Episcopacy, episcopate.

épiscopaux (episkɔpo), s.m.pl. Episcopalians.

épisode (epizɔd), s.m. [Gr. *epeisodion*] Episode.

épisodique (epizɔdik), adj. Episodic, episodical.
épisodiquement (epizɔdikmɑ̃), adv. Episodically.
épispastique (epispastik), adj. s.m. [Gr. *epispastikos*] (med.) Epispastic.
épisperme (epispɛrm), s.m. [Gr. *epi*+ *sperma*] Episperm, seed-coat.
épisser (epise), v.a. [Dutch *splissen*] To splice.
épissoir, s.m. **épissoire** (episwar), s.f. (naut.) Marline-spike.
épissure (episyr), s.f. Splice.
épistaxis (epistaksis), s.f. [Gr. *epistazein*] (med.) Epistaxis.
épistolaire (epistɔlɛr), adj. [L *epistola*] Epistolary.
épistoli-er, -ère (epistɔlje), s.m.f. Great letter-writer.
épistyle (epistil), s.m. [Gr. *epi*+*stulos*] (arch.) Epistyle; syn. ARCHITRAVE.
épitaphe (epitaf), s.f. [Gr. *epi*+*taphos*] Epitaph.
épite (epit), s.f. (naut.) Tree-nail wedge.
épithalame (epitalam), s.m. [Gr. *epi*+ *thalamos*] Epithalamium.
épithélial, -e, (aux) (epiteljal), adj. (anat.) Epithelial.
épithélium (epiteljɔm), s.m. [Gr. *epi*+ *thēlē*] (anat.) Epithelium.
épithème (epitɛm), s.m. (pharm.) Epithem.
épithète (epitɛt), s.f. [Gr. *epitheton*] Epithet; syn. ADJECTIF.
épitoge (epitɔʒ), s.f. [Gr. *epi*+L *toga*] **1.** (ant.) Mantle worn over toga; **2.** (in Fr. universities) shoulder-knot (worn over professor's gown).
épitomé (epitɔme), s.m. (rare) [Gr. wd] Epitome.
épître (epitr), s.f. [L *epistola*] Epistle; (iron.) letter, epistle; (eccles.) *le côté de l'*~, the south side of the altar, the epistle side; syn. LETTRE.
épizootie (epizɔɔsi), s.f. [Gr. *epi*+*zōon*] Murrain; epizootic disease.
épizootique (epizɔɔtik), adj. Epizootic.
éplaigner (eplɛɲe), v.a. (techn.) To smooth (cloth).
éploré, -e (eplɔre), adj. [f. *é*+L *plorare*] In tears, weeping; disconsolate.
éployé, -e (eplwaje), adj. [*é*+*ployer*] Spread; (herald.) spread (of the eagle).
épluchage (eplyʃaʒ), s.m. Peeling (of vegetables); picking, cleaning; (fig.) finding fault.
éplucher (eplyʃe), v.a. [*é*+OF *pelucher*] **1.** To peel (vegetables); **2.** to pick, to clean; **3.** to purl (wool, silk, &c.); **4.** (fig.) to sift; to examine minutely; to pick holes in, to find fault with; ~ *la vie de X*, to pry into X's private life; **s'**~, v.pr. to preen its feathers (of a bird); to clean itself; (fig.) to criticize oneself severely.
éplucheu-r, -se (eplyʃœr), s.m.f. Picker, cleaner; ~ *de pommes de terre*, scullion, (fem.) kitchen-maid; (fig.) fault-finder; hair-splitter.
éplucheir (eplyʃwar), s.m. Paring-knife; potato-peeler.
épluchure (eplyʃyr), s.f. Piece of peel; (pl.) parings; pickings, refuse.
épode (epɔd), s.f. [Gr. *epi*+*ōdē*] Epode.
époi (epwa), s.m. [f. *epieu*] (hunt.) Trochings (pl.).
épointage (epwɛ̃taʒ), s.m. Blunting (of a pencil, &c.).
épointé, -e (epwɛ̃te), p. adj. **1.** (vet.) With a broken thigh (of a dog); hip-shot (of a horse); **2.** (of pencil, tool, &c.) blunted.
épointement (epwɛ̃tmɑ̃), s.m. Bluntness.
épointer (epwɛ̃te), v.a. [f. *pointe*] To blunt, to break the point of; **s'** ~, v.pr. to grow blunt.
éponge (epɔ̃ʒ), s.f. [L *spongia*] Sponge; (fig.) *boire comme une* ~, to drink like a fish; (fig.) *passer l'*~ *sur son passé*, to wipe or blot out the past, to let bygones be bygones; (fig.) *il a pressé l'*~, he has squeezed him (or her) dry.
éponger (epɔ̃ʒe), v.a. To sponge, to clean with a sponge; **s'**~, v.pr. *s'*~ *le front*, to mop one's brow.
épontille (epɔ̃tij), s.f. (naut.) Stanchion, shore.
épontiller (epɔ̃tije), v.a. [f. *pont*] (naut.) To prop, to shore.
éponyme (epɔnim), adj. [Gr. *epi*+*onoma*] Eponym.
épopée (epɔpe), s.f. [Gr. *epopoiia*] Epic, epopee, epos.
époque (epɔk), s.f. [Gr. *epokhē*] Period, time, epoch; *à l'*~ *des croisades*, at the time of the crusades; *de l'*~ *des Tudor*, of the Tudor period; *à une* ~ *éloignée*, at a remote period; (geol.) period; ~ *tertiaire*, tertiary period; (fig.) *événement qui fait* ~, epoch-making event.
épouiller (epuje), v.a. [f. *pou*] To louse, to clean of lice.
époumoner (epumɔne), v.a. [f. *poumon*] To tire the lungs of, to exhaust, to put out of breath; *s'*~ *à répéter une chose*, to make oneself hoarse repeating a thing.
épousailles (epuzɑj), s.f.pl. Espousals, nuptials.
épouse (epuz), s.f. Wife; (archaic) spouse.
épousée (epuze), s.f. Bride.
épouser (epuze), v.a. [L *sponsare*] **1.** To marry; (fig.) to espouse; ~ *le parti de*, to espouse the cause of; **2.** (fig.) to adapt itself to, to fit exactly, to clothe tightly; ~ *la forme de*, to cover exactly, to be exactly adapted to.
épouseur (epuzœr), s.m. (colloq.) Suitor; marrying man.
époussetage (epustaʒ), s.m. Dusting.
épousseter (epuste), v.a. [f. *poussière*]

1. To dust; 2. (fam.) to leather, to give a good hiding to.
époussette (epusɛt), s.f. Dusting-brush; duster.
épouti (eputi), s.m. [*é*+*poutie*] Orts, flaw, fault (in cloth).
épouvantable (epuvɑ̃tabl), adj. Frightful, dreadful, appalling, hideous.
épouvantablement (epuvɑ̃tabləmɑ̃), adv. Frightfully, dreadfully, appallingly.
épouvantail (epuvɑ̃taj), s.m. Scarecrow; (fig.) bugbear.
épouvante (epuvɑ̃t), s.f. Terror, fright, dismay, dread, affright; *être frappé d'*~, to be terror-stricken; *porter l'*~, to spread terror or dismay.
épouvantement (epuvɑ̃tmɑ̃), s.m. Utter terror, mighty dread.
épouvanter (epuvɑ̃te), v.a. [pop. L *expaventare*] To terrify, to frighten, to appal, to dismay; to scare; **s'**~, v.pr. to be terrified, dismayed, to be appalled, to be scared; to take fright.
épou-x, -se (epu, epuz), s.m.f. [f. L *sponsus*] Husband, (fem.) wife; (pl.) husband and wife, couple; *futur* ~, intended husband.
épreindre (eprɛ̃dr), v.a. (obs.) [L *exprimere*] To squeeze out, to press.
épreinte (eprɛ̃t), s.f. (med.) Tenesmus, straining.
(s')éprendre (seprɑ̃dr), v.pr. [*é*+*prendre*] To fall in love (*de*, with).
épreuve (eprœv), s.f. [f. *éprouver*] 1. Test, ordeal, trial, sorrow; *à toute* ~, unflinching, thoroughly reliable; trusty, faithful; *nous sommes de cœur avec vous dans votre* ~, we feel for you in your sorrow; *courage à toute* ~, unflinching courage; *mettre à l'*~, to put to the test; *passer par de rudes* ~*s*, to go through terrible ordeals; *prendre à l'*~, to take on trial; *temps d'*~, probation; *j'en ai fait l'*~, I have tried it; 2. proof; *à l'*~ *de l'eau, du feu, etc.*, waterproof, fireproof, &c.; 3. (print.) proof; ~ *en placard*, or *placard*, galley proof; ~ *chargée*, foul proof; ~ *peu chargée*, clean proof; ~ *d'auteur*, author's proof; *seconde* ~ revise; ~ *d'artiste*, artist's proof; ~ *avant la lettre*, proof before letters; 4. (photo.) print.
épris, -e (epri), p. adj. [f. *éprendre*] In love (*de*, with), smitten (with), taken (with).
éprouver (epruve), v.a. [f. *prouver*] 1. To test, to put to the test, to try, to prove, to put to the proof; ~ *un canon*, to test a cannon; 2. (fig.) to feel, to experience, to meet with; to go through; ~ *des malheurs*, to meet with misfortunes; ~ *une douleur*, to feel a pain.
éprouvette (epruvɛt), s.f. Test-tube, gauge.
épsilon (epsilɔn), s.m. [Gr. wd] Epsilon.
épucer (epyse), v.a. [f. *puce*] To rid or clear of fleas.
épuisable (epɥizabl), adj. Exhaustible.
épuisant, -e (epɥizɑ̃), p. adj. Exhausting.
épuisement (epɥizmɑ̃), s.m. Draining-off; (fig.) exhaustion, impoverishment; *l'*~ *des finances*, the low state of the finances.
épuiser (epɥize), v.a. [*é*+*puiser*] To exhaust, to drain; to use up, to consume; to tire out, to enervate, to wear out; *l'édition est épuisée*, the book is out of print; *terre épuisée*, impoverished land; *je suis épuisée (de fatigue)*, I am exhausted, I am done up, fagged out, dog-tired, tired to death; **s'**~, v.pr. 1. to exhaust oneself, to wear oneself out; 2. to be sold out; to be nearly exhausted.
épuisette (epɥizɛt), s.f. 1. Landing-net; 2. bird-net; 3. baling-out can.
épulotique (epylɔtik), adj. [Gr. *epoulōtikos*] (med.) Epulotic.
épurateur (epyratœr), s.m. Refiner. ~, adj. Refining.
épurati-f, -ve, épuratoire (epyratif, epyratwar), adj. (techn.) Refining, purifying.
épuration (epyra'sjɔ̃), s.f. (lit. and fig.) Refinement, refining; purification, purifying; syn. ÉPUREMENT.
épure (epyr), s.f. [f. *épurer*] 1. Draught, working drawing (of buildings, &c.); 2. fair copy.
épurement (epyrmɑ̃), s.m. (lit. and fig.) Purifying; syn. ÉPURATION.
épurer (epyre), v.a. [f. *pur*] To refine, to clear, to clarify; (fig.) to purify, to purge; ~ *de l'or*, to refine gold; ~ *de l'eau*, to clarify water; **s'**~, v.pr. to be purified, to become pure; to grow refined (of style, &c.).
épurge (epyrʒ), s.f. [f. *purger*] (bot.) Spurge.
équarrir (ekarir), v.a. [f. OF *quarré*] 1. To square; to cut into squares; 2. to quarter; to dismember (meat, &c.).
équarrissage, équarrissement (ekarisaʒ, ekarismɑ̃), s.m. 1. Squaring; 2. quartering, dismembering; *clos d'*~, knacker's yard.
équarrisseur (ekarisœr), s.m. Knacker.
équarrissoir (ekariswar), s.m. 1. Knacker's yard; 2. knacker's knife.
équateur (ekwatœr), s.m. [f. L *aequare*] Equator.
équation (ekwa'sjɔ̃), s.f. [L *aequatio*] Equation.
équatorial, -e, (aux) (ekwatɔrjal), adj. Equatorial. ~, s.m. Equatorial.
équatori-en,-enne (ekwatɔrjɛ̃), adj. s.m.f. (Inhabitant) of the Equatorial region.
équerre (ekɛr), s.f. [LL *exquadra*] T-square, set-square, square rule; *à*

fausse ~, out of the square; bevel; *d'*~, square.
équerrer (ekɛre), v.a. To square; to bevel.
équestre (ekɛstr), adj. [L *equestris*] Equestrian.
équiangle (ekɥiɑ̃gl), adj. [L *aequus*+ Fr. *angle*] Equiangular.
équidistance (ekɥidistɑ̃s), s.f. Equal distance.
équidistant, -e (ekɥidistɑ̃), adj. [L *aequus*+Fr. *distant*] Equidistant.
équilatéral, -e, (aux) (ekɥilateral), adj. [f. L *aequus*+*latus*] Equilateral.
équilibrant, -e (ekilibrɑ̃), p. adj. Equilibrating.
équilibre (ekilibr), s.m. [L *aequus*+*libra*] Equilibrium, equipoise, poise, balance; *perdre l'*~, to lose one's balance; *l'*~ *des pouvoirs*, the balance of power; *mettre en* ~, to poise.
équilibrer (ekilibre), v.a. To balance, to poise, to equilibrate; (fig.) *esprit mal équilibré*, unbalanced mind.
équilibreur (ekilibrœr), s.m. Balancer. ~, adj. Balancing.
équilibriste (ekilibrist), s.m.f. Equilibrist.
équille (ekij), s.f. [OF *esquille*] (ichth.) Sand-eel.
équimultiple (ekɥimyltipl), s.m. Equimultiple.
équin, -e (ekɛ̃), adj. [L *equus*] Equine.
équinoxe (ekinɔks), s.m. [L *aequus*+*nox*] Equinox; *vents d'*~, equinoctial gales.
équinoxial, -e, (aux) (ekinɔksjal), adj. Equinoctial.
équipage (ekipaʒ), s.m. [f. *équiper*] **1.** Equipage, suite; **2.** carriage; *avoir* ~, to keep one's carriage; **3.** garb, turn-out, state, condition, plight; *arriver en piteux* ~, to arrive in a woful plight; **4.** (naut.) crew; *maître d'*~, boatswain; **5.** (mil.) *train des* ~*s*, baggage-train.
équipe (ekip), s.f. **1.** Gang (of workmen); *chef d'*~, foreman; **2.** (sport.) team; **3.** train (of barges, &c.).
équipée (ekipe), s.f. Freak, prank; escapade.
équipement (ekipmɑ̃), s.m. Equipment, accoutrement; outfit, kit.
équiper (ekipe), v.a. [f. ON *skipa*] To equip, to fit out; to man (a ship); **s'**~, v.pr. to equip oneself, to fit oneself out; to rig oneself out.
équipollence (ekipɔlɑ̃s), s.f. Equipollence.
équipollent, -e (ekipɔlɑ̃), adj. [L *aequipollens*] Equipollent.
équipoller (ekipɔle), v.a. [L *aeque*+ *pollere*] To render equipollent.
équisétacée (ekizetase), s.f. [f. L *equus*+ *seta*] (bot.) Equisetum.
équitable (ekitabl), adj. [f. *équité*] Equitable, fair; syn. JUSTE.
équitablement (ekitabləmɑ̃), adv. Equitably, fairly.
équitant, -e (ekitɑ̃), adj. [L *equitans*] (bot.) Equitant.
équitation (ekita'sjɔ̃), s.f. [L *equitatio*] Equitation, riding, horsemanship; *école d'*~, riding-school.
équité (ekite), s.f. [L *aequitas*] Equity; *avec* ~, equitably, fairly; syn. JUSTICE.
équivalence (ekivalɑ̃s), s.f. Equivalence.
équivalent, -e (ekivalɑ̃), adj. s.m. Equivalent.
équivaloir (ekivalwar), v.a. [L *aeque*+ *valere*] To be equivalent (*à*, to), to be tantamount (to).
équivoque (ekivɔk), adj. [L *aequus*+*vox*] Equivocal, ambiguous, suspicious, questionable, doubtful, uncertain; *phrase* ~, equivocal phrase; *vertu* ~, doubtful virtue. ~, s.f. Equivoque, ambiguity; equivocation; *user d'*~, to equivocate.
équivoquer (ekivɔke), v.n. To equivocate.
érable (erabl), s.m. [f. pop. L *acer arbor*] (bot.) Maple, maple-tree; ~ *à sucre*, sugar-maple; *sucre d'*~, maple-sugar.
éradication (eradika'sjɔ̃), s.f. [*é*+L *radix*] Eradication.
éraflement (erɑfləmɑ̃), s.m. Grazing, scratching.
érafler (erɑfle), v.a. [*é*+*rafler*] To graze, to scratch.
éraflure (erɑflyr), s.f. Graze, scratch.
éraillé, -e (erɑje), p. adj. **1.** Hoarse, husky (of the voice); **2.** frayed, puckered; **3.** bloodshot (of the eyes).
éraillement (erɑjmɑ̃), **1.** Fraying, unravelling; **2.** ectropion (of the eyes).
érailler (erɑje), v.a. [*é*+OF *roeillier*] To fray, to unravel; **s'**~, v.pr. **1.** to fray, to unravel; **2.** to become husky or hoarse (of the voice); **3.** to become bloodshot (of the eyes).
éraillure (erɑjyr), s.f. **1.** Fret, fraying; **2.** (of the skin) chafe, gall.
erbium (ɛrbjɔm), s.m. (chem.) Erbium.
erbue (ɛrby), s.f. See HERBUE.
ère (ɛr), s.f. [L *aera*] Era.
érectile (erɛktil), adj. Erectile.
erectilité (erɛktilite), s.f. Erectility.
érection (erɛksjɔ̃), s.f. [L *erectio*] Erection, erecting; establishment.
éreintant, -e (erɛ̃tɑ̃), p. adj. Exhausting; *travail* ~, killing work.
éreintement (erɛ̃tmɑ̃), s.m. Exhaustion; (fig.) slating.
éreinter (erɛ̃te), v.a. [f. *rein*] **1.** To exhaust, to knock up; *il est éreinté*, he is played out, or dog-tired; **2.** (archaic) to break the back of; **3.** (fam.) to thrash unmercifully; (fig.) to slate, to pull to pieces; (fam.) to slang; **s'**~, v.pr. **1.** to tire oneself out, to knock oneself up; to be knocked up; **2.** to toil and moil, to drudge.
éreinteur (erɛ̃tœr), s.m. adj. Savage critic.

érémitique (eremitik), adj. [f. L *eremita*] Eremitic.
érésipèle (erezipɛl), s.m. See ÉRYSIPÈLE.
éréthisme (eretism), s.m. [Gr. *erethismos*] Erethism.
erg (ɛrg), s.m. (phys.) Erg, ergon.
ergastule (ɛrgastyl), s.m. [L *ergastulum*] Slaves' prison.
ergo (ɛrgo), conj. [L wd] Ergo.
ergot (ɛrgo), s.m. [orig. unkn.] **1.** Cock-spur; spur; dew-claw (of a dog); *être sur ses ~s*, to be riding the high horse; (fig.) *se dresser sur ses ~s*, to bristle up, to fire or flare up; to strut like a bantam cock; **2.** (bot.) ergot, blight, smut.
ergotage, ergotement (ergɔtaʒ, ergɔtmɑ̃) s.m. **ergoterie** (ɛrgɔtri), s.f. (fam.) Cavilling, quibbling, quibble.
ergoté, -e (ɛrgɔte), adj. [f. *ergot*] **1.** Spurred; **2.** (bot.) blighted.
ergoter (ɛrgɔte), v.n. [L *ergo*] (fam.) To wrangle, to cavil, to chop logic.
ergoteu-r, -se (ɛrgɔtœr), adj. Cavilling. **~**, s.m.f. Caviller, wrangler.
ergotine (ɛrgɔtin), s.f. [f. *ergot*] (pharm.) Ergotine.
ergotisme (ɛrgɔtism), s.m. (obs.) **1.** Ergotism; **2.** (fig.) cavilling.
ériger (eriʒe), v.a. [L *erigere*] To erect, to raise, to rear; to set up, to institute; **s'~**, v.pr. to set up (for), to pose (as); (of buildings) to be erected or built.
érigéron (eriʒerɔ̃), s.m. (bot.) Erigeron, fleabane.
érigne, érine (eriɲ, erin), s.f. [f. L *aranea*] (surg.) Attolent, levator.
éristique (eristik), adj. s.f. [Gr. *eristikos*] Eristic.
ermin (ɛrmɛ̃), s.m. [f. *Arménien*] Customs-duty (in the Levant).
erminette (ɛrminɛt), s.f. Adze.
ermitage (ɛrmitaʒ), s.m. Hermitage.
ermite (ɛrmit), s.m. [L *eremita*] Hermit, eremite.
éroder (erɔde), v.a. [L *erodere*] To erode.
érosi-f, -ve (erozif), adj. Erosive.
érosion (erozjɔ̃), s.f. [L *erosio*] Erosion.
érotique (erɔtik), adj. [Gr. *erōs, -ōtos*] Erotic.
érotiquement (erɔtikmɑ̃), adv. Erotically.
érotisme (erɔtism), s.m. Erotism.
érotomane, érotomaniaque (erɔtɔman, erɔtɔmanjak), adj., s.m.f. Erotomaniac.
érotomanie (erɔtɔmani), s.f. Erotomania.
erpétologie, herpétologie (ɛrpetɔlɔʒi), s.f. [Gr. *herpeton+logos*] Herpetology.
erpétologique (ɛrpetɔlɔʒik), adj. Herpetological.
erpétologiste (ɛrpetɔlɔʒist), s.m. Herpetologist.
errant, -e (ɛrɑ̃), p. adj. [f. *errer*] Wandering, roving; vagrant, rambling; *chevalier ~*, knight-errant; *le juif errant*, the Wandering Jew.
erratique (ɛratik), adj. [f. L *errare*] Erratic.
erratum (ɛratɔm), s.m. (pl. *errata*) [L wd] Erratum.
erre (ɛr), s.f. [f. *errer*] Course, way; way (of a ship); (pl.) track (of a stag, &c.); (naut.) *aller à grand'~*, to go full speed, under full sail; (fig.) to do things on a large scale; *son ~ est coupée*, she is brought to; *aller sur les ~s de X*, to follow in X's footsteps or tracks; *revenir à ses anciennes ~s*, to return to one's old ways.
errements (ɛrmɑ̃), s.m.pl. (often pej.) Ways, habits; weaknesses.
errer (ɛre), v.n. [L *errare*] To wander, to stray; to range, to ramble; (fig.) to err, to go astray; to make mistakes; *~ ça et là*, to wander about, to ramble here and there.
erreur (ɛrœr), s.f. [L *error*] Error, mistake; (prov.) *~ n'est pas compte*, it is never too late to correct a misreckoning; *commettre* or *faire une ~*, to commit, or to make an error; *induire X en ~*, to mislead or to misinform X; *tirer X d'~*, to disabuse, to undeceive X; *sauf ~*, errors excepted; if I am not mistaken; *~!*, you are mistaken!, nay!; (pop). *y a pas d'~*, and no mistake!
erroné, -e (ɛrɔne), adj. [L *erroneus*] Erroneous, mistaken.
ers (ɛr), s.m. [L *ervum*] (bot.) Ers, bitter vetch.
ersatz (ɛrsats), s.m. [Germ. wd] Substitute.
erse (ɛrs), adj. [early Scotch form of *Irish*] Erse.
erse (ɛrs), s.f. **erseau,** (pl. **-x**) (ɛrso), s.m. Rope ring.
érubescence (erybɛsɑ̃s), s.f. Erubescence.
érubescent, -e (erybɛsɑ̃), adj. [L *erubescens*] Erubescent, reddening.
éructation (erykta'sjɔ̃), s.f. Eructation.
éructer (erykte), v.n. [L *eructare*] To eructate.
érudit, -e (erydi), adj. [L *eruditus*] Erudite, learned. **~**, s.m. Erudite scholar; syn. DOCTE, SAVANT.
érudition (erydisjɔ̃), s.f. [L *eruditio*] Erudition.
érugineu-x, -se (eryʒinø), adj. [f. L *aerugo*] Rust-coloured.
érupti-f, -ve (eryptif), adj. Eruptive.
éruption (erypsjɔ̃), s.f. [L *eruptio*] Eruption.
érysipèle (erizipɛl), s.m. [Gr. *erusipelas*] (pathol.) Erysipelas.
érythème (eritɛm), s.m. [Gr. *eruthēma*] (pathol.) Erythema.
ès (ɛs), prep. [f. *en les*] In, of; *bachelier ~ lettres*, bachelor of arts.
(s')esbigner (sɛsbiɲe), v.pr. (pop.) To cut and run.
esbroufe (ɛsbruf), s.f. (pop.) Swank; *faire de l'~*, to swank.

esbroufer (ɛsbrufe), v.n. (slang) To swank. ~, v.a. To swank for the benefit of, to astonish, to take advantage of; to 'do' (a person).
esbroufeur (ɛsbrufœr), s.m. (pop.) Swank, bouncer. ~, adj. Swanky, swanking.
escabeau (pl. **-x**) (ɛscabo), s.m. **escabelle** (ɛskabɛl), s.f. [L *scabellum*] Stool.
escadre (ɛskadr), s.f. [It. *squadra*] Squadron; *chef d'~*, commodore.
escadrille (ɛskadrij), s.f. Flotilla, small squadron; air squadron.
escadron (ɛskadrɔ̃), s.m. [It. *squadrone*] (mil.) Squadron (of horse); *chef d'~*, major.
escadronner (ɛskadrɔne), v.n. (obs.) To manœuvre in squadrons.
escalade (ɛskalad), s.f. [It. *scalata*] Scaling, escalade.
escalader (ɛskalade), v.a. To scale.
escale (ɛskal), s.f. [It. *scala*] **1.** Calling-place, port; *faire ~ à un port*, to touch or to call at a port; to put into port; **2.** (aeron.) landing.
escalier (ɛskalje), s.m. [L *scalaria*] Staircase, stairs, flight of stairs (interior), or steps (exterior); ~ *tournant*, winding staircase; ~ *en colimaçon*, spiral staircase; (naut.) ~ *de commandement*, accommodation ladder; (fig.) *esprit de l'~*, esprit d'escalier, wit that comes too late; *avoir l'esprit de l'~*, to be wise after the event; ~ *dérobé*, secret staircase; ~ *roulant*, moving staircase, escalator; *cage d'~*, well of the stairs, staircase; ~ *de service*, backstairs, tradesmen's entrance.
escalin (ɛskalɛ̃), s.m. [MDutch *schelling*] Dutch sixpenny piece.
escalope (ɛskalɔp), s.f. [OF *escaloppe*] Collop, veal cutlet.
escamotage (ɛskamɔtaʒ), s.m. Juggling, sleight of hand, legerdemain; filching; suppressing, withholding or withdrawing from publication or notice.
escamote (ɛskamɔt), s.f. Juggler's ball.
escamoter (ɛskamɔte), v.a. [Span. *escamotar*] **1.** To conjure away; **2.** to pilfer, to make away with; **3.** to hurry over; ~ *son travail*, to do one's work just anyhow; **4.** (fig.) to trick out of, to get out of; ~ *les difficultés*, to rush one's fences; ~ *une difficulté*, to slur over a difficulty.
escamoteu-r, -se (ɛskamɔtœr), s.m.f. **1.** Juggler; **2.** fleecer, pilferer.
escamper (ɛskɑ̃pe), v.n. (obs.) [It. *scampare*] To decamp, to scamper away.
escampette (ɛskɑ̃pɛt), s.f. [f. *escamper*] (pop.) *Prendre la poudre d'~*, to show a clean pair of heels.
escapade (ɛskapad), s.f. [It. *scappata*] Escapade, prank, freak.
escape (ɛskap), s.f. [L *scapus*] (arch.) Scape.
escarbille (ɛskarbij), s.f. [f. L *carbo*] Cinder, clinker.
escarbot (ɛskarbo), s.m. [L *scarabaeus*] (ent.) Beetle.
escarboucle (ɛskarbukl), s.f. [L *carbunculus*] Carbuncle.
escarcelle (ɛskarsɛl), s.f. [It. *scarsella*] Purse, wallet, money-bag.
escargot (ɛskargo), s.m. [Provenç. *escargol*] Snail; *escalier en ~*, spiral staircase; *aller comme un ~*, to go at a snail's pace.
escargotière (ɛskargɔtjɛr), s.f. Snail-farm.
escarmouche (ɛskarmuʃ), s.f. [It. *scaramuccia*] Skirmish.
escarmoucher (ɛskarmuʃe), v.n. To skirmish.
escarmoucheur (ɛskarmuʃœr), s.m. Skirmisher.
escarole, scarole (ɛskarɔl, skarɔl), s.f. [It. *scariola*] Endive, Batavian endive. ⚠ *Endive* (Fr. wd) = blanched chicory.
escarotique, escharotique (ɛskarɔtik), adj. s.m. Caustic.
escarpe[1] (ɛskarp), s.f. [It. *scarpa*] (fort.) Scarp, escarp.
escarpe[2] (ɛskarp), s.m. Assassin; murderous thief, ruffian.
escarpé, -e (ɛskarpe), p. adj. Steep, precipitous, scarped, abrupt.
escarpement (ɛskarpəmɑ̃), s.m. Escarpment, steep face or slope, steepness.
escarper (ɛskarpe), v.a. [f. *escarpe*] (fort.) To escarp, to counterscarp.
escarpin (ɛskarpɛ̃), s.m. [It. *scarpino*] (pl.) Pumps; dancing-slippers.
escarpolette (ɛskarpɔlɛt), s.f. [It. *scarpoletta*] Swing.
escarre, eschare (ɛskar), s.f. **1.** [Gr. *eskhara*] (med.) Slough, scab; **2.** [LL *exquadra*] (herald.) compartment of shield (a square enclosing one corner).
escarrifier (ɛskarifje), v.a. To form a scab.
eschatologie (ɛskatɔlɔʒi), s.f. [Gr. *eskhatos*+*logos*] Eschatology.
esche (ɛʃ), s.f. See AICHE.
escient (ɛsjɑ̃), s.m. [f. L *sciens*] Knowledge; *à bon ~*, *à son ~*, deliberately, knowingly, intentionally, consciously.
(s')esclaffer (sɛsklafe), v.pr. To roar with laughter, to guffaw.
esclandre (ɛsklɑ̃dr), s.m. [LL *scandalum*] Esclandre, scandal, scene; to-do; *faire un ~*, to make a scene; to give rise to scandal.
esclavage (ɛsklavaʒ), s.m. Slavery, thraldom, bondage.
esclavagiste (ɛsklavaʒist), s.m. adj. (That is a) supporter of slavery.
esclave (ɛsklav), s.m.f. Slave, bondman, bondmaid, thrall; drudge; *âme d'~*, slavish disposition. ~adj. Slavish; *être ~ de sa*

parole, to be bound by one's word; to be absolutely reliable.
esclavon, -ne (ɛsklavɔ̃), adj. s.m.f. Slavonian.
escobar (ɛskɔbar), s.m. [Span. prop. n. *Escobar y Mendoza*] Shuffler, quibbler, prevaricator, casuist.
escobarder (ɛskɔbarde), v.n. To equivocate, to prevaricate, to shuffle, to quibble.
escobarderie (ɛskɔbardəri), s.f. Prevarication, shuffling, equivocation; mental reservation.
escoffion (ɛskɔfjɔ̃), s.m. [It. *scoffione*] (obs.) Lace cap, mutch.
escogriffe (ɛskɔgrif), s.m. **1.** (obs.) Sharper; shark; **2.** ungainly, lanky fellow.
escomptable (ɛskɔ̃tabl), adj. Discountable.
escompte (ɛskɔ̃t), s.m. [It. *sconto*] Discount; *à l'~*, at a discount; *faire l'~*, to discount bills.
escompter (ɛskɔ̃te), v.a. To discount, to pay in cash before date; (fig.) to anticipate, to forestall.
escompteur (ɛskɔ̃tœr), s.m. Discounter.
escopette (ɛskopɛt), s.f. [It. *schioppetto*] Carbine (15th-16th. cent.); blunderbuss.
escorte (ɛskɔrt), s.f. [It. *scorta*] Escort; (nav.) convoy; *bateau d'~*, convoy-ship; (fig.) train, retinue; *l'ambition et son ~ de vices*, ambition and the vices it brings in its train.
escorter (ɛskɔrte), v.a. To escort, to convoy; (fig.) to escort, to accompany, to attend; *faire ~*, to send an escort with.
escot (ɛsko), s.m. [for *ascot*, f. *Aerschot*, town of Brabant] Kind of serge.
escouade (ɛskwad), s.f. [f. *escadre*] **1.** (mil.) Squad; **2.** gang.
escourgée, écourgée (ɛskurʒe, ekurʒe), [L *excoriare*] Scourge, lash; cat-o'-nine-tails.
escourgeon, écourgeon (ɛskurʒɔ̃, ekurʒɔ̃), s.m. [f. LL *scario*] (agric.) Winter barley.
escousse (ɛskus), s.f. (rare) [L *excutere*] Spring, run, start; *prendre son ~*, to take off.
escrime (ɛskrim), s.f. [OHG *skirmjan*] Fencing; *salle d'~*, fencing-school.
escrimer (ɛskrime), v.n. To fence; **s'~**, v.pr. (fig.) to try hard (*à*, to), to have a turn (at); to apply oneself, to endeavour, to peg away at.
escrimeur (ɛskrimœr), s.m. Fencer.
escroc (ɛskro), s.m. [It. *scrocco*] Swindler.
escroquer (ɛskrɔke), v.a. [It. *scroccare*] To steal; to sponge, (slang) to scrounge; *~ un dîner*, to scrounge one's dinner.
escroquerie (ɛskrɔkri), s.f. Swindling, cheating.
escroqueu-r, -se (ɛskrɔkœr), s.m.f. (rare) Swindler; scrounger.
esculape (ɛskylap), s.m. (iron.) Aesculapius, clever physician.
ésotérique (ezɔterik), adj. [Gr. *esōterikos*] Esoteric.
espace (ɛspɑs), s.m. [L *spatium*] **1.** Space, room; **2.** space, duration, time; **3.** (mus.) interval. ~ s.f. (print.) Space.
espacement (ɛspɑsmɑ̃), s.m. **1.** Interval, interspace; **2.** (print.) spacing.
espacer (ɛspɑse), v.a. **1.** To leave a space between, to spread out; **2.** to leave an interval between; *des visites espacées*, rare visits; **3.** (print.) to space.
espadon (ɛspadɔ̃), s.m. [It. *spadone*] **1.** Two-handed sword; **2.** sword-fish.
espadrille (ɛspadrij), s.f. [Provenç. *espardillo*] Bathing-shoe, sand-shoe.
espagnol, -e (ɛspaɲɔl), adj. Spanish. **~**, s.m.f. Spaniard. **~**, s.m. Spanish (language).
espagnolette (ɛspaɲɔlɛt), s.f. French-window fastener.
espalier (ɛspalje), s.m. [It. *spalliera*] Espalier.
espar, espart, épart (ɛspar, epar), s.m. [Germ. *sparren*] (naut., artill.) Spar.
esparcet, éparcet (ɛsparsɛ, eparsɛ), s.m. **esparcette, éparcette** (ɛsparsɛt, eparsɛt) s.f. (bot.) Sainfoin.
espargoute (ɛspargut), s.f. (bot.) Spurry.
espèce (ɛspɛs), s.f. [L *species*] **1.** Species, kind, sort; *l'~ humaine*, mankind, (scient.) the human species; *une ~ de* (syn. UNE SORTE DE), a sort of; (pej.) *c'est une ~ de fou*, he's more or less crazy; (fam.) *~ d'idiot!*, you blinking idiot!; **2.** (pl.) (fin.) specie; *~s sonnantes*, hard cash; *payer en ~s*, to pay in specie or in cash; **3.** (law) case in point; *dans l'~*, in this case; **4.** (pl.) (theol.) elements; *les deux ~s*, the bread and the wine.
espérable (ɛsperabl), adj. To be hoped.
espérance (ɛsperɑ̃s), s.f. [f. *espérer*] Hope, expectation, trust; *dans l'~ de*, in the expectation of; *répondre à ses ~s*, to come up to expectation; *se nourrir d'~*, to live on hope; *c'est toute mon ~*, I hope and trust it will be so; *~s*, (pl.) hopes, expectations; *grandes ~s*, great expectations; *oncle à ~s*, rich uncle; syn. ESPOIR.
espérant, -e (ɛsperɑ̃), p. adj. Hoping, trusting.
espérantiste (ɛsperɑ̃tist), adj. s.m.f. Esperantist.
espéranto (ɛsperɑ̃to), s.m. [neol., pen-name of the inventor] Esperanto (language).
espérer (ɛspere), v.a. [L *sperare*] To hope, to hope for; to expect; (iron.) *je l'espère bien!*, I should hope so, indeed!; **~**, v.n. to be hopeful, to rely on; *~ en*, to put one's trust in, to rely on.
espiègle (ɛspjɛgl), adj. [Germ. prop. n.

Eulenspiegel] Mischievous, up to mischief (of children); roguish, prankish, waggish, freakish; *que cet enfant est ~ !*, that child is always up to mischief! ~, s.m. Young imp, mischievous imp (of children); wag, madcap, practical joker.

espièglerie (ɛspjɛgləri), s.f. Mischievousness; waggery; prank, freak, roguish trick, joke.

espingole (ɛspɛ̃gol), s.f. [etym. dub.] Blunderbuss.

espion, -ne (ɛspjɔ̃), s.m.f. [It. *spione*] **1.** Spy; **2.** (racing) tout.

espionnage (ɛspjonaʒ), s.m. Spying, espionage, spy system.

espionner (ɛspjone), v.a.n. To spy upon, to pry into; to spy, to play the spy.

esplanade (ɛsplanad), s.f. [It. *spianata*] Esplanade, parade.

espoir (ɛspwar), s.m. [f. *espérer*] **1.** Hope; *sans ~*, hopeless; *avoir l'~ de*, to be in hopes of; **2.** hope (person, thing, that hope centres in); syn. ESPÉRANCE.

esponton (ɛspɔ̃tɔ̃), s.m. [It. *spuntone*] Spontoon, half-pike.

espringale (ɛsprɛ̃gal), s.f. [f. Germ. *springen*] (medieval) Ballista, sling.

esprit (ɛspri), s.m. [L *spiritus*] **1.** Spirit, ghost; inspiration; vital principle; *le Saint ~*, the Holy Ghost; *l'~ du Seigneur*, the spirit of the Lord; *rendre l'~*, to give up the ghost; *croire aux ~s*, to believe in ghosts or spirits; *~ follet*, sprite, elf, leprechaun, goblin; *~ malin*, fiend, evil spirit; *~ familier*, familiar spirit; **2.** spirit, mind; understanding; opinion; *l'~ humain*, the human mind or understanding; *~ de corps*, esprit de corps, public spirit; fraternity, devotion to one's society; *~ de parti*, party spirit; *~ public*, public interest, the mind of the public; (⚠ not 'public spirit'); *avoir l'~ sain*, to be of sound mind; *par ~ de contradiction*, from a spirit of contradiction, out of contrariness, from pure contrariness; *avoir l'~ tendu*, to be in a state of mental tension; *avoir l'~ en éveil*, to be quick-witted; to be on one's guard; *cultiver l'~*, to cultivate the mind; *avoir l'~ de travers*, to have a kink in one's mind; *avoir l'~ bien fait*, to have a good all-round intelligence; *~ dérangé*, disordered mind; *~ de suite*, consistency; perseverance; *~ borné*, narrow mind, narrow-minded person; *les grands ~s se rencontrent*, great minds think alike; *remettre dans l'~ de* (or *à*), to remind; *ne pas avoir l'~ tranquille*, to be uneasy in one's mind; *rassurer les ~s*, to set people's minds at rest; *un homme d'~*, a man of parts, a witty and reasonable man; *il m'est venu dans l'~*, it crossed my mind; *~ fort*, free-thinker, self-opinionated man; *~ fécond*, fertile mind; *~ sec*, barren intellect; *présence, absence d'~*, presence, absence of mind; *être bien dans l'~ de X*, to stand well in X's opinion; *se mettre bien dans l'~ de X*, to ingratiate oneself with X; *~ d'ordre*, orderliness; (fig.) *aliéner l'~ de quelqu'un*, to lose some one's favour; *rappeler à l'~*, to call to mind; **3.** character, disposition, spirit; *~ remuant*, restless disposition or mind; *avoir l'~ remuant*, to be active-minded, to have a restless mind; *tour d'~*, turn of mind, bent; *l'~ du siècle*, the spirit of the age; *avoir l'~ du commerce*, to have the business instinct; **4.** wit; *~ de l'escalier*, belated wit; *avoir de l'~*, to be witty; *faire de l'~*, to play the wit; *il a de l'~ jusqu'au bout des ongles*, he is as witty as they're made, he is devilish witty; *l'~ court les rues*, wit is as common as water; *un bel ~*, a wit; *il a plus d'~ qu'il n'est gros*, he is as full of wit as an egg is full of meat; **5.** meaning, sense; *saisir l'~ d'un auteur*, to enter into, or to grasp, an author's meaning; *entrer dans l'~ de son rôle*, to enter into the spirit of one's part; **6.** (usually pl. in French), wits, senses; *reprendre ses ~s*, to recover one's senses, to come to oneself; *où avait-il l'~ quand?* where were his wits when?; *avoir le bon ~ de*, to have the good sense to; *recueillir ses ~s*, to collect one's wits; **7.** (chem.) spirit, spirits; *~ de sel*, spirits of salt; *~-de-vin*, alcohol; spirits of wine (see ALCOOL); *~ de bois*, methylated spirit; **8.** (gram.) *~ rude*, aspiration mark (in Greek language), spiritus asper, rough breathing; *~ doux*, mark on inaspirate vowels; spiritus lenis, smooth breathing.

esquicher (ɛskiʃe), v.n. (obs.) **s'esquicher**, v.pr. (obs.) **1.** (cards) To throw away a trick intentionally; **2.** (fig.) to sit on the fence.

esquif (ɛskif), s.m. [It. *schifo*] (naut.) Skiff.

esquille (ɛskij), s.f. [L *schidia*] Splinter (of bone).

esquilleu-x, -se (ɛskijø), adj. Splintered.

esquinancie (ɛskinɑ̃si), s.f. [Gr. *kunagkhē*] (pathol.) Quinsy.

esquinter (ɛskɛ̃te), v.a. [Provenç. orig.] (pop.) See syn. ÉREINTER.

esquisse (ɛskis), s.f. [It. *schizzo*] Sketch, rough draft; outline, plan (of a book); (literature) survey; syn. ÉBAUCHE.

esquisser (ɛskise), v.a. To sketch, to outline; *~ une révérence*, to make a hurried bow; to bob a curtsey; syn. ÉBAUCHER.

esquiver (ɛskive), v.a. [It. *schivare*] To elude, to evade; to dodge; *~ une difficulté*, to get round a difficulty; *s'~*, v. pr. to slip off; (fam.) to skedaddle.

essai (ɛsɛ), s.m. [f. *essayer*] **1.** Trial, test;

assay, assaying; *faire l'~ de*, to make a trial of, to test; *faire l'~ d'or*, to assay gold; *prendre à l'~*, to take on trial; *faites-en l'~*, try it; **2.** essay; attempt, endeavour; *ce n'est pas son coup d'~*, that's not his first attempt; **3.** (Lit.) essay.

essaim (ɛsɛ̃), s.m. [L *examen*] Swarm (also fig.).

essaimage (ɛsɛmaʒ), s.m. Swarming, swarming-season.

essaimer (ɛsɛme), v.n. [f. *essaim*] To swarm; (fig.) to emigrate.

essanger (ɛsɑ̃ʒe), v.a. [L *exsalicare*] To soak (dirty linen, &c.).

essarder (ɛsarde), v.a. (obs.) [OF *essardre*, f. *ardre*] **1.** To burn; **2.** (naut.) to swab.

essarter (ɛsarte), v.a. To clear (land); to grub up.

essarts (ɛsar), s.m.pl. [L *exsartum*] Newly-cleared land.

essayage (ɛsɛjaʒ), s.m. **1.** Trying-on, fitting (of clothes); **2.** trying, proving, testing.

essayer (ɛsɛje), v.a. [L *exagium*] **1.** To try, to attempt, to essay; *~ une chose*, to try a thing; *~ de faire une chose*, to try to do a thing; **2.** to try on; *~ une robe*, to try on a dress, to be fitted for a dress; **3.** to make a trial of; **4.** to assay; *~ de l'or*, to assay gold; *~*, v.n. to try (*de*, to), to make an attempt (to); *~ de marcher*, to try to walk; **s'~**, v.pr. to try one's hand (*à*, at), to try one's strength or skill.

essayerie (ɛsɛjri), s.f. Assay-office.

essayeu-r, -se (ɛsɛjœr), s.m.f. **1.** Fitter; **2.** assayer.

essayiste (ɛsɛjist), s.m.f. Essayist.

esse (ɛs), s.f. [from the letter *S*] **1.** S-shaped object; **2.** linch-pin (of axle).

essence (ɛsɑ̃s), s.f. [L *essentia*] **1.** Essence; *par ~*, by its very nature; essentially; **2.** petrol; (in America) gasoline; (techn. slang) juice; (⚠ French *essence* = petrol, and French *pétrole* = petroleum, paraffin oil, paraffin; and French *paraffine* = (solid) paraffin); *bidon d'~*, petrol-can; *réservoir à ~*, petrol-tank; *~ minérale*, benzoline; *~ de térébenthine*, spirits of turpentine; **3.** (forestry) species.

essentiel, -le (ɛsɑ̃sjɛl), adj. Essential; *huile ~le*, essential oil. *~*, s.m. Essential, main or chief point.

essentiellement (ɛsɑ̃sjɛlmɑ̃), adv. Essentially.

esseulé, -e (ɛsœle), adj. [f. *seul*] Solitary, left alone, lonely.

essieu (pl. **-x**) (ɛsjø), s.m. [L *axis*] Axle-tree; spindle; pin (of a block); *boîte d'~*, axle-sleeve; axle-box; *écartement des ~x*, wheel-base, axle-base; *rupture d'~*, fracture of an axle.

essor (ɛsɔr), s.m. [f. *essorer*] Flight, soaring; (fig.) impulse, impetus, flight; swing, play; *donner de l'~ à*, to give wings to; *l'~ du génie*, the soaring of genius; *prendre son ~*, to get well started, to gather way; to take one's flight; progress; *l'~ rapide d'une ville*, the rapid growth of a city.

essorage (ɛsɔraʒ), s.m. Drying, hanging-out (of linen).

essorant, -e (ɛsɔrɑ̃), adj. (herald.) Soaring.

essorer (ɛsɔre), v.a. [L *ex+aura*] To dry (linen), to hang out to dry.

essoreuse (ɛsɔrøz), s.f. **1.** Mangle, wringer; **2.** (mech.) drying-machine.

essoriller (ɛsɔrije), v.a. [f. *oreille*] To crop the ears of.

essouchement (ɛsuʃmɑ̃), s.m. Clearing, digging up.

essoucher (ɛsuʃe), v.a. [f. *souche*] To dig up, to grub up (roots).

essoufflement (ɛsufləmɑ̃), s.m. Want of breath, panting, breathlessness.

essouffler (ɛsufle), v.a. [*es+souffler*] To put out of breath, to wind; *être tout essoufflé*, to be all out of breath; to be blown; **s'~**, v.pr. to get out of breath, to be out of breath.

essuie-main, essuie-mains (ɛsɥimɛ̃), s.m. (pl. invar.) [f. *essuyer+main*] (Hand-)towel.

essuie-plume (ɛsɥiplym), s.m. (pl. invar.) Pen-wiper.

essuyage (ɛsɥijaʒ), s.m. Dusting; wiping.

essuyer (ɛsɥije), v.a. [L *exsuccare*] **1.** To dust; to wipe, to dry; to wipe off, up, dry, or away; **2.** (fig.) to endure, to bear, to undergo, to meet with; *~ un affront*, to swallow an insult; *~ le feu de l'ennemi*, to bear the brunt of the enemy's fire; *~ un refus* or *un revers*, to meet with a check; *~ les larmes de X*, to console X; (fig.) *~ les plâtres*, to move in before the plaster is dry; *essuyez vos pieds, s.v.p.*, rub your shoes, please; **s'~**, v.pr. to wipe one's face, hands, &c.

essuyeu-r, -se (ɛsɥijœr), s.m.f. Drier, wiper, duster (person).

est (ɛst), s.m. [OE *eastan*] East; *à l'~* or *vers l'~*, to the east or eastwards; *vent d'~*, east or easterly wind; syn. ORIENT, LEVANT.

estacade (ɛstakad), s.f. [It. *steccata*, stake] Boom, jetty, breakwater.

estafette (ɛstafɛt), s.f. [It. *staffetta*] (mil.) Estafette, express messenger.

estafier (ɛstafje), s.m. [It. *staffiere*] (pej.) Armed attendant, hired ruffian; flunkey, lanky footman; armed lackey.

estafilade (ɛstafilad), s.f. [It. *staffilata*] **1.** Gash, cut; **2.** slash, rent (in clothing).

estafilader (ɛstafilade), v.a. To cut, to gash, to slash.

estagnon (ɛstaɲɔ̃), s.m. Can (for olive oil, espec. in South of France).

---

a, mal, latte; ɑ, pas; ɑ̃, *enfant*; e, fée; ɛ, père, nette; ɛ̃, *vin*, *pain*; ə, premier; g, *dogue*, *gale*; h, *héros*; i, *finir*; j, *yeux*, viens, b*aill*er; k, croire; ɲ, oi*gn*on; o, *pause*, dose;

estame (ɛstam), s.f. [L *stamen*] Worsted, knitted wool.
estaminet (ɛstaminɛ), s.m. [Walloon *staminet*] Tap-room; small beer-house, tavern; (fig. fam.) *pilier d'~*, tavern haunter.
estampage (ɛstɑ̃paʒ), s.m. Stamping (of metal, &c.).
estampe (ɛstɑ̃p), s.f. **1.** Print, engraving; *magasin d'~s*, print-shop; **2.** stamp, stamping-machine, puncher.
estamper (ɛstɑ̃pe), v.a. [Teutonic orig.] **1.** To engrave; **2.** to stamp; **3.** (slang) to rook, to have, to fleece, to overcharge.
estampeur (ɛstɑ̃pœr), s.m. **1.** Engraver; **2.** stamping-machine.
estampillage (ɛstɑ̃pijaʒ), s.m. Stamping, marking.
estampille (ɛstɑ̃pij), s.f. [Span. *estampilla*] Stamp, mark; trade-mark; (fig.) *donner son ~ à une entreprise*, to give one's sanction to an enterprise.
estampiller (ɛstɑ̃pije), v.a. To stamp, to mark.
ester (ɛste), v.n. [L *stare*] To bring an action, to appear in court, to plead.
estère (ɛstɛr), s.f. [Span. *estera*] Straw or reed mat.
esterlin (ɛstɛrlɛ̃), s.m. [12th-century Fr. form of Engl. *sterling*] Ancient gold coin; see STERLING.
esthète (ɛstɛt), s.m.f. [Gr. *aisthētēs*] Aesthete.
esthéticien, -ne (ɛstetisjɛ̃), s.m.f. Aesthetician.
esthétique (ɛstetik), s.f. Aesthetics. ~, adj. Aesthetic, aesthetical.
esthétiquement (ɛstetikmɑ̃), adv. Aesthetically.
esthonien, -ne (ɛstɔnjɛ̃), adj. s.m.f. Esthonian.
estimable (ɛstimabl), adj. Estimable.
estimat-eur, -rice (ɛstimatœr), s.m.f. Valuer; appraiser.
estimati-f, -ve (ɛstimatif), adj. Estimative; *dresser un devis ~*, to make an estimate.
estimation (ɛstima'sjɔ̃), s.f. Estimation, appraising; *faire une ~ de*, to estimate, to appraise.
estimatoire (ɛstimatwar), adj. Estimative.
estime (ɛstim), s.f. [f. *estimer*] Esteem, regard; estimation; (naut.) reckoning; *être en grande ~*, to be held in high esteem.
estimer (ɛstime), v.a.n. [L *aestimare*] To estimate, to value; to rate, to assess; (fig.) to esteem, to regard, to prize; to consider, to deem; *trop ~*, to overrate.
estivage[1] (ɛstivaʒ), s.m. (of cattle) Summering in the mountains.
estivage[2] (ɛstivaʒ), s.m. (naut.) Packing or stowing of goods.
estival, -e, (aux) (ɛstival), adj. Aestival, summer; *une robe ~e*, a summer dress.
estivandier (ɛstivɑ̃dje), s.m. Harvester, harvest-labourer.
estivation (ɛstiva'sjɔ̃), s.f. [f. L *aestas*] Aestivation.
estive (ɛstiv), s.f. [f. *estiver*] Trimming, stowing of cargo.
estiver[1] (ɛstive), v.n. [L *aestivare*] To pass the summer; ~, v.a. to drive (flocks) up the mountains for the summer.
estiver[2] (ɛstive), v.a. [L *stipare*] (naut.) To stow, to trim.
estoc (ɛstɔk), s.m. [It. *stocco*] (archaic) Tuck; small sword (15th–16th century); *frapper d'~*, to strike with the point; *frapper d'~ et de taille*, to cut and thrust, to lay about one; **2.** stump, stock (of trees); *couper à blanc ~*, to cut down at the root.
estocade (ɛstɔkad), s.f. [It. *stoccata*] Stoccado, thrust, lunge; (fig.) unexpected attack.
estomac (ɛstɔma), s.m. [L *stomachus*] Stomach; breast, chest; *le creux de l'~*, the pit of the stomach; *avoir l'~ creux*, to feel empty or hungry; *avoir l'~ dans les talons*, to be as hungry as a hunter; *mal à l'~*, stomach-ache; *avoir de l'~*, to have pluck or staying-power; (fam.) to be able to stick it.
estomaquer (ɛstɔmake), v.a. (fig.) To bowl over (with surprise); *s'~*, v.pr. **1.** (colloq.) to take offence, to be annoyed or nettled; *il s'est estomaqué*, he was put out; **2.** (rare) to exhaust oneself by speaking.
estompe (ɛstɔ̃p), s.f. [etym. dub.] **1.** (drawing) Stump; **2.** stump-drawing.
estomper (ɛstɔ̃pe), v.a. To stump, to shade off, to blur; (fig.) to tone down (a narrative, &c.).
estouffade (ɛstufad), s.f. (cook.) Dish of meat stewed in a closed saucepan; see ÉTOUFFÉE.
estourbir (ɛsturbir) v.a. (slang) To kill.
estrade (ɛstrad), s.f. Platform, stand, dais, stage; *battre l'~*, (mil.) to scout; to go marauding.
estragon (ɛstragɔ̃), s.m. [Gr. *drakontion*] (bot.) Tarragon.
estramaçon (ɛstramasɔ̃), s.m. [It. *stramazzone*] Two-edged sword.
estran, estrand (ɛstrɑ̃), s.m. [Engl. *strand*] Strand.
estrapade (ɛstrapad), s.f. [It. *strappata*] Strappado.
estrapader (ɛstrapade), v.a. To strappado; to torture.
estrapasser (ɛstrapase), v.a. [It. *strapazzare*] To override, to overwork (a horse in manège).
estrope (ɛstrɔp), s.f. [L *stroppus*] (naut.) Strop.

estropié, -e (ɛstrɔpje), p. adj. Crippled; disabled. ~ s.m.f. Cripple; disabled person.

estropier (ɛstrɔpje), v.a. [It. *stroppiare*] To cripple, to maim, to disable; (fig.) to mutilate, to distort, to mangle, to murder (a language, a verse, a name, &c.).

estuaire (ɛstɥɛr), s.m. [L *aestuarium*] Estuary.

esturgeon (ɛstyrʒɔ̃), s.m. [OHG *sturio*] (ichth.) Sturgeon.

et (e), conj. [L wd] And; ~ *vous* ~ *moi*, both you and I.

êta (ɛta), s.m. [Gr. wd] Eta.

établage (etablaʒ), s.m. [f. *étable*] Stabling.

étable[1] (etabl), s.f. [L *stabulum*] Stable; stall; cattle-shed; cow-house; ~ *à cochons*, pigsty; ~ *à moutons*, sheep-house.

étable[2] (etabl), s.m. See syn. ÉTRAVE, s.f.

établer (etable), v.a. To stable, to put up (horses, &c.).

établi (etabli), s.m. [f. *établir*] Carpenter's, joiner's, or tailor's bench.

établir (etablir), v.a. [L *stabilire*] To establish; to institute, to found; to settle, to set up; to set up in business; to assert, to lay down (a law, a principle); to prove; to strike (a balance); to impose (a tax); **s'~**, v.pr. to establish oneself, to take up one's residence; to settle down (usually in reference to marriage); to set up in business, to set up for oneself.

établissement (etablismɑ̃), s.m. **1.** Establishment; premises; *dans l'~*, on the premises; **2.** establishment, foundation; **3.** setting up in business; settlement, marriage settlement; **4.** proving, showing; **5.** imposition (of taxes); **6.** trading-post, trading-centre; *les ~s français dans l'Inde*, the French trading-posts in India.

étage (etaʒ), s.m. [f. LL *staticum*] **1.** Stor(e)y, floor; flight (of stairs); (fig.) stage; *menton à double ~*, double chin; *sot à triple ~*, consummate ass; *demeurer au troisième ~*, to live on the third floor; *monter trois ~s*, to go up three flights; **2.** degree, class, rank; *de bas ~*, of low degree, of low birth.

étagement (etaʒmɑ̃), s.m. Tiers (pl.); successive belts (pl.) (of cultivation).

étager (etaʒe), v.a. To arrange in tiers; **s'~** v.pr. to rise in tiers, to rise tier upon tier, to rise gradually one above another.

étagère (etaʒɛr), s.f. What-not; set of shelves.

étai (etɛ), s.m. [etym. dub.] Stay, shore, prop, strut; (fig.) support, stay; ~ *du grand mât*, mainstay.

étaim (etɛ̃), s.m. [L *stamen*] Fine carded wool.

étain (etɛ̃), s.m. [L *stannum*] Tin; pewter; tin-plate; *papier d'~*, tinfoil.

étainier (etɛnje), s.m. Pewter-smith; pewter merchant.

étal (etal), s.m. [OHG *stal*] Butcher's stall; butcher's shop.

étalage (etalaʒ), s.m. **1.** Display, exposure of goods for sale; window-display; goods exposed for sale; shop-window, frontage; *vol à l'~*, shop-lifting; (fig.) display, show, showing off; *faire ~ de son esprit*, to parade one's wit; **2.** stall-tax.

étalager (etalaʒe), v.a. To dress (windows), to display, to lay out (goods).

étalagiste (etalaʒist), s.m.f. **1.** Window-dresser; **2.** stall-keeper.

étale (etal), adj. [f. *étaler*] (naut.) Slack, dead; *navire ~*, ship hove to; *mer ~*, slack water. ~, s.m. Slack water.

étalement (etalmɑ̃), s.m. Displaying; parading.

étaler (etale), v.a. [f. *étal*] To expose for sale; to spread out, to unfold; ~ *une carte*, to spread out a map; (cards) to show (one's hand); (fig.) to display, to parade, to show off; ~ *ses richesses*, to parade one's wealth; **s'~**, v.pr. **1.** to stretch oneself out, to sprawl; **2.** (fam.) to measure one's length, to fall down at full length, to come a cropper.

étali-er, -ère (etalje), s.m.f. Journeyman butcher; hawking butcher.

étalinguer (etalɛ̃ge), v.a. (naut.) To clinch, to bend.

étalingure (etalɛ̃gyr), s.f. (naut.) Bend, clinch.

étalon[1] (etalɔ̃), s.m. [OF *estel*] Standard (of weights and measures); *d'~*, standard.

étalon[2] (etalɔ̃), s.m. [OHG *stal*] Stallion; ~ *de haras*, stud-horse.

étalonner (etalɔne), v.a. To stamp, to gauge.

étalonneur (etalɔnœr), s.m. Gauger, inspector of weights and measures.

étamage (etamaʒ), s.m. Plating, tinning, silvering, quicksilvering.

étambot (etɑ̃bo), s.m. [Scand. orig.] (naut.) Stern-post.

étambrai (etɑ̃brɛ), s.m. [orig. dub.] (naut.) Partners (pl.).

étamer (etame), v.a. [f. *étaim*] To plate, to tin, to quicksilver.

étameur (etamœr), s.m. Tinner, silverer; (colloq.) tinman, tinker.

étamine[1] (etamin), s.f. [f. *étaim*] **1.** Curtain-muslin; thin woollen material; **2.** (naut.) bunting; **3.** bolting-cloth, sieve; (fig.) *passer par l'~*, to sift, to go over with a comb.

étamine[2] (etamin), s.f. [L *stamen*] (bot.) Stamen.

étampe (etɑ̃p), s.f. **1.** Stamper; **2.** punching-tool, swage; heading-tool (for nails).

étamper (etɑ̃pe), v.a. [f. *estamper*] To stamp; to punch (holes).

étamperche (etɑ̃pɛrʃ), s.f. Scaffolding-pole.
étampeur (etɑ̃pœr), s.m. Stamper.
étampure (etɑ̃pyr), s.f. Splay or widening (of the hole in a horse-shoe, &c.).
étamure (etamyr), s.f. Tinning, material for tinning.
étanche (etɑ̃ʃ), adj. [f. *étancher*] Water-tight, air-tight, steam-tight, &c. ~ s.f. *A ~ d'eau*, water-tight.
étanchéité (etɑ̃ʃeite), s.f. Water-tightness.
étanchement (etɑ̃ʃmɑ̃), s.m. Stanching (of blood, &c.); quenching, slaking.
étancher (etɑ̃ʃe), v.a. [f. *étang*] **1.** To stanch, to stop; **2.** to render water-tight; **3.** (fig.) to slake, to quench; *~ sa soif*, to quench one's thirst.
étançon (etɑ̃sɔ̃), s.m. [f. OF *ester*] Prop, stay; stanchion.
étançonnement (etɑ̃sɔnmɑ̃), s.m. Propping, shoring.
étançonner (etɑ̃sɔne), v.a. [f. *étançon*] To prop, to shore, to stay, to underprop.
étang (etɑ̃), s.m. [L *stagnum*] Pond, pool; fish-pond; lake.
étape (etap), s.f. [LG *stapel*] **1.** Stage; halting-place, station; day's march; *brûler les~s*, to ride or travel without relays; (fig.) to go post-haste; **2.** (archaic) depot, mart.
étarquer (etarke), v.a. (naut.) To hoist, to tauten.
état (eta), s.m. [L *status*] **1.** State, commonwealth; estate of the realm; *affaires d'~*, affairs of State; *coup d'~*, coup d'État; *homme d'~*, statesman; *États-Unis*, United States; *raison d'~*, reason of state; (hist.) *tiers ~*, third estate; *~s généraux*, States General; **2.** state; plight, predicament; *il n'est pas en ~ de voyager*, he is not fit to travel; *être dans un triste ~*, to be in a sorry plight; (of patient) to be in a bad way; (fam.) *être dans tous ses ~s*, to be in a pretty taking, to be all in a bustle, or flurry; **3.** state, case, condition; *tenir une chose en ~*, to keep a thing in order, in good condition; *il est en ~ de payer*, he is in a position to pay; *faire peu d'~ de*, to take little account of; *mettre X en ~ de*, to enable X to; *en quelque ~ que soit l'affaire*, however the matter may stand; *en tout ~ de cause*, in any case; *~ de choses*, state of things; *mettre X hors d'~ de*, to put it out of X's power to; *être hors d'~ de*, to be unable to; *remettre en ~*, to set right; *à l'~ de neuf*, as good as new; **4.** profession, calling; station; office; *de son ~*, by profession; *~ militaire*, military profession; *bureau d'~ civil*, registrar's office; *~ civil*, civic status; **5.** account, statement, return; *~ de comptes*, statement of accounts; **6.** establishment; *tenir un grand ~*, to keep up a large establishment.
étatisme (etatism), s.m. Etatisme, State Socialism.
état-major (etamaʒɔr), s.m. (pl. *états-majors*) (mil.) Staff, general staff; staff headquarters; *carte d'~*, ordnance map.
étau (pl. -x) (eto), s.m. [MHG *stoc*] Vice; *~ d'établi*, bench-vice; *être pris* or *serré comme dans un étau*, to be held or gripped as in a vice.
étayement, étayage (etɛjmɑ̃, etɛjaʒ), s.m. Staying, propping; (fig.) supporting.
étayer (etɛje), v.a. [f. *étai*] To prop, to shore, to stay; (fig.) to support.
été (ete), s.m. [L *aestas*] Summer; *au fort de l'~*, in the height of summer; *l'~ de la vie*, the prime of life; *se mettre en ~*, to put on summer clothes; *heure d'~*, summer time; *~ de la St-Martin*, St. Martin's summer.
éteigneu-r, -se (etɛɲœr), s.m.f. Lamplighter; person employed to put out street-lamps.
éteignoir (etɛɲwar), s.m. Extinguisher; (fig.) wet blanket.
éteindre (etɛ̃dr), v.a. [L *extinguere*] **1.** To put out, to extinguish; to smother (noise); *le feu est éteint*, the fire has gone out; *~ le feu*, to put out the fire; *voix éteinte*, faint voice; *yeux éteints*, dull, lack-lustre eyes; filmy eyes (of the old); **2.** to obliterate, to exterminate; *~ une race*, to exterminate a race; **3.** to slake; to quench, to appease; *~ de la chaux*, to slake lime; *~ sa soif*, to quench one's thirst; **4.** to cancel, to annul (debts, &c.); **s'~**, v.pr. **1.** to be extinguished, to be put out or quenched; *le feu s'éteint*, the fire is going out; **2.** to diminish, to become extinct; to die out, to die away; to die peacefully; *la famille s'est éteinte*, the family has died out.
étendage (etɑ̃daʒ), s.m. Clothes-lines; drying-ground; action of hanging out to dry.
étendard (etɑ̃dar), s.m. [f. *étendre*] Standard, flag, colours (pl.), banner; *arborer*, *déployer*, or *planter un ~*, to hoist, unfurl, or plant the standard or colours.
étendoir (etɑ̃dwar), s.m. **1.** Clothes-line, clothes-pole; **2.** printer's peel (for hanging up freshly printed sheets to dry).
étendre (etɑ̃dr), v.a. [L *extendere*] To spread out; to stretch out, to extend; *~ du linge*, to hang out washing, or to spread out washing; *~ les ailes*, to spread the wings; *~ la main*, to extend one's hand; (fig.) to extend, to expand, to enlarge; *~ son commerce*, to expand one's business; *~ sa domination*, to extend one's sway; to lay on (colours); to lay; *~ un blessé sur*, to lay a wounded man upon; **s'~**, v.pr. to lie down, to stretch oneself out; *s'~ de tout son long*,

to stretch oneself at full length; to spread out, to reach; *s'~ au loin,* to spread far and wide; to expatiate, to dwell; *s'~ sur un sujet,* to expatiate upon a subject.

étendu, -e (etɑ̃dy), p. adj. Vast, wide, extensive; *plaine ~e,* vast plain; *connaissances ~es,* wide knowledge; outspread, outstretched, extended; *ailes ~es,* outstretched wings.

étendue (etɑ̃dy), s.f. Expanse; *vaste ~ de mer,* vast expanse of sea; reach, scope, length; *~ de la vue,* field of vision; duration, length (of time); development; (also fig.) extent, extensiveness; *dans toute son ~,* to the full; *l'~ des dégâts,* the extent of the damage; (phil.) extension, space.

éternel, -le (etɛrnɛl), adj. [L *aeternalis*] Eternal, everlasting, endless. *L'~,* s.m. Eternal God.

éternelle (etɛrnɛl), s.f. (bot.) Immortelle; syn. IMMORTELLE.

éternellement (etɛrnɛlmɑ̃), adv. Eternally.

éterniser (etɛrnize), v.a. **1.** To perpetuate; **2.** to drag out; (fam.) to spin out; **s'~,** v.pr. **1.** to be perpetuated; **2.** (colloq.) to remain for ever; to take root.

éternité (etɛrnite), s.f. [L *aeternitas*] Eternity; *de toute ~,* from time immemorial; from all eternity.

éternuement (etɛrnymɑ̃), s.m. Sneeze.

éternuer (eternɥe), v.n. [L *sternutare*] To sneeze.

étésien (etezjɛ̃), adj. m. [Gr. *etēsios*] Etesian.

étêter (etɛte), v.a. [f. *tête*] **1.** To lop, to pollard; **2.** to take the head off (nails, pins, &c.).

éteuf (etœf), s.m. [etym. dub.] Ball; (fig.) *renvoyer l'~,* to return the compliment; to give tit for tat.

éteule (etøl), s.f. [LL *stupila*] Stubble.

éthane (etan), s.m. (chem.) Ethane.

éther (etɛr), s.m. [Gr. *aithēr*] Ether, aether; (chem.) ether.

éthéré, -e (etere), adj. Ethereal.

éthérification (eterifika'sjɔ̃), s.f. Etherification.

éthérifier (eterifje), v.a. To etherify.

éthérisation (eteriza'sjɔ̃), s.f. Etherization.

éthériser (eterize), v.a. To etherize.

éthérisme (eterism), s.m. (med.) Etherism.

éthéromane (eterɔman), s.m.f. adj. Etheromaniac.

éthéromanie (eterɔmani), s.f. Etheromania.

éthiopien, -ne (etjɔpjɛ̃), adj. s.m.f. Ethiopian.

éthiopique (etjɔpik), adj. Ethiopic.

éthique (etik), adj. [Gr. *ēthikos*] Ethic, ethical. ~, s.f. Ethics.

ethmoïde (ɛtmɔid), adj. s.m. [Gr. *ēthmos*+*eidos*] (anat.) Ethmoid.

ethnique (ɛtnik), adj. [Gr. *ethnos*] Ethnic, ethnical.

ethnographe (ɛtnɔgraf), s.m.f. Ethnographer.

ethnographie (ɛtnɔgrafi), s.f. Ethnography.

ethnographique (ɛtnɔgrafik), adj. Ethnographical.

ethnologie (ɛtnɔlɔʒi), s.f. Ethnology.

ethnologique (ɛtnɔlɔʒik), adj. Ethnological.

ethnologue, ethnologiste (ɛtnɔlɔg, ɛtnɔlɔʒist), s.m.f. Ethnologist.

éthologie, éthographie (etɔlɔʒi, etɔgrafi), s.f. [Gr. *ēthos*+*logos, graphein*] Ethology, ethography.

éthyle (etil), s.m. (chem.) Ethyl.

étiage (etjaʒ), s.m. [f. *étier*] Low water, low-water mark.

étier (etje), s.m. [L *aestuarium*] Canal, conduit (in salt-marshes).

étincelant, -e (etɛ̃slɑ̃), p. adj. Sparkling; glistening (of moisture); glittering (usually of hard objects); flashing; *esprit ~,* sparkling wit; *yeux ~s de joie,* eyes sparkling with joy; *yeux ~s de colère,* eyes flashing with anger.

étinceler (etɛ̃sle), v.n. [f. *étincelle*] To sparkle, to twinkle, to gleam; to glisten (of moisture); to flash, to glitter; *ses yeux étincelaient de malice,* his (her) eyes were twinkling with mischief.

étincelle (etɛ̃sɛl), s.f. [L *scintilla*] Spark; (motor.) *~ d'allumage,* ignition spark; (fig.) spark, flash; brilliance; *jeter des ~s,* to throw out sparks.

étincellement (etɛ̃sɛlmɑ̃), s.m. Sparkling, twinkling, flashing; scintillation.

étiolement (etjɔlmɑ̃), s.m. Etiolation, sickliness; enfeeblement, chlorosis, emaciation; (fig.) *l'~ de l'intelligence,* intellectual anaemia.

étioler (etjɔle), v.a. [OF *étieuler*] To etiolate; to enfeeble, to weaken, to enervate; **s'~,** v.pr. (bot.) to become etiolated; to waste away (of persons); (fig.) to become enervated (of the mind).

étiologie (etjɔlɔʒi), s.f. [Gr. *aitia*+*logos*] Etiology, aetiology.

étique (etik), adj. [var. of *hectique*] Lean, lank, emaciated.

étiquetage (etiktaʒ), s.m. Ticketing, labelling.

étiqueter (etikte), v.a. To label; to ticket.

étiqueteu-r, -se (etiktœr), s.m.f. Labeller, ticketer.

étiquette (etikɛt), s.f. [f. Germ. *stechen*] **1.** Ticket, label, tag; **2.** etiquette, ceremonial; *tenir à l'~,* to be a stickler for etiquette; *observer l'~,* to stand on ceremony.

étirable (etirabl), adj. Stretchable.
étirage (etiraʒ), s.m. **1.** Stretching; **2.** wire-drawing.
étirer (etire), v.a. [*é+tirer*] To stretch, to lengthen; to draw (wire); **s'~**, v.pr. (fam.) to stretch, to stretch oneself, to stretch one's limbs.
étisie (etizi), s.f. [f. *étique*] (pathol.) Emaciation.
étoc (etɔk), s.m. var. of ESTOC.
étoffe (etɔf), s.f. [etym. dub.] **1.** Stuff, cloth, material; **2.** (fig.) quality, worth; *avoir de l'~*, to have the right stuff in one; **3.** (pl., print.) charge for wear and tear.
étoffé, -e (etɔfe), p. adj. Stuffed full, well lined; (fig.) well stocked, well furnished (mind, &c.); *voix bien ~e*, voice with plenty of body to it.
étoffer (etɔfe), v.a. To put enough stuff into; (fig.) to pad; to give body to; to enliven, to invigorate.
étoile (etwal), s.f. [L *stella*] Star; (fig.) star, fate, destiny; (theatr.) star; *à la lumière des ~s*, by starlight; *coucher à la belle ~*, to sleep out, to sleep in the open; *~ tombante* or *filante*, shooting star; *~ polaire*, pole-star; *mauvaise ~*, unlucky star; (fig.) *voir des ~s en plein midi*, to see stars; *~ de mer*, star-fish; *Monsieur Trois ~s*, Mr. Blank-Dash.
étoilé, -e (etwale), p. adj. Starry; starred, studded with stars; star-shaped.
étoilement (etwalmɑ̃), s.m. Star-shaped crack.
étoiler (etwale), v.a. To star, to stud with stars; to crack.
étole (etɔl), s.f. [L *stola*] Stole.
étonnamment (etɔnamɑ̃), adv. Surprisingly, astonishingly, amazingly.
étonnant, -e (etɔnɑ̃), p. adj. Astonishing, amazing, marvellous, wonderful; *il n'est pas ~ que*, it's no wonder that, or, no wonder that.
étonnement (etɔnmɑ̃), s.m. Astonishment, amazement; wonder; shock; *tout le monde est dans l'~*, every one is astonished; syn. SURPRISE.
étonner (etɔne), v.a. [pop. L *extonare*] **1.** To astonish, to amaze, to astound; to startle, to give a shock to (the sense was very strong in the seventeenth century, but nowadays *étonner* generally means 'to surprise'); **2.** to cause to shake; **s'~**, v.pr. to be astonished, astounded, amazed, or surprised; to wonder; *ne s'~ de rien*, to be surprised at nothing.
étouffade (etufad), s.f. See ESTOUFFADE.
étouffage (etufaʒ), s.m. Suffocating, stifling.
étouffant, -e (etufɑ̃), p. adj. Suffocating, sultry, very close; *chaleur ~e*, sweltering heat.
étouffée (etufe), s.f. *cuire à l'~*, to stew in a closed vessel.
étouffement (etufmɑ̃), s.m. Suffocation, stifling; suffocating fit; suffocating sensation.
étouffer (etufe), v.a. [OF *estouffer*; perh. f. Gr. *tuphos*] **1.** To suffocate, to stifle, to choke, to smother; *~ le feu*, to damp down or smother the fire; **2.** to deaden, to drown (sound, &c.); (fig.) to stifle, to suppress, to hush up; *~*, v.n. to choke; *~ de rire*, to choke with laughter; *on étouffe ici*, it is stifling here; **s'~**, v.pr. to choke; syn. SUFFOQUER.
étouffoir (etufwar), s.m. **1.** Cinder-pail, charcoal-box; **2.** damper (of a piano); **3.** extinguisher; **4.** (fig.) *quel ~!*, what a fug!
étoupe (etup), s.f. [L *stuppa*] Tow, oakum; *~ de coton*, cotton waste; *faire de l'~*, to pick oakum; (fig.) *mettre le feu aux ~s*, to fan or add fuel to the flame.
étouper (etupe), v.a. To stop, to bung up (with tow); (naut.) to caulk; *s'~ les oreilles*, to put cotton wool in one's ears.
étoupille (etupij), s.f. [f. *étoupe*] (artill.) Quick-match.
étoupiller (etupije), v.a. [f. *étoupe*] To prime.
étourderie (eturdəri), s.f. Thoughtlessness, heedlessness; thoughtless act, blunder.
étourdi, -e (eturdi), p. adj. Thoughtless, heedless, careless; hare-brained. *~*, s.m.f. (fam.) Giddy goat; *à l'~e*, like a heedless fool; thoughtlessly.
étourdiment (eturdimɑ̃), adv. Heedlessly, thoughtlessly, carelessly.
étourdir (eturdir), v.a. [f. OF *tourd*] **1.** To stun, to daze; to make dizzy or giddy; to deafen; **2.** (fig.) to astound, to stagger; **3.** to benumb (pain); **s'~**, v.pr. to make oneself giddy; to divert one's thoughts, to try to forget something.
étourdissant, -e (eturdisɑ̃), p. adj. Stunning, staggering; deafening; (fig.) stunning, astounding.
étourdissement (eturdismɑ̃), s.m. **1.** Giddiness, dizziness, vertigo; *avoir des ~s*, to be subject to attacks of giddiness; **2.** (fig.) amazement, stupefaction, shock; **3.** forgetfulness, distraction (from trouble).
étourneau (pl. -x) (eturno), s.m. [L *sturnus*] **1.** (ornith.) Starling; **2.** (fig.) feather-brain.
étrange (etrɑ̃ʒ), adj. [L *extraneus*] Strange, odd, queer; outlandish.
étrangement (etrɑ̃ʒmɑ̃), adv. Strangely, oddly, queerly.
étrang-er, -ère (etrɑ̃ʒe), adj. [f. *étrange*] **1.** Foreign, strange; unknown; *corps ~*, foreign body; *langue ~ère*, foreign language; **2.** irrelevant; *un fait ~ à la cause*, a fact irrelevant to the case. *~*, s.m.f. **1.** Foreigner, stranger, alien;

2. s.m. foreign parts; *à l'~*, abroad; (comm.) *à destination de l'~*, for the foreign market (of goods); going abroad or for foreign countries (of persons).

étranger (etrɑ̃ʒe), v.a. (rare, hunt.) To drive away.

étrangeté (etrɑ̃ʒte), s.f. Strangeness, oddness, queerness; strange thing.

étranglé, -e (etrɑ̃gle), p. adj. 1. Restricted, scanty, too narrow; 2. strangled, choking (voice).

étranglement (etrɑ̃gləmɑ̃), s.m. Strangling, strangulation; constriction; narrowing (of a valley, &c.).

étrangler (etrɑ̃gle), v.a. [L *strangulare*] 1. To strangle, to stifle, to throttle, to choke; 2. to constrict; 3. (fig.) to smother, to suppress, to hush up; **~**, v.n. to choke, to be choking; to be short of breath; **s'~**, v.pr. to strangle oneself; to choke.

étrangleu-r, -se (etrɑ̃glœr), s.m.f. Strangler, garotter.

étrangloir (etrɑ̃glwar), s.m. (naut.) Trail.

étranguillon (etrɑ̃gijɔ̃), s.m. (vet.) Strangles.

étrape (etrap), s.f. Small sickle.

étraper (etrape), v.a. [L *extirpare*] To cut (stubble).

étrave (etrav), s.f. [Scand. orig.] (naut.) Stem.

être (ɛtr), v. subst. [pop. L *essere* for *esse*] 1. To be, to exist; *je pense, donc je suis*, I think, therefore I exist; *il est soldat*, he is a soldier; (prov.) *on ne peut pas ~ et avoir été*, you can't have your cake and eat it; *~ à l'aise*, to be comfortable; *~ mal à l'aise*, to be uncomfortable; *~ à l'étroit*, to be cramped for room; *~ debout*, to stand, to be standing; to be up (dressed); *~ assis, -e*, to sit; *~ étendu, -e*, to lie; *ils sont trois*, there are three of them; *~ bien*, (colloq.) (*a*) to be good-looking; (*b*) to be well; *n'~ plus*, to be no more, to be dead; *~ de moitié*, to go halves; 2. [used impersonally] it is; there are; *il est vrai, évident que . . .*, it is true, obvious that . . .; *il est des gens qui . . .*, there are people who . . .; *il est à espérer, à craindre, que . . .*, it is to be hoped, feared, that . . .; *soit!*, so be it!; *ainsi soit-il!*, amen; *n'eût été que*, had it not been that; *comme si de rien n'était*, as if nothing had happened; *étant donné que . . .*, given that . . .; *toujours est-il que . . .*, the fact remains that . . .; 3. (with *ce*) it is, there are; *c'est que*, the fact is, the truth is; it is because; *c'est qu'il a peur*, the fact is, he is afraid; *s'il ne vient pas, c'est qu'il est malade*, if he does not come it is because he is ill; *c'est selon*, it depends; *ce n'est pas que*, not that; *cela est*, it is so; *qu'est-ce que c'est que cela?*, what is that?; *qu'est-ce qu'il a dit?*, what did he say?; *qu'est-ce que c'est?*, what is it?; *c'est cela*, that's it, that's right; *ce n'est pas cela*, it's wrong somewhere, it's not quite that; *si ce n'est que . . .*, except that, were it not that . . .; *serait-ce que . . .?*, can it be that . . .?; *ne fût-ce que pour . . .*, were it only for . . .; *voilà ce que c'est que de . . .*, that is what comes of . . .; *à moins que ce ne soit . . .*, unless it be . . .; *c'est à qui se plaindra*, every one is complaining; *ce que c'est que de nous!*, such is the fate of man, such is the way of all flesh!; 4. (with prep. *à*) to belong to; to be in service with, to be at or in; to be occupied with; to concern; *la maison est à lui*, the house belongs to him; *c'est à moi*, it is mine; *il est au mois*, he is employed by the month; *je suis tout à vous*, I am at your service; *~ à sa toilette*, to be getting dressed; *~ tout à sa lecture*, to be absorbed in one's book; *ils étaient à boire*, they were drinking; *il est long à venir*, he is a long time coming; *c'est à vous de parler*, it's for you to speak, it's your turn to speak; *c'est à vous à vous en occuper*, it's up to you to attend to it; 5. (with prep. *en*) to be in; to be dressed in; to be busy with; *~ en deuil*, to be in mourning; *~ en bonne, mauvaise, santé*, to be in good, bad, health; 6. (with prep. *après*) (colloq.) to pester, to fuss; *il est toujours après moi*, he is always pestering me; 7. (with prep. *avec*) *~ bien, mal, avec . . .*, to be on good, bad terms with . . .; 8. (with prep. *pour*) to favour, to be for; *il n'est pas pour nous*, he is not on our side; 9. (with prep. *de*) to come from, to be a native of, to belong to; *~ de Nice*, to come from Nice; *il est des nôtres*, he is one of us; *~ de service*, to be on duty; 10. to go, to have been; *j'ai été à Paris, en France, etc.*, I have been in Paris, in France, &c.; *il est à Paris depuis trois ans*, he has been in Paris for three years; *je fus retrouver mon ami*, I went to find my friend; 11. (used as auxiliary to the passive and to certain reflexive and neuter verbs) *j'ai été aimé*, I have been loved; *je me suis promené*, I have been for a walk; *je suis allé à Rome*, I went to Rome; 12. *en ~*, idiom. phr., *il n'en est rien*, it is nothing of the sort; *c'en est fait de*, it is all over, or up, with; *quoiqu'il en soit*, be that as it may; *en ~ là*, to have come to that; *où en êtes-vous?*, where have you got to?; *en êtes-vous encore là?*, have you got no further than that?; (fig.) do you still believe that?; *en ~ pour sa peine, ses frais*, to have wasted one's labours, one's money; *en ~ à la moitié*, to have got to the middle; *il en sera de lui comme des autres*, he will share the same fate as the others; *je ne sais plus où j'en suis,* I have lost the place (in a book); (fig.) I don't know what I am about; *je n'en suis plus,* I cry off; *en êtes-vous?,* are you game for it?; *voilà où nous en sommes,* that is how we stand; *en ~ quitte pour,* to get off with, to escape with; *j'en suis pour ce que j'ai dit,* I abide by what I have said; *s'il en est ainsi,* if that be so; *il en est de . . ., comme de . . .,* it is the same with . . ., as with . . .; *voilà ce qu'il en est,* that is how the matter stands; *il n'en a rien été,* nothing came of it; **13.** *y ~,* idiom. phr., *ça y est!,* that 's done it!, there (you are)!; *j'y suis!,* I see!, I've got it!; *vous y êtes!,* you've got it!; you've hit it!; *n'y ~ pas du tout,* to be wide of the mark; *n'y ~ plus du tout,* to have lost the thread; *y ~,* to be at home; *n'y ~ pour personne,* to be at home to nobody; *n'y ~ pour rien,* to have had no hand in it; *y ~ pour un tiers,* to come in for a third share; *j'y suis pour si peu,* I have had so little to do with it.

être (ɛtr), s.m. Being, creature; being, existence; *non-~,* nonentity.

étrécir (etresir), v.a. [f. *étroit*] To narrow; to take in (clothes); **s'~,** v.pr. to narrow, to contract.

étrécissement (etresismɑ̃), s.m. Narrowing, contraction, tightening.

étreindre (etrɛ̃dr), v.a. [L *stringere*] To clasp, to press (in the arms); to embrace; to bind, to tie up; (fig.) *l'émotion l'étreint,* his emotion overcomes him.

étreinte (etrɛ̃t), s.f. Embrace; hug; clasp, grasp; clasping, pressing.

étrenne (etrɛn), s.f. (usually in pl.) [L *strena*] **1.** (in pl.) New Year's gift; Christmas-box (for servants, &c.); **2.** gift; **3.** (comm.) first deal of the day; **4.** (sing.) first use; *en avoir l'~,* to have the first use of it.

étrenner (etrɛne), v.a. [f. *étrenne*] **1.** To be the first to buy from; **2.** to wear (clothes) for the first time; **~,** v.n. **1.** to sell first; **2.** (pop.) to catch it.

êtres, aîtres (ɛtr), s.m.pl. [L *extera*] Interior arrangement, ins and outs, parts (of a house); *connaître les ~ d'une maison,* to know the ins and outs (or the geography) of a house.

étrésillon (etrezijɔ̃), s.m. [f. *trésillon;* OF *esteser,* to stretch] (mining) Prop, pit-prop, stay.

étrésilloner (etrezijɔne), v.a. To prop, to stay.

étrier (etrije), s.m. [Germ. orig.] Stirrup; *à franc ~,* at full gallop; *coup de l'~,* stirrup-cup, parting-cup, grace-cup; *vider les ~s,* to slip one's stirrups; (by ext.) to take a toss, to be thrown; (fig.) to lose countenance; *avoir le pied à l'~,* to have one's foot in the stirrup; to have the ball at one's feet; to be booted and spurred; (fig.) *tenir l'~ à X,* to aid and abet X; to lend a helping hand to X; *être ferme sur ses ~s,* to have a firm seat; **2.** (arch.) strap; **3.** (naut.) link.

étrille (etrij), s.f. [L *strigilis*] Curry-comb.

étriller (etrije), v.a. **1.** To curry, to comb (a horse); **2.** (fig.) to dress down, to drub; **3.** (fam.) to fleece.

étripage (etripaʒ), s.m. Gutting (of fish); drawing (of fowl, &c.).

étriper (etripe), v.a. [f. *tripe*] To draw, to gut; *à étripe-cheval,* at breakneck speed.

étriqué, -e (etrike), p. adj. Scanty, skimped, scrimped, mean, stinted, curtailed; *habits ~s,* narrow, ill-cut clothes.

étriquer (etrike), v.a. [Germ. orig.] To skimp, to scrimp, to make too tight; (fig.) to fail to develop, to curtail (a speech, &c.).

étrivière (etrivjɛr), s.f. [f. *étrier*] Stirrup-leather; *donner les ~s,* to give a good leathering; (fig.) to dress down.

étroit, -e (etrwa), adj. [L *strictus*] Narrow, tight, strait; confined; limited; strict, rigorous; *esprit ~,* narrow mind; *cerveau ~,* shallow brain; *~e amitié,* close friendship; *vivre à l'~,* to live sparingly, narrowly; *habit ~,* tight coat; *être logé à l'~,* to be cramped for room; *~e obligation,* bounden duty; binding engagement.

étroitement (etrwatmɑ̃), adv. Narrowly, tightly; closely, intimately; sparingly; *~ uni,* closely united, intimately bound up (*avec,* with).

étroitesse (etrwatɛs), s.f. Narrowness, straitness; closeness, tightness; *~ d'esprit,* narrow-mindedness.

étronçonner (etrɔ̃sɔne), v.a. [f. *tronçon*] (forestry) To poll.

étrusque (etrysk), adj. s.m.f. Etruscan.

étude (etyd), s.f. [L *studium*] **1.** Study; acquirements, attainments; *cabinet d'~,* study; *avoir fait de bonnes ~s,* to have done well at school, at college; *avoir fini ses ~s,* to have finished one's education; *maître d'~,* usher; **2.** office, chambers; practice (of a notary, solicitor, &c.); *acheter une ~,* to buy a practice; **3.** essay, study, survey, scheme, sketch, treatise; (mus.) study; **4.** *à l'~,* under consideration (of plans, &c.).

étudiant, -e (etydjɑ̃), s.m.f. Student, undergraduate.

étudier (etydje), v.a. [f. *étude*] To study, to read; to study, to practise (music); to study, to watch; **~,** v.n. to study, to read; to practise (music); **s'~,** v.pr. to observe oneself; *s'~ à,* to school oneself to; SYN. APPRENDRE.

étui (etɥi), s.m. [etym. dub.] **1.** Case, box; needle-case; sheath; **2.** (naut.) tarpaulin.
étuve (etyv), s.f. [LL *stupa*] **1.** Sweating-room, hot-room (in a bath); **2.** oven, sterilizer; **3.** drying-stove.
étuvée (etyve), s.f. syn. of ÉTOUFFÉE.
étuver (etyve), v.a. **1.** (cook.) To steam, to stew, to braise; **2.** to sterilize in an oven; **3.** (med.) to wash by dabbing.
étuviste (etyvist), s.m. Bath-keeper.
étymologie (etimɔlɔʒi), s.f. [Gr. *etumos*+*logos*] Etymology.
étymologique (etimɔlɔʒik), adj. Etymological.
étymologiquement (etimɔlɔʒikmɑ̃), adv. Etymologically.
étymologiste (etimɔlɔʒist), s.m.f. Etymologist.
eubage (øbaʒ), s.m. Gaulish druid.
eucalyptus (økaliptys), s.m. [Gr. *eu*+*kaluptos*] (bot.) Eucalyptus, gum-tree.
eucharistie (økaristi), s.f. [Gr. *eukharistia*] Eucharist.
eucharistique (økaristik), adj. Eucharistic.
eucologe (økɔlɔʒ), s.m. [Gr. *eukhē*+*logos*] Euchologion, euchology.
eudémonisme (ødemɔnism), s.m. [Gr. *eudaimōn*] Eudemonism.
eudiomètre (ødjɔmɛtr), s.m. [Gr. *eudia*+*metron*] Eudiometer.
eugénique (øʒenik), s.f. **eugénisme** (øʒenism), s.m. [Gr. *eugenēs*] Eugenics, eugenism.
euh ! (ø), interj. Ah !, aha !, hum !
eunecte (ønɛkt), s.m. (zool.) Anaconda.
eunuque (ønyk), s.m. [Gr. *eunē*+*ekhein*] Eunuch.
eupatoire (øpatwar), s.f. [Gr. *eupatorion*] (bot.) Eupatorium.
eupepsie (øpɛpsi), s.f. [Gr. *eupepsia*] Eupepsia.
euphémique (øfemik), adj. Euphemistic.
euphémisme (øfemism), s.m. [Gr. *euphēmismos*] Euphemism.
euphonie (øfɔni), s.f. [Gr. *euphōnia*] Euphony.
euphonique (øfɔnik), adj. Euphonic.
euphorbe (øfɔrb), s.f. [prop. n. *Euphorbus*] (bot.) Euphorbia, spurge.
euphuïsme (øfɥism), s.m. [f. *Euphues*, Engl. novel by J. Lyly, 1580] Euphuism.
européaniser (œrɔpeanize), v.a. To Europeanize.
européen, -ne (œrɔpeɛ̃), adj. s.m.f. European.
eurythmie (øritmi), s.f. [Gr. *eu*+*rhuthmos*] Eurhythmy; eurhythmics; harmony.
eurythmique (øritmik), adj. Eurhythmic.
eustache (østaʃ), s.m. [prop. n. *Eustache* (Dubois), a cutler] Rough knife, whittle, clasp-knife.

eux (ø), pers. pron. 3rd p. m.pl. They, them; ~*-mêmes*, themselves.
E.V. = *en ville*, in town, (postage) Local.
évacuant, -e, évacuati-f, -ve (evakɥɑ̃, evakɥatif), adj. (med.) Evacuative, evacuant.
évacuation (evakɥa'sjɔ̃), s.f. Evacuation.
évacuer (evakɥe), v.a. [L *evacuare*] To evacuate.
évadé, -e (evade), p. adj. Escaped. ~, s.m.f. Escaped prisoner, convict, &c.
(s')évader (sevade), v.pr. [L *evadere*] To escape, to make one's escape; to get away; syn. S'ÉCHAPPER, S'ENFUIR.
évagation (evaga'sjɔ̃), s.f. (rare) [L *evagatio*] Evagation.
évaluable (evalɥabl), adj. Evaluable, ratable, appraisable.
évaluation (evalɥa'sjɔ̃), s.f. Evaluation, estimate, reckoning, valuation.
évaluer (evalɥe), v.a. [*é*+OF *value* for *valeur*] To value, to estimate.
évanescent, -e (evɑ̃nɛsɑ̃), adj. [L *evanescens*] Evanescent.
évangéliaire (evɑ̃ʒeljɛr), s.m. Evangelistary.
évangélique (evɑ̃ʒelik), adj. **1.** Evangelistic (of the four Evangelists); **2.** evangelical (according to the teaching of the gospel).
évangéliquement (evɑ̃ʒelikmɑ̃), adv. **1.** Evangelistically; **2.** evangelically.
évangélisateur (evɑ̃ʒelizatœr), s.m. Evangelizer.
évangélisation (evɑ̃ʒeliza'sjɔ̃), s.f. Evangelization.
évangéliser (evɑ̃ʒelize), v.a. To evangelize.
évangéliste (evɑ̃ʒelist), s.m. Evangelist.
évangile (evɑ̃ʒil), s.m. [L *evangelium*] Gospel; *côté de l'*~, gospel side, north side (of the altar); *parole d'*~, gospel truth.
(s')évanouir (sevanwir), v.pr. [L *evanescere*] **1.** To faint, to swoon, to lose consciousness; **2.** to vanish.
évanouissement (evanwismɑ̃), s.m. **1.** Fainting-fit, swoon; **2.** disappearance.
évaporable (evapɔrabl), adj. Evaporable.
évaporateur (evapɔratœr), s.m. Evaporator.
évaporation (evapɔra'sjɔ̃), s.f. Evaporation.
évaporatoire (evapɔratwar), adj. Evaporating.
évaporé, -e (evapɔre), adj. (fig.) Giddy, thoughtless; *tête* ~*e*, flighty nature. ~, s.m.f. Hare-brained creature.
évaporer (evapɔre), v.a. [L *evaporare*] To evaporate; (fig.) to give vent to; **s'**~, v.pr. to evaporate; to be dissipated; (fig.) to become dissipated, to grow flighty or heedless.

évaporomètre (evaporomɛtr), s.m. Evaporometer.
évasé, -e (evɑze), p. adj. Wide, widening, bell-shaped, bell-mouthed.
évasement (evɑzmɑ̃), s.m. Widening; bell-mouth (of guns); (arch.) splay.
évaser (evɑze), v.a. [f. *vase*] To widen, to make bell-shaped or bell-mouthed; (arch.) to splay; **s'~**, v.pr. to widen out, to spread out.
évasi-f, -ve (evazif), adj. Evasive.
évasion (evɑzjɔ̃), s.f. [L *evasio*] Evasion, escape; (fig.) evasion, shuffling excuse.
évasivement (evazivmɑ̃), adv. Evasively.
évasure (evɑ̃zyr), s.f. Widening (of an opening); (arch.) splay.
évêché (evɛʃe), s.m. [f. *évêque*] **1.** Bishopric, see; **2.** bishop's palace.
évection (evɛksjɔ̃), s.f. [L *evectio*] (astron.) Evection.
éveil (evɛj), s.m. [f. *éveiller*] **1.** Awakening; **2.** warning, hint, alarm; *donner l'~ à*, to put on his guard, to alarm; *en ~*, on the watch, on the look-out.
éveillé, -e (evɛje), p. adj. Wide awake, lively, sprightly; sharp, intelligent.
éveiller (evɛje), v.a. [LL *exvigilare*] To wake, to awaken, to rouse; to excite, to enliven; *~ des soupçons*, to arouse or excite suspicion; **s'~**, v.pr. to awake, to wake up; *s'~ en sursaut*, to awake with a start.
événement (evɛnmɑ̃), s.m. [f. L *evenire*] Event, occurrence; issue, result; sensational event, sensation; *en cas d'~*, in case of emergency; *attendre l'~*, to await the issue.
évent (evɑ̃), s.m. [f. *éventer*] Open air; vent-hole; air-hole; blow-hole (of cetaceans); (artill.) windage; (fig.) *être une tête à l'~*, to be feather-brained.
éventail (evɑ̃taj), s.m. [f. *éventer*] Fan; *en ~*, fan-shaped; *fenêtre en ~*, fan-light.
éventaillerie (evɑ̃tajri), s.f. Fan-making industry or business.
éventaillier (evɑ̃taje), s.m. Fan-seller or -maker.
éventailliste (evɑ̃tajist), s.m. Fan-maker.
éventaire (evɑ̃tɛr), s.m. [f. *éventer*] Tray-basket.
éventé, -e (evɑ̃te), p. adj. **1.** Windy; **2.** fanned, aired; draughty; **3.** flat (of wine); **4.** (fig.) flighty, feather-brained; syn. ÉVAPORÉ.
éventer (evɑ̃te), v.a. [f. *vent*] **1.** To fan; to winnow (corn); to expose to the air; **2.** to let (wine, &c.) get flat; **3.** (fig.) to discover, to get wind of; **s'~**, v.pr. **1.** to fan oneself; **2.** to be divulged; **3.** to go flat (of wine, &c.).
éventoir (evɑ̃twar), s.m. Fire-fan.
éventration (evɑ̃tra'sjɔ̃), s.f. Eventration.
éventrer (evɑ̃tre), v.a. [f. *ventre*] To disembowel; to gut (fish, &c.); (by ext.) to rip up, to break open.
éventualité (evɑ̃tɥalite), s.f. Eventuality.
éventuel, -le (evɑ̃tɥɛl), adj. [f. L *eventus*] Eventual; contingent.
éventuellement (evɑ̃tɥɛlmɑ̃), adv. Eventually, in the event of; contingently.
évêque (evɛk), s.m. [Gr. *episkopos*] Bishop.
éversi-f, -ve (evɛrsif), adj. (rare) [L *versus*] Subversive.
éversion (evɛrsjɔ̃), s.f. Overthrow.
(s')évertuer (sevɛrtɥe), v.pr. [f. *vertu*] To strive (*à*, to), to exert or bestir oneself.
éviction (eviksjɔ̃), s.f. [L *evictio*] Eviction.
évidage (evidaʒ), s.m. Scooping out, hollowing out.
évidement (evidmɑ̃), s.m. [f. *évider*] Groove; hollowing out; hollowness.
évidemment (evidamɑ̃), adv. Evidently, obviously, clearly.
évidence (evidɑ̃s), s.f. [L *evidentia*] Evidence, obviousness; plainness, clearness; conspicuousness; *se rendre à l'~*, to be convinced, to recognize the truth of something; *en ~*, conspicuous; in the limelight; *mettre en ~*, to bring forward, to make conspicuous; to make evident. ⚠ In English (law) 'evidence' means also 'information tending to establish fact', 'statement' = *témoignage*.
évident, -e (evidɑ̃), adj. Evident, obvious, clear, plain.
évider (evide), v.a. [*é+vider*] To hollow out, to scoop out, to groove.
évidoir (evidwar), s.m. Auger, gouge.
évier (evje), s.m. [OF *ève* for *eau*] (Kitchen-) sink.
évincement (evɛ̃smɑ̃), s.m. Evicting, ejecting, ousting.
évincer (evɛ̃se), v.a. [L *evincere*] To evict, to oust, to turn out. ⚠ Not to be translated by 'to evince' which = *manifester, montrer, témoigner, indiquer* (*une qualité, un défaut*, &c.).
évitable (evitabl), adj. Avoidable.
évitage (evitaʒ), s.m. **évitée** (evite), s.f. (naut.) Swinging, berth (of a ship lying at anchor).
évitement (evitmɑ̃), s.m. Avoiding; (rail.) *gare d'~, voie d'~*, siding.
éviter (evite), v.a. [L *evitare*] **1.** To avoid; to evade; to shun, to eschew; *~ la mauvaise compagnie*, to shun bad company; *~ les dangers*, to avoid danger; **2.** (used with negative) to prevent; *évitez qu'il ne vous parle*, prevent his speaking to you; ~, v.n. (naut.) to swing; **s'~**, v.pr. to avoid each other; to be avoided.
évocable (evɔkabl), adj. That may be evoked.
évocat-eur, -rice (evɔkatœr), adj. Reminiscent (of the past); suggestive, evocative.

évocation (evɔka'sjɔ̃), s.f. Evocation; raising up; recall, recollection; (law) removal.
évocatoire (evɔkatwar), adj. Evocatory.
évoluer (evɔlɥe), v.n. [f. *évolution*] To perform evolutions; (fig.) to develop, to be transformed gradually; to change one's mind gradually; to evolve.
évolution (evɔlysjɔ̃), s.f. [L *evolutio*] Evolution; development, transformation; *faire des ~s*, to go through its or one's evolutions.
évolutionnisme (evɔlysjɔnism), s.m. Evolutionism.
évolutionniste (evɔlysjɔnist), s.m. adj. Evolutionist.
évoquer (evɔke), v.a. [L *evocare*] **1.** To evoke, to call up; (magic) to conjure up (also fig.); **2.** (law) to remove (to).
évulsi-f, -ve (evylsif), adj. Evulsive.
évulsion (evylsjɔ̃), s.f. [L *evulsio*] Evulsion.
ex- (ɛks), pref. [L *ex*] Ex-.
exacerbation (egzasɛrba'sjɔ̃), s.f. [L *exacerbatio*] Exacerbation.
exact, -e (ɛgzakt), adj. [L *exactus*] Exact, accurate; regular, punctual; rigorous, precise, strictly correct; *à l'heure ~e*, punctually, to the minute; *sciences ~es*, exact sciences (mathematics).
exactement (ɛgzaktəmɑ̃), adv. Exactly, accurately; punctually, rigorously.
exacteur (ɛgzaktœr), s.m. Exactor, extorter.
exaction (ɛgzaksjɔ̃), s.f. Exaction; impost, extortion.
exactitude (ɛgzaktityd), s.f. Exactitude; exactness, accuracy; punctuality; precision.
exagérat-eur, -rice (ɛgzaʒeratœr), adj. Exaggerating. ~ s.m.f. Exaggerator.
exagérati-f, -ve (ɛgzaʒeratif), adj. Exaggerative.
exagération (ɛgzaʒera'sjɔ̃), s.f. Exaggeration; overrating.
exagéré, -e (ɛgzaʒere), p.adj. Exaggerated.
exagérer (ɛgzaʒere), v.a. [L *exaggerare*] To exaggerate.
exagéreur (ɛgzaʒerœr), s.m. See syn. EXAGÉRATEUR.
exalbuminé, -e (ɛgzalbymine), adj. (bot.) Exalbuminous.
exaltation (ɛgzalta'sjɔ̃), s.f. [f. *exalter*] Exaltation; excitement.
exalté, -e (ɛgzalte), p. adj. Over-excited, heated; exalted. ~, s.m.f. Fanatic.
exalter (ɛgzalte), v.a. [L *exaltare*] To exalt, to extol; to inflame, to over-excite; **s'~**, v.pr. to get enthusiastic, to become inflamed; (pej.) to become over-excited.
examen (ɛgzamɛ̃), s.m. [L wd] Examination; (colloq.) exam; survey, investigation, scrutiny; *~ de conscience*, self-examination; *passer un ~*, to pass an examination, to take one's degree; *faire ~ de*, to examine; *jury d'~*, board of examiners; *libre ~*, free-thought.
examinat-eur, -rice (ɛgzaminatœr), adj. Examining. ~, s.m.f. Examiner; (rare) examinator.
examiner (ɛgzamine), v.a. [L *examinare*] To examine; to survey; to investigate; to ponder; to discuss, to weigh; *~ à fond*, to make a thorough investigation of, to discuss thoroughly; *~ superficiellement*, to glance over; **s'~**, v.pr. to examine one's conscience; to study or search oneself; to examine or inspect each other.
exanthémateu-x, -se (ɛgzɑ̃tematø), adj. Exanthematic, eruptive.
exanthème (ɛgzɑ̃tɛm), s.m. [Gr. *exanthēma*] (med.) Exanthema.
exarchat (ɛgzarka), s.m. Exarchate.
exarque (ɛgzark), s.m. [Gr. *exarkhos*] Exarch.
exaspération (ɛgzaspera'sjɔ̃), s.f. Exasperation.
exaspérer (ɛgzaspere), v.a. [L *exasperare*] To exasperate, to provoke, to incense, to aggravate; **s'~**, v.pr. to become exasperated.
exaucement (ɛgzosmɑ̃), s.m. Fulfilment, granting, hearing (of prayers, &c.).
exaucer (ɛgzose), v.a. [f. *exhausser*] To fulfil, to hearken to, to grant (desires, prayers, &c.).
excavateur (ɛkskavatœr), s.m. (mech.) Excavator, steam-shovel.
excavation (ɛkskava'sjɔ̃), s.f. [f. *excaver*] Excavation.
excaver (ɛkskave), v.a. [L *excavare*] To excavate.
excédant, -e (ɛksedɑ̃), p. adj. **1.** Exceeding, excess, excessive; **2.** unbearable.
excédent (ɛksedɑ̃), s.m. Surplus, overplus, excess; *~ de bagages*, excess luggage.
excéder (ɛksede), v.a. [L *excedere*] **1.** To exceed; to surpass, to rise above; **2.** to surfeit; (fig.) to wear or tire out; to annoy; to bore to death; **s'~**, v.pr. to wear oneself out; to overwork oneself.
excellemment (ɛksɛlamɑ̃), adv. Excellently, surpassingly.
excellence (ɛksɛlɑ̃s), s.f. [f. *excellent*] Excellence, excellency; *Son ~*, His or Her Excellency; *par ~*, pre-eminently, par excellence, above all.
excellent, -e (ɛksɛlɑ̃), adj. [f. *exceller*] Excellent; delightful; (Amer. slang) O.K.
excellentissime (ɛksɛlɑ̃tisim), adj. (in titles) Most Excellent.
exceller (ɛksɛle), v.n. [L *excellere*] To excel (*à*, in).
excentricité (ɛksɑ̃trisite), s.f. [L *ex+centrum*] Eccentricity.
excentrique (ɛksɑ̃trik), adj. Eccentric. ~, s.m. (techn.) Eccentric; *collier d'~*, eccentric strap.

excentriquement (ɛksɑ̃trikmɑ̃), adv. Eccentrically.
excepté, -e (ɛksɛpte), p. adj. Excepted; *les femmes ~es*, women excepted; ~, (invar.) prep. except, excepting, but; *~ que*, except that.
excepter (ɛksɛpte), v.a. [L *exceptare*] To except, to exclude.
exception (ɛksɛpsjɔ̃), [L *exceptio*] s.f. Exception; (law) bar, demurrer; *à l'~ de*, with the exception of; *à cette ~ près*, with this exception; (prov.) *l'~ confirme la règle*, the exception proves the rule; *faire ~*, to be an exception; *faire une ~*, to make an exception; *d'~*, exceptional.
exceptionnel, -le (ɛksɛpsjɔnɛl), adj. Exceptional.
exceptionnellement (ɛksɛpsjɔnɛlmɑ̃), adv. Exceptionally.
excès (ɛksɛ), s.m. [L *excessus*] Excess; intemperance; violence; *avec ~*, *jusqu'à l'~*, *à l'~*, excessively, immoderately, to or with excess; *faire des ~*, to be guilty of excesses; to be intemperate.
excessi-f, -ve (ɛksɛsif), adj. Excessive.
excessivement (ɛksɛsivmɑ̃), adv. Excessively, to excess.
exciper (ɛksipe), v.n. [L *excipere*] To allege (as exculpation), to plead, to bring forward as an excuse, reason, or claim; *~ de sa bonne foi*, to plead one's good faith.
excipient (ɛksipjɑ̃), s.m. (pharm.) Excipient.
excise (ɛksiz), s.f. [Engl. wd] Excise.
exciser (ɛksize), v.a. [f. *excision*] To cut out, to excise.
excision (ɛksizjɔ̃), s.f. [L *excisio*] Excision.
excitabilité (ɛksitabilite), s.f. Excitability.
excitable (ɛksitabl), adj. Excitable.
excitant, -e (ɛksitɑ̃), p. adj. Exciting (to the senses); (med.) excitant. ~, s.m. Excitant.
excitat-eur, -rice (ɛksitatœr), adj. Exciting. ~, s.m. Exciter; *~ de troubles*, sower of discord; instigator; (phys.) excitator.
excitati-f, -ve (ɛksitatif), adj. Excitative.
excitation (ɛksita'sjɔ̃), s.f. Excitement, excitation.
exciter (ɛksite), v.a. [L *excitare*] To excite, to stir up, to rouse; to quicken; to spur, to prompt; **s'~**, v.pr. to get excited, to work oneself up; to spur each other on.
exclamati-f, -ve (ɛksklamatif), adj. Exclamatory, exclamative; (gram.) of exclamation.
exclamation (ɛksklama'sjɔ̃), s.f. [f. *exclamer*] Exclamation; *point d'~*, exclamation mark, note of exclamation.
(s')exclamer (sɛksklame), v.pr. [L *exclamare*] To exclaim, to cry out.
exclure (ɛksklyr), v.a. [L *excludere*] To exclude, to shut out, to debar; **s'~**, v.pr. to be mutually incompatible, to exclude each other.
exclusi-f, -ve (ɛksklyzif), adj. Exclusive.
exclusion (ɛksklyzjɔ̃), s.f. Exclusion; *à l'~ de*, to the exclusion of.
exclusivement (ɛksklyzivmɑ̃), adv. Exclusively.
exclusivisme (ɛksklyzivism), s.m. Exclusivism.
exclusiviste (ɛksklyzivist), s.m.f. Exclusivist.
exclusivité (ɛksklyzivite), s.f. Exclusiveness; *avoir l'~ de*, to possess the exclusive rights of.
excommunication (ɛkskomynika'sjɔ̃), s.f. Excommunication.
excommunier (ɛkskɔmynje), v.a. [L *excommunicare*] To excommunicate.
excoriation (ɛkskɔrja'sjɔ̃), s.f. Excoriation; barking.
excorier (ɛkskɔrje), v.a. [L *excoriare*] To bark, to excoriate; **s'~**, v.pr. to be excoriated.
excortiquer (ɛkskɔrtike), v.a. See syn. DÉCORTIQUER.
excrément (ɛkskremɑ̃), s.m. [L *excrementum*] Excrement; (fig.) *~ de la terre*, scum of the earth.
excrémenteu-x, -se, excrémentiel, -le (ɛkskremɑ̃tø, ɛkskremɑ̃sjɛl), adj. Excrementitious, excremental, excrementitial.
excréter (ɛkskrete), v.a. [f. L *excretum*] To excrete.
excrét-eur, -rice, excrétoire (ɛkskretœr, ɛkskretwar), adj. Excretive, excretory.
excrétion (ɛkskresjɔ̃), s.f. Excretion.
excroissance (ɛkskrwasɑ̃s), s.f. [f. *croissance*] Excrescence.
excursion (ɛkskyrsjɔ̃), s.f. [L *excursio*] Excursion, tour, ramble, pleasure trip; (fig.) digression.
excursionniste (ɛkskyrsjɔnist), s.m.f. Excursionist, tourist.
excusable (ɛkskyzabl), adv. Excusable, pardonable.
excuse (ɛkskyz), s.f. [f. *excuser*] Excuse; (pl.) apology; (law) plea; pretext, pretence; motive of exculpation; (pop.) *faites ~!*, excuse me!; *faire des ~s*, to apologize; *je vous présente toutes mes ~s*, I beg to apologize.
excuser (ɛkskyze), v.a. [L *excusare*] To excuse, to exculpate; to pardon; to serve as an excuse for; to apologize for; *excusez-moi*, excuse me; **s'~**, v.pr. to apologize, to make an excuse; to ask to be excused; to decline an invitation, &c.; *s'~ sur X*, to cast or lay the blame on X; *qui s'excuse s'accuse*, a guilty conscience needs no accuser.

exeat (ɛgzeat), s.m. [L wd] Exeat; (fig.) *donner à X son* ~, to permit X to leave.
exécrable (ɛgzekrabl), adj. Execrable, abominable.
exécrablement (ɛgzekrabləmɑ̃), adv. Execrably, abominably.
exécration (ɛgzekra'sjɔ̃), s.f. Execration; *avoir en* ~, to hold in execration; to abhor; *vouer à l'*~, to doom or consign to execration.
exécrer (ɛgzekre), v.a. [L *exsecrari*] To execrate, to hold in detestation.
exécutable (ɛgzekytabl), adj. Feasible, practicable.
exécutant, -e (ɛgzekytɑ̃), s.m.f. Executant, performer.
exécuter (ɛgzekyte), v.a. [L *exsequi*] **1.** To execute, to perform, to carry out, to fulfil; ~ *un arrêt*, to carry out a sentence; **2.** to execute, to put to death; **s'**~, v.pr. (*a*) to be performed, to take place; (*b*) to submit; to yield, to comply, to resign oneself; *allons, exécutez-vous !*, come, submit with a good grace!
exécut-eur, -rice (ɛgzekytœr), s.m.f. **1.** Executor, (fem.) executrix; ~ *testamentaire*, executor; **2.** executioner, hangman; ~ *des hautes œuvres*, hangman.
exécuti-f, -ve (ɛgzekytif), adj. Executive. ~, s.m. The Executive.
exécution (ɛgzekysjɔ̃), s.f. [L *executio*] **1.** Execution; fulfilment; *mettre à* ~ *un plan*, to carry out a plan; *en* ~ *de*, in pursuance of; ~ *d'un débiteur*, distraint; *homme d'*~, resolute man, man of action; **2.** execution, putting to death; *ordre d'*~, death-warrant.
exécutoire (ɛgzekytwar), adj. Executory. ~, s.m. Writ of execution.
exèdre (ɛgzɛdr), s.f. [Gr. *exedra*] (ant.) Exedra, exhedra.
exégèse (ɛgzeʒɛs), s.f. [Gr. *exēgēsis*] Exegesis.
exégète (ɛgzeʒɛt), s.m.f. Exegetist.
exégétique (ɛgzeʒetik), adj. Exegetical.
exemplaire (ɛgzɑ̃plɛr), adj. Exemplary. ~, s.m. Copy (of book, &c.); specimen; pattern, archetype.
exemplairement (ɛgzɑ̃plɛrmɑ̃), adv. Exemplarily, in an exemplary manner.
exemple (ɛgzɑ̃pl), s.m. [L *exemplum*] Example; *à l'*~ *de*, in imitation of, on the model of; *donner l'*~, to set the example; *par* ~ *!*, upon my word !; *par* ~, for example, for instance; *prêcher d'*~, to practise what one preaches; *prendre* ~ *sur*, to be guided by, to model oneself upon; *sans* ~, unparalleled.
exempt, -e (ɛgzɑ̃), adj. [L *exemptus*] Exempt.
exempt (ɛgzɑ̃), s.m. (archaic) **1.** Adjutant; **2.** police officer.
exempté, -e (ɛgzɑ̃te), p. adj. Exempted.
exempter (ɛgzɑ̃te), v.a. To exempt, to free (*de*, from); **s'**~, v.pr. to exempt oneself, to dispense (*de*, with).
exemption (ɛgzɑ̃psjɔ̃), s.f. [L *exemptio*] Exemption.
exequatur (ɛgzekwatyr), s.m. invar. [L wd] Exequatur.
exerçant, -e (ɛgzɛrsɑ̃), p. adj. Practising.
exercer (ɛgzɛrse), v.a. [L *exercere*] To exercise, to drill; to exert; to practise (of doctors, &c.), to carry on, to follow (a profession or trade); ~ *des soldats*, to drill soldiers; ~ *la patience de X*, to try X's patience; **s'**~, v.pr. to practise, to train oneself; to exert oneself; *s'*~ *à sauter*, to practise jumping, to train for jumping.
exercice (ɛgzɛrsis), s.m. [L *exercitium*] **1.** Exercise, practice, use; training; *l'*~ *des vertus*, the exercise of virtue; *se tenir en* ~, to keep oneself in practice, in training; *entrer en* ~, to enter upon one's duties; (mil.) drill; ~ *à feu*, rifle practice; *faire l'*~, to be drilled; **2.** (comm., admin.) financial year; *règlement d'un* ~, balancing of a budget; **3.** (customs) inspection.
exérèse (ɛgzerɛz), s.f. [Gr. *exairesis*] (surg.) Amputation, extraction.
exergue (ɛgzɛrg), s.m. [Gr. *ex*+*ergon*] Exergue, exergum.
exfoliation (ɛksfɔlja'sjɔ̃), s.f. Exfoliation.
exfolier (ɛksfɔlje), v.a. [L *ex*+*folium*] To exfoliate.
exhalaison (ɛgzalɛzɔ̃), s.f. Exhalation, vapour.
exhalant, -e (ɛgzalɑ̃), p. adj. (med.) Exhalant, exhaling.
exhalation (ɛgzala'sjɔ̃), s.f. Exhaling; evaporation (from the skin).
exhaler (ɛgzale), v.a. [L *exhalare*] To exhale; to emit, to give vent to; (fig.) ~ *sa colère*, to give vent to one's wrath; ~ *le dernier soupir*, to breathe one's last; **s'**~, v.pr. to be emitted, to be exhaled.
exhaussement (ɛgzosmɑ̃), s.m. Raising up, elevation; mound.
exhausser (ɛgzose), v.a. [*ex*+*hausser*] To raise, to make higher.
exhaustion (ɛgzostjɔ̃), s.f. [L *exhaustio*] Exhaustion.
exhérédation (ɛgzereda'sjɔ̃), s.f. Exheredation, disinheritance.
exhéréder (ɛgzerede), v.a. [L *exhēredere*] To exheredate, to disinherit; syn. DÉSHÉRITER.
exhiber (ɛgzibe), v.a. [L *exhibere*] To produce, to show; (law) to exhibit; ~ *ses papiers, son passeport*, to produce one's papers, one's passport; **s'**~, v.pr. to exhibit oneself; to make an exhibition of oneself.
exhibition (ɛgzibisjɔ̃), s.f. Exhibition; producing, exhibiting, display.
exhilarant, -e (ɛgzilarɑ̃), adj. [f. L *ex*+*hilaris*] Gay, hilarious, funny, sidesplitting, laughable, exhilarating. ✧ 'Ex-

hilarating' usually means *tonique, reconstituant, réconfortant,* whilst *exhilarant* = exciting laughter or hilarity.
exhortation (ɛgzɔrta'sjɔ̃), s.f. Exhortation.
exhorter (ɛgzɔrte), v.a. [L *exhortari*] To exhort, to encourage (*à*, to).
exhumation (ɛgzyma'sjɔ̃), s.f. Exhumation, disinterment.
exhumer (ɛgzyme), v.a. [L *ex+humus*] To exhume, to disinter; (fig.) to dig up, to rake up; to bring to light.
exigeant, -e (ɛgziʒɑ̃), p. adj. Exacting; over-particular, hard to please.
exigence (ɛgziʒɑ̃s), s.f. **1.** Exaction, unreasonable demand; **2.** exigency, exigence.
exiger (ɛgziʒe), v.a. [L *exigere*] To exact; to demand, to require; to call for, to necessitate; ~ *des égards,* to demand respect; ~ *des soins,* to require care.
exigibilité (ɛgziʒibilite), s.f. Exigibility, possibility of exacting, exactibility.
exigible (ɛgziʒibl), adj. Exigible, that may be exacted.
exigu, -ë (ɛgzigu), adj. [L *exiguus*] Exiguous, very small; syn. PETIT.
exiguïté (ɛgzigyite), s.f. Exiguity, exiguousness.
exil (ɛgzil), s.m. [L *exilium*] Exile (abstract sense), banishment.
exilé, -e (ɛgzile), s.m.f. Exile. ~, **e-**, p. adj. Exiled.
exiler (ɛgzile), v.a. To exile, to banish; **s'**~, v.pr. to go into (voluntary) exile; (fig.) to seclude oneself; syn. BANNIR.
existant, -e (ɛgzistɑ̃), p. adj. Existing, existent, in being; extant.
existence (ɛgzistɑ̃s), s.f. **1.** Existence, being, life; living; livelihood; *moyens d'*~, means of livelihood; **2.** (comm.) stock in hand.
exister (ɛgziste), v.n. [L *existere*] To exist, to be in existence; to be extant; to live; *il existe,* there is, there are; (colloq.) *ça n'existe pas!*, rubbish!, piffle!, it 's not worth mentioning.
ex-libris (ɛkslibris), s.m. [L wd] Exlibris.
exocet (ɛgzɔsɛ), s.m. [f. L *exocoetus*] (ichth.) Flying fish.
exode (ɛgzɔd), s.m. [Gr. *exodos*] Exodus, exodium.
exonération (ɛgzɔnera'sjɔ̃), s.f. Exoneration; exemption; ~ *d'impôt,* exemption from taxation.
exonérer (ɛgzɔnere), v.a. [L *exonerare*] To exonerate, to free from blame; to exempt; ~ *du service militaire,* to exempt from military service.
exophtalmie (ɛgzɔftalmi), s.f. [*ex*+Gr. *opththalmos*] Exophthalmia.
exophtalmique (ɛgzɔftalmik), adj. Exophthalmic.
exorable (ɛgzɔrabl), adj. [f. L *exorare*] Exorable, accessible to entreaty.
exorbitant, -e (ɛgzɔrbitɑ̃), adj. [f. *ex+orbite*] Exorbitant.
exorcisation (ɛgzɔrsiza'sjɔ̃), s.f. Exorcization.
exorciser (ɛgzɔrsize), v.a. [Gr. *exorkizein*] To exorcize, to cast out (devils, &c.); (fig.) to conjure.
exorciseur (ɛgzɔrsizœr), s.m. Exorcist.
exorde (ɛgzɔrd), s.m. [L *exordium*] Exordium.
exosmose (ɛgzɔsmoz), s.f. [Gr. *exō+ōsmos*] (phys.) Exosmosis.
exostose (ɛgzɔstoz), s.f. [Gr. *exō+osteon*] (pathol.) Exostosis.
exotérique (ɛgzɔterik), adj. [Gr. *exōterikos*] Exoteric.
exotique (ɛgzɔtik), adj. [Gr. *exōtikos*] Exotic.
exotisme (ɛgzɔtism), s.m. Exotism.
expansibilité (ɛkspɑ̃sibilite), s.f. Expansibility.
expansible (ɛkspɑ̃sibl), adj. [f. *expansion*] Expansible, stretchable.
expansi-f, -ve (ɛkspɑ̃sif), Expansile; (fig.) expansive, effusive.
expansion (ɛkspɑ̃sjɔ̃), s.f. [L *expansio*] Expansion; (fig.) expansiveness.
expatriation (ɛkspatria'sjɔ̃), s.f. Expatriation.
expatrier (ɛkspatrie), v.a. [f. L *ex+patria*] To expatriate; **s'**~, v.pr. to expatriate oneself, to leave one's country.
expectant, -e (ɛkspɛktɑ̃), adj. Expectant.
expectati-f, -ve (ɛkspɛktatif), adj. Expectative.
expectation (ɛkspɛkta'sjɔ̃), s.f. [L *expectatio*] Expectation, expectancy.
expectative (ɛkspɛktativ), s.f. Expectative, expectancy.
expectorant, -e (ɛkspɛktɔrɑ̃), adj. s.m. Expectorant.
expectoration (ɛkspɛktɔra'sjɔ̃), s.f. Expectoration; syn. CRACHEMENT.
expectorer (ɛkspɛktɔre), v.a. [L *expectorare*] To expectorate; syn. CRACHER.
expédiée (ɛkspedje), s.f. Running hand (-writing).
expédient, -e (ɛkspedjɑ̃), adj. [L *expediens*] Expedient.
expédient (ɛkspedjɑ̃), s.m. Expedient, device; last shift; *en être réduit aux* ~*s*, to be reduced to one's last shift; (pej.) *vivre d'*~*s*, to live by one's wits; syn. RESSOURCE.
expédier (ɛkspedje), v.a. [L *expedire*] **1.** To dispatch, to send off, to forward; **2.** to draw up (a deed, &c.); **3.** (fam.) to account for (to kill), to dispatch.
expédit-eur, -rice (ɛkspeditœr), s.m.f. Sender; shipper.
expéditi-f, -ve (ɛkspeditif), adj. Expeditious.

expédition (ɛkspedisjɔ̃), s.f. [L *expeditio*] **1.** Expedition, dispatch; shipment, consignment; (pl.) dispatches; *faire l'~ de,* to dispatch, to forward; *l'~ des troupes,* the expedition of troops; *homme d'~,* able or efficient man; **2.** (law) copy; drawing up; **3.** expedition, warlike enterprise, raid.

expéditionnaire (ɛkspedisjɔnɛr), s.m.f. **1.** Sender, shipper; **2.** forwarding clerk; (law) copying clerk. **~,** adj. Expeditionary.

expéditivement (ɛkspeditivmɑ̃), adv. Expeditiously, speedily.

expérience (ɛksperjɑ̃s), s.f. [L *experientia*] Experience; trial; (scient.) experiment; *homme d'~,* experienced, wise man; *par ~,* by experience; from experience.

expérimental, -e, (aux) (ɛksperimɑ̃tal), adj. Experimental.

expérimentalement (ɛksperimɑ̃talmɑ̃), adv. Experimentally.

expérimentat-eur, -rice (ɛksperimɑ̃tatœr), s.m.f. Experimenter. **~,** p. adj. Experimentative.

expérimentation (ɛksperimɑ̃ta'sjɔ̃), s.f. Experimentation.

expérimenté, -e (ɛksperimɑ̃te), p. adj. Experienced; skilled.

expérimenter (ɛksperimɑ̃te), v.a. [f. L *experimentum*] To experiment with, to test; **~,** v.n. to experiment.

expert, -e (ɛkspɛr), adj. [L *expertus*] Expert (*à*, at, in), skilled, skilful. **~,** s.m.f. Expert, appraiser, valuer, surveyer; *à dire d'~,* according to good authority.

expertement (ɛkspɛrtəmɑ̃), adv. Expertly, skilfully.

expertise (ɛkspɛrtiz), s.f. Survey, valuation, assessment (by experts); experts' report.

expertiser (ɛkspɛrtize), v.a. To value, to assess, to take an expert's advice on, or valuation of.

expiable (ɛkspjabl), adj. [L *expiabilis*] Expiable.

expiat-eur, -rice (ɛkspjatœr), adj. Expiatory.

expiation (ɛkspja'sjɔ̃), s.f. [L *expiatio*] Expiation, atonement; *en ~ de,* as an atonement for, in atonement of.

expiatoire (ɛkspjatwar), adj. Expiatory.

expier (ɛkspje), v.a. [L *expiare*] To expiate, to atone for.

expirant, -e (ɛkspirɑ̃), p. adj. Expiring.

expirateur (ɛkspiratœr), adj. (anat.) Expiratory. **~,** s.m. Expiratory muscle.

expiration (ɛkspira'sjɔ̃), s.f. Expiration; expiry, termination.

expirer (ɛkspire), v.a. [L *exspirare*] To expire, to breathe out; to exhale; **~,** v.n. to expire, to die; to expire (of leases, &c.).

explétι-f, -ve (ɛkspletif), adj. s.m. [L *expletivus*] Expletive.

explétivement (ɛkspletivmɑ̃), adv. Expletively.

explicable (ɛksplikabl), adj. Explicable.

explicateur (ɛksplikatœr), adj. Explicatory. **~,** s.m. Explainer.

explicati-f, -ve (ɛksplikatif), adj. Explicative, explanatory.

explication (ɛksplika'sjɔ̃), s.f. Explanation, explication; *avoir une ~ avec X,* to have it out with X.

explicite (ɛksplisit), adj. [L *explicitus*] Explicit.

explicitement (ɛksplisitmɑ̃), adv. Explicitly.

expliquer (ɛksplike), v.a. [L *explicare*] To explain, to account for, to expound; to construe; **s'~,** v.pr. **1.** to express oneself, one's ideas; **2.** to have an explanation with each other, to have it out; **3.** to be accounted for, to be explained.

exploit (ɛksplwa), s.m. [f. *exploiter*] **1.** Exploit, feat, achievement; (colloq.) stunt; **2.** (law) writ; *signifier un ~,* to serve a writ.

exploitable (ɛksplwatabl), adj. Exploitable, workable.

exploitant (ɛksplwatɑ̃), p. adj. Exploiting. **~,** s.m. Exploiter.

exploitation (ɛksplwata'sjɔ̃), s.f. **1.** Exploitation, working; improvement; cultivation; *en ~,* in course of exploitation; *mettre en ~,* to begin to work; *matériel d'~,* working stock; *~ rurale,* farming; **2.** exploitation, profiting (by), cheating.

exploiter (ɛksplwate), v.a. [pop. L *explicitare*] **1.** To exploit, to work (mines, &c.); to improve, to cultivate (land, &c.); **2.** to exploit, to impose upon, to take advantage of; to sweat; (rare) **~,** v.n. (law) to serve a writ.

exploiteu-r, -se (ɛksplwatœr), s.m.f. Exploiter, sweater.

explorable (ɛksplɔrabl), adj. Explorable.

explorat-eur, -rice (ɛksplɔratœr), s.m.f. Explorer. **~,** adj. Exploring, exploratory.

exploration (ɛksplɔra'sjɔ), s.f. Exploration.

explorer (ɛksplɔre), v.a. [L *explorare*] To explore, to investigate, to search.

exploser (ɛksploze), v.n.a. To explode.

exploseur (ɛksplozœr), s.m. Fuse, exploder.

explosible (ɛksplozibl), adj. Explosive.

explosi-f, -ve (ɛksplozif), adj. Exploding, explosive. **~,** s.m. Explosive.

explosion (ɛksplozjɔ̃), s.f. [L *explodere*] Explosion, bursting, blowing-up; (fig.) explosion, outbreak.

exponentiel, -le (ɛkspɔnɑ̃sjɛl), adj. [L *exponens*] (math.) Exponential.

exportable (ɛkspɔrtabl), adj. Exportable.

exportat-eur, -rice (ɛkspɔrtatœr), s.m.f. Exporter. **~,** adj. Exporting, export.

exportation (ɛksporta'sjɔ̃), s.f. Exportation, export.
exporter (ɛksporte), v.a. [L *ex+portare*] To export.
exposant, -e (ɛkspozɑ̃), s.m.f. **1.** (art) Exhibitor; **2.** (law) petitioner; **3.** s.m. (math.) index, exponent.
exposé (ɛkspoze), s.m. Statement, account, report; explanation; paper, essay, lecture; *faire un* ~, to draw up a statement; to give a (technical) lecture; *faire l'~ de*, to state, to give an account of.
exposer (ɛkspoze), v.a. [L *ex+ponere*] **1.** To expose (to view), to show, to display; ~ *en vente*, to expose for sale; *une maison exposée au midi*, a house facing south; **2.** to state, to expound, to explain; ~ *un système*, to expound a system; **3.** to expose, to hazard, to endanger, to lay open; ~ *sa vie*, to imperil one's life; **4.** (obs.) to abandon (a child); **s'~**, v.pr. to expose oneself, to lay oneself open (to); to be exposed (to).
exposition (ɛkspozisjɔ̃), s.f. **1.** Exhibition; exposure; ~ *de fleurs, de bétail*, flower-show, cattle-show; **2.** situation, orientation; **3.** (fig.) statement, explanation, exposition, account; *faire l'~ de*, to make a statement of.
expr-ès, -esse (ɛksprɛ), adj. [L *expressus*] Express, precise, formal, positive; *défense expresse de*, it is strictly forbidden to; ~, s.m. Express messenger, express courier. ~, adv. On purpose, purposely, expressly; *c'est un fait* ~, it was done on purpose.
express (ɛksprɛs), s.m. adj. [Engl. wd] Express (train).
expressément (ɛksprɛsemɑ̃), adv. Expressly, clearly, distinctly.
expressi-f, -ve (ɛksprɛsif), adj. Expressive.
expression (ɛksprɛsjɔ̃), s.f. [L *expressio*] **1.** Expression; expressiveness; utterance; *réduit à sa plus simple* ~, (math.) reduced to its lowest terms, (fig.) reduced to a minimum; **2.** squeezing.
expressivement (ɛksprɛsivmɑ̃), adv. Expressively.
exprimable (ɛksprimabl), adj. Expressible.
exprimer (ɛksprime), v.a. [L *exprimere*] **1.** (fig.) To express, to convey by words or gesture, to betoken; to utter; **2.** to squeeze out, to press out; **s'~**, v.pr. to express oneself, one's thoughts; to be expressed.
expromission (ɛkspromisjɔ̃), s.f. [L *expromissio*] Expromission.
expropriat-eur, -rice (ɛkspropriatœr), s.m.f. Expropriator. ~, adj. Expropriating.
expropriation (ɛkspropria'sjɔ̃), s.f. Expropriation.
exproprier (ɛksproprie), v.a. [f. L *ex+proprius*] To expropriate, to dispossess.
expugnable (ɛkspyɲabl), adj. [L *expugnabilis*] Expugnable.
expulser (ɛkspylse), v.a. [L *expulsare*] To expel, to eject, to drive out, to oust.
expulsi-f, -ve (ɛkspylsif), adj. Expulsive.
expulsion (ɛkspylsjɔ̃), s.f. Expulsion, expelling, ousting.
expurgation (ɛkspyrga'sjɔ̃), s.f. **1.** Expurgation; **2.** (forestry) thinning.
expurgatoire (ɛkspyrgatwar), adj. Expurgatorial; expurgatory.
expurger (ɛkspyrʒe), v.a. [L *expurgare*] To expurgate; to bowdlerize.
exquis, -e (ɛkski), adj. [L *exquisitus*] Exquisite ⚠; choice, delightful, refined, nice. ~, s.m. (abstract) Exquisiteness. ⚠ English 'exquisite' frequently = *aigu, intense*, ex.: exquisite pain; *exquis* in French is not used in this sense.
exquisement (ɛkskizmɑ̃), adv. Delightfully, exquisitely (⚠ see *exquis*).
exquisité (ɛkskizite), s.f. (rare) Exquisiteness.
exsangue (ɛksɑ̃g), adj. [L *ex+sanguis*] Bloodless; anaemic; (fig.) feeble, spiritless.
exstrophie (ɛkstrofi), s.f. [Gr. *ex+strophē*] (pathol.) Exstrophy.
exsuccion (ɛksyksjɔ̃), s.f. Sucking up or out.
exsudant, -e (ɛksydɑ̃), adj. s.m. Exudative.
exsudation (ɛksyda'sjɔ̃), s.f. Exudation, sweat, oozing out.
exsuder (ɛksyde), v.a.n. [L *exsudare*] To exude, to give off.
extase (ɛkstɑz), s.f. [Gr. *ekstasis*] Ecstasy, rapture; (fig.) *être en* ~ *devant quelqu'un* or *quelque chose*, to be in raptures over a person or thing.
(s')extasier (sɛkstɑzje), v.pr. To fall into ecstasy, to go into raptures.
extatique (ɛkstatik), adj. Ecstatic, rapturous. ~, s.m.f. Ecstatic.
extemporané, -e (ɛkstɑ̃porane), adj. [L *extemporaneus*] Extemporaneous; extemporary; extempore.
extenseur (ɛkstɑ̃sœr), adj. Extensory. ~, s.m. **1.** (anat.) Extensor; **2.** chest-expander.
extensibilité (ɛkstɑ̃sibilite), s.f. Extensibility.
extensible (ɛkstɑ̃sibl), adj. Extensible, stretchable, elastic.
extensi-f, -ve (ɛkstɑ̃sif), adj. Causing extension; extensive.
extension (ɛkstɑ̃sjɔ̃), s.f. [L *extensio*] Extension, stretching; extent.
exténuation (ɛkstenɥa'sjɔ̃), s.f. Extenuation, exhaustion.
exténuer (ɛkstenɥe), v.a. [L *extenuare*] To tire out; (archaic in French) to extenuate; ⚠ in English the most usual sense of

'to extenuate' is *diminuer, atténuer*; **s'~**, v.pr. to wear oneself out.

extérieur, -e (ɛksterjœr), adj. [L *exterior*] Exterior, external, outward; foreign; syn. EXTERNE. ~, s.m. Exterior, outside; appearance; foreign countries, abroad; *nouvelles de l'~*, news from abroad.

extérieurement (ɛksterjœrmɑ̃), adv. Externally, outwardly, exteriorly; (fig.) in appearance, superficially.

extériorisation (ɛksterjɔriza'sjɔ̃), s.f. Exteriorization.

extérioriser (ɛksterjɔrize), v.a. To exteriorize.

extériorité (ɛksterjɔrite), s.f. Exteriority.

exterminat-eur, -rice (ɛkstɛrminatœr), adj. Exterminating. ~, s.m.f. Exterminator.

extermination (ɛkstɛrmina'sjɔ̃), s.f. Extermination.

exterminer (ɛkstɛrmine), v.a. [L *exterminare*] To exterminate; to annihilate; **s'~**, v.pr. to kill each other; (pop.) to wear oneself out.

externat (ɛkstɛrna), s.m. **1.** Day-school; **2.** post of dresser (in a hospital).

externe (ɛkstɛrn), adj. [L *externus*] Exterior, outer; syn. EXTÉRIEUR. ~, s.m. **1.** Day-scholar; **2.** dresser (in hospitals).

exterritorialité (ɛkstɛritɔrjalite), s.f. Exterritoriality, extraterritoriality.

extinct-eur, -rice (ɛkstɛ̃ktœr), adj. Extinguishing. ~, s.m. Fire-extinguisher.

extincti-f, -ve (ɛkstɛ̃ktif), adj. [f. L *extinctum*] Extinctive.

extinction (ɛkstɛ̃ksjɔ̃), s.f. [f. L *extinguere*] **1.** Extinction; quenching (of fire); (mil.) *~ des feux*, lights out; *~ de voix*, loss of voice; **2.** redemption (of liabilities); **3.** liquidation, settlement (of debts); **4.** quelling (of disturbances).

extinguible (ɛkstɛ̃gibl), adj. Extinguishable, quenchable.

extirpable (ɛkstirpabl), adj. Extirpable.

extirpateur (ɛkstirpatœr), s.m. **1.** Extirpator; **2.** (agric. mach.) extirpator, weeder, weed-grubber.

extirpation (ɛkstirpa'sjɔ̃), s.f. Extirpation.

extirper (ɛkstirpe), v.a. [L *extirpare*] To extirpate; syn. DÉRACINER.

extorquer (ɛkstɔrke), v.a. [L *extorquere*] To extort, to wrest, to worm out.

extorqueu-r, -se (ɛkstɔrkœr), s.m.f. Extortioner.

extorsion (ɛkstɔrsjɔ̃), s.f. [L *extorsio*] Extortion.

extra (ɛkstra), pref. [L wd] Extra; *vin ~*, extra-special wine. ~, s.m. **1.** Extra, something extra; **2.** (domestic service) temporary or extra help; temporary job.

extracteur (ɛkstraktœr), s.m. Extractor.

extractible (ɛkstraktibl), adj. Extractable.

extracti-f, -ve (ɛkstraktif), adj. Extractive.

extraction (ɛkstraksjɔ̃), s.f. [L *extractio*] Extraction; descent, birth; *de basse ~*, of low birth, of humble extraction; *l'~ d'une dent*, the drawing of a tooth.

extrader (ɛkstrade), v.a. To extradite.

extradition (ɛkstradisjɔ̃), s.f. [L *ex*+*traditio*] Extradition.

extrados (ɛkstrado), s.m. (arch.) Extrados.

extra-fin, -fine (ɛkstrafɛ̃), adj. Superfine.

extra-fort (ɛkstrafɔr), s.m. (dressm.) Prussian binding.

extraire (ɛkstrɛr), v.a. [L *extrahere*] To extract; to make extracts from (writings, &c.); to draw, take, pull, or dig out.

extrait (ɛkstrɛ), s.m. **1.** Extract; **2.** epitome, abstract (of books, &c.); **3.** certificate; *~ authentique*, certified copy of a document; *~ de naissance, mariage, baptême*, certificate of birth, marriage, baptism; *~ mortuaire*, death certificate.

extrajudiciaire (ɛkstraʒydisjɛr), adj. Extra-judicial.

extralégal, -e, (aux) (ɛkstralegal), adj. Extra-legal.

extra-muros (ɛkstramyros), adv. [L wd] Suburban, without or outside the walls (of a city).

extraordinaire (ɛkstrɔrdinɛr), adj. [*extra*+*ordinaire*] Extraordinary, unusual, uncommon; odd, queer; (Inquisition) *question ~*, rack.

extraordinairement (ɛkstrɔrdinɛrmɑ̃), adv. Extraordinarily.

extravagance (ɛkstravagɑ̃s), s.f. Extravagance, folly, extravagant act, excessive expenditure of money; *dire des ~s*, to speak wildly.

extravagant, -e (ɛkstravagɑ̃), adj. Extravagant, wild.

extravaguer (ɛkstravage), v.n. [L *extravagari*] To rave, to talk wildly or extravagantly.

extravasation, extravasion (ɛkstravɑsa'sjɔ̃, ɛkstravɑsjɔ̃), s.f. Extravasation.

(s')extravaser (sɛkstravɑze), v.pr. [L *extra*+*vas*] To extravasate.

extrême (ɛkstrɛm), adj. [L *extremus*] Extreme, utmost. ~, s.m. Extreme, utmost point; *se jeter dans les ~s*, to run to extremes; *les ~s se touchent*, extremes meet.

extrêmement (ɛkstrɛməmɑ̃), adj. Extremely.

extrême-onction (ɛkstrɛmɔ̃ksjɔ̃), s.f. Extreme unction.

extrémiste (ɛkstremist), adj. s.m.f. Extremist.

extrémité (ɛkstremite), s.f. **1.** Extremity, end; tip; **2.** last moment, verge of death; *à l'~*, without resource; dying; **~s**, (pl.) extremities, violent actions.

extrinsèque (ɛkstrɛ̃sɛk), adj. [L *extrinsecus*] Extrinsic, extrinsical.
exubérance (egzyberɑ̃s), s.f. Exuberance.
exubérant, -e (egzyberɑ̃), adj. [L *exuberans*] Exuberant; luxuriant.
exubération (egzybera'sjɔ̃), s.f. Exuberance.
exubérer (egzybere), v.n. (rare) To exuberate.
exulcérer (egzylsere), v.a. [L *exulcerare*] To exulcerate.
exultation (egzylta'sjɔ̃), s.f. [f. *exulter*] Exultation, exultancy.
exulter (egzylte), v.n. [L *exultare*] To exult; to be exultant.
exutoire (egzytwar), s.m. [L *exutus*] (med.) Issue; (fig.) outlet.
ex-voto (ɛksvoto), s.m. invar. [L wd] Ex voto.
eyra (ɛra), s.m. (zool.) Kind of cougar.

F

F, f (ɛf), s.m. 6th letter of the alphabet. Abbrev. of *franc*, and (mus.) of *forte*.
fa (fa), s.m. [first syllable of *famuli* in second line of the 13th-cent. Hymn to John the Baptist] (mus.) fa = F; *clef de* ~, bass clef, F clef.
fabagelle (fabaʒɛl), s.f. **fabago** (fabago), s.m. (bot.) Bean-caper; *Zygophyllum fabago*.
fable (fabl), s.f. [L *fabula*] **1.** Fable, allegory, fiction, legendary tale; mythology; **2.** untruth, fib; **3.** laughing-stock; *devenir la* ~ *de la ville*, to become the laughing-stock of the town.
fabliau (pl. **-x**) (fablijo), s.m. [f. *fable*] Fabliau.
fablier (fablije), s.m. [f. *fable*] **1.** Fable-book; **2.** fabler, fabulist.
fabricant (fabrikɑ̃), s.m. [f. *fabriquer*] Manufacturer, maker.
fabricateur (fabrikatœr), s.m. (pej.) Forger, coiner, fabricator.
fabrication (fabrika'sjɔ̃), s.f. [f. L *fabricatio*] **1.** Manufacture, fabrication, making; **2.** forging.
fabricien (fabrisjɛ̃), s.m. [f. *fabrique*] Vestryman, churchwarden.
fabrique (fabrik), s.f. [f. L *faber, fabrica*] **1.** Manufacture, factory, works; *prix de* ~, cost price; *marque de* ~, trade mark; (fam.) *c'est de sa* ~, that is of his invention; **2.** fabric ⚠, property, revenue of a church; vestry-board. ⚠ 'Fabric' in English means also *édifice, structure, tissu, textile*, but *fabrique* has none of these acceptations.
fabriquer (fabrike), v.a. To manufacture, to fabricate, to make; to forge; (fam.) *qu'est-ce que vous fabriquez là?*, now what are you doing?, what are you up to?
fabuleusement (fabyløzmɑ̃), adv. Fabulously.
fabuleu-x, -se (fabylø), adj. [f. L *fabula*] Fabulous.
fabuliste (fabylist), s.m.f. Fabulist.
façade (fasad), s.f. [f. It. *facciata*] Front, frontage, façade; (fig.) appearance; *tout cela n'est que* ~, that's all sham; (slang) *refaire sa* ~, to make up, to paint one's face.
face (fas), s.f. [L *facies*] Face, visage; countenance, look; surface (of a thing); (geom.) plane surface of a solid; side; (of a coin) head; ~ *à* ~, face to face; *en* ~, to a person's face; *regardez-moi en* ~, look me full in the face; *je le leur dirai en* ~, I will tell them to their faces; *en* ~ *de*, opposite to, in front of; *de* ~, in front, with a full front, full face; *à la* ~ *de*, in the face of; ~ *de carême*, woe-begone face; *la question change de* ~, the question bears quite another aspect; *faire* ~ *à une dépense*, to meet an expenditure; *faire* ~ *au danger*, to look danger in the face; *jouer à pile ou* ~, to play at heads or tails, or pitch and toss; *faire volte-*~, to wheel round; to face about; *demi-tour* ~ *à droite!*, right about face!; about turn!; *sauver la* ~, to keep up appearances; to save one's face; *perdre la* ~, to lose face.
face-à-main (fasamɛ̃), s.m. invar. Folding eye-glass, lorgnette.
facétie (fasesi), s.f. [L *facetia*] Joke, buffoonery, jest; facetiousness.
facétieusement (fasesjøzmɑ̃), adv. Facetiously.
facétieu-x, -se (fasesjø), adj. Facetious, jocular.
facette (fasɛt), s.f. [f. *face*] Facet; *taillé à* ~*s*, cut into facets; faceted.
facetter (fasɛte), v.a. To facet.
fâché, -e (faʃe), p. adj. Displeased, offended, vexed, nettled; angry (*contre*, with); sorry (*de*, for, that); on bad terms (*avec*, with), at variance (with).
fâcher (faʃe), v.a. [f. LL *fasticare*] To anger, to offend, to displease, to make angry, to vex; *ils sont fâchés*, they are on bad terms; **se** ~, v.pr. to get angry, to take offence, to become exasperated; to fall out, to quarrel.
fâcherie (faʃri), s.f. Vexation, annoyance; quarrel.
fâcheusement (faʃøzmɑ̃), adv. Sadly, regrettably, sorrily; unpleasantly; unfortunately.
fâcheu-x, -se (faʃø), adj. Sad, grievous, vexatious, troublesome, unpleasant, untoward, regrettable, untimely. ~, s.m.f. Bore, importunate person.
facial, -e, (aux) (fasjal), adj. Facial; *angle* ~, facial angle.
facies (fasjɛs), s.m. [L wd] Facies, aspect of the face.

facile (fasil), adj. [L *facilis*] Easy, facile, natural, fluent, compliant; (pej.) loose; *de mœurs* ~*s*, abandoned.

facilement (fasilmɑ̃), adv. Easily, with facility.

facilité (fasilite), s.f. [L *facilitas*] Facility, ease, readiness of speech, &c., aptitude; accommodation, convenience, advantage; weakness, compliance; looseness.

faciliter (fasilite), v.a. To facilitate, to make easy.

façon (fasɔ̃), s.f. [L *factio*] Make, making, workmanship, fashion, shape, fashioning; manner, way, sort, kind; (agric.) dressing; *tailleur à* ~, jobbing tailor; *à la* ~ *de*, after the manner of, *à sa* ~, in one's own way; *de cette* ~, in this way, so, at this rate; *de* ~ *à*, so as to; *de* ~ *ou d'autre*, somehow or other, in some way; *de* ~ *que*, so that; *de sa* ~, of his, her, or one's making; *je lui dirai ma* ~ *de penser*, I will give him a piece of my mind; *c'est une* ~ *de parler*, it's not to be taken too literally; *de toute* ~, any way, in any case; anyhow, at any rate; *en aucune* ~, by no means, in no way; *sans* ~, unceremoniously; **4.** ceremony, ado, fuss, difficulty; *faire des* ~*s*, (*a*) to resist; (*b*) to make a great deal of fuss; (*c*) to stand upon ceremony; *j'accepte sans* ~, I accept without any ceremony.

faconde (fakɔ̃d), s.f. [L *facundia*] Fluency of speech, loquacity; (fam.) gift of the gab.

façonné (fasɔne), s.m. Figured stuff.

façonner (fasɔne), v.a. [f. *façon*] To make, to work, to make up, to fashion, to shape; to improve; to adorn; (agric.) to dress.

façonni-er, -ère (fasɔnje), adj. s.m.f. **1.** Ceremonious, formal (person); **2.** (person) working at home.

fac-similé (faksimile), s.m. [L wd] Facsimile.

factage (faktaʒ), s.m. [f. *facteur*] **1.** Porterage, carriage; letters and parcels delivery; **2.** the price to be paid for this.

fact-eur, -rice (faktœr), s.m.f. [f. L *factum, factor*] **1.** Maker (of musical instruments); **2.** factor, commission agent or salesman; **3.** postman, letter-carrier; **4.** porter, carrier (of parcels, luggage, &c.); **5.** (math.) factor; (fig.) circumstance, fact, influence, or element contributing to a result.

factice (faktis), adj. [L *facticius*] Factitious, artificial.

facticement (faktismɑ̃), adv. Factitiously.

factieu-x, -se (faksjø), adj. Factious. ~, s.m.f. Factionist.

faction (faksjɔ̃), s.f. [L *factio*] **1.** Faction; **2.** sentry, watch, guard; *être de* ~, to be on sentry-duty; *être en* ~, to stand sentinel; *relever de* ~, to relieve sentry; (fig.) long waiting, watch.

factionnaire (faksjɔnɛr), s.m. (mil.) Sentry, sentinel.

factorage (faktɔraʒ), s.m. [f. *facteur*] (comm.) Factorage.

factorie, factorerie (faktɔri, faktɔrri), s.f. [f. *facteur*] Factory (in the colonies).

factotum (faktɔtɔm), s.m. [L wd] Factotum, Jack of all trades.

factum (faktɔm), s.m. [L wd] Factum, statement, memorial, pamphlet; (pej.) libel.

facture (faktyr), s.f. [f. L *facere*] **1.** Bill, invoice; **2.** making, building (of organs, pianos); **3.** composition, literary workmanship.

facturer (faktyre), v.a. To invoice.

facturi-er, -ère (faktyrje), s.m.f. Invoice clerk; ~, s.m. invoice-book.

facule (fakyl), s.f. [L *facula*] (astr.) Facula.

facultati-f, -ve (fakyltatif), adj. Optional, facultative.

facultativement (fakyltativmɑ̃), adv. Optionally.

faculté (fakylte), s.f. [L *facultas*] **1.** Faculty, ability, aptitude; **2.** faculty, power inherent in the body, an organ, or a chemical substance; **3.** liberty, right, possibility of doing something; **4.** means, faculties, mind; **5.** faculty, department of a university.

fadaise (fadɛz), s.f. [f. Provenç. *fadeza*] Fiddle-faddle, trifle, nonsense, silly speech.

fadasse (fadas), adj. Mawkish, insipid, dull, insignificant, palish, wishy-washy.

fade (fad), adj. [f. L *vapidus*] Insipid, tasteless, vapid, mawkish, flat, insignificant.

fadé, -e, adj. (slang) In a bad way, worn out; *il est* ~, he is done for, he is a goner.

fadement (fadmɑ̃), adv. Insipidly, mawkishly, vapidly.

fadeur (fadœr), s.f. [f. *fade*] **1.** Insipidity, tastelessness, vapidness, flatness, mawkishness; **2.** silly insipid talk or compliment.

fafiot (fafjo), s.m. (colloq.) Banknote, flimsy; *des* ~*s*, flimsies.

fagne (faɲ), s.f. [etym. unkn.] Bog at the top of a mountain.

fagot (fago), s.m. [f. L *fax*, or *fagus*?] Faggot, fagot, bundle; *du vin de derrière les* ~*s*, extra-choice wine (hidden behind the fagots because of its value); *sentir le* ~, to savour of the stake, to be tainted with heresy; *il y a* ~*s et* ~*s*, there are men and men; *c'est un vrai* ~ *d'épines*, he is a regular bear; (rare) *débiter des* ~*s*, to tell idle stories, to talk nonsense.

fagotage (fagɔtaʒ), s.m. **1.** Faggotmaking; **2.** botch; **3.** ridiculous way of dressing.

fagoter (fagɔte), v.a. **1.** To faggot; **2.** to dress (a person) ridiculously or like a guy; to make a fright of; **se** ~, v.pr. to dress oneself ridiculously; to bundle oneself up.

fagoteur (fagɔtœr), s.m. Faggot-maker.

fagotin (fagɔtɛ̃), s.m. **1.** Small faggot; **2.** monkey dressed up; **3.** merry andrew, jack pudding.

fagoue (fagu), s.f. (butch.) Sweetbread, thymus; pig's pancreas.

faible (fɛbl), adj. [f. L *flebilis*] Weak, feeble, dim, wanting in strength, poor, sorry, meagre, slack, faint, faint-hearted, deficient, compliant, partial; *un ~ revenu*, a meagre income. ~, s.m. **1.** Weak person, weakling, the feeble, the poor; *protéger le ~*, to protect the feeble, the poor; *un ~ d'esprit*, a moron; **2.** weak point or side, foible; **3.** partiality, foible, predilection; *avoir un ~ pour*, to have a partiality for, to be partial to.

faiblement (fɛbləmɑ̃), adv. Feebly, weakly, faintly, slightly, poorly.

faiblesse (fɛblɛs), s.f. [f. *faible*] **1.** Weakness, feebleness, faintness, poorness, smallness, shortness, want of force, power, or character, complaisance; (extreme) indulgence; **2.** fainting-fit, swoon; *tomber en ~*, to swoon; **3.** partiality; fondness, foible.

faiblir (fɛblir), v.n. To become weak, to relent, to slacken, to flag, to abate, to give way, to yield.

faïence (fajɑ̃s), s.f. [f. *Faenza*, in Italy] Faience, earthenware, crockery.

faïencerie (fajɑ̃sri), s.f. Earthenware-manufactory; earthenware-trade.

faïencier (fajɑ̃sje), s.m. Earthenware-manufacturer; dealer in crockery.

faille (faj), s.f. **1.** Fissure, fault, excavation, dike; **2.** faille (a silk material).

failli, -e (faji), s.m.f. p. adj. [f. *faillir*] Bankrupt.

faillibilité (fajibilite), s.f. Fallibility.

faillible (fajibl), adj. Fallible.

faillir (fajir), v.n. [L *fallere*] **1.** To fail, to fall short, to miss, to be deficient; **2.** to err, to be mistaken, to do wrong, to sin; **3.** to be on the point of, to have well-nigh or nearly . . .; *j'ai failli l'oublier*, I nearly forgot it; *j'ai failli tomber*, I very nearly fell; **4.** to go bankrupt.

faillite (fajit), s.f. Failure; bankruptcy; *faire ~*, to fail, to break, to be (a) bankrupt, to become insolvent; *actif d'une ~*, assets in a bankruptcy; *déclaration de ~*, declaration of insolvency.

faim (fɛ̃), s.f. [L *fames*] Hunger; (fig.) craving appetite, eager desire, thirst; *avoir ~*, to be hungry; *apaiser sa ~*, to stay one's hunger; *avoir une ~ de loup*, to be as hungry as a hunter; to be ravenously hungry; *je meurs de ~*, I am ravenously hungry; *mourir de ~*, to starve to death, to die of starvation; *faire mourir de ~*, to starve to death; *réduire par la ~*, to starve out; *un meurt-de-~*, a starveling; *avoir ~ de gloire*, to hunger after, to long for, celebrity; *la ~ chasse le loup du bois*, hunger will break through stone walls; *~-valle*, s.f. morbidly ravenous appetite (of horses).

faîne (fɛn), s.f. [L *fagina*] Beech-nut.

fainéant, -e (fɛneɑ̃), adj. [*fait+néant*] Idle, sluggish, sluggard, lazy. ~, s.m.f. Idler, sluggard, drone, good-for-nothing, lazybones; loafer; *faire le ~*, to idle; syn. (pop.) FEIGNANT.

fainéanter (fɛneɑ̃te), v.n. To idle, to be lazy; to loaf.

fainéantise (fɛneɑ̃tiz), s.f. Idleness, laziness, slothfulness, loafing.

faînée (fɛne), s.f. [f. *faîne*] Crop of beech-mast; gathering of beech-nuts.

faire (fɛr), v.a. [L *facere*] To make, to create; to bring forth, to beget, to bear; to fabricate, to construct, to build, to form, to fashion; to do, to perform, to execute, to perpetrate; to cause, to bring; to gain, to collect, to reap, to acquire; to turn, to convert; to form, to train; to walk, to travel; to constitute, to compose, to make up, to be; to tell, to say; to imitate, to counterfeit, to pretend to be; to compel; to allow; *~ du pain*, to make bread; *l'oiseau fait son nid*, the bird builds its nest; *~ une conférence*, to give a lecture; *~ un poème*, to compose a poem; *~ un calcul*, to make a calculation; *~ son testament*, to make one's will; *~ une description*, to give a description; *~ une opération*, to perform an operation; *~ un discours*, to make a speech; *~ la guerre, la paix*, to make war, peace; *~ des excuses*, to make an apology, to apologize; *~ serment*, to take an oath; *~ une maladie*, to have an illness; *~ usage (de)*, to make use (of); *~ un lit*, to make a bed; *~ de l'argent*, to make money; *~ fortune*, to make one's fortune, to grow rich; *~ ses orges*, to feather one's nest; *~ ses délices de*, to delight in; *~ les foins*, to make hay; *~ une chambre*, to do a room; *~ la cuisine*, to do the cooking; *~ le dîner*, to cook the dinner; *~ des progrès*, to make progress; *~ du chemin*, to make way; *~ son chemin*, to make one's way in the world, to succeed; *~ un pas*, to take a step; *~ une promenade*, to take a walk; *~ un voyage*, to make a voyage, a journey; *~ 60 Km. à l'heure*, to travel or go or do 60 *Km.* an hour; *~ 10 Km. à pied*, to walk 10 *Km.*; *deux et deux font quatre*, two and two make (or are) four;

~ *nombre*, to make up a number; ~ *honneur*, to do honour; ~ *le bien, le mal*, to do good, evil; ~ *du bien à X*, to do good to X; ~ *du mal à X*, to harm X; *que faites-vous aujourd'hui?*, what are you doing to-day?; *n'avoir rien à* ~, to have nothing to do; *bonne à tout* ~, maid-of-all-work; general servant; cook-general; (naut.) ~ *de l'eau*, to take in fresh water; ~ *eau*, to spring a leak; *que voulez-vous que j'y fasse?*, how can I help it?; *que* ~*?*, what is to be done?; *je n'en ferai rien*, I shall do nothing of the sort; *qu'est-ce que cela fait?*, what does it matter?; *n'avoir que* ~ *de*, to have no need of; to have nothing to do with; not to care for; to have no use for; ~ *l'aumône*, to give alms; *ne pas* ~ *quartier*, not to give quarter; ~ *sa prière*, to say one's prayers; ~ *ses Pâques*, to receive the Sacrament at Easter; ~ *son apprentissage*, to serve one's apprenticeship; ~ *un métier*, to follow, to carry on, a trade; ~ *ses études*, to study, to be at school; ~ *sa médecine*, to study medecine; ~ *attention* (*à*), to pay attention (to), to give heed (to), to mind; ~ *l'aimable*, to affect amiability; ~ *le fou*, to play the fool; ~ *semblant de*, to pretend to; ~ *le mort*, to sham dead; ~ *le dégoûté*, to turn up one's nose (at something); ~ *son malin*, to pose as a knowing one; ~ *l'enfant*, to be foolish, to act like a child; ~ *fi* (*de*), to despise, to turn up one's nose (at); ~ *de son mieux*, to do one's best, to strive; (colloq.) *la* ~ *à la pose*, to pose, to show off; ~ *fond* (*sur*), to rely (on); ~ *honte à*, to put to shame, to shame; ~ *horreur à*, to strike with horror; ~ *part à*, to let know; ~ *peur à*, to frighten; ~ *pitié*, to excite pity; ~ *queue*, to queue, to wait at the door; *rien n'y fait*, it is all of no use; ~ *sensation*, to create a sensation; ~ *silence*, to stop talking, to keep silence; *avoir fort à* ~, to have a great deal to do, to have a hard job of it; *comment* ~*?*, what is to be done?; *en* ~ *à sa tête*, to follow one's own bent (or idea); *oui, fit-il*, yes, said he; *fasse le Ciel que*, Heaven grant that; *elle ne fait que de sortir*, she has only just gone out; ~ *appeler*, to send for; ~ *dire*, to send word; ~ ~, to get done, to have made, built, &c.; ~ *entrer*, to show in; ~ *entendre*, (*a*) to give to understand; (*b*) to produce; ~ *savoir*, to let know, to inform (of); ~ *venir*, to send for; (slang) *il sait y* ~, he is up to snuff; *il fait jour*, it is daylight; *il fait froid, chaud*, it is cold, warm, hot, &c.; *il fait du vent*, it is windy; *il va* ~ *de l'orage*, there will be a storm; *il fait meilleur ici*, it is more comfortable here; *c'en est fait* (*de*), it's all up, it is all over (with); *cela fait bien*, that looks well; *vous faites bien* (*de*), you are right (to), you do well (to); (slang) *on lui a fait son porte-monnaie*, his purse has been stolen; **se** ~, v.pr. to be made, to be done, built, &c.; to become, to form onself, to improve, to get accustomed, inured, used (to); to grow, to pretend to be, to begin; *se* ~ *religieuse*, to become a nun; *ce vin s'est fait*, this wine has matured; *se* ~ *à la fatigue*, to inure oneself to hardships; *on se fait à tout*, one gets accustomed to anything; *se* ~ *la main*, to get one's hand in, to improve; *on se fait vieux*, one grows old; *il se fait tard*, it is getting late; *se laisser* ~, to take it lying down; *elle se fait aimer*, she makes herself liked, beloved; she ingratiates herself; *se* ~ *entendre*, to make oneself heard; *si ce mariage se fait*, if this marriage takes place; *comment cela se fait-il?*, how does it happen?, how is it?; *comment se fait-il que*, how is it that; *cela ne se fait pas*, that is not done, people do not do that; *il pourrait se* ~ *que*, it might happen that; *autant que* ~ *se peut*, as far as one can, as much as possible.

faire (fɛr), s.m. Doing, making, make, execution, workmanship, technique.

faire-part (fɛrpar), s.m. invar. Note announcing a birth, a christening, wedding, burial, &c.; invitation to a ceremony.

faisable (fɛzabl), adj. [f. *faire*] Feasible, practicable, possible.

faisan, -e (fɛzɑ̃), s.m.f. [L *phasianus*] (ornith.) Pheasant; ~*e*, hen-pheasant.

faisandé, -e (fɛzɑ̃de), p. adj. [f. *faisan*] High, gamy.

faisandeau (pl. **-x**) (fɛzɑ̃do), s.m. Young pheasant.

faisander (fɛzɑ̃de), v.a. To give a flavour of venison to, to keep (game) until it is high; **se** ~, v.pr. to get high.

faisanderie (fɛzɑ̃dri), s.f. Pheasantry.

faisandi-er, -ère (fɛzɑ̃dje), s.m.f. Pheasant-breeder.

faisceau (pl. **-x**) (fɛso), s.m. [LL *fascellus*] Bundle, fascicle, (anat.) fasciculus; cluster; (ant.) fasces; (mil.) pile of arms; *former les* ~*x*, to pile arms; (opt.) pencil.

faiseu-r, -se (fɛzœr), s.m.f. [f. *faire*] **1.** Maker, doer, performer; *une robe de chez le bon* ~, a gown made by a first-class dressmaker; *un* ~ *d'embarras*, a fussy person; *un* ~ *de tours*, a mountebank; ~ *d'affaires*, company promoter; ~ *de systèmes*, system-monger; **2.** swindler, charlatan, fraud, fibber; *méfiez-vous, c'est un* ~, take care, he is a fraud, or a swindler; *faiseuse d'anges*, abortionist, woman who procures a miscarriage by unlawful practices.

faisselle (fɛsɛl), s.f. [f. L *fiscella*] Cheese-vat.

fait, -e (fɛ), p. adj. [f. *faire*] Made, done, shaped, suited, intended, grown, grown up, ripe, matured, seasoned, inured (to), &c.; *habits tout ~s*, ready-made clothes, *aussitôt dit, aussitôt ~*, no sooner said than done; *c'est bien ~*, that's as it should be, it serves him (or her, or them, &c., right); *esprit bien ~*, good or intelligent man; sound mind; *jambe bien ~e*, well shaped (or shapely) leg; *un homme ~*, a grown-up man; *c'en est ~*, it's all over now; *c'en est fait de moi*, it's all over with me; *prix ~*, set price; *c'est une affaire ~e*, it's settled; *comme vous voilà ~!*, what a state you are in!; (slang), *je suis ~!*, I am nabbed!, or copped!

fait (fɛ), s.m. Fact, deed, act, doing, truth, reality, point in question, matter, object, behaviour; *au ~*, (*a*) in fact, after all, speaking of that, well, to the point; (*b*) acquainted (*de*, with), informed (of), aware (of); *mais au ~*, but to return to the point; *dans le ~, de ~*, truly, in fact, in reality, really; *en ~ de*, in matters of, with regard to; *par le ~*, in fact, speaking of that; *tout à ~*, quite, altogether, wholly, entirely, utterly; *si ~*, yes, indeed; *~s et gestes*, sayings and doings; *hauts ~s*, great deeds, exploits; *prendre X sur le ~*, to catch X in the very act; *~ d'armes*, military exploit, feat of arms; *~s divers*, miscellaneous news; *ce n'est pas mon ~*, that does not suit me, that does not concern me; *le ~ est que*, the fact is that; it's true that, after all; *être sûr de son ~*, (*a*) to be sure of what one says, to be upon sure ground; (*b*) to be cocksure; *voies de ~*, blows, assault, violences; *prendre ~ et cause pour X*, to take X's part; to side with X; *dire son ~ à X*, to tell X some unpleasant truths; to give X a bit of one's mind; *venez au ~*, come to the point.

faîtage (fɛtaʒ), s.m. [f. *faîte*] Ridge, ridge-piece, ridge-lead.

faîte (fɛt), s.m. [f. OHG *first*, OF *feste*] Top, summit, ridge; (fig.) pinnacle, zenith, summit.

faîtière (fɛtjɛr), s.f. [f. *faîte*] Ridge-tile. ~, adj. Ridge, of the ridge.

fait-tout (fɛtu), s.m. [*fait*+*tout*] Stew-pan.

faix (fɛ), s.m. [f. L *fascis*] Burden, load.

fakir (fakir), s.m. [Arab. wd] Fakir.

falaise (falɛz), s.f. [Germ. orig.] Cliff.

falbala (falbala), s.m. [orig. uncert.] Furbelow.

fallacieusement (falasjøzmɑ̃), adv. Fallaciously.

fallacieu-x, -se (falasjø), adj. [L *fallaciosus*] Fallacious.

falloir (falwar), v. impers. [another form of *faillir*, f. L *fallere*] To be necessary, to be required, to be wanted, to need, to be needful; to be obliged; must, should, ought; *il faut manger pour vivre*, one must eat to live; *il me faut sortir*, I must go out; *il faudra voir!*, we shall see about that!; *comme il faut*, ladylike, gentlemanlike, well-bred; *faut-il que je sois bête!*, what a fool I am! **s'en ~**, v.pr. impers., to want, to be wanting, to fall short; *peu s'en faut que*, nearly; within a little; *peu s'en est fallu qu'il ne gagnât*, he was very near winning; *il s'en faut de vingt francs*, the sum is short by twenty francs; *il s'en faut de beaucoup*, very far from it; *tant s'en faut*, far from it;

falot (falo), s.m. [f. It. *falò*] Lantern, cresset.

falot, -e (falo), adj. [f. It. *falò*] Droll, ludicrous, laughable; dull, dim, weak.

falourde (falurd), s.f. [etym. unkn.] Faggot of thick sticks.

falsificat-eur, -rice (falsifikatœr), s.m.f. Falsifier, falsificator, forger, debaser, adulterator (of goods, &c.). ~, adj. That falsifies, debases, &c.

falsification (falsifika'sjɔ̃), s.f. Falsification, adulteration, sophistication; debasement (of coin).

falsifier (falsifje), v.a. [f. L *falsus*+*facere*] To falsify, to adulterate, to sophisticate; to debase (coin).

falun (falœ̃), s.m. [orig. unkn.] (geol.) Falun, shell-marl.

faluner (falyne), v.a. To manure with shell-marl.

falunière (falynjɛr), s.f. Shell-marl pit.

famé, -e (fame), adj. [f. L *fama*] Famed; *mal ~*, ill-famed, of bad repute; *bien ~*, of good repute.

famélique (famelik), adj. [L *famelicus*] Starving, famished. ~, s.m.f. Starveling.

fameusement (famøzmɑ̃), adv. Famously; (pop.) extremely, excessively, awfully, capitally.

fameu-x, -se (famø), adj. [L *famosus*] Famous, renowned, (colloq.) ripping, capital, excellent, topping, first-rate.

familial, -e, (aux) (familjal), adj. [f. L *familia*] Pertaining to family or home.

familiariser (familjarize), v.a. [f. *familier*] To familiarize, to accustom; **se ~**, v.pr. **1.** to grow or to get familiar; **2.** to get used, accustomed (*avec*, to), to familiarize oneself (with); (of animals) to grow tame.

familiarité (familjarite), s.f. **1.** Familiarity, unceremoniousness; **2.** close intercourse; **3.** ~*s*, (pl.) liberties; *se permettre des ~s*, to take liberties.

famili-er, -ère (familje), adj. [f. L *familiaris*] Familiar, intimate; well known, simple, common, usual; un-

ceremonious, free, over-free. ~, s.m. Familiar, favourite, bosom-friend.
familièrement (familjɛrmɑ̃), adv. Familiarly, unceremoniously.
familistère (familistɛr), s.m. [f. *famille*] (Fr. hist.) Familistery, phalanstery (a communist establishment after Fourier's system); syn. PHALANSTÈRE.
famille (famij), s.f. [L *familia*] Family, relatives, parentage, kin, kindred, race, group; *avoir de la* ~, to have children; *en* ~, at home; *avoir un air de* ~, to have a family likeness; *affaires de* ~, domestic concerns, family affairs, private affairs; *fils de* ~, young man of quality; gentleman's son; *mère de* ~, mother of a family; mother; *être chargé de* ~, to have a large family; *entrer dans une* ~, to enter a family; *nom de* ~, family name, surname.
famine (famin), s.f. [f. LL *famina*] Famine, hunger, scarcity or dearth of food; (fig.) *crier* ~ *sur un tas de blé*, to cry famine on a heap of corn; to complain of poverty when one has enough and to spare.
fanage (fanaʒ), s.m. [f. *faner*] Turning, tedding (of grass).
fanaison (fanɛzɔ̃) s.f. See FENAISON.
fanal (pl. **aux**) (fanal), s.m. [f. Gr. *phanos*] Lantern, ship's lantern, signal light.
fanatique (fanatik), adj. s.m.f. [L *fanaticus*] Fanatic, fanatical; ~ *de*, infatuated with.
fanatiquement (fanatikmɑ̃), adv. Fanatically.
fanatiser (fanatize), v.a. To fanaticize.
fanatisme (fanatism), s.m. Fanaticism.
fanchon (fɑ̃ʃɔ̃), s.f. [f. prop. n. *Françoise*] Kerchief; head-wrapper.
fandango (fɑ̃dɑ̃go), s.m. [Span. wd] Fandango.
fane (fan), s.f. [f. *faner*] Dead leaf, fallen leaf, leaf; top, tops (of carrots, &c.)
faner (fane), v.a.n. [f. L *fenum*] **1.** To ted, to turn (grass); **2.** to fade, to tarnish; **se** ~, v.pr. to fade, to fade away, to wither, to wilt.
faneu-r, -se (fanœr), s.m.f. Hay-maker; **~se**, s.f. tedding-machine.
fanfare (fɑ̃far), s.f. [f. *fanfaron*] Fanfare, flourish of trumpets, &c.; brass-band society; ostentatious boast.
fanfaron, -ne (fɑ̃farɔ̃), adj. [f. Span. *fanfarron*] Boasting, swaggering. ~, s.m.f. Boaster, braggart, braggadocio, swaggerer, blusterer; *faire le* ~, to play the braggart, to swagger.
fanfaronnade (fɑ̃farɔnad), s.f. Fanfaronade, brag.
fanfaronner (fɑ̃farɔne), v.n. To swagger, to boast, to utter fanfaronades.
fanfreluche (fɑ̃frəlyʃ), s.f. [f. LL *fanfaluca*] Bauble, light dress-ornaments, finery.
fange (fɑ̃ʒ), s.f. [etym. dub.] Mud, mire, dirt, filth; (fig.) vileness, filth of vice, degradation.
fangeu-x, -se (fɑ̃ʒø), adj. Muddy, miry, filthy.
fanion (fanjɔ̃), s.m. [f. *fanon*] Small flag, fanion, colour.
fanon (fanɔ̃), s.m. [f. OHG. *fano*] **1.** (obs.) Small flag; **2.** fannell, fanon; syn. MANIPULE; **3.** dewlap (of an ox, &c.); **4.** fetlock (of a horse); **5.** fin, bone (of a whale); **6.** wattle (of a turkey, cock, &c.); **7.** pendant (of a banner).
fantaisie (fɑ̃tɛzi), s.f. [f. Gr. *phantasia*] Fancy, imagination; humour, whim, caprice; something that pleases; *suivre sa* ~, to follow one's fancy; *se passer une* ~, to indulge a whim; *article de* ~, fancy article; *pain de* ~, fancy bread; *vivre à sa* ~, to live according to one's tastes; (mus.) fantasia; fantasy (⚠ only in the sense of image-making faculty = *imagination créatrice d'images fantastiques*).
fantaisiste (fɑ̃tɛzist), adj. s.m.f. Fanciful, whimsical (person).
fantasia (fɑ̃tazja), s.f. [It. wd] Fantasia, Arabian display of horsemanship.
fantasmagorie (fɑ̃tasmagɔri), s.f. [f. Gr. *phantasma*] Phantasmagoria.
fantasmagorique (fɑ̃tasmagɔrik), adj. Phantasmagoric.
fantasque (fɑ̃task), adj. [f. *fantaisie*] Fanciful, whimsical, capricious, odd; fantastic.
fantassin (fɑ̃tasɛ̃), s.m. [f. It. *fantaccino*] Foot-soldier.
fantastique (fɑ̃tastik), adj. [f. Gr. *phantastikos*] Fantastic, fantastical, fanciful; unbelievable, incredible, chimerical.
fantastiquement (fɑ̃tastikmɑ̃), adv. Fantastically, chimerically, unbelievably.
fantoche (fɑ̃tɔʃ), s.m. [f. It. *fantoccio*] Puppet, marionette; (fig.) weathercock; unreliable person.
fantomatique (fɑ̃tomatik), adj. Illusive, pertaining to a phantom.
fantôme (fɑ̃tom), s.m. [f. Gr. *phantasma*] Phantom, ghost, spectre; (fig.) shadow, chimera, wild fancy; *se faire des* ~*s*, to create chimeras.
faon (fɑ̃), s.m. [f. L *fetus*] (zool.) Fawn, doe, calf of deer.
faonner (fane), v.n. [f. *faon*] To fawn.
faquin (fakɛ̃), s.m. [f. It. *facchino*] Manikin, Turk's head; scoundrel, scamp, snob, cad.
farad (farad), s.m. [f. *Faraday*, d. 1867] Farad, electro-magnetic unit of capacity.
faradisation (faradiza'sjɔ̃), s.f. Faradization.
faramineux (faraminø), adj. See PHARAMINEUX.
farandole (farɑ̃dɔl), s.f. [Provenç. wd] Farandole (a dance).

faraud, -e (faro), adj. s.m.f. [f. *fier*] (Person) dressed with bravery (said of peasants, &c.), ostentatious, foppish, fop, (rustic) swell; *faire le* ~, to swank.
farce (fars), s.f. [f. L *farcire*] **1.** Stuffing, forcemeat; **2.** farce, comedy, joke, practical joke, trick; *faire une* ~ *à X*, to play X a trick, or to play a trick on X; *faire ses* ~*s*, to be wild, to go on the spree; to play pranks. ~, adj. Funny, droll, farcical.
farceu-r, -se (farsœr), s.m.f. **1.** Practical joker, comic fellow; buffoon, trickster; **2.** rum fellow, old blade, humbug, rogue, rake; (fem.) gay woman. ~, adj. Fond of playing tricks.
farcin (farsɛ̃), s.m. [f. L *farciminum*] (vet.) Farcy, (obs.) farcin.
farcir (farsir), v.a. [f. L *farcire*] To stuff; (archaic) to farce; to fill with forcemeat; (fig.) to cram, to stuff; ~ *un poulet*, to stuff a fowl; ~ *un discours de citations*, to cram a speech with quotations; **se** ~, v.pr. *le fatras dont je m'étais farci la tête* (Rousseau), the learned lumber with which I had filled my head.
fard (far), s.m. [f. *farder*] Paint, rouge; (fig.) false show, mask, disguise, guile; *parler sans* ~, to speak frankly; (slang) *piquer un* ~, to blush, to colour up.
farde (fard), s.f. [f. Arab. *farda*] Bale (of coffee) of 185 kg.
fardeau (pl. **-x**) (fardo), s.m. [f. *farde*] Burden, load, grievous burden.
farder (farde), v.a. [orig. uncert., f. Germ. *Farbe*?] To rouge, to paint (the face); (fig.) to dress up, to gloss over, to varnish, to disguise; ~ *sa pensée*, to disguise one's thoughts; **se** ~, v.pr. to paint one's face, to paint, to rouge one's face.
fardier (fardje), s.m. [f. *fardeau*] Truck, trolley; gill.
farfadet (farfadɛ), s.m. [etym. dub.] Hobgoblin, elf, leprechaun.
farfouiller (farfuje), v.n.a. [f. *fouiller*] To rummage, to rummage about, or among.
fargue (farg), s.f. [f. Span. *falca*] (naut.) Gunwale; wash-board.
faribole (faribɔl), s.f. [orig. unkn.] Twaddle, nonsense, idle talk, trifle, rigmarole, bosh.
faridondaine, faridondon (faridɔ̃dɛn, faridɔ̃dɔ̃), s.f. Fol-de-rol-de-lol.
farinacé, -e (farinase), adj. Farinaceous.
farine (farin), s.f. [L *farina*] Flour, meal; ~ *de froment*, wheat-flour; *fleur de* ~, fine flour; *saupoudrer de* ~, to flour; (fig.) *ce sont gens de même* ~, they are birds of a feather; *opinions de même* ~, opinions of the same stamp.
fariner (farine), v.a. To flour.
farineu-x, -se (farinø), adj. Farinaceous, mealy; covered with flour. ~, s.m. Mealy substance, farinaceous food.
farini-er, -ère (farinje), s.m.f. Flour-dealer; ~**ère**, s.f. flour-bin.
farlouse (farluz), s.f. (ornith.) Meadow pipit, titlark.
farniente (farnjɛnte), s.m. [It. wd] Farniente, idleness.
faro (faro), s.m. [Walloon wd] Faro, Belgian beer.
farouch (faruʃ), s.m. [Provenç. wd] (bot.) Crimson clover.
farouche (faruʃ), adj. [LL *forasticus*] **1.** Wild, savage, fierce, grim, sullen; *un air* ~, a grim look; **2.** shy, excessively reserved, skittish, unsociable.
farrago (farago), s.m. [L wd] Medley, hotchpotch, farrago; a mixture of grains.
fasce (fas), s.f. [L *fascia*] (herald.) Fesse, fascia.
fascé, -e (fase), adj. (herald.) Fessy.
fascicule (fasikyl), s.m. [L *fasciculus*] Number, part, tract; fascicle.
fasciculé, -e (fasikyle), adj. Fasciculate.
fascié, -e (fasje), adj. (zool.) Fasciated, streaked.
fascinat-eur, -rice (fasinatœr), adj. Fascinating. ~, s.m.f. Fascinator; charmer.
fascination (fasina'sjɔ̃), s.f. Fascination.
fascine (fasin), s.f. [L *fascina*] Fascine, faggot, bundle.
fasciner (fasine), v.a. [f. L *fascinare*] To fascinate, to charm.
fascisme (fasism), s.m. [f. It. *fascio*] Fascism; fascismo.
fasciste (fasist), s.m.f. Fascist.
faséier, faséyer, fasiller (fazeje, fazije), v.n. (naut.) To shiver (as a sail).
faséole (fazeɔl), s.f. [L *faseolus*] Kidney bean.
faste (fast), s.m. [L *fastus*] Pomp, splendour, magnificence, gorgeous display; ostentatiousness. ~, adj. Auspicious; *un jour* ~, a lucky day, a memorable day.
fastes (fast), s.m.pl. [L *fasti*] Fasti, chronological tables of the Romans; (fig.) annals, records.
fastidieusement (fastidjøzmɑ̃), adv. Tediously, irksomely. ⚠ See *fastidieux*.
fastidieu-x, -se (fastidjø), adj. [L *fastidiosus*] Tedious, irksome, dull, wearisome. ⚠ Not to be translated by 'fastidious' which means *difficile à satisfaire, raffiné*.
fastigié, -e (fastiʒje), adj. [f. L *fastigium*] (bot.) Fastigiate, tapering to a point.
fastueusement (fastɥøzmɑ̃), adv. Magnificently, gorgeously, ostentatiously.
fastueu-x, -se (fastɥø), adj. Magnificent, gorgeous, ostentatious, stately, pompous.
fat (fat), adj. m. [f. L *fatuus*] Foppish,

conceited, vainglorious, vain. ~, s.m. Fop, coxcomb, puppy, conceited man.

fatal, -e, (als) (fatal), adj. [L *fatalis*] Fatal; *le coup* ~, the fatal blow.

fatalement (fatalmɑ̃), adv. Fatally, inevitably, unhappily; by way of consequence.

fatalisme (fatalism), s.m. Fatalism.

fataliste (fatalist), adj. Fatalist, fatalistic.

fatalité (fatalite), s.f. [L *fatalitas*] Fatality; calamity.

fatidique (fatidik), adj. [L *fatidicus*] Fatidic, fatidical, prophetic.

fatigant, -e (fatigɑ̃), p. adj. Fatiguing, tiring; tiresome, wearisome, irksome.

fatigue (fatig), s.f. [f. *fatiguer*] Fatigue ⚠, weariness, lassitude; weakness; hard work; *tomber de* ~, *être rendu de* ~, to break down with exhaustion, to be knocked up. ⚠ 'Fatigue' is also used in English but not in French in the sense of *corvée militaire*; ex.: *les hommes de corvée* = the fatigue party.

fatiguer (fatige), v.a. [L *fatigare*] To tire, to weary, to wear out; to fatigue, to worry, to tease, to importune; to mix (salad); ~, v.n. to get tired, to tire oneself; to bear a weight; **se ~, v.pr.** to tire oneself, to be fatigued, to be nearly worn out; to grow weary, to take a dislike.

fatras (fatrɑ), s.m. Medley, lumber, trash, stuff, balderdash; *ce n'est qu'un* ~, that 's nothing but trash.

fatuité (fatɥite), s.f. [L *fatuitas*] Fatuity, self-conceit, foppishness, impertinence.

faubert (fobɛr), s.m. [f. Dutch *zwabber*?] (naut.) Mop, swab.

faubourg (fobur), s.m. [OF *forsbourg*] Suburb, outskirts.

faubourien, -ne (foburjɛ̃), adj. Suburban, popular, low; *accent* ~, lower-class accent.

faucard (fokar), s.m. River scythe.

faucarder (fokarde), v.a. To cut down rushes and grass in a river.

fauchage (foʃaʒ), s.m. Mowing.

fauchaison, fauche (foʃɛzɔ̃, foʃ), s.f. Mowing time, mowing.

faucher (foʃe), v.a.n. [f. *faux*] To mow, to mow down, to cut down with a scythe; (fig.) to destroy; ~, v.n. (of a horse) to dish; (slang) *je suis fauché*, I am stony broke.

fauchet (foʃɛ), s.m. Hay-rake; small scythe.

faucheu-r, -se (foʃœr), s.m.f. Mower, hay-maker; ~**se**, s.f. mowing-machine.

faucheux (foʃø), s.m. (ent.) Field-spider, spinner; daddy-long-legs.

faucille (fosij), s.f. [L *falcicula*] Sickle, reaping-hook.

faucon (fokɔ̃), s.m. [LL *falco*] (ornith.) Falcon, hawk; *chasser au* ~, to hawk; *décoiffer le* ~, to unhood the falcon.

fauconneau (pl. **-x**) (fokɔno), s.m. Eyas, young hawk; (anc. artill.) falconet.

fauconnerie (fokɔnri), s.f. **1.** Falconry; **2.** hawking.

fauconnier (fokɔnje), s.m. Falconer, hawker.

faufiler (fofile), v.a. [= *forfiler*; *fors*+*filer*] To baste, to tack; syn. BÂTIR; **se** ~, v.pr. to creep, to slink, to edge oneself, to edge, to insinuate oneself, to ingratiate oneself.

faufilure (fofilyr), s.f. Basting, tacking.

faulx (fo), s.f. See FAUX.

faune[1] (fon), s.m. [L *faunus*] Faun; fem. *faunesse*.

faune[2] (fon), s.f. Fauna.

faussaire (fosɛr), s.m.f. [f. *fausser*] Forger.

faussement (fosmɑ̃), adv. [f. *faux*] Falsely, untruly, erroneously, wrongfully.

fausser (fose), v.a. [L *falsare*] To strain, to bend to excess, to distort, to force, to warp, to violate, to strain (a voice) out of tune; ~ *l'esprit*, to warp (some one's) mind; ~ *une clé*, to bend a key; ~ *le sens d'un texte*, to strain (or distort) the sense of a text; ~ *compagnie à X*, to give X the slip; ~, v.n. to sing or play out of tune.

fausset[1] (fosɛ), s.m. [L *falsus*] Falsetto, head voice.

fausset[2] (fosɛ), s.m. Spigot.

fausseté (foste), s.f. [L *falsitas*] Falsity, falseness; falsehood, lie, (fam.) fib.

faute (fot), s.f. [f. L *fallere*, LL *fallita*] Dearth, want, scarcity; *faire* ~ *à*, to fail; *se faire* ~ *de*, to abstain from; *il ne se fait pas* ~ *de mentir*, he never sticks at a lie; ~ *de mieux*, for want of something better; mistake, error, slip, imperfection, blemish, blunder; ~ *d'impression*, misprint; ~ *d'inattention*, slip; *je viendrai sans* ~, I will come without fail; fault, transgression, offence, thing wrongly done, responsibility for something wrong; *c'est ma* ~, the fault is mine; *rejeter la* ~ *sur X*, to impute the fault to X, to throw the blame on X; *à qui la* ~?, whose fault is it?

fauter (fote), v.n. (pop.) To commit a fault, to sin, to go wrong, to let oneself be seduced, to take the wrong turning.

fauteuil (fotœj), s.m. [f. OHG *faldan*+*stuol*] Arm-chair, easy chair, elbow-chair, (theatr.) fauteuil, stall; chair; (fig.) presidency of a meeting, chair; membership of the French Academy; (colloq.) *arriver* (or *gagner*) *comme dans un* ~, to win hands down.

faut-eur, -rice (fotœr), s.m. [L *fautor*] Favourer, abettor, fomenter.

fauti-f, -ve (fotif), adj. At fault, faulty, erroneous, full of errors.

fautivement (fotivmɑ̃), adv. Erroneously, in a faulty manner, wrongly.

fauve (fov), adj. [OHG *falw*] **1.** Fawn-coloured, fallow, tawny; **2.** wild, savage. ~, s.m. Wild beast; fawn colour.
fauvette (fovɛt), s.f. [f. *fauve*] (ornith.) Warbler; ~ *à tête noire*, blackcap warbler.
faux, fausse (fo), adj. [L *falsus*] False, erroneous, untrue, unsound, inexact, inaccurate, wrong, deceitful, perfidious, insincere, artificial, sham, out of tune, discordant; *un ~ bruit*, a false report; *un calcul ~*, a false calculation; *~ comme un jeton*, as false as a brass shilling; *fausse démarche*, wrong step; *faire un ~ pas*, to stumble; (fig.) to make a mistake, to commit an error of conduct; *faire fausse route*, to be on the wrong track; *fausse couche*, miscarriage; *~ col*, collar; *c'est un ~ bonhomme*, he is a fake, a hypocrite; *fausse monnaie*, base money; *~-monnayeur*, coiner (of base money); *porter à ~*, not to rest properly on its support; (fig.) to be beside the point; *s'inscrire en ~ contre*, to deny emphatically; *~ frais*, incidental expenses; *fausses dents*, artificial teeth; *faire ~ bond à X*, to fail to keep an appointment with X; *~-fuyant*, shift, subterfuge, evasion, pretence. ~, adv. Falsely, wrongfully, out of tune; *à ~*, erroneously, falsely.
faux[1] (fo), s.m. Falsehood; forgery; imitation.
faux[2] **(faulx,** obs.) (fo), s.f. [L *falx*] Scythe; (anat.) falx.
faveur (favœr), s.f. [L *favor*] Favour, boon, goodwill, benevolence; vogue; narrow ribbon; *être en ~ de*, to be, to declare, in favour of; *faites-moi la ~ de venir*, do me the favour of coming; *billet de ~*, free ticket; *à la ~ de la nuit*, under cover of night; *en ~ de X*, in X's favour; *Jeanne accorde ses ~s à X*, Jane bestows her favours on X.
favorable (favɔrabl), adj. [L *favorabilis*] Favourable.
favorablement (favɔrabləmɑ̃), adv. Favourably.
favori, -te (favɔri), adj. s.m.f. [f. It. *favorito*] Favourite; ~, s.m. whisker.
favoriser (favɔrize), v.a. To favour, to approve; to treat with partiality.
favoritisme (favɔritism), s.m. Favouritism.
fayot, fayol (fajo, fajɔl), s.m. [L *phaseolus*] (pop.) Bean, kidney bean.
féal, -e, (aux) (feal), adj. [f. *foi*] Trusty, faithful. ~, s.m. Faithful friend, helper, or servant.
fébricitant, -e (febrisitɑ̃), adj. [f. L *febricitare*] Fevered, feverish.
fébrifuge (febrifyʒ), adj. s.m. [f. L *febris+fugare*] Febrifuge, antifebrile.
fébrile (febril), adj. [L *febrilis*] Febrile, feverish.
fébrilement (febrilmɑ̃), adv. Feverishly.
fécal, -e, (aux) (fekal), adj. [f. *fèces*] Faecal.
fèces (fɛs), s.f.pl. [L *faex*] Excrements; faeces.
fécond, -e (fekɔ̃, fegɔ̃), adj. [L *fecundus*] Fecund, prolific; fertile, fruitful, rich; (fig.) inventive.
fécondation (fekɔ̃da'sjɔ̃), s.f. Fecundation.
féconder (fekɔ̃de, fegɔ̃de), v.a. [L *fecundare*] To fecundate, to fertilize.
fécondité (fekɔ̃dite), s.f. [L *fecunditas*] Fecundity, fruitfulness, fertility, copiousness.
fécule (fekyl), s.f. [L *faecula*] Fecula, starch.
féculence (fekylɑ̃s), s.f. Feculence.
féculent, -e (fekylɑ̃), adj. s.m. Feculent; syn. FÉCULEU-X, -SE.
féculerie (fekylri), s.f. Fecula- or starch-manufacture.
fédéral, -e, (aux) (federal), adj. [f. L *foedus*] Federal, confederate.
fédéraliser (federalize), v.a. To federalize; **se** ~, v.pr. to federalize.
fédéralisme (federalism), s.m. Federalism.
fédéraliste (federalist), adj. s.m.f. Federalist.
fédérati-f, -ve (federatif), adj. Federative, federal.
fédération (federa'sjɔ̃), s.f. Federation.
fédéré, -e (federe), p. adj. s.m.f. Federate.
fédérer (federe), v.a.n. [L *foederare*] To federate; **se** ~, v.pr. to federate.
fée (fe), s.f. [L *fata*] Fairy; *conte de ~s*, fairy-tale; *travail de ~*, delicate piece of work; *avoir des doigts de ~*, to have skilful, deft hands; *une ~ Carabosse*, an old hag.
féerie (feri), s.f. Enchantment, fairy-scene, fairy-tale, fairy-art, fairyland, fairy-show.
féerique (ferik), adj. Fairy; fairy-like, wonderful, enchanting.
feignant, -e (fɛɲɑ̃), adj. [f. *fait+néant*] (colloq.) Lazybones, loafer, good-for-nothing, idle dog.
feindre (fɛ̃dr), v.a.n. [L *fingere*] To feign, to sham, to pretend, to simulate; to dissemble; ~, v.n. to limp (as a horse).
feinte (fɛ̃t), s.f. [f. *feindre*] Feint, sham, dissimulation, pretence, artifice, make-believe; (fenc.) *faire une ~*, to make a feint.
feintise (fɛ̃tiz), s.f. (obs.). See FEINTE.
feld-maréchal (fɛldmareʃal), s.m. [Germ. *Feld-Marschall*] Field-Marshal.
feldspath (fɛldspat), s.m. [Germ. wd] Feldspath, felspar.
fêlé, -e (fɛle), p. adj. Cracked; (fig.) crack-brained, crazy; *avoir le cerveau ~, le timbre ~*, to be crack-brained; (slang) to be off one's chump; (slang) to be barmy on the crumpet.

fêler (fɛle), v.a. [LL *faculare*] To crack, to fissure.
félibre (felibr), s.m.f. [Provenç. wd] (southern French literature) Man or woman of letters; hence **félibrige,** s.m. the association of the *félibres.*
félicitation (felisita'sjɔ̃), s.f. Congratulation, felicitation.
félicité (felisite), s.f. [L *felicitas*] Felicity, intense happiness, bliss; blessing; appropriateness (of a word, expression, &c.).
féliciter (felisite), v.a. To congratulate, to felicitate (on); **se ~** (*de*), v.pr. to congratulate oneself or each other (on).
félin, -e (felɛ̃), adj. [L *felinus*] Feline. **~**, s.m. Feline.
félinité (felinite) s.f. Felinity.
fellah (fɛlla), s.m. [Arab. wd] Fellah; *fellahine* (fɛlain), s.f. fellah woman; (collect.) fellaheen.
félon, -ne (felɔ̃), adj. [LL *fello*] Felon, felonious. **~**, s.m.f. Felon.
félonie (feloni), s.f. Felony, treason.
felouque (fəluk), s.f. [f. Arab. *falūka*] (naut.) Felucca.
fêlure (fɛlyr), s.f. [f. *fêler*] Crack, chink; (fig.) *avoir une* **~**, to be barmy, or crazy.
femelle (fəmɛl), s.f. [L *femella*] (zool., techn.) Female, she-, hen; ♀ (of persons, only in very disparaging sense) woman, creature, female.
féminin, -e (feminɛ̃), adj. [L *femininus*] Feminine, womanly, female, womanish. **~**, s.m. (gram.) Feminine gender; *au* **~**, in the feminine; *du* **~**, feminine; *l'éternel* **~**, the eternal feminine.
féminiser (feminize), v.a. To feminize, to make womanish; (gram.) to make, to render feminine.
féminisme (feminism), s.m. [f. *femme*] Feminism, movement in favour of women's rights.
féministe (feminist), adj. s.m.f. Feminist, supporter of women's rights.
femme (fam), s.f. [L *femina*] Woman (pl. women), female; wife. **~**, adj. Female, woman-; *~-auteur*, authoress; *~-peintre*, paintress, painter; *bonne* **~**, old woman, goody; *maîtresse* **~**, capable woman, or (pej.) managing woman; **~** *de chambre*, lady's-maid, chamber-maid, maid; **~** *de charge*, housekeeper; **~** *de ménage*, charwoman; *sage-~*, midwife; *cherchez la* **~**, there 's a woman at the bottom of it; **~** *publique*, prostitute; *prendre* **~**, to marry, to take a wife.
femmelette (famlɛt), s.f. Weak, delicate, pusillanimous woman; (fig.) effeminate, pusillanimous man.
fémoral, -e (aux) (femɔral), adj. [L *femoralis*] (anat.) Femoral.
fémur (femyr), s.m. [L *femur*] (anat.) Femur.
fenaison (fənɛzɔ̃), s.f. [f. L *fenum*] Haymaking, hay-harvest.
fendant, -e (fɑ̃dɑ̃), p. adj. s.m. Swaggering, swaggerer; *faire le* **~**, to play the bully; to be swaggering, hectoring, to talk big; see syn. FANFARON.
fendeur (fɑ̃dœr), s.m. Splitter, cleaver; (fig.) **~** *de naseaux*, braggadocio.
fendiller (fɑ̃dije), v.a. [f. *fendre*] To crack, to split; **se ~**, v.pr. to crack, to chap, to chink.
fendoir (fɑ̃dwar), s.m. Cleaver, cleaving-tool.
fendre (fɑ̃dr), v.a. [L *findere*] To split, to cleave, to slit, to rend, to rip up, to sliver; (fig.) to rend; *cela fend le cœur*, it 's heart-rending; **~** *la foule*, to squeeze, to cleave a way through the crowd; **se ~**, v.pr. (*a*) to split, to be rent asunder, to crack; (*b*) to chap; (*c*) (fenc.) to lunge; (*d*) (fam.) to spend, to fork out, to stump up (money).
fenêtrage (fənɛtraʒ), s.m. (arch.) Windows; fenestration.
fenêtre (fənɛtr), s.f. [L *fenestra*] Window; casement; *porte-~*, French window; **~** *à guillotine*, sash-window; **~** *en rotonde*, bow window; **~** *en saillie*, bay window; **~** *en ogive*, lancet window; *jeter l'argent par les* **~***s*, to be extravagant, to be a spendthrift, to squander one's money.
fenil (fəni), s.m. [f. L *fenum*] Hay-loft.
fenouil (fənuj), s.m. [L *feniculum*] (bot.) Fennel.
fenouillet (fənujɛ), s.m. (bot.) Fennel-apple.
fente (fɑ̃t), s.f. [f. *fendre*] Split, crack, slit, chink, cleft, fissure, slot, gap, cranny, crevice, rip.
fenton (fɑ̃tɔ̃), s.m. (techn.) Iron-cramp; slit iron.
fenugrec (fənygrɛk), s.m. [L *foenum graecum*] (bot.) Fenugreek, *Trigonella foenum graecum.*
féodal, -e, (aux), adj. [LL *feodalis*] Feudal.
féodalité (feɔdalite), s.f. Feudality, feudalism.
fer (fɛr), s.m. [L *ferrum*] Iron; head, point, sword, lance, weapon; forceps; rail; (of animals) shoe; (fig.) **~***s*, chains; **~** *à friser*, curling-iron; **~** *à repasser*, iron, flat-iron; *fil de* **~**, iron wire; *chemin de* **~**, railway; **~** *de lance*, head or blade of a lance; (fenc.) *engager le* **~**, to cross, to engage, swords; *il faut battre le* **~** *pendant qu'il est chaud*, you must strike while the iron is hot; *cela ne vaut pas les quatre* **~***s d'un chien*, that is not worth a rap; *tomber les quatre* **~***s en l'air*, to fall on one's back.
ferblanc (fɛrblɑ̃), s.m. Tin, tin-plate.
ferblanterie (fɛrblɑ̃tri), s.f. Tin-ware, tin-trade.

ferblantier (fɛrblɑ̃tje), s.m. Tin-smith, tinman, tinker.

férial, -e, (aux) (ferjal), adj. Ferial.

férie (feri), s.f. [L *feria*] Holiday, feria; (Cath. liturg.) weekday; *deuxième* ~, Monday.

férié, -e (ferje), adj. [f. *férie*] Kept as a holiday; *dimanches et jours* ~*s*, on Sundays and holy days.

férir (ferir), v.a. [L *ferire*] (All forms of this verb are obsolete, except the infinitive and pp. *féru*.) *Sans coup* ~, without striking a blow, without encountering resistance; *féru de*, infatuated with.

ferler (fɛrle), v.a. [etym. dub.] To furl (a sail).

fermage (fɛrmaʒ), s.m. [f. *ferme*] Rent (of a farm).

fermail (pl. **aux**) (fɛrmaj), s.m. [f. *fermer*] Clasp.

fermant, -e (fɛrmɑ̃), p. adj. Closing; *à jour* ~, at the close of day; *à portes* ~*es*, on the closing of the gates (of a fortified town).

ferme (fɛrm), adj. [L *firmus*] Firm, solid, steady, fast, fixed, resolute, steadfast, constant, bold; *de pied* ~, unflinchingly; *vente* ~, obligatory sale; *la terre* ~, the continent, the shore, terra firma. ~, adv. Fast, firmly, stoutly. ~, interj. Courage!

ferme[1] (fɛrm), s.f. [LL *firma*] Farm, farm-lease; farm-house; *prendre à* ~, to farm; *donner à* ~, to let to farm; (slang) *la* ~*!*, see FERMER.

ferme[2] (fɛrm), s.f. [f. *fermer*] (arch.) Roof-timbers; (theatr.) set piece.

fermement (fɛrməmɑ̃), adv. Firmly, fixedly, strongly, steadfastly.

ferment (fɛrmɑ̃), s.m. [L *fermentum*] Ferment, leaven; (fig.) leaven.

fermentation (fɛrmɑ̃ta'sjɔ̃), s.f. **1.** Fermentation; **2.** (fig.) ferment.

fermenter (fɛrmɑ̃te), v.n. [L *fermentum* for *fervimentum*] To ferment, to work, to rise.

fermentescibilité (fɛrmɑ̃tɛssibilite), s.f. Fermentability.

fermentescible (fɛrmɑ̃tɛssibl), adj. Fermentable.

fermer (fɛrme), v.a. [L *firmare*] To close, to shut, to shut up, to stop up, to obstruct, to lock, to fasten, to clench (the fists), to enclose; ~ *le robinet*, to turn off the tap; ~ *le gaz*, to turn off the gas; ~ *un livre*, to close a book; ~ *la porte à clé*, to lock the door; ~ *à double tour*, to double-lock; ~ *la porte au nez de X*, to shut the door in X's face; ~ *les yeux*, to close one's eyes; (fig.) ~ *les yeux sur quelque chose*, to wink at a thing, to let it pass; ~ *les yeux à X*, to close X's eyes; to be present at X's last moments; *je n'ai pu* ~ *l'œil de la nuit*, I have not been able to sleep a wink; (fig.) ~ *la bouche à X*, to stop X's mouth, to silence X; ~ *un port*, to shut up, or to block up, a harbour; ~ *la discussion*, to close the debate; ~ *la marche*, to bring up the rear; to go last; (fig.) ~ *boutique*, to stop business; ~ *ses oreilles à la médisance*, to turn a deaf ear to slander; ~, v.n. *on va* ~, it 's closing-time; *cette porte ferme bien*, this door shuts close; *le bureau ferme à six heures*, the office closes at six; **se** ~, v.pr. to shut, to close, to be shut, &c.; *la plaie commence à se* ~, the wound is beginning to close up, or to heal; (slang) *la ferme!*, or *ferme-la!* or *ferme ta boîte!*, oh! can it!; cheese it!; shut your trap!; dry up!; chuck it!; hold your jaw!

fermeté (fɛrməte), s.f. [L *firmitas*] Firmness, solidity, hardness, steadfastness, steadiness; ~ *d'âme*, fortitude.

fermeture (fɛrmətyr), s.f. **1.** Shutting, closing; **2.** fastenings, shutter, shutters; *la* ~ *de la chasse*, the end of the shooting season; ~ *éclair*, zip fastening.

fermi-er, -ère (fɛrmje), s.m.f. Farmer, farmer's wife; contractor; ~ *général*, farmer-general (of revenues).

fermoir (fɛrmwar), s.m. [f. *fermer*] Clasp, snap, hook, spring; (carp.) paring-chisel, ripping-chisel.

féroce (ferɔs), adj. [L *ferox*] Ferocious, fierce, savage, cruel; *un appétit* ~, a ravenous appetite.

férocement (ferɔsmɑ̃), adv. Ferociously, fiercely, cruelly, savagely.

férocité (ferɔsite), s.f. Ferocity, savageness, ferociousness, cruelty.

ferrade (fɛrad), s.f. [f. *fer*] Branding or marking of cattle with hot irons; rural festivity in Provence on this occasion.

ferrage (fɛraʒ), s.m. [f. *ferrer*] Shoeing (of a horse), tiring, rimming (of a wheel).

ferraille (fɛrɑj), s.f. [f. *fer*] Scrap-iron, old iron; (fig.) rubbish.

ferrailler (fɛrɑje), v.n. [f. *fer*] To fence (rather poorly); (fig.) to wrangle, to dispute.

ferrailleur (fɛrɑjœr), s.m. **1.** Dealer in old iron; **2.** fencer; fighter, bully; **3.** (fig.) wrangler, argumentative person.

ferrant (fɛrɑ̃), p. adj. *Maréchal* ~, farrier, shoeing-smith.

ferré, -e (fɛre), p. adj. Bound with iron, tipped with iron, shod (as a horse, &c.), hobnailed, ferruled; *chemin* ~, metalled, or macadamized road; *voie* ~*e*, railway; *eau* ~*e*, chalybeate water; ~ *à glace*, roughshod, frost-nailed; (fig.) *être* ~ (or ~ *à glace*) *sur quelque chose*, to be well versed (or well up) in something.

ferrement (fɛrmɑ̃), s.m. [f. *ferrer*] **1.** Putting the irons on (convicts); **2.** ironwork.

ferrer (fɛre), v.a. [f. *fer*] To bind with iron, to mount with iron; to shoe (horses, &c.); ~ *à glace*, to rough-shoe; to ring (pigs); to tag (laces); ~ *un poisson*, to give a jerk with the hook when fishing, to strike a fish.

ferret (fɛrɛ), s.m. [f. *fer*] Tag (of laces, &c.); ⚠ not 'ferret', which = *furet*.

ferreur (fɛrœr), s.m. Shoe-smith, coach-smith, tagger.

ferreux (fɛrø), adj. m. [f. *fer*] (chem.) Ferrous.

ferrique (fɛrik), adj. (chem.) Ferric.

ferronnerie (fɛrɔnri), s.f. Foundry, iron-mongery, ironwork.

ferronnier (fɛrɔnje), s.m. Iron-founder.

ferronnière (fɛrɔnjɛr), s.f. Ferroniere, frontlet, coronet (worn on the forehead).

ferrugineu-x, -se (fɛryʒinø), adj. [f. *fer*] Ferruginous, chalybeate.

ferrure (fɛryr), s.f. [f. *fer*] **1.** Shoeing, shoes (of animals); **2.** ironwork, irons.

fertile (fɛrtil), adj. [L *fertilis*] Fertile, productive, fruitful, prolific.

fertilisant, -e (fɛrtilizã), p. adj. Fertilizing. ~, s.m. Fertilizer.

fertilisation (fɛrtiliza'sjɔ̃), s.f. Fertilization.

fertiliser (fɛrtilize), v.a. To fertilize.

fertilité (fɛrtilite), s.f. [L *fertilitas*] Fertility; (fig.) abundance, resourcefulness.

féru, -e (fery), p. adj. [f. *férir*] Struck, smitten, infatuated (*de*, with); ~ *d'amour*, enamoured.

férule (feryl), s.f. [L *ferula*] **1.** (bot.) Ferula, giant fennel; **2.** ferule, rod, wooden pallet; (fig.) authority, domination, sway; *être sous la ~ de X*, to be under X's thumb or authority.

fervemment (fɛrvamã), adv. Fervently.

fervent, -e (fɛrvã), adj. [L *fervens*] Fervent.

ferveur (fɛrvœr), s.f. [L *fervor*] Fervour, fervency.

fesse (fɛs), s.f. [f. L *fissus*] Buttock; *les ~s*, the buttocks, the bottom; (naut.) tuck; *~-cahier*, s.m. quill-driver; *~-mathieu*, s.m. skinflint, miserly old hunks.

fessée (fɛse), s.f. Spanking, whipping; slapping on the buttocks, flogging.

fesser (fɛse), v.a. To spank, to flog, to whip.

fessi-er, -ère (fɛsje), adj. [f. *fesse*] (anat.) Gluteal, pertaining to the buttocks. ~, s.m. (fam.) Rump, bottom.

fessu, -e (fɛsy), adj. Broad bottomed, large breeched.

festin (fɛstɛ̃), s.m. [It. *festino*] Feast, banquet, rich repast.

festiner (fɛstine), v.a. To feast, to regale; ~, v.n. to banquet, to feast.

festival (pl. **aux**) (fɛstival), s.m. [f. L *festivus*] Festival.

festoiement (fɛstwa'mã), s.m. Feasting, entertaining.

feston (fɛstɔ̃), s.m. [It. *festone*] Festoon, garland; (embroidery) scallop; *découpé en ~s*, scalloped.

festonner (fɛstɔne), v.a. To festoon; (embroidery) to scallop; ~, v.n. (fam.) to zigzag, as a tipsy man; to reel about.

festoyer (fɛstwaje), v.n.a. To feast, to entertain, to eat sumptuously, to make good cheer; to carouse.

fêtard (fɛtar), s.m. (colloq.) Man of pleasure, rake, free-liver; one who likes to go frequently on the spree.

fête (fɛt), s.f. [L *festum*] Feast, festivity, festival, holiday, birthday, anniversary, saint's day, treat; *~-Dieu*, Corpus Christi day; *faire ~ à X*, to give X a warm reception, or a hearty welcome; *se faire une ~ de*, to look forward to with pleasure; *jour de ~*, festive day, feast-day, holiday; *souhaiter bonne ~ à X*, to wish X many happy returns of the day; *trouble-~*, wet blanket, kill-joy; *ce n'est pas tous les jours ~*, Christmas comes but once a year; *faire la ~*, to revel, to lead a gay life, to go on the spree.

fêter (fɛte), v.a. To keep as a holiday, to observe, to celebrate; to welcome, to entertain, to treat, to feast, to make much of.

fétiche (fetiʃ), s.m. [f. Port. *feitiço*] Fetish.

fétichisme (fetiʃism), s.m. Fetishism.

fétichiste (fetiʃist), adj. Fetishist.

fétide (fetid), adj. [L *foetidus*] Fetid, stinking, putrid.

fétidité (fetidite), s.f. Fetidness.

fétu (fety), s.m. [L *festuca*] Straw; *cela ne vaut* (or *pèse*) *pas un ~*, it 's not worth a straw (or a pin, or a fig).

fétuque (fetyk), s.f. [f. *fétu*] (bot.) Fescue-grass.

feu (pl. **-x**) (fø), s.m. [f. L *focus*] Fire, flame, combustion, burning; signal-light, beacon; heat, inflammation; hearth, home; (fig.) ardour, heat, passion, flame; *faire un ~*, to make or build a fire; *au ~, au ~ !*, fire !, fire !; *village de cent ~x*, a village of one hundred homesteads; *arme à ~*, fire-arm; *bouche à ~*, piece of artillery; *coup de ~*, shot, gun-shot, &c.; *faire ~*, to fire, to shoot; (fig.) *faire ~ des quatre pieds*, to do one's utmost, to strain every nerve; *faire long ~*, (*a*) to hang fire, to miscarry; (*b*) to last a long time, to live long; *faire ~ qui dure*, to last, to live long; to take care of one's health; to make one's money go a long way; *mettre le ~ à*, to light, to set on fire, to set fire to; *mettre tout à ~ et à sang*, to destroy everything with fire and sword, to put to fire and sword; *jeter ~ et flamme*, to rage, to fume; to breathe fire and slaughter; *prendre* ~, to catch or take fire, to blaze up; *n'y voir que du* ~, not to see through it; to be unable to make it out; *ce diamant jette des ~x merveilleux*, this diamond has a wonderful lustre; *être tout* ~ *tout flamme pour*, to be all on fire for, to be all enthusiasm for, to be very enthusiastic over, or about; *être pris entre deux ~x*, to be fired at before and behind, to be attacked on every side; *être sans* ~ *ni lieu*, to have neither house nor home; *jeter de l'huile sur le* ~, to throw oil on the flames; *j'en mettrais ma main au* ~, I would stake my life upon it; *ce plat va au* ~, this dish stands fire; this dish is fireproof; *aller au* ~, to go into battle; *pas de fumée sans* ~, no smoke without fire; *le supplice du* ~, the stake; *faire mourir à petit* ~, to kill by inches, to burn with a slow fire; *cuire à petit* ~, to cook on a slow fire; *à grand* ~, on a quick or hot fire; ~ *d'artifice*, fireworks (pl.); ~ *de joie*, bonfire; ~ *follet*, will-o'-the-wisp, Jack-o'-lantern, ignis fatuus; ~ *fixe*, fixed light, ~ *tournant*, revolving light; ~ *à éclipses*, intermittent fire; ~ *St-Elme*, St. Elmo's fire, corposant; ~ *grégeois*, Greek fire; *le* ~ *de ses yeux*, his or her fiery looks; the lustre of her eyes; *couronner les ~x de X*, to reward X's love; *avoir le* ~ *sacré*, to burn with a sacred fire, to be indomitable; to have genius or inspiration; *donnez-moi du* ~, give me a light; *le* ~ *des passions*, the heat of passion.

feu, -e (fø), adj. [LL *fatutus*] Late, deceased; ~ *ma tante, ma feue tante*, my deceased aunt.

feudataire (fødatɛr), s.m.f. [f. LL *feodum*] Feudatory.

feudiste (fødist), s.m. [f. LL *feodum*] Feudist.

feuillage (fœjaʒ), s.m. [f. *feuille*] Foliage, leafage, leaves.

feuillaison (fœjɛzɔ̃), s.f. [f. *feuille*] Foliation.

feuillant, -ine (fœjɑ̃), s.m.f. Feuillant; (*a*) a monk; (*b*) (Fr. hist.) a member of a Constitutional club in 1791; *~ine*, s.f. (*a*) a nun, (*b*) a kind of pastry.

feuillard (fœjar), s.m. [f. *feuille*] **1.** Hoop-wood; **2.** hoop-iron.

feuille (fœj), s.f. [L *folium*] Leaf (pl. *leaves*), blade; sheet (of paper, &c.); newspaper, list, folio; *trembler comme la* ~, to shake like a leaf; ~ *de route*, way-bill, route(-order); (bookbind.) ~ *de garde*, fly-leaf; ~ *volante*, loose sheet; ~ *morte*, dead leaf, feuillemorte (colour); ~ *de paravent*, screen-leaf; (colloq.) ~ *de chou*, unimportant daily, gutter sheet, rag; ~ *d'or*, gold-leaf; ~ *d'étain*, tinfoil; ~ *de cuivre*, sheet copper; *chute des ~s*, autumn, (Amer.) fall.

feuillé, -e (fœje), p. adj. See FEUILLU.

feuillée (fœje), s.f. Foliage, bower; *sous la* ~, under the greenwood tree.

feuiller (fœje), v.n. To leaf, to put forth leaves; (paint.) to paint foliage.

feuillet (fœjɛ), s.m. [f. *feuille*] **1.** Leaf = two pages; **2.** (zool.) manyplies.

feuilletage (fœjtaʒ), s.m. Flaky paste, puff paste; the making of this.

feuilleté, -e (fœjte), adj. **1.** Perused; **2.** made of flaky paste.

feuilleter (fœjte), v.a. [f. *feuillet*] **1.** To turn over the leaves (of a book, &c.); to thumb, to peruse; **2.** to make flaky paste.

feuilleton (fœjtɔ̃), s.m. [f. *feuillet*] Feuilleton, (in French newspapers) serial; *publié en* ~, issued in serial form.

feuillette (fœjɛt), s.f. [f. Goth. *fulli*] Cask (of 100 or 140 litres according to origin).

feuillu, -e (fœjy), adj. Leafy.

feuillure (fœjyr), s.f. [f. *feuille*] (carp. joinery) Rabbet, rebate, cheek (of a door).

feutrage (føtraʒ), s.m. [f. *feutre*] Felting, matting.

feutre (føtr), s.m. [f. OHG *vilz*] Felt; felt-cloth; felt hat, felt bonnet; padding (for saddles).

feutrer (føtre), v.a. To felt, to pad, to mat; *à pas feutrés*, stealthily; with muffled tread; like a thief in the night.

feutrier (føtrje), s.m. Felt-maker.

fève (fɛv), s.f. [L *faba*] Bean, *Faba vulgaris*, broad bean; berry; *roi de la* ~, Twelfth-night King; *trouver la* ~ *au gâteau*, to find the bean in the cake; (fig.) to hit the mark, to be lucky; *rendre* ~ *pour pois*, to give tit for tat, a Roland for an Oliver.

féverole (fevrɔl), s.f. [f. *fève*] Horse-bean, Scotch bean.

févier (fevje), s.m. (bot.) Horned acacia, *Gleditschia*.

février (fevrie), s.m. [L *Februarius*] February.

fez (fɛz), s.m. [f. *Fez* in Morocco] Fez.

fi (fi), interj. [onom.] Fy, fye, fie, for shame!; ~ *donc!*, fie! fie!; *faire* ~ *de*, to turn up one's nose at; to despise; to snap one's fingers at.

fiacre (fjakr), s.m. [f. *St Fiacre*] Hackney coach, hack, four-wheeler; (colloq.) *remiser son* ~, to kick the bucket; to die.

fiançailles (fjɑ̃saj), s.f.pl. [f. *fiancer*] Betrothal, engagement, affiancing; syn. ACCORDAILLES.

fiancé, -e (fjɑ̃se), p.p. s.m.f. Betrothed, engaged; affianced husband; affianced bride.

fiancer (fjɑ̃se), v.a. [f. OF *fier*, *fiance*] To betroth, to affiance; *il est fiancé à*, he is engaged or betrothed to; **se** ~, v.pr. to be engaged, betrothed, affianced.

fiasco (fjasko), s.m. [It. wd] Failure, fiasco; *faire* ~, to fail, to come to grief.

flasque (fjask), s.f. [f. It. *fiasco*] Flask, bottle.
fibre (fibr), s.f. [L *fibra*] Fibre; thread, filament; (fig.) texture, disposition, feeling, sensibility; *avoir la ~ sensible*, (*a*) to be easily moved; (*b*) to be touchy.
fibreu-x, -se (fibrø), adj. Fibrous.
fibrille (fibrij), s.f. Fibril, (bot.) fibrilla.
fibrine (fibrin), s.f. (chem.) Fibrin.
fibrome (fibrom), s.m. (surg.) Fibrous tumour, fibroma.
fibule (fibyl), s.f. [L *fibula*] Fibula, clasp.
fic (fik), s.m. [L *ficus*] Fig-like excrescence, (vet.) fig.
ficaire (fikɛr), s.f. [L *ficaria*] (bot.) Filewort, *Ficaria*.
ficeler (fisle), v.a. [f. *ficelle*] To tie up, to tie with string, to cord; (fam.) *il est bien mal ficelé!*, he is thoroughly badly turned out; what a guy he looks!
ficelier (fislje), s.m. String-reel; packthread-roller.
ficelle (fisɛl), s.f. [f. L *filum*] String, twine, packthread; (fig.) trick; *tenir les ~s*; to manage the puppets; to pull the wires; *connaître toutes les ~s*, to be up to every dodge, to know the game, the tricks. ~, adj. *Être très ~*, to be very tricky, cunning, cute, crafty; (subst.) *c'est une vieille ~*, he (or she) is an artful dodger.
fichant, -e (fiʃɑ̃), adj. **1.** (fort.) Darting (obs.); **2.** (colloq.) confoundedly annoying, vexatious.
fichaise (fiʃɛz), s.f. See FOUTAISE.
fiche (fiʃ), s.f. [f. *ficher*] **1.** Pin, peg, picket, surveying arrow; **2.** slip, file, reference note; *~ de consolation*, little bit of comfort; compensation.
ficher (fiʃe), v.a. (p.p. *fiché* or *fichu*), [L *figere*, LL *ficcare*] To drive in, to thrust in; (fam.) to do, to work, to shove, to place, to land, to chuck, to give, to deal (a blow), to stick; *qu'est-ce que tu fiches ici?*, what the deuce are you up to?; *va te faire fiche!*; go and be hanged!; *il n'en fiche pas lourd*, he does not do a stroke (of work); he is not working hard; he takes it easy; *fichez-moi la paix*, just let me alone; shut up!; *il l'a fichu dedans*, he got the better of him, he let him in for it; *il est bien mal fichu*, he is very badly turned out; *~ le camp*, to hop it, to clear off, to cut along; *fichez-moi le camp et plus vite que ça!*, hop it and be quick about it; sling your hook!; *il l'a fichu à la porte*, he hoofed him out; he gave him the sack; he kicked him out; *je t'en fiche!*, nonsense!; nothing of the kind!; *il est fichu*, he is done for; it's all up with him; *se ~ de*, and *se fiche de*, to laugh at; not to care for; *il s'est fiché de vous*, he has been making game of you; he was pulling your leg; *il s'en fiche pas mal!*, he does not care a rap; *je m'en fiche!*, what do I care; ⚠ *se ficher* is a euphemistic equivalent of *se foutre*.
fichier (fiʃje), s.m. [f. *fiche*] Box-file, index-box.
fichoir (fiʃwar), s.m. Peg, clothes-peg.
fichtre (fiʃtr), interj. (fam.) Hang it!, the deuce!, confound it!, bless me!, by Jove!, by Gad!, dash it!
fichtrement (fiʃtrəmɑ̃), adv. (fam.) Deucedly, awfully, confoundedly, infernally, intensely, strongly, capitally.
fichu (fiʃy), s.m. [uncert. orig.] Neckerchief, kerchief.
fichu, -e (fiʃy), p. adj. Wretched, queer, poor, sorry, ugly, pitiful. See FICHER.
fichument, (fiʃymɑ̃), adv. (fam.) Wretchedly, sorrily, deucedly, infernally.
ficoïde (fikɔid), s.f. [f. L *ficus*] (bot.) Fig-marigold, *Mesambryanthemum*.
ficti-f, -ve (fiktif), adj. Fictitious.
fiction (fiksjɔ̃), s.f. [L *fictio*] Fiction, (*a*) the act of inventing; (*b*) the thing invented; invented statement; imaginary world, or thing, or situation.
fictivement (fiktivmɑ̃), adv. Fictitiously.
fidéicommis (fideikɔmi) s.m. [L *fidei*+*commissum*] (law) Fideicommissum, trust.
fidéicommissaire (fideikɔmisɛr), s.m. (law) Transferee, trustee.
fidéjusseur (fideʒysœr), s.m. [L *fidejussor*] (law) Fidejussor, surety.
fidéjussion (fideʒysjɔ̃), s.f. Fidejussion, suretyship.
fidèle (fidɛl), adj. [L *fidelis*] Faithful, true, loyal, constant, trusty, trustworthy, accurate, exact; retentive (memory). ~, s.m. Faithful friend or follower; *les ~s*, s.m.f.pl. the true believers, the congregation, churchgoers.
fidèlement (fidɛlmɑ̃), adv. Faithfully, loyally, truly, exactly, honestly, trustily.
fidélité (fidelite), s.f. [L *fidelitas*] Fidelity, faithfulness, loyalty, trustiness, constancy; accuracy; retentiveness (of the memory); *jurer ~*, to take an oath of fidelity.
fiduciaire (fidysjɛr), adj. [L *fiduciarius*] Fiduciary; *circulation ~*, note circulation, paper circulation.
fief (fjɛf), s.m. [OHG *fihu*, Germ. *Vieh*, LL *feodum*] Fief, feud, fee; *franc ~*, freehold.
fieffé, -e (fjɛfe), p. adj. **1.** Enfeoffed; **2.** (fam.) arrant, regular, downright; *un ~ coquin*, an arrant knave.
fieffer (fjɛfe), v.a. (obs.) To enfeoff.
fiel (fjɛl), s.m. [L *fel*] Gall; (fig.) rancour, bitterness; malignity; *être sans ~*, to bear no malice; *paroles pleines de ~*, rancorous speech.
fielleu-x, -se (fjɛlø), adj. Gally, bitter, rancorous.
fiente (fjɑ̃t), s.f. [L *fimus*] Dung, excrement.

fienter (fjɑ̃te), v.n. To dung.

fier (fje), v.a. (obs., now superseded by *confier*) [L *fidere*] To entrust; **se ~** (*à*), v.pr. to trust (to), to put one's trust (in), to confide (in), to rely (on); *ne vous y fiez pas trop*, don't make too sure.

fi-er, -ère (fjɛr), adj. [L *ferus*] Proud, haughty, bold, arrogant; noble, grand, indomitable; fearless; *une âme ~e*, a lofty soul, an intrepid soul; *~ comme Artaban*, as proud as Lucifer; *~ comme un paon*, as proud as a peacock; (fam.) excessive, remarkable, rare, (in this sense, the adjective is always placed before the subst.); *vous avez un ~ culot*, you have no end of a cheek; *une ~e bêtise*, a rare piece of foolishness; *faire le ~*, to put on proud airs, to look big.

fier-à-bras (fjɛrabrɑ), s.m. Hector, bully, swaggerer, braggart.

fièrement (fjɛrmɑ̃), adv. Haughtily, proudly, arrogantly; (fam.) capitally, awfully.

fiérot, -te (fjero), adj. Proudish, uppish, stuck-up.

fierté (fjɛrte), s.f. [L *feritas*] Haughtiness, pride, spirit, boldness, intrepidity.

fièvre (fjɛvr), s.f. [L *febris*] Fever, heat, (high) temperature (of the body), ague; (fig.) heat, excitement, feverishness; *avoir la ~*, to be in a fever; *donner la ~*, to put into a fever.

fiévreusement (fjevrøzmɑ̃), adv. Feverishly, restlessly.

fiévreu-x, -se (fjevrø), adj. Feverish, restless. ~, s.m. Fever patient.

fifre (fifr), s.m. [f. Germ. *Pfeife*] Fife; fifer; *jouer du ~*, to fife.

fifrer (fifre), v.n. To fife.

figaro (figaro), s.m. [f. *Figaro*, character in Beaumarchais] Barber; go-between.

figement (fiʒmɑ̃), s.m. Congealment, coagulation, curdling.

figer (fiʒe), v.a.n., and **se ~**, v.pr. [LL *fidicare*] To congeal, to coagulate, to curdle; (fig.) to stiffen.

fignolage (fiɲɔlaʒ), s.m. Minute finishing or completing.

fignoler (fiɲɔle), v.a.n. [f. *fin*] To refine; to finish minutely, to finish off.

figue (fig) s.f. [L *ficus*] (bot.) Fig; *~ de Barbarie*, prickly pear; *d'un air moitié ~ moitié raisin*, half reluctantly, half willingly; half sweet, half sour; *faire la ~ à*, to laugh at, to dare, to mock.

figuerie (figri), s.f. Fig-orchard.

figuier (figje), s.m. (bot.) Fig-tree; *~ d'Inde, de Barbarie*, Indian fig, *Opuntia vulgaris*.

figurant, -e (figyrɑ̃), s.m.f. (theatr.) Figurant(e), accessory character, dummy.

figurati-f, -ve (figuratif), adj. Figurative; topographical. **~ve**, s.f. (gram.) Characteristic (letter).

figuration (figyra'sjɔ̃), s.f. Figuration; (theatr.) body of figurants; notation (of pronunciation).

figurativement (figyrativmɑ̃), adv. Figuratively, symbolically.

figure (figyr), s.f. [L *figura*] Form, shape, image, diagram, representation, symbol; (human) face, countenance; (danc.) steps, figure; (rhet.) metaphor, trope; (paint., sculpt.) figure; *être bien de ~*, *avoir une belle ~*, to have a handsome face; *une ~ de connaissance*, an old acquaintance; *faire une triste ~*, to cut a poor figure; *faire bonne ~*, to keep one's countenance; *faire ~ dans le monde*, to cut a brilliant figure; to cut a dash; *il lui a dit cela en pleine ~*, he said that to his face; *je parlerai sans ~s*, I will speak plainly.

figuré, -e (figyre), p. adj. Figurative, figurate, figural, figured, symbolical, ornate, florid. ~, s.m. *Au ~*, in a figurative sense.

figurer (figyre), v.a. [L *figurare*] To figure, to represent, to delineate, to typify; ~, v.n. to cut a figure; to appear, to stand, to be in view, to be prominent or conspicuous; **se ~**, v.pr. to imagine, to picture mentally; to fancy, to believe; *figurez-vous que*, would you believe that; just listen to this.

figurine (figyrin), s.f. Figurine (statuette), vignette (of a postage-stamp).

fil (fil), s.m. [L *filum*] Thread, yarn, filament, wire; edge, sharpness; stream, direction, grain; order, clue; *~ à plomb*, plumb-line; *au ~ de l'eau*, down the stream; *de ~ en aiguille*, one thing bringing on another, or leading to another; *tenir le bout du ~*, to have the clue; *ne tenir qu'à un ~*, to hang by a thread; *perdre le ~ de son discours*, to lose the thread of one's speech; *ruses cousues de ~ blanc*, tricks easily seen through; *donner du ~ à un couteau*, to whet a knife; to give an edge to a knife; *donner du ~ à retordre à X*, to cut out work for X, to give X a good deal of trouble; *tenir les ~s*, to pull the wires; *couper droit ~*, to cut straight, along the warp or the woof; *passer au ~ de l'épée*, to put to the sword; *télégraphie sans ~*, wireless telegraphy; *~ de la Vierge*, gossamer thread; (colloq.) *il n'a pas inventé le ~ à couper le beurre*, he'll never set the Thames on fire.

filage (filaʒ), s.m. [f. *filer*] Spinning.

filaire (filɛr), s.m.f. [f. *fil*] (zool.) Filaria.

filament (filamɑ̃), s.m. [L *filamentum*] Filament, thread, string, thin wire; filament (in electric lamps).

filamenteu-x, -se (filamɑ̃tø), adj. Filamentous, filamentose.

filandière (filɑ̃djɛr), s.f. adj. Spinner,

spinning woman or nun; *les sœurs ~s*, the fatal sisters, the Fates.

filandre (filɑ̃dr), s.f. [f. *fil*] **1.** String, stringy part of meat; **2.** gossamer.

filandreu-x, -se (filɑ̃drø), adj. Stringy; fibrous; tough; (fig.) prosy, diffuse, loose, verbose (as style).

filant, -e (filɑ̃), p. adj. Viscous, flowing, viscid; *étoile ~e*, shooting star, falling star.

filanzane (filɑ̃zan), s.m. Filanzane (a travelling chair, borne by four bearers, in Madagascar).

filasse (filas), s.f. [f. *fil*] Tow; *cheveux de ~*, flaxen hair.

filassi-er, -ère (filasje), s.m.f. Flax and hemp dresser.

filateur (filatœr), s.m. **1.** Spinning-mill owner; **2.** spinner.

filature (filatyr), s.f. **1.** Spinning-mill; spinning; **2.** following, shadowing; *prendre en ~*, to shadow, to follow.

file (fil), s.f. [f. *filer*] Row, file, line; *à la ~*, one after another; *à la ~ indienne*, in Indian file; *prendre la ~*, to fall in with the others, to wait for one's turn, to 'queue'; *chef de ~*, leader; *par ~ à droite!*, right file!; *une longue file d'autos*, a long line of motor-cars; *feu de ~*, running, dropping fire.

filé (file), s.m. Cotton yarn; thread of gold or silver.

filer (file), v.a.n. [L *filare*] **1.** To spin; *l'araignée file sa toile*, the spider spins its web; *~ un son*, to hold a note; *~ ses jours dans l'oisiveté*, to spin out one's time in idleness; *~ le parfait amour*, to be all love and sentiment, to philander; to bill and coo; *~ un câble*, to pay out rope; *~ dix nœuds à l'heure*, to make ten knots; *~ une scène*, to develop a scene; *~ la carte*, to play a wrong or false card surreptitiously; *du temps que Berthe filait*, in the good old times, in the days of yore, or of good queen Bess; **2.** to follow, to track, to shadow; **3.** ~, v.n. to make oneself scarce, to slip away, to be off, to bolt; (slang) to leg it; to pop off, to fade away; *faire ~*, to send off, to turn away, or out; *~ à l'anglaise*, to take French leave; *~ doux*, to be all submission, to eat humble pie, to sing small; **4.** to rope, to be ropy, viscous; **5.** to smoke, to flare (of a lamp); **6.** to shoot (of a star).

filerie (filri), s.f. Hemp-spinning mill; rope-walk; wire-drawing.

filet (filɛ), s.m. [f. *fil*] **1.** Net, network, (fig. pl.) snare; *faire tomber dans ses ~s*, to ensnare; **2.** thin thread, string, filament; **3.** fillet (of beef, fish, &c.); *contre-~*, *faux ~*, chine of beef, upper cut; **4.** streamlet, drop, streak; *un ~ de vinaigre*, a dash of vinegar; *un ~ de voix*, a thin voice; **5.** (anat.) fraenum; (colloq.) *avoir le ~*, to be tongue-tied; *avoir le ~ coupé*, to have a glib tongue; **6.** (arch.) fillet; **7.** (techn.) *~ d'une vis*, thread of a screw; **8.** (print.) rule; **9.** (riding) bridoon.

filetage (filtaʒ), s.m. Thread; thread-making (of screws, &c.); wire drawing; poaching.

fileter (filte), v.a. To cut the thread of (a screw, &c.); to wiredraw; to poach.

filial, -e, (aux) (filjal), adj. Filial.

filialement (filjalmɑ̃), adv. Filially.

filiation (filja'sjɔ̃), s.f. [L *filiatio*] Filiation, connexion.

filière (filjɛr), s.f. [f. *fil*] Draw-plate; screw-plate; (naut.) rope; (fig.) regular course, series, channel; *suivre toute la ~*, to go through all the grades of employment (in an administration, industry, &c.).

filiforme (filifɔrm), adj. Filiform, thread-like.

filigrane (filigran), s.m. [It. *filigrana*] **1.** Filigree; **2.** watermark (of paper).

filigraner (filigrane), v.a. **1.** To filigree; **2.** to watermark (paper).

filin (filɛ̃), s.m. [f. *fil*] Rope, line.

filipendule (filipɑ̃dyl), s.f. (bot.) Dropwort, *Spiraea filipendula*.

fille (fij), s.f. [L *filia*] Daughter; girl, maid, maiden, lass, spinster, servant-girl; nun; prostitute; (fig.) offspring, dependency; *rester ~*, to remain single; *belle-~*, daughter-in-law; stepdaughter; *petite-~*, grand-daughter; *arrière-petite-~*, great-grand-daughter; *~ d'honneur*, maid of honour; *~ de chambre*, chamber-maid, lady's maid; *~ de cuisine*, kitchen-maid; *~ de salle*, waitress; *~ de joie*, *~ publique*, prostitute; *~ à marier*, marriageable girl; *vieille ~*, spinster, old maid; *la France, ~ aînée de l'Église*, France, the eldest daughter of the Church; *la superstition, ~ de l'ignorance*, superstition, the daughter of ignorance.

fillette (fijɛt), s.f. **1.** Little girl, girlie, lass; **2.** half-bottle of Anjou wine.

filleul, -e (fijœl), s.m.f. [LL *filiolus*], Godson, god-daughter.

film (film), s.m. [Engl. wd] Film.

filmer (filme) v.a. To film.

filoche (filɔʃ), s.f. [f. *fil*] Network.

filon (filɔ̃), s.m. [f. *fil*] Vein, lode; (fig.) source of profits, bit of luck; windfall; soft or cushy job; *il a trouvé le ~*, he has struck a rich vein, he has found his niche; (war slang) he has got a Blighty one.

filoselle (filozɛl), s.f. [It. *filosello*] Grogram yarn, floss silk.

filou (pl. **-s**) (filu), s.m. [f. Engl. *fellow*] Pickpocket, thief, sharper, cheat, swindler.

filouter (filute), v.a. To steal, to pick the pocket of, to pinch, to swindle, to cheat; *il m'a filouté vingt francs,* he cheated me out of twenty francs.

filouterie (filutri), s.f. Pocket-picking, stealth, swindle, cheat, theft.

fils (fis), s.m. [L *filius*] Son; (fig.) son, young friend; native of a country; offspring; *petit-~*, grandson; *arrière-petit-~*, great-grandson; *beau-~*, stepson, son-in-law; *~ de famille,* young gentleman (well provided for); *~ de ses œuvres,* self-made man; *les ~ d'Apollon,* the poets; (pej.) *~ d'archevêque*, a fellow whose career is due to influential relatives; *il est bien le ~ de son père,* he is a chip of the old block.

filtrage (filtraʒ), s.m. Filtering, straining, filtration.

filtration (filtra'sjɔ̃), s.f. See syn. FILTRAGE.

filtre (filtr), s.m. [It. *filtro*] Filter, strainer, filtering-stone.

filtrer (filtre), v.a. To filter, to strain; ~, v.n. to filter, to pass through a filter, &c.

fin (fɛ̃), s.f. [L *finis*] End, close, termination, conclusion; death; aim, object, purpose; *toucher à sa ~*, to be near one's end, *arriver à ses ~s,* to gain one's end; *à quelle ~?*, to what end?; *à la ~*, in the end; finally, at last, after all; *à la ~ des ~s,* in the end, in the upshot; *en ~ de compte,* when all is said and done; *sans ~*, endless, endlessly, perpetually; *prendre ~, tirer à sa ~*, to come to an end; *mettre ~ à,* to stop, to put an end to; *à toute ~*, for all purposes; *mener à bonne ~*, to bring to a successful end, to make a success (of); *~ courant,* end of the present month; *qui veut la ~ veut les moyens,* where there 's a will there 's a way; all 's well that ends well; *~ de non-recevoir,* put-off, refusal; (law) plea-in-bar, exception; (colloq.) *faire une ~*, to turn over a new leaf; to get married; *faire une belle ~*, to die a Christian death.

fin, -e (fɛ̃), adj. Fine, refined, delicate; precious; nice; slender, thin, tenuous, minute, subtle, keen, acute, sharp; *argent, or ~*, fine silver, gold; *vin ~*, fine wine; *pierres ~es,* precious stones, gems; *~e fleur de farine,* fine flour; *écriture ~e,* small hand: *~es herbes,* savoury herbs; *des traits ~s,* delicate features; *~e (champagne),* brandy; *une ~e,* a glass of brandy; *une taille ~e,* a slender waist; *une pluie ~e,* a fine, persistent rain; *avoir l'oreille ~e,* to have a sharp or quick ear; *avoir le nez ~*, to have a good nose, (fig.) to be sagacious or far-sighted; *être un ~ connaisseur,* to be a true, or good connoisseur; *être une ~e lame,* to be a good swordsman; *être une ~e mouche,* to be a sly one; *au ~ fond de,* right at the bottom of; *le ~ du ~*, the quintessence; *jouer au plus ~*, to finesse; *voilà le ~ mot,* here is the true motive, the secret reason.

final, -e (pl. **-s**) (final), adj. [L *finalis*] Final, last, ultimate; *point ~*, final point; *cause ~e,* final cause.

finale (final), s.f. **1.** Last syllable or letter of a word; **2.** (sports, games) final, deciding heat or game. ~, s.m. (mus.) Finale.

finalement (finalmɑ̃), adv. Finally, lastly, in conclusion.

finalité (finalite), s.f. Finality.

finance (finɑ̃s), s.f. [f. OF *finer=payer*] Finance, treasury; *~s,* (pl.) cash, resources, money.

financer (finɑ̃se), v.a.n. To lay out money; to find the capital (for a business, enterprise, &c.), to invest money in; (colloq.) to pay, to fork out.

financi-er, -ère (finɑ̃sje), adj. Financial. ~, s.m. Financier, capitalist; *~ère,* s.f. (cook.) financière (sauce).

financièrement (finɑ̃sjɛrmɑ̃), adv. Financially.

finasser (finase), v.n. [f. *fin*] To finesse, to use petty tricks, to manœuvre.

finasserie (finasri), s.f. (pej.) Finesse, finessing, petty trick, craft, cunning.

finassi-er, -ère (finasje), adj. s.m.f. Petty trickster, cunning (person).

finaud, -e (fino), adj. [f. *fin*] Cunning. s.m.f. Sly or cunning person; sly-boots.

finement (finmɑ̃), adv. Finely, delicately, minutely; skilfully; shrewdly.

finesse (finɛs), s.f. Fineness, delicacy, nicety, refinement; thinness, slenderness, tenuousness; acuteness, quickness, wit, shrewdness; finesse, trick, artifice; *entendre ~ à,* to give a malicious construction to; *les ~s de la langue*; the niceties of the language; *~ cousue de fil blanc,* artifice easily seen through.

finette (finɛt), s.f. Finette, a cotton tissue.

fingard, -e (fɛ̃gar), adj. Restive.

fini, -e (fini), p. adj. Finished, ended, complete, settled, concluded; downright, arrant, thorough; ruined, done for, broken down; finite, limited, perfect; *un coquin ~*, an arrant rogue. ~, s.m. Finish; the finite; minute care; polish.

finir (finir), v.a.n. [L *finire*] To end, to finish, to put an end to, to conclude, to complete, to finish off, to cease, to come to an end; to terminate, to draw to a close, to die; *en ~*, to put an end to a thing, to settle it, to have done with it, to cut it short; *en ~ avec,* to get rid of, to have done with; *à n'en plus ~*, endless, endlessly; *cela finira mal,* that will turn out badly; *il finit par nous dire que,* in the end he told us that, he ended by telling us that; *n, i ni, c'est fini,* and that 's an end of it.

finissage (finisaʒ), s.m. Finishing, finish, completion; syn. (fam.) FINITION.
finisseu-r, -se (finisœr), s.m.f. Finisher, polisher.
finition (finisjɔ̃), s.f. See FINISSAGE.
finlandais, -e, (fɛ̃lɑ̃dɛ), adj. Finnish. s.m.f. Finlander, Finn, Finnish language; syn. FINNOIS.
finnois, -e (finwɑ), adj. s.m.f. See syn. FINLANDAIS.
fiole (fjɔl), s.f. [LL *phiola*] Phial, vial, small bottle; (slang) face, head; *tu veux te payer ma* ~, you want a laugh at my expense.
fion (fjɔ̃), s.m. (pop.) Finish, last touch; *donner un coup de* ~, to give the last touch, to smarten up.
fioriture (fjɔrityr), s.f. [It. *fioritura*] Flourish; grace-note; graces, superfluous ornament.
firmament (firmamɑ̃), s.m. [L *firmamentum*] Firmament.
firman (firmɑ̃, firman), s.m. [Turk. wd] Firman.
firme (firm), s.f. [f. L *firmus*] Firm.
fisc (fisk), s.m. [f. L *fiscus*] Public treasury, Exchequer; revenue officers.
fiscal, -e, (aux) (fiskal), adj. Fiscal.
fiscalité (fiskalite), s.f. Fiscal laws, fiscal policy; (pej.) fiscal policy tending to exaggerated taxation.
fissile (fisil), adj. [L *fissilis*] Fissile, cleavable.
fissipare (fisipar), adj. [f. L *fissus*+*parere*] Fissiparous.
fissipède (fisipɛd), adj. [f. L *fissus*+*pes, pedis*] (zool.) Fissiped.
fissirostre (fisirɔstr), adj. [f. L *fissus*+*rostrum*] (ornith.) Fissirostral. ~**s**, s.m.pl. Fissirostres.
fissuration (fisyra'sjɔ̃), s.f. Fissuring, cleavage, splitting.
fissure (fisyr), s.f. [L *fissura*] Fissure, crevice, cleft, slit, crack.
(se) fissurer (səfisyre), v.pr. To fissure, to crack, to cleave, to be cleft.
fiston (fistɔ̃), s.m. [f. *fils*] (pop.) Sonny, my boy, lad.
fistulaire (fistylɛr), adj. Fistular.
fistule (fistyl), s.f. [L *fistula*] Fistula.
fistuleu-x, -se (fistylø), adj. Fistulous, fistulose, fistular.
fixage (fiksaʒ), s.m. [f. *fixer*] (photo., techn.) Fixing.
fixat-eur, -rice (fiksatœr), adj. Fixing. ~, s.m. Fixing-bath; fixing-apparatus.
fixation (fiksa'sjɔ̃), s.f. [LL *fixatio*] Fixation, fixing, settling, determining.
fixe (fiks), adj. [L *fixus*] Fixed, firm, set, fast, steady, immovable, invariable, regular; *étoile* ~, fixed star; *avoir le regard* ~, to stare stonily, to look fixedly, to have a vacant, stony expression; *idée* ~, fixed idea, obsession; *s'assembler à jour* ~, to meet on stated days, or regularly, on a fixed day; *prix* ~, set price; *à poste* ~, resident, in a permanent way. ~*!*, interj. (mil.) Eyes front!
fixe (fiks), s.m. Fixed salary.
fixement (fiksmɑ̃), adv. Fixedly, steadfastly.
fixer (fikse), v.a. To fix, to fasten, to stick, to direct (the eye, &c.) fixedly, to stare at, to gaze steadily on; to single out with one's eyes; ~ *les yeux sur*, to look fixedly, intently on, or at; to settle, to set down, to determine, to appoint; ~ *sa résidence à Paris*, to take up one's abode in Paris; ~ *l'attention de X*, to attract (and keep) X's attention; ~ *son choix sur*, to settle one's choice, to decide upon; *je suis fixé!*, well, now I know what I have to do, or what 's what; **se** ~, v.pr. to take up one's abode, to settle down.
fixité (fiksite), s.f. Fixity, fixedness, stability.
fjord (fjɔr), s.m. [Norw. wd] Fjord, fiord.
fla (fla), s.m. invar. [onom.] Double beat of the drum; see RA.
flac (flak), interj. [onom.] Plash!, bang!, clap!
flaccidité (flaksidite), s.f. [f. L *flaccidus*] Flaccidness; flaccidity.
flache (flaʃ), s.f. [f. L *flaccus*] Wane, flaw (in wood); pool; pot-hole (in a road). ~, adj. Flawy, flawed.
flacon (flakɔ̃), s.m. [LL *flasco*] Flagon, flask, phial, vial, bottle, decanter.
flafla (flafla), s.m. (pop.) Show, dash, fuss; *faire du* ~, to show off, to make a fuss.
flagellant (flaʒɛllɑ̃), s.m. Flagellant.
flagellation (flaʒɛlla'sjɔ̃), s.f. Flagellation, scourging, flogging.
flageller (flaʒɛlle), v.a. [L *flagellare*] To flagellate, to scourge, to flog.
flageoler (flaʒɔle), v.n. [f. OF *flageol*] To tremble, to shake, to be shaky (on one's legs).
flageolet (flaʒɔlɛ), s.m. [OF wd] **1.** (mus.) Flageolet; flageolet-player; **2.** (bot.) flageolet, kidney-bean.
flagorner (flagɔrne), v.a. [orig. unkn.] To fawn upon, to flatter.
flagornerie (flagɔrnri), s.f. Base flattery, fawning.
flagorneu-r, -se (flagɔrnœr), s.m.f. Sycophant, fawner, flatterer, toad-eater. ~, adj. Sycophantic, fawning, toad-eating.
flagrant, -e (flagrɑ̃), adj. [L *flagrans*] Flagrant, glaring; *en* ~ *délit*, flagrante delicto, in the very act.
flair (flɛr), s.m. [f. *flairer*] Scent, smell; nose (of a dog); (fig.) flair, perspicacity.
flairer (flɛre), v.a. [L *fragrare*] To scent,

to smell; to smell out; (fig.) to detect, to guess at; to nose; ~ *quelque chose de suspect*, (colloq.) to smell a rat.

flamand, -e (flamɑ̃), adj. s.m.f. Flemish, pertaining to Flanders, Fleming.

flamant (flamɑ̃), s.m. [f. *flamme*] (ornith.) Flamingo.

flambage (flɑ̃baʒ), s.m. [f. *flamber*] Singeing (of a fowl, &c).

flambant, -e (flɑ̃bɑ̃), p. adj. Flaming, blazing; *tout ~ neuf*, brand-new.

flambeau (pl. **-x**) (flɑ̃bo), s.m. [f. *flamber*] Flambeau, torch, candlestick; *allumer le ~ de l'hymen*, to light the torch of hymen, to marry; *le ~ du jour*, the luminary of the world = the sun; *aux ~x*, by torch-light.

flambée (flɑ̃be), s.f. Brushwood fire, blaze, flare-up.

flamber (flɑ̃be), v.a.n. [f. OF *flambe*, *flamme*] To singe, to pass before the fire, to sterilize by flame; (slang) ~, v.n. to blaze, to blaze up, to flame; *je suis flambé!* I am done for!, I am dished, or copped.

flamberge (flɑ̃bɛrʒ), s.f. [name of Renaud de Montauban's sword] Sword, rapier; *mettre ~ au vent*, to draw the sword, (fig.) to rush to fight.

flamboiement (flɑ̃bwa'mɑ̃), s.m. Blazing, blazing up, flaring up.

flamboyant, -e (flɑ̃bwajɑ̃), p. adj. **1.** Blazing, flaming; **2.** (arch.) flamboyant.

flamboyer (flɑ̃bwaje), v.n. [f. *flamber*] To flame, to blaze, to flash, to flare.

flamine (flamin), s.m. [L *flamen*] (ant.) Flamen.

flamingant, -e (flamɛ̃gɑ̃), adj. s.m.f. (Person) speaking the Flemish language.

flamme (flam), s.f. [L *flamma*] **1.** Flame, flare, fire, blaze, heat; (fig.) ardour, love; *déclarer sa ~*, to declare one's amorous flame; *brûler d'une ~ secrète*, to burn with a secret passion; *Jeanne d'Arc périt par les ~s*, Joan of Arc was burnt to death; *jeter feu et ~*, to fret and fume; to breathe fire and slaughter; **2.** (mil., naut.) streamer, pennant, pendant, pennon; **3.** (vet.) fleam.

flammé, -e (flame), adj. **1.** Flame-shaped; **2.** glazed (as pottery, stoneware, &c.).

flammèche (flamɛʃ), s.f. [f. *flamme*] Flake (of fire), spark.

flammerole (flamrɔl), s.f. Ignis fatuus, will-o'-the-wisp.

flan (flɑ̃), s.m. [OHG *flado*] **1.** Custard; **2.** (coin.) blank, coin-plate; **3.** (print.) flong.

flanc (flɑ̃), s.m. [orig. uncert.] Flank, side; bosom, womb; *se battre les ~s*, to lash one's sides; (fig.) to flog oneself (into), to exert oneself violently; *être sur le ~*, to be laid up, to be on the sick list, to be played out; (fig.) *prêter le ~*, to lay oneself open (to attack, criticism, &c.); *par le ~ droit!*, (mil.) right turn!; (mil. slang) *tirer au ~*, to malinger, to swing the lead.

flancher (flɑ̃ʃe), v.n. To give way, to show the white feather, to sing small, to turn tail.

flanchet (flɑ̃ʃɛ), s.m. [f. *flanc*] Flank (of beef).

flanconade (flɑ̃kɔnad), s.f. (fenc.) Flanconade.

flandrin (flɑ̃drɛ̃), s.m. [f. *Flandre*] Lanky fellow, gawky man.

flanelle (flanɛl), s.f. [Engl. *flannel*] **1.** Flannel; **2.** flannel underclothing; ⚠ In English 'flannels' is frequently used in the pl. with the sense of 'cricket clothes', 'white flannel trousers' = *pantalon de tennis*. In French *flanelle* is only used for the material or for flannel underclothing.

flâner (flɑne), v.n. [orig. uncert.] To lounge, to idle, to loiter, to saunter, to loaf.

flânerie (flɑnri), s.f. Loitering, idling, loafing, sauntering, lounging.

flâneu-r, -se (flɑnœr), s.m.f. Lounger, idler, loafer, saunterer.

flanquer[1] (flɑ̃ke), v.a. [f. *flanc*] To flank.

flanquer[2] (flɑ̃ke), v.a. [f. *flaque*] To fling, to throw, to pitch, to give, to bang; ~ *X à la porte*, to bundle X out, to turn X out bag and baggage; to kick X out; (slang) ~ *une tournée à X*, to give X a drubbing, or a good licking; *se ~ par terre*, v.pr. to go sprawling, to fall heavily.

flapi, -e (flapi), adj. (colloq.) Frazzled, knocked up, wobbly, exhausted.

flaque (flak), s.f. [f. *flache*] Puddle, plash, small pool.

flaquée (flake), s.f. Dash (of liquid).

flaquer (flake), v.a. To dash, to throw (a liquid).

flasque (flask), adj. [L *flaccus*] Flaccid, flabby, slack, limp, loose, soft, feeble.

flasque (flask), s.f. [LL *flasca*] Powder-flask; (naut.) whelp (of capstan); (artill.) cheek (of gun-carriage).

flatter (flate), v.a. [f. LG *flat*] To caress, to stroke, to rub; (fig.) to flatter, to fawn upon, to humour; **se ~**, v.pr. to flatter oneself, to fancy oneself, to indulge oneself with the belief (*que*, that); to delude oneself; to pride oneself; to flatter each other.

flatterie (flatri), s.f. Caress, flattery, fawning, compliment.

flatteu-r, -se (flatœr), s.m.f. Flatterer. ~, adj. Flattering, complimentary, gratifying; caressing, fawning.

flatteusement (flatøzmɑ̃), adv. Flatteringly.

flatueu-x, -se (flatɥø), adj. [f. L *flatus*] Flatulent.

flatulence (flatylɑ̃s), s.f. Flatulence.
flatulent, -e (flatylɑ̃), adj. Flatulent.
fléau (pl. **-x**) (fleo), s.m. [f. L *flagellum*] **1.** Flail; **2.** beam (of a balance); **3.** (fig.) scourge, calamity, plague, destroyer; bore, public nuisance.
flèche (flɛʃ), s.f. [etym. dub.] **1.** Arrow, dart; (astr.) sagitta; (fig.) *faire ~ de tout bois,* to resort to any shift; **2.** (of a carriage) perch; **3.** (of a mast) pole; **4.** (of a steeple) spire.
fléchir (fleʃir), v.a. [L *flectere*] To bend, to bow; (fig.) to move, to appease, to touch; **~**, v.n. to bend, to give way, to sink, to stoop; (comm.) to fall.
fléchissement (fleʃismɑ̃), s.m. Bending, giving way; (comm.) fall.
fléchisseur (fleʃisœr), adj.m. s.m. Flexor, flector; *muscle* **~**, flexor.
flegmatique (flɛgmatik), adj. Phlegmatic.
flegmatiquement (flɛgmatikmɑ̃), adv. Phlegmatically.
flegme (flɛgm), s.m. [Gr. *phlegma*] Phlegm.
flémard, -e, flemmard (flɛmar), adj. s.m.f. (pop.) Lazy, lazybones, slacker.
flemme, flème (flɛm), s.f. (pop.) Laziness, dislike for work; *j'ai la* **~**, I feel a bit slack; I won't do a turn; I feel lazy or 'Mondayish'; *il bat sa* **~**, he is lazy, he is idling, he slacks about.
fléole (fleɔl), s.f. (bot.) Cat's-tail grass, timothy-grass.
flet (flɛ), s.m. (ichth.) Flounder.
flétan (fletɑ̃), s.m. (ichth.) Halibut.
flétrir (fletrir), v.a. [f. L *flaccere*] To wither, to fade, to blast, to blight; to brand, to stigmatize, to tarnish; to condemn; **se ~**, v.pr. to wither, to fade away.
flétrissure (fletrisyr), s.f. **1.** Withering, fading; **2.** brand, stigma, mark of infamy.
fleur (flœr), s.f. [L *flos*] Flower, bloom, blossom; (fig.) finest part; beginning, prime, pick, choice; surface; praises, eulogy; (fig.) *~ des pois,* pink of fashion, best society; *~s de rhétorique,* flowers of rhetoric; *la ~ de l'âge,* the prime of life; *avoir la ~ d'une chose,* to get a thing in its prime; *~ de soufre,* flowers of sulphur, sublimed sulphur; *~ de chevalerie, la fine ~ des chevaliers,* the flower of chivalry; *~ de lys,* fleur-de-lys, flower-de-luce; *à ~s,* flowered; *à ~ de,* on a level with, even with; *des yeux à ~ de tête,* goggle eyes.
fleuraison (flœrɛzɔ̃), s.f. See FLORAISON.
fleurdeliser (flœrdəlize), v.a. To brand, to adorn, with fleur-de-lys.
fleurer (flœre), v.n.a. [f. *fleur*] To smell, to exhale an odour.
fleuret (flœrɛ), s.m. [f. *fleur*] **1.** (fenc.) Foil; *~ démoucheté,* foil with the button off; **2.** floss silk.
fleurette (flœrɛt), s.f. Floweret; (fig.) love-speech, sweet nonsense; *conter* **~**, to make love, to flirt, to talk sweet nonsense, or sweet nothings.
fleuri, -e (flœri), p. adj. Flowery, flowering, flowered; blooming, blossoming; florid, flushed with red; ornate, flourished, florid; *un style* **~**, an ornate or florid style.
fleurir (flœrir), v.n. To flower, to blossom; to flourish; **~**, v.a. to flower, to adorn, to deck with flowers, to give flowers to.
fleurissant, -e (flœrisɑ̃), p. adj. Flowering, blooming, flowery, blossoming.
fleuriste (flœrist), s.m.f. Florist, flower-fancier, flower-maker, nursery-man, flower-seller. **~** adj. *Jardin* **~**, flower garden.
fleuron (flœrɔ̃), s.m. Fleuron, floret, flower-shaped ornament; *c'est le plus beau ~ de sa couronne,* it's the brightest jewel in his crown, it's the best of his assets.
fleuronné, -e (flœrɔne), adj. Decorated with fleurons; (bot.) having florets.
fleuve (flœv), s.m. [L *fluvius*] River (falling into the sea); (fig.) course, current, stream; (myth.) river-god.
flexibilité (flɛksibilite), s.f. Flexibility, pliancy, pliability.
flexible (flɛksibl), adj. [L *flexibilis*] Flexible, pliant, pliable.
flexion (flɛksjɔ̃), s.f. [L *flexio*] Flexion, bending; (gram.) inflexion.
flexueu-x, -se (flɛksɥø), adj. Flexuous.
flexuosité (flɛksɥozite), s.f. Flexuosity.
flibuste (flibyst), s.f. Filibustering, buccaneering.
flibuster (flibyste), v.n.a. To filibuster, to buccaneer; (pop.) to pinch, to steal.
flibusterie (flibystəri), s.f. Filibustering, piracy, robbery, swindle.
flibustier (flibystje), s.m. [f. Dutch *vrijbueter*] Filibuster, buccaneer, pirate; robber, swindler.
flic (flik), s.m. (slang) Policeman, copper, peeler.
flingot (flɛ̃go), s.m. (pop.) Soldier's rifle.
flirter (flirte, flœrte), v.n. [Engl. *to flirt*] To flirt.
floche (flɔʃ), adj. Flossy, velvety; *soie* **~**, floss silk.
flocon (flɔkɔ̃), s.m. [L *floccus*] Flake (of snow), flock (of wool, &c.), tuft; wreath (of smoke); *il neige à gros ~s,* snow is falling in great flakes.
floconneu-x, -se (flɔkɔnø), adj. Fleecy; flaky.
flonflon (flɔ̃flɔ̃), s.m. [onom.] Tol-de-rol; vulgar noisy music.
floraison (flɔrɛzɔ̃), s.f. Blossoming, flowering, florification, efflorescence; flowering season; syn. FLEURAISON.
floral, -e, (aux) (flɔral), adj. Floral; *Jeux floraux* (*de Toulouse*), Academy of Poetry (founded in Toulouse, 1323).

floralie (flɔrali), s.f. Floralia (feast in honour of the goddess Flora); flower-show.
flore (flɔr), s.f. [L *Flora*] Flora.
floréal (flɔreal), s.m. [f. L *floreus*] Floreal (from 20 April to 19 May = the eighth month in calendar of 1st French Republic).
florence (flɔrɑ̃s), s.m. [f. *Florence*, Italy] **1.** Florence, sarcenet; **2.** silkworm gut.
florentin, -e (flɔrɑ̃tɛ̃), adj. s.m.f. Florentine.
florès (flɔrɛs), s.m. [f. *fleur*] *Faire* ~, to cut a dash, to be highly successful, to be highly in vogue, to be all the go.
floriculture (flɔrikyltyr), s.f. Floriculture.
florifère (flɔrifɛr), adj. [f. L *flos, floris*+ *ferre*] Floriferous, flower-bearing.
florilège (flɔrilɛʒ), s.m. [f. L *flos, floris*+ *legere*] Florilegium, anthology.
florin (flɔrɛ̃), s.m. [It. *florino*] Florin.
florissant, -e (flɔrisɑ̃), adj. Flourishing, prosperous, thriving; *avoir une mine ~e*, to be the picture of health.
florule (flɔryl), s.f. [f. *fleur*] Floret, floscule.
flosculeu-x, -se (flɔskylø), adj. (bot.) Floscular, flosculous.
flot (flo), s.m. [OHG *fluot*] Wave, billow; tide; flood, torrent, stream, surge, immense quantity, multitude; undulation, waving; knot; float, floating; (pl.) the sea; *être à* ~, to be floating, to be afloat, to be prosperous; *mettre à* ~, to set afloat, (fig.) to set up; *remettre à* ~, to bring back into favour or prosperity (a scheme, a company, or a person); *couler à ~s*, to run in torrents, to be flowing freely; *verser des ~s de larmes*, to shed floods of tears; *fendre les ~s*, to cleave the waves; ~ *de rubans*, knot of ribbon; *des ~s de cheveux*, masses of hair.
flottabilité (flɔtabilite), s.f. Floatability, buoyancy.
flottable (flɔtabl), adj. Floatable, navigable for rafts.
flottage (flɔtaʒ), s.m. Floatage, floating of wood, rafting.
flottaison (flɔtɛzɔ̃), s.f. Flotation, water-line; *ligne de* ~, water-line.
flottant, -e (flɔtɑ̃), p. adj. Floating, flowing, waving; (fig.) irresolute, wavering, unsettled; *dette ~e*, floating debt.
flotte (flɔt), s.f. [f. *flotter*] Fleet; navy; cable-buoy; float; (slang), rain, water.
flottement (flɔtmɑ̃), s.m. **1.** Floating; **2.** undulation; (fig.) wavering, hesitation.
flotter (flɔte), v.n.a. [f. *flot*] To float, to swim, to be buoyed up, to raft (timber, &c), to be wafted; to flow, to drift, to hang loosely; (fig.) to waver, to fluctuate.
flotteur (flɔtœr), s.m. Float, float-gauge; raftsman.
flottille (flɔtij), s.f. Flotilla.
flou, -e (flu), adj. [Flemish *flauw*] Light, soft, blurred, dim, fluffy; not too precise. ~, s.m. Softness, delicacy, dimness, imprecision; the making of afternoon or evening dresses, as opposed to tailor-made dresses.
flouer (flue), v.a. (pop.) To rob, to cheat, to deceive, to take in, to diddle.
flouve (fluv), s.f. (bot.) Sweet vernal grass, *Anthoxanthum odoratum*.
fluctuation (flyktɥasjɔ̃), s.f. Fluctuation.
fluctueu-x, -se (flyktɥø), adj. [L *fluctuosus*] Fluctuating.
fluer (flɥe), v.n. To flow (of the tide).
fluet, -te (flɥɛ), adj. [f. *flou*] Thin, spare, slender, slim, not vigorous, delicate.
flueurs (flɥœr), s.f.pl. [f. L *fluor*] Menstrual flux; ~ *blanches*, fluor albus, whites, leucorrhaea.
fluide (flɥid), s.m. adj. [L *fluidus*] Fluid.
fluidité (flɥidite), s.f. Fluidity.
fluor (flɥɔr), s.m. (chem.) Fluorine; (min.) fluor, fluor-spar.
fluorescence (flɥɔrɛssɑ̃s), s.f. Fluorescence. **fluorescent, -e**, adj. Fluorescent.
fluorhydrique (flɥɔridrik), adj. Fluorhydric, hydro-fluoric: **fluorhydrate**, s.m. Fluoride.
fluorine (flɥɔrin), s.f. Native fluoride of calcium. ⚠ Not 'fluorine', which = (Fr.) *fluor*.
fluorure (flɥɔryr), s.m. Fluoride.
flûte (flyt), s.f. [orig. uncert.] **1.** Flute; flautist; **2.** small roll (of bread); **3.** champagne-glass; **4.** (naut.) *armé en* ~, armed en flute; **5.** (pl. pop.) spindle-shanks; *jouer des ~s*, to leg it; (interj.) ~ *!*, fudge !, hang !, blow !; *ce qui vient par la ~ s'en va par le tambour*, lightly come, lightly go; ill got, ill spent.
flûté, -e (flyte), p. adj. Fluted, flute-like (of sound), fluty (of the voice).
flûter (flyte), v.a.n. To flute, to play the flute; (pop.) to drink hard, to tipple, to tope.
flûtiste (flytist), s.m.f. Flautist, flute-player.
fluvial, -e, (aux) (flyvjal), adj. [L *fluvialis*] Fluvial, river-.
fluviatile (flyvjatil), adj. Fluviatile, fluviatic.
flux (fly), s.m. [L *fluxus*] Flux, flow, tide; flood; (fig.) abundance, flood, torrent; ~ *de paroles*, torrent of words.
fluxion (flyksjɔ̃), s.f. [L *fluxio*] **1.** Inflammation, fluxion, odontalgia, swollen face; ~ *de poitrine*, inflammation of the lungs; **2.** (math.) fluxion. **fluxionnaire**, adj. Fluxional.
foc (fɔk), s.m. [Scand. wd] Jib, staysail; *grand* ~, standing jib, boom jib; *petit* ~, fore-topmast staysail; *clin* ~, flying jib; ~ *d'artimon*, mizzen staysail.

focal, -e, (aux) (fɔkal), adj. [L *focus*] (opt., math.) Focal.

foène (foɛn), s.f. [L *fuscina*] (fish.) Fish-gig, eel-spear.

fœtus (fetys), s.m. [L wd] Foetus, fetus.

foi (fwa), s.f. [L *fides*] Faith, troth, belief, faithfulness, trust, credit, veracity; principles, religion; *ajouter* ~ *à*, to give credit to, to trust, to believe, to pin one's faith upon; *engager sa* ~, to pledge one's faith; *manquer à la* ~ *jurée*, to break one's pledged faith; *être de bonne* ~, to be candid, to act in good faith, or bona fide, to be sincere; *de mauvaise* ~, false, dishonest, treacherous, insincere, unfair; *en* ~ *de quoi*, in testimony whereof; *sur la* ~ *du serment*, upon oath; *n'avoir ni* ~ *ni loi*, to regard neither law nor gospel; *digne de* ~, worthy of credit; *sur la* ~ *des traités*, on the strength of treaties; *ma* ~ *!*, *par ma* ~ *!*, *sur ma* ~ *!*, upon my word !, really !, faith !, forsooth ! I declare !; ~ *d'honnête homme !*, on the honour of a gentleman, on my honour !; *faire* ~ *de*, to prove, to be evidence of.

foie (fwɑ), s.m. [f. L *ficatum*] Liver; *pâté de* ~ *gras*, goose-liver pie, 'pâté de foie gras'; (pop.) *avoir les* ~*s*, or *avoir les* ~*s blancs*, to be a coward; to suffer from cold feet; to funk; to be white- or lily-livered.

foin (fwɛ̃), s.m. [L *foenum*] Hay, grass; choke (of an artichoke); haymaking; *avoir du* ~ *dans ses bottes*, to be well off; to have feathered one's nest; *faire ses* ~*s*, to make big profits; (slang) *faire un* ~, to kick up a row, to make a fuss; *rhume des* ~*s*, hay-fever; ~ *des importuns !*, a plague on the bores !; *bête à manger du* ~, perfect idiot.

foire[1] (fwar), s.f. [L *feria*] Fair, market; *champ de* ~, market-place; *s'entendre comme larrons en* ~, to be hand and glove together, to be as thick as thieves; *à la* ~ *d'empoigne*, by robbery.

foire[2] (fwar), s.f. [f. L *forina*] (pop.) Looseness of the bowels. Hence **foirer**, v.n. to have diarrhoea; **foireu-x, -se**, adj. relaxed; (fig.) funky, cowardly, afraid.

fois (fwɑ), s.f. [f. L *vices*] Time, turn; *une* ~, once, once upon a time; *une bonne* ~, *une* ~ *pour toutes*, once for all; *pour une* ~, *pour cette* ~, for once; *une* ~ *ceci fait*, as soon as this is done; when once this is done; *une* ~ *parti, il ne reviendra plus*, once gone, he will not return; *deux* ~, twice; *il faut y regarder à deux* ~, look before you leap; *bien des* ~, many times; *à la* ~, *tout à la* ~, at a time, all at once, at the same time, together, both; *deux* ~ *par semaine*, twice a week.

foison (fwazɔ̃), s.f. [L *fusio*] Plenty, abundance; *à* ~, plentifully; in plenty; *il y a des fleurs à* ~, there are plenty of flowers.

foisonnement (fwazɔnmɑ̃), s.m. Increase, swarming.

foisonner (fwazɔne), v.n. To abound, to swarm, to increase, to multiply.

fol, -le (fɔl), adj. s.m.f. See FOU.

folâtre (fɔlɑtr), adj. [f. *fol*] Playful, frolicsome, wanton.

folâtrer (fɔlɑtre), v.n. To play, to frolic, to sport, to dally, to toy, to frisk.

foliacé, -e (fɔljase), adj. [f. L *folium*] Foliaceous.

foliation (fɔljasjɔ̃), s.f. Foliation.

folichon, -ne (fɔliʃɔ̃), adj. Frolicsome, gay, amusing. Hence **folichonner**, v.n. See syn. FOLÂTRER.

folie (fɔli), s.f. [f. *fol*] Madness, lunacy, folly, distraction; piece of folly, foolery, extravagance, nonsense; small country-house for recreation (obs.); *aimer à la* ~, to love to distraction; *faire la* ~ *de*, to be foolish enough to; *faire des* ~*s*, to be extravagant, to squander money; to play pranks; *dire, débiter des* ~*s*, to talk nonsense, to say foolish amusing things; *cela touche à la* ~, that is akin to madness; ~ *des grandeurs*, megalomania.

folié, -e (fɔlje), adj. [f. L *folium*] (bot.) Foliate.

folio (fɔljo), s.m. [L wd] Folio; *in-*~, folio.

foliole (fɔljɔl), s.f. [L *foliolum*] (bot.) Foliole.

folioter (fɔljɔte), v.a. To foliate, to paginate.

folklore (fɔlklɔr), s.m. [Engl. wd] Folk-lore.

folle (fɔl) adj. f. s.f. See FOU.

follement (fɔlmɑ̃), adv. Madly, extravagantly, distractedly, dotingly, foolishly.

follet, -te (fɔlɛ), adj. [f. *fol*] Wanton, frolicsome; *poil* ~, downy hair, fluff; *feu* ~, ignis fatuus, will-o'-the-wisp; *esprit* ~, goblin, sprite.

folliculaire (fɔlikylɛr), s.m. [L *folliculus*] Pamphleteer; cheap or hack journalist.

follicule (fɔlikyl), s.m. [L *folliculus*] (bot., anat.) Follicle.

fomentat-eur, -rice (fɔmɑ̃tatœr), s.m.f. Fomenter. ~, adj. Fomenting.

fomentation (fɔmɑ̃taˈsjɔ̃), s.f. Fomentation; (fig.) instigation.

fomenter (fɔmɑ̃te), v.a. [L *fomentare*] To foment; (fig.) to excite, to stir up, to abet.

foncé, -e (fɔ̃se), p. adj. Deep, dark (of colours); *vert* ~, dark green.

foncer (fɔ̃se), v.a. [f. *fonds*] **1.** To bottom, to line; **2.** to sink (a well); **3.** to darken, to deepen (a colour); ~, v.n. to rush, to dash, to charge down.

fonci-er, -ère (fɔ̃sje), adj. [f. *fonds*] Landed, land-; based on, or derived from land; fundamental; *propriétaire* ~, land owner; *crédit* ~, mortgage-loan society; *impôt* ~, land-tax; *qualités* ~*ères*, fundamental qualities.

foncièrement (fɔ̃sjɛrmɑ̃), adv. Fundamentally, thoroughly, at bottom.

fonction (fɔ̃ksjɔ̃), s.f. [L *functio*] Function, duty, office, employment; (math.) function; *faire* ~ *de*, to act as, to do the office of; *entrer en* ~*s*, to enter upon one's duties; *en* ~ *de*, as a consequence of, varying with.

fonctionnaire (fɔ̃ksjɔnɛr), s.m.f. Functionary, official, officer, Civil Servant.

fonctionnel, -le (fɔ̃ksjɔnɛl), adj. Functional.

fonctionnement (fɔ̃ksjɔnmɑ̃), s.m. Working, action, operation.

fonctionner (fɔ̃ksjɔne), v.n. To work, to operate, to function.

fond (fɔ̃), s.m. [L *fundus*] Bottom, ground, foundation, background; depth; end, extremity, remotest part, back; seat (of trousers); matter (as opposed to form); *à* ~, thoroughly, to the bottom; *à* ~ *de train*, at full speed; *au* ~, *dans le* ~, at bottom, in the main, on the whole; after all, in reality; at heart; *de* ~ *en comble*, from top to bottom; *faire* ~ *sur*, to rely on; *au fin* ~ *de*, at or to the very bottom of, at or to the further end of; *se détacher sur un* ~ *clair*, to stand out on a light ground; *vingt brasses de* ~, twenty fathoms of water; *au* ~ *de la Russie*, in the remotest part of Russia; *coureur de* ~, stayer. See FONDS.

fondamental, -e, (aux) (fɔ̃damɑ̃tal), adj. Fundamental.

fondamentalement (fɔ̃damɑ̃talmɑ̃), adv. Fundamentally.

fondant, -e (fɔ̃dɑ̃), p. adj. Melting, juicy, dissolving. ~, s.m. **1.** (med., chem.) Solvent, flux; **2.** fondant, sweetmeat.

fondat-eur, -rice (fɔ̃datœr), s.m.f. Founder, (fem.) foundress. ~, adj. Founding.

fondation (fɔ̃da'sjɔ̃), s.f. Foundation; founding, donation.

fondé, -e (fɔ̃de), p. adj. Founded, well founded, authorized, justified; *être* ~ *à*, to have good grounds for. ~, s.m. Person authorized to act for another; ~ *de pouvoir*, agent (acting under power of attorney); *le bien-*~ *d'une accusation*, good grounds for an accusation.

fondement (fɔ̃dmɑ̃), s.m. [f. *fonder*] Foundation, ground, groundwork, basis, cause; *un bruit sans* ~, an unfounded report; (fam.) bottom.

fonder (fɔ̃de), v.a. [L *fundare*] To found, to lay the foundation of, to build, to institute; to establish; to authorize; **se** ~, v.pr. to be grounded, to rest, to rely.

fonderie (fɔ̃dri), s.f. [f. *fondre*] Foundry, melting-house.

fondeur (fɔ̃dœr), s.m. Founder, melter.

fondoir (fɔ̃dwar), s.m. Melting-house (of butchers, &c.).

fondre (fɔ̃dr), v.a.n. [L *fundere*] To melt, to melt down or away, to found, to smelt, to cast; to dissolve, to blend, to mix, to soften; ~ *sur*, to rush or pounce upon.

fondrière (fɔ̃drjɛr), s.f. Quagmire, bog, morass, slough, drift (of snow).

fonds (fɔ̃), s.m. invar. [f. *fond*] Ground, landed property; funds, money, capital; stock in trade; (fig.) field, matter, subject, property, character; *biens-*~, landed property; *les* ~ *publics*, the public stocks; *les* ~ *secrets*, service-fund, secret service money; *être en* ~, to be in funds, to have ready money; *à* ~ *perdu*, with sunk capital; *faire* ~ *sur*, see FOND.

fondue (fɔ̃dy), s.f. [f. *fondre*] (cook.) Fondue, cheese soufflé.

fongible (fɔ̃ʒibl), adj. [L *fungibilis*] (law) Fungible.

fongosité (fɔ̃gozite), s.f. (med.) Fungosity, fungus.

fongueu-x, -se (fɔ̃gø), adj. Fungous.

fongus (fɔ̃gys), s.m. [L *fungus*] (med.) Fungus.

fontaine (fɔ̃tɛn), s.f. [L *fons*] Fountain, fount, spring, filter, cistern.

fontainier, fontenier (fɔ̃tɛnje, fɔ̃ntənje), s.m. Fountain-maker, turncock, well-sinker.

fontanelle (fɔ̃tanɛl), s.f. [f. *fontaine*] (anat.) Fontanel(le).

fontange (fɔ̃tɑ̃ʒ), s.f. [f. *Mlle de Fontanges*, 1661–81] Fontange (topknot).

fonte[1] (fɔ̃t), s.f. [f. *fondre*] **1.** Melting, thaw, thawing; smelting, casting; **2.** cast-iron, gun-metal, cast; **3.** (print.) fount.

fonte[2] (fɔ̃t), s.f. [It. *fonda*] Holster (of saddles).

fontenier (fɔ̃tənje), s.m. See FONTAINIER.

fonts (fɔ̃), s.m.pl. [L *fons*] Font; *tenir X sur les* ~ *baptismaux*, to stand godfather or godmother to X.

for (fɔr), s.m. [L *forum*] Jurisdiction; tribunal; ~ *intérieur*, conscience; ~ *extérieur*, human justice; ~ *ecclésiastique*, jurisdiction of the Church.

forage (fɔraʒ), s.m. [f. *forer*] Boring, drilling.

forain, -e (fɔrɛ̃), adj. [f. L *fors*] Non-resident, foreign, alien, itinerant; pertaining to fairs and markets; *marchand* ~, hawker, pedlar. ~, s.m. Itinerant trader, actor, or circus performer.

foraminé, -e (fɔramine), adj. [L *foramen*] Foraminated, foraminous.

forban (fɔrbɑ̃), s.m. [L *fors*+LL *banum*] Pirate, rover, freebooter, thief, swindler; (fig.) plagiarist.

forçage (fɔrsaʒ), s.m. [f. *forcer*] Forcing; (coin) overweight.

forçat (fɔrsa), s.m. [It. *forzato*] Convict; (fig.) hard-working, over-worked person.

force (fɔrs), s.f. [LL *fortia*] Strength, force, might, power, authority, strong hand, constraint; proficiency, driving power; fortitude; *~s*, pl. troops; *~ armée*, *~ publique*, the police, the troops; *céder à la ~ majeure*, to yield to superior force; *être à bout de ~s*, to be done up; *rassembler ses ~s*, to muster one's forces; *les ~s lui manquent*, his strength is failing; *un tour de ~*, a feat of strength, an extraordinary performance; an exploit; (colloq.) a stunt; *à ~*, very hard, forcibly; *à ~ de*, by dint of, by force of; *à toute ~*, absolutely, by all means, obstinately; *de ~*, forcibly, by force; *de vive ~*, by main strength, by storm, irresistibly; *de gré ou de ~*, willing or not, willy-nilly, by fair means or foul; *de ~ à*, strong enough to, able to, equal to; *de toute sa ~*, *de toutes ses ~s*, with all one's might, as hard, fast, loud, &c., as one can; *être de ~*, to be a match for each other; *par ~*, forcibly; *dans toute la ~ du terme*, in every sense of the word; *faire ~ de rames*, to row with all one's might; *faire ~ de voiles*, to crowd on all sail; *~ me fut de*, I was obliged to; *maison de ~*, house of correction; *dans la ~ de l'âge*, in one's prime, in the vigour of manhood. *~*, adj. A great deal, many.

forcé, -e (fɔrse), p. adj. Forced, affected, unnatural, far-fetched; *travaux ~s*, hard labour; *avoir la main ~e*, to have one's hand forced; *marches ~es*, forced marches; *c'était ~*, it was bound to happen.

forcement (fɔrsmɑ̃), s.m. [f. *forcer*] Forcing, compulsion.

forcément (fɔrsemɑ̃), adv. Necessarily; forcibly.

forcené, -e (fɔrsne), adj. s.m.f. [f. *fors*+ (Germ.) *Sinn*] (That is) frantic, mad, wild with rage.

forceps (fɔrsɛps), s.m. [L wd] (surg.) Forceps.

forcer (fɔrse), v.a. [f. *force*] To force, to break open, to break through; to compel, to oblige, to impel, to obtain by force; to storm, to assault, to violate; to stretch, to strain; (gard.) to force; *~ une porte*, to break a door open; *~ la main à* X, to force X's hand; *~ sa voix*, to strain one's voice; *~ la consigne*, to infringe orders; *~ le pas*, to hasten; *~ un cheval*, to strain a horse; *~ un cerf*, to hunt down a stag.

forcerie (fɔrsri), s.f. (gard.) Forcing-house.

forclore (fɔrklɔr), v.a. [*fors*+*clore*] (law) To foreclose.

forclusion (fɔrklyzjɔ̃), s.f. (law) Foreclosure.

forer (fɔre), v.a. [L *forare*] To bore, to drill, to pierce.

foresti-er, -ère (fɔrɛstje), adj. [f. *forêt*] Forestal, forest-, relating to forests; *garde ~*, forester, keeper. *~*, s.m. Forester.

forêt (fɔrɛ), s.f. [LL *forestis*] Forest; (fig.) mass, quantity; *une ~ de cheveux*, a shock of hair.

foret (fɔrɛ), s.m. [f. *forer*] Drill, borer; (artill.) foret.

forfaire (fɔrfɛr), v.n.a. def. [*fors*+*faire*] To forfeit.

forfait (fɔrfɛ), s.m. [f. *forfaire*] **1.** Crime, heinous crime; **2.** contract, job; *prendre un travail à ~*, to contract for, to take work by the job, to do job-work; *déclarer ~*, to declare forfeit.

forfaiture (fɔrfɛtyr), s.f. [f. *forfaire*] Forfeiture, prevarication, crime.

forfanterie (fɔrfɑ̃tri), s.f. [f. It. *furfanteria*] Bragging, boasting, boast.

forficule (fɔrfikyl), s.f. [LL *forficula*] (ent.) Earwig.

forge (fɔrʒ), s.f. [L *fabrica*, OF *farge*] Forge, iron-works, smithy, blacksmith's shop, farrier's shop.

forgeage (fɔrʒaʒ), s.m. Forging.

forger (fɔrʒe), v.a. [f. *forge*] To forge; (fig.) to fabricate, to invent; *se ~ des chimères*, to let one's imagination (or fears) run away with one; *~ un mot*, to coin a word.

forgeron (fɔrʒərɔ̃), s.m. Blacksmith.

forgeur (fɔrʒœr), s.m. Forger, coiner (of words). ⚠ *Forgeur* is not always pej. but 'forger' usually = *faussaire*.

forjeter (fɔrʒəte), v.n. [*fors*+*jeter*] To jut out.

forlancer (fɔrlɑ̃se), v.a. [*fors*+*lancer*] To start (stags, game).

forligner (fɔrliɲe), v.n. [*fors*+*ligne*] To degenerate, to forfeit one's honour.

(se) formaliser (səfɔrmalize), v.pr. To take offence, to take exception (to), to bristle, to be ruffled.

formalisme (fɔrmalism), s.m. [f. L *formalis*] Formalism.

formaliste (fɔrmalist), adj. Formal, ceremonious. *~*, s.m.f. Formalist, stickler for etiquette.

formalité (fɔrmalite), s.f. Formality, form.

format (fɔrma), s.m. [f. *forme*] Size (and shape) of a book, format.

format-eur, -rice (fɔrmatœr), adj. Creative, forming. *~*, s.m. Creator.

formation (fɔrma'sjɔ̃), s.f. [L *formatio*] Formation, forming, moulding, development.

forme (fɔrm), s.f. [L *forma*] Form, shape, figure, contour, aspect; (chem.) state, mould, frame; etiquette, usage, manners; *dans les ~s*, in the usual form; *en bonne et due ~*, in due form, regularly; *pour la ~*, for form's sake, *mettez-y des ~s*, be polite; *prendre ~*, to shape, to take shape; *prendre toutes sortes de ~s*, to take all kinds of shapes; *sous toutes ses ~s*, in all its aspects; *être bien en ~*, to be in excellent form; *en ~ de croissant*, crescent-shaped.

formel, -le (fɔrmel), adj. [L *formalis*] Formal, precise, express, explicit.

formellement (fɔrmɛlmɑ̃). Expressly, explicitly, formally.

former (fɔrme), v.a. To form, to shape, to create, to fashion, to conceive, to mould; to compose, to constitute; **se ~**, v.pr. to take shape, to be formed, to improve oneself.

formiate (fɔrmjat), s.m. (chem.) Formate, formiate.

formicant (fɔrmikɑ̃), adj. m. [L *formicans*] Weak and frequent (of the pulse).

formication (fɔrmika'sjɔ̃), s.f. See FOURMILLEMENT.

formidable (fɔrmidabl), adj. [L *formidabilis*] Formidable, dreadful.

formidablement (fɔrmidabləmɑ̃), adv. Formidably, dreadfully.

formique (fɔrmik), adj. [f. L *formica*] (chem.) Formic.

formulaire (fɔrmylɛr), s.m. [f. L *formula*] Formulary.

formule (fɔrmyl), s.f. [L *formula*] Formula, form, prescription; (alg.) formula.

formuler (fɔrmyle), v.a. To formulate, to draw up in due form, to express; (alg.) to reduce to a formula.

fornication (fɔrnika'sjɔ̃), s.f. Fornication.

forniquer (fɔrnike), v.n. [f. L *fornix*] To fornicate.

fors (fɔr), prep. [L *foris*] Except, but, save.

fort, -e (fɔr), adj. [L *fortis*] Strong, powerful, robust, vigorous, sturdy; copious; stiff, stout; strong-smelling; outrageous, shocking; skilful, clever; high (of wind), heavy (of soil, rain, &c.); *une ~e somme*, a considerable sum of money; *un coffre ~*, a strong-box, a safe; *de la colle ~e*, glue; *faire l'esprit ~*, to play the cynic; *être une ~e tête*, to be strong-minded, to be a thruster; *haleine ~e*, bad breath; *à plus ~e raison*, all the more reason; *voilà qui est un peu ~!*, come! I like that!; that's rather strong!; *c'est trop ~, c'est par trop ~!*, really it is too bad, that's a bit thick!; *c'est plus fort que moi!*, I cannot help it; *ça, ce n'est pas ~!*, that is not very clever!; *de plus en plus ~!*, better and better!; increasing continually; *se faire ~ de*, to feel confident of being able to; to undertake to; *se porter ~ pour X*, to answer for X; *être ~ en histoire*, to be well up in history; *être ~ aux échecs*, to be an excellent chess-player; *trouver plus ~ que soi*, to meet with more than one's match; *~ comme un Turc*, as strong as a horse; *le plus ~ est fait*, the worst is over; *en dire de ~es*, to tell spicy stories.

fort (fɔr), s.m. **1.** Stronghold, fort, fortress; **2.** strong man; *~ de la halle*, market porter; *~ en thème*, clever boy, (at school) whale for work; **3.** strong part, strong side; heart, thickest part, height; *au ~ de l'orage*, in the height of the storm; *connaître le ~ et le faible de l'affaire*, to know the ins and outs of the matter.

fort (fɔr), adv. Very, very much, highly, strongly, hard, loud, fast; *~ bien*, very well; *il pleut très ~*, it's raining fast or hard; *vous allez ~!*, you are going it strong!, you exaggerate; *avoir ~ à faire*, to have much work (and some difficulty).

forte (fɔrte), adj. s.m. [It. wd] (mus.) Forte.

fortement (fɔrtəmɑ̃), adv. Strongly, vigorously, with force, much, intensely.

forteresse (fɔrtərɛs), s.f. [f. *fort*] Fortress, stronghold.

fortifiant, -e (fɔrtifjɑ̃), p. adj. Strengthening, fortifying, invigorating, bracing. **~**, s.m. Tonic.

fortification (fɔrtifika'sjɔ̃), s.f. Fortification.

fortifier (fɔrtifje), v.a. [f. L *fortis+facere*] To strengthen, to fortify, to invigorate, to brace; to surround with fortifications, to fortify; to corroborate; **se ~**, v.pr. to grow strong; to confirm oneself (*dans*, in).

fortin (fɔrtɛ̃), s.m. [f. *fort*] Small fort.

fortissimo (fɔrtisimo), adv. s.m. [It. wd] Fortissimo.

fortrait, -e (fɔrtrɛ), adj. [f. L *fors+trahere*] (of horses) Overworked, spent.

fortraiture (fɔrtrɛtyr), s.f. (of horses) Over-fatigue.

fortuit, -e (fɔrtɥi), adj. [L *fortuitus*] Fortuitous, casual.

fortuitement (fɔrtɥitmɑ̃), adv. Fortuitously, casually.

fortune (fɔrtyn), s.f. [L *fortuna*] Fortune, chance, fate, luck, risk; wealth, property, means, prosperity; *la ~ des armes*, the fortune of war; *revers de ~*, reverses of fortune; *faire ~*, to make a fortune; *manger sa ~*, to squander one's fortune; *les caprices de la ~*, the freaks of fortune; *chercher, tenter ~*, to seek one's fortune; *faire contre mauvaise ~ bon cœur*, to put a good face on misfortune; to make the best of a bad job; *la ~ me sourit*, fortune smiles upon me; *venir dîner à la ~ du pot*, to take pot-luck; *homme à bonnes ~s*, lady-killer; *officier de ~*, (*a*) soldier of fortune; (*b*) ranker officer; *voile de ~*, lug-sail, cross-jack sail; *mât de ~*, jury-mast; *~ de mer*, sea risks.

fortuné, -e (fɔrtyne), adj. Fortunate, lucky, happy.

forum (fɔrɔm), s.m. [L wd] Forum.

forure (fɔryr), s.f. [f. *forer*] Bore, hole drilled, keyhole.

fosse (fos), s.f. [L *fossa*] Pit, hole in the ground, grave, trench; *~s nasales*, chambers of the nose, nasal fosses; *avoir un pied dans la ~*, to have one foot in the grave; *~ commune*, common grave, pauper's grave; *~ aux ours*, bear-pit; *~ d'aisances*, cesspool; *cul de basse-~*, underground prison (under a dungeon), oubliette, trap-dungeon.

fossé (fose), s.m. [L *fossa*] Ditch, trench, drain, moat, fosse; *sauter le ~*, to cast the die, to cross the Rubicon; *au bout du ~ la culbute!*, a short life and a merry one; *le ~ s'élargit entre eux*, they grow more and more estranged, the rift widens between them.

fossette (fɔsɛt), s.f. [f. *fosse*] Dimple; (game) chuck-farthing.

fossile (fɔsil), s.m. adj. [L *fossilis*] Fossil.

fossilisation (fɔsiliza'sjɔ̃), s.f. Fossilization.

fossiliser (fɔsilize), v.a. To fossilize; **se** ~, v.pr. to become fossilized.

fossoyage, fossoiement (foswajaʒ, foswamɑ̃), s.m. Grave-digging, ditching.

fossoyer (foswaje), v.a. [f. *fosse*] To ditch.

fossoyeur (foswajœr), s.m. Grave-digger; ditcher.

fou, fol (archaic), (fem.) **folle** (fu, fɔl), adj. [L *follis*] Mad, insane, senseless, foolish, wild, frolicsome, distracting, excessive, excessively fond (*de*, of); *il est ~ de musique*, he is passionately fond of music; *être ~ de joie*, to be mad with joy; *être ~ de douleur*, to be distracted with pain; *ils me feront devenir ~*, they are driving me mad; *un argent ~, un prix ~*, a heap or a mint of money, an awful price; *faire le ~*, to play the fool; *gaîté folle*, wanton gaiety; *il y a un monde ~*, there is a great crowd of people; it 's a crush; *un succès ~*, a prodigious success; *~ rire*, wild laugh, uncontrollable laughter; *il est ~ à lier*, he is raving mad; *un mal de tête ~*, a splitting headache.

fou, folle (fu, fɔl), s.m.f. **1.** Madman, madwoman, lunatic; madcap, fool; *plus on est de ~s, plus on rit*, the more the merrier; **2.** jester; **3.** (chess) bishop; **4.** (ornith.) gannet.

fouace (fwas), s.f. [LL *focacia*] Griddlecake, hearth-cake.

fouaille (fwaj), s.f. (boar-hunt.) Quarry.

fouailler (fwaje), v.a. [f. *fouet*] To lash, to whip repeatedly and brutally.

foucade (fukad), s.f. (colloq.) Whim, fad, impulse, sudden thought or action; *travailler par ~s*, to work by fits and starts.

foudre[1] (fudr), s.f. [f. L *fulgur*] Lightning, thunderbolt, bolt; *coup de ~*, clap of thunder; (fig.) love at first sight; *la ~ est tombée sur*, a thunderbolt fell on; *être frappé de la ~*, *être comme frappé de la ~*, to be thunderstruck; *lancer ses ~s*, to hurl one's thunders; ~, s.m. *un ~ de guerre*, *d'éloquence*, a great captain, a hero; a powerful orator.

foudre[2] (fudr), s.m. [f. Germ. *Fuder*] Large cask, tun.

foudroiement (fudrwamɑ̃), s.m. Thunderstroke, stroke of lightning; (fig.) utter destruction, crushing.

foudroyant, -e (fudrwajɑ̃) p. adj. Thunderstriking; (fig.) sudden and terrible, crushing, thundering, stunning.

foudroyer (fudrwaje), v.a. [f. *foudre*] To thunderstrike; to kill as by lightning; (fig.) to crush, to overwhelm, to ruin, to confound, to destroy.

fouée (fwe), s.f. [f. *feu*] **1.** Bat-fowling; **2.** oven-fire, faggot.

fouet (fwɛ), s.m. [f. *fou*, OF wd for beechtree] Whip, lash, thong, whipcord; whipping, flogging; *donner le ~ à X*, to flog X; *coup de ~*, lash, (fig.) stimulus; (artill.) *tir de plein ~*, horizontal fire, sweeping fire; (ornith.) *~ de l'aile*, tip (of the wing); *~ à œufs*, egg-whisk.

fouettement (fwɛtmɑ̃), s.m. Whipping, beating, pattering.

fouetter (fwɛte), v.a. [f. *fouet*] To whip, to lash, to flog, to beat, to cut, to horsewhip; (fig.) to patter, to strike against, to stimulate; *avoir bien d'autres chiens à ~*, to have other fish to fry; *il n'y a pas là de quoi ~ un chat*, it 's a mere trifle, it 's not worth mentioning; it 's nothing to write home about; *la pluie fouette les vitres*, the rain is beating or pattering against the windowpanes; *~ des œufs*, to beat eggs, to whisk eggs; *~ de la crème*, to whip cream; *cela fouette le sang*, that is stimulating; ~, v.n. (slang) to stink.

fougade (fugad), s.f. See FOUCADE.

fougasse (fugas), s.f. [f. It. *fugata*] (mil.) Fougasse, small mine.

fougeraie (fuʒrɛ), s.f. Fernery, fern-brake.

fougère (fuʒɛr), s.f. [f. LL *filicaria*] (bot.) Fern, fern-brake.

fougue (fug), s.f. [f. L *focus*] Impetuosity, fire, mettle, spirit.

fougueusement (fugøzmɑ̃), adv. Fierily, impetuously.

fougueu-x, -se (fugø), adj. Impetuous, fiery, hot, ardent, spirited.

fouille (fuj), s.f. [f. *fouiller*] Digging, excavation; searching; *~-au-pot*, s.m. (fig.) busybody, meddler.

fouiller (fuje), v.a.n. [L *fodicare*] To dig, to excavate; to investigate, to rummage, to pry (into); to search; *~ dans sa mémoire*, to ransack one's memory; (sculpt.) to sink, to hollow; **se** ~, v.pr. to search one's pockets; (slang) *il peut se ~*, he can whistle for it; *tu peux te ~!*, don't you wish you may get it!

fouillis (fuji), s.m. [f. *fouiller*] Medley, litter, confusion, mess.
fouine (fwin), s.f. [f. *fou* (beech)] (zool.) **1.** Marten, beech-marten; **2.** see syn. FOÈNE.
fouiner (fuine), v.n. (fam.) To pry (into), to peer inquisitively, to nose about, to nose round. Hence (colloq.) **fouinard,** adj. s.m. Nosy Parker.
fouir (fwir), v.a. [L *fodere*] To dig.
fouisseu-r, -se (fwisœr), adj. Digging.
foulage (fulaʒ), s.m. [f. *fouler*] Treading, fulling; pressure.
foulant, -e (fulɑ̃), p. adj. Pressing down, forcing; *pompe ~e,* force-pump; (slang) tiring.
foulard (fular), s.m. [orig. unkn.] **1.** Silk kerchief; **2.** foulard (silk material).
foule (ful), s.f. [f. *fouler*] **1.** Crowd, multitude, mass; *une ~ de,* a mass of, numerous; *se distinguer de la ~,* to rise above the common herd; to stand out from the crowd; *venir en ~,* to come in crowds, to crowd; **2.** fulling.
foulée (fule), s.f. **1.** Tread; **2.** stride; **3.** track, appui.
fouler (fule), v.a. [LL *fullare*] To full, to tread, to mill; to trample (on), to press, to crush; to sprain (one's ankle, &c.); (print.) to press; *~ la vendange,* to press the grapes; *~ le sol natal,* to walk on one's native soil; *~ aux pieds,* to trample upon; (colloq.) *ne pas se ~,* or *ne pas se ~ la rate,* to take it easy.
foulerie (fulri), s.f. Fulling-mill.
foulon (fulɔ̃), s.m. [L *fullo*] Fuller; *terre à ~,* fuller's earth; *moulin à ~,* fulling-mill.
foulque (fulk), s.f. [L *fulica*] (ornith.) Coot.
foulure (fulyr), s.f. Sprain, strain.
four (fur), s.m. [L *furnus*] Oven, kiln, furnace, bakehouse; (fig.) failure; *~ à chaux,* lime-kiln; *ç'a été un vrai ~,* or *un ~ noir,* it has been a dead failure, a regular take-in, a sell; *petits ~s,* petits fours, small cakes, small iced cakes, sweets; (fam.) *~ à bachot,* special school for cramming candidates for the baccalauréat.
fourbe (furb), adj. [It. *furbo*] Knavish, cheating, crafty, false. ~, s.m. Knave, rogue, cheat; ~, s.f. cheat, imposture, knavery, perfidy.
fourberie (furbəri), s.f. Cheating, imposture, deceit, knavery.
fourbi (furbi), s.m. (mil. slang, and colloq.) Kit, goods and chattels, all one's possessions; also: complicated affairs; the whole situation; *tout le ~,* lock, stock, and barrel.
fourbir (furbir), v.a. [f. OHG *furbjan*] To furbish, to polish, to rub up.
fourbissage (furbisaʒ), s.m. Furbishing; syn. FOURBISSURE, s.f.
fourbu, -e (furby), p. adj. [part. of old verb *fourboire*] Foundered, over-fatigued, knocked-up, done for.
fourbure (furbyr), s.f. (vet.) Foundering, founder.
fourche (furʃ), s.f. [L *furca*] Fork, pitch-fork, (of bicycles, &c.) fork; point of bifurcation; *~s patibulaires,* forked gibbet; *~s caudines,* Caudine Forks; *faire la ~,* to branch off.
fourchée (furʃe), s.f. Forkful.
fourcher (furʃe), v.n. To fork, to branch off; to trip (of the tongue); *la langue lui a fourché,* he made a slip of the tongue; his tongue tripped.
fourchet (furʃɛ), s.m. (vet.) Foot-rot.
fourchette (furʃɛt), s.f. [f. *fourche*] Fork, table-fork; (fam.) eater; (of a bird) merry-thought, wish-bone; frog (of a horse's hoof); *être une bonne ~,* to be a good trencherman, a hearty eater or feeder.
fourchon (furʃɔ̃), s.m. Prong (of a fork).
fourchu, -e (furʃy), p. adj. Forked; *pied~,* cloven hoof, cloven foot.
fourchure (furʃyr), s.f. Forking.
fourgon (furgɔ̃), s.m. [orig. uncert.] **1.** Wagon, baggage or ammunition wagon; delivery-van, van; **2.** oven-rake, poker.
fourgonner (furgɔne), v.a. To poke, to stir (the fire); to poke, to rummage.
fourmi (furmi), s.f. [L *formica*] (zool.) Ant; *~-lion,* formica leo, ant-lion; *avoir des ~s dans les jambes,* to have pins and needles in one's legs; *j'ai des ~s dans les jambes,* my legs have gone to sleep.
fourmilier (furmilje), s.m. (zool.) Ant-bear, ant-eater; ant-bird.
fourmilière (furmiljɛr), s.f. Ant-hill; (fig.) swarm.
fourmillement (furmijmɑ̃), s.m. **1.** Swarming; **2.** tingling, pins and needles, pricking.
fourmiller (furmije), v.n. [f. *fourmi*] To swarm; to tingle.
fournaise (furnɛz), s.f. [L *fornax*] Furnace; (fig.) hot place.
fourneau (pl. **-x**) (furno), s.m. [f. *four*] Stove, range, kitchen-range; *~ à gaz,* gas-stove, gas-ring; *~ à pétrole,* paraffin-stove; *haut ~,* blast-furnace; *~ de mine,* chamber (of a mine); *~ de pipe,* bowl (of a pipe).
fournée (furne), s.f. Baking; (fig.) batch.
fourni, -e (furni), p. adj. [f. *fournir*] Thick, bushy, well grown; supplied, stocked.
fournil (furni), s.m. [f. *four*] Bakehouse.
fourniment (furnimɑ̃), s.m. Accoutrements, belts; outfit, paraphernalia; see FOURBI.
fournir (furnir), v.a. [f. OHG *frumjan*] To furnish (with), to supply, to stock, to provide (with), to give; to afford; to produce; *~ une longue carrière,* to run a long race, to have a long career; ~ v.n. to provide (for), to pay (for); *~ aux besoins de X,* to provide for X('s expenses.)
fournissement (furnismɑ̃), s.m. Share of capital.

fournisseur (furnisœr), s.m. Supplier, purveyor, army contractor, tradesman.
fourniture (furnityr), s.f. Providing, supplying, supply, supplies; (of dressmakers, &c.) trimmings, goods, material; *~s de bureau*, office stationery. (⚠ Not 'furniture', which = *mobilier*.)
fourrage (furaʒ), s.m. [f. OF *feurre, fourre*] Fodder, forage; (dressm.) fur-lining.
fourrager (furaʒe), v.n.a. To forage, to rummage.
fourragère (furaʒɛr), s.f. **1.** Piece of land where fodder is grown; **2.** foraging-wagon; **3.** cord worn round the arm at the shoulder by members of French regiments which have seen active service. **~**, adj. Fit for fodder, fodder-.
fourrageur (furaʒœr), s.m. Forager.
fourré, -e (fure) p. adj. Furred, lined with fur; thick, full of thickets and briars, tangled; (cook.) stuffed; *coup ~*, (fenc.) blow given and received simultaneously; (fig.) underhand trick; *monnaie ~e*, plated coin. **~** s.m. Thicket.
fourreau (pl. **-x**) (furo), s.m. [f. Goth. *fodr*] Sheath, case, scabbard, cover; tight-fitting dress or underdress; *la lame a usé le ~*, the sword has worn out the scabbard; (fig.) the mind was too active for the body.
fourrer (fure), v.a. To line with fur; to plate (medals, coin, &c.); to cram, to stuff, to thrust, to shove, to force; *~ une idée dans la tête de X*, to hammer a notion into X's head; *~ dedans*, to take in, to dupe; to do brown; *~ son nez partout*, to poke one's nose everywhere; **se ~**, v.pr. to hide oneself, to thrust oneself; *ces gens-là se fourrent partout*, those people intrude themselves everywhere, or must have a finger in every pie; *il ne sait où se ~*, he does not know where to hide himself.
fourreur (furœr), s.m. Furrier.
fourrier (furje), s.m. [f. *fourrage*] Quartermaster-sergeant; (fig.) precursor, fore-runner, provider. (⚠ Not 'furrier', see *fourreur*.)
fourrière (furjɛr), s.f. [f. *fourrage*] Pound (for strayed animals); greenyard; *mettre en* (or *à la*) *~*, to impound.
fourrure (furyr), s.f. [f. *fourrer*] Fur, fur garment; (naut.) service; (herald.) vair.
fourvoyer (furvwaje), v.a. [f. *fors+voie*] To mislead, to lead astray, to baffle; **se ~**, v.pr. to stray, to go astray, to blunder badly.
foutaise (futɛz), s.f. [f. *foutre*] (slang) Rubbish, nonsense, tripe; syn. FICHAISE.
fouteau (pl. **-x**) (futo), s.m. See syn. HÊTRE.
foutre (futr), v.a.n. [f. L *futuere*] (slang, vulg.) To thrust, to shove, to deal (blows); to do; to give; *~ le camp*, to decamp; *se ~ de*, (*a*) not to care a damn for; (*b*) to mock, to make game of. *~!*, interj. Damn!, dash it!; see FICHER.
foutu, -e (futy), adj. and p.p. of *foutre*. (slang) Done; dressed; given; rotten; wretched; *un homme mal ~*, a badly dressed (or clumsily built) man; *un ~ temps*, rotten weather; *il est ~*, it's all up with him.
foyer (fwaje), s.m. [f. LL *focarium*] Hearth, hearthstone, fire, fireside, home; grate, furnace; (fig.) centre, nucleus, seat, source; (theatr.) foyer, lobby; *~ des artistes*, green-room; (techn.) focus (pl. foci).
frac (frak), s.m. Frock-coat, dress-coat.
fracas (frakɑ), s.m. [It. *fracasso*] Crash, uproar, fracas, tumult; (fig.) fuss, noise, excessive show.
fracasser (frakase), v.a. To break to pieces, to shatter, to smash.
fraction (fraksjɔ̃), s.f. [LL *fractio*] Fraction, portion; breaking; (arith.) fraction.
fractionnaire (fraksjɔnɛr), adj. Fractional, fractionary.
fractionnement (fraksjɔnmɑ̃), s.m. Dividing into fractions.
fractionner (fraksjɔne), v.a., and **se ~**, v.pr. To divide into fractions.
fracture (fraktyr), s.f. [L *fractura*] Breaking, rupture; (surg.) fracture.
fracturer (fraktyre), v.a. To fracture, to smash; to break open, to force.
fragile (fraʒil), adj. [L *fragilis*] Fragile, frail, brittle, delicate, weak, unstable.
fragilité (fraʒilite), s.f. Fragility, frailty, brittleness, weakness, instability.
fragment (fragmɑ̃), s.m. [L *fragmentum*] Fragment, piece, scrap, remnant, extract.
fragmentaire (fragmɑ̃tɛr), adj. Fragmentary.
fragmentation (fragmɑ̃ta'sjɔ̃), s.f. Division into fragments, fragmentation.
fragmenter (fragmɑ̃te), v.a. To divide into fragments.
fragon (fragɔ̃), s.m. (bot.) Knee-holly, butcher's broom.
frai (frɛ), s.m. [f. *frayer*] **1.** Spawning, spawn; spawning-season; **2.** fry (young fish); **3.** (of a medal) wear.
fraîchement (frɛʃmɑ̃), adv. Coolly, freshly; newly, lately, freshly; (fig.) without cordiality.
fraîcheur (frɛʃœr), s.f. [f. *frais*] Freshness, coolness, bloom; chill.
fraîchir (frɛʃir), v.n. To freshen, to blow fresh; (of the temperature) to get colder.
frairie (frɛri), s.f. [f. LL *fratria*] Merry-making, feast, tuck-in.
frais, fem. **fraîche** (frɛ, frɛʃ), adj. [f. Germ. *frisch*] Fresh, cool, coldish; blooming, hale; recent, new, fresh; *de fraîche date*, recent, brand-new; *peu ~*, *pas ~*, stale; *me voilà ~ maintenant!*, now I am in a pretty pickle!; *sortir à la fraîche*, to take a walk in the cool of the evening; *mettre au ~*, to put in a cool place; *œufs ~*, new-laid eggs. **~**, adv. *~ émoulu du collège*, fresh from college; *rasé de ~*, just shaved.

frais[1] (frɛ), s.m. Cool, coolness, cool place.

frais[2] (frɛ), s.m.pl. [f. OHG *fridu*] Expenses, expenditure, charges; (fig.) trouble, efforts, advances; *à peu de* ~, at a slight cost, easily; *à grands* ~, at great expense; *à mes* ~, at my cost; *sur nouveaux* ~, anew, afresh; all over again; *faire ses* ~, to get back one's expenses; *faux* ~, incidental expenses; *en être pour ses* ~, to have lost one's money (or had one's pains) for nothing; *faire les* ~ *de*, see DÉFRAYER; *faire des* ~, *se mettre en* ~, to make efforts to please.

fraise (frɛz), s.f. [L *fragum*] Strawberry; strawberry-mark; (butch.) crow; (fort.) fraise; (dressm.) ruffle, ruff; (techn.) cutting-file, fraise.

fraisement, fraisage (frɛzmɑ̃, frɛzaʒ), s.m. Fraising (of a drill-hole, &c.).

fraiser (frɛze), v.a. To plait, to ruffle; to fraise, to enlarge (a drill-hole) with a fraise; to mill; to knead (dough); *machine à* ~, or *fraiseuse*, milling-machine.

fraisier (frɛzje), s.m. (bot.) Strawberry-plant.

fraisière (frɛzjɛr), s.f. Strawberry-bed.

fraisil (frɛzi), s.m. Charcoal dust, coal dross.

framboise (frɑ̃bwaz), s.f. [etym. dub.] Raspberry.

framboiser (frɑ̃bwaze), v.a. To flavour with raspberry.

framboisier (frɑ̃bwazje), s.m. (bot.) Raspberry-cane.

framée (frame), s.f. [L *framea*] Frankish lance.

franc (frɑ̃), s.m. [f. L *Francus*] Franc, French coin.

franc, fem. **franche** (frɑ̃, frɑ̃ʃ), adj. [L *francus*] Frank, free, open, sincere, loyal, open-hearted, genuine, whole, unadulterated; arrant, mere; (hort.) ungrafted; ~ *de port*, post paid; *être* ~ *du collier, y aller* ~ *jeu*, to act with entire sincerity; *franche lippée*, a good meal without expense; *avoir son* ~ *parler*, to speak one's mind freely; to be outspoken; *un* ~ *coquin*, an arrant rogue; *dix jours* ~*s*, ten full days. ~*-alleu*, s.m. Freehold; ~*-bord*, s.m. free-board; ~*-fief*, s.m. frankfee, freehold; ~*-maçon*, s.m. freemason; ~*-maçonnerie*, s.f. freemasonry; ~ *parler*, s.m. freedom of speech; ~*-tireur*, s.m. sharp-shooter, skirmisher. ~, adv. Frankly, freely, openly; *parler* ~, to speak plainly, frankly.

franc, fem. **franque** (frɑ̃), s.m.f. adj. [f. L *Francus*] Frank, Frankish. (In the Levant all Europeans are often called Franks.)

français, -e (frɑ̃sɛ), adj. French; s.m.f. Frenchman, Frenchwoman, French (tongue); *aller au Français*, to go to the Théâtre Français; (fig.) *en bon* ~, in plain terms; *à la* ~*e*, in the French fashion; (fig.) bravely and gaily.

franc-comtois, -e (frɑ̃kɔ̃twɑ), adj. s.m.f. (Native) of Franche-Comté.

franchement (frɑ̃ʃmɑ̃), adv. Frankly, openly, freely, plainly, candidly, unreservedly, boldly; *allez-y* ~, now, go for it boldly.

franchir (frɑ̃ʃir), v.a. [f. *franc*] To clear, to jump over, to leap over, to pass over, to go beyond, to overstep, to surmount; ~ *le pas*, to take the leap; ~ *l'obstacle*, to overcome the obstacle or difficulty; ~ *le Rubicon*, to cross the Rubicon.

franchise (frɑ̃ʃiz), s.f. [f. *franc*] **1.** Exemption, immunity, freedom (of a city, &c.); franchise; (⚠ 'franchise' in English, but not in French, means also *droit de vote*;) **2.** frankness, sincerity, openness, candour, boldness; *en* ~, duty-free; ~ *postale*, post free; *en toute* ~, in all sincerity.

franchissable (frɑ̃ʃisabl), adj. Passable.

francisation (frɑ̃siza'sjɔ̃), s.f. Gallicizing, registration as a French ship.

franciscain, -e (frɑ̃siskɛ̃), s.m.f. adj. [f. *St François*] Franciscan, grey friar; (fem.) Franciscan nun.

franciser (frɑ̃size), v.a. To gallicize, to frenchify; **se** ~, v.pr. to become French or (pej.) frenchified.

francisque (frɑ̃sisk), s.f. [L *francisca*] Battle-axe, francisc.

franco (frɑ̃ko), adv. [It. wd] Free of charge, postage prepaid, post free. ~, adj. (in compounds) French-; Franco-.

francolin (frɑ̃kɔlɛ̃), s.m. (ornith.) Francolin.

francophile (frɑ̃kɔfil), adj. [f. *franc*+(Gr) *philos*] Francophil.

francophobe (frɑ̃kɔfɔb), adj. [f. *franc*+(Gr.) *phobos*] Francophobe.

frange (frɑ̃ʒ), s.f. [L *fimbria*] Fringe.

franger (frɑ̃ʒe), v.a. To fringe.

frangin, -e (frɑ̃ʒɛ̃), s.m.f. (slang) Brother, sister.

frangipane (frɑ̃ʒipan), s.f. [f. *Frangipani*, It. prop. n.] Frangipane, almond cream; a perfume.

frangipanier (frɑ̃ʒipanje), s.m. (bot.) Red jasmine.

franquette (frɑ̃kɛt), s.f. [f. *franc*] *A la bonne* ~, simply, without ceremony.

frappage (frapaʒ), s.m. Striking, stamping; coining (of money); syn. FRAPPE, s.f.

frappant, -e (frapɑ̃), p. adj. Striking, impressive.

frappe (frap), s.f. Stamp; coining; (print.) set of matrices; (slang) scamp.

frappé, -e (frape), p. adj. Struck, surprised, impressed; (of liquids) iced; coined, stamped; *ouvrage* ~ *au bon coin*, remarkably good piece of work; *être* ~ *d'une idée*, to be struck with an idea; *être*

~ *d'une amende*, to be fined, to be mulcted in a fine; (mus.) *temps* ~, down-beat.

frappement (frapmɑ̃), s.m. Striking, beating.

frapper (frape), v.a.n. [etym. dub.] To strike, to hit, to beat, to slap, to smite, to knock, to afflict, to impress, to surprise, to move; to ice (liquids); to stamp, to coin (money); to tax (goods), to impose taxes on; ~ *d'une amende*, to mulct in a fine; ~ *du pied*, to stamp; ~ *des mains*, to clap one's hands; ~ *à la porte*, to knock at the door; ~ *de terreur*, to strike with terror; **se** ~, v.pr. to scourge oneself; to be strongly and sadly impressed.

frappeu-r, -se (frapœr), s.m.f. Striker, beater, knocker. ~, adj. Striking, rapping; *esprit* ~, rapping spirit (at séance, etc.).

frasque (frask), s.f. [It. *frasca*] Prank, freak, folly, piece of extravagance; *faire des*, or *ses* ~*s*, to be up to one's pranks.

frater (fratɛr), s.m. [L wd] (fam.) Barber-surgeon, sawbones; illiterate monk.

fraternel, -le (fratɛrnɛl), adj. Fraternal, brotherly.

fraternellement (fratɛrnɛlmɑ̃), adv. Fraternally.

fraternisation (fratɛrniza'sjɔ̃), s.f. Fraternization.

fraterniser (fratɛrnize), v.n. [f. L *frater*] To fraternize.

fraternité (fratɛrnite), s.f. Fraternity, brotherhood.

fratricide (fratrisid), s.m. [f. L *frater*+*caedere*] Fratricide. ~, adj. Fratricidal.

fraude (frod), s.f. [L *fraus*] Fraud, deceit, cheat; *en* ~, fraudulently; *entrer en* ~, to smuggle in; *faire une* ~, to commit a fraud; ⚠ English 'fraud' can be said of a person, but not *fraude*.

frauder (frode), v.a. To defraud; ~, v.n. to smuggle; to cheat.

fraudeu-r, -se (frodœr), s.m.f. Defrauder, smuggler, cheater.

frauduleusement (frodyløzmɑ̃), adv. Fraudulently.

frauduleu-x, -se (frodylø), adj. Fraudulent; *banqueroute* ~*se*, fraudulent bankruptcy.

fraxinelle (fraksinɛl), s.f. [f. L *fraxinus*] (bot.) Dittany.

frayer (frɛje), v.a. [f. *fricare*] To trace out, to mark out, to open out, to beat, to prepare, to make easy; ~ *la voie à X*; to pave the way for X, to facilitate X's progress; to rub against, to wear away; ~, v.n. to spawn (of fish); to have relations (*avec*, with); **se** ~, v.pr. *se* ~ *un passage*, to clear a way for oneself.

frayeur (frɛjœr), s.f. [f. L *fragor*] Fright, fear, dread, terror.

fredaine (frədɛn), s.f. Prank, frolic; *faire des* ~*s*, to play pranks.

fredon (frədɔ̃), s.m. [etym. dub.] Trill, quaver, humming.

fredonnement (frədɔnmɑ̃), s.m. Humming.

fredonner (frədɔne), v.a.n. To hum.

frégate (fregat), s.f. [It. *fregata*] Frigate; (ornith.) frigate-bird.

frégaton (fregatɔ̃), s.m. (naut.) Frigatoon.

frein (frɛ̃), s.m. [L *frenum*] Bit (of a bridle), brake; (fig.) check, curb, restraint; *ronger son* ~, to champ the bit, to fret; *ne plus connaître de* ~, to throw off all restraint; ~ *sur le différentiel*, brake on the differential shaft; ~ *à main*, hand-brake; ~ *à pied*, foot-brake; *serrer le* ~, to brake, to apply the brake.

frelatage (frəlataʒ), s.m. Adulteration, sophistication.

frelater (frəlate), v.a. To adulterate, to sophisticate, to doctor, to falsify.

frelateur (frəlatœr), s.m. Adulterator, sophisticator.

frêle (frɛl), adj. [L *fragilis*] Weak, fragile, delicate, frail.

frelon (frəlɔ̃), s.m. [etym. uncert.] (ent.) Hornet; drone.

freluche (frəlyʃ), s.f. [OF wd] Tuft of silk, tassel.

freluquet (frəlykɛ), s.m. [f. *freluche*] Coxcomb, puppy, dandy, fribble. (⚠ *Freluquet* would not be said of a strong, powerful man.)

frémir (fremir), v.n. [L *fremere*] To rustle, to roar; to shudder, to tremble with fear, horror, shame, &c.; to quiver; to simmer, to be on the point of boiling.

frémissant, -e (fremisɑ̃), p.adj. Quivering, trembling.

frémissement (fremismɑ̃), s.m. Quiver, shudder, flutter, rustle, shake; quivering, shuddering, fluttering, tremor, rustling; simmering.

frênaie (frɛnɛ), s.f. Ash-grove, ash-plantation.

frêne (frɛn), s.m. [L *fraxinus*] (bot.) Ash-tree, ash.

frénésie (frenezi), s.f. [L. *phrenesis*] Frenzy, madness, rage, distraction, excessive activity, frantic ways.

frénétique (frenetik), adj. Frantic, frenzied, distracted.

frénétiquement (frenetikmɑ̃), adv. Frantically.

fréquemment (frekamɑ̃), adv. Frequently, often.

fréquence (frekɑ̃s), s.f. [L *frequentia*] Frequency, quickness (of the pulse).

fréquent, -e (frekɑ̃), adj. [L *frequens*] Frequent, quick (of a pulse).

fréquentati-f, -ve (frekɑ̃tatif), adj. (gram.) Frequentative.

fréquentation (frekɑ̃ta'sjɔ̃), s.f. Frequentation, company; frequent use.

fréquenter (frekɑ̃te), v.a. [L *frequentare*] To frequent, to associate with, to haunt, to keep company with, to resort to, to

visit often; *mal fréquenté*, ill famed, frequented by bad people.
frère (frɛr), s.m. [L *frater*] Brother (pl. brothers or brethren), fellow Christian, fellow member; friar, monk; ~ *aîné*, elder brother; ~ *cadet*, younger brother; *demi-~*, half-brother; ~ *utérin*, brother on the mother's side; ~ *consanguin*, brother on the father's side; *beau-~*, brother-in-law; ~ *de lait*, foster-brother; ~ *d'armes*, brother-in-arms; *faux* ~, traitor; *en ~s*, like brothers.
frérot (frero), s.m. (fam.) *Mon* ~, little brother mine.
fresque (frɛsk), s.f. [f. It. *fresco*] Fresco; *peindre à* ~, to paint in fresco.
fressure (frɛsyr), s.f. [orig. unkn.] (butch.) Pluck, fry, haslet.
fret (frɛ), s.m. [f. Dutch *vracht*] Freight; chartering.
frètement (frɛtmɑ̃), s.m. Freighting.
fréter (frete), v.a. To freight, to charter.
fréteur (fretœr), s.m. Freighter, charterer, shipowner, one who lets a vessel on contract; see AFFRÉTEUR.
frétillant, -e (fretijɑ̃), p. adj. Wriggling, lively, frisky, brisk, excited.
frétillement (fretijmɑ̃), s.m. Wriggling, frisking.
frétiller (fretije), v.n. [etym. dub.] To wriggle, to be impatient, to frisk, to get very excited, to fidget.
frétillon (fretijɔ̃), s.m. Fidgety, restless person.
fretin (frətɛ̃), s.m. [f. *frai*] Fry, young fish; (fig.) unimportant people, trash, rubbish.
frette (frɛt), s.f. [abbrev. of *ferrette*] Iron band, hoop; (arch.) fret.
fretter (frɛtte), v.a. To hoop, to bind with iron.
freux (frø), s.m. [f. OHG *hruoh*] (ornith.) Rook.
friabilité (friabilite), s.f. Friability.
friable (friabl), adj. [L *friabilis*] Friable, crumbling easily, crisp, short.
friand, -e (friɑ̃), adj. Fond (*de*, of), greedy (for); nice, dainty, appetizing; *un morceau* ~, a dainty bit; *être ~ de miel*, to be fond of honey, or greedy for honey. ~, s.m. Small patty.
friandise (friɑ̃diz), s.f. **1.** Daintiness; **2.** sweet, dainty, titbit.
fricandeau (pl. **-x**) (frikɑ̃do), s.m. (cook.) Veal stew, fricandeau.
fricassée (frikase), s.f. (cook.) Fricassee; (fig.) medley, smash, jumble.
fricasser (frikase), v.a. [f. LL *fricare*] (cook.) To fricassee; (fig.) to squander.
fricasseur (frikasœr), s.m. Bad cook; (fig.) spendthrift, rake.
friche (friʃ), s.f. [LL *friscum*] Fallow, fallow land, uncultivated or waste land; *laisser en* ~, to let lie fallow.
frichti (friʃti), s.m. (pop.) Food, grub.
fricot (friko), s.m. [f. *fricasser*] (pop.) Stew, food, (slang) grub.
fricoter (frikote), v.n. To eat, to feast; (fig.) to job (in the funds); to make illicit profits.
fricoteu-r, -se (frikɔtœr), s.m.f. Feaster, good liver, bad cook; jobber, one who makes illicit profits; (mil.) scrimshanker.
friction (friksjɔ̃), s.f. [L *frictio*] Friction, rubbing; *gants à ~s*, flesh-gloves; *embrayage à ~*, friction clutch; (fig.) disagreement.
frictionner (friksjɔne), v.a. To friction, to rub, to massage.
frigidaire (friʒidɛr), s.m. Refrigerator, ice-chest.
frigidité (friʒidite), s.f. [L *frigiditas*] Frigidity, coldness; impotency.
frigorifier (frigɔrifje), v.a. To refrigerate, to freeze; *viande frigorifiée*, or **frigo**, s.f., frozen meat.
frigorifique (frigɔrifik), adj. [f. L *frigus, frigoris+facere*] Frigorific. ~, s.m. Refrigerator.
frileu-x, -se (frilø), adj. [f. LL *frigorosus*, OF *frieleus*] Chilly, sensitive to cold.
frimaire (frimɛr), s.m. [f. *frimas*] Frimaire (third month of the calendar of the first French Republic, from 21 Nov. to 20 Dec.).
frimas (frimɑ), s.m. Rime, hoar-frost; cold weather; *la saison des~*, the wintry season.
frime (frim), s.f. [OF *frume*] Sham, make-believe, pretence, grimace.
frimousse (frimus), s.f. [f. *frime* = *mine*] (colloq.) Face, phiz (of child or young girl).
fringale (frɛ̃gal), s.f. [corrupt. of *faim+valle*] Hunger-fit.
fringant, -e (frɛ̃gɑ̃), adj. [f. *fringuer*] Brisk, frisky, lively, smart, dashing, dapper; (of a horse) prancing, mettlesome.
fringuer (frɛ̃ge), v.n. [orig. uncert.] To frisk about; to prance; (slang) to dress; *être bien fringué*, to be expensively dressed.
fripe (frip), s.f. [OF wd] Rag; (pop.) anything eaten on bread, such as butter, cheese, &c.
friper (fripe), v.a. [f. *fripe*] To rumple, to crumple, to spoil; **se** ~, v.pr. to get rumpled easily, to crush.
friperie (fripri), s.f. Frippery, second-hand clothes, old furniture; old clothes or old furniture trade or shop.
fripe-sauce (fripsos), s.m. (pop.) Greedy-guts; bad cook.
fripi-er, -ère (fripje), s.m.f. Second-hand clothes dealer or broker.
fripon, -ne (fripɔ̃), s.m.f. [f. *friper*] Rogue, cheat, rascal, gipsy; hussy. ~, adj. Roguish.
friponner (fripɔne), v.n.a. To cheat, to pilfer, to gull, to cozen.
friponnerie (fripɔnri), s.f. Roguery, knavery, robbery; piece of roguery, knavish trick.

fripouille (fripuj), s.f. Scamp, rascal, blackguard, bad lot; *c'est une fameuse* ~, he is a thorough blackguard.

friquet (frikɛ), s.m. [OF *frigue*] (ornith.) Tree-sparrow.

frire (frir), v.a.n. def. To fry; *faire* ~, to fry; (slang) *être frit*, to be done for.

frise (friz), s.f. [f. LL *frisium*] Frieze, border; (fort.) *chevaux de* ~, chevaux de frise.

frisé, -e (frize), p. adj. Curled, curly, curly-headed; *chou* ~, savoy cabbage.

friser (frize), v.a.n. To curl, to frizzle, to crisp; (fig.) to graze, to brush, to be near to; ~ *la cinquantaine*, to be getting on for fifty, to be not far off fifty; ~ *l'impertinence*, to be somewhat impertinent.

frisette (frizɛt), s.f. Frisette, small curl.

frison (frizɔ̃), s.m. Small curl.

frison, -ne (frizɔ̃), s.m.f. adj. Frisian, of Friesland.

frisotter (frizɔte), v.n.a. To frizzle, to becurl.

frisquet, -te (friskɛ), adj. [f. LL *friscus*] Chill, chilly.

frisson (frisɔ̃), s.m. [f. L *frigere*] Shiver, chill, shudder, quiver, thrill.

frissonnant, -e (frisɔnɑ̃), p. adj. Shivering, shuddering, shaking, quivering.

frissonnement (frisɔnmɑ̃), s.m. Slight shiver, shudder, &c.

frissonner (frisɔne), v.n. To shiver (*de*, with), to shudder (with), to quiver, to tremble, to feel a thrill (of).

frisure (frizyr), s.f. [f. *friser*] Curling, curls.

frit, -e (fri), p. adj. (see FRIRE) Fried. ~*es*, s.f.pl. Fried potatoes, chips.

fritillaire (fritillɛr), s.f. [f. L *fritillus*] (bot.) Fritillary.

fritte (frit), s.f. (glass-making) Frit.

friture (frityr), s.f. [f. *frire*] Frying; fried food; fried fish, fish to be fried; dripping, oil, butter, lard, fat for frying; (wireless, teleph., &c.) unpleasant noise resembling frying, or sizzling.

frituri-er, -ère (frityrje), s.m.f. Fried-fish dealer, cook who does the frying.

frivole (frivɔl), adj. [L *frivolus*] Frivolous, flimsy, trifling.

frivolement (frivɔlmɑ̃), adv. Frivolously.

frivolité (frivɔlite), s.f. **1.** Frivolity, frivolousness, flimsiness; ~*s* (pl.) trifles, frivolous things; **2.** tatting.

froc (frɔk), s.m. [LL *frocus*] Cowl, hood, frock (of a monk); *prendre le* ~, to turn monk; *jeter le* ~ *aux orties*, to throw off the cowl.

frocard (frɔkar), s.m. [f. *froc*] (iron.) Monk.

froid (frwa), s.m. [L *frigidus*] Cold, low temperature, cold weather, coldness, indifference, chill, cold fit; *transir de* ~, to be numbed with cold, to be chilled to the bone; *j'ai* ~, I am cold; *j'ai* ~ *aux pieds*, my feet are cold; *battre* ~ *à X*, to give X the cold shoulder; *un* ~ *noir*, raw cold weather; *il y a du* ~ *entre eux*, there is a certain coolness in their relations; *être en* ~ *avec X*, to be on cool terms with X; *cela a jeté un* ~, it acted as a wet blanket; *il n'a pas* ~ *aux yeux*, he does not suffer from cold feet; *cela ne fait ni chaud ni* ~, that is neither here nor there.

froid, -e (frwa), adj. Cold, cool, frigid, lifeless, lukewarm, indifferent, dull, dispassionate, chilly, chilling.

froidement (frwadmɑ̃), adv. Coldly, coolly, lukewarmly; in cold blood, dispassionately.

froideur (frwadœr), s.f. Coldness, coolness, chilliness, frigidity, unfeelingness.

froidure (frwadyr), s.f. Coldness (of the weather).

froissement (frwasmɑ̃), s.m. Rumpling, crumpling, bruising, creasing; (fig.) annoyance, vexation, ruffling, offending.

froisser (frwase), v.a. [f. pop. L *frustiare*] To rumple, to crumple, to crease, to bruise; (fig.) to offend, to ruffle, to hurt the feelings of, to annoy, to vex; **se** ~, v.pr. to take offence.

frôlement (frolmɑ̃), s.m. Grazing, light contact, rustle, brushing.

frôler (frole), v.a. [orig. unkn.] To graze, to brush, to touch lightly, to rustle against.

fromage (frɔmaʒ), s.m. [f. *forme, formage*] Cheese; ~ *à la crème*, cream cheese; ~ *de porc*, brawn; ~ *glacé*, ice-cream; *entre la poire et le* ~, at dessert (when everybody feels most convivial); (colloq.) *il a trouvé un bon* ~, he has got a soft or cushy job.

fromag-er, -ère (frɔmaʒe), s.m.f. **1.** Cheese-maker; **2.** cheese-mould; **3.** (bot.) silk-cotton tree. ~, adj. Pertaining to cheese-making.

fromagerie (frɔmaʒri), s.f. Cheese-dairy, cheese-trade.

froment (frɔmɑ̃), s.m. [L *frumentum*] Wheat; *de* ~, wheaten, of wheat.

fromental, -e, (aux) (frɔmɑ̃tal), adj. Frumentaceous. ~, s.m. Oat-grass.

fronce (frɔ̃s), s.f. [f. *froncer*] Gather, pucker, crease.

froncement (frɔ̃smɑ̃), s.m. Gathering, puckering; ~ *de sourcils*, knitting of the brows; frown.

froncer (frɔ̃se), v.a. [orig. uncert.] To gather, to pucker; to wrinkle; ~ *les sourcils*, to knit one's brows, to frown; ~ *les lèvres*, to purse one's lips.

frondaison (frɔ̃dɛzɔ̃), s.f. [f. L *frons*] Foliation; foliage.

fronde[1] (frɔ̃d), s.f. [L *funda*] Sling; (Fr. hist.) la Fronde.

fronde[2] (frɔ̃d) s.f. [f. L *frons, frondis*] (bot.) Frond.

fronder (frɔ̃de), v.a.n. To sling; to blame, to find fault with, to rail, to jeer at, to scoff at, to beard, to set at defiance.

frondeu-r, -se (frɔ̃dœr), s.m.f. **1.** Slinger; **2.** fault-finder, critic, railer, rioter, frondeur. ~, adj. Censorious, jeering, carping, daring, rebellious (and usually witty).
front (frɔ̃), s.m. [L *frons*] Forehead, brow; countenance; head, fore-part; (fig.) boldness, impudence, (pop.) brass, cheek; *courber le* ~, to bow one's head; *montrer un* ~ *sévère*, to have a stern countenance; *avoir le* ~ *de*, to have the face to, to have the cheek to; *faire* ~ *à*, to face, to confront; ~ *de bataille*, battle front; *heurter de* ~, to run counter to; *marcher de* ~, to walk abreast; *mener de* ~, to manage simultaneously.
frontal, frontail (pl. **aux**) (frɔ̃tal, frɔ̃taj), s.m. [f. *front*] Forehead strap (of harness), head-piece (of horse's armour).
frontal, -e, (aux) (frɔ̃tal), adj. Frontal.
fronteau (pl. -x) (frɔ̃to), s.m. Frontlet.
frontière (frɔ̃tjɛr), s.f. [f. *front*] Frontier, border; (fig.) confine.
frontignan (frɔ̃tiɲɑ̃), s.m. [geog. orig.] Frontignan (wine).
frontispice (frɔ̃tispis), s.m. [LL *frontispicium*] Frontispiece.
fronton (frɔ̃tɔ̃), s.m. [f. *front*] (arch.) Frontal, fronton, pediment; (naut.) poop-rail.
frottage (frɔtaʒ), s.m. [f. *frotter*] Rubbing, polishing, waxing and polishing.
frottée (frɔte), s.f. (pop.) Drubbing.
frottement (frɔtmɑ̃), s.m. Rubbing, friction, contact, interaction.
frotter (frɔte), v.a. [orig. uncert.] To rub, to polish; (colloq.) to drub, to thrash, to pommel; **se** ~, v.pr. to rub oneself, to associate (*à*, with); *ne vous y frottez pas!*, have nothing to do with it!; *qui s'y frotte s'y pique*, meddle and smart for it; *se* ~ *les mains*, to rub one's hands; (fig.) to rejoice.
frotteur (frɔtœr), s.m. Floor-polisher; scrubber.
frottis (frɔti), s.m. Thin wash of colour.
frottoir (frɔtwar), s.m. Scrubber; any rubbing-appliance; friction-surface (for matches); burnisher, planisher.
frouer (frue), v.n. [onom.] To pipe (as a decoy, in bird-catching).
frou-frou (frufru), s.m. [onom.] Rustle, rustling; *faire du* ~, to cut a dash.
froufrouter (frufrute), v.n. To rustle.
froussard (frusar), adj. s.m. (pop.) Funky (fellow).
frousse (frus), s.f. (pop.) Fright, funk; *avoir la* ~, to be in a funk; to have got the wind up.
fructidor (fryktidɔr), s.m. [f. L *fructus*+ Gr. *dōron*] Fructidor (12th month of the French Republican calendar, 18 Aug. to 16 Sept.).
fructification (fryktifika'sjɔ̃), s.f. Fructification.
fructifier (fryktifje), v.n. To fructify, to bear fruit; (fig.) to bear interest, to bring profit.
fructueusement (fryktɥøzmɑ̃), adv. Fruitfully, profitably.
fructueu-x, -se (fryktɥø), adj. Fruitful, profitable, lucrative.
frugal, -e, (aux) (frygal), adj. [L *frugalis*] Frugal.
frugalement (frygalmɑ̃), adv. Frugally.
frugalité (frygalite), s.f. Frugality.
frugivore (fryʒivɔr), adj. [f. L *frux*+ *vorare*] Frugivorous.
fruit[1] (frɥi), s.m. [L *fructus*] Fruit; (fig.) produce, result, profit; ~ *à noyau*, stone-fruit; ~ *à pépins*, pip-fruit; (fig.) ~ *sec*, dunce; failure; unsuccessful candidate; *travailler avec* ~, to work profitably; *porter son* ~, to produce its effect.
fruit[2] (frɥi), s.m. (mason.) Batter; *avoir du* ~, to batter.
fruité, -e (frɥite), adj. Fruity.
fruiterie (frɥitri), s.f. Fruit-shop, greengrocer's shop; fruit-loft.
fruiti-er, -ère (frɥitje), adj. Fruit-bearing, fruit-.
fruiti-er, -ère (frɥitje), s.m.f. Fruiterer, greengrocer. ~, s.m. Fruit-loft, fruit-case, fruit-stand.
frumentaire (frymɑ̃tɛr), adj. [f. L *frumentum*] Frumentarious.
frusques (frysk), s.f.pl. (pop.) Clothing, traps, duds, togs.
frusquin (fryskɛ̃), s.m. (pop.) *Perdre tout son saint-*~, to lose one's all.
fruste (fryst), adj. [It. *frusto*] (of medals) Worn, defaced; (fig.) unpolished, rough.
frustration (frystra'sjɔ̃), s.f. Frustration.
frustrer (frystre), v.a. [L *frustrari*] To frustrate, to defraud, to balk, to deprive.
frutescent, -e (frytɛssɑ̃), adj. [f. L *frutex*] (bot.) Frutescent.
fuchsia (fyksja, fyʃja) [f. *Fuchs*, Germ. botanist] Fuchsia.
fuchsine (fyksin), s.f. (chem.) Fuchsine.
fucus (fykys), s.m. [L wd] (bot.) Fucus.
fuégien, -ne (fɥeʒjɛ̃), adj. s.m.f. (Native) of Terra del Fuego, Fuegian.
fugace (fygas), adj. [L *fugax*] Fugaceous, fleeting.
fugacité (fygasite), s.f. Fugacity, fugaciousness.
fugiti-f, -ve (fyʒitif), adj. [L *fugitivus*] Fugitive, runaway; fleeting, transient. ~, s.m.f. Fugitive, runaway, wanderer.
fugue (fyg), s.f. [L *fuga*] **1.** (mus.) Fuga, fugue; **2.** (pop.) flight, prank, bolting; *faire une* ~, to bolt, to have a lark, to run away.
fuie (fɥi), s.f. Dovecote.
fuir (fɥir), v.a. [L *fugere*] To fly or run away (from); to shun, to avoid, to evade, to elude; ~, v.n. to flee, to fly, to run away, to escape, to take flight; to vanish; to recede; (of a vessel) to leak; *faire* ~, to put to flight; *le temps fuit*, time flies; **se** ~,

v.pr. to avoid each other; to shun each other; to fly from oneself.
fuite (fɥit), s.f. Flight, evasion, running away, escape; avoiding; leakage, crack; *prendre la* ~, to take flight; *mettre en* ~, to put to flight; ~ *de gaz*, escape of gas.
fulgurant, -e (fylgyrɑ̃), p. adj. Flashing; like lightning.
fulguration (fylgyra'sjɔ̃), s.f. [f. L *fulgur*] Lightning, fulguration, flashing.
fulgurer (fylgyre), v.n. To flash.
fuligineu-x, -se (fyliʒinø), adj. [f. L *fuligo*] Fuliginous, sooty.
fulmicoton (fylmikɔtɔ̃), s.m. Gun-cotton.
fulminant, -e (fylminɑ̃), p. adj. Fulminant, fulminating; (fig.) threatening, thundering.
fulminate (fylminat), s.m. (chem.) Fulminate.
fulmination (fylmina'sjɔ̃), s.f. Fulmination.
fulminer (fylmine), v.n.a. [L *fulminare*] To fulminate; (fig.) to threaten, to thunder, to storm, to fulmine.
fumage (fymaʒ), s.m. **1.** Manuring; **2.** smoking, curing; **3.** lacquering (of silver, &c.).
fumant, -e (fymɑ̃), p. adj. Smoking, smoky, steaming, reeking; fuming, raging.
fume-cigare, -cigarette, &c. (fymsigar), s.m. Cigar-holder, cigarette-holder, &c.
fumée (fyme), s.f. [L *fumus*] Smoke, fume, vapour, steam, reek, mist; (fig.) dream, empty vapour, phantom, idle conceit; *pas de* ~ *sans feu*, no smoke without fire; *s'en aller en* ~, to vanish in smoke; *les* ~*s du vin*, the fumes of wine.
fumer (fyme), v.a.n. [L *fumare*] To smoke, to steam, to reek; (fig.) to fume; to manure, to dung; to cure, to smoke (meat, fish).
fumerie (fymri), s.f. Smoking den; ~ *d'opium*, opium den.
fumerolle (fymrɔl), s.f. [f. *fumer*] Fumarole.
fumeron (fymrɔ̃), s.m. Smoky bit of charcoal.
fumet (fymɛ), s.m. [f. *fumée*] Scent, flavour, bouquet.
fumeterre (fymtɛr), s.f. (bot.) Fumitory.
fumeu-r, -se (fymœr), s.m.f. Smoker.
fumeu-x, -se (fymø), adj. Smoky, smoking; heady, confused, dim, hazy; *esprit* ~, hazy mind, confused brain.
fumier (fymje), s.m. [LL *fimarium*] Dung, dunghill, manure; muck.
fumigation (fymiga'sjɔ̃), s.f. Fumigation.
fumigatoire (fymigatwar), adj. Fumigating.
fumiger (fymiʒe), v.a. [L *fumigare*] To fumigate.
fumiste (fymist), s.m. [f. *fumée*] Chimney-builder; chimney-doctor; chimney-sweep; (fig.) practical joker, wag, humbug.
fumisterie (fymistəri), s.f. Chimney-sweeping, chimney-building; (fig.) foolery, imposition, joke, sell.
fumivore (fymivɔr), adj. [f. L *fumus*+ *vorare*] Smoke-consuming. ~, s.m. Smoke-consumer.
fumoir (fymwar), s.m. Smoking-shed (for curing meat or fish); smoking-room.
fumure (fymyr), s.f. [f. *fumier*] Manuring.
funambule (fynɑ̃byl), s.m.f. [f. L *funis*+ *ambulare*] Funambulist, rope-dancer.
funambulesque (fynɑ̃bylɛsk), adj. Funambulatory, grotesque.
funèbre (fynɛbr), adj. [L *funebris*] Funereal, pertaining to burial; sad, mournful, gloomy, dismal.
funérailles (fynerɑj), s.f.pl. [L *funeralia*] Funeral, obsequies, burial; syn. OBSÈQUES.
funéraire (fynerɛr), adj. [L *funerarius*] Funeral, funereal, pertaining to burial.
funeste (fynɛst), adj. [L *funestus*] Fatal, deadly, disastrous, baneful.
funiculaire (fynikylɛr), adj. [f. L *funiculus*] Funicular. ~, s.m. Rope railway; ~, s.f. (math.) catenary.
funicule (fynikyl), s.m. [L *funiculus*] (bot.) Funiculus.
fur (fyr), s.m. [L *forum*] *Au* ~ *et à mesure*, gradually, in succession, as soon (as), in proportion (to); as fast (as).
furet (fyrɛ), s.m. [LL *furittum*] (zool.) Ferret; (fig.) Paul Pry, ferreter.
fureter (fyrte), v.n. [f. *furet*] To ferret, to hunt with a ferret; (fig.) to rummage, to pry about.
fureteu-r, -se (fyrtœr), s.m.f. Ferreter, rummager, prier, hunter, (fam.) Nosy Parker. ~, adj. Prying.
fureur (fyrœr), s.f. [L *furor*] Fury, rage, madness, passion, frenzy; craze; *entrer en* ~, to get into a fury; *faire* ~, to be the rage, to be all the go.
furfuracé, -e (fyrfyrase), adj. [f. L *furfur*] Furfuraceous.
furibond, -e (fyribɔ̃), adj. [L *furibundus*] Furibund, furious, furious-looking, raging.
furie (fyri), s.f. [L *furia*] Fury, rage; fury, termagant.
furieusement (fyrjøzmɑ̃), adv. Furiously, tremendously, with a vengeance.
furieu-x, -se (fyrjø), adj. [L *furiosus*] Furious, raging, wild, fierce, enraged.
furolle (fyrɔl), s.f. Ignis fatuus.
furoncle (fyrɔ̃kl), s.m. [L *furunculus*] Furuncle, boil.
furti-f, -ve (fyrtif), adj. [f. L *furtivus*] Furtive, stealthy, secret.
furtivement (fyrtivmɑ̃), adv. Furtively, stealthily.
fusain (fyzɛ̃), s.m. [LL *fusago*] (bot.) Spindle-tree; charcoal (for drawing); charcoal drawing.
fuseau (pl. **-x**) (fyzo), s.m. [f. L *fusus*]

Spindle; *jambes de* ~, spindle-shanks; distaff, bobbin; *dentelle aux* ~*x*, bobbin-lace; (techn.) spindle, axle, stave, leaf (of a pinion), whelp (of a capstan).
fusée (fyze), s.f. [f. *fuseau*] Fuse, fusee, (fireworks) rocket, squib; spindleful, bobbinful; volley (of laughter); ~ *éclairante*, star-shell, sky-rocket; ~ *d'essieu*, steering-swivel; ~ *porte-amarre*, rocket-apparatus, life-rocket; *baguette de* ~, rocket-stick.
fuselage (fyzlaʒ), s.m. (aeron.) Fuselage, body; frame.
fuselé, -e (fyzle), adj. [f. *fuseau*] Spindle-shaped, slender.
fuser (fyze), v.n. [f. L *fusus*] To fuse, to deflagrate, to fizz, to expand, to spread.
fusibilité (fyzibilite), s.f. Fusibility.
fusible (fyzibl), adj. [L *fusus*] Fusible. ~, s.m. (electr.) Fuse, cut-out; plug fuse.
fusiforme (fyziform), adj. [f. *fuseau*] Fusiform, spindle-shaped.
fusil (fyzi), s.m. [f. LL *focile*] Gun, rifle, musket, firelock; steel (for sharpening knives); tinder-box; ~ *à aiguille*, needle-gun; ~ *à deux coups*, double-barrelled gun; ~ *rayé*, rifle; *pierre à* ~, flint; *coup de* ~, gun-shot, report of a gun, rifle, &c.; (fig.) *changer son* ~ *d'épaule*, to change one's tactics, profession, or opinions; to change one's mind; (slang) *coup de* ~, fleecing, charging an exorbitant price; *n'avoir rien dans le* ~, to have nothing in one's bread-basket.
fusilier (fyzilje), s.m. Fusilier; ~ *marin*, marine.
fusillade (fyzijad), s.f. Fusillade, volley of musketry, firing, shooting.
fusiller (fyzije), v.a. To shoot (down), to execute by shooting.
fusion (fyzjɔ̃), s.f. [L *fusio*] Fusion, melting, blending; (fig.) union.
fusionnement (fyzjɔnmɑ̃), s.m. Amalgamating, amalgamation.
fusionner (fyzjɔne), v.n. To amalgamate, to blend, to unite.
fustigation (fystiga'sjɔ̃), s.f. Whipping, flagellation, flogging.
fustiger (fystiʒe), v.a. [L *fustigare*] To whip, to flog.
fût (fy), s.m. [L *fustis*] Stock (of a gun); shaft (of a column); trunk; cask (of wine).
futaie (fytɛ), s.f. [f. *fût*] Forest (of old trees); *haute* ~, full-grown trees.
futaille (fytɑj), s.f. [f. *fût*] Cask, barrel.
futaine (fytɛn), s.f. [f. LL *fustaneum*] Fustian.
futé, -e (fyte), adj. [f. L *fustis*] Sharp, cunning, sly.
futile (fytil), adj. [L *futilis*] Futile, frivolous, trifling.
futilité (fytilite), s.f. Futility, frivolity, trifle.
futur, -e (fytyr), adj. [L *futurus*] Future, to come. ~, s.m. **1.** (gram.) Future; **2.** intended husband; ~*e*, s.f. intended wife.
fuyant, -e (fɥijɑ̃), p. adj. [f. *fuir*] Flying, fleeing; fleeting, ephemeral, fading, vanishing. *Faux-*~, s.m. evasion, shuffling excuse, shift.
fuyard, -e (fɥijar), adj. s.m.f. Fugitive, runaway.

G

G, g (ʒe), s.m. 7th letter of the alphabet.
gabare (gabar), s.f. [It. *gabarra*] (naut.) **1.** Lighter, barge, flat; **2.** drag-net; **3.** (fig.) mess.
gabarier (gabarje), s.m. Lighter-man.
gabarit (gabari), s.m. Model; size; mould; draught (of a ship); (techn.) template; (fig.) kind; syn. ACABIT.
gabegie (gabʒi), s.f. Trickery, fraud, foul play; (Amer.) graft; (colloq.) waste, mess due to fraud, disorder, &c.
gabelle (gabɛl), s.f. [Provenç. *gabela*] Salt-tax; excise.
gabelou (gablu), s.m. (obs. pop.) Exciseman; (now pej.) custom-house officer, excise-man.
gabier (gabje), s.m. (naut.) Topman; (sort of) quartermaster; ~ *breveté*, able (-bodied) seaman.
gabion (gabjɔ̃), s.m. [It. *gabbione*] Gabion (wicker basket filled with earth, for use in fortification, &c.).
gabionnage (gabjɔnaʒ), s.m. Gabionage.
gabionner (gabjɔne), v.a. To defend or cover with gabions.
gable (gɑbl), s.m. [LL *gabulum*] (arch.) Gable, gable end; syn. PIGNON.
gabord (gabɔr), s.m. (naut.) Garboard, garboard strake.
gâchage (gɑʃaʒ), s.m. [f. *gâcher*] Wasting, spoiling; (of plaster, &c.) spilling, mixing.
gâche (gɑʃ), s.f. (techn.) **1.** Staple; **2.** wall-hook; **3.** trowel, baker's spatula.
gâcher (gɑʃe), v.a. [OHG *waskan*] To mix, or temper (mortar, plaster); (fig.) to spoil, to waste, to make a mess of; ~ *le métier*, to sell under price; to be too generous.
gâchette (gɑʃɛt), s.f. [f. *gâche*] **1.** (of a lock) Catch, follower; **2.** (of a firelock) trigger.
gâcheu-r, (gɑʃœr), s.m. Bricklayer's labourer; ~, **-se**, s.m.f. (fig.) bungler, waster.
gâcheu-x, -se (gɑʃø), adj. (rare) Sloppy, miry, muddy, splashy.
gâchis (gɑʃi), s.m. Wet mortar; slop, mire, sludge, slush; (fig.) muddle, mess, hash, pickle; *un joli* ~, a nice mess; *faire du* ~, to make a mess; *le* ~ *de la politique*, the political muddle.
gade (gad), s.m. (ichth.) Cod-fish.
gadouard (gadwar), s.m. Night-man, scavenger.

gadoue (gadu), s.f. Sewage, night-soil (used as manure).

gaélique (gaelik), adj. s.m. Gaelic.

gaffe (gaf), s.f. **1.** (naut.) Boat-hook, gaff; **2.** (colloq.) blunder, bloomer, howler; *faire une* ~, to put one's foot in it; to drop a brick; to blunder; *avaler sa* ~, to kick the bucket, to die.

gaffer (gafe), **1.** v.a. To hook; **2.** ~, v.n. (colloq.) to blunder; to put one's foot in it; to drop a brick.

gaffeu-r, -se (gafœr), s.m.f. Blunderer, idiot. ~, adj. Blundering, idiotic.

gaga (gaga), adj. (colloq.) Soft-witted, doting. ~ s.m. Dotard; syn. GÂTEUX.

gage (gaʒ), s.m. [Teut. orig.] **1.** Pledge, gage, deposit, security; *prêteur sur* ~*s*, pawnbroker; *mettre en* ~, to pawn; **2.** token, testimony, proof, promise; *en* ~ *d'amitié*, in token of friendship; **3.** (games) forfeit; **4.** ~*s*, (pl.) wages, hire; *à* ~*s*, hired; *casser aux* ~*s*, to discharge, (colloq. Amer.) to fire; (pej.) *être aux* ~*s de X*, to be in the pay of X; to be a hireling of X's.

gager (gaʒe), v.a. **1.** To wager, to bet, to lay; *je gage que si*, I bet it is; *je gage que non*, I bet you it is not; *gageons qu'il le fera*, I'll warrant he will do it; **2.** to hire, to pay; **3.** to pledge, to secure by a pledge.

gagerie (gaʒri), s.f. **1.** (law) Execution by way of security; **2.** rural fair where servants and labourers are hired.

gageure (gaʒyr), s.f. [f. *gager*] Wager, bet; *c'est une* ~ *!*, it's a bet!; *tenir une* ~, to lay a wager.

gagiste (gaʒist), s.m. **1.** Hired man; (theatr.) utility man; **2.** (law) *créancier* ~, guaranteed creditor; ~, pledgee.

gagnant, -e (gaɲɑ̃), s.m.f. Winner. ~, adj. Winning.

gagne-denier (gaɲdənje), s.m. (pl. *gagne-deniers*) Day-labourer.

gagne-pain (gaɲpɛ̃), s.m. (pl. invar.) **1.** Means of subsistence, livelihood, trade, pot-boiler; **2.** bread-winner.

gagne-petit (gaɲpəti), s.m. (pl. invar.) Knife-grinder; petty trader; one who is content with low wages or small profits; (said of a shop) 'small profits and quick returns'.

gagner (gaɲe), v.a. [f. OHG *weidenen*] To gain, to earn, to get, to make; *il gagne cent francs par jour*, he earns, or makes, or gets a hundred francs a day; to win (by chance, speculation, or at play); *il m'a gagné cent francs*, he won a hundred francs from me; to obtain, to get, to gain, to gain over, to win; ~ *la bataille*, to win the battle, or the field; ~ *l'avantage sur X*, to get the better of X; to obtain success against X; *il l'a bien gagné !*, he well deserves it !; ~ *du temps*, to gain time; ~ *du terrain*, to gain ground; to get on; ~ *X*, to win X over; to win X's confidence; *gagnez-le à notre cause*, win him over to our cause; ~ *la porte*, to make for the door; ~ *du chemin*, or *du pays*, to get on; ~ *le large*, to stand out to sea; (fig.) to take to one's heels; to make oneself scarce; to scamper away; ~ *un rhume*, to catch a cold; *la faim me gagne*, I am getting hungry; *l'ennui la gagne*, she is getting bored; ~ *X de vitesse*, to overtake X, to outstrip X; ~, v.n. ~ *à être connu*, to improve upon acquaintance; *il a bien gagné*, he is much improved; *l'incendie gagne*, the fire is spreading; *tôt gagné, tôt gaspillé*, easy come, easy go; *qui gagne joue bien*, he plays well who wins; *qui épargne, gagne*, a penny saved is a penny gained; **se** ~, v.pr. to be catching, to be infectious; to be earned.

gagneu-r, -se (gaɲœr), s.m.f. Winner, gainer.

gai, -e, (ge, gɛ), adj. [Teutonic orig.] Gay; ⚠ *une femme* ~*e*, a bright, or merry, or cheerful woman (NOT 'a gay woman', which = *une femme légère*, or *une femme de mœurs légères*); lively, merry, cheerful, jolly, jovial, bright, sprightly, gleeful, mirthful; brisk, spirited; vivid, clear, bright; slightly tipsy, half seas over; elevated; ~ *comme un pinson*, as merry as a lark, or as a grig; *il se sentait fort* ~, he felt in high spirits; *spectacle* ~, light entertainment, amusing play; *des couleurs* ~*es*, vivid hues; bright colours; *avoir le vin* ~, to be merry in one's cups; *il était un peu* ~, he was rather flushed, or elevated; (iron.) ~ *comme un bonnet de nuit*, as dull as ditch-water.

gaïac (gajak), s.m. (bot.) Guaiacum, guaiac; lignum vitae.

gaiement, gaîment (gɛmɑ̃), adv. Gaily, merrily, brightly, heartily, cheerfully; see GAI.

gaieté, gaîté (gɛte), s.f. Gaiety, liveliness, merriness, cheerfulness, sprightliness; mirth, merriment, humour, mettle; merry sayings, doings; frolic, freak; *en* ~, merry, slightly elevated; *de* ~ *de cœur*, out of sheer wantonness.

gaillard, -e (gajar), adj. Hearty, brisk, gay, jovial; libertine, free, fresh, cool; buxom, healthy, up to the mark, fit, hard, smart; *frais et* ~, hale and hearty; *tenir des propos* ~*s*, to make use of free language; (naut.) *vent* ~, fresh wind.

gaillard, -e (gajar), **1.** s.m.f. Merry or jolly fellow, strapping fellow; daring chap, gay dog; (fem.) buxom, determined woman; **2.** s.m. (naut.) ~ *d'arrière*, quarter-deck; ~ *d'avant*, forecastle; **3.** s.f. (bot.) gaillardia; **4.** s.f. (print.) bourgeois; **5.** s.f. (dance) galliard.

gaillardement (gajardəmɑ̃), adv. Cheerfully, jovially, merrily; heartily, boldly, briskly; freely.
gaillardise (gajardiz), s.f. Rather free talk (or action), gaiety; jolly, mirthful expression; sprightliness, jollity; *dire des ~s*, to use free, wanton language, to tell broad stories.
gaillet (gajɛ), s.m. (bot.) Bedstraw, cheese-rennet; syn. CAILLE-LAIT.
gailletin (gajtɛ̃), s.m. Small coal; syn. TÊTE-DE-MOINEAU.
gaillette, gailleterie (gajɛt, gajɛtri), s.f. Middle-sized coal.
gain (gɛ̃), s.m. [f. *gagner*] **1.** Gain, profit, benefit, lucre, pelf; *âpre au ~*, greedy, grasping; *l'amour du ~*, love of lucre; **2.** advantage, success, winning; *avoir ~ de cause*, to gain one's cause; to win or carry the day; to be successful (in a lawsuit, a discussion, a polemic); *donner ~ de cause à X*, to decide in X's favour; *se retirer sur son ~*, to leave after winning.
gaine (gɛn), s.f. [f. L *vagina*] Sheath, case; scabbard; (arch.) pedestal; terminal.
gainer (gɛne), v.a. To sheathe, to encase, to clothe tightly.
gainerie (gɛnri), s.f. **1.** Sheath-making, case-making; **2.** the articles manufactured, jewel-cases, glove-boxes, &c.
gainier (gɛnje), s.m. Sheath- or case-maker.
gaîté (gɛte), s.f. See GAIETÉ.
gala (gala), s.m. [It. wd] Gala, festive occasion; *habits de ~*, gala dress, full dress, glad rags.
galactagogue (galaktagɔg), adj. [f. Gr. *gala, galaktos*+*agōgos*] Galactogogue.
galactomètre (galaktomɛtr), s.m. Lactometer.
galactophage (galaktɔfaʒ), adj. Galactophagous.
galamment (galamɑ̃), adv. Courteously, handsomely, with great politeness; gallantly. ⚠ The usual meaning of 'gallantly' is *bravement, courageusement*; but *galamment* is not used in that sense.
galandage (galɑ̃daʒ), s.m. Brick partition.
galanga (galɑ̃ga), s.m. (bot.) Galingale.
galant, -e (galɑ̃), adj. [OF *galer*, to rejoice] Courteous (especially to ladies), complimentary, civil, courtly, very attentive (to ladies); elegant, fashionable; gallant. ⚠ But English 'gallant' usually = *courageux, brave*; ⚠ *galante* when said of a woman = a prostitute; *un ~ homme*, a true gentleman; *un homme ~*, a fine fellow, very attentive to ladies; *une attention ~e*, a complimentary token of respect or regard.
galant (galɑ̃), s.m. Sweetheart, wooer, lover, suitor, flirt; beau, masher, gallant, lady-killer, spark; (pej.) seducer; *faire le ~*, to play the gallant, to spark; *un vert ~*, a ladies' man (no longer young); (colloq., vulg.) a caution.
galanterie (galɑ̃tri), s.f. **1.** Courtesy, politeness, attention paid to ladies; **2.** libertinism, libertinage, harlotry (cf. *femme galante*).
galanthe (galɑ̃t), s.f. (bot.) Snowdrop.
galantin (galɑ̃tɛ̃), s.m. Dangler, elderly beau.
galantine (galɑ̃tin), s.f. (cook.) Galantine.
galapiat (galapja), s.m. (colloq.) Scamp; street boy, urchin. [Galatia.
galate (galat), adj. s.m.f. Galatian, of
galaxie (galaksi), s.f. Galaxy, milky way; (fig.) galaxy, brilliant company; gathering of celebrities.
galbanum (galbanɔm), s.m. (bot.) Galbanum (a resin); (fig.) blarney, humbug, gammon.
galbe (galb), s.m. [It. *garbo*] Outline, contour, sweep, curve; (arch.) entasis; (fig.) elegance, dash, line, style.
galbeu-x, -se (galbø), adj. Having a graceful, elegant outline; (fig.) elegant, stylish.
gale (gal), s.f. [etym. dub.] **1.** Itch; scab; mange; **2.** (bot.) scurf; **3.** (fig. of persons) a pestilent nuisance; *elle est méchante comme la ~*, she is a very devil; *il n'a pas la ~ aux dents*, he likes good cooking. (⚠ Not 'gale', which = *tempête, ouragan.*)
galéasse (galeas), s.f. [OF *galée*; It. *galeazza*] (naut.) Venetian galley, galliass.
galée (gale), s.f. (print.) Galley. [galega.
galéga (galega), s.m. (bot.) Goat's rue,
galéjade (galeʒad), s.f. (southern France wd.) Yoke; cock and bull story.
galène (galɛn), s.f. [Gr. *galēnē*] Galena, lead ore, lead-glance; *poste à ~*, crystal set (wireless).
galère (galɛr), s.f. [Span. *galera*] **1.** Galley; *qu'allait-il faire dans cette ~?*, what business had he there?, what on earth induced him to get into that fix?; *vogue la ~!*, let her rip!; come what may!; here goes!; **2.** *~s*, (pl.) galleys, hard labour, penal servitude; (fig.) drudgery; wretched life or place; **3.** mason's hand-truck.
galerie (galri), s.f. [LL *galeria*] **1.** Gallery, passage, large lobby; **2.** (mining) drift, gallery, adit; **3.** cornice, rim (of furniture); **4.** (of a car) luggage-grid; **5.** (theatr.) tier, circle, spectators, company; *jouer pour la ~*, to play to the gallery; *ceci n'est pas pour la ~*, this is not just showing-off; *faire ~*, to be a wall-flower; *~ de tableaux*, picture-gallery.
galérien (galerjɛ̃), s.m. Galley-slave.
galet (galɛ), s.m. [OF *gal*] **1.** Pebble, pebble-stone, cobble, cobble-stone, shingle; *plage de ~s*, shingly beach;

2. shovel-board; 3. (mech.) friction roller; bowl; slide.

galetas (galtɑ), s.m. [f. *Galata*, Constantinople] Garret, attic; wretched lodging, den.

galette (galɛt), s.f. **1.** Flat cake; *plat comme une* ~, as flat as a pancake; **2.** (slang) money, dibs, cash, tin, rhino; *filer avec la* ~, to bolt with the dibs.

galeu-x, -se (galø), adj. [f. *gale*] Itchy, scabby, mangy; (bot.) scurfy. ~, s.m. Scabby fellow; *qui se sent* ~ *se gratte*, if the cap fits, wear it; *brebis* ~*se*, scabby sheep, (fig.) black sheep.

galgal (galgal), s.m. [Gael. wd] Tumulus, cairn.

galhauban (galobɑ̃), s.m. (naut.) Backstay; ~*s volants*, shifting backstays; *rides de* ~*s*, lanyards of the backstays.

galibot (galibo), s.m. Tram-boy (in coal-mines).

galicien, -ne (galisjɛ̃), adj. s.m.f. Galician (of Galicia (*Galice*) in Spain; or Galicia (*Galicie*) in Central Europe).

galiléen, -ne (galileɛ̃), adj. s.m.f. Galilean.

galimafrée (galimafre), s.f. Hotchpotch, hash, badly-prepared food; (fig.) gallimaufry.

galimatias (galimatjɑ), s.m. [etym. dub.] Galimatias, gibberish, balderdash, bosh; *pompeux* ~, bombast.

galion (galjɔ̃), s.m. [f. OF *galée*] (naut.) Galleon.

galiote (galjɔt), s.f. (naut.) Galliot, half-galley; ~ *à bombes*, bomb-ketch.

galipette (galipɛt), s.f. (slang) Caper, trick, gambol, frolic.

galipot (galipo), s.m. Galipot, white resin.

galipoter (galipɔte), v.a. To tar, to pitch (a boat) with resin.

galle (gal), s.f. [L *galla*] Gall, gall-nut; ~ *de chêne*, oak-apple, oak-gall; *noix de* ~, (pl.) nutgalls.

gallérie (galleri), s.f. (ent.) Bee-moth.

gallican, -e (gallikɑ̃), adj. s.m.f. [L *gallicanus*] Gallican.

gallicanisme (gallikanism), s.m. Gallicanism.

gallicisme (gallisism), s.m. [f. L *gallicus*] Gallicism.

gallinacé, -e (gallinase), adj. [f. L *gallina*] Gallinaceous. ~**s**, s.m.pl. Gallinaceae.

gallique (gallik), adj. [f. L *Gallia*] Gallic, of the Gauls.

gallium (galljɔm), s.m. (chem.) Gallium (a rare metal).

gallois, -e (gallwɑ), adj. Welsh, of Wales. ~**-e**, s.m.f. Welshman, Welshwoman; the Welsh language.

gallomane (gallɔman), adj. s.m.f. [f. L *Gallus*] Gallomaniac.

gallomanie (gallɔmani), s.f. Gallomania.

gallon (galɔ̃), s.m. Gallon, four quarts, = 4·54 *litres*.

gallophobe (gallɔfɔb), adj. s.m.f. Gallophobe.

gallophobie (gallɔfɔbi), s.f. [f. L *Gallus*+ Gr. *phobos*] Gallophobia.

galoche (galɔʃ), s.f. [Gr. *kalopous*] Clog; *menton de* ~, nut-cracker chin; (naut.) open snatch-block.

galon (galɔ̃), s.m. [etym. dub.] Galloon, lace, braid; (mil., navy) stripe; *avoir ses* ~*s*, to become a corporal; *quand on prend du* ~ *on n'en saurait trop prendre*, as well be hanged for a sheep as a lamb; one can never have too much of a good thing.

galonner (galɔne), v.a. To adorn with gold or silver lace; to lace; to trim with braid; *les galonnés*, (pej.) *les galonnards*, the officers.

galonni-er, -ère (galɔnje), s.m.f. Gold-lace maker.

galop (galo), s.m. [etym. dub.] **1.** Gallop, galloping; *petit* ~, canter; *grand* ~, full gallop; *un temps de* ~, a short gallop; **2.** (danc.) gallopade; **3.** (pop.) blowing-up; *je lui ai flanqué un* ~, I gave him a rare dressing down; (fig.) *j'écris au* ~, I am writing in great haste.

galopade (galɔpad), s.f. Gallop, galloping; (fig.) rush, helter-skelter, rushing. ⚠ Not 'gallopade' which = *galop* (a dance).

galopant, -e (galɔpɑ̃), p. adj. (med.) Rapid; *phtisie* ~*e*, rapid phthisis, galloping consumption.

galoper (galɔpe), v.n. To gallop, to move fast, to run about; *il fait tout en galopant*, or *à la galopade*, he does everything in a hurry; ~, v.a. to gallop (a horse); (fam.) *les agents le galopent*, the police are after him.

galopin (galɔpɛ̃), s.m. **1.** Scamp, imp, urchin; **2.** errand-boy, young apprentice.

galoubet (galubɛ), s.m. Three-hole flute; tabor pipe.

galuchat (galyʃa), s.m. [f. inventor's name] Sharkskin or dogfish skin prepared for vanity bags, sheaths, &c.

galurin (galyrɛ̃), s.m. (colloq.) Hat, 'tile'.

galvanique (galvanik), adj. Galvanic.

galvanisation (galvaniza'sjɔ̃), s.f. Galvanization.

galvaniser (galvanize), v.a. [f. *Galvani*, discoverer] To galvanize; (fig.) to galvanize into life, to stimulate, to rouse.

galvano (galvano). In compounds: galvano-; ex.: *galvanoplastie*, s.f. galvanoplasty; *galvanoplastique*, adj. galvanoplastic; *galvanoscope*, s.m. galvanoscope.

galvanomètre (galvanɔmɛtr), s.m. Galvanometer.

galvauder (galvode), v.a. [etym. unkn.]

To spoil, to botch, to bungle, to disgrace; **se** ~, v.pr. to degrade oneself.

galvaudeu-x, -se (galvodø), s.m.f. **1.** Drudge, wretch, vagabond, good-for-nothing; scamp, knock-about; **2.** jobbing porter.

gambade (gɑ̃bad), s.f. [It. *gambata*] Gambol, caper; *faire des ~s*, to gambol; *payer en ~s*, to pay in excuses.

gambader (gɑ̃bade), v.n. To gambol, to caper, to frisk about, to romp, to skip.

gambe (gɑ̃b), s.f. [f. It. *gamba*] **1.** (naut.) (pl.) Shrouds; **2.** (mus.) *viole de ~*, viola da gamba.

gambette (gɑ̃bɛt), s.m. (ornith.) Red-shank, sandpiper.

gambiller (gɑ̃bije), v.n. [Provenç. *gambilha*] To frisk about, to kick about; to dance.

gambit (gɑ̃bi, gɑ̃bit), s.m. (chess) Gambit.

gamelle (gamɛl), s.f. [It. *gamella*] (mil.) Mess-tin; porringer, platter, bowl; *manger à la ~*, to mess with the rank and file; *camarade de ~*, mess mate.

gamin, -e (gamɛ̃), s.m.f. [etym. dub.] **1.** Mere boy or girl, youngster; **2.** street urchin, street arab, hoyden, brat, chit. ~, adj. Saucy.

gaminer (gamine), v.n. To romp about, to be hoydenish.

gaminerie (gaminri), s.f. Prank, antics, joke, boyish trick.

gamme (gam), s.f. [3rd Gr. letter, *gamma*] **1.** (mus.) Gamut, scale; **2.** range, scale, tone; *hors de ~*, in a fix; *changer de ~*, to alter one's tone, to lower one's pretensions; to come down a peg; *monter une ~ à X*, to blow up X, to rate X soundly.

gamopétale (gamopetal), adj. [f. Gr. *gamos*+Fr. *pétale*] (bot.) Gamopetalous.

ganache (ganaʃ), s.f. [It. *ganascia*] **1.** Lower jaw (of a horse); **2.** blockhead, old fogy; **3.** well padded chair.

gandin (gɑ̃dɛ̃), s.m. [f. *boulevard de Gand*, now *des Italiens*, in Paris] Swell, fop, dandy, nut.

ganga (gɑ̃ga), s.m. (ornith.) Sand-grouse.

ganglion (gɑ̃gliɔ̃), s.m. [Gr. *gagglion*] Ganglion.

ganglionnaire (gɑ̃gliɔnɛr), adj. Ganglionic, ganglionary.

gangrène (gɑ̃grɛn), s.f. [Gr. *gaggraina*] (pathol.) Gangrene, necrosis; (fig.) canker, corruption.

gangrener (gɑ̃grəne), v.a. To gangrene; **se** ~, v.pr. to become affected with gangrene; (fig.) to canker, to get corrupted.

gangréneu-x, -se (gɑ̃grenø), adj. Gangrenous, cankerous.

gangue (gɑ̃g), s.f. [Germ. *Gang*] Gangue, vein, vein-stone, matrix-ore.

ganse (gɑ̃s), s.f. [It. *gancio*] Cord, braid, twist, band, edging; loop (of diamonds).

ganser (gɑ̃se), v.a. To braid, to trim with silk cord or edging, &c.

gant (gɑ̃), s.m. [f. OHG *want*] Glove; gauntlet; ~ *bourré*, boxing or fencing glove; *souple comme un ~*, easily managed; as pliant as a wand; *cela me va comme un ~*, that suits me to a T; *se donner les ~s de*, to claim the credit of; *elle ne prend pas de ~s pour lui parler*, she handles him without gloves; *je n'ai pas pris de ~s pour lui dire*, I told him point-blank; *jeter le ~*, to throw down the gauntlet; to challenge; *relever le ~*, to take up the challenge.

gantelée (gɑ̃tle), s.f. (bot.) Foxglove, columbine, throatwort; syn. GANT DE NOTRE DAME, DIGITALE.

gantelet (gɑ̃tlɛ), s.m. Gauntlet.

ganter (gɑ̃te), v.a. To glove, to put gloves on; (fig.) to fit, to suit to a T; ~ *du sept*, to take sevens in gloves; **se** ~, v.pr. to put on one's gloves; to get one's gloves (*chez*, at).

ganterie (gɑ̃tri), s.f. Glove-making; glove-trade; glove-shop.

ganti-er, -ère (gɑ̃tje), s.m.f. Glover.

garage (garaʒ), s.m. [f. *garer*] **1.** Garage; **2.** shunting into the siding; siding; putting into wet dock; *voie de ~*, siding.

garagiste (garaʒist), s.m.f. Owner of a garage.

garance (garɑ̃s), s.f. [LL *varantia*] Madder, madder-root, garance; madder red, garancin.

garancière (garɑ̃sjɛr), s.f. **1.** Madder-ground; **2.** madder-dying establishment.

garant, -e (garɑ̃), s.m.f. [OHG *werento*, OF *guarant*] **1.** Voucher; *être, se porter ~*, to vouch for, to be answerable for, to be surety for; **2.** (law) guarantee, warrantor, surety; **3.** authority, pledge, proof; *ceci est vrai, j'ai eu de bons ~s*, this is true, I have it on good authority.

garantie (garɑ̃ti), s.f. **1.** Guarantee; warranty; warrant; *sans ~*, unwarranted; *sous la ~ de*, guaranteed by; ~ *de droit*, implied warranty; *sans ~ du gouvernement* (abbrev. S.G.D.G.), the government does not guarantee the patent; **2.** security, pledge; *quelles ~s?*, what security?; *je veux de bonnes ~s*, I must have good security; *donner des ~s à X contre Z*, to secure X against Z.

garantir (garɑ̃tir), v.a. **1.** To guarantee; to warrant; to vouch for; to secure; to answer for; *garanti deux ans*, warranted for two years; *cela, je vous le garantis*, as to that, I'll vouch for it, or answer for it; **2.** to certify, to attest, to assure, to declare; **3.** to keep, to protect, to safeguard, to shield, to screen, to shelter; ~ *du froid*, to keep warm; ~ *contre le malheur*, to shield against misfortune; ~ *contre le feu*, to protect against fire; *se ~ contre*, to guard, shield oneself against; to avoid.

garbure (garbyr), s.f. [local wd, SW. of France] (cook.) Soup of cabbage, bacon, goose-meat, &c.

garce (gars), s.f. [fem. of *gars, garçon*] (a very offensive term) Strumpet, wretch, hussy, trollop; wench.

garcette (garsɛt), s.f. [Span. *garceta*] (naut.) Gasket, cat-o'-nine-tails, rope's end; *~ de ris*, reef-point.

garçon (garsɔ̃), s.m. [LL *garcio*, OF *guerchon, gaçon*] **1.** Boy, lad; stripling, youth, young man; **2.** bachelor, single man; *vivre en ~*, to live single, to carry on as if unmarried; **3.** fellow, man; *beau ~*, fine fellow, handsome man; *joli ~*, (often pej.) good-looking fellow; *brave ~*, good fellow, honest lad; *être, se faire petit ~*, to be, to make oneself, very small; *~ d'honneur*, best man; *faire le mauvais ~*, to bluster; **4.** waiter, assistant, shop-boy, groom, messenger, servant; *premier ~*, foreman; *~ de ferme*, farm-hand; *~ de café, de salle*, waiter.

garçonne (garsɔn), s.f. [neol.] (pej.) Boyish, mannish, easy-mannered woman.

garçonnet (garsɔnɛ), s.m. Little boy, youngster.

garçonnie-r, -ère (garsɔnje), adj. Hoydenish, mannish, boyish; *elle a des allures ~ères*, (*a*) she is a regular tomboy; (*b*) she has mannish, free ways. **~ère**, s.f. Bachelor's apartments or rooms.

gardable (gardabl), adj. That keeps; easy to keep.

garde[1] (gard), s.f. [f. *garder*] **1.** Guard, keeping; defence; protection; *avoir la ~ de*, to have the keeping of (a house, a library, a collection, &c.); to be entrusted with the care of (a child, an invalid, &c.); *confier à la ~ de*, to entrust to; *à la ~ de Dieu*, in God's keeping; (fam.) happen what may!; **2.** watch, state of vigilance, attention, caution, care, heed; *prenez ~!*, look out!, mind!; *prenez ~ de tomber*, take care not to fall; *prenez ~ aux voleurs!*, beware of pickpockets; *prendre ~ à*, to notice, to beware of; *prendre ~ que*, to remember, to note; to contrive or to mind not to; *prenez ~ que vous êtes étroitement surveillé*, remember you are closely watched; *prenez ~ qu'on ne vous surveille, voie, entende*, take care not to be watched, seen, heard; *se donner ~ de*, to beware of, to take care not to; *il n'a ~ d'écrire en français*, no fear of his writing in French; he cannot write in French; *n'avoir ~ de*, to be far from; to be careful not to; to be too wise, prudent, clever to; to have no wish to, to be unable to; *être de ~*, to be on guard; *faire bonne, mauvaise, ~*, to keep good, bad, watch; *se tenir sur ses ~s*, to be on the watch; *chien de ~*, watch-dog; **3.** police, watch, duty, (mil.) guard; *~ à vous!*, attention!; *en ~!*, guard!; *monter la ~*, to mount guard; *descendre la ~*, to come off guard, to be relieved; *être de ~*, to be on guard, on duty; *avant-~*, vanguard; *arrière-~*, rearguard; *~ bourgeoise, nationale*, militia; *corps-de-~*, guard-house, guard-room; *~ de police*, barrack-guard, *~ à pied, à cheval*, foot-guards, horse-guards; **4.** wardress, sick-nurse, nurse; **5.** hilt; *jusqu'à la ~*, up to the hilt; (fig.) *s'en donner jusqu'à la ~*, to take one's fill of it; to go the whole hog; **6.** (bookbind.) fly-leaf; **7.** (pl.) wards (of a lock).

garde[2] (gard), s.m. **1.** Warden, guardian, keeper, watchman, attendant; guardsman, guard; (In compounds *garde*, when it applies to a man or woman, takes an *s* in the plural; ex.: *des gardes-chiourmes, des gardes-malades*. In other compounds *garde* is a verb. stem and is invar.; ex.: *des garde-fous, des garde-meubles*.) *~ champêtre*, s.m. rural constable; *~ du corps*, s.m., see CORPS; *~-barrière*, s.m.f. crossing-keeper, gate-keeper; *~-boue*, s.m. mudguard; splash-board; *~-cendres*, s.m. fender; *~-chasse*, s.m. game-keeper; *~-corps*, s.m. hand-rail; rail; *~-côte*, s.m. coast-guard; coast-guard ship; *~-crotte*, s.m. splash-board; *~-feu*, s.m. fire-guard; *~-fou*, s.m. parapet, hand-rail; *~-frein*, s.m. brakesman; *~-magasin*, s.m. warehouse-keeper; *~ malade*, s.f.m. sick-nurse, attendant; *~-manger*, s.m. meat-safe; *~-meuble*, s.m. storehouse, repository, lumber-room; *~-pêche*, s.m. river-keeper, water-bailiff; *~-robe*, s.f. (*a*) wardrobe; (*b*) water closet; (*c*) dejection, stool, faecal matter; *~-chiourme*, s.m. warder; *~-vue*, s.m. shade; *Garde des Sceaux*, s.m. Minister of Justice; (in England) Lord Chancellor.

gardénia (gardenja), s.m. (bot.) Gardenia.

garder (garde), v.a. [OHG *wardon*] To keep; to take care of, to preserve; to attend, to attend to, to look after, to heed; to watch; *ayez l'obligeance de ~ ma place*, kindly keep my seat; *elle le garde la nuit*, she sits up with him at night; to keep, to guard, to protect, to defend; to maintain, to preserve, to withhold, to retain, to hold, to uphold; *Dieu m'en garde!*, God forbid!; *~ à vue*, to keep a strict watch on; *~ les vaches, les moutons*, to tend cows, sheep; *nous n'avons pas gardé les cochons ensemble, n'est-ce pas?*, please don't be so familiar; *~ les bienséances*, to observe etiquette; *gardez-vous de faire cela*, mind you don't do that; *gardez cela pour vous*, don't tell; mum's the word; *il s'en gardera bien*, he will know better than to do that; *~ ran-*

cune à X, to bear X a grudge; ~ *le lit, la chambre*, to keep one's bed, one's room; ~ *une poire pour la soif*, see POIRE; ~ *sa poudre sèche*, see POUDRE; ~ *rancune*, to bear, to owe, a grudge; *je la garde bonne à X*, I have a rod in pickle for X; *je lui garde une dent; je lui garde un chien de ma chienne*, I owe him a grudge; *en donner à* ~ *à X*, to impose upon X, to get X to hold the dog; *il vous en donne à* ~, he takes you for a fool; **se** ~, v.pr. to keep; to keep or be kept on; to guard (against), to beware; *se* ~ *de*, to take care not to; to beware, to forbear, to avoid, to abstain from, to keep from; *cela se garde-t-il bien?*, does it keep?; *gardez-vous en bien*, mind you don't do that; don't you do that; do nothing of the kind; *je m'en garderai bien*, I will take good care not to do that; *gardez-vous des systèmes*, avoid systematization.

garderie (gardəri), s.f. Infant's school; syn. CRÈCHE.

gardeu-r, -se (gardœr), s.m.f. Keeper, herd.

gardien, -ne (gardjɛ̃), s.m.f. adj. Guardian, warden, keeper; warder, wardress; caretaker; door-keeper; watchman; ~ *judiciaire*, bailiff's man; ~ *de la paix*, (Paris) policeman, constable; *ange* ~, guardian angel.

gardiennage (gardjɛnaʒ), s.m. Guardianship; wardenship, keepership; keeping, caretaking.

gardon (gardɔ̃), s.m. [LL *gardio*] (ichth.) Ide, roach; *frais comme un* ~, as fit as can be, as sound as a roach.

gare (gar), s.f. [f. *garer*] Station; depot; *chef de* ~, station-master; ~ *des marchandises*, goods station; (of rivers, canals, &c.) siding-station, basin; (slang) *à la* ~*!*, away with you!, out you go!, enough of that!

gare! (gar), interj. Look out!, make way!, take care!, out of the way there!, mind!; ~ *à votre tête*, mind your head!; *sans crier* ~, without warning; without the slightest warning.

garenne (garɛn), s.f. [OF *warrenne*] Warren; *lapin de* ~, wild rabbit; *comme lapins en* ~, like rabbits in a warren.

garer (gare), v.a. [OHG *waron*] (rail.) To shunt; to put under shelter; to put out of the way; (naut.) to dock; (motor.) to garage, to park; **se** ~, v.pr. to move out of the way, to shield (*contre*, against).

gargantua (gargɑ̃tɥa), s.m. [f. prop. n. in Rabelais] Gargantua, glutton, enormous eater.

(se) gargariser (səgargarize), v.pr. [Gr. *gargarizein*] To gargle; (fig.) *se* ~ *de*, to relish (words, sounds, praise, &c.), to delight in.

gargarisme (gargarism), s.m. Gargle, gargling; the liquid used for this.

gargote (gargɔt), s.f. Cheap eating-house; cook-shop; (pej.) wretched restaurant.

gargoter (gargɔte), v.n.a. (rare) [OF *gargate* = throat] **1.** To eat in low cook-shops; **2.** to cook slovenly, wretchedly.

gargoti-er, -ère (gargɔtje), s.m.f. Cook-shop keeper; wretched cook.

gargouillade (gargujad), s.f. **1.** (singing) Vulgar quivering or warbling; **2.** old dance.

gargouille (garguj), s.f. [LL *gargulia*] Gargoyle, water-spout.

gargouillement, gargouillis (gargujmɑ̃, garguji), s.m. **1.** Gurgling; **2.** rumbling (in the stomach, (colloq.) collywobbles.

gargouiller (garguje), v.n. **1.** To gurgle; **2.** to rumble; **3.** to paddle.

gargoulette (gargulɛt), s.f. Porous water-jug.

gargouillis (garguji), s.m. See GARGOUILLEMENT.

gargousse (gargus), s.f. [corrupt. of *cartouche*] Cartridge, cannon cartridge.

garigue, garrigue (garig), s.f. [Provenç. wd] Waste land.

garnement (garnəmɑ̃), s.m. Scapegrace, scamp, good-for-nothing; *mauvais* ~, dangerous vagabond, bad boy.

garni (garni), s.m. [f. *garnir*] Furnished lodgings; lodging-house; *vivre en* ~, to live in furnished lodgings; *louer en* ~, to let lodgings. ~, adj. and pp. Filled, trimmed, garnished, furnished, provided; *avoir la bourse bien* ~*e*, to have one's purse well lined; *bifteck* ~, beefsteak with potatoes (or water-cress).

garnir (garnir), v.a. [OHG *warnjan*] **1.** To furnish, to provide, to stock, to store, to fit up, to fit out; ~ *une chambre*, to furnish a room; ~ *une bibliothèque*, to stock a library; ~ *un nécessaire*, to fit up a work-box; **2.** to adorn, to decorate, to trim, to line, to fur, to mount (with diamonds, &c); (cook., &c.) to garnish; **3.** to fill, to cover; *salle bien* ~*e*, well-filled house (room); **se** ~, v.pr. to furnish oneself (with); to fill, to be filling; (theatr.) *la salle se garnit*, the house is filling; *ceci se garnit de*, this is meant to be lined (or trimmed) with.

garnisaire (garnizɛr), s.m. [f. *garnison*] (mil.) **1.** Garrisoned soldier; **2.** bailiff's man.

garnison (garnizɔ̃), s.f. Garrison; *troupes en* ~, garrisoned troops; *ville de* ~, garrison town.

garnissage (garnisaʒ), s.m. Trimming; garnishing; padding.

garnisseu-r, -se (garnisœr), s.m.f. Trimmer.

garniture (garnityr), s.f. [f. *garnir*] **1.** Fittings, requisites, appointments; **2.** ornaments, trimming, lining, garnishing;

mounting, setting; ~ *de cheminée*, set of chimney ornaments; ~ *de toilette*, toilet-set, toilet-ware; ~ *de foyer*, set of fire-irons; **3.** (cook.) garnish, dressing; **4.** (naut.) rigging.

garou (garu), s.m. (bot.) Spurge-flax, garou-bush; (pharm.) garou bark; *loup-~*, werewolf; (fig.) regular bear.

garousse, jarrousse (garus, ʒarus), s.f. (bot.) Lentil of Spain.

garrigue (garig), s.f. See GARIGUE.

garrot (garo), s.m. [etym. dub.] **1.** Tightener, packing-stick; **2.** (vet.) withers; *blessé au ~*, wither-galled.

garrotte (garɔt), s.f. [Span. *garrote*] Garotte, strangulation.

garrotter (garɔte), v.a. [f. *garrot*] To bind down, to tie down, to pinion, to handcuff; to garotte.

garrulité (garylite), s.f. [f. L *garrire*] Garrulity.

gars, gas (gɑ), s.m. Lad, boy, chap, stripling; *un mauvais, un bon ~*, a bad, a good fellow.

gascon, -ne (gaskɔ̃), adj. s.m.f. Gascon, of Gascony; (fig.) boaster, braggart.

gasconnade (gaskɔnad), s.f. Brag, boast, gasconade.

gasconner (gaskɔne), v.n. To brag, to boast; to speak with a Gascon accent.

gaspillage (gaspijaʒ), s.m. [f. *gaspiller*] Waste, squandering.

gaspiller (gaspije), v.a. [etym. dub.] To waste, to squander away, to spoil.

gaspilleu-r, -se (gaspijœr), adj. Wasting. ~, s.m.f. Squanderer, spendthrift, waster.

gastéropode (gasterɔpɔd), s.m. [f. Gr. *gastēr*+*pous, podos*] (zool.) Gast(e)ropod.

gastralgie (gastralʒi), s.f. [f. Gr. *gastēr*+ *algos*] Gastralgia.

gastrique (gastrik), adj. Gastric.

gastrite (gastrit), s.f. (pathol.) Gastritis.

gastronome (gastrɔnɔm), s.m.f. Epicure, gastronome, good liver.

gastronomie (gastrɔnɔmi), s.f. Gastronomy.

gastronomique (gastrɔnɔmik), adj. Gastronomic, gastronomical.

gat, ghât (gɑ), s.m. [Hindi *ghāt*] Landing-steps, steps cut in rocky slope, ghaut.

gâte (gɑt), [f. *gâter*] In compounds: spoiler; *~-cuir*, s.m. cobbler; *~-métier*, s.m. underseller, blackleg, rat; *~-papier*, s.m. scribbler; *~-sauce*, s.m. scullion, bad cook; *~-tout*, s.m. mar-all.

gâté, -e (gɑte), p. adj. Damaged, tainted; spoilt; decayed, gone bad; *un enfant ~*, a spoilt child; *de la viande ~e*, tainted meat.

gâteau (pl. **-x**) (gɑto), s.m. Cake; (fig.) profit, booty; *avoir part au ~*, to share in the booty; *se partager le ~*, to divide the spoil; *~ des Rois*, Twelfth-night cake; *~ de miel*, honeycomb; *un papa-~*, a father who spoils his child.

gâter (gɑte), v.a. [L *vastare*] **1.** To waste, to spoil, to injure, to impair, to damage, to hurt, to deteriorate, to mar, to deform, to disfigure, to harm; *enfant gâté*, spoilt child; *fruit gâté*, rotten fruit; *ce qui ne gâte rien*, which is all the better; *se ~ la main*, to spoil one's workmanship (by doing inferior work); *vue gâtée*, impaired eyesight; **2.** to taint, to soil; to corrupt, to deprave, to foul; *la chaleur gâte la viande*, heat taints meat; **3.** to waste, to use prodigally; *vous gâtez trop de plâtre*, you are wasting plaster; *~ du papier*, to scribble; *il a gâté son affaire*, he has spoilt his chances; **se ~**, v.pr. to go wrong, to decay, to go bad, to break, to get tainted; *ses affaires se gâtent*, his business is going wrong; (in a discussion) *çà va se ~*, this is getting pretty hot; they will come to blows; *le temps se gâte*, the weather is breaking up; syn. GASPILLER, GÂCHER, ABÎMER, DÉTÉRIORER, CORROMPRE.

gâterie (gɑtri), s.f. Spoiling, over-petting; foolish indulgence; pleasure given, gift, attention paid.

gâteu-x, -se (gɑtø), adj. Decrepit; helpless and unclean. ~, s.m.f. Dotard, old fool, idiot.

gâtine (gɑtin), s.f. Waste land, swampy ground, especially in Vendée.

gâtisme (gɑtism), s.m. Dotage, idiocy, feeble-mindedness (espec. from old age).

gatte (gat), s.f. (naut.) Manger.

gattilier (gatilje), s.m. (bot.) Agnus castus.

gauche (goʃ), adj. [f. *gauchir*] **1.** Left; *à ~!*, left!; *tournez à ~*, turn left; *tenez votre ~*, keep to your left (when driving); *mariage de la main ~*, illegal union; left-handed marriage; **2.** crooked, ill-shaped; awkward, clownish, clumsy, gawky, uncouth, ungainly; *à l'air ~*, awkward-looking; gawky; *manières ~s*, clumsy, uncouth manners; (Lit.) *une tournure ~*, a clumsy expression; (fig.) on the wrong side; (colloq.) *passer l'arme à ~*, to die, to kick the bucket.

gauche (goʃ), s.f. Left side; left hand; (mil.) left wing; (polit.) radical benches; *extrême ~*, most 'advanced' parties; *jusqu'à la ~*, up to the hilt; to the bitter end; to the finish; (slang) *ton copain jusqu'à la ~!*, yours to a cinder.

gauchement (goʃmɑ̃), adv. Clumsily, awkwardly.

gauch-er, -ère (goʃe), adj. Left-handed. ~, s.m.f. Left-handed person.

gaucherie (goʃri), s.f. **1.** Awkwardness, clumsiness; **2.** blunder, bungle.

gauchir (goʃir), v.a.n. [OHG *wenkjan*] To warp, to put out of shape; to dodge, to turn aside, to shuffle; **se ~**, v.pr. to warp, to get out of shape.

gauchissement (goʃismɑ̃), s.m. Warping.
gaude (god), s.f. [OHG *walda*] **1.** (bot.) Dyer's weed; weld; **2.** hominy; maize hasty-pudding.
(se) gaudir (səgodir), v.pr. [L *gaudere*] To rejoice, to make merry; *se ~ de X*, to make game of X, to deride X.
gaudissart (godisar), s.m. [f. prop. n. in Balzac] Bagman, wag.
gaudriole (godrijɔl), s.f. [f. *gaudir*] Broad jest, licentious humour.
gaufrage (gofraʒ), s.m. Goffering, crimping, fluting.
gaufre (gofr), s.f. [f. Dutch *wafel*] **1.** Waffle, wafer; **2.** honeycomb; **3.** (slang) *être la ~ d'une affaire*, to be the dupe, the fool, in a transaction; **4.** (slang) *se sucrer la ~*, to powder one's face.
gaufrer (gofre), v.a. To goffer, to crimp, to emboss; *fer à ~*, goffering-iron.
gaufrette (gofrɛt), s.f. Small wafer, sugar wafer.
gaufreu-r, -se (gofrœr), s.m.f. Gofferer, crimper.
gaufrier (gofrie), s.m. Waffle-iron.
gaufroir (gofrwar), s.m. Goffering-iron.
gaufrure (gofryr), s.f. Embossing, goffering.
gaulage (golaʒ), s.m. Beating (of trees); knocking down (of fruit).
gaule (gol), s.f. [etym. dub.; Goth. *walus*?] Pole, long pole; rod, fishing-rod; switch.
gauler (gole), v.a. To beat (trees); to knock down (fruit, nuts, &c.) with a pole.
gaulois, -e (golwɑ), adj. [f. *Gaule*] **1.** Gallic, Gaulish; **2.** free, rather coarse, frank; *plaisanterie ~e*, broad joke, Rabelaisian story. **~, -e**, s.m.f. Gaul; *à la ~e*, in the old French fashion.
gauloiserie (golwazri), s.f. Broad joke, rather coarse witty saying.
gaupe (gop), s.f. (pop.) Slut, trollop, drab.
gauss (gos), s.m. [f. *K. M. Gauss*, German mathematician, 1777–1855] Gauss, a unit of intensity of a magnetic field.
(se) gausser (səgose), v.pr. To jeer, to banter; *se ~ de X*, to deride X, to make game of X, to scoff derisively at X; syn. *faire des gorges chaudes de X*.
gavage (gavaʒ), s.m. (lit. and fig.) Cramming.
gave (gav), s.m. (in the Pyrenees) Torrent, river.
gaver (gave), v.a. (lit. and fig.) To cram; **se ~**, v.pr. to cram or stuff oneself (*de*, with); to gorge.
gavial (pl. **-s**) (gavjal), s.m. (zool.) Gavial, gharrial.
gaviot (gavjo), s.m. (pop.) Throat.
gavotte (gavɔt), s.f. [Provenç. wd] Gavotte (dance and tune).
gavroche (gavrɔʃ), s.m. [f. prop. n. in Victor Hugo] (Paris) street arab, urchin, saucy, witty boy.
gayal (pl. **-s**) (gajal), s.m. (zool.) Gayal.
gaz (gɑz), s.m. [word invented by Van Helmont (1578–1644) from Gr. *khaos*] **1.** Gas; **2.** coal-gas; gas-light; gas company; *bec de ~*, gas-burner, gas-light, gas-lamp; *tuyau à ~*, gas-pipe; *compteur à ~*, gas-meter; *fourneau à ~*, gas-ring, gas-stove; *fuite de ~*, escape of gas; *usine à ~*, gas-works; *fermer le ~*, to turn off the gas; *ouvrir le ~*, to turn on the gas; **3.** (med.) flatus, wind; **4.** (motor.) gas, petrol; *mettre les ~*, to step on the gas; *masque à ~*, gas-mask, gas-helmet.
gaze (gɑz), s.f. [f. *Gaza* in Syria] Gauze.
gazé, -e (gɑze), p. adj. **1.** Softened, toned down, veiled; **2.** gassed, affected with gas-poisoning.
gazéifier (gɑzeifje), v.a. To gasify, to convert into gas.
gazelle (gazɛl), s.f. [Arab. *ghazāl*] (zool.) Gazelle, small antelope.
gazer (gɑze), v.a.n. **1.** To veil, to tone down, to gloss over, to soften down (an expression, a tale); **2.** (pop.) to go full steam ahead, to make things rip; *ça va ~*, (*a*) there's going to be trouble; look out for squalls!; (*b*) (motor.) let's step on the gas!; **3.** (chiefly in the p.p.) to gas, to poison with gas. ⚠ *Gazer* has never the sense of 'to gas' = to talk emptily, boastfully and abundantly, which = *débagouler*.
gazeti-er, -ère (gaztje), s.m.f. (obs.) Gazetteer, newsmonger.
gazette (gazɛt), s.f. [It. *gazetta*] Gazette, newspaper, news-sheet; (by ext.) newsmonger.
gazeu-x, -se (gɑzø), adj. Gaseous; aerated, effervescent; *eau ~se*, soda-water, soda.
gazier (gɑzje), s.m. Gas-fitter; **~, -ère**, s.m.f. gauze-maker.
gazogène (gazoʒɛn), s.m. Gazogene. **~**, adj. Effervescent.
gazolène, gazoléine, gazoline (gazɔlɛn, gazɔlein, gazolin), s.f. Gasolene.
gazomètre (gazɔmɛtr), s.m. Gasometer.
gazon (gɑzɔ̃), s.m. [OHG *waso*] Grass, short grass; sward, sod, turf; lawn, green-sward, grass-plot; *~ d'Angleterre*, cat's-tail grass; ladies' cushion; *~ d'Espagne*, thrift; *ne marchez pas sur le ~*, keep off the grass.
gazonnant, -e (gɑzɔnɑ̃), p. adj. Turfy, giving the effect of a lawn.
gazonner (gɑzone), v.a. To turf, to lay with turf.
gazonneu-x, -se (gɑzɔnø), adj. Turfy.
gazouillant, -e (gazujɑ̃), adj. Warbling, chirping, prattling.
gazouillement (gazujmɑ̃), s.m. **1.** Warbling, twittering, chirping; **2.** purling,

murmur, babbling, babble, prattle, lisping; syn. GAZOUILLIS.

gazouiller (gazuje), v.n.a. [OF *gaser* = *jaser*] **1.** To warble, to chirp, to chirrup, to twitter; **2.** to purl, to murmur, to babble, to prattle, to lisp.

gazouillis (gazuji), s.m. See GAZOUILLEMENT.

geai (ʒe, ʒɛ), s.m. [etym. dub.] (ornith.) Jay; *le ~ paré des plumes du paon*, the daw in peacock's feathers.

géant, -e (ʒeɑ̃), s.m.f. [f. Gr. *gigas, gigantos*] Giant, (fem.) giantess, colossus; *à pas de ~*, with giant strides. ~, adj. Gigantic, giantlike.

gecko (ʒeko), s.m. (zool.) Gecko.

géhenne (ʒeɛn), s.f. [Hebr. *gēhinnōm*] Gehenna, hell; (fig.) torture, torment, misery.

geignant, -e, geignard, -e (ʒɛɲɑ̃, ʒɛɲar), adj. Whining, complaining, moaning. ~, s.m.f. Whiner, grouser, croaker.

geignement (ʒɛɲmɑ̃), s.m. Moan, moaning, whine.

geindre (ʒɛ̃dr), v.n. [L *gemere*] To moan, to whine; to complain, to grouse.

geindre (ʒɛ̃dr), s.m. See GINDRE.

gel (ʒɛl), s.m. Frost, freezing; syn. GELÉE.

gélatine (ʒelatin), s.f. [f. L *gelatus*] Gelatine.

gélatineu-x, -se (ʒelatinø), adj. Gelatinous.

gelée (ʒəle), s.f. [f. *geler*] **1.** Frost; *forte ~*, hard frost; *~ blanche*, hoar-frost, white frost; **2.** (cook.) jelly.

geler (ʒəle), v.n.a. [L *gelare*] To freeze; to congeal; to get frost-bitten; to feel bitterly cold; *il gèle à pierre fendre*, it is freezing very hard; *gelé*, frost-bitten, frozen; ice-cold.

géli-f, -ve (ʒelif), adj. [f. *geler*] **1.** Freezable, damageable through frost; *pierre ~ve*, building-stone not frost-proof; **2.** frost-cleft.

géline (ʒelin), s.f. [L *gallina*] Hen; syn. POULE.

gélinotte (ʒelinɔt), s.f. [f. L *gallina*] (ornith.) **1.** Hazel grouse; **2.** (rare) fattened pullet.

gélivure (ʒelivyr), s.f. Crack caused by frost.

gémeaux (ʒemo), s.m.pl. [L *gemelli*] (astr.) The Twins; Gemini.

géminé, -e (ʒemine), adj. [f. L. *geminare*] Geminate, double; *colonnes ~es*, geminate columns; (law) reiterated.

gémir (ʒemir), v.n. [L *gemere*] To groan, to moan, to whine, to bewail, to complain, to lament, to bemoan, to repine; *faire ~ la presse*, to print away; to keep the press going; *les gonds gémissaient*, the hinges creaked.

gémissant, -e (ʒemisɑ̃), p. adj. Groaning, moaning, complaining, lamenting.

gémissement (ʒemismɑ̃), s.m. Groan, moan, groaning, moaning; (fig.) wail, complaint, lament; (pej.) whine, whining, bewailing.

gemmage (ʒemmaʒ), s.m. Incising pine-trees to get resin.

gemmation (ʒɛmma'sjɔ̃), s.f. [f. L *gemma*] Budding, gemmation.

gemme (ʒɛm), s.f. [L *gemma*] Gem, precious stone; syn. PIERRE PRÉCIEUSE; ~, adj. *sel ~*, rock-salt.

gemmé, -e (ʒemme), p. adj. Adorned with gems; gemmate.

gemmer (ʒɛmme), v.a.n. **1.** To incise (pine-trees to get rosin); **2.** to gemmate, to put forth buds; **3.** to adorn with gems.

gemmule (ʒɛmmyl), s.f. (bot.) Gemmule.

gémonies (ʒemɔni), s.f.pl. [L *gemoniae*] (Rom. ant.) Gemoniae; (fig.) pillory; *vouer aux ~*, to curse, to pillory, to doom to misery.

génal, -e, (aux) (ʒenal), adj. [f. L *gena*] (anat.) Of the cheek, pertaining to the cheek.

gênant, -e (ʒɛnɑ̃), p. adj. Troublesome, in the way, inconvenient, embarrassing, awkward, annoying, irksome.

gencive (ʒɑ̃siv), s.f. [L *gingiva*] Gum (of the teeth).

gendarme (ʒɑ̃darm), s.m. [*gens-d'armes*] **1.** Gendarme (*not* policeman); (obs.) man-at-arms; guardsman; *dormir en ~*, to sleep with one eye open; *sommeil de ~*, cat-nap; **2.** bear, Turk, surly fellow; **3.** (fig.) virago, termagant; **4.** flaw, spot (in diamonds); **5.** spark (of fire); **6.** red herring.

(se) gendarmer (səʒɑ̃darme), v.pr. To make a violent protest; to kick (*contre*, against), to fire up; to resist.

gendarmerie (ʒɑ̃darməri), s.f. **1.** Gendarmerie (rural police or constabulary, mounted or on foot); **2.** the body of French gendarmes; **3.** station or barracks for gendarmes.

gendre (ʒɑ̃dr), s.m. [L *gener*] Son-in-law.

gêne (ʒɛn), s.f. [f. OF *gehir*] **1.** Inconvenience; trouble; uncomfortableness; discomfort; difficulty; embarrassment; **2.** constraint, restraint, uneasiness; *sans ~*, free and easy, cool, impudent, off-handed, unceremonious, at home; (iron.) *où il y a de la ~, il n'y a pas de plaisir*, nothing like making oneself at home!; **3.** need, penury, scarcity, want, straitened circumstances; straits; *être dans la ~*, to be hard-up; **4.** (slightly archaic) rack, torture; *être à la ~*, to be on the rack; *se mettre l'esprit à la ~*, to rack one's brains.

gêné, -e (ʒɛne), p. adj. [f. *gêner*] Inconvenienced, uneasy, constrained; stiff, self-conscious, embarrassed; *avoir un air ~*, to have a constrained look; short

of cash; *n'être pas* ~, to know how to make oneself at home; *on se sent* ~, one does not feel at ease; *qui est* ~ *est gênant*, a man ill at ease makes others uneasy.
généalogie (ʒenealɔʒi), s.f. [f. Gr. *genea*+*logos*] Genealogy, pedigree.
généalogique (ʒenealɔʒik), adj. Genealogical; *arbre* ~, genealogical or family tree.
généalogiste (ʒenealɔʒist), s.m.f. Genealogist.
génépi (ʒenepi), s.m. (bot.) Alpine mugwort.
gêner (ʒɛne), v.a. [f. *gêne*] To inconvenience, to disturb, to trouble, to embarrass, to be in the way of, to make uneasy or uncomfortable; *si cela ne vous gêne pas*, if that does not inconvenience you; *ses souliers le gênaient*, his shoes were too tight, or pinched him; to constrain, to restrain, to cramp; to obstruct, to hinder, to impede; (obs.) to torture, to rack; **se** ~, v.pr. to inconvenience (or trouble, or disturb, &c.) oneself or each other, to squeeze oneself; to put oneself out; to pinch or stint oneself; (often iron.) *ne vous gênez pas!*, make yourself quite at home!, don't mind me!; *c'est un homme qui ne se gêne guère*, or *pas*, he is a cool customer; he is apt to take liberties.
général, -e, (aux) (ʒeneral), adj. [L *generalis*] General. ~, s.m. General; ~ *de brigade*, brigadier-general; ~ *de division*, lieutenant general, major-general; ~*e*, s.f. 1. general's wife; 2. (mil.) drum-beat; *battre la* ~*e*, to beat to arms. *en* ~, adv. Generally, usually; mainly, on the whole, for the most part, in a general sense, in general.
généralat (ʒenerala), s.m. Generalship (office of general, not strategy).
généralement (ʒeneralmɑ̃), adv. Generally, usually, in general, in a general sense; ~ *admis*, current.
généralisable (ʒeneralizabl), adj. Generalizable.
généralisat-eur, -rice (ʒeneralizatœr), adj. Generalizing.
généralisation (ʒeneraliza'sjɔ̃), s.f. Generalization.
généraliser (ʒeneralize), v.a.n. To generalize; **se** ~, v.pr. to become widespread.
généralissime (ʒeneralisim), s.m. Generalissimo.
généralité (ʒeneralite), s.f. Generality.
générat-eur, -rice (ʒeneratœr), adj. Generating, generative. ~, s.m. Generator, begetter; generator, apparatus for producing gases, steam, electricity, &c.
génération (ʒenera'sjɔ̃), s.f. [L *generatio*] Generation, procreation; generation, single step in descent or pedigree.
généreusement (ʒenerøzmɑ̃), adv. Generously, nobly; bountifully, abundantly, plentifully; gallantly, courageously.
généreu-x, -se (ʒenerø), adj. [L *generosus*] Generous, noble; bountiful, generous, abundant, plentiful, fertile, liberal; courageous; *un don* ~, a handsome gift; *un oncle* ~, a generous uncle; *un sol* ~, fertile soil, a rich or fruitful country; *être d'un sang* ~, to be well born, to have a noble and impetuous nature, to have innate courage or gallantry.
générique (ʒenerik), adj. [f. L *genus, generis*] Generic.
générosité (ʒenerozite), s.f. Generosity, magnanimity, bounteousness, liberality; nobility of temper; act of generosity, gift; *être en veine de* ~, to be lavishly disposed.
genèse (ʒənɛz), s.f. [Gr. *genesis*] Genesis; origination.
génésiaque (ʒenezjak), adj. Genetic, pertaining to genesis or the book of Genesis.
génésique (ʒenezik), adj. Genetic, pertaining to generation or procreation.
genestrolle (ʒənɛstrɔl) s.f. (bot.) Dyer's greenweed, dyer's broom.
genet (ʒənɛ), s.m. [Span. *jinete*] Jennet; Spanish horse. ⚠ Not 'genet', which = *civette, belette, genette (fourrure)*.
genêt (ʒənɛ), s.m. [L *genista*] (bot.) Broom; ~ *anglais*, needle-furze.
genette (ʒənɛt), s.f. [Span. *gineta*] 1. (zool.) Genet, civet-cat; 2. Turkish bit, ring curb; *aller à la* ~, to ride with short stirrups.
gêneu-r, -se (ʒɛnœr), s.m.f. Intruder, bore, kill-joy.
genevois, -e (ʒənəvwɑ), adj. s.m.f. Genevese, Genevan, of Geneva.
genévrier (ʒənevrie), s.m. (bot.) Juniper-tree, juniper.
génial, -e, (aux) (ʒenjal), adj. Having or denoting genius; highly original; wonderfully clever. ⚠ Not English 'genial', which = (*a*) *réjouissant, bienfaisant, réconfortant, jovial, sociable, d'heureuse disposition*; (*b*) (rare) *génésique, nuptial*.
génialement (ʒenjalmɑ̃), adv. In a way characterized by genius, in a wonderfully clever way. ⚠ Not 'genially', which = *jovialement, sociablement, de manière réjouissante*, &c.
géniculé, -e (ʒenikyle), adj. Geniculate, knee-shaped.
génie (ʒeni), s.m. [L *genius*] 1. Genius (pl. genii), tutelary spirit, sprite, goblin; *elle a été son mauvais* ~, she has been his evil genius; 2. genius (pl. geniuses), nature, character, bent, native disposition; *le* ~ *d'une langue*, the genius of a language; 3. genius (no pl.), exalted

intellectual power, wonderful ability, creative power; *une idée de ~*, a wonderful idea; **4.** engineering, (mil.) corps of engineers; *soldat du ~*, sapper (and miner).
genièvre (ʒənjɛvr), s.m. [L *juniperus*] **1.** Juniper; **2.** gin, geneva.
génisse (ʒenis), s.f. [L *junix*] Heifer, young cow.
génital, -e, (aux) (ʒenital), adj. Genital.
génitif (ʒenitif), s.m. [L *genitivus*] Genitive; *au ~*, in the genitive.
genou (pl. **-x**) (ʒənu), s.m. [L *geniculum*] Knee; *à ~x*, kneeling; down on one's knees; *se mettre à ~x*, to kneel down; *se mettre à ~x devant X*, to go down on one's knees to X; to throw oneself at X's feet; *mettre ~ en terre*, to bend the knee; (fig.) *je le ferai mettre à ~x*, I will bring him to his knees; *chauve comme un ~*, bald as a bladder, as a billiard-ball, or as a coot; *il était dans l'eau jusqu'au ~*, he was knee-deep in the water.
genouillère (ʒənujɛr), s.f. [f. *genou*] Knee-guard; knee-pad; knee-piece (of armour), knee-cap.
génovéfain (ʒenɔvefɛ̃), s.m. [f. L *genovefa*] Canon of the order of St. Geneviève.
genre (ʒɑ̃r), s.m. [L *genus, generis*] **1.** Genus, kind, species, sort, class, order, description; *le ~ humain*, mankind; style, manner, way, taste, fashion; *un ~ de vie*, a manner of life; *un grand homme dans son ~*, a great man in his way; *de mauvais ~*, bad form; *se donner un ~*, to give oneself airs; to pose; *grand ~*, pink of fashion; (pop.) *avoir du ~*, to have elegance, chic, style; *peinture de ~*, genre painting; *faire du ~*, to pose, to have high-falutin airs; **2.** (gram.) gender.
gens (ʒɑ̃), s.m.f. pl. [L *gens*] (When an adj. is placed before *gens*, it is in the fem., when placed after, it is masc.: ex. *des gens vertueux, les vieilles gens.*) **1.** People, folk, folks, persons, men, women; *vieilles ~*, old people, old folks; *sottes ~*, silly people; *petites ~*, common people; *~ du monde*, society people, fashionable people; *de braves ~*, good honest people; *des ~ braves*, courageous people; *~ de lettres*, men of letters, literati; *les honnêtes ~*, respectable people; *les jeunes ~*, young men; *~ d'affaires*, business men; *~ de robe*, men of the law, lawyers; *~ d'église*, clergy; *droit des ~*, law of nations; *il n'y a pas de sot métier, il n'y a que de sottes ~*, there is no stupid calling, only stupid people; **2.** servants, attendants, fellows; *sonner ses ~s*, to ring for one's servants.
gent (ʒɑ̃), s.f. [L *gens*] Race, tribe, people, nation; (poet.) *la ~ ailée*, the winged tribe; *la ~ trotte-menu*, rats and mice.
gent, -e (ʒɑ̃), adj. (obs.) [f. L *genitus*] Fair, pretty, sweet.
gentiane (ʒɑ̃sjan), s.f. [L *gentiana*] (bot.) Gentian.
gentil, -le (ʒɑ̃ti, fem. ʒɑ̃tij), adj. [L *gentilis*] Gentle, nice, pleasant, amiable, pretty, kind; agreeable; (colloq.) *vous voilà ~ !*, well, you are in a pretty pickle !; *faire le ~*, to affect pretty ways; to ingratiate oneself.
gentil (ʒɑ̃ti), s.m. (not used in the fem., but usually in the m. pl.) Gentile.
gentilhomme (ʒɑ̃tijɔm), s.m. (pl. *gentilshommes*) Nobleman, gentleman.
gentilhommerie (ʒɑ̃tijɔmri), s.f. Nobility; (pej.) small gentry, (slang) nobs.
gentilhommière (ʒɑ̃tijɔmjɛr), s.f. Small country seat, small manor.
gentillâtre (ʒɑ̃tijɑtr), s.m. Squireen, lordling.
gentillesse (ʒɑ̃tijɛs), s.f. Prettiness, gracefulness, amiability, kindness; pretty trick, pretty speech, polite act, kindness; (iron.) blarney, fine words; abuse.
gentillet, -te (ʒɑ̃tijɛ), adj. Prettyish.
gentiment (ʒɑ̃timɑ̃), adv. Gently, prettily, gracefully, amiably, kindly, pleasantly.
génuflexion (ʒenyflɛksjɔ̃), s.f. [f. L *genu+flectere*] Genuflexion, kneeling.
géocentrique (ʒeosɑ̃trik), adj. Geocentric.
géode (ʒeɔd), s.f. [f. Gr. *geōdēs*] (min.) Geode.
géodésie (ʒeɔdezi), s.f. [f. Gr. *gē+daiein*] Geodesy.
géodésique (ʒeɔdezik), adj. Geodesic, geodetic, geodetical.
géographe (ʒeɔgraf), s.m.f. Geographer.
géographie (ʒeɔgrafi), s.f. [f. Gr. *gē+graphein*] Geography.
géographique (ʒeɔgrafik), adj. Geographic, geographical.
géographiquement (ʒeɔgrafikmɑ̃), adv. Geographically.
geôle (ʒol), s.f. [LL *caveola*, OF *gayole*] Jail, gaol, prison; jailer's lodge.
geôli-er, -ère (ʒolje), s.m.f. Gaoler, jailer.
géologie (ʒeɔlɔʒi), s.f. [f. Gr. *gē+logos*] Geology.
géologique (ʒeɔlɔʒik), adj. Geologic, geological.
géologue (ʒeɔlɔg), s.m.f. Geologist.
géomancie (ʒeɔmɑ̃si), s.f. [f. Gr. *gē+manteia*] Geomancy.
géométral, -e, (aux) (ʒeɔmetral), adj. Geometrical, to scale, plan- (not perspective). *Plan ~*, or *~*, s.m. ground plan.
géomètre (ʒeɔmɛtr), s.m.f. Geometer; *arpenteur ~*, land surveyor.
géométrie (ʒeɔmetri), s.f. [f. Gr. *gē+metron*] Geometry.
géométrique (ʒeɔmetrik), adj. Geometric, geometrical; *progression ~*, geometrical progression.
géométriquement (ʒeɔmetrikmɑ̃), adv. Geometrically.

géophage (ʒeɔfaʒ), adj. Earth-eating, geophagous.
géophagie (ʒeɔfaʒi), s.f. [f. Gr. *gē+phagia*] Geophagy.
géorama (ʒeɔrama), s.m. [f. Gr. *gē+orama*] Georama.
géorgien, -ne (ʒeɔrʒjɛ̃), adj. s.m.f. Georgian, (*a*) of Georgia, Caucasus; (*b*) of Georgia, U.S.A.
géorgique (ʒeɔrʒik), adj. [f. Gr. *gē+ergon*] Georgic, rural, pertaining to agriculture. *Les ~s*, s.f.pl. The Georgics.
géotropisme (ʒeotrɔpism), s.m. [f. Gr. *gē +trepein*] (bot.) Geotropism.
gérance (ʒerɑ̃s), s.f. Management, managership; editorship.
géranium (ʒeranjɔm), s.m. [f. Gr. *geranos*] (bot.) Geranium.
gérant, -e (ʒerɑ̃), s.m.f. [f. *gérer*] Manager, manageress; acting partner; (of a journal) editor; *directeur ~*, managing director; *armateur ~*, ship's husband.
gerbe (ʒɛrb), s.f. [f. OHG *garba*] Sheaf (pl. sheaves), bundle; (fireworks) gerbe; (of water) jet, spout.
gerbée (ʒɛrbe), s.f. Wheat-sheaf only half thrashed.
gerber (ʒɛrbe), v.a. To bind up in sheaves.
gerbier (ʒɛrbje), s.m. Small stack; stook of corn.
gerboise (ʒɛrbwaz), s.f. (zool.) Jerboa.
gerce (ʒɛrs), s.f. [f. *gercer*] **1.** Crack, chap (of the skin); **2.** clothes-moth; woodlouse; **3.** (slang) prostitute.
gercement (ʒɛrsmɑ̃), s.m. Chapping, cracking.
gercer (ʒɛrse), v.a.n. and **se~**, v.pr. [etym. dub.] To chap, to crack.
gerçure (ʒɛrsyr), s.f. Chap, crack; syn. GERCE.
gérer (ʒere), v.a. [L *gerere*] To manage, to conduct, to administer, to carry on.
gerfaut (ʒɛrfo), s.m. [OHG orig.] (ornith.) Gerfalcon.
germain, -e (ʒɛrmɛ̃), adj. [L *germanus*] German; *cousin ~*, first cousin; *cousin issu de ~*, second cousin; *sœur ~e*, own sister (of the whole blood).
germain, -e (ʒɛrmɛ̃), adj. s.m.f. Germanic, German, of ancient Germany.
germandrée (ʒɛrmɑ̃dre), s.f. [LL *germandra*] (bot.) Germander.
germanique (ʒɛrmanik), adj. Germanic.
germaniser (ʒɛrmanize), v.a. To germanize.
germanisme (ʒɛrmanism), s.m. **1.** Germanism; **2.** German idiom.
germaniste (ʒɛrmanist), s.m.f. Germanist.
germanium (ʒɛrmanjɔm), s.m. (chem.) Germanium.
germe (ʒɛrm), s.m. [L *germen*] **1.** Germ, seed; bud; embryo; **2.** shoot, sprout (of a bulbous root); **3.** cicatricule, tread (of an egg); **4.** principle, origin, beginning, dawn.
germer (ʒɛrme), v.n. [f. *germe*] To germinate, to sprout, to shoot; (fig.) to spring up.
germinal (ʒɛrminal), s.m. [f. L *germen*] Germinal (7th month in Fr. Republican calendar, from 21 March to 19 April).
germinati-f, -ve (ʒɛrminatif), adj. Germinal, germinative.
germination (ʒɛrmina'sjɔ̃), s.f. Germination.
germoir (ʒɛrmwar), s.m. Malt-house.
gérondif (ʒerɔ̃dif), s.m. [f. L *gerere*] Gerund.
géronte (ʒerɔ̃t), s.m. [Gr. *gerōn*] Foolish old man, dotard.
gérontocratie (ʒɛrɔ̃tokrasi), s.f. [f. Gr. *gerōn+kratos*] Gerontocracy, government by old men.
gésier (ʒezje), s.m. [L *gigerium*] Gizzard.
gésine (ʒezin), s.f. (obs.) [f. *gésir*] Childbed, confinement, lying-in.
gésir (ʒezir), v.n. [L *jacere*] To lie (used only in the forms: *il gît, nous gisons, vous gisez, ils gisent, je gisais, tu gisais, il gisait, nous gisions, vous gisiez, ils gisaient, gisant*); *ci-gît*, here lies; *c'est là que gît le lièvre*, that 's the point, that 's the crux.
gesse (ʒɛs), s.f. (bot.) Vetch; everlasting pea.
gestation (ʒɛsta'sjɔ̃), s.f. [L *gestatio*] Gestation.
gestatoire (ʒɛstatwar), adj. [f. L *gestare*] Gestatorial.
geste[1] (ʒɛst), s.m. [L *gestus*] **1.** Gesture, motion, sign; **2.** action, feat, geste; *faits et ~s*, actions and conduct; sayings and doings; *faire des ~s*, to gesticulate; *joignant le ~ à la parole*, suiting the action to the word.
geste[2] (ʒɛst), s.f. [L *gesta*] Heroic action, deed, exploit; heroic story; *chansons de ~*, French epic poems of the early Middle Ages.
gesticulation (ʒɛstikyla'sjɔ̃), s.f. Gesticulation.
gesticuler (ʒɛstikyle), v.n. [L *gesticulari*] To gesticulate.
gestion (ʒɛstjɔ̃), s.f. [L *gestio*] Management, administration, conduct (of business, &c.).
gestionnaire (ʒɛstjɔnɛr), adj. Managing. ~, s.m.f. Manager, manageress; caterer.
geyser (ʒezɛr, gezɛr) s.m. [Icelandic *geysir*] Geyser, intermittent spring of hot water. ⚠ In English, but not in French, the word is also used as the name of an apparatus for heating water = *chauffe-bain*.
ghetto (gɛtto), s.m. [It. wd] Ghetto.
gibbeu-x, -se (ʒibø), adj. [f. L *gibbus*] Gibbous, hump-backed.
gibbon (ʒibbɔ̃), s.m. (zool.) Gibbon.
gibbosité (ʒibbozite), s.f. Gibbosity.
gibecière (ʒibsjɛr), s.f. [f. *gibier*] Game-bag, pouch, poke, satchel, conjurer's bag; *tours de ~*, conjuring tricks.

gibelin, -e (ʒiblɛ̃), adj. Ghibelline.
gibelotte (ʒiblɔt), s.f. [f. *gibier*] (cook.) Rabbit-stew.
giberne (ʒibɛrn), s.f. [It. *giberna*] Cartridge-pouch; *avoir le bâton de maréchal dans sa ~*, to have a foot on the ladder.
gibet (ʒibɛ), s.m. [OF *gibet*, dim. of *gibe*] Gibbet, gallows.
gibier (ʒibje), s.m. [etym. dub.] Game; *~ à plumes*, wildfowl, game-birds; *~ à poil*, venison, rabbits, hares, game-animals; *~ de braconnage*, poached game; *pièce de ~*, head of game; *menu~*, small game; *gros ~*, big game; (fig.) *~ de potence*, gallows bird.
giboulée (ʒibule), s.f. Sudden shower; *~ de mars*, April shower.
giboyer (ʒibwaje), v.n. (rare) To go shooting.
giboyeu-x, -se (ʒibwajø), adj. Abounding in game.
gibus (ʒibys), s.m. [f. inventor's name] Opera hat, crush-hat, gibus.
gicler (ʒikle), v.n. To splash; to spurt out, to squirt.
gicleur (ʒiklœr), s.m. (motor.) Nozzle, jet, spray-nozzle; *~ principal*, main jet; *~ auxiliaire*, auxiliary jet; *chapeau de ~*, main jet cap.
gifle (ʒifl), s.f. [OF *giffle* = *joue*] Smack, slap; box on the ear; *tête à ~s*, repulsive face.
gifler (ʒifle), v.a. To slap in the face; *~ X*, to give X a slap in the face; *ils sont à ~*, they want smacking.
gigantesque (ʒigɑ̃tɛsk), adj. [f. L *gigas, gigantem*] Gigantic, colossal, tremendous.
gigantisme (ʒigɑ̃tism), s.m. Gigantism.
gigogne (ʒigɔɲ), s.f. [n. of character in puppet theatre] *La mère ~*, the old woman who lived in a shoe; *une mère ~*, a woman with many children; *table ~*, nest of tables.
gigolo (ʒigɔlo), s.m. Ladies' man, fancy man, gigolo; **gigolette**, s.f. fast girl.
gigot (ʒigo), s.m. [etym. dub.] Hind leg; (pop.) shank, leg; *~ de mouton*, leg of mutton; *manches à ~*, leg-of-mutton sleeves.
gigoter (ʒigɔte), v.n. To keep kicking about, to kick, to fidget with one's legs; (pop.) to dance, to shake a leg.
gigue (ʒig), s.f. [OF *gigue*, kind of fiddle] **1.** Hind leg; (pop.) shank, stump, leg; **2.** (dance and tune) jig; **3.** (pop.) *une grande ~*, a big gawky girl.
gilet (ʒilɛ), s.m. [f. *Gille*, a character in the old comedy, who wore a sleeveless vest? or f. Turk. *jelek*?] Waistcoat, vest; *~ d'escrime*, fencing-jacket; *~ de flanelle*, flannel vest; *~ de force*, strait-jacket; *~ de sauvetage*, life-jacket; *~ de tricot*, cardigan; jersey; sweater; pull-over; *~ croisé*, double-breasted waistcoat; *~ droit*, single-breasted waistcoat.
gileti-er, -ère (ʒiltje), s.m.f. Waistcoat-maker. *~, -ère*, adj. *Une chaine~ère*, an Albert watch-chain.
gille (ʒil), s.m. [see *gilet*] **1.** Ninny, simpleton, clown; *faire le ~*, to play the fool; *faire ~*, to slip off; **2.** large fishing-net.
gimblette (ʒɛ̃blɛt), s.f. [dialect wd] Cracknel, ring-biscuit.
gindre, geindre (ʒɛ̃dr), s.m. [f. L *junior*] Baker's man.
gingas (ʒɛ̃gɑ), s.m. (obs.) Tick, ticking.
gingembre (ʒɛ̃ʒɑ̃br), s.m. [L *gingiber*] Ginger.
gingival, -e, (aux) (ʒɛ̃ʒival), adj. (anat.) Gingival.
gingivite (ʒɛ̃ʒivit), s.f. [f. L *gingiva*] Gingivitis, inflammation of the gums.
ginglyme (ʒɛ̃glim), s.m. [Gr. *gigglumos*] (anat.) Ginglymus, hinge-like joint.
ginguet, -te (ʒɛ̃gɛ), adj. (obs.) Poor, sorry, wretched; (of wine) thin, sour.
girafe (ʒiraf), s.f. [Arab. *zarāfa*] (zool.) Giraffe.
girande (ʒirɑ̃d), s.f. [It. *girandа*] Sheaf of water-jets; (fireworks) bouquet, gerbe.
girandole (ʒirɑ̃dɔl), s.f. [It. *girandola*] **1.** Chandelier; **2.** sprig (of diamonds, &c.).
girasol (ʒirasɔl), s.f. [It. *girasole*] Girasol(e), fire-opal.
giration (ʒira'sjɔ̃), s.f. [f. L *gyrare*] Gyration.
giratoire (ʒiratwar), adj. Gyratory.
giraumon(t) (ʒiromɔ̃), s.m. (bot.) Pumpkin.
girie (ʒiri), s.f. (pop.) Captious complaint, jeremiad; fuss; *faire des ~s*, to make no end of fuss.
girofle (ʒirɔfl), s.m. [Gr. *karuophullon*] (bot.) Cloves; *un clou de ~*, a clove.
giroflée (ʒirɔfle), s.f. (bot.) Stock, gilliflower; *~ ravenelle*, wall-flower; (pop.) *~ à cinq feuilles*, slap in the face.
giroflier (ʒirɔflje), s.m. (bot.) Clove-tree.
girolle (ʒirɔl), s.f. (bot.) Chanterelle (mushroom), edible agaric.
giron (ʒirɔ̃), s.m. [etym. dub.] Lap; bosom; (fig.) pale; *le ~ de l'Église*, the bosom of the Church.
Gironde (ʒirɔ̃d), s.f. [f. geog. n.] (Fr. hist.) The party of the Gironde; the moderate republicans. *~*, adj. f. (slang) Pretty.
girondin, -e (ʒirɔ̃dɛ̃), adj. Of the Gironde. *~*, s.m. Girondist (member of the Girondist party, 1st Fr. Republic).
gironné (ʒirɔne), adj. s.m. (herald.) Gyronny.
girouette (ʒirwɛt), s.f. [f. L *gyrare*] Vane, weather-cock; (fig.) time-server, turncoat.
gisant, -e (ʒizɑ̃), p. adj. [f. *gésir*] Lying down.
gisement (ʒizmɑ̃), s.m. (geol., min.) Bearing, bed, stratum; (naut.) bearing, lie (of coast, &c.).

gît (ʒi). See GÉSIR.
gitane (ʒitan), s.f. [Span. *gitana*] Gipsy.
gîte (ʒit), s.m. [f. *gésir*] **1.** Home, lodging, shelter, halting-place, quarters, refuge; (of a hare) form; **2.** (geol.) layer, bed; **3.** (butch.) ~ *à la noix*, silverside; **4.** ~, s.f. (naut.) heeling, heel, list.
gîter (ʒite), v.n. To lodge, to sleep, to take shelter; **se** ~, v.pr. to lodge, to take shelter; to conceal oneself.
givre (ʒivr), s.m. **1.** Rime, hoar-frost; **2.** see GUIVRE.
givré, -e (ʒivre), adj. Frosted, rimy.
glabre (glabr), adj. [L *glaber*] Glabrous, smooth-skinned; clean-shaven.
glaçage (glasaʒ), s.m. Glazing.
glaçant, -e (glasɑ̃), p. adj. (lit. and fig.) Freezing, chilling, icy.
glace (glas), s.f. [L *glacies*] **1.** Ice; (fig.) coldness; ~ *flottante*, ice-floe, ice-field, iceberg; *pris dans les* ~*s*, ice-bound; ~ *à rafraîchir*, rough ice; *boire à la* ~, to drink iced; *ferrer à* ~, to rough-shoe; (fig.) *rompre la* ~, to break the ice; **2.** freezing-point; **3.** ice, ice-cream; **4.** glazing; **5.** plate-glass; mirror, looking-glass; window (of a carriage), glass window; **6.** flaw (of a diamond).
glacé, -e (glase), p. adj. **1.** Iced, frozen, icy cold, chilled; chilling; *il a les mains* ~*es*, his hands are ice-cold; *je suis* ~, I am chilled to the marrow; *un accueil* ~, a chilly reception; **2.** glazed; *papier* ~, glazed paper; covered with icing sugar, iced. ~, s.m. Glaze.
glacer (glase), v.a. **1.** To freeze, to congeal, to ice, to chill; (fig.) to freeze, to chill, to paralyse, to depress; ~ *le sang*, to freeze one's blood; to make one's blood run cold; ~ *d'horreur*, to strike dumb with horror; **2.** to glaze; to cover with sugar-icing, to ice.
glacerie (glasri), s.f. Mirror- and glass-making.
glaciaire (glasjɛr), adj. (geol.) Glacial; *période* ~, ice-age, glacial epoch.
glacial, -e (pl. -s) (glasjal), adj. (lit. and fig.) Glacial, icy, frozen, freezing; *vent* ~, biting wind; *un accueil* ~, a freezing reception.
glacier (glasje), s.m. **1.** Glacier, mass of ice; **2.** dealer in ices, lemonade, drinks.
glacière (glasjɛr), s.f. Refrigerator; ice-chest, ice-house.
glacis (glasi), s.m. **1.** (fort.) Glacis; **2.** (paint., &c.) glazing.
glaçon (glasɔ̃), s.m. Icicle; floe; piece of ice.
glaçure (glasyr), s.f. Glazing.
gladiateur (gladjatœr), s.m. [L *gladiator*] Gladiator.
glaïeul (glajœl), s.m. [L *gladiolus*] (bot.) Gladiolus, corn-flag, iris.
glaire (glɛr), s.f. [f. L *clarus*] Glair.
glairer (glɛre), v.a. To glair, to smear with glair or white of egg.
glaireu-x, -se (glɛrø), adj. Glairy, glairous.
glaise (glɛz), s.f. [f. LL *glis*] Clay, marl, potter's earth, loam; *terre* ~, potter's clay; syn. ARGILE.
glaiser (glɛze), v.a. To marl.
glaiseu-x, -se (glɛzø), adj. Clayey, marly. syn. ARGILEUX.
glaisière (glɛzjɛr), s.f. Marl-pit, clay-pit.
glaive (glɛv), s.m. [L *gladius*] (poet., fig.) Sword, blade, steel; *tirer le* ~, to wage war.
glanage (glanaʒ), s.m. [f. *glaner*] Gleaning.
gland (glɑ̃), s.m. [L *glans*] **1.** Acorn; **2.** tassel; **3.** (anat.) gland.
glandage (glɑ̃daʒ), s.m. Pannage.
glande (glɑ̃d), s.f. [L *glandula*] (anat.) Gland; (pop.) swollen glands.
glandé, -e (glɑ̃de), adj. (vet.) Glandered.
glandée (glɑ̃de), s.f. Pannage, crop of acorns.
glandulaire, glanduleu-x, -se (glɑ̃dylɛr, glɑ̃dylø), adj. Glandular, glandulous.
glandule (glɑ̃dyl), s.f. (anat.) Glandule.
glane (glan), s.f. [f. *glaner*] Gleaning; small sheaf, wisp of straw, handful of ears of corn; ~ *d'oignons*, rope of onions.
glaner (glane), v.a.n. [LL *glenare*] To glean; (fig.) to cull from, to select.
glaneu-r, -se (glanœr), s.m.f. Gleaner.
glanure (glanyr), s.f. Gleanings (pl.).
glapir (glapir), v.n. [L *glattire*] To yelp; (of fox) to bark; (of rabbits) to squeak; (fig.) to screech, to scream, to squeak.
glapissant, -e (glapisɑ̃), p. adj. Yelping, barking, screeching.
glapissement (glapismɑ̃), s.m. Yelping, barking, screeching, squeaking.
glas (glɑ), s.m. [L *classicum*] Knell, passing bell, tolling; *sonner le* ~, to toll the knell.
glaucome (glokom), s.m. (pathol.) Glaucoma.
glauque (glok), adj. [Gr. *glaukos*] Glaucous, pale sea-green.
glèbe (glɛb), s.f. [L *gleba*] Glebe, land, ground, soil; clod, sod; *attaché à la* ~, attached to the soil.
gléchome (glekom), s.m. (bot.) Ground ivy.
glène (glɛn), s.f. [Gr. *glēnē*] (anat.) Glene, socket; (naut.) coil.
glénoïde, glénoïdal, -e, (aux) (glenɔid, glenɔidal), [f. *glène*] Glenoid.
glette (glɛt), s.f. (chem.) Litharge; syn. LITHARGE.
glissade (glisad), s.f. Slide, sliding; slip; (danc.) glissade; *faire une* ~, to have a slide, to glissade; to slip.
glissant, -e (glisɑ̃), p. adj. Slippery; (fig.) ticklish, hazardous; *il fait* ~, it is slippery walking.

ɔ, n*o*te, gl*o*tte; ɔ̃, m*on*ter, r*on*de; ø, f*eu*, cr*eu*x; œ, p*eu*r, s*œu*r; œ̃, *un*; ʃ, *ch*ez, s*ch*isme; u, t*ou*t; w, *ou*i, d*oi*t, d*ou*aire; y, m*u*r, p*u*; ɥ, h*u*ile, m*u*ette; z, *z*èle, ro*s*e; ʒ, dé*j*à, *g*entil.

glissé (glise), s.m. (danc.) Slide, glissade, gliding step.
glissement (glismɑ̃), s.m. Slipping, sliding, gliding motion.
glisser (glise), v.n. [OF *glier*, OHG *glitan*, Germ. *gleiten*] **1.** To slide, to practise sliding, to move smoothly along; to glide; to make no impression; **2.** to slip, to glissade; to slip away, to slip out; *cela m'a glissé des mains*, it slipped out of my hands; *le pied lui a glissé, il a glissé du pied*, his foot slipped; **3.** (with *sur*) to glide over; to slip over, to pass over, to touch lightly on; to slur over; to glance at; *glissons là-dessus*, enough said, no more of that, let us pass over that; ~, v.a. to slip; *il a glissé la main dans ma poche*, he slipped his hand into my pocket; ~ *un mot dans une phrase*, to slip a word into a sentence; *je lui en ai glissé un mot*, I gave him a hint about it; I dropped (or whispered) a word of it into his ear; *il me glissa que*, he insinuated that; **se** ~, v.pr. to slip, to glide, to creep or steal, to insinuate oneself; *il se glissa le long du mur*, he stole along the wall; *il s'est glissé une coquille dans*, a misprint has slipped into.
glisseu-r, -se (glisœr), s.m.f. adj. Slider, glider, sliding, gliding; *hydro-*~, seaplane, sea-glider.
glissière (glisjɛr), s.f. Guide, slide-bar.
glissoir (gliswar), s.m. Guide block; ~*e*, s.f. slide; sliding or skating ground.
global, -e, (aux) (glɔbal), adj. Lump, total, entire, whole; *une somme* ~*e*, a lump sum.
globalement (glɔbalmɑ̃), adv. In the lump, taken in the lump.
globe (glɔb), s.m. [L *globus*] **1.** Globe, sphere, orb; *le* ~ *de l'œil*, the eyeball; ~ *de feu*, fireball; **2.** earth, world, our planet; *sur toute la surface du* ~, all over the earth; **3.** glass case (on a clock, &c.); glass shade.
globulaire (glɔbylɛr), adj. Globular.
globule (glɔbyl), s.m. [L *globulus*] Globule.
globuleu-x, -se (glɔbylø), adj. Globulous, globular, globose.
gloire (glwar), s.f. [L *gloria*] Glory, fame, renown; vanity, pride, glorification; *mettre sa* ~ *à, se faire* ~ *de*, or *une* ~ *de*, to pride oneself upon; to glory in; (archaic) honour, reputation.
glomérule (glɔmeryl), s.m. [f. L *glomus*] Glomerule.
gloria (glɔria), s.m. **1.** (liturg.) gloria; **2.** (pop., dial.) coffee with brandy.
gloriette (glɔrjɛt), s.f. Summer-house, pavilion, arbour; syn. TONNELLE.
glorieusement (glɔrjøzmɑ̃), adv. Gloriously.
glorieu-x, -se (glɔrjø), adj. **1.** Glorious, illustrious, **2.** proud, conceited, vainglorious; *faire le* ~, to be a braggart; to brag, to swank, to swagger; **3.** (theol.) glorified, blessed.
glorification (glɔrifika'sjɔ̃), s.f. Glorification.
glorifier (glɔrifje), v.a. To glorify, to honour; **se** ~ **de**, v.pr. to glory in; to boast of.
gloriole (glɔrjɔl), s.f. Vainglory, vanity, petty pride, conceit; *plein de* ~, eaten up with vanity; ⚠ not 'gloriole', which = *auréole*.
glose (gloz), s.f. [f. Gr. *glōssa*] **1.** Comment, gloss, paraphrase, explanation; **2.** misrepresentation, carping; malevolent comment or criticism; **3.** interlinear translation; glossary.
gloser (gloze), v.n.a. **1.** To comment on, to gloss; **2.** ~ *sur*, to carp at, to find fault with.
glossaire (glɔsɛr), s.m. Glossary.
glossateur (glɔsatœr), s.m. Commentator (*de*, on); glossator.
glotte (glɔt), s.f. [f. Gr. *glōtta*] (anat.) Glottis.
glottique (glɔtik), adj. Glottal, glottic.
glouglou (gluglu), s.m. [onom.] Gurgling, gurgle; (of turkeys) gobbling.
glouglouter (gluglute), v.n. (of turkeys) To gobble.
gloussement (glusmɑ̃), s.m. Clucking, cluck.
glousser (gluse), v.n. [onom.] To cluck.
glouteron (glutrɔ̃), s.m. (bot.) Burdock, burr; syn. BARDANE, CAILLE-LAIT.
glouton, -ne (glutɔ̃), adj. [L *glutto*] Gluttonous, greedy. ~, s.m.f. Glutton; (zool.) wolverene, glutton.
gloutonnement (glutɔnmɑ̃), adv. Gluttonously, greedily, ravenously.
gloutonnerie (glutɔnri), s.f. Gluttony, greediness.
glu (gly), s.f. [L *glus*] Bird-lime, glue; ~ *marine*, marine glue; *prendre à la* ~, to snare; *avoir de la* ~ *aux doigts*, to be light-fingered, thievish.
gluant, -e (glɥɑ̃), adj. Sticky, slimy, gluey, adhesive; syn. POISSEUX.
gluau (pl. **-x**) (glɥo), s.m. Lime-twig; (fig.) snare.
glucinium (glysinjɔm), s.m. (chem.) Glucinum, beryllium.
glucose, glycose (glykoz, glikoz), s.f. and m. [f. Gr. *glukus*] Glucose.
glucoside (glykozid), s.m. (chem.) Glucoside.
gluer (glɥe), v.a. To smear with glue, to lime; to make sticky, to clog, to bedaub.
glui (glɥi), s.m. Rye-straw, thatching-straw.
glume (glym), s.f. [L *gluma*] (bot.) Glume; husk, chaff.
gluten (glytɛn), s.m. [L wd] Gluten.
glutineu-x, -se (glytinø), adj. Glutinous, viscous.

glutinosité (glytinozite), s.f. Glutinosity, viscidity, stickiness.
glycérine (gliserin), s.f. [f. Gr. *glukeros*] Glycerine.
glycériner (gliserine), v.a. To glycerinate.
glycine (glisin), s.f. (bot.) Wistaria.
glycogène (glikoʒɛn), s.m. (chem.) Glycogen.
glycol (glikɔl), s.m. (chem.) Glycol.
glycose (glikoz), s.f. and m. See GLUCOSE.
glycosurie (glikɔsyri), s.f. (pathol.) Glycosuria.
glyphe (glif), s.m. [Gr. *gluphē*] Glyph.
glyptique (gliptik), s.f. Glyptics. ~, adj. Glyptic.
glyptodon (gliptɔdɔ̃), s.m. (zool.) Glyptodon.
gnaf, gniaf (ɲaf), s.m. (pop.) Cobbler; syn. BOUIF.
gnangnan (ɲɑ̃ɲɑ̃), adj. Namby-pamby, mildly sentimental; slow, sluggish, spiritless. ~, s.m.f. Milksop, dawdler, slowcoach.
gneiss (gnɛs), s.m. [Germ. wd] (geol.) Gneiss.
gniole (ɲɔl), s.f. (slang) Brandy.
gnognote (ɲɔɲɔt), s.f. (pop.) Rubbish, small beer.
gnome (gnom), s.m., fem. (rare) **gnomide,** [wd invented by Paracelsus] Gnome, goblin, leprechaun; syn. NAIN, LUTIN.
gnomique (gnomik), adj. [f. Gr. *gnōmikos*] Gnomic, sententious.
gnomon (gnɔmɔ̃), s.m. [Gr. wd] Gnomon, pin or triangular plate of a sundial.
gnomonique (gnɔmɔnik), adj. Gnomonic. ~, s.f. Gnomonics, art of making sundials.
gnose (gnoz), s.f. [Gr. *gnōsis*] **1.** Gnosis; **2.** gnosticism.
gnosticisme (gnɔstisism), s.m. (phil.) Gnosticism.
gnon (ɲɔ̃), s.m. (pop.) Blow, biff, clout.
gnou (gnu), s.m. [Hottentot wd] (zool.) Gnu.
(tout de) go (tudəgo), adv.loc. Offhand, at once, straight off; *allez-y tout de* ~, no more ado.
gobe (gɔb), s.f. [f. *gober*] Fattening ball (for fowls); pellet of poison; large pill.
gobelet (gɔblɛ), s.m. Goblet, tumbler, mug, cup; *tour de* ~, thimble-rigging; *joueur de* ~, juggler, thimble-rigger, mountebank.
gobeleterie (gɔblɛtri), s.f. Cup-making.
gobeletier (gɔblɛtje), s.m. Cup-maker.
gobelins (gɔblɛ̃), s.m. [f. prop. n. of founder of factory in Paris] Gobelins (tapestry).
gobeloter (gɔblɔte), v.n. To tipple.
gobeloteur (gɔblɔtœr), s.m. Tippler.
gobe-mouches (gɔbmuʃ), s.m. **1.** Simpleton, gull, ninny, booby; **2.** (bot.) catch-fly; fly-trap; **3.** (ornith.) fly-catcher.
gober (gɔbe), v.a. [Celt. orig.] To gobble up, to gulp down, to swallow, to bolt; (fig.) to accept with ready credulity, to swallow; (slang) to like, to be potty on; **se** ~, v.pr. to suffer from swelled head, to fancy oneself.
(se) goberger (səgɔbɛrʒe), v.pr. (pop.) **1.** To stuff and swill; to guzzle, to eat greedily; **2.** (obs.) to amuse or enjoy oneself, to lounge; syn. (FAIRE) RIPAILLE, S'EMPIFFRER.
gobet (gɔbɛ), s.m. (obs.) Gull.
gobeu-r, -se (gɔbœr), s.m.f. Gull, simpleton.
gobichonner (gɔbiʃɔne), v.n. To junket, to feast; syn. (FAIRE) BOMBANCE.
gobie (gɔbi), s.m. (ichth.) Goby.
godage, (gɔdaʒ), s.m. Bagging, puckering (of clothes, &c.).
godaille (gɔdɑj), s.f. (colloq.) Swilling, tippling, feasting, spree; syn. RIBOTE.
godailler (gɔdɑje), v.n. To swill, to tipple, to guzzle, to go on the spree.
godailleu-r, -se (gɔdɑjœr), s.m.f. (colloq.) Guzzler, swiller.
godan, godant (gɔdɑ̃), s.m. Fib, lie, imposture, humbug, tommy-rot, gas; *donner dans le* ~, to swallow the lie, to be taken in.
godasse (gɔdas), s.f. (slang) Shoe, boot, clod-crusher.
godelureau (pl. **-x**) (gɔdlyro), s.m. [OF *goguelureau*] Coxcomb, village beau, popinjay.
godenot (gɔdno), s.m. [etym. dub.] Juggler's puppet; (fig.) dwarf, ill-built man.
goder (gɔde), v.n. To pucker, to crease, to bag.
godet (gɔdɛ), s.m. [etym. dub.] Cup, mug, drinking-horn, cup (of lamp), pan (of colours), saucer; bucket (of dredger, noria, &c.); jet (of foundry); calyx (of flowers); (dressm.) godet.
godiche, godichon, -ne (gɔdiʃ, gɔdiʃɔ̃), adj. Awkward, clumsy, gawky, silly. ~, s.m.f. Simpleton, booby, muff, flat, bumpkin; *une grande* ~, a big gawk.
godille (gɔdij), s.f. (naut.) Scull, stern-oar; *avancer à la* ~, to scull.
godiller (gɔdije), v.n. To scull.
godilleur (gɔdijœr), s.m. Sculler.
godillot (gɔdijo), s.m. [f. name of boot manufacturer who contracted for the French army in 1870] (pop.) Boot, heavy boot, beetle-crusher, clod-crusher.
godiveau (pl. **-x**) (gɔdivo), s.m. (cook.) Force-meat pie.
godron (gɔdrɔ̃), s.m. [etym. dub.] Gadroon; goffered pleat, goffer, &c.
godronner (gɔdrɔne), v.a. To gadroon; to goffer.
goéland (gɔelɑ̃), s.m. [Bret. *gwēlan*] (ornith.) Sea-gull; ~ *tridactyle*, kittiwake.
goélette (gɔelɛt), s.f. (naut.) Schooner; ~ *carrée*, topsail schooner.

goémon (gɔemɔ̃), s.m. [Celt. wd] (bot.) Wrack, sea-weed; syn. VRAIC.

goétie (gɔesi), s.f. [Gr. *goēteia*] Goety, sorcery.

gogaille (gɔgɑj), s.f. Junketing; see syn. GODAILLE.

gogo (gogo), s.m. [etym. dub.] (pop.) Mug, flat, credulous person, gull, pigeon.

(à) gogo (agogo), adv.loc. (fam.) Plenty and to spare, in plenty, in clover; to one's heart's content; *en avoir à* ~, to have one's fill of it.

goguenard, -e (gɔgnar), adj. Jeering, chaffing, sneering.

goguenarder (gɔgnarde), v.n. [etym. dub.] To jeer, to banter, to sneer.

goguenot, gogue (gɔgno, gɔg), s.m. (pop.) (usually in the pl.) Privy.

goguette (gɔgɛt), s.f. (colloq.) *En* ~, in a merry mood, in his cups, on the spree, fresh.

goinfre (gwɛ̃fr), s.m. Glutton, (pop.) greedy-guts, gormandizer; syn. GOULIAFRE.

goinfrer (gwɛ̃fre), v.n. To stuff; to gormandize; syn. BÂFRER.

goinfrerie (gwɛ̃frəri), s.f. Gormandizing, gluttony, stuffing, guttling.

goitre (gwɑtr), s.m. [f. L *guttur*] (pathol.) Goitre, wen.

goitreu-x, -se (gwɑtrø), adj. Goitred, goitrous.

golfe (gɔlf), s.m. [It. *golfo*] Gulf, bay; *le* ~ *du Lion*, the Gulf of Lyons; *le* ~ *de Gascogne*, the Bay of Biscay.

gommage (gɔmaʒ), s.m. Gumming.

gomme (gɔm), s.f. [L *gummi*] Gum; india-rubber; ~ *para*, Para rubber; ~ *gutte*, gamboge; ~ *arabique*, gum arabic; ~ *élastique*, indiarubber; ~ *à encre*, ink-eraser; (obs. slang) *la* ~, the pink of society.

gommer (gɔme), v.a. **1.** To gum; **2.** to mix with gum.

gommeu-x, -se (gɔmø), adj. Gummous, gummy. ~, s.m. (pop.) Toff, masher, swell, (k)nut; ~, s.f. dashing girl, swell.

gommier (gɔmje), s.m. (bot.) Gum-tree, gum-acacia.

gomphose (gɔ̃foz), s.f. [Gr. *gomphōsis*] (anat.) Gomphosis.

gond (gɔ̃), s.m. [Gr. *gomphos*] Hinge; *hors des* ~*s*, unhinged; (fig.) beside oneself with rage; *cela me fait sortir des* ~*s*, that exasperates me.

gondolage (gɔ̃dɔlaʒ), s.m. Warping.

gondolant, -e (gɔ̃dɔlɑ̃), p. adj. (slang) Killing, very comical, side-splitting.

gondole (gɔ̃dɔl), s.f. [It. *gondola*] Gondola.

gondoler (gɔ̃dɔle), v.n. To warp; **se** ~, v.pr. **1.** to warp; **2.** (slang) to shake with laughter.

gondolier (gɔ̃dɔlje), s.m. Gondolier.

gonfalon (gɔ̃falɔ̃), s.m. [It. *gonfalone*] Gonfalon, banner.

gonfalonier (gɔ̃falɔnje), s.m. Gonfalonier.

gonflé, -e (gɔ̃fle), p. adj. Swollen, inflated; *des yeux* ~*s*, swollen eyes; (fig.) ~ *d'orgueil*, eaten up with pride, bursting with pride.

gonflement (gɔ̃fləmɑ̃), s.m. Swelling, inflation, distension; blowing-up, pumping-up (of tires).

gonfler (gɔ̃fle), v.a. [f. L *conflare*] To swell, to inflate, to distend, to puff up, to bloat; ~ *un pneu*, to inflate or to pump up a tire; ~, v.n. and **se** ~, v.pr. to get swollen, to swell, to be puffed up.

gong (gɔ̃g), s.m. [Malay wd] Gong.

gongorisme (gɔ̃gɔrism), s.m. [f. *Gongora*, Span. author] Gongorism (resembling euphuism in Engl.).

gonin (gɔnɛ̃), s.m. (obs. except in:) *un maître* ~, a knowing card, a deep old rascal, a sly dog.

goniomètre (gɔnjɔmɛtr), s.m. [f. Gr. *gōnia*+*metron*] Goniometer.

goniométrie (gɔnjɔmetri), s.f. Goniometry.

goniométrique (gɔnjɔmetrik), adj. Goniometric(al).

gonne (gɔn), s.f. Cask, (tar-)barrel.

gonorrhée (gɔnɔre), s.f. [Gr. *gonorrhoia*] (pathol.) Gonorrhoea.

gord (gɔr), s.m. [LL *gordum*] Fishing weir; kiddle.

gordien (gɔrdjɛ̃), adj.m. [f. *Gordius*, who tied the knot cut by Alexander the Great] Gordian; *le nœud* ~, the Gordian knot.

goret (gɔrɛ), s.m. [OF *gore* = sow] **1.** Young pig, pig; (fig., pop.) dirty pig; **2.** (naut.) hog, scrub-broom.

gorge (gɔrʒ), s.f. [L *gurges*] **1.** Throat, gullet; *mal de* ~, sore throat; *avoir mal à la* ~, to have a sore throat; *prendre X à la* ~, *sauter à la* ~ *de X*, to collar X; *ce brouillard prend à la* ~, this fog nearly chokes one; *à pleine* ~, at the top of one's voice; *rire à* ~ *déployée*, to split one's sides with laughing; *faire des* ~*s chaudes de*, to make fun of, to laugh or chuckle at; *rendre* ~, to disgorge, to stump up; *faire rentrer à X ses paroles dans la* ~, to make X eat his words; ~*-de-pigeon*, ~, adj. invar. iridescent, shot, columbine; **2.** breast, bosom, neck and shoulders; **3.** pass, defile, strait, cañon, gorge, gully; **4.** groove (of pulley); **5.** (bot.) mouth, orifice; **6.** (arch., fort.) gorge. ⚠ 'Gorge' in English also = *le contenu de l'estomac, ce qui a été avalé.*

gorgée (gɔrʒe), s.f. Draught, gulp, mouthful, sip; (fig.) drop; *boire à petites* ~*s*, to sip.

gorger (gɔrʒe), v.a. To gorge, to cram, to glut; to load (*de*, with); **se** ~, v.pr. to gorge oneself (*de*, with), to stuff.

gorgerette (gɔrʒərɛt), s.f. [f. *gorge*] Lady's ruffle, gorget, wimple; (armour) gorget.
gorgerin (gɔrʒərɛ̃), s.m. (armour) Gorget, neckpiece.
gorgone (gɔrgɔn), s.f. [f. Gr. myth.] Gorgon.
gorgonie (gɔrgɔni), s.f. Gorgonia, sea-fan, kind of polyp.
gorille (gɔrij), s.m. [African for 'wild man' in Gr. account of Hanno's voyage, 5th or 6th cent. B.C.] (zool.) Gorilla.
gosier (gozje), s.m. [etym. dub.] Throat, gullet; windpipe; *avoir le ~ en pente*, or *avoir une éponge dans le ~*, to be fond of a glass; *avoir le ~ blindé*, to have a cast-iron throat; *s'humecter le ~*, to wet one's whistle; *s'éclaircir le ~*, to clear one's throat; *coup de ~*, bawling; *chanter à plein ~*, to sing at the top of one's voice.
gosse (fem. **gosse** or **gosseline**) (gɔs), s.m.f. (pop.) Brat, kid, urchin; sweetheart, girl. ~, adj. Young, green, immature.
gotha (gɔta), s.m. **1.** Almanach de Gotha; (fig.) the cream of society; **2.** German aeroplane, gotha.
gothique (gɔtik), adj. [L *gothicus*] Gothic, pertaining to the Goths; (fig.) antiquated; (print., writ.) German, black-letter (type), black; (arch.) gothic, ogival.
goton, gothon (gɔtɔ̃), s.f. [abbrev. of *Margoton*] Rustic wench, lass; (pej.) strumpet.
gouache (gwaʃ), s.f. [f. It. *guazzo*] Gouache (kind of painting).
gouailler (gwɑje), v.n.a. To jeer, to chaff, to banter, to tease, to sneer at; syn. RAILLER, BLAGUER.
gouaillerie (gwɑjri), s.f. Chaff, joke, sneers, bantering, sharp raillery, rallying.
gouailleu-r, -se (gwɑjœr), adj. Flouting, mocking, jeering. ~, s.m.f. Chaffer, joker, quiz, jeerer.
goualer (gwale), v.a.n. (slang) To sing, to bawl.
goualeu-r, -se (gwalœr), s.m.f. (slang) Singer, street-singer.
gouape (gwap), s.f. (pop.) Lazy brute, foul-mouthed scoundrel, cad, blackguard; (though *gouape* is fem. it is usually said of a man, ex.: *X, c'est une vraie ~*, X is a lazy brute, a regular cad).
goudron (gudrɔ̃), s.m. [Arab. *qaṭrān*] Tar, pitch.
goudronnage (gudrɔnaʒ), s.m. Tarring, pitching; (naut.) paying.
goudronner (gudrɔne), v.a. To tar, to pitch, (naut.) to pay; *eau goudronnée*, tar-water; *toile goudronnée*, tarpaulin.
goudronneu-x, -se (gudrɔnø), adj. Tarry.
gouffre (gufr), s.m. [f. *golfe*] Gulf, abyss, chasm, pit; whirlpool; (fig.) anything absorbing, insatiable, ruinous; *un ~ d'iniquités*, a hellish man; *un ~ d'argent*, a ghoul for money; a 'gold-digger'; a bottomless pit; a ruinous enterprise; *quel ~!*, what a glutton!
gouge (guʒ), s.f. [LL *gubia*] **1.** Gouge, concave bladed chisel; **2.** jade.
gouger (guʒe), v.a. To gouge (wood, &c.).
goujat (guʒa), s.m. **1.** Skunk, cad, stinking contemptible fellow, dirty dog; **2.** mason's hodman, mortar-boy; **3.** (obs.) soldier's servant, camp follower.
goujaterie (guʒatri), s.f. Dirty trick, mean behaviour, action of a cad, utterly bad manners.
goujon[1] (guʒɔ̃), s.m. [f. *gouge*] Gudgeon, coupling-bolt; (carp.) dowel; *~ de chaîne*, link-pin; *~ d'embrayage*, clutch bolt.
goujon[2] (guʒɔ̃), s.m. [L *gobio*] (ichth.) Gudgeon. ⚠ ~ in French is not used figuratively, as in English for a credulous person.
goule (gul), s.f. [Arab. *ghoul*] **1.** Ghoul; **2.** var. of *gueule*] (dialect) big mouth.
goulée (gule), s.f. [f. *goule, gueule*] Gulp, draught, mouthful (of water, wine, &c.).
goulet (gulɛ), s.m. [f. *goule, gueule*] Narrow pass, gullet, water channel, strait, defile.
gouliafre (guljafr), s.m. Glutton; see syn. GOINFRE.
goulot (gulo), s.m. [f. *goule, gueule*] Neck (of bottle, &c.); (pop.) throat, mouth, gizzard; *repousser du ~*, to have foul breath; *se rincer le ~*, to wet one's whistle.
goulu, -e (guly), adj. [f. *goule, gueule*] Greedy, voracious, gluttonous. ~, s.m.f. Glutton.
goulûment (gulymɑ̃), adv. Greedily, voraciously, gluttonously.
goum (gum), s.m. [Arab. wd] (mil.) Native contingent in North Africa.
goumier (gumje), s.m. [f. *goum*] Native cavalryman in French North Africa.
goupil (gupi), s.m. [L *vulpecula*] (obs.) Fox.
goupille (gupij), s.f. [etym. dub.] (mech.) Pin, split pin, cotter; *chasse-~*, nail-punch.
goupiller (gupije), v.a. (mech.) To pin; *~ un écrou*, to fix a nut with a split pin; (pop.) to arrange, to contrive; **se ~**, v.pr. (colloq.) to shape, to be managed; *ça ne se goupille pas bien*, things are not shaping well, I don't see how to manage it.
goupillon (gupijɔ̃), s.m. [f. OF *goupil*] **1.** Aspersorium, holy-water sprinkler; (fig.) *le sabre et le ~*, the army and the clergy, or the Church; **2.** bottle-brush, brush, cylinder brush.
gourbi (gurbi), s.m. [Alger. wd] Hut, cabin.
gourd, -e (gur), adj. [L *gurdus*] Benumbed, swollen, numb. ⚠ Not English 'gourd' which = *gourde*.

gourde (gurd), s.f. [L *cucurbita*] (bot.) **1.** Gourd, calabash; **2.** wicker bottle, travelling-flask or -bottle; **3.** (pej.) stupid girl or fellow; silly idiot; *quelle ~!*, what a duffer!

gourdin (gurdɛ̃), s.m. [It. *cordino*] Cudgel, thick stick.

goure (gur), s.f. [f. Arab. *gharra* = to deceive] (old Fr. thieves' cant) Take-in; vitiated preparation or ingredient.

gourer (gure), v.a. (slang) To take in, to deceive; **se ~**, v.pr. to be mistaken, to deceive oneself; (vulg.) *tu te goures!*, you are quite out, or altogether out.

gourgandine (gurgɑ̃din), s.f. **1.** Strumpet, whore, street-walker; **2.** (obs.) a kind of open-breasted corsage.

gourgane (gurgan), s.f. (bot.) Horse-bean.

gourmade (gurmad), s.f. [f. *gourmer*] Punch, blow in the face, smack.

gourmand, -e (gurmɑ̃), adj. [etym. dub.] Greedy, fond of choice food, epicurean. **~**, s.m.f. **1.** Epicure, gourmand, gastronomist, connoisseur of table delicacies; (⚠ Not 'gormandizer' which = *glouton*; in French a *gourmand* is more voracious than a *gourmet*, but less so than a *glouton*); **2.** **~**, s.m. (hort.) shoot, parasitic growth.

gourmander (gurmɑ̃de), v.a. To rebuke sharply, to reprove harshly, to give a good blowing-up to.

gourmandise (gurmɑ̃diz), s.f. **1.** Indulgence in good eating, greedy relish of choice food; (⚠ Not 'gormandizing', which = *gloutonnerie, voracité*); **2.** dainty, sweet dish, titbit, dainty bit.

gourme (gurm), s.f. (vet.) Strangles; (of children) scabs; (fig.) *jeter sa ~*, to sow one's wild oats, to have one's fling.

gourmé, -e (gurme), adj. Stiff, formal, starched, frozen, solemn.

gourmer (gurme), v.a. **1.** To punch, to hit, to pommel, to pitch into; **2.** to curb (a horse); **se ~**, v.pr. **1.** to pitch into each other; **2.** to stiffen, to be starched, to grow stiff, or formal.

gourmet (gurmɛ), s.m. [OF *gourmet* = wine-taster's assistant] Gourmet, epicure, connoisseur of table delicacies, wines, &c.

gourmette (gurmɛt), s.f. **1.** (harness) Curb chain, curb; (fig.) rope; *lâcher la ~* (or *la bride*) *à X*, to give X a freer hand, to give X more scope; **2.** watch-chain, wristlet chain, bracelet chain.

gournable (gurnabl), s.f. Tree-nail.

goussant, goussaut (gusɑ̃, guso), s.m. Thick-set horse.

gousse (gus), s.f. [etym. dub.] Pod, shell, husk, cod; *une ~ d'ail*, a clove of garlic.

gousset (gusɛ), s.m. [f. *gousse*] **1.** Fob, pocket; **2.** gusset; **3.** bracket; *vide-~*, pickpocket; *avoir le ~ bien rempli*, to be well off.

goût (gu), s.m. [L *gustus*] Taste; savour, relish, flavour, smell; liking, taste, bent, inclination; *avoir le goût de*, to taste like, to taste of; *ce pain a bon ~*, this bread tastes nice; *relever le ~ de*, to give a relish to; *de haut ~*, high-flavoured, rich; highly-seasoned; *est-ce à votre ~?*, is this to your taste?; *des ~s et des couleurs, il ne faut point disputer*, there is no accounting for tastes; *chacun son ~*, tastes differ; *chacun à son ~*, every one to his liking; *avoir du ~ pour*, to like, to have a liking for, to favour; *avoir le ~ difficile*, to be hard to please, to be particular; *trouver à son ~*, to fancy; to be partial to; *de bon ~*, in good taste; *de mauvais ~*, vulgar, in bad taste; *prendre ~ à*, to take a liking to; *~ dépravé*, perverted taste; *dans le ~ de*, in the style or manner of.

goûter (gute), v.a. **1.** To taste; to try; *goûtez de ce vin*, try this wine; *goûtez notre vin*, try our wine; **2.** to appreciate, to relish, to approve of, to enjoy, to delight in, to feel; *je ne goûte pas ces plaisanteries*, I do not appreciate that sort of joke; *ce peintre est fort goûté dans certains milieux*, this painter is much liked in certain circles; *goûtez-vous la grâce de ces vers?*, do you feel the charm of these lines?; **~**, v.n. to have tea; to take a light lunch, or collation (in the afternoon); **se ~**, v.pr. to be tasted, tried, taken in small quantity.

goûter (gute), s.m. Tea, light repast (in the afternoon), five-o'clock tea; *à l'heure du ~*, at tea-time.

goutte (gut), s.f. [L *gutta*] **1.** Drop; dram, nip; *une ~ d'eau*, a drop of water; *boire la ~*, to have a drop (of liquor, not wine); *boire une ~*, to have a nip; (vulg.) *payer la ~*, to stand a drink; *~ à ~*, drop by drop; *~ à ~ on emplit la cave*, many a little makes a mickle; *ils se ressemblent comme deux ~s d'eau*, they are as like as two peas; **2.** (pathol.) gout; *il a la ~*, he is gouty; *~ militaire*, gleet; *~ sciatique*, sciatica; **3.** jot, bit. **~**, adv. In the least, at all, anything; *je n'y vois ~*, I do not see at all; *il n'y entend ~*, he does not understand a bit, or a jot, or in the least; he knows nothing about it.

gouttelette (gutlɛt), s.f. [dim. of *goutte*] Little drop, drip.

goutter (gute), v.n. To drip; to leak.

goutteu-x, -se (gutø), adj. (pathol.) Gouty. **~**, s.m.f. Gouty person.

gouttière (gutjɛr), s.f. [f. *goutter*) Gutter (⚠ of a roof, not of a street; the street-gutter = *le ruisseau*; also in fig. sense); *chat de ~*, stray cat; spout; fore-edge (of a book); groove (of a bone); (surg.) hollow splint.

gouvernable (guvɛrnabl), adj. Governable; manageable.

gouvernail (pl. **-s**) (guvɛrnaj), s.m. [L *gubernaculum*] Rudder, helm; ~ *vertical* or *azimutal*, vertical rudder (for azimuth steering); ~ *horizontal* or *d'altitude* or *de profondeur*, horizontal rudder (for altitude steering); dipping plane; ~ *avant*, bow-rudder; ~ *arrière*, stern-rudder; ~ *compensé*, balanced rudder; (fig.) *tenir le* ~, to be at the helm.

gouvernance (guvɛrnɑ̃s), s.f. (obs.) Governorship (in France before the Revolution).

gouvernant, -e (guvɛrnɑ̃), p. adj. Governing, ruling; *les classes* ~*es*, the ruling classes. *Les* ~*s*, s.m.pl. The rulers, the government.

gouvernante (guvɛrnɑ̃t), s.f. **1.** Governess; **2.** housekeeper (of a widower or bachelor). ⚠ Nowadays not 'governor's wife', which = *la femme du gouverneur*.

gouverne (guvɛrn), s.f. Guidance, direction, line of conduct; *ceci soit dit pour votre* ~, let me tell you that for your guidance; take your cue, remember that.

gouvernement (guvɛrnəmɑ̃), s.m. **1.** Government, rule, sway; management, conduct, direction; **2.** governorship, government; **3.** body of governing people, government, the Cabinet; *un* ~ *de droite, de gauche*, a conservative, a radical government; **4.** government house.

gouvernemental, -e, (aux) (guvɛrnəmɑ̃tal), adj. Governmental.

gouverner (guvɛrne), v.a. [L *gubernare*] **1.** To govern, to rule, to control, to direct; ~ *un pays*, to govern (or rule over) a country; ~ *sa maison*, to direct one's household; *il a su* ~ *sa barque*, he has cleverly managed his affairs; (gram.) ~ *l'accusatif*, to govern the accusative; **2.** to manage, to husband; ~ *sa dépense*, to husband one's revenue, one's resources, one's provisions; **3.** to steer (*sur*, for); ~, v.n. to answer the helm; *ce bateau gouverne bien*, this boat steers well; she answers, or feels, the helm; *le navire ne gouverne plus*, the boat does not answer the helm; **se** ~, v.pr. to govern or control oneself; to manage one's own affairs; to be governed; to answer the helm.

gouverneur (guvɛrnœr), s.m. **1.** Governor, ruler, head, manager; **2.** tutor, preceptor (in royal or aristocratic families). ⚠ *Gouverneur* is not used like 'governor' in the (colloq.) sense of 'father', *père*, nor in the (obs.) sense of 'steersman' = *homme de barre, barreur*, nor in the sense of 'employer', 'boss' = *patron*.

gouvernorat (guvɛrnɔra), s.m. Governorship.

goyave (gwajav), s.f. (bot.) Guava.

goyavier (gwajavje), s.m. (bot.) Guava-tree.

grabat (graba), s.m. [L *grabatus*] Pallet, wretched bed, truckle-bed; (fig.) *mourir sur un* ~, to die in utter destitution.

grabuge (grabyʒ), s.m. [It. *garbuglio*] A card-game; (fig.) squabble, row, brawl; *il va y avoir du* ~, there will be ructions; we are in for a hot time.

grâce (grɑs), s.f. [L *gratia*] **1.** Grace; favour; pardon, mercy; *demander* ~, to cry mercy, to crave quarter (*à*, from); *accorder* ~, to grant mercy, to forgive, to pardon (*à*, to); *demander, accorder, une* ~, to ask, to grant, a favour; *faire* ~ *à*, to let off, to spare, to forgive; *faire une* ~ *à X*, to do X a favour; *faites-moi la* ~ *de*, do me the favour of; *faire* ~ *de*, to remit, to dispense with, to let off; *l'an de* ~, the year of grace, in the year of our Lord; *coup de* ~, finishing stroke, death-blow; *à la* ~ *de Dieu!*, in God's hands!, at random; come what may!; ~ *à Dieu!*, thank God!; *de* ~*!*, pray!, for mercy's sake!; *de bonne* ~, readily, willingly, with a good grace; *de mauvaise* ~, reluctantly, grudgingly, with a bad grace; *être dans les bonnes* ~*s de*, to be liked, or trusted by; to be on good terms with, to be in the good graces of; *rentrer en* ~, to get into favour again; *par* ~, for mercy's sake; *par* ~ *pour*, for the sake of; *vous auriez mauvaise* ~ *à* (or *de*), it would ill become you to; ~ *d'état*, moral privilege; self-delusion; **2.** (pl.) thanks; prayer, thanksgiving; grace (after meat); *actions de* ~*s*, thanksgiving; *rendre* ~*s à*, to return thanks to; *je vous rends* ~*s pour*, I thank you for; **3.** gracefulness, elegance, charm, blandishment; (pej.) *faire des* ~*s*, to be full of airs and graces; *bonne* ~, kind reception, welcome; *une* ~ *captivante*, a winning charm; (myth.) *les trois Grâces*, the three Graces.

gracier (grasje), v.a. (law) To pardon, to reprieve.

gracieusement (grasjøzmɑ̃), adv. **1.** Graciously, kindly, gratuitously, by grace; **2.** gracefully, with grace.

gracieuseté (grasjøzte), s.f. **1.** Act of courtesy, of kindness, affability; **2.** gratuity.

gracieu-x, -se (grasjø), adj. **1.** Gracious, gratuitous, courteous; *à titre* ~, by free grant; **2.** graceful.

gracile (grasil), adj. [L *gracilis*] Gracile, slender and fragile, delicate, slim.

gracilité (grasilite), s.f. Gracility, slender fragility, delicate slimness.

gradation (grada'sjɔ̃), s.f. [L *gradatio*] Gradation; *par* ~*s insensibles*, by imperceptible degrees.

grade (grad), s.m. [L *gradus*] **1.** Rank, grade (⚠ not (as in U.S.A.) 'grade', 'gradient' = *pente*); *monter en* ~, to be promoted; (slang) *en prendre pour son* ~, to get it hot (according to one's responsibility); **2.** (math., geom.) grade = $\frac{1}{400}$ part of the circle.

gradé (grade), s.m. (mil). Non-commissioned officer.

gradin (gradɛ̃), s.m. [It. *gradino*] Step, ledge, shelf, bench, tier; *en ~s*, in tiers.

graduation (gradɥa'sjɔ̃), s.f. Graduating, graduation. ⚠ Not in the sense of taking or conferring academic degrees.

gradué, -e (gradɥe), p. adj. **1.** Graduated; progressive, gradual; **2.** (rare, also s.m.f.) graduate (of a university).

graduel, -le (gradɥɛl), adj. Gradual.

graduellement (gradɥɛlmɑ̃), adv. Gradually.

graduer (gradɥe), v.a. **1.** To graduate, to mark divisions or degrees on; **2.** to increase (difficulty, &c.). ⚠ Not used in the sense of to take or confer an academic degree.

graillement (grɑjmɑ̃), s.m. Huskiness, hoarseness.

grailler (grɑje), v.n. [f. *graille*, dialect wd for *corneille* = crow] **1.** To speak hoarsely; **2.** (hunt.) to sound the horn to recall the hounds.

graillon (grɑjɔ̃), s.m. [f. *gras*] **1.** Fat, burnt fat, remnants of badly cooked food; greaves; *sentir le ~*, to smell of badly cooked food or of burnt fat; **2.** thick expectoration, phlegm.

graillonner (grɑjɔne), v.n. **1.** To hawk up phlegm; to breathe as if hawking; **2.** to smell of bad food.

grain (grɛ̃), s.m. [L *granum*] **1.** Grain, berry, corn; *gros ~s*, wheat and rye; winter corn; *menus ~s*, barley, oats, spring corn; *en ~s*, in berries, whole; *poulets de ~*, corn-fed pullets; *~ de raisin*, grape; *~ de grêle*, hailstone; *~ de beauté*, mole; *~ de plomb*, shot; **2.** jot, bit, dash, touch; *un ~ de folie*, a touch of madness; *sans un ~ d'esprit, de bon sens*, without the slightest sense of humour, entirely devoid of common sense; **3.** bead; *~ de chapelet*, rosary bead; **4.** (of skin, of silk and other textiles) grain; *ruban gros ~*, petersham ribbon; *à gros ~*, coarse-grained; **5.** squall, shower; *essuyer un ~*, to be in a squall; (fig.) *veiller au ~*, to keep a sharp look-out; to practise strict economy; *risquer un ~* to risk a wrangle, to be in for a breeze; (slang) *avoir un ~*, to have a bee in one's bonnet, to be a little cracked, or crazy; **6.** (obs. and pharm.) grain, small weight ($\frac{1}{7000}$ of lb.).

graine (grɛn), s.f. Seed; *~ d'épinards*, bullions (of epaulets); *monter en ~*, to run to seed; (fig.) to be growing into an old maid; to be on the shelf; (fig.) *mauvaise ~*, bad lot; *~ de vers à soie*, silkworm eggs; *~ de lin*, linseed.

graineterie (grɛntri), s.f. Seed-trade.

graineti-er, -ère (grɛntje), s.m.f. Seedsman or woman; corn-chandler; syn. GRAINIER.

graissage (grɛsaʒ), s.m. Greasing, oiling, lubrication; *~ par bagues centrifuges*, lubrication by means of splash rings; *huile de ~*, lubricating oil; *~ sous pression*, forced lubrication.

graisse (grɛs), s.f. [L *crassus*] **1.** Fat, grease, lard; tallow; *~ de rôti*, dripping; *~ de rognon*, suet; *~ à friture*, lard; *~ de boucherie*, rough fat; *~ de porc*, pig's fat; lard; (mech.) oil; grease; *~ consistante*, thick or consistent grease; (colloq.) *~ de prison*, unhealthy fatness; *prendre de la ~*, to get fat.

graisser (grɛse), v.a. To oil, to grease, to lubricate; to dirty; to smear; *~*, v.n. (of wine) to get ropy; *~ la patte à X*, to grease X's palm; to tip or bribe X; *~ le marteau*, to tip the porter; *~ ses bottes*, to get ready (for kingdom come).

graisseur (grɛsœr), s.m. Lubricator; *~ à compression*, grease-squirt, lubrication-pump, grease-gun.

graisseu-x, -se (grɛsø), adj. Greasy; fat, fatty; (pathol.) *dégénérescence ~ du cœur*, fatty degeneration of the heart.

gramen (gramɛn), s.m. [L wd] (bot.) Grass; (U.S.A.) grama.

graminée (gramine), s.f. Gramineous plant.

grammaire (grammɛr), s.f. [Gr. *grammatikē*] Grammar; *~ comparée*, comparative grammar.

grammairien, -ne (grammɛrjɛ̃), s.m.f. Grammarian.

grammatical, -e, (aux) (grammatikal), adj. Grammatical.

grammaticalement (grammatikalmɑ̃), adv. Grammatically.

grammatiste (grammatist), s.m.f. (obs.) Grammarian, teacher.

gramme (gram), s.m. [Gr. *gramma*] Gramme, gram = 15·432 Troy grains.

gramophone (gramɔfɔn), s.m. [arbitrary modern formation] Gramophone, phonograph.

grand, -e (grɑ̃), adj. [L *grandis*] **1.** Great; large, big, tall; high, lofty, wide; capacious; *un ~ homme*, a great man; *un homme ~*, a tall man; *un ~ gaillard roux*, a tall, red-haired fellow; *une ~e bringue*, a big, gawky girl; *un ~ vieillard*, a grand old man; *une ~e personne*, a grown-up; *au ~ air*, in the open air; *de ~s airs*, airs of grandeur; *~ jour*, broad daylight; *~ livre*, ledger; *~'route*, high road; *~es eaux*, floods, fountains in full play at Versailles or St-Cloud; *~'messe*, high mass; *~ ressort*, mainspring; *en ~*, on a large scale; **2.** full; severe; intense; hard; *en ~ uniforme*, in full dress; *une ~e chaleur*, intense heat; *un ~ froid*, severe cold; *une ~e gelée*, a hard frost; **3.** capital (of letters); **4.** grand, great, noble, majestic; fashionable; *le ~ monde*, society; the fashionable world; *en ~ style*, in grand style, in a noble manner; *en ~ apparat*, with full ceremony; *en ~ habit*, in full dress; *trancher du ~*, to give oneself grand airs; **5.** main, open; *la ~e entrée*, the main entrance; *voleur de ~ chemin*; highwayman; *~ ouvert*, wide open; *grand aumônier*, s.m. grand almoner; *grand cordon*, s.m. grand cordon; *~'croix*, s.f. grand cross; s.m. Grand-Cross, Knight Grand-Cross; *~-duc*, s.m. grand duke; (ornith.) great horn-owl, eagle owl; *~-duché*, s.m. grand duchy; *~e-duchesse*, s.f. grand duchess; *~'garde*, s.f. (mil.) main guard; *~'maman*, s.f. grandmamma, granny; *~'mère*, s.f. grandmother; (of animals) grandam; *~-oncle*, s.m. great-uncle; *~-père*, grandfather; (of animals) grandsire; *~'tante*, s.f. great-aunt; *cela ne vaut pas ~'chose*, that is not up to much; *un pas ~'chose*, a bad lot.

grand (grɑ̃), s.m. **1.** (sing.) Greatness, grandeur, sublimity; **2.** high personage, magnate, lord, grandee; (at school) *un ~*, a big boy, a pupil in the upper forms; *une ~e*, a big girl, one of the senior pupils; *un ~ d'Espagne*, a Spanish grandee; *les ~s*, great folks, the great people; the lords and ladies; (slang) the nobs.

grandelet, -te (grɑ̃dəlɛ), adj. Biggish, pretty tall, tallish.

grandement (grɑ̃dmɑ̃), adv. Greatly, largely, highly, vastly; grandly, handsomely; *faire ~ les choses*, to treat guests, friends, &c., handsomely; to do things well; *il est ~ temps de partir*; it's high time to go.

grandesse (grɑ̃dɛs), s.f. Grandeeship.

grandeur (grɑ̃dœr), s.f. [f. *grand*] Size, bulk, magnitude, extent, length, breadth, tallness, height; greatness, dignity, grandeur, nobleness; (title) his Lordship; *~ d'âme*, magnanimity; (*de*) *~ naturelle* or *~ nature*, life-size; *par ordre de ~*, according to size; *regarder X du haut de sa ~*, to look down upon X.

grandiloquence (grɑ̃dilɔkɑ̃s), s.f. Grandiloquence.

grandiloquent, -e (grɑ̃dilɔkɑ̃), adj. [L *grandiloquus*] Grandiloquent, pompous, bombastic (language).

grandiose (grɑ̃djoz), adj. Grandiose, grand.

grandir (grɑ̃dir), v.n. To grow, to grow up, to grow big, to grow tall; to increase, to rise; *cet enfant grandit trop*; *il sort de ses habits*, that child is growing too fast, he is growing out of his clothes; ~, v.a. to magnify, to exaggerate; **se ~**, v.pr. to make oneself appear taller, or greater, or important.

grandissement (grɑ̃dismɑ̃), s.m. Increase; growing; magnifying.

grandissime (grɑ̃disim), adj. Very great, tremendous.

grand'mère, grand'messe, grand-père, &c. See GRAND.

grange (grɑ̃ʒ), s.f. [LL *granica*] Barn. ⚠ Not 'grange', which (nowadays) = *petit château, résidence de campagne.*

granit (granit, grani), s.m. [It. *granito*] Granite; (fig.) *cœur de ~*, heart of stone.

granité, -e (granite), adj. Granité, grained. ~, s.m. Granité (linen or woollen material).

granitique (granitik), adj. Granitic.

granitoïde (granitɔid), adj. Granitoid.

granivore (granivɔr), adj. [f. L *granum*+ *vorare*] Granivorous.

granulaire (granylɛr), adj. [f. L *granum*] Granular.

granulation (granyla'sjɔ̃). s.f. Granulation.

granule (granyl), s.m. [f. L *granulum*] Granule.

granuler (granyle), v.a. To granulate; *granulé, -e*, granulated.

granuleu-x, -se (granylø), adj. Granulous.

graphie (grafi), s.f. **graphisme** (grafism), s.m. [f. Gr. *graphē*] Writing, system of writing, using letters, signs, or symbols.

graphique (grafik), adj. Graphic; ⚠ see *graphiquement*. ~, s.m. (geom., and sciences) Diagram, record, explanatory drawing, graph.

graphiquement (grafikmɑ̃), adv. Graphically, by writing; with the help of diagrams. ⚠ Not used figuratively in French; in English 'graphically' often means 'vividly' = *d'une manière nette et précise.*

graphite (grafit), s.m. (min.) Graphite, plumbago.

graphologie (grafɔlɔʒi), s.f. [Gr. *graphē*+ *logos*] Graphology.

graphologique (grafɔlɔʒik), adj. Graphological.

graphophone. (grafɔfɔn), s.m. See syn. GRAMOPHONE.

grappe (grap), s.f. [Germ. orig.] Bunch, cluster; *~ de raisin*, bunch of grapes; *~ de fleurs*, cluster of flowers; *en ~*, in a bunch; (fig.) *mordre à la ~*, to jump at it; to swallow the bait. ⚠ *Grappe* must not be translated by 'grape' which = *grain de raisin, raisin.*

grappillage (grapijaʒ), s.m. Vine-gleaning; (fig.) pickings, petty pilfering.

grappiller (grapije), v.a.n. To glean (grapes); (fig.) to pick up a trifle, to get pickings, to pilfer in a small way.

grappilleu-r, -se (grapijœr), s.m.f. Pilferer.

grappillon (grapijɔ̃), s.m. Small bunch of grapes.
grappin (grapɛ̃), s.m. [OF *grape*, hook] Grapnel, grappling-iron, hook; (fig.) *jeter* or *mettre le ~ sur*, to hook, to clutch; to get into one's clutches; to buttonhole; *elle a mis le ~ sur lui*, she has got her claws into him.
gras, -se (grɑ), adj. [L *crassus*] **1.** Fat, fleshy, fatty; *gros et ~*, fat and lusty; *~ comme un moine*, as fat as a pig; *tuer le veau ~*, to kill the fatted calf; **2.** oily; waxy, sticky; *chiffons ~*, oily rags, **3.** thick, slippery, heavy; rich, fertile; *terres ~ses*, rich lands, fertile fields; *terre ~se*, argillaceous (clayey) soil; *le terrain, le chemin était ~*, the ground was slippery; the road was greasy; **4.** made with meat; juicy, dressed with meat-gravy; *soupe ~se, potage ~*, meat-soup; **5.** shrove; les *jours ~*, Shrovetide, flesh-days; *mardi ~*, Shrove Tuesday; **6.** broad, spicy; *un conte ~*, a spicy tale, a licentious story; **7.** (of wine) ropy; *tourner au ~*, to get ropy; (of cheese) rich; (of the voice) oily, thick; *parler ~*, to speak with a burr; (of a cough) loose; (of coal) caking; *faire la ~se matinée*, to get up very late.
gras (grɑ), s.m. Fat, fat part; *le ~ de la jambe*, the calf; *faire ~*, not to fast, to eat meat; *riz au ~*, rice cooked with meat or with gravy; *~-double*, s.m. tripe.
grassement (grasmɑ̃), adv. Plentifully; liberally, handsomely; comfortably, in plenty, in clover; *être payé ~*, to draw a large salary; *payer ~*, to pay generously; *vivre ~*, to live on the fat of the land.
grasset (grasɛ), s.m. (of horses) Stifle.
grasseyement (grasɛjmɑ̃), s.m. [f. *gras*] Burr, speaking with a burr, guttural pronunciation of the *r*, usual in France north of the Loire.
grasseyer (grasɛje), v.n. To speak with a burr; (the opposite way is '*rouler les r*').
grassouillet, -te (grasujɛ), adj. Chubby, plump.
grateron (gratrɔ̃), s.m. (bot.) Goose-grass, cleavers.
graticuler (gratikyle), v.a. [It. *graticolare*] To divide (a drawing) into squares (in order to reproduce it on a smaller or larger scale).
gratification (gratifika'sjɔ̃), s.f. Gratuity, present, tip, reward, extra pay. ⚠ Not 'gratification' which = *satisfaction, contentement, indulgence.*
gratifier (gratifje), v.a. [L *gratificari*] To favour (*de*, with), to bestow on; *~ X d'un coup de poing*, to favour X with a blow.
gratin (gratɛ̃), s.m. [f. *gratter*] (cook.) Gratin; *au ~*, au gratin, gratine, browned, dressed with bread-crumbs and grated cheese and baked; (fig.) *le ~*, the upper ten, the cream of society; the most exclusive set.
gratiner (gratine), v.a.n. (cook.) **1.** To brown, to prepare au gratin; **2.** to catch, to burn slightly.
gratiole (grasjɔl), s.f. (bot.) Hyssop; hedge-hyssop.
gratis (gratis), adv. [L wd] Free, without any charge, gratuitously, gratis; *entrée ~*, free admittance; syn. GRATUITEMENT.
gratitude (gratityd), s.f. [L *gratitudo*] Gratitude, thankfulness.
grattage (grataʒ), s.m. [f. *gratter*] Scratching, scraping; scratching out, erasing.
gratte (grat), s.f. **1.** (gard., naut.) Scraper; **2.** pickings, cabbage, graft, illicit small profits; **3.** (comp.) *~-ciel*, s.m. sky-scraper; (bot.) *~-cul*, s.m. hip, dog-rose berry; *~-papier*, s.m. quill-driver.
gratter (grate), v.a.n. [Germ. *kratzen*] **1.** To scrape, to scratch; to scrape off, to scratch out; *trop ~ cuit, trop parler nuit*, least said, soonest mended; *~ X où ça lui démange*, or, *~ X au bon endroit*, to flatter X's weakness; **2.** to overtake; *il gratte tout le monde sur la route*, he overtakes all cars on the road; **3.** to pilfer in a small way, to make small profits (generally illicit) or small economies; **se ~**, v.pr. to scratch oneself, to rub oneself; *se ~ la tête*, to scratch one's head; *qui se sent galeux se gratte*, let him whom the cap fits wear it.
grattoir (gratwar), s.m. Eraser, scratching-knife; (gard.) scraper.
gratuit, -e (gratɥi), adj. [L *gratuitus*] Gratuitous, free; *supposition ~e*, gratuitous inference.
gratuité (gratɥite), s.f. Gratuitousness. ⚠ Not 'gratuity' which = *gratification.*
gratuitement (gratɥitmɑ̃), adv. Gratuitously, gratis, free of charge.
grau (gro), s.m. (in South of France) Channel connecting a salt lake or river with the sea.
gravatier (gravatje), s.m. Rubbish-carrier.
gravats (gravɑ), s.m.pl [f. *grève*] Rubbish, stones and old plaster; syn. GRAVOIS.
grave (grav), adj. [L *gravis*] Grave, heavy, serious; solemn, ponderous; serious, severe; weighty, momentous; *prendre un air ~*, to assume a solemn air; *accent ~*, grave accent; *blessure ~*, dangerous wound; *note ~*, low note; *ton ~*, deep tone; *du ~ au doux, du plaisant au sévère*, from grave to gay.
gravé, -e (grave), p.adj. Engraved, carved; pitted, pock-marked.
graveler (gravəle), v.a. To strew with gravel.
graveleu-x, -se (gravlø), adj. **1.** Sandy, gritty; **2.** suffering from gravel; **3.** smutty.
gravelle (gravɛl), s.f. [f. *grève*] (pathol.) Gravel.

gravelure (gravlyr), s.f. Smutty talk, obscenity, spicy bit.

gravement (gravmɑ̃), adv. Gravely, seriously, solemnly; deeply, severely; ~ *blessé*, dangerously wounded; ~ *offensé*, grievously offended.

graver (grave), v.a. [OHG *graban*] To engrave; to impress, to imprint; ~ *à l'eau-forte*, to etch; ~ *au burin*, to engrave; ~ *en creux*, to sink; ~ *en relief*, to emboss; ~ *quelque chose dans la mémoire de X*, to impress something on X's mind; **se** ~, v.pr. to get engraved, impressed; *cette leçon se grava dans sa mémoire*, that experience remained vivid in his memory.

graves (grav), s.f.pl. (In the Bordeaux region) Sandy and stony ground; ~, s.m. Graves wine.

graveur (gravœr), s.m. Engraver, etcher; die-sinker.

gravier (gravje), s.m. [f. *grève*] Gravel, grit.

gravir (gravir), v.a. [f. L *gradi*] To climb, to clamber up, to scale, to ascend.

gravitation (gravita'sjɔ̃), s.f. [f. modern L *gravitare*] Gravitation.

gravité (gravite), s.f. [L *gravitas*] **1.** Gravity, seriousness, solemnity, sedateness; **2.** gravity, weight, importance, grievousness; deepness (of a sound); **3.** gravity; *centre de* ~, centre of gravity.

graviter (gravite), v.n. To gravitate.

gravois (gravwa), s.m.pl. See syn. GRAVATS.

gravure (gravyr), s.f. [f. *graver*] Engraving, print; ~ *sur bois*, woodcut; ~ *au trait*, line-engraving; ~ *à l'eau-forte*, also *eau-forte*, s.f., etching; (colloq.) illustration, picture.

gré (gre), s.m. [L *gratum*] Will, pleasure, inclination, liking, taste; consent, agreement; gratitude; *à votre* ~*!*, as you please!; *est-ce à votre* ~*?*, is this to your liking?; *rien n'était à son* ~, nothing would suit him; nothing was to his taste; nothing was good enough for him; *à son* ~, *tout était médiocre*, according to him everything was second-rate; *bon* ~ *mal* ~, or *de* ~ *ou de force*, willy-nilly; *de plein* ~, willingly; of his own free will; *contre son* ~, unwillingly; against the grain; by compulsion; *prendre en* ~, to take a liking to; to regard favourably; *de bon* ~, of one's own accord; *de mauvais* ~, grudgingly, reluctantly; *vendre de* ~ *à* ~, to sell by private contract; (antonym: *vendre par adjudication*, to sell by auction); *je lui en sais* ~ (or *bon* ~), I feel grateful to him; *sachons lui* ~ *de cela*, let us count that to his credit; *savoir mauvais* ~ *à X de*, to take it ill that X should; to resent X doing; *au* ~ *des flots*, at the mercy of the waves.

gréage (greaʒ), s.m. [f. *gréer*] Rigging (of a boat).

grèbe (grɛb), s.m. (ornith.) Grebe.

grec, -que (grɛk), adj. [Gr. *graikoi*, L *graecus*] Greek, Grecian (rare except of architecture, facial outline or attitude), Hellenic; *calendes* ~*ques*, Greek calends. ~, **-que**, s.m.f. Greek, Hellene; ~, s.m. (the) Greek (language); sharper; ~**que**, s.f. Greek key-pattern, fret, grecque; (bookbind.) bookbinder's saw.

gréciser (gresize), v.a. To hellenize.

gréco-romain, -e (grekorɔmɛ̃), adj. Graeco-Roman.

grecque (grɛk), s.f. See GREC.

grecquer (grɛke), v.a. (bookbind.) To notch with the saw (*grecque*).

gredin, -e (grədɛ̃), s.m.f. Scoundrel, villain, scamp, bad lot.

gredinerie (grədinri), s.f. Villainy, knavery, rascally trick, dirty trick.

gréement (gremɑ̃), s.m. (naut.) Rigging.

gréer (gree), v.a. [f. ON *greidi*] (naut.) To rig.

greffage (grɛfaʒ), s.m. Grafting (of trees, vines, &c.).

greffe[1] (grɛf), s.m. [f. Gr. *grapheion*] Record-office, registry; registrar's office.

greffe[2] (grɛf), s.f. [f. Gr. *grapheion*] (hort.) **1.** Graft, grafting; **2.** graft, bud, shoot, scion; ~ *en couronne*, crown-grafting; ~ *en écusson*, graft by gems, or budding; ~ *en fente*, cleft grafting; ~ *par rapprochement*, graft by approach; inarching; (surg.) graft.

greffer (grɛfe), v.a. To graft; syn. ENTER; **se** ~, v.pr. to be grafted.

greffeu-r, -se (grɛfœr), s.m.f. Grafter.

greffier (grɛfje), s.m. Clerk of the Court; registrar; recorder; ~*-municipal*, town clerk.

greffoir (grɛfwar), s.m. Grafting-knife.

greffon (grɛfɔ̃), s.m. Graft, bud, shoot, scion (to be inserted).

grégaire (gregɛr), adj. [L *gregarius*] Gregarious.

grège (grɛʒ), adj. [It. *greggia*] (of silk only) Raw.

grégeois (greʒwɑ), adj. m. *Feu* ~, Greek fire.

grégorien, -ne (gregɔrjɛ̃), adj. [f. Pope *Gregory* I] Gregorian; *chant* ~, Gregorian chant, plain-chant; *calendrier* ~, Gregorian calendar.

grègues (grɛg), s.f.pl. (old) [f. *grecque*] Breeches; *tirer ses* ~*s*, to scamper off, to take to one's heels.

grêle (grɛl), adj. [L *gracilis*] Slender, delicate, slim; thin; (of sound) piping, thin; *intestin* ~, small intestine; *aux jambes* ~*s*, spindle-shanked; syn. FLUET, MENU, GRACILE.

grêle (grɛl), s.f. [OF *gresle*; orig. unkn.] Hail, hailstorm, hail-shower; hailstone; ~ *de coups*, hail of blows; *méchant comme la* ~, as wicked as sin.

grêler (grɛle), v.n. To hail; *il grêle*, it is hailing; *être grêlé*, (*a*) to be ravaged or damaged by hail; (*b*) to be pitted with smallpox, to be pock-marked.

grelin (grəlɛ̃), s.m. (naut.) Hawser, small cable, warp, cablet.

grêlon (grɛlɔ̃), s.m. Hail-stone.

grelot (grəlo), s.m. Small round bell, horse-bell, sheep-bell, toy bell, hawk-bell; (fig.) *attacher le* ~, to bell the cat, to take the initiative; *trembler le* ~, to shiver, to shake till one's teeth chatter.

grelotter (grəlɔte), v.n. To shiver with cold, to shake till one's teeth chatter.

greluchon (grəlyʃɔ̃), s.m. (colloq., pej.) Young paramour, 'amant de cœur' of a kept woman; a lover who lives at the expense of a woman.

grémial (pl. **aux**) (gremjal), s.m. [f. L *gremium*] Gremial (bishop's apron).

grémil (gremil), s.m. (bot.) Gromwell.

grémille (gremij), s.f. (ichth.) Ruff.

grenache (grənaʃ), s.m. A kind of vine, in Languedoc and Roussillon; the wine made from this.

grenade (grənad), s.f. [Span. *granada*, f. L *granatum*] **1.** (bot.) Pomegranate; **2.** (mil.) grenade.

grenadier (grənadje), s.m. **1.** (bot.) Pomegranate-tree; **2.** (mil.) grenadier; (fig., of a woman) *c'est un vrai* ~, she is a regular termagant.

grenadière (grənadjɛr), s.f. **1.** (of a musket) Middle band, ring; *mettre à la* ~, to sling (a rifle); **2.** grenade-pouch.

grenadille (grənadij), s.f. (bot.) Passion-flower, granadilla.

grenadin, -e (grənadɛ̃), adj. s.m.f. (Native) of Granada. ~, s.m. **1.** (cook.) Grenadine (a dish of glazed veal or poultry fillets); **2.** (ornith.) African finch; **3.** (bot.) a kind of carnation; ~**e**, s.f. **1.** grenadine (silk); **2.** pomegranate syrup.

grenaille (grənɑj), s.f. [f. *grain*] **1.** Small shot, granulated metal; **2.** refuse grain, tailings; ~ *de riz*, rice-dust.

grenailler (grənɑje), v.a. To granulate (metal).

grenat (grəna), s.m. [L *granatum*] Garnet. ~, adj. m. Garnet-red, claret.

grener (grəne), v.n. To run to seed, to seed; ~, v.a. **1.** to granulate; **2.** to grain (leather, &c.); **3.** (engr.) to stipple.

grènetis (grɛnti), s.m. (of coins) Milling, milled edge.

grenier (grənje), s.m. [L *granarium*] Loft, granary, warehouse; garret, attic, lumber-room; ~*s d'abondance*, public store-house; ~ *à foin*, hay-loft; *de la cave au* ~, from garret to cellar; (fig.) large room or study on upper floor, as in *le Grenier des Goncourt*.

grenouille (grənuj), s.f. [L *ranula*] Frog; (pop.) *manger la* ~, to run away with the till.

grenouillère (grənujɛr), s.f. Froggery; swamp, marsh, damp place.

grenouillet (grənujɛ), s.m. (bot.) Solomon's seal; syn. SCEAU DE SALOMON.

grenouillette (grənujɛt), s.f (bot.) Frog-bit, water-crowfoot; (pathol.) ranula, tumour of the tongue.

grenu, -e (grəny), adj. **1.** Grainy; **2.** grained (as leather, skin, marble, &c.); **3.** clotted (as oil).

grès (grɛ), s.m. [f. OHG *grioz*] **1.** Sandstone; gritstone; ~ *à meule*, millstone grit; **2.** stoneware.

gréseu-x, -se (grezø), adj. Gritty, of the nature of gritstone.

grésière (grezjɛr), s.f. Sandstone quarry.

grésil (grezil), s.m. [f. *grès*] Sleet, small hail.

grésillement (grezijmɑ̃), s.m. Crackling, noisy shrivelling; pattering (as of sleet); sizzling, sputtering sound (as of frying).

grésiller (grezije), v.n. To sleet; to crackle, to sizzle; to patter; to shrivel up (in the heat).

grésillon (grezijɔ̃), s.m. Small-size coals.

grève (grɛv), s.f. [LL *grava*] **1.** Strand, beach; place of execution; (in Rom. antiq. the place of execution was the strand; cf. *Place de Grève* in Paris, near the Seine); **2.** strike; *faire* ~, or *se mettre en* ~, to strike, or to go out on strike; *être en* ~, to be on strike, to be out on strike; *briseurs de* ~, strike-breakers; ~ *générale*, general strike; ~ *de sympathie*, sympathetic strike.

grever (grəve), v.a. [L *gravare*] To burden, to encumber (*de*, with).

gréviste (grevist), s.m.f. Striker.

grianneau (pl. **-x**) (griano), s.m. (ornith.) Young grouse.

gribouillage (gribujaʒ), s.m. Scrawl; (paint.) daub.

gribouille (gribuj), s.m. [n. of a character in old farces] Booby, simpleton, noodle.

gribouiller (gribuje), v.a.n. To scrawl, to scribble; to daub.

gribouillette (gribujɛt), s.f. (game) Scramble; *à la* ~, at random, in a scramble.

gribouilleu-r, -se (gribujœr), s.m.f. Scrawler, scribbler; sorry draughtsman.

gribouillis (gribuji), s.m. Scrawl, illegible scribbling.

grief (griɛf), s.m. [OF *gref*, f. *grever*] **1.** Grievance; injury, wrong; **2.** complaint, cause of complaint; *faire* ~ *à X de*, to count as a grievance against X, to lay blame on X for, to impute an injury to X; *je ne vous en fais pas* ~, I do not charge you with that; I do not condemn you on that score; *redresser*

un ~, to redress a grievance. ⚠ Not English 'grief', which = *chagrin*.
gri-ef, -ève (griɛf), adj. (rare) [L *gravis*] Grievous, severe, dangerous.
grièvement (griɛvmɑ̃), adv. Grievously, dangerously; ~ *blessé*, severely wounded.
grièveté (griɛvte), s.f. (obs.) Grievousness.
griffade (grifad), s.f. Scratch, clawing.
griffe (grif), s.f. [f. OHG *grifan*] **1.** Claw; talon (espec. of bird of prey); (fig., pl.) clutches; *coup de* ~, scratch; (fig.) ill turn, sharp word; *tomber sous la* ~ *de X* or *dans les* ~*s de X*, to fall into X's clutches; **2.** signature, stamp, facsimile of signature; *revêtu de ma* ~, bearing my signature; **3.** (agric.) root (of asparagus); offset tuber (of anemones, &c.); **4.** (mech.) ~ *d'accouplement*, dog or claw of the coupling.
griffer (grife), v.a. To scratch, to claw.
griffon (grifɔ̃), s.m. [L *gryphus*] **1.** (myth., herald.) Griffin, griffon, gryphon; **2.** griffon (dog); **3.** a kind of tap, in watering places.
griffonnage (grifɔnaʒ), s.m. Scrawl; syn. GRIBOUILLAGE.
griffonner (grifɔne), v.a.n. To scrawl, to scribble.
griffonneu-r, -se (grifɔnœr), s.m.f. Scribbler, scrawler.
griffu, -e (grify), adj. Clawed, taloned, having claws or talons.
griffure (grifyr), s.f. Scratch.
grigne (griɲ), s.f. [f. *grigner*] Pucker; slit in breadcrust.
grigner (griɲe), v.n. [OHG *grinan*] (sewing, dressm.) To pucker, to be uneven.
grignon (griɲɔ̃), s.m. Crust end of French loaf of bread.
grignoter (griɲɔte), v.a. To nibble, to gnaw; to peck at; (fig.) to use up little by little; to acquire gradually.
grignotis (griɲɔti), s.m. (engr.) Dotting.
grigou (grigu), s.m. (pop.) Skinflint, miser, screw, tight-wad.
gril (gri), s.m. Gridiron, grill; toaster; (fig.) *être sur le* ~, to be on tenter-hooks, or upon thorns, or in a stew.
grillade (grijad), s.f. (cook.) Grill, broiled meat.
grillage (grijaʒ), s.m. **1.** Grilling, toasting, broiling; singeing (of hair, fowls, pigs, &c.); **2.** (metall.) roasting; **3.** wire-work, wire-netting, wire-lattice, railing.
grillager (grijaʒe), v.a. To fit or enclose with wire-netting or with a wooden lattice; to lattice.
grillageur (grijaʒœr), s.m. Wire-worker.
grille (grij), s.f. [L *craticula*] **1.** Iron gate, iron railing; **2.** grate, grating; **3.** fire-bars; **4.** cipher, key to secret writing, frame.
grille-pain (grijpɛ̃), s.m. invar. Toaster.
griller (grije), v.a. **1.** To grill, to toast, to broil, to burn; to singe; (metall.) to roast; ~ *une cigarette*, (pop.) *en* ~ *une*, to smoke a cigarette; ~ *un moteur*, to overheat an engine; *grillé par le soleil*, scorched, parched by the sun; *il grille d'envie de*, he is burning, or longing to; **2.** to enclose with iron railing, to rail in, to lattice, to grate.
grillon (grijɔ̃), s.m. [L *gryllus*] (ent.) Cricket; ~ *domestique*, house cricket; ~*-taupe*, mole-cricket, fen-cricket. ⚠ Note that French *criquet* = locust.
grimaçant, -e (grimasɑ̃), p. adj. Grinning, wry, distorted, twisted.
grimace (grimas), s.f. [etym. dub.] Grimace, grin, wry face, face; sham, humbug, affectation, airs and graces; *faire la* ~ *à*, to make faces at; (fig.) to show reluctance to; *faire des* ~*s*, to make faces; (fig.) to simper, to give oneself airs.
grimacer (grimase), v.n. To make wry faces, to grimace, to grin; to pucker; *un gilet qui grimace*, a waistcoat that puckers.
grimaci-er, -ère (grimasje), adj. Grimacing, mincing, simpering; shamming, canting, finical. ~, s.m.f. Grimacer, simperer, humbug.
grimage (grimaʒ), s.m. (theatr.) Make-up.
grimaud, -e (grimo), adj. Grim, peevish, cross, ill-tempered. ~, s.m. Dunce, fool, scribbler.
grime (grim), s.m. [f. It. *grimo*] (theatr.) Old fogy, dotard; actor playing such a part. ⚠ Not English 'grime' which = *suie, crasse*.
grimer (grime), v.a. To make up, to paint the face of; **se** ~, v.pr. to make up, to paint one's face, to wrinkle one's face, to make oneself unrecognizable (with paint, false hair, &c.).
grimoire (grimwar), s.m. [corrupt. of *grammaire*] Conjuring book, black book; (now fig.) illegible scrawl, unintelligible document, double Dutch, gibberish, jargon.
grimpant, -e (grɛ̃pɑ̃), p. adj. Climbing, creeping; *plante* ~*e*, creeper. ~, s.m. (slang) Trousers, pants, slacks, bags.
grimper (grɛ̃pe), v.n.a. [f. *gripper*] To climb, to clamber up, to scale, to mount; (of plants) to creep up; (colloq.) *faire* ~ *X*, to pull X's leg.
grimpereau (pl. **-x**) (grɛ̃pro), s.m. (ornith.) Tree-creeper.
grimpeu-r, -se (grɛ̃pœr), adj. Climbing. ~, s.m.f. Climber; *les* ~*s*, (ornith.) the climbers (woodpecker, parrot, &c.).
grincement (grɛ̃smɑ̃), s.m. Grating, grinding, grating sound, gnashing (of teeth); *il y aura des pleurs et des* ~*s de dents*, there will be weeping and gnashing of teeth.

grincer (grɛ̃se), v.n.a. [etym. dub.] To grind, to grate, to creak, to gnash; *ce bruit me fait ~ des dents*, this noise sets my teeth on edge, or grates on me; *la fenêtre grince*, the window is grating (on its hinges).

grincheu-x, -se (grɛ̃ʃø), adj. [f. *grincer*] Grumpy, surly, crabbed, peevish. ~, s.m.f. Grumbler.

gringalet (grɛ̃galɛ), s.m. Puny fellow, undersized man, whipster. ~, adj. Puny, undersized.

griot (grijo), s.m. **1.** Seconds (of meal or flour); **2.** ~, *-te*, s.m.f. witch-doctor in Africa.

griotte (grijɔt), s.f. **1.** (bot.) Egriot cherry; **2.** a kind of marble, with red and brown spots.

grippage, grippement (gripaʒ, gripmɑ̃), s.m. (mech., motor., &c.) Seizing; jam, jamming, excessive friction, overheating, insufficient oiling.

grippe (grip), s.f. [f. *gripper*] **1.** Influenza, (colloq.) flu; **2.** dislike; *prendre X en ~*, to take a dislike to X; (jest.) to take a scunner at X; to get one's knife into X.

grippé, -e (gripe), p. adj. **1.** Ill with influenza; **2.** (mech.) seized.

grippeminaud (gripmino), s.m. Grimalkin, hypocrite, dissembling rascal.

gripper (gripe), v.a. [f. OLG *gripan*] To pounce upon, to snatch up, to clutch; to grip, to grasp or hold tightly; ~, v.n. **1.** (mech.) to seize, to jam, to stop (because of insufficient oiling, overheating, &c.); **2.** (dressm.) to pucker, to wrinkle, to shrivel, to shrink.

grippe-sou (gripsu), s.m. (pl. *grippe-sous*) Skinflint, miser, pinch-penny, curmudgeon, screw, money-grubber.

gris, -e (gri, fem. griz), adj. [OHG wd] Grey; gray; grey-haired; grizzled, grizzly; *faire ~e mine à X*, to give X black looks; *il lui en fait voir de ~es*, he gives him a warm time of it; he leads him a dance; *la nuit tous les chats sont ~*, when lights are away all cats are grey; *un homme à cheveux ~*, a grey-haired man; (print.) *lettres ~es*, flourished letters. ~, s.m. **1.** Grey; *~ cendré*, ash-grey; *~ perle*, pearl-grey; *~ pommelé*, dapple-grey; **2.** tipsy, fuddled, drunk; *il est ~ comme un Polonais*, he is as drunk as a lord.

grisaille (grizɑj), s.f. Grisaille; black and white check.

grisailler (grizɑje), v.n.a. To paint in grey or grisaille.

grisâtre (grizɑtr), adj. Greyish.

griser (grize), v.a. [f. *gris*] **1.** To fuddle, to make tipsy; (fig.) to intoxicate, to exalt; *il se grise de mots*, he gets carried away by his own eloquence; *ses premiers succès l'ont grisé*, his first successes have turned his head; **se ~**, v.pr. to get drunk (*de*, on); to intoxicate oneself (with); **2.** to paint grey, to tone down (a picture).

griserie (grizri), s.f. Tipsiness; (fig.) intoxication, exaltation.

griset (grizɛ), s.m. **1.** (ornith.) Young goldfinch; **2.** (ichth.) a kind of large shark.

grisette (grizɛt), s.f. (obsolescent) Coquettish work-girl or shop-girl.

grisgris, grigri (grigri), s.m. African negro's amulet.

grisoller (grizɔle), v.n. (of larks) To carol, to warble.

grison (grizɔ̃), s.m. **1.** Greybeard; **2.** donkey; **3.** (obs.) valet, dressed in grey and employed as secret messenger.

grisonnant, -e (grizɔnɑ̃), p. adj. Turning grey; grizzled.

grisonner (grizɔne), v.n. To turn grey, to grow grey.

grisou (grizu), s.m. [Walloon wd] Fire-damp; *coup de ~*, explosion of fire-damp.

grive (griv), s.f. (ornith.) Thrush; *saoul comme une ~*, as drunk as a fiddler, or as a lord; (prov.) *faute de ~s, on mange des merles*, half a loaf is better than no bread.

grivelé, -e (grivle), adj. [f. *grive*] Speckled, dappled.

griveler (grivle), v.n.a. To consume drink or food without having money to pay for it; to pilfer.

grivèlerie (grivɛlri), s.f. Consuming food or drink without having money to pay for it.

grivois, -e (grivwɑ), adj. Broad, spicy, rather smutty; *conte ~*, broad story; *chanson ~e*, spicy ditty.

grivoiserie (grivwazri), s.f. Broad, spicy talk or story.

groenlandais, -e (grɔɛnlɑ̃dɛ), adj. s.m.f. Of Greenland, Greenlander.

grog (grɔg), s.m. [Engl. wd] Grog, toddy.

grognard (grɔɲar), adj. s.m. Grumbling, grumbler; veteran (espec. of Napoleonic wars).

grognement (grɔɲəmɑ̃), s.m. Groan, grunt, grunting, growl, growling, snarl, snarling; (fig.) grumbling.

grogner (grɔɲe), v.n. [L *grunnire*] To grunt, to groan, to growl, to snarl; (fig.) to grumble.

grogneu-r, -se (grɔɲœr), adj. s.m.f. Grumbling, grumbler.

grognon (grɔɲɔ̃), adj. (usually invar. in the fem.) [f. *grogner*] Grumbling, sullen; *une fille ~*, a sullen girl. ~, s.m.f. Grumbler, growler, croaker, peevish sullen person, morose person.

grognonner (grɔɲɔne), v.n.a. To grumble, to mutter unpleasantly, to grunt.

groin (grwɛ̃), s.m. Snout (of a hog); bestial face. ⚠ Not English 'groin', which = *aine*.

grole, grolle (grɔl), s.f. [L *gracula*] (ornith.) Rook.
grommeler (grɔmle), v.n.a. [Germ. *grummeln*] To mutter, to grumble, to growl.
grommellement (grɔmɛlmɑ̃), s.m. Growl, grumble; muttering.
grondant, -e (grɔ̃dɑ̃), p. adj. Roaring, rumbling, booming; (fig.) threatening.
grondement (grɔ̃dmɑ̃), s.m. Roar, roaring; rumbling; booming; pealing, peal.
gronder (grɔ̃de), v.n. [L *grundire*] To roar; to rumble, to boom; to growl; to snarl; ~, v.a. to scold, to chide, to reprimand.
gronderie (grɔ̃dri), s.f. Reprimand, scolding, chiding.
grondeu-r, -se (grɔ̃dœr), adj. Scolding, grumbling, grousing, nagging. ~, s.m.f. Scold, regular grumbler, fault-finder.
grondin (grɔ̃dɛ̃), s.m. (ichth.) Red gurnet, gurnard.
groom (grum), s.m. [Engl. wd] Boy servant, lad; 'buttons', page. ⚠ In French *groom* is only used for a young manservant, especially in hotels, while in English it has other senses, ex.: groom of the Chamber = *gentilhomme de la Chambre (du roi)*; the bridegroom = *le marié*; groomsman = *garçon d'honneur*. English 'groom' in the sense manservant is archaic or obsolete; now it means a servant who looks after the horses and stables.
gros, -se (gro), adj. [LL *grossus*] Large, big, stout, bulky, great, thick, swollen; fat, corpulent, stout, obese, coarse, broad, loud, plain; ~ *bétail*, cattle, bovines; ~*se caisse*, big drum; *avoir le cœur* ~, to be heavy-hearted, or deeply affected; *en avoir* ~ *sur le cœur*, to have had as much as one can bear; *une* ~*se femme*, a stout woman; *une femme* ~*se*, a pregnant woman; *un* ~ *papa*, or ~ *père*, or ~ *pépère*, a fat jolly fellow, a fatty; *de* ~ *mots*, high words; ~*se plaisanterie*, coarse joke; ~ *rire*, coarse laugh; *du* ~ *drap*, coarse thick cloth; *un* ~ *marchand*, a wealthy merchant; *une* ~*se somme*, a large sum of money; *de* ~ *souliers*, heavy shoes; *un* ~ *rhume*, a bad or severe cold; *la mer est* ~*se*, the sea runs high; *par* ~*se mer*, in a heavy sea; ~ *temps*, foul, dirty weather; *jouer* ~ *jeu*, to play high; *une* ~*se voix*, a loud voice; *c'est de l'esprit un peu* ~, it's witty, but not very subtle; *il y a* ~ *à parier que*, the odds are that; *le* ~ *bon sens*, plain common sense; *les* ~ *bonnets*, the big-wigs; the nobs; (vulg.) *les grosses légumes* (though *légume* is masc.), the nobs; ~*se* (fem.) **1.** all senses of *gros*; **2.** pregnant.
gros (gro), s.m. Bulk, main part, mass; wholesale, wholesale trade; *le* ~ *de son armée*, the main body of his troops; *le* ~ *de ses affaires*, the bulk of his trade; *faire le* ~ *de la besogne*, to do the spadework; *en* ~ *et en détail*, wholesale and retail; *commerce de* ~, wholesale trade; *en* ~, in the lump; *écrire* ~ or *en* ~, to write in a large hand; ~ *de Naples*, ~ *de Tours*, gros de Naples, de Tours. ~, adv. Much, a good deal; *gagner* ~, to gain much; *perdre* ~, to lose heavily; *risquer* ~, to risk much, to take great risks.
gros-bec (grobɛk), s.m. (ornith.) Hawfinch, grosbeak.
groseille (grozɛj), s.f. [f. LL *acricella*] (bot.) Red currant; ~ *à maquereau*, gooseberry; *gelée de* ~*s*, red-currant jelly; ~, s.m. red-currant colour, a light vivid red.
groseillier (grozɛje), s.m. (bot.) Currant-bush or -tree; ~ *à maquereau*, gooseberry-bush.
gros-grain (grogrɛ̃), s.m. Petersham (ribbon).
gros-jean (groʒɑ̃), s.m. Hodge; *rester* ~ *comme devant*, to be no better off; to find oneself come down again to one's former condition (after great hopes of betterment); *c'est* ~ *qui en remontre à son curé*, it's teaching one's grandmother to suck eggs.
grosse (gros), s.f. Gross (12 dozen): (writing) large hand; (law) engrossed text, draft, copy; engrossment; (comm., naut.) bottomry; *contrat à la* ~, bottomry bond; *prêt à la* ~, bottomry loan; (pej.) *fait à la* ~, not minutely or carefully done.
grossesse (grosɛs), s.f. Pregnancy.
grosseur (grosœr), s.f. **1.** Size, bulk, thickness, stoutness; *de la* ~ *d'un œuf*, the size of an egg; **2.** tumour, swelling.
grossi-er, -ère (grosje), adj. **1.** Coarse, thick, gross; *erreur* ~*ère*, gross mistake; **2.** homely, plain, common; clumsy, rough, rude, blunt, uncouth; unmannerly; *mœurs* ~*ères*, rough ways; *d'un air* ~, rudely; *sur un ton* ~, in an uncivil manner, bluntly; *drap* ~, coarse cloth.
grossièrement (grosjɛrmɑ̃), adv. Grossly, coarsely, rudely, roughly; *répondre* ~, to answer coarsely or rudely; ~ *esquissé*, roughly sketched; ~ *sculpté* or *taillé*, roughly hewn.
grossièreté (grosjɛrte), s.f. **1.** Coarseness, grossness; boorishness, churlishness; **2.** roughness, plainness, rudeness; **3.** rude word, coarse expression, scurrility.
grossir (grosir), v.a. To make bigger; to enlarge; to increase; to augment; to magnify, to exaggerate, to make appear stouter; ~, v.n. to grow bigger, to swell out, to grow fat or stout; **se** ~, v.pr. to grow bigger, to increase, to augment, to gather.

grossissant, -e (grosisɑ̃), p. adj. **1.** Increasing; **2.** magnifying; *verre* ~, magnifying glass.

grossissement (grosismɑ̃), s.m. **1.** Increase; swelling out; **2.** magnifying; magnifying power; enlargement; exaggeration.

grossiste (grosist), s.m.f. Wholesaler.

grosso-modo (grɔsomɔdo), adv. loc. [L wd] Roughly, at a rough estimate.

grossoyer (grɔswaje), v.a.n. To engross (a document, &c.).

grotesque (grɔtɛsk), adj. [It. *grottesco*] Grotesque, ludicrous. ~, s.m. The grotesque; grotesque figure, caricature, buffoon, ludicrous character.

grotesquement (grɔtɛskəmɑ̃) adv. Grotesquely, ludicrously.

grotte (grɔt), s.f. [It. *grotta*] Cave, cavern; (artificial) grotto; syn. CAVERNE.

grouillant, -e (grujɑ̃), p. adj. Swarming (*de*, with); seething, stirring, moving about, active; crawling.

grouillement (grujmɑ̃), s.m. Swarming, stirring, crawling, seething; rumbling.

grouiller (gruje), v.n. To swarm, to crawl, to stir, to be alive (with); *les rues grouillent de monde*, the streets are swarming with people; (vulg.) ~, and **se** ~, v.pr. to bestir oneself, to hurry up; *grouillez-vous!*, stir your stumps!, get a move on!, look alive!

group (grup), s.m. (rare) [It. *gruppo*] Sealed bag of money.

groupe (grup), s.m. [It. *gruppo*] Group, cluster; (politics) group, section, wing; sub-party; (Lit.) school, coterie, set, circle.

groupement (grupmɑ̃), s.m. Grouping, group, association, organized group; (Lit., art, politics) ~ *d'avant-garde*, advanced school, group, or set.

grouper (grupe), v.a. To group, to gather, to collect, to form into a group, to arrange; **se** ~, v.pr. to form a group or groups, to assemble; to be grouped.

gruau (pl. **-x**) (gryo), s.m. [LL *grutum*] **1.** Corn, grain incompletely ground; oatmeal, groats; **2.** (abbrev. of *farine de* ~ *de blé, d'avoine*, &c.), best flour; *pain de* ~, finest wheaten bread; **3.** gruel; *tisane de* ~, water gruel; **4.** (ornith.) young crane; also *gruon*.

grue (gry), s.f. [L *grus*] **1.** (ornith.) Crane; *faire le pied de* ~, to dance attendance, to wait about a long time, to kick one's heels; **2.** (mech.) crane; **3.** fast woman, tart.

gruger (gryʒe), v.a. [Dutch *gruizen*] To crunch, to eat up, to devour, to scrunch; (fig.) ~ *X*, to devour X's substance; to eat X out of house and home.

grume (grym), s.f. [L *gluma*] Bark (left on felled trees); *en* ~, in the log, unbarked, rough. ⚠ Not English 'grume', which = *caillot, grumeau*.

grumeau (pl. **-x**) (grymo), s.m. [L *grumus*] Clot, lump; *en* ~*x*, clotted.

(se) grumeler (səgrymle), v.pr. To clot.

grumeleu-x, -se (grymlø), adj. Clotted, grumous, rugged, rough, uneven.

gruon. See GRUAU **4.**

gruyère (gryjɛr), s.m. [geog. Swiss orig.] Gruyère cheese.

guano (gɥano), s.m. [Peruvian *huanu*] Guano.

guatémaltèque (gwatemaltɛk), adj. s.m.f. Guatemalan.

gué (ge), s.m. [L *vadum*] Ford; *passer une rivière à* ~, to ford a river.

gué (ge), interj. [corrupt. of *gai*] Used in burden of popular songs: *la bonne aventure ô gué!*, your fortune hey ho, your fortune!

guéable (geabl), adj. Fordable.

guèbre (gɛbr), adj. s.m.f. [Pers. *gabr*] Guebre, Zoroastrian.

guède (gɛd), s.f. [Germ. orig.] Woad, dyer's woad, pastel.

guéer (gee), v.a. **1.** To ford (a river); **2.** to water (a horse, &c.); to rinse (linen, &c.) in a stream.

guelfe (gɛlf), s.m.f. [It. *Guelfo*] Guelph. ~, adj. Guelphic.

guelte (gɛlt), s.f. [f. Germ. *Geld*] Percentage on sales, commission allowed to shop assistants.

guenille (gənij), s.f. [etym. dub.] Rag, tatter; *en* ~*s*, tattered, in rags; (fig., by ext.) skin, body; ~ *si l'on veut, ma* ~ *m'est chère*, however destitute, poor number one is dear to me; syn. HAILLON.

guenilleu-x, -se (gənijø), adj. In rags, tattered. ~, s.m.f. Ragamuffin.

guenillon (gənijɔ̃), s.m. Small rag.

guenipe (gənip), s.f. [etym. unkn.] Slut, slattern, trollop.

guenon (gənɔ̃), s.f. [etym. unkn.] She-monkey; (fig.) fright.

guenuche (gənyʃ), s.f. [f. *guenon*] Young she-monkey; (fig.) fright, chattering minx.

guépard (gepar), s.m. (zool.) Cheetah, guepard.

guêpe (gɛp), s.f. [L *vespa*] (ent.) Wasp; ~ *frelon*, hornet; *à taille de* ~, wasp-waisted.

guêpier (gɛpje), s.m. Wasps' nest, hornets' nest; (ornith.) bee-eater; (fig.) *tomber dans un* ~, to bring a hornets' nest about one's ears.

guerdon (gɛrdɔ̃), s.m. [f. OHG *widarlon*] (poet.) Reward, guerdon.

guère (gɛr), adv. [OHG *weigaro*] But little, not much, not very; but few, not many; hardly, scarcely, barely; hardly anyone but, hardly anything but, hardly ever; *il ne tardera* ~, he won't be long; *je ne le connais* ~, I hardly know him; *je ne le vois* ~, I hardly ever see him; *il ne s'en faut* ~, it wants but little; ~ *moins*, little less; ~ *plus*, little more; *il ne sait ~ ce qu'il dit*, he speaks at random; syn. PEU.

guéret (gerɛ), s.m. [L *vervactum*] Ploughed land, fallow; (poet.) *les ~s*, the fields.

guéridon (geridɔ̃), s.m. [f. prop. n. in an old comedy] Small round table, loo-table, centre-table, stand.

guérilla (gerilla), s.f. [Span. wd] Guerrilla warfare.

guérir (gerir), v.a. [OHG *warjan*] To cure, to heal; (fig.) to help, to recover, to remedy, to rid, to free; ~ *X d'une mauvaise habitude*, to rid, or cure X of a bad habit; *les rhumes guérissent facilement*, colds are easy to cure; '*je le pansai, Dieu le guarit*' (old form of *guérit*; well-known saying of Ambroise Paré), I doctored that man, but it was God who cured him; ~, v.n. to be or get cured, to get well again; **se ~**, v.pr. to recover; to be cured, healed; to get rid (*de*, of); *Médecin, guéris-toi toi-même*, Physician, heal thyself.

guérison (gerizɔ̃), s.f. Recovery, cure, healing; syn. CURE.

guérissable (gerisabl), adj. Curable.

guérisseu-r, -se (gerisœr), s.m.f. Healer, curer; (pej.) quack doctor.

guérite (gerit), s.f. [etym. dub.] Sentry-box; signalman's box.

guerre (gɛr), s.f. [OHG *werra*] **1.** War, warfare; hostilities; *faire la ~ à*, to make war against or upon; to wage war upon; to be at war with; *déclarer la ~*, to declare war (*à*, upon); *allumer la ~*, to kindle war; *état de ~*, state of war; *être en ~ avec*, to be at war with; *porter la ~ en pays ennemi*, to carry the war into the enemy's country; *il a fait toute la ~ avec X*, he served with X throughout the war; *sur le pied de ~*, on a war footing; ~ *civile*, civil war; ~ *sainte*, holy war; (fig.) ~ *au couteau*, war to the knife; *bateau de ~*, warship; *cri de ~*, war-cry; war-whoop; *petite ~*, skirmishing; field practice; *foudre de ~*, great warrior; (colloq.) hero, thunderbolt; *hommes* or *gens de ~*, soldiers, military men; *un grand homme de ~*, a great captain; ~ *d'épuisement*, war of attrition; ~ *de tranchées*, trench warfare; ~ *sous-marine, navale, aérienne, chimique*, submarine, naval, aerial, chemical warfare; ~ *de positions*, strategic war; *d'avant-~*, pre-war; *d'après-~*, post-war; *à la ~ comme à la ~*, let 's take things as they come, the rough with the smooth; no harm in roughing it a bit; *à la ~ comme en amour*, in love and war; *de ~ lasse*, for the sake of peace and quiet; from sheer weariness; *c'est de bonne ~*, it 's fair play; *qui terre a, ~ a*, much coin, much care; *je lui fais la ~ pour le débarrasser de cette habitude*, I keep nagging at him to rid him of this habit; **2.** War Office, War Department; *passez à la Marine et à la ~*, call at the Admiralty and the War Office.

guerri-er, -ère (gɛrje), adj. Warlike, martial; *danse ~ère*, war-dance. **~, -ère**, s.m.f. Warrior, soldier; female warrior, amazon; syn. BELLIQUEUX, MARTIAL.

guerroyant, -e (gɛrwajɑ̃), p. adj. Combative, pugnacious, fighting.

guerroyer (gɛrwaje), v.n. To make or wage war (frequently); (colloq.) to scrap.

guerroyeur (gɛrwajœr), adj. s.m. Addicted to war; regular warrior, man fond of fighting.

guet (gɛ), s.m. [f. *guetter*] Watch, watching; night-patrol; *faire le ~*, to be on the watch, to stand or keep watch; to mount guard; *avoir l'œil au ~*, to keep a sharp look-out; *l'oreille au ~*, listening intently; *crier au ~*, to call the watch; *mot du ~*, watchword, password.

guet-apens (gɛtapɑ̃), s.m. (pl. *guets-apens*) Ambuscade, ambush, trap, snare; felonious attack, foul play; *tomber dans un ~*, to fall into a trap, or ambuscade; to be treacherously attacked.

guêtre (gɛtr), s.f. [etym. dub.] Gaiter, legging; ~ (*courte*), spat; (colloq.) *tirer ses ~s*, to hook it; *traîner ses ~s*, to lounge, to dawdle about.

guêtrer (gɛtre), v.a. To put gaiters on, to gaiter; **se ~**, v.pr. to put on one's gaiters or leggings.

guetter (gɛte), v.a. [OHG *wahta*] To watch for, to be on the look-out for; to lie in wait for; to keep an eye on.

guetteur (gɛtœr), s.m. Watchman, observer, signalman, look-out man; night-watchman.

gueulard (gəlar), s.m. [f. *gueule*] Bawler; furnace-mouth; gully-hole; (naut.) speaking-trumpet. **~, -e**, adj. Bawling.

gueule (gœl), s.f. [L *gula*] **1.** Mouth of animals, jaws, chops; (vulg.) mouth of persons; **2.** (vulg., pop.) mug, head; palate, throat; gabble, talk, jaw; *quelle sale ~!*, what a snouty face!, what a repulsive mug!; *c'est un fort-en-~*, he is full of jaw; he is foul-mouthed; (slang) *ta ~!*, dry up!; *fine ~*, epicure, gastronomist; *les ~s cassées*; soldiers wounded in the face; ~ *de canon*, muzzle; *avoir la ~ pavée*, to have a cast-iron throat; *la ~ de bois*, parched mouth (after a bout of drinking); *avoir la ~ de bois*, to feel like the morning after the night before; *il est venu la ~ enfarinée*, he came as mealy-mouthed as they are made; *être sur la ~*, to be particular about one's food; to appreciate good cooking; *taire sa ~*, to shut one's jaw; *casser la ~ à X*, to knock X's head off; **3.** aperture, opening, mouth; ~ *du four*, furnace-mouth.

gueule-de-loup (gœldəlu), s.f. (pl. *gueules-de-loup*) (bot.) Snapdragon; syn. MUFLIER.

gueuler (gœle), v.n.a. (pop.) To bawl, to shout, to yell, to mouth; to shriek.

gueules (gœl), s.m. [f. L *gulae*] (herald.) Gules.

gueuleton (gœltɔ̃), s.m. (colloq.) Square meal, blow-out, tuck-in.

gueuletonner (gœltɔne), v.n. To tuck in, to feast.

gueusaille (gøzɑj), s.f. [f. *gueux*] Rabble.

gueusailler (gøzɑje), v.n. To associate with beggars, vagabonds, &c.

gueusard (gøzar), s.m. Ragamuffin, vagabond, loafer.

gueuse[1] (gøz), s.f. **1.** Tatterdemalion, wretch, miserable woman; **2.** bad woman, bad lot, drab, slut.

gueuse[2] (gøz), s.f. [f. Germ. *Guss*] Pig-iron; sow.

gueuser (gøze), v.n.a. To beg, to loaf, to go begging.

gueuserie (gøzri), s.f. Beggary, beggarliness, sluttishness; rubbish.

gueu-x, -se (gø), adj. [OF wd, name adopted by revolted nobles and merchants in the Netherlands, 1590] Beggarly, destitute, miserable, sluttish; ~ *comme un rat d'église*, as poor as a church mouse. ~, **-se**, s.m.f. Ragamuffin, tatterdemalion, loafer, tramp, pauper; scoundrel, rascal; *vivre comme un* ~, to live like a pauper; *s'habiller comme un* ~, to dress like a tramp; syn. BESOGNEUX, HAILLONNEUX, MENDIANT, INDIGENT, CHEMINEAU.

gui[1] (gi), s.m. [L *viscum*] (bot.) Mistletoe.

gui[2] (gi), s.m. [OF *guie*] (naut.) Spanker-boom; main boom, boom; ~ *de foc*, jig-boom.

guibolle (gibɔl), s.f. (pop.) Leg, pin, stump; *jouer des* ~*s*, to hook it, to leg it.

guibre (gibr), s.f. (naut.) Cutwater.

guiche (giʃ), s.f. [etym. dub.] **1.** Shield strap; **2.** curl of hair worn over the ear or on the cheek.

guichet (giʃɛ), s.m. [Scand. orig.] Wicket-gate, small window in a door; ticket window; counter (in post-office); booking-office; cashier's desk.

guichetier (giʃtje), s.m. Turnkey.

guide[1] (gid), s.m. [f. *guider*] **1.** Guide; **2.** guide-book; **3.** (mil.) guide, fugleman; **4.** (naut.) guide; halyard; **5.** (mech.) controlling tool, gauge, bar, rod, guide; ~ *d'écrou*, guide for steering nut; ~*-rope*, s.m. guide-rope; *laisser filer le* ~*-rope*, to drop the guide-rope; ~*-âne*, s.m. guide, directions; guide-lines; ~*-main*, s.m. hand-guide.

guide[2] (gid), s.f. [It. *guida*] Rein; *conduire à grandes* ~*s*, to drive four-in-hand; (fig.) *mener la vie à grandes* ~*s*, (*a*) to live in grand style, or in dashing style; (*b*) to live a fast life.

guider (gide), v.a. [Goth. *witan*] To guide, to lead, to direct; to steer; *mal guidé*, misguided; **se** ~, v.pr. to guide oneself, to be guided; to go (*sur*, by); syn. CONDUIRE, MENER.

guidon (gidɔ̃), s.m. [f. *guider*] Handle-bar (of cycle); (mil.) guidon, pennant; (naut.) broad pennant or pendant; sight (of fire-arms).

guignard (giɲar), s.m. (ornith.) Dotterel.

guigne (giɲ), s.f. **1.** Sweet cherry; **2.** (colloq.) bad luck; *c'est la* ~ *noire*, it's hard cheese; deuced bad luck!; *porter la* ~, to bring bad luck; syn. GUIGNON.

guigner (giɲe), v.a. To peep at; to have an eye on; to covet.

guignier (giɲe), s.m. (bot.) Sweet cherry-tree.

guignol (giɲɔl), s.m. [name of a character in 18th-century Fr. puppet shows] Punch and Judy show, puppet show; (pej.) a ridiculously dressed person.

guignolet (giɲɔlɛ), s.m. Sweet cherry liqueur.

guignon (giɲɔ̃), s.m. Bad luck; see syn. GUIGNE.

guillage (gijaʒ), s.m. Working, fermentation (of beer).

guillaume (gijom), s.m. Rabbet-plane.

guilledou (gijdu), s.m. Only used in *courir le* ~, to go on the spree, to go wenching.

guillemet (gijmɛ), s.m. Inverted comma, quotation-mark; *mettre entre* ~*s*, to put between inverted commas.

guillemeter (gijmɛte), v.a. To put between inverted commas.

guillemot (gijmo), s.m. (ornith.) Guillemot.

guiller (gije), v.n. To ferment (of beer).

guilleret, -te (gijrɛ), adj. [etym. dub.] Sprightly, brisk, merry, lively; *il a l'air* ~, he looks quite lively.

guilleri (gijri), s.m. Chirping (of sparrows).

guillochage (gijɔʃaʒ), s.m. Engine-turning, adorning with guilloche; chasing.

guillocher (gijɔʃe), v.a. To engine-turn, to adorn with guilloche, to chase (silver, &c.).

guillochis (gijɔʃi), s.m. Guilloche; guilloche work.

guillotine (gijɔtin), s.f. [f. Dr. *Guillotin*, inventor or adapter of machine for beheading] Guillotine; *fenêtre à* ~, sash-window.

guillotinement (gijɔtinmɑ̃), s.m. Beheading.

guillotiner (gijɔtine), v.a. To guillotine, to behead.

guimauve (gimov), s.f. (bot.) Marsh-mallow; (fig.) *à la* ~, or *à la pâte de* ~, milk and water . . ., milk for babes, soppy, mawkish.

guimbarde (gɛ̃bard), s.f. **1.** Rickety old carriage, shandrydan; **2.** jew's-harp; wretched guitar; **3.** small plane (tool).
guimpe (gɛ̃p), s.f. [OHG *wimpal*] Chemisette, tucker, neckerchief; (of nuns) wimple.
guindage (gɛ̃daʒ), s.m. Hoisting.
guindal (pl. **aux**) (gɛ̃dal), s.m. See GUINDEAU.
guindant (gɛ̃dɑ̃), s.m. (naut.) Hoist; height of flags.
guindé, -e (gɛ̃de), p. adj. Stiff, formal, stuck up; strained, stilted, affected.
guindeau (pl. **-x**) (gɛ̃do), s.m. (naut.) Windlass; *taquets de ~*, whelps.
guinder (gɛ̃de), v.a. [OHG *windan*] To hoist, to hoist up; to strain, to force, to make affected or stiff; **se ~**, v.pr. to force one's talent, to become affected, stiff, formal; to be stilted.
guinderesse (gɛ̃drɛs), s.f. (naut.) Mast-rope, top-tackle pennant.
guinée (gine), s.f. [Engl. *guinea*] **1.** Guinea; **2.** cotton cloth for export to West African countries.
guingan (gɛ̃gɑ̃), s.m. [Malay orig., etym. dub.] Gingham. ⚠ Colloquially 'gingham' = umbrella, *parapluie*.
guingois (gɛ̃gwɑ), s.m. Crookedness; *de ~*, awry, crookedly; *aller tout de ~*, to walk crookedly.
guinguette (gɛ̃gɛt), s.f. [etym. dub.] Small suburban tavern (generally with a garden).
guipure (gipyr), s.f. [Goth. *weipan*] Guipure, lace.
guirlande (girlɑ̃d), s.f. [It. *ghirlanda*] Garland, wreath; (fig.) *tresser des ~s à X*, to praise X to the skies.
guise (giz), s.f. [OHG *wisa*] Way, manner, guise, wise; humour, fancy, choice; *à votre ~*, as you like; *il n'en fait qu'à sa ~*, he will listen to no advice, he never does but what he likes; he will have his own way; *en ~ de*, by way of, instead of. ⚠ 'Guise' in English has usually the sense of external appearance = *aspect*, and often of garb = *vêture*.
guitare (gitar), s.f. [Span. *guitarra*] Guitar; (colloq.) *assez de cette ~*, enough of this; do not harp always on the same string.
guitariste (gitarist), s.m.f. Guitar-player.
guitoune (gitun), s.f. [war neolog.] Dug-out.
guivre (givr), s.f. [f. L *vipera*] Serpent; (herald.) wyvern.
gustati-f, -ve (gystatif), adj. Gustatory.
gustation (gysta'sjɔ̃), s.f. [f. L *gustare*] Tasting, gustation.
gutta-percha (gyttapɛrka), s.f. [Malay wd.] Gutta-percha.
gutte, gomme-gutte (gyt, gomgyt), s.f. [Malay *getah*] Gamboge.
guttural, -e, (aux) (gytyral), adj. [f. L *guttur*] Guttural, throaty.
gymnase (ʒimnɑz), s.m. [Gr. *gumnasion*] Gymnasium, building for practice of gymnastics (not a secondary school as in Germany).
gymnasiarque (ʒimnɑzjark), s.m. Gymnasiarch.
gymnaste (ʒimnast), s.m.f. Gymnast.
gymnastique (ʒimnastik), s.f. Gymnastics. **~**, adj. Gymnastic.
gymnique (ʒimnik), s.f. Gymnics, gymnastics. **~**, adj. Gymnic.
gymnosophie (ʒimnosɔfi), s.f. Gymnosophy.
gymnosophiste (ʒimnosɔfist), s.m.f. [f. Gr. *gumnos+sophos*] Gymnosophist, ascetic naked mystic.
gymnosperme (ʒimnospɛrm), adj. s.f. [Gr. *gumnos+sperma*] (bot.) Gymnospermous (plant).
gymnote (ʒimnɔt), s.m. (ichth.) Gymnotus, electric eel.
gynandre (ʒinɑ̃dr), adj. [Gr. *gunandros*] (bot.) Gynandrous.
gynécée (ʒinese), s.f. [Gr. *gunaikeion*] Gynaeceum.
gynécocratrie (ʒinekokrasi), s.f. [Gr. *gunē+kratein*] Gynaecocracy.
gynécologie (ʒinekɔlɔʒi), s.f. [f. Gr. *gunē+logos*] Gynaecology.
gynécologue (ʒinekɔlɔg), s.m.f. adj. Gynaecologist, specialist in diseases of women.
gypaète (ʒipaɛt), s.m. [Gr. *gupo+aetos*] (ornith.) Bearded vulture.
gypse (ʒips), s.m. [Gr. *gupsos*] (geol.) Gypsum, plaster of Paris.
gypseu-x, -se (ʒipsø), adj. Gypseous, gypsous.
gypsophile (ʒipsɔfil), s.f. (bot.) Gypsophila.
gyratoire (ʒiratwar), adj. See GIRATOIRE.
gyromancie (ʒiromɑ̃si), s.f. [f. Gr. *guros +manteia*] Gyromancy.
gyromètre (ʒirɔmɛtr), s.m. [Gr. *guros+metron*] Gyrometer.
gyroscope (ʒirɔskɔp), s.m. [f. Gr. *guros+skopein*] Gyroscope.
gyroscopique (ʒirɔskɔpik), adj. Gyroscopic.

H

When the h must be slightly aspirated the phonetic spelling begins with an h; in that case there is no liaison and no elision.

H, h (aʃ), s.m. and often f. 8th letter of the alphabet.
ha (ha), interj. Ah!, now!
habile (abil), adj. [L *habilis*] Able, clever, adroit, skilful, cunning; (law) qualified, competent. **~**, s.m.f. (pej.) Knowing one.

habilement (abilmɑ̃), adv. Ably, cleverly, adroitly, skilfully, dexterously.
habileté (abilte), s.f. Skill, dexterousness, expertness, cleverness, talent; ability.
habilitation (abilita'sjɔ̃), s.f. (law) Qualification.
habilité (abilite), s.f. (law) Competency, qualification.
habiliter (abilite), v.a. (law) To render competent, to qualify.
habillage (abijaʒ), s.m. Dressing; (cook.) dressing, trussing (of poultry, &c.).
habillé, -e (abije), p. adj. **1.** Dressed; *tout* ~, fully clad, in one's clothes; **2.** dressy, elegant; *robe* ~*e*, gown, party frock, afternoon dress.
habillement (abijmɑ̃), s.m. **1.** (The act of) clothing; **2.** clothes, clothing, suit.
habiller (abije), v.a. [f. *habit*] To dress, to clothe; to dress up, to wrap up; to supply with clothes; to fit, to sit well on; (pop.) to abuse; **s'**~, v.pr. to dress, to put on one's clothes; to attire oneself; to buy one's clothes, to have one's clothes made (*chez*, at).
habilleu-r, -se (abijœr), s.m.f. Dresser (of actors).
habit (abi), s.m. [f. L *habitus*] Coat, dress-coat, full dress, garb, attire, habit; ~**s**, s.m.pl. clothes, clothing, (colloq.) togs, toggery; *marchand d'*~*s*, seller of clothes, old-clo'man; ~ *de cheval*, (for ladies) riding-habit; (for men) riding-kit, riding-breeches and coat; ~ *à la française*, cutaway coat; ~ *à queue de morue*, dress coat (with swallow-tails); *prendre l'*~, to turn monk; *en* ~*s de deuil*, in mourning; *en* ~, in evening clothes, in dress clothes; *dois-je venir en* ~*?*, (fam). must I put on a boiled shirt?
habitable (abitabl), adj. [f. *habiter*] Habitable, inhabitable. ⚠ In French *inhabitable* has the opposite sense = unfit to be lived in, uninhabitable.
habitacle (abitakl), s.m. [L *habitaculum*] Abode; (naut.) binnacle.
habitant, -e (abitɑ̃), s.m.f. Inhabitant, dweller, resident, inmate; (poet.) denizen; native; (pl.) people.
habitat (abita), s.m. Habitat.
habitation (abita'sjɔ̃), s.f. [L *habitatio*] Habitation, dwelling, abode, residence, house; inhabitation, the act of inhabiting; (obs.) settlement.
habiter (abite), v.a.n. [L *habitare*] To inhabit, to dwell in, to reside in, to occupy, to live in, to live; *où habitez-vous?*, where do you live?; *elle habite avec sa mère*, she lives with her mother.
habitude (abityd), s.f. [L *habitudo*] Habit, use, practice, custom, way, trick; *prendre, contracter, de mauvaises* ~*s*, to contract bad habits; *par* ~, from habit; *avoir l'*~ *de*, to be accustomed to; *d'*~, usual; (adv.) usually; *l'*~ *est une seconde nature*, habit is second nature; *faire perdre à X cette mauvaise* ~, to break X of this bad habit.
habitué, -e (abitɥe), s.m.f. Frequenter, regular customer.
habituel, -le (abitɥɛl), adj. Habitual, customary, usual, wonted; *à la façon* ~*le*, in the usual way.
habituellement (abitɥɛlmɑ̃), adv. Habitually, usually, customarily, generally; as a rule.
habituer (abitɥe), v.a. [f. L *habitus*] To habituate, to accustom, to inure; **s'**~, v.pr. to get accustomed (*à*, to), to accustom oneself, to get inured, to train oneself (*à*, to), to grow familiar (*à*, with).
hâbler (hɑble), v.n. [Span. *hablar*] To boast, to brag, to talk big.
hâblerie (hɑbləri), s.f. Boasting, bragging.
hâbleu-r, -se (hɑblœr), s.m.f. Boaster, braggart, bouncer. ~, **-se**, adj. Boasting, bragging.
hache (haʃ), s.f. [OHG *happa*] Axe, hatchet; ~ *d'abordage*, boarding-axe; ~ *d'armes*, battle-axe; ~ *de bûcheron*, felling-axe; *périr sous la* ~, to die on the block; *visage fait à coups de* ~, roughly-hewn, rugged features.
hachement (haʃmɑ̃), **hachage** (aʃaʒ), s.m. Cutting, mincing, hashing; hacking.
hacher (haʃe), v.a. To chop, to hack, to mince, to hash, to cut up, to cut to pieces; ~ *menu*, to chop small; (of troops) *se faire* ~ *jusqu'au dernier*, to die to the last man; *il se ferait* ~ *plutôt que de céder*, he would suffer anything rather than give in. *Hache* in comp. = cutter; the comp. is always masc. and invar.: *hache-paille*, chaff-cutter; ~*-viande*, meat-cutter, or -mincer.
hachereau (pl. **-x**) (haʃro), s.m. Hatchet.
hachette (haʃɛt), s.f. Hatchet.
hachis (haʃi), s.m. [f. *hacher*] Hash, mincemeat.
hachish, haschisch (haʃiʃ), s.m. [Arab. wd] Hashish.
hachoir (haʃwar), s.m. **1.** Chopping-knife, cleaver, mincing-machine; **2.** chopping-board.
hachure (haʃyr), s.f. (drawing) Hatching, cross-hatching, shading line.
hagard, -e (hagar), adj. [orig. uncert.] Haggard, wild looking.
hagiographe (aʒjɔgraf), s.m.f. [f. Gr. *hagios*+*graphein*] Hagiographer. ~, adj. Hagiographic.
hagiographie (aʒjɔgrafi), s.f. Hagiography.
haie (hɛ), s.f. [f. OLG *haga*] Hedge; hedgerow, fence, hurdle; ~ *vive*, quickset hedge; *faire, former la* ~, to stand in a line; *entourer d'une* ~, to hedge in, to fence in.

haillon (hɑjɔ̃), s.m. [f. OHG *hadel*] Rag, tatter; *en ~s*, tattered.
haillonneu-x, -se (hɑjɔnø), adj. Tattered, in rags.
haine (hɛn), s.f. [f. *haïr*] Hatred, hate, abhorrence; *en ~ de*, out of hatred of.
haineusement (hɛnøzmɑ̃), adv. Hatefully, malevolently, malignantly.
haineu-x, -se (hɛnø), adj. Full of hatred, malevolent, malignant.
haïr (hair), v.a. (irreg.: *je hais, nous haïssons, haï*), [f. OHG *hatjan*] To hate, to loathe.
haire (hɛr), s.f. [f. OHG *harre*] Hair-shirt, hair-cloth.
haïssable (haisabl), adj. Heinous, odious, hateful.
haïtien, -ne (aisjɛ̃), adj. s.m.f. Haïtian, of Haïti.
halage (halaʒ), s.m. [f. *haler*] Towage, towing, hauling; *chemin de ~*, towing-path.
halbran (halbrɑ̃), s.m. [f. Germ. *halb+Ente*] Young wild duck.
halbrené, -e (halbrəne), adj. Ragged-feathered; (fig.) over-fatigued.
hâle (hɑl), s.m. [f. *hâler*] Sunburn; dry wind.
hâlé, -e (hɑle), p. adj. Sunburnt, tanned, swarthy.
haleine (alɛn), s.f. [LL *halena*] Breath, wind; *hors d'~*, winded, out of breath; *courir à perdre ~*, to run so fast that one is out of breath; to run oneself out of breath; *retenir son ~*, to hold one's breath; *reprendre ~*, to recover one's breath; (fig.) *tenir en ~*, to keep in practice, to keep in suspense, to keep in play; *tout d'une ~*, in the same breath; at a stretch; running; *œuvre de longue ~*, long piece of work, work of time; *avoir l'~ courte*, to be short-winded.
halenée (alne), s.f. [f. *haleine*] Breath, whiff.
haler (hale), v.a. [f. OScand. *hala*] To haul, to tow.
hâler (hɑle), v.a. [f. OHG *hal*] To burn, to tan; **se** ~, v.pr. to get sunburnt.
haletant, -e (haltɑ̃), adj. [f. *haleter*] Out of breath, winded, breathless, panting.
halètement (halɛtmɑ̃), s.m. [f. *haleter*] Panting, puffing.
haleter (halte), v.n. [etym. dub.] To pant, to gasp for breath, to puff.
haleur (halœr), s.m. Hauler, boat-tower.
halicot (aliko), s.m. See HARICOT.
halieutique (aljøtik), adj. [f. Gr. *halieutikos*] Halieutic. ~, s.f. Halieutics (art of fishing).
halitueu-x, -se (alitɥø), adj. [f. L *halitus*] Moist, halituous.
hallage (halaʒ), s.m. [f. *halle*] Market dues.
hallali (halali), s.m. [onom.] (stag-hunt.) Halloo, whoop, tally-ho; death of the stag.
halle (hal), s.f. [OHG *halla*] Market-hall, market-place; *fort de la ~*, market-porter; *langage des ~s*, billingsgate.
hallebarde (halbard), s.f. [f. MHG *helmbarde*] Halberd; *il tombe des ~s*, it 's raining cats and dogs.
hallebardier (halbardje), s.m. Halberdier.
hallier (halje), s.m. **1.** Thicket; **2.** (rare) market-keeper.
hallucination (allysina'sjɔ̃), s.f. Hallucination, delusion; *avoir des ~s*, to be subject to hallucinations.
halluciné, -e (allysine), adj. s.m.f. (Person) suffering from hallucinations, deluded (person).
halluciner (allysine), v.a. [L *hallucinari*] To hallucinate, to delude.
halo (halo), s.m. [Gr. *halōs*] Halo.
halogène (alɔʒɛn), adj. [f. Gr. *hals, halos +gennan*] Halogenous.
haloïde (alɔid), s.m. adj. (chem.) Haloid.
hâloir (hɑlwar), s.m. Drying-room for hemp.
halot (halo), s.m. [orig. unkn.] Rabbit-burrow.
halotechnie (halotɛkni), s.f. [f. Gr. *hals+tekhnē*] (chem.) Preparation of salts.
halte (halt), s.f. [Germ. *Halt*] Halt, halting-place; (interj.), *~!, ~ là!* halt!, stop!, stand!; *faire ~*, to stop, to make a halt, to halt.
haltère (altɛr), s.m. [Gr. *haltēr*] Dumb-bell.
hamac (hamak), s.m. [Span. *hamaca*] Hammock; (naut.) cot.
hamadryade (amadrjad), s.f. [Gr. *hamadruas*] Hamadryad, wood-nymph.
hamadryas (amadrjɑs), s.m. (zool.) Hamadryad, Abyssinian baboon.
hamamélis (amamelis), s.m. (bot.) Witch-hazel.
hameau (pl. **-x**) (hamo), s.m. [OF *hamel, hamelet*] Hamlet.
hameçon (amsɔ̃), s.m. [L *hamus*] Hook, fish-hook; (fig.) bait; *mordre à l'~*, to take the bait.
hampe (hɑ̃p), s.f. [L *ampla*] Staff, stem, flower-stalk, handle.
hamster (hamstɛr), s.m. [Germ. wd] (zool.) Hamster.
han (hɑ̃), s.m. [onom.] Han (guttural grunt uttered when striking a heavy blow).
hanap (hanap), s.m. [OHG *hnapf*] Hanap, goblet, tankard.
hanche (hɑ̃ʃ), s.f. [LGerm. *hanke*] Hip; haunch; quarter (of horses, &c.); *les poings sur les ~s*, with arms akimbo.
handicap (hɑ̃dikap), s.m. [Engl. wd] Handicap.
handicaper (hɑ̃dikape), v.a. To handicap.
hangar (hɑ̃gar), s.m. [LL *angarium*]

Shed, hangar, outhouse, pent-house, shanty; (aeron.) hangar.

hanneton (hantɔ̃), s.m. [f. Germ. *Hahn*] (ent.) Cockchafer, May-bug, May-beetle; (fig.) giddy goose; *étourdi comme un* ~, as giddy as a goose.

hanovrien, -ne (hanɔvrjɛ̃), adj. s.m.f. Hanoverian.

hanse (hɑ̃s), s.f. [OHG *hansa*] Hanse; Hanse towns.

hanséatique (hɑ̃seatik), adj. Hanseatic.

hanter (hɑ̃te), v.a. [f. L *habitare*?] To frequent, to haunt; *dis-moi qui tu hantes, je te dirai qui tu es*, birds of a feather flock together; a man is known by his company; *être hanté par un souvenir*, to be obsessed or haunted by a memory.

hantise (hɑ̃tiz), s.f. **1.** Obsession, haunting memory, feeling, or impression; **2.** (obs.) frequentation, frequenting.

happe (hap), s.f. Cramp-iron.

happelourde (haplurd), s.f. Imitation gem.

happer (hape), v.a. [f. Dutch *happen*] To snap up, to bite, to snatch, to seize, to lay hold of, to nab, to bag, to bone; ~, v.n. to adhere.

haquenée (hakne), s.f. [OF wd] Ambling saddle-mare; hackney.

haquet (hakɛ), s.m. [orig. unkn.) Dray.

harangue (harɑ̃g), s.f. [f. OHG *hring*, OF *arenge*] Speech, harangue, address, oration.

haranguer (harɑ̃ge), v.a.n. To harangue, to address, to make a speech.

harangueu-r, -se (harɑ̃gœr), s.m.f. Haranguer, speaker, orator, speech-maker.

haras (harɑ), s.m. [f. Arab. *faras* = horse] Breeding-stud.

harasse (haras), s.f. Crate (for packing china-ware).

harassement (harasmɑ̃), s.m. Harassment, extreme fatigue.

harasser (harase), v.a. [orig. unkn.] To harass, to weary, to tire out.

harcèlement (harsɛlmɑ̃), s.m. Worrying, harassing.

harceler (harsle), v.a. [f. OF *herce*, *herse*] To worry, to harass, to molest.

harde (hard), s.f. [f. Goth. *hairda*] **1.** Herd (of deer), flock; **2.** (hunt.) leash.

harder (harde), v.a. (hunt.) To leash (dogs).

hardes (hard), s.f.pl. [f. OF *fardes*] (usually pej.) Clothes, togs, things, toggery, wearing-apparel.

hardi, -e (hardi), adj. [f. Germ. *hard*] Bold, daring, fearless, hasty, rash, dauntless; impudent; ~ *comme un page*, as bold as brass; *des manières* ~*es*, forward manners. ⚠ One must avoid translating *hardi* by 'hardy', save in exceptional cases; 'hardy' = *vigoureux*, *résistant*, *endurci*, *intrépide*: a hardy plant = *une plante rustique*. ~ *!*, interj. Courage !, go it !, cheerly !, cheer up !

hardiesse (hardjɛs), s.f. Boldness, daring, fearlessness, intrepidity, hardihood (see HARDI); impudence, rashness, freedom, licence.

hardiment (hardimɑ̃), adv. Boldly, daringly, fearlessly; impudently.

harem (harɛm), s.m. [Arab. *ḥarīm*] Harem.

hareng (harɑ̃), s.m. [f. OHG *hâring*] Herring; bloater, bloated herring; ~ *saur*, kippered herring, kipper; *la caque sent toujours le* ~, what is bred in the bone will come out in the flesh; *serrés comme* ~*s en caque*, packed like sardines.

harengaison (harɑ̃gɛzɔ̃), s.f. Herring fishing; herring season.

harengère (harɑ̃ʒɛr), s.f. Fish-woman, fish-wife, fish-fag; (fig.) loud-voiced, vulgar woman.

harenguet (harɑ̃gɛ), s.m. (ichth.) Sprat.

hargne (harɲ), s.f. Peevishness, grumpiness.

hargneu-x, -se (harɲø), adj. [f. OF *hargne*] Peevish, surly, morose, cross-grained, grumpy, churlish; (of dogs) snarling.

haricot (hariko), s.m. [orig. unkn.] Bean, kidney bean, haricot bean; ~*s verts*, French beans; ~ *d'Espagne*, scarlet runner; (bot.) *Phaseolus*; ~ or *halicot de mouton*, Irish stew, mutton stew.

haridelle (haridɛl), s.f. [orig. unkn.] Worn-out hack, jade, sorry horse; (fig., pop.) gawky woman.

harmonica (armɔnika), s.m. [f. Gr. *harmonicon*] Harmonica.

harmonie (armɔni), s.f. [Gr. *harmonia*] Harmony; harmonics; (fig.) concord, harmony, peace.

harmonieusement (armɔnjøzmɑ̃), adv. Harmoniously.

harmonieu-x, -se (armɔnjø), adj. Harmonious, melodious, harmonizing; proportionate, peaceful.

harmonique (armɔnik), adj. s.m.f. Harmonic; (math.) harmonic.

harmoniser (armɔnize), v.a. To harmonize (*avec*, with); **s'**~, v.pr. to harmonize, to match well.

harmoniste (armɔnist), s.m.f. Harmonist.

harmonium (armɔnjɔm), s.m. Harmonium.

harnachement (harnaʃmɑ̃), s.m. Harness, trappings; (fig.) rig-out, working equipment.

harnacher (harnaʃe), v.a. To harness; (fig.) to rig out.

harnais (harnɛ), s.m. [orig. unkn., OF *harnois*] Harness, trappings; armour, equipment; (fig.) *blanchi sous le* ~ or *harnois*, grown grey in the service.

haro (haro), s.m. [orig. unkn.] Hue and cry; *crier* ~ *sur X*, to cry shame upon X.

harpagon (arpagɔ̃), s.m. [character in Molière's *L'Avare*] Miser, skinflint.

harpail (harpaj), s.m. Herd of young stags.

harpaye (harpɛj), s.f. (ornith.) Moor-buzzard, marsh-harrier.

harpe[1] (harp), s.f. [OHG *harfa*] Harp; (ichth.) harp-shell; ~ *éolienne*, Aeolian harp; *pincer de la* ~, to play the harp.

harpe[2] (harp), s.f. [Gr. *harpē*] **1.** Toothing (in masonry); **2.** hook.

harpeau (pl. **-x**) (harpo), s.m. [f. *harpe*][2] (naut.) Grappling-iron.

harpie (harpi), s.f. [Gr. *harpuia*] Harpy; (fig.) shrew; (ornith.) harpy-eagle.

harpin (harpɛ̃), s.m. [f. *harpe*[2]] (naut.) Boat-hook.

harpiste (harpist), s.m.f. Harpist.

harpon (harpɔ̃), s.m. [f. Gr. *harpē*] Harpoon, spear; cramp-iron.

harponnage (harpɔnaʒ), s.m. Harpooning.

harponner (harpɔne), v.a. To harpoon, to spear.

harponneur (harpɔnœr), s.m. Harpooner.

hart (har), s.f. [etym. dub.] **1.** Withe, fagot-band; **2.** rope, halter; *mériter la* ~, to deserve hanging.

hasard (hazar), s.m. [f. Arab. *az-zahr*] Hazard, risk, chance, hap, peril; *à tout* ~, at all hazards, at all events; *au* ~, at a venture, at random; *par* ~, by chance, (archaic) peradventure; accidentally, fortuitously; *le connaîtriez-vous, par* ~ ?, do you happen to know him?; *courir le* ~, to run the risk; *ne rien laisser au* ~, to leave nothing to chance; *un coup de* ~, a stroke of fortune; *s'en remettre au* ~, to leave it to chance; *corriger le* ~, to cheat at play, to assist fortune.

hasardé, -e (hazarde), p. adj. Hazardous, risky, rash.

hasarder (hazarde), v.a. [f. *hasard*] To hazard, to risk, to venture, to stake; *se* ~ *à*, to take the risk of, to venture to.

hasardeusement (hazardøzmɑ̃), adv. Hazardously.

hasardeu-x, -se (hazardø), adj. Risky, venturesome, hazardous, unsafe.

haschisch, hachish (haʃiʃ), s.m. [Arab. wd] Hashish.

hase (hɑz), s.f. [Germ. wd] Doe-hare, doe-rabbit.

hast (ast), s.m. (obs.) [L *hasta*] Spear; *arme d'*~, long-hafted weapon.

haste (hast), s.f. (obs.) [L *hasta*] Spear.

hasté, -e (haste), adj. Lance-shaped.

hâte (hɑt), s.f. [f. Goth. *haifsts*] Haste, hurry, speed, precipitation; *à la* ~, in a hurry; *avoir* ~ (*de*), to be in a hurry (to), to be anxious (to), to long (to); *en toute* ~, with all possible speed; *trop de* ~ *gâte tout*, more haste, less speed.

hâtelet (hatlɛ), s.m. [f. *hâte*] **1.** (cook.) Small skewer; **2.** piece of meat roasted on it.

hâter (hɑte), v.a. To hasten, to haste, to hurry, to urge on, to forward; ~ *le pas*, to quicken one's pace; (hort.) to force; **se** ~, v.pr. to hurry, to be in a hurry, to make haste, to hasten.

hâtier (hɑtje), s.m. Spit-rack; kitchen andiron.

hâti-f, -ve (hɑtif), adj. [f. *hâte*] Precocious, forward, early, premature, hasty; *pois* ~*s*, early peas; *fruits* ~*s*, (archaic) hastings, early fruit.

hâtivement (hɑtivmɑ̃), adv. Early; hastily, in haste, prematurely.

hâtiveté (hɑtivte), s.f. Earliness, forwardness.

hauban (hobɑ̃), s.m. [Flemish *hoband*] (naut.) Shroud.

haubaner (hobane), v.a. (naut.) To prop (a mast).

haubergeon (hobɛrʒɔ̃), s.m. Small hauberk, habergeon.

haubert (hobɛr), s.m. [OHG *halsberg*] Hauberk; coat of mail.

hausse (hos), s.f. [f. *hausser*] Rise; (print.) overlay; (of a rifle) back-sight; sight; *en* ~, rising; *jouer à la* ~, to speculate on a rise; *joueur à la* ~, bull.

hausse-col (hoskɔl), s.m. (pl. *hausse-cols*) (armoury) Gorget, neck-piece.

haussement (hosmɑ̃), s.m. Raising, lifting, shrugging, shrug (*d'épaules*, of the shoulders).

hausser (hose), v.a.n. [f. LL *altiare*] To raise, to lift up, to increase; to shrug (*les épaules*, the shoulders); *la rente hausse*, the funds are going up; *les actions haussent*, the price of shares is rising; ~ *la voix*, to raise one's voice; ~, (of the weather) to clear up; **se** ~, v.pr. to raise oneself, to rise, to be raised; *se* ~ *sur la pointe des pieds*, to stand on tiptoe.

haussier (hosje), s.m. (fin.) Bull, speculator on a rise.

haussière, aussière (osjɛr), s.f. Hawser.

haut, -e (ho), adj. [L *altus*] High, lofty, tall, raised, elevated, upright, erect, uplifted, eminent, grand; loud; upper; *navire de* ~ *-bord*, man-of-war; *le* ~ *bout de la table*, the upper end of the table; *jeter les* ~*s cris*, to raise an outcry, to complain loudly; *être* ~ *en couleur*, to be of a ruddy complexion; *avoir une* ~*e idée de soi-même*, to have a high opinion of oneself; ~*s faits*, great deeds; *en* ~*e mer*, out to sea, on the high seas; *exécuteur des* ~*es œuvres*, executioner; *le* ~ *Niger*, the upper Niger; *le Très-Haut*, the Most High; *de* ~*e taille*, very tall; *crime de* ~*e trahison*, crime of high treason; *avoir le verbe* ~, to talk very loud; to be peremptory or arrogant in speech; *à voix* ~*e*, aloud; *viande de* ~ *goût*, highly-seasoned meat. ~, adv. High, highly, aloft, up, at a high price, aloud; *porter ~ la tête* (or *le front*), to walk with head erect; to carry one's head high; *pendu ~ et court*, fairly hanged; *~ la main*, off-hand, easily; *~ le pied!*, be off!; *machine ~ le pied*, light engine, railway engine driven without a train; *personnes ~ placées*, people of high rank; *le prendre de ~*, to talk big, to be haughty; *reprendre de plus ~*, to begin farther back; *en ~*, at the top; above; upstairs; *de ~ en bas*, from top to bottom; (fig.) haughtily, contemptuously, arrogantly; *là-~*, up there, in heaven; *prenez par en ~*, take the upper way; *tout ~*, aloud. ~, s.m. Top, height, summit, upper part, high notes; *tomber de son ~*, to fall down flat; (fig.) to be thunderstruck; *avoir quatre mètres de ~*, to be four metres high; *des ~s et des bas*, ups and downs; *les Hauts de Meuse*, the Heights of Meuse; *~-de-chausses*, s.m. breeches, trunk-hose; (mus.) *~e-contre*, s.f. counter-tenor; *~-le-cœur*, s.m. nausea, retching; *~-le-corps*, s.m. start, bound; *~-mal*, s.m. epilepsy; *~ relief*, s.m. high relief.

hautain, -e (hotɛ̃), adj. Haughty, proud, lofty, arrogant, supercilious.

hautainement (hotɛnmɑ̃), adv. Haughtily, superciliously.

hautbois (hobwɑ), s.m. [*haut*+*bois*] Oboe; oboe-player, oboist.

hautboïste (hobɔist), s.m.f. Oboist.

hautement (hotmɑ̃), adv. Highly, resolutely, boldly, stoutly, aloud.

(sa) hautesse (sahotɛs), s.f. (His) Highness (the Sultan).

hauteur (hotœr), s.f. Height, altitude, elevation, hill, loftiness, haughtiness; *~s*, heights, uplands; *être à la ~ de Noirmoutier*, to be off Noirmoutier; (geom.) *~ d'un triangle, parallélogramme, etc.*, altitude of a triangle, &c.; *se montrer à la ~ des circonstances*, to come up to scratch; *être à la ~ de sa tâche*, to be equal to one's task; *être à la ~ de X*, to be a match for X; *répondre avec ~*, to answer haughtily.

haut-fourneau (hofurno), s.m. (pl. *hauts-fourneaux*) Blast-furnace.

hauturi-er, -ère (hotyrje), adj. (naut.) Of the high seas; *pilote ~*, sea pilot, proper pilot, as distinct from coasting or river pilot.

havanais, -e (havanɛ), adj. s.m.f. **1.** (Native) of Havana; **2.** a small dog.

havane (havan), s.m. Havana cigar. ~, adj. Cigar-coloured; light brown.

hâve (hɑv), adj. [orig. unkn.] Emaciated, wan, pale.

haveneau (pl. **-x**) (havno), s.m. (fish.) Purse-net.

havir (havir), v.a. To scorch the outside of (meat); ~, v.n. (of meat) to scorch on the outside.

havre (hɑvr), s.m. [f. OHG *hafen*] Haven, harbour, port.

havresac (hɑvrəsak), s.m. [f. Germ. *Habersack*] Knapsack, haversack, tool-wallet, bag.

hayon (hajɔ̃), s.m. Rear part of body of a motor-car or wagon, which may be lowered to give access from the back.

hé! (he), interj. Ho!; halloo!; hoy; I say!; there!; now!

heaume (hom), s.m. [f. OHG *helm*] Helm, helmet.

hebdomadaire (ɛbdɔmadɛr), adj. [f. Gr. *hebdomas*] Weekly. ~, s.m. Weekly (paper).

hebdomadairement (ɛbdɔmadɛrmɑ̃), adv. Weekly.

hebdomadi-er, -ère (ɛbdɔmadje), s.m.f. adj. Hebdomadary; (one) on duty for a week.

héberge (ebɛrʒ), s.f. [OHG *heriberga*] **1.** (law) Point of disjunction; **2.** point at which a party wall ceases to be common.

hébergement (ebɛrʒəmɑ̃), s.m. Lodging.

héberger (ebɛrʒe), v.a. [f. Germ. *Herberge*] To lodge, to harbour, to entertain.

hébété, -e (ebete), p. adj. Dulled, stupefied, besotted, stupid. ~, s.m.f. Dullard, sot, dunce, blockhead, moron.

hébètement (ebɛtmɑ̃), s.m. Dullness, sottishness, stupidity.

hébéter (ebete), v.a. [L *hebetare*] To dull, to besot, to hebetate, to make stupid.

hébétude (ebetyd), s.f. Dullness, stupidity, hebetude.

hébraïque (ebraik) adj. [f. Gr. *hebraios*] Hebraic, Hebrew.

hébraïsant, -e, hébraïste (ebraizɑ̃, ebraist), adj. s.m.f. Hebraist.

hébraïsme (ebraism), s.m. Hebraism.

hébreu (pl. **-x**) (ebrø), fem. **hébraïque,** adj. Hebrew. ~, s.m. Hebrew; Hebrew language; (fig.) *c'est de l'~ pour moi!*, it's Greek to me; it is impossible for me to understand it.

hécatombe (ekatɔ̃b), s.f. [f. Gr. *hekaton* +*bous*] Hecatomb.

hectare (ɛktar), s.m. [f. Gr. *hekaton*+ (Fr.) *are*] Hectare (= 2 acres, 1 rood, 35 perches, or 2·4711 acres).

hectique (ɛktik), adj. [f. Gr. *hektikos*] Hectic.

hectisie (ɛktizi), s.f. [f. *hectique*] Hectic fever.

hecto-, hect- (ɛkto, ɛkt), pref. [Gr. *hekaton*] (in comp.) Hecto- (= 100 times the unit).

hectogramme (ɛktɔgram), s.m. Hectogramme (abbrev.: hg.).

hectolitre (ɛktɔlitr), s.m. Hectolitre (abbrev.: hl.).

hectomètre (ɛktɔmɛtr), s.m. Hectometre (= 109 yards; abbrev. hm.).

hectowatt (εktɔwat), s.m. Hectowatt (= 100 watts).
hédonisme (edonism), s.m. [f. Gr. *hēdonē*] (phil.) Hedonism.
hégélianisme (eʒeljanism, egeljanism) s.m. [f. prop. n. *Hegel*] (phil.) Hegelianism.
hégélien, -ne (eʒeljɛ̃, egeljɛ̃), adj. Hegelian.
hégémonie (eʒemɔni), s.f. [Gr. *hēgemonia*] Hegemony.
hégire (eʒir), s.f. [Arab. *hijra*] Hegira.
heiduque (εdyk), s.m. [Magyar *hajduk*] Heyduck, Hungarian soldier.
hein (hɛ̃), interj. Hey!, what?, now then!
hélas (elɑ, elɑs), interj. [*hé*+*las*] Alas. ~, s.m. Alas, sigh, moan, exclamation.
héler (hele), v.a. [f. Engl. *to hail*] To hail, to call, to speak (a ship).
hélianthe (eljɑ̃t), s.m. [f. Gr. *hēlios*+*anthos*] (bot.) Helianthus, sunflower.
héliaque (eljak), adj. Heliacal.
hélice (elis), s.f. [f. Gr. *helissein, helix*] Screw, air-screw, helix; propeller; *bateau à* ~, screw-steamer; *escalier en hélice*, spiral staircase; *pale d'*~, blade.
hélicoïdal, -e, (aux) (elikɔidal), adj. Helicoidal, spiral.
hélicoïde (elikɔid), s.m. Helicoid.
hélicon (elikɔ̃), s.m. (mus.) Helicon (kind of horn).
hélicoptère (elikɔptεr), s.m. [f. Gr. *helix* +*pteron*] Helicopter.
héliocentrique (eljosɑ̃trik), adj. [f. Gr. *hēlios*+*kentron*] Heliocentric.
héliographe (eljograf), s.m. [f. Gr. *hēlios* +*graphein*] Heliograph; syn. HÉLIOSTAT.
héliogravure (eljogravyr), s.f. Heliogravure.
hélioscopie (eljoskɔpi), s.f. [f. Gr. *hēlios*+*skopein*] Helioscopy.
héliothérapie (eljoterapi), s.f. [f. Gr. *hēlios* +*therapeia*] Heliotherapy.
héliotrope (eljotrɔp), s.m. [f. Gr. *hēlios*+*trepein*] (bot., min.) Heliotrope.
héliotypie (eljotipi), s.f. Heliotypy.
hélium (eljɔm), s.m. [f. Gr. *hēlios*] (chem.) Helium (symbol: He).
hélix (eliks), s.m. [Gr. wd] (anat., zool.) Helix.
hellébore (εllebɔr), s.f. See ELLÉBORE.
hellène (εllεn), adj. s.m.f. [f. Gr. *Hellēnes* (pl.)] Hellenic, Hellene.
hellénique (εllenik), adj. Hellenic.
hellénisme (εllenism), s.m. Hellenism.
helléniste, hellénisant, -e (εllenist, εllenizɑ̃), s.m.f. Hellenist.
hellénistique (εllenistik), adj. Hellenistic (said of the period in Greece between Alexander's conquest and the Roman conquest).
helminthe (εlmɛ̃t), s.m. [f. Gr. *helmins*] (med.) Helminth.
helvétien, -ne (εlvetjɛ̃), adj. s.m.f. Helvetian; (in the plural subst. *les Helvètes* is the more frequent form).
helvétique (εlvetik), adj. Helvetic, Swiss; *les Alpes* ~*s*, the Swiss Alps.
hem! (hεm), interj. Hem!, I say!
hématie (emati), s.f. [f. Gr. *haima, -atos*] Blood-vesicle, globule of the blood.
hématite (ematit), s.f. (min.) Haematite.
hématologie (ematɔlɔʒi), s.f. [f. Gr. *haima*+*logos*] Haematology.
hématose (ematoz), s.f. [Gr. *haimatōsis*] (physiol.) Haematosis, conversion of venous blood into arterial blood.
hématurie (ematyri), s.f. [f. Gr. *haima*+*ouron*] (med.) Haematuria.
hémélytre (emelitr), s.m. [f. Gr. *hēmi-*+*elutron*] (ent.) Hemielytrum (pl. hemielytra).
hémérocalle (emerɔkal), s.f. [f. Gr. *hēmera*+*kallos*] (bot.) Hemerocallis, day-lily.
hémicycle (emisikl), s.m. [f. Gr. *hēmi-*+*kuklos*] Hemicycle.
hémione (emjɔn), s.m. [f. Gr. *hēmi-*+*onos*] (zool.) *Equus hemionus*, hemione, dziggetai.
hémiplégie (emipleʒi), s.f. [f. Gr. *hēmi-*+*plēssein*] (pathol.) Hemiplegia.
hémiptère (emiptεr), adj. [f. Gr. *hēmi-*+*pteron*] (ent.) Hemipterous, hemipteral. ~, s.m. Hemipter.
hémisphère (emisfεr), s.m. [f. Gr. *hēmi-*+*sphaira*] Hemisphere.
hémisphérique (emisferik), adj. Hemispherical.
hémistiche (emistiʃ), s.m. [f. Gr. *hēmi-*+*stikhos*] (pros.) Hemistich.
hémoglobine (emoglɔbin), s.f. [f. Gr. *haima*] Haemoglobin.
hémoptysie (emoptizi), s.f. [f. Gr. *haima*+*ptusis*] (pathol.) Haemoptysis, spitting of blood.
hémorragie (emɔraʒi), s.f. [f. Gr. *haima* +*rēgnunai*] (pathol.) Haemorrhage.
hémorragique (emɔraʒik), adj. Haemorrhagic.
hémorrhée (emɔre), s.f. [f. Gr. *haima*+*rhein*] (pathol.) Haemorrhaea.
hémorroïdes (emɔrɔid), s.f.pl. [f. Gr. *haima*+*rhein*] (pathol.) Haemorrhoids, piles.
hémostase (emostɑz), s.f. [f. Gr. *haima*+*stasis*] (pathol.) Haemostasia.
hémostatique (emostatik), adj. s.m. Haemostatic.
hendécagone, endécagone (ɑ̃dekagɔn), s.m. adj. [f. Gr. *hendeka*+*gōnia*] Hendecagon.
henné (hεnne), s.m. [Arab. *ḥinna'*] Henna.
hennin (hεnnɛ̃), s.m. Hennin (a feminine head-dress, 15th century).
hennir (hεnir), v.n. [L *ḥinnire*] To neigh, to whinny.

hennissement (hɛnismɑ̃), s.m. Neighing, neigh.
hépatique (epatik), adj. [f. Gr. *hēpar*] Hepatic. ~, s.f. (bot.) Liverwort.
hépatite (epatit), s.f. [f. Gr. *hēpar*] **1.** (pathol.) Hepatitis; **2.** (min.) hepatite.
heptacorde (ɛptakɔrd), s.m. [f. Gr. *hepta*) Heptachord.
heptaèdre (ɛptaɛdr), s.m. adj. [f. Gr. *hepta+hedra*] Heptahedral.
heptagonal, -e, (aux) (ɛptagɔnal), adj. Heptagonal.
heptagone (ɛptagɔn), s.m. [f. Gr. *hepta+gōnia*] Heptagon.
heptagyne (ɛptaʒin), adj. [f. Gr. *hepta+gunē*] (bot.) Heptagynian, heptagynous.
heptamètre (ɛptamɛtr), s.m. adj. [f. Gr. *hepta+metron*] (pros.) Heptameter.
heptandre (ɛptɑ̃dr), adj. [f. Gr. *hepta+anēr*] (bot.) Heptandrian, heptandrous.
heptarchie (ɛptarʃi), s.f. [f. Gr. *hepta+archē*] Heptarchy.
héraldique (eraldik), adj. [f. LL *heraldus*] Heraldic. ~, s.f. Heraldry.
héraut (hero), s.m. [LL *heraldus*] Herald; (poet.) harbinger.
herbacé, -e (ɛrbase), adj. Herbaceous.
herbage (ɛrbaʒ), s.m. [f. *herbe*] **1.** Herbage, herbs, grass, green food; **2.** pasture-ground, meadow.
herbag-er, -ère (ɛrbaʒe), s.m.f. Grazier. ~, adj. Meadow.
herbager (ɛrbaʒe), v.a. To graze (cattle).
herbe (ɛrb), s.f. [L *herba*] Herb, grass, blade of grass, wort, weed, simple; *brin d'~*, blade of grass; *blé en ~*, corn in the blade; *fines ~s*, herbs, savoury herbs; *~s potagères*, pot-herbs; *~ de la St-Jean*, St. John's wort, mugwort; (fig.) *avoir toutes les ~s de la St-Jean*, to have all the necessary ingredients, to be ready for any eventuality; (fig.) *manger son blé en ~*, to eat the calf in the cow's belly, to anticipate one's income; *avocat en ~*, future barrister; *couper l'~ sous le pied à X*, to supplant X, to take the wind out of X's sails; *vous vous êtes laissé couper l'~ sous le pied*, you have let your nose be put out of joint; *sur quelle ~ a-t-il marché?*, what is the matter with him?, what has put him out?; *mauvaise ~ croît toujours*, ill weeds grow apace; *~ à éternuer*, sneezewort; *~ aux chats*, catmint; *~ aux gueux*, clematis; &c.
herbeiller (ɛrbɛje), v.n. To graze (of boars).
herber (ɛrbe), v.a. [f. *herbe*] To bleach (linen) on the grass.
herberie (ɛrbəri), s.f. **1.** Bleaching-ground; **2.** herb-market.
herbette (ɛrbɛt), s.f. Short grass, turf, greensward; *danser sur l'~*, to dance on the green.
herbeu-x, -se (ɛrbø), adj. Herbose, grassy, weedy.
herbier (ɛrbje), s.m. **1.** Grass-shed; **2.** herbarium, herbal.
herbière (ɛrbjɛr), s.f. Herb-woman.
herbivore (ɛrbivɔr), adj. [f. L *herba+vorare*] Herbivorous. ~, s.m., Herbivore.
herborisateur, herboriseur (ɛrbɔrizatœr, ɛrbɔrizœr), s.m., (fem.) **herborisatrice**, Herborizer.
herborisation (ɛrbɔriza'sjɔ̃), s.f. Herborization, herborizing.
herboriser (ɛrbɔrize), v.n. To herborize.
herboriste (ɛrbɔrist), s.m.f. Herbalist, dealer in medicinal herbs and simples, toilet wares, &c.
herboristerie (ɛrbɔristəri), s.f. Herb-shop, herbalist's shop.
herbu, -e (ɛrby), adj. Grass-grown.
hercher (hɛrʃe), v.n. (mining) To cart (ore).
hercheur (hɛrʃœr), s.m. Ore-carter.
hercule (ɛrkyl), s.m. [f. myth. *Hercules*] Hercules, athletic man, man of herculean strength.
herculéen, -ne (ɛrkyleɛ̃), adj. Herculean.
hère (hɛr), s.m. [orig. dub.] **1.** Wretch; *pauvre ~*, sorry fellow, poor devil; **2.** young stag.
héréditaire (ereditɛr), adj. Hereditary.
héréditairement (ereditɛrmɑ̃), adv. Hereditarily.
hérédité (eredite), s.f. [L *hereditas*] Heredity, hereditary transmission, inheritance.
hérésiarque (erezjark), s.m. Heresiarch.
hérésie (erezi), s.f. [Gr. *hairesis*] Heresy.
hérétique (eretik), adj. Heretical. ~, s.m.f. Heretic.
hérissé, -e (herise), p. adj. [f. *hérisson*] Bristling, shaggy; on end; studded (*de*, with), covered (*de*, with); *cheveux ~s* or *tête ~e*, shaggy mane; *un devoir ~ de fautes*, an exercise full of mistakes; *une affaire ~e de difficultés*, an affair bristling with difficulties.
hérissement (herismɑ̃), s.m. Bristling; (fig.) stiffening, getting on the defensive, getting one's back up.
hérisser (herise), v.a. [f. *hérisson*] To bristle, to erect, to arm; to bristle up; to garnish (*de*, with), to lard, to fill, to cover (*de*, with); **se** ~, v.pr. to bristle up, to stand on end; (fig.) to be cross-grained, to stiffen, to have one's back up.
hérisson (herisɔ̃), s.m. [L *ericius*] **1.** Hedgehog; (fig.) gruff or crusty person; **2.** sweep's machine; rotary gill; **3.** (fort.) herisson; (techn.) sprocket-wheel; **4.** (bot.) chestnut-burr.
héritage (eritaʒ), s.m. Inheritance, heritage, patrimony; *faire* or *recueillir un ~*, to inherit property.

hériter (erite), v.a.n. [L *hereditare*] To inherit; ~, v.n. to succeed.

hériti-er, -ère (eritje), s.m.f. Heir, (fem.) heiress; ~ *légitime*, heir-at-law; ~ *naturel*, heir of one's body; *être* ~ *de son oncle*, to be heir to one's uncle.

hermaphrodisme (ɛrmafrɔdism), s.m. Hermaphroditism.

hermaphrodite (ɛrmafrɔdit), s.m. adj. [f. *Hermès*+*Aphrodite*] Hermaphrodite.

herméneutique (ɛrmenøtik), adj. [f. Gr. *hermēneuein*] Hermeneutic. ~, s.f. Hermeneutics.

hermès (ɛrmɛs), s.m. [Gr. *Hermēs*] Hermes, head of Mercury.

hermétique (ɛrmetik), adj. [f. myth. *Hermēs*] Hermetic; *la science* ~, the hermetic science; alchemy.

hermétiquement (ɛrmetikmɑ̃), adv. Hermetically, closely, tightly.

hermine (ɛrmin), s.f. [f. *Armenia*] (zool.) Ermine, ermine fur; (herald.) ermine.

hermitage, hermite (ɛrmitaʒ, ɛrmit), s.m. See ERMITAGE, ERMITE.

herniaire (hɛrnjɛr), adj. Hernial, pertaining to hernia.

hernie (hɛrni), s.f. [L *hernia*] (pathol.) Hernia.

hernutes (hɛrnyt), s.m.pl. [f. *Herrnhut*, Saxony] Moravians, United Brethren, Herrnhuters.

héroï-comique (erɔikɔmik), adj. Heroi-comic, heroi-comical, mock-heroic.

héroïde (erɔid), s.f. Heroid.

héroïne (erɔin), s.f. [f. Gr. *hērōs*] **1.** Heroine, heroic woman; **2.** heroine, principal female personage in a poem, play, or novel; **3.** (chem.) heroin (a derivative of morphine).

héroïque (erɔik), adj. [f. *héros*] Heroic; epic; (fig.) drastic, violent and efficacious.

héroïquement (erɔikmɑ̃), adv. Heroically.

héroïsme (erɔism), s.m. Heroism.

héron (herɔ̃), s.m. [f. OHG *heiger*] (ornith.) Heron.

héronneau (pl. **-x**) (herɔno), s.m. Young heron.

héronnière (herɔnjɛr), s.f. Heronry.

héros (hero), s.m. [Gr. *hērōs*] Hero.

herpes (hɛrp), s.f.pl. Natural treasures of the sea; sea-wreckage.

herpès (ɛrpɛs), s.m. [f. Gr. *herpein*] (pathol.) Herpes.

herpétique (ɛrpetik), adj. Herpetic.

hersage (hɛrsaʒ), s.m. Harrowing.

herse (hɛrs), s.f. [L *irpex*] **1.** (agric.) Harrow; **2.** (fort.) herse, portcullis; **3.** (theatr.) batten-lights.

hersement (hɛrsmɑ̃), s.m. See HERSAGE.

herser (hɛrse), v.a. (agric.) To harrow.

hertzien, -ne (hɛrtzjɛ̃), adj. [f. *Hertz*, Germ. physicist, 1857-94] Hertzian; *ondes* ~*nes*, Hertzian waves.

hésitant, -e (ezitɑ̃), p. adj. Hesitating, wavering, undecided; faltering.

hésitation (ezita'sjɔ̃), s.f. Hesitation, uncertainty; faltering, stammering.

hésiter (ezite), v.n. [L *haesitare*] To hesitate, to waver, to falter, to stammer; *sans* ~, unhesitatingly; *il faut le faire, il n'y a pas à* ~, it's got to be done, and the sooner the better; it's got to be done, no doubt about it.

hessois, -e (hɛswɑ), adj. s.m.f. Hessian.

hétaïre (etair), s.f. [Gr. *hetaira*] Courtesan, hetaira.

hétéroclite (eterɔklit), adj. [Gr. *heteroklitos*] Heteroclite, odd, whimsical, queer, irregular, abnormal.

hétérodoxe (eterɔdɔx), adj. [Gr. *heteros*+*doxa*] Heterodox.

hétérodoxie (eterɔdɔksi), s.f. Heterodoxy.

hétérogène (eterɔʒɛn), adj. [Gr. *heteros*+*genos*] Heterogeneous, heterogeneal, heterogene.

hétérogénéité (eterɔʒeneite), s.f. Heterogeneousness, heterogeneity.

hetman (hɛtman), s.m. [Polish wd] Hetman.

hêtraie (hɛtrɛ), s.f. (bot.) Beech-grove.

hêtre (hɛtr), s.m. [f. OHG *hester*] Beech, beech-tree.

heu! (hø), interj. Hum!, well!, now!, oh!

heur (œr), s.m. [L *augurium*] Hap, luck, (obs. exc. in: *tout n'est qu'*~ *et malheur*, life has its little ups and downs; and: *si j'ai eu l'heur de vous plaire*, if I have had the good hap to please you).

heure (œr), s.f. [L *hora*] Hour, time; moment, appointed time; ~*s* (pl.) prayer-book, book of hours; *une demi-*~, half an hour; *un quart d'*~, a quarter of an hour; *quelle* ~ *est-il?*, what o'clock is it?; what time is it?; *il est quatre* ~*s moins le quart*, it's a quarter to four; *quatre* ~*s*, four o'clock; *quatre* ~*s un quart*, a quarter past four; *quatre* ~*s et demie*, half past four; *à cinq* ~*s tapant*, at five sharp; *à cette* ~, *à l'*~ *qu'il est*, at the present time, by this time; *à la bonne* ~*!*, well and good!, that's right!, all right!; *à l'*~, (*a*) by the hour; (*b*) at the right time; *de bonne* ~, early; *de meilleure* ~, earlier; *d'*~ *en* ~, hourly; gradually; every hour; *tout à l'*~, (*a*) directly, in a moment; presently; (*b*) just a moment ago; *il travaille à ses* ~*s*, he chooses his own time for work; *partir sur l'*~, to leave immediately; *son* ~ *est venue*, his last hour has come; *votre* ~ *viendra*, your turn will come; *mettre sa montre à l'*~, to set one's watch; *le quart d'*~ *de Rabelais*, paying-time, the time for settling; *l'*~ *d'été*, summer time.

heureusement (œrøzmɑ̃), adv. Happily, fortunately; successfully, safely.

heureu-x, -se (œrø), adj. [f. *heur*] Happy,

blissful, fortunate, blest, successful, lucky, auspicious, prepossessing, pleasing; felicitous, happy; *repartie ~se*, witty rejoinder; *mémoire ~se*, faithful memory; *~ naturel*, happy disposition; *une ~se étoile*, a happy star. ~, s.m. Happy man; *les ~ de ce monde*, the happy ones of the world; the lucky ones.
heurt (hœr), s.m. [f. *heurter*] Knock, shock, collision, clash; bruise.
heurtement (hœrtmɑ̃), s.m. Clash, clashing.
heurter (hœrte), v.a. [orig. uncert.] To knock against, to hit, to strike, to run against, to jostle, to shock, to offend, to clash with, to jar; ~, v.n. to knock, to rap; **se** ~ (*à*), v.pr. to run against, or counter to; to jostle each other, to clash together; *se ~ la tête contre*, to knock one's head against.
heurtoir (hœrtwar), s.m. Knocker; stop-stone.
hexaèdre (ɛkzaɛdr), adj. [Gr. *hex*+*hedra*] Hexahedral. ~, s.m. Hexahedron.
hexagonal, -e, (aux) (ɛkzagɔnal), adj. [f. Gr. *hex*+*gōnia*] Hexagonal.
hexagone (ɛkzagɔn), s.m. Hexagon.
hexamètre (ɛkzamɛtr), s.m. [f. Gr. *hex*+*metron*] Hexameter.
hiatus (jatys), s.m. [f. L *hiare*] Hiatus.
hibernal, -e, (aux) (ibɛrnal), adj. Wintry, hibernal; syn. HIVERNAL.
hibernant, -e (ibɛrnɑ̃), p. adj. (zool.), Hibernating.
hibernation (ibɛrna'sjɔ̃), s.f. (zool.) Hibernation.
hiberner (ibɛrne), v.n. [L *hibernare*] To hibernate.
hibou (pl. -x) (hibu), s.m. [orig. uncert.] Owl; (fig.) solitary bird, moper.
hic (hik), s.m. [L wd] Rub, difficulty; *voilà le ~*, there 's the rub.
hideur (hidœr), s.f. [f. *hideux*] Hideousness.
hideusement (hidøzmɑ̃), adv. Hideously, horribly, dreadfully, shockingly.
hideu-x, -se (hidø), adj. [f. OF *hide* = fright] Hideous, frightful, dreadful, shocking, ghastly.
hie (hi), s.f. [f. Germ. *Heie*] Paving-rammer or beetle; syn. DEMOISELLE.
hièble (iɛbl), s.f. [L *ebulum*] (bot.) Dwarf elder, danewort; *Sambucus ebulus*.
hiémal, -e, (aux) (jemal), adj. (poet.) [L *hiemalis*] Wintry.
hier (jɛr), adv. [L *heri*] Yesterday; ~ *matin*, yesterday morning; *avant-~*, the day before yesterday.
hiérarchie (hjerarʃi), s.f. [f. Gr. *hieros*+*archē*] Hierarchy, subordination.
hiérarchique (hjerarʃik), adj. Hierarchical.
hiérarchiquement (hjerarʃikmɑ̃), adv. Hierarchically.
hiératique (jeratik), adj. [f. Gr. *hieros*] Hieratic, sacerdotal; *écriture ~*, hieratic writing.
hiéroglyphe (jerɔglif), s.m. [f. Gr. *hieros*+*gluphō*] Hieroglyph, hieroglyphic.
hiéroglyphique (jerɔglifik), adj. Hieroglyphic, hieroglyphical.
hiérophante (jerɔfɑ̃t), s.m. [f. Gr. *hieros*+*phainō*] Hierophant.
hilarant, -e (ilarɑ̃), adj. [f. L *hilarans*] Hilarious, exhilarating, enlivening; (chem.) *gaz ~*, laughing-gas.
hilare (ilar), adj. Hilarious, laughing, cheerful.
hilarité (ilarite), s.f. [L *hilaritas*] Hilarity, loud laughter, mirth, cheerfulness.
hile (hil), s.m. [L *hilum*] (bot.) Hilum.
hiloire (ilwar), s.f. [Span. *eslora*] (naut.) Binding-strake (of the deck).
hindou, -e (ɛ̃du), adj. s.m.f. Hindu.
hindoustani (ɛ̃dustani), s.m. Hindustani (language).
hippiâtre (ipjɑtr), s.m. [f. Gr. *hippos*+*iatros*] Veterinary surgeon.
hippique (ipik), adj. [f. Gr. *hippos*] Of horses, horse-, relating to horses; *concours ~*, horse-show.
hippocampe (ipokɑ̃p), s.m. (myth.) Hippocamp, hippocampus; (ichth.) hippocampus.
hippocentaure (iposɑ̃tɔr), s.m. [Gr. *hippos*+*kentauros*] Hippocentaur; centaur.
hippocratique (ipokratik), adj. Hippocratic, of or relating to Hippocrates.
hippocratisme (ipokratism), s.m. Hippocratism; system of Hippocrates.
hippodrome (ipɔdrom), s.m. [f. Gr. *hippos*+*dromos*] Hippodrome, circus, race-ground.
hippogriffe (ipɔgrif), s.m. [f. Gr. *hippos* +L *gryphus*] Hippogriff.
hippophage (ipɔfaʒ), adj. [f. Gr. *hippos*+*phagō*] Hippophagous.
hippophagique (ipɔfaʒik), adj. Hippophagic.
hippopotame (ipɔpɔtam), s.m. [f. Gr. *hippos*+*potamos*] (zool.) Hippopotamus.
hirondelle (irɔ̃dɛl), s.f. [L *hirundo*] Swallow; martin; *~ de cheminée*, chimney-swallow; *~ des fenêtres*, house-martin; *une ~ ne fait pas le printemps*, one swallow does not make a summer.
hirsute (irsyt), adj. [L *hirsutus*] Hirsute, shaggy, hairy, unkempt (hair).
hispanique (ispanik), adj. [f. L *Hispania*] Hispanic, Spanish.
hispanisme (ispanism), s.m. Hispanicism, Spanish idiom.
hispide (ispid), adj. [L *hispidus*] Hispid, bristly.
hisser (hise), v.a. [f. Scand. *hissa*] To hoist, to haul up (sails), to run up (a flag); **se** ~, v.pr. to raise oneself, to hoist oneself.

histogénie (istoʒeni), s.f. [f. Gr. *histos*+*genos*] Histogeny.
histoire (istwar), s.f. [L *historia*] History, story, tale, account; fuss, bustle, difficulty, ado, disturbance, trouble; fib; *le plus beau de l'*~, the cream of the story, the plum; *que d'*~*s !*, what a fuss !; *cela va faire des* ~*s*, that's going to make trouble, or a fine fuss; ~ *de rire*, for the fun of the thing; just for fun.
histologie (istɔlɔʒi), s.f. [f. Gr. *histos*+*logos*] Histology.
historicité (istɔrisite) s.f. Historic truth, historic value.
historié, -e (istɔrje), p. adj. Historiated, embellished, adorned.
historien, -ne (istɔrjɛ̃), s.m.f. Historian.
historier (istɔrje), v.a. To historiate, to adorn, to embellish.
historiette (istɔrjɛt), s.f. [f. *histoire*] Short tale or story, anecdote.
historiographe (istɔrjɔgraf), s.m.f. Historiographer.
historique (istɔrik), adj. Historic, historical; *c'est* ~, it's a fact. ~, s.m. History, recital (of facts); *faire l'*~ *d'une affaire*, to give a chronological account of a business; to relate the developments of an affair.
historiquement (istɔrikmɑ̃), adv. Historically, chronologically.
histrion (istrjɔ̃), s.m. [L *histrio*] Histrion; (fig.) histrion, mountebank.
hiver (ivɛr), s.m. [f. L *hibernus*] Winter; *d'*~, winter, wintry; *sports d'*~, winter sports.
hivernage (ivɛrnaʒ), s.m. **1.** Wintering, winter season; **2.** winter harbour; **3.** (agric.) winter fallowing, winter fodder.
hivernal, -e, (aux) (ivɛrnal), adj. Wintry, hibernal; (poet.) hyemal.
hiverner (ivɛrne), v.n. [f. *hiver*] To winter; ~, v.a. (agric.) to winter-fallow.
hobereau (pl. **-x**) (hɔbro), s.m. [OF *hobe* = bird of prey] **1.** Small hawk, hobby; **2.** squireen.
hocco (hɔko), s.m. [Guiana native wd] (ornith.) Hocco, curassow, *Crax*.
hoche (hɔʃ), s.f. Notch.
hochement (hɔʃmɑ̃), s.m. Toss (of the head), shake.
hochepot (hɔʃpo), s.m. [*hoche*+*pot*] (cook.) Hotchpotch, hotchpot.
hochequeue (hɔʃkø), s.m. [*hoche*+*queue*] (ornith.) Wagtail.
hocher (hɔʃe), v.a. [orig. uncert.] **1.** To toss, to shake, to wag; **2.** to notch, to nick, to indent.
hochet (hɔʃɛ), s.m. [f. *hocher*] Child's rattle; (fig.) toy, bauble.
hodomètre (ɔdɔmɛtr), s.m. [f. Gr. *hodos* +*metron*] Hodometer, odometer.
hoir (war), s.m. [L *heres*] Heir.
hoirie (wari), s.f. [f. *hoir*] Inheritance.
holà ! (hɔla, hola), interj. Halloo !, holloa !, holla !, ho ! ~, s.m. *Mettre le* ~ *à*, to put a stop to; to put one's foot down on.
hollandais, -e (hɔlɑ̃dɛ), adj. s.m.f. Dutch, Dutchman, Dutchwoman, Dutch language.
hollande (hɔlɑ̃d), s.m. Dutch cheese. ~, s.f. Large potato; holland (linen).
holocauste (ɔlɔkost), s.m. [Gr. *holocaustos*] Holocaust, burnt offering.
holothurie (ɔlɔtyri), s.f. [Gr. *holothourion*] (zool.) Holothurian.
homard (hɔmar), s.m. [f. Scand. *humarr*] Lobster.
hombre (ɔ̃br), s.m. [Span. wd] Ombre (card-game).
homélie (ɔmeli), s.f. [eccles. L *homilia*] Homily.
homéopathie (ɔmeɔpati), s.f. [f. Gr. *homoios*+*pathos*] Homœopathy.
homéopathique (ɔmeɔpatik), adj. Homoeopathic.
homérique (ɔmerik), adj. Homeric.
homicide (ɔmisid), s.m. [f. L *homo*+*caedere*] Homicide, manslaughter, murder; murderer. ~, adj. Homicidal, murderous, killing.
hommage (ɔmaʒ), s.m. [f. *homme*] Homage, respect, service, compliment; ~ *de l'auteur*, with the author's compliments; *faire* ~ *à X de*, to present X with; *présenter ses* ~*s à X*, to pay one's respects to X; *rendre* ~ *à la vérité*, to do homage to truth.
hommasse (ɔmas), adj. (of a woman) Manlike, masculine, heavy-built.
homme (ɔm), s.m. [L *homo*] Man; adult; human creature, mankind; husband, lover; vassal, dependant; soldier; workman; ~ *d'affaires*, business man; ~ *d'armes*, soldier; ~ *d'argent*, rapacious man; ~ *de bien*, honest, virtuous man, generous man; *brave* ~, good fellow; ~ *de cheval*, horseman, gentleman rider; ~ *de cœur*, generous man; ~ *d'Église*, ecclesiastic; ~ *d'état*, statesman; ~ *de journée*, day-labourer; ~ *de lettres*, literary man, man of letters; ~ *de loi*, lawyer; ~ *de métier*, professional; ~ *du monde*, man of the world; man about town; ~ *de paille*, dummy, man of straw, ~ *du peuple*, man of the lower classes; ~ *de plume*, writer; ~ *de qualité*, gentleman, nobleman; ~ *comme il faut*, gentleman; ~ *de robe*, gentleman of the long robe; ~ *à tout faire*, Jack of all trades; *voilà mon* ~, that is the man for me; *il n'est pas* ~ *à faire cela*, he is not the sort of man to act like that; *un* ~ *averti en vaut deux*, forewarned, forearmed; *le Fils de l'*~, the Son of Man.
homocentrique (ɔmosɑ̃trik), adj. [f. Gr. *homo*-+*kentron*] (geom.) Homocentric.

homogène (ɔmɔʒɛn), adj. [f. Gr. *homo-* +*genos*] Homogeneous, homogene.
homogénéité (ɔmɔʒeneite), s.f. Homogeneity, homogeneousness.
homologation (ɔmɔlɔga'sjɔ̃), s.f. Homologation, confirmation.
homologue (ɔmɔlɔg), adj. Homologous. ~, s.m. Homologue.
homologuer (ɔmɔlɔge), v.a. [f. Gr. *homo-* +*logos*] To homologate, to confirm.
homoncule (ɔmɔ̃kyl), s.m. [L *homunculus*] Homunculus, dwarf.
homonyme (ɔmɔnim), adj. [f. Gr. *homo* +*onuma*] Homonymous. ~, s.m. Homonym; ~, s.m.f. namesake.
homonymie (ɔmɔnimi), s.f. Homonymy.
homosexuel, -le (ɔmɔsɛksɥɛl), adj. s.m.f. Homosexual.
hongre (hɔ̃gr), adj. [f. *Hongrie*, Hungary] Gelded. ~, s.m. Gelding.
hongrer (hɔ̃gre), v.a. To geld.
hongreur (hɔ̃grœr), s.m. Gelder.
hongrois, -e (hɔ̃grwɑ), adj. s.m.f. Hungarian.
honnête (ɔnɛt), adj. [L *honestus*] Honest, loyal, respectable, honourable, fair; proper, seemly, decent, reasonable, moderate; polite, civil; ~ *homme*, honest man; (in the 17th c. and still frequently) cultivated man, gentleman; *un homme* ~, an honest man; *une* ~ *femme*, a respectable woman; *des paroles bien* ~*s*, obliging words; *maintien* ~, decent bearing; *récompense* ~, suitable reward.
honnêtement (ɔnɛtmɑ̃), adv. Honestly; properly; politely, civilly, kindly, suitably.
honnêteté (ɔnɛtəte), s.f. Honesty, probity, integrity; propriety, decency, politeness, civility, attention; *braver l'*~, to offend against propriety.
honneur (ɔnœr), s.m. [L *honor*] Honour, credit, repute; (pl.) honours, preferments; *dame d'*~, lady-in-waiting; *demoiselle d'*~, bridesmaid; *garçon d'*~, best man, groomsman; *avoir l'*~ *de*, to have the honour of, to beg leave to; *faire* ~ *à X*, to do honour to X, to honour X; *faire* ~ *de*, to ascribe the honour of; *faire* ~ *à ses engagements, à sa signature*, to honour one's engagements, one's signature; to pay everybody honestly their own; *faire* ~ *à sa famille*, to be a credit to one's family; *cela vous fait beaucoup d'*~, that is much to your credit; *faire les* ~*s*, to do the honours; *tenir à* ~ *de*, to deem it a point of honour to; *engager son* ~, to stake one's honour; *être engagé d'*~, to be bound by honour; *rendre de grands* ~*s à*, to pay great honours to; *se piquer d'*~, to make it a point of honour; to do something zealously; *se faire* ~ *de*, to take to oneself the credit of; to glory in; *être en* ~, to be in honour, to be in favour; *en tout bien tout* ~, with honourable intentions; honour bright; *s'en tirer à son* ~, to come off with honour; *ne jouer que pour l'*~, to play for love; *affaire d'*~, duel; *champ d'*~, battle-field; *point d'*~, point of honour; *parole d'*~, word of honour; *parole d'*~ *!, sur mon* ~ *!*, upon my honour!
honnir (hɔnir), v.a. [f. OHG *haunjan*] To brand, to disgrace, to cover with shame; *honni soit qui mal y pense*, evil be to him who evil thinks.
honorabilité (ɔnɔrabilite), s.f. Honourableness, respectability.
honorable (ɔnɔrabl), adj. Honourable, respectable, creditable.
honorablement (ɔnɔrabləmɑ̃), adv. Honourably, respectably, creditably.
honoraire (ɔnɔrɛr), adj. [L *honorarius*] Honorary. ~**s**, s.m.pl. Honorarium, fee, fees, emoluments, stipend.
honorer (ɔnɔre), v.a. [L *honorare*] To honour, to pay honour to, to do credit to, to be an honour to; *s'*~ *de*, to deem it an honour to.
honorifique (ɔnɔrifik), adj. Honorary, honorific, gratuitous, honour-giving.
honte (hɔ̃t), s.f. [f. OHG *haunita*] Shame, disgrace, confusion, bashfulness; *avoir* ~ *de*, to be ashamed to; *avoir toute* ~ *bue*, to be lost to all sense of shame; *faire* ~ *à X*, to shame X; to make X ashamed of himself; *être* (or *faire*) *la* ~ *de sa famille*, to disgrace one's family; *fausse* ~, bashfulness, sheepishness; *s'en revenir avec sa courte* ~, to come home baulked and looking foolish.
honteusement (hɔ̃tøzmɑ̃), adv. Shamefully, disgracefully; bashfully.
honteu-x, -se (hɔ̃tø), adj. Shameful, disgraceful, disreputable; ashamed, abashed, looking foolish; *un pauvre* ~, a poor man, ashamed to beg; *le morceau* ~, the last bit going begging.
hôpital (pl. **aux**) (ɔpital), s.m. [f. L *hospes*] Hospital.
hoplite (ɔplit), s.m. [f. Gr. *hoplitēs*] Hoplite.
hoquet (hɔkɛ), s.m. [orig. uncert.; perhaps onom.] Hiccup; *avoir le* ~, to hiccough, to hiccup, to have the hiccups.
horaire (ɔrɛr), adj. [L *horarius*] Horary, relating to hours. ~, s.m. Time-table.
horde (hɔrd), s.f. [f. Turki *orda*] Horde, rabble.
horion (hɔrjɔ̃), s.m. [orig. unkn.] Buffet, blow, thump, thwack, bruiser; *recevoir des* ~*s*, to get knocked about.
horizon (ɔrizɔ̃), s.m. [Gr. *horizōn*] Horizon.
horizontal, -e, (aux) (ɔrizɔ̃tal), adj. Horizontal.
horizontalement (ɔrizɔ̃talmɑ̃), adv. Horizontally.
horloge (ɔrlɔʒ), s.f. [f. Gr. *hōra*, L *horo-*

logium] Clock, turret-clock, church-clock; ~ *à eau*, water-clock, clepsydra; *j'ai attendu trois heures d'*~, I waited three full hours, or three hours by the clock; *réglé comme une* ~, as regular as clockwork.

horloger (ɔrlɔʒe). s.m. Watch-maker, clock-maker.

horlogerie (ɔrlɔʒri), s.f. Horology, clock- and watch-making; clockwork.

hormis (ɔrmi), prep. [*hors*+*mis*] Except, but, save, with the exception of.

horographie (ɔrɔgrafi), s.f. [f. Gr. *hōra*+*graphein*] Horography; syn. GNOMONIQUE.

horométrie (ɔrɔmetri), s.f. [f. Gr. *hōra*+*metron*] Horometry.

horoscope (ɔrɔskɔp), s.m. [f. Gr. *hōra*+*skopein*] Horoscope; *faire l'*~ *de X*, to cast X's nativity; *se faire tirer son* ~, to have one's fortune told.

horreur (ɔrœr), s.f. [L *horror*] Horror, shuddering, dread, abhorrence, hatred, disgust; dreadful thing, shocking thing, horrid words, slander; (fig.) hideous person; *avoir* ~ *de*, to abhor, to have a horror of; to hate; *faire* ~ *à*, to horrify, to make (one) shudder, to disgust.

horrible (ɔribl), adj. [L *horribilis*] Horrible, horrid, hideous, dreadful, shocking.

horriblement (ɔribləmɑ̃), adv. Horribly, horridly, dreadfully, awfully, shockingly.

horrifier (ɔrifje), v.a. To horrify, to shock, to disgust.

horrifique (ɔrifik), adj. [L *horrificus*] Horrific, horrid, frightful.

horripilant, -e (ɔripilɑ̃), p. adj. Annoying, irritating.

horripilation (ɔripila'sjɔ̃), s.f. Horripilation; irritation, setting on edge; (fam.) goose-flesh.

horripiler (ɔripile), v.a. [f. L *horrere*+*pilus*] To set on edge, to irritate, to make one's flesh creep.

hors (hɔr), adv. [f. L *foris*] Out, outside. ~, prep. Out of, outside, without, beside, save, except; ~ *de*, out of; ~ *d'ici!*, away with you!; ~ *de là*, beyond that; ~ *de chez soi*, away from home; *être* ~ *de soi*, to be beside oneself; ~ *d'affaire, de danger*, out of danger; ~ *de combat*, disabled; ~ *d'haleine*, out of breath, breathless; ~ *ligne*, matchless; ~ *de prix*, awfully expensive; ~ *de service*, worn out, unfit for use.

hors-d'œuvre (hɔrdœvr), s.m. invar. Hors-d'œuvre, side-dish; (arch.) outwork; (fig). digression; excrescence, superfluous thing.

hortensia (ɔrtɑ̃sja), s.m. (bot.) Hydrangea.

horticole (ɔrtikɔl), adj. Horticultural.

horticulteur (ɔrtikyltœr), s.m. Horticulturist, gardener.

horticulture (ɔrtikyltyr), s.f. [f. L *hortus*+*cultura*] Horticulture; *exposition d'*~, flower-show.

hosanna (hozana), s.m. [Hebr. wd] Hosanna; (fig.) song of praise and joy.

hospice (ɔspis), s.m. [f. L *hospes, hospitium*] Hospice, asylum, refuge, monastery, hospital.

hospitali-er, -ère (ɔspitalje), adj. [L *hospitalis*] **1.** Hospital, relating to hospitals; **2.** hospitable. ~, s.m. Hospitaller.

hospitalièrement (ɔspitaljɛrmɑ̃), adv. Hospitably.

hospitalité (ɔspitalite), s.f. [L *hospitalitas*] Hospitality, hospitableness; *donner l'*~ *à X*, to welcome X; to lodge X.

host (ɔst), s.m. See OST.

hostie (ɔsti), s.f. [L *hostia*] Host; (consecrated) wafer; (antiq.) victim, offering.

hostile (ɔstil), adj. [L *hostilis*] Hostile, inimical.

hostilement (ɔstilmɑ̃), adv. In a hostile manner, hostilely.

hostilité (ɔstilite), s.f. [f. *hostile*] Hostility (*contre*, to), animosity, ill-will, opposition; act of warfare; *commencer les* ~*s*, to begin hostilities; *manifester de l'*~ *contre X*, to show ill will or hostility towards X, to oppose X.

hôte, hôtesse (ot, otɛs), s.m.f. [L *hospes*] **1.** Host, hostess (one who entertains another at his or her own house); **2.** guest; visitor; **3.** (poet.) denizen; **4.** host, landlord, innkeeper, hostess; *table d'*~, ordinary, table-d'hote. ⚠*Hôtesse* is only used in senses **1** and **4**; in sense **2** *hôte* is used, even for a woman.

hôtel (otɛl), s.m. [L *hospitale*] Hotel; town mansion, large house; public building, hall; ~ *des Postes*, General Post-Office; ~ *de Ville*, Town Hall; ~ *des Ventes*, auction mart; ~ *meublé*, lodging-house; *descendre à l'*~, to put up at an hotel; *maître d'*~, butler, steward.

hôteli-er, -ère (otəlje), s.m.f. Innkeeper, landlord, (fem.) landlady. ~, adj. Hotel-, pertaining to hotels and hotel-keeping; *l'industrie* ~*ère*, the hotel-keeping business.

hôtellerie (otɛlri), s.f. [f. *hôtel*] Hostelry, inn.

hotte (hɔt), s.f. [Germ. orig.] **1.** Back-basket, dosser; **2.** chimney-funnel, over-mantel.

hottée (hɔte), s.f. Basketful.

hottentot, -e (hɔtɑ̃to), adj. s.m.f. Hottentot.

hottereau (pl. **-x**) (hɔtro), s.m. Small back-basket.

hotteur (hɔtœr), s.m. Back-basket carrier.

hou! (hu), interj. Bo!, hi!, hoo!, down with.

houache (hwaʃ), s.f. [Scand. orig.] Wake (of a ship).
houblon (hublɔ̃), s.m. [f. MDutch *hommel*] Hop; *perche à ~*, hop-pole.
houblonni-er, -ère (hublɔnje), adj. Hop-, pertaining to the hop.
houblonnière (hublɔnjɛr), s.f. Hop-plantation.
houe (hu), s.f. [f. OHG *houwa*] Hoe.
houer (hue), v.a. To hoe.
houille (huj), s.f. [Walloon wd] Coal, pit-coal; *la ~ blanche*, water-power; *mine de ~*, coal-pit, colliery, coal-mine.
houill-er, -ère (huje), adj. Coal; *terrain ~*, coal-field; *formation ~ère*, coal-series, coal-measures.
houillère (hujɛr), s.f. Colliery, coal-mine.
houilleur (hujœr), s.m. adj. Collier.
houilleu-x, -se (hujø), adj. Coaly, containing coal.
houle (hul), s.f. [Bret. *houl*] Swell, surge, billows.
houlette (hulɛt), s.f. [f. OF verb *houler* = *lancer*] Crook, shepherd's crook, crosier; trowel.
houleu-x, -se (hulø), adj. Swelling, rough, rolling; (fig.) agitated, hostile.
houp! (hup), interj. Gee-up!, move on!, jump!, away with you!
houppe (hup), s.f. [orig. uncert.] Tuft, top-knot, puff; *~ à poudre*, powder-puff.
houppelande (huplɑ̃d), s.f. [orig. uncert.] Overcoat, greatcoat, upper coat.
houpper (hupe), v.a. To tuft, to comb (wool, silk, &c.).
houppette (hupɛt), s.f. Small tuft; powder-puff.
hourdage, hourdis (hurdaʒ, hurdi), s.m. Rough-walling.
hourder (hurde), v.a. To rough-wall, to pug.
houret (hurɛ), s.m. Worthless hound, cur.
houri (huri), s.f. [Pers. wd] Houri.
hourra (hura), s.m. [Engl. *hurrah*] Hurrah.
hourvari (hurvari), s.m. [onom.] **1.** (hunt.) Cry to call back the hounds; **2.** (fam.) tumult, hubbub, uproar.
housard (uzar), s.m. (obs.). See HUSSARD.
houseau (pl. **-x**) (huzo), s.m. Legging, gaiter, spatterdash.
houspiller (huspije), v.a. [OF *housse-pigner*] To worry, to pull about, to maul, to tug, to handle roughly, to rate, to egg on.
houssaie (husɛ), s.f. (bot.) Holly-grove.
housse (hus), s.f. [OF *houce*] (loose) Cover, case, dust-sheet, horse-cloth, saddle-cloth; *~ de fauteuil*, arm-chair cover.
houssine (husin), s.f. [f. *houx*] Switch, rod.
houssiner (husine), v.a. To switch, to beat, to cane.
houssoir (huswar), s.m. Whisk, dusting-broom, holly-broom.
housson (husɔ̃), s.m. (bot.) Knee-holly, butcher's broom.
houx (hu), s.m. [f. OGerm. *huls*] Holly, holly-tree.
hova (hɔva), adj. s.m.f. Hova.
hoyau (pl. **-x**) (hwajo), s.m. [f. *houe*] Mattock, grubbing-axe.
hublot (hyblo), s.m. [OF *hulot*] Small port-hole, scuttle, port-hole.
huche (hyʃ), s.f. [LL *hutica*] Kneading-trough, bread-bin.
hucher (hyʃe), v.a.n. [LL *huccare*] (hunt.) To call, to whistle.
huchet (hyʃɛ), s.m. Call-horn, hunting-horn.
hue! (hy), interj. [onom.] Gee!, pull up!, go on!
huée (hye), s.f. Hooting, hoot, hue and cry; *il fut accueilli par des ~s*, they set up a hue and cry when they saw him.
huer (hɥe), v.a. To hoot, to hoot after, to cry down, to boo; ~, v.n. to hoot (of an owl).
huguenot, -e (hygno), s.m.f. adj. [orig. uncert.; f. Germ. *Eidgenossen* or f. *Hugues*] Huguenot. *~e*, s.f. Low cooking-stove.
hui (ɥi), adv. [f. L *hodie*] (obs. exc. in *aujourd'hui*). To-day, this day; *aujourd'~*, to-day; (obs.) *d'~ en un an*, in a year from to-day.
huilage (ɥilaʒ), s.m. Oiling.
huile (ɥil), s.f. [L *oleum*] Oil; *~ de table*, *~ comestible*, salad-oil, table-oil; *~ à brûler*, lamp-oil, *~ de ricin*, castor oil; *~ de foie de morue*, cod-liver oil; *~ à graisser*, lubricating-oil; *peindre à l'~*, to paint in oils; *~ de coude*, elbow-grease; *jeter de l'~ sur le feu*, to add fuel to the flame; *~ de cotret*, cudgelling; *faire tache d'~*, to spread indefinitely; *les Saintes Huiles*, Holy Oils.
huiler (ɥile), v.a. To oil, to anoint with oil; to grease.
huilerie (ɥilri), s.f. Oil-works, oil-shop.
huileu-x, -se (ɥilø), adj. Oily, greasy.
huilier (ɥilje), s.m. **1.** Cruet-stand, cruet; **2.** oil-man. ~, adj. Pertaining to the oil trade.
huis (ɥi), s.m. (obs.) [L *ostium*] Door; *à ~ clos*, with closed doors, in private, privately; *demander le ~ clos*, to demand the exclusion of the public.
huisserie (ɥisri), s.f. Door-frame.
huissier (ɥisje), s.m. [f. *huis*] Usher, sheriff's officer, bailiff, tipstaff (of courts); process-server; beadle, door-keeper.
huit (ɥit, ɥi before a consonant), num. adj. s.m. [L *octo*] Eight, the eighth; *de demain en ~*, to-morrow week; *il y a ~ jours*, a week ago, it is a week since; *il y a eu mardi ~ jours*, last Tuesday week.

huitain (ɥitɛ̃), s.m. Stanza of eight lines or verses.
huitaine (ɥitɛn), s.f. **1.** (collectively) Eight; **2.** eight days, a week; *dans la* ~, in the course of the week; *dans une* ~, in a week or so; *à* ~, this day week.
huitième (ɥitjɛm), ord. adj. s.m. Eighth. ~, s.f. Eighth form.
huitièmement (ɥitjɛməmɑ̃), adv. Eighthly.
huître (ɥitr), s.f. [L *ostrea*] Oyster; *écaille d'*~, oyster-shell; *banc d'*~*s*, oyster-bed; *bourriche d'*~*s*, barrel of oysters; ~ *perlière*, pearl-oyster; (fig.) booby, dunce; *raisonner comme une* ~, to reason like a fool.
huîtri-er, -ère (ɥitrije), adj. Relating to oysters, oyster-.
hulan (ylɑ̃), s.m. See UHLAN.
hulotte (hylɔt), s.f. [L *ulula*] Wood-owl, tawny owl.
hululer (ylyle), v.n. See ULULER.
humain, -e (ymɛ̃), adj. [L *humanus*] **1.** Human; *le genre* ~, mankind; *la nature* ~*e*, human nature; *au-dessus des forces* ~*es*, above human power; *n'avoir plus figure* ~*e*, not to look any longer like a human being; **2.** humane, kind, merciful; *sentiments* ~*s*, humane feelings; *respect* ~, excessive care for public opinion; *il s'abstient par respect* ~, he won't do it for fear of what people will say. ~**s**, s.m.pl. Mankind, mortals, men, human beings.
humainement (ymɛnmɑ̃), adv. Humanly; humanely, in a humane manner, mercifully, kindly.
humaniser (ymanize), v.a. To render human; to humanize; to render humane, kind; **s'**~, v.pr. to grow humane, to become more tractable, to soften down, to become more sociable.
humanisme (ymanism), s.m. Humanism, study of the humanities.
humaniste (ymanist), s.m.f. Humanist, classical scholar.
humanitaire (ymanitɛr), adj. Humanitarian, philanthropic.
humanité (ymanite), s.f. [L *humanitas*] **1.** Humanity, human nature; **2.** humanity, mankind; **3.** benevolence, kindness, mercy, humanity; **4.** ~*s*, (pl.) humanities.
humble (œ̃bl), adj. [L *humilis*] Humble, lowly, meek; *se faire* ~, to take a back seat.
humblement (œ̃bləmɑ̃), adv. Humbly, submissively, meekly.
humectant, -e (ymɛktɑ̃), p. adj. Humective, moistening, refreshing.
humectation (ymɛkta'sjɔ̃), s.f. Humectation, wetting, moistening.
humecter (ymɛkte), v.a. [L *humectare*] To humect, to wet, to moisten, to damp; (fam.) *s'*~ *le gosier*, to have a drop of something, to wet one's whistle.
humer (hyme), v.a. [orig. uncert.] To suck in, to inhale, to snuff, to sniff up.
huméral, -e, (aux) (ymeral), adj. [f. *humérus*] (anat.) Humeral.
humérus (ymerys), s.m. [L wd] (anat.) Humerus.
humeur (ymœr), s.f. [L *humor*] Humour, disposition, temper, mood; ill humour; *être de bonne* ~, to be in a good humour; *être de mauvaise* ~, to be in a temper, to be ill-tempered, to be ill-humoured; *avec* ~, peevishly, crossly; *d'*~ *douce*, sweet-tempered; *être d'*~ *à*, to be disposed to, to be in the mood for; *prendre de l'*~, to get out of temper; ~*s froides*, scrofula; ~ *noire*, spleen.
humide (ymid), adj. [L *humidus*] Humid, damp, wet, moist, watery; *yeux* ~*s*, tearful eyes.
humidifier (ymidifje), v.a. To wet, to make moist.
humidité (ymidite), s.f. Humidity, dampness, wetness, moisture.
humiliant, -e (ymiljɑ̃), p. adj. Humiliating, mortifying, humbling.
humiliation (ymilja'sjɔ̃), s.f. Humiliation, abasing, abasement, humbling.
humilier (ymilje), v.a. [L *humiliare*] To humiliate, to humble, to abase, to mortify; **s'**~, v.pr. to abase oneself, to humble oneself.
humilité (ymilite), s.f. [L *humilitas*] Humility, humbleness, meekness, lowliness; *avec* ~, humbly.
humoral, -e, (aux) (ymɔral), adj. [f. L *humor*] (med.) Humoral.
humoriste (ymɔrist), s.m.f. [f. *humour*] Humorist, satirist. ~, adj. Humorous, witty.
humoristique (ymɔristik), adj. Humoristic, humorous, witty, satirical.
humour (ymur), s.m. [f. L *humor*] Humour.
humus (ymys), s.m. [L wd] Humus, vegetable mould.
Hun (hœ̃), s.m. (usually pl. *les Huns*; no feminine) Hun.
hune (hyn), s.f. [Scand. *hunn*] (naut.) Top; *grand'*~, main-top; ~ *d'artimon*, mizzen-top; ~ *de misaine*, foretop; *mât de* ~, topmast.
hunier (ynje), s.m. (naut.) Topsail; *grand* ~, main topsail; *petit* ~, fore topsail.
huppe (hyp), s.f. [L *upupa*] **1.** Tuft (of feathers); **2.** (ornith.) hoopoe.
huppé, -e (hype), p. adj. Tufted, crested; (fig.) topping, crack, rich, fashionable, tiptop.
hure (hyr), s.f. [orig. unkn.] Head (of boar, pig, &c.).
hurlement (hyrləmɑ̃), s.m. Howling,

howl, yelling, yell, roaring, roar, shrieking, shriek; *pousser des ~s de rage*, to howl with rage.

hurler (hyrle), v.n.a. [f. L *ululare*] To howl, to yell, to shriek, to roar; ~ *de douleur*, to howl with pain; *il faut ~ avec les loups*, when you are at Rome, you must do as the Romans do.

hurleu-r, -se (hyrlœr), s.m.f. Howler. ~, adj. Howling.

hurluberlu (yrlybɛrly), s.m. [orig. unkn.] Harebrained fellow, harum-scarum.

huron, -ne (hyrɔ̃), s.m.f. adj. Huron.

hussard (hysar), s.m. [Hungarian *huszar*] Hussar; *à la hussarde*, in the hussar fashion, hussar-like, by plunder, roughly.

hussite (hysit), s.m.f. [f. *J. Huss*] Hussite.

hutin (hytɛ̃), adj. (obs.) Stubborn, headstrong, quarrelsome.

hutte (hyt), s.f. [f. OGerm. *hutta*] Hut, log hut, cabin, hovel.

(se) hutter (səhyte), v.pr. To make a hut, to lodge in a hut.

hyacinthe (jasɛ̃t), s.f. [Gr. *huakinthos*] (gem) Hyacinth, jacinth; (bot.) hyacinth; see JACINTHE, more usual.

hyalin, -e (jalɛ̃), adj. [f. Gr. *hualos*] Hyaline.

hyaloïde (jalɔid), adj. Hyaloid, vitriform.

hyalotechnie (jalotɛkni), s.f. [f. Gr. *hualos+tekhnē*] Art of working glass.

hybridation (ibrida'sjɔ̃), s.f. Hybridizing.

hybride (ibrid), adj. s.m. [L *hybrida*] Hybrid, mongrel.

hydne (idn), s.m. (bot.) [f. Gr. *hudnon*] A kind of mushroom, hydnum.

hydrate (idrat), s.m. [f. Gr. *hudōr*] (chem.) Hydrate.

hydraté, -e (idrate), p. adj. (chem.) Hydrated.

hydraulique (idrolik), s.f. Hydraulics. ~, adj. Hydraulic, hydraulical.

hydravion (idravjɔ̃), s.m. Seaplane.

hydre (idr), s.f. [f. Gr. *hudra*] Hydra; (zool.) water-snake; (fig.) hydra.

hydrocarbure (idrokarbyr), s.m. (chem.) Hydrocarburet, carburetted hydrogen.

hydrocéphale (idrosefal), adj. s.m.f. [*hydro*+(Gr.) *kephalē*] Hydrocephalous, (person) affected with hydrocephalus.

hydrofuge (idrofyʒ), adj. [pref. *hydro*+(L) *fugare*] Siccative, drying.

hydrogène (idrɔʒɛn), s.m. [pref. *hydro*+(Gr.) *gennān*] Hydrogen.

hydrographe (idrograf), s.m. [pref. *hydro* +(Gr.) *graphein*] Hydrographer. ~, adj. Hydrographic.

hydrographie (idrografi), s.f. Hydrography.

hydrographique (idrografik), adj. Hydrographic.

hydrologie (idrolɔʒi), s.f. [pref. *hydro*+(Gr.) *logos*] Hydrology.

hydromel (idrɔmɛl), s.m. [Gr. *hudromeli*] Hydromel.

hydromètre (idrɔmɛtr), s.m. Hydrometer.

hydrométrie (idrometri), s.f. [pref. *hydro* +(Gr.) *metron*] Hydrometry.

hydrophobe (idrofɔb), adj. s.m.f. (Person) affected with hydrophobia.

hydrophobie (idrofɔbi), s.f. [Gr. *hudrophobia*] Hydrophobia; syn. RAGE.

hydropique (idrɔpik), adj. [Gr. *hudrōpikos*] Hydropic, dropsical.

hydropisie (idrɔpizi), s.f. Dropsy.

hydroscope (idrɔskɔp), s.m. [pref. *hydro* +(Gr.) *skopein, skopos*] Dowser, bletonist, finder of springs, water-diviner.

hydroscopie (idroskɔpi), s.f. Bletonism, dowsing.

hydrostatique (idrostatik), s.f. [f. Gr. *hudrostatēs*] Hydrostatics. ~, adj. Hydrostatic, hydrostatical.

hydrothérapie (idrɔterapi), s.f. [pref. *hydro*+(Gr.) *therapeia*] Hydrotherapeutics, hydrotherapy, hydropathy, water-cure.

hydrothérapique (idrɔterapik), adj. Hydropathic.

hydrure (idryr), s.m. (chem.) Hydride, hydruret.

hyémal, -e, (aux) (jemal), adj. See HIÉMAL.

hyène (iɛn), s.f. [Gr. *huaina*] (zool.) Hyena, hyaena.

hygiène (iʒjɛ̃n), s.f. [Gr. *hugiainein*] Hygiene, hygienics.

hygiénique (iʒjenik), adj. Hygienic.

hygiéniquement (iʒjenikmɑ̃), adv. Hygienically.

hygiéniste (iʒjenist), s.m.f. Hygienist, physician.

hygromètre (igrɔmɛtr), s.m. [f. Gr. *hugros+metron*] Hygrometer.

hygrométrie (igrometri), s.f. Hygrometry.

hygrométrique (igrometrik), adj. Hygrometric.

hymen (imɛn), s.m. [Gr. *humēn*] **1.** Hymen; **2.** hymen, marriage; *le flambeau de l'~*, the torch of Hymen.

hyménée (imene), s.m. Hymen, marriage.

hyménoptère (imenɔptɛr), adj. [f. Gr. *humēn+pteron*] (ent.) Hymenopterous, hymenopteral. ~, s.m. Hymenopteran, hymenopter.

hymne (imn), s.m. [Gr. *humnos*] Hymn, anthem; (fig.) hymn, song of praise; ~, s.f. (Church) Hymn.

hyoïde (iɔid), adj. s.m. [Gr. *huoeidēs*] (anat.) Hyoid.

hypallage (ipalaʒ), s.f. [Gr. wd] (gram.) Hypallage.

hyperbate (ipɛrbat), s.f. [Gr. *huperbaton*] Hyperbaton.

hyperbole (ipɛrbɔl), s.f. [Gr. *huperbolē*] (geom.) Hyperbola; (rhet.) hyperbole.

hyperbolique (ipɛrbɔlik), adj. Hyperbolic, hyperbolical.

hyperboliquement (ipɛrbɔlikmɑ̃), adv. Hyperbolically.
hyperboloïde (ipɛrbɔlɔid), s.m. (geom.) Hyperboloid.
hyperboréen, -ne (ipɛrbɔreɛ̃), adj. [f. L *hyperboreus*] Hyperborean.
hypercritique (ipɛrkritik), s.m. [f. Gr. *huper+kritikos*] Hypercritic; ~, s.f. hypercriticism. ~, adj. Hypercritical.
hyperdulie (ipɛrdyli), s.f. [f. Gr. *huper+douleia*] Hyperdulia.
hyperesthésie (ipɛrɛstezi), s.f. [f. Gr. *huper+aisthēsis*] (med.) Hyperaesthesia.
hypertrophie (ipɛrtrɔfi), s.f. [f. Gr. *huper +trophē*] Hypertrophy.
hypertrophier (ipɛrtrɔfje), v.a. To hypertrophy; **s'~**, v.pr. to become hypertrophied.
hypèthre (ipɛtr), adj. [Gr. *hupaithros*] (arch.) Hypaethral; without a roof.
hypnose (ipnɔz), s.f. [Gr. *hupnos*] Hypnosis.
hypnotique (ipnɔtik), adj. Hypnotic.
hypnotiser (ipnɔtize), v.a. To hypnotize.
hypnotiseur (ipnɔtizœr), s.m. Hypnotizer.
hypnotisme (ipnɔtism), s.m. Hypnotism.
hypo (ipo), pref. [f. Gr. *hupo*] Hypo-.
hypocondre (ipɔkɔ̃dr), s.m. [f. Gr. *hupo +khondros*] (anat.) Hypochondrium. ~, adj. Hypochondriac.
hypocondriaque (ipɔkɔ̃drjak), adj. Hypochondriac, splenetic.
hypocondrie (ipɔkɔ̃dri), s.f. Hypochondria; spleen.
hypocras (ipɔkrɑs), s.m. [f. L *hippocraticum vinum*] Hippocras.
hypocrisie (ipɔkrizi), s.f. [Gr. *hupokrisis*] Hypocrisy.
hypocrite (ipɔkrit), s.m.f. Hypocrite. ~, adj. Hypocritical.
hypocritement (ipɔkritmɑ̃), adv. Hypocritically.
hypodermique (ipɔdɛrmik), adj. [f. Gr. *hupo+derma*] Hypodermic.
hypogastre (ipɔgastr), s.m. [Gr. *hupogastrion*] Hypogastrium.
hypogastrique (ipogastrik), adj. Hypogastric.
hypogée (ipɔʒe), s.m. [f. Gr. *hupo+gē*] Hypogeum.
hypophosphate (ipofɔsfat), s.m. (chem.) Hypophosphate.
hypostase (ipɔstɑz), s.f. [Gr. *hupo+stasis*] (theol.) Hypostasis.
hypostyle (ipɔstil), adj. [Gr. *hupostulos*] (arch.) Hypostyle.
hyposulfate (iposylfat), s.m. (chem.) Hyposulphate.
hyposulfite (iposylfit), s.m. (chem.) Hyposulphite.
hypoténuse (ipɔtenyz), s.f. [Gr. *hupoteinousa*] (geom.) Hypotenuse.
hypothécaire (ipɔtekɛr), adj. On mortgage, mortgage; *créancier ~*, mortgagee; *débiteur ~*, mortgager; *prêt ~*, mortgage loan.
hypothénar (ipɔtenar), adj. invar. [f. Gr. *hupo+thenar*] (anat.) Hypothenar.
hypothèque (ipɔtɛk), s.f. [Gr. *hupothēkē*] Mortgage; *avoir ~ sur*, to have a mortgage on; *grevé d'~*, mortgaged; *libre d'~*, unmortgaged.
hypothéqué, -e (ipɔteke), p. adj. Mortgaged; (fig.) *il est bien ~*, he is in very bad health; he is in a very bad way, nearly infirm, threatened with infirmity.
hypothéquer (ipɔteke), v.a. To mortgage.
hypothèse (ipɔtɛz), s.f. [Gr. *hupothesis*] Hypothesis, supposition; *par ~*, hypothetically.
hypothétique (ipɔtetik), adj. Hypothetical.
hypothétiquement (ipɔtetikmɑ̃), adv. Hypothetically.
hypotypose (ipɔtipoz), s.f. [Gr. *hupotupōsis*] (rhet.) Hypotyposis.
hypsomètre (ipsɔmɛtr), s.m. [f. Gr. *hupsos+metron*] Hypsometer.
hyrcanien, -ne (irkanjɛ̃), adj. Hyrcanian.
hysope (izɔp), s.f. [Gr. *hussōpos*] (bot.) Hyssop.
hysterie (isteri), s.f. [f. Gr. *hustera*] Hysteria, hysterics. ⚠ In French *hystérie* has always a pathological sense; in English 'hysterics' is often used with the sense of exaggerated nervous laughter, or tears; in that case it must not be rendered by *hystérie*, but by *crise de fou rire, accès de larmes*, &c.
hystérique (isterik), adj. Hysteric, hysterical. ⚠ See HYSTÉRIE.

I

I, i (i), s.m. 9th letter of the alphabet; *droit comme un I*, as straight as an arrow; *mettre les points sur les I*, to dot one's i's; to leave nothing unsaid, or unexplained; to be very precise.
ïambe (iɑ̃b), s.m. [Gr. *iambos*] Iambus, iamb; *~s*, (pl.) satiric piece.
ïambique (iɑ̃bik), adj. Iambic.
ibère (ibɛr), s.m.f. Iberus (pl. Iberi).
ibérien, -ne (iberjɛ̃), adj. Iberian, of Spain.
ibérique (iberik), adj. Iberic, Iberian.
ibidem (ibidɛm), adv. [L wd] Ibidem.
ibis (ibis), s.m. [Egypt. orig.] (ornith.) Ibis.
icarien, -ne (ikarjɛ̃), adj. s.m.f. [f. myth. *Ikaros*] Icarian.
iceberg (isbɛrg), s.m. [Scand. wd] Iceberg.
icelui, icelle (pl. **iceux, icelles**) (islɥi, isɛl; isø, isɛl), dem. adj. pron. [f. L *ecce+ille*] (obs. exc. law) This, these, the said, the aforesaid.

ichneumon (iknømɔ̃), s.m. [Gr. wd] (zool.) **1.** Ichneumon; **2.** ichneumon fly.
ichnographie (iknɔgrafi), s.f. [f. Gr. *ikhnos+graphein*] Ichnography, ground-plan.
ichtyologie (iktjɔlɔʒi), s.f. [f. Gr. *ikhthus +logos*] Ichthyology.
ichtyophage (iktjɔfaʒ), adj. [f. Gr. *ikhthus +phagein*] Ichthyophagous. ~, s.m.f. Ichthyophagist.
ichtyophagie (iktjɔfaʒi), s.f. Ichthyophagy.
ichtyosaure (iktjɔzor), s.m. [f. Gr. *ikhthus +sauros*] Ichthyosaurus.
ici (isi), adv. [f. L *ecce+hic*] Here, in this place; hither; now, this time; *~-bas*, here, in this (lower) world; here below; *c'est* ~, this is the place; here we are; *d'*~, hence, from here; *d'~ à ce que*, by the time that; *d'~ trois jours*, within three days; *d'~ là*, in the meantime, by that time; till this point is reached; *~ et là, d'~ de là*, hither and thither; *jusqu'*~, hitherto, till now, as yet, up to this time; *par* ~, this way, by here, through here; thereabout; *~ près*, close by, hard by, near by; (fam.) *vous voyez ça d'*~, you can just picture it.
icoglan (ikɔglɑ̃), s.m. [Turk. wd] Icoglan.
icone (ikon), s.f. [Gr. *eikōn*] Icon.
iconoclaste (ikɔnɔklast), s.m.f. [f. Gr. *eikōn+klaein*] Iconoclast. ~, adj. Iconoclastic.
iconolâtrie (ikɔnɔlɑtri), s.f. [f. Gr. *eikōn +latreuein*] Iconolatry, image-worship.
iconostase (ikɔnɔstɑz), s.f. [f. Gr. *eikōn+stasis*] Iconostasis (large triple screen used in Greek churches).
icosaèdre (ikɔzaɛdr), s.m. [f. Gr. *eikosi* (= 20)+*hedra*] Icosahedron.
ictère (iktɛr), s.m. [Gr. *ikteros*] (pathol.) Icterus, jaundice; syn. JAUNISSE.
idéal, -e, (aux) (ideal), adj. Ideal, unreal, imaginary; perfect. ~, s.m. (pl. **als** or **aux**) Ideal.
idéalement (idealmɑ̃), adv. Ideally, completely and perfectly; *~ belle*, perfectly beautiful.
idéalisation (idealiza'sjɔ̃), s.f. Idealization.
idéaliser (idealize), v.a. To idealize.
idéalisme (idealism), s.m. Idealism.
idéaliste (idealist), s.m.f. Idealist. ~, adj. Idealistic.
idéalité (idealite), s.f. Ideality.
idée (ide), s.f. [Gr. *idea*] Idea, notion, conception; purpose, intention, plan; mind; *~ lumineuse*, bright idea; *~ fixe*, obsession; *~s noires*, blues; *changer d'*~, to change or to alter one's mind; *se mettre dans l'*~, to take it into one's head; *a-t-on ~ d'une chose pareille?*, did you ever hear of such a thing?; *il m'est venu à l'*~, it occurred to me; *quelle ~!*, what an idea!; well, I never!; *j'ai ~ que*, I rather think that; I fancy that; *se faire des ~s*, to conjure up idle fancies, to imagine things; *avoir une haute ~ de*, to esteem highly, to value much; (colloq.) *ajouter une ~ de cognac*, to add just a drop of brandy; *une ~ de derrière la tête*, (*a*) a secret design; (*b*) a lurking suspicion.
idem (idɛm), adv. [L wd] Idem, ditto.
identification (idɑ̃tifika'sjɔ̃), s.f. Identification.
identifier (idɑ̃tifje), v.a. [f. L *idem+facere*] To identify; **s'**~, v.pr. to identify oneself.
identique (idɑ̃tik), adj. [f. L *idem*] Identical, the same, the very same, self-same; (math.) identical.
identiquement (idɑ̃tikmɑ̃), adv. Identically.
identité (idɑ̃tite), s.f. [LL *identitas*] Identity; sameness, identicalness.
idéographie (ideɔgrafi), s.f. [f. Gr. *idea+graphein*] Ideography.
idéologie (ideɔlɔʒi), s.f. [f. Gr. *idea+logos*] Ideology.
idéologique (ideɔlɔʒik), adj. Ideological.
idéologue (ideɔlɔg), s.m.f. Ideologist.
ides (id), s.f.pl. [L *idus*] Ides.
idiomatique (idjɔmatik), adj. Idiomatic.
idiome (idjom), s.m. [Gr. *idiōma*] Language, dialect; idiom. ⚠ In English 'idiom' is generally used in the sense of: form of expression peculiar to a language = *idiotisme*.
idiosyncrasie (idjosɛ̃krazi), s.f. [Gr. *idiosunkrasia*] Idiosyncrasy.
idiot, -e (idjo), adj. [Gr. *idiōtēs*] Idiotic. ~, s.m.f. Idiot. ⚠ In French the sense is stronger; the word cannot be used as freely as in English. To call somebody *idiot* gives offence.
idiotie (idjɔsi), s.f. **1.** Idiocy, idiotcy, imbecility, mental deficiency; **2.** act or saying of an idiot or a fool.
idiotisme (idjɔtism), s.m. Idiom.
idoine (idwan), adj. [L *idoneus*] Proper, fitting.
idolâtre (idɔlɑtr), adj. [f. Gr. *eidōlon*] Idolatrous, idolizing. ~, s.m.f. Idolater, idolatress.
idolâtrer (idɔlɑtre), v.a. To idolize, to worship; ~, v.n. (obs.) to idolatrize, to practise idolatry.
idolâtrie (idɔlɑtri), s.f. [f. Gr. *eidolon+latreuein*] Idolatry; (fig.) excessive fondness; *il l'aime à l'*~, he idolizes her.
idolâtrique (idɔlɑtrik), adj. Idolatrous.
idole (idɔl), s.f. [Gr. *eidōlon*] Idol; *faire son ~ de*, to idolize, to make a god of; *être l'~ de*, to be worshipped by, to be idolized by.
iduméen, -ne (idymeɛ̃), adj. s.m.f. Idumean.
idylle (idil), s.f. [Gr. *eidullion*] Idyll.

idyllique (idillik), adj. Idyllic.

if (if), s.m. [Celt. or Germ. orig.] (bot.) **1.** Yew, yew-tree; **2.** triangular stand for holding lamps for illuminations, &c.

igname (ignam), s.f. [Span. *ñame*] (bot.) Yam.

ignare (iɲar), adj. s.m.f. [L *ignarus*] Ignorant, ignoramus, dunce.

igné, -e (igne), adj. [L *igneus*] Igneous.

ignifuge (ignifyʒ), adj. Fireproof.

ignifuger (ignifyʒe), v.a. [L *ignis+fugare*] To render fireproof.

ignition (ignisjɔ̃), s.f. [f. L *ignis*] Ignition; *entrer en* ~, to ignite.

ignivore (ignivɔr), adj. Fire-eating.

ignoble (iɲɔbl), adj. [L *ignobilis*] Ignoble, vile, base, mean, filthy.

ignoblement (iɲɔbləmɑ̃), adv. Ignobly, vilely.

ignominie (iɲɔmini), s.f. [L *ignominia*] Ignominy, shame, baseness.

ignominieusement (iɲɔminjøzmɑ̃), adv. Ignominiously.

ignominieu-x, -se (iɲɔminjø), adj. Ignominious.

ignorance (iɲɔrɑ̃s), s.f. [L *ignorantia*] Ignorance; *être dans l'~ de*, to be ignorant of, to be unaware of; *par* ~, from ignorance; ~ *crasse*, gross ignorance; *croupir dans l'~*, to wallow in ignorance.

ignorant, -e (iɲɔrɑ̃), adj. Ignorant, illiterate; unacquainted (*de*, with); uninformed (of). ~, s.m.f. Ignoramus, dunce.

ignorantin (iɲɔrɑ̃tɛ̃), adj.m. s.m. Ignorantine (friar).

ignorantisme (iɲɔrɑ̃tism), s.m. Ignorantism.

ignorantissime (iɲɔrɑ̃tisim), adj. Most ignorant.

ignoré, -e (iɲɔre), p. adj. Unknown, concealed, secluded.

ignorer (iɲɔre), v.a. [L *ignorare*] To be ignorant of, not to know, not to be aware of, to be unaware of, not to be acquainted with, to be unconscious of; (fam.) to snub (somebody by affecting not to see him or her); **s'~**, v.pr. not to know oneself, to be ignorant or unconscious of one's own capabilities or possibilities. ⚠ Note that English 'ignore' = *ignorer à dessein, ne pas tenir compte de; refuser de connaître.*

iguane (igɥan), s.m. [Caribbean Span. orig.] (zool.) Iguana.

iguanodon (igɥanɔdɔ̃), s.m. (zool.) Iguanodon.

il (il), pron. m. (fem. **elle**, pl. **ils, elles**) [L *ille*] He, it, pl. they; there; ~ *pleut*, it is raining; ~ *est arrivé beaucoup de monde*, many people have arrived; ~ *fut un temps où*, there was a time when.

île (il), s.f. [L *insula*] Island; isle; *l'~ de France*, Mauritius; *les ~s*, the West Indies; the Antilles; *les ~s sous le Vent*, the Leeward Islands; *les ~s du Vent*, the Windward Islands; *les ~s Britanniques*, the British Isles.

iléon (ileɔ̃), s.m. [L *ilia*] (anat.) Ileum.

iles (il), s.m.pl. [L *ilia*] (anat.) Ilia.

îlet (ilɛ), s.m. [f. *île*] Very small island; syn. ÎLOT.

iléus (ileys), s.m. (pathol.) Occlusion of the intestine, ileus.

iliade (iljad), s.f. [f. *Ilion*] Iliad.

iliaque (iljak), adj. [f. L *ilia*] (anat.) Iliac.

illégal, -e, (aux) (illegal), adj. Illegal, unlawful.

illégalement (illegalmɑ̃), adv. Illegally.

illégalité (illegalite), s.f. Illegality; illegal act.

illégitime (illeʒitim), adj. Illegitimate; unlawful, unjust, spurious; *enfant* ~, illegitimate child.

illégitimité (illeʒitimite), s.f. Illegitimacy.

illettré, -e (illɛtre), adj. Illiterate, ignorant.

illicite (illisit), adj. [L *illicitus*] Illicit, unlawful.

illicitement (illisitmɑ̃), adv. Illicitly, unlawfully.

illico (illiko), adv. [L wd] (fam.) At once, forthwith, there and then, in a trice.

illimitable (illimitabl), adj. Illimitable.

illimité, -e (illimite), adj. Unlimited, boundless, unbounded.

illisibilité (illizibilite), s.f. Illegibility.

illisible (illizibl), adj. Illegible; unreadable.

illisiblement (illiziblәmɑ̃), adv. Illegibly.

illogicité (illɔʒisite), s.f. See ILLOGISME.

illogique (illɔʒik), adj. Illogical.

illogiquement (illɔʒikmɑ̃), adv. Illogically.

illogisme (illɔʒism), s.m. Illogicalness, illogicality.

illuminant, -e (illyminɑ̃), p. adj. Illuminating.

illuminateur (illyminatœr), s.m. Illuminator.

illuminati-f, -ve (illyminatif), adj. Illuminative.

illumination (illymina'sjɔ̃), s.f. Illumination; display of lights.

illuminé, -e (illymine), p. adj. Illuminated; enlightened. ~, s.m.f. Visionary; illuminato, illuminee (pl. illuminati).

illuminer (illymine), v.a. [L *illuminare*] To illuminate, to light up; to illumine, to enlighten, to brighten up. ⚠ *Illuminer* cannot be used, like 'to illuminate', in the sense of: to decorate a manuscript, initial letters, &c. with paint and gold; in that sense *enluminer* is the word to use.

illusion (illyzjɔ̃), s.f. [L *illusio* f. *illudere*] Illusion, delusion, fallacy, chimera, hallucination; *être plein d'~s*, to be given to illusion; *être dans l'~*, to be labouring under a delusion; *faire ~ à X*, to delude X, to impose upon X; *se faire ~ à soi-même*, to delude, to deceive oneself; *~ d'optique*, optical illusion.

illusionner (illyzjɔne), v.a. (rare) To delude; **s'~**, v.pr. to delude oneself.

illusionniste (illyzjɔnist), s.m.f. Illusionist, conjurer; syn. PRESTIDIGITATEUR.

illusoire (illyzwar), adj. Illusory, illusive, delusive, fallacious.

illusoirement (illyzwarmɑ̃), adv. Illusively, delusively, fallaciously.

illustrateur (illystratœr), s.m. Illustrator, draughtsman.

illustration (illystra'sjɔ̃), s.f. **1.** Illustration, illustriousness, celebrity; **2.** illustrious person; **3.** illustration, picture, engraving; **4.** example, instance.

illustre (illystr), adj. [L *illustris*] Illustrious, famous, renowned, world-renowned.

illustrer (illystre), v.a. To render illustrious, to illustrate; to explain, to illustrate, to make clear; to adorn with pictures, engravings, &c.; to illuminate (manuscripts); **s'~**, v.pr. render oneself illustrious, add fame and glory to one's name.

illustrissime (illystrisim), adj. [It. *illustrissimo*] Most illustrious.

illuter (illyte), v.a. [f. L *il+lutum*] (med.) To lute, to mix with mud.

illyrien, -ne (illirjɛ̃), adj. s.m.f. Illyrian.

îlot (ilo), s.m. [f. *île*] Islet; (fig.) block (of buildings).

ilote (ilɔt), s.m. [Gr. *heilōtēs*] Helot.

ilotisme (ilɔtism), s.m. Helotism.

image (imaʒ), s.f. [L *imago*] Image, likeness, picture, effigy, imagery, print; (fig.) semblance, representation in the mind; (rhet.) metaphor, simile, comparison; (opt.) image; *Dieu créa l'homme à son ~*, God made man after his own likeness, or: created man in his own image; *voir son ~ dans l'eau*, to see one's reflection in the water; *cela fait ~*, that's striking; *livre d'~s*, picture-book; *sage comme une ~*, as quiet as a mouse. ♤ In English 'image' also = *statue*.

imagé, -e (imaʒe), p. adj. Full of images, imaged; *langage ~*, (colloq.) truculent words; vivid style; picturesque language.

imager (imaʒe), v.a. To adorn with images.

imagerie (imaʒri), s.f. Picture-trade.

imaginable (imaʒinabl), adj. Imaginable.

imaginaire (imaʒinɛr), adj. Imaginary, fantastic, unreal. **~**, s.f. (math.) Imaginary.

imagi-er, -ère (imaʒje), adj. Pertaining to imagery. ~, s.m.f. Person who makes or sells images; also, as in the Middle Ages, sculptor, woodcarver, painter.

imaginati-f, -ve (imaʒinatif), adj. Full of imagination, imaginative. **~ve,** (fam.) s.f. Imagination.

imagination (imaʒina'sjɔ̃), s.f. [L *imaginatio*] **1.** Imagination, fancy, creative faculty; **2.** fancy, conceit, chimera, imagination; *c'est une pure ~*, that is all fancy.

imaginer (imaʒine), v.a. [L *imaginari*] To imagine, to conceive, to fancy, to invent, to contrive, to surmise; **s'~**, v.pr. to believe, to imagine, to fancy, to surmise, to persuade oneself, to get into one's head.

iman, imam (imɑ̃, imam), s.m. [Arab. wd] Imam.

imbattable (ɛ̃batabl), adj. Unbeatable; matchless.

imbécile (ɛ̃besil), adj. [L *imbecillis*] Imbecile, foolish. **~**, s.m.f. Imbecile, idiot, fool.

imbécillité (ɛ̃besilite), s.f. Imbecility, idiocy, foolishness, foolish act or talk.

imberbe (ɛ̃bɛrb), adj. [L *imberbis*] Beardless, unbearded; (fig.) very young, raw, green.

imbiber (ɛ̃bibe), v.a. [L *imbibere*] To soak, to imbue, to wet, to cause to imbibe; **s'~** (*de*), v.pr. to imbibe, to be soaked (in), to be steeped (in), to be permeated (with); (colloq.) to drink, to tipple. ♤ 'To imbibe' means frequently: *s'imprégner de, être imbu de, se pénétrer de.*

imbibition (ɛ̃bibisjɔ̃), s.f. Imbibition.

imbrication (ɛ̃brika'sjɔ̃), s.f. Imbrication, overlapping.

imbrifuge (ɛ̃brifyʒ), adj. [f. L *imber+fugare*] Rainproof, waterproof.

imbriqué, -e (ɛ̃brike), p. adj. [L *imbricatus*] Imbricated.

imbriquer (ɛ̃brike), v.a. To imbricate, to overlap.

imbroglio (ɛ̃brɔgljo), s.m. [It. wd] Imbroglio.

imbu, -e (ɛ̃by), adj. [f. obs. *imboire*] Imbued; *~ de préjugés*, imbued with prejudices.

imbuvable (ɛ̃byvabl), adj. Undrinkable.

imitable (imitabl), adj. Imitable.

imitat-eur, -rice (imitatœr), adj. Imitative. **~**, s.m.f. Imitator.

imitati-f, -ve (imitatif), adj. Imitative; *harmonie ~ve*, imitative harmony.

imitation (imita'sjɔ̃), s.f. [L *imitatio*] Imitation, copy, mimicry; *à l'~ de*, in imitation of.

imiter (imite), v.a. [L *imitari*] To imitate, to copy, to mimic, to be like, to look like; to counterfeit.

immaculé, -e (immakyle), adj. [*im+maculé*] Immaculate, spotless.

immanence (immanɑ̃s), s.f. Immanence.

immanent, -e (immanɑ̃), adj. [L *immanens*] Immanent.

immangeable (ɛ̃mɑ̃ʒabl, immɑ̃ʒabl), adj. Uneatable.

immanquable (immɑ̃kabl, ɛ̃mɑ̃kabl), adj. Certain, infallible, sure.

immanquablement (immɑ̃kabləmɑ̃, ɛ̃mɑ̃kabləmɑ̃), adv. Infallibly, unfailingly.

immarcescible (immarsɛsibl), adj. [f. L *in+marcescere*] Incorruptible, unfading.
immatérialité (immaterjalite), s.f. Immateriality.
immatériel, -le (immaterjɛl), adj. Immaterial, insubstantial, not consisting of matter. ⚠ In French *immatériel* has never the sense of 'unimportant', 'irrelevant' (= *sans importance*), which is a usual acceptation of 'immaterial'.
immatériellement (immaterjɛlmɑ̃), adv. Immaterially, incorporeally.
immatriculation (immatrikyla'sjɔ̃), s.f. Matriculation.
immatricule (immatrikyl), s.f. Registering, matriculation.
immatriculer (immatrikyle), v.a. To matriculate, to register; *se faire ~*, to get one's name entered.
immaturité (immatyrite), s.f. Immaturity, unripeness.
immédiat, -e (immedja), adj. [L *immediatus*] Immediate, instantaneous.
immédiatement (immedjatmɑ̃), adv. Immediately; directly, forthwith, instantaneously, instantly, at once.
immémorial, -e, (aux) (immemɔrjal), adj. Immemorial; *de temps ~*, for ages, from time immemorial.
immense (immɑ̃s), adj. [L *immensus*] Immense, huge, immeasurable, vast, boundless.
immensément (immɑ̃semɑ̃), adv. Immensely, vastly, hugely; ~ *de*, an immense amount of.
immensité (immɑ̃site), s.f. [L *immensitas*] Immensity, vastness, infinity, boundlessness, hugeness.
immerger (immɛrʒe), v.a. [L *immergere*] To immerse.
immérité, -e (immerite), adj. Undeserved, unjust, unmerited.
immersion (immɛrsjɔ̃), s.f. [L *immersio*] Immersion.
immesurable (ɛ̃məzyrabl), adj. Immeasurable.
immeuble (immœbl), adj. [L *immobilis*] Fixed, real (of estate); immovable. ~, s.m. Real estate, landed property, building.
immigrant, -e (immigrɑ̃), s.m.f. p. adj. Immigrant.
immigration (immigra'sjɔ̃), s.f. Immigration.
immigrer (immigre), v.n. [L *immigrare*] To immigrate.
imminence (imminɑ̃s), s.f. Imminence.
imminent, -e (imminɑ̃), adj. [L *imminens*] Imminent, impending.
immiscer (immise), v.a. [L *immiscere*] To introduce, to mix up; **s'~** (*dans*), v.pr. to interfere (in), to thrust oneself (into), to meddle (with).
immixtion (immikstjɔ̃), s.f. Interfering, meddling.
immobile (immɔbil), adj. [L *immobilis*] Immobile, motionless, immovable, unmoved.
immobili-er, -ère (immɔbilje), adj. Real, landed (estate), immovable; *société ~ère*, building society; real-estate agency.
immobilisation (immɔbiliza'sjɔ̃), s.f. Immobilization, stop, tying up, fastening; converting into real estate.
immobiliser (immɔbilize), v.a. To immobilize, to stop, to tie up, to fasten; to convert into real estate.
immobilité (immɔbilite), s.f. Immobility, fixedness, inactivity, supineness, stillness.
immodération (immɔdera'sjɔ̃), s.f. Immoderation.
immodéré, -e (immɔdere), adj. Immoderate.
immodérément (immɔderemɑ̃), adv. Immoderately.
immodeste (immɔdɛst), adj. Immodest, indecent.
immodestement (immɔdɛstəmɑ̃), adv. Immodestly, indecently.
immodestie (immɔdɛsti), s.f. Immodesty.
immolation (immɔla'sjɔ̃), s.f. Immolation.
immoler (immɔle), v.a. [L *immolare*] To immolate, to sacrifice, to kill; **s'~**, v.pr. to sacrifice oneself.
immonde (immɔ̃d), adj. [L *immundus*] Filthy, unclean, foul, disgusting, ignoble, vile.
immondice (immɔ̃dis), s.f. [L *immunditia*] Filth, dirt.
immoral, -e, (aux) (immɔral), adj. Immoral.
immoralement (immɔralmɑ̃), adv. Immorally.
immoralité (immɔralite), s.f. Immorality.
immortaliser (immɔrtalize), v.a. To immortalize, to perpetuate the memory of.
immortalité (immɔrtalite), s.f. [L *immortalitas*] Immortality.
immortel, -le (immɔrtɛl), adj. Immortal, everlasting. ~, s.m. (fam.) Member of the French Academy; **~s**, s.m.pl. the gods; **~le**, s.f. (bot.) immortelle, everlasting flower.
immortellement (immɔrtɛlmɑ̃), adv. Immortally.
immuabilité (immɥabilite), s.f. See syn. IMMUTABILITÉ.
immuable (immɥabl), adj. [L *immutabilis*] Immutable, immovable, steadfast.
immuablement (immɥabləmɑ̃), adv. Immutably, invariably.
immuniser (immynize), v.a. [f. L *immunis*] To immunize.
immunité (immynite), s.f. [L *immunitas*] Immunity.
immutabilité (immytabilite), s.f. [f. L *immutabilis*] Immutability; syn. IMMUABILITÉ.

impact (ɛ̃pakt), s.m. [f. L *impactus*] Impact, collision.
impair, -e (ɛ̃pɛr), adj. [L *impar*] (arith.) Odd, uneven; (anat.) single, singular. ~, s.m. Blunder; *commettre un ~*, to blunder; (colloq.) to put one's foot in it.
impalpabilité (ɛ̃palpabilite), s.f. Impalpability.
impalpable (ɛ̃palpabl), adj. [LL *impalpabilis*] Impalpable.
impardonnable (ɛ̃pardɔnabl), adj. Unpardonable.
imparfait, -e (ɛ̃parfɛ), adj. Imperfect, incomplete, defective. ~, s.m. (gram.) Imperfect (tense).
imparfaitement (ɛ̃parfɛtmɑ̃), adv. Imperfectly, incompletely, not entirely.
imparité (ɛ̃parite), s.f. [L *imparitas*] Imparity, oddness.
impartageable (ɛ̃partaʒabl), adj. Indivisible.
impartial, -e, (aux) (ɛ̃parsjal), adj. Impartial, unprejudiced, unbiassed.
impartialement (ɛ̃parsjalmɑ̃), adv. Impartially.
impartialité (ɛ̃parsjalite), s.f. Impartiality.
impartir (ɛ̃partir), v.a. [L *impartiri*] To grant, to allow, to impart. ⚠ English 'to impart' usually means to communicate as knowledge or information, to share (knowledge, a secret, &c.) = *faire part*, *communiquer*, *faire savoir*.
impassable (ɛ̃pasabl), adj. Impassable.
impasse (ɛ̃pɑs), s.f. Blind alley, blocked way; (fig.) deadlock, fix, inextricable difficulty or entanglement; (whist, bridge) finesse.
impassibilité (ɛ̃pasibilite), s.f. Impassibility, phlegm, impassivity, impassiveness.
impassible (ɛ̃pasibl), adj. [L *impassibilis*] Impassible, impassive.
impassiblement (ɛ̃pasibləmɑ̃), adv. Impassively.
impatiemment (ɛ̃pasjamɑ̃), adv. Impatiently.
impatience (ɛ̃pasjɑ̃s), s.f. [L *impatiens*] Impatience, restlessness, longing, (colloq.) fidgets; *donner de l'~ à X*, to put X out of all patience.
impatient, -e (ɛ̃pasjɑ̃), adj. Impatient, restless, fidgety, anxious, eager.
impatientant, -e (ɛ̃pasjɑ̃tɑ̃), p. adj. Provoking, tiresome, irksome.
impatienter (ɛ̃pasjɑ̃te), v.a. To put out of patience, to provoke; **s'~**, v.pr. to get impatient, to lose patience, to fidget, to fret.
impatroniser (ɛ̃patrɔnize), v.a. [f. *patron*] To put in authority or possession; **s'~**, v.pr. to assume authority.
impayable (ɛ̃pɛjabl), adj. Invaluable, priceless, capital; exceedingly funny, too good to be true.
impayé, -e (ɛ̃pɛje), adj. Unpaid.
impeccabilité (ɛ̃pɛkabilite), s.f. Impeccability, unimpeachableness.
impeccable (ɛ̃pɛkabl), adj. [f. L *peccare*] Impeccable, unerring; perfectly correct, faultless, unimpeachable.
impeccablement (ɛ̃pɛkabləmɑ̃), adv. Impeccably, unimpeachably, faultlessly.
impedimenta, impédiments (ɛ̃pedimɛnta, ɛ̃pedimɑ̃), s.m.pl. [L wd] Impedimenta.
impénétrabilité (ɛ̃penetrabilite), s.f. Impenetrability, imperviousness.
impénétrable (ɛ̃penetrabl), adj. Impenetrable, impervious, inscrutable; (of a person) close.
impénétrablement (ɛ̃penetrabləmɑ̃,) adv. Impenetrably, inscrutably.
impénitence (ɛ̃penitɑ̃s), s.f. Impenitence; *mourir dans l'~ finale*, to die impenitent.
impénitent, -e (ɛ̃penitɑ̃), adj. Impenitent.
impense (ɛ̃pɑ̃s), s.f. [L *impensa*] Expense (for repairs and improvements to an estate).
impérati-f, -ve (ɛ̃peratif), adj. [L *imperativus*] Imperative, commanding. ~, s.m. (gram.) Imperative.
impérativement (ɛ̃perativmɑ̃), adv. Imperatively.
impératoire (ɛ̃peratwar), s.f. (bot.) Masterwort.
impératrice (ɛ̃peratris), s.f. [L *imperatrix*] Empress.
imperceptibilité (ɛ̃pɛrsɛptibilite), s.f. Imperceptibility.
imperceptible (ɛ̃pɛrsɛptibl), adj. Imperceptible, indistinguishable, insignificant.
imperceptiblement (ɛ̃pɛrsɛptibləmɑ̃), adv. Imperceptibly.
imperdable (ɛ̃pɛrdabl), adj. That cannot be lost.
imperfectibilité (ɛ̃pɛrfɛktibilite), s.f. Imperfectibility.
imperfectible (ɛ̃pɛrfɛktibl), adj. Imperfectible.
imperfection (ɛ̃pɛrfɛksjɔ̃), s.f. Imperfection, imperfectness; defect, blemish.
impérial, -e, (aux) (ɛ̃perjal), adj. [L *imperialis*] Imperial.
impériale (ɛ̃perjal), s.f. **1.** (of a coach, carriage, bus, tramcar) Top, roof, outside; **2.** (game of cards) all-fours; **3.** imperial (beard).
impérialement (ɛ̃perjalmɑ̃), adv. Imperially.
impérialisme (ɛ̃perjalism), s.m. Imperialism.
impérialiste (ɛ̃perjalist), adj. s.m.f. Imperialist.
impérieusement (ɛ̃perjøzmɑ̃), adv. Imperiously.
impérieu-x, -se (ɛ̃perjø), adj. [L *imperiosus*] Imperious, domineering, overbearing.

impérissable (ɛ̃perisabl), adj. Imperishable, everlasting.

impéritie (ɛ̃perisi), s.f. [L *imperitia*] Incapacity, inefficiency.

imperméabiliser (ɛ̃pɛrmeabilize), v.a. To make waterproof.

imperméabilité (ɛ̃pɛrmeabilite), s.f. Impermeability, imperviousness.

imperméable (ɛ̃pɛrmeabl), adj. Impermeable, impervious, waterproof, water-tight, air-tight. ~, s.m. Rain-coat, mackintosh, waterproof.

impersonnalité (ɛ̃pɛrsɔnalite), s.f. Impersonality.

impersonnel, -le (ɛ̃pɛrsɔnɛl), adj. Impersonal.

impersonnellement (ɛ̃pɛrsɔnɛlmɑ̃), adv. Impersonally.

impertinemment (ɛ̃pɛrtinamɑ̃), adv. Impertinently, insolently.

impertinence (ɛ̃pɛrtinɑ̃s), s.f. Impertinence, insolence, rudeness; impertinent act or talk, pertness.

impertinent, -e (ɛ̃pɛrtinɑ̃), adj. [L *impertinens*] Impertinent, insolent, pert, rude, saucy, arrogant.

imperturbabilité (ɛ̃pɛrtyrbabilite), s.f. Imperturbability.

imperturbable (ɛ̃pɛrtyrbabl), adj. [f. L *perturbare*] Imperturbable.

imperturbablement (ɛ̃pɛrtyrbabləmɑ̃), adv. Imperturbably.

impétigo (ɛ̃petigo), s.m. [L wd] (med.) Impetigo.

impétrant, -e (ɛ̃petrɑ̃), s.m.f. Candidate; (law) grantee.

impétrer (ɛ̃petre), v.a. [L *impetrare*] To impetrate, to obtain.

impétueusement (ɛ̃petɥøzmɑ̃), adv. Impetuously.

impétueu-x, -se (ɛ̃petɥø), adj. [L *impetuosus*] Impetuous, vehement, violent, boisterous.

impétuosité (ɛ̃petɥozite), s.f. Impetuosity, violence, vehemence.

impie (ɛ̃pi), adj. [L *in+pius*] Impious, godless, ungodly. ~, s.m.f. Impious person, heathen, infidel.

impieté (ɛ̃piete), s.f. Impiety, ungodliness; act of impiety or wickedness; *dire des ~s*, to utter impieties.

impitoyable (ɛ̃pitwajabl), adj. Pitiless, unpitying, ruthless, relentless, unmerciful, hard-hearted, inexorable.

impitoyablement (ɛ̃pitwajabləmɑ̃), adv. Pitilessly, ruthlessly, unrelentingly, inexorably.

implacabilité (ɛ̃plakabilite), s.f. Implacability.

implacable (ɛ̃plakabl), adj. [L *implacabilis*] Implacable, irreconcilable, relentless, inexorable.

implacablement (ɛ̃plakabləmɑ̃), adv. Implacably.

implantation (ɛ̃plɑ̃ta'sjɔ̃), s.f. Implantation.

implanter (ɛ̃plɑ̃te), v.a. To implant, to plant; (fig.) to introduce, to establish, to instil, to inculcate; **s'~**, v.pr. to be implanted, to take root, to grow.

implexe (ɛ̃plɛks), adj. (rare) [L *implexus*] Implex, intricate.

implication (ɛ̃plika'sjɔ̃), s.f. Implication, involving; (log.) contradiction, discrepancy. ⚠ 'Implication' in English, but not in French, may also mean *insinuation*.

implicite (ɛ̃plisit), adj. [L *implicitus*] Implicit, implied, tacitly comprised; *volonté ~*, implied will; *foi ~*, implicit belief.

implicitement (ɛ̃plisitmɑ̃), adv. Implicitly, impliedly.

impliquer (ɛ̃plike), v.a. [L *implicare*] To implicate, to involve, to entangle, to imply; *on a impliqué X dans cette accusation*, X was implicated in this accusation; ~ *contradiction*, to imply contradiction.

imploration (ɛ̃plɔra'sjɔ̃), s.f. Imploration, supplication.

implorer (ɛ̃plɔre), v.a. [L *implorare*] To implore, to supplicate, to beseech, to crave, to beg; ~ *la clémence du vainqueur*, to implore the conqueror to be clement; ~ *l'appui de X*, to beseech X to help.

impoli, -e (ɛ̃pɔli), adj. Uncivil, rude, discourteous, impolite. ~, s.m.f. Uncivil person.

impoliment (ɛ̃pɔlimɑ̃), adv. Uncivilly, rudely, impolitely.

impolitesse (ɛ̃pɔlitɛs), s.f. Incivility, rudeness, impoliteness, act of rudeness; *faire une ~*, to behave rudely.

impolitique (ɛ̃pɔlitik), adj. Impolitic, unwise.

impolitiquement (ɛ̃pɔlitikmɑ̃), adv. Impoliticly, impolitically, unwisely.

impondérabilité (ɛ̃pɔ̃derabilite), s.f. Imponderability.

impondérable (ɛ̃pɔ̃derabl), adj. s.m. Imponderable.

impopulaire (ɛ̃pɔpylɛr), adj. Unpopular.

impopularité (ɛ̃pɔpylarite), s.f. Unpopularity.

importable (ɛ̃pɔrtabl), adj. Importable.

importance (ɛ̃pɔrtɑ̃s), s.f. [f. *importer*] Importance, moment, worth, purport, consequence; authority, credit; self-conceit; *avoir de l'~*, to be of importance or of moment; *attacher de l'~ à*, to consider important, to attach importance to; *c'est de peu d'~*, it 's of slight importance; *sans ~*, of no moment, of no consequence, of no importance, unimportant; *on l'a rossé d'~*, they gave him a fine thrashing; *se donner des airs d'~*, to play the consequential.

important, -e (ɛ̃pɔrtɑ̃), adj. Important, momentous, of consequence, weighty.

chief, essential; *peu ~*, unimportant. ~, s.m. The essential, the main point; consequential man; *faire l'~*, to give oneself airs, to set up for a man of importance; *l'~ est de savoir*, the main point is to know.

importat-eur, -rice (ɛ̃portatœr), s.m.f. Importer. ~, adj. Importing.

importation (ɛ̃porta'sjɔ̃), s.f. Importation; *~s*, imports.

importer[1] (ɛ̃porte), v.a. [L *importare*] To import; (fig.) to introduce, to bring in.

importer[2] (ɛ̃porte), v.n. def. (used only in the inf. and the 3rd pers.) To import, to be of moment, to matter, to signify; *il importe que ce soit fait immédiatement*, it is important that this should be done at once; *il importe peu que*, it signifies but little that; *peu importe*, it does not matter much; *cela m'importe beaucoup*, that matters a good deal to me; *que m'~?*, what is that to me?; *qu'importe?*, what does it matter?; it is of no consequence; *n'importe*, no matter, never mind; *n'importe comment*, no matter how; *n'importe lequel*, no matter which; *n'importe où*, anywhere; *n'importe quand*, at any time; (colloq.) anywhen; *n'importe qui*, any one; *n'importe quoi*, anything.

importun, -e (ɛ̃portœ̃), adj. [L *importunus*] Importunate, tiresome, troublesome; ill-timed, obtrusive. ~, s.m.f. Intruder, bore, dun, hanger-on, importunate person.

importuner (ɛ̃portyne), v.a. To importune, to annoy, to pester, to harass, to trouble, to inconvenience, to tease, to molest, to intrude on.

importunité (ɛ̃portynite), s.f. Importunity.

imposable (ɛ̃pozabl), adj. Taxable.

imposant, -e (ɛ̃pozɑ̃), p. adj. Imposing, impressive, commanding, grand.

imposé, -e (ɛ̃poze), p. adj. Imposed, taxed. ~, s.m.f. Tax-payer, rate-payer.

imposer (ɛ̃poze), v.a. [L *imponere*] To lay (hands); to impose, to inflict, to thrust (upon), to force (on); to levy; to tax; (print.) to impose; *~ la loi aux vaincus*, to impose laws on the conquered; *~ silence à*, to impose silence on; to silence; to hush; to control; *~ une punition*, to inflict a punishment; *~ le sucre*, to tax sugar; ~, v.n. to awe, to be overawing; *en ~ à X*, to impose on X; to overawe X; to impress X; **s'~**, v.pr. to obtrude; to be imposed, to force oneself or itself; to be evident; to tax oneself.

imposition (ɛ̃pozisjɔ̃), s.f. Imposition; laying on (of hands); inflicting, infliction; tax, assessment; (print.) imposition; *percevoir les ~s*, to collect the taxes. ⚠ In English, but not in French, 'imposition' means also *pensum* = work set as punishment at school.

impossibilité (ɛ̃posibilite), s.f. Impossibility; *de toute ~*, utterly impossible; *être, se trouver, dans l'~ de faire quelque chose*, to find it impossible to do something.

impossible (ɛ̃posibl), adj. [L *impossibilis*] Impossible, impracticable, fabulous, inadmissible; *si, par ~*, if against all probability. ~, s.m. That which is impossible; *je ferai l'~ pour lui*, I will do my very utmost for him; (prov.) *à l'~ nul n'est tenu*, there is no doing impossibilities; what cannot be cured must be endured; *viser l'~*, to aim at impossibilities.

imposte (ɛ̃post), s.f. [It. *imposta*] (arch.) Impost, fan-light.

imposteur (ɛ̃postœr), s.m. [L *impostor*] Impostor, cheat, deceiver, swindler.

imposture (ɛ̃postyr), s.f. Imposture, deception, deceit, cheat, lie, swindle.

impôt (ɛ̃po), s.m. [L *impositum*] Tax, duty, impost, taxation, rate; *~s directs*, direct taxes; *~ sur le revenu*, income-tax; *frapper d'un ~*, to tax; *l'assiette de l'~*, the assessment of the taxes; *percevoir les ~s*, to collect the taxes; syn. CONTRIBUTIONS.

impotence (ɛ̃potɑ̃s), s.f. [L *impotentia*] Impotence, impotency.

impotent, -e (ɛ̃potɑ̃), adj. Impotent, crippled; powerless. ~, s.m.f. Cripple. ⚠ 'Impotent' in English means also 'wholly lacking in sexual power'; in this acceptation it must be translated by *impuissant*.

impraticabilité (ɛ̃pratikabilite), s.f. Impracticability.

impraticable (ɛ̃pratikabl), adj. Impracticable, unpassable, unmanageable, unfeasible.

imprécation (ɛ̃preka'sjɔ̃), s.f. [L *imprecatio*] Imprecation, curse, public denunciation; *lancer, faire, des ~s contre X*, to curse X, to utter imprecations against X.

imprécatoire (ɛ̃prekatwar), adj. Imprecatory.

imprécis, -e (ɛ̃presi), adj. Imprecise, inaccurate, vague, blurred.

imprécision (ɛ̃presizjɔ̃), s.f. Want of precision, vagueness, inaccuracy.

imprégnation (ɛ̃preɲa'sjɔ̃), s.f. Impregnation.

imprégner (ɛ̃preɲe), v.a. [L *impraegnare*] To impregnate; **s'~** (*de*), v.pr. to become impregnated, imbued (with).

imprenable (ɛ̃prənabl), adj. Impregnable, inexpugnable.

impresario (ɛ̃prezarjo), s.m. [It. wd] Impresario, manager.

imprescriptibilité (ɛ̃prɛskriptibilite), s.f. Imprescriptibility.

imprescriptible (ɛ̃prɛskriptibl), adj. Imprescriptible, indefeasible.

impresse (ɛ̃prɛs), adj. f. [L *impressus*] (phil.) Impressed.

impression (ɛ̃prɛsjɔ̃), s.f. [L *impressio*] Impression; impress, impressing, stamping; printing, print, issue, edition; (paint.) priming; *être à l'~*, to be in the printer's hands; to be gone to press; *faute d'~*, misprint; *faire ~*, to be impressive, to make or leave an impression; *avoir, garder une mauvaise ~ de*, to be unfavourably impressed by.
impressionnabilité (ɛ̃prɛsjɔnabilite), s.f. Impressionability, nervousness, receptiveness, excitableness.
impressionnable (ɛ̃prɛsjɔnabl), adj. Impressionable, sensitive, nervous, receptive, excitable.
impressionnant, -e (ɛ̃prɛsjɔnɑ̃), p. adj. Impressive.
impressionner (ɛ̃prɛsjɔne), v.a. To impress, to make an impression on; to move, to affect; **s'~**, v.pr. (colloq.) to be affected.
impressionnisme (ɛ̃prɛsjɔnism), s.m. Impressionism.
imprévisible (ɛ̃previzibl), adj. Impossible to foresee.
imprévision (ɛ̃previzjɔ̃), s.f. Want of foresight.
imprévoyance (ɛ̃prevwajɑ̃s), s.f. Improvidence, carelessness, want of foresight.
imprévoyant, -e (ɛ̃prevwajɑ̃), adj. Improvident, careless, unforeseeing, unwary.
imprévu, -e (ɛ̃prevy), adj. Unforeseen, unexpected. **~**, s.m. The unforeseen; *en cas d'~*, for contingencies; in an emergency; *sauf ~*, except or barring the unforeseen; barring accidents.
imprimable (ɛ̃mprimabl), adj. Printable.
imprimatur (ɛ̃primatyr), s.m. invar. [L wd] Imprimatur, official licence to print.
imprimé (ɛ̃prime), s.m. Printed matter.
imprimer (ɛ̃prime), v.a. [L *imprimere*] To impress, to imprint, to communicate, to impart, to instil; to stamp; to print, to put in print, to publish; (paint.) to prime; *~ un mouvement à*, to give motion to, to set in motion; *se faire ~*, to set up for an author.
imprimerie (ɛ̃primәri), s.f. Art of printing, printing; printing office or house; *caractère d'~*, type.
imprimeur (ɛ̃primœr), s.m. Printer.
imprimeuse (ɛ̃primøz), s.f. Printing machine.
improbabilité (ɛ̃prɔbabilite), s.f. Improbability, unlikelihood.
improbable (ɛ̃prɔbabl), adj. Improbable, unlikely.
improbat-eur, -rice (ɛ̃prɔbatœr), adj. Disapprobatory.
improbation (ɛ̃prɔba'sjɔ̃), s.f. Disapproval, disapprobation.
improbité (ɛ̃prɔbite), s.f. Improbity, dishonesty.
improducti-f, -ve (ɛ̃prɔdyktif), adj. Unproductive.
improductivité (ɛ̃prɔdyktivite), s.f. Barrenness, unproductiveness.
impromptu (ɛ̃prɔ̃pty), adv. adj. invar. [L *in promptu*] Impromptu, off-hand, extempore, without preparation. **~**, s.m. Impromptu.
imprononçable (ɛ̃prɔnɔ̃sabl), adj. Unpronounceable.
impropre (ɛ̃prɔpr), adj. Unfit, inaccurate, wrong; improper; *~ au service militaire*, unfit for military service; *expression ~*, inaccurate or wrong expression. ⚠ 'Improper' means also *inconvenant, indécent.*
improprement (ɛ̃prɔprәmɑ̃), adv. Unsuitably, inaccurately, wrongly.
impropriété (ɛ̃prɔpriete), s.f. Unfitness, inaccuracy; impropriety. ⚠ See IMPROPRE.
improuver (ɛ̃pruve), v.a. To disapprove of.
improvisat-eur, -rice (ɛ̃prɔvizatœr), s.m.f. Improvisator, improviser, extemporizer.
improvisation (ɛ̃prɔviza'sjɔ̃), s.f. Improvisation; (mus.) voluntary, impromptu.
improviser (ɛ̃prɔvize), v.a.n. [f. L *in+provisus*] To improvise, to utter or compose extempore; to do something hastily without the necessary preparation.
(à l')improviste (alɛ̃prɔvist), adv. loc. All of a sudden, unexpectedly; *survenir à l'~*, to come unawares.
imprudemment (ɛ̃prydamɑ̃), adv. Imprudently, incautiously, indiscreetly.
imprudence (ɛ̃prydɑ̃s) s.f. [*im+prudence*] Imprudence, heedlessness, unwariness, indiscretion; imprudent act or speech; *commettre une ~*, to be guilty of an indiscretion; *faire des ~s*, to act imprudently or daringly; *quelle ~!*, how imprudent!
imprudent, -e (ɛ̃prydɑ̃), adj. Imprudent, heedless, incautious, unwary, foolhardy, daring; unwise, indiscreet.
impubère (ɛ̃pybɛr), adj. [L *impubes*] Not arrived at puberty.
impudemment (ɛ̃pydamɑ̃), adv. Impudently, shamelessly.
impudence (ɛ̃pydɑ̃s), s.f. Impudence, shamelessness, effrontery, sauciness, brazenness, cheek; *quelle ~!*, what cheek!
impudent, -e (ɛ̃pydɑ̃), adj. [f. L *pudens*] Impudent, shameless, saucy, brazen, cheeky.
impudeur (ɛ̃pydœr), s.f. Immodesty, indecency, impudicity; extreme impudence.
impudicité (ɛ̃pydisite), s.f. [f. *impudique*] Impudicity, unchastity, lewdness.
impudique (ɛ̃pydik), adj. [f. L *im+pudicus*] Immodest, unchaste, lewd.
impudiquement (ɛ̃pydikmɑ̃), adv. Immodestly, unchastely, lewdly.

impuissance (ɛ̃pɥisɑ̃s), s.f. Powerlessness, impotence, inability, incapacity; (pathol.) impotence.

impuissant, -e (ɛ̃pɥisɑ̃), adj. Powerless, unable, ineffectual; (pathol.) impotent; *être ~ à*, to be unable to.

impulsi-f, -ve (ɛ̃pylsif), adj. [f. L *impulsus*] Impulsive; impellent.

impulsion (ɛ̃pylsjɔ̃), s.f. [L *impulsio*] Impulsion, impulse, impetus.

impunément (ɛ̃pynemɑ̃), adv. With impunity, without inconvenience.

impuni, -e (ɛ̃pyni), adj. Unpunished; *laisser un affront ~*, to put up with an insult.

impunité (ɛ̃pynite), s.f. [L *impunitas*] Impunity.

impur, -e (ɛ̃pyr), adj. Impure, foul, unclean, unchaste, lewd; adulterated.

impurement (ɛ̃pyrmɑ̃), adv. Impurely.

impureté (ɛ̃pyrte), s.f. Impurity; foulness; admixture of foreign matter.

imputable (ɛ̃pytabl), adj. Imputable, chargeable (*sur*, to, on).

imputation (ɛ̃pyta'sjɔ̃), s.f. Imputation, charge, deduction, accusation.

imputer (ɛ̃pyte), v.a. [L *imputare*] To impute, to ascribe, to charge, to deduct; *~ à crime*, to impute as a crime; *n'imputez mon silence qu'à mon peu de loisir*, do not impute my silence to anything but my want of time.

imputrescible (ɛ̃pytrɛsibl), adj. Imputrescible.

inabordable (inabɔrdabl), adj. Inaccessible, unapproachable.

inabrité, -e (inabrite), adj. Unsheltered.

inabrogeable (inabrɔʒabl), adj. Unrepealable.

inacceptable (inaksɛptabl), adj. Unacceptable.

inacceptation (inaksɛpta'sjɔ̃), s.f. Non-acceptance.

inaccessibilité (inaksɛsibilite), s.f. Inaccessibility.

inaccessible (inaksɛsibl), adj. Inaccessible, unattainable, unapproachable; (fig.) insensible, unmoved; *un cœur ~ à la pitié*, a heart which cannot be moved by pity.

inaccomplissement (inakɔ̃plismɑ̃), s.m. Non-fulfilment, inexecution.

inaccordable (inakɔrdabl), adj. **1.** Unallowable, ungrantable; **2.** irreconcilable; **3.** untunable.

inaccoutumé, -e (inakutyme), adj. Unaccustomed, unwonted, unusual.

inachevé, -e (inaʃve), adj. Unfinished, incomplete.

inachèvement (inaʃɛvmɑ̃), s.m. Incompletion, incompleteness, unfinished state.

inacti-f, -ve (inaktif), adj. Inactive, inert, sluggish, unemployed.

inaction (inaksjɔ̃), s.f. Inaction, inertness; *rester dans l'~*, to remain inactive.

inactivité (inaktivite), s.f. Inactivity.

inadmissibilité (inadmisibilite), s.f. Inadmissibility.

inadmissible (inadmisibl), adj. Inadmissible.

inadmission (inadmisjɔ̃), s.f. Non-admission.

inadvertance (inadvɛrtɑ̃s), s.f. Inadvertence, oversight; *par ~*, inadvertently.

inaliénabilité (inaljenabilite), s.f. Inalienability.

inaliénable (inaljenabl), adj. Inalienable, untransferable.

inalliable (inaljabl), adj. (of metals) That cannot be alloyed; (fig.) incompatible.

inaltérabilité (inalterabilite), s.f. Inalterability, unalterableness, immutability, unchangeableness.

inaltérable (inalterabl), adj. Inalterable, unchangeable, immutable, unchanging; unspoilable.

inamical, -e, (aux) (inamikal), adj. Unfriendly, inimical.

inamovibilité (inamɔvibilite), s.f. Irremovability, permanency.

inamovible (inamɔvibl), adj. Irremovable, permanent, for life.

inanimé, -e (inanime), adj. Inanimate, lifeless, senseless, spiritless.

inanité (inanite), s.f. [L *inanitas*] Inanity, emptiness, nothingness, vanity.

inanition (inanisjɔ̃), s.f. [L *inanitio*] Inanition, starvation; *tomber d'~*, to faint for want of food; (colloq.) to be ravenously hungry.

inapaisable (inapɛzabl), adj. Unappeasable, implacable, unquenchable.

inapaisé, -e (inapɛze), adj. Unappeased, unquenched, unpacified.

inaperçu, -e (inapɛrsy), adj. Unperceived, unseen, unnoticed, unheeded.

inappétence (inapetɑ̃s), s.f. Inappetence, want of appetite.

inapplicable (inaplikabl), adj. Inapplicable, unfit, irrelevant, inexecutable.

inapplication (inaplika'sjɔ̃), s.f. Inapplication, inattention.

inappliqué, -e (inaplike), adj. Inattentive, heedless, unmindful; not carried out.

inappréciable (inapresjabl), adj. **1.** Inestimable, invaluable; **2.** unnoticeable, inappreciable.

inappréciablement (inapresjabləmɑ̃), adv. Inappreciably, invaluably; unnoticeably.

inapprivoisable (inaprivwazabl), adj. Untamable.

inapte (inapt), adj. Inapt, unqualified, unfit.

inaptitude (inaptityd), s.f. Inaptitude, unfitness.

inarticulé, -e (inartikyle), adj. Inarticulate.

inassermenté, -e (inasɛrmɑ̃te), adj. Unsworn; syn. INSERMENTÉ.
inasservi, -e (inasɛrvi), adj. Unenslaved, unsubdued.
inassimilable (inasimilabl), adj. Unassimilable.
inassouvi, -e (inasuvi), adj. Unsatiated, unquenched, ungratified.
inattaquable (inatakabl), adj. Unassailable, inexpugnable; (fig.) unimpeachable, irreproachable, unquestionable.
inattendu, -e (inatɑ̃dy), adj. Unexpected, unlooked for, unforeseen.
inattenti-f, -ve (inatɑ̃tif), adj. Inattentive, unmindful, heedless.
inattention (inatɑ̃sjɔ̃), s.f. Inattention, heedlessness, inadvertency.
inaudible (inodibl), adj. Inaudible.
inaugural, -e, (aux) (inogyral), adj. Inaugural, opening.
inauguration (inogyra'sjɔ̃), s.f. Inauguration, opening.
inaugurer (inogyre), v.a. [L *inaugurare*] To inaugurate, to open, to institute, to usher in; to mark the beginning of.
inauthenticité (inotɑ̃tisite), s.f. Want of authenticity.
inauthentique (inotɑ̃tik), adj. Unauthentic, not genuine.
inavouable (inavwabl), adj. Unavowable, not to be acknowledged; shameful.
incalculable (ɛ̃kalkylabl), adj. Incalculable, countless; impossible to foresee, unreckonable.
incalculablement (ɛ̃kalkylabləmɑ̃), adv. Incalculably.
incandescence (ɛ̃kɑ̃dɛssɑ̃s), s.f. [f. L *incandescere*] Incandescence.
incandescent, -e (ɛ̃kɑ̃dɛssɑ̃), adj. Incandescent, white-hot.
incantation (ɛ̃kɑ̃ta'sjɔ̃), s.f. [L *incantatio*] Incantation.
incapable (ɛ̃kapabl), adj. Incapable, unable, unfit; unqualified, incompetent; *être ~ de marcher*, to be unable to walk; *c'est un ~*, he is an incapable; *les mineurs sont ~s de disposer de leurs biens*, persons under age are not qualified to dispose of their property.
incapacité (ɛ̃kapasite), s.f. Incapacity, incapability, inability, unfitness; (law) disqualification, incompetence; *frapper d'~*, to incapacitate.
incarcération (ɛ̃karsera'sjɔ̃), s.f. Incarceration.
incarcérer (ɛ̃karsere), v.a. [f. L *carcer*] To incarcerate, to imprison.
incarnadin, -e (ɛ̃karnadɛ̃), adj. [It. *incarnatino*] Incarnadine, flesh-coloured.
incarnat, -e (ɛ̃karna), adj. Incarnadine, bright red, rose-red; *trèfle ~*, crimson clover. ~, s.m. Incarnate colour, crimson colour; (bot.) crimson clover.
incarnati-f, -ve (ɛ̃karnatif), adj. (med.) Incarnative, generating flesh.
incarnation (ɛ̃karna'sjɔ̃), s.f. Incarnation; (fig.) embodiment; (of a nail) ingrowth.
incarner (ɛ̃karne), v.a. [L *incarnare*] To incarnate; to embody in flesh; *c'est un diable incarné!*, he is a devil incarnate!; *un ongle incarné*, an ingrowing nail; **s'~**, v.pr. to become incarnate, to be embodied; (of a nail) to grow in.
incartade (ɛ̃kartad), s.f. [Span. *encartada*] Petulant insult; prank, folly, frolic.
incassable (ɛ̃kɑsabl), adj. Unbreakable.
incendiaire (ɛ̃sɑ̃djɛr), s.m.f. adj. Incendiary.
incendie (ɛ̃sɑ̃di), s.m. [L *incendium*] Fire, conflagration; *pompe à ~*, fire-engine; *maîtriser l'~*, to get the fire under.
incendier (ɛ̃sɑ̃dje), v.a. To set fire to, to burn down.
incertain, -e (ɛ̃sɛrtɛ̃), adj. Uncertain, questionable, undecided, unsettled, wavering; indistinct, vague, faint.
incertitude (ɛ̃sɛrtityd), s.f. Uncertainty, doubt, incertitude, suspense; fickleness; *laisser X dans l'~*, to leave X in suspense.
incessamment (ɛ̃sɛsamɑ̃), adv. At once, directly; incessantly, unceasingly.
incessant, -e (ɛ̃sɛsɑ̃), adj. Incessant, ceaseless, unceasing, continual, repeated.
incessibilité (ɛ̃sɛsibilite), s.f. Inalienability.
incessible (ɛ̃sɛsibl), adj. Untransferable, inalienable.
inceste (ɛ̃sɛst), s.m. [L *incestus*] Incest.
incestueusement (ɛ̃sɛstɥøzmɑ̃), adv. Incestuously.
incestueu-x, -se (ɛ̃sɛstɥø), adj. Incestuous.
inchavirable (ɛ̃ʃavirabl), adj. Uncapsizable.
inchoati-f, -ve (ɛ̃kɔatif), adj. [f. L *inchoare*] (gram.) Inceptive, inchoative.
incidemment (ɛ̃sidamɑ̃), adv. Incidentally, casually.
incidence (ɛ̃sidɑ̃s), s.f. Incidence; *angle d'~*, angle of incidence.
incident, -e (ɛ̃sidɑ̃), adj. [f. L *incidere*] Incidental, fortuitous, casual; incident, falling on. **~e**, s.f. (gram.) Relative clause.
incident (ɛ̃sidɑ̃), s.m. Incident, occurrence, event; small difficulty; episode; subordinate action.
incinération (ɛ̃sinera'sjɔ̃), s.f. Incineration, cremation.
incinérer (ɛ̃sinere), v.a. [f. L *in+cinerare*] To incinerate, to cremate.
incirconcis (ɛ̃sirkɔ̃si), adj. m. Uncircumcised.
incise (ɛ̃siz), s.f. [f. L *incisus*] (gram.) Short subordinate sentence, parenthetical phrase.
inciser (ɛ̃size), v.a. [f. L *incidere*] To

make an incision, to incise, to gash, to tap.
incisi-f, -ve (ɛ̃sizif), adj. Incisive, sharp, cutting. ~ve, s.f. Incisor, incisive tooth.
incision (ɛ̃sizjɔ̃), s.f. Incision, cut, gash, notch.
incitant, -e (ɛ̃sitɑ̃), p. adj. Inciting, stimulating.
incitat-eur, -rice (ɛ̃sitatœr), adj. Inciting. ~, s.m.f. Inciter.
incitation (ɛ̃sita'sjɔ̃), s.f. Incitation, incitement, incentive.
inciter (ɛ̃site), v.a. [L *in+citare*] To incite, to urge, to stir up; ~ *le peuple à la révolte*, to incite the people to rebellion.
incivil, -e (ɛ̃sivil), adj. Uncivil, rude, unmannerly.
incivilité (ɛ̃sivilite), s.f. Incivility, rudeness; *commettre une* ~, to behave rudely.
incivique (ɛ̃sivik), adj. Unpatriotic.
incivisme (ɛ̃sivism), s.m. Incivism, want of good citizenship.
inclassable (ɛ̃klɑsabl), adj. Unclassifiable, nondescript.
inclémence (ɛ̃klemɑ̃s), s.f. Inclemency.
inclément, -e (ɛ̃klemɑ̃), adj. Inclement.
inclinaison (ɛ̃klinɛzɔ̃), s.f. [f. *incliner*] Inclination, incline, gradient; dip, dipping; bow.
inclination (ɛ̃klina'sjɔ̃), s.f. [f. *incliner*] Inclination, bow, nod; bent, propensity, attachment, love; *mariage d'*~, love-match; *par* ~, from inclination.
incliner (ɛ̃kline), v.a.n. [L *inclinare*] To incline, to bend, to bow, to stoop; to slope, to dip; to be inclined (*à*, to), to be disposed; to have a tendency (to); **s'**~, v.pr. to bow down; to bend, to stoop; (geol.) to dip, to tilt.
inclure (ɛ̃klyr), v.a. [L *includere*] To include, to enclose.
inclus, -e (ɛ̃kly), adj. Enclosed; *ci-*~, herein enclosed.
inclusi-f, -ve (ɛ̃klyzif), adj. Inclusive.
inclusion (ɛ̃klyzjɔ̃), s.f. Inclusion.
inclusivement (ɛ̃klyzivmɑ̃), adv. Inclusively.
incoercible (ɛ̃kɔɛrsibl), adj. Incoercible.
incognito (inkɔgnito), adv. [It. wd] Incognito.
incohérence (ɛ̃kɔerɑ̃s), s.f. Incoherence.
incohérent, -e (ɛ̃kɔerɑ̃), adj. Incoherent. ⚠ English 'incoherent' also = *hétéroclite, hétérogène.*
incohésion (ɛ̃kɔezjɔ̃), s.f. (phys.) Incoherence.
incolore (ɛ̃kɔlɔr), adj. Colourless.
incomber (ɛ̃kɔ̃be), v.n. [L *incumbere*] To be incumbent; *cette tâche incombe à X*, this duty is incumbent on X.
incombustibilité (ɛ̃kɔ̃bystibilite), s.f. Incombustibility.
incombustible (ɛ̃kɔ̃bystibl), adj. Incombustible, fire-proof.
incomestible (ɛ̃kɔmɛstibl), adj. Uneatable, inedible.
incommensurabilité (ɛ̃kɔmmɑ̃syrabilite), s.f. Incommensurability.
incommensurable (ɛ̃kɔmmɑ̃syrabl), adj. Incommensurable; (colloq.) huge, enormous.
incommodant, -e (ɛ̃kɔmɔdɑ̃), p. adj. Annoying, troublesome, inconvenient.
incommode (ɛ̃kɔmɔd), adj. Inconvenient, incommodious, troublesome, tiresome, uncomfortable, unhandy.
incommodément (ɛ̃kɔmɔdemɑ̃), adv. Uncomfortably, incommodiously.
incommoder (ɛ̃kɔmɔde), v.a. To incommode, to inconvenience, to make unwell, to disagree with, to annoy, to trouble, to disturb; *se sentir incommodé*, to be rather unwell, to feel indisposed.
incommodité (ɛ̃kɔmɔdite), s.f. Inconvenience, trouble, indisposition, discomfort, ailment, infirmity.
incommunicable (ɛ̃kɔmynikabl), adj. Incommunicable.
incommutabilité (ɛ̃kɔmytabilite), s.f. Incommutability.
incommutable (ɛ̃kɔmytabl), adj. (law) Inalienable, that cannot legally be dispossessed. ⚠ Not English 'incommutable', which = *immuable.*
incomparable (ɛ̃kɔ̃parabl), adj. Incomparable, matchless, unequalled.
incomparablement (ɛ̃kɔ̃parabləmɑ̃), adv. Incomparably.
incompatibilité (ɛ̃kɔ̃patibilite), s.f. Incompatibility, inconsistency.
incompatible (ɛ̃kɔ̃patibl), adj. Incompatible, inconsistent.
incompétence (ɛ̃kɔ̃petɑ̃s), s.f. Incompetence, incompetency.
incompétent, -e (ɛ̃kɔ̃petɑ̃), adj. Incompetent.
incompl-et, -ète (ɛ̃kɔ̃plɛ), adj. Incomplete, imperfect.
incomplètement (ɛ̃kɔ̃plɛtmɑ̃), adv. Incompletely.
incompréhensibilité (ɛ̃kɔ̃preɑ̃sibilite), s.f. Incomprehensibility.
incompréhensible (ɛ̃kɔ̃preɑ̃sibl), adj. Incomprehensible, unintelligible, inconceivable.
incompressibilité (ɛ̃kɔ̃prɛsibilite), s.f. Incompressibility.
incompressible (ɛ̃kɔ̃prɛsibl), adj. Incompressible.
incompris, -e (ɛ̃kɔ̃pri), adj. Not understood, unappreciated.
inconcevable (ɛ̃kɔ̃səvabl), adj. Inconceivable; (colloq.) very remarkable, unheard of, incredible.
inconcevablement (ɛ̃kɔ̃səvabləmɑ̃), adv. Inconceivably.
inconciliable (ɛ̃kɔ̃siljabl), adj. Irreconcilable, incompatible, inconsistent.

inconduite (ɛ̃kɔ̃dɥit), s.f. Misconduct, immoral behaviour.

incongru, -e (ɛ̃kɔ̃gry), adj. [L *incongruus*] Incongruous, out of place, unseemly.

incongruité (ɛ̃kɔ̃grɥite), s.f. Incongruity, incongruousness.

inconnu, -e (ɛ̃kony), adj. Unknown. ~, s.m. The unknown; *~e*, s.f. (math.) unknown quantity; ~, s.m.f. unknown person, stranger; nobody, person whose name is not known or famous.

inconsciemment (ɛ̃kɔ̃sjamɑ̃), adv. Unconsciously, unknowingly.

inconscience (ɛ̃kɔ̃sjɑ̃s), s.f. Unconsciousness.

inconscient, -e (ɛ̃kɔ̃sjɑ̃), adj. Unconscious, not conscious.

inconséquemment (ɛ̃kɔ̃sekamɑ̃), adv. Inconsequently, inconsistently.

inconséquence (ɛ̃kɔ̃sekɑ̃s), s.f. Inconsequence, inconsistency, imprudence, thoughtless act or words.

inconséquent, -e (ɛ̃kɔ̃sekɑ̃), adj. Inconsequent, inconsistent, imprudent, indiscreet.

inconsidération (ɛ̃kɔ̃sidera'sjɔ̃), s.f. Inconsiderateness, unconsideredness.

inconsidéré, -e (ɛ̃kɔ̃sidere), adj. Unconsidered, inconsiderate, hasty, incautious, rash. ⚠ 'Inconsiderate' now nearly always means without consideration for other people's feelings, rights, &c. = *irrévérencieux, manquant d'égards.*

inconsidérément (ɛ̃kɔ̃sideremɑ̃), adv. Inconsiderately, thoughtlessly, incautiously, rashly.

inconsistance (ɛ̃kɔ̃sistɑ̃s), s.f. Inconsistency.

inconsistant, -e (ɛ̃kɔ̃sistɑ̃), adj. Inconsistent, unstable, flimsy, not firm.

inconsolable (ɛ̃kɔ̃sɔlabl), adj. Disconsolate, inconsolable.

inconsolé, -e (ɛ̃kɔ̃sole), adj. Unconsoled, uncomforted.

inconstance (ɛ̃kɔ̃stɑ̃s), s.f. Inconstancy, fickleness, changeableness.

inconstant, -e (ɛ̃kɔ̃stɑ̃), adj. Inconstant, fickle, unsteady, flighty.

inconstitutionnalité (ɛ̃kɔ̃stitysjɔnalite), s.f. Unconstitutionality.

inconstitutionnel, -le (ɛ̃kɔ̃stitysjɔnɛl), adj. Unconstitutional.

inconstitutionnellement (ɛ̃kɔ̃stitysjɔnɛlmɑ̃), adv. Unconstitutionally.

incontestable (ɛ̃kɔ̃tɛstabl), adj. Incontestable, indisputable, unquestionable.

incontestablement (ɛ̃kɔ̃tɛstabləmɑ̃), adv. Incontestably, unquestionably.

incontesté, -e (ɛ̃kɔ̃tɛste), adj. Uncontested, unquestioned, undisputed.

incontinence (ɛ̃kɔ̃tinɑ̃s), s.f. Incontinence.

incontinent, -e (ɛ̃kɔ̃tinɑ̃), adj. [L *incontinens*] Incontinent.

incontinent (ɛ̃kɔ̃tinɑ̃), adv. [L *in continenti* (*tempore*)] At once, forthwith, immediately, on the spot.

incontrôlable (ɛ̃kɔ̃trolabl), adj. Uncontrollable.

inconvenance (ɛ̃kɔ̃vnɑ̃s), s.f. Impropriety, unseemliness; unseemly act, breach of good manners, impropriety; *quelle ~ !*, how very improper !, shocking !

inconvenant, -e (ɛ̃kɔ̃vnɑ̃), adj. Improper, unseemly, shocking.

inconvénient (ɛ̃kɔ̃venjɑ̃), s.m. [f. L *in*+ *conveniens*] Inconvenience, disadvantage, objection, harm; *je ne vois pas d'~ à cela*, I see no objection to that; *tout système a ses ~s*, every system has its disadvantages. ⚠ English 'inconvenient', adj., = *incommode, intempestif, gênant, déplacé.*

inconvertible (ɛ̃kɔ̃vɛrtibl), adj. Inconvertible.

incorporation (ɛ̃korpɔra'sjɔ̃), s.f. Incorporation.

incorporel, -le (ɛ̃kɔrpɔrɛl), adj. Incorporeal.

incorporer (ɛ̃kɔrpɔre), v.a. [L *incorporare*] To incorporate (*à*, with), to combine, to fuse, to mix; to enrol; to embody.

incorrect, -e (ɛ̃kɔrɛkt), adj. Incorrect, inaccurate, faulty; unseemly.

incorrectement (ɛ̃kɔrɛktəmɑ̃), adv. Incorrectly, inaccurately, wrongly.

incorrection (ɛ̃kɔrɛksjɔ̃), s.f. Incorrectness, inaccuracy; breach of manners; *commettre une ~*, to be guilty of a breach of manners.

incorrigible (ɛ̃koriʒibl), adj. Incorrigible, irreclaimable, bad beyond hope of amendment; arrant, confirmed.

incorruptibilité (ɛ̃kɔryptibilite), s.f. Incorruptibility.

incorruptible (ɛ̃kɔryptibl), adj. Incorruptible.

incrédibilité (ɛ̃kredibilite), s.f. Incredibility.

incrédule (ɛ̃kredyl), adj. Incredulous, unbelieving. ~, s.m.f. Unbeliever, infidel.

incrédulité (ɛ̃kredylite), s.f. Incredulity, unbelief.

incréé, -e (ɛ̃kree), adj. Increate, uncreated.

incriminable (ɛ̃kriminabl), adj. Incriminable, liable to prosecution, impeachable.

incrimination (ɛ̃krimina'sjɔ̃), s.f. Incrimination, charge.

incriminer (ɛ̃krimine), v.a. [f. L *in*+ *crimen*] To incriminate, to impeach, to charge (*d'un crime*, with a crime).

incroyable (ɛ̃krwajabl), adj. Incredible, past belief; unheard of; astounding. ~, s.m. Fop (under the French Directory), Incroyable.

incroyablement (ɛ̃krwajabləmɑ̃), adv. Incredibly.

incroyant, -e (ɛ̃krwajɑ̃), s.m.f. Unbeliever.
incrustation (ɛ̃krysta'sjɔ̃), s.f. Incrustation, inlaid work, inlaying.
incruster (ɛ̃kryste), v.a. [L *incrustare*] To incrust, to encrust, to inlay; **s'~**, v.pr. to become encrusted, to be inlaid; (colloq.) to fasten on to something, to have come to stay, to outstay one's welcome, to take root.
incubateur (ɛ̃kybatœr), s.m. Incubator; syn. COUVEUSE.
incubation (ɛ̃kyba'sjɔ̃), s.f. [f. L *incubare*] Incubation.
incube (ɛ̃kyb), s.m. [L *incubus*] Incubus.
inculpable (ɛ̃kylpabl), adj. Chargeable.
inculpation (ɛ̃kylpa'sjɔ̃), s.f. Inculpation, charge.
inculpé, -e (ɛ̃kylpe), s.m.f. Accused, defendant.
inculper (ɛ̃kylpe), v.a. [L *inculpare*] To inculpate, to charge (*de*, with), to accuse (of).
inculquer (ɛ̃kylke), v.a. [L *inculcare*] To inculcate, to teach, to instil.
inculte (ɛ̃kylt), adj. [L *incultus*] Uncultivated, untilled; (fig.) unkempt, neglected, rude, unpolished, uneducated, incult.
incunable (ɛ̃kynabl), adj. [L *incunabulum*] Early printed, incunabular. **~**, s.m. Incunabulum (pl. incunabula), early printed book.
incurabilité (ɛ̃kyrabilite), s.f. Incurability.
incurable (ɛ̃kyrabl), adj. Incurable; hopeless. **~**, s.m. Incurable; *les Incurables*, s.m.pl. hospital for incurables in France.
incurablement (ɛ̃kyrabləmɑ̃), adv. Incurably, hopelessly.
incurie (ɛ̃kyri), s.f. [L *incuria*] Carelessness, negligence, dereliction of duty.
incuriosité (ɛ̃kyrjozite), s.f. Incuriosity.
incursion (ɛ̃kyrsjɔ̃), s.f. [L *incursio*] Incursion, inroad, raid, foray.
incurvation (ɛ̃kyrva'sjɔ̃), s.f. [L *incurvatio*] Incurvation, curvature.
incurver (ɛ̃kyrve), v.a. [L *incurvare*] To curve inward, to bend, to incurvate.
incuse (ɛ̃kyz), adj. s.f. [L *incusa*] Badly struck (medal).
indébrouillable (ɛ̃debrujabl), adj. Inextricable; inexplicable.
indécemment (ɛ̃desamɑ̃), adv. Indecently, improperly.
indécence (ɛ̃desɑ̃s), Indecency, impropriety, obscenity; indecent act or speech.
indécent, -e (ɛ̃desɑ̃), adj. Indecent, immodest, unseemly, improper, obscene.
indéchiffrable (ɛ̃deʃifrabl), adj. Undecipherable, illegible; (fig.) unintelligible, incomprehensible, inexplicable.
indéchirable (ɛ̃deʃirabl), adj. Untearable.
indécis, -e (ɛ̃desi), adj. [f. L *in+decisus*] Uncertain, irresolute, wavering; indistinct, blurred, undefined, doubtful; *un homme ~*, an irresolute man; *une victoire ~e*, a doubtful victory.
indécision (ɛ̃desizjɔ̃), s.f. Indecision, irresoluteness; doubt.
indéclinable (ɛ̃deklinabl), adj. Indeclinable.
indécomposable (ɛ̃dekɔ̃pozabl), adj. Indecomposable.
indécousable (ɛ̃dekuzabl), adj. That will not come unsewn.
indécrottable (ɛ̃dekrɔtabl), adj. Uncleanable; (fig.) unteachable, incorrigible, boorish, rude; inveterate.
indéfectible (ɛ̃defɛktibl), adj. Indefectible, unfailing.
indéfectiblement (ɛ̃defɛktibləmɑ̃), adv. Indefectibly, unfailingly.
indéfendable (ɛ̃defɑ̃dabl), adj. Indefensible, untenable.
indéfini, -e (ɛ̃defini), adj. Indefinite, unlimited, undefined, undetermined; *article ~*, indefinite article; *passé ~*, perfect tense.
indéfiniment (ɛ̃definimɑ̃), adv. Indefinitely; to an indefinite time; sine die; endlessly.
indéfinissable (ɛ̃definisabl), adj. Undefinable, unaccountable, nondescript.
indéformable (ɛ̃defɔrmabl), adj. That will not come out of shape.
indélébile (ɛ̃delebil), adj. Indelible, ineffaceable.
indélibéré, -e (ɛ̃delibere), adj. Undeliberate, unpremeditated.
indélicat, -e (ɛ̃delika), adj. Indelicate, unhandsome, unscrupulous. ⚠ English 'indelicate' means usually *inconvenant, grossier, ordurier*.
indélicatement (ɛ̃delikatmɑ̃), adv. Indelicately, unscrupulously.
indélicatesse (ɛ̃delikatɛs), s.f. Indelicacy; indelicate act, unscrupulous act.
indemne (ɛ̃dɛmn), adj. [L *indemnis*] Uninjured, unscathed, unharmed, safe and sound.
indemnisation (ɛ̃dɛmniza'sjɔ̃), s.f. Indemnification.
indemniser (ɛ̃dɛmnize), v.a. To indemnify, to make good; (law) to recoup; *~ X d'une perte*, to compensate X for a loss.
indemnité (ɛ̃dɛmnite, ɛ̃damnite), s.f. Indemnity; compensation; expenses; *~ de route*, travelling expenses; *~ de chômage*, unemployment benefit, dole.
indémontrable (ɛ̃demɔ̃trabl), adj. Undemonstrable.
indéniable (ɛ̃denjabl), adj. Undeniable, unquestionable, evident.
indentation (ɛ̃dɑ̃ta'sjɔ̃), s.f. Indentation, notch.
indépendamment (ɛ̃depɑ̃damɑ̃), adv. Independently; *~ de*, beyond, in addition to.

indépendance (ɛ̃depɑ̃dɑ̃s), s.f. Independence, freedom, sovereignty, self-government, self-direction.
indépendant, -e (ɛ̃depɑ̃dɑ̃), adj. Independent; free, self-governing; not obsequious; self-willed; unconnected (*de*, with).
indéracinable (ɛ̃derasinabl), adj. Ineradicable.
indescriptible (ɛ̃dɛskriptibl), adj. Indescribable.
indésirable (ɛ̃dezirabl), adj. s.m.f. Undesirable (person).
indestructibilité (ɛ̃dɛstryktibilite), s.f. Indestructibility.
indestructible (ɛ̃dɛstryktibl), adj. Indestructible.
indéterminable (ɛ̃detɛrminabl), adj. Indeterminable, unascertainable.
indétermination (ɛ̃detɛrmina'sjɔ̃), s.f. Indetermination; indefiniteness; irresolution.
indéterminé, -e (ɛ̃detɛrmine), adj. Indeterminate, vague, unascertained; irresolute; (math.) indeterminate.
index (ɛ̃dɛks), s.m. (invar.) [L *index*] **1.** Forefinger; **2.** index, table of contents; **3.** (Cath. Church) Index; *mettre à l'~*, to prohibit, to condemn, to forbid.
indicat-eur, -rice (ɛ̃dikatœr), adj. Indicatory, indicating; *poteau ~*, sign-post. ~, s.m. Indicator; gauge, meter, guide; railway time-table; (police) informer.
indicati-f, -ve (ɛ̃dikatif), adj. Indicative. ~, s.m. (gram.) Indicative mood.
indication (ɛ̃dika'sjɔ̃), s.f. Indication, information, direction, sign, token, symptom; hint, pointer.
indice (ɛ̃dis), s.m. [L *indicium*] Sign, token, mark, symptom; (math., phys.) index; *~ de réfraction*, index of refraction.
indicible (ɛ̃disibl), adj. Unspeakable, ineffable, indescribable, unutterable.
indiciblement (ɛ̃disibləmɑ̃), adv. Unspeakably, ineffably.
indict (ɛ̃dikt), s.m., **indiction** (ɛ̃diksjɔ̃), s.f. [L *indictio*] Indiction.
indien, -ne (ɛ̃djɛ̃), adj. s.m.f. Indian.
indienne (ɛ̃djɛn), s.f. Printed cotton, printed calico.
indifféremment (ɛ̃diferamɑ̃), adv. Indifferently, equally, alike, impartially. ⚠ 'Indifferently' has often the sense of 'passably', 'poorly' = *passablement, médiocrement.*
indifférence (ɛ̃diferɑ̃s), s.f. Indifference, unconcern.
indifférent, -e (ɛ̃diferɑ̃), adj. Indifferent, unconcerned; immaterial, unimportant. ⚠ In English 'indifferent' has often the sense of *passable, médiocre.*
indigénat (ɛ̃diʒena), s.m. **1.** Denizenship; **2.** (collect.) the natives.
indigence (ɛ̃diʒɑ̃s), s.f. [f. *indigent*] Indigence, extreme poverty; (fig.) need, want, poverty; *tomber dans l'~*, to become a pauper; *~ d'idées*, poverty of ideas.
indigène (ɛ̃diʒɛn), adj. s.m.f. [L *indigena*] Native; *plante ~*, native plant.
indigent, -e (ɛ̃diʒɑ̃), adj. Indigent, poor, needy, destitute. ~, s.m.f. Pauper; *les ~s*, the submerged tenth.
indigeste (ɛ̃diʒɛst), adj. Indigestible; (fig.) crude, confused, heavy, incoherent, unreadable.
indigestion (ɛ̃diʒɛstjɔ̃), s.f. Indigestion; (fig.) extreme satiety.
indignation (ɛ̃diɲa'sjɔ̃), s.f. Indignation.
indigne (ɛ̃diɲ), adj. Unworthy (*de*, of); (law) debarred (from); worthless, undeserving; infamous; *~ de vivre*, unworthy to live; *une conduite ~*, infamous behaviour.
indigné, -e (ɛ̃diɲe), p. adj. Indignant, shocked, revolted.
indignement (ɛ̃diɲmɑ̃), adv. Unworthily; infamously, shamefully, scandalously.
indigner (ɛ̃diɲe), v.a. [L *indignari*] To rouse the indignation of; **s'~**, v.pr. to be indignant, to be angry, to be exasperated or revolted.
indignité (ɛ̃diɲite), s.f. Unworthiness, worthlessness; vileness, baseness, indignity; outrage; (law) disqualification.
indigo (ɛ̃digo), s.m. [Span. wd] Indigo.
indigoterie (ɛ̃digɔtri), s.f. Indigo works.
indigotier (ɛ̃digɔtje), s.m. (bot.) Indigo-plant.
indiquer (ɛ̃dike), v.a. [L *indicare*] To indicate, to point out, to show; to inform of, to denote, to betoken; *~ à*, to direct to, to acquaint with; to name, to recommend; to appoint; to sketch lightly; *indiquez-lui votre maison*, direct him to your house; *à l'heure indiquée*, at the appointed time; *c'était tout indiqué*, it was obvious; it was obviously the thing to do.
indirect, -e (ɛ̃dirɛkt), adj. Indirect; (of evidence) circumstantial; (of heirs) collateral.
indirectement (ɛ̃dirɛktəmɑ̃), adv. Indirectly.
indiscernable (ɛ̃disɛrnabl), adj. Indiscernible.
indisciplinable (ɛ̃disiplinabl), adj. Indisciplinable, unruly.
indiscipline (ɛ̃disiplin), s.f. Indiscipline, insubordination.
indiscipliné, -e (ɛ̃disipline), adj. Undisciplined, unruly.
indiscr-et, -ète (ɛ̃diskrɛ), adj. Indiscreet, inconsiderate, inquisitive, prying; obtrusive, intrusive, free. ~, s.m.f. Indiscreet person, babbler, tell-tale; prying person. ⚠ In English 'indiscreet' often = *manquant de discernement, irréfléchi.*

indiscrètement (ɛ̃diskrɛtmɑ̃), adv. Indiscreetly, inconsiderately, obtrusively, freely, inquisitively.
indiscrétion (ɛ̃diskresjɔ̃), s.f. Indiscretion, indiscreetness, imprudence, piece of indiscretion, inquisitiveness; *serait-ce une* ~ (or *y aurait-il* ~) *de ma part de demander*, would it be indiscreet of me to ask; *commettre une* ~, to commit an indiscretion, to be guilty of an indiscretion. ⚠ English 'indiscretion' frequently means *acte contraire à la probité, indélicatesse*.
indiscutable (ɛ̃diskytabl), adj. Indisputable, incontestable, unquestionable.
indispensable (ɛ̃dispɑ̃sabl), adj. Indispensable. ~, s.m. The indispensable, necessaries.
indispensablement (ɛ̃dispɑ̃sabləmɑ̃), adv. Indispensably.
indisponible (ɛ̃disponibl), adj. Undisposable, unavailable; (law) entailed.
indisposé, -e (ɛ̃dispoze), p. adj. Indisposed, unwell, poorly.
indisposer (ɛ̃dispoze), v.a. To indispose, to make unwell; to disincline, to cause to be unfavourable, to prejudice, to set (*contre*, against); *on l'a indisposé contre moi*, they have prejudiced him against me.
indisposition (ɛ̃dispozisjɔ̃), s.f. Indisposition, slight ailment.
indisputable (ɛ̃dispytabl), adj. Indisputable.
indissolubilité (ɛ̃disɔlybilite), s.f. Indissolubility.
indissoluble (ɛ̃disɔlybl), adj. Indissoluble.
indissolublement (ɛ̃disɔlybləmɑ̃), adv. Indissolubly.
indistinct, -e (ɛ̃distɛ̃kt), adj. Indistinct.
indistinctement (ɛ̃distɛ̃ktəmɑ̃), adv. Indistinctly, indiscriminately, impartially, equally.
individu (ɛ̃dividy), s.m. [f. L *individuus*] Individual, fellow, person; *un drôle d'*~, a queer fellow; *avoir soin de son* ~, to take care of number one, or of oneself.
individualisme (ɛ̃dividɥalism), s.m. Individualism.
individualité (ɛ̃dividɥalite), s.f. Individuality; individual, personality.
individuel, -le (ɛ̃dividɥɛl), adj. Individual.
individuellement (ɛ̃dividɥɛlmɑ̃), adv. Individually; separately; severally.
indivis, -e (ɛ̃divi), adj. [L *indivisus*] Undivided; *par* ~, jointly.
indivisibilité (ɛ̃divizibilite), s.f. Indivisibility.
indivisible (ɛ̃divizibl), adj. Indivisible; inseparable.
indivision (ɛ̃divizjɔ̃), s.f. Wholeness; joint-ownership.
in-dix-huit (indizɥit, ɛ̃dizɥit), s.m. Decimo-octavo; 18mo.
indo-chinois, -e (ɛ̃doʃinwa), adj. s.m.f. Indo-Chinese.
indocile (ɛ̃dɔsil), adj. Indocile, unmanageable, disobedient, unruly.
indocilité (ɛ̃dɔsilite), s.f. Indocility.
indolemment (ɛ̃dɔlamɑ̃), adv. Indolently, lazily.
indolence (ɛ̃dɔlɑ̃s), s.f. [L *indolentia*] Indolence, listlessness, sloth, sluggishness, indifference.
indolent, -e (ɛ̃dɔlɑ̃), adj. [L *indolens*] Indolent, lazy, sluggish, indifferent.
indolore (ɛ̃dɔlɔr), adj. [*in*+(L) *dolor*] Not painful.
indomptable (ɛ̃dɔ̃tabl), adj. Indomitable, untamable, unmanageable, ungovernable.
indompté, -e (ɛ̃dɔ̃te), adj. Untamed, wild, uncontrolled, unbroken, unsubdued.
indou, -e (ɛ̃du), adj. s.m.f. See HINDOU.
in-douze (ɛ̃duz, induz), s.m. adj. invar. Duodecimo, 12mo.
indu, -e (ɛ̃dy), adj. Undue, unseasonable, not right; *rentrer à une heure* ~*e*, to come home at a very late hour; *somme* ~*e*, sum not due. ~, s.m. Amount which is not due.
indubitable (ɛ̃dybitabl), adj. [f. L *in*+ *dubitabilis*] Indubitable, unquestionable, beyond doubt.
indubitablement (ɛ̃dybitabləmɑ̃), adv. Indubitably, unquestionably.
induct-eur, -rice (ɛ̃dyktœr), adj. Inductive. ~, s.m. Inductor.
inducti-f, -ve (ɛ̃dyktif), adj. Inductive.
induction (ɛ̃dyksjɔ̃), s.f. [L *inductio*] Induction; inference; (electr.) induction; *bobine d'*~, induction coil. ⚠ English 'induction' also = *installation d'un clergyman*.
induire (ɛ̃dɥir), v.a. [L *inducere*] To induce, to lead, to infer; ~ *en erreur, en tentation*, to lead into error, into temptation; (phys., electr.) to induce; *courant induit*, induced current.
induit (ɛ̃dɥi), s.m. (electr.) Armature; induced current.
indulgemment (ɛ̃dylʒamɑ̃), adv. Indulgently.
indulgence (ɛ̃dylʒɑ̃s), s.f. Indulgence, forbearance, leniency; *user d'*~ *envers X*, to show indulgence to X; to treat X indulgently; (Cath. Church) remission of punishment after sacramental absolution. ⚠ English 'indulgence' also = *mollesse, laisser-aller*.
indulgent, -e (ɛ̃dylʒɑ̃), adj. [f. L *indulgere*] Indulgent, lenient, forbearing.
indûment (ɛ̃dymɑ̃), adv. Unduly.
induration (ɛ̃dyra'sjɔ̃), s.f. (med.) Induration.
indurer (ɛ̃dyre), v.a. [L *indurare*] (pathol.) To indurate, to harden; **s'**~, v.pr. to grow indurate, abnormally hard. ⚠ *In-*

durer is not used in the fig. sense like 'to indurate' = *endurcir* (*le cœur*, &c.).

industrialisme (ɛ̃dystrialism), s.m. Industrialism.

industrie (ɛ̃dystri), s.f. [L *industria*] **1.** Industry, dexterity, skill, ingenuity, diligence, good management; **2.** branch of trade or manufacture; business, industry, work; (pej.) *chevalier d'~*, swindler, sharper.

industriel, -le (ɛ̃dystrjɛl), adj. Industrial. ~, s.m. Manufacturer.

industriellement (ɛ̃dystrjɛlmɑ̃), adv. Industrially; (manufactured) in large quantities.

industrieusement (ɛ̃dystrjøzmɑ̃), adv. Industriously, skilfully.

industrieu-x, -se (ɛ̃dystriø), adj. Industrious, ingenious, skilful, clever, hard-working.

induvie (ɛ̃dyvi), s.f. [L *induvia*] (bot.) Induvia.

inébranlable (inebrɑ̃labl), adj. Immovable, unshakable, firm, steady, constant.

inébranlablement (inebrɑ̃labləmɑ̃), adv. Immovably, steadily, resolutely.

inédit, -e (inedi), adj. [L *ineditus*] Inedited, unpublished. ~, s.m. Unpublished work; (fig.) novelty.

ineffable (inɛfabl), adj. [L *ineffabilis*] Ineffable, unutterable, exquisite, unspeakable.

ineffablement (inɛfabləmɑ̃), adv. Ineffably, unspeakably.

ineffaçable (inɛfasabl), adj. Indelible, ineradicable, ineffaceable.

ineffaçablement (inɛfasabləmɑ̃), adv. Indelibly, ineffaceably.

inefficace (inɛfikas), adj. Inefficacious, ineffectual.

inefficacement (inefikasmɑ̃), adv. Inefficaciously, ineffectually.

inefficacité (inɛfikasite), s.f. Inefficacity, ineffectiveness, inefficiency.

inégal, -e, (aux) (inegal), adj. Unequal; uneven, rough; partial; disproportioned; irregular; (fig.) fickle; *pouls ~*, irregular pulse.

inégalement (inegalmɑ̃), adv. Unequally, unevenly, irregularly, partially.

inégalité (inegalite), s.f. Inequality, unevenness, irregularity, roughness.

inélastique (inelastik), adj. Inelastic.

inélégamment (inelegamɑ̃), adv. Inelegantly.

inélégance (inelegɑ̃s), s.f. Inelegance.

inélégant, -e (inelegɑ̃), adj. Inelegant.

inéligibilité (inelizibilite), s.f. Ineligibility.

inéligible (inelizibl), adj. Ineligible.

inéluctable (inelyktabl), adj. [L *ineluctabilis*] Ineluctable, unavoidable, inevitable.

inéluctablement (inelyktabləmɑ̃), adv. Ineluctably, unavoidably, inevitably.

inéludable (inelydabl), adj. Ineludible.

inemployé, -e (inɑ̃plwaje), adj. Not in use; vacant, unutilized; unused; unemployed. ⚠ *Inemployé* is generally said of things, rarely of persons; 'unemployed', on the contrary, is more often said of persons than of things.

inénarrable (inenarabl), adj. Unspeakable, indescribable; (colloq.) too funny for words.

inepte (inɛpt), adj. [L *ineptus*] Inept, silly, absurd.

ineptement (inɛptəmɑ̃), adv. Ineptly, stupidly.

ineptie (inɛpsi), s.f. [L *ineptia*] Ineptitude, ineptness, foolish absurdity.

inépuisable (inepɥizabl), adj. Inexhaustible.

inépuisablement (inepɥizabləmɑ̃), adv. Inexhaustibly.

inerme (inɛrm), adj. [L *inermis*] (bot.) Thornless, inerm.

inerte (inɛrt), adj. [L *iners*] Inert; dull, sluggish, inactive, irresponsive.

inertie (inɛrsi), s.f. Inertia; inertness, inactivity, sluggishness; *force d'~*, vis inertiae.

inespéré, -e (inɛspere), adj. Unhoped for; unlooked for.

inestimable (inɛstimabl), adj. Inestimable, priceless, invaluable.

inétendu, -e (inetɑ̃dy), adj. Unextended.

inévitable (inevitabl), adj. Inevitable, unavoidable.

inévitablement (inevitabləmɑ̃), adv. Inevitably, unavoidably.

inexact, -e (inɛgzakt), adj. Inexact, inaccurate; unpunctual.

inexactement (inɛgzaktəmɑ̃), adv. Inaccurately, incorrectly; unpunctually.

inexactitude (inɛgzaktityd), s.f. Inexactitude, inexactness, inaccuracy; unpunctuality.

inexcusable (inɛkskyzabl), adj. Inexcusable, unwarrantable, unpardonable.

inexécutable (inɛkzekytabl), adj. Inexecutable, impracticable.

inexécuté, -e (inɛkzekyte), adj. Unexecuted, unperformed, undone, not carried out.

inexécution (inɛkzekysjɔ̃), s.f. Inexecution, non-performance, neglect.

inexercé, -e (inɛgzɛrse), adj. Unexercised, unpractised.

inexigible (inɛgzizibl), adj. Not demandable, not due.

inexistant, -e (inɛgzistɑ̃), adj. Unexisting, not in being; (colloq.) insignificant, of no value, of no import.

inexorable (inɛgzɔrabl), adj. [L *inexorabilis*] Inexorable, unrelenting, inflexible, pitiless.

inexorablement (inɛgzɔrabləmɑ̃), adv. Inexorably, pitilessly.

inexpérience (inɛksperjɑ̃s), s.f. Inexperience.
inexpérimenté, -e (inɛksperimɑ̃te), adj. Inexperienced, untried; (colloq.) green, raw; *procédé* ~, untried process.
inexpiable (inɛkspjabl), adj. Inexpiable; (obs.) irreconcilable, pitiless.
inexplicable (inɛksplikabl), adj. Inexplicable, unaccountable, puzzling.
inexpliqué, -e (inɛksplike), adj. Unexplained, unaccounted for.
inexploitable (inɛksplwatabl), adj. Unworkable, uncultivable.
inexploité, -e (inɛksplwate), adj. Unworked, uncultivated.
inexploré, -e (inɛksplɔre), adj. Unexplored.
inexplosible (inɛksplozibl), adj. Unexplosive, inexplosive.
inexpressible (inɛksprɛsibl), adj. Inexpressible, indescribable.
inexpressi-f, -ve (inɛksprɛsif), adj. Inexpressive, lacking expression.
inexprimable (inɛksprimabl), adj. Inexpressible, unspeakable, unutterable.
inexpugnable (inɛkspyɲabl), adj. [f. L *in+ex+pugnare*] Inexpugnable, impregnable.
inextensible (inɛkstɑ̃sibl), adj. Inextensible.
inextinguible (inɛkstɛ̃gibl), adj. Inextinguishable, unquenchable; irrepressible, uncontrollable.
inextricable (inɛkstrikabl), adj. [f. L *in+extricare*] Inextricable.
inextricablement (inɛkstrikabləmɑ̃), adv. Inextricably.
infaillibilité (ɛ̃fajibilite), s.f. Infallibility.
infaillible (ɛ̃fajibl), adj. Infallible, certain, sure to happen, certain of success.
infailliblement (ɛ̃fajibləmɑ̃), adv. Infallibly.
infaisable (ɛ̃fɛzabl), adj. Unfeasible, not to be done, impossible, impracticable.
infamant, -e (ɛ̃famɑ̃), adj. Infamous, degrading, ignominious; *peine ~e*, degrading punishment.
infâme (ɛ̃fɑm), adj. [L *infamis*] Infamous, ignominious; squalid, filthy, of ill fame. ~, s.m.f. Infamous person.
infamie (ɛ̃fami), s.f. Infamy, infamous action, baseness, infamous dealings or words.
infant, -e (ɛ̃fɑ̃), s.m.f. [Span. *infante*] Infante, infanta.
infanterie (ɛ̃fɑ̃tri), s.f. [It. *infanteria*] Infantry; ~ *de marine*, marines, marine light infantry.
infanticide (ɛ̃fɑ̃tisid), s.m. [f. L *infans+caedere*] **1.** Infanticide; **2.** child-murderer; (fem.) child-murderess. ~, adj. Infanticidal.
infantile (ɛ̃fɑ̃til), adj. Infantile, child-.
infatigable (ɛ̃fatigabl), adj. Indefatigable.
infatigablement (ɛ̃fatigabləmɑ̃), adv. Indefatigably.
infatuation (ɛ̃fatɥa'sjɔ̃), s.f. Infatuation.
infatuer (ɛ̃fatɥe), v.a. [f. L *in+fatuus*] To infatuate; **s'~** (*de*), v.pr. to be infatuated (with).
infécond, -e (ɛ̃fekɔ̃, ɛ̃fegɔ̃), adj. Unfruitful, barren, sterile.
infécondité (ɛ̃fekɔ̃dite), s.f. Unfruitfulness, barrenness, sterility.
infect, -e (ɛ̃fɛkt), adj. [L *infectus*] Foul, stinking, infected, filthy; (fig.) foul, base, vile; (colloq.) *un livre* ~, an awful or disgusting book; *un ~ individu*, a putrid fellow; *un temps* ~, beastly weather.
infecter (ɛ̃fɛkte), v.a. To infect, to taint, to pollute, to corrupt; ~, v.n. to stink. ⚠ In English 'to infect' means often *communiquer à*, ex.: to infect X with one's mirth, *communiquer sa gaîté à X*. In French *infecter* means always 'to pollute', 'to contaminate'.
infectieu-x, -se (ɛ̃fɛksjø), adj. Infectious, contagious.
infection (ɛ̃fɛksjɔ̃), s.f. Infection, contagion, corruption; stench; (fig., pej.) moral contagion.
inféodation (ɛ̃feɔda'sjɔ̃), s.f. Infeudation, enfeoffment; (fig.) subjection.
inféoder (ɛ̃feɔde), v.a. To enfeoff; **s'~** (*à*), v.pr. to give oneself (to); to attach oneself (to).
infère (ɛ̃fɛr), adj. (bot.) Lower.
inférence (ɛ̃ferɑ̃s), s.f. Inference.
inférer (ɛ̃fere), v.a. [f. L *in+ferre*] To infer (*de*, from).
inférieur, -e (ɛ̃ferjœr), adj. [L *inferior*] Inferior, lower, under; *vallée ~e*, lower valley; nether, subordinate, petty; *de qualité ~e*, of inferior quality. ~, s.m. Inferior, subaltern.
inférieurement (ɛ̃ferjœrmɑ̃), adv. In an inferior manner, in a low degree.
infériorité (ɛ̃ferjɔrite), s.f. Inferiority.
infernal, -e, (aux) (ɛ̃fɛrnal), adj. [L *infernalis*] Infernal, hellish; *pierre ~e*, lunar caustic; *machine ~e*, bomb, infernal machine.
infernalement (ɛ̃fɛrnalmɑ̃), adv. Infernally.
infertile (ɛ̃fɛrtil), adj. Infertile, barren.
infertilité (ɛ̃fɛrtilite), s.f. Infertility; barrenness, aridity.
infester (ɛ̃fɛste), v.a. [L *infestare*] To infest, to haunt, to spoil, to invade, to raid; *maison infestée de rats*, house swarming with rats.
infidèle (ɛ̃fidɛl), adj. Unfaithful, faithless, false, disloyal, inaccurate; unbelieving. ~, s.m. Infidel, unbeliever; unfaithful (person).
infidèlement (ɛ̃fidɛlmɑ̃), adv. Unfaithfully, untruly, inaccurately.
infidélité (ɛ̃fidelite), s.f. Infidelity, un-

faithfulness, faithlessness; inaccuracy; *faire des ~s à X*, to be unfaithful to X.
infiltration (ɛ̃filtra'sjɔ̃), s.f. Infiltration.
(s')infiltrer (sɛ̃filtre), v.pr. To infiltrate, to percolate; (fig.) to spread, to creep.
infime (ɛ̃fim), adj. [L *infimus*] Lowest, extremely trifling.
infini, -e (ɛ̃fini), adj. Infinite, boundless, endless, numberless. ~, s.m. Infinite, infinity; *à l'~*, to infinity, endlessly, ad infinitum.
infiniment (ɛ̃finimɑ̃), adv. Infinitely, endlessly, exceedingly; (math.) ~ *petit*, infinitesimal.
infinité (ɛ̃finite), s.f. Infinity, infiniteness, infinitude; multitude; (colloq.) no end (of).
infinitésimal, -e, (aux) (ɛ̃finitezimal), adj. Infinitesimal.
infiniti-f, -ve (ɛ̃finitif), adj. s.m. [f. L *infinitivus*] (gram.) Infinitive; *à l'~*, in the infinitive.
infirmati-f, -ve (ɛ̃firmatif), adj. Invalidating, annulling.
infirmation (ɛ̃firma'sjɔ̃), s.f. Invalidation, annulment.
infirme (ɛ̃firm), adj. [f. L *in+firmus*] Infirm, crippled. ~, s.m.f. Cripple, invalid.
infirmer (ɛ̃firme), v.a. To invalidate, to nullify; to weaken, to quash.
infirmerie (ɛ̃firməri), s.f. Infirmary, sick-ward.
infirmi-er, -ère (ɛ̃firmje), s.m.f. Hospital attendant, (fem.) nurse.
infirmité (ɛ̃firmite), s.f. Infirmity, weakness, failing, chronic disease.
inflammabilité (ɛ̃flamabilite), s.f. Inflammability.
inflammable (ɛ̃flamabl), adj. Inflammable; (fig., iron.) passionate, easily falling in love.
inflammation (ɛ̃flama'sjɔ̃), s.f. Inflammation.
inflammatoire (ɛ̃flamatwar), adj. Inflammatory.
inflation (ɛ̃fla'sjɔ̃), s.f. [f. L *in+flare*] Inflation.
infléchir (ɛ̃fleʃir), v.a. To inflect, to bend; s'~, v.pr. to be inflected, to bend.
inflexibilité (ɛ̃flɛksibilite), s.f. Inflexibility.
inflexible (ɛ̃flɛksibl), adj. Inflexible, unbending, unrelenting, inexorable.
inflexiblement (ɛ̃flɛksibləmɑ̃), adv. Inflexibly, inexorably.
inflexion (ɛ̃flɛksjɔ̃), s.f. Inflection, inflexion, bend; modulation (of voice).
infliger (ɛ̃fliʒe), v.a. [L *in+fligere*] To inflict, to impose.
inflorescence (ɛ̃flɔrɛsɑ̃s), s.f. Inflorescence.
influençable (ɛ̃flɥɑ̃sabl), adj. Easily influenced.
influence (ɛ̃flɥɑ̃s), s.f. [f. *influer*] Influence, authority, power, sway, action; *avoir de l'~ sur X*, to have influence over X; *avoir quelque ~*, to be influential.
influencer (ɛ̃flɥɑ̃se), v.a. To influence, to sway.
influent, -e (ɛ̃flɥɑ̃), adj. Influential.
influenza (ɛ̃flɥɛnza), s.f. [It. wd] Influenza, flu.
influer (ɛ̃flɥe), v.n. [f. L *in+fluere*] To exert influence (*sur*, on); ~ *sur*, to influence.
influx (ɛ̃fly), s.m. Influx.
in-folio (infɔljo, ɛ̃fɔljo), s.m. adj. invar. [L wd] Folio.
informat-eur, -rice (ɛ̃fɔrmatœr), s.m.f. Informer, informant. ~, adj. Informing.
information (ɛ̃fɔrma'sjɔ̃), s.f. Information, news; inquiry; inquest; *aller aux ~s*, *prendre des ~s*, to make inquiries. ⚠ English 'information' also = *dénonciation, accusation*.
informe (ɛ̃fɔrm), adj. Shapeless, formless, misshapen; imperfect; (law) informal.
informé (ɛ̃fɔrme), s.m. (law) Inquiry; *jusqu'à plus ample ~*, until further inquiry has been made.
informer (ɛ̃fɔrme), v.a. [L *in+formare*] To inform, to tell, to acquaint; s'~, v.pr. to inquire, to investigate; ~, v.n. (law) to institute an inquiry.
infortune (ɛ̃fɔrtyn), s.f. Misfortune, adversity.
infortuné, -e (ɛ̃fɔrtyne), adj. Unfortunate, ill-fated.
infraction (ɛ̃fraksjɔ̃), s.f. [f. L *infringere*] Infraction, infringement, breach.
infranchissable (ɛ̃frɑ̃ʃisabl), adj. Impassable, insurmountable.
infra-rouge (ɛ̃fraruʒ), adj. (opt.) Infrared.
infrastructure (ɛ̃frastryktyr), s.f. Infrastructure.
infréquenté, -e (ɛ̃frekɑ̃te), adj. Unfrequented.
infructueusement (ɛ̃fryktɥøzmɑ̃), adv. In vain, to no purpose, fruitlessly.
infructueu-x, -se (ɛ̃fryktɥø), adj. Vain, unfruitful, fruitless, unavailing, unsuccessful.
infumable (ɛ̃fymabl), adj. Unsmokable.
infus, -e (ɛ̃fy), adj. [L *infusus*] Inborn, innate, intuitive.
infuser (ɛ̃fyze), v.a. [f. L *infundere*] To infuse; to steep; s'~, v.pr. (of tea) to draw, to be infused.
infusible (ɛ̃fyzibl), adj. Infusible, unmeltable.
infusion (ɛ̃fyzjɔ̃), s.f. Infusion.
infusoires (ɛ̃fyzwar), s.m.pl. [f. L *infusus*] Infusoria.
ingambe (ɛ̃gɑ̃b), adj. [f. It. *gamba*] Brisk, alert, nimble, agile.
(s')ingénier (sɛ̃ʒenje), v.pr. [f. L *ingenium*]

To tax one's ingenuity, to set one's wits to work, to contrive.
ingénieur (ɛ̃ʒenjœr), s.m. Engineer; ~ *des Arts et Manufactures*, civil engineer; ~ *des constructions navales*, naval architect, shipbuilder; ~ *des mines*, mining engineer; ~ *des ponts et chaussées*, civil engineer (under government) for bridges and roads, in France.
ingénieusement (ɛ̃ʒenjøzmɑ̃), adv. Ingeniously, cleverly, adroitly.
ingénieu-x, -se (ɛ̃ʒenjø), adj. [L *ingeniosus*] Ingenious, clever, adroit, witty, well contrived.
ingéniosité (ɛ̃ʒenjozite), s.f. Ingenuity (⚠ see INGÉNUITÉ); clever contrivance; *mécanisme d'une grande* ~, very cleverly contrived mechanism.
ingénu, -e (ɛ̃ʒeny), adj. [L *ingenuus*] Ingenuous, candid, guileless, unsophisticated. **~es**, s.f. (theatr.) *Jouer les ~es*, to act the part of the very young unsophisticated girl.
ingénuité (ɛ̃ʒenɥite), s.f. Ingenuousness, candour, frankness, openness, artlessness. ⚠ *Ingénuité* cannot be translated by 'ingenuity' which = *ingéniosité*.
ingénument (ɛ̃ʒenymɑ̃), adv. Ingenuously, candidly, artlessly.
ingérence (ɛ̃ʒerɑ̃s), s.f. Meddling, interference.
ingérer (ɛ̃ʒere), v.a. [L *in+gerere*] To ingest; **s'~**, v.pr. to interfere, to meddle (*dans*, with).
ingestion (ɛ̃ʒɛstjɔ̃), s.f. Ingestion.
inglorieusement (ɛ̃glɔrjøzmɑ̃), adv. Ingloriously.
inglorieu -x, -se (ɛ̃glɔrjø), adj. Inglorious.
ingouvernable (ɛ̃guvɛrnabl), adj. Ungovernable, unruly.
ingrat, -e (ɛ̃gra), adj. [L *ingratus*] Ungrateful, unthankful; thankless; unprofitable; unpromising, sterile, unpleasant. **~**, s.m.f. Ungrateful person, ingrate.
ingratitude (ɛ̃gratityd), s.f. Ingratitude, ungratefulness, thanklessness; unprofitableness.
ingrédient (ɛ̃gredjɑ̃), s.m. [L *ingrediens*] Ingredient.
inguéable (ɛ̃geabl), adj. [f. *gué*] Unfordable.
inguérissable (ɛ̃gerisabl), adj. Incurable.
inguinal, -e, (aux) (ɛ̃gɥinal), adj. [f. L *inguinis*] Inguinal.
ingurgitation (ɛ̃gyrʒita'sjɔ̃), s.f. Ingurgitation.
ingurgiter (ɛ̃gyrʒite), v.a. [f. L *gurges*] To ingurgitate.
inhabile (inabil), adj. Unskilful, unskilled, inexpert; (law) unqualified, disqualified, incompetent.
inhabilement (inabilmɑ̃), adv. Unskilfully, awkwardly.
inhabileté (inabilte), s.f. Unskilfulness; inability, incompetence.
inhabilité (inabilite), s.f. (law) Incompetency, disability.
inhabitable (inabitabl), adj. Uninhabitable. ⚠ English 'inhabitable' = French *habitable*.
inhabité, -e (inabite), adj. Uninhabited.
inhabitude (inabityd), s.f. Want of habit.
inhalateur (inalatœr), s.m. Inhalator.
inhalation (inala'sjɔ̃), s.f. Inhalation.
inhaler (inale), v.a. [L *in+halare*] To inhale.
inharmonie (inarmɔni), s.f. Lack of harmony.
inharmonieu-x, -se (inarmɔnjø), adj. Inharmonious, discordant.
inhérence (inerɑ̃s), s.f. Inherence.
inhérent, -e (inerɑ̃), adj. [L *inhaerens*] Inherent.
inhibition (inibisjɔ̃), s.f. [f. L *inhibere*] Inhibition.
inhospitali-er, -ère (inɔspitalje), adj. Inhospitable, forbidding, unfriendly.
inhumain, -e (inymɛ̃), adj. Inhuman, cruel. **~e**, s.f. Cruel fair one.
inhumainement (inymɛnmɑ̃), adv. Inhumanely.
inhumanité (inumanite), s.f. Inhumanity, cruelty.
inhumation (inyma'sjɔ̃), s.f. Burial, inhumation, interment.
inhumer (inyme), v.a. [f. L *in+humus*] To bury, to inhume, to inter.
inimaginable (inimaʒinabl), adj. Unimaginable, inconceivable.
inimitable (inimitabl), adj. Inimitable.
inimitié (inimitje), s.f. [L *inimicitia*] Enmity, feud, hatred, aversion; *avoir de l'~ pour X*, to bear enmity towards X, to have an aversion to, or for, X.
ininflammable (inɛ̃flamabl), adj. Uninflammable.
inintelligemment (inɛ̃tɛliʒamɑ̃), adv. Unintelligently.
inintelligence (inɛ̃tɛliʒɑ̃s), s.f. Lack of intelligence.
inintelligent, -e (inɛ̃tɛliʒɑ̃), adj. Unintelligent.
inintelligible (inɛ̃tɛliʒibl), adj. Unintelligible.
inintentionnellement (inɛ̃tɑ̃sjɔnɛlmɑ̃), adv. Unintentionally.
ininterrompu, -e (inɛ̃tɛrɔ̃py), adj. Uninterrupted, unbroken.
inique (inik), adj. [f. L *in+aequus*] Iniquitous.
iniquement (inikmɑ̃), adv. Iniquitously.
iniquité (inikite), s.f. Iniquity, sin, unrighteousness; injustice, inequity.
initial, -e, (aux) (inisjal), adj. [f. L *initium*] Initial. **~e**, s.f. Initial, initial letter.

initiat-eur, -rice (inisjatœr), s.m.f. Initiator. ~, adj. Initiating.
initiation (inisja'sjɔ̃), s.f. Initiation.
initiative (inisjativ), s.f. Initiative; *prendre l'~*, to take the initiative.
initié, -e (inisje), p. adj. Initiated. ~, s.m.f. Initiate, one of the initiated.
initier (inisje), v.a. [L *initiare*] To initiate, to teach, to admit. ⚠ English 'initiate' also = *entreprendre, mettre en train, provoquer.*
injecté, -e (ɛ̃ʒɛkte), p. adj. Bloodshot, injected.
injecter (ɛ̃ʒɛkte), v.a. [L *injicere*] To inject; **s'~**, v.pr. to become bloodshot; to inject oneself (with).
inject-eur, -rice (ɛ̃ʒɛktœr), adj. Injecting. ~, s.m. Injector.
injection (ɛ̃ʒɛksjɔ̃), s.f. Injection.
injonction (ɛ̃ʒɔ̃ksjɔ̃), s.f. [L *injunctio*] Injunction, order; *faire ~ à X*, to enjoin upon X.
injouable (ɛ̃ʒuabl), adj. Unplayable, unactable.
injure (ɛ̃ʒyr), s.f. [L *injuria*] Injury, insult, wrong, offence, abuse; *dire des ~s à X*, to abuse X; *faire ~ à X*, to wrong X.
injurier (ɛ̃ʒyrje), v.a. To abuse, to call names, to revile. ⚠ Not 'to injure' which = *blesser, endommager, nuire à.*
injurieu-x, -se (ɛ̃ʒyrjø), adj. Injurious, insulting, abusive.
injuste (ɛ̃ʒyst), adj. Unjust, unfair, wrong, undeserved, unequal.
injustement (ɛ̃ʒystəmɑ̃), adv. Unjustly, unfairly, wrongly, undeservedly.
injustice (ɛ̃ʒystis), s.f. Injustice, wrong, act of injustice.
injustifiable (ɛ̃ʒystifjabl), adj. Unjustifiable, unwarrantable.
injustifié, -e (ɛ̃ʒystifje), adj. Unjustified, unwarranted.
inlassable (ɛ̃lɑsabl), adj. Untirable, indefatigable.
innavigable (innavigabl), adj. Innavigable.
inné, -e (inne), adj. [L *innatus*] Innate, inborn.
innégociable (innegɔsjabl), adj. Not negotiable.
innéité (inneite), s.f. Innateness.
innervation (innɛrva'sjɔ̃), s.f. Innervation.
innerver (innɛrve), v.a. To innervate.
innocemment (inɔsamɑ̃), adv. Innocently, candidly; foolishly.
innocence (inɔsɑ̃s), s.f. Innocence, guiltlessness; artlessness, purity, candid simplicity.
innocent, -e (inɔsɑ̃), adj. [L *in*+*nocens*] Innocent, guiltless, harmless, not guilty; pure and candid; unsophisticated, simple, foolish; weak-minded. ~, s.m. Innocent person; person not guilty; simpleton, idiot; babe, infant; *faire l'~*, to sham innocence, to play the fool.
innocenter (inɔsɑ̃te), v.a. To declare innocent, to find not guilty, to acquit.
innocuité (inɔkɥite), s.f. Innocuousness, harmlessness.
innombrable (innɔ̃brabl), adj. Innumerable, numberless.
innomé, -e (innɔme), adj. See INNOMMÉ.
innominé, -e (innɔmine), adj. [f. L *nomen*] Nameless, unnamed; innominate.
innommable (innɔmabl), adj. Unspeakable, foul, disgusting, unmentionable.
innommé, -e (innɔme), adj. Nameless, unnamed; innominate.
innovat-eur, -rice (innɔvatœr), s.m.f. Innovator. ~, adj. Innovating.
innovation (innɔva'sjɔ̃), s.f. Innovation.
innover (innɔve), v.n. [L *innovare*] To innovate, to make innovations.
inobservance (inɔpsɛrvɑ̃s), s.f. Non-observance, neglect.
inobservation (inɔpsɛrva'sjɔ̃), s.f. Non-observance, breach, non-execution.
inobservé, -e (inɔpsɛrve), adj. Unnoticed, unobserved, overlooked.
inoccupation (inɔkypa'sjɔ̃), s.f. Inoccupation.
inoccupé, -e (inɔkype), adj. Unoccupied, idle, unemployed; empty, vacant.
in-octavo (inɔktavo), s.m. adj. invar. [f. L *in*+*octavus*] Octavo, 8vo.
inoculable (inɔkylabl), adj. Inoculable.
inoculation (inɔkyla'sjɔ̃), s.f. Inoculation.
inoculer (inɔkyle), v.a. [L *inoculare*] To inoculate.
inodore (inɔdɔr), adj. Inodorous, scentless, free from smell.
inoffensi-f, -ve (inɔfɑ̃sif), adj. Inoffensive, harmless.
inofficieu-x, -se (inɔfisjø), adj. (law) Inofficious.
inondation (inɔ̃da'sjɔ̃), s.f. Inundation, deluge, flood, overflow; (fig.) multitude.
inonder (inɔ̃de), v.a. [L *inundare*] To inundate, to flood, to deluge, to overflow; to drench; (fig.) to overspread, to overwhelm.
inopérant, -e (inɔperɑ̃), adj. Inoperative.
inopiné, -e (inɔpine), adj. [f. L *opinari*] Unexpected, sudden.
inopinément (inɔpinemɑ̃), adv. Unexpectedly, suddenly, unawares.
inopportun, -e (inɔpɔrtœ̃), adj. Inopportune, untimely.
inopportunité (inɔpɔrtynite), s.f. Inopportuneness, unseasonableness.
inorganique (inɔrganik), adj. Inorganic.
inoubliable (inublijabl), adj. Unforgettable.
inouï, -e (inwi), adj. [*in*+*ouï*] Unheard of, unprecedented; extraordinary.
inoxydable (inɔksidabl), adj. Inoxidizable, rustless.

in petto (inpɛtto), adv. [It. wds] Inwardly.
inqualifiable (ɛ̃kalifjabl), adj. Unqualifiable, for which no name is too bad.
inquart (ɛ̃kar), s.m. **inquartation** (ɛ̃karta'sjɔ̃), **quartation** (karta'sjɔ̃), s.f. Quartation.
in-quarto (inkwarto, ɛ̃kwarto), s.m. adj. invar. [f. L *quartus*] Quarto, 4to.
inqui-et, -ète (ɛ̃kjɛ), adj. [*in*+L *quietus*] Uneasy, disquieted, anxious, restless, fidgety.
inquiétant, -e (ɛ̃kjetɑ̃), p. adj. Disquieting, alarming.
inquiéter (ɛ̃kjete), v.a. To disquiet, to alarm, to make uneasy, to trouble, to worry; **s'~**, v.pr. to make oneself uneasy, to be anxious, to fret, to chafe, to worry.
inquiétude (ɛ̃kjetyd), s.f. Disquiet, disquietude, anxiety, uneasiness, concern; restlessness, fidgets; *avoir des ~s*, to be uneasy; *donner de l'~*, to cause anxiety, to make uneasy; *soyez sans ~ à ce sujet*, make yourself easy on that score.
inquisiteur (ɛ̃kizitœr), s.m. Inquisitor. ~, adj. Inquisitive.
inquisition (ɛ̃kizisjɔ̃), s.f. [L *inquisitio*] Inquisition.
inquisitorial, -e, (aux) (ɛ̃kizitɔrjal), adj. Inquisitorial.
insaisissable (ɛ̃sɛzisabl), adj. **1.** Unseizable, not distrainable; **2.** imperceptible, indiscernible.
insalubre (ɛ̃salybr), adj. Insalubrious, unhealthy, unwholesome.
insalubrité (ɛ̃salybrite), s.f. Insalubrity, unhealthiness, unwholesomeness.
insanité (ɛ̃sanite), s.f. [f. L *insanus*] Insanity, madness; foolish speech, idiocy.
insapide (ɛ̃sapid), adj. See INSIPIDE.
insatiabilité (ɛ̃sasjabilite), s.f. Insatiability.
insatiable (ɛ̃sasjabl), adj. [L *insatiabilis*] Insatiable, unquenchable.
insatiablement (ɛ̃sasjabləmɑ̃), adv. Insatiably.
insciemment (ɛ̃sjamɑ̃), adv. Unknowingly, unconsciously.
inscription (ɛ̃skripsjɔ̃), s.f. [L *inscriptio*] Inscription, inscribing, writing; registration, matriculation, entry, record; ~ *hypothécaire*, registry of mortgage; ~ *maritime*, divisions of seamen liable to be called up for service; *prendre ses ~s*, to enter for the term; (approxim. = to matriculate).
inscrire (ɛ̃skrir), v.a. To inscribe, to write down, to enter, to register, to set down; (geom.) to inscribe; **s'~**, v.pr. to inscribe one's name, to matriculate, to enter one's name; *s'~ en faux contre*, to deny the truth of, to protest against. ⚠ English 'to inscribe a book to X' = *dédier un livre à X*.
inscrit, -e (ɛ̃skri), p. adj. (geom.) Inscribed. ~ (*maritime*), s.m. Seaman liable to be called up for service.
inscrutable (ɛ̃skrytabl), adj. Inscrutable.
insecte (ɛ̃sɛkt), s.m. [L *insectum*] Insect.
insecticide (ɛ̃sɛktisid), adj. s.m. [f. L *insectum*+*caedere*] Insect-destroying, insecticide.
insectivore (ɛ̃sɛktivɔr), adj. [f. L *insectum*+*vorare*] Insectivorous. ~, s.m. Insectivore.
insécurité (ɛ̃sekyrite), s.f. Insecurity.
in-seize (insɛz, ɛ̃sɛz), s.m. adj. invar. Sixteen-mo, 16mo.
insensé, -e (ɛ̃sɑ̃se), adj. Insane, senseless, mad, absurd, extravagant.
insensibilisat-eur, -rice (ɛ̃sɑ̃sibilizatœr), adj. s.m. Anaesthetic.
insensibilisation (ɛ̃sɑ̃sibiliza'sjɔ̃), s.f. Anaesthesia.
insensibiliser (ɛ̃sɑ̃sibilize), v.a. To anaesthetize.
insensibilité (ɛ̃sɑ̃sibilite), s.f. Insensibility, unconsciousness, unfeelingness, callousness; anaesthesia.
insensible (ɛ̃sɑ̃sibl), adj. Insensible; unconscious, unfeeling, callous; imperceptible.
insensiblement (ɛ̃sɑ̃sibləmɑ̃), adv. Insensibly, gradually, by degrees, imperceptibly.
inséparabilité (ɛ̃separabilite), s.f. Inseparableness.
inséparable (ɛ̃separabl), adj. Inseparable; ~, s.m.f. (colloq.) love-bird.
inséparablement (ɛ̃separabləmɑ̃), adv. Inseparably.
insérer (ɛ̃sere), v.a. [f. L *in*+*serere*] To insert, to put in; to print.
insermenté (ɛ̃sɛrmɑ̃te), adj. m. Recusant, unsworn.
insertion (ɛ̃sɛrsjɔ̃), s.f. Insertion.
insidieusement (ɛ̃sidjøzmɑ̃), adv. Insidiously.
insidieu-x, -se (ɛ̃sidjø), adj. [L *insidiosus*] Insidious.
insigne (ɛ̃siɲ), adj. [L *insignis*] Signal, notorious, arrant.
insigne (ɛ̃siɲ), s.m. Badge, token, insignia (pl.); (slang) tag.
insignifiance (ɛ̃siɲifjɑ̃s), s.f. Insignificance.
insignifiant, -e (ɛ̃siɲifjɑ̃), adj. Insignificant, that does not matter.
insinuant, -e (ɛ̃sinɥɑ̃), p. adj. Insinuating, persuasive.
insinuation (ɛ̃sinɥa'sjɔ̃), s.f. Insinuation, hint, suggestion, innuendo.
insinuer (ɛ̃sinɥe), v.a. [L *insinuare*] To insinuate; to hint, to suggest; **s'~**, v.pr. to insinuate oneself, to worm one's way; to steal (into).
insipide (ɛ̃sipid), adj. [L *insipidus*] Insipid, tasteless; dull, flat.

insipidité (ɛ̃sipidite), s.f. Insipidity, tastelessness, dullness.

insistance (ɛ̃sistɑ̃s), s.f. Insistence, persistence.

insister (ɛ̃siste), v.n. [L *in+sistere*] To insist, to persist, to dwell, to lay stress (*sur*, on).

insociabilité (ɛ̃sɔsjabilite), s.f. Unsociableness.

insociable (ɛ̃sɔsjabl), adj. Unsociable.

insolation (ɛ̃sɔla'sjɔ̃), s.f. [L *insolatio*] Insolation, sunstroke.

insolemment (ɛ̃sɔlamɑ̃), adv. Insolently, saucily, impudently.

insolence (ɛ̃sɔlɑ̃s), s.f. Insolence, sauciness, rudeness.

insolent, -e (ɛ̃sɔlɑ̃), adj. [L *insolens*] Insolent, saucy, rude; unheard of, extraordinary. ~, s.m.f. Insolent fellow or person.

insolite (ɛ̃sɔlit), adj. [L *in+solitus*] Unusual, unwonted.

insolubilité (ɛ̃sɔlybilite), s.f. Insolubility.

insoluble (ɛ̃sɔlybl), adj. (chem.) Insoluble; insolvable, unsolvable, irresolvable; that cannot be solved or explained.

insolvabilité (ɛ̃sɔlvabilite), s.f. Insolvency.

insolvable (ɛ̃sɔlvabl), adj. Insolvent. ⚠ Not English 'insolvable' which = *insoluble.*

insomnie (ɛ̃sɔmni), s.f. [f. L *in+somnus*] Sleeplessness, insomnia.

insondable (ɛ̃sɔ̃dabl), adj. Unfathomable.

insouciamment (ɛ̃susjamɑ̃), adv. Carelessly.

insouciance (ɛ̃susjɑ̃s), s.f. [f. *souci*] Carelessness, heedlessness, unconcern.

insouciant, -e (ɛ̃susjɑ̃), adj. Careless, heedless, unmindful, regardless.

insoucieu-x, -se (ɛ̃susjø), adj. Careless, regardless, free from care.

insoumis, -e (ɛ̃sumi), adj. Refractory, unsubdued, unruly. ~, s.m. (mil.) Defaulter.

insoumission (ɛ̃sumisjɔ̃), s.f. Insubordination.

insoupçonnable (ɛ̃supsɔnabl), adj. Above suspicion.

insoupçonné, -e (ɛ̃supsɔne), adj. Unsuspected.

insoutenable (ɛ̃sutnabl), adj. Indefensible, untenable, unbearable.

inspecter (ɛ̃spɛkte), v.a. [L *inspectare*] To inspect, to survey, to scan.

inspect-eur, -rice (ɛ̃spɛktœr), s.m.f. Inspector, (fem.) inspectress; surveyor, superintendent; visitor.

inspection (ɛ̃spɛksjɔ̃), s.f. Inspection, survey; inspectorship, surveyorship; *faire l'~ de*, to examine, to inspect.

inspirat-eur, -rice (ɛ̃spiratœr), s.m.f. Inspirer. ~, adj. Inspiring; (anat.) inspiratory.

inspiration (ɛ̃spira'sjɔ̃), s.f. Inspiration; suggestion; *quelle bonne ~!*, what a capital idea!; (physiol.) inhaling, inspiration.

inspiré, -e (ɛ̃spire), p. adj. s.m.f. Inspired (person), prophet.

inspirer (ɛ̃spire), v.a. [L *inspirare*] **1.** To inspire, to suggest, to instil; to advise, to incite, to urge; **2.** to inhale, to inspire; **s'~** (*de*), v.pr. to draw one's inspiration (from), to imitate.

instabilité (ɛ̃stabilite), s.f. Instability, want of stability; fickleness, changeableness, unsteadiness.

instable (ɛ̃stabl), adj. Unstable, unsteady; fickle.

installation (ɛ̃stalasjɔ̃), s.f. Installation; fitting up; establishment; (U.S.A.) fixings.

installer (ɛ̃stale), v.a. [f. *stalle*] To install; to fit up; to establish, to inaugurate; to settle, to place; to fix; **s'~**, v.pr. to establish oneself, to take up one's abode, to settle, to put up (at an hotel).

instamment (ɛ̃stamɑ̃), adv. Earnestly, eagerly.

instance (ɛ̃stɑ̃s), s.f. [L *instantia*] Entreaty, instance, instancy, solicitation; *avec ~*, earnestly, pressingly; *se rendre aux ~s de X*, to yield to X's entreaties; (law) instance; *tribunal de première ~*, court of first instance, inferior court; *être en ~ de divorce*, to be in process of obtaining a divorce. ⚠ In French *instance* has never the sense of *exemple* = example, which is common in English.

instant, -e (ɛ̃stɑ̃), adj. [L *instans*] Instant, urgent, pressing, eager; imminent.

instant (ɛ̃stɑ̃), s.m. Instant, moment, *à l'~*, instantly, at once; *dans un ~*, in a few minutes; in a moment; *en un ~*, in a trice; *à tout ~*, continually, frequently; *d'un ~ à l'autre*, at any time, imminently; *un ~!*, stop; wait a bit; that won't do!; *dès l'~ que*, since.

instantané, -e (ɛ̃stɑ̃tane), adj. Instantaneous. ~, s.m. (photo.) Snapshot.

instantanéité (ɛ̃stɑ̃taneite), s.f. Instantaneousness.

instantanément (ɛ̃stɑ̃tanemɑ̃), adv. Instantaneously, in an instant, without delay, in a trice; syn. SUR-LE-CHAMP.

(à l')instar (de) (alɛ̃stardə), prep. loc. [L *instar*] Like, in imitation of, after, after the fashion of.

instauration (ɛ̃stɔra'sjɔ), s.f. Establishment.

instaurer (ɛ̃store), v.a. [L *instaurare*] To establish, to found.

instigat-eur, -rice (ɛ̃stigatœr), s.m.f. [f. L *instigare*] Instigator, inciter.

instigation (ɛ̃stiga'sjɔ̃), s.f. Instigation, suggestion, incitement; *agir à l'~ de X*, to act at X's instigation.

instiguer (ɛ̃stige), v.a. (rare) [L *instigare*] To instigate, to incite.

instillation (ɛ̃stila'sjɔ̃), s.f. Instillation.

instiller (ɛ̃stile), v.a. [L *instillare*] To instil.

instinct (ɛ̃stɛ̃), s.m. [L *instinctus*] Instinct; *d'~*, *par ~*, instinctively.
instincti-f, -ve (ɛ̃stɛ̃ktif), adj. Instinctive.
instinctivement (ɛ̃stɛ̃ktivmɑ̃), adv. Instinctively.
instituer (ɛ̃stitɥe), v.a. [L *instituere*] To institute, to establish, to found, to settle.
institut (ɛ̃stity), s.m. Institute, institution; (religious) order; *l'Institut*, the five French Academies.
institutes (ɛ̃stityt), s.f.pl. (Justinian's) Institutes.
institut-eur, -rice (ɛ̃stitytœr) [L *institutor*] Teacher, schoolmaster; (fem.) schoolmistress (in elementary schools); governess.
institution (ɛ̃stitysjɔ̃), s.f. Institution, foundation, establishment; boarding-school, seminary, academy; organized society, established order, law and customs.
instructeur (ɛ̃stryktœr), adj. s.m. Instructing, instructor; *sergent ~*, drill-sergeant.
instructi-f, -ve (ɛ̃stryktif), adj. Instructive.
instruction (ɛ̃stryksjɔ̃), s.f. [L *instructio*] **1.** Instruction, tuition, education, teaching; knowledge, learning; *manquer d'~*, to be wanting in education; to be uneducated; *avoir beaucoup d'~*, to be learned; **2.** direction, instructions, orders; *donner des ~s*, to give directions; **3.** (law) examination, inquiry; *juge d'~*, examining magistrate, coroner.
instruire (ɛ̃strɥir), v.a. [L *instruere*] To instruct, to teach, to educate, to train; (law) to examine, to investigate; **s'~**, v.pr. to learn, to study, to improve oneself.
instruit, -e (ɛ̃strɥi), p. adj. Well educated, learned, well informed.
instrument (ɛ̃strymɑ̃), s.m. [L *instrumentum*] Instrument, implement, tool; agent; deed, treaty, document; *~s aratoires*, agricultural implements; (mus.) *~ à cordes*, stringed instruments; *~s à vent*, wind instruments; *servir d'~*, to be instrumental, to be the agent.
instrumentaire (ɛ̃strymɑ̃tɛr), adj. (law) To or of a deed or legal instrument.
instrumental, -e, (aux) (ɛ̃strymɑ̃tal), adj. Instrumental, pertaining to musical instruments. ⚠ *Instrumental* in French usually means 'pertaining to musical instruments'; the sense of 'agent-', 'used to an end', is rare and old; *instrumental* has never in French the sense of 'useful' 'efficacious' =*utile, efficace*, which, though obsolete, is to be met with in English literature.
instrumentation (ɛ̃strymɑ̃ta'sjɔ̃), s.f. (mus.) Instrumentation.
instrumenter (ɛ̃strymɑ̃te), v.a. (mus.) To instrument; ~, v.n. **1.** to compose instrumental music (syn. ORCHESTRER); **2.** (law) to instrument, to draw up instruments, deeds; to proceed.
instrumentiste (ɛ̃strymɑ̃tist), s.m.f. Instrumentalist, musician.
insu (ɛ̃sy), s.m. [*in+su*] Unknowingness, unawareness; *à l'~ de X*, unknown to X.
insubmersible (ɛ̃sybmɛrsibl), adj. Unsinkable, insubmergible.
insubordination (ɛ̃sybɔrdina'sjɔ̃), s.f. Insubordination.
insubordonné, -e (ɛ̃sybɔrdɔne), adj. Insubordinate.
insuccès (ɛ̃syksɛ), s.m. Failure, want of success, miscarriage.
insuffisamment (ɛ̃syfizamɑ̃), adv. Insufficiently.
insuffisance (ɛ̃syfizɑ̃s), s.f. Insufficiency, deficiency, incompetency.
insuffisant, -e (ɛ̃syfizɑ̃), adj. Insufficient, deficient, incompetent, inadequate.
insufflation (ɛ̃syfla'sjɔ̃), s.f. Insufflation, inflation.
insuffler (ɛ̃syfle), v.a. [L *insufflare*] To insufflate.
insulaire (ɛ̃sylɛr), adj. [f. L *insula*] Insular. ~, s.m.f. Islander, insular.
insularité (ɛ̃sylarite), s.f. Insularity.
insultant, -e (ɛ̃syltɑ̃), p. adj. Insulting, abusive.
insulte (ɛ̃sylt), s.f. Insult, affront; *faire une ~ à X*, to offer an insult to X, to insult X; *souffrir une ~*, to brook an insult; *laver une ~*, to take vengeance for an insult, to wipe out an affront.
insulter (ɛ̃sylte), v.a.n. [L *insultare*] To insult, to offer an insult.
insulteur (ɛ̃syltœr), s.m. Insulter, offender.
insupportable (ɛ̃sypɔrtabl), adj. Insupportable, insufferable, unbearable.
insupportablement (ɛ̃sypɔrtabləmɑ̃), adv. Insupportably, insufferably, unbearably.
insurgé, -e (ɛ̃syrʒe), s.m.f. p. adj. Insurgent.
(s')insurger (sɛ̃syrʒe), v.pr. [L *in+surgere*] To rebel, to revolt, to rise in insurrection.
insurmontable (ɛ̃syrmɔ̃tabl), adj. Insurmountable, insuperable, unconquerable.
insurrection (ɛ̃syrɛksjɔ̃), s.f. Insurrection, rising, revolt, mutiny.
insurrectionnel, -le (ɛ̃syrɛksjɔnɛl), adj. Insurrectional, insurrectionary.
intact, -e (ɛ̃takt), adj. [L *intactus*] Intact, untouched, entire, unblemished, whole, inviolate.
intaille (ɛ̃taj), s.f. [f. It. *intagliare*] Intaglio.
intangibilité (ɛ̃tɑ̃ʒibilite), s.f. Intangibility.

intangible (ɛ̃tɑ̃ʒibl), adj. [LL *intangibilis*] Intangible.
intarissable (ɛ̃tarisabl), adj. Inexhaustible.
intarissablement (ɛ̃tarisabləmɑ̃), adv. Inexhaustibly.
intégrable (ɛ̃tegrabl), adj. (math.) Integrable, that may be integrated.
intégral, -e, (aux) (ɛ̃tegral), adj. [f. L *integer*] Integral, whole, entire; (math.) integral. **~e**, s.f. (math.) Integral.
intégralement (ɛ̃tegralmɑ̃), adv. Integrally, wholly, in full.
intégralité (ɛ̃tegralite), s.f. Integrality, wholeness, completeness.
intégrant, -e (ɛ̃tegrɑ̃), p. adj. Integrant, integral; *faire partie ~e de*, to be an integral part of; (colloq.) to be part and parcel of.
intégration (ɛ̃tegra'sjɔ̃), s.f. (math.) Integration.
intègre (ɛ̃tɛgr), adj. [L *integer*] Upright, honest.
intègrement (ɛ̃tɛgrəmɑ̃), adv. Honestly, uprightly.
intégrer (ɛ̃tegre), v.a. To integrate.
intégrité (ɛ̃tegrite), s.f. Integrity, honesty, probity, uprightness; soundness, entireness.
intellect (ɛ̃tɛlɛkt), s.m. [L *intellectus*] Intellect, understanding, brains.
intellecti-f, -ve (ɛ̃tɛlɛktif), adj. Intellective.
intellectuel, -le (ɛ̃tɛlɛktɥɛl), adj. s.m. Intellectual.
intellectuellement (ɛ̃tɛlɛktɥɛlmɑ̃), adv. Intellectually.
intelligemment (ɛ̃tɛliʒamɑ̃), adv. Intelligently, cleverly.
intelligence (ɛ̃tɛliʒɑ̃s), s.f. [L *intelligentia*] Intelligence, understanding, brains, cleverness, skill, ability; means of information, secret correspondence; *avoir des ~s avec l'ennemi*, to hold secret intercourse with the enemy; *avoir des ~s dans la place*, to have one's own means of information; to have spies on the spot; *vivre en bonne ~ avec X*, to live, or to be, on good terms, or on friendly terms, with X; *être d'~ avec X*, to be in league with X; to be hand and glove with X; *~ bornée*, narrow understanding. ⚠ English 'intelligence' also = *renseignements, information*; ex.: Intelligence officer, *officier du Service des Renseignements*.
intelligent, -e (ɛ̃tɛliʒɑ̃), adj. Intelligent, quick, clever, sharp, shrewd.
intelligibilité (ɛ̃tɛliʒibilite), s.f. Intelligibility.
intelligible (ɛ̃tɛliʒibl), adj. Intelligible, distinct, clear; *à haute et ~ voix*, aloud and distinctly.
intelligiblement (ɛ̃tɛliʒibləmɑ̃), adv. Intelligibly, distinctly.
intempérance (ɛ̃tɑ̃perɑ̃s), s.f. Intemperance, excess.
intempérant, -e (ɛ̃tɑ̃perɑ̃), adj. [L *intemperans*] Intemperate.
intempéré, -e (ɛ̃tɑ̃mpere), adj. Ill-regulated.
intempérie (ɛ̃tɑ̃peri), s.f. (usually in the pl.) [L *in+temperies*] Inclemency (of the weather).
intempesti-f, -ve (ɛ̃tɑ̃pɛstif), adj. [L *intempestivus*] Intempestive, unseasonable, untimely.
intempestivement (ɛ̃tɑ̃pɛstivmɑ̃), adv. Unseasonably, inopportunely.
intenable (ɛ̃tənabl), adj. Untenable.
intendance (ɛ̃tɑ̃dɑ̃s), s.f. Management, direction, intendancy, (mil.) commissariat.
intendant, -e (ɛ̃tɑ̃dɑ̃), s.m.f. [f. L *intendens*] Intendant, manager, steward, commissioner, comptroller, (mil.) commissariat officer.
intense (ɛ̃tɑ̃s), adj. [L *intensus*] Intense, extreme, vehement, strained, excessive.
intensi-f, -ve (ɛ̃tɑ̃sif), adj. Intensive.
intensité (ɛ̃tɑ̃site), s.f. Intensity, violence, severity.
intenter (ɛ̃tɑ̃te), v.a. [L *intentare*] To bring (an action).
intention (ɛ̃tɑ̃sjɔ̃), s.f. [L *intentio*] Intention, intent, purpose, design; *à l'~ de X*, on X's account; for X's sake; *avec ~*, intentionally, on purpose; *dans l'~ de*, with a view to; *avoir l'~ de*, to intend to; *l'enfer est pavé de bonnes ~s*, hell is paved with good intentions.
intentionné, -e (ɛ̃tɑ̃sjɔne), adj. Intentioned, disposed, meaning; *mal ~*, ill-intentioned, evil-disposed, evil-minded; *bien ~*, well-meaning.
intentionnel, -le (ɛ̃tɑ̃sjɔnɛl), adj. Intentional; done, said, &c. on purpose.
intentionnellement (ɛ̃tɑ̃sjɔnɛlmɑ̃), adv. Intentionally, purposely, on purpose, with a definite purpose, purposefully.
intercadence (ɛ̃tɛrkadɑ̃s), s.f. (med.) Irregular beating of the pulse.
intercalaire (ɛ̃tɛrkalɛr), adj. Intercalary.
intercalation (ɛ̃tɛrkala'sjɔ̃), s.f. Intercalation.
intercaler (ɛ̃tɛrkale), v.a. [L *intercalare*] To intercalate, to interpolate, to interpose, to insert.
intercéder (ɛ̃tɛrsede), v.n. [L *intercedere*] To intercede.
intercepter (ɛ̃tɛrsɛpte), v.a. [f. L *intercipere*] To intercept.
interception (ɛ̃tɛrsɛpsjɔ̃), s.f. Interception, intercepting.
intercesseur (ɛ̃tɛrsɛsœr), s.m. Intercessor, interceder (*auprès de*, with).
intercession (ɛ̃tɛrsɛsjɔ̃), s.f. Intercession.
interchangeable (ɛ̃tɛrʃɑ̃ʒabl), adj. Interchangeable.

intercostal, -e, (aux) (ɛ̃tɛrkɔstal), adj. [f. L *inter+costa*] (anat.) Intercostal.
interdiction (ɛ̃tɛrdiksjɔ̃), s.f. [L *interdictio*] Interdiction, prohibition; deprivation (of rights); *frapper d'~*, to lay under an interdict.
interdire (ɛ̃tɛrdir), v.a. [L *interdicere*] (conjugated like *dire*, except in 2nd pers. pl. indic. and imper. *interdisez*] To interdict, to prohibit, to refuse, to forbid, to suspend; to lay under an interdict; to confound, to nonplus, to dumbfound, to stun.
interdit (ɛ̃tɛrdi), s.m. Interdict; person interdicted; *frapper X d'~*, to lay X under an interdict.
interdit, -e (ɛ̃tɛrdi), p. adj. **1.** Interdicted; **2.** abashed, nonplussed, speechless, dumbfounded, stunned, overwhelmed.
intéressant, -e (ɛ̃terɛsɑ̃), p. adj. **1.** Interesting; **2.** deserving pity and help; **3.** (colloq.) *être dans une position ~e*, to be with child, to be pregnant, (pop.) to be in the family way, to be in an interesting condition.
intéressé, -e (ɛ̃terɛse), p. adj. **1.** Interested, concerned, having an interest (in). **~, -e**, s.m.f. Interested party; *les ~s*, those concerned; **2.** adj. covetous, mercenary, miserly; *motif ~*, selfish motive.
intéresser (ɛ̃terɛse), v.a.n. [f. *intérêt*] **1.** To interest; **2.** to give an interest or share to; **3.** to concern, to affect; **s'~**, v.pr. to take an interest (*à*, in); to be concerned.
intérêt (ɛ̃terɛ), s.m. [L *interest*] Interest; concern, share; *~s composés*, compound interest; *avoir ~ à*, to have an interest in; *avoir un ~ en jeu*, to have an axe to grind; *j'ai ~ à rester*, it's to my advantage to stay; *prendre les ~s de X*, to defend X's interests; *mettre X dans mes ~s*, to bring X into my interest, or on to my side; *dommages et ~s*, damages; *livre dénué d'~*, thoroughly uninteresting book.
interférence (ɛ̃tɛrferɑ̃s), s.f. (phys.) Interference.
interférer (ɛ̃tɛrfere), v.n. [L *inter+ferre*] (phys.) To interfere.
interfolier (ɛ̃tɛrfɔlje), v.a. [f. L *inter+folium*] To interleave (a book, &c.).
intérieur, -e (ɛ̃terjœr), adj. [L *interior*] Interior, inner, internal, inward, inside; inland; *la vie ~e*, the inner life.
intérieur (ɛ̃terjœr), s.m. Inside, interior, inner part; home, private life; inland part of a country; *à l'~*, inside, indoors, inwards, inland; *être un homme d'~*, to be a family man; *se plaire dans son ~*, to be fond of one's home; *à l'~ de la voiture*, inside; *une ville de l'~*, an inland town; *Ministre de l'Intérieur*, Home Secretary; *tableau d'~*, scene of home life, interior.
intérieurement (ɛ̃terjœrmɑ̃), adv. Internally, inwardly, within.
intérim (ɛ̃terim), s.m. [L wd] Interim; *par ~*, ad interim; *dans l'~*, meanwhile.
intérimaire (ɛ̃terimɛr), adj. Temporary, ad interim. **~**, s.m.f. Interim functionary.
interjection (ɛ̃tɛrʒɛksjɔ̃), s.f. Interjection; (law) lodging (of an appeal).
interjeter (ɛ̃tɛrʒəte), v.a. [*inter+jeter*] (law) To lodge (an appeal).
interligne (ɛ̃tɛrliɲ), s.m. Space between two lines; interlining; **~**, s.f. (print.) lead, space between lines.
interligner (ɛ̃tɛrliɲe), v.a. To interline; (print.) to space out, to lead.
interlinéaire (ɛ̃tɛrlineɛr), adj. Interlinear; interlineal.
interlocut-eur, -rice (ɛ̃tɛrlɔkytœr), s.m.f. [f. L *inter+locutum*] Interlocutor, speaker.
interlocutoire (ɛ̃tɛrlɔkytwar), adj. Interlocutory. **~**, s.m. Interlocutory decree or judgement.
interlope (ɛ̃tɛrlɔp), adj. [f. Engl. *interloper*] **1.** Interloping, intruding, meddling; contraband; **2.** equivocal, of bad repute, of the underworld, flash. ⚠ Sense No. **2** is the more usual in French; in English the sense corresponding to No. **1** is the only one for the subst. 'interloper'.
interloquer (ɛ̃tɛrlɔke), v.a. [f. L *interloqui*] (law) To subject to an interlocutory decree; to nonplus, to disconcert.
intermède (ɛ̃tɛrmɛd), s.m. [It. *intermedio*] Interlude; (chem.) intermediate, medium.
intermédiaire (ɛ̃tɛrmedjɛr), adj. [f. L *intermedium*] Intermediate, intervening, interposed. **~**, s.m.f. Intermediary, middle-man, agent, medium, go-between; *par l'~ de*, through the medium of.
interminable (ɛ̃tɛrminabl), adj. Interminable, endless; *quel discours ~!*, what a long-winded speech!
interminablement (ɛ̃tɛrminabləmɑ̃), adv. Endlessly.
intermittence (ɛ̃tɛrmitɑ̃s), s.f. Intermission, intermittence; *par ~s*, intermittently.
intermittent, -e (ɛ̃tɛrmitɑ̃), adj. [f. L *intermittere*] Intermittent.
internat (ɛ̃tɛrna), s.m. **1.** Boarding-school; state of being a boarder; **2.** office of house-surgeon (in a French hospital).
international, -e, (aux) (ɛ̃tɛrnasjɔnal), adj. International.
internationalisme (ɛ̃tɛrnasjɔnalism), s.m. Internationalism.
interne (ɛ̃tɛrn), adj. [L *internus*] Internal, inward, interior, resident. **~**, s.m.f. Boarder (at school); *~ d'hôpital*, house-surgeon (of a hospital).
internement (ɛ̃tɛrnəmɑ̃), s.m. Internment.
interner (ɛ̃tɛrne), v.a. [f. *interne*] To intern, to confine within the limits (of town, country, or lunatic asylum).

internissable (ɛ̃tɛrnisabl), adj. Untarnishable.
internonce (ɛ̃tɛrnɔ̃s), s.m. Internuncio.
interpellat-eur, -rice (ɛ̃tɛrpɛlatœr), s.m.f. Interpellator, questioner.
interpellation (ɛ̃tɛrpɛlaˈsjɔ̃), s.f. Interpellation; (in parliament) question; summons; apostrophe, call.
interpeller (ɛ̃tɛrpɛle), v.a. To interpellate, to question, to summon; to put a question to; to call, to apostrophize.
interpolation (ɛ̃tɛrpolaˈsjɔ̃), s.f. Interpolation.
interpoler (ɛ̃tɛrpole), v.a. [L *interpolare*] To interpolate.
interposer (ɛ̃tɛrpoze), v.a. To interpose; **s'~**, v.pr. to interpose, to come forward.
interposition (ɛ̃tɛrpozisjɔ̃), s.f. Interposition, intervention.
interprétation (ɛ̃tɛrpretaˈsjɔ̃), s.f. Interpretation, construction, explanation, rendering; *donner une mauvaise* or *fausse ~ à mes paroles*, to misconstrue my words; *~ originale*, original rendering.
interprète (ɛ̃tɛrprɛt), s.m.f. Interpreter.
interpréter (ɛ̃tɛrprete), v.a. [f. L *interpretari*] To interpret, to expound, to construe; to render.
interrègne (ɛ̃tɛrrɛɲ), s.m. [L *interregnum*] Interregnum.
interrogant, -e (ɛ̃tɛrɔgɑ̃), adj. Inquisitive.
interrogat-eur, -rice (ɛ̃tɛrɔgatœr), adj. Interrogative, questioning, searching. **~**, s.m.f. Interrogator, questioner, examiner.
interrogati-f, -ve (ɛ̃tɛrɔgatif), adj. Interrogative; (law) interrogatory.
interrogation (ɛ̃tɛrɔgaˈsjɔ̃), s.f. Interrogation; *point d'~*, point, note, or mark of interrogation.
interrogativement (ɛ̃tɛrɔgativmɑ̃), adv. Interrogatively, questioningly.
interrogatoire (ɛ̃tɛrɔgatwar), s.m. Examination, interrogatory.
interroger (ɛ̃tɛrɔʒe), v.a. [L *interrogare*] To interrogate, to examine, to cross-examine, to question; **s'~**, v.pr. to examine oneself; to question each other.
interrompre (ɛ̃tɛrɔ̃pr), v.a. [L *interrumpere*] To interrupt; to stop, to suspend, to cut off, to break in upon; **s'~**, v.pr. to break off, to stop.
interrupt-eur, -rice (ɛ̃tɛryptœr), s.m.f. Interrupter; (electr.) switch, contact-breaker. **~**, adj. Interrupting.
interruption (ɛ̃tɛrypsjɔ̃), s.f. Interruption.
intersection (ɛ̃tɛrsɛksjɔ̃), s.f. Intersection.
interstellaire (ɛ̃tɛrstɛlɛr), adj. Interstellar.
interstice (ɛ̃tɛrstis), s.m. [L *interstitium*] Interstice, chink, crevice.
interstitiel, -le (ɛ̃tɛrstisjɛl), adj. Interstitial.
intertropical, -e, (aux) (ɛ̃tɛrtrɔpikal), adj. Intertropical.
intervalle (ɛ̃tɛrval), s.m. [L *intervallum*] Interval; interstice, gap; meantime; *par ~s*, at intervals; *dans l'~*, (between two dates) in the meantime.
intervenant, -e (ɛ̃tɛrvənɑ̃), p. adj. Intervening. **~**, s.m.f. Intervening party.
intervenir (ɛ̃tɛrvənir), v.n. [L *intervenire*] To intervene, to interfere, to interpose, to act as mediator; to occur, to happen; (law) to interplead.
intervention (ɛ̃tɛrvɑ̃sjɔ̃), s.f. Intervention, interference, mediation.
interversion (ɛ̃tɛrvɛrsjɔ̃), s.f. Inversion, reversal, change of order.
intervertir (ɛ̃tɛrvɛrtir), v.a. [f. L *inter+vertere*] To invert, to change the order of, to reverse.
interview (ɛ̃tɛrvju), s.f. and m. [Engl. wd] Interview.
intestat (ɛ̃tɛsta), s.m. adj. invar. [L *intestatus*] Intestate.
intestin (ɛ̃tɛstɛ̃), s.m. [L *intestinum*] Intestine, bowel, gut; *~ grêle*, small intestine; *gros ~*, large intestine.
intestin, -e (ɛ̃tɛstɛ̃), adj. Intestine, internal, domestic, civil.
intestinal,- e, (aux) (ɛ̃tɛstinal), adj. Intestinal.
intimation (ɛ̃timaˈsjɔ̃), s.f. Notification, notice, intimation. ⚠ English 'intimation' also = *insinuation, suggestion*.
intime (ɛ̃tim), adj. [L *intimus*] Intimate, inmost, deep, secret, confidential, private; *ami ~*, intimate friend; *la nature ~ des choses*, the inward, or essential, nature of things.
intimé, -e (ɛ̃time), s.m.f. adj. (law) Appellee, defendant.
intimement (ɛ̃timəmɑ̃), adv. Intimately, privately, deeply, closely, familiarly.
intimer (ɛ̃time), v.a. [L *intimare*] To notify, to enjoin, to give notice of appeal to.
intimidant, -e (ɛ̃timidɑ̃), p. adj. Intimidating.
intimidation (ɛ̃timidaˈsjɔ̃), s.f. Intimidation.
intimider (ɛ̃timide), v.a. [f. LL *in+timidare*] To intimidate; to scare, to browbeat; **s'~**, v.pr. or *se laisser ~*, to be easily intimidated.
intimité (ɛ̃timite), s.f. Intimacy, close connexion; *dans l'~*, in the home, privately, informally, in a simple way.
intitulé, -e (ɛ̃tityle), p. adj. Entitled. **~**, s.m. Title.
intituler (ɛ̃tityle), v.a. [f. L *in+titulus*] To entitle, to name; **s'~**, v.pr. to call oneself.
intolérable (ɛ̃tɔlerabl), adj. Intolerable, unbearable.
intolérablement (ɛ̃tɔlerabləmɑ̃), adv. Intolerably.

intolérance (ɛ̃tɔlerɑ̃s), s.f. Intolerance.
intolérant, -e (ɛ̃tɔlerɑ̃), adj. Intolerant.
intolérantisme (ɛ̃tɔlerɑ̃tism), s.m. Intoleration, intolerance.
intonation (ɛ̃tɔna'sjɔ̃), s.f. [f. L *in*+*tonus*] Intonation.
intoxication (ɛ̃tɔksika'sjɔ̃), s.f. Intoxication, poisoning. ⚠ English 'intoxication' also = *ivresse, griserie, enivrement.*
intoxiquer (ɛ̃tɔksike), v.a. [L *intoxicare*] To intoxicate; **s'~**, v.pr. to intoxicate oneself, to drug oneself, to indulge in narcotics, alcohol, &c.
intrados (ɛ̃trado), s.m. (arch.) Intrados.
intraduisible (ɛ̃tradɥizibl), adj. Untranslatable.
intraitable (ɛ̃trɛtabl), adj. Unmanageable, intractable, headstrong, unruly, unyielding.
intra-muros (ɛ̃tramyros), adv. loc. [L wd] Within the walls, within the town.
intransigeance (ɛ̃trɑ̃ziʒɑ̃s), s.f. Uncompromisingness, irreconcilableness, intolerance.
intransigeant, -e (ɛ̃trɑ̃ziʒɑ̃), adj. [f. L *transigere*] Intransigent, uncompromising, intolerant.
intransiti-f, -ve (ɛ̃trɑ̃zitif), adj. (gram.) Intransitive.
intransportable (ɛ̃trɑ̃sportabl), adj. Untransportable, too ill to be moved.
in-trente-deux (intrɑ̃tdø, ɛ̃trɑ̃tdø), s.m. adj. invar. Trigesimo-secundo, 32mo.
intrépide (ɛ̃trepid), adj. [f. L *trepidus*] Intrepid, dauntless, fearless, undaunted.
intrépidement (ɛ̃trepidmɑ̃), adv. Intrepidly, fearlessly.
intrépidité (ɛ̃trepidite), s.f. Intrepidity, fearlessness.
intrigant, -e (ɛ̃trigɑ̃), s.m.f. Schemer, wire-puller, intriguer. ~, adj. Intriguing, scheming.
intrigue (ɛ̃trig), s.f. [f. L *intricare*; It. *intrigo*] Intrigue; plot (of a novel, play, &c.).
intriguer (ɛ̃trige), v.n.a. To intrigue, to plot; to puzzle, to perplex, to arouse the curiosity of.
intrinsèque (ɛ̃trɛ̃sɛk), adj. [L *intrinsecus*] Intrinsic.
intrinsèquement (ɛ̃trɛ̃sɛkmɑ̃), adv. Intrinsically.
introduct-eur, -rice (ɛ̃trɔdyktœr), s.m.f. Introducer, usher, gentleman usher.
introducti-f, -ve (ɛ̃trɔdyktif), adj. Introductive, (law) introductory.
introduction (ɛ̃trɔdyksjɔ̃), s.f. Introduction; preamble; introducing.
introduire (ɛ̃trɔdɥir), v.a. [L *introducere*] To introduce, to put in, to insert, to thrust in; to show in, to introduce, to usher in, to let in, to bring in; **s'~**, v.pr. to introduce oneself, to creep in, to worm oneself in.
introït (intrɔit), s.m. [L *introitus*] Introit.
intronisation (ɛ̃trɔniza'sjɔ̃), s.f. Enthroning, enthronement.
introniser (ɛ̃trɔnize), v.a. [f. *trône*] To enthrone; to establish.
introuvable (ɛ̃truvabl), adj. Not to be got or found; matchless.
intrus, -e (ɛ̃try), adj. [L *intrusus*] Intruding. ~, s.m.f. Intruder, interloper, unwanted or unwelcome person.
intrusion (ɛ̃tryzjɔ̃), s.f. Intrusion, intruding.
intuiti-f, -ve (ɛ̃tɥitif), adj. Intuitive.
intuition (ɛ̃tɥisjɔ̃), s.f. [f. L *in*+*tueri*] Intuition.
intuitivement (ɛ̃tɥitivmɑ̃), adv. Intuitively.
intumescence (ɛ̃tymɛssɑ̃s), s.f. Intumescence.
intumescent, -e (ɛ̃tymɛssɑ̃), adj. [L *intumescens*] Intumescent, swelling up.
intussusception (ɛ̃tysysɛpsjɔ̃), s.f. [L *intus*+*susceptio*] (physiol.) Intussusception.
inule (inyl), s.f. [L *inula*] (bot.) Inula, elecampane.
inusable (inyzabl), adj. Everlasting, that will not wear out; of everlasting wear.
inusité (inyzite), adj. Unusual, not in use, rare.
inutile (inytil), adj. Useless, of no use, unnecessary, needless, vain, no good; good for nothing, worthless; ~ *de vous dire que*, needless to say; I need not say that.
inutilement (inytilmɑ̃), adv. Uselessly, vainly, in vain, needlessly, to no purpose.
inutilisé, -e (inytilize), adj. Inutilized, not made use of.
inutilité (inytilite), s.f. Inutility, uselessness; useless thing.
invaincu, -e (ɛ̃vɛ̃ky), adj. Unvanquished, unconquered.
invalidation (ɛ̃valida'sjɔ̃), s.f. Invalidation.
invalide (ɛ̃valid), adj. [L *invalidus*] Invalid, infirm, disabled. ~, s.m.f. Invalid, cripple; military or naval pensioner.
invalidement (ɛ̃validmɑ̃), adv. Invalidly.
invalider (ɛ̃valide), v.a. To invalidate; (naut.) to invalid; (law) to nullify.
invalidité (ɛ̃validite), s.f. Invalidity; (law) nullity.
invariabilité (ɛ̃varjabilite), s.f. Invariability.
invariable (ɛ̃varjabl), adj. Invariable.
invariablement (ɛ̃varjabləmɑ̃), adv. Invariably.
invasion (ɛ̃va'zjɔ̃), s.f. [f. L *invasio*] Invasion, invading, inroad, irruption; encroachment.
invective (ɛ̃vɛktiv), s.f. [f. L *invectivus*] Invective, abuse.
invectiver (ɛ̃vɛktive), v.a.n. To revile, to inveigh (*contre*, against).

invendable (ɛ̃vɑ̃dabl), adj. Unsaleable.
invendu, -e (ɛ̃vɑ̃dy), adj. Unsold.
inventaire (ɛ̃vɑ̃tɛr), s.m. [L *inventarium*] Inventory, stock-taking; *faire l'~*, to take stock, to take an inventory (*de*, of); *sous bénéfice d'~*, without liability for debts beyond the assets of the estate; (fig.) only if it pays to do it.
inventer (ɛ̃vɑ̃te), v.a. [f. L *invenire, inventum*] To invent, to devise, to contrive, to imagine, to fabricate; *il n'a pas inventé la poudre*, or *il n'a pas inventé la ficelle à couper le beurre*, he will never set the Thames on fire.
inventeur (ɛ̃vɑ̃tœr), s.m. Inventor.
inventi-f, -ve (ɛ̃vɑ̃tif), adj. Inventive.
invention (ɛ̃vɑ̃sjɔ̃), s.f. Invention, discovery, contrivance; fabrication, device; inventiveness, ingenuity; fiction, untruth; *brevet d'~*, patent; *quelle ~ !*, what a fib !
inventorier (ɛ̃vɑ̃tɔrje), v.a. To inventory, to draw up an inventory of, to catalogue.
inversable (ɛ̃vɛrsabl), adj. That cannot be upset.
inverse (ɛ̃vɛrs), adj. [L *inversus*] Inverse, inverted; contrary; *en sens ~*, in the opposite direction. ~, s.m. Reverse; *à l'~ de*, contrariwise to; counter to; *en raison ~ de*, in inverse ratio to.
inversement (ɛ̃vɛrsəmɑ̃), adv. Inversely.
inversion (ɛ̃vɛrsjɔ̃), s.f. Reversal; (gram.) inversion.
invertébré, -e (ɛ̃vɛrtebre), adj. s.m. Invertebrate.
invertir (ɛ̃vɛrtir), v.a. [L *in+vertere*] To invert, to reverse.
investigat-eur, -rice (ɛ̃vɛstigatœr), adj. Investigating, searching, scrutinizing. ~, s.m.f. Investigator, inquirer.
investigation (ɛ̃vɛstiga'sjɔ̃), s.f. [L *investigatio*] Investigation, research, inquiry, scrutiny.
investir (ɛ̃vɛstir), v.a. [L *investire*] To invest; to surround.
investissement (ɛ̃vɛstismɑ̃), s.m. Investment (♤ only in the mil. sense).
investiture (ɛ̃vɛstityr), s.f. Investiture.
invétéré, -e (ɛ̃vetere), p. adj. [f. L *in+veterare*] Inveterate, confirmed, arrant.
(s')invétérer (sɛ̃vetere), v.pr. To grow inveterate.
invincibilité (ɛ̃vɛ̃sibilite), s.f. Invincibleness, invincibility.
invincible (ɛ̃vɛ̃sibl), adj. [L *invincibilis*] Invincible; unconquerable, insurmountable.
invinciblement (ɛ̃vɛ̃sibləmɑ̃), adv. Invincibly.
inviolabilité (ɛ̃vjɔlabilite), s.f. Inviolability.
inviolable (ɛ̃vjɔlabl), adj. [L *inviolabilis*] Inviolable.
inviolablement (ɛ̃vjɔlabləmɑ̃), adv. Inviolably.
invisibilité (ɛ̃vizibilite), s.f. Invisibility, invisibleness.
invisible (ɛ̃vizibl), adj. [L *in+visibilis*] Invisible.
invisiblement (ɛ̃viziblәmɑ̃), adv. Invisibly.
invitation (ɛ̃vita'sjɔ̃), s.f. Invitation.
invite (ɛ̃vit), s.f. Card played to indicate to partner what his lead should be (at bridge); (fig.) inducement, suggestion, incentive, incitement; hint.
invité, -e (ɛ̃vite), s.m.f. Guest, invited guest.
inviter (ɛ̃vite), v.a. [L *invitare*] To invite, to beg, to request; to engage; to incite, to induce, to allure; *~ à dîner*, to ask to dinner; *cela invite au sommeil*, this invites sleep, or induces sleep.
invocation (ɛ̃vɔka'sjɔ̃), s.f. Invocation.
invocatoire (ɛ̃vɔkatwar), adj. Invocatory.
involontaire (ɛ̃vɔlɔ̃tɛr), adj. Involuntary.
involontairement (ɛ̃vɔlɔ̃tɛrmɑ̃), adv. Involuntarily.
involucre (ɛ̃vɔlykr), s.m. [L *involucrum*] (bot.) Involucre.
involution (ɛ̃vɔlysjɔ̃), s.f. [L *involutio*] Involution.
invoquer (ɛ̃vɔke), v.a. [L *invocare*] To invoke, to cry to, to appeal to, to implore, to call for.
invraisemblable (ɛ̃vrɛsɑ̃blabl), adj. Unlikely, improbable, unbelievable.
invraisemblablement (ɛ̃vrɛsɑ̃blabləmɑ̃), adv. Improbably, unlikely.
invraisemblance (ɛ̃vrɛsɑ̃blɑ̃s), s.f. Unlikelihood, improbability; unlikely thing.
invulnérabilité (ɛ̃vylnerabilite), s.f. Invulnerability.
invulnérable (ɛ̃vylnerabl), adj. [f. L *invulnerabilis*] Invulnerable.
iode (jɔd), s.m. [f. Gr. *iōdēs*] Iodine; *teinture d'~*, tincture of iodine.
ioder (jɔde), v.a. To iodize.
iodeux (jɔdø), adj. (chem.) Iodous.
iodhydrique (jɔdidrik), adj. (chem.) Hydriodic.
iodifère (jɔdifɛr), adj. Iodiferous.
iodler (jɔdle), v.n.a. See IOULER.
iodoforme (jɔdɔfɔrm), s.m. Iodoform.
iodure (jɔdyr), s.m. (chem.) Iodide.
ioduré, -e (jɔdyre), adj. Combined or impregnated with iodine.
ion (jɔ̃), s.m. [Gr. wd] Ion.
ionien, -ne (jɔnjɛ̃), adj. s.m.f. Ionian.
ionique (jɔnik), adj. Ionic; *l'ordre ~*, the Ionic order.
ionisation (jɔniza'sjɔ̃), s.f. Ionization.
ionone (jɔnɔn), s.f. (chem.) Ionone.
iota (jɔta), s.m. [Gr. letter] Iota; (fig.) jot, iota, tittle.
iotacisme (jɔtasism), s.m. Iotacism.
iouler (jule), v.n.a. [onom.] To yodel; syn. JODLER.

ipécacuanha (ipekakɥana) (also **ipéca**), s.m. (pharm.) Ipecacuanha.
iradé (irade), s.m. [Turk. wd] Irade, written decree of the Sultan.
iranien, -ne (iranjɛ̃), adj. s.m.f. Iranian.
irascibilité (irassibilite), s.f. Irascibility.
irascible (irassibl), adj. [L *irascibilis*] Irascible.
ire (ir), s.f. (obs.) [L *ira*] Wrath, anger, ire.
iridectomie (iridɛktɔmi), s.f. [f. Gr. *iris*+ *ektomē*] (surg.) Iridectomy.
iridées (iride), s.f.pl. (bot.) Iridaceae.
iridescent, -e (iridɛssɑ̃), adj. Iridescent.
iridium (iridjɔm), s.m. (chem.) Iridium.
iris (iris), s.m. [Gr. wd] (bot.) Iris; rainbow; (anat.) iris.
irisation (iriza'sjɔ̃), s.f. Irisation, iridescence.
irisé, -e (irize), adj. Irisated, iridescent, rainbow-coloured.
iriser (irize), v.a. To give the colours of the rainbow to; **s'~**, v.pr. to become iridescent.
irlandais, -e (irlɑ̃dɛ), adj. s.m.f. Irish, Irishman, Irishwoman, Irish language.
ironie (irɔni), s.f. [f. Gr. *eirōneia*] Irony.
ironique (irɔnik), adj. Ironical.
ironiquement (irɔnikmɑ̃), adv. Ironically.
ironiste (irɔnist), s.m.f. Ironist.
iroquois, -e (irɔkwɑ), adj. s.m.f. Iroquois; (fig.) rum one, queer fish.
irrachetable (irraʃtabl), adj. Irredeemable.
irradiation (irradjasjɔ̃), s.f. Irradiation.
irradier (irradje), v.a. [L *irradiare*] To irradiate, to radiate.
irraisonnable (irrɛzɔnabl), adj. See DÉRAISONNABLE.
irraisonné, -e (irrɛzɔne), adj. Unreasoning, spontaneous.
irrationnel, -le (irrasjɔnɛl), adj. Irrational; (math.) irrational.
irréalisable (irrealizabl), adj. Unrealizable, irrealizable, unattainable, unfeasible.
irrecevabilité (irrəsəvabilite), s.f. Inadmissibility.
irrecevable (irrəsəvabl), adj. Inadmissible, that cannot be accepted.
irréconciliable (irrekɔ̃siljabl), adj. Irreconcilable.
irrécouvrable (irrekuvrabl), adj. Irrecoverable.
irrécusable (irrekyzabl) Irrecusable, unexceptionable.
irrécusablement (irrekyzabləmɑ̃), adv. Irrecusably.
irréductibilité (irredyktibilite), s.f. Irreducibility.
irréductible (irredyktibl), adj. Irreducible.
irréel, -le (irreɛl), adj. Unreal.
irréfléchi, -e (irrefleʃi), adj. Thoughtless, inconsiderate, unguarded.
irréflexion (irreflɛksjɔ̃), s.f. Thoughtlessness.
irréfragable (irrefragabl), adj. Irrefragable; irrefutable.
irréfutable (irrefytabl), adj. Irrefutable.
irréfutablement (irrefytabləmɑ̃), adv. Irrefutably.
irrégularité (irregylarite), s.f. Irregularity, unevenness.
irréguli-er, -ère (irregylje), adj. Irregular.
irrégulièrement (irregyljɛrmɑ̃), adv. Irregularly.
irréligieu-x, -se (irreliʒjø), adj. Irreligious.
irréligion (irreliʒjɔ̃), s.f. Irreligion.
irrémédiable (irremedjabl), adj. Irremediable, irretrievable.
irrémédiablement (irremedjabləmɑ̃), adv. Irremediably, irretrievably.
irrémissible (irremisibl), adj. Irremissible, unpardonable.
irrémissiblement (irremisibləmɑ̃), adv. Irremissibly.
irréparable (irreparabl), adj. Irreparable, irretrievable.
irréparablement (irreparabləmɑ̃), adv. Irreparably, irretrievably.
irrépréhensible (irrepreɑ̃sibl), adj. Irreprehensible, unimpeachable.
irrépressible (irreprɛsibl), adj. Irrepressible.
irréprochable (irreprɔʃabl), adj. Irreproachable, unexceptionable.
irréprochablement (irreprɔʃabləmɑ̃), adv. Irreproachably.
irrésistible (irrezistibl), adj. Irresistible.
irrésistiblement (irrezistibləmɑ̃), adv. Irresistibly.
irrésolu, -e (irrezɔly), adj. Irresolute, wavering.
irrésolution (irrezɔlysjɔ̃), s.f. Irresolution, indecision.
irrespectueusement (irrɛspɛktɥøzmɑ̃), adv. Disrespectfully.
irrespectueu-x, -se (irrɛspɛktɥø), adj. Disrespectful.
irrespirable (irrɛspirabl), adj. Unbreathable.
irresponsabilité (irrɛspɔ̃sabilite), s.f. Irresponsibility.
irresponsable (irrɛspɔ̃sabl), adj. Irresponsible.
irrétrécissable (irretresisabl), adj. Unshrinkable.
irrévérence (irreverɑ̃s), s.f. Irreverence; (colloq.) cheek.
irrévérencieusement (irreverɑ̃sjøzmɑ̃), adv. Irreverently, disrespectfully.
irrévérencieu-x, -se (irreverɑ̃sjø), adj. Irreverent, disrespectful, cheeky.
irrévocable (irrevɔkabl), adj. Irrevocable.
irrévocablement (irrevɔkabləmɑ̃), adv. Irrevocably.

irrigable (irigabl), adj. Irrigable.
irrigateur (irigatœr), s.m. Watering-engine; irrigator, enema, syringe.
irrigation (iriga'sjɔ̃), s.f. Irrigation.
irriguer (irige), v.a. [f. L *irrigare*] To irrigate.
irritabilité (iritabilite), s.f. Irritability, irritableness, touchiness.
irritable (iritabl), adj. Irritable, touchy.
irritant, -e (iritɑ̃), p. adj. Irritating, provoking; (med.) irritant. ~, s.m. Irritant.
irritation (irita'sjɔ̃), s.f. Irritation.
irriter (irite), v.a. [L *irritare*] To irritate, to annoy, to vex, to provoke, to anger, to incense; to inflame.
irroration (irrɔra'sjɔ̃), s.f. [f. L *irrorare*] Irroration, bedewing, dew-bath.
irruption (irrypsjɔ̃), s.f. [f. L *irruptum*] Irruption, invasion, violent entry; *faire ~ dans*, to invade; to burst into.
isabelle (izabɛl), adj. [f. prop. n. *Isabelle*] Isabel-coloured, dun-coloured. ~, s.m. Isabel (colour).
isard (izar), s.m. (zool.) Izard, chamois of the Pyrenees.
isatis (izatis), s.m. [etym. dub.] (zool.) Isatis, blue fox, arctic fox.
isba (isba), s.f. [Russ. wd] Isba.
ischémie (iskemi), s.f. [f. Gr. *iskhein*+*haima*] Ischaemia.
ischiatique (iskjatik), adj. (anat.) Ischiatic, sciatic.
ischion (iskjɔ̃), s.m. [Gr. wd] (anat.) Ischium, ischion.
ischurie (iskyri), s.f. [f. Gr. *iskhein*+*ouron*] Ischuria.
isiaque (izjak), adj. Isiac; pertaining to Isis.
islam (islam), s.m. [Arab. wd] Islam.
islamique (islamik), adj. Islamic.
islamisme (islamism), s.m. Islamism.
islamite (islamit), adj. s.m.f. Islamite.
islandais, -e (islɑ̃dɛ), adj. Icelandic. ~, s.m.f. Icelander; Icelandic (language).
ismaélite (ismaelit), s.m.f. Ishmaelite. ~, adj. Ishmaelitic.
isobare (izɔbar), **isobarique** (izɔbarik), adj. [f. Gr. *isos*+*baros*] (meteor.) Isobar, isobaric, isobarometric.
isocèle (izɔsɛl), adj. [Gr. *isoskelēs*] Isosceles.
isochimène (izɔkimɛn), adj. [f. Gr. *isos*+*kheimainein*] Isochimenal.
isochromatique (izɔkrɔmatik), adj. [f. Gr. *isos*+*khrōma*] Isochromatic.
isochrone (izɔkron), adj. [f. Gr. *isos*+*khronos*] Isochronal, isochronous.
isocline (izɔklin), adj. [f. Gr. *isos*+*klei-nein*] Isoclinal.
isogone (izɔgɔn), adj. [f. Gr. *isos*+*gōnia*] Isogonic.
isolant, -e (izɔlɑ̃), p. adj. Insulating. ~, s.m. Insulator.
isolat-eur, -rice (izɔlatœr), adj. Insulating. ~, s.m. Insulator.
isolation (izɔla'sjɔ̃), s.f. Insulation. ⚠ English 'isolation' = *isolement*.
isolé, -e (izɔle), p. adj. Isolated, lonely, solitary; (electr.) insulated.
isolement (izɔlmɑ̃), s.m. **1.** Loneliness, isolation, solitude; *vivre dans l'~*, to live in retirement; **2.** (electr.) insulation.
isolément (izɔlemɑ̃), adv. Separately; solitarily.
isoler (izɔle), v.a. [f. It. *isolare*] To isolate, to separate, to cut off, to seclude, to segregate; (electr.) to insulate.
isoloir (izɔlwar), s.m. **1.** Insulator; **2.** polling booth.
isomère (izɔmɛr), adj. [f. Gr. *isos*+*meros*] Isomeric.
isomorphe (izɔmɔrf), adj. [f. Gr. *isos*+*morphē*] Isomorphous.
isoscèle (izɔsɛl), adj. See ISOCÈLE.
isotherme (izɔtɛrm), adj. [f. Gr. *isos*+*thermos*] Isothermal. ~, s.f. Isotherm.
isotrope (izɔtrɔp), adj. [f. Gr. *isos*+*tropos*] Isotropic.
israélite (izraelit), adj. Israelitish, Israelitic. ~, s.m.f. Israelite.
issant, -e (isɑ̃) [pres. part. of (obs.) *issir*] (herald.) Issuant.
issir (isir), v.n. (obs.) [L *exire*] To issue, to go forth.
issu, -e (isy), adj. [p.p. of (obs.) *issir*] Born, descended, sprung (*de*, from, of); *cousin ~ de germain*, second cousin.
issue (isy), s.f. [f. *issu*] **1.** Issue, egress, outlet, way out, end; *à l'~ du combat*, at the end of the fight; **2.** *~s*, pl. pollard, refuse grain, bran; **3.** offal (of slaughtered animals). ⚠ English 'issue' also = *publication, livraison, numéro d'un périodique*; and *débat, discussion*; ex. the point at issue, *le point en litige, la question, la chose en question*.
isthme (ism), s.m. [Gr. *isthmos*] Isthmus.
isthmique (ismik), adj. Isthmian.
itacisme (itasism), s.m. [f. Gr. *ēta*] Itacism.
itague (itag), s.f. (naut.) Runner-tie.
italianiser (italjanize), v.a. To Italianize.
italianisme (italjanism), s.m. Italianism.
italien, -ne (italjɛ̃), adj. s.m.f. Italian.
italique (italik), adj. Italic. ~, s.m. Italic (type, letter); *mettre en ~s*, to italicize.
item (itɛm), adv. [L wd] Moreover, item, also, ditto. ~, s.m. (invar.) Item.
itérati-f, -ve (iteratif), adj. [f. L *iterum*] Iterative.
itération (itera'sjɔ̃), s.f. Iteration, repetition.
itérativement (iterativmɑ̃), adv. Repeatedly.
ithos (itos), s.m. (obs.) [f. Gr. *ēthos*] Ethics.

itinéraire (itinerɛr), adj. [f. L *iter*] Itinerary. ~, s.m. Itinerary, route, guide-book.
itou (itu), adv. [f. L *hic talis*] Also, likewise; *et moi* ~, and I, too.
iule (jyl), s.m. (zool.) Millepede, iulus.
ivoire (ivwar), s.m. [L *eboreus*] Ivory; ivory-work; bone (of the teeth); *en* ~, *d'*~, ivory.
ivoirerie (ivwarri), s.f. Ivory-carving, ivory-trade.
ivoirier (ivwarje), s.m. Ivory-carver.
ivoirin, -e (ivwarɛ̃), adj. Ivory, shining like ivory.
ivorine (ivɔrin), s.f. Ivorine, artificial ivory.
ivraie (ivrɛ), s.f. [L *ebriaca herba*] (bot.) Darnel, rye-grass, tare; (fig.) tares; *séparer l'~ d'avec le bon grain*, to separate the wheat from the tares.
ivre (ivr), adj. [L *ebrius*] Drunk, intoxicated, inebriated, tipsy; *à moitié* ~, half seas over; ~ *mort*, dead-drunk; ~ *de joie*, beside oneself with joy; ~ *de sang*, thirsting for blood, drunk with blood.
ivresse (ivrɛs), s.f. Drunkenness; inebriation, frenzy, rapture, enthusiasm.
ivrogne (ivrɔɲ), s.m. Drunkard. ~, adj. Given to drink.
ivrogner (ivrɔɲe), v.n. and **s'**~, v.pr. To get drunk often, to booze.
ivrognerie (ivrɔɲəri), s.f. Drunkenness, frequent inebriety.
ivrognesse (ivrɔɲɛs), s.f. Drunken woman.
ixia (iksjɑ), s.f. (bot.) Ixia.
izard (izar), s.m. See ISARD.

J

J, j (ʒi), s.m. 10th letter of the alphabet; *j'*, contraction of *je*.
ja (ʒa), adv. (obs.) Already.
jable (ʒabl), s.m. (tech.) Stave-groove; grooved stave-ends.
jaborandi (ʒabɔrɑ̃di), s.m. [Braz. wd] Jaborandi.
jabot (ʒabo), s.m. [orig. unkn.] Crop, maw (of a bird); frill (of a shirt, dress, &c.); (colloq.) *se remplir le* ~, to have a blow-out.
jabotage (ʒabɔtaʒ), s.m. Chattering, jabbering, prattle.
jaboter (ʒabɔte), v.n. To jabber, to chatter, to prattle; to jaw.
jaboteu-r, -se (ʒabɔtœr), s.m.f. Chatterer, jabberer, chatterbox.
jacasse (ʒakas), s.f. [imit.] Magpie; (fig.) chatterbox.
jacasser (ʒakase), v.n. To chatter, to prattle, to cackle, to jabber; ~ *comme une pie borgne*, to chatter like a magpie.
jacasserie (ʒakasri), s.f. Prattle, chatter, chattering.
jacée (ʒase), s.f. (bot.) Knapweed; ~ *des blés*, cornflower.
jacent, -e (ʒasɑ̃), adj. [f. L *jacere*] (law) In abeyance; *sous-*~, immediately under.
jachère (ʒaʃɛr), s.f. [LL *gascaria*] Fallow, fallow ground; *être en* ~, to lie fallow; *laisser une parcelle en* ~, to let a plot lie fallow.
jacinthe (ʒasɛ̃t), s.f. [L *hyacinthus*] (bot.) Hyacinth; ~ *des prés*, bluebell. ⚠ English 'jacinth' = French *hyacinthe*, a gem, a variety of zircon.
jaco, jacot, jacquot (ʒako), s.m. (colloq.) Pretty Poll, Poll parrot.
jacobée (ʒakɔbe), s.f. (bot.) Ragwort.
jacobin (ʒakɔbɛ̃), s.m. [LL *jacobinus*] **1.** Jacobin friar; **2.** Jacobin (Radical Revolutionist of the 1st Fr. Republic). ⚠ Not 'Jacobite'.
jacobinisme (ʒakɔbinism), s.m. Jacobinism.
jacobite (ʒakɔbit), s.m. adj. [f. *Jacobus* = James II] Jacobite.
jaconas (ʒakɔnɑ), s.m. [f. Urdu *Jagannathi*] Jaconet.
jacquard (ʒakar), s.m. [f. Fr. inventor's n.] Jacquard loom.
jacquerie (ʒakri), s.f. [f. *Jacques*, *Jacques Bonhomme* = Fr. peasant] Jacquerie, rising of peasantry, espec. that of 1357–8.
Jacques (ʒɑk), s.m. [L *Jacobus*] James, Jim; ~ *Bonhomme*, symbolic name for the French peasant, as John Bull for the traditional Englishman; Hodge, Jack Frog; *maître* ~, Jack of all trades; *faire le* ~, to play the fool.
jacquet (ʒakɛ), s.m. Backgammon.
jacquot (ʒako), s.m. See JACO.
jactance (ʒaktɑ̃s), s.f. [L *jactantia*] Boasting, bragging, bounce, swagger; *plein de* ~, boastful.
jaculatoire (ʒakylatwar), adj. [L *jaculari*] Ejaculatory; *prière* ~, short, unspoken, impromptu prayer.
jade (ʒad), s.m. [f. Span. *ijada*] Jade (a hard, translucent stone). ⚠ In English 'jade' also means 'worn-out horse' and 'unpleasant woman' = *rosse*.
jadis (ʒɑdis), adv. [f. L *jam*+*dies*] Of old, in olden times, once upon a time, whilom, formerly; *au temps* ~, in the good old days, in days of old, of yore; in auld lang syne.
jaguar (ʒagɥar), s.m. (zool.) Jaguar.
jaillir (ʒajir), v.n. [etym. dub.] To spout, to gush (out), to burst forth, to spurt out, to spring up, to spirt, to splash; *il a fait* ~ *de la boue sur*, he has splashed mud on.
jaillissant, -e (ʒajisɑ̃), p. adj. Spouting, gushing, springing, bursting, rushing.
jaillissement (ʒajismɑ̃), s.m. Gushing, spouting, splashing, &c.; see JAILLIR.
jais (ʒɛ), s.m. [OF *jaiet*] Jet; *noir comme le* ~, jet-black.

jalap (ʒalap), s.m. [Span. *jalapa*] (pharm.) Jalap.
jale (ʒal), s.f. Large bowl or tub.
jalet (ʒalɛ), s.m. (obs.) Pebble; *arc à* ~, stone-bow.
jalon (ʒalɔ̃), s.m. Surveying staff, stake, pole, landmark, beacon; (fig.) landmark.
jalonnement (ʒalɔnmɑ̃), s.m. Staking-out, marking-out.
jalonner (ʒalɔne), v.a.n. To mark out, to stake out, to peg out (a claim); to place landmarks.
jalonneur (ʒalɔnœr), s.m. Marker, pointer.
jalousement (ʒaluzmɑ̃), adv. Jealously.
jalouser (ʒaluze), v.a. To be jealous of, to envy; **se** ~, v.pr. to envy each other.
jalousie (ʒaluzi), s.f. [f. LL *zelosus*, OF *gelosi*] **1.** Jealousy; envy; *donner de la* ~ *à X*, to make X jealous; **2.** Venetian blind, jalousie, shutter; **3.** (bot.) sweet-william.
jalou-x, -se (ʒalu), adj. [OF *gelos*] **1.** Jealous; envious; **2.** solicitous to preserve rights, affection, &c.; ~ *de plaire*, anxious to please; ~ *de son origine*, proud of one's extraction; ~ *de ses privilèges*, jealous of one's privileges. ~, s.m.f. Jealous person, envious person; *faire des* ~, to excite envy.
jamais (ʒamɛ), adv. [*ja*+*mais*] Never, ever, at any time; *à* ~, *pour* ~, for ever; *à tout* ~, for ever and ever; *au grand* ~, to all eternity; never by any chance; ~ *de la vie!*, no fear!; *plus vite que* ~, faster than ever; *presque* ~, hardly ever; *si* ~, if ever; ~ *plus*, never more; ~ *trop tard pour bien faire*, never too late to mend.
jambage (ʒɑ̃baʒ), s.m. **1.** (writing) Down-stroke; **2.** (arch.) jamb (of a door).
jambe (ʒɑ̃b), s.f. [LL *gamba*] Leg, shank, stem (of a glass); ~ *de bois*, wooden leg; *j'ai les* ~*s en coton*, my legs feel like cotton wool; *avoir les* ~*s en manche de veste*, to be bow-legged; *le gros de la* ~, the calf of the leg; ~ *de force*, prop, stay; *jouer des* ~*s*, *prendre ses* ~*s à son cou*, to take to one's heels; *faire quelque chose par-dessous la* ~, to do something easily, negligently, off-handedly; *tirer dans les* ~*s à X*, to run counter to X's plans; (iron.) *ça vous fait une belle* ~*!*, and a lot of good that will do you!; *courir à toutes* ~*s*, to run at top speed; *en aurai-je la* ~ *mieux faite?*, shall I be any the better for it?
jambé, -e (ʒɑ̃be), adj. Legged; *bien* ~, with well-shaped legs; *haut* ~, long-legged.
jambière (ʒɑ̃bjɛr), s.f. Legging, shin-guard; (armour) greave.
jambon (ʒɑ̃bɔ̃), s.m. Ham.
jambonneau (pl. **-x**) (ʒɑ̃bɔno), s.m. Shoulder (of pork); small ham.
janissaire (ʒanisɛr), s.m. [Turk. *yeni-tsheri*] Janissary.
janot (ʒano), s.m. Jack-pudding, tomfool, ninny, simpleton.
janoterie (ʒanɔtri), s.f. Nonsense, bull, tomfoolery.
jansénisme (ʒɑ̃senism), s.m. [f. Cornelius *Jansen* (*Jansenius*) d. 1638] Jansenism.
janséniste (ʒɑ̃senist), adj. s.m.f. Jansenist.
jante (ʒɑ̃t), s.f. [etym. dub.; perh. It. *gambita*] Rim (of a wheel), felloe, felly; *frein sur* ~, rim-brake.
jantille (ʒɑ̃tij), s.f. Paddle (of a water-wheel); syn. PALETTE.
janvier (ʒɑ̃vje), s.m. [L *Januarius*] January.
japon (ʒapɔ̃), s.m. Japan paper; Japan ware.
japonais, -e (ʒapɔnɛ), adj. s.m.f. Japanese.
japonaiseries (ʒapɔnɛzri), s.f.pl. Japanese curios of small value.
japonner (ʒapɔne), v.a. (rare) To japan.
jappement (ʒapmɑ̃), s.m. Yelping.
japper (ʒape), v.n. [onom.] To yelp, to yap.
jaquemart (ʒakmar), s.m. [f. *Jacques*] Jack-of-the-clock, jack (a figure of a man which strikes the bell of a clock).
jaquette (ʒakɛt), s.f. (Man's) morning-coat; *complet* ~, morning suit; (woman's) coat (of a tailor-made coat and skirt); jacket. ⚠ English '(man's) jacket' means a short coat without tails; it does not translate the French *jaquette d'homme*. In English 'jacket' means also *couverture volante d'un livre*; *pelage d'animal*; potatoes boiled in their jackets = *pommes de terre en robe de chambre*.
jaquier (ʒakje), s.m. (bot.) Breadfruit-tree.
jar (ʒar), s.m. See JARS.
jard (ʒar), s.m. [etym. dub.] River-gravel.
jarde (ʒard), s.f. [It. *giarda*] (vet.) Bone-spavin.
jardin (ʒardɛ̃), s.m. [OF *gardin*, f. Teut.; cf. Germ. *Garten*; Engl. *garth*, *yard*] Garden; ~ *potager*, kitchen-garden; ~ *anglais*, ornamental grounds; ~ *des Plantes*, Botanical Gardens; ~ *d'Acclimatation*, Zoological Gardens, Zoo; *le* ~ *de la France*, i.e. la Touraine; ~ *de curé*, small country garden, old-fashioned and well tended.
jardinage (ʒardinaʒ), s.m. Gardening.
jardiner (ʒardine), v.n. To garden.
jardinet (ʒardinɛ), s.m. Very small garden.
jardineu-x, -se (ʒardinø), adj. (of precious stones) Spotty.
jardini-er, -ère (ʒardinje), s.m.f. Gardener; ~ *fleuriste*, horticulturist; ~ *maraîcher*, market-gardener; ~*ère*, s.f. flower-stand, plant-stand; (cook.) *à la* ~*ère*, or ~*ère*, dressed with vegetables, esp. carrots, green peas, &c. ~, adj. Garden-; *plantes* ~*ères*, garden plants.

jargon (ʒargɔ̃), s.m. [etym. dub.] **1.** Jargon; lingo, gibberish, technical language, slang; debased, barbarous, or unintelligible language; **2.** [f. It. *giargone*] jargon, jargoon, translucent or smoky zircon.

jargonner (ʒargɔne), v.n.a. To jargon, to jabber, to talk unintelligibly.

jarnac (ʒarnak), s.m. [f. *baron de Jarnac*, who killed an adversary in a duel by an unexpected blow, 1547] *Coup de* ~, treacherous attack; underhand blow.

jarni! (ʒarni), interj. (obs.) Zounds!

jarosse (ʒarɔs), s.f. (bot.) Vetch.

jarre (ʒar), s.f. [Arab. *jarrah*] Jar, earthenware vessel, large basin, vat.

jarret (ʒarɛ), s.m. [Celt. *garr*] Ham, hock, hough, hamstring; (cook.) knuckle (of veal); shin or leg (of beef); *tendon du* ~, hamstring; *couper le* ~ *à*, to hamstring; *avoir du* ~, to be a good walker; *être ferme sur ses* ~*s*, to stand firm, erect; (fig.) to be in a good situation; *tendre le* ~, to walk with a springy gait.

jarreté, -e (ʒarte), adj. (vet.) *Bien* ~, close-hammed.

jarretelle (ʒartɛl), s.f. Stocking suspender.

jarretière (ʒartjɛr), s.f. [f. *jarret*] Garter; *il ne lui va pas à la* ~, he is not fit to hold a candle to him.

jars (ʒar), s.m. Gander; *dévider le* ~, to speak slang; *entendre le* ~, to be up to snuff.

jaser (ʒɑze), v.n. **1.** To chatter, to gossip, to prate, to prattle; to talk, to criticize; *on commence à* ~, people are beginning to talk; *on jase sur vous*, you are being talked about; **2.** to blab; *n'allez pas* ~, don't go and blab; don't let the cat out of the bag.

jaserie (ʒɑzri), s.f. Prattle, chatter, tittle-tattle.

jaseron (ʒɑzrɔ̃), s.m. Thin gold chain.

jaseu-r, -se (ʒɑzœr), s.m.f. Prater, chatterer, chatterbox, windbag; ~, s.m. (ornith.) waxwing. ~, adj. Babbling; *le ruisseau* ~, the babbling brook.

jasmin (ʒasmɛ̃), s.m. [Arab. f. Pers. *yâsmin*] (bot.) Jasmine, jessamine.

jaspe (ʒasp), s.m. [Gr. *iaspis*] Jasper.

jasper (ʒaspe), v.a. To marble; to vein; to sprinkle; (bookbinding) *jaspé sur tranche*, sprinkled, with marbled edges.

jaspiner (ʒaspine), v.n. (colloq.) To chatter, to talk.

jaspure (ʒaspyr), s.f. Marbling, sprinkling, veins, variegating.

jatte (ʒat), s.f. [L *gabata*] Bowl; platter, porringer, basin; dessert-stand; glass bowl; *cul-de-*~, (legless) cripple.

jauge (ʒoʒ), s.f. [etym. dub.] Gauge, gauging-rod; ~ *à huile*, oil gauge; (naut.) tonnage, burthen; ~ *officielle*, register tonnage; (hort.) trench for storing plants.

jaugeage (ʒoʒaʒ), s.m. Gauging, measurement.

jauger (ʒoʒe), v.a. To gauge, to measure the capacity of; (fig.) to size up, to estimate, to gauge; (naut.) to draw, to be (so many tons) register; *ce cargo jauge x pieds*, this cargo draws x feet.

jaugeur (ʒoʒœr), s.m. Gauger.

jaumière (ʒomjɛr), s.f. (naut.) Rudder-hole; *trou de* ~, helm-port.

jaunâtre (ʒonɑtr), adj. Yellowish.

jaune (ʒon), adj. [L *galbinus*] Yellow; ~ *comme un coing*, as yellow as a guinea. ~, s.m. **1.** Yellow; **2.** yolk (of an egg); **3.** blackleg, non-unionist workman.

jauneau (pl. **-x**) (ʒono), s.m. (bot.) Buttercup; bachelor's button; ~ *d'eau*, yellow water-lily.

jaunet (ʒonɛ), s.m. (pop.) Yellow boy (gold coin).

jaunir (ʒonir), v.a. To make yellow, to paint or dye yellow; ~ v.n. to grow or turn yellow.

jaunissant, -e (ʒonisɑ̃), p. adj. Turning yellow; ripening, golden.

jaunisse (ʒonis), s.f. (pathol.) Jaundice.

jaunissement (ʒonismɑ̃), s.m. Yellowing, turning yellow.

javanais, -e (ʒavanɛ), adj. s.m.f. Javanese.

javart (ʒavar), s.m. (vet.) Quittor, ulcer on pastern.

javeau (pl. **-x**) (ʒavo), s.m. [etym. dub., prob. Celt.] Sand-bank.

javel (ʒavɛl), or *eau de* ~, s.f. [f. *Javel*, a quarter of Paris; sometimes wrongly spelt *eau de javelle*] Bleaching liquid, eau de Javelle.

javelage (ʒavlaʒ), s.m. Laying in swathes or loose sheaves.

javeler (ʒavle), v.a.n. To lay in swathes or loose sheaves.

javelle (ʒavɛl), s.f. [etym. dub., prob. Celt. orig.] Swath, loose sheaf; handful, bundle (of ears).

javelot (ʒavlo), s.m., **javeline** (ʒavlin), s.f. Javelin.

je, j' (ʒə), pers. pron. I; *je suis*, I am; *suis-je?*, am I?

jeannette (ʒanɛt), s.f. **1.** Small gold cross (hung at the neck, once worn by peasant girls); **2.** sleeve-board (for ironing sleeves, &c.).

jeannot, janot (ʒano), s.m. Booby, ninny, simpleton; *c'est comme le couteau de* ~, that 's like the Irishman's gun (said of any object that has been mended so often as to have nothing of the original left).

jectisses, jetisses (ʒɛktis, ʒɛtis), adj. f. pl. [f. *jeter*] *Terres* ~, made earth, loose soil; *pierres* ~, building-stones, movable by hand.

je-m'en-fichisme (or **-foutisme**) (ʒəmɑ̃fiʃism, ʒəmɑ̃futism), loc. [f. *se ficher, se foutre*] (colloq.) Casualness, utter indifference; hence **je-m'en-fichiste,** adj. s.m.f.

jenny (ʒɛni), s.f. (Spinning-)jenny.

jérémiade (ʒeremjad), s.f. [f. *Jérémie*, Jeremiah] Jeremiad, lamentation.

jersey (ʒɛrze), s.m. [f. *Jersey* island] Jersey, (*a*) close-fitting knitted woollen tunic, bodice, or garment; (*b*) machine-made knitted woollen material.

jersiais, -e (ʒɛrzjɛ), adj. Of Jersey. **~, -e,** s.m.f. Jerseyman, Jerseywoman.

jésuite (ʒezɥit), s.m. adj. [f. *Jésus*] Jesuit; *~ de robe courte*, lay Jesuit.

jésuitique (ʒezɥitik), adj. (pej.) Jesuitical.

jésuitiquement(ʒezɥitikmɑ̃),adv. Jesuitically.

jésuitisme (ʒezɥitism), s.m. (pej.) Jesuitism, hypocrisy.

Jésus (ʒezy), s.m. Jesus; *papier jésus* or ~, long royal (paper), super-royal (about 0·72 m. × 0·55 m.); *grand ~*, imperial.

jet (ʒɛ), s.m. [cf. *jeter*] Throw, throwing; cast, casting; jet, gush, spurt (of water); shoot, sprout (of plants); ray, stream (of light); toss, tossing; sketch; *~ d'eau*, fountain; *~ d'abeilles*, swarm of bees; *d'un seul ~*, at one stroke, with a single effort; *c'est un premier ~*, that is a first sketch; *~ à la mer*, jettisoning; *à un ~ de pierre*, at a stone's throw.

jeté (ʒəte), s.m. (danc.) Jeté.

jetée (ʒəte), s.f. Jetty, mole, pier.

jeter (ʒəte), v.a. [L *jactare*, pop. L *jettare*] **1.** To throw; to throw away, out, or down; to cast, to fling, to hurl, to dash, to toss, to pitch; to emit, to shoot; *~ l'ancre*, to cast anchor; *~ les yeux sur*, to cast one's eyes on; to select (a person); *~ un cri*, to utter a cry; *~ des vapeurs*, to emit, to belch smoke and steam; *~ un soupir*, to heave a sigh; *~ le manche après la cognée*, to throw the rope after the bucket; *~ son bonnet par-dessus les moulins*, to throw off all restraint, to lose all sense of modesty; (slang) *n'en jetez plus, la cour est pleine !*, don't go on, that will do !; come off it !, draw it mild!; (fig.) *~ sa gourme*, to sow one's wild oats; *~ de l'huile sur le feu*, to add fuel to the flame; *~ son argent par les fenêtres*, to play ducks and drakes with one's money; *~ des racines*, to strike root; *le sort en est jeté*, the die is cast; *~ les fondations de*, to lay the foundation of; *~ un coup d'œil à*, to give a look to, to look at; **2.** (med.) to discharge; *~ du pus*, to run, to suppurate; **se ~**, v.pr. to throw oneself, to fling oneself, to fall upon, to pounce upon, to rush; *se ~ à corps perdu*, to rush headlong (*dans, sur*, into, against); (of rivers, &c.) to disembogue, to empty (*dans*, into).

jeton (ʒtɔ̃, ʒətɔ̃), s.m. Mark, counter; *faux comme un ~*, as false as a brass shilling.

jeu (pl. **-x**) (ʒø), s.m. [L *jocum*] **1.** Game, play, sport, pastime, amusement, frolic; *ce n'est pas de* (or *du*) *~*, that 's not fair; that 's not cricket; *c'est le ~*, that 's the game; *être à deux de ~*, (*a*) to be even, to be a match for each other; (*b*) to share risks and interests; *ne me mettez pas en ~*, do not mix me up in it; *sa tête est en ~*, his life is at stake; *c'est bien vieux ~*, it 's quite old-fashioned; *~ de mains, ~ de vilain !*, no horse-play !; rough play often ends in tears; *avoir du ~*, to get good cards; *avoir beau, mauvais, ~*, to have a good, poor, hand; *avoir du bonheur au ~*, to have luck at play; (fig.) *il cache son ~*, he covers his designs; *jouer gros ~*, to play for high stakes, to play high; (fig.) to risk much; *faire le ~ de X*, to play into X's hands; *faire bonne mine à mauvais ~*, to make the best of a bad job; to put a good face on the matter; *se piquer au ~*, to persist (in a game, enterprise, &c.); to set one's jaw; to warm up; to get keener; *à beau ~ beau retour*, one good turn deserves another; *maison de ~*, gambling-house; *jeux de société*, indoor games, round games; *~ de mots*, pun; *~ d'esprit*, witticism; *cela passe le ~*, that is beyond a joke; *le ~ n'en vaut pas la chandelle*, the game is not worth the candle; **2.** set, suit, pack (of cards); *~ de clefs, d'avirons, d'aiguilles*, set of spanners, oars, needles; *~x d'orgues*, organ-stops; *un ~ de quilles*, a set of ninepins; *~ d'échecs*, (*a*) chessboard; (*b*) set of chess-men; (*c*) chess game; **3.** (mech.) play, looseness; *la direction a du ~*, there is some play in the gear; *corriger le ~*, to take up the play, to take up the slack; *mettre en ~*, to start; to bring to bear; **4.** expression, manner of acting; *~x de physionomie*, facial play, changing expressions.

jeudi (ʒødi), s.m. [f. L *Jovis dies*] Thursday; *~ gras*, Sheer Thursday, Maundy Thursday; *~ saint*, Maundy Thursday; *la semaine des quatre ~s*, a month of Sundays; Tib's eve.

(à) jeun (aʒœ̃), adv. [L *jejunus*] Fasting, on an empty stomach; *prenez celà à ~*, take this on an empty stomach, or before breakfast.

jeune (ʒœn), adj. [L *juvenis*] **1.** Young, youthful; immature; (fam.) green; *un homme ~*, a man still young; *un ~ homme*, a young man; *un très ~ homme*, a youth; *un visage ~*, a young, youthful, face; *dans mon ~ temps*, in my youth; *son essai est un peu ~*, his essay is rather immature; *vous êtes bien ~, mon ami*, you are very green, my friend; *un ~ vin*, young, immature, raw wine; **2.** younger, junior; *mon ~ fils*, my younger son; *Dumas le ~*, Dumas the younger; *Leblanc ~ et Cie*, Leblanc junior and Co.; *jouer les ~s premiers*, to act the lovers' parts; to play the juvenile lead.

jeûne (ʒøn), s.m. Fast, fasting, abstinence.

jeûner (ʒøne), v.n. [L *jejunare*] To fast.

jeunesse (ʒœnɛs), s.f. **1.** Youth, youthful days; *dans sa* ~, in his youth; in his young days; *dans sa première* ~, in his early youth; *elle n'est plus de la première* ~, she is no chicken; *de* ~, *dès sa* ~, from early youth, from youth onwards; *il faut que* ~ *se passe*, youth will be served; boys will be boys; **2.** youth, young people; *la* ~ *du village*, the youth of the village; *enseigner la* ~, to teach young people; ~ *dorée*, gilded youth; *si* ~ *savait!*, if youth but knew!; **3.** youthfulness (of appearance, heart); **4.** (fam.) young lass, wench.

jeunet, -te (ʒœnɛ), adj. Very young, youthful, of tender age; green, raw.

jeûneu-r, -se (ʒønœr), s.m.f. One who fasts, faster.

jiu-jitsu (ʒjyʒitsy), s.m. [Japan. wd] Jiu-jitsu.

joaillerie (ʒɔɑjri), s.f. [f. *joyau*] **1.** Jewellery, jewelry, gems, jewels; **2.** jewellery trade.

joailli-er, -ère (ʒɔɑje), s.m.f. Jeweller.

job (ʒɔb), s.m. [abbrev. of *jobard*] (slang) *Monter le* ~ *à X*, to cod X, to humbug X; *se monter le* ~, (*a*) to delude oneself; (*b*) to work oneself up.

jobard (ʒɔbar), s.m. [OF *jobe*] (fam.) Booby, ninny, noodle.

jobarder (ʒɔbarde), v.a. (fam.) To bamboozle, to gull.

jobarderie (ʒɔbardri), s.f. Gullibility, credulity; nonsensical talk, foolish jabbering.

joc (ʒɔk), s.m. (techn.) Non-working state (of mill); *mettre un moulin à* ~, to stop a mill.

jocasse (ʒɔkɑs), s.f. (ornith., fam.) Misselthrush.

jockey (ʒɔke), s.m. [Engl. wd] Jockey; *Jockey Club*, Jockey Club.

jocko (ʒɔko), s.m. (fam.) Pongo, jacko.

jocrisse (ʒɔkris), s.m. [prop. n. of a character in old farces] Dupe, gull, ninny.

jocrisserie (ʒɔkrisri), s.f. (theatr. fam.) Gullibility; clownishness.

jodler (jɔdle), v.a. [Germ. *jodeln*, onom.] To yodel; syn. IOULER, IODLER.

joie (ʒwɑ), s.f. [L *gaudium*] Joy, joyfulness, gladness, delight; *ne pas se tenir de* ~, to be overwhelmed, beside oneself, with joy; *faire la* ~ *de X*, to be X's joy; *pleurer de* ~, to weep for joy; *se faire une* ~ *de*, to take delight in; to look forward to; pleasure, enjoyment; *renoncer aux* ~*s de ce monde*, to renounce the pleasures of this world; *nager dans la* ~, to be overjoyed; *un rabat-*~, a kill-joy; a wet blanket.

joignant (ʒwaɲɑ̃), prep. Next to, contiguous to, adjoining; *la maison joignant la nôtre*, the house next to, adjoining, ours.

joindre (ʒwɛ̃dr), v.a.n. [L *jungere*] To join, unite, put together, connect; to enclose, to add; ~ *les deux bouts d'une ficelle*, to join the two ends of a piece of string; ~ *les pieds*, to put one's feet together; ~ *les mains*, to clasp one's hands; ~ *l'utile à l'agréable*, to combine usefulness with pleasure; *le canal qui joint les deux mers*, the canal which connects the two seas; *l'amitié qui les joint*, the friendship which unites them; (fam.) *avoir de la peine à* ~ *les deux bouts*, to have difficulty in making both ends meet; (of things) to be next to, contiguous to, to adjoin; *notre maison joignait l'église*, our house adjoined, was next to, the church; (of persons) to join, to overtake; *il va* ~ *son régiment*, he is going to join his regiment; *je n'avais pas de difficulté à les* ~, I had no difficulty in overtaking them; *les fenêtres ne joignent pas bien*, the windows do not fit well; **se** ~, v.pr. to meet, to join; to be united; to be adjoining.

joint (ʒwɛ̃), p. adj. Joined, united, connected, close together; *pieds* ~*s*, feet close together; *mains* ~*es*, clasped hands; *ci-*~, herewith, enclosed herewith, annexed; *vous trouverez ci-*~ *une copie de notre lettre*, you will find herewith a copy of our letter; ~ *à cela que*, added to which, besides which.

joint (ʒwɛ̃), s.m. (anat.) Joint, articulation; (fam.) *trouver le* ~, to hit on the best way of tackling something; (geol.) joint, fissure; (techn.) joint; ~ *à la cardan*, cardan-joint; ~ *coudé*, toggle-joint; ~ *à recouvrement*, lap-joint; join, seam; *ouvrage de menuiserie où on ne voit pas les* ~*s*, piece of carpentry in which the joins are invisible.

jointé (ʒwɛ̃te), adj. (vet.) Jointed; *court-*~, short-jointed; *long-*~, long-jointed.

jointée (ʒwɛ̃te), s.f. Double handful.

jointement (ʒwɛ̃tmɑ̃), s.m. Joining; jointing.

jointi-f, -ve (ʒwɛ̃tif), adj. (of slats, boards, &c.) Close together, touching, joining.

jointoiement (ʒwɛ̃twajmɑ̃), s.m. (mason.) Pointing, grouting (of walls).

jointout (ʒwɛ̃tu), s.m. (techn.) Jointing-plane.

jointoyer (ʒwɛ̃twaje), v.a. (techn.) To point, to grout.

jointoyeur (ʒwɛ̃twajœr), s.m. (techn.) Workman employed on pointing.

jointure (ʒwɛ̃tyr), s.f. Join, joint; (anat.) joint, articulation.

joli, -e (ʒɔli), adj. (of person, face, voice, &c.) Pretty, pleasing; (of things) pretty, nice, (fam.) sweet; *il a de* ~*s meubles*, he has some nice furniture; *un* ~ *chapeau*, a pretty hat, (fam.) a sweet hat; *dire de* ~*es choses*, to say pleasant things; (fam.) *faire le* ~ *cœur*, to do the pretty; (of income, property, &c.) comfortable, fine, (fam.) decent, jolly good; *il a un ~ poste*, he has a jolly good billet; (iron.) fine, nice, pretty; *vous voilà dans un ~ état !*, you are in a nice pickle !; *en voilà une ~e façon de traiter ses amis !*, that 's a fine way to treat one's friends !

joliet, -te (ʒɔliɛ), adj. **1.** Pretty-pretty, affectedly pretty; **2.** rather pretty.

joliment (ʒɔlimɑ̃), adv. Prettily, nicely; (iron.) nicely, finely; *on vous a ~ triché*, you have been nicely had; (fam.) extremely, tremendously, excessively, very much; *il est ~ riche*, he is enormously, tremendously, rich; *il est ~ malhonnête*, he is extremely rude; *vous vous êtes ~ trompé*, you are very much mistaken.

joliveté (ʒɔlivte), s.f. Pretty bauble.

jomarin (ʒɔmarɛ̃), s.m. [corrupt. of *jonc marin*] (bot., fam.) Furze, gorse.

jonc (ʒɔ̃), s.m. [L *juncus*] **1.** (bot.) Rush; *panier de ~*, rush basket; (fam.) *droit comme un ~*, straight as a die; **2.** rattan cane, Malacca cane; **3.** guard-ring, keeper.

joncacées (ʒɔ̃kase), s.f.pl. (bot.) Juncaceae, rushes.

joncer (ʒɔ̃se), v.a. (rare) To rush-bottom (a chair), to rush (a chair-bottom).

jonchaie (ʒɔ̃ʃɛ), s.f. Bed of rushes.

jonchée (ʒɔ̃ʃe), s.f. **1.** Scattering, strewing, of flowers; **2.** heap (of things) on the ground; **3.** cream cheese, made in rush baskets.

jonchement (ʒɔ̃ʃmɑ̃), s.m. Scattering, strewing (of a road with flowers, &c.); littering (of the ground with dead leaves, &c.); covering, strewing (of a battle-field with corpses, &c.).

joncher (ʒɔ̃ʃe), v.a. [f. *jonc*] To scatter, to strew (a road with flowers, &c.); *les feuilles mortes jonchent le sol*, the ground is strewn, littered, with dead leaves; *le champ de bataille était jonché de cadavres*, the battle-field was strewn, covered, with corpses.

jonchets (ʒɔ̃ʃɛ), s.m.pl. Spillikins.

joncier (ʒɔ̃sie), s.m. (bot.) Spanish broom, *Spartium junceum, Cytisus junceus.*

jonction (ʒɔ̃ksjɔ̃), s.f. [L *junctio*] Junction; joining (of two rivers, &c.); *point de ~*, meeting-point, junction. ⚠ English 'junction', when meaning the place or station on a railway where lines meet and unite, must be translated by *embranchement.*

jongler (ʒɔ̃gle), v.n. [L *joculari*] To juggle; to play sleight-of-hand tricks.

jonglerie (ʒɔ̃gləri), s.f. Jugglery, juggling; sleight-of-hand tricks; (fam.) duplicity, trickery; fraud, jugglery.

jongleur (ʒɔ̃glœr), s.m. **1.** Juggler; conjuror; (fam.) trickster; **2.** (hist.) minstrel.

jonque (ʒɔ̃k), s.f. [Javanese *djong*] (Chinese) Junk.

jonquille (ʒɔ̃kij), s.f. [Span. *junquillo*] (bot.) Jonquil. ~, adj. Jonquil colour, pale yellow.

joseph (ʒozef), adj. **1.** *Papier ~*, tissue paper; **2.** (colloq.) *faire son ~*, to affect chaste, virtuous airs; not to respond to a woman's advances.

jottereaux (ʒɔtro), s.m.pl. (naut.) Cheeks.

jouable (ʒwabl), adj. Playable.

jouailler (ʒwɑje), v.n. (fam.) **1.** To play for low stakes; **2.** to strum (on a piano), to scrape (on a violin).

joubarbe (ʒubarb), s.f. (bot.) Houseleek.

joue (ʒu), s.f. [L *gabata*] **1.** (anat.) Cheek; *aux ~s rouges*, red-cheeked; *aux ~s creuses*, hollow-cheeked; *embrasser quelqu'un sur les deux ~s*, to kiss some one on either cheek; *coucher en ~, mettre en ~*, to take aim at; (mil.) *en ~ !*, present !; **2.** (techn.) cheek (of pulley, &c.).

jouée (ʒue), s.f. (arch.) Reveal (of doorway, recess).

jouer (ʒwe), v.a.n. [L *jocari*] **1.** To play, (of children, young animals) to gambol, to sport, to frolic; *~ au tennis, aux cartes*, to play tennis, cards; *il joue bien au football*, he is good at football; *~ à la poupée*, to play with dolls; *c'est à vous à ~*, it is your turn to play; *~ sur les mots*, to quibble, to equivocate; *~ une carte*, to play, to lay down, a card; *~ de malheur*, to have a run of bad luck; *~ à la hausse*, to speculate on a rise; *~ sa fortune, sa vie*, to stake one's fortune, to risk one's life; (theatr.) to play, to act; *~ le rôle de*, to play, to take the part of; *on joue 'Horace' au théâtre*, they are playing, acting, *Horace* at the theatre, *Horace* is on at the theatre; *~ la surprise*, to simulate, to feign, surprise; *étoffe qui joue la soie*, stuff which imitates, looks like, silk; **2.** (of mechanism, key in lock, &c.) to play, to move freely; *serrure qui ne joue pas*, lock which does not act, work; *faire ~ une machine*, to set a machine going or working, to start a machine; *faire ~ une mine*, to spring a mine; (of woodwork) to warp, to become warped, to spring; (of wind) to veer; *~ X, se ~ de X*, to deceive X, to play X false; **se ~ (de)**, v.pr. to make game of, to sport with; *se ~ des lois*, to disregard, to snap one's fingers at, the law; *se ~ des difficultés*, to overcome difficulties with the utmost ease; *en se jouant*, with the utmost ease.

jouet (ʒwɛ), s.m. Toy, plaything; (fig.) victim, laughing-stock; *le ~ du destin*, the victim of Fate; *le ~ de toute la ville*, the laughing-stock, sport, of the whole town.

joueu-r, -se (ʒwœr), s.m.f. Player; *les ~s de tennis*, the tennis-players; player, performer, actor; *un ~ de violon*, a violin-player; gambler, gamester; (fin.) stock-jobber; *~ à la hausse*, bull; *~ à la baisse*, bear. ~, adj. Playful, sportive, frolicsome, fond of play.

joufflu, -e (ʒufly), adj. (fam.) Chubby, chubby-cheeked, plump-faced.

joug (ʒug, ʒu), s.m. [L *jugum*] Yoke; *mettre les bœufs au ~*, to yoke the oxen; *faire passer sous le ~*, to pass, send, under the yoke; (fig.) yoke, domination; (techn.) beam (of a balance); *le ~ de l'opinion*, the heavy yoke of opinion.

jougoslave (jugoslav), adj. s.m.f. Jugoslav, Yugoslav.

jouir (ʒwir), v.n. [L *gaudere*] *~ de*, To enjoy, to rejoice in, to revel in, to be delighted at; *~ de la vie*, to enjoy life; *~ du bonheur d'un ami*, to rejoice in, to be delighted at, a friend's happiness; to enjoy, to be in possession of, to have the use of; *~ de l'estime de tout le monde*, to possess or enjoy the esteem of everybody; *~ de toutes ses facultés*, to be in possession of, to have the use of, all one's faculties.

jouissance (ʒwisɑ̃s), s.f. **1.** Enjoyment, pleasure, joy, delight; *trouver une ~ à servir X*, to take pleasure in, to enjoy, serving X; **2.** enjoyment, possession, use; *avoir la ~ de certains privilèges*, to enjoy, to have the enjoyment of, certain privileges; *entrer en ~ d'une propriété*, to enter into possession of a property; *pendant sa ~ d'office*, during his tenure of office; **3.** usufruct (of a property); (fin.) dividend payable, interest payable.

jouissant, -e (ʒwisɑ̃), p. adj. (law) In possession; *~ de tous ses droits*, in possession of, enjoying, his full rights.

jouisseu-r, -se (ʒwisœr), s.m.f. Sensualist, sybarite.

joujou (pl. **-x**) (ʒuʒu), s.m. Small toy or plaything.

jour (ʒur), s.m. [L *diurnum*] **1.** Day; *~ de fête*, holiday; *~ ouvrable*, working day, work-day; *pendant le ~*, during the day, in the daytime; *beauté d'un ~*, transient beauty; *dans ces ~s-là*, in those days; *à un de ces ~s!*, I hope to see you again soon; so long!; *je m'en vais pour huit ~s*, I am going away for a week; *quinze ~s*, a fortnight; *tous les ~s*, every day; *tous les deux ~s*, every other day; day about; *vêtements de tous les ~s*, everyday clothes; *dans huit ~s*, this day week; *dans quinze ~s*, in a fortnight; *jours caniculaires*, dog days; *les jours gras*, Shrovetide; *ce n'est pas tous les ~s fête*, Christmas comes but once a year; *~ des rois*, Twelfth Night; *dix francs par ~*, ten francs a day; *à ~*, up to date; *mettre à ~*, to bring up to date; *un ~ ou l'autre*, some day, sooner or later; *d'un ~ à l'autre*, gradually, little by little; *du ~ au lendemain*, from day to day; *on l'attend de ~ en ~*, we are expecting him everyday, from day to day; *vivre au ~ le ~*, (*a*) to live for the present; (*b*) to live from hand to mouth; *au premier ~*, at the first opportunity; *à chaque ~ suffit sa peine*, sufficient unto the day is the evil thereof; *à bon ~ bonne œuvre*, the better the day the better the deed; *bonjour!* good morning! good afternoon! good day!; (fam.) *c'est le ~ et la nuit*, they are as different as chalk from cheese; **2.** to-day; *les enfants du ~*, children of to-day; *nouvelles du ~*, to-day's news; *fruits du ~*, freshly-gathered fruit; **3.** time; *à court ~*, short-dated (bills, &c.); *à long ~*, long-dated; **4.** daylight; *plein ~*, *grand ~*, broad daylight; *il fait ~*, it is daylight; *il commence à faire ~*; it is beginning to get light; *le ~ se lève*, the sun is rising; *la pointe du ~*, dawn, daybreak; *demi-~*, *petit ~*, twilight, half-light; *la chute du ~*, nightfall; *beau comme le ~*, as fair as the day; **5.** light; *un ~ blafard*, a wan light; *le ~ baisse*, dusk is coming on; *avoir le ~ dans les yeux*, to have the light in one's eyes; (fam.) *clair comme le ~*, perfectly plain, as clear as day; *montrer les choses sous un autre ~*, to show things in a different light; *jeter du ~ sur un sujet*, to throw some light on a subject; *regarder quelque chose dans un ~ favorable*, to look at something in a favourable light; *mettre un ouvrage au ~*, to publish a book; **6.** life, lifetime; *pendant les ~s de votre père*, during your father's lifetime; *voir le ~*, to be born; to come to light; to come out; *sauver les ~s de X*, to save X's life; *sur ses vieux ~s*, in his old age; *donner le ~ à*, to give birth to; **7.** aperture, gap, opening, (of house) window; *pratiquer des ~s à une pièce*, to make windows to a room; *percé à ~*, pierced through and through, openwork; *bas à ~*, openwork stockings; *~ de souffrance*, window opening on a neighbour's estate, under certain conditions; borrowed light; **8.** at-home day; *c'est aujourd'hui son ~*, it is her at-home day to-day; *quel est votre ~?*, which day are you at home?

journal (pl. **aux**) (ʒurnal), s.m. [L *diurnalis*] **1.** Journal, diary; (comm.) journal, day-book; (naut.) *~ de bord*, log-book; **2.** newspaper, paper; *lire les ~x*, to read the papers.

journali-er, -ère (ʒurnalje), adj. [f. L *diurnalis*] Daily, quotidian, diurnal; *sa tâche ~ère*, his daily task; uncertain, transient, changeable. ~, s.m. Day-labourer.

journalisme (ʒurnalism), s.m. Journalism.

journaliste (ʒurnalist), s.m.f. Journalist.

journée (ʒurne), s.f. [LL *diurnata*] **1.** Day; *passer une bonne ~*, to spend a nice day; *travailler toute la ~*, to work the whole day long; (fam.) *toute la sainte ~*, the whole blessed day; *travailler à la* ~, to work by the day; (fam.) *à petites* ~*s*, little by little, by easy stages; daytime, day; *travailler pendant la* ~, to work during the daytime; **2.** daily wage, day's wages; day's work; *il a fait une bonne* ~, he has done a good day's work; *la* ~ *de huit heures*, the eight-hour day; *aller en* ~, to work by the day, to do daywork; *homme de* ~, day-labourer; *femme de* ~, charwoman; daily maid; *c'est à une* ~ *d'ici*, it is a day's journey from here; **3.** day, battle, contest; *la* ~ *de Valmy*, the battle of Valmy; *gagner la* ~, to carry, win, the day; *perdre la* ~, to lose the day.

journellement (ʒurnɛlmɑ̃), adv. Every day, daily; *le docteur fait sa visite* ~, the doctor visits daily; *cela se voit* ~, it is a thing one sees daily, it is an everyday occurrence.

journoyer (ʒurnwaje), v.n. (pop.) To fritter away one's day.

joute (ʒut), s.f. Joust, tilt, tilting-match; (of cocks) fight, main; (fig.) (oratorical, &c.) contest.

jouter (ʒute), v.n. [LL *juxtare*] To joust, to tilt; (of cocks) to fight; (fig.) to contest, to contend.

jouteur (ʒutœr), s.m. Jouster, tilter; (fig.) adversary, antagonist (in games, discussion, &c.).

jouvence (ʒuvɑ̃s), s.f. [L *juventa*] Youth; *la fontaine de* ~, the fountain of youth; *élixir de* ~, elixir of youth.

jouvenceau (pl. **-x**) (ʒuvɑ̃so), s.m. [L *juvenculus*] (fam.) Youth, lad, young fellow.

jouvencelle (ʒuvɑ̃sɛl), s.f. [L *juvencella*] (fam., often iron. or pej.) Lass, maid, maiden, damsel, wench.

jovial, -e (pl. **aux** and **als**) (ʒɔvjal), adj. [L *jovialis*] Jovial, convivial, jolly, merry.

jovialement (ʒɔvjalmɑ̃), adv. Jovially, convivially, merrily.

jovialité (ʒɔvjalite), s.f. Joviality, conviviality, jollity.

joyau (ʒwajo), s.m. [OF *joel*] Jewel.

joyeusement (ʒwajɔ̃zmɑ̃), adv. Joyfully, joyously, merrily, delightedly.

joyeuseté (ʒwajøzte), s.f. (fam.) Jest, joke.

joyeu-x, -se (ʒwajø) adj. Joyful, joyous, merry, delighted, jolly; *une* ~*se nouvelle*, joyful news; *bande* ~*se*, merry crew; *il était tout* ~ *de vous voir*, he was delighted to see you. ~, s.m. (pop.) Soldier serving in the *Bataillons d'Afrique*, or *'bat' d'Af'* (punishment regiment in Fr. N. Africa).

jubé (ʒybe), s.m. [L *jube*] (arch.) Rood-loft, rood-screen; (fam.) *venir à* ~, to give in, to submit.

jubilaire (ʒybilɛr), adj. (of year, &c.) Jubilee, of the jubilee; (of person) who has reached his fiftieth year of service.

jubilant, -e (ʒybilɑ̃), p. adj. Jubilant, joyful.

jubilation (ʒybilaˈsjɔ̃), s.f. Jubilation, joy, rejoicing.

jubilé (ʒybile), s.m. [Hebr. *yobel*] (Jew. hist., R.C. Ch.) Jubilee; (of person, &c.) jubilee, fiftieth anniversary; (of married couple) golden wedding.

jubiler (ʒybile), v.n. [L *jubilare*] To exult, to jubilate, to rejoice.

juchée (ʒyʃe), s.f. Pheasant's perch or roost.

jucher (ʒyʃe), v.n. [f. OF *juc* = *juchoir*] (of birds) To roost, to go to roost; (fam.) to live in a high story; to perch oneself up; ~, v.a. to perch (a thing) up high; **se** ~ v.pr. to perch, to perch oneself.

juchoir (ʒyʃwar), s.m. Roost, perch, roosting-place.

judaïque (ʒydaik), adj. [L *judaeus*] Judaic, Judaical, Jewish; *interprétation* ~, pharisaical interpretation.

judaïquement (ʒydaikmɑ̃), adv. Judaically, Jewishly.

judaïsant, -e (ʒydaizɑ̃), p. adj. Judaizing, that follows Jewish customs.

judaïser (ʒydaize), v.a.n. To judaize.

judaïsme (ʒydaism), s.m. Judaism.

judas (ʒydɑ), s.m. **1.** (fam.) Judas, traitor; betrayer; *baiser de* ~, Judas kiss; *poil de* ~, carroty hair; **2.** judas, peep-hole.

judicature (ʒydikatyr), s.f. [L *judicaturus*] Judicature.

judiciaire (ʒydisjɛr), adj. [L *judiciarius*] Judicial, forensic, legal; *débats* ~*s*, forensic discussions; *vente* ~, sale by order of the Court; *combat* ~, trial by combat; *poursuites* ~*s*, legal proceedings. ~, s.f. Judgement, discernment, sense, judiciousness.

judiciairement (ʒydisjɛrmɑ̃), adv. Judicially, legally, by act of justice, forensically.

judicieusement (ʒydisjøzmɑ̃), adv. Judiciously, sensibly, discerningly, wisely, discreetly.

judicieu-x, -se (ʒydisjø) Judicious, sensible, discerning, wise, discreet.

jugal, -e, (aux) (ʒygal), adj. [f. L *jugalis*] (anat.) Cheek-, jugal, zygomatic (bone, &c.); syn. ZYGOMATIQUE.

juge (ʒyʒ), s.m. [L *judex*] (jur.) Judge; magistrate, justice; ~ *de paix*, justice of the peace, magistrate; ~ *consulaire*, judge for commercial cases; ~ *d'instruction*, examining magistrate, police magistrate; (fam.) judge, arbiter, arbitrator, umpire; *être* ~ *et partie*, to be judge of one's own cause; *le souverain* ~, the supreme arbiter, God.

jugé (ʒyʒe), s.m. (used only in certain phrases) *Bien* ~, just sentence; *mal* ~, unjust sentence; *tirer au* ~, to shoot or make a shot by guess; *au* ~, or *au juger*, at a guess.

jugeable (ʒyʒabl), adj. Capable of being judged, amenable to a tribunal.

jugement (ʒyʒmɑ̃), s.m. **1.** (law) Judg(e)ment, sentence; *prononcer le* ~, to pass sentence; *mettre en* ~, to bring to trial; *rendre un* ~ *contre un malfaiteur*, to deliver judgement against, to sentence, a malefactor; ~ *par défaut*, judgement by default; *subir un* ~, to undergo sentence; *le* ~ *dernier*, doomsday, the Day of Judgement; **2.** judgement, discernment; *avoir un* ~ *droit*, to have sound judgement; *faire preuve de* ~, to show good sense; judgement, opinion, estimate; *je m'en rapporte à votre* ~, I leave it to you; *donner son* ~ *sur une chose*, to give one's opinion about, one's estimate of, a thing.

jugeote (ʒyʒɔt), s.f. (fam.) Gumption, nous, good sense, discernment, judgement.

juger (ʒyʒe), v.a.n. [L *judicare*] To judge, to give judgement on, to pronounce sentence on; to form an opinion about; to criticize; to deem; ~ *nécessaire de*, to deem it necessary to; *mal* ~, to misjudge; ~ *sur l'étiquette du sac*, to judge by appearances; *au* ~: see JUGÉ; **se** ~, v.pr. (*a*) to judge oneself; to judge each other; (*b*) to be tried; *l'affaire se jugera demain*, the case will be heard to-morrow.

jugeu-r, -se (ʒyʒœr), s.m.f. (pej.) Faultfinder, caviller.

jugulaire (ʒygylɛr), s.f. [f. L *jugulum*] (anat.) Jugular (vein); (mil.) chin-strap. ~, adj. Jugular.

juguler (ʒygyle), v.a. [L *jugulare*] To strangle, to jugulate; (fig.) to arrest course of.

jui-f, -ve (ʒɥif), adj. [L *judaeus*] Jewish. ~, s.m.f. Jew, (fem.) Jewess; *le* ~ *errant*, the wandering Jew; *le petit* ~, the funnybone (in elbow).

juillet (ʒɥije), s.m. [L *julius*] July.

juin (ʒɥɛ̃), s.m. [L *junius*] June.

juiverie (ʒɥivri), s.f. Jewry, set of Jews; ghetto; Jewish trick.

jujube (ʒyʒyb), s.m. [f. Gr. *zizuphon*] Jujube.

jujubier (ʒyʒybje), s.m. (bot.) Jujube-tree.

julep (ʒylɛp), s.m. [Arab. *julāb*] (pharm.) Julep.

julien, -ne (ʒyljɛ̃), adj. [f. *Julius Caesar*] Julian; *calendrier* ~, Julian calendar.

julienne (ʒyljɛn), s.f. **1.** (bot.) Rocket; **2.** (cook.) julienne (vegetables cut in small pieces, for soup).

jumeau (ʒymo), (pl. **-x**), fem. **jumelle**, adj. [L *gemellus*] Twin, twin-born; double, alike; *cerises jumelles*, double cherries. ~ s.m.f. Twin.

jumelé, -e (ʒymle), p. adj. Geminate, double, twin; *bandages* ~*s*, twin tyres; (herald.) gemel.

jumeler (ʒymle), v.a. To geminate, to couple, to double, to link, to strengthen with cheeks.

jumelles (ʒymɛl), s.f.pl. **1.** Twin sisters; **2.** opera-glasses, binoculars, field-glasses; **3.** (carp.) cheeks, side-beams; **4.** (herald.) gemel.

jument (ʒymɑ̃), s.f. [L *jumentum*] Mare.

jungle (ʒɔ̃gl), s.f. [Sansk. *jangala*] Jungle.

junte (ʒɔ̃t), s.f. [Span. *junta*] Junta.

jupe (ʒyp), s.f. [Arab. *jubba*] Skirt; *il est toujours pendu aux* ~*s de sa mère*, he is always tied to his mother's apron-strings.

jupon (ʒypɔ̃), s.m. Petticoat, underskirt.

jurande (ʒyrɑ̃d), s.f. (obs.) Wardenship of a guild.

jurassien, -ne (ʒyrasjɛ̃), adj. s.m.f. Jurassian, (native) of the Jura.

jurassique (ʒyrasik), adj. (geol.) Jurassic.

jurat (ʒyra), s.m. [L *juratus*] (obs.) Jurat, municipal officer in south of France before the Revolution.

juratoire (ʒyratwar), adj. (law) Juratory.

juré, -e (ʒyre), p. adj. Sworn; *ennemis* ~*s*, sworn enemies.

juré (ʒyre), s.m. [f. *jurer*] Juryman, juror; *récuser un* ~, to challenge a juror.

jurement (ʒyrmɑ̃), s.m. [f. *jurer*] Oath, swearing.

jurer (ʒyre), v.a.n. [L *jurare*] **1.** To swear, to state (something) on oath, to take an oath, to vow, to promise; **2.** to swear, to blaspheme; ~ *comme un charretier*, to swear like a trooper; **3.** to clash, to jar, to be out of keeping (*avec*, with); *le vert jure avec le bleu*, green clashes with blue; or green does not go with blue; *il ne faut* ~ *de rien*, you never can tell.

jureur (ʒyrœr), s.m. (rare) Swearer.

juridiction (ʒyridiksjɔ̃), s.f. [L *jurisdictio*] Jurisdiction.

juridictionnel, -le (ʒyridiksjɔnɛl), adj. Jurisdictional.

juridique (ʒyridik), adj. Judicial, legal, juridical.

juridiquement (ʒyridikmɑ̃), adv. Juridically.

jurisconsulte (ʒyriskɔ̃sylt), s.m. [L *jurisconsultus*] Jurist, lawyer, jurisconsult.

jurisprudence (ʒyrisprydɑ̃s), s.f. [L *jurisprudentia*] Jurisprudence.

juriste (ʒyrist), s.m. [f. L *jus*] Jurist.

juron (ʒyrɔ̃), s.m. Oath, profane oath; blasphemy; *lâcher un* ~, to rap out an oath; to use strong language.

jury (ʒyri), s.m. [Engl. wd] Jury; *chef du* ~, foreman of the jury; *dresser la liste du* ~, to empanel a jury; *il est du* ~, he is on the jury; ~ *d'examen*, board of examiners.

jus (ʒy), s.m. [L wd] Juice; gravy; (mil. slang) coffee; (techn. slang) electric current; juice; *le* ~ *de la treille*, wine.

jusant (ʒyzɑ̃), s.m. [f. L *jusum*] (naut.) Ebb-tide; *au* ~, at ebb-tide.

jusée (ʒyze), s.f. Tan-liquor.

jusque (ʒysk), prep. [LL *deusque*] Till,

---

a, mal, latte; **ɑ**, pas; **ɑ̃**, *enfant*; **e**, *fée*; **ɛ**, *père*, nette; **ɛ̃**, *vin*, *pain*; **ə**, *premier*; **g**, *dogue*, *gale*; **h**, *héros*; **i**, *finir*; **j**, *yeux*, *viens*, *bailler*; **k**, *croire*; **ɲ**, *oignon*; **o**, *pause*, *dose*;

until, as far as; *jusqu'à ce que, jusqu'à tant que* (with subj.), till; *jusqu'à ce qu'il vienne,* till he comes; *jusqu'ici,* till now, so far, as far as here; *~-là,* till then, up to that point; *jusqu'alors,* till then, until now; *jusqu'à présent,* till now; *jusqu'à quand?,* how long?; *jusqu'où?,* how far?, to what extent?; *jusques à quand?,* till when?, how long?; *il n'est pas jusqu'aux animaux qui ne l'aiment,* the very beasts love him; *il jouerait jusqu'à sa chemise,* he would stake his very shirt; *du premier jusqu'au dernier,* from the first to the last; *jusqu'au bout,* to the end; through and through, to a finish; hence: *jusqu'auboutiste,* s.m.f. (war-time slang) whole-hogger, die-hard; (slang) *copains jusqu'à la mort,* pals till hell freezes.

jusquiame (ʒyskjam), s.f. [Gr. *huoskuamos*] (bot.) Henbane.

jussion (ʒysjɔ̃), s.f. [L *jussio*] (Royal) command.

justaucorps (ʒystokɔr), s.m. [*juste-au-corps*] Jerkin, close-fitting body-garment; long corselet-bodice.

juste (ʒyst), adj. [L *justus*] **1.** Just, equitable, right, righteous, fair, legitimate; *~ récompense,* just reward; **2.** just, accurate, exact, true, sound, correct; *avoir l'oreille ~,* to have a correct ear; *le total est ~,* the sum is accurate, or correct; *cette pendule est ~,* this clock is right; **3.** tight, narrow; barely enough; *des souliers trop ~s,* shoes which are too small; *100 francs, c'est bien ~,* 100 frs, that 's barely enough; *au plus ~,* at the lowest; *comme de ~,* of course; *je ne puis le dire au ~,* I cannot tell exactly; *c'est ~,* that 's right; *~ ciel!, ~s cieux!,* heavens! ~, s.m.f. The just; upright or righteous man or woman. ~, adv. *~ en cet endroit,* just at that spot; *il est ~ trois heures,* it 's just three o'clock; *j'ai passé tout ~,* I just managed to pass.

justement (ʒystəmɑ̃), adv. **1.** Justly, equitably, fairly, rightly; **2.** just, exactly; indeed.

juste-milieu (pl. -x) (ʒystəmiljø), s.m. Happy medium, golden mean.

justesse (ʒystɛs), s.f. Justness, accuracy, precision, correctness, propriety; (mus.) correctness; *de ~,* with precision; by a hairbreadth.

justice (ʒystis), s.f. [L *justitia*] Justice; fairness, equitableness, righteousness, impartiality; courts of justice; jurisdiction; *aller en ~,* to go to law; *appeler X en ~,* to go to law with X; *citer X en ~,* to sue X; *rendre ~ à X,* to do justice to X; *faire ~ de X,* to treat X as he or it deserves; *cour de ~,* court of law; *que ~ soit faite,* let execution be done; *rendre la ~,* to administer justice; *bois de ~,* gallows, framework of guillotine; *se faire ~ à soi-même,* to take the law into one's own hands; *réclamer ~,* or *demander ~,* to seek redress. ⚠ English 'justice' also = 'magistrate', *magistrat, juge*; ex. Justice of the Peace = *juge de paix.*

justiciable (ʒystisjabl), adj. Justiciable, amenable. ~, s.m.f. Justiciable.

justicier (ʒystisje), s.m. Justiciary, administrator of justice; lover of justice; one who redresses wrong. ~ adj. Justiciary.

justicier (ʒystisje), v.a. To execute judgement on, to punish.

justifiable (ʒystifjabl), adj. Justifiable, warrantable.

justifiablement (ʒystifjabləmɑ̃), adv. Warrantably.

justifiant, -e (ʒystifjɑ̃), p. adj. (theol.) Justifying.

justificat-eur, -rice (ʒystifikatœr), adj. Justificatory.

justificati-f, -ve (ʒystifikatif), adj. Justificative; *mémoire ~,* voucher; document in proof, documentary memo.

justification (ʒystifika'sjɔ̃), s.f. [f. L *justificare*] Justification, proof; (print.) adjustment of line, length of line.

justifier (ʒystifje), v.a. [L *justificare*] To justify, to manifest, to prove, to clear, to vindicate, to legitimate, to make good; (print.) to adjust (lines); *~ de,* v.n. to give satisfactory proof of; **se ~,** v.pr. to justify oneself, to clear oneself; (of things) to be justified.

jute (ʒyt), s.m. [f. Sansk. *juṭa*] Jute.

juter (ʒyte), v.n. [f. *jus*] To give juice; to spirt.

juteu-x, -se (ʒytø), adj. Juicy. ~, s.m. (mil. slang) Adjutant.

juvénile (ʒyvenil), adj. [f. L *juvenis*] Juvenile, youthful.

juvénilement (ʒyvenilmɑ̃), adv. Youthfully, boyishly.

juvénilité (ʒyvenilite), s.f. Juvenility.

juxtalinéaire (ʒykstalineɛr), adj. [f. L *juxta+linea*] Juxtalinear, line for line.

juxtaposer (ʒykstapoze), v.a. [f. L *juxta+* (Fr.) *poser*] To juxtapose.

juxtaposition (ʒykstapozisjɔ̃), s.f. Juxtaposition; (techn.) *par simple ~,* butt-jointed.

K

K, k (kɑ), s.m. 11th letter of the alphabet.

kabyle (kabil), adj. s.m.f. Kabyle, Berber.

kaïnite (kainit), s.f. (chem.) Kainite.

kakatoès (kakatoɛs), s.m. [Malay *kakatoua*] (ornith.) Cockatoo; syn. CACATOIS.

kaki (kaki), s.m. (bot.) [Jap. wd] Japanese persimmon, kaki (fruit).

kaléidoscope (kaleidɔskɔp), s.m. [f. Gr. *kalos+eidos+skopein*] Kaleidoscope.

kali (kali), s.m. **1.** (bot.) Saltwort; **2.** kali, soda.
kamichi (kamiʃi), s.m. (ornith.) Horned screamer.
kan, khan (kɑ̃), s.m. [Turki wd] **1.** Khan, prince; **2.** khan, caravanserai.
kanat, khanat (kana), s.m. Khanate.
kangourou (kɑ̃guru), s.m. (zool.) Kangaroo.
kantien, -ne (kɑ̃tjɛ̃), adj. [f. Immanuel *Kant*] Kantian.
kantisme (kɑ̃tism), s.m. [f. *Kant*] Kantism; hence: *kantiste*, kantist.
kaolin (kaɔlɛ̃), s.m. [Chinese wd] Kaolin.
kaoliniser (kaɔlinize), v.a. To kaolinize.
kappa (kapa), s.m. Kappa, 10th letter of Greek alphabet.
karagan (karagɑ̃), s.m. (zool.) Karagan, a species of Siberian fox.
karakul (karakyl), s.m. See CARACUL.
karatas (karatɑs), s.m. (bot.) Karatas (tropical plant of the family *Bromeliaceae*).
karpathique (karpatik), adj. Carpathian.
kayac (kajak), s.m. [Eskimo wd] Kayak (canoe).
képi (kepi), s.m. [f. Germ.-Swiss *Käppi*] Kepi, cap.
kératine (keratin), s.f. Keratin.
kératose (keratoz), s.f. [f. Gr. *keras, keratos*] (pathol.) Keratose.
kermès (kɛrmɛs), s.m. [Arab. *kirmiz*] (ent.) Kermes.
kermesse (kɛrmɛs), s.f. [Flem. wd] Kermis.
ketmie (kɛtmi), s.f. (bot.) Ketmia.
keuper (køpɛr), s.m. (obs.) (geol.) Keuper (upper trias).
khamsin (kamsin), s.m. [Arab. *khamsīn*] Khamsin (wind).
khan (kɑ̃), s.m. See KAN.
khédivat (kediva), s.m. Khedivate.
khédive (kediv), s.m. [Turk. wd] Khedive.
khédivial, -e, (aux) (kedivjal), adj. Khedival.
kief (kjɛf), s.m. [Arab. *kaif*] Kef, kief, drowsy state, complete rest of Orientals.
kif-kif (kifkif), adv. loc. (pop.) *C'est* ~, or *c'est* ~ *bourriquot*, it 's six of one and half a dozen of the other; it 's much of a muchness; it comes to the same.
kilo- (kilo), pref. [f. Gr. *khilioi* = 1000] In comb. = 1000. ~, s.m. (abbrev. of *kilogramme*) Kilogram (10 kilograms = about 22 lb.).
kilogramme (kilɔgram), s.m. [*kilo+gramme*] Kilogram (abbrev. kg.).
kilogrammètre (kilɔgramɛtr), s.m. [*kilo+gramme+mètre*] Kilogrammetre.
kilojoule (kilɔʒul), s.m. [*kilo+joule*] Kilojoule (abbrev. kj.).
kilolitre (kilɔlitr), s.m. [*kilo+litre*] Kilolitre.
kilométrage (kilɔmetraʒ), s.m. Measuring by kilometres.
kilomètre (kilɔmɛtr), s.m. [*kilo+mètre*] Kilometre (= ⅝ of a mile; abbrev. km.).
kilométrer (kilɔmetre), v.a. To measure by kilometres; to mark distances in kilometres on road, railway, &c.
kilométrique (kilɔmetrik), adj. Kilometric, kilometrical.
kilowatt (kilɔwat), s.m. [*kilo+watt* = 1000 *watts*] (electr.) Kilowatt.
kimono (kimɔno), s.m. [Jap. wd] Kimono, Japanese dressing-gown.
kinétoscope (kinetɔskɔp), s.m. [f. Gr. *kinein*] Kinetoscope.
King-Charles (kingʃarl), s.m. King Charles's spaniel.
kinkajou (kɛ̃kaʒu), s.m. (zool.) Kinkajou.
kino (kino), s.m. (pharm.) Kino (gum of various trees, used as astringent).
kiosque (kjɔsk), s.m. [f. Turk. *kiūshk*] Kiosk; news-stall; ~ *à musique*, bandstand.
kirsch, kirschwasser (kirʃ, kirʃvasœr), s.m. [Germ. wd] Kirsch, kirschwasser.
klaxon (klaksɔ̃, klaksɔn), s.m. [neol.] Motor-horn.
klephte (klɛft), s.m.f. Klepht.
kleptomane (klɛptɔman), adj. s.m.f. Kleptomaniac.
kleptomanie (klɛptɔmani), s.f. [Gr. *kleptēs+mania*] Kleptomania.
knout (knut), s.m. [Russ. wd] Knout.
kobold (kɔbɔld), s.m. [Germ. myth.] Kobold.
kodak (kɔdak), s.m. [trade name] Kodak, photographic camera.
kohl, kohol (kol), s.m. [Arab. wd] Kohl.
kola (kɔla), s.m. [f. West African native wd] (bot.) Kola, cola; *noix de* ~, cola-nut.
konak (kɔnak), s.m. [Serb. wd] King's palace in Serbia.
kopeck (kɔpɛk), s.m. [Russ. wd] Kopeck, copeck.
kopje (kɔpj), s.m. [Dutch wd] Kopje, small hill in South Africa.
korrigan, -e (kɔrigɑ̃), s.m.f. [Bret. wd] Korrigan, leprechaun, sprite.
krach (krak), s.m. [Germ. wd] Krach, financial crash.
krypton (kriptɔ̃), s.m. [f. Gr. *krupton*] (chem.) Krypton (a rare gas, discovered by Ramsay in 1898).
ksar (pl. **ksour**) (ksar), s.m. [Berber wd] Ksar, fortified place.
Kugelhopf, kouglof (kuglɔf), s.m. Kugelhopf, an Alsatian cake.
kummel (kymɛl), s.m. [Germ. wd] Kümmel (liqueur).
kurde (kyrd), adj. Of Kurdistan. ~ s.m.f. Kurd.
kwass (kvas), s.m. [Russ. wd] Kvass (liqueur).
kymrique, cymrique (kimrik, simrik), adj. s.m. Cymric.

kyrie (kirie), s.m. [Gr. wd] Kyrie, kyrie eleison.
kyrielle (kirjɛl), s.f. [f. Gr. *kurie*] Litany; (colloq.) string, lot, list, long string of words.
kyste (kist), s.m. [Gr. *kustis*] (pathol.) Cyst.
kysteu-x, -se, kystique (kistø, kistik), adj. Cystous.

L

L, l (ɛl), s.m. 12th letter of the alphabet.
l' (contr. of *le* and *la* before vowels and silent aitches) The; him, her, it.
la (la), art. f. sing. [L *illa*] The. ~, pron. Her, it; *je ~ verrai*, I shall see her; *ce fut une faute, je veux l'oublier*, it was a mistake, I wish to forget about it.
la (la), s.m. [1st syllable of *labii*, in ancient hymn] (mus.) La, A; (fig.) *donner le ~*, to set the fashion.
là (la), adv. [L *illac*] There, thither, here; *çà et ~*, here and there; to and fro; everywhere; *celui-~, celle-~*, that one; that; he, she; *cet homme-~*, that man there, this man; *ces gens-~*, those people; *à ce point-~*, to this degree; *restons-en ~*, that 's enough; let 's stop there; *à dix milles de ~*, ten miles away; ten miles off; *il en est ~, vraiment !*, really ! so this is what he has come to !; *que dites-vous ~ !*, now, what are you saying ! ; *elle n'est pas ~*, she is out; she is not here; *~-bas*, down there, yonder, over there; *~-dedans*, in there, within; *~-dessous*, under there, underneath; *il y a quelque chose ~-dessous*, there is a snake in the grass; I smell a rat; *~-dessus*, up there; thereupon; *~-dessus il salua et partit*, thereupon he raised his hat and went; *~-haut*, up there; (fig.) in Paradise, in heaven; *~ même*, in that very place; ~,~, now, now; easy, gently; (excl.) *oh ~ ~ !*, oh ! dear me !; *tout est ~*, that 's the main point; (slang) *il est un peu ~*, he is all there; he is not the man to be overlooked; *qui va ~ ?*, who goes there ?; *par ~*, that way.
label (labɛl), s.m. [Engl. wd] (comm.) Label. ⚠ In French *label* is only used in the sense of special trade-union mark.
labelle (labɛl), s.m. [L *labellum*] (bot.) Labellum.
labeur (labœr), s.m. [L *labor*] Labour, work, toil, pains; (print.) book-work long numbers.
labial, -e, (aux) (labjal), adj. [f. L *labium*] Labial. ~e, s.f. (phon.) Labial.
labiatiflore (labjatiflɔr), adj. [L *labium*+*flos*] (bot.) Labiate (plant).
labié, -e (labje), adj. (bot.) Labiate.
labile (labil), adj. [L *labilis*] Labile; unstable, liable to fail.
laboratoire (labɔratwar), s.m. [f. L *laborare*] Laboratory.
laborieusement (labɔrjøzmɑ̃), adv. Laboriously, with difficulty, painfully.
laborieu-x, -se (labɔrjø), adj. [L *laboriosus*] **1.** Laborious; hard-working, industrious; **2.** toilful, showing signs of toil, not facile, not fluent, painful.
labour (labur), s.m. Tillage, ploughing; ploughed land; *donner un labour à*, to till, to plough; *bœufs de ~*, plough-oxen. ⚠ Not English 'labour' which = *labeur, peine, dur travail*, and also *accouchement, douleurs*.
labourable (laburabl), adj. Fit for tillage; arable.
labourage (laburaʒ), s.m. Ploughing; dressing (of vines); art of husbandry.
labourer (labure), v.a.n. [L *laborare*] To plough, to dig; to dress (vines); (fig.) to cut, to rip up; *la balle lui a labouré le visage*, the bullet ripped up his face; (naut.) to drag; *~ le fond*, to graze the bottom; to toil and moil, to drudge.
laboureur (laburœr), s.m. Ploughman; husbandman. ⚠ Not English 'labourer', which = *travailleur, journalier, manœuvre*; ex. a bricklayer's labourer = *un manœuvre de maçon*.
laboureuse (laburøz), s.f. Steam-plough.
labre (labr), s.m. [L *labrum*] **1.** (anat., zool.) Upper lip; **2.** (ichth.) rock-fish; syn. VIEILLE DE MER.
labyrinthe (labirɛ̃t), s.m. [Gr. *laburinthos*] **1.** Labyrinth, maze; **2.** (anat.) labyrinth.
labyrinthodon (labirɛ̃tɔdɔ̃), s.m. [Gr. *laburinthos*+*odous*] (zool.) Labyrinthodon.
lac (lak), s.m. [L *lacus*] Lake; (fig., colloq.) *l'affaire est dans le ~*, it 's all up; it 's a complete failure.
laçage, lacement (lasaʒ, lasmɑ̃), s.m. [f. *lacer*] Lacing.
laccase (lakaz), s.f. (chem.) Laccin.
laccifère (laksifɛr), adj. (bot.) Lacciferous.
lacé (lase), s.m. [f. *lacer*] Lace-glass.
lacédémonien, -ne (lasedemɔnjɛ̃), adj. s.m.f. Lacedaemonian.
lacer (lase), v.a. [L *laqueare*] To lace; to interlace; (naut.) to fasten (sails) together; *se ~*, to tighten one's stays.
lacération (lasera'sjɔ̃), s.f. Laceration, tearing up.
lacérer (lasere), v.a. [L *lacerare*] To lacerate, to tear up.
laceron (lasrɔ̃), s.m. See LAITERON.
lacertiens, lacertiliens (lasɛrtjɛ̃, lasɛrtiljɛ̃), s.m.pl. [f. L *lacerta*] (zool.) Lacertians, *Lacertilia*.
lacet (lasɛ), s.m. [f. *lacs*] Lace; braid; bowstring; snare; sharp bend; (fig.) snare, toils; *route en ~s*, a zigzag road; a road with numerous sharp bends; *ferrer un ~*, to tag a lace; *mouvement de ~*, rocking; *poser des ~s*, to set toils.
lâchage (lɑʃaʒ), s.m. Letting go; (fam.) jilting, giving the slip, dropping.

lâche (lɑʃ), adj. [f. *lâcher*] **1.** Loose, slack; **2.** cowardly, slothful, mean-spirited, dastardly, base. ~, s.m. Coward, poltroon, sluggard.
lâché, -e (lɑʃe), p. adj. [f. *lâcher*] Slackly done, carelessly or slothfully done.
lâchement (lɑʃmɑ̃), adv. In a dastardly, cowardly way; feebly, without vigour, without spirit; loosely; slothfully.
lâcher (lɑʃe), v.a. [L *laxare*] To loosen, to slacken, to relax, to loose, to loose one's hold of, to let slip, to let go, to release, to liberate; ~ *sa proie*, to let one's prey escape; ~ *un coup de fusil*, to discharge a gun; (fam.) ~ *ses alliés*, to abandon one's allies; ~ *une sottise*, to blurt out a foolish remark; ~ *prise*, to let go; ~ *pied*, to give ground, to flee; *elle l'a lâché*, she has jilted him; *vous n'allez pas nous ~?*, you won't leave us in the lurch?
lâcher (lɑʃe), s.m. [f. *lâcher*] The act of letting go, of releasing; *un ~ de pigeons*, the release of a flight of pigeons.
lâcheté (lɑʃte), s.f. [f. *lâche*] Cowardice, faint-heartedness; meanness, baseness; *commettre une ~*, to commit an act of cowardice or of meanness.
lâcheu-r, -se (lɑʃœr), s.m.f. [f. *lâcher*] (fam.) Turncoat; shirker; one who abandons his friends.
lacinié, -e (lasinje), adj. [L *laciniatus*] (bot.) Laciniate, jagged.
lacis (lasi), s.m. [f. *lacer*] **1.** Network; **2.** (anat.) plexus.
laçon (lasɔ̃), s.m. Wire snare.
laconique (lakɔnik), adj. [Gr. *lakōnikos*] Laconic, concise.
laconiquement (lakɔnikmɑ̃), adv. Laconically.
laconisme (lakɔnism), s.m. Laconism, conciseness, brevity.
lacryma-christi (lakrima kristi), s.m. [L wds] Lachryma Christi (wine).
lacrymal, -e (pl. **aux**) (lakrimal), adj. [L *lacryma*] (anat.) Lachrymal.
lacrymatoire (lakrimatwɑr), s.m. adj. [L *lacryma*] Lachrymatory.
lacrymogène (lakrimɔʒɛn), adj. Tear-producing; *gaz ~*, tear-gas.
lacs (lɑ), s.m.pl. [L *laqueus*] Noose, snare; toils; cord; *tendre des ~ à X*, to lay snares for X; ~ *d'amour*, love-knot.
lactaire (laktɛr), adj. [LL *lactaris*] Lactary. ~, s.m. (bot.) A kind of mushroom.
lactate (laktat), s.m. [L *lac*] (chem.) Lactate.
lactation (lakta'sjɔ̃), s.f. Lactation.
lacté, -e (lakte), adj. Milky; lacteous; *diète ~e*, milk diet; (astrol.) *la voie ~e*, the Milky Way.
lactescence (laktessɑ̃s), s.f. Lactescence, milkiness.
lactescent, -e (laktessɑ̃), adj. [L *lactescere*] Lactescent, milky.
lactifère (laktifɛr), adj. [L *lactifer*] Lactiferous.
lactique (laktik), adj. Lactic.
lactomètre (laktɔmɛtr), s.m. Lactometer.
lactose (laktoz), s.f. Lactose.
lactucarium (laktykarjɔm), s.m. [f. L *lactuca*] (pharm.) Lactucarium.
lacune (lakyn), s.f. [L *lacuna*] Lacuna; gap, hiatus, missing link, blank, omission, deficiency; *combler une ~*, to fill a blank or gap; to meet a want.
lacuneu-x, -se (lakynø), adj. Deficient, lacunal, lacunary, lacunose.
laçure (lasyr), s.f. [f. *lacer*] Lacing.
lacustre (lakystr), adj. [f. L *lacus*] Lacustrine; *cité ~*, lake village.
ladanum (ladanɔm), s.m. [Gr. *ladanon*] Ladanum, gum-resin.
ladre (ladr), adj. [f. *Lazarus*] **1.** Leprous; **2.** (fig.) mean, stingy; close-fisted, shabby, scurvy. ~, s.m. **1.** Leper; lazar; **2.** (fig.) miser; curmudgeon.
ladrerie (ladrəri), s.f. **1.** Leprosy, leper-hospital, lazar-house; **2.** measles (in pigs); **3.** avarice, stinginess, sordidness.
lagan (lagɑ̃), s.m. (obs.) Feudal due of lagan.
lagon (lagɔ̃), s.m. (small) Lagoon; pool on the shore.
lagopède (lagɔpɛd), s.m. [Gr. *lagōs*+L *pes*] (ornith.) Lagopode, ptarmigan.
lagophtalmie (lagɔftalmi), s.f. [Gr. *lagōphthalmon*] (pathol.) Lagophthalmia.
laguis (lagis), s.m. Slip-knot, noose.
lagune (lagyn), s.f. [It. *laguna*] Lagoon.
lai (lɛ), s.m. [OF wd, orig. dub.] Lay, a short narrative poem.
lai, -e (lɛ), adj. [eccles. L *laicus*] Lay. ~, s.m.f. Lay brother, (fem.) lay sister; layman.
laïc (laik), adj. s.m. See LAÏQUE.
laiche (lɛʃ), s.f. [Germ. *Liesch*] (bot.) Sedge.
laïcisation (laisiza'sjɔ̃), s.f. Secularisation.
laïciser (laisize), v.a. [f. *laic*] To laicize, to secularize.
laïcité (laisite), s.f. Secularity.
laid, -e (lɛ), adj. [OHG *leid*] Ugly, ill-looking, ill-featured, ill-favoured, plain, unsightly; naughty; disagreeable; improper; ~ *comme un pou*, ugly as sin. *Le* ~, s.m. Ugliness, the ugly side.
laidement (lɛdmɑ̃), adv. In an unsightly, disagreeable, unpleasant manner.
laideron (lɛdrɔ̃), s.m.f. Plain woman, unattractive creature, plain Jane.
laideur (lɛdœr), s.f. Ugliness, plainness; unsightliness, deformity; unseemliness.
laie (lɛ), s.f. **1.** Sow; **2.** bridle-path; **3.** stone-cutter's hammer.
lainage (lɛnaʒ), s.m. Woollen goods; fleece, wool; woollens; teaseling.
laine (lɛn), s.f. [L *lana*] Wool; worsted;

woolly hair; *bêtes à* ~, sheep; ~ *filée*, worsted; ~ *à quatre fils*, four-ply wool; *pure* ~, all wool; *se laisser manger la* ~ *sur le dos*, to let oneself be eaten out of house and home.

lainer (lɛne), v.a. (techn.) To tease, to dress. ~, s.m. Pile, texture.

lainerie (lɛnri), s.f. Manufacture of wool, woollen trade; woollen goods.

laineu-r, -se (lɛnœr), s.m.f. **1.** Woollen-worker; **2.** ~**se**, s.f. (mech.) gig, gig-mill.

laineu-x, -se (lɛnø), adj. **1.** Woolly, fleecy; **2.** (bot.) downy.

laini-er, -ère (lɛnje), adj. Of wool, woollen. ~, s.m.f. Woollen-worker; wool-merchant.

laïque, laïc (laik), fem. **laïque,** adj. [eccles. L *laicus*] Lay, laic, secular. ~, s.m.f. Layman, (fem.) laywoman; lay brother, (fem.) lay sister; *les laïques*, the laity.

lais (lɛ), s.m.pl. [f. *laisser*] Staddle; alluvium.

laisse (lɛs), s.f. **1.** Leash, lead, strings; **2.** hatband; **3.** (naut.) alluvium, mud-bank; seawrack; tide-mark.

laissées (lɛse), s.f.pl. (hunt.) Dung.

laissé-pour-compte (lɛsepurkɔ̃t), s.m. Article left on the dealer's hands.

laisser (lɛse), v.a. [L *laxare*] To leave, to quit; to give up; to let alone; to leave behind; to leave off; to discard; to abandon; to forget; to entrust; to bequeath; to allow, to permit; *laissez donc!*, leave off!, don't bother; ~ *aller*, to let go, to neglect; ~ *à désirer*, to leave room for improvement; *il y a à prendre et à* ~, there is enough to pick and choose; *c'est à prendre ou à* ~, you may take it or leave it; it's a case of Hobson's choice; ~ *là*, to leave in the lurch; *il est pauvre, mais il ne laisse pas d'être honnête homme*, he is poor, but nevertheless honest; ~ *tomber*, to let fall, to drop; to utter negligently (words); (slang) to drop (a person); to chuck up (a thing); ~ *faire*, to let things drift; to refrain from interference; *laissez-moi la paix*, let me alone; ~ *à l'abandon*, to leave, or to let lie about, in disorder; to neglect completely; **se** ~, v.pr. to let oneself; *se* ~ *aller*, to let oneself go; to let oneself be disheartened; to be careless, to let things drift; *se* ~ *aller à mentir*, to allow oneself to become a liar; *se* ~ *éblouir*, to let oneself be dazzled; *je me suis laissé dire que*, I have been given to understand that; *se* ~ *faire*, not to resist.

laisser aller (lɛseale), s.m. invar. Taking things easy, easy-goingness; lack of constraint; slackness; indifference, neglect, carelessness, listlessness.

laisser-courre (lɛsekur), s.m. invar. (hunt.) The uncoupling; the starting-place.

laisser faire (lɛsefɛr), s.m. invar. Policy of non-intervention.

laisser-passer, laissez-passer (lɛsepɑse), s.m. invar. Pass, permit.

lait (lɛ), s.m. [L *lac*] **1.** Milk; *frère de* ~, foster-brother; *dents de* ~, milk-teeth; *fièvre de* ~, milk fever; *battre le* ~, to churn; *petit* ~, or ~ *clair*, whey; ~ *coupé*, milk and water; ~ *de poule*, egg flip, milk with sugar and yolk of egg; *au* ~, made with milk; (fig.) *sucer avec le* ~, to imbibe in childhood; **2.** liquid resembling milk; white of egg; ~ *d'amandes*, milk of almonds; ~ *de chaux*, white lime; (fig.) *boire du* ~, to experience keen satisfaction; to find something intensely gratifying; *il monte comme une soupe au* ~, he is like touchwood, or tinder; he flares up in a jiffy; he is very short-tempered; *vache à* ~, (lit. and fig.) milch cow.

laitage (lɛtaʒ), s.m. Milk foods; milk diet.

laitance, laite (lɛtɑ̃s, lɛt), s.f. Milt, soft roe.

laité, -e (lɛte), adj. Soft-roed.

laiterie (lɛtri), s.f. Dairy; milk-house; dairy-farm; milk-shop; milk-trade.

laiteron (lɛtrɔ̃), s.m. (bot.) Sow-thistle; hare's-lettuce.

laiteu-x, -se (lɛtø), adj. Milky, lacteal; milk-white.

laiti-er, -ère (lɛtje) **1.** s.m.f. Milkman, dairyman; (fem.) milkmaid, dairymaid. ~, adj. Pertaining to milk, having milk; *vache* ~*ère*, milch cow; **2.** s.m. (metall.) slag, dross.

laiton (lɛtɔ̃), s.m. Brass; alloy of copper and zinc; *fil de* ~, brass wire; hence **laitonner,** (lɛtɔne) v.a. to trim with brass wire.

laitue (lɛty), s.f. [L *lactuca*] (bot.) Lettuce; ~ *romaine*, cos lettuce; ~ *pommée*, cabbage lettuce; ~ *d'âne*, wild teasel; ~ *de chien*, dandelion.

laïus (lajys), s.m. (school slang) Speech, lecture; *piquer un* ~, to spout; to speechify; *faire du* ~, to speak for speaking's sake; hence **laïusser,** (lajyse) v.n. to spout, to speechify.

laize (lɛz), s.f. [LL *latia*] Width (of material).

lakiste (lakist), s.m. [f. Engl. *lake*] Lake poet; *les* ~*s*, the Lake poets.

lama (lama), s.m. **1.** [Peruv. *llama*] (zool.) Llama; **2.** [Tibet. *blama*] Lama.

lamaïque (lamaik), adj. Lamaic, Lamaistic.

lamaïsme (lamaism), s.m. Lamaism.

lamaïste (lamaist), s.m.f. adj. Lamaist.

lamanage (lamanɑʒ), s.m. (naut.) Piloting, pilotage; harbour-pilotage.

lamaneur (lamanœr), s.m. [Flemish *lotman*] (naut.) Pilot; harbour-pilot.

lamantin (lamɑ̃tɛ̃), s.m. (zool.) Lamantin, sea-cow, manatee.

lamaserie (lamazri), s.f. [f. Tibet. *blama*] Lamasery.

lambda (lɑ̃bda), s.m. [Gr. wd] Lambda, 11th letter of Greek alphabet.
lambdacisme (lɑ̃bdasism), s.m. Lambdacism; lallation.
lambeau (pl. -**x**) (lɑ̃bo), s.m. [etym. dub.] Rag, tatter, strip, shred; piece, part, fragment; remains, remnant; scrap, bit, morsel; *en* ~*x*, in rags and tatters; *mettre en* ~*x*, to tear to shreds.
lambel (lɑ̃bɛl), s.m. [etym. dub.] (herald.) Label.
lambick (lɑ̃bik), s.m. Lambick (Belgian beer).
lambin, -e (lɑ̃bɛ̃), s.m.f. [f. *lambiner*] Dawdler, loiterer, slow-coach. ~, adj. Dawdling, loitering, slothful, slow.
lambiner (lɑ̃bine), v.n. [f. prop. n. *Lambin*] To dawdle, to loiter; to trifle, to waste time; to dilly-dally.
lambourde (lɑ̃burd), s.f. **1.** (carp.) Joist; **2.** (mason.) soft building-stone, marlstone.
lambre (lɑ̃br), s.m. (zool.) Spider-crab.
lambrequin (lɑ̃brəkɛ̃), s.m. [f. Flemish *lamper*] **1.** (arch.) Lambrequin, scallop, festoon; **2.** (herald.) lambrequin, mantle; **3.** valance, fringe.
lambris (lɑ̃bri), s.m. [L *labrusca*] Panelling, wainscot, lining; (arch.) roof, ceiling; (poet.) canopy; abode, dwelling; ~ *d'appui*, dado.
lambrissage (lɑ̃brisɑʒ), s.m. Wainscoting, panelling, lining.
lambrisser (lɑ̃brise), v.a. [f. *lambris*] To wainscot, to panel, to line.
lambruche, lambrusque (lɑ̃bryʃ, lɑ̃brysk), s.f. [L *labrusca*] Wild vine.
lame (lam), s.f. [L *lamina*] **1.** (metall.) Plate, sheet; foil; wire; (techn.) plate or leaf; ~ *de ressort*, leaf of a spring; blade; sword; (by ext.) swordsman; *une fine* ~, a first-rate swordsman or fencer; *avoir un visage en* ~ *de couteau*, to be hatchet-faced; **2.** (naut.) wave, billow; swell, surge; *creux de la* ~, trough of the wave.
lamé, -e (lame), adj. Spangled, lamé. ~, s.m. Lamé, brocade woven with raised pattern in gold or silver; cloth of gold or silver, Indian cloth.
lamellaire (lamɛllɛr), adj. Lamellar.
lamelle (lamɛl), s.f. [L *lamella*] Lamella, thin plate; strip.
lamellé, -e, lamelleu-x, -se (lamɛlle, lamɛllø), adj. Lamellate, lamellated, lamellose.
lamellibranche (lamɛllibrɑ̃ʃ), adj. s.m. Lamellibranch, bivalve (mollusc.); having lamellar bivalvular shell.
lamellicorne (lamɛllikɔrn), adj. s.m. (ent.) Lamellicorn.
lamelliforme (lamɛllifɔrm), adj. Lamelliform.
lamellirostre (lamɛllirɔstr), adj. (ornith.) Lamellirostral. ~, s.m. Lamelliroster.
lamentable (lamɑ̃tabl), adj. [L *lamentabilis*] Lamentable, deplorable, pitiable, pitiful; sorry.
lamentablement (lamɑ̃tabləmɑ̃), adv. Lamentably, deplorably, pitifully.
lamentation (lamɑ̃ta'sjɔ̃), s.f. [L *lamentatio*] Lamentation, lament, lamenting; wailing, wail, whine.
(se) lamenter (səlamɑ̃te), v.pr. To lament (*sur*, for, over), to bewail, to whine, to moan.
lamette (lamɛt), s.f. [f. *lame*] Lametta, lamina; small blade or plate.
lamie (lami), s.f. [L *lamia*] **1.** Lamia; **2.** (ichth.) lamia, lamna, white shark; syn. CHIEN-DAUPHIN.
lamier (lamje), s.m. (bot.) Dead-nettle, blind-nettle; syn. ORTIE.
laminage (laminaʒ), s.m. Lamination, laminating, rolling.
laminaire (laminɛr), s.f. [f. L *lamina*] (bot.) Laminaria, sea-girdle.
laminer (lamine), v.a. [f. L *lamina*] To laminate, to roll or beat (metal) into thin plates.
laminerie (laminri), s.f. Rolling-mills.
lamineur (laminœr), s.m. Roller, flatter.
lamineu-x, -se (laminø), adj. Laminose.
laminoir (laminwar), s.m. Rolling-mill, flatting-mill; (fig.) *passer X au* ~, to crush X, to sit upon X, to reduce X to abject submission.
lampadaire (lɑ̃padɛr), s.m. [f. Gr. *lampas*] Candelabrum, lampstand, lampadary.
lampadéphore (lɑ̃padefɔr), s.m. [Gr. *lampas*+*phoros*] Torch-bearer.
lampant, -e (lɑ̃pɑ̃), adj. (of mineral oil) Well purified.
lampas[1] (lɑ̃pɑ), s.m. [f. *lamper*] **1.** (pop.) Throat; *s'arroser le* ~, to wet one's whistle; **2.** (vet.) lampas.
lampas[2] (lɑ̃pɑ), s.m. [etym. dub.] Lampas, silk orig. from China.
lampassé, -e (lɑ̃pɑse), adj. (herald.) Langued.
lampe (lɑ̃p), s.f. [Gr. *lampas*] **1.** Lamp; ~ *à alcool*, spirit-lamp or -stove; ~ *à arc*, arc-lamp; ~ *à huile*, oil-lamp; ~ *à pétrole*, paraffin- or petrol-lamp; ~ *électrique*, electric lamp; ~ *portative*, portable lamp; ~ *de sûreté* or *de mineur* or *de Davy*, safety-lamp; **2.** (slang) belly; *s'en coller plein la* ~, to blow oneself out, to guzzle.
lampée (lɑ̃pe), s.f. Large gulp (of drink), swill, swig.
lamper (lɑ̃pe), v.a. [var. of *laper*] To drink greedily, to toss off, to swig.
lamperon (lɑ̃prɔ̃), s.m. [f. *lampe*] Wick-holder (of a lamp).
lampion (lɑ̃pjɔ̃), s.m. [f. *lampe*] Lampion, lamp used for illuminations; (by ext.) Chinese lantern.
lampiste (lɑ̃pist), s.m.f. **1.** Lamp-maker; **2.** lamp-trimmer.

lampisterie (lɑ̃pistəri), s.f. **1.** Lamp-manufacture, lamp-trade; **2.** lamp-room.
lampourde (lɑ̃purd), s.f. (bot.) Bur-weed.
lamprillon (lɑ̃prijɔ̃), s.m. (ichth.) Small lamprey.
lamproie (lɑ̃prwɑ), s.f. [L *lampetra*, LL *lampreda*] (ichth.) Lamprey; ~ *de rivière*, lampern, river lamprey.
lampyre (lɑ̃pir), s.m. (ent.) Glow-worm, lampyris; syn. VER LUISANT.
lançage (lɑ̃saʒ), s.m. See syn. LANCEMENT.
lancastrien, -ne (lɑ̃kastrjɛ̃), adj. s.m.f. Lancastrian.
lance (lɑ̃s), s.f. [L *lancea*] **1.** Lance, spear; lancer; **2.** nozzle, spout, branch-pipe; (mil., obs.) ~ *à feu*, portfire-stick; (fig.) *rompre une* ~ *pour X*, to take up the cudgels for X; ~*-bombes*, s.m. bomb-thrower; ~*-pierres*, s.m. catapult; ~*-torpilles*, s.m. torpedo-tube.
lancement (lɑ̃smɑ̃), s.m. [f. *lancer*] Throwing, flinging, hurling, casting, cast; (naut.) launching; (fig.) launching, starting, start, pushing (of goods) by advertisement, press, &c.; syn. LANÇAGE.
lancéole (lɑ̃seɔl), s.f. [f. L *lancea*] (bot.) Lanceola.
lancéolé, -e (lɑ̃seɔle), adj. Lanceolate, shaped like spear-head.
lancer (lɑ̃se), v.a. [f. *lance*] To throw, to fling, to hurl, to cast, to dart, to toss; to shoot forth; to emit; to issue (*un mandat d'arrêt*, a warrant); ~ *une gifle à X*, to fetch X a box on the ear; ~ *un regard en arrière*, to throw a glance backwards; (hunt.) ~ *un cerf*, to start a stag; (naut.) ~ *un navire*, to launch a ship; (comm.) ~ *ses produits*, to push, to advertise one's goods; *être très lancé*, to be quite in the swim, to be 'well away'; **se** ~, v.pr. to dart, to rush, to venture, to make a start, to launch out; *se* ~ *à la poursuite de*, to rush in pursuit of; *se* ~ *dans le monde*, to launch out into society. ⚠ 'To lance' is only used poetically in the sense of *lancer*; the usual sense is *percer, ouvrir d'un coup de lancette*.
lancer (lɑ̃se), s.m. Throw, throwing, cast; cast of fishing-line; *pêche au* ~, rod-fishing; (hunt.) starting (of stag, deer, &c.). ⚠ Not 'lancer', which = *lancier*.
lanceron, lançon (lɑ̃srɔ̃, lɑ̃sɔ̃), s.m. (ichth.) Young pike; syn. ÉQUILLE.
lance-torpille (lɑ̃stɔrpij), s.m. Torpedo-tube; pl. *lance-torpilles*.
lancette (lɑ̃sɛt), s.f. (surg.) Lancet; (arch.) *ogive à* ~, lancet arch.
lanceu-r, -se (lɑ̃sœr), s.m.f. Person who starts or launches undertakings; publicity agent; company promoter; pushing person.
lanche (lɑ̃ʃ), s.f. [Span. *lancha*] (naut.) Two-masted boat.
lancier (lɑ̃sje), s.m. (mil.) Lancer; (danc.) *quadrille des* ~*s*, lancers.
lanciforme (lɑ̃sifɔrm), adj. Spear-shaped.
lancinant, -e (lɑ̃sinɑ̃), p. adj. [f. L *lancinare*] Lancinating, shooting; *douleur* ~*e*, shooting pain, twinges of pain.
lancination (lɑ̃sina'sjɔ̃), s.f. Twinge, shooting.
lanciner (lɑ̃sine), v.n. [L *lancinare*] To shoot, to twinge, to be lancinating.
landais, -e (lɑ̃dɛ), adj. s.m.f. Belonging to Les Landes, (inhabitant) of the Landes (France).
landamman (lɑ̃damɑ̃), s.m. [Germ. *Land* +*Amtmann*] Landamman (in Switzerland).
landau (pl. **-s**) (lɑ̃do), s.m. [Germ. geog. orig. *Landau*] Landau.
landaulet (lɑ̃dolɛ), s.m. Landaulet.
lande (lɑ̃d), s.f. [Celt. *landa*] Heath, moor, wasteland; (pl.) dunes; barren tracts.
landgrave (lɑ̃dgrav), s.m. [Germ. *Landgraf*] Landgrave.
landgraviat (lɑ̃dgravja), s.m. Landgraviate.
landier (lɑ̃dje), s.m. [OF *andier*] **1.** Andiron, fire-dog; **2.** (pop.) gorse, furze.
laneret (lanrɛ), s.m. [f. *lanier*] (ornith.) Lanneret.
langage (lɑ̃gaʒ), s.m. [f. *langue*] Language, tongue; speech, dialect; diction; talk, words; style; expression; tone; *changer de langage*, to change one's tone; to sing small; *beau* ~, fine talk.
lange (lɑ̃ʒ), s.m. [L *laneus*] Swaddling-cloth; swathing-band; swathe; napkin; (print.) blanket.
langer (lɑ̃ʒe), v.a. To swaddle.
langoureusement (lɑ̃gurøzmɑ̃), adv. Languishingly, languorously, amorously, longingly, yearningly.
langoureu-x, -se (lɑ̃gurø), adj. [f. *languer*] Languishing; pining; languid, yearning, longing, sentimental.
langouste (lɑ̃gust), s.f. [L *locusta*] (crust.) Spiny lobster; rock lobster.
langoustière (lɑ̃gustjɛr), s.f. Lobster-net.
langoustine (lɑ̃gustin), s.m. (crust.) Prawn.
langue (lɑ̃g), s.f. [L *lingua*] Tongue; strip, neck, tongue, narrow oblong thing; language; speech, talk; style; ~ *verte*, (syn. *argot*) slang; *coup de* ~, epigram; slanderous remark; sarcasm; *jeter sa* ~ *aux chiens*, to give it up, to give up guessing; *avaler sa* ~, to hold one's tongue; *tirer la* ~, put out one's tongue (*à*, at); (fig.) to show signs of exhaustion; *se mordre la* ~, (*a*) to stop short when about to say something silly, or untimely; (*b*) to repent of what one has said; *avoir la* ~ *bien pendue* or *affilée*, to have the gift of the gab, to have a glib tongue; *avoir la*

~ *affilée*, to have a sharp tongue; *avoir la ~ trop longue*, to have a long tongue; to be unable to keep a secret; *prendre ~*, to get into conversation (*avec*, with); *avoir la ~ liée*, to be tongue-tied; *avoir un mot sur le bout de la ~*, to have a word on the tip of one's tongue; *être une mauvaise ~*, to be a back-biter or slanderer; *la ~ lui a fourché*, he made a slip of the tongue; *elle n'a pas sa ~ dans sa poche*, she is never at a loss for a reply; she has a ready tongue; ~ *mère*, primitive language; ~ *maternelle*, native tongue, mother tongue; ~ *morte*, dead language; ~ *vivante*, living language; ~ *de chat*, s.f. thin finger-biscuit; ~ *de terre*, narrow strip of land.

languedocien, -ne (lɑ̃gdosjɛ̃), adj. s.m.f. (Native) of Languedoc.

languette (lɑ̃gɛt), s.f. Small tongue; tongue-shaped object; needle (of a balance); tongue (of a musical instrument); stem (of a key); partition (in a chimney); (naut.) wedge; (techn.) flat key; feather.

langueur (lɑ̃gœr), s.f. [L *languor*] Languor; languidness; debility, lassitude, weakness, listlessness, apathy; *maladie de ~*, decline, lingering disease, consumption.

languide (lɑ̃gid), adj. [L *languidus*] Languid; weary; weak; listless; dull; apathetic.

languier (lɑ̃gje), s.m. Smoked hog's tongue.

languir (lɑ̃gir), v.n. [L *languere*] To languish; to waste away; to wither; to long; to pine; to droop; to flag; to be dull, to be inactive; ~ *d'amour*, to pine away for love; *elle se languit*, she is pining away. (In the south of France the v.pr. *se languir* is most usual.)

languissamment (lɑ̃gisamɑ̃), adv. Languidly; feebly, weakly; languishingly; apathetically; listlessly; wearily.

languissant, -e (lɑ̃gisɑ̃), p. adj. Languishing, languid, languorous; drooping, pining; flagging; weak; slow, slack; dull, flat, heavy; spiritless, listless, apathetic.

languissement (lɑ̃gismɑ̃), s.m. Drooping, declining, decline, languishing.

laniaire (lanjɛr), adj. [L *laniarius*] Laniary, canine; lacerating. ~, s.f. Canine tooth.

lanice (lanis), adj. f. Of wool; *bourre ~*, wool flocks.

lanier (lanje), s.m. [f. L *laniarius*] (ornith.) Lanner.

lanière (lanjɛr), s.f. [etym. dub.] Thong; lash; strap.

lanifère, lanigère (lanifɛr, lanigɛr), adj. [L *lana*+*ferre* or *gerere*] Wool-bearing; laniferous, lanigerous.

laniste (lanist), s.m. [L *lanista*] Master of the Gladiators (in Rom. ant.).

lanlaire (lɑ̃lɛr). Only in *envoyer faire ~*, to send about one's business, or to Jericho; *va te faire ~ !*, go to Jericho!

lanoline (lanɔlin), s.f. [f. L *lana*] Lanolin.

lansquenet (lɑ̃skənɛ), s.m. [Germ. *Landsknecht*] Lansquenet.

lantanier (lɑ̃tanje), s.m. (bot.) Lantana; wild sage.

lanterne (lɑ̃tɛrn), s.f. [L *lanterna*] Lantern; lamp; lanthorn; street-lamp; (arch.) lantern tower; lantern, light-chamber of lighthouse; (mech.) lantern-wheel, trundle; (naut.) powder-box; ~ *sourde*, dark lantern; ~*s que tout cela*, that's all rubbish; *à la ~ !*, lynch him!; string him up to the lamp-post!; *prendre des vessies pour des ~s*, to believe the moon is made of green cheese; ~ *magique*, magic lantern; ~ *vénitienne*, Chinese lantern.

lanterneau (pl. -x), **lanternon** (lɑ̃tɛrno, lɑ̃tɛrnɔ̃), s.m. Lantern-light; small lantern tower.

lanterner (lɑ̃tɛrne), v.n. (fam.) To dally, to trifle, to dawdle; to fool one's time away; ~, v.a. to delude with empty words; to keep (a person) dancing attendance; to make a fool of; to put off; to weary, to bore.

lanternerie (lɑ̃tɛrnri), s.f. (fam.) Dilly-dallying, trifling; twaddle, nonsense; trifles.

lanternier (lɑ̃tɛrnje), s.m. **1.** Lantern-maker; lamp-lighter; **2.** dawdler, trifler, babbler.

lanthane (lɑ̃tan), s.m. [f. Gr. *lanthanein*] (chem.) Lanthanum.

lantiponnage (lɑ̃tipɔnaʒ), s.m. Stuff and nonsense; rigmarole.

lantiponner (lɑ̃tipɔne), v.a.n. To talk nonsense; to delude with empty words; to tease, to annoy, to bore.

lanturlu, lanturelu (lɑ̃tyrly), s.m. ~ *!*, (interj.) fudge!; pooh!; no fear!; go on!; stuff and nonsense!

lanugineu-x, -se (lanyʒinø), adj. [L *lanuginosus*] Woolly; downy, lanuginous.

lapalissade (lapalisad), s.f. [f. old song, *M. de la Palisse*] Obvious truth, truism, humorous platitude; syn. VÉRITÉ DE LA PALISSE.

laparotomie (laparɔtomi), s.f. [Gr. *lapara* +*tomē*] (surg.) Laparotomy.

lapement (lapmɑ̃), s.m. Lapping.

laper (lape), v.a.n. [Germ. *lappen*] To lap; to lap up; to lick up.

lapereau (pl. -x) (lapro), s.m. [f. *lapin*] Young rabbit.

lapicide (lapisid), adj. [L *lapis*+*caedere*] (of a plant) That thrusts its roots between stones or rocks. ~, s.m. Stone-engraver, lapicide.

lapidaire (lapidɛr), s.m. adj. [f. L *lapis*]

Lapidary; *style* ~, (lit.) style of an inscription in stone; (fig.) terse style, concise and vivid expression.

lapidairerie (lapidɛrri), s.f. Lapidary workshop.

lapidation (lapida'sjɔ̃), s.f. Stoning.

lapider (lapide), v.a. [L *lapidare*] To stone; to stone to death; (fig.) to abuse, to slate, to run down.

lapidification (lapidifika'sjɔ̃), s.f. Lapidification, petrefaction.

lapidifier (lapidifje), v.a. To lapidify, to petrify; to turn into stone; **se** ~, v.pr. to become petrified; to turn into stone.

lapidifique (lapidifik), adj. Lapidific, petrific.

lapilleu-x, -se (lapijø), adj. [f. L *lapillus*] Stony (of fruit).

lapilli (lapili), s.m.pl. [L wd] (geol.) Lapilli (fragments of stone ejected from volcanoes).

lapin (lapɛ̃), s.m. [etym. dub.] Rabbit; ~ *de garenne*, wild rabbit; ~ *de chou*, tame rabbit; *courir comme un* ~, to run like a hare; *c'est un fameux* ~, he's an artful dog, or hot stuff, or a regular brick; he's a knowing one; *en* ~, squeezed, or on the flap seat; ~ *du Brésil*, guinea-pig; ~*e*, s.f. doe-rabbit; (colloq.) *poser un* ~ *à X*, to keep X dancing attendance in vain; to fail to turn up at a rendez-vous with X; *Jeannot* ~, Bunny.

lapiner (lapine), v.n. (of doe-rabbits) To litter.

lapinière (lapinjɛr), s.f. Rabbit-farm; rabbit-hutch.

lapis, lapis lazuli (lapislazyli), s.m. [LL wd] (min.) Lapis lazuli.

lapon, -e (lapɔ̃), adj. s.m.f. Lapp.

laps, -e (laps), adj. [L *lapsus*] Falling away from faith, or into heresy.

laps (laps), s.m. Lapse, space (of time). ⚠ English 'lapse' also = *lapsus* and *faute, erreur de conduite.*

lapsus (lapsys), s.m. [L wd] Lapse, slip, error, mistake; ~ *calami*, slip of the pen; ~ *linguae*, slip of the tongue.

laptot (lapto), s.m. Senegalese soldier.

laquais (lakɛ), s.m. [Span. *lacayo*] Lackey; flunkey; footman; *mentir comme un* ~, to be a confirmed liar.

laque (lak), s.f. [Pers. *lak*] Lacquer, lac, shellac; ~, s.m. lacquer; lacquer-work.

laquer (lake), v.a. To lacquer; to japan.

laquet (lakɛ), s.m. Small lake.

laqueton (laktɔ̃), s.m. (obs.) Foot-boy; page-boy, buttons.

laqueur (lakœr), s.m. Lacquer-worker.

laqueu-x, -se (lakø), adj. Of the colour or nature of lac.

laraire (larɛr), s.m. [L *lararium*] (ant.) Shrine of the Lares.

larbin (larbɛ̃), s.m. (pej. or iron.) Flunkey.

larcin (larsɛ̃), s.m. [L *latrocinium*] Larceny, petty theft, pilfering; stolen article; plagiarism.

lard (lar), s.m. [L *lardum*] Pork (flesh), pork fat, bacon; *une tranche de* ~, a slice of bacon; *être gras à* ~, to be as fat as a pig; (pop.) *faire du* ~, to get fat with idleness; *flèche de* ~, flitch of bacon. ⚠ Not English 'lard' which = *saindoux.*

lardacé, -e (lardase), adj. Lardaceous; like lard.

larde (lard), s.f. Meat larded with bacon.

larder (larde), v.a. **1.** (cook.) To lard, to stuff; **2.** (fig.) to interlard, to garnish; **3.** to stab, to pierce, to run through; **4.** to assail; to jeer at; **5.** (naut.) to thrum; *aiguille à* ~, larding-needle.

larderasse (lardras), s.f. (naut.) Thick hemp rope.

lardeu-x, -se, lardiforme (lardø, lardiform), adj. Fat, lardlike.

lardoire (lardwar), s.f. **1.** Larding-pin or -needle; **2.** (eng.) iron shoe.

lardon (lardɔ̃), s.m. **1.** Rasher of bacon; small piece of bacon inserted in meat before cooking; **2.** gibe, jeer, taunt, lampoon; **3.** (slang, very vulgar) brat, child, infant.

lardonner (lardɔne), v.a. **1.** To cut in strips; **2.** (fig.) to taunt, to jeer at.

lare (lar), s.m. adj. [L *lar*] (ant.) Lar, household god; ~*s*, household gods; home; *les dieux* ~*s*, the household gods, the Lares.

larenier (larnje), s.m. See more usual form **larmier.**

large (larʒ), adj. [L *largus*] Broad, wide, extensive, ample; big; generous, liberal; lax, loose, free, easy, unscrupulous; abundant, large, copious; grand, bold; *conscience* ~, accommodating conscience; ~ *de deux mètres*, two metres wide. ~, s.m. Breadth, width; (naut.) open sea, the offing; *courir au* ~, to run for the offing; *passer au* ~, to sheer off, to give a wide berth to; *vent du* ~, sea-breeze; *au* ~, (*a*) (interj.) keep off!; (*b*) spaciously, comfortably; at one's ease; *en long et en* ~, in both length and breadth; *marcher* or *aller de long en* ~, to go, or pace, to and fro, or up and down; (fig.) *prendre le* ~, to leg it, to run away; (colloq.) *il n'en mène pas* ~, he feels, or looks, very small; he cuts a sorry figure.

largement (larʒəmɑ̃), adv. Extensively, largely, widely, amply, abundantly, copiously; generously, liberally, bountifully; boldly, in the grand manner.

largesse (larʒɛs), s.f. Liberality, bounty, munificence, money bestowed; (arch.) largesse.

largeur (larʒœr), s.f. Breadth, width; (rail.) gauge; ~ *d'idées*, breadth of mind; (slang) *je me suis fait estamper dans les* *grandes* ~*s*, I have been done brown; *dans les grandes* ~*s*, on a large scale; in grand style; with a vengeance; completely.

larghetto (largɛtto), adv. s.m. [It. wd] (mus.) Larghetto.

largo (largo), adv. s.m. [It. wd] (mus.) Largo.

largue (larg), adj. adv. (naut.) Slack, flowing, loose; *vent* ~, with a large wind; with the wind on the quarter or abaft the beam; *courir* ~, to beat out to sea. ~, s.m. High sea, offing.

larguer (large), v.a. (naut.) To slack, to let go, to loosen; to let run (rope); to let out; to let fly; to cast off.

larigot (larigo), s.m. [etym. dub.] Flute, pipe, shawm; *boire à tire-*~, to drink like a fish; to drink hard.

larix (lariks), s.m. [L wd] (bot.) Larch-tree; syn. MÉLÈZE.

larme (larm), s.f. [L *lacryma*] Tear; drop; *être en* ~*s*, to be in tears; *fondre en* ~*s*, to melt or burst into tears; *pleurer à chaudes* ~*s*, to cry one's eyes out; to weep copiously; to dissolve in tears; *être touché aux* ~*s*, to be moved to tears; *verser des* ~*s*, to shed tears; *les* ~*s aux yeux*, with tears in his eyes; *avoir la* ~ *à l'œil*, to be moved; to have tears in one's eyes; to be in a sentimental mood; *avec des* ~*s dans la voix*, in a tremulous voice; tremulously; *rire aux* ~*s*, to cry with laughing, to laugh till the tears come; *avoir le don des* ~*s*, to be able to cry at will; ~*s de crocodile*, crocodile tears; (chem.) ~*s bataviques*, Prince Rupert's drops; *une* ~ *de vin*, a drop of wine.

larmier (larmje), s.m. **1.** (arch.) Drip, larmier, corona; **2.** (anat.) angle of eye nearest to nose; tear-bag; (of horses) eye-vein; syn. LARENIER.

larmoiement (larmwamɑ̃), s.m. Watering or running of the eyes; (fig.) whining, whimpering.

larmoyant, -e (larmwajɑ̃), p. adj. Watering (of the eyes); weeping, tearful, in tears, lachrymose; (fig.) sentimental and pathetic, maudlin.

larmoyer (larmwaje), v.n. To water (of the eyes); to weep, to shed tears, to cry, to whimper, to snivel.

larmoyeu-r, -se (larmwajœr), s.m.f. Whimperer; sniveller; person prone to tears.

larron, -nesse (larɔ̃), s.m.f. [L *latro*] Thief, robber, pilferer; ~, s.m. (print.) bite, blank space (due to faulty printing); dog's ear; *s'entendre comme* ~*s en foire*, to be as thick as thieves; *quand les* ~*s se battent, les larcins se découvrent*, when thieves fall out honest folks come by their own; *le mauvais* ~, the impenitent thief; *l'occasion fait le* ~, opportunity makes the thief; keep yourself from opportunities and God will keep you from sins.

larronneau (pl. -x) (larɔno), s.m. Petty thief; pilferer.

larvaire (larvɛr), adj. Larval.

larve (larv), s.f. [L *larva*] (zool.) Larva, grub; (ant.) spectre, ghost, phantom.

larvé, -e (larve), adj. (med.) Larvated, masked.

larvicole (larvicɔl), adj. [f. L *larva*+*colere*] Living in the body of the larvae, larvicolous.

laryngé, -e, laryngien, -ne (larɛ̃ʒe, larɛ̃ʒjɛ̃), adj. (anat.) Laryngeal, laryngean.

laryngectomie (larɛ̃ʒɛktɔmi), s.f. [Gr. *larugx*+*ektomē*] (surg.) Laryngectomy.

laryngite (larɛ̃ʒit), s.f. (med.) Laryngitis.

laryngologie (larɛ̃gɔlɔʒi), s.f. [Gr. *larugx*+*logos*] Laryngology.

laryngoscope (larɛ̃gɔskɔp), s.m. Laryngoscope.

laryngoscopie (larɛ̃gɔskɔpi), s.f. [Gr. *larugx*+*skopein*] Laryngoscopy.

laryngotome (larɛ̃gɔtɔm), s.m. [Gr. *larugx*+*tomē*] Laryngotome, instrument for operating on the larynx.

laryngotomie (larɛ̃gɔtɔmi), s.f. Laryngotomy.

larynx (larɛ̃ks), s.m. [Gr. *larugx*] (anat.) Larynx.

las (lɑs), interj. Alas!; poet. syn. of HÉLAS.

las, -se (lɑ, lɑs), adj. [L *lassus*] Tired, weary (*de*, of), bored (with), sick (of), disgusted, fed up; *de guerre* ~*se*, for the sake of peace and quiet.

lasagne (lazɑgn), s.f. [It. *lasagna*] (cook.) Lasagna.

lascar (laskar), s.m. [Hindu *lashkar*] Lascar; (colloq.) fellow, strapping fellow; blighter; knowing one.

lasci-f, -ve (lassif), adj. [L *lascivus*] Lascivious, lustful.

lascivement (lassivmɑ̃), adv. Lasciviously.

lascivité, lasciveté (lassivite, lassivte), s.f. Lasciviousness.

lassant, -e (lɑsɑ̃), p. adj. Tiring, tiresome, fatiguing; tedious, boring, wearisome.

lasser (lɑse), v.a. To tire, to fatigue, to wear out; to bore; ~, v.n. to be tiring; **se** ~, v.pr. to get tired, to grow weary (*de*, of).

lassis (lɑsi), s.m. Silk-floss.

lassitude (lɑsityd), s.f. [L *lassitudo*] Lassitude, fatigue, weariness; languor; (fig.) boredom; weariness.

lasso (laso), s.m. [Span. *lazo*] Lasso, lariat.

last, laste (last), s.m. [Dutch *last*] (naut.) Last (= 4000 lb.).

lasting (lastɛ̃g), s.m. [Engl. wd] Lasting (woollen cloth).

latanier (latanje), s.m. (bot.) Latania; Bourbon palm; macaw-tree.
latent, -e (latɑ̃), adj. [L *latens*] Latent; hidden, concealed; dormant, secret; not visible; not apparent.
latéral, -e, (aux) (lateral), adj. [L *latus*] Lateral; side.
latéralement (lateralmɑ̃), adv. Laterally, sideways.
latex (latɛks), s.m. [L wd] (bot.) Latex; sap.
lathyrus (latirys), s.m. [Gr. *lathuros*] (bot.) Lathyrus, vetch; syn. GESSE.
laticifère (latisifɛr), adj. [L *latex+ferre*] (bot.) Laticiferous.
laticlave (latiklav), s.m. [L *latus+clavus*] (ant.) Laticlave.
latifolié, -e (latifɔlje), adj. [L *latus+folium*] (bot.) Latifoliate; broad-leaved.
latifundia (latifɔ̃dja), s.m. [L pl. wd] Latifundia; large private estates.
latin, -e (latɛ̃), adj. s.m.f. [L *latinus*] Latin; Roman; ~ *de cuisine*, dog Latin; *y perdre son* ~, to rack one's brain in vain; to be unable to make head or tail of it; *être au bout de son* ~, to be at one's wit's end; (naut.) *voile* ~*e*, lateen sail.
latinisant, -e (latinizɑ̃), p. adj. Of Roman church in Greek countries; latinizing. ~, -e, s.m.f. Member of Roman church in Greek countries.
latinisation (latiniza'sjɔ̃), s.f. Latinization.
latiniser (latinize), v.a. To latinize.
latinisme (latinism), s.m. Latinism; Latin idiom.
latiniste (latinist), s.m.f. Latinist.
latinité (latinite), s.f. Latinity; *basse* ~, low Latin.
latirostre (latirostr), adj. [L *latus+rostrum*] (ornith.) Latirostrous; broad-beaked.
latitude (latityd), s.f. [L *latitudo*] Latitude; climate; space, room; (fig.) latitude; freedom, tolerance, scope. ⚠ In English but not in French 'latitude' means also *largeur, ampleur*; ex. (joc.) a hat with great latitude of brim, *un chapeau à vastes bords*.
latitudinaire (latitydinɛr), adj. s.m. (theol.) Latitudinarian.
latitudinal, -e, (aux) (latitydinal), adj. Latitudinal.
latomie (latɔmi), s.f. [L *latomia*] (ant.) Quarry used as prison.
latrie (latri), s.f. [Gr. *latreia*] Worship; adoration, latria.
latrines (latrin), s.f.pl. [L *latrina*] Latrine, privy.
latrodecte (latrɔdɛkt), s.m. [Gr. *lathrodēktēs*] (ent.) Poisonous spider.
lattage (lataʒ), s.m. Lathing; lath-work.
latte (lat), s.f. [Germ. orig.] **1.** Lath; **2.** sword, broadsword.
latter (late), v.a. To lath.
lattis (lati), s.m. Lathwork, lathing.
laudanisé, -e (lodanize), adj. Containing laudanum.
laudanum (lodanɔm), s.m. Laudanum.
laudati-f, -ve (lodatif), adj. [f. L *laudare*] Laudatory.
laudes (lod), s.f.pl. [L wd] (eccles.) Lauds.
lauracées (lorase), s.f.pl. (bot.). See LAURINÉES.
lauré, -e (lore), adj. [L *laureatus*] (numism.) Crowned with laurel.
lauréat, -e (lorea), adj. s.m.f. Laureate.
laurelle (lorɛl), s.f. (bot.) Oleander.
laurentie (lorɑ̃si), s.f. (bot.) Campanula.
lauréole (loreɔl), s.f. [L *laureola*] (bot.) Daphne; syn. DAPHNÉ.
laurier (lorje), s.m. [L *laurus*] (bot.) Laurel; (fig.) honour; glory; *se reposer sur ses* ~*s*, to rest on one's laurels or on one's oars; to rest and be thankful; *se couvrir de* ~*s*, to cover oneself with glory; *flétrir ses* ~*s*, to sully one's honour; ~*-cerise*, cherry-laurel; ~*-rose*, oleander; ~*-sauce*, bay-tree; ~*-tin*, laurustinus.
laurinées (lorine), s.f.pl. (bot.) Lauraceae; syn. LAURACÉES.
lavable (lavabl), adj. Washable.
lavabo (lavabo), s.m. [L wd] **1.** (eccles.) Lavabo; linen towel; **2.** wash-basin; wash-stand, lavatory.
lavage (lavaʒ), s.m. Washing; (med.) lotion; slop; wish-wash.
lavallière (lavaljɛr), s.f. [f. *Mlle de La Vallière*] Loose fancy necktie.
lavande (lavɑ̃d), s.f. [LL *lavendula*] (bot.) Lavender.
lavanderie (lavɑ̃dri), s.f. Wash-house; washing-place.
lavandier (lavɑ̃dje), s.m. (obs.) Yeoman of the laundry.
lavandière (lavɑ̃djɛr), s.f. **1.** Washer-woman; laundress; ~ *belge*, washing-machine; **2.** (ornith.) wagtail.
lavaret (lavarɛ), s.m. (ichth.) Lavaret; coregonus; freshwater herring.
lavasse (lavas), s.f. Wish-wash; swill; slop, belly wash, soup or beverage diluted with too much water, tasteless sloppy soup or sauce; (rare) heavy rain.
lavatère (lavatɛr), s.f. (bot.) Cultivated mallows.
lave (lav), s.f. [It. *lava*] Lava.
lavé, -e (lave), adj. Washed; (paint.) pale, faint, light.
lave-mains (lavmɛ̃), s.m. invar. Wash-basin, wash-hand-basin.
lavement (lavmɑ̃), s.m. **1.** Enema; clyster; **2.** (obs.) washing.
laver (lave), v.a. [L *lavare*] To wash; to cleanse; to wash away; to bathe; (fig.) to absolve, to purify; to clear; to expiate; (paint.) to colour-wash; *il faut* ~ *son linge sale en famille*, dirty linen should not be

---

ɔ, note, glɔtte; ɔ̃, monter, ronde; ø, feu, creux; œ, peur, sœur; œ̃, un; ʃ, chez, schisme; u, tout; w, oui, doit, douaire; y, mur, pu; ɥ, huile, muette; z, zèle, rose; ʒ, déjà, gentil.

washed in public; it 's an ill bird that fouls its own nest; *s'en* **~** *les mains*, to wash one's hands of it; **~** *la tête à quelqu'un*, to give some one a dressing-down; (slang) to sell (at any price, for want of money); **se ~**, v.pr. to wash oneself, to wash one's face, or hands, &c.; (fig.) to justify oneself, to clear oneself (*de*, of).

laverie (lavri), s.f. Washing-place; scullery.

lavette (lavɛt), s.f. Dish-cloth.

laveu-r, -se (lavœr), s.m.f. Washer; washerwoman; scourer; *~se de vaisselle*, scullery-maid, dish-washer; **~se**, s.f. washing-machine.

lavique (lavik), adj. (geol.) Lavic.

lavis (lavi), s.m. (paint.) Colour-wash; *dessin au* **~**, Indian-ink sketch; wash drawing.

lavoir (lavwar), s.m. Washing-place; wash-house; (metall.) washing-trough; (artill.) scouring-rod.

lavure (lavyr), s.f. Dish-water (also fig., fam.); pig-wash; (metall.) washing, scouring; *~s*, sweepings, washings.

laxati-f, -ve (laksatif), adj. [f. L *laxare*] (med.) Laxative. **~**, s.m. Laxative.

laxité (laksite), s.f. [f. L *laxus*] Laxity, laxness; looseness; slackness.

layer (lɛye), v.a. [f. *laie*] To cut (a path); to blaze (trees).

layetier (lɛjtje), s.m. Box-maker; case-maker; trunk-maker; *~-emballeur*, packing-case maker.

layette (lɛjɛt), s.f. **1.** Baby-linen, layette; **2.** light wooden box or case.

layeur (lɛjœr), s.m. (forestry) Path-maker; blazer.

layon (lɛjɔ̃), s.m. [f. *laie*] (hunt.) Narrow track or path in coverts.

lazaret (lazarɛ), s.m. [It. *lazzaretto*] Lazaretto, lazaret; quarantine-hospital; quarantine-dock.

lazariste (lazarist), s.m. (eccles.) Lazarist; Lazarite.

lazulite (lazylit), s.m. See syn. LAPIS.

lazzi (lazi), s.m.pl. [It. wd] Gibes, witty sarcasms, jeers, or taunts. ⚠ *Lazzi* has in Italian the sense of buffoonery = *pantomime comique*, but not usually in the French.

le, la, l', les (lə, la, lɛ), def. art. [f. L *ille, illa*] The; a; *trois frs. la livre*, three frs. a pound; *deux fois l'an*, twice a year; *la nuit*, during the night, nightly, at night. **le, la, l', les**, pron. Him, her, it, them; *je le veux bien*, I am willing or agreeable; I consent; *vous le direz*, you will say it; *je le crois*, I think so; *je le punirai*, I will punish him.

lé (lɛ), s.m. [L *latus*] **1.** Breadth, width (of material); **2.** towing-path.

lèche (lɛʃ), s.f. [f. *lecher*] Thin slice; (slang) fawning, flattery, back-scratching, licking the dust; *faire de la* **~**, to play the toady; to suck up (*à*, to).

léché, -e (leʃe), adj. Licked; (fig.) laboured; highly finished; *c'est un ours mal* **~**, he wants licking into shape; he is an unlicked cub; *une peinture* **~e**, a laboured picture.

lèchefrite (lɛʃfrit), s.f. (cook.) Dripping-pan.

lèchement (lɛʃmɑ̃), s.m. Licking.

lécher (leʃe), v.a. [Germ. *lecken*] To lick; to lap; (fig.) to labour, to overdo, to polish; **~** *la poussière*, to lick the dust; *s'en* **~** *les doigts*, to lick one's chops or lips over it; to smack one's lips; **~** *les bottes de X*, to suck up to X; to fawn upon or cringe to X; to lick X's shoes.

lécheu-r, -se (leʃœr), s.m.f. Gormandizer, glutton; (fig.) flatterer, parasite, toady, toad-eater, sucker-up.

lécithine (lesitin), s.f. [f. Gr. *lekithos*] Lecithin.

leçon (ləsɔ̃), s.f. [L *lectio*] Lesson; lecture; reading (of a text), lection; **~** *de choses*, object-lesson; punishment, warning; lecture, reprimand; failure; *que cela vous serve de* **~**, let that be a lesson to you; *il donne des* **~s**, he gives private lessons; *prendre des* **~s** *de X*, to take lessons from X; *faire la* **~** *à X*, (*a*) to dictate to X (what he must do); (*b*) to take X to task; *je n'ai pas de* **~** *à recevoir de vous*, I won't be dictated to by you.

lect-eur, -rice (lɛktœr) s.m.f. [L *lector*] Reader; lector; proof-reader; lecturer (in a foreign university).

lecture (lɛktyr), s.f. [L *lectura*] Reading; proof-correcting. ⚠ Not English 'lecture' which = (*a*) *conférence, leçon*; (*b*) *remontrance, blâme*.

lédon (ledɔ̃), s.m. [Gr. *lēdon*] (bot.) Ledum.

légal, -e, (aux) (legal), adj. [L *legalis*] Legal, lawful; legitimate; forensic. ⚠ In English 'legal'=also: *qui a rapport au Droit*; ex. 'my legal friend' = *mon ami l'avocat*, or *le juge*, or *le professeur de Droit*, &c.

légalement (legalmɑ̃), adv. Lawfully, legally, legitimately.

légalisable (legalizabl), adj. Legalizable.

légalisation (legaliza'sjɔ̃), s.f. Legalization; authentication.

légaliser (legalize), v.a. To legalize; to authenticate.

légalité (legalite), s.f. Legality; lawfulness; *rester dans la* **~**, to keep within the law.

légat (lega), s.m. [L *legatus*] Legate.

légataire (legatɛr), s.m.f. [f. L *legare*] Legatee; **~** *universel*, residuary legatee.

légation (lega'sjɔ̃), s.f. [L *legatio*] (diplom.) Legation; (eccles.) legateship.

legato (legato), adv. s.m. [It. wd] (mus.) Legato.

lège (lɛʒ), adj. [Dutch *leeg*] (naut.) Light; not deeply laden; in ballast.

légendaire (leʒɑ̃dɛr), adj. Legendary; fabulous. ~, s.m. Collection of legends; writer of legends.

légende (leʒɑ̃d), s.f. [L *legenda*] **1.** Legend, myth; story, fable; record, narrative; **2.** key; reference; explanation; **3.** inscription, motto.

lég-er, -ère (leʒe), adj. [f. L *levis*] Light; slight, trifling; loose; airy; nimble, agile, swift, fleet; gentle, soft; slender, small, moderate, unimportant; light-armed; unencumbered; buoyant; clear; flimsy, delicate; superficial, fickle, inconsiderate, thoughtless, wanton; *à la ~ère*, inconsiderately, thoughtlessly, carelessly, wantonly, unwisely; *d'un cœur ~*, with a clear conscience; *avoir la main ~ère*, (*a*) to be light-handed, to be dexterous; (*b*) to be prone to give blows, &c.; *avoir la tête ~ère*, to be hare-brained; *~ à la course*, nimble- or swift-footed; (fig.) *avoir le pied ~*, to be always on the move. ⚠ 'Legerdemain' used in English is not used in French = *tour de passe-passe*.

légèrement (leʒɛrmɑ̃), adv. Lightly; loosely; slightly; softly; nimbly, with agility; swiftly; buoyantly; flimsily, delicately; thoughtlessly; wantonly; cursorily; slightingly; *il a agi très ~*, he acted very inconsiderately; *se vêtir ~*, to dress lightly, to be lightly, thinly, clad; *~ blessé*, slightly wounded.

légèreté (leʒɛrte), s.f. Lightness; nimbleness; swiftness; slightness; buoyancy; levity; airiness, fickleness; thoughtlessness, inconsiderateness, imprudence, carelessness; facility, ease; slight fault.

légiférer (leʒifere), v.n. [f. L *legifer*] To legislate; to make laws.

légion (leʒjɔ̃), s.f. [L *legio*] (ant.) Legion; host, multitude; *~ d'honneur*, Legion of Honour; *~ Étrangère*, Foreign Legion (body of foreign volunteers in modern, especially Fr., armies).

légionnaire (leʒjɔnɛr), s.m. Legionary; soldier of *Légion Étrangère*; member of *Légion d'Honneur*.

législat-eur, -rice (leʒislatœr), s.m.f. [L *legislator*] Legislator; (fem. rare) legislatress; law-giver. ~, adj. Legislating, lawgiving, law-making.

législati-f, -ve (leʒislatif), adj. Legislative.

législation (leʒisla'sjɔ̃), s.f. Legislation; body of laws.

législativement (leʒislativmɑ̃), adv. By legislation.

législature (leʒislatyr), s.f. Legislature; time of office of a legislative body.

légiste (leʒist), s.m.f. Legist; jurisconsult.

légitimaire (leʒitimɛr), adj. Legitimate; fixed by law.

légitimation (leʒitima'sjɔ̃), s.f. Legitimation; legal recognition, legitimization.

légitime (leʒitim), adj. [L *legitimus*] Legitimate; born in wedlock; lawful, rightful; justifiable, allowable. ~, s.f. (colloq.) Wife.

légitimé, -e (leʒitime), adj. s.m.f. Legitimated.

légitimement (leʒitimmɑ̃), adv. Legitimately, lawfully, legally; rightfully; justifiably.

légitimer (leʒitime), v.a. To legitimize; to legitimate; to recognize; to justify; to serve as justification for.

légitimisme (leʒitimism), s.m. Legitimism.

légitimiste (leʒitimist), s.m.f. adj. Legitimist.

légitimité (leʒitimite), s.f. Legitimacy; lawfulness, justifiableness.

legs (lɛ), s.m. [f. L *legatum*] Legacy, bequest; *faire un ~*, to leave a legacy.

léguer (lege), v.a. [L *legare*] To bequeath, to leave; to transmit, to give by will.

légume (legym), s.m. [L *legumen*] Vegetable; (bot.) pod, pulse, leguminous plant; (colloq.) *les grosses ~s*, the big-wigs, big bugs, or big pots.

légumi-er, -ère (legymje), adj. Vegetable. ~, s.m. Vegetable-dish.

légumine (legymin), s.f. (chem.) Legumin.

légumineu-x, -se (legyminø), adj. (bot.) Leguminous. **~ses**, s.f.pl. (bot.) Leguminous plants.

légumiste (legymist), s.m.f. (rare) **1.** Market-gardener; **2.** vegetarian.

leitmotiv (laitmɔtif), s.m. [Germ. wd] (mus.) Leitmotiv, character-theme; (fig.) motto, frequent repetition, shibboleth, byword, favourite saying, catchword.

lemme (lɛm), s.m. [Gr. *lēmma*] (math.) Lemma.

lemming (lɛmming), s.m. (zool.) Lemming.

lemna (lɛmna), s.f. [Gr. wd] (bot.) Lemna; duckweed.

lemnacées (lɛmnase), s.f.pl. (bot.) Lemnaceae.

lemniscate (lɛmniskat), s.f. [Gr. *lēmniskos*] Lemniscate.

lémur (lemyr), s.m. (zool.) Lemur.

lémures (lemyr), s.m.pl. [L *lemures*] (ant.) Lemures; manes; ghosts.

lémuriens (lemyrjɛ̃), s.m.pl. (zool.) Lemuridae.

lendemain (lɑ̃dmɛ̃), s.m. [*l'endemain*] Next day, following day, day after; *remettre au ~*, to put off till to-morrow; *le plus beau ~ ne nous rend pas la veille*, what 's past is gone for ever; *il n'y a pas de bonne fête sans ~*, all good things must come to an end; *penser au ~*, to think of the morrow; *une chose décidée du jour au ~*, a matter settled somewhat hastily; *au ~ de la guerre*, on the morrow of the

war; *le ~ de*, the day after; *le ~ matin*, the next morning.
lendit (lɑ̃di), s.m. [f. L *indictum*] Lendit; fair at St. Denis (obs.); schools athletic competition.
lendore (lɑ̃dɔr), s.m.f. (obs.) Dawdler, sleepy-head.
lénifier (lenifje), v.a. [L *lenis*+*facere*] To soothe, to mitigate, to attenuate, to assuage.
léniti-f, -ve (lenitif), adj. [L *lenitivus*] Lenitive; emollient. ~, s.m. Lenitive; emollient; soothing drug; (fig.) mitigation, palliative.
lent, -e (lɑ̃), adj. [L *lentus*] Slow, tardy; remiss, backward; dull, sluggish; indolent; (med.) low; *d'esprit ~*, slow-witted; *~ à la colère*, slow to anger; *avoir la parole ~e*, to be slow of speech; *combustion ~e*, slow combustion.
lente (lɑ̃t), s.f. [L *lens*] Nit.
lentement (lɑ̃tmɑ̃), adv. Slowly, tardily; dully; sluggishly, indolently.
lenteur (lɑ̃tœr), s.f. Slowness; dullness; sluggishness; indolence; delay; procrastination; dilatoriness.
lenticelle (lɑ̃tisɛl), s.f. (bot.) Lenticel.
lenticellé, -e (lɑ̃tisɛlle), adj. (bot.) Lenticellate, having lenticels on the bark.
lenticulaire, lenticulé, -e (lɑ̃tikylɛr, lɑ̃tikyle), adj. [f. L *lenticula*] Lenticular.
lenticule (lɑ̃tikyl), s.f. (bot.) Lemna, duckweed.
lentiforme (lɑ̃tifɔrm), adj. [L *lens, lentis* +*forma*] Lentiform; lens-shaped.
lentigo (lɑ̃tigɔ), s.m. [f. L *lens*] (med.) Lentigo.
lentille (lɑ̃tij), s.f. [L *lenticula*] **1.** Lentil; (colloq.) *plat de ~s*, (Esau's) mess of pottage; **2.** (bot.) duckweed; **3.** (opt.) lens; magnifying-glass; **4.** (med.) lentigo; **5.** (horol.) bob.
lentilleu-x, -se (lɑ̃tijø), adj. Lentiginous; freckled.
lentillon (lɑ̃tijɔ̃), s.m. Small lentil.
lentisque (lɑ̃tisk), s.m. [L *lentiscus*] (bot.) Lentisk, lentiscus; mastic-tree.
lento (lɛntɔ), adv. s.m. [It. wd] (mus.) Lento.
léonin, -e (leɔnɛ̃), adj. [L *leoninus*] Leonine; lion-like.
léontine (leɔ̃tin), s.f. (obs.) Lady's watch-chain.
léonure, léonurus (leɔnyr, leɔnyrys), s.m. [L *leo*+Gr. *oura*] (bot.) Motherwort; syn. QUEUE-DE-LION.
léopard (leɔpar), s.m. [L *leopardus*] (zool.) Leopard, cheetah; (herald.) leopard, lion passant guardant as in arms of England.
léopardé, -e (leɔparde), adj. Spotted; (herald.) léopardé.
lépicène (lepisɛn), s.f. (bot.) Husk, chaff, glume.
lépidodendron (lepidɔdɛ̃drɔ̃), s.m. (bot.) Lepidodendrum.
lépidolithe (lepidɔlit), s.m. [Gr. *lepis*+ *lithos*] (min.) Lepidolite.
lépidoptère (lepidɔptɛr), s.m. [Gr. *lepis*+ *pteron*] (ent.) Lepidopteran; *~s*, s.m.pl. Lepidoptera. ~, adj. Lepidopterous.
lépidosirène (lepidɔsirɛn), s.m. (ichth.) Lepidosiren.
lépiote (lepjɔt), s.f. (bot.) Kind of mushroom.
lépisme (lepism), s.m. (ent.) Lepisma; mite; bookworm.
léporide (lepɔrid), s.m. [L *lepus, -oris*+ Gr. *eidos*] (zool.) Leporide.
léporidés (lepɔride), s.m.pl. (zool.) Leporidae.
lèpre (lɛpr), s.f. [L *lepra*] Leprosy.
lépreu-x, -se (leprø), s.m.f. Leper. ~, adj. Leprous.
léproserie (leprozri), s.f. Leper-house.
lepte (lɛpt), s.m. (ent.) Leptus; *~ automnal*, harvest-bug.
leptinotarse (lɛptinotars), s.f. (ent.) Colorado beetle.
leptologie (lɛptɔlɔʒi), s.f. [f. Gr. *leptos*+ *logos*] Leptology, euphuism, excessive subtlety of style.
lepture (lɛptyr), s.f. (ent.) Leptora.
lequel, laquelle, lesquels, lesquelles (ləkɛl, lakɛl, lɛkɛl), rel. pron. [*le*+*quel*] Who, whom, which, that; (int.) which one?, who?; *~ préférez-vous?*, which one do you prefer?; *~ de vous a dit?*, which of you was it who said?; *il l'a envoyé à Jones lequel l'a fait passer à Smith*, he sent it to Jones, who passed it on to Smith; *à laquelle avez-vous parlé?*, whom did you speak to?, to whom have you spoken?; *duquel* (for *de lequel*) *est-il le fils?*, whose son is he?
lérot (lero), s.m. [f. *loir*] (zool.) Garden dormouse.
les (lɛ), art. pron. See LE.
lès, lez (lɛ), prep. [L *latus*] Near, next to; ex. *Sotteville-lès-Rouen*, *Plessis-lès-Tours*.
lesbien, -ne (lɛsbjɛ̃), adj. Lesbian; pertaining to Lesbian vice. ~ s.m.f. Lesbian.
lèse (lɛz) [f. L *laesa*] In comp.: *~-majesté*, s.f. lese-majesty; *~-humanité*, s.f. treason against society.
léser (leze), v.a. [f. *lèse*] To wrong, to injure.
lésinant, -e (lezinɑ̃), p. adj. Stingy, mean, niggardly; parsimonious; close-fisted.
lésine (lezin), s.f. [It. *lesina*] Stinginess, niggardliness, meanness; parsimony; close-fistedness.
lésiner (lezine), v.n. To be stingy, mean, niggardly, parsimonious; to haggle; to chaffer; to pinch and scrape, to stand higgling (*sur*, over).
lésinerie (lezinri), s.f. See LÉSINE.

lésineu-r, -se (lezinœr), adj. Stingy, mean, parsimonious, close-fisted. ~ s.m.f. Miser, niggard, haggler.

lésion (lezjɔ̃), s.f. [L *laesio*] Lesion, injury, hurt; (law) breaking (of a contract); wrong, damage.

lésionnaire (lezjɔnɛr), adj. Injurious; wrongful.

lessivage (lɛsivaʒ), s.m. Washing, lye-washing.

lessive (lɛsiv), s.f. [L *lixiva*] **1.** (chem.) Lixivium; lye; soda, sodium carbonate, &c.; **2.** washing, wash; dirty linen; *faire la* ~, to wash and boil linen; *envoyer à la* ~, to send to the wash; *jour de* ~, washing-day; **3.** (fam.) losses.

lessiver (lɛsive), v.a. To wash in lye; to wash and boil (linen).

lessiveuse (lɛsivøz), s.f. Laundry boiler, copper, washing-machine, lye-washer, lye-washing machine; see MACHINE À LAVER.

lessonie (lɛsoni), s.f. (bot.) Lessonia; giant seaweed.

lest (lɛst), s.m. [Germ. *Last*] Ballast; *sac de* ~, ballast-sack, sand-bag; *navire sur* ~, ship in ballast; *jeter du* ~, to throw or heave out ballast; (fig.) to lower one's pretensions; to give up one thing for the sake of another that is better or more urgent; to come down a peg or two.

lestage (lɛstaʒ), s.m. Ballasting.

leste (lɛst), adj. [It. *lesto*] Lively, brisk, agile, nimble, light-footed, smart; quick; skilful; free, saucy; indecorous, improper; *avoir la main* ~, to be too ready to come to blows.

lestement (lɛstəmɑ̃), adv. Briskly, lightly, nimbly; smartly; quickly, skilfully; freely, indecorously; thoughtlessly.

lester (lɛste), v.a. (naut.) To ballast; **se** ~, v.pr. (colloq.) to tuck in, to line one's stomach; to make a good square meal.

lesteur (lɛstœr), s.m. (naut.) Ballast-lighter; ballast-heaver; plumb, plumb-line.

léthargie (letarʒi), s.f. [Gr. *lēthē*+*argos*] Lethargy.

léthargique (letarʒik), adj. Lethargic, lethargical.

léthifère (letifɛr), adj. [L *letum*+*ferre*] Lethiferous; deadly, mortal.

lette, letton, lettique (lɛt, lɛtɔ̃, lɛtik), s.m. Lettish, Lett (language). **letton, -e,** adj. s.m.f. Lett.

lettrage (lɛtraʒ), s.m. Lettering.

lettre (lɛtr), s.f. [L *littera*] Letter; (print.) type, character; note; epistle; ~*s*, pl. learning; letters; literature; arts; *à la* ~, literally, to the letter; word for word; *en toutes* ~*s*, plainly; in full; *prendre au pied de la* ~, to take literally; *avoir des* ~*s*, to be learned, to have a cultivated mind; *grande* ~, capital letter; *petite* ~, small letter; ~ *d'avis*, advice note; ~ *de change*, bill of exchange; ~ *de crédit*, letter of credit; (Fr. hist.) ~ *de cachet*, arbitrary warrant of arrest or imprisonment; (naut.) ~ *de mer*, sea-letter, pass; ~*s de marque*, letters of mark; ~*s patentes*, letters patent; ~ *de voiture*, way-bill; ~*s d'introduction*, credentials, letters of introduction; *jeter une* ~ *à la boîte*, to post a letter; ~ *chargée*, ~ *recommandée*, registered letter; *les belles* ~*s*, literature, belles-lettres; *homme de* ~*s*, writer, literary man; *femme de* ~*s*, writer, authoress; (fig.) *c'est* ~ *close*, it's a secret; ~ *morte*, dead letter, law no longer observed; *pèse-*~*s*, letter-balance; *traduire à la* ~, to render word for word; *gravure* or *épreuve avant la* ~, proof before letters; *boîte aux* ~*s*, letter-box.

lettré, -e (lɛtre), adj. Learned; literate; literary. ~, s.m. Literary man, scholar, cultivated person; *les* ~*s*, the literati.

lettrine (lɛtrin), s.f. (print.) Reference letter; heading, head-lettering.

leu (lø), s.m. [old form of *loup*] Wolf (only used in the phrase *à la queue* ~ ~, in single file, one after another, in Indian file).

leucocyte (løkɔsit), s.m. [Gr. *leukos*+ *kutos*] (anat.) Leucocyte; white corpuscle.

leucocythémie, leucémie (løkɔsitemi, løsemi), s.f. (med.) Leucocythaemia, leucocytosis.

leucoma, leucome (løkɔma, løkɔm), s.m. [Gr. *leukōma*] (med.) Leucoma.

leucomaïne (løkɔmain), s.f. Leucomaine (alkaloid found in living tissues).

leucorrhée (løkɔre), s.f. Leucorrhoea; whites.

leude (lød), s.m. [LL *leudis*, Germ. *Leute*] Liege lord; great vassal.

leur (pl. **-s**) (lœr), poss. adj. [L *illorum*] Their. ~, pers. pron. (invar.) To them, them; *donnez-le-*~, give it to them; *ne* ~ *faites pas de mal*, don't harm them; *le* or *la* ~, *les* ~*s*, poss. pron. theirs, their own; *les pauvres ont leurs peines, les riches ont aussi les* ~*s*, poor people have their troubles, but rich people have also theirs. ~, s.m. *Quelques-uns y mettent du* ~, some bring some of their own; or give a helping hand; *les* ~*s*, their relations, friends, allies; *il n'est pas des* ~*s*, he is not one of them.

leurre (lœr), s.m. [MHG *luoder*] (falc.) Lure, decoy; (fish.) bait; (fig.) decoy; delusion, allurement, bait; *c'était un* ~, it was a delusion.

leurrer (lœre), v.a. (falc.) To draw to a lure; (fig.) to entice; to allure; to decoy; **se** ~, v.pr. to delude oneself.

levage (ləvaʒ), s.m. Raising, lifting; *appareils de* ~, hoisting or lifting devices, cranes, jacks, &c.

levain (ləvɛ̃), s.m. Leaven; (fig.) leaven,

ferment; ~ *de bière*, yeast; *pain sans* ~, unleavened bread.
levant (ləvɑ̃), s.m. East; Levant. ~, adj. Rising; *le soleil* ~, the rising sun; (fig.) the coming power. ⚠ 'To levant' in English = *prendre la fuite, filer sans payer; lever le pied.*
levantin, -e (ləvɑ̃tɛ̃), adj. s.m.f. Levantine. ~**e**, s.f. Levantine (cloth).
lève (lɛv), s.f. [f. *lever*] Mallet, bat.
levé, -e (ləve), p.adj. Raised, hoisted, lifted, erect; *au pied* ~, at a moment's notice, unawares, unexpectedly; *tête* ~*e*, with head erect; fearlessly; *dessin à main* ~*e*, freehand drawing.
levée (ləve), s.f. Raising; removal; abandoning; levy; rising; collection; crop; harvest; (cards) trick; (naut.) swell; (eng.) embankment, dyke, causeway; breaking-up; ~ *postale*, collection of letters, from pillar-box or in post-office; clearing of letters. ⚠ Not English 'levee', which = *réception à la Cour*; however in U.S.A. 'levee' has also the meaning of 'embankment' = *levée (le long d'un fleuve)*.
lever (ləve), v.a. [L *levare*] To lift, to lift up, to raise, to elevate, to hoist, to set up, to take up, to heave up; to haul up, to weigh (anchor); to levy, to gather, to call up, to collect; (hunt.) to start; to break up, to close; to abolish; to copy; (print.) to compose; to remove (a difficulty, &c.); to clear; ~, v.n. to rise, to come up, to spring up, to grow; ~ *l'ancre*, to weigh anchor; ~ *une armée*, to levy troops, or an army; ~ *la main sur X*, to lift up one's hand against X; to strike X; to threaten X; ~ or *hausser les épaules*, to shrug one's shoulders; ~ *la boîte aux lettres*, to clear the letter-box; ~ *le camp*, to break up, or strike, camp; ~ *le masque*, to throw off the mask; (fig.) ~ *le pied*, to abscond with the cash-box; ~ *la séance*, to close the meeting; to end the sitting; ~ *un lièvre*, to start a hare; (fig.) to raise or moot a ticklish question; ~ *un plan*, to make a survey, to draw a plan; (vulg. slang) ~ *une femme*, to make an easy conquest, to 'pick up' a woman; *poudre à faire* ~ *la pâte*, baking-powder; **se** ~, v.pr. to rise, to get up, to stand up, to spring up, to get out of bed, to be raised, to be collected, to be levied; *à qui se lève matin, Dieu prête la main*, it's the early bird that catches the worm; *le soleil se lève*, the sun rises, or is rising; *se* ~ *de table*, to leave the (dinner) table; *le vent se lève*, the wind rises.
lever (ləve), s.m. Getting up; rising; levee; *le* ~ *du soleil*, sunrise; *le* ~ *du rideau*, rise of the curtain; *le* ~*-dieu*, the elevation of the host; ~ *des plans*, land-surveying; (theatr.) ~ *de rideau*, curtain-raiser.
leveu-r, -se (ləvœr), s.m.f. Worker in a paper-factory; (print.) compositor.
levier (ləvje), s.m. [f. *lever*] (mech.) Lever; crowbar; handspike; ~ *de commande* or *des vitesses*, gear-lever; change-speed lever; (aeron.) steering-lever; joystick; rudder-bar; ~ *de frein à main*, brake hand-lever, hand-brake; ~ *démonte-pneu*, tyre-lever; *point d'appui du* ~, fulcrum; (fig.) power, motive, influence.
lévigation (leviga'sjɔ̃), s.f. Levigation.
léviger (levige), v.a. [L. *levigare*] To levigate; to grind fine.
lévirat (leviraɑ), s.m. [f. L *levir*] Levirate law.
lévirostres (levirɔstr), s.m.pl. [f. L *levis, rostrum*] (ornith.) Levirostres.
lévitation (levita'sjɔ̃), s.f. [L *levitas*] Levitation.
lévite (levit), s.m. [Hebr. *Levi*] Levite; ~, s.f. surcoat, long coat.
lévogyre (levɔʒir), adj. [f. L *laevus+gyrare*] (chem.) Laevo-rotatory.
levrauder (ləvrode), v.a. (obs.) To harass, to worry, to run down.
levraut (ləvro), s.m. Young hare, leveret.
lèvre (lɛvr), s.f. [L *labrum*] Lip; (surg.) edge; *du bout des* ~*s*, mincingly; disdainfully; half-heartedly; *sur le bord des* ~*s*, on the tip of the tongue; *avoir le cœur sur les* ~*s*, (*a*) to have one's heart in one's mouth; (*b*) to be open-hearted, to wear one's heart on one's sleeve (in this sense *avoir le cœur sur la main* is better).
levrette (ləvrɛt), s.f. Greyhound bitch; Italian greyhound. ⚠ Not 'leveret' which = *levraut*.
levretté (ləvrɛte), adj. Of the build of a greyhound.
levretter (ləvrɛte), v.n. (of a greyhound bitch) To whelp; ~, v.a. to course.
lévrier (levrije), s.m. Greyhound, harrier.
levron, -ne (ləvrɔ̃), s.m.f. Greyhound or harrier pup.
lévulose (levyloz), s.f. [f. L *laevus*] (chem.) Levulose, laevulose; fruit-sugar.
levure (ləvyr), s.f. Yeast, barm, leaven.
levurier (ləvyrie), s.m. Yeast-maker; yeast-merchant.
lexicographe (lɛksikɔgraf), s.m.f. [Gr. *lexikon+graphein*] Lexicographer.
lexicographie (lɛksikɔgrafi), s.f. Lexicography.
lexicographique (lɛksikɔgrafik), adj. Lexicographical.
lexicologie (lɛksikɔlɔʒi), s.f. [Gr. *lexikon +logos*] Lexicology.
lexicologique (lɛksikɔlɔʒik), adj. Lexical.
lexicologue (lɛksikɔlɔg), s.m.f. Lexicologist.
lexique (lɛksik), s.m. Lexicon; abridged dictionary.
lez (lɛ), prep. [L *latus*] Near (obs. exc. in place names); see LÈS.

lézard (lezar), s.m. [L *lacertus*] Lizard; *faire le* ~, to bask in the sun; ~ *d'eau*, newt.

lézarde (lezard), s.f. [f. *lézard*] **1.** Crevice, crack, chink; **2.** gold or silver braid.

lézardé, -e (lezarde), p. adj. Cracked, full of crevices or chinks.

lézarder (lezarde), v.a. To make cracks or crevices in; ~, v.n. to idle, to bask; **se** ~, v.pr. to crack, to crumble.

liage (liaʒ), s.m. Binding, fastening.

liais (liɛ), s.m. (geol.) Lias, freestone; *pierre de* ~, Portland stone.

liaison (ljɛzɔ̃), s.f. [f. *lier*] Joining, junction, joint; binding together; union, unity; connexion; tie, bond; intimacy; love affair; (mil.) liaison; (build.) mortar, pointing; (cook.) thickening; (mus.) slur, tie, bind, ligature; liaison (between words); (writing) stroke; *officier de* ~, liaison officer; *rompre une* ~, to break off an attachment or love-affair; *en* ~ *avec*, jointly with.

liaisonner (ljɛzone), v.a. (build.) To point, to grout; to lay (bricks).

liane (ljan), s.f. (bot.) Liana; bindweed, tropical creeper.

liant, -e (ljɑ̃), p. adj. Sociable, engaging, affable, friendly, pliant, yielding, supple; soft; flexible; pliable; compliant, gentle, courteous. ~, s.m. Pliancy; suppleness; flexibility; compliance; gentleness; affability.

liard (ljar), s.m. [etym. dub.] (obs.) Coin worth a quarter of a sou; (fig.) farthing; rap; *n'avoir pas un rouge* ~, not to have a brass farthing; *couper un* ~ *en quatre*, to nip a raisin; to skin flints.

liarder (ljarde), v.n. To be a skinflint; to haggle; to screw; to pay in driblets.

liardeur (liardœr), s.m. Skinflint; miser; haggler, stingy or close-fisted fellow.

lias (liɑs), s.m. [OF *liois*] (geol.) Lias.

liasique (liɑzik), adj. (geol.) Liassic.

liasse (ljas), s.f. [f. *lier*] Bundle; file (of papers).

libage (libaʒ), s.m. [OF *libe*] (build.) Ashlar; rough stone.

libation (liba'sjɔ̃), s.f. [L *libatio*] Libation; (joc.) potation.

libelle (libɛl), s.m. [L *libellus*] Lampoon; libel.

libellé (libɛlle), s.m. Wording; contents; drawing-up; account, report.

libeller (libɛlle), v.a. To draw up, to word.

libelliste (libɛllist), s.m. (rare) Lampoonist; author of libels.

libellule (libɛllyl), s.f. [f. L *libella*] (ent.) Libellula; dragonfly.

libellulidés (libɛllylide), s.m.pl. (ent.) Libellulidae.

liber (libɛr), s.m. [L wd] (bot.) Liber; bast.

libera (libera), s.m. [L wd] (eccles.) Prayer for the dead.

libérable (liberabl), adj. That may be liberated or discharged, due to be released or liberated.

libéral, -e, (aux) (liberal), adj. [L *liberalis*] Liberal; ample; free, generous; openhanded; directed to general enlargement of mind; favourable to democratic reforms; *les professions libérales*, the learned professions; *avoir des idées* ~*es*, to be broad-minded. ~, s.m. Liberal; member of the Liberal party.

libéralement (liberalmɑ̃), adv. Liberally; generously, amply; broad-mindedly.

libéralisme (liberalism), s.m. Liberalism.

libéralité (liberalite), s.f. Liberality; generosity; donation; gift.

libérat-eur, -rice (liberatœr), s.m.f. [L *liberator*] Liberator; deliverer; rescuer. ~, adj. Liberating, releasing, freeing, rescuing.

libération (libera'sjɔ̃), s.f. Liberation; deliverance, rescue; setting free; exemption, release; discharge; ~ *conditionnelle*, ticket-of-leave.

libératoire (liberatwar), adj. Liberating; freeing; clearing from debt.

libéré, -e (libere), p. adj. Freed; released, discharged; *forçat* ~, released convict; *action* ~*e*, paid-up share.

libérer (libere), v.a. [L *liberare*] To liberate, to free; to discharge, to release; to clear; to pay off; **se** ~, v.pr. to arrange to be at liberty, to disengage oneself; to rid oneself (*de*, of), to clear oneself of debt; to be discharged.

libérien, -ne (liberjɛ̃), adj. (bot.) Liberian, of the liber, or bast.

libertaire (libɛrtɛr), s.m.f. adj. Libertarian; anarchist.

liberté (libɛrte), s.f. [L *libertas*] Liberty, freedom; independence; ease; licence; franchise; privilege; boldness; *en* ~, free; *mettre* or *remettre en* ~, to free, to set at liberty, to liberate; ~ *naturelle*, natural liberty; ~ *civile*, civil liberty; ~ *de conscience*, liberty of conscience; ~ *d'esprit*, ease of mind, leisure; *mettre en* ~ *provisoire*, to discharge conditionally; *prendre la* ~ *de faire*, to take the liberty of doing, or to presume to do; *prendre des* ~*s*, to take liberties, to be unduly familiar.

liberticide (libɛrtisid), adj. s.m.f. [f. L *libertas*+*caedere*] Liberticide.

libertin, -e (libɛrtɛ̃), s.m.f. [L *libertinus*] **1.** Libertine, rake; **2.** free-thinker; libertine. ~, adj. **1.** Libertine, licentious; **2.** free-thinking, libertine.

libertinage (libɛrtinaʒ), **1.** s.m. Dissoluteness, libertinage; **2.** (obs.) free-thinking.

libertiner (libɛrtine), (rare) v.n. To lead a dissolute life, to be a libertine.

libidineu-x, -se (libidinø), adj. [f. L *libido*] Libidinous, lascivious, lustful.

libouret (liburɛ), s.m. (fish.) Mackerel-line.
libraire (librɛr), s.m.f. [L *librarius*] Bookseller; ~-*éditeur*, bookseller and publisher. ⚠ Not 'librarian' which = *bibliothécaire*.
librairie (librɛri), s.f. Book-trade; bookshop; (obs.) library (⚠ which nowadays = *bibliothèque*).
libration (libra'sjɔ̃), s.f. [f. L *librare*] (astr.) Libration.
libre (libr), adj. [L *liber*] Free; at liberty; exempt; disengaged; unoccupied; unemployed; unattached; private (of schools); unstamped (of paper); irregular (of verse); frank; open; broad; ~ *à vous de*, you are quite free to; it's up to you to; you may if you like; ~ *de tout lien*, quite free, disengaged, quite at liberty; *avoir le champ* ~, to have free scope; *à l'air* ~, in the open (air); *avoir l'esprit* ~, to be free of cares; *des propos un peu* ~*s*, rather risky talk. ~ *arbitre*, s.m. Free will; ~-*échange*, s.m. free trade; ~-*échangiste*, free-trader; ~ *penseu-r, -se*, s.m.f. adj. (that is a) free-thinker; ~-*passage*, s.m. right of way, free passage.
librement (librəmɑ̃), adv. Independently, freely; boldly; familiarly; *en user* ~, to make free with.
librettiste (librɛttist), s.m.f. Librettist.
libretto (librɛtto), s.m. [It. wd] Libretto.
lice (lis), s.f. [OHG *lista*] **1.** Lists; (fig.) arena, field of action; (lit. and fig.) *entrer dans la* ~, to enter the lists; **2.** stile, wooden fence; **3.** (hunt.) bitch hound; **4.** *lice* or *lisse*, warp; *haute* ~, high warp; *basse* ~, low warp. ⚠ Not English 'lice', which = *poux*.
licence (lisɑ̃s), s.f. [L *licentia*] **1.** Licence; leave, permission; liberty; **2.** licentiousness; **3.** master's degree; (see **licencié**).
licencié, -e (lisɑ̃sje), s.m.f. Licentiate (no exact equivalent in Engl.); ~ *ès lettres*, M.A. (Master of Arts); ~ *ès sciences*, B.Sc. (Bachelor of Science); ~ *en droit*, person having a diploma permitting him or her to practise law. ~, **-e**, p. adj. Discharged, dismissed; *tous les commis ont été* ~*s*, all the clerks have been dismissed.
licenciement (lisɑ̃simɑ̃), s.m. Disbanding; breaking-up; dismissal.
licencier (lisɑ̃sje), v.a. To disband; to break up; to dismiss, to discharge.
licencieusement (lisɑ̃sjøzmɑ̃), adv. Licentiously.
licencieu-x, -se (lisɑ̃sjø), adj. Licentious, dissolute.
licet (lisɛt), s.m. [L wd] Permission, leave (to).
liceuse (lisøs), s.f. [f. *lice*] Warp-maker.
lichen (likɛn), s.m. [Gr. *leikhēn*] (bot.) Lichen.
lichéneu-x, -se (likenø), adj. Lichenous.
lichénicole (likenikɔl), adj. Lichenicolous.
lichénoïde (likenoid), adj. Lichenoid, lichenous.
licher (liʃe), v.a. [f. *lécher*] (pop.) To lick; to eat gluttonously, to drink; to tipple.
licheu-r, -se (liʃœr), s.m.f. Tippler.
licier (lisje), s.m. Warp-weaver.
licitation (lisita'sjɔ̃), s.f. [L *licitatio*] Sale by auction.
licitatoire (lisitatwar), adj. Of auction, pertaining to auction.
licite (lisit), adj. [L *licitus*] Licit, lawful, allowable.
licitement (lisitmɑ̃), adv. Licitly, legally, lawfully.
liciter (lisite), v.a. To auction; to sell by auction.
licorne (likɔrn), s.f. [L *unicornis*] Unicorn; ~ *de mer*, narwhal.
licou, licol (liku, likɔl), s.m. [f. *lier*+*col*] Halter; head-stall.
licteur (liktœr), s.m. [L *lictor*] (ant.) Lictor.
lie (li), s.f. [perhaps of Celt. orig.] (lit. and fig.) Dregs; lees; grounds; scum; *boire le calice jusqu'à la* ~, to drink the cup to the very dregs. ⚠ Not English 'lie' which = *mensonge*.
lie (li), adj. f. (obs.) [L *laeta*] Merry, gay, jolly; *faire chère* ~, to make merry, to make good cheer; to eat and drink merrily, to have a good old blow-out.
liège (liɛʒ), s.m. [L *levis*] Cork; (bot.) *chêne*-~, cork-oak.
liégeu-x, -se (ljeʒø), adj. Corky.
liement (limɑ̃), s.m. Binding.
lien (ljɛ̃), s.m. [L *ligamen*] Bond, tie; band, strap, cord, string; ligament, ligature; link, chain; fetter, shackle. ⚠ Not English 'lien' which = *droit de gage sur une propriété, nantissement*.
lientérie (ljɑ̃teri), s.f. [Gr. *leienteria*] (med.) Lientery.
lientérique (ljɑ̃terik), adj. Lienteric.
lier (lje), v.a. [L *ligare*] To bind, to tie, to tie up; to fasten; to connect, to link up; to bind down; (cook.) to thicken; (mus.) to slur; to enter into, to engage in; *ils sont très liés*, they are intimate friends, they are thick as thieves; ~ *conversation*, to enter into conversation; (fig.) *avoir les mains liées*, to have one's hands tied; **se** ~, v.pr. (fig.) to bind oneself; to form a connexion (with); to associate oneself (with).
lierre (ljɛr), s.m. [L *hedera*] (bot.) Ivy; ~ *terrestre*, ground ivy.
liesse (ljɛs), s.f. [L *laetitia*] Joy, mirth, merriment.
lieu (pl. **-x**) (ljø), s.m. [L *locus*] Place, spot; ground; reason, occasion; position, place; family, extraction; source, authority; dwelling-place; stead, lieu; turn; ~*x*, (*a*) premises; (*b*) privy; *au* ~ *de*, instead of; in lieu of; *au* ~ *que*, whereas; *avoir* ~, to

take place, to happen; *avoir tout ~ de*, to have every reason to; *donner ~ à*, to give rise to; *tenir ~ de*, to take the place of, to serve as; *en haut ~*, in high quarters; *en ~ sûr*, in a place of safety; *en dernier ~*, lastly; *en premier ~*, in the first place; *en quelque ~ que*, wherever; *en tout ~*, everywhere; *mauvais ~*, house of ill fame; *n'avoir ni feu ni ~*, to be homeless; *au ~ et place de*, or *en son ~ et place*, as a substitute for; *en temps et ~*, at the right time; *~ commun*, commonplace, platitude, trite saying; *être sur les ~x*, to be on the spot; *aller aux ~x*, to go to the W.C.

lieue (ljø), s.f. [L *leuca*] League; *~ kilométrique* = 4 kilometers = $2\frac{1}{2}$ Engl. miles; *être à cent ~s de penser que*, to be miles off thinking; to be very far from thinking that.

lieu-r, -se (ljœr), s.m.f. Binder; trusser.

lieutenance (ljœtnɑ̃s), s.f. Lieutenancy.

lieutenant (ljœtnɑ̃), s.m. [*lieu+tenant*] Lieutenant; *sous-~*, sub-lieutenant; *~-colonel*, lieutenant-colonel; (naut.) *~ de vaisseau*, lieutenant R.N.; *~ (d'un navire de commerce)* second mate; *~ de port*, deputy harbour-master; (fig.) substitute, deputy, person acting for another; *vous serez mon ~*, you will be my assistant, you will act as my substitute.

lieutenante (ljœtnɑ̃t), s.f. (obs.) Wife of a lieutenant(-governor); (fam.) wife of a lieutenant.

lièvre (ljɛvr), s.m. [L *lepus*] (zool.) Hare; (fig.) *lever le* or *un ~*, to raise a ticklish question; *avoir une mémoire de ~*, to have a memory like a sieve; *courir le même ~*, to have the same axe to grind; *bec de ~*, harelip; *pour faire un civet, prenez un ~*, first catch your hare, then cook it; *il ne faut pas courir deux ~s à la fois*, you must not have too many irons in the fire.

lièvreteau (pl. **-x**) (liɛvrəto), s.m. Young hare; syn. LEVRAUT.

ligament (ligamɑ̃), s.m. [L *ligamentum*] (anat.) Ligament.

ligamenteu-x, -se (ligamɑ̃tø), adj. Ligamental.

ligature (ligatyr), s.f. [L *ligatura*] Ligature; bandage; (print.) ligature; (hort.) binding.

ligaturer (ligatyre), v.a. To bind.

lige (liʒ), adj. [LL *liticus*] (feudal) Liege.

ligement (liʒmɑ̃), adv. (obs.) With liege homage.

lignage (liɲaʒ), s.m. Lineage; race; family, descent.

lignager (liɲaʒe), s.m. Man of the same lineage, kinsman.

lignard (liɲar), s.m. (pop.) Soldier of the line.

ligne (liɲ), s.f. [L *linea*] Line; row, rank; formation; outline; fishing-line; (naut.) twine; (geog.) equator, line; *passer la ~*, to cross the line; (rail.) line; *grande ~*, main line; *~ à plomb*, plumb-line; *~ électrique*, electric line; *en ~*, in a row; *~ de sonde*, lead-line; *faire entrer en ~ de compte*, to take into account; *hors ~*, beyond comparison; *en ~ !*, fall in !; *aller à la ~*, to begin a new paragraph; *troupes de ~*, troops of the line; *vaisseau de ~*, man-o'-war, ship of the line, or line-of-battle ship; *vaisseaux en ~*, ships in line abreast; *~ de feu*, line of fire; *~ de conduite*, line of conduct; *~ d'arrivée*, winning-post; *~ de flottaison*, water-line; *pêcher à la ~*, to angle; *en droite ~*, straight, straight across.

lignée (liɲe), s.f. **1.** Lineage, line, descent, race; **2.** offspring, descendants.

ligner (liɲe), v.a. To draw lines on; to chalk.

lignerolle (liɲrɔl), s.f. (naut.) Thin twine.

lignette (liɲɛt), s.f. Net-twine.

ligneul (liɲœl), s.m. [LL *lineolum*] Wax-thread, wax end, shoemaker's end.

ligneu-x, -se (liɲø), adj. [f. L *lignum*] (bot.) Woody; ligneous. ~, s.m. Lignin.

lignicole (liɲikɔl), adj. Living in wood.

lignification (liɲifika'sjɔ̃), s.f. (bot.) Lignification.

(se) lignifier (səliɲifje), v.pr. [L *lignum+facere*] (bot.) To lignify.

lignine (liɲin), s.f. (chem.) Lignin.

lignite (liɲit, lignit), s.m. Lignite; fossil wood.

ligotage (ligɔtaʒ), s.m. Binding; fettering.

ligoter (ligɔte), v.a. [etym. dub.] To bind tightly; to secure; to fetter, to lash.

ligroïne (ligrɔin), s.f. (chem.) Ligroin, petroleum ether; syn. ÉTHER DE PÉTROLE.

ligue (lig), s.f. [It. *liga*] League; confederation; association; coalition; *en ~ avec*, in league with.

liguer (lige), v.a. To unite; to band together; *ligué avec*, leagued with or leagued together; **se ~**, v.pr. to form a league, to league together.

ligueu-r, -se (ligœr), s.m.f. Leaguer; confederate; (Fr. hist.) member of the League formed against the Huguenots in the time of Henri III.

ligule (ligyl), s.f. [L *ligula*] (bot., ent.) Ligula.

ligulé, -e (ligyle), adj. (bot.) Ligulated.

liguliflore (ligyliflɔr), adj. With ligulated flowers.

liguliforme (ligylifɔrm), adj. Liguliform; strap-shaped.

ligurien, -ne (ligyrjɛ̃), adj. s.m.f. Ligurian.

lilas (lilɑ), s.m. [Span. *lilac*] (bot.) Lilac; lilac colour. ~, adj. invar. Lilac.

liliacées (liljase), s.f.pl. [f. L *lilium*] (bot.) Liliaceae.

lilial, -e (liljal), adj. Lily-like.

lilliputien, -ne (lilipysjɛ̃), adj. Lilliputian, tiny.

limace (limas), s.f. [L *limax*] Slug; (mech.) Archimedean screw.
limacien, -ne (limasjɛ̃), adj. Limaceous.
limaçon (limasɔ̃), s.m. (zool.) Snail; (mech.) screw; (anat.) cochlea; *escalier en* ~ (or rather *en colimaçon*), spiral staircase; syn. COLIMAÇON.
limaçonnière (limasɔnjɛr), s.f. Snail-farm.
limage (limaʒ), s.m. Limation; filing.
limaille (limɑj), s.f. Filings.
liman (limɑ̃), s.m. [Russ. wd] Lagoon (near the Black Sea).
limande (limɑ̃d), s.f. (ichth.) Dabfish; (naut.) parcelling.
limbaire (lɛ̃bɛr), adj. (bot.) Limbate.
limbe (lɛ̃b), s.m. [L *limbus*] (math.) Limb, edge, border; halo; (bot.) edge, limb, blade, lamina; ~**s**, pl. limbo. ⚠ In English 'limb' means also *membre, partie du corps.*
lime (lim), s.f. [L *lima*] **1.** File; **2.** (bot.) sweet lime (fruit). ⚠ Not English 'lime', which = **1.** *chaux*; **2.** *glu*; **3.** *tilleul*; **4.** *limon*².
limer (lime), v.a. To file; to polish; (fig.) to put the finishing touch to.
limettier (limɛtje), s.m. Sweet lime tree.
limeu-r, -se (limœr), s.m.f. Filer, polisher.
limier (limje), s.m. [f. L *ligamen*] Bloodhound; bear-hound; (fig.) policeman; detective; spy.
liminaire (liminɛr), adj. [f. L *limen*] Preliminary; introductory; prefatory.
limitable (limitabl), adj. Limitable.
limitati-f, -ve (limitatif), adj. Limitative, limiting, restricting, specifying.
limitation (limita'sjɔ̃), s.f. Limitation; restriction. ⚠ In French *limitation* means always the act of limiting or restricting; it cannot be used as in the English expression: 'he has his limitations' = *il a ses côtés faibles.*
limite (limit), s.f. [L *limes*] Bound, bounds, border, boundary; limit. ⚠ *Limite* in French cannot apply to persons as in the English slang expression: 'he is the limit!' = *il est vraiment impossible!, on n'a jamais vu un être pareil!*
limité, -e (limite), p. adj. Limited, restricted, bounded.
limiter (limite), v.a. To limit, to restrict; to restrain.
limitrophe (limitrɔf), adj. [L *limitrophus*] Limitrophe, bordering upon; adjacent to.
limnée (limne), s.f. (zool.) Limnaea.
limon¹ (limɔ̃), s.m. [L *limus*] Mud, slime, sediment, ooze, alluvium; (fig.) origin.
limon² (limɔ̃), s.m. [Arab. *laiūmn*] Lime (fruit).
limon³ (limɔ̃), s.m. (techn.) **1.** Shaft, thill; **2.** (arch.) notch-board (of stairs).
limonade (limɔnad), s.f. **1.** Lemonade; ~ *gazeuse*, aerated lemonade; **2.** retail of drinks.
limonadi-er, -ère (limɔnadje), s.m.f. **1.** Seller of lemonade; **2.** café-keeper.
limonage (limɔnaʒ), s.m. (agric.) Mud-manuring.
limonène (limɔnɛn), s.m. (chem.) Carburetted hydrogen.
limoneu-x, -se (limɔnø), adj. Muddy, slimy; alluvial.
limonier¹ (limɔnje), s.m. Lemon-tree.
limonier² (limɔnje), s.m. Shaft-horse, thiller.
limonière (limɔnjɛr), s.f. Shafts; four-wheeled carriage; wagon.
limonite (limɔnit), s.f. (min.) Limonite.
limoselle (limɔzɛl), s.f. (bot.) Mudwort.
limosinage (limɔzinaʒ), s.m. [f. *limousin*] (build.) Rough-walling; ashlar-work.
limousin, -e (limuzɛ̃), adj. s.m. Of Limoges, of Limousin. ~, s.m. Rough-waller; ~**e**, s.f. **1.** limousine; **2.** wagoner's cloak.
limousiner (limuzine), v.a. To rough-wall.
limpide (lɛ̃pid), adj. [L *limpidus*] Limpid; clear, pure; (fig.) simple; lucid.
limpidité (lɛ̃pidite), s.f. Limpidness; clearness; (fig.) simplicity; lucidity.
limule (limyl), s.m. [f. L *limus*] (zool.) King-crab.
limure (limyr), s.f. Limation, filing; filings.
lin (lɛ̃), s.m. [L *linum*] (bot.) Flax; linen.
linacé, -e (linase), adj. Like flax.
linaigrette (linɛgrɛt), s.f. (bot.) Cotton-grass.
linaire (linɛr), s.f. (bot.) Toad-flax; flax-weed.
linceul (lɛ̃sœl), s.m. [L *linteolum*] Shroud, winding-sheet.
linçoir (lɛ̃swar), s.f. (carp.) Assembling-piece.
lindor (lɛ̃dɔr), s.m. (cards) Seven of diamonds in Pope Joan.
linéaire (lineɛr), adj. [L *linearis*] Linear.
linéal, -e, (aux) (lineal), adj. Linear, lineal. ⚠ The sense of: 'in the direct line of descent or ancestry' is rare in French, but frequent in English.
linéament (lineamɑ̃), s.m. [L *lineamentum*] Lineament; feature; line; outline; rudiment, beginnings.
linette (linɛt), s.f. Flax-seed; linseed.
linge (lɛ̃ʒ), s.m. [L *lineum*] Linen; ~ *de maison*, household linen; ~ *de fantaisie*, fancy linen; ~ *de table*, table-linen; ~ *de corps*, underlinen; *sac à* ~ (*sale*), linen-bag; *changer de* ~, to change one's linen; (fig.) *il faut laver son* ~ *sale en famille*, dirty linen should be washed at home; it's an ill bird that fouls its own nest.
ling-er, -ère (lɛ̃ʒe), s.m.f. Linen-draper; ~**ère**, s.f. linen-maid, sempstress.
lingerie (lɛ̃ʒri), s.f. **1.** Linen-trade; linen-manufacture; **2.** linen room; **3.** lingerie, ladies' underclothing, frills, collars, &c.

lingette (lɛ̃ʒɛt), s.f. Norman serge; flannelette.
lingot (lɛ̃go), s.m. [f. Engl. *ingot*] **1.** Ingot; bullion; **2.** slug; **3.** (print.) piece of type, clump.
lingotière (lɛ̃gɔtjɛr), s.f. Ingot-mould.
lingual, -e, (aux) (lɛ̃gwal), adj. Lingual.
linguet (lɛ̃gɛ), s.m. (naut.) Pawl.
linguiforme (lɛ̃gɥifɔrm), adj. Tongue-shaped; linguiform.
linguiste (lɛ̃gɥist), s.m.f. [f. L *lingua*] Linguist.
linguistique (lɛ̃gɥistik), s.f. Linguistics; philology. ~, adj. Linguistic.
lini-er, -ère (linje), adj. Linen; *industrie ~ère*, linen-trade. **~ère,** s.f. Field of flax.
liniment (linimɑ̃), s.m. [f. L *linire*] Liniment; embrocation.
linition (linisjɔ̃), s.f. [L *linitio*] Anointing, smearing.
linographie (linɔgrafi), s.f. [Gr. *linon*+*graphein*] Printing on cloth.
linoléum (linɔleɔm), s.m. [Fr. *lin*+L *oleum*] Linoleum, oil-cloth, floor-cloth, lino.
linon (linɔ̃), s.m. [etym. dub.] Lawn (cloth).
linot (lino), s.m., **linotte** (linɔt), s.f. (ornith.) Linnet; *avoir une tête de linotte*, to be hare-brained; to be feather-brained.
linotype (linɔtip), s.f. (print.) Linotype.
linotypiste (linɔtipist), s.m.f. Linotypist.
linsang (lɛ̃sɑ̃), s.m. [Javanese wd] (zool.) Linsang.
linteau (pl. -x) (lɛ̃to), s.m. [f. LL *limitale*] Lintel.
lion (ljɔ̃), s.m. [L *leo*] Lion; (fig.) lion; dandy; (astrol.) Leo; *la part du ~*, the lion's share; *l'âne couvert de la peau du ~*, the ass in the lion's skin; *le ~ du jour*, the lion of the day, the lion; *Richard Cœur de Lion*, Richard Cœur de Lion, Richard the Lion-hearted.
lionçeau (pl. -x) (ljɔ̃so), s.m. Lion cub.
lionne (ljɔn), s.f. Lioness; (fig., obs.) fashionable woman (in the middle of 19th century).
lioube (ljub), s.f. Notch, groove, mortise.
lipoïde (lipɔid), adj. [f. Gr. *lipos*+*eidos*] Fatty, fat-like.
lipome (lipom), s.m. [f. Gr. *lipos*] (surg.) Lipoma; fatty tumour.
lipothymie (lipɔtimi), s.f. [Gr. *leipein*+*thumos*] (med.) Lipothymia.
lippe (lip), s.f. [Germ. wd] Thick underlip; *faire la ~*, to pout.
lippée (lipe), s.f. Mouthful; *franche ~*, free meal, regular blow-out.
lippu, -e (lipy), adj. Thick-lipped.
liquation (likwa'sjɔ̃), s.f. [L *liquatio*] (metall.) Liquation.
liquéfaction (likefaksjɔ̃), s.f. [f. L *liquefactum*] Liquefaction.
liquéfiable (likefjabl), adj. Liquefiable.
liquéfiant, -e (likefjɑ̃), p. adj. Liquefying.
liquéfier (likefje), v.a. [L *liquere*+*facere*] To liquefy.
liquette (likɛt), s.f. (slang, fam.) Shirt; chemise.
liqueur (likœr), s.f. [L *liquor*] Liquid; liquor; liqueur; *vin de ~*, sweet wine; *verre à ~*, liqueur-glass; *~ titrée*, standard solution.
liquidambar (likidɑ̃bar), s.m. [f. L *liquidus*+LL *ambar*] (bot.) Liquidambar.
liquidateur (likidatœr), s.m. Liquidator. ~, adj. Liquidating.
liquidati-f, -ve (likidatif), adj. Of liquidation.
liquidation (likida'sjɔ̃), s.f. (law) Liquidation; clearance sale; settling-up; winding-up; *~ judiciaire*, voluntary liquidation.
liquide (likid), adj. [L *liquidus*] Liquid; smooth, clear. ~, s.m. Liquid, humour, fluid; liquor; ~, s.f. (phon.) liquid.
liquider (likide), v.a. To liquidate; to settle; to wind up; to sell off; **se ~**, v.pr. to settle one's affairs; to pay one's debts; to be settled, liquidated.
liquidité (likidite), s.f. Fluidity.
liquoreu-x, -se (likɔrø), adj. [f. *liqueur*] Sweet, luscious.
liquoriste (likɔrist), s.m. Dealer in spirits.
lire (lir), s.f. [It. *lira*] Lira.
lire (lir), v.a. [L *legere*] To read; *~ la musique*, to read music at sight; *~ dans la pensée de quelqu'un*, to read some one's thoughts; *dans l'espoir* or *l'attente de vous ~*, hoping to hear from you; awaiting your reply.
lis, lys (lis), s.m. [L *lilium*] (bot.) Lily; (naut.) edge of sail; *teint de ~*, lily-white; *fleurs de ~*, (herald.) fleurs-de-lis; (poet.) kingdom of France.
lise (liz), s.f. Quicksands.
lisérage (lizeraʒ), s.m. Piping; welting; outlining.
liséré (lizere), s.m. Piping; cording; welting; binding; narrow striped border.
lisérer (lizere), v.a. [f. *lisière*] To bind, to pipe.
liseron (lizrɔ̃), s.m. (bot.) Bindweed; convolvulus.
lisette (lizɛt), s.f. Soubrette; (pop. catchword) *pas de ça ~ !*, nothing doing !, don't try it on me !
liseu-r, -se (lizœr), s.m.f. Reader; ~, s.f. book-marker.
lisibilité (lizibilite), s.f. Legibility; readable quality (of a book).
lisible (lizibl), adj. Legible; readable.
lisiblement (liziblәmɑ̃), adv. Legibly, clearly.
lisière (lizjɛr), s.f. Border, selvage, list; edge (of a forest); **~s**, s.f.pl. leading-strings; *être toujours tenu en ~s*, to be always tied to one's mother's apron-strings; *chaussons de ~s*, list slippers.

lissage (lisaʒ), s.m. Smoothing; glossing; glazing.
lisse (lis), adj. Smooth; glossy; polished.
lisse,[1] **lice** (lis), s.f. (naut.) Line; ribband; rail; *~s de couronnement*, taffrail; hand-rail.
lisse[2] (lis), s.f. Warp; see LICE.
lissé, -e (lise), p. adj. Smooth; glossy; polished; sleek. ~, s.m. (cook.) A certain point reached when boiling sugar.
lisser (lise), v.a. To smooth; to glaze; to polish; (naut.) to fit with rails.
lisseu-r, -se (lisœr), s.m.f. Polisher; *~se*, s.f. polishing-machine; rolling-machine.
lissoir (liswar), s.m. Polishing-tool; burnisher; glazing-machine.
liste (list), s.f. [OHG *lista*] List; roll; catalogue; *~s électorales*, register of voters; *scrutin de ~*, vote by list; *~ civile*, civil list.
listel, listeau, liston (listɛl, listo, listɔ̃), s.m. [It. *listello*] Listel, fillet; moulding; small rail; (naut.) filing; moulded circle round edge of a coin.
lit (li), s.m. [L *lectus*] Bed; (river-)bed; layer, stratum; (naut.) *~ du vent*, the wind's eye; (fig.) marriage; *aller au ~*, to go to bed; *se mettre au ~*, (*a*) to go to bed; (*b*) to take to one's bed; *garder le ~*, to keep one's bed; *~ de camp*, camp-bed; *~ à colonnes*, four-poster (bed); *~ de douleur*, bed of sickness; *~ de mort*, death-bed; *~ pliant*, folding bed; *~ de Procuste*, Procrustean bed; *chambre à deux ~s*, double bedroom; *faire ~ à part*, not to sleep together; *~ de parade*, bed of State; (obs.) *~ de justice*, seat of justice; *~ de plume*, feather-bed; *faire un ~*, to make a bed; *comme on fait son ~ on se couche*, as you make your bed, so you must lie on it; *enfant du premier ~*, child by the first wife; *~ clos*, cupboard-bed.
litanies (litani), s.f.pl. [Gr. *litaneia*] Litany; **litanie,** s.f.sing. rigmarole; tale of woe.
liteau (pl. **-x**) (lito), s.m. **1.** Stripe (in linen); **2.** (carp.) wooden bracket; **3.** wolf's lair.
litée (lite), s.f. Lair, haunt; litter.
liter (lite), v.a. [f. *lit*] To pack (salt fish) in barrels.
literie (litri), s.f. Bed and bedding.
litham (litam), s.m. Turkish veil.
litharge (litarʒ), s.f. [Gr. *lithos+arguros*] (chem.) Litharge.
lithargé, -e, lithargyré, -e (litarʒe, litarʒire), adj. Adulterated with litharge.
lithiase, lithiasie (litiɑz, litiɑzi), s.f. (med.) Lithiasis, lithia; stone.
lithine (litin), s.f. (chem.) Oxide of lithium.
lithium (litjɔm), s.m. (chem.) Lithium.
lithochromie (litɔkrɔmi), s.f. [Gr. *lithos+khroma*] Chromolithography.
lithochromographie (litɔkrɔmɔgrafi), s.f. Chromolithography.
lithocolle (litɔkɔl), s.f. [Gr. *lithos+kolla*] Lithocolla; stone cement.
lithoglyphie (litɔglifi), s.f. [Gr. *lithos+gluphein*] Lithoglyphics.
lithographe (litɔgraf), s.m. [Gr. *lithos+graphein*] Lithographer.
lithographie (litɔgrafi), s.f. Lithography; lithograph.
lithographier (litɔgrafje), v.a. To lithograph.
lithographique (litɔgrafik), adj. Lithographic.
lithoïde (litɔid), adj. [Gr. *lithos+eidos*] Stone-like; lithoid.
lithologie (litɔlɔʒi), s.f. [Gr. *lithos+logos*] Lithology.
lithologue (litɔlɔg), s.m. Lithologist.
lithophage (litɔfaʒ), adj. [Gr. *lithos+phagein*] (zool.) Lithophagous.
lithophanie (litɔfani), s.f. [Gr. *lithos+phainein*] Lithophany.
lithophyte (litɔfit), s.m. [Gr. *lithos+phuton*] (zool.) Lithophyte.
lithotome (litɔtom), s.m. (surg.) Lithotome.
lithotomie (litɔtɔmi), s.f. [Gr. *lithos+tomē*] (surg.) Lithotomy; cystotomy.
lithotomiste (litɔtɔmist), s.m. Lithotomist.
lithotriteur (litɔtritœr), s.m. [Gr. *lithos*+L *tritor*] (surg.) Lithotriptor.
lithotritie (litɔtriti), s.f. (surg.) Lithotripsy.
lithotypographie (litotipɔgrafi), s.f. Lithograph-printing.
lithuanien, -ne (lityanjɛ̃), adj. s.m.f. Lithuanian.
litière (litjɛr), s.f. [f. *lit*] Stable-litter; litter (carriage); *faire ~ de ses scrupules*, to throw one's scruples to the winds.
litigant, -e (litigɑ̃), s.m.f. Litigant.
litige (litiʒ), s.m. [L *litigium*] Litigation; lawsuit; strife.
litigieu-x, -se (litiʒjø), adj. Disputable; contested.
litispendance (litispɑ̃dɑ̃s), s.f. [L *lis + pendere*] Pending judgement; pendency.
litorne (litɔrn), s.f. (ornith.) Litorn; fieldfare.
litote (litɔt), s.f. [Gr. *lītotēs*] (rhet.) Litotes.
litre[1] (litr), s.m. Litre (measure).
litre[2] (litr), s.f. Black band on hatchment, litre.
litron (litrɔ̃), s.m. Litron (obs.), $\frac{1}{16}$ bushel.
littéraire (litɛrɛr), adj. Literary.
littérairement (litɛrɛrmɑ̃), adv. From a literary point of view; in a literary manner.
littéral, -e (aux) (litɛral), adj. [f. L *littera*] **1.** Literal; **2.** written.
littéralement (litɛralmɑ̃), adv. Literally.

littérateur (litɛratœr), s.m. Man of letters.

littérature (litɛratyr), s.f. Literature; knowledge of literature.

littoral, -e (aux) (litɔral), adj. [f. L *litus*] Littoral; coastal. ~, s.m. Coast; coast-line; sea-shore; seaboard.

littorine (litɔrin), s.f. (zool.) Littorina.

liturgie (lityrʒi), s.f. [Gr. *leitourgia*] Liturgy; ritual.

liturgique (lityrʒik), adj. Liturgical.

liturgiste (lityrʒist), s.m. Liturgist.

lituus (lityys), s.m. [L wd] Augur's wand.

liure (liyr), s.f. [L *ligatura*] Cart-rope; roping; cord.

livarde (livard), s.f. (naut.) Sprit; *voile à* ~, sprit-sail.

livarot (livaro), s.m. [f. *Livarot*, Calvados] Livarot cheese.

livèche (livɛʃ), s.f. [LL *levisticum*] (bot.) Lovage.

livet (livɛ), s.m. (naut.) Bridge-line, marked on the framework of a ship during construction.

livide (livid), adj. [L *lividus*] Livid; very pale, of an ashen paleness.

lividité (lividite), s.f. Lividness.

livie (livi), s.f. (ent.) Marsh-fly.

livrable (livrabl), adj. Ready for delivery; to be delivered.

livraison (livrɛzɔ̃), s.f. **1.** Delivery; *voiture de* ~, delivery-van. **2.** (book) volume, part, number, issue.

livre (livr), s.m. [L *liber*] Book; work; register; ~ *de bord* or *journal du bord*, log-book; ~ *de comptes*, account-book; *grand-*~, ledger; *Grand-Livre* (*de la Dette Publique*), Register of the National Debt; ~ *d'heures*, prayer-book, book of hours; ~ *de lecture*, reading-book; ~ *jaune* (diplomatic records), Blue book; ~ *de loch*, ship's log; log-book; *traduire à* ~ *ouvert*, to translate at sight; *placer sur le Grand* ~, to invest in public funds; *publier* or *faire paraître un* ~, to publish a book; ~ *épuisé*, book out of print; (fam.) *parler comme un* ~, to speak like a book; *tenue de livres en partie double*, book-keeping by double entry.

livre (livr), s.f. [L *libra*] **1.** Livre (an old Fr. money of account); **2.** franc; *avoir cinquante mille* ~*s de rente*, to have an income of 50,000 francs; **3.** pound sterling; **4.** (current use) half-kilogramme = 500 gr.

livrée (livre), s.f. Livery; (fig.) outward signs; colours; *en* ~, in livery. ⚠ In English, 'livery' has also the senses of: (*a*) *aliments et effets distribués aux dépendants*; (*b*) *nourriture à forfait d'un cheval*; (*c*) *location de chevaux*, ex.: livery stable; (obs.) a horse at livery = *un cheval en pension*.

livrer (livre), v.a. [L *liberare*] To deliver; to hand over; to surrender; to give up, to betray; to abandon, to give over; to entrust, to confide; ~ *bataille*, to offer or give battle; **se** ~, v.pr. to give oneself over (*à*, to); to give way (to); to devote one's attention (to).

livresque (livrɛsk), adj. Bookish; learnt from books.

livret (livrɛ), s.m. Small book; booklet; libretto, book of words; catalogue; guide; hand-book; bank-book; memorandum-book; certificate-book; licence; ~ *de Caisse d'Épargne*, Savings Bank depositor's book.

livreu-r, -se (livrœr), adj. s.m.f. Deliverer; messenger.

lixiviateuse (liksivjatøz), s.f. (rare) [f. L *lixivium*] Washing-machine.

lixiviation (liksivja'sjɔ̃), s.f. (chem.) Lixiviation.

lixiviel, -le (liksivjɛl), adj. (rare) Lixivial.

lizarique (lizarik), adj. (chem.) Alizaric (acid).

llano (lano), s.m. Llano (South Amer. plain).

lloyd (lɔid), s.m. [f. prop. n.] Lloyd's (as a name of shipping or underwriting corporations).

lobe (lɔb), s.m. [Gr. *lobos*] (anat., bot.) Lobe; (arch.) cusp, foil.

lobé, -e (lɔbe), adj. Lobed, lobate.

lobélie (lɔbeli), s.f. (bot.) Lobelia.

lobulaire (lɔbylɛr), adj. Lobular.

lobule (lobyl), s.m. Lobe, lobule.

lobuleu-x, -se (lɔbylø), adj. Lobular.

local (pl. **aux**) (lɔkal), s.m. Local, spot, premises, quarters. ⚠ In English 'local' means also *habitant d'un lieu, professionnel exerçant en un certain lieu*; *timbre valable dans le district*; *train desservant les stations du district*.

local, -e, (aux) (lɔkal), adj. [f. L *locus*] Local; *couleur* ~*e*, local colour.

localement (lɔkalmɑ̃), adj. Locally; on the spot.

localisation (lɔkaliza'sjɔ̃), s.f. Localization.

localiser (lɔkalize), v.a. [f. *local*] **1.** To localize; **2.** to locate; **se** ~, v.pr. to be localized.

localité (lɔkalite), s.f. Place, spot; locality.

locataire (lɔkatɛr), s.m.f. Tenant, lodger; lessee; householder.

locat-eur, -rice (lɔkatœr), s.m.f. (rare) [L *locator*] Owner, (fem.) landlady.

locati-f, -ve (lɔkatif), adj. Pertaining to tenancy; *valeur* ~*ve*, letting value, value of the rent; *réparations* ~*ves*, repairs for which the tenant is liable.

locati-f, -ve (lɔkatif), adj. s.m. (gram). Locative (case).

location (lɔka'sjɔ̃), s.f. [L. *locatio*] **1.** Letting out; **2.** hiring, renting; *donner en* ~, to let out; *prendre en* ~, to hire; to rent; to have (seats) reserved; *agent de* ~, house-agent; (theatr.) *bureau de* ~, box-office. ⚠ Not English 'location', which = (*a*) *détermination d'un lieu, situation, repérage*; (*b*) *réserve, concession, emplacement; ferme, station, établissement.*

locatis (lɔkati), s.m. [f. *location*] (fam., slightly pej.) **1.** Hack; hired conveyance; **2.** rented room or lodging.

loch (lɔk), s.m. [Engl. *log*] (naut.) Log; *filer le* ~, to heave the log; *naviguer au* ~, to sail by the log; *ligne de* ~, log-line; *livre de* ~ or *livre de bord*, log-book; *table de* ~, log-board.

loche (lɔʃ), s.f. (zool.) **1.** Loach; **2.** slug.

locher (lɔʃe), v.n. [Germ. orig.] To be loose; ~, v.a. to shake.

locomobile (lɔkɔmɔbil), adj. [L *locus* +*mobile*] Movable, locomotive, portable. ~ s.f. Locomotive, traction-engine, portable engine.

locomot-eur, -rice (lɔkɔmɔtœr), adj. Locomotive; *muscles* ~*s*, locomotor muscles.

locomoti-f, -ve (lɔkɔmɔtif), adj. Locomotive; of locomotion; locomotory. ⚠ 'Locomotive' in English can be said jestingly of a person but not in French; 'a locomotive person' = *une personne qui a la bougeotte; qui est constamment en voyage, qui a le pied léger.*

locomotion (lɔkɔmɔsjɔ̃), s.f. [L *locus*+ *motus*] Locomotion, power of motion; way (espec. mechanical) of travelling.

locomotive (lɔkɔmɔtiv), s.f. Locomotive engine, steam-engine, electric engine. ⚠ See LOCOMOTIF, adj.

loculaire, loculé, -e, loculeu-x, -se (lɔkylɛr, lɔkyle, lokylø), adj. [f. L *loculus*] (zool., bot.) Locular.

locuste (lɔkyst), s.f. [L *locusta*] (ent.) Locust.

locution (lɔkysjɔ̃), s.f. [L *locutio*] Locution, style of speech, idiom, word or phrase.

loden (lɔdɛn), s.m. [geog. orig.] Loden (waterproof and windproof woollen material).

lods (lo), s.m.pl. [f. LL *laudes*] (obs.) Only used in: *lods et ventes* (feud. law), lord's due.

loess (løs), s.m. [Germ. *Löss*] (geol.) Loess.

lof (lɔf), s.m. [Scand. orig.] (naut.) Luff; windward; *virer* ~ *pour* ~, to veer, to tack; *aller au* ~, to luff; ~ *de grand'voile*, weather tack of the mainsail; *lever les* ~*s*, to raise tacks and sheets.

lofer (lɔfe), v.n. (naut.) To luff; *lofe tout!*, luff all!

logarithme (lɔgaritm), s.m. [Gr. *logos*+ *arithmos*] Logarithm, log.; *table de* ~*s*, table of logarithms.

logarithmique (lɔgaritmik), adj. Logarithmic.

loge (lɔʒ), s.f. [f. OHG. *laubja*] Cell, den, hut, woodman's cabin; (theatr.) (*a*) box; (*b*) dressing-room; (fig.) *aux premières* ~*s* (*pour*), in a capital place (for); (freemasonry) lodge; porter's room; keeper's lodge (at gates of park or grounds of large house). ⚠ 'Lodge' is nowadays frequently used in the sense of *maison de campagne*, even if it is a large one; but *loge* cannot be used in this acceptation.

logeable (lɔʒabl), adj. Fit to live in.

logement (lɔʒmɑ̃), s.m. **1.** Lodgings, quarters, (cheap) dwelling-place, hired rooms; **2.** lodging, placing, quartering; billeting; **3.** (mil.) lodgement; *billet de* ~, billet, billet-ticket.

loger (lɔʒe), v.n. [f. *loge*] To live (in), to reside, to lodge, to put up; ~ v.a. to lodge, to house, to accomodate, to receive as guest or inmate, to take in; to place; ~ *le diable dans sa bourse*, to have an empty purse; ~ *chez X*, to live with X; ~ *à la belle étoile*, to sleep in the open. ⚠ *Loger* has not like 'to lodge' the sense of 'to leave', 'to deposit' (a statement, complaint &c.) = *déposer une plainte*, nor 'to leave with a person for security' = *confier à*; se ~, v.pr. (*a*) to take lodgings; to take up one's abode; (*b*) to fix itself, to lodge itself, to remain.

logette (lɔʒɛt), s.f. Small cell; small hut or cabin, small den.

logeu-r, -se (lɔʒœr), s.m.f. Lodging-house keeper, landlord, (fem.) landlady.

logicien, -ne (lɔʒisjɛ̃), s.m.f. Logician.

logique (lɔʒik), s.f. [Gr. *logikē*] Logic, logicality. ~, adj. Logical.

logiquement (lɔʒikmɑ̃), adv. Logically.

logis (lɔʒi), s.m. [f. *loger*] Home, dwelling, abode, house, lodging; *trouver X au* ~, to find X at home; (fig.) *la folle du* ~, fancy, imagination; *maréchal des* ~, quartermaster of cavalry; *corps de* ~, a main part of a building.

logistique (lɔʒistik), s.f. Logistics. ~, adj. Logistical.

logographe (lɔgɔgraf), s.m.f. [f. Gr. *logos* +*graphein*] Logograph.

logographie (lɔgɔgrafi), s.f. Logography.

logogriphe (lɔgɔgrif), s.m. [Gr. *logos*+ *grīphos*] Logogriph.

logomachie (lɔgɔmaʃi), s.f. [Gr. *logomakhia*] Logomachy, dispute about words.

logos (lɔgos), s.m. [Gr. wd] Logos.

loi[1] (lwɑ), s.f. [L *lex*] Law, the law, rule, statute, decree, act; sway; command; *avoir force de*~, to be law; to have the force of law; *faire* ~, to be law; *faire des* ~*s*, to make, or enact, laws; *faire la* ~ *à X*, to dictate to X, to lay down the law to X, to hector X; *homme de* ~, lawyer, law-officer; *hors la* ~, outlawed, outlaw;

mettre hors la ~, to outlaw; *se faire une* ~ *de*, to make a point of; *les* ~*s du mouvement*, the laws of motion; *les* ~*s de la grammaire*, the rules of grammar; *nécessité n'a pas de* ~, necessity knows no law; *n'avoir ni foi ni* ~, to be without honour or honesty; *projet de* ~, Bill, draft of proposed Act of Parliament; *présenter un projet de* ~, to bring in a Bill.

loi[2] (lwɑ), s.f. [f. *aloi*] Standard (of coins).

loin (lwɛ̃), adv. [L *longe*] Far, far off, away, a long way off; *au* ~, far away; *bien* ~, very far, a long way off; *bien* ~ *de me plaindre, je veux . . .*, far be it from me to complain, but I intend . . .; *de* ~, from afar; from a distance; *venez-vous de* ~*?*, do you come from far?; (fig.) *je vous vois venir de* ~, I can see what you are aiming at; *il revient de* ~, he has had a narrow escape; he comes back from the borderland, or death's door; *a beau mentir qui vient de* ~, travellers tell fine tales; *de* ~ *en* ~, at long intervals; *vous êtes* ~ *de compte!*, you are out in your reckoning; ~ *des yeux*, ~ *du cœur*, out of sight, out of mind; *du plus* ~ or *d'aussi* ~ *que je me souvienne*, as far back as I can remember; *voir* ~, to be far-sighted; *aller* ~, to go far; (fig.) *vous allez trop* ~*!*, this is beyond a joke; you are going too far!, you exaggerate; (slang) you are coming it rather strong; *ce garçon ira* ~, this young man has a future before him, or will go far; ~ *de moi une pareille pensée!*, far be it from me to have such a thought!; *cela remonte* ~, that's long past; that dates far back; that can be traced far back; that began long ago.

lointain, -e (lwɛ̃tɛ̃), adj. Remote, distant, far off. ~, s.m. Distance; background; *dans le* ~, in the distance, far off.

loir (lwar), s.m. [L *glis*] (zool.) Dormouse; *dormir comme un* ~, to sleep like a log.

loisible (lwazibl), adj. Permissible, licit, allowable; *il vous est* ~ *de partir quand vous voudrez*, you have a perfect right to leave when you choose.

loisir (lwazir), s.m. [f. L *licere*] Leisure, spare time, time; *à* ~, at leisure; *avoir des* ~*s*, to have leisure; *je le ferai à mes heures de* ~, I will do it in my spare time; *employer ses* ~*s*, to use one's spare time; *êtes-vous de* ~*?*, are you at leisure?

lolo (lolo), s.m. [child. wd] Milk.

lombago (lɔ̃bago), s.m. See LUMBAGO.

lombaire (lɔ̃bɛr), adj. [f. *lombes*] (anat.) Lumbar, of the loins.

lombard, -e (lɔ̃bar), adj. s.m.f. Lombard.

lombes (lɔ̃b), s.m.pl. [L *lumbi*] (anat.) Loins.

lombric (lɔ̃brik), s.m. [L *lumbricus*] (zool.) Earth-worm; syn. VER DE TERRE.

lombrical, -e, (aux) (lɔ̃brikal), adj. (anat.) Lumbrical (muscle).

lomentacé, -e (lɔmɑ̃tase), adj. [f. L *lomentum*] (bot.) Lomentaceous.

londonien, -ne (lɔ̃dɔnjɛ̃), adj. Of London. ~, s.m.f. Londoner.

londrès (lɔ̃drɛs), s.m. [f. *Londres*] Havana cigar (originally made for Londoners).

long, -ue (lɔ̃), adj. s.m.f. [L *longus*] Long; *au* ~ *de*, alongside of; *tout au* ~, all along; the whole yarn; in full; *à la* ~*ue*, in the long run; after a time; *trois mètres de* ~, three metres long; *de* ~ *en large*, to and fro; up and down; *de* ~*ue main*, a long time in advance; slowly and carefully prepared; of long standing; *en savoir* ~, to know all about it; *en savoir trop* ~, to know too much; *cela en dit* ~, that speaks volumes; *étendu tout de son* ~, lying at full length; *avoir la vue* ~*ue*, to be far-sighted; *avoir la mine* ~*ue*, to make, pull, or wear a long face; *sauce trop* ~*ue*, too thin or watery sauce; *en* ~, lengthwise, lengthways; (phon.) *une (syllabe)* ~*ue*, a long (syllable); *vous avez eu la langue trop* ~*ue*, you have been talking too much; your tongue has been running too fast; you said too much; *il a le bras* ~, he has a long arm; is very influential; can make his power felt; *capitaine au* ~ *cours*, ocean- or seagoing captain; *de* ~*s mois*, many months.

longanime (lɔ̃ganim), adj. [L *longus*+*animus*] Patient, forbearing.

longanimité (lɔ̃ganimite), s.f. Longanimity, forbearance, long-suffering.

long-courrier (lɔ̃kurje), adj. m. Ocean-going. ~, s.m. Ocean-going ship.

longe[1] (lɔ̃ʒ), s.f. [LL *longa*] Tether, thong, leading-rein.

longe[2] (lɔ̃ʒ), s.f. [f. LL *lumbea*] Loin; ~ *de veau*, loin of veal.

longer (lɔ̃ʒe), v.a. [f. *long*] To run along (by), to coast along; to lie or extend along.

longeron (lɔ̃ʒrɔ̃), s.m. Longitudinal bearer; sole-bar, longeron.

longévité (lɔ̃ʒevite), s.f. [L *longus*+*aevum*] Longevity.

longicorne (lɔ̃ʒikɔrn), adj. [L *longus*+*cornu*] (zool.) Longicorn.

longirostre (lɔ̃ʒirɔstr), adj. [L *longus*+*rostrum*] [zool.] Longirostral.

longitude (lɔ̃ʒityd), s.f. [L *longitudo*] Longitude; *le Bureau des Longitudes*, in Paris, corresponds to the Nautical Almanac Office in England, and to the Cambridge Observatory in U.S.A.

longitudinal, -e, (aux) (lɔ̃ʒitydinal), adj. Longitudinal.

longitudinalement (lɔ̃ʒitydinalmɑ̃), adv. Longitudinally; lengthways, lengthwise.

long-jointé, -e (lɔ̃ʒwɛ̃te), adj. Long in the pastern, long-limbed, long-legged.

longtemps (lɔ̃tɑ̃), adv. [*long*+*temps*] Long, a long time, a long while; *depuis* ~, long ago, long since; for a long time past; *c'est fini depuis* ~, it has been fininished a long time; *il a mis* ~ *à trouver*, he was long finding out; *avant* ~, before long; *il n'en a plus pour* ~, he is not long for this world; *aussi* ~ *que*, as long as; *je n'attendrai pas plus* ~, I shall not wait any longer.

longue (lɔ̃g), adj. See LONG. ~, s.f. Long (syllable, or vowel); *à la* ~, in the long run.

longuement (lɔ̃gmɑ̃), adv. Long, at (full or some) length, lengthily; *trop* ~, at too great length.

longuerine, longrine (lɔ̃grin), s.f. Railway sleeper; syn. TRAVERSE.

longuet, -te (lɔ̃gɛ), adj. Rather too long, longish. ~, s.m. Stick-shaped roll of bread.

longueur (lɔ̃gœr), s.f. [f. *long*] Length; duration; slowness; prolixity; *en* ~, lengthwise, lengthways; *gagner par trois* ~*s*, to win by three lengths; *de six mètres de* ~, or *d'une* ~ *de six m.*, six metres in length, or six m. long; *il y a des* ~*s dans ce morceau*, there are wordy, lengthy parts in this passage (of prose or poetry); *traîner en* ~, to be long drawn-out; to be unduly prolonged, to drag on.

longue-vue (lɔ̃gvy), s.f. (pl. *longues-vues*) Glass, spyglass, telescope.

looch (lɔk), s.m. [Arab. *lahok*] Potion, draught.

lopin (lɔpɛ̃), s.m. [etym. dub.] Bit, portion, patch (usually of ground); ~ *de terre*, patch of ground.

loquace (lɔkwas), adj. [L. *loquax*] Loquacious, talkative.

loquacité (lɔkwasite), s.f. Loquacity, loquaciousness, talkativeness.

loque (lɔk), s.f. [orig. dub.] Rag, tatter; *en* ~*s*, in rags and tatters.

loquèle (lɔkɛl), s.f. [L *loquela*] Gab, flow of words; gift of the gab, loquacity.

loquet (lɔkɛ), s.m. [HGerm. orig.] Latch; *fermer la porte au* ~, to latch the door. ⚠ Not 'locket', which = *médaillon*.

loqueteau (pl. **-x**) (lɔkto), s.m. Small latch.

loqueteu-x, -se (lɔktø), adj. Ragged. ~, s.m.f. Beggar, ragged fellow or woman, person.

loquette (lɔkɛt), s.f. Small rag.

lord-maire (lɔrmɛr), s.m. [f. Engl. *lord mayor*] Lord Mayor.

lordose (lɔrdoz), s.f. [Gr. *lordōsis*] (pathol.) Lordosis.

lorette (lɔrɛt), s.f. (obs.) [f. *N.-D.-de-Lorette*, a quarter in Paris] Gay woman.

lorgner (lɔrɲe), v.a. [f. OF *lorgne*, squinting] To look at through one's lorgnette or opera-glass; (fig.) to covet, to have an eye on.

lorgnette (lɔrɲɛt), s.f. Opera-glass; field-glass. ⚠ Not English 'lorgnette' which = *face-à-main*; syn. JUMELLES. [PINCE-NEZ.

lorgnon (lɔrɲɔ̃), s.m. Eye-glasses; syn.

lori[1] (lɔri), s.m. [Engl. *lorry*] Lorry, small truck used on railways and tramways. ⚠ English 'lorry' now usually means a motor-truck = *camion* (*automobile*).

lori[2] (lɔri), s.m. [Malay *lūri*] (ornith.) Lory.

loriot (lɔrjo), s.m. [f. L *aureolus*] (ornith.) Golden oriole, oriole.

loris (lɔris), s.m. (zool.) [etym. dub.] Loris.

lorrain, -e (lɔrɛ̃), adj. Of Lorraine, Lorrainian; ~, s.m.f. Lorrainer.

lors (lɔr), adv. [L *illa+hora*] Then; *dès* ~, thenceforth, from that time; *depuis* ~, since then, thenceforth; ~ *même que*, even though; ~ *de*, at the time of; *pour* ~, in that case, then, so.

lorsque (lɔrsk), conj. When, whilst; *lorsqu'il parla*, when he spoke; ~ *vous viendrez*, when you come.

los (los), s.m. [L *laus*] Praise, laud; *entonner un* ~ *pour*, to sing the praises of.

losange (lɔzɑ̃ʒ), s.m. [OF. *losenge*] Lozenge, rhomb, diamond figure; *en* ~, diamond-shaped, lozenge-shaped. ⚠ *Losange* is not used like 'lozenge' in the sense of medicinal tablet of flavoured sugar = *pastille, comprimé*, &c.

losangé, -e (lɔzɑ̃ʒe), p. adj. (herald.) Lozenged.

losanger (lɔzɑ̃ʒe), v.a. To divide into lozenges.

lot (lo), s.m. [f. Teut. wd] Lot, portion, share; fate; prize; *gagner le gros* ~, to win the big prize (in a lottery); (fig.) to carry the day, to carry it, to be very lucky or successful; *le* ~ *qui lui est échu*, the portion that has fallen to his share; *c'est le* ~ *commun*, that's the common fate. ⚠ 'Lot' in Engl. means also: *sort* (draw or cast lots = *tirer au sort*); *impôt, taxe* (scot and lot); *individu* (bad lot = *triste personnage*); *grande quantité de* (lots of friends).

loterie (lɔtri), s.f. [It. *lotteria*] Lottery, raffle; (fig.) lottery.

loti, -e (lɔti), p. adj. [f. *lot*] Provided for, favoured, portioned; (iron.) *le voilà bien* ~ *!*, or *bien mal* ~ *!*, now he is in a sorry plight; *bien* ~, well portioned; *mal* ~, ill-favoured.

lotier (lɔtje), s.m. [f. L *lotus*] (bot.) Bird's-foot trefoil; melilot.

lotion (lɔsjɔ̃), s.f. [L *lotio*] Lotion. ⚠ In English (slang) 'lotion' means also alcoholic drink = *liqueur, petit verre*.

lotionner (lɔsjɔne), v.a. To lotion, to bathe, to wash.

lotir (lɔtir), v.a. To portion out, or off, to divide into lots, to allot; see LOTI.

lotissement (lɔtismɑ̃), s.m. **1.** Allotting, allotment, apportioning; **2.** plot, the ground allotted.

loto (lɔto), s.m. [It. *lotto*] Lotto; *avoir des yeux en boules de* ~, to be goggle-eyed.
lotos (lɔtos), s.m. See LOTUS.
lotte (lɔt), s.f. (ichth.) **1.** (freshwater fish) Burbot, eel-pout; **2.** (sea fish), conger-eel.
lotus, lotos (lɔtys, lɔtos), s.m. [Gr. *lōtos*] (bot.) Lotus, lotos.
louable (lwabl), adj. Praiseworthy, commendable, laudable.
louablement (lwabləmɑ̃), Laudably, in a praiseworthy manner.
louage (lwaʒ), s.m. [f. *louer*²] **1.** Letting out; **2.** hiring; rent; *de* ~, hired.
louange (lwɑ̃ʒ), s.f. [f. *louer*¹] Praise, commendation; extolling; glorification; *chanter les* ~*s de X*, to sing X's praises; *donner des* ~*s à X*, to bestow praise on X; *digne de* ~, praiseworthy; *mériter des* ~*s*, to deserve praise; *c'est à sa* ~, it does him credit.
louanger (lwɑ̃ʒe), v.a. To praise, to bestow praise on, to extol.
louangeu-r, -se (lwɑ̃ʒœr), adj. Laudatory, eulogistic; *paroles* ~*ses*, laudatory words. ~, s.m.f. Flatterer.
louche (luʃ), adj. [f. L *luscus*] Squinting, squint-eyed; (fig.) equivocal, dubious-looking, suspicious, shady; *c'est bien* ~ *cette affaire-là*, this looks very suspicious indeed.
louche (luʃ), s.f. [LL *lucia*] Soup-ladle, ladle; (techn.) wimble.
louchement (luʃmɑ̃), s.m. Squinting.
loucher (luʃe), v.n. To squint; (fig.) ~ *sur*, to covet, to have an eye on; to have a squint at.
louchet (luʃɛ), s.m. [f. *louche*] Spade.
loucheu-r, -se (luʃœr), s.m.f. Squinter, squint-eyed person.
louchir (luʃir), v.n. (of liquids) To get muddy.
louer¹ (lwe), v.a. [L *laudare*] To praise, to bestow praise on, to commend; to extol, to eulogize; **se** ~, v.pr. to praise oneself; *se* ~ *de*, to be thoroughly satisfied with; to rejoice in; to be pleased with; *j'ai sujet de me* ~ *de lui*, or *je n'ai qu'à me* ~ *de lui*, I have reason to be satisfied with him; I am thoroughly satisfied with him.
louer² (lwe), v.a. [L *locare*] **1.** To let out, to let, to hire out; to let on lease; ~ *sa maison*, to let one's house; *maison à* ~, house to let; **2.** to rent; to hire; ~ *une maison*, to rent a house; ~ *un cheval*, to hire a horse.
loueu-r, -se (lwœr), s.m.f. Hirer, letter; ~ *de voitures*, livery-stable keeper, job-master, carriage-hirer.
loufoque (lufɔk), adj. (slang, colloq.) Cranky, cracked, crazy, crack-brained. ~, s.m.f. Crank; syn. LOUF and LOUFTINGUE.
loufoquerie (lufɔkri), s.f. Craziness.
lougre (lugr), s.m. [Engl. *lugger*] (naut.) Lugger.
louis (lwi), s.m. [f. name of Fr. kings] Louis, gold coin = 20 francs.
louise-bonne (lwizbɔn), s.f. Louise-bonne pear.
loulou (lulu), s.m. **1.** Pomeranian (dog); **2.** term of endearment; *mon* ~, ducky, darling.
loup (lu), s.m., **louve** (luv), fem. [L *lupus*] **1.** Wolf; (fig.) defect, misfit; *aller à pas de* ~, to walk or tread stealthily; *avoir une faim de* ~, to be ravenously hungry; *avoir vu le* ~, to know what is what; *connu comme le* ~ *blanc*, well known to everybody; *un vieux* ~ *de mer*, an old salt; an old sea-dog; *enfermer le* ~ *dans la bergerie*, to shut up the wolf in the sheep-fold; to set the fox to keep the geese; *tenir le* ~ *par les oreilles*, to hold or have the wolf by the ears (= to be in a situation in which one can neither retreat, advance, nor stop); *hurler avec les* ~*s*, when we are at Rome, we must do as Rome does; he who kennels with wolves must howl; *les* ~*s ne se mangent pas entre eux*, there is honour among thieves; dog doesn't eat dog; *se jeter dans la gueule du* ~, to rush into the lion's mouth; *quand on parle du* ~ *on en voit la queue*, talk of the Devil and he is sure to appear; *entre chien et* ~, at dusk; in the twilight (when it is impossible to distinguish between a wolf and a dog); *tête de* ~, wall-broom (Turk's-head shape, with long pole); *saut de* ~, sunk fence, ha-ha; *mon* ~, my darling, ducky; *crier au* ~, to cry wolf; **2.** velvet mask.
loup-cervier (lusɛrvje), s.m. (pl. *loups-cerviers*) [f. L *lupus*+*cervarius*] (zool.) Lynx; syn. LYNX.
loupe (lup), s.f. [orig. dub.] **1.** Magnifying glass, lens; *vu à la* ~, magnified; **2.** (pathol.) wen, tumour; **3.** (slang) laziness; **4.** (in wood) bole, beautifully veined bole of hardwood.
louper (lupe), v.a. (slang) **1.** To bungle, to make a mess of, to do badly; **2.** to miss.
loup-garou (lugaru), s.m. (pl. *loups-garous*) [f. *loup*+OHG *werawolf*] Werewolf; (fig.) regular bear, surly fellow.
loupiot (lupjo), s.m. (slang, very vulg.) Brat, child, urchin.
lourd, -e (lur), adj. [Celt. orig.] Heavy, weighty; (fig.) dull, thick, clumsy, gross, oppressive, close; drowsy; *avoir la main* ~*e*, to be heavy-handed; *le temps est* ~, the weather is sultry; *avoir la tête* ~*e*, to feel heavy, drowsy, to have a headache; *aliment* ~, heavy food; *artillerie* ~*e*, heavy artillery; *une* ~*e faute*, a gross mistake or blunder.

lourdaud, -e (lurdo), adj. Heavy, clumsy, awkward. ~, s.m.f. Blockhead, lout, clown, clumsy fellow, rustic.
lourdement (lurdəmɑ̃), adv. Heavily; grossly.
lourderie, lourdise (lurdəri, lurdiz), s.f. See BALOURDISE.
lourdeur (lurdœr), s.f. Heaviness; dullness, tediousness.
loure (lur), s.f. (mus.) **1.** Loure, kind of bagpipe; **2.** a dance played on the loure.
lourer (lure), v.a. (mus.) To tie (notes).
loustic (lustik), s.m. [f. Germ. *lustig*] Wag, facetious fellow, joker.
loutre (lutr), s.f. [L *lutra*] (zool.) Otter; otter-fur, otter-skin.
louvart, louvat (luvar, luva), s.m. Young wolf.
louve (luv), s.f. **1.** She-wolf, **2.** (techn.) clips; lewis; sling; claw.
louver (luvɛ), v.a. (techn.) To lift (with a sling, claw, &c.).
louvet, -te (luvɛ), adj. (of horses) Wolf-coloured.
louveteau (pl. **-x**) (luvto), s.m. Wolf-cub.
louveter (luvte), v.n. (of she-wolves) To whelp.
louveterie (luvtri, luvɛtri), s.f. Wolf-hunting; wolf-hunting equipage; *lieutenant de* ~, officer in charge of wolf-hunting.
louvetier (luvtje), s.m. Master of the wolf-hounds; officer of the wolf-hunt; wolf-hunter.
louviers (luvje), s.m. [f. *Louviers*, in France] Louviers cloth.
louvoyer (luvwaje), v.n. [f. *lof*] (naut.) To tack, to tack about; (fig.) to manœuvre, to dodge, to evade answering, yielding, &c.
lovelace (lɔvlas), s.m. [f. prop. n. of character in *Clarissa Harlowe*] Lovelace, rake.
lover (love), v.a. (naut.) To coil (a rope).
loxodromie (lɔksodrɔmi), s.f. [f. Gr. *loxodromos*] (naut.) Loxodromics.
loxodromique (lɔksodrɔmik), adj. (naut.) Loxodromic.
loyal, -e, (aux) (lwajal), adj. [L *legalis*] Loyal, true, faithful, sincere, fair-dealing, straightforward; (comm.) unadulterated.
loyalement (lwajalmɑ̃), adv. Loyally, truthfully, fairly, honestly.
loyalisme (lwajalism), s.m. Loyalism.
loyaliste (lwajalist), adj. s.m.f. Loyalist.
loyauté (lwajote), s.f. Honesty, fairness, fair dealing; loyalty. ⚠ The most frequent sense of 'loyalty', nowadays, is *loyalisme, fidélité.*
loyer (lwaje), s.m. [L *locarium*] Rent, house-rent; hire, wages; (fig.) reward; *donner à* ~, to let; *payer un gros* ~, to pay a high rent.
lubie (lybi), s.f. [f. L *lubere*] Whim, fad, crotchet; *quelle* ~ *vous prend?*, what's this new whim?
lubricité (lybrisite), s.f. Lubricity, lewdness. ⚠ 'Lubricity' means also *glissant, état de lubrification, huilage.*
lubrifiant, -e (lybrifjɑ̃), p. adj. Lubricant, lubricating.
lubrification (lybrifika'sjɔ̃), s.f. Lubrication.
lubrifier (lybrifje), v.a. [f. L *lubricare*] To lubricate.
lubrique (lybrik), adj. [L *lubricus*] Lubricious, lewd.
lucane (lykan), s.m. (ent.) Stag-beetle; syn. CERF-VOLANT.
lucarne (lykarn), s.f. [Goth. *lukarn*] Skylight; dormer-window; garret-window.
lucide (lysid), adj. [L *lucidus*] Lucid, clear, sane. ⚠ In English 'lucid' = also *brillant, limpide, lumineux.*
lucidement (lysidmɑ̃), adv. Lucidly, clearly.
lucidité (lysidite), s.f. Lucidity.
lucifuge (lysifyʒ), adj. [L *lucifugus*] Lucifugous.
luciole (lysjɔl), s.f. [It. *lucciola*] (ent.) Fire-fly.
lucrati-f, -ve (lykratif), adj. [L *lucrativus*] Lucrative, profitable.
lucrativement (lykrativmɑ̃), adv. Lucratively.
lucre (lykr), s.m. [L *lucrum*] Lucre, profit.
ludion (lydjɔ̃), s.m. [L *ludio*] (phys.) Ludion.
luette (lɥɛt), s.f. [f. L *uva*] (anat.) Uvula.
lueur (lɥœr), s.f. [f. L *lucere*] Glimmer, gleam, faint light; (fig.) gleam, ray; *une* ~ *d'espoir*, a gleam of hope.
luge (lyʒ), s.f. [Swiss wd] Luge, toboggan.
luger (lyʒe), v.n. To luge, to toboggan.
lugubre (lygybr), adj. [L *lugubris*] Lugubrious, dismal.
lugubrement (lygybrəmɑ̃), adv. Lugubriously, dismally.
lui (lɥi), pers. pron. Him, her, it; to or at him, her, it; he, it; *je* ~ *ai dit*, I said to him, or I told him; *c'est* ~, it's he; *c'est* ~ *qui parlera*, it is he who is going to speak; *je suis plus vieux que* ~, I am older than he.
luire (lɥir), v.n. [L *lucere*] To shine, to gleam, to glitter, to glisten; to dawn, to appear.
luisant, -e (lɥizɑ̃), p. adj. Shining; shiny, glossy, bright; *ver* ~, glow-worm. ~, s.m. Shine.
lumachelle (lymaʃɛl), s.f. [It. *lumachella*] Shell-marble.
lumbago (lɔ̃bago), s.m. [L wd] Lumbago.
lumen (lymɛn), s.m. [L wd] Lumen, unit of light; abbrev. *lu*.
lumière (lymjɛr), s.f. [L *luminaria*] Light; daylight, day; luminary, lamp, candle;

(fig.) enlightenment, knowledge, civilization; luminary, person of intellectual eminence; (paint.) light; *à la ~*, by artificial light; *voir la ~* or *le jour*, to be born; *mettre en ~*, to bring to light, to elucidate, to throw light on; to stress; *avoir des ~s sur*, to have information about; (techn.) *~ d'admission*, steam-port; *~ d'échappement*, exhaust-port; *~ de distribution*, ignition-port.

lumignon (lymiɲɔ̃), s.m. Snuff, candle-end; faint light or lamp.

luminaire (lyminɛr), s.m. [L *luminaria*] Lights, luminary. ⚠ 'Luminary', but not *luminaire*, can apply to a person; in that case the French word is *lumière*; ex. *une lumière de la science.*

luminescence (lyminɛssɑ̃s), s.f. Luminescence, power of emitting light.

luminescent, -e (lyminɛssɑ̃) adj. Luminescent, luminiferous.

lumineusement (lyminøzmɑ̃), adv. Luminously; clearly.

lumineu-x, -se (lyminø), adj. [L *luminosus*] Luminous, bright, shining; (fig.) luminous, clear.

luminosité (lyminozite), s.f. Luminosity.

lunaire (lynɛr), adj. Lunar.

lunaire (lynɛr), s.f. (bot.) Lunary, moonwort.

lunaison (lynɛzɔ̃), s.f. Lunation.

lunatique (lynatik), adj. s.m.f. [L *lunaticus*] Whimsical, capricious, eccentric person; ⚠ and sometimes 'lunatic'; but the usual meaning of 'lunatic' is *fou, aliéné.*

lunch (lœnʃ), s.m. [Engl. wd] Wedding breakfast; light afternoon meal, with cakes, sandwiches, tea, champagne, &c. (at a wedding party, &c.). ⚠ Not 'luncheon', which = *déjeuner.*

lundi (lœ̃di), s.m. [f. L *luna+dies*] Monday; *faire le ~*, or *fêter la Saint-Lundi*, not to work on Mondays.

lune (lyn), s.f. [L *luna*] Moon; *pleine ~*, full moon; *nouvelle ~*, new moon; *~ rousse*, April moon; *~ de miel*, honeymoon; *clair de ~*, moonlight, moonshine; (fig.) *être toujours dans la ~*, to go wool-gathering; to be absent-minded or a day-dreamer; *faire un trou à la ~*, to shoot the moon, to run from one's creditors; *vouloir prendre la ~ avec ses dents*, to attempt impossibilities; *demander la ~*, to demand the impossible; to cry for the moon; *avoir des ~s*, to have whims; (bot.) *~ d'eau*, white water-lily.

luné, -e (lyne), adj. **1.** Lunate; **2.** in a certain humour; *bien ~*, well disposed; *mal ~*, in a bad humour.

lunetier (lyntje, lynɛtje), s.m. Spectacle-maker or seller, optician.

lunette (lynɛt), s.f. [f. *lune*] **1.** Telescope, spyglass; *~ d'approche*, telescope; **2.** *~s* (pl.) spectacles, specs; *~ d'auto*, goggles; **3.** (fort., arch.) lunette; **4.** merry-thought (bone); **5.** seat (of a water-closet); **6.** aperture of the *guillotine.*

lunetterie (lynɛtri), s.f. Spectacle-trade, spectacle-making.

lunettier (lynɛtje), s.m. See LUNETIER.

lunisolaire (lynisɔlɛr), adj. Lunisolar.

lunulaire (lynylɛr), adj. Lunular, crescent-shaped.

lunule (lynyl), s.f. [L *lunula*] Lunula; (geom.) lunula, crescent-shaped figure.

lunulé, -e (lynyle), adj. Lunulate.

lupanar (lypanar), s.m. [L wd] Brothel; syn. BORDEL.

lupercales (lypɛrkal), s.f.pl. [L *lupercalia*] (Rom. ant.) Lupercalia.

lupin (lypɛ̃), s.m. [L *lupinus*] (bot.) Lupin.

lupinelle (lypinɛl), s.f. (bot.) Sainfoin, trefoil.

lupuline (lypylin), s.f. (bot.) Hop-trefoil.

lupus (lypys), s.m. [L wd] (pathol.) Lupus.

lurette (lyrɛt), s.f. (colloq.) Only used in: *il y a belle ~ que*, it's a long time since.

luron, -ne (lyrɔ̃), s.m.f. Jolly fellow, regular brick; (fem.) buxom woman, bouncing girl.

lustrage (lystraʒ), s.m. Glossing.

lustral, -e, (aux) (lystral), adj. [L *lustralis*] Lustral.

lustration (lystra'sjɔ̃), s.f. [L *lustratio*] Lustration.

lustre[1] (lystr), s.m. [It. *lustro*] **1.** Gloss, lustre, refulgence, brilliance; **2.** chandelier, lustre, sconce, pendant, electrolier.

lustre[2] (lystr), s.m. [L *lustrum*] Lustrum, period of five years.

lustrer (lystre), v.a. To gloss, to glaze, to give a gloss to.

lustrine (lystrin), s.f. Linenette, lustrine (glossy cotton fabric).

lut (lyt), s.m. (chem.) Lute, luting.

lutation (lyta'sjɔ̃), s.f. Luting.

luter (lyte), v.a. [f. L *lutum*] To lute.

luth (lyt), s.m. [f. Arab. *al'ūd*] (mus.) Lute.

luthéranisme (lyteranism), s.m. Lutheranism.

lutherie (lytri), s.f. Musical-instrument making or trade or (rare) shop.

luthérien, -ne (lyterjɛ̃), adj. s.m.f. Lutheran.

luthier (lytje), s.m. Musical-instrument maker or seller.

lutin (lytɛ̃), s.m. [f. OF *netun*, f. *Neptune*] Elf, goblin, sprite, leprechaun; naughty child, pickle.

lutin, -e (lytɛ̃), adj. (obs.) Sprightly.

lutiner (lytine), v.a. To tease, to caress, to excite.

lutrin (lytrɛ̃), s.m. [f. LL *lectrum*] Lectern.

lutte (lyt), s.f. [f. *lutter*] Wrestling; struggle, contest, strife; *de haute ~*, by main force; with a high hand.

lutter (lyte), v.n. [L *luctari*] To wrestle; to grapple (*avec*, with), to struggle, to strive, to vie.
lutteu-r, -se (lytœr), s.m.f. Wrestler; (fig.) adversary, champion.
lux (lyks), s.m. Lux, unit of light.
luxation (lyksa'sjɔ̃), s.f. Luxation, dislocation.
luxe (lyks), s.m. [L *luxus*] Luxury, sumptuousness, splendour, superabundance; *de* ~, sumptuous; 'de luxe', costly, choice, magnificently got up; *édition de* ~, library edition; *train de* ~, Pullman-car express; *objets de* ~, luxury articles; fancy goods, luxuries.
luxer (lykse), v.a. [L *luxare*] To luxate, to dislocate; *se* ~ *le bras*, to luxate or dislocate one's arm.
luxueusement (lyksɥøzmɑ̃), adv. Luxuriously, sumptuously, magnificently, richly.
luxueu-x, -se (lyksɥø), adj. Luxurious, sumptuous, magnificent, costly, rich.
luxure (lyksyr), s.f. [L *luxuria*] Lust, lewdness.
luxuriance (lyksyrjɑ̃s), s.f. Luxuriance, exuberance.
luxuriant, -e (lyksyrjɑ̃), adj. Luxuriant, exuberant, abundant.
luxurieusement (lyksyrjøzmɑ̃), adv. Lustfully, lewdly. ⚠ Not 'luxuriously', which = *luxueusement*.
luxurieu-x, -se (lyksyrjø), adj. Lustful, lewd. ⚠ Not 'luxurious', which = *luxueux*.
luzerne (lyzɛrn), s.f. [Provenç. *luzerno*] (bot.) Lucern(e).
luzernière (lyzɛrnjɛr), s.f. Lucern-field.
luzule (lyzyl), s.f. (bot.) Wood rush, *Luzula*.
lycanthrope (likɑ̃trɔp), s.m. Lycanthrope; see syn. LOUP-GAROU.
lycanthropie (likɑ̃trɔpi), s.f. [Gr. *lukanthrōpia*] Lycanthropy, transformation of person into a wolf.
lycée (lise), s.m. [Gr. *lukeion*] State secondary school in France.
lycéen, -ne (liseɛ̃), s.m.f. Pupil attending a *lycée*; collegian; schoolboy, (fem.) schoolgirl; syn. COLLÉGIEN,-NE.
lychnide, s.f., **lychnis**, s.m. (liknid, liknis) [Gr. *lukhnis*] (bot.) Lychnis, campion, ragged robin.
lycopode (likɔpɔd), s.m. [f. Gr. *lukos*+ *pous, podos*] (bot.) Lycopod, lycopodium.
lyddite (lidit), s.f. [f. *Lydd*, in Kent] (chem.) Lyddite.
lydien, -ne (lidjɛ̃), adj. Lydian; of Lydia. ~ s.m.f. Lydian.
lymphatique (lɛ̃fatik), adj. Lymphatic.
lymphatisme (lɛ̃fatism), s.m. Lymphatism.
lymphe (lɛ̃f), s.f. [L *lympha*] Lymph; (bot.) sap.
lynchage (lɛ̃ʃaʒ), s.m. Lynching.
lyncodon (lɛ̃kɔdɔ̃), s.m. (zool.) Lyncean.
lyncher (lɛ̃ʃe), v.a. [f. U.S.A. *lynch*] To lynch.
lynx (lɛ̃ks), s.m. [Gr. *lugx*] (zool.) Lynx; (fig.) *il a des yeux de* ~, or *un œil de* ~, he is lynx-eyed, or sharp-sighted.
lyonnais, -e (ljɔnɛ, ljɔnɛz), adj. Of Lyons, s.m.f. Native of Lyons.
lyre (lir), s.f. [L *lyra*] Lyre; (fig.) poetic talent, poetry; (astr.) Lyra; (colloq.) *toute la* ~ *alors!*, and the whole show; the whole caboodle; the whole bag of tricks; the whole boiling; *oiseau-*~, lyre-bird.
lyrique (lirik), adj. Lyric, lyrical; (fig.) enthusiastic, poetic, lofty, high-flown.
lyrisme (lirism), s.m. Lyricism; (fig.) high-flown sentiments or expressions.
lysimachie, lysimaque (lizimaki, lizimak), s.f. [Gr. *lusimakhion*] (bot.) Loosestrife, lysimachia.

M

M, m (ɛm), s.m. Thirteenth letter of the alphabet; M = one thousand; M., abbrev. of *Monsieur*.
ma (ma), poss. adj. f. My, my own (*mon* is used instead of *ma* before a vowel or mute *h*; ex.: *mon amie*, my friend, *ma chère amie*, my dear friend).
maboul, -e (mabul), adj. [Arab. *makhboul*] (slang) Loony, cracked, having a screw loose, a little wrong in the upper story, daft, off one's nut.
macabre (makabr), adj. [probably f. OF *Macabé*] Macabre; grim, gruesome, dismal, lugubrious, deathly, ghastly; *la danse* ~, the dance of death.
macadam (makadam), s.m. [f. prop. n. *John McAdam* (1756–1836)] Macadam, macadam road, macadamized road.
macadamisage (makadamizaʒ), s.m. Macadamization.
macadamiser (makadamize), v.a. To macadamize.
macaque (makak), s.m. [Port. *macaco*] (zool.) Macaco; (fig.) hideous man.
macareux (makarø), s.m. (ornith.) Puffin, coulterneb, Labrador auk.
macaron (makarɔ̃), s.m. [It. *maccarone*] Macaroon.
macaronée (makarɔne), s.f. (poet.) Macaronic verse.
macaroni (makarɔni), s.m. [It. *maccaroni*] Macaroni; (colloq. pej.) Italian, dago.
macaronique (makarɔnik), adj. Macaronic.
macchabée, machabée, macchab (makabe, makab), s.m. [f. prop. n. in Hebr. hist.] (slang) Dead body, corpse.
macédoine (masedwan), s.f. (cook.) Macédoine, dish of mixed vegetables or fruit; (fig.) medley, miscellany, hotch-potch, olio.

macédonien, -ne (masedɔnjɛ̃), adj. s.m.f. Macedonian.

macératé, macéré (maserate, masere), s.m. Liquid product of maceration.

macérat-eur -rice (maseratœr), adj. Macerating. ~, s.m. Macerator.

macération (masera'sjɔ̃), s.f. Maceration; (fig.) mortification.

macérer (masere), v.a. [L. *macerare*] To macerate; **se ~**, v.pr. to be macerated; (fig.) to macerate one's body, to mortify oneself; *les ermites se macéraient pour l'amour de Dieu*, the hermits mortified the flesh for the love of God.

maceron (masrɔ̃), s.m. [It. *macerone*] (bot.) Alexanders, horse-parsley.

macfarlane (makfarlan), s.m. [f. Scottish prop. n.] Inverness cape.

machaon (makaɔ̃), s.m. (ent.) Machaon, swallow-tailed butterfly.

mâche (mɑʃ), s.f. (bot.) Corn-salad, lamb's-lettuce.

mâche-bouchon, mâche-bouchons (mɑʃbuʃɔ̃), s.m. Cork-presser, cork-squeezer.

mâchefer (mɑʃfɛr), s.m. [*mâche*+*fer*] Slag, dross (of iron), clinkers, cinders, hammerslag; (fig.) braggart, boaster.

mâcheli-er, -ère (mɑʃəlje), adj. [L *maxillaris*] Of the jaw, grinding, molar; *dents ~ères*, grinders. **~ère**, s.f. Molar, grinder.

mâchement (mɑʃmɑ̃), s.m. [f. *mâcher*] Chewing, munching, mastication.

mâcher (mɑʃe), v.a. [L. *masticare*] **1.** To chew, to masticate, to munch; to bite, to bite at, to tear; to grind, to mince, to reduce to a pulp; (obs.) to eat gluttonously; to champ (the bit); to mumble (one's words); **2.** (fig.) to cut out, to prepare; to explain; **3.** (fig.) to mince (matters); *ne pas ~ ses mots*, not to mince matters; *~ à vide*, to move one's jaws up and down, to chew the air; (fig.) to live on hope, to delude oneself with false expectations; *on lui avait mâché toute sa besogne*, the work was all cut and dried for him; *ne pas ~ ce qu'on pense*, not to mince matters, to speak one's mind.

mâcheu-r, -se (mɑʃœr), s.m.f. (obs.) Chewer, muncher; great eater.

machiavélique (makjavelik), adj. [f. prop. n. *Machiavelli*] Machiavellian; cunning; crafty in politics.

machiavélisme (makjavelism), s.m. Machiavellianism; cunning, artifice, double-dealing.

machiavéliste (makjavelist), s.m. (rare) Machiavel, Machiavellian.

mâchicatoire (mɑʃikatwar), s.m. adj. See MASTICATOIRE.

mâchicoulis (mɑʃikuli), s.m. [LL *machicolare*] (fort.) Machicolations (pl.).

mâchiller (mɑʃije), v.a. To chew, to munch slowly.

machin, -e (maʃɛ̃), s.m.f. [f. *machine*] (colloq.) What's-his-name, thingumbob, so-and-so, thingummy, thing; *c'est ~ qui l'a dit*, what's-his-name said so.

machinal, -e, (aux) (maʃinal), adj. Mechanical, automatic, instinctive.

machinalement (maʃinalmɑ̃), adv. Mechanically, automatically, instinctively.

machinateur (maʃinatœr), s.m. Machinator, plotter, contriver.

machination (maʃina'sjɔ̃), s.f. Machination, plot, scheme, intrigue.

machine (maʃin), s.f. [L. *machina*, f. Gr. *mēkhanē*] Machine, engine, implement, piece of machinery, piece of mechanism; machinery, mechanism, apparatus, appliance, contrivance, system; frame (of the body); machination, intrigue, plot, scheme; *~ à battre*, thrashing-machine; *~ à coudre*, sewing-machine; *~ à écrire*, typewriter; *~ à vapeur*, steam-engine; *~ de guerre*, engine of war; *~-outil*, tool, machine-tool; *~ pneumatique*, air-pump; *~ de vingt chevaux*, twenty h.p. engine; *~ infernale*, infernal machine; *la ~ ne fonctionne plus*, the engine is out of order; *faire ~ en arrière*, to reverse the engine; *c'est une simple ~*, he is a mere machine; *la ~ animale*, the animal system; *la ~ ronde*, the earth, the globe; *chambre des ~s*, engine-room; *~s agricoles*, agricultural implements.

machiner (maʃine), v.a. [L *machinari*] To machinate, to plot, to plan, to contrive; (theatr.) to arrange (scenery); *il machine votre perte*, he is plotting your ruin; *~ une féerie*, to arrange a transformation scene.

machinerie (maʃinri), s.f. Machinery; machine-factory; -machine or engine-room; contrivance; plant. ⚠ *Machinerie* must not be confused with 'machinery' in its wider and figurative sense = *système*, *régime*, *dispositif*, *procédure*, *mécanisme*, and in literary work *le merveilleux*.

machiniser (maʃinize), v.a. (rare) To mechanize, to make mechanical.

machinisme (maʃinism), s.m. Mechanism, machinery.

machiniste (maʃinist), s.m.f. Machinist; driver, bus-driver, engine-driver; engineer; (theatr.) stage-carpenter, scene-shifter; *faire signe au ~*, to signal to the driver.

mâchoire (mɑʃwar), s.f. [f. *mâcher*] Jaw, jawbone; chap, chop (of animals); (fig.) blockhead, fathead, dolt; *~ supérieure*, upper jaw; *~ inférieure*, lower jaw; *jouer des ~s*, to eat, to munch; *c'est une véritable ~*, he is a regular blockhead; *les ~s d'un étau*, the jaws of a vice; *~ de frein*, brake-cheek or -block.

mâchonnement (maʃɔnmɑ̃), s.m. Chewing, munching; mumbling.
mâchonner (maʃɔne), v.a. To chew with difficulty, to munch; to mumble; *que mâchonnez-vous entre vos dents?*, what are you mumbling between your teeth?
mâchure (maʃyr), s.f. Defect, flaw (in material); bruise (in fruit).
mâchurer (maʃyre), v.a. To daub, to smear, to smudge, to blot, to blacken; (print.) to blacken, to spoil (a sheet).
macis (masi), s.m. [orig. dub.] Mace (of nutmeg).
maclage (maklaʒ), s.m. Mixing of glass (in furnace).
macle (makl), s.f. [L *macula*] **1.** (chem.) **1.** Macle, twin crystal; **2.** (herald.) mascle; **3.** (fish.) large net; **4.** (min.) macula.
maclé, -e (makle), p. adj. (min.) Maculated, marked with maculae.
macler (makle), v.a. (glass-making) To mix or stir (melted glass).
mâcon (makɔ̃), s.m. [f. *Mâcon* in France] Red wine from Mâcon.
maçon (masɔ̃), s.m. [LL *macio*] Mason, bricklayer, builder; freemason; (fig.) bungler; *maître* ~, master mason; *franc-*~, freemason; ~, **-ne,** adj. (zool.) mason (of animals).
maçonnage (masɔnaʒ), s.m. Mason's work, stonework, masonry.
maçonner (masɔne), v.a. To build; to wall up, to brick, to plaster up, to stop up; to block up; (fig.) to bungle, to botch.
maçonnerie (masɔnri), s.f. Masonry; stonework, brickwork; *franc-*~, s.f. freemasonry.
maçonnique (masɔnik), adj. Masonic.
macouba (makuba), s.m. [f. *Macouba*, Martinique] Macouba tobacco.
macque (mak), s.f. (techn.) Tewing-beetle, brake (for beating hemp).
macquer (make), v.a. To tew, to beat, to brake (hemp).
macramé (makrame), s.m. [f. Turk. *maqrama*] Macramé.
macre (makr), s.f. (bot.) Water-caltrop, water-chestnut.
macreuse (makrøz), s.f. **1.** (ornith.) Scoter, surf-duck, widgeon; black diver; **2.** (butch.) part of shoulder of beef.
macro-, macr- (makrɔ), pref. [Gr. *makros*] Long, large.
macrobe, macrobien, -ne (makrɔb, makrɔbjɛ̃), adj. [Gr. *makros*+*bios*] Macrobiotic.
macrocéphale (makrɔsefal), adj. [Gr. *makros*+*kephalē*] Macrocephalic.
macrocéphalie (makrɔsefali), s.f. Macrocephaly.
macrocosme (makrɔkɔsm), s.m. [Gr. *makros*+*kosmos*] Macrocosm.
macrodactyle (makrɔdaktil), adj. [Gr. *makros*+*daktulos*] Macrodactylic.
macropode[1] (makrɔpɔd), adj. s.m. [Gr. *makros*+*pous, podos*] (zool.) Macropod; (bot.) macropodous, macropodal.
macropode[2] (makrɔpɔd), s.m. (ichth.) Macropod.
macropodes, macropodiens, macropodites (makrɔpɔd, makrɔpɔdjɛ̃, makrɔpɔdit), s.m.pl. (zool.) Macropodians.
macroscélide (makrɔselid), s.m. (zool.) Macroscelid.
macroscopique (makrɔskɔpik), adj. [Gr. *makros*+*skopein*] Macroscopic.
macrosporange (makrɔspɔrɑ̃ʒ), s.m. (bot.) Macrosporangium.
macrospore (makrɔspɔr), s.f. [Gr. *makros*+*spora*] (bot.) Macrospore.
macroure (makrur), adj. [Gr. *makros*+*oura*] (zool.) Macrurous; (bot.) spiked. **~s,** s.m.pl. (zool.) Macrura.
maculage (makylaʒ), s.m. **maculation,** (makyla'sjɔ̃), s.f. [L *maculatio*] Maculation, spotting, staining, blotting.
maculature (makylatyr), s.f. [f. L *maculare*] (print.) Maculature, waste proof-sheet; coarse brown paper.
macule (makyl), s.f. [L *macula*] Stain, spot, blemish, blur; (print.) blur, mackle; (astr.) macula, sun-spot; *un agneau sans* ~, a lamb without blemish.
maculer (makyle), v.a. [L *maculare*] To maculate; to blot, to spot, to stain; ~, v.n. to become maculated, spotted, stained.
maculiforme (makylifɔrm), adj. [L *macula*+*forma*] Maculiform.
madame (madam), s.f. (pl. *mesdames*) [*ma*+*dame*] Madam, ma'am; wife; Mrs., mistress; lady; my lady; your or her ladyship; ~ *la duchesse*, the duchess; your or her grace; ~ *votre mère*, your mother; ~ *est servie*, lunch, dinner, is ready, or served, madam; ~ *vaut bien monsieur*, she is as good as he is, the wife is as good as the husband, it is six of one and half a dozen of the other; *faire la* ~, to give oneself airs; *jouer à la* ~, to play at lords and ladies.
madapolam (madapɔlam), s.m. [f. *Madapollam*, Madras] Madapollam.
madécasse (madekas), adj. [f. *Madagascar*] Of Madagascar. ~, s.m.f. Madagass, Madecass.
madéfaction (madefaksjɔ̃), s.f. [f. *madéfier*] Madefaction, wetting, humectation.
madéfier (madefje), v.a. [L *madefacere*] (chem.) To madefy (obs.), to wet, to moisten, to humect.
madeleine (madlɛn), s.f. **1.** Cake, sponge-cake; **2.** early pear, plum, peach; **3.** Magdalen, repentant prostitute.
madelonnette (madlɔnɛt), s.f. **1.** Small madeleine (cake); **2.** repentant prostitute; *les* ~*s*, female penitentiary asylum (in Paris).

mademoiselle (madmwazɛl), s.f. (pl. *mesdemoiselles*) [*ma*+*demoiselle*] Miss (only used without name by servants, etc.); this, or the, young lady; ~ *désire-t-elle attendre?*, would you like to wait, Miss?; ~ *votre sœur*, your sister.
madère (madɛr), s.f. Madeira (the island); ~, s.m. Madeira (wine).
madi (madi), s.m. **madie** s.f. [Chil. *madi*] (bot.) Madia.
madone (madɔn), s.f. [It. *madonna*] Madonna.
madrague (madrag), s.f. [Arab. orig.] (fish.) Crawl, tunny-net, kettle-net.
madras (madrɑ), s.m. [geog. orig.] Madras; bandanna, bandanna handkerchief.
madre (madr), s.m. [OHG *masar*] Mottled or speckled wood.
madré, -e (madre), adj. [f. *madre*] **1.** Cunning, crafty, sly, deep, sharp; *un renard* ~, a sly fox; syn. RUSÉ; **2.** (techn.) speckled, spotted, mottled.
madréporaires (madrepɔrɛr), s.m.pl. (zool.) Madreporaria.
madrépore (madrepɔr), s.m. [It. *madrepora*] (zool.) Madrepore.
madréporique, madréporien, -ne (madrepɔrik, madrepɔrjɛ), adj. (zool.) Madreporic.
madrier (madrije), s.m. [f. L *materin*] Thick plank, joist.
madrigal (pl. **aux**) (madrigal), s.m. [It. *madrigale*] Madrigal.
madrilène (madrilɛn), adj. [f. *Madrid*] s.m.f. (Native) of Madrid.
madrure (madryr), s.f. [f. *madré*] Speck, spot, speckling, spotting, mottling.
maërl (maɛrl), s.m. Sea-sand.
maestoso (maɛstozo), adv. [It. wd] (mus.) Maestoso, majestically.
maestria (maɛstrija), s.f. [It. wd] Mastery; dash; *exécuté avec* ~, dashingly done; brilliantly interpreted, or executed.
maestro (maɛstro), s.m. [It. wd] (mus.) Maestro.
mafflu, -e (mafly), adj. (fam.) Chubby, chubby-faced, chubby-cheeked.
magasin (magazɛ̃), s.m. [Arab. *makhāzin*] Shop, store; emporium, warehouse, storehouse, storeroom; stock; magazine; basket (of coach); *marchandises en* ~, goods in stock; *avoir des marchandises en* ~, to have stock in hand; *mettre en* ~, to warehouse, to store; *courir les* ~*s*, to go shopping; ~ *de nouveautés*, linen-draper's; fancy-goods shop; ~ *de poudre*, powder-magazine; *inspecteur de* ~, shop-walker; *garçon de* ~, shop-boy; *demoiselle de* ~, shop-girl; *tenir un* ~, to keep a shop.
magasinage (magazinaʒ), s.m. Warehousing; storage; warehouse-rent; *droits de* ~, warehouse-rent.
magasinier (magazinje), s.m. Warehouse-man, warehouse-keeper; store-keeper.
magazine (magazin), s.m. [Engl. wd] Magazine.
magdalénien, -ne (magdalenjɛ̃), adj. [f. *La Madeleine*, Dordogne] (archaeol.) Magdalenian.
magdaléon (magdaleɔ̃), s.m. [Gr. *magdalia*] (pharm.) Magdaleon.
mage (maʒ), s.m. [L *magus*] Magian, mage, magus, magician; *les rois* ~*s*, the Magi, the three wise men of the East.
mage, maje (maʒ), adj. m. [L *major*] (obs.) Chief; *juge* ~, chief justice.
magenta (maʒɛ̃ta), adj. s.m. [f. *Magenta*, Italy] Magenta (colour).
maghzen (magzen), s.m. [Arab. wd] Moorish government, court.
magicien, -ne (maʒisjɛ̃), s.m.f. Magician, enchanter, necromancer, sorcerer, (fem.) sorceress, witch.
magie (maʒi), s.f. [Gr. *mageia*] Magic; (fig.) magic, charm, enchantment; ~ *blanche, naturelle*, white or natural magic; ~ *noire*, black art, black magic, witchcraft; *la* ~ *des nuits en pleine mer*, the charm of nights at sea.
magique (maʒik), adj. Magic, magical; (fig.) enchanting, wonderful, surprising; *baguette* ~, magic wand, conjuring wand; *lanterne* ~, magic lantern.
magiquement (maʒikmɑ̃), adv. Magically.
magisme (maʒism), s.m. Magianism.
magister (maʒistɛr), s.m. [L wd] Village schoolmaster, dominie; (fig.) pedant.
magistère (maʒistɛr), s.m. [L *magisterium*] Grand-mastership of the Order of Malta; (pharm.) magistery.
magistral, -e, (aux) (maʒistral), adj. [L *magistralis*] Magistral, of masters, of a master; authoritative, dictatorial; principal, sovereign; clever, brilliant, masterly; *œuvre* ~*e*, masterly work; *ligne* ~*e*, principal outline; *médicament* ~, magistral remedy; *remède* ~, sovereign remedy; *parler d'un ton* ~, to speak in an authoritative tone.
magistrale (maʒistral), s.f. (fort.) Magistral, top line of fortifications.
magistralement (maʒistralmɑ̃), adv. With masterliness, wonderfully, brilliantly; completely.
magistrat (maʒistra), s.m. [L *magistratus*] Magistrate, judge, justice; civic officer, town councillor.
magistrature (maʒistratyr), s.f. Magistracy, magistrature, bench; ~ *assise*, judges, the bench; ~ *debout*, body of public prosecutors; *entrer dans la* ~, to become a magistrate.
magma (magma), s.m. [Gr. wd] Magma.
magnan (maɲɑ̃), s.m. [Provenç. wd] Silkworm (from S. of France).

magnanarelle (maɲanarɛl), s.f. [f. *magnan*] Silk-worm breeder, woman who tends silk-worms.
magnanerie (maɲanri), s.f. [f. *magnan*] Silk-worm nursery.
magnani-er, -ère (maɲanje), s.m.f. Silkworm breeder or rearer.
magnanime (maɲanim), adj. [L *magnanimus*] Magnanimous, generous, high-souled.
magnanimement (maɲanimmɑ̃), adv. Magnanimously.
magnanimité (maɲanimite), s.f. Magnanimity.
magnat (magna), s.m. [f. L *magnus*] Magnate.
(se) magner (səmaɲe), v.pr. (slang) To hurry; to bestir oneself; *allons, magne-toi!*, stir your stumps!
magnes (maɲ), s.f.pl. (slang) Fuss, high-faluting airs; *assez de ~!*, none of your airs! come off it!
magnésie (maɲezi), s.f. [Gr. *magnēsia*] (chem.) Magnesia; *sulfate de ~*, Epsom salts.
magnésien, -ne (maɲezjɛ̃), adj. (chem.) Magnesian.
magnésique (maɲezik), adj. (chem.) Magnesic.
magnésite (maɲezit), s.f. (min.) Magnesite.
magnésium (maɲeziɔm), s.m. (chem.) Magnesium.
magnétique (maɲetik), adj. [Gr. *magnēs*] Magnetic; mesmeric; (fig.) attractive, compelling, magnetic; *barreau ~*, artificial magnet; *faisceau ~*, magnetic battery; *il y a quelque chose de ~ dans son regard*, there is something magnetic in his look.
magnétiquement (maɲetikmɑ̃), adv. Magnetically.
magnétisable (maɲetizabl), adj. Magnetizable.
magnétisation (maɲetiza'sjɔ̃), s.f. Magnetization, mesmerization.
magnétiser (maɲetize), v.a. To magnetize; (obs.) to mesmerize, to hypnotize.
magnétiseur (maɲetizœr), s.m. Magnetist; magnetizer, mesmerizer, mesmerist, hypnotizer.
magnétisme (maɲetism), s.m. (phys.) Magnetism; mesmerism, hypnotism; (fig.) magnetism, attraction; *~ terrestre*, terrestrial magnetism; *~ animal*, animal magnetism, mesmerism.
magnétite (maɲetit), s.f. (min.) Magnetite.
magnéto (maɲeto), s.f. (mach.) Magneto; *~ à induit tournant*, magneto with rotating armature.
magnéto-électrique (maɲetoelɛktrik), adj. (phys.) Magneto-electric, electromagnetic.
magnétomètre (maɲetɔmɛtr), s.m. [*magnéto*+*mètre*] (phys.) Magnetometer.
magnificat (magnifikat), s.m. [L wd] Magnificat.
magnificence (maɲifisɑ̃s), s.f. [L *magnificentia*] Magnificence, splendour, luxury, lavishness, grandeur, pomp, stateliness; generosity; magnificent things.
magnifier (maɲifje), v.a. [L *magnificare*] To magnify; to praise, to extol, to exalt, to laud, to glorify, to exaggerate, to aggrandize.
magnifique (maɲifik), adj. [L *magnificus*] Magnificent, splendid, grand, stately, sumptuous; munificent, generous, liberal; pompous, lavish, ostentatious, vain; lofty, sublime, noble; brilliant, fine; *un temps ~*, glorious weather.
magnifiquement (maɲifikmɑ̃), adv. Magnificently.
magnitude (magnityd), s.f. [L *magnitudo*] Magnitude; size.
magnolia, magnolier (magnolja, magnolje), s.m. [f. Pierre *Magnol*, botanist, 1638–1715] (bot.) Magnolia; *~ glauque*, white bay; *~ bleu*, beaver-wood; *~ des marais*, swamp sassafras; *~ à grandes fleurs*, big laurel; *~ parasol*, umbrella-tree; *~ de la Chine*, yulan, Chinese magnolia.
magnoliacées (magnoljase), s.f.pl. (bot.) Magnoliaceae.
magot[1] (mago), s.m. [f. *Magog*] **1.** (zool.) Magot, Barbary ape, baboon; **2.** grotesque figure (of china); ugly man, ill-favoured person; fright; *c'est un véritable ~*, he is a regular fright. ⚠ *Magot* has never the sense of English 'maggot', which = *ver blanc* and (fig.) *lubie, caprice.*
magot[2] (mago), s.m. [OF *mugot*] (fam.) Hoard (of money), hidden treasure; (slang) *avoir le ~*, to be well off; to have the dibs; *croquer son ~*, to squander one's money.
mahaleb (maalɛb), s.m. [Arab. *maḥlab*] (bot.) Mahaleb, black-cherry tree.
maharajah (maaraʒa), s.m. [Hindi wd] Maharajah.
mahdi (mɑdi), s.m. [Arab. wd] Mahdi.
mahdisme (mɑdism), s.m. Mahdism.
mahdiste (mɑdist), s.m. Mahdist.
mahométan, -e (maɔmetɑ̃), adj. s.m.f. Mohammedan.
mahométisme (maɔmetism), s.m. Mohammedanism.
mahonie (maɔni), s.f. **mahonia** (maɔnja), s.m. [f. *Bernard McMahon*] (bot.) Mahonia.
mahonnais, -e (maɔnɛ), adj. s.m.f. From Mahon (Minorca), Mahonian, Minorcan.
mahonne (maɔn), s.f. [Turk. *māwuna*] (naut.) Mahone.

mahout (mau), s.m. [Hind. *mahaut*] Mahout, elephant-driver; syn. CORNAC.
mahratte (marat), adj. s.m.f. [Hind. *Marhaṭṭa*] Mahratta.
mai (mɛ), s.m. [L *maius*] May; may-pole; *le premier ~*, May-day; (Fr. hist.) *champ de ~*, assembly of the nation held in May; (bot.) *bois de ~*, hawthorn, may; *pomme de ~*, may-apple; *lis de ~*, May-lily, lily-of-the-valley; *planter le ~*, to set up the may-pole; *en avril ne te découvre pas d'un fil, en ~ je ne sais*, cast not a clout till May be out.
maie (mɛ), s.f. [L *magide*] Kneading-trough; bread-bin; trough.
maïeur (maiœr), s.m. (obs.) [L *major*] Mayor.
maigre (mɛgr), adj. [L *macer*] Lean, thin, spare, gaunt; skinny, scraggy, lanky; poor, sorry, scanty, meagre; barren; (arch.) slender; uninflammable, close-burning (coal); *devenir ~*, to grow thin; (fam.) *~ échine*, lanky-bones; *~ comme un chat de gouttière, un hareng, un clou*, as thin as a lath, as a herring, as a whipping-post; nothing but skin and bone; *une bourse ~*, a lean purse; *de la viande ~*, lean meat; *jour ~*, fast-day, day of abstinence; *faire ~*, to fast, to abstain from meat; *soupe ~*, vegetable soup; *repas ~*, fish meal, meal without meat; *faire ~ chère*, to fare badly; *~ chère*, poor fare, poor living; *un ~ repas*, a poor meal; *un sol ~*, a barren soil; *une ~ réception*, a cold reception; *colonne ~*, slender column. ~, s.m. Lean; fish and vegetable food; light diet; *donnez-moi du ~*, give me some lean.
maigre (mɛgr), s.m. (ichth.) Maigre.
maigrelet, -te (mɛgrəlɛ), adj. Thin, thinnish, lean, spare.
maigrement (mɛgrəmɑ̃), adv. Meagrely; poorly, sparely; sparingly, sorrily.
maigreur (mɛgrœr), s.f. Leanness, thinness, spareness; meagreness, poorness, scantiness, barrenness; (arch.) slenderness.
maigrichon, -ne (mɛgriʃɔ̃), adj. (fam.) Thin, thinnish, a bit thin. ~, s.m.f. Lean person.
maigrir (mɛgrir), v.n. To grow lean, to get thin, to waste away; *il maigrit à vue d'œil*, he is visibly wasting away; ~, v.a. to make look thin.
mail (maj), s.m. [L *malleus*] **1.** (obs.) Mallet, mall, pall-mall (implement, game); **2.** promenade, mall, sheltered walk.
mail-coach (mɛlkotʃ), s.m. [Engl. wd] Mail-coach.
maille[1] (mɑj), s.f. [L *macula*] Stitch; knot; mesh; ring, link (of mail); speck, speckle, spot (on bird's wings); web (in the eye); *~ tombée*, dropped stitch; *cotte de ~s*, coat of mail; *~ à ~ se fait le haubergeon*, every little helps.
maille[2] (mɑj), s.f. [L *metallia*] Maille (old copper coin); (fig.) doit, stiver, farthing; rush, straw; *cela ne vaut pas la ~*, that is not worth a straw; *n'avoir ni sou ni ~*, to be without a farthing in the world; to be as poor as a church mouse; *à sou ~ et denier*, to a farthing; *avoir ~ à partir avec X*, to have a crow to pluck, a bone to pick with X; *bonne est la ~ qui sauve le denier*, take care of the pence and the pounds will take care of themselves.
maillé, -e (mɑje), p. adj. Stitched; mailed; reticulated; speckled; *fer ~*, wire netting.
mailler (mɑje), v.a. [f. *maille*] To make network, to reticulate; to lace (a studding sail); to mail, to arm with mail; ~, v.n. to bud (of vines); to grow speckled (of partridges).
maillet (majɛ), s.m. [f. *mail*] Mallet; beetle; (pop.) hammer-head (shark).
mailletage (majtaʒ), s.m. (naut.) Sheathing (ship's bottom) with scupper-nails.
mailleter (majte), v.a. (naut.) To sheathe with scupper nails.
mailleton (majtɔ̃), s.m. First-year bud.
mailloche (majɔʃ), s.f. [f. *mail*] Big mallet; beetle; mall, maul; mace; drum-stick (for big drum).
maillon (majɔ̃), s.m. Shackle, ring, link (of chain); stitch; noose, slip, running knot.
maillonner (majɔne), v.a. To link.
maillot (majo), s.m. Swaddling band, swaddling clothes, long clothes; (fig.) infancy; under-vest, jersey; tights (of a dancer); *~ de bain*, bathing-costume; *enfant au ~*, infant, child in arms.
maillotin (majɔtɛ̃), s.m. [f. *maillet*] Olive-press; mallet; *les ~s*, rebel inhabitants of Paris under Charles VI.
maillure (mɑjyr), s.f. Spot (in wood); speck, speckle (on a hawk, &c.).
main (mɛ̃), s.f. [L *manus*] Hand, fist; handwriting; lead, trick, deal (at cards); hook, ring (at end of well-rope), holder, handle, grapple; hand-shovel, scoop; quire (of paper); authority, power, help; (bot.) cirrus, tendril; *à deux ~s, des deux ~s*, with both hands, for two hands, two-handed; (mus.) *à quatre ~s*, duet for piano; *à la main*, in his or her hand, or their hands; by hand; to hand, handy; *à la portée de la ~*, within reach; *à ~ armée*, by main force; *à pleines ~s, à belles ~s*, by handfuls, largely, liberally, plentifully; *à toutes ~s*, fit for anything, of all trades, of all work; *avoir une belle ~*, to write a good hand; *avoir la ~*, to have the lead, to deal, to play first (at cards); *avoir les ~s liées*, to have one's hands tied, to be unable to do anything; *avoir la main légère*, to be skilful, to be light-handed; *il n'y va pas de ~ morte*, he does not do

things by halves; *de toute ~*, from any one, anyhow; *battre des ~s*, to clap, to applaud; *cheval de ~*, led horse; *coup de ~*, (*a*) help; (*b*) unexpected attack; *donner un coup de ~ à*, to help, to assist; *de la ~ à la bouche se perd souvent la soupe*, there is many a slip 'twixt the cup and the lip; *demander la ~ de*, to ask the hand of (in marriage); *de la ~ à la ~*, direct from one person to another; *de longue ~*, of long standing, long since; *de ~ en ~*, from hand to hand; *donner la ~ à quelqu'un*, to give a hand to some one; *donner les ~s à une chose*, to consent to something; *lever la ~*, to take one's oath, to swear; *lever la ~ sur X*, to raise one's hand against X; *en ~*, in hand, at one's disposal; *en ~s propres*, into one's own hands, personally; *en un tour de ~*, in a twinkling; *en venir aux ~s*, to come to blows, to close (with), to come to close quarters; *faire ~ basse sur*, to lay violent hands on; to plunder; to seize upon; *frapper dans la ~*, to strike a bargain; *fait à la ~*, hand-made; made by hand; *l'argent lui fond dans la ~*, money slips through his fingers; *froides ~s, chaudes amours*, cold hands, a warm heart; *avoir la ~ heureuse, bonne*, to be lucky; *il en a les ~s nettes*, his hands are clean of it; *être en bonnes ~s*, to be in good hands; *être sous la ~ de*, to be under the thumb of, in the power of; *forcer la main de*, to compel, to force the hand of; *haut la ~*, with a high hand, with authority; easily, dashingly; *mener un cheval haut la ~*, to hold a tight rein; *avoir la haute ~ sur*, to command; *haut les ~s*, hands up; (fig.) *se laver les ~s de*, to wash one's hands of; *lâcher la ~*, to give head, to give rope; to lower one's pretensions; *j'en mettrais ma ~ au feu*, I would stake my life on it; (game) *~ chaude*, hot cockles; *~ de papier*, a quire of paper; *mettre la dernière ~ à quelque chose*, to put the finishing touch to something; (fig.) *mettre la ~ à la pâte*, to put one's shoulder to the wheel; *mettre la ~ à quelque chose*, to set one's hand to something; *mettre la ~ sur*, to lay hands on; *perdre la ~*, to lose one's skill through want of practice; *savoir de bonne ~*, to know on good authority, from a good source; *se donner la ~*, to shake hands, to go hand in hand, to join hands; *se faire la ~*, to get one's hand in; to try one's hand; *s'entretenir la ~*, to keep one's hand in; *se perdre la ~*, to get rusty; *sous la ~*, at hand, on the spot; *sous ~*, underhand, secretly, clandestinely; *tendre la ~*, to hold out one's hand; to lend a helping hand; to make an offer of conciliation; to beg; *tenir la ~ à*, to see to, to attend to, to see that; *les ~s m'en tombent*, I am astounded; *tour de ~*, sleight of hand; *~ courante*, (*a*) (arch.) hand-rail; (*b*) (comm.) day-book; *allons, la ~ et que ce soit fini!*, now shake hands, and not a word more about it!; (colloq.) *passer la ~ dans le dos à X*, to soft-soap X, to butter X up; *prendre X la ~ dans le sac*, to catch X red-handed.

main-d'œuvre (mɛ̃dœvr), s.f. (pl. *mains-d'œuvre*) [*main+œuvre*] Work, workmanship; the workers; manual labour; payment for work done.

main-forte (mɛ̃fɔrt), s.f. invar. [*main+forte*] Help, assistance; *prêter ~*, to lend assistance.

mainlevée (mɛ̃lve), s.f. [*main+levée*] (law) Withdrawal, replevin.

mainmise (mɛ̃miz), s.f. [*main+mise*] (law) Seizure.

mainmortable (mɛ̃mɔrtabl), adj. [f. *mainmorte*] Subject to mortmain; inalienable.

mainmorte (mɛ̃mɔrt), s.f. [*main+morte*] (law) Mortmain.

maïnote (mainɔt), adj. s.m.f. (Native) of Maïna (S. Peloponnesus).

maint, -e (mɛ̃), adj. Many a, many; *~es fois*, many a time; *~ homme*, many a man.

maintenance (mɛ̃tnɑ̃s), s.f. (obs.) Maintenance. ⚠ Not used in the common English sense of 'that which is necessary to keep alive', as in 'board and maintenance', 'an order for maintenance', &c.

maintenant (mɛ̃tnɑ̃), adv. [*main+tenant*] Now, at present, at this time, nowadays; *de ~*, of this time; *dès ~*, henceforth, henceforward.

mainteneur (mɛ̃tnœr), s.m. [f. *maintenir*] (obs.) Maintainer, keeper; official at floral games at Toulouse.

maintenir (mɛ̃tnir), v.a. [*main+tenir*] To uphold, to sustain; to defend; to support; to keep together; to keep in order; to maintain, to keep up; to enforce; to preserve; *~ le bon ordre*, to keep order; **se ~**, v.pr. to keep up, to remain; to be kept up, to be sustained; to last, to subsist, to continue; to hold out, to stand one's ground, to maintain one's position; to remain in force; *se ~ en bonne santé*, to keep in good health; *les prix se maintiennent*, prices keep up. ⚠ *Maintenir* cannot be used like 'to maintain', in the sense of: *soutenir, subvenir aux besoins de, entretenir*.

maintenue (mɛ̃tny), s.f. (law) Confirmation of possession.

maintien (mɛ̃tjɛ̃), s.m. Maintenance, preservation, keeping up; carriage, deportment, bearing, attitude, demeanour, behaviour.

maire (mɛr), s.m. [L *major*] Mayor; *~ du palais*, Mayor of the Palace, chief officer of state under Merovingian kings; *adjoint du* ~, deputy mayor.

mairesse (mɛrɛs), s.f. Mayoress.

mairie (mɛri), s.f. **1.** Mayoralty; **2.** town hall.

mais (mɛ), conj. [L *magis*] But; why; ~ *encore*, but yet; ~ *non*, indeed not; no indeed; no, of course; ~ *oui*, ~ *si*, but of course, yes indeed; *eh!* ~, why!; *je n'en puis* ~, I cannot help it; I can do no more; *je ne veux pas de vos* ~, I'll have none of your buts.

maïs (mais), s.m. [Span. *maiz*] (bot.) Maize, Indian corn; (U.S.A.) corn; syn: BLÉ DE TURQUIE.

maison (mɛzɔ̃), s.f. [L *mansio*] House, residence; home; household, family; establishment, firm, agency; shop, warehouse, premises; ~ *d'arrêt, de force*, gaol, prison; ~ *de campagne*, rural villa, detached house; country house; small country residence; ~ *de chasse*, hunting-box, shooting-lodge; ~ *de commerce*, firm; ~ *de commission*, commission agency; ~ *garnie, meublée*, furnished house, furnished rooms; ~ *de jeu*, gambling-house; ~ *mortuaire*, residence of the deceased; ~ *religieuse*, convent; ~ *du roi*, the king's household, household troops; ~ *rustique*, cottage; ~ *de santé*, asylum, nursing home; *état, train de* ~, establishment; *à la* ~, at home; indoors; *par-dessus les* ~*s*, beyond all reason; *faire* ~ *nette*, to make a clean sweep, to turn out all one's servants; *faire* ~ *neuve*, to change all one's servants; *garder la* ~, to stay at home, to remain indoors, to mind the house; *tenir* ~, to keep house; *tenir la* ~, to manage the house; *Petites* ~*s*, lunatic asylum; *c'est un ami de la* ~, he is a friend of the family; *la* ~ *d'Autriche*, the house of Austria; *les* ~*s empêchent de voir la ville*, you cannot see the wood for the trees; *avoir* ~ *ouverte*, to keep open house; ~ *close*, or ~ *de tolérance*, licensed brothel; ~ *de correction*, reformatory; ~ *de garde*, (*a*) porter's lodge; (*b*) watchman's cottage; *il est de bonne* ~, he is of a good family, or stock.

maisonnée (mezɔne), s.f. Whole house, household, family.

maisonnette (mezɔnɛt), s.f. Small house, cottage, lodge, little cot.

maistrance (mɛstrɑ̃s), s.f. [f. *maistre*] (naut.) Body of petty officers.

maître (mɛtr), s.m. [L *magister*, f. *major*] Master; ruler, lord; owner, proprietor, landlord; instructor, teacher, tutor; governor, director; chief, head; (law) Mr. (as a title of barristers, notaries, &c.); (naut.) boatswain, second mate; *premier* ~, chief petty officer; *second* ~, or *quartier* ~, second-class petty officer; *être passé* ~ *en*, to have obtained the degree of master in; (colloq.) to be proficient, skilled, a past master in; *petit* ~, fop, dandy, spark, beau; ~ *d'armes*, fencing master; ~ *de ballet*, ballet-master; ~ *de chapelle*, precentor; ~ *d'école*, schoolmaster; (naut.) ~ *d'équipage*, boatswain; ~ *d'étude*, usher; ~ *de forges*, ironmaster; ~ *d'hôtel*, steward, butler, major-domo, head cook; ~ *Jacques*, Jack-of-all-trades, factotum; ~ *de maison*, master of the house; host; housemaster; *coup de* ~, a masterly or master-stroke; *de main de* ~, in a masterly fashion; *frapper en* ~, to knock hard; *trouver son* ~, to find one's match, or one's master; *se rendre* ~ *des esprits*, to win over men's minds, to persuade men; *se rendre* ~ *de l'émeute*, to quell the riot; *se rendre* ~ *du feu*, to get the fire under; *se rendre* ~ *de son sujet*, to master one's subject; *tel* ~, *tel valet*, like master, like man; ~ *des hautes œuvres*, executioner, hangman. ~, adj. Arrant, notorious; clever, superior; principal, main, grand, high; *un* ~ *sot*, an arrant fool; *un* ~ *fripon*, a thorough scamp; *un* ~ *homme*, a clever man; *le* ~*-autel*, the high altar.

maîtresse (mɛtrɛs), s.f. **1.** Mistress; ruler, lady; owner, proprietress, landlady; teacher, governess, head, principal; **2.** sweetheart, lady-love, mistress; *petite* ~, woman of affected elegance. ~, adj. Clever, superior; main; important; *une* ~ *femme*, a superior, efficient woman, who knows what she is about, or what's what; *la poutre* ~, the main beam.

maîtrisable (mɛtrizabl), adj. Governable, controllable, masterable.

maîtrise (mɛtriz), s.f. **1.** Mastership, authority; mastery, control; freedom (of a corporation); ~ *de soi-même*, self-control; **2.** choir-school; choir.

maîtriser (mɛtrize), v.a. [f. *maître*] To master, to govern, to rule, to control; to subdue, to overcome, to keep down, to get the better of; to lord it over; ~ *ses passions*, to control one's passions; **se** ~, v.pr. to control or curb oneself; to restrain oneself.

majesté (maʒɛste), s.f. [L *majestas*] Majesty, dignity, stateliness; *Sa* ~ *Très Chrétienne*, His most Christian Majesty, the king of France; *Sa* ~ *Catholique*, the king of Spain; *Leurs* ~*s*, Their Majesties; *crime de lèse-*~, high treason.

majestueusement (maʒɛstɥøzmɑ̃), adv. Majestically.

majestueu-x, -se (maʒɛstɥø), adj. Majestic, stately, magnificent.

majeur, -e (maʒœr), adj. [L *major*] Major, greater; superior, main, chief, most important; (law) of age; major; (mus.) major; (at cards) major; (naut.) main, principal; *la* ~*e partie*, the greater part; *force ~e*, superior force, absolute necessity; *une fille ~e*, a daughter of age; (mus.) *tierce ~e*, major third. ~ s.m. **1.** (law) Major, male of full age; **2.** the middle finger; **3.** (mus.) major; **4.** ~**e**, s.f. (logic) major premiss.

majolique, maïolique (maʒɔlik, maiɔlik), s.f. [It. *majolica*] Majolica, earthenware from Majorca.

major (maʒɔr), s.m. [L wd] (mil.) Major; army doctor, major, surgeon-major; *état-~*, staff, staff-officers, headquarters; *sergent-~*, sergeant-major; *tambour-~*, drum-major.

majorat (maʒɔra), s.m. (law) Majorat; right of primogeniture; entailed estate.

majoration (maʒɔra'sjɔ̃), s.f. Over-estimation; increase (in price); *~ temporaire de 40%*, temporary increase of 40%.

majordome (maʒɔrdɔm), s.m. [L *major*+ *domus*] Major-domo.

majorer (maʒɔre), v.a. To over-estimate, to over-value; to increase (price).

majoritaire (maʒɔritɛr), s.m. adj. (By) absolute majority.

majorité (maʒɔrite), s.f. [L *majoritas*] **1.** Majority; coming of age, full age; *atteindre sa ~*, to come of age; **2.** majority; *à la ~ de deux voix*, by a majority of two; *la ~ des hommes le pensent*; most people think so; *~ absolue*, absolute majority. ⚠ *La majorité* has not in French the sense of 'the dead' = *les morts*, whilst 'majority' is frequently used in that sense: 'to join the majority' = *mourir*.

majorquin, -e (maʒɔrkɛ̃), adj. s.m.f. (Native) of Majorca.

majuscule (maʒyskyl), adj. [L *majusculus*] Capital, large. ~, s.f. Capital letter.

maki (maki), s.m. [Malagasy *maka*] (zool.) Maki, lemur.

mal (pl. **maux**) (mal, mo), s.m. [L *malum*] Evil, ill, wrong, mischief, sin; ache, pain, harm, hurt, sore, soreness, sickness, ailment; hardship, misfortune, trouble, toil, difficulty, inconvenience, dislike, repugnance; *avoir ~ à*, to have a pain in; *j'ai ~ au doigt*, I have a sore finger; *j'ai ~ aux dents*, I have toothache; *j'ai ~ à la tête*, I have a headache; my head aches; *j'ai ~ au pied*, my foot hurts; my foot is sore; *j'ai le ~ de mer*, I feel sea-sick; *j'ai ~ au cœur*, I feel sick; *j'ai le ~ du pays*, I am homesick; *il a eu plus de peur que de ~*, he was more frightened than hurt; *il n'y a que demi ~*, no great misfortune; not much harm in that; *~ d'enfant*, pains of childbirth, labour; *haut ~*, epilepsy; *induire à ~*, to lead into evil; *faire ~*, to hurt; to ache; to cause pain; *vous me faites ~*, you hurt me; *cela fait ~*, it hurts; *faire le ~*, to sin, to do or commit evil; *évitez le ~ et faites le bien*, shun evil and do good; *faire du ~ à X*, to injure X, to harm X; *prendre ~*, to catch cold; *dire du ~ de X*, to speak ill of X; to slander X; *donner du ~*, to give trouble, to cause trouble; to be difficult to achieve; *se donner beaucoup de ~*, or *un ~ de chien*, or *un ~ de tous les diables*, to take pains; to try hard, to strive, to leave no stone unturned, to take a great deal of trouble; *mettre à ~*, (*a*) to beat severely; (*b*) to ruin; (*c*) to seduce; *vouloir du ~ à X*, to wish X harm; *raconter ses maux*, to tell one's troubles; *quel ~ y a-t-il à cela?* or *quel ~ voyez-vous à cela?*, what harm is there in that?; *chacun sent bien son ~*, nobody knows where the shoe pinches so well as he who wears it; *rendre le bien pour le ~*, to return good for evil; *de deux maux il faut choisir le moindre*, of two evils, choose the less; *aux grands maux les grands remèdes*, desperate cases call for desperate remedies.

mal (mal), adv. [L *male*] Wrong, amiss, badly; ill; uncomfortably; at variance, on bad terms; out of favour, in disgrace; bad-looking, ugly, plain; badly off; *prendre ~ quelque chose*, to put a wrong construction on something (said or done); to take offence; *cela va ~*, things are going badly; *ce chapeau vous va ~*, this hat does not suit you; *de ~ en pis*, from bad to worse; *être au plus ~*, to be past recovery, at the point of death; *être fort ~*, to be very ill; *être ~ avec X*, to be on bad terms with X; *être ~ vu de X*, to be out of favour with X; *être ~ dans ses affaires*, to be in a bad way, in low water; *mal à propos*, unseasonably, out of place; *~ gérer*, to mismanage; *n'être pas ~*, to be not bad-looking; *se trouver ~*, to faint, to feel faint, to swoon; *trouver ~*, to find amiss; *tourner ~*, to go to the bad; to go wrong; *pas ~ de*, quite a number of, quite a lot of; not a few; *vous vous y prenez ~*, you go the wrong way to work.

mal, -e (mal), adj. [L *malus*] Bad, fatal; *bon gré, ~ gré*, willing or not, willy-nilly; *bon an ~ an*, one year with another; year in, year out.

malabar, -e (malabar), adj. Of Malabar.

malachite (malakit), s.f. [f. Gr. *malakhē*] (min.) Malachite.

malacie (malasi), s.f. [Gr. *malakia*] (med.) Depraved appetite.

malacoderme (malakɔdɛrm), adj. [Gr. *malakos*+*derma*] (zool.) Malacoderm.

malacologie (malakɔlɔʒi), s.f. [Gr. *malakos*+*logos*] (zool.) Malacology.

malacoptérygien, -ne (malakɔpteriʒjɛ̃), adj. [Gr. *malakos* + *pterux*] (ichth.) Malacopterygian.

malacostracés (malakɔstrase), s.m.pl. [Gr. *malakos*+*ostrakon*] (zool.) Malacostraca.

malade (malad), adj. [f. L *male* + *habitus*] Sick, ill, poorly, unwell; sickly, ailing, infirm, diseased, unhealthy; affected, attacked, disordered; in a bad way or plight; *tomber* ~, to fall ill; *se sentir* ~, to feel ill; ~ *à la mort*, sick unto death; *rendre* ~, to make ill; *avoir un bras* ~, to have a sore arm; *la vigne est* ~, the vine is diseased; *avoir l'esprit* ~, to be sick in mind; *ce livre est bien* ~, that book is in a bad state. ~, s.m.f. Sick person, invalid, patient, sufferer; *soigner un* ~, to nurse a sick person; *faire le* ~, to feign illness; (mil.) *se faire porter* ~, to ask to be put on the sick-list.

maladie (maladi), s.f. [f. *malade*] Illness, sickness, malady; disease, complaint, ailment, disorder; distemper; passion, mania; *faire une* ~, to have an illness; *la* ~ *de la vigne*, phylloxera; *la* ~ *des chiens*, distemper; *avoir la* ~ *des vieux meubles*, to have a passion for old furniture; (colloq.) *il en fera une* ~ *!*, he will be terribly worried; he will fret and fume!

maladi-f, -ve (maladif), adj. Sickly, ailing, unhealthy, frail-looking, puny.

maladivement (maladivmɑ̃), adv. Unhealthily, morbidly.

maladrerie (maladrəri), s.f. [*malade*+ *ladrerie*] Leper-hospital, lazaretto (Middle Ages).

maladresse (maladrɛs), s.f. Awkwardness, unskilfulness, clumsiness; awkward thing, blunder.

maladroit, -e (maladrwa), adj. [*mal*+ *adroit*] Awkward, unskilful, clumsy, bungling; (fig.) stupid, foolish, blundering. ~, s.m.f. Awkward person, blunderer.

maladroitement (maladrwatmɑ̃), adv. Clumsily, awkwardly, unskilfully; (fig.) foolishly, stupidly, blunderingly.

malaga (malaga), s.m. Malaga (wine, grapes).

malaguette, maniguette (malagɛt, manigɛt), s.f. Guinea-pepper.

malaire (malɛr), adj. [f. L *mala*] (anat.) Malar, of the cheek.

malais, -e (malɛ), adj. s.m.f. Malay.

malaise (malɛz), s.m. [*mal*+*aise*] Uncomfortableness, discomfort; (fig.) uneasiness; (rare) straitened circumstances; *avoir un* ~, to feel ill, to feel unwell.

malaisé, -e (malɛze), adj. Hard, difficult, rough, toilsome, troublesome, fatiguing, inconvenient; in straitened circumstances, hard up, needy.

malaisément (malɛzemɑ̃), adv. With difficulty, with trouble.

malandre (malɑ̃dr), s.f. [L *malandria*] **1.** Malanders (in horses); **2.** rotten knot (in wood).

malandreu-x, -se (malɑ̃drø), adj. Having dead knots (of wood); (slang) queer.

malandrin (malɑ̃drɛ̃), s.m. [It. *malandrino*, 14th-century robber]; robber, highwayman, marauder, villain, ruffian.

malappris, -e (malapri), adj. Ill-bred, ill-mannered, unmannerly, uncivil. ~ s.m.f. Ill-bred person, malapert.

malaptérure (malapteryr), s.m. (ichth.) Thunder-fish.

malard, malart, (malar), s.m. [etym. dub.] (ornith.) Mallard, wild drake.

malaria (malarja), s.f. [It. wd] Malaria.

malate (malat), s.m. (chem.) Malate.

malavisé, -e (malavize), adj. Ill-advised, imprudent, rash, unwise, ill-judged. ~, s.m.f. Imprudent person.

malaxage (malaksaʒ), s.m. **malaxation** (malaksa'sjɔ̃), s.f. Malaxation.

malaxer (malakse), v.a. [L *malaxare*] To malaxate.

malaxeur (malaksœr), s.m. Mixer, kneader. ~, adj. m. Kneading.

malbâti, -e (malbɑti), adj. Ill-shaped, ungainly, gawky. ~, s.m.f. Ungainly person.

malchance, malechance (malʃɑ̃s), s.f. [f. *mal*+*chance*] Ill-luck, mishap, mischance.

malchanceu-x, -se (malʃɑ̃sø), adj. Unlucky.

malcomplaisant, -e (malkɔ̃plɛzɑ̃), adj. Disobliging, uncivil.

malcontent, -e (malkɔ̃tɑ̃), adj. Discontented, dissatisfied, malcontent. ~, s.m.f. Discontented person, malcontent; *coiffé à la* ~, with cropped hair; *les* ~*s*, (Fr. hist.) the Malcontents (name of a party at court of Charles IX).

maldisant, -e (maldizɑ̃), adj. Syn. of MÉDISANT.

maldonne (maldɔn), s.f. [*mal*+*donner*] (at cards) Misdeal; *faire* ~, to misdeal.

mâle (mɑl), s.m. [L *masculus*] Male; he, cock, buck, dog, bull, ram, jack, tom, he-man. ~, adj. Masculine, manly; virile, energetic; *une voix* ~, a manly voice.

malebête (malbɛt), s.f. [*male*+*bête*] (obs.) Dangerous person.

malédiction (malediksjɔ̃), s.f. [L *maledictio*] Malediction, curse; *donner sa* ~ *à*, to curse.

malefaim (malfɛ̃), s.f. [*male*+*faim*] (obs.) Gnawing hunger.

maléfice (malefis), s.m. [L *maleficium*] Spell; witchcraft, sorcery; *jeter un* ~ *sur*, to cast a spell over.

maléficié, -e (malefisje), adj. (rare) Bewitched; (fig.) disgraced; injured, afflicted, broken down.

maléfique (malefik), adj. [L *maleficus*] Hurtful, weird and malignant, malevolent, uncanny and harmful.

malemort (malmɔr), s.f. [*male*+*mort*] Tragic death, bad end.

malencombre (malɑ̃kɔ̃br), s.m. (obs.) Mischance, unfortunate occurrence.

malencontre (malɑ̃kɔ̃tr), s.f. (fam.) Mischance, mishap, untoward accident.

malencontreusement (malɑ̃kɔ̃trøzmɑ̃), adv. Unluckily, unfortunately, untowardly, inopportunely, unseasonably.

malencontreu-x, -se (malɑ̃kɔ̃trø), adj. Unlucky, untoward, inopportune.

malendurant, -e (malɑ̃dyrɑ̃), adj. [*mal+endurant*] Unenduring, not very enduring.

mal-en-point (malɑ̃pwɛ̃), adv. loc. Badly off; in a sorry plight.

malentendu (malɑ̃tɑ̃dy), s.m. Misunderstanding, mistake, misapprehension.

malepeste (malpɛst), interj. [*male+peste*] Plague on it!

mal-être (malɛtr), s.m. (rare) Uncomfortableness, discomfort; uneasiness; straitened circumstances.

malévole (malevɔl), adj. [L *malevolus*] (rare) Malevolent, ill-disposed.

malfaçon (malfasɔ̃), s.f. Bad work; defect in work; bungled or botched work.

malfaire (malfɛr), v.n. (used in the pres. inf. only) To do ill, to do harm, to do mischief.

malfaisance (malfɛzɑ̃s), s.f. Evil-doing, wrongdoing, wrong, malfeasance.

malfaisant, -e (malfɛzɑ̃), p. adj. Malfeasant, mischievous, malicious; injurious, noxious, hurtful, unwholesome.

malfait-eur, -rice (malfɛtœr), s.m.f. Scoundrel, criminal, thief; malefactor, evil-doer.

malfamé, -e (malfame), adj. Ill-famed, disreputable.

malformation (malforma'sjɔ̃), s.f. [*mal +formation*] Malformation.

malgache (malgaʃ), adj. s.m.f. From Madagascar; Malagasy; *la langue* ~, the Malagasy language.

malgracieusement (malgrasjøzmɑ̃), adv. Ungraciously, rudely, uncivilly.

malgracieu-x, -se (malgrasjø), adj. Uncivil, rude, ungracious.

malgré (malgre), prep. [*mal+gré*] In spite of, despite; notwithstanding; ~ *tout*, for all that; in spite of everything, nevertheless; *il l'a fait ~ moi*, he did it in spite of me, or against my will; ~ *le mauvais temps*, notwithstanding the bad weather; ~ *que j'en aie*, in spite of myself.

malhabile (malabil), adj. Unskilful, awkward, clumsy.

malhabilement (malabilmɑ̃), adv. Unskilfully, awkwardly, clumsily.

malhabileté (malabilte), s.f. (rare) Unskilfulness, awkwardness.

malherbe (malɛrb), s.f. (bot.) Deadly carrot, thapsia.

malheur (malœr), s.m. [*mal+heur*] Unhappiness; misfortune, ill luck; mischance, mishap; calamity, disaster, accident; woe, misery, adversity, poverty; disgrace; *à quelque chose ~ est bon*, it is an ill wind that blows nobody any good; *tomber dans le* ~, to fall into misfortune; *faire le ~ de*, to bring misfortune on; *tout n'est qu'heur et ~ en ce monde*, that's the way of the world; hap and mishap govern the world; *jouer de* ~, to be unlucky, to have a run of bad luck; *par* ~, unhappily, unfortunately; *oiseau de* ~, bird of ill omen; *pour comble, pour surcroît de* ~, to crown all; *un ~ ne vient jamais seul*, misfortunes never come singly, it never rains but it pours; *porter* ~, to bring bad luck; *il vous arrivera* ~, you will come to grief; *faire un* ~, to commit some fatal violence; to cause an accident.

malheureusement (malœrøzmɑ̃), adv. Unhappily, unfortunately, unluckily; badly, miserably, wretchedly.

malheureu-x, -se (malœrø), adj. Unfortunate, unlucky, ill-starred, hapless; unsuccessful, disastrous, fatal; ill-omened, untoward, ominous; unpleasant, disagreeable; miserable, wretched, sorry, paltry; beggarly, poor; *être ~ comme les pierres*, to be as wretched as can be; to be like a dying duck in a thunderstorm; *il est né* ~, he was born under an unlucky star; *te voilà! ça n'est pas ~!*, here you are, at last! ~ s.m.f. Poor wretch; wretch, rogue, villain; naughty child; *les* ~, the poor; the submerged tenth; (colloq.) *qu'allais-tu faire ~!*, dear me!, what were you going to embark on!; what the deuce were you about?, what business was that of yours?

malhonnête (malɔnɛt), adj. **1.** Dishonest, fraudulent, knavish; **2.** rude, uncivil, impolite, unmannerly. ~, s.m.f. Rude person.

malhonnêtement (malɔnɛtmɑ̃), adv. **1.** Dishonestly; **2.** rudely, uncivilly.

malhonnêteté (malɔnɛtte), s.f. **1.** Dishonesty, want of integrity; dishonest action; **2.** rudeness, incivility; rude action.

malice (malis), s.f. [L *malitia*] Malice ⚠; maliciousness, spite, mischief, mischievousness, harm; roguishness, archness, slyness; prank, trick, witty trick, dodge; *faire des ~s à quelqu'un*, to play tricks on some one; *entendre ~ à quelque chose*, to find a sly meaning in; *n'y pas entendre* ~, to do a thing in all innocence, to mean, to see no harm in a thing; *une ~ cousue de fil blanc*, a trick which is easily seen through. ⚠ The English word 'malice' is nearer to the old meaning of the French word *malice* = *méchanceté, rancune*. In law it must be translated by *intention criminelle*. 'With malice prepense', 'with malice aforethought' = *avec prémédita-*

tion. The French *malice* is more usually to be translated 'mischievousness'.

malicieusement (malisjøzmɑ̃), adv. Maliciously; archly, roguishly, slily.

malicieux, -se (malisjø), adj. s.m.f. Malicious (⚠ see *malice*); sly, arch, witty, roguish, mischievous (person).

malignement (maliɲmɑ̃), adv. Malignantly, malignly, maliciously.

malignité (maliɲite), s.f. [L *malignitas*] Malignity, malignancy; spite, malice.

malin (fem.) **maligne** (malɛ̃), adj. Malicious, malignant, mischievous; evil, ill; sly, cunning, artful, sharp, shrewd, deep; clever; satirical, witty, roguish, arch, saucy, cute; *fièvre maligne,* malignant fever; *ce n'est pas* ~, that is easy enough; *l'esprit* ~, the devil; *le* ~, the devil, Satan. ~, s.m.f. A shrewd or cute one.

malines (malin), s.f. [f. *Malines,* Belgium] Mechlin lace.

malingre (malɛ̃gr), adj. [etym. dub.] Sickly, ailing, weakly, puny. ⚠ The English words 'to malinger', 'malingerer', differ totally in meaning from the French *malingre.* The verb = *faire le malade,* (mil. slang) *tirer au flanc, se faire porter pâle.* The noun 'malingerer' = *un simulateur, un tire-au-flanc.*

malingrerie (malɛ̃grəri), s.f. (rare) Sickliness.

malintentionné, -e (malɛ̃tɑ̃sjɔne), adj. Evil-minded, ill-disposed; *il est* ~ *à votre égard,* he is ill-disposed towards you. ~ s.m.f. Ill-disposed person.

malique (malik), adj. [L *malum*] (chem.) Malic.

malitorne (malitɔrn), adj. s.m. [f. L *male*+ *tornatus*] Rude, coarse, uncouth (fellow).

mal-jugé (malʒyʒe), s.m. Erroneous judgement.

mallard (malar), s.m. (techn.) Small grindstone, knife-grinder's stone.

malle (mal), s.f. [OHG *malaha*] Trunk; pedlar's box; mail; mail-coach, mail-steamer, mail-train; *faire, défaire sa* ~, to pack, to unpack.

malléabiliser (malleabilize), v.a. (rare) To render malleable.

malléabilité (malleabilite), s.f. Malleability, malleableness.

malléable (malleabl), adj. [f. L *malleus*] Malleable; (fig.) supple, docile, compliant, tractable.

malléer (mallee), v.a. [f. L *malleus*] To malleate (rare), to hammer into a sheet, to beat flat.

malléolaire (malleɔlɛr), adj. (anat.) Malleolar.

malléole (malleɔl), s.f. [L *malleolus*] (anat.) Malleolus, ankle-bone.

malle-poste (malpɔst), s.f. (pl. *malles-poste*) Mail-coach, mail, mail-train.

malletier (maltje), s.m. [f. *malle*] Trunk-maker.

mallette (malɛt), s.f. **1.** Small trunk, portmanteau, attaché case, box; **2.** (bot.) shepherd's-purse.

mallier (malje), s.m. (obs.) [f. *malle*] Post-horse.

malmener (malməne), v.a. [*mal*+*mener*] To maltreat, to handle or use roughly; to abuse, to insult, to rate.

malotru, -e (malɔtry), adj. [OF *malastru,* f. LL *maleastrucum*] Rough, rude, uncivil, ill-bred; coarse. ~, s.m. Ruffian, rough, boor, lout, bear.

malouin, -e (maluɛ̃), adj. s.m.f. (Native) of St. Malo.

malpeigné, -e (malpɛɲe), s.m.f. (colloq.) Unkempt, slovenly, dirty creature.

malpighiacées (malpigjase), s.f.pl. (bot.) Malpighiaceae.

malpighie (malpigi), s.f. (bot.) Malpighia.

malplaisant, -e (malplɛzɑ̃), adj. s.m.f. Unpleasant, disagreeable (person).

malpropre (malprɔpr), adj. [*mal*+*propre*] Unclean, dirty, filthy, untidy; indecent; unfit; dishonest.

malproprement (malprɔprəmɑ̃), adv. Uncleanly, dirtily, nastily; clumsily; badly; in a dishonest way, fraudulently.

malpropreté (malprɔprəte), s.f. Dirtiness, uncleanness, nastiness, slovenliness, filth; indecency; dishonesty.

malsain, -e (malsɛ̃), adj. [*mal*+*sain*] Unhealthy; unwholesome, injurious, dangerous; (fig.) immoral, corrupting, demoralizing.

malséance (malseɑ̃s), s.f. Unseemliness, impropriety.

malséant, -e (malseɑ̃), adj. Unseemly, unbecoming, unsuitable; improper, indecorous.

malsonnant, -e (malsɔnɑ̃), adj. Ill-sounding, offensive, scandalous, obnoxious.

malt (malt), s.m. [Engl. wd] Malt.

maltage (maltaʒ), s.m. Malting.

maltais, -e (maltɛ), adj. s.m.f. [f. *Malta*] Of Malta, Maltese.

malterie (maltəri), s.f. Malt-house.

malteur (maltœr), adj. s.m. Maltman, maltster.

malthusianisme (maltyzjanism), s.m. [f. *Malthus,* 1766–1835] Malthusianism.

malthusien, -ne (maltyzjɛ̃), adj. s.m.f. Malthusian.

maltose (maltoz), s.f. (chem.) Maltose.

maltôte (maltot), s.f. (obs.) [f. L *male*+ *tollere*] (Fr. hist.) Tax levied in 1292, &c. for the wars in Flanders; exaction, extortion; tax-collecting; (collectively) tax-gatherers.

maltôtier (maltotje), s.m. Extortioner; (pej.) tax-gatherer.

maltraiter (maltrɛte), v.a. To maltreat, to ill-treat, to ill-use, to abuse, to handle roughly; to injure, to wrong, to damage, to deal harshly with; (fig.) to rate, to slate.
malvacées (malvase), s.f.pl. [L *malva*] (bot.) Malvaceae.
malveillamment (malvɛjamɑ̃), adv. Malevolently, spitefully, maliciously, with ill will.
malveillance (malvɛjɑ̃s), s.f. Malevolence, ill will; spite, malice.
malveillant, -e (malvɛjɑ̃), adj. [for *malveuillant*] Malevolent, ill-disposed, evil-disposed, evil-minded; spiteful. ~, s.m.f. Evil-minded, malevolent person.
malvenant, -e (malvənɑ̃), adj. Unwelcome; stunted (of plants, &c.).
malvenu, -e (malvəny), adj. Unjustified, unwarranted, wrong, unwelcome, ill-advised; *être ~ à se plaindre*, not to be justified in complaining, to have no good grounds for complaining; to complain ill-advisedly.
malversation (malvɛrsa'sjɔ̃), s.f. Malversation, peculation, embezzlement.
malverser (malvɛrse), v.n. (rare) [L *male +versari*] To peculate, to embezzle, to be guilty of malversation.
malvoisie (malvwazi), s.f. [f. *Malvasia* in Greece] Malmsey wine.
malvoulu, -e, mal voulu, -e (malvuly), adj. (rare) Disliked, detested; cut, avoided.
mamamouchi (mamamuʃi) [Burlesque Turkish wd] Mock Turkish title in Molière's *Bourgeois Gentilhomme*; official, Jack-in-office.
maman (mamɑ̃), s.f. [onom.] Mother, mamma, mammy, mummy, mum; *grand-* or *bonne ~*, grandmamma, granny.
mamelé, -e (mamle), adj. Mammate, having nipples, teats, dugs.
mamellaire (mamɛlɛr), adj. Mamillary.
mamelle (mamɛl), s.f. [L *mamilla*] Breast; (of animals) udder; (fig.) bosom; heart; lactation, infancy; (bot.) *herbe aux ~s*, nipplewort; *un enfant à la ~*, a child at the breast; *porter un cœur sous la ~*, to be warm-hearted.
mamelliforme (mamɛlliform), adj. Mamilliform.
mamelon (mamlɔ̃), s.m. Nipple, teat, pap; dug (of animals); (fig.) pap, hummock, rounded eminence, hill, hillock, mound.
mamelonné, -e (mamlɔne), adj. Mamillated; covered with rounded protuberances or elevations.
mamelu, -e (mamly), adj. (pop.) Full-breasted.
mameluk (mamluk), s.m. [Arab. wd] Mameluke.
m'amie (mami), s.f. [archaic abbrev. for *ma amie*] My love, my darling.
mamillaire (mamillɛr), adj. [f. L *mamma*] Mamillary, mamilliform.
mammaire (mamɛr), adj. [f. L *mamma*] Mammary.
mammalogie (mamalɔʒi), s.f. Mammalogy.
mammalogique (mamalɔʒik), adj. Mammalogical.
mammifère (mammifɛr), adj. [L *mamma +ferre*] Mammiferous. ~, s.m. Mammifer, mammal (pl. mammalia.)
mammite (mamit), s.f. [f. L *mamma*] (pathol.) Mastitis, mammitis.
mammouth (mamut), s.m. [f. Russ. *mammot*] Mammoth.
m'amour, mamour (mamur), s.f. [f. *ma+amour*] My love, my darling; *faire des mamours à X*, to coax, to wheedle, to cajole X.
mam'selle, mam'zelle (mamzɛl) [pop. abbrev. of *mademoiselle*] Miss.
man (mɑ̃), s.m. (ent.) Larva of the cockchafer, grub.
manager (manədʒer), s.m. [Engl. wd] Manager.
manant (manɑ̃), s.m. (feud. law) Peasant, villain, serf; (nowadays pej.) peasant, rustic, clodhopper, bumpkin, clown; rustic, ill-bred man.
manc-eau, -elle (pl. *manceaux*) (mɑ̃so), adj. s.m.f. (Native) of Le Mans (France).
mancelle (mɑ̃sɛl), s.f. Tug, thill-tug (of harness).
mancenille (mɑ̃snij), s.f. [Span. *manzanilla*] (bot.) Manchineel.
mancenillier (mɑ̃snilje), s.m. (bot.) Manchineel-tree.
manche (mɑ̃ʃ), s.m. [L *manicum*] Handle, holder, haft, helve; stick, stock, shaft, pole, rod; neck (of a violin); tail (of a plough); loom (of an oar); knuckle-bone (of meat); *~ à balai*, broomstick; (aeron.) joystick, steering-lever; *~ à gigot*, bone-holder (for carving mutton); *~ de gigot*, knuckle-bone of leg of mutton; *jeter le ~ après la cognée*, to throw the helve after the hatchet; *branler au ~*, *branler dans le ~*, to waver, to hesitate, to be shaky, to be unsafe, in a parlous state; to totter; *se mettre du côté du ~*, to side with the strongest; to side with the party in power.
manche (mɑ̃ʃ), s.f. [L *manica*] Sleeve; flexible pipe, hose; strait, channel; rubber, game, heat; *avoir quelqu'un dans sa ~*, to have some one (influential) as patron or protector; *tirer la ~ à quelqu'un*, to beg a person to do something; *avoir la ~ large*, to be very indulgent on questions of morality; *on ne se mouche plus sur sa ~*, the world has grown wiser; *c'est une autre paire de ~s*, that is quite another pair of shoes, or another thing; that's a horse of another colour; *~ à ~*,

even (at play); *j'ai gagné la première* ~, I have won the first rubber, game, heat; ~ *à gigot*, leg-of-mutton sleeve; ~ *à vent*, (*a*) wind-sail; (*b*) air-shaft; *la Manche*, the English Channel, the Channel; name of a (Fr.) department.

mancheron (mɑ̃ʃrɔ̃), s.m. **1.** Handle (of a plough); **2.** short sleeve.

manchette (mɑ̃ʃɛt), s.f. [f. *manche*] **1.** Cuff, wristband, ruffle; (fig.) handcuff; **2.** (print.) side-note; headline (in newspaper).

manchon (mɑ̃ʃɔ̃), s.m. [f. *manche*] Muff; cylindrical coupler for tubes, axles, &c.; gas-mantle; roller; *chien de* ~, lap-dog; ~ *d'accouplement*, coupling-box; muff coupling.

manchot (mɑ̃ʃo), adj. s.m. [L *mancus*] One-handed, one-armed (person); (ornith.) penguin; *il n'est pas* ~, he is no fool, there are no flies on him.

mancipation (mɑ̃sipa'sjɔ̃), s.f. [L *mancipatio*] (Roman law) Mancipation.

mandant, -e (mɑ̃dɑ̃), s.m.f. Constituent, elector.

mandarin, -e (mɑ̃darɛ̃), adj. s.m.f. [Sansk. *mantrin*] Mandarin.

mandarinat (mɑ̃darina), s.m. Mandarinate.

mandarine (mɑ̃darin), s.f. Mandarin orange; tangerine.

mandarinier (mɑ̃darinje), s.m. (bot.) Mandarin-orange tree.

mandarinisme (mɑ̃darinism), s.m. Mandarinism.

mandat (mɑ̃da), s.m. [L *mandatum*] Mandate, authority; commission, charge; warrant, writ; draft, cheque, money-order, order; ~ *d'arrêt*, ~ *d'amener*, warrant for arrest; ~ *de comparution*, summons to appear; ~ *de dépôt*, commitment; ~ *de perquisition*, search-warrant; ~*-poste*, money order, postal order; *s'acquitter d'un* ~, to carry out one's orders, one's duties, to discharge one's obligations. ⚠ In English 'mandate' also = *ordre, injonction*: Sir, I obey the mandate = *Monsieur, j'obéis à cet ordre.*

mandataire (mɑ̃datɛr), s.m. [L *mandatarius*] Mandatory; proxy, attorney, representative, agent.

mandat-carte (mɑ̃dakart), s.m. (pl. *mandats cartes*) Money order sent in post-card form.

mandatement (mɑ̃datmɑ̃), s.m. The sending of money by a money order.

mandater (mɑ̃date), v.a. To deliver an order for the payment of.

mandati-f, -ve (mɑ̃datif), adj. Mandatory.

mandchou, -e (mɑ̃dʃu), adj. s.m.f. Manchu.

mandement (mɑ̃dmɑ̃), s.m. Mandate, mandamus; charge (of a bishop).

mander (mɑ̃de), v.a. [L *mandare*] **1.** To inform, to acquaint with, to let know, to tell; to write, to write to say; to send, to send word; **2.** to send for; to summon, to call, to call for; to order; *on a mandé le médecin*, the doctor was sent for.

mandibulaire (mɑ̃dibylɛr), adj. (anat.) Mandibular.

mandibule (mɑ̃dibyl), s.f. [L *mandibula*] Mandible, jaw.

mandille (mɑ̃dij), s.f. (obs.) [Span. *mandil*] Mandil, livery-coat.

mandoline (mɑ̃dɔlin), s.f. [It. *mandolino*] (mus.) Mandolin.

mandore (mɑ̃dɔr), s.f. [f. It. *mandora*] (mus.) Mandore, mandola.

mandragore (mɑ̃dragɔr), s.f. [L *mandragora*] (bot.) Mandragora, mandrake.

mandrill (mɑ̃drij), s.m. (zool.) Mandril.

mandrin (mɑ̃drɛ̃), s.m. **1.** (techn.) Mandrel, chuck, drift, punch, strike, former; **2.** [f. famous robber] robber, ruffian.

manducabilité (mɑ̃dykabilite), s.f. (rare) Manducability, fitness to be eaten.

manducable (mɑ̃dykabl), adj. [L *manducare*] Eatable, manducable.

manducation (mɑ̃dyka'sjɔ̃), s.f. Manducation, eating, chewing.

manéage (maneaʒ), s.m. [f. OF *maneier*] Unpaid work by merchant sailors.

manécanterie (manekɑ̃tri), s.f. [L *mane* + *cantare*] Parish choir-school.

manège (manɛʒ), s.m. [f. It. *maneggiare*] **1.** Manège, horsemanship; training of horses; riding, riding-school; **2.** roundabout, merry-go-round; horse-mill; **3.** (fig.) trick, play, manœuvre, intrigue. ⚠ Not English 'manage', though 'to manage' is etymologically allied to the French *manège* rather than to *ménage*. The verb 'to manage' corresponds to French *manier* though it has been influenced to a certain extent by *ménage, ménager*. Its chief meanings are: *manier, conduire, diriger, soumettre, mater, venir à bout de*; *enjôler, enbobiner, amadouer*; *ménager* (*son bien*); he knows how to manage, *il sait bien s'y prendre*; my mother was the only one who could ever manage him, *ma mère était la seule qui pût jamais en venir à bout.*

manéger (maneʒe), v.a. To break in, to train, to exercise (a horse); to perform feats of horsemanship.

mânes (mɑn), s.m.pl. [L *manes*] (used only in pl.) (myth.) Manes, ghosts, shades.

manette (manɛt), s.f. [f. *main*] Hand-lever, grip, small handle; (naut.) spoke (of steering-wheel).

manganate (mɑ̃ganat), s.m. (chem.) Manganate.

manganèse (mɑ̃ganɛz), s.m. [It. *manganese*] (chem.) Manganese.

manganésien, -ne (mɑ̃ganezjɛ̃), adj. Manganesian.

manganésifère (mɑ̃ganezifɛr), adj. Manganiferous.
manganeux (mɑ̃ganø), adj. (chem.) Manganous.
mangeable (mɑ̃ʒabl), adj. Eatable, palatable.
mangeaille (mɑ̃ʒɑj), s.f. Food (for animals); (fam.) food, victuals, grub, eatables.
mangeant, -e (mɑ̃ʒɑ̃), p. adj. Eating; *être bien* ~, to be a hearty eater.
mangeoire (mɑ̃ʒwar), s.f. Manger, crib, trough.
mangeoter, mangeotter (mɑ̃ʒɔte), v.a. To eat little, to nibble.
manger (mɑ̃ʒe), v.a.n. [L *manducare*] To eat, to eat up or away; to devour, to consume; to take, to absorb; to corrode, to destroy, to ruin; to run through; to spend, to squander; to chew, to nibble, to gnaw, to bite; to clip; to swallow (words); *les gros poissons mangent les petits*, might overcomes right; ~ *son blé en herbe*, to anticipate one's income; ~ *son pain blanc le premier*, to have one's best time first; ~ *la consigne*, to break bounds, to disobey orders; ~ *X des yeux*, to devour X with one's eyes; ~ *son bien*, to squander one's fortune; *salle à* ~, dining-room; *ce poêle mange beaucoup de charbon*, this stove requires, or consumes, a lot of coal; ~ *ses mots*, to swallow one's words; ~ *de la vache enragée*, to have a hard time, to have a rough time of it; ~ *un morceau*, to take a snack; (fig.) ~ *le morceau*, to let on; to reveal the secret; to turn informer, (slang) to blow the gaff; *donnez-moi à* ~, give me something to eat; ~ *du bout des dents*, to nibble; to pick at one's food; to be dainty or nice in eating; *on mange bien ici*, the cooking is good here; **se** ~, v.pr. to be eaten, to eat each other up, to devour each other; (gram.) to be elided. ~, s.m. Eating; food; dish; grub; *il en perd le boire et le* ~, it takes away his appetite; *à petit* ~ *bien boire*, a small eater, a great drinker.
mangerie (mɑ̃ʒri), s.f. (fam.) Eating, guzzling; (fig.) exaction, extortion.
mange-tout (mɑ̃ʒtu), s.m. invar. **1.** (bot.) Bean or pea the pod of which is good to eat; **2.** spendthrift, squanderer, prodigal.
mangeu-r, -se (mɑ̃ʒœr), s.m.f. Eater, great eater, trencherman; exploiter, extortioner; spendthrift; ~ *de charrettes, de petits enfants*, braggart; ~ *de livres*, bookworm.
mangeure (mɑ̃ʒyr), s.f. (rare) Part eaten or nibbled away.
mangle (mɑ̃gl), s.f. [Malay *mangghi*] (bot.) Mangrove, mangle.
manglier (mɑ̃glje), s.m. (bot.) Mangrove-tree.
mangonneau (pl. -x) (mɑ̃gɔno), s.m. (mil., obs.) Mangonel.
mangoustan (mɑ̃gustɑ̃), s.m. [Malay *mangustan*] (bot.) Mangosteen.
mangouste (mɑ̃gust), s.f. [Span. *mangosta*] (zool.) Ichneumon, mongoose; (bot.) mangosteen.
mangue (mɑ̃g), s.f. [Malay *mangga*] (bot.) Mango; (ichth.) mango-fish.
manguier (mɑ̃gje), s.m. (bot.) Mango-tree.
maniabilité (manjabilite), s.f. Suppleness, pliability; manageableness, tractability.
maniable (manjabl), adj. Easy to handle, easily handled, supple, pliable; manageable, ductile, tractable, handy.
maniage (manjaʒ), s.m. (rare) Handling.
maniaque (manjak), adj. Maniac, mad, eccentric, faddy, crotchety. ~, s.m.f. Maniac, lunatic, eccentric person. ⚠ 'Mania', 'maniac' have in English kept their primitive meaning: 'mania' = *aliénation, transport, délire, égarement d'esprit*; but *manie* merely implies *travers d'esprit, goût porté jusqu'à l'excès*, and usually *maniaque* = faddy.
manichéen, -ne (maniʃeɛ̃), adj. s.m.f. Manichean.
manichéisme (maniʃeism), s.m. Manicheism.
manichordion (manikɔrdjɔ̃), s.m. [for *monochordon*] (mus.) Manichord, clavichord.
manicle, manique (manikl, manik), s.f. [L *manicula*] (ant.) Hand-leather, gauntlet; long sleeve covering the wrist.
manicure, manucure (manikyr, manykyr), s.m.f. [L *manus*+*curare*] Manicure.
manie (mani), s.f. [L and Gr. *mania*] Mania; passion, rage; whim, fancy, fad, eccentricity; hobby. ⚠ See MANIAQUE.
maniement (manimɑ̃), s.m. [f. *manier*] Handling, fingering, touching; management, use, conduct; handling (of money); (butch.) certain parts of an animal from which its fatness can be judged by handling.
manier (manje), v.a. [f. L *manus*] To handle, to touch, to finger; to use, to wield, to ply, to work; to manage, to govern; ~ *une épée*, to wield a sword; *il manie bien la langue*, he expresses himself well. ~, s.m. Touch, feel; *au* ~, by the feel, by the touch.
manière (manjɛr), s.f. [f. *main*] Manner, way, fashion, style; sort, kind; affectation, mannerism; (pl.) manners; *chacun a sa* ~, every one does things in his own way; *de la même* ~, in the same way; *à la manière de*, after the style of; *une* ~ *de parler*, a way of speaking; *de la bonne* ~, handsomely; *il y a la* ~, there's a way of doing it; *il a de mauvaises* ~*s*, he has no manners, he is ill-mannered;

~ *d'être*, attitude, bearing, deportment; ~ *de voir*, view, opinion; *avoir des ~s distinguées*, to have good manners; (fam.) *faire des ~s*, to be affected; (loc.) *de ~ à*, so as to; *de ~ que*, or *de ~ à ce que*, so that.

maniéré, -e (manjere), p. adj. Affected, unnatural, forced, simpering, mincing, la-di-da, lackadaisical.

maniérer (manjere), v.a. To force, to strain, to make unnatural.

maniérisme (manjerism), s.m. Mannerism.

manieu-r, -se (manjœr), s.m.f. Handler; (pej.) ~ *d'argent*, money-dealer, stock-jobber.

manifestant, -e (manifɛstɑ̃), s.m.f. Manifester, person who takes part in public demonstration (for or against something or somebody).

manifestat-eur, -rice (manifɛstatœr), adj. (rare) Manifestative.

manifestation (manifɛsta'sjɔ̃), s.f. Manifestation, demonstration, public expression of opinion, feeling, &c.

manifeste (manifɛst), adj. [L *manifestus*] Manifest, evident, obvious, clear, plain.

manifeste (manifɛst), s.m. Manifesto, declaration; (naut.) manifest.

manifestement (manifɛstəmɑ̃), adv. Manifestly, evidently, obviously, plainly.

manifester (manifɛste), v.a. To manifest, to make known, to make clear; **se ~**, v.pr. to manifest oneself, or itself, to make oneself known; to be made manifest.

manigance (manigɑ̃s), s.f. (fam.) Manœuvre, underhand dealing, trick, intrigue.

manigancer (manigɑ̃se), v.a. (fam.) To plot, to contrive.

manille[1] (manij), s.f. [Span. *malilla*] (cards) Manille; a kind of card-game.

manille[2] (manij), s.m. [f. *Manille*, Manila] **1.** Manilla cigar; **2.** hat made of manilla straw.

manille[3] (manij), s.f. [f. L *manicula*] Anklet, ring; shackle; wooden peg.

maniller (manije), v.a. (naut.) To join with shackles.

manillon (manijɔ̃), s.m. (cards) Each of the four aces in the game of manille.

manioc (manjok), s.m. [Amer. orig.] (bot.) Manioc, cassava.

manipulaire (manipylɛr), adj. [L *manipularis*] Manipular. ~, s.m. (ant.) Commander of a maniple.

manipulat-eur, -rice (manipylatœr), s.m.f. Manipulator.

manipulation (manipyla'sjɔ̃), s.f. Manipulation; (fig.) intrigue; *~s électorales*, gerrymandering.

manipule (manipyl), s.m. [L *manipulus*] (Cath. relig., Rom. ant.) Maniple.

manipuler (manipyle), v.a [f. L *manus*] To manipulate, to work, to operate, to handle.

manique (manik), s.f. See MANICLE.

manitou (pl. -s) (manitu), s.m. [N. Amer. Indian wd] Manitou, god of certain North American Indians; (fig.) *le grand ~*, the boss of the show.

maniveau (pl. -x) (manivo), s.m. [f. *manne*[2]] Punnet, wicker basket.

manivelle (manivɛl), s.f. [f. *main*] Handle, winch; crank, starting-handle.

manne[1] (man), s.f. [Heb. *mān*, Arab. *mann*] Manna; abundant food; substance exuding from certain ash-trees; (fig.) *la ~ céleste*, spiritual food.

manne[2] (man), s.f. [Low Germ. wd] Hamper, basket; ~ *d'enfant*, wicker cradle.

mannée (mane), s.f. Basketful, hamperful.

mannequin[1] (mankɛ̃), s.m. [f. *manne*[2]] Long basket, hamper.

mannequin[2] (mankɛ̃), s.m. [Dutch *manneken*] **1.** Manikin; lay figure, dummy; scarecrow; puppet, bust, dress-stand; automaton; *c'est un vrai ~*, he is a regular automaton; **2.** mannequin, girl who shows off dresses at a dressmaker's.

mannequinage (mankinaʒ), s.m. Kind of sculpture used for decorating buildings.

mannequiné, -e (mankine), adj. (art) Stiff, unnatural, lifeless.

mannequiner (mankine), v.a. (rare) To pose (one's figures) stiffly, unnaturally.

mannette (manɛt), s.f. [f. *manne*[2]] Small basket.

mannite (manit), s.f. (chem.) Mannite.

manœuvre[1] (manœvr), s.f. [L *manus*+*opera*] Action, working; proceeding; drill, drilling (of soldiers); manœuvre; working (of a ship); (fig.) contrivance, trick, stratagem, move; (pl.) rigging, ropes; *grandes ~s*, field practice, field manœuvres; *~s courantes*, running rigging; ~ *dormantes*, standing rigging; *faire une fausse ~*, to make a false move.

manœuvre[2] (manœvr), s.m. Labourer, navvy, mason's labourer, hodman; (fig.) literary hack, hodman.

manœuvrer (manœvre), v.a.n. [f. *manœuvre*] To work, to manœuvre, to handle, to manage; to work the ship, to steer; to drill; *faire ~ des soldats*, to drill soldiers; to manœuvre; to manage cleverly; *il a bien manœuvré dans cette affaire*, he managed that affair cleverly.

manœuvrier (manœvrje), s.m. (naut.) Able seaman; (mil.) clever officer; (fig.) clever polemist, tactician. ~, adj. Manœuvring.

manoir (manwar), s.m. [f. L *manere*] Manor, manor-house; dwelling.

manola (manɔla), s.f. [Span. wd] Spanish working-girl.

manomètre (manɔmɛtr), s.m. [Gr. *manos* +*metron*] Manometer.

manométrique (manometrik), adj. Manometric, manometrical.

manoque (manɔk), s.f. (naut.) Small bundle of marline, log-line, span yarn, &c. of about 30 to 60 fathoms; small bundle of tobacco leaves.

manouvri-er, -ère (manuvrje), s.m.f. Day labourer, workman, (fem.) workwoman.

manquant, -e (mɑ̃kɑ̃), p. adj. Missing, absent, wanting; short. ~ s.m.f. Defaulter, absentee.

manque (mɑ̃k), s.m. [f. *manquer*] Want, lack, need, deficiency; shortcoming, failure, defect, breach; miss; (rid.) stumble; ~ *d'argent*, want of money; *c'est le ~ d'instruction qui vous a perdu*, it was the lack of education that undid you; ~ *de parole*, breach of one's word; ~ *de*, *par ~ de*, for want of; ~ *de touche*, ~ *à toucher*, miss (at billiards); (slang) *un financier à la ~*, a sham financier.

manqué, -e (mɑ̃ke), p. adj. Defective, imperfect; unsuccessful; miscarried, abortive; lost, spoiled, missed, to no purpose, would-be; *une affaire ~e*, an unsuccessful affair; *un poète ~*, a would-be poet; *un vêtement ~*, a misfit.

manquement (mɑ̃kmɑ̃), s.m. Omission, oversight, slip; lack, shortcoming, failure, want; failing, fault; miss, missing, breach; *un ~ de respect*, a lack of respect.

manquer (mɑ̃ke), v.n.a. [It. *mancare*, f. L *mancus*] To miss, to fail, to go wrong; to be wanting, to be lacking, to be deficient; to give way, to slip; to miss fire; to be short, to stand in need (*de*, of); to be wanting in respect; to be regardless or unfaithful; to be insolvent, to go bankrupt; to miscarry; *un fusil qui manque*, a gun that misses fire; *il a manqué de tomber*, he nearly fell; *il manque de tout*, he is destitute; *il ne manque de rien*, he lacks nothing; *il ne manquait plus que cela*, that is the last straw, that crowns all; *il manque deux personnes*, two people are missing; *je n'y manquerai pas*, I will not fail, I will not forget; *l'affaire a manqué*, the affair has fallen through; *l'argent lui manque*, he is short of money; *le cœur lui manque*, his heart fails him; ~ *de respect à X*, to be disrespectful to X; ~ *à sa parole*, to break one's word; ~ *à son devoir*, to fail in one's duty; *vous me manquez*, I miss you; ~, v.a. to miss, to lose, to spoil; ~ *son coup*, to miss one's aim, (fig.) to fail; ~ *son train*, to miss one's train; **se** ~, v.pr. to miss each other.

mansarde (mɑ̃sard), s.f. [f. *Mansard*, Fr. architect] **1.** Garret window, attic window; **2.** garret, attic; *fenêtre en ~*, attic window; *toit en ~*, curb-roof, mansard-roof; *elle habite une humble ~*, she lives in a tiny attic.

mansardé, -e (mɑ̃sarde), adj. With attics, with a sloping roof; sloping (of roofs).

manse (mɑ̃s), s.m. [LL *mansus*] (feud. law) House with a certain amount of land attached; farm, estate.

mansion (mɑ̃sjɔ̃), s.f. [L *mansio*] (Rom. ant.) Halting-place. ⚠ Not English 'mansion', which = *importante résidence*, *hôtel particulier de grandes dimensions*, *château*, *résidence officielle*.

mansionnaire (mɑ̃sjɔnɛr), s.m. (Rom. ant.) Steward; (eccles.) sexton, verger.

mansuétude (mɑ̃sɥetyd), s.f. [L *mansuetudo*] Mansuetude, meekness, gentleness, mildness, forbearance.

mante (mɑ̃t), s.f. [Provenç. *manta*] **1.** Mantle; **2.** [Gr. *mantis*] (ent.) mantis; ~ *religieuse*, praying mantis.

manteau (pl. **-x**) (mɑ̃to), s.m. [L *mantellum*] Cloak, mantle, coat, great-coat; mantel, mantelpiece; (herald.) mantling; mantle; (fig.) mask, pretence; *sous le ~*, under the rose; sub rosa; clandestinely; *le ~ royal*, the royal mantle; ~ *de cheminée*, mantelpiece.

mantelé, -e (mɑ̃tle), adj. Mantled; hooded (of crows).

mantelet (mɑ̃tlɛ), s.m. Short coat or cloak; apron, canopy-front (of coach); carriage-pad, pad (of horse); (fort.) mantlet; (naut.) lid.

manteline (mɑ̃tlin), s.f. (obs.) Short cloak worn by countrywomen.

mantelure (mɑ̃tlyr), s.f. Different coloured hair (on dog's back).

mantille (mɑ̃tij), s.f. [Span. *mantilla*] Mantilla.

mantisse (mɑ̃tis), s.f. (math.) Mantissa.

manucode (manykɔd), s.m. (ornith.) Manucode; a kind of bird of paradise; syn. PARADISIER.

manucure (manykyr), s.f. See MANICURE.

manuel, -le (manɥɛl), adj. [L *manualis*] Manual; *travail ~*, manual labour. ~, s.m. Manual, hand-book.

manuellement (manɥɛlmɑ̃), adv. Manually, by hand.

manufacturable (manyfaktyrabl), adj. Manufacturable.

manufacture (manyfaktyr), s.f. [f. L *manus* + *facere*] Manufacture, making; factory, mill, works; hands, employers. ⚠ The English 'manufacture' has lost the meaning of *établissement* (i.e. the building). It now signifies *fabrication* (*d'un article*), and *produit manufacturé*. In a bad sense it signifies *fabrication machinale* (i.e. mechanical work or production).

manufacturer (manyfaktyre), v.a. To manufacture, to make, to fabricate.

manufacturi-er, -ère (manyfaktyrje), s.m.f. Manufacturer. ~, adj. Manufacturing.

manuluve, maniluve (manylyv, manilyv), s.m. Hand-bath.

manumission (manymisjɔ̃), s.f. [L *manumissio*] (Rom. and feud. law) Manumission, enfranchisement.

manuscrit, -e (manyskri), adj. [f. L *manus+scriptus*] Manuscript. ~, s.m. Manuscript; (print.) copy.

manutention (manytɑ̃sjɔ̃), s.f. [f. L *manus +tenere*] Administration, management; manipulation (of goods, &c.); (mil., nav.) commissariat, army store, bakehouse.

manutentionnaire (manytɑ̃sjɔnɛr), s.m. **1.** Manager; army store-keeper, army baker; **2.** workman or employee who handles goods.

manutentionner (manytɑ̃sjɔne), v.a. **1.** To manufacture (stores), to supply (bread) for the army; **2.** to handle (goods).

manuterge (manytɛrʒ), s.m. [L *manus+tergere*] (eccles.) Manutergium.

mappemonde (mapmɔ̃d), s.f. [L *mappa +mundi*] Map of the world; ~ *céleste*, map of the heavens, planisphere.

maqueraison (makrɛzɔ̃), s.f. Mackerel season.

maquereau[1] (pl. -x) (makro), s.m. [etym. dub.] (ichth.) Mackerel.

maquereau,[2] **-elle** (pl. -x) (makro), s.m.f. (pej.) Pimp, pander, bully, procurer.

maquette (makɛt), s.f. [It. *macchietta*] (sculp.) Small rough model; (paint.) rough sketch, small lay figure; sketch (of scenery, of large picture) (print.) lay-out.

maquignon (makiɲɔ̃), s.m. Horse-dealer, horse-jobber; (fig. pej.) jobber, go-between.

maquignonner (makiɲone), v.a. To bishop, to jockey (a horse for sale); to job, to make up, to arrange in an underhand way.

maquillage (makijaʒ), s.m. Rouging, painting one's face, make-up.

maquiller (makije), v.a. To paint the face, to rouge, to make up; (fig.) to fake, to change, to disguise, to hide; *se* ~, to paint one's face, to rouge, to make up.

maquilleur (makijœr), s.m. Mackerel boat.

maquilleuse (makijøz), s.f. [f. *maquiller*] (theatr.) Face-painter, maker-up.

maquis, makis (maki), s.m. [It. *macchia*] Scrub, wild bushy land (in Corsica), jungle, maquis.

marabout (marabu), s.m. [Arab. *murābiṭ*] **1.** Marabout (Mussulman ascetic); marabout mosque or chapel; **2.** big-bellied kettle or coffee-pot; **3.** marabou-stork; marabou-feathers.

maraîch-er, -ère (marɛʃe), adj. [f. *marais*] Of market-gardening. ~, s.m.f. Market-gardener.

marais (marɛ), s.m. [Germ. orig.] Marsh, swamp, fen, bog, moor, morass; market-garden; ~ *salant*, salt-marsh; *dessécher un* ~, to drain a marsh; *le quartier du Marais*, an old part of Paris, once a very fashionable neighbourhood.

marante (marɑ̃t), s.f. (bot.) Maranta.

marasme (marasm), s.m. [Gr. *marasmos*] Marasmus, consumption; atrophy, emaciation; (fig.) *les affaires sont dans le* ~, business is slack.

marasque (marask), s.f. [It. *marasca*] (bot.) Marasca cherry.

marasquin (maraskɛ̃), s.m. [It. *maraschino*] Maraschino.

marâtre (marɑtr), s.f. [LL *matrastra*, f. L *mater*] Step-mother; unkind, harsh mother; (fig.) harsh woman.

maraud, -e (maro), s.m.f. (obs.) Rogue, knave, rascal, scoundrel; (fem.) jade, hussy.

maraudage (marodaʒ), s.m. Marauding, plundering.

maraude (marod), s.f. [f. *maraud*] Marauding, plundering (of soldiers in war); stealing from gardens, orchards, &c.; (of taxicabs) *faire la* ~, to drive slowly looking for fares; to 'crawl'.

marauder (marode), v.n. To maraud, to go marauding, to go about pilfering.

maraudeu-r, -se (marodœr), s.m.f. Plunderer, marauder, pilferer, trespasser.

maravédis (maravedi), s.m. [Arab. *murābiṭīn*] Maravedi (old Spanish copper coin); *il n'a plus un* ~, he is ruined, or (colloq.) cleaned out.

marayon, maragon (marɛjɔ̃, maragɔ̃), s.m. Man who exploits a salt-marsh.

marbre (marbr), s.m. [L *marmor*] Marble; marble slab; marble-work; marble statue; grinding-stone; (print.) imposing stone; (bookbind.) marbling; (fig.) *être froid comme du* ~, to be hard-hearted, insensible; *demeurer comme un* ~, to remain stock-still, motionless; (naut.) ~ *du gouvernail*, barrel of the steering-wheel; (print.) *sur le* ~, in type.

marbré, -e (marbre), p. adj. Marbled, veined like marble; *du papier* ~, marbled, mottled paper.

marbrer (marbre), v.a. To marble, to mottle; to beat black and blue.

marbrerie (marbrəri), s.f. Marble-cutting, marble-work; marble-yard, marble-works.

marbreu-r, -se (marbrœr), s.m.f. Paper-marbler.

marbrier (marbrije), s.m. Marble-cutter; marble-polisher; marble-dealer; marble-grainer; tombstone-cutter, dealer in funeral ornaments.

marbrière (marbrijɛr), s.f. Marble-quarry.

marbrure (marbryr), s.f. Marbling, marble-graining; black and blue marks, weals (on the skin), bruises.

marc[1] (mar), s.m. [f. *marcher*] Residuum, residue (of fruit, &c., after pressing); grounds, dregs, husks, skins, grains; ~ *de raisin*, skins of grapes (after pressing); ~ *de café*, coffee-grounds.

marc[2] (mar), s.m. [Germ. wd] Mark (coin); *au* ~ *le franc*, so many shillings in the pound.

marcairie (markɛri), s.f. [etym. dub.] Cow-house; cattle (in E. France).

marcassin (markasɛ̃), s.m. Young wild boar.

marcassite (markasit), s.f. [Arab. *marqashitha*] (min.) Marcasite.

marceline (marsəlin), s.f. **1.** Marceline, a thin silk fabric; **2.** (min.) marceline: red silicate of manganese.

marcescence (marsɛssɑ̃s), s.f. [f. *marcescent*] (bot.) Marcescence.

marcescent, -e (marsɛssɑ̃), adj. [f. L *marcescere*] (bot.) Marcescent.

marcescible (marsɛssibl), adj. [L *marcescibilis*] (bot.) Marcescible.

marchage (marʃaʒ), s.m. Preparation of potter's clay by treading it underfoot.

marchand, -e (marʃɑ̃), s.m.f. [LL *mercatans* f. *mercari*] Merchant, dealer, trader; shop-keeper, shopman, tradesman, (fem.) tradeswoman, storekeeper; salesman; buyer; (auctions) bidder; ~ *de*..., ...-dealer, ...-vendor, ...-monger, ...-merchant; ~ *d'habits*, old-clothes man; ~*e à la toilette*, dealer in ladies' left-off clothing, wardrobe dealer; ~(*e*) *des quatre saisons*, costermonger; ~ *en gros*, wholesale dealer, merchant; ~ *en détail*, retail dealer, retailer; ~ *de nouveautés*, linen-draper; (fig. pej.) ~ *de soupe*, headmaster of a boarding-school, a regular Squeers; *en être le mauvais* ~, to have made a bad bargain over it; *trouver* ~, to find a purchaser; *y-a-t'il* ~ ?, is there a bidder?; (prov.) *n'est pas* ~ *qui toujours gagne*, we must expect losses sometimes; (prov.) *de* ~ *à* ~ *il n'y a que la main*, one thief is as bad as another.

marchand, -e (marʃɑ̃), adj. Merchantable, marketable, saleable, vendible; mercantile, trading, merchant, commercial; good for trade, fit for trade; navigable (of a river); wholesale; *marine* ~*e*, merchant service, mercantile marine; *vaisseau, navire* ~, merchantman; *matelot* ~, merchant-seaman; *place* ~*e*, a good place for trade; *prix* ~, trade price.

marchandage (marʃɑ̃daʒ), s.m. Bargaining; haggle, haggling; sub-letting of piece-work; sub-contract.

marchandailler (marʃɑ̃dɑje), v.n. To haggle.

marchander (marʃɑ̃de), v.a.n. To bargain for; to haggle over or about; to stand bargaining over; to beat down; (fig.) to spare, to grudge; to hesitate, to expose; to sub-let, to put on job-contract work; *ne pas* ~ *sa peine*, not to grudge one's trouble; to go all lengths; to go the whole hog; ~ *les éloges*, to praise with some reluctance; ~ *les consciences*, to bribe; ~, v.n. to haggle, to chaffer, to bargain; (fig.) to hesitate, to be irresolute; *sans* ~, without hesitating; *il n'y a pas à* ~, it's either the one or the other; you may take it or leave it.

marchandeu-r, -se (marʃɑ̃dœr), s.m.f. Bargainer, haggler; contractor, job-contractor; middleman; task-master, sweater.

marchandise (marʃɑ̃diz), s.f. Merchandise, goods, wares, commodity; article; *faire valoir sa* ~, to push one's goods; to show off one's goods, (fig.) to set oneself off; *faire métier et* ~ *d'une chose*, to trade in, (fig.) to be used to a thing, to be in the habit of doing a thing; (prov.) ~ *qui plaît est à demi vendue*, please the eye and pick the purse; ~ *de contrebande*, smuggled goods; *le pavillon couvre la* ~, the flag covers the merchandise.

marchant, -e (marʃɑ̃), p. adj. Walking, moving, going, proceeding.

marchantiacées (marʃɑ̃tjase), s.f.pl. (bot.) Marchantiaceae.

marchantie (marʃɑ̃ti), s.f. [f. pr. n. *Marchant*] (bot.) Marchantia.

marche[1] (marʃ), s.f. [f. *marcher*] Walk, walking; gait; march, distance, journey; marching; progress, advance; procession; course; movement, working (of machines), sailing, steaming (of ships); move (at chess); conduct, way of proceeding; (hunt.), spoor of deer; (mus.) march; *une* ~ *forcée*, a forced march; *fermer la* ~, to close the procession, to bring up the rear; *ouvrir la* ~, to lead the way; *ce navire a une* ~ *avantageuse*, that vessel is a fast sailer; *être construit pour la* ~, to be built for speed; *avoir la* ~ *sur*, to outsail; *gagner une* ~ *sur*, to steal a march on; *mettre en* ~, to set going, to start working; *se mettre en* ~, to start out, to set off; ~ *funèbre*, dead march; *la* ~ *de la civilisation*, the progress of civilization; *la mise en* ~, the starting; *une* ~ *de deux heures*, a two hours' walk; *c'est à deux heures de* ~, it's two hours' walk from here; *gêner la* ~ *de*, to impede the march, progress, or advance of; *voici la* ~ *à suivre*, this is the course to follow; this is the way to proceed; *suivre la* ~ *de la maladie*, to observe the progress of the disease; ~ *arrière*, reverse.

marche[2] (marʃ), s.f. Stair, step; treadle (of a lathe); (fig.) *être sur les* ~*s du trône*, to be the next heir to the throne.

marche[3] (marʃ), s.f. [Teut. *marka*] March, border, frontier.

marché (marʃe), s.m. [L *mercatus*]

Market; market-place; mart, emporium, fair; bargain, purchase; price, rate; agreement, contract, treaty; *faire son* ~, to go marketing; *le cours du* ~, the market price; ~ *encombré*, overstocked market; ~ *languissant*, dull market; ~ *aux fleurs*, flower market; *voici un chapeau bon* ~, here is a cheap hat; *en voici un qui est meilleur* ~, here is a cheaper one; *faire un* ~ *avantageux*, to make a good bargain; *rompre un* ~, to break off a bargain; ~ *au comptant*, cash transaction; ~ *à terme*, for future settlement on a specific account day; (fig.) *être quitte à bon* ~, to come off better than one expected; *avoir bon* ~ *de*, to get the better of easily; *je lui ai mis le* ~ *à la main*, I told him he could take it or leave it; I have driven him into a corner, he must take it or leave it; *faire bon* ~ *d'une chose*, to hold cheap, to think little of; *il ne sera pas quitte à si bon* ~, he will not get off so easily; *conclure un* ~, to strike a bargain; *un* ~ *d'or*, a great bargain; *on n'a jamais bon* ~ *de mauvaise marchandise*, a bad article is dear at any price; *par-dessus le* ~, into the bargain; besides that.

marchepied (marʃəpje), s.m. Step, stair; footboard, running-board; pair of steps; (fig.) stepping-stone; footpath; *servir de* ~, to serve as a stepping-stone.

marcher (marʃe), v.n. [f. L *marcus*] To walk, to go on foot; to step, to tread; to go, to travel, to march; to work (of machines); to sail, to run, to ply (of ships); to advance, to proceed, to move on, to progress; to behave; *cette montre ne marche pas bien*, this watch does not keep good time; *faire* ~, to set going, to start working; (slang) to humbug; ~ *à grands pas*, to stride along; ~ *à l'ennemi*, to march against the enemy; ~ *dans l'eau*, to wade; ~ *à pas de loup*, to walk stealthily; to creep; ~ *à quatre pattes*, to go on all fours; ~ *sur la pointe des pieds*, to walk on tiptoe; ~ *à pas comptés*, to pace gravely; ~ *à tâtons*, to grope one's way; ~ *droit*, to walk straight; (fig.) to behave properly; (fam.) *il veut vous faire* ~, he is pulling your leg; *je ne marche pas !*, nothing doing !; I am not having any !; ~ *sur les pas de* or *sur les traces de X*, to follow in X's footsteps, to follow X's example; (fig.) *il ne se laisse pas* ~ *sur le pied*, he will not allow himself to be sat on; ~, v.a. (rare) to tread, to trample; (hat-making) to press, to felt, to full. ~, s.m. Walk, gait, step, pace, tread; walking, ground (on which one walks).

marcheu-r, -se (marʃœr), adj. s.m.f. Walking; pedestrian, walker; sailer; *un bon* ~, (a) a good walker; (b) a fast sailer; (fam., pej.) *un vieux* ~, an old rip.

marcottage (markɔtaʒ), s.m. (hort.) Layering.

marcotte (markɔt), s.f. (hort.) Layer, runner.

marcotter (markɔte), v.a. (hort.) To layer.

mardelle (mardɛl), s.f. See MARGELLE.

mardi (mardi), s.m. [L *mars*+*dies*] Tuesday; ~ *gras*, Shrove Tuesday.

mare (mar), s.f. [LL *mara*] Pool, pond.

marécage (marekaʒ), s.m. [f. *maresc*, old form of *marais*] Marsh, bog, fen, swamp, morass.

marécageu-x, -se (marekaʒø), adj. Marshy, swampy, boggy.

maréchal (mareʃal), s.m. (pl. *maréchaux*), [OHG *marahscalh* (OTeut. *marhos* +*skalkoz*)] Farrier, shoeing-smith; marshal, field-marshal; ~ *ferrant*, farrier, shoeing-smith; ~ *de France*, field-marshal; ~ *des logis*, non-commissioned officer (of cavalry).

maréchalat (mareʃala), s.m. Marshalship.

maréchale (mareʃal), s.f. Field-marshal's wife.

maréchalerie (mareʃaləri), s.f. Farriery; farrier's shop.

maréchaussée (mareʃose), s.f. (obs.) Marshalsea; constabulary, mounted police.

marée (mare), s.f. [f. L *mare*] Tide, flood; fresh sea-fish; ~ *basse*, low tide; ~ *haute*, high tide; ~ *morte*, neap tide; *grande* ~, spring tide; ~ *des équinoxes*, equinoctial tide; ~ *montante*, rising tide; ~ *descendante*, ebbing tide; *la* ~ *monte*, the tide is coming in; *la* ~ *descend*, the tide is going out; *prendre la* ~, to take advantage of the tide; (fig.) *aller contre vents et* ~*s*, to pursue one's course in spite of all opposition; *marchand de* ~, fishmonger; *la* ~ *est abondante*, there is fish in abundance; *arriver comme* ~ *en carême*, to arrive most opportunely; *la* ~ *n'attend personne*, time and tide wait for no man; *ce qui vient de flot s'en retourne de* ~, lightly come, lightly go; *train de* ~, fish train.

marégramme (maregram), s.m. Marigram.

marégraphe, maréographe, maréomètre (maregraf, mareɔgraf, mareɔmɛtr), s.m. Marigraph, tide-gauge.

marègue (marɛg), s.f. Thick woollen material.

marelle (marɛl), s.f. [f. *méreau*] Hopscotch (a game).

maremmatique (marɛmatik), adj. Maremmatic.

maremme (marɛm), s.f. [It. *maremma*] Maremma.

marengo (marɛ̃go), s.m. Speckled cloth; Oxford mixture; pepper and salt (colour); *poulet à la* ~, chicken dressed with mushrooms and olive oil.

mareyage (marɛjaʒ), s.m. Fish-trade.
mareyeu-r, -se (marɛjœr), s.m.f. Fish-salesman, fish-carrier, fish-tranter.
margarine (margarin), s.f. Margarine.
margarique (margarik), adj. [f. Gr. *margaron*] (chem.) Margaric.
margay (margɛ), s.m. (zool.) Margay, tiger-cat.
marge (marʒ), s.f. [L *margo*] Margin (of paper, books, &c.); border; (fig.) latitude, scope, room, time; *laisser assez de ~ à X*, to give X sufficient scope; *nous avons de la ~*, we have time to spare.
margelle (marʒɛl), s.f. (Rom. ant.) Puteal; curb, kerb, brink, edge (of a well).
marger (marʒe), v.a. (print.) To regulate the margin of; to feed (a printing-press).
margeu-r, -se (marʒœr), s.m.f. (print.) Layer-on.
marginal, -e, (aux) (marʒinal), adj. Marginal.
marginer (marʒine), v.a. To write in the margin of.
margot (margo), s.f. [f. prop. n.] Magpie; gossip, chatterbox, talkative wench.
margota, margotas (margɔtɑ), s.m. Flat-bottomed barge.
margoter, margotter (margɔte), v.n. To cry (of a quail).
margotin (margɔtɛ̃), s.m. [f. *Margot*?] Small faggot, bundle of firewood.
margouillis (marguji), s.m. [etym. dub.] Puddle, slush, slop; (fig.) mess, lurch; *laisser X dans le ~*, to leave X in the lurch.
margoulette (margulɛt), s.f. [f. OF *goule* = *gueule*] (slang) Mouth, mug, jaw; *casser la ~ à X*, to break X's jaw, to damage X's looks.
margrave (margrav), s.m.f. [Germ. *Markgraf*] Margrave.
margraviat (margravja), s.m. Margraviate.
margriette, margrillette (margrjɛt, margrijɛt), s.f. Thick glass-ware sold by European traders along the coast of Africa.
marguerite (margərit), s.f. [L *margarita*] (bot.) Daisy, marguerite, ox-eye daisy; (obs.) pearl; (naut.) messenger; *faire ~*, to heave with a messenger; *reine-~*, China aster; *jeter des ~s aux pourceaux*, to cast pearls before swine; (as prop. n.) Margaret. ⚠ *Reine-marguerite* corresponds to the English 'aster'. The French *aster* = Michaelmas daisy.
marguillerie (margijri), s.f. **1.** Churchwardenship; **2.** church register.
marguillier (margije), s.m. [L *matricularius*] Churchwarden.
mari (mari), s.m. [L *maritus*] Husband; spouse.
mariable (marjabl), adj. Marriageable.
mariage (marjaʒ), s.m. [f. *marier*] Marriage, matrimony, wedlock; match; wedding, nuptial ceremony; union, (fig.) blending; (naut.) lashing; *~ d'inclination*, love-match; *~ de convenance* or *de raison*, match arranged in view of position or money; *contrat de ~*, marriage settlement, or articles; *prendre en ~*, to take to wife; *promettre ~ à*, to promise to marry; *demander quelqu'un en ~*, to ask for a person's hand; *apporter une grosse dot en ~*, to have a big dowry.
marianisme (marjanism), s.m. [f. *Vierge Marie*] Mariolatry; exaggerated cult of the Virgin Mary.
marié, -e (marje), p. adj. Married; (fig.) matched, blended, linked. **~, -e** s.m.f. Bridegroom, married man; (fem.) bride, married woman; *se plaindre que la ~e est trop belle*, to complain of a good bargain; *les nouveaux ~s* (pl.), the bride and bridegroom, the newly-married couple.
marier (marje), v.a. [L *maritare*] To marry, to join together in wedlock; to give in marriage; (fig.) to match, to join, to blend, to unite; (naut.) to lash; *il a marié sa fille au plus riche fermier du canton*, he married his daughter to the richest farmer in the district; *~ des couleurs*, to blend colours; (hort.) *~ deux variétés de roses*, to cross two kinds of roses; *~ sa voix au son d'un instrument*, to mingle one's voice with the sound of an instrument; (naut.) *~ des cordages*, to lash ropes together; **se ~**, v.pr. to marry, to get married, to marry each other; (fig.) to match, to blend, to pair, to combine (*avec*, with). ⚠ In English 'to marry' is a transitive verb. In French *marier* is transitive only in the sense of 'to give in marriage': he married his cousin = *il a épousé sa cousine*.
marie-salope (marisalɔp), s.f. (pl. *maries-salopes*). (naut.) Dredger; mud-barge, mud-lighter.
marieu-r, -se (marjœr), s.m.f. Match-maker.
marigot (marigo), s.m. Marigot: in W. Africa, the side channel of a river.
marin, -e (marɛ̃), adj. [L *marinus*, f. *mare*] Marine; sea-faring, sea-going; nautical; found in the sea; *avoir le pied ~*, to have good sea-legs, (fig.) to keep one's head in a difficulty. **~**, s.m. Seaman, seafarer, sailor, mariner; *~ d'eau douce*, freshwater sailor, landlubber.
marinade (marinad), s.f. (cook.) Marinade, pickle; fry of pickled meat.
marinage (marinaʒ), s.m. Pickling.
marine (marin), s.f. [f. *marin*] Marine; sea service, naval service; naval administration; Admiralty; navy, fleet, naval forces; shipping, craft; smell, taste of the sea; (paint.) seascape, sea-piece; *~ marchande*, merchant or mer-

cantile marine, merchant service; ~ *militaire*, navy, (in England) Royal Navy; *infanterie de* ~, colonial infantry. ⚠ 'Marine' in English also means *fusilier marin*. 'Tell that to the marines' may be translated: *à d'autres!*, *chansons que tout cela*. The slang expression 'a dead marine' = *une bouteille vide*, and a 'marine' in naval slang = *un lourdaud, un niais, une gourde, un cornichon*.

mariner (marine), v.a. To cure, to pickle; to preserve; to souse; ~, v.n. to be in pickle; (fig.) *laisser* ~ *X*, to keep X kicking his heels.

maringouin (marɛ̃gwɛ̃), s.m. [f. Brazil. *marigoui*] Mosquito.

marini-er, -ère (marinje), adj. Marine; *officier* ~, petty officer. ~, s.m. Bargeman, lighterman, waterman, boatman.

marinisme (marinism), s.m. [f. It. *Marini*] Marinism.

mariolâtrie (marjɔlɑtri), s.f. Mariolatry.

marionnette (marjɔnɛt), s.f. [f. *Marion*] Marionette, puppet; (fig.) frivolous, weak-minded person; mere puppet; (techn.) vertical pulley; ~**s**, pl. puppet-show.

mariste, marianite (marist, marjanit), (Rom. Cath.) Marist.

marital, -e, (aux) (marital), adj. [L *maritalis*] Marital.

maritalement (maritalmɑ̃), adv. Maritally, matrimonially; as husband and wife.

maritime (maritim), adj. [L *maritimus*] Maritime, sea; nautical, naval; *législation* ~, maritime law, navigation laws; *puissances* ~*s*, maritime powers; *ville* ~, maritime town.

maritorne (maritɔrn), s.f. [f. name of servant-girl in Cervantes' *Don Quixote*] Slattern, slut, wench, maid-of-all-work.

marivaudage (marivodaʒ), s.m. [f. *Marivaux*, 1688–1763] Affected style after the manner of Marivaux; far-fetched gallantry.

marivauder (marivode), v.n. [f. *Marivaux*] To imitate the style of Marivaux; to affect refinement, to make pretty speeches; to flirt.

marjolaine (marʒɔlɛn), s.f. [LL *majorana*] (bot.) Sweet marjoram.

marjolet (marʒɔlɛ), s.m. (obs.) Fop, little coxcomb.

mark (mark), s.m. Mark (German money).

marli (marli), s.m. Scotch gauze, thread gauze; fillet bordering the inside of a plate, &c.

marlou (pl. -**s**) (marlu), s.m. (slang) Bully, pimp.

marmaille (marmɑj), s.f. [f. *marmot*] (colloq.) Brats, crowd of brats.

marmelade (marməlad), s.f. [f. Gr. *melimēlon*] Marmalade, preserve of fruits, jam; *viande en* ~, meat cooked to a jelly; (fig.) *avoir la figure en* ~, to have one's face smashed to a jelly. ⚠ In English 'marmalade' nearly always means *marmelade d'oranges*; it is rarely used of a preserve made of other fruit (except lemons and grape-fruit).

marmenteau (pl. -**x**) (marmɑ̃to), s. adj.m. [f. OF *mairement*] Ornamental (growing) timber, on an estate, not to be cut by lessees.

marmitage (marmitaʒ), s.m. Bombarding with heavy shells.

marmite (mɑrmit), s.f. Copper, boiler; saucepan, pot, porridge-pot; potful; digester; (fig.) heavy shell; ~ *de Papin*, Papin's digester; (fig.) *faire bouillir la* ~, to keep the pot boiling; *écumer la* ~, to skim the pot, (fig.) to sponge; *écumeur de* ~*s*, sponger, parasite; *la* ~ *est renversée*, they give no more parties; *nez en pied de* ~, prominent upturned nose; (geol.) ~ *de géants*, huge hollow in the rocks, worn away by water; 'pot-hole'.

marmitée (marmite), s.f. Potful.

marmiter (marmite), v.a. To bombard with heavy shells.

marmiteu-x, -se (marmitø), adj. Pitiful, wretched, miserable; ~ s,m.f. poor fellow, tatterdemalion.

marmiton (marmitɔ̃), s.m. [f. *marmite*] Scullion, scullery-boy.

marmonner (marmɔne), v.n. To mutter, to mumble, to murmur.

marmoréen, -ne (marmɔreɛ̃), adj. Marmoreal; (fig.) cold, icy, marmorean.

marmorisation (marmɔriza'sjɔ̃), s.f. Marmorization.

marmoriser (marmɔrize), v.a. To marmorize.

marmot (marmo), s.m. [f. *marmotte*] Brat, little boy, little chap; (obs.) small monkey; grotesque figure; (fig.) *croquer le* ~, to dance attendance, to kick or cool one's heels.

marmottage (marmɔtaʒ), s.m. Mumbling, muttering.

marmotte (marmɔt), s.f. **1.** (zool.) Marmot; *dormir comme une* ~, to sleep like a top; **2.** woman's kerchief worn round the head; **3.** box of samples; **4.** (naut.) match-tub; **5.** (bot.) kind of plum.

marmottement (marmɔtmɑ̃), s.m. Murmuring, muttering, mumbling.

marmotter (marmɔte), v.a. [etym. dub.] To mutter, to mumble, to murmur.

marmotteu-r, -se (marmɔtœr), s.m.f. Mumbler, mutterer.

marmottier (marmɔtje), s.m. (bot.) Kind of plum-tree.

marmouset (marmuzɛ), s.m. [etym. dub.] **1.** Grotesque figure; **2.** urchin, small boy; **3.** fire-dog, andiron; ⚠ Not 'marmoset', which = *ouistiti*.

marnage (marnaʒ), s.m. (agric.) Marling, claying.

marner (marne), v.a. (agric.) To marl; ~, v.n. (naut.) to rise beyond the usual level (of tides).

marneur (marnœr), adj. s.m. (agric.) Marler, marl-digger.

marneu-x, -se (marnø), adj. Marly, marlaceous.

marnière (marnjɛr), s.f. Marl-pit.

marocain, -e (marɔkɛ̃), adj. s.m.f. (Native) of Morocco; Moroccan; (material) marocain, moracain.

marolles (marɔl), s.m. [Fr. geog. orig.] Cheese made at Maroilles.

maronite (marɔnit), adj. s.m.f. Maronite.

maronner (marɔne), v.n. (colloq.) To grumble, to growl, to mutter.

maroquin (marɔkɛ̃), s.m. [f. *Maroc*] Morocco, morocco-leather; roan; *papier* ~, morocco-paper.

maroquinage (marɔkinaʒ), s.m. Preparation of morocco-leather.

maroquiner (marɔkine), v.a. To morocco, to dress like morocco-leather.

maroquinerie (marɔkinri), s.f. **1.** Morocco-leather dressing; **2.** morocco-leather factory; **3.** morocco-leather trade or shop; **4.** leather goods.

maroquinier (marɔkinje), s.m. Morocco-leather dresser, tanner, leather-goods maker, leather-goods dealer.

marotique (marɔtik), adj. [f. *Clément Marot*] Marotic, in the style of Marot.

marotte (marɔt), s.f. [dim. of *Marie*] Fool's bauble; (fig.) fancy, whim, hobby, folly; (millinery, hairdressing) dummy head, model; *chacun a sa* ~, every one has his fads; *caresser sa* ~, to ride one's hobby-horse.

marouflage (maruflaʒ), s.m. (paint.) Lining, pasting.

maroufle[1] (marufl), s.m. Clodhopper, bumpkin, boor, clown, rustic; rascal, scoundrel.

maroufle[2] (marufl), s.f. (paint.) Painter's glue, lining-paste.

maroufler (marufle), v.a. (paint.) To line, to paste.

maroute, marouette (marut, maruɛt), s.f. (bot.) Stinking camomile.

marprime (marprim), s.f. Sail-makers' punch; awl.

marquage (markaʒ), s.m. Marking.

marquant, -e (markɑ̃), p. adj. Of note; conspicuous; striking; remarkable; *cartes* ~*es*, cards that count; *personnes* ~*es*, notabilities; (fam.) nobs.

marque (mark), s.f. [f. *marquer*] Mark ⚠, imprint, stamp; cipher, trade-mark, private mark; brand, branding-iron; print, trace (of footsteps); testimony, proof, token; counter (at play); mole, scar, pit (on the skin); note, distinction; (naut.) marque; *donner à X une* ~ *d'estime*, to give X a proof of esteem; *la* ~ *d'une charge*, the emblem of office; *un homme de* ~, a man of note; *liqueurs de* ~, liqueurs of superior quality; ~ *de fabrique*, trade-mark; (naut.) *lettre de* ~, letter of marque. ⚠ In English 'mark' means also: *cible*; *point* (at school, examinations, &c.); *niveau moyen*, *qualité minimum indispensable*; (naut.) *amer*.

marqué, -e (marke), p. adj. Marked, stamped, branded; evident, conspicuous, obvious; decided, fixed, determined; *avoir les traits* ~*s*, to have strongly-marked features; *le moment* ~, the appointed time; *papier* ~, stamped paper; *il est né* ~, he was born with a mole; (theatr.) *rôles* ~*s*, parts taken by actors no longer young; ~ *à l'A*, first-class, A1; ~ *de la petite vérole*, pitted with small-pox; *un succès* ~, a marked success; *une tendance très* ~*e*, a strongly marked tendency; (colloq.) *elle est un peu* ~*e*, she looks rather old.

marquer (marke), v.a. [Germ. orig.] To mark; to stamp; to brand, to stigmatize; to indicate, to betoken, to denote; to appoint, to state, to tell, to mention; to show marks of, to testify; to score; *encre à* ~, marking-ink; *je lui ai marqué que*, I wrote to him that; ~ *à X ce qu'il doit faire*, to tell X what he must do; ~ *à X sa reconnaissance*, to show one's gratitude to X; ~ *ses points*, to mark one's points (at play); ~, v.n. to make one's mark; to mark, to be remarked, to be remarkable, to attract notice, to be conspicuous, to be evident; to date; to show the time (of sundials, clocks, &c.); to show the age by the teeth (of horses); (colloq.) *cela marquerait trop*, that would be too noticeable, would attract too much attention; (pop.) ~ *bien*, to have a good, or stylish, appearance; ~ *mal*, to have a bad appearance.

marqueter (markəte), v.a. To spot, to speckle; to inlay, to tessellate.

marqueterie (markɛtri), s.f. Marquetry, inlaid-work, inlaying, mosaic; (fig.) patchwork, miscellany.

marqueteur (markətœr), s.m. Inlayer.

marquette (markɛt), s.m. Cake (of virgin wax).

marqueu-r, -se (markœr), s.m.f. Marker; scorer, tally-keeper.

marquis (marki), s.m. [LL *marcha*] (obs.) Marcher, one who guarded a March; marquis, marquess; (iron.) *c'est un* ~ *de Carabas*, he is a great landowner.

marquisat (markiza), s.m. Marquisate.

marquise (markiz), s.f. **1.** Marchioness; **2.** marquee, awning; settee; porch, verandah; **3.** parasol; **4.** marquise ring; **5.** kind of pear.

marquoir (markwar), s.m. Stylus, bodkin; marker (used by tailors); sampler; counter (at card-games, &c.).

marraine (marɛn), s.f. [LL *matrina*, f. L *mater*] Godmother; sponsor, introducer; proposer (for membership of a club, &c.).

marrant (marɑ̃), adj. (slang) **1.** Amusing; **2.** boring, annoying, dull. ⚠ The expression *c'est marrant* has two opposite meanings: (*a*) (more usual) it's very amusing; (*b*) it's very boring. Only the tone of voice implies the difference of meaning; *en avoir marre* means always 'to be fed up with it'.

(se) marrer (səmare), v.pr. (slang.) **1.** To enjoy oneself immensely; **2.** to be bored. ⚠ As in the case of *marrant*, the verb *se marrer* has two opposite meanings, but the first is the more usual.

marri, -e (mari), adj. [Teut. *marrjan*] Sorry, grieved, troubled, penitent, repentant.

marron (marɔ̃), s.m. Chestnut, Spanish chestnut; cracker (of fireworks); (mil.) mark, tally; check; curl tied with ribbon; chestnut colour; (slang) blow; *~ d'Inde*, horse-chestnut; *tirer les ~s du feu*, to serve as catspaw. ~, adj. invar. Chestnut-colour.

marron, -ne (marɔ̃), adj. [Span. *cimarron*] Fugitive, runaway (of slaves); run wild (of animals that have been tame); (comm.) unlicensed, interloping, clandestine; *nègre ~*, runaway slave; *cochon ~*, wild boar; *courtier ~*, unlicensed broker.

marronnage (marɔnaʒ), s.m. Running away (of slaves); carrying on the business of a broker without a licence.

marronner[1] (marɔne), v.a. (obs.) To curl (the hair).

marronner[2] (marɔne), v.n. **1.** (colloq.) To grumble, to grouse; **2.** to be a runaway slave, to maroon; to carry on business without a licence. ⚠ English 'to maroon' may also mean *camper pendant plusieurs jours* (U.S.A.). Transitively it signifies *abandonner (quelqu'un) dans une île déserte.*

marronnier (marɔnje), s.m. Horse-chestnut-tree, Spanish chestnut-tree; *~ d'Inde*, horse-chestnut-tree. ⚠ The edible *marron* or *grosse châtaigne* is the fruit of the *châtaignier* = 'chestnut-tree'; *le marronnier* is usually the horse-chestnut-tree.

marrube (maryb), s.m. [L *marrubium*] (bot.) Horehound; *~ aquatique*, water-horehound, gipsywort.

mars (mars), s.m. [L *martius*, f. *Mars*] March; (myth.) Mars; (fig.) war; (pl.) spring corn; *arriver comme ~ en carême*, to be sure to happen; *champ de ~*, large open space, drilling-ground.

marsault, marseau (pl. **-x**) (marso), s.m. (bot.) Sallow, marsh willow.

marseillais, -e (marsɛjɛ), adj. s.m.f. (Native) of Marseilles; *~e*, s.f. French national song.

marsouin (marswɛ̃), s.m. [Germ. *Meerschwein*] Porpoise, sea-hog; (colloq.) marine; (fig.) ugly, dirty man; (naut.) forecastle awning.

marsupial, -e, (aux) (marsypjal), adj. [f. L *marsupium*] (zool.) Marsupial, marsupiate. ~, s.m.pl. (zool.) Marsupialia.

martagon (martagɔ̃), s.m. [Span. wd] (bot.) Martagon, Turk's-cap.

marte (mart), s.f. See MARTRE.

marteau (pl. **-x**) (marto), s.m. [L *martulus*] Hammer; knocker (of a door); (ichth.) hammer-headed shark, hammer-fish; (anat.) malleus; *~ à deux mains*, *~ de forge*, sledge-hammer; (colloq.) *avoir un coup de ~*, or *être ~*, to be gone in the upper story, to be barmy on the crumpet, to have bats in the belfry, to have a bee in one's bonnet, to have a screw loose; *être entre le ~ et l'enclume*, to be between the devil and the deep sea; *graisser le ~*, to tip the porter; *il vaut mieux être ~ qu'enclume*, better be biter than bit.

marteau-pilon (martopilɔ̃), s.m. (pl. *marteaux-pilons*) Steam-hammer.

martel (martɛl), s.m. (obs.) Hammer; *avoir*, or *se mettre ~ en tête*, to be very uneasy, to be worried.

martelage (martəlaʒ), s.m. Hammering; marking (of trees).

marteler (martəle), v.a. To hammer; to mark (trees); (fig.) to labour, to strain; to accentuate (a syllable).

martelet (martəlɛ), s.m. Small hammer.

marteleur (martəlœr), s.m. Hammerer; hammerman; hammersmith.

martellerie (martɛlri), s.f. Workshop, forge where metals are hammered.

martial, -e, (aux) (marsjal), adj. [L *martialis*, f. *Mars*] Martial, warlike; military; (med., obs.) applied to medicaments containing iron; *cour ~e*, court martial; *loi ~e*, martial law.

martialement (marsjalmɑ̃), adv. Martially.

martien, -ne (marsjɛ̃), adj. Of, from Mars. ~, s.m.f. Martian.

martin[1] (martɛ̃), s.m. **1.** (ornith.) Martin, grackle; **2.** Neddy; (U.S.A.) Jack (donkey); **3.** Bruin (bear).

Martin[2] (martɛ̃), s.m. (prop. n.) Martin; *faute d'un point M~ perdit son âne*, a miss is as good as a mile; *la Saint-~*, Martinmas; *faire la Saint-~*, to indulge in good living; *été de la Saint-~*, St. Martin's summer.

martinet[1] (martinɛ), s.m. [f. *Martin*] (ornith.) Swift, martin.

martinet[2] (martinɛ), s.m. [f. *marteau*] **1.** Tilt-hammer; **2.** taws(e), cat-o'-nine-tails, whip; cloth whisk; **3.** flat candle-stick with handle. ⚠ Not English 'martinet' which = *personne ayant autorité et assurant une discipline rigide.*

martineur (martinœr), s.m. Syn. of MARTELEUR.

martingale (martɛ̃gal), s.f. [Provenç. *martegalo,* f. *Martigues*] **1.** (harness) Martingale; **2.** (naut.) martingale; **3.** (at cards) martingale; **4.** (dressm.) strap-belt (at the back only).

martingaler (martɛ̃gale), v.n. To play a martingale.

martin-pêcheur (martɛ̃pɛʃœr), s.m. (pl. *martins pêcheurs*) (ornith). Kingfisher.

martin-sec (martɛ̃sɛk), s.m. (pl. *martins-secs*) (bot.) Kind of pear.

martin-sire (martɛ̃sir), s.m. (pl. *martins-sires*) (bot.) Kind of pear.

martoire (martwar), s.m. [f. *marteau*] Double-faced hammer.

martre, marte (martr, mart), s.f. [Germ. orig.] (zool.) Marten; ~ *blanche,* ermine; ~ *zibeline,* sable; *fourrure de* ~, sable; (fig.) *prendre* ~ *pour renard,* to take a cow for a bull, to be misled by a resemblance.

martyr, -e (martir), s.m.f. adj. [Gr. *martus*] Martyr; (fig.) *le commun des* ~*s,* the common herd.

martyre (martir), s.m. [eccles. L *martyrium*] Martyrdom; (fig.) great physical or moral suffering; *souffrir le* ~, to suffer martyrdom.

martyriser (martirize), v.a. To martyrize; (fig.) to torment, to persecute, to torture.

martyrium (martirjɔm), s.m. [L wd] Church or chapel dedicated to or containing the tomb of a martyr.

martyrologe (martirɔlɔʒ), s.m. [eccles. L *martyrologium*] Martyrology.

marum (marɔm), s.m. (bot.) Catmint.

marxisme (marksism), s.m. [f. *Karl Marx,* 1818–1883] Marxism, doctrines of Karl Marx.

marxiste (marksist), adj. s.m.f. Marxian.

maryland (marilɑ̃d), s.m. Virginia tobacco.

mas (mɑ, mɑs), s.m. [Provenç. wd] Farm, cottage in S. of France; house.

mascarade (maskarad), s.f. [It. *mascherata*] Masquerade, mask; maskers; disguise, pretence, hypocrisy.

mascaret (maskarɛ), s.m. [Gascon orig.] Bore, eagre (at mouth of rivers).

mascaron (maskarɔ̃), s.m. [It. *mascherone*] (arch.) Mask; grotesque figure.

mascotte (maskɔt), s.f. [Provenç. *masco*] Mascot.

masculin, -e (maskylɛ̃), adj. [L *masculinus*] Masculine, male, manly; (gram.) masculine; *rime* ~*e,* masculine rhyme. ~, s.m. (gram.) The masculine, masculine gender; *au* ~, in the masculine.

masculiniser (maskylinize), v.a. To make masculine.

masculinité (maskylinite), s.f. Masculinity, masculineness.

masque (mask), s.m. [It. *maschera*] Mask; respirator, box-respirator; (fig.) blind, cloak, disguise, pretence; masquerader, masker, mummer; (fenc.) face-guard; cast, death-mask; (fig.) face, countenance, expression, physiognomy; ugly person, fright; (arch.) mascaron; (naut.) smoke-sail, screen; ~, s.f. hag, witch, ugly woman; *lever* or *jeter le* ~, to unmask; to throw off the mask; *arracher le* ~ *à X,* to unmask X; *prendre le* ~ *de la vertu,* to pretend to be virtuous; ~ *à gaz,* box-respirator; *la petite* ~ *!,* the minx!

masqué, -e (maske), p. adj. Masked; disguised; hidden, concealed; *bal* ~, masked ball, masquerade, fancy-dress ball; *la porte était* ~*e par des arbres,* trees concealed the door; *batterie* ~*e,* masked battery.

masquer (maske), v.a. To mask; to cloak, to disguise; to camouflage; to conceal, to hide; (naut.) to take aback (sails); **se** ~, v.pr. to mask, to mask oneself; to put on a mask, to be disguised; to hide oneself, to conceal oneself.

massacrant, -e (masakrɑ̃), p. adj. (colloq.) Cross, peevish, disagreeable; *il est d'une humeur* ~*e,* he is as cross as two sticks; he is in an unbearable temper.

massacre (masakr), s.m. [OF *maçacre,* orig. dub.] Massacre, butchery, slaughter; (fig.) havoc; waste; squandering, spoiling; smashing, mangling, hacking; bungler, botcher; (herald., hunt.) head (of a stag); *jeu de* ~, Aunt Sally (game).

massacrer (masakre), v.a. To massacre, to slaughter, to murder, to butcher; to mangle, to destroy; to waste, to squander, to smash, to hack; to spoil, to bungle; (theatr.) ~ *son rôle,* to murder one's part; ~ *l'anglais,* to murder the King's English.

massacreur (masakrœr), s.m. Slaughterer, slayer; botcher, bungler.

massage (masaʒ), s.m. Massage; rubbing.

massaliote (masaljɔt), adj. s.m.f. [f. *Massilia,* old name for Marseilles] (Person) from or of old Marseilles.

masse[1] (mas), s.f. [L *massa*] Mass, heap, lump; bulk, aggregate; mob; capital, stock, common fund; stakes (at play); *en* ~, in a body, in the mass, in great numbers or quantity; by bulk; *les* ~*s,* the masses, the people; *soulever les* ~*s,* to stir up the people; *une* ~ *de,* a mass of; a lot of; ~ *de manœuvre,* mass of

manœuvre; (phys.) *la ~ d'un corps*, the mass of a body; (electr.) earth.
masse[2] (mas), s.f. [pop. L *matea*] Mace; sledge-hammer; rammer; *~ d'armes*, mace; (bot.) *~ d'eau*, reed-mace, cat's-tail.
massé (mase), s.m. (billiards) Massé, push-stroke, stroke made with cue held perpendicular.
masselotte (maslɔt), s.f. (metall.) Small mass of superfluous metal remaining attached to an object after it is cast.
massepain (maspɛ̃), s.m. [It. *marzapane*] Marzipan, marchpane; round almond cake.
masser[1] (mase), v.a. [Arab. *massa*] To massage, to rub.
masser[2] (mase), v.a. [f. *masse*] To mass, to group together (troops); (billiards) to strike with a push-stroke; **se ~**, v.pr. to group together, to crowd together.
masséter (masetɛr), s.m. adj. (anat.) Masseter.
massette[1] (masɛt), s.f. [f. *masse*] (bot.) Reed-mace, cat's-tail, bulrush.
massette[2] (masɛt), s.f. [f. *masse*] Sledge-hammer; wooden mace.
masseu-r, -se (masœr), s.m.f. Masseur, (fem.) masseuse.
massicot (masiko), s.m. **1.** (metall.) Massicot, yellow oxide of lead; **2.** guillotine (for cutting paper, &c.). See MASSIQUOT.
massier[1] (masje), s.m. [f. *masse*] Mace-bearer.
massi-er[2], **-ère** (masje), s.m.f. Pupil who collects the monthly subscriptions and pays the general expenses of a studio.
massi-f, -ve (masif), adj. [f. *masse*] Massive, bulky, solid; (fig.) lumpish, clumsy, heavy; *avoir l'esprit ~*, to be slow-witted; *argent ~*, solid silver. ~, s.m. Group, clump, cluster (of trees, flowers); thicket, grove; (arch.) solid mass, block (of masonry), wall, pier, pile; chain, group (of mountains).
massiquot, massicot (masiko), s.m. [f. name of inventor] (techn.) Guillotine (for cutting paper, &c.).
massivement (masivmɑ̃), adv. Massively, heavily, solidly.
massiveté (masivte), s.f. Massiveness.
massore, massorah (masɔr, masɔra), s.f. [Hebr. *massōreth*] Masorah, Masora, Massora (Jewish critical compilation on the Hebrew Bible).
massorète (masɔrɛt), s.m. Mas(s)orete.
massorétique (masɔretik), adj. Masoretic, Masoretical.
massue (masy), s.f. [f. *masse*] Club; *coup de ~*, knock-out blow; (fig.) calamity, catastrophe; *prendre une ~ pour écraser une fourmi*, or *une mouche*, to use a sledge-hammer to crack a nut; to crush a fly upon the wheel.
mastic (mastik), s.m. [Gr. *mastikhē*] Mastic; putty; cement; (bot.) mastic, species of thyme. ~, adj. Mastic-coloured.
masticage (mastikaʒ), s.m. Cementing, puttying.
masticateur (mastikatœr), adj. Masticator, masticating. ~, s.m. Mincing-machine.
mastication (mastika'sjɔ̃), s.f. [f. L *masticare*] Mastication.
masticatoire (mastikatwar), s.m. adj. Masticatory.
mastiff (mastif), s.m. Mastiff (dog).
mastigadour (mastigadur), s.m. (obs.) (vet.) Slabbering-bit.
mastiquer[1] (mastike), v.a. To cement, to putty.
mastiquer[2] (mastike), v.a.n. [L *masticare*] To masticate, to chew.
mastoc (mastɔk), s.m. adj. [Germ. *mastochs*] Heavy, lumpish, clumsy (fellow).
mastodonte (mastɔdɔ̃t), s.m. [Gr. *mastos* +*odous*] (zool.) Mastodon.
mastodynie (mastɔdini), s.f. (med.) Mastodynia.
mastoïde (mastɔid), adj. [Gr. *mastos*+ *eidos*] (anat.) Mastoid; *apophyse ~*, mastoid process.
mastoïdien, -ne (mastɔidjɛ̃), adj. (anat.) Mastoidean, mastoideal, mastoid.
mastoïdo-huméral, -e, (aux) (mastɔidoymeral), adj. (anat.) Mastoid-humeral.
mastoquin (mastɔkɛ̃), s.m. (naut.) Post of helm-port.
mastroquet (mastrɔke), s.m. (fam.) Keeper of a pub; pub; wine-shop keeper.
masulipatam, mazulipatam (mazylipatɑ̃), s.m. [Indian geog. orig.] Indian calico.
masure (mazyr), s.f. [LL *mansura*] Hovel, tumbledown dwelling, ramshackle hut.
mat (mat), s.m. adj. (invar.) [Pers. *māt*] (chess) Mate; *échec et ~*, checkmate; *faire X échec et ~*, to checkmate X.
mat, -e (mat), adj. [same orig. as *mat* s.m.] Mat(t), dull, lustreless, unpolished; dead, dull-sounding; flat, insipid; heavy, sodden; *coloris ~*, dull colouring; *or ~*, unpolished gold; *son ~*, dull muffled sound. ~, s.m. Dull side, dull part.
mât (mɑ), s.m. [Germ. *mast*] Mast, spar, pole; *le grand ~*, the mainmast; *~ de fortune*, jury-mast; *~ de pavillon*, flag-mast, flagstaff; *~ de rechange*, spare mast; *~ d'artimon*, mizzen-mast; *~ de beaupré*, bowsprit; *~ de misaine*, fore-mast; ⚓ see MISAINE; *abaisser un ~*, to strike a mast; *~ de cocagne*, greasy pole.
matacher (mataʃe), v.a. To tattoo.
matador (matadɔr), s.m. [Span. wd] Matador; (slang) bigwig, magnate; (cards) principal cards in games of *hombre* and *quadrille*.

matage (mataʒ), s.m. [f. *mat*] The use of a tarnisher on gilt; the painting of gilt with gum to protect it.
mâtage, mâtement (mɑtaʒ, mɑtmɑ̃), s.m. [f. *mât*] The fixing of the lower masts of a ship.
matamore (matamɔr), s.m. [Span. *matamoros*] Hector, bully, braggart; *faire le* ~, to bully.
matassin (matasɛ̃), s.m. [Span. *matachin*] (obs.) Dancer.
match (matʃ), s.m. [Engl. wd] Match (in sport). ⚠ *Match* has not in French the sense of *mariage*; 'a love-match' = *un mariage d'inclination*; a tennis match = *un match de tennis*.
maté (mate), s.m. (bot.) Maté; Paraguay tea.
matelas (matlɑ), s.m. [It. *materasso*] Mattress; cushion, pad; squab; ~ *à air*, air-bed; ~ *à eau*, water-bed.
matelasser (matlase), v.a. To stuff, to pad, to line with cushions; to cover with a mattress.
matelassi-er, -ère (matlasje), s.m.f. Mattress-maker.
matelassure (matlasyr), s.f. Padding, wadding, stuffing, padded lining.
matelot (matlo), s.m. [Dutch *mategenoot*] Sailor, seaman; shipmate, mariner, messmate; consort-ship; child's sailor-suit; *bon* ~, able-bodied seaman (abbrev. A.B.)
matelotage (matlotaʒ), s.m. Seamanship; seaman's wages, pay.
matelote (matlɔt), s.f. **1.** (rare) Seaman's wife; **2.** matelote, fish cooked with wine and onions; **3.** hornpipe; *à la* ~, seaman-like, sailor fashion.
mater (mate), v.a. (chess) To checkmate; (fig.) to subdue, to humble, to bring down.
mâter (mɑte), v.a. [f. *mât*] (naut.) To mast, to supply with masts.
mâtereau (pl. **-x**) (mɑtro), s.m. [f. *mât*] (naut.) Small mast; spar, pole.
matérialisation (materjaliza'sjɔ̃), s.f. Materialization.
matérialiser (materjalize), v.a. To materialize.
matérialisme (materjalism), s.m. Materialism.
matérialiste (materjalist), s.m.f. Materialist. ~, adj. Materialistic.
matérialité (materjalite), s.f. Materiality, materialness.
matériaux (materjo), s.m.pl. [f. LL *materia*] Materials; material.
matériel, -le (materjɛl), adj. [L *materialis*] Material, heavy, of the body, dull; sensuous, sensual. ~, s.m. **1.** That which is material or concerned with the matter; matter; **2.** material, stores; stock-in-trade; working-stock, rolling-stock, plant; implements, apparatus; furniture, fittings, equipment, requisites; (colloq.) *assurer la* ~*le*, to keep the pot boiling.
matériellement (materjɛlmɑ̃), adv. Materially; positively, to all intents and purposes, in fact; sensually.
maternel, -le (matɛrnɛl), adj. [L *maternus*, f. *mater*] Maternal, motherly; *langue* ~*le*, mother-tongue; *parents* ~*s*, relations on the mother's side. **la** ~**le**, s.f. Infants' school, crèche, kindergarten.
maternellement (matɛrnɛlmɑ̃), adv. Maternally, in a motherly fashion.
maternité (matɛrnite), s.f. Maternity, motherhood; lying-in hospital; *service de la* ~, maternity department (in hospital).
mateu-r, -se (matœr), s.m.f. Workman who deadens gold or silver or takes off the soldering mark.
mâteur (mɑtœr), s.m. [f. *mât*] Experienced seaman in charge of the hoisting and lowering of the masts.
mathématicien, -ne (matematisjɛ̃), s.m.f. Mathematician.
mathématique (matematik), adj. [L *mathematicus*, f. Gr. *mathēmatikē*] Mathematic, mathematical. ~, s.f. Mathematics; ~*s pures*, pure mathematics, ~ *mixtes*, or *appliquées*, mixed or applied mathematics.
mathématiquement (matematikmɑ̃), adv. Mathematically; rigorously.
mathurin[1] (matyrɛ̃), s.m. (colloq.) Sailor, jack tar.
mathurin[2] (matyrɛ̃), s.m. Mathurin, monk of the Order of Trinitarians.
matico (matiko), s.m. [Span. dim. of *Mateo* = Matthew] (bot.) Matico.
matière (matjɛr), s.f. [L *materia*] Matter; material, substance; (fig.) subject-matter, theme, subject; cause, reason, motive, grounds; contents; *en* ~ *de*, in matters of; *entrer en* ~, to broach the subject; ~ *première*, raw material; ~*s d'or et d'argent*, bullion; ~ *médicale*, materia medica; ~ *à procès, à poursuite*, grounds for a lawsuit, an action; (iron.) *s'élever au-dessus de la* ~, to soar above material things, to rise superior to material considerations; ~ *imposable*, taxable article.
matin (matɛ̃), s.m. [L *matutinum*] Morning; forenoon, dawn; (fig.) prime, youth; *un beau* ~, one fine morning; *un de ces quatre* ~*s*, one of these (fine) days; *être du* ~ *et du soir*, to be up early and late; (prov.) *rouge au soir, blanc au* ~, *c'est la journée du pèlerin*, evening red and morning gray, sets the pilgrim on his way; *quand il pleut le* ~, *continue ton chemin*, a misty morning may turn out a fine day; *tel rit le matin qui pleure le soir*, laughter is akin to tears; after sweet meat, sour sauce. ~, adv. Early, early in the morning; *se lever* ~, to get

up early; *de bon ~*, very early; (prov.) *ce n'est pas tout de se lever ~, il faut arriver à l'heure*, it is one thing to hurry, and another to succeed; *qui se lève ~, se repose de bonne heure*, early sow, early mow.

mâtin[1] (mɑtɛ̃), s.m. [pop. L *mansuetinus*] Mastiff; cur; mongrel dog.

mâtin[2], **-e** (mɑtɛ̃), s.m.f. (colloq., not always pej.) Scoundrel, fellow, rascal, hussy; *sacré ~ !*, by Jove!

matinal, -e, (aux or **als)** (matinal), adj. Morning; early, early rising; matutinal; *une personne ~e*, an early riser; *une visite ~e*, an early call.

matinalement (matinalmɑ̃), adv. (rare) Early, early in the morning.

mâtiné, -e (mɑtine), p. adj. [f. *mâtin*] (of dogs, and fig.) Crossed, mongrel, not of pure race; mixed or blended (*de*, with).

mâtineau (pl. **-x**) (mɑtino), s.m. [f. *mâtin*] Small or young mastiff.

matinée (matine), s.f. [f. *matin*] **1.** Morning, forenoon; *dormir la grasse ~, faire la grasse ~*, to lie abed late; **2.** morning's work; theatrical performance, social gathering or concert taking place in the afternoon instead of the evening, matinée; **3.** dressing-jacket.

mâtiner (mɑtine), v.a. [f. *mâtin*] To cross-breed; to serve, to cover (of dogs); (fig. rare) to abuse, to snub, to disparage.

matines (matin), s.f.pl. Matins.

matineu-x, -se (matinø), adj. [f. *matin*] Early, early rising; *être ~*, to be an early riser.

matini-er, -ère (matinje), adj. Morning, of the morning; (used only in: *l'étoile ~e*, the morning star).

matir (matir), v.a. [f. *mat*] To deaden (gold, silver); to take off the soldering mark.

matité (matite), s.f. Deadness, dullness, drabness; heaviness.

matoir (matwar), s.m. Tool for deadening metals.

matois, -e (matwɑ), adj. [f. OF slang *mate* = meeting-place of Parisian thieves] Cunning, sly, artful, deep, crafty. ~, s.m.f. Cunning person, sly dog, sly puss, sly fellow; *c'est un fin ~* he's an artful blade.

matoisement (matwazmɑ̃), adv. (rare) Slyly, cunningly, artfully.

matoiserie (matwazri), s.f. Cunning, slyness, craftiness.

matou (pl. **-s**) (matu), s.m. Tom-cat; (fig.) disagreeable fellow, baboon.

matraque (matrak), s.f. [Arab. *miṭraq*] Cudgel, bludgeon.

matras (matra), s.m. **1.** Bolt (from crossbow); **2.** (chem.) matrass.

matriarcal, -e, (aux) (matriarkal), adj. Matriarchal.

matriarcat (matriarka), s.m. [L *mater*+ Gr. *arkhē*] Matriarchy.

matricaire (matrikɛr), s.f. (bot.) Matricaria, feverfew, motherwort.

matrice (matris), s.f. [L *matrix*] **1.** (anat.) Matrix, womb; **2.** original register; original weight or measure; mould; block; die.

matricide (matrisid), s.m. [L *mater*+ *caedere*] Matricide: (*a*) the crime; (*b*) the murderer.

matriciel, -le (matrisjɛl), adj. (admin.) Belonging to, according to, the official tax-registers.

matriculaire (matrikylɛr), adj. Entered on the register, matriculate.

matricule (matrikyl), s.f. [L *matricula*] Register, roll, rolls; certificate of matriculation. ~, adj. Matriculation. ~, s.m. Matriculation number.

matriculer (matrikyle), v.a. To register, to enter in the register; to mark something with a matriculation number. ⚠ Not English 'to matriculate', which = (*a*) *admettre* (*un étudiant*) *à l'université*; (*b*) *être admis à l'université*.

matrimonial, -e, (aux) (matrimɔnjal) adj. Matrimonial.

matrimonialement (matrimɔnjalmɑ̃), adv. (rare) Matrimonially.

matrone (matrɔn), s.f. [L *matrona*] Matron, elderly and stout woman; midwife. ⚠ Colloq. *matrone* is often pejorative; not so in English. 'Matron' has several meanings in English: *femme mariée qui est femme de bien*; *sainte qui a été mariée*; *femme chargée d'assurer les soins domestiques dans une institution publique*; *infirmière-en-chef d'un hôpital* (*même non mariée*).

matte (mat), s.f. (metall.) Matte.

matthiole (matiɔl), s.f. (bot.) Mathiola; ~ *blanchâtre*, stock-gilliflower.

maturati-f, -ve (matyratif), adj. [f. L *maturare*] (med.) Maturative. ~, s.m. Maturative, maturant.

maturation (matyra'sjɔ̃), s.f. [L. *maturatio*] Maturation, ripening; (med.) suppuration.

mâture (mɑtyr), s.f. [f. *mât*] Masting, masts, spars; wood for masts; art of masting; masting-sheers; mast-shed, mast-store.

maturément (matyremɑ̃), adv. With, after, full deliberation.

maturité (matyrite), s.f. [L *maturitas*] Maturity, ripeness, mellowness; mature age; completion; circumspection, consideration befitting mature age; *avec ~*, maturely, with consideration; *venir à ~*, to ripen; to come to maturity.

matutinal, -e, (aux) (matytinal), adj. [L *matutinus*] Matutinal.

maubèche (mobɛʃ), s.f. (ornith.) Sandpiper.

maudire (modir), v.a. [L *male*+*dicere*] To curse, to execrate; to hate, to rue;

to reprove, to censure; ~ *X du haut de la chaire,* to curse X with bell, book, and candle.

maudissable (modisabl), adj. Execrable, detestable.

maudit, -e (modi), p. adj. Cursed, accursed; horrible, detestable, abominable, wretched, cursed, confounded; ~ *soit!,* curse it!, confound it! ~, s.m. *Le* ~, Satan, the Accursed; *les* ~*s,* the damned.

mauge, maugère (moʒ, moʒɛr), s.f. (naut.) Scupper-hose.

maugré (mogre), prep. Old form of *malgré.*

maugréer (mogree), v.n. [*mal+gré*] To grumble, to growl; to fret and fume, to curse and swear; *sans* ~, without grumbling.

maupiteu-x, -se (mopitø), adj. s.m.f. (obs.) Cruel (person); that does not merit pity.

maure, more (mɔr), adj. s.m. (for fem. see *mauresque*) Moor; Moorish; *traiter X de Turc à* ~, to deal hardly with X, to treat X badly.

maurelle (mɔrɛl), s.f. (bot.) Dyer's croton.

mauresque, moresque (mɔrɛsk), adj. s.f. Moresque, Moorish woman; loose Oriental trousers; Moorish dance; arabesque.

mausolée (mozɔle), s.m. [f. prop. n. *Mausole,* Mausolus] Mausoleum.

maussade (mosad), adj. [L *male+ sapidus*] Sulky, sullen, cross; disagreeable, unpleasant; dull, tedious.

maussadement (mosadmɑ̃), adv. Disagreeably, sullenly, peevishly.

maussaderie (mosadri), s.f. Crossness, sulkiness, sourness, sullenness.

mauvais, -e (movɛ), adj. Bad, ill, evil; wicked, evil-minded, naughty; mischievous, injurious, hurtful, wrong, amiss, foul, unpleasant; sinister, unpropitious; contrary, adverse; wretched, sorry, cheap, poor; nasty; (print.) battered; hard, difficult; unsound (of doctrines); *passer un* ~ *quart d'heure,* to have a bad quarter of an hour; to have a short but unpleasant experience; to catch it; *avoir* ~*e mine,* to look ill; *les temps sont* ~, the times are bad; *il est très* ~*e langue,* he is a regular backbiter; he has a sharp tongue; ~*e nouvelle,* bad news; ~ *sujet,* black sheep, rogue; ~*e tête,* hot-headed fellow; *faire* ~ *visage à X,* to treat X coldly; *il fait* ~, the weather is bad; *trouver* ~ *que,* to take it amiss that; *prendre en* ~*e part,* to take in bad part; *mer* ~*e,* rough sea; *pas* ~, not bad, pretty good; ~*e herbe pousse toujours,* ill weeds grow apace; *il la trouve* ~*e!,* he is disgusted!, that's a wretched experience for him; he is sick of it. ~, s.m. Bad; *discerner le bon du* ~, to distinguish good from bad; *il faut prendre le bon avec le* ~, you must take the rough with the smooth. ~, adv. Badly, wrong, amiss, ill; *sentir* ~, to smell nasty.

mauvaisement (movɛzmɑ̃), adv. (rare) Badly, wrongly, nastily, naughtily.

mauvaiseté (movɛzte), s.f. Badness, naughtiness; nastiness; wickedness; sly trick.

mauve (mov), s.f. [L *malva*] (bot.) Mallow; (ornith.) gull, sea-mew. ~, s.m. Mauve (colour). ~, adj. Mauve.

mauvéine (movein), s.f. (chem.). Syn. of ANILINE.

mauviette (movjɛt), s.f. (ornith.) Lark, field-lark; (colloq.) lath, stick (thin, small person); *manger comme une* ~, to eat like a sparrow.

mauvis (movi), s.m. (ornith.) [etym. dub.] Mavis; redwing.

maxillaire (maksilɛr), adj. [L *maxilla*] Maxillary. ~, s.m. Maxilla, jaw(-bone); ~ *supérieur,* upper jaw; ~ *inférieur,* lower jaw.

maxima (maksima), s.m.pl. [pl. of *maximum*] Maxima; *thermomètre à* ~ *et à minima,* maximum and minimum thermometer, register, self-registering thermometer.

maximaliste (maksimalist), s.m.f. Maximalist.

maxime (maksim), s.f. [L *maxima*] Maxim; *tenir ou avoir pour* ~, to hold as a maxim.

maximer (maksime), v.a. (obs.) **1.** To fix the maximum of; **2.** to establish as a maxim.

maximum (maksimɔm), s.m. [L wd] Maximum; highest point, price, &c.; the most, the height, the acme; *au* ~, at the most, at the highest. ~, adj. Highest, greatest, maximum.

maye (mɛ), s.f. [f. *maie*] Stone trough into which oil pours from the press.

mayonnaise (majɔnɛz), s.f. [etym. dub., perh. f. *Mahon?*] (cook.) Mayonnaise (sauce).

mazagran (mazagrɑ̃), s.m. Coffee served cold in a glass; the glass in which it is served.

mazarinade (mazarinad), s.f. [f. Cardinal *Mazarin*] Libel written against Mazarin during the wars of the Fronde.

mazdéisme (mazdeism), s.m. [Avestic *mazda*] Mazdaism, Zoroastrianism.

mazéage (mazeaʒ), s.m. (metall.) The first operation in refining cast iron; syn. FINAGE.

mazeau (pl. -x) (mazo), s.m. (metall.) Sheet of cast iron refined for the first time.

mazer (maze), v.a. (metall.) To refine cast iron.

mazerie (mazri), s.f. Place where cast iron is refined.

mazette (mazɛt), s.f. Poor hack, sorry horse, tit; (fig.) milksop, poor creature, duffer; *~!*, good heavens! you don't say so.

mazout (mazu), s.m. [Russ. wd] Heavy oil, fuel oil.

mazurka (mazyrka), s.f. [Pol. wd] Mazurka.

me, m' (mə), pers. pron. [L wd] Me, to me; myself, to myself; ~ *voici*, here I am.

mé-, més- (mə, mez), [OHG *missi-*] Prefix used in an unfavourable sense.

mea-culpa (meakylpa), s.m. [L wds] Mea culpa; *dire, faire son* ~, to cry peccavi; to plead guilty.

méandre (meɑ̃dr), s.m. [f. n. of a winding river in Asia Minor] Meander, winding, maze.

méandrine (meɑ̃drin), s.f. (zool.) [f. *méandre*] Meandrina, genus of corals.

méat (mea), s.m. [L *meatus*] (anat.) Meatus, duct, passage.

mec (mɛk), s.m. (slang) Pimp, pander; (colloq. jest) bloke, cove.

mécanicien, -ne (mekanisjɛ̃), adj. s.m.f. Mechanician; ~, s.m. machinist, mechanic; engine-builder; engine-man, engine-driver, car-driver, chauffeur; ~, adj. *ingénieur* ~, mechanical engineer; *le* ~ *(du train)*, the engine-driver; *ouvrière ~ne*, sewing-machinist.

mécanique (mekanik), adj. [Gr. *mēkhanē*] Mechanic, mechanical; machine-made, made by machinery. ~, s.f. Mechanics; mechanism, machinery; machine, piece of machinery; brake; (fig.) intrigue; *la* ~ *céleste*, the structure of the heavens; ~ *appliquée*, applied mechanics.

mécaniquement (mekanikmɑ̃), adv. Mechanically.

mécaniser (mekanize), v.a. To render mechanical, to turn into a machine; (colloq.) to tease, to plague; ~ *les hommes*, to use men as mere machines.

mécanisme (mekanism), s.m. Mechanism, machinery; structure; contrivance; (fig.) arrangement, handling (of an instrument); *il comprend le* ~ *du langage*, he understands the mechanism of language; *il a un* ~ *remarquable*, he has remarkable (piano) technique.

mécanothérapie (mekanoterapi), s.f. [Gr. *mēkhanē+therapeia*] (med.) Mecanotherapy.

mécène (mesɛn), s.m. [f. prop. n. *Maecenas*] Maecenas, patron of literature or art.

méchage (meʃaʒ), s.m. [f. *mèche*] Sulphuring (a cask).

méchamment (meʃamɑ̃), adv. Wickedly; spitefully, maliciously, ill-naturedly; mischievously.

méchanceté (meʃɑ̃ste), s.f. [f. *méchant*] Wickedness; spite, spitefulness, malice, maliciousness; perverseness, waywardness, mischievousness, naughtiness; ill-natured action, reflection, slander, base action.

méchant, -e (meʃɑ̃), adj. [OF *meschéant*, f. *meschoir*] Wicked, evil, bad; ill-natured, spiteful, malicious; wayward, naughty, mischievous; wretched, worthless; sorry, paltry, poor; unpleasant, disagreeable; vicious (of a horse); ugly, bad-looking; *un* ~ *poète*, a sorry poet; *une ~e affaire*, an unpleasant affair; *il n'est pas si* ~ *qu'il en a l'air*, his bark is worse than his bite; *il n'est nul si* ~ *qui ne trouve sa ~e*, every Jack has his Jill. ~, s.m.f. Wicked person, evil-doer, reprobate; (pl.) the wicked; *faire le* ~, to be fractious (of a child).

mèche (mɛʃ), s.f. [etym. dub.] Wick (of lamp, candle, &c.); tinder, match, fuse, linstock; whiplash; lock (of hair); tuft, tassel; screw, bit, drill; worm (of a corkscrew); (surg.) tent; ~ *anglaise*, centre-bit; *découvrir, éventer la* ~, (mil.) to discover the enemy's mine by means of a counter-mine; (fig.) to discover a plot; (colloq.) *vendre la* ~, to let the cat out of the bag; *être de* ~ *avec X*, to be hand and glove with X, to be X's accomplice; (fam.) *il n'y a pas* ~, it is no go, it is impossible, nothing doing.

méchef (meʃɛf), s.m. (obs.) [*mé+chef*] Mishap, mischance, mischief; harm; catastrophe.

mécher (meʃe), v.a. To fumigate with brimstone; to sulphur (a cask).

mécheu-x, -se (meʃø), adj. Forming a cord (of raw wool).

mecklembourgeois, -e (mɛklɑ̃burʒwɑ), adj. s.m.f. [f. *Mecklembourg*] Mecklenburger.

mécompte (mekɔ̃t), s.m. Miscalculation; mistake, error; (fig.) disappointment, disillusionment; *vous aurez un grave* ~, you will have a bitter disappointment.

(se) mécompter (səmekɔ̃te), v. pr. (rare) To miscalculate, to be out in one's reckoning; to be disappointed.

méconium (mekɔnjɔm), s.m. [L wd] Meconium.

méconnaissable (mekɔnɛsabl), adj. Unrecognizable, not to be recognized.

méconnaissance (mekɔnɛsɑ̃s), s.f. Unthankfulness, disregard, ingratitude; not recognizing or knowing again.

méconnaissant, -e (mekɔnɛsɑ̃), p. adj. (rare) Unmindful, ungrateful, thankless.

méconnaître (mekɔnɛtr), v.a. Not to recognize, not to know again, to fail to recognize; to disown, to deny; to disregard, to slight, to ignore; to misappreciate, to misunderstand, to misjudge; ~ *ses parents*, to disown one's relations; **se** ~, v.pr. not to know oneself, to forget what one has been; to misunderstand each other.

mécontent, -e (mekɔ̃tɑ̃), adj. Displeased, dissatisfied, discontented; *il est ~ de vous*, he is displeased with you; *vous êtes ~ de tout*, you are discontented with everything. **~, -e**, s.m.f. Malcontent, dissatisfied person.

mécontentement (mekɔ̃tɑ̃tmɑ̃), s.m. Displeasure, dissatisfaction; discontent; *donner du ~ à*, to displease.

mécontenter (mekɔ̃tɑ̃te), v.a. To displease, to dissatisfy.

mécréance (mekreɑ̃s), s.f. Disbelief, incredulity, unbelief; infidelity.

mécréant, -e (mekreɑ̃), p. adj. [pref. *mé*+OF *créant*] Unbelieving, infidel; incredulous, sceptical. **~**, s.m.f. Unbeliever, infidel.

mécroire (mekrwar), v.a.n. (rare) To disbelieve.

médaille (medaj), s.f. [It. *medaglia*] Medal; (arch.) medallion; metal badge or ticket; licence; *~ d'honneur*, prize-medal; *le revers de la ~*, the reverse of the medal, (fig.) the dark side of the picture; *toute ~ a son revers*, there is a dark side to every picture; *tourner la ~*, to look at the other side; *la ~ est renversée*, the tables are turned.

médaillé, -e (medaje), p. adj. Medalled, with a medal, rewarded with a medal. **~** s.m.f. Medallist, prizewinner.

médailler (medaje), v.a. To award a medal to, to reward with a medal; to authorize, to license.

médailleur (medajœr), s.m. Medal-engraver, die-sinker.

médaillier (medaje), s.m. Cabinet of medals, collection of medals.

médailliste (medajist), s.m. Collector of medals; medal-engraver.

médaillon (medajɔ̃), s.m. Medallion; locket.

Mède (mɛd), adj. s.m.f. [f. *Médie*] Median; Mede.

médecin (medsɛ̃), s.m. [L *medicus*] Doctor, physician, medical attendant; adviser, medical man; (fig.) healer; *~ consultant*, physician; *~ chirurgien*, general practitioner; surgeon; *faire venir le ~*, to send for the doctor; *il est abandonné des ~s*, the doctors have given him up; *le temps est un grand ~*, time cures all ills, time is the great healer.

médecine (medsin), s.f. [L *medicina*] Medicine, physic; medical science; the Faculty; remedy, draught, purge; *étudiant, docteur en ~*, student, doctor of medicine; *~ légale*, forensic or legal medicine, medical jurisprudence; *~ noire*, black draught; *~ de cheval*, violent remedy, extra large dose; *~ opératoire*, surgery; (fig.) *avaler sa ~*, to make the best of it; (prov.) *il ne faut pas prendre la ~ en plusieurs verres*, disagreeable things must be done quickly.

médeciner (mɛdsine), v.a. (rare) To physic, to doctor; **se ~**, v.pr. to doctor oneself.

médial, -e, (aux) (medjal), adj. s.m.f. [L *medialis*] (gram.) Medial.

médialement (medjalmɑ̃), adv. Medially.

médian, -e (medjɑ̃), adj. [L *medianus*] Median, middle; *veines ~es*, median veins. **~e**, s.f. (geom.) Median.

médianoche (medjanoʃ), s.m. [f. Span. *medio*+*noche*] Midnight supper after fast.

médiante (medjɑ̃t), s.f. [L *medians*] (mus.) Mediant.

médiastin (medjastɛ̃), s.m. [L *mediastinus*] (anat.) Mediastinum.

médiat, -e (medja), adj. [L *mediatus*] Mediate.

médiatement (medjatmɑ̃), adv. (rare) Mediately.

médiat-eur, -rice (medjatœr), s.m.f. [L *mediator*] Mediator; (fem.) mediatrix, mediatress. **~**, adj. Mediating, mediatory.

médiation (medja'sjɔ̃), s.f. Mediation.

médiatisation (medjatiza'sjɔ̃), s.f. Mediatization.

médiatiser (medjatize), v.a. To mediatize.

médical, -e, (aux) (medikal), adj. Medical; *matière ~e*, materia medica.

médicalement (medikalmɑ̃), adv. Medically.

médicament (medikamɑ̃), s.m. [L *medicamentum*] Medicament, medicine, remedy.

médicamentaire (medikamɑ̃tɛr), adj. Medicamental.

médicamentation (medikamɑ̃ta'sjɔ̃), s.f. Syn. of MÉDICATION.

médicamenter (medikamɑ̃te), v.a. To medicate; to doctor, to physic; **se ~**, v.pr. to doctor oneself.

médicamenteu-x, -se (medikamɑ̃tø), adj. Medicinal, medicamental.

médicastre (medikastr), s.m. [It. *medicastro*] Quack, medicaster.

médicat-eur, -rice (medikatœr), adj. Medicative.

médication (medika'sjɔ̃), s.f. [L *medicatio*] Medication.

médicinal, -e, (aux) (medisinal), adj. Medicinal.

médicinier (medisinje), s.m. Jatropha: a genus of plants of the order Euphorbiaceae.

médico-légal, -e, (aux) (medikolegal), adj. Medico-legal, pertaining to forensic medicine.

médiéval, -e, (aux) (medjeval), adj. [L *medium*+*aevum*] Medieval.

médiévisme (medjevism), s.m. Medievalism.
médiéviste (medjevist), s.m.f. Medievalist.
médimne (medimn), s.m. [Gr. *medimnos*] (ant.) Medimno.
médiocre (medjɔkr), adj. [L *mediocris*] Mediocre, middling; moderate, passable, indifferent. ~, s.m. Mediocrity.
médiocrement (medjɔkrəmɑ̃), adv. Middlingly, moderately; tolerably, passably; poorly; hardly, barely.
médiocrité (medjɔkrite), s.f. [L *mediocritas*] Mediocrity; moderate fortune; indifference, mediocre talent, inferior ability; want of cleverness; *un ramassis de ~s*, a crowd of nobodies.
médique (medik), adj. Median, pertaining to the Medes.
médire (medir), v.n. [pref. *mé+dire*] To slander, to speak ill or slightingly of, to traduce; to disparage; *~ de son prochain*, to speak ill of one's neighbour.
médisance (medizɑ̃s), s.f. [f. *médire*] Slander, scandal, backbiting, piece of scandal.
médisant, -e (medizɑ̃), p. adj. Slanderous, scandalous. ~, s.m.f. Slanderer, scandalmonger, backbiter.
méditati-f, -ve (meditatif), adj. Meditative, contemplative, pensive.
méditation (medita'sjɔ̃), s.f. Meditation, musing, reverie.
méditer (medite), v.a. [L *meditari*] To meditate, to think over, to consider; to contemplate, to plan, to project; *~ la ruine de X*, to plot X's ruin; ~, v.n. to meditate, to contemplate; *il passe sa vie à ~*, he spends his life in meditation.
méditerrané, -e (meditɛrane), adj. [f. L *medius+terra*] Midland, inland; *une mer ~e*, a mediterranean sea; *la Méditerranée*, the Mediterranean Sea.
méditerranéen, -ne (meditɛraneɛ̃), adj. Mediterranean.
médium (medjɔm), s.m. [L *medius*] Medium. ⚠ In English 'medium' has frequently the sense of *intermédiaire, truchement*; in French it is only used (colloquially) in the sense of person claiming ultra-physical perception.
médius (medjys), s.m. [L *medius*] Middle finger.
médoc (medɔk), s.m. [Fr. geog. orig.] Medoc wine (claret).
médullaire (medyllɛr), adj. [f. L *medulla*] (anat.) Medullar, medullary.
médulleu-x, -se (medyllø), adj. Medullary, containing marrow or pith.
méduse (medyz), s.f. [Gr. *Medousa*] (zool.) Medusa, jelly-fish; (myth.) Medusa; (fig.) *tête de ~*, ugly face, ghastly object.
méduser (medyze), v.a. [f. *méduse*] (fam.) To petrify, to nonplus, to stupefy, to astound, to dumbfound.
meeting (mitiŋ, metɛ̃g), s.m. [Engl. wd] Meeting; race-meeting; assembly. ⚠ In French *meeting* does not mean 'meeting with another person', *rencontre entre deux personnes*, but numerous assembly = *réunion populaire nombreuse*.
méfaire (mefɛr), v.n. (rare) [pref. *mé+faire*] To do evil, to do wrong, to do harm.
méfait (mefɛ), s.m. [f. *méfaire*] Misdeed, misdoing, crime; damage.
méfiance (mefjɑ̃s), s.f. Mistrust, distrust; suspicion; caution; (prov.) *~ est mère de sûreté*, safe bind, safe find.
méfiant, -e (mefjɑ̃), p. adj. Mistrustful, distrustful; suspicious, cautious.
(se) méfier (səmefje), v.pr. [pref. *mé+fier*] To be suspicious (*de*, of); to mistrust, to distrust; to suspect; to beware, to mind, to look out, to be on one's guard; *il se méfie de moi*, he mistrusts me; *il ne se méfie de rien*, he does not suspect anything.
még-, méga- (meg, mega), pref. [Gr. *megas*] Prefix indicating multiplication of a unit by a million; (fig.) prefix indicating largeness, great quantity.
mégadyne (megadin), s.f. (phys.) Megadyne.
mégajoule (megaʒul), s.m. (phys.) Megajoule.
mégalithe (megalit), s.m. Megalith.
mégalithique (megalitik), adj. Megalithic.
mégalocéphale (megalɔsefal), adj. s.m.f. Megalocephalic, megacephalic.
mégalogone (megalɔgɔn), adj. (min.) Megalogonal.
mégalomane (megalɔman), adj. s.m.f. Megalomaniac.
mégalomanie (megalɔmani), s.f. Megalomania.
mégalosaure (megalɔsor), s.m. (zool.) Megalosaurus.
mégamètre (megamɛtr), s.m. Megametre = 1,000,000 metres.
mégaphone (megafɔn), s.m. Megaphone, speaking-trumpet.
mégaptère (megaptɛr), s.m. (zool.) Megapter.
mégarde (megard), s.f. [pref. *mé+garde*] Inadvertence, inadvertency; *par ~*, inadvertently, unawares.
mégascope (megaskɔp), s.m. (obs.) Megascope.
mégathérium (megaterjɔm), s.m. (zool.) Megatherium.
mégère (meʒɛr), s.f. [L *megaera*] Shrew, vixen, termagant; *La ~ apprivoisée*, 'The Taming of the Shrew'.
mégie (meʒi), s.f. Tawing, leather-dressing.

mégir, mégisser (meʒir, meʒise), v.a. [L *medicare*] To taw (leather).
mégis (meʒi), s.m. Bath for dressing skins; (adj.) *veau* ~, tawed calf-leather.
mégisserie (meʒisri), s.f. Tawing, leather-dressing.
mégissier (meʒisje), s.m. Tawer, leather-dresser.
mégohm (megom), s.m. (phys.) Megohm.
mégot (mego), s.m. (slang) Cigar-stump, cigarette-end.
méhari (meari), s.m. [Arab. wd] Kind of dromedary.
méhariste (mearist), s.m. adj. Man, soldier, officer riding a dromedary.
meilleur, -e (mɛjœr), adj. [L *melior*] (compar. of *bon*) Better, preferable; *de ~e heure*, earlier; *le* ~ (superlative of *bon*), best, the best; *c'est mon ~ ami*, he is my best friend; *~ marché*, or *à ~ marché*, cheaper. ~, s.m.f. The best, the cream; *la raison du plus fort est toujours la ~e*, might is right; *le ~ n'en vaut rien*, bad is the best; *boire du* ~, to drink the best wine.
meistre, mestre (mɛstr), s.m. [f. *maître*] (naut.) Mainmast.
méjuger (meʒyʒe), v.n. [*mé+juger*] To misjudge.
mékhitariste (mekitarist), s.m. [f. *Mekhitar* (18th c.)] Mekhitarist.
mélampyre (melɑ̃pir), s.m. [Gr. *melas+pūros*] (bot.) Cow-wheat.
mélancolie (melɑ̃kɔli), s.f. [Gr. *melas+kholē*] Melancholy, sadness, gloom, dejection; *chasser la* ~, to drive away the spleen; *ne pas engendrer la* ~, to be a gay fellow; to make merry.
mélancolique (melɑ̃kɔlik), adj. Melancholy; dismal, sad, gloomy, mournful; *être* ~, to be in a brown study.
mélancoliquement (melɑ̃kɔlikmɑ̃), adv. Melancholily, mournfully, gloomily; sadly.
mélanémie (melanemi), [Gr. *melas+haima*] s.f. (med.) Melanaemia.
mélanésien, -ne (melanezjɛ̃), adj. s.m.f. [f. *Mélanésie*] Melanesian.
mélange (melɑ̃ʒ), s.m. [f. *mêler*] Mixture, mixing, mingling; blending, medley, jumble; crossing, intermixture (of breeds); alloy (of chemicals); mash (for brewing); ~s, pl. miscellaneous works, miscellanea; ~ *confus*, jumble; *sans* ~, unmixed, unblended, (fig.) pure, unalloyed.
mélangeoir (melɑ̃ʒwar), s.m. Movable receptacle in which to grind and mix certain substances.
mélanger (melɑ̃ʒe), v.a. To mix, to mingle, to blend, to cross, to intermix.
mélangeu-r, -se (melɑ̃ʒœr), s.m.f. Mixer, blender.
mélanippe (melanip), s.f. (ent.) Genus of lepidopterous insects.
mélanocétus (melanosetys), s.m. (ichth.) Genus of short-bodied fish with very large heads found in the Atlantic.
mélanose (melanoz), s.f. [f. Gr. *melas*] (med.) Melanosis.
mélasse (melas), s.f. [Span. *melaza*] Molasses, treacle; (slang) trouble, misfortune, misery, fix, pickle.
mélastomacées (melastɔmase), s.f.pl. (bot.) Melastomaceae.
mélastome (melastɔm), s.m. (bot.) Melastoma.
melchite (mɛlkit), s.m. (eccles. hist.) Melchite.
mêlé, -e (mɛle), p. adj. Mixed; miscellaneous; *sang* ~, mixed blood.
mêlée (mɛle), s.f. Scrimmage, tussle, conflict, fray, hand-to-hand fight; free fight; scuffle; altercation, squabble, quarrel; (Rugby football) scrimmage, scrum.
mêler (mɛle), v.a. [LL *misculare*, f. L *miscere*] To mix, to mingle, to blend, to cross; to mix up, to jumble; to entangle, to implicate, to involve; to shuffle (cards); ~ *de l'eau avec du vin*, to mix water with wine; ~ *les fils*, to entangle the threads; ~ *une serrure*, to force a lock; **se** ~, v.pr. to mingle, to be mingled, to be mixed, to intermingle, to mingle together; to interfere; to have a hand in; to get entangled, to get mixed up (*dans*, in); *de quoi vous mêlez-vous?*, what business is that of yours?; *mêlez-vous de vos affaires*, mind your own business; *le diable s'en mêle*, the devil is in it; *se ~ dans la foule*, to mingle with the crowd; *se ~ de politique*, to meddle with politics; *il faut toujours qu'il se mêle des affaires des autres*, he must have a finger in other people's pie.
mélèze (melɛz), s.m. [L *mel*] (bot.) Larch, European larch.
mélia (melja), s.m. (bot.) Melia.
méliacées (meljase), s.f.pl. (bot.) Meliaceae.
mélilot (melilo), s.m. (bot.) Melilot.
méli-mélo (melimelo), s.m. (colloq.) Medley, jumble.
mélinite (melinit), s.f. [Gr. *mēlinos*] Melinite.
mélique (melik), s.f. (bot.) Melic-grass.
mélique (melik), adj. [f. Gr. *melos*] Melic.
mélisse (melis), s.f. [Gr. *melissa*] (bot.) Balm, balm-mint; *eau de* ~, extract of balm.
mélitte (melit), s.f. (bot.) Bastard balm.
mellifère (mɛllifɛr), adj. Melliferous.
mellification (mɛllifika'sjɔ̃), s.f. [f. L *mel+facere*] Mellification.
mellifique (mellifik), adj. Mellific.
melliflue (mɛllifly), adj. [L *mellifluus*] Mellifluous; (fig. obs.) honeyed, soft; *des paroles ~s*, honeyed words.

mellite (mɛllit), s.m. [f. L *mel*] (med.) Medicament prepared with honey.
mélo (melo), s.m. abbrev. of *mélodrame.*
mélodie (melɔdi), s.f. [Gr. *melōdia*] Melody; (fig.) melodiousness, sweetness.
mélodieusement (melɔdjøzmɑ̃), adv. Melodiously; musically, sweetly, harmoniously, tunefully.
mélodieu-x, -se (melɔdjø), adj. Melodious; musical, sweet, harmonious, tuneful.
mélodique (melɔdik), adj. (mus.) Melodic.
mélodiste (melɔdist), s.m.f. Melodist.
mélodium (melɔdjɔm), s.m. (mus.) Melodeon, harmonium.
mélodramatique (melɔdramatik), adj. Melodramatic.
mélodramatiser (melɔdramatize), v.a. To melodramatize.
mélodrame (melɔdram), s.m. [Gr. *melos* +*drama*] Melodrama.
méloé (meloe), s.m. (ent.) Meloe, May-beetle, oil-beetle.
mélographe (melɔgraf), s.m. [Gr. *melos*+ *graphein*] (mus.) Melograph.
mélographie (melɔgrafi), s.f. Melography.
mélomane (melɔman), s.m.f. adj. Melomaniac.
mélomanie (melɔmani), s.f. Melomania.
melon (məlɔ̃), s.m. [L *melo*] **1.** (bot.) Melon; ~ *d'eau,* water-melon; ~ *cantaloup,* cantaloup melon; **2.** bowler hat.
melongène (məlɔ̃ʒɛn), s.f. Syn. of AUBERGINE.
mélonide (melɔnid), adj. [Gr. *mēlon*+ *eidos*] (bot.) Apple-shaped.
melonné, -e (məlɔne), adj. Melon-shaped. ~**e,** s.f. Variety of pumpkin.
melonnière (məlɔnjɛr), s.f. Melon-bed.
mélopée (melɔpe), s.f. [f. Gr. *melos*+ *poiein*] Melopœia; melody; recitative chant; (Gr. ant.) rules for song-composition.
méloplaste (melɔplast), s.m. [Gr. *melos*+ *plastos*] (mus.) Meloplast.
mélotrope (melɔtrɔp), s.m. [Gr. *melos*+ *tropein*] (mus.) Melotrope.
membrane (mɑ̃bran), s.f. [L *membrana*] (anat.) Membrane; film; ~ *interdigitale,* web (of water-bird's foot); ~ *muqueuse,* mucous membrane; ~ *séreuse,* serous membrane.
membraneu-x, -se (mɑ̃branø), adj. Membranous.
membraniforme (mɑ̃branifɔrm), adj. Membraniform.
membranule (mɑ̃branyl), s.f. Small membrane.
membre (mɑ̃br), s.m. [L *membrum*] Member; limb; organ of virility; (naut.) rib-timber, part of frame; ~ *de l'Association,* member of the Association; *il est traité comme un des* ~*s de la famille,* he is treated as one of the family; *il a mal dans tous ses* ~*s,* he aches in every limb; (colloq.) *se saigner aux quatre* ~*s pour X,* to work oneself to the bone for X.
membré, -e (mɑ̃bre), adj. Membered, limbed; *être bien* ~, to be strong-limbed, to be well-built.
membru, -e (mɑ̃bry), adj. Strong, stout-limbed, large-limbed.
membrure (mɑ̃bryr), s.f. Frame, the human frame; ribs, timbers (of a ship); (carp.) panel-frame.
même (mɛm), adj. [LL *metipsimus,* f. *egometipse*] Same; self-same, very same; self, himself, herself, itself; *la* ~ *chose,* the same thing; *le jour* ~, the self-same day; *lui-*~, himself; *elle a fait cela d'elle-*~, she did that of her own accord; *eux-*~*s,* themselves; *c'est cela* ~, that is just the point; *Marie? c'est la bonté même!,* Mary? she is goodness itself (or incarnate). ~, s.m. Same, the same; *cela revient au* ~, that comes to the same thing. ~, adv. Even, also, likewise; *il a* ~ *tué son fils,* he even killed his son; *être à* ~ *de,* to be in a position to; to be able to; *boire à* ~, to drink out of the bottle; *manger à* ~, to eat off the dish; *de* ~, likewise, in the same way; *faites de* ~, do the same; *de* ~ *que,* just as, as well as, in the same way as; *mettre à* ~ *de,* to enable; *quand* ~ *il me l'aurait dit,* even if he had told me; *vous êtes à* ~ *de me rendre service,* you are in a position to do me a service; *tout de* ~, all the same; in the same way.
mêmement (mɛmmɑ̃), adv. (obs.) Likewise, in the same way.
mémento (memɛ̃to), s.m. [L wd] Memento; agenda; memorandum-book; synopsis, epitome; prayer.
mémoire[1] (memwar), s.f. [L *memoria*] Memory; recollection, remembrance; commemoration; fame; *à la* ~ *de,* in memory of; *avoir une* ~ *de lièvre,* to have a short memory; *conserver la* ~ *de,* to remember; *en* ~ *de,* in memory of; *de* ~ *d'homme,* within the memory of man; *je n'en ai pas la moindre* ~, I have not the slightest recollection of it; *une* ~ *fidèle,* a retentive memory; *rappeler quelque chose à la* ~ *de quelqu'un,* to remind somebody of something; *si j'ai bonne* ~, if I remember rightly; *jouer de* ~, to play from memory; *conserver quelque chose dans la* ~, to bear something in mind; *pour* ~, as a reminder; for information.
mémoire[2] (memwar), s.m. Memorandum; bill, statement of account; report, treatise; memorial; (pl.) memoirs; *dresser un* ~, to draw up an account; ~ *acquitté,* receipted bill; ~ *d'apothicaire,* exorbitant bill.
mémorable (memɔrabl), adj. [L *memorabilis*] Memorable.

mémorablement (memɔrabləmɑ̃), adv. Memorably.

mémorandum (memɔrɑ̃dɔm), s.m. [L wd] Memorandum; memorandum-book, memo.

mémorati-f, -ve (memɔratif), adj. Mindful.

mémorial (pl. **aux**) (memɔrjal), s.m. Memorial; (comm.) waste-book; memoirs.

mémorialiste (memɔrjalist), s.m.f. Memorialist.

mémorisation (memɔriza′sjɔ̃), s.f. Memorization.

menaçant, -e (mənasɑ̃), p. adj. Threatening, menacing.

menace (mənas), s.f. [L *minacia*] Menace, threat; *~s en l'air*, empty or idle threats.

menacer (mənase), v.a. To threaten; (Lit.) to menace; to forebode; to portend; to impend; *~ ruine, ~ de tomber*, to totter, to be on the point of ruin; *~ du poing*, to shake one's fist at.

ménade (menad), s.f. [Gr. *mainas*] Maenad, bacchante; (fig.) dissolute or passionate woman.

ménage (menaʒ), s.m. [LL *mansionaticum*] Housekeeping, housewifery; household, house, family; household goods, set of furniture; married couple, couple, husband and wife; housework; management, good management; thrift, saving, economy; *elle entend bien le ~*, she is a good housewife; *se mettre en ~*, to set up house, to marry; to live together as married people; *faire bon ~*, to get on well together; *faire le ~*, to do the housework; to clean up; *femme de ~*, charwoman; *jeune ~*, young couple; *pain de ~*, home-made, ordinary bread; *~ de garçon*, bachelor's household; *~ à trois*, three-cornered establishment, the eternal triangle.

ménageable (menaʒabl), adj. That should be taken care of or looked after.

ménagement (menaʒmɑ̃), s.m. Regard, consideration; tenderness; circumspection, discretion; caution, care; *sans ~s*, unsparingly; *je lui ai expliqué la chose sans ~s*, I explained the case to him most plainly.

ménager (menaʒe), v.a. [f. *ménage*] To husband, to be sparing of, to save, to economize; to take care of, to be careful of, to treat with caution; to treat kindly, to treat with respect, to take care not to offend, to humour; to reserve; to procure; to contrive, to manage; to arrange, to prepare, to bring about; *~ X*, to treat X kindly, tactfully; *~ ses forces*, to spare one's strength; *~ ses ressources*, to husband one's resources; *~ une agréable surprise à X*, to prepare a pleasant surprise for X; *~ une étoffe*, to make the most of a piece of material; *~ un escalier dans une maison*, to contrive a staircase in a house; *~ ses paroles*, to speak little; *~ la chèvre et le chou*, to run with the hare and hunt with the hounds; (prov.) *qui veut aller loin ménage sa monture*, he who wishes to live long avoids excess; slow and steady wins the race; **se ~**, v.pr. to take care of oneself, to spare oneself; to behave with caution; to have regard for one another's feelings; to keep on good terms with each other.

ménag-er, -ère (menaʒe), adj. Economical, saving, thrifty, careful; frugal, sparing; *eaux ~ères*, slops. **~ère**, s.f. **1.** Housewife, housekeeper; *elle est bonne ~*, she is a good housewife; **2.** cruet-stand.

ménagerie (menaʒri), s.f. [f. *ménager*] Menagerie; (obs.) poultry-yard.

ménageu-r, -se (menaʒœr), s.m.f. Time-server.

mendaïte, mandaïte, mendéen (mɑ̃dait, mɑ̃deɛ̃), adj. s.m. (relig.) Mandaean.

mendiant, -e (mɑ̃djɑ̃), s.m.f. Beggar, mendicant; *les quatre ~s*, (*a*) the four orders of mendicant friars: Jacobins, Augustins, Franciscans, Carmelites; (*b*) dessert of hazel-nuts, figs, almonds, raisins.

mendicité (mɑ̃disite), s.f. Beggary, mendicity, begging, vagrancy; beggars, mendicancy.

mendier (mɑ̃dje), v.a. [L *mendicare*] To beg, to beg for; (fig.) to solicit, to implore; *~ son pain*, to beg one's bread; *~ sa vie*, to live by begging; *~ l'appui de X*, to solicit X's help; *~*, v.n. to beg.

mendole (mɑ̃dol), s.f. [It. wd] (ichth.) Mendole, cackerel.

meneau (pl. **-x**) (mɛno), s.m. [etym. unkn.] (arch.) Mullion.

ménechme (menɛkm), s.m. [f. *Les Ménechmes* of Plautus] Person bearing an extraordinary resemblance to another.

menée (məne), s.f. [f. *mener*] (hunt.) Track of a stag; (fig., usually in pl.) underhand dealing, conspiracy, plot, intrigue, scheming.

mener (məne), v.a. [L *minare*] To guide, to conduct, to lead; to drive (a carriage); to steer; to bring, to convey, to carry, to take; to lead (a dance, &c.); to manage, to administer, to govern, to carry on; to draw, to trace, to introduce; *mené par sa femme*, hen-pecked; *~ à bonne fin*, to carry out, to bring to a successful issue; *~ bien sa barque*, to manage one's affairs well; *~ de front*, to carry on simultaneously; *~ grand train*, to cut a dash; *~ une vie déréglée*, to lead an irregular life; *~ X rudement*, to treat X badly; *~ X par le nez*, to lead X by the nose; *~ à la baguette*, to rule with a high hand; *~ grand deuil de quelque chose*, to regret something bitterly.

ménestrel (menɛstrɛl), s.m. [L *ministerialis*] Minstrel.
ménétrier (menetrie), s.m. [L *ministerialis*] Fiddler.
meneu-r, -se (mənœr), s.m.f. Conductor, leader; ring-leader; **~se,** s.f. (rare) agent for wet-nurses.
menhir (mɛnir), s.m. [Celt. *men+hir*] (archaeol.) Menhir.
méniane (menjan), s.f. [L *maenianum*] (arch.) Verandah, balcony (in Italy).
ménil, mesnil (menil), s.m. [L *manere*] (obs.) Abode, habitation, village.
ménille (menij), s.f. Handle used by paper-makers; ring to which convicts were chained.
menin (mənɛ̃), s.m. [Span. *menino*] (in Spain) Young nobleman chosen as companion to the children of the royal family; (in France) gentleman attached to the person of the Dauphin; (by ext.) (pej.) minion, favourite.
ménine (menin), s.f. [Span. *menina*] Lady of quality attached to the person of a Spanish princess.
méninge (menɛ̃ʒ), s.f. [Gr. *mēnigx*] (anat.) Meninx.
méningite (menɛ̃ʒit), s.f. (med.) Meningitis.
ménispermacées, ménispermées (menispɛrmase, menispɛrme), s.f.pl. (bot.) Menispermaceae.
ménisque (menisk), s.m. [Gr. *mēniskos*] (opt.) Meniscus; crescent-shaped ornament.
mennonite (mɛnɔnit), s.m. [f. *Menno* Simons (1492-1559)] (relig.) Mennonite.
ménologe (menɔlɔʒ), s.m. [Gr. *mēn+logos*] Menology.
menon (mənɔ̃), s.m. Ram that leads herd to new pastures; kind of goat found in the Levant, the skin of which is made into morocco leather.
ménopause (menɔpoz), s.f. [Gr. *mēn+pausis*] (physiol.) Menopause.
menotte (mənɔt), s.f. [f. *main*] (colloq.) Little hand, tiny hand (of children); **~s,** pl. handcuffs, manacles; *mettre les ~s à*, to handcuff, (fig.) to hamper.
menotter (mənɔte), v.a. To handcuff, to manacle.
mense (mɑ̃s), s.f. [L *mensa*] Income, revenue, stipend (of abbey, ecclesiastic); (obs.) table, board.
mensonge (mɑ̃sɔ̃ʒ), s.m. [LL *mentionica*] Lie, falsehood, untruth, fib, story; (fig.) fiction, fable; illusion, delusion; vanity; *débiter des ~s*, to tell lies; *la poésie vit de ~s*, poetry is all fiction; *tout n'est que ~*, all is vanity.
mensong-er, -ère (mɑ̃sɔ̃ʒe), adj. Lying, untrue, deceitful; false, illusory.
mensongèrement (mɑ̃sɔ̃ʒɛrmɑ̃), adv. Untruly, falsely, deceitfully.
menstrues (mɑ̃stry), s.f.pl. [L *menstruus*] (physiol.) Catamenia, menses, menstrual flow.
mensualité (mɑ̃sɥalite), s.f. Monthly payment; monthly allowance; monthly instalment; *payer par ~s*, to pay by monthly instalments.
mensuel, -le (mɑ̃sɥɛl), adj. [L *mensualis*] Monthly.
mensuellement (mɑ̃sɥɛlmɑ̃), adv. Monthly.
mensurabilité (mɑ̃syrabilite), s.f. [f. *mensurable*] Mensurability.
mensurable (mɑ̃syrabl), adj. [f. L *mensura*] Mensurable, measurable.
mensurateur (mɑ̃syratœr), s.m. adj. That measures; *appareil ~*, measuring apparatus.
mensuration (mɑ̃syra'sjɔ̃), s.f. [L *mensuratio*] Mensuration.
mentagre (mɑ̃tagr), s.f. [L *mentagra*] (med.) Mentagra.
mental, -e, (aux) (mɑ̃tal), adj. [f. L *mens*] Mental; *calcul ~*, mental arithmetic; *aliénation ~e*, insanity; *maladie ~e*, disease of the mind.
mentalement (mɑ̃talmɑ̃), adv. Mentally.
mentalité (mɑ̃talite), s.f. [f. *mental*] Mentality.
menterie (mɑ̃tri), s.f. [f. *mentir*] (colloq.) Story, fib, falsehood.
menteu-r, -se (mɑ̃tœr), s.m.f. Liar, story-teller, fibber. **~,** adj. Lying, false, deceitful.
menteusement (mɑ̃tøzmɑ̃), adv. Deceitfully, falsely.
menthe (mɑ̃t), s.f. [L *mentha*] (bot.) Mint; peppermint; *~ poivrée, anglaise*, peppermint; *~ verte*, spearmint; *~ aquatique*, watermint; *~ coq*, tansy; *~ pouliot*, penny-royal; *~ de chat*, catmint; *pastilles de ~*, peppermint drops, peppermints; *crème de ~*, crème de menthe, liqueur flavoured with peppermint.
menthol (mɑ̃tɔl), s.m. (chem.) Menthol.
mentholé, -e (mɑ̃tɔle), adj. (chem.) Mentholated, containing menthol.
mentiane (mɑ̃sjan), s.f. (bot.) Guelder rose; syn. VIORNE.
mention (mɑ̃sjɔ̃), s.f. [L *mentio*] Mention; *faire ~ de*, to mention; *~ honorable*, distinction, honourable mention (in an examination).
mentionner (mɑ̃sjɔne), v.a. To mention, to make mention of; to name; *mentionné ci-dessus*, above mentioned.
mentir (mɑ̃tir), v.n. [L *mentiri*] To lie, to tell a lie, an untruth; to fib, to tell stories; *a beau ~ qui vient de loin*, travellers tell fine tales; *faire ~ le proverbe*, to belie the proverb; *il en a menti*, he lied; *à ne point ~*, to tell the truth; *bon sang ne peut ~*, true blue will never stain.

menton (mɑ̃tɔ̃), s.m. [L *mentum*] Chin; *un double ~, un ~ à double étage*, a double chin; *~ de galoche*, turned-up chin, nut-cracker chin.

mentonnet (mɑ̃tɔnɛ), s.m. Catch (of lock, wheel, &c.).

mentonnière (mɑ̃tɔnjɛr), s.f. Chin-band, chin-piece (of helmet); chin-strap; chin-bandage.

mentor (mɑ̃tɔr), s.m. [f. Gr. prop. n. *Mentor*] Mentor, guide, tutor.

menu, -e (məny), adj. [L *minutus*] Slim, slender, spare, thin, small, fine; inconsiderable, petty, lesser, minor; common; *le ~ peuple*, the lower classes, the common people; *~s frais*, small expenses, sundry expenses; *~e monnaie*, small change; *~s grains*, small grain (oats, barley, &c.); *~ plomb*, small shot; *~ gibier*, small game; *~s plaisirs*, pocket-money, pin-money. *~*, adv. Small, fine, minutely; *hacher ~*, to mince; *écrire ~*, to write small; *pleuvoir dru et ~*, to rain thick and fast; *marcher, trotter ~*, to walk with quick short steps; *la gent trotte-~* (in La Fontaine), rats and mice.

menu (məny), s.m. Minute detail; particulars; bill of fare, menu; lower class; small linen; *par le ~*, minutely, at great length, with all particulars; *des gens du ~*, people of the lower class; *le ~ d'un repas*, the bill of fare.

menuaille (mənɥɑj), s.f. (rare) [f. *menu*] Small change, small money; small fish, small fry; trash.

menuet (mənɥɛ), s.m. [f. *menu*] Minuet.

menuisage (mənɥizaʒ), s.m. [f. *menuiser*] Sawing; carpentering, joining.

menuise, menuisaille (mənɥiz, mənɥizɑj), s.f. Small shot; small fish.

menuiser (mənɥize), v.n. To cut, to saw, to hew; to do carpenter's or joiner's work.

menuiserie (mənɥizri), s.f. Carpentry, woodwork, joinery, joiner's work.

menuisier (mənɥizje), s.m. adj. Joiner, carpenter; *~ en bâtiments*, house-carpenter.

ménure (menyr), s.f. (ornith.) Lyre-bird.

menu-vair (mənyvɛr), s.m. Minever, miniver; syn. PETIT-GRIS.

ményanthe (menjɑ̃t), s.m. (bot.) Marsh trefoil, buckbean.

méphistophélique (mefistɔfelik), adj. [f. *Méphistophélès*] Mephistophelian.

méphitique (mefitik), adj. [L *mephiticus*] Mephitic.

méphitisme (mefitism), s.m. Mephitis.

méplat, -e (mepla), adj. [*mé+plat*] Thicker on one side than on the other; (paint.) *lignes ~es*, lines forming the transition from one plane to another. *~*, s.m. Any one of the planes which together form the surface of a body.

(se) méprendre (səmeprɑ̃dr), v.pr. [*mé+prendre*] To mistake, to make a mistake, to be mistaken; to misapprehend; *c'est à ne pas s'y ~*, you cannot make a mistake; *c'est son père à s'y ~*, he is the very image of his father; *vous vous méprenez*, you are mistaken.

mépris (mepri), s.m. [f. *mépriser*] Contempt, scorn, disregard, disrespect; (pl.) contemptuous treatment, contumelious language; *avoir du ~ pour X*, to despise X; *au ~ de*, in defiance of, in contempt of; *la familiarité engendre le ~*, familiarity breeds contempt.

méprisable (meprizabl), adj. Contemptible, despicable.

méprisablement (meprizabləmɑ̃), adv. Contemptibly, despicably.

méprisant, -e (meprizɑ̃), p. adj. Contemptuous, scornful.

méprise (mepriz), s.f. Mistake, oversight, error, misunderstanding; *faire une lourde ~*, to make a great mistake; *par ~*, by mistake.

mépriser (meprize), v.a. [*mé+priser*] To scorn, to despise; to set at naught, to slight, to disregard; *se ~*, to despise oneself; to despise each other.

mer (mɛr), s.f. [L *mare*] Sea; deep, main, ocean, tide; (fig.) a vast quantity or extent of; *par ~*, by sea; *une goutte d'eau dans la ~*, a drop in the ocean; *un homme à la ~*, a man overboard; (fig.) a man who has lost his reputation; *aller au bord de la ~*, to go to the seaside; *ce n'est pas la ~ à boire*, it is not such a formidable thing!, it's easy enough!; *chercher X par ~ et par terre*, to look for X high and low; *d'outre-~*, from across the seas; (naut.) *embarquer un coup de ~*, to ship a sea; *en pleine ~*, in the open sea, on the high seas; *gens de ~*, seafaring men; *homme de ~*, seafaring man, sailor; *jeter à la ~*, to throw overboard; *tomber à la ~*, to fall overboard; *pleine ~, haute ~*, open sea, high sea; *basse ~*, low tide; *~ intérieure*, inland sea; *loup de ~*, Jack Tar, old salt; *mal de ~*, seasickness; *avoir le mal de ~*, to be seasick; *mettre à la ~*, to put to sea; to launch; *porter de l'eau à la ~*, to carry coals to Newcastle; *tenir la ~*, to be seaworthy (of a ship); to keep out at sea; (fig.) to rule the waves; *prendre la ~*, to go to sea; (naut.) *un coup de ~*, a sea; *grosse ~*, heavy sea; *la ~ moutonne*, the sea is foaming; there are white horses; *la ~ est étale*, it is slack water; (fig.) *une ~ de tribulations*, a sea of troubles.

mercanti (mɛrkɑ̃ti), s.m. [wd originally applied to Algerian traders following troops] Profiteer, unscrupulous tradesman; bazaar-merchant; camp-follower.

mercantile (mɛrkɑ̃til), adj. [It. *mercantile*] Mercantile, commercial; mercenary.

mercantilisme (mɛrkɑ̃tilism), s.m. (often pej.) Mercantilism, trade spirit; commercialism.

mercaptan (mɛrkaptɑ̃), s.m. [f. L *mercurium+captans*] (chem.) Mercaptan.

mercenaire (mɛrsənɛr), adj. [L *mercenarius*] Mercenary, venal, paid, hired. ~, s.m. Hired soldier, labourer, hireling; mercenary; ~, s.f. hired working woman.

mercenariat (mɛrsənarja), s.m. Profession of a mercenary or hired soldier.

mercenarisme (mɛrsənarism), s.m. Mercenariness.

mercerie (mɛrsri), s.f. [f. LL *merciarius*] Mercery, haberdashery.

merci (mɛrsi), s.f. [L *merces*] Mercy, discretion, will, pleasure, pity; *crier, implorer* ~, to cry for mercy; *sans* ~, merciless, pitiless; *être à la* ~ *de X*, to be at the mercy of X. ~, s.m. interj. Thanks, thank you, no thank you; *Dieu* ~, thank God; *grand* ~, *mille* ~*s*, many thanks.

merci-er, -ère (mɛrsje), s.m.f. [LL *merciarius*, f. L *merx*] Haberdasher; mercer. ⚠ Usually 'mercer' = *marchand de tissus, soieries, nouveautés de luxe*.

mercredi (mɛrkrədi), s.m. [L *Mercurii dies*] Wednesday; *le* ~ *des cendres*, Ash-Wednesday.

mercure (mɛrkyr), s.m. [L *Mercurius*], Mercury, quicksilver; (astr.) Mercury.

mercureux (mɛrkyrø), adj. m. (chem.) Mercurous.

mercuriale[1] (mɛrkyrjal), s.f. [f. L *Mercurius*] Market-prices (of grain).

mercuriale[2] (mɛrkyrjal), s.f. [f. L *Mercurii dies*] Rebuke, reprimand; (obs.) judicial assembly held every Wednesday in Paris; speech, harangue pronounced on this occasion.

mercuriale[3] (mɛrkyrjal), s.f. [L *mercurialis herba*] (bot.) Mercury; ~ *vivace*, dog's-mercury.

mercuriel, -le (mɛrkyrjɛl), adj. Mercurial. ⚠ *Mercuriel* is not used like 'mercurial' with the fig. meanings: *vif d'esprit, animé, prompt à la repartie; changeant, capricieux, évaporé*.

mercurique (mɛrkyrik), adj. m. Mercuric.

merde (mɛrd), s.f. [L *merda*] (very vulg., to be avoided) Excrement (of man, animals); (interj.) ~*!*, you be blowed!, blast you!

merdeu-x, -se (mɛrdø), adj. (very vulg., to be avoided) Filthy, nasty.

mère (mɛr), s.f. [L *mater*] Mother; dam (of animals); hen (of birds); (fig.) parent, cause, source, reason; the chief, the head; matrix, mould (in pottery); *la révérende* ~, the Reverend Mother (superior of a convent); *notre* ~ *commune*, mother earth; *notre première* ~, Eve; ~ *patrie*, mother country; *belle-*~, step-mother, mother-in-law; *la Grèce a été la* ~ *des beaux-arts*, Greece was the cradle of the fine arts; ~ *de famille*, mother of a family; ~ *nourrice*, foster-mother; ~ *de vinaigre*, mother (produced by fermentation of vinegar). ~, adj. Mother; first, chief, principal; *la reine* ~, the queen mother; *langue* ~, mother tongue; *l'idée* ~, the chief idea or principal idea.

mère (mɛr), adj. f. [f. L *merus*] Pure, fine; ~ *goutte*, wine from unpressed grapes; ~ *laine*, fine lamb's-wool.

méreau (pl. -x) (mero), s.m. [LL *merellus*] Token, counter, check; disk (used at hopscotch).

mérétrice, mérétrix (meretris, meretriks), s.f. [L *meretrix*] (zool.) Genus of mollusca.

mergule (mɛrgyl), s.m. [f. L *mergus*] (ornith.) Guillemot, goosander.

méridien, -ne (meridjɛ̃), adj. [L *meridianus*] Meridian, meridional; *hauteur méridienne*, meridian altitude; *ligne méridienne*, meridian line. ~, s.m. Meridian; *premier* ~, first meridian; ~ *magnétique*, magnetic meridian. ~**ne**, s.f. **1.** Meridian line; **2.** siesta, midday nap; *faire la* ~, to take an afternoon nap.

méridional, -e, (aux) (meridjɔnal), adj. Meridional, southern. ~, s.m. Southerner, inhabitant of the south.

meringue (mərɛ̃g), s.f. [etym. dub.] Meringue.

meringuer (mərɛ̃ge), v.a. (cook.) To make a meringue of, to make into a meringue; to cover with meringue.

mérinos (merinos), s.m. [Span. *merino*] Merino sheep; merino wool; merino (material).

merise (məriz), s.f. (bot.) Wild cherry.

merisier (mərizje), s.m. Wild cherry-tree.

méritant, -e (meritɑ̃), p. adj. Meritorious, deserving, worthy.

mérite (merit), s.m. [L *meritum*] Merit, worth; desert, due; talent, ability, capacity, attainments; *il sera traité selon ses* ~*s*, he shall be dealt with according to his deserts; *se donner le* ~ *de quelque chose*, to give oneself the credit of having done something; *se faire un* ~ *de*, to glory in.

mériter (merite), v.a. [f. *mérite*] To merit, to deserve; to earn, to gain; to need, to require; ~ *des éloges*, to merit praise; *cette nouvelle mérite confirmation*, that news requires confirmation; ~, v.n. to be praiseworthy, to be meritorious, to be deserving; *cela ne mérite pas qu'on en parle*, that is not worth talking about; *il a bien mérité de sa patrie*, he has deserved well of his country; *il mérite d'être récompensé*, he deserves to be rewarded.

méritoire (meritwar), p. adj. Meritorious, deserving.

méritoirement (meritwarmɑ̃), adv. Meritoriously.

merl, maerl (mɛrl), s.m. [dialect form of *marne*] Marl.

merlan (mɛrlɑ̃), s.m. [f. *merle*] (ichth.) Whiting; (colloq.) hairdresser, barber.

merle (mɛrl), s.m. [L *merula*] (ornith.) Blackbird; (colloq.) fellow; *un fin ~*, a cunning blade; *un vilain ~*, (or, iron.) *un beau ~*, a cad; a disagreeable fellow; *un dénicheur de ~s*, a sharper; *un ~ blanc*, a mare's nest; an extraordinary fellow; something impossible, incredible.

merleau (pl. **-x**) (mɛrlo), s.m. Young blackbird.

merlette (mɛrlɛt), s.f. Hen blackbird; (herald.) martlet.

merlin[1] (mɛrlɛ̃), s.m. [LL *martellinus*] Pole-axe; axe; cleaver, chopper.

merlin[2] (mɛrlɛ̃), s.m. [Flemish *maarline*] (naut.) Marline.

merlon (mɛrlɔ̃), s.m. [It. *merlone*] (fort.) Merlon.

merluche (mɛrlyʃ), s.f. **merlus** (mɛrly), s.m. (ichth.) Hake; stockfish.

mérovingien, -ne (merovɛ̃ʒjɛ̃), adj. [f. *Mérovée*] Merovingian.

merrain, mairain (mɛrɛ̃), s.m. [LL *materiamen*] Stave-wood, clap-board; beam (of deer's antlers).

merveille (mɛrvɛj), s.f. [L *mirabilia*] Wonder, marvel, miracle, prodigy; *faire ~*, to do wonderfully well, to do remarkably well; *faire des ~s*, to do wonders; *promettre monts et ~s*, to promise wonders; *les sept ~s du monde*, the seven wonders of the world; *à ~*, adv. loc. admirably, wonderfully well, capitally, marvellously; *tout va à ~*, everything is going swimmingly; *je me porte à ~*, I am in splendid health; I am very fit.

merveilleusement (mɛrvɛjøzmɑ̃), adv. Wonderfully, marvellously, splendidly.

merveilleu-x, -se (mɛrvɛjø), adj. Wonderful, wondrous, marvellous; excellent, superior, capital; strange. ~, s.m. The wonderful, the marvellous, the wonderful part; the supernatural; ~, s.m.f. dandy, beau, fop, (fem.) affected lady (under the Directory, 1795).

mérycisme (merisism), s.m. [Gr. *mērukismos*] (med.) Merycism.

mes (mɛ), adj. poss. pl. of *mon, ma*. See MON.

més- (me), pref. See MÉ.

mésair, mézair (mezɛr), s.m. [It. *mezzaria*] (riding) Canter.

mésaise (mezɛz), s.m. [*més*+*aise*] (obs.) Malaise, uncomfortableness, uneasiness; lack (of money).

mésalliance (mezaljɑ̃s), s.f. Misalliance, bad match.

mésallier (mezallje), v.a. [pref. *més*+*allier*] To misally; (fig.) to lower, to disparage; **se ~**, v.pr. to marry beneath one.

mésange (mezɑ̃ʒ), s.f. [f. OHG *meisa*] (ornith.) Titmouse, tomtit, tit.

mésangette (mezɑ̃ʒɛt), s.f. Bird-trap.

mésarriver (mezarive), v. impers. (rare) [*més*+*arriver*] To turn out ill, to happen ill, to come to grief; *il vous en mésarrivera*, you will come to grief through it, or, on that account.

mésavenance (mezavnɑ̃s), s.f. (rare) Disagreeableness; unlucky event.

mésavenant, -e (mezavnɑ̃), adj. (rare) Displeasing, disagreeable.

mésavenir, mésadvenir (mezavnir, mezadvənir), v. impers. (rare) [*més*+*advenir*] To turn out ill.

mésaventure (mezavɑ̃tyr), s.f. Mischance, misadventure, mishap.

mesdames, mesdemoiselles (mɛdam, mɛdmwazɛl), s.f.pl. (pl. of *madame, mademoiselle*) Ladies; *mesdames et messieurs*, ladies and gentlemen.

mésentente (mezɑ̃tɑ̃t), s.f. [pref. *més*+*entente*] Misunderstanding, disagreement.

mésentère (mezɑ̃tɛr), s.m. [Gr. *mesos*+*enteron*] (anat.) Mesentery.

mésentérique (mezɑ̃terik), adj. (anat.) Mesenteric.

mésentérite (mezɑ̃terit), s.f. (med.) Mesenteritis.

mésestimation (mezɛstima'sjɔ̃), s.f. [*més*+*estimation*] Wrong estimation.

mésestime (mezɛstim), s.f. [pref. *més*+*estime*] Disesteem, discredit, disrepute.

mésestimer (mezɛstime), v.a. [pref. *més*+*estimer*] To disesteem, to think little of; to underrate, to undervalue, to underestimate.

mésintelligence (mezɛ̃tɛliʒɑ̃s), s.f. [*més*+*intelligence*] Misunderstanding, disagreement, discord, variance.

mésinterprétation (mezɛ̃tɛrpreta'sjɔ̃), s.f. [pref. *més*+*interprétation*] Misinterpretation.

mésinterpréter (mezɛ̃tɛrprete), v.a. To misinterpret.

mesmérien, -ne (mɛsmerjɛ̃), adj. Mesmeric. ~, s.m. Mesmerist.

mesmérisme (mɛsmerism), s.m. [f. prop. n. *Mesmer*] Mesmerism.

méso- (mezo), pref. [Gr. *mesos*] Middle.

mésocarpe (mezokarp), s.m. [Gr. *mesos*+*karpos*] (bot.) Mesocarp.

mésocéphale (mezosefal), adj. [Gr. *mesos*+*kephalē*] (anat.) Mesocephalic.

mésoderme (mezodɛrm), s.m. [Gr. *mesos*+*derma*] (anat.) Mesoderm.

mésoffrir (mezofrir), v.t. [pref. *més*+*offrir*] (rare) To underbid.

mésologie (mezoloʒi), s.f. [Gr. *meson*+*logos*] (biol.) Mesology.

mésologique (mezoloʒik), adj. (biol.) Mesological.

mésophyte (mezɔfit), s.m. [Gr. *mesos*+*phuton*] (bot.) Mesophyte.

mésopotamien, -ne (mezɔpɔtamjɛ̃), adj. s.m.f. [f. *Mésopotamie*] Mesopotamian.

mésopotamique (mezɔpɔtamik), adj. [f. *Mésopotamie*] Mesopotamian.

mésothorax (mezɔtɔraks), s.m. [Gr. *mesos* +*thōrax*] (anat., zool.) Mesothorax.

mésozoïque (mezɔzɔik), adj. [Gr. *mesos*+*zōon* (geol.) Mesozoic.

mesquin, -e (mɛskɛ̃), adj. [It. *meschino*] Shabby; paltry, poor, pitiful; mean, stingy, niggardly; illiberal, narrow; *une chambre ~e*, a shabby room; *des idées ~es*, narrow ideas; *être ~*, to be stingy.

mesquinement (mɛskinmɑ̃), adv. Shabbily, meanly; stingily.

mesquinerie (mɛskinri), s.f. Meanness, shabbiness, poorness; stinginess; shabby trick.

mess (mɛs), s.m. [Engl. *mess*, f. Fr. *mets*] Mess, officers' table.

message (mɛsaʒ), s.m. [LL *missaticum*] Message; official communication; *porter un ~*, to carry or take a message.

messag-er, -ère (mɛsaʒe), s.m.f. Messenger, carrier; coach, stage-coach; (fig.) harbinger, herald, forerunner; (ornith.) secretary-bird; *un ~ d'État*, a messenger of State; *le ~ des dieux*, the messenger of the gods (Mercury); *l'Aurore, la ~ère du jour*, Aurora, the harbinger of day.

messagerie (mɛsaʒri), s.f. [f. *message*] Stage-coach, coach, stage, carrier's cart; stage-coach office; (rail.) goods traffic, goods department, goods office; *les ~s maritimes*, steam-packet service.

messe (mɛs), s.f. [L *missa*] (R. Cath. relig.) Mass; music sung or played at high mass; *~ basse*, low mass; *grand'~*, high mass; *~ de minuit*, midnight mass; *livre de ~*, prayer-book; *dire la ~*, to say mass.

messéance (mɛsseɑ̃s), s.f. Unseemliness, unbecomingness, impropriety.

messéant, -e (mɛsseɑ̃), adj. Unseemly, unbecoming, improper.

messénien, -ne (mɛsenjɛ̃), adj. s.m.f. [f. *Messénie*] Messenian.

messeoir (mɛsswar), v.n. impers. [pref. *més*+*seoir*] To be unseemly, to be unbecoming, to be unfitting.

messer (mɛsɛr), s.m. [It. *messere*] (obs.) Master; *~ gaster*, the stomach.

messianique (mɛsianik), adj. Messianic.

messianisme (mɛsianism), s.m. Messianism.

messidor (mɛsidɔr), s.m. [L *messis*+Gr. *dōron*] Messidor (10th month in calendar of First French Republic, 20 June = 19 July).

messie (mɛsi), s.m. [Hebr. *māshīaḥ*] Messiah.

messier (mɛsje), s.m. [LL *messarius*, f. L *messis*] Keeper (of fields and vineyards), harvest-watcher.

messieurs (mɛsjø), (pl. of *monsieur*) Gentlemen.

messin, -e (mɛsɛ̃), adj. s.m.f. (Native) of Metz.

messire (mɛsir), s.m. Sir, sire, master, squire; *~ Jean*, a kind of pear.

mestre (mɛstr), s.m. [old form of *maître*] Master; (obs. mil.) *~ de camp*, colonel.

mesurable (məzyrabl), adj. Measurable.

mesurage (məzyraʒ), s.m. Measurement, measuring; metage.

mesure (məzyr), s.f. [L *mensura*] Measure gauge, standard; measurement, size, bounds, dimension, capacity, limit, compass; (fig.) calculation, reckoning; moderation, decorum, propriety; prudence, precaution; (mus.) bar; (pros.) metre; (fenc.) distance; *faire bonne ~*, to give good measure; *à la ~*, by measure, on draught; (mus.) *~ à trois temps*, triple time; *battre la ~*, to beat time; *aller en ~*, to keep time; *à ~*, in proportion, according; *à ~ que*, in proportion as, according as; *à ~ que l'un avançait, l'autre reculait*, as fast as one advanced, the other retreated; *au fur et à ~*, in proportion (*que*, as), successively; *manquer de ~*, to lack moderation; *outre ~*, beyond all measure, excessively; *la ~ du possible*, the bounds of possibility; *combler la ~*, to go to extremes; *prendre ses ~s*, to take one's precautions; *donner sa ~*, to show one's capabilities; *sans ~*, beyond all measure, without any bounds; *ne point garder de ~ avec X*, to have no consideration for X; *se mettre en ~ de*, to get ready to, to prepare to.

mesuré, -e (məzyre), p. adj. Measured; regular, proportioned; (fig.) cautious, circumspect, guarded, prudent; *il est très ~ dans ses discours*, he is very guarded in what he says.

mesurément (məzyremɑ̃), (rare) adv. Prudently, moderately, guardedly.

mesurer (məzyre), v.a. [LL *mensurare*] To measure; to measure out; to proportion, to calculate; to compare, to consider, to weigh, to examine; *il mesure chaque parole*, he weighs every word; **se ~**, v.pr. to be measured, to be proportioned; to try one's strength, to measure swords; (fig.) to vie, to contend, to cope.

mesureur (məzyrœr), s.m. Measurer; meter.

mésusage (mezyzaʒ), s.m. Misuse, abuse.

mésuser (mezyze), v.n. [*més*+*user*] To misuse, to abuse; *~ de la liberté*, to misuse liberty.

meta (meta), s.f. [L wd] (Rom. ant.) Meta.

métabole (metabɔl), s.f. [Gr. *metabolē*], Metabola.

métacarpe (metakarp), s.m. [Gr. *meta* +*karpos*] (anat.) Metacarpus.

métacarpien, -ne (metakarpjɛ̃), adj. (anat.) Metacarpal.
métacentre (metasɑ̃tr), s.m. [Gr. *meta*+*kentron*] (naut.) Metacentre.
métacentrique (metasɑ̃trik), adj. (naut.) Metacentric.
métachronisme (metakrɔnism), s.m. [Gr. *meta*+*khronos*] Metachronism.
métagramme (metagram), s.m. [Gr. *meta*+*gramma*] Metagram.
métairie (metɛri), s.f. [f. *métayer*] Farm, the produce of which is shared by landlord and tenant; small farm, dairy farm.
métal (pl. **aux**) (metal), s.m. [Gr. *metallon*] Metal; ~ *anglais*, electro-plate; Britannia metal; ~ *blanc*, German silver; ~ *précieux*, precious metal. ⚠ *Métaux* can never be used in the sense of the English 'metals' = *rails*: 'the train left the metals' = *le train a quitté les rails*.
métalepse (metalɛps), s.f. [Gr. *metalēpsis*] (rhet.) Metalepsis.
métalléité (metaleite), s.f. [f. *métal*] Metalleity.
métallifère (metalifɛr), adj. [L *metallum* +*ferre*] Metalliferous.
métallin, -e (metallɛ̃), adj. Metalline.
métallique (metallik), adj. Metallic.
métalliquement (metallikmɑ̃), adv. Metallically.
métallisation (metalliza'sjɔ̃), s.f. Metallization.
métalliser (metallize), v.a. To metallize.
métallochromie (metallɔkrɔmi), s.f. [f. *métal*+Gr. *khrōma*] Metallochromy.
métallographie (metallɔgrafi), s.f. [f. *métal*+Gr. *graphein*] Metallography.
métallographique (metallɔgrafik), adj. Metallographic.
métalloïde (metallɔid), s.m. [*métal*+Gr. *eidos*] Metalloid.
métalloïdique (metallɔidik), adj. Metalloid.
métallothérapie (metallɔterapi), s.f. (med.) Metallotherapy.
métallurgie (metallyrʒi), s.f. [f. Gr. *metallon*+*ergon*] Metallurgy.
métallurgique (metallyrʒik), adj. Metallurgical.
métallurgiste (metallyrʒist), s.m. Metallurgist.
métamère (metamɛr), adj. [Gr. *meta*+*meros*] Metameric. ~, s.m. (zool.) Metamere.
métamérie (metameri), s.f. [f. *métamère*] (chem.) Metamerism.
métamorphique (metamɔrfik), adj. (geol.) Metamorphic.
métamorphisme (metamɔrfism), s.m. (geol.) Metamorphism.
métamorphosable (metamɔrfozabl), adj. Metamorphosable.
métamorphose (metamɔrfoz), s.f. [f. *métamorphoser*] Metamorphosis.
métamorphoser (metamɔrfoze), v.a. [f. Gr. *meta*+*morphē*] To metamorphose, to change, to transform.
métaphore (metafɔr), s.f. [Gr. *metaphora*] (rhet.) Metaphor, image.
métaphorique (metafɔrik), adj. Metaphoric, metaphorical.
métaphoriquement (metafɔrikmɑ̃), adv. Metaphorically.
metaphoriser (metafɔrize), v.a. To metaphorize.
métaphosphate (metafɔsfat), s.m. (chem.) Metaphosphate.
métaphosphorique (metafɔsfɔrik), adj. (chem.) Metaphosphoric.
métaphrase (metafrɑz), s.f. [Gr. *metaphrasis*] Metaphrase, metaphrasis.
métaphraste (metafrast), s.m. Metaphrast.
métaphysicien, -ne (metafizisjɛ̃), s.m.f. Metaphysician.
métaphysique (metafisik), s.f. [Gr. *(ta) meta (ta) phusika*] (phil.) Metaphysics. ~, adj. Metaphysical.
métaphysiquement (metafizikmɑ̃), adv. Metaphysically.
métaplasme (metaplasm), s.m. [Gr. *metaplasmos*] (gram.) Metaplasm.
métaplastique (metaplastik), adj. (gram.) Metaplastic.
métargon (metargɔ̃), s.m. (chem.) Metargon.
métastase (metastɑz), s.f. [Gr. *metastasis*] (med., rhet.) Metastasis.
métatarse (metatars), s.m. [Gr. *meta*+*tarsos*] (anat.) Metatarsus.
métatarsien, -ne (metatarsjɛ̃), adj. s.m. (anat.) Metatarsal.
métathèse (metatɛz), s.f. [Gr. *metathesis*] (gram., med.) Metathesis.
métathorax (metatɔraks), s.m. [Gr. *meta* +*thōrax*] (ent.) Metathorax.
métayage (metɛjaʒ), s.m. Metayage.
métay-er, -ère (metɛje), s.m.f. [LL *medietarius*] Metayer (farmer holding land on condition that half the produce is given to the landlord); farmer; labourer.
métazoaire (metazɔɛr), s.m. [f. Gr. *meta* +*zōon*] (zool.) Metazoon.
méteil (metɛj), s.m. [f. L *mixtus*] (agric.) Maslin (mixture of wheat and rye).
métempsycose (metɑ̃psikoz), s.f. [Gr. *meta*+*en*+*psukhē*] Metempsychosis.
météore (meteɔr), s.m. [Gr. *meteōros*] Meteor; (fig.) dazzling person or event.
météorique (meteɔrik), adj. Meteoric.
météorisation (meteɔriza'sjɔ̃), s.f. See MÉTÉORISME.
météoriser (meteɔrize), v.a. [Gr. *meteōrizein*] (med.) To distend with flatulence.
météorisme (meteɔrism), s.m. **météorisation** (meteɔrizasjɔ̃), s.f. (med.) Meteorism, flatulence.

météorite (meteɔrit), s.f. Meteorite.
météorologie (meteɔrɔlɔʒi), s.f. [Gr. *meteōros*+*logos*] Meteorology.
météorologique (meteɔrɔlɔʒik), adj. Meteorological.
météorologiste, météorologue (meteɔrɔlɔʒist, meteɔrɔlɔg), s.m.f. Meteorologist.
météoromancie (meteɔrɔmɑ̃si), s.f. [Gr. *meteōros*+*manteia*] Meteoromancy.
métèque (metɛk), s.m. [Gr. *metoikos*] (Gr. ant.) Stranger living in Athens; (by ext., pej.) foreigner living in another country.
méthane (metan), s.m. (chem.) Methane.
méthode (metɔd), s.f. [Gr. *methodos*] Method, system, way, custom, habit; rudiments, elementary treatise; *il fait tout avec* ~, he does everything methodically; *chacun a sa* ~, every one has his own method; ~ *de piano*, pianoforte method.
méthodique (metɔdik), adj. Methodical.
méthodiquement (metɔdikmɑ̃), adv. Methodically.
méthodisme (metɔdism), s.m. Methodism.
méthodiste (metɔdist), s.m.f. adj. Methodist.
méthyle (metil), s.m. [f. Gr. *methu*+*hulē*] (chem.) Methyl.
méthylène (metylɛn), s.m. (chem.) Methylene.
méthylique (metilik), adj. (chem.) Methylic.
méticuleusement (metikyløzmɑ̃), adv. Meticulously.
méticuleu-x, -se (metikylø), adj. [L *meticulosus*] Meticulous, fastidious, nice, over-scrupulous.
méticulosité (metikylozite), s.f. Meticulousness, fastidiousness, over-niceness.
métier (metje), s.m. [L *ministerium*] **1.** Trade, handicraft; business, profession, calling; employment, occupation, work; *apprendre un* ~, to learn a trade; *exercer un* ~, to follow a trade; *corps de* ~, guild, corporation; *arts et* ~*s*, arts and crafts; *le* ~ *des armes*, the military profession; *être du* ~, to be in the trade, to be one of the cloth; *servir un plat de son* ~, to play a trick, to show what one can do; *faire* ~ *de*, to make a trade of; *de son* ~, by trade, by profession; (prov.) *chacun son* ~ *et les vaches seront bien gardées*, every one to his trade; *il n'est si petit* ~ *qui ne nourrisse son maître*, keep thy shop and thy shop will keep thee; *il n'est point de sot* ~, all professions are good in their way; **2.** loom, frame; (fig.) anvil, stocks; ~ *à bas*, stocking-frame; ~ *à main*, hand-loom; ~ *mécanique*, power-loom; ~ *à tapisserie*, tapestry-frame; *avoir plusieurs ouvrages sur le* ~, to have several works on hand.
métis, -se (metis), adj. [L *mixticius*, f. *mixtus*] Mixed, half-bred, half-caste (of persons); mongrel, cross-bred (of animals); hybrid (of plants). ~, s.m.f. Half-breed, half-caste (person); mongrel, cross-breed (animals); hybrid (plants).
métissage (metisaʒ), s.m. [f. *métis*] Cross-breeding.
métisser (metise), v.a. To cross (animals, plants).
métonien (metɔnjɛ̃), adj. m. [f. *Méton*, Athenian astronomer] (astr.) Metonic; *cycle* ~, metonic cycle.
métonomasie (metɔnɔmazi), s.f. [Gr. *meta*+*onoma*] Metonomasy.
métonymie (metɔnimi), s.f. [Gr. *metōnumia*] Metonymy.
métope (metɔp), s.f. [Gr. *metopē*] (arch.) Metope.
métoposcope (metɔpɔskɔp), s.m. Metoposcopist.
métoposcopie (metɔpɔskɔpi), s.f. [Gr. *metōpon*+*skopia*] Metoposcopy.
métoposcopique (metɔpɔskɔpik), adj. Metoposcopic.
métrage (metraʒ), s.m. Measurement, length in metres.
mètre (mɛtr), s.m. [Gr. *metron*] Metre (=1·093633 English yards); (pros.) metre; metrical foot.
métré (metre), s.m. Measurement in metres.
métrer (metre), v.a. To measure by the metre.
métreur (metrœr), s.m. adj. Measurer, surveyor; appraiser.
métrique (metrik), adj. [Gr. *metrikos*] Metric, metrical; *système* ~, metric system.
métrique (metrik), s.f. [f. Gr. *metron*] Versification, prosody; scansion.
métrite (metrit), s.f. (med.) Metritis.
métro (metro), s.m. Abbrev. for the Paris Metropolitan Railway; underground; tube.
métrologie (metrɔlɔʒi), s.f. [Gr. *metron* +*logos*] Metrology.
métrologique (metrɔlɔʒik), adj. Metrological.
métrologiste, métrologue (metrɔlɔʒist, metrɔlɔg), s.m. Metrologist.
métromane (metrɔman), s.m. [Gr. *metron* +*mania*] Metromaniac.
métromanie (metrɔmani), s.f. [f. *métromane*] Metromania.
métronome (metrɔnɔm), s.m. [Gr. *metron* +*nomos*] Metronome.
métropole (metrɔpɔl), s.f. [Gr. *mētēr*+*polis*] Mother country; metropolis, capital; metropolitan see.
métropolitain, -e (metrɔpɔlitɛ̃), adj. Metropolitan; archiepiscopal; *église* ~*e*, mother-church. ~, s.m. **1.** Archbishop, metropolitan; **2.** metropolitan railway, tube, underground railway.

métropolite (metrɔpɔlit), s.m. (Gr. Church) Metropolitan.
mets (mɛ), s.m. [L *missum*] Dish, viand, mess, food.
mettable (mɛtabl), adj. Wearable, fit to be worn.
mettage (mɛtaʒ), s.m. Preparation for a piece of work.
metteur (mɛtœr), s.m. Putter, layer; ~ *en œuvre*, mounter, setter (of jewels); (fig.) one who carries out other people's ideas; ~ *en scène*, stage-manager; (print.) ~ *en pages*, clicker, maker-up.
mettre (mɛtr), v.a. [L *mittere*] To put, to set, to place; to put in, to introduce; to put on, to wear; to bring; to employ; to contribute, to devote, to expend; to suppose, to imagine; ~ *la clef dans la serrure*, to put the key in the lock; ~ *sa robe*, to put on one's dress; ~ *son argent à la caisse d'épargne*, to put one's money into the Savings Bank; ~ *cent francs à un chapeau*, to spend a hundred francs on a hat; *mettez du soin dans tout ce que vous faites*, be careful in all you do; *j'ai mis une heure à y aller*, it took me an hour to get there; *mettez le reste du bœuf en bouillon*, make the rest of the beef into soup; *mettez que je n'ai rien dit*, suppose I have said nothing; ~ *le couvert*, to lay the table; ~ *une terre en blé*, to sow a field with corn; ~ *la main à la pâte*, to put one's shoulder to the wheel; ~ *la main sur X*, to arrest X; ~ *la main sur quelque chose*, to discover something; ~ *la dernière main à un travail*, to put the finishing touches to a piece of work; ~ *la main à la plume*, to take up one's pen; ~ *un vaisseau à la mer*, to launch a ship; ~ *de côté*, to put on one side; to save; ~ *en pièces*, to break, to crush; ~ *à sec*, to dry up, to empty; ~ *à l'épreuve*, to prove; ~ *à même de*, to enable; *y* ~ *du sien*, to make concessions, to meet (some one) half way; ~ *X au pied du mur*, to corner X; ~ *des paroles en musique*, to set words to music; ~ *en ordre*, to set in order; (print.) ~ *en pages*, to make up; ~ *la charrue devant les bœufs*, to put the cart before the horse; ~ *par écrit*, to set down in writing; ~ *à l'amende*, to fine; ~ *dehors*, to turn out; ~ *X au fait*, to inform X of the state of affairs; ~ *un livre au jour*, to publish a book; (mil.) ~ *aux arrêts*, to put under arrest; *mettez cela dans votre poche, et votre mouchoir par-dessus*, put that in your pipe and smoke it; (slang) ~ *les voiles*, or *les* ~, to be off; to hop it; to cut along; **se** ~, v.pr. to put or place oneself; to sit down; to lie down; to stand up; to dress; *se* ~ *à*, to begin, to set about; to take to, to apply oneself, to turn one's thoughts to; to go, to get; to break out; *se* ~ *à table*, to sit down to table; (slang) to avow; to own up; *se* ~ *à travailler*, to begin work; *se* ~ *au régime*, to follow a diet; *se* ~ *en colère*, to get angry; *se* ~ *à son aise*, to put oneself at one's ease; *se* ~ *bien*, to dress well; *se* ~ *en frais*, to incur expenses; *se* ~ *en tête*, to take it into one's head; *se* ~ *à tout*, to turn one's hand to anything; *se* ~ *à la fenêtre*, to stand at the window; *se* ~ *bien avec*, to get on good terms with; *se* ~ *dans le commerce*, to go into business; *se* ~ *du fard*, to make up; *se* ~ *en route*, to start off, to start out; *se* ~ *mal avec X*, to fall out with X; *se* ~ *sur son quant-à-soi*, to give oneself airs; *s'y* ~, to set about it, to turn to, to buckle to.
meublant, -e (mœblɑ̃), p. adj. Fit for furnishing, effective, achieving an effect of a well furnished place, filling; *meubles* ~*s*, movables, furniture.
meuble (mœbl), adj. [L *mobilis*] Movable, loose, personal; *sol* ~, light soil; fine mould; *biens* ~*s*, personal property; movables. ~, s.m. Piece of furniture, set of furniture; *se mettre dans ses* ~*s*, to set up house; to furnish apartments or a house of one's own.
meubler (mœble), v.a. To furnish; to stock, to store; *chambre meublée*, furnished room; ~ *sa mémoire*, to store one's memory (*de*, with); *avoir la bouche bien meublée*, to have a fine set of teeth; **se** ~, v.pr. to purchase furniture.
meuglement (møgləmɑ̃), s.m. Bellowing. See syn. BEUGLEMENT.
meugler (møgle), v.n. See syn. BEUGLER.
meulard (mølar), s.m. Large grindstone.
meule (mœl), s.f. [L *mola*] Millstone; grindstone; wheel; (of hay, &c.) rick; *mettre en* ~, to stack; ~ *de fromage*, a cheese (round and flat like a millstone).
meulerie (mølri), s.f. Millstone yard.
meulier (mølje), s.m. Millstone maker.
meuli-er, -ère (mølje), adj. Pertaining to millstone or grindstone; *pierre* ~*ère*, millstone; millstone grit. ~**ère**, s.f. Millstone quarry.
meulon (mølɔ̃), s.m. Small (hay)cock, small stack.
meunerie (mønri), s.f. Milling trade; (collect.) millers.
meuni-er, -ère (mønje), s.m.f. [L *molinarius*] Miller, (fem.) miller's wife, mistress of a mill; *mésange* ~*ère*, long-tailed titmouse.
meurt-de-faim (mœrdəfɛ̃), s.m. invar. Starveling, starved wretch.
meurtre (mœrtr), s.m. [f. Germ. *Mord*] Murder, manslaughter; (fig.) crime.
meurtri-er, -ère (mœrtrie), s.m.f. Murderer, murderess. ~, adj. Murderous, sanguinary, deadly.
meurtrière (mœrtrijɛr), s.f. **1.** Murderess; **2.** (fort.) loophole.

meurtrir (mœrtrir), v.a. To bruise; to make black and blue, to injure, to batter; *des fruits meurtris*, bruised fruit; *tout meurtri*, covered with bruises.

meurtrissure (mœrtrisyr), s.f. Bruise, contusion.

meute (møt), s.f. [LL *movita*, f. L *movere*] Pack (of hounds); *chef de ~*, leader of the pack, whipper-in.

mévente (mevɑ̃t), s.f. Sale at a loss; slackness of trade, lack of sale.

mexicain, -e (mɛksikɛ̃), adj. s.m.f. Mexican.

mézéréon (mezereɔ̃), s.m. (bot.) Mezereon; *Daphne mezereum*.

mezzanine (mɛdzanin), s.f. [It. *mezzanino*] (arch.) Mezzanine, mezzanine floor, mezzanine window.

mezzo-soprano (mɛdzosoprano), s.m. [It. wd] Mezzo-soprano.

mezzo-tinto (mɛdzotinto), s.m. [It. wd] Mezzotint.

mi (mi), s.m. [1st syllable of wd 'Mira' in hymn of St. John the Baptist] (mus.) Mi = E, the third note of the scale.

mi (mi), pref. invar. [f. L *medius*] Half, demi, mid, in the middle; *la ~-août*, the middle of August; *à ~-chemin*, half way; *à ~-corps*, up to the waist; *à ~-côte*, half way up (the hill); *à ~-jambe*, half way up the leg; *à ~-mât*, half-mast high, *~-parti*, equally divided; composed of two dissimilar halves.

miaou (mjau), s.m. [onom.] Miaow, mew, mewing, caterwaul.

miasmatique (mjasmatik), adj. Miasmatic, miasmal.

miasme (mjasm), s.m. [Gr. *miasma*] Miasma.

miaulement (mjolmɑ̃), s.m. Mewing.

miauler (mjole), v.n. [onom.] To mew; to caterwaul.

mica (mika), s.m. [L wd] Mica.

micacé, -e (mikase), adj. Micaceous.

mi-carême (mikarɛm), s.f. Mid-Lent.

micaschiste (mikaʃist), s.m. [*mica*+ *schiste*] Micaschist, mica-slate.

miche (miʃ), s.f. [MDutch *micke*] Loaf, round loaf.

micmac (mikmak), s.m. [etym. dub.] Trick, scheme, intrigue, stratagem, dodge.

micocoulier (mikokulje), s.m. (bot.) Nettle-tree, *Celtis australis*.

microbe (mikrɔb), s.m. [f. Gr. *mikros*+ *bios*] Microbe.

microbicide (mikrɔbisid), adj. [*microbe*+ (L) *caedere*] Microbicidal, germicidal.

microbien, -ne (mikrɔbjɛ̃), adj. Microbial.

microbiologie (mikrobiɔlɔʒi), s.f. [*microbe* + (Gr.) *logos*] Microbiology.

microcéphale (mikrosefal), adj. [Gr. *mikros*+*kephalē*] Microcephalous. ~, s.m.f. Microcephalous person.

microcosme (mikrokom), s.m. [Gr. *mikros* +*kosmos*] Microcosm.

micrographie (mikrografi), s.f. [f. Gr. *mikros*+*graphein*] Micrography.

micrométrie (mikrometri), s.f. [f. Gr. *mikros*+*metron*] Micrometry.

micron (mikrɔ̃), s.m. [Gr. wd] Micron (the millionth of a metre).

micro-organisme (mikroorganism), s.m. Micro-organism.

microphone (mikrɔfɔn), s.m. [f. Gr. *mikros*+*phonē*] Microphone.

microscope (mikrɔskɔp), s.m. [f. Gr. *mikros*+*skopein*] Microscope.

microscopique (mikrɔskɔpik), adj. Miscroscopic; (fig.) minute, extremely small.

microthermie (mikrotɛrmi), s.f. [f. Gr. *mikros* + (Fr.) *thermie*] Therm, the millionth of a *thermie*; syn. PETITE CALORIE.

microzoaire (mikrozoɛr), s.m. [Gr. *mikros* +*zōon*] Microzoon; infusorian; microscopic animalcule.

miction (miksjɔ̃), s.f. [L *mictio*] Urination, making water.

midi (midi), s.m. [f. L *medius*+*dies*] Noon, midday, twelve o'clock, noontide; south; southern aspect or direction; *une fenêtre au ~*, a window facing south; *passer l'hiver dans le ~*, to spend the winter in the South (of France); *il a sonné ~*, or *~ est sonné*, it has struck twelve; *sur le coup de ~*, on the stroke of twelve; *chercher ~ à quatorze heures*, to make difficulties where there are none; to look for knots in a bulrush.

midinette (midinɛt), s.f. (colloq.) Dressmaker's apprentice or work-girl (who comes out at noon to get her light luncheon).

mie[1] (mi), s.f. [L *mica*] **1.** Crumb; **2.** (obs.) little bit.

mie[2] (mi), s.f. [abbrev. of *amie*] Dearest; *ma ~*, my darling, my love, honey.

mie (mi), adv. [L *mica*] None, not at all; *je n'en veux ~*, I won't have any of that.

miel (mjɛl), s.m. [L *mel*] Honey; *rayon de ~*, honeycomb; *être tout ~ et tout sucre*, to be all sugar and honey, to be honey-tongued; to be mealy-mouthed; to be all gentleness; *lune de ~*, honeymoon; *mouche à ~*, honey-bee; *on prend plus de mouches avec du ~ qu'avec du vinaigre*, more is done by kindness than by harshness.

miellé, -e (mjɛle), adj. Honeyed; honey-sweet.

mielleusement (mjɛløzmɑ̃), adv. Blandly, with honeyed tongue; lusciously; fawningly, unctuously, insinuatingly.

mielleu-x, -se (mjɛlø), adj. Honey, honey-like; (fig.) honeyed, honey-tongued, mawkish, oily, insinuating, hypocritical.

mien, -ne (mjɛ̃), poss. adj. poss. pron. [L *meus*] Mine, my own, of mine; *un ~ cousin,* a cousin of mine; *les ~s,* my relations, my family, my people.

miette (mjɛt), s.f. [f. *mie*] Small crumb, least bit, particle; *réduire en ~s,* to smash to atoms, to smash to smithereens.

mieux (mjø), adv. [L *melius*] Better; *à qui ~ ~,* in emulation of each other, vying or striving with each other; *de ~ en ~,* better and better; *j'aimerais ~,* I would rather; I would prefer; *je ne demande pas ~,* nothing would please me better; I am quite willing; *on ne peut ~,* as well as possible; *rien de ~,* nothing better; *tant ~!,* so much the better!

mieux (mjø), s.m. Best, the best, best way, best thing, something better; *le ~ est l'ennemi du bien,* leave well alone; *il est au ~ avec X,* he is on the best terms with X; *faire pour le ~,* to act for the best; *faire de son ~,* to do one's best (*pour,* to); *faute de ~,* for want of something better; *le ~ est de,* it is best to; *le ~ continue,* the improvement continues.

mièvre (mjɛvr), adj. [orig. unkn.] Dainty, mincing, affectedly gentle, niminy-piminy, prim; (of speech) all prunes and prisms. ⚠ Nowadays *mièvre* cannot be translated by 'arch', 'roguish' (=*espiègle, vif*); this sense is quite obsolete.

mièvrement (mjɛvrəmɑ̃), adv. Affectedly, daintily, demurely, mincingly.

mièvrerie (mjɛvrəri), s.f. Affected daintiness.

mignard, -e (miɲar), adj. [f. *mignon*] Affectedly pretty or dainty.

mignarder (miɲarde), v.a. To coddle.

mignardise (miɲardiz), s.f. **1.** Daintiness, affected delicacy, pretty ways; **2.** (bot.) *œillet ~,* feathered pink; **3.** a kind of narrow braid.

mignon, -ne (miɲɔ̃), adj. [f. Celt. *min*] Delicately pretty, dainty, tiny and graceful; *argent ~,* spare money; pocket-money; *péché ~,* favourite sin, besetting sin; foible. **~,** s.m.f. **1.** Darling; *mon ~, ma ~ne,* my darling, my treasure; my precious; **2.** (historic pej.) minion; **~ne,** s.f. (print.) emerald, minion.

mignonnette (miɲɔnɛt), s.f. **1.** Mignonette lace; **2.** ground pepper; **3.** (photo.) midget; **4.** (bot.) a variety of pink. ⚠ In English 'mignonette' = *réséda.*

mignoter (miɲɔte), v.a. To coddle, to fondle.

migraine (migrɛn), s.f. [f. Gr. *hēmikrania*] Sick headache; *avoir la ~,* to have a headache.

migraineu-x, -se (migrɛnø), adj. Headachy.

migrat-eur, -rice (migratœr), adj. Migrant, migrating, migratory.

migration (migra'sjɔ̃), s.f. [L *migratio*] Migration.

migratoire (migratwar), adj. Migratory.

mijaurée (miʒore), s.f. [orig. unkn.] Affected woman, prudish person; *faire la ~,* to put on side; to simper, to be a mass of affectation.

mijoter (miʒɔte), v.a.n. [orig. unkn.] To simmer, to stew gently; *faire ~,* to let simmer; (fig.) to plot, to devise, to invent, to organize, to hatch.

mikado (mikado), s.m. Mikado.

mil[1] (mil), s.m. [etym. dub.] Indian club.

mil[2] (mij), s.m. See syn. MILLET.

mil (mil), num. adj. See MILLE.

mi-laine (milɛn), adj. (of material) Not pure wool.

milan (milɑ̃), s.m. [L *milvus*] (ornith.) Kite.

mildiou (mildju), s.m. [f. Engl. *mildew*] Mildew (on vines).

milésien, -ne (milezjɛ̃), adj. s.m.f. [(*a*) f. *Milet,* Asia Minor; (*b*) f. *Milesius*] Milesian.

miliaire (miljɛr), adj. [L *miliarius*] Miliary.

milice (milis), s.f. [L *militia*] Militia; (Fr. hist.) train-bands, citizen-soldiers; (fig.) *les ~s célestes,* the heavenly host.

milicien (milisjɛ̃), s.m. Militiaman.

milieu (pl. **-x**) (miljø), s.m. [*mi*+*lieu*] Middle, centre, midst, medium, heart; circle, environment, society, sphere; mean; *au ~ de,* in the middle of; in the midst of; among; *au beau ~, en plein ~,* right in the middle; *juste ~,* golden mean; happy medium; *il n'y a pas de ~,* there is no middle course, it must be the one or the other; *l'Empire du ~,* the Middle Kingdom; *tenir le ~ entre,* to be the golden mean between; *vivre au ~ des plaisirs,* to live in the midst of pleasures; *le ~ où il vit,* the society to which he belongs.

militaire (militɛr), adj. [L *militaris*] Military; army-; of the army; of war; martial; *faire son service ~,* to serve one's time in the army; to serve in the army; *heure ~,* sharp, punctually; **~,** s.m. **1.** Soldier; **2.** the soldiers, military, soldiery.

militairement (militɛrmɑ̃), adv. In soldierly style, with rigid discipline.

militant, -e (militɑ̃), adj. s.m.f. Militant.

militarisation (militariza'sjɔ̃), s.f. Militarization.

militariser (militarize), v.a. To militarize.

militarisme (militarism), s.m. Militarism.

militer (milite), v.n. [L *militare*] To militate.

mille (mil), num. adj. s.m. invar. [L wd] Thousand, a thousand; *l'an ~,* the year one thousand; *l'an mil* (note orthography) *huit cents*, the year 1800; ~ *fois merci*, ~ *remerciements*, a thousand thanks.

mille (mil), s.m. [L wd] Mile = 1609 metres; ~ *marin* = 1852 metres.

mille-feuille (milfœj), s.f. (pl. *mille-feuilles*) **1.** (bot.) Milfoil, yarrow; **2.** mille-feuille cake.

mille-fleurs (milflœr), s.f. Extract of many flowers.

millénaire (millenɛr), s.m. [L *millenarius*] Millenary. ~, adj. Millenary, millenial, millenarian.

mille-pattes (milpat), s.m. (ent.) Millepede, millipede; wood-louse; centipede.

mille-pertuis (milpɛrtɥi), s.m. (bot.) St. John's wort.

millépore (millepɔr), s.m. Millepore (a genus of corals).

millésime (millezim), s.m. [L. *millesimus*] Millesimal; date (on coins, medals, &c.).

millet, mil (mijɛ, mij), s.m. [L *milium*] (bot.) Canary-seed; millet, millet-grass.

milliaire (miljɛr), adj. [L *milliarius*] Miliary; ~, s.m. or *pierre* ~, milestone.

milliard (miljar), s.m. 1000 millions, milliard.

milliardaire (miljardɛr), adj. s.m.f. Multi-millionaire.

milliardième (miljardjɛm), s.m. One-thousand-millionth part.

milliasse (miljas), s.f. (obs.) Thousands, swarms.

millième (miljɛm), s.m. Thousandth, one-thousandth part.

millier (milje), s.m. Thousand; ten hundredweight; *on les trouve par* ~*s*, they are to be found in thousands.

milligramme (milligram), s.m. Milligramme = 0·0154 grain.

millilitre (millilitr), s.m. Millilitre; the thousandth part of a litre.

millime (millim), s.m. One thousandth of a franc.

millimètre (millimɛtr), s.m. Millimetre, the thousandth part of a metre.

million (miljɔ̃), s.m. Million.

millionième (miljɔnjɛm), s.m. adj. Millionth.

millionnaire (miljɔnɛr), s.m.f. adj. Millionaire.

millithermie (millitɛrmi), s.f. 1000 Therms = thousandth part of a *thermie*; (abbrev. mth.) syn. GRANDE CALORIE.

milord (milɔr), s.m. [f. Engl. *my lord*] **1.** Lord; (colloq.) nabob; **2.** four-wheeled carriage, phaeton.

milouin (milwɛ̃), s.m. (ornith.) Pochard (sea-duck).

mime (mim), s.m. [Gr. *mimos*] Mime; mimic.

mimer (mime), v.a. To mimic.

mimétisme (mimetism), s.m. [Gr. *mimesthai*] Mimetism.

mimeu-x, -se (mimø), adj. (bot.) Contractile; sensitive.

mimique (mimik), adj. Mimic, mimetic. ~, s.f. Mimicry, art of mimicry; ~, s.m. mimographer.

mimodrame (mimodram), s.m. Mimodrame.

mimographe (mimograf), s.m.f. Mimographer.

mimosa (mimoza), s.m. [mod. L wd] (bot.) Mimosa.

minable (minabl), adj. [f. *miner*] **1.** That may be mined; **2.** pitiable, shabby, down at heel, dilapidated, seedy, shabby-genteel.

minage (minaʒ), s.m. Corn-measuring; corn-duty.

minaret (minarɛ), s.m. [Arab. *manarat*] Minaret.

minauder (minode), v.n. [f. *mine*] To simper, to smirk, to be lackadaisical.

minauderie (minodri), s.f. Simpering, airs, lackadaisical manners, affected ways.

minaudi-er, -ère (minodje), adj. Simpering, minikin, affected, lackadaisical, full of airs.

mince (mɛ̃s), adj. [orig. unkn.] Thin, slim, slender; insignificant, inconsiderable, scanty; (vulg.) ~ *!* interj., ~ *alors!*, gee whiz!, oh my!, my eye!, that's something to look at!, ain't that nice!, what swank!

minceur (mɛ̃sœr), s.f. Thinness; slenderness, slimness.

mine[1] (min), s.f. [Celt. orig.] Look, mien, countenance, bearing; *avoir bonne* ~, to look well; *avoir mauvaise* ~, to look ill; *un homme de bonne* ~, a good-looking man, a man of good appearance, a man looking like a gentleman; *un homme de mauvaise* ~, an evil-looking man; *faire* ~ *de*, to look as if, to pretend to; *faire la* ~, to look displeased, to pout, to sulk, to scowl; *faire des* ~*s*, to ogle, to smirk; *faire bonne* ~ *à X*, to receive X well, to greet X pleasantly; *faire bonne* ~ *à mauvais jeu*, to put a good face on a bad business; *faire grise* ~ *à X*, to look sour (or black) at X; *il ne paye pas de* ~, his appearance is against him; *payer de* ~, to be all outside show; *juger sur la* ~, to judge by appearances.

mine[2] (min), s.f. [Celt. orig.] Mine, pit; mine, torpedo; (naut.) *champ de* ~*s*, mine-field; *navire poseur de* ~*s*, mine-layer; *navire dragueur de* ~*s*, mine-sweeper; (min.) ore; (fig.) source, store; *c'est une* ~ *d'or*, it's a treasure; it's a gold-mine; ~ *de plomb*, black lead, plumbago; *faire jouer une* ~, to spring a mine; (fig.) *éventer la* ~, to baffle someone's designs; *puits de* ~, shaft.

mine[3] (min), s.f. [Gr. *mna*] **1.** Mina

(Greek coin = 100 drachms); **2.** [f. Gr. *hēmina*] mine (old Fr. measure of corn).

miner (mine), v.a. [f. *mine*[2]] To mine, to undermine, to sap; (fig.) to wear away, to waste gradually; to prey upon; *ce chagrin le mine,* this sorrow preys upon him.

minerai (minrɛ), s.m. Ore.

minéral, (aux) (mineral), s.m. [f. LL *minera*] Mineral, ore.

minéral, -e, (aux) (mineral), adj. Mineral; *eau ~e,* mineral water, soda-water.

minéralisation (mineraliza'sjɔ̃), s.f. Mineralization.

minéraliser (mineralize), v.a. To mineralize.

minéralogie (mineralɔʒi), s.f. [f. *minéral* +Gr. *logos*] Mineralogy.

minéralogique (mineralɔʒik), adj. Mineralogical.

minéralogiste (mineralɔʒist), s.m.f. Mineralogist.

minerval, -e (aux), minervien, -ne (minɛrval, minɛrvjɛ̃), adj. Pertaining to Minerva.

minerve (minɛrv), s.f. [f. prop. n. *Minerva*] (print.) Minerva machine, Minerva press.

minerviste (minɛrvist), adj. s.m.f. (Printer) using a Minerva machine.

minet, -te (minɛ), s.m.f. [etym. dub.] (fam.) Cat, pussy, puss.

mineur (minœr), s.m. adj. [f. *miner*] **1.** (that is a) Miner, pitman, collier; **2.** sapper, miner.

mineur, -e (minœr), adj. [L *minor*] Lesser, minor; under age; *il est ~,* he is under age; (mus.) *mode ~,* minor mode; *tierce ~e,* minor third; *les quatre ordres ~s,* the four minor (ecclesiastical) orders; *l'Asie ~e,* Asia Minor; *poètes ~s,* minor poets; *frère ~,* Minorite. **~, -e,** s.m.f. Minor, person under age; **~e,** s.f. (logic) minor term; minor premiss; **~,** s.m. (mus.) minor (key).

miniature (minjatyr), s.f. [It. *miniatura*] Miniature; *en ~,* on a small scale, miniature, in miniature, tiny.

miniaturiste (minjatyrist), adj. s.m.f. Miniature-painter, miniaturist.

mini-er, -ère (minje), adj. Pertaining to mines; *l'industrie ~ère,* the mining industry. **~ère,** s.f. Open mine.

minimant, -e (minimɑ̃), adj. Arriving at its minimum.

minime (minim), adj. [L *minimus*] Minimal, very small, trifling, minute. **~,** s.m. Minim.

minimum (minimɔm), s.m. [L wd] Minimum, least; *au ~,* at the least, as little as may be.

ministère (ministɛr), s.m. [L *ministerium*] Ministry, charge, office, function, department; medium; *~ des Affaires Étrangères,* Foreign Office; *~ de l'Intérieur,* Home Office; *remplir les devoirs de son ~,* to discharge the duties of one's office; *~ public,* public prosecutor; (colloq.) *cela n'est pas de mon ~,* that does not belong to my province.

ministériel, -le (ministerjɛl), adj. Ministerial; *officiers ~s,* notaries, attorneys, &c.; (colloq.) *les ~s,* the supporters of the government.

ministrable (ministrabl), adj. (colloq.) Standing a fair chance of becoming a Minister (of State).

ministre (ministr), s.m. [L *minister*] Minister, agent, instrument; clergyman, rector, vicar, parson; *~ plénipotentiaire,* plenipotentiary minister; *premier ~,* premier; prime minister; *~ du Commerce,* President of the Board of Trade; *~ de l'Instruction Publique,* President of the Board of Education; *~ de l'Intérieur,* Home Secretary; *~ de la Guerre,* Secretary for War; *~ de la Marine,* First Lord of the Admiralty; *~ des Finances,* Chancellor of the Exchequer.

ministresse (ministrɛs), s.f. (colloq., slightly iron.) Wife of a Minister (of State).

minium (minjɔm), s.m. [L wd] Minium, red lead.

minois (minwɑ), s.m. [f. *mine*] Face, pretty face, phiz.

minon (minɔ̃), s.m. (fam.) Cat, puss, pussy.

minorati-f, -ve (minɔratif), adj. s.m. [f. L *minorare*] Laxative.

minorité (minɔrite), s.f. [LL *minoritas*] **1.** Minority; **2.** nonage; minority; *en ~,* in a minority.

minorquin, -e (minɔrkɛ̃), adj. s.m.f. Minorcan; (native) of Minorca.

minot (mino), s.m. [f. *mine*] (obs.) **1.** Old French measure (= 39 litres); **2.** (naut.) bumkin.

minoterie (minɔtri), s.f. [f. *minot*] Flour trade; flour-mill.

minotier (minɔtje), s.m. Miller; flour merchant, flour dealer.

minuit (minɥi), s.m. inv. [*mi+nuit;* this wd was fem. until 17th c.] Midnight, twelve o'clock at night; *sur le ~,* at the hour of midnight; *~ et demi,* half-past twelve.

minuscule (minyskyl), adj. [L *minusculus*] Diminutive, tiny, minuscule. **~,** s.f. Minuscule, small letter.

minute (minyt), s.f. [f. L *minutus*] **1.** Minute (sixtieth part of an hour or of a degree); *aiguille des ~s,* minute hand; (fig.) instant, very short time; *je reviens dans une ~,* I will be back in no time; (excl.) *~ !,* one minute !, half a moment !; *ponctuel à la ~,* punctual to the minute; **2.** minute, original document, rough draft, memorandum; **3.** small writing, small hand.

minuter (minyte), v.a. **1.** To draft (a document, scheme, &c.); **2.** to record in minutes, to find the exact time of.
minuterie (minytri), s.f. **1.** Minute wheels; **2.** contrivance connecting two parts of an electric circuit, thus producing electric light, and breaking the circuit automatically after a certain number of minutes.
minutie (minysi), s.f. [L *minutia*] **1.** Minutia (pl. minutiae), trifle; **2.** extreme care, accuracy.
minutieusement (minysjøzmɑ̃), adv. Minutely, meticulously, accurately.
minutieu-x, -se (minysjø), adj. Meticulous, minute, accurate, precise, extremely careful, particular.
miocène (miɔsɛn), adj. [f. Gr. *meiōn*+*kainos*] (geol.) Miocene.
mioche (mjɔʃ), s.m.f. (colloq.) Brat, chit, urchin, kid.
mi-parti, -e (miparti), adj. [*mi*+*parti*] Half and half; bipartite.
mirabelle (mirabɛl), s.f. [Fr. geog. orig.] (bot.) Mirabelle plum.
miracle (mirɑkl), s.m. [L *miraculum*] Miracle, wonder, marvel, prodigy; miracle play; *opérer des ~s*, to work miracles; *à ~*, to a miracle, wonderfully well; *par ~*, by a miracle; *crier au ~*, to extol; to praise to the skies; to declare a thing a miracle; *faiseur de ~s*, miracle-worker.
miraculé, -e (mirakyle), adj. Cured by a miracle; that has been the object of a miracle.
miraculeusement (mirakyløzmɑ̃), adv. Miraculously, wonderfully.
miraculeu-x, -se (mirakylø), adj. Miraculous; wonderful.
mirage (miraʒ), s.m. [f. *mirer*] Mirage; (fig.) mirage, delusion.
mire (mir), s.f. [f. *mirer*] Sight, aim; land-surveyor's pole; *ligne de ~*, line of sight; *point de ~*, aim, mark; object in view; (fig.) *elle était le point de ~ de tous*, she was stared at by all; she had made herself conspicuous.
mirer (mire), v.a. [f. L *mirari*] To look at, to aim at; *~ des œufs*, to look through eggs with the aid of a strong light (to judge their freshness); **se ~**, v.pr. to look at oneself, to be reflected; to admire oneself, to take pride in oneself.
mirette (mirɛt), s.f. **1.** Mason's pointing tool; **2.** (fam.) peeper, eye.
mirifique (mirifik), adj. [L *mirificus*] (iron.) Marvellous, wonderful, mirific.
mirifiquement (mirifikmɑ̃), adv. (iron.) Marvellously, wonderfully, grandly.
mirliflore (mirliflor), s.m. [orig. unkn.] (iron.) Regular fop, swell, jack-a-dandy, blade, toff.
mirliton (mirlitɔ̃), s.m. [orig. unkn.] Reed-pipe; *vers de ~*, doggerel.
mirmidon (mirmidɔ̃), s.m. See MYRMIDON.
mirobolamment (mirɔbɔlamɑ̃), adv. (iron.) Astoundingly, stupendously, marvellously, splendidly.
mirobolant, -e (mirɔbɔlɑ̃), adj. [f. *myrobalan*] (iron.) Stunning, top-hole, marvellous, scrumptious.
miroir (mirwar), s.m. [f. *mirer*] Mirror, looking-glass; (fig.) mirror; *œufs au ~*, eggs cooked with a little butter; *~ ardent*, burning glass; *~ à alouettes*, revolving mirror used to catch larks; (fig.) catch-penny.
miroitant, -e (mirwatɑ̃), p. adj. Glistening, glittering, flashing, sparkling, shining.
miroité, -e (mirwate), p. adj. (of a horse's coat) Shiny, dappled.
miroitement (mirwatmɑ̃), s.m. Flash, glistening, glisten, glitter, reflection of light.
miroiter (mirwate), v.n. To flash, to glisten, to glitter, to reflect light; *faire ~ (quelque chose) aux yeux de X*, to dazzle, or allure X with (something).
miroiterie (mirwatri), s.f. Mirror-trade; looking-glass manufactory.
miroitier (mirwatje), s.m. Looking-glass maker; looking-glass dealer.
miroton (mirɔtɔ̃), s.m. [orig. unkn.] (cook.) Hash, stew.
mis, -e (mi), p. adj. [part. of *mettre*] Dressed; *un homme bien ~*, a well-dressed man.
misaine (mizɛn), s.f. [f. It. *mezzana*] Foremast; *voile de ~*, foresail. ⚠ English 'mizen' = *mât d'artimon*, not *misaine*.
misanthrope (mizɑ̃trɔp), adj. [f. Gr. *misein*+*anthrōpos*] Misanthropic. ~, s.m.f. Misanthrope, misanthropist.
misanthropie (mizɑ̃trɔpi), s.f. Misanthropy.
misanthropique (mizɑ̃trɔpik), adj. Misanthropic.
miscellanées (misɛllane), s.f.pl. [L *miscellanea*] Miscellanea; syn. MÉLANGES.
miscibilité (misibilite), s.f. Miscibility.
miscible (misibl), adj. [f. L *miscere*] Miscible, mixable.
mise (miz), s.f. [f. *mettre, mis*] Putting, setting, laying; stake, outlay; dress, manner or style of dressing; *cela ne serait pas de ~*, that would not be suitable; *~ négligée*, careless way of dressing, slovenly appearance; *~ en accusation*, indictment; *~ en arrestation*, arrest, apprehension; *~ en action*, bringing out, bringing into use, realization; *~ en cause*, implication, involving; *~ en court-circuit*, short-circuiting; *~ en demeure*, demand, urgent claim; request in due form of law; *~ à l'eau*, *~ à flot*, launching; *~ à exécution*, carrying out, realization; *~ de fonds*, outlay, investment, disbursement; *~ à jour*, putting in order (up to date); *~ au jour*, bringing to light; *~ en jugement*, bringing to trial; *~ en liberté*,

release, discharge; ~ *en marche*, starting; ~ *au monde*, giving birth to; bringing forth; producing; ~ *en œuvre*, bringing into use or application; (print.) ~ *en pages*, making-up; ~ *à pied*, dismissal; ~ *en place*, placing, setting, laying; ~ *en pli*, (of hair) setting; ~ *au point*, focussing; (fig.) re-stating (facts, &c. in their true light and proportion); ~ *en pratique*, application; ~ *à prix*, (*a*) setting a price on (a person's head); (*b*) estimating; (*c*) (at auction sale), upset price; ~ *en scène*, staging, getting up; ~ *en train*, starting, launching; (print.) making ready; ~ *en valeur*, development, improvement; ~ *en vigueur*, enforcement; ~ *en vente*, putting up for sale; ~ *bas*, (of animals) bringing forth.

miser (mize), v.a.n. To stake (at play); to bid (at an auction); (fig.) ~ *sur les deux tableaux*, to hold with the hare and run with the hounds.

misérable (mizerabl), adj. [L *miserabilis*] Miserable, pitiful, wretched, sorry, worthless, insufficient; contemptible, villainous; *une existence* ~, a wretched life; *un salaire* ~, insufficient wages; starvation wages. ~, s.m.f. Villain; scoundrel, criminal, wretch.

misérablement (mizerabləmɑ̃), adv. Wretchedly, miserably, pitifully.

misère (mizɛr), s.f. [L *miseria*] Misery, distress, extreme poverty, wretchedness; *cent francs ! une* ~ *!*, a hundred francs !, it's a mere nothing !; *crier* ~, to complain of bad times; *faire des* ~*s à X*, to plague X, to tease, to worry X; *tomber dans une affreuse* ~, to be reduced to extreme poverty; *chacun a ses petites* ~*s*, every one has his own little troubles.

miséreu-x, -se (mizerø), adj. s.m.f. Wretchedly poor (person).

miséricorde (mizerikɔrd), s.f. [L *misericordia*] Mercy; *demander* ~, to beg, to cry for mercy; *faire* ~, to show mercy; *à tout péché* ~, there is pardon for every sin; ~ *!*, mercy on us !, mercy on me !; (naut.) *ancre de* ~, sheet-anchor.

miséricordieusement (mizerikɔrdjøzmɑ̃) adv. Mercifully.

miséricordieu-x, -se (mizerikɔrdjø), adj. Merciful.

misogyne (mizɔʒin), adj. [f. Gr. *misein*+ *gunē*] Misogynous. ~, s.m. Misogynist, woman-hater.

missel (misɛl), s.m. [f. L *missa*] Missal.

mission (misjɔ̃), s.f. [L *missio*] Mission; *envoyer en* ~, to send on a mission; *remplir une* ~, to perform a mission.

missionnaire (misjɔnɛr), adj. s.m.f. Missionary.

missive (misiv), adj. s.f. [f. L *missus*] Missive.

mistelle (mistɛl), s.f. [f. L *mustum*] Mistelle (must of which the fermentation has been stopped).

mistoufle (mistufl), s.f. (colloq.) Scurvy trick.

mistral (pl. **-s**) (mistral), s.m. Mistral (wind).

mitaine (mitɛn), s.f. [etym. dub.] Mitten; (fig.) *je n'ai pas pris de* ~*s pour le remettre à sa place*, I made no bones about telling him off.

mitan (mitɑ̃), s.m. (obs.) Middle.

mite (mit), s.f. [Germ. orig.] **1.** Moth; (in cheese) mite; *mangé des* ~*s*, moth-eaten; **2.** mite (coin of the smallest value). ⚠ 'Mite' in English also = *toute petite chose, très petit enfant*, 'a wee mite of a child' = *un tout petit*.

mité, -e (mite), adj. Moth-eaten.

miteu-x, -se (mitø), adj. (colloq.) Moth-eaten; wretched, shabby.

mithridate (mitridat), s.m. [f. Gr. prop. n.] Mithridate; old name for *thériaque*, theriac; *vendeur de* ~, quack.

mithridatisation (mitridatiza'sjɔ̃), s.f. Gradual immunization against poison, mithridatism.

mitigati-f, -ve (mitigatif), adj. Mitigatory.

mitigation (mitiga'sjɔ̃), s.f. Mitigation.

mitigé, -e (mitiʒe), p. adj. Mitigated; alleviated, moderate.

mitiger (mitiʒe), v.a. [f. L *mitis, mitigare*] To mitigate, to moderate, to alleviate, to reduce the severity of.

miton (mitɔ̃), s.m. **1.** Long mitten; **2.** (colloq.) *onguent* ~ *mitaine*, chip in porridge, addition which does neither good nor harm; **3.** [f. *mie*] crumb.

mitonner (mitɔne), v.a.n. [f. *miton* (3)] To simmer gently; (fig.) to contrive, to prepare, to let ripen; (colloq.) to fondle, to coddle, to pet.

mitoyen, -ne (mitwajɛ̃), adj. [f. *moitié*] Party, partition, middle; *mur* ~, party-wall; *cloison* ~*ne*, partition wall.

mitoyenneté (mitwajɛnte), s.f. Party right, party property.

mitraillade (mitrɑjad), s.f. Volley of grape-shot.

mitraille (mitrɑj), s.f. [f. *mite*] Mitraille, grape-shot, canister-shot; hail of shot; scrap-iron; (colloq.) coppers, small change.

mitrailler (mitrɑje), v.a.n. To fire into (with machine-gun), to fire mitraille.

mitrailleur (mitrɑjœr), s.m. Mitrailleuse gunner, machine-gunner.

mitrailleuse (mitrɑjøz), s.f. Machine-gun, mitrailleuse.

mitral, -e, (aux) (mitral), adj. Mitral, mitre-shaped.

mitre (mitr), s.f. [Gr. *mitra*] Mitre; mitre-shaped chimney-pot.

mitré, -e (mitre), adj. Mitred.

mitron (mitrɔ̃), s.m. [f. *mitre*] Baker's man, journeyman baker.

(à) mi-voix (amivwɑ), adv. loc. Under one's breath; in an undertone; in a low voice, in a muffled voice, between one's teeth.

mixte (mikst), adj. [L *mixtus*] Mixed; composite; *école* ~, mixed school.

mixtion (mikstjɔ̃), s.f. [L *mixtio*] Mixing; mixture.

mixture (mikstyr), s.f. Mixture.

mnémonique (mnemɔnik), adj. [Gr. *mnēmonikos*] Mnemonic.

mnémotechnie (mnemɔtɛkni), s.f. [Gr. *mnēmē+tekhnē*] Mnemotechny.

mnémotechnique (mnemɔtɛknik), adj. Mnemotechnic.

mobile (mɔbil), adj. [L *mobilis*] Mobile, movable; changeable, unsettled, changing, excitable, unsteady; *garde* ~, (Fr.) militia (1868–71). ~, s.m. **1.** Mover, moving power, spring, incentive; **2.** body in motion; **3.** soldier of the *garde mobile*; syn. (of 3) MOBLOT.

mobili-er, -ère (mɔbilje), adj. Movable; of personal property; *vente ~ère*, sale of furniture; *valeurs ~ères*, transferable securities; *crédit* ~, loan on personal security.

mobilier (mɔbilje), s.m. Furniture, movables; suite; ~ *de salon*, drawing-room suite.

mobilisable (mɔbilizabl), adj. Mobilizable.

mobilisation (mɔbiliza'sjɔ̃), s.f. Mobilization.

mobiliser (mɔbilize), v.a.n. To mobilize.

mobilité (mɔbilite), s.f. [f. *mobile*] Mobility, movability; (fig.) instability; liveliness; fickleness.

moblot (mɔblo), s.m. [pop. abbrev. of *garde mobile*, see MOBILE (3)] Moblot, soldier of the *garde mobile*.

mocassin (mɔkasɛ̃), s.m. [N. Amer. Indian wd] Moccasin.

moche (mɔʃ), adj. (slang) Ugly, dowdy, rotten, worn out.

modal, -e, (aux) (mɔdal), adj. Modal; ~, s.f. (logic) Modal proposition.

modalité (mɔdalite), s.f. Modality.

mode[1] (mɔd), s.f. [f. L *modus*] Fashion, mode, vogue; way, custom; millinery; *à la* ~, in fashion, chic; *mettre à la* ~, to bring into fashion; *passer de* ~, to get out of fashion; *la dernière* ~, the latest; *magasin de ~s*, milliner's shop; *cousin à la ~ de Bretagne*, cousin once removed; *bœuf à la* ~, à la mode beef.

mode[2] (mɔd), s.m. [L *modus*] Mode, way; (gram.) mood, mode; (log., mus.) mode; ~ *d'emploi*, directions for use.

modelage (mɔdlaʒ), s.m. Modelling.

modèle (mɔdɛl), s.m. [It. *modello*] Model; pattern, design; ~ *déposé*, patent, patented; ~ *d'écriture*, copy; *grand* ~, large size; ~ *de vertu*, paragon or model of virtue. ~, adj. Exemplary.

modelé (mɔdle), s.m. Relief, modelling, model.

modeler (mɔdle), v.a. To model, to shape; **se** ~ *sur*, v.pr. to take pattern by, to take for one's model.

modeleur (mɔdlœr), s.m. adj. Modeller.

modéliste (mɔdelist), s.m.f. Pattern-maker, designer (in dressmaking).

modénature (mɔdenatyr), s.f. [f. It. *modano*] (arch.) Profile of a cornice.

modérantisme (mɔderɑ̃tism), s.m. Moderatism.

modérantiste (mɔderɑ̃tist), adj. s.m.f. Moderatist.

modérat-eur, -rice (mɔderatœr), adj. Moderating. ~, s.m.f. Moderator.

modération (mɔdera'sjɔ̃), s.f. Moderation, moderating; moderateness.

modéré, -e (mɔdere), p. adj. Moderate. ~, s.m.f. (politics) Moderate.

modérément (mɔderemɑ̃), adv. Moderately.

modérer (mɔdere), v.a. [L *moderari*] To moderate, to mitigate, to restrain, to curb, to check, to slacken (*vitesse*, speed); to abate; **se** ~, v.pr. to moderate or restrain oneself, to control oneself.

moderne (mɔdɛrn), adj. [L *modernus*] Modern; (iron.) new-fangled; *à la* ~, in the modern style. ~, s.m. Modern style; **~s**, s.m.pl. the moderns; modern authors, scientists, or artists.

modernisation (mɔdɛrniza'sjɔ̃), s.f. Modernization.

moderniser (mɔdɛrnize), v.a. To modernize.

modernisme (mɔdɛrnism), s.m. Modernism.

modernité (mɔdɛrnite), s.f. Modernity, modernness.

modeste (mɔdɛst), adj. [L *modestus*] Modest, unassuming, bashful, chaste; moderate.

modestement (mɔdɛstəmɑ̃), adv. Modestly; moderately.

modestie (mɔdɛsti), s.f. Modesty, simplicity; moderation.

modicité (mɔdisite), s.f. [LL *modicitas*] Smallness, modicum, moderateness.

modifiable (mɔdifjabl), adj. Modifiable.

modificat-eur, -rice (mɔdifikatœr), adj. Modificatory.

modificati-f, -ve (mɔdifikatif), adj. (gram.) Modifying.

modification (mɔdifika'sjɔ̃), s.f. Modification, alteration.

modifier (mɔdifje), v.a. [L *modificare*] To modify, to alter; to tone down; (gram.) to modify, to qualify the sense of.

modillon (mɔdijɔ̃), s.m. [It. *modiglione*] (arch.) Modillion.

modique (mɔdik), adj. [L *modicus*] Small, moderate.

modiquement (mɔdikmɑ̃), adv. Moderately.

modiste (mɔdist), s.f. Milliner, modiste. ⚠ Not dressmaker.

modulation (mɔdyla'sjɔ̃), s.f. Modulation.

module (mɔdyl), s.m. [L *modulus*] (arch., &c.) Module, standard, unit.

moduler (mɔdyle), v.a.n. [L *modulari*] To modulate; to pass from key to key.

moelle (mwal), s.f. [L *medulla*] Marrow; (fig.) pith, marrow; *jusqu'à la ~ des os*, to the marrow; *~ épinière*, spinal marrow; *os à ~*, marrowbone; (bot.) *courge à la ~*, vegetable marrow; *pourri jusqu'aux ~s*, rotten to the core.

moelleusement (mwaløzmɑ̃), adv. Softly, mellowly.

moelleu-x, -se (mwalø), adj. Marrowy, mellow, soft, elastic, rich, comfortable, springy. ~, s.m. Mellowness, springiness.

moellon (mwalɔ̃), s.m. (mason.) Ragstone, ashlar, rubble, roughstone.

mœurs (mœrs, also mœr), s.f.pl. [L *mores*] Manners, habits, customs, ways; morals; *sans ~*, unprincipled; *avoir de bonnes ~*, to be a moral person; *cela n'est plus dans nos ~*, that is not done nowadays; *autre temps, autres ~*, manners change with the times.

mofette, moufette (mɔfɛt, mufɛt), s.f. Choke-damp, noxious fumes.

mogol (mɔgɔl), s.m. [Pers. *mughal*] Mogul.

mohair (mɔɛr), s.m. [Engl. wd, f. Arab.] Mohair.

moi (mwa), pers. pron. [L *me*] Me, to me; I, for my part; *à ~ !*, help !; *c'est à ~*, it is mine; it belongs to me; it is my turn; *c'est ~*, it is I; *de vous à ~*, between you and me; *~ je crois que*, for my part I believe that; *ni ~ non plus*, neither do I; *~-même*, myself. ~, s.m. Ego, self.

moignon (mwaɲɔ̃), s.m. [orig. unkn.] Stump.

moindre (mwɛ̃dr), adj. [L *minor*] Less, lesser, smaller, lower, inferior; *le ~*, the least, the smallest, the slightest; *au ~ bruit il s'effraie*, the least noise frightens him; *je n'en ai pas gardé le ~ souvenir*, I have not the least recollection of it, or of him, her.

moindrement (mwɛ̃drəmɑ̃), adv. *Pas le ~*, not in the least.

moine (mwan), s.m. [Gr. *monakhos*] Monk, friar; bed-warmer, warming-pan; (print.) friar; *l'habit ne fait pas le ~*, the cowl does not make the monk; the coat does not make the gentleman; *gras comme un ~*, as fat as a pig.

moineau (pl. -x) (mwano), s.m. [f. *moine*] Sparrow; *tirer* or *brûler sa poudre aux ~x*, to waste powder and shot; (fig.) *un vilain ~*, a queer-looking fellow; a queer bird; a bad egg.

moinerie (mwanri), s.f. Monks (collectively), (pej.) shavelings.

moinillon (mwanijɔ̃), s.m. Petty monk or friar.

moins (mwɛ̃), adv. s.m. [L *minus*] Less (*que, de*, than); fewer (*de*, than); not so, not so many (*que*, as); (math.) minus; *le ~*, the least; *à ~ de*, for less than, unless; *à ~ que*, unless; *au ~*, at least, at any rate; mind !; *de ~*, less; too little; *de ~ en ~*, less and less; *du ~*, at any rate; *en ~ de rien*, in less than no time; *pour le ~*, to say the least; *ni plus ni ~*, neither more nor less; *non ~ que*, as well as; *pas le ~ du monde*, not in the least; *pour le ~*, at least; *rien ~ que*, anything but; nothing less than; *tout au ~*, *à tout le ~*, at the very least; *midi ~ le quart*, a quarter to twelve; *je ne suis rien ~ que certain de cela*, I am anything but convinced of that; *elle n'est rien ~ que jolie*; she is anything but pretty; *il ne s'agit de rien ~ que sa fortune*, nothing less than his fortune is at stake; *10 ~ 5 = 5*, 10 minus 5 = 5; (slang) *c'est ~ cinq*, it's a near shave; (colloq.) *c'est bien le ~ !*, it's the least he can do !; *~ 3 degrés*, minus 3°, or 3° below zero.

moins-value (mwɛ̃valy), s.f. Decrease in value, falling off.

moirage (mwaraʒ), s.m. Watering (of silk, &c.).

moire (mwar), s.f. [f. Engl. *mohair*] Watered silk.

moiré, -e (mware), p. adj. Watered, moiré.

moirer (mware), v.a. To give a watered or moiré appearance to, to moiré.

mois (mwɑ), s.m. [L *mensis*] Month; monthly allowance or pay; *payé au ~*, paid by the month; *au ~ de*, in the month of; *par ~*, monthly; a month; *tous les 36 du ~*, once in a blue moon.

moise (mwaz), s.f. [f. L *mensa*] (carp.) Tie-piece, brace; half-timber; strut.

moïse (mɔiz), s.m. [f. prop. n. *Moïse*] Bassinet(te).

moisi, -e (mwazi), p. adj. Mouldy, musty. ~, s.m. Mould, mustiness; *odeur de ~*, fusty smell.

moisir (mwazir), v.a.n. [L *mucere*] To grow mouldy or musty; to make mouldy; (colloq.) *je ne vais pas ~ ici*, I am not going to stop here long; I am not going to stay here and moulder; **se ~**, v.pr. to grow mouldy.

moisissure (mwazisyr), s.f. Mouldiness, mustiness, mould, mouldy part.

moissine (mwasin), s.f. Vine-branch with grapes hanging (for preserving).

moisson (mwasɔ̃), s.f. [f. L *messis*] Harvest, crop; harvest-time; *faire la ~*, to harvest, to gather in the harvest.

moissonner (mwasɔne), v.a. To harvest, to reap, to gather in the harvest; *~ un*

champ, to reap a field; *qui sème le vent moissonne la tempête*, he who sows the wind shall reap the whirlwind.
moissonneu-r, -se (mwasɔnœr), s.m.f. Harvester, reaper.
moite (mwat), adj. [L *mucidus*] Moist, clammy, damp.
moiteur (mwatœr), s.f. Moisture, clamminess, dampness.
moitié (mwatje), s.f. [L *medietas*] Half; (colloq.) wife, better half; (law, Lit.) moiety (⚠ 'moiety' means also: one of two parts into which a thing is divided, the parts not necessarily being equal); *à* ~, half; *se mettre de* ~ *avec X*, to go halves with X; *à* ~ *prix*, for half price; *à* ~ *route*, half way.
moitir (mwatir), v.a.n. To moisten; to grow moist.
moka (mɔka), s.m. [f. *Moka*, Arabia] **1.** Mocha; **2.** mocha cake.
mol, -le (mɔl), adj. See MOU.
molaire (mɔlɛr), s.f. adj. [L *molaris*] Molar tooth, molar, grinder.
molard (mɔlar), s.m. (colloq., vulg.) Gob, expectoration; hence *molarder*, v.n. to spit.
moldave (mɔldav), adj. s.m.f. Moldavian.
môle (mol), s.m. [L *moles*] Pier, mole (⚠ not in the sense of *taupe*.)
moléculaire (mɔlekylɛr), adj. Molecular.
molécule (mɔlekyl), s.f. [f. L *moles*] Molecule.
molène (mɔlɛn), s.f. (bot.) Mullein.
moleskine (mɔlɛskin), s.f. [f. Engl. *moleskin*] American cloth. ⚠ Not 'moleskin' which = *fourrure de taupe*.
molestation (mɔlɛsta'sjɔ̃), s.f. Molestation, annoyance, annoying.
molester (mɔlɛste), v.a. [f. L *molestus*] To molest, to annoy.
molette (mɔlɛt), s.f. [f. L *mola*] **1.** Muller (for mixing and grinding colours); **2.** rowel (of spur); **3.** (techn., motor.) roller wheel; *clé à* ~, spanner.
molinisme (mɔlinism), s.m. [f. *Luis Molina*, Jesuit, 1535–1600] Molinism.
moliniste (mɔlinist), adj. s.m.f. Molinist.
mollah (mɔla), s.m. [Arab. *maula*] Mullah.
mollasse (mɔlas), adj. [f. *mol*] Flabby; (fig.) apathetic. ~, s.f. (geol.) Molasse, a rock composed of limestone, sand, and clay, which hardens when exposed to the air. ⚠ Not 'molasses', which = *mélasse*.
mollement (mɔlmɑ̃), adv. Softly, loosely; indolently, apathetically, slackly, tamely, effeminately, not firmly.
mollesse (mɔlɛs), s.f. Softness, flabbiness, laxity, slackness, indolence, tameness.
mollet (mɔlɛ), s.m. Calf (of the leg).
mollet, -te (mɔlɛ), adj. Soft, soft-boiled, light.
molletière (mɔltjɛr), s.f. Legging, puttee.
molleton (mɔltɔ̃), s.m. [f. *mol*] Molleton, swanskin; ~ *de laine*, soft thick flannel.
mollification (mɔllifika'sjɔ̃), s.f. Mollification.
mollifier (mɔlifje), v.a. To soften; (fig.) to mollify.
mollir (mɔlir), v.n. [L *mollire*] To soften, to grow soft, to slacken; (of wind) to abate; to give way; (slang) *mollis!*, do not insist!, let things go.
mollusque (mɔlysk), s.m. [f. L *molluscus*] Mollusc.
moloch (mɔlɔk), s.m. [f. name of Canaanite god] (zool.) Moloch, thorn-lizard.
molosse (mɔlɔs), s.m. [f. *Molossia* in ancient Greece] Mastiff, watch-dog, large dog.
moly (mɔli), s.m. [Gr. *mōlu*] (bot.) Moly.
molybdène (mɔlibdɛn), s.m. [f. Gr. *molubdos*] (chem.) Molybdenum.
môme (mom), s.m.f. (slang) Kid, brat, urchin; girl.
moment (mɔmɑ̃), s.m. [L *momentum*] Moment, instant; (mech.) moment; *j'étais occupé à ce* ~*-là*, I was busy at the moment; *dans un* ~, *un petit* ~, *un* ~*!*, half a moment!, one moment!; *c'est le bon* ~, now is the time; *saisir le* ~ *favorable*, to seize the opportunity; *à tout* ~, every moment, momently, at any time; *à tous* ~*s*, at every turn; *au* ~ *de*, on the point of; *au* ~ *où*, *au* ~ *que*, the instant that; *par* ~*s*, at times, now and then; *de* ~ *en* ~, *d'un* ~ *à l'autre*, from moment to moment; momently; any instant; any time; every moment; *il l'a assisté à ses derniers* ~*s*, he was with him when he breathed his last; *je le ferai à mes* ~*s perdus*, I will do it in my spare time, or, whenever I have a moment to spare; *du* ~ *que*, (*a*) from the instant that; the moment that; (*b*) since; *abuser de vos* ~*s*, to trespass on your time. ⚠ 'Moment' in English means also *importance*; ex.: 'a matter of no moment' = *une question sans importance*; hence: 'momentous' = *de grande importance*.
momentané, -e (mɔmɑ̃tane), adj. Momentary, transitory.
momentanément (mɔmɑ̃tanemɑ̃), adv. Momentarily, for the time being.
mômerie (momri), s.f. [f. OF *momer*, f. Germ. *mummen*] Mummery, antics (pl.).
momie (mɔmi), s.f. [Arab. *mūmia*] Mummy.
momification (mɔmifika'sjɔ̃), s.f. Mummification.
momifier (mɔmifje), v.a. To mummify.
momot (mɔmo), s.m. (ornith.) Motmot.
mon, (fem.) **ma,** (pl.) **mes** (mɔ̃, ma, mɛ), poss. adj. [f. L *meus*] My (*mon* is used instead of *ma*, in the feminine, before a vowel or unaspirated *h*; ex.: *mon âme*, *ma pauvre âme*; *mon héroïne*, *ma pure héroïne*).

monacal, -e, (aux), (mɔnakal), adj. [f. Gr. *monakhos*] Monac(h)al, monastic.
monachisme (mɔnaʃism), s.m. Monachism.
monaco (mɔnako), s.m. Money (struck by the Prince of Monaco); (slang) ~*s*, oof, pelf, cash, money.
monade (mɔnad), s.f. [f. Gr. *monas*] Monad.
monadelphe (mɔnadɛlf), adj. [f. Gr. *monos*+*adelphos*] (bot.) Monadelphous.
monandre (mɔnɑ̃dr), adj. [f. Gr. *monos*+ *anēr, andros*] (bot.) Monandrous.
monarchie (mɔnarʃi), s.f. [Gr. *monarkhia*] Monarchy.
monarchique (mɔnarʃik), adj. Monarchical.
monarchiste (mɔnarʃist), adj. s.m.f. Monarchist.
monarque (mɔnark), s.m. [Gr. *monarkhēs*] Monarch, sovereign.
monastère (mɔnastɛr), s.m. [Gr. *monastērion*] Monastery, convent.
monastique (mɔnastik), adj. Monastic, monachal; monkish.
monastiquement (mɔnastikmɑ̃), adv. Monastically, monkishly.
monaut (mɔno), adj. m. [Gr. *monōtos*] One-eared (animal).
monceau (pl. **-x**) (mɔ̃so), s.m. [L *monticellus*] Heap, pile, stack; (fig.) mass, heaps (pl.).
mondain, -e (mɔ̃dɛ̃), adj. [L *mundanus*] Worldly, worldly-minded; society (man or woman); mundane, earthly. ~, s.m.f. Man about town, man or woman in society.
mondanité (mɔ̃danite), s.f. Worldliness; mundanity; ~*s*, social events.
monde (mɔ̃d), s.m. [L *mundus*] World, universe; mankind, people; society, company, folks; lot of people, crowd; *venir au* ~, to be born; *mettre au* ~, to give birth to; *il habite au bout du* ~, he lives at the other end of the world; *si vous en tirez dix francs, c'est tout le bout du* ~, if you get ten francs for that, it is the utmost; *se moquer du* ~, to take people for a pack of fools; to act impudently; *rien au* ~, nothing in the world; *pour rien au* ~, not on any account; *il y a beaucoup de* ~, there is a lot of people, there is a crowd; it's full; *tout le* ~, everybody, every one; anybody; *il n'y a pas grand* ~, there are not many people present; *le grand* ~, (colloq.) *le beau* ~, the nobs, the higher circles, the fashionable world, the best society; *un homme du* ~, a gentleman, a society man, a man about town; *une femme du* ~, a lady; *le petit* ~, (*a*) the young people, the children; (*b*) people of modest origin; small fry; *l'autre* ~, the next or other world; the hereafter; *c'est vieux comme le* ~, it is as old as the hills; *renoncer au* ~, to renounce the world; *on ne peut contenter tout le* ~ *et son père*, one cannot satisfy all the world and his wife; *connaître* or *savoir son* ~, (*a*) to know whom one has to deal with; to know one's customers; (*b*) to have good manners.
monde (mɔ̃d), adj. (obs.) [L *mundus*] Clean, pure (of food).
monder (mɔ̃de), v.a. [L *mundare*] To cleanse; to husk, to shell, to hull (beans, &c.), to blanch (almonds).
mondial, -e, (aux) (mɔ̃djal), World-wide.
mondifier (mɔ̃difje), v.a. [L *mundificare*] (surg.) To cleanse.
monégasque (mɔnegask), adj. s.m.f. Monegasque, (native) of Monaco.
monère (mɔnɛr), s.f. [G. *monērēs*] (biol.) Moner, moneron, (pl.) monera.
monétaire (mɔnetɛr), adj. [f. L *moneta*] Monetary.
monétisation (mɔnetiza'sjɔ̃), s.f. Monetization; syn. MONNAYAGE.
monétiser (mɔnetize), v.a. To monetize; syn. MONNAYER.
mongol, -e (mɔ̃gɔl), adj. s.m.f. Mongolian, Mongol.
mongolique (mɔ̃gɔlik), adj. Mongolian.
monisme (mɔnism), s.m. [f. Gr. *monos*] Monism.
monit-eur, -rice (mɔnitœr), s.m.f. [L *monit-or, -rix*] Monitor; adviser, guide; prefect; (word sometimes used as title of newspaper).
monition (mɔnisjɔ̃), s.f. [L *monitio*] Monition.
monitoire (mɔnitwar), s.m. adj. Monitory.
monitor (mɔnitɔr), s.m. (naut.) Monitor.
monitorial, -e, (aux) (mɔnitɔrjal), adj. Monitory.
monnaie (mɔnɛ), s.f. [f. Roman goddess Juno *Moneta*] Coin, money, change; mint; currency; *ne pas avoir de* ~, to have no small change; *faites-moi la* ~ *de cent francs*, give me change for a hundred francs; *papier-*~, paper money; ~ *légale*, legal tender; *Hôtel de la* ~, Mint; *payer en* ~ *de singe*, to blarney one's creditors; *fausse* ~, counterfeit coin; *battre* ~, to coin money; (fig.) *il lui a rendu la* ~ *de sa pièce*, he paid him back in his own coin; (bot.) ~ *du pape*, moneywort; syn. LUNAIRE.
monnayage (mɔnɛjaʒ), s.m. Coining, coinage, minting.
monnayer (mɔnɛje), v.a. To coin, to mint; (fig.) to exploit (one's talents, &c.).
monnayeur (mɔnɛjœr), s.m. Coiner, minter; *faux* ~, counterfeiter, coiner (of counterfeit money).
mono- (mɔno), pref. [Gr. *monos*] Mono-.
monobasique (mɔnobɑzik), adj. Monobasic.
monocarpien, -ne (mɔnokarpjɛ̃), adj. Monocarpous, monocarpic.
monochrome (mɔnokrom), adj. Monochrome.

monocle (mɔnɔkl), s.m. [f. *mono*+L *oculus*] (Single) eyeglass, monocle.
monocorde (mɔnɔkɔrd), s.m. (mus.) Monochord. ~, adj. (fig.) Monotonous, tedious.
monocotylédone (mɔnɔkɔtiledɔn), adj. (bot.) Monocotyledonous.
monodie (mɔnɔdi), s.f. [Gr. *monōdia*] Monody.
monogame (mɔnogam), adj. Monogamous.
monogamie (mɔnogami), s.f. Monogamy.
monogamique (mɔnogamik), adj. Monogamous.
monogramme (mɔnogram), s.m. Monogram.
monographie (mɔnografi), s.f. Monograph.
monographique (mɔnografik), adj. Monographic.
monoïque (mɔnɔik), adj. [f. Gr. *monos*+*oikos*] (bot.) Monoecian, monoecious.
monolithe (mɔnolit), adj. Monolithic. ~, s.m. Monolith.
monologue (mɔnɔlɔg), s.m. Monologue, soliloquy.
monologuer (mɔnɔlɔge), v.n. To soliloquize, to monologize.
monomane, monomaniaque (mɔnɔman, mɔnomanjak), adj. s.m.f. Monomaniac.
monomanie (mɔnomani), s.f. Monomania.
monôme (mɔnom), s.m. (alg.) Monomial; (colloq.) students' processional rag (in single file).
monomètre (mɔnomɛtr), adj. Monometric.
monopétale (mɔnopetal), adj. (bot.) Monopetalous.
monoplan (mɔnɔplɑ̃), s.m. Monoplane.
monopode (mɔnɔpɔd), adj. Monopodous.
monopole (mɔnɔpɔl), s.m. [Gr. *monopōlion*] Monopoly, exclusive possession.
monopolisation (mɔnɔpɔliza'sjɔ̃), s.f. Monopolization.
monopoliser (mɔnɔpɔlize), v.a. To monopolize.
monoptère (mɔnɔptɛr), adj. Monopteral.
monorail (mɔnoraj), s.m. adj. Monorail.
monorime (mɔnorim), adj. Monorhyme, having the same rhyme throughout.
monosépale (mɔnosepal), adj. (bot.) Monosepalous.
monosperme (mɔnospɛrm), adj. (bot.) Monospermous.
monostique (mɔnɔstik), adj. [f. Gr. *monos*+*stikhos*] (pros.) Monostich.
monosyllabe (mɔnosillab), s.m. Monosyllable. ~, adj. Monosyllabic.
monosyllabique (mɔnosillabik), adj. Monosyllabic.
monothéique (mɔnoteik), adj. Monotheistic.
monothéisme (mɔnoteism), s.m. Monotheism.
monothéiste (mɔnoteist), adj. Monotheistic. ~, s.m.f. Monotheist.
monotone (mɔnɔtɔn), adj. Monotonous, wearisome.
monotonement (mɔnɔtɔnmɑ̃), adv. Monotonously.
monotonie (mɔnɔtɔni), s.f. Monotony, monotonousness.
monotrème (mɔnɔtrɛm), s.m. (zool.) Monotreme.
monotype (mɔnotip), s.m. Monotype.
monovalent, -e (mɔnovalɑ̃), adj. (chem.) Monovalent.
monoxyle (mɔnoksil), adj. s.m. Monoxylous, monoxylon, (boat) made from one piece of timber.
mons. (mɔ̃s), s.m. [abbrev. of *monsieur*] (in derision, or jest.) Master, sir.
monseigneur (mɔ̃sɛɲœr) s.m. [*mon*+*seigneur*] (pl. *messeigneurs, nosseigneurs*), My lord, your lordship, your Grace; ~, s.m., also *pince-*~, s.f. jemmy, crowbar.
monseigneuriser (mɔ̃sɛɲœrize), v.a. To belord.
monsieur (məsjø), s.m. (pl. *messieurs*), [*mon*+*sieur*] Gentleman; *M.*, Mr. (mister); sir; the master (of the house); (hist.) the eldest brother of the King of France; *ce* ~, this gentleman; *cher* ~, dear sir; ~ *le Président*, Mr. President; ~ *le Maire*, Mr. Mayor, your Worship; *un vilain* ~, a dirty dog; a swine of a fellow; a low bounder; *prune de* ~, Orleans plum.
monstrance (mɔ̃strɑ̃s), s.f. (Cath. Church) Monstrance.
monstre (mɔ̃str), s.m. [L *monstrum*] Monster; (fig.) monster. ~, adj. (colloq.) huge; *un succès* ~, a huge success.
monstrueusement (mɔ̃stryøzmɑ̃), adv. Monstrously.
monstrueu-x, -se (mɔ̃stryø), adj. Monstrous, outrageous, atrocious; (of crime, deed, &c.) heinous.
monstruosité (mɔ̃stryozite), s.f. Monstrosity; monstrousness.
mont (mɔ̃), s.m. [L *mons*] Mountain, mount; *les* ~*s des Pyrénées*, the Pyrenees; *par* ~*s et par vaux*, up hill and down dale; *promettre* ~*s et merveilles*, to promise no end of wonders; ~*-de-Piété* (now called *Crédit Municipal*), official pawnbroking establishment; *mettre au* ~*-de-Piété*, to pawn.
montage (mɔ̃taʒ), s.m. **1.** Carrying up, lifting; **2.** mounting, setting; mount; fitting-up.
montagnac (mɔ̃taɲak), s.m. [f. prop. n.] Montagnac (a thick woollen stuff).
montagnard, -e (mɔ̃taɲar), s.m.f. Mountaineer; highlander; (Fr. hist.) member of *la Montagne*. ~, adj. Of the mountains, montane.

montagne (mɔ̃taɲ), s.f. [f. LL *montania*] Mountain; mount, highland; (Fr. hist.) *la Montagne,* an ultra-revolutionary party; *chaîne de ~s,* mountain-chain; *pays de ~,* mountainous country; *~s russes,* switchback, scenic railway.

montagneu-x, -se (mɔ̃taɲø), adj. Mountainous, hilly.

montaison (mɔ̃tɛzɔ̃), s.f. (fish.) Migration of salmon up the rivers.

montanisme (mɔ̃tanism), s.m. [f. *Montanus*] Montanism.

montant, -e (mɔ̃tɑ̃), p. adj. Ascending, uphill; *rue ~e,* uphill street; *un astre ~,* a rising star; *une robe ~e,* a high-necked dress; *un col ~,* a stand-up collar; *marée ~e,* flood tide; *train ~,* up train.

montant (mɔ̃tɑ̃), s.m. **1.** Upright (of ladder, &c.); **2.** post (of door); **3.** (naut.) stanchion; **4.** amount, total; **5.** high flavour, pungency; (fig.) piquancy, causticity, verve.

monte (mɔ̃t), s.f. **1.** Serving, covering (of animals); **2.** riding; way of riding; **3.** rising (of silk-worms).

monté, -e (mɔ̃te), p. adj. **1.** Mounted (on horseback); **2.** provided (*en,* with), supplied; *bien ~ en souliers,* well set up with shoes; **3.** *un coup ~,* a pre-arranged affair; a put-up job; a put-up trick; **4.** *il est très ~ contre vous,* he is very cross with you.

monte-charge (mɔ̃tʃarʒ), s.m. Lift, hoist, elevator, service-lift.

montée (mɔ̃te), s.f. Slope, rise, ascent, acclivity; (arch.) height; going up, ascending.

monténégrin, -e (mɔ̃tenegrɛ̃) adj. s.m.f. Montenegrin.

monte-plats (mɔ̃tplɑ), s.m. (pl. *monte-plats*) Service-lift.

monter (mɔ̃te), v.n.a. [f. *mont*] To go up, to come up, to ascend, to climb, to mount; to rise, to slope up; to ride; to amount (*à,* to); to stock, to furnish, to equip, to fit out, to fit up; to set, to mount; to boil up; to grow up, to shoot; to get on, to prosper; *~ à un arbre,* to climb up a tree; *~ à bicyclette,* to ride a bicycle; *~ à cheval,* to ride; *~ à l'échelle,* to climb up a ladder; to go up the ladder; (fig. colloq.) *vous voulez me faire ~ à l'échelle,* you would like to get a rise out of me; *~ à sa chambre,* to go up to one's room; *~ sur le trône,* to ascend the throne; *~ à l'assaut de,* to storm; (colloq.) *~ sur ses grands chevaux,* to be on one's high horse; to show one is really angry; *~ sa montre,* to wind up one's watch; *~ une machine,* to set up, to fit up, a machine; *la marée monte,* the tide is coming in, the tide is rising; *~ l'escalier,* to go upstairs; *~ en graine,* to run to seed; (fig.) to become an old maid; *ce vin monte à la tête,* this wine flies to one's head; this wine is heady; *~ sa maison,* to furnish one's house; *~ un magasin,* to stock a shop (*en,* with); *~ un diamant,* to set a diamond; *~ une cabale,* to get up a cabal; *~ la tête à X,* to excite X, to work X up; *faire ~ M. X,* to show Mr. X up; (colloq.) to get a rise out of Mr. X; *le total monte,* or *se monte à 500 frs.,* the total amounts to 500 frs.; *la rente monte,* the funds are going up; the stocks are rising; **se ~,** v.pr. **1.** to provide oneself (*en,* with); **2.** to amount (*à,* to); **3.** to get excited or angry.

monteu-r, -se (mɔ̃tœr), s.m.f. Setter; mounter, fitter.

montgolfière (mɔ̃gɔlfjɛr), s.f. [f. inventor's name, *Montgolfier*] Fire-balloon, Montgolfier balloon.

monticole (mɔ̃tikɔl), adj. [f. L *mons*+*colere*] Monticolous, growing in the mountains.

monticule (mɔ̃tikyl), s.m. Hillock, knoll, little mount, mound.

mont-joie (mɔ̃ʒwɑ), s.f. Cairn, heap of stones; (Fr. hist.) *M~ St Denis !,* a war-cry.

montmorency (mɔ̃mɔrɑ̃si), s.f. [Fr. geog. orig.] A variety of cherry.

montoir (mɔ̃twar), s.m. Horse-block, upping stone; *côté du ~,* near side (left side of horse).

montrable (mɔ̃trabl), adj. Presentable, showable.

montre[1] (mɔ̃tr), s.f. [f. *montrer*] Watch; *~-bracelet,* wrist watch; *~ à répétition,* repeater.

montre[2] (mɔ̃tr), s.f. [f. *montrer*] Show, display; show-window, show-case; *en ~,* in the window; (fig.) *faire ~ de son savoir,* to show off one's learning.

montrer (mɔ̃tre), v.a. [L *monstrare*] To show, to display, to point out, to exhibit, to manifest, to evince; to teach; to prove; *~ la corde,* to be threadbare; (fig.) *~ le chemin,* to set an example; *~ X au doigt,* to point at X; *~ du sangfroid,* to show presence of mind; *~ qu'on a raison,* to prove one is right; (lit. and fig.) *~ les dents,* to show one's teeth; **se ~,** v.pr. to show oneself, to appear; to prove oneself to be; (colloq.) to show spirit.

montreu-r, -se (mɔ̃trœr), s.m.f. Shower, showman; *~ d'ours,* bear-leader.

montueu-x, -se (mɔ̃tɥø), adj. Steep, hilly.

monture (mɔ̃tyr), s.f. **1.** Mount, horse, donkey, camel, &c., animal for riding; beast, nag; *qui veut aller loin ménage sa ~,* fair and softly goes far in a day; slow and steady wins the race; **2.** setting, mounting, frame; stock (of a gun).

monument (mɔnymɑ̃), s.m. [L *monumentum*] Monument; *~ public,* public building.

monumental, -e, (aux) (mɔnymɑ̃tal), adj. Monumental, grand, (fig.) stupendous.

moque (mɔk), s.f. [orig. dub.; Dutch *mok*?] (naut.) Heart, dead-eye.

(se) moquer (səmɔke), v.pr. [etym. dub.] To laugh (*de*, at), to make game or fun (of), to jeer (at); to ridicule; not to care; to care nothing (for); *je m'en moque comme de l'an quarante* or *je m'en moque pas mal*, I don't care a rap for it; *se ~ du tiers et du quart*, not to care a rap for the opinion of Tom, Dick, and Harry; *on se moque de lui*, they are laughing at him; he is being bamboozled; *la pelle se moque du fourgon*, the pot is calling the kettle black; *se faire ~ de soi*, to make a fool of oneself; *vous vous moquez!*, you are jesting.

moquerie (mɔkri), s.f. Mockery, jeer, scoff, derision.

moquette (mɔkɛt), s.f. [OF *mocade*, orig. dub.] **1.** Velvet-pile carpet; **2.** decoy-bird.

moqueu-r, -se (mɔkœr), adj. Mocking, scoffing, jeering, jesting, teasing. ~, s.m.f. Mocker, jeerer, scoffer, wag.

moqueusement (mɔkøzmɑ̃), adv. Mockingly.

morailles (mɔrɑj), s.f.pl. (techn.) Barnacles (for restive horses).

moraillon (mɔrɑjɔ̃), s.m. [f. *morailles*] Hasp.

moraine (morɛn), s.f. [Provenç. *mourreno*] Moraine.

moraïte (morait), adj. s.m.f. Morean.

moral, -e, (aux) (moral), adj. [L *moralis*] Moral, of good morals, righteous; spiritual, intellectual; *un livre ~*, a moral book; *préceptes ~aux*, moral precepts; *une victoire ~e*, a moral victory; *certitude ~e*, moral certainty. ~, s.m. Morale; mind, spirit, mental faculties; *remonter le ~ à X*, to cheer X up; ⚠ See MORALE, s.f.

morale (mɔral), s.f. Ethics, moral science, morality, moral teaching (of fable, &c.); *il m'a fait de la ~*, he has been lecturing me; *la ~ de cette histoire c'est que . . .*, the moral to be drawn from all this is that . . .; *la ~ chrétienne*, Christian morality. ⚠ Note that English 'morale' = *moral* and that English 'moral' frequently = *morale*; ex.: 'to draw the moral of', *tirer la morale de.*

moralement (mɔralmɑ̃), adv. Morally.

moralisat-eur, -rice (mɔralizatœr), adj. Edifying, moralizing, improving, uplifting.

moralisation (mɔraliza'sjɔ̃), s.f. Moralization.

moraliser (mɔralize), v.a. To moralize, to improve; to lecture; ~, v.n. to coin moral precepts, to moralize.

moraliste (mɔralist), s.m.f. Moralist, moral philosopher.

moralité (mɔralite), s.f. Morality, morals, moral sense, integrity; morality play.

morasse (mɔras), s.f. (print.) Final proof of a newspaper. ⚠ Not to be translated by 'morass' which = *marécage.*

moratoire (mɔratwar), adj. [L *moratorius*] Moratory. ~, s.m. Moratorium.

moratorium (mɔratɔrjɔm), s.m. [L wd] Moratorium.

morbide (mɔrbid), adj. [L *morbidus*] Morbid.

morbidement (mɔrbidmɑ̃), adv. Morbidly.

morbidesse (mɔrbidɛs), s.f. [It. *morbidezza*] Morbidezza.

morbidité (mɔrbidite), s.f. Morbidness, morbidity.

morbifique (mɔrbifik), adj. [L *morbificus*] Morbific.

morbleu (mɔrblø), interj. [f. *mordieu*] The deuce!, hang it!, damn!

morceau (pl. **-x**) (mɔrso), s.m. [f. L *morsus*] Piece, morsel, bit, snack, fragment; *manger un ~*, to eat a mouthful; (fig.) *manger le ~*, to give the show away; to blab; (slang) to blow up the whole caboodle; *un fin ~, un ~ délicat*, a tit-bit; (mus.) *~ à quatre mains*, pianoforte piece for four hands; *~x choisis*, select pieces (of poetry, literature, &c.).

morceler (mɔrsəle), v.a. To parcel out, to cut up, to divide into portions.

morcellement (mɔrsɛlmɑ̃), s.m. Parcelling out, subdivision.

mordache (mɔrdaʃ), s.f. [f. *mordax*] (mech.) Box-clamps; vice-clamps.

mordacité (mɔrdasite), s.f. [f. L *mordax*] Mordacity; (fig.) causticity.

mordant, -e (mɔrdɑ̃), p. adj. Mordant, caustic, biting, corrosive, pungent, cutting. ~, s.m. **1.** Mordant causticity, pungency, corrosiveness; **2.** (mus.) mordent (𝆕 or 𝆕𝆕).

mordelle (mɔrdɛl), s.f. (ent.) Mordella.

mordicant, -e (mɔrdikɑ̃), adj. [f. L *mordicare*] Corrosive, mordant, caustic; see syn. MORDANT.

mordicus (mɔrdikys), adv. [L wd] Doggedly, tenaciously, tooth and nail.

mordienne (mɔrdjɛn), interj. [f. *mordieu*] Hang it!, *à la grosse ~*, unceremoniously, bluntly.

mordieu (mɔrdjø), interj. (archaic) [*mort + de + Dieu*] (archaic) 'Sdeath!; damn!, hang it!

mordillage (mɔrdijaʒ), s.m. Nibbling.

mordiller (mɔrdije), v.a. [f. *mordre*] To nibble, to bite at.

mordoré, -e (mɔrdɔre), adj. [f. *More+doré*] Mordoré, bronze. ~, s.m. Mordoré shade.

mordorer (mɔrdɔre), v.a. To give a mordoré or bronze shade to.

mordorure (mɔrdɔryr), Giving a mordoré or bronze shade; this colour.

mordre (mɔrdr), v.a. [L *mordere*] To bite, to bite off; to gnaw; to corrode; ~ *la poussière*, to bite the dust; ~ *au latin*, to take to Latin; ~ *à l'hameçon*, to nibble at the bait; (colloq.) *ça ne mord pas*, no go, nothing doing; **se** ~, v.pr. *il s'en mord la langue*, he repents bitterly what he said; *vous vous en mordrez les doigts*, you shall rue it; *la lime mord l'acier*, the file eats away the steel.

more, moresque (mɔr, mɔrɛsk), adj. s.m.f. See syn. MAURE, MAURESQUE.

mor-eau, -elle (mɔro), adj. [f. *More*] Jet black, black and shining.

morelle (mɔrɛl), s.f. [f. *moreau*] (bot.) Morel, nightshade.

morfil (mɔrfil), s.m. Wire-edge.

morfondre (mɔrfɔ̃dr), v.a. [f. *morve*+*fondre*] To chill; **se** ~, v.pr. to be chilled; (fig.) to cool one's heels, to dance attendance, to waste one's time, to be waiting and bored.

morfondure (mɔrfɔ̃dyr), s.f. (vet.) Catarrh (of horses).

morganatique (mɔrganatik), adj. [f. Germ. *Morgengabe*] Morganatic.

morganatiquement (mɔrganatikmɑ̃), adv. Morganatically.

morgeline (mɔrʒəlin), s.f. [f. *mordre*+*géline*] (bot.) Chickweed.

morgue (mɔrg), s.f. [orig. unkn.] **1.** Haughtiness, arrogance; **2.** mortuary.

moribond, -e (mɔribɔ̃), adj. s.m.f. [L *moribundus*] Moribund, dying, at the point of death.

moricaud, -e (mɔriko), s.m.f. Darky, sambo, blackamoor.

morigéner (mɔriʒene), v.a. [LL *morigenare*] To chide, to lecture, to take to task; (colloq.) to blow up.

morille (mɔrij), s.f. (bot.) Morel (mushroom.

morillon (mɔrijɔ̃), s.m. **1.** Black grape; **2.** tufted duck; **3.** (pl.) brown emeralds.

morio (mɔrjo), s.m. (ent.) Camberwell beauty.

morion (mɔrjɔ̃), s.m. [Span. *morrión*] Morion.

mormon, -e (mɔrmɔ̃), adj. s.m.f. [f. the Book of *Mormon* (imaginary author)] Mormon.

mormonisme (mɔrmɔnism), s.m. Mormonism.

morne (mɔrn), adj. [Germ. orig.] Gloomy, dismal, dejected, dull.

morne (mɔrn), s.m. [f. Span. *morro*] Isolated hill (in West Indies).

morné, -e (mɔrne), adj. (herald.) Blunted.

mornifle (mɔrnifl), s.f. Slap in the face; (vulg.) one on the jaw.

morose (mɔroz), adj. [L *morosus*] Morose, sullen, peevish, gloomy.

morosité (mɔrozite), s.f. Moroseness, sullenness, gloominess.

morphine (mɔrfin), s.f. [f. *Morphée*] Morphia; *piqûre de* ~, hypodermic injection of morphia.

morphinisme (mɔrfinism), s.m. Morphinism.

morphinomane (mɔrfinɔman), adj. s.m.f. Morphinomaniac.

morphinomanie (mɔrfinɔmani), s.f. Morphinomania.

morphologie (mɔrfolɔʒi), s.f. [f. Gr. *morphē*+*logos*] Morphology.

morphologique (mɔrfolɔʒik), adj. Morphological.

morpion (mɔrpjɔ̃), s.m. [*mord*+*pion*] (ent.) Crab-louse.

mors (mɔr), s.m. [L *morsus*] Bit (of bridle); (fig.) check; *prendre le* ~ *aux dents*, to bolt, to run away; (fig.) to take the bit between one's teeth, (colloq.) to go off one's chump.

morse[1] (mɔrs), s.m. [f. Lapp. *morsa*] Walrus, morse.

morse[2], **Morse** (mɔrs), adj. s.m. [f. inventor's name] Morse (alphabet).

morsure (mɔrsyr), s.f. Bite, biting; sting; ~ *de chien*, bite of a dog; ~ *de puce*, flea-bite.

mort (mɔr), s.f. [L *mors*] Death; decease; *combattre à* ~, to fight to the death; *guerre à* ~, war to the knife; *condamner à* ~, to sentence to death; *être à l'article de la* ~, to be at the point of death; *lit de* ~, death-bed; *mourir de sa belle* ~, to die a natural death; *mettre à* ~, to put to death; *se donner la* ~, to commit suicide; *la* ~ *sans phrases*, death and no remarks, death without heroics; *avoir la* ~ *dans l'âme*, to be grieved to death, to be sick at heart; to be in the dumps; *souffrir mille* ~*s*, to suffer a thousand deaths, to suffer agonies; *à la vie, à la* ~ *!*, for ever; in life and death; ~ *aux rats*, vermin-killer; *une* ~ *douce*, an easy death.

mort, -e (mɔr), adj. [L *mortuus*] Dead; lifeless, inanimate, inert; benumbed, insensible, hardened (*à*, against); obsolete, past, extinct; dull, lustreless; *eaux* ~*es*, stagnant waters; *langue* ~*e*, dead language; (naut.) *œuvres* ~*es*, upper works; dead works; (paint.) *nature* ~*e*, still life; (mech.) *point* ~, dead point; dead centre; *il n'y va pas de main* ~*e*, he strikes hard; he does not do things by halves; ~*e la bête*, ~ *le venin*, dead men tell no tales; ~*e-saison*, slack time, dead season. ~, s.m. Dead person, deceased, corpse, defunct; (at games) dummy; *jour des* ~*s*, All Souls' Day; *office des* ~*s*, burial-service; *faire le* ~, to sham dead; (fig.) to keep quiet; to let oneself be forgotten; to lie low.

mortadelle (mɔrtadɛl), s.f. [It. *mortadella*] Bologna sausage, polony.

mortaillable (mɔrtɑjabl), adj. [Fr. feud. law] Subject to *mortaille*.

mortaille (mɔrtɑj), s.f. [f. *mort*+*tailler*]

(Fr. feud. law) Right to the goods of a deceased serf.

mortaisage (mortɛzaʒ), s.m. Mortising.

mortaise (mortɛz), s.f. [orig. unkn.] Mortise.

mortaiser (mortɛze), v.a. To mortise.

mortaiseuse (mortɛzøz), s.f. Mortising-machine.

mortalité (mortalite), s.f. [L *mortalitas*] **1.** Mortality; **2.** death-rate.

morte-eau (morto), s.f. Neap-tide.

mortel, -le (mortɛl), adj. Mortal; deadly; (colloq.) boring, tedious, mortal; *coup ~*, death-blow; *dépouille ~le*, mortal remains; *ennemi ~*, mortal foe; *haine ~le*, deadly, implacable hatred; *maladie ~le*, fatal illness, mortal disease; *péché ~*, mortal sin; *attendre deux ~les heures*, to wait two mortal hours. ~, s.m.f. Mortal; *le commun des ~s*, the common herd.

mortellement (mortɛlmɑ̃), adv. Mortally; (colloq.) awfully, extremely.

morte-saison (mortəsɛzɔ̃), s.f. (pl. *mortes-saisons*) Slack time.

mort-gage (morgaʒ), s.m. (pl. *morts-gages*) (law) Mortgage.

morticole (mortikol), s.m. [neol.] Saw-bones, doctor.

mortier (mortje), s.m. [L *mortarium*] (vessel) Mortar; (artill.) mortar; (mason.) mortar; mortier, mortier-cap.

mortifiant, -e (mortifjɑ̃), p. adj. Mortifying; humiliating.

mortification (mortifika'sjɔ̃), s.f. Mortification.

mortifier (mortifje), v.a. [L *mortificare*] To mortify; to make (meat) tender; (fig.) to humiliate.

mortinatalité (mortinatalite), s.f. Ratio of still to live births.

mort-né, -e (morne), adj. (pl. *mort-nés*, or *-nées*) Still-born, born dead.

mortuaire (mortɥɛr), adj. [L *mortuarius*] Funerary, mortuary, pertaining to burial; *domicile ~*, house of the deceased; *drap ~*, pall; *registre ~*, register of deaths.

morue (mory), s.f. [LL *moluta*] Cod, cod-fish; *huile de foie de ~*, cod-liver oil.

morutier (morytje), s.m. Cod-fishing boat; cod fisher.

morvand-eau, -elle, morvandieau (morvɑ̃do, morvɑ̃djo), adj. s.m.f. (Native) of Morvan.

morve (morv), s.f. [etym. dub.] (vet.) Glanders; (colloq.) snot.

morveu-x, -se (morvø), adj. Glandered; snotty. ~, s.m.f. (colloq.) Brat, urchin, raw youth, greenhorn; *qui se sent ~ se mouche*, if the cap fits wear it.

mosaïque (mozaik), s.f. [It. *mosaico*] Mosaic, mosaic work, tessellated pavement; (fig.) mosaic, miscellany, medley.

mosaïque (mozaik), adj. Mosaic, relating to Moses.

mosaïsme (mozaism), s.m. Mosaism.

mosaïste (mozaist), adj. s.m.f. Mosaic-maker, mosaicist.

moscatelle (moskatɛl), s.f. (bot.) Moschatel, hollow-root.

moscouade (moskwad), s.f. [f. Span. *mascabado*] Muscovado (unrefined sugar).

moscovite (moskovit), adj. s.m.f. [f. *Moscou*] Muscovite.

mosette (mozɛt), s.f. [It. *mozzetta*] Camail, mozzetta.

mosquée (moske), s.f. [f. Arab. *mesjid*] Mosque.

mot (mo), s.m. [f. L *muttum*] Word; saying; short note; answer (to a riddle); *~ à ~*, word for word; *~ pour ~*, word for word; *bon ~*, witticism, joke, pun; *gros ~s*, abuse; coarse, obscene, or bad language; *savoir le fin ~ de tout cela*, to know the long and short of it all; to know the inner meaning of it all; *au bas ~*, at the least; at the lowest (estimate); *comprendre à demi-~*, to take the hint; *à ~s couverts*, ambiguously; *~ d'ordre*, watchword, order; *~ de passe*, password; *avoir toujours le ~ pour rire*, to be jocose; to be always ready with a joke; *deux ~s, je vous prie*, a word with you, please; *envoyez-moi un ~*, just drop me a line; *c'est là mon dernier ~*, I will not take less than that, and there's an end of it; that is my last word; *je l'ai pris au ~*, I took him at his word; *tranchons le ~!*, in plain words; not to mince matters; to put it plainly; *qui ne dit ~ consent*, silence gives consent; *ils s'étaient donné le ~*, they had passed the word round; they had arranged it all beforehand; *n'en soufflez pas ~!*, do not breathe a word!; *en un ~*, in one word; briefly; *en deux ~s comme en cent*, to cut a long story short; *il ne mâche pas ses ~s*, he does not mince matters; he calls a spade a spade; *elle veut dire son ~*, she will have her say; *ils ont eu des ~s ensemble*, they have had (high) words; *avoir le dernier ~*, to have the last word; *le ~ de l'énigme*, the explanation of the riddle, the key; *je lui en toucherai un ~*, I will mention it to him.

motet (motɛ), s.m. [f. *mot*] (mus.) Motet.

mot-eur, -rice (motœr), adj. [L *motor*] Propelling, motive, moving, driving; *force ~rice*, motive power; *arbre ~*, driving-shaft; *essieu ~*, driving-axle, live axle; (anat.) *muscle ~*, motor. ~, s.m. Motor, engine, moving power, propeller; *~ à double effet*, double-acting motor; *~ à essence*, petrol-motor; *~ à explosion*, internal-combustion engine; *~ à deux temps*, two-stroke engine; *~ à vapeur*, steam-engine; *~ à pétrole*, oil-engine; *~ Diesel*, Diesel engine; *refroidissement du ~*, engine-cooling.

motif (mɔtif), s.m. [L *motivus*] Motive, incentive; cause, reason, explanation; (mus., &c.) motif, theme; *pour quel ~?*, on what ground?; *sans ~*, without a motive, motiveless; (colloq.) *pour le bon ~*, with a view to matrimony, with honourable intentions.

motilité (mɔtilite), s.f. Motility.

motion (mosjɔ̃), s.f. [L *motio*] **1.** Motion, moving, movement; **2.** motion, formal proposal in deliberative assembly. ⚠ 'Motion' in English means also 'evacuation of bowels' = *selle*, but never has this sense in French.

motiver (mɔtive), v.a. To state the reason for; to be the motive or cause of, to motivate, to justify.

motoculture (mɔtokyltyr), s.f. [f. *moteur* +*culture*] Agriculture utilizing motor-ploughs and other implements.

motocyclette (mɔtosiklɛt), s.f. [f. *moteur* +*bicyclette*] (colloq. abbrev, *moto*) Motor-bicycle, motor-cycle, motor-bike.

motocycliste (mɔtosiklist), s.m.f. Motor-cyclist.

motrice (mɔtris), adj. s.f. See masc. MOTEUR; often used nowadays as s.f. in the sense of electric locomotive.

motte (mɔt), s.f. [orig. unkn.] Lump, clod, ball of earth; mound; *~ à brûler*, dried tan, peat, turf; *~ de gazon*, sod; *~ de beurre*, roll of butter.

mottereau (pl. **-x**) (mɔtro), s.m. (ornith.) Sand-martin.

motteux (mɔtø), s.m. (ornith.) Wheatear.

motus (motys), interj. [f. *mot*] Hush!, mum!, do not breathe a word of that!, mum's the word!

mou (*mol* before a word beginning with a vowel or mute *h*), **molle** (mu, mɔl), adj. [L *mollis*] Soft, yielding, slack, loose, mellow, flaccid, lax; indolent, slack-twisted, effeminate, tame-spirited; *temps ~*, close weather; *style ~*, nerveless style. ~, s.m. (naut.) Slack.

mou (mu), s.m. Lights (pl.); lungs (of sheep, bullocks, &c.); (slang) *rentrer dans le ~ à X*, to slip into X; to belabour X; *bourrer le ~ à X*, to kid X, to hoax X, to stuff X with false stories or notions.

mouchard (muʃar), s.m. [f. *mouche*] Spy, police-spy, nark, informer; sneak, tell-tale; (Amer.) stool-pigeon.

mouchardage (muʃardaʒ), s.m. Sneaking, spying, telling tales, peaching.

moucharder (muʃarde), v.n.a. To spy, to inform, to sneak, to peach.

mouche (muʃ), s.f. [L *musca*] Fly; blister-fly; patch; beauty-spot; button (of foil); short imperial (on chin); bull's-eye (of target); spy, informer; *c'est une fine ~*, she is a sly one; he is a sly dog; *elle a pris la ~*, she is in a huff; she got offended; she has taken umbrage; *faire ~*, to hit the bull's-eye; *quelle ~ vous pique?*, what's the matter with you?, what whim have you got into your head?; *de véritables pattes de ~*, a quite illegible scrawl; *chiures de ~*, fly-blows; *couvert de chiures de ~s*, fly-blown; *~ à viande*, blowfly; *~ bleue*, bluebottle fly; *~ à miel*, honey-bee; *c'est la ~ du coche*, he (or she) is a regular busybody; he (or she) is a fussy good-for-nothing; he or she is a fly on the coach wheel; *on prend plus de ~s avec du miel qu'avec du vinaigre*, more is done by kindness than by harshness; gently does the trick; (naut.) (*a*) (obs.) river passenger-boat; (*b*) advice-boat.

moucher (muʃe), v.a. [f. L *mucus*] To wipe (somebody's nose); to snuff (a candle); (fig.) to reprimand, (colloq.) to wipe the floor with (a person); to set down; **se ~**, v.pr. to blow one's nose; (slang) *il ne se mouche pas du pied*, he does things in grand style; he won't be satisfied with second best; he won't play second fiddle.

moucherolle (muʃrɔl), s.m. [f. *mouche*] (ornith.) Flycatcher.

moucheron (muʃrɔ̃), s.m. Midge; (of candle) snuff.

mouchet (muʃɛ), s.m. (ornith.) Hedge-sparrow.

moucheté, -e (muʃte), p. adj. Spotted, speckled, flecked; *chat ~*, tabby cat; *fleuret ~*, capped foil.

moucheter (muʃte), v.a. To spot, to speckle, to fleck; to cap, to button (foils).

mouchette (muʃɛt), s.f. **1.** (arch.) Listel, beading; **2.** (pl.) candle-snuffers.

moucheture (muʃtyr), s.f. Spot, speckle; spottedness; spotting.

mouchoir (muʃwar), s.m. Handkerchief, neckerchief, kerchief; (fig.) *jeter le ~*, to choose, to throw the handkerchief.

mouchure (muʃyr), s.f. Running mucus of nose; snuff, candle snuff.

moudre (mudr), v.a. (irreg.) [L *molere*] To grind; (fig.) *être moulu*, to be dead tired; to be bruised all over.

moue (mu), s.f. [Germ. orig.] Pouting; *faire la ~*, to pout; to make a lip.

mouette (mwɛt), s.f. (ornith.) Sea-gull, sea-mew.

mouffette (mufɛt), s.f. (zool.) Skunk.

mouflard, -e (muflar), s.m.f. Fat-face, chubby-cheeks.

moufle[1] (mufl), s.f. [etym. dub.] **1.** Mitten (glove with thumb and no fingers); **2.** tackle-block, pulley-block.

moufle[2] (mufl), s.m. (chem.) Muffle.

mouflon (muflɔ̃), s.m. (zool.) Moufflon.

mouillage (mujaʒ), s.m. **1.** Watering, soaking, mixing with water; **2.** (naut.) anchoring; *être au ~*, to lie at anchor.

mouillement (mujmɑ̃), s.m. Watering, soaking, wetting, mixing with water; anchoring.
mouiller (muje), v.a.n. [L *mollire*] To soak, to water, to wet, to mix with water; to anchor; to pronounce the letters *ll* liquid, to palatalize the letters *ll*; *mouillé jusqu'aux os*, dripping wet, drenched to the skin.
mouillette (mujɛt), s.f. Sippet, finger of bread (to eat with boiled eggs).
mouilleur (mujœr), s.m. Stamp-damper; *bateau ~ de mines*, mine-layer.
mouilloir (mujwar), s.m. Water-can (for spinners).
mouillure (mujyr), s.f. Wetting, wet, dampness.
mouise (mwiz), s.f. (slang) Poverty; *être dans la ~*, to be frightfully hard up; to be in Queer Street; syn. PURÉE.
moujik (muʒik), s.m. [Russ. wd] Muzhik, moujik.
moukère (mukɛr), s.f. (slang) Dancing girl; prostitute (espec. in North Africa).
moulage (mulaʒ), s.m. **1.** Casting, moulding, cast; **2.** grinding.
moule[1] (mul), s.m. [L *modulus*] Mould, form, cast, matrix; *faire un ~*, to take a cast; *~ à gâteaux*, mould, pastry-mould; (fig.) *le ~ en est perdu*, there are no more of the sort; *fait au ~*, (fig.) beautifully shaped.
moule[2] (mul), s.f. [L *musculus*] Mussel; (colloq.) duffer.
moulé, -e (mule), p. adj. Close-fitting; closely-fitted; well-shaped; *lettre ~e*, print; writing like print.
mouler (mule), v.a. To cast, to mould; to shape, to form; to show the shape of, to follow the curves of; **se ~** (*sur*, on), v.pr. to be shaped (after something), to fit exactly; to model oneself; to take as a model.
mouleur (mulœr), s.m. Moulder. ~, adj. That is a moulder.
moulière (muljɛr), s.f. [f. *moule*[2]] Mussel-bed.
moulin (mulɛ̃), s.m. [L *molinum*] Mill; *~ à bras*, hand-mill; *~ à eau*, water-mill; *~ à vent*, windmill; *~ à vapeur*, steam-mill; *~ à café*, coffee-mill; (mil. slang) machine-gun; *~ à paroles*, chatterbox; *faire venir l'eau au ~*, to bring grist to the mill; *jeter son bonnet par-dessus les ~s*, (of women) to throw off all restraint; to take the plunge, and not to care a straw what people may think of your bad conduct.
moulinage (mulinaʒ), s.m. Silk-throwing.
mouliner (muline), v.a. To throw (silk).
moulinet (mulinɛ), s.m. Small windlass; small mill; drum; (fishing) reel, spinning reel; (fenc.) flourish; *faire des ~s avec son épée, sa canne*, to flourish one's sword, one's stick.
moulineu-r, -se, moulini-er, -ère (mulinœr, mulinje), s.m.f. Silk-thrower.
moult (mult), adv. (archaic) [L *multum*] Much.
moulu, -e (muly), p. adj. [f. *moudre*] Ground; bruised all over; *or ~* or *ormolu*, ground gold (for gilding), ormolu.
moulure (mulyr), s.f. (arch., join.) Moulding.
moulurer (mulyre), v.a. To adorn with mouldings.
mourant, -e (murɑ̃), p. adj. Dying, expiring; (fig.) faltering, languishing, fading, very pale. ~, s.m.f. Dying person.
mourir (murir), v.n. [f. L *mori*] To die; to expire, to breathe one's last, to perish, to die away; (of fire, light) to go out; *~ au péché*, to die unto sin; *à ~ de rire*, too funny for words; killing; side-splitting; *~ de faim*, to starve, to starve to death; (fig.) *~ d'envie de*, to have a great mind to; to be dying to; to wish very much to; *faire ~*, to kill; *faire ~ à petit feu*, to kill by inches; *faire ~ X de chagrin*, to break X's heart; **se ~**, v.pr. to be dying; *le jour se meurt*, the day is dying; the daylight is fading.
mouron (murɔ̃), s.m. (bot.) Chickweed; pimpernel; groundsel.
mourre (mur), s.f. [It. *morra*] Mor(r)a (game).
mousquet (muskɛ), s.m. [It. *moschetto*] Musket.
mousquetade (muskətad), s.f. Musket volley.
mousquetaire (muskətɛr), s.m. Musketeer.
mousqueterie (muskɛtri), s.f. Musketry; musket-fire.
mousqueton (muskətɔ̃), s.m. Musketoon; carbine; *porte-~*, swivel.
moussaillon (musɑjɔ̃), s.m. Small ship-boy.
mousse[1] (mus), s.m. [It. *mozzo*] Young sailor under 16 years old; ship-boy; cabin-boy.
mousse[2] (mus), s.f. [OHG *mos*] **1.** (bot.) Moss; *couvert de ~*, moss-grown; (prov.) *pierre qui roule n'amasse pas ~*, a rolling stone gathers no moss; **2.** [f. L *mulsa*] froth, scum, foam, lather; effervescence; surge; (slang) *se faire de la ~*, to fret, to worry.
mousse (mus), adj. [It. *mozzo*] Blunt, not sharp.
mousseline (muslin), s.f. [f. *Mossoul*, (It.) *Mussolo, mussolina*] Muslin; *~ de soie*, chiffon.
mousser (muse), v.n. To froth, to foam, (of wine) to sparkle; (fig.) *faire ~*, (*a*) to praise; to puff up; to crack up; (*b*) (slang) to rile, to make angry.
mousseron (musrɔ̃), s.m. (bot.) Button-mushroom.
mousseu-x, -se (musø), adj. Foaming, frothy; (of wines, &c.) sparkling; *rose ~se*, moss-rose.

moussoir (muswar), s.m. Chocolate stick (to make chocolate frothy).

mousson (musɔ̃), s.f. [f. Arab. *mausim*] Monsoon.

moussu, -e (musy), adj. Mossy, moss-grown.

moustache (mustaʃ), s.f. [It. *mostaccio*] Moustache, (of cats) whiskers.

moustachu, -e (mustaʃy), adj. Moustached.

moustérien, -ne (musterjɛ̃), adj. [f. *Le Moustier*, Dordogne, France] (archaeol.) Mousterian.

moustille (mustij), s.f. [f. L *mustum*] Strength, sparkle (of wine).

moustiquaire (mustikɛr), s.f. Mosquito-net.

moustique (mustik), s.m. [Span. *mosquito*] Mosquito.

moût (mu), s.m. [L *mustum*] Must (unfermented wine); wort (of beer).

moutard (mutar), s.m. [orig. unkn.] (pop.) Brat, urchin.

moutarde (mutard), s.f. [f. *moût*] Mustard; (colloq.) *la ~ lui monte au nez*, he is getting really angry; his monkey is up; *c'est comme de la ~ après dîner*, it comes a day after the fair.

moutardier (mutardje), s.m. Mustard-pot; mustard-maker; (colloq.) *il se croit le premier ~ du pape*, he thinks no small beer of himself.

moutier, moustier (mutje), s.m. (obs.) [L *monasterium*] Monastery.

mouton (mutɔ̃), s.m. [LL *multo*] (alive) Sheep; (as meat) mutton; (fig.) lamb; *doux comme un ~*, as gentle as a lamb; *troupeau de ~s*, flock of sheep; *tonte des ~s*, sheep-shearing; *pieds de ~*, sheep's trotters; *relié en peau de ~*, bound in basan, in basil; *peau de ~*, sheepskin; basan; basil; *la mer a des ~s*, the waves are crested with white horses; (fig.) *revenons à nos ~s*, but to return to our subject, (jest.) to our muttons; *faire le ~*, to act as decoy; (techn.) rammer, monkey, beetle.

moutonnement (mutɔnmɑ̃), s.m. Billowing, foaming (of sea).

moutonner (mutɔne), v.n.a. To billow, to foam, to break into foam or white horses; to make curly, fleecy.

moutonneu-x, -se (mutɔnø), adj. Billowy, foam-crested.

moutonni-er, -ère (mutɔnje), adj. Sheep-like, sheepish.

mouture (mutyr), s.f. [LL *molitura*] Grinding; grist; mixture of wheat, rye, and barley; (fig.) *tirer d'un sac deux ~s*, to get a double profit out of something.

mouvance (muvɑ̃s), s.f. [f. *mouvoir*] (feud. law) Tenure.

mouvant, -e (muvɑ̃), p. adj. Moving, shifting, ever-changing; (fig.) fickle; (herald.) issuant; *sables ~s*, quicksands.

mouvement (muvmɑ̃), s.m. [f. *mouvoir*] Movement, motion, gesture, move; impulse; agitation, sensation; (horol.) works; traffic; (admin.) series of appointments or promotions; *sans ~*, lifeless, limp, inanimate; *mettre en ~*, to start; *se mettre en ~*, to start; to move; to bestir oneself; *être en ~*, to be in motion; *avoir un ~ d'humeur*, to have a fit of temper; *~ de pitié*, impulse of pity; *c'est le premier ~ qui est le bon*, the first impulse is the best; *les ~s de l'âme*, the emotions of the soul, the passions; (mus.) *le ~ d'un morceau*, the tempo of a piece of music; *~ oratoire*, sway of eloquence; rhetorical action; *~ perpétuel*, perpetual motion; *il y a beaucoup de ~ dans cette rue*, there is a good deal of traffic in this street; *le ~ maritime*, shipping intelligence; shipping traffic; *faire une chose de son propre ~*, to do something of one's own accord; *il n'est plus dans le ~*, he is a back number; he is no longer in the swim.

mouvementé, -e (muvmɑ̃te), p. adj. Animated, agitated, bustling, full of variety, incident, ups and downs, or sudden turns; (of ground) broken; undulating.

mouvementer (muvmɑ̃te), v.a. To give animation or movement to.

mouver (muve), v.a. To stir.

mouvoir (muvwar), v.a. irreg. [L *movere*] To move, to start, to prompt; *mû par la vapeur*, driven by steam; **se ~**, v.pr. to be in motion, to move; to stir.

moxa (mɔksa), s.m. [Jap. *mokusa*] (med.) Moxa.

moye (mwa), s.f. [f. *moyer*] Layer of soft stone.

moyen, -ne (mwajɛ̃), adj. [f. L *medianus*] Mean, middle, middle-sized, average; medium; (log.) *~ terme*, middle term, mean; (math.) *terme ~*, middle term, mean; *le ~ âge*, the Middle Ages; *une femme d'âge ~*, a middle-aged woman.

moyen (mwajɛ̃), s.m. [L *medianum*] Means, way, manner, medium, contrivance, ability, possibility; *~s*, (pl.) means, pecuniary resources; power; abilities; *au ~ de*, by means of; *par tous les ~s*, by all manner of means; *il n'y a pas ~!*, it cannot be done; *employer les grands ~s*, to resort to drastic measures; to resort to desperate remedies; *je n'en ai pas les ~s*, I cannot afford it.

moyenâgeu-x, -se (mwajɛnaʒø), adj. Medieval, of the Middle Ages.

moyennant (mwajɛnɑ̃), prep. By means of; in consideration of; on condition of, in return for; *~ que*, conj. loc. on condition that.

moyenne (mwajɛn), s.f. Average, mean, medium; *en ~*, on the average; *prendre la ~ de*, to take the average of.

moyennement (mwajɛnmɑ̃), adv. Moderately; on an average, middling, middlingly; fairly well.
moyer (mwaje), v.a. [f. L *mediare*] To saw (freestone) in two halves.
moyère (mwajɛr), s.f. Reed-grown marsh.
moyette (mwajɛt), s.f. Shock (of corn, &c.), stook.
moyeu (mwajø), s.m. [L *modiolus*] **1.** (of a wheel) Nave, hub; **2.** (of egg) yolk; **3.** preserved plum.
mozarabe (mɔzarab), s.m. adj. [Span. wd] Mozarab.
mozette (mɔzɛ̃t), s.f. See MOSETTE.
muabilité (mɥabilite), s.f. Mutability, changeableness.
muable (mɥabl), adj. Mutable, changeable.
muance (mɥɑ̃s), s.f. [f. *muer*] (mus.) Changing a note; breaking of the voice.
mucilage (mysilaʒ), s.m. [L *mucilago*] Mucilage.
mucilagineu-x, -se (mysilaʒinø), adj. Mucilaginous.
mucosité (mykozite), s.f. [f. L *mucus*] Mucus, mucosity.
mucron (mykrɔ̃), s.m. [L *mucro*] (bot.) Mucro.
mucus (mykys), s.m. [L wd] Mucus.
mue (my), s.f. [f. *muer*] **1.** Moulting, moulting season; **2.** breaking (of human voice); **3.** coop, mew.
mue (my), adj. fem. [f. L *muta*] *Rage* ~, mute rage (of dogs).
muer (mɥe), v.n. [L *mutare*] **1.** To moult; to shed or cast feathers, horns, skin, &c.; **2.** to break (as the voice); **3.** to change; **se** ~, v.pr. to change oneself or itself, to be transformed (*en*, into).
muet, -te (mɥɛ), adj. [L *mutus*] Dumb, mute; speechless, voiceless, silent; *sourd-*~, deaf and dumb; *la frayeur l'a rendu* ~, terror struck him dumb; *scène* ~*te*, dumb show; *la loi est* ~*te sur ce point*, the law is silent on the point. ~, s.m.f. Dumb person, mute; ~**te**, s.f. mute letter.
muette (mɥɛt), s.f. [f. *meute*] Hunting-lodge.
mufle (myfl), s.m. [orig. unkn.] Snout, muzzle; (fig. of persons) cad, rotter, skunk, boor, dirty dog, bounder; *quel* ~, what a pig; (bot.) ~ *de veau*, snapdragon. ~, adj. Piggish.
muflerie (myfləri), s.f. Caddish action, ungentlemanly conduct or speech; dirty trick, boorishness.
muflier (myflje), s.m. (bot.) Snapdragon.
muge, mulet (myʒ, mylɛ), s.m. [f. L *mugil*] (ichth.) Mullet.
mugir (myʒir), v.n. [L *mugire*] To bellow, to low; (fig.) to roar.
mugissement (myʒismɑ̃), s.m. Bellowing, lowing, roaring, roar.
muguet (mygɛ), s.m. **1.** (bot.) Lily of the valley; **2.** (obs.) dandy, beau; **3.** (med.) thrush.
mugueter (mygte), v.a.n. To flirt, to play the gallant.
muid (mɥi), s.m. [f. L *modius*] Hogshead (obs. measure = about 59 galls.).
muire (mɥir), s.f. [L *muria*] Salt water (of salt-marshes).
mulard, -e (mylar), s.m.f. adj. (A kind of) Duck.
mulassi-er, -ère (mylasje), adj. Pertaining to mule-rearing.
mulâtre, -sse (mylɑtr, mylɑtrɛs), s.m.f. adj. [Span. *mulato*] Mulatto.
mule[1] (myl), s.f. [L *mula*] Mule, she-mule.
mule[2] (myl), s.f. [L *mulleus*] Slipper.
mulet (mylɛ), s.m. [L *mulus*] **1.** Mule, he-mule; *têtu comme un* ~, as stubborn as a mule; mulish, mulishly obstinate; **2.** (ichth.) mullet.
muletier (myltje), s.m. Muleteer.
mulle (myl), s.m. (ichth.) Surmullet.
mulot (mylo), s.m. [Germ. orig.] (zool.) Field-mouse.
mulsion (mylsjɔ̃), s.f. [L *mulsio*] Milking.
mult-, multi- (mylt, mylti), pref. [L *multus*] Mult-, multi-; *multiarticulé, -e*, adj. multiarticulate; &c.
multicolore (myltikɔlɔr), adj. Multicolour, multi-coloured.
multifide (myltifid), adj. Multifid.
multiflore (myltiflɔr), adj. Multiflorous.
multiforme (myltifɔrm), adj. Multiform.
multimillionnaire (myltimiljɔnɛr), adj. s.m.f. Multi-millionaire.
multipare (myltipar), adj. (biol.) Multiparous.
multiple (myltipl), adj. s.m. [L *multiplex*] Multiple; *plus petit commun* ~, least common multiple.
multiplex (myltiplɛks), adj. s.m. (techn.) Multiplex.
multipliable (myltiplijabl), adj. Multipliable.
multipliant, -e (multiplijɑ̃), p. adj. Multiplying.
multiplicande (myltiplikɑ̃d), s.m. Multiplicand.
multiplicateur (myltiplikatœr), s.m. Multiplier, multiplicator.
multiplicati-f, -ve (myltiplikatif), adj. Multiplicative, multiplying.
multiplication (myltiplika'sjɔ̃), s.f. **1.** Multiplication; *table de* ~ or *de Pythagore*, multiplication table; **2.** (bicyc.) gear.
multiplicité (myltiplisite), s.f. Multiplicity, manifold variety.
multiplier (myltiplie), v.a.n. [L *multiplicare*] To multiply; to increase in number by procreation; **se** ~, v.pr. to multiply; (fig.) to be everywhere; to exert oneself to the utmost.

multipolaire (myltipolɛr), adj. (physiol.) Multi-polar.
multitubulaire (myltitybylɛr), adj. Multitubular.
multitude (myltityd), s.f. [L *multitudo*] Multitude, crowd.
municipal, -e, (aux) (mynisipal), adj. Municipal; *Conseiller* ~, member of the town council; *garde* ~, soldier of the Municipal Guard.
municipalité (mynisipalite), s.f. Municipality, town administration; town council; town hall.
municipe (mynisip), s.m. [L *municipium*] (Rom. ant.) Municipium.
munificence (mynifisɑ̃s), s.f. [L *munificentia*] Munificence, bounteousness.
munificent, -e (mynifisɑ̃), adj. Munificent, generous, bountiful, bounteous.
munir (mynir), v.a. [L *munire*] To provide (*de*, with); to arm; **se** ~, v.pr. to provide oneself (*de*, with).
munition (mynisjɔ̃), s.f. [L *munitio*] Munition, ammunition, equipment; *pain de* ~, regulation bread, ration bread.
munitionnaire (mynisjɔnɛr), s.m. Commissary, munitioner.
munitionner (mynisjɔne), v.a. To munition.
muntjac (møntʒak), s.m. [Sunda *minchak*] (zool.) Muntjak (small Asiatic deer).
muqueu-x, -se (mykø), adj. [L *mucosus*] Mucous. **~se**, s.f. Mucous membrane.
mur (myr), s.m. [L *murus*] Wall; ~ *d'appui*, parapet; ~*s d'enceinte*, walls (pl.); ~ *de soutènement*, retaining wall; ~ *mitoyen*, party wall; (fig.) *mettre X au pied du* ~, to drive X into a corner; (fig.) *quand on est au pied du* ~, when one has one's back to the wall.
mûr, -e (myr), adj. [L *maturus*] Ripe, matured; (fig.) mature; *fruits* ~*s*, ripe fruit; *âge* ~, mature age; *abcès* ~, ripe abscess; *esprit* ~, mature mind, serious mind; *après* ~*e délibération*, after careful consideration; *étoffe trop* ~*e*, worn-out material; (fam.) *être* ~, to be mellow or drunk.
murage (myraʒ), s.m. Walling, walling up.
mûraie (myrɛ), s.f. Mulberry plantation.
muraille (myrɑj), s.f. Wall, partition; (naut.) side (of ship); ~*s*, ramparts; *la Grande* ~, the Great Wall of China.
muraillement (myrɑjmɑ̃), s.m. Walling.
murailler (myrɑje), v.a. To wall.
mural, -e, (aux) (myral), adj. Mural.
mûre (myr), s.f. [L *morum*] (bot.) Mulberry; ~ *de ronce*, blackberry.
mûrement (myrmɑ̃), adv. Thoroughly, deeply, profoundly, maturely.
murène (myrɛn), s.f. [L *muraena*] (ichth.) Muraena, marine eel, (sea-)lamprey.
murer (myre), v.a. To wall, to wall up, to brick up, to wall in; to immure.
murex (myrɛks), s.m. [L wd] Murex.
muriate (myrjat), s.m. (chem.) Muriate.
muriatique (myrjatik), adj. (chem.) Muriatic.
mûrier (myrje), s.m. (bot.) Mulberry-tree; mulberry-bush.
mûrir (myrir), v.a.n. To ripen, to mature.
mûrissant, -e (myrisɑ̃), p. adj. Ripening.
murmurant, -e (myrmyrɑ̃), p. adj. Murmuring, babbling, purling (waters).
murmure (myrmyr), s.m. [L *murmur*] Murmur, whispering, purl, purling; (fig.) grumbling.
murmurer (myrmyre), v.n.a. To murmur, to whisper, to purl (as water), to mutter; (fig.) to grumble.
mûron (myrɔ̃), s.m. [f. *mûre*] Blackberry.
murrhin, -e (myrɛ̃), adj. [L *murrhinus*] Murrhine (vase).
musagète (myzaʒɛt), adj. [f. Gr. *mousagetēs*] (of Apollo) Leading the Muses.
musaraigne (myzarɛɲ), s.f. [f. L *mus*+*araneus*] (zool.) Shrew-mouse.
musard, -e (myzar), adj. [f. *muser*] Loitering. ~, s.m.f. Loiterer.
musarder (myzarde), v.n. To loiter.
musarderie, musardise (myzardəri, myzardiz), s.f. Loitering, trifling.
musc (mysk), s.m. [L *muscus*] **1.** (zool.) Musk-deer; **2.** musk.
muscade (myskad), s.f. Nutmeg.
muscadelle (myskadɛl), s.f. Musk-pear.
muscadet (myskadɛ), s.m. **1.** Muscatel wine; **2.** a small acid apple.
muscadier (myskadje), s.m. (bot.) Nutmeg-tree.
muscadin (myskadɛ̃), s.m. [It. *moscardino*] **1.** Fop, dandy; **2.** musk lozenge.
muscardin (myskardɛ̃), s.m. (zool.) Small dormouse.
muscardine (myskardin), s.f. Muscardine (silk-worm disease).
muscat (myska), s.m. [f. *muscade*] Muscatel grape; muscatel wine.
muscidées (myside), s.f.pl. (ent.) Muscidae (dipterous family).
muscle (myskl), s.m. [L *musculus*] Muscle.
musclé, -e (myskle), adj. Muscular, having well-developed muscles.
muscoïde (myskoid), adj. Moss-like.
musculaire (myskylɛr), adj. Muscular.
musculature (myskylatyr), s.f. Musculature.
musculeu-x, -se (myskylø), adj. Muscular, musculous, having well-developed muscles.
muse (myz), s.f. [L *musa*] Muse.
museau (pl -x) (myzo), s.m. [LL *musus*] Muzzle, snout; (fig.) face.
musée (myze), s.m. [Gr. *mouseion*] Museum, picture- or art-gallery.
museler (myzle), v.a. To muzzle; (fig.) to silence, to muzzle.

muselière (myzəljɛr), s.f. Muzzle.
musellement (myzɛlmɑ̃), s.m. Muzzling; silencing.
muser (myze), v.n. [etym. dub.] To loiter, to stand idling, to moon, to trifle.
muserolle (myzrɔl), s.f. (harness) Noseband.
musette (myzɛt), s.f. [OF *muse*] **1.** Bagpipe, musette; *bal* ~, dance to bagpipes; popular dance-hall; **2.** nose-bag (for horse); **3.** bag, haversack.
muséum (myzeɔm), s.m. [L wd] Museum.
musical, -e, (aux) (myzikal) adj. Musical. ⚠ 'Musical' in English has all the senses of *musical* in French and also the sense of 'fond of music', 'skilled in music', which must be translated by *musicien, musicienne*: are you musical? = *êtes-vous musicien?*; in French *musical* is only applied to things, voices, &c., never to persons.
musicalement (myzikalmɑ̃), adv. Musically.
musicien, -ne (myzisjɛ̃), s.m.f. Musician. ~, adj. Musical.
musicographe (myzikɔgraf), s.m.f. Musicograph.
musicomane (myzikɔman), s.m.f. Musicomaniac.
musique (myzik), s.f. [L *musica*] Music; band; *la* ~ *du régiment*, the regimental band; ~ *de chambre*, chamber-music; *mettre en* ~, to set to music; *faire de la* ~, to play, to have music; *nous ferons de la* ~ *ensemble*, we shall play together; we shall have some music; *chef de* ~, bandmaster; *réglé comme un papier de* ~, as regular as clockwork; (fam.) *il en a fait une* ~ *!*, he did make a row!
musiquer (myzike), v.n. To play, to make or have music, to strum.
musiquette (myzikɛt), s.f. Easy unpretentious music.
musoir (myzwar), s.m. (naut.) Pierhead; jetty-head.
musqué, -e (myske), p. adj. Musked, perfumed with musk; musk-; *rat* ~, musk-rat.
musquer (myske), v.a. To perfume with musk.
(à) musse-pot (amyspo), adv. loc. Underhand, secretly.
(se) musser (səmyse), v.pr. [f. L *mussare*] (archaic) To hide.
mussi-f, -ve (mysif), adj. [L *musivum*] (chem.) Mosaic; *or* ~, mosaic gold; ormolu.
mussitation (mysitaˈsjɔ̃), s.f. [f. L *mussitare*] Mussitation, muttering, speaking in a low voice, weakness of the voice.
mustang (mystɑ̃), s.m. [Span. *mestengo*] Mustang.
mustélidés (mystelide), s.m.pl. [f. L *mustela*] (zool.) Mustelidae.
musulman, -e (myzylmɑ̃), adj. s.m.f. Mussulman, Mohammedan.
mutabilité (mytabilite), s.f. Mutability, changeableness.
mutable (mytabl), adj. Mutable.
mutacisme (mytasism), s.m. [L *mutacismus*] Mutation (of letters *b* and *p* when pronouncing).
mutage (mytaʒ), s.m. Mutage (checking fermentation of wine).
mutation (mytaˈsjɔ̃), s.f. [L *mutatio*] Mutation, change; (law) transfer; *droits de* ~, transfer duty.
muter (myte), v.a. **1.** To check the fermentation of (grapes); **2.** to transfer.
mutilateur (mytilatœr), s.m. Mutilator.
mutilation (mytilaˈsjɔ̃), s.f. Mutilation, maiming, mangling.
mutilé, -e (mytile), s.m.f. adj. Mutilated (person), disabled (soldier, &c.).
mutiler (mytile), v.a. [L *mutilare*] To mutilate, to maim, to disable.
mutin, -e (mytɛ̃), adj. s.m.f. [f. OF *meute*] **1.** Mutinous, mutineer (⚠ nowadays in French only the noun is used in this sense); **2.** sprightly, arch, roguish.
mutiner (mytine), v.a. To excite to rebellion; **se** ~, v.pr. to rebel, to mutiny.
mutinerie (mytinri), s.f. Mutiny, riot; archness, roguishness.
mutisme (mytism), s.m. [f. L *mutus*] Mutism, dumbness, silence.
mutité (mytite), s.f. [f. L *mutus*] Dumbness.
mutualité (mytɥalite), s.f. Mutuality.
mutuel, -le (mytɥɛl), adj. [f. L *mutuus*] Mutual; reciprocal; *société de secours* ~*s*, friendly society, (mutual) benefit society.
mutuellement (mytɥɛlmɑ̃), adv. Mutually.
mutule (mytyl), s.f. [L *mutulus*] (arch.) Mutule.
mycélium (miseljɔm), s.m. (bot.) Mycelium.
mycoderme (mikɔdɛrm), s.m. [f. Gr. *mukēs*+*derma*] Mycoderm.
mycologie, mycétologie (mikɔlɔʒi, misetɔlɔʒi), s.f. [f. Gr. *mukēs*+*logos*] (bot.) Mycology.
mycose (mikoz), s.f. (pathol.) Mycosis.
myélite (mielit), s.f. [f. Gr. *muelos*] (pathol.) Myelitis.
mygale (migal), s.f. (zool.) Mygale (a kind of spider).
myologie (miɔlɔʒi), s.f. [f. Gr. *mus*+*logos*] Myology.
myope (mjɔp), adj. s.m.f. [Gr. *muōps*] Myopic, short-sighted (person).
myopie (mjɔpi), s.f. Short-sightedness, myopia.
myosotis (mjɔzɔtis), s.m. [f. Gr. *mus*+*ōtos*] (bot.) Forget-me-not; syn. NE M'OUBLIEZ PAS.
myotomie (mjɔtɔmi), s.f. [f. Gr. *mus*+*tomē*] Myotomy.

myriade (mirjad), s.f. [f. Gr. *murias*] Myriad.
myriagramme (mirjagram), s.m. = 10,000 grammes.
myriamètre (mirjamɛtr), s.m. = 10,000 metres.
myriapode (mirjapɔd), s.m. (zool.) Myriapod.
myrica (mirika), s.m. [Gr. *murikē*] (bot.) Myrica.
myrmidon (mirmidɔ̃), s.m. [Gr. *Murmidones*] Myrmidon.
myrobalan, myrobolan (mirɔbalɑ̃, myrɔbɔlɑ̃), s.m. [Gr. *murobalanos*] (bot.) Myrobalan.
myrrhe (mir), s.f. [Gr. *murrha*] (bot.) Myrrh.
myrtacées (mirtase), s.f.pl. (bot.) Myrtaceae.
myrte (mirt), s.m. [L *myrtus*] (bot.) Myrtle.
myrtille (mirtil), s.f. (bot.) Bilberry, whortleberry; *Vaccinium myrtillus*; syn. AIRELLE.
mystagogie (mistagɔʒi), s.f. [Gr. *mustagōgos*] Mystagogy.
mystagogue (mistagɔg), s.m.f. Mystagogue.
mystère (mistɛr), s.m. [Gr. *mustērion*] Mystery, secret; miracle-play, mystery; *faire un* ~ *de*, to make a mystery of; *environné de* ~, wrapt in mystery.
mystérieusement (misterjøzmɑ̃), adv. Mysteriously.
mystérieu-x, -se (misterjø), adj. Mysterious.
mysticisme (mistisism), s.m. [f. L *mysticus*] Mysticism.
mysticité (mistisite), s.f. Mysticalness.
mystifiable (mistifjabl), adj. Easy to mystify.
mystificat-eur, -rice (mistifikatœr), adj. Mystifying; ~ s.m.f. Mystifier, hoaxer.
mystification (mistifika'sjɔ̃), s.f. Mystification, hoax.
mystifier (mistifje), v.a. To mystify, to hoax.
mystique (mistik), adj. s.m.f. [L *mysticus*] Mystic; ~, s.f. mystic system or science.
mystiquement (mistikmɑ̃), adv. Mystically.
mythe (mit), s.m. [Gr. *muthos*] Myth, fabulous thing; fiction.
mythique (mitik), adj. Mythical.
mythologie (mitɔlɔʒi), s.f. Mythology.
mythologique (mitɔlɔʒik), adj. Mythological.
mythologiste, mythologue (mitɔlɔʒist, mitɔlɔg), s.m.f. Mythologist.
mytiliculture (mitilikyltyr), s.f. [Gr. *mutilos*] Mussel breeding.
myxomycètes (miksɔmisɛt), s.m.pl. [Gr. *muxa+mukēs*] (bot.) Myxomycetes.

N

N, n (ɛn), s.m. 14th letter of the alphabet.
na (na), interj. [onom.] There; there it is; there you are!; I don't care.
nabab (nabab), s.m. [Arab. *nuwwāb*] Nabob; (fig.) nabob, wealthy luxurious person.
nababie (nababi), s.f. Nabobship; nabob's territory.
nable (nabl), s.m. [Dutch *nagel*] (naut.) Scuttle-hole, plug-hole, boat-hole; *bouchon de* ~, plug.
nabot (nabo), s.m. [orig. dub.] (pej.) Dwarf, shrimp; dandiprat, manikin, Tom Thumb; syn. AVORTON, MALBÂTI, CRIQUET, BOUT D'HOMME.
nacarat (nakara), adj. s.m. [Span. *nacarado*] Nacarat.
nacelle (nasɛl), s.f. [L *navicella*] **1.** Skiff, wherry, cockle, cockle-shell, cockle boat; **2.** car; gondola (of airship); **3.** (arch.) scotia.
nacre (nakr), s.f. [Span. *nácar*] Nacre, mother of pearl.
nacré, -e (nakre), p. adj. Nacreous, nacred, pearly.
nacrer (nakre), v.a. To nacre; to give a pearly gloss to.
nacrure (nakryr), s.f. Nacreous whiteness.
nadir (nadir), s.m. [Arab. *naḍir*] (astr.) Nadir.
naevus (pl. *naevi*) (nevys), s.m. [L wd] Naevus, birth-mark; syn. ENVIE, TACHE DE VIN.
nafé (nafe), s.m. (bot.) Gombo; *pâte de* ~, *sirop de* ~, pectoral syrup or jelly made from this.
naffe (naf), s.f. [Arab. *nafḥa*] Naphe; *eau de* ~ orange-flower water.
nage (naʒ), s.f. **1.** Swimming; *à la* ~, by swimming; *se jeter à la* ~, to jump into the water; *traverser, passer à la* ~, to swim across, over; **2.** (naut.) rowing, paddling, sculling; *chef de* ~, stroke, stroke-oar; *donner la* ~, to give the stroke, to row stroke; **3.** perspiration; *être tout en* ~, to be all in a perspiration, to be drenched with sweat.
nagée (naʒe), s.f. Stroke (in swimming).
nageoire (naʒwar), s.f. [f. *nager*] **1.** (of fish) Fin; **2.** cork, bladder, float for swimming; **3.** board (round piece of wood placed in a pail to keep the water steady).
nageoter (naʒɔte), v.n. To swim about, to splash in the water.
nager (naʒe), v.n. [f. L *navigare*] **1.** To swim, to float, to be buoyed up; ~ *entre deux eaux*, to swim under water; **2.** (naut.) to row, to pull; **3.** to swim (in), to be immersed (in); **4.** (fig.) to welter, to roll; ~ *dans l'opulence*, to be rolling in riches; ~ *dans la joie*, to be overjoyed; (slang)

il sait ~, he is up to snuff; he knows what's what.

nageu-r, -se (naʒœr), s.m.f. **1.** Swimmer; **2.** (naut.) oarsman. ~, adj. Swimming, natatorial.

naguère, naguères (nagɛr), adv. [contr. of *n'a guère = il n'y a guère de temps que*] But lately, not long ago, formerly, erewhile, whilom, time was when.

naïade (najad), s.f. [f. Gr. *naias*] **1.** (myth.) Naiad, water-nymph; **2.** (bot.) naiad.

naïadées (najade), s.f.pl. (bot.) Naiadaceae.

naï-f, -ve (naif), adj. [f. L *nativus* (cf. doublet: *natif*)] Artless, naïve, unaffected, candid; (pej.) credulous, unsuspecting, silly, green. ~, s.m.f. Naïve, credulous person; booby, mug, simpleton, muff.

nain, -e (nɛ̃), s.m.f. [L *nanus*] Dwarf. ~, adj. Dwarf, dwarfish; puny; (card-game) ~ *jaune*, Pope Joan; *arbre* ~, dwarf tree. See LINDOR.

naissain (nɛsɛ̃), s.m. Spawn of shell-fish, spat.

naissance (nɛsɑ̃s), s.f. [f. *naître*] Birth, extraction, descent, lineage, rise, springing up, beginning, root, dawn; *de* ~, from one's birth; by birth; *muet de* ~, born dumb; *anniversaire de* ~, *jour de* ~, birthday; *lieu de* ~, birth-place; ~ *de N.S.*, Nativity; *donner* ~ *à X*, to give birth to X; *donner* ~ *à quelque chose*, to give rise to something; *prendre* ~, to take its rise, to originate (in); *de haute* ~, high-born; *de basse* ~, low-born; *seconde* ~, conversion, turning to God; *la* ~ *du jour*, daybreak; *ce fleuve, à sa* ~, this river, at its source; *la* ~ *d'une voûte*, the spandrel; *la* ~ *de la gorge*, the part of the (female) body where the throat joins the breasts.

naissant, -e (nɛsɑ̃), p. adj. New-born, just beginning to grow, springing up, rising, dawning, budding; (chem.) nascent.

naître (nɛtr), v.n. (very irreg.: *je naquis, né, naissant*) [L *nascere*] To be born (*de*, of); to come into the world; to spring (from), to begin, to arise (from), to originate (in), to spring up; to bud; *je naquis à Londres*, I was born in London; *encore à* ~, unborn; *faire* ~, to give birth to; to cause to grow, to bring forth; to raise, to give rise to, to call into existence, to start, to suggest; *faire* ~ *des soupçons*, to give rise to suspicion; *avoir vu* ~ *X*, (*a*) to have known X from infancy; (*b*) to be X's birthplace; *qui vient de* ~, new-born.

naïvement (naivmɑ̃), adv. Naïvely, artlessly, candidly, ingenuously, innocently; credulously.

naïveté (naivte), s.f. Artlessness, ingenuousness, candour, innocence, naïveté; (pej.) silliness; *dire des* ~*s*, to say silly, childish things; to speak foolishly.

naja (naʒa), s.m. [f. Hindi *nāg*] (zool.) Naja, naia.

nanan (nanɑ̃), s.m. (child. wd) Goodies, sweets, something very pleasant, lollipop.

nandou (pl. **-s**) (nɑ̃du), s.m. [Braz. wd] (ornith.) Nandu, American ostrich.

nanisation (naniza'sjɔ̃), s.f. [f. *nain*] (hort.) Dwarfing.

naniser (nanize), v.a. (hort.) To dwarf.

nanisme (nanism), s.m. Dwarfishness.

nankin (nɑ̃kɛ̃), s.m. [f. *Nankin(g)*, China] Nankeen; *pantalon de* ~, nankeens (pl.). ~, adj. Light yellow, pale buff.

nanocéphale (nanɔsefal), adj. [Gr. *nanos* +*kephalē*] Nanocephalous.

nanocéphalie (nanɔsefali), s.f. Nanocephaly.

nansouk (nɑ̃suk), s.m. [Hind. *nainsukh*] Nainsook.

nantir (nɑ̃tir), v.a. [f. OF *nant* = security, guarantee] To give security to, to give as a pledge; to provide (*de*, with); **se** ~, v.pr. to provide oneself (*de*, with); to take possession; (fig.) to feather one's nest.

nantissement (nɑ̃tismɑ̃), s.m. Pledge, security, mortgage; *donner en* ~, to give as a pledge or security.

napée (nape), s.f. [Gr. *napaia*] (myth.) Napaea, nymph of wooded dells.

napel (napɛl), s.m. [L *napellus*] **1.** (bot.) Wolf's-bane, aconite, monks-hood; **2.** nightshade.

naphtaline (naftalin), s.f. (chem.) Naphthalene.

naphte (naft), s.m. [Pers. orig., L *naphtha*] (chem.) Naphtha; ~ *brut*, crude naphtha.

naphtol (naftɔl), s.m. (pharm.) Naphthol.

napiforme (napifɔrm), adj. [f. L *napus*] Napiform, turnip-shaped.

napoléon (napɔleɔ̃), s.m. Napoleon (gold coin of 20 francs).

napoléonien, -ne (napɔleɔnjɛ̃), adj. Napoleonic, Napoleon's; Napoleonistic.

napolitain, -e (napɔlitɛ̃), adj. s.m.f. Neapolitan; ~**e**, s.f. kind of woollen stuff.

nappage (napaʒ), s.m. Napery, table-linen sold by the yard or metre.

nappe (nap), s.f. [f. L *mappa*] Table-cloth, cloth; ~ *d'autel*, communion-cloth; ~ (*d'eau*), sheet (of water); (fish.) net; (geom.) nappe; *mettre la* ~, to lay the cloth; *ôter la* ~, to remove the cloth; *éclair en* ~, sheet-lightning.

napperie (napri), s.f. Linen-room. ⚠ Not 'napery', which = *linge de table*; *nappage*.

napperon (naprɔ̃), s.m. Tray-cloth; slip; upper cloth; doily.

narcéine (narsein), s.f. [f. Gr. *narkē*] (chem.) Narceine, narceia.

narcisse (narsis), s.m. [Gr. *narkissos*] (bot.)

Narcissus, daffodil, (fig.) narcissistic, self-worshipping man; hence **narcissisme,** s.m. narcissism.
narcose (narkoz), **s.f.** [f. Gr. *narkē*] (med.) Narcosis.
narcotique (narkotik), **adj.** [Gr. *narkōtikos*] Narcotic; soporific. **~,** s.m. Narcotic; opiate.
narcotisme (narkotism), s.m. Narcotism.
nard (nar), s.m. [L *nardus*] Nard, spikenard; ~ *sauvage*, asarabacca.
narghileh, narguilé (nargile), s.m. [Pers. *nargileh*] Narghile, nargileh.
nargue (narg), s.f. [orig. unkn.] Scorn, sneer, fling; ~ *de*, ~ *pour*, a fig for!, hang!; *dire* ~ *de*, to speak contemptuously of; *faire* ~ *à*, to defy, to set at defiance, to laugh at, to beard.
narguer (narge), v.a. To beard, to defy, to snap one's fingers at, to laugh to scorn.
narine (narin), s.f. [LL *narina*] Nostril.
narquois, -e (narkwɑ), adj. Cunning, sneering, sly, mocking, jeering.
narquoisement (narkwazmɑ̃), adv. Jeeringly, mockingly, slyly.
narrat-eur, -rice (naratœr), s.m.f. [L *narrator*] Narrator, story-teller, relater.
narrati-f, -ve (naratif), adj. Narrative.
narration (narra'sjɔ̃), s.f. [L *narratio*] Narration, narrative, story, relation, tale.
narré (nare), s.m. Narrative, relation, account; statement.
narrer (nare), v.a. [L *narrare*] To narrate, to relate, to tell, to recount; syn. RACONTER.
narthex (nartɛks), s.m. [Gr. wd] (arch.) Narthex.
narval (narval), s.m. [Scand. orig.] (zool.) Narwhal, sea-unicorn.
nasal, -e, (aux) (nazal), adj. [f. L *nasus*] Nasal. ~, s.m. (anc. armour) Nasel, nasal; ~e, s.f. (gram.) nasal.
nasalement (nazalmɑ̃), adv. Nasally.
nasalisation (nazaliza'sjɔ̃), s.f. Nasalization.
nasaliser (nazalize), v.n.a. To nasalize.
nasalité (nazalite), s.f. Nasality; twang.
nasarde (nazard), s.f. [f. L *nasus*] Fillip on the nose; (fig.) taunt, scoff; saucy retort; snub, set-down, rebuff.
nasarder (nazarde), v.a. (archaic) To fillip on the nose, to jeer at; to rebuff.
naseau (pl. **-x**) (nazo), s.m. (of an animal) Nostril; *fendeur de ~x*, braggart.
nasicorne (nazikorn), adj. [L *nasus*+*cornu*] (zool.) Nasicornous.
nasière (nazjɛr), s.f. Nose-ring.
nasillard, -e (nazijar), adj. Nasal, snuffling. ~, s.m.f. Snuffler.
nasillement (nazijmɑ̃), s.m. Snuffling, speaking with a nasal sound; twang; twangle.
nasiller (nazije), v.n. To speak through the nose, to snuffle, to have a twang.
nasilleu-r, -se (nazijœr), s.m.f. Snuffler.
nasillonnement (nazijɔnmɑ̃), s.m. See NASILLEMENT.
nasique (nazik), s.m. [f. L *nasus*] (zool.) Proboscis-monkey.
nasse (nas), s.f. [L *nassa*] (fish.) Bow-net, weel, eel-basket, lobster-basket; (fig.) noose, snare; *être dans la* ~, to be caught in the noose.
natal, -e, (als or aux) (natal), adj. [L *natalis*] Natal, native, birth . . .; *ciel* ~, native clime; *lieu* ~, birthplace; *ma terre ~e*, my native land, my country.
natalité (natalite), s.f. Natality; birth-rate.
natation (nata'sjɔ̃), s.f. [L *natatio*] Swimming, natation.
natatoire (natatwar), adj. Natatory, swimming.
nati-f, -ve (natif), adj. s.m.f. [L *nativus*, cf. doublet: *naïf*] Native.
nation (na'sjɔ̃), s.f. [L *natio*] Nation, people, race; *Société des ~s*, League of Nations.
national, -e, (aux) (nasjɔnal), adj. National; native. **~aux,** s.m.pl. Nationals, fellow-countrymen.
nationalement (nasjɔnalmɑ̃), adv. Nationally.
nationalisation (nasjɔnaliza'sjɔ̃), s.f. Nationalization.
nationaliser (nasjɔnalize), v.a. To nationalize.
nationalisme (nasjɔnalism), s.m. Nationalism.
nationaliste (nasjɔnalist), s.m.f. adj. Nationalist.
nationalité (nasjɔnalite), s.f. Nationality; *acte de* ~ (*de navire*), ship's certificate.
nationaux (nasjɔno), s.m.pl. See NATIONAL.
nativement (nativmɑ̃), adv. Natively.
nativité (nativite), s.f. [L *nativitas*] Nativity, birth (of Jesus Christ).
natron, natrum (natrɔ̃, natrɔm), s.m. [Arab. *natroun*] (chem.) Natron, soda.
nattage (nataʒ), s.m. Matting, plaiting, twisting.
natte (nat), s.f. [f. L *matta*] **1.** Plait, tress, plaited tress; **2.** mat, matting, rush mat, straw mat.
natter (nate), v.a. To plait, to braid, to mat, to twist.
natti-er, -ère (natje), s.m.f. Mat-maker, mat-seller.
(in) naturalibus [L adv. loc.] Without any clothes on, in a state of nature, in puris naturalibus, stark naked.
naturalisation (natyraliza'sjɔ̃), s.f. [f. L *naturalis*] Naturalization.
naturaliser (natyralize), v.a. **1.** To naturalize; *se faire* ~, to obtain letters of naturalization; **2.** to stuff (a dead animal).
naturalisme (natyralism), s.m. Naturalism.

naturaliste (natyralist), s.m.f. Naturalist. ~, adj. Naturalistic.

naturalité (natyralite), s.f. Citizenship, status of a native or naturalized person.

nature (natyr), s.f. [L *natura*] Nature, kind, sort, essence, constitution, temper, disposition; *d'après* ~, from life; *de sa* ~, by nature, in its nature; *de* ~ *à*, calculated to, of a kind to; *payer en* ~, to pay in kind; *contre* ~, monstrous, unnatural; *état de* ~, natural state; state of nature; ~ *morte*, still life; *grandeur* ~, life-size. ~, adj. Plain, unadorned, natural, unadulterated; *café* ~, coffee without milk or liqueurs.

naturel, -le (natyrɛl), adj. Natural, native, innate, inborn, artless, genuine, ingenuous, free, genial, congenial, easy; *grandeur* ~*le*, life-size; *la loi* ~*le*, the law of Nature; *fils* ~, illegitimate son.

naturel (natyrɛl), s.m. Naturalness, simplicity, native ease, genuineness, native disposition; *au* ~, to the life; plain; *d'un bon* ~, good-natured; *d'un mauvais* ~, ill-natured; *un heureux* ~, a happy disposition; *chassez le* ~, *il revient au galop*, what is bred in the bone will not out of the flesh; ~, **-le**, s.m.f. native.

naturellement (natyrɛlmɑ̃), adv. Naturally; by nature; artlessly, candidly; as a matter of course; (excl.) of course!

nauclée (nokle), s.f. (bot.) Nauclea, grapple-plant, uncaria.

naucler, nauclerc, nauclère (noklɛr), s.m. (ornith.) Swallow-tailed hawk.

naucore (nokɔr), s.f. (ent.) Kind of aquatic hemipter.

naufrage (nofraʒ), s.m. [L *naufragium*] Shipwreck, wreck; *faire* ~, to be shipwrecked.

naufragé, -e (nofraʒe), adj. Shipwrecked. ~, s.m.f. Shipwrecked person; wrecked sailor, castaway.

naufrager (nofraʒe), v.n. To be shipwrecked.

naufrageur (nofraʒœr), s.m. Wrecker, plunderer.

naulage (nolaʒ), s.m. [f. L *naulum*] (naut.) Freight; syn. FRET, NOLIS.

naumachie (nomaʃi), s.f. [f. Gr. *naumakhia*] Naumachia, mock sea-fight.

nauséabond, -e (nozeabɔ̃), adj. [L *nauseabundus*] Nauseous, nauseating, stinking; (fig.) loathsome.

nausée (noze), s.f. [L *nausea*] Nausea; sea-sickness, retching; (fig.) disgust; *cela vous donne la* ~, or *des* ~*s*, it makes one sick.

nauséeu-x, -se (nozeø), adj. Nauseous; retching.

nautile (notil), s.m. [L *nautilus*] **1.** (zool.) Nautilus; **2.** swimming-belt, life-belt.

nautique (notik), adj. Nautical; *l'art* ~, seamanship; *carte* ~, sea-chart.

nautoni-er, -ère (notɔnje), s.m.f. [f. LL *nautonem*, f. L *nauta*; OF *notonier*] (poet.) Mariner, pilot, boatman, (fem.) boatwoman; *le* ~ *des sombres bords*, the grim ferryman of Hell (Charon).

navaja (navaʒa), s.f. [Span. wd] Navaja, Spanish cutlass.

naval, -e (pl. -s) (naval), adj. [L *navalis*] Naval, sea-, nautical, maritime.

navarin (aux pommes) (navarɛ̃), s.m. (cook.) Irish stew; mutton stew with potatoes and turnips.

navarrais, -e, navarrin, -e (navarɛ, navarɛ̃), adj. s.m.f. Navarrese.

navée (nave), s.f. (obs.) [f. L *navis*, LL *navata*] Boatload.

navet (navɛ), s.m. [f. L *napus*] Turnip; *chou-*~, Swedish turnip; *il a du sang de* ~, he is as white as a sheet; (paint.) *c'est un* ~, it is a daub.

navetier (navtje), s.m. Shuttle-maker.

navette (navɛt), s.f. [f. *nef*] **1.** Shuttle; **2.** (bot.) rape; **3.** incense-box; **4.** kind of pulley; **5.** Indian canoe; *faire la* ~ (*entre*), to go or run to and fro (between) several times; to ply (between); *point de* ~, lock-stitch; *huile de* ~, rape-oil.

navicelle (navisɛl), s.f. [f. L *navis*] (arch.) Antique boat-shaped fountain.

naviculaire (navikylɛr), adj. Navicular.

navicule (navikyl), s.f. (bot.) Kind of sea-weed.

naviforme (navifɔrm), adj. [f. L *navis*] Naviform; boat-shaped.

navigabilité (navigabilite), s.f. Navigability; sea-worthiness.

navigable (navigabl), adj. Navigable, sea-worthy; affording passage for ships; open; controllable.

navigant, -e (navigɑ̃), p. adj. Navigating.

navigateur (navigatœr), s.m. [L *navigator*] Mariner, navigator, voyager, sailor, seafaring man; aeronaut, balloonist. ⚠ Not 'navigator' in the sense of 'navvy', which = *terrassier*. ~, adj. (fem. *navigatrice*) Navigating, sea-faring.

navigation (naviga'sjɔ̃), s.f. Navigation, sailing, shipping, voyage.

naviguer (navige), v.a.n. [doublet of *nager*, L *navigare*] To navigate, to sail, to voyage, to row, to go over; (fig.) *ici il nous faut* ~ *avec prudence*, here we must tread lightly.

naville (navij), s.f. [f. It. *naviglio*] Small irrigation canal.

navire (navir), s.m. [f. L *navigium*] Ship (⚠ in Engl. ships are frequently referred to, especially by sailors, as 'she'); vessel, boat; ~ *de guerre*, man-of-war; ~ *marchand*, merchantman; *les* ~*s*, (collect.) the shipping.

navrant, -e (nɑvrɑ̃), p. adj. Distressing, heart-rending, harrowing, causing great grief.

navré, -e (nαvre), p. adj. Distressed, broken-hearted; (colloq.) *je suis ~ de vous avoir fait attendre*, I am awfully sorry to have kept you waiting.
navrer (nαvre), v.a. [etym. dub., OHG *narwe*?] To distress; to cause grief to. ⚠ In Old French *navrer* had a stronger sense than it has nowadays, meaning 'to wound'.
nazaréen, -ne (nazareɛ̃), adj. s.m.f. Nazarean, Nazarene, Nazarite.
ne (**n'** before vowel or unaspirated *h*) (nə), adv. **1.** as negative: Not, no, never (usually constr. with *pas* or *point*; *ne* is placed before the verb, *pas* or *point* after the verb, except in the infinitive; ex.: *je ~ mange pas*; *~ pas manger*); **2.** as expletive, with verbs like *craindre, douter*, and with comparatives, ex.: *je crains qu'il ~ soit parti*, I am afraid he will be gone; *plus amoureux que je ~ fus jamais*, more devoted than I ever was; **3.** *~ . . . que = seulement*, only, but, nothing but, no one but, none but, anything but, any one but, no more than, no other than; *je ~ le vois ni l'entends*, I neither see nor hear him; *vous ~ pouvez pas ~ pas le faire*, you cannot but do it; *je me soucierais fort peu de tout ce qu'ils peuvent dire, n'était l'artifice*, I would not care a pin about what they might say, were it not for their insidiousness; *il agit autrement qu'il ~ parle*, he does not act in accordance with his speeches.
né, -e (ne), p. adj. [f. *naître*] Born, descended; produced, foaled; *~ poète*, a poet born; *il est ~ Français*, he is French by birth; *Madame X, née Y*, Mrs. X, whose maiden name was Y; *un ennemi-~ de*, a born enemy of; *bien ~*, of good birth, of good family; well constituted, well balanced, noble, generous, brave; *mort-~*, still-born; *nouveau-~*, new-born; *premier-~*, first-born.
néanmoins (neɑ̃mwɛ̃), adv. [*néant*+ *moins*] However, nevertheless, notwithstanding, yet, for all that, still.
néant (neɑ̃), s.m. [etym. dub., prob. f. L *ne* and *inde*] Nothingness, nonentity, vacancy, worthlessness, emptiness; annihilation; nil; *réduire à ~*, to reduce to nothing, to knock to pieces, to annihilate, to set at naught; *tirer du ~*, to draw out of nothing; *le témoignage de notre ~*, the token of our nothingness; *le ~ des grandeurs*, the worthlessness of glory. *~*, adv. Nothing, naught, nil.
néantise (neɑ̃tiz), s.f. Worthlessness, extreme indolence.
nébalie (nebali), s.f. Kind of crustacean.
nèble (nɛbl), s.m. [L *nebula*] (agric.) Mist, blight; (vet.) rot.
nébride (nebrid), s.f. [Gr. *nebris*] (Of Bacchus, &c.) Fawn-skin, nebris.
nébulaire (nebylɛr), adj. Nebular.
nébuleusement (nebyløzmɑ̃), adv. Nebulously.
nébuleu-x, -se (nebylø), adj. [L *nebulosus*] **1.** Nebulous; **2.** hazy, vague, obscure. *~se*, s.f. Nebula (pl. nebulae).
nébulosité (nebylozite), s.f. **1.** Nebulosity; **2.** haziness, cloudiness, obscurity, vagueness.
nécessaire (nesɛsɛr), adj. [f. L *necessarius*] Necessary, indispensable, requisite; unavoidable, needful; *~ à* (or *pour*), necessary to; *il est ~ que vous fassiez cela*, it is necessary that you should do that; or, it is necessary for you to do that; *se rendre ~*, to make oneself indispensable, or necessary; *il n'y a pas d'homme ~*, nobody is indispensable; *rendre ~s des mesures énergiques*, to call for strong measures.
nécessaire (nesɛsɛr), s.m. **1.** Necessaries, what is necessary; *il manque même du ~*, he lacks or wants the first necessaries of life; *se refuser le ~*, to deny oneself necessaries; *il fait le ~*, he makes a fuss, he is a busybody; *pour cette affaire, je ferai le ~*, I will do all that is needed in the matter; **2.** dressing-case, box, work-box; *~ de réparations*, repairing-outfit.
nécessairement (nesɛsɛrmɑ̃), adv. Necessarily; fatally, inevitably, of course, unavoidably.
nécessarien (nesɛsarjɛ̃), s.m. Necessarian, necessitarian.
nécessitant, -e (nesɛsitɑ̃), p. adj. Compelling, compulsory, absolute.
nécessité (nesɛsite), s.f. [L *necessitas*] Necessity; necessariness, exigency; need, want, pinch; *faire de ~ vertu*, to make a virtue of necessity; *être* (or *se trouver*) *dans la ~ de faire*, to be (or to lie) under the necessity of doing; *de toute ~*, necessarily; unavoidably, of necessity; *c'est une ~ que de*, it is necessary to (infin.); *~ fait loi*, necessity knows no law.
nécessiter (nesɛsite), v.a. To necessitate, to render or make necessary; to compel, to force, to imply, to oblige.
nécessiteu-x, -se (nesɛsitø), adj. s.m.f. Necessitous, needy, poor.
nécrologe (nekrɔlɔʒ), s.m. [f. Gr. *nekros*+ *logos*] Necrology, death-roll; obituary.
nécrologie (nekrɔlɔʒi), s.f. Necrology, obituary notice; death-roll.
nécrologique (nekrɔlɔʒik), adj. Necrological.
nécrologue (nekrɔlɔg), s.m. Necrologist.
nécromancie (nekrɔmɑ̃si), s.f. [f. Gr. *nekromanteia*] Necromancy.
nécromancien, -ne (nekrɔmɑ̃sjɛ̃), s.m.f. Necromancer; syn. NÉCROMANT.
nécrophage (nekrɔfaʒ), adj. [f. Gr. *nekros*+ *-phagos*] (zool.) Necrophagous. *~*, s.m. Necrophagan.
nécrophore (nekrɔfɔr), s.m. [f. Gr.

nekros+-phoros] (ent.) Burying-beetle; necrophore; sexton-beetle.
nécropole (nekrɔpɔl), s.f. [f. Gr. *nekros+polis*] Necropolis, cemetery; charnel-house; burial-ground.
nécropsie, nécroscopie (nekrɔpsi, nekrɔskɔpi), s.f. Necropsy, necroscopy, post-mortem examination; syn. AUTOPSIE.
nécrose (nekroz), s.f. [Gr. *nekrōsis*] (pathol.) Necrosis.
nécroser (nekroze), v.a. (med.) To necrose; **se** ~, v.pr. to become necrosed.
nectaire (nɛktɛr), s.m. (bot.) Nectary.
nectar (nɛktar), s.m. [Gr. *nektar*] (lit. and fig.) Nectar.
nectaré, -e, nectaréen, -ne (nɛktare, nektareɛ̃), adj. Nectared, nectarean, nectarous.
néerlandais, -e (neɛrlɑ̃dɛ), adj. Netherlandish, Dutch. ~, s.m.f. Netherlander, Dutchman, (fem.) Dutchwoman.
nef (nɛf), s.f. [L *navis*] **1.** (obs.) Ship, vessel; **2.** (of church) nave.
néfaste (nefast), adj. [L *nefastus*] Woful, inauspicious, unlucky.
nèfle (nɛfl), s.f. [f. L *mespilus*] (bot.) Medlar; (slang) *des ~s!*, nothing doing!; you be blowed!; don't you wish you may get it!
néflier (neflje), s.m. (bot.) Medlar-tree.
négat-eur, -rice (negatœr), adj. Denying. ~, s.m.f. Denier.
négatif (negatif), s.m. (photo.) Negative.
négati-f, -ve (negatif), adj. Negative.
négation (nega'sjɔ̃), s.f. [L *negatio*] Negation; *répondre par une* ~, to answer in the negative.
négative (negativ), s.f. Negative, denial, refusal; *répondre par la* ~, to answer in the negative.
négativement (negativmɑ̃), adv. Negatively, in the negative.
négligé (neglíʒe), s.m. **1.** Négligé, morning dress; loose garment; déshabillé, undress; **2.** carelessness, negligence, freedom from restraint or artificiality. ~, p. adj. Neglected, unadorned, unstudied, careless, slovenly, loose, &c.
négligeable (negliʒabl), adj. Negligible, unimportant, not to be taken into account, that may be omitted, or neglected; *quantité* ~, negligible quantity.
négligement (negliʒmɑ̃) (obs.), s.m. Neglect, negligence.
négligemment (negliʒamɑ̃), adv. Carelessly, negligently, neglectfully, remissly, (archaic) slovenly.
négligence (negliʒɑ̃s), s.f. [L *negligentia*] **1.** Neglect, negligence, remissness; **2.** instance of neglect, short-coming, mistake, oversight, inaccuracy; **3.** carelessness, slovenliness, negligence; *par ma* ~, through my neglect; *il y a en cela de la* ~ *de votre part*, you have been careless in this matter.
négligent, -e (negliʒɑ̃), adj. Neglectful, negligent, careless, remiss, inaccurate.
négliger (negliʒe), v.a. [f. L *negligere*] To neglect, to omit, to be careless of, to leave out, to overlook, to slight, to disregard; **se** ~, v.pr. *elle se néglige*, she neglects herself, she is careless of her person; *il se sont longtemps négligés* (*mutuellement*), they have long neglected each other.
négoce (negɔs), s.m. [L *negotium*] Trade; business-agency; intervention, mediation.
négociabilité (negɔsjabilite), s.f. Negotiability.
négociable (negɔsjabl), adj. Negotiable, convertible into cash or notes.
négociant, -e (negɔsjɑ̃), s.m.f. Merchant, trader; ~ *en vins*, wine-merchant.
négociat-eur, -rice (negɔsjatœr), s.m.f. Negotiator, (fem.) negotiatrix; mediator, (fem.) mediatrix.
négociation (negɔsja'sjɔ̃), s.f. [L *negotiatio*] Negotiation, transaction, mediation, palaver; compromise, discussion (in order to bring about an arrangement); business; *engager des ~s*, to enter into negotiations.
négocier (negɔsje), v.a.n. To negotiate, to trade; to discuss. ⚠ In English one may 'negotiate' a fence, a corner, &c.: *on franchit, on réussit à franchir une haie, un tournant, etc.*, but *négocier* cannot be used in this sense.
nègre (nɛgr), s.m. adj. [f. L *niger*, Span. *negro*] Negro (fem. negress), black; nigger; (fig.) hack, ghost, a sweated contributor; *travailler comme un* ~, to work like a nigger; *parler petit* ~, to speak French as it is spoken by the Blacks in the French colonies, or 'pidgin French'.
nègrerie (nɛgrəri), s.f. Barracoon, negro-jail, negro-barrack.
négresse (negrɛs), s.f. Negress, negro woman. ~ adj. f. Negro, black.
négrier (negrije), s.m. Slave-ship, slave-trader; *capitaine* ~, captain of a slave-ship.
négrillon, -ne (negrijɔ̃), s.m.f. Negro boy, negro girl, (jest.) sambo, blacky, nigger.
négroïde (negrɔid), adj. Negro, black, negroid.
négrophile (negrɔfil), adj. s.m.f. Negrophil.
négus (negys), s.m. Negus (sovereign of Abyssinia).
neige (nɛʒ), s.f. [f. L *nix*] **1.** Snow; **2.** (fig.) whiteness; *d'un blanc de* ~, of a snowy whiteness, snow-white; *une boule de* ~, a snow-ball; *il était tombé beaucoup de* ~, it had snowed very hard; *faire boule de* ~, to increase rapidly; *où sont les ~s d'antan?*, where are the snows of yester-year?; *perce-*~, snowdrop; *œufs à la* ~, floating

islands; *œufs battus en* ~, eggs whipped to a froth; *bloqué par les* ~*s*, snowbound.
neiger (nεʒe), v.n. To snow; (fig.) *il a neigé sur sa tête*, his head is white with age; (fig.) *il neigeait des pétales*, the earth was sprinkled with petals, there was a shower of petals.
neigeu-x, -se (nεʒø), adj. Snowy.
nelumbo (nelymbo), s.m. (bot.) Nelumbo.
nématode (nematɔd), s.m. [f. Gr. *nēma*] (zool.) Nematode; ~ *de la betterave*, beetroot-worm.
nématoïde (nematɔid), adj. Worm-shaped, nematoid.
néméen, -ne (nemeɛ̃), adj. Nemean; *les Néméennes*, (Gr. Lit.; Pindar's) Nemean odes.
némophile (nemɔfil), s.f. [f. Gr. *nemos*+*philos*] (bot.) Nemophila.
némoral, -e, (aux) (nemɔral), adj. [f. L *nemus*] Nemoral, of the woods.
ne m'oubliez pas (nəmublijepɑ), s.m. (bot.) Forget-me-not; syn. MYOSOTIS.
nénais (nenε), s.m. (fam.) Bubby.
néné (nene), s.m. (slang) *Les* ~*s*, charlies, woman's breasts.
nénies (neni), s.f.pl. [f. L *nenia*] Greek funeral songs.
nenni (nεnni), adv. [f. L *non*+*ille*] (fam.) Nay, no, not at all; *que* ~*!*, no indeed, certainly not!
nénufar, nénuphar (nenyfar), s.m. [f. Arab. *nīnūfar*] (bot.) Nenuphar, water-lily.
néo- (neo), (pref.) [Gr. *neos*] (in comps.) Neo-.
néo-calédonien, -ne (neokaledɔnjɛ̃), s.m.f. adj. New Caledonian.
néo-catholicisme (neokatɔlisism), s.m. Neo-Catholicism.
néo-celtique (neosεltik), adj. (of language) Neo-Celtic, of Celtic origin.
néo-christianisme (neokristjanism), s.m. Neo-Christianity.
néocomien, -ne (neokɔmjɛ̃), adj. s.m. [f. LL *Neocomium*, latinized form of Neuchâtel] (geol.) Neocomian.
néo-cor (neokɔr), s.m. Kind of cornet.
néographe (neograf), s.m.f. Neographer.
néographisme (neografism), s.m. [Gr. *neo*+*graphe*] Neography, new system of orthography.
néo-grec, -que (neogrεk), adj. Neo-Greek, modern Greek.
néo-latin, -e (neolatɛ̃), adj. Neo-Latin.
néolithique (neolitik), adj. [f. Gr. *neos*+*lithos*] Neolithic.
néologisme (neolɔʒism), s.m. [f. Gr. *neos*+*logos*] Neologism.
néologiste, néologue (neolɔʒist, neolɔg), s.m.f. Neologist.
néo-malthusianisme (neomaltyzjanism), s.m. Neo-Malthusianism.
néon (neɔ̃), s.m. [f. Gr. *neos*] Neon.
néophobe (neofɔb), s.m.f. [f. Gr. *neos*+*phobos*] Neophobe. ~, adj. Neophobic.
néophobie (neofɔbi), s.f. Neophobia.
néophron (neofrɔ̃), s.m. (ornith.) Neophron.
néophyte (neofit), s.m.f. adj. [f. Gr. *neos*+*phutos*] Neophyte; (fig.) beginner, tiro, novice, neophyte.
néoplasme (neoplasm), s.m. [f. Gr. *neos*+*plasma*] Neoplasm (tumour).
néo-platonicien, -ne (neoplatɔnisjɛ̃), adj. Neoplatonic; ~, s.m.f. Neoplatonist.
néo-platonisme (neoplatɔnism), s.m. Neo-platonism.
néorama (neorama), s.m. [f. Gr. *neos* +*orama*] Neorama.
néotérique (neoterik), adj. [f. Gr. *neoterikos*] Neoteric, new-fangled.
néozoïque (neɔzɔik), adj. [Gr. *neos*+*zōon*] (geol.) Neozoic.
népâlais, -e (nepalε), adj. s.m.f. Nepalese.
nèpe (nεp), s.f. [L *nepa*] (ent.) Water-scorpion.
népenthès (nepɛ̃tεs), s.m. [Gr. *nēpenthes*] **1.** (bot.) Nepenthes, pitcher-plant; **2.** (ant.) nepenthes, nepenthe (drug capable of banishing grief or trouble).
néphalie (nefali), s.f. Temperance festivity.
néphalien, -ne (nefaljɛ̃), adj. s.m.f. (that is a) Nephalist, teetotaller, abstainer.
néphalisme (nefalism), s.m. [f. Gr. *nēphalios*] Nephalism, teetotalism, temperance.
néphralgie (nefralʒi), s.f. [f. Gr. *nephros* +*algos*] Nephralgia.
néphrétique, néphritique (nefretik), adj. Nephritic.
néphrite (nefrit), s.f. (pathol.) **1.** Nephritis; **2.** (min.) nephrite, jade.
népotisme (nepɔtism), s.m. [f. L *nepos*] Nepotism.
neptunien, -ne (nεptynjɛ̃), adj. Neptunian.
néréides (nereid), s.f. [f. L *nereis*] (myth.) Nereid; (zool.) nereid.
nerf (nεrf) (the *f* is mute in the plural *nerfs* and in *nerf de bœuf*), s.m. [L *nervus*] **1.** Nerve; **2.** sinew, tendon; **3.** (fig.) vigour, strength, stamina, vim, energy; ~ *de bœuf*, lash, scourge; *vous me portez sur les* ~*s*, you get on my nerves, you worry me; *avoir une attaque de* ~*s*, to have a fit of hysterics; *l'argent, c'est le* ~ *de la guerre*, money is the sinews of war; *manquer de* ~, to lack energy; (colloq.) *avoir les* ~*s en pelote*, to have one's nerves all on edge.
nerf-férure (nεrferyr), s.f. (pl. *nerfs-férures*) (vet.) Inflammation of the flexor tendons, overreach.
nérinée (nerine), s.f. (zool.) Fossil mollusc.

nérite (nerit), s.f. [L *nerita*] (moll.) Nerite, nerita.
néroli (nerɔli), s.m. [from the name of an Italian princess] Neroli, essential oil distilled from bitter-orange flowers.
néronien, -ne (nerɔnjɛ̃), adj. Neronian; cruel, licentious.
nerprun (nɛrprœ̃), s.m. [f. L *niger*+ *prunum*] (bot.) Buckthorn.
nerval, -e, (aux) (nɛrval), adj. (med.) Neural, nervine.
nervation (nɛrva'sjɔ̃), s.f. Nervation, neuration.
nervé, -e (nɛrve), p. adj. Nerved, nervous, (bot.) nervate.
nerver (nɛrve), v.a. To nerve, to cover with strips; (bookbind.) to cord, to band.
nerveusement (nɛrvøzmɑ̃), adv. Nervously, dryly, energetically.
nerveu-x, -se (nɛrvø), adj. Nervous; irritable; sinewy, nervy, wiry, strong; (of style) terse, vigorous, nervous.
nervin (nɛrvɛ̃), adj. Nervine. ~, s.m. Nerve-tonic.
nervosisme (nɛrvozism), s.m. Morbid nervousness, nervous diathesis, nervous disorder.
nervosité (nɛrvozite), s.f. Nervousness.
nervure (nɛrvyr), s.f. (bot.) Rib, nervure; (arch.) nervure, rib; (bookbind.) cording, cords, bands, slips; (needlework) piping.
nestor (nɛstɔr), s.m. [f. prop. n.] Nestor, senior, elder, adviser, wise old man.
nestorianisme (nɛstɔrjanism), s.m. Nestorianism.
nestorien, -ne (nɛstɔrjɛ̃), adj. s.m. (eccles. hist.) Nestorian.
net, -te (nɛt), adj. [L *nitidus*] Clean, neat, clear, tidy, sharp, distinct, free, plain, frank, point-blank, empty, blameless; (of price) net; (lit. and fig.) *avoir les mains ~tes*, to have clean hands; *avoir l'esprit ~*, to be clear-headed; *j'en aurai le cœur ~*, I am resolved to know the truth about it; *faire maison ~te* or *faire place ~te*, to clear one's house (of unpleasant people); to make a clean sweep (of); *revenu ~*, net income; *bénéfice ~*, net profit; *mettre au ~ (quelque chose)*, to make a fair copy of. ~, adv. Flatly, plainly, point-blank; *refuser ~*, to refuse point-blank, to decline flatly.
nettement (nɛtəmɑ̃), adv. Neatly, cleanly, clearly, sharply, purely, frankly, flatly, point-blank.
netteté (nɛtəte, nɛtte), s.f. Neatness, cleanness, cleanliness, clearness, distinctness, sharpness, plainness, tidiness.
nettoiement, nettoyage (nɛtwamɑ̃, nɛtwajaʒ), s.m. Cleaning, cleansing, clearing, scouring, sweeping, wiping, French-cleaning; *appareil de ~ par le vide*, vacuum-cleaner; see syn. ASPIRATEUR.
nettoyable (nɛtwajabl), adj. Cleanable, cleansable.
nettoyer (nɛtwaje), v.a. To clean, to cleanse, to clear, to scour, to sweep, to wipe; *donner un vêtement à ~*, to send a garment to be dry-cleaned; (games) *~ le tapis*, to sweep the board; *se ~ les mains*, to wash one's hands; *se ~*, to wash and dry oneself; (colloq.) *se faire ~*, to be cleaned out, stripped of one's money.
nettoyeu-r, -se (nɛtwajœr), s.m.f. Cleaner, scourer, picker.
nettoyure (nɛtwajyr), s.f. Cleansings, sweepings.
neuf (nœf), num. adj. s.m. [L *novem*] Nine; *le ~ janvier*, the ninth of January, or Jan. ninth; *deux ~*, two nines; *Louis Neuf*, Louis the Ninth; *un ~ de carreau*, a nine of diamonds.
neu-f, -ve (nœf), adj. [L *novus*] **1.** New, fresh; *battant ~*, brand-new; *remettre à ~*, to do up like new; **2.** (fig.) raw, inexperienced, innocent, green, fresh. ~, s.m. What is new; novelty; *elle ne veut porter que du ~*, she will wear nothing but new clothes; *quoi de ~?*, what's the news?
neufchâtel (nøʃɑtɛl), s.m. Neufchâtel cheese (cream cheese).
neume (nøm), s.m. [f. Gr. *pneuma*] Neum (group of notes sung to single syllable in plain-song).
neurasthénie (nørasteni), s.f. Neurasthenia.
neurasthénique (nørastenik), adj. Neurasthenic.
neuro-, neur-, (nœro, nœr), (in comps.) pref. [f. Gr. *neuron*] Neuro-, neur-; ex.: *neurectomie*, neurectomy; *neurologie*, neurology; *neuropathologie*, neuropathology, *neurotomie*, neurotomy, &c.
neustrien, -ne (nøstrjɛ̃), adj. Neustrian.
neutralement (nøtralmɑ̃), adv. Neutrally.
neutralisant, -e (nøtralizɑ̃), p. adj. Neutralizing.
neutralisation (nøtraliza'sjɔ̃), s.f. Neutralization.
neutraliser (nøtralize), v.a. To neutralize; **se** ~, v.pr. to neutralize each other, to become neutral.
neutralité (nøtralite), s.f. Neutrality.
neutre (nøtr), adj. m.f. s.m. [L *neuter*] Neutral, neuter; *rester ~*, to remain neutral; (gram.) *au ~*, in the neuter; *de teinte ~*, neutral-tinted.
neuvaine (nœvɛn), s.f. (Cath. liturgy) Novena, neuvaine, prayers for nine days.
neuvième (nœvjɛm), adj. s.m. Ninth, ninth part, ninth regiment; ~, s.f. (mus.) ninth.
neuvièmement (nœvjɛmmɑ̃), adj. Ninthly.
névé (neve), s.m. [f. L *nix*] Glacier-snow, névé.
neveu (pl. **-x**; fem. **nièce**) (nəvø), s.m. [L *nepos*] Nephew; *petit-~*, grand-nephew;

~ *à la mode de Bretagne*, cousin once removed; (fig.) *~x, arrière-~x*, (pl.) posterity, descendants.

névralgie (nevralʒi), s.f. [f. Gr. *neuron*+*algos*] Neuralgia.

névralgique (nevralʒik), adj. Neuralgic.

névraxe (nevraks), s.m. (anat.) Neural axis.

névrite (nevrit), s.f. (med.) Neuritis.

névritique (nevritik), adj. (med.) Neurotic, nervine.

névro- (in comps.) (nevro, nevrɔ) Neuro- (see *neuro-*); *~graphe, -graphie*, neurograph, -graphy; *~logue, -logie, -logique*, neurologist, -logy, -logical; *~pathe, -pathie, -pathique*, neuropath, -pathy, -pathic; &c.

névrome (nevrom), s.m. (med.) Nervous tumour.

névroptère (nevrɔptɛr), adj. [f. Gr. *neuron*+*pteron*] Neuropterous, neuropteral. ~, s.m. Neuropteran, neuropter.

névrose (nevroz), s.f. [f. Gr. *neuron*] (pathol.) Neurosis (pl. neuroses).

névrosé, -e (nevroze), adj. s.m.f. (Person) suffering from neurosis; (fig.) ill-balanced, nervous (person).

newtonianisme (njutɔnjanism), s.m. Newtonian philosophy.

newtonien, -ne (njutɔnjɛ̃), adj. s.m.f. Newtonian.

new-yorkais, -e (nujɔrkɛ), adj. Of New York. ~, s.m.f. New-Yorker.

nez (ne), s.m. [L *nasus*] **1.** Nose, nostrils; **2.** nose, smell; (of dogs) scent, nose; **3.** (arch.) nosing; **4.** (naut.) nose, bow, head; *il saigne du ~*, his nose bleeds; *~ à ~*, face to face; *~ en pied de marmite*, pug-nose (with thick turned-up end); *au ~ et à la barbe de X*, under X's very nose; (fig.) *se casser le ~*, to be disappointed, to find nobody at home; to be frustrated; (fig.) *donner sur le ~*, to mortify, to humiliate, to scold; *il fait un ~!* or *un ~ d'une aune!*, he pulls a long face, he looks foolish; (fig.) *il a fait un pied de ~*, he cut a snook, he mocked (at); *à vue de ~*, by rule of thumb; *il met son ~ partout*, or *il fourre le ~ partout*, he pokes his nose into everything, he is a regular Nosy Parker; *cela lui pend au ~*, he may expect that; *il m'a ri au ~*, he laughed in my face; *on voulait lui tirer les vers du ~*, they wished to pump him; *marcher le ~ au vent*, to walk with one's nose in the air; *il me regarda sous le ~*, he stared me in the face; *il me l'a jeté au ~*, he cast it in my teeth; *mettre le ~ dessus*, to guess right, to discover or nose the important (hidden) point; *je lui fermai la porte au ~*, I shut the door in his face; *elle le mène par le bout du ~*, she leads him by the nose, she knows how to manage him; *donner du ~ en terre*, to fall on one's face; to fail; to come a nasty cropper; *avoir le ~ fin* or *avoir du ~*, to have a good nose; to be far-sighted, sagacious, perspicacious; *qui coupe son ~ dégarnit son visage*, it is an ill bird that fouls its own nest; *si vous crachez en l'air, cela vous retombera sur le ~*, curses come home to roost; *parler du ~*, to speak through the nose; (colloq.) *se manger le ~*, to quarrel bitterly, to fight; *se piquer le ~*, to booze, to be a confirmed drinker; (aeron.) *piquer du ~*, to nose-dive.

ni (ni) conj. [L *nec*] Neither . . . nor; either . . . or; *~ plus ~ moins*, neither more nor less; *~ moi non plus*, nor I neither.

niable (njabl), adj. Deniable, that can be denied.

niais, -e (njɛ), adj. s.m.f. [f. L *nidus*] Silly, foolish, spoony; ninny, simpleton, booby; *faire le ~*, to act the simpleton.

niaisement (njɛzmɑ̃), adv. Sillily, foolishly.

niaiser (njɛze), v.n. To trifle; to dawdle; to play the fool.

niaiserie (njɛzri), s.f. Silliness, foolishness; nonsense, foolery, trifle.

nicaise, nicodème (nikɛz, nikɔdɛm) s.m. [prop. names used as mild insult] Noodle, simpleton, booby; *grand Nicodème va!*, what a fool! you fool!

nice (nis) (obs.), adj. [f. L *nescius*] Silly, foolish. ♤ Same orig. as English 'nice' which nowadays means *plaisant, joli, agréable*.

niche (niʃ), s.f. [f. It. *nicchia*] **1.** Niche, recess, alcove, retreat; **2.** (dog-)kennel; **3.** trick, prank; *il m'a fait une ~*, he played a trick upon me.

nichée (niʃe), s.f. [f. *nicher*] Nest, nestlings, brood; (fig.) set, lot.

nicher (niʃe), v.n. [f. LL *nidicare*] To nestle, to build a nest; (fig.) to lodge; ~, v.a. (fig.) to nestle, to place, to settle, to thrust; **se** ~, v.pr. to nestle, to place oneself, to lie, to lodge or hide oneself; *où la vertu va-t-elle se ~!*, in what strange places is virtue to be found!

nichet (niʃɛ), s.m. Nest-egg.

nicheu-r, -se (niʃœr), adj. Nest-building.

nichoir (niʃwar), s.m. Breeding-cage.

nichons (niʃɔ̃), s.m.pl. (extremely vulgar) Bosom, breasts.

nickel (nikɛl), s.m. [Germ. wd] (chem.) Nickel.

nickelage, nickelisage, (niklaʒ, niklizaʒ), s.m. **nickelure** (niklyr), s.f. Nickeling, nickelizing, nickel-plating.

nickelé, nickelisé (nikle, niklize), p. adj. Nickeled, nickelized, nickel-plated.

nickeler (nikle), v.a. To nickel, to coat with nickel.

nickeleur (niklœr), s.m. Nickel-plater.

nickelifère (niklifɛr), adj. Nickeliferous.

nicodème (nikɔdɛm), s.m. See syn. NICAISE.

niçois, -e (niswa), adj. s.m.f. (Native) of Nice.
nicotiane (nikɔsjan), s.f. (bot.) Nicotian.
nicotianine (nikɔsjanin), s.f. (chem.) Nicotianine.
nicotine (nikɔtin), s.f. [f. J. *Nicot*, Frenchman who first imported tobacco] (chem.) Nicotine.
nicotiniser (nikɔtinize), v.a. To nicotinize; *dé~*, to de-nicotinize.
nictation, nictitation (nikta'sjɔ̃), s.f. Nictation, nictitation.
nicter (nikte), v.n. [L *nictare*] (vet.) To nictitate, to wink.
nictitant, -e (niktitɑ̃), adj. Nictitating; *paupière ~e*, nictitating eyelid, membrane.
nid (ni), s.m. [L *nidus*] Nest; hole; berth, den, retreat, post; *petit à petit l'oiseau fait son ~*, little strokes fell great oaks; *~ à rats*, rat-hole; *à chaque oiseau son ~ est beau*, home is home, be it never so homely; *revenir au ~*, to come home; *trouver la pie au ~*, to make a lucky discovery, to strike lucky.
nidification (nidifika'sjɔ̃), s.f. Nidification, nest-building.
nidifier (nidifje), v.n. To nidificate, to build a nest.
nidoreu-x, -se (nidɔrø), adj. [f. L *nidor*] Nidorous.
nidulant, -e (nidylɑ̃), p. adj. Nidulant, nest-building.
nièce (njɛs), s.f. [LL *neptia*] Niece (see NEVEU); *~ à la mode de Bretagne*, cousin once removed; *petite-~*, grand-niece.
niellage (njɛlaʒ), s.m. Niello-work.
nielle[1] (njɛl), s.m. [f. It. *niello*] Niello, niello-work.
nielle[2] (njɛl), s.f. [f. L *nigella*] **1.** (bot.) Ear-cockles, corn-cockle, fennel-flower; **2.** purples, smut; black rust.
nieller (njɛle), v.a. **1.** To smut, to blight; **2.** to niello, to inlay with niello.
nielleur (njɛlœr), s.m. Niellist, niello-worker. ~, adj. m. Niello-working.
niellure (njɛlyr), s.f. **1.** Smut, blight; **2.** niello-work.
nier (nje), v.a. [f. L *negare*] To deny, to disown; *cela ne peut se ~*, it is undeniable; *~ une dette*, to refuse to acknowledge a debt.
nigaud, -e (nigo), adj. [f. L *nequam*?] Silly, foolish. ~, s.m.f. **1.** Simpleton, booby, block-head; **2.** (ornith.) green cormorant.
nigaudement (nigodmɑ̃), adv. Sillily.
nigauder (nigode), v.n. To play the fool.
nigauderie (nigodri), s.f. Silliness, foolishness, foolery.
nigaudinos (nigodinos), s.m. (pop.) Great noodle, great booby.
nigelle (niʒɛl), s.f. [L *nigella*] (bot.) Fennel-flower.
nigrescent, -e (nigrɛssɑ̃), adj. Nigrescent.
nigrin, -e (nigrɛ̃), adj. Coal-black.
nigritique (nigritik), adj. Nigritian, of Nigritia.
nihilisme (niilism), s.m. [f. L *nihil*] Nihilism.
nihiliste (niilist), adj. Nihilistic. ~, s.m.f. Nihilist.
nilgaut (nilgo), s.m. [f. Hindustani *nilgao*] (zool.) Nylghau, nilgai.
nille (nij), s.f. (motor.) Ring of starting-handle.
nilomètre (nilɔmɛtr), s.m. [Gr. *Neilometrion*] Nilometer.
nilométrique, nilotique (nilɔmetrik, nilɔtik), adj. Nilometric, nilotic.
nimbe (nɛ̃b), s.m. [L *nimbus*] Glory, halo, nimbus.
nimber (nɛ̃be), v.a. To halo; (fig.) *nimbé de vertus*, haloed with virtues.
nimbus (nɛ̃bys), s.m. [L wd] Nimbus, rain-cloud.
ninivite (ninivit), s.m.f. adj. Ninevite.
nippe (nip), s.f. (usually pl.) [orig. unkn.] Clothes, article of apparel, duds, togs.
nipper (nipe), v.a. To tog, to provide with clothes; **se** ~, v.pr. to buy new clothes.
nique (nik), s.f. [f. Germ. *nicken*] Sign of mockery; *faire la ~ à*, to bemock, to bite one's thumb at, to baffle.
niquedouille (nikduj) (obs.), s.m. [f. *nique+andouille*] Booby.
nisco (nisko), interj. (pop.) Nix!, nothing doing!, no such thing!, not a bit of it!, no use!
nitée (nite), s.f. [var. of *nichée*] Brood, nestlings.
nitescence (nitɛssɑ̃s), s.f. [f. L *nitescere*] Dim light.
(sainte) nitouche (sɛ̃tnituʃ), s.f. [*ne+y+touche*] (fam.) Demure-looking chit; *elle fait la ~*, she looks as if butter would not melt in her mouth.
nitrate (nitrat), s.m. Nitrate.
nitraté, -e (nitrate), p. adj. Nitrated.
nitre (nitr), s.m. [L *nitrum*] Nitre, saltpetre.
nitré, -e (nitre), p. adj. Nitred.
nitreu-x, -se (nitrø), adj. Nitrous.
nitrière (nitrjɛr), s.f. Nitre-bed, saltpetre-bed.
nitrification (nitrifika'sjɔ̃), s.f. Nitrification.
nitrifier (nitrifje), v.a. and **se** ~, v.pr. To nitrify.
nitrique (nitrik), adj. Nitric.
nitrite (nitrit), s.m. Nitrite.
nitro- (nitro), (in comps.) Nitro-; ex. *~benzine*, *~glycérine*, &c.
nivéal, -e, (aux) (niveal), adj. [f. L *nix*] Winter- (said of plants that flower in winter).
niveau (pl. **-x**) (nivo), s.m. [f. L *libella*] Level; *être de ~ avec*, or *au ~ de*, to be level with; *~ d'eau*, water-level;

~ *des eaux*, water-mark; ~ *de maçon* or *à plomb*, plumb-level; ~ *à bulle d'air*, spirit-level; *il est au* ~ *des plus grands peintres*, he is on a par with the best painters.

niveler (nivle), v.a. To level, to make equal, to make even; **se** ~, v.pr. to be levelled.

niveleu-r, -se (nivlœr), s.m.f. Leveller. ~, adj. Levelling.

nivellement (nivɛlmɑ̃), s.m. Levelling.

nivéole (niveɔl), s.f. [f. L *niveus*] (bot.) Snow-flake, snowdrop.

nivereau (pl. **-x**) (nivro) s.m.f. **niverolle** (nivrɔl), s.f. (ornith.) Snow-finch.

nivernais, -e (nivɛrnɛ), adj. s.m.f. (Native) of Nevers; *carottes à la* ~*e*, carrot-stew.

nivet (nivɛ), s.m. (pop.) Illicit or illegal profit; bribe, secret tip.

nivôse (nivoz), s.m. [f. L *nivosus*] Nivose (month of the French Republican calendar from 21 Dec. to 19 Jan.).

nixe (niks), s.f. [f. Scand. *nix*] (myth.) Nixie, water-elf.

nizeré (nizre), s.m. Essence of white roses.

nobiliaire (nɔbiljɛr), adj. Nobiliary, patrician, of the nobility. ~, s.m. (in England) Peerage (book); book containing list of aristocratic families of a country.

nobilissime (nɔbilisim), adj. Most noble.

noble (nɔbl), adj. [L *nobilis*] Noble, high, lofty, noble-minded, elevated; of noble birth or descent. ~, s.m.f. **1.** Noble, nobleman, (fem.) noblewoman; (fam.) nob; **2.** old gold coin; ~ *à la rose*, rose-noble.

noblement (nɔbləmɑ̃), adv. Nobly, honourably, generously.

noblesse (nɔblɛs), s.f. **1.** Nobility, noblesse, (fam.) the nobs; *petite* ~, gentry; ~ *oblige*, rights imply duties; noblesse oblige; **2.** nobleness.

nobliau (pl. **-x**) (nɔblijo), s.m. Lordling, petty nobleman.

noce, noces (nɔs), s.f. [L *nuptiae*] **1.** (sing. or pl.) Wedding, nuptials, wedding-feast; **2.** (sing.) drinking-bout, revelry, carousal, orgy; *gâteau de* ~*s*, wedding-cake; *il n'avait jamais été à pareille* ~, he had never had such a time of it; *elle avait épousé X en premières* ~*s*, she was X's wife by a first marriage; *en secondes* ~*s*, by a second marriage; ~*s d'argent*, silver wedding; ~*s d'or, de diamant*, golden, diamond wedding; *n'être pas à la* ~, to have a bad time of it; *faire la* ~, to go on the spree.

nocer (nɔse), v.n. (pop.) To lead a gay life, to go on the spree.

noceu-r, -se (nɔsœr), s.m.f. Reveller, rake, libertine, (fem.) debauchee, gay or fast woman.

nocher (nɔʃe), s.m. [f. LL *nauticarius*] (poet.) Mariner, pilot; *le* ~ *des Enfers*, Charon, Hell's ferryman.

noci-f, -ve (nɔsif), adj. [L *nocivus*] Noxious, poisonous, harmful, unwholesome.

nocivité (nɔsivite), s.f. Noxiousness.

noctambule (nɔktɑ̃byl), adj. [f. L *nox*+ *ambulare*] Night-walking, noctambulant. ~, s.m.f. Noctambulist, somnambulist; night-walker, night-rover.

noctambuler (nɔktɑ̃byle), v.n. To noctambulate; to walk in one's sleep.

noctambulisme (nɔktɑ̃bylism), s.m. Noctambulism, noctambulation, somnambulism.

noctiflore (nɔktiflɔr), adj. Noctiflorous, night-flowering.

noctilion (nɔktiljɔ̃), s.m. [f. L *nox*] (zool.) Noctilio (bat).

noctilucque (nɔktilyk), s.m. (zool.) Noctiluca.

noctuéliens (nɔktɥeljɛ̃), s.m.pl. [f. L *nox*] (ent.) Genus of nocturnal lepidoptera.

noctuelle (nɔktɥɛl), s.f. (ent.) Little owl, owl-moth.

noctule (nɔktyl), s.f. (zool.) Noctule (bat).

nocturne (nɔktyrn), adj. [L *nocturnus*] Nocturnal, of night, nightly, night-. ~, s.m. (zool.) Nocturnal; (music) nocturne; (Cath. liturg.) nocturn.

nocturnement (nɔktyrnəmɑ̃), adv. Nocturnally, by night.

nocuité (nɔkɥite), s.f. [f. L *nocuus*] Noxiousness.

nodal, -e, (aux) (nɔdal), adj. (physiol.) Nodal.

nodosité (nɔdozite), s.f. [f. L *nodus*] Nodosity, node, knot.

nodule (nɔdyl), s.m. [L *nodulus*] Nodule.

noduleu-x, -se (nɔdylø), adj. Nodulous, nodular.

nodus (nɔdys), s.m. [L wd] (med.) Node.

noël (nɔɛl), s.m.f. [f. L *natalis*] Christmas; Yule; Nowel; Christmas carol, Christmas hymn; *à la* ~, at Christmas; *bûche de* ~, Yule log; *fêtes de* ~, Christmas holidays; *quand* ~ *est vert, Pâques seront blanches, qui voit à* ~ *les moucherons, verra à Pâques les glaçons*, when the winter is mild, the spring will be wintry; a green Christmas means a white Easter; *la veillée de* ~, Christmas eve; (obs.), ~*!* ~*!*, Hurrah! Hurrah!; *tant crie-t'on* ~ *qu'il vient* (Villon), long looked for comes at last.

nœud (nø), s.m. [L *nodus*] **1.** Knot, bow, tie; *trancher le* ~ *gordien*, to cut the Gordian knot; ~ *d'ajut*, two bowlines; ~ *d'anguille*, running bowline; ~ *de bouline*, outside clinch; ~ *coulant*, slip-knot; ~ *d'écoute*, sheet-knot; clew; ~ *de fouet*, rolling hitch; ~ *de grappin*, fisherman's bend; ~ *de hauban*, French shroud-knot; ~ *d'orin*, buoy-rope knot;

~ *plat*, reef-knot, square knot; ~ *de ride*, Matthew Walker knot; ~ *de trésillon*, marlin-spike hitch; **2.** (naut.) knot; *le navire file dix* ~*s*, the ship is doing ten knots; **3.** (in wood, &c.) knot, joint; (fig.) knotty point, difficulty, rub; main point; **4.** tie, bond, fetters, knot; **5.** (slang) *filer son* ~, (*a*) to be off; (*b*) to die, to peg out.

noir, -e (nwar), adj. [L *niger*] Black; swarthy, sable, negro, dark, smutty, coal-black; (fig.) dirty, dark, gloomy, dismal, wicked, base; (slang) drunk; *du pain* ~, black bread, rye-bread; *du café* ~, strong or black coffee (without milk); ~ *comme un four, comme dans un four*, pitch-dark; *il voit tout en* ~, he is gloomy, he sees everything in a bad light, he looks on the dark side; *viandes* ~*es*, brown meat (game); *c'est ma bête* ~*e*, I hate the sight of him; *un froid* ~, bitter cold; a black frost; *gravure à la manière* ~*e*, mezzotint; *il est dans ses humeurs* ~*es*, he is in a melancholy mood; ~ *de coups*, all black and blue; *un point* ~, a dark spot, a cloud; *une* ~*e ingratitude*, black ingratitude; *une action* ~*e*, a black deed; *faire une peinture bien* ~*e de la situation*, to give a gloomy view of the case.

noir (nwar), s.m. Black, negro, nigger; (fig.) gloom, spleen, the blue devils, the dismals; ~*-animal*, bone-black; ~ *de fumée*, lamp-black; smut; ~ *d'ivoire*, ivory-black; *être en* ~, to be dressed in black, to wear black; *broyer du* ~, to have the blues, to be gloomy, to be in the dumps; *mettre dans le* ~, to hit the bull's-eye; *deux* ~*s ne font pas un blanc*, two wrongs do not make a right; ~, s.f. (mus.) crotchet.

noirâtre (nwarɑtr), adj. Blackish.

noiraud, -e (nwaro), adj. Swarthy, swarthy-looking, black.

noirceur (nwarsœr), s.f. Blackness, darkness, (fig.) gloominess, wickedness, baseness, heinousness, atrocity, base trick or act, slander.

noircir (nwarsir), v.a. To blacken, to black; (fig.) to blacken, to slander, to defame; **se** ~, v.pr. to blacken oneself; to defame each other.

noircissement (nwarsismɑ̃), s.m. Blackening, blacking.

noircisseu-r, -se (nwarsisœr), adj. s.m.f. Blackener; ~ *de papier*, scribbler.

noircissure (nwarsisyr), s.f. Black spot, smudge, blackening.

noire (nwar), s.f. (mus.) Crotchet.

noirement (nwarmɑ̃), adv. Blackly, wickedly.

noise (nwaz), s.f. [orig. dub., L *nausea*?] Quarrel (obs. except in *chercher* ~ *à X*, to pick a quarrel with X).

noiseraie (nwazrɛ), s.f. Walnut-grove.

noisetier (nwaztje), s.m. (bot.) Hazel-tree.

noisette (nwazɛt), s.f. [f. L *nux*] Hazel-nut. ~, adj. Hazel-coloured.

noix (nwɑ), s.f. [L *nux*] Walnut, nut; *coquille de* ~, nut-shell; (fig.) small light vessel; ~ *du genou*, knee-cap; ~ *de moulin*, cogwheel, cone; (carp.) rule-joint; ~ *d'Amérique*, Brazil nut; ~ *de coco*, coco-nut; ~ *de galle*, gall-nut; (slang) *à la* ~, worthless; *boniments à la* ~, empty talk, nonsense, eyewash.

noli me tangere s.m. [L wds] (bot.) Touch-me-not; noli me tangere; syn. GRANDE BALSAMINE; **2.** (pathol.) noli me tangere, erosine ulcer, lupus.

nolis (nɔlis), s.m. (naut.) Freight; syn. FRET.

nolisateur, noliseur (nɔlizatœr, nɔlizœr), s.m. Charterer, freighter.

nolisement (nɔlizmɑ̃), s.m. Chartering, freighting.

noliser (nɔlize), v.a. [It. *noleggiare*] To charter, to freight.

nolition (nɔlisjɔ̃), s.f. Nolition.

nom (nɔ̃), s.m. [L *nomen*] **1.** Name, surname; ~ *de famille*, surname, family name; ~ *de baptême, petit* ~, Christian name; *petit* ~ *d'amitié*, pet name; ~ *de jeune fille*, ~ *de demoiselle*, maiden name; ~ *de guerre*, pseudonym, assumed name, alias; ~ *de plume*, pen-name; ~ *propre*, proper name; ~ *de théâtre*, stage name; ~ *marchand*, trade-name; *avoir* ~, to be called; *porter le* ~ *de, le prénom de*, to be called after, to be named; *porter un beau* ~, to bear a great name; *sans* ~, nameless; *de* ~, by name, nominally; *au* ~ *de*, in the name of, for the sake of; **2.** reputation, fame, title; *se faire un* ~, to win a name for oneself; *il n'était roi que de* ~, he was king only in name; **3.** (gram.) noun; ~ *commun*, common noun; ~ *propre*, proper noun, proper name; ~ *de nombre*, numeral noun; **4.** (in oaths) ~ *de* ~ *!*, ~ *d'un petit bonhomme !, d'un chien !, d'une pipe !, d'un tonnerre !*, hang it!, confound it!, by Jove!, by Jingo!; ~ *de Dieu!*, damn!, by God!

noma (nɔma), s.m. [L wd] (med.) Noma.

nomade (nɔmad), adj. [f. Gr. *nomas*] Nomad, nomadic, wandering, migrating. ~, s.m.f. Nomad.

nomadisme (nɔmadism), s.m. Nomadism.

nomarque (nɔmark), s.m. [f. Gr. *nomos*+ *arkhein*] Nomarch. **nomarcat**, s.m. Nomarchy.

nombles (nɔ̃bl), s.m.pl. [f. L *lumbulus*] Numbles.

nombrable (nɔ̃brabl), adj. Numerable, countable.

nombrant (nɔ̃brɑ̃), p. adj. m. (math.) Abstract.

nombre (nɔ̃br), s.m. [L *numerus*] **1.** Number; ~ *entier*, whole number, integer; ~ *d'or*, golden number; ~ *cardinal*, cardinal number; ~ *ordinal*, ordinal number; ~ *pair*, even number; ~ *impair*, odd number; **2.** number(s), quantity; *au* ~ *de*, to the number of; *bon* ~ *de gens*, a great many people; *en* ~, in great numbers; *être en* ~ *suffisant*, to form a quorum; *pour faire* ~, to make up a number; *être au* ~ *des élus*, to be numbered with the elect; *dans le* ~, among the number; *tout fait* ~, every little helps; *sans* ~, numberless, innumerable; **3.** (Lit.) harmony, cadence; **4.** (gram.) number; *le grec a trois* ~*s*, Greek has three numbers; *le* ~ *pluriel*, the plural number.

nombrer (nɔ̃bre), v.a. To number, to count; **se** ~, v.pr. to be numbered; to count each other; **nombré, -e,** p. adj. numbered, concrete.

nombreusement (nɔ̃brøzmɑ̃), adv. Numerously, harmoniously.

nombreu-x, -se (nɔ̃brø), adj. Numerous, large, many; multifarious, manifold; (Lit.) harmonious, numerous; *réunion peu* ~*se*, small party; *pendant de* ~*ses générations*, for many generations; *une prose* ~*se*, a rhythmic or harmonious prose; *un vers* ~, a rhythmical or numerous line.

nombril (nɔ̃bri), s.m. [f. L *umbilicus*] Navel; (bot.) eye.

nome (nom), s.m. [f. Gr. *nomos*] Nome (ancient Gr. form of musical composition); (ant.) nome (province).

nôme (nom), s.m. [f. Gr. *nomos*] (math.) Nome, nomial; *monôme, binôme, trinôme*, monomial, binomial, trinomial.

nomenclat-eur, -rice (nɔmɑ̃klatœr), s.m.f. Nomenclator.

nomenclature (nɔmɑ̃klatyr), s.f. [L *nomenclatura*] Nomenclature.

nominal, -e, (aux) (nɔminal), adj. Nominal, of names; *faire l'appel* ~, to call over the names; *appel* ~, roll-call. ~, s.m. (phil.) Nominalist. **~isme**, s.m. Nominalism. **~iste**, adj. Nominalistic. **~iste**, s.m.f. Nominalist.

nominalement (nɔminalmɑ̃), adv. Nominally, in name only, not effectively.

nominataire (nɔminatɛr), s.m.f. Nominee.

nominat-eur, -rice (nɔminatœr), s.m.f. Nominator, appointer, presenter.

nominati-f, -ve (nɔminatif), adj. Nominative; (of shares) registered, personal. ~, s.m. (gram.) Nominative, nominative case.

nomination (nɔmina'sjɔ̃) s.f., [L *nominatio*] Nomination, appointment. ⚠ In English 'nomination' has also the sense of *désignation, proposition d'un nom pour une élection ou une nomination.*

nominativement (nɔminativmɑ̃), adv. By name.

nommé, -e (nɔme), p. adj. **1.** Named; *un* ~ *Smith*, one Smith; *le* ~ *Smith*, the man named Smith, the said Smith; *ah! il est bien* ~, he deserves his name!; **2.** appointed, designate, elect; *à point* ~, in the nick of time; at just the right time; *à jour* ~, on the appointed day.

nommément (nɔmemɑ̃), adv. Namely, particularly, especially.

nommer (nɔme), v.a. [L *nominare*] **1.** To name, to call, to nickname, to mention; *sans* ~ *personne*, without mentioning any names, naming no names; *surnommer*, to nickname; **2.** to appoint, to nominate (⚠ see *nomination*); to designate, to elect; *faire nommer X à*, to obtain X's appointment to; **se** ~, v.pr. **1.** to be named or called; **2.** to give one's name, to introduce oneself. See S'APPELER.

nomographe (nɔmɔgraf), s.m. [f. Gr. *nomos+graphein*] Nomographer; **nomographie,** s.f. nomography.

non (nɔ̃), adv. [L *non*] No, not; ~ *pas*, no, not so; ~ *point!*, by no means!; ~ *pas que* (with subj.), not that; ~ *plus*, either; *ni moi* ~ *plus*, nor I neither; ~ *plus que*, no more than; *que* ~*!*, no indeed, dear me, no!, certainly not!; *jurer que* ~, to swear that it is not so; (used in the same way as *n'est-ce pas*) *vous ne parlerez pas,* ~*?*, you won't speak, will you? (*oui* is also used in this sense); *il a fait cela?* ~*?*, he has done it!, is it true?, is it possible?; (in comps.) non-, un-, in-, im-, ex. ~*-activité*, non-activity; ~*-acceptation*, non-acceptance; *non-combattant*, non-combatant; ~*-conducteur*, non-conducting; ~*-conformisme*, nonconformity; *verdict de* ~*-culpabilité*, verdict of not guilty; ~*-être*, non-existence, nonentity; *ordonnance de* ~*-lieu*, verdict of no true bill, throwing out of accusation; ~*-moi*, non-ego; *fin de* ~*-recevoir*, (jur.) plea in bar, exception; (fig.) put-off; ~*-valeur*, valueless person or thing, waste; ~*-sens*, nonsense, absurdity.

nonagénaire (nɔnaʒenɛr), adj. s.m.f. Nonagenarian.

nonante (nɔnɑ̃t), num. adj. (obs.) [f. L *nonaginta*] Ninety; **nonantième,** ord. adj. ninetieth.

nonce (nɔ̃s), s.m. [L *nuntius*, It. *nunzio*] Nuncio.

nonchalamment (nɔ̃ʃalamɑ̃), adv. Negligently, lazily, carelessly, supinely, heedlessly.

nonchalance (nɔ̃ʃalɑ̃s), s.f. **nonchaloir** (nɔ̃ʃalwar), s.m. [f. OF *non+chaloir*] Nonchalance, listlessness, laziness, carelessness, supineness, sluggishness, heedlessness.

nonchalant, -e (nɔ̃ʃalɑ̃), adj. Lazy, listless, careless, heedless, supine, sluggish.

nonciature (nɔ̃sjatyr), s.f. Nunciature; nuncio's residence.
none (nɔn), s.f. [L *nona*] (Cath. liturg.) Nones (ninth hour).
nonidi (nɔnidi), s.m. [f. L *nonus+dies*] (obs.) Nonidi (ninth day of the decade in French republican calendar).
nonius (nɔnjys), s.m. [f. name of Portuguese mathematician] Nonius, vernier.
nonne, nonnain (nɔn, nɔnɛ̃), s.f. [f. L *nonna*] Nun; (in mod. French *nonnain* is only used jestingly).
nonnette (nɔnɛt), s.f. **1.** (obs.) Young nun; **2.** small round gingerbread cake.
nonobstant (nɔnɔbstɑ̃), prep. [f. L *non+obstans*] Notwithstanding, in spite of. ~, adv. Notwithstanding.
nonpareil, -le (nɔ̃parɛj), adj. [*non+pareil*] Matchless, peerless, unequalled, nonpareil. **~le,** s.f. **1.** Nonpareil (very small article, tiny sweets); **2.** (print.) nonpareil; **3.** (bot.) nonesuch.
nonuple (nɔnypl), adj. Ninefold.
nonupler (nɔnyple), v.a. To repeat nine times.
nopal (nɔpal), s.m. (bot.) Nopal, cochineal fig; *Cactus opuntia.*
nord (nɔr), s.m. [f. OE *north*] North; northern countries; (department of France) Nord; *faire le* ~, to steer northwards; *au* ~, *vers le* ~, northwards, to, in, at, the North; *du* ~, northern, northerly, from the North; *~-est,* northeast, north-easter (wind); *~-ouest,* or *norois, noroit,* north-west, north-wester (wind); (fig.) *perdre le* ~, to lose one's presence of mind; *ne pas perdre le* ~, to keep one's wits about one. ~, adj. Northern, north; northerly; *pôle* ~, north pole; *latitude* ~, north latitude.
nordique (nɔrdik), adj. Nordic, Scandinavian.
nordir (nɔrdir), v.n. To veer to the north.
noria (nɔrja), s.f. [Span. wd, f. Arab. *nā'ūra*] Noria.
normal, -e, (aux) (nɔrmal), adj. [f. L *norma*] **1.** Normal, regular; **2.** (geom.) perpendicular. **~e,** s.f. **1.** Normality, usual state, average quantity; **2.** abbrev. for *École Normale Supérieure,* highest French school for teachers; **3.** (geom.) perpendicular line.
normalement (nɔrmalmɑ̃), adv. Normally.
normalien, -ne (nɔrmaljɛ̃), s.m.f. **1.** Pupil of a normal school; **2.** pupil or ex-pupil of *École Normale Supérieure.*
normand, -e (nɔrmɑ̃), adj. s.m.f. **1.** Norman, of Normandy; **2.** (hist.) Northman, native of Scandinavia; **3.** (fig.) crafty, sly, ambiguous, evasive; *à* ~, ~ *et demi,* set a thief to catch a thief; *réponse de Normand,* evasive, cunning answer.
norme (nɔrm), s.f. [L *norma*] Norm, rule, pattern, standard, type.
norois, -e, norrois, -e, normannique (nɔrwɑ, nɔrmanik), adj. Norse; of the Northmen.
norois, noroit (nɔrwɑ), s.m. North-west wind, north-wester, nor'-wester.
nos (no), poss. adj. m.f.pl. Our, our own. See NOTRE.
nosseigneurs (nosɛɲœr), s.m.pl. (pl. of *monseigneur*) Our lords, my lords.
nostalgie (nɔstalʒi), s.f. [f. Gr. *nostos+algos*] Nostalgia, home-sickness. **Nostalgique,** adj. Nostalgic.
nota (nɔta), s.m. (pl. *nota*) [L wd] Note, observation; ~ *bene,* kindly note, nota bene.
notabilité (nɔtabilite), s.f. **1.** Notableness, notability; **2.** notable person; (fam.) nob, big pot.
notable (nɔtabl), adj. [L *notabilis*] Notable, important. ~, s.m.f. Notable person, worthy, leading man or woman; (fam.) nob, big pot, big bug.
notablement (nɔtabləmɑ̃), adv. Much, considerably, notably.
notaire, -sse, s.m.f. [L *notarius*] Notary, notary-public, solicitor; (fem.) wife of a *notaire.*
notamment (nɔtamɑ̃), adv. Especially, particularly, among others.
notarial,-e, (aux) (nɔtarjal), adj. Notarial.
notariat (nɔtarja), s.m. Function, profession, of a notary.
notarié, -e (nɔtarje), adj. Drawn up, or done by a notary.
notation (nɔta'sjɔ̃), s.f. [L *notatio*] Notation.
note (nɔt), s.f. [L *nota*] **1.** Note, mark, remark, observation, minute; *prendre* ~ *de,* to note down; **2.** bill, account; ~ *d'hôtel,* hotel bill; **3.** (mus.) note; *fausse* ~, wrong note; (fig.) discordance; *donner la* ~, to strike the note, (fig.) to lead the fashion; *être bien dans la* ~, to do the right thing in the right place; to harmonize. ⚠ 'Note' in English, but not in French, has also the sense of *lettre, missive, billet.*
noter (nɔte), v.a. To note, to note down, to make a memorandum of, to observe, to notice; to mark, to give marks to; (mus.) to prick, to set to music; *personne bien notée,* person of good repute; *il est mal noté,* he has a black mark against his name.
notice (nɔtis), s.f. [L *notitia*] Notice, review, account, list; ~ *biographique,* biographical notice, or sketch.
notification (nɔtifika'sjɔ̃), s.f. Notification, notice.
notifier (nɔtifje), v.a. To notify.
notion (nosjɔ̃), s.f. [L *notio*] Notion, idea, element, knowledge.

notoire (notwar), adj. [LL *notorius*] Notorious, evident, publicly known.

notoirement (notwarmɑ̃), adv. Notoriously.

notoriété (notorjete), s.f. Notoriety, notoriousness; *il est de ~ publique que*, it is notorious that; it is well known that.

notre (notr), poss. adj. [L *noster*] Our, our own.

nôtre (notr), pron. poss. Ours, our own; *le ~, la ~, les ~s*, our, our own, ours. *Le ~*, s.m. Our property; our part; *il faut y mettre du ~*, we must do something to help; *les ~s*, s.m.pl. our relations; our compatriots; our friends; our fellow-partisans; our side; *serez-vous des ~s?*, will you join us?

Notre-Dame (notrədam), s.f. **1.** Our Lady; **2.** cathedral of Paris.

notule (notyl), s.f. Short note or annotation.

nouage (nuaʒ), s.m. [f. *nouer*] Knotting.

nouba (nuba), s.f. [Arab. orig.] Military music of the French North-African troops; (fig.) piece of merriment, frolic; *faire la grande ~*, to go on the spree; to paint the town red.

noue (nu), s.f. [LL *nauda*] **1.** (agric.) Pasture-land; **2.** gutter, gutter-lead, gutter-tile.

noué, -e (nue), p. adj. [f. *nouer*] **1.** Knotted; **2.** (of fruit) set; **3.** (pathol.) rickety.

nouer (nue), v.a. [L *nodare*] To knot, to tie; (fig.) *~ une intrigue*, to scheme, to plot; *~ des relations*, to form an acquaintance, or friendship; **se ~**, v.pr. to be tied; to form knots; (of fruits) to set; (pathol.) to grow rickety.

nouet (nuɛ), s.m. [f. *nouer*] Little rag tied and enclosing sugar or other substance.

noueu-x, -se (nuø), adj. Knotty, knotted, nodose, gnarled.

nougat (nuga), s.m. [f. LL *nucatum*] Nougat, almond cake.

nouilles (nuj), s.f.pl. [f. Germ. *Nudel*] Nouilles, noodles; ribbon vermicelli; (dim.) **nouillettes**, (nujət), s.f.pl. small noodles.

noumène (numɛn), s.m. [f. Gr. *nooumenon*] (phil.) Noumenon (pl. -ena).

nounou (pl. **-s**) (nunu), s.f. [child. wd] Nurse, wet-nurse, nanny.

nourrain (nurɛ̃), s.m. [L *nutrimen*] Young fish, young fry.

nourrice (nuris), s.f. [L *nutricia*] Nurse, wet-nurse; *en ~*, at nurse, out at nurse, as a baby; *mettre en ~*, to put out to nurse.

nourrici-er, -ère (nurisje), adj. Nutritive, nourishing; *père ~*, foster-father.

nourrir (nurir), v.a. [L *nutrire*] To nourish, to feed, to nurture, to keep, to maintain, to foster, to suckle, to board (as pupils); (fig.) to foment, to encourage, to entertain, to provide; *feu nourri*, brisk steady fire; *~ un espoir*, to entertain hopes; *~*, v.n. to be nourishing; **se ~**, v.pr. to feed, to live (on), to maintain oneself, to thrive.

nourrissage (nurisaʒ), s.m. Rearing and feeding (of cattle).

nourrissant, -e (nurisɑ̃), p. adj. Nutritive, nourishing, nutritious.

nourrisseur (nurisœr), s.m. Cattle-feeder, grazier, breeder.

nourrisson (nurisɔ̃), s.m. Nursling, foster-child.

nourriture (nurityr), s.f. Nourishment, food, diet, maintenance; nursing, suckling.

nous (nu), pers. pr. [L *nos*] (in the nominative) We; (as direct or indirect object) us; *~ voici*, here we are; (reciprocal) each other; *~ ~ convenons*, we suit each other; *à ~*, ours, our own, our turn; *à ~ deux*, let's have a go at it; *~-même*, ourself; *~-mêmes*, ourselves.

nouure (nuyr), s.f. (pathol.) Rickets; setting (of fruits).

nouveau (pl. **-x**), **nouvel, -le** (nuvo, nuvɛl), adj. [f. L *novus, novellus*] New, fresh, novel, additional, recent, new-fangled; *le nouvel an*, the New Year. *~*, adv. New, newly; *les ~x mariés*, the newly married couple; *un ~ venu*, a new-comer; *à ~*, anew, afresh, again; *de ~*, anew, again, over again, once more; *quoi de ~?*, what news? *~*, s.m. Novelty, new thing, new man, new pupil; *tout ~ tout beau*, a new broom sweeps clean; all that is new is fair.

nouveau-né, -e (nuvone), loc. s.m.f. New-born child; *une fille ~e*, a new-born daughter.

nouveauté (nuvote), s.f. [L *novellitas*] Novelty, newness, change, innovation; new thing, latest fashion, new idea, new publication, new play, &c.; early fruit or vegetable; linen-drapery; *magasin de ~s*, linen-draper's shop; draper's; *haute ~*, latest fashion.

nouvelle (nuvɛl), s.f. [LL *novella*] **1.** News, tidings, fresh information, intelligence; *vous m'en direz des ~s!*, you will be surprised at it!; you will be highly pleased with it!; *donnez-moi de vos ~s*, let me hear from you; **2.** short story, tale; ⚠ not 'novel', which = *roman*; **3.** (slang) *la Nouvelle*, the penal settlement of New Caledonia.

nouvellement (nuvɛlmɑ̃), adv. Newly, recently, lately.

nouvelliste (nuvɛlist), s.m.f. Newsmonger, reporter.

novale (noval), s.f. [L *novalis*] Newly cleared land.

novat-eur, -rice (novatœr), s.m.f. [f. L *novator*] Innovator. *~*, adj. Innovating.

novembre (novɑ̃br), s.m. [L *november*] November.

novice (nɔvis), s.m.f. [L *novitius*] **1.** Novice, probationer; neophyte; **2.** (fig.) apprentice, green hand, greenhorn. **~,** adj. Raw, inexperienced, green.

noviciat (nɔvisja), s.m. **1.** Novitiate, time of probation; **2.** novices' quarters; **3.** (fig.) apprenticeship.

noyade (nwajad), s.f. [f. *noyer*] Drowning, noyade.

noyale, noyalle (nwajal), s.f. [f. *Noyal-sur-Velaine,* France] Sail-cloth, sack-cloth.

noyau (pl. **-x**) (nwajo), s.m. [L *nucale*] **1.** Stone; *fruits à ~,* stone-fruit; *il faut casser le ~ pour avoir l'amande,* he must crack the nut that would have the kernel; **2.** nucleus, central part, origin, core; **3.** (arch.) newel (of stairs).

noyé, -e (nwaje), p. adj. Drowned, flooded, deluged, bathed; *des yeux ~s de larmes,* eyes swimming in tears. **~,** s.m.f. Drowned person.

noyer (nwaje), v.a. [L *necare*] To drown, to flood, to immerse, to drench, to dilute; (fig.) to lose (*dans,* in), to forget (in), to overwhelm; *~ son chagrin dans le vin,* to drown one's sorrows in wine; *~ sa pensée dans le verbiage,* to water down or dilute one's thought in a torrent of words; (fig.) *~ le poisson,* to confuse issues (purposely); **se ~,** v.pr. to be drowning, to drown oneself; (fig.) to wallow, to lose oneself, to go to ruin.

noyer (nwaje), s.m. [f. L *nux*] (bot.) Walnut-tree, walnut-wood.

nu, -e (ny), adj. [L *nudus*] Naked, stark naked, bare, uncovered, undressed; plain, unadorned; *bras ~s,* with bare arms; *jambes ~es, ~-jambes,* bare-legged; *~-pieds, pieds ~s,* bare-footed; *~-tête, tête ~e,* bare-headed; *~e propriété,* bare ownership; property without the usufruct; *à ~,* bare, laid bare; (fig.) openly, frankly; *monter à ~,* to ride bare-back.

nu (ny), s.m. (paint.) Nude, naked figure.

nuage (nɥaʒ), s.m. [f. *nue*] Cloud, mist, (fig.) shadow, quarrel, threat to happiness or good accord; *il est toujours dans les ~s,* he is always wool-gathering, or in the clouds, or absent-minded.

nuageusement (nɥaʒøsmɑ̃), adv. Cloudily, hazily, vaguely.

nuageu-x, -se (nɥaʒø), adj. Cloudy, clouded; (fig.) vague, obscure, hazy.

nuance (nɥɑ̃s), s.f. [f. *nuer*] **1.** Shade, hue, tint, nuance; (mus.) modification of time and expression; **2.** difference, distinction, gradation; *oh! il y a une ~!,* oh! but that is different!; observe the shades of meaning; *observer les ~s,* to mark the shades; to render the shades of expression; *une ~ de mépris,* a touch, or shade, of contempt.

nuancement (nɥɑ̃smɑ̃), s.m. Shading, shadowing.

nuancer (nɥɑ̃se), v.a. To shade, to tint; to vary, to variegate.

nubécule (nybekyl), s.f. [L *nubecula*] (med.) Nubecula.

nubien, -ne (nybjɛ̃), adj. s.m.f. Nubian.

nubile (nybil), adj. [L *nubilis*] Nubile, marriageable.

nubilité (nybilite), s.f. Nubility, marriageableness.

nucléal, -e, (aux) (nykleal), adj. Nucleal, nucleolar.

nucléole (nykleɔl), s.m. [f. L *nucleolus*] Nucleolus.

nudité (nydite), s.f. [L *nuditas*] **1.** Nakedness, nudity; **2.** (fig.) bareness, nakedness; **3.** (pl.) naked parts, naked figures; the nude; nudities.

nue (ny), s.f. [L *nubes*] Cloud, sky; *tomber des ~s,* to be astounded, to be thunderstruck; to be taken aback; *porter aux ~s,* to praise or extol to the skies; (fig., lit.) *se perdre dans les ~s,* to be lost in the clouds.

nuée (nɥe), s.f. [f. *nue*] **1.** Cloud, rain-cloud, storm, shower; **2.** swarm, host, multitude; flight (of birds).

nuer (nɥe), v.a. [see *nuancer,* more usual but not exactly syn.] To shade, to shade off, to graduate.

nuire (nɥir), v.n. [L *nocere*] To harm, to injure, to hurt, to wrong, to be harmful, injurious, hurtful, noxious; **~ à,** to hurt, to wrong, to spoil, to hinder, to be in the way of; **se ~,** v.pr. to harm oneself or each other; *ne ~ en rien,* to do no harm at all; *se ~ à soi-même,* to injure oneself; *se ~ l'un l'autre,* to harm each other; *ce qui nuit à l'un sert l'autre,* one man's meat is another man's poison.

nuisible (nɥizibl), adj. Harmful, hurtful, injurious, noxious, detrimental.

nuisiblement (nɥiziblǝmɑ̃), adv. Injuriously, harmfully.

nuit (nɥi), s.f. [L *nox*] Night, night-time; darkness, dark; *il (se) fait ~,* it is night, it is getting dark; *de ~,* by night, nightly; *toute la ~,* all night long; *la ~ des temps,* time immemorial; *~ blanche,* sleepless night; *à la ~ tombante,* at nightfall; *~ close, ~ noire,* night, pitch-dark; *la ~,* at night; *faire une bonne ~,* to have a good night's rest; *passer la ~,* to spend the night; to sit up all night; *la ~ porte conseil,* sleep on it; seek advice of your pillow; time will show a plan; *la ~, tous les chats sont gris,* all cats are grey in the dark; *bonne ~,* good night; *chemise de ~,* nightgown; *vase de ~,* chamber-pot, chamber; *c'est le jour et la ~,* it's quite different, one is the reverse of the other; *il ne passera pas la ~,* he will be dead before morning.

nuitamment (nɥitamɑ̃), adv. Nightly, by night, in the night.

ɔ, note, glotte; **ɔ̃,** monter, r*on*de; **ø,** f*eu*, cr*eux*; **œ,** p*eu*r, s*œu*r; **œ̃,** *un*; **ʃ,** *ch*ez, s*ch*isme; **u,** t*ou*t; **w,** *ou*i, d*oi*t, d*ou*aire; **y,** m*u*r, p*u*; **ɥ,** h*u*ile, m*u*ette; **z,** *z*èle, ro*s*e; **ʒ,** dé*j*à, *g*entil.

nuitée (nɥite), s.f. Night, one night's work; one night's lodging.
nul, -le (nyl), adj. [L *nullus*] **1.** No, not one, not any; **2.** null, ineffectual, ignorant, of no worth, nil; ~ *et non avenu*, null and void; *c'est un coup* ~, that stroke goes for nothing; *partie* ~*le*, drawn game; *il est* ~, he is a dunce, or a cipher, or a dud. ~, pron. No one, nobody; ~ *n'est prophète en son pays*, no man is a prophet in his own country.
nullement (nylmɑ̃), adv. In no way, by no means, not at all, nowise.
nullification (nyllifika'sjɔ̃), s.f. (Amer. polit.) Nullification.
nullifier (nyllifje), v.a. To nullify.
nullité (nyllite), s.f. **1.** Nullity; **2.** incapacity, worthlessness, total want, nonentity, cipher, nobody.
nûment (nymɑ̃), adv. Frankly, openly, plainly.
numéraire (nymerɛr), adj. [L *numerarius*] Legal (of money values). ~, s.m. Specie, hard cash, coin.
numéral, e, (aux) (nymeral), adj. Numeral.
numérateur (nymeratœr), s.m. [L *numerator*] Numerator.
numération (nymera'sjɔ̃), s.f. [L *numeratio*] Numeration.
numérique (nymerik), adj. Numerical.
numériquement (nymerikmɑ̃), adv. Numerically.
numéro (nymero), s.m. [It. *numero*] **1.** Number, size, sort; *être du bon* ~, to be of good quality; *c'est mon* ~ *deux*, it is my second-best (hat, &c.); *tirer un mauvais* ~, to be unlucky; *c'est un* ~ *!*, he is a queer bird!; **2.** ticket; **3.** copy, issue; number; **4.** turn, stunt.
numérotage (nymerɔtaʒ), s.m. **numérotation** (nymerɔta'sjɔ̃), s.f. Numbering.
numéroter (nymerɔte), v.a. **1.** To number; **2.** to page.
numéroteur (nymerɔtœr), s.m. Numberer, numbering-machine, paging-machine. ~, adj. Numbering.
numide (nymid), s.m.f. adj. Numidian.
numidique, numidien, -ne (nymidik, nymidjɛ̃), adj. Numidian.
numismate (nymismat), s.m.f. Numismatist.
numismatique (nymismatik), s.f. [f. Gr. *nomisma* and L *numisma*] Numismatics. ~, adj. Numismatic.
numismatologie (nymismatolɔʒi), s.f. Numismatology.
nummulaire (nymylɛr), adj. [L *nummularius*] Nummular. ~, s.f. (bot.) Moneywort.
nummuline (nymylin), s.f. (fossil) Nummulite.
nuncupati-f, -ve (nɔ̃kypatif), adj. (law) Nuncupative.
nunnation (nynna'sjɔ̃), s.f. (phon.) Nunnation.
nuptial, -e, (aux) (nypsjal), adj. [L *nuptialis*] Nuptial, wedding-; *anneau* ~, wedding-ring; *bénédiction* ~*e*, marriage service.
nuque (nyk), s.f. [Arab. orig.] Nape (of the neck).
nutriti-f, -ve (nytritif), adj. Nutritive, nutritious, nourishing.
nutrition (nytrisjɔ̃), s.f. [f. L *nutrire*] Nutrition.
nutritivité (nytritivite), s.f. Nutritiveness.
nyctalope (niktalɔp), s.m.f. adj. [f. Gr. *nuctalōps*] Nyctalops.
nyctalopie (niktalɔpi), s.f. Nyctalopia, night-sight.
nymphale (nɛ̃fal), s.m. [f. Gr. *numphē*] Nymphalid, nymphal.
nymphe (nɛ̃f), s.f. [f. Gr. *numphē*] Nymph; (ent.) nympha.
nymphéa (nɛ̃fea), s.m. (bot.) Nymphaea, water-lily, nenuphar.
nymphéacées (nɛ̃fease), s.f.pl. (bot.) Nymphaeaceae.
nymphée (nɛ̃fe), s.m. [f. Gr. *numphaion*] Nymphaeum, grotto, marble fountain.
nystagme (nistagm), s.m. [Gr. *nystagmos*] Nystagmus.

O

O, o (ɔ, o), s.m. Fifteenth letter of the alphabet; **ô** (interj.) O!, Oh!
oasis (ɔazis), s.f. invar. [Gr. wd, prob. of Egypt. orig.] (lit. and fig.) Oasis (pl. oases).
obédience (ɔbedjɑ̃s), s.f. [L *obedientia*] Obedience; *lettre d'*~, teaching-certificate (granted by religious superior to member of a teaching order).
obéir (ɔbeir), v.n. [L *obedire*] To obey, to be obedient (*à*, to); to yield (to), to comply (with); to be pliant, to bend; *se faire* ~ *de*, to get obedience from; ~ *au mors, à la barre*, to answer the bit, the helm.
obéissance (ɔbeisɑ̃s), s.f. Obedience; dutifulness; allegiance; dominion, authority; pliancy; *par* ~ *à*, in obedience to; *jurer* ~ *à*, to swear allegiance to; *sous l'*~ *de*, under the authority of. ⚠ Not 'obeisance', which = *révérence, profond salut*.
obéissant, -e (ɔbeisɑ̃), p. adj. Obedient, dutiful, pliant, docile; *peu* ~, disobedient; *votre fils* ~, your dutiful son; *nature* ~*e*, pliable disposition.
obélisque (ɔbelisk), s.m. [Gr. *obeliskos*] Obelisk.
obérer (ɔbere), v.a. [L *obaerare*] To involve in debt, to burden; *être fort obéré*, to be deeply involved; **s'**~, v.pr. to involve oneself in debt, to run into debt.

obèse (ɔbɛz), adj. [L *obesus*] Corpulent, fat, stout, obese.

obésité (ɔbezite), s.f. [L *obesitas*] Corpulence, obesity.

obier (ɔbje), s.m. (bot.) Guelder-rose; syn. BOULE-DE-NEIGE.

obit (ɔbit), s.m. [L *obitus*] (Cath. liturg.) Obit, memorial service.

obituaire (ɔbitɥɛr), s.m. adj. [f. *obit*] Obituary.

objecter (ɔbʒɛkte), v.a. [L *objectare*] To object (*que*, that); to put forward as an objection (*à*, to); *on lui objecta sa jeunesse*, they objected to him on account of his youth.

objecti-f, -ve (ɔbʒɛktif), adj. Objective. ~, s.m. Objective, object, objective point, point aimed at; (opt.) object-glass; (photo.) lens.

objection (ɔbʒɛksjɔ̃), s.f. Objection; *faire des ~s à*, to raise objections to, to object to; *aller au-devant d'une ~*, to meet an objection; *je n'y vois pas d'~*, I see no objection (to that); (colloq.) I am agreeable.

objectivation (ɔbʒɛktiva'sjɔ̃), s.f. Objectification, objectivation.

objectivement (ɔbʒɛktivmɑ̃), adv. Objectively.

objectiver (ɔbʒɛktive), v.a. To objectify, to objectivate.

objectivité (ɔbʒɛktivite), s.f. Objectivity, objectiveness.

objet (ɔbʒɛ), s.m. [L *objectum*] **1.** Object, thing, article, matter, subject; *grandir les ~s*, to magnify things; *~s de première nécessité*, articles of everyday use; *un ~ d'art*, a work of art; *~ de risée*, laughing-stock; **2.** (phil.) object; **3.** object, purpose, aim, end; subject, object, purport; *sans ~*, without an object; *il avait pour ~*, his object was; he aimed at; *ces choses ont toutes le même ~*, these things all aim at the same object.

objurgation (ɔbʒyrga'sjɔ̃), s.f. [f. L *objurgare*] Reproof, objurgation, violent upbraiding.

objurgatoire (ɔbʒyrgatwar), adj. Objurgatory.

oblat (ɔbla), s.m. [L *oblatus*] Oblate.

oblation (ɔbla'sjɔ̃), s.f. Oblation, offering; *faire une ~*, to make an oblation; *~ du pain et du vin*, offering of bread and wine.

obligataire (ɔbligatɛr), s.m.f. [f. L *obligare*] Bond-holder, debenture-holder.

obligation (ɔbliga'sjɔ̃), s.f. [L *obligatio*] **1.** Obligation, bounden duty; *c'est une ~ pour vous de le faire*, it is your bounden duty to do it; *avoir des ~s à X*, to lie under an obligation to X; to be beholden to X; *n'avoir aucune ~ à X*, to be under no obligation to X; *je vous en aurai une grande ~*, I shall be greatly obliged to you; *malgré les ~s que je vous ai*, much as I am obliged to you; *remplir ses ~s*, to fulfil one's obligations; **2.** (law) recognizance, obligation, bond; *souscrire une ~ en due forme*, to enter into recognizances for; *porteur d'~s*, bond-holder; **3.** (fin.) bond, debenture, preference share.

obligatoire (ɔbligatwar), adj. Compulsory, binding, incumbent, obligatory; *acte ~*, act of obligation.

obligé, -e (ɔbliʒe), p. adj. **1.** Obliged, bound; *vous y êtes ~*, you are bound to do it; **2.** necessary; **3.** grateful, obliged, beholden; *être bien ~ à X de quelque chose*, to be greatly obliged (or beholden) to X for something.

obligé, -e (ɔbliʒe), s.m.f. Obligee, debtor; *un de vos ~s*, a person you have obliged, one who is under an obligation to you.

obligeamment (ɔbliʒamɑ̃) adv. Obligingly, kindly, courteously.

obligeance (ɔbliʒɑ̃s), s.f. Obligingness; *d'une extrême ~*, most obliging; *ayez l'~ de*, be so kind as to, be good enough to.

obligeant, -e (ɔbliʒɑ̃), p. adj. Obliging, kind (*pour*, to); *paroles ~es*, kind words.

obliger (ɔbliʒe), v.a. [L *obligare*] **1.** To oblige (*à*, *de*, to), to compel, to bind, to call upon; *votre devoir vous y oblige*, you are in duty bound to do it; *votre intérêt vous y oblige*, it is to your interest to do so; *j'obligerai X à partir*, I will compel X to leave; **2.** to oblige, to please, to gratify, to do a service to; *vous m'obligerez en faisant cela immédiatement*, you will oblige me by doing that immediately; **s'~**, v.pr. **1.** to oblige or bind oneself (*à*, to); **2.** to bind or compel one another (*à*, to); **3.** to oblige each other.

oblique (ɔblik), adj. [L *obliquus*] Oblique, slanting; (fig.) indirect, underhand, oblique; *conduite ~*, crooked behaviour; double-dealing; (gram.) oblique.

obliquement (ɔblikmɑ̃), adv. Obliquely, slantingly, askew, slantwise; (fig.) unfairly, in an underhand way, indirectly, crookedly.

obliquer (ɔblike), v.a.n. To become oblique, to make oblique, to turn, to change one's direction or opinion; *~ à droite*, to bear or slant off to the right, to turn or swerve to the right.

obliquité (ɔblikɥite), s.f. Obliquity, obliqueness, slant; (fig.) insincerity, crookedness.

oblitération (ɔblitera'sjɔ̃), s.f. Obliteration.

oblitérer (ɔblitere), v.a. [L *obliterare*] To obliterate, to destroy, to wipe out, to render (stamps, &c.) valueless; **s'~**, v.pr. to become obliterated, to disappear.

oblong, -ue (ɔblɔ̃), adj. [L *oblongus*] Oblong.

obole (ɔbɔl), s.f. [Gr. *obolos*] Obole, obolus;

(fig.) farthing, mite, small gift or contribution; *l'~ de la veuve*, the widow's mite; *n'avoir pas une ~*, not to be worth a groat or stiver; *je n'en donnerais pas une ~*, I would not give a straw for it; *je vous apporte mon ~*, here is my small contribution.

obscène (ɔbsɛn), adj. [L *obscenus*] Lewd, obscene, foul. ⚠ 'Obscene' in English is often used in the sense of *répugnant, hideux*; but *obscène* in French implies always lewdness, indecency, smuttiness, lubricity, &c.

obscénité (ɔbsenite), s.f. Obscenity, obsceneness, lewdness, lubricity, smutty talk.

obscur, -e (ɔbskyr), adj. [L *obscurus*] Dark, dim, dingy, gloomy; (fig.) obscure, abstruse, not clear; hidden, unnoticed, humble, doubtful; *faire ~*, to be dark; to grow dark; *naissance ~e*, humble birth; *clair-~*, chiaroscuro, light and shade.

obscurantisme (ɔbskyrɑ̃tism), s.m. Obscurantism.

obscurantiste (ɔbskyrɑ̃tist), adj. s.m.f. Obscurant, obscurantist.

obscuration (ɔbskyra'sjɔ̃), s.f. (astr.) Obscuration.

obscurcir (ɔbskyrsir), v.a. To obscure, to cloud, to darken, to dim; (fig.) to dim, to obscure; *le chagrin a obscurci sa raison*, sorrow has clouded (or dimmed) his mind; **s'~**, v.pr. to grow dark, obscure, or dim.

obscurcissement (ɔbskyrsismɑ̃), s.m. Dimness, darkening, obscuration.

obscurément (ɔbskyremɑ̃), adv. **1.** Dimly, darkly, obscurely, humbly.

obscurité (ɔbskyrite), s.f. Darkness, obscurity, gloom; dimness; (fig.) obscurity, unintelligibleness; humbleness; *dans une complète ~*, in utter darkness; *dans l'~*, in the dark; *vivre dans l'~*, to live in obscurity; *l'~ de sa naissance*, the humbleness of his birth (or extraction); *un discours rempli d'~s*, an unintelligible speech.

obsécration (ɔksekra'sjɔ̃), s.f. [L *obsecratio*] (rhet.) Obsecration.

obséder (ɔbsede), v.a. [L *obsidere*] To beset, to haunt; to obsess, to torment; to importune, to prey upon; *obsédé par une idée fixe*, obsessed by a fixed idea; *~ X de sollicitations*, to importune X with entreaties.

obsèques (ɔbsɛk), s.f.pl. [L *obsequiae*] Obsequies (pl.), funeral.

obséquieusement (ɔbsekɥijøzmɑ̃), adv. Obsequiously, fawningly.

obséquieu-x, -se (ɔbsekɥijø), adj. [L *obsequiosus*] Obsequious, fawning.

obséquiosité (ɔbsekɥijozite), s.f. Obsequiousness.

observable (ɔbsɛrvabl), adj. Observable.

observance (ɔbsɛrvɑ̃s), s.f. Observance, rule; keeping or performance of a law, custom, duty, ritual.

observat-eur, -rice (ɔbsɛrvatœr), s.m.f. Observer, watcher, spy, spectator; looker-on. ~, adj. Observant, observing; heedful, attentive; *peu ~*, little given to observation, unobservant.

observation (ɔbsɛrva'sjɔ̃), s.f. [L *observatio*] Observation, look-out; observance; (naut.) sight, watch; objection, remark, notice, hint, slight reproof; *faire une ~*, to make an observation, to observe; (astr.) to take an observation; *faire une ~ à*, to reprimand slightly, to admonish, to give a warning to; *assez d'~s !*, that will do !; (mil.) *corps d'~*, reconnoitring corps ; *être en ~*, (*a*) to be on the look-out; (*b*) to be placed under observation.

observatoire (ɔbsɛrvatwar), s.m. Observatory.

observer (ɔbsɛrve), v.a.n. [L *observare*] **1.** To observe, to examine, to watch, to look at; to remark, to notice, to perceive; *je lui ai fait ~ que*, I pointed out to him that; I reminded him that; **2.** to comply with; to fulfil; to obey; to keep; *~ le silence*, to keep silent; **s'~**, v.pr. to be on one's guard, to behave cautiously; to observe each other; to be observed, to occur; *cela s'observe fréquemment*, that occurs frequently; that 's often seen.

obsession (ɔbsɛsjɔ̃), s.f. [L *obsessio*] Obsession; possession; importunity; *je ne puis me délivrer de cette ~*, I cannot rid myself of this obsession.

obsidiane (ɔbsidjan), s.f. [L *obsidianus*, f. *Obsidius, Obsius*, prop. n.] (geol.) Obsidian, a dark, vitreous lava.

obsidional, -e, (aux) (ɔbsidjɔnal), adj. [f. L *obsidio*] Obsidional.

obsolète (ɔbsɔlɛt), adj. [L *obsoletus*] Obsolete.

obstacle (ɔbstakl), s.m. [L *obstaculum*] Obstacle, hindrance, obstruction, impediment; bar; *mettre* or *faire ~ à*, to hinder; to stand in the way of; *course d'~s*, obstacle race.

obstétrical, -e, (aux) (ɔbstetrikal), adj. Obstetric(al), pertaining to midwifery or child-birth.

obstétrique (ɔbstetrik), s.f. [f. L *obstetrix*] Obstetrics, midwifery.

obstination (ɔbstina'sjɔ̃), s.f. [L *obstinatio*] Obstinacy, stubbornness, self-will, wilfulness; syn. ENTÊTEMENT.

obstiné, -e (ɔbstine), p. adj. Obstinate, stubborn, self-willed, wilful; syn. OPINIÂTRE.

obstinément (ɔbstinemɑ̃), adv. Obstinately, stubbornly.

(s')obstiner (sɔbstine), v.pr. [L *obstinare*] To be obstinate, to persist (*à*, in); *il s'obstine au silence*, he keeps obstinately silent; he persists in keeping silent.

obstructi-f, -ve (ɔbstryktif), adj. [f. L *obstructus*] Obstructive; (med.) obstruent.

obstruction (ɔbstryksjɔ̃), s.f. [L *obstructio*] Obstruction, stoppage, blocking.

obstructionnisme (ɔbstryksjɔnism), s.m. Obstructionism.

obstructionniste (ɔbstryksjɔnist), adj. s.m.f. Obstructionist.

obstruer (ɔbstrɥe), v.a. [L *obstruere*] To obstruct, to stop up, to block up, to be in the way of; **s'~**, v.pr. to get obstructed, stopped, or blocked.

obtempérer (ɔbtɑ̃pere), v.n. [L *obtemperare*] To obey, to submit (*à*, to), to comply (with); *~ à un ordre*, to obey an order.

obtenir (ɔbtənir), v.a. [L *obtinere*] To obtain, to get, to gain, to procure, to come by; *faire ~ à X*, to get, to procure for X; **s'~**, v.pr. to be obtained; *cela s'obtient*, that may be obtained.

obtention (ɔbtɑ̃sjɔ̃), s.f. Obtainment, obtaining, getting.

obturant, -e (ɔbtyrɑ̃), p. adj. Stopping.

obturat-eur, -rice (ɔbtyratœr), adj. Stopping, closing. ~, s.m. (anat.) Obturator; (photo.) shutter; (techn.) stop-valve, stop-cock; puncture stop; breech-plug.

obturation (ɔbtyra'sjɔ̃), s.f. Obturation, stopping-up, shutting; (dentist.) stopping.

obturer (ɔbtyre), v.a. [L *obturare*] To obturate, to stop up, to stop (a tooth); to close, to seal.

obtus, -e (ɔbty), adj. [L *obtusus*] Obtuse, dull, blunt; *angle ~*, obtuse angle; *~angle*, obtuse-angled; *d'esprit ~*, slow-witted, dull-minded, stupid, obtuse.

obus (ɔbys, ɔby), s.m. [f. Germ. *Haubitze*] Shell; *~ à balles*, shrapnel-shell.

obusier (ɔbyzje), s.m. Howitzer, field howitzer.

obvenir (ɔbvənir), v.n. [L *obvenire*] (law) To escheat, to revert by escheat.

obvers, obverse (ɔbvɛr, ɔbvɛrs), s.m. [L *obversus*] Obverse, face (of a coin); syn. AVERS.

obvier (à) (ɔbvje), v.n. [L *obviare*] To obviate, to prevent; *~ à un inconvénient*, to obviate an inconvenience; syn. PARER (À).

oc (ɔk), adv. [f. L *hoc*] (obs.) Yes; *langue d'~*, the dialect (spoken south of the Loire in the Middle Ages) in which this affirmative adv. was used; langue d'Oc. See OÏL.

ocarina (ɔkarina), s.m. [f. It. *oca*] (mus.) Ocarina.

occase (ɔkɑz), adj.f. [L *occasus*] (astr.) Westerly; *amplitude ~*, arc of horizon between the point where a star sets and the true west.

occase (ɔkɑz), s.f. (slang) Opportunity, occasion; *tomber sur la fine ~*, to strike oil.

occasion (ɔkazjɔ̃), s.f. [f. L *occidere*, *occasio*] Occasion, opportunity, suitable juncture; (good) bargain; cause, reason, motive; *à l'~*, if need be, eventually, (up)on occasion; *en toute ~*, on all occasions, at all times; whenever need arises; *dans quelle ~?*, in what circumstances?; *être l'~ de*, to bring about, to cause; *dans les grandes ~s*, on special occasions; *profiter d'une ~*, to improve an opportunity, to get a bargain; *saisir l'~ aux cheveux*, to seize time by the forelock; *voiture d'~*, second-hand car.

occasionnel, -le (ɔkazjɔnɛl), adj. Occasional; chance.

occasionnellement (ɔkazjɔnɛlmɑ̃), adv. Occasionally.

occasionner (ɔkazjɔne), v.a. To occasion, to cause, to bring about.

occident (ɔksidɑ̃), s.m. [L *occidens*] Occident, west; *d'~*, western, occidental; syn. PONANT.

occidental, -e, (aux) (ɔksidɑ̃tal), adj. Occidental, western, westerly, west. ~, s.m.f. Occidental.

occipital, -e, (aux) (ɔksipital), adj. (anat.) Occipital.

occiput (ɔksipyt), s.m. [L wd] (anat.) Occiput.

occire (ɔksir), v.a. [L *occidere*] To kill, to slay.

occlure (ɔklyr), v.a. [L *occludere*] To occlude, to stop up.

occlusi-f, -ve (ɔklyzif), adj. Occluding, shutting, stopping up.

occlusion (ɔklyzjɔ̃), s.f. Occlusion, shutting up.

occultation (ɔkylta'sjɔ̃), s.f. [f. L *occultare*] (astr.) Occultation.

occulte (ɔkylt), adj. [L *occultus*] Occult, esoteric, recondite.

occultisme (ɔkyltism), s.m. Occultism, science of occult things.

occupant, -e (ɔkypɑ̃), p. adj. **1.** Occupying, engrossing; **2.** (law) concerned as the attorney. ~, s.m.f. Occupier, occupant; *le droit du premier ~*, the rights of the first settler or occupier.

occupation (ɔkypa'sjɔ̃), s.f. [L *occupatio*] **1.** Occupation, pursuit; employment, business, work; *être sans ~*, (*a*) to have nothing to do; (*b*) to be unemployed; **2.** (law) occupancy; **3.** (mil.) occupation, taking possession of or holding a country or district; *armée d'~*, army of occupation.

occupé, -e (ɔkype), p. adj. Occupied, busy, engaged; preoccupied, engrossed (*de*, with).

occuper (ɔkype), v.a. [L *occupare*] To occupy, to take up, to employ; to engross, to preoccupy; to take possession of (a country, town, &c.); to reside in; **s'~**, v.pr. to busy oneself (*de*, with), to occupy oneself; to apply oneself (*à*, *de*, to); to be employed or engaged; to think (*de*, of), to take notice (*de*, of), to trouble oneself; to attend (*de*, to).

occurrence (ɔkyrɑ̃s), s.f. [f. L *occurrere*] Occurrence, happening, event; *en l'~*, in this case.

occurrent, -e (ɔkyrɑ̃), adj. Occurring, occurrent.

océan (ɔseɑ̃), s.m. [L *oceanus*] Ocean; (fig.) oceans, immense expanse or quantity of anything.

océane (ɔsean), adj.f. (archaic) *Mer ~*, high sea, the ocean.

océanide (ɔseanid), s.f. (myth.) Oceanid; sea-nymph.

océanien, -ne (ɔseanjɛ̃), adj. s.m.f. Oceanian.

océanique (ɔseanik), adj. Oceanic.

océanographie (ɔseanɔgrafi), s.f. Oceanography.

océanographique (ɔseanɔgrafik), adj. Oceanographic(al).

ocellation (ɔsɛlla'sjɔ̃), s.f. Ocellation, ocellus.

ocelle (ɔsɛl), s.m. [L *ocellus*] Ocellus.

ocellé, -e (ɔsɛlle), adj. Ocellated, ocellate.

ocelot (ɔslo), s.m. [f. Mexic. *tlalocelotl*] (zool.) Mexican wild cat, ocelot.

ochlocratie (ɔklɔkrasi), s.f. [Gr. *okhlokratia*] Ochlocracy, mob-rule.

ocre (ɔkr), s.f. [Gr. *ōkhra*] (min.) Ochre.

ocreu-x, -se (ɔkrø), adj. Ochreous, ochrous, ochry.

oct, octa, octi, octo (ɔkt, ɔkta, ɔkti, ɔkto), pref. [f. Gr. *oktō*] Oct-, octa-, octo-.

octacorde (ɔktakɔrd), s.m. adj. (mus.) Octachord, eight-stringed (instrument).

octaèdre (ɔktaɛdr), s.m. [Gr. *oktahedron*] (geom.) Octahedron. ~, adj. Octahedral.

octaédrique (ɔktaedrik), adj. Octahedral.

octaétéride (ɔktaeterid), s.f. [Gr. *oktaeteris*] Period of 8 years.

octandre (ɔktɑ̃dr), adj. (bot.) Octandrous, octandrian.

octandrie (ɔktɑ̃dri), s.f. Octandria.

octant (ɔktɑ̃), s.m. [L *octans*] Octant, ⅛ of circumference of a circle; ⅛ of area of a circle contained within two radii and arc; (astr.) point in planet's apparent course 45° distant from given point; graduated eighth of circle used in astronomy and navigation.

octante (ɔktɑ̃t), num. adj. (archaic) Eighty.

octantième (ɔktɑ̃tjɛm), adj. (archaic) Eightieth.

octastyle (ɔktastil), s.m. adj. (arch.) Octastyle, having eight columns.

octateuque (ɔktatøk), s.m. [Gr. *octateukhos*] Octateuch, first eight books of the Old Testament.

octave (ɔktav), s.f. [L *octavus*] **1.** (mus.) Octave, octave-flute, piccolo; **2.** octave interval, octave; **3.** (Cath. Church) octave, eighth day after religious festival; also the whole week after religious festival.

octavier (ɔktavje), v.n.a. (mus.) To overblow, to play an octave higher.

octavin (ɔktavɛ̃), s.m. (mus.) Octave-flute, piccolo.

octavo (ɔktavo), adv. Eighthly; *in-~*, octavo.

octavon, -ne (ɔktavɔ̃), s.m.f. adj. Octoroon, offspring of quadroon and white.

octennal, -e, (aux) (ɔktɛnnal), adj. (rare) Octennial.

octidi (ɔktidi), s.m. [pref. *octi* + L *dies*] Octidi (eighth day of the decade in the calendar of the first French republic).

octobre (ɔktɔbr), s.m. [L *october*] October.

octogénaire (ɔktɔʒenɛr), adj. s.m.f. Octogenarian.

octogonal, -e, (aux) (ɔktɔgɔnal), adj. Octagonal.

octogone (ɔktɔgɔn), s.m. [f. Gr. *oktō*+ *gōnia*] (geom.) Octagon. ~, adj. Octagonal.

octosyllabe, octosyllabique (ɔktɔsillab, ɔktɔsillabik), adj. Octosyllabic.

octroi (ɔktrwɑ), s.m. **1.** Grant, concession, *faire l'~ de quelque chose à X*, to grant something to X; **2.** town-due, toll, city-toll, duty; **3.** toll-house, toll-office.

octroyer (ɔktrwaje), v.a. [LL *auctoricare*] To grant; to concede; *~ un privilège*, to grant a privilege.

octuor (ɔktɥɔr), s.m. (mus.) Octet.

octuple (ɔktypl), s.m. [L *octuplus*] Octuple. ~, adj. Octuple, eightfold.

octupler (ɔktyple), v.a.n. To octuple, to increase eightfold.

oculaire (ɔkylɛr), adj. [f. L *oculus*] Ocular; eye-; *témoin ~*, eye-witness. ~, s.m. Eye-glass, eye-piece.

ocularisté (ɔkylarist), s.m.f. Ocularist; maker of artificial eyes.

oculi (ɔkyli), s.m. [L wd] Oculi, third Sunday in Lent.

oculiste (ɔkylist), s.m.f. [f. L *oculus*] Oculist, ophthalmic surgeon, eye-doctor.

odalisque (ɔdalisk), s.f. [Turk. *odalik*] Odalisk, odalisque.

ode (ɔd), s.f. [Gr. *ōdē*] Ode.

odelette (ɔdlɛt), s.f. Little ode.

odéon (ɔdeɔ̃), s.m. [Gr. *ōdeion*] Odeum, Odéon (name of a theatre in Paris).

odeur (ɔdœr), s.f. [L *odor*] Odour; smell; scent; perfume; fragrance; (fig.) repute; *mourir en ~ de sainteté*, to die in the odour of sanctity; *il n'est pas en ~ de sainteté auprès de son curé*, he is not in his curé's good graces; he does not stand very high in the opinion of his curé.

odieusement (ɔdjøzmɑ̃), adv. Odiously, hatefully, invidiously.

odieu-x, -se (ɔdjø), adj. [L *odiosus*] Odious, hateful; invidious. ~, s.m. Odium, odiousness.

odomètre (ɔdɔmɛtr), s.m. [Gr. *hodos*+ *metron*] Odometer, podometer; syn. PODOMÈTRE.

odontalgie (ɔdɔ̃talʒi), s.f. [Gr. *odous*+ *algos*] Odontalgia, odontalgy, toothache.

odontalgique (ɔdɔ̃talʒik), adj. Odontalgic.

odontologie (ɔdɔ̃tɔlɔʒi), s.f. [Gr. *odous*+ *logos*] Odontology, dentistry.

odorant, -e (ɔdɔrɑ̃), p. adj. Odorous, fragrant, scented, sweet-scented, sweet-smelling, sweet.

odorat (ɔdɔra), s.m. Smell, sense of smell.

odorer (ɔdɔre), v.a.n. (rare) [L *odorare*] To smell; syn. SENTIR.

odoriférant, -e (ɔdɔriferɑ̃), adj. [L *odor*+ *ferre*] Odoriferous, &c. (see syn. ODORANT).

odyssée (ɔdise), s.f. [Gr. *Odusseia*, f. prop. n. *Odusseus*] Odyssey, narrative of adventures; eventful travels, series of wanderings.

œcuménicité (ekymenisite), s.f. Oecumenicity.

œcuménique (ekymenik), adj. [f. Gr. *oikoumenē*] Oecumenical; of or representing the whole (Christian) world.

œdémateu-x, -se (edematø), adj. (med.) Oedematous.

œdème (edɛm), s.m. [Gr. *oidēma*] (med.) Oedema.

œdicnème (ediknɛm), s.m. (ornith.) Oedicnemus.

œdipe (edip), s.m. [f. *Oidipous*, prop. n. in Gr. myth.] Oedipus; solver of riddles.

œil (œj) (pl. **yeux**, jø), s.m. [L *oculus*] **1.** Eye; **2.** sight, eye; **3.** hole (in cheese, bread, &c.), eyelet; **4.** lustre (of gems); **5.** bubble, speck (of soup); **6.** face (of letters); *~-de-bœuf*, (*a*) bull's-eye; (*b*) oval window; *~-de-chat*, cat's-eye; *~ d'aigle*, eagle's eye; sharp eyesight; *clin d'~*, wink, twinkling of an eye; *coup d'~*, (*a*) glance; (*b*) peep; (*c*) survey; (*d*) view; (*e*) ogle; *au premier coup d'~*, at first sight, at a glance; *à vue d'~*, visibly, apace; *avoir l'~*, to be wide awake, to be on one's guard; (pop.) *à l'~*, on tick; gratis; without paying; on the free list; *avoir X à l'~*, *avoir l'~ sur X*, to have one's eye on X, to keep a close watch on X; *avoir l'~ à*, to mind; *avoir de l'~*, to look well, to be chic, stylish, smart; *s'en battre l'~*, not to care a fig (or a straw or a hang) for it; *donner dans l'~ à X*, to dazzle X, to take X's fancy; *faire de l'~ à*, to ogle, to make eyes at; *se fourrer le doigt dans l'~*, to be quite out; to deceive oneself blindly; to be grossly mistaken; *voir d'un bon ~*, to look favourably (upon); *mauvais ~*, evil eye; *avoir le mauvais ~*, to bring bad luck; *avoir le compas dans l'~*, to have a good eye for distances; *ouvrez l'~, et le bon*, look out !; *il a un ~ de lynx*, he has the eyes of a lynx, he can see through a brick wall; *un ~ au beurre noir*, *un ~ poché*, a black eye; an eye in mourning; *à l'~ nu*, with the naked eye; *tourner de l'~*, (*a*) to be sea-sick; to be sick; (*b*) to die, to kick the bucket, to go west; *~ de perdrix*, (*a*) corn between the toes; soft corn; (*b*) kind of huckaback material, diaper; *entre quatre (z')yeux*, privately, between you and me and the door-post; *par-dessus les yeux*, over head and ears; *elle lève les yeux*, she raises her eyes; *pour ses beaux yeux*, gratuitously, for love; *il n'a pas froid aux yeux*, he is plucky; he is not a coward; he is not short of cheek; *fermer les yeux sur*, to shut one's eyes to; to wink at; to tolerate; to connive at; *faire les yeux doux à*, to look lovingly at, to ogle, to gloat over; to look sweet at; to give the glad eye to; *à mes yeux*, to my mind; *ouvrir de grands yeux*, to stand staring, to look astonished; to stare in astonishment; *tout voir par ses propres yeux*, to see everything with one's own eyes; to keep an eye on everything; *il n'a d'yeux que pour elle*, he sees nothing but her; *je l'ai regardé dans le blanc des yeux*, I looked him full in the face; *cela saute aux yeux*, that is obvious; that 's as clear as noonday; *jeter les yeux sur*, to cast one's eyes on; to look; (fig.) to select; *faire des yeux furieux*, to cast furious looks (*à*, upon); *cela coûte les yeux de la tête*, it costs a mint of money; *elle n'a pas les yeux dans sa poche*, she is wide awake, clear-sighted, observant; *je suis tout yeux*, I am all eyes, expectant, keenly attentive; *couver des yeux*, to look covetously, greedily, or passionately at; *voir avec les yeux de la foi*, believe blindly; *je l'ai vu de mes yeux*, I have seen it with my own eyes; *il voit tout par les yeux de X*, he sees everything through X's eyes; *loin des yeux, loin du cœur*, out of sight, out of mind; *faire des yeux de merlan frit*, look like a dying duck in a thunderstorm; *en mettre plein les yeux* (or *la vue*) *à X*, try to come it over X; *yeux bridés*, slit-like eyes, slanting eyes.

œillade (œjad), s.f. [f. *œil*] Glance, sly look, wink, ogle, leer, sweet look, sheep's eyes.

œillère (œjɛr), s.f. [f. *œil*] **1.** Eye-tooth; **2.** blinker; piece of harness, eye-flap; **3.** eye-bath, eye-glass.

œillet (œjɛ), s.m. [f. *œil*] **1.** Eyelet, eyelet-hole; **2.** (bot.) pink, carnation; *~ de poète*, sweet-william; *~ d'Inde*, African marigold; *~ des prés*, ragged robin.

œilleton (œjtɔ̃), s.m. (hort.) Sucker, offshoot; layer; young bud.

œillette (œjɛt), s.f. (bot.) Oil-poppy, white poppy; opium-poppy; *huile d'~*, poppy-seed oil.

œnanthe (enɑ̃t), s.f. (bot.) Oenanthe.

œnanthique (enɑ̃tik), adj. Oenanthic.

œnologie (enɔlɔʒi), s.f. [f. Gr. *oinos*+ *logos*] Oenology; science of wine-making.
œnomètre (enɔmɛtr), s.m. Oenometer.
œnophile (enɔfil), s.m.f. [f. Gr. *oinos*+ *philos*] Oenophile, oenophilist. ~, **adj.** Oenophilic, wine-loving.
œnophore (ɛnɔfɔr), s.m. [Gr. *oinos*+ *phoros*] **1.** (anc.) Wine-vessel, wine-jar; **2.** cup-bearer.
œsophage (ɛzɔfaʒ), s.m. [Gr. *oisophagos*] (anat.) Oesophagus.
œsophagien, -ne (ɛzɔfaʒjɛ̃), adj. Oesophageal, pertaining to the oesophagus.
œsophagite (ɛzɔfaʒit), s.f. (pathol.) Oesophagitis, inflammation of the oesophagus.
œstre (ɛstr), s.m. [f. Gr. *oistros*] (ent.) Oestrus, gad-fly, bot-fly.
œuf (œf) (pl. **-s**, ø), s.m. [L *ovum*] Egg; (of fish) roe, spawn; anything egg-shaped; *~s à la coque*, (soft-)boiled eggs; *~s durs*, hard-boiled eggs; *~s sur le plat*, eggs cooked with fresh butter in the dish in which they are served; *~s à la neige*, snow eggs, beaten white of eggs boiled in milk and served on custard; *~s pochés*, poached eggs; *~s frits*, fried eggs; *~ brouillés*, scrambled eggs; *~ de Pâques*, Easter egg; Easter gift; *~ clair*, wind-egg; *blanc d'~*, white of egg; *jaune d'~*, egg-yolk; *donner un ~ pour avoir un bœuf*, to throw a sprat to catch a mackerel; to give a sprat to catch a herring; (prov.) *qui vole un ~ vole un bœuf*, he who steals an ounce will steal a pound; *marcher sur des ~s*, to walk or skate on thin ice; *tondre sur un ~*, to skin a flint; *mettre tous ses ~s dans le même panier*, to venture one's all in an enterprise, to have or put all one's eggs in one basket; *plein comme un ~*, (*a*) chock-full; (*b*) as drunk as a lord.
œufrier (œfrje), s.m. Egg-boiler.
œuvé, -e (œve), adj. (of fish) Hard-roed.
œuvre (œvr), s.f. [L *opera*] **1.** Work, labour; *ne faire ~ de ses dix doigts*, to do nothing on earth; *à l'~!*, to work!; *se mettre à l'~*, to set to work; *faire ~ de*, to behave as; **2.** piece of work; production of the mind; *un fils de ses ~s*, a self-made man; *à l'~ on connaît l'artisan* (or *l'ouvrier*), a man is known by what he does, the proof of the pudding is in the eating; *les plus belles ~s de Chopin*, Chopin's finest compositions; *être à l'~*, to be busy with, or engaged on something; *~s posthumes*, posthumous works; *~s inédites*, unpublished works; **3.** moral deed, act of charity; *~s pies*, acts of piety; **4.** charitable society, social work; charity committee; **5.** fabric (of a church; *banc d'~*, churchwarden's pew; **6.** (jewellery) mounting, setting; *mettre en ~*, to work up; to set (a jewel); (fig.) to carry out (an idea); to set going; *mettre tout en ~*, to leave no stone unturned; **7.** (naut.) *~s mortes*, topsides; (naut.) *~s vives*, bottom, quick works. ~, s.m. **1.** The complete works of a great author, painter, musician, &c.; *tout l'~ de Chopin*, the whole of Chopin's compositions or works; **2.** (arch.) *le gros ~*, the foundations; *dans ~*, inside; *hors d'~*, outside; *à pied d'~*, at hand, in the neighbourhood; *reprendre en sous-~*, to underpin; **3.** (alchemy) *le grand ~*, the search for the philosophers' stone.
œuvrer (œvre), v.n. To work (in a fervent, artistic way).
œuvrette (œvrɛt), s.f. (Lit., mus.) Little work.
offensant, -e (ɔfɑ̃sɑ̃), p. adj. Offensive, insulting.
offense (ɔfɑ̃s), s.f. [L *offensa*] **1.** Offence, abuse, insult; **2.** transgression, offence, trespass, wrong; *Seigneur, pardonnez-nous nos ~s*, Lord, forgive us our trespasses.
offensé, -e (ɔfɑ̃se), p. adj. Offended. **~**, s.m.f. Offended party.
offenser (ɔfɑ̃se), v.a. [f. *offense*] **1.** To offend, to shock, to injure; to give offence to; to be offensive to; *soit dit sans vouloir vous ~*, no offence meant; no offence, I hope; *il n'y a que la vérité qui offense*, the greater the truth, the greater the libel; **2.** to offend against, to sin against, to trespass against, to transgress; **s'~**, v.pr. to take offence, to be offended (*de*, with); to take exception, to be angry.
offenseur (ɔfɑ̃sœr), s.m. Offender. ⚠ 'Offender' frequently means *délinquant*, *criminel*, *pécheur*, but *offenseur* has not this acceptation.
offensi-f, -ve (ɔfɑ̃sif), adj. Offensive, aggressive, attacking. **~ve**, s.f. Offensive; *prendre l'~ve*, to take the offensive; to attack.
offensivement (ɔfɑ̃sivmɑ̃), adv. Offensively.
offert, -e (ɔfɛr), p.p. of *offrir*.
offerte, offertoire (ɔfɛrt, ɔfɛrtwar), s.f. Offertory.
office[1] (ɔfis), s.m. [L *officium*] **1.** Divine service; mass; *l'~ des morts*, burial service, office for the dead, prayers for the dead; **2.** office, post, duty, functions, turn; agency; department; board; *d'~*, (*a*) in virtue of one's office; (*b*) officially; (*c*) of one's own accord; *faire ~ de*, to serve as; *rendre de bons ~s à X*, to do X a good turn or friendly office; *~ d'hygiène publique*, Board of Public Health; *exercer un ~*, to hold an office.
office[2] (ɔfis), s.f. Pantry, offices; (fig.) servants' hall or room, servants' quarters, the servants collectively; *ragots d'~*, servants' gossip.

official (ɔfisjal), s.m. Official (presiding officer of an ecclesiastical court).
officialité (ɔfisjalite), s.f. Officiality; ecclesiastical court.
officiant, -e (ɔfisjɑ̃), p. adj. s.m. Officiating (priest).
officiat (ɔfisja), s.m. Surgical degree, certificate of *officier de santé.*
officie-l, -lle (ɔfisjɛl), adj. Official; (colloq. pej.) red-tape. ~, s.m. = *Le Journal Officiel,* the official record of new laws, and of sittings of the Senate and Chamber of Deputies, published and sold daily; *les ~s,* (colloq.) the authorities, the big bugs.
officiellement (ɔfisjɛlmɑ̃), adv. Officially.
officier (ɔfisje), v.n. [f. *office*] (eccles.) To officiate.
officier (ɔfisje), s.m. [f. LL *officiarius*] Officer; *être ~,* to be an officer; (mil.) ~ *général,* general officer; ~ *supérieur,* field officer; ~ *de compagnie* or *de corps,* company officer; ~ *d'ordonnance,* orderly officer; *sous-~,* non-commissioned officer; (hist.) ~ *de bouche, du gobelet,* officer of the Household; (naut.) ~ *de port,* harbour-master; ~ *de marine,* naval officer; ~ *général,* flag-officer; ~ *de quart,* officer of the watch; ~ *de santé,* surgeon (who has not taken all examinations); (law) ~ *civil,* ~ *de justice,* officer of the law; law-officer; *~s ministériels,* legal officers (attorneys, solicitors, &c.).
officieusement (ɔfisjøzmɑ̃), adv. **1.** Officiously, non-officially; semi-officially; **2.** kindly; **3.** in a meddlesome way.
officieu-x, -se (ɔfisjø), adj. [L *officiosus*] **1.** Unofficial, semi-official, informal; **2.** obliging; **3.** officious, meddlesome, given to offering service that is not wanted.
officinal, -e, (aux) (ɔfisinal), adj. [LL *officinalis*] Officinal, used in medicine.
officine (ɔfisin), s.f. [L *officina*] **1.** Laboratory; **2.** (fig.) a place where mysterious (political or other) things are concocted.
offrande (ɔfrɑ̃d), s.f. [L *offerenda*] **1.** Offering, oblation; **2.** present.
offrant (ɔfrɑ̃), s.m. p. adj.m. Bidder; bidding; *au plus ~ et dernier enchérisseur,* to the highest bidder.
offre (ɔfr), s.f. [f. *offrir*] Offer, tender; *faire une ~ de,* to make an offer or tender of; *les lois de l'~ et la demande,* the laws of supply and demand.
offrir (ɔfrir), v.a. [L *offerre*] **1.** To offer, to present, to hold out, to proffer; ~ *ses souffrances à Dieu,* to offer up one's sorrows to God; *ceci n'offre pas de difficultés,* this presents no difficulties; **2.** to afford, to exhibit, to expose to view; *cette campagne offre des aspects agréables,* this countryside presents pleasant aspects; **3.** to bid; **s'~,** v.pr. to propose oneself, to offer; *le premier chemin qui s'offre,* the first path that offers; *jamais pareille occasion ne s'offrira,* you will never have such an opportunity again.
offusquer (ɔfyske), v.a. [L *offuscare*] **1.** To cloud, to obscure; to dazzle; **2.** to give offence to; to stand in (one's) light; **s'~,** v.pr. to be offended, shocked, to take exception, to take offence.
ogival, -e, (aux) (ɔʒival), adj. (arch.) Ogival, lancet, gothic.
ogive (ɔʒiv), s.f. [etym. dub.] Ogive, diagonal groin or rib of vault; Gothic arch; *en ~,* shaped as a pointed arch; ogival.
ognon (ɔɲɔ̃), s.m. See OIGNON.
ogre, -sse (ɔgr, ɔgrɛs), s.m.f. [etym. dub.] Ogre; (fem.) ogress; man-eating giant; (fig.) blusterer, hector, bear, brute; *manger comme un ~,* to eat like a wolf.
oh ! (o), interj. Oh !, O !, ho !, indeed !
ohé ! (oe), interj. Halloo !, hi !, I say !; (naut.) ahoy !; *~ ! du canot, du navire,* boat ahoy !, ship ahoy !
ohm (om), s.m. [after G. S. *Ohm,* German physicist, 1787–1854] Ohm, unit of electrical resistance; hence *~mètre,* s.m. ohmmeter.
oïdium (ɔidjɔm), s.m. [f. Gr. *ōon*] Oidium, vine-mildew.
oie (wɑ), s.f. [LL *auca*] Goose (pl. geese); (fig.) silly girl; *patte d'~,* goose-foot; (fig.) (*a*) crow's foot, (*b*) crossing, intersection; *jeu de l'~,* the game of Goose; *elle est bête comme une ~,* she is a regular goose, a simpleton; *une ~ blanche,* a girl excessively innocent and credulous.
oignon, ognon (waɲɔ̃, ɔɲɔ̃), s.m. [L *unio*] **1.** Onion; **2.** (bot.) bulb, bulbous root; **3.** (pop.) large watch, turnip; *regretter les ~s d'Égypte,* to hanker after the flesh-pots of Egypt; *en rang d'~s,* in a row; (slang) *c'est pas tes ~s ça !,* it 's none of your business.
oignonière (waɲɔnjɛr), s.f. Onion-bed.
oïl (ɔil), adv. [f. L *hoc+ille*; OF *oïl* = yes]; *Langue d'~,* the langue d'Oil, the old French language spoken north of the Loire, while the *langue d'Oc* was spoken south of the Loire.
oindre (wɛ̃dr), v.a. irreg. [L *ungere*] To anoint; *oignez vilain, il vous poindra, poignez vilain, il vous oindra,* save a thief from the gallows, and he will be the first to cut your throat; *l'oint du Seigneur,* the Lord's Anointed.
oiseau (pl. -x) (wazo), s.m. [L *aucellus*] **1.** Bird; fowl; hawk; *à vol d'~,* as the crow flies; *comme l'~ sur la branche,* temporarily, in an unsettled way, always on the move; *~x de passage,* migratory birds, birds of passage; *l'~ de Junon,* Juno's bird (the peacock); *l'~ de Minerve,* the owl; *~-mouche,* humming bird; ~ *de proie,* bird of prey; *~x de basse-cour,* fowls, poultry; *un ~ de mauvais augure,*

a bird of ill omen, a bearer of sad news; *petit à petit l'~ fait son nid*, little strokes fell great oaks; many a little makes a mickle; take care of the pence and the pounds will take care of themselves; *vilain ~, celui qui salit son nid!*, it's an ill bird that fouls its own nest; **2.** (mason.) hod; **3.** (fig. pej.) fellow, bird, customer; *un drôle d'~*, a queer customer.

oiseler (wazle), v.n. [f. OF *oisel*] To catch birds; ~, v.a. to train (a hawk).

oiselet (wazlɛ), s.m. Little bird.

oiseleur (wazlœr), s.m. Fowler, bird-catcher.

oiselier (wazlje), s.m. Bird-breeder, bird-dealer, bird-seller.

oisellerie (wazɛlri), s.f. **1.** Bird-catching; **2.** bird-shop; bird-trade.

oiseusement (wazøzmɑ̃), adv. Idly, uselessly, vainly.

oiseu-x, -se (wazø), adj. [L *otiosus*] Idle; useless, vain, trifling; *détails ~*, useless details; *paroles ~ses*, idle words, empty talk.

oisi-f, -ve (wazif), adj. [f. L *otium*] Idle, unoccupied, unemployed; useless, lying idle. ~, s.m.f. Idler.

oisillon (wazijɔ̃), s.m. Little bird, young bird, fledg(e)ling.

oisivement (wazivmɑ̃), adv. Idly.

oisiveté (wazivte), s.f. Idleness; leisure hours, vacant hours; *un jour d'~*, a day of leisure, a holiday; *l'~ est mère de tous les vices*, idleness is the root of all evil, Satan finds some mischief still for idle hands to do.

oison (wazɔ̃), s.m. Gosling; (fig.) goose, ninny.

okapi (ɔkapi), s.m. [Central African native wd] (zool.) Okapi (a West African ruminant with resemblances to giraffe, deer, and zebra, discovered in 1900).

oléacées, oléinées (ɔlease, ɔleine), s.f.pl. (bot.) Oleaceae.

oléagineu-x, -se (ɔleaʒinø), adj. [f. L *olea*] Oleaginous, oily.

oléandre (ɔleɑ̃dr), s.m. [f. LL *lorandrium*] (bot.) Oleander.

oléate (ɔleat), s.m. (chem.) Oleate.

oléiculture (ɔleikyltyr), s.f. Olive-growing.

oléine (ɔlein), s.f. [f. L *oleum*] (chem.) Olein.

oléique (ɔleik), adj. Oleic.

oléomètre (ɔleɔmɛtr), s.m. Oleometer.

olfacti-f, -ve (ɔlfaktif), adj. [f. L *olfactus*] Olfactory, olfactive.

olfaction (ɔlfaksjɔ̃), s.f. Olfaction, smelling, sense of smell.

olibrius (ɔlibriys), s.m. [f. name of a 5th-century governor of Gaul] Braggart; swaggerer; queer and obtrusive fellow.

olifant (ɔlifɑ̃), s.m. [f. L *elephantus*] Oliphant; Roland's horn, horn of ivory.

oligarchie (ɔligarʃi), s.f. [Gr. *oligarkhia*] Oligarchy.

oligarchique (ɔligarʃik), adj. Oligarchic(al).

olim (ɔlim), s.m. [L wd] Registers of Paris Parliament 1254–1318.

olivacé, -e (ɔlivase), adj. Olivaceous.

olivaie (ɔlivɛ), s.f. Olive-plantation or -grove.

olivaire (ɔlivɛr), adj. [f. L *olivarius*] Olive-like, olivary.

olivaison (ɔlivɛzɔ̃), s.f. Olive season, olive-gathering.

olivâtre (ɔlivɑtr), adj. Olive-coloured or -hued, sallow.

olive (ɔliv), s.f. [L *oliva*] **1.** Olive; any olive-shaped thing; **2.** (fig.) olive-branch; **3.** (arch.) olive-moulding, olive-head. ~, adj. Olive-coloured.

oliverie (ɔlivri), s.f. Olive-oil works or mill.

olivette (ɔlivɛt), s.f. **1.** Olive-grove or -plantation; **2.** a kind of grape; **3.** ~s, pl. olivettes (dance after the olive-gathering).

olivier (ɔlivje), s.m. (bot.) Olive-tree, olive; *le Jardin des ~s*, the Garden of Olives; (fig.) *tendre la branche d'~*, to hold out the olive-branch; to make overtures for reconciliation.

olivine (ɔlivin), s.f. Olivine (a precious stone, a kind of chrysoprase).

olla-podrida (ɔllapɔdrida), s.f. [Span. wds] Olla podrida; (fig.) hotchpotch, salmagundi, medley.

olographe (ɔlɔgraf), adj. [Gr. *holos*+*graphein*] Holograph, holographic.

olympe (ɔlɛ̃p), s.m. [f. *Olympus*, Thessalian mountain] Olympus; (fig.) heaven, divine abode; the Gods.

olympiade (ɔlɛ̃pjad), s.f. [f. Gr. *olumpias*] Olympiad.

olympien, -ne (ɔlɛ̃pjɛ̃), adj. s.m. Olympian.

olympique (ɔlɛ̃pik), adj. Olympic; *jeux ~s*, Olympic games.

ombelle (ɔ̃bɛl), s.f. [L *umbella*] (bot.) Umbel.

ombellé, -e (ɔ̃bɛlle), adj. (bot.) Umbellate, umbellated, umbellar.

ombellifère (ɔ̃bɛllifɛr), adj. [f. Fr. *ombelle*+L *ferre*] (bot.) Umbelliferous. ~, s.f. Umbellifer (pl. umbelliferae).

ombelliforme (ɔ̃bɛllifɔrm), adj. Umbelliform.

ombellule (ɔ̃bɛllyl), s.f. (bot.) Umbellet, umbellule.

ombilic (ɔ̃bilik), s.m. [L *umbilicus*] **1.** Navel; umbilicus; (bot.) hilum; **2.** (geom.) umbilicus, point of surface through which all the lines of curvature pass.

ombilical, -e, (aux) (ɔ̃bilikal), adj. Navel-shaped; umbilical; pertaining to the navel.

ombiliqué, -e, (ɔ̃bilike), adj. Umbilicate, navel-shaped.

omble, omble chevalier (ɔ̃bl), s.m. [f. L

amula] s.m. (zool.) Char, hill-trout; grayling; umber; syn. OMBRE CHEVALIER.

ombon (ɔ̃bɔ̃), s.m. [L *umbo*] Umbo, boss in centre of shield.

ombrage (ɔ̃braʒ), s.m. [f. *ombre*] **1.** Shade; (poet.) umbrage; *les verts ~s*, the verdant shades; **2.** (fig.) umbrage, sense of slight; *faire, porter ~ à X*, to give umbrage (or offence) to X.

ombragé, -e (ɔ̃braʒe), p. adj. Shaded, shady, leafy.

ombrager (ɔ̃braʒe), v.a. To shade; to cover, to shelter; to conceal, to hide, to adorn.

ombrageu-x, -se (ɔ̃braʒø), adj. Suspicious, distrustful, easily offended or frightened; (of horses) shy, skittish, difficult.

ombre[1] (ɔ̃br), s.f. [L *umbra*] **1.** Shade, shadow; *les ~s du soir*, the shades of night; *c'est l'~ au tableau*, it is the dark side of the picture; *il a peur de son ~*, he is afraid of his own shadow; *il n'y a pas l'~ d'un doute*, there is not a shadow of doubt; *sans l'~ d'un doute*, without a shadow of doubt; *il n'est plus que l'~ de lui-même*, he is but the shadow of his former self; **2.** spirit, ghost; **3.** obscurity, darkness, dark, gloom; *il vaut autant laisser cela dans l'~*, it would be just as well to take no notice of that; (colloq.) *mettre un homme à l'~*, to put a man into prison; **4.** (fig.) protection, shelter, cover; **5.** (min.) umber.

ombre[2] (ɔ̃br), s.m. [L *umbra*] **1.** (ichth.) Grayling, umber; *~ chevalier*, char, salmo-salvelinus, hill-trout (see syn. OMBLE).

ombre[3], **hombre** (ɔ̃br), s.m. See HOMBRE.

ombrelle (ɔ̃brɛl), s.f. [It. *ombrello*] Parasol, sunshade. ⚠ Not 'umbrella', which = *parapluie*.

ombrer (ɔ̃bre), v.a. To shade, to darken parts of a drawing, to give effects of light and shade.

ombreu-x, -se (ɔ̃brø), adj. Shady, shaded, shadowy; (poet.) umbrageous.

ombrien, -ne (ɔ̃brijɛ̃), adj. s.m.f. Umbrian.

ombrine (ɔ̃brin), s.m. (ichth.) A Mediterranean fish.

oméga (omega), s.m. [last letter of Gr. alphabet] Omega; *l'alpha et l'~ de quelque chose*, the beginning and the end; the whole of something; the alpha and omega.

omelette (ɔmlɛt), s.f. [f. OF *alumelle*, a tin plate] Omelet; *~ aux fines herbes*, savoury omelet; *on ne fait pas d'~ sans casser des œufs*, you can't make an omelet without breaking eggs.

omettre (ɔmɛtr), v.a. [L *omittere*] To omit; to leave out, to pass over; *une lettre omise*, a letter left out; *j'ai omis de l'avertir*, I omitted, or neglected, to warn him.

omission (ɔmisjɔ̃), s.f. Omission, oversight; *sauf erreur ou ~*, errors and omissions excepted.

omnibus (ɔmnibys), s.m. [L wd] Omnibus; (fam.) bus. ~, adj. **1.** Slow; *train ~*, slow or omnibus train; **2.** general, of all work.

omnipotence (ɔmnipɔtɑ̃s), s.f. [f. L *omnis+potentia*] Omnipotence.

omnipotent, -e (ɔmnipɔtɑ̃), adj. [L *omnis+potens*] Omnipotent.

omniprésence (ɔmniprezɑ̃s), s.f. Omnipresence.

omniprésent, -e (ɔmniprezɑ̃), adj. Omnipresent.

omniscience, s.f. [L *omnis+scientia*] Omniscience.

omnium (ɔmnjɔm), s.m. [L wd] **1.** (fin.) Omnium, company transacting various kinds of business; **2.** (turf) consolation stakes.

omnivore (ɔmnivɔr), adj. [f. L *omnis+vorare*] Omnivorous.

omophage (ɔmɔfaʒ), adj. s.m.f. [f. Gr. *ōmos+phagein*] Omophagous, that eats raw meat; omophagist.

omophagie (ɔmɔfaʒi), s.f. Habit of eating raw meat, omophagia.

omoplate (ɔmɔplat), s.f. [f. Gr. *ōmos+platē*] Shoulder-blade, scapula.

on (ɔ̃), ind. pron. [f. L *homo*] One, we, people (pl.); a woman, a man, you; they; somebody; some one (often construed with a passive verb in English); *~ doit aimer son pays*, one is bound to love one's country, we ought to love our country; *~ dit*, they say, it is said, people say; *~ me dit que*, they tell me that; I am told that; I hear that; *quand ~ est jeune, ~ est généreux*, when one (or a man) is young, one (or he) is generous; *~ pardonne tant que l'~ aime*, we forgive as long as we love; *~ ferme !*, closing time!; *~ bâtit un pont superbe*, they are building a magnificent bridge; *~ vous appelle*, somebody is calling you; *~ y va*, coming !; *~ demande*, wanted; *~ s'imagine que*, people think that; *~ assure que*, it is stated that; *~ croirait que*, one would think that; *~ sonne*, there 's a ring; *~ frappe*, there 's a knock at the door; *~ n'en sait rien*, nobody knows; *un ~-dit*, a rumour, a hearsay.

onagre, s.m. [Gr. *onagros*] (zool.) Onager, wild ass; ~, s.f. (bot.) evening primrose; syn. ONAGRAIRE, ŒNOTHÈRE.

onanisme (ɔnanism), s.m. [f. *Onan*, Genesis xxxviii] Onanism, self-pollution, masturbation.

once[1] (ɔ̃s), s.f. [L *uncia*] (weight) Ounce; (fig.) grain, bit; *il n'a pas une ~ de vanité*, he has not an atom of vanity.

once[2] (ɔ̃s), s.f. [L *lyncea*] (zool.) Ounce, snow-leopard.
oncial, -e, (aux) (ɔ̃sjal), adj. s.f. [L *uncialis*] Uncial.
oncirostre (ɔ̃sirɔstr), adj. [f. L *uncus*+*rostrum*] Having a hooked beak.
oncle (ɔ̃kl), s.m. [L *avunculus*] Uncle.
oncques, onc (ɔ̃k), adv. (obs.) [L *unquam*] Ever, never.
onction (ɔ̃ksjɔ̃), s.f. [L *unctio*] Unction; anointing; (fig.) unction; soothing, flattering eloquence or persuasiveness, mellifluous eloquence; *l'extrême* ~, extreme unction, the last sacrament (Catholic Church).
onctueusement (ɔ̃ktɥøzmɑ̃), adv. Unctuously; in a soothing, mellifluous way.
onctueu-x, -se (ɔ̃ktɥø), adj. Unctuous, oily; (fig.) unctuous, mellifluous, smooth; soothing; (pej.) oily.
onctuosité (ɔ̃ktɥozite), s.f. Unctuousness, oiliness.
onde (ɔ̃d), s.f. [L *unda*] **1.** Wave; undulation; water, the sea; (fig. pl.) waves; ~ *électrique*, electric wave; *longueur d'*~, wave-length; *l'*~ *amère*, the briny wave; *l'*~ *noire*, the Stygian lake.
ondé, -e (ɔ̃de), adj. Undulated, wavy, waved; watered (as silk, moire, &c.); grained (as wood).
ondée (ɔ̃de), s.f. [f. *onde*] (Light) shower.
ondin, -e (ɔ̃dɛ̃), s.m.f. [f. *onde*] Undine, water-sprite.
ondoiement (ɔ̃dwa'mɑ̃), s.m. **1.** Undulatory motion; waving; undulation; **2.** private baptism.
ondoyer (ɔ̃dwaje), v.n. **1.** To undulate, to wave, to meander; **2.** ~, v.a. to baptize privately.
ondulation (ɔ̃dyla'sjɔ̃), s.f. [L *undula*] Undulation, waving, flowing; (of hair) waving, Marcel waving; ~ *permanente*, or *permanente*, permanent waving.
ondulatoire (ɔ̃dylatwar), adj. Undulatory.
onduler (ɔ̃dyle), v.n.a. To undulate, to wave, to flow gently, to ripple; ~, v.a. to wave (hair); *tôle ondulée*, corrugated iron.
onduleu-x, -se (ɔ̃dylø), adj. Undulating, waving, wavy.
onéraire (ɔnerɛr), adj. [L *onerarius*] Acting (not honorary).
onéreu-x, -se (ɔnerø), adj. [L *onerosus*] Onerous; (fig.) burdensome, heavy, expensive; *à titre* ~, burdened with certain conditions, subject to certain payments.
onérosité (ɔnerozite), s.f. Onerousness.
ongle (ɔ̃gl), s.m. [L *ungula*] **1.** Nail (of human fingers or toes); *ciseaux à* ~*s*, nail-scissors; *brosse à* ~*s*, nail-brush; (fig.) *il a de l'esprit jusqu'au bout des* ~*s*, he is witty to his finger-tips; he is extremely witty; *payer rubis sur l'*~, to pay cash, to pay on the nail, to pay readily enough; *avoir les* ~ *en deuil*, to have dirty finger-nails; ~ *incarné*, in-growing nail; **2.** (animal's) claw, hoof; **3.** (bird's) talon, claw; (fig.) *rogner les* ~*s à X*, to pare X's claws; (fig.) *il a bec et* ~*s*, he will fight tooth and nail.
onglée (ɔ̃gle), s.f. [f. *ongle*] Painful numbness of the finger-tips (from cold); *j'ai l'*~, my fingers are aching and quite numb.
onglet (ɔ̃glɛ), s.m. (bookbind., print.) Guard, stub; two-page cancel; slip of paper or cardboard; (techn.) notch; mitre; *tailler à* ~, to mitre.
onglette (ɔ̃glɛt), s.f. Flat graver.
onglier (ɔ̃glije), s.m. Manicure-case, manicure-set.
onglon (ɔ̃glɔ̃), s.m. Each division of (ruminant's) hoof.
onguent (ɔ̃gɑ̃), s.m. [L *unguentum*] Ointment, unguent, salve; *de l'*~ *miton mitaine*, eyewash; *dans les petits pots les bons* ~*s*, small parcels hold fine wares.
onguicule (ɔ̃gɥikyl), s.m. Small nail or claw.
onguiculé, -e (ɔ̃gɥikyle), adj. Unguicular, unguiculate.
onguiforme (ɔ̃gɥifɔrm), adj. Unguiform.
ongulé, -e (ɔ̃gyle), adj. Ungulate.
onirocritie (ɔnirokrisi), s.f. [f. Gr. *oneiros* +*kritēs*] Oneirocriticism.
oniromancie (ɔniromɑ̃si), s.f. [f. Gr. *oneiros*+*manteia*] Oneiromancy.
onomastique (ɔnɔmastik), adj. [f. Gr. *onoma*] Onomastic, pertaining to proper names.
onomatopée (ɔnɔmatɔpe), s.f. [Gr. *onomatopoiia*] Onomatopoeia, onomatopoeic word; onomatop(e).
ontogénèse (ɔ̃tɔʒenɛz), s.f. [f. Gr. *ontos*+*genesis*] Ontogenesis.
ontologie (ɔ̃tɔlɔʒi), s.f. [f. Gr. *ontos*+*logos*] Ontology.
ontologique (ɔ̃tɔlɔʒik), adj. Ontological (pertaining to the essence of things or being).
onyx (ɔniks), s.m. [Gr. *onux*] **1.** (min.) Onyx; **2.** (med.) onyx, pterygion.
onze (ɔ̃z), num. adj. s.m. [L *undecim*] Eleven; eleventh; *le* ~ *avril*, April eleventh, or, the eleventh of April.
onzième (ɔ̃zjɛm), num. ord. adj. Eleventh. ~, s.m. Eleventh part.
onzièmement (ɔ̃zjɛmmɑ̃), adv. Eleventhly.
oolithe (ɔɔlit), s.m. [Gr. *ōon*+*lithos*] (geol.) Oolite, roestone.
oolithique (ɔɔlitik), adj. Oolitic.
opacité (ɔpasite), s.f. [L *opacitas*] Opacity, opaqueness.
opale (ɔpal), s.f. [L *opalus*] Opal.
opalescence (ɔpalɛssɑ̃s), s.f. Opalescence.
opalescent, -e (ɔpalɛssɑ̃), adj. Opalescent.

opalin, -e (ɔpalɛ̃), adj. Opaline.
opaque (ɔpak), adj. [L *opacus*] Opaque; (fig.) not lucid, dark, obscure.
opéra (ɔpera), s.m. [It. *opera*] **1.** Opera; **2.** opera-house, in Paris; *grand ~*, grand opera; *~-comique*, comic opera; *~ bouffe*, opera bouffe.
opérable (ɔperabl), adj. Operable, that can be cured by a surgical operation.
opérat-eur, -rice (ɔperatœr), s.m.f. Operator.
opération (ɔpera'sjɔ̃), s.f. [L *operatio*] Operation; working; performance; surgical operation; (math.) operation; *c'est le Docteur X qui fera l'~*, Dr. X will operate; *salle d'~*, operating-room or -theatre; *table d'~*, operating-table; *subir une ~*, to undergo an operation; *une ~ commerciale*, a business transaction; (mil.) *le théâtre des ~s*, the zone in which strategic movements of troops, ships, &c., take place; *l'~ du Saint-Esprit*, the working of the Holy Spirit; (colloq.) *par l'~ du Saint-Esprit*, of itself, miraculously; *faire une ~ d'arithmétique*, to perform an arithmetical operation.
opératoire (ɔperatwar), adj. Of surgical operations, operative; *médecine ~*, surgery.
operculaire (ɔpɛrkylɛr), adj. Opercular, operculate, operculated.
opercule (ɔpɛrkyl), s.m. [L *operculum*] Operculum; fish's gill-cover; lid-like structure in plants.
operculé, -e (ɔpɛrkyle), adj. Operculate, operculated.
opéré, -e (ɔpere), p. adj. Under surgical treatment. ~, s.m.f. Patient.
opérer (ɔpere), v.a.n. [L *operari*] To operate; to work, to work out, to effect, to bring about; to operate upon; *se faire ~*, to undergo an operation; *~ X*, to operate upon X; *~ un kyste*, to extirpate a cyst; *~ des merveilles*, to work wonders; *le remède opère*, the remedy is acting, or, is having the desired effect.
opérette (operɛt), s.f. [f. *opéra*] Operetta (light opera).
opes (ɔp), s.m.pl. [L *opa*] (build.) Scaffold-holes.
ophicléide (ɔfikleid), s.m. [f. Gr. *ophis*+ *kleis*] (mus.) Ophicleide.
ophidien, -ne (ɔfidjɛ̃), adj. s.m. [f. Gr. *ophis*+*eidos*] Ophidian, serpent; *les ~s*, s.m.pl. the ophidia.
ophioglosse (ɔfjɔglɔs), s.f. [f. Gr. *ophis*+ *glōssa*] (bot.) Adder's-tongue, ophioglossum.
ophiolâtrie (ɔfjɔlatri), s.f. [f. Gr. *ophis*+ *latreia*] Serpent-worship.
ophiologie (ɔfjɔlɔʒi), s.f. [f. Gr. *ophis*+ *logos*] Ophiology.
ophiophage (ɔfjɔfaʒ), adj. [f. Gr. *ophis*+ *phagein*] Ophiophagous.
ophite (ɔfit), s.m. [Gr. *ophis*] (min.) Ophite, serpentine marble.
ophrys (ɔfris), s.f. (bot.) Ophrys, orchis.
ophtalmie (ɔftalmi), s.f. [f. Gr. *ophthalmos*] (pathol.) Ophthalmia.
ophtalmique (ɔftalmik), adj. Ophthalmic.
ophtalmologie (ɔftalmɔlɔʒi), s.f. [Gr. *ophthalmos*+*logos*] Ophthalmology.
ophtalmologique (ɔftalmɔlɔʒik), adj. Ophthalmological.
ophtalmoscope (ɔftalmɔskɔp), s.m. Ophthalmoscope, instrument for inspecting retina.
opiacé, -e (ɔpjase), adj. s.m. (pharm.) Opiate.
opiacer (ɔpjase), v.a. [f. *opium*] (pharm.) To opiate.
opiat (ɔpja), s.m. [f. *opium*] (pharm.) **1.** Opiate, sleeping-draught; **2.** tooth-paste.
opilati-f, -ve (ɔpilatif), adj. (med.) Obstruent, obstructive, oppilative.
opilation (ɔpila'sjɔ̃), s.f. (med.) Obstruction, oppilation.
opiler (ɔpile), v.a. [L *oppilare*] (med.) To obstruct, to oppilate; **s'~**, v.pr. to be or become obstructed.
opimes (ɔpim), adj. f.pl. [f. L *opimus*] Rich; *dépouilles ~s*, spolia opima (arms stripped from hostile general by Roman commander).
opinant, -e (ɔpinɑ̃), s.m.f. Speaker; one who states an opinion.
opiner (ɔpine), v.n. [L *opinari*] To opine, to be of opinion, to give one's opinion; *~ du bonnet*, to nod assent.
opiniâtre (ɔpinjɑtr), adj. [f. *opinion*] Opinionated; obstinate, stubborn; unyielding, steady, persevering; *rhume ~*, stubborn cold; *une résistance ~*, an obstinate (or stout) resistance.
opiniâtrément (ɔpinjɑtremɑ̃, ɔpinjatrəmɑ̃), adv. Obstinately, stubbornly.
opiniâtrer (ɔpinjɑtre), v.a. To render obstinate; **s'~**, v.pr. to be obstinate.
opiniâtreté (ɔpinjɑtrəte), s.f. [f. *opiniâtre*] Obstinacy, stubbornness, self-will, wilfulness, resolution, steadiness, obduracy.
opinion (ɔpinjɔ̃), s.f. [L *opinio*] Opinion, belief, judgement, provisional conviction; public opinion, views prevalent among people in general; formal statement by expert; *c'est affaire d'~*, it's a matter of opinion; *se faire une ~*, to form an opinion; *ils sont de la même ~*, they are of the same opinion; (fam.) they row in the same boat; *il a trop bonne ~ de lui-même*, he has too high an opinion of himself; *l'~ publique*, public opinion; *avoir le courage de son ~*, to have the courage of one's convictions; *braver l'~*, to defy or scorn public opinion.
opiomane (ɔpjɔman), s.m.f. adj. (One) given to the opium habit.

opisthodome (ɔpistɔdɔm), s.m. [f. Gr. *opisthen+domos*] (anc. arch.) Opisthodomos.

opium (ɔpjɔm), s.m. [Gr. *opion*] Opium.

opoponax (ɔpɔpɔnaks), s.m. [Gr. wd] (bot.) Opopanax.

opossum (ɔpɔsɔm), s.m. (zool.) Opossum; opossum fur.

opothérapie (ɔpoterapi), s.f. [f. Gr. *opos* +*therapeia*] Opotherapy, treatment by means of extracts of an organ or organs.

opportun, -e (ɔpɔrtœ̃), adj. [L *opportunus*] Opportune, timely, well-timed, seasonable, favourable, expedient, convenient; *en temps* ~, opportunely, timely, seasonably; *au moment* ~, at the right moment.

opportunément (ɔpɔrtynemɑ̃), adv. Opportunely, timely, seasonably, in good time, at the right moment.

opportunisme (ɔpɔrtynism), s.m. Opportunism.

opportuniste (ɔpɔrtynist), s.m.f. adj. Opportunist.

opportunité (ɔpɔrtynite), s.f. [L *opportunitas*] Opportunity; favourable juncture, opening; opportuneness, timeliness, seasonableness.

opposabilité (ɔpozabilite), s.f. Opposability (*du pouce*, of the thumb).

opposable (ɔpozabl), adj. Opposable.

opposant, -e (ɔpozɑ̃), p. adj. Opposing, adverse. ~, s.m.f. Opponent, adversary.

opposé, -e (ɔpoze), p. adj. s.m. Opposite, contrary in position (*à*, to), facing, face to face, back to back, opposed (to), of contrary kind; adverse (to), hostile (to); *c'est tout l'~!*, it's quite the reverse!; *fermement ~ à la prohibition*, firmly opposed to prohibition.

opposer (ɔpoze), v.a. [L *opponere*] To oppose; to place opposite (*à*, to); to compare (with), to plead (*que*, that); to stand in the way of; **s'~**, v.pr. to be opposed, to oppose, to resist, to object (*à*, to), to set oneself (against); *je m'y oppose*, I am against this; I won't have it; I strongly object to this.

opposite (ɔpozit), s.m. Opposite, reverse; *à l'~ de*, opposite, facing.

opposition (ɔpozisjɔ̃), s.f. [L *oppositio*] Opposition, antagonism, resistance, hindrance, stop; antithesis, contrast; (law) garnishment; opposition; caveat; (polit.) the party in opposition, the opposition; *les bancs de l'~*, the opposition benches; *mettre ~ sur le salaire de X*, to lodge an objection to X's wages; *je n'y mets aucune ~*, I offer no opposition to it; *sans ~*, nemine contra.

oppresser (ɔprɛse), v.a. [L *opprimere, oppressum*] To oppress; (fig.) to lie heavy on; *il est très oppressé*, he is breathing with much difficulty. ⚠ In the sense of overwhelming with superior numbers or power, governing tyrannically, 'to oppress' would be best translated by *opprimer*.

oppresseur (ɔprɛsœr), s.m. Oppressor, tyrant. ~, adj. Tyrannical, cruel, oppressive.

oppressi-f, -ve (ɔprɛsif), adj. Oppressive.

oppression (ɔprɛsjɔ̃), s.f. **1.** Oppression, tyranny; **2.** difficulty in breathing; *avoir de l'~*, to have a weight on the chest.

opprimer (ɔprime), v.a. [L *opprimere*] To oppress, to crush down, to govern tyrannically, to keep under by coercion.

opprimé, -e, p. adj. Down-trodden; **les ~s**, s.m.pl. the oppressed, the down-trodden.

opprobre (ɔprɔbr), s.m. [L *opprobrium*] Opprobrium, shame, disgrace, obloquy; *il est l'~ de sa famille*, he is the shame of his family; *mourir dans l'~*, to die in disgrace.

optati-f, -ve (ɔptatif), adj. s.m. [L *optativus*] Optative.

opter (ɔpte), v.n. [L *optare*] To choose (*entre*, between).

opticien, -ne (ɔptisjɛn), s.m.f. Optician.

optime (ɔptim), adv. [L wd] **1.** Very well, capitally; **2.** first-rate.

optimisme (ɔptimism), s.m. [f. L *optimus*] Optimism.

optimiste (ɔptimist), adj. Optimistic. ~, s.m.f. Optimist.

option (ɔpsjɔ̃), s.f. [f. L *optare*] Option, choice, choosing.

optique (ɔptik), s.f. (science) Optics (pl.); aspect, perspective, illusion; *étudier l'~*, to study optics; *l'~ du théâtre*, stage (or theatrical) illusion. ~, adj. Optical; optic; *le nerf ~*, the optic nerve.

optiquement (ɔptikmɑ̃), adv. Optically.

optomètre (ɔptɔmɛtr), s.m. (optics) Optometer, opsiometer.

opulemment (ɔpylamɑ̃), adv. Opulently.

opulence (ɔpylɑ̃s), s.f. [L *opulentia*] Opulence, wealth, affluence; (colloq.) *nager dans l'~*, to be rolling in money; to wallow in riches.

opulent, -e (ɔpylɑ̃), adj. Opulent, wealthy, rich, affluent.

opuscule (ɔpyskyl), s.m. [L *opusculum*] Opuscule, opusculum.

or (ɔr), conj. [L *hora*] Now; but; well; ~ *ça*, now then; ~ *donc*, well.

or (ɔr), s.m. [L *aurum*] Gold; gold ornament; gold money; gold colour; ~, adj. gold-coloured, gold; (fig.) golden; ~ *vierge*, native gold; ~ *en barre*, gold in bar; *lingot d'~*, gold-ingot; ~ *en feuille*, gold-leaf; ~ *filé*, spun gold; *d'or, en ~*, gold, of gold; (fig.) golden; *une montre en ~*, or *d'~*, a gold watch; *il a un cœur d'~*, he has a heart of gold; *au poids de l'~*, for its weight in gold; (fig.) very dear; *parler d'~*, to speak like an angel; to give capital advice; *être tout cousu d'~*, to be made of money; *rouler sur l'~*, to be rolling in money; (prov.) *le silence est d'~*, silence is golden; *tout ce qui brille n'est pas ~*, all is not gold that glitters; *vaisselle d'~*, gold plate; *c'est de l'~ en barre*, (*a*) she, or he, is pure gold; (*b*) it 's as safe as the Bank of England; *on n'en peut avoir ni pour ~ ni pour argent*, it cannot be had for love or money; *noces d'~*, golden wedding; *nombre d'~*, golden number; *âge d'~*, golden age; *on lui a offert un pont d'~*, he was offered splendid terms, or a heavy bribe.

oracle (ɔrɑkl), s.m. [L *oraculum*] Oracle.

orage (ɔraʒ), s.m. [f. L *aura*] Thunder-storm, storm, tempest; (fig.) storm; *le temps est à l'~*, the weather is stormy; *il va faire de l'~*, there 's going to be a storm; there 's a storm brewing; *laisser passer l'~*, to let the storm blow over.

orageusement (ɔraʒøzmɑ̃), adv. Stormily.

orageu-x, -se (ɔraʒø), adj. Stormy, tempestuous; (fig.) stormy; *une vie ~se*, a riotous life; *une discussion ~se*, a stormy debate.

oraison (ɔrɛzɔ̃), s.f. [L *oratio*] **1.** (obs.) Oration, speech; *~ funèbre*, funeral oration; **2.** orison, prayer; *faire ~*, to say prayers; *l'~ dominicale*, the Lord's Prayer.

oral, -e, (aux) (ɔral), adj. [f. L *os*] Oral, verbal, by word of mouth.

oralement (ɔralmɑ̃), adv. Orally.

orange (ɔrɑ̃ʒ), s.f. [Arab. *naranj*] Orange; *fleur d'~*, orange flower; *~ sanguine*, blood-orange. ~, adj. Orange-coloured, orange.

orangé, -e (ɔrɑ̃ʒe), p. adj. Orange-coloured, orange.

orangeade (ɔrɑ̃ʒad), s.f. Orangeade, orange-juice.

orangeat (ɔrɑ̃ʒa), s.m. Candied orange-peel.

oranger (ɔrɑ̃ʒe), s.m. Orange-tree; *eau de fleur d'~*, orange-flower water; *fleur d'~*, orange-blossom.

orangère (ɔrɑ̃ʒɛr), s.f. Orange-woman, orange-girl.

orangerie (ɔrɑ̃ʒri), s.f. **1.** Orangery, orange-house; **2.** orange-grove or -plantation.

orangette (ɔrɑ̃ʒɛt), s.f. Orange-berry (the orange gathered before maturity and used in confectionery, or crystallized).

orang-outang (ɔrɑ̃gutɑ̃), s.m. [Malay wd] (zool.) Orang-outang.

orat-eur, -rice (ɔratœr), s.m.f. [L *orator*] Orator, speaker; spokesman, (fem.) spokeswoman; mouth-piece (of a body of people), pleader; *n'être pas ~*, to be no orator; *Cicéron fut le plus grand ~ de Rome*, Cicero was the greatest orator of Rome.

oratoire (ɔratwar), adj. Oratorical, of public speaking; *art ~*, the art of public speaking, oratory.

oratoire (ɔratwar), s.m. Oratory, private chapel; *l'Oratoire du Louvre*, the principal Protestant church in Paris.

oratoirement (ɔratwarmɑ̃), (rare) adv. Oratorically.

oratorien (ɔratɔrjɛ̃), s.m. adj.m. Oratorian.

oratorio (ɔratɔrjo), s.m. [It. wd] (mus.) Oratorio.

orbe (ɔrb), s.m. [L *orbis*] Orb, orbit; sphere, globe. ~, adj. **1.** (arch.) Dead or blind (wall); **2.** (of blows) contusing, bruising.

orbicole (ɔrbikɔl), adj. [f. L *orbis+colere*] Growing everywhere.

orbiculaire (ɔrbikylɛr), adj. [f. L *orbiculus*] (anat.) Orbicular. ~, s.m. Orbicular muscle.

orbitaire (ɔrbitɛr), adj. Orbital.

orbital, -e, (aux) (ɔrbital), adj. Orbital.

orbite (ɔrbit), s.f. [L *orbita*] **1.** (astr.) Orbit; **2.** (anat.) orbit, socket (of the eye).

orcanète (ɔrkanɛt), s.f. [f. *arcanne*] (bot.) Orcanet, alkanet.

orchestique (ɔrkɛstik), adj. [Gr. *orkhêstikos*] (Gr. ant.) Orchestic, of dancing.

orchestral, -e, (aux) (ɔrkɛstral), adj. Orchestral.

orchestration (ɔrkɛstra'sjɔ̃), s.f. (mus.) Orchestration, scoring.

orchestre (ɔrkɛstr), s.m. [Gr. *orkhēstra*] **1.** Orchestra, band; the musicians; *chef d'~*, conductor, band-master, leader of the band (or orchestra); **2.** orchestra stalls (in theatre or concert-hall).

orchestrer (ɔrkɛstre), v.a. (mus.) To orchestrate, to arrange or score for orchestral performance.

orchidée (ɔrkide), s.f. (bot.) Orchid; *les ~s*, the orchidaceae.

orchis (ɔrkis), s.m. [Gr. wd] (bot.) Orchis.

orchite (ɔrkit), s.f. (pathol.) Orchitis, inflammation of the testicles.

ord, -e (ɔr), adj. (obs.) [L *horridus*] Dirty, foul, nasty.

ordalie (ɔrdali), s.f. [f. Anglo-Saxon *ordāl*] Ordeal (old form of trial in Middle Ages).

ordinaire (ɔrdinɛr), adj. [L *ordinarius*] Ordinary, common, usual, customary; vulgar. ~, s.m. **1.** The usual way; **2.** usual fare; **3.** (mil.) mess; *à l'~, comme à l'~*, as usual; *d'~, pour l'~*, usually; *au-dessus de l'~*, above the common run.

ordinairement (ɔrdinɛrmɑ̃), adv. Ordinarily, commonly, usually, generally, mostly.

ordinal, -e, (aux) (ɔrdinal), adj. [L *ordinalis*] Ordinal.

ordinand (ɔrdinɑ̃), s.m. [L *ordinandus*] Candidate for holy orders, ordinand.

ɔ, note, glotte; **ɔ̃**, monter, ronde; **ø**, feu, creux; **œ**, peur, sœur; **œ̃**, un; **ʃ**, chez, schisme; **u**, tout; **w**, oui, doit, douaire; **y**, mur, pu; **ɥ**, huile, muette; **z**, zèle, rose; **ʒ**, déjà, gentil.

ordinant (ɔrdinɑ̃), s.m. [L *ordinans*] Ordaining bishop, ordinant.
ordination (ɔrdinaˈsjɔ̃), s.f. [L *ordinatio*] Ordination.
ordo (ɔrdo), s.m. Ordo, church calendar.
ordonnance (ɔrdɔnɑ̃s), s.f. [f. *ordonner*] **1.** Order, array, disposition; **2.** ordering; regulation; ~ *de police,* police regulation; **3.** (law) statute; *prendre une* ~, to issue an order; **4.** (med.) prescription; *l'*~ *du médecin,* the doctor's prescription; **5.** (mil.) orderly; *officier d'*~, orderly officer; *l'*~ *de cet officier,* this officer's orderly.
ordonnancement (ɔrdɔnɑ̃smɑ̃), s.m. [f. *ordonnancer*] Order for payment.
ordonnancer (ɔrdɔnɑ̃se), v.a. To write an order for the payment of.
ordonnat-eur, -rice (ɔrdɔnatœr), s.m.f. Manager, ruler, master of the ceremonies; *commissaire* ~, pay commissioner; ~ *des cérémonies,* master of ceremonies.
ordonné, -e (ɔrdɔne), p. adj. **1.** Well-regulated, ordered; **2.** orderly, methodical, well behaved, fond of order.
ordonnée (ɔrdɔne), s.f. (geom.) Ordinate.
ordonner (ɔrdɔne), v.a.n. [L *ordinare*] **1.** To order, to set in order, to dispose, to array; *il a bien ordonné sa vie,* he has ordered his life well; **2.** to enjoin, to order, to direct, to provide; **3.** to ordain (a priest); **4.** (med.) to prescribe; *le médecin lui ordonne le repos,* the doctor prescribes rest.
ordre (ɔrdr), s.m. [L *ordo*] **1.** Order; disposition, array; (mil.) line, order; sequence; *avec* ~, in good order; methodically; *avoir de l'*~, to be orderly; *n'avoir pas d'*~, to be disorderly; *mettre en* ~ *ses idées,* to arrange one's ideas; *l'*~ *et le désordre,* order and disorder; *dans un* ~ *parfait,* in perfect order; in apple-pie order; *rentrer dans l'*~, to be quiet again; *faire rentrer dans l'*~, to put to rights; to restore peace and order; *j'y mettrai bon* ~, I'll see to that; I'll set that straight; I'll put a stop to that; *numéro d'*~, reference number; *en* ~ *de bataille,* in order of battle; **2.** command, behest, order, direction; writ, order, regulation, mandate; rule, duty; *par* ~, (*a*) by order; on duty; (*b*) in regular order, each in his turn; ~ *du jour,* order of the day; resolution; programme; *passer à l'*~ *du jour,* to pass to the order of the day; *à l'*~ *!, à l'*~ *!,* order! order!; *rappeler à l'*~, to call to order; *mot d'*~, password; *il reçut l'*~ *d'avancer,* he was ordered to advance; *jusqu'à nouvel* ~, until further orders; until one hears to the contrary; *d'*~ *et pour compte de,* by order and on account of; *en sous-*~, subordinate, subordinately, under another; *mettre* or *citer à l'*~ *du jour de l'armée,* to proclaim to the army; to mention in the general orders; *billet à* ~, promissory note; **3.** (natural) order (group below class, and subdivided into genera); class, tribe, corporation, category; **4.** (religious, etc.) order; fraternity; *entrer dans les* ~*s,* to take orders; *les* ~*s mineurs,* minor orders; *l'*~ *de la Jarretière,* the Order of the Garter; *l'*~ *les Templiers,* the order of Templars; *les bases de l'*~ *social,* the basis of social order; *de premier* ~, of the highest order; first-class; (colloq.) A 1; O.K.; (arch.) *les cinq* ~*s classiques,* the five classical orders (Tuscan, Doric, Ionic, Corinthian, and Composite).
ordure (ɔrdyr), s.f. [f. L *horridus,* OF *ord*] Ordure, dung, excrement; household refuse, filth; (fig.) obscenity, foul language, ribaldry; *boîte aux* ~*s,* dust-bin; *jeter aux* ~*s,* to throw into the dust-bin; *défense de déposer des* ~*s,* commit no nuisance; no rubbish to be shot here.
orduri-er, -ère (ɔrdyrje), adj. Filthy, ribald, foul, obscene.
oréade (ɔread), s.f. [Gr. *oreias*] (myth.) Oread, mountain-nymph.
orée (ɔre), s.f. [f. L *ora*] Edge, border, skirt (espec. of wood, forest, &c.).
oreillard, -e (ɔrɛjar), adj. Lop-eared. ~, s.m. (zool.) Small bat.
oreille (ɔrɛj), s.f. [L *auricula*] Ear; hearing; dog's-ear (in a book); ear-lap (of a cap); tongue (of a shoe); fluke (of an anchor); breast, mould-board (of a plough); any ear-shaped appendage or thing; (bot.) ~ *d'ours,* auricula, bear's ear; *avoir l'*~ *fine, bonne,* to have a quick ear, to be quick of hearing; *avoir l'*~ *dure,* to be hard of hearing; *avoir de l'*~, to have a good ear (for music); *aux longues* ~*s,* long-eared; *avoir mal à l'*~, to have ear-ache; *prêter l'*~ *à,* to listen to, to lend an ear to, to attend to; *faire la sourde* ~, to turn a deaf ear; *dormir sur les deux* ~*s,* to sleep quietly, or soundly; to have an easy mind; *de toutes ses* ~*s,* with all one's ears; *dire un mot à l'*~ *de X,* to whisper a word in X's ear; *se faire tirer l'*~, to be most unwilling, to hang back; to need pressing; *il ne se fit pas tirer l'*~, he did not need much entreaty; (fig.) *montrer le bout de l'*~, to show oneself as one is; to show the cloven hoof; *il n'entend pas de cette* ~*-là,* he is deaf on that side; (fig.) he won't listen, or consent, to that, he won't have it; *il se retira l'*~ *basse,* he went away crestfallen, or with his tail between his legs, or looking rather down; *j'ai les* ~*s rebattues de cela,* I am sick of hearing that; *il n'écoute que d'une* ~, he pays very little attention to what is being said; *ne venez pas ainsi me corner aux* ~*s,* do not come and din it into my ears in that way; *par-dessus les* ~*s,* over head and ears; *autant lui en pend à l'*~,

he may expect the same (something unpleasant); *les* ~*s ont dû vous corner* (or *tinter*), your ears must have burned; *je lui frotterai les* ~*s*, I will twist his tail (or pull his ears) for him; (fig.) *échauffer les* ~*s à X*, to irritate X; *dresser l'*~, to prick one's ears; (fig.) to smell a rat; *fendre l'*~ *à X*, (mil.) to pension off, to cashier; to dismiss from service; to sack; *ventre affamé n'a pas d'*~*s*, the hungry belly has no ears.

oreiller (ɔrɛje), s.m. Pillow; *taie d'*~, pillow-case; pillow-slip.

oreillette (ɔrɛjɛt), s.f. **1.** Ear-lap (of a cap); **2.** (anat.) auricle; **3.** ~**s**, pl. a kind of fried cake, made in Southern France.

oreillon (ɔrɛjɔ̃), s.m. Ear; small ear, handle (bot., &c.); ~**s**, pl. (pathol.) mumps.

oremus (ɔremys), s.m. [L wd] Prayer, orison.

ores (ɔr), adv. [L *hora*] *D'*~ *et déjà*, from this moment; henceforth, thenceforth.

orfèvre (ɔrfɛvr), s.m. [L *aurum*+*faber*] Goldsmith, silversmith; (fig.) *vous êtes* ~, *M. Josse*, you are in the trade, my dear sir; that is not disinterested advice.

orfèvrerie (ɔrfɛvrəri), s.f. **1.** Gold- or silversmith's art, trade, or work; **2.** gold or silver plate or jewellery.

orfévri, -e, orfévré, -e (ɔrfevri, ɔrfevre), adj. (rare) Wrought by a gold- or silversmith.

orfraie (ɔrfrɛ), s.f. [L *ossifraga*] (ornith.) Osprey.

orfroi (ɔrfrwɑ), s.m. [L *aurum Phrygium*] Orphrey, orfray.

organdi (ɔrgɑ̃di), s.m. [etym. dub.] Organdie.

organe (ɔrgan), s.m. [Gr. *organon*] **1.** (Bodily) organ; *aucun des* ~*s essentiels*, no vital part; *l'*~ *de la parole*, the organs of speech; **2.** voice; *un bel* ~, a good voice; **3.** spokesman, agent, agency, mouthpiece (of a body of people); means, organ, medium of communication; newspaper, magazine or review representing cause, party, pursuit, &c. ⚠ Not 'organ', musical instrument, which = *orgue*.

organeau (pl. **-x**) (ɔrgano), s.m. (naut.) Anchor-ring.

organique (ɔrganik), adj. Organic, of the bodily organs, vital; (pathol., chem.) organic.

organiquement (ɔrganikmɑ̃), adv. Organically.

organisable (ɔrganizabl), adj. Organizable.

organisat-eur, -rice (ɔrganizatœr), s.m.f. Organizer, steward. ~, adj. Organizing.

organisation (ɔrganiza'sjɔ̃), s.f. [f. *organiser*] Organization, formation, arrangement, structure; nature, being, individual; organized body, system, or society; mind; *chargé de l'*~ *des secours*, entrusted with making arrangements for help.

organisé, -e (ɔrganize), p. adj. Organized; systematically arranged; constituted; *une tête bien* ~*e*, a well-balanced mind.

organiser (ɔrganize), v.a. [LL *organizare*] To organize, to get up, to form, to draw up, to arrange, to settle; **s'**~, v.pr. to become organized; to get settled, to settle.

organisme (ɔrganism), s.m. Organism, system, constitution, arrangement.

organiste (ɔrganist), s.m.f. Organist.

organsin (ɔrgɑ̃sɛ̃), s.m. [It. *organzino*] Organzine.

orgasme (ɔrgasm), s.m. [f. Gr. *organ*] Orgasm.

orge (ɔrʒ), s.f. [L *hordeum*] Barley (*orge* is masc. in: ~ *mondé*, husked, or hulled barley; Scotch barley; and ~ *perlé*, pearl barley); *faire ses* ~*s*, to mow barley; (fig.) to feather one's nest; *tisane d'*~, barley-water.

orgeat (ɔrʒɑ), s.m. Orgeat (a sweet drink made of barley or almonds, sugar, and orange-flower water).

orgelet (ɔrʒəlɛ), s.m. [L *hordeolum*] Stye (on the eye).

orgiaque (ɔrʒjak), adj. [Gr. *orgiastikos*] Orgiastic.

orgie (ɔrʒi), s.f. [Gr. *orgia*] Orgy; drinking-bout, revelry, debauchery; (fig.) riotous wealth, extravagance; excess; *faire une* ~, to have a drinking-bout; *une* ~ *de fleurs*, a profusion of flowers.

orgue (ɔrg), s.m. (but fem. in the plural) [L *organum*] **1.** Organ; *jeu d'*~, organ-stop; *buffet d'*~, organ-case; ~ *de Barbarie* [corrupt. of *Barberi*, inventor] street-organ, barrel-organ; ~ *à pédales*, pedal-organ; (mus.) *point d'*~, 𝄐, pause; **2.** organ-loft; **3.** (obs. fort.) portcullis; **4.** (naut.) tub.

orgueil (ɔrgœj), s.m. [f. OHG *urgoli*] Pride, arrogance; *avec* ~, (*a*) proudly; (*b*) haughtily; *faire l'*~ *de*, to be the pride of; *nous devrions mettre notre* ~ *à*, it should be our pride to.

orgueilleusement (ɔrgɛjøzmɑ̃), adv. Proudly; haughtily, arrogantly, boastingly.

orgueilleu-x, -se (ɔrgɛjø), adj. s.m.f. **1.** Proud (person); **2.** arrogant, haughty (person); *les* ~, the proud, proud people; *c'est une* ~*se*, she is vain and haughty.

orichalque (ɔrikalk), s.m. [Gr. *oros*+*khalkos*] (ant.) Orichalc, a precious metal; also pure copper, latten, and bronze.

orient (ɔrjɑ̃), s.m. [L *oriens*] **1.** The East, the Orient; *d'*~ *en occident*, from east to west; *de l'*~, eastern, of the east; *les portes de l'*~, the gates of the East; *en* ~, in the East; *l'Extrême* ~, the Far East; *le proche* ~, the near East; *le Grand* ~, the Grand Lodge (of freemasons); **2.** (of pearls) water, orient, lustre.

oriental, -e, (aux) (ɔrjɑ̃tal), adj. s.m.f.

Oriental, eastern, easterly; east; *à l'~e*, in the Eastern fashion.
orientalisme (ɔrjɑ̃talism), s.m. Orientalism.
orientaliste (ɔrjɑ̃talist), s.m.f. Orientalist.
orientation (ɔrjɑ̃ta'sjɔ̃), s.f. **1.** Orientation, finding the cardinal points; **2.** position, bearings; **3.** (naut.) trimming (of sails, yards).
orientement (ɔrjɑ̃tmɑ̃), s.m. **1.** Orientation; **2.** (naut.) trim (of sails).
orienter (ɔrjɑ̃te), v.a. **1.** To orientate, to set towards the east; **2.** (fig.) to direct; **3.** to trim (a sail, a yard); **s'~**, v.pr. to orientate oneself, to find out in what direction the east is; to ascertain one's position; to take one's bearings; to see what one is about.
orifice (ɔrifis), s.m. [L *orificium*] Orifice, opening, aperture, hole, mouth; nozzle (of a hose, atomizer, pipe, &c.).
oriflamme (oriflɑm), s.f. [L *aurea*+ *flamma*] Oriflamme.
origan (ɔrigɑ̃), s.m. [Gr. *origanon*] (bot.) Wild marjoram, origan, origanum; syn. MARJOLAINE.
originaire (ɔriʒinɛr), adj. **1.** ~ *de*, coming originally from; native of; *vous n'êtes pas ~ de ce pays*, you are not a native of this country; **2.** original, first, primitive, innate.
originairement (ɔriʒinɛrmɑ̃), adv. Originally, primitively.
original, -e, (aux) (ɔriʒinal), adj. [L *originalis*] **1.** Original, model, primitive, first; innate, initial, earliest; **2.** original, novel in character, not imitative; **3.** strange, queer, singular, peculiar, eccentric, quaint. ~, s.m.f. **1.** Eccentric person, original; odd fellow; **2.** the model, the thing which has been imitated, copied, or represented; *dans l'~*, in the original; *est-ce un ~ ou une reproduction?*, is it an original (drawing or picture) or a reproduction?
originalement (ɔriʒinalmɑ̃), adv. Originally.
originalité (ɔriʒinalite), s.f. **1.** Originality; **2.** eccentricity, oddness, oddity, quaintness, singularity.
origine (ɔriʒin), s.f. [L *origo*] Origin, source, starting-point, beginning, derivation, extraction; descent, birth; *dès l'~*, from the very beginning; *à l'~*, originally; *avoir son ~ dans, tirer son ~ de*, (of a thing) to take (or have) its rise in, to originate in; (of a person) to draw one's origin from; *d'~ illustre*, of illustrious descent; *d'~ française*, French by extraction, French by birth; (of things) made in France; French made; of French origin; *emballage d'~*, original package; *quelle est l'~ de ce mot?*, what's the origin of this word?
originel, -le (ɔriʒinɛl), adj. Original, primitive; *péché ~*, original sin.
originellement (ɔriʒinɛlmɑ̃), adv. Originally, primitively.
orignal (pl. **-s**) (ɔriɲal), s.m. [Basque *orégnac*] (zool.) Canadian elk.
orillon (ɔrijɔ̃), s.m. See OREILLON.
orin (ɔrɛ̃), s.m. (naut.) Buoy-rope (of an anchor).
oripeau (pl. **-x**) (ɔripo), s.m. [OF *orie* (= golden)+*peau*] **1.** Dutch leaf, Dutch gold, foil, tinsel; **2.** gaudy clothes, tinselled or faded finery; showy rags; **3.** (by ext.) tawdry ornaments, tawdry style, anything showy but worthless.
orle (ɔrl), s.m. [It. *orlo*] (arch., herald.) Orle.
orléanais, -e (ɔrleanɛ), adj. s.m.f. Of Orleans, (native) of Orleans. ~, s.m. Orleanais (old French province).
orléaniste (ɔrleanist), adj. s.m.f. Orleanist, supporter of the Orleans princes (as claimants to the French throne).
orléans (ɔrleɑ̃), s.m. [f. *Orléans*, Fr. town] **1.** Orleans (a fabric with cotton warp and worsted weft); **2.** Orleans wine.
ormaie, ormoie (ɔrmɛ, ɔrmwɑ), s.f. [f. *orme*] Elm-grove, elm-plantation.
orme (ɔrm), s.m. [L *ulmus*] (bot.) Elm; ~ *tilleul*, broad-leaved elm; ~ *de montagne*, wych-elm; *attendez-moi sous l'~!*, you may wait for me till doomsday.
ormeau (pl. **-x**) (ɔrmo), s.m. Young elm, elm.
ormille (ɔrmij), s.f. Very young elm, elm-sapling; plantation of young elms.
orne (ɔrn), s.f. [L *ornus*] (bot.) Flowering ash.
ornemaniste (ɔrnəmanist), s.m.f. Ornamentalist, sculptor or painter of ornaments, decorator.
ornement (ɔrnəmɑ̃), s.m. [L *ornamentum*] Ornament, adornment, decorative feature; knick-knack, tracery, moulding, embroidery; (mus.) grace, grace-note, embellishment; *d'~*, ornamental, decorative; *sans ~*, unadorned.
ornemental, -e, (aux) (ɔrnəmɑ̃tal), adj. Ornamental, decorative.
ornementation (ɔrnəmɑ̃ta'sjɔ̃), s.f. Ornamentation, adornment, decoration.
ornementer (ɔrnəmɑ̃te), v.a. To ornament, to decorate, to adorn, to beautify.
orner (ɔrne), v.a. [L *ornare*] To adorn, to ornament, to decorate; (fig.) to grace, to embellish; ~ *de fleurs*, to decorate with flowers; ~ *son esprit*, to adorn one's mind; *style orné*, ornate style.
ornière (ɔrnjɛr), s.f. [from dialect wd *orne*] Rut; (fig.) beaten track, old way, groove, path.
ornithogale (ɔrnitɔgal), s.m. [f. Gr. *ornis*] (bot.) Star of Bethlehem, ornithogalon.
ornithologie (ɔrnitɔlɔʒi), s.f. [f. Gr. *ornithos*+*logos*] Ornithology.

ornithologiste, ornithologue (ɔrnitɔlɔʒist, ornitɔlɔg), s.m.f. Ornithologist.
ornithomancie (ɔrnitɔmɑ̃si), s.f. Ornithomancy.
ornithorynque (ɔrnitɔrɛ̃k), s.m. (zool.) Ornithorhynchus, duck-billed platypus.
orobanche (ɔrɔbɑ̃ʃ), s.f. (bot.) Broom-rape.
orobe (ɔrɔb), s.m. [Gr. *orobos*] (bot.) Orobus, bitter vetch; black pea.
orographie (ɔrɔgrafi), s.f. [f. Gr. *oros*+*graphein*] Orography, oreography; syn. OROLOGIE.
orographique (ɔrɔgrafik), adj. Orographical; syn. OROLOGIQUE.
oronge (ɔrɔ̃ʒ), s.f. (bot.) Orange-milk mushroom; imperial mushroom; orange agaric; *fausse* ~, toadstool, fly-agaric; *Amanita muscaria.*
orpailleur (ɔrpɑjœr), s.m. Gold-seeker, gold-finder, gold-washer.
orphelin, -e (ɔrfəlɛ̃), s.m.f. [L *orphanus*] Orphan; *enfant* ~ *de père,* fatherless child; ~ *de mère,* motherless child.
orphelinat (ɔrfəlina), s.m. Orphanage, orphan-asylum, institution for education of orphans.
orphéon (ɔrfeɔ̃), s.m. [f. *Orpheus*] Orpheon, choral society.
orphéonique (ɔrfeɔnik), adj. Orpheonic; of choral singing or music.
orphéoniste (ɔrfeɔnist), s.m. Orpheonist, member of a choral society.
orphie (ɔrfi), s.f. (ichth.) Garfish, sea-pike, sea-needle, horn-fish.
orphique (ɔrfik), adj. [f. *Orpheus*] Orphic. **~s**, s.m.pl. Votaries of Orpheus; Orphic poems; **~s**, s.f.pl. Orphic mysteries.
orpiment (ɔrpimɑ̃), s.m. [L *auripigmentum*] Orpiment.
orpin (ɔrpɛ̃), s.m. **1.** (bot.) Stonecrop; **2.** (min.) orpiment.
orque (ɔrk), s.f. (ichth.) Grampus, orc, springer.
orseille (ɔrsɛj), s.f. **1.** (bot.) Orchil; **2.** red dye extracted from orchil.
ort (ɔrt), adj. invar., adv. (comm.) Gross, gross weight. ⚠ Not English 'ort', which = *restes, petits débris, rebut.*
orteil (ɔrtɛj), s.m. [f. L *articulus*] Toe; *le gros* ~, the great toe.
orthodoxe (ɔrtɔdɔks), adj. s.m.f. [f. Gr. *orthos*+*doxa*] Orthodox; (fig.) correct, approved; *l'Église* ~, the Orthodox Church.
orthodoxie (ɔrtɔdɔksi), s.f. Orthodoxy.
orthogonal, -e, (aux) (ɔrtɔgɔnal), adj. [f. Gr. *orthos*+*gōnia*] Orthogonal.
orthographe (ɔrtɔgraf), s.f. [Gr. *orthos*+*graphē*] Orthography, spelling; *faute d'*~, spelling mistake; mis-spelling, wrong or bad spelling, mis-spelt word; *savoir l'*~, to know how to spell; to spell correctly; *bonne* ~, good spelling; *il a une* ~ *déplorable,* his spelling is shocking.
orthographie (ɔrtɔgrafi), s.f. Elevation, plan; orthography.
orthographier (ɔrtɔgrafje), v.a. To spell; **s'~**, v.pr. to be spelt.
orthographique (ɔrtɔgrafik), adj. Orthographic(al).
orthographiquement (ɔrtɔgrafikmɑ̃), adv. Orthographically.
orthopédie (ɔrtɔpedi), s.f. [f. Gr. *orthos*+*paideia*] Orthopaedy.
orthopédique (ɔrtɔpedik), adj. Orthopaedic.
orthopédiste (ortɔpedist), s.m.f. adj. Orthopaedist.
orthoptère (ɔrtɔptɛr), adj. [f. Gr. *orthos*+*pteron*] (ent.) Orthopterous, orthopteral. ~, s.m. Orthopteran, orthopter (pl. orthoptera).
ortie (ɔrti), s.f. [L *urtica*] (bot.) Nettle; stinging nettle; ~ *blanche,* dead-nettle; *jeter le froc aux* ~*s,* (of monks) to be unfrocked.
ortier (ɔrtje), v.a. To nettle, to sting.
ortive (ɔrtiv), adj.f. [L *ortivus*] (astr.) Rising, of the rising of a heavenly body; *amplitude* ~, arc of horizon between the true East and the centre of rising star.
ortolan (ɔrtɔlɑ̃), s.m. [L *hortulanus*] (ornith.) Ortolan, garden-bunting.
orvale (ɔrval), s.f. [etym. unkn.] (bot.) Clary.
orvet (ɔrvɛ), s.m. [etym. unkn.] (zool.) Slow-worm, blind-worm.
orviétan (ɔrvjetɑ̃), s.m. [It. *orvietano*] Orvietan, Venice treacle; (fig.) quack medicine, nostrum; *marchand d'*~, quack; (fig.) swindler, humbug.
oryx (ɔriks), s.m. [Gr. *orux*] (zool.) Oryx, genus of large straight-horned African antelopes.
os (os, pl. o and os), s.m. invar. [L wd] Bone; *il ne fera pas de vieux* ~, he'll never make old bones; he will not live long; *n'avoir que les* ~ *et la peau,* to be nothing but skin and bone; *trempé jusqu'aux* ~, drenched to the skin; *un* ~ *à ronger,* a bone to pick; something to do; *les* ~ *lui percent la peau,* his bones stick through his skin.
oscillation (ɔssilla'sjɔ̃), s.f. Oscillation, swing, sweep; (fig.) fluctuation, wavering.
oscillatoire (ɔssillatwar), adj. Oscillatory.
osciller (ɔssille), v.n. [L *oscillare*] To oscillate, to swing, to sweep; to fluctuate, to waver, to hesitate.
osculat-eur, -rice (ɔskylatœr), adj. (geom.) Osculatory.
osculation (ɔskyla'sjɔ̃), s.f. [f. L *osculari*] (geom.) Osculation. ⚠ Not used in French as it is sometimes in English in the sense of kiss, kissing.
osé, -e (oze), p. adj. Bold, daring; venturesome, hazardous; *être assez* ~ *pour,* to be

bold enough to; *vous êtes bien ~*, you are very bold; *une entreprise ~e*, a daring venture; a risky undertaking.

oseille (ozɛj), s.f. [L *oxalis*] (bot.) Sorrel; *sel d'~*, oxalate of potash; salts of sorrel.

oser (oze), v.a.n. [L *audere*] To dare, to venture, to attempt; to be daring, to be bold enough to; to presume; *si j'ose le dire*, if I may venture to say so; *il n'oserait pas!*, he would not dare!

oseraie (ozrɛ), s.f. Osier-ground, osier-plot, osier-bed, osier-holt.

oseu-r, -se (ozœr), s.m.f. Bold man; (fem.) bold woman. ~, adj. Bold, daring.

osier (ozje), s.m. [LL *ausaria*] Osier, water-willow; wicker, withy, basket-work; *panier d'~*, wicker basket; *voiture en ~*, basket carriage.

osmanli (ɔsmɑ̃li), s.m. adj. (usually in the pl.) [Turk. wd] Osmanli, ottoman.

osmium (ɔsmjɔm), s.m. [f. Gr. *osmē*] (chem.) Osmium.

osmologie (ɔsmɔlɔʒi), s.f. [f. Gr. *osmē*+*logos*] Osmology; science of smells.

osmonde (ɔsmɔ̃d), s.f. (bot.) Osmund, osmund royal, royal fern, flowering fern.

osmose (ɔsmoz), s.f. [f. Gr. *ōsmos*] Osmose, osmosis.

osmotique (ɔsmɔtik), adj. Osmotic.

ossature (ɔssatyr), s.f. [f. *os*] Osseous frame; bony structure; skeleton; (fig.) framework, frame, build, structure.

osséine (ɔssein), s.f. Osteine.

osselet (ɔslɛ), s.m. [f. *os*] **1.** Ossicle, small bone; **2.** knuckle-bone; *jouer aux ~s*, to play knuckle-bones; **3.** (vet.) knee-splint.

ossements (ɔsmɑ̃), s.m.pl. [f. *os*] Bones (of dead bodies).

osseu-x, -se (ɔsø), adj. [f. *os*] Osseous, bony.

ossianique (ɔsjanik), adj. [f. prop. n. *Ossian*, 3rd c.] Ossianic; of Ossian, Ossian's.

ossification (ɔsifika'sjɔ̃), s.f. Ossification.

ossifier (ɔsifje), v.a. [f. *os*] To ossify; **s'~**, v.pr. to ossify, to turn into bone.

ossu, -e (ɔsy), adj. Bony; large-boned; big-boned.

ossuaire (ɔsɥɛr), s.m. [L *ossuarium*] Ossuary, charnel-house.

ost, host (ɔst), s.m. (obs.) [f. L *hostis*] **1.** Army; **2.** camp.

ostéine (ɔstein), s.f. [f. Gr. *osteon*] Osteine; syn. OSSÉINE.

ostéite (ɔsteit), s.f. (pathol.) Osteitis; inflammation of the osseous substance.

ostensible (ɔstɑ̃sibl), adj. [f. L *ostendere*] Apparent.

ostensiblement (ɔstɑ̃sibləmɑ̃), adv. Openly.

ostensoir (ɔstɑ̃swar), s.m. [f. L *ostensus*] (Cath. Church) Monstrance; ostensory.

ostentation (ɔstɑ̃ta'sjɔ̃), s.f. [L *ostentatio*] Ostentation, show, vain display; *faire ~ de*, to make a show of.

ostéocolle (ɔsteokɔl), s.f. [Gr. *osteon*+*kolla*] Osteocolla, bone-glue.

ostéogénie (ɔsteoʒeni), s.f. [Gr. *osteon*+*genos*] Osteogenesis, formation of bone.

ostéologie (ɔsteolɔʒi), s.f. [Gr. *osteon*+*logos*] Osteology.

ostracé, -e (ɔstrase), adj. [f. Gr. *ostrakon*] Ostraceous, shell-like, oyster-like.

ostraciser (ɔstrasize), v.a. To ostracize.

ostracisme (ɔstrasism), s.m. [f. Gr. *ostrakon*] Ostracism; *frapper d'~*, to ostracize.

ostréicole (ɔstreikɔl), adj. [f. L *ostrea*+*colere*] Pertaining to oyster-breeding.

ostréiculteur (ɔstreikyltœr), s.m. Oyster-farmer, oyster-breeder.

ostréiculture (ɔstreikyltyr), s.f. Ostreiculture, oyster-breeding.

ostrogoth, -e (ɔstrogɔt), s.m.f. Ostrogoth; (fig.) Goth, rude uncivilized person, rough fellow.

otage (ɔtaʒ), s.m. [LL *obsidaticum*] Hostage; pledge; *en ~*, as a hostage.

otalgie (ɔtalʒi), s.f. [f. Gr. *ous*+*algos*] Otalgia, ear-ache.

otarie (ɔtari), s.f. [f. Gr. *ous*, *ōtos*] (zool.) Eared seal, otary.

ôté (ote), prep. [f. *ôter*] Except for, save for, bating, but, barring; *un bon livre, ~ deux chapitres*, a good book except for two chapters.

ôter (ote), v.a. [f. L *obstare*] To take away; to remove; to take off; to take, to snatch; to strip off, to take off, to pull off (one's clothes); to cut off; to take away (*de*, *à*, from), to deprive of; to relieve, or to rid of; *ôtez votre manteau*, take off your cloak; *on lui a ôté son emploi*, he has been dismissed; *ôtez-lui cette idée de la tête*, get this nonsense out of his head; *il faut bien ~ son chapeau devant cet homme-là*, one has to take off one's hat to such a man; *de six ôtez deux*, take (or subtract) two from six; *ôtez-moi cette incertitude*, relieve me of this doubt; *il me l'a ôté des mains*, he snatched it out of my hands; *on lui a ôté tout espoir*, he has been deprived of all hope; they did not give him the least hope; **s'~**, v.pr. **1.** to remove oneself; (colloq.) *ôte-toi de là, que je m'y mette*, you get out and let me in; make room for your betters; **2.** to rid oneself of; *je ne puis m'~ cela de la tête*, I cannot get that idea out of my mind; **3.** to stint oneself; *s'~ le pain de la bouche pour X*, to stint oneself to support X.

otite (ɔtit), s.f. [f. Gr. *ous*, L *otos*] (pathol.) Otitis, inflammation of the ear.

ottoman, -e (ɔtɔmɑ̃), adj. s.m.f. Ottoman. ~e, s.f. Ottoman (sofa).

ou (u), conj. [L *aut*] Or, either, else, otherwise; *~ bien*, or else, or otherwise; *ce sera lui ~ moi*, it will be either he or I.

où (u), adv. [L *ubi*] Where, whither; whence, which, at which, in which, from which, to which; when; that; *d'~*, whence, from which; where . . . from; how; ~ *allez-vous?*, where are you going?; ~ *allons-nous si la baisse continue?*, where shall we be if prices go on falling?; *d'~ venez-vous?*, where do you come from?; ~ *en êtes-vous de cette affaire?*, how are you getting on with that business?; *d'~ vient la nouvelle?*, where does this news come from?; *voilà par ~ j'ai passé*, (*a*) that's the way I came; (*b*) that's what I have had to endure; *dans l'état ~ il est*, in the condition in which he is; *dans le cas ~*, in case; *c'est là ~ je voulais en venir*, that's what I was driving at; *d'~ vient que*, how is it that; *par ~?*, which way?; ~ *que vous alliez*, wherever you may go.

ouaille (wɑj), s.f. [L *ovicula*] (fig.) Sheep; (pl.) flock, sheep.

ouais (wɛ), interj. Well now!, now then!, what!, how now!, indeed!, why!, bless me!, bless my soul!, dear me!

ouate (wat), s.f. Cotton wool; cotton padding; wadding; (fig.) softness, whiteness; ~ *hydrophile*, absorbent cotton wool.

ouater (wate), v.a. To wad, to pad, to line with wadding; (fig.) *ouaté*, velvety, soft, softened.

oubli (ubli), s.m. Forgetting, forgetfulness; oblivion, oversight, inadvertence, neglect, omission, slip, breach; pardon, forgiveness; *par ~*, by an oversight; *mettre en ~*, to forget; ~ *de soi-même*, abnegation, forgetfulness of self; *tomber dans l'~*, to fall into oblivion; *l'~ de ses devoirs*, neglect of one's duty; *réparer un ~*, to redeem an act of neglect; to make up for one's neglect.

oubliable (ublijabl), adj. Forgettable.

oublie (ubli), s.f. [L *oblata*] Wafer (biscuit).

oublier (ublije), v.a.n. [f. L *oblitus*] To forget, to overlook, to neglect, to omit; *faisant ~ jusqu'au nom*, causing the very name to be forgotten; *faire ~ à X*, to make X forget; *oubliant toute décence, toute prudence*, forgetful of all decency, setting aside prudence; *oublions le passé*, let bygones be bygones; *j'ai oublié mon mouchoir*, I forgot to take a handkerchief; *j'ai oublié mon parapluie chez vous*, I left my umbrella at your house; **s'~**, v.pr. **1.** to neglect one's own interests; to be unselfish, forgetful of self; **2.** to forget oneself, to act unbecomingly; to lose self-consciousness; **3.** to be (easily) forgotten.

oubliettes (ublijɛt), s.f.pl. Oubliette (secret dungeon); (fig.) *mettre aux ~s*, to consign to oblivion.

oublieu-r, -se (ublijœr), s.m.f. [f. *oublie*] Wafer-maker.

oublieusement (ublijøzmɑ̃), adv. Forgetfully.

oublieu-x, -se (ublijø), adj. Forgetful, unmindful.

ouche (uʃ), s.f. [pop. L *olca*] Small garden or orchard adjoining house; small plot where the soil is especially fertile.

oued (wɛd), s.m. (pl. *ouadi*) [Arab. *wādī*] North African river-bed or ravine; wadi.

ouest (wɛst), s.m. [etym. dub.; L *vesper*?, Anglo-Saxon *west*] West; *vent d'~*, west wind; westerly wind; *à l'~*, to or in the west; west, westward, westerly; *vers l'~*, westward.

ouf (uf), interj. (of relief) Oh!, phew!, thank heaven!

oui (wi), adv. s.m. [f. OF *oïl*] Yes, yea, ay; so?, indeed?, eh?; ~ *vraiment!*, yes indeed!; *que ~!*, yes, to be sure!; *dire ~*, to say yes; to say 'I will' (be married); *dire que ~*, to say that it is so; *ne dire ni ~ ni non*, to give no positive answer; not to say either yes or no; *pour un ~, pour un non*, for the least thing; ~ *da!*, yes, to be sure!; *vous irez, ~?*, you will go, will you not?; *cela se garde, ~?*, that keeps, does it not?

ouï, -e (wi), p. adj. [f. *ouïr*] (archaic) Heard, having heard, having been heard; *j'ai ~ dire*, I have heard; *par ~-dire*, by hearsay.

ouiche (wiʃ), **ouat** (wat), interj. (pop.) Pooh!, ah!, not a bit of it!, don't you believe it!

ouïe (wi), s.f. [f. *ouïr*] **1.** Hearing; *avoir l'~ fine*, to be sharp of hearing; **2.** sound-hole (of musical instrument); **3.** **~s**, pl. (of fish) gills.

ouillage (ujaʒ), s.m. (of a cask of wine) Filling up, ullage.

ouiller (uje), v.a. [f. L *dolium*] To ullage.

ouïr (wir), v.n.a. (archaic) [L *audire*] To hear; *j'ai ouï (dire)*, I have heard it said.

ouistiti (wistiti), s.m. (zool.) Ouistiti, marmoset.

ouragan (uragɑ̃), s.m. [Span. *huracan*] Hurricane, (fig.) explosion (of temper); *un ~ politique*, a political storm; *arriver comme un ~*, to arrive like a whirlwind.

ourdir (urdir), v.a. [L *ordiri*] To warp; to weave; (fig.) to plot, to contrive, to brew, to hatch, to form, to frame; ~ *une toile*, to warp a cloth; ~ *un complot*, to hatch a plot; ~ *la perte de X*, to plot X's downfall.

ourdissage (urdisaʒ), s.m. Warping.

ourdisseu-r, -se (urdisœr), s.m.f. Warper.

ourdissoir (urdiswar), s.m. Warp-beam; warping-mill.

ourler (urle), v.a. To hem; ~ *à jour*, to hemstitch.

ourlet (urlɛ), s.m. [f. L *ora*; OF *orle*] Hem; ~ *à jour*, open hem, hemstitching; *faire un ~*, to make a hem.

ours (urs), s.m. [L *ursus*] Bear, he-bear, (fig.) unsociable, disagreeable (or ill-bred) man; regular bear; ~ *gris*, grizzly bear; (fig.) *c'est un ~ mal léché*, he is an ill-licked cub, or a rough, rude fellow; *c'est le pavé de* *l'~*, it was well meant, but disastrous; save me from my friends; *prenez mon ~*, there is nothing like leather; *il ne faut pas vendre la peau de l'~ avant de l'avoir tué*, don't count your chickens before they are hatched.

ourse (urs), s.f. She-bear; (astr.) Ursa; *la Grande* **~**, the Great Bear, Ursa Major; *la Petite* **~**, the Little Bear, Ursa Minor.

oursin (ursɛ̃), s.m. **1.** (zool.) Sea-urchin, sea-hedgehog; **2.** bear-skin.

ourson (ursɔ̃), s.m. Bear-cub.

oust, ouste (ust), interj. Away with you !, off you go !

outarde (utard), s.f. [L *avistarda*] (ornith.) Bustard.

outardeau (pl. **-x**) (utardo), s.m. Young bustard.

outil (uti), s.m. [L *utensile*] Tool; implement, instrument; (slang) *va donc eh! ~!*, get away with you, you silly duffer.

outillage (utilaʒ), s.m. Stock or set of tools or implements; tools, implements, machinery, gear, plant.

outiller (utije), v.a. To supply, furnish, or stock with tools or instruments; *mal outillé*, badly supplied with tools; badly equipped.

outrage (utraʒ), s.m. [f. L *ultra*] Insult, outrage, abuse, offence, injury, ravages; *~ sanglant*, gross outrage; *faire ~ à X*, to outrage X; to commit an outrage on X; to commit an offence against X; *l'~ des ans*, the ravages of time.

outrageant, -e (utraʒɑ̃), p. adj. Outrageous, insulting.

outrager (utraʒe), v.a. To outrage, to insult, to abuse, to offend against; to shock.

outrageusement (utraʒøzmɑ̃), adv. outrageously.

outrageu-x, -se (utraʒø), adj. Outrageous.

outrance (utrɑ̃s), s.f. [f. L *ultra*] Excess; *à ~, à toute ~*, to excess, beyond all measure, to the utmost, to a finish; desperately, furiously, unsparingly, unmercifully, to the bitter end; *se battre à ~*, to fight most desperately; *guerre à ~*, war to the knife, to the bitter end, to the death.

outranci-er, -ère (utrɑ̃sje), adj. Carrying things to extremes or to excess; extreme, excessive, exaggerated, out-and-out.

outre (utr), s.f. [L *uter*] Skin, goat's skin; leather bottle.

outre (utr), prep. adv. [L *ultra*] **1.** Beyond, farther, further; **2.** besides, in addition to; *d'~ en ~*, through and through; *passer ~*, to go beyond, to go any further, to go on, to pass on, to proceed; (fig.) to take no notice; *~-mer*, beyond the seas; *d'~-mer*, from beyond the seas; *d'~ tombe*, from beyond the tomb; posthumous; *en ~*, besides, moreover; *~ que*, besides, notwithstanding that, added to this.

outré, -e (utre), p. adj. **1.** Exaggerated, carried to excess, &c. (see OUTRER), excessive, extreme, out-and-out, wild, overstrained, extravagant; **2.** out of patience, beside oneself, furious, mad; *je suis ~ de tant d'impertinence*, I am out of patience, or I have not patience with such impertinences.

outrecuidance (utrəkɥidɑ̃s), s.f. [f. *outrecuidant*] Overweening conceit, presumption, audacity, arrogance; bumptiousness; (fam.) cheek.

outrecuidant, -e (utrəkɥidɑ̃), adj. [f. *outre*+OF *cuider*] Overweening, presumptuous, bumptious, (fam.) cheeky.

outrément (utremɑ̃) (rare) adv.; Excessively; with exaggeration; eccentrically.

outremer (utrəmɛr), s.m. Ultramarine, lapis lazuli; *bleu d'~*, ultramarine blue. ~, adj. Ultramarine.

outrepasse (utrəpas), s.f. Extra cuttings (of woods).

outrepasser (utrəpase), v.a. To overstep, to transgress; to go beyond, to exceed; *~ ses pouvoirs*, to exceed one's powers.

outrer (utre), v.a. [f. *outre*] **1.** To overdo, to carry too far, to overstrain, to exaggerate; **2.** to exasperate, to incense, to put out of all patience.

ouvert, -e (uvɛr), adj. [f. *ouvrir*] Open; unfortified; unprotected, unsheltered; free; (fig.) open-hearted, frank, sincere, ready, free; *à bras ~s*, cordially, heartily; with open arms; *à bureau ~*, on presentation; *à ciel ~*, open, in the open; *grand ~*, wide open; *traduire à livre ~*, to translate at sight; *en guerre ~e*, at war; *port ~*, open harbour; *en pays ~*, in open country; *la politique de la porte ~e*, the open-door policy; *les yeux ~s*, with open eyes; *l'exposition est ~e*, the show is open; *à cœur ~*, unreservedly, openheartedly; *un esprit ~*, an open-minded person; *un compte ~*, a running account.

ouvertement (uvɛrtəmɑ̃), adv. Openly; frankly.

ouverture (uvɛrtyr), s.f. [f. *ouvert*] **1.** Opening, aperture, orifice, mouth, inlet, gap, hole, passage; **2.** beginning, opening, commencement; *l'~ de la chasse*, the opening of the shooting season; **3.** (chess) opening; **4.** (pl.) overtures, proposal, opening of negotiations; *faire des ~s à X*, to make overtures to X; **5.** (mus.) overture; **6.** (arch.) opening, span, width of door, window, &c.; *un homme d'une grande ~ d'esprit*, a very large-minded or open-minded man; *~ d'une succession*, proving of a will; time when an inheritance can be acquired or received.

ouvrable (uvrabl), adj. **1.** Workable; **2.** working; *jours ~s*, work-days, working days.

ouvrage (uvraʒ), s.m. [f. *ouvrer*] Work, piece of work; workmanship; performance; fortification; ~ *d'art*, engineering work, outwork, bridge, tunnel, &c. (⚠ Not 'work of art', which = *œuvre d'art*); *avoir du cœur à l'~*, to work with a will; *n'avoir pas d'~, être sans ~*, to be out of employment (or work), to be unemployed; *se mettre à l'~*, to set to work; *laisser l'~*, to leave off working; (fam.) to knock off work; (fort.) *~s extérieurs*, outworks; ~ *à l'aiguille*, ~ *de dame*, needlework; *panier à ~*, work-basket; *c'est le meilleur ~ que vous ayez fait*, it is the best work you have written; *un savant ~*, a learned work.

ouvragé, -e (uvraʒe), p. adj. Wrought, figured.

ouvrager (uvraʒe), v.a. To work, to figure; to decorate, to chisel, to finish; to embellish.

ouvraison (uvrɛzɔ̃), s.f. Working.

ouvrant, -e (uvrɑ̃), p. adj. Opening; *à jour ~*, at dawn, at day-break; *à portes ~es*, on the opening of the gates.

ouvre- (uvr), (in comp.) [f. *ouvrir*] Opener; *~-gants*, s.m. glove-stretcher; *~-huîtres*, s.m. oyster-opener, oyster-knife.

ouvré, -e (uvre), p. adj. Wrought; diapered; *linge ~, toile ~e*, diaper huckaback, damask linen.

ouvrée (uvre), s.f. (obs.) Extent of ground that a man can work (plough, &c.) in one day.

ouvrer (uvre), v.n. [L *operare*] To work; ~, v.a. **1.** to work, to chisel, to chase; **2.** to damask, to diaper (linen, &c.).

ouvreu-r, -se (uvrœr), s.m.f. Opener; (theatr.) **~se**, s.f. box-opener.

ouvri-er, -ère (uvrije), s.m.f. [L *operarius*] Workman, artisan, operative, worker; handicraftsman, journeyman; workwoman; hand; maker; *premier ~*, foreman; *première ~ère*, forewoman; ~ *à la journée*, day-labourer; journeyman; *~ère en journée*, seamstress; ~ *agricole*, agricultural labourer; *mauvais ~ n'a jamais de bons outils*, a bad workman always blames his tools. ~, adj. Working, labouring, operative; of working men, of work-people; trade-; *la classe ~ère*, the working class; *jour ~*, working day; *la question ~ère*, the labour question; (fig.) *la cheville ~ère*, the mainspring; the working part; *habitations ~ères*, workmen's dwellings.

ouvrir (uvrir), v.a.n. [L *aperire*] To open, to open up, to unclose, to unlock, to set open, to break open, to throw open; to spread, to unfold; to uncork; to sharpen; to begin, to start; to propose, to broach; ~ *de grands yeux*, to stare; *ouvrez l'œil, et le bon !*, look out !; ~ *une boutique, un commerce*, to open a shop, a business; ~ *le feu*, to open fire, to begin shooting; ~ *de belles perspectives*, to open up good prospects; ~ *le débat*, to open the debate, or the case; *ce salon ouvre sur la pelouse*, this drawing-room opens on to the lawn; *la session est ouverte*, the session is opened; *on devrait lui ~ les yeux*, somebody ought to enlighten him; ~ *une souscription*, to start a subscription; ~ *un compte à X*, to open an account with X; to open an account for X; ~ *l'appétit*, to sharpen the appetite; ~ *son cœur à X*, to unbosom oneself to X; **s'~**, v.pr. to be opened, to open; to expand; (fig.) to open oneself, to open one's mind; to unbosom oneself; to disclose one's intentions; *s'~ un passage*, to make or force one's way.

ouvroir (uvrwar), s.m. Working place (for poor unemployed girls or women).

ovaire (ɔvɛr), s.m. [f. L *ovum*] (anat., bot.) Ovary.

ovalaire (ɔvalɛr), adj. Oval.

ovale (ɔval), adj. s.m. [f. L *ovum*] Oval.

ovarien, -ne (ɔvarjɛ̃), adj. [f. *ovaire*] Ovarian.

ovation (ɔva'sjɔ̃), s.f. [L *ovatio*] Ovation, enthusiastic reception; *faire une ~ à X*, to receive X in triumph.

ove (ɔv), s.m. [f. L *ovum*] (arch.) Ovum, egg.

ové, -e (ɔve), adj. Ovate.

ovibos (ɔvibos), s.m. (zool.) Ovibovine, musk-ox.

oviducte (ɔvidykt), s.m. (anat.) Oviduct.

ovine (ɔvin), adj.f. [f. L *ovis*] Ovine; *bêtes ~s*, sheep.

ovipare (ɔvipar), adj. [L *ovum+parere*] Oviparous.

ovoïde (ɔvɔid), adj. s.m. [f. L *ovum*] Ovoid.

ovovivipare (ɔvovivipar), adj. Ovoviviparous.

ovulaire (ɔvylɛr), adj. Ovular.

ovule (ɔvyl), s.m. [f. L *ovum*] Ovule.

oxalate (ɔksalat), s.m. (chem.) Oxalate.

oxalide (ɔksalid), s.f. (bot.) Oxalis, wood-sorrel.

oxalique (ɔksalik), adj. (chem.) Oxalic.

oxhydrique (ɔksidrik), adj. Oxyhydrogen (for blow-pipes).

oxycrat (ɔksikrat), s.m. Oxycrate, mixture of vinegar and water.

oxydable (ɔksidabl), adj. (chem.) Oxidizable.

oxydation (ɔksida'sjɔ̃), s.f. (chem.) Oxidation, oxidization.

oxyde (ɔksid), s.m. [f. L, Gr. *oxus*] (chem.) Oxide.

oxyder (ɔkside), v.a. To oxidize; **s'~**, v.pr. to become oxidized.

oxygénation (ɔksiʒena'sjɔ̃), s.f. (chem.) Oxygenation.

oxygène (ɔksiʒɛn), s.m. adj. [Gr. *oxus*+*genēs*] Oxygen.
oxygéné, -e (ɔksiʒene), p. adj. Oxygenated.
oxygéner (ɔksiʒene), v.a. To oxygenate.
oxymel (ɔksimɛl), s.m. Oxymel, mixture of vinegar, honey, and water.
oxyton (ɔksitɔ̃), s.m. [f. Gr. *oxus*+*tonos*] Oxytone, word with acute accent on last syllable.
oxyure (ɔksjyr), s.f. (zool.) Worm, nematode.
oyant, -e (wajɑ̃), p. adj. (archaic) Hearing. ~, s.m.f. (law) Hearer (of an account).
ozone (ɔzɔn), s.m. [f. Gr. *ozein*] Ozone.
ozoné, -e (ɔzɔne), adj. Ozonized.
ozoniseur (ɔzɔnizœr), s.m. Ozonizer.
ozonomètre (ɔzɔnɔmɛtr), s.m. Ozonometer.

P

P, p (pe), s.m. The 16th letter of the alphabet.
pacage (pakaʒ), s.m. [f. L *pascuum*] Pasture-ground, pasturage, pasture.
pacager (pakaʒe), v.a.n. To pasture, to graze.
pacha (paʃa), s.m. [Turk. wd] Pasha.
pachalik (paʃalik), s.m. Pashalic; syn. VILAYET.
pachyderme (pakidɛrm, paʃidɛrm), adj. [f. Gr. *pakhus*+*derma*] (zool.) Pachydermatous. ~, s.m. Pachyderm; *les* ~*s*, the pachydermata.
pacificat-eur, -rice (pasifikatœr), s.m.f. Pacificator, pacifier, peace-maker. ~, adj. Pacifying, peace-making.
pacification (pasifika'sjɔ̃), s.f. Pacification, peace-making, appeasement.
pacifier (pasifje), v.a. [L *pacificare*] To pacify, to appease (person, country, anger, &c.).
pacifique (pasifik), adj. [L *pacificus*] Pacific, peaceful, peaceable, quiet, gentle, mild; *l'Océan* ~, the Pacific Ocean; *d'humeur* ~, in peaceful mood, of a peaceful disposition.
pacifiquement (pasifikmɑ̃), adv. Peacefully, in peace, quietly, peaceably.
pacifisme (pasifism), s.m. Pacifism.
pacifiste (pasifist), adj. s.m.f. Pacifist, advocate of peace.
pacotille (pakɔtij), s.f. [f. *paquet*] Small stock of goods; cheap wares; shoddy, slop goods; pack, bale.
pacquage (pakaʒ), s.m. Packing (of fish).
pacquer (pake), v.a. To pack (fish).
pacte (pakt), s.m. [L *pactum*] Pact, compact, contract, covenant, agreement, treaty; (fig.) bargain; *le* ~ *de Locarno*, the Locarno Pact; (hist.) *le* ~ *de famille*, the Family Compact; *faire un* ~ *avec*, to enter into an agreement with; *il a un* ~ *avec le diable*, he has made a bargain with the devil.
pactiser (paktize), v.n. To make an agreement, to come to terms; (fig.) to compound, to compromise (*avec*, with).
Pactole (paktɔl), s.m. [f. the river *Pactolus*] Source of wealth; *il a trouvé le* ~, he has found a gold-mine; he has found the philosophers' stone.
padischah (padiʃa), s.m. [Pers. wd] Padishah.
padou (padu), s.m. (obs.) [f. *Padua*] Ferret, tape.
padouan, -e (paduɑ̃), adj. s.m.f. Paduan.
pæan (peɑ̃), s.m. See PÉAN.
paf (paf), adj. invar. (colloq.) Tight, drunk, blotto. ~*!*, interj. Bang!
pagaie (pagɛ), s.f. [Malay wd] **1.** Paddle; **2.** (also *pagaïe, pagaille, pagaye*) disorder, mess; *quelle* ~*!*, what a mess!
paganisme (paganism), s.m. [f. L *paganus*] Paganism, heathenism.
pagayer (pagɛje), v.n. [f. *pagaie*] To paddle.
page[1] (paʒ), s.f. [L *pagina*] Page; *à la* ~ *20*, at the 20th page, or on page 20; *mettre en* ~*s*, to make up; *mise en* ~, making-up; *la plus belle* ~ *de sa carrière*, the brightest page in his life; (colloq.) *ne pas être à la* ~, not to be in the know; not to know what's o'clock; *être à la* ~, to be in the swim; to be up to date.
page[2] (paʒ), s.m. [orig. dub., perhaps LL *pagius*] Page; *effronté comme un* ~, cheeky as a robin; bold as brass; *être hors de* ~, to be one's own master (to have served one's time as a page). ⚠ In English, but not in French, 'page', 'page-boy', is used nowadays in the sense of *jeune garçon en livrée, chasseur*.
pagination (paʒina'sjɔ̃), s.f. Pagination, paging.
paginer (paʒine), v.a. To paginate, to page.
pagne (paɲ), s.m. [Span. *paño*] Loincloth (of savages or negroes).
pagnon (paɲɔ̃), s.m. [f. prop. n.] Fine black Sedan broadcloth.
(se) pagnoter (səpaɲɔte), v.pr. (slang) To go to bed.
pagode (pagɔd), s.f. [Port. *pagode*] **1.** Pagoda, pagod; **2.** pagoda, a gold coin formerly current in India.
paie (pɛ), s.f. Wages, salary; see PAYE.
paiement (pɛmɑ̃), s.m. See PAYEMENT.
païen, -ne (pajɛ̃), adj. [L *paganus*] Pagan, heathen, heathenish. ~, s.m.f. Pagan, heathen, infidel.
paillage (pɑjaʒ), s.m. [f. *paille*] **1.** Cane bottoming; **2.** (agric.) mulching.
paillard, -e (pɑjar), adj. [f. *paille*] Lewd, wanton, lecherous. ~, s.m.f. Lewd person; ~*e*, s.f. bawd.
paillarder (pɑjarde), v.n. To practise lewdness, to play the rake.
paillardise (pɑjardiz), s.f. Lewdness, wantonness.

paillasse[1] (pajas), s.f. [f. *paille*] **1.** Straw mattress, straw palliasse; pallet; **2.** (jest.) body, carcass; **3.** (vulg.) lewd woman.

paillasse[2] (pajas), s.m. [f. prop. n.] Clown, merry andrew; (fig.) mountebank; weathercock, turncoat.

paillasson (pajasɔ̃), s.m. [f. *paille*] Straw mat, mat, matting.

paille (pɑj, paj), s.f. [L *palea*] **1.** Straw, chaff; *botte de* ~, bundle (or truss) of straw; (fig.) *un feu de* ~, a short-lived blaze; *mettre X sur la* ~, to reduce X to beggary; *il mourra sur la* ~, he will die in the gutter; *tirer à la courte* ~, to draw lots; *rompre la* ~ *avec X*; to fall out with X; *mettre de la* ~ *dans ses souliers*, to feather one's nest; *homme de* ~, man of straw, man who lends his name to some shady transaction, agent; *des gants* ~, straw-coloured gloves; **2.** flaw, mote; *voir la* ~ *dans l'œil de son prochain et ne pas voir la poutre dans le sien*, to see the mote in our neighbour's eye, but not to see a beam in our own; **3.** tittle, jot; *une* ~ *!*, or *c'est une* ~ *!*, a mere trifle !

paille-en-queue (pɑjɑ̃kø), s.m. (ornith.) Tropical bird, phaeton, ring-tail.

pailler (pɑje), s.m. Farmyard, straw-heap or -rick; dung-hill; (fig.) stronghold.

pailler (pɑje), v.a. **1.** To straw-bottom; **2.** (agric. hort.) to mulch.

paillet (pɑjɛ), adj. m. (of red wine) Pale. ~, s.m. **1.** Heap of straw; **2.** (naut.) mat, fender.

pailleté, -e (pajte), p. adj. Spangled, bespangled.

pailleter (pajte), v.a. To spangle.

paillette (pajɛt), s.f. [f. *paille*] **1.** Spangle; **2.** grain (of gold); (fig.) spark (of wit); **3.** flaw (in a gem).

pailleu-r, -se (pɑjœr), s.m.f. **1.** Dealer in straw; **2.** straw-carrier; **3.** chair-bottomer.

pailleu-x, -se (pɑjø), adj. (metall.) Flawy, flawed.

paillis (paji, pɑji), s.m. (agric., hort.) Mulch.

paillon (pɑjɔ̃), s.m. **1.** Straw wrapping (for bottles); **2.** large spangle, foil, tinsel; **3.** piece of solder.

paillot (pajo), s.m. Small palliasse or straw mattress.

pain (pɛ̃), s.m. [L *panis*] **1.** Bread, loaf, loaf of bread; *petit* ~, roll; *du* ~ *blanc*, white bread; ~ *bis*, brown bread; ~ *rassis*, stale bread; ~ *de munition*, regulation bread; ~ *à cacheter*, wafer; *faire son* ~, to bake, to make bread; ~ *d'épice*, gingerbread; (bibl.) ~*s de proposition*, shewbread; ~ *bénit*, consecrated bread; *c'est* ~ *bénit !*, it serves him right !; *manger son* ~ *blanc le premier*, to take the easiest first; to eat one's cake first; *faire passer le goût du* ~ *à X*, to kill X, to do for X; to send X to kingdom come; *avoir du* ~ *sur la planche*, (*a*) to have goods in store; to have saved up against a rainy day; (*b*) to have plenty on hand; to have one's work cut out; *il ne vaut pas le* ~ *qu'il mange*, he is not worth his salt; *long comme un jour sans* ~, as long as a week of Sundays, or as a day in Lent, or as a wet Sunday; *gagner son* ~, to earn one's living; *je ne mange pas de ce* ~*-là*, I don't go in for that sort of thing; **2.** (of colour, soap, wax, &c.) cake, tablet, lump, roll; ~ *de sucre*, sugar-loaf; **3.** (slang) biff, clout; *coller un* ~ *sur la gueule à X*, to land X one on the mug.

pair (pɛr), s.m. [f. L *par*] Peer; equal; (of birds) mate; *traiter X de* ~ *à compagnon*, to be hail fellow well met with X.

pair, -e (pɛr), adj. [L *par*] Equal, even; *nombre* ~, even number; *aller de* ~ *avec*, to be on an equal footing with; to be cheek by jowl with; *être hors de* ~, to be beyond all comparison, to be peerless, matchless; ~, s.m. *au* ~, 'au pair' (= without salary, for board and lodging only); (Stock Exchange) par; *le* ~ *du change*, the par of exchange; *au* ~, at par; *au-dessus du* ~, above par; ~**e**, s.f. pair, couple; brace (of game birds); *ils font bien la* ~ *!*, they are well matched !; that's a fine couple for you !; *une* ~ *de pistolets*, a brace of pistols; *une* ~ *de gants*, a pair of gloves; *une* ~ *d'amis*, good chums; *une* ~ *de ciseaux*, a pair of scissors; scissors.

pairesse (pɛrɛs), s.f. Peeress.

pairie (pɛri), s.f. Peerage.

pairle (pɛrl), s.m. (herald.) Pall.

paisible (pɛzibl), adj. [f. *paix*] Peaceful, peaceable, quiet, placid.

paisiblement (pɛzibləmɑ̃), adv. Peacefully, peaceably, placidly.

paissance (pɛsɑ̃s), s.f. (rare) [f. *paître*] Pasturing.

paissant, -e (pɛsɑ̃), p. adj. Grazing.

paisson (pɛsɔ̃), s.f. Pasture, pasturing.

paître (pɛtr), v.n.a. [L *pascere*] To graze, to pasture, to feed; ~ *l'herbe nouvelle*, to graze new grass; *paissez mes agneaux*, feed my lambs; (colloq.) *je l'ai envoyé* ~, I sent him about his business; I sent him to Jericho, or to the right-about.

paix (pɛ), s.f. [L *pax*] Peace, quiet, calm; ~ *!*, be quiet !, shut up !, that will do !; *faire la* ~, to make peace; *faire sa* ~ *avec X*, to make one's peace with X; *laissez-le en* ~ (or, slang) *fichez-lui la* ~, leave him alone, let him alone; ~ *fourrée*, insincere, delusive peace, hollow peace; *traité de* ~, peace treaty; *juge de* ~, justice of the peace; ~ *à ses cendres*, peace to his ashes; *calumet de* ~, pipe of peace.

pal (pal), s.m. [L *palus*] **1.** Pale, stake, empalement; **2.** (herald.) pale.

palabre (palabr), s.f. [Span. *palabra*] Palaver.

palabrer (palabre), v.n. To palaver.
paladin (paladɛ̃), s.m. [f. L *palatinus*] Paladin, champion.
palais[1] (palɛ), s.m. [L *palatium*] Palace; ~ *de justice* (and abbrev.) *Palais*, Law Courts, Bar; *style de* ~, law jargon.
palais[2] (palɛ), s.m. [L *palatum*] Palate, roof (of the mouth); (fig.) taste.
palan (palɑ̃), s.m. [f. It. *palanco*] Tackle, hoisting-gear.
palanche (palɑ̃ʃ), s.f. [Gr. *phalagx*] Yoke (for carrying two pails, &c.).
palançon (palɑ̃sɔ̃), s.m. Prop (to support mud walls).
palanque (palɑ̃k), s.f. [It. *palanca*] Timber stockade.
palanquin (palɑ̃kɛ̃), s.m. [Port. *palanquim*] Palanquin, palankeen.
palastre (palastr), s.m. [f. L *pala*] Lock-plate.
palatal, -e, (aux) (palatal), adj. [f. L *palatum*] (phon.) Palatal.
palatial, -e, (aux) (palasjal), adj. [f. L *palatium*] Palatial, magnificent.
palatin,[1] **-e** (palatɛ̃), adj. [L *palatinus*] Palatine; pertaining to the palace.
palatin,[2] **-e** (palatɛ̃), adj. [f. L *palatum*] Palatal, pertaining to the palate.
palatinat (palatina), s.m. Palatinate.
palatine (palatin), s.f. Fur tippet (made fashionable by Princess Palatine, 1676).
pale[1] (pal), s.f. [L *pala*] Blade (of an oar); float, paddle-board; sluice; (aeron.) ~ *d'hélice*, blade (of propeller).
pale[2] (pal), s.f. [L *palla*] (Cath. liturg.) Linen cover for chalice.
pâle (pɑl), adj. [L *pallidus*] Pale, pallid, wan, palish, ghastly; (fig.) colourless, tame; ~ *comme un linge*, as pale as death, as white as a sheet; *bleu* ~, pale blue; *un style bien* ~, a tame, or a colourless, style; (mil. slang) *se faire porter* ~, to parade for medical treatment, to go sick.
palée (pale), s.f. Row of stakes or pales.
palefrenier (palfrənje), s.m. [f. *palefroi*] Groom, stable-man, ostler.
palefroi (palfrwɑ), s.m. [LL *palafredus*] Palfrey.
palémon (palemɔ̃), s.m. (zool.) Palaemon, prawn.
paléographe (paleɔgraf), s.m.f. Palaeographer. ~, adj. Palaeographic.
paléographie (paleɔgrafi), s.f. [f. Gr. *palaios+graphē*] Palaeography.
paléographique (paleɔgrafik), adj. Palaeographical.
paléolithique (paleɔlitik), adj. [f. Gr. *palaios+lithos*] Palaeolithic.
paléontologie (paleɔ̃tɔlɔʒi), s.f. [f. Gr. *palaios+onta+logos*] Palaeontology.
paléontologique (paleɔ̃tɔlɔʒik), adj. Palaeontological.
paleron (palrɔ̃), s.m. [f. L *pala*] (butch.) Shoulder-blade.
palestine (palɛstin), s.f. (print.) Fount of type of double pica size.
palestre (palɛstr), s.f. [Gr. *palaistra*] Palaestra.
palet (palɛ), s.m. [f. L *pala*] Quoit; *jouer au* ~, to play at quoits.
paletot (palto), s.m. [orig. dub.; ODutch *palt-rok*, Middle Engl. *paltok*] Overcoat.
palette (palɛt), s.f. [f. L *pala*] Pallet, paddle, float-board; battledore; (paint.) palette; (fig.) colouring, style; (butch.) shoulder-blade.
palétuvier (paletyvje), s.m. (bot.) Mangrove-tree.
pâleur (pɑlœr), s.f. Pallor, wanness, pallidness.
pali (pali), s.m. Pali (language).
palier (palje), s.m. [orig. uncert.] Landing, stair-head; (mech.) plummer-block; bearings; ~ *de butée*, thrust bearing; ~ *à rouleaux*, roller bearing; *vitesse en* ~, speed on the flat; *par* ~*s successifs*, gradually.
palière (paljɛr), adj. f. (of a step) Top; *marche* ~, top step.
palifier (palifje), v.a. [f. *pal*] To strengthen with piles.
palikare (palikar), s.m. [mod. Gr. *palikari*] Palikar.
palimpseste (palɛ̃psɛst), s.m. adj. [f. Gr. *palin+psēstos*] Palimpsest.
palingénésie (palɛ̃ʒenezi), s.f. [f. Gr. *palin+genesis*] Palingenesy, revival.
palinodie (palinɔdi), s.f. [Gr. *palinōdia*] Palinode, palinody, recantation. ⚠ *Palinodie* in French is usually pejorative and means turning one's coat, changing one's opinion (to one's own advantage). In English 'palinode' is nearer the Greek sense, retractation of a former expression of feelings by a poet or believer; also repetition of a song.
pâlir (pɑlir), v.n.a. To turn or grow pale; to blench, to wane; to pale, to grow dim, to be on the wane; ~ *sur ses livres*, to pore over books; *son étoile pâlit*, his star is on the wane; he is losing credit.
palis (pali), s.m. [f. *pal*] Stake, pale; paling.
palissade (palisad), s.f. [f. *palis*] Palisade, paling, hoarding.
palissader (palisade), v.a. To palisade, to fence, to rail in, to stockade.
palissage (palisaʒ), s.m. (hort.) Nailing up, paling.
palissandre (palisɑ̃dr), s.m. (bot.) Rosewood, palisander, jacaranda; violet wood.
pâlissant, -e (pɑlisɑ̃), p. adj. Turning pale, on the wane.
palisser (palise), v.a. [f. *palis*] To nail up, to train (vine, wall-tree, &c.).
palisson (palisɔ̃), s.m. (furrier's) Softening iron.
palladium[1] (palladjɔm), s.m. [L wd] Palladium; (fig.) palladium, safeguard.

palladium (palladjɔm), s.m. (chem.) Palladium.
palliati-f, -ve (paljatif), adj. s.m. Palliative.
palliation (palja'sjɔ̃), s.f. Palliation.
pallier (palje), v.a. [L *palliare*] To palliate, to mitigate, to alleviate.
palmaire (palmɛr), adj. (anat.) Palmar; of, or in the palm of the hand.
palmarès (palmarɛs), s.m. [f. L *palma*] Prize-list, list of honours.
palme[1] (palm), s.f. [L *palma*] Palm-branch; palm-tree; palm, success; *à vous la ~!*, you are the cleverest; we all bow to you; you surpass them all; *remporter la ~*, to bear away the palm; *la ~ du martyre*, the crown of martyrdom; *les ~s (d'académie)*, insignia of Fr. order.
palme[2] (palm), s.m. [L *palmus*, f. *palma*] (ant.) Palm, handbreadth (a measure = 0·225m.).
palmé, -e (palme), adj. Palmate, palmed.
palmeraie (palmərɛ), s.f. Palmery, palm-tree plantation or grove.
palmette (palmɛt), s.f. Palmette, honeysuckle ornament.
palmier (palmje), s.m. Palm-tree, great palm, date-tree, *Phoenix dactylifera*; *~ nain*, dwarf palm-tree, palmetto, *Chamaerops humilis*.
palmipède (palmipɛd), adj. s.m. [f. L *palma+pedis*] Palmiped.
palmiste (palmist), s.m. (bot.) Cabbage-tree, cabbage-palm, palmetto.
palmite (palmit), s.f. Palm-marrow.
palmure (palmyr), s.f. (ornith.) Web (of palmipeds).
palois, -e (palwɑ), adj. s.m.f. (Native) of Pau (France).
palombe (palɔ̃b), s.f. [L *palumbes*] Ring-dove, wood-pigeon.
palonnier (palɔnje), **palonneau** (pl. **-x**) (palɔno), s.m. Swing bar (of a carriage), pole.
palot (palo), s.m. Fishing-shovel.
pâlot, -te (pɑlo), adj. Rather pale, palish, wannish.
palourde (palurd), s.f. Cockle (shell-fish).
palpabilité (palpabilite), s.f. Palpability, palpableness.
palpable (palpabl), adj. Palpable, tangible; obvious.
palpablement (palpabləmɑ̃), adv. Palpably.
palpation (palpa'sjɔ̃), s.f. Palpation.
palpe (palp), s.f. Palp, feeler (of insects, &c.).
palpébral, -e, (aux) (palpebral), adj. [f. L *palpebra*] (anat.) Palpebral, pertaining to the eyelids.
palper (palpe), v.a. [L *palpare*] To palpate, to handle, to finger; (colloq.) to pocket, to receive (money).
palpitant, -e (palpitɑ̃), adj. **1.** Palpitating, throbbing; **2.** exciting, thrilling (story, novel, &c.).
palpitation (palpita'sjɔ̃), s.f. Palpitation, throb, throbbing.
palpiter (palpite), v.n. [L *palpitare*] To palpitate, to throb; to be thrilled.
palplanche (palplɑ̃ʃ), s.f. [*pal+planche*] Pile, coffer-dam plank.
palsambleu (palsɑ̃blø), interj. (obs.) [corrupt. of *par le sang de Dieu*] Zounds!, by jingo!
paltoquet (paltɔkɛ), s.m. [f. *paletot*] Lout, churl, bumpkin; bloke.
paludéen, -ne (palydeɛ̃), adj. [f. L *palus, paludis*] Marshy, marsh-, paludal, malarial; *fièvre ~ne*, marsh fever, malaria.
paludier (palydje), s.m. Salt-maker.
paludisme (palydism), s.m. Impaludism.
palus (paly), s.m. [L wd] Marsh, fen.
palustre (palystr), adj. Palustral.
pâmer, v.n. **se pâmer**, v.pr. (pɑme) [f. Gr. *spasma*] To swoon, to faint away; to be enraptured; *se ~ d'admiration*, to be overcome or transported with admiration; to praise something up to the skies; *se ~ de rire*, to nearly die with laughing; *c'est à ~ de rire!*, it 's killing!, it 's enough to make one die with laughing.
pâmoison (pɑmwazɔ̃), s.f. Swoon, fainting-fit; *tomber en ~*, to fall into a swoon, to faint away.
pampa (pɑ̃pa), s.f. [Span. wd] Pampa.
pampe (pɑ̃p), s.f. [f. *pampre*] Blade (of corn, &c.).
pamphlet (pɑ̃flɛ), s.m. [f. *Pamphilet* (title of medieval love-poem)] Pamphlet. ⚠ *Un pamphlet* in French = a short satirical, vehement work; it is often used pejoratively; a 'pamphlet' in Engl. is a small unbound treatise, espec. on a subject of current interest = *une brochure d'actualité*.
pamphlétaire (pɑ̃fletɛr), s.m.f. Pamphleteer. ⚠ See PAMPHLET.
pampille (pɑ̃pij), s.f. Drop: small light tassel.
pamplemousse (pɑ̃pləmus), s.m. (bot.) Grape-fruit, shaddock, pompelmoose; *Citrus decumana*, the fruit of this.
pampre (pɑ̃pr), s.m. [L *pampinus*] Vine-branch; (arch.) vine-branch.
pan (pɑ̃), s.m. [L *pannus*] Flap, lappet, loose part of a garment; side, pane, face; *les ~s d'un écrou*, the sides of a nut; piece, section (of a wall, &c.); *~ coupé*, cant; *à ~s coupés*, cantwise.
pan (pɑ̃), interj. Bang!
panabase (panabɑz), s.f. (chem.) Panabase, grey copper.
panacée (panase), s.f. [Gr. *panakeia*] Panacea; (pej.) nostrum.
panache (panaʃ), s.m. [It. *pennachio*] Tuft, plume; top; triangular part of pendentive of an arch; (fig.) panache;

faire ~, (on horseback) to come a cropper; (of a motor-car) to turn right over, to turn a somersault; *avoir du* ~, to be dashing; (colloq.) *avoir son* ~, to be screwed, drunk.

panaché, -e (panaʃe), p. adj. Variegated, streaked, motley, mixed; see EMPANACHÉ.

panacher (panaʃe), v.a.n. To plume; to streak, to variegate, to mix; **se** ~, v.pr. to become variegated, streaked.

panachure (panaʃyr), s.f. Streak, variegation, stripe.

panade (panad), s.f. [f. *pain*, Provenç. *panada*] Panada, bread soup; (colloq.) *être dans la* ~, to be hard up; to be in the soup, or in a mess, or in the cart.

panais (panɛ), s.m. [L *pastinaca*] Parsnip; (colloq.) *des* ~ *!*, not much !, not likely !

panama (panama), s.m. [geog. orig.] Panama hat, panama.

paname (panam), [prop. n.] (slang) Paris.

panard, -e (panar), adj. (of horses) With out-turned toes.

panaris (panari), s.m. [L *panaricium*] (pathol.) Whitlow.

panathénées (panatene), s.f.pl. Panathenaea.

pancarte (pɑ̃kart), s.f. [Gr. *pan*+L *charta*] Placard, bill, show-card.

pancrace (pɑ̃kras), s.m. [Gr. *pagkration*] (ant.) Pancratium (wrestling and boxing contest).

pancréas (pɑ̃kreɑs), s.m. [Gr. *pagkreas*] Pancreas, sweetbread.

pancréatique (pɑ̃kreatik), adj. Pancreatic.

panda (pɑ̃da), s.m. Panda, red bear-cat; (a rodent of the Himalayas).

pandectes (pɑ̃dɛkt), s.f.pl. [L wd] Pandects.

pandémonium (pɑ̃demɔnjɔm), s.m. [wd coined by Milton f. Gr. *pan*+*daimōn*] Pandemonium, utter confusion.

pandit (pɑ̃di), s.m. [Hind. *pandit*] Pundit, a learned Brahmin.

pandore (pɑ̃dɔr), s.m. (colloq.) Bobby, copper (policeman).

pandour (pɑ̃dur), s.m. [Serbo-Croatian wd] Pandour; (fig.) brute, plunderer, coarse, brutal man, bully.

pané, -e (pane), p. adj. [f. *pain*] Breaded, covered with bread-crumbs; (colloq.) hard up (see PANNÉ).

panégyrique (paneʒirik), s.m. [Gr. *panēgurikos*] Panegyric, eulogy.

panégyriste (paneʒirist), s.m.f. Panegyrist.

paner (pane), v.a. [f. *pain*] To bread, to cover with bread-crumbs.

panerée (panre), s.f. [f. *panier*] Basketful.

paneterie (pantri), s.f. [f. *pain*] Pantry, bread-room.

panetier (pantje), s.m. Pantler.

panetière (pantjɛr), s.f. [f. *pain*] **1.** Shepherd's satchel; **2.** bread-cupboard; **3.** small sideboard.

paneton (pantɔ̃), s.m. [f. *pain*] Wicker mould for a loaf of bread.

pangolin (pɑ̃gɔlɛ̃), s.m. [Malay wd] (zool.) Scaly ant-eater, pangolin.

panic (panik), s.m. [L *panicum*] (bot.) Panic-grass, pannicle, millet.

panicaut (paniko), s.m. (bot.) Field eryngo.

panicule (panikyl), s.m. [L *panicula*] (bot.) Panicle.

paniculé, -e (panikyle), adj. Paniculate.

panier (panje), s.m. [L *panarium*] Basket, hamper, wicker basket; pannier (for beast of burden); hoop petticoat, pannier; ~ *à salade*, salad-net, salad-basket; (colloq.) prison van, Black Maria; (fig.) ~ *percé*, spendthrift; *faire danser l'anse du* ~, to take the market penny (immoderately); *le dessus du* ~, the pick of the basket; ~ *à ouvrage*, work-basket; ~ *à papier*, waste-paper basket; *adieu* ~*s, vendanges sont faites*, it's all over.

panifiable (panifjabl), adj. That can be converted into bread.

panification (panifika'sjɔ̃), s.f. Panification.

panifier (panifje), v.a. [f. L *panis*+*facere*] To turn into bread.

panique (panik), adj. [f. the god *Pan*] Panic. ~, s.f. Panic, sudden infectious fright; (of animals) stampede.

panne (pan), s.f. [f. L *penna*] **1.** Plush, silk shag; **2.** pantile; **3.** fat (of a pig); **4.** [f. Germ. *Bahn*] pane (of a hammer); **5.** purlin (of a roof); **6.** poverty, need; *être dans une* ~ *noire*, to be terribly hard up; *être en* ~, (naut.) to lie to; (of a motor-car) to be disabled, to have a break-down; (naut.) *mettre en* ~, to bring to; **7.** (colloq.) (*a*) failure; (*b*) unimportant part in a play.

panné, -e (pane), adj. Hard-up, penniless, in Queer Street; syn. (slang) FAUCHÉ.

panneau (pl. **-x**) (pano), s.m. [f. *pan*] Panel; (naut.) hatch; (hort.) glass-frame; snare, trap; *donner dans le* ~, to fall into the snare.

pannequet (pankɛ), s.m. [f. Engl. *pancake*] A cake, sort of crisp pancake.

panneton (pantɔ̃), s.m. [f. *pennon*] Key-bit; catch (of a window-fastening).

pannicule (panikyl), s.m. [L *panniculus*] (pathol.) Panniculus carnosus.

panonceau (pl. **-x**) (panɔ̃so), s.m. [f. *pennon*] Escutcheon.

panoplie (panɔpli), s.f. [f. Gr. *panoplia*, f. *hopla*] Panoply; trophy of arms.

panoptique (panɔptik), s.m. Panopticon.

panorama (panɔrama), s.m. [*pan*+Gr. *horama*] Panorama.

panoramique (panɔramik), adj. Panoramic.

pansage (pɑ̃saʒ), s.m. Grooming, dressing-down (of a horse).

panse (pɑ̃s), s.f. [L *pantex*] **1.** Paunch (the first stomach of ruminants); **2.** (fam.) paunch, belly, corporation, pot-belly; brim (of a bell); belly (of a bottle); (fig.) *une ~ d'a*, a single stroke, the least bit of work.

pansement (pɑ̃smɑ̃), s.m. Dressing (of a wound).

panser (pɑ̃se), v.a. [L *pensare*] To dress (a wound); to groom (a horse).

pansu, -e (pɑ̃sy), adj. Pot-bellied; bulging, fat.

pantagruélique (pɑ̃tagrɥelik), adj. [f. *Pantagruel*, in Rabelais] Pantagruelian.

pantalon (pɑ̃talɔ̃), s.m. [It. *Pantalone*] **1.** Trousers, pair of trousers, pantaloons, pants; **2.** (women's) drawers; **3.** an old dance.

pantalonnade (pɑ̃talɔnad), s.f. Pantaloonery, buffoonery; sham, false demonstration.

pante (pɑ̃t), s.m. (slang) Flat, cove, bloke.

pantelant, -e (pɑ̃tlɑ̃), p. adj. Panting, gasping, palpitating, quivering.

panteler (pɑ̃tle), v.n. [f. LL *phantasiare*] To pant, to gasp, to quiver, to palpitate.

pantenne, pantène (pɑ̃tɛn), s.f. [Provenç. wd] Draw-net; wicker tray; (naut.) *en ~*, apeak (as a sign of mourning).

panthée (pɑ̃te), adj. f. [f. Gr. *pan*+*theos*] Bearing the symbols of several deities together.

panthéisme (pɑ̃teism), s.m. [f. Gr. *pan*+ *theos*] Pantheism.

panthéistique, panthéiste (pɑ̃teistik, pɑ̃teist), adj. Pantheistical, pantheist.

panthéon (pɑ̃teɔ̃), s.m. [Gr. wd] Pantheon.

panthère (pɑ̃tɛr), s.f. [L *panthera*] Panther.

pantière (pɑ̃tjɛr), s.f. [f. L *panther*] Draw-net (for catching birds); game-net, game-bag.

pantin (pɑ̃tɛ̃), s.m. [etym. dub.] Puppet, dancing-jack; (fig.) trimmer, time-server; guy.

panto- (pɑ̃to), pref. [Gr. *pas, pantos*] Panto-.

pantographe (pɑ̃tɔgraf), s.m. [*panto*+ (Gr.) *graphein*] Pantograph.

pantois, -e (pɑ̃twɑ), adj. [f. LL *phantasiare*] (obs.) Panting; (now) astounded, nonplussed, aghast, amazed.

pantomime (pɑ̃tomim), s.m. [*panto*+Gr. *mimos*] Pantomimist; ~, s.f. pantomime, dumb show.

pantouflard (pɑ̃tuflar) s.m. (colloq.) Slipshod man, easy-going fellow who values his comfort beyond all things.

pantoufle (pɑ̃tufl), s.f. [orig. unkn.] Slipper; *être en ~s*, to be in slippers; *raisonner comme ma ~*, to reason like a jackass.

pantoufler (pɑ̃tufle), v.n. **1.** (fam.) To talk, to chatter at random; **2.** to reason like a jackass.

panure (panyr), s.f. [f. *pain*] Bread-crumbs (sprinkled over meat, fish, &c.).

paon (pɑ̃), s.m. [L *pavo*] **1.** (ornith.) Peacock, peafowl; **2.** (ent.) peacock butterfly, emperor-moth; (fig.) vain fellow; *se parer des plumes du ~*, to deck oneself in borrowed plumes.

paonne (pan), s.f. Pea-hen.

paonneau (pl. -x) (pano), s.m. Pea-chick.

paonner (pane), v.n. (of a peacock) To spread its tail; (fig.) to show off.

papa (papa), s.m. [Gr. *pappas*] Father, daddy, dad, papa; *bon ~*, grandpapa, grandad; *à la ~*, familiarly, easy, good-naturedly, offhand.

papable (papabl), adj. Eligible for the papacy.

papal, -e, (aux) (papal), adj. Papal.

papas (papɑs), s.m. [Gr. wd] Papas (Greek priest).

papauté (papote), s.f. Papacy, popedom, pontificate.

papavéracées (papaverase), s.f.pl. (bot.) Papaveraceae.

papaye (papɛj), s.f. [Span. *papaya*] Papaw.

papayer (papaje), s.m. (bot.) Papaw-tree.

pape (pap), s.m. [Gr. *pappas*] Pope.

papegai (papgɛ), s.m. [Arab. *babbagha*] (ornith.) Popinjay.

papelard, -e (paplar), adj. [etym. dub.] Hypocritical, sanctimonious.

papelardise (paplardiz), s.f. Hypocrisy.

paperasse (papras), s.f. Old waste-paper, scribbled paper; red tape.

paperasser (paprase), v.n. To rummage among old papers; to scribble.

paperassi-er, -ère (paprasje), adj. s.m.f. Scribbling; red tape, red tapist, scribbler, preserver of old useless papers.

papesse (papɛs), s.f. Popess, papess; *la ~ Jeanne*, Pope Joan.

papeterie (papɛtri), s.f. [f. *papier*] **1.** Paper-manufactory, paper-mill; **2.** paper-making; paper-trade; **3.** stationery; **4.** stationer's shop; **5.** writing-case.

papeti-er, -ère (paptje), s.m.f. **1.** Stationer; **2.** paper-maker.

papier (papje), s.m. [L *papyrus*] Paper; document; *~ buvard*, blotting-paper; *~ à calquer*, tracing-paper; *~ d'emballage*, brown paper; *~ à lettres*, note-paper; *~-monnaie*, paper money; *~ de verre* (or *verré* or *émeri*), glass-paper, sand-paper, emery-paper; *~ de soie*, tissue paper; *~ de tournesol*, litmus paper; *~ mâché*, papier mâché; *être dans les petits ~s de X*, or *être bien dans les ~s de X*, to be in X's good books; *rayez cela de vos ~s*, leave that out of your reckoning; do not count on that !; *il est réglé comme un ~ de musique*, he is as regular as clock-work; *presse-~*, paper-weight; *le ~ souffre tout*, any lie can be put on paper; *avez-vous vos ~s?*, have you got your identity papers? (passports, identity cards, &c.).

papilionacé, -e (papiljɔnase), adj. (bot.) Papilionaceous. **~es,** s.f.pl. Papilionaceae.

papillaire (papilɛr), adj. Papillary.

papille (papij), s.f. [L *papilla*] Papilla.

papillon (papijɔ̃), s.m. [L *papilio*] **1.** Butterfly; (fig.) *~s noirs*, blues, gloomy thoughts; *~ de nuit*, moth; **2.** (of gas) fish-tail burner; **3.** (in a book, &c.) detachable inset.

papillonner (papijɔne), v.n. To flutter about; (fig.) to trifle, to flirt.

papillotage (papijɔtaʒ), s.m. Blinking (of the eyes); dazzle, glitter, tinsel (of style); (print.) slurring.

papillote (papijɔt), s.f. [orig. dub.] **1.** Curl-paper; **2.** comfit wrapped in paper, cracker; **3.** buttered paper in which meat is broiled.

papilloter (papijɔte), v.n. To blink; to dazzle; to be gaudy.

papisme (papism), s.m. Popery, papism.

papiste (papist), s.m.f. Papist.

papotage (papɔtaʒ), s.m. [onom.] Prattle, gossip; chatter, small talk, tittle-tattle.

papoter (papɔte), v.n. To prattle, to chatter.

papule (papyl), s.f. [L *papula*] Papula, papule, pimple.

papuleu-x, -se (papylø), adj. Papulous.

papyracé, -e (papirase), adj. Papyraceous.

papyrus (papirys), s.m. [Gr. *papuros*] Papyrus.

pâque (pɑk), s.f. [L *pascha*, f. Hebr. wd] Passover; see PÂQUES.

paquebot (pakbo), s.m. [f. Engl. *packet-boat*] Packet-boat, mail-boat, liner, steamer, steam packet.

pâquerette (pɑkrɛt), s.f. [f. *Pâques*] Daisy, Easter daisy.

Pâques (pɑk), s.m.pl. Easter; *à ~ prochain*, next Easter; *~*, s.f.pl. Easter; *~ fleuries*, Palm Sunday; *faire ses ~*, to receive the Sacrament at Easter; *œufs de ~*, Easter eggs.

paquet (pakɛ), s.m. [Engl. *packet*] Packet, parcel, bundle; mail; (print.) slip; lump, mass; *embarquer un ~ de mer*, to ship a heavy sea; *faire un ~*, to make a parcel; *faire ses ~s*, to pack up, to be off; *recevoir son ~*, to get the sack, to be hoofed out; *risquer le ~*, to chance it.

paquetage (paktaʒ), s.m. Packing up; (mil.) kit, outfit.

paqueter (pakte), v.a. To tie up in a parcel, to pack up.

paquetier (paktje), s.m. (print.) Slip-compositor.

pâquis (pɑki), s.m. [f. L *pascere*] Pasture-ground.

par (par), prep. [L *per*] By, by means of, through, across, per, for every; for the sake of; *couper ~ morceaux*, to cut into pieces; *tant ~ tête*, so much per head, so much a head; *cinq francs ~ personne*, five francs a person; five francs each; *voyager ~ eau*, to travel by sea; *se promener ~ la ville*, to walk about the town; *~ monts et ~ vaux*, over hill and dale; *tomber ~ terre*, to fall on or to the ground; *tenir ~ la main*, to hold by the hand; *~ curiosité*, out of curiosity; *~ pitié!*, for pity's sake!; *regarder ~ la fenêtre*, to look out of the window; *page ~ page*, page after page; *commencer ~ dire*, to begin by saying; *de ~ le roi*, in the King's name; *~ ailleurs*, in other respects, besides; *~-ci ~-là*, here and there, hither and thither, now and then; *~ delà*, beyond; *~ derrière*, from behind; *~ devant*, before, forwards; *~ trop*, far too much.

para (para), s.m. Small Turkish coin.

parabase (parabɑz), s.f. [Gr. *parabasis*] Parabasis.

parabole (parabɔl), s.f. [Gr. *parabolē*] **1.** Parable, allegory; **2.** (geom.) parabola.

parabolique (parabɔlik), adj. Parabolic.

paraboliquement (parabɔlikmɑ̃), adv. By way of parable; parabolically.

paraboloïde (parabɔlɔid), s.m. (geom.) Paraboloid.

parachèvement (paraʃɛvmɑ̃), s.m. Finishing, completion, bringing to perfection.

parachever (paraʃve), v.a. [*par+achever*] To finish, to complete, to bring to perfection.

parachronisme (parakrɔnism), s.m. [Gr. *para+khronos*] Parachronism.

parachute (paraʃyt), s.m. [f. *parer+chute*] Parachute.

paraclet (paraklɛ), s.m. [Gr. *paraklētos*] Paraclete.

parade (parad), s.f. [Span. *parada*] Parade, show, display, pageant, state; farce or show given in the open air (at a fair); (fenc.) parrying, parry; *faire la ~*, to parade; *faire ~ de son luxe*, to make a parade of luxury, to be ostentatious; *chambre de ~*, state room; *lit de ~*, bed of state; *il n'est pas heureux à la ~*, he is a bad hand at repartee.

parader (parade), v.n. To show off; *faire ~ un cheval*, to show off the paces of a horse.

paradigme (paradigm), s.m. [Gr. *paradeigma*] Paradigm, model.

paradis (paradi), s.m. [Gr. *paradeisos*] Paradise; (theatr.) upper gallery; (hort.) apple-stock used for grafting on; (millinery) bird of paradise; *vous ne l'emporterez pas en ~!*, you wait, I will get even with you; *oiseau de ~*, bird of paradise.

paradisiaque (paradizjak), adj. Paradisiac.
paradisier (paradizje), s.m. Bird of paradise.
parados (parado), s.m. [f. *parer*+*dos*] (fort.) Parados.
paradoxal, -e, (aux) (paradɔksal), adj. Paradoxical.
paradoxalement (paradɔksalmɑ̃), adv. Paradoxically.
paradoxe (paradɔks), s.m. [f. Gr. *para*+ *doxa*] Paradox.
paradoxisme (paradɔksism), s.m. (rhet.) Paradoxy.
parafe, paraphe (paraf), s.m. [f. Gr. *paragraphos*] Paraph, flourish (after one's signature or initials).
parafer, parapher (parafe), v.a. To paraph, to sign with a flourish, to initial.
paraffine (parafin), s.f. [f. L *parum*+ *affinis*] Paraffin. ⚠ In English 'paraffin' is also used for paraffin oil = *pétrole*.
paraffiner (parafine), v.a. To cover with paraffin.
parafoudre (parafudr), s.m. [*pare*+*à*+ *foudre*] Lightning-conductor (especially one employed to protect electrical apparatus).
parage (paraʒ), s.m. (usually in the plural) [f. Port. *paragem*] **1.** Quarter, locality, parts, place; **2.** [f. *pair*?] extraction, descent, quality; *une dame de haut* ~, a lady of high degree, a lady of quality.
paragraphe (paragraf), s.m. [f. Gr. *para*+ *graphein*] Paragraph.
paragrêle (paragrɛl), adj. [*pare*+*à*+*grêle*] Paragrandine (a contrivance for averting hailstorms).
paraître (parɛtr), v.n. and impers. [f. LL *parescere*] To appear, to come in sight, to show oneself, or itself; to become visible; to seem, to look like; to come out, to be published; to cut a figure, to make a show; *il paraît cinquante ans*, he looks fifty; *elle a quarante ans, mais ne les paraît pas*, she is forty but she does not look her age; *cela paraît satisfaisant*, this seems quite all right; *chercher à* ~, to try to cut a figure; *à ce qu'il paraît*, as it would seem; *sans qu'il y paraisse*, (*a*) although it does not look like it; (*b*) without its being seen; *il y paraît*, it's easy to see; *il n'y paraît pas*, one would not have thought it; there are no signs of it; *il paraît qu'il l'a dit*, it appears he said so; *il paraîtrait que vous avez tort*, it seems you are wrong; *vient de* ~, just published, just out; *faire* ~, to show; to publish.
paralipse (paralips), s.f. [Gr. *paraleipsis*] (rhet.) Paralipsis.
parallactique (paralaktik), adj. (astr.) Parallactic.
parallaxe (paralaks), s.f. [Gr. *parallaxis*] (astr.) Parallax.
parallèle (paralɛl), adj. [Gr. *parallêlos*] Parallel. ~, s.f. Parallel; ~, s.m. (astr., geog.) parallel, (fig.) parallel, simile, comparison; *mettre en* ~ *avec*, to draw a parallel between; *montage en* ~, multiple connexion.
parallèlement (paralɛlmɑ̃), adv. In a parallel way.
parallélépipède, parallélipipède (paralelepipɛd, paralelipipɛd), s.m. Parallelepiped.
parallélisme (paralelism), s.m. Parallelism.
parallélogramme (paralelɔgram), s.m. Parallelogram.
paralogisme (paralɔʒism), s.m. [Gr. *paralogismos*] Paralogism.
paralysant, -e (paralizɑ̃), p. adj. Paralysing.
paralyser (paralize), v.a. To paralyse, to render powerless.
paralysie (paralizi), s.f. [Gr. *paralusis*] Paralysis, palsy; *attaque de* ~, paralytic stroke.
paralytique (paralitik), adj. Paralysed, palsied, paralytic. ~, s.m.f. Paralytic.
paramètre (paramɛtr), s.m. Parameter.
parangon (parɑ̃gɔ̃), s.m. [Span. wd] Paragon, model of excellence; flawless diamond, pearl, &c.; (print.) double pica; *mettre en* ~, to compare.
parangonner (parɑ̃gɔne), v.a. (print.) To adjust, to range.
parapet (parapɛ), s.m. [It. *parapetto*] Parapet, breastwork.
paraphe (paraf), s.m. See PARAFE.
parapher (parafe), v.a. See PARAFER.
paraphernal, -e, (aux) (parafɛrnal), adj. (law) Paraphernal; *biens paraphernaux*, paraphernalia, wife's property.
paraphrase (parafrɑz), s.f. [Gr. *paraphrasis*] Paraphrase, lengthy commentary.
paraphraser (parafrɑze), v.a. To paraphrase.
paraphrastique (parafrɑstik), adj. Paraphrastic, not literal.
parapluie (paraplɥi), s.m. [*pare*+*à*+ *pluie*] Umbrella; *manche de* ~, umbrella handle.
parasélène (paraselɛn), s.f. [Gr. *para*+ *selênê*] (astr.) Paraselene.
parasitaire (parazitɛr), adj. Parasitical.
parasite (parazit), s.m. [Gr. *para*+*sitos*] Parasite. ~, adj. Parasitic, parasitical.
parasiticide (parazitisid), adj. Parasiticide.
parasitique (parazitik), adj. Parasitic, parasitical.
parasitisme (parazitism), s.m. Parasitism.
parasol (parasɔl), s.m. [It. *parasole*] Parasol.
parasolerie (parasɔlri), s.f. Umbrella- and parasol-making and trade.
paratonnerre (paratɔnɛr), s.m. [f. *parer*+

tonnerre] Lightning-conductor, lightning-rod.

paravent (paravɑ̃), s.m. [It. *paravento*] Screen, folding screen.

parbleu (parblø), interj. [for *par Dieu*] Indeed !, by Jove ! (Amer.) sure !, you bet !, forsooth !

parc (park), s.m. [Germ. orig.] Park; fold, sheep-fold, pen, cattle-run, paddock; vivarium, bed (of oysters); pleasure grounds, ground; (artill.) park.

parcage (parkaʒ), s.m. (of sheep) Folding; (of cattle) penning; (of oysters) laying down.

parcellaire (parsɛlɛr), adj. By small portions, in detail.

parcelle (parsɛl), s.f. [L *particula*] Part, particle, portion, parcel, patch (of land).

parcellement (parsɛlmɑ̃), s.m. Portioning out, parcelling.

parceller (parsɛle), v.a. To parcel, to portion out.

parce que (parsəkə), conj. loc. [*par*+*ce*+*que*] Because, on account of; ⚠ not to be confused with *par ce que*, by that which, from what.

parchemin (parʃəmɛ̃), s.m. [geog. orig. from *Pergame*] Parchment; (fig.) title of nobility.

parcheminé, -e (parʃəmine), p. adj. Parchment-like.

parcheminer (parʃmine), v.a. To render parchment-like.

parcheminerie (parʃminri), s.f. Parchment-making or -trade.

parchemini-er, ère (parʃminje), s.m.f. Parchment-maker.

parcimonie (parsimɔni), s.f. [L *parcimonia*] Parsimony.

parcimonieusement (parsimɔnjøzmɑ̃), adv. Parsimoniously.

parcimonieu-x, -se (parsimɔnjø), adj. Parsimonious.

parcourir (parkurir), v.a. To travel over or through, to run about, to scour, to wander over; (fig.) to survey, to run over; ~ *des yeux*, to survey, to glance over; ~ *un livre*, to run through a book, to read cursorily, to peruse.

parcours (parkur), s.m. Course, run, distance, line, journey, way; (of a river) course; *libre* ~, right of way; *effectuer le* ~, to cover the distance.

pardessus (pardəsy), s.m. [*par*+*dessus*] Overcoat, great-coat.

pardi, pardieu. See syn. PARBLEU.

pardon (pardɔ̃), s.m. [f. *pardonner*] Pardon, forgiveness, condonation; (in Brittany) pilgrimage; *je vous demande* ~, I beg your pardon; pardon me; excuse me; ~ *!*, I beg your pardon !; stop !, now look here !; **~s**, s.m.pl. indulgences.

pardonnable (pardɔnabl), adj. Pardonable, excusable.

pardonner (pardɔne), v.a. [L *perdonare*] To pardon, to forgive, to condone, to excuse, to overlook; to spare; *Dieu me pardonne !*, God forgive me; *une maladie qui ne pardonne pas*, a fatal disease.

paré, -e (pare), p. adj. Adorned, trimmed, dressed; (naut.) ready, clear; *bal* ~, full-dress ball; (law) *titre* ~, title in due form; (naut.) ~ *!*, ready !

pare-brise (parbriz), s.m. Wind-screen.

pare-choc (parʃɔk), s.m. (motor-car) Fender.

pare-éclats (pareklɑ), s.m. Splinter-screen.

pare-étincelles (paretɛ̃sɛl), s.m. Spark-guard.

parégorique (paregɔrik), adj. [f. Gr. *parēgorein*] Paregoric.

pareil, -le (parɛj), adj. [f. L *par*] Like, alike, similar, such, like that, identical, same; *dire une chose* ~*le !*, to say such a thing !; *une méchanceté sans* ~*le*, an unheard-of wickedness; *il n'a pas son* ~ *pour*, he has not his equal for, there is nobody like him for, (fam.) he is the one for. ~, s.m. Equal, match; ~*le*, s.f. the like, tit for tat; *lui rendre la* ~*le*, to give tit for tat.

pareillement (parɛjmɑ̃), adv. Similarly, likewise, in like manner; too.

parelle (parɛl), s.f. (bot.) Parella (a lichen).

parement (parmɑ̃), s.m. [f. *parer*] **1.** Altar-cloth; **2.** cuff; **3.** facing (of dress, coat, &c.); **4.** (build.) facing of stone; **5.** kerb-stone.

parementer (parmɑ̃te), v.a. (build.) To face.

parenchyme (parɑ̃ʃim), s.m. [Gr. *paregkhuma*] Parenchyma.

parénétique (parenetik), adj. [f. Gr. *parainesis*] Parenaetical, hortatory.

parent, -e (parɑ̃), s.m.f. [L *parens*] Relative, relation, kinsman; (fem.) kinswoman; **~s**, s.m.pl. parents (father and mother), relatives, relations, kindred, family; *grands-~s*, s.m.pl. grand-parents; *c'est un ~ du côté maternel*, he is a relation on the mother's side; *proche* ~, near relative. **~, -e**, adj. Related.

parentage (parɑ̃taʒ), s.m. Parentage, kindred, family, relations.

parenté (parɑ̃te), s.f. Relationship, consanguinity; kinship; kindred, relatives, kith and kin.

parentèle (parɑ̃tɛl), s.f. (rare) [L *parentela*] Kindred, relatives, kith and kin.

parenthèse (parɑ̃tɛz), s.f. [Gr. *parenthesis*] Parenthesis; (fig.) interlude; *entre* ~*s*, in parenthesis; *par* ~, *entre* ~*s*, by the way.

parer (pare), v.a. [L *parare*] To adorn, to dress, to embellish, to set off, to attire, to bedizen, to trim; to pare; to parry, to ward off; ~ *à*, to remedy; (naut.) to make ready; **se** ~, v.pr. to adorn oneself, to be adorned, decked; to plume oneself (*de*, on), to boast (of); *se ~ des plumes du paon*, to deck oneself in borrowed plumes.

paresse (parɛs), s.f. [f. L *pigritia*] Laziness, sloth, idleness, sluggishness, indolence; dullness, atony.

paresser (parɛse), v.n. To idle, to fritter away one's time.

paresseusement (parɛsøzmɑ̃), adv. Lazily, idly, slothfully.

paresseu-x, -se (parɛsø), adj. Lazy, idle, slothful, sluggish, indolent, slow; (of the stomach, bowels, &c.) sluggish, weak, slow. **~**, s.m.f. Idler, sluggard, lazy person; **~**, s.m. (zool.) ai, three-toed sloth.

parfaire (parfɛr), v.a. [*par+faire*] To complete, to finish, to perfect; to make up (a sum of money).

parfait, -e (parfɛ), adj. [L *perfectus*] Perfect, finished, complete, faultless, accomplished; (fam.) capital, first-rate; *~!* or *c'est ~!* capital!, all right! **~**, s.m. Perfection; (gram.) perfect (syn. PASSÉ DÉFINI); *plus que ~*, pluperfect.

parfaitement (parfɛtmɑ̃), adv. Perfectly, completely, thoroughly, quite; *~!*, quite so!, yes yes, decidedly!, exactly!, certainly!

parfilage (parfilaʒ), s.m. Unravelling, unweaving.

parfiler (parfile), v.a. [*par+filer*] To unravel, to unweave.

parfois (parfwɑ), adv. [*par+fois*] Sometimes, occasionally, now and then; syn. QUELQUEFOIS.

parfum (parfœ̃), s.m. [f. L *pro+fumus*] Perfume, scent, fragrance, odour, flavour; (of wines) bouquet.

parfumer (parfyme), v.a. To perfume, to scent, to sweeten, to deodorize; **se ~**, v.pr. to use perfumes, to scent oneself.

parfumerie (parfymri), s.f. Perfumery; perfumes.

parfumeu-r, -se (parfymœr), s.m.f. Perfumer.

parhélie, parélie (pareli), s.m. [f. Gr. *para+hēlios*] (astr.) Parhelion.

pari (pari), s.m. [f. *parier*] Bet, wager, stake; *faire un ~*, to lay a bet; *tenir, accepter un ~*, to take a bet; *~-mutuel*, betting in which all the stakes, less a percentage, are divided among the backers of the winning horse.

paria (parja), s.m. [f. Tamil *paṛaiyar*] Pariah, outcast.

pariade (parjad), s.f. [f. L *par*] Pairing, pairing-time (of birds).

parian (parjɑ̃), s.m. [f. *Paros*] Parian (porcelain).

parier (parje), v.a. [L *pariare*] To bet, to wager, to stake; *il y a gros à ~ que*, the odds are that; *~ à coup sûr*, to bet on a certainty; *~ pour X*, to back X.

pariétaire (parjetɛr), s.f. [f. L *paries*], (bot.) Pellitory.

pariétal, -e, (aux) (parjetal), adj. [f. L *paries*] Parietal. **~**, s.m. Parietal bone.

parieu-r, -se (parjœr), s.m.f. Wagerer, better, betting man or woman.

parigot, -e (parigo), s.m.f. (slang) Parisian.

parisette (parizɛt), s.f. (bot.) Herb-paris, true love, *Paris quadrifolia*.

parisianiser (parizjanize), v.a. To render Parisian.

parisianisme (parizjanism), s.m. Parisian habits or customs, Parisian elegance.

parisien, -ne (parizjɛ̃), adj. s.m.f. Parisian.

parité (parite), s.f. [L *paritas*] Parity, equality.

parjure (parʒyr), s.m. [L *perjurium*] Perjury; **~**, s.m.f. perjurer. **~**, adj. Perjured, forsworn.

(se) parjurer (səparʒyre), v.pr. To perjure oneself, to forswear oneself.

parlage (parlaʒ), s.m. Idle talk.

parlant, -e (parlɑ̃), p. adj. Speaking, talking; (fig.) speaking, lifelike, expressive; *un portrait ~*, a speaking likeness; (herald.) allusive, canting; *cinéma ~*, talkies (pl.), sound film.

parlé, -e (parle), p. adj. Spoken, colloquial.

parlement (parləmɑ̃), s.m. [f. *parler*] Parliament.

parlementaire (parləmɑ̃tɛr), adj. Parliamentary; civil, courteous. **~**, s.m. **1.** bearer of a flag of truce; **2.** parliamentarian; **3.** member of Parliament.

parlementarisme (parləmɑ̃tarism), s.m. Parliamentary institutions or system.

parlementer (parləmɑ̃te), v.n. To parley, to come to terms, to negotiate.

parler (parle), v.n.a. [LL *parabolare, paraulare*] To speak, to talk, to converse; (*de*, of), to treat, to mention; to express oneself; *sans ~ de*, not to mention; to say nothing of; besides; *trouver à qui ~*, to find some one to talk to, to find one's match; to catch a tartar; *faire ~ de soi*, to be much talked about, to get oneself a name; to get a bad name; *il sait ce que ~ veut dire*, he understands what is meant; he can take a hint; he knows what's what; *~ à bâtons rompus*, to talk desultorily; *~ du nez*, to speak through the nose; *~ à l'oreille de X*, to speak in X's ear; *~ d'abondance*, to speak extempore; *~ d'or*, to speak wisely; *~ en l'air*, to talk at random; *~ haut*, to speak loud; to speak firmly; *~ au cœur*, to move the heart; *~ à son bonnet*, to speak to oneself; *cela ne vaut pas la peine d'en ~*, it is not worth mentioning; don't mention it; (excl.) *parlez-moi de cela!*, now, that's something!; *vous en parlez bien à votre aise!*, it's easy for you to say so; *~ trois langues*, to speak three languages; ~

affaires, to talk about business, to talk shop; (prov.) *trop ~ nuit*, least said, soonest mended; (slang) *tu parles!*, rather!; not half!; (Amer.) you said it!; **se ~**, v.pr. to speak to each other; to be spoken.

parler (parle), s.m. Speech, utterance, way of speaking or pronouncing; parlance; *avoir son franc ~*, to be able to speak one's mind.

parleu-r, -se (parlœr), s.m.f. Talker, speech-maker, speaker; *être beau ~*, to be tongue-valiant; to have a glib tongue; to be honey-mouthed; *haut ~*, (wireless) loud speaker.

parloir (parlwar), s.m. Parlour.

parlote (parlɔt), s.f. (colloq.) Resort of gossips; (iron.) debating society; palaver.

parmélie (parmeli), s.f. (bot.) Parmelia, yellow wall-lichen.

parmesan, -e (parməzɑ̃), adj. s.m.f. [f. *Parma*] Parmesan. ~, s.m. Parmesan cheese.

parmi (parmi), prep. [*par+mi* (= *moitié*)] Among, amongst, amid, amidst, with.

parnasse (parnas), s.m. [geog. orig.] Parnassus, poetry, anthology of Parnassian verse.

parnassien, -ne (parnasjɛ̃), adj. Parnassian.

parodie (parɔdi), s.f. [Gr. *parōdia*] Parody.

parodier (parɔdje), v.a. To parody, to mimic.

parodiste (parɔdist), s.m.f. Parodist.

paroi (parwɑ), s.f. [L *paries*] Wall, partition, side, face, facing; (anat.) coat, wall.

paroir (parwɑr), s.m. Paring-knife.

paroisse (parwas), s.f. [L *parochia*] Parish; parish church; parishioners.

paroissial, -e, (aux) (parwasjal), adj. Parochial, parish.

paroissien, -ne (parwasjɛ̃), s.m.f. Parishioner; (colloq.) *c'est un drôle de ~!*, he is a queer fellow!; ~, s.m. prayer-book.

parole (parɔl), s.f. [LL *parabola*] Speech, utterance, voice, tone; language; word; sentence, saying; word of honour; *avoir la ~*, to have leave to speak; *prendre la ~*, to speak; *demander la ~*; to ask leave to speak; *la ~ est à X*, it's X's turn to speak; *couper la ~ à X*, to cut X short; to interrupt X; *perdre la ~*, to lose the use of one's tongue; *un honnête homme n'a qu'une ~*, an honest man's word is as good as his bond; *la ~ est d'argent, mais le silence est d'or*, speech is silver, silence is gold; *donner sa ~*, *engager sa ~*, to pledge one's word; *c'est un homme de ~*, he is a man of his word; *manquer de ~*, *manquer à sa ~*, to go from one's word; to break one's word; *tenir sa ~*, to keep one's word; *rendre sa ~ à X*, to release X from his promise; *reprendre sa ~*, to withdraw one's word; *prisonnier sur ~*, prisoner on parole; *la ~ de Dieu*, the word of God; *ma ~!*, upon my word!

paroli (parɔli), s.m. [It. wd] Paroli, double stake; *faire ~*, to double.

paroli-er, -ère (parɔlje), s.m.f. Librettist, song-writer.

paronomase (parɔnɔmɑz), s.f. [Gr. *paronomasia*] (rhet.) Word-play, paronomasia (ex. *qui vivra verra, qui se ressemble s'assemble*).

paronomasie (parɔnɔmɑzi), s.f. Paronomasia; resemblance between words of different languages.

paronymie (parɔnimi), [Gr. *para+onoma*] Paronymy (ex. *abstraire, distraire*).

parotide (parɔtid), s.f. adj. [f. Gr. *parōtis*] (anat.) Parotid (gland).

parotidien, -ne (parɔtidjɛ̃), adj. Parotid.

paroxysme (parɔksism), s.m. [Gr. *paroxusmos*] Paroxysm.

parpaillot, -e (parpajo), s.m.f. [Provenç. wd] Huguenot; (colloq.) unbeliever (in the Roman Catholic faith), independent mind.

parpaing (parpɛ̃), s.m. [etym. dub.; f. L *per+pangere*?] (build.) Perpend-stone, perpender; (also) block of artificial stone.

parquer (parke), v.a. [f. *parc*] To pen, to pen up (cattle); to fold (sheep); to bed (oysters); to enclose, to imprison; (artill.) to park.

parquet (parkɛ), s.m. [f. *parc*] **1.** Bar (of a court of justice) public prosecutor's offices; the prosecuting magistrates; **2.** floor, flooring, parquet floor; French flooring; **3.** stockbrokers' ring.

parquetage (parkətaʒ), s.m. Flooring, making a floor.

parqueterie (parkɛtri), s.f. Floor-making.

parqueteur (parkətœr), s.m. Floor-layer.

parrain (parɛ̃), s.m. [L *patrinus*] Godfather, sponsor; introducer; (colloq.) namesake.

parrainage (parɛnaʒ), s.m. Sponsorship.

parricide (parisid), s.m. [L *parricidium*] **1.** Parricide, murder; **2.** s.m.f. parricide, murderer. ~, adj. Parricidal.

parsemer (parsəme), v.a. [*par+semer*] To strew, to sprinkle, to intersperse, to dot, to stud, to spangle; to be strewn on.

parsi, -e (parsi), s.m.f. adj. [Pers. wd] Parsee.

part[1] (par), s.m. [L *partus*] **1.** Child, infant; birth; **2.** parturition of animals.

part[2] (par), s.f. [L *pars*] Share, part, portion; side; *avoir ~ à*, to share in; to partake of; *prendre ~ à*, to have a hand in, to take part in, to participate in, to be a party to; to sympathize with; *prendre X à ~*, to take X aside; *prendre en bonne ~*, to take in good part; *prendre en mauvaise ~*, to take amiss; *faire la ~ de*, to make allowance for; *faire la ~ du feu*, to circumscribe the fire; (fig.) to sacrifice something in order to save more; *faire ~ de . . . à X*, to acquaint X of; to inform X of; *lettre de faire ~*, or *faire-~*, s.m. card, (wedding card); formal announcement of birth, wedding, death, &c.; *à ~*, aside, apart; *à ~ soi*, inwardly; *de ~ en ~*, through and through; *de ~ et d'autre*, on both sides; *d'une ~*, on the one hand; *d'autre ~*, on the other hand; besides; *de toutes ~s*, on all sides; *de la ~ de X*, in X's name; on X's part; from X; *nulle ~*, nowhere; *quelque ~*, somewhere; *je le tiens de bonne ~*, I have it on good authority.

partage (partaʒ), s.m. [f. OF *partir*] Sharing, dividing, division, dealing out, apportionment, partition; share, lot, portion; *être le ~ de*, to be the lot of; *il eut en ~ la force et la bonté*, strength and goodness fell to his lot; *ligne de ~ des eaux*, dividing ridge, watershed.

partagé -e (partaʒe), p. adj. Portioned, divided; *les avis sont ~s à ce sujet*, the votes are divided on this point; *un amour ~*, a reciprocal love.

partageable (partaʒabl), adj. Divisible into shares.

partager (partaʒe), v.a. [f. *partage*] To divide, to share out, to portion, to parcel, to distribute, to deal out; to share, to partake of, to participate in, to go shares in; to gift, to endow; *la nature l'a bien mal partagé*, nature has treated him badly; *il est joliment bien partagé!*, his bread is well buttered; the fates have been most kind to him; *~ la joie de X*, to share X's joy; *~ la poire en deux*, to split the difference; *~ l'opinion de X*, to be of the same opinion as X; **se ~**, v.pr. to divide, to be divided.

partageu-x, -se (partaʒø), s.m.f. (colloq.) Sharer, communist.

partance (partɑ̃s), s.f. (naut.) Readiness to sail, departure; *navire en ~*, ship ready to sail.

partant (partɑ̃), conj. Consequently, therefore, thus.

partant, -e (partɑ̃), s.m.f. Goer; (racing) starter; *liste des ~s probables*, list of probable starters.

partenaire (partənɛr), s.m.f. [Engl. *partner*] Partner, associate; (colloq. U.S.A.) pard.

parterre (partɛr), s.m. [*par+terre*] Flower-bed, flower-garden, parterre; (theatr.) pit; (fig.) audience.

parthe (part), adj. s.m.f. Parthian; *la flèche du ~*, the Parthian shaft.

parthénogénèse (partenoʒenɛz), s.f. [Gr. *parthenos+genesis*] Parthenogenesis; reproduction without sexual union.

parti (parti), s.m. [f. *partir* = *partager*] Party, side, cause, part; decision, course; *~ pris*, foregone conclusion, prepossession; *de ~ pris*, intentionally, designedly; match, person to be married; *épouser un bon ~*, to make a good match, to marry a rich wife (or husband); advantage, profit; *tirer bon ~ de*, to turn to good account; *tirer ~ de tout*, to make a profit out of everything; *esprit de ~*, party spirit; *les ~s politiques*, the political parties; *en prendre son ~*, to reconcile oneself to the inevitable; to make the best of it; *faire un mauvais ~ à X*, to handle X roughly; to murder X; *il a pris le ~ de filer*, he chose to be off; *prendre le ~ de X*, or *prendre ~ pour X*, to side with X; to take X's part; to espouse X's cause; *il faut prendre un ~*, you must come to a decision; *c'est le seul ~ à prendre*, or *il n'y a qu'un ~ à prendre*, there 's only one course open.

parti, -e or **-te** (parti), p. adj. **1.** Divided, parted; parti-coloured; (herald.) party; **2.** (colloq.) (*a*) half-seas-over, drunk; (*b*) asleep.

partiaire (parsjɛr), adj. [L *partiarius*] That pays part of rent in produce.

partial, -e, (aux) (parsjal), adj. [f. *parti*] Partial (*pour*, to); biased, unfair.

partialement (parsjalmɑ̃), adv. Partially.

partialité (parsjalite), s.f. Partiality, bias.

participant, -e (partisipɑ̃), s.m.f. adj. Participant, sharer; participator; participating, contributing, concerned.

participation (partisipaˈsjɔ̃), s.f. Participation (*à*, in), share, partaking (of), knowledge, privity.

participe (partisip), s.m. [L *participium*] (gram.) Participle; *~ présent*, present participle; *~ passé*, past participle.

participer (partisipe), v.n. [L *pars+capere*] To participate (*à*, in), to partake (of), to share, to be a party to, to have a share (in); to have something of.

particulariser (partikylarize), v.a. To particularize, to specify.

particularisme (partikylarism), s.m. Particularism.

particularité (partikylarite), s.f. Peculiarity, particularity, particular.

particule (partikyl), s.f. [L *particula*] **1.** Particle; **2.** *~ nobiliaire*, the word *de*, *du*, *de la*, or *des* preceding one's name (a mark of nobility); **3.** (gram.) a small invariable word or prefix; ex. as *dé* in *déplaire*.

particuli-er, -ère (partikylje), adj. [L *particularis*] Particular, peculiar, specific, special, circumstantial; private, personal, intimate. ~, s.m.f. Private person, civilian; fellow, bloke; *en ~*, apart, privately; in particular, specially; *en mon ~*, for my own part. ⚠ *Particulier* is not used like 'particular' in the sense of fastidious, scrupulously exact.

particulièrement (partikyljɛrmɑ̃), adv. Particularly, in particular, especially, chiefly; apart, peculiarly, singly.

partie (parti), s.f. [f. OF *partir*] Part, portion; match, game; party, gathering, excursion, amusement; line of business, profession, special pursuit; (comm.) lot, goods; litigant, party; (mus.) part; *être juge et* ~, to be one's own judge; *prendre à* ~, (law), to sue; (colloq.) to take to task, to attack; (law) *se porter* ~ *civile*, to appear against; *avoir affaire à forte* ~, to have a powerful opponent; *tenir les livres en* ~ *double*, to keep books by double entry; *en* ~ *simple*, by single entry; *avoir* ~ *liée avec*, to be jointly liable with, to share risks and profits with; *la* ~ *est perdue!*, it's all up!; *la* ~ *est remise, c'est* ~ *remise*, the pleasure is only deferred; ~ *nulle*, drawn game; *la* ~ *n'est pas égale*, it's not an equal match; *perdre la* ~, to lose the game; *voulez-vous être de la* ~*?*, will you be one of us?; *faire* ~ *de*, to belong to; to form part of; to be a member of; *faire une* ~ *de piquet*, to play a game of piquet; *en* ~, partly, in part; ~ *carrée*, party of four (two men and two women); ~ *fine*, spree, junket.

partiel, -le (parsjɛl), adj. Partial, not total, in parts; *éclipse* ~*le*, partial eclipse.

partiellement (parsjɛlmɑ̃), adv. Partially, in parts, by instalments.

partinium (partinjɔm), s.m. (chem.) Partinium (a metallic alloy).

partir (partir), v.n. [L *partire*] To start, to set out, to leave, to go, to be off, to depart; (of birds) to spring up; (of firearms) to go off; to pop; to dart; *à* ~ *de*, from, reckoning from; *faire* ~, to send off, to dispatch; to wipe off (a stain); ~ *d'un grand éclat de rire*, to burst out laughing; *cela part d'un bon cœur*, that comes from a kind heart; ~, v.a. (obs.); to divide; *avoir maille à* ~ *avec*, to have a bone to pick with.

partisan (partizɑ̃), s.m. [It. *partigiano*] Partisan, stickler (for), favourer (of); *je suis assez* ~ *de*, I am rather in favour of.

partiti-f, -ve (partitif), adj. Partitive.

partition (partisjɔ̃), s.f. [L *partitio*] Partition, division; (mus.) score; musical composition. ⚠ In English 'partition' means also a slight wall = *une cloison*, but in French *partition* is not used in that sense.

partout (partu), adv. Everywhere; ~ *où*, wherever, wheresoever, whenever; ~ *ailleurs*, everywhere else, in any other place.

parturition (partyrisjɔ̃), s.f. [L *parturitio*] Parturition.

parure (paryr), s.f. Attire, dress, ornament; finery; set (of undergarments); ~ *de diamants*, set of diamonds; paring, parings (of skins, &c.).

parution (parysjɔ̃), s.f. Publication, issuing; *dès la* ~ *de ce livre*, as soon as this book is out.

parvenir (parvənir), v.n. [f. L *pervenire*] (conjug. like *venir*, with auxil. *être*) To attain (*à*, to), to reach, to obtain, to succeed, to rise (to); to gain access (to); *faire* ~, to forward.

parvenu, -e (parvəny), s.m.f. (pej.) Upstart, parvenu.

parvis (parvi), s.m. [f. L *paradisus*] Parvis, outer sanctuary, parvise; (poet.) *les célestes* ~, the Heavens.

pas (pɑ), s.m. [L *passus*] Step; pace; tread, gait, stride; progress; footprint, trace; passage, strait, difficulty, trouble; *porter ses* ~ *vers*, to turn one's steps towards; ~ *à* ~, step by step; *au* ~, at a walking pace; in time; *à* ~ *comptés*, with measured steps; *à grands* ~, *à* ~ *de géant*, with long strides, with giant strides; at a great pace; *à* ~ *lents*, at a slow pace; slowly; *emboîter le* ~ *à X*, to tread in X's footsteps; (fig.) *à* ~ *de loup*, stealthily; with stealthy steps; ~ *accéléré*, quick step; ~ *de charge*, double quick step; ~ *gymnastique*, double march; *faux* ~, false step, trip, stumble, (fig.) slip, fault, mistake; *se tirer d'un mauvais* ~, to get out of a scrape; *sauter* or *franchir le* ~, to take a resolution, to take the leap, to submit; (pop.) to die; *marquer le* ~, to mark time; (fig.) to wait; *faire les cent* ~, to pace to and fro; to do sentry-go; *mettre au* ~, to walk (a horse); *mettre X au* ~, to discipline X, to bring X into line, to make X obey; *attention, il y a un* ~, take care, there's one step; *le* ~ *de la porte*, the threshold; (comm.) ~ *de porte*, goodwill; *j'y vais de ce* ~, I am going there directly; *prendre le* ~ *sur X*, to take precedence of X; *retourner sur ses* ~, to retrace one's steps; ~ *de clerc*, blunder; ~ *de vis*, pitch of screw.

pas (pɑ), adv. (neg.) No, not, not any; ~ *du tout*, not at all; *presque* ~, hardly, scarcely any.

pascal, -e, (aux) (paskal), adj. [L *paschalis*] Paschal, of the Jewish Passover; of Easter.

pasquinade (paskinad), s.f. [It. *pasquinata*] Lampoon, pasquinade.

passable (pasabl), adj. [f. *passer*] Passable, tolerable, middling, decent, fairly good, that will pass muster; indifferent; *santé* ~, indifferent health.

passablement (pasabləmɑ̃), adv. Passably, tolerably, middlingly; somewhat.

passacaille (pasakɑj), s.f. [Span. *pasacalle*] (mus., danc.) Passacaglia.

passade (pasad), s.f. [f. *passer*] **1.** Short stay; **2.** passing fancy, brief intimacy, amour, short-lived love-affair (this sense is the most usual); **3.** (rid.) passade; **4.** (swimming) ducking, dip.

passage (pasaʒ), s.m. [f. *passer*] Passing; passage, corridor; way, thoroughfare, lane; crossing; passage-money; transition; passage (of a book, &c.); (rail.) ~ *à niveau*, level crossing; *guetter au* ~, to lie in wait for; *barrer le* ~, to bar the way; *s'ouvrir un* ~, to make or force one's way through; *oiseaux de* ~, birds of passage; migratory birds; *je suis de* ~, I am only passing through.

passag-er, -ère (pasaʒe), adj. Passing, transient, transitory, migratory, short-lived; (colloq.) *rue* ~*ère*, much-frequented street. ~, s.m.f. Passenger.

passagèrement (pasaʒɛrmɑ̃), adv. Momentarily, transiently, fleetingly.

passant, -e (pɑsɑ̃), p. adj. Much-frequented; *en* ~, by the way; cursorily, (chess) en passant; (herald.) passant. ~, s.m.f. Passer-by.

passation (pɑsa'sjɔ̃), s.f. Drawing-up (of a title-deed, contract, &c.).

passavant (pɑsavɑ̃), s.m. (naut.) Gangway; (customs) pass, permit.

passe (pɑs), s.f. [f. *passer*] **1.** Pass, passage; **2.** odd money; **3.** (fenc.) passado, thrust; **4.** (print.) overplus; extra sheets; **5.** (naut.) channel, pass, passage; **6.** act of sexual intercourse; **7.** (fig.) situation; **8.** magnetic influence; *faire des* ~*s magnétiques à*, to hypnotize; *être en* ~ *d'arriver*, to be in a fair way of succeeding; to stand a good chance of getting on; *être dans une mauvaise* ~, to be in a fix; *mot de* ~, pass-word; *maison de* ~, disorderly house; (disguised) brothel; ~, in comp. (f. v. *passer*): ~*-boules*, s.m. game with a figure-head, into the mouth of which balls are thrown; ~*-debout*, s.m. (invar.) permit for transit (of wines, &c.); ~*-droit*, s.m. illegitimate favour; injustice; wrong; ~*-lacet*, s.m. bodkin; ~*-méteil*, s.m. maslin; ~*-montagne*, s.m. Balaclava helmet, flying helmet; ~*-parole*, s.m. (mil.) running order; ~*-partout*, s.m. pass-key, master-key; (engr.) passe-partout; ~-~, s.m. sleight of hand; *tour de* ~-~, sleight of hand trick; ~*-pied*, s.m. a Breton dance; ~*-purée*, s.m. potato-masher, colander; (bot.) ~*-rose*, s.f. hollyhock; ~*-temps*, s.m. pastime; ~*-thé*, s.m. tea-strainer.

passé, -e (pɑse), p. adj. Past, gone, dead, vanished; faded, withered; *la semaine* ~*e*, last week; *il est dix heures* ~*es*, it 's past ten; *il a trente ans* ~*s*, he is over thirty. ~, s.m. Past, time past, things past; (gram.) past tense; *comme par le* ~, as before; (poet.) as in days of yore.

passé (pɑse), prep. After; beyond; ~ *dix heures*, after ten.

passée (pɑse), s.f. Flight (of woodcock, &c.).

passement (pasmɑ̃), s.m. [f. *passer*] Lace (of gold, silk, wool, &c.); braid; trimming.

passementer (pasmɑ̃te), v.a. To lace, to trim with gold, &c.

passementerie (pasmɑ̃tri), s.f. Lace; lace-making; lace-trade; trimmings, braid.

passementi-er, -ère (pasmɑ̃tje), s.m.f. adj. (That is a) maker or seller of lace or trimmings.

passepoil (pɑspwal), s.m. Piping, edging (for clothes).

passeport (pɑspɔr), s.m. Passport; (fig.) recommendation.

passer (pɑse), v.n.a. [LL *passare*] (takes the auxil. *être* when condition is implied and *avoir* when action is implied) To pass, to pass along, through, by, over, across; to become; to go, to move on; to disappear, to fade, to pass away, to die; to look in, to call; to be considered, to be received, to be deemed; to pass muster; to hand; to circulate; to be examined; to overlook, to omit, to forgive; to sift, to strain; to draw up, to enter upon; *en* ~ *par là*, to submit to it, to put up with it; ~ *pour*, to pass for, to be considered, to be deemed; ~ *outre*, to go on, to take no notice, to proceed; *y* ~, to pass, to submit to it, to go through it; *cela me passe*, that beats me, that 's beyond my understanding; *cela m'a passé de l'esprit*, it has slipped my memory; ~ *sur une peccadille*, to overlook a peccadillo; *cela peut* ~, that 's tolerable; *cela se passera*, that won't last; ~ *une rivière à la nage*, to swim across a river; ~ *à gué*, to ford; *passez-moi du sel*, pass the salt, please; ~ *un marteau*, to hand a hammer; ~ *une pièce de monnaie*, to pass a coin; ~ *un contrat*, to draw up a deed; *passez votre chemin*, go your way; ~ *de la farine*, to sift flour; ~ *du bouillon*, to strain broth; ~ *sous silence*, to take no notice of, to omit; ~ *son envie de*, to gratify one's desire of; *l'envie m'en a passé*, I have no desire for it now; (pop.) *faire* ~ *le goût du pain à X*, to kill X; ~ *les bornes, la mesure*, to be beyond all limits, all measure, to go too far, (slang) to be the limit; ~ *un examen*, to take or undergo an examination; *cela fait* ~ *une heure ou deux*, that whiles away an hour or two; ~ *au fil de l'épée*, to put to the sword; ~ *par les armes*, to shoot; *je passerai chez lui*, I will call on him; *on ne passe pas*, no thoroughfare; stop !; *passons !*, let us change the subject; *passe pour une fois, mais*, let it pass, for once, but; ~ *l'été à la campagne*, to spend the summer in the country; ~ *à tabac*, to thrash; **se** ~, v.pr. to happen; to disappear; to be spent; to do without; *il ne peut se* ~ *de vin*, he cannot do without his wine; *que se passe-t-il ?*, what 's going on ?, what 's happening ?; *la moitié de la vie se passe en sommeil*, half our life is spent in sleep; *vous souffrez ? cela se passera !*, does it hurt ? it won't last long.

passerage (pɑsraʒ), s.f. [*passe*+*rage*] (bot.) Pepperwort, *Lepidium*.

passereau (pl. **-x**) (pɑsro), s.m. [f. L *passer*] (ornith.) Sparrow.

passerelle (pasrɛl), s.f. [f. *passer*] Foot-bridge; (naut.) bridge; gangway.
passerine (pasrin), s.f. (ornith.) Passerine.
passeu-r, -se (pasœr), s.m.f. Ferry-man, (fem.) ferry-woman.
passibilité (pasibilite), s.f. Passibility, liability.
passible (pasibl), adj. [L *passibilis*] Passible, liable (*de*, to).
passi-f, -ve (pasif), adj. **1.** Passive, not active; **2.** on the debit side; *dettes ~ves*, liabilities; (gram.) passive.
passif (pasif), s.m. Debts, liabilities; (gram.) passive.
passiflore (pasiflɔr), s.f. [f. L *passio*+*flos*] (bot.) Passion-flower.
passion (pasjɔ̃), s.f. [L *passio*] Passion, agony; deep or strong emotion; fondness, craze, love; the object of one's passion; *avoir la ~ du tennis*, to have a craze for tennis; *souffrir mort et ~*, to suffer excruciating pains.
passionnant, -e (pasjɔnɑ̃), p. adj. Thrilling, exciting.
passionné, -e (pasjɔne), p. adj. Passionate, doting (*pour*, on), passionately fond (*de*, of); impassioned.
passionnel, -le (pasjɔnɛl), adj. Passional, due to love.
passionnément (pasjɔnemɑ̃), adv. Passionately, fondly, ardently, vehemently.
passionner (pasjɔne), v.a. To impassion; to interest powerfully, to move with passion; **se ~** (*pour*), v.pr. to become impassioned (of), to be deeply interested (in); to give way to passion (for).
passivement (pasivmɑ̃), adv. Passively.
passiveté, passivité (pasivte, pasivite), s.f. Passivity.
passoire (paswar), s.f. [f. *passer*] Colander, strainer.
pastel[1] (pastɛl), s.m. [It. *pastello*] Pastel; pastel-drawing.
pastel[2] (pastɛl), s.m. (bot.) Woad, *Isatis tinctoria*.
pastelliste (pastɛlist), s.m.f. Pastellist.
pastèque (pastɛk), s.f. [Arab. *baṭikh*] (bot.) Water-melon.
pasteur (pastœr), s.m. [L *pastor*] Shepherd; pastor, clergyman, (Protestant) minister; *Le Bon Pasteur*, Jesus Christ, the Good Shepherd.
pasteurisation (pastœriza'sjɔ̃), s.f. [f. *Louis Pasteur*] Pasteurization, sterilization (of milk, &c.).
pasteuriser (pastœrize), v.a. To pasteurize, to sterilize (milk, &c.).
pastiche (pastiʃ), s.m. [It. *pasticcio*] Pasticcio, pastiche, imitation.
pasticher (pastiʃe), v.a. [f. *pastiche*] To imitate, to make a pastiche of.
pasticheu-r, -se (pastiʃœr), s.m.f. Imitator, author of a pastiche.
pastille (pastij), s.f. [f. L *pastillus*] Pastille, lozenge, drop.
pastoral, -e, (aux) (pastɔral), adj. Pastoral. **~e**, s.f. Pastoral (play, poem, or piece of music).
pastorat (pastɔra), s.m. Pastorate, pastorship.
pastour, pastoureau (pl. **-x**) (pastur, pasturo) (obs. or local) s.m. Shepherd boy.
pastourelle (pasturɛl), s.f. **1.** Shepherdess; **2.** old French dance.
pat (pat), adj. m. (at chess) Stale-mate; *faire ~*, to stale-mate.
patache (pataʃ), s.f. [Span. wd] **1.** (naut.) Lugger, revenue-cutter, barge (in these senses the Fr. word is obsolete); **2.** public conveyance; rickety old coach or carriage.
patachon (pataʃɔ̃), s.m. Steersman or driver of a *patache* (obs. except in: *vie de ~*, knockabout life, boisterous, jolly life).
patafioler (patafjɔle), v.a. [orig. unkn.] (obs. except in): *que le bon Dieu* (*or le diable*) *te patafiole!*, may God confound you!, the devil take you!
patagon, -ne (patagɔ̃), adj. s.m.f. Patagonian.
patapouf (patapuf), s.m. **1.** Podge, podgy man; **2.** heavy and comical fall.
pataquès (patakɛs), s.m. [corrupt. of *Je ne sais pas-t-à qui est-ce*] Fault in speaking (ex. sounding a *t* for an *s* or vice versa); dreadful slip; mistake, bloomer, howler.
patarafe (pataraf), s.f. [corrupt. of *parafe*] Scrawl.
patard, patar (patar), s.m. [Provenç. orig.] Farthing; *n'avoir plus un ~*, to be broke; to be in low water; to be on the rocks; to be in Queer Street.
patarouf (pataruf), s.m. (colloq.) Hubbub, sensation, fuss.
patate (patat), s.f. [Span. *patata*] Batata, sweet potato; (colloq.) potato.
patati, patata (patatipatata) Onom. wd applied to endless, rapid, small talk or gossiping; tittle-tattle.
patatras (patatra), interj. [onom.] Bang!, crash!
pataud, -e (pato), adj. [f. *patte*] Clumsy, awkward. **~**, s.m. Pup; large-pawed dog.
patauger (patoʒe), v.n. [f. *pataud*] To flounder, to splash, to wade, to paddle (in the mud); (fig.) to make a mess (*dans*, of), to become entangled (in).
patchouli (patʃuli), s.m. [Tamil wd] (bot.) Patchouli; (perfume) patchouli.
pâte (pat), s.f. [LL *pasta*] Dough, batter; paste; pulp; (fig.) constitution, temper; *~ brisée*, short paste; *~ feuilletée*, puff paste, flaky paste; (fig.) *mettre la main à la ~*, to put one's shoulder to the wheel, to set one's hand to the work; *vivre comme un coq en ~*, to live in clover; *c'est une bonne ~*, he (or she) is a good sort.

pâté (pɑte), s.m. **1.** Pie, pasty, patty; ~ *de maisons,* block (of buildings); *cela s'enlève* or *se vend comme des petits ~s,* it sells like hot cakes; **2.** blot (of ink); *faire un ~ (sur son papier),* to make a blot (on one's paper).

pâtée (pɑte), s.f. Bran-mash, mess (for dogs), paste (for fattening poultry).

patelin, -e (patlɛ̃), adj. [f. the hero of *La Farce de Pathelin*] Wheedling, crafty, sly, artfully meek; *un air ~,* sneaking ways. ~, s.m. **1.** Wheedler; **2.** (colloq.) small place, village; birth-place, home-town; 'the old home'.

patelinage (patlinaʒ), s.m. [f. *patelin*] Wheedling; sneaky, flattering ways.

patelle (patɛl), s.f. [L *patella*] **1.** (ant.) Patella; **2.** (zool.) limpet.

patène (patɛn), s.f. [L *patena*] Paten.

patenôtre (pɑtənotr), s.f. [f. L *Pater noster*] Paternoster; (colloq.) *dire ses ~s,* to tell one's beads; to mutter prayers; (fig.) to mutter unintelligibly.

patent, -e (patɑ̃), adj. [L *patens*] Patent, obvious; *lettres ~es,* letters patent.

patentable (patɑ̃tabl), adj. Liable to pay a licence-fee; that requires a licence.

patente (patɑ̃t), s.f. [f. *patent*] Patent, trade-licence; licence-tax; (naut.) bill of health; *~ nette,* clean bill of health.

patenté, -e (patɑ̃te), p. adj. Licensed, patented, patent.

patenter (patɑ̃te), v.a. To license; *faire ~ une invention,* to patent an invention; to obtain a patent for an invention.

pater (pɑtɛr), s.m. [L wd] Paternoster; great bead (of a chaplet).

patère (patɛr), s.f. [L *patera*] **1.** (ant.) Patera; **2.** clothes-peg, hat-peg; round curtain-hook.

paterne (patɛrn), adj. [f. L *paternus*] Hypocritical, mawkish, mealy-mouthed, affectedly paternal.

paternel, -le (patɛrnɛl), adj. [f. L *paternus*] Paternal, fatherly, on the father's side. ~, s.m. (colloq.) Father; *voilà le ~* or *mon ~,* here comes the guv'nor, or the pater.

paternellement (patɛrnɛlmɑ̃), adv. Paternally, in a fatherly manner.

paternité (patɛrnite), s.f. Paternity, fatherhood; (fig.) authorship.

pâteu-x, -se (pɑtø), adj. [f. *pâte*] Pasty, clammy, doughy, sticky, viscous; thick (of the voice); milky (of gems); heavy (of style).

pathétique (patetik), adj. [Gr. *pathētikos*] Pathetic, moving, touching. ~, s.m. Pathos, pathetic.

pathétiquement (patetikmɑ̃), adv. Pathetically.

pathogène (patɔʒɛn), adj. [f. Gr. *pathos*+ *gennan*] Pathogenic, pathogenous.

pathologie (patɔlɔʒi), s.f. [f. Gr. *pathos*+ *logos*] Pathology.

pathologique (patɔlɔʒik), adj. Pathological.

pathos (patos), s.m. [Gr. wd] Affected pathos; bathos, bombast, rant. ⚠ *Pathos* in French is pej. and is syn. of *emphase, phébus, galimatias,* whereas English 'pathos' = *le pathétique, l'émouvant.*

patibulaire (patibylɛr), adj. [f. L *patibulum*] Patibulary, of the gallows; *fourches ~s,* the gallows; *une mine ~,* a hang-dog look.

patiemment (pasjamɑ̃), adv. Patiently.

patience (pasjɑ̃s), s.f. [L *patientia*] Patience, forbearance, endurance, fortitude; puzzle; game of patience; *être à bout de ~,* to be out of patience; *prenez ~,* be patient; have patience; *perdre ~,* to lose patience; *exercer la ~ de X,* to try X's patience; ~!, wait a bit!, have patience!; *prendre son mal en ~,* to bear one's misfortune patiently.

patient, -e (pasjɑ̃), adj. Patient, forbearing, enduring. ~, s.m.f. **1.** Sufferer (under medical treatment); patient; **2.** culprit (about to be executed); condemned person.

patienter (pasjɑ̃te), v.n. To have patience, to be patient.

patin (patɛ̃), s.m. [f. *patte*] **1.** Skate; **2.** (obs.) patten, clog; **3.** chair (of rail); **4.** sill (of a staircase); *~s à roulettes,* roller skates; *~s d'aéroplane,* slippers, sleigh runners; (motor.) *~ d'essieu,* spring plate, spring pad or block.

patinage (patinaʒ), s.m. **1.** Skating; **2.** sliding, slipping (of an engine).

patine (patin), s.f. [etym. dub.] Patina.

patiner (patine), v.n. **1.** To skate; **2.** to skid, to slide (of wheels); ~, v.a. to give a patina to.

patineu-r, -se (patinœr), s.m.f. Skater.

pâtir (pɑtir), v.n. [L *pati*] To suffer.

pâtis (pɑti), s.m. [L *pastus*] Pasture-ground, common.

pâtisser (pɑtise), v.n.a. To make pastry; to make into pastry.

pâtisserie (pɑtisri), s.f. [f. *pâte*] **1.** Pastry; **2.** pastry-making; **3.** pastry-shop; **4.** pastry-trade.

pâtissi-er, -ère (pɑtisje), s.m.f. Pastry-cook.

pâtissoire (pɑtiswar), s.f. Pastry-board.

pâtisson (pɑtisɔ̃), s.m. (bot.) Squash-melon.

patito (patito), s.m. [It. wd] Cicisbeo.

patoche (patɔʃ), s.f. [f. *patte*] **1.** (colloq.) Paw, large hand; **2.** stroke of ferule.

patois (patwɑ), s.m. [etym. dub.] Patois, dialect; jargon, brogue, lingo.

patoiser (patwaze), v.n. To speak patois.

pâton (pɑtɔ̃), s.m. Paste, bolus (for fattening poultry).

patouiller (patuje), v.n. [f. *patte*] To dabble.

patraque (patrak), s.f. [orig. unkn.] Worn-out or badly-made machine, clock, &c.; worn-out, sickly person. ~, adj. Worn-out; sickly, seedy, poorly; *se sentir* ~, to feel poorly, to feel knocked up.

pâtre (pɑtr), s.m. [L *pastor*] Shepherd, herdsman.

patriarcal, -e, (aux) (patriarkal), adj. Patriarchal.

patriarcalement (patriarkalmɑ̃), adv. Patriarchally.

patriarcat (patriarka), s.m. Patriarchate.

patriarche (patriarʃ), s.m. [L *patriarcha*] Patriarch.

patrice (patris), s.m. [L *patricius*] Patrician (a title of dignity created by the Emperor Constantine); see syn. PATRICIEN.

patriciat (patrisja), s.m. Patriciate.

patricien, -ne (patrisjɛ̃), s.m.f. adj. Patrician; (fig.) nobleman; aristocrat(ic); *des mains ~nes*, aristocratic hands.

patrie (patri), s.f. [L *patria*] Fatherland, native country, country, birth-place, home.

patrimoine (patrimwan), s.m. [L *patrimonium*] Patrimony, inheritance.

patrimonial, -e, (aux) (patrimɔnjal), adj. Patrimonial.

patriotard, -e (patriɔtar), adj. (colloq.) Jingo.

patriote (patriɔt), s.m.f. Patriot. ~, adj. Patriotic.

patriotique (patriɔtik), adj. Patriotic.

patriotiquement (patriɔtikmɑ̃), adv. Patriotically.

patriotisme (patriɔtism), s.m. Patriotism.

patristique (patristik), **patrologie** (patrɔlɔʒi), s.f. [f. Gr. *pater*] Patristic, patrology (study of the life and writings of the Fathers of the Church).

patron,[1] **-ne** (patrɔ̃), s.m.f. [L *patronus*] Patron, patron saint; employer, (colloq.) boss, guv'nor, principal, manager, (fem.) manageress, mistress, head, boss; skipper, master of a vessel, coxswain; proprietor (of a small hotel); (colloq.) *demandez ça à la ~ne*, ask my wife; ask the missis.

patron[2] (patrɔ̃), s.m. Pattern, model; stencil; standard; *dès ~-minet*, or *dès potron-minet*, by daybreak, at peep of day, very early.

patronage (patrɔnaʒ), s.m. **1.** Patronage, support, countenance; **2.** advowson; **3.** benevolent society for protection of young people; its premises.

patronal, -e, (aux) (patrɔnal), adj. Patronal; *fête ~e*, patron saint's day.

patronat (patrɔna), s.m. Patronate, protection, mastership; the employers.

patronne (patrɔn), s.f. Guardian saint; mistress, employer; (colloq.) wife, housewife, 'the missis'.

patronner (patrɔne), v.a. To patronize, to protect; (rare) to trace by a pattern.

patronnesse (patrɔnɛs), s.f. adj. f. (That is a) patroness.

patronnet (patrɔnɛ), s.m. Young pastry-cook.

patronymique (patrɔnimik), adj. [f. Gr. *patēr+onoma*] Patronymic.

patrouille (patruj), s.f. [f. *patte*] (mil.) Patrol.

patrouiller (patruje), v.n.a. To patrol; (fig.) to paddle, to mess about, to dabble; to paw.

patte (pat), s.f. [etym. dub.] Paw (of animals), foot (of birds), leg (of insects); (fig.) clutches, claws; (colloq.) human hand, paw, human foot; fluke (of an anchor), strap, band, flap, tab; end (of braces); bracket, holdfast, hook, cramp, foot (of a spoke); (fig.) *~s de mouche*, scrawl; hooks and hangers; ill-formed, minute writing; *coup de ~*, slily given blow, slap; (fig.) dart, shaft, fling; *faire ~ de velours*, to draw in its claws; to cajole, to flatter, to be all smirks and smiles; *montrer ~ blanche*, to say the password, to prove one's right to be admitted; to use the shibboleth; *~s de lapin*, very short whiskers; *marcher à quatre ~s*, to go on all fours; *mille-~s*, centipede; *graisser la ~ à X*, to bribe X, to grease X's palm; *à bas les ~s !*, hands off !; none of your games !; *tomber sous la ~ de X*, to fall into X's clutches; (slang) *se tirer des ~s*, to take oneself off, to trot off, to make oneself scarce; to flee, to escape, to run away; *~ d'oie*, (*a*) crow's-foot (wrinkle); (*b*) cross-roads; *~-pelu*, s.m. wolf in sheep's clothing; *~-fiche*, s.m. cramp, holdfast; *je ne puis lire ses ~s de mouches*, I am unable to read his (or her) scrawl.

pattu, -e (paty), adj. Large-pawed, broad-footed; feather-legged (of pigeons).

pâturage (pɑtyraʒ), s.m. Pasture, pasture-ground, pasturage, grazing-land.

pâture (pɑtyr), s.f. [L *pastura*] Food (for animals), fodder; pasture, pasturage; *servir de ~ à*, to become the prey of; *droit de vaine ~*, common of pasture.

pâturer (pɑtyre), v.n.a. To pasture, to graze, to feed, to feed on.

pâturin (pɑtyrɛ̃), s.m. (bot.) Meadow-grass.

paturon (patyrɔ̃), s.m. [f. OF *pâture* = fetter] Pastern (of a horse).

paucité (posite), s.f. [L *paucitas*] Paucity, smallness of number.

paulownia (polonja), s.m. (bot.) Paulownia (tree).

paume (pom), s.f. [L *palma*] **1.** Palm (of the hand); **2.** tennis, tennis-court.

paumelle (pomɛl), s.f. **1.** (bot.) Two-rowed barley; **2.** hinge; French-window handle, hand-guard.
paumer (pome), v.a. To smack, to slap; (slang) to lay hold of, to scrounge; *se faire* ~, to get nabbed, caught.
paumure (pomyr), s.f. Palm (of a deer's antlers).
paupérisme (poperism), s.m. [f. L *pauper*] Pauperism.
paupière (popjɛr), s.f. [L *palpebra*] Eyelid; (fig.) *ouvrir la* ~, to wake up; *fermer la* ~, to go to sleep.
pause (poz), s.f. [L *pausa*] Pause, stop; (mus.) bar rest, semibreve rest; *demi-*~, minim rest.
pauser (poze), v.n. To pause.
pauvre (povr), adj. [L *pauper*] Poor, needy, necessitous, indigent, unfortunate, destitute; wretched, sorry, paltry, pitiful, mean; barren, sterile; dear; *le* ~ *homme!*, poor devil!; ~ *d'esprit*, (*a*) poor in spirit; (*b*) weak-minded, moron; *un sol* ~, a barren soil; *mon* ~ *ami*, my dear friend; *un* ~ *sire*, a poor wight, a wretched fellow. ~, s.m. (see *pauvresse*, s.f.) Poor person, pauper; *un* ~ *honteux*, a poor man who is ashamed to beg.
pauvrement (povrəmɑ̃), adv. Poorly, wretchedly, shabbily.
pauvresse (povrɛs), s.f. Extremely poor woman, beggar-woman, woman in rags.
pauvret (povrɛ), adj. Poor, shabby. ~, s.m.f. Poor little thing, poor creature.
pauvreté (povrəte), s.f. Poverty, indigence; wretchedness; barrenness; poorness; sorry thing, stupid saying; ~ *n'est pas vice*, poverty is no crime; *dire des* ~*s*, to deal in platitudes; syn. INDIGENCE.
pavage (pavaʒ), s.m. Paving; pavement.
pavane (pavan), s.f. [Span. *pavana*, f. L *pavo*] Pavan (dance).
(se) pavaner (səpavane), v.n. To strut, to flaunt; to show off.
pavé (pave), s.m. [f. *paver*] Paving-stone; pavement; (fig.) street; *se trouver sur le* ~, to be out of work, to be without a home, to be utterly destitute; *tenir le haut du* ~, to take the wall, to take precedence, to hold the first rank, to show off; *battre le* ~, to idle about town; *brûler le* ~, to tear along; *tâter le* ~, to proceed cautiously; *le* ~ *du roi*, the king's highway.
pavement (pavmɑ̃), s.m. Paving; pavement.
paver (pave), v.a. [L *pavire*] To pave; *pavé de bonnes intentions*, paved with good intentions.
paveur (pavœr), s.m. Pavior, paviour, paver.
pavie (pavi), s.f. [f. *Pavie*, Italy] (bot.) Clingstone peach.
pavillon (pavijɔ̃), s.m. [f. L *papilio*] **1.** Pavilion, tent, summer-house, lodge, box, detached house, wing of a house, outhouse; **2.** bell (of a trumpet, &c.); **3.** flag, colours; *amener le* ~, to haul down the colours; *hisser le* ~, to hoist the colours; (fig.) *baisser* ~, to yield, to surrender, to sing small, to give in.
pavois (pavwɑ), s.m. [It. *pavese*] Shield, pavise; (naut.) bulwark, armour; flags arranged in a certain order; (fig.) *élever sur le* ~, to laud to the skies.
pavoisement (pavwazmɑ̃), s.m. Decking, dressing with flags.
pavoiser (pavwaze), v.a. To deck, to dress with flags.
pavot (pavo), s.m. [L *papaver*] (bot.) Poppy; *tête de* ~, poppy-head.
payable (pɛjabl), adj. Payable, due; ~ *à vue*, payable at sight.
payant, -e (pɛjɑ̃), p. adj. Paying; paid for; *billets* ~*s*, paid-for tickets; ~, s.m.f. Payer.
paye, paie (pɛj, pɛ), s.f. Pay, wages; (colloq.) debtor; *haute* ~, extra pay; *jour de* ~, pay-day.
payement, paiement (pɛjmɑ̃, pɛmɑ̃), s.m. Payment; *moyennant le* ~ *de*, on payment of; *faute de* ~, for or in case of non-payment; *faire face à un* ~, to meet a payment; *suspendre ses* ~*s*, to suspend payment; (fig.) *voilà le* ~ *de vos peines!*, that is to reward you for all your trouble.
payen, -ne (pajɛ̃), adj. s.m.f. (obs.) See PAÏEN.
payer (pɛje), v.a. [f. L *pacare*] To pay, to pay for, to pay off; to pay down, to pay away; to repay; to discharge; to reward; to atone for; ~ *d'audace* or *d'effronterie*, to brazen it out; to put a bold face on it; ~ *comptant*, to pay cash down, to pay cash; ~ *de sa personne*, to exert oneself, to expose oneself; *je leur ai laissé la note à* ~, I left them to foot the bill; *je suis payé pour le savoir*, I know it to my cost; ~ *les violons*, to pay the piper; ~ *son écot*, to pay one's share; *se faire* ~, to obtain or to enforce payment; ~ *de retour*, to pay back; *il me le paiera!*, I will make him smart for it; he shall pay for this; **se** ~, v.pr. to be paid; to treat oneself to; *se* ~ *une automobile*, to treat oneself to a motor-car; *il veut se* ~ *ma tête*, he wishes to have the laugh of me, he wants to pull my leg; *se* ~ *de mots*, to be the dupe of empty words.
payeu-r, -se (pɛjœr), s.m.f. Payer; paymaster. ~, adj. Paying.
pays (pei), s.m. [f. L *pagus*] Country, land, region; home, birth-place, fatherland; nation; (colloq.) fellow-countryman, (fem.) *payse*, countrywoman, compatriot; *avoir le mal du* ~, to be home-sick; *voir du* ~, to travel; (fig.) *faire voir du* ~ *à X*, to lead X a pretty dance; *battre le* ~, to rove about, (fig.) to wander; *se trouver en*

~ *de connaissance,* to be among friends; to know one's ground; ~ *perdu,* out-of-the-way place; *être bien de son* ~, (*a*) to be a simpleton; (*b*) to have all the characteristics of one's race; *tiens! voilà une* ~*e!*, hallo! here is a girl from my country (or village)!; *nul n'est prophète en son* ~, no man is a prophet in his own country.

paysage (peizaʒ), s.m. Landscape, scenery; landscape-painting; (Lit.) description of landscape.

paysagiste (peizaʒist), s.m. Landscape-painter. ~, adj. Landscape.

paysan, -ne (peizɑ̃), s.m.f. [f. *pays*] Peasant, rustic, countryman, (fem.) countrywoman; *les* ~*s*, the peasantry. ~, adj. Rustic, country-; *à la mode* ~*ne*, in country fashion, peasant-like.

paysannerie (peizanri), s.f. Rusticity; peasantry; pastoral play or novel.

payse (peiz), s.f. See PAYS.

péage (peaʒ), s.m. [f. L *pes*, LL *pedaticum*] Toll.

péag-er, -ère (peaʒe), s.m.f. Toll-gatherer, toll-collector.

péan, pæan (peɑ̃), s.m. [Gr. *paian*] Pæan, song of praise or triumph.

peau (pl. **-x**) (po), s.f. [L *pellis*] Skin; hide; peel, rind; leather; *risquer sa* ~, to risk one's skin, or one's life; *vendre cher sa* ~, to sell one's life dearly; *faire* ~ *neuve,* to turn over a new leaf; to turn one's coat; *sur la* ~, or *à même la* ~, next one's skin; *il mourra dans la* ~ *d'un imbécile,* he will be a fool as long as he lives; *n'avoir que les os et la* ~, to be as thin as a lath; to be nothing but skin and bone; *il ne faut pas vendre la* ~ *de l'ours avant de l'avoir tué,* first catch your hare; do not count your chickens before they are hatched; *Peau-Rouge,* redskin, Red Indian; *il a juré d'avoir sa* ~, he swore he would do for him, he has sworn to kill him; (slang) *avoir la* ~ *trop courte,* to be lazy; *avoir X dans la* ~, to be violently in love with X; *la* ~*!*, I'll give you nothing, no go! you won't get any.

peaucier (posje), adj. s.m. (anat.) Cutaneous (muscle).

peausserie (posri), s.f. Leather-dressing, fur-trade, peltry, skin-trade.

peaussier (posje), s.m. Skin-dresser, leather-dealer, fell-monger. ~, adj. Pertaining to skins.

pec (pɛk), adj. m. [Dutch *pekel*] Newly-salted (herring).

pécaïre (pekair), interj. [in South of France] Dear me!, now then!, &c.

pécari (pekari), s.m. [Carib *pakira*] (zool.) Peccary, Mexican hog.

peccable (pɛkabl), adj. [f. L *peccare*] Peccable, liable to sin.

peccadille (pɛkadij), s.f. [Span. *pecadillo*] Peccadillo.

peccant, -e (pɛkɑ̃), adj. (obs. med.) Peccant, morbid, not healthy.

peccavi (pɛkavi), s.m. [L wd] Peccavi; *faire son* ~, to acknowledge one's offences; to cry peccavi.

pechblende (pɛʃblɑ̃d), s.m. [Germ. wd] (min.) Pitchblende (an ore of uranium).

pêche[1] (pɛʃ), s.f. [f. L *persicum*] (bot.) Peach.

pêche[2] (pɛʃ), s.f. [f. *pêcher*] Fishing, angling; ~ *à la ligne,* angling; *canne à* ~, fishing-rod; *ligne de* ~, fishing-line; *aller à la* ~, to go fishing; *vendre sa* ~, to sell one's catch; *articles de* ~, fishing-tackle; *bateau de* ~, fishing-boat; *grande* ~, deep-sea fishing; ~ *à la dérive,* drift-net fishing.

péché (peʃe), s.m. [L *peccatum*] Sin, transgression, trespass, offence; *commettre un* ~ *mortel,* to commit a mortal sin; ~ *véniel,* venial sin; ~ *mignon,* besetting sin, favourite sin, foible; *racheter ses* ~*s*, to redeem one's sins; *à tout* ~ *miséricorde,* forgive and forget; we must not desire the death of the sinner; ~ *avoué est à demi pardonné,* a fault confessed is half redressed.

pécher (peʃe), v.n. [L *peccare*] To sin, to transgress; to be deficient; *ce raisonnement pèche par la base,* this reasoning is fundamentally false; *ce n'est pas par là qu'il pèche,* that is not his failing; ~ *contre les convenances,* to offend against decency.

pêcher (pɛʃe), s.m. (bot.) Peach-tree.

pêcher (pɛʃe), v.a.n. [L *piscari*] To fish, to angle; to fish up; to fish for, to drag out; (fig.) to get hold of; ~ *en eau trouble,* to fish in troubled waters; **se** ~, v.pr. to be fished, to be found.

pécheresse (peʃrɛs), s.f. See PÉCHEUR.

pêcherie (pɛʃri), s.f. Fishery, fishing-ground, fisheries.

péch-eur, -eresse (peʃœr), s.m.f. Sinner.

pêcheu-r, -se (pɛʃœr), s.m.f. Fisher, angler, fisherman, (fem.) fisherwoman; ~ *à la ligne,* angler.

pécore (pekɔr), s.f. [f. L *pecora*] Affected goose, ass, stupid woman, pretentious silly girl, dunce.

pecque (pɛk), (obs.) s.f. Silly conceited woman.

pectiné, -e (pɛktine), adj. [f. L *pecten*] (anat.) Pectinate, comb-shaped (muscle).

pectoral, -e (aux) (pɛktɔral), adj. [f. L *pectus, pectoris*] Pectoral; *pastilles* ~*es*, cough lozenges. ~, s.m. Pectoral, breast-plate.

péculat (pekyla), s.m. [L *peculatus*] Peculation, embezzlement.

pécule (pekyl), s.m. [L *peculium*] Savings, hoard.

pécune (pekyn), s.f. [L *pecunia*] Money, (slang) brass.

pécuniaire (pekynjɛr), adj. Pecuniary; *aide* ~, pecuniary aid.

pécunieu-x, -se (pekynjø), adj. Moneyed, well-off.
pédagogie (pedagɔʒi), s.f. [Gr. *paidagōgia*] Pedagogy.
pédagogique (pedagɔʒik), adj. Pedagogic.
pédagogue (pedagɔg), s.m.f. Pedagogue (often used, in Fr. as in Engl., in a pejorative sense).
pédale (pedal), s.f. [It. *pedale*] Pedal; (mus.) pedal-note; ~ *forte*, loud pedal; ~ *faible*, soft pedal; (fig.) cycling.
pédalé, -e (pedale), adj. (bot.) Pedate, palmate, pedal-shaped.
pédaler (pedale), v.n. To pedal; (fig.) to cycle.
pédalier (pedalje), s.m. (mus.) Pedal-board; (cycle) crank-gear.
pédant, -e (pedɑ̃), adj. [It. *pedante*] Pedantic. ~, s.m.f. Pedant.
pédanterie (pedɑ̃tri), s.f. Pedantry; syn. PÉDANTISME, s.m.
pédantesque (pedɑ̃tɛsk), adj. Pedantic.
pédantesquement (pedɑ̃tɛskəmɑ̃), adv. Pedantically.
pédantiser (pedɑ̃tize), v.n. To pedantize, to play the pedant.
pédantisme (pedɑ̃tism), s.m. Pedantry; syn. PÉDANTERIE, s.f.
pédéraste (pederast), s.m. [Gr. *paiderastēs*] Paederast.
pédérastie (pederasti), s.f. Paederasty.
pédestre (pedɛstr), adj. [L *pedester*] Pedestrian, foot-; walking.
pédestrement (pedɛstrəmɑ̃), adv. On foot.
pédicelle (pedisɛl), s.m. [f. L *pediculus*] (bot.) Pedicel.
pédiculaire (pedikylɛr), adj. Pedicular, lousy (disease). ~, s.f. (bot.) Lousewort; syn. HERBE AUX POUX.
pédicule (pedikyl), s.m. [L *pediculus*] (bot., zool.) Pedicle, peduncle.
pédiculé, -e (pedikyle), adj. Pedunculate, pedicellate.
pédicure (pedikyr), s.m.f. [f. L *pes, pedis* +*curare*] Pedicure, chiropodist.
pédieu-x, -se (pedjø), adj. [f. L *pes, pedis*] Pertaining to the foot; *artère ~se*, dorsalis pedis artery.
pédiluve (pedilyv), s.m. (med.) Foot-bath.
pédimane (pediman), adj. [L *pes, pedis*+ *manus*] (zool.) Pedimane, pedimanous.
pédomètre, podomètre (pedɔmɛtr, pɔdɔmɛtr), s.m. [L *pes, pedis*+Gr. *metron*] Pedometer.
pédonculaire (pedɔ̃kylɛr), adj. (bot.) Peduncular.
pédoncule (pedɔ̃kyl), s.m. [L *pedunculus*] (bot.) Peduncle, stalk; (anat.) appendix of the encephalon.
pédonculé, -e (pedɔ̃kyle), adj. Pedunculate.
pègre (pɛgr), s.f. [South dialectal orig.] (slang) Light-fingered gentry, fraternity of thieves; *haute ~*, swell mob; *basse ~*, lower class of thieves.
pégriot (pegrjo), s.m. (slang) Pilferer.
peignage (pɛɲaʒ), s.m. Combing; wool-combing.
peigne (pɛɲ), s.m. [L *pecten*] Comb; ~ *à grosses dents*, large-tooth comb; *donner un coup de ~*, to comb hastily; *sale comme un ~*, filthy dirty.
peignée (pɛɲe), s.f. **1.** Cardful (of wool); **2.** (slang) drubbing, set-to, thrashing.
peigner (pɛɲe), v.a. [f. *peigne*] To comb; to card (wool, &c.); (fig.) to polish, to adorn; (slang) to thrash, to drub; *un jardin bien peigné*, a well-kept garden; ~ *son style*, to polish one's style; **se ~**, v.pr. to comb one's hair.
peigneu-r, -se (pɛɲœr), s.m.f. Comber, wool-comber; ~**se**, s.f. carding-machine.
peignoir (pɛɲwar), s.m. Wrapper, dressing-gown, bath towel.
peignures (pɛɲyr), s.f.pl. Combings.
peille (pɛj), s.f. Rags (for paper-making).
peindre (pɛ̃dr), v.a.n. [L *pingere*] To paint; to stain; to portray, to describe, to depict, to express; *à ~*, very handsome, very picturesque; *se faire ~*, to sit for one's portrait, *la terreur se peint* (or *est peinte*) *sur son visage*, terror is written on his face; *elle se peint*, she paints her face, she rouges her face.
peinard (pɛnar), adj. (slang) Quiet; *se tenir ~*, to lie doggo, to keep on the Q.T.
peine (pɛn), s.f. [L *poena*] Punishment; pain, grief, sorrow, affliction, misery, anxiety; labour, trouble, pains, toil; difficulty, ado; *à ~*, hardly, scarcely; *à grand ~*, with much difficulty; *cela fait ~*, it hurts one to see that; *ce n'est pas la ~*, it's not worth while; don't bother about it; *être en ~ de*, to be concerned with; to be anxious to; *en être pour sa ~*, to have had one's trouble for nothing; to lose one's labour; *être dans la ~*, to be in trouble; to be afflicted; *faire de la ~ à X*, to pain X; *il a de la ~ à marcher*, he walks with difficulty; he is scarcely able to walk; *sous ~ de*, at the risk of; *sous ~ de mort*, on (or under) pain of death; *mourir à la ~*, to die in harness; to work oneself to death; *se donner de la ~*, to take pains; *prenez la ~ de vous asseoir*, pray take a seat; *toute ~ mérite salaire*, the labourer is worthy of his hire. ⚠ Fr. *peine* cannot be said of physical suffering like Engl. 'pain'.
peiné, -e (pɛne), p. adj. Pained, afflicted, grieved.
peiner (pɛne), v.a. To pain, to grieve, to make uneasy, to fatigue; ~, v.n. to labour hard, to toil; **se ~**, v.pr. to pain oneself; to take pains.
peintre (pɛ̃tr), s.m. [f. L *pictor*] Painter; ~ *en bâtiments*, house-painter; ~ *d'enseignes*,

sign-painter; *femme* ~, woman painter, paintress.
peintresse (pɛ̃trɛs), s.f. Paintress (*peintresse* is pej. and rarely used nowadays, *femme peintre* is more frequent).
peinture (pɛ̃tyr), s.f. Painting; paint; picture; (fig.) description, picture; ~ *à l'huile*, oil-painting; ~ *à l'aquarelle*, water-colour; (colloq.) *je ne peux pas le voir en* ~ *!*, I can't bear the sight of him.
peinturlurage (pɛ̃tyrlyraʒ), s.m. Daubing, daub.
peinturlurer (pɛ̃tyrlyre), v.a. To daub, to paint roughly, badly.
péjorati-f, -ve (peʒɔratif), adj. [f. L *pejor*] Pejorative.
pékan (pekɑ̃), s.m. [Amer. Indian *pékané*] (zool.) Pekan, Pennant's marten, a quadruped of the weasel family; pekan-fur.
pékin (pekɛ̃), s.m. **1.** Pekin (a Chinese tissue); **2.** (colloq.) civilian; philistine; *en* ~, in mufti; in civies.
pelade (pəlad), s.f. [f. *peler*] Scurf, alopecia.
pelage (pəlaʒ), s.m. [f. *poil*] Coat, fur, hair.
pélagianisme (pelaʒjanism), s.m. [f. *Pelagius*, a monk of the 4th–5th c.] Pelagianism.
pélagien, -ne (pelaʒjɛ̃), adj. **1.** Pelagian; of Pelagius or his doctrines; **2.** [f. Gr. *pelagos*] pelagian, pelagic, of the open sea.
pélagique (pelaʒik), adj. [f. Gr. *pelagos*] Pelagic, of the open sea.
pelard (pəlar), adj. m. Barked (wood).
pelardeau (pl. **-x**) (pəlardo), s.m. Wooden plug.
pélargonium (pelargɔnjɔm), s.m. [f. Gr. *pelargos*] (bot.) Pelargonium. (In Fr. pop. called *géranium*, in Engl. 'geranium'.)
pélasgien, -ne (pelaʒjɛ̃), adj. [f. L *Pelasgi*, n. of ancient Eastern Mediterranean race] Pelasgic, Pelasgian.
pelé, -e (pəle), p. adj. Bald, bald-headed; naked, bare; peeled; threadbare, shabby; *il n'y avait que quatre* ~*s et un tondu*, there was nothing but the ragtag and bobtail.
pêle-mêle (pɛlmɛl), s.m. Jumble, pell-mell, medley, disorder. ~, adv. Pell-mell, helter-skelter, promiscuously, in disorder or confusion.
peler (pəle), v.a.n. [f. L *pilare*] To skin, to peel, to peel off, to pare, to pare off, to strip of hair; ~ *une poire*, to peel a pear; **se** ~, v.pr. to peel, to peel off, to come off, to be peeled, &c.
pèlerin, -e (pɛlrɛ̃), s.m.f. [L *peregrinus*] Pilgrim; traveller; (colloq.) fellow; ~ *de St Jacques*, (shell) scallop.
pèlerinage (pɛlrinaʒ), s.m. Pilgrimage; *aller en* ~, *faire un* ~, to go on a pilgrimage.
pèlerine (pɛlrin), s.f. [f. *pèlerin*] Pelerine, tippet, cape.
pélican (pelikɑ̃), s.m. [L *pelecanus*] **1.** (ornith.) Pelican; **2.** (techn.) holdfast; (obs.) dentist's forceps.
pelisse (pəlis), s.f. [f. LL *pellicia*] Pelisse, greatcoat, fur-lined coat or cloak.
pellagre (pɛlagr), s.f. [It. *pellagra*] (med.) Pellagra.
pelle (pɛl), s.f. [L *pala*] Shovel, spade, scoop; blade (of an oar); spoon (for salt, sugar, ice, &c.); (slang) *ramasser une* ~, to come a cropper; to fall (from one's bicycle, horse, &c.); *remuer à la* ~, to shovel; (fig.) *remuer l'argent à la* ~, to have heaps of money; to be rolling in riches; *la* ~ *se moque du fourgon*, it is a case of the pot calling the kettle black.
pellée, pelletée (pɛle, pɛlte), s.f. Shovelful.
pelleter (pɛlte), v.a. To shovel.
pelleterie (pɛltri), s.f. [f. L *pellis*] Peltry, furriery; skins; fur-trade.
pelleteur (pɛltœr), s.m. Shoveller; shovelling-machine.
pelleti-er, -ère (pɛltje), s.m.f. Furrier. ~, adj. Fur-.
pellicule (pɛlikyl), s.f. [L *pellis, pellicula*] **1.** Pellicle, scurf, dandruff; **2.** (photo.) film.
pelliculeu-x, -se (pɛlikylø), adj. Scurfy.
pellucide (pɛllysid), adj. [f. L *per*+ *lucidus*] Pellucid.
péloponésien, -ne (pelɔpɔnezjɛ̃), adj. s.m.f. Peloponnesian.
pelotage (plɔtaʒ), s.m. Winding skeins into balls; loose play at billiards; (colloq.) cuddling, canoodling, fondling.
pelote (plɔt), s.f. [f. L *pila*] **1.** Ball, pincushion; **2.** (on the forehead of a horse) star, blaze; **3.** pelota, Basque game; the ball used in this game; **4.** (fig.) hoard, round sum; *faire sa* ~, to feather one's nest; to make one's pile.
peloter (plɔte), v.a. **1.** To wind into a ball; **2.** (colloq.) to pet, to cuddle, to fondle, to caress, to paw; to flatter; **3.** (colloq.) to bang, to beat, to handle roughly; **se** ~, v.pr. **1.** to bill and coo; **2.** to bang each other; ~, v.n. to play Basque tennis; ~ *en attendant partie*, to keep one's hand in till the game begins, to knock up balls.
peloton (plɔtɔ̃), s.m. Ball; group, knot, cluster; (mil.) platoon, half-company; *feu de* ~, platoon-firing.
pelotonner (plɔtɔne), v.a. To wind into balls; **se** ~, v.pr. to roll oneself (or itself) up, to curl oneself up, to nestle.
pelouse (pəluz), s.f. [f. *poil*] Lawn, grass-plot, greensward.
pelu, -e (pəly), adj. [f. *poil*] Hairy; (see doublet: POILU).
peluche (plyʃ), s.f. [f. *poil*] Plush, shag.
peluché, -e, pelucheu-x, -se (plyʃe, plyʃø), adj. Shaggy, plushy.
pelucher (plyʃe), v.n. To wear rough, to become shaggy.

pelure (pəlyr), s.f. Rind, peel, paring; (jest.) clothes; ~ *d'oignon*, onion-peel; ~*s de pommes de terre*, potato-parings; *papier* ~, foreign-post paper, India paper.
pelvien, -ne (pɛlvjɛ̃), adj. [f. L *pelvis*] (anat.) Pelvic.
pelvis (pɛlvis), s.m. [L wd] (anat.) Pelvis.
pemmican (pɛmikɑ̃), s.m. [Engl. wd, f. Cree Indian *pimecan*] Pemmican.
penaille (pənɑj), s.f., **penaillon** (pənɑjɔ̃), s.m. (obs.) Rag.
pénal, -e, (aux) (penal), adj. [f. L *poena*] Penal.
pénalement (penalmɑ̃), adv. Penally.
pénalité (penalite), s.f. Penalty; penal law.
pénates (penat), s.m.pl. [L wd] Penates; (fig.) home, fireside.
penaud, -e (pəno), adj. [f. *peine*] Abashed, crestfallen, sheepish, embarrassed.
penchant (pɑ̃ʃɑ̃), s.m. Declivity, slope, slant; (fig.) tendency, bent, inclination, taste, propensity; fondness; decline, decay; *suivre ses* ~*s* (or *son* ~), to follow one's bent; *dans le* ~ *de l'âge*, in the decline of life.
penchement (pɑ̃ʃmɑ̃), s.m. Slant, sloping, stooping.
pencher (pɑ̃ʃe), v.a.n. [f. L *pendere*] To incline, to bend, to stoop, to droop, to be bent; to lean (towards); ~ *un vase*, to incline a vase; *faire* ~, to weigh down; ~ *vers la ruine*, to be on the verge of ruin; ~ *vers* (or *à*) *l'indulgence*, to incline towards leniency; *marcher, la tête penchée*, to walk with bent head; **se** ~, v.pr. to bend, to lean, to stoop.
pendable (pɑ̃dabl), adj. Deserving hanging, abominable; *cas* ~, hanging matter; (jest.) *jouer un tour* ~ *à X*, to play X an abominable trick.
pendaison (pɑ̃dɛzɔ̃), s.f. Hanging (on the gallows).
pendant, -e (pɑ̃dɑ̃), p. adj. Hanging, drooping, pendent; (fig.) pending, undecided.
pendant (pɑ̃dɑ̃), s.m. [f. *pendre*] **1.** Pendant; frog (of a sword-belt); anything hanging by way of ornament; ear-drop; **2.** counterpart, match; *faire* ~, to match.
pendant (pɑ̃dɑ̃), prep. During; ~ *que*, while, whilst.
pendard, -e (pɑ̃dar), s.m.f. (colloq.) Rascal, rogue; (fem.) jade, hussy.
pendeloque (pɑ̃dlɔk), s.f. Pendant, drop, hanging ornament; tatter, shred.
pendentif (pɑ̃dɑ̃tif), s.m. (arch.) Pendentive; **2.** hanging jewel, pendant.
penderie (pɑ̃dri), s.f. Hanging wardrobe; dressing-room with hanging wardrobes.
pendiller (pɑ̃dije), v.n. To dangle.
pendre (pɑ̃dr), v.a.n. [L *pendere*] To hang, to hang up, to hang on the gallows, to suspend; to hang down, to dangle, to be hanging, to be pending, to be suspended, to droop, to sag; *il a dit pis que* ~ *de vous*, he said everything that was bad of you; *cela lui pend au nez*, he may expect as much.
pendu, -e (pɑ̃dy), p. adj. s.m.f. Hung, hanging; hanged; hanged man or woman; *avoir la langue bien* ~*e*, to have a well-oiled tongue; to have the gift of the gab; *avoir de la corde de* ~ *dans sa poche*, to have the devil's own luck; *je veux bien être* ~ *si*, I'll be hanged if.
pendule[1] (pɑ̃dyl), s.m. [L *pendulus*] Pendulum.
pendule[2] (pɑ̃dyl), s.f. Clock, time-piece; *remonter une* ~, to wind up a clock.
pêne (pɛn), s.m. [f. L *pessulus*] Bolt (of a lock).
pénétrabilité (penetrabilite), s.f. Penetrability.
pénétrable (penetrabl), p. adj. Penetrable; (fig.) distinguishable, intelligible.
pénétrant, -e (penetrɑ̃), p. adj. Penetrative, penetrating, piercing; shrewd, keen, acute, searching, sagacious; *un froid* ~, piercing cold; *un esprit* ~, a sagacious, or penetrating, or shrewd mind.
pénétration (penetraˈsjɔ̃), s.f. Penetration; acuteness, shrewdness.
pénétré, -e (penetre), p. adj. Impregnated; deeply impressed, concerned, affected; full (*de* of); imbued (with).
pénétrer (penetre), v.a.n. [L *penetrare*] To penetrate, to pierce, to go through; to pervade, to imbue; to search, to fathom, to understand, to divine, to see through, to unravel; **se** ~, v.pr. to penetrate each other; to convince oneself, to be penetrated or filled (*de*, with).
pénible (penibl), adj. [f. *peine*] Painful, laborious, troublesome, uneasy, hard, difficult, toilsome; distressing.
péniblement (peniblәmɑ̃), adv. Painfully, laboriously, distressingly.
péniche (peniʃ), s.f. [f. Engl. *pinnace*] Pinnace, barge, shallop, lighter; pram (in Baltic lands and Scandinavia).
pénil (penil), s.m. [f. L *pecten*] (anat.) Pubes, mons Veneris.
péninsulaire (penɛ̃sylɛr), adj. Peninsular.
péninsule (penɛ̃syl), s.f. [L *paene*+*insula*] Peninsula.
pénis (penis), s.m. [L wd] (anat.) Penis.
pénitence (penitɑ̃s), s.f. [L *paenitencia*] Penitence, penance; punishment; penalty (in games); *faire* ~, to do penance; *mettre en* ~, to punish, to put in the corner.
pénitencier (penitɑ̃sje), s.m. Penitentiary, reformatory, house of correction, prison.
pénitent, -e (penitɑ̃), adj. Penitent, repentant, contrite. ~, s.m.f. Penitent.
pénitentiaire (penitɑ̃sjɛr), adj. Penitentiary.

pénitenti-aux, -elles (penitɑ̃sjo), adj. pl. Penitential, of penitence or penance.
penne (pɛn), s.f. [L *penna*] **1.** Feather (of the tail or wing); **2.** (naut.) peak (of a lateen sail).
penné, -e (pɛne), adj. (bot.) Pinnate.
pennon (pɛnɔ̃), s.m. [f. *penne*] Pennon.
pénombre (penɔ̃br), s.f. [f. L *paene*+*umbra*] Penumbra, dim or subdued light.
penon (pənɔ̃), s.m. (naut.) Dog-vane.
pensant, -e (pɑ̃sɑ̃), p. adj. Thinking; *bien* ~, (colloq., jest.) right-thinking, well-disposed (in religious and political matters, according to one party); *il est très bien* ~, he is a supporter of the (Roman Catholic) Church; he is a reactionary or a Conservative.
pensée (pɑ̃se), s.f. Thought, thinking, mind, meaning, opinion, conception, idea; maxim, sentence; (bot.) pansy, heartsease; *rendre sa* ~, to express one's thought; *parler contre sa* ~, to speak against one's mind; *il me vient dans la* ~ *que*, it comes into my mind that; *entrer dans la* ~ *de X*, to follow X's train of thought; *lire dans la* ~ *de X*, to read X's thoughts.
penser (pɑ̃se), v.n.a. [L *pensare*] To think, to cogitate, to think of, to reflect, to consider, to conceive; to be near, to be on the point; *cela donne à* ~, that gives food for reflection, or for thought; *je ne sais que* ~ *de cela*, I do not know what to think of that; *il pense comme moi*, he agrees with me; *dire sa façon de* ~ *à X*, to give X a piece of one's mind; *à quoi pensez-vous ?*, what are you thinking of ?; *sans y* ~, unintentionally; *faites-moi* ~ *à*, remind me to; *pensez à votre mère*, think of your mother; *pensez à votre santé*, take care of your health; *vous n'y pensez pas !*, surely you don't mean it !; *pensez donc !*, just think of it !; *que pensez-vous de cela ?*, what do you think of (or say to) that ? *honni soit qui mal y pense*, evil be to him who evil thinks; *il a pensé mourir*, he nearly lost his life; *j'ai pensé tomber*, I was near falling.
penser (pɑ̃se), s.m. (poet.) Thought, train of thought.
penseu-r, -se (pɑ̃sœr), s.m.f. Thinker. ~, adj. Thinking.
pensi-f, -ve (pɑ̃sif), adj. Pensive, thoughtful.
pension (pɑ̃sjɔ̃), s.f. [L *pensio*] Pension, allowance, annuity; board, board and lodging; boarding-house; boarding-school; ~ *de famille*, family boarding-house; *prendre en* ~, to receive as boarder (or paying guest); *mettre en* ~, (*a*) to send to a boarding-school; (*b*) to entrust; ~ *viagère*, life annuity.
pensionnaire (pɑ̃sjɔnɛr), s.m.f. Boarder; paying guest; schoolboy, schoolgirl at boarding-school; pensioner; *prendre des* ~*s*, to take in boarders; to receive paying guests.
pensionnat (pɑ̃sjɔna), s.m. Boarding-school.
pensionner (pɑ̃sjɔne), v.a. To pension, to grant an allowance to.
pensivement (pɑ̃sivmɑ̃), adv. Pensively.
pensum (pɛ̃sɔm), s.m. [L wd] Imposition, extra task (at school).
pentacle (pɛ̃takl), s.m. [LL *pentaculum*] Pentacle.
pentacorde (pɛ̃takɔrd), s.m. [f. Gr. *pente* = 5] (mus. ant.) Pentachord.
pentadactyle (pɛ̃tadaktil), adj. [Gr. *pente* (=5)+*dactulos*] Pentadactylous, five-fingered.
pentaèdre (pɛ̃taɛdr), s.m. [Gr. *pente*+*hedra*] Pentahedron. ~, adj. Pentahedral.
pentagonal, -e (aux) (pɛ̃tagɔnal), adj. Pentagonal.
pentagone (pɛ̃tagɔn), s.m. [Gr. *pente* (=5) +*gōnia*] Pentagon.
pentamètre (pɛ̃tamɛtr), s.m. [f. Gr. *pente* (=5)+*metron*] (pros.) Pentameter.
pentarchie (pɛ̃tarʃi), s.f. [f. Gr. *pente* (=5) +*archē*] Pentarchy.
pentateuque (pɛ̃tatøk), s.m. [Gr. *pente*+*teukhos*] Pentateuch.
pente (pɑ̃t), s.f. [f. L *pendere*] Declivity, slope, descent; ascent; pitch (of roofs); side, wall (of tents); valance (of a bed); incline, gradient; (fig.) bent, propensity; *une rue en* ~, a sloping street; *la* ~ *naturelle de l'esprit*, the natural bent of the mind; *avoir le gosier en* ~, to be fond of the bottle, to be a tippler.
Pentecôte (pɑ̃tkot), s.f. [Gr. *pentēkostē*] Whitsuntide, Pentecost; *dimanche de* ~, Whit Sunday; *lundi de* ~, Whit Monday.
pentstémon (pɛ̃tstemɔ̃), s.m. [f. Gr. *pente* +*stēmōn*] (bot.) Pentstemon.
penture (pɑ̃tyr), s.f. [LL *penditura*] Hinge, iron brace.
pénultième (penyltjɛm), adj. [f. L *paene* +*ultimus*] Last but one, penultimate. ~, s.f. Penultima.
pénurie (penyri), s.f. [L *penuria*] Scarcity, dearth, want, penury.
péon (peɔ̃), s.m. [f. LL *pedo*] Peon (a labourer in South America; a foot-soldier in India).
péotte (peɔt), s.f. [It. *peotta*] Peotta (large gondola).
pépère (pepɛr), s.m. (colloq.) **1.** Quietly jovial old fellow; **2.** territorial soldier. (slang) ~, adj. Ripping, A 1, O.K., first-rate; snug, comfy.
pépètes, pépettes (pepɛt), s.f.pl. (slang) Money, brass, tin.
pépie (pepi), s.f. [LL *pipita*] Pip, roup (disease of fowls); (colloq.) *avoir la* ~, to be always dry, to be tremendously thirsty; to be fond of wetting one's whistle.

pépiement (pepimɑ̃), s.m. Chirping, chirp.
pépier (pepje), v.n. [L *pipire*] To chirp.
pépin (pepɛ̃), s.m. [orig. uncert.] Pip, kernel, stone (of grapes); ~ *de raisin*, grape-stone; (slang) **1.** umbrella, gamp, gingham; **2.** hitch, difficulty; *il y a un* ~, there 's a hitch; **3.** love; *j'ai un* ~ *pour lui*, I am sweet on him.
pépinière (pepinjɛr), s.f. [f. *pépin*] Nursery (garden).
pépiniériste (pepinjerist), s.m. Nurseryman.
pépite (pepit), s.f. [Span. *pepita*] Nugget; (slang) *il n'a plus une* ~, he is stony broke.
peplum (peplɔm), s.m. [L wd] Peplum.
pepsine (pɛpsin), s.f. [f. Gr. *pepsis*] Pepsin.
peptone (pɛptɔn), s.f. Peptone.
perçage (pɛrsaʒ), s.m. Piercing, boring.
percale (pɛrkal), s.f. [Pers. *pargala*] Cambric, cambric muslin, percale.
percaline (pɛrkalin), s.f. Glazed calico, percaline, chintz.
perçant, -e (pɛrsɑ̃), p. adj. Piercing, sharp, keen, shrill (voice), acute; *froid* ~, piercing cold; *vue* ~*e*, keen sight; *yeux* ~*s*, piercing eyes; *cris* ~*s*, piercing or shrill cries; *un esprit* ~, an acute, shrewd, or penetrating mind.
perce (pɛrs), s.f. Piercer, borer; hole (in flute, &c.); *mettre en* ~, to broach (a cask of wine), to tap (a cask).
percé, -e (pɛrse), p. adj. Pierced, bored, perforated, in holes, out at elbows; opened, tapped; (fig.) pierced, afflicted; (fig.) ~ *à jour*, seen through; *panier* ~, spendthrift; *des bas* ~*s*, stockings with holes in them.
percée (pɛrse), s.f. Opening, vista, glade.
percement (pɛrsmɑ̃), s.m. Piercing, boring, perforation, opening.
perce-muraille (pɛrsəmyrɑj), s.f. (bot.) Pellitory of the wall, *Sarietaria officinalis*.
perce-neige (pɛrsənɛʒ), s.f. (bot.) Snowdrop, *Galanthus nivalis*.
percentage (pɛrsɑ̃taʒ), s.m. [f. L *per*+ (Fr.) *cent*] Percentage.
perce-oreille (pɛrsɔrɛj), s.m. (ent.) Earwig; syn. FORFICULE.
perce-pierre (pɛrsəpjɛr), s.f. (bot.) **1.** Samphire, *Crithmum maritimum*; **2.** field lady's mantle, *Alchemilla arvensis*.
percepteur (pɛrsɛptœr), s.m. [L *perceptor*] Collector, tax-gatherer.
perceptibilité (pɛrsɛptibilite), s.f. Perceptibility.
perceptible (pɛrsɛptibl), adj. Perceptible; collectible, leviable; audible.
perceptiblement (pɛrsɛptibləmɑ̃), adv. Perceptibly, perceivably.
percepti-f, -ve (pɛrsɛptif), adj. Perceptive.
perception (pɛrsɛpsjɔ̃), s.f. **1.** Perception, faculty of perceiving; **2.** perception; collecting, gathering; collectorship; collector's office.
percer (pɛrse), v.a.n. [LL *pertusiare*] To pierce, to bore, to drill, to perforate; to open; to tap, to broach; to break through, to tunnel; to soak through; to come into notice, to attain to fame; to cut a passage through; ~ *de coups*, to cover with wounds; ~ *une fenêtre*, to make a window; *les os lui percent la peau*, his bones are coming through his skin, he is nothing but skin and bone; ~ *d'un coup d'épée*, to run through the body; ~ *l'avenir*, to dive into the future; ~ *un mystère*, to solve a mystery; ~ *un abcès*, to lance an abscess; *cela perce le cœur*, it 's heartrending; *la pluie m'a percé jusqu'aux os* (or more frequently, *transpercé*), the rain has soaked me through; *l'enfant perce ses dents*, the child is cutting his teeth; *ce garçon percera*, this young man will get on; *l'ennemi n'a pu* ~, the enemy has been unable to break through.
perceu-r, -se (pɛrsœr), s.m.f. Borer; ~*se*, s.f. boring-machine.
percevable (pɛrsəvabl), adj. Collectible; perceivable.
percevoir (pɛrsəvwar), v.a. [L *percipere*] To perceive; to collect, to gather (taxes).
perche[1] (pɛrʃ), s.f. [L *perca*] (ichth.) Perch.
perche[2] (pɛrʃ), s.f. [L *pertica*] Perch, pole, rod; old land measure; (fig.) *tendre la* ~ *à X*, to help X out of a difficulty.
percher (pɛrʃe), v.n., **se** ~, v.pr. To perch, to roost; (colloq.) *où perchez-vous?*, where are you staying (or living)?
percheron, -ne (pɛrʃərɔ̃), adj. s.m.f. (Native) of the Perche; horse or mare (from the Perche); Percheron.
percheu-r, -se (pɛrʃœr), adj. Perching; roosting.
perchlorate (pɛrklɔrat), s.m. (chem.) Perchlorate.
perchlorique (pɛrklɔrik), adj. Perchloric.
perchlorure (pɛrklɔryr), s.m. Perchloride.
perchoir (pɛrʃwar), s.m. [f. *percher*] Roost, perch, stand.
perclus, -e (pɛrkly), adj. [L *praeclusus*] Crippled, impotent, disabled, paralysed; (fig.) slow (of mind).
perçoir, -e (pɛrswar), s.m.f. Piercer (to tap casks, &c.), fret; borer.
percolateur (pɛrkɔlatœr), s.m. [f. L *per*+ *colare*] Percolator.
percussion (pɛrkysjɔ̃), s.f. [L *percussio*] Percussion.
percutant, -e (pɛrkytɑ̃), p. adj. Percussive, producing percussion; *fusée* ~*e*, percussion-fuse.
percuter (pɛrkyte), v.a. To percuss, to strike.

percuteur (pɛrkytœr), s.m. Striker (of a gun hammer), percutient.
perdable (pɛrdabl), adj. Losable.
perdant, -e (pɛrdɑ̃), s.m.f. **1.** Loser; **2.** s.m. (naut.) ebb-tide. **~**, p. adj. Losing.
perdition (pɛrdisjɔ̃), s.f. Perdition, destruction, wreck; *navire en ~*, ship in distress; sinking ship; *âme en ~*, soul in danger of ruin, on the road to damnation.
perdre (pɛrdr), v.a. [L *perdere*] To lose, to be deprived of, to waste, to mislead, to be the ruin of, to destroy, to corrupt, to spoil, to get rid of; (naut.) to carry away; *~ ses forces*, to lose one's strength; *~ du* (or *son*) *sang*, to lose blood; *~ la santé*, to lose one's health; *~ patience*, to lose patience, *~ l'équilibre*, to lose one's balance; *courir à ~ haleine*, to tear along; to run till one is out of breath; *~ la tête*, *~ la carte*, *~ le nord*, to lose one's wits; to become confused, bewildered; *y ~ son latin*, to be at one's wit's end; *~ le fil de son discours*, to stop short, to be nonplussed, to lose the thread of one's discourse; *~ X de réputation*, to defame X, to ruin X's reputation; *~ de vue*, to lose sight of; *il y a longtemps que je l'ai perdu de vue*, it 's quite a long time since I heard of him; *le jeu le perdra*, gambling will be the ruin of him; *~ pied*, to get out of one's depth; *~ du terrain*, to lose ground; to give way; *~ un pari*, to lose a wager; **~**, v.n. to lose, to be a loser, to deteriorate, to fall, to fail; *jouer à qui perd gagne*, to play a losing game; (naut.) to ebb; **se ~**, v.pr. to lose one's way, to get lost; to disappear; to vanish; to blend; to spoil, to be wasted, disused; *cet usage se perd*, this custom is falling into disuse; to ruin oneself, to be ruined; to lower oneself; to go to perdition; *je m'y perds*, I cannot make head or tail of it; it beats me; I am bewildered; (naut.) *se ~ corps et biens*, to founder with all hands.
perdreau (pl. **-x**) (pɛrdro), s.m. Young partridge.
perdrix (pɛrdri), s.f. [L *perdix*] (ornith.) Partridge; *une couple de ~*, a brace of partridges; *~ rouge*, red-legged partridge; *œil-de-~*, s.m. (*a*) soft corn; (*b*) huckaback (material).
perdu, -e (pɛrdy), p. adj. Lost, ruined, undone, dead, destroyed, doomed, spoiled, wasted; invisible; forlorn, stray; *à corps ~*, headlong, desperately; *à vos moments ~s*, in your spare time; *crier, courir comme un ~*, to shout, to run, like mad; *sentinelle ~e*, advanced sentry; *pour un de ~ dix de retrouvés*, there 's as good fish in the sea as ever came out of it; *salle des pas ~s*, outer hall, waiting-hall; *placer de l'argent à fonds ~*, to sink one's money in an annuity; *pays ~*, out-of-the-way place.
père (pɛr), s.m. [L *pater*] Father, sire, parent; (pl.) forefathers; old or senior fellow; creator, inventor; *beau-père*, father-in-law, stepfather; *~ nourricier*, foster-father; *le ~ Smith*, old Smith; *tel ~ tel fils*, like father like son; *de ~ en fils*, from father to son; *on ne peut contenter tout le monde et son ~*, one cannot please all the world and his wife.
pérégrin, -e (peregrɛ̃), adj. (obs.) [L *peregrinus*] Peregrine, wandering.
pérégrination (peregrina'sjɔ̃), s.f. Peregrination, wandering.
péremption (perɑ̃psjɔ̃), s.f. (law) Nonsuit; limitation.
péremptoire (perɑ̃ptwar), adj. (law) That precludes all debate; decisive; peremptory; *d'un ton ~*, peremptorily.
péremptoirement (perɑ̃ptwarmɑ̃), adv. Peremptorily.
pérennité (perɛnite), s.f. [f. L *perennis*] Perenniality.
péréquation (perekwa'sjɔ̃), s.f. [L *peraequatio*] Equal distribution; equalization; increasing in due proportion; making proportional, putting on an equal basis; adjusting (retiring pensions, &c.).
perfectibilité (pɛrfɛktibilite), s.f. Perfectibility.
perfectible (pɛrfɛktibl), adj. Perfectible.
perfection (pɛrfɛksjɔ̃), s.f. [L *perfectio*] Perfection, completeness; completion; *à la ~*, to perfection; *~s*, qualities, virtues.
perfectionnement (pɛrfɛksjɔnmɑ̃), s.m. Improvement; finishing.
perfectionner (pɛrfɛksjɔne), v.a. To bring to perfection, to improve, to improve upon; **se ~**, v.pr. to improve oneself, to improve; to perfect oneself.
perfide (pɛrfid), adj. [L *perfidus*] Perfidious, treacherous. **~**, s.m.f. Traitor, (fem.) traitress.
perfidement (pɛrfidmɑ̃), adv. Perfidiously, falsely, treacherously.
perfidie (pɛrfidi), s.f. Perfidy, treachery, act of perfidy.
perfolié, -e (pɛrfɔlje), adj. [f. L *folium*] (bot.) Perfoliate.
perforant, -e (pɛrfɔrɑ̃), p. adj. Perforating, perforative.
perforat-eur, -rice (pɛrfɔratœr), adj. Perforative. **~rice**, s.f. Perforating-machine.
perforation (pɛrfɔra'sjɔ̃), s.f. Perforation.
perforer (pɛrfɔre), v.a. [L *perforare*] To perforate, to bore.
performance (pɛrfɔrmɑ̃s), s.f. [Engl. wd] Performance (of race-horse, &c.).
pergola (pɛrgɔla), s.f. [It. wd] Pergola.
péri (peri), s.m.f. [Pers. wd] Peri, fairy, genius.
périanthe (perjɑ̃t), s.m. [Gr. *peri*+*anthos*] (bot.) Perianth.
péricarde (perikard), s.m. [Gr. *peri*+ *kardia*] (anat.) Pericardium.

péricarpe (perikarp), s.m. (bot.) Pericarp, seed-vessel.
péricliter (periklite), v.n. [L *periclitare*] To be in jeopardy, to threaten to fall, to go to ruin.
péridot (perido), s.m. [etym. dub.] (min.) Peridot, chrysolite.
périgée (periʒe), s.m. [Gr. *peri+gē*] (astr.) Perigee.
périgourdin, -e (perigurdɛ̃), adj. s.m.f. (Native) of Perigord.
périhélie (perieli), s.m. [Gr. *peri+hēlios*] Perihelion.
péril (peril), s.m. [L *periculum*] Peril, danger, hazard, jeopardy, risk; *être en ~ de*, to be in danger of; *mettre en ~*, to put in jeopardy, to endanger; *au ~ de sa vie*, at his peril, at the risk (or hazard) of his life; *faire cela à ses risques et ~s*, to take all the risks of it; to do it at one's peril; *il n'y a pas ~ en la demeure*, there is no need to hurry.
périlleusement (perijøzmɑ̃), adv. Perilously.
périlleu-x, -se (perijø), adj. Perilous, hazardous, risky.
périmer (perime), v.n. [L *perimere*] To be barred by limitation, to pass out of date, to lapse; (fig.) to abolish.
périmètre (perimɛtr), s.m. [Gr. *peri+metron*] Perimeter.
périnéal, -e, (aux) (perineal), adj. (anat.) Perineal.
périnée (perine), s.m. [Gr. *perineos*] (anat.) Perineum.
période (perjɔd), s.f. [Gr. *periodos*] Period; (gram., mus.) period; ~, s.m. pitch; turning; acme.
périodicité (perjɔdisite), s.f. Periodicity.
périodique (perjɔdik), adj. Periodic, periodical; (arith.) recurring; circulating. ~, s.m. Periodical, newspaper, magazine, &c.
périodiquement (perjɔdikmɑ̃), adv. Periodically.
périoste (perjɔst), s.m. [Gr. *peri+osteon*] (anat.) Periosteum.
périostite (perjɔstit), s.f. (pathol.) Periostitis.
péripatéticien, -ne (peripatetisjɛ̃), adj. s.m.f. [f. Gr. *peripatētikos*] Peripatetic.
péripatétisme (peripatetism), s.m. Peripateticism.
péripétie (peripesi), s.f. [Gr. *peripeteia*] Peripeteia, sudden turn of fortune, vicissitude.
périphérie (periferi), s.f. [f. Gr. *peri+pherein*] Periphery.
périphérique (periferik), adj. Peripheral.
périphrase (perifrɑz), s.f. [f. Gr. *peri+phrazein*] Periphrase, periphrasis, roundabout way of speaking.
périphraser (perifrɑze), v.n. To periphrase, to speak or write periphrastically.
périple (peripl), s.m. [Gr. *periplous*] Periplus.
périptère (periptɛr), s.m. [Gr. *peri+pteron*] Peripter. ~, adj. Peripteral.
périr (perir), v.n. (always takes the auxiliary *avoir*) [L *perire*] To perish, to die, to be wrecked, ruined, lost; to be destroyed; (law) to lapse; *faire ~*, to put to death; *~ de froid*, to perish with cold; *~ d'ennui*, to be bored to death.
périsciens (perisjɛ̃), s.m.pl. [f. Gr. *peri+skia*] Periscians, periscii.
périscope (periskɔp), s.m. [f. Gr. *peri+skopein*] Periscope.
périsperme (perispɛrm), s.m. (bot.) Perisperm.
périssable (perisabl), adj. Perishable; *denrées ~s*, perishable foodstuffs.
périssoire (periswar), s.f. [f. *périr*] Kind of canoe.
péristaltique (peristaltik), adj. [f. Gr. *peri+stellein*] (physiol.) Peristaltic.
péristyle (peristil), s.m. [f. Gr. *peri+stulos*] Peristyle.
périsystole (perisistɔl), s.f. (med.) Perisystole.
péritoine (peritwan), s.m. [Gr. *peritonaion*] (anat.) Peritoneum.
péritonite (peritɔnit), s.f. (pathol.) Peritonitis.
perle (pɛrl), s.f. [etym. dub., f. LL *pirula*?] Pearl, bead; (fig.) cream, best, jewel; *~ fine*, real pearl; *~ en tube*, bugle; *nous ne sommes pas ici pour enfiler des ~s*, we are not here to trifle our time away; *c'est la ~ des maris*, he is the best of husbands.
perlé, -e (pɛrle), p. adj. **1.** Pearled, adorned with pearls; **2.** pearly; **3.** finished to perfection; brilliantly executed; **4.** *orge ~*, pearl-barley.
perler (pɛrle), v.a. To bead, to adorn with pearls; to pearl (barley); to finish to perfection, to execute brilliantly; ~, v.n. to pearl, to drop, to glisten; *la sueur lui perlait au front*, sweat stood in drops on his forehead.
perli-er, -ère (pɛrlje), adj. Pearl-bearing; *huître ~ère*, pearl oyster.
perlimpinpin (pɛrlɛ̃pɛ̃pɛ̃), s.m. *Poudre de ~*, quack powder, charlatan's nostrum.
perlot (pɛrlo), s.m. (colloq.) Tobacco, (vulg.) baccy.
permanence (pɛrmanɑ̃s), s.f. Permanence, permanency; *en ~*, permanently, holding permanent sittings.
permanent, -e (pɛrmanɑ̃), adj. [L *permanens*] Permanent, standing; *armée ~e*, standing army.
permanganate (pɛrmɑ̃ganat), s.m. (chem.) Permanganate.
perme (pɛrm), s.f. [abbrev. of *permission*] (mil. slang) Leave, furlough.
perméabilité (pɛrmeabilite), s.f. Permeability.

perméable (pɛrmeabl), adj. [f. L *permeare*] Permeable.
permettre (pɛrmɛtr), v.a. [L *permittere*] To allow, to permit, to let, to authorize; to suffer, to put up with; to enable, to afford room for or the possibility of; *permettez!*, allow me!; wait a bit!; *permettez-moi de*, allow me to ; **se ~**, v.pr. to indulge in, to allow oneself; to be suffered or tolerated.
permis (pɛrmi), s.m. Permit, licence, pass, permission; ~ *de chasse*, shooting-licence.
permission (pɛrmisjɔ̃), s.f. Permission, leave; leave of absence; *avec votre* ~, with your leave.
permissionnaire (pɛrmisjɔnɛr), s.m.f. Permittee; soldier (or schoolboy, schoolgirl) on leave.
permixtion (pɛrmikstjɔ̃), s.f. Permixtion.
permutable (pɛrmytabl), adj. Permutable.
permutant, -e (pɛrmytɑ̃), s.m.f. Permuter.
permutation (pɛrmyta'sjɔ̃), s.f. Permutation, exchange; (math.) permutation.
permuter (pɛrmyte), v.n. [L *per+mutare*] To permute, to exchange one's post or function with another.
pernicieusement (pɛrnisjøzmɑ̃), adv. Perniciously.
pernicieu-x, -se (pɛrnisjø), adj. [f. L *pernicies*] Pernicious, hurtful, noxious, injurious; nefarious.
péroné (perɔne), s.m. [Gr. wd] (anat.) Fibula, perone.
péronnelle (perɔnɛl), s.f. [f. L *Petronilla*] Hussy, silly wench, saucy baggage.
péroraison (perɔrɛzɔ̃), s.f. [L *peroratio*] Peroration.
pérorer (perɔre), v.n. [L *perorare*] To perorate, to speechify, (fam.) to spout, to jaw, to gas.
péroreu-r, -se (perɔrœr), s.m.f. Speechifier, spouter, gasser.
pérot (pero), s.m. [f. *père*] Sapling (left after two thinnings-out of growing trees).
peroxyde (perɔksid), s.m. (chem.) Peroxide.
peroxyder (perɔkside), v.a. (chem.) To peroxidize.
perpendiculaire (pɛrpɑ̃dikylɛr), adj. s.f. [f. L *per+pendere*] Perpendicular, normal; *abaisser une* ~, to let fall a perpendicular; *élever une* ~, to raise a perpendicular; syn. NORMALE.
perpendiculairement (pɛrpɑ̃dikylɛrmɑ̃), adv. Perpendicularly.
perpendicularité (pɛrpɑ̃dikylarite), s.f. Perpendicularity.
perpendicule (pɛrpɑ̃dikyl), s.m. Plumb-line; syn. FIL-À-PLOMB.
perpétration (pɛrpetra'sjɔ̃), s.f. Perpetration, committing.
perpétrer (pɛrpetre), v.a. [L *perpetrare*] To perpetrate, to commit.
perpétuation (pɛrpetɥa'sjɔ̃), s.f. Perpetuation.
perpétuel, -le (pɛrpetɥɛl), adj. Perpetual, permanent; for life, life-; endless.
perpétuellement (pɛrpetɥɛlmɑ̃), adv. Perpetually, endlessly, everlastingly.
perpétuer (pɛrpetɥe), v.a. [L *perpetuare*] To perpetuate.
perpétuité (pɛrpetɥite), s.f. Perpetuity; *à* ~, for ever; for life; *travaux forcés à* ~, penal servitude for life.
perpignan (pɛrpiɲɑ̃), s.m. [f. *Perpignan*, town] Rod or handle of a whip; (by ext.) carter's whip.
perplexe (pɛrplɛks), adj. [L *perplexus*] Perplexed, irresolute, puzzled.
perplexité (pɛrplɛksite), s.f. Perplexity, bewilderment.
perquisition (pɛrkizisjɔ̃), s.f. [L *perquisitio*] Investigation, search; (law) search; *lancer un mandat de* ~, to issue a search-warrant.
perquisitionner (pɛrkizisjɔne), v.n. To search, to make a search; ~ *dans un appartement*, to search a flat.
perré (pɛre), s.m. [f. *pierre*] Stone facing to an earth wall.
perrière (pɛrjɛr), s.f. (obs.) (artill.) Swivel-gun, perrier.
perron (pɛrɔ̃), s.m. [f. *pierre*] Perron; flight of stone steps before a house.
perroquet (pɛrɔkɛ), s.m. [Span. *periquito*, It. *parrochetto*] **1.** Parrot; *réciter comme un* ~, to parrot, to talk like a parrot; **2.** (naut.) topgallant sail; *grand* ~, main topgallant sail; *petit* ~, fore topgallant sail; ~ *volant*, royal sail.
perruche (pɛryʃ), s.f. **1.** Hen-parrot; **2.** parakeet; **3.** (naut.) mizzen topgallant sail.
perruque (pɛryk), s.f. [It. *perruca*] Wig, periwig, peruke; (fig.) *vieille* ~, *tête à* ~, old fogy.
perruqui-er, -ère (pɛrykje), s.m.f. Wigmaker, peruke-maker, hairdresser, barber.
pers, -e (pɛr), adj. [orig. dub.] Bluish-green, perse; *la déesse aux yeux* ~, Minerva.
persan, -e (pɛrsɑ̃), adj. s.m.f. Persian.
perse (pɛrs), s.f. [f. *Perse*, Persia] Unglazed chintz, heavy cretonne.
perse (pɛrs), adj. s.m.f. Persian (*perse* is used instead of *persan* in reference to ancient Persia; ex. *les rois perses*).
persécutant, -e (pɛrsekytɑ̃), p. adj. Tiresome, annoying, importunate.
persécuter (pɛrsekyte), v.a. [f. L *persequi*] To persecute, to harass, to torment; to importune, to annoy; to bore; to dun.
persécut-eur, -rice (pɛrsekytœr), s.m.f. Persecutor, tormentor.

persécution (pɛrsekysjɔ̃), s.f. Persecution, annoyance, tormenting.
persévéramment (pɛrseveramɑ̃), adv. Perseveringly.
persévérance (pɛrseverɑ̃s), s.f. Perseverance, steadiness, persistence, constancy.
persévérant, -e (pɛrseverɑ̃), p. adj. Persevering, perseverant, persistent, steady, steadfast.
persévérer (pɛrsevere), v.n. [L *perseverare*] To persevere, to persist, to hold on, to continue steadfastly.
persicaire (pɛrsikɛr), s.f. [f. L *persicus*] (bot.) Persicaria, peachwort.
persienne (pɛrsjɛn), s.f. [f. *Perse*] Venetian shutter, louvre-shutter, persienne, outside wooden or iron window-blinds.
persiflage (pɛrsiflaʒ), s.m. Quizzing, banter, chaff, chaffing, persiflage.
persifler (pɛrsifle), v.a. [f. *siffler*] To quiz, to rally, to chaff, to banter, to mock.
persifleu-r, -se (pɛrsiflœr), s.m.f. Quiz, chaffer, banterer. **~**, adj. Quizzing, mocking.
persil (pɛrsi), s.m. [L *petroselinum*] (bot.) Parsley.
persillade (pɛrsijad), s.f. **1.** (cook.) Seasoning made of oil, vinegar, and chopped parsley; **2.** (by ext.) a dish, usually cold beef, seasoned with *persillade*.
persillé, -e (pɛrsije), adj. Green-spotted (cheese); spotted with fat (meat).
persique (pɛrsik), adj. Persian, of ancient Persia; *le golfe Persique*, the Persian Gulf.
persistance (pɛrsistɑ̃s), s.f. Persistence, persistency; persisting.
persistant, -e (pɛrsistɑ̃), p. adj. Persistent, persisting.
persister (pɛrsiste), v.n. [L *persistere*] To persist, to hold out, to maintain one's opinion, to continue; to last.
personnage (pɛrsɔnaʒ), s.m. Personage, person, great person, somebody; individual, fellow; *un grossier ~!*, an ill-mannered fellow; character, dramatis persona.
personnalité (pɛrsɔnalite), s.f. Personality, individuality, personal character; personage, important person; (obs.) egoism.
personne[1] (pɛrsɔn), s.f. [L *persona*] Person, one's person, individual, body, external appearance; (gram.) person; *payer de sa ~*, not to spare oneself; *c'est la bonté en ~*, she (or he) is kindness itself; *j'irai en ~*, I will go in person; *il soigne sa petite ~*, he looks after number one; *jeune ~*, young girl, young lady; *sans acception de ~*, without respect of persons.
personne[2] (pɛrsɔn), indef. pron. m. sing. Any one, anybody; no one, nobody; *~ n'est parfait*, nobody is perfect; *je doute que ~ vienne*, I doubt whether anybody will come; *je n'ai trouvé ~*, I found nobody at home; nobody was there.
personnel, -le (pɛrsɔnɛl), adj. Personal; (obs. sense) egoistic; *pronom ~*, personal pronoun. **~**, s.m. Staff (of servants, officials, &c.), personnel, hands.
personnellement (pɛrsɔnɛlmɑ̃), adv. Personally, in person.
personnification (pɛrsɔnifika'sjɔ̃), s.f. Personification.
personnifier (pɛrsɔnifje), v.a. To personify, to impersonate.
perspecti-f, -ve (pɛrspɛktif), adj. [f. L *perspicere*] Perspective. **~ve**, s.f. Perspective, view, vista, prospect; expectation; *avoir la ~ d'un bel avenir*, to have the prospect of a successful career; *en ~*, in the distance; in expectation.
perspicace (pɛrspikas), adj. [L *perspicax*] Perspicacious, shrewd.
perspicacité (pɛrspikasite), s.f. Perspicacity, shrewdness.
perspicuité (pɛrspikɥite), s.f. (obs.) Perspicuity.
perspirable (pɛrspirabl), adj. Perspirable.
perspiration (pɛrspira'sjɔ̃), s.f. (med.) Insensible perspiration. ⚠ Note that 'perspiration' in English = *transpiration* in French.
persuader (pɛrsɥade), v.a. [L *persuadere*] To persuade, to convince, to induce, to satisfy; **se ~**, v.pr. to persuade oneself, to be persuaded, to imagine, to get into one's mind, to be of opinion; to persuade each other.
persuasi-f, -ve (pɛrsɥazif), adj. Persuasive, convincing.
persuasion (pɛrsɥazjɔ̃), s.f. Persuasion, conviction, belief; persuading, persuasiveness.
persuasivement (pɛrsɥazivmɑ̃), adv. Persuasively, convincingly.
perte (pɛrt), s.f. [f. L *perdita*] Loss, privation, ruin, fall, wreck; waste; perdition; leak, escape; (med.) flooding; *à ~ de vue*, as far as the eye can reach; *à ~*, at a loss; *être en ~*, to be a loser; *en pure ~*, uselessly, to no purpose; *à ~ d'haleine*, out of breath (see PERDRE); *profits et ~s*, profit and loss; *~ sèche*, dead loss; *vendre à ~*, to sell at a loss.
pertinacité (pɛrtinasite), s.f. [f. L *pertinax*] Pertinacity.
pertinemment (pɛrtinamɑ̃), adv. Pertinently.
pertinence (pɛrtinɑ̃s), s.f. Pertinence, pertinency.
pertinent, -e (pɛrtinɑ̃), adj. [L *pertinens*] Pertinent.
pertuis (pɛrtɥi), s.m. [f. L *pertusus*] Opening, sluice, hole; (geog.) straits; pass (in the Jura).
pertuisane (pɛrtɥizan), s.f. [It. *partegiana*] Partisan, halberd.

perturbat-eur, -rice (pɛrtyrbatœr), s.m.f. Disturber, perturber, agitator. ~, adj. Disturbing.
perturbation (pɛrtyrba'sjɔ̃), s.f. Disturbance, perturbation.
perturber (pɛrtyrbe), v.a. [L *perturbare*] To disturb, to perturb.
péruvien, -ne (peryvjɛ̃), adj. s.m.f. Peruvian.
pervenche (pɛrvɑ̃ʃ), s.f. [L *pervinca*] (bot.) Periwinkle.
pervers, -e (pɛrvɛr), adj. [L *perversus*] Perverse, froward, obstinate in the wrong, depraved, wicked. ⚠ In French the sense of *pervers* is chiefly: depraved, wicked; it is more precise and more pejorative than English 'perverse', which often means obstinate, fickle, contrary, cross-grained, &c. = *contrariant, capricieux, entêté, difficultueux, déraisonnable.*
perversion (pɛrvɛrsjɔ̃), s.f. Perversion.
perversité (pɛrvɛrsite), s.f. Perversity, perverseness. ⚠ See PERVERS.
pervertir (pɛrvɛrtir), v.a. [L *pervertere*] To pervert, to lead astray, to corrupt, to deprave; **se** ~, v.pr. to get corrupted, to be perverted.
pervertissable (pɛrvɛrtisabl), adj. Pervertible.
pervertisseu-r, -se (pɛrvɛrtisœr), adj. Perverting. ~, s.m.f. Corrupter, perverter.
pesade (pəsad), s.f. [f. It. *posata*] (rid.) Pesade, rearing.
pesage (pəzaʒ), s.m. **1.** Weighing; **2.** (turf) weighing-paddock, paddock.
pesamment (pəzamɑ̃), adv. Heavily; (fig.) ponderously, clumsily.
pesant, -e (pəzɑ̃), p. adj. Heavy, weighty, weighing; ponderous, clumsy, burdensome, sluggish, slow. ~, s.m. Weight; *il vaut son ~ d'or*, he is worth his weight in gold.
pesanteur (pəzɑ̃tœr), s.f. Weight, heaviness, dullness, sluggishness, ponderousness; (phys.) gravity, gravitation; *lois de la ~*, laws of gravitation.
pèse (pɛz), s.m. invar. (in comps.:) *~-acide*, acidimeter; *~-lait*, lactometer; *~-lettre*, letter-scales; *~-liqueur*, alcoholometer, &c.
pesée (pəze), s.f. **1.** Weighing; amount weighed at one time; **2.** pressure, bearing with weight or force on something.
peser (pəze), v.a. [L *pensare*] To weigh; (fig.) to estimate, to ponder, to weigh; *pesez bien vos paroles*, weigh your words carefully; to exert pressure, to bear with weight or force; to be heavy, to lie heavy, to lay stress, to dwell; *cela vous pèse sur le cœur*, that lies heavy upon your heart; **se** ~, v.pr. to weigh oneself, to be weighted.
pesette (pəzɛt), s.f. Assay-scales.
peseu-r, -se (pəzœr), s.m.f. Weigher.
peson (pəzɔ̃), s.m. Spring-balance; steelyard.
pessaire (pɛsɛr), s.m. [LL *pessarium*] Pessary.
pesse (pɛs), s.f. **pessereau** (pɛsro), s.m. (bot.) Mare's-tail, *Equisetum.*
pessimisme (pɛsimism), s.m. [f. L *pessimus*] Pessimism.
pessimiste (pɛsimist), s.m.f. Pessimist. ~, adj. Pessimistic.
peste (pɛst), s.f. [L *pestis*] Pestilence, plague, scourge; (fig.) pest, torment, nuisance, bore; ~ *noire*, Black Death; *la ~ soit de X !*, a plague upon X!; *~ !*, bless me! (interj. which often expresses admiration or envy).
pester (pɛste), v.n. To storm, to fret and fume, to inveigh, to curse and swear, to grumble.
pestifère (pɛstifɛr), adj. [f. L *pestis*+*ferre*] Pestiferous.
pestiféré, -e (pɛstifere), adj. Plague-stricken; pestiferous. ~, s.m.f. Person infected with the plague.
pestilence (pɛstilɑ̃s), s.f. Pestilence; (fig.) corruption.
pestilent, -e (pɛstilɑ̃), adj. Pestilent.
pestilentiel, -le (pɛstilɑ̃sjɛl), adj. Pestilential.
pet (pɛ), s.m. [L *peditus*] Fart; (pastry) ~ *de nonne*, fritter; (colloq.) *un ~-en-l'air*, a bum-freezer, a short jacket.
pétale (petal), s.m. [Gr. *petalon*] Petal.
pétalisme (petalism), s.m. [Gr. *petalismos*] (ant.) Petalism, form of ostracism.
pétarade (petarad), s.f. [f. *pet*] (indecent) Farting; cracking, noise of crackers; useless cannonade; fireworks.
pétard (petar), s.m. [f. *péter*] Petard; cracker; (colloq.) *faire du ~*, to protest vehemently, to kick up a row.
pétarder (petarde), v.a. To blow up with a petard.
pétardier (petardje), s.m. Petardier.
pétase (petɑz), s.m. [Gr. *petasos*] Petasus.
pétaudière (petodjɛr), s.f. [f. *roi Pétaud*] Disorderly, noisy assembly; bear garden; Bedlam broken loose.
pet-en-l'air (pɛtɑ̃lɛr), s.m. (vulg.) Bum-freezer; short morning jacket (to be worn in the bedroom).
péter (pete), v.n. (indecent) To fart, to break wind; to crackle, to crack, to make a loud report, to snap, to explode; ~ *dans la main*, to fail, to come to nothing; (colloq.) *un pète-sec*, a man with dry, sharp ways.
péteux (petø), s.m. (vulg.) Farter; (colloq.) sorry fellow, wretch.
pétillant, -e (petijɑ̃), p. adj. Crackling; (lit. and fig.) sparkling.
pétillement (petijmɑ̃), s.m. Crackling; sparkling.
pétiller (petije), v.n. [f. *péter*] To crackle, to sparkle; *ses yeux pétillent*, his eyes are

sparkling; ~ *d'impatience*, to boil with impatience, to be all eagerness; *ce livre pétille d'esprit*, this book sparkles with wit.

pétiole (pesjɔl), s.m. [L *petiolus*] Petiole.

pétiolé, -e (pesjɔle), adj. Petiolate.

petit, -e (pəti), adj. [orig. dub.] Small, little, diminutive, tiny, wee, short, young, junior; unimportant, slight, trifling; low, shabby, mean, humble; *être aux ~s soins pour X*, to be all attention to X; ~ *à* ~, little by little, by degrees; (prov.) ~ *à* ~ *l'oiseau fait son nid*, little strokes fell great oaks; *en* ~, on a small scale; (prov.) *~e cervelle, prompte colère*, a little pot is soon hot; *un ~ esprit*, a narrow-minded person; *le ~ peuple*, the common people; *se faire ~ devant X*, to abase oneself before X; *~e-fille*, grand-daughter; *~-fils*, grandson; *~-gris*, miniver, Siberian squirrel; *~-lait*, whey; *~-maître*, dandy, fop, beau; *~-neveu*, grand-nephew; *~e-nièce*, grand-niece; *~s-enfants*, grand-children. ~, s.m.f. *Les ~s de ce monde*, the poor, the humble; *faire des ~s*, to bring forth young ones, to multiply; to breed, to pup, to kitten, to farrow, &c.; *les ~s*, (at school) the juniors.

petitement (pətitmɑ̃), adv. In small quantity; poorly; meanly.

petitesse (pətitɛs), s.f. **1.** Smallness, littleness, shortness; lowness, insignificance; **2.** meanness, piece of meanness; ~ *d'esprit*, narrowness of mind, narrow-mindedness.

pétition (petisjɔ̃), s.f. [L *petitio*] Petition, request; ~ *de principe*, petitio principii.

pétitionnaire (petisjɔnɛr), s.m.f. Petitioner.

petitionnement (petisjɔnmɑ̃), s.m. Petition, petitioning.

pétitionner (petisjɔne), v.n. To petition.

pétitoire (petitwar), adj. [L *petitorius*] (law) Petitory. ~, s.m. Claim of ownership.

peton (pətɔ̃), s.m. [f. *pied*] (colloq.) Tiny foot.

pétoncle (petɔ̃kl), s.m. [L *pectunculus*] (zool.) Scallop, shell-fish.

pétré, -e (petre), adj. [f. L *petra*] (geog.) Stony; *Arabie ~e*, Arabia Petraea.

pétrel (petrɛl), s.m. (ornith.) Petrel, storm-petrel, stormy petrel.

pétreu-x, -se (petrø), adj. [f. L *petra*] Stony, rocky, stonelike.

pétri, -e (petri), p. adj. Kneaded; (fig.) full; ~ *d'esprit*, full of wit.

pétrifiant, -e (petrifjɑ̃), p. adj. Petrifying, petrifactive.

pétrification (petrifika'sjɔ̃), s.f. Petrifaction, petrification.

pétrifier (petrifje), v.a. [f. L *petra+facere*] To petrify, to turn into stone, to stupefy; *pétrifié de crainte*, petrified with fear.

pétrin (petrɛ̃), s.m. [L *pistrinum*] Kneading-trough; (fig.) scrape, hot water, mess, fix; *il s'est mis dans le ~*, he has put himself in a fix, he has got himself into a scrape.

pétrir (petrir), v.a. [LL *pistrire*] To knead; (fig.) to form, to mould.

pétrissage (petrisaʒ), s.m. Kneading.

pétrisseu-r, -se (petrisœr), s.m.f. adj. Kneader; **~se**, s.f. kneading-machine.

pétrole (petrɔl), s.m. [f. L *petra+oleum*] Petroleum; paraffin oil, paraffin. ⚠ Not 'petrol', which = *essence* (for motors, &c.).

pétroler (petrɔle), v.a. To set fire to by means of petroleum.

pétrolerie (petrɔlri), s.f. Petroleum-works.

pétroleu-r, -se (petrɔlœr), s.m.f. Incendiary (using petroleum).

pétroli-er, -ère (petrɔlje), adj. Petroleum-; pertaining to petroleum; *navire ~*, petroleum ship, oil-tanker.

pétrolifère (petrɔlifɛr), adj. Petroliferous.

pétulance (petylɑ̃s), s.f. Petulance, petulancy, sprightliness, sauciness.

pétulant, -e (petylɑ̃), adj. [L *petulantem*] Petulant, saucy, sprightly.

petun (pətœ̃), s.m. (obs.) [Brazil. wd] Tobacco, snuff.

pétuner (petyne), v.n. (obs.) To smoke; to take snuff.

pétunia (petynja), s.m. (bot.) Petunia.

pétunsé (petœ̃se), s.m. [Chinese wd] Petuntse, China-stone.

peu (pø), adv. [L *paucus*] Little, not much; few, not many; not very; *à ~ près*, *à ~ de chose près*, about; nearly; *d'ici ~*, *sous ~*, in a few days; shortly; before long; *depuis ~*, lately; not long ago; recently; a little while ago; ~ *à* ~, by degrees; little by little; by little and little; *quelque ~*, somewhat; *tant soit ~*, ever so little; *pour ~ que*, if . . . only; if . . . ever so little; if . . . in the least; *si ~ que*, however, how . . . soever; *si ~ que rien*, a mere nothing; *très ~*, *fort ~*, *bien ~*, very little; ~ *aimable*, not too amiable; ~ *de livres*, few books; *parler ~*, to speak little; ~ *ou prou*, little or much; *vivre de ~*, to live on next to nothing; *homme de ~*, a common sort of man; low-class man; *se contenter de ~*, to be content with little. ~, s.m. Little, bit, few; *attendez un ~*, wait a bit; *encore un ~*, a little longer; a little more; (iron.) *excusez du ~*, how modest!; *un petit ~*, a little bit, a little while; *un ~ mieux*, a little better; *le ~ qu'il sait*, the little he knows.

peulven (pølvɛn), s.m. [Bret. wd] Menhir.

peuplade (pœplad), s.f. Tribe, horde, colony, people.

peuple (pœpl), s.m. [L *populus*] People, nation, tribe, race; population, common people, crowd, lower classes; working classes; *le bas* ~, the rabble, the mob; *un grand concours de* ~, a great crowd. ~, adj. Vulgar, common.

peuplement (pœpləmɑ̃), s.m. Peopling; stocking (of a poultry-yard, pond, &c.).

peupler (pœple), v.a. To people; to stock (with animals); to populate, to furnish with settlers; ~, v.n. to multiply, to breed.

peuplier (pœplje), s.m. [L *populus*] (bot.) Poplar.

peur (pœr), s.f. [L *pavor*] Fear, fright, dread, terror; *avoir* ~, to be afraid; (slang) to be funky; *avoir grand'*~, to be in great fear; (slang) to have the wind up; to be in a blue funk; *à faire* ~, frightful, frightfully; *faire* ~ *à X*, to frighten X; (slang) to put the wind up X; *mourir de* ~, to die of fright; (fig.) to be frightened to death; *en être quitte pour la* ~, to come off with nothing worse than a fright; *avoir* ~ *de son ombre*, to be afraid of one's shadow, to be afraid of everything; *avoir plus de* ~ *que de mal*, to be more frightened than hurt; *de* ~ *de*, for fear of; *de* ~ *que*, lest, for fear that; *sans* ~, fearless; fearlessly.

peureusement (pœrøzmɑ̃), adv. Fearfully, timorously, cowardly.

peureu-x, -se (pœrø), adj. Fearful, timorous, timid, shy, easily frightened, funky. ~, s.m.f. Trembler, coward, poltroon.

peut-être (pøtɛtr), adv. Maybe, perhaps, perchance, possibly, peradventure.

pèze (pɛz), s.m. (slang) Money, rhino.

phaéton (faetɔ̃), s.m. [f. *Phaeton*, myth. n.] **1.** (iron.) Driver, coachman; **2.** phaeton (a light four-wheeled carriage).

phagocyte (fagɔsit), s.m. [Gr. *phagein*+ *kutos*] Phagocyte.

phagocytose (fagɔsitoz), s.f. Phagocytosis.

phalange (falɑ̃ʒ), s.f. [Gr. *phalagx*] **1.** Phalanx; army, host; **2.** (anat.) phalanx.

phalanger (falɑ̃ʒe), s.m. (zool.) Phalanger.

phalangette (falɑ̃ʒɛt), s.f. (anat.) Third phalanx.

phalangien, -ne (falɑ̃ʒjɛ̃), adj. Of the phalanx.

phalangine (falɑ̃ʒin), s.f. (anat.) Second phalanx.

phalanstère (falɑ̃stɛr), s.m. [word coined by Fourier, 1772–1837] Phalanstery.

phalanstérien, -ne (falɑ̃sterjɛ̃), adj. Phalansterian.

phalène (falɛn), s.f. (ent.) Phalæna, moth.

phallique (falik), adj. Phallic.

phallus (falys), s.m. [Gr. *phallos*] Phallus.

phanérogame (fanerɔgam), adj. [Gr. *phaneros*+*gamos*] (bot.) Phanerogamous. ~, s.f. Phanerogamous plant, phanerogam.

pharamineu-x, -se (faraminø), adj. Stupendous, amazing, astounding; immense.

pharaon (faraɔ̃), s.m. **1.** Pharaoh; **2.** faro (card-game).

pharaonique (faraɔnik), adj. Pharaonic.

phare (far), s.m. [f. Gr. *Pharos*, n. of an island] Lighthouse; phare; beacon; (motor.) headlight; search-light; (fig.) guide.

pharillon (farijɔ̃), s.m. Small lighthouse; fire-pan used for fishing at night; fishing with this.

pharisaïque (farizaik), adj. Pharisaic, pharisaical, hypocritical.

pharisaïsme (farizaism), s.m. Pharisaism.

pharisien, -ne (farizjɛ̃), s.m.f. Pharisee; self-righteous person.

pharmaceutique (farmasøtik), adj. Pharmaceutical. ~, s.f. Pharmaceutics.

pharmacie (farmasi), s.f. [f. Gr. *pharmakon*] Pharmacy, pharmaceutics; chemist's shop, apothecary's trade, druggist's shop; dispensary; medicine-chest; drugs.

pharmacien, -ne (farmasjɛ̃), s.m.f. Chemist, druggist, apothecary; pharmaceutist, pharmacologist.

pharmacologie (farmakɔlɔʒi), s.f. Pharmacology.

pharmacologique (farmakɔlɔʒik), adj. Pharmacological.

pharmacopée (farmakɔpe), s.f. Pharmacopoeia.

pharyngien, -ne (farɛ̃ʒjɛ̃), adj. Pharyngeal.

pharyngite (farɛ̃ʒit), s.f. Pharyngitis.

pharynx (farɛ̃ks), s.m. [Gr. *pharugx*] Pharynx.

phase (fɑz), s.f. [Gr. *phasis*] Phasis (of planet); phase, aspect, stage, period, turn.

phébus (febys), s.m. [f. *Phoebus Apollo*] **1.** The sun; **2.** bombast, fustian, rant; *donner dans le* ~, to write bombast.

phénicien, -ne (fenisjɛ̃), adj. s.m.f. Phoenician.

phénique (fenik), adj. (chem.) Carbolic.

phénix (feniks), s.m. [Gr. *phoinix*] Phoenix; (fig.) phoenix; paragon; wonderful person.

phénol (fenɔl), s.m. [f. Gr. *phainein*] (chem.) Phenol; carbolic acid.

phénoménal, -e, (aux) (fenɔmenal), adj. Phenomenal; (fig.) prodigious.

phénoménalement (fenɔmenalmɑ̃), adv. Amazingly, phenomenally, prodigiously.

phénomène (fenɔmɛn), s.m. [Gr. *phainomenon*] Phenomenon; (fig.) wonder, wonderful person or event; (iron.) queer fellow; card; caution, (slang) oner.

philanthrope (filɑ̃trɔp), s.m.f. [Gr. *philos* +*anthrōpos*] Philanthropist.

philanthropie (filɑ̃trɔpi), s.f. Philanthropy.

philanthropique (filɑ̃trɔpik), adj. Philanthropic.
philatélie (filateli), s.f. [Gr. *philos*+ *ateleia*] Philately, stamp-collecting.
philatéliste (filatelist), s.m.f. Philatelist.
philharmonie (filarmɔni), s.f. [f. Gr. *philos* + (Fr.) *harmonie*] Love of, or devotion to, music.
philharmonique (filarmɔnik), adj. Philharmonic.
philhellène (filɛlɛn), s.m.f. [Gr. *philos*+ *hellēn*] Philhellene.
philippine (filipin), s.f. [f. prop. n.] Philippina.
philippique (filipik), s.f. Philippic; (fig.) bitter invective.
philistin, -e (filistɛ̃), s.m.f. Philistine.
philologie (filɔlɔʒi), s.f. [Gr. *philos*+*logos*] Philology.
philologique (filɔlɔʒik), adj. Philological.
philologue (filɔlɔg), s.m.f. Philologist, philologer.
philomathique (filɔmatik), adj. [f. Gr. *philos*+*manthanein*] Philomathic.
philomèle (filɔmɛl), s.f. [Gr. *philomēla*] Philomela; nightingale.
philosophale (filɔzɔfal), adj. *Pierre* ~, philosophers' stone.
philosophe (filɔzɔf), s.m.f. [Gr. *philos*+ *sophos*] Philosopher. ~, adj. Philosophical.
philosopher (filɔzɔfe), v.n. To philosophize.
philosophie (filɔzɔfi), s.f. [Gr. *philos*+ *sophia*] Philosophy; *prenez cela avec* ~, bear it philosophically; take it quietly.
philosophique (filɔzɔfik), adj. Philosophic, philosophical.
philosophiquement (filɔzɔfikmɑ̃), adv. Philosophically, resignedly.
philotechnique (filɔtɛknik), adj. Philotechnic.
philtre (filtr), s.m. [Gr. *philtron*] Philtre, love-potion.
phlébite (flebit), s.f. [f. Gr. *phleps*] (pathol.) Phlebitis.
phlébotomie (flebɔtɔmi), s.f. Phlebotomy.
phlegmasie (flɛgmazi), s.f. (pathol.) Phlegmasia.
phlegme (flɛgm), s.m. See FLEGME.
phlegmon (flɛgmɔ̃), s.m. [Gr. *phlegmonē*] (pathol.) Phlegmon.
phlegmoneu-x, -se (flɛgmɔnø), adj. Phlegmonous.
phlogistique (flɔʒistik), s.m. [Gr. *phlogistos*] Phlogiston.
phlox (flɔks), s.m. [Gr. *phlox*] (bot.) Phlox.
phobie (fɔbi), s.f. [f. Gr. *phobos*] Phobia.
phocéen, -ne (fɔseɛ̃), adj. s.m.f. Phocaean.
phœnix (feniks), s.m. (bot.) Phoenix, palm-tree. See PHÉNIX.
pholade (fɔlad), s.f. [f. Gr. *phōlas*] (zool.) Pholas, stone-borer.
phonation (fɔna'sjɔ̃), s.f. Phonation.
phonétique (fɔnetik), adj. [f. Gr. *phōnē*] Phonetic. ~, s.f. Phonetics.
phonétiquement (fɔnetikmɑ̃), adv. Phonetically.
phonographe, phono (fɔnɔgraf, fɔno), s.m. [f. Gr. *phōnē*+*graphein*] Phonograph, gramophone; syn. GRAMOPHONE.
phonographie (fɔnɔgrafi), s.f. Phonography.
phonographique (fɔnɔgrafik), adj. Phonographic.
phoque (fɔk), s.m. [L *phoca*] (zool.) Seal; *peau de* ~, sealskin.
phormium (fɔrmjɔm), s.m. (bot.) Phormium, New Zealand flax.
phosphate (fɔsfat), s.m. (chem.) Phosphate.
phosphaté, -e (fɔsfate), p. adj. Phosphated.
phosphène (fɔsfɛn), s.m. [f. Gr. *phōs*+ *phainein*] Phosphene.
phosphite (fɔsfit), s.m. (chem.) Phosphite.
phosphore (fɔsfɔr), s.m. [f. Gr. *phōs*+ *phoros*] (chem.) Phosphorus.
phosphoré, -e (fɔsfɔre), p. adj. Phosphorated, phosphuretted.
phosphorescence (fɔsfɔrɛssɑs), s.f. Phosphorescence.
phosphorescent, -e (fɔsfɔrɛssɑ̃), adj. Phosphorescent.
phosphoreux (fɔsfɔrø), adj. m. (chem.) Phosphorous.
phosphorique (fɔsfɔrik), adj. (chem.) Phosphoric.
phosphorite (fɔsfɔrit), s.f. Phosphorite; native phosphate of lime.
phosphure (fɔsfyr), s.m. (chem.) Phosphide, phosphuretted . . .; ~ *d'hydrogène*, phosphuretted hydrogen.
photo (fɔto), s.f. [abbrev. of *photographie*] Photo; snapshot; portrait.
photo (fɔto) (in comps.) [f. Gr. *phōs, photos*] Photo-; *photochimie*, s.f. photo-chemistry; *photochromie*, s.f. photochromy, &c.
photogénique (fɔtɔʒenik), adj. Photogenic.
photographe (fɔtɔgraf), s.m.f. Photographer.
photographie (fɔtɔgrafi), s.f. **1.** Photography; **2.** photograph, snapshot; portrait.
photographier (fɔtɔgrafje), v.a. To photograph, to take a snapshot of; *se faire* ~, to have one's photograph taken.
photographique (fɔtɔgrafik), adj. Photographic; *appareil* ~, camera.
photographiquement (fɔtɔgrafikmɑ̃), adv. Photographically.
photogravure (fɔtɔgravyr), s.f. Photo-engraving, photogravure.
photolithographie (fɔtɔlitɔgrafi), s.f. Photolithography.
photométrie (fɔtɔmetri), s.f. Photometry.
photosphère (fɔtɔsfɛr), s.f. (astr.) Photosphere.

phototypie (fototipi), s.f. Collotype.
phrase (frɑz), s.f. [Gr. *phrasis*] Phrase, sentence; ~ *musicale*, musical phrase; *sans* ~, straight out, plainly; (gram.) *membre de* ~, clause; *faire des* ~*s*, to spin fine-sounding phrases; *faiseur de* ~*s*, phrase-monger.
phraséologie (frɑzeɔlɔʒi), s.f. Phraseology.
phraser (frɑze), v.n.a. **1.** To spin fine-sounding sentences; **2.** (mus., poet.) to mark the phrases of.
phraseu-r, -se (frɑzœr), s.m.f. Phrase-monger, would-be fine speaker.
phrénologie (frenɔlɔʒi), s.f. [f. Gr. *phrēn* +*logos*] Phrenology.
phrénologiste (frenɔlɔʒist), s.m.f. **phrénologue** (frenɔlɔg), s.m. Phrenologist.
phrygane (frigan), s.f. (ent.) Phryganea.
phrygien, -ne (friʒjɛ̃), adj. s.m.f. Phrygian; *bonnet* ~, Phrygian cap.
phtisie (ftizi), s.f. [Gr. *phthisis*] Phthisis, consumption.
phtisique (ftizik), adj. s.m.f. Phthisical, consumptive (person).
phylactère (filaktɛr), s.m. [Gr. *phulaktērion*] (ant.) Phylactery, amulet, charm.
phylloxera (filɔksera), s.m. [f. Gr. *phullon* +*xēros*] (ent.) Phylloxera.
physalis (fizalis), s.m. (bot.) Physalis, winter-cherry; syn. ALKÉKENGE.
physicien, -ne (fizisjɛ̃), s.m.f. Physicist. ⚠ Note that 'physician' does not mean *physicien*, but *docteur en médecine*.
physiognomonie (fizjɔgnɔmɔni), s.f. Physiognomy, physiognomics.
physiologie (fizjɔlɔʒi), s.f. [f. Gr. *phusis*+ *logos*] Physiology.
physiologique (fizjɔlɔʒik), adj. Physiological.
physiologiste (fizjɔlɔʒist), s.m.f. Physiologist.
physionomie (fizjɔnɔmi), s.f. [f. Gr. *phusis*+*gnōmōn*] Physiognomy, countenance, appearance, look, characteristic features; face; (colloq.) phiz; *abîmer la* ~ *à*, to hit in the face.
physionomiste (fizjɔnɔmist), s.m. Physiognomist.
physique (fizik), adj. [Gr. *phusikos*] Physical, material, bodily; absolute, real. ~, s.f. Physics; ~, s.m. constitution, body, physique.
physiquement (fizikmɑ̃), adv. Physically, materially, bodily.
pi (pi), s.m. [Greek letter] Pi, π, the symbol representing the ratio of the circumference of a circle to the diameter, $= 3{\cdot}1416$.
piaculaire (pjakylɛr), adj. [L *piacularis*] Piacular, expiatory.
piaffe (pjaf), s.f. [f. *piaffer*] (colloq.) Show, ostentation, dash.
piaffement (pjafmɑ̃), s.m. Pawing the ground, prancing; (fig.) fidgeting.
piaffer (pjafe), v.n. [orig. unkn.] To paw the ground, to prance; (fig.) to fidget, to move restlessly; to make a show, to be ostentatious.
piaffeu-r, -se (pjafœr), adj. Prancing; (fig.) ostentatious.
piaillard, -e (pjɑjar), adj. Bawling, squalling.
piailler (pjɑje), v.n. [f. *pie*] To chirp shrilly; (fig.) to bawl, to squall.
piaillerie (pjɑjri), s.f. Shrill chirping; (fig.) bawling, squalling, outcry.
piailleu-r, -se (pjɑjœr), adj. Chirping. ~, s.m.f. Bawler, squaller.
piane-piane (pjanpjan), adv. [f. It. *piano*] Softly, gently.
pianino (pjanino), s.m. [It. wd] Pianette, pianino, cottage piano.
pianiste (pjanist), s.m.f. [f. *piano*] Pianist.
piano, forte-piano, pianoforte (pjano, fɔrtepjano, pjanofɔrte), s.m. [It. wds] Piano, pianoforte; ~ *droit*, upright piano; cottage piano; ~ *à queue*, grand piano; ~ *crapaud*, baby grand; ~ *mécanique*, piano-player; piano-organ; *toucher du* ~, to play the piano.
piano (pjano), adv. [It. wd] Softly, not loud; gently.
pianoter (pjanɔte), v.n. To strum, to thrum.
piastre (pjastr), s.f. [It. *piastra*] Piastre (coin).
piaulement (pjolmɑ̃), s.m. Puling, piping (of chickens, &c.); whining.
piauler (pjole), v.n. [onom.] To pule (as chickens); to whine, to whimper; to cry.
piaulis (pjoli), s.m. Puling (of birds).
(à) pible (apibl), adv. Of one piece; *mât à* ~, pole-mast.
pic[1] (pik), s.m. [L *picus*] (ornith.) Woodpecker; *pic-vert, pivert*, green woodpecker.
pic[2] (pik), s.m. [Germ. orig.] Pick, pick-axe; poker; (naut.) peak; peak, summit; (at piquet) pique; *faire* ~, to pique; *à* ~, (*a*) perpendicularly, (*b*) (naut.) apeak; (*c*) (colloq.) in the nick of time; just at the right time.
picador (pikadɔr), s.m. [Span. wd] Picador.
picaillon (pikɑjɔ̃), s.m. A small copper coin in Savoy = farthing; (fig.) money, tin; *avoir des* ~*s*, to be well off.
picard, -e (pikar), adj. s.m.f. Picard.
picaresque (pikarɛsk), adj. [f. Span. *picaro*] Picaresque.
pichenette (piʃnɛt), s.f. Fillip; syn. CHIQUENAUDE.
pichet (piʃɛ), s.m. [orig. dub., LL *becarium* ?] Jug, pitcher, mug.
picholine (piʃɔlin), s.f. Picholine (olive).
picorée (pikɔre), s.f. [f. Span. *pecorea*] Pilfering; *aller à la* ~, to go pilfering.

picorer (pikɔre), v.a.n. To peck; to pick up food; (fig.) to go pilfering, to pilfer.

picot (piko), s.m. [f. *pic*] **1.** Edging, purl (of lace), picot; **2.** small splinter (of wood); **3.** pick-hammer; **4.** (fish.) net for catching flat fish.

picoté, -e (pikɔte), p. adj. Marked; pitted; dotted, spotted; pricked.

picotement (pikɔtmɑ̃), s.m. Pricking; pins and needles.

picoter (pikɔte), v.a. To prick; to peck; to tease; to pick up (food); to dot.

picotin (pikɔtɛ̃), s.m. Peck of oats; feed of corn.

picrate (pikrat), s.m. (chem.) Picrate.

picrique (pikrik), adj. [f. Gr. *pikros*] (chem.) Picric.

pictural, -e, (aux) (piktyral), adj. [f. L *pictura*] Pictural, pictorial.

picvert, pivert (pivɛr), s.m. Green woodpecker.

pie (pi), s.f. [L *pica*] Magpie, pie; (jest.) *trouver la ~ au nid,* to make a profitable discovery; *jaser comme une ~ borgne,* to prattle like a magpie; *bavarder comme une ~,* to chatter nineteen to the dozen; *~-grièche,* (*a*) shrike; (*b*) (of a person) shrew. ~, adj. Piebald (horse).

pie (pi), adj. [L *pius*] Pious; *œuvre ~,* alms-deed; act of piety.

pièce (pjɛs), s.f. [orig. dub., perh. Celt.] Piece, fragment, part, length, portion, bit; document, paper, instrument; gun; coin; play; trick; room, apartment; joint (of meat), dish; cask; *mettre, tailler en ~s,* to break to pieces, to rout (an army); *de ~s et de morceaux,* of odds and ends; of shreds and patches; *~ à ~,* bit by bit, piecemeal; *faire ~ à X,* to play a trick upon X; *vin en ~,* wine in the cask, or in the wood; *de toutes ~s,* entirely, wholly, at all points; *tout d'une ~,* all of a piece; (fig.) as stiff as a poker; *donner la ~ à,* to tip; *travailler aux ~s,* to work by the job, to do piece-work, to be paid by the piece; (fig.) *rendre à X la monnaie de sa ~,* to give X tit for tat; *être près de ses ~s,* to be low in cash; *ah la bonne ~!,* mischievous creature!, cunning blade!; *~s de rechange,* spare parts.

piécette (pjesɛt), s.f. **1.** Small piece (of money); **2.** peseta.

pied (pje), s.m. [L *pes, pedis*] Foot; leg; stalk, plant; head (of celery); *à ~,* on foot, foot-; dismounted, on Shanks's mare; *à ~ d'œuvre,* near at hand; *à ~s joints,* with feet together; *à ~ sec,* dry-shod, on dry land; *au petit ~,* on a small scale; *au ~ levé,* without a moment's notice; *au ~ de la lettre,* literally; *de ~ en cap,* from top to toe; cap-à-pie; *de ~ ferme,* unflinchingly; *doigt de ~,* toe; *portrait en ~,* full-length likeness; *machine haut le ~,* light engine; *sur ~,* on foot; on one's feet; well again; alive, awake, up and about; *sur le ~ de,* on the footing of; *sur quel ~ êtes-vous avec lui?,* on what footing are you with him?; *sur le ~ de paix,* on a peace footing; *sur ce ~-là,* on that footing; at that rate; *sur la pointe du ~,* or *des ~s,* on tiptoe; *avoir ~,* to be in one's depth; *avoir le ~ marin,* to have one's sea-legs, to be a good sailor; *avoir bon ~ bon œil,* to be hale and hearty; *faire le ~ de grue,* to dance attendance; *frapper du ~,* to stamp; *lâcher ~,* to give way, to run away; (fig.) *lever le ~,* to take to one's heels, to abscond, to decamp; to run away with the till; *marcher sur les ~ à X,* to tread on X's toes; to be rude to X; *se lever du ~ gauche,* to get out of bed on the wrong side; *mettre ~ à terre,* to dismount; to alight; *je ne mettrai plus les ~s chez lui,* I will never again set foot in his house; *mettre les ~s dans le plat,* to put one's foot in it; to make a blunder; *mettre à ~,* to dismount; (fig.) to dismiss, to discharge, to suspend; *faire un ~ de nez,* to make a long nose (at); to cut a snook (in derision); *perdre ~,* to get out of one's depth, to be carried off one's feet, to go under; (fig.) to be lost, ruined; *prendre ~,* to get into one's depth; to gain a footing; *~ à ~,* step by step, inch by inch; *couper l'herbe sous le ~ à X,* to forestall X; to take the wind out of X's sails; *sécher sur ~ d'impatience,* to pine away with restless eagerness; *aller ~s nus,* to go barefoot; *ne savoir sur quel ~ danser,* not to know which way to turn; *tenir ~,* to stand one's ground, to stand firm; *coup de ~,* kick; *mettre X au ~ du mur,* to corner X, to drive X into a corner; (bot.) *~-d'alouette,* s.m. larkspur, delphinium; *~-de-biche,* s.m. hind's foot; iron lever, claw lever; *~-bot,* s.m. club-footed man; *~-de-chèvre,* s.m., crowbar; *~ à coulisse,* sliding callipers; *~-droit,* s.m. (arch.) piedroit; *~-à-terre,* s.m. small flat, temporary lodging; *~ plat,* s.m. flat foot; (fig.) mean wretch; *partir du bon ~,* to put one's best foot foremost; *faire des ~s et des mains,* to move heaven and earth; to do one's utmost; *le ~ m'a manqué,* my foot slipped; *travailler d'arrache-~,* to work unremittingly, strenuously; *~s et poings liés,* tied hand and foot; *il ne se mouche pas du ~,* he gives himself airs; he does things on a grand scale; he thinks no small beer of himself; *de plain-~,* on the same level; on a level (*avec,* with).

piédestal (pl. **aux**) (pjedɛstal), s.m. [It. *piedestallo*] Pedestal.

piédouche (pjeduʃ), s.m. [It. *pieduccio*] Piedouche, small pedestal.

piège (pjɛʒ), s.m. [L *pedica*] Trap; snare, (fig.) snare; *prendre au ~,* to entrap, to ensnare, to catch in a trap; *donner dans* *le* ~, to be caught in a trap; *tendre un* ~, to set a trap.

piégeage (pjeʒaʒ), s.m. Setting traps.

pie-grièche (pigriɛʃ), s.f. Shrike; (fig.) shrew.

pie-mère (pimɛr), s.f. [L *pia mater*] (anat.) Pia mater.

piémontais, -e (pjemɔ̃tɛ), adj. s.m.f. Piedmontese.

piéride (pjerid), s.f. (ent.) Pieris, butterfly.

pierraille (pjɛrɑj), s.f. Small stones, broken stones, rocky, stony soil.

pierre (pjɛr), s.f. [L *petra*] Stone, flint, rock, grit; ~ *à aiguiser*, whetstone; ~ *de taille*, freestone; ~ *infernale*, lunar caustic; ~ *philosophale*, philosophers' stone; ~ *à plâtre*, gypsum; ~ *d'attente*, toothing-stone; ~ *de touche*, touchstone; ~ *précieuse*, precious stone, gem; *jeter la* ~ *à X*, to accuse X, to condemn X; *une* ~ *dans mon jardin!*, that's aimed at me!; that's a dig at me; ~ *d'achoppement*, stumbling-block; ~ *de l'angle*, chief corner-stone; (prov.) ~ *qui roule n'amasse pas mousse*, a rolling stone gathers no moss; *malheureux comme les* ~*s*, acutely unhappy; as wretched as can be; *faire d'une* ~ *deux coups*, to kill two birds with one stone; *maladie de la* ~, calculus stone; *poser la première* ~, to lay the foundation-stone.

pierrée (pjɛre), s.f. Stone drain.

pierreries (pjɛrri), s.f.pl. Gems, precious stones.

pierrette (pjɛrɛt), s.f. **1.** Woman dressed as a pierrot, pierrette; **2.** (rare) small stone.

pierreu-x, -se (pjɛrø), adj. Stony, flinty, gritty; (pathol.) calculous; **~se**, s.f. (obs.) loose woman.

pierrier (pjɛrje), s.m. **1.** Swivel-gun; **2.** (obs.) gun for firing stones.

pierrot (pjɛro), s.m. [f. *Pierre*] **1.** Pierrot merry andrew; **2.** house-sparrow.

pierrure (pjɛryr), s.f. Burr (at base of deer's horns).

piété (pjete), s.f. [L *pietas*] Piety; godliness; ~ *filiale*, filial devotion; *mont-de-*~, municipal pawn-shop.

piéter (pjete), v.n. [f. *pied*] **1.** (at bowls) To foot the mark; **2.** (of game, espec. partridges) to walk instead of flying; ~, v.a. to set (*contre*, against).

piétinement (pjetinmɑ̃), s.m. Trampling, pawing the ground; (mil.) marking time.

piétiner (pjetine), v.a.n. To trample, to stamp, to paw the ground; ~ *de colère*, to dance with rage.

piétisme (pjetism), s.m. [f. *piété*] Pietism.

piétiste (pjetist), s.m.f. Pietist.

piéton (pjetɔ̃), s.m. Pedestrian, walker, foot-passenger; (obs.) rural postman.

piètre (pjɛtr), adj. [L *pedestris*] Paltry, sorry, shabby, wretched.

piètrement (pjɛtrəmɑ̃), adv. Wretchedly, poorly, sorrily, shabbily.

pieu (pl. **-x**) (pjø), s.m. [L *palus*] Stake, post, pale, pile, strong stick; (slang) bed; *aller au* ~ (or *se pieuter*), to go to bed; (mil. slang) to go to kip.

pieusement (pjøzmɑ̃), adv. Piously, devoutly.

pieuvre (pjøvr), s.f. [f. L *polypus*] Octopus, poulpe, devil-fish; (fig.) vampire; syn. POULPE.

pieu-x, -se (pjø), adj. [L *pius*] Pious, devout.

piézomètre (pjezomɛtr), s.m. [f. Gr. *piezein*+*metron*] (physiol.) Piezometer (for measuring the compressibility of liquids).

pif (pif), s.m. (slang) Bottle-nose, large nose, boko, beak.

piffre (pifr), s.m. [It. *piffero*] Glutton.

pif-paf (pifpaf), excl. [onom.] Slap! bang!, flick! flack!

pigamon (pigamɔ̃), s.m. (bot.) Meadow-rue, thalictrum.

pige (piʒ), s.f. (slang) *Faire la* ~ *à X*, to surpass X, to duff X; to lick X.

pigeon, -ne (piʒɔ̃), s.m.f. [L *pipio*] Pigeon, dove; (slang) dupe, gull, simpleton; ~ *ramier*, wood-pigeon; ~ *culbutant*, tumbler; ~ *voyageur*, carrier-pigeon; homing pigeon, homer; *gorge de* ~, dove-coloured; shot; (fig.) *plumer le* ~, to pluck a pigeon, to pigeon or gull a person.

pigeonneau (pl. **-x**) (piʒɔno), s.m. Young pigeon; gull, simpleton.

pigeonnier (piʒɔnje), s.m. Pigeon-house, pigeonry, dovecot; (colloq.) shooting-box; unimportant house built on a hilltop.

piger (piʒe), v.a. (slang) To squint at; to look at; to appreciate; to catch (a cold), to lay hold of; to understand; *je n'ai rien pigé de ce qu'il a dit*, or *je n'y ai rien pigé*, I did not understand a word of what he said; *pige-moi cette robe!*, just cast your eye on that frock!; *se faire* ~, to get nabbed; ~ *un rhume*, to catch a cold.

pigment (pigmɑ̃), s.m. [L *pigmentum*] Pigment.

pigmentaire (pigmɑ̃tɛr), adj. Pigmentary, pigmental.

pigmentation (pigmɑ̃ta'sjɔ̃), s.f. Pigmentation.

pigne (piɲ), s.f. Pine-cone; pine-kernel.

pignocher (piɲɔʃe), v.a. **1.** To nibble at; **2.** to paint badly, with too tiny strokes.

pignon[1] (piɲɔ̃), s.m. [f. L *pinna*] **1.** Gable, gable-end; *avoir* ~ *sur rue*, to have a house of one's own; **2.** pinion (cog-wheel); *grand* ~, chain-wheel; *petit* ~, sprocket-wheel; ~ *conique*, bevel pinion; ~ *à rochet*, ratchet-wheel; ~ *à roue libre*, free wheel; ~ *de marche arrière,* reverse-gear wheel.

pignon[2] (piɲɔ̃), s.m. [f. L *pinea*] Kernel of fir-cone, pine-kernel.

pignorati-f, -ve (piɲɔratif), adj. [f. L *pignorare*] (law) Pignorative (said of a sale with power of redemption).

pignouf (piɲuf), s.m. (colloq.) Cad, vulgar fellow.

pilaire (pilɛr), adj. See PILEUX.

pilastre (pilastr), s.m. [It. *pilastro*] Pilaster.

pilau, pilaf (pilo, pilaf), s.m. [Turk. wd] Stewed rice with meat, pilau, pilaff.

pile (pil), s.f. [L *pila*] **1.** Pile, heap; **2.** pier (of bridge), mole (of masonry); pounding stone; **3.** (electr.) battery, pile; **4.** (colloq.) thrashing; *flanquer une ~ à X,* to give X a drubbing; **5.** (coin, medals, &c.) pile, reverse; *jouer à ~ ou face,* to toss up; to play at heads or tails; to play pitch and toss. ⚠ In French *pile* has never the sense of funeral pile, *bûcher de funérailles;* nor the sense of *argent, fortune, magot,* as in: to make one's pile; nor the sense of pointed stake, or post, or beam = *madrier, pilot.*

piler (pile), v.a. To pound, to crush.

pilet (pilɛ), s.m. (ornith.) Pintail duck.

pileu-x, -se (pilø), adj. [L *pilus, pilosus*] Pilous, pilose, hairy; syn. PILAIRE.

pilier (pilje), s.m. [f. *pile*] Pillar, post, column; (fig.) support, pillar, prop; constant frequenter; *c'est un ~ de cabaret,* he is a pub-loafer.

pilifère (pilifɛr), adj. Piliferous.

pillage (pijaʒ), s.m. Pillage, plunder; spoil; *livrer au ~,* to give up to plunder.

pillard, -e (pijar), s.m.f. Pillager, plunderer. ~, adj. Pillaging, plundering, pilfering.

piller (pije), v.a.n. [LL *piliare*] To pillage, to plunder, to ransack, to pilfer, to steal, to take from; (of dogs) to seize; *pille! pille!,* seize him!

pillerie (pijri), s.f. Pillage, pilfering.

pilon (pilɔ̃), s.m. [f. *piler*] **1.** Pestle; beetle, stamper, crusher, rammer; *mettre au ~,* to destroy (books); **2.** (of a fowl) drumstick; **3.** artificial (wooden) leg.

pilonnage (pilɔnaʒ), s.m. Pounding, ramming.

pilonner (pilɔne), v.a. To pound, to ram, to crush, to mill.

pilori (pilɔri), s.m. [orig. dub.; OF *pellori*] Pillory; *mettre X au ~,* to pillory X, to defame X.

pilorier (pilɔrje), v.a. To pillory, to expose, to unmask (a person's villainy).

piloselle (pilozɛl), s.f. [f. L *pilosus*] (bot.) Mouse-ear hawkweed, *Hieracium pilosella.*

pilot (pilo), s.m. [f. *pile*] **1.** Pile, stake; **2.** conical heap of salt; **3.** rags (used for making paper). ⚠ Not Engl. 'pilot', which = *pilote.*

pilotage (pilɔtaʒ), s.m. **1.** Pile-driving; **2.** (naut.) piloting, pilotage.

pilote (pilɔt), s.m. [f. It. *pilota*] **1.** Pilot; (fig.) guide; **2.** pilot-fish.

piloter (pilɔte), v.a. **1.** To drive piles into; **2.** to pilot, to steer; (fig.) to guide.

pilotin (pilɔtɛ̃), s.m. Pilot's apprentice.

pilotis (pilɔti), s.m. Pile-work; series of piles forming a foundation.

pilou (pilu), s.m. [f. L *pilus*] Thick flannelette.

pilulaire (pilylɛr), adj. Pilular. ~, s.m. Tube for giving pills to horses, cattle, &c.

pilule (pilyl), s.f. [L *pilula*] Pill; (fig.) *dorer la ~,* to gild the pill.

pimbêche (pɛ̃bɛʃ), s.f. [orig. dub.] Pretentious silly shrew; a woman who is at the same time stupid, insolent, and affected.

piment (pimɑ̃), s.m. [f. Span. *pimienta*] Pimento; (fig.) piquancy.

pimenter (pimɑ̃te), v.a. To flavour with pimento; (fig.) to give piquancy to; *une comédie très pimentée,* a highly piquant and spicy comedy.

pimpant, -e (pɛ̃pɑ̃), adj. [f. OF *pimper = piper*] Sprightly and smart, spruce, natty, trim.

pimprenelle (pɛ̃prənɛl), s.f. (bot.) Burnet, *Poterium;* ⚠ Not Engl. 'pimpernel', which nowadays = *mouron.*

pin (pɛ̃), s.m. [L *pinus*] Pine-tree, Scotch fir; *~-pignon,* stone-pine; *pomme de ~,* pine-cone.

pinacle (pinakl), s.m. [L *pinaculum*] Pinnacle; *mettre* or *porter X au ~,* to praise X to the skies.

pinacothèque (pinakɔtɛk), s.f. [f. Gr. *pinax+thēkē*] Picture-gallery.

pinard (pinar), s.m. [f. *pineau,* a kind of vine] (slang) Wine.

pinasse, pinace (pinas), s.f. [f. L *pinus*] Pinnace.

pinastre (pinastr), s.m. (bot.) Pinaster; syn. PIN MARITIME.

pinçage (pɛ̃saʒ), s.m. Pinching; nipping off (buds, &c.); syn. PINCEMENT.

pinçard, -e (pɛ̃sar), adj. (said of a horse) Wearing the shoe at the toe.

pince (pɛ̃s), s.f. [f. *pincer*] Pinch, pinching; hold, grip; pincers, nippers, pliers, forceps, tongs, tweezers; claw (of a lobster); front of a horse-shoe; crowbar; (dressm.) dart; *~ coupante,* cutting-pliers; *~ à glace,* ice-tongs; *~ plate,* flat-nosed pliers; *~ ronde,* round-nosed pliers; *~ à sucre,* sugar-tongs; *~-monseigneur,* jemmy; (slang) hand, flipper.

pincé, -e (pɛ̃se), p. adj. Affected, prim, stiff, pursed, pinched; *lèvres ~es,* thin lips; pursed mouth.

pinceau (pl. **-x**) (pɛ̃so), s.m. [L *penicillum*] Brush, paint-brush; pencil; style of painting; pencil of rays; *coup de ~*, stroke, brush-stroke.

pincée (pɛ̃se), s.f. Pinch (of snuff, &c.).

pincelier (pɛ̃slje), s.m. [f. *pinceau*] Dip-cup (for painting).

pince-maille (pɛ̃smɑj), s.m.f. Skinflint, miser, pinch-penny.

pincement (pɛ̃smɑ̃), s.m. Pinching, pinch, twisting, slight pain; nipping (of buds, &c.). See PINÇAGE.

pince-nez (pɛ̃sne), s.m. (invar.) Pince-nez, spring double eyeglass; syn. LORGNON, BINOCLE.

pincer (pɛ̃se), v.a. To pinch, to compress, to squeeze, to grip; to nip, to nip off, to clip; (colloq.) to catch; *se faire ~*, to get caught; to get found out or nabbed; to be pinched; (slang) *en ~ pour X*, to be sweet on X, to be gone on X; (U.S.A.) to be dippy about X; *se ~ le doigt*, to pinch one's finger; *~ de la harpe*, to play upon the harp; *~*, v.n. *le froid pince dur*, it's bitingly cold.

pince-sans-rire (pɛ̃ssɑ̃rir), s.m. (invar.) Dry joker.

pincette (pɛ̃sɛt), s.f. *~* or *~s*, Tongs; *il n'est pas à prendre avec des ~s!*, you would not touch him with a pair of tongs; (fig.) he is like a bear with a sore head.

pinchard, -e (pɛ̃ʃar), adj. Said of a horse with an iron-grey coat.

pinçon (pɛ̃sɔ̃), s.m. Pinch; mark left by a pinch.

pindarique (pɛ̃darik), adj. [f. *Pindare*] Pindaric.

pinéal, -e, (aux) (pineal), adj. [f. L *pinea*] (anat.) Pineal.

pineau, pinot (pino), s.m. A kind of vine.

pinède (pinɛd), **pineraie** (pinrɛ), s.f. Pine-grove, pine or fir plantation.

pingouin (pɛ̃gwɛ̃), s.m. (ornith.) Penguin.

pingre (pɛ̃gr), s.m. [orig. dub.] Skinflint, miser, curmudgeon; (U.S.A. slang) tight-wad. ~, adj. m.f. Avaricious, close-fisted, stingy.

pingrerie (pɛ̃grəri), s.f. Stinginess, close-fistedness; meanness.

pinière (pinjɛr), s.f. See PINÈDE.

pinne (pin), **pinne marine** (pinmarin), s.f. [f. L *pinna*] (zool.) Pinna, wing-shell.

pinné, -e (pine), adj. (bot.) Pinnate.

pinnule (pinyl), s.f. [L *pinnula*] Pinnula, sight-vane (of alidad).

pinque (pɛ̃k), s.f. [Middle Dutch *pincke*] (naut.) Pink (three-masted ship, used chiefly in the Mediterranean).

pinson (pɛ̃sɔ̃), s.m. [LL *pincio*] (ornith.) Finch, chaffinch; *gai comme un ~*, gay as a lark; playful as a kitten, merry as a grig.

pintade (pɛ̃tad), s.f. [Span. *pintada*] (ornith.) Guinea-fowl, guinea-hen.

pintadeau (pl. -x) (pɛ̃tado), s.m. Guinea-chick.

pinte (pɛ̃t), s.f. [orig. dub.] Pint; *se faire une ~ de bon sang*, to have a good laugh, to enjoy oneself highly.

pinter (pɛ̃te), v.a.n. (colloq.) To drink immoderately; to tipple.

piochage (pjɔʃaʒ), s.m. Digging.

pioche (pjɔʃ), s.f. [f. *pic*] Pick-axe, mattock.

piochement (pjɔʃmɑ̃), s.m. Digging.

piocher (pjɔʃe), v.a.n. To dig; (fig.) to work hard, to fag, to swot; to study sedulously.

piocheu-r, -se (pjɔʃœr), s.m.f. Digger; (fig.) hard-working student, swot.

piolet (pjɔlɛ), s.m. [Alpine dialect wd] Piolet, ice-axe.

pion (pjɔ̃), s.m. [f. LL *pedo*] **1.** Pawn (at chess); piece (at draughts); (fig.) *damer le ~ à X*, to outdo X; **2.** usher, under-master (at a school); **3.** (in India) peon.

pioncer (pjɔ̃se), v.n. (slang) To sleep, to have a nap, to snooze, to have forty winks.

pioncette (pjɔ̃sɛt), s.f. (slang) Nap, forty winks.

pionner (pjɔne), v.n. (at chess, draughts) To play so as to take and lose many pawns.

pionni-er, -ère (pjɔnje), s.m.f. (lit. & fig.) Pioneer.

piot (pjo), s.m. (obs.) Wine; *humer le ~*, to drink, to tipple.

pioupiou (pjupju), s.m. (colloq.) Tommy, foot-soldier.

pipa (pipa), s.m. [Surinam negro wd] (zool.) Pipa, Surinam toad.

pipe (pip), s.f. [f. *piper*] **1.** (obs.) Pipe, cask (a measure for wine, &c.); **2.** pipe; *allumer sa ~*, to light one's pipe; *fourneau de ~*, bowl of a pipe; *tuyau de ~*, pipe-stem; (colloq.) *casser sa ~*, to kick the bucket, to hop the twig, to die, to go west.

pipeau (pl. -x) (pipo), s.m. [f. *piper*] **1.** Reed-pipe; bird-call; **2.** lime-twigs, snare (for birds).

pipée (pipe), s.f. Bird-catching (by decoy); *prendre à la ~*, to catch birds with a bird-call; (fig.) to entice, to ensnare, to take in, to cozen, to beguile.

pipelet, -te (piplɛ), s.m.f. [from a character in *Les Mystères de Paris*, by Eug. Sue] (pej.) Porter, concierge; (U.S.A.) janitor.

piper (pipe), v.a. [f. L *pipare*] To catch (birds, with a bird-call), to deceive, to beguile; to cheat; to cog (dice), to mark, to prepare (cards).

pipéracées (piperase), s.f.pl. (bot.) Piperaceae.

piperie (pipri), s.f. Cheating, trick, deceit.

pipette (pipɛt), s.f. [f. *pipe*] (chem.) Pipette; wine-taster.

pipi (pipi), s.m. [child. wd] Piddle, water, urine; *faire ~*, to piddle.

pipit, or farlouse (pipit, farluz), s.m. (ornith.) Tit-lark, pipit.
pipistrelle (pipistrɛl), s.f. (zool.) Pipistrel; common bat.
piquage (pikaʒ), s.m. Stitching.
piquant, -e (pikɑ̃), p. adj. Prickling, prickly, stinging, sharp, pungent, piercing, biting; (fig.) piquant, pointed, lively, spicy, witty; *une beauté ~e*, a piquant beauty; *un froid ~*, biting cold; *des mots ~s*, pointed words; witty words.
piquant (pikɑ̃), s.m. Prickle, thorn, sting, stinging-nettle; quill (of porcupine); (fig.) piquancy, pungency, zest, point, cream.
pique (pik), s.f. [f. *piquer*] **1.** Pike, spear (of a pike); **2.** (obs.) pike-length; *être à cent ~s au-dessus de*, to be far above; **3.** pique, grudge, offence; ~, s.m. spade (at cards).
piqué (pike), s.m. Piqué, a ribbed cotton fabric; quilting.
piqué, -e (pike), p. adj. Pricked; stitched, quilted; larded; worm-eaten; fly-blown; (of wine) pricked, sour; (slang) crazy, crack-brained, cracked; *cela n'est pas ~ des vers*, that's not to be sneezed at.
pique-assiette (pikasjɛt), s.m. (invar.) Parasite, sponger, dinner-hunter.
pique-bœuf (pikbœf), s.m. (ornith.) Beefeater (bird).
pique-nique (piknik), s.m. [etym. dub.] Picnic; *faire un ~*, to have a picnic.
pique-notes (piknɔt), s.m. Bill-file.
piquer (pike), v.a.n. [f. *pic*] To prick, to sting; to lard; to stitch, to quilt; to goad, to spur, to excite, to stimulate; to pique, nettle; to pin; *~ la curiosité de X*, rouse X's curiosity; *quelle mouche vous pique?*, what's up with you?; (U.S.A.) what's biting you?; *~ des deux*, to gallop off; *~ une tête*, to take a header; (aeron.) *~ du nez*, to nose-dive; (slang) *~ un soleil*, or *un fard*, to blush; **se ~**, v.pr. to pretend (*de*, to), to pride oneself (on); to get piqued; *X s'est piqué d'honneur*, X was put on his mettle; X made it a point of honour; *il se pique d'avoir plus d'esprit que X*, he pretends to be more witty than X; *il se pique d'un rien*, he takes offence at the slightest thing; (colloq.) *se ~ le nez*, to tipple; *se ~ au jeu*, to persist in playing although losing; to get excited and obstinate.
piquet (pikɛ), s.m. [f. *pique*] Stake, peg; (mil.) picket; (game) piquet; *être au ~*, (at school) to be standing in a corner, as punishment; *~ de fleurs*, cluster of flowers.
piquetage (piktaʒ), s.m. Marking with stakes or pegs.
piqueter (pikte), v.a. To mark with stakes or pegs; to dot.
piquette (pikɛt), s.f. Thin wine; inferior wine, piquette.
piqueur (pikœr), s.m. Huntsman, whipper-in; outrider, stud-groom; wine-taster; ~,
piqueuse, s.m.f. Stitcher, sewer. ~, adj. m. *Marteau ~*, mining-drill; drill.
piquier (pikje), s.m. Pikeman.
piqûre (pikyr), s.f. Prick, pricking, sting, bite; puncture; worm-hole; stitching, quilting, stitched seam; (med.) injection, hypodermic injection (of morphia, serum, &c.).
pirate (pirat), s.m. [Gr. *peiratês*] Pirate; (fig.) pirate, plagiarist.
pirater (pirate), v.n. To commit piracy, to play the pirate.
piraterie (piratri), s.f. Piracy, act of piracy; (fig.) plunder, plagiarism.
pire (pir), adj. [L *pejor*] Worse; *le remède est ~ que le mal*, the remedy is worse than the disease; (preceded by the definite article) worst; *le ~ ennemi*, the worst enemy. ~, s.m. *Souvent qui choisit prend le ~*, pick and choose and take the worst; *en mettant les choses au ~*, even if the worst comes to the worst.
piriforme (piriform), adj. [f. L *pirum*] Piriform, pear-shaped.
pirogue (pirɔg), s.f. [Carib. wd] (naut.) Pirogue, dug-out, canoe.
pirouette (pirwɛt), s.f. Pirouette; whirligig; (fig.) sudden change of opinion.
pirouetter (pirwɛte), v.n. To pirouette, to whirl about.
pis (pi), s.m. [f. L *pectus*] Udder.
pis (pi), adv. [L *pejus*] Worse; *~ aller*, the worst, the last resource, or shift; *au ~ aller*, at the worst; *aller de mal en ~*, to go from bad to worse; *qui ~ est*, what is worse; *de ~ en ~*, worse and worse. ~, s.m. *Mettons les choses au ~*, let's suppose the worst; *le ~ qui puisse arriver*, the worst that can happen; *tant ~!*, it can't be helped!, come what may!
pisciculteur (pisikyltœr), s.m. Pisciculturist.
pisciculture (pisikyltyr), s.f. [f. L *piscis+cultor*] Pisciculture, fish-culture.
piscine (pissin), s.f. [L *piscina*] Piscina.
piscivore (pissivɔr), adj. Piscivorous.
pisé (pize), s.m. (mason.) Pisé.
piser (pize), v.a. To build of pisé.
pissat (pisa), s.m. Urine.
pissement (pismɑ̃), s.m. (indecent) Pissing.
pissenlit (pisɑ̃li), s.m. (bot.) Dandelion.
pisser (pise), v.n.a. (indecent) To piss, to make water, to urinate, to piddle.
pisseu-x, -se (pisø), adj. Stained with urine, piss-burnt.
pissoir (piswar), s.m. Urinal.
pissotière (pisɔtjɛr), s.f. Street water-closet, urinal.
pistache (pistaʃ), s.f. [Gr. *pistakion*] Pistachio-nut.
pistachier (pistaʃje), s.m. (bot.) Pistachio-tree.
piste (pist), s.f. [It. *pista*] Track, trail, trace; scent; piste, race-course, ring; *être*

à la ~ *de*, to be after; to be on the trail of; *suivre à la* ~, to follow in the track of, to track.
pisteur (pistœr), s.m. Tout, hotel tout.
pistil (pistil), s.m. [f. L *pistillus*] (bot.) Pistil.
pistole (pistɔl), s.f. [f. It. *pistola*] **1.** Pistole; **2.** separate ward in prison, in which the prisoners may buy their food.
pistolet (pistɔlɛ), s.m. [It. *pistolese*] **1.** Pistol; *coup de* ~, pistol-shot; **2.** fellow, (slang) bloke; *quel drôle de* ~*!*, what a queer fellow!; **3.** (naut.) boomkin; **4.** drawing-instrument with various curves.
piston (pistɔ̃), s.m. [f. L *pistare*] **1.** Piston; sucker; *coup de* ~, stroke of the piston; *course du* ~, travel of the piston; *segment de* ~, piston-ring; *tige de* ~, piston-rod; *fusil à* ~, percussion-gun; **2.** (mus.) cornet; **3.** (colloq.) recommendation, partial protection, favour; *avoir du* ~, to be able to pull wires; to be pushed.
pistonner (pistɔne), v.a. **1.** (colloq.) To recommend, to protect, to favour, to back up, to shove, to push; **2.** (obs.) to worry.
pitance (pitɑ̃s), s.f. [f. *pitié*] Pittance, daily allowance of food.
pitchpin (pitʃpɛ̃), s.m. (bot.) Pitch-pine.
pite (pit), s.f. [f. LL *picta*] Mite (a very small coin); ~, (bot.) kind of agave.
piteusement (pitøzmɑ̃), adv. Piteously, woefully, pitiably, miserably, disgracefully.
piteu-x, -se (pitø), adj. [f. L *pietosus*] Piteous, pitiable, paltry, sorry, disgraceful.
pithécanthrope (pitekɑ̃trɔp), s.m. [f. Gr. *pithēkos*+*anthrōpos*] Pithecanthrope.
pitié (pitje), s.f. [L *pietas*] Pity; object of pity; *à faire* ~, pitifully; wretchedly; *ayez* ~ *de moi!*, have pity upon me!; *par* ~, for pity's sake; out of pity; *prendre X en* ~, to take pity on X; *quelle* ~*!*, what a pity!; that's too bad!; *sans* ~, pitiless.
piton (pitɔ̃), s.m. Screw-ring; peak (of mountain).
pitoyable (pitwajabl), adj. Pitiable, pitiful, merciful; paltry, wretched, poor.
pitoyablement (pitwajabləmɑ̃), adv. Pitifully, mercifully; wretchedly, sorrily, miserably.
pitre (pitr), s.m. [etym. dub.] Clown, buffoon, merry andrew, jack pudding.
pitrerie (pitrəri), s.f. Buffoonery, clownery, drollery, antics; *faire des* ~*s*, to perform antics, to clown.
pittoresque (pitɔrɛsk), adj. [It. *pittoresco*] Picturesque, vivid, graphic, pictorial. ~, s.m. Picturesque, picturesqueness.
pittoresquement (pitɔrɛskəmɑ̃), adv. Picturesquely.
pituitaire (pitɥitɛr), adj. Pituitary.
pituite (pitɥit), s.f. [L *pituita*] Pituita.
pituiteu-x, -se (pitɥitø), adj. Pituitous.
pivert, picvert (pivɛr), s.m. [*pic*+*vert*] (ornith.) Green woodpecker.
pivoine (pivwan), s.f. [L *paeonia*] **1.** (bot.) Peony; **2.** (rare) ~, s.m. bullfinch.
pivot (pivo), s.m. [orig. dub.] Pivot, hinge; (fig.) pivot, main point or part.
pivotant, -e (pivɔtɑ̃), p. adj. **1.** Revolving; **2.** (bot.) tap-rooted; *racine* ~*e*, tap-root.
pivoter (pivɔte), v.n. To turn on a pivot, to revolve.
placabilité (plakabilite), s.f. Placability.
placable (plakabl), adj. [L *placabilis*] Placable.
placage (plakaʒ), s.m. [f. *plaquer*] Veneering.
placard (plakar), s.m. [f. *plaquer*] **1.** Placard, poster, bill, libel; **2.** cupboard (in a wall); **3.** (print.) slip; *épreuves en* ~*s*, slip-proofs.
placarder (plakarde), v.a. **1.** To post (a placard, &c.); **2.** to lampoon.
place (plas), s.f. [L *platea*] Place, spot, room, seat, space, stand, square, market-place; (comm.) mart, market, exchange; charge, office, function; situation; rank; (mil.) place, fortress, stronghold, parade ground; *à sa* ~, in his, her, its place; *à votre* ~, if I were you; *faire* ~ *à*, to make room for; to give way to; *faire la* ~, to canvass for orders; *entrer en* ~, to get a situation; *prenez* ~, sit down, take a seat; *quitter la* ~, to give up one's place; to leave; *retenir sa* ~, to secure one's seat; *tenir* ~ *de*, to stand instead of; to do instead of; to take the place of; *se tenir à sa* ~, to know one's station; *sur* ~, on the spot; *demeurer sur* ~, to remain still; ~*s s'il vous plaît?*, fares, please!; *remettre X à sa* ~, to put X in his place; to give X a good dressing-down; to tell X off.
placement (plasmɑ̃), s.m. Placing; investing; *bureau de* ~, registry-office.
placenta (plasɛ̃ta), s.m. [f. Gr. *plakous*] (med.) Placenta.
placentaire (plasɛ̃tɛr), adj. (med.) Placental.
placer (plase), v.a. [f. *place*] To place, to put, to set, to lay, to invest (money), to put out, to put at interest; to get (a person) into a situation; to sell, to dispose of; to introduce, to edge in; *bien* ~ *sa confiance*, to bestow one's confidence wisely; **se** ~, v.pr. to get a situation (as servant); to be placed, &c.
placer (plasɛr), s.m. [Span. wd] Placer, diggings.
placet (plasɛ), s.m. [L wd] Placet, petition.
placeu-r, -se (plasœr), s.m.f. Registry-office keeper; (theatr., cinema) box-opener.
placide (plasid), adj. [L *placidus*] Placid.
placidement (plasidmɑ̃), adv. Placidly.

placidité (plasidite), s.f. Placidity, placidness.
placi-er, -ère (plasje), s.m.f. Placer; agent, commercial traveller, (U.S.A.) drummer. See PLACEUR.
plafond (plafɔ̃), s.m. [*plat+fond*] Ceiling; (colloq.) *avoir une araignée dans le* ~, to have a bee in one's bonnet.
plafonnage (plafɔnaʒ), s.m. Ceiling; the act of ceiling.
plafonner (plafɔne), v.a.n. To ceil; (aeron., v.n.) to fly at a high altitude.
plafonneur (plafɔnœr), s.m. Plasterer, ceiling-maker.
plafonnier (plafɔnje), s.m. Ceiling-lamp, pendant.
plage (plaʒ), s.f. [L *plaga*] Beach, seashore; (naut.) ~ *arrière*, aftermost deck (of ship).
plagiaire (plaʒjɛr), s.m.f. Plagiarist. ~, adj. Plagiarizing.
plagiat (plaʒja), s.m. Plagiarism, plagiary.
plagier (plaʒje), v.a. [f. L *plagiarius*] To plagiarize.
plaid (plɛ), s.m. **1.** (obs.) [f. L *placitum*] Plea; court sitting; **2.** [Engl. wd] ~ *écossais*, plaid, travelling-rug.
plaider (plɛde), v.a.n. To plead, to argue; to allege; to go to law, to sue; ~ *le faux pour savoir le vrai*, to use a draw to elicit truth, to elicit truth by alleging a falsehood; ~ *coupable*, to plead guilty.
plaideu-r, -se, plaidant, -e (plɛdœr, plɛdɑ̃), s.m.f. Litigant, suitor.
plaidoirie (plɛdwari), s.f. Pleading, address, speech.
plaidoyer (plɛdwaje), s.m. Speech (for the defence), address, pleading; appeal.
plaie (plɛ), s.f. [L *plaga*] Wound, sore; (fig.) hurt, evil, plague; *panser une* ~, to dress a wound; *ne rêver que* ~*s et bosses*, to think the more mischief the better sport; (fig.) *mettre le doigt sur la* ~, to put one's finger on the evil; *les* ~*s d'Égypte*, the plagues of Egypt.
plaignant, -e (plɛɲɑ̃), s.m.f. Plaintiff, prosecutor, complainant. ~, p. adj. Complaining.
plain, -e (plɛ̃), adj. [L *planus*] Plane, level, flat; *de* ~*-pied*, on a level, on the same floor; on a footing of equality; smoothly, easily. ⚠ Not English 'plain' in the sense of ugly, unattractive = *laid*.
plain-chant (plɛ̃ʃɑ̃), s.m. (pl. *plains-chants*) Plain-song, plain-chant.
plaindre (plɛ̃dr), v.a. [L *plangere*] **1.** To pity, to feel compassion for, to commiserate; *elle est à* ~, she is to be pitied; **2.** to repine at; to grudge, to be sparing of; ~ *sa peine*, to grudge one's trouble; **se** ~, v.pr. to complain, to lament, to moan, to grumble, to groan; to lodge a complaint.
plaine (plɛn), s.f. [f. *plain*] Plain, field, level ground.
plainte (plɛ̃t), s.f. Complaint, plaint, lamentation; wail, wailing, groan, moan; *porter* ~, *déposer une* ~ *contre X*, to lodge a complaint against X.
plainti-f, -ve (plɛ̃tif), adj. Plaintive, wailing, mournful, moanful; querulous.
plaintivement (plɛ̃tivmɑ̃), adv. Plaintively, moanfully; querulously.
plaire (plɛr), v.n. [L *placere*] To please, to be pleasant, pleasing, to appeal to; ~ *à X*, to please X; *à Dieu ne plaise*, God forbid; *comme il vous plaira*, as you please; as you like; *vous plaît-il de?*, would you like to?; *plaise à Dieu, plût au ciel, qu'il en soit ainsi*, would to God it were so; *plaît-il?*, what do you say?, I beg your pardon?; *s'il vous plaît*, if you please; please; by your leave; pray; *cela vous plaît à dire*, you are pleased to say so; **se** ~ v.pr. to please each other; to take pleasure; to thrive; *ils se sont plu à me tourmenter*, they delighted in tormenting me; *la vigne se plaît sur les coteaux*, the vine thrives on the slopes of small hills.
plaisamment (plɛzamɑ̃), adv. Pleasantly, agreeably, humorously, merrily; comically, funnily.
plaisance (plɛzɑ̃s), s.f. Pleasance, pleasure (obs. except in the phrase *de* ~); *bateau de* ~, pleasure-boat; *maison de* ~, country-seat.
plaisant, -e (plɛzɑ̃), p. adj. Pleasant, pleasing, nice, agreeable; comical, funny, humorous, jocose, ludicrous. ~, s.m. **1.** Jester, joker, wag; *mauvais* ~, sorry jester, trickster, mischievous wag; **2.** comical side, humour, laughable part, fun; *le* ~ *de l'aventure*, the fun of it.
plaisanter (plɛzɑ̃te), v.n.a. To jest, to joke, to banter, to chaff, to sport, to trifle; *c'est un homme qui ne plaisante pas*, he is not a man to be trifled with; *il ne plaisante pas là-dessus*, he does not joke about that; he is in downright earnest in that matter; *en plaisantant*, jokingly.
plaisanterie (plɛzɑ̃tri), s.f. Joke, jest, facetiousness, humour, witticism; practical joke; trifling, derision, mockery; *faire des* ~*s*, to crack jokes; *tourner tout en* ~, to make fun of everything; *entendre la* ~, to know how to take a joke; *cela passe la* ~, that is beyond a joke; ~ *à part*, jesting aside; seriously; *par* ~, by way of a joke; *quelle* ~ *!*, what a mockery !; that 's going too far !
plaisantin (plɛzɑ̃tɛ̃), s.m. (pej.) Wag, facetious man, jester, joker.
plaisir (plɛzir), s.m. [f. L *placere*] **1.** Pleasure, delight, gratification; diversion, amusement, pastime; consent, agreeableness, agreement, kindness; *à* ~, wantonly, plentifully; *avec* ~, with pleasure; *au* ~ *(de vous revoir) !*, bye-bye; well, so long!; *avoir, trouver*, or *prendre du* ~ *à*, to

delight in; *cela me fait* ~, that gives me pleasure; that's a pleasure to me; *faites-moi le* ~ *de*, do me the favour of; *pour vous faire* ~, to please you; (prov.) *pas de* ~ *sans peine*, no pleasure without pain; no joy without alloy; *à son bon* ~, at his (or her) own sweet will; *régime du bon* ~, absolute monarchy; *menus* ~*s*, amusements; (by ext.) pocket-money; **2.** a kind of wafer, rolled in the shape of a cone.

plamée (plame), s.f. (tanning) Lime-water.

plamer (plame), v.a. [f. *plain*] To treat or dress (raw hides) with lime.

plan, -e (plɑ̃), adj. [L *planus*] Level, even, flat, plane; *surface* ~*e*, plane surface; *angle* ~, plane angle.

plan (plɑ̃), s.m. [f. *plan*, adj.] **1.** (geom.) Plane; ~ *incliné*, inclined plane; **2.** plan, map, drawing, diagram, draught; *levée des* ~*s*, surveying; **3.** design, plan, scheme, project; **4.** (paint.) plane, ground, distance; **5.** (Lit.) plan, composition; *au premier* ~, in the foreground, to the fore; *reléguer au second* ~, *à l'arrière-*~, to put in the background; *laisser en* ~, to leave unfinished; to give (a person) the slip, to leave in the lurch.

planaire (planɛr), s.f. (zool.) Planaria, planarian worm.

planche (plɑ̃ʃ), s.f. [L *planca*] Board, plank, shelf; (engr.) plate; (theatr.) boards, stage, theatrical profession; (gard.) bed; (swimming) *faire la* ~, to float, or swim on one's back; ~ *de salut*, sheet-anchor; (motor., aeron.) ~ *de tablier*, or *de bord*, dashboard; *monter sur les* ~*s*, to tread the boards, to become an actor or actress.

planchéiage (plɑ̃ʃejaʒ), s.m. Boarding, flooring.

planchéier (plɑ̃ʃeje), v.a. To board, to floor, to plank.

plancher (plɑ̃ʃe), s.m. [f. *planche*] Floor, flooring; ceiling; *sauter jusqu'au* ~, to jump to the ceiling; (fig.) to have the shock of one's life; (colloq.) *le* ~ *des vaches*, dry land; *vider* or *débarrasser le* ~, to clear out; to make oneself scarce.

planchette (plɑ̃ʃɛt), s.f. Small board; plane-table (for surveying).

plançon (plɑ̃sɔ̃), s.m. Shoot (used as a cutting); sapling.

plan-concave (plɑ̃kɔ̃kav), adj. Plano-concave; **plan-convexe,** plano-convex.

plancton (plɑ̃ktɔ̃), s.m. [Gr. *plagktos*] (biol.) Plankton.

plane[1] (plan), s.f. [L *plana*] Spoke-shave; drawing-knife, cutting-tool; paring-knife. ⚠ Not English 'plane' which = *rabot*.

plane[2] (plan), s.m. [L *platanus*] (bot.) Plane-tree, Norway maple; *Acer platanoides*.

planer[1] (plane), v.a. [L *planare*] To plane, to pare off, to smooth.

planer[2] (plane), v.n. [f. *plain*] To soar, to hover; (fig.) to look down; ~ *au-dessus des difficultés*, to soar above difficulties; (aeron.) to glide; *vol plané*, glide; planed flight.

planétaire (planetɛr), adj. Planetary.

planète (planɛt), s.f. [Gr. *planētēs*] Planet.

planeur (planœr), s.m. **1.** Planisher; **2.** glider (motorless aeroplane).

planisphère (planisfɛr), s.m. Planisphere.

plankton (plɑ̃ktɔ̃), s.m. See PLANCTON.

planquer (plɑ̃ke), v.a. (slang) To conceal; **se** ~, v.pr. to hide, to take cover.

plant (plɑ̃), s.m. [f. *planter*] Plant, slip, sapling; bed, plantation; seedlings.

plantage (plɑ̃taʒ), s.m. Planting, plantation.

plantain (plɑ̃tɛ̃), s.m. [L *plantago*] (bot.) Plantain; *Plantago*.

plantaire (plɑ̃tɛr), adj. Plantar, of the sole of the foot.

plantation (plɑ̃ta'sjɔ̃), s.f. Planting; plantation.

plante (plɑ̃t), s.f. [L *planta*] **1.** Plant; *Jardin des Plantes*, Botanic Gardens; ~*s grasses*, succulent plants; **2.** sole (of the foot). ⚠ *Plante* in French is not used like 'plant' in the sense of fixtures, implements, machinery (= *matériel*, *installation industrielle*), machinery of intellectual work (= *moyens d'accomplissement d'une œuvre intellectuelle*), planned swindle, hoax (= *machination*, *escroquerie*, *coup monté*), detective, picket of detectives (= *policier*, *police*).

planter (plɑ̃te), v.a. [L *plantare*] To plant; to set, to fix, to drive in; to set up, to station; ~ *un clou*, to drive a nail; *il m'a planté là*, he has given me the slip; he left me in the lurch; *un garçon bien planté*, a well-set-up fellow; a stalwart, sturdy lad; **se** ~, v.pr. to station oneself; to stand, to place oneself; to be planted, to be set.

planteur (plɑ̃tœr), s.m. Planter; owner of a colonial plantation.

plantigrade (plɑ̃tigrad), adj. s.m. (zool.) Plantigrade.

plantoir (plɑ̃twar), s.m. Dibble; planting-tool, setting-stick.

planton (plɑ̃tɔ̃), s.m. (mil.) Orderly; *être de* ~, to be on duty, to be stationed.

plantule (plɑ̃tyl), s.f. (bot.) Plantule; embryo of a plant.

plantureusement (plɑ̃tyrøzmɑ̃), adv. Abundantly, copiously, plentifully, luxuriantly.

plantureu-x, -se (plɑ̃tyrø), adj. [f. OF *plenteure* = plenty] Abundant, copious, plentiful, luxuriant; fertile; fleshy.

planure (planyr), s.f. Shaving (of wood, &c.).

plaque (plak), s.f. [f. Dutch *plakke*] Plate, slab, sheet; veneer; plaque, badge, star; (photo.) plate; ~ *de blindage*, ~ *de cheminée*, back of a chimney; also draught-sheet, drawer, blower; (rail.) ~ *tournante*, turntable; ~ *d'accumulateur*, (accumulator) plate or electrode; (motor.) ~ *réglementaire, à numéro*, regulation number-plate.

plaqué (plake), s.m. Plated metal, electro-plate. ~, p. adj. Veneered (wood).

plaqueminier (plakminje), s.m. (bot.) Ebony-tree, persimmon-tree; *Diospyros.*

plaquer (plake), v.a. [f. *plaque*] To plate; to veneer; to lay on, to lay down; (mus.) ~ *des accords*, to thump out chords on the piano; (colloq.) ~ *quelqu'un* or *quelque chose*, to abandon, to jilt, to leave in the lurch; to cast off, to chuck up; *j'ai bonne envie de tout* ~, I feel like chucking everything up.

plaquette (plakɛt), s.f. Booklet; thin book; small plaque; (obs.) small coin.

plaqueu-r, -se (plakœr), s.m.f. adj. Plater; veneerer; (colloq.) one who leaves you in the lurch.

plasticité (plastisite), s.f. Plasticity.

plastique (plastik), adj. [Gr. *plastikos*] Plastic. ~, s.f. Plastic art; modelling; (colloq.) physique, bodily structure or development.

plastron (plastrɔ̃), s.m. [f. It. *piastra*] Breastplate, (fenc.) plastron; pad; (clothes) front, shirt-front; (fig.) butt, laughing-stock.

plastronner (plastrɔne), v.n. To pose; to make a brave show; to brave it out.

plat (pla), s.m. [f. *plat*, adj.] Dish; collection-plate; flat part, (of oars, &c.) blade; (naut.) mess; ~*s*, (bookbinding) sides; *mettre les petits* ~*s dans les grands*, to spare nothing; to turn the house out of windows; to make great preparations; to kill the fatted calf; *mettre les pieds dans le* ~, to put one's foot in it; *il nous a servi un* ~ *de sa façon*, he played us one of his tricks; ~ *allant au feu*, fireproof dish.

plat, -e (pla), adj. [LL *plattus*] Flat, level; plain, dull, vapid, spiritless, pithless; (of colours) uniform; (of hair) straight; *à* ~, flat; *à* ~ *ventre*, flat on the ground; (fig.) *être à* ~ *ventre devant X*, to fawn on X, to be buttering up to X; to cringe (to X); *battre à* ~*e couture*, to rout utterly; *un style* ~, a dull style, a pithless style; *vaisselle* ~*e*, plate; (naut.) *calme* ~, dead calm.

platane (platan), s.m. [Gr. *platanos*] (bot.) Plane-tree.

plat-bord (plabɔr), s.m. (pl. *plats-bords*) (naut.) Gunwale.

plateau (pl. **-x**) (plato), s.m. [f. *plat*] Tray, salver; (of a balance) scale; tableland, plateau, upland; platform; *les hauts* ~*x*, the uplands.

plate-bande (platbɑ̃d), s.f. (pl. *plates-bandes*] Flower-bed, narrow garden bed; (arch.) lintel.

platée (plate), s.f. **1.** Dishful; **2.** (arch.) foundations (of a building).

plateforme (platfɔrm), s.f. Platform; ~ *électorale*, electoral platform, (by ext.) platform oratory.

plate-longe (platlɔ̃ʒ), s.f. (pl. *des plates-longes*) (harness) Kicking-strap.

platement (platmɑ̃), adv. Dully, flatly, plainly, spiritlessly.

platine[1] (platin), s.m. [f. Span. *plata*] (chem.) Platinum.

platine[2] (platin), s.f. **1.** (of firearms) Lock-plate; (of a key-lock) plate; (of a microscope) stage-plate; (of watches, &c.) plate; (print.) platen; **2.** (slang) gift of the gab, tongue; *quelle* ~ *!*, what a tongue!

platiner (platine), v.a. To platinize; ***vis** platinée*, contact screw.

platitude (platityd), s.f. Flatness, dullness, platitude, meanness.

platonicien (platɔnisjɛ̃), adj. Platonic. ~, s.m.f. Platonist.

platonique (platɔnik), adj. Platonic.

platoniquement (platɔnikmɑ̃), adv. Platonically; (colloq.) disinterestedly.

platonisme (platɔnism), s.m. [f. *Plato*] Platonism.

plâtrage (plɑtraʒ), s.m. Plastering, plaster-work, lath and plaster; flimsy work.

plâtras (plɑtrɑ), s.m. Old plaster, rubbish.

plâtre (plɑtr), s.m. [f. Gr. *emplastron*] Plaster; plaster cast, plaster figure; ~ ***fin***, plaster of Paris; *essuyer les* ~*s*, to live in a newly-built (damp) house; *battre comme* ~, to beat to a jelly; to thrash pitilessly.

plâtrer (plɑtre), v.a. To plaster; (agric.) to manure (with gypsum); (colloq.) **se** ~, v.pr. to paint one's face.

plâtreu-x, -se (plɑtrø), adj. Chalky, plastery.

plâtrier (plɑtrje), s.m. Plasterer.

plâtrière (plɑtrjɛr), s.f. Gypsum-quarry; plaster-kiln.

plausibilité (plozibilite), s.f. Plausibility, plausibleness, credibility.

plausible (plozibl), adj. [f. L *plaudere, plausum*] Plausible.

plausiblement (plozibləmɑ̃), adv. Plausibly.

plèbe (plɛb), s.f. [L *plebs, plebis*] Common people.

plébéien, -ne (plebejɛ̃), adj. Plebeian.

plébiscitaire (plebissitɛr), adj. Plebiscitary.

plébiscite (plebissit), s.m. [f. L *plebs*] Plebiscite.

plectre (plɛktr), s.m. [Gr. *plēktron*] (mus.) Plectrum.

pléiade (plejad), s.f. [f. Gr. *pleias*] Pleiad; (fig.) pleiad.

plein, -e (plɛ̃), adj. [L *plenus*] Full (*de*, of), filled (*de*, with), replete, whole, fraught, solid, complete, thorough, copious; *à* ~, *en* ~, fully, entirely; right in the middle of; *à ~es mains*, freely, liberally, abundantly, *à ~es voiles*, in full sail; all sails set; *en ~ jour*, in broad daylight; *en ~ hiver*, in the depth of winter; *en ~e mer*, on the open sea; *en ~ midi*, (*a*) at noon, in the heat of day; (*b*) facing full south; *faire une ~e eau*, to dive (in deep water); *en ~ champ*, in the open fields; *en ~e terre*, in the open ground; in free soil; *en ~e classe*, before the whole class; *arbre fruitier en ~ vent*, standard fruit-tree; *un jour* ~, a whole day; *un mois* ~, a whole month; *~e lune*, full moon; *~e mer*, high tide; *la mer est ~e*, it is high tide; *~ de son sujet*, full of one's subject, engrossed with one's subject; *~ de soi-même*, self-conceited; *~ d'inquiétude*, full of anxiety; *en ~e lumière*, in full light; *de son ~ gré*, of one's own free will; *~ de vin*, or ~, (colloq.) drunk, full up; *en bois* ~, in solid wood; *donner ~s pouvoirs*, to give full powers; *avoir le cœur* ~, to have one's heart full, to be sad, to be full of grief; (naut.) *porter* ~, to keep the sails full; full sail; *tout* ~, (*a*) quite full; (*b*) many; *avoir tout ~ d'amis*, to have many friends; *avoir de l'argent ~ ses poches*, to have plenty of money; *il en a ~ la bouche*, he is full of it; he talks of nothing else, he is brimming over with it.

plein (plɛ̃), s.m. Full part, plenum, solid part, middle; (writing) thick stroke; (naut.) full tide, high tide; *battre son* ~, to be in full swing; *faire son ~ d'essence*, to have one's tank filled with petrol; *faire le* ~, to fill up (with petrol).

pleinement (plɛnmɑ̃), adv. Fully, entirely, thoroughly; *être ~ d'accord*, to agree completely, to be in complete agreement.

pléni-er, -ère (plenje), adj. [f. *plein*] Plenary.

plénipotentiaire (plenipɔtɑ̃sjɛr), adj. s.m. Plenipotentiary.

plénitude (plenityd), s.f. Plenitude, fullness, completeness.

pléonasme (pleɔnasm), s.m. [Gr. *pleonasmos*] Pleonasm.

pléonastique (pleɔnastik), adj. Pleonastic.

plésiosaure (plezjɔzɔr), s.m. (zool.) Plesiosaurus.

plessis (plɛsi), s.m. [Norman wd] Close, domain, estate.

plet (plɛ), s.m. (naut.) Coil (of a cable).

pléthore (pletɔr), s.f. [Gr. *plēthōrē*] Plethora.

pléthorique (pletɔrik), adj. Plethoric.

pleur (plœr), s.m. [f. *pleurer*] Tear; *verser, répandre des ~s*, to shed tears; *essuyer ses ~s*, to dry one's tears.

pleural, -e, (aux) (plœral), adj. (anat.) Pleural.

pleurard, -e (plœrar), adj. Whimpering. ~, s.m.f. Whimperer, blubberer.

pleurer (plœre), v.n.a. [L *plorare*] To weep, to cry, to shed tears; to bewail, to lament, to mourn (over, for); to bleed (as vines, &c.); *~ à chaudes larmes, ~ comme une madeleine, ~ comme un veau*, to cry one's eyes out, to weep abundantly; *~ de joie*, to weep for joy; *~ X*, to mourn for X.

pleurésie (plœrezi), s.f. (pathol.) Pleurisy.

pleurétique (plœretik), adj. Pleuritic.

pleureu-r, -se (plœrœr), s.m.f. Weeper, whimperer, mourner. ~, adj. Weeping, whimpering; *saule* ~, weeping willow.

pleurnicher (plœrniʃe), v.n. To whimper, to whine, to snivel.

pleurnicherie (plœrniʃri), s.f. Whimpering, whining, snivelling.

pleurnicheu-r, -se (plœrniʃœr), s.m.f. Whimperer, sniveller. ~, adj. Snivelling.

pleurodynie (plœrodini), s.f. (pathol.) Pleurodynia.

pleuronecte (plœrɔnɛkt), s.m. (ichth.) Pleuronectid.

pleutre (pløtr), s.m. Dastard, coward, contemptible wretch. ~, adj. Cowardly.

pleutrerie (pløtrəri), s.f. Cowardice, act of cowardice.

pleuvoir (plœvwar), impers. v. [L *pluere*] To rain; to pour, to shower down; (fig.) to come thick, to fall, to come abundantly; *il pleut à verse*, or *à seaux*, it is pouring (in buckets); *il pleut des hallebardes*, it is raining cats and dogs; *comme s'il en pleuvait*, freely, in quantities, easily; *les coups pleuvaient*, it rained blows; blows were falling in a shower.

plèvre (plɛvr), s.f. [f. Gr. *pleuron*] (anat.) Pleura.

plexus (plɛksys), s.m. [L wd] (anat.) Plexus.

pleyon (plɛjɔ̃), s.m. [f. *ployer*] Osier tie; curved fruiting-branch.

pli (pli), s.m. [f. *plier*] Fold, crease, tuck, pleat; rumple; wrinkle, inequality, difficulty; envelope, letter, message; habit, bend, routine; *cela ne fera pas un* ~, there will not be the slightest difficulty about that; *il a pris un mauvais* ~, he has contracted bad habits, or a bad habit; *un faux* ~, a crease, a false pleat; *sous ce* ~, enclosed; herein; *un ~ de terrain*, an undulation of the ground; *un ~ au front*, a wrinkle on the forehead.

pliable (pliabl), adj. Pliable, flexible.

pliage (pliaʒ), s.m. Folding.

pliant, -e (pliɑ̃), p. adj. Flexible, supple, pliant; folding. ~, s.m. Folding chair, camp-stool, folding seat, deck-chair.

plie (pli), s.f. (ichth.) Plaice.

pliement (plimɑ̃), s.m. Bending, folding.

plier (plie), v.a.n. [doublet of *ployer*, f. L *plicare*] To fold, to fold up, to bend; (fig.) to curb, to bring under; ~ *bagage*, to decamp; to be off, bag and baggage; to pack off; ~ *les genoux*, to kneel; to bend the knee; ~ *devant la volonté de X*, to yield to X's authority; **se** ~, v.pr. to submit (*à*, to), to yield (to), to comply (with); to be folded, to be bent.

plieu-r, -se (pliœr), s.m.f. Folder; **~se**, s.f. folding-machine.

plinthe (plɛ̃t), s.f. [Gr. *plinthos*] Plinth.

pliocène (pliɔsɛn), adj. s.m. [Gr. *pleiōn*+*kainos*] Pliocene.

plioir (plijwar), s.m. Paper-knife; folder.

plique (plik), s.f. [f. L *plicare*] (pathol.) Plica.

plissage (plisaʒ), s.m. Plaiting, pleating, tucking.

plissé (plise), s.m. Frill, frilling, pleated part (of a garment, &c.).

plissement (plismɑ̃), s.m. Folding, pleating; (geol.) corrugation, folding.

plisser (plise), v.a.n. To plait, to fold, to pleat, to tuck, to kilt, to crease, to crumple; to wrinkle, to pucker; (geol.) to corrugate.

plisseu-r, -se (plisœr), s.m.f. Plaiter, pleater.

pliure (pliyr), s.f. Folding; fold.

ploc (plɔk), s.m. [Dutch *plok*] (naut.) Sheathing hair.

ploiement (plwamɑ̃), s.m. Bending; ~ *des genoux*, kneeling.

plomb (plɔ̃), s.m. [L *plumbum*] Lead; shot; plumb-line; plummet; sink; leaden seal; (fig.) ballast, weight; *dormir d'un sommeil de* ~, to sleep heavily, soundly, like a log; (fig.) *avoir du* ~ *dans l'aile*, to be on one's last legs; to be crippled; to be half ruined; to be winged; *saumon de* ~, pig-lead; ~ *de chasse*, shot; *il lui faudrait un peu de* ~ *dans la tête*, he wants a little ballast; *fil à* ~, plumb-line, plummet; *les* ~*s de Venise*, the leads of Venice; the jails of Venice; *mine de* ~, plumbago, blacklead; *à* ~, perpendicularly; right, just in time, opportunely; *en* ~, leaden.

plombage (plɔ̃baʒ), s.m. **1.** Stopping (of teeth); **2.** plumbing, loading; **3.** sealing.

plombagine (plɔ̃baʒin), s.f. Plumbago, black-lead.

plombé, -e (plɔ̃be), p. adj. Loaded (of sticks, &c.); stopped (of teeth); sealed; leaden-hued, livid.

plomber (plɔ̃be), v.a. **1.** To load, to cover with lead; **2.** to seal, to stamp with lead; **3.** to stop (a tooth); **4.** to plumb; ~ *un mur*, to plumb a wall; **se** ~, v.pr. to take on a leaden hue, to become livid.

plomberie (plɔ̃bri), s.f. Plumbery; lead works.

plombier (plɔ̃bje), s.m. Plumber.

plombifère (plɔ̃bifɛr), adj. Plumbiferous.

plongeant, -e (plɔ̃ʒɑ̃), p. adj. Plunging; diving; downward; *tir* ~, downward firing, plunging fire.

plongée (plɔ̃ʒe), s.f. Dive, diving, immersion, submersion (of submarine); (fort.) glacis.

plongement (plɔ̃ʒmɑ̃), s.m. Plunging, dip; immersion.

plongeon (plɔ̃ʒɔ̃), s.m. **1.** Dive, diving, plunge; *faire un* ~, to dive; **2.** (ornith.) diver, loon.

plonger (plɔ̃ʒe), v.a.n. [LL *plumbicare*] To plunge, to immerse, to dip, to thrust; to dive, to pitch (of ships), to rush in; **se** ~, v.pr. to plunge, to yield (to grief, &c.) to rush (*dans*, into), to revel (in), to sink (into), to immerse oneself (in).

plongeu-r, -se (plɔ̃ʒœr), s.m.f. **1.** Diver; **2.** dish-washer, scullery-boy (in hotels, &c.); **3.** (ornith.) diver.

ploquer (plɔke), v.a. [f. *ploc*] (naut.) To felt, to sheath (a ship's bottom) with hair.

ploutocrate (plutɔkrat), s.m. [Gr. *ploutos* +*kratos*] Plutocrat.

ploutocratie (plutɔkrasi), s.f. Plutocracy.

ploutocratique (plutɔkratik), adj. Plutocratic.

ployer (plwaje), v.a.n. [L *plicare*; see doublet *plier*] To bend, to bow, to fold, to fold up; (fig.) to curb, to submit, to give way; ~ *sous le faix*, to give way under the burden; **se** ~, v.pr. to yield, to submit, to give way; to be folded.

pluche (plyʃ), s.f. See PELUCHE.

pluie (plɥi), s.f. [L *pluvia*] Rain; shower, downpour; abundance; *jour de* ~, rainy day; *le temps est à la* ~, it looks like rain; *petite* ~ *abat grand vent*, a little rain lays a great dust; *ennuyeux comme la* ~, as dull as ditch-water; *après la* ~ *le beau temps*, every cloud has a silver lining; *une* ~ *d'or*, a golden shower; *faire la* ~ *et le beau temps*, to rule the roost; to be the boss of the show; *parler de la* ~ *et du beau temps*, to talk of indifferent things.

plumage (plymaʒ), s.m. Plumage, feathers.

plumard (plymar), s.m. Feather broom; (colloq.) bed; (mil. slang) *aller au* ~ (or *au pieu*) to go to kip.

plumasserie (plymasri), s.f. Feather-trade.

plumassi-er, -ère (plymasje), s.m.f. adj. Plumassier, feather-dresser, feather-dealer.

plume (plym), s.f. [L *pluma*] Feather, plume, quill; pen; (fig.) style of writing; ~ *d'oie*, goose-quill; *lit de* ~, feather bed; *tenir la* ~, to write; *prendre la* ~, to write; *dessin à la* ~, pen-and-ink sketch; *guerre de* ~, paper war; *il y a laissé des* ~*s*, he has lost money; he has been fleeced; *écrire au courant de la* ~, to write off-hand; *trait de* ~, dash, stroke of the pen.

plumeau (pl. **-x**) (plymo), s.m. [f. *plume*] Feather duster.

plumer (plyme), v.a. To pluck (a bird, &c.); (fig.) to pluck, to fleece, to ruin; ~ *la poule sans la faire crier*, to fleece the sheep without making it bleat.

plumet (plymɛ), s.m. Plume, plume of feathers; (colloq.) *avoir son* ~, to have had enough; to be slightly tipsy; to be slightly oiled; to be slightly binged. ⚠ Not 'plummet', which = *plomb de sonde*.

plumetis (plymti), s.m. (embroidery) Feather-stitch, satin-stitch; *brodé au* ~, feather-stitched.

plumeu-x, -se (plymø), adj. Feathery, plumose, plumous.

plumier (plymje), s.m. Pencil-box, pen-box.

plumitif (plymitif), s.m. Quill-driver, scribbler; (law) minute-book.

plumule (plymyl), s.f. (bot., zool.) Plumule; syn. GEMMULE.

(la) plupart (laplypar), s.f. [*plus+part*] Most, the greatest part, the majority, most people; *la* ~ *du temps*, mostly, generally; *la* ~ *des gens disent*, most people say; *pour la* ~, mostly; *les femmes sont, pour la* ~, *curieuses*, most women are curious.

plural-e, (aux) (plyral), adj. Plural.

pluralité (plyralite), s.f. [f. L *pluralis*] Plurality.

pluriel, -le (plyrjɛl), adj. Plural. ~, s.m. Plural.

plus (ply), adv. [L *plus*] More, most, further, farther, longer, any more, any longer; the more; (~ marks the comparative in French; with def. art. it marks the superlative, ~ *cher*, dearer; *le* ~ *long*, the longest, &c.); (math.) plus: +; *ne* . . . ~, no more, no longer, not again, never again, never more; *au* ~, *tout au* ~, at most, at the utmost; *d'autant* ~, the more so; *bien* ~, much more, more than that; *de* ~, moreover, besides; *de* ~ *en* ~, more and more; *de* ~ *en* ~ *mal*, worse and worse; *de* ~ *en* ~ *fort!*, worse and worse!; better and better!; *en* ~, in addition (to), besides, more, over, extra; *le* ~, the most; ~ *malheureux que X*, more unhappy than X; *je n'ai* ~ *que cela*, I have nothing left but that; *ni* ~ *ni moins*, neither more nor less; ~ *ou moins*, more or less; *qui* ~ *est*, what is more; *sans* ~, without any more; only; *sans* ~ *tarder*, without further delay; *tant et* ~, abundantly; enough and to spare; *il n'est* ~ *temps*, it is too late; ~ *tard*, later; later on; *il n'est* ~, he is dead; ~ *on est de fous* ~ *on rit*, the more the merrier; ~ *le jour est long* ~ *la nuit est courte*, the longer the day, the shorter the night; *il n'en peut* ~, he is nearly done, he is tired out; *je n'ai* ~ *qu'à vous remercier*, it only remains for me to thank you; *deux fois* ~, twice as much; doubly; *six fois* ~, six times more; ~ *tôt*, earlier, sooner; (*see* PLUTÔT). ~, s.m. The most, the maximum; *qui peut le* ~ *peut le moins*, he who can achieve what is difficult can do what is easy.

plusieurs (plyzjœr), adj. m.f. pl. [LL *plusiores*] Several, many, some, a few. ~, pron. pl. Several people, some people.

plus-pétition (plypetisjɔ̃), s.f. (law term) Exorbitant demand.

plus-que-parfait (plyskəparfɛ), s.m. (pl. *plus-que-parfaits*) (gram.) Pluperfect.

plus-value (plyvaly), s.f. (pl. *plus-values*) Increase in value, increment.

plutonien, -ne (plytɔnjɛ̃), adj. [Gr. myth. n. *Ploutōn*] Plutonian, Plutonic.

plutôt (plyto), adv. (not to be confounded with *plus tôt*) Rather, sooner, preferably; ~ *que*, rather than; ~ *souffrir que mourir*, better to suffer than to die; *voyez* ~, see for yourself.

pluvial (plyvjal), s.m. (Cath. liturg.) Pluvial (a cope).

pluviale (plyvjal), adj. f. Rain-; of rain, rainy; *eau* ~, rain-water.

pluvier (plyvje), s.m. (ornith.) Plover.

pluvieu-x, -se (plyvjø), adj. Rainy, pluvious, wet.

pluviomètre (plyvjɔmɛtr), s.m. Pluviometer, rain-gauge.

pluviôse (plyvjoz), s.m. [f. L *pluvia*] Fifth month of calendar of first French Republic (20 Jan. to 18 or 19 Feb.).

pneu (pnø), s.m. [abbrev. of *pneumatique*] **1.** Tyre, tire; *un* ~ *crevé*, a punctured tyre; *un* ~ *éclaté*, a burst tyre; **2.** express letter.

pneumatique (pnømatik), adj. [f. Gr. *pneuma*] Pneumatic. ~, s.f. Pneumatics; ~, s.m. (also *pneu*) **1.** tyre; **2.** express letter.

pneumatologie (pnømatɔlɔʒi), s.f. [f. Gr. *pneuma+logos*] Pneumatology.

pneumonie (pnømɔni), s.f. [Gr. *pneumonia*] (pathol.) Pneumonia.

pochade (pɔʃad), s.f. (paint.) Rough sketch; (also Lit.) sketch, amusing short piece.

pochard, -e (pɔʃar), s.m.f. Drunkard; (slang) drunk, toper. (Hence colloq.) *se pocharder*, v.pr. to get drunk.

poche (pɔʃ), s.f. [orig. dub.] **1.** Pocket; *argent de* ~, pocket-money; *dictionnaire de* ~, pocket-dictionary; *elle n'a pas ses yeux dans sa* ~, she 's got eyes in her head; *connaître comme sa* ~, to know like the palm or back of one's hand; *mettez ça dans votre* ~ *et votre mouchoir par-dessus*, you may put that in your pipe and smoke it; *il met X complètement dans sa* ~, he is too strong for X; he throws X completely into the shade; he twists X round his little finger; *fouiller dans ses* ~*s*, to search one's pockets; **2.** pouch, bag, sack; *acheter chat* *en* ~, to buy a pig in a poke; **3.** crop (of birds); **4.** rabbit-net; **5.** (rare) soup-ladle.

pocher (pɔʃe), v.a. To poach (eggs, &c.); to bruise (the eyes); *il m'a poché l'œil,* he has given me a black eye.

pochetée (pɔʃte), s.f. Pouchful; pocketful; (slang) *quelle* ~ *!,* or *il en a une* ~ *!,* what a stupid fellow !, you duffer !

pochette (pɔʃɛt), s.f. **1.** Small pocket; **2.** pochette; **3.** small fiddle; **4.** small handkerchief.

pocheuse (pɔʃøz), s.f. (cook.) Poacher, poaching strainer.

pochoir (pɔʃwar), s.m. Stencil-plate.

pochon (pɔʃɔ̃), s.m. Soup-ladle; (colloq.) punch, bruise.

podagre (pɔdagr), s.m. [Gr. *podagra*] Gouty person; (fig.) grumpy old person. ~, adj. Gouty. ~, s.f. Gout, podagra (in the feet).

podestat (pɔdɛsta), s.m. [f. L *potestas*] Podesta.

podomètre (pɔdɔmɛtr), s.m. [Gr. *pous, podos+metron*] Pedometer; instrument for estimating distance by recording number of steps taken.

poêle[1] (pwɑl), s.m. [L *pallium*] Pall, canopy.

poêle[2] (pwɑl), s.m. [f. L *pensilis*] Stove.

poêle[3] (pwɑl), s.f. [L *patella*] Frying-pan; (fig.) *tenir la queue de la* ~, to be the boss; to boss the show; *sauter de la* ~ *dans la braise,* to jump out of the frying-pan into the fire.

poêlée (pwɑle), s.f. Panful.

poêlier (pwɑlje), s.m. Stove-maker, stove-dealer.

poêlon (pwɑlɔ̃), s.m. Saucepan; pipkin.

poème (pɔɛm), s.m. [Gr. *poiēma*] Poem.

poésie (pɔezi), s.f. [Gr. *poiēsis*] Poetry; poesy; piece of poetry.

poète (pɔɛt), s.m. adj. [Gr. *poiētēs*] Poet.

poétereau (pl. -x) (pɔetro), s.m. Wretched poet, poetaster.

poétesse (pɔetɛs), s.f. Poetess.

poétique (pɔetik), adj. Poetical. ~, s.f. Poetics.

poétiquement (pɔetikmɑ̃), adv. Poetically.

poétiser (pɔetize), v.a. **1.** To make poetical; **2.** (rare) to versify.

pognon (pɔɲɔ̃), s.m. (slang) Money, dibs, brass, tin, splosh, oof, chink.

pogrom (pɔgrɔm), s.m. [Russ. wd] Pogrom, mass murder.

poids (pwɑ), s.m. [L *pensum*] Weight, heaviness; (phys.) gravity; burden, (fig.) importance, purport, weight; *un* ~ *de 5 kg.,* a weight of 5 kg.; ~ *brut,* gross weight; ~ *net,* net weight; *un homme de* ~, an important man; *vendre au* ~, to sell by weight; *vendre au* ~ *de l'or,* to sell very dear; *son opinion est d'un grand* ~, his opinion has much weight.

poignant, -e (pwaɲɑ̃), p. adj. [f. *poindre*] Poignant.

poignard (pwaɲar), s.m. [f. *poing*] Poniard, dagger; (fig.) *mettre le* ~ *sur la gorge à X,* to drive X into a corner, to force X to do something under threat; *signer le* ~ *sur la gorge,* to sign under coercion.

poignarder (pwaɲarde), v.a. To stab; (fig.) to stab to the heart.

poigne (pwaɲ), s.f. [f. *poing*] Grip, grasp; (fig.) strong will, energy; *un homme à* ~, a strong-handed man, a masterful man; (colloq. U.S.A.) a he-man.

poignée (pwaɲe), s.f. Handful; handle, hilt (of a sword), holder; (fig.) small number, handful; *à* ~*s,* by handfuls; ~ *de main,* handshake; *donner une* ~ *de main à X,* to shake hands with X.

poignet (pwaɲɛ), s.m. Wrist; wristband, cuff; (fig.) *à la force du* ~, by one's own energy.

poil (pwal), s.m. [L *pilus*] (of persons and animals) Hair; bristle; down, wool; (of cloth, hats, &c.) nap; (of horses) coat, colour; (fig.) beard; courage; *un brave à trois* ~*s,* a hero of the first water; *avoir un* ~ *dans la main,* to have no liking for work; to feel Mondayish; *à* ~, (*a*) (of a horse) bareback; (*b*) (slang) (of a person) naked; *à contre-*~, against the grain; (slang) *faire le* ~ *à X,* to give X a drubbing; *reprendre du* ~ *de la bête,* to have another go at it; not to lose heart.

poilu, -e (pwaly), adj. Hairy, shaggy; (bot.) pilose. ~, s.m. (since the war of 1914) Tommy, French infantryman.

poinçon (pwɛ̃sɔ̃), s.m. [L *punctio*] Bodkin, punch, awl, point; (cask) puncheon; (build.) king-post; (coining) stamp.

poinçonnage (pwɛ̃sɔnaʒ), s.m. Stamping.

poinçonner (pwɛ̃sɔne), v.a. To stamp, to punch.

poinçonneuse (pwɛ̃sɔnøz), s.f. Punching-machine.

poindre (pwɛ̃dr), v.n. [f. L *pungere*] To appear, to come up, to break, to dawn; ~, v.a. (obs.) to cudgel, to maltreat, to sting; *oignez vilain, il vous poindra, poignez vilain, il vous oindra,* flatter the low and they will treat you roughly, cudgel them, and they will lick your boots.

poing (pwɛ̃), s.m. [L *pugnus*] Fist, (closed) hand; *coup de* ~, blow with the fist, fisticuff, punch; *pieds et* ~*s liés,* bound hand and foot; *serrer les* ~*s,* to clench one's fist; *coup-de-*~ *américain,* knuckle-duster; *dormir à* ~*s fermés,* to sleep soundly, or like a top.

point (pwɛ̃), s.m. [L *punctum*] Point, dot, speck; stitch; stop, full stop; *deux* ~*s,* colon; ~ *et virgule,* semi-colon; ~ *d'interrogation,* note of interrogation, question-mark; ~ *d'exclamation,* note of exclamation; *à ~*, (*a*) just in time; at the right moment; (*b*) (of roasted meat) done to a turn; (*c*) (of fruit) ripe; *à ~ nommé*, most opportunely; in the nick of time; just when wanted; *à quel ~?*, to what extent?, how far?; *au ~*, in focus; *au ~ où nous en sommes*, as matters stand; matters having reached that point; *venir au ~*, to come to the point; *au dernier ~*, in the highest degree; *de ~ en ~*, minutely, in all particulars; gradually; *de tout ~, en tout ~*, in every respect; *sur le point de . . .*, on the verge of, just before . . ., very near . . .; *à tel ~ que*, to such a degree that; *jusqu'à un certain ~*, to a certain extent; *~ d'arrêt*, stopping-place; *~ arrière*, back-stitch; *~ de boutonnière*, buttonhole-stitch; *~ de chaînette*, chain-stitch; *~ de contact*, point of contact; *~ de chausson*, herring-bone-stitch; *~ de croix*, cross-stitch; *~ de côté*, hem-stitch; *avoir un ~ de côté*, to have a stitch in one's side; *~ devant*, running-stitch; *~ de départ*, starting-point; *~ d'épine*, feather-stitch; *~ de fait*, point of fact; *~ de fuite*, point of sight; vanishing-point; *~ de fusion*, fusing-point; *~ de congélation*, freezing-point; *~ d'intersection*, point of intersection; *le ~ du jour*, the dawn; *~ d'honneur*, point of honour; *~ de jonction*, meeting-point; (artill.) *~ de mire*, sight; (colloq.) aim, target, object; *~ mort*, dead point, dead centre; (mus.) *~ d'orgue*, pause; *~ de vue*, point of view, opinion; (U.S.A.) view-point; *à ce ~ de vue*, in that light; *un beau ~ de vue*, a fine view; *les ~s cardinaux*, the cardinal points; (naut.) *faire le ~*, to take the bearings; *un ~ fait à temps en sauve mille*, a stitch in time saves nine; *il vous rendrait des ~s*, he is more than a match for you; he can give you points (and a beating); *un ~ noir à l'horizon*, breakers ahead, a black cloud on the horizon; *mettez les ~s sur les i*, cross your *t*s and dot your *i*s; *un ~ c'est tout*, there 's an end of it.

point (pwɛ̃), adv. No, not, not at all, not any, none, no such thing; *je n'en veux ~*, I won't have any.

pointage (pwɛ̃taʒ), s.m. **1.** Pointing, aiming, levelling; **2.** checking, ticking off.

pointe (pwɛ̃t), s.f. [LL *puncta*] Point, head, tip, top; nail, tack; cape, ness, foreland; peak, pinnacle; (fig.) pungency, sharpness, flavour, zest; witticism; touch; *pousser une ~*, to make an advance; *pousser sa ~*, to press one's point; *à la ~ du jour*, at the break of day; (fig.) *à la ~ de l'épée*, forcibly; by main force, by storm; *une ~ d'ironie*, a touch of irony; *sur la ~ des pieds*, on tiptoe; (danc.) *faire des ~s*, to dance standing on the toes; *lancer des ~ à X*, to rail at X, to tease X, to plague X with pointed witticisms.

pointeau (pl. **-x**) (pwɛ̃to), s.m. **1.** (motor.) Needle; *joint de siège de ~*, needle valve; **2.** centre-punch.

pointer (pwɛ̃te), v.a.n. **1.** To point (a gun, &c.), to aim; **2.** to check, to tick off; **3.** (of a horse) to rear; *~ les oreilles*, to prick up its ears; **4.** to begin, to appear, to break (as the dawn, &c.); **5.** (mus.) to dot (a note).

pointeur (pwɛ̃tœr), s.m. Pointer, gunner; marker, checker.

pointillé, -e (pwɛ̃tije), p. adj. Dotted; *ligne ~e*, dotted line. ~, s.m. Dotted drawing, dotted line or outline; stippled engraving.

pointiller (pwɛ̃tije), v.a. To dot, to stipple, to perforate; ~, v.n. to cavil, to tease, to contest, to enter into detailed argument.

pointilleu-x, -se (pwɛ̃tijø), adj. Captious, punctilious, nice; cavilling, irascible.

pointilliste (pwɛ̃tijist), adj. s.m.f. Pointilliste (painter).

pointu, -e (pwɛ̃ty), adj. Sharp, pointed, peaked, peaky, acute; (fig.) pointed, sharp, captious, subtle; (of voice) shrill.

pointure (pwɛ̃tyr), s.f. **1.** (of shoes, gloves, &c.) Size; **2.** (print.) point.

poire (pwar), s.f. [L *pirum*] Pear; powder-flask; bulb; any pear-shaped object; (colloq.) (*a*) head, face; (*b*) simpleton, juggins, gullible fool; *faire sa ~*, to try to show off; *il ne faudrait pas me prendre pour une ~*, you must not think me a juggins; you won't see any green in my eye; *coupons la ~ en deux*, let us split the difference; *garder une ~ pour la soif*, to lay up something for a rainy day.

poiré (pware), s.m. Perry.

poireau, porreau (pl. **-x**) (pwaro, pɔro), s.m. Leek, wart; (fig. colloq.) decoration of *Mérite Agricole*; (slang) *faire son ~*, to show off.

poireauter (pwarɔte), v.n. (colloq., slang) To wait, to be kept waiting, to kick one's heels, to be kept hanging about.

poirée (pware), s.f. (bot.) White beet; syn. BETTE.

poirier (pwarje), s.m. (bot.) Pear-tree.

pois (pwɑ), s.m. [L *pisum*] **1.** (bot.) Pea; (pl. peas and (obs.) pease); *petits ~*, green peas; *~ cassés*, split peas; *~ chiches*, chick peas; *~ de senteur*, sweet peas; *ce n'est pas la fleur des ~*, (of a person) he (or she) has a bad reputation; he (or she) is not in the best society; **2.** spot; *satinette à ~*, spotted sateen.

poison (pwazɔ̃), s.m. [L *potio*] Poison, [venom.

poissard, -e (pwasar), adj. [f. *poix*] Vulgar, billingsgate, low. *~e*, s.f. Fish-wife, vulgar loud-voiced woman.

poisse (pwas), s.f. [f. *poisser*] (slang) Bad luck, annoyance; *quelle ~!*, how provoking!, bother!, damn!

poisser (pwase), v.a.n. [f. *poix*] To pitch; to make sticky, to be sticky; (slang) (*a*) to annoy; (*b*) to scrounge; *se faire* ~, (very vulgar) to get caught or nabbed, to catch it, to be arrested.

poisseu-x, -se (pwasø), adj. Sticky, gluey, pitchy.

poisson (pwasɔ̃), s.m. [LL *piscio*] Fish; (obs.) quartern, gill; ~ *d'avril*, catch for April fools; April fool's errand, or take-in; *faire un* ~ *d'avril à X*, to make X an April fool; ~ *rouge*, goldfish; *ni chair ni* ~, neither fish, flesh, nor fowl; *être comme le* ~ *dans l'eau*, to be in one's element; to have every comfort; *cela finit en queue de* ~, that ends in nothing; it is petering out; ~ *de rivière*, freshwater fish; ~ *de mer*, sea fish; (astr.) *les* ~*s*, Pisces; (fig.) *noyer le* ~, to confuse (voluntarily) the issue.

poissonnaille (pwasɔnɑj), s.f. Small fish, small fry; syn. FRETIN.

poissonnerie (pwasɔnri), s.f. Fish-market, fishmonger's shop, fish department.

poissonneu-x, -se (pwasɔnø), adj. Abounding in fish.

poissonni-er, -ère (pwasɔnje), s.m.f. Fish-monger, fish-woman.

poissonnière (pwasɔnjɛr), s.f. Fish-kettle.

poitevin, -e (pwatvɛ̃), adj. s.m.f. (Native) of Poitou.

poitrail (pl. **-s**) (pwatraj), s.m. [f. *poitrine*] **1.** Breast, chest (of a horse); breastplate, breast-strap (of harness); **2.** (build.) breastsummer, bressummer.

poitrinaire (pwatrinɛr), adj. s.m.f. Consumptive.

poitrine (pwatrin), s.f. [f. L *pectus, pectoris*] Chest; breast, breasts, bosom; lungs; (butch.) brisket; *maladie de* ~, consumption; *voix de* ~, chest voice; (fig.) *se frapper la* ~, to cry peccavi.

poivrade (pwavrad), s.f. [f. *poivre*] Poivrade (sauce).

poivre (pwavr), s.m. [L *piper*] Pepper; ~ *de Cayenne*, Cayenne pepper; ~ *long*, Jamaica pepper, pimento; (fig.) piquancy, smutty witticism; ~ *et sel*, grizzly, grey, greyish; pepper-and-salt.

poivrer (pwavre), v.a. To pepper; (fig.) to make highly spiced or salacious.

poivrier (pwavrie), s.m. **1.** (bot.) Pepper-plant; **2.** pepper-box.

poivrière (pwavriɛr), s.f. **1.** Pepper-plantation; **2.** pepper-box; **3.** (arch.) corner-turret.

poivrot (pwavro), s.m. (colloq.) Drunkard, boozer.

poix (pwɑ), s.f. [L *pix*] Pitch; shoemaker's wax; *enduire de* ~, to pitch; ~*-résine*, resin.

poker (pokɛr), s.m. [Engl. wd] Poker (card-game).

polaire (polɛr), adj. [f. *pole*] Polar; *l'étoile* ~, the pole-star.

polaque, polacre (polak, polakr), (obs.) s.m. Polish cavalryman (18th c.); ~, s.f. (naut.) polacca.

polarimètre (polarimɛtr), s.m. Polarimeter.

polarisation (polariza'sjɔ̃), s.f. Polarization.

polariser (polarize), v.a. To polarize.

polarité (polarite), s.f. Polarity.

polder (poldɛr), s.m. [Dutch wd] Polder.

pôle (pol), s.m. [f. Gr. *polos*] Pole; ~ *magnétique*, magnetic pole; ~ *nord, boréal*, or *arctique*, North Pole; ~ *sud, austral*, or *antarctique*, South Pole; ~ ~ *positif, négatif*, positive, negative pole (of electric cell, battery, &c.).

polémarque (polemark), s.m. (ant.) Polemarch.

polémique (polemik), s.f. [f. Gr. *polemos*] Controversy, polemic; polemics. ~, adj. Polemic, polemical, controversial.

polémiste (polemist), s.m.f. Polemist, controversialist.

polenta (polɛnta), s.f. [It. wd] Polenta, Italian porridge.

poli, -e (poli), p. adj. [f. *polir*] **1.** Polished, glossy; **2.** polite; civil. ~, s.m. Polish, finish.

police (polis), s.f. [Gr. *politeia*] **1.** Police; police regulations; *bonnet de* ~, forage cap; *agent de* ~, policeman; constable, inspector; *commissaire de* ~, (district) superintendent of police (there is no exact equivalent in English); (mil.) *salle de* ~, guard-room; *tribunal de simple* ~, police-court; *faire la* ~, to maintain order; **2.** policy; ~ *d'assurance*, insurance policy.

policer (polise), v.a. To civilize, to refine, to polish; ⚠ rarely 'to police', which = *administrer, contrôler au moyen de la police.*

polichinelle (poliʃinɛl), s.m. [It. *Pulcinella*] Punch, merry andrew, buffoon; (fig.) upstart, puppet, buffoon; *c'est le secret de* ~, it is an open secret; *la pratique de* ~, the squeaker of the Punch and Judy man.

polici-er, -ère (polisje), adj. Pertaining to the police. ~, s.m. Police inspector.

poliment (polimɑ̃), adv. Politely, civilly.

polir (polir), v.a. [L *polire*] To polish; to civilize, to refine, to give a finish to; **se** ~, v.pr. to be polished.

polissage (polisaʒ), s.m. Polishing.

polisseu-r, -se (polisœr), s.m.f. Polisher.

polissoir (poliswar), s.m. Polisher; ~**e**, s.f. polishing-brush.

polisson, -ne (polisɔ̃), adj. Licentious, loose. ~, s.m.f. Scamp, scapegrace, young rascal.

polissonnerie (polisɔnri), s.f. **1.** Blackguardly trick, mischievous trick, broad joke; **2.** indecent, licentious talk, drawing, or piece of writing. ⚠ ~ may be said of a child's mischievous pranks or tricks;

it is not very pejorative in this case; but the sense is quite different and strongly pejorative when it is said of an adult's actions or writings, drawings, &c.
polissure (pɔlisyr), s.f. Polishing.
politesse (pɔlitɛs), s.f. [It. *politezza*] Politeness, good breeding, civility; act of civility; *brûler la ~ à X*, to leave X abruptly, to give X the slip; *faire une ~ à X*, to do X a kindness.
politicien, -ne (pɔlitisjɛ̃), s.m.f. adj. Politician.
politique (pɔlitik), s.f. [Gr. *politikē*] Politics; policy; *parler ~*, to talk politics; *soutenir la ~ de X*, to support X's policy; *la ~ extérieure*, foreign policy; ~, s.m. politician.
politique (pɔlitik), adj. Political; politic, prudent, crafty, wise; *droits ~s*, political rights.
politiquement (pɔlitikmɑ̃), adv. Politically; cunningly, shrewdly, wisely.
polka (pɔlka), s.f. [Polish orig.] Polka (dance).
polker (pɔlke), v.n. To dance the polka, to polk.
pollen (pɔlɛn), s.m. [L wd] Pollen.
pollicitation (pɔlisita'sjɔ̃), s.f. [f. L *polliceri*] (law) Pollicitation, promise not yet formally accepted, and therefore revocable.
pollinique (pɔlinik), adj. (bot.) Pollinic.
pollinisation (pɔliniza'sjɔ̃), s.f. (bot.) Pollination.
polluer (pɔllɥe), v.a. [L *polluere*] To pollute.
pollution (pɔllysjɔ̃), s.f. Pollution.
polo (pɔlo), s.m. [f. Engl. wd] **1.** Polo; **2.** a round brimless cap.
polochon (pɔlɔʃɔ̃), s.m. (colloq.) Bolster.
polonais, -e (pɔlɔnɛ), adj. Polish. ~ s.m. Pole; *saoul comme un ~*, as drunk as a lord; ~e, s.f. **1.** Polish woman; **2.** polonaise (a dance); **3.** polonaise (a garment).
poltron, -ne (pɔltrɔ̃), adj. [It. *poltrone*] Coward, chicken-hearted, cowardly. ~, s.m.f. Coward, poltroon.
poltronnerie (pɔltrɔnri), s.f. Cowardice, poltroonery.
polyandrie (pɔliɑ̃dri), s.f. [f. Gr. *polus+andros*] Polyandry, polyandria.
polychrome (pɔlikrom), adj. [Gr. *polukhrōmos*] Polychrome, polychromic, polychromous, polychromatic.
polyèdre (pɔliɛdr), adj. (also *polédrique*) [f. Gr. *poluedros*] Polyhedral, polyhedrous. ~, s.m. Polyhedron.
polygame (pɔligam), s.m.f. [Gr. *polugamos*] Polygamist. ~, adj. Polygamous, polygamic.
polygamie (pɔligami), s.f. Polygamy.
polyglotte (pɔliglɔt), adj. [Gr. *poluglōttos*] Polyglot, polyglottal, polyglottic. ~, s.m.f. Polyglot.
polygonal, -e, (aux) (pɔligɔnal), adj. Polygonal.
polygone (pɔligɔn), s.m. [Gr. *polugōnos*] Polygon.
polygraphe (pɔligraf), s.m. [Gr. *polus+graphein*] Polygraph; versatile author.
polymorphe (pɔlimɔrf), adj. [Gr. *polus+morphē*] Polymorphous, multiform.
polynésien, -ne (pɔlinezjɛ̃), adj. s.m.f. Polynesian.
polynôme (pɔlinom), s.m. [Gr. *polus+* L *nomen*] (alg.) Polynomial, polynome.
polype (pɔlip), s.m. [f. Gr. *polus+pous*] Polyp; (pathol.) polypus.
polypétale (pɔlipetal), adj. (bot.) Polypetalous.
polypier (pɔlipje), s.m. (nat. hist.) Polypier, polypary.
polypode (pɔlipɔd), adj. s.m. [f. Gr. *polus+pous, podos*] Polypod.
polysyllabique (pɔlisillabik), adj. Polysyllabic.
polytechnicien (pɔlitɛknisjɛ̃), s.m. Student of *École polytechnique.*
polytechnique (pɔlitɛknik), adj. [f. Gr. *polutekhnos*] Polytechnic.
polythéisme (pɔliteism), s.m. [f. Gr. *polutheos*] Polytheism.
polythéiste (pɔliteist), adj. Polytheistic.
pommade (pɔmad), s.f. [f. *pomme*] Pomade, pomatum, ointment; (fig.) flattery, soft sawder, blarney.
pommader (pɔmade), v.a. To pomade, to apply ointment or brilliantine.
pomme (pɔm), s.f. [L *pomum*] Apple; pippin; any apple-shaped object; *~ d'Adam*, Adam's apple; *mériter la ~*, to deserve the palm; *~ de canne*, head of a stick; *~ à cidre*, cider-apple; (fig.) *~ de discorde*, bone of contention; apple of discord; *~ de chou*, head of a cabbage; *~ de pin*, pine-cone; *~ de terre*, potato; *~ d'arrosoir*, rose of a watering-can.
pommé, -e (pɔme), p. adj. Grown to a round head; (colloq. fig.) complete, downright, regular, out and out; *une bêtise ~e*, a horrible floater; a shocking blunder, a bloomer.
pommeau (pl. -x) (pɔmo), s.m. [f. *pomme*] Pommel; knob.
pomme de terre (pɔmdətɛr), s.f. Potato; *~s de terre en robe de chambre*, potatoes cooked in their jackets.
pommelé, -e (pɔmle), adj. Dappled, dapple; *cheval gris ~*, dapple-grey horse; *ciel ~*, dappled sky; mackerel sky.
(se) pommeler (səpɔmle), v.pr. To become dappled.
pommelle (pɔmɛl), s.f. Strainer (over a drain-pipe).
pommer (pɔme), v.n. To grow to a head, to cabbage.
pommeraie (pɔmrɛ), s.f. Apple-orchard.

pommette (pɔmɛt), s.f. [f. *pomme*] Cheek-bone; pommel.
pommier (pɔmje), s.m. (bot.) Apple-tree.
pomologie (pɔmɔlɔʒi), s.f. [f. L *pomum*+ Gr. *logos*] Pomology.
pompe[1] (pɔ̃p), s.f. [Gr. *pompē*] Pomp, state, ceremony; *~s funèbres*, funeral ceremony; funeral company, undertaker; *en grande ~*, in state; *renoncer au monde et à ses ~s*, to renounce the world and all its pomps.
pompe[2] (pɔ̃p), s.f. [orig. dub., Dutch *pomp*?] Pump, pumping-machine, exhaust-pump, suction-pump; *~ à incendie*, fire-engine; *~ à air*, air-pump, tyre air-pump, inflator; *~ foulante*, force-pump; *~ aspirante et foulante*, lift- and force-pump; *~ à bière*, beer-engine; *~ d'arrosage*, watering-engine.
pomper (pɔ̃pe), v.a. To pump; to suck up.
pompette (pɔ̃pɛt), adj. (colloq.) Slightly tipsy, half-seas-over, fresh, squiffy.
pompeusement (pɔ̃pøzmɑ̃), adv. Pompously, in state.
pompeu-x, -se (pɔ̃pø), adj. Pompous, stately, grand.
pompier (pɔ̃pje), s.m. Fireman; (rare) pump-maker. ~, adj. Conventional, philistine, academic and old-fashioned.
pompon (pɔ̃pɔ̃), s.m. Pompon, top-knot, tuft, tassel; (colloq.) *avoir son ~* or *son plumet*, to be slightly oiled; to have had a drop too much.
pomponner (pɔ̃pɔne), v.a. [f. *pompon*] To deck out, to bedeck, to dress up, to titivate, to bedizen; **se** ~, v.pr. to dress up with much care, to titivate.
ponant (pɔnɑ̃), s.m. [It. *ponente*] West; syn. OCCIDENT.
ponçage (pɔ̃saʒ), s.m. Pumicing; pouncing (of drawings).
ponce (pɔ̃s), s.f. [L *pumex*] Pumice; (drawing) pounce; *pierre ~*, pumice-stone.
ponceau[1] (pl. **-x**) (pɔ̃so), s.m. [f. *pont*] Small bridge; culvert.
ponceau[2] (pl. **-x**) (pɔ̃so), s.m. [f. *paon, paonceau*] Corn-poppy. ~, adj. invar. Flame-coloured, poppy-red.
poncer (pɔ̃se), v.a. To pumice; (drawing) to pounce.
poncif (pɔ̃sif), s.m. [f. *poncer*] Pattern (for pounced drawing), (fig.) trite, conventional thought or saying, hackneyed expression.
poncire (pɔ̃sir), s.m. [f. *pomme*+(L) *citreum*] Poncire-lemon.
poncis (pɔ̃si), s.m. Pounced drawing.
ponction (pɔ̃ksjɔ̃), s.f. [L *punctio*] (surg.) Puncture, tapping.
ponctionner (pɔ̃ksjɔne), v.a. (surg.) To puncture, to tap.
ponctualité (pɔ̃ktɥalite), s.f. Punctuality.
ponctuation (pɔ̃ktɥa'sjɔ̃), s.f. Punctuation.
ponctué, -e (pɔ̃ktɥe), p. adj. Punctuated; dotted.
ponctuel, -le (pɔ̃ktɥɛl), adj. [LL *punctualis*] Punctual, exact.
ponctuellement (pɔ̃ktɥɛlmɑ̃), adv. Punctually.
ponctuer (pɔ̃ktɥe), v.a. [LL *punctuare*] To punctuate, to mark, to dot.
pondérabilité (pɔ̃derabilite), s.f. Ponderability.
pondérable (pɔ̃derabl), adj. [L *ponderabilis*] Ponderable.
pondérat-eur, -rice (pɔ̃deratœr), adj. Balancing, moderating.
pondération (pɔ̃dera'sjɔ̃), s.f. Ponderation; equipoise; moderation, weight.
pondérer (pɔ̃dere), v.a. [f. L *ponderare*] To balance; to give weight and poise to; to moderate.
pondeuse (pɔ̃døz), s.f. Good layer. ~, adj. Laying; (fig.) prolific, productive.
pondoir (pɔ̃dwar), s.m. Laying-place; laying-basket.
pondre (pɔ̃dr), v.a.n. [L *ponere*] To lay eggs, to lay; (fig.) to produce, to be prolific, to publish; *~ un article*, to deliver oneself of an article.
ponette (pɔnɛt), s.f. She-pony.
poney (pɔne), s.m. [Engl. wd] Pony.
pongo (pɔ̃go), s.m. (zool.) Pongo, ape.
pont (pɔ̃), s.m. [L *pons*] Bridge; deck; *~ tournant*, swing bridge; *~ suspendu*, suspension-bridge; *premier ~*, lower deck; *deuxième ~*, upper deck; *faux ~*, spar-deck; *vaisseau à trois ~s*, three-decker; *pantalon à ~*, trousers with side fastening (without a fly); *~ aux ânes*, pons asinorum; bridge of asses; *faire un ~ d'or à X*, to make great pecuniary concessions to X; *il passera encore beaucoup d'eau sous les ~s avant que*, many things may happen before; no hurry; *couper les ~s*, to take the decisive step, to burn one's boats, to cut off one's own retreat; *faire le ~*, to keep holiday on a working day between two holidays; *ingénieur des Ponts et Chaussées*, State civil engineer; *tout le monde sur le ~!*, all hands on deck; *se porter comme le Pont-Neuf*, to be as sound as a rock; to be as fit as a fiddle; to enjoy splendid health; *c'est vieux comme le Pont-Neuf*, it's as old as the hills; Queen Anne is dead; (slang) *couper dans le ~*, to be deceived, to be taken in; to fall into a snare.
pont-arrière (pɔ̃tarjɛr), s.m. (motor.) Rear axle, differential casing.
ponte[1] (pɔ̃t), s.m. [Span. *punto*] Punter (at baccara, &c.).
ponte[2] (pɔ̃t), s.f. [f. *pondre*] Laying (of eggs).
ponté, -e (pɔ̃te) p. adj. (naut.) Decked.
ponter (pɔ̃te), v.a. (naut.) To deck; ~, v.n. to punt (at games).

ɔ, note, glotte; ɔ̃, *monter, ronde*; ø, *feu, creux*; œ, *peur, sœur*; œ̃, *un*; ʃ, *chez, schisme*; u, *tout*; w, *oui, doit, douaire*; y, *mur, pu*; ɥ, *huile, muette*; z, *zèle, rose*; ʒ, *déjà, gentil*.

pontet (pɔ̃tɛ), s.m. [f. *pont*] **1.** Trigger-guard; **2.** saddle-tree.
pontife (pɔ̃tif), s.m. [L *pontifex*] Pontiff; (fig.) a self-important ponderous critic, author, or artist; *le souverain* ~, the Pope, the sovereign Pontiff.
pontifical, -e, (aux) (pɔ̃tifikal), adj. Pontifical.
pontificalement (pɔ̃tifikalmɑ̃), adv. Pontifically.
pontificat (pɔ̃tifika), s.m. Pontificate.
pontifier (pɔ̃tifje), v.n. To pontificate; (fig.) to pontify, to play the pontiff; to speak or act pompously, to show off.
pontin, -e (pɔ̃tɛ̃), adj. Pontine; *les Marais* ~*s*, the Pontine Marshes.
pont-levis (pɔ̃ləvi), s.m. (pl. *ponts-levis*) Draw-bridge.
ponton (pɔ̃tɔ̃), s.m. [L *ponto*] Bridge of boats; pontoon; hulk, convict-ship; landing-pier.
pontonnier (pɔ̃tɔnje), s.m. Pontonier, pontoon-soldier.
pope (pɔp), s.m. [Russ. *pop*] Pope (parish priest of Greek church in Russia).
popeline (pɔplin), s.f. [It. *papalina*] Poplin.
poplité, -e (pɔplite), adj. [f. L *poples*] (anat.) Popliteal.
popote (pɔpɔt), s.f. (colloq.) Cooking, food, grub; mess; (colloq.) *faire la* ~, to do the cooking; to get the grub ready; *faire* ~ *ensemble*, to grub together, to share the damages; (mil.) to mess together; ~ *d'officiers*, officers' mess.
populace (pɔpylas), s.f. [It. *popolaccio*] Populace, mob, rabble.
populaci-er, -ère (pɔpylasje), adj. Low, vulgar, of the rabble; billingsgate.
populage (pɔpylaʒ), s.m. (bot.) Marsh-marigold.
populaire (pɔpylɛr), adj. [f. L *populus*] **1.** Popular; **2.** vulgar, common; *expression* ~, vulgar or common expression; *se rendre* ~, to make oneself popular.
populairement (pɔpylɛrmɑ̃), adv. Popularly; commonly.
populariser (pɔpylarize), v.a. To popularize; to spread among the people; to make popular.
popularité (pɔpylarite), s.f. Popularity.
population (pɔpylaˈsjɔ̃), s.f. Population.
populeum (pɔpyleɔm), s.m. [f. L *populus*] (pharm.) Poplar ointment.
populeu-x, -se (pɔpylø), adj. Populous.
populo (pɔpylo), s.m. (colloq.) The common people, the lower classes, the rabble.
poquet (pɔkɛ), s.m. [f. *poche*] Small hole in the ground in which beans or certain other seeds are sown.
porc (pɔr and pɔrk), s.m. [L *porcus*] Hog, pig, swine; pork; (fig.) filthy swine; *côtelettes de* ~, pork chops.
porcelaine (pɔrslɛn), s.f. [It. *porcellana*] Porcelain, china, chinaware. ~, adj. Ivory-coloured; (of horses) blue-grey.
porcelaini-er, -ère (pɔrslɛnje), adj. Pertaining to china or porcelain. ~, s.m.f. Porcelain-maker, porcelain-dealer.
porcelet (pɔrslɛ), s.m. Young pig, porket.
porc-épic (pɔrkepik), s.m. (zool.) Porcupine; (fig.) very touchy person; Tartar.
porche (pɔrʃ), s.m. [L *porticus*] Porch, portal.
porch-er, -ère (pɔrʃe), s.m.f. Swine-herd, pig-driver.
porcherie (pɔrʃri), s.f. Pigsty; piggery.
porcin, -e (pɔrsɛ̃), adj. Porcine.
pore (pɔr), s.m. [Gr. *poros*] Pore.
poreu-x, -se (pɔrø), adj. Porous.
porion (pɔrjɔ̃), s.m. Overseer (in coal-mines).
porisme (pɔrism), s.m. [Gr. *porisma*] (math.) Porism.
pornographe (pɔrnɔgraf), s.m.f. adj. Pornographer, pornographic.
pornographie (pɔrnɔgrafi), s.f. [Gr. *pornē*+*graphē*] Pornography.
pornographique (pɔrnɔgrafik), adj. Pornographic, obscene.
porosité (pɔrozite), s.f. Porosity.
porphyre (pɔrfir), s.m. [Gr. *porphura*] Porphyry.
porphyriser (pɔrfirize), v.a. To porphyrize, to grind, to pulverize.
porque (pɔrk), s.f. [It. *porca*] (naut.) Rider.
porracé, poracé (pɔrase), adj. [L *porraceus*] Porraceous, greenish.
porreau (pɔro) s.m. See POIREAU.
port[1] (pɔr), s.m. [L *portus*] Harbour, haven, port, sea-port town; (fig.) haven, refuge, shelter; *arriver à bon* ~, to arrive safely; (fig.) *mener à bon* ~, to bring to a happy issue; (fig.) *faire naufrage au* ~, to be lost at the eleventh hour; to fall at the last fence; ~ *de guerre*, naval base; ~ *marchand*, commercial harbour.
port[2] (pɔr), s.m. [f. *porter*] **1.** Bearing, gait, mien, presence; **2.** carrying; wearing; *être au* ~ *d'armes*, to shoulder arms; **3.** (naut.) burden (of a ship); **4.** carriage (of parcels), postage (of letters); *franco de* ~, carriage-paid; ~-*salut*, Port Salut cheese.
portable (pɔrtabl), adj. Portable; wearable.
portage (pɔrtaʒ), s.m. Carriage, porterage, transport; portage.
portail (pl. **-s**) (pɔrtaj), s.m. [LL *portale*] Portal, gate, gateway.
portant, -e (pɔrtɑ̃), p. adj. Bearing, carrying; in health; *bien* ~, in good health; *mal* ~, in bad health, unwell; *à bout* ~, close; at point-blank range; (fig.) point-blank; to one's face.
portant (pɔrtɑ̃), s.m. (theatr.) Prop of set-piece, piece of side-scenery, wing.
portati-f, -ve (pɔrtatif), adj. Portative, portable, hand-, pocket-.

porte (pɔrt), s.f. [L *porta*] Door, doorway, entrance; pass, defile; Porte; eye (for a hook); *à la ~!*, away with you!, out with you!; *mettre à la ~*, to turn out; *être aux ~s du tombeau*, to be at death's door; *l'ennemi est à nos ~s*, the enemy is at our gates; *de ~ en ~*, from door to door; *fermer* (or *refuser*) *sa ~ à X*, not to be at home to X; to forbid X the house; *frapper à la ~*, to knock at the door; (fig.) *frapper à toutes les ~s*, to leave no stone unturned; (fig.) *mettre la clef sous la ~*, to abscond; *prendre la ~*, to leave the room, to slip out, to go out; *à ~s ouvrantes*, at the opening of the gates; *~ à deux battants*, folding doors; *~ cochère*, carriage entrance; *~ à coulisse*, sliding door; *~ de derrière*, *~ de service*, back door, back-entrance; *la Sublime Porte*, the Sublime Porte; (fig.) *il faut qu'une ~ soit ouverte ou fermée*, it must be either one thing or the other.

porte (pɔrt), adj. f. (anat.) Portal; *veine ~*, portal vein.

porté, -e (pɔrte), p. adj. Inclined (*à*, to), disposed (to), prone (to); projected; *ombre ~e*, projected shadow; *bien ~*, in good taste.

porte-affiches (pɔrtafiʃ), s.m. invar. Advertising board.

porte-aiguilles (pɔrtɛgɥij), s.m. invar. Needle-case.

porte-allumettes (pɔrtalymɛt), s.m. invar. Match-box, match-holder.

porte-amarre (pɔrtamar), s.m. invar. Line-rocket.

porte-assiettes (pɔrtasjɛt), s.m. invar. Plate-stand.

porte-baïonnette (pɔrtbajɔnɛt), s.m. invar. Bayonet-frog.

porte-balle (pɔrtbal), s.m. invar. Pedlar.

porte-bonheur (pɔrtbɔnœr), s.m. invar. **1.** Bringer of good luck, mascot; **2.** bangle.

porte-bouquet (pɔrtbukɛ), s.m. invar. Bouquet-holder.

porte-bouteilles (pɔrtbutɛj), s.m. invar. Bottle-rack, bottle-carrier.

porte-cartes (pɔrtəkart), s.m. invar. Card-case.

porte-chapeaux (pɔrtʃapo), s.m. invar. Hat-stand, hat-rack.

porte-cigare (pɔrtsigar), s.m. invar. Cigar-holder; *~s*, cigar-case.

porte-cigarettes (pɔrtsigarɛt), s.m. invar. Cigarette-holder; *~s*, cigarette-case.

porte-clefs (pɔrtəkle), s.m. invar. **1.** Turnkey; **2.** key-ring.

porte-couteau (pɔrtəkuto), s.m. invar. Knife-rest.

porte-crayon (pɔrtəkrɛjɔ̃), s.m. invar. Pencil-holder.

porte-drapeau (pɔrtədrapo), s.m. invar. Colour-sergeant, ensign.

portée (pɔrte), s.f. **1.** Litter, brood; **2.** reach, range; *à ~*, within reach; *à ~ de la voix*, within call; **3.** capacity, range, ability, comprehension, level; *se mettre à la ~ de X*, to come down to X's level; **4.** importance, bearing; **5.** (build.) bearing, length; **6.** (mus.) stave; **7.** (naut.) burden, tonnage.

porte-enseigne (pɔrtɑ̃sɛɲ), s.m. invar. Colour-sergeant, ensign.

porte-épée (pɔrtepe), s.m. invar. Sword-belt.

porte-étendard (pɔrtetɑ̃dar), s.m. invar. Standard-bearer, cornet.

porte-étrier (pɔrtetrie), s.m. invar. Stirrup-strap.

portefaix (pɔrtəfɛ), s.m. invar. Street-porter, porter.

porte-fenêtre (pɔrtfənɛtr), s.f. (pl. *portes-fenêtres*) French window.

portefeuille (pɔrtəfœj), s.m. [*porte*+*feuille*] Portfolio; pocket-book, note-case; (fig.) ministry; (fin.) bills and acceptances, commercial bills; (slang) bed; *se fourrer au ~*, to go to bed; *mettre un lit en ~*, to make an apple-pie bed.

porte-flambeau (pɔrtəflɑ̃bo), s.m. invar. Torch-bearer.

porte-malheur (pɔrtəmalœr), s.m. invar. Bird of ill omen, bringer of bad luck.

portemanteau (pl. **-x**) (pɔrtmɑ̃to), s.m. **1.** Coat-stand, coat-peg; coat-hanger; **2.** (obs.) portmanteau, suit-case; **3.** (naut.) davit.

portement (pɔrtəmɑ̃), s.m. Carrying (only used in the loc. *~ de croix*, Christ's carrying of the Cross).

porte-mine (pɔrtəmin), s.m. invar. Pencil-case, pencil-holder.

porte-monnaie (pɔrtmɔnɛ), s.m. invar. Purse.

porte-montre (pɔrtəmɔ̃tr), s.m. invar. Watch-stand.

porte-mousqueton (pɔrtmuskətɔ̃), s.m. invar. Swivel, swivel-hook.

porte-musique (pɔrtmyzik), s.m. invar. **1.** Music-case; **2.** canterbury, music-stand.

porte-parapluies (pɔrtparaplɥi), s.m. invar. Umbrella-stand.

porte-parole (pɔrtəparɔl), s.m. invar. Spokesman; mouthpiece.

porteplume (pɔrtəplym), s.m. Pen-holder; *~ réservoir*, fountain-pen.

porter (pɔrte), v.a. [L *portare*] To bear, to support; to carry, to convey, to bring; to wear, to have on; to hold, to have, to carry; to induce, to incline; *portez armes!*, shoulder arms!; *~ les armes*, to carry (or to bear) arms, to serve as a soldier; *~ bonheur*, to bring luck; *~ le bras en écharpe*, to carry or wear one's arm in a sling; *~ les cheveux longs*, to wear one's hair long; *~ X dans son cœur*, to love X; *la nuit porte conseil*, sleep on it; *c'est sa femme qui porte la culotte*, it 's his wife that rules the roost, his wife wears the breeches; *~ la coupe à* *ses lèvres*, to carry the cup to one's lips; ~ *sa croix*, to bear one's cross; ~ *le deuil de X*, to be in mourning for X; ~ *envie à X*, to envy X; ~ *des fruits*, to bear fruit; *vous portez tout à l'extrême*, you always carry things to extremes; ~ *intérêt*, (*a*) to yield interest; (*b*) to show interest or solicitude; ~ *un jugement sur*, to pass judgement upon; ~ *la main sur X*, to strike X; ~ *malheur*, to bring bad luck, or ill luck; ~ *X aux nues*, to praise X up to the skies; ~ *ombrage*, to give umbrage; ~ *la parole*, to be the spokesman; ~ *préjudice à X*, to be prejudicial to X, to harm X; ~ *ses pas vers*, to bend one's steps towards; *il en portera la peine*, he will suffer for it; ~ *ses regards sur*, to look towards, to glance at, to glance over; (fig.) ~ *la robe*, to be a magistrate; (fig.) ~ *la soutane*, to be a priest; ~ *la santé de X*, to drink X's health; ~ *témoignage*, to bear witness; ~ *la tête haute*, to carry one's head high; ~ *X en terre*, to carry X to his last home; ~ *un toast à X*, to toast X; *ce navire porte bien la toile*, this ship can carry a lot of sail; *il porte bien le vin*, he can drink a good deal (without getting drunk); ~ *du velours*, to wear velvet; ~, v.n. **1.** to bear, to be supported, to rest; *tout l'édifice porte sur ces colonnes*, these columns bear the whole weight of the building; ~ *à faux*, to bear false, to be out of the perpendicular; **2.** (of animals) to be with young, to bear; **3.** (artill.) to reach, to carry; (fig.) to get home; *cet argument n'a pas porté*, this argument did not hit the mark; it did not tell; *ce fusil porte à . . .*, this rifle carries . . .; **4.** (naut.) to stand, to bear off; *laisser* ~, to bear away; *ce vin* ~ *à la tête*, this wine goes to the head; *sa tête a porté contre le mur*, his head struck against the wall; **se** ~, v.pr. to be worn, to be carried; to go, to resort, to move, to rush, to affect; *tout le monde se porte de ce côté*, everybody goes in that direction; to be, to do; *comment vous portez-vous?*, how do you do?; *se bien* ~, to be well; to be in good health; *se mal* ~, to be unwell, to be in poor health; to stand forth, to assume the character (of); *se* ~ *partie civile contre X*, to appear against X; *se* ~ *garant pour X*, to answer for X.

porter (pɔrtœr), s.m. [Engl. wd] Porter (beer).

porte-respect (pɔrtərɛspɛ), s.m. invar. **1.** Defensive weapon; **2.** chaperon; person of imposing appearance.

porteu-r, -se (pɔrtœr), s.m.f. Carrier, porter, bearer; holder; *titres au* ~, bonds payable to bearer; bearer securities; *cheval* ~, near-side horse; *chaise à* ~*s*, sedan-chair; ~ *de chaise*, chair-man; ~ *d'eau*, water-carrier.

porte-serviettes (pɔrtsɛrvjɛt), s.m. invar. Towel-horse.

porte-veine (pɔrtəvɛn), s.m. See syn. PORTE-BONHEUR.

porte-verge (pɔrtəvɛrʒ), s.m. invar. Verger, beadle.

porte-voix (pɔrtəvwɑ), s.m. invar. Speaking-trumpet, megaphone.

porti-er, -ère (pɔrtje), s.m.f. Porter, door-keeper, janitor.

portière (pɔrtjɛr), s.f. **1.** Door-keeper (woman); syn. CONCIERGE; **2.** carriage door, portière, door-curtain.

portière (pɔrtjɛr), adj. f. (of cows, &c.) Of an age to bear.

portillon (pɔrtijɔ̃), s.m. Small gate, postern.

portion (pɔrsjɔ̃), s.f. [L *portio*] Portion, (⚠ not nowadays in the sense of inheritance, marriage portion); part, share, lot; *être réduit à la* ~ *congrue*, to have enough to live on and no more.

portique (pɔrtik), s.m. [L *porticus*] Portico, porch; (gymn.) cross-bar; (ant.) Porch.

porto (pɔrto), s.m. [f. *Oporto*] Port wine, port, porto.

portor (pɔrtɔr), s.m. [f. It. *porta oro*] Portor (a kind of marble).

portraire (pɔrtrɛr), v.a. [f. L *protrahere*] (rare) To portray.

portrait (pɔrtrɛ), s.m. [f. *portrait*] Portrait, likeness, picture; (fig.) description, image, semblance; (slang) face; *cet enfant est le* ~ *de son père*, that child is the very image of his father; (slang) *il lui a abîmé le* ~, he spoiled his beauty for him; he has battered his dial.

portraitiste (pɔrtrɛtist), s.m.f. Portrait-painter.

portraiturer (pɔrtrɛtyre), v.a. [f. L *protrahere*] To paint the portrait of, to portray; (fig.) to depict.

port-salut (pɔrsaly), s.m. [geog. orig.] Port Salut cheese.

portugais, -e (pɔrtygɛ), adj. s.m.f. Portuguese. ~*e*, s.f. Portuguese oyster.

portulan (pɔrtylɑ̃), s.m. [It. *portolano*] Portulan, portolano, book of sea-ports, ancient nautical map; sailing directions.

portune (pɔrtyn), s.m. (zool.) A kind of crab.

posage (pozaʒ), s.m. Placing, laying, putting, fixing, fitting.

pose (poz), s.f. **1.** Placing, laying, fixing, fitting; **2.** attitude; posture; pose; **3.** showing off; affectation; side, posing; **4.** (photo.) exposure; (slang) *la faire à la* ~, to show off; to put on trimmings; to put on side.

posé, -e (poze), p. adj. **1.** Staid, sober, steady; influential; **2.** admitted; *ceci* ~, *il en découle que*, this being granted, it follows that.

posément (pozemɑ̃), adv. Sedately, staidly, slowly, quietly.

poser (poze), v.a.n. [L *pausare*] To place, to lay down, to set, to put; to post up, to apply; to post (sentries); to state, to admit, to declare; (arith.) to put down; (mus.) to pitch; (at dominoes) to pose; (techn.) to fit, to fix up, to hang, to affix; to sit (for one's portrait); to wait; *il m'a fait ~ longtemps*, he has kept me waiting a long time; to pose, to attitudinize, to show off; **se ~**, v.pr. to perch, to pitch; (fig.) to play the part (*en*, of); *se ~ en victime*, to play the martyr.

poseu-r, -se (pozœr), s.m.f. **1.** Layer, setter, &c.; **2.** poser, snob, humbug, prig, conceited fellow.

positi-f, -ve (pozitif), adj. [L *positivus*] Positive, certain, actual; matter-of-fact, practical; *pôle ~*, positive pole; *c'est ~ !*, it 's a fact !

positif (pozitif), s.m. Positive, reality; (gram., photo.) positive; (mus.) choir organ.

position (pozisjɔ̃), s.f. Position, situation, station; attitude; status; standing; case; circumstances; *il est en ~ de*, he is in a position to; he is able to; *être dans une bonne ~*, to be well off; *perdre sa ~*, to lose one's employment; to get the sack; to lose one's rank or social status; (colloq.) *être dans une ~ intéressante*, to be in the family way, an interesting condition.

positivement (pozitivmɑ̃), adv. Positively, expressly, explicitly.

positivisme (pozitivism), s.m. **1.** Positivism; **2.** matter-of-factness.

positiviste (pozitivist), s.m.f. adj. Positivist.

possédé, -e (pɔsede), p. adj. Possessed, infatuated; dominated; possessed by a devil. ~, s.m.f. Mad person, maniac; *se démener comme un ~*, to rampage like a madman.

posséder (pɔsede), v.a. [f. L *possidere*] To possess, to own, to have; to enjoy, to be master of, to know thoroughly, to dominate; to be possessed of; *être possédé d'une idée*, to be possessed by (or with) an idea; *l'ambition le possède*, he is eaten up with ambition; *l'ambition qu'il possède*, the ambition he is possessed of; *~ une femme*, to enjoy a woman; *~ son sujet*, to have a thorough command of one's subject; **se ~**, v.pr. to have self-control, to be master of one's passions; *il ne se possède pas de joie*, he is beside himself with joy.

possesseur (pɔsɛsœr), s.m. Possessor, owner, holder, occupier.

possessi-f, -ve (pɔsɛsif), adj. Possessive. ~, s.m. (gram.) Possessive case.

possession (pɔsɛsjɔ̃), s.f. [L *possessio*] **1.** Possession, ownership; *être en ~ de*, to own; *mettre en ~ de*, to give possession of; to invest with; *prendre ~ de*, to take possession of; **2.** property; *les ~s françaises en Afrique*, the French colonies (or possessions) in Africa; **3.** possession, madness, state of being possessed by the devil.

possessionnel, -le (pɔsɛsjɔnɛl), adj. (law) Possessionary.

possessoire (pɔsɛswar), adj. (law) Possessory. ~, s.m. Right of possession.

possibilité (pɔsibilite), s.f. Possibility.

possible (pɔsibl), adj. [L *possibilis*] Possible; *c'est bien ~*, that may be; *pas ~ !*, you don't say so !, well I never !; *le plus ~*, as much as possible; *le plus tôt ~*, as soon as possible; *si ~*, if possible; *le moins ~*, the least possible; as few . . . as possible; as little as can be; *vous est-il ~ de venir ?*, can you possibly come ? ~, s.m. Possible, possibility, what is possible; *au ~*, extremely; *je ferai tout mon ~*, I will do my best.

postal, -e, (aux) (pɔstal), adj. Postal; *carte ~e*, post-card; *colis ~*, postal packet, parcel post.

postdater (pɔstdate), v.a. To post-date.

poste[1] (pɔst), s.f. [f. L *posita*] Post, (relay) post, post-office, mail, postal service; *maître de ~*, postmaster; *courir la ~*, to go post-haste; to ride post, to travel post; *chevaux de ~*, post-horses; *chaise de ~*, post-chaise; *mettre une lettre à la ~*, to post a letter; *bureau de ~*, post-office; *timbre ~*, stamp; *Directeur des Postes*, Postmaster General; *lettre ~ restante*, letter to be kept till called for, poste-restante letter.

poste[2] (pɔst), s.m. [It. *posto*] Post, station, employment, place, berth, office; (naut.) quarters; (mil., police) guard-house, station-house, police-station; *mourir à son ~*, to die at one's post; *à ~ fixe*, permanently; *~ isolé*, detached post; *~ d'incendie*, fire-station; *être conduit au ~*, to be arrested; to be taken to the police-station; *passer la nuit au ~*, to be kept a prisoner till morning at the police-station, or in the lock-up; *~ de T.S.F.*, wireless-set.

poster (pɔste), v.a. **1.** To station, to post; **2.** to send by post, to post.

postérieur, -e (pɔsterjœr), adj. [L *posterior*] Posterior, later, subsequent; back, hind. ~, s.m. Posteriors, bottom, buttocks, behind.

postérieurement (pɔsterjœrmɑ̃), adv. Posteriorly, subsequently, later, afterwards.

postériorité (pɔsterjɔrite), s.f. Posteriority.

postérité (pɔsterite), s.f. [L *posteritas*] Posterity, issue.

postes (pɔst), s.f.pl. (arch.) Vitruvian scroll.

posthume (pɔstym), adj. [L *postumus*] Posthumous.
postiche (pɔstiʃ), adj. [It. *posticcio*] Superadded, false, artificial, sham. ~, s.m. False hair, wig.
posti-er, -ère (pɔstje), s.m.f. **1.** Postman, post-office servant; **2.** post-horse.
postillon (pɔstijɔ̃), s.m. [It. *postiglione*] Postilion, post-boy; (colloq.) *envoyer des ~s* or *postillonner*, to splutter a spray of saliva while talking.
postillonner (pɔstijɔne), v.n. (very fam.) To splutter or sputter a spray of saliva while talking; *méfiez-vous, il va vous ~ dans la figure!*, umbrellas up!
postscolaire (pɔstskɔlɛr), adj. *Enseignement ~*, continuation classes.
post-scriptum (pɔstskriptɔm), s.m. invar. [L wd] Postscript; P.S.
postulant, -e (pɔstylɑ̃), s.m.f. Applicant, postulant, candidate.
postulat (pɔstyla), s.m. [L *postulatum*] Postulate.
postuler (pɔstyle), v.a. [L *postulare*] To apply for, to postulate; ~, v.n. (law term) to conduct a suit.
posture (pɔstyr), s.f. [It. *postura*] Posture, attitude; situation; *être en bonne ~ pour*, to be in a fair way to; *être en mauvaise ~*, to be in a bad way; to be in an awkward position.
pot (po), s.m. [LL *pottus*] Pot, jug, tankard, can, jar, vessel; *un ~ à eau*, a water-jug; *un ~ d'eau*, a jug of water; *~-au-feu*, boiled beef and broth; (fig.) *mettre la poule au ~*, to have a good meal, to eat fowl (once a week); *~ à colle*, glue-pot; *~ au lait*, milk-jug; *~ de chambre*, chamber-pot; chamber; (fig.) *~ de vin*, bribe; *payer les ~s cassés*, to stand the racket, to pay the damage, to face the music; (fig.) *tourner autour du ~*, to beat about the bush; *sourd comme un ~*, as deaf as a post; (fig.) *découvrir le ~ aux roses*, to find out the (nasty) secret; (fig.) *c'est le ~ de terre contre le ~ de fer*, it's a most unequal combat; it's the weak against the strong; *venez dîner, à la fortune du ~*, come and take pot-luck with us; (fig.) *faire le ~ à deux anses*, to have a lady on each arm; (fig.) *~ au noir*, dark, doubtful circumstances; (fig.) *faire bouillir le ~* (or *la marmite*), to keep the pot boiling; *il n'y a si vilain ~ qui ne trouve son couvercle*, every Jack must have his Jill; *~-pourri*, medley, pot-pourri.
potable (pɔtabl), adj. [L *potabilis*] Potable, drinkable; *eau ~*, drinking-water; (fig.) tolerable.
potache (pɔtaʃ), s.m. (colloq.) Schoolboy.
potage (pɔtaʒ), s.m. [f. *pot*] Soup; (fig.) *pour tout ~*, all told.
potager (pɔtaʒe), s.m. **1.** Vegetable or kitchen garden; **2.** kitchen stove, charcoal-stove. **potag-er, -ère,** adj. Comestible, culinary; *plantes ~ères*, pot-herbs, vegetables.
potamot (pɔtamo), s.m. (bot.) Pond-weed.
potard (pɔtar), s.m. [f. *pot*] (colloq., slightly pej.) Chemist, druggist.
potasse (pɔtas), s.f. [Dutch *potasch*] Potash.
potasser (pɔtase), v.a.n. (school slang) To study hard, to grind, to swot (at).
potassique (pɔtasik), adj. Potassic.
potassium (pɔtasjɔm), s.m. (chem.) Potassium.
pote (pɔt), adj. f. Swollen. ~, s.m. (slang) see POTEAU.
poteau (pl. **-x**) (pɔto), s.m. [f. L *postis*] Post, stake; starting-post; *~ télégraphique*, telegraph-pole; (slang) (also *pote*) comrade, pal, chum, old bean.
potée (pɔte), s.f. **1.** Jugful, potful; **2.** emery-dust; putty-powder; **3.** (metall.) luding loam.
potelé, -e (pɔtle), adj. Plump, chubby.
potelet (pɔtlɛ), s.m. Small post, prop.
potence (pɔtɑ̃s), s.f. [L *potentia*] Potence, gallows, gibbet; bracket; *gibier de ~*, jail-bird, gallows-bird.
potentat (pɔtɑ̃ta), s.m. [f. L *potens*] Potentate.
potentiel, -le (pɔtɑ̃sjɛl), adj. s.m. Potential.
potentiellement (pɔtɑ̃sjɛlmɑ̃), adv. Potentially.
potentille (pɔtɑ̃tij), s.f. (bot.) Potentilla, cinquefoil.
poterie (pɔtri), s.f. Pottery, earthenware; earthenware pipe; pottery works.
poterne (pɔtɛrn), s.f. [L *posterula*] Postern.
potiche (pɔtiʃ), s.f. [f. *pot*] Chinese or Japanese porcelain vase.
potier (pɔtje), s.m. Potter; earthenware-dealer; *~ d'étain*, pewterer.
potin[1] (pɔtɛ̃), s.m. [f. *pot*] Pinchbeck (alloy of copper, tin, pewter, &c.).
potin[2] (pɔtɛ̃), s.m. **1.** Hubbub, noise, din, pother; *faire du ~*, to kick up a row; **2.** piece of gossip, tittle-tattle, society rumours.
potiner (pɔtine), v.n. To prattle, to gossip.
potini-er, -ère (pɔtinje), adj. Gossipy. **potinière,** s.f. Centre of gossip; also name of a theatre in Paris.
potion (pɔsjɔ̃), s.f. [L *potio*] Potion, draught.
potiron (pɔtirɔ̃), s.m. (bot.) Pumpkin.
potron-jaquet, potron-minet (pɔtrɔ̃ʒakɛ, pɔtrɔ̃minɛ), s.m. [etym. dub.] Dawn; *dès le ~*, at peep of day.
pou (pl. **-x**) (pu), s.m. [L *pediculus*] Louse; *laid comme un ~*, as ugly as sin; (fig.) *chercher des ~x à X*, to pick a quarrel with X.
pouacre (puakr), adj. s.m.f. [f. *podagre*] Nasty, filthy (person).

pouah ! (pwa), interj. Faugh !, ugh !, nasty thing !

poubelle (pubɛl), s.f. [f. *M. Poubelle*, Préfet de la Seine 1883–96] Dust-bin.

pouce (pus), s.m. [L *pollex*] Thumb; big toe; inch; *mettre les ~s*, to give in; to throw up the sponge; to knuckle under; *manger sur le ~*, to take a snack; *s'en mordre les ~s*, to repent bitterly of; to suffer for it; (slang) *et le ~ !*, and a good bit more !; *se tourner les ~s*, to twirl or twiddle one's thumbs.

Poucet (Petit) [prop. n.] (in fairy-tales) Hop-o'-my-thumb.

poucettes (pusɛt), s.f.pl. Thumbscrew, manacles.

poucier (pusje), s.m. **1.** Thumb-stall; **2.** latch.

pou-de-soie, poult-de-soie (pudəswɑ), s.m. [etym. dub.] Paduasoy.

pouding (puding), s.m. [Engl. *pudding*] **1.** Pudding; **2.** pudding-stone.

poudre (pudr), s.f. [L *pulver*] Powder, dust; gunpowder; *sucre en ~*, castor sugar; *~ de chasse*, shooting-powder; *~ de riz*, rice-powder, powder; *~ de perlimpinpin*, nostrum; quack powder; *coton ~*, gun-cotton; *soute aux ~s*, powder-room; *jeter de la ~ aux yeux*, to impose on any one, to throw dust into people's eyes; *mettre le feu aux ~s*, to put everything in a blaze; *il n'a pas inventé la ~*, he will never set the Thames on fire; *prendre la ~ d'escampette*, to make oneself scarce; to skedaddle; to bolt; *faire parler la ~*, to wage war; *tirer sa ~ aux moineaux*, to waste powder and shot; *réduire en ~*, to grind; *faire mordre la ~* or *la poussière*, to vanquish, to kill.

poudrer (pudre), v.a. To powder, to sprinkle with powder; **se ~**, v.pr. to powder one's face (or nose or hair).

poudrerie (pudrəri), s.f. Powder-works.

poudrette (pudrɛt), s.f. Dried night-soil.

poudreu-x, -se (pudrø), adj. Dusty, powdery.

poudrier (pudrije), s.m. **1.** Gunpowder-maker; **2.** sand-box; **3.** powder-box.

poudrière (pudrijɛr), s.f. Powder-magazine; powder-mill; powder-flask.

poudroiement (pudrwamɑ̃), s.m. Covering with dust, or powder; puffs of dust or coloured powders; rising of dust.

poudroyer (pudrwaje), v.n. To be dusty, to fall to dust, to rise in dust.

pouf ! (puf), interj. Plump !

pouf (puf), s.m. **1.** Centre ottoman, ottoman seat, pouffe; **2.** pad, bustle (in dress).

pouffer (pufe), v.n. *~ de rire*, to burst out laughing; to guffaw.

poufflasse (pufjas), s.f. (vulg.) Slut, harlot, street-walker.

pouillard (pujar), s.m. Young partridge; young pheasant.

pouilles (puj), s.f.pl. (colloq.) *Chanter ~ à X*, to abuse X.

pouillerie (pujri), s.f. [f. *pou*] Squalid poverty, filthy, miserly habits; dirty hole.

pouilleu-x, -se (pujø), adj. Lousy, filthy, wretched; *Champagne Pouilleuse*, barren Champagne. **~**, s.m.f. Wretched person, lousy fellow.

pouillot (pujo), s.m. (ornith.) Willow-warbler.

poulailler (pulɑje), s.m. **1.** Hen-house, hen-roost, fowl-house; **2.** poulterer; **3.** (fig., theatr.) upper gallery.

poulain (pulɛ̃), s.m. [f. L *pullus*, LL *pullamen*] **1.** Foal, colt; **2.** timber slide-way for casks, &c.

poulaine (pulɛn), s.f. [f. *Pologne*, OF *Poulaine*] **1.** Ship's prow; ship's latrine; **2.** medieval fashion for shoes; *souliers à la ~*, long pointed shoes.

poularde (pulard), s.f. Fattened pullet.

poule (pul), s.f. [L *pulla*] **1.** Hen; fowl; **2.** pool (at cards) or tournament (billiards); **3.** third figure of French quadrille; *c'est une ~ mouillée*, he is a chicken-hearted fellow; he is a milksop; *~ d'Inde*, turkey-hen; *~ d'eau*, moor-hen; *tuer la ~ aux œufs d'or*, to kill the goose that lays the golden eggs; *j'ai la chair de ~*, my flesh creeps; *cela donne la chair de ~*; it gives one the creeps; that gives one gooseflesh; *lait de ~*, mulled egg; (vulg.) **~**, gay woman; *sa ~*, his girl.

poulet (pulɛ), s.m. **1.** Chicken; fowl; *~ de grain*, corn-fed chicken; **2.** love-letter, short note; (iron.) unpleasant news brought by a short note.

poulette (pulɛt), s.f. Pullet; (fig. vulg.) lass; *sauce ~*, a kind of white sauce.

pouliche (puliʃ), s.f. Filly.

poulie (puli), s.f. [f. Gr. *polos*] Pulley; block.

pouliner (puline), v.n. (of mares) To foal.

poulinière (pulinjɛr), adj. f. s.f. Brood-(mare).

pouliot (puljo), s.m. [L *pulegium*] (bot.) Pennyroyal.

poulot, -te (pulo), s.m.f. (fam.) Darling, chick.

poulpe (pulp), s.m. [Gr. *polupous*] (zool.) Octopus.

pouls (pu), s.m. [L *pulsus*] Pulse; *tâter le ~ à X*, to feel X's pulse; (fig.) to gauge X's strength.

poumon (pumɔ̃), s.m. [L *pulmo*] Lung, lungs; *à pleins ~s*, freely, breathing deeply; with full lungs.

poupard, -e (pupar), s.m.f. Chubby doll or baby. **~**, adj. *Figure ~e*, chubby face.

poupe (pup), s.f. [L *puppis*] Stern, poop; *avoir le vent en ~*, to sail before the wind; (fig.) to be in luck's way; to be in favour.

poupée (pupe), s.f. [L *pupa*] Doll;

milliner's figure or block; bunch of hemp or flax; (fig.) puppet, vain girl.

poupin, -e (pupɛ̃), adj. Chubby, ruddy, childish; *figure ~e*, chubby face.

poupon, -ne (pupɔ̃), s.m.f. Infant, baby, chubby baby.

pouponnière (puponjɛr), s.f. Public nursery, infants' home.

poupoule (pupul), s.f. (very vulg.) Darling, chickabiddy.

pour (pur), prep. [L *pro*] For, for the sake of, on account of; in favour of; on the part of; towards; as for, as to; instead of; in order to; *faites cela ~ moi*, do it for my sake; *~ ainsi dire*, as it were; *~ ce qui est de cela*, about this; concerning that; as regards that; *~ moi, je pense que*, for my part, I think that; *en avoir ~ son argent*, to have one's money's worth; *il en a acheté ~ 1.000 francs*, he has bought 1,000 francs' worth of it; *on l'a laissé ~ mort*, he was left for dead; *~ cent*, per cent; *œil ~ œil, dent ~ dent*, an eye for an eye, a tooth for a tooth; *jour ~ jour*, to a day; *~ ce qui me regarde*, as far as I am concerned; *être ~ partir*, to be about to start; *assez jeune ~ apprendre*, young enough to learn; *~ grand que*, however great; *~ peu que*, if ever, if ever so little; *~ que*, in order that; for . . . to; *~ lors*, then; *~ ce que* (obs.), because (of). *~*, s.m. Pro; *le ~ et le contre*, the pros and cons.

pourboire (purbwar), s.m. [*pour+boire*] Tip; gratuity.

pourceau (pl. **-x**) (purso), s.m. [L *porcellus*] Hog, pig, swine; (fig.) beast, filthy person.

pour-cent (pursɑ̃), s.m. Percentage (*un tant-pour-cent* is more frequent than *un pour-cent*).

pourcentage (pursɑ̃taʒ), s.m. Percentage.

pourchas (purʃɑ), s.m. [f. *pourchasser*] Chase, pursuit; research; ⚠ not 'purchase', which = *achat*.

pourchasser (purʃase), v.a. [*pour+chasser*] To pursue eagerly, to chase, to hunt after, to dog.

pourchasseur (purʃasœr), s.m. Hunter, seeker, pursuer.

pourfendeur (purfɑ̃dœr), s.m. Killer, swaggerer, braggart, braggadocio.

pourfendre (purfɑ̃dr), v.a. [*pour+fendre*] **1.** To cleave asunder; **2.** to pierce with a sword, to run (a man) through the body, to transfix.

pourlécher (purleʃe), v.a. [*pour+lécher*] To lick all over; **se ~**, v.pr. to lick one's lips; to lick the chops.

pourparler (purparle), s.m. [*pour+parler*] (usually in plural) Parley, negotiation, palaver; *entrer en ~s*, to enter into negotiations.

pourpier (purpje), s.m. [OF *poulpied, porpié*] (bot.) Purslane.

pourpoint (purpwɛ̃), s.m. [f. OF *pourpoindre* = to stitch] Doublet; *à brûle-~*, point-blank.

pourpre (purpr), s.f. [L *purpura*] Purple-red ⚠; (fig.) purple, sovereign dignity; (herald.) purpure; (pathol.) purpura, purples; (zool.) purple-fish. ⚠ In English 'purple' usually = *violet* (*légèrement rougeâtre*).

pourpre (purpr), adj. Purple-red, dark red. ⚠ In English the most usual sense of 'purple' is *violet, magenta*; for instance *lèvres pourpres* cannot be translated by 'purple lips'. This would mean the bluish lips of a diseased person; the correct equivalent would be 'ruby lips'; a purple dress can be worn as half mourning but *une robe pourpre* cannot.

pourpré, -e (purpre), adj. Purple, ruby, red; (see POURPRE ⚠) *lèvres ~es*, ruby lips; *fièvre ~e*, purpura.

pourpris (purpri), s.m. (obs.) Abode, enclosure, home; *le céleste ~*, Heaven.

pourquoi (purkwa), conj. and adv. Why; what for; for what reason; *c'est ~*, that's why; *~ pas?*, why not? *~*, s.m. The reason why; the why and the wherefore.

pourri, -e (puri), adj. Rotten; *être ~ de préjugés*, to be stiff with prejudices; *temps ~*, dirty weather.

pourrir (purir), v.n. [L *putrescere*] To rot, to grow rotten, to corrupt; **se ~**, v.pr. to get rotten.

pourriture (purityr,) s.f. Rottenness, rot, putrefaction, rotten thing.

poursuite (pursɥit), s.f. Pursuit, chase; (law) *~s*, suit, indictment, action, proceedings.

poursuivant, -e (pursɥivɑ̃), s.m.f. **1.** Applicant; suitor, prosecutor, plaintiff; **2.** pursuer.

poursuivre (pursɥivr), v.a. To pursue, to chase, to seek; to sue, to prosecute, to proceed against; *~ son chemin*, to go one's way; *~ son discours*, to proceed with one's speech; *~ X en justice*, to prosecute X at law; to sue X.

pourtant (purtɑ̃), adv. [L *pro tanto*] However, yet, still.

pourtour (purtur), s.m. Circumference, periphery; (theatr.) pit-tier.

pourvoi (purvwa), s.m. (law) Appeal.

pourvoir (purvwar), v.n.a. [L *providere*] To provide (*à*, for), to make provision; to supply, to attend (*à*, to), to endow; **se ~**, v.pr. to provide oneself; (law) to appeal, to petition.

pourvoyeu-r, -se (purvwajœr), s.m.f. Provider, caterer, purveyor.

pourvu que (purvykə), loc. conj. Provided, provided that.

poussah (pusa), s.m. [Chinese wd] Chinese plaything in the shape of a fat man; (fig.) obese ugly person.

pousse (pus), s.f. [f. *pousser*] Shoot, sprout; (vet.) heaves, broken wind; (of wines) over-fermentation; *~-café*, s.m. (colloq.) liqueur; *~-cailloux*, s.m. (colloq.) tommy, foot-slogger.

poussée (puse), s.f. Push, pushing, shove, thrust; pressure.

pousse-pousse (puspus), s.m. Rickshaw.

pousser (puse), v.a.n. [L *pulsare*] To push, to shove, to impel, to drive on, to carry, to extend; to grow, to shoot, to put forth; *~ un soupir*, to fetch a sigh, to heave a sigh; *~ son cheval*, to urge one's horse; *~ X à bout*, to provoke X beyond endurance; *~ X à se remuer*, to goad X into action; (slang) *en ~ une*, to sing a song; *à la va comme je te pousse*, in a happy-go-lucky way; **~**, v.n. **1.** to grow; **2.** to make way.

poussier (pusje), s.m. Coal-dust.

poussière (pusjɛr), s.f. [OF *pous* = dust] Dust; (fig.) *mordre la ~*, to bite the dust.

poussiéreu-x, -se, adj. Dusty.

poussi-f, -ve (pusif), adj. Broken-winded.

poussin (pusɛ̃), s.m. Chick, chicken.

poussinière (pusinjɛr), s.f. Chicken-coop.

poussoir (puswar), s.m. Push, button (of bell, &c.).

poutre (putr), s.f. [LL *pullitra*] Beam; (aeron.) girder.

poutrelle (putrɛl), s.f. Small beam.

pouvoir (puvwar), v.a.n. [f. L *posse*] To be able (can), to have power, to be allowed (may); *n'en plus ~*, *n'en ~ mais*, to be done up, to be worn out; *il peut tout sur vous*, he has power over you; *je n'y puis rien*, I cannot help it; I can do nothing in the matter; *il est on ne peut plus aimable*, he is always as nice as can be; **se ~**, v. impers. pr. to be possible; *cela se peut*, that may be.

pouvoir (puvwar), s.m. Power, might, force, ability, capacity, authority; government, command, authorities; (law) power of attorney; *je ferai tout ce qui est en mon ~*, I will do my utmost; *abuser de son ~*, to abuse one's power; *arriver au ~*, to come into power; to achieve power.

pouzzolane (pudzɔlan), s.f. [It. *pozzolana*] Pozzolana.

pragmatique (pragmatik), adj. [Gr. *pragmatikos*] Pragmatic.

pragmatisme (pragmatism), s.m. Pragmatism.

prairial (prɛrjal), s.m. [f. *prairie*] Prairial (9th month of the calendar of first French Republic, 20 May to 18 June).

prairie (prɛri), s.f. [f. *pré*] Meadow, grassland. ⚠ Not 'prairie', which is used in English of the immense North-American grass-lands, partly uncultivated and partly used for the cultivation of wheat; *~ artificielle*, a meadow in which clover, lucern, &c., have been sown.

praline (pralin), s.f. [f. *M. de Plessis-Praslin*] Burnt almond, praline.

praliné (praline), s.m. Chocolate almonds, chocolate and almonds ground and made into a paste.

praliner (praline), v.a. To bake (almonds) in sugar.

prame (pram), s.f. [f. Dutch *praam*] Pram, flat-bottomed boat.

praticabilité (pratikabilite), s.f. Practicability.

praticable (pratikabl), adj. [f. *pratiquer*] Practicable. **~**, s.m. (theatr.) Frame of scenery, real (not illusive) stage requisite.

praticien, -ne (pratisjɛ̃), s.m.f. **1.** Practitioner; **2.** figure-carver (the workman who reduces the block for the artist).

pratiquant, -e (pratikɑ̃), p. adj. Church-going, practising, observant. **~**, s.m.f. Church-goer, practising churchman.

pratique (pratik), s.f. [Gr. *praktikos*] **1.** Practice, execution, dealing, way of doing things, observance, experience, performance; habit, routine; underhand practices; intercourse; (naut.) pratique; *avoir la libre ~*, to take or have pratique; *donner libre ~*, to admit to pratique; *mettre en ~*, to put into practice; to carry out; **2.** practice, custom; customer; *avoir beaucoup de ~s*, to have many customers; to do good business; **3.** Punch's whistle; **4.** (slang) bad lot, rogue.

pratique (pratik), adj. Practical, matter-of-fact; convenient, practicable, feasible; experienced, skilful.

pratiquement (pratikmɑ̃), adv. Practically.

pratiquer (pratike), v.a. To practise, to carry out, to exercise; to frequent, to associate with; to make, to open, to execute; *~ la vertu*, to practise virtue; *~ la médecine*, to practise medicine; *~ un chemin*, to open a road; *~ une opération*, to perform an operation; *évitez de ~ les méchants*, avoid association with the wicked; **se ~**, v.pr. to be done, to be customary, to be practised.

pré (pre), s.m. [L *pratum*] Meadow, mead; (fig.) *aller sur le ~*, to fight a duel; *~ salé*, salt-marsh; salt-marsh sheep (or mutton).

préachat (preaʃa), s.m. Prepayment.

préadamite (preadamit), adj. s.m.f. Preadamite.

préalable (prealabl), adj. [*pré+aller*] Previous, preliminary; *au ~*, first; previously; before going any further.

préalablement (prealabləmɑ̃), adv. First, previously.

préambule (preɑ̃byl), s.m. [f. L *prae+ambulare*] Preamble.

préau (pl. **-x**) (preo), s.m. [f. L *pratum*] Courtyard, covered playground.

préavis (preavi), s.m. [*pré*+*avis*] Forewarning.
prébende (prebɑ̃d), s.f. [L *praebenda*] Prebend; prebendaryship.
prébendier (prebɑ̃dje), s.m. Prebendary.
précaire (prekɛr), adj. [L *precarius*] Precarious, uncertain.
précairement (prekɛrmɑ̃), adv. Precariously.
précarité (prekarite), s.f. Precariousness.
précaution (prekosjɔ̃), s.f. [L *praecautio*] Precaution, foresight, caution, prudence, care, wariness; *prendre ses ~s,* to take one's precautions; to play for safety; *user de ~s,* to proceed warily, to behave cautiously.
précautionner (prekosjɔne), v.a. To warn, to forewarn, to caution; **se ~,** v.pr. to take precautions, to guard (*contre,* against).
précautionneu-x, -se (prekosjɔnø), adj. Wary, cautious.
précédemment (presedamɑ̃), adv. Previously, before.
précédence (presedɑ̃s), s.f. Precedence, precedency, priority.
précédent, -e (presedɑ̃), adj. [L *praecedens*] Previous, precedent, former. **~,** s.m. Precedent, previous case taken as example or justification.
précéder (presede), v.a.n. [L *prae*+*cedere*] To precede, to happen before, to go before; to take precedence of; *les mots qui précèdent,* the words that precede (this sentence); *précédés de* (or *par*) *notre guide,* preceded by our guide.
préceinte (presɛ̃t), s.f. [OF *pourceinte*] (naut.) Wale (of ship).
précepte (presɛpt), s.m. [L *praeceptum*] Precept.
précept-eur, -rice (presɛptœr), s.m.f. Tutor; (rare) preceptor, teacher, preceptress.
préceptoral, -e, (aux) (presɛptɔral), adj. Tutorial, preceptorial.
préceptorat (presɛptɔra), s.m. Tutorship, preceptorship.
précession (presɛsjɔ̃), s.f. [LL *praecessio*] Precession; *~ des équinoxes,* precession of the equinoxes.
prêche (prɛʃ), s.m. [f. *prêcher*] Sermon, preaching; (colloq.) lecture.
prêcher (prɛʃe), v.a.n. [L *praedicare*] To preach, to preach upon, to preach up, to praise, to extol; to sermonize; *~ l'Évangile,* to preach the Gospel; *~ d'exemple,* to practise what one preaches; *~ pour son saint,* to have an eye to one's own interest; *~ dans le désert,* to preach in the desert, to talk for nothing, or in vain.
prêcheu-r, -se (prɛʃœr), adj. Preaching, predicant; (colloq.) preachy. **~,** s.m.f. **1.** Preacher; **2.** sermonizer, fault-finder.
prêchi-prêcha (prɛʃiprɛʃa), s.m. (onom.) Tiresome repetition, mumbling, preachifying; *il m'ennuie avec son éternel ~,* he bores me to death, he is always preachifying.
précieuse (presjøz), s.f. [Fr. 17th cent.] Woman of affected literary tastes.
précieusement (presjøzmɑ̃), adv. **1.** Preciously; *garder ~,* to treasure up; **2.** affectedly.
précieu-x, -se (presjø), adj. [L *pretiosus*] **1.** Precious, valuable, costly, rare, esteemed; *pierres ~ses,* precious stones; gems; **2.** affected, too elaborate; mincing; niminy-piminy. **~,** s.m. Affectedness, affected style.
préciosité (presjozite), s.f. Preciosity, affectedness, affectation, exaggerated elaborateness; finicalness.
précipice (presipis), s.m. [L *praecipitium*] Precipice, abyss, chasm, deep gorge; (fig.) ruin, disaster.
précipitamment (presipitamɑ̃), adv. Hastily, precipitately, rashly.
précipitant (presipitɑ̃), s.m. (chem.) Precipitant.
précipitation (presipita'sjɔ̃), s.f. [L *praecipitatio*] Precipitation, haste, hurry, precipitancy; (chem.) precipitation; *avec trop de ~,* too rashly.
précipité (presipite), s.m. (chem.) Precipitate.
précipité, -e (presipite), p. adj. Precipitate, precipitated, hurried, hasty, sudden, headlong; *départ ~,* hurried departure; *course ~e,* headlong flight; *à pas ~s,* with hurried steps.
précipiter (presipite), v.a. [L *praecipitare*] **1.** To precipitate, to hurl, to fling, to throw or dash down, to plunge; **2.** to hasten, to hurry, to urge, to quicken; *~ ses pas,* to hurry along; *il ne faut rien ~,* never do things in a hurry; **se ~,** v.pr. **1.** to throw oneself headlong; to rush down; **2.** to rush on, to hasten, to hurry, to be precipitate.
préciput (presipy), s.m. [L *praecipuum*] (law) Preference legacy.
précis, -e (presi), adj. [L *praecisus*] Precise, accurate, exact, fixed, formal, concise, terse. **~,** s.m. Summary, epitome, compendium, manual.
précisément (presizemɑ̃), adv. Precisely, exactly; just so, accurately.
préciser (presize), v.a. To state precisely, to specify.
précision (presizjɔ̃), s.f. Precision, preciseness, accuracy; *armes de ~,* arms of precision.
précité, -e (presite), p. adj. Aforementioned, above-mentioned, aforesaid.
précoce (prekɔs), adj. [L *praecox*] Precocious, early; forward; premature; *fruits ~s,* early fruit; *mort ~,* premature

death; *esprit* ~, precocious mind, precociousness.
précocement (prekɔsmɑ̃), adv. Precociously; prematurely.
précocité (prekɔsite), s.f. Precociousness, precocity.
précompte (prekɔ̃t), s.m. Previous deduction.
préconception (prekɔ̃sɛpsjɔ̃), s.f. Preconception.
préconcevoir (prekɔ̃svwar), v.a. To preconceive.
préconçu, -e (prekɔ̃sy), p. adj. Preconceived.
préconisation (prekɔniza'sjɔ̃), s.f. Preconization, commendation.
préconiser (prekɔnize), v.a. [f. L *praeconium*] To preconize, to advocate; to commend, to extol; to sanction the appointment of.
précordial, -e, (aux) (prekɔrdjal), adj. (anat.) Praecordial.
précurseur (prekyrsœr), s.m. [L *prae+cursor*] Forerunner, harbinger, precursor. ~, adj. m. Precursory, premonitory.
prédécédé, -e (predesede), p. adj. s.m.f. Predeceased.
prédécéder (predesede), v.n. To predecease another, to die first.
prédécès (predesɛ), s.m. Predecease.
prédécesseur (predesɛsœr), s.m. Predecessor.
prédestination (predɛstina'sjɔ̃), s.f. [LL *praedestinatio*] Predestination.
prédestiné, -e (predɛstine), p. adj. Predestined; predetermined; reserved (for), prepared (for), elect. ~, s.m.f. One of the elect or predestined.
prédestiner (predɛstine), v.a. To predestinate, to foredoom; to predetermine, to preordain, to predestine.
prédétermination (predetɛrmina'sjɔ̃), s.f. Predetermination.
prédéterminer (predetɛrmine), v.a. To predetermine.
prédicable (predikabl), adj. [L *praedicabilis*] Predicable.
prédicant (predikɑ̃), s.m. Preacher (usually protestant); predicant.
prédicat (predika), s.m. [LL *praedicatum*] (gram., logic) Predicate.
prédicat-eur, -rice (predikatœr), s.m.f. Preacher, religious orator; predicant.
prédication (predika'sjɔ̃), s.f. Preaching; sermon, predication.
prédiction (prediksjɔ̃), s.f. [L *praedictio*] Prediction, foretelling, foreboding, prophecy.
prédilection (predilɛksjɔ̃), s.f. [LL *praedilectio*] Predilection, preference, partiality; foible, weakness; *avoir une ~ pour X*, to be partial to X; *mes livres de ~*, my favourite books.
prédire (predir), v.a. [*pré+dire*] To predict, to foretell; *je vous l'avais prédit*, I forewarned you; (v.n.) to prophesy.
prédisposer (predispoze), v.a. To predispose (*à*, to), to render liable or subject (*à*, to), to incline (to).
prédisposition (predispozisjɔ̃), s.f. Predisposition (*à*, to); previous fitness, propensity.
prédominance (predɔminɑ̃s), s.f. Predominance, prevalence, ascendency.
prédominant, -e (predɔminɑ̃), p. adj. Predominant, prevalent, prevailing.
prédominer (predɔmine), v.n.a. [L *prae+dominari*] To predominate, to prevail (over), to have control (over).
prééminence (preeminɑ̃s), s.f. Preeminence, precedence.
prééminent, -e (preeminɑ̃), adj. Preeminent.
préempti-f, -ve (preɑ̃ptif), adj. Preemptive.
préemption (preɑ̃psjɔ̃), s.f. [L *prae+emptio*] Pre-emption.
préétabli, -e (preetabli), p. adj. Pre-established, original, primitive, preordained.
préétablir (preetablir), v.a. To pre-establish, to pre-ordain.
préexcellence (preɛksɛlɑ̃s), s.f. Preexcellence, superiority.
préexistant, -e (preɛgzistɑ̃), p. adj. Preexistent.
préexistence (preɛgzistɑ̃s), s.f. Preexistence.
préexister (preɛgziste), v.n. To pre-exist.
préface (prefas), s.f. [L *praefatio*] Preface, introduction (to book).
préfacer (prefase), v.a. To preface.
préfectoral, -e, (aux) (prefɛktɔral), adj. Prefectorial, prefectoral, pertaining to a French *préfet*.
préfecture (prefɛktyr), s.f. [L *praefectura*] Prefecture; residence of a *préfet* = county town; ~ *de police*, police head-quarters.
préférable (preferabl), adj. Preferable, better, worthy of preference.
préférablement (preferabləmɑ̃), adv. Preferably.
préféré, -e (prefere), p. adj. s.m.f. Favourite, preferred, darling.
préférence (preferɑ̃s), s.f. Preference; mark of preference; taste; *de ~*, preferably.
préférer (prefere), v.a. [L *praeferre*] To prefer (⚠ not in the sense 'to promote', which = *faire avancer, donner de l'avancement à*, nor 'to submit', which = *soumettre*); to regard or value more than another person or thing, to choose, to like better.
préfet (prefɛ), s.m. [L *praefectus*] Prefect, head, chief administrator of a district or county (in France); ~ *des études*, vice-principal in a school; prefect; ~ *maritime*,

naval commander-in-chief (of a district); port-admiral; ~ *de police* (in Paris), head of Paris police, prefect of police.
préfète (prefɛt), s.f. Wife of a *préfet*.
préfix, -e (prefiks), adj. [L *praefixus*] Prefixed, appointed; *jour* ~, appointed day.
préfixe (prefiks), s.m. [L *praefixus*] (gram.) Prefix.
préfixer (prefikse), v.a. To prefix, to appoint.
préfixion (prefiksjɔ̃), s.f. Prefixion, appointment, previous settling.
prégnant, -e (preɲɑ̃), adj. [L *praegnans*] Pregnant.
préhenseur (preɑ̃sœr), adj. m., **préhensile** (preɑ̃sil), adj. [f. L *prehensum*] (zool.) Prehensile.
préhension (preɑ̃sjɔ̃), s.f. [L *prehensio*] Prehension.
préhistoire (preistwar), s.f. Prehistory.
préhistorique (preistɔrik), adj. Prehistoric, primeval.
préjudice (preʒydis), s.m. [L *praejudicium*] Damage, detriment, wrong, hurt, harm, injury, prejudice; *porter* ~ *à X*, to wrong X; *le* ~ *qu'on lui a causé*, the harm which has been done to him; *au* ~ *de X*, to X's prejudice; *sans* ~ *de mes droits*, without prejudice to my claims. ⚠ Note that the usual meaning of English 'prejudice' is *préjugé*.
préjudiciable (preʒydisjabl), adj. Detrimental, prejudicial (*à*, to), injurious.
préjudiciel, -le (preʒydisjɛl), adj. (law) Interlocutory.
préjudicier (preʒudisje), v.n.a. To be detrimental (to), to harm, to wrong.
préjugé (preʒyʒe), s.m. Presumption, prejudice, prepossession; (law) precedent; *exempt de* ~*s*, free from prejudice.
préjuger (preʒyʒe), v.a. [f. L *prae*+ *judicare*] To prejudge, to decide beforehand or hastily.
prélart (prelar), s.m. [orig. unkn.] (naut.) Tarpaulin; syn. BÂCHE.
(se) prélasser (səprelɑse), v.pr. [f. *prélat*] To take one's ease, to lounge, to enjoy utter comfort; (rarely) to strut.
prelat (prela), s.m. [L *praelatus*] Prelate.
prélation (prela'sjɔ̃), s.f. [L *praelatio*] (law) Prelation, preference (given to lessee to purchase).
prélature (prelatyr), s.f. Prelature; prelates collectively.
prèle (prɛl), s.f. (bot.) [f. *âpre, âprelle*] Horsetail, *Equisetum*.
prélegs (prelɛ), s.m. Preferential legacy.
prélèvement (prelɛvmɑ̃), s.m. Previous deduction; the substance or sum taken or deducted.
prélever (preləve), v.a. [L *praelevare*] To deduct previously, to take first, to reserve, to levy.
préliminaire (preliminɛr), adj. [f. L *prae*+*limen*] Preliminary, previous. ~, s.m. Preliminary.
préliminairement (preliminɛrmɑ̃), adv. Preliminarily.
prélude (prelyd), s.m. [L *praeludium*] (mus.) Prelude; (fig.) prelude.
préluder (prelyde), v.n. To prelude; to tune up.
prématuré, -e (prematyre), adj. [L *prae*+*maturus*] Premature; hurried, untimely.
prématurément (prematyremɑ̃), adv. Prematurely, too soon.
prématurité (prematyrite), s.f. (rare) Prematurity.
préméditation (premedita'sjɔ̃), s.f. Premeditation; (law) malice prepense; *avec* ~, wilfully; with malice aforethought.
préméditer (premedite), v.a. To premeditate.
prémices (premis), s.f.pl. [L *primitiae*] First-fruits; (fig.) beginning, first results, first-fruits, first choice.
premi-er, -ère (prəmje), adj. [L *primarius*] First, former (of two), foremost, best; prime; primeval, early; leading, principal; (math.) prime; *nombres* ~*s entre eux*, numbers prime to each other; *au* ~ *abord*, at first sight; *en* ~ *lieu*, in the first place; *matières* ~*es*, raw materials; *de* ~*e main*, first hand; ~*-né*, first-born; *le* ~ *venu*, the first comer; any one; the man in the street. ~, s.m. **1.** First floor; *demeurer au* ~, to live on the first floor; **2.** the first of the month; **3.** (theatr.) *jeune* ~, lover, actor playing usually the lover's part; ~*e*, s.f. **1.** (dressm.) (for ~*e main*) head worker in a dressmaking establishment; **2.** first night, first performance of a play; **3.** first class in a carriage, bus, train, &c. (in this sense ~*e* is often used in the plural: *en premières, les premières*).
premièrement (prəmjɛrmɑ̃), adv. Firstly, in the first place.
prémisse (premis), s.f. [L *praemissa*] (log.) Premise.
prémonitoire (premɔnitwar), adj. Premonitory.
prémontré (premɔ̃tre), s.m. Premonstrant, Premonstratensian.
prémunir (premynir), v.a. [L *praemunire*] To caution, to forewarn, to forearm; to provide; **se** ~, v.pr. to provide oneself (*de*, with; *contre*, against).
prenable (prənabl), adj. Pregnable, to be taken, to be won; seizable.
prenant, -e (prənɑ̃), p. adj. Taking, receiving; prehensile; *queue* ~*e*, prehensile tail; *partie* ~*e*, payee.
prendre (prɑ̃dr), v.a.n. [L *prehendere*] To take, to take up, to grasp, to lay hold, to seize, to snatch; to apprehend, to catch;

to receive, to accept; to deal with; to manage; to adopt, to contract; to put on, to wear; to choose, to appoint, to name (a day); to charge (money); to begin to burn, to ignite, to catch, to draw (as fires), to thicken (as mayonnaise, &c.); to curdle; to take root; to succeed; ~ *d'assaut*, to take by storm; *à tout* ~, on the whole; *autant de pris sur l'ennemi*, so much saved out of the fire; so much to the good; ~ *les armes*, to take up arms; ~ *la balle au bond*, to take the ball on the rebound; to seize the opportunity; *bien lui a pris de*, he was lucky to; ~ *garde*, to take care, to mind, to be upon one's guard; ~ *place*, to take a seat; to take place, to happen; ~ *soin de*, to look after; ~ *pied*, to get a footing; *que je vous y prenne!*, let me catch you at it!; *qu'est-ce qui vous prend?*, what's the matter with you?, what's up now?; *mal vous en prendra*, evil will betide you; *je sors d'en* ~, you will not catch me again so soon; *prenez-le comme vous voudrez*, you can take it as you like; *c'est à* ~ *ou à laisser*, there it is, take it or leave it; *ces allumettes ne prennent pas*, these matches don't strike; ~ *son parti de quelque chose*, to make the best of something; ~ *son parti*, to make up one's mind; ~ *parti pour X*, to side with X; *prenez que je n'aie rien dit*, let's suppose I said nothing; ~ *par le plus court*, to go the shortest way; ~ *naissance*, to take its rise, to begin, to start; (colloq.) *ça ne prend pas!*, it's no use!, that's no go!, that won't wash! (vulg.) no bon!, nope!; (slang) *qu'est-ce qu'il va* ~*?*, he'll get it hot!; *prenez patience*, have patience; ~ *en mauvaise part*, to take amiss; ~ *en main*, to take in hand, to undertake, to manage; *au fait et au* ~, when it comes to the scratch; ~ *X par son faible*, to get round X; ~ *X au mot*, to take X at his word; ~ *X en flagrant délit*, to catch X in the very act, or red-handed; *l'envie a pris X de*, X was seized with a desire to; *la glace n'est pas assez prise*, the ice won't hold; *pris de vin*, tipsy; **se** ~, v.pr. to be taken, to be caught; to act; to congeal, to thicken, to curdle; *vous ne savez pas vous y* ~, you do not know how to set about it; *elle se prit à pleurer*, she began to cry; *ils se sont pris d'amitié*, they have taken a liking to each other; *s'en* ~ *à X*, to lay the blame at X's door; *ne vous en prenez qu'à vous-même*, you have only yourself to thank for it.

preneu-r, -se (prənœr), s.m.f. Taker; buyer, payee; lessee; purchaser; catcher.

prénom (prenɔ̃), s.m. [L *praenomen*] Christian name; syn. PETIT NOM, NOM DE BAPTÊME.

prénommé, -e (prenɔme), adj. Above-named; named, christened.

préoccupation (preɔkypa'sjɔ̃), s.f. Preoccupation, anxiety, care; mental absorption, engrossment.

préoccupé, -e (preɔkype), p. adj. Preoccupied, thoughtful, absorbed, engrossed (*de*, in).

préoccuper (preɔkype), v.a. [L *praeoccupare*] To engross, to absorb the thoughts of, to trouble, to preoccupy; **se** ~, v.pr. to trouble oneself (*de*, about), to set about (doing something).

préopinant, -e (preɔpinɑ̃), s.m.f. Previous speaker.

préparat-eur, -rice (preparatœr), s.m.f. Preparer, preparator, assistant.

préparatif (preparatif), s.m. (usually in the plur.) Preparations; *faire ses* ~*s*, to make one's preparations.

préparation (prepara'sjɔ̃), s.f. Preparation; *sans* ~, extempore.

préparatoire (preparatwar), adj. Preparatory.

préparer (prepare), v.a. [L *praeparare*] To prepare, to make ready, to dispose; **se** ~, v.pr. to make oneself ready, to prepare oneself, to get ready; *un orage se prépare*, there is a storm brewing; *il se prépare quelque chose*, there is something brewing.

prépondérance (prepɔ̃derɑ̃s), s.f. Preponderance.

prépondérant, -e (prepɔ̃derɑ̃), adj. [f. L *praeponderare*] Preponderant; *voix* ~*e*, casting vote.

préposé, -e (prepoze), s.m.f. Person in charge; officer; overseer; keeper.

préposer (prepoze), v.a. To set over; to put in charge; to appoint.

prépositi-f, -ve (prepozitif), adj. (gram.) Prepositive.

préposition (prepozisjɔ̃), s.f. (gram.) Preposition.

prépotence (prepɔtɑ̃s), s.f. [L *praepotentia*] Ruling power, predominance.

prépuce (prepys), s.m. [L *praeputium*] (anat.) Prepuce, foreskin.

prérogative (prerɔgativ), s.f. [L *praerogativus*] Prerogative.

près (prɛ), adv. [L *pressus*] Near, by, hard by, close, close by; nearly, on the point of; *à beaucoup* ~, by a good deal, not nearly so; *à cela* ~, except for that; save that; *à peu de chose* ~, nearly; to within a trifle; about; *à peu* ~, nearly, nearly so, almost; pretty much; tolerably; *c'est à peu* ~ *la même chose*, it is much the same thing; *au plus* ~, (naut.) close to the wind; *de* ~, close, near, intimately; (fig.) *ne pas y regarder de si* ~, not to be too particular; *rasé de* ~, clean-shaven; *serrer de* ~, to be hard upon, to press hard; to be very pressing, very bold (in an improper way); *de* ~ *et de loin*, near and far; *tout* ~, close by, quite near. ~, prep. Near, close to, in the vicinity of; *avoir la tête ~ du bonnet*, to be hot-headed; *il est ~ de trois heures*, it is nearly three; *~ de finir*, near the end; *~ de cent francs*, about one hundred francs.

présage (prezaʒ), s.m. [L *praesagium*] Presage, omen; foreboding, conjecture.

présager (prezaʒe), v.a. To presage, to forebode; to conjecture.

pré-salé (presale), s.m. Salt-marsh sheep or mutton.

presbyte (prɛsbit), s.m.f. [Gr. *presbutēs*] Far-sighted, presbyopic person (who cannot see clearly at a short distance). ~, adj. Presbytic, presbyopic.

presbytéral, -e, (aux) (prɛsbiteral), adj. Of the priest, presbyteral, presbyterial; *maison ~e*, parsonage, vicarage.

presbytère (prɛsbitɛr), s.m. [f. Gr. *presbuteros*] Parsonage, vicarage, presbytery.

presbytérianisme (prɛsbiterjanism), s.m. Presbyterianism.

presbytérien, -ne (prɛsbiterjɛ̃), adj. s.m.f. [f. Gr. *presbuteros*] Presbyterian.

presbytisme (prɛsbitism), s.m. **presbytie** (prɛsbiti), s.f. [see PRESBYTE] Presbyopia.

prescience (prɛssjɑ̃s), s.f. [L *praescientia*] Prescience, foreknowledge, foresight.

prescient, -e (prɛssjɑ̃), adj. Prescient.

prescriptible (prɛskriptibl), adj. (law) Prescriptible.

prescription (prɛskripsjɔ̃), s.f. [L *praescriptio*] Prescription; (med.) prescript, prescription; (law) limitation; prescription.

prescrire (prɛskrir), v.a. [L *praescribere*] To prescribe; (law) to bar; **se ~**, v.pr. **1.** to prescribe for oneself; **2.** (law) to be lost by limitation.

préséance (prezeɑ̃s), s.f. Precedence; *avoir la ~ sur*, to take precedence of.

présence (prezɑ̃s), s.f. [L *praesentia*] Presence, attendance; *faire acte de ~*, to put in an appearance; *jeton de ~*, fee for attendance; *en ~*, face to face, facing each other; in each other's presence; *en ~ de*, in the presence of; in view of; *~ d'esprit*, presence of mind; wits; consciousness. ⚠ *Présence* has never, like English 'presence', the sense of ceremonial attendance on a person of royal rank, nor that of commanding appearance.

présent[1] (prezɑ̃), s.m. [f. *présenter*] Gift, present; *faire ~ de*, to give as a present; to give, to make a present of, to present (X) with.

présent[2] (prezɑ̃), s.m. Present time, present; (gram.) present tense; *au ~*, in the present tense.

présent, -e (prezɑ̃), adj. [L *praesens*] Present, actual, current; attentive, present to; *dans le cas ~*, in the present case; *votre image sans cesse est ~e à mon âme*, your image is ever before my mind; *par les ~es (lettres)*, by these present letters, by these presents; *à ~*, at present, now; *dès à ~*, from this moment; *jusqu'à ~*, till now; *pour le ~*, for the time being.

présentable (prezɑ̃tabl), adj. Presentable, fit to be seen.

présentation (prezɑ̃ta'sjɔ̃), s.f. Presentation, introduction; *à ~*, on presentation; *faire les ~s*, to introduce people to each other.

présentement (prezɑ̃tmɑ̃), adv. For the present, now; ⚠ not nowadays 'presently', which = *bientôt, tout à l'heure*.

présenter (prezɑ̃te), v.a. [L *praesentare*] To present, to offer, to hold out, to introduce, to show, to bring forward; to deliver; *~ X à Y*, to introduce X to Y; *~ une requête*, to present or deliver a petition; **se ~**, v.pr. to present oneself, to appear, to occur; *une difficulté s'est présentée*, a difficulty arose; *l'affaire se présente bien*, this business promises well.

préservat-eur, -rice (prezɛrvatœr), adj. s.m. Preservative.

préservati-f, -ve (prezɛrvatif), adj. s.m. Preservative.

préservation (prezɛrva'sjɔ̃), s.f. Preservation, preserving from injury or destruction; keeping.

préserver (prezɛrve), v.a. [L *praeservare*] To preserve, to keep from harm; to save, to defend; *que le ciel m'en préserve!*, heaven forbid!; *Dieu vous préserve de ce malheur!*, may God preserve you from this misfortune! ⚠ French *préserver* is not used in the sense of preparing fruit, meat, &c., by boiling with sugar, pickling, &c., which = *mettre en conserve*.

présidence (prezidɑ̃s), s.f. Presidency, chairmanship.

président, -e (prezidɑ̃), s.m.f. [L *praesidens*] President, chairman, presiding judge; *~ du conseil*, prime minister, Premier.

présidentiel, -le (prezidɑ̃sjɛl), adj. Presidential.

présider (prezide), v.a.n. [L *praesidere*] To preside over; to take the chair, to be in the chair; (fig.) to watch over, to superintend.

présidial, (aux) (obs.) (prezidjal), s.m. adj. Presidial.

presle (prɛl), s.f. See PRÈLE.

présompti-f, -ve (prezɔ̃ptif), adj. [f. L *praesumptus*] Presumptive, apparent; *héritier ~*, heir apparent.

présomption (prezɔ̃psjɔ̃), s.f. **1.** Presumption, supposition; **2.** conceit, conceitedness, presumptuousness.

présomptueusement (prezɔ̃ptɥøzmɑ̃), adv. Presumptuously, conceitedly.

présomptueu-x, -se (prezɔ̃ptɥø), adj. [L *praesumptuosus*] Presumptuous, conceited, presuming.

presque (prɛsk), adv. [*près*+*ce*+*que*] Almost, nearly, all but; ~ *jamais*, scarcely ever, ~ *pas*, scarcely; hardly, scarcely any; ~ *toujours*, almost always; ~ *personne*, hardly any one; *il n'y en a* ~ *plus*, there is hardly any left.

presqu'île (prɛskil), s.f. Peninsula.

pressage (prɛsaʒ), s.m. Pressing.

pressant, -e (prɛsɑ̃), p. adj. Pressing, earnest, vehement, importunate, insistent; urgent; *affaires* ~*es*, urgent matters.

presse (prɛs), s.f. [f. *presser*] **1.** Crowd, throng; **2.** haste, urgency; **3.** press; printing-press; *mettre sous* ~, to put into press; ~ *à copier*, copying-machine (or -press); **4.** press (newspapers collectively); *il a une mauvaise* ~, the papers are down on him; **5.** in comp. ~*-citron*, s.m. lemon-squeezer; ~*-étoupe*, s.m. stuffing-box (in a steam-engine); ~*-papier*, s.m. paper-weight; ~*-purée*, s.m. potato-masher; strainer.

pressentiment (prɛsɑ̃timɑ̃), s.m. Presentiment, foreboding; misgiving.

pressentir (prɛsɑ̃tir), v.a. **1.** To have a presentiment of, to have some idea of; to guess, to feel (something) coming; **2.** to sound, to ascertain the opinion of.

presser (prɛse), v.a. [f. L *pressum*] To press, to squeeze, to crush, to jam; to hurry, to hasten, to urge, to urge on, to importune, to harass; *ce qui presse le plus*, what is most urgent; *pressez-vous !*, hurry up !, make haste !; *rien ne presse*, there is no hurry; ~ *une orange*, to squeeze an orange; ~ *X de questions*, to ply X with questions; ~ *X de partir*, to urge X to leave; *il faut* ~ *X d'accepter*, we must insist on X's acceptance, or that X should accept.

pression (prɛsjɔ̃), s.f. Pressure, steam-pressure; *machine à basse* ~, low-pressure engine; (fig.) *exercer une* ~ *sur X*, to bring pressure to bear on X; *boutons* ~, or ~*s*, press-fasteners.

pressis (prɛsi), s.m. Juice (pressed out by a machine).

pressoir (prɛswar), s.m. Press, wine-press, cider-press; press-house.

pressurage (prɛsyraʒ), s.m. Pressing; squeezing.

pressurer (prɛsyre), v.a. **1.** To press, to squeeze; **2.** (fig.) to oppress, to grind, to screw, to overtax, to exhaust.

prestance (prɛstɑ̃s), s.f. [L *praestantia*] Commanding appearance, bearing, carriage, presence, deportment, portliness.

prestant (prɛstɑ̃), s.m. (mus.) Diapason (of an organ).

prestation (prɛsta'sjɔ̃), s.f. [f. L *praestare*] Prestation; tax consisting either of money or of labour on the public roads; ~ *de serment*, taking an oath.

preste (prɛst), adj. [It. *presto*] Agile, nimble, quick. ~ *!* (interj.) Quick !, sharp !

prestement (prɛstəmɑ̃), adv. Nimbly, quickly.

prestesse (prɛstɛs), s.f. Agility, nimbleness, quickness.

prestidigitateur (prɛstidiʒitatœr), s.m. [f. *preste*+(L) *digitus*] Conjuror, juggler.

prestidigitation (prɛstidiʒita'sjɔ̃), s.f. Legerdemain, sleight-of-hand; *tour de* ~, conjuring trick.

prestige (prɛstiʒ), s.m. [L *praestigium*] Fascination; illusion; magic spell; prestige, magic, influence; *avoir du* ~, to have prestige.

prestigieu-x, -se (prɛstiʒjø), adj. Fascinating; impressive.

presto, prestissimo (prɛsto, prɛstisimo), adv. [It. wds] Presto, quick, sharp.

prestolet (prɛstɔlɛ), s.m. Priestling, unimportant young priest.

présumable (prezymabl), adj. Presumable.

présumer (prezyme), v.a. [f. L *prae*+*sumere*] To suppose, to expect; to presume (*de*, upon). ⚠ French *présumer* has not the sense of to take the liberty of, to venture, to behave arrogantly.

présupposer (presypoze), v.a. To presuppose.

présure (prezyr), s.f. [It. *presura*] Rennet (for curdling milk).

prêt (prɛ), s.m. [f. *prêter*] Loan; advance pay.

prêt, -e (prɛ), adj. [LL *praestus*] Ready, prepared; ~ *à partir*, ready to go.

prêtable (prɛtabl), adj. Lendable.

prétantaine, prétentaine (pretɑ̃tɛn), s.f. [orig. unkn.] *Courir la* ~, to gad about; to be on the loose.

prêté (prɛte), s.m. Thing lent; *c'est un* ~ *pour un rendu*, it is tit for tat; a Roland for an Oliver.

prétendant, -e (pretɑ̃dɑ̃), s.m.f. Claimant, applicant; (s.m.) suitor, wooer; pretender (to the throne).

prétendre (pretɑ̃dr), v.a.n. [L *praetendere*] To pretend, to claim; to aspire (*à*, to); to intend, to mean, to affirm, to assert, to mean to say; *que prétendez-vous* (*obtenir*) *de moi ?*, what do you think you can expect from me ?; *il prétend partir demain*, he means to start to-morrow; *on prétend que*, it is said that; it is rumoured that. ⚠ 'To pretend' has often a more pejorative sense than *prétendre*, as to allege falsely, to simulate, to counterfeit = *simuler*, *contrefaire*, *faire croire*.

prétendu, -e (pretɑ̃dy), p. adj. Supposed, alleged, so-called, would-be. ~, s.m. Suitor, wooer (intending marriage).

prête-nom (prɛtnɔ̃), s.m. Person lending his or her name, man of straw, agent; syn. HOMME DE PAILLE.

prétentaine. See PRÉTANTAINE.

prétentieusement (pretɑ̃sjøzmɑ̃), adv. Pretentiously, affectedly.

prétentieu-x, -se (pretɑ̃sjø), adj. Pretentious, affected; ostentatious; stilted (of style).

prétention (pretɑ̃sjɔ̃), s.f. [f. *prétendre*] **1.** Pretension, claim (*à*, to); **2.** affectedness, pretentiousness.

prêter (prɛte), v.a. [L *praestare*] To lend; to attribute, to ascribe; ~ *le flanc à*, to lay oneself open to; ~ *la main à quelque chose*, to lend a hand with something; ~ *l'oreille*, to listen; to lend an ear; ~ *serment*, to take the oath; *ce cuir prête bien*, this leather stretches easily; **se** ~, v.pr. to submit, to lend oneself (*à*, to), to countenance, to accept.

prétérit (preterit), s.m. [L *praeteritum*] (gram.) Preterite.

prétérition (preterisjɔ̃), s.f. [L *praeterio*] (rhet.) Preterition.

préteur (pretœr), s.m. (Rom. hist.) Praetor.

prêteu-r, -se (prɛtœr), s.m.f. Lender; ~ *sur gages*, pawnbroker. ~, adj. Of a lending disposition, generous.

prétexte (pretɛkst), s.m. [L *praetextus*] Pretext, pretence; *sous* ~ *que*, under the pretence that; *sous* ~ *de partir*, under the pretence of leaving.

prétexte (pretɛkst), s.f. [Rom. ant.] Pretexta. ~, adj. *La robe* ~, the pretexta.

prétexter (pretɛkste), v.a. To make a pretext of, to allege.

prétintaille (pretɛ̃taj), s.f. (obs.) [orig. dub.] Fingle-fangle.

prétoire (pretwar), s.m. [L *praetorium*] Praetorium; (fig.) tribunal, court.

prétorien, -ne (pretɔrjɛ̃), adj. Praetorian; ~, s.m. (fig.) soldier.

prêtraille (prɛtraj), s.f. (pej.) The clerical crew.

prêtre (prɛtr), s.m. [Gr. *presbuteros*] Priest; *grand* ~, high priest; *se faire* ~, to take (holy) orders.

prêtresse (prɛtrɛs), s.f. Priestess.

prêtrise (prɛtriz), s.f. Priesthood; priests collectively; *recevoir la* ~, to take orders.

préture (pretyr), s.f. Praetorship.

preuve (prœv), s.f. [L *proba*] Proof, evidence, token; (math.) proof; *faire* ~ *de*, to show; *faire ses* ~*s*, to give proof of one's ability; to show one's mettle.

preux (prø), adj. [LL *prodis*] Gallant, valiant. ~, s.m. Gallant knight.

prévaloir (prevalwar), v.n. To prevail; **se** ~ (*de quelque chose*), v.pr. to avail oneself (of something).

prévaricat-eur, -rice (prevarikatœr), adj. That betrays his office.

prévarication (prevarika'sjɔ̃), s.f. Betrayal of trust or office. ⚠ Engl. 'prevarication' = *réponse évasive, faux-fuyant*; *tromperie*.

prévariquer (prevarike), v.n. [L *praevaricari*] To betray or abuse one's trust, or office. ⚠ Not 'to prevaricate'; see PRÉVARICATION.

prévenance (prevnɑ̃s), s.f. Kind attention, obligingness.

prévenant, -e (prevnɑ̃), p. adj. Obliging, nice, attentive, kind, engaging, prepossessing.

prévenir (prevnir), v.a. [L *praevenire*] To anticipate, to get the start of, to forestall; to prevent, to ward off; to forewarn, to apprise of, to inform; to prepossess, to anticipate, to bias; *mieux vaut* ~ *que guérir*, prevention is better than cure; *vous étiez prévenu*, you were warned; *il a prévenu tous ses concurrents*, he got the start of all competitors; ~ *les désirs de X*, to anticipate X's wishes; *son visage prévient en sa faveur*, his (or her) face is prepossessing.

préventi-f, -ve (prevɑ̃tif), adj. Preventive; *faire de la prison* ~*ve*, to be detained on suspicion (or before trial).

prévention (prevɑ̃sjɔ̃) s.f. Bias, prejudice, prepossession; *avoir des* ~*s contre X*, to be prejudiced against X; (law) *en état de* ~, committed; *être en* ~ *de conseil de guerre*, to be committed for trial before a court-martial.

préventivement (prevɑ̃tivmɑ̃), adv. Preventively, previously; on suspicion, before trial.

prévenu, -e (prevny), p. adj. Preceded, forestalled, anticipated; informed, forewarned; accused, committed for trial. ~, s.m.f. The accused.

prévision (previzjɔ̃), s.f. Prevision, anticipation, conjecture; forecast; prophecy; *en* ~ *de*, in anticipation of; in expectation of; *en* ~ *des mauvais jours*, against a rainy day.

prévoir (prevwar), v.a. [*pré*+*voir*] To foresee, to anticipate, to conjecture, to forecast, to look forward to; to provide for.

prévôt (prevo), s.m. [f. L *praepositus*] Provost; ~ *des marchands*, provost of the gilds; ~ *d'armes*, fencing-master's assistant; (mil.) provost-marshal.

prévôtal, -e, (aux) (prevotal), adj. Pertaining to a provost.

prévôtalement (prevotalmɑ̃), adv. Without appeal.

prévôté (prevote), s.f. Provostship.

prévoyance (prevwajɑ̃s), s.f. [f. *prévoir*] Foresight, forethought, caution; *société de* ~, provident society.

prévoyant, -e (prevwajɑ̃), p. adj. Prudent, far-seeing, provident, cautious, careful.

priapée (priape), s.f. [f. *Priape*, Priapus] Obscene poem, Priapics. ~**s** (plur.) Priapus' feasts.

prié, -e (prie) p. adj. Invited.

prie-dieu (pridjø), s.m. invar. Prie-dieu; prayer-stool; devotional chair.

prier (prie), v.a.n. [L *precari*] To pray, to beg, to ask, to beseech; to invite, to ask; *je vous en prie,* I beg of you; pray; ~ *Dieu,* to pray to God; *donnez-moi du pain je vous prie,* give me some bread, if you please; *j'ai prié dix personnes à dîner,* I have invited ten guests to dinner; *elle veut se faire* ~, she likes to be pressed; *il ne s'est pas fait* ~ *pour,* he did not have to be asked twice to.

prière (priɛr), s.f. [f. *prier*] Prayer, request, entreaty, petition, supplication; ~ *de répondre,* kindly answer; *à la* ~ *de X,* by the desire of X.

prieur, -e (priœr), s.m.f. [L *prior*] Prior, superior, prioress.

prieuré (priœre), s.m. Priory.

primaire (primɛr), adj. [L *primarius*] Primary; elementary; *école* ~, elementary school.

primat (prima), s.m. [L *primas*] Primate. ⚠ Not to be confounded with French *primate,* which = monkey, of the order of primates.

primate (primat), s.m. (zool.) Primate, member of the primates.

primatial, -e, (aux) (primasjal), adj. Primatial.

primatie (primasi), s.f. Primacy.

primauté (primote), s.f. [f. L *primus*] Primacy, supremacy, pre-eminence.

prime (prim), s.f. [L *praemium*] Premium; bonus, bounty, prize; *faire* ~, to be highly appreciated; ~ *d'assurance,* insurance premium. ⚠ Not 'prime', which = *état de perfection, fraîcheur première; atome;* (fenc.) *parade de prime.*

prime (prim), adj. [L *primus*] First, early; *la* ~ *jeunesse,* early youth; *de* ~ *abord,* at first sight; *de* ~ *saut,* at the first try; at once; (alg.) accented, prime; A^1 = A prime, A^1.

primer (prime), v.a. **1.** To surpass, to excel, to beat; *sagesse prime richesse,* wisdom is better than riches; **2.** to award a medal or prize to; *taureau primé,* prize bull.

primerose (primroz), s.f. (bot.) Hollyhock. ⚠ Not 'primrose', which = *primevère;* syn. PASSEROSE, ROSE TRÉMIÈRE.

primesauti-er, -ère (primsotje), adj. Impulsive, off-hand, spontaneous, quick-witted; sprightly.

primeur (primœr), s.f. [f. L *primus*] Beginning, early fruit, first (of anything); freshness, newness, bloom; *vous en aurez la* ~, you will be the first to enjoy it; ~**s**, (plur.) early vegetables.

primevère (primvɛr), s.f. [L *primus*+*ver*] (bot.) Primrose. ⚠ 'Primrose' is not the same flower as *primerose,* which = hollyhock.

primidi (primidi), s.m. [L *primus*+*dies*] First day of decade in calendar of the 1st French Republic.

primiti-f, -ve (primitif), adj. [L *primitivus*] Primitive, original, first, primeval; pristine, simple, uncultivated, unrefined. ~, s.m. **1.** (gram.) Primitive; **2.** (painter) Primitive.

primitivement (primitivmɑ̃), adv. Primitively, originally; excessively simply, without refinement or comfort.

primo (primo), adv. [L wd] Firstly, in the first place, first.

primogéniture (primoʒenityr), s.f. [f. L *primus*+*genitus*] Primogeniture; syn. AÎNESSE.

primordial, -e, (aux) (primɔrdjal), adj. [L *primordialis*] Primordial, primeval, primary.

primordialement (primɔrdjalmɑ̃), adv. Primordially.

primulacées (primylase), s.f.pl. (bot.) Primulaceae.

prince (prɛ̃s), s.m. [f. L *princeps*] Prince, sovereign; (fig.) first in rank or merit; *se montrer bon* ~, to be kindly, to prove easy to get on with; to play the good fellow; *vivre en* ~, to live like a prince; *le fait du* ~, arbitrary act of government; *le* ~ *des ténèbres,* the Prince of Darkness.

princeps (prɛ̃sɛps), adj. [L wd] Earliest; *édition* ~, earliest edition.

princesse (prɛ̃sɛs), s.f. Princess; (fig., colloq.) the State; *aux frais de la* ~, at the expense of the State; free.

princi-er, -ère (prɛ̃sje), adj. Princely, of a prince.

princièrement (prɛ̃sjɛrmɑ̃), adv. Like a prince; sumptuously.

principal, -e, (aux) (prɛ̃sipal), adj. [L *principalis*] Principal, chief, head, capital, essential, main. ~, s.m. **1.** (money) Capital, principal; **2.** (person) chief, head; head master, principal; **3.** main thing, principal thing; *le* ~ *c'est d'être honnête,* the chief thing is to be honest.

principalat (prɛ̃sipala), s.m. Head-mastership (in a school).

principalement (prɛ̃sipalmɑ̃), adv. Principally, essentially, chiefly, mainly.

principat (prɛ̃sipa), s.m. [L *principatus*] Principate, sovereignty.

principauté (prɛ̃sipote), s.f. **1.** Principality; **2.** princedom.

principe (prɛ̃sip), s.m. [L *principium*] Principle, source, beginning, origin; basis, reason, elements; essential matter; natural agent; principle, rule; *dès le* ~, from the beginning; from the outset; *les* ~*s de la géométrie,* the rudiments of geometry; *c'est un homme sans* ~*s,* he is an unprincipled man; *par* ~, on principle.

principicule (prɛ̃sipikyl), s.m. Petty prince, princeling.

printani-er, -ère (prɛtanje), adj. Spring-like, vernal, spring.

printemps (prɛ̃tɑ̃), s.m. [f. (L) *primus*+(Fr.) *temps*] Spring, springtime; (fig.) springtime, bloom, prime.

priorat (priora), s.m. Priorship.
(à) priori (apriori), adv. s.m. [L wd] A priori.
priorité (priorite), s.f. [f. L *prior*] Priority, precedence.
pris, -e (pri), p. adj. [f. *prendre*] Taken; smitten; caught; frozen, congealed, set; ~ *de vin*, tipsy; *bien* ~, well shaped; ~ *dans les glaces*, ice-bound; *nez* ~, stuffed-up nose.
prisable (prizabl), adj. Estimable, valuable.
prise (priz), s.f. [f. *prendre*] Taking, capture; *la* ~ *de Rome*, the taking of Rome; prize, capture, the thing taken; *une bonne* ~, a good capture; a lawful prize; *lâcher* ~, to let go one's hold; to let go; *amariner une* ~, to man a prize; *on n'a pas de* ~, it's difficult to get a hold; ~ *de tabac*, pinch of snuff; ~ *de bec*, quarrel, tiff, set-to, wrangling, slanging match; *être aux* ~*s*, to be at grips; *mettre aux* ~*s*, to set one against the other; to set by the ears; *je leur ai donné* ~ *sur moi*, I gave them a hold over me; ~ *de corps*, arrest, imprisonment; ~ *d'armes*, (*a*) taking up arms; (*b*) military ceremony; ~ *d'eau*, intake of water; ~ *d'air*, air-hole; ~ *de possession*, taking possession; *Tribunal des* ~*s*, Prize Court; (electr.) ~ *de courant*, wall-plug.
prisée (prize), s.f. Appraisement.
priser[1] (prize), v.a. [LL *pretiare*] To appraise, to estimate, to value, to set a high price on.
priser[2] (prize), v.a. [f. *prise*] To take snuff.
priseu-r, -se (prizœr), s.m.f. **1.** Snuff-taker; **2.** appraiser; *commissaire* - ~, auctioneer.
prismatique (prismatik), adj. Prismatic.
prisme (prism), s.m. [Gr. *prisma*] Prism; (opt.) prism.
prison (prizɔ̃), s.f. [L *prensio*] Prison, gaol, jail, imprisonment; *faire de la* ~, to do time, to be in prison.
prisonni-er, -ère (prizɔnje), s.m.f. adj. Prisoner, captive.
privati-f, -ve (privatif), adj. (gram.) Privative.
privation (priva'sjɔ̃), s.f. Privation, deprivation, want, hardship; *vivre de* ~*s*, to lead a miserable life; to be hard up; to suffer many privations.
privauté (privote), s.f. [f. *privé*] Excessive familiarity; *se permettre des* ~*s*, to take liberties.
privé, -e (prive) p. adj. Private; familiar; tame; privy; *vie* ~*e*, private life; *de son autorité* ~*e*, on one's own authority; *oiseau* ~, tame bird. ~, s.m. Private life; *dans le* ~, in private life; in the home; ~**s**, s.m.pl. (colloq.) water-closet.
privément (privemɑ̃), adv. Privately, intimately; unformally, informally.
priver (prive), v.a. [L *privare*] **1.** To deprive; **2.** to tame (animals); ~ *X de sa liberté*, to deprive X of his liberty; **se** ~, v.pr. to deprive oneself; to abstain; to stint oneself.
privilège (privilɛʒ), s.m. [L *privilegium*] Privilege, prerogative; licence.
privilégié, -e (privileʒje), p. adj. Privileged, licensed; preferential (share); entitled to preference. ~, s.m.f. Privileged person.
privilégier (privileʒje), v.a. To privilege, to grant a privilege to; to license.
prix (pri), s.m. invar. [L *pretium*] Price, cost, value, worth; prize, reward; stakes; *au* ~ *de*, (*a*) at the cost of; (*b*) in comparison with; *à bas* ~, at a low price, cheap; *à* ~ *coûtant*, at cost price; ~ *de gros*, wholesale price; ~ *fixe*, fixed price, net price; *hors de* ~, extravagantly dear; *à tout* ~, at any price; at any cost; *à vil* ~, dirt-cheap; *une chose sans* ~, an invaluable thing; *mettre à* ~ *la tête de X*, to set a price upon X's head; *remporter un* ~, to carry off a prize; *disputer un* ~, to contend for a prize; *décerner le* ~, to award the prize; *j'attache beaucoup de* ~, *à*, I set great value upon, I value highly; (colloq.) *au* ~ *où est le beurre*, as things are; (slang) *dans les grands* ~, capitally, on a large scale; to the backbone; with a vengeance; in grand style.
probabilisme (prɔbabilism), s.m. Probabilism.
probabilité (prɔbabilite), s.f. Probability, likelihood; (math.) probability.
probable (prɔbabl), adj. [L *probabilis*] Probable, likely; *c'est bien* ~, it is very likely.
probablement (prɔbabləmɑ̃), adv. Probably, very likely.
probant, -e (prɔbɑ̃), adj. Convincing, conclusive.
probation (prɔba'sjɔ̃), s.f. [L *probatio*] Probation.
probatoire (prɔbatwar), adj. Probatory.
probe (prɔb), adj. [L *probus*] Honest, upright. ⚠ Not English 'probe', which = *instrument de chirurgie servant à l'exploration des plaies*.
probité (prɔbite), s.f. [L *probitas*] Probity, honesty, uprightness, integrity.
problématique (prɔblematik), adj. Problematic(al), doubtful, questionable.
problématiquement (prɔblematikmɑ̃), adv. Problematically, doubtfully.
problème (prɔblɛm), s.m. [Gr. *problēma*] Problem; (fig.) problem, puzzle; *résoudre un* ~, to solve a problem.
proboscidien, -ne (prɔbɔssidjɛ̃), adj. [f. Gr. *proboskis*] Proboscidian. ~**s**, s.m.pl. Proboscidea, proboscidians.
procédé (prɔsede), s.m. [f. *procéder*] Proceeding, behaviour, dealing, trick;

process, system, operation; (billiards) cue-tip; *il a toujours eu de bons ~s à mon égard*, he has always behaved well to me.

procéder (prɔsede), v.n. [L *procedere*] To proceed (*de*, from), to arise (from), to originate (in); to proceed, to behave, to operate, to do, to go on, to act, to deal; (law) to take proceedings; *bien des maladies procèdent d'une mauvaise hygiène*, many diseases come from bad hygiene; *procédons avec ordre*, let us proceed with order, or methodically; *on va ~ à l'examen de*, they are going to examine; *~ criminellement contre X*, to prosecute X.

procédure (prɔsedyr), s.f. Procedure, practice, proceedings.

procéduri-er, -ère (prɔsedyrje), adj. s.m.f. Pettifogging, litigious (person).

procès (prɔsɛ), s.m. [L *processus*] Lawsuit, suit, trial; process (♤ Engl. 'process' means also *progrès, développement, processus, procédé*); (anat.) process; *faire* or *intenter un ~ à X*, to bring an action against X; to prosecute X; to sue X; *gagner son ~*, to win one's case; *perdre son ~*, to lose one's case; *être en ~ avec X*, to be at law with X; *~-verbal*, police report; written report of proceedings; *dresser ~-verbal à X*, to lodge an information against X; (fig.) *faire le ~ de* (person or thing), to criticize, to blame, to find fault with; *sans autre forme de ~*, without further ceremony.

processi-f, -ve (prɔsɛsif), adj. Litigious, pettifogging.

procession (prɔsɛsjɔ̃), s.f. [L *processio*] Procession; *aller en ~*, to go or walk in procession.

processionnaire (prɔsɛsjɔnɛr), s.f. (ent.) Processionary caterpillar.

processionnal (pl. **aux**) (prɔsɛsjɔnal), s.m. Processional.

processionnel, -le (prɔsɛsjɔnɛl), adj. Processional.

processionnellement (prɔsɛsjɔnɛlmɑ̃), adv. In procession.

processionner (prɔsɛsjɔne), v.n. To walk in procession, to procession.

processus (prɔsɛsys), s.m. [L wd] Processus, process.

procès-verbal (pl. **aux**) (prɔsɛvɛrbal), s.m. **1.** Written report of proceedings, minutes; **2.** (law) written statement of facts in support of charge; *dresser ~ à X*, to lodge an information against X.

prochain (prɔʃɛ̃), s.m. Neighbour, brother, fellow-creature.

prochain, -e (prɔʃɛ̃), adj. Near, nearest, next, coming, approaching, near at hand; (phil.) proximate; *l'année ~e*, next year; *sentant sa fin ~e*, feeling that death was near; *au ~ village*, in the neighbouring village.

prochainement (prɔʃɛnmɑ̃), adv. Shortly, soon.

proche (prɔʃ), adj. [L *propius*] Neighbouring, near, approaching, close at hand; *de ~ en ~*, step by step; from place to place; nearer and nearer. **~s**, s.m.pl. Near relatives, kindred.

proclamation (prɔklama'sjɔ̃), s.f. Proclamation.

proclamer (prɔklame), v.a. [L *proclamare*] To proclaim, to announce, to publish.

proclitique (prɔklitik), adj. s.m. [Gr. *pro+klitikos*] Proclitic (word).

proconsul (prɔkɔ̃syl), s.m. (Rom. ant.) Proconsul.

proconsulaire (prɔkɔ̃sylɛr), adj. Proconsular.

proconsulat (prɔkɔ̃syla), s.m. Proconsulate.

procréat-eur, -rice (prɔkreatœr), adj. Procreative.

procréation (prɔkrea'sjɔ̃), s.f. Procreation, generation.

procréer (prɔkree), v.a.n. [L *procreare*] To procreate, to beget, to generate.

procurateur (prɔkyratœr), s.m. [L *procurator*] Procurator.

procuratie (prɔkyrasi), s.f. Procuracy; procurator's palace.

procuration (prɔkyra'sjɔ̃), s.f. [L *procuratio*] Procuration, proxy; *donner ~*, to empower; *par ~*, by proxy.

procuratrice (prɔkyratris), s.f. (Woman) proxy, attorney, procurator, steward.

procurer (prɔkyre), v.a. [L *procurare*] To procure, to get (for somebody), to acquire, to obtain; *~ une situation*, to get a situation (*à*, for somebody); *cela lui a procuré bien des désagréments*, this has caused him much unpleasantness.

procureur (prɔkyrœr), s.m. (fem. see *procuratrice* and (obs.) *procureuse*) Attorney, solicitor, procurator, proxy, agent; *~ général*, Attorney General; *~ de la République*, public prosecutor. ♤ *Procureur* must not be translated by 'procurer', which commonly means go-between, pander, person who procures women for the gratification of another's lust = *proxénète*.

procureuse (prɔkyrøz), s.f. Procuress; bawd. ♤ Also sometimes: wife of attorney—but this is obsolete and better avoided.

prodigalement (prɔdigalmɑ̃), adv. Lavishly, extravagantly, prodigally.

prodigalité (prɔdigalite), s.f. Prodigality, lavishness, extravagance; *avec ~*, lavishly.

prodige (prɔdiʒ), s.m. [L *prodigium*] Prodigy, marvel, wonder; *cela tient du ~*, that is prodigious.

prodigieusement (prɔdiʒjøzmɑ̃), adv. Prodigiously, wonderfully.

prodigieu-x, -se (prɔdiʒjø), adj. Prodigious, wonderful, stupendous, tremendous.

prodigue (prɔdig), adj. [L *prodigus*] Prodigal, lavish, extravagant, wasteful; *l'enfant* ~, the prodigal son. ~, s.m. Spendthrift, squanderer.
prodiguer (prɔdige), v.a. To squander, to be lavish of, to throw away, to give freely or lavishly.
prodrome (prɔdrom), s.m. [Gr. *prodromos*] Premonitory symptom, prodrome; introduction, preamble.
product-eur, -rice (prɔdyktœr), s.m.f. Producer. ~, adj. Producing, creative.
productibilité (prɔdyktibilite), s.f. Productibility, productivity.
productible (prɔdyktibl), adj. Producible.
producti-f, -ve (prɔdyktif), adj. Productive.
production (prɔdyksjɔ̃), s.f. [L *productio*] **1.** Production, producing, exhibition; **2.** produce; ~*s littéraires*, literary productions or works.
productivité (prɔdyktivite), s.f. Productiveness, productivity.
produire (prɔdɥir), v.a. [L *producere*] To produce, to bring forth, to bear, to make, to create; to exhibit, to show; to cause, to beget; to yield, to bring; ~ *intérêt*, to yield interest; *la guerre produit de grands maux*, war causes great evils, or much misery; *cela n'a produit aucun effet*, it has had no effect; ~ *un titre*, to show one's title-deeds; **se** ~, v.pr. **1.** to occur, to happen; **2.** to exhibit oneself.
produit (prɔdɥi), s.m. Produce, production; product, result; profit, yield; exhibit; (math.) product.
proéminence (prɔeminɑ̃s), s.f. **1.** Prominence; **2.** protuberance.
proéminent, -e (prɔeminɑ̃), adj. Prominent, protuberant.
profanat-eur, -rice (prɔfanatœr), s.m.f. Profaner.
profanation (prɔfana'sjɔ̃), s.f. Profanation; defilement.
profane (prɔfan), adj. [L *profanus*] **1.** Profane (⚠ more pejorative in English than in French), impious; **2.** secular. ~, s.m.f. Uninitiated person.
profaner (prɔfane), v.a. To profane; to pollute, to violate, to defile.
proférer (prɔfere), v.a. [L *proferre*] To utter. ⚠ Not 'to proffer', which = *offrir, tendre.*
prof-ès, -esse (prɔfɛ), adj. Professed (monk, or nun).
professer (prɔfɛse), v.a.n. [f. L *professus*] To profess, to avow, to acknowledge, to declare; to practise; to teach, to be a professor of; ~ *une opinion, une religion*, to profess an opinion, a religion; ~ *le métier de*, to practise the calling of; ~ *l'histoire*, to teach history.
professeur (prɔfɛsœr), s.m.f. Teacher, master, professor, lecturer. ⚠ 'Professor' = *professeur de l'Enseignement Supérieur* or *professeur de faculté*; whilst master, schoolmaster, teacher = (approxim.) *professeur de lycée*, or *de collège*, or *d'Écoles Normales*, &c.; lecturer = *professeur chargé de cours*; also *lecteur, conférencier, maître de conférences.*
profession (prɔfɛsjɔ̃), s.f. [L *professio*] **1.** Profession, declaration; ~ *de foi*, profession of faith; credo; declaration of opinion; *faire* ~ *de*, to boast of being, to set up for; **2.** profession, calling, business; *quelle est sa* ~*?*, what is he doing?; what is his profession?
professionnel, -le (prɔfɛsjɔnɛl), adj. s.m.f. Professional (as distinct from an amateur); *École* ~*le*, technical school.
professoral, -e, (aux) (prɔfɛsɔral), adj. Professorial.
professorat (prɔfɛsɔra), s.m. Professorship, professorate, teaching, lectureship.
profil (prɔfil), s.m. [It. *profilo*] Profile; section; *tête de* ~, side-face; *vue de* ~, side-view; *vu et dessiné de* ~, seen and drawn in profile.
profiler (prɔfile), v.a. To represent the profile of, to profile; **se** ~, v.pr. to appear, to stand out in profile.
profit (prɔfi), s.m. [f. L *profectus*] Profit, advantage, gain; account; *au* ~ *de X*, in aid of X, for the benefit of X, on X's behalf; *faites-en votre* ~, make the best of it; profit by it; let that be of profit to you; *cela fait beaucoup de* ~, that is very profitable; *mettre à* ~, to turn to account; *retirer du* ~ *de*, to benefit by; ~*s et pertes*, profit and loss.
profitable (prɔfitabl), adj. Profitable, advantageous.
profitablement (prɔfitabləmɑ̃), adv. Profitably.
profiter (prɔfite), v.n. To profit, to benefit, to avail oneself; to improve; to grow; *bien mal acquis ne profite point*, ill-gotten goods never prosper; ~ *des circonstances*, to make the best of circumstances; *les arbres fruitiers ne profitent pas bien dans ce sol*, fruit-trees do not thrive well in this soil; ~ *en sagesse*, to increase in wisdom.
profiteu-r, -se (prɔfitœr), s.m.f. Profiteer; syn. MERCANTI. ~, adj. Profiteering.
profond, -e (prɔfɔ̃), adj. [L *profundus*] Deep, profound; dark; ~ *sommeil*, sound sleep; ~*e révérence*, low bow or curtsy; *un esprit* ~, a profound mind; *une voix* ~*e*, a deep voice; *un* ~ *soupir*, a deep sigh; *une nuit* ~*e*, a pitch-dark night; *une solitude* ~*e*, perfect solitude; *un* ~ *scélérat*, a consummate rascal; *peu* ~, shallow. (slang) ~e, s.f. Pocket.
profondément (prɔfɔ̃demɑ̃), adv. Deeply, profoundly, soundly, utterly; *dormir* ~, to sleep soundly; to sleep like a log, or a top.
profondeur (prɔfɔ̃dœr), s.f. Depth;

profundity; *10 mètres de ~*, 10 m. in depth; *une pensée d'une grande ~*, a thought of great profundity; (aeron.) *gouvernail de ~*, elevator, joy-stick.

profus, -e (profy), adj. [L *profusus*] Profuse.

profusément (profyzemɑ̃), adv. Profusely.

profusion (profyzjɔ̃), s.f. [L *profusio*] Profusion, lavishness; *à ~*, in profusion, lavishly.

progéniture (proʒenityr), s.f. [f. L *progenitus*] Progeny, offspring.

prognathe (prognat), adj. [Gr. *pro+ gnathos*] Prognathous.

prognathisme (prognatism), s.m. Prognathism.

prognostique (prognostik), adj. See PRONOSTIQUE.

programme (program), s.m. [Gr. *pro+ gramma*] Program(me); scheme, play-bill; political statement. ♤ 'Program(me)' is often used in colloquial English in the sense of *carnet de bal*.

progrès (progrɛ), s.m. [L *progressus*] Progress, improvement; progression; *faire des ~*, to make progress (sing.); to improve. ♤ 'Progress' in English frequently means development, advance = *développement, avance, mouvement en avant*; *progrès* in French usually implies improvement; road repairs in progress = *travaux en cours*, not *travaux en progrès*.

progresser (progrɛse), v.n. To progress, to get on, to improve. ♤ See PROGRÈS.

progressi-f, -ve (progrɛsif), adj. Progressive; gradual.

progression (progrɛsjɔ̃), s.f. [L *progressio*] Progression, advancement; progress; (math., mus.) progression (geometrical, harmonic, &c.).

progressiste (progrɛsist), adj. Progressive. *~*, s.m.f. Progressionist (rather conservative in Fr. politics).

progressivement (progrɛsivmɑ̃), adv. Progressively; gradually.

prohiber (proibe), v.a. [L *prohibere*] To prohibit, to forbid; *chasse prohibée*, (*a*) no trespassers; (*b*) close time; *armes prohibées*, prohibited weapons.

prohibiti-f, -ve (proibitif), adj. Prohibitive, prohibitory.

prohibition (proibisjɔ̃), s.f. Prohibition.

prohibitionnisme (proibisjonism), s.m. Prohibitionism.

prohibitionniste (proibisjonist), adj. s.m.f. Prohibitionist.

proie (prwɑ), s.f. [L *praeda*] Prey; booty, victim; *oiseau de ~*, bird of prey; *être en ~ à l'anxiété*, to be a prey to anxiety; *les poules sont souvent la ~ du renard*, the fowls often fall a prey to the fox; *lâcher la ~ pour l'ombre*, to lose the substance for the shadow.

projecteur (proʒɛktœr), s.m. [f. L *projectum*] Searchlight; (motor.) headlight.

projecti-f, -ve (proʒɛktif), adj. Projective.

projectile (proʒɛktil), s.m. [f. L *projectus*] Projectile, missile.

projection (proʒɛksjɔ̃), s.f. [L *projectio*] Projection ♤; throwing; (geom.) projection; projected image; projecting rays of light; *conférence avec ~s*, lecture with lantern-slides, lantern-lecture. ♤ In English the most usual sense of 'projection' is jut, protruding (thing) = *saillie, chose qui fait saillie, en saillie*; in French this sense is rare.

projecture (proʒɛktyr), s.f. Projection, jutting.

projet (proʒɛ), s.m. [L *projectus*] Project, scheme, design, idea, plan; *faire des ~s*, to form projects; *un homme à ~s*, a schemer.

projeter (proʒte), v.a. **1.** To project, to throw, to hurl, to fling; **2.** to scheme, to intend, to plan, to contemplate.

prolégomènes (prolegomɛn), s.m.pl. [Gr. *prolegomena*] Prolegomena, prefatory matter.

prolepse (prolɛps), s.f. [Gr. *prolēpsis*] (rhet.) Prolepsis.

proleptique (prolɛptik), adj. Proleptic.

prolétaire (proletɛr), s.m. [L *proletarius*] Proletarian.

prolétariat (proletarja), s.m. Proletariat.

prolétarien, -ne (proletarjɛ̃), adj. Proletarian.

prolifération (prolifera'sjɔ̃), s.f. Proliferation, multiplying.

prolifère (prolifɛr), adj. [f. L *proles+ferre*] Proliferous.

prolifique (prolifik), adj. [L *proles+ facere*] Prolific.

proligère (proliʒɛr), adj. [L *proles+ gerere*] Proligerous, generative.

prolixe (proliks), adj. [L *prolixus*] Prolix, verbose, wordy.

prolixement (proliksəmɑ̃), adv. Prolixly, at great length, verbosely.

prolixité (proliksite), s.f. Prolixity.

prologue (prolog), s.m. [Gr. *pro+logos*] Prologue.

prolongation (prolɔ̃ga'sjɔ̃), s.f. Prolongation; lengthening, extension of time, or delay; postponement; protraction. See PROLONGEMENT.

prolonge (prolɔ̃ʒ), s.f. (artill.) Ammunition-wagon.

prolongement (prolɔ̃ʒmɑ̃), s.m. Lengthening, extension. ♤ In matters of time *prolongation* is generally used; and *prolongement* is more usual when space is concerned.

prolonger (prolɔ̃ʒe), v.a. [L *prolongare*] To prolong, to lengthen, to extend;

(geom.) to extend, to produce, to draw out in length; (naut.) to sail along (a coast).

promenade (prɔmnad), s.f. **1.** Walk, stroll, constitutional; (*en voiture, en auto*) drive; (*à cheval, en auto*) ride; *faire une* ~, to go for a walk, drive, ride; **2.** walk; the place where one goes for a stroll; *une* ~ *plantée d'arbres*, a tree-bordered promenade (or walk).

promener (prɔmne), v.a. [f. *mener*] To take out for a walk; to take out walking; to lead; ~ *ses regards sur*, to let one's eyes wander over; *envoyer* ~ *X*, to send X about his business; **se** ~, v.pr. to go for a walk, stroll, drive, &c.; *se* ~ *de long en large*, to walk up and down; *allez vous* ~!; *va te* ~!, be off with you!

promeneu-r, -se (prɔmnœr), s.m.f. Walker, promenader, stroller.

promenoir (prɔmnwar), s.m. Covered walk; (theatr.) gallery; promenade.

promesse (prɔmɛs), s.f. [L *promissa*] Promise; promissory note, note of hand; *faire des* ~*s*, to make promises; *tenir sa* ~, to keep one's promise; *violer sa* ~, to break one's promise.

prometteu-r, -se (prɔmɛtœr), adj. **1.** Tempting, promising; **2.** quick at promising.

promettre (prɔmɛtr), v.a. [L *promittere*] To promise, to announce, to forebode; to give hopes of; ~ *et tenir font deux*, it is one thing to promise, another to perform; fair words butter no parsnips; ~ *monts et merveilles*, to promise wonders; *un enfant qui promet*, (*a*) a promising child; (*b*) (iron.) a future scoundrel; *le temps promet de l'orage*, this weather forebodes a storm; **se** ~, v.pr. to promise oneself, to resolve; to promise each other; to look forward to.

promis, -e (prɔmi), p. adj. Promised; *la Terre* ~*e*, the promised land; *chose* ~*e*, *chose due*, promises should be kept. ~, **-e**, s.m.f. Betrothed, bride, bridegroom.

promiscue (prɔmisky), adj. f. Promiscuous.

promiscuité (prɔmiskɥite), s.f. [f. L *promiscuus*] Promiscuity, mixing, promiscuousness. ⚠ In English the sense is less pejorative than in French; it does not always imply sexual relations or possibilities; ex. a promiscuous massacre = *un massacre en bloc, sans acception de personnes*; 'promiscuous hospitality' = *hospitalité peu exclusive*.

promission (prɔmisjɔ̃), s.f. [L *promissio*] Promise; *terre de* ~, promised land; land of promise.

promontoire (prɔmɔ̃twar), s.m. [L *promontorium*] Promontory, headland.

promot-eur, -rice (prɔmɔtœr), s.m.f. [f. L *pro*+*movere*] Promoter.

promotion (prɔmɔsjɔ̃), s.f. [L *promotio*] Promotion, preferment; (collect.) persons promoted.

promouvoir (prɔmuvwar), v.a. defect. [L *promovere*] To promote, to advance.

prompt, -e (prɔ̃), adj. [L *promptus*] Prompt, quick, sudden, swift; *avoir l'esprit* ~, to have a quick understanding; *avoir la répartie* ~*e*, to be quick at repartee; *avoir l'humeur* ~*e*, to be quick-tempered.

promptement (prɔ̃tmɑ̃), adv. Promptly, quickly, swiftly.

promptitude (prɔ̃tityd), s.f. Promptitude, swiftness, quickness, readiness.

promptuaire (prɔ̃ptɥɛr), s.m. [L *promptuarium*] Promptuary, manual.

promu, -e (prɔmy), p. adj. [f. *promouvoir*] Promoted.

promulgation (prɔmylga'sjɔ̃), s.f. Promulgation.

promulguer (prɔmylge), v.a. [L *promulgare*] To promulgate.

pronation (prɔna'sjɔ̃), s.f. [f. L *pronare*] Pronation.

prône (pron), s.m. [orig. dub.] Sermon, homily; (fig.) homily; (colloq.) *recommander X au* ~, to complain of X (to his superiors).

prôner (prone), v.a. To lecture; to extol, to cry up, to crack up, to praise.

pronom (prɔnɔ̃), s.m. [L *pronomen*] (gram.) Pronoun; ~ *personnel*, personal pronoun; ~ *relatif*, relative pronoun; ~ *possessif*, possessive pronoun; ~ *indéfini*, indefinite pronoun; ~ *interrogatif*, interrogative pronoun.

pronominal, -e, (aux) (prɔnɔminal), adj. Pronominal.

prononçable (prɔnɔ̃sabl), adj. Pronounceable, utterable.

prononcé, -e (prɔnɔ̃se), p. adj. Pronounced; marked, decided; prominent. ~, s.m. Delivering (of judgement).

prononcer (prɔnɔ̃se), v.a.n. [L *pronuntiare*] To pronounce, to utter, to deliver, to declare; to decide; **se** ~, v.pr. **1.** to declare oneself, to speak out, to make one's choice; **2.** to be pronounced.

prononciation (prɔnɔ̃sja'sjɔ̃), s.f. [L *pronuntiatio*] **1.** Pronunciation; **2.** delivery.

pronostic (prɔnɔstik), s.m. [Gr. *prognōstikon*] Prognostic, prognostication, prognosis.

pronostique (prɔnɔstik), adj. Prognostic.

pronostiquer (prɔnɔstike), v.a. To prognosticate; to foretell.

pronostiqueu-r, -se (prɔnɔstikœr), s.m.f. Prognosticator.

propagande (prɔpagɑ̃d), s.f. [L *propaganda*] Propaganda; *faire de la* ~, to carry on propaganda.

propagandiste (prɔpagɑ̃dist), s.m.f. Propagandist.

propagat-eur, -rice (prɔpagatœr), s.m.f. Propagator, spreader. ~, adj. Propagating, spreading.

propagation (prɔpaga'sjɔ̃), s.f. Propagation, spreading.

propager (prɔpaʒe), v.a. [L *propagare*] To propagate, to spread.

propane (prɔpan), s.m. (chem.) Propane.

propension (prɔpɑ̃sjɔ̃), s.f. [L *propensio*] Propensity, tendency, propension, inclination, bent.

prophète, prophétesse (prɔfɛt), s.m.f. [L *propheta*] Prophet, prophetess; *nul n'est ~ en son pays*, no man is a prophet in his own country; *~ de malheur*, prophet of evil; bird of ill omen; Cassandra.

prophétie (prɔfesi), s.f. Prophecy; prophetic utterance.

prophétique (prɔfetik), adj. Prophetic, prophetical.

prophétiquement (prɔfetikmɑ̃), adv. Prophetically.

prophétiser (prɔfetize), v.a.n. To prophesy; to foretell.

prophylactique (prɔfilaktik), adj. Prophylactic.

prophylaxie (prɔfilaksi), s.f. [f. Gr. *pro+ phulaxis*] Prophylaxis.

propice (prɔpis), adj. [L *propitius*] Propitious, favourable; suitable; *le ciel vous soit ~*, may fortune smile on you; *rendre ~*, to propitiate.

propitiation (prɔpisja'sjɔ̃), s.f. [L *propitiatio*] Propitiation.

propitiatoire (prɔpisjatwar), adj. Propitiatory.

propolis (prɔpɔlis), s.m. [Gr. wd] Propolis, bee-glue.

proportion (prɔpɔrsjɔ̃), s.f. [L *proportio*] Proportion, (math.) ratio, proportion; extent; *~s*, s.f.pl. proportions, dimensions of athlete, body, building, &c.; *en* (or *à*) *~ de*, in proportion to; *en ~*, proportionally; *toutes ~s gardées*, with due proportion; everything considered; all allowances being made; *la catastrophe prit de grandes ~s*, the disaster developed to a great magnitude; *la ~ des naissances par rapport à la population*, the proportion of births to the population.

proportionnalité (prɔpɔrsjɔnalite), s.f. Proportionality.

proportionné, -e (prɔpɔrsjɔne), p. adj. Proportioned, proportionate.

proportionnel, -le (prɔpɔrsjɔnɛl), adj. Proportional.

proportionnellement (prɔpɔrsjɔnɛlmɑ̃), adv. Proportionally; in proportion (*à*, to).

proportionner (prɔpɔrsjɔne), v.a. To proportion, to adjust, to accommodate.

propos (prɔpo), s.m. [L *propositum*] **1.** Purpose, resolution; **2.** talk, remark, discourse, idle talk; *à ~*, opportunely; in good time, seasonable, pertinent, pertinently; by the way; *à ~, viendrez-vous ce soir?*, by the way, are you coming tonight?; *à ~ de*, about; in reference to; with regard to; speaking of; *à ~ de bottes*, with reference to nothing in particular; *à quel ~?*, what about?, for what reason?; what are you referring to?; *à tout ~*, continually, at every turn, on every occasion; *mal à ~*, at the wrong time; unseasonably; inopportunely; *de ~ délibéré*, of set purpose, on purpose, purposely; deliberately; *hors de ~*, unseasonably; not to the purpose. **à ~**, s.m. **1.** Opportuneness; **2.** a short occasional play or poem.

proposable (prɔpozabl), adj. That may be brought forward or offered for consideration.

proposant, -e (prɔpozɑ̃), p. adj. Proposing. ~, s.m. Protestant student in divinity.

proposer (prɔpoze), v.a. [f. L *proponere*] To propose, to offer; to propound, to move; *~ X en exemple*, to set X up as a model; **se ~**, v.pr. **1.** to offer oneself; **2.** to resolve, to intend, to mean; *je me propose de rester quelques jours ici*, I intend staying (or to stay) a few days here; *nous nous proposons de partir*, we intend to go.

proposition (prɔpozisjɔ̃), s.f. [L *propositio*] Offer, proposal; (gram., rhet., math.) proposition; statement; (comm.) job; wares, special offer; *pains de ~*, shewbread; *faire des ~ de paix*, to make proposals or overtures of peace.

propre (prɔpr), adj. [L *proprius*] Own, characteristic, very, same, self-same, proper, peculiar; clean, neat; suitable (*à*, for); *chaque être a ses qualités ~s*, each creature has its characteristic qualities; *ce sont là ses ~s paroles*, these are his very words; *remettre en main ~*, to be delivered into the person's own hands; *sa ~ fille*, his own daughter; *le sens ~ d'un mot*, (*a*) the right meaning of a word; (*b*) the literal sense of a word; *un nom ~*, a proper name; a proper noun; *bois ~ à la construction*, timber suitable for building; *biens ~s*, personal property; *un ~ à rien*, a good-for-nothing; *~ à tout et bon à rien*, Jack-of-all-trades and master of none; *il ne possède rien en ~*, he has nothing of his own; *~ comme un sou neuf*, as clean as a whistle; as neat as a new pin; *vous voilà ~*, now you are in a pretty mess. ~, s.m. Characteristic, nature, peculiar quality; *le ~ de l'homme est de penser*, it is in the nature of man to think; *au ~ et au figuré*, in the literal as in the figurative sense; *eh bien, c'est du ~!*, a fine thing indeed!, what a shame!

proprement (prɔprəmɑ̃), adv. Properly, exactly, cleanly, decently; rightly; *à ~ parler*, properly speaking; *~ dit*, properly so called.

propret, -te (prɔprɛ), adj. Neat, tidy, spruce, natty, prim.

propreté (prɔprəte), s.f. Cleanliness, neatness.

propriétaire (prɔprietɛr), s.m.f. Owner, proprietor, proprietress, landlord, landlady, landowner; ~ *foncier*, landowner; *nu* ~, bare owner, owner without the usufruct of his property.

propriété (prɔpriete), s.f. [L *proprietas*] **1.** Ownership; **2.** property, estate, landed property; **3.** characteristic quality, particular virtue; **4.** (gram.) propriety, correctness; *nue* ~, bare ownership; property the usufruct of which belongs to another person; ~ *littéraire*, copyright.

proprio (prɔprio), s.m. (colloq.) Owner, landlord.

propulseur (prɔpylsœr), s.m. Propeller. ~, adj. Propelling, propulsive.

propulsi-f, -ve (prɔpylsif), adj. Propulsive.

propulsion (prɔpylsjɔ̃), s.f. [f. L *propulsus*] Propulsion.

propylée (prɔpile), s.m. [Gr. *propulaion*] Propylaeum.

prorata (prɔrata), s.m. invar. [L wd] Proportion; *au* ~ *de*, in proportion to.

prorogati-f, -ve (prɔrɔgatif), adj. Prorogating.

prorogation (prɔrɔga'sjɔ̃), s.f. Prorogation, adjournment.

proroger (prɔrɔʒe), v.a. [L *prorogare*] To prorogue, to adjourn; to prolong.

prosaïque (prozaik), adj. [f. *prose*] Prosaic, commonplace.

prosaïquement (prozaikmɑ̃), adv. Prosaically.

prosaïsme (prozaism), s.m. Prosaism, commonplaceness.

prosateur (prozatœr), s.m. Prose-writer (though this word is masculine, it can be used of a woman; ex. *Colette est un de nos plus grands prosateurs*).

proscripteur (prɔskriptœr), s.m. Proscriber, banisher.

proscription (prɔskripsjɔ̃), s.f. [L *proscriptio*] Proscription, banishment; abolition.

proscrire (prɔskrir), v.a. [L *proscribere*] To proscribe, to banish, to exile, to outlaw; to forbid, to abolish.

proscrit, -e (prɔskri), p. adj. Proscribed, banished, abolished, forbidden. ~, s.m.f. Exile, outcast, refugee, outlaw.

prose (proz), s.f. [L *prosa*] Prose; *mettre en* ~, to turn into prose.

prosecteur (prɔsɛktœr), s.m. Prosector.

prosélyte (prozelit), s.m.f. [L *proselytus*] Proselyte.

prosélytisme (prozelitism), s.m. Proselytism.

prosodie (prɔzɔdi), s.f. [f. Gr. *pros*+*ōdē*] Prosody.

prosodique (prɔzɔdik), adj. Prosodic.

prosopopée (prɔzɔpɔpe), s.f. [f. Gr. *prosōpon*] Prosopopœia.

prospect (prɔspɛk), s.m. [L *prospectus*] Prospect, view.

prospecter (prɔspɛkte), v.a. [f. L *prospectus*] To prospect.

prospecteur (prɔspɛktœr), s.m. Prospector.

prospection (prɔspɛksjɔ̃), s.f. Prospection, prospecting.

prospectus (prɔspɛktys), s.m. [L wd] Prospectus, hand-bill.

prospère (prɔspɛr), adj. [L *prosperus*] Prosperous, thriving, flourishing, successful.

prospérer (prɔspere), v.n. To prosper, to thrive, to be successful.

prospérité (prɔsperite), s.f. Prosperity, success, prosperousness; *avoir une face de* ~, to have a face like a full moon.

prostate (prɔstat), s.f. [Gr. *prostatēs*] (anat.) Prostate.

prosternation (prɔstɛrna'sjɔ̃), s.f.; **prosternement** (prɔstɛrnəmɑ̃), s.m. Prostration, obeisance.

prosterner (prɔstɛrne), v.a. [L *pro*+*sternere*] To prostrate; **se** ~, v.pr. to prostrate oneself, to bow very low.

prosthèse (prɔstɛz), s.f. [Gr. *prosthesis*] (gram.) Prosthesis.

prostituée (prɔstitɥe), s.f. Prostitute, harlot, whore, street-walker, strumpet.

prostituer (prɔstitɥe), v.a. [L *prostituere*] To prostitute; **se** ~, v.pr. to prostitute oneself.

prostitution (prɔstitysjɔ̃), s.f. Prostitution.

prostration (prɔstra'sjɔ̃), s.f. [L *prostratio*] Prostration; mental or physical exhaustion. ⚠ 'Prostration' in English means also *prosternation*; *prostration* means almost always nervous breakdown, dejection, low spirits, despondency.

prostré, -e (prɔstre), adj. [L *prostratus*] Reduced to utter dejection; dispirited, prostrate, physically exhausted.

prostyle (prɔstil), s.m. [Gr. *prostulos*] (arch.) Prostyle.

protagoniste (prɔtagɔnist), s.m. [Gr. *prōtagōnistēs*] Protagonist.

prote (prɔt), s.m.f. [f. Gr. *prōtos*] (print.) Overseer.

protect-eur, -rice (prɔtɛktœr), s.m.f. [L *protector*] Protector, protectress, patron, patroness. ~, adj. Patronizing; protective, protecting; *droits* ~*s*, protective taxes.

protection (prɔtɛksjɔ̃), s.f. [L *protectio*] Protection, support, shelter; patronage; protectionism.

protectionnisme (prɔtɛksjɔnism), s.m. Protectionism.

protectionniste (prɔtɛksjɔnist), adj. s.m.f. Protectionist.

protectorat (prɔtɛktɔra), s.m. Protectorate.

protée (prɔte), s.m. [Gr. *Prōteus*] Proteus; (fig.) turncoat; (bot.) protea; (zool.) proteus, amoeba.

protégé, -e (prɔteʒe), s.m.f. Protégé, protégée, dependant.

protéger (prɔteʒe), v.a. [L *protegere*] To protect, to shield, to shelter, to defend; to patronize, to encourage.

protéiforme (prɔteifɔrm), adj. Protean, proteiform.

protéine (prɔtein), s.f. (chem.) Protein.

protéique (prɔteik), adj. (chem.) Proteinic.

protestable (prɔtɛstabl), adj. Protestable, that can be protested.

protestant, -e (prɔtɛstɑ̃), s.m.f. adj. [f. *protester*] Protestant.

protestantisme (prɔtɛstɑ̃tism), s.m. Protestantism.

protestataire (prɔtɛstatɛr), s.m.f. adj. Protester, protestor, person who protests (against something).

protestation (prɔtɛsta'sjɔ̃), s.f. Protestation, protest; *~s d'amitié*, profession of friendship, marks of affection, polite effusions.

protester (prɔtɛste), v.n.a. [L *protestari*] To protest, to make a formal declaration (against something); to affirm; *~ une traite*, to protest a bill; *~ de son innocence*, to affirm one's innocence.

protêt (prɔtɛ), s.m. [f. *protester*] Protest (for non-payment).

prothèse (prɔtɛz), s.f. [Gr. *prothesis*] (surg.) Prothesis (supplying artificial substitutes for a deficient organ).

prothorax (prɔtɔraks), s.m. (ent.) Prothorax.

proto- (prɔto), pref. [Gr. *prōtos*] (in compounds, chem.) Proto-.

protocolaire (prɔtɔkɔlɛr), adj. Formal, in keeping with etiquette, in the approved way.

protocole (prɔtɔkɔl), s.m. [Gr. *prōtokollon*] **1.** Protocol, formulary; **2.** etiquette.

protonotaire (prɔtonɔtɛr), s.m. Protonotary.

protoplasme (prɔtɔplasm), s.m. Protoplasm.

prototype (prɔtɔtip), s.m. Prototype.

protoxyde (prɔtɔksid), s.m. Protoxide.

protozoaire (prɔtɔzɔɛr), s.m. [Gr. *prōtos*+*zōon*] Protozoan, protozoon; *~s* (pl.) protozoa.

protubérance (prɔtyberɑ̃s), s.f. [f. L *pro*+*tuber*] Protuberance.

protubérant, -e (prɔtyberɑ̃), adj. Protuberant, bulging out.

prou (pru), adv. [OF *proust*] Much; *peu ou ~*, little or much; to a certain extent; *ni peu ni ~*, not at all.

proue (pru), s.f. [L *prora*] (naut.) Prow, stem.

prouesse (pruɛs), s.f. [f. *preux*] Prowess, feat, exploit.

prouvable (pruvabl), adj. Provable.

prouver (pruve), v.a. [L *probare*] To prove, to give proof of, to show; *cela prouve sa bonne volonté*, this shows his good intention; *qui prouve trop ne prouve rien*, to prove too much is to prove nothing.

provéditeur (prɔveditœr), s.m. (in Venice) Proveditor.

provenance (prɔvnɑ̃s), s.f. Origin, source, place of production; goods; *en ~ de*, coming from.

provenant, -e (prɔvnɑ̃), p. adj. Coming (*de*, from).

provençal, -e, (aux) (prɔvɑ̃sal), adj. s.m.f. Provençal, Provençal language.

provende (prɔvɑ̃d), s.f. [L *praebenda*] Provision; victuals; (for animals) provender.

provenir (prɔvnir), v.n. [L *pro*+*venire*] To come (*de*, from), to have its source, to issue, to spring, to arise, to proceed, to result.

proverbe (prɔvɛrb), s.m. [L *proverbium*] Proverb, saying; *passer en ~*, to become a proverb, or proverbial.

proverbial, -e, (aux) (prɔvɛrbjal), adj. Proverbial.

proverbialement (prɔvɛrbjalmɑ̃), adv. Proverbially.

providence (prɔvidɑ̃s), s.f. [L *providentia*] Providence.

providentiel, -le (prɔvidɑ̃sjɛl), adj. Providential.

providentiellement (prɔvidɑ̃sjɛlmɑ̃), adv. Providentially.

provignage, provignement (prɔviɲaʒ, prɔviɲmɑ̃), s.m. Layering (of vines, rose-trees, &c.); syn. MARCOTTAGE.

provigner (prɔviɲe), v.a. [f. *provin*] To layer (vines, rose-trees, &c.); ~, v.n. to multiply; syn. MARCOTTER.

provin (prɔvɛ̃), s.m. [L *propago*] Layer.

province (prɔvɛ̃s), s.f. [L *provincia*] Province, shire, country; *une dame de ~*, a lady from the provinces; *gens de ~*, country people.

provincial, -e, (aux) (prɔvɛ̃sjal), adj. Provincial, of the provinces; countrified. ~, s.m. Provincial (of religious order).

provincialisme (prɔvɛ̃sjalism), s.m. Provincialism.

proviseur (prɔvizœr), s.m. [L *provisor*] Head master, principal.

provision (prɔvizjɔ̃), s.f. [L *provisio*] Provision, store, stock; sum prepared for a payment; *aller aux ~s*, to do one's marketing, to provide oneself with necessaries; *faire ~ de patience*, to take patience; *verser une ~ à X*, to pay X a

guarantee, to make a provisional payment to X.
provisionnel, -le (prɔvizjɔnɛl), adj. Provisional.
provisoire (prɔvizwar), adj. [L *provisorius*] Provisional, temporary. ~, s.m. Makeshift; provisional state.
provisoirement (prɔvizwarmɑ̃), adv. Temporarily, provisionally, in the meantime, for the time being.
provisorat (prɔvizɔra), s.m. Headmastership.
provocant, -e (prɔvɔkɑ̃), adj. **1.** Provocative, exciting, alluring; **2.** provoking.
provocat-eur, -rice (prɔvɔkatœr), s.m.f. Provoker, instigator, aggressor. ~, adj. Provoking; *agent* ~, hired agitator, nark.
provocation (prɔvɔka'sjɔ̃), s.f. Provocation, instigation.
provoquer (prɔvɔke), v.a. [L *provocare*] To provoke, to rouse, to stir up; to challenge, to incite (*à*, to); to bring on, to cause; ~ *un adversaire*, to challenge an adversary; ~ *à boire*, to urge to drink; ~ *la sueur*, to cause to perspire.
proxénète (prɔksenɛt), s.m.f. [Gr. *proxenētēs*] Go-between, procurer, procuress, proxenete. ⚠ *Proxénète* in French is always an infamous name; in English the word 'proxenete' had often the sense of marriage agent, honest go-between; but it is now obsolete.
proxénétisme (prɔksenetism), s.m. Procuring; the doings of go-betweens, procurers, &c.; making profits out of other persons' vices.
proximité (prɔksimite), s.f. [f. L *proximitas*] Proximity, propinquity, nearness; near relationship; *à* ~ *de*, near; in the neighbourhood of.
proyer (prwaje), s.m. (ornith.) Bunting.
prude (pryd), adj. [OF wd] Prudish. ~, s.f. Prude.
prudemment (prydamɑ̃), adv. Prudently, cautiously, warily.
prudence (prydɑ̃s), s.f. [L *prudentia*] Prudence, caution, wariness, discretion.
prudent, -e (prydɑ̃), adj. [L *prudens*] Prudent, cautious, wary, discreet.
pruderie (prydri), s.f. Prudishness, prudery.
prud'homie (prydɔmi), s.f. Probity, integrity, experience of business.
prud'homme (prydɔm), s.m. [f. *preux*+ *homme*] **1.** Wise, honest man; member of a board of arbitration between employers and workers: *Conseil des* ~*s*; **2.** (colloq.) *Monsieur* ~, canting man, given to uttering grandiloquent platitudes.
prud'hommesque (prydɔmɛsk), adj. [f. *Monsieur Prud'homme*] Pompous and hackneyed.
pruine (prɥin), s.f. [L *pruina*] (bot.) Pruina; dust or bloom of fruit, mushrooms, &c.
prune (pryn), s.f. [L *prunum*] Plum; ~ *de Damas*, damson; ~ *de Monsieur*, Orleans plum; ~ *de reine-Claude*, greengage; (fig.) *pour des* ~*s*, for nothing. ⚠ English 'prune' = *pruneau*, not *prune*.
pruneau (pl. -x) (pryno), s.m. Prune, dried plum; (colloq.) shot, bullet.
prunelle (prynɛl), s.f. **1.** (bot.) Prunella, sloe; **2.** (anat.) eyeball, pupil; apple of the eye; (fig.) *il y tient comme à la* ~ *de ses yeux*, he values it as the apple of his eye; *jouer de la* ~, to ogle; **3.** prunella, a woollen material.
prunellier (prynɛlje), s.m. (bot.) Sloe-tree; blackthorn.
prunier (prynje), s.m. (bot.) Plum-tree.
prurigineu-x, -se (pryriʒinø), adj. (pathol.) Pruriginous.
prurigo (pryrigo), s.m. [L wd] (pathol.) Prurigo.
prurit (pryri, pryrit), s.m. Pruritus, itching.
prussien, -ne (prysjɛ̃), adj. s.m.f. Prussian.
prussique (prysik), adj. (chem.) Prussic.
prytanée (pritane), s.m. [Gr. *prutaneion*] Prytaneum, military school.
psallette (psalɛt), s.f. [f. Gr. *psallein*] Singing-school (in churches, convents).
psalliote (psaljɔt), s.f. (bot.) A kind of mushroom.
psalmiste (psalmist), s.m. [L *psalmista*] Psalmist.
psalmodie (psalmɔdi), s.f. [f. Gr. *psalmos* +*ōdē*] Psalmody; (fig.) sing-song.
psalmodier (psalmɔdje), v.a.n. To chant, to sing psalms; (fig.) to drone out.
psaltérion (psalterjɔ̃), s.m. [Gr. wd] (mus.) Psaltery.
psaume (psom), s.m. [Gr. *psalmos*] Psalm.
psautier (psotje), s.m. Psalm-book, psalter.
pseudo (psødo), pref. [f. Gr. *pseudēs*] Pseudo-.
pseudonyme (psødɔnim), s.m. [*pseudo*+ (Gr.) *onuma*] Pseudonym. ~, adj. Pseudonymous.
psitt ! (psit), interj. (onom.) Hello !; look here!; hi !, hey !, I say !
psittacidés (psitaside), s.m.pl. [f. Gr. *psittakos*] (ornith.) Psittacidae.
psoas (psɔɑs), s.m. [Gr. *psoa*] (anat.) Psoas (muscle).
psora (psɔra), s.f. [Gr. wd] (pathol.) Psora, the itch.
psoriasis (psɔrjazis), s.m. (pathol.) Psoriasis.
psyché (psiʃe), s.f. Cheval-glass, psyche.
psychanalyse (psikanaliz), s.f. (neol.) Psycho-analysis.
psychiatre (psikjɑtr), s.m.f. [Gr. *psukhē*+ *iatros*] Psychiater, alienist.
psychiatrie (psikjɑtri), s.f. Psychiatry.

psychique (psiʃik), adj. [Gr. *psukhikos*] Psychical, psychic.
psychologie (psikɔlɔʒi), s.f. [Gr. *psukhē*+ *logos*] Psychology.
psychologique (psikɔlɔʒik), adj. Psychological; (colloq.) *le moment* ~, the opportune time, the favourable occasion, the psychological moment.
psychologiquement (psikɔlɔʒikmɑ̃), adv. Psychologically.
psychologue (psikɔlɔg), s.m.f. Psychologist.
psychose (psikoz), s.f. (pathol.) Psychosis.
psychothérapie (psikoterapi), s.f. Psychotherapy.
psychromètre (psikrɔmɛtr), s.m. (techn.) Psychrometer, hygrometer.
psylle (psil), s.m. Snake-charmer.
ptéro (ptero), pref. [f. Gr. *pteron*] Ptero-.
ptérodactyle (pterodaktil), s.m. [f. Gr. *pteron*+*daktulos*] (zool.) Pterodactyl.
ptéropode (pteropɔd), adj. [Gr. *pteron*+ *pous*] (zool.) Pteropodous. ~*s*, s.m.pl. Pteropoda.
ptolémaïque (ptɔlemaik), adj. (hist.) Ptolemaic.
ptomaïne (ptomain), s.f. (bio-chem.) Ptomaine.
ptose (ptoz), s.f. [Gr. *ptōsis*] (pathol.) Ptosis.
ptyaline (ptialin), s.f. [f. Gr. *ptualon*] (bio-chem.) Ptyalin.
pu (py), p.p. of *pouvoir*; see that verb.
puant, -e (pɥɑ̃), p. adj. Stinking; (fig.) impudent; *bête* ~*e*, skunk.
puanteur (pɥɑ̃tœr), s.f. Stink, stench.
pubère (pybɛr), adj. [L *puber*] Arrived at puberty; pubescent.
puberté (pybɛrte), s.f. [L *pubertas*] Puberty.
pubescence (pybɛssɑ̃s), s.f. (bot.) Pubescence.
pubescent, -e (pybɛssɑ̃), adj. (bot.) Pubescent.
pubien, -ne (pybjɛ̃), adj. (anat.) Pubic.
pubis (pybis), s.m. [L *pubes*] (anat.) Pubis.
publi-c, -que (pyblik), adj. [L *publicus*] Public, common; *la chose* ~*que*, the general weal, the State; *l'intérêt* ~, the public (or common) interest; *le bien* ~, the public welfare; *le bruit* ~, public opinion; public rumour; open secret; *fille* ~*que*, prostitute; *maison* ~*que*, brothel. ⚠ *Maison* ~*que* must not be translated by 'public house', which = *bar, cabaret, brasserie, marchand de vins, bistro.* ~, s.m. Public; audience; *en* ~, publicly, in public.
publicain (pyblikɛ̃), s.m. Publican; (colloq.) extortioner; stockbroker. ⚠ In Engl. the usual sense of 'publican' is keeper of a public house = *tavernier*.
publication (pyblika'sjɔ̃), s.f. Publication, issuing; book, magazine, &c., issued; proclamation; ~ *périodique*, periodical.
publiciste (pyblisist), s.m.f. Publicist; syn. JOURNALISTE.
publicité (pyblisite), s.f. **1.** Publicity, publicness; **2.** advertising; *faire beaucoup de* ~, to advertise lavishly.
publier (pyblie), v.a. [L *publicare*] To publish, to make public; ~ *quelque chose sur les toits*, to trumpet something, to proclaim something from the housetops; to publish, to issue (books), to bring out.
publiquement (pyblikmɑ̃), adv. Publicly.
puce (pys), s.f. [L *pulex, pulicis*] Flea; (colloq.) *cela lui a mis la* ~ *à l'oreille*, that made him feel uneasy; that has awakened his attention or suspicion; (colloq.) *secouer les* ~*s à X*, to give X a drubbing. ~, adj. Puce-coloured.
puceau (pl. **-x**) (pyso), s.m. [LL *pulicellus*] Intact youth.
pucelage (pyslaʒ), s.m. Maidenhood, virginity.
pucelle (pysɛl), s.f. [f. L *puella*] Maid, maiden, virgin; *la* ~ *d'Orléans*, the Maid of Orleans, Joan of Arc. ~, adj. Maiden.
puceron (pysrɔ̃), s.m. [f. *puce*] (ent.) Puceron, aphis, blight insect, green fly, plant-louse.
puche (pyʃ), s.f. Shrimp-net.
pucier (pysje), s.m. (slang, esp. mil.) Bed, flea-bag.
puddlage (pydlaʒ), s.m. (metall.) Puddling.
puddler (pydle), v.a. [Engl. wd] To puddle.
puddleur (pydlœr), s.m. Puddler.
pudeur (pydœr), s.f. [L *pudor*] Modesty, bashfulness; decency; *sans* ~, shameless.
pudibond, -e (pydibɔ̃), adj. [L *pudibundus*] Bashful.
pudibonderie (pydibɔ̃dri), s.f. Excessive bashfulness, exaggerated, affected modesty.
pudicité (pydisite), s.f. Modesty, chastity, purity, pudency.
pudique (pydik), adj. Chaste, modest, bashful, pudic.
pudiquement (pydikmɑ̃), adv. Chastely, modestly, bashfully.
puer (pɥe), v.n.a. [L *putere*] To stink; ~ *le vin*, to smell strongly of wine.
puériculture (pɥerikyltyr), s.f. [L *puer*+ Fr. *culture*] Rearing of children, infant management.
puéril, -e (pɥeril), adj. [L *puerilis*] Puerile, childish; trifling.
puérilement (pɥerilmɑ̃), adv. Childishly, puerilely.
puérilité (pɥerilite), s.f. Puerility, childishness.
puerpéral, -e, (aux) (pɥɛrperal), adj. [f. L *puerpera*] Puerperal.
puffisme (pɥfism), s.m. [f. Engl. *puff*] Puffing, impudent advertisement.

pugilat (pyʒila), s.m. [L *pugilatus*] Pugilism, boxing; fight, boxing-contest.
pugiliste (pyʒilist), s.m. Pugilist, boxer.
puîné, -e (pɥine), adj. [*puis+né*] Younger, second, next.
puis (pɥi), adv. [L *postea*] Then, after that, afterwards, besides; *et* ~, and then; *et* ~?, what next?
puisage (pɥizaʒ), s.m. Drawing up, pumping.
puisard (pɥizar), s.m. Cesspool; (min.) sump.
puisatier (pɥizatje), s.m. Well-sinker.
puiser (pɥize), v.a. [f. *puits*] To draw, to fetch up (a liquid); (fig.) to fetch, to take, to borrow.
puisque (pɥisk), conj. [*puis+que*] As, since, because.
puissamment (pɥisamɑ̃), adv. Powerfully, forcibly, mightily.
puissance (pɥisɑ̃s), s.f. [f. *puissant*] Power, might, force; sway, authority, command; (math.) power; *à la 4e* ~, to the 4th power; State, government, nation; *traiter de* ~ *à* ~, to treat on a footing of equality; *il est en ma* ~, he is in my power; *la* ~ *paternelle*, the parental authority; ~ *en chevaux*, horse-power.
puissant, -e (pɥisɑ̃), adj. Powerful, mighty, influential; (colloq.) stout, corpulent; *le tout-*~, the Almighty; *les* ~*s*, s.m.pl. the mighty; the magnates, the great; (colloq.) the big bugs.
puits (pɥi), s.m. [L *puteus*] Well; pit; ~ *artésien*, artesian well; ~ *d'aération*, air-shaft; ~ *de mine*, pit; (colloq.) ~ *de science*, walking encyclopaedia; budget of information.
pulicaire (pylikɛr), s.f. [f. L *pulex*] (bot.) Fleawort; *Pulicaria*.
pullulation (pylyla'sjɔ̃), s.f. Pullulation, swarming.
pulluler (pylyle), v.n. [L *pullulare*] To pullulate, to swarm, to multiply rapidly.
pulmonaire (pylmɔnɛr), s.f. (bot.) Lungwort, pulmonary; *Pulmonaria*; syn. CONSOUDE.
pulmonaire (pylmɔnɛr), adj. [f. L *pulmo*] Pulmonary.
pulmonique (pylmɔnik), adj. s.m.f. Pulmonic, consumptive.
pulpe (pylp), s.f. [L *pulpa*] Pulp.
pulper (pype), v.a. To reduce to pulp, to pulp.
pulpeu-x, -se (pylpø), adj. Pulpous, pulpy.
pulsati-f, -ve (pylsatif), adj. Pulsative, pulsatory.
pulsatille (pylsatij), s.f. (bot.) Pasque-flower, pulsatilla.
pulsation (pylsa'sjɔ̃), s.f. [f. L *pulsare*] Pulsation; throbbing, beating (of the pulse); vibration.
pultacé, -e (pyltase), adj. [f. L *puls*] (pathol.) Pultaceous.
pulvérisateur (pylverizatœr), s.m. Pulverizator, vaporizer, spray.
pulvérisation (pylveriza'sjɔ̃), s.f. Pulverization, pulverizing.
pulvériser (pylverize), v.a. [L *pulverizare*] **1.** To pulverize, to reduce to spray; **2.** to pulverize, to reduce to powder; (fig.) to crush, to grind to powder.
pulvérulent, -e (pylverylɑ̃), adj. Pulverulent, in dust.
puma (pyma), s.m. (zool.) Puma, cougar.
punais, -e (pynɛ), adj. [f. L *putidus+nasus*] Stinking (of mouth or nose).
punaise (pynɛz), s.f. [f. *punais*] **1.** (ent.) Bug; *plat comme une* ~, as flat as a flounder; **2.** drawing-pin.
punch (pɔ̃ʃ), s.m. [Engl. wd] Punch, toddy.
puni, -e (pyni), p. adj. Punished.
punique (pynik), adj. [L *punicus*] Punic; (fig.) *la foi* ~, Punic faith, disloyalty.
punir (pynir), v.a. [L *punire*] To punish, to chastise; to avenge; ~ *de mort*, to punish with death; *faire* ~ *X*, to have X punished; *il est puni par où il a péché*, he found his punishment in his sin itself.
punissable (pynisabl), adj. Punishable, liable to punishment or sanction.
punition (pynisjɔ̃), s.f. Punishment; *en* ~, for a punishment; as a punishment.
pupe (pyp), s.f. (ent.) Pupa, pupe, chrysalis.
pupillaire (pypillɛr), adj. (law) Pupillary; (anat.) pupillary.
pupillarité (pypillarite), s.f. Pupilarity, pupilage, wardship.
pupille (pypil), s.m.f. [L *pupillus*] **1.** Ward, pupil, minor in charge of a guardian; **2.** ~, s.f. [L *pupilla*] (anat.) pupil.
pupitre (pypitr), s.m. [L *pulpitum*] Desk, reading-desk; writing-desk, davenport; music-stand. ⚠ The English word 'pulpit', though of the same origin, now means *chaire* (in churches).
pur, -e (pyr), adj. [L *purus*] Pure, unmingled, unalloyed, unadulterated, genuine, true, chaste, innocent, unsullied; clean, spotless; sheer, downright; *ciel* ~, clear sky; ~*e bêtise*, downright foolishness; *par* ~*e malice*, for or out of sheer malice; *un* ~ *caprice*, a mere whim; *une voix* ~*e*, a clear voice; *du vin* ~, wine without water; *conscience* ~*e*, clear conscience; *cheval* ~*-sang*, blood-horse, thoroughbred; *c'est la* ~*e vérité*, it 's the plain unvarnished truth; *en* ~*e perte*, to no purpose, in vain; in mere waste.
purée (pyre), s.f. (cook.) Mash, purée; ~ *de pommes de terre*, mashed potatoes; (fig., colloq.) *être dans la* ~, to be hard up, to be in Queer Street, or on the rocks.
purement (pyrmɑ̃), adv. Purely, merely, cleanly; ~ *et simplement*, unconditionally, simply, solely, exclusively.
pureté (pyrte), s.f. Purity, pureness, genuineness; innocence, chastity.

purgati-f, -ve (pyrgatif), adj. Purgative, purging. ~, s.m. Purgative.
purgation (pyrga'sjɔ̃), s.f. Purgation, purge.
purgatoire (pyrgatwar), s.m. [L *purgatorium*] Purgatory.
purge (pyrʒ), s.f. **1.** Purge; **2.** (law) paying off (a mortgage); **3.** (techn.) clearing; *robinet de* ~, blow-off cock.
purger (pyrʒe), v.a. [L *purgare*] To purge, to purify, to cleanse, to clear, to wipe off; to blow off; ~ *sa peine*, to serve one's time; **se** ~, v.pr. to take physic, to purge oneself.
purgeur (pyrʒœr), s.m. (techn.) Blow-cock.
purifiant, -e (pyrifjɑ̃), p. adj. Purifying.
purificat-eur, -rice (pyrifikatœr), adj. Purifying. ~, s.m.f. Purificator.
purification (pyrifika'sjɔ̃), s.f. Purification, purifying; Candlemas.
purificatoire (pyrifikatwar), s.m. (Cath. liturg.) Purificator.
purifier (pyrifje), v.a. [L *purificare*] To purify; to cleanse; to refine (gold, &c.).
puriforme (pyriform), adj. (med.) Puriform; resembling pus.
purin (pyrɛ̃), s.m. Liquid manure; dung water.
purisme (pyrism), s.m. [f. *pur*] Purism.
puriste (pyrist), s.m.f. adj. Purist.
puritain, -e (pyritɛ̃), s.m.f. adj. [f. L *puritas*] Puritan.
puritanisme (pyritanism), s.m. Puritanism.
puron (pyrɔ̃), s.m. Whey.
purot (pyro), s.m. Dung-water pit.
purotin (pyrotɛ̃), s.m. (slang) Down-at-heel fellow, pauper.
purpurin, -e (pyrpyrɛ̃), adj. [f. L *purpura*] Reddish, ruby-coloured, purplish; *lèvres* ~*es*, ruby lips. See POURPRE ⚶.
purpurine (pyrpyrin), s.f. Purpurin; bronze powder.
purulence (pyrylɑ̃s), s.f. Purulence.
purulent, -e (pyrylɑ̃), adj. Purulent.
pus (py), s.m. [L wd] (pathol.) Pus, matter.
pusillanime (pyzillanim), adj. [L *pusillus* + *animus*] Pusillanimous.
pusillanimité (pyzillanimite), s.f. Pusillanimity.
pustule (pystyl), s.f. [L *pustula*] Pustule, pimple.
pustuleu-x, -se (pystylø), adj. Pustulous.
putain (pytɛ̃), s.f. [f. OF *pute*] Prostitute, street-walker, whore, harlot.
putati-f, -ve (pytatif), adj. [f. L *putare*] (law) Putative, reputed, supposed.
putois (pytwɑ), s.m. [f. L *putidus*] (zool.) Polecat.
putréfacti-f, -ve (pytrefaktif), adj. Putrefactive.
putréfaction (pytrefaksjɔ̃), s.f. Putrefaction.
putréfiable (pytrefjabl), adj. Liable to putrefy.
putréfier (pytrefje), v.a. [L *putrefieri*] To putrefy; **se** ~, v.pr. to putrefy, to rot.
putrescence (pytrɛssɑ̃s), s.f. Putrescence.
putrescent, -e (pytrɛssɑ̃), adj. Putrescent.
putrescibilité (pytrɛssibilite), s.f. Putrescibility.
putrescible (pytrɛssibl), adj. Putrescible.
putride (pytrid), adj. [L *putridus*] Putrid.
putridité (pytridite), s.f. Putridity.
puy (pɥi), s.m. [L *podium*] Mountain, conical peak (in Auvergne).
pygargue (pigarg), s.m. [Gr. *pugargos*] (ornith.) Pygarg; sea-eagle; osprey.
pygmée (pigme), s.m. [f. Gr. *pugmē*] Pygmy; (fig.) dwarf.
pygméen, -ne (pigmeɛ̃), adj. Pygmaean.
pyjama (piʒama), s.m. [Hindustani wd of Pers. orig.] Pyjama, pajama.
pylône (pilon), s.m. [Gr. *pulōn*] Pylon.
pylore (pilɔr), s.m. [f. Gr. *pulōros*] (anat.) Pylorus.
pyorrhée (piɔrre), s.f. [f. Gr. *puon* + *rhein*] (med.) Pyorrhoea; discharge of pus.
pyracanthe (pirakɑ̃t), s.f. [Gr. *purakantha*] (bot.) Pyracanth; syn. BUISSON ARDENT.
pyrale (piral), s.f. [Gr. *puralis*] (ent.) Pyralis.
pyramidal, -e, (aux) (piramidal), adj. Pyramidal; (fig.) astounding, tremendous.
pyramide (piramid), s.f. [Gr. *puramis*] Pyramid.
pyramider (piramide), v.n. To rise like a pyramid; to tower up; to taper.
pyramidon (piramidɔ̃), s.m. **1.** Top of an obelisk; **2.** (med., chem.) pyramidon.
pyrénéen, -ne (pireneɛ̃), adj. Pyrenean; pertaining to the Pyrenees.
pyrénéite (pireneit), s.f. (min.) Pyreneite, a variety of garnet.
pyrèthre (pirɛtr), s.m. [Gr. *purethron*] (bot.) Pyrethrum; *poudre de* ~, insect-powder.
pyrexie (pirɛksi), s.f. [f. Gr. *puressein*] (pathol.) Pyrexia; febrile disease.
pyrique (pirik), adj. [f. Gr. *pur*] Pyrotechnic.
pyrite (pirit), s.f. (chem.) Pyrites.
pyriteu-x, -se (piritø), adj. Pyritous.
pyro- (piro), pref. [Gr. *pur*] (in comp.) Pyro-.
pyrogallique (pirogalik) adj. (chem.) Pyrogallic.
pyrogravure (pirɔgravyr), s.f. Pyrogravure; poker-work.
pyrolâtrie (pirɔlɑtri), s.f. [f. Gr. *pur* + *latreia*] Pyrolatry, worship of fire.
pyroligneux (pirɔliɲø) adj. m. [f. Gr. *pur* + L *lignum*] (chem.) Pyroligneous.

pyromètre (pirɔmɛtr), s.m. [Gr. *pur*+*metron*] Pyrometer.
pyroscaphe (pirɔskaf), s.m. (obs.) [Gr. *pur*+*skaphos*] (old name for) Steamboat, steamer.
pyroscope (pirɔskɔp), s.m. [Gr. *pur*+*skopein*] Pyroscope.
pyrosis (pirozis), s.m. [Gr. *purōsis*] (med.) Pyrosis, water-brash.
pyrotechnie (pirɔtɛkni), s.f. [Gr. *pur*+*tekhnē*] Pyrotechnics.
pyrotechnique (pirɔtɛknik), adj. Pyrotechnic(al).
pyroxène (pirɔksɛn), s.m. [Gr. *pur*+*xenos*] (min.) Pyroxene, a metal occurring in lavas.
pyroxylé, -e (pirɔksile) adj. [Gr. *pur*+*xulon*] (chem.) *Poudre ~e*, pyroxyle powder, smokeless powder; gun-cotton.
pyroxyline (pirɔksilin), s.f. (chem.) Pyroxylin; gun-cotton.
pyrrhique (pirik), adj. [f. Gr. *Purrhos*] Pyrrhic. ~, s.f. Pyrrhic dance.
pyrrhonien, -ne (pirɔnjɛ̃), adj. s.m.f. Pyrrhonian, Pyrrhonic.
pyrrhonisme (pirɔnism), s.m. [f. Gr. *Purrhōn*] Pyrrhonism.
pythagoricien, -ne (pitagɔrisjɛ̃), adj. s.m.f. [f. Gr. *Puthagoreios*] Pythagorean.
pythagorique (pitagɔrik), adj. Pythagorean.
pythagorisme (pitagɔrism), s.m. Pythagorism.
pythie (piti), s.f. (ant.) Pythia.
pythien, -ne (pitjɛ̃), adj. Pythian.
python (pitɔ̃), s.m. [f. Gr. *puthōn*] (zool.) Python (snake).
pythonisse (pitɔnis), s.f. [L *pythonissa*] (ant.) Pythoness; (colloq.) fortune-teller, prophetess.
pyxide (piksid), s.f. [f. Gr. *puxis*] (zool.) Madagascar tortoise; (bot.) pyxidium.

Q

Q, q (ky), s.m. The seventeenth letter of the alphabet.
qu'. See QUE.
quadragénaire (kadraʒenɛr), adj. s.m.f. [L *quadragenarius*] Quadragenarian.
quadragésimal, -e, (aux) (kadraʒezimal), adj. Quadragesimal, pertaining to Lent.
quadragésime (kadraʒezim, kwadraʒezim), s.f. [L fem. of *quadragesimus*] Quadragesima; *dimanche de la ~*, Quadragesima Sunday, first Sunday in Lent.
quadrangle (kadrɑ̃gl, kwadrɑ̃gl), s.m. Quadrangle.
quadrangulaire (kadrɑ̃gylɛr, kwadrɑ̃gylɛr), adj. [f. L *quadrangulus*] Quadrangular.
quadrant (kadrɑ̃, kwadrɑ̃), s.m. Quadrant.
quadrat, cadrat (kadra), s.m. (print.) Quadrat, quad.
quadratique (kwadratik), adj. (math.) Quadratic.
quadratrice (kwadratris), s.f. (geom.) Quadratrix.
quadrature (kadratyr, kwadratyr), s.f. [L *quadratura*] Quadrature; (fig.) *chercher la ~ du cercle*, to try to square the circle, to pursue an impossible research.
quadri (kadri, kwadri), pref. [L comb. form] Four-; ex. *quadricolore*, four-coloured.
quadricorne (kadrikɔrn), adj. (bot.) Quadricornous.
quadricycle (kadrisikl), s.m. Quadricycle.
quadriennal, -e, (aux) (kadriɛnal, kwadriɛnal), adj. Quadrennial, four-yearly.
quadrifide (kadrifid), adj. (bot.) Quadrifid, cleft into four divisions or lobes.
quadrifolié, -e (kadrifɔlje, kwadrifɔlje), (bot.) Quadrifoliate.
quadrige (kadriʒ, kwadriʒ), s.m. [L *quadriga*] Quadriga.
quadrijumeaux (kadriʒymo), adj. m. pl. (anat.) Quadrigeminal.
quadrilatéral, -e, (aux) (kadrilateral, kwadrilateral), adj. Quadrilateral, four-sided.
quadrilatère (kadrilatɛr, kwadrilatɛr), s.m. adj. [L *quadri*+*latus*] Quadrilateral.
quadrillage (kadrijaʒ), s.m. Chequer-work.
quadrille (kadrij), s.m. [f. Span. *cuadrilla*] **1.** Quadrille (dance); ~, s.f. troop of horsemen (at a tournament); **2.** ~, s.m. [f. Span. *cuartillo*] quadrille (card-game).
quadrillé, -e (kadrije), p. adj. (of materials) Chequered; (of paper) ruled in squares.
quadriller (kadrije), v.a. To rule in squares.
quadrilobé, -e (kadrilɔbe), adj. (bot.) Quadrilobate.
quadrinôme (kadrinom), s.m. (alg.) Quadrinomial.
quadrisaïeul, -e (kadrizajœl), s.m.f. Ancestor in the fourth degree.
quadrisyllabe (kadrisilab), s.m. Quadrisyllable.
quadrisyllabique (kadrisilabik), adj. Quadrisyllabic.
quadrumane (kadryman, kwadryman), s.m. [f. L *quadru*+*manus*] Quadrumane; *ordre des ~s*, the Quadrumana. ~, adj. Quadrumanous.
quadrupède (kadrypɛd, kwadrypɛd), s.m. adj. [L *quadru*+*pes*] Quadruped.
quadruple (kadrypl, kwadrypl), adj. [L *quadruplus*] Quadruple; fourfold. ~, s.m. **1.** Quadruple; **2.** double pistole (Spanish coin).
quadruplement (kadrypləmɑ̃), (also kwadrypləmɛ̃), s.m. Increasing fourfold; quadruplication. ~, adv. Quadruply.
quadrupler (kadryple, kwadryple) To quadruple, to increase fourfold.

quai (ke), s.m. [Celt. *cai*] Quay, wharf; (rail.) platform; *droit de ~*, wharfage; *le Quai d'Orsay*, the French Foreign Office.

quaiche (kɛʃ), s.f. [Engl. *ketch*] (naut.) Ketch.

qualifiable (kalifjabl), adj. That can be qualified, described, or appreciated; *une conduite qui n'est pas ~*, behaviour for which there is no name.

qualificateur (kalifikatœr), s.m. (Rom. Cath. Church) Qualificator, theologian who deals with offences in ecclesiastical courts.

qualificati-f, -ve (kalifikatif), adj. (gram.) Qualificative; qualificatory. ~, s.m. Epithet; significant appellation.

qualification (kalifika'sjɔ̃), s.f. Appellation, title; epithet; qualification. ⚠ *Qualification* in French has never the sense of 'modification', 'restricting or limiting circumstance', 'detraction from completeness' = *modification, restriction, réserves, mitigation*, which is in English the usual sense of 'qualification'; but it has sometimes as in English the sense of quality fitting a person (for a post, &c.).

qualifié, -e (kalifje), p. adj. **1.** Qualified (for doing, to do); **2.** *vol ~*, theft with aggravating circumstances.

qualifier (kalifje), v.a. [L *qualis+facere*] To qualify; to attribute some quality to; to describe as; *~ X de scélérat*, to call X a scoundrel. ⚠ *Qualifier* has not like 'to qualify' the sense of 'to modify', 'to make less absolute', 'to mitigate' = *modifier, restreindre, mitiger, rendre moins absolu*.

qualitati-f, -ve (kalitatif), adj. Qualitative.

qualitativement (kalitativmɑ̃), adv. Qualitatively.

qualité (kalite), s.f. [L *qualitas*] Quality, characteristic, trait; attribute; excellence, skill, accomplishment; high rank, nobility; title; *un vin de ~*, a choice wine; *il a les défauts de ses ~s*, he has the defects of his qualities; *en ~ de*, in the capacity of; as; under the name of.

quand (kɑ̃), adv. conj. [L *quando*] When, whenever; what time?; while, whilst; though, even though, although; *depuis ~?*, how long is it since?, from when does it date?; *jusqu'à ~ pouvez-vous rester?*, till when can you stay?; *~ bien même*, even though; *~ même*, all the same, nevertheless.

quant, -e (kɑ̃), adj. [L *quantum*] (Obs. except in:) *toutes et ~es fois*, whenever.

quant à (kɑ̃ta), prep. [L *quantum*] As for, with regard to, respecting; *~ moi, je le ferai*, for my part, I have decided to do it.

quant-à-soi (kɑ̃taswa), s.m. Reserve, dignity; *se tenir sur son ~*, to stand on one's dignity; to behave with reserve.

quantième (kɑ̃tjɛm), adj. s.m. Which (number), which day (of the month).

quantitati-f, -ve (kɑ̃titatif), adj. Quantitative.

quantitativement (kɑ̃titativmɑ̃), adv. Quantitatively.

quantité (kɑ̃tite), s.f. [L *quantitas*] Quantity; great deal, amount, abundance, numbers; (math.) quantity; (pros.) quantity; *~ de gens disent que*, quite a number of persons say that; a great many persons say that; *on trouve ces animaux en ~*, these animals are found in quantities; *on peut voir des ~s d'étoiles*, we can see numberless stars; *acheter par grandes ~s*, to buy in large quantities.

quantum (pl. **quanta**) (kwɑ̃tɔm), s.m. [L wd] Quantum; *théorie des quanta*, (math.) quantum theory.

quarantaine (karɑ̃tɛn), s.f. **1.** Forty, some forty; age of forty, fortieth year; **2.** quarantine; *mettre en ~*, to quarantine; to send to Coventry; **3.** (bot.) stock.

quarante (karɑ̃t), adj. num. [L *quadraginta*] Forty; *je m'en moque comme de l'an ~*, I don't care a straw about it; *les ~*, the French Academicians.

quarantenaire (karɑ̃tnɛr), adj. **1.** Of forty years; **2.** (naut.) pertaining to quarantine.

quarantième (karɑ̃tjɛm), adj. s.m.f. Fortieth; fortieth part.

quarderonner (kardərɔne), v.a. [f. *quart-de-rond*] (arch.) To round off (an angle).

quarré (kare), adj. s.m. (obs.) see CARRÉ.

quart (kar), s.m. [L *quartus*] Fourth part, quarter; quart (an Engl. measure = roughly 1 *litre*); (naut.) (*a*) watch; (*b*) point of the compass; *~ de cercle*, quadrant; *~ d'heure*, quarter of an hour; *pour le ~ d'heure*, for the present, presently; *passer un mauvais ~ d'heure*, to have a bad time of it; *le ~ d'heure de Rabelais*, the moment of payment or reckoning, the critical moment; the moment for forking out; *les trois ~s du temps*, most of the time, mostly, usually; *aux trois ~s ivre*, three parts drunk; (arch.) *~ de rond*, quarter-round, ovolo; (mus.) *~ de soupir*, semiquaver rest; *deux heures un ~*, a quarter past two; *deux heures trois ~s* or *trois heures moins le ~*, a quarter to three; *officier de ~*, officer of the watch; *maître de ~*, boatswain's mate; *être de ~*, *faire le ~*, to keep a watch. ~, -e, adj. (med.) *Fièvre ~e*, quartan fever or ague.

quartanier (kartanje), s.m. Wild boar four years old.

quartaut (karto), s.m. (obs.) Octave, quarter-cask (a measure for wine, &c.).

quarte (kart), adj. Quartan; *fièvre ~*, quartan fever or ague. ~, s.f. **1.** (mus.) Fourth; **2.** (fenc. and piquet) carte, quart; **3.** (obs.) half gallon.

quartenier (kartənje), s.m. (obs.) Police officer (in charge of a quarter).

quarteron[1] (kartərɔ̃), s.m. [f. *quart*] The fourth part of a hundred; 25.

quarteron[2], **-ne** (kartərɔ̃), s.m.f. [f. Span. *cuarteron*] Quadroon.

quartidi (kwartidi), s.m. Fourth day of the decade (in calendar of 1st French Republic).

quartier (kartje), s.m. [f. *quart*] Quarter; piece, portion, slice, block; lump; gammon (of bacon); *mettre en ~s*, to tear to pieces; *faire ~ à*, to spare; to give quarter; *demander ~*, to cry for quarter; *1er ~ de lune*, 1st quarter of the moon; *~-général*, head-quarters; (naut.) *~-maître*, quartermaster; *elle est la gazette du ~*, she is the gossip of the neighbourhood; *~ de selle*, saddle-flap; *prendre ses ~s d'hiver*, to take up one's winter quarters.

quarto (kwarto), adv. [L wd] Quarto; fourthly. *in-~*, s.m. Quarto; 4to.

quartz (kwarts), s.m. [Germ. wd] Quartz.

quartzeu-x, -se (kwartsø), adj. Quartzose.

quasi (kazi), s.m. (butch.) Thick end of loin of veal.

quasi, quasiment (kazi, kazimɑ̃), adv. Almost; so to speak, as it were, quasi; *~-contrat*, quasi-contract; *~-délit*, unintentional petty offence.

quasimodo (kazimədo), s.f. [L wds] Low Sunday; Quasimodo Sunday.

quassia (kwasja), s.m. (bot.) Quassia; syn. QUASSIER.

quaternaire (kwatɛrnɛr), adj. [L *quaternarius*] Quaternary.

quaterne (kwatɛrn), s.m. [L *quaterni*] Quaternion (at games).

quaterné, -e (kwatɛrne), adj. (bot.) Quaternate.

quaternion (kwatɛrnjɔ̃), s.m. [L *quaternio*] (math.) Quaternion.

quatorze (katɔrz), adj. num. [L *quatuordecim*] Fourteen; fourteenth.

quatorzième (katɔrzjɛm), adj. num. ord. Fourteenth. ~, s.m. The fourteenth.

quatorzièmement (katɔrzjɛmmɑ̃), adv. Fourteenthly.

quatrain (katrɛ̃), s.m. [f. *quatre*] Quatrain; four-line stanza.

quatre (katr), adj. num. [L *quatuor*] Four; *Henri IV*, Henry the Fourth; *travailler comme ~*, to work like a nigger; *il se mettrait en ~ pour X*, he would go through fire and water for X; *faire le diable à ~*, to kick up a terrible row; *il se tenait à ~ pour ne pas répondre*, it was as much as he could do not to answer; *descendre* (or *monter*) *~ à ~*, to run down (or up) the stairs in great haste, four steps at a time; *tiré à ~ épingles*, dressed up to the nines; looking as if he had just come out of a bandbox; spruce; *marcher à ~ pattes*, to go on all fours; *marchande des ~ saisons*, costermonger; *fraise des ~-saisons*, a variety of strawberry; *~-Temps*, Ember days.

quatre-vingtième (katrəvɛ̃tjɛm), adj. num. ord. s.m. Eightieth.

quatre-vingts (katrəvɛ̃), adj. num. Eighty, fourscore; (the final *s* is suppressed when ~ is followed by another number: *quatre-vingt-neuf*, eighty-nine); *~-dix*, ninety; *~-quinze*, ninety-five.

quatrième (katrjɛm), adj. ord. Fourth. ~, s.m. Fourth; fourth floor; fourth player. ~, s.f. Fourth form or class (at school); the fourth.

quatrièmement (katrijɛmmɑ̃), adv. Fourthly.

quatriennal, -e, (aux) (katriɛnal), adj. Quadrennial; syn. QUADRIENNAL.

quatrillion (katriljɔ̃), s.m. One thousand (Fr.) *trillions*, 1 with 15 ciphers; ⚠ not 'quadrillion', which = 1 with 24 ciphers.

quatuor (kwatɥɔr), s.m. [L wd] Quartet, quartette, quatuor.

quayage (kɛjaʒ), s.m. [f. *quai*] Wharfage, quayage.

que, qu' (kə, k), rel. pron. [L *quem*] Whom, which, that, of which, at which; (*que* is often untranslated: *le fils qu'elle aimait*, the son whom she loved; the son she loved; *voici le livre ~ vous cherchiez*, here is the book you were looking for); *il ne sait ~ faire*, he does not know what to do; *il n'a rien fait de mal ~ je sache*, he has not committed any wrong that I know of; *je ne sais ce ~ vous voulez dire*, I don't know what you mean; *faites ce ~ bon vous semble*, do what you like; do as you like; *~ dites-vous?*, what are you saying?; *~ devenir?*, what will become of me?; what shall I do?; *le jour qu'il mourut*, the day he died; *qu'est-ce ~ c'est?*, what is it?

que (kə), adv. How much, how many; *~ vous êtes bon!*, how kind you are!; *~ de difficultés!*, what a lot of difficulties!; *~ si!*, rather!, of course!; *~ non!*, not a bit of it!

que, qu' (kə, k), conj. [L *quid*] That, than, as, if, whether, in order that, as though, although, so that, &c.; (often left untranslated, as: *je crois qu'il est honnête*, I believe he is an honest man); *vous dites ~ oui*, you say yes; you say it is so; you say that it is so; *il croit ~ non*, he thinks not; *est-il possible ~ vous partiez?*, is it possible that you are really going?; *qu'il accepte ou non*, whether he agrees or no; *~ son nom soit béni*, blessed be his name; *qu'il fasse comme il lui plaît*, let him do as he likes; *qu'il me soit permis de*, might I be allowed to; *tant ~ je vivrai*, as long as I live; *on m'en ferait cadeau ~ je n'en voudrais pas!*, I wouldn't have it as a gift!; *venez ici, ~ je vous voie*, come nearer, that I may see your face; *êtes-vous malade ~*

vous ne mangez pas?, you are eating nothing, are you unwell?; *n'attendez pas qu'il pleuve*, do not wait until the rain begins; *de peur* ~, lest; for fear (that); *encore* ~, though; *ne . . . que*, but; only.

quel, -le (kɛl), adj. [L *qualis*] What; which; whatever; *~le heure est-il?*, what time is it?, what is the time?; *je ne sais ~le robe choisir*, I do not know which dress to choose; ~ *que*, *~le que*, *~s que*, *~les que* (of persons), whoever, whosoever; (of things) whatever, whichever; ~ *que soit le résultat*, whatever the result may be.

quelconque (kɛlkɔ̃k), adj. ind. [L *qualiscumque*] Whatever; any; some or other; ordinary; without characteristics; *en un point ~ de*, anywhere on (or in); *un livre* ~, any book; *il faut donner une raison* ~, you must give a reason of some sort; *d'une manière* ~, anyhow; *ce livre est très* ~, this book is quite an ordinary one, has no specially good points.

quellement (kɛlmɑ̃), adv. (unusual, except in:) *Tellement* ~, so-so; indifferently.

quelque (kɛlk(ə)), adj. ind. [*quel*+*que*] Some, any, a few; ~ *indiscret aura dit cela*, some busybody has probably said that; ~ *jour*, some day or other; *il a dû avoir ~ sujet de se plaindre*, very likely he had some grievance, or some ground for complaint; *~s amis*, a few friends; *ces ~s lignes*, these few lines; ~ *chose*, something; ~ *part*, somewhere; ~ *peu*, somewhat; *il y a ~s années*, some few years ago; a few years ago. ~, adv. (invar.) About, some, nearly; *avoir ~ cinquante ans*, to be about fifty; ~ *. . . que*, however . . .; ~ *grands qu'ils soient*, however great they may be.

quelquefois (kɛlkəfwɑ), adv. Sometimes; syn. PARFOIS.

quelqu'un, -e (kɛlkœ̃), ind. pron. [*quelque*+*un*] Somebody, some one; anybody, any one; *se croire* ~, to think oneself somebody; to be conceited; *quelques-uns de mes amis*, a few of my friends.

quémander (kemɑ̃de), v.a. To beg, to beg for, to solicit, to go cringing and begging for.

qu'en-dira-t-on (kɑ̃diratɔ̃), s.m. invar. What people say; public talk; *se moquer du* ~, not to care a rap for what people say.

quenelle (kənɛl), s.f. [Germ. *Knödel*] (cook.) Quenelle; forcemeat- or fish-ball.

quenotte (kənɔt), s.f. [Germ. orig.] (colloq.) Tooth, 'peggy'.

quenouille (kənuj), s.f. [f. L *colus*] **1.** Distaff; (fig.) *tomber en* ~, to be ruled by women; **2.** pyramid-shaped fruit-tree.

quenouillée (kənuje), s.f. Distaff-ful.

quérable (kerabl), adj. [f. *quérir*] (law) Demandable.

quercitron (kɛrsitrɔ̃), s.m. [L *quercus*+ Fr. *citron*] (bot.) Quercitron; dyer's oak.

querelle (kərɛl), s.f. [L *querela*] Quarrel, quarrelling, row, brawl; *chercher ~ à X*, to pick a quarrel with X; ~ *d'Allemand*, groundless quarrel; *n'épousez pas sa* ~, do not take up his quarrel; *vider une* ~, to fight it out; to settle a dispute.

quereller (kərɛle), v.a.n. To quarrel with, to pick a quarrel with; to scold; se ~, v.pr. to wrangle, to have words, to fall out, to quarrel.

querelleu-r, -se (kərɛlœr), adj. Quarrelsome.

quérimonie (kwerimɔni), s.f. [L *querimonia*] Plaint, complaint, querimoniousness.

quérir (kerir), v.a. (only used in the infinitive) [L *quaerere*] To fetch; *aller* ~, to go and fetch; *envoyer* ~, to send for.

questeur (kwɛstœr, kɛstœr), s.m. [L *quaestor*] Quaestor; questor (one of the treasurers in the French National Assembly).

question (kɛstjɔ̃), s.f. [L *quaestio*] Question; query; point, matter, issue; rack, torture; *mettre à la* ~, to put on the rack; *mettre en* ~, to call in question; *de quoi est-il ~?*, what is the matter?; *il n'est pas ~ de cela*, (*a*) that is not the point; (*b*) do not count on that, there is no possibility of it; *vous sortez de la* ~, you do not stick to the point; *là n'est pas la* ~, that 's not the point, or the question; *la ~ préalable*, the previous question; *faire, poser une ~ à X*, to ask X a question; *ensuite, il fut ~ du mariage*, next, the question of the wedding came up; *qu'il n'en soit plus ~!*, (*a*) let bygones be bygones; let us say no more about it; (*b*) do not bother me any more; *c'est une ~ de vie ou de mort*, it 's a question of life and death; *c'est une ~ de temps*, it 's a question of time.

questionnaire (kɛstjɔnɛr), s.m. **1.** Questionary, list of questions; **2.** torturer.

questionner (kɛstjɔne), v.a. To question, to interrogate. ⚠ Note that *questionner* has never the sense of 'throw doubt upon' = *mettre en question, jeter le doute sur*, which is a very usual sense of 'to question' in English.

questionneu-r, -se (kɛstjɔnœr), adj. Inquisitive.

questure (kwɛstyr), s.f. [L *quaestura*] Quaestorship; office of the *questeurs* (in French parliament).

quête (kɛt), s.f. [f. L *quaerere*] **1.** Quest, search; (hunt.) beating about; **2.** collection; begging; *faire la* ~, to make a collection (⚠ see *collection*); *se mettre en ~ de quelque chose*, to go in quest of something; to look for something.

quêter (kɛte), v.a.n. **1.** To go in quest of,

to look for, to seek; **2.** to beg, to collect money (in church), to make a collection.

quêteu-r, -se (kɛtœr), s.m.f. Collector, collectress; *quêteuse,* (at a wedding) bridesmaid; *moine* ~, mendicant friar.

quetsche (kwɛtʃ), s.f. [Alsac. *quatsch*] Mussel-plum.

queue (kø), s.f. [L *cauda*] Tail; tail-piece, pigtail; any appendix shaped like a tail; latter end, fag end; rear; queue, string; handle; stalk, stem (of plants, fruit, flowers, &c.); label (of documents); train (of a dress); cue (billiards); *à la* ~, in a file, behind the others; *à la* ~ *leu leu,* one after another; in Indian file; *en* ~, in the rear; *faire* ~, to stand one behind the other, waiting; to queue; to wait one's turn; *finir en* ~ *de poisson,* to fizzle out; to end miserably; to peter out, to end in a fiasco; *cela n'a ni* ~ *ni tête,* that has neither head nor tail; *tirer le diable par la* ~, to live from hand to mouth; to be hard up; *piano à* ~, grand piano; *demi-*~, semi-grand; *piano à* ~ *crapaud,* baby grand piano; (fig.) *tenir la* ~ *de la poêle,* to be the boss; (techn.) ~*-d'aronde,* dovetail; ~ *de cheveux,* pigtail; *porte-*~, train-bearer; *à la* ~ *gît le venin,* the sting is in the tail; *habit à* ~ *de morue,* swallow-tail coat.

queuter (køte), v.n. (at billiards, croquet, &c.) To make a push-stroke.

queux[1] (kø), s.m. (obs.) [L *coquus*] Cook; (only used in *maître* ~).

queux[2] (kø), s.f. [L *cos*] Whetstone.

qui (ki), rel. pron. [L wd] Who, whom, which, that, whoever, whomsoever, he who, she who; *à* ~, to whom; *à* ~ *est ce livre?,* whose book is this?; *à* ~ *de droit,* to the proper party; *à* ~ *mieux mieux,* in eager rivalry; each louder (or quicker, or better, &c.) than the other; *pour* ~ *s'y connaît,* to any one who knows; *c'est à* ~ *le fera,* they all wish to do it; *je ne sais* ~ *vous voulez dire,* I do not know whom you mean; *je n'ai parlé à* ~ *que ce soit,* I spoke to nobody; *aimez* ~ *vous aime,* love those who love you; *à* ~ *le tour?,* whose turn is it?; ~ *avez-vous vu?,* whom have you seen?; ~ *est là?,* who is there?; ~ *vive?,* who goes there?; *ils s'échappèrent* ~ *par la porte,* ~ *par la fenêtre,* some escaped through the door, others through the window; ~ *perd, gagne,* he who loses, wins.

(à) quia (akɥia), adv. [L wd] In a quandary; *être à* ~, to be at a loss; *être réduit à* ~, to be in a quandary; to be nonplussed; to be reduced to 'because'; to have one's back to the wall; to be brought to bay.

quibus (kɥibys), s.m. [L wd] (colloq.) Money; cash; tin; the needful.

quiche (kiʃ), s.f. [local wd] (cook.) A sort of thick custard, speciality of Lorraine.

quiconque (kikɔ̃k), ind. pron. [L *quicumque*] Whoever, whosoever, whomsoever, any one who.

quidam (kwidam, kidɑ̃), s.m. [L wd] Quidam, individual, fellow, chap, some one, bloke.

quiddité (kɥiddite), s.f. [f. L *quid*] (phil.) Quiddity.

quiet, quiète (kɥiɛ), adj. [L *quietus*] Quiet, tranquil, calm.

quiètement (kɥiɛtmɑ̃), adv. Quietly, tranquilly, calmly.

quiétisme (kɥietism), s.m. Quietism.

quiétiste (kɥietist), adj. s.m.f. Quietist.

quiétude (kjetyd, kɥietyd), s.f. Quietude, repose, tranquillity, calmness.

quignon (kiɲɔ̃), s.m. [f. *coin*] Hunch (of bread).

quille (kij), s.f. [Germ. orig.] **1.** Skittle, ninepin; *jeu de* ~*s,* game of skittles; *reçu comme un chien dans un jeu de* ~*s,* as welcome as a dog at a wedding, or as a dog on a racecourse; **2.** (slang) leg, shank; *jouer des* ~*s,* to run away; to take to one's heels; (U.S.) to absquatulate; **3.** (naut.) keel; *fausse* ~, false keel.

quiller (kije), v.n. To throw for first play at skittles.

quillette (kijɛt), s.f. Osier-cutting.

quillier (kije), s.m. Skittle-alley.

quilloir (kijwar), s.m. [f. *quille*] (naut.) Rod used for turning a capstan, &c.; also in rope-making.

quillon (kijɔ̃), s.m. Cross-bar (of a sword).

quinaire (kɥinɛr), adj. [L *quinarius*] Quinary.

quinaud, -e (kino), adj. [etym. dub.] Abashed, nonplussed, ashamed; *rester* ~, to be nonplussed.

quincaille (kɛ̃kɑj), s.f. [f. *clinquant, clinquaille*] Ironmongery, hardware; (slang) cash, tin, money, copper.

quincaillerie (kɛ̃kɑjri), s.f. Ironmongery, hardware, ironmongery shop or trade.

quincaillier (kɛ̃kɑje), s.m. Ironmonger.

quinconce (kɛ̃kɔ̃s), s.m. [L *quincunx*] Quincunx; *en* ~, quincuncial; planted in fives, or in quincunxes.

quine (kin), s.m. (at backgammon) Two fives.

quiné, -e (kine), adj. (bot.) Quinate.

quinine (kinin), s.f. [f. Span. *quina*] (pharm.) Quinine, sulphate of quinine; quinia.

quinquagénaire (kɛ̃kaʒenɛr), adj. s.m.f. [L *quinquagenarius*] Fifty years old; quinquagenarian.

quinquagésime (kwɛ̃kwaʒezim), s.f. Quinquagesima Sunday.

quinquennal, -e, (aux) (kɛ̃kɛnal), adj. [L *quinquennalis*] Quinquennial.

quinquérème (kɥɛ̃kɥerɛm), s.f. (ant. naut.) Quinquereme.

quinquet (kɛ̃kɛ), s.m. [f. *Quinquet,* name of first maker] Argand lamp, lamp.

quinquina (kɛ̃kina), s.m. [Peruvian *kina-kina*] Peruvian bark, quinquina, cinchona; *vin de* ~, quinine wine.

quint (kɛ̃), adj. m. [L *quintus*] The Fifth; *Charles-*~, Charles the Fifth.

quintaine (kɛ̃tɛn), s.f., **quintan** (kɛ̃tɑ̃), s.m. Quintain.

quintal, (pl. **aux**) (kɛ̃tal), s.m. Quintal, hundredweight (50 kilogr.); ~ *métrique* = 100 kilogr.

quinte (kɛ̃t), s.f. [f. L *quintus*] **1.** (mus.) Fifth; **2.** tenor violin; **3.** (fenc.) quinte; **4.** fit (of coughing); **5.** freak, whim.

quintefeuille (kɛ̃tfœj), s.f. (bot.) Cinquefoil.

quintessence (kɛ̃tɛssɑ̃s), s.f. [*quinte+essence*] Quintessence; pith.

quintessencié, -e (kɛ̃tɛssɑ̃sje), p. adj. Hypercritical, quintessential, over-subtilized.

quintessencier (kɛ̃tɛssɑ̃sje), v.a. To extract the quintessence of, to subtilize, to refine excessively.

quintette (kɥɛ̃tɛt), s.m. [It. *quintetto*] (mus.) Quintet.

quinteu-x, -se (kɛ̃tø), adj. Peevish, whimsical, crotchety, freakish, (colloq.) contrary; *avoir l'humeur* ~*se*, to be peevish; to be querulous, contrary, &c.

quintidi (kɥɛ̃tidi), s.m. Quintidi, fifth day of the decade (in calendar of 1st French Republic).

quintillion (kɥɛ̃tiljɔ̃), s.m. One thousand (Fr.) *quatrillions* (1 with 18 ciphers); ⚠ not (Engl.) 'quintillion', which = fifth power of million = 1 with 30 ciphers.

quinto (kɥinto), adv. [L wd] Quinto; fifthly.

quintuple (kɛ̃typl, kɥɛ̃typl), s.m. adj. [L *quintuplex*] Quintuple, fivefold.

quintupler (kɛ̃typle), v.a. To quintuple, to increase fivefold.

quinzaine (kɛ̃zɛn), s.f. Fifteen, about fifteen; fortnight; the fourteenth day after; *remettre à* ~, to put off for a fortnight.

quinze (kɛ̃z), adj. num. [L *quindecim*] Fifteen; fifteenth; *d'aujourd'hui en* ~, this day fortnight; *de demain en* ~, tomorrow fortnight; *de mardi en* ~, next Tuesday fortnight; *il y a eu* ~ *jours hier*, a fortnight yesterday; *tous les* ~ *jours*, every fortnight; once a fortnight.

Quinze-Vingts (kɛ̃zvɛ̃), s.m.pl. Hospital in Paris for the blind.

quinzième (kɛ̃zjɛm), adj. num. ord. s.m. Fifteenth; fifteenth part.

quinzièmement (kɛ̃zjɛmmɑ̃), adv. Fifteenthly.

quiproquo (kiprɔko), s.m. [L *quid pro quod*] Mistake, misunderstanding; cross questions and crooked answers.

quittance (kitɑ̃s), s.f. [f. *quitte*] Receipt, discharge; (fig.) *donner* ~, to hold quit.

quittancer (kitɑ̃se), v.a. To give a receipt for; to receipt.

quitte (kit), adj. [f. L *quietus*] Quit, free, discharged, clear, out of debt; *me voilà* ~ *envers vous*, I owe you nothing now; now we are quits; let us cry quits; *il en est* ~ *à bon marché*, he comes off cheap; *elle en est* ~ *pour la peur*, she escapes with a good fright; *je le ferai,* ~ *à être puni*, I shall do it and chance the punishment; *jouer* ~ *ou double*, to play double or quits; ~ *à* ~, quits; *tenir* ~, to hold quit.

quitter (kite), v.a. To leave, to abandon, to give up, to renounce, to forsake; to hold quit, to quit, to discharge; ~ *la place*, to leave, to make oneself scarce; to give up; *il ne la quitte pas des yeux*, he does not take his eyes off her; ~ *ses habits*, to take off one's clothes; ~ *la partie*, to leave the game; (fig.) to renounce; ~ *la vie*, to depart (this life); ~ *prise*, to let go one's hold; ~ *le deuil*, to go out of mourning. ⚠ 'To quit' has also the sense of to repay, to requite = *répondre à, récompenser, payer de retour*.

quitus (kɥitys), s.m. [LL wd] Discharge, receipt in full.

qui va là ? (kivala), interj. Who goes there?, who is there?

qui-vive ? (kiviv), interj. Who goes there? ~, s.m. Alert; *être toujours sur le* ~, to be constantly on the look-out; to be always on the alert.

quoi (kwɑ), rel. pron. [L *quid*] What, which; *à* ~ *pensez-vous?*, what are you thinking of?; *à propos de* ~*?*, what is it about?; with respect to what?; *ce à* ~ *je fais allusion*, that which I am alluding to; *il n'y a pas de* ~ *rire*, it's no laughing matter; *il n'y a pas de* ~ *pleurer*, it is not worth crying about; (colloq.) *il n'y a pas de* ~*!*, don't mention it; there is no offence; *il n'a pas de* ~ *vivre*, he has not enough to live on; *de* ~ *vous mêlez-vous?*, what business is that of yours?; *c'est en* ~ *vous vous trompez*, that is just where you are mistaken; *en* ~ *puis-je vous servir?*, what can I do for you?, in what way can I serve you?; ~*! vous partez?*, what are you really going?; ~*? que dites-vous?*, what? what do you say?; I beg your pardon, what did you say?; *un je ne sais* ~, an indefinable something; (at the end of an enumeration) *et je ne sais* ~ *encore*, and I don't know what all; ~ *que ce soit*, anything whatever; ~ *qu'il en soit*, be that as it may; ~ *qu'il fasse*, whatever he may do; ~ *qu'il en ait*, whatever he may wish.

quoique (kwak), conj. (the verb after *quoique* must be in the subj.) [*quoi+que*] Although, though; ~ *il soit pauvre, il est honnête*, he is honest, although he is poor.

quolibet (kɔlibɛ), s.m. [f. L *quod libet*] Quibble, low joke, offensive epithet.

quorum (kɔrɔm, kwɔrɔm), s.m. [L wd] Quorum.
quote-part (kɔtpar), s.f. [L *quota+pars*] Share, portion; quota.
quotidien, -ne (kɔtidjɛ̃), adj. [f. L *quotidie*] Daily, quotidian; *fièvre ~ne*, quotidian ague; *notre pain ~*, our daily bread. **~**, s.m. Daily (newspaper).
quotidiennement (kɔtidjɛnmɑ̃), adv. Daily.
quotient (kɔsjɑ̃), s.m. [L *quotiens*] Quotient.
quotité (kɔtite), s.f. [f. L *quotus*] Quota.

R

R, r (ɛr), s.m. The eighteenth letter of the alphabet; a few abbrev.: R., *Réaumur* (thermometer); r., *rue*, street; R.F., *République Française*, French Republic; R.P., (*a*) *Réponse payée*, reply paid; (*b*) *Représentation Proportionnelle*, proportional representation; (*c*) *Le Révérend Père*, Reverend Father; R.S.V.P., *réponse s'il vous plaît*, please answer.
ra (ra), s.m. (onom.) Ruffle (of a drum).
rabâchage (rabɑʃaʒ), s.m. Tiresome repetition, twaddle.
rabâcher (rabɑʃe), v.a.n. [orig. dub.] To repeat over and over again, to twaddle.
rabâcheu-r, -se (rabɑʃœr), s.m.f. Twaddler, eternal repeater, tiresome babbler.
rabais (rabɛ), s.m. [f. *rabaisser*] Reduction in price, abatement, rebate, allowance, discount; *au ~*, at a reduced price; (also, fig. and pej.) meanly, niggardly.
rabaissement (rabɛsmɑ̃), s.m. Lowering, depreciation; humiliation.
rabaisser (rabɛse), v.a. [*re+abaisser*] To lower, to depreciate, to disparage, to belittle; *~ l'orgueil de X*, to humble X's pride; *~ les prétentions de X*, to lower X's pretentions; *~ les mérites de X*, to disparage X's merit.
raban (rabɑ̃), s.m. [Dutch *raaband*] (naut.) Rope-band, lanyard, furling-line, gasket, roband; *~ de cabestan*, swiftlet.
rabaner (rabane), v.a. To fit (a sail) with rope-bands and earings, ready for bending it to its yard; to pass a gasket round.
rabat (raba), s.m. [f. *rabattre*] Bands (worn by priests, &c.); *~-joie*, damper, kill-joy, wet blanket, spoil-sport.
rabattage (rabataʒ), s.m. Beating for game (and fig., for customers).
rabattement (rabatmɑ̃), s.m. **1.** Deduction, discount, rebate; **2.** lowering, bringing down; turning down; **3.** (geom.) projection.
rabatteur (rabatœr), s.m. (hunt.) Beater.
rabattre (rabatr), v.a. [*re+abattre*] To beat down, to bring down, to put down, to turn down; to lower, to reduce, to rebate; (techn.) to flange, to flatten; (hunt.) to beat up; to humble, to disparage; *il vous faut en ~*, you must come down a peg or two; *~ une couture*, to turn down a seam; *~ le caquet à X*, to stop X's jaw; *se ~ sur*, to fall back on.
rabbi (rabi), s.m. [Hebr. *rabh*] Rabbi.
rabbin (rabɛ̃), s.m. [Hebr. *rabh*] Rabbi; *grand ~*, Chief Rabbi.
rabbinique (rabinik), adj. Rabbinical.
rabbinisme (rabinism), s.m. Rabbinism.
rabdomancie (rabdɔmɑ̃si), s.f. [Gr. *rhabdos+manteia*] Rhabdomancy.
rabdomancien, -ne (rabdɔmɑ̃sjɛ̃), s.m.f. Rhabdomancer, water-diviner, dowser.
rabelaisien, -ne (rablɛzjɛ̃), adj. [f. *Rabelais*] Rabelaisian.
rabibocher (rabibɔʃe), v.a. To mend, to repair, to reconcile; (colloq.) **se ~**, v.pr. to make it up.
rabiole (rabjɔl), s.f. (bot.) Field turnip; kohlrabi.
rabiot, rabiau (rabjo), s.m. (mil. slang) Remains of food or drink; supplementary period of service in the army; (fig. colloq.) small bonus, windfall, something to the good, surplus.
rabique (rabik), adj. [f. L *rabies*] Rabid.
râble (rɑbl), s.m. **1.** [f. L *rapulum*] Back (of hare, &c.); **2.** [f. L *rutabulum*] rake, iron bar, fire-hook.
râblé, -e (rɑble), adj. (of hare, &c.) Thick-backed; (of persons) broad-backed, strong-backed; (fig.) sturdy.
râblure (rɑblyr), s.f. (naut.) Rabbet (of the keel).
rabonnir (rabɔnir), v.a. [f. *bon*] To improve.
rabot (rabo), s.m. [orig. unkn.] Plane, scraper.
rabotage, rabotement (rabɔtaʒ, rabɔtmɑ̃), s.m. Planing.
raboter (rabɔte), v.a. To plane; (fig.) to polish; to improve (the character of a person).
raboteur (rabɔtœr), s.m. Planer; *raboteuse*, s.f. planing-machine.
raboteu-x, -se (rabɔtø), adj. Knotty, rugged, rough, uneven; (fig.) harsh, unpolished.
rabougri, -e (rabugri), p. adj. Stunted.
rabougrir (rabugrir), v.n.a. [*re*+(OF) *abougrir*] To stunt; to be stunted; **se ~**, v.pr. to grow stunted.
rabougrissement (rabugrismɑ̃), s.m. Stuntedness, sickliness, etiolation.
rabouiller (rabuje), v.a. [local wd f. Berri] To trouble (the water) with a branch in order to catch fish.
rabouillère (rabujɛr), s.f. Rabbit's hole, nest, or burrow.
rabouilleu-r, -se (rabujœr), s.m.f. Fisherman or -woman who troubles the water in order to catch fish.

rabouter, raboutir (rabute, rabutir), v.a. [*re+abouter*] To join end to end; to piece.

raboutissage (rabutisaʒ), s.m. Joining, piecing together.

rabrouer (rabrue), v.a. [orig. dub.] To snub, to rebuke, to chide, to set (X) down, to give (X) a dressing-down, or a talking-to.

racage (rakaʒ), s.m. [f. *raque*] (naut.) Parrel.

racahout (rakau), s.m. [Arab. wd] Racahout, a mixture of salep, cocoa, sugar, &c., used as a light nutritive food for invalids and infants.

racaille (rakɑj), s.f. [etym. dub.] Rabble, riff-raff.

raccommodable (rakɔmɔdabl), adj. Mendable.

raccommodage (rakɔmɔdaʒ), s.m. Mending, darning, repairing.

raccommodement (rakɔmɔdmɑ̃), s.m. Reconciliation; making it up again.

raccommoder (rakɔmɔde), v.a. [*re+accommoder*] To mend, to darn, to repair, to patch; to reconcile; *se ~ avec X*, v.pr. to make it up with X.

raccommodeu-r, -se (rakɔmɔdœr), s.m.f. Mender.

raccord (rakɔr), s.m. **1.** Joining, junction, joint; levelling; **2.** pipe-connexion, socket; nipple; *bride de ~*, joint-flange; **3.** (theatr., lit., paint.) *faire un ~*, to re-connect, to join and harmonize disconnected speeches, pieces, or parts.

raccordement (rakɔrdəmɑ̃), s.m. Junction, joining, levelling, connecting.

raccorder (rakɔrde), v.a. [*re+accorder*] To join, to connect; to set to rights.

raccourci, -e (rakursi), p. adj. Shortened, abridged; *tomber à bras ~s sur X*, to assault X; to strike X with all one's might; *en ~*, in miniature; briefly. ~, s.m. Short cut; epitome, abridgement; (perspective) foreshortening.

raccourcir (rakursir), v.a.n. [f. *court*] To shorten, to abridge, to curtail; (perspective) to foreshorten; (slang) to guillotine, to behead; *les jours raccourcissent*, the days are drawing in; **se ~**, v.pr. to get shorter, to shrink.

raccourcissement (rakursismɑ̃), s.m. Shortening, abridging, shrinking; (colloq.) beheading.

raccoutrer (rakutre), v.a. [*re+accoutrer*] To mend; (fig.) to reconcile.

raccoutumer, réaccoutumer (rakutyme, reakutyme), v.a. To reaccustom; **se ~**, v.pr. to reaccustom oneself, to get used again (*à*, to).

raccroc (rakro), s.m. Lucky stroke (at billiards), (fig.) fluke; *par ~*, by a lucky hit; by chance, by a stroke of good luck; *un beau coup!—oh, par ~ seulement*, a fine hit!—oh, only a fluke!; *faire le ~*, to solicit (as a prostitute).

raccrocher (rakrɔʃe), v.a.n. To hook up again; to hang up again; to pick up; to solicit (as a prostitute); **se ~** (*à*), v.pr. to clutch hold (of), to grasp tightly; (fig.) *se ~ à cet espoir*, to cling to that hope.

race (ras), s.f. [It. *razza*] Race; stock, breed; line, lineage, family; kind; *de ~ pure*, thoroughbred; *~ bovine*, cattle; *~ chevaline*, horse species; (prov.) *bon chien chasse de ~*, breeding tells; like sire, like son; it runs in the blood; *croiser les ~s*, to cross the breeds; *animal de (bonne) race*, pure-bred animal.

racème (rasɛm), s.m. [L *racemus*] (bot.) Raceme.

racer (rase), v.n. To breed; *bien racé, -e*, thoroughbred; true-born.

rachat (raʃa), s.m. [*re+achat*] Buying in, repurchase, redeeming; (moral) redemption; recovery; ransom; *vendre avec faculté de ~*, to sell with power of redemption.

rachetable (raʃtabl), adj. Redeemable.

racheter (raʃte), v.a. [*re+acheter*] To buy back, to buy again, to buy off, to buy in; to repurchase; (fig.) to redeem, to ransom, to atone for; *~ des captifs*, to ransom prisoners; *~ un défaut par bien des qualités*, to atone for one's faults by many virtues; **se ~**, v.pr. to redeem oneself; to buy one's freedom; to be compensated; to be atoned for.

rachidien, -ne (raʃidjɛ̃), adj. (anat.) Rachidian, spinal.

rachis (raʃi), s.m. [Gr. wd] (anat.) Rachis, spinal column.

rachitique (raʃitik), adj. Rachitic, rickety.

rachitisme (raʃitism), s.m. Rachitis, rickets.

racinage (rasinaʒ), s.m. **1.** Esculent roots; **2.** walnut-root, -bark, or -leaves in decoction; **3.** (bookbind.) dendroid pattern, root figuring.

racinal (pl. **aux**) (rasinal), s.m. (carp.) Beam, rafter, sleeper.

racine (rasin), s.f. [f. L *radix*] Root; (fig.) root, beginning, origin; (math.) *~ carrée*, square root; *~ cubique*, cube root; *~ quatrième*, fourth, or biquadratic root; *couper le mal dans sa ~*, to eradicate the evil; to get to the very root of the evil; *prendre ~*, to take root, to root; (fig.) (*a*) to establish oneself; (*b*) to cling like a limpet; to have come to stay; to stick.

raciner (rasine), v.n. **1.** To root, to strike root; **2.** to dye with roots; **3.** (bookbind.) to make a dendroid pattern on.

racinien, -ne (rasinjɛ̃), adj. After the style of Racine.

rack. See ARACK.

râclage (rɑklaʒ), s.m. Scraping.

râcle, râclette (rɑkl, rɑklɛt), s.f. Scraper; squeegee.

râclée (rɑkle), s.f. (colloq.) Drubbing, licking, thrashing, dressing-down.
râcler (rɑkle), v.a. [L *radere*, Prov. *rasclar*] To scrape; ~ *du violon*, to scrape on the violin.
râcloir, s.m., **râcloire,** s.f. (rɑklwar) Scraper; strike.
râclure (rɑklyr), s.f. Scrapings (plur.).
racolage (rakɔlaʒ), s.m. **1.** Recruiting; **2.** soliciting.
racoler (rakɔle), v.a. [*re*+*accoler*] **1.** To recruit, to entice to enlist, to crimp; **2.** to solicit, to pick up; **3.** to tout for.
racoleu-r, -se (rakɔlœr), s.m.f. adj. **1.** Crimp, recruiting-sergeant; **2.** tout; **3.** street-walker, prostitute.
racontable (rakɔ̃tabl), adj. Relatable, fit to be told.
racontage (rakɔ̃taʒ), s.m. Gossip, scandal, chit-chat; twaddle.
racontar (rakɔ̃tar), s.m. Gossip, scandal, rumour, report, hearsay, statement of doubtful accuracy.
raconter (rakɔ̃te), v.a. [*re*+*conter*] To tell, to relate, to narrate; *qu'est-ce que vous racontez là?*, what are you talking about?; *il en raconte de belles!*, he tells fine tales!; *il raconte bien*, he is a good story-teller; *allons donc! vous voulez m'en* ~*!*, now then! you are pulling my leg!, tell that to the marines!
raconteu-r, -se (rakɔ̃tœr), s.m.f. Story-teller.
racornir (rakɔrnir), v.a. [f. *corne*] To harden, to shrivel; **se** ~, v.pr. to shrivel, to dry up; to become hard and shrivelled; (fig.) to grow callous; to be a back number, to grow old-fashioned.
racornissement (rakɔrnismɑ̃), s.m. Hardening, shrivelling; (fig.) callousness.
racquitter (rakite), v.a. To recover; **se** ~, v.pr. to win back.
rade (rad), s.f. [Scand. orig.] (naut.) Roads, roadstead; *en* ~, in the roads; ~ *foraine*, open roadstead; *grand'*~, outer roadstead; *petite* ~, or ~ *intérieure*, inner roadstead, inner roads.
radeau (pl. **-x**) (rado), s.m. [f. L *ratis*] Raft, float.
rader[1] (rade), v.a. To bring (a ship) into the roads; to anchor . . . in the roads.
rader[2] (rade), v.a. [L *radere*] To strike (a measure of grain).
radiaire (radjɛr), adj. [f. L *radius*] Radiate.
radial, -e, (aux) (radjal), adj. (anat.) Radial.
radiant, -e (radjɑ̃), p. adj. Radiant. ~, s.m. (astr.) Radiant point, apparent focal point of meteoric shower.
radiateur (radjatœr), s.m. Radiator; *bouchon de* ~, radiator-cap; ~ *nid d'abeille*, honeycomb radiator.
radiation[1] (radjasjɔ̃), s.f. [f. *radier*] Radiation, irradiation.
radiation[2] (radjasjɔ̃), s.f. [f. LL *radiare*] Striking-out, obliteration, cancelling.
radical, -e, (aux) (radikal), adj. [f. L *radix*] Radical, of the roots; radical, thorough. ~, s.m. **1.** (gram.) Radical; **2.** (polit.) member of the *Parti Radical*; **3.** (math., chem.) radical.
radicalement (radikalmɑ̃), adv. Radically.
radicalisme (radikalism), s.m. Radicalism.
radicant, -e (radikɑ̃), adj. (bot.) Radicant, radicating.
radicelle (radisɛl), s.f. (bot.) Radicle, rootlet, radicel.
radicivore (radisivɔr), adj. [L *radix*+*vorare*] (zool.) Radicivorous.
radiculaire (radikylɛr), adj. Radicular.
radicule (radikyl), s.f. [L *radicula*] (bot.) Radicle.
radié, -e (radje), p. adj. [L *radiatus*] Radiate, radiant, radiated.
radier (radje), v.n.a. **1.** To irradiate, to radiate, to shine, to beam; **2.** to strike out, to obliterate, to cancel.
radier (radje), s.m. (build.) Floor, apron, inverted arch.
radieu-x, -se (radjø), adj. [L *radiosus*] Radiant, beaming (with joy), shining; dazzling, splendid; *ciel* ~, cloudless sky, glorious weather.
radiner (radine), v.n. (slang) To turn up, to come back, to arrive.
radio-acti-f, -ve (radjoaktif), adj. Radio-active.
radio-activité (radjoaktivite), s.f. Radio-activity.
radiogramme (radjɔgram), s.m. Radiogram; wireless telegram.
radiographie (radjɔgrafi), s.f. Radiography; X-ray photography.
radiographier (radjɔgrafje), v.a. To radiograph.
radiologie (radjɔlɔʒi), s.f. [L *radius*+Gr. *logos*] Radiology.
radiomètre (radjɔmɛtr), s.m. Radiometer.
radioscopie (radjɔskɔpi), s.f. [L *radius*+Gr. *skopein*] Radioscopy.
radiothérapie (radjɔterapi), s.f. [L *radius*+Gr. *therapeia*] Radiotherapy.
radis (radi), s.m. [It. *radice*] Radish; (fig.) *il n'a plus un* ~, he has not a brass farthing left.
radium (radjɔm), s.m. Radium.
radius (radjys), s.m. [L wd] (anat.) Radius.
radoire (radwar), s.f. [f. L *radere*] Strike (for levelling measures of corn).
radotage (radɔtaʒ), s.m. Nonsense, silly twaddle, drivel, silly repetition.
radoter (radɔte), v.n. To rave, to dote, to

twaddle, to drivel, to wander, to talk nonsense.
radoteu-r, -se (radɔtœr), s.m.f. Dotard, driveller.
radoub (radu), s.m. Repairing; *bassin de* ~, graving-dock; *en* ~, under repair.
radouber (radube), v.a. [*re*+*adouber*] (naut.) To refit, to repair, to grave; *se* ~, to go into dock.
radoucir (radusir), v.a. [*re*+*adoucir*] To soften, to make milder, to mitigate; **se** ~, v.pr. to grow milder, to soften, (fig.) to be softened; *le temps se radoucit*, it is getting milder.
radoucissement (radusismɑ̃), s.m. Softening; (of the weather) change for the better; relenting, abatement.
rafale (rafal), s.f. [orig. dub.] Squall, gust of wind, flaw, blast; *souffler en* ~, to blow in gusts.
raffermir (rafɛrmir), v.a. [*re*+*affermir*] To strengthen, to make firmer, to fortify; ~ *le courage de X*, to fortify X's courage; **se** ~, v.pr. to grow stronger; to improve; to harden, to get firm; to set.
raffermissement (rafɛrmismɑ̃), s.m. Hardening, strengthening; (cook.) setting; (fig.) improvement, fortifying.
raffinade (rafinad), s.f. Best refined sugar.
raffinage (rafinaʒ), s.m. Refining, refinement (of gold, sugar, &c.). ⚠ ~ is not used in the figurative sense, see RAFFINEMENT.
raffiné, -e (rafine), p. adj. Refined, nice, subtle, exquisite. ~, s.m.f. Refined person, exquisite.
raffinement (rafinmɑ̃), s.m. Refinement; subtlety; extreme ingenuity.
raffiner (rafine), v.a. [*re*+*affiner*] To refine; ~, v.n. to be over-fine, to split hairs, to refine; ~ *sur le point d'honneur*, to be over-fine on the point of honour.
raffinerie (rafinri), s.f. Refinery; sugar-refinery.
raffineu-r, -se (rafinœr), s.m.f. Refiner; sugar-refiner; sugar-boiler.
raffoler (rafɔle), v.n. [*re*+*affoler*] To dote (*de*, on); to be passionately fond (of).
raffut (rafy), s.m. (colloq.) Shindy, row, dust, violent protests; *un* ~ *du diable*, a devil of a row; *faire du* ~, to kick up a dust; *quel* ~ *!*, what a dust-up !
raffûter (rafyte), v.a. [*re*+*affûter*] To re-sharpen.
rafiau, rafiot (rafjo), s.m. [orig. unkn.] Skiff, small boat with a lateen sail; (also pej.) wretched boat; tub; basket.
rafistolage (rafistɔlaʒ), s.m. (colloq.) Patching-up, make-up.
rafistoler (rafistɔle), v.a. [OF] To mend somehow, to patch up, to do up, to tinker up.
rafle (rɑfl), s.f. **1.** Police raid; **2.** sweeping-off; **3.** grape-stalk; **4.** (at dice) pair royal.
rafler (rɑfle), v.a. [etym. dub.] To sweep off; to carry away, to make a clean sweep of; *ils ont tout raflé*, they have made a clean sweep of everything; they have bagged everything. ⚠ Not 'to raffle', which = *mettre en loterie*.
rafraîchir (rafrɛʃir), v.a. [*re*+*fraîchir*] To refresh, to cool, to freshen; to renovate, to repair, to do up; to trim, to clip (the hair); *je vais lui* ~ *la mémoire !*, I will refresh his memory for him!; ~ *les cheveux*, to trim the hair; ~ *le sang*, to cool the blood; ~ *du vin*, to cool wine; ~ *une robe*, to renovate a dress; **se** ~, v.pr. **1.** to get cooler; *le temps se rafraîchit*, it 's getting cooler; **2.** to have a drink, take some refreshment.
rafraîchissant, -e (rafrɛʃisɑ̃), p. adj. Refreshing, cooling; (med.) laxative, aperient.
rafraîchissement (rafrɛʃismɑ̃), s.m. Refreshment; cooling, cooling effect; renovating; **~s**, s.m.pl., refreshments, drinks; (mil.) fresh supplies.
rafraîchissoir (rafrɛʃiswar), s.m. Wine-cooler, refrigerator; syn. GLACIÈRE.
ragaillardir (ragajardir), v.a. To cheer (X) up, to enliven.
rage (raʒ), s.f. [L *rabies*] Rage, rabidness; hydrophobia; *accès de* ~, fit of madness; *être fou de* ~, to be mad with rage; *faire* ~, (*a*) to storm, to rage, to run riot; (*b*) to be all the rage; *écumer de* ~, to foam at the mouth; *avoir la* ~ *d'écrire*, to have a mania for writing; *une* ~ *de dents*, a violent toothache.
rager (raʒe), v.n. To fume, to be in a passion, to be enraged.
rageu-r, -se (raʒœr), adj. Ill-tempered, passionate, peevish, fretful. ~, s.m. Spitfire.
rageusement (raʒøzmɑ̃), adv. Angrily, peevishly, passionately.
raglan (raglɑ̃), s.m. [f. *Raglan*, prop. name] Raglan coat; *manches* ~, raglan sleeves.
ragot (rago), s.m. [orig. unkn.] **1.** Gossip, tittle-tattle, chit-chat, twaddle; slander, calumny; **2.** two-year-old wild boar; **3.** cramp-iron.
ragot, -e (rago), adj. [orig. unkn.] Dumpy, thick-set, stumpy.
ragoter (ragɔte), v.a.n. To grumble (at), to quarrel (with); to talk scandal; syn. FAIRE DES RAGOTS.
ragotin (ragɔtɛ̃), s.m. [f. *ragot* ?] Stumpy little man.
ragoût (ragu), s.m. [f. *ragoûter*] Ragout, stew; (fig.) zest, piquancy, relish; ~ *de mouton*, Irish stew; *ce livre a au moins le* ~ *de la nouveauté*, this book possesses, if nothing else, the flavour of novelty.
ragoûtant, -e (ragutɑ̃), p. adj. Tempting, pleasing; *un aspect peu* ~, a not too tempting look.

---

o, note, glotte; ɔ̃, monter, ronde; ø, feu, creux; œ, peur, sœur; œ̃, un; ʃ, chez, schisme; u, tout; w, oui, doit, douaire; y, mur, pu; ɥ, huile, muette; z, zèle, rose; ʒ, déjà, gentil.

ragoûter (ragute), v.a. [*re+à+goûter*] To stimulate the appetite of, to please, to tempt.

ragrafer (ragrafe), v.a. [*re+agrafer*] To hook again, to clasp again.

ragrandir (ragrɑ̃dir), v.a. To enlarge; to make wider or bigger.

ragréement (ragremɑ̃), s.m. Finishing-off; renovation; refitting; syn. RAGRÉAGE (naut.) dubbing.

ragréer (ragree), v.a. [*re+gréer*] (build.) To finish off (a wall, &c.); to refit; (naut.) to dub.

raguer (rage), v.a.n. [f. Engl. *to rag*] (naut.) To chafe, to gall, to rub; to be chafed.

rai (rɛ), s.m. [f. L *radium*] Ray; spoke.

raid (rɛd), s.m. [Engl. wd] Flight, raid.

raide (rɛd), adj. [L *rigidus*] Stiff, rigid, tight, taut; (fig.) inflexible, stiff, rather too strong; exorbitant; broad, free, coarse; *c'est un peu ~!*, that's coming it rather strong!; *le procédé est plutôt ~!*, that's rather stiff!; *une pente ~*, a steep slope; *tomber ~ mort*, to fall stone dead; *il en dit de ~s*, his jests are rather broad!; *danser sur la corde ~*, to dance on the tight-rope; *~ comme une barre de fer*, as stiff as a poker.

raidement (rɛdmɑ̃), adv. Stiffly, rigidly, steeply.

raideur (rɛdœr), s.f. Stiffness, rigidity, inflexibility, tightness; swiftness; steepness.

raidillon (rɛdijɔ̃), s.m. Steep short cut, steep path.

raidir, roidir (rɛdir, rwadir), v.a. To stiffen, to make rigid, to tighten; (naut.) to haul taut; **se ~**, v.pr. to stiffen, to grow stiff or rigid; to harden oneself (*contre*, against).

raidissement (rɛdismɑ̃), s.m. Stiffening; tightening.

raidisseur (rɛdisœr), s.m. Wire-tightener.

raie[1] (rɛ), s.f. [LL *riga*] Line, stripe, stroke, streak; parting (of the hair); *à ~s*, striped; (opt.) ray (of spectrum).

raie[2] (rɛ), s.f. [L *raja*] (ichth.) Ray(-fish), skate-fish; *~ bouclée*, ray-maid; (*nœud*) *gueule de ~*, cat's-paw (knot).

raifort (rɛfor), s.m. [L *radix+fortis*] (bot.) Horse-radish.

rail (raj), s.m. [Engl. wd] Rail. ⚠ *Rail* in French is only used in the sense of iron rail for trains, tram-cars, &c.; in English 'rail' means also any horizontal or inclined bar, or continuous series of bars, of wood or metal, used to hang things on, as top of banisters, part of fence, &c.

railler (rɑje), v.a.n. To mock, to rail at, to jeer at, to rally, to deride, to scoff at, to laugh at; *se ~ de*, to laugh at, to make game of. ⚠ 'To rail at' has generally a stronger sense than *railler*, and can often be translated by *invectiver*, or *chanter pouilles à*.

raillerie (rɑjri), s.f. Raillery, piece of raillery, banter, joke, chaff, mock, scoff; *entendre ~*, to know how to take a joke.

railleu-r, -se (rɑjœr), adj. Rallying, jesting, scoffing, satirical. **~**, s.m.f. Joker, rallier, scoffer, banterer.

railleusement (rɑjøzmɑ̃), adv. Mockingly, jeeringly, scoffingly.

raine (rɛn), s.f. See syn. RAINETTE.

rainer (rɛne), v.a. [f. *rainure*] To groove.

rainette (rɛnɛt), s.f. [L *rana*] **1.** Tree-frog, frog; **2.** rennet apple; see REINETTE.

rainure (rɛnyr), s.f. [orig. dub.] Groove; *~ de graissage*, oil-groove.

raiponce (rɛpɔ̃s), s.f. [f. L *radix pontica*] (bot.) Rampion.

raire, réer (rɛr, ree), v.n. [L *radere*] To troat, to bell (of bucks, &c.).

rais (rɛ), s.m. [L *radius*] Spoke (of a wheel); beam, ray (of light).

raisin (rɛzɛ̃), s.m. [L *racemus*] Grape, grapes (usually grapes, pl.); *~s secs*, raisins; *grain de ~*, grape; *grappe de ~*, bunch of grapes; *~s de Corinthe*, currants, *~s de Smyrne*, sultanas; (paper-mak.) *grand-~*, royal (paper).

raisiné (rɛzine), s.m. A jam made of pears, sugar, and grape-juice.

raison (rɛzɔ̃), s.f. [L *ratio*] Reason; good sense, judgement; sanity; (math.) ratio; rate; *~ sociale*, style of firm; *à ~ de*, at the rate of; *à plus forte ~*, a fortiori; all the more reason; with still more reason; and much more so; *~ de plus*, all the more reason; *comme de ~*, as is reasonable; *en ~ de*, (*a*) in proportion to; (*b*) in consideration of; *par la ~ que*, because; *avoir ~*, to be right; to be in the right; to have satisfaction (for); *avoir ~ de*, to get the better of; *avoir des ~s avec X*, to have words with X; *avoir de bonnes ~s pour*, to have good ground to; *donner ~ à X*, to decide in X's favour, to side with X; *entendre ~, se rendre à la ~*, to listen to reason, to be amenable, tractable; *se faire une ~*, to accept something resignedly, to reconcile oneself to one's fate; *faire ~ de*, to give satisfaction for; *demander ~ d'une insulte*, to demand satisfaction for an insult; *mettre X à la ~*, to bring X to his senses; *parler ~*, to talk sense; *plus que de ~*, more than is reasonable; *la ~ du plus fort est toujours la meilleure*, God is on the side of the big battalions; might is right; *perdre la ~*, to lose one's reason, to become insane, to go mad; *point tant de ~s*, do not argue so much; *la ~ d'être*, the end and justification; *vous m'en rendrez ~!*, you will answer to me for that!; *cela n'a ni rime ni ~*, there is neither rhyme nor reason in that; that's perfect nonsense; *ce qu'elle a fait n'a ni rime ni ~*, she did it without rhyme or reason.

raisonnable (rɛzɔnabl), adj. Reasonable,

rational, thinking; moderate, adequate, suitable.

raisonnablement (rɛzɔnabləmɑ̃), adv. Reasonably, rationally; sensibly, moderately, adequately, suitably, tolerably.

raisonné, -e (rɛzɔne), p. adj. Rational, methodical; deliberate.

raisonnement (rɛzɔnmɑ̃), s.m. Reasoning, line of argument; reason, judgement.

raisonner (rɛzɔne), v.n.a. To reason; to argue, to consider; to raise objections; to bring to reason, to induce by reasoning; (naut.) see ARRAISONNER.

raisonneu-r, -se (rɛzɔnœr), adj. Reasoning, arguing, objecting, fault-finding, not submissive. ~, s.m.f. Reasoner, arguer, dialectician; answerer, fault-finder.

rajah (raʒa), s.m. [Hind. wd] Rajah.

rajeunir (raʒœnir), v.n. To grow young again, to recover one's freshness; ~ v.a. to make young again; to give the appearance of youth; to renew, to modernize; **se** ~, v.pr. to understate one's age; to make oneself look young again.

rajeunissant, -e (raʒœnisɑ̃), p. adj. Giving a youthful appearance.

rajeunissement (raʒœnismɑ̃), s.m. Growing young again, rejuvenation; modernizing, revival, renovation.

rajouter (raʒute), v.a. To add . . . again; to add . . . more.

rajustement (raʒystəmɑ̃), s.m. Readjustment, setting to rights again, readaptation; making it up.

rajuster (raʒyste), v.a. To readjust, to put to rights, to readapt; **se** ~, v.pr. (*a*) to rearrange one's clothes; (*b*) to make it up.

râle (rɑl), s.m. [orig. dub.] (ornith.) Rail; ~ *d'eau*, water-rail; ~ *des genêts*, land-rail.

râle, râlement (rɑl, rɑlmɑ̃), s.m. [orig. dub.] Rattle, death-rattle, gasp.

ralentir (ralɑ̃tir), v.a.n. [f. *lent*] To slow down, to slacken, to reduce speed; to ease; to lessen; to moderate, to abate; ~ *le pas*, to slacken one's pace; **se** ~, v.pr., to relent; to reduce one's speed; *au ralenti*, at reduced speed.

ralentissement (ralɑ̃tismɑ̃), s.m. Slackening; easing; abatement, relenting; flagging; (fig.) cooling.

râler (rɑle), v.n. [f. *râle*] To have the death-rattle; to be in the throes of death; (slang) to fume, to be angry; (hence *râleur, râleuse*, grouser, bad-tempered fellow).

ralingue (ralɛ̃g), s.f. [Scand. orig.] (naut.) Bolt-rope; (of a tent) pitch-rope; *mettre en* ~, to shiver; to luff and shake her.

ralinguer (ralɛ̃ge), v.a.n. **1.** To sew the bolt-ropes to a sail; **2.** to shiver; to fly loose to the wind; to be all in the wind; to be all alive.

ralliement (ralimɑ̃), s.m. Rallying, rally; joining (a cause, a party); *mot de* ~, rallying-cry; *point de* ~, rallying-point; rallying-place; *signe de* ~, rallying-sign.

rallier (ralje), v.a. [*re*+*allier*] **1.** To rally, to bring together; **2.** (naut., &c.) to stand for, to return to; ~ *le bord*, to return on board; ~ *la terre*, to stand into the land; to haul in; ~ *le navire au vent*, to haul the ship into the wind; ~ *son poste*, to return to one's post; **se** ~, v.pr. to rally, to join; *se* ~ *à*, to adhere to; (naut.) *se* ~ *à terre*, to hug the shore.

rallonge (ralɔ̃ʒ), s.f. Lengthening-piece, eking-piece; ~ *de table*, leaf.

rallongement (ralɔ̃ʒmɑ̃), s.m. Lengthening.

rallonger (ralɔ̃ʒe), v.a. [*re*+*allonger*] To lengthen.

rallumer (ralyme), v.a. [*re*+*allumer*] To relight; (fig.) to rekindle, to kindle again, to revive; ~ *la colère de X*, to rekindle X's anger; **se** ~, v.pr. to be lighted again, to be rekindled, to rekindle, to revive, to burst out again; *la guerre se ralluma*, war broke out again.

rallye-paper (ralipepœr), s.m. [Engl. orig.] Paper-chase.

Ramadan (ramadɑ̃), s.m. [Arab. wd] Ramadan.

ramage (ramaʒ), s.m. [f. L *ramus*] **1.** Branched pattern, flower-pattern; **2.** warbling, chirping (of birds); (fig.) prattle.

ramager (ramaʒe), v.a.n. **1.** (v.a.) To flower (stuffs, &c.); **2.** to warble, to chirp; to prattle.

ramaigrir (ramɛgrir), v.a.n. To make thin again; to grow thin again.

ramas (ramɑ), s.m. [f. *ramasser*] Heap, lot, set, mass; *un* ~ *de bandits*, a pack of robbers; *un* ~ *d'erreurs*, a mass of mistakes; see syn. RAMASSIS.

ramassage (ramɑsaʒ), s.m. Gathering, picking up.

ramasse (ramɑs), s.f. Mountain sledge.

ramassé, -e (ramɑse), p. adj. Thick-set, squat, dumpy; syn. TRAPU, -E.

ramasse-miettes (ramɑsmjɛt), s.m. invar. Crumb-scoop, crumb-brush and -tray.

ramasser (ramɑse), v.a. [*re*+*amasser*] To gather up, to collect; to gather together; to pick up; to take up; ~ *ses forces*, to muster all one's strength; ~ *une bûche* or *une pelle*, to come a cropper; (fig. colloq.) ~ *X*, to give it X hot; to pepper X; to bite X's nose off; to wipe the floor with X; **se** ~, v.pr. to roll oneself up, to roll itself up; to gather oneself up; to get up again (after a fall), to pick oneself up.

ramasseu-r, -se (ramɑsœr), s.m.f. **1.** Gatherer, collector; **2.** mountain sledge-driver.

ramassis (ramɑsi), s.m. Heap, lot, mass; rabble, gang; see syn. RAMAS.

Ramazan (ramazɑ̃), s.m. See RAMADAN.

rambarde (rɑ̃bard), s.f. [It. *rambata*] (naut.) Hand-rail.
rambour (rɑ̃bur), s.m. [geog. orig.] Rambure, a kind of apple.
rame[1] (ram), s.f. [f. OGerm. *rama*] **1.** Prop, stick; **2.** oar; *faire force de ~s*, to ply the oars; *bateau à six ~s*, six-oared boat.
rame[2] (ram), s.f. [f. Span. *resma*, f. Arab.] Ream (of paper) = 500 *feuilles* = 20 *mains*.
rame[3] (ram), s.f. Train; *~ de bateaux*, convoy; *~ de wagons*, train (of carriages or trucks).
ramé, -e (rame), p. adj. *Pois ~s*, peas trained on sticks; *boulets ~*, (obs.) bar-shot, chain-shot; (herald.) ramé, attired.
rameau (pl. **-x**) (ramo), s.m. [L *ramus*] Bough, branch; sprig; (fig.) branch, subdivision; ramification; *Dimanche des ~x*, Palm Sunday; (fig.) *~ d'olivier*, olive-branch.
ramée (rame), s.f. Green boughs, branches, arbour; *danser sous la ~*, to dance under the greenwood tree.
ramenable (ramnabl), adj. Amenable, reclaimable.
ramender (ramɑ̃de), v.a. (obs.) To manure again; to mend (gilding, &c.); to lower the price of.
ramener (ramne), v.a. [*re+amener*] To bring back, to bring home, to bring again, to bring round, to restore; *~ la prospérité*, to restore prosperity; *la faim le ramène au logis*, hunger brings him home; *~ son châle sur ses épaules*, to pull one's shawl round one's shoulders.
ramequin (ramkɛ̃), s.m. [Germ. *Rähmchen*] (cook.) Ramikin.
ramer[1] (rame), v.a. To stick (peas), to prop (plants).
ramer[2] (rame), v.n. To row, to pull at the oars, to pull.
ramereau (pl. **-x**) (ramro), s.m. (ornith.) Young ring-dove.
ramette (ramɛt), s.f. **1.** Ream (of note-paper); **2.** (print.) job-chase.
rameu-r, -se (ramœr), s.m.f. Rower, oarsman, oarswoman. [ramose.
rameu-x, -se (ramø), adj. Branchy,
ramie (rami), s.f. (bot.) Ramee, grass-cloth plant.
ramier (ramje), s.m. [f. L *ramus*] **1.** (ornith.) Wood-pigeon, ring-dove; **2.** branches; syn. RAMÉE.
ramification (ramifika'sjɔ̃), s.f. [LL *ramificatio*] Ramification.
ramifier (ramifje), v.a. To ramify; **se ~**, v.pr. to ramify, to branch out, to divide.
ramille (ramij), s.f. Twig.
ramingue (ramɛ̃g), adj. [It. *ramingo*] (of horses) Restive.
ramoindrir (ramwɛ̃drir), v.a. [*re+amoindrir*] To lessen, to depreciate, to cheapen.
ramoitir (ramwatir), v.a. To moisten again.
ramolli, -e (ramɔli), p. adj. Grown soft; (fig. colloq.) potty, soft, soft-headed, soft-witted; *il est ~*, he has gone potty. ~, s.m.f. Softy.
ramollir (ramɔlir), v.a. [f. *mou*] To soften; (fig.) to soften, to enervate, to lessen; **se ~**, v.pr. to soften, to grow soft; to grow soft-witted.
ramollissement (ramɔlismɑ̃), s.m. Softening; (pathol.) softening of the brain. [besom.
ramon (ramɔ̃), s.m. [OF *raim*] Broom,
ramonage (ramɔnaʒ), s.m. Chimney-sweeping.
ramoner (ramɔne), v.a. [f. *ramon*] To sweep (a chimney).
ramoneur (ramɔnœr), s.m. Sweep, chimney-sweep.
rampant, -e (rɑ̃pɑ̃), p. adj. Crawling, creeping; (herald.) rampant; (fig.) servile, grovelling, fawning, cringing; (arch.) sloping. ⚠ In English 'rampant' has not only the heraldic sense, but means also raging, violent, dangerous, threatening, rampaging; ex. the spirit of democracy is rampant, *le souffle de la démocratie est menaçant*.
rampe (rɑ̃p), s.f. **1.** Banisters; stair hand-rail; (slang) *lâcher la ~*, to peg out; to kick the bucket; to die; **2.** slope, incline, gradient; ramp; **3.** (theatr.) footlights.
rampement (rɑ̃pmɑ̃), s.m. Crawling, creeping.
ramper (rɑ̃pe), v.n. [f. OHG *rampon*] To crawl, to creep; to crouch; (fig.) to grovel, to cringe; (arch.) to ramp, to slope. ⚠ Not 'to ramp', which = *se dresser sur ses pattes de derrière*; *prendre une attitude menaçante*.
ramponneau (pl. **-x**) (rɑ̃pɔno), s.m. (slang) Blow, shock.
rams (rams), s.m. [Germ. *Ramsch*] Skat (card-game); ramsch (in game of skat).
ramure (ramyr), s.f. [f. L *ramus*] **1.** Branches, green boughs, foliage; **2.** antlers (of a stag).
rancart (rɑ̃kar), s.m. [orig. dub.] Refuse; *mettre au ~*, to throw aside; (colloq.) *on a mis X au ~*, X has been put on the shelf.
rance (rɑ̃s), adj. [L *rancidus*] Rancid, rank, stale; (fig.) out of date; passé; behind the times. ~, s.m. Rancidness; *sentir le ~*, to smell rancid.
ranche (rɑ̃ʃ), s.f. [etym. dub.] Rung (of a pole-ladder).
rancher (rɑ̃ʃe), s.m. Pole-ladder.
rancidité (rɑ̃sidite), s.f. Rancidness, rancidity.
rancio (rɑ̃sjo), s.m. [Span. wd] Rancio (wine).
rancir (rɑ̃sir), v.n. [f. *rance*] To grow rancid or stale.
rancissement (rɑ̃sismɑ̃), s.m. Growing rancid; rancidness, rancidity.

rancœur (rɑ̃kœr), s.f. [L *rancor*] Rancour, bitterness.

rançon (rɑ̃sɔ̃), s.f. [f. L *redemptio*] Ransom; *payer ~ pour X*, to ransom X.

rançonnement (rɑ̃sɔnmɑ̃), s.m. Extortion, taxation; (colloq.) fleecing; sticking it on.

rançonner (rɑ̃sɔne), v.a. To set a ransom upon; to exact ransom from; (fig.) to fleece, to exploit; to make pay through the nose. ⚠ Not 'to ransom', which usually = *payer rançon pour.*

rançonneu-r, -se (rɑ̃sɔnœr), s.m.f. Extortioner.

rancune (rɑ̃kyn), s.f. [L *rancor*] Rancour, spite, grudge; *sans ~!*, let bygones be bygones; no ill feeling; bearing no grudge; *il garde ~ à X*, he owes or bears X a grudge.

rancuni-er, -ère (rɑ̃kynje), adj. Rancorous, spiteful, resentful.

randonnée (rɑ̃dɔne), s.f. [orig. dub., f. OHG *rando*?] **1.** (hunt.) Circuit (of game); **2.** long walk, long ride, long tour.

rang (rɑ̃), s.m. [f. OHG *hring*] Row, line, rank, range; place, station, order; (print.) frame; (theatr.) tier, row; *un ~ de perles*, a string of pearls; *un ~ de soldats*, a rank of soldiers; *à son ~*, at one's place; *garder* or *tenir son ~*, to keep one's place, to live up to one's station in society; *se mettre sur les ~s*, to enter the lists; to compete, to come forward as a candidate; *mettre X au ~ de*, to reckon X among; to value X as much as; *une personne de haut ~*, a person of rank; *rompre les ~s*, to break rank; *rentrer dans le ~*, to return to one's place among the rank and file; (naut.) *vaisseau de 1er ~*, ship of the first rate; *en ~ d'oignons*, all in a line.

rangé, -e (rɑ̃ʒe), p. adj. In good order, tidy; (fig.) steady, leading a serious life; *bataille ~e*, pitched battle.

rangée (rɑ̃ʒe), s.f. Row, line, array, file, tier, set, string.

rangement (rɑ̃ʒmɑ̃), s.m. Putting in order, tidying, classifying, arranging.

ranger (rɑ̃ʒe), v.a. [f. *rang*] To put in order, to put in its place; to arrange, to array; to range, to count (*parmi*, among), to put aside, to keep back; to tidy; to bring under, to subdue; (naut.) to sail close to; *~ un pays sous sa loi*, to bring a country under one's law, to subdue a country; **se ~**, v.pr. **1.** to settle down; to sober down (after sowing one's wild oats); **2.** to side (*du côté de*, with); **3.** to make room; **4.** to fall in (*à l'avis de X*, with X's opinion); **5.** *se ~ en bataille*, to be drawn up in order of battle.

ranimer (ranime), v.a. [*re*+*animer*] To revive, to restore to life; (fig.) to stir up, to enliven; *~ les couleurs de*, to revive the colour of; **se ~**, v.pr. to revive, to come to life again; (fig.) to brighten up, to cheer up.

ranz (rɑ̃ts), s.m. [Swiss wd] Tune; *~ des vaches*, Swiss herdsmen's melody.

raout (raut), s.m. [f. Engl. *rout*] Evening party, party; rout. ⚠ Though *raout* is a form of 'rout', the sense is different. In English the most usual sense of 'rout' is: *réunion tumultueuse de buveurs, beuverie, 'partouze'; rixe; troubles; défaite*; the sense of 'evening party' is archaic. In French *raout* has only the sense of 'party', but is becoming obsolete.

rapace (rapas), adj. [L *rapax*] Rapacious, greedy. **~**, s.m. Rapacious bird; bird of prey.

rapacité (rapasite), s.f. Rapacity; *avec ~*, rapaciously.

rapatelle (rapatɛl), s.f. A kind of hair cloth.

rapatriage (rapatriaʒ), s.m. (colloq.) Making it up, reconciliation.

rapatriement (rapatrimɑ̃), s.m. **1.** Repatriation, sending back to one's native country; **2.** reconciliation.

rapatrier (rapatrie), v.a. [f. *patrie*] To repatriate, to send back to one's native country; to reconcile; **se ~**, v.pr. (colloq.) to make it up.

râpe (rɑp), s.f. [f. *râper*] Grater; scraper; rasp. ⚠ Not 'rape', which = *viol.*

râpé, -e (rɑpe), p. adj. **1.** Grated; *fromage ~*, grated cheese; **2.** shabby, threadbare, worn out.

râpé (rɑpe), s.m. **1.** Rape-wine; **2.** grated cheese.

râper (rɑpe), v.a. [It. *raspare*] To grate; to rasp; to wear out.

rapetasser (raptase), v.a. (colloq.) [Provenç. wd.] To patch up, to mend, to botch, to tinker.

rapetissement (raptismɑ̃), s.m. Shortening; belittling; shrinking.

rapetisser (raptise), v.a.n. [f. *petit*] To shorten, to make smaller, to become shorter, to make appear smaller; to shrink; (fig.) to belittle.

raphia (rafja), s.m. (bot.) Raffia.

rapide (rapid), adj. [L *rapidus*] Rapid, speedy, fleet, swift; fast; steep. **~**, s.m. **1.** (geog.) Rapid; **2.** (rail.) fast train, express.

rapidement (rapidmɑ̃), adv. Rapidly, swiftly, fast; steeply.

rapidité (rapidite), s.f. Rapidity, swiftness, speed; steepness.

rapiéçage, rapiécement (rapjesaʒ, rapjesmɑ̃), s.m. Piecing, patching, botching; also RAPIÉCETAGE (obs.).

rapiécer (rapjese), v.a. [*re*+*à*+*pièce*] To piece, to patch up, to botch; also RAPIÉCETER (obs.).

rapière (rapjɛr), s.f. [orig. dub.] Rapier.

rapin (rapɛ̃), s.m. (colloq.) Art student, dauber.

rapine (rapin), s.f. [f. L *rapere*] Plundering, rapine, robbery; spoil, plunder.
rapiner (rapine), v.a.n. To plunder, to pillage.
rapointir (rapwɛ̃tir), v.a. To resharpen.
rappareiller (raparɛje), v.a. To rematch.
rappariement (raparimɑ̃), s.m. Rematching.
rapparier (raparje), v.a. To rematch.
rappel (rapɛl), s.m. Recall, recalling; repeal; ~ *à l'ordre*, call (to order); *battre le* ~, to beat to arms; (fig.) to gather, to summon, to cause to assemble, to call up.
rappeler (raple), v.a. [*re+appeler*] To recall, to call back; to call home; to repeal; to bring back (*à*, to); to summon up; to muster; ~ *à la vie*, to restore to life; ~ *X à l'ordre*, to call X to order; *rappelez-moi à son souvenir*, kindly remember me to him; **se** ~, v.pr. to remember, to recollect, to recall to mind; *rappelle-toi cela*, remember that.
rappliquer (raplike), v.a. [*re+appliquer*] **1.** To apply again; **2.** (slang) ~, v.n. to return, to come back, to come home.
rapport (rapɔr), s.m. [f. *rapporter*] **1.** Product, revenue; *en plein* ~, producing abundantly; **2.** report, account, statement; *faire un* ~, to draw up a report; **3.** relation, connexion, correspondence; *à quoi cela a-t-il* ~?, what does it relate to?; *sous ce* ~, in this respect; *sous tous les* ~*s*, in every respect; **4.** (plur.) intercourse; *mettre X en* ~ *avec Z*, to bring X into touch with Z; **5.** ratio; *par* ~ *à*, on account of; in proportion to, in regard to.
rapportable (rapɔrtabl), adj. Repealable.
rapporter (rapɔrte), v.a. [*re+apporter*] **1.** To bring back, to bring home; to return, to refund; **2.** to produce, to yield, to bring in; **3.** to add, to eke out with; **4.** to report, to state, to give an account of, to tell, to quote; **5.** to repeal (a law, &c.); ~, v.n. to tell tales; (pop.) to peach, to split (on somebody); **se** ~, v.pr. to concern, to relate (to), to correspond; *je m'en rapporte à vous*, I leave it to you; *cela se rapporte à une ancienne affaire*, that relates to an old story.
rapporteu-r, -se (rapɔrtœr), s.m.f. **1.** Tell-tale, one who peaches; informer; **2.** reporter; **3.** (geom.) protractor.
rapprendre (raprɑ̃dr), v.a. [*re+apprendre*] To learn anew.
rapprochement (raprɔʃmɑ̃), s.m. Bringing together; drawing closer; (fig.) reconciliation; comparison; parallel.
rapprocher (raprɔʃe), v.a. To bring nearer or closer, to make appear nearer; to bring together; to reconcile; to compare; **se** ~, v.pr. to draw nearer or closer, to be brought together, to become reconciled; to approximate, to approach.
rapsode, rhapsode (rapsɔd), s.m. [Gr. *rhapsōdos*] Rhapsode, rhapsodist.
rapsodie, rhapsodie (rapsɔdi), s.f. Rhapsody.
rapt (rapt), s.m. [L *raptus*] Abduction, rape.
râpure (rɑpyr), s.f. Raspings, scrapings.
raquette (rakɛt), s.f. [f. Arab. *raḥa*] **1.** Racket; racquet, battledore; **2.** snowshoe, racket.
raquettier (rakɛtje), s.m. Racket-maker.
rare (rar), adj. [L *rarus*] Rare, exceptional, unusual; of uncommon excellence; rarefied; *vous vous faites bien* ~, we see very little of you; you are quite a stranger.
raréfaction (rarefaksjɔ̃), s.f. Rarefaction, rarefication.
raréfiant, -e, raréfacti-f, -ve (rarefjɑ̃, rarefaktif), adj. Rarefying.
raréfier (rarefje), v.a. [L *rarus+facere*] To rarefy; **se** ~, v.pr. to become rarefied.
rarement (rarmɑ̃), adv. Rarely, seldom, unusually.
rareté (rarte), s.f. Rarity, scarcity; great value (caused by rarity).
rarissime (rarisim), adj. Most rare.
ras, -e (rɑ (fem. rɑz)), adj. [L *rasus*] Close-cropped, close-shaven, bare, smooth, flat; *faire table* ~*e*, to clear the board; (fig.) to sweep away all preconceptions; to begin anew; *en* ~*e campagne*, in open country; *à poil* ~, short-haired.
ras (rɑ), s.m. **1.** Level; *au* ~ *de l'eau*, close to the water; level with the water; **2.** short-napped cloth; **3.** (naut.) ~ *de carène*, floating stage; **4.** [Arab. wd] ras, chief; **5.** [Breton wd] ~ *de marée* (also *raz*), bore; tidal wave.
rasade (rɑzad), s.f. Bumper; *boire force* ~*s*, to drink bumper after bumper.
rasage (rɑzaʒ), s.m. Shaving.
rasant, -e (rɑzɑ̃), p. adj. [f. *raser*] **1.** Grazing, rasant; *feu* ~, grazing fire; **2.** (slang) boring, dull, tiring; *cet orateur est* ~, this speaker is a perfect bore.
rascasse (raskas), s.f. (ichth.) Scorpaena (a Mediterranean fish).
rasement (rɑzmɑ̃), s.m. Demolishing, pulling to the ground; levelling, razing to the ground.
raser (rɑze), v.a. **1.** To shave; **2.** to graze, just to touch; to skim; (naut.) ~ *la côte*, to hug the coast; **3.** to pull down, to demolish; to raze to the ground; **4.** (slang) to bore, to tire, to worry; **se** ~, v.pr. **1.** to shave; **2.** to crouch, to squat close to the ground; **3.** (slang) to be bored.
raseu-r, -se (rɑzœr), s.m.f. **1.** Shaver; **2.** (colloq.) bore; *quel* ~!, what a bore he is!
rasibus (rɑzibys), adv. Quite close.
rasière (rɑzjɛr), s.f. An old measure for potatoes; 1 ~ = roughly 70 litres.
rasoir (rɑzwar), s.m. Razor; ~ *de sûreté*,

safety razor; *cuir à ~*, razor-strop; (colloq.) bore.

rassade (rasad), s.f. Glass beads (for trading with negroes).

rassasiement (rasazimã), s.m. Satiety, satiating.

rassasier (rasazje), v.a. [*re*+(L)*ad*+*satiare*] To sate, to fill, to satiate, to gorge; to surfeit; *être rassasié de*, to have one's fill of; to be sick of; to be fed up with; *~ sa curiosité, ses yeux*, to satisfy one's curiosity, one's eyes; **se ~**, v.pr. to take one's fill; to be satiated.

rasse (ras), s.f. Coal-basket.

rassemblement (rasãbləmã), s.m. Gathering, assembling, mustering, collecting; assemblage, gathering, crowd, great concourse, mob; *disperser les ~s*, to disperse the crowd or the mob.

rassembler (rasãble), v.a. [*re*+*assembler*] To gather, to assemble, to muster, to call up, to collect, to put together; *~ ses pensées*, to collect one's thoughts; *~ ses forces*, to muster up one's strength; *~ des troupes*, to muster troops; *~ un cheval*, to gather up a horse (for a jump); **se ~**, v.pr. to assemble, to congregate, to muster.

rasseoir (raswar), v.a. [*re*+*asseoir*] To reseat, to put in its place again; *~ ses idées*, to collect one's thoughts, to calm one's senses; **se ~**, v.pr. to sit down again; to settle (of liquids); to become composed again, to calm down.

rasséréner (raserene), v.a. [f. *serein*] To clear up, to calm down, to restore serenity to, to cheer up; **se ~**, v.pr. to clear up, to brighten up, to recover one's serenity.

rassis, -e (rasi), p. adj. [f. *rasseoir*] Settled; calm, sedate; stale (of bread); *homme d'esprit ~*, sober-minded man; calm and collected man.

rassortiment, réassortiment (rasɔrtimã, reasɔrtimã), s.m. Matching (colours, &c.); restocking (goods, &c.).

rassortir, réassortir (rasɔrtir, reasɔrtir), v.a. To match; to restock.

rassoter (rasɔte), v.a. To infatuate again.

rassurant, -e (rasyrã), p. adj. Reassuring, tranquillizing.

rassurer (rasyre), v.a. [*re*+*assurer*] To reassure, to tranquillize, to cheer; **se ~**, v.pr., to feel or be reassured, to take heart again; to settle, to grow composed again; *rassurez-vous*, don't be afraid; set your mind at rest.

rastaquouère, rasta (rastakwɛr, rasta), s.m. [Span.-American *rastracuero*] Suspicious gentleman from abroad; fishy adventurer; swindler; showy person; ostentatious and dubious individual.

rat (ra), s.m. [orig. dub.] Rat; (colloq.) close-fisted person, miser; *~ de cave*, (*a*) excise-man; (*b*) taper; *~ d'opéra*, ballet-dancer; *~ d'église*, regular church-goer; *~ d'hôtel*, hotel-thief; *~ d'eau*, water-rat; *~des champs*, field-rat; *queue de ~*, s.f. narrow braid; *mort aux ~s*, s.f. ratsbane; *à bon chat bon ~*, set a thief to catch a thief; *avoir des ~s dans la tête*, to have whims.

rata (rata), s.m. [f. *ratatouille*] (mil. slang.) Stew, grub, food.

ratafia (ratafja), s.m. Ratafia (liqueur).

ratatiné, -e (ratatine), p. adj. Dried up, shrivelled.

ratatiner (ratatine), v.a. [orig. unkn.] To shrivel, to shrink; **se ~**, v.pr. to shrink, to shrivel up.

ratatouille (ratatuj), s.f. [Provenç. wd] Irish stew, sorry food, mess.

rate[1] (rat), s.f. [etym. dub.] (anat.) Spleen; (colloq.) *ne pas se fouler la ~*, not to work too hard, to take things easy; *se désopiler la ~*, to drive away the spleen, to laugh fit to split; to make merry; *se décharger la ~*, to vent one's choler. ⚠ Not 'rate' which = *taux; cours, vitesse*.

rate[2] (rat), s.f. Female rat.

raté (rate), s.m. [f. *rater*] **1.** Misfire; *avoir des ~s*, (motor, aeroplane, &c.) to misfire; **2.** unsuccessful man, failure. **~, -e**, p. adj. Missed, miscarried, defective, spoiled, lost, unsuccessful.

râteau (pl. **-x**) (rɑto), s.m. [L *rastellus*] Rake; rack.

ratel (ratɛl), s.m. [etym. dub.] (zool.) Ratel, honey-badger.

râteler (rɑtle), v.a. To rake; syn. RATISSER.

râteleu-r, -se (rɑtlœr), s.m.f. Raker.

râtelier (rɑtlje), s.m. **1.** Rack (in stables); (pej.) *manger à plusieurs ~s*, to eat at more than one manger; to get money from different sources, to be paid by more than one master; to serve God and Mammon; **2.** set of teeth.

rater (rate), v.n.a. [f. *rat*] (of fire-arms, motors, &c.) To miss fire; to fail, to miscarry; ~, (v.a.) to bungle, to fail to accomplish, to miss; *l'affaire a raté*, the thing fell through; *~ son effet*, to bungle one's effect, to miss one's aim or object; *ne ratez pas cette occasion*, don't lose this opportunity.

ratiboiser (ratibwaze), v.a. (colloq.) To take the whole of; to clean out; *je suis ratiboisé*, I am cleaned out.

ratichon (ratiʃɔ̃), s.m. (pop.) Priest, sky-pilot, devil-dodger.

ratier (ratje), s.m. adj. Rat-catcher (dog), ratter.

ratière (ratjɛr), s.f. Rat-trap.

ratification (ratifika'sjɔ̃), s.f. Ratification.

ratifier (ratifje), v.a. [f. L *ratus*+*facere*] To ratify.

ratine (ratin), s.f. [orig. unkn.] Ratteen, sponge-cloth, pilot-cloth, petersham.

⚠ Nowadays the word 'petersham' is used for what the French call *ruban gros grain*.
ratiner (ratine), v.a. To frieze.
ratiocination (rasjɔsina'sjɔ̃), s.f. (pej.) Ratiocination.
ratiociner (rasjɔsine), v.n. [L *ratiocinari*] To ratiocinate.
ration (rasjɔ̃), s.f. [L *ratio*] Ration, allowance; *mettre à la* ~, to allowance; *mettre à la demi-*~, to put upon half allowance.
rational (rasjɔnal), s.m. (Jewish) high priest's breastplate.
rationaliser (rasjɔnalize), v.a. To rationalize.
rationalisme (rasjɔnalism), s.m. Rationalism.
rationaliste (rasjɔnalist), adj. s.m.f. Rationalist.
rationalité (rasjɔnalite), s.f. Rationality.
rationnaire (rasjɔnɛr), adj. That receives an allowance.
rationnel, -le (rasjɔnɛl), adj. Rational; (math., astr.) rational.
rationnellement (rasjɔnɛlmɑ̃), adv. Rationally.
rationnement (rasjɔnmɑ̃), s.m. Rationing, allowancing; putting on short allowance.
rationner (rasjɔne), v.a. [f. *ration*] To ration; to put on short allowance.
ratissage (ratisaʒ), s.m. Raking, scraping.
ratisser (ratise), v.a. [f. L *radere*] To rake, to scrape; (colloq.) to sweep off, to take all the money of, to clean out.
ratissoire (ratiswar), s.f. Scraper.
ratissure (ratisyr), s.f. Scrapings.
raton (ratɔ̃), s.m. [f. *rat*] **1.** (zool.) Raccoon; **2.** young rat; (fig.) pet, darling.
rattachage, rattachement (rataʃaʒ, rataʃmɑ̃), s.m. Tying up again, reconnexion, re-fastening.
rattacher (rataʃe), v.a. [*re+attacher*] To tie up again, to re-fasten, to re-connect; to reunite; **se ~ à,** v.pr. to be connected with, to belong to; to join, to adhere to.
rattrapage (ratrapaʒ), s.m. Making up for, mending, correcting.
rattraper (ratrape), v.a. [*re+attraper*] To catch again, to re-capture; to catch up, to overtake; to recover; to get even with; ~ *le temps perdu*, to make up for lost time; *bien fin qui m'y rattrapera*, once bitten twice shy; they won't catch me doing that again; *il va vite mais je le rattraperai*, he is walking fast but I think I shall overtake him; **se** ~, v.pr. to catch hold (*à*, of), to recover, to make up for.
rature (ratyr), s.f. Erasure, crossing out (a word, &c.).
raturer (ratyre), v.a. [f. L *radere*] To erase, to cross out, to scratch out; *tout raturé*, full of erasures; syn. BIFFER.
raucité (rosite), s.f. Hoarseness, raucity, roughness.
rauque (rok), adj. [L *raucus*] Hoarse; harsh, raucous.
ravage (ravaʒ), s.m. [f. *ravir*] Ravages (plur.), devastation, havoc, spoil, ruin; *faire des ~s*, to commit ravages, to cause havoc.
ravager (ravaʒe), v.a. [f. *ravage*] To ravage, to spoil, to devastate, to ruin, to lay waste.
ravageur (ravaʒœr), s.m. Spoiler, plunderer, ravager; (obs.) mudlark.
ravalement (ravalmɑ̃), s.m. **1.** Rough-casting; **2.** reduction in thickness; **3.** (fig.) disparaging; humbling; abasement.
ravaler (ravale), v.a. [*re+avaler*] **1.** To swallow again, to gulp down again; **2.** to rough-cast (a wall, &c.); **3.** (fig.) to disparage, to abase, to run down; *c'est ~ l'homme au niveau de la brute*, it means abasing man to the level of the beast; **4.** to eat, to keep back; *on lui a fait ~ ses paroles*, he was obliged to eat his words; he had to retract; **se** ~, v.pr. to lower oneself, to debase oneself.
ravaudage (ravodaʒ), s.m. Mending, patching up, botching, darning; (obs.) talking nonsense.
ravauder (ravode), v.a.n. [etym. dub.] To mend, to darn, to botch up; (colloq. obs.) to scold, to abuse; to talk rot.
ravauderie (ravodri), s.f. Nonsense, talking rot.
ravaudeuse (ravodøz), s.f. Woman who darns stockings, &c.; mender; (colloq.) silly talker, wrangling woman.
rave (rav), s.f. [L *rapa*] (bot.) French turnip, field-turnip; *chou-*~, kohlrabi; *céleri* ~, celeriac, turnip-rooted celery.
ravelin (ravlɛ̃), s.m. (fort.) Ravelin.
ravenelle (ravnɛl), s.f. (bot.) Wallflower.
ravier (ravje), s.m. [f. *rave*] Hors-d'œuvre dish.
ravière (ravjɛr), s.f. Ground planted with field-turnips.
ravigote (ravigɔt), s.f. (cook.) Ravigote sauce, shallot sauce.
ravigoter (ravigɔte), v.a. [for *ravigorer*] To pick up, to revive, to enliven, to cheer up, to put new life into.
ravin (ravɛ̃), s.m. [f. *raviner*] Ravine, gully.
ravine (ravin), s.f. [L *rapina*] Small mountain stream; ravine, gully.
ravinement (ravinmɑ̃), s.m. Wearing away, gullying, hollowing out.
raviner (ravine), v.a. [f. L *rapina*] To gully, to wear away, to hollow out, to plough out.
ravir (ravir), v.a. [L *rapere*] **1.** To carry off, to take away, to rob of, to ravish; **2.** to enrapture, to transport, to delight, to ravish; *à* ~, wonderfully well, to admiration, admirably; *je suis ravi de vous voir*, I am delighted to see you;

la mort lui a ravi ce qu'il avait de plus cher, death has robbed him of his dearest treasure.

ravisement (ravizmɑ̃), (obs.) s.m. Changing one's mind.

(se) raviser (səravize), v.pr. [*re+aviser*] To change one's mind, to think better of it.

ravissant, -e (ravisɑ̃), p. adj. **1.** (rare) Rapacious; **2.** ravishing, delightful, lovely, exquisite, enrapturing.

ravissement (ravismɑ̃), s.m. **1.** Rape; **2.** rapture, delight; *être dans le* ~, to be enraptured; to be in raptures, in ecstasies.

ravisseur (ravisœr), s.m. Ravisher, spoiler.

ravitaillement (ravitɑjmɑ̃), s.m. Revictualling, supplying, purveying.

ravitailler (ravitɑje), v.a. [f. *victuailles*] To re-victual, to provide, to supply (*de*, with).

raviver (ravive), v.a. [*re+aviver*] To revive, to rouse, to enliven, to brace; to quicken.

ravoir (ravwar), v.a. (only used in the infinitive) [*re+avoir*] To get back; *vous ne pourrez pas le* ~, you won't be able to get it back.

rayage (rɛjaʒ), s.m. Rifling (of guns); streaking; scratching; syn. RAYEMENT.

rayé, -e (rɛje), p. adj. Streaked, striped; (of fire-arms) rifled.

rayement (rɛjmɑ̃), s.m. See RAYAGE.

rayer (rɛje), v.a. [f. *raie*] To scratch; to streak, to rule; to rifle; to scratch out, to cross out (a word, &c.).

rayère (rɛjɛr), s.f. [f. *raie*] Loop-hole.

rayon (rɛjɔ̃), s.m. [f. *rai*] Ray, beam; radius; spoke (of wheel); shelf; department (of a shop, &c.); *dix mètres de* ~, ten metres in radius; ~*s X*, Röntgen rays, X-rays; ~ *de miel*, honeycomb; ~ *d'espérance*, ray of hope; (colloq.) *ce n'est pas de mon* ~, that's not within my province.

rayonnage (rɛjɔnaʒ), s.m. Shelving; shelves.

rayonnant, -e (rɛjɔnɑ̃), p. adj. Radiating; radiant, beaming (*de*, with); (arch.) rayonnant, late Gothic.

rayonnement (rɛjɔnmɑ̃), s.m. Radiation; radiance.

rayonner (rɛjɔne), v.n. To radiate; to beam, to shine; ~ *de joie*, to beam with joy.

rayonnés (rɛjɔne), s.m.pl. (zool.) Radiata.

rayonneur (rɛjɔnœr), s.m. Cultivator (garden implement).

rayure (rɛjyr), s.f. [f. *rayer*] Stripe, striping; rifling (of fire-arms); scratch, scratching; crossing out, scratching out.

raz (rɑ), s.m. [ON *ras*] Race, tide-race; ~ *de marée*, bore, tidal wave.

razzia (razzja, radzja), s.f. [Arab. *rhaziat*] Razzia.

razzier (razzje), v.a. To plunder, to make a clean sweep of.

ré (re), s.m. [1st syllable of L *resonare*] (mus.) Re, D.

réa (rea), s.m. Sheave (of a pulley).

réabonner (reabɔne), v.a. [*re+abonner*] To renew (a person's) subscription; **se** ~, v.pr. to renew one's subscription.

réabsorber (reapsɔrbe), v.a. To reabsorb.

réabsorption (reapsɔrpsjɔ̃), s.f. Reabsorption.

réaccoutumer (reakutyme), v.a. To reaccustom; **se** ~, v.pr. to re-accustom oneself.

réacti-f, -ve (reaktif), adj. s.m. Reactive, reagent.

réaction (reaksjɔ̃), s.f. Reaction; (polit.) reaction, retrograde tendency.

réactionnaire (reaksjɔnɛr), adj. s.m.f. Reactionary.

réadmettre (readmɛtr), v.a. To re-admit, to admit again.

réadmission (readmisjɔ̃), s.f. Readmission.

réagir (reaʒir), v.n. [*re+agir*] To react.

réajourner (reajurne), v.a. To readjourn.

réal, (aux) (real), s.m. [Span. wd] Real (Span. coin).

réal, -e, (aux) (real), adj. [Span. wd] Royal.

réalgar (realgar), s.m. (chem.) Realgar.

réalisable (realizabl), adj. Realizable, feasible.

réalisation (realiza'sjɔ̃), s.f. Realization; conversion into money; fulfilment; materialization.

réaliser (realize), v.a. [f. L *realis*] To realize, to fulfil, to materialize; to convert into money; (new acceptation) ~, v.a.n. to realize, to understand.

réalisme (realism), s.m. Realism.

réaliste (realist), adj. Realistic. ~, s.m.f. Realist.

réalité (realite), s.f. Reality; *en* ~, in fact; in reality.

réapparaître (reaparɛtr), v.n. To reappear.

réapparition (reaparisjɔ̃), s.f. Reappearance.

réappeler (reaple), v.a. To call anew; ~, v.n. to appeal a second time.

réapprovisionner (reaprɔvizjɔne), v.a. To supply again, to re-stock.

réargenter (rearʒɑ̃te), v.a. To re-silver, to re-plate.

réassortiment, (reasɔrtimɑ̃) s.m. **réassortir** (reasɔrtir), v.a.n. See RASSORTIMENT, &c.

réassurance (reasyrɑ̃s), s.f. Reinsurance.

réassurer (reasyre), v.a. To reinsure. ⚠ Not 'to reassure' in the sense of to restore the confidence of, to confirm again in an opinion, &c., which = *rassurer*.

rebaptiser (rəbatize), v.a. To rebaptize.

rébarbati-f, -ve (rebarbatif), adj. [f. OF *se rebarber*, to face the enemy] Surly, stern, forbidding; grim-looking.
rebâtir (rəbɑtir), v.a. To rebuild.
rebattre (rəbatr), v.a. To beat again; to shuffle (cards) again; to repeat, to say over and over again; *ne me rebattez plus les oreilles de cela*, stop dinning it into my ears.
rebattu, -e (rɛbaty), adj. (fig.) Hackneyed; stale; oft-told; *sujet* ~, hackneyed matter or motive.
rebec (rəbɛk), s.m. [Arab. *rebab*] (mus.) Rebeck.
rebelle (rəbɛl), adj. [L *rebellis*] Rebellious, rebelling, refractory; disobedient. ~, s.m.f. Rebel.
(se) rebeller (sərəbɛlle), v.pr. To rebel (*contre*, against).
rébellion (rebɛlljɔ̃), s.f. [L *rebellio*] Rebellion, revolt.
(se) rebéquer (sərəbeke), v.pr. [f. *bec*] (colloq.) To answer saucily, pertly, or arrogantly.
(se) rebiffer (sərəbife), v.pr. To be refractory, not to submit, not to yield; to champ the bit, to kick over the traces, to turn restive.
reboisement (rəbwazmɑ̃), s.m. Replanting, re-afforestation, re-timbering.
reboiser (rəbwaze), v.a. To replant, to re-afforest.
rebond (rəbɔ̃), s.m. Rebound.
rebondi, -e (rəbɔ̃di), p. adj. Chubby, plump, buxom.
rebondir (rəbɔ̃dir), v.n. To rebound.
rebondissement (rəbɔ̃dismɑ̃), s.m. Rebounding, rebound.
rebord (rəbɔr), s.m. Edge, brim, rim, ledge, raised edge, brink; border; hem.
reborder (rəbɔrde), v.a. To put a new border on, to re-hem, to re-edge.
(se) rebotter (sərəbɔte), v.pr. To put one's boots on again.
reboucher (rəbuʃe), v.a. To stop up again; to cork again.
rebours (rəbur), adj. [LL *reburrus*] Cross-grained. ~, s.m. Wrong way, wrong side; reverse, opposite; *à* ~, *au* ~, against the grain, against the nap; backwards; *au* ~ *de*, contrary to, against; *il prend tout ce qu'on dit au* ~, he misconstrues everything one says.
reboutement (rəbutmɑ̃), s.m. Bone-setting.
rebouter (rəbute), v.a. [f. *bout*] To set (bones).
rebouteu-r, -se, rebouteu-x, -se (rəbutœr, rəbutø), s.m.f. Bone-setter.
reboutonner (rəbutɔne), v.a. To re-button; **se** ~, v.pr. to button up one's clothes again; (fig. colloq.) to become cautious and reticent again, to retire into one's shell.
rebroder (rəbrɔde), v.a. To embroider (an already ornate material).
rebroussement (rəbrusmɑ̃), s.m. Turning back, stroking backwards; (geom.) inflection, retrogression (of a curve).
rebrousser (rəbruse), v.a. To turn back, to stroke backwards, to turn up (hair); ~ *chemin*, to retrace one's steps; *à rebrousse poil*, against the hair, against the nap; (fig.) against the grain, the wrong way.
rebuffade (rəbyfad), s.f. [It. *ribuffo*] Rebuff, rebuke, set-down; *essuyer des* ~*s*, to meet with a rebuff; to catch it, to be rebuked.
rébus (rebys), s.m. [f. L *res, rebus*] Rebus; (fig.) riddle, enigma, puzzle.
rebut (rəby), s.m. [f. *rebuter*] **1.** (rare) Rebuke; *essuyer des* ~*s*, to meet with a rebuff; **2.** refuse, rubbish, waste; *mettre au* ~, to throw aside (as waste); *lettre tombée au* ~, letter sent to the dead-letter office; *le* ~ *du genre humain*, the scum of the earth; *marchandises de* ~, rubbishy goods.
rebutant, -e (rəbytɑ̃), p. adj. Repulsive, disgusting; tedious, discouraging, disheartening.
rebuter (rəbyte), v.a. [*re*+*buter*] To repel, to rebuke; to dishearten; to disgust, to shock; *il me rebute toujours*, he is always rebuking me; *ses manières vous rebutent*, his manners are disgusting; **se** ~, v.pr. *il se rebute facilement*, he is easily discouraged. ⚠ Engl. 'to rebut' = *repousser, réfuter*.
recacheter (rəkaʃte), v.a. To seal again.
récalcitrant, -e (rekalsitrɑ̃), p. adj. Refractory, recalcitrant, rebellious, obstinate, resisting.
récalcitrer (rekalsitre), v.n. [f. L *calx, calcis*] To resist, to recalcitrate, to be recalcitrant.
recaler (rəkale), v.a. [*re*+*caler*] **1.** To wedge again; **2.** (colloq.) to pluck (in an examination); *il s'est encore fait* ~, he managed to get plucked (or ploughed) again.
récapitulati-f, -ve (rekapitylatif), adj. Recapitulatory.
récapitulation (rekapityla'sjɔ̃), s.f. Recapitulation, summing up.
récapituler (rekapityle), v.a. [f. L *capitulum*] To recapitulate, to sum up.
recarreler (rəkarle), v.a. To pave (a floor) anew.
recasser (rəkɑse), v.a. To break again.
recauser (rəkoze), v.n. To talk again; *nous en recauserons*, we shall speak about that again, let 's discuss that later.
recéder (rəsede), v.a. To cede again, to yield again, to sell (something) one had bought for oneself. ⚠ Not 'to recede', which = *reculer*.

recel, recèlement (rəsɛl, rəsɛlmɑ̃), s.m. Receiving stolen goods.

recéler (rəsele), v.a. [*re+celer*] To receive (stolen goods); to conceal; to contain hidden; to keep in safety; ~ *des marchandises*, to receive stolen goods; *la terre recèle des trésors*, the earth contains hidden treasures.

receleu-r, -se (rəselœr), s.m.f. Receiver (of stolen goods).

récemment (resamɑ̃), adv. [f. *récent*] Lately, recently; freshly, newly.

recensement (rəsɑ̃smɑ̃), s.m. Census, statistical return.

recenser (rəsɑ̃se), v.a. [f. L *re+censere*] To take the census of; to check off; to count (votes).

recenseur (rəsɑ̃sœr), s.m. Official who takes the census.

recension (rəsɑ̃sjɔ̃), s.f. Recension, collation (of texts, &c.).

récent, -e (resɑ̃), adj. [L *recens*] Recent, fresh, late, new.

recépage (rəsepaʒ), s.m. Cutting down (of vines, &c.) close to the ground.

recéper (rəsepe), v.a. [f. *cep*] To cut down close to the ground.

récépissé (resepise), s.m. [L wd] Receipt, acknowledgement.

réceptacle (resɛptakl), s.m. [f. L *receptum*] Receptacle; (bot.) thalamus.

récepteur (resɛptœr), s.m. Receiver, receiving instrument.

récepti-f, -ve (resɛptif), adj. Receptive.

réception (resɛpsjɔ̃), s.f. [L *receptio*] Reception; receiving, taking over, admission; welcoming; party, entertainment, levee; *accuser* ~ *de*, to acknowledge receipt of; *poste de* ~ (*T.S.F.*), (wireless) receiving station (or set).

réceptionnaire (resɛpsjɔnɛr), s.m.f. adj. Receiver, reception (clerk).

réceptionner (resɛpsjɔne), v.a. (comm. neol.) To receive and verify (goods); to take over; to check.

réceptivité (resɛptivite), s.f. Receptivity.

réceptrice (resɛptris), adj. f. Receiving (machine).

recerclage (rəsɛrklaʒ), s.m. Re-hooping.

recercler (rəsɛrkle), v.a. To put new hoops on.

recette (rəsɛt), s.f. [L *recepta*] **1.** Receipt, return, takings; *faire* ~, to give good returns; *la pièce ne fait pas* ~, the play is not a box-office success; **2.** (med., cook.) recipe; **3.** collector's office; receivership; *garçon de* ~, collector.

recevabilité (rəsəvabilite), s.f. Receivability, receivableness.

recevable (rəsəvabl), adj. Receivable.

receveu-r, -se (rəsəvœr), s.m.f. Receiver; money-taker; collector; postmaster; (tram-car) conductor; ~ *des contributions*, tax-collector.

recevoir (rəsəvwar), v.a. [L *recipere*] To receive, to admit, to take, to take in, to accept; to welcome; to meet with; ~, v.n. to entertain; to be at home; *ils reçoivent beaucoup*, they entertain a good deal; *recevrez-vous demain?*, will you be at home to-morrow?; ~ *un cadeau*, to receive a present; ~ *un mauvais accueil*, to meet with a bad reception; ~ *les excuses de X*, to accept X's apologies; *se faire* ~ *avocat*, to be called to the bar; (comm.) *reçu votre lettre du 20 courant*, your letter of the 20th to hand.

réchampir (reʃɑ̃pir), v.a. (paint.) To pick out (with another colour); to set off.

rechange (rəʃɑ̃ʒ), s.m. Change; *objet de* ~, spare part; *roue de* ~, spare wheel; change (*de*, of).

rechanger (rəʃɑ̃ʒe), v.a. To change again.

rechanter (rəʃɑ̃te), v.a. To sing again; to repeat.

réchapper (reʃape), v.n. To escape scot free (from a danger); to recover (from an illness); *un réchappé de la potence*, a gallows-bird.

rechargement (rəʃarʒəmɑ̃), s.m. Reloading, re-lading, re-shipment; remetalling (of roads).

recharger (rəʃarʒe), v.a. **1.** To re-load, to re-last; to re-ship; **2.** to re-load (fire-arms); **3.** to re-metal (roads); **4.** to charge (the enemy) again.

réchaud (reʃo), s.m. Dish-warmer; chafing-dish; methylated-spirit stove, spirit-lamp; small charcoal stove.

réchauffage (reʃofaʒ), s.m. Warming up again.

réchauffé (reʃofe), s.m. Food which has been warmed up again; (fig.) stale stuff; *c'est du* ~*!*, that's an old tale!, Queen Anne 's dead!, that 's stale news!

réchauffement (reʃofmɑ̃), s.m. Warming up; (hort.) lining a hotbed anew.

réchauffer (reʃofe), v.a. [*re+chauffer*] To warm up again; to stir up, to rekindle, to revive (enthusiasm, courage, &c.); (hort.) to line (a hotbed) anew; ~ *un serpent dans son sein*, to nurse a viper in one's bosom; **se** ~, v.pr. to get warm again.

réchauffoir (reʃofwar), s.m. Warmer; dish-warmer.

rechausser (rəʃose), v.a. To put shoes or stockings on (a person) again; (agric.) to bank up; **se** ~, v.pr. to put one's shoes on again.

rèche (rɛʃ), adj. [orig. dub.] Rough, harsh.

recherche (rəʃɛrʃ), s.f. Research, investigation; search, quest, pursuit, inquiry, examination; suit, courtship; studied elegance, refinement; affectation; *faire des* ~*s*, to undertake researches, to carry out investigations; *aller à la* ~ *de*, to go in quest of; to search for; *s'habiller* *avec* ~, to dress with studied elegance; ~ (*en mariage*), suit.

recherché, -e (rəʃɛrʃe), adj. Refined, choice, fastidious, exquisite; much sought after; *une expression trop ~e,* a far-fetched or affected expression.

rechercher (rəʃɛrʃe), v.a. [*re+chercher*] To seek again, to look for again; to research into; to make the subject of research; to seek after, to search for; to inquire after; to woo, to court, to solicit in marriage; ~ *l'amitié de X,* to wish for X's friendship; *tout le monde la recherche,* she is very much sought after.

rechigné, -e (rəʃiɲe) p. adj. Cross, surly, sullen, grim; *visage* ~, cross-looking face; *d'un ton* ~, crossly.

rechigner (rəʃiɲe), v.n. [f. OGerm. *kinan*] To turn restive, to look surly, to sulk, to be cross; *en rechignant,* with a bad grace; crossly.

rechute (rəʃyt), s.f. Relapse; fresh fall; *avoir une* ~, to have a relapse.

rechuter (rəʃyte), v.n. To have a relapse, to relapse.

récidive (residiv), s.f. [f. L *recidivus*] Repetition of the offence; relapse into crime; relapse (of an illness).

récidiver (residive), v.n. To repeat the offence, to offend again, to relapse.

récidiviste (residivist), s.m.f. Relapser, old offender, recidivist.

récidivité (residivite), s.f. Propensity to relapse.

récif (resif), s.m. [f. Span. *arrecife*] Reef (of rocks).

récipé (resipe), s.m. (obs.) [f. L *recipe*] Recipe; medical prescription.

récipiendaire (resipjɑ̃dɛr), s.m.f. [f. L *recipiendus*] New member, member elect; recipiendary.

récipient (resipjɑ̃), s.m. [f. L *recipiens*] Receptacle, receiver, vessel; cistern. ⚠ Not 'recipient', which nowadays = (*a*) *personne qui reçoit quelque chose;* (*b*) *angle rentrant.*

réciprocité (resiprɔsite), s.f. Reciprocity, reciprocation.

réciproque (resiprɔk), adj. [L *reciprocus*] Reciprocal, mutual; (math.) reciprocal; inverse; *raison* ~, inverse ratio. ~, s.f. (log.) Converse, reciprocal proposition; (colloq.) the opposite, return; *rendre la* ~, to give tit for tat, a Roland for an Oliver, to return the like.

réciproquement (resiprɔkmɑ̃), adv. Reciprocally, mutually, vice-versa; (math.) conversely.

récit (resi), s.m. [f. *réciter*] Tale; recital, report, account, narration, relation; *faites-moi le ~ de ce qui s'est passé,* give me an account of what happened; (mus.) recitative.

récital (pl. **-s**) (resital), s.m. [Engl. wd] Recital.

récitant, -e (resitɑ̃), p. adj. (mus.) Solo. ~, s.m.f. Reciter; soloist.

récitateur (resitatœr), s.m. Reciter.

récitatif (resitatif), s.m. (mus.) Recitative.

récitation (resita'sjɔ̃), s.f. Recitation, reciting, recital.

réciter (resite), v.a. [L *recitare*] To recite, to repeat (lessons), to tell, to relate.

réclamant, -e (reklamɑ̃), s.m.f. Claimant.

réclamation (reklama'sjɔ̃), s.f. Claim, complaint, demand, protest; *faire une* ~, to put in a claim, to lodge a complaint.

réclame (reklam), s.f. Advertisement, advertising, puff, publicity; *faire de la* ~, to advertise largely, to puff; (print.) catchword; ~, s.m. (hawking) bird call.

réclamer (reklame), v.a.n. [L *reclamare*] To claim, to demand, to require; to complain, to protest (*contre,* against); to object (to); **se ~ *de,*** v.pr. to refer to, to make use of the name of; *réclamez-vous de moi,* make use of my name.

reclouer (rəklue), v.a. To nail again.

reclure (rəklyr), v.a. def. (used only in the infinitive and comp. tenses) [L *recludere*] To shut up, to confine; **se ~,** v.pr. to confine oneself.

reclus, -e (rəkly), p. adj. Shut up, sequestered, secluded. ~, s.m.f. Recluse.

réclusion (reklyzjɔ̃), s.f. Reclusion, seclusion, confinement; (law) solitary imprisonment.

recogniti-f, -ve (rəkɔɲitif), adj. (law) Recognitory.

recognition (rəkɔɲisjɔ̃), s.f. [L *recognitio*] Recognition.

recoiffer (rəkwafe), v.a. To dress (the head or hair) again; to cap (a bottle, &c.); **se ~,** v.pr. to dress one's hair again.

recoin (rəkwɛ̃), s.m. [*re+coin*] Corner; (fig.) innermost recess.

récolement (rekɔlmɑ̃), s.m. **1.** Verification; **2.** (law) re-examination (of witnesses).

récoler (rekɔle), v.a. [L *recolere*] **1.** To verify; **2.** to read his previous evidence to (a witness).

recollage (rəkɔlaʒ), s.m. Pasting or gluing again.

récollection (rekɔlɛksjɔ̃), s.f. (rare) Contemplation. ⚠ Not Engl. 'recollection', which = *souvenir, acte de se souvenir.*

recollement (rəkɔlmɑ̃), s.m. See RECOLLAGE.

recoller (rəkɔle), v.a. [*re+coller*] To paste again, to glue again, to mend; **se ~,** v.pr. to join up (of the edges of a wound, &c.).

récollet, -te (rekɔlɛ), s.m.f. [f. L *recollectus*] Recollect (monk or nun).

recoloration (rəkɔlɔra'sjɔ̃), s.f. Reviving the colour.

recolorer (rəkɔlɔre), v.a. To revive the colour of.

récolte (rekɔlt), s.f. [It. *ricolta*] Harvest, crop, gathering; (fig.) harvest, collection; *~s sur pied*, standing crops; *faire rentrer la ~*, to get in the harvest.

récolter (rekɔlte), v.a. To get in, to reap; to harvest, to gather in; to receive.

recommandable (rəkɔmɑ̃dabl), adj. Commendable, worthy of commendation; respectable.

recommandation (rəkɔmɑ̃da'sjɔ̃), s.f. Recommendation, introduction; reference; injunction, advice, order; (post-office) registration.

recommander (rəkɔmɑ̃de), v.a. [*re+commander*] To recommend, to introduce, to commend; to enjoin, to order, to request, to exhort, to beg, to advise; to register; *lettre recommandée*, registered letter; **se ~**, v.pr. to implore the help or protection (*à*, of); *se ~ de X*, to make use of X's name; to give X's name as reference.

recommencement (rəkɔmɑ̃smɑ̃), s.m. Recommencement, beginning anew.

recommencer (rəkɔmɑ̃se), v.a.n. To recommence, to begin or start again; *c'est toujours à ~*, there 's no end to it; *~ sur nouveaux frais*, to begin all over again.

récompense (rekɔ̃pɑ̃s), s.f. Reward; recompense, compensation; *en ~ de*, in return for; *recevoir une juste ~*, to be justly rewarded.

récompenser (rekɔ̃pɑ̃se), v.a. [*re+compenser*] To reward, to repay, to recompense; to compensate; *~ X selon son mérite*, to reward X according to his deserts; *~ les services de X*, to reward X for his services.

recomposer (rəkɔ̃poze), v.a. To recompose.

recomposition (rəkɔ̃pɔzisjɔ̃), s.f. Recomposition.

recompter (rəkɔ̃te), v.a. To count again.

réconciliable (rekɔ̃siljabl), adj. Reconcilable.

réconciliat-eur, -rice (rekɔ̃siljatœr), s.m.f. Reconciler.

réconciliation (rekɔ̃silja'sjɔ̃), s.f. Reconciliation; reconcilement; making it up; (theol.) atonement, expiation.

réconcilier (rekɔ̃silje), v.a. [L *reconciliare*] To reconcile (*avec*, to, with); *~ deux amis*, to reconcile two friends; *je l'ai réconcilié avec X*, I have reconciled him with (or to) X; **se ~**, v.pr. to be reconciled; to make it up; to kiss and be friends; to heal the breach. ⚠ *Réconcilier* is said of persons only, while 'to reconcile' applies also to ideas, notions, statements, &c.

reconduction (rəkɔ̃dyksjɔ̃), s.f. (law) Renewal of a lease.

reconduire (rəkɔ̃dɥir), v.a. [*re+conduire*] To take back; to see home; to accompany to the door; to show out; to drive back, to drive out.

réconfort (rekɔ̃fɔr), s.m. Comfort, relief, help, consolation; *apporter un grand ~ à X*, to comfort X greatly.

réconfortant, -e (rekɔ̃fɔrtɑ̃), p. adj. Comforting, relieving, consolatory, reviving.

réconfortation (rekɔ̃fɔrta'sjɔ̃), s.f. Consolation; cheering up.

réconforter (rekɔ̃fɔrte), v.a. [*re+conforter*] To comfort, to help, to relieve, to console, to revive, to fortify, to cheer up.

reconnaissable (rəkɔnɛsabl), adj. Recognizable.

reconnaissance (rəkɔnɛsɑ̃s), s.f. [f. *reconnaître*] Recognition; gratitude, thankfulness; acknowledgement; (mil.) reconnoitring, reconnaissance; *témoigner sa ~*, to show one's gratitude; *manquer de ~*, to be ungrateful; *en ~ de vos services*, in recognition of your services; (mil.) *faire une ~*, to go out reconnoitring, to make a reconnaissance; *~ du mont de piété*, pawn-ticket.

reconnaissant, -e (rəkɔnɛsɑ̃), p. adj. Grateful, thankful.

reconnaître (rəkɔnɛtr), v.a. [*re+connaître*] To recognize, to know, to identify; to find out; to acknowledge; to admit, to be grateful, to make return for; (mil.) to reconnoitre; *vous devez ~ que*, you must acknowledge that, or admit that; *son innocence a été reconnue*, his innocence has been recognized; *se faire ~*, to make oneself known; *je vous reconnais bien là*, that 's just like you; **se ~**, v.pr. to know oneself, to know each other; to be recognized; *je ne m'y reconnais plus*, I don't know what I am about; I am at sea; *se ~ coupable*, to admit one's guilt; *donnez-moi le temps de me ~*, give me time to take my bearings.

reconquérir (rəkɔ̃kerir), v.a. To reconquer, to recover, to regain, to win again.

reconstituant, -e (rəkɔ̃stitɥɑ̃), p. adj. Tonic, bracing, invigorating. **~**, s.m. Tonic.

reconstituer (rəkɔ̃stitɥe), v.a. To reconstitute, to re-create, to restore, to re-establish, to reconstruct.

reconstitution (rəkɔ̃stitysjɔ̃), s.f. Reconstitution, reconstruction, restoration, reorganization.

reconstruction (rəkɔ̃stryksjɔ̃), s.f. Reconstruction, rebuilding.

reconstruire (rəkɔ̃strɥir), v.a. To reconstruct, to rebuild.

reconvention (rəkɔ̃vɑ̃sjɔ̃), s.f. (law) Cross-action.

reconventionnel, -le (rəkɔ̃vɑ̃sjɔnɛl), adj. (law) Cross.

recopier (rəkɔpje), v.a. To copy over again, to make a duplicate of, to re-copy.

recoquiller (rəkɔkije), v.a. To turn up, to dog's-ear (pages); **se ~**, v.pr. to curl up, to shrivel, to cockle.

record (rəkɔr), s.m. [Engl. wd] Record; *détenir un ~*, to hold a record; *battre le ~*, to break the record. ⚠ In French *record* has never the sense of report, piece of recorded evidence, gramophone record, &c.; it is only used in the sense of best performance (in sports, &c.).

recorder[1] (rəkɔrde), v.a. (obs.) [L *recordare*] To recall (*à*, to); to remind of (something).

recorder[2] (rəkɔrde), v.a. [*re+corder*] To tie up again, to cord again. ⚠ Not 'to record', which = *conserver par écrit, relater*.

recors (rəkɔr), s.m. [f. *recorder*] Bailiff's man, bumbailiff.

recoucher (rəkuʃe), v.a. To put to bed again; to lay down again; **se ~**, v.pr. to go to bed again, to lie down again.

recoudre (rəkudr), v.a. To sew up again, to sew again; (fig.) to mend; to gather, to join up.

recoupe (rəkup), s.f. **1.** Coarse flour, seconds; **2.** stone chips; **3.** shreds (of cloth, &c.), clippings.

recoupement (rəkupmɑ̃), s.m. **1.** (build.) Set-off; **2.** verification, test (by comparison of information from different sources), cross-examination. ⚠ *Recoupement* cannot be translated by 'recoupment', which means recompensing, being recouped for loss or expense = *compensation*.

recouper (rəkupe), v.a. To cut again; to blend (wines); (at cards) to cut again. ⚠ Not 'to recoup'. See RECOUPEMENT.

recoupette (rəkupɛt), s.f. Sharps (coarse flour).

recourber (rəkurbe), v.a. To bend, to bend round, to bend back; **se ~**, v.pr. to be curved, to bend, to curl.

recourir (rəkurir), v.n. [f. *recours*] **1.** To run again, to race again; **2.** to have recourse (*à*, to); to turn (to).

recours (rəkur), s.m. [L *recursus*] Recourse; resource, refuge; (law) appeal; *avoir ~ à*, to have recourse to, to turn to; *~ en grâce*, recommendation to mercy.

recouvrable (rəkuvrabl), adj. Recoverable.

recouvrage (rəkuvraʒ), s.m. Covering again; re-covering; changing the cover of.

recouvrance (rəkuvrɑ̃s), s.f. (obs.) Recovery.

recouvrement (rəkuvrəmɑ̃), s.m. **1.** Covering again, re-covering; **2.** overlapping; **3.** recovery; recovery of debts; *~ des impôts*, collection of taxes; *~s*, debts collected.

recouvrer (rəkuvre), v.a. [L *recuperare*] To recover, to collect, to regain.

recouvrir (rəkuvrir), v.a. To re-cover, to cover over, to hide, to conceal; to overlap.

recracher (rəkraʃe), v.a.n. To spit out again.

récréance (rekreɑ̃s), s.f. [f. OF *recroire = rendre*] Provisional possession; *lettres de ~*, letters of recall.

récréati-f, -ve (rekreatif) adj. Recreative, amusing.

récréation (rekreasjɔ̃), s.f. [L *recreatio*] Recreation, amusement; pastime; playtime, play-hours.

recréer (rəkree), v.a. [*re+créer*] To recreate, to create anew.

récréer (rekree), v.a. [L *recreare*] To amuse, to divert; **se ~**, v.pr. to amuse oneself.

récrément (rekremɑ̃), s.m. [L *recrementum*] (physiol.) Recrement.

récrémenteu-x, -se (rekremɑ̃tø), adj. Recremental.

recrépissage (rəkrepisaʒ), s.m. Replastering, second pargeting.

recrépir (rəkrepir), v.a. [*re+crépir*] To re-plaster, to parget anew; (colloq.) *~ son visage*, to paint one's face; (fig.) to patch up, to dress up (an old story, &c.).

recreuser (rəkrøze), v.a. To dig up again, to hollow out deeper.

(se) récrier (sərekrije), v.pr. To cry out (*contre*, against; *sur*, upon), to exclaim; to cry up, to extol; to cry down, to disparage; to cry shame upon; *dès qu'il ouvre la bouche, tout le monde se récrie d'admiration*, as soon as he opens his mouth everybody cries out with admiration.

récrimination (rekrimina'sjɔ̃), s.f. Recrimination, reproach.

récriminatoire (rekriminatwar), adj. Recriminatory.

récriminer (rekrimine), v.n. [f. *re*+(L) *crimen*] To recriminate.

récrire (rekrir), v.a. [*re+écrire*] To write again, to rewrite.

recroiser (rəkrwaze), v.a. [*re+croiser*] To cross again, to overlap again.

recroquevillé, -e (rəkrɔkvije), p. adj. Shrivelled up.

(se) recroqueviller (sərəkrɔkvije), v.pr. To shrivel up, to curl up.

recru, -e (rəkry), p. adj. [f. OF *se recroire*] Knocked up, jaded, tired out.

recrû (rəkry), s.m. [f. *recroître*] Growth of the year, new shoots.

recrudescence (rəkrydɛssɑ̃s), s.f. [f. L *recrudescere*] Recrudescence.

recrudescent, -e (rəkrydɛssɑ̃), adj. Recrudescent.

recrue (rəkry), s.f. [f. *recroître*] **1.** Recruiting; **2.** recruit.

recrutement (rəkrytmɑ̃), s.m. Recruiting, recruitment.

recruter (rəkryte), v.a. To recruit, to enlist; to enrol; **se ~**, v.pr. to be recruited, to be enlisted.

recruteur (rəkrytœr), s.m. Recruiter, recruiting officer.
recta (rɛkta), adv. [L wd] Exactly, punctually.
rectal, -e, (aux), (rɛktal), adj. (anat.) Rectal.
rectangle (rɛktɑ̃gl), adj. [f. L *rectus*+ (Fr.) *angle*] Rectangular, right-angled; *triangle* ~, right-angled triangle. ~, s.m. Rectangle.
rectangulaire (rɛktɑ̃gylɛr), adj. Rectangular.
recteur (rɛktœr), s.m. [L *rector*] Rector, Head (of university); (in Brittany ~ = *curé*, Catholic priest).
rect-eur, -rice (rɛktœr), adj. [L *rector, rectrix*] Directing. **~rices,** s.f.pl. (ornith.) Tail feathers.
rectifiable (rɛktifjabl), adj. Rectifiable.
rectificateur (rɛktifikatœr), s.m. (chem.) Rectifier.
rectificati-f, -ve (rɛktifikatif), adj. Rectifying.
rectification (rɛktifika'sjɔ̃), s.f. [L *rectificatio*] Rectification.
rectifier (rɛktifje), v.a. [f. L *rectus*+ *facere*] To rectify; to correct, to redress, to straighten; to refine, to purify.
rectiligne (rɛktiliɲ), adj. Rectilinear.
rectitude (rɛktityd), s.f. [L *rectitudo*] Rectitude, integrity, uprightness.
recto (rɛkto), s.m. [L wd] Recto, right-hand page of open book, front of leaf.
rectoral, -e, (aux) (rɛktoral), adj. Rectorial.
rectorat (rɛktora), s.m. Rectorship, rectorate.
rectum (rɛktɔm), s.m. [L wd] (anat.) Rectum.
reçu (rəsy), s.m. [f. *recevoir*] Receipt, written acknowledgement; *au ~ de votre lettre*, on receipt of your letter. ~, -e, p. adj. Usual, customary, accepted; *les usages ~s*, the approved manner, the good old customs.
recueil (rəkœj), s.m. [f. *recueillir*] Collection, miscellany.
recueillement (rəkœjmɑ̃), s.m. **1.** Silent reflection, devout silence, composure, concentration of thought, collectedness; **2.** (rare) gathering, collecting.
recueilli, -e (rəkœji), p. adj. Concentrated, devout, silent, collected.
recueillir (rəkœjir), v.a. [L *recolligere*] To gather, to collect; to reap, to receive; to shelter, to harbour; to inherit; **se** ~, v.pr. to concentrate one's thoughts, to meditate devoutly.
recuire (rəkɥir), v.a. To bake again; to anneal, to re-heat (glass, metals, &c.).
recuit (rəkɥi), s.m. **recuite** (rəkɥit), s.f. Re-heating, annealing.
recul (rəkyl), s.m. [f. *reculer*] Recoil; backing, backward movement; (of fire-arms) kick, recoil, drawing back; space or time necessary for judging rightly an object, a picture, an action.
reculade (rəkylad), s.f. Backing, falling back; (fig.) retreat, climb down; *une honteuse ~*, a shameful retreat, or climb-down; *faire une ~*, to beat a retreat, to turn tail.
reculé, -e (rəkyle), p. adj. Distant, remote.
reculée (rəkyle), s.f. Space for moving back; *feu de ~*, roasting fire.
reculement (rəkylmɑ̃), s.m. Backing, drawing back; (harness) breeching, breech-band.
reculer (rəkyle), v.a.n. [f. *cul*] To draw back, to back, to move back, to go backwards; to put off, to delay, to postpone; to fall back, to back out, to retreat, to recoil, to shrink, to flinch; (of fire-arms) to recoil, to kick; *~ sa chaise*, to draw one's chair back; *ne ~ devant rien*, to stick at nothing; *il n'est plus temps de ~*, there is no going back now; (fig.) *~ pour mieux sauter*, (*a*) to avoid a small evil only to fall into a greater; (*b*) to go back in order to take a better leap.
(à) reculons (arəkylɔ̃), adv. loc. Backwards; *entrer à ~ dans*, to back into.
récupérable (rekyperabl), adj. Recoverable, retrievable.
récupération (rekypera'sjɔ̃), s.f. Recuperation, recovery.
récupérer (rekypere), v.a. [L *recuperare*] To recover, to retrieve; ⚠ rarely 'to recuperate', v.n.a., which = *guérir, se rétablir, retrouver* (*ses forces, son argent*); **se** ~, v.pr. to recoup oneself; *se ~ de ses pertes*, v.pr. to retrieve one's losses.
récurage (rekyraʒ), s.m. Scouring, scrubbing.
récurer (rekyre), v.a. [*re*+*écurer*] To scour, to scrub.
récurrence (rekyrɑ̃s), s.f. [f. L *re*+ *currere*] Recurrence.
récurrent, -e (rekyrɑ̃), adj. Recurrent.
récursoire (rekyrswar), adj. (law) That can give rise to an appeal.
récusable (rekyzabl), adj. Exceptionable, challengeable.
récusation (rekyza'sjɔ̃), s.f. (law) Challenge (of judges, jurors, &c.); exception.
récuser (rekyze), v.a. [L *recusare*] (law) To challenge; to take exception to; not to admit; **se** ~, v.pr. to excuse oneself, to decline (to judge, pronounce, &c.).
rédact-eur, -rice (redaktœr), s.m.f. [f. L *redactus*] Writer, author, editor; clerk; contributor; *~ en chef*, (chief) editor; *~ gérant*, sub-editor.
rédaction (redaksjɔ̃), s.f. [f. L *redactus*] Drawing up (of a deed, &c.); wording, writing; editing (newspapers); the editors, editorial staff.
redan, redent (rədɑ̃), s.m. (fort.) Redan; (arch.) skewback.

reddition (rɛddisjɔ̃), s.f. [L *redditio*] Surrender; ~ *d'une ville*, surrender of a town; ~ *de comptes*, rendering of accounts.
redéfaire (rədefɛr), v.a. To undo again.
redemander (rədəmɑ̃de), v.a. To ask . . . back again, to ask for . . . again, to demand again; to ask for a second helping of.
rédempteur (redɑ̃ptœr), s.m. [f. L *redemptum*] Redeemer, Saviour. ~, **rédemptrice**, adj. Redeeming, redemptory, redemptive.
rédemption (redɑ̃psjɔ̃), s.f. [L *redemptio*] Redemption.
rédemptoriste (redɑ̃ptɔrist), s.m. Redemptorist.
redent (rədɑ̃), s.m. See REDAN.
redescendre (rədɛssɑ̃dr), v.n. To come down again, to take down again.
redevable (rədəvabl), adj. Indebted (*de*, for; *à*, to).
redevance (rədəvɑ̃s), s.f. Rent, quit-rent, dues, royalty.
redevenir (rədəvənir), v.a. To become . . . again.
redevoir (rədəvwar), v.a. To owe still, to be indebted for.
rédhibition (redibisjɔ̃), s.f. [f. L *redhibitum*] (law) Redhibition.
rédhibitoire (redibitwar), adj. Redhibitory; that annuls the transaction.
rédiger (rediʒe), v.a. [L *redigere*] To draw up, to write out, to word, to indite, to write; to edit (a newspaper).
rédimer (redime), v.a. [L *redimere*] To redeem; **se** ~, v.pr. to redeem oneself; to buy oneself off.
redingote (rədɛ̃gɔt), s.f. [f. Engl. *riding-coat*] Frock coat.
redire (rədir), v.a. To tell again, to say again, to repeat; *trouver à* ~ *à tout*, to find fault with everything; *il n'y a rien à* ~ *à cela*, there is nothing amiss in that.
redite (rədit), s.f. Repetition, tautology.
redondance (rədɔ̃dɑ̃s), s.f. Redundancy, redundance, bombast.
redondant, -e (rədɔ̃dɑ̃), p. adj. [L *redundans*] Redundant, bombastic.
redonder (rədɔ̃de), v.n. [L *redundare*] To be redundant, to superabound.
redonner (rədɔne), v.a.n. To give back again, to restore; ~ *dans*, to deal (cards) again; to fall into . . . again.
redorer (redɔre), v.a. To regild.
redormir (rədɔrmir), v.n. To sleep again, to go to sleep again.
redoublé, -e (rəduble), p. adj. Redoubled, accelerated, intensified; (mil.) *au pas* ~, at double-quick pace, at the double; *frapper à coups* ~*s*, to beat unmercifully.
redoublement (rədubləmɑ̃), s.m. Redoubling; increase; intensification, repetition; reduplication; paroxysm.
redoubler (rəduble), v.a.n. **1.** To redouble, to increase; ~ *d'efforts*, to come on with redoubled force; to redouble one's efforts; ~ *de soins*, to be doubly attentive; *la tempête redouble*, the storm is increasing; **2.** to line anew; to new-line.
redoul (rədul), s.m. (bot.) Tanner's sumach, coriaria.
redoutable (rədutabl), adj. Formidable, terrible, redoubtable, dreadful, forbidding.
redoute (rədut), s.f. [It. *ridotto*] (fort.) **1.** Redoubt, ridotto; **2.** party, dancing-party, dancing-establishment.
redouter (rədute), v.a. [*rɛ*+*douter*] To dread, to fear; *vous n'avez rien à* ~, you have nothing to fear; you have nothing to be afraid of.
redowa (redɔva), s.f. [f. Czech wd] Redowa (dance).
redresse (rədrɛs), s.f. (naut.) Righting tackle; (slang) *un type à la* ~, a cute fellow, a fellow quite up to snuff; one not to be trifled with.
redressement, redressage (rədrɛsmɑ̃, rədrɛsaʒ), s.m. Straightening; righting; (fig.) redressing, redress, righting.
redresser (rədrɛse), v.a. [*re*+*dresser*] To straighten, to make straight again; to right (a ship); (fig.) to redress, to reform, to put right; (fam.) to set to rights; **se** ~, v.pr. to become straight again, to stand erect; to hold up one's head; (of a ship) to right herself.
redresseur (rədrɛsœr), s.m. Redresser, righter; ~ *de torts*, redresser of wrongs, regular Don Quixote.
redû (rədy), s.m. [f. *redevoir*] Balance due.
réduct-eur, -rice (redyktœr), adj. Reducing. ~, s.m. (chem.) Reducer.
réductibilité (redyktibilite), s.f. Reducibleness.
réductible (redyktibl), adj. Reducible.
réduction (redyksjɔ̃), s.f. [L *reductio*] Reduction, reducing; conversion; (arith.) reduction; (surg.) reduction; diminution, abatement; subjugation, conquest; *échelle de* ~, reducing scale, scale of reduction; (log.) ~ *à l'absurde*, reductio ad absurdum.
réduire (redɥir), v.a. [f. L *reducere*] To reduce, to diminish, to abate, to curtail, to bring down; to transform, to condense; to boil down; to subjugate, to drive, to compel; (surg.) to reduce; ~ *en poudre, en cendres*, to reduce to dust, to ashes; ~ *ses dépenses*, to reduce, to curtail, one's expenses; ~ *les rebelles*, to subdue the rebels; ~ *X au silence*, to silence X; ~ *X au désespoir*, to drive X to despair; ~ *au même dénominateur*, to reduce to a common denominator; **se** ~, v.pr. to be reduced, to reduce oneself; to reduce one's expenditure; to diminish, to dwindle, to consume away; to amount; *tout cela se réduit à peu de chose*, all this amounts to very little.
réduit (redɥi), s.m. Little nook, hole;

hovel; corner, poor lodging; sty; (fort.) reduit.
réduplicati-f, -ve (redyplikatif), adj. Reduplicative.
réduplication (redyplika'sjɔ̃), s.f. Reduplication.
réédification (reedifika'sjɔ̃), s.f. Rebuilding.
réédifier (reedifje), v.a. To rebuild.
rééditer (reedite), v.a. To republish, to reissue.
réédition (reedisjɔ̃), s.f. New edition, republishing, reissuing.
rééducation (reedyka'sjɔ̃), s.f. Re-education, training anew.
réel, -le (reɛl), adj. [L *realis*] Real, actual; (law) relating to things, not to persons; in esse. ~, s.m. Reality, the real.
réélection (reelɛksjɔ̃), s.f. Re-election.
rééligible (reeliʒibl), adj. Re-eligible.
réélire (reelir), v.a. To re-elect.
réellement (reɛlmɑ̃), adv. Really, actually, in reality, truly; in fact.
réengagement (reɑ̃gaʒmɑ̃), s.m., **réengager** (reɑ̃gaʒe), v.a. See RENGAGEMENT, RENGAGER.
réensemencement (reɑ̃smɑ̃smɑ̃), s.m. Resowing.
réensemencer (reɑ̃smɑ̃se), v.a. To resow, to sow again.
réer (ree), v.n. See RAIRE.
réescompte (reɛskɔ̃t), s.m. Rediscount.
réescompter (reɛskɔ̃te), v.a. To rediscount.
réexpédier (reɛkspedje), v.a. To send on, to forward; to send back.
réexpédition (reɛkspedisjɔ̃), s.f. Forwarding, sending on; sending back.
réexportation (reɛkspɔrta'sjɔ̃), s.f. Re-exportation, re-export.
réexporter (reɛkspɔrte), v.a. To re-export.
réfaction (refaksjɔ̃), s.f. (comm.) Allowance, rebate.
refaire (rəfɛr), v.a. To do again, to make again, to remake, to do over again; to restore, to renew; (colloq.) to take in, to deceive; **se** ~, v.pr. to recruit one's strength; to pick up; to retrieve one's losses.
refait, -e (rəfɛ), p. adj. (fam.) Taken in, deceived, cheated, done, dished; *j'ai été* ~, I have been done brown. ~, s.m. **1.** New horns (of deer); **2.** drawn game.
réfection (refɛksjɔ̃), s.f. [L *refectio*] **1.** Rebuilding, repairs; **2.** collation, repast.
réfectoire (refɛktwar), s.m. [LL *refectorium*] Refectory, dining-room, dining-hall.
refend (rəfɑ̃), s.m. [f. *refendre*] Splitting, division; *bois de* ~, sawn timber; *mur de* ~, partition wall.
refendre (rəfɑ̃dr), v.a. [*re*+*fendre*] To cleave, to split, to saw lengthwise.
référé (refere), s.m. (law) Plea of urgency; *en* ~, provisionally.
référence (referɑ̃s), s.f. [f. *référer*] **1.** Reference; **2.** ~*s* (pl.), character, references.
référendaire (referɑ̃dɛr), adj. [f. L *referre*] Referendary; *conseiller* ~, referendary.
referendum (referɑ̃dɔm), s.m. [L wd] Referendum.
référer (refere), v.a.n. [f. L *referre*] To refer, to attribute, to ascribe; *en* ~ *à X*, to refer to X; **se** ~, v.pr. *s'en* ~ *à l'avis de X*, to leave the matter to X's decision.
refermer (rəfɛrme), v.a. To shut again, to close again, to reclose; (surg.) to close; **se** ~, v.pr. to close again.
referrer (rəfɛre), v.a. To shoe again, to new-shoe (horses, &c.).
refiler (rəfile), v.a. (slang) To hand over, to pass off; to palm off; *il m'a refilé une pièce fausse*, he palmed off a bad coin on me.
réfléchi, -e (refleʃi), p. adj. Deliberate; reflected; thoughtful; well considered; (gram.) reflexive.
réfléchir (refleʃir), v.a. [L *reflectere*] To reflect, to reflect back, to throw back; to reverberate; ~, v.n. to think, to ponder, to reflect, to consider; *réfléchissez à cela*, think it over; **se** ~, v.pr. to be reflected.
réfléchissant, -e (refleʃisɑ̃), p. adj. Reflecting.
réfléchissement (refleʃismɑ̃), s.m. Reflection (of light, &c.).
réflecteur (reflɛktœr), s.m. Reflector. ~, adj. Reflecting.
reflet (rəflɛ), s.m. [f. L *reflexus*] Reflection; flash; (paint.) reflex; reflected light; ~ *des glaces*, ice-blink; (fig.) reflection, reflex, replica, duplicate, reproduction, secondary manifestation.
refléter (rəflete), v.a. [f. *reflet*] To reflect; **se** ~, v.pr. to be reflected.
refleurir (rəflœrir), v.n. To blossom again, to flower again; (fig.) to flourish again, to re-flourish; *faire* ~, to revive.
refleurissement (rəflœrismɑ̃), s.m. Blossoming again, reflorescence.
réflexe (reflɛks), adj. [L *reflexus*] Reflex. ~, s.m. Reflex.
réflexibilité (reflɛksibilite), s.f. Reflexibility.
réflexible (reflɛksibl), adj. Reflexible.
réflexion (reflɛksjɔ̃), s.f. [L *reflexio*] **1.** Reflection; *angle de* ~, angle of reflection; **2.** thought, consideration; ~ *faite*, on thinking it over; on second thoughts; *faire ses* ~*s*, to consider the matter; to reflect; *plongé* or *abîmé dans de profondes* ~*s*, sunk in deep thought; *cela mérite* ~, that 's worth thinking about.
refluer (rəflɥe), v.n. [L *refluere*] To flow back; to ebb; (fig.) to flow back, to be driven back; *faire* ~, to drive back.

reflux (rəfly), s.m. [f. *refluer*] Reflux, ebb; refluence, flowing back; *le flux et le* ~, the ebb and flow.

refondre (rəfɔ̃dr), v.a. To refound, to recast; to recoin; (fig.) to recast, to remodel, to improve.

refonte (rəfɔ̃t), s.f. Recasting, refounding; recoinage; (fig.) remodelling, remoulding, reform, overhauling.

réformable (refɔrmabl), adj. Reformable, that can be altered.

réformat-eur, -rice (refɔrmatœr), s.m.f. Reformer. ~, adj. Reforming.

réformation (refɔrma'sjɔ̃), s.f. [f. *réformer*] Reform, reformation, amendment.

réforme (refɔrm), s.f. Reform, reformation, amendment; (mil.) invaliding, discharge; putting on half pay; (of horses) selling off; (hist.) Reformation.

réformé, -e (refɔrme), p. adj. Amended, improved; invalided, discharged; reformed; *la religion ~e*, the protestant religion.

reformer (rəfɔrme), v.a. To form again, to re-form; **se** ~, v.pr. to re-form.

réformer (refɔrme), v.a. [L *reformare*] To reform, to amend, to improve; (mil.) to invalid, to discharge, to put on half pay; ~ *les lois*, to reform laws; ~ *sa conduite*, to reform one's life; **se** ~, v.pr. to amend, to turn over a new leaf.

refouillement (rəfujmɑ̃), s.m. Deepening; chiselling.

refoulement (rəfulmɑ̃), s.m. Driving back, forcing back; compression, pressure; repression, inhibition.

refouler (rəfule), v.a. [*re*+*fouler*] To drive back, to force back; to ebb; to repel, to compress; (artill.) to ram (a gun).

refouloir (rəfulwar), s.m. Rammer (for guns).

réfractaire (refraktɛr), adj. [f. L *refractarius*] Refractory (*à*, to); rebellious, obstinate; *argile* ~, fire-clay. ~, s.m. Defaulter.

réfracter (refrakte), v.a. [f. L *refringere*] To refract; **se** ~, v.pr. to be refracted; syn. RÉFRANGER.

réfracteur (refraktœr), s.m. adj. m. Refractor, refracting.

réfracti-f, -ve (refraktif), adj. Refractive.

réfraction (refraksjɔ̃), s.f. [L *refractio*] (phys.) Refraction.

refrain (rəfrɛ̃), s.m. [f. OF *refraindre*, to break] Burden (of a song), refrain; chorus; (by ext.) *toujours le même ~!*, the same old story again!

réfranger (refɑ̃ʒe), v.a. Syn. of RÉFRACTER.

réfrangibilité (refrɑ̃ʒibilite), s.f. Refrangibility.

réfrangible (refrɑ̃ʒibl), adj. Refrangible.

refrapper (rəfrape), v.a.n. To strike again; to knock again; to re-stamp (coin).

refréner (rəfrene), v.a. [L *refrenare*] To curb, to bridle, to master.

réfrigérant, -e (refriʒerɑ̃), p. adj. Cooling, refrigerant, freezing; (fig.) freezing, chilling, distant; *mélange* ~, freezing mixture. ~, s.m. **1.** Refrigerant; **2.** refrigerator.

réfrigération (refriʒera'sjɔ̃), s.f. Refrigeration.

réfrigérer (refriʒere), v.a. [L *refrigerare*] To refrigerate, to cool, to freeze, to congeal; (fig.) to chill, to freeze, to paralyse.

réfringence (refrɛ̃ʒɑ̃s), s.f. (phys.) Refractive power.

réfringent, -e (refrɛ̃ʒɑ̃), adj. [f. L *refringere*] Refracting, refractive.

refrogner (rəfrɔɲe), v.a.n. See RENFROGNER.

refroidir (rəfrwadir), v.a.n. [f. *froid*] To cool, to get cold, to chill; (fig.) to chill, to damp, to discourage; (slang) to murder; ~ *l'enthousiasme de X*, to damp X's enthusiasm; **se** ~, v.pr. to cool, to get cold; to get chilly, to catch cold.

refroidissement (rəfrwadismɑ̃), s.m. **1.** Cooling, refrigeration; *à ~ par eau, par air*, water-cooled (motor or engine), air-cooled (engine); **2.** coolness, estrangement; **3.** chill, cold; *prendre un* ~, to catch a chill.

refuge (rəfyʒ), s.m. [L *refugium*] Refuge, shelter; (fig.) protection, consolation; *chercher* ~, to seek refuge.

réfugié, -e (refyʒje), p. adj. s.m.f. Refugee.

(se) réfugier (sərefyʒje), v.pr. [f. *refuge*] To take shelter, to seek refuge; (fig.) to have recourse.

refuir (rəfɥir), v.n. (hunt.) To double.

refuite (rəfɥit), s.f. (hunt.) Doubling, shift, dodging; (fig.) shift.

refus (rəfy), s.m. Refusal, denial; *essuyer un* ~, to meet with a flat refusal; (colloq. fam.) *ce n'est pas de* ~, I won't say no to that; *je n'accepte pas de* ~, I won't take no for an answer.

refuser (rəfyze), v.a. [f. L *refundere, refusum*] To refuse, to decline to accept, to decline, to deny; ~ *sa porte à X*, to deny X admittance; ~ *une offre*, to decline an offer; ~ *son consentement*, to refuse one's consent; ~ *une invitation*, to decline an invitation; *ce candidat a été refusé*, this candidate failed to satisfy the examiners; this candidate has been plucked; ~ *un candidat*, to plough a candidate; **se** ~, v.pr. to deny oneself, to grudge oneself; *se ~ à faire cela*, to refuse to do that; to object to doing that.

réfutable (refytabl), adj. Refutable.

réfutation (refyta'sjɔ̃), s.f. [L *refutatio*] Refutation.

réfuter (refyte), v.a. [L *refutare*] To refute, to confute.

regagner (rəgaɲe), v.a. To regain, to recover, to win back; to make up for; ~ *son logis*, to go home; ~ *la grande route*, to get back to the high road; ~ *la confiance de X*, to win back X's confidence; ~ *le temps perdu*, to make up for lost time.

regain (rəgɛ̃), s.m. [*re*+*gain*] Aftermath, second crop of grass; (fig.) renewal, revival.

régal (pl. **-s**) (regal), s.m. [It. *regalo*] Feast, treat; *c'est un vrai ~ pour moi de*, it 's a real treat for me to.

régalade (regalad), s.f. Giving a treat, regaling; *boire à la ~*, to pour (wine, &c., from a bottle) down one's throat, without putting the bottle to one's lips.

régalant (regalɑ̃), p. adj. Entertaining, pleasant; *ce n'est pas très ~*, it 's no great fun.

régale (regal), adj. [L *regalis*] Royal; *eau ~*, aquaregia. ~, s.f. Right of French kings to receive revenues of vacant bishoprics; ~, s.m. regal (an organ stop).

régalement (regalmɑ̃), s.m. Levelling (ground).

régaler (regale), v.a. [f. *régal*] To regale, to treat, to entertain; **se ~**, v.pr. give oneself a treat.

régalien, -ne (regaljɛ̃), adj. [f. L *regalis*] Regal, royal; *droits ~s*, regalia.

regard (rəgar), s.m. [f. *regarder*] **1.** Look, glance; notice, attention; *attirer tous les ~s*, to attract everybody's attention; *lancer des ~s furieux*, to cast angry looks; to look as black as thunder; to glare; *suivre du ~*, to follow with one's eyes; *fixer, attacher ses ~s sur X*, to look fixedly at X, to stare at X; *abaisser son ~ sur*, to look down at; *d'un seul ~*, at a glance; *en ~*, opposite, on the opposite page; *au ~ de*, in comparison with; with regard to; **2.** opening, man-hole. ⚠ Not 'regard' in the senses of *considération, estime, compliments*.

regardant, -e (rəgardɑ̃), p. adj. Particular, nice; close-fisted, stingy, niggardly, near, (colloq.) as mean as they make them.

regarder (rəgarde), v.a. [*re*+*garder*] To look at, to glance at, to look on, to gaze at, to see; to face; to mind, to consider; to concern; *cela ne me regarde pas*, that does not concern me; *cela ne vous regarde pas*, that 's not your business; *cette maison regarde le sud*, this house faces south; ~ *X de travers*, to scowl at X; to frown at X; ~ *fixement X*, to stare at X; ~ *d'un bon œil*, to look benevolently upon; ~ *curieusement*, to peer at; *je le regarde comme mon principal ennemi*, I consider him my chief enemy; *vous allez vous faire ~*, you will attract notice; ~, v.n. *il regarde à deux sous*, he looks at every penny he spends; *j'y regarderai à deux fois*, I shall think twice before doing it; *regardez !*, look !; **se ~**, v.pr. **1.** to look at oneself, to examine oneself; **2.** to look at each other; **3.** to front, to face each other.

regarnir (rəgarnir), v.a. To trim again, to furnish again, to stuff again; (cook.) to garnish again; to refill.

régate (regat), s.f. [It. *regatta*] **1.** Regatta; **2.** a kind of necktie.

regazonner (rəgazɔne), v.a. To re-turf.

regel (rəʒɛl), s.m. Renewed frost, freezing again.

regeler (rəʒle), v.a.n. To freeze again.

régence (reʒɑ̃s), s.f. **1.** Regency; **2.** (Fr. hist.) Regency of Philippe d'Orléans, 1715–23; *style ~*, French style of this period, early 18th c.

régénérat-eur, -rice (reʒeneratœr), adj. Regenerating. ~, s.m.f. Regenerator.

régénération (reʒenera'sjɔ̃), s.f. Regeneration.

régénérer (reʒenere), v.a. [L *regenerare*] To regenerate; (fig.) to renew; to make to be born again; to amend.

régénérescence (reʒenerɛssɑs), s.f. Regeneration.

régent, -e (reʒɑ̃), s.m.f. [L *regens*] **1.** Regent; **2.** Philippe d'Orléans, Regent of France 1715–23; **3.** a celebrated diamond of the French crown; **4.** master (in a college, &c.); **5.** one of the fifteen governors of the Bank of France.

régenter (reʒɑ̃te), v.a.n. [f. *régent*] To govern; (fig.) to lord it over; to tyrannize over.

régicide (reʒisid), s.m. [f. L *rex*+*caedere*] **1.** Regicide; murderer of a king; **2.** regicide, murder of a king; king-killing.

régie (reʒi), s.f. [f. *régir*] Excise; administration, State management.

regimbement (rəʒɛ̃bmɑ̃), s.m. Resistance, kicking.

regimber (rəʒɛ̃be), v.n. To kick, to resist, to kick (against), to kick up; to kick over the traces.

régime (reʒim), s.m. [L *regimen*] **1.** Regimen, diet; *suivre un ~, être au ~*, to be on a diet; **2.** form of government; administration; rules; ~ *dotal*, dotal system; **3.** (of bananas) cluster; **4.** (gram.) object; ~ *direct*, direct object; ~ *indirect*, indirect object; **5.** (techn., motors, &c.) normal speed, normal working; *le ~ d'un fleuve*, the rate of flow of a river.

régiment (reʒimɑ̃), s.m. [f. L *regimen*] Regiment.

régimentaire (reʒimɑ̃tɛr), adj. Regimental.

réginglette (reʒɛ̃glɛt), s.f. Small spring trap for birds.

région (reʒjɔ̃), s.f. [L *regio*] Region; (anat.) part of the body.

régional, -e, (aux) (rɛʒjɔnal), adj. Local, regional, of the district.

régionalisme (reʒjɔnalism), s.m. Regionalism.
régir (reʒir), v.a. [L *regere*] To rule, to govern, to manage, to administer; (gram.) to govern.
régisseur (reʒisœr), s.m. Steward, bailiff; (theatr.) manager.
registre (rəʒistr), s.m. [L *regestum*] Register, account-book; (colloq.) *il est sur mes ~s*, I have him on my books; (mus.) register; (techn.) damper (in chimneys), register valve.
registrer (rəʒistre), v.a. To record, to register; syn. ENREGISTRER.
réglable (reglabl), adj. Adjustable.
réglage (reglaʒ), s.m. Ruling (of paper); regulating, timing, adjusting; *vis de ~*, adjusting screw; *à ~ automatique*, self-regulating.
règle (rɛgl), s.f. [L *regula*] Rule; ruler; order, pattern; principle, law; *il est de ~ que*, it is customary to; *en ~*, in order, right, correct, regular; *dans toutes les ~s*, according to rule; *l'exception confirme la ~*, the exception proves the rule; *~ de trois*, rule of three; *~ à calcul*, slide-rule; *en ~ générale*, as a rule; *~s*, monthly courses.
réglé, -e (regle), p. adj. Regular, steady, well-ordered; *des habitudes ~es*, regular habits.
règlement (rɛgləmɑ̃), s.m. Ruling; rule, regulation; settlement; *~ de comptes*, settlement of an account; squaring; *~s de police*, police regulations.
réglementaire (regləmɑ̃tɛr), adj. Regulation; regular, correct, standard; *coiffure ~*, regulation cap.
réglementairement (regləmɑ̃tɛrmɑ̃), adv. According to regulations.
réglementation (regləmɑ̃ta'sjɔ̃), s.f. Strict regulation; system of regulation; *~ de la prostitution*, systematic organization and control of prostitution by the police.
réglementer (regləmɑ̃te), v.a. To regulate, to rule, to make regulations for.
régler (regle), v.a. [f. *règle*] To rule (paper, &c.), to regulate, to arrange, to order; to time, to set, to adjust; *une affaire réglée*, a settled matter; *~ un compte*, to settle an account; *il est réglé comme papier à musique*, he is as regular as clockwork; *~ sa montre*, to set one's watch; *~ ses désirs*, to control one's aspirations; *~ sa dépense*, to moderate one's expenses; *~ les préséances*, to fix the order of precedence; (techn.) *~ la carburation*, to get the proper mixture; *~ l'allumage*, to time the ignition; **se ~**, v.pr. to regulate oneself, to take pattern (from), to be guided; *je me règlerai sur vous*, I shall go by what you say; *le compte s'est réglé par un bénéfice en ma faveur*, the account has been settled by a balance in my favour.
réglet (reglɛ), s.m. (techn., print.) Rule.
réglette (reglɛt), s.f. Small ruler, reglet.
réglisse (reglis), s.f. [Gr. *glukurrhiza*] Liquorice; *jus de ~*, Spanish liquorice; *bois de ~*, root liquorice.
réglure (reglyr), s.f. Ruling (of paper).
régnant, -e (reɲɑ̃), p. adj. Reigning, prevailing, usual, predominant, current, prevalent; *la famille ~e*, the reigning family; *le goût ~*, the prevailing fashion.
règne (rɛɲ), s.m. [L *regnum*] Reign; sway; (fig.) vogue, predominance, reign; (nat. hist.) kingdom; *~ animal*, animal kingdom; *sous le ~ de Napoléon*, in the reign of Napoleon.
régner (reɲe), v.n. [L *regnare*] To reign; to be prevalent, to prevail, to hold sway; (arch.) to run; (of diseases) to rage, to be rife, to be prevailing; *le désordre qui règne*, the disorder and confusion which exist.
régnicole (reɲikɔl), adj. s.m.f. [f. L *regnum + colere*] Native, denizen.
regonfler (rəgɔ̃fle), v.a.n. To re-inflate; to swell again.
regorgeant, -e (rəgɔrʒɑ̃), p. adj. Overflowing, brimming (*de*, with).
regorger (rəgɔrʒe), v.n. To overflow, to brim (*de*, with); to disgorge; (fig.) to be plentiful, to brim (with), to abound, to be crowded, to be glutted, to be replete, to possess an excess (of); to wallow (in).
regrat (rəgra), s.m. [f. *regratter*] Huckstering, second-hand dealing.
regrattage (rəgrataʒ), s.m. Scraping again, re-scraping.
regratter (rəgrate), v.a. To re-scrape; to regrate; to huckster.
regratterie (rəgratri), s.f. Huckstering, huckster's trade.
regratti-er, -ère (rəgratje), s.m.f. adj. Huckster, petty second-hand dealer; regrater.
regréer (rəgree), v.a. To re-rig (a ship).
regreffer (rəgrɛfe), v.a. To regraft, to graft again.
régressi-f, -ve (regrɛsif), adj. [f. L *regressus*] Regressive.
régression (regrɛsjɔ̃), s.f. [L *regressio*] Regression.
régressivement (regrɛsivmɑ̃), adv. Regressively.
regret (rəgrɛ), s.m. [f. *regretter*] Regret; yearning, repining; repentance, sorrow; *à ~*, reluctantly; *avoir du ~*, to feel regret, to feel sorry; *tous mes ~s*, I am very sorry; (fam.) awfully sorry; *exprimez vos ~s*, make your apologies; *être aux ~s*, to feel sorry.
regrettable (rəgrɛtabl), adj. Regrettable, deplorable, to be regretted; *~ erreur*, sad mistake.
regretter (rəgrɛte), v.a. [f. Goth. *gretan*] To regret, to lament, to grieve for, to miss, to be sorry to have lost, to be sorry for; to repent; *le regretté X*, the lamented X; *je la regrette*, I miss her.

regros (rəgro), s.m. Thick bark of oak-tree.

régularisation (regylariza'sjɔ̃), s.f. Putting in order, regulating, regularization.

régulariser (regylarize), v.a. [f. L *regularis*] To regularize, to regulate.

régularité (regylarite), s.f. Regularity.

régulat-eur, -rice (regylatœr), adj. Regulating, standard. ~, s.m. Regulator; governor; throttle; ~ *à boules*, governor.

régulation (regyla'sjɔ̃), s.f. Regulating, adjusting, regulation.

régule (regyl), s.m. [f. L *regulus*] (chem.) Regulus; (aeron.) Babbitt metal.

réguli-er, -ère (regylje), adj. [L *regularis*] Regular; right, correct; punctual. ~, s.m. Regular (monk, soldier).

régulièrement (regyljɛrmɑ̃), adv. Regularly; correctly; every time, always.

régurgitation (regyrʒita'sjɔ̃), s.f. Regurgitation.

régurgiter (regyrʒite), v.a. [L *regurgitare*] To regurgitate.

réhabilitation (reabilita'sjɔ̃), s.f. Rehabilitation.

réhabiliter (reabilite), v.a. [*re*+*habiliter*] To rehabilitate; **se** ~, v.pr. to rehabilitate oneself, to recover one's good name.

réhabituer (reabitɥe), v.a. To reaccustom; **se** ~, v.pr. to grow reaccustomed.

rehaussement (rəosmɑ̃), s.m. Raising up, raising; heightening, enhancing, increase (in value); (paint.) touching up.

rehausser (rəose), v.a. To raise up; to heighten, to enhance; to enrich; to touch up.

rehaut (rəo), s.m. (paint.) Light, lights.

reillère (rɛjɛr), s.f. Conduit bringing water to the wheel of the mill.

réimportation (reɛ̃pɔrta'sjɔ̃), s.f. Reimportation, re-import.

réimporter (reɛ̃pɔrte), v.a. To reimport.

réimposer (reɛ̃poze), v.a. To reassess (taxes); (print.) to reimpose.

réimposition (reɛ̃pozisjɔ̃), s.f. Further assessment; (print.) reimposition.

réimpression (reɛ̃prɛsjɔ̃), s.f. Reprinting, reprint, reimpression.

réimprimer (reɛ̃prime), v.a. To reprint, to print again.

rein (rɛ̃), s.m. [L *ren*] Kidney; ~*s*, (plur.) loins; (arch.) extrados (of arch); *se casser les* ~*s*, to break one's back; (fig.) to ruin oneself, to do for oneself; *ceindre ses* ~*s*, to gird up one's loins; *la chute des* ~*s*, the small of the back; *avoir les* ~*s solides*, to be strong-backed; (fig.) to have a long purse; *poursuivre l'ennemi l'épée dans les* ~*s*, to follow close on the enemy's heels; *il s'est donné un tour de* ~*s*, he sprained his back. ⚠ Not 'rein', which = *guide, rêne*.

réincarcération (reɛ̃karsera'sjɔ̃), s.f. Reincarceration.

réincarcérer (reɛ̃karsere), v.a. To reincarcerate.

réincorporer (reɛ̃kɔrpɔre), v.a. To reincorporate.

reine (rɛn), s.f. [L *regina*] Queen; (at chess) queen; ~ *des abeilles*, queen bee; *la rose est la* ~ *des fleurs*, the rose is the queen of flowers; (bot.) ~*-claude*, greengage; (bot.) ~*-marguerite*, China aster; ~ *mère*, queen mother; (bot.) ~ *des prés*, meadow-sweet.

reinette (rɛnɛt), s.f. Rennet (apple). See RAINETTE.

réinstallation (reɛ̃stala'sjɔ̃), s.f. Re-establishment, reinstalment; resettling.

réinstaller (reɛ̃stale), v.a. To reinstall, to re-establish; to refurnish (a flat, &c.), to resettle; **se** ~, v.pr. to reinstall oneself, to settle again.

reinté, -e (rɛ̃te), adj. Strong-backed, broad-backed.

réintégration (reɛ̃tegra'sjɔ̃), s.f. Reinstatement.

réintégrande (reɛ̃tegrɑ̃d), s.f. (law) Restoration, reinstalment, recovery of possession.

réintégrer (reɛ̃tegre), v.a. To reinstate, to take back, to bring back, to return to; ~ *X dans ses droits*, to reinstate X in his rights; ~ *le domicile conjugal*, to return to the conjugal residence, to go back to one's husband or wife; to go home. ⚠ Engl. 'to reintegrate' and 'to redintegrate' = *rétablir dans son intégralité*.

reis (rɛis), s.m. **1.** [Arab. orig.] Chief; **2.** [Port. wd] reis (a coin).

réitérati-f, -ve (reiteratif), adj. Reiterative.

réitération (reitera'sjɔ̃), s.f. Reiteration.

réitérer (reitere), v.a. [L *re*+*iterare*] To reiterate, to repeat.

reître (rɛtr), s.m. [Germ. *Reiter*] Reiter; (fig.) hardened rough soldier.

rejaillir (rəʒajir), v.n. To spurt up, out, to gush out, to fly; to rebound (*contre*, against), to be reflected.

rejaillissement (rəʒajismɑ̃), s.m. Gushing up, spurting out, spouting; rebounding, rebound; reflection.

rejet (rəʒɛ), s.m. [f. *rejeter*] **1.** Rejection; carrying, transfer; **2.** new shoot (of plant, tree); **3.** (pros.) enjambment; running on into the next line.

rejetable (rəʒətabl), adj. Rejectable.

rejeteau (pl. **-x**) (rəʒəto), s.m. Weatherboard (at bottom of window or door).

rejeter (rəʒəte), v.a. [*re*+*jeter*] To reject, to throw out, to throw or fling back; to set aside; to dismiss, to refuse; to throw up (food); ~ *un projet de loi*, to throw out a bill; ~ *un pourvoi*, to dismiss an appeal; ~ *sa responsabilité sur X*, to cast the responsibility upon X.

rejeton (rəʒətɔ̃), s.m. [f. *rejet*] Shoot, offshoot, runner; (fig.) offspring, scion.
rejoindre (rəʒwɛ̃dr), v.a. [*re+joindre*] To join again, to reunite; to overtake; to rejoin (one's regiment). ⚠ In English 'to rejoin' frequently means to answer = *répondre, répliquer*; hence rejoinder = *réplique*; **se ~**, v.pr. to meet, to reunite, to be reunited; to close.
rejointoiement (rəʒwɛ̃twamɑ̃), s.m. Rejointing.
rejointoyer (rəʒwɛ̃twaje), v.a. [f. *joint*] (mason.) To re-joint; to point the joints of (a wall).
rejouer (rəʒwe), v.n.a. To play again; to gamble again, to speculate again.
réjoui, -e (reʒwi), p. adj. Cheerful, merry, jolly; *un gros ~*, a jolly fat fellow.
réjouir (reʒwir), v.a. [*re+*OF *esjouir*] To cheer, to rejoice, to enliven, to gladden, to please, to delight; *~ la vue*, to please the eyes; **se ~**, v.pr. to rejoice, to be delighted (*de*, at, with); to enjoy oneself; to make merry.
réjouissance (reʒwisɑ̃s), s.f. Rejoicing; rejoicings, merry-making, amusement, festivities; (butch.) make-weight (of bones thrown in by the butcher); *en signe de ~*, as a token (or sign) of rejoicing.
réjouissant, -e (reʒwisɑ̃), p. adj. Jolly, amusing, cheering, merry, jovial.
relâchant, -e (rəlɑʃɑ̃), p. adj. s.m. Laxative, aperient.
relâche (rəlɑʃ), s.m. Respite, remission, interruption; relaxation, intermission; *travailler sans ~*, to work unremittingly; *donnez-vous un ~*, take some rest; have a respite; *son mal ne lui laisse pas de ~*, his pain gives him no respite; (theatr.) no performance; *faire ~*, to have no performance.
relâche (rəlɑʃ), s.f. (naut.) Putting into port; stay; *faire ~ à Durban*, to put into Durban.
relâché, -e (rəlɑʃe), p. adj. Loose, lax, slack.
relâchement (rəlɑʃmɑ̃), s.m. Relaxation, slackness, slackening, loosening; falling-off; laxness; looseness (of the bowels); intermission, respite, abatement; *le ~ des muscles*, the relaxation of the muscles; *le ~ des mœurs*, the looseness or laxity of living, or of morals; *~ de la discipline*, laxity of discipline.
relâcher (rəlɑʃe), v.a. [*re+lâcher*] To loosen, to slacken; to release, to set at liberty; to abate; (naut.), v.n. to put into port; **se ~**, v.pr. to slacken, to get loose; to get milder; to relax, to fall off; to unbend.
relais (rəlɛ), s.m. [f. *relayer*] Relay; stage; change of horses; posting-house; (hunt.) relay.
relancer (rəlɑ̃se), v.a. [*re+lancer*] To throw back, to throw again; (hunt.) to start again; (fig.) to importune, to hunt out, to beset.
relaps, -e (rəlaps), adj. s.m.f. [L *relapsus*] Relapsed (person), apostate (for the second time). ⚠ In English 'relapse' (s.) means the act of relapsing, sinking again into wrong-doing = *l'acte de retomber dans l'hérésie, le mal*; also: deterioration in a patient's condition after partial recovery = *rechute*.
rélargir (relarʒir), v.a. [*re+élargir*] To let out (clothes); to widen.
relater (rəlate), v.a. [f. L *relatum*] To tell, to narrate, to state, to mention, to relate. ⚠ In English 'to relate' has also the sense of connecting, bringing into relation, concerning = *se rapporter à*; ex. he notices nothing but what relates to himself, *il ne fait attention qu'à ce qui le concerne*.
relati-f, -ve (rəlatif), adj. [L *relativus*] Relative, relating (*à*, to); (gram.) relative (pronoun, adjective, &c.). ⚠ In English 'relative' (s.) = *parent, parente*.
relation (rəla'sjɔ̃), s.f. [L *relatio*] Relation, connexion, correspondence; proportion; narration, narrative, statement; *~s*, (pl.) **1.** acquaintances, friends; *avoir de belles ~s*, to be well connected; **2.** intercourse; *être en ~s avec X*, to have friendly intercourse with X; to be acquainted with X; *avoir eu des ~s coupables avec X*, to have had immoral intercourse with X. ⚠ In English 'relations' has also very frequently the sense of family, kinsfolk; near relations = *proches parents*.
relativement (rəlativmɑ̃), adv. Relatively, comparatively; *~ à*, concerning.
relativisme (rəlativism), s.m. Relativism.
relativité (rəlativite), s.f. Relativity, relativeness; *doctrine de la ~*, theory of relativity.
relaver (rəlave), v.a. To wash again.
relaxation (rəlaksa'sjɔ̃), s.f. **1.** Relaxation; **2.** releasing (of a prisoner, &c.).
relaxe (rəlaks), s.f. Relaxation; release.
relaxer (rəlakse), v.a. [L *relaxare*] To release, to relax.
relayer (rəlɛje), v.a.n. [f. OF *layer*] To relay, to relieve, to take the place of; to change horses; **se ~**, to relieve each other, to take it in turns.
relégation (rəlega'sjɔ̃), s.f. Relegation, banishment to a certain place, exile, imprisonment in a remote place.
reléguer (rəlege), v.a. [L *relegare*] To relegate, to exile, to banish, to shut up, to seclude, to keep in a remote place. ⚠ 'To relegate' has also the sense of: to transfer (matter) for decision, to refer (person) for information = *renvoyer (à)*.
relent (rəlɑ̃), s.m. [etym. dub.] Musty smell; nasty smell.

relevailles (rələvaj), s.f.pl. [f. (*se*) *relever*] Churching (of a woman); *faire ses* ~, to be churched.
relève (rəlɛv), s.f. Shift, relief.
relevé, -e (rələve), p. adj. High, exalted, lofty, refined; (cook.) highly seasoned. ~, s.m. Statement, abstract, list, return, summary; (cook.) 1st dish after the soup; ~**e**, s.f. afternoon; *à 3 heures de* ~*e*, at three in the afternoon.
relèvement (rəlɛvmɑ̃), s.m. Raising; abstract, statement; (naut.) bearings; moral salvation, moral rescue, redemption, preservation.
relever (rələve), v.a. [*re*+*lever*] To raise again, to lift up again; to pick up, to set up; to heighten, to set off, to enhance; to exalt, to improve, to restore, to revive, to dignify; to point out, to praise, to remark; to take up, to snap up; to liberate, to release, to set free; to achieve the moral rescue of; (cook.) to season; to turn up (one's collar, &c.), to draw up; ~ *la tête*, to hold up one's head again; to regain one's self-confidence; ~ *le courage de X*, to raise X's courage; ~ *le gant*, to take up the gauntlet; to accept the challenge; *une mouche relève le teint*, a patch enhances the complexion; ~ *une côte*, to take the bearings of a coast; ~ *une sentinelle*, to relieve a sentry; ~ *X de ses vœux*, to release X from his vows; ~, v.n. **1.** to depend, to be dependent (*de*, on), to rest (with); *cela relève de la justice*, that rests with the judge; **2.** to recover; ~ *de maladie*, to have just recovered from an illness; **se** ~, v.pr. to get up again, to rise again, to recover, to retrieve one's losses; (naut.) to right itself; to recover one's self-respect.
releveur (rələvœr), s.m. (anat.) Levator, elevator.
reliage (rəljaʒ), s.m. Hooping (of casks).
relief (rəljɛf), s.m. [f. *relever*] Relief, relievo, embossment; set-off; enhancement; ~*s*, (pl.) scraps; ~ *des montagnes*, relief of the mountains; *avoir du* ~, to stand out; *donner du* ~ *à*, to set off, to give relief to; *manquer de* ~, to be flat, dull; *bas-*~, low relief; *demi-*~, demi-relief, *haut-*~, high relief; *en* ~, in relief; raised. ⚠ 'Relief' in English has frequently the sense of alleviation = *soulagement*.
relier (rəlje), v.a. [*re*+*lier*] To bind again, to connect, to unite; to bind (books); to hoop (casks).
relieu-r, -se (rəljœr), s.m.f. Bookbinder; ~**se**, s.f. binding-machine.
religieusement (rəliʒjøzmɑ̃), adv. Religiously, devoutly, scrupulously.
religieu-x, -se (rəliʒjø), adj. Religious, devout, pious; scrupulous. ~, s.m. Monk; ~*se*, s.f. nun.
religion (rəliʒjɔ̃), s.f. [L *religio*] Religion; *entrer en* ~, to take one's vows; to become a monk or a nun; *se faire une* ~ *de*, to make it a matter of conscience to; to consider it one's bounden duty to; *surprendre la* ~ *de X*, to take advantage of X's good faith.
religionnaire (rəliʒjɔnɛr), (obs.) s.m.f. Huguenot.
religiosité (rəliʒjozite), s.f. Religiosity.
reliquaire (rəlikɛr), s.m. [f. *reliques*] Reliquary, shrine.
reliquat (rəlika), s.m. [L *reliqua*] Balance, rest, remainder.
reliquataire (rəlikatɛr), s.m.f. Debtor owing a balance.
relique (rəlik), s.f. [f. L *reliquiae*] Relic.
relire (rəlir), v.a. [*re*+*lire*] To read again, to read over again, to re-read.
reliure (rəljyr), s.f. [f. *relier*] Bookbinding.
relocation (rəlɔka'sjɔ̃), s.f. Reletting.
relouage (rəluaʒ), s.m. [etym. dub.] Spawning of herrings.
relouer (rəlue), v.a. To re-let, to let again; to sub-let.
reluire (rəlɥir), v.n. To shine, to glisten, to be bright; *faire*~, to polish; *tout ce qui reluit n'est pas or*, all is not gold that glitters.
reluisant, -e (rəlɥizɑ̃), p. adj. Shining, glittering; (fig.) chic, flattering.
reluquer (rəlyke), v.a. [f. OF *luquer*] (fam.) To peer at, to ogle, to have an eye upon, to keep eyeing; (fig.) to covet.
remâcher (rəmɑʃe), v.a. To chew again; (fig.) to ruminate, to revolve in one's mind, to chew; to nurse; ~ *un grief*, to nurse a grievance.
remailler (rəmɑje), v.a. See REMMAILLER.
remaniement (rəmanimɑ̃), s.m. Altering, rearrangement, doing over again.
remanier (rəmanje), v.a. [*re*+*manier*] To alter, to handle again, to rearrange, to do . . . again; (print.) to overrun.
remariage (rəmarjaʒ), s.m. Marrying again, remarriage.
remarier (rəmarje), v.a. To marry . . . again; **se** ~, v.pr. to marry again, to remarry.
remarquable (rəmarkabl), adj. Remarkable, noticeable.
remarquablement (rəmarkabləmɑ̃), adv. Remarkably.
remarque (rəmark), s.f. [f. *remarquer*] Remark, observation, notice, note; mark.
remarquer (rəmarke), v.a. [*re*+*marquer*] To remark, to notice, to observe, to distinguish; to mark again; *remarquez !*, mind you !; *faire* ~, to point out; to call attention to; *se faire* ~, to distinguish oneself; (pej.) to attract notice.
remballer (rɑ̃bale), v.a. [*re*+*emballer*] To repack, to pack up again.
rembarquement (rɑ̃barkəmɑ̃), s.m. Reembarking; reshipment.

rembarquer (rɑ̃barke), v.a.n. [*re+embarquer*] To re-embark, to reship; **se ~**, v.pr. to go on board again; (fig.) to start (something) again.
rembarrer (rɑ̃bare), v.a. [f. *barre*] To rebuke, to repulse, to set down, to snub; (fam.) *se faire ~*, to get sat on.
remblai (rɑ̃blɛ), s.m. [f. *remblayer*] Embanking; embankment.
remblaver (rɑ̃blave), v.a. [*re+emblaver*] To sow again (with corn).
remblayage (rɑ̃blɛjaʒ), s.m. Filling up, embanking.
remblayer (rɑ̃blɛje), v.a.n. [*re+emblayer*] To fill up, to embank.
remboîtement (rɑ̃bwatmɑ̃), s.m. Resetting (of a bone, &c.).
remboîter (rɑ̃bwate), v.a. [*re+emboîter*] To reset (a bone, &c.).
rembouger (rɑ̃buʒe), v.a. [f. *re+en+bouge*] To fill up, to keep full (a vase, or cask, &c.).
rembourrage (rɑ̃buraʒ), s.m. Stuffing, padding.
rembourrer (rɑ̃bure), v.a. [*re+bourrer*] To stuff, to pad (*de*, with); (fam.) *être bien rembourré*, to be well upholstered.
remboursable (rɑ̃bursabl), adj. Repayable; reimbursable, redeemable.
remboursement (rɑ̃bursəmɑ̃), s.m. Repayment, reimbursement; *contre ~*, cash on delivery.
rembourser (rɑ̃burse), v.a. [*re+embourser*] To repay, to reimburse, to refund; *~ une somme*, to repay a sum of money; *~ une rente*, to redeem an annuity; *~ un créancier*, to pay a creditor.
rembrunir (rɑ̃brynir), v.n.a. To make or become a darker brown; (fig.) to darken, to sadden; **se ~**, v.pr. to grow sombre, to be gloomy, to cloud over.
rembucher (rɑ̃byʃe), v.a. To pursue into covert; **se ~**, v.pr. to return to covert.
remède (rəmɛd), s.m. [L *remedium*] Remedy; cure, medicine; *porter ~ à*, to remedy; *~ de bonne femme*, old wives' remedy; *aux grands maux les grands ~s*, desperate diseases require desperate remedies.
remédier (rəmedje), v.n. To provide or be a remedy (*à*, for); *~ à un mal*, to remedy an evil; *~ à*, to remedy, to help, to remove, to put right.
remêler (rəmɛle), v.a. To mix again; to shuffle again (cards).
remémorati-f, -ve (rəmemɔratif), adj. Rememorative, commemorative.
remémorer (rəmemɔre), v.a. [L *rememorari*] To remind, to put in mind; **se ~**, to recollect, to remember.
remerciement, remercîment (rəmɛrsimɑ̃), s.m. Thanks (pl.) (*de, pour*, for); *exprimer des ~s*, to return thanks, to express one's thanks.
remercier (rəmɛrsje), v.a. [f. *merci*] **1.** To thank (*de*, for); **2.** to dismiss, to discharge, to sack.
réméré (remere), s.m. [*re*+(L) *emere*] (law) Right of repurchase; *vente à ~*, sale with faculty of redemption.
remesurer (rəməzyre), v.a. To measure again.
remettre (rəmɛtr), v.a. [L *remittere*] To put back, to put back again; to put on again; to set (a bone, &c.); to bring, to deliver, to hand over; to entrust; to remit (a sum of money, a sin); to postpone, to put off, to adjourn; to cure, to make right again; to reconcile; to recall; **se ~**, v.pr. to be all right again, to recover oneself, to grow composed again; to get reconciled; *je m'en remets à vous*, I leave it to you; *se ~ à*, to set about again.
rémige (remiʒ), s.f. [L *remex*] Remex (pl. remiges), quill-feather (of the wing).
réminiscence (reminissɑ̃s), s.f. [f. L *reminisci*] Reminiscence, unconscious recollection.
remisage (rəmizaʒ), s.m. Housing, putting into the coach-house; (fig.) pushing out of the way; stowing away, shelving.
remise (rəmiz), s.f. [f. *remettre*] **1.** Putting back; **2.** delivery; **3.** allowance, rebate, commission, discount; **4.** postponement; delay, deferring, adjournment; **5.** remission, pardon, forgiveness; **6.** coach-house or -shed; *voiture de ~*, hired carriage.
remiser (rəmize), v.a. [f. *remise*] To house, to put in the coach-house; (fig.) to stow away, to push out of the way; to shelve.
remisier (rəmizje), s.m. (Stock Exchange) Broker's agent; half-commission man.
rémissibilité (remisibilite), s.f. Remissibility.
rémissible (remisibl), adj. Remissible.
rémission (remisjɔ̃), s.f. [L *remissio*] Remission, forgiveness; (med.) abatement.
rémittent, -e (remitɑ̃), adj. [L *remittens*] (med.) Remittent.
remmaillage (rɑ̃mɑjaʒ), s.m. Taking up or picking up a ladder (in stockings, &c.); restitching.
remmailler (rɑ̃mɑje), v.a. [f. *maille*] To take up or pick up a ladder (in stockings, &c.); to restitch.
remmailloter (rɑ̃majɔte), v.a. [f. *maillot*] To rewrap (an infant).
remmancher (rɑ̃mɑ̃ʃe), v.a. [f. *manche*] To put a new handle to.
remmener (rɑ̃mne), v.a. [*re+emmener*] To take back again.
rémois, -e (remwɑ), adj. s.m.f. (Native) of Rheims.
rémolade (remɔlad), s.f. See REMOULADE.
remole (rəmɔl), s.f. [f. Provenç. *remoulin* f. L *remoliri*] Dangerous eddy.

remontage (rəmɔ̃taʒ), s.m. Resetting; remounting, putting together again; winding up (of a clock, &c.).

remontant, -e (rəmɔ̃tɑ̃), p. adj. **1.** (hort.) Flowering twice in the year; perpetual flowering; **2.** invigorating, bracing, tonic.

remonte (rəmɔ̃t), s.f. **1.** Going up stream; **2.** remounting, remount.

remonter (rəmɔ̃te), v.n.a. [*re*+*monter*] To go up stream, to go up again, to reascend, to remount; to set up again; to bring up again; to set again; to wind up (clocks, &c.); to put together again; to vamp (boots); to new-front; to trace back; to stock again; *la rente remonte*, the stocks are rising; ~ *au déluge*, to go back to the Flood; ~ *le moral à X*, to cheer X up, to restore X's self-confidence; ~ *sa maison*, to furnish one's house; ~ *un magasin*, to restock a warehouse; **se** ~, v.pr. to get a new horse; to stock oneself again (*de*, with); to recover one's strength or spirits.

remontoir (rəmɔ̃twar), s.m. Keyless action, lever escapement; *montre à* ~, keyless watch, lever watch.

remontrance (rəmɔ̃trɑ̃s), s.f. Remonstrance, reproof.

remontrer (rəmɔ̃tre), v.a.n. To point out, to show or demonstrate again; *en* ~ *à*, to instruct, to teach, to remonstrate with; *c'est Gros-Jean qui en remontre à son curé*, it is teaching one's grandmother to suck eggs; **se** ~, v.pr. to show oneself again, to appear again.

rémora (remɔra), s.m. (ichth.) Remora; sucking fish; (fig.) hindrance, obstacle.

remords (rəmɔr), s.m. [f. L *remorsus*] Remorse; *avoir des* ~, to feel remorse; to be remorseful; *sans* ~, remorseless; remorselessly; *étouffer ses* ~, to stifle remorse.

remorquage (rəmɔrkaʒ), s.m. Towing, hauling.

remorque (rəmɔrk), s.f. Towing, tow, hauling; tow-rope, towing-hawser; (motor.) trailer; *prendre en* ~, to take in tow; *larguer la* ~, to cast off the tow-rope; *se mettre à la* ~ (*de*), to get into tow; (fig.) to let oneself be led (by), to follow in the wake (of), to be under the thumb of.

remorquer (rəmɔrke), v.a. [It. *rimorchiare*] To tow, to haul, to take in tow; to drag, to tug.

remorqueu-r, -se (rəmɔrkœr), adj. Towing, hauling. ~, s.m. Tug, steam-tug.

remoudre (rəmudr), v.a. To grind again.

rémoudre (remudr), v.a. [*re*+*émoudre*] To whet again, to resharpen, to reset.

remouiller (rəmuje), v.a. **1.** To wet again; **2.** to anchor again.

rémoulade, rémolade (remulad, remɔlad), s.f. [It. *remolata*] Remoulade sauce; sharp sauce.

remouler (rəmule), v.a. To remould.

rémouleur (remulœr), s.m. Grinder, knife-grinder.

remous (rəmu), s.m. [Provenç. wd] Eddy, eddy-water, whirl; (aeron.) ~ *d'air*, back-wash.

rempaillage (rɑ̃pɑjaʒ), s.m. Chair-bottoming.

rempailler (rɑ̃pɑje), v.a. [*re*+*empailler*] To rebottom (chairs).

rempailleu-r, -se (rɑ̃pɑjœr), s.m.f. Chair-mender, chair-bottomer.

rempaqueter (rɑ̃pakte), v.a. [*re*+*empaqueter*] To repack, to pack up again.

rempart (rɑ̃par), s.m. [f. OF *remparer*] Rampart; (fig.) bulwark, safeguard, help, defence.

rempiler (rɑ̃pile), v.n. (mil. slang) To re-enlist for military service.

remplaçable (rɑ̃plasabl), adj. Replaceable, interchangeable.

remplaçant, -e (rɑ̃plasɑ̃), s.m.f. Substitute, deputy.

remplacement (rɑ̃plasmɑ̃), s.m. Replacing, substituting, replacement, substitution, change; *en* ~ *de*, in the place of.

remplacer (rɑ̃plase), v.a. [f. *re*+*en*+*place*] To replace, to substitute, to take or fill the place of, to supersede, to do instead of; to reinvest; *se faire* ~, to find a substitute.

remplage (rɑ̃plaʒ), s.m. (build.) Filling up; rubble.

rempli (rɑ̃pli), s.m. Tuck, taking in, fold.

remplier (rɑ̃plie), v.a. To take in, to tuck up; to turn in.

remplir (rɑ̃plir), v.a. [*re*+*emplir*] To fill, to fill up, to refill, to replenish; to cram, to crowd; to fulfil, to perform; to answer; to complete; *bien* ~ *son temps*, to employ one's time well; ~ *ses promesses*, to fulfil one's promises; ~ *sa tâche*, to perform one's duty; ~ *l'attente de X*, to fulfil X's expectations; **se** ~, v.pr. to fill or cram oneself, to be filled, to be thronged, to be crowded.

remplissage (rɑ̃plisaʒ), s.m. Filling; filling up; filling in; (fig.) rubbish, trash, padding, verbiage, platitude.

remplisseuse (rɑ̃plisøz), s.f. Lace-mender, filler-in.

remploi (rɑ̃plwa), s.m. [f. *remployer*] (law) Reinvestment.

remployer (rɑ̃plwaje), v.a. To use again; (law) to reinvest.

(se) remplumer (sərɑ̃plyme), v.pr. (of birds) To get new feathers; (colloq.) to put on flesh, to pick up again (in health, spirits, money, &c.).

rempocher (rɑ̃pɔʃe), v.a. [*re*+*empocher*] To pocket again.

rempoissonnement (rɑ̃pwasɔnmɑ̃), s.m. Restocking with fish.

rempoissonner (rɑ̃pwasɔne), v.a. To restock with fish.

remporter (rɑ̃pɔrte), v.a. To take back again; to carry off; to get, to obtain; ~ *la victoire*, to win the victory; ~ *le prix*, to carry off the prize; ~ *la palme*, to carry the day; to bear away the palm.

rempotage (rɑ̃pɔtaʒ), s.m. Repotting.

rempoter (rɑ̃pɔte), v.a. To repot, to put in pots again.

remuable (rəmɥabl), adj. Movable.

remuage (rəmɥaʒ), s.m. Moving, stirring, turning.

remuant, -e (rəmɥɑ̃), p. adj. Turbulent, restless, brisk, moving, active, bustling, busy, enterprising, pushing.

remue-ménage (rəmymenaʒ), s.m. Bustle, stir, fuss, ado, confusion, excitement, sensation.

remuement (rəmymɑ̃), s.m. Moving, removing, stir, stirring.

remuer (rəmɥe), v.a.n. [*re*+*muer*] To move, to keep moving, to fidget, to stir, to turn, to stir up, to shake; to affect, to touch; to wag (the tail); to shake (the head); ~ *ciel et terre*, to move heaven and earth; to leave no stone unturned; *ne* ~ *ni pied ni patte*, to be quite motionless, not to move a muscle; (fig.) ~ *l'argent à la pelle*, to be disgustingly rich; **se** ~, v.pr. to bestir oneself, to be busy, to move, to take pains.

remueuse (rəmɥøz), s.f. (obs.) Under-nurse; woman who rocks the cradle.

remugle (rəmygl), s.m. [f. Normandy dialect *mucre* = damp] Mustiness, musty smell.

rémunérat-eur, -rice (remyneratœr), adj. Remunerative, paying, profitable. ~, s.m. Rewarder.

rémunération (remynera'sjɔ̃), s.f. Remuneration, reward, payment, repayment.

rémunératoire (remyneratwar), adj. (law) Remuneratory.

rémunérer (remynere), v.a. [L *remunerari*] To remunerate, to reward, to repay.

renâcler (rənɑkle), v.n. [f. OF *renasquer*] To snuffle, to snort; (fig.) to resist, to show reluctance, to hang back.

renaissance (rənɛsɑ̃s), s.f. [f. *renaître*] Renascence; revival, renewal, regeneration; Renaissance (16th c.).

renaissant, -e (rənɛsɑ̃), p. adj. Renascent, revived, reviving, recurring, returning.

renaître (rənɛtr), v.n. [*re*+*naître*] To be born again, to revive, to spring up again, to rise again, to reappear, to return, to be restored (*à*, to).

rénal, -e, (aux) (renal), adj. [L *renalis*] (anat.) Renal.

renard (rənar), s.m. [f. prop. n. in *Le Roman de Renart*] Fox; fox-skin; (fig.) sly fox, cunning fellow, deep dog; blackleg; *Maître* ~, Reynard the fox.

renarde (rənard), s.f. [f. *renard*] She-fox, vixen.

renardeau (pl. -x) (rənardo), s.m. Young fox, fox-cub.

renarder (rənarde), v.n. To play the fox, to act cunningly; (slang) to vomit.

renardier (rənardje), s.m. Fox-catcher.

renardière (rənardjɛr), s.f. Fox's hole, earth.

rencaisser (rɑ̃kɛse), v.a. **1.** To put again into boxes, or tubs; **2.** to put back into the cash-box.

renchaîner (rɑ̃ʃɛne), v.a. [*re*+*enchaîner*] To enchain again, to tie again.

renchéri, -e (rɑ̃ʃeri), p. adj. Particular, over-nice, finicky; *faire la* ~*e*, to give oneself airs.

renchérir (rɑ̃ʃerir), v.a.n. To raise the price of, to make dearer; to become dearer, to rise in price; ~ *sur*, to outdo, to improve upon; to go one better than.

renchérissement (rɑ̃ʃerismɑ̃), s.m. Rise (in price).

rencogner (rɑ̃kɔɲe), v.a. [f. *coin*] To drive into a corner; **se** ~, v.pr. to draw back into a corner.

rencontre (rɑ̃kɔ̃tr), s.f. Meeting, encounter, hit; collision, duel, fight; conjuncture, juncture, occasion; *aller à la* ~ *de X*, to go to meet X; *faire une mauvaise* ~, to have an unpleasant encounter; to meet with thieves (or dangerous persons); *en toute* ~, on any occasion; (horol.) *roue de* ~, balance wheel; *marchandise de* ~, second-hand goods; *gîte de* ~, chance night's lodging.

rencontrer (rɑ̃kɔ̃tre), v.a. [*re*+*encontrer*] To meet, to meet with, to encounter, to come across; to hit upon; to run into, to collide with; to experience; ~ *beaucoup de difficultés*, to encounter many difficulties, to meet with much trouble; *vous avez rencontré juste*, you have hit the right nail on the head; you have been lucky; **se** ~, v.pr. to meet, to meet each other; to collide, to come into collision; to be met with, to be found; to be of the same mind (*avec*, with); to arrive at the same result; *les grands esprits se rencontrent*, great wits meet each other half-way, or jump together; great minds think alike; *cela ne se rencontre pas tous les jours*, that is not to be met with every day.

rendement (rɑ̃dmɑ̃), s.m. Yield, output, return(s).

rendez-vous (rɑ̃devu), s.m. invar. Appointment, tryst, rendezvous; clandestine meeting; appointed place of meeting; *donner, fixer, un* ~ *à X*, to make an appointment with X; ~ *de chasse*, hunting-lodge; *arriver le premier au* ~, to be first at the meeting-place.

rendormir (rɑ̃dɔrmir), v.a. [*re*+*endormir*] To send to sleep again; **se** ~, v.pr. to go to sleep again.

rendosser (rɑ̃dose), v.a. [*re*+*endosser*] To put on (clothes) again.

rendre (rɑ̃dr), v.a. [L *reddere*] To give back, to return, to restore; to bring in, to yield; to cast up, to vomit; to exhale, to emit; to express, to convey, to translate; *~ l'âme*, to give up the ghost; *~ un arrêt*, to issue a decree; *~ à César ce qui est à César*, to render unto Caesar the things that are Caesar's; *~ compte*, to render an account; *~ gorge*, to disgorge; *~ grâce (à)*, to thank, to return thanks (to); *~ hommage à*, to render homage to; *~ la justice*, to dispense justice; *~ justice à X*, to do X justice; *rendre sa parole à X*, to release X from his promise; *~ service à X*, to do X a good turn; *~ témoignage*, to bear witness; *~ visite à X*, to pay X a visit; to call on X; *il m'en rendra raison*, he will have to apologise for that; *Dieu vous le rende!*, may God reward you!; (abs.) to yield; **se ~**, v.pr. to go (*à*, to); to surrender, to yield; to make oneself; to be translated; *se ~ maître de*, to master; *se ~ agréable*, to make oneself pleasant; *je me rends à vos raisons*, I admit you are right; I yield to your arguments; *tous les fleuves se rendent à la mer*, all rivers flow into the sea; *cela ne peut se rendre en français*, that cannot be accurately translated into French.

rendu, -e (rɑ̃dy), p. adj. Rendered, brought back, returned; tired out, exhausted, spent; knocked up, done up; arrived at one's destination; *compte ~*, s.m. account, report; *~*, s.m. **1.** return, returned thing; *un prêté pour un ~*, tit for tat, a Roland for an Oliver; **2.** finish, execution (of a work of art).

rêne (rɛn), s.f. [f. L *retinere*] Rein; (fig.) rein; *tenir les ~s du gouvernement*, to hold the reins of government; *lâcher les ~s*, to give the horse his head.

renégat, -e (rənega), adj. s.m.f. [It. *rinegato*] Renegade, turncoat.

rêner (rɛne), v.a. To bridle, to rein, to rein in.

rénette (renɛt), s.f. [f. *rouanne*] (techn.) Paring-knife.

renettoyer (rənɛtwaje), v.a. To clean again.

renfaîter (rɑ̃fɛte), v.a. [f. *faîte*] To repair the ridge of (a roof), to new-ridge.

renfermé (rɑ̃fɛrme), s.m. [f. *renfermer*] Fustiness, stuffiness; *sentir le ~*, to smell fusty, to be stuffy.

renfermer (rɑ̃fɛrme), v.a. [*re+enfermer*] To lock up again, to confine, to shut up; to contain, to comprise, to include; to conceal, to restrict; **se ~**, v.pr. to confine oneself, to limit oneself; *se ~ en soi-même*, to retire into oneself; to keep one's thoughts to oneself.

renfiler (rɑ̃file), v.a. [*re+enfiler*] To thread again.

renflammer (rɑ̃flame), v.a. [*re+enflammer*] To rekindle; **se ~**, v.pr. to flare up again; (fig.) to fall in love again, to be enamoured again.

renflé, -e (rɑ̃fle), p. adj. Swollen, swelling out; *colonne ~e*, swelling column; (bot.) inflated.

renflement (rɑ̃fləmɑ̃), s.m. Swelling; (arch.) entasis.

renfler (rɑ̃fle), v.a.n. [*re+enfler*] To swell, to enlarge; **se ~**, v.pr. to swell, to be swollen.

renflouage (rɑ̃fluaʒ), **renflouement** (rɑ̃flumɑ̃), s.m. Getting afloat again; refloating.

renflouer (rɑ̃flue), v.a. [f. *re+en+flot*] To set afloat again, to refloat; to raise.

renfoncement (rɑ̃fɔ̃smɑ̃), s.m. Hollow; dinting in, knocking in, blow; (print.) indention.

renfoncer (rɑ̃fɔ̃se), v.a. To drive deeper, to sink; to pull down (a hat, &c.); (techn.) to indent; to new-bottom (a cask).

renforçage, renforcement (rɑ̃fɔrsaʒ, rɑ̃fɔrsmɑ̃), s.m. Strengthening, reinforcement; (photo.) intensifying.

renforcé, -e (rɑ̃fɔrse), p. adj. Downright, arrant, regular; concentrated; *un sot ~*, a downright fool; *un célibataire ~*, a confirmed bachelor.

renforcer (rɑ̃fɔrse), v.a. [f. *force*] To strengthen, to reinforce, to intensify, to confirm, to concentrate.

renfort (rɑ̃fɔr), s.m. [f. *renforcer*] Reinforcement, fresh strength, help, relief; *de ~*, extra, additional; *à grand ~ de*, by dint of, with the aid of.

renfrognement (rɑ̃frɔɲmɑ̃), s.m. Scowl, frown, frowning.

renfrogner (rɑ̃frɔɲe), v.a. [etym. dub.] (obs. *refrogner*) To contract one's face in a frown; **se ~**, v.pr. to frown, to scowl, to look sullen.

rengagé (rɑ̃gaʒe), s.m. (mil.) One who has re-enlisted.

rengagement (rɑ̃gaʒmɑ̃), s.m. Re-enlistment; re-engagement; pawning again.

rengager (rɑ̃gaʒe), v.a.n. To re-enlist; to re-engage; to pawn again; **se ~**, v.pr. to re-enlist; syn. (slang) REMPILER.

rengaine (rɑ̃gɛn), s.f. Tiresome repetition, hackneyed story; *encore la même ~!*, we have heard all that before!, the same old story again and again!

rengainer (rɑ̃gɛne), v.a. [f. *re+en+gaine*] To put up (one's sword), to sheathe; (fig.) to pocket, to forbear, to suppress; *rengainez vos compliments*, pocket your compliments; keep your flatteries, or soft words.

rengorgement (rɑ̃gɔrʒəmɑ̃), s.m. Bridling up, carrying one's head high, airs.

(se) rengorger (sərɑ̃gɔrʒe), v.pr. [f. *gorge*] To give oneself airs, to carry one's head high, to strut.

rengraisser (rɑ̃grɛse), v.a.n. [*re+engraisser*] To put on flesh again, to grow fat again; to fatten, to feed.

rengrener (rɑ̃grəne), v.a. **1.** To fill (the hopper) again with corn; **2.** (techn.) to put in gear again, to re-engage.
reniement (rənimɑ̃), s.m. Denying, disowning, denial.
renier (rənje), v.a. [*re+nier*] To deny, to disown, to forswear; *Pierre renia trois fois Jésus*, Peter denied Jesus three times.
reniflement (rəniflәmɑ̃), s.m. Sniffling, sniff, snivelling.
renifler (rənifle), v.n.a. [f. OF *nifler*] To sniffle, to sniff, to snivel; to nose; ~ *du tabac*, to take snuff; ~ *une vilaine affaire*, to suspect foul dealing; (fig.) ~ *sur*, to turn up one's nose at.
renifleu-r, -se (rəniflœr), adj. s.m.f. Sniffling, sniffer.
réniforme (renifɔrm), adj. Reniform, kidney-shaped.
rénitence (renitɑ̃s), s.f. (med.) Renitency.
rénitent, -e (renitɑ̃), adj. (med.) Renitent.
renne (rɛn), s.m. [Scand. wd] Reindeer.
renoircir (rənwarsir), v.a. To blacken again.
renom (rənɔ̃), s.m. [f. *renommer*] Reputation, repute, renown; *de mauvais* ~, of ill repute; *en* ~, famous, reputed, fashionable.
renommé, -e (rənɔme), p. adj. Renowned, famed, celebrated, noted (*pour*, for), well known, reputed.
renommée (rənɔme), s.f. Renown, fame, celebrity; *bonne* ~ *vaut mieux que ceinture dorée*, a good name is better than riches; *la* ~ *aux cent bouches*, hundred-mouthed Fame.
renommer (rənɔme), v.a. To name again, to nominate again, to re-elect; to make famous.
renonce (rənɔ̃s), s.f. [f. *renoncer*] (at cards) Revoke.
renoncement (rənɔ̃smɑ̃), s.m. Renouncement, renunciation; ~ *à* (or *de*) *soi-même*, self-denial; abnegation.
renoncer (rənɔ̃se), v.n.a. [L *renuntiare*] To renounce, to give up, to relinquish; (at cards) to revoke; ~ *à une succession*, to give up an inheritance; ~ *à une entreprise*, to give up an enterprise, to give up doing something; *j'y renonce!*, I give it up!; ~ *sa foi*, to abjure one's faith; to disown one's belief. ⚠ 'To renounce' is more solemn than *renoncer à*.
renonciataire (rənɔ̃sjatɛr), s.m.f. Person in favour of whom one gives up something.
renonciat-eur, -rice (rənɔ̃sjatœr), s.m.f. Renouncer.
renonciation (rənɔ̃sja'sjɔ̃), s.f. Renunciation, renouncement, self-denial.
renonculacées (rənɔ̃kylase), s.f.pl. (bot.) Ranunculaceae.
renoncule (rənɔ̃kyl), s.f. [f. L *ranuncula*] (bot.) Ranunculus, buttercup, crowfoot, spearwort; ~ *bouton d'or*, buttercup.
renouée (rənwe), s.f. (bot.) Knot-grass; polygonum; spotted persicaria.
renouement (rənumɑ̃), s.m. Tying again; renewal (of friendship, &c.).
renouer (rənwe), v.a. To tie again, to bind again; to renew, to resume; ~ *la conversation*, to resume the conversation; ~ *amitié*, to renew friendship; ~, v.n. to resume relations (*avec*, with).
renouveau (pl. **-x**) (rənuvo), s.m. Springtime.
renouvelable (rənuvlabl), adj. Renewable; that may be replaced.
renouveler (rənuvle), v.a. [f. *re+nouveau*] To renew, to renovate; to revive, to regenerate; to repeat, to do again; to replace; **se** ~, v.pr. to be revived, renewed, refreshed; to occur again; to change, to be replaced.
renouvellement (rənuvɛlmɑ̃), s.m. Renewal, renewing; renovating; replacing, refurnishing, restocking; repetition.
rénovat-eur, -rice (renɔvatœr), adj. s.m.f. Renovating, renovator.
rénovation (renɔva'sjɔ̃), s.f. [L *renovatio*] Renovation, renewal, refreshing; restoration.
rénover (renɔve), v.a. [L *renovare*] To renovate, to revive; to restore.
renseignement (rɑ̃sɛɲəmɑ̃), s.m. Information, indication, account; intelligence; *fournir des* ~*s sur*, to give information about; *aller aux* ~*s*, to make inquiries, to seek information.
renseigner (rɑ̃sɛɲe), v.a. [*re+enseigner*] To give information to, to direct; **se** ~, v.pr. to seek information, to make inquiries.
rensemencer (rɑ̃smɑ̃se), v.a. To re-sow.
rente (rɑ̃t), s.f. [L *reddita*] Yearly income, rent (⚠ not in the sense of *loyer*); income, revenue dividends; ~ *viagère*, life annuity; *vivre de ses* ~*s*, to live on one's income; ~*s sur l'État*, government stock; *faire une* ~ *à X*, to allow a pension to X.
renté (rɑ̃te), p. adj. That has an income; endowed; *être bien* ~, to be well off, to have a good income.
renter (rɑ̃te), v.a. To endow. ⚠ Not 'to rent', which = *louer, prendre en location*.
renti-er, -ère (rɑ̃tje), s.m.f. Stockholder; person who lives on his or her income; man (or woman) of property.
rentoilage (rɑ̃twalaʒ), s.m. Putting new canvas (to a picture).
rentoiler (rɑ̃twale), v.a. To put new canvas to (a picture); to put new linen to (shirts, &c.), to patch.
rentrage (rɑ̃traʒ), s.m. Taking in, housing, carrying home.
rentraire (rɑ̃trɛr), v.a. [f. L *re+intrahere*] To mend (invisibly), to sew up.
rentraiture (rɑ̃trɛtyr), s.f. Invisible mending or sewing.

---

a, m*a*l, l*a*tte; ɑ, p*a*s; ɑ̃, *en*fant; e, f*é*e; ɛ, p*è*re, n*e*tte; ɛ̃, v*in*, p*ain*; ə, pr*e*mier; g, do*gue*, *g*ale; h, *h*éros; i, f*i*n*i*r; j, *y*eux, v*i*ens, bai*ll*er; k, *c*roire; ɲ, oi*gn*on; o, p*au*se, d*o*se;

rentrant, -e (rɑ̃trɑ̃), p. adj. Re-entrant, pointing inwards; *angle* ~, re-entrant angle. ~, s.m. New player.

rentrayage (rɑ̃trɛjaʒ), s.m. Fine-drawing; invisible mending; sewing up.

rentrayeu-r, -se (rɑ̃trɛjœr), s.m.f. Fine-drawer.

rentré, -e (rɑ̃tre), p. adj. Driven in; suppressed, restrained, checked; *sueur* ~*e*, checked perspiration; *colère* ~*e*, suppressed indignation.

rentrée (rɑ̃tre), s.f. Re-entering; reappearance; reopening (of schools, &c.); *à la* ~ *des classes*, at the beginning of term; coming home; ~*s tardives*, late hours; gathering in, getting in, housing; (money matters) return, payment, getting in (of taxes, &c.); *attendre des* ~*s*, to expect to receive some payments; (at cards) cards taken in.

rentrer (rɑ̃tre), v.n. [*re*+*entrer*] To re-enter, to go in, to come or go home; to get back, to recover; ~ *dans son bien*, to recover one's property; ~ *dans l'ordre*, to restore to order; ~ *en grâce*, to come into favour again; ~ *en possession de*, to recover, to regain possession of; ~ *en soi-même*, to reflect, or consider seriously; to commune with oneself; *cela ne rentre pas dans mes attributions*, that does not come into my rights; that is no part of my duties; that 's not my province; *faire* ~ *X sous terre*, to humiliate X; to overwhelm X; ~, v.a. to gather in, to bring home, to bring back, to get in, to house; to check, to suppress; ~ *les foins*, to get in the hay; *rentrez vos larmes*, check your tears; stop crying; *rentrez les avirons*, ship the oars; (slang) *il va lui* ~ *dedans*, or *lui* ~ *dans le chou*, he will pitch into him.

rentr'ouvrir (rɑ̃truvrir), v.a. To reopen slightly.

renversable (rɑ̃vɛrsabl), adj. Easily upset; reversible.

renversant, -e (rɑ̃vɛrsɑ̃), p. adj. (fig.) Startling, stunning, stupendous, stupefying.

renverse (rɑ̃vɛrs), s.f. Reversal; *tomber à la* ~, to fall on one's back; (fig. fam.) to be struck all of a heap, to be bowled over.

renversé, -e (rɑ̃vɛrse), p. adj. Reversed, inverted; turned upside down; overthrown; lying on one's back; discomposed, utterly disconcerted; *avoir une figure* ~*e*, to look overcome with grief, staggered; *c'est le monde* ~*!*, everything is upside down!, things have come to a pretty pass!

renversement (rɑ̃vɛrsmɑ̃), s.m. Overturning, upsetting, turning upside down; inversion, reversing; subversion, destruction, ruin, overthrow; (mus.) inverting; *mécanisme de* ~, reversing gear.

renverser (rɑ̃vɛrse), v.a. [f. *envers*] To upset, to overturn, to overthrow, to turn upside down, to knock down; to spill (liquids); to reverse; (mus., arith.) to invert; (fig.) to stupefy, to astound, to amaze, to disarange, to turn topsy-turvy, to turn (a person's head); ~ *la vapeur*, to reverse the engine, or steam; **se** ~, v.pr. to be upset, overturned, to throw oneself back, to fall back; to capsize.

renvi (rɑ̃vi), s.m. [f. *renvier*] Overstake (at cards).

renvidage (rɑ̃vidaʒ), s.m. (techn.) Winding up.

renvider (rɑ̃vide), v.a. [*re*+*envider*] To wind upon the bobbins (in spinning).

renvier (rɑ̃vje), v.n. To increase one's stakes (at cards).

renvoi (rɑ̃vwa), s.m. [f. *renvoyer*] Returning, return, sending back; dismissal, turning out, discharge; postponement, adjournment, reference; reverberation (of sound); (med., and fam.) rising, eructation.

renvoyer (rɑ̃vwaje), v.a. [*re*+*envoyer*] To return, to send back; to dismiss, to discharge; to turn out, (colloq.) to hoof out; to put off, to postpone, to adjourn, to refer; to reverberate, to reflect, to throw back; **se** ~, v.pr. *se* ~ *la balle*, to bandy compliments, jokes, sallies, &c.

réoccupation (reɔkypa'sjɔ̃), s.f. Re-occupation.

réoccuper (reɔkype), v.a. To reoccupy.

réorganisation (reɔrganiza'sjɔ̃), s.f. Re-organization.

réorganiser (reɔrganize), v.a. To re-organize.

réouverture (reuvɛrtyr), s.f. Reopening.

repaire (rəpɛr), s.m. [f. OF *repairer*] Lair; den, haunt; ~ *de brigands*, den of thieves.

repaître (rəpɛtr), v.n.a. To feed, to nourish, to entertain; *se* ~, to feast (*de*, upon); *se* ~ *de chimères*, to live on chimeras, to delight in idle fancies.

répandre (repɑ̃dr), v.a. [*re*+*épandre*] To pour, to shed, to spill, to sprinkle; to spread, to scatter, to diffuse, to propagate; to exhale; to lavish, to distribute; ~ *des larmes, des pleurs*, to shed tears; ~ *un parfum*, to exhale a fragrance, a scent; ~ *l'alarme*, to spread the alarm; ~ *l'Évangile*, to propagate the Gospel; ~ *l'instruction*, to diffuse instruction; ~ *de faux bruits*, to spread (or circulate) false reports; ~ *son sang*, to shed one's blood; **se** ~, v.pr. to spread, to be scattered, to be propagated, diffused; to run out, to burst out; *se* ~ *en invectives*, to burst into invective; *se* ~ *dans le monde*, to go out into society; *le bruit se répand que*, it is rumoured that.

répandu, -e (repɑ̃dy), p. adj. Rumoured, propagated, spread, widespread; poured out, spilt; prevalent; *l'opinion la plus* ~*e*, the prevalent opinion; *un homme très* ~, a man well known in society circles.

réparable (reparabl), adj. Reparable, that may be mended or repaired.

reparaître (rəparɛtr), v.n. To reappear, to make one's reappearance.

réparat-eur, -rice (reparatœr), adj. Restorative, refreshing. ~, s.m.f. Repairer, restorer, mender.

réparation (repara'sjɔ̃), s.f. Repair, mending, repairing; reparation, atonement, amends, indemnification, compensation, retractation; *~s courantes*, running repairs; *en* ~, under repair; *atelier de ~s*, repair shop; *demander ~ à X*, to demand satisfaction or reparation from X; *~ par les armes*, duel.

réparer (repare), v.a. [L *reparare*] To repair, to mend; to make amends for; to make up for; to restore, to retrieve; to make reparation for; to redress (wrongs).

reparler (rəparle), v.n. To speak again; *nous en reparlerons*, we shall see about that; let us think it over; we'll discuss that later.

répartement (repartəmɑ̃), s.m. [f. *répartir*] Assessment (of taxes).

repartie (rəparti), s.f. Repartee, rejoinder, retort, reply; *avoir la ~ prompte, être prompt à la* ~, to be quick at repartee.

repartir[1] (rəpartir), v.a.n. To answer, to retort, to rejoin.

repartir[2] (rəpartir), v.n. To leave again, to set out again; (of a train) to start again.

répartir (repartir), v.a. [*re+partir = partager*] To distribute, to assess (taxes), to allot, to portion out, to divide.

répartiteur (repartitœr), s.m. Assessor (of taxes).

répartition (repartisjɔ̃), s.f. Distribution, assessment (of taxes); allotment, apportionment.

repas (rəpɑ), s.m. [f. L *repascere*] Meal, repast.

repassage (rəpɑsaʒ), s.m. **1.** Ironing (of linen, &c.); **2.** sharpening, grinding (of knives, &c.); **3.** passing again.

repasser (rəpɑse), v.n. To pass again, to cross, to cross again, to come again, to look in again, to call again; ~, v.a. to iron (linen), to sharpen, to grind, to set (knives, &c.), to strop (razors); *~ une leçon*, to look over a lesson; *~ un examen*, to undergo or take an examination again; *~ quelque chose dans son esprit*, to revolve something in one's mind; *~ les Alpes*, to recross the Alps.

repasseur (rəpɑsœr), s.m. Grinder; *~ de couteaux*, knife-grinder.

repasseuse (rəpɑsøz), s.f. Ironer, laundress.

repaver (rəpave), v.a. To repave.

repayer (rəpɛje), v.a. To pay over again.

repêchage (rəpɛʃaʒ), s.m. Fishing up again; (fig.) help (at examination, &c.); supplementary examination for candidates who have previously failed, consolation race.

repêcher (rəpɛʃe), v.a. To fish up again; (fig.) to help out of a difficulty.

repeindre (rəpɛ̃dr), v.a. To paint again.

repeint (rəpɛ̃), s.m. Retouched part (of a picture).

repenser (rəpɑ̃se), v.n.a. To think again (of something), to think over, to reconsider.

repentance (rəpɑ̃tɑ̃s), s.f. Repentance, contrition, compunction.

repentant, -e (rəpɑ̃tɑ̃), p. adj. Repentant, penitent.

repenti, -e (rəpɑ̃ti), p. adj. Repentant, penitent.

(se) repentir (sərəpɑ̃tir), v.pr. [f. L *re+poenitere*] To repent, to rue; *se ~ de ses fautes*, to repent one's sins; *se ~ d'avoir fait cela*, to repent having done that; *il s'en repentira*, he shall repent this, or of this; he shall repent; *je l'en ferai* ~, I will make him rue it.

repentir (rəpɑ̃tir), s.m. Repentance, remorse, contrition; (colloq.) alteration, correction (in painting); *~s*, ringlets, curls.

repérage (rəperaʒ), s.m. [f. *repérer*] Fitting to a mark, finding the bearings, taking up guiding marks, identifying the origin or the spot (*de*, of); making a guiding mark.

repercer (rəpɛrse), v.a. To pierce again, to bore again.

répercussi-f, -ve (repɛrkysif), adj. (med.) Repercussive, repellent, astringent.

répercussion (repɛrkysʃɔ̃), s.f. [L *repercussio*] Repercussion, reverberation; (fig.) consequence.

répercuter (repɛrkyte), v.a. [L *re+percutere*] To repercuss, to reverberate, to echo.

reperdre (rəpɛrdr), v.a. To lose again, to miss again.

repère (rəpɛr), s.m. [f. L *reperire*] Guiding mark; joining mark, bench mark; landmark; *point de* ~, guiding mark, landmark; (fig.) landmark, indication.

repérer (rəpere), v.a. [f. L *repatriare*] To mark; to adjust; to discover; *~ une batterie*, to discover the exact position of a battery.

répertoire (repɛrtwar), s.m. [L *repertorium*] Repertory, catalogue, index; (theatr.) stock plays, repertory; *un vivant* ~, a walking encyclopaedia.

répertorier (repɛrtɔrje), v.a. To index.

repeser (rəpəze), v.a. To weigh again; (fig.) to reconsider.

répéter (repete), v.a. [L *repetere*] To repeat, to say again, to tell again; to rehearse (a play, part, &c.); to do again, to recommence; to dispose symmetrically;

to reflect; (law) to demand back; *il ne se l'est pas fait* ~ *deux fois*, he did not wait to be told twice; ~ *une expérience*, to repeat an experiment; **se** ~, v.pr. to repeat oneself, to tautologize, to say the same thing over and over again; to occur again; to be repeated.

répétit-eur, -rice (repetitœr), s.m.f. Private teacher, coach, tutor, assistant teacher.

répétition (repetisjɔ̃), s.f. [L *repetitio*] **1.** Repetition, repeating; *montre à* ~, repeater; recurrence, reiteration; *fusil à* ~, magazine-rifle; **2.** rehearsal; **3.** private lesson; **4.** (law) claim for recovery of money.

répétitorat (repetitɔra), s.m. Tutorship.

repétrir (rəpetrir), v.a. To knead again; (fig.) to re-create, to mould again.

repeuplement (rəpœpləmɑ̃), s.m. Repeopling, restocking; ~ *d'un étang*, restocking of a pond.

repeupler (rəpœple), v.a. To repeople, to restock.

repic (rəpik), s.m. (at piquet) Repique.

repincer (rəpɛ̃se), v.a. To pinch again, to nip again; (fig.) to catch again; *si je t'y repince*, if I catch you at it again.

repiquage (rəpikaʒ), s.m. **1.** Transplanting; **2.** picking up, repair (of roads).

repiquer (rəpike), v.a. **1.** To prick again; **2.** to transplant; **3.** to pick up, to dig up, to repair (roads); **4.** (naut.) ~ *dans le vent*, to haul into the wind again.

répit (repi), s.m. [f. L *respectus*] Respite, rest, breathing-space, delay; *sans* ~, without respite, unceasingly, unremittingly.

replacement (rəplasmɑ̃), s.m. Replacing, reinvestment.

replacer (rəplase), v.a. To replace, to put back again; to reinvest (funds); **se** ~, v.pr. to get a new situation (as servant).

replantation (rəplɑ̃ta'sjɔ̃), s.f. **replantage** (rəplɑ̃taʒ), s.m. Replanting.

replanter (rəplɑ̃te), v.a. To replant.

replâtrage (rəplatraʒ), s.m. Plastering up, botching up; botch; (fig.) patched-up reconciliation.

replâtrer (rəplatre), v.a. To new-plaster, to plaster up; (fig.) to botch up, to patch up.

repl-et, -ète (rəplɛ), adj. [L *repletus*] Stout, fat, fatty, obese. ⚠ Not to be translated by 'replete', which means, full, filled, stocked with, gorged, sated = *rempli, plein* (*de*, with).

répléti-f, -ve (repletif), adj. Replenishing.

réplétion (replesjɔ̃), s.f. [L *repletio*] **1.** Obesity, stoutness; **2.** repletion, plethora.

repleuvoir (rəplœvwar), v.n. impers. To rain again.

repli (rəpli), s.m. [f. *replier*] Fold, crease, turn, coil (of a serpent); (fig.) recess (of the soul).

repliement (rəplimɑ̃), s.m. Folding back; (mil.) falling back (of troops).

replier (rəplie), v.a. To fold up again, to turn in, to turn back; **se** ~, v.pr. to twist oneself, to bend, to coil; (mil.) to fall back; to fall back upon one's own thoughts; to meditate; to retire within oneself.

réplique (replik), s.f. [f. *répliquer*] **1.** Retort, rejoinder, repartee, reply, answer; *argument sans* ~, unanswerable reason; (theatr.) cue; *donner la* ~, to give the cue; **2.** (mus.) repeat; replica.

répliquer (replike), v.a.n. To reply, to retort, to answer.

replisser (rəplise), v.a. To pleat again.

reploiement (rəplwamɑ̃), s.m. See syn. REPLIEMENT.

replonger (rəplɔ̃ʒe), v.a.n. To plunge again, to dip again; to re-immerse; **se** ~, v.pr. to plunge again, to plunge oneself again, to be immersed, (fig.) involved, absorbed (in debt, thought, difficulties, &c.).

reployer (rəplwaje), v.a. See syn. REPLIER.

repolir (rəpɔlir), v.a. To repolish; to retouch.

repolissage (rəpɔlisaʒ), s.m. Repolishing.

répondant, -e (repɔ̃dɑ̃), s.m.f. Respondent; surety, bail, bondsman, referee; (at church) clerk.

répondre (repɔ̃dr), v.n.a. [L *respondere*] To answer, to reply (*à*, to), to write back; to respond to, to correspond (*à*, with), to be in accordance (with); to be security, to be bail, to be answerable, to be responsible (*de*, for); to come up (*à*, to); to give a suitable return; to echo, to be in proportion, to be symmetrical; to argue, to allege reasons; *il ne sait que* ~, he does not know what to answer; *le succès n'a pas répondu à mes espérances*, the result fell short of my expectations; ~ *à la tendresse de X*, to return X's love; *votre vie me répond de la sienne*, your life will answer for his; *je réponds de son honnêteté*, I will answer for his probity; *je vous en réponds*, take my word for it; I will be bound it is !; I should think so indeed !; ~ *pour X*, to go bail for X; to be surety for X; to answer for X; *la douleur me répond à la tête*, I feel the pain in my head; se ~, v.pr. to answer each other; to correspond, to be symmetrical.

répons (repɔ̃), s.m. [L *responsum*] (Cath. liturgy) Response.

réponse (repɔ̃s), s.f. [L *responsa*] Answer, reply, retort, response, rejoinder; *avoir* ~ *à tout*, never to be at a loss for an answer; *rendre* ~, to return an answer; ~ *de Normand*, equivocal or shuffling answer; (mus.) response (in a fugue).

repopulation (rəpɔpyla'sjɔ̃), s.f. Repeopling, repopulation.
report (rəpɔr), s.m. Carrying forward, bringing forward; amount brought forward; (Stock Exchange) continuation, contango. ⚠ Not Engl. 'report', which = *rapport, compte rendu, bulletin trimestriel, coup (de fusil)*, &c.
reportage (rəpɔrtaʒ), s.m. Reporting (for newspapers).
reporter (rəpɔrtœr), s.m. [Engl. wd] Reporter.
reporter (rəpɔrte), v.a. [*re*+*porter*] To carry back, to take back, to bring back; to transfer; (book-keep.) to bring (or carry) forward; (Stock Exchange) to carry over; (⚠ not 'to report', which = *rendre compte de, faire un rapport, constater*); **se** ~, v.pr. to be carried back; to go back (in imagination, memory, &c.); to refer.
repos (rəpo), s.m. [f. *reposer*] Rest, repose, quiet, respite; peace, sleep; (mus., pros.) pause, caesura; (mil.) ~ *!*, stand at ease !; *au* ~, at rest, when resting; *champ du* ~, churchyard; *avoir l'esprit en* ~, to be easy in one's mind; *mettre sa conscience en* ~, to ease one's conscience; *laissez-moi en* ~, let me alone; *valeurs de tout* ~, gilt-edged securities, perfectly safe bonds; *mettre un fusil au* ~, to half-cock a gun.
reposé, -e (rəpoze), p. adj. Refreshed, rested; *à tête* ~*e*, coolly, at leisure, deliberately; after thinking it over.
reposée (rəpoze), s.f. (hunt.) Lair.
reposer (rəpoze), v.a. **1.** [*re*+*poser*] To lay again, to put or place again, to set back; **2.** [L *re*+*pausare*] to rest, to give repose to; ~, v.n. to rest, to repose, to sleep; to lie; to be based, to be established (*sur*, on), to be built; to settle (as liquids); *ici repose X*, here lies X; **se** ~, v.pr. to place oneself again; (of birds, &c.) to light, to alight again; to rest, to repose, to take rest; to rely (*sur*, upon).
reposoir (rəpozwar), s.m. [L *repositorium*] Temporary altar, street altar.
repoussant, -e (rəpusɑ̃), p. adj. Repulsive, repellent, loathsome.
repoussé (rəpuse), p. adj. s.m. Repoussé.
repoussement (rəpusmɑ̃), s.m. Repulsion; recoil (of fire-arms).
repousser (rəpuse), v.a. **1.** To push back, to push away; to repulse, to repel; to throw away; to drive back; ~ *un tiroir*, to push back a drawer; ~ *l'ennemi*, to drive back the enemy; to repulse the enemy; ~ *une demande*, to reject a demand; ~ *un projet de loi*, to throw out a bill; **2.** (v.n.) (of fire-arms) to recoil, to kick; **3.** (v.n.a.) to grow again, to shoot again; *ses cheveux repoussent*, his hair is growing again.
repoussoir (rəpuswar), s.m. **1.** Driving-bolt; **2.** (fig.) set-off, contrast.
répréhensible (repreɑ̃sibl), adj. [L *reprehensibilis*] Reprehensible.
répréhensi-f, -ve (repreɑ̃sif), adj. Reprehensive.
répréhension (repreɑ̃sjɔ̃), s.f. [L *reprehensio*] Reprehension.
reprendre (rəprɑ̃dr), v.a.n. [L *reprehendere*] To take back, to get back, to retake, to recover, to resume possession of, to catch again; to take up, to go on; to find fault with, to reprove; to begin again; to resume; to answer, to rejoin; to take root again, to grow again, to get well again; ~ *haleine*, to recover one's breath; to take breath; (fig.) to get a respite; to pause; ~ *courage*, to pluck up courage; to take heart again; ~ *le dessus*, to get the upper hand again; to regain self-control; ~ *des forces*, to recover one's strength; *la goutte l'a repris*, he is suffering from gout again; ~ *ses habits d'été*, to take to one's summer clothes again; ~ *connaissance*, to recover consciousness; ~ *ses esprits*, to recover one's senses; *reprenez de ce plat*, have some more; *on ne m'y reprendra pas de sitôt*, they won't catch me at it again; ~ *en sous-œuvre*, to underpin; to stay up; *ah ! reprit-elle*, ah ! she replied; *le froid a repris*, the cold has set in again; *il faut* ~ *les enfants avec douceur*, children must be reproved with kindness; *on n'y trouve rien à* ~, there's nothing to find fault with; ~ *sa parole*, to take back one's word; **se** ~, v.pr. to regain self-control; to correct oneself; to stop oneself.
représaille (rəprezɑj), s.f. [LL *represalia*] (generally used in the plural) Reprisal; retaliation; *user de* ~*s*, to retaliate.
représentant, -e (rəprezɑ̃tɑ̃), s.m.f. Representative, delegate, deputy; ~ *de commerce*, commercial traveller, bagman.
représentati-f, -ve (rəprezɑ̃tatif), adj. Representative.
représentation (rəprezɑ̃ta'sjɔ̃), s.f. Exhibition, show, production; performance; likeness, image, picture; display, show, entertainment; remonstrance; *faire des* ~*s à X*, to remonstrate with X; *frais de* ~, money allowed for official entertaining; *la* ~ *nationale*, the national representation; the Members of Parliament.
représenter (rəprezɑ̃te), v.a.n. [L *repraesentare*] To present again, to represent; to show, to display; to picture, to offer the likeness of, to portray, to describe, to typify, to symbolize; to act, to perform, to personate; to be the delegate of, to stand in the place of; (comm.) to travel for; to appear prosperous; to make some show; to keep a large establishment; **se** ~, v.pr. to imagine, to picture to oneself; to present oneself again; to occur again.
répressible (reprɛsibl), adj. Repressible.

répressi-f, -ve (represif), adj. [f. L *repressus*] Repressive.
répression (represjɔ̃), s.f. Repression.
réprimandable (reprimɑ̃dabl), adj. That may or must be reprimanded.
réprimande (reprimɑ̃d), s.f. [L *reprimenda*] Reprimand, rebuke, blame.
réprimander (reprimɑ̃de), v.a. To reprimand, to reprove, to upbraid.
réprimant, -e (reprimɑ̃), p. adj. Repressive.
réprimer (reprime), v.a. [L *reprimere*] To repress, to restrain, to curb, to quell, to check, to hold in check.
repris (rəpri), s.m. ~ *de justice*, old offender.
reprisage (rəprizaʒ), s.m. Darning, mending.
reprise (rəpriz), s.f. [f. *reprendre*] Retaking, recapture, resumption, renewal, revival, improvement; (theatr.) re-performance, revival; (mus.) repeat; darning, mending; *faire des ~s*, to darn; (build.) underpinning; (law) reprisal; (boxing) round; (fenc.) bout; *à plusieurs ~s*, several times, over and over again; *à trois ~s*, thrice, three times; *à deux ~s*, twice.
repriser (rəprize), v.a. To darn, to mend.
réprobat-eur, -rice (reprɔbatœr), adj. Reproachful, reproving.
réprobation (reprɔba'sjɔ̃), s.f. [L *reprobatio*] Reprobation.
reprochable (rəprɔʃabl), adj. Reproachable.
reproche (rəprɔʃ), s.m. [f. *reprocher*] Reproach, blame; *faire un ~ à X de*, to reproach X with; *sans ~*, blameless; above reproach; *sans peur et sans ~*, fearless and blameless; *soit dit sans ~*, without intending any reproach.
reprocher (rəprɔʃe), v.a. [LL *repropiare*] To reproach, to charge (*de*, with); to cast in the teeth (*à*, of); (law) to take exception to; ~ *ses torts à X*, to reproach X with his faults; (law) ~ *des témoins*, to take exception to witnesses; ~ *sa nourriture à X*, to grudge X his food; **se ~**, v.pr. to reproach oneself.
reproduct-eur, -rice (rəprɔdyktœr), adj. Reproductive.
reproduction (rəprɔdyksjɔ̃), s.f. [f. *reproduire*] Reproduction; imitation; republication; copy; reproducing, reprinting; breeding (of stock), procreation.
reproduire (rəprɔdɥir), v.a. [*re+produire*] To reproduce; to imitate, to copy; to republish, to reprint; **se ~**, v.pr. to be reproduced; to reappear, to occur again, to recur; to breed, to procreate, to generate offspring; to propagate; to multiply.
réprouvable (repruvabl), adj. Reprehensible, reprovable.
réprouvé, -e (repruve), p. adj. Reprobate, (theol.) damned. ~, s.m.f. Reprobate, outcast.
réprouver (repruve), v.a. [L *reprobare*] To reprobate, to condemn, to disapprove of.
reps (rɛps), s.m. Rep (silk or woollen).
reptation (rɛpta'sjɔ̃), s.f. [L *reptatio*] Reptation, creeping, crawling.
reptatoire (rɛptatwar), adj. Of reptation, crawling, reptant.
reptile (rɛptil), s.m. [L *reptilis*] Reptile; (fig.) crawling wretch, toad-eater, fawning cur, grovelling fellow.
repu, -e (rəpy), p. adj. [f. *repaître*] Satiated.
républicain, -e (repyblikɛ̃), adj. s.m.f. Republican.
républicaniser (repyblikanize), v.a. To republicanize.
républicanisme (repyblikanism), s.m. Republicanism.
republier (rəpyblie), v.a. To republish, to reissue.
république (repyblik), s.f. [L *res publica*] Republic, commonwealth.
répudiable (repydjabl), adj. Repudiable.
répudiation (repydja'sjɔ̃), s.f. Repudiation.
répudier (repydje), v.a. [L *repudiare*] To repudiate; to renounce.
répugnance (repyɲɑ̃s), s.f. Repulsion, repugnance, reluctance, aversion, unwillingness; *avec ~*, unwillingly, reluctantly; *avoir de la ~ à faire cela*, to be lo(a)th to do that.
répugnant, -e (repyɲɑ̃), p. adj. Repugnant, repulsive, disgusting.
répugner (repyɲe), v.n. [L *repugnare*] To be repugnant, repulsive, &c., to feel repugnance, to feel lo(a)th (*à*, to); *il répugne à faire cela*, he feels lo(a)th to do that; *cela me répugne*, I find that disgusting; I loathe doing that; it turns my stomach.
répulsi-f, -ve (repylsif), adj. Repulsive.
répulsion (repylsjɔ̃), s.f. [L *repulsio*] Repulsion, disgust, aversion.
réputation (repyta'sjɔ̃), s.f. [L *reputatio*] Reputation, repute, character, name, fame; *perdu de ~*, disreputable; disgraced; of tarnished reputation; *avoir la ~ de*, to pass for, to be known for; *connaître X de ~*, to know X by report.
réputé, -e (repyte), p. adj. Reputed, considered, known (*pour*, for), famous, renowned, in repute.
réputer (repyte), v.a. [L *reputare*] To deem, to esteem, to repute, to hold, to account.
requérable (rəkerabl), adj. (law) To be demanded.
requérant, -e (rəkerɑ̃), p. adj. Claiming, suing. ~, s.m.f. Applicant, petitioner, plaintiff.
requérir (rəkerir), v.a.n. [L *requirere*] To require, to ask, to summon, to call upon; to request; ~ *X de faire cela*, to require or

to summon X to do that; to bid X do that; to fetch, to summon, to call in; ~ *la force publique*, to call in the police.
requête (rəkɛt), s.f. [f. *requérir*] Request, demand, petition, application; *présenter sa* ~, to present a petition; to make a request; *Maître des Requêtes*, Master of Requests (in Fr. *Conseil d'État*).
requêter (rəkɛte), v.a. (hunt.) To search again.
requiem (rekɥiɛm), s.m. [L wd] Requiem.
requin (rəkɛ̃), s.m. [orig. dub.] Shark; (fig.) shark, sharper, swindler.
requinquer (rəkɛ̃ke), v.a. [etym. dub.] (colloq.) To smarten up; **se** ~, v.pr. **1.** to smarten oneself up; **2.** to recover health, strength, spirits, &c., to pick up.
requis, -e (rəki), p. adj. Required; *l'âge* ~, the required age; *les conditions* ~*es*, the required conditions or circumstances.
réquisition (rekizisjɔ̃), s.f. [L *requisitio*] Requisition, demand, application, summons; levy; *à la* ~ *de X*, on the demand of X; *mettre en* ~, to put in requisition, to requisition, to commandeer.
réquisitionnement (rekizisjɔ̃nmɑ̃), s.m. Requisitioning, levy.
réquisitionner (rekizisjɔne), v.a. To requisition, to levy, to commandeer.
réquisitoire (rekizitwar), s.m. Speech for the prosecution, list of charges; list of grievances, indictment.
rescinder (rɛsɛ̃de), v.a. [L *rescindere*] (law) To rescind.
rescision (rɛssizjɔ̃), s.f. [L *rescissio*] (law) Rescission; (surg.) cutting off.
rescapé, -e (rɛskape), p. adj. s.m.f. [dialect form of *réchappé*] Surviving, survivor.
rescisoire (rɛssizwar), adj. (law) Rescissory.
rescousse (rɛskus), s.f. [f. OF *recourre, rescoure*] Renewed attack; *venir à la* ~, to come to the rescue; to bring fresh forces.
rescription (rɛskripsjɔ̃), s.f. [L *rescriptio*] Rescription, money order.
rescrit (rɛskri), s.m. [L *rescriptum*] Rescript.
réseau (pl. **-x**) (rezo), s.m. [f. L *retiolum*] Net, network; (fig.) web, tangle, system; (arch.) tracery; ~ *de fils barbelés*, barbed-wire entanglements; ~ *de chemins de fer*, railway system, network of railways.
résection (resɛksjɔ̃), s.f. [f. L *resecare*] (surg.) Resection, cutting off.
réseda (rezeda), s.m. (bot.) Mignonette.
réséquer (reseke), v.a. [L *resecare*] (surg.) To resect, to cut off.
réservation (rezɛrva'sjɔ̃), s.f. (law) Reservation.
réserve (rezɛrv), s.f. [f. *réserver*] Reserve, reservation; guardedness; discretion, reticence, wariness, coyness; store, reserve; (hunt.) preserve; (mil.) reserves; *faire des* ~*s*, to make reservations; *à la* ~ *de*, except; with reservation of; *mettre en* ~, to lay by, to put by; *se tenir sur la* ~, to be on one's guard; to be reticent; *sans* ~*s*, without any reserve, unreservedly; *sous toutes* ~*es*, with all proper reserves.
réservé, -e (rezɛrve), p. adj. Reserved, guarded, reticent, cautious; private; engaged.
réserver (rezɛrve), v.a. [L *reservare*] To reserve, to lay by, to keep back; to spare, to set apart; to keep in store; **se** ~, v.pr. to reserve for oneself; to bide one's time; to wait for an opportunity; *je me réserve de le lui dire quelque jour*, I intend to tell him myself, some day.
réserviste (rezɛrvist), s.m. (mil.) Reservist.
réservoir (rezɛrvwar), s.m. Tank, cistern, reservoir; *plume à* ~, fountain-pen; ~ *à essence*, petrol-tank; ~ *à huile*, oil-box, oil-tank.
résidence (rezidɑ̃s), s.f. [L *residentia*] Residence, dwelling, abode; residency; *établir sa* ~, to take up one's abode, or one's residence.
résident (rezidɑ̃), s.m. Resident.
résider (rezide), v.n. [L *residere*] To reside, to have one's home or residence; to consist, to lie; *la difficulté réside en ceci*, the difficulty lies in this.
résidu (rezidy), s.m. [L *residuum*] Residue; (chem.) residuum; (arith.) remainder.
résignant, -e (reziɲɑ̃), s.m.f. Resigner.
résignataire (reziɲatɛr), s.m.f. Resignee.
résignation (reziɲa'sjɔ̃), s.f. [L *resignatio*] Resignation; resigning; resignation, submission; *avec* ~, resignedly.
résigné, -e (reziɲe), p. adj. Resigned, submissive.
résigner (reziɲe), v.a. [L *resignare*] To resign; **se** ~, v.pr. to resign oneself, to submit, to be resigned; *se* ~ *à l'inévitable*, to resign oneself to the inevitable.
résiliation (rezilja'sjɔ̃), s.f. **résiliement** (rezilimɑ̃), s.m. Cancelling.
résilier (rezilje), v.a. [L *resilire*] To cancel, to annul.
résille (rezij), s.f. [f. *réseau*] Hair-net; network; lead bars (in stained-glass window).
résine (rezin), s.f. [L *resina*] Resin, rosin.
résiner (rezine), v.a. **1.** To extract resin from (pines); **2.** to rosin; to rub over with rosin.
résineu-x, -se (rezinø), adj. Resinous.
résini-er, -ère (rezinje), s.m. Person who extracts resin from pines. ~, adj. Pertaining to rosin, resin, or (obs.) rosen.
résinifère (rezinifɛr), adj. Resiniferous.
résipiscence (rezipisɑ̃s), s.f. [f. L *resipiscere*] Resipiscence, repentance; *venir à* ~, to amend, to return to one's senses, to repent.

résistance (rezistɑ̃s), s.f. [f. *résister*] Resistance, opposition, resisting, impeding or stopping effect; (electr.) resistance; *bobine de* ~, resistance-coil; *boîte de* ~, resistance-box; *faire* ~, to offer resistance, to resist, to rebel; *éprouver une* ~, to meet with some resistance; *sans* ~, unresistingly; *pièce de* ~, main course (of meal); *prendre la ligne de moindre* ~, to take the line of least resistance.

résistant, -e (rezistɑ̃), p. adj. Unyielding, resisting; strong, lasting, firm, tough.

résister (reziste), v.n. [L *resistere*] To offer resistance (*à*, to); ~ *à*, to resist, to oppose, to withstand; to endure, to bear, to hold out; ~ *à la fatigue*, to be proof against fatigue; to resist the strain; ~ *à l'ennemi*, to hold out against the enemy; to resist the enemy; ~ *à la tentation*, to withstand or resist temptation.

résolu, -e (rezɔly), p. adj. [f. *résoudre*] Resolute, unwavering, determined, firm of purpose; (of problems, difficulties, &c.) resolved, solved.

résoluble (rezɔlybl), adj. **1.** Resolvable; **2.** cancellable.

résolument (rezɔlymɑ̃), adv. Resolutely, firmly, boldly, stoutly.

résoluti-f, -ve (rezɔlytif), adj. s.m. Resolutive, resolvent, discutient.

résolution (rezɔlysjɔ̃), s.f. [L *resolutio*] Resolution, solution, solving; (med., pros., mus., techn.) resolution; (math.) resolution, reduction (of an equation); ~ *d'un contrat*, cancelling of an agreement; *prendre la* ~ *de*, to make up one's mind to; *changer de* ~, to change one's mind; *agir avec* ~, to act resolutely; *manquer de* ~, to be wanting in resolution, to be irresolute; *prendre de bonnes* ~*s*, to form or make good resolutions.

résolutoire (rezɔlytwar), adj. (law) Cancelling, resolutive.

résolvant, -e (rezɔlvɑ̃), p. adj. s.m. See syn. RÉSOLUTIF.

résonance (rezɔnɑ̃s), s.f. [L *resonantia*] Resonance.

résonateur (rezɔnatœr), s.m. Resonator.

résonnant, -e (rezɔnɑ̃), p. adj. Resonant, resounding, echoing; sonorous.

résonnement (rezɔnmɑ̃), s.m. Resounding, echoing.

résonner (rezɔne), v.n. [L *resonare*] To resound, to ring (*de*, with), to be sonorous; (fig.) to produce a sensation, to be much talked of; to be filled (with), to resound (with).

résorber (rezɔrbe), v.a. [f. L *re*+*sorbere*] To reabsorb, to resorb; **se** ~, v.pr. to be resorbed.

résorcine (rezɔrsin), s.f. (chem.) Resorcin.

résorption (rezɔrpsjɔ̃, rezɔrbsjɔ̃), s.f. [f. L *resorbere*] Resorption, reabsorption.

résoudre (rezudr), v.a. irreg. [L *resolvere*] **1.** To resolve, to solve, to dissolve, to disintegrate, to melt, to dissipate, to break up into parts, to convert (into), to reduce by mental analysis; to cancel; *un problème résolu*, a solved problem; *je résous une équation*, I resolve, or reduce, an equation; *cela ne résout pas la question*, that does not settle the question; *nous avons résolu notre bail*, we have cancelled our lease; **2.** v.n. to resolve, to make up one's mind (*de*, to), to decide upon; *il a résolu qu'il irait demain*, he has made up his mind to go to-morrow; he is resolved upon going to-morrow; **se** ~, v.pr. **1.** to bring oneself (*à*, to); to resolve, to make up one's mind (to); to resign oneself (to); **2.** to be resolved, to be dissolved or converted; *la tumeur se résoudra*, the tumour will resolve, or be resolved; *l'eau se résout en vapeur*, water is resolved into vapour.

respect (rɛspɛ), s.m. [f. L *respectus*] Respect, reverence, regard; *porter* ~ *à X*, to have respect for X; ~ *humain*, regard for public opinion; *présenter ses* ~*s à X*, to pay one's respects to X; *manquer de* ~ *à X*, to be wanting in respect towards X; to slight X; to fail in courtesy towards X; *tenir X en* ~, to awe X; to keep X in awe; to intimidate X; *sauf votre* ~, with all deference to you. ⚠ In French *respect* cannot now be used as in English in the sense of 'reference', 'relation'; ex. in many respects = *à bien des égards*; admirable in respect of style = *admirable au point de vue du style*, &c.; though in the 17th cent. *respect* was used frequently in that acceptation.

respectabilité (rɛspɛktabilite), s.f. [f. Engl. wd] Respectability.

respectable (rɛspɛktabl), adj. Respectable; important; *une somme* ~, a pretty large sum, a respectable amount.

respectablement (rɛspɛktabləmɑ̃), adv. Respectably.

respecter (rɛspɛkte), v.a. To respect, to have respect for; to spare, to respect, to refrain from damaging, offending, interrupting, &c.; **se** ~, v.pr. to respect oneself; to respect each other.

respecti-f, -ve (rɛspɛktif), adj. Respective; reciprocal.

respectivement (rɛspɛktivmɑ̃), adv. Respectively.

respectueusement (rɛspɛktɥøzmɑ̃), adv. Respectfully, deferentially.

respectueu-x, -se (rɛspɛktɥø), adj. Respectful, deferential.

respirable (rɛspirabl), adj. Respirable, fit to be breathed, breathable.

respiration (rɛspira'sjɔ̃), s.f. [f. *respirer*] Respiration, breathing; *difficulté de* ~, shortness of breath; *avoir la* ~ *coupée*, to be out of breath; *ce vent vous coupe la* ~, this wind takes one's breath away.

respiratoire (rɛspiratwar), adj. Respiratory.

respirer (rɛspire), v.n.a. [L *respirare*] To breathe, to respire; to live; to exhale; to express, to manifest; to rest, to have a respite; *ah! je respire!*, ah, that's better!; *il a de la peine à* ~, he breathes with difficulty; *laissez-moi* ~, let me take breath; give me some respite; *elle respire la santé*, she is the living embodiment of health; *il ne respire que vengeance*, he thirsts for vengeance.

resplendir (rɛsplɑ̃dir), v.n. [L *resplendere*] To be resplendent (*de*, with), to shine.

resplendissant, -e (rɛsplɑ̃disɑ̃), p. adj. Resplendent (*de*, with), dazzling, bright, shining.

responsabilité (rɛspɔ̃sabilite), s.f. Responsibility; liability.

responsable (rɛspɔ̃sabl), adj. [f. L *respondere*] Responsible, accountable, liable (*de*, for; *envers*, to).

responsi-f, -ve (rɛspɔ̃sif), adj. (law) Responsive, respondent.

resquilleur (rɛskijœr), s.m. (slang) Gate-crasher.

ressac (rəsak), s.m. [Provenç. wd] Surf; undertow.

ressaisir (rəsɛzir), v.a. [*re*+*saisir*] To seize again, to catch again, to recover, to regain; **se** ~, v.pr. to regain one's self-control; *se* ~ *de quelque chose*, to recapture, to regain possession of something.

ressasser (rəsase), v.a. **1.** To resift; **2.** to keep on repeating, to say over and over again.

ressasseur (rəsasœr), s.m. Tiresome repeater.

ressaut (rəso), s.m. [f. OF *ressaillir*] Projection; abrupt fall, dip, difference of level.

ressauter (rəsote), v.n. To leap again; (colloq.) to protest, to kick, to show fight, to resist.

ressayer (rɛsɛje), v.a.n. To try again.

resseller (rəsɛle), v.a. To resaddle.

ressemblance (rəsɑ̃blɑ̃s), s.f. Resemblance, likeness.

ressemblant, -e (rəsɑ̃blɑ̃), p. adj. Like, similar, very much alike; true to life; *ce portrait est très* ~, the likeness is very good, or striking.

ressembler (rəsɑ̃ble), v.n. [*re*+*sembler*] To resemble, to be like, to be alike; *votre portrait ne vous ressemble pas*, your portrait is not very like you; *comme vous ressemblez à votre mère!*, how like your mother you are!; how you resemble your mother!; *cela ne ressemble à rien*, it is like nothing on earth; I can make neither head nor tail of it; **se** ~, to be very much alike; *ils se ressemblent comme deux gouttes d'eau*, they are as like as two peas; *qui se ressemble s'assemble*, birds of a feather flock together.

ressemelage (rəsəməlaʒ), s.m. Resoling.

ressemeler (rəsəmle), v.a. [f. *semelle*] To resole.

ressentiment (rəsɑ̃timɑ̃), s.m. Resentment, grievance.

ressentir (rəsɑ̃tir), v.a. [*re*+*sentir*] To feel; **se** ~, v.pr. to be felt; to be experienced; to feel the effects (*de*, of); *elle se ressent encore de sa chute*, she still feels the effects of her fall.

resserre (rəsɛr), s.f. Lock-up store, store-room.

resserré, -e (rəsɛre), p. adj. Narrow; *un vallon* ~, a narrow dell.

resserrement (rəsɛrmɑ̃), s.m. Tightening, tightness; confinement; oppression; constipation.

resserrer (rəsɛre), v.a. To contract, to tighten; to abridge, to condense; (med.) to bind, to be binding; to lock up again, to put back again in its place; ~ *les liens de l'amitié*, to strengthen the bonds of friendship.

resservir (rəsɛrvir), v.n.a. To be used again; to serve again; to hand (dishes, coffee, &c.) again.

ressort (rəsɔr), s.m. [f. *ressortir*] **1.** Spring, elasticity; (fig.) energy, means; ~ *à boudin*, coil-spring; ~ *de choc*, buffer-spring; *main de* ~, shackle; ~ *de rappel*, reaction-spring; *faire jouer tous les* ~*s*, to set every wheel in motion; to pull the wires; to leave no stone unturned; **2.** jurisdiction, department, province; *cela n'est pas de mon* ~, that does not come within my province; that is not in my line; *en dernier* ~, in the last resort; without appeal.

ressortir[1] (rəsɔrtir), v.n. [*re*+*sortir*] To go or come out again; to stand out; to result; *il ressort chaque soir*, he goes out again every night; *le noir fait* ~ *les couleurs*, black makes other colours stand out; black throws colours into relief.

ressortir[2] (rəsɔrtir), v.n. To be under the jurisdiction of; to pertain (*à*, to), to relate; *cette affaire ressortit au juge de paix*, this case falls under the jurisdiction of the magistrate.

ressortissant, -e (rəsɔrtisɑ̃), p. adj. s.m.f. (Person) under the jurisdiction (*à*, of).

ressouder (rəsude), v.a. To solder again; to unite again.

ressource (rəsurs), s.f. **1.** Resource, device, shift, expedient; *un homme de* ~, a resourceful man; **2.** ~*s*, (pl.) resources, money, means, fortune; *se trouver sans* ~*s*, to be without means; to be impoverished; (colloq.) to be stony broke.

ressouvenance (rəsuvnɑ̃s), s.f. Remembrance.

ressouvenir (rəsuvnir), s.m. See syn. RESSOUVENANCE.

(se) ressouvenir (sərəsuvnir), v.pr. To remember; *se ~ de*, to call to mind again; *faire ~*, to remind.

ressuage (rəsɥaʒ), s.m. (metall.) Eliquation.

ressuer (rəsɥe), v.n. [*re*+*suer*] To sweat again; to run with moisture; (metall.) *faire ~*, to liquate.

ressui (rɛsɥi), s.m. [f. *ressuyer*] (hunt.) Lair (where animals dry themselves after rain, &c.).

ressusciter (rɛsysite), v.a. [L *resuscitare*] To resuscitate, to revive, to restore to life, consciousness, vigour, &c.; ~, v.n. to revive, to return to life, to resuscitate, to be resuscitated.

ressuyer (rɛsɥije), v.a. To dry again, to dry.

restant, -e (rɛstɑ̃), p. adj. Left, remaining, surviving; *poste ~e*, 'poste restante'. ~, s.m. Rest, remainder.

restaurant (rɛstorɑ̃), s.m. **1.** Restaurant, eating-house, dining-room; **2.** restorative.

restaurat-eur, -rice (rɛstoratœr), s.m.f. **1.** Restorer, repairer; **2.** eating-house keeper, restaurant keeper.

restauration (rɛstora'sjɔ̃), s.f. [f. *restaurer*] Restoration; nutrition; repair, restoration, bringing back to original state.

restaurer (rɛstore), v.a. [L *restaurare*] To restore, to re-establish, to repair; **se** ~, v.pr. to take refreshment, food, &c. ⚠ Note that 'to restore' has also in English the sense of to give back, to return = *rendre, rapporter, restituer*, as well as that of to re-establish; ex. his hat was restored to him = *son chapeau lui fut rendu*; *restaurer* cannot be used in this sense.

reste (rɛst), s.m. [f. *rester*] Rest, residue, remainder, remnant, remains; leavings; remnants; (math.) remainder; *paix à ses ~s*, peace to his ashes; *être en ~ avec*, to owe to, to be indebted to; *je ne veux pas être en ~ avec vous*, I do not want to do less for you than you have done for me; *il est parti sans demander son ~*, he took himself off without waiting for anything more; *jouir de son ~*, to make the most of what is left to one (of time, money, life, &c.); *jouer son ~*, to stake all that is left to one; *j'en ai de ~*, I have more than enough; *il a de la bonté de ~*, it 's a case of misplaced kindness! *au ~*, *du ~*, besides, nevertheless, yet, also, furthermore.

rester (rɛste), v.n. [L *restare*] To remain, to stay; (archaic) to rest; to be left; to continue, to stand, to last, to keep, to endure; *une œuvre qui restera*, a work which will live; *~ debout*, to remain standing; *~ court*, not to know what to say; to stop short; *~ stupéfait*, to stand astounded; *Mme X restera chez elle le mardi 15 octobre*, Mrs. X will be at home on Tuesday, October 15th; *~ sur la bonne bouche*, to keep something nice for the finish; *reste à savoir si*, it remains to be seen whether; *voilà tout ce qui me reste*, that is all I have left; *il ne me reste que 20 francs*, I have only 20 fr. left; *il ne me reste qu'à vous remercier*, I have only to thank you; *je reste votre fidèlement dévoué*, I remain yours truly; *restons-en là*, let us stop at that; that will do; let us say no more about it; *j'en étais resté à*, I had just been telling (or saying); *elle n'en restera pas là*, she will not be content with that; *comme vous êtes resté longtemps!* how long you have been!; (motor.) *~ en panne*, to break down.

restituable (rɛstitɥabl), adj. Repayable, refundable.

restituer (rɛstitɥe), v.a. [L *restituere*] To restitute; to restore, to return, to give back.

restitution (rɛstitysjɔ̃), s.f. [L *restitutio*] Restitution; restoring; reparation; *opérer la ~ de*, to make restitution of.

restreindre (rɛstrɛ̃dr), v.a. [L *restringere*] To restrict, to limit, to shorten, to restrain; **se** ~, v.pr. to restrain oneself; to retrench (one's expenses).

restricti-f, -ve (rɛstriktif), adj. Restrictive.

restriction (rɛstriksjɔ̃), s.f. [L *restrictio*] Restraint, restriction; reserve, reservation; *~ mentale*, mental reservation; *sans ~s*, without restriction.

restringent, -e (rɛstrɛ̃ʒɑ̃), adj. (med.) Astringent.

résultant, -e (rezyltɑ̃), adj. Resulting. *~e*, s.f. (math., phys.) Resultant.

résultat (rezylta), s.m. Result, issue, consequence, outcome; (math.) result; *sans ~*, without result, in vain, fruitless, fruitlessly; (sport, games) *match sans ~*, draw.

résulter (rezylte), v.n. [L *resultare*] To result (*de*, from), to follow, to be the outcome (*de*, of).

résumé (rezyme), s.m. Summary, epitome, abstract, synopsis, abridgement, compendium; *faire le ~ de*, to sum up; *au ~*, *en ~*, on the whole, after all; in brief.

résumer (rezyme), v.a. [L *resumere*] To sum up, to recapitulate, to abridge, to give a summary of, to summarize, to resume; ⚠ the most usual sense of 'to resume' is: *reprendre, continuer* (*un discours, une conversation*), *réoccuper*; ex. to resume work = *reprendre le travail*; to resume one's seat = *reprendre son siège*; he resumed the thread of his discourse = *il reprit le fil de son discours*; *résumer* is not used in this sense; **se** ~, v.pr. to sum up; to be summed up.

resurgir (rəsyrʒir), v.n. To resurge; to occur again.
résurrection (rezyrɛksjɔ̃), s.f. [L *resurrectio*] Resurrection, revival, resurrecting.
résurrectionniste (rezyrɛksjɔnist), s.m. Resurrectionist.
rétable (retabl), s.m. [f. L *retro*+Fr. *table*] Retable, reredos.
rétablir (retablir), v.a. To re-establish, to restore, to repair, to retrieve, to readjust; ~ *la discipline*, to restore discipline; ~ *ses affaires*, to retrieve one's losses; ~ *sa santé*, to recover one's health; ~ *la vérité*, to correct false statements; to state the real truth; to establish the truth; **se** ~, v.pr. to recover one's health; to be re-established or restored.
rétablissement (retablismɑ̃), s.m. Re-establishment, restoration, recovery, recovery of health; revival; (gymn.) lifting oneself on the hands.
retaille (rətɑj), s.f. [f. *tailler*] Parings, cuttings, shreds, waste bits.
retailler (rətɑje), v.a. To cut again.
rétamage (retamaʒ), s.m. Re-tinning, mending of saucepans, &c.; re-silvering (of glass).
rétamer (retame), v.a. [*re*+*étamer*, f. *étain*] To re-tin; to re-silver (glass); to tinker.
rétameur (retamœr), s.m. Tinker.
retaper (rətape), v.a. [*re*+*taper*] (colloq.) To do up (hats); to mend, to renew; **se** ~, v.pr. to recover.
retard (rətar), s.m. Delay, slowness; *être en* ~, *avoir du* ~, to be late; to be behind time; to be overdue; *être en* ~ *de dix minutes*, to be ten minutes late; *votre montre est en* ~ *de cinq minutes*, your watch is five minutes slow; (techn., motor.) ~ *à l'allumage*, retarded ignition.
retardataire (rətardatɛr), adj. Late, behindhand, in arrear. ~, s.m.f. Late comer, loiterer, lagger.
retardat-eur, -rice (rətardatœr), adj. (phys., techn.) Retarding.
retardation (rətarda'sjɔ̃), s.f. (phys.) Retardation.
retardement (rətardəmɑ̃), s.m. Delay, putting off; retardment.
retarder (rətarde), v.a.n. [L *retardare*] To retard, to delay, to be slow, to be late, to keep back; to lag, to fall behind; to be old-fashioned, to be behind the times; to be antiquated, to be a fossil; ~ *sa montre*, to put back one's watch; *vous retardez de 10 minutes*, you are 10 minutes slow; *vous êtes en retard de 10 minutes*, you are 10 minutes late; *ces gens-là retardent!*, those people are behind the times.
retâter (rətɑte), v.a. [*re*+*tâter*] To touch again; (fig.) to enjoy again, to taste again.
reteindre (rətɛ̃dr), v.a. [*re*+*teindre*] To dye again.
retendre (rətɑ̃dr), v.a. [*re*+*tendre*] To stretch again; ~ *un piège à rats*, to reset a rat-trap.
retenir (rətənir), v.a. [*re*+*tenir*] To keep back, to make stay, to hold back, to withhold, to delay; to remember, to recollect; to hold in, to check, to prevent, to hinder; to deduct; to secure (seats); to engage (servants, &c.), to bespeak; (arith.) to carry; ~ *X à dîner*, to make X stay to dinner; ~ *ses larmes*, to keep back one's tears; ~ *sa langue*, to hold one's tongue; ~ *sa colère*, to restrain one's anger; *je ne sais ce qui me retient de parler*, I don't know what prevents me from speaking; *retenez bien ceci*, be sure to remember this; *donner et* ~ *ne vaut*, one cannot have one's cake and eat it; one cannot give and keep at the same time; *un rhume le retient au lit*, a cold confines him to his bed; (arith.) *je pose 3 et je retiens 1*, I put down 3 and carry 1; (colloq.) *je le retiens celui-là!*, I'll get my own back on him!; **se** ~, v.pr. to restrain oneself, to keep back, to refrain (*de*, from) to control oneself; to catch hold (*à*, of), to clutch, to cling; to stop.
rétent-eur, -rice (retɑ̃tœr), **rétenti-f, -ve** (retɑ̃tif), adj. Retentive.
rétention (retɑ̃sjɔ̃), s.f. [L *retentio*] Retention, reservation; keeping back; (arith.) carrying over.
rétentionnaire (retɑ̃sjɔnɛr), s.m.f. Detainer.
retentir (rətɑ̃tir), v.n. [f. L *re*+*tinnire*] To resound, to ring, to re-echo; to have a repercussion.
retentissant, -e (rətɑ̃tisɑ̃), p. adj. Resounding, ringing, sonorous, echoing; (fig.) sensational.
retentissement (rətɑ̃tismɑ̃), s.m. Resounding, ringing; echo, fame, sensation; *avoir un grand* ~, to create a deep impression; to be much talked of.
retentum (retɑ̃tɔm), s.m. [L wd] (law) Tacit clause or proviso; (colloq.) secret reservation.
retenue (rətəny), s.f. [f. *retenir*] Reserve, moderation, modesty, discretion; caution, self-control, wariness; stoppage of pay; (at school) *être en* ~, to be kept in; (arith.) deduction; *et 3 de* ~, and 3 to carry; (techn.) *palan de* ~, relieving-tackle. ⚠ Not 'retinue', which = *suite*.
reterçage, retersage (rətɛrsaʒ), s.m. Fourth dressing of vines.
retercer, reterser (rətɛrse), v.a. [*re*+*tercer*] To give the fourth dressing to (vines).
rétiaire (resjɛr), s.m. [L *retiarius*] (Rom. ant.) Retiarius.
réticence (retisɑ̃s), s.f. [L *reticentia*] Reticence, reserve, voluntary omission, reservation.
réticulaire (retikylɛr), adj. [f. L *reticulum*] Reticular.

réticule (retikyl), s.m. [L *reticulum*] Vanity bag, bag; (archaic) hair-net; (opt.) reticle.
réticulé, -e (retikyle), adj. [f. L *reticulum*] Reticulated.
réti-f, -ve (retif), adj. Restive; (fig.) restive, unmanageable, mulish.
rétine (retin), s.f. [f. L *rete*] (anat.) Retina.
retirade (rətirad), s.f. (fort.) Retirade.
retiration (rətira'sjɔ̃), s.f. (print.) Backing; *presse à* ~, perfecting-machine.
retiré, -e (rətire), p. adj. Isolated, remote, secluded, retired; *un endroit* ~, a remote place; *vivre très* ~, to lead a retired life; ~ *des affaires*, retired from business.
retirement (rətirmɑ̃), s.m. (surg.) Contraction; withdrawal; secluded life, seclusion.
retirer (rətire), v.a. [*re*+*tirer*] To pull back again, to draw back; to extract, to draw out, to get, to obtain, to derive; to withdraw; to take back, to remove; to retract, to recall; ~ *grand profit de*, to profit greatly by; ~ *sa parole*, to go back on one's word; ~ *ses paroles*, to retract one's words; ~ *son vêtement*, to take off one's cloak, mantle, &c.; **se** ~, v.pr. to retire, to withdraw, to retreat, to recede; to go home; to go to bed; to ebb; to go away; *retirez-vous!*, leave the room! away with you! be off!; *se* ~ *des affaires*, to retire from business; *cette étoffe se retire au lavage*, this material shrinks in the washing.
retombée (also **retombe**) (rətɔ̃be), s.f. (arch.) Springing (of arches).
retomber (rətɔ̃be), v.n. [*re*+*tomber*] To fall again; to have a relapse; to hang down; ~ *dans le même travers*, to relapse into the same fault; *son sang retombera sur vous*, his blood will be visited on your head; ~ *toujours sur ses pieds*, always to fall on one's feet.
retondre (rətɔ̃dr), v.a. To shear again; (arch.) to clean off.
retoquer (rətɔke), v.a. [*re*+*toquer*] (colloq.) To plough (a candidate in an examination); to knock again.
retordement (rətɔrdəmɑ̃), s.m. Retwisting.
retordeu-r, -se (rətɔrdœr), s.m.f. Twister.
retordoir (rətɔrdwar), **retorsoir** (rətɔrswar), s.m. (weaving) Doubling and twisting machine.
retordre (rətɔrdr), v.a. [*re*+*tordre*] To retwist, to twist; (fig.) *donner du fil à* ~ *à X*, to give X a good deal of trouble; to cut out work for X.
rétorque (retɔrk), s.f. Retort, repartee, (Amer.) come-back; *une* ~ *écrasante*, a crushing retort.
rétorquer (retɔrke), v.a.n. [L *retorquere*] To retort, to make an argument tell against its user.
retors, -e (rətɔr), adj. [f. *retordre*] Twisted; artful, cunning, shrewd; *un homme* ~, a cute one, a deep customer.
rétorsi-f, -ve (retɔrsif), adj. Retortive.
rétorsion (retɔrsjɔ̃), s.f. [L *retortio*] Retorting; retorsion.
retouche (rətuʃ), s.f. Retouch, retouching; after-touch; touching up.
retoucher (rətuʃe), v.a. To touch again; to touch up, to retouch; to improve.
retoucheu-r, -se (rətuʃœr), s.m.f. (photo.) Retoucher.
retour (rətur), s.m. [f. *retourner*] Return, coming back, coming home; repetition, recurrence; winding; decline, wane; reciprocity; (arch.) return; vicissitude; *billet d'aller et* ~, return ticket; *son amour n'est pas payé de* ~, his love is not returned, or reciprocated; *sans esprit de* ~, for good; irretrievably; *perdu sans* ~, past all hope; *il n'est pas encore de* ~, he is not yet back; *à votre* ~, on your return; *en* ~, in return (*de*, for); *faire* ~ *à*, to revert to; *faire un* ~ *sur soi-même*, to look into one's heart; to examine one's conscience; *les* ~*s de la fortune*, the vicissitudes of fortune; *les tours et* ~*s de la rivière*, the windings and turnings of the river; *chargement de* ~, return cargo; *par* ~ (*du courrier*), by return (of post); *être sur le* ~, to be on the shady side of forty; to be on the wane; *beauté sur le* ~, beauty on the wane; (fig.) *un vieux cheval de* ~, an old offender; a deep customer; ~ *d'âge*, menopause; *en* ~ *d'équerre*, at right angles; (motor.) ~ *de manivelle*, back-stroke; kicking back (of the starting-crank); ~ *de flamme*, burning-back; ~ *de gaz*, blow-back. ⚠ *Retour* has not, like 'return', the sense of profit, interest; restitution.
retourne (rətuгn), s.f. Card turned up (in certain games).
retournement (rəturnəmɑ̃), s.m. Turning.
retourner (rəturne), v.a.n. [*re*+*tourner*] To turn again, to turn back, to send back; to turn over; to return, to go back; to be brought back, to be returned; to turn up (cards); ~ *sur ses pas*, to retrace one's steps; ~ *un manuscrit*, to send back a manuscript; ~ *un vêtement*, to turn a garment; ~ *sa casaque*, to turn one's coat; to change sides; *je sais de quoi il retourne*, I know how matters stand; I know what is going on; **se** ~, v.pr. to turn round; (fig.) to know how to manage; *s'en* ~, to go back.
retracer (rətrase), v.a. To retrace; to relate, to picture. ⚠ *Retracer* has not the sense of Engl. 'to retrace' in: to retrace one's steps, which = *revenir sur ses pas*.
rétractable (retraktabl), adj. Retractable.
rétractation (retrakta'sjɔ̃), s.f. Retractation.
rétracter (retrakte), v.a. [f. L *retractare*] To retract; to unsay, to withdraw, to

recall, to recant; **se ~**, v.pr. to retract, to eat one's words.
rétractile (retraktil), adj. Retractile.
rétractilité (retraktilite), s.f. Retractility.
rétraction (retraksjɔ̃), s.f. Retraction, contraction, drawing-in.
retraduire (rətradɥir), v.a. To retranslate.
retraire (rətrɛr), v.a. [L *retrahere*] (law) To redeem.
retrait, -e (rətrɛ), p. adj. Shrunk, contracted, retracted; (law) redeemed.
retrait (rətrɛ), s.m. Shrinkage, contraction; withdrawal; (law) redemption; closet; ~ *d'un projet de loi*, withdrawal of a bill; ~ *d'emploi*, dismissal, discharge; *mettre en disponibilité par ~ d'emploi*, to retire (a person) from office; *en ~*, receding, retreating, withdrawn, back from alignment.
retraite (rətrɛt), s.f. [f. L *retrahere*] Retreat, retiring; shelter, seclusion; superannuation; retiring pension; retirement (from business, world, &c.); (mil.) (*a*) retreat; (*b*) drum-beat or bugle-call as the signal for retreat; *battre en ~*, to beat a retreat, to retreat; *battre la ~*, to beat the tattoo; *sonner la ~*, to sound the retreat; *mettre à la ~*, to pension off; *mise à la ~*, superannuation; *prendre sa ~*, to retire on a pension; *en ~*, retired; *couper la ~ à X*, to cut off X's retreat; *vivre dans la ~*, to live in retirement; *donner ~ à X*, to harbour X; to shelter X; *~s pour la vieillesse*, old-age pensions; *~ de voleurs*, den of thieves; *quelle délicieuse ~!*, what a lovely retreat (or resort, abode)!
retraité, -e (rətrɛte), p. adj. Pensioned off, on the retired list, retired, superannuated. ~, s.m.f. One who is pensioned off, &c.
retraiter (rətrɛte), v.a. To pension off.
retranchement (rətrɑ̃ʃmɑ̃), s.m. Retrenchment, suppression; curtailment; (mil.) entrenchment, retrenchment.
retrancher (rətrɑ̃ʃe), v.a. To retrench, to cut off, to suppress, to curtail; (arith.) to deduct, to subtract; (mil.) to entrench; **se ~**, v.pr. to entrench oneself, to intrench oneself; (fig.) to defend oneself; to screen oneself; to shelter oneself (*derrière un prétexte*, behind a pretext).
retranscrire (rətrɑ̃skrir), v.a. To copy out again.
retravailler (rətravaje), v.a.n. To work again or anew; to polish, to finish.
retraverser (rətravɛrse), v.a.n. To cross again, to go over again, to go through again.
rétréci, -e (retresi), p. adj. Narrow, shrunk, limited; narrow-minded.
rétrécir (retresir), v.a.n. [*re*+*étrécir*] To narrow, to taper, to straiten, to make narrower; to shrink, to take in; ~ *l'esprit*, to narrow the mind; *ce tissu ne rétrécit pas au lavage*, this material does not shrink in the wash.
rétrécissement (retresismɑ̃), s.m. Narrowing, shrinking, contraction; (med.) stricture.
retremper (rətrɑ̃pe), v.a. To soak again, to steep again; (metall.) to temper again, to harden; (fig.) to strengthen, to reinvigorate; **se ~**, v.pr. (fig.) to recruit oneself, to be reinvigorated, to harden.
rétribuer (retribɥe), v.a. [L *retribuere*] To remunerate, to pay, to reward.
rétribution (retribysjɔ̃), s.f. [L *retributio*] Remuneration, fee, pay, salary, reward; (fig.) reward, retribution. ⚠ In English 'retribution' is not used as a synonym of fee, salary, &c. (*salaire*), but means generally recompense for evil (rarely for good) done, vengeance, requital; ex. the day of retribution = *le jour du jugement*; *l'heure du châtiment*.
rétro- (retro), pref. [L *retro*] Retro-; ~, s.m. (billiards) screw-back-stroke.
rétroacti-f, -ve (retroaktif), adj. Retroactive.
rétroaction (retroaksjɔ̃), s.f. Retroaction.
rétroactivement (retroaktivmɑ̃), adv. Retroactively.
rétroactivité (retroaktivite), s.f. Retroactivity.
rétrocéder (retrosede), v.a. [*retro*+*céder*] To retrocede, to cede back again. ⚠ The usual meaning of 'to retrocede' is *se retirer, reculer*.
rétrocessi-f, -ve (retrosɛsif), adj. Retrocessive.
rétrocession (retrosɛsjɔ̃), s.f. Retrocession.
rétrogradation (retrograda'sjɔ̃), s.f. Retrogradation, retrogression.
rétrograde (retrɔgrad), adj. Retrograde, backward, reverting to an inferior state, reactionary.
rétrograder (retrograde), v.n.a. To retrograde, to go backwards, to revert to an inferior state.
rétrogression (retrogrɛsjɔ̃), s.f. Retrogression.
rétropédalage (retropedalaʒ), s.m. Back-pedalling.
rétrospecti-f, -ve (retrɔspɛktif), adj. Retrospective.
rétrospectivement (retrɔspɛktivmɑ̃), adv. Retrospectively.
retroussé, -e (rətruse), p. adj. Turned up, tucked up; *un nez ~*, a turned-up nose.
retroussement (rətrusmɑ̃), s.m. Turning up, tucking up.
retrousser (rətruse), v.a. [*re*+*trousser*] To turn up, to tuck up; **se ~**, v.pr. to tuck up one's dress; to be turned up.
retroussis (rətrusi), s.m. [f. *retrousser*] Tucking-up; facing, cock (of a hat), top (of a boot).

retrouver (rətruve), v.a. [*re+trouver*] To find again, to recover, to meet again, to recognize; ~ *son chemin*, to find one's way again; **se** ~, v.pr. to find each other again, to meet again; to find one's way again; *je n'arrive pas à m'y* ~, I don't know what I am about; I cannot make head or tail of it; I am all at sea.

rétroversion (retrovɛrsjɔ̃), s.f. [f. L *retro+ versum*] Retroversion.

rets (rɛ), s.m. (invar.) [L *rete*] Net; (fig.) snare, toils; *pris dans les* ~, ensnared.

réunion (reynjɔ̃), s.f. Reunion, collection, body, gathering; meeting, party, joining again, junction; reconciliation; ~ *politique*, political meeting; ~ *de famille*, family gathering or party.

réunir (reynir) v.a. [*re+unir*] To reunite, to join together, to join again, to join; to gather, to assemble, to muster; to collect; to bring together; to reconcile; to connect; **se** ~, v.pr. to gather, to meet, to assemble, to be reunited; to concur.

réussi, -e (reysi), p. adj. Successful, well done.

réussir (reysir), v.n. [f. It. *riuscire*] To be successful, to be a success, to succeed; to turn out well; to prosper, to thrive; ~ *à passer*, to succeed in getting through; *tout lui a réussi*, he succeeded in everything; ~, v.a. to perform well, to do successfully, to carry out well.

réussite (reysit), s.f. [f. *réussir*] **1.** Success, upshot, happy issue or result; **2.** (card-game) patience; syn. PATIENCE.

revaccination (rəvaksina'sjɔ̃), s.f. Revaccination.

revacciner (rəvaksine), v.a. [*re+vacciner*] To revaccinate.

revaloir (rəvalwar), v.a. To return, to repay; *je lui revaudrai ça*, I shall make him pay for it; I will be even with him; I will pay him out.

revanche (rəvɑ̃ʃ), s.f. [f. *revancher*] Revenge, return, return match; *à charge de* ~, on condition of a like return; one good turn deserves another; *en* ~, in return; on the other hand; *prendre sa* ~, to take one's revenge; to play the return match; to have another try at it.

revancher (rəvɑ̃ʃe), v.a. [var. of *revenger*] To defend; **se** ~, v.pr. to take one's revenge, to have one's turn.

rêvasser (rɛvase), v.n. [f. *rêver*] To dream idly; to keep dreaming; to have confused dreams, to muse, to go wool-gathering.

rêvasserie (rɛvasri), s.f. Idle dreaming, musing; wool-gathering.

rêvasseu-r, -se (rɛvasœr), s.m.f. Idle dreamer, muser, wool-gatherer.

rêve (rɛv), s.m. [f. *rêver*] Dream; idle fancy, day-dream, illusion, reverie.

revêche (rəvɛʃ), adj. [etym. dub.] Harsh, cross-grained, peevish, contrary, as cross as two sticks, rough, crabbed.

réveil (revɛj), s.m. [f. *réveiller*] Waking, awakening, awaking; alarum (clock); (mil.) reveille; revival; (fig.) awakening; disillusionment; *à mon* ~, *au* ~, on waking.

réveille-matin (revɛjmatɛ̃), s.m. Alarum-clock, alarm-clock; (bot.) a variety of spurge.

réveiller (revɛje), v.a. [*re+éveiller*] To wake, to wake up, to rouse; to stir up, to revive, to quicken, to recall; ~ *la douleur*, to quicken the pain; ~ *des souvenirs*, to reawaken memories; **se** ~, v.pr. to wake, to wake up, to be roused, to be revived.

réveillon (revɛjɔ̃), s.m. Christmas eve (midnight) supper.

réveillonner (revɛjɔne), v.n. To revel at Christmas eve midnight supper.

révélat-eur, -rice (revelatœr), adj. Revealing, tell-tale, divulging. ~, s.m.f. Informer; detecter; (photo.) developer.

révélation (revela'sjɔ̃), s.f. [L *revelatio*] Revelation, disclosure, discovery; thing disclosed.

révéler (revele), v.a. [L *revelare*] To reveal, to disclose, to betray; (photo.) to develop; **se** ~, v.pr. to reveal itself, to show itself, to be disclosed.

revenant, -e (rəvənɑ̃), p. adj. Prepossessing; *physionomie* ~*e*, prepossessing appearance. ~*-bon*, s.m. Unexpected profit, bonus; ~, s.m. ghost; *des histoires de* ~*s*, ghost stories.

revendeu-r, -se (rəvɑ̃dœr), s.m.f. Retail dealer, second-hand dealer; ~*se à la toilette*, second-hand clothes dealer.

revendication (rəvɑ̃dika'sjɔ̃), s.f. Revendication, claiming, claim.

revendiquer (rəvɑ̃dike), v.a. [f. L *re+ vindicare*] To claim, to enter a claim to; (fig.) to lay claim to.

revendre (rəvɑ̃dr), v.a. [*re+vendre*] To resell, to sell again, to sell what one has bought; *en* ~ *à X*, to be more than a match for X; *de l'esprit? elle en a à* ~*!*, yes, she has wit enough and to spare!

revenez-y (rəvənezi), subst. loc. (colloq.) *Avoir un petit goût de* ~, to taste moreish; to make one wish to help oneself again; to taste excellent.

revenir (rəvənir), v.n. [*re+venir*] To come back, to return, to come again, to come on again, to come round again; to cost; to please; to be equivalent to; ~ *à soi*, to come to oneself, to come to; to revive; to recover consciousness; *son nom ne me revient pas*, I cannot remember his name; *voilà des façons qui ne me reviennent pas*, these manners do not please me; *cela revient au même*, it comes to the same thing; *cela revient à dire que*, that amounts to saying that; *je n'en reviens pas!* I cannot get over it; I am lost in astonishment!;

that beats me; *n'y revenez plus*, do not do that again; *il n'y a pas à y ~*, that is definitely settled; *vous en revenez toujours là*, you are always harping on that string; *il revient de loin*, he had a narrow escape; that was a hair-breadth escape; he very nearly died; *je suis bien revenu sur son compte*, I have lost all the illusions I had about him; *mais revenons à nos moutons*, but to return to our subject; *la parole lui est revenue*, he can speak again, he has recovered his speech; *dès qu'elle fut un peu revenue de sa surprise*, as soon as she had a little got over her surprise; *elle est revenue de sa frayeur*, she has got over her fright; *quand on l'a vexé il ne revient pas facilement*, when once he is offended he cannot be easily pacified; *il me revient que*, I hear that, I am told that; *ce qui m'en revient est bien peu de chose*, the profit I get from it is pretty small; *sa maison lui revient à*, his house costs him; *il s'en revenait tout doucement*, he was coming back very slowly; (cook.) *faire ~ de la viande*, to fry meat in butter or fat, so as to brown it slightly (1st operation in making a stew); *il revient sur ce qu'il avait dit*, he retracts what he said; *cet aliment revient*, this food repeats (in the stomach); *~ sur ses pas*, to retrace one's steps; *~ à la charge*, to return to the charge; *elle s'est évanouie, on a eu grand'-peine à la faire ~*, she fainted, and it was hard work to bring her round again.

revente (rəvɑ̃t), s.f. Resale; selling again.

revenu (rəvəny), s.m. [f. *revenir*] Income; (*~ d'État*) revenue; *impôt sur le ~*, income-tax.

revenue (rəvəny), s.f. Young growth (of wood).

rêver (rɛve), v.n.a. [OF *resver*, orig. dub.] To dream (*de*, of); to muse, to ponder, to think deeply; to rave, to be delirious; *~ tout éveillé*, to dream with one's eyes open; to indulge in day-dreams; *il ne rêve que plaies et bosses*, he is always hankering after a black eye; *vous rêvez !*, you are dreaming !; *je crois ~ !*, really I believe it is all a dream !, I must be dreaming!

réverbération (revɛrbera'sjɔ̃), s.f. Reverberation.

réverbère (revɛrbɛr), s.m. [f. *réverbérer*] **1.** Reverberator; **2.** street lamp, lamp-post; *four à ~*, reverberatory furnace.

réverbérer (revɛrbere), v.a. [L *reverberare*] To reverberate (light or heat); to reflect. ⚠ In Engl. 'to reverberate' is also used of sound = *répercuter*.

reverdir (rəvɛrdir), v.n. To grow green again; (fig.) to reblossom, to grow young again; ~, v.a. to paint green again.

reverdissement (rəvɛrdismɑ̃), s.m. Growing green again.

révéremment (reveramɑ̃), adv. Reverently.

révérence (reverɑ̃s), s.f. [L *reverentia*] **1.** Reverence; *~ parler, sauf ~*, saving your reverence; **2.** curtsy, curtsey, courtesy, bow, obeisance; *faire la ~*, to curtsy; *je leur ai tiré ma ~*, I made my bow and trotted off.

révérenciel, -le (reverɑ̃sjɛl), adj. Reverential.

révérencieusement (reverɑ̃sjøzmɑ̃), adv. Reverentially, reverently.

révérencieu-x, -se (reverɑ̃sjø), adj. Reverential.

révérend, -e (reverɑ̃), adj. s.m.f. [L *reverendus*] Reverend; (Reverend, of clergyman; Very R., of dean; Right R., of bishop; Most R., of archbishop); *mon ~*, Reverend sir; your Reverence.

révérendissime (reverɑ̃disim), adj. Right reverend, most reverend.

révérer (revere), v.a. [L *revereri*] To revere, to honour, to venerate.

rêverie (rɛvri), s.f. [f. *rêver*] Reverie, day-dream, musing, idle dreaming, idle fancy; chimera; *s'abandonner à la ~*, to give oneself up to reverie; to go wool-gathering.

revers (rəvɛr), s.m. invar. [f. L *reversus*] Back, reverse, other side, wrong side, counterpart; (tailor.) lapel, facing; (of boots) top; (tennis) back-stroke, back-hander; misfortune, reverse, disaster, ruin, losses of money; *le ~ de la médaille*, the reverse of the medal, the dark side of the picture; *à ~*, on the other side; *prendre l'ennemi à ~*, to outflank the enemy; to attack the enemy in the rear; *éprouver de grands ~*, to meet with great reverses; to suffer great losses. ⚠ In English 'reverse' has also frequently the sense of the contrary = *le contraire*; ex. he made remarks the reverse of complimentary = *il fit des commentaires qui n'étaient rien moins que flatteurs*.

réversal, -e, (aux) (revɛrsal), adj. (comm.) Of mutual concession.

reversement (rəvɛrsmɑ̃), s.m. (naut.) Transhipment.

reverser (rəvɛrse), v.a. [*re*+*verser*] To pour out again, to pour into the same vessel, bottle, &c.; to transfer, to carry over; to pay back; (naut.) to tranship. ⚠ Not 'to reverse', which = *renverser, invertir, annuler*.

reversi (rəvɛrsi), s.m. [It. *rovescino*] Reversi (card-game).

réversibilité (revɛrsibilite), s.f. Reversibility.

réversible (revɛrsibl), adj. Revertible, reversible (*sur*, to).

réversion (revɛrsjɔ̃), s.f. [L *reversio*] Reversion.

reversoir (rəvɛrswar), s.m. Dam, weir.

revertier (rəvɛrtje), s.m. [orig. unkn.] Variety of backgammon.

revêtement (rəvɛtmɑ̃), s.m. [f. *revêtir*] Revetment, facing (of masonry), retaining wall; veneering.
revêtir (rəvɛtir), v.a. [*re+vêtir*] To put on; to clothe; to cover, to coat; ~ *un habit*, to put on a coat; *revêtu de son armure*, clad in armour; *mur revêtu de marbre*, wall faced with marble; ~ *une apparence*, to assume the appearance; *l'autorité dont il est revêtu*, the authority he is invested with; ~ *ses pensées d'un style étincelant*, to clothe one's thoughts in brilliant language; **se** ~ *de*, v.pr. to put on; to assume.
rêveu-r, -se (rɛvœr), adj. Dreamy, musing. ~, s.m.f. Dreamer.
rêveusement (rɛvøzmɑ̃), adv. Dreamily, pensively.
revidage (rəvidaʒ), s.m. **1.** Emptying again; **2.** settlement between dealers who have had goods knocked down to them at auctions.
revider (rəvide), v.a. [*re+vider*] **1.** To empty again; **2.** see REVIDAGE.
revient (rəvjɛ̃), s.m. Cost; *prix de* ~, cost price.
revif (rəvif), s.m. Rising tide.
revirement (rəvirmɑ̃), s.m. [f. *virer*] (naut.) Tacking about; sudden change, complete change; changing sides, turning round; ~ *d'opinion*, complete change of opinion; (comm.) transfer.
revirer (rəvire), v.n. (naut.) To tack, to tack about; to change sides, to turn round.
révisable (revizabl), adj. Revisable.
réviser (revize), v.a. [*re*+L *visere*] To revise, to examine anew, to reconsider.
réviseur (revizœr), s.m. Reviser; proof-reader; comptroller.
révision (revizjɔ̃), s.f. [L *revisio*] Revision, revisal, reconsideration; ~ *d'un procès*, rehearing of a case (in law court); (mil.) *Conseil de* ~, medical examination board for recruits.
revivification (rəvivifika'sjɔ̃), s.f. Revivification.
revivifier (rəvivifje), v.a. To revivify, to vivify, to revive, to regenerate.
reviviscence (rəvivissɑ̃s), s.f. [f. L *reviviscere*] Viviscence, reviviscence.
reviviscent, -e (rəvivissɑ̃), adj. Reviviscent.
revivre (rəvivr), v.n.a. [*re+vivre*] To come to life again; to live . . . again; *faire* ~, to revive, to bring to life again; to restore; ~ *sa jeunesse*, v.a. to live one's youth again, to recall one's youth to mind.
révocable (revɔkabl), adj. Revocable.
révocation (revɔka'sjɔ̃), s.f. [L *revocatio*] Revocation, dismissal, removal from office; repeal, annulment.
révocatoire (revɔkatwar), adj. Revocatory.
revoici, revoilà (rəvwasi, rəvwala), prep. (colloq.) Here is again, there is . . . again; *me* ~, here I am again.
revoir (rəvwar), v.a. [*re+voir*] To see again, to examine again, to meet again, to behold again; *à* ~, to be re-examined; **se** ~, v.pr. to meet again; to be again on good terms. ~, s.m. Meeting again; *au* ~, good-bye for the present; fare-you-well; (colloq.) so long!; bye-bye; *adieu jusqu'au* ~, farewell till we meet again.
revoler (rəvɔle), v.n. [*re+voler*] To fly back, to fly again.
revolin (rəvɔlɛ̃), s.m. (naut.) Eddy-wind, whirlwind.
révoltant, -e (revɔltɑ̃), p. adj. Revolting, shocking.
révolte (revɔlt), s.f. [f. *révolter*] Revolt, rebellion, mutiny; indignation.
révolté, -e (revɔlte), s.m.f. Rebel, mutineer.
révolter (revɔlte), v.a. [It. *rivoltare*] To revolt; to cause to revolt, to make rebel, to shock, to arouse indignation in; ~ *la conscience*, to be revolting to the conscience; **se** ~, v.pr. to revolt, to rebel, to mutiny, to rise (*contre*, against); to be shocked, to feel indignant.
révolu, -e (revɔly), adj. [L *revolutus*] Revolved, past, accomplished, full, completed; *il a trente ans* ~*s*, he has completed his 30th year; *époques* ~*es*, past ages.
revoluté, -e (rəvɔlyte), adj. (bot., arch.) Revolute.
révoluti-f, -ve (revɔlytif), adj. Revolute; pertaining to revolution.
révolution (revɔlysjɔ̃), s.f. [L *revolutio*] Revolution; revolving motion; complete change; *surface de* ~, surface of revolution; *les planètes font leurs* ~*s autour du soleil*, the planets revolve round the sun; *la* ~ *russe*, the Russian revolution.
révolutionnaire (revɔlysjɔnɛr), adj. Revolutionary. ~, s.m.f. Revolutionary, revolutionist.
révolutionnairement (revɔlysjɔnɛrmɑ̃), adv. In a revolutionary manner.
révolutionner (revɔlysjɔne), v.a. To revolutionize.
revolver (revɔlvɛr), s.m. [Engl. wd] Revolver, browning.
revomir (rəvɔmir), v.a. To vomit again, to throw up again.
révoquer (revɔke), v.a. [L *revocare*] To repeal, to annul, to revoke (⚠ not in the sense *faire une renonce* (whist or bridge)); to rescind, to withdraw; to dismiss, to remove from office, to recall; ~ *en doute*, to question, to call in question.
revoyure (rəvwajyr), s.f. (pop. form of *revoir*) *A la bonne* ~ *!*, see you again!, so long!
revue (rəvy), s.f. [f. *revoir*] Review, reviewing; magazine; survey, revising, inspection; (theatr.) revue; (mil.) *passer*

en ~, to review; *faire la* ~ *de*, to look over, to examine one after the other; (colloq.) *nous sommes gens de* ~, *nous sommes de* ~, we shall see each other again before long; ~ *hebdomadaire*, weekly review; weekly.
revuiste (rəvɥist), s.m. Revuist, author of a revue (satirical play about recent events).
révulser (revylse), v.a. [f. L *revulsus*] To displace, to contract, to twist, to repel, to divert.
révulsi-f, -ve (revylsif), adj. s.m. Revulsive.
révulsion (revylsjɔ̃), s.f. [L *revulsio*] Revulsion.
rez (rɛ), prep. [L *rasus*] On a level with; *à* ~ *de*, at the level of.
rez-de-chaussée (redʃose), s.m. Ground floor, ground level; *au* ~, on the ground floor.
rhabdomancie (rabdɔmɑ̃si), s.f. [Gr. *rhabdomanteia*] Rhabdomancy.
rhabillage, rhabillement (rabijaʒ, rabijmɑ̃), s.m. Mending, botching, recoating; putting on one's clothes again.
rhabiller (rabije), v.a. To dress again; to mend, to repair; to clothe; **se** ~, v.pr. to dress again, to put on one's clothes again.
rhabilleu-r, -se (rabijœr), s.m.f. Mender, repairer.
rhapsode (rapsɔd), s.m. See RAPSODE.
rhénan, -e (renɑ̃), adj. Rhenish.
rhéomètre (reɔmɛtr), s.m. [f. Gr. *rheos*+*metron*] Rheometer.
rhéophore (reɔfɔr), s.m. [f. Gr. *rheos*+*phoros*] (phys.) Rheophore.
rhéostat (reɔsta), s.m. [f. Gr. *rheos*+L *statos*] (electr.) Rheostat.
rhéteur (retœr), s.m. [Gr. *rhētōr*] Rhetor, rhetorical orator; (iron.) spouter, speechifier.
rhétien, -ne (retjɛ̃), adj. (geol.) Rhaetic.
rhétique (retik), adj. (geog.) Rhaetian.
rhétoricien (retɔrisjɛ̃), s.m. **1.** Rhetorician; **2.** student in the rhetoric class.
rhétorique (retɔrik), s.f. [Gr. *rhētorikē*] Rhetoric; (fig., pej.) fine words, bombast; *figure de* ~, rhetorical figure; rhetorique, highest form before *baccalauréat* in Fr. *lycées* (approxim. equivalent: Upper Vth).
rhinalgie (rinalʒi), s.f. [f. Gr. *rhis*+*algos*] (med.) Rhinalgia.
rhinanthe (rinɑ̃t), s.m. (bot.) Rhinanthus, yellow rattle.
rhingrave (ringrav, rɛ̃grav), s.m. [f. Germ. *Rhein*+*Graf*] Rhinegrave, count of the Rhine.
rhinocéros (rinɔseros), s.m. [f. Gr. *rhis, rhinos*+*keras*] (zool.) Rhinoceros.
rhinoplastie (rinɔplasti), s.f. (surg.) Rhinoplasty.
rhinoscopie (rinɔskɔpi), s.f. (med.) Rhinoscopy.
rhizocarpé, -e (rizokarpe), adj. (bot.) Rhizocarpous.
rhizome (rizom), s.m. [f. Gr. *rhiza*] (bot.) Rhizoma.
rhizophage (rizɔfaʒ), adj. [f. Gr. *rhiza*+*phagein*] Rhizophagous, feeding on roots.
rhodanien, -ne (rɔdanjɛ̃), adj. (geog.) Rhodanian, of the Rhone.
rhodien, -ne (rɔdjɛ̃), adj. s.m. (geog.) Rhodian, of Rhodes.
rhodium (rɔdjɔm), s.m. [f. Gr. *rhodon*] (chem.) Rhodium, Rh.
rhododendron (rɔdɔdɛ̃drɔ̃), s.m. (bot.) Rhododendron.
rhombe (rɔ̃b), s.m. [Gr. *rhombos*] Rhomb, rhombus.
rhomboèdre (rɔ̃bɔɛdr), s.m. [f. Gr. *rhombos*+*hedra*] (geom.) Rhombohedron.
rhomboïdal, -e, (aux) (rɔ̃bɔidal) adj. Rhomboidal.
rhomboïde (rɔ̃bɔid), s.m. (geom.) Rhomboid.
rhubarbe (rybarb), s.f. [L *rha barbarum*] Rhubarb; *passe-moi la* ~ *je te passerai le séné*, one good turn deserves another; you scratch my back and I will scratch yours.
rhum (rɔm), s.m. [f. Engl. *rum*] Rum.
rhumatisant, -e (rymatizɑ̃), adj. Affected with rheumatism.
rhumatismal, -e, (aux) (rymatismal), adj. Rheumatic.
rhumatisme (rymatism), s.m. [Gr. *rheumatismos*] Rheumatism.
rhumb. See RUMB.
rhume (rym), s.m. [f. Gr. *rheuma*] Cold; ~ *de cerveau*, cold in the head; *attraper un* ~, to catch cold; *un gros* ~, a violent cold; (slang) *qu'est-ce qu'il a pris pour son* ~ *!*, a nice talking-to he 's got!, he has caught it!
rhummerie (rɔmri), s.f. Rum distillery.
rhythme (ritm), s.m. See RYTHME.
rhyton (ritɔ̃), s.m. [f. Gr. *rhein*] Rhyton (a Greek drinking-cup).
riant, -e (rjɑ̃), p. adj. Smiling, cheerful, pleasant, prepossessing; *visage* ~, smiling face, prepossessing face; *paysage* ~, pleasant landscape or view.
ribambelle (ribɑ̃bɛl), s.f. [etym. dub.] Swarm, string, lot, tremendous lot, whole batch, host, shoals.
ribaud, -e (ribo), s.m.f. adj. [LL *ribaldus*] Ribald.
ribauderie (ribodri), s.f. Ribaldry.
ribord (ribɔr), s.m. [f. *bord*] (naut.) Garboard (strake), bottom planking.
ribordage (ribɔrdaʒ), s.m. (naut.) Damage by fouling.
ribote (ribɔt), s.f. [orig. unkn.] Drunken bout; *être en* ~, to be fuddled, to be tight; to be on the spree; *faire* ~, to have a drunken bout, to be keeping it up.
riboter (ribɔte), v.n. See (FAIRE) RIBOTE.
riboteu-r, -se (ribɔtœr), s.m.f. Boozer; regular old tippler.
ribouis (ribwi), s.m. (slang) Boot.

ricanement (rikanmɑ̃), s.m. Sneering, tittering, sneer, chuckle.
ricaner (rikane), v.n. [f. OF *rechaner*] To sneer, to titter, to giggle, to chuckle.
ricaneu-r, -se (rikanœr), s.m.f. Sneerer. ~, adj. Sneering, giggling.
ric-à-rac (rikarak), (obs.) **ric-rac** (rikrak), loc. adv. Strictly, exactly, sharply.
richard, -e (riʃar), s.m.f. Rich fellow, moneyed man, nabob, money-bags.
riche (riʃ), adj. [Germ. *reich*] Rich, wealthy, well off; copious, abundant, fertile; costly, valuable; *une ~ moisson*, an abundant harvest; *une langue ~*, a rich language; *une rime ~*, a rich or double rhyme; *vous avez perdu une ~ occasion de vous taire*, you lost a good opportunity of holding your tongue; *il est ~ à millions*, he is rolling in riches. ~, s.m. Rich person; *on ne prête qu'aux ~s*, people only lend to the rich; money begets money; it never rains but it pours.
richement (riʃmɑ̃), adv. Richly, copiously, abundantly, sumptuously.
richesse (riʃɛs), s.f. [f. *riche*] Richness; riches (pl.); wealth, opulence; fertility, abundance; *~ d'une langue*, copiousness (or richness) of a language; *la ~ publique*, the public wealth; *contentement passe ~*, enough is as good as a feast; content is better than riches.
richissime (riʃisim), adj. Rolling in money; abominably rich.
ricin (risɛ̃), s.m. [L *ricinus*] (bot.) Castor-oil plant; *huile de ~*, castor oil.
ricocher (rikɔʃe), v.n. [orig. dub.] To ricochet, to rebound.
ricochet (rikɔʃɛ), s.m. Ricochet; ducks and drakes (stone skimming on water); *faire des ~s*, to play ducks and drakes; (mil.) *tir à ~*, ricochet firing; *par ~*, in an indirect way; roundabout.
rictus (riktys), s.m. [L wd] Grin, rictus.
ride (rid), s.f. [f. *rider*] Wrinkle; ripple (on water); (naut.) laniard; *nœud de ~*, Matthew Walker knot, stopper knot. ⚠ Not 'ride', which = *course, chevauchée*.
ridé, -e (ride), p. adj. Wrinkled, shrivelled; rippled, ripply, covered with ripples (as water); corrugated.
rideau (pl. **-x**) (rido), s.m. [f. *rider*] Curtain; (fig.) screen, veil; (theatr.) curtain; *baisser le ~*, to drop the curtain; (theatr.) *un lever de ~*, a short opening play; a curtain-raiser; *tirer le ~*, to draw the curtain; *un ~ de peupliers*, a screen of poplars; a long line of poplars.
ridée (ride), s.f. Lark-net.
ridelle (ridɛl), s.f. Standard side, stave-side, rack (forming side of a cart).
rider (ride), v.a. [f. MDutch *ride*] To wrinkle; to shrivel; to ripple (water); to corrugate; **se ~**, v.pr. to get wrinkled, to shrivel; (of water) to ripple.
ridicule (ridikyl), adj. [L *ridiculus*] Ridiculous; *se rendre ~*, to make oneself ridiculous. ~, s.m. Ridicule, ridiculousness; *cela est d'un ~ achevé*, this is perfectly ridiculous; *tomber dans le ~*, to become ridiculous; *tourner X en ~*, to ridicule X; *le ~ qu'il se donne*, the ridicule he brings upon himself.
ridiculement (ridikylmɑ̃), adv. Ridiculously.
ridiculiser (ridikylize), v.a. To ridicule.
rien (rjɛ̃), ind. pron. [f. L *res, rem*] Anything, nothing, nought, not anything; *~ autre, ~ d'autre*, nothing else; *~ de moins*, nothing less; *~ moins que*, nothing less than; no less than; anything but; *en moins de ~, en un ~ de temps*, in a trice; in a jiffy; in less than no time; *moins que ~*, next to nothing; *pour ~*, (*a*) for nothing; for no reason; (*b*) dirt cheap; for a song; given away; *ce n'est ~*, it's nothing; *cela ne fait ~*, it does not matter; *il n'en est ~*, nothing of the kind; *ne faire semblant de ~*, to pretend not to notice something; *cela ne vaut ~*, it's worth nothing; *il n'est ~ moins que sot*, he is anything but a fool; *~ moins que cela*, anything but that; *n'en faites ~*, do nothing of the sort; *cela ne servira à ~*, that will be no use; that will be in vain; *n'aboutir à ~*, to come to nothing; *un homme de ~*, a nobody; *un propre-à-~*, a good-for-nothing; *il ne faut jurer de ~*, you never can tell; never prophesy unless you know; *il ne sait ~ de ~*, he knows absolutely nothing; *qui ne risque ~ n'a ~*, nothing venture, nothing win; *pour ~ au monde*, not for anything; not to save my life!; *il n'y a ~ à dire à cela*, there is nothing to be said to that; that is a clincher; *si peu que ~*, next to nothing; *il ne reste plus ~*, there is nothing left; *~ au monde ne me fera oublier cela*, nothing in the world will make me forget that; *y a-t-il rien qui vous plaise ici?*, is there anything here that you like?; *~ que d'y penser, j'en ai le frisson*, I shudder at the mere thought of it; *il est parti de ~*, he rose from nothing; *~ de tel que la santé*, there is nothing like health; (slang) *elle est ~ moche*, she is frightfully ugly; *il est ~ saoul*, he is as drunk as a lord. ~, s.m. Mere nothing, veriest trifle, nothingness; *c'est un ~*, it's a trifle; *~s*, s.m.pl., trifles; *s'amuser à des ~s*, to amuse oneself with trifles.
rieu-r, -se (rjœr), adj. Laughing, merry. ~, s.m. Laugher; *avoir les ~s de son côté*, to have the laugh on one's side.
rieuse (rjøz), s.f. (ornith.) Kind of sea-gull.
riflard (riflar), s.m. **1.** (carp.) Jack-plane; **2.** (mason.) paring-chisel; **3.** longest unprepared wool; **4.** rough file (for metals); **5.** (colloq.) umbrella, brolly, gamp.

rifler (rifle), v.a. To plane, to file.
rigaudon, rigodon (rigodɔ̃), s.m. [f. *Rigaud*, dancing-master] Rigadoon.
rigide (riʒid), adj. [L *rigidus*] Rigid, stiff; (fig.) rigid, strict, austere, severe.
rigidement (riʒidmɑ̃), adv. Rigidly.
rigidité (riʒidite), s.f. Rigidity, stiffness; (fig.) rigidity, strictness, severity, austerity.
rigolade (rigɔlad), s.f. (pop.) Lark, fun, good time, good laugh, revelry, carousal, buffoonery. Hence *rigolard, rigolboche*, &c., adj., very funny; fond of fun.
rigole (rigɔl), s.f. [orig. dub.] Small trench, gutter, rill, irrigating canal.
rigoler (rigɔle), v.n. [orig. dub.] To have a good laugh, to have great fun, to have a lark, to go on the spree; to carouse, to revel, to frolic, to romp.
rigolo, -te (rigɔlo), adj. (pop.) Funny, jolly, comic. ~, s.m. **1.** Wag; **2.** revolver.
rigorisme (rigɔrism), s.m. Rigorism, rigour, strictness.
rigoriste (rigɔrist), adj. Rigorist.
rigoureusement (rigurøzmɑ̃), adv. Rigorously, strictly, exactly.
rigoureu-x, -se (rigurø), adj. [f. *rigueur*] Rigorous, strict, exact; severe, harsh, inclement (winter, &c.); *châtiment* ~, severe punishment; *démonstration* ~*se*, exact, rigorous, or accurate demonstration; *un climat* ~, an inclement climate.
rigueur (rigœr), s.f. [L *rigor*] Rigour, strictness, accuracy; harshness, inclemency; *à la* ~, (*a*) strictly; strictly speaking; in ever so small a degree; (*b*) in case of absolute necessity; *de* ~, indispensable; *l'habit est de* ~, evening dress must be worn; *tenir* ~ *à X*, to remain severe towards X; to refuse to forgive X; to continue to frown upon X.
rillettes (rijɛt), s.f.pl. [OF *rille* = slice] Rillettes (minced pork cooked in fat, special dish of Touraine).
rillons (rijɔ̃), s.m.pl. Rillons (pieces of pork or goose-meat cooked in fat).
rimailler (rimɑje), v.n.a. [f. *rime*] To write doggerel verse.
rimaillerie (rimɑjri), s.f. Doggerel.
rimailleur (rimɑjœr), s.m. Doggerel rhymester, sorry rhymer, poetaster.
rime (rim), s.f. [f. L *rhythmus*] Rhyme; ~*s croisées*, alternate masculine and feminine rhymes; *cela n'a ni* ~ *ni raison*, there is neither rhyme nor reason in that; that is incoherent, or unaccountable, or at cross purposes.
rimer (rime), v.n. To rhyme; to write verse; *cela ne rime à rien*, there is no sense in that; *à quoi cela rime-t-il?*, what can you make of that?, what 's the meaning of that? [poetaster.
rimeur (rimœr), s.m. Rhymer, rhymester,
rinçage (rɛ̃saʒ), s.m. Rinsing.
rinceau (pl. **-x**) (rɛ̃so), s.m. [L *ramuscellus*] Scroll pattern, foliage ornament.
rince-bouche (rɛ̃sbuʃ), **rince-doigts** (rɛ̃sdwɑ), s.m. invar. Finger-bowl.
rincer (rɛ̃se), v.a. [etym. dub., f. L *recens*?] To rinse, to wash out; (slang) *se* ~ *l'œil*, to take a good look, to be all eyes; *se* ~ *la dalle*, to wet one's whistle.
rinceu-r, -se (rɛ̃sœr), s.m.f. Rinser, washer.
rinçoir (rɛ̃swar), s.m. Rinsing-tub.
rinçure (rɛ̃syr), s.f. Rinsings, slops.
ringard (rɛ̃gar), s.m. Fire-rake, clinker-bar.
riocher (riɔʃe), v.n. [f. *rire*] To giggle, to titter.
ripaille (ripɑj), s.f. [orig. dub.] Feast, feasting, carousal, revelry; *faire* ~, to feast, to carouse.
ripailler (ripɑje), v.n. To feast, to carouse.
ripatons (ripatɔ̃), s.m.pl. (slang) Boots, shoes (espec. old ones); syn. RIBOUIS.
ripe (rip), s.f. [f. ON *rispa*] **1.** Scraper (for stone); **2.** chip (of wood).
riper (ripe), v.a. To scrape.
ripopée (ripɔpe), s.f. Slops, swipes (of wine), (fig.) mishmash.
riposte (ripɔst), s.f. [It. *risposta*] (fenc.) Riposte, parry and thrust; (fig.) repartee, smart reply; counterstroke, retort; *prompt à la* ~, quick at repartee.
riposter (ripɔste), v.n. [f. *riposte*] To ripost, to parry and thrust; (fig.) to retort, to answer smartly.
ripuaire (ripɥɛr), adj. [f. L *ripa*] Riparian; *droits* ~*s*, riparian rights.
riquiqui (rikiki), s.m. (pop.) **1.** Dram, spirit, liqueur; **2.** undersized person, whippersnapper; **3.** smallest finger.
rire (rir), v.n. [L *ridere*] To laugh; to smile, to look pleasant, auspicious; *aimer à* ~, to like fun; to like a joke; to like a good time; *c'est à mourir de* ~, it 's enough to make one die of laughing; it 's too funny for words; ~ *aux anges*, to laugh alone and without reason; ~ *aux larmes*, to laugh till the tears come; ~ *aux éclats, à gorge déployée*, to roar with laughter; *éclater de* ~, to burst out laughing; ~ *sous cape*, to laugh in one's sleeve; *il a toujours le mot pour* ~, he is ever ready with a joke; *il lui a ri au nez*, he laughed in his face; ~ *du bout des lèvres*, ~ *jaune*, to force a laugh; to laugh on the wrong side of one's mouth; *rira bien qui rira le dernier*, he laughs best who laughs last; *faire* ~, to make people laugh; to raise a laugh; ~ *aux dépens de X*, to laugh at X's expense; *se pâmer de* ~, to be ready to die with laughing; *se tordre de* ~, to split one's sides with laughing; *pour* ~, for fun; not seriously; in jest; *histoire de* ~, for fun; *vous voulez* ~*!*, you are not serious; *il n'y a pas de quoi* ~, it 's nothing to laugh at; it 's no

laughing matter; **se ~** *de*, v.pr. to laugh at; to make game of.

rire (rir), s.m. Laugh, laughing, laughter; *accès de* ~, fit of laughter; *éclat de* ~, burst of laughter; peal of laughter; *un gros* ~, a loud laugh, a guffaw; a horse-laugh; *un* ~ *étouffé*, a suppressed laugh; *fou* ~, wild laugh, uncontrollable laughter, hysterical laughter; *avoir le fou* ~, to be convulsed with laughter.

ris[1] (ri), s.m. [L *risus*] Laugh, laughter, smile.

ris[2] (ri), s.m. [Scand. orig.] (naut.) Reef; *prendre un* ~, to take in a reef; *prendre le bas* ~, to close-reef; *avec deux* ~ *aux huniers*, with double-reefed topsails.

ris[3] (ri), s.m. [orig. dub.] (butch.) Sweetbread.

risban (risbɑ̃), s.m. [Dutch *rijsbank*] Harbour fort.

risée (rize), s.f. Laugh, guffaw; derision; laughing-stock; *être un objet de* ~, to be a laughing-stock; *s'enfuir sous les huées et les* ~*s*, to be driven away by the general derision and hooting; (naut.) squall, gust; cat's-paw, flurry.

risette (rizɛt), s.f. [f. *ris*] Pretty little smile; *faire* ~, to smile prettily.

risible (rizibl), adj. Risible, laughable.

risiblement (riziblǝmɑ̃), adv. Laughably, ridiculously.

risquable (riskabl), adj. That may be risked.

risque (risk), s.m. [It. *risco*] Risk, hazard; *au* ~ *de*, at the risk of; *à tout* ~, at all hazards; *à ses* ~*s et périls*, at one's own risk; *courir le* ~ *de*, to run the risk of; *j'en courrai le* ~, I will chance it.

risquer (riske), v.a. [f. *risque*] To risk, to run the risk of, to hazard, to chance; ~ *sa vie*, to risk one's life; ~ *la bataille*, to chance the fight; *qui ne risque rien n'a rien*, nothing venture nothing have; ~ *le tout pour le tout*, to risk all to win all; (colloq.) ~ *le paquet*, to chance it; to venture all; *risqué*, (*a*) hazardous; (*b*) improper; *risque-tout*, dare-devil.

rissole (risɔl), s.f. [f. L *russeolus*] **1.** (cook.) Rissole, fritter; **2.** (fish.) anchovy-net.

rissoler (risɔle), v.a.n. (cook.) To brown; (fig.) to get sunburnt.

ristourne (also **ristorne**) (risturn), s.f. [It. *ristorno*] Return, premium; rebate on accepted price; partial cancelling of an insurance, for the benefit of insurer.

rit, rite (rit), s.m. [L *ritus*] Rite.

ritournelle (riturnɛl), s.f. [It. *ritornello*] (mus.) Ritornello, burden; (colloq.) tiresome repetition.

ritte (rit), s.f. [etym. unkn.] A kind of plough.

ritualisme (ritɥalism), s.m. Ritualism.

ritualiste (ritɥalist), adj. s.m.f. Ritualist.

rituel, -le (ritɥɛl), adj. [L *ritualis*] Ritual. ~, s.m. Prayer-book; ritual.

rivage (rivaʒ), s.m. [f. L *ripa*] Strand, beach, shore, rivage, bank, coast.

rival, -e, (aux) (rival), adj. [L *rivalis*] Rival. ~, **-e**, s.m.f. Rival; *sans* ~, without a rival, unrivalled.

rivaliser (rivalize), v.n. To rival, to compete (*avec*, with); ~ *d'adresse avec X*, to vie in skill with X.

rivalité (rivalite), s.f. Rivalry, rivalship, competition, emulation.

rive (riv), s.f. [L *ripa*] Bank, shore, beach, coast; border, edge, skirt; ~ *droite d'une rivière*, right bank of a river; *la* ~ *gauche* (in Paris), the left bank, the part of the city lying south of the Seine; *à la* ~ *du bois*, in line with the border of the wood.

rivelaine (rivlɛn), s.f. Miner's pick.

rivement (rivmɑ̃), s.m. Riveting.

river (rive), v.a. [etym. dub.] To rivet; (fig.) *il lui a rivé son clou*, he gave him a clincher; he gave it to him sharply; he gave him his quietus.

riverain, -e (rivrɛ̃), adj. [f. *rive*] Riparian, riverside, adjoining (a road, &c.). ~, s.m.f. Owner of riverside property; owner of property bordering wood, road, street.

rivet (rivɛ), s.m. [f. *river*] Rivet.

rivetage (rivtaʒ), s.m. Riveting.

riveter (rivte), v.a. To rivet.

riveu-r, -se (rivœr), s.m.f. Riveter; ~*se*, riveting-machine.

rivière (rivjɛr), s.f. [LL *riparia*] River, stream; ~ *de diamants*, diamond necklace; *les petits ruisseaux font les grandes* ~*s*, little strokes fell great oaks; many a little makes a mickle.

rivoir (rivwar), s.m. Riveting-hammer.

rivulaire (rivylɛr), adj. (bot.) Growing on the banks of rivers; aquatic, aquatile.

rivure (rivyr), s.f. **1.** Riveting, clenching; **2.** hinge-pin.

rixe (riks), s.f. [L *rixa*] Brawl, row, scuffle, fight, quarrel, affray, squabble.

riz (ri), s.m. [It. *riso*] Rice; *eau de* ~, rice-water; *poudre de* ~, rice-powder; ~*-pain-sel*, nickname of commissariat officers and soldiers (military Supply and Food Department).

rizière (rizjɛr), s.f. Rice-plantation, rice-field.

rizotto (rizɔtɔ), s.m. [It. *risotto*] (cook.) Risotto, curried rice.

rob[1] (rɔb), s.m. [Arab. wd] (pharm.) Rob.

rob,[2] **robre** (rɔb, rɔbr), s.m. [Engl. *rubber*] Rubber (at whist and bridge).

robe (rɔb), s.f. [f. OF *rober*; OHG *roub*] Gown, dress, frock, robe ♤; (of clergyman) cloth; (of animals) coat; *noblesse de* ~, nobility of the long robe; ~ *de chambre*, dressing-gown; ~ *décolletée*, low dress; ~ *montante*, high-necked dress;

un cheval de ~ brune, a horse with a brown coat; *des pommes de terre en ~ de chambre*, potatoes boiled in their jackets. ⚠ 'Robe' in English is very frequently used for garment worn as indication of wearer's rank, office, profession, ex. the long robe = *la soutane* or *la robe d'avocat, de juge*; gentlemen of the robe = *avocats, magistrats* = *gens de robe*; also used poetically for long garment.

rober (rɔbe), v.a. **1.** To bark (madder); **2.** to wrap (cigars).

robin (rɔbɛ̃), s.m. (colloq.) 'Limb of the law', lawyer, gentleman of the long robe.

robine, roubine (rɔbin, rubin), s.f. [dialect. orig.] (chiefly in South of France) Irrigation-canal; canal.

robinet (rɔbinɛ), s.m. Tap, cock; *fermer le ~*, to turn off the tap or cock; *ouvrir le ~*, to turn on the tap or cock; *~ d'admission*, inlet-tap; admission-tap; *~ d'alimentation*, feed-tap; *~ de vidange*, waste-cock; (fig.) *~ d'eau tiède*, proser; prosy fellow; driveller.

robinetier (rɔbinɛtje), s.m. Cock-maker.

robinetterie (rɔbinɛtri), s.f. Cock-making; cock trade.

robinier (rɔbinje), s.m. (bot.) Robinia, false acacia.

roborati-f, -ve (rɔbɔratif), adj. [f. L *roborare*] (med.) Roborant, invigorating.

robre (rɔbr), s.m. See ROB[2].

robuste (rɔbyst), adj. [L *robustus*] Robust, sturdy, strong, hardy. ⚠ Not 'robustious', which means boisterous, self-assertive = *bruyant, turbulent, suffisant*.

robustement (rɔbystəmɑ̃), adv. Robustly, sturdily.

robustesse (rɔbystɛs), s.f. Robustness.

roc (rɔk), s.m. [LL *rocca*] Rock; *avoir un cœur de ~*, to be hard-hearted, to have a heart of flint. ⚠ Engl. 'roc' = Fr. *rock*.

rocaille (rɔkɑj), s.f. [f. *roc*] Rockwork, grotto-work; *style ~*, rococo style.

rocailleur (rɔkajœr), s.m. Rockwork-maker.

rocailleu-x, -se (rɔkajø), adj. Stony, pebbly; (fig.) harsh, rough.

rocambeau (pl. **-x**) (rɔkɑ̃bo), s.m. (naut.) Traveller (iron ring for holding sails).

rocambole (rɔkɑ̃bɔl), s.f. [Germ. *Rockenbolle*] **1.** Rocambole; **2.** (bot.) Spanish garlic.

roccella, rocelle (rɔksɛla, rɔsɛl), s.f. (bot.) Archil, orchil.

roche (rɔʃ), s.f. [LL *rocca*] Rock, boulder; (fig.) rock, flint, stone; *clair comme de l'eau de ~*, as clear as crystal; *cristal de ~*, rock crystal; *un homme de la vieille ~*, a man of the old school; a man who belongs to the good old stock; *il y a anguille sous ~*, there is a snake in the grass; I smell a rat; there is more here than meets the eye; there is something brewing; *il a un cœur de ~*, he has a heart of flint.

rocher (rɔʃe), s.m. Rock, crag, boulder, cliff; *~ branlant*, logan-stone, rocking-stone; (zool.) mure; (anat.) hard part of temporal bone.

rocher (rɔʃe), v.n. [f. *roche*] To froth.

rochet[1] (rɔʃɛ), s.m. [f. OF *froc, roc*] Rochet (surplice).

rochet[2] (rɔʃɛ), s.m. [f. Germ. *Rocken*] **1.** Bobbin (for silk); **2.** ratchet, *roue à ~*, ratchet-wheel.

rocheu-x, -se (rɔʃø), adj. Rocky, abounding in rocks.

rock (rɔk), s.m. [Arab. *rukh*] Roc (fabulous bird).

rococo (rɔkoko), s.m. [f. *rocaille*] Rococo, rococo style. ~, adj. Antiquated, old-fashioned.

rocou, roucou (rɔku, ruku), s.m. [Carib. *rucu*] Anatta; roucou (a dye).

rocouyer (rɔkuje), s.m. (bot.) Anatta-tree, roucou(-tree).

rodage (rɔdaʒ), s.m. (techn.) Grinding-in; smoothing by friction; *en ~*, being run in.

roder (rɔde), v.a. [f. L *rodere*] To grind in; to smooth by friction; *~ des soupapes*, to grind in valves.

rôder (rode), v.n. [L *rotare*] To prowl, to rove, to ramble, to roam, to wander.

rôdeu-r, -se (rodœr), s.m.f. Prowler, rover, vagrant.

rodomont (rɔdɔmɔ̃), s.m. [from name of a character in Ariosto's *Orlando Furioso*] Braggadoccio, rodomontader, braggart, blustering fellow; *faire le ~*, to bully, to hector; to swagger.

rodomontade (rɔdɔmɔ̃tad), s.f. [f. *rodomont*] Rodomontade, bluster, bounce, swagger.

rogation (rɔgaˈsjɔ̃), s.f. [L *rogatio*] Rogation; *~s*, (pl.) Rogation days.

rogatoire (rɔgatwar), adj. [f. L *rogare*] Of inquiry; *commission ~*, judicial commission of inquiry.

rogaton (rɔgatɔ̃), s.m. [f. L *rogatum*] Scraps, rubbish, broken meat, leavings.

rognage (rɔɲaʒ), s.m. Paring, clipping.

rogne (rɔɲ), s.f. **1.** Scab, mange; **2.** (colloq.) ill humour; *être en ~, se mettre en ~*, to be vexed, to get angry, to get cross, to be ratty, to get up on one's hind legs; to fret, to chafe.

rogne-pied (rɔɲpje), s.m. invar. Farrier's knife.

rogner (rɔɲe), v.a. [LL *rotundiare*] To clip, to pare, to cut, to curtail.

rogneu-r, -se (rɔɲœr), s.m.f. Cutter, clipper; *~se*, s.f. clipping-machine.

rogneu-x, -se (rɔɲø), adj. Mangy, scurvy.

rognoir (rɔɲwar), s.m. (bookbind.) Plough, cutting-press.

rognon (rɔɲɔ̃), s.m. [LL *renio*] Kidney.

a, mal, latte; ɑ, pas; ɑ̃, enfant; e, fée; ɛ, père, nette; ɛ̃, vin, pain; ə, premier; g, dogue, gale; h, *h*éros; i, finir; j, yeux, viens, bailler; k, croire; ɲ, oignon; o, pause, dose;

rognonner (rɔɲɔne), v.n. (colloq.) To grumble, to growl.

rognure (rɔɲyr), s.f. Paring, clipping, scraps, leavings, shavings.

rogomme (rɔgɔm), s.m. (pop.) Spirits; *une voix de ~*, gin-croak; raucous voice.

rogue (rɔg), adj. [ON *hrokr*] Arrogant, haughty, stiff.

rogue (rɔg), s.f. [Dan. *rogn*] Cod's roe.

rohart (rɔar), s.m. Hippopotamus or walrus ivory.

roi (rwa), s.m. [L *rex*] King; *~ d'armes*, king-at-arms; *~ de la nature*, lord of creation; *~ de cœur*, king of hearts; *de par le ~*, in the king's name; *en ~*, like a king; *les ~s, le jour des ~s*, Twelfth Night; *tirer* (or *fêter*) *les ~s*, to keep Twelfth Night; *pour le ~ de Prusse*, for nothing; having one's trouble for one's pains; *morceau de ~*, dish fit for a king; *vive le ~!*, long live the king!

roide, roideur, roidir (rwad, rwadœr, rwadir) See syn. RAIDE, RAIDEUR, RAIDIR.

roitelet (rwatlɛ), s.m. **1.** Petty king; **2.** (ornith.) wren.

rôle (rol), s.m. [L *rotulus*] Roll, list, catalogue; (theatr.) part, role; *à tour de ~*, in turn, by turns; (naut.) *~ d'équipage*, muster-roll; register of the ship's company; *~ de combat*, quarter-bill; *~ des contributions*, roll; *jouer un vilain ~*, to act an odious part.

rôlet (rolɛ), s.m. **1.** Small roll; **2.** small part.

rollier (rɔlje), s.m. (ornith.) Roller.

romain, -e (rɔmɛ̃), adj. s.m.f. Roman; *chiffres ~s*, Roman numerals; *l'Église Catholique Romaine*, the Roman Catholic Church; (print.) roman, primer; *~e*, s.f. **1.** steel-yard; **2.** Cos lettuce.

romaïque (rɔmaik), adj. s.m. Romaic, modern Greek.

roman, -e (rɔmɑ̃), adj. (philol.) Romance, romanic; (arch.) romanesque. ⚠ 'Romanesque' in English has a very different meaning from *romanesque* in French, which must be translated by romantic, sentimental, quixotic, &c.

roman (rɔmɑ̃), s.m. [OF *romanz*] Novel, work of fiction; (arch.) romanesque; *~-feuilleton*, serial; *héros de ~*, hero of romance; hero of chivalry; *cela tient du ~*, this is like a romance. ⚠ Not 'Roman', which = *Romain*.

romance (rɔmɑ̃s), s.f. [Span. wd] Song, ballad song, romanza. ⚠ *Romance* cannot be translated by the English 'romance', which means medieval tale = *roman de chevalerie*; vernacular language of Old France = *langue romane*; and work of fiction with scene and incidents remote from everyday life = *œuvre romanesque, légende, conte bleu, histoire à dormir debout.*

romancé, -e (rɔmɑ̃se), adj. In the form of a novel.

romanche (rɔmɑ̃ʃ), s.m. [LL *romanicum*] Romansh, language spoken in the Grisons, Tyrol, and Frioul.

romanci-er, -ère (rɔmɑ̃sje), s.m.f. Novelist.

romand, -e (rɔmɑ̃), adj. *Suisse ~e*, French Switzerland.

romanée (rɔmane), s.f. Romanée (a red Burgundy wine.)

romanesque (rɔmanɛsk), adj. Romantic, quixotic, imaginative, passionate. *~*, s.m. Romanticness, romanticism, romance. ⚠ Not the English 'romanesque', which describes the architectural style of the period between classical and Gothic and = *style roman, architecture romane.*

romanesquement (rɔmanɛskəmɑ̃), adv. Romantically.

romanichel, -le (rɔmaniʃɛl), s.m.f. adj. Gipsy, Tzigane.

romaniser (rɔmanize), v.a. [f. L *romanus*] To romanize; *~*, v.n. to become a Roman Catholic.

romaniste (rɔmanist), s.m.f. Romanist, philologist versed in Romance languages.

romantique (rɔmɑ̃tik), adj. s.m. Romantic.

romantiquement, (rɔmɑ̃tikmɑ̃), adv. Romantically.

romantisme (rɔmɑ̃tism), s.m. Romanticism.

romarin (rɔmarɛ̃), s.m. [L *ros marinus*] (bot.) Rosemary.

rombière (rɔ̃bjɛr), s.f. (slang, pej.) Oldish woman; moll.

rompre (rɔ̃pr), v.a.n. [L *rumpere*] To break, to break asunder, to snap; to interrupt, to divert, to break the force of; to deaden; (med.) to rupture; *être rompu aux affaires*, to have experience and skill in business, to be a good business man; *~ ses chaînes*, to break one's chains; *~ un entretien*, to interrupt a conversation; (hunt.) *~ les chiens*, to call off the hounds; (fig.) to change the subject, to divert the conversation; *~ le fil de son discours*, to break the thread of one's discourse; (lit. and fig.) *~ la glace*, to break the ice; (fig.) *~ une lance avec X*, to break a lance with X; *~ une lance pour X*, to defend X; to say a good word for X; to take up the cudgels for X; *~ son ménage, son établissement*, to break up one's household; *~ un mariage*, to break off a marriage; (fenc.) *~*, to draw back; (fenc.) *ne pas ~ d'une semelle*, not to draw back one step; *~ la tête à X*, to split X's head; *ne me rompez plus la tête avec vos plaintes*, do not importune me any more with your grievances; *~ avec X*, to break with X; to fall out with X; *~ à l'amiable*, to part friends; to part on good terms; ~ *en visière à X*, to come to an open quarrel with X; *rompez!*, off with you!, that will do!; *rompu de fatigue*, tired out; ~ *des couleurs*, to blend colours; *applaudir à tout* ~, to applaud frantically; to bring the house down with applause; *à bâtons rompus*, by fits and starts; by snatches; **se** ~, v.pr. to be broken, to be interrupted, to break; to part, to be refracted; *se* ~ *le cou*, to break one's neck; (fig.) to be ruined; *se* ~ *la tête*, to rack one's brains; *se* ~ *à la fatigue*, to accustom oneself to fatigue.

rompu, -e (rɔ̃py), p. adj. Broken; tired out.

ronce (rɔ̃s), s.f. [L *rumex*] (bot.) Bramble, blackberry-bush, *Rubus*; (fig.) thorn, obstacle, briar; (metall.) barbed wire; (in wood) round vein, streak.

ronceraie (rɔ̃srɛ), s.f. Brake, brambly ground.

ronceu-x, -se, (rɔ̃sø), adj. Brambly, thorny; (of wood) veiny, streaky.

ronchonner (rɔ̃ʃone), v.n. (colloq.) To grumble, to grouse, to growl, to mumble, to mutter between one's teeth.

ronchonneu-r, -se (rɔ̃ʃonœr), s.m.f. Grumbler, growler, bear.

roncier (rɔ̃sje), s.m. Bramble-bush.

rond, -e (rɔ̃), adj. [L *rotundus*] Round, circular, rounded, rotund; plump; frank, open; even; *un compte* ~, an even account, an even sum; *en nombres* ~*s*, in round numbers; *être* ~ (or *carré*) *en affaires*, to be plain-dealing and brisk; to be business-like and frank; *un petit homme tout* ~, a plump little man, a fat little fellow; (colloq.) *il est* ~, he is tipsy.

rond (rɔ̃), s.m. Round, ring, circle, orb, disk; (slang) sou, money; *danser en* ~, to dance in a ring; *tourner en* ~, to turn round and round; *s'asseoir en* ~, to sit in a circle; ~ *de cuir*, leather sitting pad; (fig.) quill-driver; ~ *de serviette*, napkin-ring; (slang) *il n'a plus un* ~, he has no money left; he is penniless; he is stony broke.

rondache (rɔ̃daʃ), s.f. Round shield, round buckler.

ronde (rɔ̃d), s.f. Round, patrol; (dance, mus.) round, roundelay; (mus.) semi-breve, o; (writing) round hand; *à la* ~, round about; around; all round; *passer à la* ~, to hand round; *faire la* ~, to go the rounds; *faire sa* ~, to make one's round, to inspect; *à 10 lieues à la* ~, 10 leagues round.

rondeau (pl. -x), **rondel** (rɔ̃do, rɔ̃dɛl), s.m. Roundelay, rondeau; (mus.) rondo; (agric.) roller.

rondelet, -te (rɔ̃dlɛ), adj. Plump, plumpish, rounded; *fortune* ~*te*, pretty large fortune.

rondelette (rɔ̃dlɛt), s.f. Sail-cloth.

rondelle (rɔ̃dɛl), s.f. Ring, rondelle, rundle; round shield; roundel; (techn., motor., &c.) collar, washer; ~ *d'amiante*, asbestos washer; ~ *fendue*, split washer.

rondement (rɔ̃dmɑ̃), adv. Roundly, promptly, briskly, frankly, bluntly, thoroughly; *y aller* ~, not to dilly-dally; to make things hum.

rondeur (rɔ̃dœr), s.f. Roundness, rotundity; (fig.) plain dealing, briskness.

rondin (rɔ̃dɛ̃), s.m. Round log; cudgel.

rond-point (rɔ̃pwɛ̃), s.m. Circus (at intersection of roads); (arch.) apse.

ronflant, -e (rɔ̃flɑ̃), adj. (fig.) Sonorous, high-sounding; loud and deceitful, exaggerated.

ronflement (rɔ̃fləmɑ̃), s.m. Snore, snoring; roar, rumbling, boom, roaring (of wind), humming (of top).

ronfler (rɔ̃fle), v.n. [orig. dub.] To snore; to roar, to boom, to rumble, to snort, to hum (as tops); (colloq.) *il faut que ça ronfle!*, things have got to hum a bit!; we have got to make things hum!; put some vim, or ginger, into it!; look alive!

ronfleu-r, -se (rɔ̃flœr), s.m.f. Snorer.

rongeant, -e (rɔ̃ʒɑ̃), adj. Gnawing, corroding; tormenting; *soucis* ~*s*, tormenting cares; anxieties.

ronge-maille (rɔ̃ʒmaj), s.m. invar. [f. *La Fontaine*] Nibbler (=rat).

rongement (rɔ̃ʒmɑ̃), s.m. Gnawing, corroding, torment.

ronger (rɔ̃ʒe), v.a. [L *rumigare*] To gnaw, to nibble, to eat; to corrode, to wear away; ~ *son mors*, or *son frein* (of a horse) to champ the bit; (fig.) to fret, to chafe with impatience; ~ *ses ongles*, to bite one's nails; **se** ~, v.pr. to fret, to chafe; to be corroded.

rongeu-r, -se (rɔ̃ʒœr), adj. Gnawing; corroding; heart-consuming. ~, s.m. Rodent.

ronron (rɔ̃rɔ̃), s.m. [onom.] Purr, purring, *faire* ~, to purr.

ronronner (rɔ̃rone), v.n. To purr.

roquefort (rɔkfɔr), s.m. [Fr. geog. orig.] Roquefort cheese.

roquelaure (rɔklor), s.f. (obs.) [f. prop. n.] Roquelaure (a cloak worn by men in the 17th c.).

roquentin (rɔkɑ̃tɛ̃), s.m. [orig. unkn.] **1.** (obs.) Old soldier on half-pay; **2.** old beau, old fogey.

roquer (rɔke), v.n. [f. *roc*, rook (in chess)] To castle.

roquet (rɔkɛ), s.m. [orig. dub.] Cur, little mongrel; (fig.) cur.

roquette (rɔkɛt), s.f. (bot.) Rocket.

rorqual (rɔrkwal), s.m. [Scand. wd] (zool.) Rorqual.

rosace (rozas), s.f. [f. *rose*] Rose, rose-window.

rosacé, -e (rozase), adj. [L *rosaceus*] (bot.) Rosaceous. **~es**, s.f.pl. (bot.) Rosaceae.

rosaire (rozɛr), s.m. [f. *rose*] Rosary.
rosaniline (rozanilin), s.f. (chem.) Rosaniline.
rosat (roza), adj. invar. [L *rosatus*] Of roses; *miel* ~, honey of roses.
rosâtre (rozatr), adj. Pinkish.
rosbif (rɔsbif), s.m. [f. Engl. *roast beef*] Piece of beef for roasting (usually from the leg (*tranche*)); piece of roast beef.
rose (roz), s.f. [L *rosa*] Rose, rose-window, rose diamond; ~ *des vents*, compass-card; *l'aurore aux doigts de* ~, the rosy-fingered Dawn; *ne pas être sur un lit de* ~*s*, not to lie on a bed of roses; *découvrir le pot aux* ~*s*, to find out the secret, to unmask the intrigue, to reveal the foul play; *des lèvres de* ~, rosy lips; *pas de* ~ *sans épines*, there is no rose without a thorn; *bois de* ~, tulip-wood; ~ *trémière*, hollyhock; *diamant taillé en* ~, rose-cut diamond. ~, s.m. Rose-colour, pink; *voir tout en* ~, to see only the bright side of things; to wear rose-coloured spectacles; *le* ~ *vous va bien*, rose-colour suits you.
rose (roz), adj. Rosy, pink, rose, rose-coloured, roseate; *tout n'est pas* ~ *en ce monde*, all is not sunshine in this world; life is not a bed of roses.
rosé, -e (roze), adj. Rosy, roseate, pink, light pink; *vin* ~, wine of a very light red colour.
roseau (pl. **-x**) (rozo), s.m. [Goth. orig.] (bot.) Reed.
rose-croix (rozkrwa), s.f. Rosicrucian brotherhood. ~, s.m. Rosicrucian.
rosée (roze), s.f. [f. L *ros*] Dew; *goutte de* ~, dewdrop.
roselet (rozlɛ), s.m. (comm.) Ermine.
roséole (rozeɔl), s.f. [f. *rosé*] Roseola; German measles, rose-rash.
roser (roze), v.a. To make pink or rose-coloured; to rose; to give a roseate tint to.
roseraie (rozrɛ), s.f. Rose-garden, rosery.
rosette (rozɛt), s.f. Rosette; bow-knot; order of Légion d'honneur; red chalk, red ink; red copper.
rosier (rozje), s.m. (bot.) Rose-tree, rose-bush.
rosière (rozjɛr), s.f. Winner of the rose as the best-behaved girl of her village.
rosiériste (rozjerist), s.m.f. Rose-grower.
rosir (rozir), v.n. To grow pink, to paint pink, to blush.
rossard (rɔsar), s.m. [f. *rosse*] Broken-down hack; (fig.) jade, lazy-bones, idler, scamp, ne'er-do-well.
rosse (rɔs), s.f. [MHG *ros*] Miserable hack, worn-out old horse; (fig.) jade, shrew, lazy-bones; regular brute. ~, adj. Malicious, malignant, spiteful, ironic; satirical, cruel.
rossée (rɔse), s.f. Thrashing, licking, drubbing; syn: ROULÉE.
rosser (rɔse), v.a. [f. *rosse*] To thrash, to lick, to belabour, to give a drubbing to.
rossignol (rɔsiɲɔl), s.m. [L *lusciniola*] **1.** Nightingale; **2.** picklock; **3.** waste, dead stock, unsaleable wares.
rossinante (rɔsinɑ̃t), s.f. [f. Span. *Rocinante*, name of Don Quixote's horse] Jade, worn-out hack, sorry horse.
rossolis (rɔsɔli), s.m. [f. L *ros solis*] (liqueur) Rosoglio, rosolio; sundew.
rostral, -e, (aux) (rɔstral), adj. [f. L *rostrum*] Rostral.
rostre (rɔstr), s.m. [L *rostrum*] Rostrum.
rostré, -e (rɔstre), adj. Rostrate.
rot (ro), s.m. [f. *roter*] Belch, eructation, *faire un* ~, to belch.
rôt (ro), s.m. See syn. RÔTI.
rotacé, -e (rɔtase), adj. [f. L *rota*] (bot.) Rotate.
rotang (rɔtɑ̃g), s.m. (bot.) Rattan. See syn. ROTIN.
rotat-eur, -rice (rɔtatœr), adj. [f. L *rotare*] Rotatory. ~, s.m. (anat.) Rotator.
rotati-f, -ve (rɔtatif), adj. [f. L *rotare*] Rotary, rotative, rotatory.
rotation (rɔta'sjɔ̃), s.f. [L *rotatio*] Rotation.
rotatoire (rɔtatwar), adj. Rotatory.
rote (rɔt), s.f. **1.** (Cath. Church) Rota; **2.** (mus. instr.) rote. ⚠ Not English 'rote' in the sense of repetition, unintelligent memory, which = *routine*.
roter (rɔte), v.n. [L *ructare*] To belch.
rôti (roti), s.m. Roast meat, roast; syn. RÔT.
rôtie (roti), s.f. Slice of toast, toast; ~ *beurrée*, buttered toast.
rotifères (rɔtifɛr), s.m.pl. (zool.) Rotifera.
rotin (rɔtɛ̃), s.m. [Malay *rōtan*] Rattan, rattan cane, rattan stick; (colloq.) penny, money; *n'avoir pas un* ~, not to have a brass farthing.
rôtir (rotir), v.a. [f. OHG *rôstjan*] To roast, to bake, to broil; to toast (bread); to wither (in the sunshine); *faire* ~, to roast, to bake, to broil; **se** ~, v.pr. to be roasted, to roast oneself.
rôtissage (rotisaʒ), s.m. Roasting.
rôtisserie (rotisri), s.f. Cook-shop.
rôtisseu-r, -se (rotisœr), s.m.f. Roaster; cook-shop keeper.
rôtissoire (rotiswar), s.f. Roaster, Dutch oven, meat-screen.
rotogravure (rɔtɔgravyr), s.f. [f. *rotative*+*gravure*] Rotogravure, intaglio.
rotonde (rɔtɔ̃d), s.f. [f. L *rotundus*] **1.** (arch.) Rotunda; **2.** round cloak.
rotondité (rɔtɔ̃dite), s.f. Rotundity, roundness; plumpness.
rotor (rɔtɔr), s.m. (electr.) Rotor.
rotule (rɔtyl), s.f. [L *rotula*] (anat.) Knee-cap, patella; (techn.) knuckle end, ball-shaped end; ball-head; *joint à* ~, ball-joint; *cardan à* ~, universal ball-joint.

rotulien, -ne (rɔtyljɛ̃), adj. (anat.) Pertaining to the knee-cap, patellar.
roture (rɔtyr), s.f. [f. LL *ruptura*] Roture, plebeian condition, yeomanry.
roturi-er, -ère (rɔtyrje), s.m.f. adj. Plebeian, roturier, commoner.
rouage (ruaʒ), s.m. [f. *roue*] Wheel, wheelwork, machinery; (horol.) movement; (fig.) machinery, means; *les ~s de l'administration*, the machinery of administration.
rouan, -ne (ruɑ̃), adj. [etym. dub.] (of horses) Roan; ~, s.m. Roan horse.
rouanne (ruan), s.f. [f. Gr. *rukanē*] Brand-iron (for casks); gouge; wimble.
roublard, -e (rublar), adj. [orig. dub.] Deep, knowing, sharp, cute, cunning, double-dealing. ~, s.m. Cunning fellow, artful dodger, crafty person, cute one.
roublardise (rublardiz), s.f. Cunning, trickery, double-dealing, craftiness.
rouble (rubl), s.m. [Russ. wd] Rouble.
roucoulement (rukulmɑ̃), s.m. [onom.] Cooing.
roucouler (rukule), v.n.a. [onom.] To coo; (fig.) to coo, to bill and coo; ~ *une romance*, to warble a song.
roue (ru), s.f. [L *rota*] Wheel; (torture) wheel; *faire la ~*, to strut about; to show off; (fig.) *mettre des bâtons dans les ~s à X*, to put a spoke into X's wheel; *pousser à la ~*, to put one's shoulder to the wheel; *Cartouche périt sur la ~*, Cartouche was broken on the wheel; *une cinquième ~ de carrosse*, a thing of no use; a fifth wheel; ~ *libre*, free wheel; ~ *dentée*, cog-wheel, toothed wheel; ~ *motrice*, driving wheel; ~ *de rechange*, spare wheel; ~ *voilée*, buckled wheel; ~ *avant*, front wheel; ~ *arrière*, back or rear wheel; *moyeu de ~*, wheel boss or hub; *bloquer les ~s*, to jam, or skid, the wheels; *centrer une ~*, to true up a wheel; ~ *à aubes*, paddle-wheel.
roué, -e (rue), adj. Crafty; broken; ~ *de coups*, beaten unmercifully. ~, s.m. Roué, rake, debauchee, profligate.
rouelle (ruɛl), s.f. [f. *roue*] Round slice, ~ *de veau*, fillet of veal (middle part of leg of veal, boned).
rouennerie (ruanri), s.f. [f. *Rouen*] Cotton print.
rouer (rue), v.a. [L *rotare*] **1.** To break upon the wheel; **2.** ~ *de coups*, to beat unmercifully.
rouerie (ruri), s.f. Cunning, trickiness, artfulness, sharp practice, double-dealing.
rouet (ruɛ), s.m. [f. *roue*] **1.** Spinning-wheel; **2.** (naut.) (*a*) sheave (of a block); (*b*) winding-machine; **3.** (fire-arms) wheel lock.
rouette (ruɛt), s.f. Osier-band, twig, withe.
rouf (ruf), s.m. [f. Flemish *roef*] (naut.) House on deck, round-house, coach, break; ~ *central*, or ~ *passerelle*, bridge-house.
rouflaquette (ruflakɛt), s.f. [Norman orig.] (said only of men's hair) Lock of hair on temple; Newgate knocker; spit-curl.
rouge (ruʒ), adj. [L *rubeus*] Red; red-hot, ruddy, flushed; *perdrix ~*, red-legged partridge; ~ *de honte, de colère*, red with shame, with rage; *fer ~*, red-hot iron; *se fâcher tout ~*, to get downright angry; *voir ~*, to see red, to be mad with rage; *devenir tout ~*, to turn quite red; *les Peaux-Rouges*, the Red Indians. *~-bord*, s.m. Bumper (of red wine); *~-gorge*, s.m. (ornith.) robin redbreast; *~-queue*, s.m. (ornith.) redstart.
rouge (ruʒ), s.m. Red colour, red, redness; rouge, paint; Red Republican; plate-powder, jewellers' rouge; *le ~ lui monte au visage*, he is turning red (with shame), he is blushing scarlet; *chauffé au ~*, red-hot; *bâton de ~*, lip-stick, lip-salve; *se mettre du ~*, to rouge one's cheeks, lips, &c.
rougeâtre (ruʒatr), adj. Reddish.
rougeaud, -e (ruʒo), adj. Ruddy, red-faced.
rougeole (ruʒɔl), s.f. [f. *rouge*] Measles (plur.).
rougeoyer (ruʒwaje), v.n. To turn red, to burn red, to glow.
rouget (ruʒɛ), s.m. **1.** [ichth.] Red mullet, surmullet, red gurnet, red gurnard; **2.** (ent.) harvest-bug.
rougette (ruʒɛt), s.f. (zool.) Bat of Madagascar.
rougeur (ruʒœr), s.f. [f. *rouge*] Redness, blush, flush, glow; *~s*, (pl.) pimples, inflamed spots on the skin.
rougir (ruʒir), v.n.a. To turn red, to redden, to tinge with red, to make red, to paint red; to blush, to colour; to rouge (one's cheeks, face, &c.); (fig.) to be ashamed (*de*, of); *eau rougie*, water tinged with wine; *vous la faites ~*, you put her to the blush; ~ *jusqu'au blanc des yeux*, to blush up to the eyes; *ne rougissez pas de votre naissance*, do not be ashamed of your birth.
rougissant, -e (ruʒisɑ̃), p. adj. Blushing, reddening.
roui (rui), s.m. (of flax) Retting; *sentir le ~*, to have a rancid smell.
rouille (ruj), s.f. [L *robigo*] Rust, rustiness; (of plants) rust, mildew, blight. ~, adj. Red-brown, russet.
rouiller (ruje), v.n.a. To rust, to get rusty, to make rusty; to blight; **se ~**, v.pr. (lit. and fig.) to become rusty.
rouilleu-x, -se (rujø), adj. Rusty, rust-coloured.

rouillure (rujyr), s.f. Rustiness; (agric.) rust.
rouir (ruir), v.a. [OGerm. *rotjan*] To ret (flax); to steep.
rouissage (ruisaʒ), s.m. Retting (of flax); steeping, macerating.
roulade (rulad), s.f. [f. *rouler*] Rolling; (mus.) roulade.
roulage (rulaʒ), s.m. Rolling; carting, cartage, carriage of goods; heavy traffic; *voiture de* ~, wagon, dray.
roulant, -e (rulɑ̃), p. adj. **1.** Rolling; *matériel* ~, rolling-stock; *feu* ~, running fire; **2.** (fam.) screamingly funny, killing.
rouleau (pl. -x) (rulo), s.m. Roll, roller, rolling-pin; scroll; (of wall-paper) piece; (for roads) steam-roller; *essuie-mains à* ~, jack-towel, roller-towel; (fig.) *être au bout de son* ~, to be at the end of one's tether; to be at one's wit's end; ~ *à pâtisserie*, rolling-pin.
roulée (rule), s.f. See syn. ROSSÉE.
roulement (rulmɑ̃), s.m. Rolling, roll, circulation, rotation; tread; rumbling, rattle; ~ *de tambour*, roll of drums; ~ *de tonnerre*, rumbling of thunder; ~ *à billes*, ball-bearings; *fonds de* ~, working capital.
rouler (rule), v.a.n. [LL *rotulare*] To roll, to roll up, to wind up, to run, to revolve, to turn, to rest, to ramble, to travel, to drive, to circulate; to get the better of, to do (a person), to let in; to rumble, to rattle; ~ *carrosse*, to keep a carriage; ~ *sa bosse*, to knock about a good deal; ~ *un projet dans sa tête*, to revolve, or turn over, a plan in one's mind; ~ *un compétiteur*, to get the better of a competitor; ~ *un champ*, to roll a field; ~ *sur l'or*, to roll in riches; *tout roule là-dessus*, all turns upon that; *son discours roule sur la morale*, his speech turns on morals; *nous avons roulé toute la nuit*, we drove on through the night; *ce bâteau roule beaucoup*, this ship rolls a good deal; (prov.) *pierre qui roule n'amasse pas mousse*, a rolling stone gathers no moss; *allez! roulez!*, all right! go ahead!; *faire* ~, to keep going; *faire* ~ *les écus*, to squander one's money; *se* ~, to roll oneself, to roll itself; to wallow; to wrap oneself.
roulet (rulɛ), s.m. Hatter's roller.
roulette (rulɛt), s.f. [f. *roue*] Small wheel; roulette (game); roll; castor (of arm-chairs, etc.), trundle, roller, truckle; *comme sur des* ~*s*, as right as a trivet; swimmingly; like one o'clock; quite smoothly; ~ *à patrons*, pattern-marker, marking-wheel; ~ *à pâte*, pastry-wheel; *patin à* ~*s*, roller-skate; *lit à* ~*s*, bedstead on castors.
rouleu-r, -se (rulœr), adj. Rolling; that rolls; *bâteau* ~, ship that rolls; rolling ship. ~, s.m. roller; (ent.) vine-grub, weevil.
rouli-er, -ère (rulje), adj. Pertaining to cartage; traffic. ~, s.m. Carter, wagoner, haulier. ~*e*, s.f. Wagoner's smock.
roulis (ruli), s.m. [f. *rouler*] Rolling; *coup de* ~, roll.
roulotte (rulɔt), s.f. [f. *rouler*] Gipsy's van, caravan; showman's wagon.
roulure (rulyr), s.f. **1.** Rolling; **2.** disease of trees causing splitting; **3.** trollop, prostitute.
roumain, -e (rumɛ̃), adj. s.m.f. Rumanian.
roumi (rumi), s.m. [f. *Romain*] Rumi (name given by Arabs to any Christian).
roupie[1] (rupi), s.f. [f. Sansk. *rūpya*] Rupee.
roupie[2] (rupi), s.f. [L *rupida*] Drop (of the nose), snot.
roupiller (rupije), v.n. (colloq.) To doze, to snooze, to slumber, to sleep.
roupillon (rupijɔ̃), s.m. (slang) Nap, forty winks, snooze, short sleep, doze; *piquer un* ~, to snooze, to have forty winks.
rouquin, -e (rukɛ̃), adj. s.m.f. [f. *roux*] (colloq.) Red-haired person, ginger, carrots.
roure (rur), s.m. See ROUVRE.
rouspétance (ruspetɑ̃s), s.f. (slang) Violent protest, opposition, rebellion; *faire de la* ~, to kick over the traces; *pas de* ~!, keep quiet!, don't answer back!, don't resist!
rouspéter (ruspete), v.n. [etym. dub.] (slang) To grouse, to answer back, to protest violently, to kick over the traces, to show fight, to chew the fat.
roussâtre (rusɑtr), adj. Russet, reddish.
rousse (rus), adj. [fem. of *roux*] Russet, red (hair). ~, s.f. Red-haired girl; (slang) *la* ~, the bobbies, the police.
rousseau (pl. -x) (ruso), s.m. Red-haired fellow; carrots.
rousselet (ruslɛ), s.m. (bot.) Russet pear.
rousserole (rusrɔl), s.f. (ornith.) Great sedge-warbler; reed-warbler.
roussette (rusɛt), s.f. [f. *roux*] **1.** A kind of mushroom; **2.** dog-fish; **3.** large bat; **4.** hedge-warbler.
rousseur (rusœr), s.f. Redness, russet colour; *taches de* ~, freckles; *avoir des taches de* ~, to be freckled.
roussi (rusi), s.m. Burnt smell, scorching; *sentir le* ~, to smell of burning.
roussin (rusɛ̃), s.m. [etym. unkn.] Thick-set horse; (slang) police spy, nark.
roussir (rusir), v.a. [f. *roux*] To redden, to brown; to burn superficially, to scorch, to singe; ~ *du linge avec un fer trop chaud*, to scorch linen with too hot an iron; *faire* ~ *de la viande*, to brown meat. See (FAIRE) REVENIR.
roussissement (rusismɑ̃), s.m. Scorching, singeing; reddening.
routailler (rutaje), v.a. [f. *route*] To track with hounds.

route (rut), s.f. [L *rupta*] Road; highway; way, course, orbit, direction, path, (poet.) pathway, track; *en* ~, on the way; on one's way; go ahead!, let us start!; *faire* ~ *pour*, to make for; to steer for; *faire fausse* ~, to take the wrong road; (fig.) to take a wrong step; to bark up the wrong tree; to blunder; *se mettre en* ~, to set out, to start; *mettre en* ~, to start; (mil.) *feuille de* ~, route(-order); *la* ~ *lui a été tracée*, his course has been marked out for him; *la* ~ *du soleil*, the course of the sun; *la* ~ *des Indes*, the way to India.

routier (rutje), s.m. **1.** (naut.) Charts and sailing directions; **2.** wheelman, cyclist racing on public roads; **3.** old hand, old stager; *un vieux* ~ *de la politique*, an old hand at politics; **4.** (Middle Ages) mercenary soldier.

routi-er, -ère (rutje), adj. Of roads, road-; *carte* ~*ère*, road-map; *machine* ~*ère*, traction-engine.

routin (rutɛ̃), s.m. Path, way.

routine (rutin), s.f. [f. *route*] Routine, rote, practice, tradition, custom; *par* ~, by rote; by routine.

routini-er, -ère (rutinje), adj. Of routine; 'red tape'; doing everything by routine; of habit. ~, s.m.f. Routinist, routineer.

routoir (rutwar), s.m. Retting-pond (for flax, &c.).

rouverin (ruvrɛ̃), adj. m. [etym. unkn.] (of iron) Brittle, hot-short.

rouvieu-x, -se (ruvjø), adj. [etym. unkn.] Mangy. ~, s.m. Mange.

rouvraie (ruvrɛ), s.f. Plantation of English oaks.

rouvre, roure (ruvr, rur), s.m. [L *robur*] (bot.) English oak.

rouvrir (ruvrir), v.a. [*re*+*ouvrir*] To reopen.

rou-x, -sse (ru), adj. [L *russus*] Russet, red, red-haired, reddish, reddish-brown; *la lune* ~*sse*, April moon. ~, s.m. **1.** Russet colour; **2.** (cook.) brown butter sauce, roux; **3.** red-haired man. See ROUSSE.

royal, -e, (aux) (rwajal), adj. [L *regalis*] Royal, kingly, kinglike, regal; (fig.) splendid, fit for a king; *prince* ~, crown prince. ~**e**, s.f. Tuft of beard below underlip.

royalement (rwajalmɑ̃), adv. Royally; in a kingly manner, regally; (fig.) in a princely manner, splendidly.

royalisme (rwajalism), s.m. Royalism.

royaliste (rwajalist), adj. s.m.f. Royalist; (fig.) *être plus* ~ *que le roi*, to out-Herod Herod.

royaume (rwajom), s.m. Kingdom, realm; *le* ~ *des Cieux*, the Kingdom of Heaven; *le sombre* ~, Hades; *le* ~*-uni*, the United Kingdom.

royauté (rwajote), s.f. Royalty; kingship; monarchy.

ru (ry), s.m. [f. L *rivus*] Tiny stream or channel, rivulet.

ruade (rɥad), s.f. [f. *ruer*] Kick (of horse), kicking.

rubace, rubicelle (rybas, rybisɛl), s.f. Rubicelle (yellow or orange-red spinel); artificial ruby.

ruban (rybɑ̃), s.m. [orig. dub.] Ribbon; (techn.) band, tape; narrow strip; (fig.) decoration; (fig.) *le* ~ *rouge*, the Légion d'honneur; *scie à* ~, band-saw; ~ *de cotton*, cotton tape; ~ *gros grain*, Petersham; *un long* ~ *de route*, a long road, a long strip of road; (bot.) ~ *d'eau*, ribbon-grass; bur-reed.

rubané, -e (rybane), p. adj. **1.** Covered with ribbons; **2.** striped, streaked; *canon* ~, (fire-arms) twisted gun-barrel.

rubaner (rybane), v.a. To trim with ribbons; (techn.) to roll (iron) into strips.

rubanerie (rybanri), s.f. Ribbon-weaving; ribbon-trade; ribbon-manufacture.

rubani-er, -ère (rybanje), adj. Pertaining to ribbons. ~, s.m.f. Ribbon-maker, ribbon-weaver.

rubéfaction (rybefaksjɔ̃), s.f. (med.) Rubefaction.

rubéfiant, -e (rybefjɑ̃), adj. Rubefacient.

rubéfier (rybefje), v.a. [L *rubeus*+*facere*] (med.) To rubify.

rubellite (rybɛlit), s.f. [L *rubellus*] (min.) Rubellite (a kind of tourmaline).

rubescent, -e (rybɛssɑ̃), adj. Reddish; growing red, rubescent.

rubiacées (rybjase), s.f.pl. (bot.) Rubiaceae, the madder family.

rubican (rybikɑ̃), adj. m. [Span. *rabicano*] Flecked with white and grey (of a horse).

rubicond, -e (rybikɔ̃), adj. [L *rubicundus*] Rubicund, ruddy.

rubidium (rybidjɔm), s.m. [f. L *rubidus*] (chem.) Rubidium, Rb.

rubigineu-x, -se (rybiʒinø), [f. L *rubigo*] Rubiginous.

rubine (rybin), s.f. (obs.) [f. L *rubus*] (chem.) Red powder; ~ *d'arsenic*, realgar.

rubis (rybi), s.m. [f. L *ruber*] Ruby; *faire* ~ *sur l'ongle*, to drink to the last drop; *payer* ~ *sur l'ongle*, to pay to the last farthing; to pay on the nail; ~ *balais*, balas-ruby; (horol.) *monté sur* ~, jewelled.

rubricateur (rybrikatœr), s.m. Rubricator.

rubrique (rybrik), s.f. [L *rubrica*] **1.** Rubric, head, chapter-heading, heading, (U.S.) caption; **2.** red chalk, ruddle; **3.** ~*s*, (pl.) rubric (directions for conduct of divine service); **4.** (print.) imprint; **5.** (pop.) tricks; *il en sait des* ~*!*, he is up to all sorts of tricks.

rubriquer (rybrike), v.a. To rubricate; to mark with red.
ruche (ryʃ), s.f. [presumably of Celtic orig.] **1.** Hive, bee-hive; ~ *à cadres*, frame-hive; (fig.) swarm, numerous and busy company, body, congregation; **2.** ruche, ruching, frilling, quilling.
ruchée (ryʃe), s.f. Hiveful, swarm of bees from one hive.
rucher (ryʃe), s.m. Apiary, shed for hives, row of hives.
rucher (ryʃe), v.a. To ruche, to quill, to goffer.
rude (ryd), adj. [L *rudis*] Rough, harsh, rugged; violent, strong; famous; shapeless; unpolished, discourteous, rude. ⚠ 'Rude' in English has not so wide a sense as *rude*; it is not often applied to things; it means principally discourteous, primitive, insulting = *impoli, grossier*; *une étoffe rude* must not be rendered by 'a rude material', but by 'a rough or a coarse material'; *rude* in French is often used to express admiration, ex.: *c'est un rude jouteur*, he is a powerful and redoubtable antagonist; (slang) *un ~ lapin !*, a regular brick !, plucky fellow !
rudement (rydmɑ̃), adv. Roughly, harshly, rudely (see RUDE ⚠); (colloq.) extremely, awfully, like anything; *il travaille ~ !*, he works like anything ! (= wonderfully well and quickly), he works like the dickens !; *je me suis ~ amusé !*, I had a jolly good time !
rudenté, -e (rydɑ̃te), adj. [L *rudens*] (arch.) Cabled.
rudenture (rydɑ̃tyr), s.f. (arch.) Cabling.
rudesse (rydɛs), s.f. Roughness, harshness, unevenness, ruggedness; severity, fierceness; rudeness (see RUDE ⚠).
rudiment (rydimɑ̃), s.m. [L *rudimentum*] Rudiment.
rudimentaire (rydimɑ̃tɛr), adj. Rudimentary, primitive; imperfectly developed; elementary.
rudoiement (rydwa'mɑ̃), s.m. Ill usage, bullying, rough handling.
rudoyer (rydwaje), v.a. To use roughly, to bully, to ill-treat, to treat harshly.
rue[1] (ry), s.f. [L *ruga*] Street; *courir les ~s*, to run about the streets; (fig.) to be in everybody's mouth; *vieux comme les ~s*, as old as the hills; *~ barrée*, no thoroughfare; *~ écartée*, back or side street; *les ~s en sont pavées*, it is as common as dirt.
rue[2] (ry), s.f. [L *ruta*] (bot.) Rue. ⚠ Not 'rue' in the sense of repentance, regret.
ruée (rɥe), s.f. [f. *se ruer*] **1.** Rush, charge, onslaught, inrush; stampede; **2.** straw mixed with manure.
ruelle (rɥɛl), s.f. [f. *rue*] **1.** Narrow street, lane, alley; **2.** space between bed and wall.
ruer (rɥe), v.n. [f. L *ruere*] To kick (as horse, &c.); **se ~**, v.pr. to rush (*sur*, upon), to charge, to attack impetuously, to dash; to stampede.
ruffian (ryfjɑ̃), s.m. [It. *ruffiano*] Ruffian, rough, debauchee, rake, hooligan, desperado, bully.
rugine (ryʒin), s.f. [LL *rugina*] (surg.) Raspatory, rasp.
rugir (ryʒir), v.n.a. [L *rugire*] To roar; to bellow; (fig.) to roar.
rugissant, -e (ryʒisɑ̃), p.adj. Roaring.
rugissement (ryʒismɑ̃), s.m. Roar, roaring.
rugosité (rygozite), s.f. Rugosity, roughness, rough spot.
rugueu-x, -se (rygø), adj. [L *rugosus*] Rugged, rugose, rough, uneven; (fig.) rough, harsh.
ruine (rɥin), s.f. [L *ruina*] Ruin; (fig.) ruin; *en ~s*, in ruins; *courir à sa ~*, to go to one's ruin; *menacer ~*, to threaten to fall in ruins; *tomber en ~s*, to fall in ruins; *être en ~s*, to lie in ruins; *cela causera sa ~*, that will be the ruin of him; *elle n'est plus qu'une ~*, she is a ruin, she is the wreck of what she was.
ruiner (rɥine), v.a. To ruin, to destroy, to spoil, to overthrow; to bring to ruin; **se ~**, v.pr. to ruin oneself, to go to ruin. ⚠ *Ruiner* cannot be used in the sense of to seduce: to ruin a girl = *séduire* (not *ruiner*) *une jeune fille*.
ruineusement (rɥinøzmɑ̃), adv. Ruinously.
ruineu-x, -se (rɥinø), adj. Disastrous, bringing ruin; excessively expensive; ruinous.
ruinure (rɥinyr), s.f. [f. *ruiner*] (carp.) Notch; housing.
ruisseau (pl. **-x**) (rɥiso), s.m. [f. L *rivus*] Stream, brook, creek, rivulet; (in the street) gutter; (fig.) stream, floods; *des ~x de larmes*, floods of tears; *les petits ~x font les grandes rivières*, many a little makes a mickle.
ruisselant, -e (rɥislɑ̃), p. adj. Streaming, running (*de*, with).
ruisseler (rɥisle), v.n. [f. *ruisseau*] To stream, to run, to pour down, to run in streams; to be very wet; to trickle down; *~ de sueur*, to perspire abundantly.
ruisselet (rɥislɛ), s.m. Rivulet, brooklet.
ruissellement (rɥisɛlmɑ̃), s.m. Streaming, running, pouring down, dripping.
rumb, rhumb, (rɔ̃b), s.m. (naut.) Rhumb; *~ du vent*, air-line.
rumen (rymɛn), s.m. (zool.) Rumen, paunch.
rumeur (rymœr), s.f. [L *rumor*] Confused noise, uproar; (fig.) rumour, report; *la ~ publique l'accuse*, it is rumoured that he is guilty; he is rumoured to be guilty.
rumex (rymɛks), s.m. (bot.) Rumex, dock.

ruminant, -e (rymiṅɑ̃), p. adj. Ruminant, ruminating. ~, s.m. Ruminant.
rumination (rymina'sjɔ̃), s.f. Rumination; chewing the cud.
ruminer (rymine), v.a.n. [L *ruminare*] To ruminate, to chew the cud; (fig.) to meditate, to ponder, to muse on, to ruminate; ~ *un projet*, to ruminate a plan or a scheme.
rumsteck, romsteak (rɔmstɛk), s.m. [f. Engl. wd] Rump steak.
runes (ryn), s.f.pl. [Goth. *runa*] Runes, runic letters.
runique (rynik), adj. Runic.
ruolz (rɥɔls), s.m. [f. Fr. inventor's name] Plated metal, electro-plate; *en* or *de* ~, electro-plated.
rupestre (rypɛstr), adj. [f. L *rupes*] (bot.) Rupestrine, rupestral, rock.
rupicole (rypikɔl), s.f. (ornith.) Cock of the rock, grouse. Syn. COQ DE ROCHE.
rupin, -e (rypɛ̃), adj. (slang) (*a*) Of things: fine, dashing, A 1, natty, out and out; (*b*) of persons: rich, swell, well-groomed. ~, s.m.f. Swell, toff, nut, gent; *les* ~*s*, the nobs.
rupiner (rypine), v.n. (slang, espec. school) To do excellently, to excel, to be a success.
rupteur (ryptœr), s.m. (electr.) Contact-breaker; ~ *à commande électrique*, electrically actuated break.
rupture (ryptyr), s.f. [L *ruptura*] Rupture, breaking, bursting, fracture, breach, (fig.) rupture, breaking-off; *la* ~ *d'une digue*, the breaking of a dam; ~ *de la paix*, breach of peace; *la* ~ *d'un mariage*, the breaking-off of a match; *la* ~ *d'une veine*, the rupture of a vein; *en* ~ *de ban*, breaking bounds; *ils en sont venus à une* ~, it has come to a break between them.
rural, -e, (aux) (ryral), adj. [f. L *rus, ruris*] Rural, country. ~, s.m. Countryman; *les ruraux*, the peasantry, the countryside.
ruse (ryz), s.f. [f. *ruser*] Craft, cunning, guile, wile; ruse, stratagem, feint, trick, dodge; *recourir à une* ~ *grossière*, to have recourse to a stratagem easily seen through; ~ *de guerre*, stratagem of war; ~*s innocentes*, harmless tricks.
rusé, -e (ryze), adj. Wily, sly, rusé, artful, cunning, deep, cute; *un* ~ *compère*, a knowing card.
ruser (ryze), v.n. [f. L *recusare*, LL *refusare*] To use stratagem, to use cunning or deceit, to dodge, to fall back upon a dodge, to finesse; (hunt.) to double.
russe (rys), adj. s.m.f. Russian. ⚠ In French the usual feminine is *Russe*, but when speaking of Russian women from certain parts of Russia the fem. *Russienne* is used, ex.: *une Petite-Russienne* = a woman from *Petite-Russie*, a Little Russian.
russien, -ne (rysjɛ̃), adj. s.m.f. Russian (espec. from Little Russia).
russifier (rysifje), v.a. To russify.
russule (rysyl), s.f. [f. *roux*] (bot.) A kind of reddish poisonous mushroom.
rustaud, -e (rysto), adj. [f. L *rusticus*] Boorish, rustic, clownish, coarse. ~, s.m.f. Boor, rustic, clod-hopper, clown.
rustauderie (rystodri), s.f. Boorishness, rusticity, churlishness, coarseness, rustic manners.
rusticage (rystikaʒ), s.m. Rough-casting, rough coat (for walls), rustication.
rusticité (rystisite), s.f. [f. *rustique*] Rusticity, simplicity; boorishness; (of plants) hardiness.
rustique (rystik), adj. [L *rusticus*] Rustic, rural, country; homely, simple, unrefined; boorish; (of plants) hardy; *des travaux* ~*s*, rural work; *des manières un peu trop* ~*s*, rather boorish manners; *un siège* ~, a rustic seat; *une maison* ~, a country cottage; *des plaisirs* ~*s*, rustic pastimes. ~, s.m. Mason's hammer.
rustiquement (rystikmɑ̃), adv. Rustically.
rustiquer (rystike), v.a. To rusticate, to rough-cast (a wall, etc.). ⚠ Not 'to rusticate' in the sense of *se retirer à la campagne*; to rusticate (an undergraduate) = *renvoyer pour quelque temps de l'Université*.
rustre (rystr), s.m. [f. L *rusticus*] Rustic; churl, boor, lout, bumpkin, coarse fellow, clown.
rut (ryt), s.m. [L *rugitus*] Rut, rutting, rut-time; *être en* ~, to rut.
rutabaga (rytabaga), s.m. [Swedish orig.] (bot.) Rutabaga, Swedish turnip. Syn. CHOU-NAVET.
rutacées (rytase), s.f.pl. (bot.) Rutaceae.
ruthénium (rytenjɔm), s.m. (chem.) Ruthenium.
rutilant, -e (rytilɑ̃), p. adj. [L *rutilans*] Glowing, shining, bright red; ruddy.
rutile (rytil), s.m. [L *rutilus*] (chem). Rutile (an ore of titanium).
rutiler (rytile), v.n. [L *rutilare*] To glow, to shine, to glitter.
rythme (ritm), s.m. [Gr. *rhuthmos*] Rhythm.
rythmer (ritme), v.a. To give rhythm to; to scan.
rythmique (ritmik), adj. Rhythmical.

S

S, s (ɛs), s.m.f. 19th letter of the alphabet; a few abbrev.: S.A. = *Son Altesse*, His or Her Highness; S.E. = *Son Excellence*, His or Her Excellency; S.G.D.G. = *sans garantie du gouvernement*, without government guarantee (of patents); S.D.N. = *Société des Nations*, League of Nations;

S.M. = *Sa Majesté*, His or Her Majesty; S.O.S., wireless code signal of extreme distress; S.P. = *Saint-Père*, Holy Father; S.S. = *Sa Sainteté*, His Holiness; S.V.P. = *s'il vous plaît*, please.

sa (sa), adj. poss. f. (see SON) His, her, its.

sabayon (sabajɔ̃), s.m. [It. *zabaione*] (cook.) Sabayon (a mixture of yolks of eggs, wine, sugar, &c.).

sabbat (saba), s.m. [Heb. *schabbāth*] **1.** Sabbath; **2.** sabbath, nocturnal revels (of witches, &c.); tumult, uproarious gaiety; caterwauling; shindy, racket; *faire un* ~, to kick up a shindy.

sabbataire (sabatɛr), s.m. Sabbatarian.

sabbatique (sabatik), adj. Sabbatic(al).

sabéen, -ne (sabeɛ̃), adj. s.m.f. [f. *Saba*] Sabaean, Sabean.

sabéisme (sabeism), s.m. [f. Heb. *çĕbā*] Sabaism, star-worship.

sabelle (sabɛl), s.f. (zool.) Sabella (a genus of sea-worms).

sabellianisme (sabɛljanism), s.m. [f. *Sabellius*, 3rd-c. heresiarch] Sabellianism.

sabellien, -ne (sabɛljɛ̃), adj. Sabellian.

sabin, -e (sabɛ̃), adj. s.m.f. (ant.) Sabine.

sabine (sabin), s.f. [L *sabina*] (bot.) Savin, *Juniperus sabina*.

sabir (sabir), s.m. Dialect spoken in Algeria and Near East, a mixture of French, Spanish, Italian, Arabic; gibberish, jargon; lingua franca.

sable[1] (sabl), s.m. [L *sabulum*] Sand; (med.) gravel; ~*s mouvants*, quicksands; *banc de* ~, sandbank; (fig.) *bâtir sur le* ~, to build on sand; (fig.) *avoir du* ~ *dans les yeux*, to be sleepy.

sable[2] (sabl), s.m. [Russ. *sobol*] **1.** (herald.) Sable, black; **2.** sable (fur); syn. MARTRE ZIBELINE. ⚠ French *sable* is a technical word, *martre* and *zibeline* being the terms in ordinary use, but English 'sable' (freq. in pl.) is in common currency.

sablé, -e (sable), adj. Sanded, covered with sand; *allée* ~*e*, gravel walk. ~, s.m. (cook.) A kind of shortbread.

sabler (sable), v.a. **1.** To cover with sand, to sand, to gravel; **2.** to drink, to gulp down, to quaff, to toss off; ~ *le champagne*, to drink champagne freely.

sableu-x, -se (sablø) adj. Sandy, gravelly, containing sand.

sablier (sablie), s.m. **1.** Sand-glass, hourglass, egg-glass; **2.** sand-box (for drying wet ink).

sablière (sablier), s.f. **1.** Sand-pit, gravel-pit; **2.** (carp.) wall-plate; raising-piece; **3.** sand-box (in tram-cars, &c.).

sablon (sablɔ̃), s.m. Fine white sand; scouring-sand.

sablonner (sablɔne), v.a. To scour with fine sand.

sablonneu-x, -se (sablɔnø), adj. Sandy.

sablonnier (sablɔnje), s.m. Sand-dealer.

sablonnière (sablɔnjɛr), s.f. Sandpit (of fine sand).

sabord (sabɔr), s.m. [orig. dub.] (naut.) Port-hole; port; ~ *de charge*, raft-port; *contre-*~, deadlight.

saborder (sabɔrde), v.a. (naut.) To scuttle (a ship).

sabot (sabo), s.m. [Arab. orig.] **1.** Wooden shoe, clog, sabot; **2.** (of animals) hoof; **3.** whipping-top; **4.** (techn.) skid, shoe, brake-block; *frein à* ~, shoe-brake; ~ *du frein*, brake-shoe, brake-block; **5.** (pej.) sorry ship; sorry fiddle; *dormir comme un* ~, to sleep like a top; *il a mis du foin dans ses* ~*s*, he has feathered his nest; (bot.) ~ *de Vénus*, lady's slipper.

sabotage (sabɔtaʒ), s.m. **1.** Wooden-shoe making; **2.** sabotage (wilful damaging of plant, wares, &c., by workmen); scamped work.

saboter (sabɔte), v.n. To clatter with one's wooden shoes; ~, v.a. to botch, to scamp (work); to do wilful damage to (plant, &c.).

saboterie (sabɔtri), s.f. Wooden-shoe manufacture.

saboteu-r, -se (sabɔtœr), s.m.f. **1.** Saboteur, wilful damager of plant, materials, &c.; **2.** bungler, bad workman, botcher.

saboti-er, -ère (sabɔtje), s.m.f. Wooden-shoe maker, sabot-maker; ~*ère*, dance (in wooden shoes), clog-dance.

sabouler (sabule), v.a. (colloq.) To scold, to rate, to haul over the coals.

sabre (sabr), s.m. [Germ. *Sabel*] Sabre; (fig.) military domination; *traîneur de* ~, braggadocio, swaggerer, slasher, swashbuckler; (interj.) ~ *de bois!*, zounds!, hang it!; *coup de* ~, sabre-cut; ~-*baïonette*, sword-bayonet; ~ *au clair*, with drawn sabre; (colloq.) *le* ~ *et le goupillon*, the army and the church.

sabrer (sabre), v.a. To strike with a sabre, to slash about, to cut, to sabre; (fig.) to blot out, to strike out, to cut down; to bungle, to botch; ~ *un article*, to make drastic cuts in a paper or article.

sabretache (sabrətaʃ), s.f. [f. Germ. *Säbeltasche*] Sabretache.

sabreur (sabrœr), s.m. Swordsman, slasher, hard fighter, swashbuckler, dashing cavalry soldier; (fig.) bungler, botcher, brutal fellow.

saburral, -e, (aux) (sabyral), adj. (med.) Saburral.

saburre (sabyr), s.f. [L *saburra*] (med.) Saburra (foul granular matter in stomach).

sac[1], (sak), s.m. [L *saccus*] Bag, sack, pouch; (of a soldier, mountaineer, &c.) knapsack; ~ *à main*, lady's hand-bag;

~ *de voyage*, wallet, bag, valise, leather bag; ~ *à ouvrage*, work-bag; (fig.) ~ *à vin*, regular drunkard; *prendre X la main dans le* ~, to catch X red-handed, or in the very act; *donner le* ~ *à X*, to give X the sack, to sack X; *ils sont à mettre dans le même* ~, they are birds of a feather; they can go and live in the same hotel; *votre affaire est dans le* ~, your business is getting on swimmingly; the matter is as good as done; *un homme de* ~ *et de corde*, a regular ruffian, a downright villain; *vider son* ~, to have one's say out; *tirer d'un* ~ *deux montures*, (fig.) to make double profits; ~ *à papier !*, by George !, zounds !, bless me !; *avoir le* ~, to be rich; *épouser un* ~, to marry money; to marry for money.

sac[2] (sak), s.m. [It. *sacco*] Sack, sacking, plunder, pillage; *mettre une ville à* ~, to sack a town.

saccade (sakad), s.f. [orig. dub.] Jerk, check, saccade; *par* ~*s*, by fits and starts.

saccadé, -e (sakade), p. adj. Jerky, by jerks, irregular, broken; (fig.) abrupt (style).

saccader (sakade), v.a. To jerk, to check.

saccage (sakaʒ), s.m. Devastation.

saccager (sakaʒe), v.a. [f. *sac*] To devastate; to plunder; to throw into complete confusion, to ransack.

saccharification (sakarifika'sjɔ̃), s.f. Saccharification; conversion into sugar.

saccharifier (sakarifje), v.a. [f. LL *saccharum*] To saccharify.

saccharimètre (sakarimɛtr), s.m. Saccharimeter.

saccharine (sakarin), s.f. Saccharine.

saccule (sakyl), s.m. (anat.) Saccule.

sacculiforme (sakylifɔrm), **sacciforme** (saksifɔrm), adj. Bag-shaped, sacciform.

sacerdoce (sasɛrdɔs), s.m. [L *sacerdotium*] Sacerdocy, priesthood; (collectively) the priests.

sacerdotal, -e, (aux) (sasɛrdɔtal), adj. Sacerdotal.

sacerdotalisme (sasɛrdɔtalism), s.m. Sacerdotalism.

sachée (saʃe), s.f. Bagful, sackful.

sachem (saʃɛm), s.m. [Amer. Ind. wd] Sachem (Indian chief).

sachet (saʃɛ), s.m. [f. *sac*] Sachet, scented bag, perfume cushion.

sacoche (sakɔʃ), s.f. [f. *sac*] Satchel; money-bag; courier's bag, saddle-bag, tool-bag.

sacolève (sakɔlɛv), s.f. [It. *saccaleva*] Sackalever, sacoleva (Levantine cargo-boat).

sacquer (sake), v.a. (colloq.) To sack, to give the sack to, to dismiss, to hoof out.

sacramentaire (sakramɑ̃tɛr), adj. Sacramentarian. ~, s.m. Sacramentary; (pl., theol.) Sacramentarians.

sacramentel, -le (sakramɑ̃tɛl), adj. Sacramental.

sacramentellement (sakramɑ̃tɛlmɑ̃), adv. Sacramentally.

sacrarium (sakrarjɔm) [L wd] (ant.) Sacrarium.

sacre[1] (sakr), s.m. [f. *sacrer*] Coronation (of a king); consecration (of a bishop).

sacre[2] (sakr), s.m. [Arab. wd] (ornith.) Saker (kind of falcon); (fig.) blackguard, villain.

sacré, -e (sakre), p. adj. Sacred, holy, consecrated; *les livres* ~*s*, Holy Writ; *musique* ~*e*, sacred music; (anat.) sacral; (colloq.) damned, blessed, precious, confounded, blooming, cursed; *avoir le feu* ~, to have the sacred flame; to warm up; to be keen (on something); to be all enthusiasm.

sacrebleu (sakrəblø), interj. [corrupt. of *sacre-dieu*] Damn it !, dash it !, by Gad !; syn. SACRÉDIÉ, SAPRELOTTE, SACRISTI, &c.

sacré-cœur (sakrekœr), s.m. (Cath. Church) Heart of Jesus; great Catholic basilica in Paris.

sacrement (sakrəmɑ̃), s.m. [L *sacramentum*] Sacrament; *recevoir les derniers* ~*s*, to receive the last sacraments; *le saint* ~, the holy Sacrament; *fréquenter les* ~*s*, to go to confession and communion regularly.

sacrer (sakre), v.a. [L *sacrare*] To anoint; to consecrate; to crown; ~, v.n. to curse and swear.

sacret (sakrɛ), s.m. (ornith.) Sakeret, young tercel; syn. TIERCELET.

sacrificateur (sakrifikatœr), s.m. Sacrificer; *Grand* ~, High Priest.

sacrificatoire (sakrifikatwar), adj. Sacrificial.

sacrificature (sakrifikatyr), s.f. (rare) The office of sacrificer or sacrificial priest.

sacrifice (sakrifis), s.m. [f. L *sacrificium*] Sacrifice, offering; *il faut savoir faire des* ~*s*, one must be prepared to make sacrifices.

sacrifier (sakrifje), v.a.n. [L *sacrificare*] To sacrifice, to immolate, to offer up; *il a tout sacrifié à son ambition*, he sacrificed everything to his ambition; ~ *à la mode*, to sacrifice to fashion; **se** ~, v.pr. to sacrifice oneself.

sacrilège (sakrilɛʒ), s.m. [L *sacrilegium*] Sacrilege. ~, adj. Sacrilegious.

sacripant (sakripɑ̃), s.m. [f. *Sacripante*, prop. n. in Boiardo and Ariosto] Downright rascal, blackguard, rodomont, good-for-nothing scamp.

sacristain (sakristɛ̃), s.m. [LL *sacristanus*] Sexton, sacristan, vestry-keeper.

sacristi, sapristi (sakristi, sapristi), interj. Bless me !, by Jove !, Great Scott !

sacristie (sakristi), s.f. [LL *sacristia*] Vestry, sacristy.

sacristine (sakristin), s.f. Vestry nun, sacristine.

sacro-saint, -e (sakrosɛ̃), adj. Sacrosanct (often used ironically in Fr. as in Engl.).
sacrum (sakrɔm), s.m. [L wd] (anat.) Sacrum.
sadducéen, -ne (sadyseɛ̃), p. adj. s.m.f. Sadducean, Sadducee.
safran (safrɑ̃), s.m. [Arab. *çafrā*] **1.** (bot.) Saffron; **2.** (naut.) cheek, after-piece. ~, adj. Saffron-coloured.
safrané, -e (safrane), p. adj. Saffron-coloured, saffroned.
safraner (safrane), v.a. To saffron.
safranière (safranjɛr), s.f. Saffron plantation.
safre (safr), s.m. [It. *zaffera*] (chem.) Zaffre; (fig., obs.) glutton.
saga (saga), s.f. [Scand. wd] Saga, epic.
sagace (sagas), adj. [L *sagax*] Sagacious, shrewd, clever.
sagacité (sagasite), s.f. Sagacity.
sagaie, zagaie (sagɛ), s.f. [Arab. orig.] Assegai.
sage (saʒ), adj. [LL *sapius*] Wise, sage, prudent, discreet, judicious, sensible; good, well-behaved; chaste, modest; (to children) *soyez ~s!*, be good!; *un enfant ~*, a well-behaved child; *une loi ~*, a wise law. ~, s.m. Sage (often iron.). ⚠ Not 'sage' (bot.), which = *sauge*.
sage-femme (saʒfam), s.f. (pl. *des sages-femmes*) Midwife.
sagement (saʒmɑ̃), adv. Wisely, prudently, judiciously; well, discreetly, virtuously, chastely.
sagesse (saʒɛs), s.f. [f. *sage*] Wisdom, good sense, judiciousness, discretion; good behaviour, goodness; gentleness; chastity, virtue.
sagette (saʒɛt), s.f. (obs.) [L *sagitta*] Arrow.
sagittaire (saʒitɛr), s.m. [f. L *sagitta*] (Rom. ant.) Sagittarius, archer; (astr.) the Archer, Sagittarius; ~, s.f. (bot.) arrow-head.
sagittal -e, (aux) (saʒital), adj. Arrow-shaped; (anat.) sagittal.
sagou (sagu), s.m. [Malay wd] Sago.
sagouin (sagwɛ̃), s.m. [Guarani *sagui*] (zool.) Sagoin, squirrel-monkey; (fig.) slovenly, dirty fellow.
sagoutier, sagouier (sagutje, saguje), s.m. (bot.) Sago-tree.
sagum (sagɔm), s.m. **saie** (sɛ), s.f. [L *sagum*] (ant.) Sagum, cloak.
saï (sai), s.m. [Brazil. wd] (zool.) Sai, kind of (South American) monkey.
saie (sɛ), s.f. Goldsmith's brush.
saïga (saiga), s.m. [Russ. wd] (zool.) Saiga (kind of antelope).
saignant, -e (sɛɲɑ̃), p. adj. Bleeding, bloody; (cook.) underdone; (Amer.) rare.
saignée (sɛɲe), s.f. Blood-letting, bleeding, phlebotomy; bend of the arm, small of the arm; (fig.) drain on the purse, heavy sacrifice; (tech.) irrigation trench.
saignement (sɛɲəmɑ̃), s.m. Bleeding; ~ *de nez*, bleeding of the nose, nose-bleeding.
saigner (sɛɲe), v.a. [L *sanguinare*] To bleed, to kill by bleeding; (fig.) to drain, to exact heavy payment from; ~ *à blanc*, to bleed to death; ~, v.n. to bleed; ~ *du nez*, to bleed at the nose; **se** ~, v.pr. (fig.) to drain one's purse; to make heavy sacrifices.
saigneur (sɛɲœr), s.m. Bleeder, killer (of pigs, &c.).
saigneu-x, -se (sɛɲø), adj. Bloody; *bout ~*, scrag-end.
saillant, -e (sajɑ̃), p. adj. Projecting, jutting out; (herald.) salient; (fig.) striking, remarkable, noticeable, prominent. ~, s.m. Salient.
saillie (saji), s.f. **1.** Standing out, jutting out, projection, ledge, salient; *en ~*, sticking out; *faire ~*, to jut out; **2.** start, spurt, flash; witticism, sally; gush; **3.** (of animals) copulation, covering.
saillir (sajir), v.n. irreg. To stand out, to project, to jut out; *faire ~*, to bring out; to gush, to spurt; ~, v.a. (of animals) to cover, to serve.
sain, -e (sɛ̃), adj. [L *sanus*] Sound, hale, healthy; wholesome, salubrious; ~ *d'esprit*, sane; ~ *et sauf*, safe and sound; *jugement ~*, sound judgement; *nourriture ~e*, wholesome food; *climat ~*, salubrious climate; (naut.) *côte ~e*, clear coast.
sainbois (sɛ̃bwɑ), s.m. (bot.) Spurge-flax; garou-bark.
saindoux (sɛ̃du), s.m. [OF *saim+doux*] Lard.
sainement (sɛnmɑ̃), adv. Soundly; wholesomely, healthily, salubriously; (fig.) judiciously, sanely. ⚠ English 'sane, sanely' apply only to the mind, while *sain, sainement* in French apply to the body as well.
sainfoin (sɛ̃fwɛ̃), s.m. [*sain+foin*] (bot.) Sainfoin.
saint, -e (sɛ̃), adj. [L *sanctus*] Holy, sacred, consecrated, saintly, sainted, sanctified; *S. André*, Saint Andrew; *l'Écriture Sainte*, Holy Writ, the Scriptures; *le Saint-Esprit*, the Holy Ghost; *c'était une ~e femme*, she was a saintly woman; *toute la ~e journée*, the whole blessed day; *la terre ~e*, the Holy Land. ~, -e, s.m.f. Saint; *ne savoir à quel ~ se vouer*, not to know which way to turn; *le ~ des ~s*, holy of holies; *chacun prêche pour son ~*, every one tries to further his own interests; *coiffer Ste Catherine*, to be 25 and unmarried; (fig.) *~-Crépin*, s.m. paraphernalia; personal belongings; *~-cyrien*, s.m. military cadet (of St. Cyr school); ~-*frusquin*, s.m. personal belongings and money; one's all; *on lui a pris tout son ~-*

frusquin, they took everything he had; *un ~-honoré*, s.m. a kind of cream cake; *la ~-Jean*, s.f. midsummer; *la ~-Médard*, s.f. St. Swithin's day; *c'est une ~e-Nitouche*, s.f. she is a smooth hypocrite; she looks as if butter would not melt in her mouth; *la ~-Michel*, s.f. Michaelmas; *le ~-office*, s.m. the Holy Office; *le ~-Père*, s.m. the Holy Father, the Pope; *le ~-Siège*, s.m. the Holy See; *~-Simonien, -ne*, adj. St. Simonian; *~-Simonisme*, s.m. St. Simonianism; (colloq.) *Ste Touche*, pay-day; *faire la ~ Lundi*, to take Monday off; *à la ~ Glinglin*, on Tib's eve; never; *jusqu'à la ~ Glinglin*, till the cows come home; till two Sundays come together.

saintement (sɛ̃tmɑ̃), adv. Holily, sacredly, saintlily, piously, righteously.

sainteté (sɛ̃tәte), s.f. Holiness, sacredness, sanctity, saintliness; *Sa ~*, His Holiness, the Pope.

saïque (saik), s.m. [Turk. *shāīgā*] (naut.) Saic (Levantine cargo-vessel).

saisi (sɛzi), s.m. Debtor distrained upon.

saisi, -e (sɛzi), p. adj. **1.** Seized; struck, dumbfounded, strongly impressed, startled; **2.** cognizant (of), called upon to consider; **3.** (law) distrained.

saisie (sɛzi), s.f. Seizure (⚠ not in the sense of *apoplexie*); execution, distraint; *~-arrêt*, attachment; *~-brandon*, execution on crops; *~-exécution*, execution, distraint; *~-gagerie*, distraint; *~-revendication*, seizure under prior claim.

saisine (sɛzin), s.f. [f. *saisir*] **1.** (law) Seizing; **2.** (naut.) gripe, slings, lashing.

saisir (sɛzir), v.a. [f. LL *sacire*] **1.** To seize; to seize upon, to grasp, to lay hold of, to catch, to snatch; *~ l'occasion*, to seize the opportunity; *~ un prétexte*, to avail oneself of a pretext; to understand, to perceive; *je n'ai pas bien saisi*, I did not quite catch; **2.** to strike with amazement, to give a shock to, to startle, to strike dumb, to overwhelm; *elle en est restée toute saisie*, she was struck all of a heap; she was awe-struck; she was dumbfounded; **3.** to make cognizant (*de*, of); *~ de*, to put in the hands of; to bring before, to call upon . . . to consider; *le tribunal en est saisi*, it has been laid before the Court; **4.** (law) to seize, to attach, to distrain; **5.** (naut.) to stow, to secure; to gripe; **se ~**, v.pr. to seize, to snatch (*de*, at), to lay hold (of), to possess oneself (of); *se ~ de*, to arrest.

saisissable (sɛzisabl), adj. **1.** That can be seized, distrainable; **2.** perceptible.

saisissant, -e (sɛzisɑ̃), p. adj. Striking, thrilling, startling; (of cold) piercing. *~*, s.m. (law) Distrainer.

saisissement (sɛzismɑ̃), s.m. Shock, pang, violent or strong impression.

saison (sɛzɔ̃), s.f. [L *satio*] Season; *de ~*, in season; (fig.) well-timed, seasonable; *hors de ~*, out of season; (fig.) ill-timed, unseasonable; *arrière-~*, s.f. autumn; (U.S.A.) fall; *la morte ~*, the dead season, the slack time; *la ~ nouvelle*, springtime; *marchand des quatre ~s*, costermonger; *faire une ~ à Vichy*, to take the waters at Vichy.

saisonni-er, -ère (sɛzɔnje), adj. Periodical, following the seasons.

sajou (saʒu), s.m. [f. Tupi wd] (zool.) Sajou, a kind of South American monkey.

saké, saki (sake, saki), s.m. [Japanese wd] Saké, fermented liquor made from rice.

salace (salas), adj. [L *salax*] Salacious, lustful.

salacité (salasite), s.f. Salacity, salaciousness, lustfulness.

salade[1] (salad), s.f. [f. *saler*] Salad; (fig.) medley, mess, hotch-potch, salmagundi, farrago; *fatiguer la ~*, to mix the salad thoroughly; *panier à ~*, salad-washer, wire strainer or basket; (colloq.) police van, Black Maria.

salade[2] (salad), s.f. [It. *celata*] Sallet, helmet.

saladier (saladje), s.m. Salad-bowl, salad-dish.

salage (salaʒ), s.m. Salting; (obs.) salt-tax.

salaire (salɛr), s.m. [L *salarium*] Wages, pay, fees; (fig.) salary ⚠, reward. ⚠ In French *salaire* is chiefly used for the pay of manual workers or persons earning low wages. English 'salary', on the other hand, is the fixed periodical payment made for professional or clerical work; the best French equivalents are *traitement, émoluments*.

salaison (salɛzɔ̃), s.f. Salting; *~s*, (pl.) salt food.

salamalec (salamalɛk), s.m. [f. Arab. *salaam+aleikoum* = hail to you] Salaam (Turkish greeting); (fig.) kotow, exaggerated politeness; *faire des ~s à n'en plus finir*, to kotow endlessly, to prostrate oneself.

salamandre (salamɑ̃dr), s.f. [Gr. *salamandra*] **1.** (zool.) Salamander; **2.** patent slow-combustion stove.

salangane (salɑ̃gan), s.f. (ornith.) Salangane, esculent swallow.

salanque (salɑ̃k), s.f. Salt-marsh; syn. MARAIS SALANT.

salant (salɑ̃), adj. m. *Marais ~*, salt-marsh.

salariat (salarja), s.m. Status or condition of a wage-earner. ⚠ See SALAIRE.

salarié, -e (salarje), adj. Wage-earning; hired. *~*, s.m. Wage-earner, hireling. ⚠ See SALAIRE.

salarier (salarje), v.a. To give wages to, to hire, to pay, to have in one's pay.

salaud, -e (salo), s.m.f. (of a person) Dirty beast, rotter, skunk.

sale (sal), adj. [MHG *sal*] Dirty, foul, unclean, perilous, filthy; (fig.) low, smutty, indecent, obscene. ⚠ *Obscène* in French has a much stronger and more precise sense than 'obscene' in English.

salé, -e (sale), p. adj. Salt, salted, briny; (fig.) **1.** broad, obscene, smutty, coarse, pickled, strong, stiff; **2.** awfully dear, stiff; *il a payé ça 100 francs, c'est ~!*, they charged him 100 francs for that, I call that a bit stiff !; *petit ~*, s.m. boiled salt pork; (slang, vulgar) ~, s.m. brat, baby.

salement (salmɑ̃), adv. Dirtily, filthily, nastily; (colloq.) very much; *je suis ~ ennuyé*, I am awfully worried; I am in a fix.

salep (salɛp), s.m. [Turk. wd] (bot.) Salep.

saler (sale), v.a. [f. L *sal*] To salt, to preserve with salt, to sprinkle with salt; (fig.) to overcharge, to fleece, to salt.

saleron (salrɔ̃), s.m. Salt-bowl, salt-cellar.

saleté (salte), s.f. Dirt, filth, dirtiness, filthiness, dirty thing; dirty trick; coarse expression, obscenity, indecency; (colloq.) nasty trick.

saleu-r, -se (salœr), s.m.f. Salter.

salicaire (salikɛr), s.f. [f. L *salix*] (bot.) Spiked purple loosestrife; *Lythrum salicaria.*

salicine (salisin), s.f. (chem.) Salicin.

salicinées (salisine), s.f.pl. (bot.) Salicaceae.

salicole (salikɔl), adj. [f. L *sal+colere*] Salt-producing.

salicoque (salikɔk), s.f. (zool.) Small shrimp.

salicorne (salikɔrn), s.f. (bot.) Saltwort, *Salicornia.*

saliculture (salikyltyr), s.f. Salt-manufacture.

salicylate (salisilat), s.m. (chem.) Salicylate.

salicylique (salisilik), adj. (chem.) Salicylic.

salière (saljɛr), s.f. **1.** Salt-cellar, salt-box; **2.** salt-cellar, hollow behind the collar-bone.

salification (salifika'sjɔ̃), s.f. (chem.) Salification.

salifier (salifje), v.a. (chem.) To convert into a salt.

saligaud, -e (saligo), s.m.f. [f. *sale*] Filthy beast, rotter, skunk.

salignon (saliɲɔ̃), s.m. Salt-deposit, salt-cat.

salin, -e (salɛ̃), adj. [f. L *sal*] Saline, salt; briny. ~, s.m., ~**e**, s.f. Salt-marsh.

salinage (salinaʒ), s.m. **1.** Place where salt is gathered; **2.** alkali; **3.** salt-making by evaporation.

saline (salin), s.f. **1.** Salt-marsh; **2.** salt-mine, salt-pit.

salinier (salinje), s.m. Salt-manufacturer, salt-worker.

salinité (salinite), s.f. Salinity.

salique (salik), adj. [f. *Francs Saliens*] Salic.

salir (salir), v.a. To dirty, to soil, to stain, to foul; (fig.) to defile, to defame, to sully, to disgrace.

salissant, -e (salisɑ̃), p. adj. Easily soiled; that dirties, dirty (of work, &c.).

salisson (salisɔ̃), s.f. Little slut.

salissure (salisyr), s.f. Soil, stain, spot of dirt.

salivaire (salivɛr), adj. Salivary.

salivant, -e (salivɑ̃), p. adj. Salivant, producing unusual secretion of saliva.

salivation (saliva'sjɔ̃), s.f. Salivation.

salive (saliv), s.f. [L *saliva*] Saliva; spittle; (fig., colloq.) *perdre sa ~*, to speak in vain, to waste one's breath.

saliver (salive), v.n. To salivate.

saliveu-x, -se (salivø), adj. Saliva-like.

salle (sal), s.f. [OHG *sal*] Hall, large room, assembly room; ward (in hospitals); (theatr.) house; *faire crouler la ~*, to bring down the house; *~ d'armes*, (*a*) armoury; (*b*) fencing-school; *~ de bain*, bath-room; *~ d'attente*, waiting-room; *~ d'audience*, audience-chamber; *~ d'études*, school-room; *~ de cours*, lecture-room; *~ à manger*, dining-room; *~ des pas perdus*, entrance-hall (of courts of justice, &c.); (mil.) *~ de police*, guard-house, military prison; *~ des ventes*, auction-room, auction-mart or -hall.

salmigondis (salmigɔ̃di), s.m. [orig. dub.] (cook.) Hotch-potch, salmagundi; (fig.) medley, farrago, hotch-potch, mishmash.

salmis (salmi), s.m. (cook.) Salmi, ragout of game.

salmonidés (salmɔnide), s.m.pl. Salmonidae (family of fishes of the salmon kind).

saloir (salwar), s.m. Salting-tub, salting-house.

salon (salɔ̃), s.m. [It. *salone*] Drawing-room, parlour; salon, annual art exhibition; show; saloon. ⚠ 'Saloon' is used only of public places, not of a room in a private house; saloon car = *wagon salon*; dining-saloon = *salle de restaurant*; shaving-saloon = *salon de coiffure pour hommes*; saloon (in U.S.A.) = *bar*; saloon-keeper = *bistro, marchand de vin.*

salope (salɔp), s.f. [f. *sale*] Slut, trollop; harlot; (naut.) *Marie-~*, dredger.

saloper (salɔpe), v.a. To bungle, to spoil (one's work).

saloperie (salɔpri), s.f. Dirty trick; beastliness; smutty thing, filthy thing; rubbish, trash; *~ de temps!*, filthy weather !

salopette (salɔpɛt), s.f. (workmen's) Overalls, slops.

salpêtre (salpɛtr), s.m. [f. L *sal+petrae*] Saltpetre.

salpêtrer (salpɛtre), v.a. To cover with

saltpetre, to saltpetre; **se** ~, v.pr. to become covered with saltpetre.

salpêtrerie (salpɛtrəri), s.f. Saltpetre-works.

salpêtreu-x, -se (salpɛtrø), adj. Saltpetrous.

salpêtrier (salpɛtrje), s.m. Saltpetre-maker.

salpêtrière (salpɛtrjɛr), s.f. Saltpetre-works; *La Salpêtrière,* hospital in Paris for mentally affected persons.

salpicon (salpikɔ̃), s.m. [Span. wd] (cook.) Salpicon (a ragout of various meats, chopped and spiced, often used as stuffing or garnishing).

salpingite (salpɛ̃ʒit), s.f. [f. Gr. *salpigx*] (pathol.) Salpingitis.

salse (sals), s.f. [f. L *salsus*] Salse, small volcano (throwing out salt water and mud).

salsepareille (salsparɛj), s.f. [Span. *zarzaparrilla*] (bot.) Sarsaparilla.

salsifis (salsifi), s.m. [It. *sassefrica*] Salsify.

saltarelle (saltarɛl), s.f. [It. *saltarello*] Saltarello (a dance).

saltation (salta'sjɔ̃), s.f. [L *saltatio*] Saltation.

saltigrade (saltigrad), adj. [f. L *saltus*+*gradi*] Hopping, leaping, saltigrade.

saltimbanque (saltɛ̃bɑ̃k), s.m.f. [f. It. *saltare in banco*] Mountebank, buffoon, juggler, travelling circus clown or girl; (fig.) humbug, buffoon, unreliable fellow.

salubre (salybr), adj. [L *salubris*] Salubrious, healthy, bracing, wholesome.

salubrité (salybrite), s.f. Salubrity, healthfulness, wholesomeness; ~ *publique,* Public Health.

saluer (salɥe), v.a.n. [L *salutare*] To bow to, to pay one's respects to, to take off one's hat to; to greet, to offer one's greetings or compliments, to proclaim, to hail; (naut.) to salute; ~ *de 21 coups de canon,* to fire a salute of 21 guns in honour of; *j'ai bien l'honneur de vous* ~, (*a*) (to end a letter) yours very sincerely; (*b*) (speaking) good-bye (it may be said in a stiff manner, implying no sympathy); *saluez-le de ma part,* remember me to him.

salure (salyr), s.f. Saltness, brine.

salut (saly), s.m. [f. L *salus*] **1.** Preservation, salvation, escape, safety; *il n'a dû son* ~ *qu'à sa fuite,* he found safety in flight; he only just escaped; *travailler à son* ~, to work out one's (moral) salvation; *Armée du Salut,* Salvation Army; **2.** bow, greeting, salute, salutation; ~*!,* good day !; (poet.) hail !; *faire un* ~, to bow, to nod; *à bon entendeur* ~*!,* a word to the wise; **3.** (Cath. liturg.) benediction.

salutaire (salytɛr), adj. [L *salutaris*] Salutary, wholesome, useful, beneficial, advantageous.

salutairement (salytɛrmɑ̃), adv. To good purpose, usefully, advantageously, wholesomely.

salutation (salyta'sjɔ̃), s.f. Salutation, greeting, salute.

salutiste (salytist), s.m.f. Salvationist.

salvage (salvaʒ), s.m. [Engl. wd] Salvage; *droit de* ~, salvage money.

salvation (salva'sjɔ̃), s.f. [L *salvatio*] Salvation.

salve (salv), s.f. [It. *salva*] Volley, salvo, salute; (fig.) ~ *d'applaudissements,* round of applause.

samaritain, -e (samaritɛ̃), adj. s.m.f. Samaritan.

sambuque (sɑ̃byk), s.f. [L *sambuca*] (mus.) Sambuc, sambuca.

samedi (samdi), s.m. [f. L *sabbati dies*] Saturday; ~ *Saint,* Easter Eve.

samien, -ne (samjɛ̃), adj. s.m.f. Samian, of Samos.

samole (samɔl), s.m. (bot.) Samolus.

samovar (samɔvar), s.m. [Russ. wd] Samovar.

samoyède (samwajɛd), adj. s.m.f. Samoyed.

sampan (sɑ̃pɑ̃), s.m. Sampan (a Chinese small boat).

sanatorium (sanatɔrjɔm), s.m. (pl. *sanatoriums* or *sanatoria*) [f. L *sanare*] Sanatorium (pl. -ia), health resort.

san-benito (sɑ̃benito), s.m. [Span. wd] Sanbenito.

sancir (sɑ̃sir), v.n. (naut.) To founder, to sink by the bows.

sanctifiant, -e (sɑ̃ktifjɑ̃), adj. Sanctifying.

sanctificat-eur, -rice (sɑ̃ktifikatœr), adj. Sanctifying. ~, s.m.f. Sanctifier.

sanctification (sɑ̃ktifika'sjɔ̃), s.f. Sanctification.

sanctifier (sɑ̃ktifje), v.a. [f. L *sanctus*+*facere*] To sanctify, to hallow.

sanction (sɑ̃ksjɔ̃), s.f. [L *sanctio*] Sanction.

sanctionner (sɑ̃ksjɔne), v.a. To sanction; to approve of, to ratify.

sanctuaire (sɑ̃ktɥɛr), s.m. [L *sanctuarium*] Sanctuary, chancel (of church); (fig.) sanctuary.

sandal (sɑ̃dal), s.m. See SANTAL.

sandale (sɑ̃dal), s.f. [L *sandalium*] Sandal.

sandaraque (sɑ̃darak), s.f. [Gr. *sandarakē*] Sandarac.

sandwich (sɑ̃dwiʃ), s.m. [Engl. wd] Sandwich.

sang (sɑ̃), s.m. [L *sanguis*] Blood; (fig.) race, parentage, kindred, lineage, consanguinity; *à* ~ *froid,* cold-blooded; *à* ~ *chaud,* warm-blooded; *coup de* ~, stroke, congestion of the brain; *en* ~, *tout en* ~, covered with blood; ~ *bleu,* blue blood; *buveur de* ~, bloodthirsty man; (fig.) *avoir le* ~ *chaud,* to be ardent, to be hot-tempered; *il n'a pas de ~ dans les veines,* or *il a du ~ de navet,* he is chicken-hearted, he dare not call his soul his own; he is lily-livered; *cela fait bouillir le ~,* it makes one's blood boil; *cela glace le ~,* it curdles one's blood; *suer ~ et eau,* to strain every nerve; to sweat blood; to drudge; *le ~ lui monte à la tête,* the blood rushes to his head; *se faire une pinte de bon ~,* to have a jolly time; *se faire du mauvais ~,* to fret, to worry; to be down in the mouth; (pop.) *mon ~ n'a fait qu'un tour,* I was struck all of a heap; *mettre à feu et à ~,* to put to fire and sword; *prince du ~,* prince of the blood; *pur ~,* thoroughbred; *la voix du ~,* the call of the blood; *bon ~ ne peut mentir,* good breeding always tells; like father like son; *il a cela dans le ~,* it runs in his blood; *se battre au premier ~,* to fight till blood is drawn; *verser, répandre le ~,* to shed blood.

sang-dragon (sãdragɔ̃), s.m. Dragon's blood (a resin).

sang-froid (sãfrwa), s.m. invar. Coolness, sang-froid, composure, self-control; *de ~,* coolly, in cold blood; *garder son ~,* to keep cool; *perdre son ~,* to lose one's presence of mind, one's head, or one's self-control.

sanglant, -e (sãglã), adj. Bloody; bleeding, blood-covered, blood-stained; attended with bloodshed; (fig.) *faire de ~s reproches à X,* to reproach X sharply. ⚠ English 'bloody' is a word to be avoided, as it is used in very vulgar expressions.

sangle (sãgl), s.f. [L *cingula*] Girth, saddle-girth; strap, belt; sacking, webbing; *lit de ~,* folding bedstead (not made of metal).

sangler (sãgle), v.a. To gird, to bind with a girth, to lace tightly; to deal a blow (with a strap), to lash; **se ~,** v.pr. to lace oneself tightly.

sanglier (sãglje), s.m. [f. L *singularis*] Wild boar.

sanglot (sãglo), s.m. [L *singultus*] Sob; *éclater en ~s,* to burst into tears, to burst out sobbing.

sangloter (sãglɔte), v.n. To sob.

sangsue (sãsy), s.f. [L *sanguisuga*] (zool.) Leech; (fig.) bloodsucker, leech.

sanguification (sãgɥifika'sjɔ̃), s.f. Sanguification.

sanguin, -e (sãgɛ̃), adj. [L *sanguineus*] Of blood, pertaining to blood; sanguine; (⚠ in English 'sanguine' = French *sanguin* when used in a scientific sense; otherwise it generally means bright, hopeful, expecting things to go well = *optimiste, plein de vitalité*); *vaisseaux ~s,* blood-vessels; *orange ~e,* blood-orange. **~e,** s.f. Red chalk, red chalk drawing.

sanguinaire (sãginɛr), adj. Sanguinary, bloodthirsty. **~,** s.f. (bot.) Bloodwort.

sanguine (sãgin), s.f. **1.** Red chalk; red-chalk drawing; **2.** bloodstone.

sanguinelle (sãginɛl), s.f. (bot.) Cornel, dogwood.

sanguinolent, -e (sãginɔlã), adj. Tinged with blood.

sanhedrin (sanedrɛ̃), s.m. [Gr. *sunedrion*] Sanhedrim.

sanicle (sanikl), s.f. (bot.) Sanicle, *Sanicula.*

sanie (sani), s.f. [L *sanies*] (pathol.) Sanies.

sanieu-x, -se (sanjø), adj. Sanious.

sanitaire (sanitɛr), adj. [f. L *sanitas*] Sanitary, pertaining to health; *train ~,* ambulance train; *police ~,* health police; *cordon ~,* cordon sanitaire, sanitary cordon.

sans (sã), prep. [L *sine*] Without, were it not for, but for; (in compounds) -less; *~ ailes,* wingless; *~ amis,* friendless; *~ cesse,* incessantly, unceasingly, repeatedly; *~ cela, ~ quoi,* otherwise; *~ doute,* doubtless, no doubt; *~ que,* without, unless; *~ que je le sache,* without my knowing it; *~ plus,* without anything more; *cela va ~ dire,* of course; *dites cela ~ rire,* say that without laughing; *ne le dites pas ~ qu'on vous le demande,* don't say it unless you are asked.

sans-cœur (sãkœr), s.m.f. Heartless person.

sanscrit, -e (sãskri), adj. s.m. [Sansk. *saṃskṛita*] Sanskrit.

sanscritiste (sãskritist), s.m.f. Sanskrit scholar.

sans-culotte (sãkylɔt), s.m. (pl. *sans-culottes*) (Fr. hist.) Sans-culotte, ultra-violent republican.

sans-culottide (sãkylɔtid), s.f. adj. Each of the five complementary days of French Republican calendar; the festivals held during these days.

sans-façon (sãfasɔ̃), s.m. invar. Off-handedness, cheek, bluntness; familiarity; *c'est d'un ~ !,* I say, that 's rather cool!

sans-gêne (sãʒɛn), s.m. invar. Unceremoniousness, off-handedness, coolness, cheek, free-and-easy ways.

sansonnet (sãsɔnɛ), s.m. (ornith.) Starling, *Sturmis vulgaris.*

sans-souci (sãsusi), s.m.f. invar. Careless, easy-going person; free-and-easy person; happy-go-lucky fellow.

sans-travail (sãtravaj), s.m. invar. Unemployed.

santal (pl. -s) (sãtal), s.m. [Arab. *çandal*] (bot.) Sandalwood. Syn. SANDAL.

santé (sãte), s.f. [L *sanitas*] Health; (naut.) *patente de ~,* bill of health; *avoir une bonne ~,* to enjoy good health; *une ~ de fer,* an iron constitution; *être de ~ faible, avoir une faible ~,* to be delicate; *un air de ~,* a healthy look; *maison de ~,*

nursing home, private hospital; private asylum; *comment va la ~?*, how is your health?; *porter la ~ de X*, to drink X's health; to toast X; *à votre ~!*, your health!; (colloq.) *il en a une ~!*, (*a*) what nerve! (*b*) what cheek!
santoline (sɑ̃tɔlin), s.f. [orig. unkn.] (bot.) Lavender-cotton, santolina.
santon (sɑ̃tɔ̃), s.m. [Span. wd] Santon, Mohammedan monk or hermit, marabout.
santonine (sɑ̃tɔnin), s.f. (bot.) Santonica; (chem.) santonin.
sanve (sɑ̃v), s.f. [L *sinapis*] (bot.) Charlock; syn. MOUTARDE DES CHAMPS.
saoul, -e (su), adj. [L *satullus*] Full, drunk; (fig.) sick of, satiated (*de*, with), surfeited (with); see syn. SOÛL.
saouler (sule), v.a. To make drunk; to intoxicate; (fig.) to satiate, to surfeit (*de*, with).
sapa (sapa), s.m. [L wd] (pharm.) Grape-jelly.
sapajou (pl. **-s**) (sapaʒu), s.m. (zool.) Sapajou (South American monkey); (fig.) baboon, monkey, small ugly man.
sapan (sapɑ̃), s.m. [Malay wd] Sapan-wood.
sape (sap), s.f. [It. *zappa*] Sap, sapping, undermining, mine; (fig.) gradual ruin or destruction by underhand methods.
sapement (sapmɑ̃), s.m. Sapping, undermining, (fig.) gradual destruction.
sapèque (sapɛk), s.f. A Chinese small coin.
saper (sape), v.a. [f. *sape*] To sap, to undermine; (fig.) to destroy insidiously; *la science a sapé la base des vieilles superstitions*, science has sapped the foundations of old superstitious beliefs.
sapeur (sapœr), s.m. [f. *saper*] Sapper; *~-pompier*, fireman.
saphène (safɛn), adj. s.f. [LL *saphena*] (anat.) Saphena (vein).
saphique (safik), adj. [f. *Sapho*] Sapphic.
saphir (safir), s.m. [f. Arab. *çafīr*] Sapphire.
saphirine (safirin), s.f. Blue chalcedony.
sapide (sapid), adj. [L *sapidus*] Sapid, palatable.
sapidité (sapidite), s.f. Sapidity.
sapience (sapjɑ̃s), s.f. [L *sapientia*] Sapience, wisdom; syn. SAGESSE.
sapientiaux (sapjɑ̃sjo), adj. m. pl. s.m. pl. (Bibl.) Sapiential (books).
sapin (sapɛ̃), s.m. [L *sapinus*] Fir, fir-tree; *bois de ~*, deal; (colloq. obs.) four-wheeler, cab; coffin; *sentir déjà le ~*, to have one foot in the grave; *~ de Noël*, Christmas-tree.
sapine (sapin), s.f. Deal plank, deal board; (build.) scaffold for crane, scaffold-pole.
sapinière (sapinjɛr), s.f. Fir-plantation, fir-grove.
saponacé, -e (sapɔnase), adj. Saponaceous.
saponaire (sapɔnɛr), s.f. [f. L *sapo, saponis*] (bot.) Saponaria, soapwort.
saponification (sapɔnifika'sjɔ̃), s.f. Saponification.
saponifier (sapɔnifje), v.a. [f. L *sapo*] To saponify.
saponine (sapɔnin), s.f. (chem.) Saponin.
sapotille (sapɔtij), s.f. [Span. *zapotilla*] (bot.) Sapodilla.
sapotillier (sapɔtije), s.m. (bot.) Sapodilla-tree.
sapristi (sapristi), **saprelotte** (saprəlɔt), interj. Dear me!, by Jove!, hang it, by Jingo; other forms: *saperlotte, saperlipopette! sacristi!*, &c.
sarabande (sarabɑ̃d), s.f. [Span. *zarabanda*] Saraband.
sarbacane (sarbakan), s.f. [f. Arab. *zabaṭana*] Pea-shooter, blow-pipe.
sarcasme (sarkasm), s.m. [Gr. *sarkasmos*] Sarcasm, gibe, taunt.
sarcastique (sarkastik), adj. Sarcastic.
sarcelle (sarsɛl), s.f. [L *querquedula*] (ornith.) Teal.
sarclage (sarklaʒ), s.m. Weeding.
sarcler (sarkle), v.a. [L *sarculare*] To weed.
sarcloir (sarklwar), s.m. Weeding-hook, hoe.
sarclure (sarklyr), s.f. Weedings.
sarcocarpe (sarkokarp), s.m. adj. (bot.) Sarcocarp.
sarcocèle (sarkosɛl), s.f. [f. Gr. *sarkos*+*kēlē*] (pathol.) Sarcocele.
sarcocolle (sarkokɔl), s.f. (bot.) Sarcocol, sarcocolla.
sarcologie (sarkolɔʒi), s.f. [f. Gr. *sarkos*+*logos*] Sarcology.
sarcomateu-x, -se (sarkomatø), adj. Sarcomatous.
sarcome (sarkom), s.m. [Gr. *sarkōma*] (pathol.) Sarcoma.
sarcophage (sarkɔfaʒ), adj. [f. Gr. *sarkos*+*phagein*] Sarcophagous, corrosive. ~, s.m. Sarcophagus.
sarcopte (sarkɔpt), s.m. (ent.) Sarcopte, itch-mite.
sardanapalesque (sardanapalɛsk), adj. Sardanapalian.
sardine (sardin), s.f. [late Gr. *sardēnē*] Sardine; pilchard; (mil.) N.C.O.'s stripe.
sardini-er, -ère (sardinje), adj. Pertaining to sardine fishing or packing. ~, s.m.f. Sardine fisherman, sardine packer; sardine-fishing boat.
sardoine (sardwan), s.f. [Gr. *sardonux*] Sardonyx.
sardonique (sardɔnik), adj. [Gr. *sardonios*] Sardonic.
sardoniquement (sardɔnikmɑ̃), adv. Sardonically.
sargasse (sargas), s.f. [Port. *sargaço*]

Sargasso, gulf-weed; *Mer des ~s*, Sargasso Sea.
sarigue (sarig), s.m.f. [Brazil. *sarigueya*] (zool.) Sarigue, S. American opossum.
sarisse (saris), s.f. [Gr. *sarissa*] (ant.) Sarissa, the long lance of the Macedonian phalanx.
sarment (sarmɑ̃), s.m. [L *sarmentum*] Vine-branch, vine-shoot; sarmentum.
sarmenteu-x, -se (sarmɑ̃tø), adj. Sarmentous.
saronide (sarɔnid), s.m. [Gr. *sarōnis*] Druid.
saros (saros), s.m. (astr.) Saros (cycle of 18 years and 10⅔ days).
sarracénique (sarasenik), adj. [L *sarracenus*] Saracenic.
sarrasin (sarazɛ̃), s.m. (bot.) Saracen corn, buckwheat; syn. BLÉ NOIR.
sarrasin, -e (sarazɛ̃), s.m.f. [L *sarracenus*] Saracen. ~, adj. Saracenic.
sarrasine (sarazin), s.f. (arch.) Portcullis.
sarrau (pl. **-x**) (saro), s.m. [Arab. orig.] Smock; child's pinafore.
sarriette (sarjɛt), s.f. (bot.) Savory; *Satureia hortensis*.
sarro (saro), s.m. See SARRAU.
sas (sɑ), s.m. [f. L *saeta*] Sieve; *~ à farine*, bolter; *~ d'écluse*, lock-chamber.
sassafras (sasafrɑ), s.m. (bot.) Sassafras.
sasse (sas), s.f. [Provenç. *sasso*] Scoop, skeet.
sasser (sase), v.a. **1.** To sift; **2.** to pass (boats) through a lock; *~ et resasser quelque chose*, to examine something repeatedly and carefully.
satané, -e (satane), adj. [f. *Satan*] Infernal, confounded, damned, the devil of, regular, arrant.
satanique (satanik), adj. [f. *Satan*] Satanic, diabolical.
satellite (satɛllit), s.m. [L *satelles*] Satellite; (fig.) follower, bodyguard, henchman, hanger-on, underling.
satiété (sasjete), s.f. [L *satietas*] Satiety; *jusqu'à ~*, to satiety.
sati-f, -ve (satif), adj. [L *sativus*] (bot.) Sown or planted; cultivated, not wild.
satin (satɛ̃), s.m. [It. *setino*] Satin.
satinage (satinaʒ), s.m. Satining, glazing, hot-pressing.
satiné, -e (satine), adj. Satin-like, satiny, glazed, hot-pressed (paper), high-glazed. ~, s.m. Satin-like gloss.
satiner (satine), v.a. To satin; to glaze (paper), to put a gloss on.
satinette (satinɛt), s.f. Sateen.
satire (satir), s.f. [L *satira*] Satire; lampoon.
satirique (satirik), adj. Satirical. ~, s.m. Satirist.
satiriquement (satirikmɑ̃), adv. Satirically.
satiriser (satirize), v.a.n. To satirize.
satisfaction (satisfaksjɔ̃), s.f. [L *satisfactio*] **1.** Satisfaction, gratification, contentment; **2.** satisfying, indulging, indulgence; fulfilment of obligation; (theol.) atonement; *exiger ~*, to demand satisfaction.
satisfactoire (satisfaktwar), adj. (theol.) Satisfactory, atoning, serving as atonement.
satisfaire (satisfɛr), v.a.n. [L *satis+facere*] To satisfy, to gratify, to please, to answer, to appease, to give satisfaction, to indulge; to make reparation; *~ à ses engagements*, to meet or to fulfil one's obligations; *~ son père*, to give satisfaction to one's father, to please one's father; *~ sa faim*, to satisfy one's hunger; *~ sa curiosité, sa passion*, to gratify one's curiosity, one's passion; **se ~**, v.pr. to satisfy oneself, to indulge oneself, to gratify oneself.
satisfaisant, -e (satisfɛzɑ̃), p. adj. Satisfying, satisfactory, pleasing, gratifying.
satisfait, -e (satisfɛ), p. adj. Satisfied, pleased, gratified, contented, appeased.
satisfecit (satisfesit), s.m. [L wd] Testimonial of complete satisfaction.
satrape (satrap), s.m. [Gr. *satrapēs*] Satrap; (fig.) satrap, nabob (with implication of voluptuous luxury).
satrapie (satrapi), s.f. Satrapy.
saturable (satyrabl), adj. Saturable.
saturant, -e (satyrɑ̃), p. adj. Saturating.
saturation (satyra'sjɔ̃), s.f. Saturation.
saturer (satyre), v.a. [L *saturare*] To saturate; (fig.) to satiate, to surfeit.
saturnales (satyrnal), s.f.pl. [L *Saturnalia*] Saturnalia.
saturne (satyrn), s.m. Saturn (old name of lead); *extrait de ~*, saturated solution of sub-acetate of lead.
saturnien, -ne (satyrnjɛ̃), adj. Saturnian.
saturnin, -e (satyrnɛ̃), adj. Saturnine, pertaining to lead; *colique ~e*, lead colic. ⚠ Not English 'saturnine' in the (usual) sense of gloomy and grim, which = *sombre, taciturne*.
saturnisme (satyrnism), s.m. Saturnism, lead-poisoning.
satyre (satir), s.m. [Gr. *saturos*] Satyr; lustful and beastly-minded man.
satyrion (satirjɔ̃), s.m. (bot.) Satyrium, kind of orchis.
satyrique (satirik), adj. Satyric, pertaining to satyrs.
sauce (sos), s.f. [LL *salsa*] Sauce; (fig.) *on le met à toutes les ~s*, he is put to all sorts of work; they think him capable of everything; (fig.) *la ~ fait manger le poisson*, the details are better than the thing itself; *trop de cuisiniers gâtent la ~*, too many cooks spoil the broth; *un gâte-~*, s.m. a young scullion; (slang) *être dans la ~*, to be in the soup.

saucé, -e (sose) p. adj. (colloq.) Wet through, drenched, soused; (numism.) thinly plated (medals).
saucer (sose), v.a. **1.** To dip in sauce; to cover with sauce, to garnish with sauce; **2.** to drench, to sop, to souse; *être saucé*, (*a*) to be drenched; (*b*) to be sharply scolded, to be blown up.
saucier (sosje), s.m. Sauce-maker, cook specializing in sauces; (naut.) saucer (of capstan); sauce-tureen; socket, saucer.
saucière (sosjɛr), s.f. Sauce-tureen; sauce-boat.
saucisse (sosis), s.f. [LL *salsicia*] Sausage; (fig.) *il n'attache pas ses chiens avec des ~s*, he would skin a flint; he is as stingy as can be; (mil.) kite balloon, sausage.
saucisson (sosisɔ̃), s.m. [It. *salsiccione*] Saucisson, German sausage; Bologna sausage (*saucisson* is always eaten thinly sliced and cold); (mil.) fascine.
sauf (fem. **sauve**) (sof, sov), adj. Safe, unhurt, unscathed; *sain et ~*, safe and sound; *il a eu la vie sauve*, his life was spared; *l'honneur est ~*, honour is safe. *~-conduit*, s.m. Safe-conduct.
sauf (sof), prep. Save, except, reserving, but, under, excepting, excepted; *~ correction*, under correction; *~ erreur*, errors excepted; *~ à corriger plus tard*, reserving corrections for later; *il a tout vendu ~ sa maison*, he sold everything except his house; *~ votre respect*, saving your presence.
sauge (soʒ), s.f. (bot.) Sage; salvia.
saugrenu, -e (sogrəny), adj. Absurd, irrelevant, ridiculous, far-fetched.
saulaie (solɛ), s.f. Willow-grove.
saule (sol), s.m. [OHG *salaha*] Willow; *~ pleureur*, weeping willow.
saulée (sole), s.f. Row of willows.
saumâtre (somɑtr), adj. [L *salmacidus*] Brackish, briny.
saumon (somɔ̃), s.m. [L *salmo*] **1.** Salmon; grilse, peel (young salmon that has been only once to the sea); kelt (young salmon that has not been to sea but has already spawned); **2.** (metall.) pig, block; *~ de fonte*, pig-iron. ~, adj. Salmon-coloured.
saumoné, -e (somone), adj. Salmon; *truite ~e*, salmon trout.
saumoneau (pl. -x) (somono), s.m. Young salmon, salmonet, smolt, parr.
saumure (somyr), s.f. Brine, pickle.
saumurer (somyre), v.a.n. To brine, to pickle.
saunage (sonaʒ), s.m. **saunaison** (sonɛzɔ̃), s.f. Extraction of salt from sea-water; *faux ~*, illicit salt trade.
sauner (sone), v.n. [L *salinare*] To extract salt from sea-water.
saunerie (sonri), s.f. Salt-works; salt extraction.
saunier (sonje), s.m. Salt-maker, salt-trader; *faux ~*, salt-smuggler.
saupiquet (sopikɛ), s.m. (cook.) Sharp sauce.
saupoudrer (sopudre), v.a. [f. *sel+ poudrer*] To sprinkle (*de*, with); (fig.) to interlard, to intersperse.
saur (sor), adj. m. [f. Dutch *zoor*] Smoked, red, dried; *hareng ~*, smoked or red herring, bloater, bloated herring.
saure (sor), adj. [LL *saurus*] Sorrel.
saurer, saurir (sore, sorir), v.a. To bloat, to smoke (herrings, &c.).
saurien (sorjɛ̃), s.m. [f. Gr. *saura*] Saurian; *les ~s*, the Sauria.
saurin (sorɛ̃), s.m. Freshly-smoked herring.
saurir (sorir), v.a. See SAURER.
saurissage (sorisaʒ), s.m. Smoking, bloating (herrings).
saurisserie (sorisri), s.f. Place where herrings are smoked or bloated.
saussaie (sosɛ), s.f. See SAULAIE.
saut (so), s.m. [L *saltus*] Jump, leap, bound, hop, skip; fall, waterfall; *faire un ~*, to take a leap; *au ~ du lit*, the minute one gets out of bed; on first getting up; *~ de lit*, morning wrap, dressing-gown, kimono, wrapper; *de plein ~*, at once, suddenly, frankly; *faire le ~*, (*a*) to take the plunge; (*b*) to kick the bucket; *jouer à ~ de mouton*, to play leap-frog; *~ de carpe*, big jump (caused by surprise, &c.); *~ de loup*, ha-ha; *~ du Niagara*, Niagara Falls; *~ périlleux*, somersault; *par ~s et par bonds*, by leaps and bounds.
saute (sot), s.f. Sudden change; *~ de vent*, sudden shift of the wind; *~s d'humeur*, whims, caprices, freaks; *~-en-barque*, s.m. boating jacket, blazer; *~-mouton*, leap-frog; *~-ruisseau*, errand-boy.
sauté, -e (sote), adj. (cook.) Fried, sauté. ~, s.m. Sauté dish, sauté.
sautée (sote), s.f. Leap, space cleared in leaping.
sauteler (sotle), v.n. See SAUTILLER.
sautelle (sotɛl), s.f. Vine-shoot.
sauter (sote), v.n.a. [L *saltare*] To leap, to jump, to hop, to skip, to spring; to blow up, to explode; to miss out, to omit, to skip, to drop (a stitch); to veer, to shift; *~ au collet de X*, *~ à la gorge de X*, to fly at X's throat, to collar X; *~ à la corde*, to skip; *faire ~ la cervelle à X*, to blow X's brains out; *~ au cou de X*, to fall on X's neck, to embrace X, to welcome X affectionately; *il s'est fait ~ le caisson*, he blew his brains out; *~ d'un sujet à un autre*, to skip from one subject to another; *faire ~ la coupe* (at cards), to shift the cut; *cela saute aux yeux*, that is as clear as noonday; it strikes one at once; *faire ~ la banque*, to break the bank; *~ à bas du lit*, to jump out of bed; *faire ~ une poudrière*, to blow up a powder-magazine;

vous m'avez fait ~, you made me jump; *faire* ~ *un employé*, to oust an employee, to cause him to be dismissed; *faire* ~ *un poulet*, to fry and toss up a fowl; ~ *le fossé*, to clear the ditch; ~ *une ligne*, to leave out or skip a line; *reculer pour mieux* ~, (*a*) to bide one's time; (*b*) to stoop to conquer; (*c*) to avoid a small evil to fall into a greater; ~ *le pas*, (*a*) to take an important decision; (*b*) to kick the bucket; to go west; *le vent a sauté au nord*, the wind has shifted (or veered) to the north.

sauterelle (sotrɛl), s.f. Grasshopper; locust (in Africa); (techn.) bevel.

sauterie (sotri), s.f. Hop, dance, small informal dancing-party.

sauternes (sotɛrn), s.m. (geog. orig.) Sauternes (wine).

sauteu-r, -se (sotœr), adj. Leaping, jumping. ~, s.m.f. Leaper, jumper, (fig.) mountebank, bounder, turncoat, unreliable person, weathercock.

sauteuse (sotøz), s.f. Flat stew-pan.

sautillant, -e (sotijɑ̃), p. adj. Dropping, skipping; jerky.

sautillement (sotijmɑ̃), s.m. Skipping, hopping (of birds).

sautiller (sotije), v.n. To skip; to hop (as birds); (fig.) to skip.

sautoir (sotwar), s.m. **1.** Long watch-chain, long string of pearls; **2.** (cook.) syn. of SAUTEUSE, flat stew-pan; *en* ~, crosswise, over one's shoulder, saltirewise, slung over the shoulder.

sauvage (sovaʒ), adj. [L *silvaticus*] Savage, wild, untamed; (of plants) wild; unsociable, shy; ferocious, brutal, barbarous, savage, ferocious. ~, s.m.f. Savage; (fig.) unsociable person.

sauvagement (sovaʒmɑ̃), adv. Savagely, wildly; unsociably, shyly; barbarously, ferociously, fiercely.

sauvageon (sovaʒɔ̃), s.m. Wild stock, seedling, self-sown tree; (fig.) shy young person.

sauvagerie (sovaʒri), s.f. Wildness; unsociableness, shyness; ferocity, savageness.

sauvagesse (sovaʒɛs), s.f. [fem. of *sauvage*] Savage woman; unsociable woman, lacking education and manners.

sauvagin, -e (sovaʒɛ̃), adj. Fishy (taste); *sentir le* ~, to taste fishy (said of certain sea-birds and water-fowls). ~**e**, s.f. (ornith.) Wild water-fowl.

sauvegarde (sovgard), s.f. [*sauve*+*garde*] Safeguard, protection; safe-conduct; safety-rope, rail, &c.

sauvegarder (sovgarde), v.a. To protect, to safeguard, to guard, to shield.

sauve-qui-peut (sovkipø), s.m. Panic, stampede, headlong flight. ~*!* interj. Every man for himself !; save himself who can !

sauver (sove), v.a. [L *salvare*] To save (*de*, from), to rescue, to deliver, to spare; to bring back to life; *la forme sauve le fond*, the form redeems the subject from mediocrity; *ses yeux sauvent son visage*, her eyes redeem her face from ugliness; *il m'a sauvé la vie*, he saved my life; ~ *les apparences*, to save appearances; ~ *les défauts de*, to conceal the imperfections of; ~ *la situation*, to save the situation; **se** ~, v.pr. to save oneself; to make one's escape; to take refuge; (U.S.A. slang) to absquatulate; to run away, to abscond; to work out one's salvation; (colloq.) *je me sauve !*, I am off !; *se* ~ *à la nage*, to save oneself by swimming.

sauvetage (sovtaʒ), s.m. Rescue, saving; (of wares, &c.) salvage; *bateau de* ~, life-boat; *bouée de* ~, life-buoy; *ceinture de* ~, life-belt; *échelle de* ~, fire-escape.

sauveteur (sovtœr), adj. m. Saving. ~, s.m. Rescuer.

sauveur (sovœr), s.m. Saver, deliverer, rescuer; saviour, redeemer; *Notre* ~, Our Saviour.

sauve-vie (sovvi), s.f. (bot.) Wall-rue.

savamment (savamɑ̃), adv. Learnedly; cleverly, knowingly.

savane (savan), s.f. [Span. *sabana*] Savanna(h); (in N. America) prairie.

savant, -e (savɑ̃), adj. [f. *savoir*] Learned, clever, well-informed, expert; *une* ~*e dissertation*, a learned dissertation; *un chien* ~, a performing dog; *une femme* ~*e*, (*a*) a learned woman; (*b*) (iron.) a blue-stocking = *un bas-bleu*. ~, **-e**, s.m.f. Man or woman of learning; scholar; *les* ~*s*, the learned, the literate, the scientists.

savantasse (savɑ̃tas), s.m.f. Learned fogy, pedant.

savantissime (savɑ̃tisim), adj. (colloq.) Most learned.

savarin (savarɛ̃), s.m. [f. *Brillat-Savarin*] A kind of ring-shaped sponge-cake steeped in syrup and rum.

savate (savat), s.f. [It. *ciabatta*] Down-at-heel slipper; savate (a kind of boxing in which chiefly the feet are used); *traîner la* ~, to be slovenly and very poor; (naut.) shoe (of anchor).

saveter (savte), v.a. See SABOTER.

savetier (savtje), s.m. Cobbler; (fig., pej.) regular bungler.

saveur (savœr), s.f. [L *sapor*] Savour, flavour, savouriness, taste; (fig.) savour, smack; ~ *de préciosité*, smack of preciosity.

savoir (savwar), v.a. irreg., pr.p. *sachant*, p.p. *su* [L *sapere*] To know, to be informed of, to be aware of, to be practised in, to be trained in, to understand, to be acquainted with; to be able to, to manage to, to know how to; ~ *l'anglais*, to know English; ~ *son métier*, to know one's business; *savez-vous danser?*, can you dance?; *je n'en sais rien*, I don't know at all; I don't know anything about it; *à ~*, namely, to wit; *c'est à ~*, *reste à ~*, that remains to be seen; *pour autant que je sache*, to the best of my belief; as far as I know; *un je ne sais quoi*, a something, an indefinable something; *on fait ~ que*, notice is hereby given that; *nous croyons ~*, we have reason to believe; it is rumoured; *X lui en sait gré*, X is grateful to him; *je ne saurais flatter*, do not expect flattery from me; *c'est un homme qui sait vivre*, he is a man who knows how to behave; *pas que je sache*, not that I know of; not to my knowledge; (colloq.) *il n'a rien voulu ~*, he is unwilling; he would not hear of it; *il en sait trop long*, he knows too much; *sans le ~*, unwittingly, unconsciously; *Dieu sait que*, God knows that; *Dieu sait comme*, goodness knows how; *je suis tout je ne sais comment*, I am rather out of sorts; *faites-lui ~ que*, let him know that; *je vous sais incapable de mentir*, I know you are incapable of lying; *tout se sait à la longue*, truth is sure to come out; everything gets known in the long run.

savoir (savwar), s.m. Knowledge, erudition, learning; *~-faire*, s.m. ability, skilful management (often with a slightly pej. sense); *il ne manque pas de savoir-faire*, he knows how to manage people; he has his wits about him; *~-vivre*, s.m. good manners, good breeding, politeness; *avoir du savoir-vivre*, to know how to behave.

savoisien, -ne (savwazjɛ̃), also **savoyard, -e** (savwajar), adj. s.m.f. Of Savoy, Savoyard.

savon (savɔ̃), s.m. [L *sapo*] Soap; cake of soap; *bulle de ~*, soap-bubble; *eau de ~*, soap-suds; *pain de ~*, cake of soap; (colloq.) dressing-down, blowing-up; *donner* or *flanquer un ~ à X*, to blow X up; to give X beans; to haul X over the coals.

savonnage (savɔnaʒ), s.m. Washing with soap; soaping.

savonner (savɔne), v.a. To wash with soap; to soap; to lather (for shaving); (colloq.) to blow up, to give beans to, to rebuke, to scold; **se ~**, v.pr. (*a*) to wash oneself with soap; (*b*) to stand washing.

savonnerie (savɔnri), s.f. Soap-works; soap-trade; *tapis de la Savonnerie*, 'Savonnerie' carpet.

savonnette (savɔnɛt), s.f. Cake of soap, shaving-soap, shaving-stick; *montre à ~*, hunting-watch; (colloq.) *~ à vilain*, office purchased in order to ennoble the holder.

savonneu-x, -se (savɔnø), adj. Soapy; *terre ~se*, fuller's earth.

savonni-er, -ère (savɔnje), adj. Pertaining to soap-manufacturing. ~, s.m. **1.** Soap-manufacturer; **2.** soapberry-tree.

savourer (savure), v.a. [f. *saveur*] To taste, to relish slowly and intensely; (fig.) to enjoy, to take delight in. ⚠ Exceptionally 'to savour', which usually = *avoir le goût de, sentir*, (fig.) *suggérer, sentir*, and is somewhat archaic in the sense of 'to relish'.

savoureusement (savurøzmɑ̃), adv. Savourily; with relish, with gusto.

savoureu-x, -se (savurø), adj. Savoury, tasty, full of relish, relishable.

savoyard, -e, (savwajar), adj. s.m.f. See syn. SAVOISIEN.

saxatile (saksatil), adj. [f. L *saxum*] (bot.) Saxatile, growing among rocks.

saxe (saks), s.m. [geog. orig.] Saxe (porcelain), Dresden china.

saxhorn (sakshɔrn), s.m. [Germ. wd] (mus.) Saxhorn.

saxifrage (saksifraʒ), s.f. [f. L *saxum*+*frangere*] (bot.) Saxifrage.

saxon, -ne (saksɔ̃), adj. s.m.f. Saxon, of Saxony.

saxophone (saksɔfɔn), s.m. (mus.) Saxophone.

saynète (sɛnɛt), s.f. [f. Span. *sainete*] Short play, drawing-room comedy.

sayon (sɛjɔ̃), s.m. [f. *saie*] Sagum (Gaulish woollen cloak).

sbire (sbir), s.m. [It. *sbirro*] **1.** Sbirro; **2.** (colloq.) bumbailiff, myrmidon, police spy.

scabieuse (skabjøz), s.f. [f. L *scabies*] (bot.) Scabious, *Scabiosa*.

scabieu-x, -se (skabjø), adj. [f. L *scabies*] Scabious, scabby.

scabreu-x, -se (skɑbrø), adj. [L *scabrosus*] Scabrous, objectionable, risky; rugged; *chemin ~*, rugged path; *conte ~*, scabrous tale.

scaferlati (skafɛrlati), s.m. [etym. dub.] Scaferlati (tobacco).

scalde (skald), s.m. [Scand. wd] Skald (Scandinavian bard).

scalène (skalɛn), adj. [Gr. *skalēnos*] Scalene (triangle, cone, muscle, &c.).

scalp (skalp), s.m. [Engl. wd] Scalp.

scalpel (skalpɛl), s.m. [L *scalpellum*] Scalpel.

scalper (skalpe), v.a. [f. *scalp*] To scalp.

scammonée (skamɔne), s.f. [Gr. *skammōnia*] (bot.) Scammony.

scandale (skɑ̃dal), s.m. [Gr. *skandalon*] Scandal, public exposure, shame, offence to public opinion; *causer, faire du ~*, to give rise to scandal, to make a scandalous scene; *au grand ~ des honnêtes gens*, to the horror of honest people; *c'est un ~ que de pareilles choses soient possibles*, it is a scandal that such things should be possible; *pierre de ~*, stumbling-block. ⚠ In English 'scandal' has also the sense of malicious gossip, backbiting = *calomnie, médisance, diffamation*. In French *scandale* cannot be used in that sense.

scandaleusement (skɑ̃daløzmɑ̃), adv. Scandalously.

scandaleu-x, -se (skɑ̃dalø), adj. Scandalous, shameful.

scandaliser (skɑ̃dalize), v.a. To scandalize; **se** ~, v.pr. to be scandalized, to take offence, to be shocked.

scander (skɑ̃de), v.a. [L *scandere*] To scan.

scandinave (skɑ̃dinav), adj. s.m.f. Scandinavian.

scansion (skɑ̃sjɔ̃), s.f. Scansion, scanning.

scaphandre (skafɑ̃dr), s.m. [f. Gr. *skaphē* + *anēr*] Diving-suit or -dress, diving-apparatus.

scaphandrier (skafɑ̃drije), s.m. Diver (working under water).

scaphoïde (skafɔid), adj. s.m. [f. Gr. *skaphē*+*eidos*] (anat.) Scaphoid.

scapulaire (skapylɛr), s.m. [f. L *scapula*] Scapular, scapulary. ~, adj. (anat.) Scapular.

scapulo-huméral, -e, (aux) (skapyloymeral), adj. (anat.) Scapulo-humeral.

scarabée (skarabe), s.m. [L *scarabaeus*] (ent.) Scarabaeus, beetle, scarab.

scare (skar), s.m. [Gr. *skaros*] (ichth.) Scarus, parrot-fish.

scarificateur (skarifikatœr), s.m. [f. *scarifier*] (surg.) Scarificator, scarifier; (agric.) hoeing-machine.

scarification (skarifika'sjɔ̃), s.f. Scarification.

scarifier (skarifje), v.a. [L *scarificare*] To scarify.

scarlatine (skarlatin), s.f. [It. *scarlattina*] Scarlet fever, scarlatina.

scarole, escarole (skarɔl, ɛskarɔl), s.f. (bot.) Batavian endive. ⚠ English 'endive' = French *chicorée*, and *scarole*, while French *endive* = English (espec. cook.) chicory; but in English chicory means also, like French *chicorée*, the blue-flowered plant cultivated for its root, which dried and ground may be mixed with ground coffee.

scatologie (skatɔlɔʒi), s.f. [f. Gr. *skatos*+*logos*] Scatology.

scatologique (skatɔlɔʒik), adj. Scatological.

sceau (pl. **-x**) **scel** (so, sɛl), s.m. [L *sigillum*] Seal; *mettre le ~ à*, to seal; *porter le ~ du génie*, to be stamped with the marks of genius; *sous le ~ du secret*, under the seal of secrecy; *le Garde des Sceaux*, the Lord Chancellor; (bot.) *~ de Salomon*, Solomon's seal.

scélérat, -e (selera), adj. [L *sceleratus*] Villainous, wicked. ~, s.m.f. Rascal, villain, scoundrel; (colloq.) rascal, miscreant.

scélératesse (seleratɛs), s.f. Villainy, rascality, wickedness.

scellé (sɛle), s.m. Seal; *apposer les ~s*, to affix the seals; *lever les ~s*, to take off the seals.

scellement (sɛlmɑ̃), s.m. Fastening, fixing; sealing.

sceller (sɛle), v.a. [f. *scel*] **1.** To seal, to seal up; **2.** to fix, to fasten; (fig.) to close, to ratify, to confirm.

scelleur (sɛlœr), s.m. Sealer; cement-maker.

scénario (senarjo), s.m. [It. wd] Scenario.

scène (sɛn), s.f. [f. Gr. *skēnē*] **1.** Scene, stage, scenery; theatre, the boards; *être en ~*, to be on the stage; *mettre en ~*, to get up (a play); *mise en ~*, (*a*) staging, getting up; (*b*) scenery; **2.** row, quarrel, scene; *faire une ~ à X*, to have a row with X; to abuse X; to go for X; to turn violently on X.

scénique (senik), adj. Scenic, theatrical, picturesque, telling.

scénographie (senɔgrafi), s.f. Scenography, scene-painting.

scepticisme (sɛptisism), s.m. [f. Gr. *skepsis*] Scepticism; (phil.) scepsis.

sceptique (sɛptik), adj. [Gr. *skeptikos*] Sceptical. ~, s.m.f. Sceptic.

sceptiquement (sɛptikmɑ̃), adv. Sceptically.

sceptre (sɛptr), s.m. [Gr. *skēptron*] Sceptre; (fig.) sovereignty, sway; *tenir le ~ des élégances*, to be the arbiter of fashion; *~ de fer*, rod of iron.

schabraque, chabraque (ʃabrak), s.f. Shabrack.

schah, shah, chah (ʃa), s.m. [Pers. wd] Shah.

schako (ʃako), s.m. See SHAKO.

schapska, chapska (ʃapska), s.f. (mil.) Polish cap.

schelem (ʃlɛm), s.m. See CHELEM.

schelling (ʃeling), s.m. See SCHILLING.

schéma, schème, (ʃema, ʃɛm), s.m. [Gr. wd] Schema, diagram; scheme. ⚠ 'Scheme' in English is very frequently used in the sense of project, plan, systematic arrangement = *projet*, *ensemble*, *idée*; also artful or underhand design = *machination*; while in French it is only used in the scientific sense: simplified figuration or representation, draft of work, speech, law, &c.

schématique (ʃematik), adj. Schematic.

schématiquement (ʃematikmɑ̃), adv. Schematically.

scherzo (skɛrzo), s.m. [It. wd] Scherzo.

schibboleth (ʃibɔlɛt), s.m. [Hebr. wd] Shibboleth; (fig.) shibboleth, test word.

schiedam (skidam), s.m. [geog. orig., f. Netherlands town] Schiedam, Hollands gin.

schilling, schelling (ʃiling), s.m. [Germ. wd] Schilling (an old German coin, not to be confused with the English shilling).

ɔ, note, glotte; ɔ̃, monter, ronde; ø, feu, creux; œ, peur, sœur; œ̃, un; ʃ, chez, schisme; u, tout; w, oui, doit, douaire; y, mur, pu; ɥ, huile, muette; z, zèle, rose; ʒ, déjà, gentil.

schismatique (ʃismatik), adj. s.m.f. Schismatic.
schisme (ʃism), s.m. [Gr. *skhisma*] Schism.
schiste (ʃist), s.m. [Gr. *skhistos*] (min.) Schist.
schisteu-x, -se (ʃistø), adj. Schistose.
schistoïde (ʃistɔid), adj. Schistlike, schistoid.
schizophrène (ʃizɔfrɛn, skizɔfrɛn), adj. s.m.f. (Person) attacked with schizophrenia.
schizophrénie (ʃizɔfreni, skizɔfreni), s.f. Schizophrenia, dementia praecox.
schlague (ʃlag), s.f. [f. Germ. *schlagen*] Flogging.
schlich (ʃliʃ), s.m. [Germ. wd] (metall.) Schlich, pulverized ore.
schlittage (ʃlitaʒ), s.m. Transport of felled trees in a *schlitte.*
schlitte (ʃlit), s.f. [f. Germ. *schlitten*] Sledge (on timber trackway).
schlitter (ʃlite), v.a. To transport (timber) in a *schlitte.*
schlitteur (ʃlitœr), s.m. Timber-carrier (espec. in Alsace).
schnick (ʃnik), s.m. [f. Germ.] Spirits of a low quality, schnaps.
schooner (ʃunœr), s.m. [Engl. wd] (naut.) Schooner.
sciable (sjabl), adj. That can be sawn.
sciage (sjaʒ), s.m. Sawing; *bois de* ~, sawn timber.
sciara (sjara), s.f. (ent.) Sciara, a genus of midges.
sciant, -e (sjɑ̃), p. adj. (slang) Boring, tedious, annoying.
sciatique (sjatik), adj. [f. Gr. *iskhion*] Sciatic. ~, s.f. (pathol.) Sciatica.
scie (si), s.f. [f. *scier*] Saw; ~ *à main*, hand-saw; ~ *circulaire*, circular saw; ~ *à ruban*, ribbon saw; ~ *de scieur de long*, pit-saw, whip-saw; *trait de* ~, saw-notch; *lame de* ~, saw-blade; (colloq.) (*a*) bother, trouble, tiresome thing; *quelle* ~ *!*, what a bother !; (*b*) catchword; *quelle est la dernière* ~ *à Paris?*, what's the latest catchword in Paris, or latest tune that everybody sings in Paris?; (ichth.) saw-fish.
sciemment (sjamɑ̃), adv. Knowingly, deliberately, wittingly, purposely.
science (sjɑ̃s), s.f. [L *scientia*] Science, knowledge, learning; *avoir la* ~ *infuse*, to know everything intuitively; *un homme de* ~, a scientist; a scientific man, a scholar; ~*s appliquées*, applied sciences; ~*s exactes*, exact sciences; *savoir de* ~ *certaine*, to know for a certainty; (fig.) *un puits de* ~, a budget of learning, a walking encyclopaedia.
sciène (sjɛn), s.f. (ichth.) Sciaena.
scientifique (sjɑ̃tifik), adj. Scientific.
scientifiquement (sjɑ̃tifikmɑ̃), adv. Scientifically.
scientisme (sjɑ̃tism), s.m. [f. *science*] Scientism.
scientiste (sjɑ̃tist), s.m.f. Scientist, adept of scientism.
scier (sje), v.a. [f. L *secare*] **1.** To saw, to saw off; **2.** (naut.) to hold water, to back; **3.** (slang) to bore; ~ *le dos à* X, to bore X horribly.
scierie (siri), s.f. Saw-mill, saw-yard.
scieur (sjœr), s.m. Sawyer; ~ *de long*, sawyer; *fosse de* ~ *de long*, saw-pit.
scille (sij), s.f. (bot.) Squill, *Scilla.*
scindement (sɛ̃dmɑ̃), s.m. Dividing.
scinder (sɛ̃de), v.a. [L *scindere*] To divide, to split up.
scinque (sɛ̃k), s.m. [L *scincus*] (zool.) Skink, a kind of lizard.
scintillant, -e (sɛ̃tijɑ̃), adj. Scintillant, scintillating, sparkling; twinkling.
scintillation (sɛ̃tija'sjɔ̃), s.f. **scintillement** (sɛ̃tijmɑ̃), s.m. Scintillation, sparkling, twinkling (of stars).
scintiller (sɛ̃tije), v.n. [L *scintillare*] To scintillate, to sparkle; to twinkle (as a star).
sciographie (sjografi), s.f. [f. Gr. *skia*+*graphein*] Skiagraphy.
sciographique (sjografik), adj. Skiagraphical.
scion (sjɔ̃), s.m. [etym. dub.] **1.** Scion, shoot; **2.** top part of fishing-rod. ⚠ In English 'scion' means also descendant, young member of (espec. noble) family = *descendant, héritier.*
sciotte (sjɔt), s.f. Stone-cutter's saw.
scirpe (sirp), s.m. (bot.) Club-rush.
scissile (sisil), adj. [L *scissilis*] Scissile, that may be divided.
scission (sisjɔ̃), s.f. [L *scissio*] Scission, split, secession; (biol.) fission; *faire* ~, to secede; to split off.
scissionnaire (sisjɔnɛr), adj. Seceding. ~, s.m.f. Seceder.
scissipare (sisipar), adj. (zool.) Fissiparous.
scissiparité (sisiparite), s.f. [L *scissus*+*parere*] Fission, fissiparity, scissiparity.
scissure (sisyr), s.f. [L *scissura*] Fissure, cleft, scissure.
sciure (sjyr), s.f. [f. *scier*] Sawdust.
scléreu-x, -se (sklerø), adj. (path.) Sclerous.
sclérose (skleroz), s.f. [f. Gr. *sklēros*] (pathol.) Sclerosis.
sclérotique (sklerɔtik), s.f. [Gr. *sklērotēs*] (anat.) Sclerotic.
scolaire (skɔlɛr), adj. [f. L *schola*] School-; of schools, pertaining to schools; academic; scholastic; *année* ~, school year; academic year. ⚠ Not 'scholar', which = *savant; élève boursier d'Université.*
scolarité (skɔlarite) s.f. Course of study; time spent at college, school, &c.; *frais de* ~, school fees.

scolastique (skɔlastik), adj. [L *scholasticus*] Scholastic, of schools, academic. ~, s.f. Scholasticism; ~, s.m. scholastic.
scolastiquement (skɔlastikmɑ̃), adv. Scholastically.
scoliaste (skɔljast), s.m. [Gr. *skholiastēs*] Scholiast.
scolie (skɔli), s.f. [Gr. *skholion*] Scholium; ~, s.m. (math.) scholium.
scoliose (skɔljoz), s.f. [f. Gr. *skolios*] (pathol.) Scoliosis.
scolopendre (skɔlɔpɑ̃dr), s.f. 1. (bot.) Hart's-tongue; 2. (ent.) scolopendra, centipede.
scombéroïdes (skɔ̃berɔid), s.m.pl. (ichth.) Scombridae, scombroids, (mackerel, &c.).
scombre (skɔ̃br), s.m. [L *scomber*] (ichth.) Mackerel.
sconse (skɔ̃s) s.m. See SKUNKS.
scops (skɔps), s.m. [Gr. *skōps*] (ornith.) Scops owl, horned owl.
scorbut (skɔrbyt), s.m. [f. Dutch *scheurbuik*] Scurvy.
scorbutique (skɔrbytik), adj. Scorbutic.
scorie (skɔri), s.f. [Gr. *skōria*] Scoria, dross, slag; ~*s*, clinkers.
scorification (skɔrifika'sjɔ̃), s.f. Scorification, scorifying.
scorifier (skɔrifje), v.a. To scorify.
scorpène (skɔrpɛn), s.f. (ichth.) Scorpaena.
scorpion (skɔrpjɔ̃), s.m. [Gr. *skorpios*] (ent.) Scorpion; (astr.) Scorpio.
scorsonère (skɔrsɔnɛr), s.f. [It. *scorzonera*] (bot.) Scorzonera, black salsify.
scotie (skɔsi), s.f. [L *scotia*] (arch.) Scotia.
scouffin (skufɛ̃), s.m. Syn. COUFFIN.
scribe (skrib), s.m. [L *scriba*] Scribe; (iron.) quill-driver.
scriptural, -e, (aux) (skriptyral), adj. Scriptural.
scrofulaire (skrɔfylɛr), s.f. (bot.) Figwort, *Scrophularia*.
scrofule (skrɔfyl), s.f. [L *scrofula*] (pathol.) Scrofula; syn. ÉCROUELLES, s.f.pl.
scrofuleu-x, -se (skrɔfylø), adj. Scrofulous.
scrotal, -e, (aux) (skrɔtal), adj. (anat.) Scrotal.
scrotum (skrɔtɔm), s.m. (anat.) Scrotum.
scrupule (skrypyl), s.m. [L *scrupulus*] Scruple, doubt, qualm; *ne vous faites pas tant de ~s à ce propos*, have no scruples about that; *il a trop de ~s*, he is over-scrupulous; *je m'en ferais ~*, I would scruple to do that.
scrupuleusement (skrypyløzmɑ̃), adv. Scrupulously, strictly.
scrupuleu-x, -se (skrypylø), adj. Scrupulous, strict, exact, precise.
scrutateur (skrytatœr), s.m. [L *scrutator*] Scrutineer, searcher, investigator. ~, adj. Searching.
scruter (skryte), v.a. [L *scrutari*] To search, to scrutinize, to pry into, to investigate.
scrutin (skrytɛ̃), s.m. [L *scrutinium*] Ballot, poll; ~ *de liste*, simultaneous ballot for a number of names; *dépouiller le ~*, to count the votes; ~ *secret*, secret ballot.
scrutiner (skrytine), v.n. To vote by ballot.
sculpté, -e (skylte), p. adj. Carved; engraved; chiselled.
sculpter (skylte), v.a. [L *sculpere*] To sculpture, to carve, to engrave, to chisel; (colloq.) to sculp.
sculpteur (skyltœr), s.m. Sculptor, carver; (fem.) sculptress.
sculptural, -e, (aux) (skyltyral), adj. Sculptural, sculpturesque.
sculpture (skyltyr), s.f. [L *sculptura*] Sculpture, carving (of wood); carved work.
scutellaire (skytɛlɛr), s.f. [f. L *scutellum*] (bot.) Scutellaria, skull-cap.
scutiforme (skytifɔrm), adj. [f. L *scutum*] Shield-shaped.
scytale (sital), s.f. [Gr. *skutalē*] (antiq.) Scytale.
scyte (sit), adj. s.m.f. Scythian.
scythique (sitik), adj. Scythian, pertaining to Scythia.
se, s' (sə), pr. (invar.) Himself, herself, itself, oneself, each other; (often translated by verb in the passive: *ce mot ~ prononce*, this word is pronounced; *cela ~ conçoit facilement*, that's easily conceived or understood; ~ *marier*, to get married).
séance (seɑ̃s), s.f. [f. *seoir*] Sitting, meeting; *prendre ~*, to take one's seat; *en ~*, sitting; *lever la ~*, to close the meeting; *suspendre la ~*, to adjourn the meeting; ~ *tenante*, on the spot; there and then; forthwith; ~ *(pour un portrait)*, sitting.
séant, -e (seɑ̃), adj. [f. *seoir*] 1. Sitting; 2. fitting, decent, seemly, proper; cf. doublet SEYANT.
séant (seɑ̃), s.m. Bottom, sitting part, posterior, behind; sitting posture; *il se mit sur son ~*, he sat up.
seau (pl. -x) (so), s.m. [L *situlus*] Pail, bucket; slop-pail; ~ *à charbon*, coal-scuttle; *il pleut à ~x*, or *à verse*, it is raining in torrents, it's coming down in buckets.
sébacé, -e (sebase), adj. [f. L *sebum*] Sebaceous.
sébeste (sebɛst), s.m. (fruit) Sebesten.
sébestier (sebɛstje), s.m. (bot.) Sebesten-tree.
sébile (sebil), s.f. [orig. dub.] Wooden bowl.
séborrhée (sebɔre), s.f. Seborrhoea.
sec, (f.) sèche (sɛk, sɛʃ), adj. [L *siccus*] Dry, dried up, arid, hard; stiff, harsh. curt; lean, thin, gaunt, spare; *avoir la gorge sèche*, to have a parched throat;

avoir la bouche sèche, to have a dry mouth; *boire ~,* to drink hard; *un bruit ~,* a snap; *avoir le cœur ~,* to be hard-hearted; to be unfeeling; (fig.) *fruit ~,* (of a person) failure; *mettre au pain ~,* to put on dry bread; *à pied ~,* dry-shod; *un merci tout ~,* a curt thank you; *un homme grand et ~,* a gaunt fellow; *à ~,* dried up; *mettre un étang à ~,* to drain a pond; *perte sèche,* dead loss; (colloq.) *rester ~,* to be unable to answer, to be nonplussed; (colloq.) *être à ~,* to be broke; to be hard up; to be in low water; to be in Queer street; to be on the rocks; *tout ~,* hard and fast; (naut.) *à ~ de toile,* under bare poles; *au ~,* high and dry; (colloq.) *en cinq ~,* in a jiffy; in double-quick time. **sèche,** s.f. (slang) Cig, cigarette, gasper; *griller une ~,* to smoke a fag.

sécant, -e (sekɑ̃), adj. [f. L *secare*] (geom.) Secant. **~e,** s.f. (geom.) Secant.

sécateur (sekatœr), s.m. Pruning-scissors; pruning-shears, secateurs.

sécession (sesɛsjɔ̃), s.f. [L *secessio*] Secession.

sécessionniste (sesɛsjɔnist), adj. s.m.f. Secessionist; seceder.

séchage (seʃaʒ), s.m. Drying; seasoning (of wood).

sèchement (sɛʃmɑ̃), adv. Dryly; curtly, harshly.

sécher (seʃe), v.a.n. [L *siccare*] To dry, to dry up; to season (wood); (fig.) to wither, to pine away; (fig.) *~ les larmes de X,* to dry X's tears, to console X; *~ sur pied,* to eat one's heart out; to pine away; *~ d'envie,* to be green with envy; (slang) to dry up, to be unable to answer a question, or to go on with one's speech; *~ un cours,* to cut a lecture; **se ~,** v.pr. to dry oneself; to dry, to be dried.

sécheresse (seʃrɛs), s.f. Dryness, drought; barrenness; (fig.) dryness, curtness, harshness.

sécherie (seʃri), s.f. Drying-house.

séchoir (seʃwar), s.m. Drying-room; dryer, towel-horse, linen-airer, clothes-airer, drying-apparatus.

second, -e (səgɔ̃), (before a vowel the d is sounded like a t), adj. [L *secundus*] Second, other; assistant; *au ~ étage; au ~,* on the second floor; *voyager en ~e (classe),* to travel second (class); *de ~e main,* second-hand; *en ~,* second in command; *en ~ lieu,* in the second place; *au ~ plan,* in the middle distance; *un ~ Alexandre,* another Alexander. **~,** s.m. Second officer; second floor; second object; *ne venir qu'en ~,* to play second fiddle.

secondaire (sɛgɔ̃dɛr), adj. Secondary, accessory, subservient.

secondairement (səgɔ̃dɛrmɑ̃), adv. Secondarily, accessorily.

seconde (səgɔ̃d), s.f. Second; (mus.) second; (at schools) second = (in England) fifth form; (fenc.) seconde; *attendez une ~,* wait a minute; (math., geom., astr., geog.) second.

secondement (səgɔ̃dmɑ̃), adv. Secondly, in the second place, secundo.

seconder (səgɔ̃de), v.a. [L *secundare*] To second, to assist, to help, to support, to back.

secouement (səkumɑ̃), s.m. Shaking, jolting.

secouer (səkwe), v.a.n. [L *subcutere*] To shake, to shake off, to discard, to jolt, to toss; to rouse, to blow up; *il a été bien secoué par cette maladie,* he has been very much shaken by this illness; *secouez-le donc un peu!,* stir him up a bit!; **se ~,** v.pr. to shake oneself; (fig.) to bestir or to exert oneself.

secourable (səkurabl), adj. Helpful, willing to relieve; *tendre une main ~,* to give a helping hand.

secourir (səkurir), v.a. [L *succurrere*] To succour, to help, to assist, to relieve.

secours (səkur), s.m. Help, succour, assistance, relief, aid; subsidy; *au ~!,* help!; *crier au ~,* to cry for help; *donner, accorder un ~,* to give a subsidy; *venir au ~ de X,* to come to X's help, to give assistance to X; to back X; *Société de ~ Mutuels,* benefit society; sick-fund; *train de ~,* breakdown train.

secousse (səkus), s.f. [f. *secouer*] Shake, jolt, shock, jog, jerk; tremor; *une ~ de tremblement de terre,* an earthquake shock; (aeron. slang) yank; (slang) *il n'en fiche pas une ~,* he does not do a stroke of work.

secr-et, -ète (səkrɛ), adj. [L *secretus*] Secret, hidden, private, inward; close-tongued, reserved, reticent, discreet; *fonds ~s,* Secret Service money; *en ~,* secretly.

secret (səkrɛ), s.m. [L *secretum*] Secret; secrecy, mystery; explanation, trick; secret recipe; close confinement; *je ne suis pas du ~,* I am not in the secret; *gardez-moi le ~,* keep it secret; *c'est le ~ de Polichinelle,* it's an open secret; *confier un ~ à X,* to entrust X with a secret; *trahir un ~,* to betray a secret, to let out a secret; *mettre dans le ~,* to let into the secret; *mettre au ~,* to keep in close custody; *avoir le ~ de plaire,* to have the gift of pleasing everybody.

secrétaire (səkretɛr), s.m.f. **1.** Secretary; **2.** **~,** s.m. writing-desk, davenport; **3.** (ornith.) secretary-bird.

secrétariat (səkretarja), s.m. Secretariate; secretaryship; secretary's office.

secrètement (səkrɛtmɑ̃), adv. Secretly, in secret, privately, discreetly, inwardly.

sécréter (sekrete), v.a. [LL *secretare*] To

secrete; to produce by secretion; to exude. ⚠ *Sécréter* cannot be used like English 'to secrete' in the sense of to put (object, person, oneself) into place of concealment = *cacher, garder secret, dérober, se cacher.*

sécréteu-r, -se (also (f.) **sécrétrice**) (sekretœr), adj. Secretory.

sécrétion (sekresjɔ̃), s.f. Secretion, exuding.

sécrétoire (sekretwar), adj. Secretory.

sectaire (sɛktɛr), s.m.f. adj. [f. *secte*] Sectarian; sectary.

sectat-eur, -rice (sɛktatœr), s.m.f. [L *sectator*] Follower, disciple, votary.

secte (sɛkt), s.f. [L *secta*] Sect; *faire* ~, to form a sect; to differ from most people.

secteur (sɛktœr), s.m. [L *sector*] (geom.) Sector; section; (motor.) sector; quadrant; segment; ~ *denté*, toothed sector; ~ *à crans*, notched locking quadrant; ~ *à crans pour le réglage de l'allumage*, quadrant, or segment, for adjusting ignition.

section (sɛksjɔ̃), s.f. [L *sectio*] Section, cutting, sectioning; section, the part cut off; section, division; ~ *conique*, conic section; ~ *de tramway, autobus,* &c., stage; ~ *de vote*, polling-station; (mil.) section.

sectionnement (sɛksjɔnmɑ̃), s.m. Sectioning, dividing, division into parts or stages.

sectionner (sɛksjɔne), v.a. To section, to divide into sections.

séculaire (sekylɛr), adj. Secular; occurring once in a century; that has stood for centuries, time-honoured, ancient, venerable; *année* ~, the last year in a century. ⚠ In English 'secular' means also *séculier*, q.v., *laïque*.

séculairement (sekylɛrmɑ̃), adv. From age to age.

sécularisation (sekylariza'sjɔ̃), s.f. Secularization.

séculariser (sekylarize), v.a. [f. L *saeculum*] To secularize.

sécularité (sekylarite), s.f. Secularity.

séculi-er, -ère (sekylje), adj. [f. L *saeculum*] Secular; *le bras* ~, the secular arm, the secular jurisdiction. ⚠ In English 'secular' means also *séculaire*, q.v.

séculièrement (sekyljɛrmɑ̃), adv. Secularly.

secundo (səgɔ̃do), adv. [L wd] Secundo, secondly.

sécurité (sekyrite), s.f. [L *securitas*] Security, safety, confidence. ⚠ In English 'security' means also guarantee = *garantie*; thing deposited as pledge = *sûreté, caution, gage*; certificate of stock, bond, &c. = *valeurs, obligation,* &c.

sedan (sədɑ̃), s.m. [geog. orig.] Sedan-cloth. ⚠ English 'sedan', sedan-chair = *chaise à porteurs*; (U.S.A.) sedan = *berline*; convertible sedan = *berline transformable.*

sédati-f, -ve (sedatif), adj. s.m. [f. L *sedare*] Sedative.

sédation (seda'sjɔ̃), s.f. (med.) Sedation.

sédentaire (sedɑ̃tɛr), adj. [f. L *sedere*] Sedentary, fixed, (mil.) stationary.

sédentairement (sedɑ̃tɛrmɑ̃), adv. Sedentarily.

sédiment (sedimɑ̃), s.m. [L *sedimentum*] Sediment.

sédimentaire (sedimɑ̃tɛr), adj. Sedimentary.

sédimentation (sedimɑ̃ta'sjɔ̃), s.f. Sedimentation.

séditieusement (sedisjøzmɑ̃), adv. Seditiously.

séditieu-x, -se (sedisjø), adj. Seditious, rebellious, mutinous.

sédition (sedisjɔ̃), s.f. [L *seditio*] Sedition, rebellion, mutiny.

séduct-eur, -rice (sedyktœr), s.m.f. Seducer, deluder, enticer. ~, adj. Seductive, deluding, enticing.

séduction (sedyksjɔ̃), s.f. [L *seductio*] Seduction, enticement, allurement, ensnaring; seducing; bribing, subornation.

séduire (sedɥir), v.a. [L *seducere*] To seduce, to entice, to allure, to delude, to ensnare, to win over; to bribe, to suborn.

séduisant, -e (sedɥizɑ̃), adj. Seductive, fascinating, charming, bewitching, prepossessing; tempting; *des offres* ~*es*, a tempting offer.

ségala (segala), s.f. Rye-field.

segment (sɛgmɑ̃), s.m. [L *segmentum*] (geom.) Segment; (motor.) segment; ring; ~ *de piston*, piston-ring.

segmentaire (sɛgmɑ̃tɛr), adj. Segmental.

segmenter (sɛgmɑ̃te), v.a. To segment.

ségrégati-f, -ve (segregatif), adj. Segregative.

ségrégation (segrega'sjɔ̃), s.f. [f. L *segregare*] Segregation.

seiche (sɛʃ), s.f. [f. L *sepia*] (zool.) Cuttle-fish; *os de* ~, cuttle-bone.

séide (seid), s.m. [Arab. orig.] Blind supporter, satellite, devoted partisan; (U.S.A.) heeler.

seigle (sɛgl), s.m. [L *secale*] Rye; ~ *ergoté*, spurred rye.

seigneur (sɛɲœr), s.m. [f. L *senior*] Lord, squire, noble, nobleman; *le Seigneur (Dieu)*, the Lord; *Notre Seigneur*, Our Lord; *trancher du grand* ~, *faire le grand* ~, (*a*) to put on lordly airs; (*b*) to be very generous; *en grand* ~, lordly, lordlike; *à tout* ~, *tout honneur*, honour to whom honour is due.

seigneurial, -e, (aux) (sɛɲœrjal), adj. Lordly, manorial; *les droits* ~*aux*, the seigniorial rights.

seigneurie (sɛɲœri), s.f. Seigniory, lordship, manor; *votre* ~, your lordship.

seille (sɛj), s.f. [L *situla*] Pail, bucket.
seime (sɛm), s.f. (vet.) Sandcrack.
sein (sɛ̃), s.m. [L *sinus*] Breast; bosom; (fig.) bosom, midst, heart, womb, depths, bowels; *donner le ~ à un enfant*, to give a child the breast; to suckle a child; to nurse a child; *se percer le ~*, to stab oneself; *réchauffer un serpent dans son ~*, to cherish, to foster, a snake in one's bosom; *vivre au ~ de l'opulence*, to live in the midst of riches; *dans le ~ de sa famille*, in the bosom of one's family; home; (jest.) *je suis dans le ~ d'Abraham*, I am utterly comfortable; I am pleased as Punch; I am in clover; *le ~ de l'Église*, the bosom of the Church; the fold.
seine, senne (sɛn), s.f. [L *sagena*] Seine, ground-seine; triangular drag-net.
seing (sɛ̃), s.m. [L *signum*] Signature, sign manual; *sous ~ privé*, by private deed; *blanc-~*, signature in blank.
séisme (seism), s.m. [Gr. *seismos*] Earthquake, seism.
séismique (seismik), adj. Seismic, seismal.
seize (sɛz), num. adj. [L *sedecim*] Sixteen; sixteenth; *Louis ~*, Louis the sixteenth.
seizième (sɛzjɛm), adj. Sixteenth. ~, s.m. Sixteenth, sixteenth part.
seizièmement (sɛzjɛmmɑ̃), adv. Sixteenthly.
séjour (seʒur), s.m. **1.** Stay, sojourn, visit; *faire un court ~ à Londres*, to make a short stay in London; **2.** abode, residence, regions; *un ~ délicieux*, an enchanting abode; *le céleste ~*, the celestial regions; the abode of the gods.
séjourner (seʒurne), v.n. [f. L *subtus*+*diurnum*] To stay, to sojourn, to dwell temporarily, to remain.
sel (sɛl), s.m. [L *sal*] Salt; *~ fin*, table salt; *gros ~*, coarse salt; (plur.) *~s*, volatile salts; smelling-salts; sal volatile; Epsom salts; (fig.) wit, piquancy, pungency, humour; *le ~ attique*, Attic salt; *plaisanterie au gros ~*, coarse jest.
sélacien, -ne (selasjɛ̃), adj. [f. Gr. *selakhos*] (ichth.) Selachian.
sélagine (selaʒin), s.f. (bot.) Selaginella.
sélam (selam), s.m. [f. Arab. *salam*] Selam, emblematic nosegay.
sélection (selɛksjɔ̃), s.f. [f. L *selectus*] Selection, choice.
séléniate (selenjat), s.m. (chem.) Seleniate, selenate.
sélénieux (selenjø), **sélénique** (selenik), adj. m. (chem.) Selenious; selenic.
sélénium (selenjɔm), s.m. (chem.) Selenium.
sélénographie (selenografi), s.f. [f. Gr. *selênê*+*graphein*] Selenography.
self (sɛlf), s.f. [f. Engl. *self-induction*] Self-induction coil; syn. BOBINE DE SELF (INDUCTION).
sellage (sɛlaʒ), s.m. Saddling.
selle (sɛl), s.f. [L *sella*] **1.** Saddle; *cheval de ~*, saddle-horse; *demeurer en ~*, to keep in the saddle; *sauter en ~*, to spring into the saddle; (fig.) *se remettre en ~*, to re-establish one's position; *remettre X en ~*, to lend X a helping hand, to see X through; **2.** (med.) opening of the bowels, motion, evacuation; *aller à la ~*, to go to stool, to have a motion.
seller (sɛle), v.a. To saddle; (fig.) to saddle (with).
sellerie (sɛlri), s.f. Saddlery; harness-room.
sellette (sɛlɛt), s.f. Culprit's stool; stool of repentance; (fig.) *tenir X sur la ~*, to cross-question X; to haul X over the coals.
sellier (sɛlje), s.m. Saddle-maker, saddler.
selon (səlɔ̃), prep. [LL *sublungum*] According to; after; pursuant to; *~ moi*, to my mind; (colloq.) *c'est ~*, that depends; *~ que*, according as.
semaille (usually in the plural) (səmaj), s.f. [L *seminalia*] Sowing; seed-time, sowing-time.
semaine (səmɛn), s.f. [L *septimana*] Week; week's wages; *à la ~*, by the week, *une livre par ~*, a pound a week; *il le fera la ~ des quatre jeudis*, he will do it in a week of Sundays; or when two Sundays come together; or when pigs fly; *la ~ prochaine*, next week; *être de ~*, to be on duty for the week; *jours de ~*, working-days; week-days; *prêter à la petite ~*, to lend money at a high rate of interest for a short time.
semainier (səmɛnje), s.m. **1.** Person on duty for the week; **2.** armlet made of seven rings; **3.** case of seven razor-blades.
sémantique (semɑ̃tik), adj. [Gr. *sēmantikos*] Semantic. ~, s.f. Semantics.
sémaphore (semafɔr), s.m. [Gr. *sēma*+*phoros*] Semaphore, signal-post.
sémaphorique (semafɔrik), adj. Semaphoric.
semblable (sɑ̃blabl), adj. [f. L *similis*] Alike, like, such, similar; (geom.) similar; fellow; *a-t-on jamais vu rien de ~ ?*, did you ever see such a thing ?; *rien de ~ !*, nothing of the sort ! ~, s.m. Fellow creature.
semblablement (sɑ̃blabləmɑ̃), adv. Similarly, likewise, also, in like manner.
semblant (sɑ̃blɑ̃), s.m. Semblance, outward appearance; *faux ~*, false show; *faire ~ de*, to pretend to; *ne faites ~ de rien*, don't appear to take any notice.
sembler (sɑ̃ble), v.n. [L *similare*] To appear, to seem, to look; *si bon vous semble*, if you think fit; if it is your wish; *il semble que*, it appears that; it looks as if; *il me semble le voir*, I fancy I see him; *c'est ce qu'il me semble*,

that's precisely what I thought; *à ce qu'il me semble,* to my mind; in my opinion; *comme bon vous semblera,* just as you please; *que vous en semble?,* what do you think of that?

semé, -e (səme), adj. Sown; strewn (*de,* with), sprinkled, spangled, interspersed; (herald.) semée.

séméiologie (semejoloʒi), s.f. [Gr. *semeion+logos*] Semeiology.

semelle (səmɛl), s.f. [orig. unkn.] Sole (of a shoe); (fig.) *ne pas reculer d'une ~,* not to budge an inch; *battre la ~,* to stamp one's feet (in order to warm them); (fenc.) step; *rompre la ~,* to retire in parrying.

semence (səmɑ̃s), s.f. [L *sementis*] Seed; semen, sperm; (fig.) seed, germ; (ironmong.) tacks.

semen-contra (semɛnkɔ̃tra), s.m. [L wd] Semen contra, worm-seed.

semer (səme), v.a. [L *seminare*] To sow; to strew, to sprinkle, to scatter; (colloq.) to lose; (fig.) *~ la discorde,* to sow discord; *~ la terreur,* to spread panic; *qui sème le vent récolte la tempête,* he who sows the wind shall reap the whirlwind; gather thistles, expect prickles; *~ l'argent follement,* to squander one's money.

semestre (səmɛstr), s.m. [L *semestris*], Half year; semester; *par ~,* half-yearly; half-year's pay.

semestriel, -le (səmɛstrjɛl), adj. Half-yearly.

semeu-r, -se (səmœr), s.m.f. Sower.

semi- (səmi), pref. [L pref.] Semi-; half-.

sémillant, -e (semijɑ̃), adj. Sprightly, lively, brisk, frisky.

séminaire (seminɛr), s.m. [L *seminarium*] Seminary.

séminal, -e, (aux) (seminal), adj. [L *seminalis*] Seminal.

séminariste (seminarist), s.m. Seminarist.

sémination (semina'sjɔ̃), s.f. (bot.) Semination.

semis (səmi), s.m. Sowing; seed-bed; seedlings.

sémite (semit), s.m.f. Semite.

sémitique (semitik), adj. Semitic.

semi-voyelle (səmivwajɛl), s.f. Semi-vowel.

semnopithèque (sɛmnɔpitɛk), s.m. (zool.) Semnopithecus.

semoir (səmwar), s.m. Seed-lip, seed-bag; sowing-machine.

semonce (səmɔ̃s), s.f. [f. *semondre*] Reprimand, lecture, talking-to, wigging, dressing-down, set-down, trimming.

semoncer (səmɔ̃se), v.a. To reprimand, to rebuke, to lecture, to give a dressing-down to.

semondre (səmɔ̃dr), v.a. (obs.) [L *submonere*] To summon; to reprimand.

semoule (səmul), s.f. [It. *semola*] Semolina.

sempiternel, -le (sɛ̃pitɛrnɛl), adj. [L *sempiternus*] Everlasting, sempiternal.

sempiternellement (sɛ̃pitɛrnɛlmɑ̃), adv. Everlastingly, sempiternally.

sénat (sena), s.m. [L *senex, senatus*] Senate.

sénateur (senatœr), s.m. Senator.

sénatorial, -e, (aux) (senatɔrjal), adj. Senatorial.

sénatorien (senatɔrjɛ̃), adj. (antiq.) Senatorian.

senatus-consulte (senatyskɔ̃sylt), s.m. [L *senatus consultum*] Senatus-consultum; decree of the Senate.

senau (səno), s.m. [Dutch *snauw*] (naut.) Snow (a vessel); *voile de ~,* try-sail.

séné (sene), s.m. [Arab. orig.] (bot.) Senna; (fig.) *passe-moi la casse, je te passerai le ~,* yield me this point, and I will yield you that; scratch my back and I will scratch yours.

sénéchal (pl. **aux**) (seneʃal), s.m. [L *senescalus*] Seneschal.

sénéchaussée (seneʃose), s.f. Court or jurisdiction of a seneschal.

séneçon (sensɔ̃), s.m. (bot.) Groundsel, *Senecio.*

sénestre (senɛstr), adj. [f. L *sinister*] Left. ~, s.f. Left hand.

sénevé (senve), s.m. [L *sinapis*] (bot.) Mustard; black mustard.

sénile (senil), adj. [L *senilis*] Senile.

sénilité (senilite), s.f. Senility.

senne (sɛn), s.f. See syn. SEINE.

sénonien, -ne (senɔnjɛ̃), adj. s.m.f. (Native) of Sens (French town).

sens (sɑ̃s), s.m. [L *sensus*] **1.** Sense, senses; *les cinq sens,* the five senses; *cela tombe sous les ~,* that's obvious; that's self-evident; **2.** judgement, interpretation, meaning, opinion; *à mon ~,* in my opinion; *j'abonde dans votre ~,* I quite agree with you; *le bon ~,* good sense; *il n'est pas dans son bon ~,* he is out of his mind; (colloq.) he is not quite all there; *cela n'a pas le ~ commun,* that's absurd; *cet homme n'a pas le ~ commun,* that man has no common sense; *expression à double ~,* ambiguous expression; double-entendre; *~ figuré,* figurative sense; *~ propre,* proper meaning; *un homme de ~ rassis,* a staid, sober man; **3.** direction, way; *dans le ~ de la longueur,* lengthways; *~ devant derrière,* hind part foremost; wrong side first; *~ dessus dessous,* upside down; *ils s'enfuient dans tous les ~,* they are running away in all directions; (*rue à*) *~ unique,* one-way street.

sensation (sɑ̃sa'sjɔ̃), s.f. [L *sensatio*] Sensation, excitement; *faire ~,* to make a sensation; *à ~,* sensational.

sensationnel, -e (sɑ̃sasjɔnɛl), adj. Sensational, thrilling, exciting.

sensé, -e (sɑ̃se), adj. Sensible, judicious, of sense, sound, reasonable.
sensément (sɑ̃semɑ̃), adv. Sensibly, reasonably, soundly.
sensibiliser (sɑ̃sibilize), v.a. To sensitize; to make sensitive.
sensibilité (sɑ̃sibilite), s.f. [L *sensibilitas*] Sensibility, sensitiveness, feeling.
sensible (sɑ̃sibl), adj. [L *sensibilis*] Sensible, perceptible, appreciable; sensitive (*à*, to); tender, sore; (mus.) *note ~*, leading note. ⚠ In English 'sensible' has also and very frequently the sense of reasonable, judicious, moderate, practical, of good sense = *raisonnable, sensé, pondéré, de bon sens*; ex. be sensible = *soyez raisonnable*. In French *sensible* is never used in this sense.
sensiblement (sɑ̃sibləmɑ̃), adv. Perceptibly, visibly, considerably.
sensiblerie (sɑ̃sibləri), s.f. Maudlin sentimentality; mawkish tenderness.
sensiti-f, -ve (sɑ̃sitif), adj. Sensitive.
sensitive (sɑ̃sitiv), s.f. (bot.) Sensitive plant.
sensitivité (sɑ̃sitivite), s.f. Sensitivity.
sensorial, -e, (aux) (sɑ̃sɔrjal), adj. Sensorial.
sensoriel, -le (sɑ̃sɔrjɛl), adj. Sensorial.
sensorium (sɑ̃sɔrjɔm), s.m. [L wd] (anat.) Sensorium.
sensualisme (sɑ̃sɥalism), s.m. Sensualism.
sensualité (sɑ̃sɥalite), s.f. Sensuality.
sensuel, -le (sɑ̃sɥɛl), adj. Sensual, voluptuous.
sensuellement (sɑ̃sɥɛlmɑ̃), adv. Sensually.
sente (sɑ̃t), s.f. [L *semita*] Path.
sentence (sɑ̃tɑ̃s), s.f. [L *sententia*] Sentence; aphorism, maxim; judgement, verdict; *rendre une ~*, to pass sentence; to bring in a verdict. ⚠ Nowadays English 'sentence' usually = *phrase*, i.e. set of words complete in itself, containing subject and predicate; the sense of pithy saying, maxim, proverb, &c., is archaic; but not so in French.
sentencieusement (sɑ̃tɑ̃sjøzmɑ̃), adv. Sententiously.
sentencieu-x, -se (sɑ̃tɑ̃sjø), adj. Sententious.
senteur (sɑ̃tœr), s.f. Scent, perfume, smell; (bot.) *pois de ~*, sweet pea.
senti, -e (sɑ̃ti), p. adj. Heartfelt, deeply felt; strongly expressed, strongly worded; *quelques paroles bien ~es ont suffi*; a strongly worded warning was enough.
sentier (sɑ̃tje), s.m. [f. *sente*] Path, footpath; (fig.) track, path; road; *~s battus*, beaten tracks; hackneyed ways.
sentiment (sɑ̃timɑ̃), s.m. [f. *sentir*] Feeling, sense, sentiment, impression, sensation; opinion; *avoir le ~ de sa force*, to be conscious of one's strength; *je voudrais savoir votre ~ là-dessus*, I would like to know what you think of that; *juger par ~*, to judge by one's feeling; *être animé de bons ~s*, to be well-meaning.
sentimental, -e, (aux) (sɑ̃timɑ̃tal), adj. Sentimental.
sentimentalement (sɑ̃timɑ̃talmɑ̃), adv. Sentimentally.
sentimentalité (sɑ̃timɑ̃talite), s.f. Sentimentality.
sentine (sɑ̃tin), s.f. [L *sentina*] Well-room (of a ship); sink; (fig.) sink; *~ d'iniquité*, sink of iniquity.
sentinelle (sɑ̃tinɛl), s.f. [It. *sentinella*] Sentinel, sentry; *être en ~, faire ~*, to stand sentry; to mount guard; (fig.) to be on the watch.
sentir (sɑ̃tir), v.a. [L *sentire*] **1.** To feel, to perceive, to be conscious of, to be affected by, to experience; *~ sa propre faiblesse*, to be conscious of one's weakness; *~ des remords*, to feel remorse; *~ la faim*, to feel hungry; **2.** to smell, to scent, to savour of; to perceive the smell of, to detect by smell; (fig.) to find out, to suspect, to detect; *cela sent bon*, this smells nice; *cela sent mauvais ici*, there is a bad smell here; (fig.) *cela ne sent pas bon*, I don't like the look of it, that does not look promising; *~ l'ail*, to smell of garlic; *cette viande sent*, this meat is beginning to go bad, it smells; (fig.) *je ne peux pas le ~*, I cannot bear, or stand, him; I hate the sight of him; *~ le fagot*, to be tainted with heresy; **se ~**, v.pr. to feel, to be conscious of one's situation; to make itself felt; *je ne me sens pas bien*, I don't feel quite well; *il s'est senti mourir*, he was conscious that he was dying; *elle ne se sent pas de joie*, she is beside herself with joy; *les effets s'en font encore ~*, the consequences are still making themselves felt; *je me sens beaucoup de courage*, I feel very brave; *on se sent toujours de sa première éducation*, one always feels the effects of one's early upbringing.
seoir[1] (swar), v.n. defect. [L *sedere*] To sit (only used in *séant, sis, sise, sieds-toi*).
seoir[2] (swar), v.n. defect. [f. L *sedere*], (*sied, seyant*) To suit, to be becoming or fitting; *ce chapeau vous sied*, or *vous est seyant*, this hat is becoming and suits you well; *il vous sied mal de parler ainsi*, it ill becomes you to speak in that way.
sep (sɛp), s.m. Wooden frame of plough.
sépale (sepal), s.m. [wd made from *séparer+pétale*] (bot.) Sepal.
séparable (separabl), adj. Separable.
séparation (separa'sjɔ̃), s.f. Separation, parting, severing; *mur de ~*, partition-wall; *~ de biens*, separate maintenance; *~ de corps et de biens*, judicial separation.

séparatisme (separatism), s.m. Separatism.
séparatiste (separatist), adj. s.m. Separatist.
séparé, -e (separe), p. adj. Separate, distinct, apart.
séparément (separemɑ̃), adj. Separately, apart.
séparer (separe), v.a. [L *separare*] To separate, to part, to divide, to disunite, to disjoin, to set apart, to sever; ~ *le bon grain de l'ivraie,* to separate the wheat from the tares; ~ *les cheveux sur le front,* to part the hair on the forehead; ~ *les combattants,* to part the combatants; *la rivière sépare les deux provinces,* the river divides the two provinces; **se** ~, v.pr. to part; to break up, to part company; to be judicially separated.
sépia (sepja), s.f. [Gr. *sēpia*] Sepia; sepia drawing.
seps (sɛps), s.m. [Gr. *sēps*] (zool.) Seps, serpent-lizard.
sept (sɛt), adj. num. [L *septem*] Seven; the seventh.
septain (ʃɛtɛ̃), s.m. Seven-lined stanza.
septante (sɛptɑ̃t), adj. num. (obs.) Seventy; *la Version des* ~, the Septuagint.
septembral, -e, (aux) (sɛptɑ̃bral), adj. of September; *la purée* ~*e,* wine.
septembre (sɛptɑ̃br), s.m. [L *september*] September.
septembriseur (sɛptɑ̃brizœr), s.m. Septembrist (agent of the massacres in France in September 1792).
septénaire (sɛptenɛr), s.m. adj. Septenary.
septennal, -e, (aux) (sɛptɛnal), adj. Septennial.
septennat (sɛptɛna), s.m. Seven years' presidency (or power or mandate).
septentrion (sɛptɑ̃trjɔ̃), s.m. [L *septentriones*] North; (astr.) Ursa Minor; the Little Bear.
septentrional, -e, (aux) (sɛptɑ̃trjonal), adj. North, northern.
septicémie (sɛptisemi), s.f. [Gr. *sēptikos*+*haima*] (pathol.) Septicaemia, blood-poisoning.
septicité (sɛptisite), s.f. Septicity, septic condition or quality.
septidi (sɛptidi), s.m. [f. L *septimus*+*dies*] Septidi (7th day of the ten-day week of the French Republican calendar).
septième (sɛtjɛm), adj. num. ord. Seventh; (fig.) *être au* ~ *ciel,* to be in heaven, to be in the seventh heaven; to be enraptured; to walk on air. ~, s.m. Seventh floor; seventh part; ~, s.f. (mus.) seventh; (at school) = seventh form.
septièmement (sɛtjɛmmɑ̃), adv. Seventhly, in the seventh place; syn. SEPTIMO.
septique (sɛptik), adj. [Gr. *sēptikos*] Septic.
septuagénaire (sɛptɥaʒenɛr), adj. s.m.f. Septuagenarian.
septuagésime (sɛptɥaʒesim), s.f. [L wd] Septuagesima.
septuor (sɛptɥɔr), s.m. (mus.) Septuor, septet.
septuple (sɛptypl), adj. s.m. [L *septuplus*] Septuple, sevenfold.
septupler (sɛptyple), v.a. To septuple, to increase sevenfold.
sépulcral, -e, (aux) (sepylkral), adj. Sepulchral.
sépulcre (sepylkr), s.m. [L *sepulcrum*] Sepulchre.
sépulture (sepyltyr), s.f. [L *sepultura*] Sepulture, vault, tomb; burial.
séquanais, -e (sekwanɛ), adj. s.m.f. (Native of) *Grande Séquanaise* (Rom. Gaul).
séquanien, -ne (sekwanjɛ̃), adj. s.m. (geol.) Sequanian.
séquelle (sekɛl), s.f. (pej.) [L *sequela*] Gang, crew, set; (of things) string, series, results. ⚠ 'Sequel' in English has no pejorative sense and means only what follows after, continuation or resumption of a story, process, &c., after-effect, logical inference, conclusion = *suite; conséquence, déduction.*
séquence (sekɑ̃s), s.f. [f. L *sequi*] **1.** (at cards) Sequence; **2.** (Cath. lit.) sequence.
séquestration (sekɛstra'sjɔ̃), s.f. Sequestration, confinement.
séquestre (sekɛstr), s.m. [L *sequestrum*] (law) **1.** Sequestration; **2.** sequestrator.
séquestrer (sekɛstre), v.a. To sequester, to confine, to isolate, to shut up illegally. ⚠ In English the sense of to 'sequester' is wider than in French; ex. a sequestered place = *un endroit écarté.*
sequin (səkɛ̃), s.m. [It. *zecchino*] Sequin.
sequoia (səkwaja), s.m. (bot.) Sequoia.
sérac (serak), s.m. **1.** Serac, a Swiss cheese; **2.** serac (in glaciers, ice pillar formed by intersection of crevasses).
sérail (pl. **-s**) (seraj), s.m. [Turk *seraī*] Seraglio.
séran (serɑ̃), s.m. Flax-comb, hackle.
sérancer (serɑ̃se), v.a. [f. Germ. *schrenzen*] To hackle, to dress (flax).
sérancolin (serɑ̃kolɛ̃), s.m. A kind of Pyrenean marble.
séraphin (serafɛ̃), s.m. [Hebr. *serāphīm*] Seraph.
séraphique (serafik), adj. Seraphic, angelic.
serbe (sɛrb), adj. s.m.f. Servian, Serb.
serein (sərɛ̃), s.m. [f. *soir*] Night dew, evening damp.
serein, -e (sərɛ̃), adj. [L *serenus*] Serene, calm, undisturbed, clear, tranquil, happy; *jours* ~*s,* halcyon days.

sérénade (serenad), s.f. [It. *serenata*] Serenade; *donner une ~ à X*, to serenade X.
sérénissime (serenisim), adj. (as a title) Most Serene.
sérénité (serenite), s.f. Serenity, calmness, placidity.
séreu-x, -se (serø), adj. [f. L *serum*] Serous.
ser-f, -ve (sɛrf), adj. [L *servus*] In bondage, slave, servile. ~, s.m.f. Serf.
serfouette (sɛrfwɛt), s.f. Hoe.
serfouir (sɛrfwir), v.a. [L *circum+fodere*] To hoe.
serfouissage (sɛrfwisaʒ), s.m. Hoeing.
serge (sɛrʒ), s.f. [L *serica*] Serge.
sergé (sɛrʒe), s.m. Cotton serge.
sergent (sɛrʒɑ̃), s.m. **1.** [f. L *serviens*] Sergeant; *~ d'armes*, sergeant-at-arms; *~ de ville*, policeman; *~ fourrier*, quartermaster-sergeant; *~ instructeur*, drill-sergeant; *~-major*, sergeant-major; (in former times) bailiff; **2.** [corrupt. of *serre-joint*] (join.) cramp; (naut.) holdfast.
sergot (sɛrgo), s.m. [f. *sergent de ville*] (slang) Policeman, bobby, copper, slop.
séricicole (serisikɔl), adj. [L *sericum+colere*] Silk-producing, pertaining to sericiculture.
sériciculture (serisikyltyr), s.f. Sericiculture, sericulture, silkworm-breeding.
série (seri), s.f. [L *series*] Series; (math.) series.
sérier (serje), v.a. To classify, to sort, to arrange in series, to file.
sérieusement (serjøzmɑ̃), adv. Seriously, in earnest, earnestly, severely.
sérieu-x, -se (serjø), adj. [f. L *serius*] Serious, earnest, grave; momentous, important, severe; thorough. ~, s.m. Seriousness, gravity; *garder son ~*, to keep one's countenance; to refrain from laughing; *prendre au ~*, to take seriously; (colloq.) *alors c'était ~?*, was that straight? (Amer.) was it on the level?
serin, -e (srɛ̃), s.m.f. Canary; (fig. pej.) greenhorn; fool, ninny, gull, muff, moron.
seriner (sərine), v.a. To teach (a bird) with the bird-organ; (fig.) to din it into, to teach by repeating over and over again.
serinette (sərinɛt), s.f. Bird-organ; (fig.) sorry singer.
seringa, seringat (sərɛ̃ga), s.m. (bot.) Syringa.
seringue (sərɛ̃g), s.f. [Gr. *surigx*] Syringe, squirt.
seringuer (sərɛ̃ge), v.a. To syringe, to squirt.
serment (sɛrmɑ̃), s.m. [L *sacramentum*] Oath, swearing; *prêter ~*, to take one's oath; to be sworn; *faire prêter ~ à X*, to put X on his oath; *faire ~*, to swear; *faux ~*, false oath; *violer ses ~s*, to break one's oaths; *~ d'ivrogne*, drunkard's oath.
sermon (sɛrmɔ̃), s.m. [L *sermo*] Sermon, homily; (fig.) lecture; admonition, reprimand; *faire un ~*, to preach a sermon; to lecture.
sermonner (sɛrmɔne), v.a. To lecture, to sermonize.
sermonneu-r, -se (sɛrmɔnœr), s.m.f. Sermonizer, lecturer, fault-finder.
sérosité (serozite), s.f. [f. *sérum*] Serosity.
sérothérapie (seroterapi), s.f. Serotherapy.
sérotine (serɔtin), s.f. (zool.) Serotine, a chestnut-coloured bat.
serpe (sɛrp), s.f. [f. LL *sarpa*] Bill-hook; *taillé à la ~*, rough(ly) hewn.
serpent (sɛrpɑ̃), s.m. [L *serpens*] Snake, serpent; (mus.) serpent; (zool.) *~ à sonnettes*, rattlesnake; *la prudence du ~*, the wariness of the snake; *avoir une langue de ~*, to have a spiteful or venomous tongue; *réchauffer un ~ dans son sein*, to cherish a snake in one's bosom.
serpentaire (sɛrpɑ̃tɛr), s.m. (ornith.) Serpent-eater, secretary-bird; ~, s.f. (bot.) serpentaria, snake-weed, *Aristolochia serpentaria*.
serpente (sɛrpɑ̃t), s.f. Tissue-paper.
serpenteau (pl. -x) (sɛrpɑ̃to), s.m. Young serpent; (pyrot.) squib.
serpenter (sɛrpɑ̃te), v.n. To wind in and out, to meander; *chemin qui monte en serpentant*, path that winds up-hill.
serpentin (sɛrpɑ̃tɛ̃), s.m. **1.** Worm (of a still); tube-coil; **2.** paper streamer. ~, -e, adj. Wavy, sinuous, meandering.
serpentine (sɛrpɑ̃tin), s.f. **1.** Serpentine stone, serpentine marble; **2.** (bot.) snake-wood; **3.** a narrow denticulate lace.
serpette (sɛrpɛt), s.f. Pruning-knife; small bill-hook.
serpillière (sɛrpiljɛr), s.f. **1.** Packing-cloth; coarse apron; **2.** (ent.) mole-cricket.
serpolet (sɛrpɔlɛ), s.m. [L *serpullum*] (bot.) Serpolet, wild thyme.
serrage (sɛraʒ), s.m. Tightening; fastening, pressing; putting on (brakes); *vis de ~*, tightening-screw.
serrate (sɛrat), adj. [L *serratus*] Serrated, notched on the edge (of coins).
serratule (sɛratyl), s.f. (bot.) Saw-wort, *Serratula*.
serre (sɛr), s.f. [f. *serrer*] **1.** (of birds of prey) Talon, claw; (fig.) clutch, grip; **2.** hot-house, green-house, conservatory; **3.** pressing.
serré, -e (sɛre), p. adj. Tight, close, serried, concise, compact; (fig.) close-fisted; *avoir le cœur ~*, to have a heavy heart, to be heavy-hearted, or down-hearted; *marcher en rangs ~s*, to march in serried ranks; *jouer ~*, to play a cautious game; *un tissu ~*, a closely woven material; *un nœud ~*, a tight knot.

serre-file (sɛrfil), s.m. invar. Person bringing up the rear; (naut.) sternmost vessel.

serre-fils (sɛrfil), s.m. invar. (electr.) Terminal, connecting-screw.

serre-frein (sɛrfrɛ̃), s.m. invar. Brakesman.

serre-joint (sɛrʒwɛ̃), s.m. invar. (join.) Cramp, clamp; syn. SERGENT.

serrement (sɛrmɑ̃), s.m. Pressing, squeezing; ~ *de cœur*, pang, heaviness of heart, anguish; ~ *de mains*, hand-shake.

serre-nez (sɛrne), s.m. invar. (for horses) Twitch.

serrer (sɛre), v.a. [LL *serrare*] To press, to squeeze, to crush, to jam, to tighten, to put close together, to crowd, to close; to pass close to; to condense, to shorten; to put away, to put by, to stow away, to lock up; ~ *la main à X*, to shake hands with X; ~ *les dents*, to clench one's teeth; *cela serre le cœur*, that's heart-rending; ~ *les rangs*, to close the ranks; (naut.) ~ *le vent*, to haul close to the wind; ~ *la terre*, to hug the land; to keep close in to shore; ~ *une femme dans son corset*, to lace a woman tight; ~ *de près*, to press hard; ~ *du linge*, to put away linen; ~ *son argent*, to lock up one's money; ~ *son style*, to condense one's style; ~ *son jeu*, to play a cautious game; ~ *un nœud*, to tighten a knot; **se** ~, v.pr. to lace oneself tight; to crowd, to press each other close; to stint oneself; to pull in a bit.

serre-tête (sɛrtɛt), s.m. invar. Head-band.

serricorne (sɛrikɔrn), adj. (ent.) Serricorn.

serrure (sɛryr), s.f. [f. L *sera*] Lock; ~ *de sûreté*, safety-lock; *crocheter une* ~, to pick a lock; *regarder par le trou de la* ~, to look through the key-hole.

serrurerie (sɛryrəri), s.f. Locksmith's trade, locksmith's work.

serrurier (sɛryrje), s.m. Locksmith.

serte (sɛrt), s.f. Setting (of jewels).

sertir (sɛrtir), v.a. [f. LL *sartire*] To set, to mount.

sertissage (sɛrtisaʒ), s.m. Setting, mounting. [mounter.

sertisseu-r, -se (sɛrtisœr), s.m.f. Setter,

sertissure (sɛrtisyr), s.f. Setting.

sérum (serɔm), s.m. [L wd] **1.** (med.) Serum; **2.** (therap.) solution of drug for injection.

servage (sɛrvaʒ), s.m. [f. L *servus*] Serfdom, servitude, bondage. [cat.

serval (pl. **-s**) (sɛrval), s.m. (zool.) Tiger-

servant (sɛrvɑ̃), p. adj. m. Serving, in waiting; *chevalier* ~, follower, lover, cicisbeo. ~, s.m. Servant; (artill.) gunner, member of gun crew.

servante (sɛrvɑ̃t), s.f. Servant, maid-servant, serving-maid; (fig.) handmaid; dumb-waiter; side-table, dinner-wagon.

serve (sɛrv), s.f. See m. SERF.

serveu-r, -se (sɛrvœr), s.m.f. **1.** (tennis) Server; **2.** hired waiter or waitress.

serviabilité (sɛrvjabilite), s.f. Obligingness, serviceableness.

serviable (sɛrvjabl), adj. Obliging, serviceable, helpful.

serviablement (sɛrvjabləmɑ̃), adv. Obligingly.

service (sɛrvis), s.m. [L *servitium*] Service, duty, attendance; help; function, office; disposal; set; course; supply; *au* ~ *de*, in the service of; *être de* ~, to be on duty; *à votre* ~, at your disposal; at your service; *faire le* ~, to perform duty; to wait at table; to ply (as coaches); *hors de* ~, worn out, out of use; *escalier de* ~, back stairs; *en* ~ (*domestique*), in service; *entrer en* ~, to go into service; to become a servant; to get a situation; *entrer au* ~, to enlist; *faire son* ~ *militaire*, to serve one's time in the army; *qu'y a-t-il pour votre* ~*?*, what can I do for you?; *rendez-moi le* ~ *de*, kindly do me the favour of; *rendre un mauvais* ~ *à X*, to do X a bad turn; *vous m'avez rendu un grand* ~, you did me a great service; ~ *divin*, divine service; ~ *public*, civil service, public administration; *repas à 3* ~*s*, three-course meal; ~ *de porcelaine*, china service; ~ *à thé*, tea-service.

serviette (sɛrvjɛt), s.f. [f. *servir*] **1.** Towel, napkin, serviette; ~ *de table*, table-napkin; ~*-éponge*, Turkish towel; (⚠ In English 'serviette' is now usually regarded as slightly vulgar; napkin = *serviette de table* and also *couche de bébé*; towel = *serviette de toilette*, *serviette de bain*, &c.); **2.** leather portfolio, (limp) writing-case, lawyer's bag, dispatch-case, document-case.

servile (sɛrvil), adj. [L *servilis*] Servile; (fig.) slavish, cringing, mean-spirited, time-serving.

servilement (sɛrvilmɑ̃), adv. Servilely, basely.

servilité (sɛrvilite), s.f. Servility, slavishness, baseness, servileness.

servir (sɛrvir), v.a.n. [L *servire*] To serve; to wait upon, to attend, to be in the service of; to supply one's customers with; to serve up, to place (dishes) on the table, to wait at table; to be serviceable, to be of use; ~ *à*, to be used for; *à quoi cela servira-t-il?*, what is the use of that?; *cela ne sert à rien*, that is of no use; *il ne sert à rien de parler*, it is useless to talk; *elle m'a servi de mère*, she has been a mother to me; *elle ne sert pas à table*, she does not wait at table; *servez à 8 heures*, serve up at 8 o'clock; send in the dinner at 8 o'clock; *Madame est servie*, dinner is ready; dinner is served;

servez chaud!, serve up hot!; ~ *une pompe*, to work a pump; ~ *une rente*, to pay an annuity; ~ *de jouet à X*, to serve as X's plaything; *il a servi dans la marine*, he has served in the navy; ~ *de prétexte*, to serve as a pretext; *que ceci vous serve de leçon*, let this be a lesson to you; *que vous sert de pleurer?*, what's the use of crying?; ~ *à boire à X*, to fill X's glass; ~ *la messe*, to serve the mass; **se** ~, v.pr. to help oneself; to do for oneself; to be served up; *se* ~ *de*, to use, to make use of; to avail oneself of; *se* ~ *chez X*, to be a regular customer of X's.

serviteur (sɛrvitœr), s.m. Servant, man-servant; (fig.) *je suis votre humble* ~, your humble servant; (iron.) ~!, excuse me; I am off; nothing of the kind for me; nothing doing!

servitude (sɛrvityd), s.f. [L *servitudo*] **1.** Servitude, slavery; **2.** conditions, charge (upon an estate, &c.).

ses (sɛ), adj. poss. (plur. of *son, sa*) His, her, its, one's.

sésame (sezam), s.m. [L *sesamum*] (bot.) Sesame; ~ *ouvre-toi!*, open sesame!

sésamoïde (sezamɔid), adj. (anat.) Sesamoid.

séséli (sezeli), s.m. (bot.) Seseli; meadow saxifrage, hartwort.

sesqui- (sɛskɥi), pref. [L pref.] Sesqui-.

sesquialtère (sɛskɥialtɛr), adj. (math.) Sesquialter.

sessile (sɛsil), adj. [L *sessilis*] (bot.) Sessile.

session (sɛsjɔ̃), s.f. [f. L *sedere*] Session; sitting (of a religious council).

sesterce (sɛstɛrs), s.m. [L *sestertius*] (ant.) Sesterce.

sétacé, -e (setase), adj. [f. L *seta*] Setaceous, bristle-shaped.

setier (sətje), s.m. [f. L *sextarius*] An obsolete French measure for liquids (2 gallons) and grain (12 bushels).

sétifère (setifɛr), adj. Setiferous, bristle-bearing.

séton (setɔ̃), s.m. [f. L *seta*] Seton.

seuil (sœj), s.m. [f. L *solum*] Sill, door-sill, threshold; (fig.) threshold, dawn, beginning, entrance.

seul, -e (sœl), adj. [L *solus*] Alone, single, lonely, only, unaided, sole, mere, bare; ~ *à* ~, face to face, by ourselves, by themselves; *il tremble au* ~ *nom de la mort*, the mere mention of death makes him tremble; *il est le* ~ *qui l'ait vu*, he alone saw him. ~, adv. One only, only a; ~ *un héros ferait cela*, only a hero, none but a hero, would do it; (colloq.) *ça n'a pas été* (or *marché*) *tout* ~, it was not all plain sailing; it has been an uphill job; it was no easy matter.

seulement (sœlmɑ̃), adv. Only; solely, merely; only just; but, yet; *non* ~, not only.

seulet, -te (sœlɛ), adj. All alone; isolated.

sève (sɛv), s.f. [L *sapa*] Sap; (fig.) pith, vigour, strength, vitality, stamina.

sévère (sevɛr), adj. [L *severus*] Severe, austere, rigid, harsh, stern, strict. ⚠ In English 'severe' means also violent, extreme, trying = *violent, extrême, intense, pénible*; ex. a severe attack of gout = *une violente crise de goutte*.

sévèrement (sevɛrmɑ̃), adv. Severely, austerely, rigidly, harshly, sternly. ⚠ See SÉVÈRE.

sévérité (severite), s.f. Severity, austerity, rigour, rigidness, harshness; inclemency (of climate, season, &c.). ⚠ See SÉVÈRE.

sévices (sevis), s.m.pl. [L *saevitia*] Ill treatment, cruelty.

sévir (sevir), v.n. [L *saevire*] **1.** ~ *contre*, To punish severely, to treat rigorously; **2.** to rage, to prevail.

sevrage (səvraʒ), s.m. Weaning.

sevrer (səvre), v.a. [f. L *separare*] To wean; (fig.) to deprive (*de*, of).

sèvres (sɛvr), s.m. [f. Fr. town] Sèvres (porcelain).

sexagénaire (sɛgzaʒenɛr), adj. s.m.f. [L *sexagenarius*] Sexagenarian.

sexagésime (sɛgzaʒezim), s.f. Sexagesima.

sexdigitaire (sɛksdiʒitɛr), adj. Sexdigitate, six-fingered.

sexe (sɛks), s.m. [L *sexus*] Sex; *le beau* ~, the fair sex; *le* ~ *fort*, the sterner sex.

sexennal, -e, (aux) (sɛksɛnal), adj. [f. L *sex+annus*] Sexennial.

sexennalité (sɛksɛnalite), s.f. Sexenniality.

sextant (sɛkstɑ̃), s.m. [L *sextans*] (naut.) Sextant.

sexte (sɛkst), s.f. Sext, the 6th hour; the office of the 6th hour, recited at noon.

sextidi (sɛkstidi), s.m. [L *sextus+dies*] 6th day of the decade (in French Republican calendar).

sextil, -e (sɛkstil), adj. [L *sextilis*] (astr.) Sextile.

sexto (sɛksto), adv. [L wd] Sixthly, in the sixth place.

sextolet (sɛkstɔlɛ), s.m. (mus.) Sextole, sextolet.

sextuor (sɛkstɥɔr), s.m. (mus.) Sextet, sestet.

sextuple (sɛkstypl), adj. [LL *sextuplus*] Sextuple, sixfold. ~, s.m. Sextuple.

sextupler (sɛkstyple), v.a. To sextuple, to increase sixfold, to multiply by six.

sexualité (sɛksɥalite), s.f. [f. L *sexus*] Sexuality.

sexué, -e (sɛksɥe), p. adj. Sexuate.

sexuel, -le (sɛksɥɛl), adj. Sexual.

seyant, -e (sɛjɑ̃), adj. [f. *seoir*] Becoming.

sgraffite (sgrafit), s.m. [It. *sgraffito*] Sgraffito.

shah (ʃa), s.m. See SCHAH.

shako (ʃako), s.m. [Hungar. wd] Shako.
shampooing (ʃɑ̃pwɛ̃), s.m. [f. Engl. *shampoo*, Hindi orig.] Shampoo, shampooing.
shérif (ʃerif), s.m. [Engl. *sheriff*] Sheriff.
shunter (ʃœ̃te), v.a. [Engl. *to shunt*] (electr.) To shunt.
si (si), conj. [L *si*] If, whether, whether or not; were it not for; suppose that; ~ *ce n'est que*, unless; *il viendra* ~ *cela est nécessaire*, he will come if necessary; *je ne sais s'il* (*si il*) *viendra*, I don't know whether he will come; ~ *ce n'était la crainte de vous déplaire*, were it not for the fear of displeasing you. ~, s.m. *Des si et des mais*, ifs and buts.
si (si), adv. [L *sic*] So, so much, such, however, however much; yes, yes indeed; *que* ~ *!*, yes, to be sure!; *une si belle femme!*, so beautiful a woman!, such a beautiful woman!; *je gage que* ~, I bet it is so.
si (si), s.m. [Initials of *Sancte Johannes*] (mus.) Si, B.
siamois, -e (sjamwɑ), adj. s.m.f. Siamese; *frères* ~, Siamese twins. ~**e**, s.f. Siamese calico.
sibérien, -ne (siberjɛ̃), adj. s.m.f. Siberian; *un froid* ~, biting cold.
sibilant, -e (sibilɑ̃), adj. [f. L *sibilare*] Sibilant, hissing.
sibylle (sibil), s.f. [Gr. *sibulla*] Sibyl.
sibyllin, -e (sibillɛ̃), adj. Sibylline.
sicaire (sikɛr), s.m. [L *sicarius*] Hired assassin, bravo.
siccati-f, -ve (sikatif), adj. [f. L *siccare*] Siccative, desiccative. ~, s.m. Siccative.
siccité (siksite), s.f. [f. L *siccus*] Siccity, dryness.
sicilien, -ne (sisiljɛ̃), adj. s.m.f. Sicilian.
sicle (sikl), s.m. [Hebr. *shekel*] Shekel (a coin).
sidéral, -e, (aux) (sideral), adj. [f. L *sidus, sideris*] Sidereal, pertaining to stars.
sidération (sidera'sjɔ̃), s.f. Sideration.
sidéré, -e (sidere), adj. Dumbfounded, nonplussed, confounded, (colloq.) struck all of a heap.
sidéritis (sideritis), s.m. (bot.) Ironwort, *Sideritus*.
sidérurgie (sideryrʒi), s.f. [f. Gr. *sidēros*+*ergon*] Siderurgy, iron metallurgy.
sidérurgique (sideryrʒik), adj. Iron-; siderurgical, pertaining to iron metallurgy.
sidi (sidi), s.m. [Arab. wd] (mil. slang) Native soldier in N. Africa; (by ext.) native of N. Africa; fellow, blighter.
siècle (sjɛkl), s.m. [L *saeculum*] Century; age, period, world; *le* ~ *de Périclès*, the age of Pericles; *il y a un* ~ *que nous ne vous avons vu*, we have not seen you for ages; *au* ~ *des* ~*s*, for ever and ever; (fig.) *vivre dans le* ~, to live in the world (not in religious seclusion); *le* ~ *où nous vivons*, the age we live in; (fig.) *fin-de-*~, adj. decadent.
siège (sjɛʒ), s.m. [f. L *sedes*] Seat; box (of a coach); bench (of a tribunal); (eccles.) see; (mil.) siege; (anat.) seat, bottom; *prenez un* ~, sit down; ~ *d'arrière* or *spider*, dickey; *le Saint-*~, the Holy See; *bain de* ~, hip-bath; *mettre le* ~ *devant une ville*, to besiege a town; *lever le* ~, to raise the siege; *mettre en état de* ~, to lay under martial law; ~ *social d'une société*, registered offices of a society; head office; *le* ~ *du mal*, the seat of the malady.
siéger (sjeʒe), v.n. To sit; (of a bishop) to hold a see; to lie, to be seated, to be located.
sien, -ne (sjɛ̃), poss. adj. His, hers, its, one's; ~, pron. *le* ~, *la* ~*ne*, his own, her own, his, hers; *il fait encore des siennes*, he is up to his old tricks again; *un* ~ *parent*, a relative of his; *aimer les* ~*s*, to love one's own people; *il faut que chacun y mette du sien*, (*a*) we must split the difference; (*b*) every one of us must help, or must pay his share.
sieste (sjɛst), s.f. [Span. *siesta*] Nap, siesta; (colloq.) forty winks; *faire la* ~, to take one's afternoon nap.
sieur (sjœr), s.m. [f. L *senior*] Mr.; *le* ~ *X*, the said X.
sifflant, -e (siflɑ̃), adj. Hissing, sibilant, wheezing.
sifflement (sifləmɑ̃), s.m. Hiss, hissing, whistling, whizz; wheezing.
siffler (sifle), v.n.a. [L *sibilare*] To whistle, to whizz, to hiss; ~ *un chanteur*, to hiss a singer; ~ *un air*, to whistle a tune; ~ *son chien*, to whistle to one's dog; (colloq.) ~ *un verre de vin*, to tip off a glass of wine.
sifflet (siflɛ), s.m. Whistle; *un coup de* ~, a whistle, a boatswain's call; *couper le* ~ *à X*, to silence X; to put the quietus on X; *coupé en* ~, wedgewise.
siffleu-r, -se (siflœr), adj. s.m.f. Whistling, whistler.
sifflotement (siflɔtmɑ̃), s.m. Gentle whistling.
siffloter (siflɔte), v.n.a. To whistle softly.
sigillaire (siʒilɛr), adj. [f. L *sigillum*] Of seals, pertaining to seals. ~, s.f. (bot.) Sigillaria.
sigillé, -e (siʒile), adj. [f. L *sigillum*] (bot.) Sigillate.
sigillographie (siʒillɔgrafi), s.f. [f. L *sigillum*+Gr. *graphein*] Sigillography.
sigisbée (siʒisbe), s.m. [It. *cicisbeo*] Cicisbeo, lover, gallant.
sigle (sigl), s.m. [L *sigla*] Group of initial letters.
signal (pl. **aux**) (siɲal), s.m. [f. L *signum*] Signal; *donner le* ~ *de*, to give the signal for, to start; *faire des signaux*, to make signals, to signal.

signalé, -e (siɲale), p. adj. Signal, remarkably good, conspicuous, memorable; *un service ~*, a signal service.
signalement (siɲalmɑ̃), s.m. Description (of a person, &c.).
signaler (siɲale), v.a. [f. L *signum*] To signal; to point out, to call attention to, to take the description of; to notify, to show; **se ~**, v.pr. to signalize oneself; to distinguish oneself.
signalétique (siɲaletik), adj. Descriptive.
signaleur (siɲalœr), s.m. Signaller, signalman.
signalisation (siɲaliza'sjɔ̃), s.f. Marking with sign-posts, signals, buoys, &c.; *appareil de ~*, signalling-apparatus.
signaliser (siɲalize), v.a. To mark with signals, signposts, notice-boards, buoys, &c.; to buoy.
signataire (siɲatɛr), s.m.f. Signer; subscriber; signatory.
signature (siɲatyr), s.f. Signature, signing; *honorer sa ~*, to honour one's signature.
signe (siɲ), s.m. [L *signum*] Sign, token, mark; nod; beck, wink; *faire ~*, to wink, to make signs; *faire ~ de la main*, to beckon with the hand; *faire un ~ de tête*, to nod; *faire le ~ de la croix*, to make the sign of the cross.
signer (siɲe), v.a.n. [L *signare*] To sign; **se ~**, v.pr. to cross oneself, to make the sign of the cross.
signet (siɲɛ), s.m. Book-mark, signet.
significati-f, -ve (siɲifikatif), adj. Significant, significative, tell-tale.
signification (siɲifika'sjɔ̃), s.f. Signification, meaning, import, sense, significance; (law) legal notice.
signifier (siɲifje), v.a. [L *significare*] To signify, to mean, to have the sense of, to notify; (law) to serve. ⚠ 'To signify' has also frequently the sense of to be of importance, to matter = *importer, avoir beaucoup d'importance. Signifier* cannot be used in that sense; ex. it does not signify = *cela n'a aucune importance.*
sil (sil), s.m. [L wd] Ochre.
silence (silɑ̃s), s.m. [L *silentium*] Silence, stillness; secrecy; (mus.) rest; *garder le ~*, to keep silence; *faire ~*, to be silent; *passer sous ~*, to pass over without any mention, to omit; *réduire X au ~*, or *imposer ~ à X*, to silence X; *rompre le ~*, to break silence; *en ~*, silently; *~ !*, not a word !, mum's the word !; *la parole est d'argent mais le ~ est d'or*, speech is silver, silence is gold.
silencieusement (silɑ̃sjøzmɑ̃), adv. Silently.
silencieu-x, -se (silɑ̃sjø), adj. Silent; noiseless, still. **~**, s.m. (motor.) Silencer; exhaust-box; muffler.
silène (silɛn), s.f. (bot.) Catch-fly, silene.
silésien, -ne (silezjɛ̃), adj. s.m.f. Silesian. **~ne**, s.f. Silesia (a silky cotton material used for linings).
silex (silɛks), s.m. [L wd] Silex, flint.
silhouette (silwɛt), [f. prop. n.] Silhouette, outline, profile.
silhouetter (silwɛte), v.a. To outline, to silhouette.
silicate (silikat), s.m. (chem.) Silicate.
silice (silis), s.f. [L *silicea*] (chem.) Silica.
siliceu-x, -se (silisø), adj. Silicious, siliceous.
silicique (silisik), adj. (chem.) Silicic.
silicium (silisjɔm), s.m. (chem.) Silicium, silicon.
silicule (silikyl), s.f. (bot.) Silicula, silicle.
silique (silik), s.f. [L *siliqua*] (bot.) Siliqua.
sillage (sijaʒ), s.m. [f. *siller*] (naut.) Wake, track, course; headway; (fig.) wake.
sille (sil), s.m. [Gr. *sillos*] Greek satiric poem.
siller (sije), v.n. (naut.) To make headway.
sillet (sijɛ), s.m. Nut (of a violin-bow).
sillon (sijɔ̃), s.m. [etym. dub.] Furrow; track, wrinkle; (poet.) fields, plains; (anat.) groove.
sillonner (sijɔne), v.a. To plough; to furrow; to wrinkle (the face); *les navires sillonnent les mers*, the ships plough the seas; *l'éclair sillonne la nue*, lightning flashes through the cloud.
silo (silo), s.m. [Span. wd] (agric.) Silo.
silure (silyr), s.m. [Gr. *silouros*] (ichth.) Silurus, sheat-fish.
silurien, -ne (silyrjɛ̃), adj. s.m. (geol.) Silurian.
silves (silv), s.f.pl. [f. L *silva*] Collection of Latin poems.
simagrée (simagre), s.f. [etym. dub.] Grimace, affectation, pretence, fuss, affected ways.
simarre (simar), s.f. [It. *cimarra*] Long gown, cymar; justice's robe.
simaruba (simaryba), s.m. [Carib wd] (bot.) Simaruba.
simbleau (pl. **-x**) (sɛ̃blo), s.m. (carp.) Radius line.
simiesque (simjɛsk), **simien, -ne** (simjɛ̃), adj. [f. L *simius*] Simian, apish, monkeyish.
similaire (similɛr), adj. [f. L *similis*] Similar, like.
similarité (similarite), s.f. Similarity, likeness.
simili- (simili), pref. s.m. [f. L *similis*] Simili-, imitation; imitation diamonds.
similitude (similityd), s.f. [L *similitudo*] Similitude, likeness, resemblance, analogy, similarity; simile, comparison; *parler par ~s*, to talk in similitudes.
simoniaque (simɔnjak), adj. Simoniacal. **~**, s.m. Simoniac.
simonie (simɔni), s.f. [f. *Simon Magus*] Simony.

simoun (simun), s.m. [Arab. *semūm*] Simoon, simoom.
simple (sɛ̃pl), adj. [L *simplex*] Simple, not compound, onefold; elementary, unsophisticated; single, only, plain, easy, unadorned; artless, sincere, simple-hearted; weak in intellect, silly, naïve, credulous, foolish. ~, s.m. **1.** The simple, simplicity; **2.** **~s**, s.m.pl. simples, medicinal plants; **3.** simpleton, moron; weak-minded person, half-witted person.
simplement (sɛ̃pləmɑ̃), adv. Simply; solely, merely, barely, plainly; only; with simplicity.
simplesse (sɛ̃plɛs), s.f. Simpleness, artlessness.
simplet, -te (sɛ̃plɛ), adj. Rather simple, naïve.
simplicité (sɛ̃plisite), s.f. [L *simplicitas*] **1.** Simplicity; plainness; artlessness; **2.** silliness, simpleness.
simplifiable (sɛ̃plifjabl), adj. That can be simplified.
simplificat-eur, -rice (sɛ̃plifikatœr), adj. Simplifying. ~, s.m.f. Simplifier.
simplification (sɛ̃plifika'sjɔ̃), s.f. Simplification.
simplifier (sɛ̃plifje), v.a. To simplify.
simplisme (sɛ̃plism), s.m. Simplism.
simpliste (sɛ̃plist), adj. Simplist, simplistic, exaggeratedly simplified.
simulacre (simylakr), s.m. [L *simulacrum*] Simulacrum, image, phantom, semblance; *un ~ de combat*, a sham fight.
simulat-eur, -rice (simylatœr), s.m.f. Simulator.
simulation (simyla'sjɔ̃), s.f. Simulation, feigning, feint.
simulé, -e (simyle), p. adj. Sham, feigned, counterfeit, fictitious.
simuler (simyle), v.a. [L *simulare*] To simulate, to feign; to pretend to be, to have, or to feel; to sham.
simultané, -e (simyltane), adj. [f. L *simul*] Simultaneous.
simultanéité (simyltaneite), s.f. Simultaneity, simultaneousness.
simultanément (simyltanemɑ̃), adv. Simultaneously.
sinapisé, -e (sinapize), adj. Infused with mustard.
sinapisme (sinapism), s.m. [Gr. *sinapisma*] Sinapism.
sincère (sɛ̃sɛr), adj. [L *sincerus*] Sincere, true, truthful, ingenuous, honest, candid, frank, genuine, open-hearted.
sincèrement (sɛ̃sɛrmɑ̃), adv. Sincerely, candidly, frankly.
sincérité (sɛ̃serite), s.f. Sincerity, truthfulness, frankness, open-heartedness, ingenuousness, candour.
sincipital, -e, (aux) (sɛ̃sipital), adj. (anat.) Sincipital.
sinciput (sɛ̃sipyt), s.m. [L *semi+caput*] (anat.) Sinciput (head from forehead to top, front part of skull).
sindon (sɛ̃dɔ̃), s.m. [Gr. wd] **1.** Sindon, Christ's shroud; **2.** (surg.) sindon, pledget.
sinécure (sinekyr), s.f. [L *sine+cura*] Sinecure.
singe (sɛ̃ʒ), s.m. [L *simius*] Monkey, ape; (mech., naut.) windlass, hoist; (fig.) ape; *payer X en monnaie de ~*, to pay X with promises; to let X whistle for his money; (war slang) ~, tinned beef; (slang) boss, master, guv'nor.
singer (sɛ̃ʒe), v.a. [f. *singe*] To ape, to mimic; to imitate servilely.
singerie (sɛ̃ʒri), s.f. Apish trick, antic, buffoonery, grimace, mimicry, monkey trick; *faire des ~s*, to play monkey tricks.
singeu-r, -se (sɛ̃ʒœr), s.m.f. Ape, silly imitator, person that apes.
singleton (sɛ̃glətɔ̃), s.m. [Engl. wd] Singleton.
singulariser (sɛ̃gylarize), v.a. [f. *singulier*] To singularize, to make appear singular, odd; **se ~**, v.pr. to make oneself conspicuously singular, deliberately to attract notice.
singularité (sɛ̃gylarite), s.f. [L *singularitas*] Singularity, peculiarity, queerness, oddness.
singuli-er, -ère (sɛ̃gylje), adj. [L *singularis*] Singular, peculiar, queer, odd; *combat ~*, single combat; duel. ~, s.m. (gram.) Singular number; *au ~*, in the singular.
singulièrement (sɛ̃gyljɛrmɑ̃), adv. Singularly, strangely, queerly, oddly; particularly.
sinistre (sinistr), adj. [L *sinister*] Sinister, inauspicious; evil, wicked; of ill omen, foreshowing disaster. ~, s.m. Disaster.
sinistré, -e (sinistre), adj. s.m. That has suffered disaster; *les ~s*, the sufferers, the victims (of an earthquake, fire, &c.).
sinistrement (sinistrəmɑ̃), adv. Sinisterly, dismally, inauspiciously.
sinologie (sinɔlɔʒi), s.f. Sinology.
sinologue (sinɔlɔg), s.m.f. [f. Gr. *Sinai* (the Chinese) + *logos*] Sinologue, sinologist.
sinon (sinɔ̃), conj. [*si+non*] Else, or else, otherwise, if not; save, except; *je n'ai plus rien su ~ qu'il a été tué*, I did not hear anything more, except that he was killed.
sinople (sinɔpl), s.m. [L *sinopis*] (herald.) Vert, sinople.
sinué, -e (sinɥe), adj. [L *sinuatus*] (bot.) Sinuate, wavy-edged.
sinueu-x, -se (sinɥø), adj. [f. L *sinus*] Sinuous, winding, undulating, flexuous, meandering.
sinuosité (sinɥozite), s.f. Sinuosity, winding, bend.
sinus (sinys), s.m. [L wd] (anat.) Sinus; (geom.) sine.

sinusite (sinyzit), s.f. (pathol.) Inflammation of the sinus.
sinusoïdal, -e, (aux) (sinyzoidal), adj. Sinusoidal.
sinusoïde (sinyzoid), s.f. (geom.) Sinusoid.
sionisme (sjonism), s.m. Zionism.
siphon (sifɔ̃), s.m. [Gr. wd] Siphon; waterspout; bottle of Seltzer water.
sire (sir), s.m. [f. L *senior*] Sir, lord; sire; (colloq.) fellow; *un pauvre* ~, a poor wretch, a poor shaver; *un triste* ~, a villain. ⚠ In English, but not in French, 'sire' means also male parent of beast, espec. stallion.
sirène (sirɛn), s.f. [f. myth.] **1.** Siren, mermaid; (fig.) siren, charmer; **2.** (naut., motor., &c.) hooter, fog-horn, siren; (acoustics) siren.
siroco (sirɔko), s.m. [It. wd] Sirocco.
sirop (siro), s.m. [LL *sirupus*] Syrup.
siroter (sirɔte), v.a. To sip, to drink leisurely; to tipple.
sirupeu-x, -se (sirypø), adj. Syrupy.
sirvente (sirvɑ̃t), s.m. Sirvente (poem of Provenç. troubadours).
sis, -e (si), adj. [f. *seoir*] Situated, situate.
sismal, -e, (aux) (sismal), adj. Seismal.
sismique, séismique (sismik, seismik), adj. [f. Gr. *seismos*] Seismic.
sismographe (sismɔgraf), s.m. [f. Gr. *seismos*+*graphein*] Seismograph.
sismologie (sismɔlɔʒi), s.f. Seismology.
sison (sizɔ̃), s.m. (bot.) Stonewort.
sistre (sistr), s.m. [L *sistrum*] (mus.) Sistrum.
sisymbre (sizɛ̃br), s.m. (bot.) Sisymbrium; hedge-mustard.
site (sit), s.m. [f. L *situs*] Site.
sitôt (sito), adv. [*si*+*tôt*] As soon, so soon; ~ *pris* ~ *pendu*, caught and hanged forthwith; ~ *que*, as soon as; *il ne reviendra pas de* ~, it will be some time before he comes back.
sittelle, sittèle (sitɛl), s.f. (ornith.) Nuthatch.
situation (sitɥa'sjɔ̃), s.f. Situation, site, position; state, state of affairs, predicament; paid office, domestic place, living, livelihood; (naut.) bearing. ⚠ In English 'situation' is very frequently used in the sense of paid domestic employment = *place*; ex. cook is looking for another situation = *la cuisinière cherche une autre place*. In this particular sense it must not be translated by French *situation*; *une cuisinière cherche une place, un homme d'affaires cherche une situation.*
situer (sitɥe), v.a. [f. L *situs*] To place, to seat; to assign a place to.
sium (sjɔm), s.m. (bot.) Sium; syn. ACHE D'EAU.
six (sis, si (before a consonant)), num. adj. [L *sex*] Six, the sixth; ~-*huit*, (mus.) $\frac{6}{8}$, six-eight; *à la* ~ *quatre deux*, (colloq.) slapdash; happy-go-lucky, helter-skelter.
sixain, sizain (siksɛ̃, sizɛ̃), s.m. Stanza of six lines.
sixième (sizjɛm), adj. s.m.f. Sixth. ~, s.m. Sixth part; sixth floor; sixth class (in England second form).
sixièmement (sizjɛməmɑ̃), adv. Sixthly, in the sixth place.
sixte (sikst), s.f. (mus.) Sixth; (fenc.) sixte.
ski (ski), s.m. [Scand. wd] Ski, skee.
skieur (skiœr), s.m. Ski-runner.
skunks, sconse, skungs (skɔ̃gs), s.m. (zool.) Skunk; skunk fur.
slave (slav), adj. s.m.f. Slav.
slavisme (slavism), s.m. Slavism.
slavon, -ne (slavɔ̃), adj. s.m.f. Slavonic, Slavonian.
sloop (slup), s.m. [Engl. wd] Sloop.
sloughi (slugi), s.m. (zool.) Saluki, African greyhound.
smalah (smala), s.f. [Arab. wd] Smalah; (fig.) tribe, family.
smalt (smalt), s.m. [It. *smalto*] Smalt (blue glass).
smaragdin, -e (smaragdɛ̃), adj. [f. L *smaragdus*] Smaragdine, emerald green.
smérinthe (smerɛ̃t), s.m. (ent.) Hawk-moth.
smilax (smilaks), s.m. (bot.) Smilax.
smille (smij), s.f. [Gr. *smilē*] (techn.) Scappling-hammer; pick.
smiller (smije), v.a. To scapple.
smoking (smɔking), s.m. [Engl. wd] Dinner-jacket.
snob (snɔb), s.m. [Engl. wd] Snob.
snobisme (snɔbism), s.m. Snobbishness, snobbery.
sobre (sɔbr), adj. [L *sobrius*] Sober, temperate in regard to drink; well balanced, tranquil, moderate, quiet, inconspicuous. ⚠ In English 'sober' often means not drunk (at the moment) = *non ivre*; a man can be sober at 10 in the morning, and drunk at 12. In French *sobre* means *habituellement tempérant* = abstemious, temperate, having temperate habits.
sobrement (sɔbrəmɑ̃), adv. Soberly, temperately, moderately, charily, sparingly.
sobriété (sɔbriete), s.f. [L *sobrietas*] Sobriety (see ⚠ *sobre*); temperance; moderation.
sobriquet (sɔbrikɛ), s.m. [orig. dub.] Nickname.
soc (sɔk), s.m. [Celt. orig.] Plough-share, share.
sociabilité (sɔsjabilite), s.f. Sociability.
sociable (sɔsjabl), adj. [f. L *socius*] Sociable, companionable.
sociablement (sɔsjabləmɑ̃), adv. Sociably.
social, -e, (aux) (sɔsjal), adj. [L *socialis*] Social; *raison* ~*e*, style (of firm).

socialement (sɔsjalmɑ̃), adv. Socially.
socialisation (sɔsjalizaˈsjɔ̃), s.f. Socialization.
socialiser (sɔsjalize), v.a. To socialize.
socialisme (sɔsjalism), s.m. Socialism.
socialiste (sɔsjalist), adj. s.m.f. Socialist.
sociétaire (sɔsjetɛr), s.m.f. Member (of society), fellow; (comm.) partner; shareholder.
sociétariat (sɔsjetarja), s.m. Membership.
société (sɔsjete), s.f. [L *societas*] Society; association; company, firm, partnership; *~ à responsabilité limitée*, limited (liability) company.
socinianisme (sɔsinjanism), s.m. [f. *Laelius* and *Faustus Socinus*, 16th c.] Socinianism.
socinien, -ne (sɔsinjɛ̃), adj. s.m.f. Socinian.
sociologie (sɔsjɔlɔʒi), s.f. Sociology.
sociologique (sɔsjɔlɔʒik), adj. Sociological.
sociologue (sɔsjɔlɔg), s.m.f. Sociologist.
socle (sɔkl), s.m. [f. It. *zoccolo*] Socle, stand, pedestal, plinth, base.
socque (sɔk), s.m. [L *soccus*] Clog, patten; (fig., as symbol of classical comedy) sock.
socquette (sɔkɛt), s.f. Sock (usually worn over stockings).
socratique (sɔkratik), adj. [f. *Socrates*] Socratic.
sodé, -e (sɔde), adj. Containing soda.
sodium (sɔdjɔm), s.m. (chem.) Sodium: Na.
sodomie (sɔdɔmi), s.f. [f. *Sodome*] Sodomy.
sœur (sœr), s.f. [L *soror*] Sister; *belle-~*, sister-in-law; *~ de lait*, foster-sister; *~ de charité*, sister of mercy, sister of charity; *petites ~s des pauvres*, Little Sisters of the Poor; *les neuf ~s*, the Muses; *les trois ~*, the Fates.
sœurette (sœrɛt), s.f. (colloq.) Little sister, sissie; (Amer.) kid.
sofa, sopha (sɔfa), s.m. [Arab. wd] Sofa.
soffite (sɔfit), s.m. [It. *soffita*] (arch.) Soffit.
sofi, soufi (sɔfi, sufi), s.m. Sufi, sophy; ancient title of the King of Persia.
soi (swa), pron. [L *se*] Oneself, himself, herself, itself; *en ~*, in itself; *avoir son argent sur ~*, to have money about, or on, one; *chacun pour ~*, every man for himself; *chez ~*, at home; *un chez ~*, a home; *prendre sur ~*, to make oneself responsible for; to take upon oneself; *rentrer en ~-même*; to withdraw into oneself; *revenir à ~*, to come to, to come round; *cela va de ~*, that goes without saying; of course; *ne penser qu'à ~*, to think only of oneself.
soi-disant (swadizɑ̃), adj. (invar.) Would-be; so-called; pretended; self-styled.
soie (swa), s.f. [L *seta*] Silk; bristle; tang (of a knife); tongue (of a sword); *de ~*, *en ~*, silk, silken; *papier de ~*, tissue paper; *ver à ~*, silkworm; *des jours tissés d'or et de ~*, halcyon days; a bright and happy time; (jest.) *un habillé de ~*, a pig.
soierie (swari), s.f. Silk stuff, silks; silk trade; *marchand de ~*, silk-mercer.
soif (swaf), s.f. [L *sitis*] Thirst; *avoir ~*, to be thirsty; *étancher sa ~*, to quench one's thirst; *avoir ~ de*, to thirst for; *garder une poire pour la ~*, to put by for a rainy day; *la ~ de l'or*, thirst for gold; (colloq.) *jusqu'à plus ~*, endlessly; world without end.
soiffard, -e (swafar), s.m.f. adj. Boozer, tippler, soaker.
soigné, -e (swaɲe), p.adj. Carefully done, well finished, elaborate, well got up; (colloq.) first-rate, capital.
soigner (swaɲe), v.a. [LL *soniare*] To take care of, to look after, to do (something) carefully; to attend to, to see to; to nurse; **se ~**, v.pr. to take care of oneself; (colloq.) to do oneself well.
soigneusement (swaɲøzmɑ̃), adv. Carefully.
soigneu-x, -se (swaɲø), adj. Careful, mindful, attentive, solicitous.
soin (swɛ̃), s.m. [f. *soigner*] Care, attention; attendance, nursing; *avec ~*, carefully; *avoir ~ de*, *prendre ~ de*, to take care of; *aux bons ~s de*, care of, to the care of, c/o ; *être aux petits ~s pour X*, to be full of attentions for X, to curry favour with X; to fawn upon X.
soir (swar), s.m. [L *serum*] Evening; afternoon; *à ce ~*, good-bye till this evening; *bon ~*, good evening, good night; *du matin au ~*, from morning till night; *au ~ de la vie*, in the evening of life; *vers le ~*, *sur le ~*, towards evening; *hier au ~*, last evening, last night.
soirée (sware), s.f. Evening; afternoon; evening party, soirée; *passer la ~ ensemble*, to spend the evening together.
soit (swa, swat (before vowel or absolutely)), conj. [abbrev. of *que cela soit*] Be it so, let it be so; agreed, well and good; viz.; say; suppose; either . . . or; *~ l'un, ~ l'autre*, either one or the other; *~ trois à multiplier par cinq*, say three to be multiplied by five; *~ qu'il le dise ou non*, whether he says it or not; *ainsi ~-il*, so be it; amen.
soixantaine (swasɑ̃tɛn), s.f. Sixty, about sixty; some sixty (years of age).
soixante (swasɑ̃t), adj. num. [L *sexaginta*] Sixty; *~-dix*, seventy.
soixantième (swasɑ̃tjɛm), adj. num. ord., s.m. Sixtieth, sixtieth part.
sol (sɔl), s.m. [L *solum*] **1.** Soil, ground; *cloué au ~*, rooted to the spot; **2.** [f. L *solidus*] (obs.) sou, penny.
sol (sɔl), s.m. [f. *solve*] (mus.) Sol, G; *clé de ~*, G clef.
solaire (sɔlɛr), adj. [L *solaris*] Solar; *cadran ~*, sun-dial; *éclipse ~*, solar eclipse.

ɔ, n*o*te, gl*o*tte; ɔ̃, m*on*ter, r*on*de; ø, f*eu*, cr*eu*x; œ, p*eu*r, s*œu*r; œ̃, *un*; ʃ, *ch*ez, *sch*isme;
u, t*ou*t; w, *ou*i, d*o*it, d*ou*aire; y, m*u*r, p*u*; ɥ, h*u*ile, m*u*ette; z, *z*èle, ro*s*e; ʒ, dé*j*à, *g*entil.

solanées (sɔlane), s.f.pl. (bot.) Solanaceae.
solbature (sɔlbatyr), s.f. (vet.) Surbating, foundering, soreness (of horses' feet).
soldanelle (sɔldanɛl), s.f. (bot.) Soldanel, soldanella.
soldat (sɔlda), s.m. [It. *soldato*] Soldier, private; syn. TROUPIER, and (slang) TROUFION. ⚠ *Troupier* = private, tommy; but in English 'trooper' means private soldier in cavalry = *cavalier, soldat de cavalerie.*
soldatesque (sɔldatɛsk), s.f. (pej.) Soldiery, unruly troop of soldiers. ~, adj. Soldierly.
solde[1] (sɔld), s.f. [It. *soldo*] Pay; *demi-~*, half-pay; *être à la ~ de X*, to be in X's pay.
solde[2] (sɔld), s.m. (comm.) **1.** Settlement, cash balance; *pour ~ de tout compte*, in full settlement of all demands; **2.** clearance sale, job lot, surplus stock, goods sold 'at a sacrifice'; *journée des ~s*, bargain-day.
solder (sɔlde), v.a. **1.** To pay, to have in one's pay; **2.** to settle (an account), to pay; **3.** to sell at a reduced price, to sell off, to clear; **se** ~, v.pr. to be balanced; to result (*par*, in).
sole[1] (sɔl), s.f. [L *solum*] (agric.) Sole (portion of ground to receive a succession of different crops).
sole[2] (sɔl), s.f. [L *solea*] Sole (of animal's foot); (ichth.) sole; (techn.) sole, sleeper.
soléaire (soleɛr), adj. [f. *sole*] (anat.) Solear; *muscle ~*, soleus.
solécisme (sɔlesism), s.m. [Gr. *soloikismos*] Solecism.
soleil (sɔlɛj), s.m. [f. L *sol*] Sun, sunshine; (bot.) sunflower; (fireworks) catherine-wheel; *au ~*, in the sun; *se chauffer au ~*, to sun oneself; to bask in the sun; *au ~ couchant*, at sunset; (fig.) *avoir du bien au ~*, to have landed property; *coup de ~*, sunstroke; *il fait du ~*, the sun is shining; *rien de nouveau sous le ~*, nothing new under the sun; (colloq.) *piquer un ~*, to blush suddenly and intensely.
solen (sɔlɛn), s.m. [Gr. *sōlēn*] (ichth.) Solen, razor-shell; syn. MANCHE DE COUTEAU.
solennel, -le (sɔlanɛl), adj. [L *solemnis*] Solemn, formal; official.
solennellement (sɔlanɛlmɑ̃), adv. Solemnly, formally, in state, officially.
solennisation (sɔlaniza'sjɔ̃), s.f. Solemnization.
solenniser (sɔlanize), v.a. To solemnize.
solennité (sɔlanite), s.f. Solemnity, ceremony, celebration.
solénoïde (sɔlenɔid), s.m. (phys.) Solenoid.
solfatare (sɔlfatar), s.f. [It. *solfatara*] Solfatara.
solfège (sɔlfɛʒ), s.m. [It. *solfeggio*] (mus.) Solfeggio, sol-fa.
solfier (sɔlfje), v.a. (mus.) To sol-fa.
solidaire (sɔlidɛr), adj. [f. L *solidus*] Jointly and severally answerable, jointly responsible; solidary.
solidairement (sɔlidɛrmɑ̃), adv. Jointly and severally, solidarily.
solidariser (sɔlidarize), v.a. To render jointly liable; **se** ~, v.pr. to join together in liability; (fig.) *se ~ avec X*, to espouse X's cause.
solidarité (sɔlidarite), s.f. Solidarity.
solide (sɔlid), adj. [L *solidus*] Solid, strong, substantial, firm, stout, robust, true, weighty; *un esprit ~*, a sound mind; *de ~s raisons*, sound arguments; *il est ~ au poste*, he is to be depended upon. ~, s.m. Solid; (fig.) real, reality, that which is permanent.
solidement (sɔlidmɑ̃), adv. Solidly, firmly, strongly; soundly.
solidification (sɔlidifika'sjɔ̃), s.f. Solidification.
solidifier (sɔlidifje), v.a. To solidify; **se** ~, v.pr. to become solid, to solidify.
solidité (sɔlidite), s.f. Solidity; solidness; firmness, strength; soundness.
soliloque (sɔlilɔk), s.m. [f. L *solus*+*loqui*] Soliloquy.
solin (sɔlɛ̃), s.m. [f. *sole*[2]] (build.) Space between rafters.
solipède (sɔlipɛd), adj. s.m. [L *solus*+*pes*] Soliped.
soliste (sɔlist), s.m.f. Soloist, solo player, solo singer.
solitaire (sɔlitɛr), adj. [L *solitarius*] Solitary; isolated; alone; lonely; *ver ~*, tapeworm, taenia. ~, s.m. **1.** Hermit; **2.** solitaire (diamond); **3.** old boar; **4.** solitaire (game).
solitairement (sɔlitɛrmɑ̃), adv. Solitarily.
solitude (sɔlityd), s.f. [L *solitudo*] Solitude, loneliness, isolation; *rechercher la ~*, to seek solitude.
solivage (sɔlivaʒ), s.m. The joists.
solive (sɔliv), s.f. [f. *sole*[2]] Joist.
soliveau (pl. **-x**) (sɔlivo), s.m. Small joist; (fig.) blockhead, dunce, moron, chump.
sollicitation (sɔllisita'sjɔ̃), s.f. Entreaty, solicitation, request.
solliciter (sɔllisite), v.a. [L *sollicitare*] To incite; to entreat, to solicit, to request, to beg, to beseech, to ask earnestly. ⚠ In English 'to solicit' is also frequently used in the sense of to importune, to entice = *racoler, raccrocher.*
solliciteu-r, -se (sɔllisitœr), s.m.f. Petitioner, person going a-begging (for situation, money, favour, &c.).
sollicitude (sɔllisityd), s.f. [L *sollicitudo*] Solicitude, care, concern.
solo (sɔlo), s.m. [It. wd] Solo.
solognot, -e (sɔlɔɲo), adj. s.m.f. (Native) of Sologne (French province).
solstice (sɔlstis), s.m. [f. L *solstitium*] Solstice.

solsticial, -e, (aux) (sɔlstisjal), adj. Solstitial.

solubilité (sɔlybilite), s.f. Solubility.

soluble (sɔlybl), adj. [L *solubilis*] Soluble; solvable; *problème* ~, problem that can be solved.

solution (sɔlysjɔ̃), s.f. [L *solutio*] **1.** Solution, dissolving; **2.** solution, mixture containing a substance dissolved in a solvent; **3.** resolution, solution; solving, answer (to problem, enigma, &c.); **4.** separation; ~ *de continuité*, solution of continuity; (motor.) ~ *anti-gel*, anti-freezing mixture.

solvabilité (sɔlvabilite), s.f. Solvency.

solvable (sɔlvabl), adj. [f. L *solvere*] Solvent; ⚠ not 'solvable', which = *soluble*; *explicable*.

somatique (sɔmatik), adj. [f. Gr. *sōma*] Somatic, bodily, corporeal.

somatologie (sɔmatɔlɔʒi), s.f. [f. Gr. *sōmat(ikos)* + *logos*] Somatology.

sombre (sɔ̃br), adj. [f. L *sub*+*umbra*] Dark; sombre, gloomy, cloudy, overcast, melancholy, dismal; *rouge* ~, dark red; *humeur* ~, gloomy disposition; *de* ~*s perspectives*, sombre prospects.

sombrer[1] (sɔ̃bre), v.n. (naut.) To founder, to go down, to sink; (fig.) to collapse, to fail, to go to ruin; (mus.) ~ *sa voix*, to make one's voice sound deep and soft and tragic.

sombrer[2] (sɔ̃bre), v.a. (agric.) To give a first dressing to.

sombrero (sɔ̃brero), s.m. [Span. wd] Sombrero.

sommaire (sɔmɛr), adj. [L *summarius*] Summary, abridged, compendious, sketchy; *justice* ~, summary justice. ~, s.m. Summary, epitome, abstract, abridgement.

sommairement (sɔmmɛrmɑ̃), adv. Summarily, briefly, sketchily.

sommation (sɔma'sjɔ̃), s.f. Summons; *faire une* ~ *à X*, to summon X; *faire les trois* ~*s*, to read the Riot Act; (math.) summation.

somme[1] (sɔm), s.f. [L *summa*] Sum, total, amount; summa, summary, a title of books; compendium; *en* ~, ~ *toute*, on the whole, finally, after all.

somme[2] (sɔm), s.f. [f. LL *salma*] Burden; *bête de* ~, beast of burden.

somme[3] (sɔm), s.m. [L *somnus*] Nap, sleep; *faire un petit* ~, to have forty winks.

sommeil (sɔmɛj), s.m. [L *somniculus*] Sleep; *avoir* ~, to be sleepy; *avoir le* ~ *léger* (*dur*), to be a light (heavy) sleeper; *tomber de* ~, to be overcome with sleep; *dormir de son dernier* ~, to sleep one's last sleep; *dormir d'un* ~ *de plomb*, to sleep like a log; to sleep like a top.

sommeiller (sɔmɛje), v.n. To slumber, to doze; (fig.) to lie dormant.

sommeli-er, -ère (sɔmlje), s.m.f. Butler, cellarman.

sommer (sɔmme), v.a. To summon, to call upon; ~ *une place de se rendre*, to summon a fortress to surrender.

sommet (sɔmɛ), s.m. [L *summum*] Top, summit; (fig.) acme, pinnacle; (bot.) apex; (geom.) vertex.

sommier (sɔmje), s.m. Spring mattress, upholstered or box spring mattress; (arch.) summer, breastsummer; beast of burden; (comm.) day-book.

sommité (sɔmite), s.f. [L *summitas*] Top, head; prominent people, leader, influential person.

somnambule (sɔmnɑ̃byl), s.m.f. [L *somnus*+ *ambulare*] Somnambulist.

somnambulisme (sɔmnɑ̃bylism), s.m. Somnambulism.

somnifère (sɔmnifɛr), adj. [L *somnus*+ *ferre*] Somniferous, soporific. ~, s.m. Opiate, soporific.

somnolence (sɔmnɔlɑ̃s), s.f. [L *somnolentia*] Somnolence, drowsiness.

somnolent, -e (sɔmnɔlɑ̃), adj. Somnolent, drowsy.

somnoler (sɔmnɔle), v.n. To doze.

somptuaire (sɔ̃ptɥɛr), adj. [f. L *sumptus*] Sumptuary.

somptueusement (sɔ̃ptɥøzmɑ̃), adv. Sumptuously, magnificently.

somptueu-x, -se (sɔ̃ptɥø), adj. [f. L *sumptus*] Sumptuous, magnificent, gorgeous.

somptuosité (sɔ̃ptɥozite), s.f. Sumptuousness, magnificence, gorgeousness.

son, sa (pl. **ses**) (sɔ̃, sa, sɛ), adj. poss. His, her, its, one's; (before a vowel or a silent h *son* is used for the fem. instead of *sa*, ex. *son amie*, *son héroïne*).

son[1] (sɔ̃), s.m. [L *sonus*] Sound.

son[2] (sɔ̃), s.m. [LL *seonnum*] Bran; *taches de* ~, freckles.

sonate (sɔnat), s.f. [It. *sonata*] Sonata.

sondage (sɔ̃daʒ), s.m. (naut.) Sounding; (min.) boring; (med.) probing; *faire un* ~, to sound; (fig.) to sound, to probe.

sonde (sɔ̃d), s.f. [f. *sonder*] (naut.) Sounding-line, sounding-rod, lead; (min.) bore; (surg.) probe; *jeter la* ~, to heave the lead.

sonder (sɔ̃de), v.a. [LL *subundare*] To sound, to probe, to try, to fathom; (naut.) to sound, to take soundings in; (fig.) ~ *X*, to sound X; ~ *les intentions de X*, to sound or probe X's intentions; ~ *le terrain*, to feel one's ground, to see how the land lies.

sondeur (sɔ̃dœr), s.m. Leadsman.

songe (sɔ̃ʒ), s.m. [L *somnium*] Dream; *en* ~, in a dream; ~*-creux*, s.m. wool-gatherer, dreamer, visionary.

songer (sɔ̃ʒe), v.n. [L *somniare*] **1.** To dream, to have dreams, to think idly, to muse; **2.** to think (*à*, of), to intend, to purpose; *songez à ce que vous dites*, think of

what you are saying; *songez à ce que vous allez faire*, mind what you are about; *maintenant que j'y songe*, now that I think of it; *vous n'y songez pas!*, you don't mean it!; you would not think of such a thing!; *il songe à se marier*, he thinks of getting married.
songerie (sɔ̃ʒri), s.f. Day-dream, musing, reverie.
songeu-r, -se (sɔ̃ʒœr), adj. Dreamy, pre-occupied, thoughtful, lost in thought. ~, s.m.f. Dreamer, thinker, thoughtful person.
sonnaille (sɔnɑj), s.f. Bell, cattle-bell.
sonnailler (sɔnɑje), v.n. To keep ringing. ~, s.m. Bell-wether.
sonnant, -e (sɔnɑ̃), p. adj. Sounding, ringing; *à 6 heures ~es*, at 6 o'clock sharp; *espèces ~es*, hard cash.
sonné, -e (sɔne), p. adj. Past; *il est 6 heures ~es*, it has struck 6; *il a 50 ans ~s*, he is turned 50 years old; he has turned 50; he is over 50.
sonner (sɔne), v.a.n. [L *sonare*] To ring, to sound, to tinkle, to strike, to ring for; *les cloches sonnent*, the bells are ringing; *on sonne*, there is a ring at the door; *midi sonne*, it is striking 12; *ce mot sonne mal*, this word sounds unpleasant; *faire ~ ses mérites*, to sound one's own praises; to trumpet one's own merits; *cela sonne creux*, that sounds hollow; *sonnez la femme de chambre*, ring for the housemaid; (mil.) *~ la charge*, to sound the charge; *il n'a plus sonné mot*, after that he did not utter a word; (slang) to kill or stun a person by striking his head against a wall or the ground.
sonnerie (sɔnri), s.f. Ring, ringing, chime; striking apparatus (of clock); bells, set of bells.
sonnet (sɔnɛ), s.m. [It. *sonetto*] Sonnet.
sonnette (sɔnɛt), s.f. Bell, house-bell, electric bell; (mech.) pile-driving engine.
sonneur (sɔnœr), s.m. Bell-ringer.
sonomètre (sɔnɔmɛtr), s.m. [L *sonus*+ (Gr.) *metron*] Sonometer.
sonore (sɔnɔr), adj. [L *sonorus*] Sonorous, resonant, loud-sounding; (fig.) emphatic, high-sounding.
sonorité (sɔnɔrite), s.f. Sonorousness, sonority.
sopha (sɔfa), s.m. See SOFA.
sophi (sɔfi), s.m. See SOFI.
sophisme (sɔfism), s.m. [Gr. *sophisma*] Sophism, fallacious argument.
sophiste (sɔfist), s.m.f. Sophist.
sophistication (sɔfistikaˈsjɔ̃), s.f. Sophistication, adulteration.
sophistique (sɔfistik), adj. Sophistical. ~, s.f. Sophistry.
sophistiquer (sɔfistike), v.n. To subtilize to excess; ~, v.a. to adulterate.
sophora (sɔfɔra), s.m. (bot.) Sophora.
soporati-f, -ve, soporifique (sɔpɔratif, sɔpɔrifik), adj. [f. L *sopor*] Soporiferous, soporific; (fig.) tedious, soporific.
sopraniste (sɔpranist), s.m. Soprano; treble singer.
soprano (sɔprano), s.m. [It. wd] Soprano, treble.
sorbe (sɔrb), s.f. Sorb-apple.
sorbet (sɔrbɛ), s.m. [Turk. *shorbat*] Sorbet, sherbet.
sorbétière (sɔrbɛtjɛr), s.f. Ice-mould, ice-pail.
sorbier (sɔrbje), s.m. (bot.) Sorb-tree, service-tree; *~ des oiseaux*, mountain-ash, rowan-tree.
sorbonique (sɔrbɔnik), adj. [f. *R. de Sorbon*] Pertaining to the Sorbonne.
sorboniste (sɔrbɔnist) (obs.), s.m. Student or doctor of the University of Paris, *la Sorbonne*.
sorcellerie (sɔrsɛlri), s.f. [f. *sorcier*] Witchcraft, sorcery.
sorcier (sɔrsje), s.m. [LL *sortiarius*] Sorcerer, wizard, enchanter, magician, conjuror; *il n'est pas grand ~*, he won't set the Thames on fire. (colloq.) ~, adj. invar. *Vous avez trouvé cela, ce n'était pas bien ~!*, you found that out, it was not very difficult!
sorcière (sɔrsjɛr), s.f. [fem. of *sorcier*] Witch, sorceress, enchantress, conjuror; (fig.) *une vieille ~*, an old hag; *faite comme une ~*, dressed in sordid, unbecoming garments.
sordide (sɔrdid), adj. [L *sordidus*] Sordid, mean.
sordidement (sɔrdidmɑ̃), adv. Sordidly, meanly, stingily, miserably.
sordidité (sɔrdidite), s.f. Sordidness.
sore (sɔr), s.m. [Gr. *sōros*] (bot.) Sorus (reproductive organ in ferns).
sorgho (sɔrgo), s.m. [It. *sorgo*] (bot.) Sorghum; Indian millet.
sorite (sɔrit), s.m. [Gr. *sōreitēs*] (log.) Sorites.
sornette (sɔrnɛt), s.f. Nonsense, idle talk, stupid talk; *~s que tout cela!*, nonsense!
sort (sɔr), s.m. [L *sors*] Fate, lot, destiny, state, chance; spell, charm; hazard, chance; *jeter un ~ à X*, to cast a spell over X; *le ~ en est jeté!*, the die is cast!; *tirer au ~*, to draw lots; *améliorer son ~*, to improve one's condition; *le ~ des armes*, the chances of war; *faire un ~ à X*, to provide for X; *faire un ~ à tous les mots*, to lay emphasis upon each word. ⚠ Not 'sort', which = *sorte*.
sortable (sɔrtabl), adj. Suitable, acceptable.
sortant, -e (sɔrtɑ̃), adj. Outgoing, leaving office; drawn (of a number in lottery, &c.). *Les entrants et les ~s*, those coming in and those going out.
sorte (sɔrt), s.f. [L *sors*] Sort, kind,

species; manner, way; *toutes ~s de*, all kinds of; *de toute ~*, of every kind; of every description; *une ~ de*, a kind of; *de la ~*, thus, in this way; *de telle ~*, in such a manner; *de la bonne ~*, properly, firmly; *d'aucune ~*, in no wise; *de ~ que, en ~ que*, so that, in such a way that; *en quelque ~*, in a way, in some sort, in some degree.

sortie (sɔrti), s.f. Going out, coming out; (theatr.) exit; way out; egress; outlet; sally, outburst, tirade; *faire une ~ à X*, to give it to X; to blow X up; *faire une fausse ~*, to make a sham exit; *se ménager une ~*, to manage so as to be able to back out; *droit de ~*, export duty; *~ de bal*, opera-cloak.

sortilège (sɔrtilɛʒ), s.m. [f. L *sors+legere*] Witchcraft, charm, spell.

sortir (sɔrtir), v.n. [orig. dub.] To go out, to come out, to come forth, to leave, to leave the room, to make one's exit, to depart; to emerge, to issue, to spring, to take rise, to have origin; (paint.) to stand out; to go frequently to parties, dinners, &c.; *il sort d'ici*, he has just gone out; *~ de l'enfance*, to be no longer a child; to be growing up; *~ de maladie*, to recover from an illness; *~ de son sujet, de la question*, to wander from one's subject, from the question; *~ de Polytechnique*, to have been a pupil of the *École Polytechnique*; *~ d'une bonne famille*, to come of a good family; *il le fait ~ des gonds*, he makes him fly into a passion; *les yeux lui sortent de la tête*, his eyes are starting out of their sockets; *vous en êtes bien sorti!*, you came out of it all right; *mais d'où sortez-vous?*, where have you come from?; don't you know that?; ~, v.a. to bring out, to pull out, to extricate; (law) to have, to obtain. ~, s.m. Coming out; *au ~ de l'enfance*, on ceasing to be a child; *au ~ du lit*, on getting out of bed.

sosie (sozi), s.m. [prop. n. in Molière's *Amphitryon*] Very image, double, second self.

sotie (sɔti), s.f. [f. *sot*] Satirical farce.

sot, -te (so, sɔt), adj. [LL *sottus*] Foolish, silly, senseless, ridiculous; sheepish; *demeurer tout ~*, to look rather foolish; *à ~te question point de réponse*, a silly question deserves no answer. ~, -te, s.m.f. Fool, blockhead, dolt; *un ~ en trois lettres*, a downright fool. ⚠ Not English 'sot' in the sense of confirmed drunkard, which = *ivrogne invétéré*.

sot-l'y-laisse (solilɛs), s.m. Parson's nose (titbit over a roast fowl's rump).

sottement (sɔtmɑ̃), adv. Foolishly, stupidly, sillily.

sottise (sɔtiz), s.f. Foolishness, silliness, stupidity; foolery, nonsense, silly trick, stupid blunder; abuse, insult; *dire des ~s à X*, to abuse X; to call X names; *commettre une ~*, to do a foolish thing, to make a foolish blunder, to blunder stupidly.

sou (pl. -s) (su), s.m. [L *solidus*] Sou, copper; *~ à ~*, a penny at a time; *n'avoir pas le ~, être sans le ~, n'avoir pas un ~ vaillant*, to be penniless; *il n'a pas le ~*, he has not a copper; *une petite robe de quatre ~s*, a cheap little frock; *cela vaut 100 francs comme un ~*, it's worth 100 francs if it's worth a sou; *le ~ du franc*, 5 per cent. commission.

soubassement (subɑsmɑ̃), s.m. Base, basement; valance (of bedstead).

soubresaut (subrəso), s.m. [L *super+saltus*] Start, jolt, shock, jerk.

soubrette (subrɛt), s.f. [Provenç. orig.] Soubrette, lady's-maid; (theatr.) abigail.

soubreveste (subrəvɛst), s.f. (obs.) Sleeveless upper coat.

souche (suʃ), s.f. [orig. dub.] **1.** Stump; **2.** counterfoil; **3.** chimney-stack; **4.** (fig.) stock, root, origin, family; *faire ~*, to found a family, to be the first of a line; **5.** blockhead.

souchet (suʃɛ), s.m. [f. OF *souchever*] **1.** (bot.) Galingale; **2.** (mason.) rag stone; **3.** shoveller duck.

souchetage (suʃtaʒ), s.m. Counting the stumps (of felled timber).

soucheteur (suʃtœr), s.m. Surveyor of woods.

souci[1] (susi), s.m. [f. *soucier*] Care, anxiety, concern, trouble, solicitude; *c'est là le moindre* (or *le cadet*) *de mes ~s*, that is the least of my worries; I don't care a fig for that; *être en ~ de X*, to be anxious about X; *cela lui cause du ~*, that makes him uneasy; *sans ~*, free from care; *dévoré de ~s*, care-laden, care-worn.

souci[2] (susi), s.m. [L *solsequia*] (bot.) Marigold; *~ d'eau*, marsh marigold.

(se) soucier (səsusje), v.pr. [f. L *sollicitare*] To care (*de*, for, about); to concern oneself (*de*, with); *il s'en soucie comme de l'an quarante* or *comme de sa première chemise*, he does not care a straw for it.

soucieusement (susjøzmɑ̃), adv. Carefully, anxiously, concernedly, with deep concern.

soucieu-x, -se (susjø), adj. Full of care, concerned, anxious, thoughtful, uneasy, care-laden.

soucoupe (sukup), s.f. [*sous+coupe*] Saucer.

soudain (sudɛ̃), adj. [L *subitaneus*] Sudden. ~, adv. Suddenly, all of a sudden.

soudainement (sudɛnmɑ̃), adv. Suddenly, all of a sudden, unexpectedly.

soudaineté (sudɛnte), s.f. Suddenness.

soudanien, -ne (sudanjɛ̃), **soudanais, -e** (sudane), adj. s.m.f. Sudanese, Soudanese.

soudard (sudar), s.m. [f. *solde*, OF *soude*] (pej.) Mercenary, hardened soldier, ruffian, rough soldier.

soude (sud), s.f. [LL *soda*] (bot.) Salsola, kali, saltwort; (chem.) soda.

souder (sude), v.a. [L *solidare*] To solder; to braze, to weld; (fig.) to unite, to join; **se ~**, v.pr. to unite, to be soldered, joined; *fer à ~*, soldering-iron.

soudoyer (sudwaje), v.a. [f. *solde*] To keep in one's pay; to hire, to subsidize; to bribe.

soudure (sudyr), s.f. **1.** Solder; **2.** soldering; welding; (fig.) joining; *~ autogène*, autogenous welding.

soue (su), s.f. [f. L *sus*] Pigsty.

soufflage (suflaʒ), s.m. **1.** Glass-blowing; **2.** (naut.) sheathing, furring.

souffle (sufl), s.m. Breath, puff; expiration; exhalation; gentle breeze, effluvium; (fig.) inspiration; *il n'a plus que le ~*, he is at the point of death; *il n'y a pas un ~ de vent*, there is not a breath of air; *jusqu'à mon dernier ~*, till my last breath; *être à bout de ~*, to be winded; to be out of breath; (fig.) to be exhausted; *retenir son ~*, to hold one's breath.

soufflé, -e (sufle), s.m. (cook.) Soufflé dish, soufflé. ~, p. adj. Puffed.

souffler (sufle), v.n.a. [L *sufflare*] To breathe, to blow, to blow out, to pant, to catch one's breath; (theatr.) to prompt; (games) to huff; (naut.) to sheathe; (colloq.) to do somebody out of (something); *~ la bougie*, to blow out the candle; *laissez-le ~!*, let him take breath a moment!; *~ le feu*, to blow the fire; (fig.) to make things worse; *~ le chaud et le froid*, to blow both hot and cold; *~ l'orgue*, to blow the organ; *~ le verre*, to blow glass; *il n'a pas soufflé mot*, he did not utter a word; *surtout n'en soufflez mot à personne*, be sure not to breathe a word of that to anybody; *regarder d'où souffle le vent*, to see which way the wind blows; *~ une dame*, to huff a queen; *on vous soufflera cette affaire*, somebody is sure to do you out of this bargain; you will be forestalled.

soufflerie (sufləri), s.f. Bellows (of an organ, &c.); blast apparatus.

soufflet (suflɛ), s.m. **1.** Bellows (plur.); (of a carriage) hood; **2.** slap in the face; box on the ear; (fig.) affront, mortification, rebuke; *donner un ~ à Vaugelas*, to murder the King's English; *elle a reçu là un rude ~*, it was a mortifying blow for her.

souffleter (sufləte), v.a. To slap, to box the ears of, to give a slap in the face to; (fig.) to insult, to outrage.

souffleur (suflœr), s.m. (theatr.) Prompter; (techn.) blower; (ichth.) blower.

soufflure (suflyr), s.f. (techn.) Blow-hole, air-hole; flaw.

souffrance (sufrɑ̃s), s.f. [f. *souffrir*] Suffering, pain, ache; sufferance, delay, suspense; *en ~*, in suspense, at a standstill; *jour de ~*, borrowed light.

souffrant, -e (sufrɑ̃), p. adj. Unwell, ill, sickly; suffering, long-suffering, ailing; patient; *il n'est pas d'humeur ~e*, he is not of a very patient temper; *elle est toujours ~e*, she is perpetually ailing.

souffre-douleur (sufrədulœr), s.m. invar. Butt, laughing-stock, drudge, victim.

souffreteu-x, -se (sufrətø), adj. [f. L *suffractus*] Miserable, ailing, sickly, weakly.

souffrir (sufrir), v.a.n. [L *sufferre*] To suffer, to bear, to endure, to stand; to allow, to tolerate, to put up with, to admit of; *~ la soif*, to endure thirst; *~ mort et passion*, *~ le martyre*; to endure excruciating pain; to be on the rack; to be racked with pain; *elle ne peut ~ la vue du sang*, she cannot bear the sight of blood; *souffrez que je vous aide*, allow me to help you; *vous ne devez pas ~ cela*, you must not put up with this; *cette affaire ne souffre aucun retard*, this matter admits of no delay; *ma jambe me fait ~*, my leg is aching; *pourquoi me faites-vous ~ ainsi?*, why are you paining me so?; *ils ne peuvent se ~*, they cannot bear each other.

soufrage (sufraʒ), s.m. Sulphuring.

soufre (sufr), s.m. [L *sulphur*] Sulphur: S; brimstone; *fleur de ~*, flower of sulphur.

soufrer (sufre), v.a. To sulphur, to dip in brimstone, to fumigate or sprinkle with sulphur.

soufrière (sufriɛr), s.f. Sulphur-mine.

soufroir (sufrwar), s.m. Sulphuring-stone (for wool).

souhait (suɛ), s.m. [f. *souhaiter*] Wish, desire; *~s de nouvel an*, best wishes for a happy new year; *à ~*, capitally; awfully well; as one would have it; (after somebody has sneezed) *à vos ~s!*, God bless you!

souhaitable (suɛtabl), adj. Desirable.

souhaiter (suɛte), v.a. [f. OF *haiter* = to cheer] To wish, to wish for, to desire; *~ le bonjour*, to say good morning; *souhaitez-lui le bonjour de ma part*, remember me to him; *~ la gloire*, to wish for fame; (colloq.) *je t'en souhaite!*, don't you wish you may get it!

souillard (sujar), s.m. Hole, sink.

souillarde (sujard), s.f. Scullery.

souille (suj), s.f. [f. L *suile*] **1.** (hunt.) Wallowing-place (of wild boar, &c); **2.** (naut.) bed (of ship.)

souiller (suje), v.a. [f. *souille*] To soil, to dirty; to pollute, to sully, to defile.

souillon (sujɔ̃), s.f.m. Scullion; slut; sloven, slattern.

souillure (sujyr), s.f. Stain, dirt; defilement, pollution; (fig.) blot, taint, defilement.

soûl, -e, saoul, -e (su), adj. [L *satullus*] Full, drunk; (fig.) glutted, satiated; sick (of); surfeited (*de*, with); ~ *comme une grive* or *un Polonais*, as drunk as a lord; *laissez-le parler tout son* ~, let him talk to his heart's content.

soulagement (sulaʒmɑ̃), s.m. Alleviation, ease, relief, comfort, solace; *apporter du* ~, to give some relief, to comfort.

soulager (sulaʒe), v.a. [L *sublevare*] To relieve, to alleviate, to comfort, to solace, to ease, to allay, to help, to assist; **se** ~, v.pr. to relieve oneself; (colloq.) to make water; to have a motion.

soûlard, -e (sular), s.m.f. Drunkard.

soûler, saouler (sule), v.a. [f. *soûl*] To make drunk; (fig.) to surfeit, to glut, to intoxicate; **se** ~, v.pr. to get drunk; to satiate oneself (*de*, with).

soûlerie, saoulerie (sulri), s.f. Drinking-bout.

soulèvement (sulɛvmɑ̃), s.m. Rising, swelling, heaving, upheaval; riot, revolt, insurrection.

soulever (sulve), v.a. [*sous*+*lever*] To raise, to lift; to take up; to excite, to agitate, to stir up, to rouse, to provoke, to urge to insurrection; *cela me soulève le cœur, le cœur me soulève*, this turns my stomach; it makes me sick; ~ *une question*, to raise a point; **se** ~, v.pr. to revolt, to rise in rebellion.

soulier (sulje), s.m. [LL *subtelare*] Shoe; *être dans ses petits* ~*s*, to be on pins and needles, to be uneasy in one's mind; ~*s ferrés*, hobnailed shoes.

soulignement (suliɲmɑ̃), s.m. Underlining.

souligner (suliɲe), v.a. To underline; (fig.) to lay stress on, to make conspicuous.

souloir (sulwar), v.n. [L *solere*] (obs.) To be in the habit of.

soulte (sult), s.f. [f. L *solvere*] Balance, compensation.

soumettre (sumɛtr), v.a. [*sous*+*mettre*] To submit, to subdue, to overcome, to bring into subjection; to make to undergo; to subject; ~ *la question à X*, to submit the matter to X; **se** ~, v.pr. to submit, to yield, to surrender, to give way, to comply.

soumis, -e (sumi), p. adj. Submissive, obedient, humble, dutiful; *fille* ~*e*, registered prostitute.

soumission (sumisjɔ̃), s.f. [L *submissio*] **1.** Submissiveness; **2.** surrender; **3.** tender for a contract.

soumissionnaire (sumisjonɛr), s.m.f. Tendering party.

soumissionner (sumisjone), v.a.n. To tender (*à*, for).

soupape (supap), s.f. Valve; ~ *d'admission*, inlet-valve; intake; ~ *d'alimentation*, supply-valve; ~ *d'arrêt*, check-valve, ~ *d'aspiration*, suction-valve; ~ *d'échappement*, exhaust-valve; ~ *qui fuit*, leaky valve; ~ *à gorge*, throttle-valve; ~ *de sûreté*, safety-valve; ~ *à tiroir*, slide-valve; ~*s commandées*, mechanically operated valves; (fig.) safety-valve.

soupçon (supsɔ̃), s.m. [L *suspectio*] Suspicion; surmise, conjecture; (colloq.) very small quantity, the least drop; *un* ~ *d'ail*, a touch of garlic; *un* ~ *de fièvre*, a slight touch of fever; *concevoir des* ~*s*, to entertain or have suspicions; (U.S.A. colloq.) to suspicion.

soupçonner (supsone), v.a. To suspect, to regard with suspicion, to have a suspicion of, to surmise; *on ne peut le* ~, he cannot be suspected; (U.S.A. colloq.) to suspicion.

soupçonneusement (supsonøzmɑ̃), adv. Suspiciously.

soupçonneu-x, -se (supsonø), adj. Suspicious, distrustful.

soupe (sup), s.f. [f. *souper*] Soup; ~ *grasse*, meat soup, broth; ~ *maigre*, vegetable soup; *assiette à* ~, soup-plate; *assiette de* ~, plate of soup; *tailler la* ~, to slice bread for the soup; *tremper la* ~, to pour the soup over the slices of bread; (fig.) *monter comme une* ~ *au lait*, to flare up like a bonfire; to fly into a passion without warning; *trempé comme une* ~, drenched to the skin.

soupente (supɑ̃t), s.f. Loft, garret; braces (of a coach).

souper (supe), s.m. Supper.

souper (supe), v.n. [OF *soper*] To have supper, to take supper; (colloq., vulg.) *j'en ai soupé!*, I am fed up with it (or him, her, &c.), I have had more than enough of it.

soupeser (supəze), v.a. [*sous*+*peser*] To try the weight of; to heft.

soupeu-r, -se (supœr), s.m.f. Person having supper.

soupière (supjɛr), s.f. [f. *soupe*] Soup-tureen.

soupir (supir), s.m. [f. *soupirer*] Sigh, gasp; (mus.) crotchet rest; *demi-* ~, quaver rest; *quart de* ~, semi-quaver rest; *pousser de profonds* ~*s*, to fetch deep sighs; *rendre le dernier* ~, to breathe one's last.

soupirail, (pl. **aux**) (supiraj), s.m. Air-hole.

soupirant (supirɑ̃), s.m. Wooer, suitor, lover, cicisbeo.

soupirer (supire), v.n. [L *suspirare*] To sigh, to fetch sighs, to breathe; to long; ~ *après la liberté*, to long for freedom; ~ *de chagrin*, to sigh for grief.

souple (supl), adj. [L *supplex*] Supple, pliant, flexible, lissom; (bookbind.) limp; (fig.) yielding, pliant, tractable, docile; *avoir l'échine* ~, to cringe, to be servile.

souplement (supləmɑ̃), adv. Pliantly, flexibly, adroitly, agilely, supplely.

souplesse (suplɛs), s.f. Suppleness, flexibility, litheness; ready compliance, pliancy.
souquenille (sukənij), s.f. Smock-frock; old long coat.
souquer (suke), v.n.a. [etym. dub.] (naut.) To stiffen, to row hard, to pull away; *souquez!*, swing on!
source (surs), s.f. [f. *sourdre*] Source, spring, fountain; fount, rise; origin; *avoir, prendre, sa ~ à*, to take its rise at; (fig.) *couler de ~*, to flow naturally; *eau de ~*, spring-water; *je tiens cela de bonne ~*, I have it on good authority; *remonter à la ~ du mal*, to trace the evil back to its origin.
sourcier (sursje), s.m. Spring-finder, water-diviner, dowser.
sourcil (sursi), s.m. [L *supercilium*] Eyebrow; *froncer les ~s*, to knit one's brow, to frown.
sourcili-er, -ère (sursilje), adj. (anat.) Superciliary.
sourciller (sursije), v.n. To frown, to wince; *il a écouté cela sans ~*, he heard it without wincing, or without moving a muscle of his face.
sourcilleu-x, -se (sursijø), adj. Supercilious, haughty, lofty; towering.
sourd, -e (sur), adj. [L *surdus*] Deaf; muffled; (fig.) deaf, insensible; underhand; vague; *un bruit ~*, a muffled sound; *douleur ~e*, dull pain; *faire la ~e oreille*, to turn a deaf ear; *de ~es menées*, underhand dealings; *lanterne ~e*, dark lantern; *crier comme un ~*, to speak too loud; *frapper comme un ~*, to beat or strike unmercifully; *~ comme un pot*, as deaf as a post; *il n'est pire ~ que celui qui ne veut pas entendre*, none so deaf as those who will not hear; *être ~ à la pitié*, to be insensible, to be deaf, to pity; to be pitiless; *une voix ~e*, a dull voice, a muffled tone.
sourdement (surdəmɑ̃), adv. Indistinctly, rumblingly; secretly.
sourdine (surdin), s.f. (mus.) Mute, sordine; damper; *jouer en ~*, to play pianissimo; (fig.) *mettre une ~ à son langage*, to moderate one's way of speaking; *en ~*, on the sly.
sourd-muet, sourde-muette (surmɥɛ), s.m.f. Deaf and dumb person.
sourdre (surdr), v.n. [L *surgere*] To spring up, to rise, to gush forth.
souriant, -e (surjɑ̃), p. adj. Smiling; prepossessing, attractive.
souriceau (pl. -x) (suriso), s.m. Little mouse.
souricière (surisjɛr), s.f. Mouse-trap; (fig.) snare, police-trap.
souriquois, -e (surikwa), adj. (infrequent) Of mice; *la gent ~e*, the mouse tribe; the murine race.
sourire (surir), v.n. [L *subridere*] To smile (*de*, at); *cela me sourit assez*, this takes my fancy; I rather like this; *la fortune lui sourit toujours*, fortune always smiles on him.
sourire (surir), s.m. Smile; *~ moqueur*, sneer; (colloq.) *tout prendre avec le ~*, to put a good face on the matter.
souris[1] (suri), s.m. invar. Slight graceful smile.
souris[2] (suri), s.f. invar. [L *sorex*] Mouse (pl. mice); *éveillée comme une ~*, as brisk as a bee; *gris ~*, mouse-grey, mouse-colour; *on entendrait trotter une ~*, you could hear a pin drop; *~ qui n'a qu'un trou est bientôt prise*, it is well to have more than one string to one's bow; *trou de ~*, mouse-hole; *~ d'hôtel*, hotel-thief (woman).
sournois, -e (surnwa), adj. [orig. dub.] Sly, deep, hypocritical; underhand; (colloq.) *petit ~!*, slyboots!
sournoisement (surnwazmɑ̃), adv. Slyly, cunningly; underhand.
sournoiserie (surnwazri), s.f. Slyness, dissembling, hypocrisy, trickery.
sous (su), prep. [L *subtus*] Under; beneath, before; *~ les armes*, under arms; *avoir quelque chose ~ la main*, to have something close at hand; *regardez X ~ le nez*, to stare X in the face; *~ peu de jours, ~ peu*, in a few days, in a short time; shortly; soon; *~ prétexte de*, on the pretence of, under the pretext of; *~ le sceau du secret*, under the seal of secrecy; *~ serment*, upon oath; *~ peine de mort*, upon pain of death; *~ peine d'amende*, under penalty of a fine; *~ presse*, in the press; *~ un faux nom*, under a borrowed name; *cela s'est passé ~ mes yeux*, it happened under my own eyes; *mettre ~ les yeux de X*, to put before X; (in comp.) ~- . . . , under-, sub-, deputy-, assistant.
sous-affermer (suzafɛrme), v.a. To sublet; to take as sub-tenant.
sous-amendement (suzamɑ̃dmɑ̃), s.m. Amendment to an amendment.
sous-barbe, soubarbe (subarb), s.f. invar. **1.** Under-jaw of a horse; **2.** piece of harness; **3.** (naut.) bobstay.
sous-bibliothécaire (subibliotekɛr), s.m.f. Assistant librarian.
sous-bois (subwa), s.m. invar. Undergrowth; (paint.) forest landscape.
sous-bras (subra), s.m. invar. Dress-preserver.
sous-chef (suʃɛf), s.m. Deputy head clerk; *~ de gare*, deputy station-master.
sous-clavi-er, -ère (suklavje), adj. (anat.) Subclavian.
sous-commissaire (sukɔmisɛr), s.m. Under-commissary; assistant commissary.
sous-commission (sukɔmisjɔ̃), s.f. Sub-committee.

souscripteur (suskriptœr), s.m. Subscriber.
souscription (suskripsjɔ̃), s.f. **1.** Subscription, signature; **2.** subscription, share-list; **3.** subscribing; **4.** amount subscribed.
souscrire (suskrir), v.a.n. [L *sub*+ *scribere*] To sign, to put one's name down (for), to subscribe, to take shares (in); (fig.) to agree (*à*, to), to give consent or assent (to); ~ *pour cent francs*, to subscribe 100 francs; ~ *à un choix*, to agree to a choice.
sous-cutané, -e (sukytane), adj. Subcutaneous.
sous-délégué, -e, sub-délégué, -e (sudelege, sybdelege), s.m.f. Subdelegate.
sous-direct-eur, -rice (sudirɛktœr), s.m.f. Under-manager,under-manageress; assistant head master or head mistress.
sous-dominante (sudɔminɑ̃t), s.f. (mus.) Subdominant.
sous-entendre (suzɑ̃tɑ̃dr), v.a. To imply.
sous-entendu (suzɑ̃tɑ̃dy), s.m. Implication; double meaning; double entendre; mental reservation.
sous-entente (suzɑ̃tɑ̃t), s.f. Mental reservation; double meaning.
sous-faîte (sufɛt), s.m. (build.) King-post; under-ridgeboard.
sous-ferme (sufɛrm), s.f. Sub-lease.
sous-garde (sugard), s.f. Guard (of trigger in fire-arms).
sous-genre (suʒɑ̃r), s.m. Subgenus.
sous-gorge (sugɔrʒ), s.f. Throat-band (of harness).
sous-jacent, -e (suʒasɑ̃), adj. Subjacent, underlying.
sous-lieutenant (suljœtnɑ̃), s.m. Second lieutenant; sub-lieutenant; ensign.
sous-locataire (sulɔkatɛr), s.m.f. Under-tenant, subtenant.
sous-location (sulɔka'sjɔ̃), s.f. Under-letting, sub-letting; subtenancy.
sous-louer (sulue), v.a. **1.** To sub-let; **2.** to rent from the tenant, to take as subtenant.
sous-main (sumɛ̃), s.m. invar. Blotting-pad, writing-pad.
sous-maître, -sse (sumɛtr), s.m.f. Assistant master; usher; assistant mistress.
sous-marin, -e (sumarɛ̃), adj. Submarine. ~, s.m. Submarine (boat).
sous-maxillaire (sumaksillɛr), adj. (anat.) Submaxillary.
sous-multiple (sumyltipl), adj. s.m. Submultiple.
sous-normale (sunɔrmal), s.f. (geom.) Subnormal.
sous-œuvre (suzøvr), s.m. Underpinning, shoring up; *reprendre en* ~, to underpin.
sous-officier (suzɔfisje), s.m. Non-commissioned officer; (colloq.) *sous-off*, non-com., N.C.O.
sous-ordre (suzɔrdr), s.m. **1.** Subordinate; **2.** (nat. hist.) suborder; *en* ~, in a subordinate capacity.
sous-perpendiculaire (supɛrpɑ̃dikylɛr), s.f. See syn. SOUS-NORMALE.
sous-pied (supje), s.m. Trouser-strap, gaiter-strap.
sous-préfecture (suprefɛktyr), s.f. Sub-prefecture.
sous-préfet (suprefɛ), s.m. (French admin.) Sub-prefect; sous-préfet; *sous-préfète*, wife of a sous-préfet.
sous-produit (suprɔdɥi), s.m. By-product.
sous-secrétaire, (susəkretɛr), s.m.f. Under-secretary.
sous-secrétariat (susəkretarja), s.m. Under-secretaryship, under-secretariat(e).
sous-seing (susɛ̃), s.m. Private deed.
soussigné, -e (susiɲe), adj. s.m.f. Undersigned; *Je*, ~, I, the undersigned; *les* ~*s*, the undersigned.
sous-sol (susɔl), s.m. **1.** Basement; **2.** subsoil, substratum.
sous-tangente (sutɑ̃ʒɑ̃t), s.f. (geom.) Subtangent.
sous-tendre (sutɑ̃dr), v.a. (geom.) To subtend.
sous-titre (sutitr), s.m. Sub-title, sub-head.
soustracti-f, -ve (sustraktif), adj. (alg.) Subtractive.
soustraction (sustraksjɔ̃), s.f. Abstraction; taking away; theft; (arith.) subtraction.
soustraire (sustrɛr), v.a. [L *sub*+*trahere*] To abstract, to take away, to remove, to purloin; to steal; to withdraw, to lead away, to protect, to shield, to screen, to save; (arith.) to subtract, to deduct; *des papiers ont été soustraits*, documents have been stolen; ~ *X au châtiment*, to save X from punishment; **se** ~, v.pr. to get away (*à*, from), to escape, to flee; *se* ~ *à la justice*, to abscond from justice.
sous-traitant (sutrɛtɑ̃), s.m. Sub-contractor.
sous-traité (sutrɛte), s.m. Sub-contract.
soustylaire (sustilɛr), s.f. Substyle (of sun-dial).
sous-ventrière (suvɑ̃triɛr), s.f. (harness) Belly-band.
sous-verge (suvɛrʒ), s.m. invar. Led horse on off side of another carrying a rider.
soutache (sutaʃ), s.f. [f. Hungar. *szuszak*] Braid.
soutacher (sutaʃe), v.a. To braid.
soutane (sutan), s.f. [It. *sottana*] Cassock; (fig.) *la* ~, the cloth; *prendre la* ~, to become a priest.
soutanelle (sutanɛl), s.f. Short cassock.
soute (sut), s.f. [f. L *substare*] (naut.) Bunker; coal-bunker; store-room; ~ *aux poudres*, powder-magazine.

soutenable (sutənabl), adj. Tenable; tolerable; sustainable.
soutenance (sutnɑ̃s), s.f. Sustaining, defence, maintaining (of a thesis).
soutenant, -e (sutnɑ̃), s.m.f. Sustainer, defender (of a thesis).
soutènement (sutɛnmɑ̃), s.m. Prop, support; *mur de* ~, retaining-wall, breast-wall.
souteneur (sutnœr), s.m. Bully, pimp.
soutenir (sutnir), v.a. [L *sustinere*] To support, to maintain, to sustain, to keep up, to bear up; to prop, to prop up; to uphold, to affirm, to maintain, to back, to countenance, to stand by; ~ *la conversation*, to keep up the conversation, ~ *sa famille*, to support one's family, to maintain one's family; ~ *un siège*, to sustain a siege; ~ *une thèse*, to sustain, to defend, a thesis; **se** ~, v.pr. to support oneself, to hold out, to help each other; to be defended.
soutenu, -e (sutny), p. adj. Sustained; lofty, grand, noble; steady, unfailing, constant.
souterrain, -e (sutɛrɛ̃), adj. [f. L *sub*+*terra*] Subterranean; underground; (fig.) underhand. ~, s.m. Underground passage, vault, dug-out; tunnel.
souterrainement (sutɛrɛnmɑ̃), adv. Underground; (fig.) underhand.
soutien (sutjɛ̃), s.m. Support, mainstay, prop; supporter, upholder.
soutier (sutje), s.m. [f. *soute*] (naut.) Stoker; trimmer.
soutirage (sutiraʒ), s.m. Drawing-off (of wine, &c.), decanting.
soutirer (sutire), v.a. [*sous*+*tirer*] To draw off; to decant; (colloq.) to worm out, to extract; ~ *de l'argent à X*, to extract money from X, to squeeze money out of X; ~ *un shilling*, to cadge a bob.
souvenance (suvnɑ̃s), s.f. Remembrance, distant recollection; *douce* ~, sweet memories.
souvenir (suvnir), s.m. Remembrance, recollection, memory, reminder, souvenir, keepsake, token of remembrance; memorial; *rappelez-moi au bon* ~ *de X*, remember me to X; *garder un bon* ~ *de . . .*, to remember . . . with pleasure; *mes bons* ~*s à X*, remember me kindly to X.
(se) souvenir (səsuvnir), v.pr. To remember, to recollect, to call to mind, to bear in mind; *vous souvenez-vous d'avoir dit cela?*, do you remember having said that?; *vous souvient-il que?*, do you remember that?; *autant qu'il m'en souvienne, autant que je puis m'en* ~, to the best of my recollection; *faire* ~ *X de cela*, to remind X of it.
souvent (suvɑ̃), adv. [L *subinde*] Often; *assez* ~, rather often, not infrequently; *le plus* ~, mostly, most frequently; *peu* ~, rarely; (slang) *plus* ~, I dare say!, not if I know it!
souventefois, souventesfois (suvɑ̃tfwa), adv. (obs.) Often, oft-times.
souverain, -e (suvrɛ̃), adj. [LL *superanus*] Sovereign, supreme, paramount; final, without appeal; *remède* ~, infallible remedy, sovereign remedy; ~ *bien*, sovereign good, summum bonum; *cour* ~*e*, *tribunal* ~, supreme court; *avec un* ~ *mépris*, with sovereign contempt.
souverain, -e (suvrɛ̃), s.m.f. **1.** Sovereign, monarch; **2.** s.m. sovereign (coin).
souverainement (suvrɛnmɑ̃), adv. Supremely, superlatively, utterly.
souveraineté (suvrɛnte), s.f. Sovereignty, supremacy, infallibility; dominions.
soya (soja), s.m. (bot.) Soya-pea, soya-bean, soja.
soyeu-x, -se (swajø), adj. Silky, silken.
spacieusement (spasjøzmɑ̃), adv. Spaciously.
spacieu-x, -se (spasjø), adj. [f. L *spatium*] Spacious, vast, roomy.
spadassin (spadasɛ̃), s.m. [It. *spadaccino*] Bravo, bully, hired ruffian; swash-buckler.
spadice (spadis), s.f. [L *spadix*] (bot.) Spadix.
spahi (spai), s.m. [f. Persian *sipāhī*] Spahi (Algerian trooper).
spalax (spalaks), s.m. (zool.) Spalax; syn. RAT-TAUPE.
spalt (spalt), s.m. (min.) Spalt.
sparadrap (sparadra), s.m. Sticking-plaster, cere-cloth.
spart, sparte, (spart), s.m. [Gr. *sparton*] (bot.) Esparto, mat-weed, *Lygeum Spartum.*
sparterie (spartəri), s.f. Esparto goods; manufacture of esparto.
spartiate (sparsjat), adj. s.m.f. Spartan.
spasme (spasm), s.m. [Gr. *spasmos*] Spasm.
spasmodique (spasmɔdik), adj. Spasmodic.
spasmodiquement (spasmɔdikmɑ̃), adv. Spasmodically.
spath (spat), s.m. [Germ. wd] (min.) Spar.
spatial, -e, (aux) (spasjal), adj. [f. L *spatium*] Spatial.
spatule (spatyl), s.f. [L *spathula*] **1.** Spatula; **2.** (ornith.) spoonbill.
spécial, -e, (aux) (spesjal), adj. [f. L *species*] Special, especial, particular, peculiar.
spécialement (spesjalmɑ̃), adv. Specially, especially, particularly, peculiarly.
spécialisation (spesjaliza'sjɔ̃), s.f. Specialization.
spécialiser (spesjalize), v.a. To specialize; **se** ~, v.pr. to specialize, to become a specialist.

spécialiste (spesjalist), s.m.f. adj. Specialist; technician.
spécialité (spesjalite), s.f. Specialty, peculiarity, speciality; line of business; patent medicine.
spécieusement (spesjøzmɑ̃), adv. Speciously.
spécieu-x, -se (spesjø), adj. [L *speciosus*] Specious, right only in appearance.
spécification (spesifika'sjɔ̃), s.f. Specification, specifying, detailed description or enumeration.
spécificité (spesifisite), s.f. Specificity.
spécifier (spesifje), v.a. [L *specificare*] To specify.
spécifique (spesifik), adj. [f. L *species*] Specific. ~, s.m. Specific.
spécifiquement (spesifikmɑ̃), adv. Specifically.
spécimen (spesimɛn), s.m. [L wd] Specimen.
spéciosité (spesjozite), s.f. Speciousness.
spectacle (spɛktakl), s.m. [L *spectaculum*] Spectacle, show, sight, scene, performance, parade, pageant, exhibition; (theatr.) play, playhouse; *se donner en* ~, to make oneself conspicuous; *aller au* ~, to go to the theatre.
spectat-eur, -rice (spɛktatœr), s.m.f. Spectator, spectatress, looker-on, bystander, eye-witness; *les* ~*s*, the audience.
spectral, -e, (aux) (spɛktral), adj. **1.** Spectral, ghostly; **2.** spectral, pertaining to the spectrum; *analyse* ~*e*, spectrum analysis.
spectre (spɛktr), s.m. [L *spectrum*] **1.** Spectre, ghost, phantom; **2.** (phys.) spectrum.
spectroscope (spɛktrɔskɔp), s.m. [L *spectrum*+Gr. *skopein*] Spectroscope.
spectroscopie (spɛktrɔskɔpi), **spectrométrie** (spɛktrɔmetri), s.f. Spectroscopy.
spéculaire (spekylɛr), adj. [L *specularis*] (min.) Specular. ~, s.f. (bot.) Specularia.
spéculat-eur, -rice (spekylatœr), s.m.f. Speculator, gambler; ~ *à la baisse*, bear; ~ *à la hausse*, bull.
spéculati-f, -ve (spekylatif), adj. [f. L *speculari*] Speculative.
spéculation (spekyla'sjɔ̃), s.f. **1.** Speculation, meditation; **2.** speculation, speculative investment, business gambling.
spéculativement (spekylativmɑ̃), adv. Speculatively.
spéculer (spekyle), v.n. [L *speculari*] To speculate, to meditate; to speculate, to make investments that involve risk; to gamble; ~ *sur le sucre*, to speculate in sugar; ~ *sur l'origine du monde*, to speculate on the origin of the universe; ~ *à la baisse*, to speculate for a fall; ~ *à la hausse*, to speculate for a rise.
speculum (spekylɔm), s.m. [L wd] (surg.) Speculum.
speiss (spɛs), s.m. [Germ. orig.] (min.) Speiss.
spéléologie (speleɔlɔʒi), s.f. [f. Gr. *spēlaion* +*logos*] Spelaeology.
spergule (spɛrgyl), s.f. (bot.) Spurrey.
spermaceti (spɛrmaseti), s.m. [Gr. *sperma*+L *ceti*] Spermaceti; syn. BLANC DE BALEINE.
spermatocèle (spɛrmatosɛl), s.f. Spermatocele.
spermatozoaire (spɛrmatozɔɛr), s.m. Spermatozoon (pl. -zoa).
sperme (spɛrm), s.m. [Gr. *sperma*] Sperm; seed.
spermophile (spɛrmɔfil), s.m. (zool.) Gopher.
sphacèle (sfasɛl), s.m. [Gr. *sphakelos*] (pathol.) Sphacelus.
sphénoïdal, -e, (aux) (sfenɔidal), adj. Sphenoidal.
sphénoïde (sfenɔid), s.m. [Gr. *sphēn*+*eidos*] (anat.) Sphenoid.
sphère (sfɛr), s.f. [Gr. *sphaira*] Sphere, globe, ball; (fig.) sphere, field of action or influence, circle.
sphéricité (sferisite), s.f. Sphericity.
sphérique (sferik), adj. Spherical. ~, s.m. Balloon.
sphériquement (sferikmɑ̃), adv. Spherically.
sphéristère (sferistɛr), s.m. (ant.) Ball-play, spheristerion.
sphéroïdal, -e, (aux) (sferɔidal), adj. Spheroidal, spheroidical.
sphéroïde (sferɔid), s.m. Spheroid.
sphéromètre (sferɔmɛtr), s.m. Spherometer.
sphérométrie (sferɔmetri), s.f. Spherometry.
sphérule (sferyl), s.f. Spherule.
sphex (sfɛks), s.m. (ent.) Sphex.
sphincter (sfɛ̃ktɛr), s.m. [Gr. wd] (anat.) Sphincter.
sphinx (sfɛ̃ks), s.m. [Gr. wd] Sphinx; (fig.) sphinx, enigmatic person; (ent.) hawk-moth.
sphygmographe (sfigmɔgraf), s.m. [f. Gr. *sphugmos*+*graphein*] Sphygmograph.
spic (spik), s.m. also **aspic** [L *spica*] (bot.) Spike-lavender; *huile de* ~, spike-oil.
spica (spika), s.m. [L wd] (surg.) Spica-bandage.
spiciforme (spisiform), adj. Spike-shaped.
spicule (spikyl), s.m. [L *spicula*] Spicule.
spider (spidɛr), s.m. [Engl. wd] Dickey, back seat in a motor-car. ⚠ Not 'spider', which = *araignée*; but in S. Africa and U.S.A. the word 'spider', or 'spider-cart' is used for a lightly-built trap, usually provided with a back seat for groom or servant.
spinal, -e, (aux) (spinal), adj. [f. L *spina*] Spinal.
spinelle (spinɛl), s.m. adj. [It. *spinella*] Spinel (ruby).

spinozisme (spinozism), s.m. [f. prop. n. *Spinoza*] Spinozism.
spinule (spinyl), s.f. (bot.) Spinule.
spiral, -e, (aux) (spiral), adj. Spiral. ~, s.m. Hair-spring (of watches).
spirale (spiral), s.f. [f. *spire*] (geom.) Spiral; *en* ~, spirally, spiral.
spirant, -e (spirɑ̃), adj. s.f. (phon.) Spirant; syn. FRICATIVE.
spiration (spira'sjɔ̃), s.f. [L *spiratio*] (theol.) Spiration.
spire (spir), s.f. [Gr. *speira*] Spiral, coil, spire. ⚠ Not 'spire' in the sense of *clocher*.
spirée (spire), s.f. (bot.) Spiraea, meadow-sweet. Syn. REINE DES PRÉS.
spirite (spirit), s.m.f. [f. L *spiritus*] Spirit-rapper, spiritist. ~, adj. Pertaining to spiritism, spiritualistic (see ⚠ SPIRITUALISME).
spiritisme (spiritism), s.m. Spiritism, spiritualism (see ⚠ SPIRITUALISME).
spiritualiser (spiritɥalize), v.a. To spiritualize.
spiritualisme (spiritɥalism), s.m. Spiritualism (phil. doctrine). ⚠ In English 'spiritualism' means also belief that departed spirits communicate with and show themselves to men, especially at séances, by means of spirit-rappings, &c. = French *spiritisme*. In French *spiritualisme* cannot be used in this sense.
spiritualiste (spiritɥalist), adj. Spiritualistic. ~, s.m.f. Spiritualist (see ⚠ SPIRITUALISME).
spiritualité (spiritɥalite), s.f. Spirituality.
spirituel, -le (spiritɥɛl), adj. [L *spiritualis*] **1.** Spiritual; sacred; **2.** witty, sprightly, lively; *une femme ~le*, a witty woman; *une réponse ~le*, a witty retort.
spirituellement (spiritɥɛlmɑ̃), adv. **1.** Spiritually; **2.** wittily.
spiritueu-x, -se (spiritɥø), adj. Spirituous. ~, s.m. Spirit, spirits.
spiroïdal, -e, (aux) (spirɔidal), adj. Spiry, spiroidal.
spiromètre (spirɔmɛtr), s.m. Spirometer.
splanchnique (splɑ̃knik), adj. Splanchnic.
splanchnologie (splɑ̃knɔlɔʒi), s.f. [f. Gr. *splagkhnon*] Splanchnology.
spleen (splin), s.m. [Engl. wd] Spleen, lowness of spirits. ⚠ Not 'spleen', the organ producing certain modifications in the blood, which in French is *la rate*.
splendeur (splɑ̃dœr), s.f. [L *splendor*] Splendour, magnificence.
splendide (splɑ̃did), adj. Splendid, magnificent, sumptuous, gorgeous, glorious.
splendidement (splɑ̃didmɑ̃), adv. Splendidly.
splénétique (splenetik), adj. Splenetic.
splénique (splenik), adj. (anat.) Splenic, pertaining to the spleen.
splénite (splenit), s.f. (pathol.) Splenitis.
splénius (splenjys), s.m. [f. Gr. *splēnion*] (anat.) Splenius (muscle).
spode (spɔd), s.f. [etym. dub.] Spodium, calcined ivory.
spoliat-eur, -rice (spɔljatœr), s.m.f. Despoiler, spoliator; spoiler.
spoliation (spɔlja'sjɔ̃), s.f. Spoliation, despoiling; extortion.
spolier (spɔlje), v.a. [L *spoliare*] To despoil, to deprive, to rob, to frustrate.
spondaïque (spɔ̃daik), adj. Spondaic.
spondée (spɔ̃de), s.m. [Gr. *spondeion*] Spondee.
spondyle (spɔ̃dil), s.m. [Gr. *spondulos*] (anat.) Spondyl, vertebra.
spongiaires (spɔ̃ʒjɛr), s.m.pl. (zool.) Spongia.
spongieu-x, -se (spɔ̃ʒjø), adj. [f. L *spongia*] Spongy, spongious; easily soaked.
spongiosité (spɔ̃ʒjozite), s.f. Sponginess.
spongite (spɔ̃ʒit), s.f. (min.) Spongite.
spontané, -e (spɔ̃tane), adj. [f. L *sponte*] Spontaneous.
spontanéité (spɔ̃taneite), s.f. Spontaneity, spontaneousness.
spontanément (spɔ̃tanemɑ̃), adv. Spontaneously.
sporadicité (spɔradisite), s.f. Sporadicalness, sporadicness.
sporadique (spɔradik), adj. [Gr. *sporadikos*] Sporadic, sporadical.
sporadiquement (spɔradikmɑ̃), adv. Sporadically.
sporange (spɔrɑ̃ʒ), s.m. [f. Gr. *spora*] (bot.) Sporangium.
spore (spɔr), s.f. [Gr. *spora*] (bot.) Spore.
sporidie (spɔridi), s.f. (bot.) Sporidium.
sport (spɔr), s.m. [Engl. wd] Sport; *les ~s*, sport. ⚠ In French *sport* is only used for organized athletic games or outdoor pastimes; in English it means also amusement, fun = *plaisir, amusements*; to make sport of X = *tourner X en ridicule; s'amuser aux dépens de X.*
sporti-f, -ve (spɔrtif), adj. Sporting, sportsmanlike, relating to sport.
sportule (spɔrtyl), s.f. [L *sportula*] (ant.) Dole, alms.
spume (spym), s.m. [L *spuma*] Spume, froth.
spumescent, -e (spymɛsɑ̃), adj. Spumescent.
spumeu-x, -se (spymø), adj. Spumy, spumous, frothy.
sputation (spyta'sjɔ̃), s.f. [f. L *sputare*] Spitting, expectoration.
squale (skwal), s.m. [L *squalus*] Shark; dog-fish; flake.
squame (skwam), s.f. [L *squama*] Squama; scale.
squameu-x, -se (skwamø), adj. Squamose, squamous, scaly.

square (skwar), s.m. [Engl. wd] Enclosed public garden, square. ⚠ In French *square* means always an enclosed public garden, whatever its shape; it is not used like English 'square' in the sense of equilateral rectangle = *rectangle équilatéral*, nor 'open space surrounded by buildings', which = *place*, nor product of a number multiplied by itself = *carré*, *carré parfait d'un nombre*.

squelette (skəlɛt), s.m. [Gr. *skeletos*] Skeleton.

squelettique (skəlɛtik), adj. Skeleton-like; *maigreur* ~, extreme thinness.

squille (skij), s.f. (zool.) Mantis-shrimp, squill, squilla.

squirre (skir), s.m. [Gr. *skirros*] (pathol.) Scirrhus, scirrhosity.

stabilisat-eur, -rice (stabilizatœr), adj. Stabilizing. ~, s.m. Stabilizer; balancer; (aeron.) ~ *horizontal, vertical*, horizontal, vertical stabilizer.

stabilisation (stabiliza'sjɔ̃), s.f. Stabilization; steadying.

stabiliser (stabilize), v.a. [f. L *stabilis*] To stabilize.

stabilité (stabilite), s.f. Stability, stableness; durability, steadfastness.

stable (stabl), adj. [L *stabilis*] Stable, firm, durable; steadfast, permanent, lasting.

stabulation (stabyla'sjɔ̃), s.f. [f. L *stabulum*] Stabulation, stabling.

stade (stad), s.m. [Gr. *stadion*] Stadium; (fig.) period, stage.

stadia (stadja), s.m. Stadium (instrument for measuring distances).

staff (staf), s.m. [Engl. wd] Staff (building-material of plaster mixed with fibre, for temporary ornamental work).

stage (staʒ), s.m. [LL *stagium*] Term of probation; probation. ⚠ Not 'stage', which = *scène, estrade*, &c.

stagiaire (staʒjɛr), s.m.f. adj. One keeping his or her terms; probationer; young licentiate in law.

stagnant, -e (stagnɑ̃), p. adj. [f. L *stagnum*] Stagnant.

stagnation (stagna'sjɔ̃), s.f. Stagnation.

stalactite (stalaktit), s.f. [f. Gr. *stalaktos*] Stalactite.

stalagmite (stalagmit), s.f. [f. Gr. *stalagmos*] Stalagmite.

stalle (stal), s.f. [f. It. *stallo*] Stall, seat; stall, box (for horses).

staminé, -e (stamine), adj. [f. L *stamen*] (bot.) Staminate.

stance (stɑ̃s), s.f. [It. *stanza*] Stanza. ⚠ Not 'stance', which = *position (d'un joueur de golf), emplacement, terrain à bâtir*.

stand (stɑ̃d), s.m. [Engl. wd] Stand, stall; enclosure; shooting-gallery.

standardisation (stɑ̃dardiza'sjɔ̃), s.f. [Engl. wd] Standardization.

standardiser (stɑ̃dardize), v.a. [f. Engl. *standard*] To standardize.

stannate (stanat), s.m. (chem.) Stannate.

stannifère (stanifɛr), adj. (min.) Stanniferous.

stannique (stanik), adj. (chem.) Stannic.

staphisaigre (stafizɛgr), s.f. (bot.) Stavesacre; larkspur; *Delphinium staphisagria*.

staphylin (stafilɛ̃), s.m. [Gr. *staphulinos*] (ent.) Devil's coach-horse.

staphylin, -e (stafilɛ̃), adj. [f. Gr. *staphulē*] (anat.) Staphyline.

staphylocoque (stafilɔkɔk), s.m. [f. Gr. *staphulē*] Staphylococcus (kind of bacteria).

staphylôme (stafilom), s.m. (pathol.) Staphyloma.

staroste (starɔst), s.m. [Russ. *starosta*] Starosta.

stase (stɑz), s.f. [Gr. *stasis*] (pathol.) Stasis (stagnation of the blood or other body-fluids).

statère (statɛr), s.m. [Gr. *statēr*] (ant.) Stater, Greek coin, Greek weight.

stathouder (statudɛr), s.m. [Dutch wd] Stadtholder.

stathoudérat (statudera), s.m. Stadtholderate.

statice (statis), s.m. (bot.) Statice; thrift.

station (sta'sjɔ̃), s.f. [f. L *stare*] Standing, pause, short stay, halt; station; stand; railway station; ~ *d'hiver*, winter resort; ~ *thermale*, health resort, spa, watering-place; *faire une longue* ~, to make a long stay; ~ *verticale*, standing.

stationnaire (stasjɔnɛr), adj. At a standstill, stationary; *rester* ~, to remain at a standstill. ~, s.m. (naut.) Block-ship, guard-ship.

stationnement (stasjɔnmɑ̃), s.m. Stationing, standing still, standing; (of motor-cars) parking, remaining long on the same spot; *droit de* ~, garage or parking fee.

stationner (stasjɔne), v.n. To stop, to stand about, to stand still. ⚠ 'To station' cannot translate *stationner*; it means to assign a post or station to somebody = *poster, placer*; ex. he is stationed at Calcutta = *il est en garnison à Calcutta*.

statique (statik), adj. [f. Gr. *statikos*] Static. ~, s.f. Statics.

statisticien, -ne (statistisjɛ̃), s.m.f. Statistician.

statistique (statistik), s.f. [f. Gr. *statizein*] Statistics. ~, adj. Statistical.

statuaire (statɥɛr), s.m.f. Statuary, sculptor; ~, s.f. statuary. ~, adj. Statuary.

statue (staty), s.f. [L *statua*] Statue.

statuer (statɥe), v.a.n. [L *statuere*] To rule, to decree, to enact; to come to a decision (*sur*, upon).

statuette (statɥɛt), s.f. Statuette.

stature (statyr), s.f. [L *statura*] Stature.

statut (staty), s.m. [L *statutum*] Statute, bye-law, regulation.
statutaire (statytɛr), adj. Statutory.
stéarine (stearin), s.f. [f. Gr. *stear*] Stearin.
stéarique (stearik), adj. Stearic.
stéatite (steatit), s.f. (min.) Steatite.
stèle (stɛl), s.f. [Gr. *stēlē*] Stele.
stellaire (stɛllɛr), adj. [f. L *stella*] Stellar, stellary, of stars. ~, s.f. (bot.) Stellaria.
stellionat (stɛljɔna), s.m. [LL *stellionatus*] Fraudulent selling, pledging, &c.; stellionate.
stellionataire (stɛljɔnatɛr), s.m.f. adj. Person guilty of stellionate.
stemmate (stɛmmat), s.m. [f. Gr. *stemma*] (zool.) Stemma; syn. OCELLE.
sténographe (stenɔgraf), s.m.f. [f. Gr. *stenos*+*graphein*] Stenographer, shorthand writer.
sténographie (stenɔgrafi), s.f. Stenography, shorthand.
sténographier (stenɔgrafje), v.a. To take down in shorthand, to report.
sténographique (stenɔgrafik), adj. Stenographic, shorthand; *compte rendu* ~, verbatim report.
stentor (stɑ̃tɔr), s.m. [prop. n. in Homer] Stentor; *voix de* ~, stentorian voice.
steppe (stɛp), s.m.f. [Russ. wd] Steppe.
stérage (steraʒ), s.m. Measuring of wood (in steres).
stercoraire (stɛrkɔrɛr), adj. [L *stercorarius*] Stercoraceous.
stercoral, -e, (aux) (stɛrkɔral), adj. Stercoral.
stercoration (stɛrkɔra'sjɔ̃), s.f. [f. L *stercus, stercoris*] Stercoration.
stère (stɛr), s.m. [f. Gr. *stereos*] Stere (French measure for wood = 1 cubic metre).
stéréobate (stereɔbat), s.m. (arch.) Stereobate.
stéréographie (stereografi), s.f. Stereography.
stéréographique (stereografik), adj. Stereographic.
stéréomètre (stereomɛtr), s.m. Stereometer.
stéréoscope (stereɔskɔp), s.m. [Gr. *stereos* +*skopein*] Stereoscope.
stéréoscopique (stereɔskɔpik), adj. Stereoscopic; *vue* ~, stereoscopic slide.
stéréotomy (stereɔtɔmi), s.f. [Gr. *stereos* +*tomē*] Stereotomy.
stéréotype (stereɔtip), adj. [Gr. *stereos*+*tupos*] Stereotype, printed by stereotype.
stéréotyper (stereɔtipe), v.a. To stereotype; (fig.) to stereotype, to impart monotonous regularity to.
stéréotypeur (stereɔtipœr), s.m. Stereotyper.
stéréotypie (stereɔtipi), s.f. Stereotyping, stereotypy.
stérer (stere), v.a. To measure in steres.
stérile (steril), adj. [L *sterilis*] Sterile, barren, unfruitful, fruitless, vain; *pays* ~, barren country; *année* ~, unfruitful year; year of dearth; *efforts* ~*s*, vain, sterile efforts; *discussion* ~, sterile discussion or debate.
stérilement (sterilmɑ̃), adv. Sterilely, barrenly, unfruitfully, vainly.
stérilisation (steriliza'sjɔ̃), s.f. Sterilization.
stériliser (sterilize), v.a. To sterilize; *lait stérilisé*, sterilized milk.
stérilité (sterilite), s.f. Sterility, barrenness, unfruitfulness.
sterlet (stɛrlɛ), s.m. [f. Russ. *sterlyad'*] (ichth.) Sterlet.
sternal, -e, (aux) (stɛrnal), adj. (anat.) Sternal.
sternum (stɛrnɔm), s.m. [Gr. *sternon*] (anat.) Sternum; breast-bone.
sternutatoire (stɛrnytatwar), adj. [f. L *sternutare*] Sternutatory.
stéthoscope (stetɔskɔp), s.m. [Gr. *stēthos* +*skopein*] Stethoscope.
stibié, -e (stibje), adj. [f. L *stibium*] Containing antimony, stibious, antimonious.
stibine (stibin), s.f. (chem.) Stibnite.
stick (stik), s.m. [Engl. wd] Cane, walking-stick.
stigmate (stigmat), s.m. [Gr. *stigma*] Stigma, scar, mark, branded mark; (theol.) ~*s*, (pl.) stigmata; (bot.) stigma; (ent.) spiracle.
stigmatiser (stigmatize), v.a. To stigmatize.
stil-de-grain (stildəgrɛ̃), s.m. (paint.) Yellow lake.
stillation (stilla'sjɔ̃), s.f. [L *stillatio*] Dripping, falling drop by drop.
stimulant, -e (stimylɑ̃), p. adj. Stimulating. ~, s.m. Stimulus, stimulant.
stimulat-eur, -rice (stimylatœr), adj. Stimulating.
stimuler (stimyle), v.a. [L *stimulare*] To stimulate, to urge, to spur on.
stipe (stip), s.m. [L *stipes*] Stipe, stem.
stipendiaire (stipɑ̃djɛr), s.m. adj. Stipendiary, hired, mercenary.
stipendié, -e (stipɑ̃dje), p. adj. (pej.) Hired, paid.
stipendier (stipɑ̃dje), v.a. [f. L *stipendium*] To keep in one's pay, to hire.
stipulation (stipyla'sjɔ̃), s.f. [f. *stipulatio*] Stipulation.
stipule (stipyl), s.f. [L *stipula*] (bot.) Stipule.
stipuler (stipyle), v.a. [L *stipulari*] To stipulate (*que*, that).
stock (stɔk), s.m. [Engl. wd] Stock(-in-trade).
stoïcien, -ne (stɔisjɛ̃), adj. s.m.f. [Gr. *stōikos*] Stoic.
stoïcisme (stɔisism), s.m. Stoicism.

stoïque (stɔik), adj. Stoical, stoic.
stoïquement (stɔikmɑ̃), adv. Stoically.
stolon (stɔlɔ̃), s.m. (bot.) Stolon (bud).
stomacal, -e, (aux) (stɔmakal), adj. [f. L *stomachus*] Stomachal.
stomachique (stɔmaʃik), adj. s.m. Stomachic.
stomatique (stɔmatik), adj. [f. Gr. *stoma*] Stomatic.
stomatite (stɔmatit) s.f. (pathol.) Stomatitis.
stoppage (stɔpaʒ), s.m. [Engl. wd] Invisible mending, needle-weaving. ⚠ Not English 'stoppage', which = *arrêt, obstruction, obstacle.*
stopper (stɔpe), **1.** v.n. To stop; **2.** v.a. to mend in an invisible way, to close-darn; syn. RENTRAIRE.
stoppeu-r, -se (stɔpœr), s.m.f. Darner; one who does invisible mending.
storax (stɔraks), s.m. (bot.) Storax.
store (stɔr), s.m. [It. *stora*] Blind, Venetian blind, outside blind; *baisser un ~*, to let down a blind. ⚠ Not 'store', which = *approvisionnement; magasin,* &c.
strabisme (strabism), s.m. [f. Gr. *strabos*] Strabismus, squinting, squint.
strabotomie (strabɔtɔmi), s.f. Strabotomy.
stradivarius (stradivarjys), s.m. [f. prop. n.] Violin made by Stradivarius of Cremona (d. 1737); (colloq.) Strad.
stramoine (stramwan), s.f. (bot.) Stramonium, stramony, thorn-apple.
stramonine (stramɔnin), s.f. Stramonine, a poison obtained from stramony.
strangulation (strɑ̃gyla'sjɔ̃), s.f. [f. L *strangulare*] Strangulation, strangling.
strapontin (strapɔ̃tɛ̃), s.m. [It. *strapuntino*] Bracket-seat, flap-seat.
strass (strɑs), s.m. [f. *Strasser*, the inventor] Paste, strass.
strasse (stras), s.f. [f. It. *straccio*] Refuse-silk, floss silk.
stratagème (strataʒɛm), [Gr. *stratēgēma*] Stratagem, device, trickery; *user d'un ~*, to use a stratagem; to contrive a stratagem.
stratège (stratɛʒ), s.m. [Gr. *stratos*+ *agōgos*] (ant.) Strategus.
stratégie (strateʒi) s.f. Strategy, strategics.
stratégique (strateʒik), adj. Strategic; *mouvement ~*, strategic movement or move.
stratégiquement (strateʒikmɑ̃), adv. Strategically.
stratégiste (strateʒist), s.m. Strategist.
stratification (stratifika'sjɔ̃), s.f. Stratification.
stratifier (stratifje), v.a. [L *stratum*+ *facere*] To stratify.
stratigraphie (stratigrafi), s.f. Stratigraphy.
stratus (stratys), s.m. [L wd] Stratus (cloud).
streptocoque (strɛptɔkɔk), s.m. (bacteriology) Streptococcus (pl. streptococci).
strette (strɛt), s.f. [It. *stretto*] (mus.) Stretto, finale of a fugue.
striation (stria'sjɔ̃), s.f. [f. L *stria*] Striation.
strict, -e (strikt), adj. [L *strictus*] Strict.
strictement (striktəmɑ̃), adv. Strictly.
strident, -e (stridɑ̃), adj. Shrill, strident, harsh, screeching.
stridulation (stridyla'sjɔ̃), s.f. Stridulation.
strie (stri), s.f. [L *stria*] Stria; flute (on column); streak, stripe.
strié, -e (strie), p. adj. Striate, fluted; striped, streaked.
strier (strie), v.a. To striate.
strige (striʒ), s.f. [L *striga*] Vampire, ghoul.
strigile (striʒil), s.m. [f. L *strigilis*] (ant.) Strigil.
striure (striyr), s.f. Striation, stria.
strix (striks), s.m. (ornith.) Screech-owl.
strobile (strɔbil), s.m. [Gr. *strobīlos*] Strobile, pine-cone.
strobiliforme (strɔbiliform), adj. Strobiliform, strobile-shaped.
strontiane (strɔ̃sjan), s.f. (chem.) Strontia.
strontium (strɔ̃sjɔm), s.m. (chem.) Strontium: Sr.
strophe (strɔf), s.f. [Gr. *strophē*] Strophe, stanza; syn. STANCE.
structure (stryktyr), s.f. [L *structura*] Structure, make, arrangement, disposition, build.
strumeu-x, -se (strymø), adj. [L *strumosus*] (pathol.) Strumous, strumose.
strychnine (striknin), s.f. [f. Gr. *strukhnos*] Strychnine, strychnia.
stuc (styk), s.m. [It. *stucco*] Stucco.
stucateur (stykatœr), s.m. Stuccoer.
studieusement (stydjøzmɑ̃), adv. Studiously.
studieu-x, -se (stydjø), adj. [f. L *studium*] Studious, painstaking.
stupéfaction (stypefaksjɔ̃), s.f. Amazement, great astonishment, stupefaction. ⚠ Not English 'stupefaction' in the sense of making stupid or torpid, which = *engourdissement.*
stupéfait, -e (stypefɛ), adj. Amazed, dumbfounded, astounded; astonished; stupefied; see ⚠ STUPÉFIER.
stupéfiant, -e (stypefjɑ̃), p. adj. Stupefying, stupefactive; astounding, amazing. ~, s.m. Narcotic, stupefier.
stupéfier (stypefje), v.a. [f. L *stupor*+ *facere*] **1.** To stupefy; **2.** to astound, to amaze. ⚠ In English 'to stupefy' has generally the sense of to make stupid or torpid, or to stun = *mettre dans un état*

d'inertie physique et morale. In French it is also frequently used in the sense of to amaze = *plonger dans l'étonnement.*
stupeur (stypœr), s.f. [L *stupor*] **1.** Stupor; **2.** helpless amazement.
stupide (stypid), adj. Stupid, in a state of stupor; obtuse, crass, slow-witted, unintelligent.
stupidement (stypidmɑ̃), adv. Stupidly.
stupidité (stypidite), s.f. Stupidity, piece of stupidity.
stupre (stypr), s.m. [L *stuprum*] Stupre, defilement of a woman, lechery.
stuquer (styke), v.a. To stucco.
style (stil), s.m. [L *stilus*] **1.** Style; ~ *épique*, epic style; ~ *sublime*, lofty style; ~ *Louis XV*, *Tudor*, &c., style of Louis XV, Tudor style, &c.; *en grand* ~, on grand lines; in style; with magnificence, lavishly; in a stately manner; **2.** (bot.) style; **3.** style, gnomon of sun-dial. ⚠ In English 'style' means also title = *titre*; ex. entitled to the style of Right Honourable = *ayant droit au titre de*, &c.
styler (stile), v.a. To train, to form; *domestique bien stylé*, well-trained servant. ⚠ Not 'to style', which = *désigner spécifiquement.*
stylet (stilɛ), s.m. [f. It. *stiletto*] Stiletto, stylet.
styliste (stilist), s.m.f. Master of style, stylist.
stylite (stilit), adj. s.m. [f. Gr. *stulos*] Stylite.
stylobate (stilɔbat), s.m. [Gr. *stulos*+ *bainein*] (arch.) Stylobate.
stylographe (stilɔgraf), s.m. [Gr. *stulos*+ *graphein*] Stylograph, fountain pen.
stylographie (stilɔgrafi), s.f. Stylography.
stylographique (stilɔgrafik), adj. Stylographic.
styloïde (stilɔid), adj. Styloid.
styptique (stiptik), adj. [Gr. *stuptikos*] Styptic; that checks bleeding. ~, s.m. Styptic.
styrax (stiraks), s.m. (bot.) Styrax.
su (sy), s.m. [f. *savoir*] Knowledge; *au* ~ *de X*, to the knowledge of X; *au vu et au* ~ *de tous*, as everybody knows; to everybody's knowledge.
suage (sɥaʒ), s.m. Humidity oozing from a log of wood, &c.; (naut.) tallowing a vessel.
suaire (sɥɛr), s.m. [f. L *sudarium*] Shroud, winding-sheet.
suant, -e (sɥɑ̃), adj. Sweating, perspiring, dripping with moisture.
suasion (sɥazjɔ̃), s.f. [f. L *suadere*] Suasion, persuading.
suave (sɥav), adj. [L *suavis*] Suave, sweet, soft, delicate, pleasant, delicious, charming, bland.
suavement (sɥavmɑ̃), adv. Suavely, sweetly, gently.
suavité (sɥavite), s.f. Suavity, sweetness, delicate charm.
subaigu, -ë (sybɛgy), adj. (med.) Subacute.
subalpin, -e (sybalpɛ̃), adj. Sub-alpine.
subalterne (sybaltɛrn), adj. s.m.f. [f. L *sub*+*alter*] Subaltern, subordinate.
subconscient, -e (sybcɔ̃sjɑ̃), adj. Subconscious. ~, s.m. Subconsciousness.
subdéléguer (sybdelege), v.a. To subdelegate.
subdiviser (sybdivize), v.a. To subdivide; **se** ~, v.pr. to be subdivided.
subdivision (sybdivizjɔ̃), s.f. Subdivision.
subir (sybir), v.a. [L *subire*] To undergo, to go through, to submit to, to bear, to sustain; ~ *sa destinée*, to submit to one's fate; ~ *une opération*, *un examen*, to undergo an operation, an examination; to take an examination.
subit, -e (sybi), adj. [L *subitus*] Sudden.
subitement (sybitmɑ̃), adv. Suddenly, all of a sudden.
subito (sybito), adv. [It. wd] All of a sudden, all at once, in a jiffy.
subjacent, -e (sybʒasɑ̃), adj. See syn. SOUS-JACENT.
subjecti-f, -ve (sybʒɛktif), adj. s.m. [f. L *subjectus*] Subjective.
subjection (sybʒɛksjɔ̃), s.f. [L *subjectio*] (rhet.) Subjection (answer by speaker to his own question). ⚠ Not English 'subjection' in the sense of *subjugation.*
subjectivement (sybʒɛktivmɑ̃), adv. Subjectively.
subjectivité (sybʒɛktivite), s.f. Subjectivity.
subjoncti-f, -ve (sybʒɔ̃ktif), adj. s.m. [f. L *subjungere*] Subjunctive; *au* ~, in the subjunctive.
subjugation (sybʒyga'sjɔ̃), s.f. Subjugation.
subjuguer (sybʒyge), v.a. [f. L *sub*+ *jugum*] To subjugate; to subdue, to overcome, to master, to vanquish.
subjugueu-r, -se (sybʒygœr), s.m.f. (rare) Subjugator.
sublimation (syblima'sjɔ̃), s.f. Sublimation.
sublimatoire (syblimatwar), s.m. Sublimatory.
sublime (syblim), adj. [L *sublimis*] Sublime, grand, noble, lofty, of the most exalted kind. ~, s.m. The sublime.
sublimé (syblime), s.m. (chem.) Sublimate; ~ *corrosif*, corrosive sublimate.
sublimement (syblimәmɑ̃), adv. Sublimely.
sublimer (syblime), v.a. (chem., and fig.) To sublimate.
sublimité (syblimite), s.f. Sublimity.
sublingual, -e, (aux) (syblɛ̃gɥal), adj. [f. L *sub*+*lingua*] Sublingual.

sublunaire (syblynɛr), adj. [f. L *sub*+ *luna*] Sublunary.
submerger (sybmɛrʒe), v.a. [L *sub*+ *mergere*] To submerge, to swamp, to put under water, to flood with water; (fig.) to submerge.
submersible (sybmɛrsibl), adj. Submersible. ~, s.m. Submarine; syn. SOUS-MARIN.
submersion (sybmɛrsjɔ̃), s.f. Submersion; sinking.
subodorer (sybɔdɔre), v.a. [L *sub*+*odorari*] To scent at a distance, to smell from afar; (fig.) to guess, to suspect.
subordination (sybɔrdina'sjɔ̃), s.f. Subordination.
subordonné, -e (sybɔrdɔne), p. adj. Subordinate (*à*, to); (gram.) *proposition ~e*, subordinate clause. ~, s.m.f. Subordinate.
subordonner (sybɔrdɔne), v.a. [*sub*+ *ordonner*] To subordinate (*à*, to).
subornation (sybɔrna'sjɔ̃), s.f. Subornation, bribery.
suborner (sybɔrne), v.a. [L *sub*+*ornare*] To suborn, to bribe, to corrupt.
suborneu-r, -se (sybɔrnœr), s.m.f. Suborner, briber. ~, adj. Suborning, bribing.
subrécargue (sybrekarg), s.m. [Span. *sobre*+ *cargo*] Supercargo.
subreptice (sybrɛptis), adj. [f. L *subreptum*] Surreptitious, stealthy, furtive.
subrepticement (sybrɛptismɑ̃), adv. Surreptitiously, furtively.
subreption (sybrɛpsjɔ̃), s.f. [L *subreptio*] Subreption.
subrogation (sybrɔga'sjɔ̃), s.f. Subrogation, surrogation.
subrogatoire (sybrɔgatwar), adj. Subrogatory.
subrogé, -e (sybrɔʒe), p. adj. Surrogated, surrogate; ~ *tuteur*, trustee, surrogate guardian.
subroger (sybrɔʒe), v.a. [f. L *sub*+*rogare*] To substitute, to surrogate.
subséquemment (sybsekamɑ̃), adv. Subsequently.
subséquence (sybsekɑ̃s), s.f. Subsequence.
subséquent, -e (sybsekɑ̃), adj. [L *subsequens*] Subsequent.
subside (sybsid), s.m. [L *subsidium*] Subsidy.
subsidiaire (sybsidjɛr), adj. Subsidiary, additional, accessory.
subsidiairement (sybsidjɛrmɑ̃), adv. Furthermore, subsidiarily.
subsistance (sybzistɑ̃s), s.f. Subsistence, sustenance, maintenance, what one lives on; *~s*, s.f.pl. provisions, supplies; victualling department.
subsister (sybziste), v.n. [L *subsistere*] To subsist, to continue to exist, to keep oneself alive; to be kept alive; to hold good.
substance (sybstɑ̃s), s.f. [L *substantia*] Substance; *en ~*, in short, in the main, substantially.
substantiel, -le (sybstɑ̃sjɛl), adj. Substantial.
substantiellement (sybstɑ̃sjɛlmɑ̃), adv. Substantially.
substanti-f, -ve (sybstɑ̃tif), adj. [L *substantivus*] Substantive. ~, s.m. Substantive, noun; syn. NOM.
substantivement (sybstɑ̃tivmɑ̃), adv. Substantively, as a noun.
substituer (sybstitɥe), v.a. [f. L *sub*+ *statuere*] To substitute; (law) to entail; to appoint; ~ *une chose à une autre*, to replace one thing by another; **se ~ *à***, v.pr. to substitute oneself for; to supersede, to supplant, to oust.
substitut (sybstity), s.m. [f. L *substitutus*] Substitute, deputy.
substituti-f, -ve (sybstitytif), adj. (med.) Substitutive.
substitution (sybstitysjɔ̃), s.f. [L *substitutio*] Substitution; (law) entail.
substratum (sybstratɔm), s.m. [L wd] Substratum, foundation.
substruction (sybstryksjɔ̃), s.f. [f. L *substruere*] Substructure, substruction.
subterfuge (sybtɛrfyʒ), s.m. [f. L *subter*+ *fugere*] Subterfuge, shift; *user de ~*, to resort to subterfuge.
subtil, -e (sybtil), adj. [L *subtilis*] Subtle, subtile, evasive, tenuous, fine; nice, refined; acute, subtle, keen, crafty, smart; *avoir la vue ~e*, to be sharp-sighted; *avoir l'ouïe ~e*, to have a quick ear; *un charme ~*, a subtle charm; *un esprit ~*, a subtle mind; *une distinction ~e*, a subtle distinction.
subtilement (sybtilmɑ̃), adv. Subtly, with subtlety, cleverly; cunningly, smartly.
subtilisation (sybtiliza'sjɔ̃), s.f. (chem.) Subtilization; (colloq.) stealing, pinching.
subtiliser (sybtilize), v.a.n. **1.** To subtilize; to refine; **2.** (colloq.) to steal, to pilfer, to pinch.
subtilité (sybtilite), s.f. Subtlety, subtileness.
subulé, -e (sybyle), adj. [f. L *subula*] Subulate, awl-shaped.
suburbain, -e (sybyrbɛ̃), adj. [f. L *sub*+ *urbs*] Suburban.
subvenir (sybvənir), v.n. [L *subvenire*] To provide (*à*, for); ~ *aux besoins de X*, to provide for X's wants.
subvention (sybvɑ̃sjɔ̃), s.f. Subvention, subsidy, grant of money.
subventionner (sybvɑ̃sjɔne), v.a. To subsidize, to endow, to grant a subvention to.
subversi-f, -ve (sybvɛrsif), adj. [f. L *sub*+*vertere*] Subversive.

subversion (sybvɛrsjɔ̃), s.f. Subversion; overthrow.
subversivement (sybvɛrsivmɑ̃), adv. Subversively.
subvertir (sybvɛrtir), v.a. [L *subvertere*] To subvert, to overthrow, to upset.
suc (syk), s.m. [L *succus*] Juice; (fig.) essence, pith, quintessence.
succédané, -e (syksedane), adj. [L *succedaneus*] Acting as a succedaneum or substitute. ~, s.m. Succedaneum (pl. succedanea).
succéder (syksede), v.n. [L *succedere*] To succeed (*à*, to), to follow, to come next; **se** ~, v.pr. to succeed each other, to follow one another. ⚠ 'To succeed' has also the sense of to achieve success, to be successful = *réussir*, but *succéder* cannot (nowadays) be used in this sense, it would sound excessively archaic.
succès (syksɛ), s.m. [L *successus*] Success, result, issue; *mauvais* ~, unsuccess; ~ *fou*, tremendous success; ~ *d'estime*, passably cordial reception given to performance, from respect rather than appreciation; *sans* ~, without success, unsuccessfully; *rien ne réussit comme le* ~, nothing succeeds like success; *cela eut beaucoup de* ~, that was quite a success; that was very much appreciated.
successeur (syksɛsœr), s.m. Successor.
successibilité (syksɛsibilite), s.f. Right of succession.
successible (syksɛsibl), adj. Capable of inheriting.
successi-f, -ve (syksɛsif), adj. Successive, running, following one another.
succession (syksɛsjɔ̃), s.f. [f. L *successio*] Succession, series; following in order; sequel; succeeding (to the throne); inheritance; *recueillir une* ~, to receive an inheritance; *renoncer à une* ~, to give up one's right to a succession; *prendre la* ~ *de X*, to take over X's business; *droits de* ~, estate duties, legacy duties.
successivement (syksɛsivmɑ̃), adv. Successively, in succession.
successoral, -e, (aux) (syksɛsoral), adj. Successional.
succin (syksɛ̃), s.m. [L *succinum*] Yellow amber; syn. AMBRE.
succinct, -e (syksɛ̃), adj. [L *succinctus*] Succinct, terse, concise, short.
succinctement (syksɛ̃ktəmɑ̃), adv. Succinctly, concisely, briefly.
succinique (syksinik), adj. (chem.) Succinic.
succion (syksjɔ̃), s.f. [f. L *suctus*] Suction, sucking.
succomber (sykɔ̃be), v.n. [L *succumbere*] To succumb, to be overcome, to yield; to give way (*à*, to), to die, to perish; ~ *à la tentation*, to yield to temptation.
succube (sykyb), s.m. [L *succuba*] Succuba, succubus.
succulemment (sykylamɑ̃), adv. Succulently.
succulence (sykylɑ̃s), s.f. Succulence.
succulent, -e (sykylɑ̃), adj. [L *succulentus*] Succulent, rich, juicy.
succursale (sykyrsal), s.f. [f. L *succursus*] Branch establishment, local branch; chapel of ease, subsidiary church.
succussion (sykysjɔ̃), s.f. [L *succussio*] (med.) Succussion, shake.
sucement (sysmɑ̃), s.m. Sucking, suck.
sucer (syse), v.a. [f. L *sugere*, LL *suctiare*] To suck, to suck in, to exhaust, to drain; (fig.) to imbibe, to suck in.
sucette (sysɛt), s.f. Unperforated teat (for infants), 'dummy'.
suceu-r, -se (sysœr), s.m.f. Sucker. ~, **-se**, adj. Sucking.
suçoir (syswar), s.m. Sucker.
suçon (sysɔ̃), s.m. (pop.) Sucking-mark, red spot left on skin by prolonged kiss; a kind of boiled sweet.
suçoter (sysɔte), v.a. To keep sucking.
sucrage (sykraʒ), s.m. Sweetening, sugaring.
sucre (sykr), s.m. [Gr. *saccharon*, Arab. *sukkar*] Sugar; ~ *candi*, sugar-candy; ~ *de canne*, cane sugar; ~ *cristallisé*, crystallized sugar; ~*-glace*, icing-sugar; ~ *de lait*, lactose; ~ *d'orge*, barley sugar; ~ *de pomme*, barley sugar with apple flavouring; *pain de* ~, sugar-loaf; ~ *en poudre*, powdered sugar, castor sugar; *il est tout* ~ *et tout miel*, he is all honey; (fig.) *casser du* ~ (*sur la tête de X*), to denigrate (X), (jest.) to backbite (X), to damn (X) with faint praise; to run (X) down.
sucré, -e (sykre), p. adj. Sugared, sweetened; (fig.) demure, prim; *faire la* ~*e*, to affect demureness, to be niminy-piminy.
sucrer (sykre), v.a. To sugar, to sweeten.
sucrerie (sykrəri), s.f. Sugar-works; ~*s*, s.f.pl. sweetmeats, comfits.
sucri-er, -ère (sykrie), adj. Pertaining to the sugar industry. ~, s.m. **1.** Sugar-basin or -bowl; **2.** sugar-maker.
sucrin (sykrɛ̃), s.m. (bot.) Sweet melon.
sud (syd), s.m. [Anglo-Sax. *suth*] South. ~, adj. south, southerly, southern; *du* ~, southern; southerly; *au* ~, *vers le* ~, southward; *le pôle* ~, the south pole; *la Croix du* ~, the Southern Cross; ~*-est*, south-east, south-easterly; ~*-ouest*, south-west, south-westerly.
sudation (syda'sjɔ̃), s.f. [L *sudatio*] Sudation, sweating.
sudatoire (sydatwar), adj. Sudatory.
sudorifique (sydɔrifik), adj. [f. L *sudor*+*facere*] Sudorific.
sudoripare (sydɔripar), **sudorifère** (sydɔrifɛr), adj. (anat.) Sudoriferous.

suédois, -e (sɥedwa), s.m.f. Swede. ~, -e, adj. Swedish.
suée (sɥe), s.f. Sweating; (pop., fig.) sudden fright.
suer (sɥe), v.n.a. [L *sudare*] To sweat, to perspire, to be in a sweat; ~ *à grosses gouttes*, to perspire profusely; (vulg.) *vous me faites* ~, you bother me; you make me sick; I am fed up with you; (fig.) ~ *sang et eau*, to toil and moil; to strain every nerve; (vulg., colloq.) *en* ~ *une*, to dance a dance.
suette (sɥɛt), s.f. Sweating-sickness; ~ *miliaire*, miliary fever, sweating-fever.
sueur (sɥœr), s.f. Sweat, perspiration; *à la* ~ *de son front*, by the sweat of one's brow.
suffète (syfɛt), s.m. [L *suffes*] (ant.) Suffete, magistrate of ancient Carthage.
suffire (syfir), v.n. [L *sufficere*] To suffice, to be sufficient, to be enough, to do; *cela suffit*, that will do; *suffit que*, suffice it to say that; *à chaque jour suffit sa peine*, sufficient unto the day is the evil thereof; *il suffit que*, it will suffice that; it is enough that; *qu'il suffise de vous le dire*, let it be enough to tell you this; *il me suffit de peu*, I am content with little; **se** ~, v.pr. to shift for oneself, to provide for oneself; to be enough in itself.
suffisamment (syfizamɑ̃), adv. Sufficiently, enough.
suffisance (syfizɑ̃s), s.f. **1.** Sufficiency; **2.** self-conceit, conceitedness; *en* ~, sufficiently, enough.
suffisant, -e (syfizɑ̃), p. adj. [f. *suffire*] **1.** Sufficient, enough; **2.** conceited.
suffixe (syfiks), s.m. [f. L *sub*+*fixus*] Suffix.
suffocant, -e (syfɔkɑ̃), p. adj. Suffocating, stifling.
suffocation (syfɔka'sjɔ̃), s.f. Suffocation, choking, stifling.
suffoquer (syfɔke), v.n.a. [L *suffocare*] To suffocate, to choke; ~ *de colère*, to choke with anger; *les sanglots la suffoquent*, sobs are stifling her; she is suffocated with grief.
suffragant (syfragɑ̃), s.m. adj. Suffragan.
suffrage (syfraʒ), s.m. [L *suffragium*] Suffrage, vote; (fig.) approbation, approval, consent; ~ *universel*, universal suffrage.
suffragette (syfraʒɛt), s.f. (jest.) Suffragette.
suffusion (syfyzjɔ̃), s.f. [L *suffusio*] Suffusion.
suggérer (sygʒere), v.a. [L *suggerere*] To suggest, to hint, to insinuate; to inspire, to prompt.
suggestibilité (sygʒɛstibilite), s.f. Suggestibility.
suggesti-f, -ve (sygʒɛstif), adj. Suggestive.
suggestion (sygʒɛstjɔ̃), s.f. [L *suggestio*] Suggestion, hint, suggesting, incitement; *à la* ~ *de X*, at X's instigation.
suggestionner (sygʒɛstjɔne), v.a. To influence by (hypnotic) suggestion; to suggest.
suicide (sɥisid), s.m. [f. L *sui*+*caedere*] Suicide.
(se) suicider (səsɥiside), v.pr. To commit suicide, to kill oneself.
suie (sɥi), s.f. [Celt. orig.] Soot.
suif (sɥif), s.m. [L *sebum*] Tallow; (colloq.) *donner un* ~ *à X*, to give X a good blowing-up; to give it hot (to X).
suiffer (sɥife), v.a. To tallow, to grease, to smear with tallow.
suint (sɥɛ̃), s.m. [f. *suer*] Grease (of sheep's-wool).
suintement (sɥɛ̃tmɑ̃), s.m. Oozing, running, leaking, trickling.
suinter (sɥɛ̃te), v.n.a. To ooze, to leak, to run, to trickle.
suisse (sɥis), adj. Swiss. ~, s.m. (f. **suissesse**) Swiss; ~, s.m. beadle; porter; Swiss Guard; *un petit* ~, a small fresh cream cheese; (colloq.) *faire* ~, to drink alone, without standing treat; not to 'stand Sam'.
suite (sɥit), s.f. [LL *sequita*] **1.** Retinue, train, attendants; **2.** suite, sequel, sequence, continuation; what follows; course; coherence; consequence, result; *à la* ~ *de*, after; following close upon; in consequence of; *et ainsi de* ~, and so on; *de* ~, in succession, uninterruptedly; *tout de* ~, at once, directly, immediately; *par* ~, consequently; *par* ~ *de*, in consequence of; *attendons la* ~, let us see what happens; *cela peut avoir des* ~*s* (*fâcheuses*), that may be attended with (unpleasant) consequences; *dans la* ~, afterwards; later on; *donner* ~ *à un projet*, to carry out one's intention; *faire* ~ *à*, to be a continuation of, to follow; *la* ~ *au prochain numéro*, to be continued in our next; *il n'a pas de* ~ *dans les idées*, he has no steadiness of mind; he keeps at nothing long, he is inconsistent; *tenir des propos sans* ~, (*a*) to talk in a desultory, nonsensical way; (*b*) to talk in an incoherent, rambling way (as a madman). ⚠ Not 'suite' (of rooms, furniture, &c.) = *série*; *meuble* (*de salon*, &c.); nor 'suit', which = *complet* (*veston*); *requête*; *procès*; *recherche en mariage*, &c.
suivant (sɥivɑ̃), prep. According to, in proportion to; *coupe* ~ *AB*, section from A to B; ~ *que*, as, according as.
suivant, -e (sɥivɑ̃), p. adj. Following, next, subsequent. ~, s.m. Follower, attendant, partisan, disciple; ~*e*, s.f. waiting-maid, soubrette; (theatr.) abigail.
suivi, -e (sɥivi), p. adj. Coherent, consistent, steady, persevering; popular, sought after, well attended.
suivre (sɥivr), v.a.n. [L *sequi*] To follow, to come after, to go after, to keep up

with; to attend, to accompany; to observe, to understand, to practise (a profession); ~ *une affaire,* to follow up a matter; *à* ~, to be continued; *à faire* ~, to be forwarded; *prière de faire* ~, please forward; ~ *un cours,* to attend a class; *faire* ~ *X,* to have X followed; ~ *de loin,* to follow at a distance; ~ *de près,* to follow close on the heels of; to examine closely; ~ *son chemin,* to go one's way; *il suit de là que,* it follows from this that; it follows that; *voyez ce qui suit,* see what follows; **se ~, v.pr.** to follow one another, to follow in order; to come in succession; to be coherent.

sujet, -te (syʒɛ), adj. [L *subjectus*] Subjected, liable (*à*, to); addicted (to); ~ *à caution,* not to be depended upon, not reliable.

sujet, -te (syʒɛ), s.m.f. Subject; ~, s.m. subject, topic, matter, theme; ground, cause; (gram.) subject; *bon* ~, good fellow; *mauvais* ~, bad lot; *avoir* ~ *de se plaindre,* to have cause to complain; *assez sur ce* ~, let us say no more on that matter; ~ *de discussion,* subject of discussion; *sortir de son* ~, to wander from one's subject; *au* ~ *de,* about.

sujétion (syʒesjɔ̃), s.f. [L *subjectio*] Subjection, liability, bondage.

sulfatage (sylfataʒ), s.m. Sulphating.

sulfate (sylfat), s.m. (chem.) Sulphate.

sulfaté, -e (sylfate), p. adj. Sulphated.

sulfater (sylfate), v.a. To sulphate, to steep in copper sulphate, to syringe with sulphate.

sulfhydrate (sylfidrat), s.m. Hydrosulphate.

sulfhydrique (sylfidrik), adj. (chem.) Hydrosulphuric.

sulfite (sylfit), s.m. (chem.) Sulphite.

sulfocarbonique (sylfokarbɔnik), adj. (chem.) Sulphocarbonic.

sulfosel (sylfozɛl), s.m. (chem.) Sulphosalt.

sulfuration (sylfyra'sjɔ̃), s.f. Sulphuration.

sulfure (sylfyr), s.m. [L *sulfur*] (chem.) Sulphide, sulphuret.

sulfuré, -e (sylfyre), adj. (chem.) [Sulphuretted.

sulfureu-x, -se (sylfyrø), adj. Sulphureous, sulphur-; sulphurous (acid).

sulfurique (sylfyrik), adj. (chem.) Sulphuric.

sultan (syltɑ̃), s.m. [Arab. wd] Sultan.

sultanat (syltana), s.m. Sultanate.

sultane (syltan), s.f. Sultana; (ornith.) sultana; *poule* ~, sultana hen. ⚠ Not 'sultana' (raisin), which = *raisin de Smyrne.*

sultani, sultanin (sultani, syltanɛ̃), s.m. Sultanin, sultany (Egyptian coin).

sumac (symak), s.m. (bot.) Sumac, sumach.

summum (sɔmmɔm), s.m. [L wd] Summum, acme, summit, highest point or degree.

sunna (syna), s.f. [Arab. wd] Sunna(h) (Mohammedan book of precepts).

sunnite (synit), s.m. Sunnite, Sunni (orthodox Mohammedan).

super (sype), v.a. [f. Engl. *sup*] To suck, to sup.

superbe (sypɛrb), adj. [L *superbus*] Superb, grand-looking, stately, splendid. ~, s.m. Vainglorious or proud person; ~, s.f. vainglory, haughtiness, arrogance.

superbement (sypɛrbəmɑ̃), adv. Superbly, splendidly, magnificently.

supercherie (sypɛrʃəri), s.f. [It. *soperchieria*] Deceit, cheat, trickery, fraud.

supère (sypɛr), adj. [L *superus*] (bot.) Superior, placed above.

superfétation (sypɛrfeta'sjɔ̃), s.f. [f. L *super*+*fetus*] Superfetation; excrescence.

superfétatoire (sypɛrfetatwar), adj. Superfetatious, superfluous.

superficialité (sypɛrfisjalite), s.f. Superficialness, superficiality.

superficie (sypɛrfisi), s.f. [f. L *super*+ *facies*] Superficies, area, surface; (geom.) superficies.

superficiel, -le (sypɛrfisjɛl), adj. Superficial, of the surface; on the surface.

superficiellement (sypɛrfisjɛlmɑ̃), adv. Superficially.

superfin, -e (sypɛrfɛ̃), adj. Superfine, A1, extra.

superflu, -e (sypɛrfly), adj. [f. L *superfluere*] Superfluous, needless; redundant. ~, s.m. Superfluity, excess, unnecessary luxuries.

superfluité (sypɛrflɥite), s.f. Superfluity, superfluousness.

supérieur, -e (syperjœr), adj. [L *superior*] Superior, upper, higher; *les étages* ~*s*, the upper stories; *les classes* ~*es*, the upper classes; *se montrer* ~ *à son destin,* to rise superior to one's fate. ~, s.m. Superior, chief.

supérieurement (syperjœrmɑ̃), adv. In a superior style, superlatively, in a masterly way.

supériorité (syperjɔrite), s.f. Superiority, excellence, pre-eminence.

superlati-f, -ve (sypɛrlatif), adj. [L *superlativus*] Superlative. ~, s.m. (gram.) Superlative; *au* ~, in the superlative.

superlativement (sypɛrlativmɑ̃), adv. Superlatively.

superphosphate (sypɛrfɔsfat), s.m. Superphosphate.

superposable (sypɛrpozabl), adj. Superposable.

superposer (sypɛrpoze), v.a. [f. L *super* + (Fr.) *poser*] To superpose, to lay upon something.

superposition (sypɛrpozisjɔ̃), s.f. Superposition.

superstitieusement (sypɛrstisjøzmɑ̃), adv. Superstitiously.

superstitieu-x, -se (sypɛrstisjø), adj. Superstitious.
superstition (sypɛrstisjɔ̃), s.f. [f. L *superstare*] Superstition.
superstructure (sypɛrstryktyr), s.f. Superstructure.
supin (sypɛ̃), s.m. [L *supinum*] (gram.) Supine.
supinateur (sypinatœr), adj. s.m. [f. L *supinatus*] (anat.) Supinator (muscle).
supination (sypina'sjɔ̃), s.f. Supination.
supplantation (syplɑ̃ta'sjɔ̃), s.f. Supplantation, superseding.
supplanter (syplɑ̃te), v.a. [L *supplantare*] To supplant, to supersede.
suppléance (sypleɑ̃s), s.f. Deputyship; filling vacancy as a substitute.
suppléant, -e (sypleɑ̃), p. adj. s.m.f. Deputy; assistant; substitute.
suppléer (syplee), v.a. [L *supplere*] To do duty for, to take the place of; to make up for; to supplement, to complete; *se faire ~*, to find a substitute (for oneself).
supplément (syplemɑ̃), s.m. [L *supplementum*] Supplement, additional quantity; extra charge; (geom.) supplement.
supplémentaire (syplemɑ̃tɛr), adj. Supplementary, additional, extra.
supplémentairement (syplemɑ̃tɛrmɑ̃), adv. Supplementarily; in addition, additionally.
suppléti-f, -ve (sypletif), adj. [f. L *suppletus*] Suppletive, suppletory.
suppliant, -e (sypliɑ̃), p. adj. Supplicating, beseeching, entreating, suppliant. ~, s.m.f. Supplicant, suppliant.
supplication (syplika'sjɔ̃), s.f. [L *supplicatio*] Supplication, entreaty.
supplice (syplis), s.m. [L *supplicium*] Punishment; torment, torture; *le dernier ~*, the extreme penalty; death; (fig.) *il est au ~*, he is on the rack; *vous me mettez au ~*, you torture me; you put me on thorns; *c'est le ~ de Tantale*, it is the torture of Tantalus; it's tantalizing.
supplicié, -e (syplisje), s.m.f. Executed criminal.
supplicier (syplisje), v.a. To torture, to torment, to execute (a criminal), to put to death; (fig.) to put on thorns, to put upon the rack.
supplier (syplie), v.a. [L *supplicare*] To beseech, to entreat, to implore, to beg, to pray, to supplicate; *je vous supplie de faire cela*, I beg of you to do that.
supplique (syplik), s.f. Petition, entreaty, supplication; *présenter une ~*, to make humble petition; to petition.
support (sypɔr), s.m. [f. *supporter*] Prop, stand, stay, rest, pillar; (fig.) support, pillar, prop; (herald.) supporter; *servir de ~ à X*, to be X's support; *sans ~, sans amis, sans retraite*, without help, without friends, without a refuge; *avoir besoin de ~*, to require support.
supportable (sypɔrtabl), adj. Bearable, tolerable, endurable.
supportablement (sypɔrtabləmɑ̃), adv. Tolerably.
supporter (sypɔrte), v.a. [L *supportare*] To bear, to support, to prop, to sustain, to uphold; (fig.) to suffer, to stand, to endure, to bear with, to put up with, to tolerate; *cela ne supporte pas l'examen*, that does not stand close examination; that's easily seen through; *cela ne saurait se ~*, that cannot be tolerated; *ils ne peuvent se ~*, they cannot bear each other. ⚠ 'To support' in English is very generally used for *appuyer, soutenir, corroborer, se rallier à*, and *subvenir aux besoins de*; 'to support a resolution' must NOT be translated by *supporter une motion*, but by *appuyer une motion*.
supposable (sypozabl), adj. Supposable.
supposé, -e (sypoze), p. adj. **1.** Pretended, counterfeit, supposititious; **2.** supposed, admitted; *~ qu'il le fasse*, supposing that he does it; suppose he does so.
supposer (sypoze), v.a. [f. L *sub*+(Fr.) *poser*] To suppose, to conjecture, to assume, to take for granted, to presume; to imply; to substitute for what is genuine, to forge.
suppositi-f, -ve (sypozitif), adj. Supposititious, suppositive, assumed, hypothetical.
supposition (sypozisjɔ̃), s.f. **1.** Supposition, conjecture, hypothesis; **2.** supposititiousness, forgery, substitution.
suppositoire (sypozitwar), s.m. (pharm.) Suppository.
suppôt (sypo), s.m. [L *suppositus*] Instrument, tool, agent; *un ~ de Satan*, an imp of the devil, a tool, or (dialect) limb of Satan.
suppression (syprɛsjɔ̃), s.f. Suppressing, suppression, abolition.
supprimer (syprime), v.a. [L *supprimere*] To suppress, to stop, to abolish, to cut off, to omit, to do away with; *~ des impôts*, to take off taxes; *~ une phrase*, to take out a sentence.
suppurant, -e (sypyrɑ̃), p. adj. Suppurating.
suppurati-f, -ve (sypyratif), adj. s.m. Suppurative.
suppuration (sypyra'sjɔ̃), s.f. Suppuration.
suppurer (sypyre), v.n. [L *suppurare*] To suppurate.
supputation (sypyta'sjɔ̃), s.f. Calculation, computation.
supputer (sypyte), v.a. [L *supputare*] To calculate, to compute, to reckon; to weigh.
suprasensible (syprasɑ̃sibl), adj. Suprasensible, supersensible.

suprématie (sypremasi), s.f. [f. Engl. *supremacy*] Supremacy.

suprême (syprɛm), adj. [L *supremus*] Supreme, highest, last, crowning; *au ~ degré*, in the highest degree; *les honneurs ~s*, the last honours, funeral ceremonies; *volontés ~s*, last will (of a dying person).

suprême (syprɛm), s.m. (cook.) Suprême (a dish of poultry).

suprêmement (syprɛmmɑ̃), adv. Supremely, superlatively.

sur (syr), prep. [L *super*] On, upon, above, over; on to, towards; out of, in; concerning, respecting; *avoir de l'argent ~ soi*, to have money about or on one; *une fenêtre qui donne ~ un jardin*, a window which looks out upon a garden; *je compte ~ vous*, I rely on you; *un ~ cent*, one out of, or in, a hundred; *je prends cela ~ moi*, I take it upon myself; *~ le fait*, in the act; red-handed; *~ le moment*, at once, at first; *~ le tard*, rather late; late at night; *~ les 3 heures*, about three o'clock; *~ lest*, in ballast; *~ mer*, by sea; *juger ~*, to go by; to judge from; *~ ce sujet*, on this matter; concerning this; *trois mètres ~ quatre*, three metres by four; *revenir ~ ses pas*, to retrace one's steps; *tourner ~ la gauche*, to turn left; *~ le tout*, *~ toute chose*, above all; *~ la fin*, towards the end; *il est ~ son départ*, he is on the point of leaving.

sur, -e (syr), adj. [Germ. orig.] Sour, acid.

sûr, -e (syr), adj. [L *securus*] Certain, sure, positive, unerring; secure, steady, safe; *un ami ~*, a trustworthy friend; a trusty friend; *avoir le pied ~*, to be sure-footed; *le temps n'est pas ~*, the weather is uncertain; *mettre en lieu ~*, to put in a place of safety; *avoir le goût ~*, to have good taste; *le plus ~ est de*, the safest course is to; *être ~ de son fait*, to be sure of a thing; to know what one is talking about; *à coup ~*, (*a*) surely, certainly, assuredly; (*b*) to a certainty; with certainty; (fam.) *pour ~!*, to be sure!; sure enough; I should think so!; and no mistake; you bet your life!; *j'en suis ~ et certain*, I am positive about that; I am perfectly sure of that; *soyez ~ que*, you may be perfectly sure that. ⚠ 'Be sure to do that' must be translated by *ne manquez pas de faire cela*.

surabondamment (syrabɔ̃damɑ̃), adv. Superabundantly.

surabondance (syrabɔ̃dɑ̃s), s.f. Superabundance.

surabondant, -e (syrabɔ̃dɑ̃), p. adj. Superabundant.

surabonder (syrabɔ̃de), v.n. [*sur+abonder*] To superabound.

surah (syra), s.m. [f. *Surat*, India] Surah, twilled silk.

suraigu, -ë (syrɛgy), adj. Over-shrill, over-sharp; intense.

surajouter (syraʒute), v.a. To superadd.

suralimentation (syralimɑ̃ta'sjɔ̃), s.f. Intensive feeding.

suralimenter (syralimɑ̃te), v.a. [*sur+alimenter*] To feed up; to give (temporarily) excessive quantities of food to.

surannation (syrana'sjɔ̃), s.f. [f. *surrané*] (law) Expiration, superannuation.

suranné, -e (syrane), adj. [f. *sur+an*] Out of date, antiquated; old-fashioned; obsolete; (law) expired, superannuated.

surate (syrat), s.f. [Arab. wd] Sura (chapter of the Koran).

surbaissé, -e (syrbɛse), p. adj. Surbased (vault); very low; (motor.) *chassis ~*, dropped frame.

surbaisser (syrbɛse), v.a. To surbase.

surbau (pl. -x) (syrbo), s.m. (naut.) Frame of hatchway; coaming, combing.

surcharge (syrʃarʒ), s.f. **1.** Overload, overloading, added burden, overplus, excess; **2.** word written over another.

surcharger (syrʃarʒe), v.a. [*sur+charger*] **1.** To overload, to overburden; **2.** to write (a word) over another.

surchauffe (syrʃof), s.f. Overheating; superheating.

surchauffer (syrʃofe), v.a. [*sur+chauffer*] To overheat, to superheat.

surchauffeur (syrʃofœr), s.m. (techn.) Superheater.

surchoix (syrʃwɑ), s.m. Prime quality, first choice.

surcomposé, -e (syrkɔ̃poze), p. adj. [*sur +composé*] (gram.) Double compound.

surcot (syrko), s.m. [*sur+cotte*] Surcoat.

surcoupe (syrkup), s.f. [f. *sur+coupe*] (cards) Over-trumping.

surcouper (syrkupe), v.a.n. To over-trump.

surcroît (syrkrwa), s.m. [f. *sur+croître*] Addition, increase, surplus, overmeasure; *par ~*, in addition; to boot; moreover; *pour ~ de malheur*, to add to my (or your, or his, her, &c.) misfortune; to make matters still worse.

surcroître (syrkwɑtr), v.n.a. [*sur+croître*] To grow excessively, to increase beyond measure.

surdent (syrdɑ̃), s.f. Gag-tooth; wolf's tooth (in horses).

surdi-mutité (syrdimytite), s.f. Deaf-mutism.

surdité (syrdite), s.f. [L *surditas*] Deafness.

surdorer (syrdɔre), v.a. To double-gild.

surdos (syrdo), s.m. [*sur+dos*] (harness) Back-strap.

sureau (pl. -x) (syro), s.m. [f. L *sabucus*] (bot.) Elder, elder-tree.

surélévation (syreleva'sjɔ̃), s.f. **1.** Increase, raising higher; **2.** raised part (of building, &c.).

surélever (syrelve), v.a. [*sur*+*élever*] To raise higher; to increase.
surelle (syrɛl), s.f. [f. *sur*, adj.] (bot.) Sorrel; wood sorrel.
sûrement (syrmɑ̃), adv. 1. Surely, certainly; 2. safely, securely.
suréminent, -e (syreminɑ̃), adj. Supereminent.
surémission (syremisjɔ̃), s.f. Over-issue.
surenchère (syrɑ̃ʃɛr), s.f. Higher bid; *faire une* ~ *sur*, to outbid.
surenchérir (syrɑ̃ʃerir), v.n. [*sur*+*enchérir*] To bid higher, (fig.) to go one better; ~ *sur X*, to outbid X.
surenchérisseur (syrɑ̃ʃerisœr), s.m. Overbidder.
surérogation (syrerɔga'sjɔ̃), s.f. [L *supererogatio*] Supererogation.
surérogatoire (syrerɔgatwar), adj. Supererogatory.
surestarie (syrɛstari), s.f. [Span. *sobrestaria*] (naut.) Demurrage.
surestimation (surɛstima'sjɔ̃), s.f. Overvaluation, overestimate.
surestimer (syrɛstime), v.a. To overvalue, to overestimate.
suret, -te (syrɛ), adj. [f. *sur*] Sourish, acid.
sûreté (syrte), s.f. [f. L *securitas*] Safety, secureness; security, surety, warrant; certainty; *serrure de* ~, safety lock; *mettre en* ~, to put in safe keeping; to put out of harm's way; ~ *de main*, steadiness of hand; *en* ~ *de conscience*, with a safe conscience; *prendre ses* ~*s*, to take every precaution.
surexcitable (syrɛksitabl), adj. Overexcitable.
surexcitation (syrɛksita'sjɔ̃), s.f. Overexcitement.
surexciter (surɛksite), v.a. To overexcite, to excite greatly.
surface (syrfas), s.f. [*sur*+*face*] Surface, superficies, area; (fig.) surface, outside, appearance, first show; ~ *portante*, (aeron.) supporting surface.
surfaire (syrfɛr), v.a.n. To overrate, to overpraise, to overcharge, to charge too much; (colloq.) to stick it on.
surfaix (syrfɛ), s.m. (harness) Surcingle, girth.
surfilage (syrfilaʒ), s.m. Overcasting.
surfiler (surfile), v.a. [*sur*+*filer*] To overcast, to stitch over (edge) to prevent unravelling.
surfin, -e (surfɛ̃), adj. [*sur*+*fin*] Superfine.
surgeon (syrʒɔ̃), s.m. [f. L *surgere*] Sucker, shoot (of tree). ⚠ Not English 'surgeon', which = *chirurgien*.
surgir (syrʒir), v.n. [f. L *surgere*] To spring up, to arise, to surge, to appear; *faire* ~, to bring about; to cause to appear.
surgissement (syrʒismɑ̃), s.m. Arising, appearing.
surhaussement (syrosmɑ̃), s.m. Raising.
surhausser (syrose), v.a. To raise; to force up the price of.
surhomme (syrɔm), s.m. Superman.
surhumain, -e (syrymɛ̃), adj. Superhuman.
suricate (syrikat), s.m. (zool.) Suricate.
surimposer (syrɛ̃poze), v.a. To increase the tax on; to overtax.
surin (syrɛ̃), s.m. 1. Young apple-tree; 2. thief's knife; hence *suriner*, v.a. to knife, to murder.
surintendance (syrɛ̃tɑ̃dɑ̃s), s.f. Superintendence; superintendent's office or residence.
surintendant (syrɛ̃tɑ̃dɑ̃), s.m. Superintendent, overseer; ~**e**, s.f. (woman) superintendent.
surir (syrir), v.n. To turn sour.
surjaler (syrʒale), v.a. (naut.) To foul (an anchor); ~, v.n. to clear (the anchor).
surjet (syrʒɛ), s.m. (needlework) Overcasting, whipping.
surjeter (syrʒəte), v.a. To overcast, to whip.
surlendemain (syrlɑ̃dmɛ̃), s.m. [*sur*+*lendemain*] Second day after; *le* ~ *de son départ*, the second day after he left.
surlonge (syrlɔ̃ʒ), s.f. (butch.) Sirloin.
surmenage (syrmənaʒ), s.m. Overwork, mental or physical strain.
surmener (syrməne), v.a. [*sur*+*mener*] To overwork, to overdrive; **se** ~, v.pr. to overwork.
surmontable (syrmɔ̃tabl), adj. Surmountable, that can be overcome, conquerable.
surmonter (syrmɔ̃te), v.a. [*sur*+*monter*] To surmount, to overcome, to conquer; to rise above.
surmouler (syrmule), v.a. To cast in a mould taken from a moulded object.
surmoût (syrmu), s.m. Must (new wine).
surmulet (syrmylɛ), s.m. [*sur*+*mulet*] (ichth.) Surmullet; ~ *rouget*, red mullet.
surmulot (syrmylo), s.m. [*sur*+*mulot*] (zool.) Brown rat, Norway rat.
surnager (syrnaʒe), v.n. [*sur*+*nager*] To float, or to swim on the surface; (fig.) to survive, to remain.
surnaturel, -le (syrnatyrɛl), adj. Supernatural; supranatural, preternatural, miraculous. ~, s.m. Supernatural.
surnaturellement (syrnatyrɛlmɑ̃), adv. Supernaturally.
surnom (syrnɔ̃), s.m. Surname (archaic), cognomen, nickname, pet name. ⚠ Not 'surname' in the now usual sense of name common to all members of a family, which = *nom, nom de famille*.
surnombre (synɔ̃br), s.m. Excess, surplus.
surnommer (syrnɔme), v.a. To surname, to nickname.

surnuméraire (syrnymerɛr), adj. s.m.f. [f. L *super+numerus*] Supernumerary.

surnumérariat (syrnymerarja), s.m. Supernumerary time or service.

suroît (syrwɑ), s.m. (corrupt. of *sud-ouest*] (naut.) **1.** Sou'wester (wind); **2.** sou'wester (waterproof hat or garment).

suros (syro), s.m. (vet.) Splint (of horses).

suroxydation (syrɔksida'sjɔ̃), s.f. (chem.) Superoxidation.

suroxyder (syrɔkside), v.a. (chem.) To superoxidate.

surpasser (syrpɑse), v.a. [*sur+passer*] To be higher than, to surpass, to exceed; to excel, to outdo; (colloq.) *cela me surpasse*, that amazes me; **se** ~, v.pr. to surpass oneself.

surpaye (syrpɛj), s.f. Extra pay.

surpayer (syrpɛje), v.a. [*sur+payer*] To overpay, to pay too dear for; to pay (a person) too much.

surpeuplement (syrpœpləmɑ̃), s.m. Overpopulation, overstocking with inhabitants.

surpeuplé, -e (syrpœple), p. adj. [*sur+peuplé*] Over-populated, overcrowded.

surplis (syrpli), s.m. [L *superpellicium*] Surplice.

surplomb (syrplɔ̃), s.m. Overhang; *en* ~, overhanging; jutting out.

surplombement (syrplɔ̃bmɑ̃), s.m. Overhanging.

surplomber (syrplɔ̃be), v.n.a. [*sur+plomber*] To overhang.

surplus (syrply), s.m. [*sur+plus*] Surplus, excess, overplus; remainder, rest; *au* ~, moreover; furthermore; besides.

surprenant, -e (syrprənɑ̃), p. adj. Surprising, amazing, astonishing.

surprendre (syrprɑ̃dr), v.a. [*sur+prendre*] To surprise, to take by surprise, to amaze, to astonish; to entrap, to deceive; to obtain by artifice; to beguile; to intercept, to detect, to find out, to perceive; *la mort nous surprend*, death overtakes us; ~ *la bonne foi de X*, to abuse X's good faith; **se** ~, v.pr. to catch oneself; to surprise each other.

surprise (syrpriz), s.f. [f. *surprendre*] Surprise, amazement; *revenir de sa* ~, to recover from one's surprise; *prendre par* ~, to come upon unawares; to take by surprise; to startle; to take (something) unexpectedly and suddenly; *ménager une* ~ *à X*, to prepare a surprise for X; *boîte à* ~, jack-in-the-box.

surproduction (syrprɔdyksjɔ̃), s.f. Overproduction.

surrénal, -e, (aux) (syrrenal), adj. [*sur+rénal*] (anat.) Surrenal, above the kidneys.

sursaturation (syrsatyra'sjɔ̃), s.f. (chem.) Supersaturation.

sursaturer (syrsatyre), v.a. [*sur+saturer*] (chem.) To supersaturate.

sursaut (syrso), s.m. [*sur+saut*] Start; *se réveiller en* ~, to wake with a start.

sursauter (syrsote), v.n. To start up, to start aside, to spring.

surséance (syrseɑ̃s), s.f. [f. *surseoir*] Delay, suspension.

sursemer (syrsəme), v.a. To sow over again.

surseoir (syrswar), v.n.a. [*sur+seoir*] To suspend, to postpone, to delay, to put off; ~ *à des poursuites*, to put off proceedings; ~ *une délibération*, to postpone a deliberation.

sursis (syrsi), s.m. [f. *surseoir*] Delay (of execution), respite; suspension; reprieve.

sursitaire (syrsitɛr), s.m.f. One who has been granted a delay, or respite.

sursolide (syrsɔlid), adj. (math.) Sursolid, fourth power of a number.

surtaux (syrto), s.m. [*sur+taux*] Over-assessment, excessive rate.

surtaxe (syrtaks), s.f. Surtax, extra tax; exorbitant tax.

surtaxer (syrtakse), v.a. [*sur+taxer*] To put an extra tax on, to overtax.

surtout (syrtu), s.m. **1.** Overcoat, overall; **2.** (~ *de table*) épergne, centre-piece; **3.** light luggage-cart.

surtout (syrtu), adv. [*sur+tout*] Above all, especially.

surveillance (syrvɛjɑ̃s), s.f. Superintendence, supervision, watch, inspection; ~ *de la police*, police supervision.

surveillant, -e (syrvɛjɑ̃), s.m.f. Overseer, superintendent, guardian, watcher, watchman, keeper; (in schools) usher, master on duty.

surveille (syrvɛj), s.f. [*sur+veille*] Two days before, the day before the eve; *la* ~ *de*, two days before; syn. AVANT-VEILLE.

surveiller (syrvɛje), v.a. [*sur+veiller*] To superintend, to watch, to keep an eye on, to see to, to watch over, to look after.

survenance (syrvənɑ̃s), s.f. Unforeseen arrival; (law) unexpected birth.

survenant, -e (syrvənɑ̃), p. adj. Coming unexpectedly. ~, s.m.f. Chance comer.

survenir (syrvənir), v.n. [*sur+venir*] To arrive unexpectedly, to happen unexpectedly, to occur, to arise; (colloq.) to turn up.

survente (syrvɑ̃t), s.f. **1.** Sale at too high a figure; **2.** (naut.) increase of wind, excessive wind.

surventer (syrvɑ̃te), v.n. [*sur+venter*] (naut.) To blow a gale, to blow with increased or excessive violence.

survider (syrvide), v.a. [*sur+vider*] To pour out the over-fullness of (a vessel).

survie (syrvi), s.f. Survival, outliving, survivorship.

survivance (syrvivɑ̃s), s.f. Survival; reversion (of office).

survivanci-er, -ère (syrvivɑ̃sje), s.m.f. Reversioner (of an office).

survivant, -e (syrvivɑ̃), p. adj. Surviving. ~, s.m.f. Survivor.
survivre (syrvivr), v.n. [*sur*+*vivre*] To survive; ~ *à X*, to outlive X; *se* ~ *à soi-même*, to outlive one's faculties.
survoler (syrvɔle), v.a. To fly over.
survoltage (syrvɔltaʒ), s.m. Survoltage.
survolter (syrvɔlte), v.a. [*sur*+*volter*] To increase the voltage of.
sus (sy), prep. [LL *susum*] Upon; *courir* ~ *à l'ennemi*, to fall upon the enemy; ~ *!* ~ *!*, courage!, to arms!, up and at 'em!; come on!; *en* ~, above; in addition; extra; to boot.
susceptibilité (sysɛptibilite), s.f. Susceptibility, capacity, capability of admitting; susceptibility, touchiness, irritability; *blesser la* ~ *de X*, to hurt X's susceptibilities or feelings.
susceptible (sysɛptibl), adj. [f. L *suscipere, susceptum*] Susceptible, capable of; susceptible, touchy, irritable, easily offended.
susception (sysɛpsjɔ̃), s.f. Taking (of holy orders), reception, susception.
suscitation (sysita'sjɔ̃), s.f. [L *suscitatio*] Suscitation, instigation.
susciter (sysite), v.a. [L *suscitare*] To suscitate, to raise up; to stir up.
suscription (syskripsjɔ̃), s.f. [f. L *superscriptio*] Superscription, address.
susdénommé, -e (sysdenɔme), p. adj. [*sus*+*dénommé*] Above-mentioned.
susdit, -e (sysdi), p. adj. s.m.f. Aforesaid.
susmentionné, -e (sysmɑ̃sjɔne), adj. Above-mentioned.
susnommé, -e (sysnɔme), p. adj. s.m.f. Above-named.
suspect, -e (syspɛkt, syspɛ), adj. [L *suspectus*] Suspicious, suspected, suspect; *cela me semble* ~, I don't like the look of it; I smell a rat. ~, s.m.f. Suspect, suspected person.
suspecter (syspɛkte), v.a. To suspect; (U.S.A.) to suspicion.
suspendre (syspɑ̃dr), v.a. [L *suspendere*] To hang up; to suspend, to interrupt, to postpone, to delay.
suspendu, -e (syspɑ̃dy), p. adj. Suspended, hung up, hanging, delayed, postponed; *être* ~ *aux lèvres de X*, to be all attention to what X is saying, to hang on X's lips; *pont* ~, suspension bridge; *voiture non* ~*e*, carriage without springs.
suspens (syspɑ̃), adj. invar. [L *suspensus*] Suspended. ~, s.m. suspense; *en* ~, in suspense.
suspense (syspɑ̃s), s.f. (obs.) Suspension (of an ecclesiastic). ⚠ Not 'suspense', which = *incertitude, suspens.*
suspenseur (syspɑ̃sœr), adj. m. (anat.) Suspensory, suspending.
suspensi-f, -ve (syspɑ̃sif), adj. Suspensive, suspending; (gram.) *points* ~*s*, points of suspension.
suspension (syspɑ̃sjɔ̃), s.f. Suspension, interruption; hanging lamp; ~ *à la Cardan*, gimbals, gimbal frame; ~ *sur ressorts*, spring suspension; *points de* ~, dots (indicating a break in continuity or meaning).
suspensoir (syspɑ̃swar), s.m. Suspensory bandage, sling.
suspente (syspɑ̃t), s.f. (naut.) Sling (of a yard).
suspicion (syspisjɔ̃), s.f. [L *suspicio*] Suspicion; *tenir en* ~, to distrust.
suspied (sypje), s.m. [*sus*+*pied*] Strap (of spur).
sustentation (systɑ̃ta'sjɔ̃), s.f. Sustentation, support, maintenance.
sustenter (systɑ̃te), v.a. [f. L *sustentare*] To sustain, to support, to maintain, to nourish; **se** ~, v.pr. to support or nourish oneself.
susurration (sysyra'sjɔ̃), s.f. **susurrement** (sysyrmɑ̃), s.m. Susurration, whispering.
susurrer (sysyre), v.a.n. [L *susurrare*] To murmur, to whisper, to buzz.
sutural, -e, (aux) (sytyral), adj. (anat.) Sutural.
suture (sytyr), s.f. [L *sutura*] Suture, seam, joint.
suturer (sytyre), v.a. To suture, to join.
suzerain, -e (syzrɛ̃), s.m.f. Suzerain. ~, adj. Paramount, sovereign.
suzeraineté (syzrɛnte), s.f. Suzerainty, lordship, sovereignty.
svastika (svastika), s.m. [Sansk. wd] Swastika.
svelte (svɛlt), adj. [It. *svelto*] Svelte, slender, lissom, slim, lithe.
sveltesse (svɛltɛs), s.f. Slenderness, litheness, lissomness.
s.v.p. (ɛsvepe), [abbrev. of *s'il vous plaît*] If you please, please.
sybarite (sibarit), adj. [f. *Sybaris*] Sybaritic. ~, s.m.f. Sybarite.
sybaritique (sibaritik), adj. Sybaritic, sybaritical.
sybaritisme (sibaritism), s.m. Sybaritism.
sycomore (sikɔmɔr), s.m. [f. Gr. *sukon*+*moron*] (bot.) Sycamore.
sycophante (sikɔfɑ̃t), s.m. [f. Gr. *sukophantēs*] Sycophant, impostor, knave, rogue.
syénite (sjenit), s.f. [f. *Syène*, Egypt] (min.) Syenite.
syllabaire (sillabɛr), s.m. Spelling-book.
syllabe (sillab), s.f. [Gr. *sullabē*] Syllable.
syllabique (sillabik), adj. Syllabic.
syllabisme (sillabism), s.m. Syllabic writing.
syllabus (sillabys), s.m. [mod. L wd] Syllabus.
syllepse (sillɛps), s.f. [Gr. *sullēpsis*] (rhet.) Syllepsis.

sylleptique (sillɛptik), adj. Sylleptical.
syllogisme (sillɔʒism), s.m. [Gr. *sullogismos*] Syllogism.
syllogistique (sillɔʒistik), adj. Syllogistic, syllogistical.
sylphe (silf), s.m. [mod. L *sylphes*] Sylph.
sylphide (silfid), s.f. Sylph, sylphid.
sylvain (silvɛ̃), s.m. [f. L *sylva*] Sylvan.
sylvestre (silvɛstr), adj. [f. L *sylva*] Sylvan, pertaining to forests, growing in forests.
sylvicole (sylvikɔl), adj. [f. L *sylva*+*colere*] Pertaining to forestry.
sylviculture (silvikyltyr), s.f. Sylviculture, forestry.
sylvie (silvi), s.f. **1.** (ornith.) Warbler; **2.** (bot.) sylvia, a small white anemone growing in woods.
sylvinite (silvinit), s.f. (chem., agric.) Sylvine, sylvite, native potassium chloride.
symbiose (sɛ̃bjoz), s.f. [f. Gr. *sun*+*bios*] (biol.) Symbiosis.
symbole (sɛ̃bɔl), s.m. [Gr. *sumbolon*] Symbol; ~ *des Apôtres*, Apostles' Creed; (chem., math., &c.) symbol.
symbolique (sɛ̃bɔlik), adj. Symbolic, symbolical. ~, s.f. Symbology.
symboliquement (sɛ̃bɔlikmɑ̃), adv. Symbolically.
symbolisation (sɛ̃bɔliza'sjɔ̃), s.f. Symbolization.
symboliser (sɛ̃bɔlize), v.a. To symbolize.
symbolisme (sɛ̃bɔlism), s.m. Symbolism.
symboliste (sɛ̃bɔlist), adj. s.m.f. Symbolist.
symétrie (simetri), s.f. [Gr. *sun*+*metron*] Symmetry.
symétrique (simetrik), adj. Symmetrical.
symétriquement (simetrikmɑ̃), adv. Symmetrically.
sympathie (sɛ̃pati), s.f. [f. Gr. *sun*+*pathein*] Sympathy, fellow-feeling.
sympathique (sɛ̃patik), adj. Sympathetic; congenial; likeable; (anat.) *grand* ~, sympathetic nerve; *encre* ~, sympathetic ink.
sympathiquement (sɛ̃patikmɑ̃), adv. Sympathetically, congenially.
sympathiser (sɛ̃patize), v.n. To sympathize.
symphonie (sɛ̃fɔni), s.f. [f. Gr. *sun*+*phōnē*] Symphony.
symphonique (sɛ̃fɔnik), adj. Symphonic.
symphoniste (sɛ̃fɔnist), s.m.f. Symphonist.
symphyse (sɛ̃fiz), s.f. [Gr. *sun*+*phusis*] (anat.) Symphysis.
symptomatique (sɛ̃ptɔmatik), adj. Symptomatic.
symptomatologie (sɛ̃ptɔmatɔlɔʒi), s.f. Symptomatology.
symptôme (sɛ̃ptom), s.m. [Gr. *sumptōma*] Symptom.
synagogue (sinagɔg), s.f. [Gr. *sunagōgē*] Synagogue.
synalèphe (sinalɛf), s.f. [f. Gr. *sunaleiphein*] Synaloepha, coalescence of two syllables in pronunciation.
synallagmatique (sinalagmatik), adj. [f. Gr. *sunallagma*] (law) Synallagmatic, reciprocal.
synanthérées (sinɑ̃tere), s.f.pl. [f. Gr. *sun* + (Fr.) *anthère*] (bot.) Compositae, synanthereae.
synanthérique (sinɑ̃terik), adj. (bot.) Synanthereous.
synarthrose (sinartroz), s.f. [f. Gr. *sun*+*arthrōsis*] (pathol.) Synarthrosis.
synchrone (sɛ̃kron), adj. [f. Gr. *sun*+*khronos*] Synchronous, simultaneous, coeval.
synchronique (sɛ̃krɔnik), adj. Synchronical, synchronal, synchronous.
synchronisme (sɛ̃krɔnism), s.m. Synchronism.
syncopal, -e, (aux) (sɛ̃kɔpal), adj. Syncopal; syncopated.
syncope (sɛ̃kɔp), s.f. [Gr. *sugkopē*] Syncope, swoon, fainting-fit; *tomber en* ~, to faint away; (gram., mus.) syncopation.
syncoper (sɛ̃kɔpe), v.a. To syncopate.
syncrétisme (sɛ̃kretism), s.m. [f. Gr. *sugkrētizein*] (phil.) Syncretism.
syndactile (sɛ̃daktil), adj. [f. Gr. *sun*+*dactulos*] (zool.) Syndactylous.
syndic (sɛ̃dik), s.m. [f. Gr. *sun*+*dikē*] Syndic; official assignee (in bankruptcy); official trustee.
syndical, -e, (aux) (sɛ̃dikal), adj. Pertaining to syndicates; *chambre* ~, trade committee, trade union committee.
syndicalisme (sɛ̃dikalism), s.m. Syndicalism, trade unionism.
syndicaliste (sɛ̃dikalist), adj. s.m.f. Syndicalist, trade unionist.
syndicat (sɛ̃dika), s.m. Syndicate, trade union.
syndicataire (sɛ̃dikatɛr), adj. Pertaining to syndicates or trade unions.
syndiqué, -e (sɛ̃dike), p. adj. s.m.f. (Member) of a syndicate; syndicated; union-; unionist.
syndiquer (sɛ̃dike), v.a. To form into a syndicate; to syndicate; **se** ~, v.pr. to form themselves into a syndicate, to join a syndicate.
syndrome (sɛ̃drom), s.m. [Gr. *sundromē*] Syndrome, set of concurrent symptoms in a disease.
synecdoche, synecdoque (sinɛkdɔk), s.f. [Gr. wd] (rhet.) Synecdoche, a figure by which a more comprehensive term is used for a less comprehensive or vice versa.
synérèse (sinerɛz), s.f. [f. Gr. *sun*+*airein*] Synaeresis; contraction of two syllables into one.
synergie (sinɛrʒi), s.f. [f. Gr. *sun*+*ergon*] (physiol.) Synergy, joint working.

syngénésie (sɛ̃ʒenezi), s.f. [f. Gr. *sun*+ *genesis*] (bot.) Syngenesia.
syngnathe (sɛ̃gnat), s.m. [f. Gr. *sun*+ *gnathos*] (ichth.) Syngnathus, pipe-fish.
synodal, -e, (aux) (sinɔdal), adj. Synodic, synodal, of the Synod.
synode (sinɔd), s.m. [Gr. *sunodos*] Synod.
synodique (sinɔdik), adj. Synodic, synodal, synodical.
synonyme (sinɔnim), s.m. [f. Gr. *sun*+ *onoma*] Synonym. ~, adj. Synonymous.
synonymie (sinɔnimi), s.f. Synonymy.
synonymique (sinɔnimic), adj. Synonymic, pertaining to synonymy.
synoptique (sinɔptik), adj. [f. Gr. *sun*+ *optomai*] Synoptic. *Les ~s*, s.m.pl. the Synoptic Gospels, the Synoptics.
synovial, -e, (aux) (sinɔvjal), adj. (anat.) Synovial.
synovie (sinɔvi), s.f. [mod. L *synovia* (invented by Paracelsus)] (anat.) Synovia.
syntaxe (sɛ̃taks), s.f. [f. Gr. *sun*+*taxis*] Syntax.
syntaxique, syntactique (sɛ̃taksik, sɛ̃taktik), adj. Syntactic, syntactical.
synthèse (sɛ̃tɛz), s.f. [Gr. *sunthesis*] Synthesis (pl. syntheses).
synthétique (sɛ̃tetik), adj. Synthetic(al).
synthétiquement (sɛ̃tetikmɑ̃), adv. Synthetically.
synthétiser (sɛ̃tetize), v.a. To synthesize, to synthetize.
syphiligraphie (sifiligrafi), s.f. Syphiligraphy.
syphilis (sifilis), s.f. [f. *Syphilus*, character in 16th-c. Latin poem] (pathol.) Syphilis, pox.
syphilitique (sifilitik), adj. s.m.f. Syphilitic.
syriaque (sirjak), adj. s.m. Syriac (language).
syrien, -ne (sirjɛ̃), adj. s.m.f. Syrian.
syringa (sirɛ̃ga), s.m. [mod. L wd] (bot.) **1.** (cf. **seringa**) Syringa, mock orange; **2.** botanical name for lilac.
syringe, syrinx (sirɛ̃ʒ, sirɛks), s.f. [Gr. *surigx*] Syrinx.
syrte (sirt), s.f. [L *syrtis*] Syrtis (pl. syrtes), quicksand.
systaltique (sistaltik), adj. (physiol.) Systaltic.
systématique (sistematik), adj. Systematic.
systématiquement (sistematikmɑ̃), adv. Systematically.
systématiser (sistematize), v.a. To systematize.
système (sistɛm), s.m. [Gr. *sustēm*] System; *par ~*, systematically; (slang) *courir* or *taper sur le ~ à X*, to get on X's nerves; to exasperate X.
systole (sistɔl), s.f. [Gr. *sustolē*] (physiol.) Systole.
systyle (sistil), adj. s.m. [f. Gr. *sun*+ *stulos*] (arch.) Systyle.
syzygie (siziʒi), s.f. [f. Gr. *sun*+*zugos*] (astr.) Syzygy.

T

T, t (te), s.m. Twentieth letter of the alphabet; often used for euphony as in: *a-t-on pris?, ne voilà-t-il pas; t.s.v.p.* = *tournez s'il vous plaît*, please turn over, P.T.O.
t', contr. of *te*.
ta, ta, ta! (ta, ta, ta), interj. Tut, tut, now!
tabac (taba), s.m. [Span. *tabaco*] Tobacco, snuff; *~ à chiquer*, chewing-tobacco; *~ en carotte, en corde*, pigtail tobacco; *~ à fumer*, smoking-tobacco; *~ en poudre, à priser*, snuff; *~ râpé*, rappee; *~ de la régie*, tobacco supplied by the Fr. Government; *bureau* or *débit de ~*, tobacconist's shop; *marchand de ~*, tobacconist; *boîte à ~*, tobacco-box; *blague à ~*, tobacco-pouch; *pot à ~*, tobacco-jar; (colloq.) *passer à ~*, to handle roughly, to rough-handle, to drub; (U.S.A.) to soak; (fig.) *ce n'est pas le même ~*, that's another pair of shoes.
tabagie (tabaʒi), s.f. Low smoking-room; room where the atmosphere is vile with tobacco-smoke.
tabard (tabar), s.m. [etym. dub.] (Middle Ages) Tabard.
tabarin (tabarɛ̃), s.m. [prop. n. in old farces] Merry andrew, buffoon; *faire le ~*, to play the buffoon.
tabarinade (tabarinad), s.f. Buffoonery.
tabatière (tabatjɛr), s.f. Snuff-box; (gun) breech-block; *fenêtre à ~*, sky-light.
tabellaire (tabɛlɛr), adj. [f. L *tabella*] Tabular.
tabellion (tabɛlljɔ̃), s.m. [L *tabellio*] (obs.) Scrivener.
tabernacle (tabɛrnakl), s.m. [L *tabernaculum*] Tabernacle.
tabès (tabɛs), s.m. [L wd] (pathol.) Tabes.
tabescence (tabɛsɑ̃s), s.f. (pathol.) Tabescence.
tabis (tabi), s.m. [Arab. *attabiy*] Tabby, watered silk.
tabiser (tabize), v.a. To tabby, to water (silk).
tablature (tablatyr), s.f. [f. L *tabula*] (mus.) Tablature; *donner de la ~ à X*, to get X into trouble; to cut out X's work for him; *entendre la ~*, to be up to snuff.
table (tabl), s.f. [L *tabula*] Table, board, slab, food, &c.; *~ alphabétique*, alphabetical list, index; *~ à coulisse*, table with sliding leaves, expanding table; *~ d'hôte*, table d'hôte, ordinary; *~ à jouer*, card-table; *~ à ouvrage*, work-table; *~ à rallonges*, extending table; *~ de dix*

couverts, table laid for ten; ~ *de cuisine*, kitchen table; ~ *d'harmonie*, sound-board; ~ *de jeu*, card-table, gaming-table; ~ *des matières*, table of contents; index; ~ *de multiplication* or *de Pythagore*, multiplication table; ~ *de nuit*, bedside table; ~ *de travail*, study-table; *la sainte* ~, communion-table, Holy Communion; ~*s tournantes*, table-turning; ~ *volante*, occasional table; ~ *gigogne*, nest of tables; *aimer la* ~, to be fond of good living; *avoir une* ~ *frugale*, to live frugally; *avoir la* ~ *et le logement chez X*, to board and lodge with X; *bénir la* ~, to say grace before meat; *dresser la* ~, to set the table; *faire* ~ *rase*, to make a clean sweep; *jouer cartes sur* ~, to act openly, above board; *se lever de* ~, *sortir de* ~, *quitter la* ~, to rise from table; *mettre la* ~, to lay the cloth, to set the table; *se mettre à* ~, to sit down to table; (colloq.) *se mettre à* ~, to blow the gaff, to inform against one's accomplices; *tenir* ~ *ouverte*, to keep open house; *propos de* ~, table-talk; *le dos au feu, le ventre à* ~, with every comfort; *haut bout de la* ~, head of the table.

tableau (pl. **-x**) (tablo), s.m. [dim. of *table*] Picture, painting, scene, scenery, view; list, catalogue, board, (law) rolls, panel, (rail.) time-table; (hunt.) list of game killed; ~ *d'annonces*, advertising-board; ~ *de chevalet*, easel-piece; (electr.) ~ *de distribution*, switch-board; ~ *noir*, blackboard; (law) *rayé du* ~, struck off the rolls; (fam.) ~ *!*, tableau!; then followed a scene!; there's a picture for you!; ~ *vivant*, tableau; *une ombre au* ~, a dark side to the picture.

tableautin (tablotɛ̃), s.m. Small picture.

tablée (table), s.f. Table, company at table.

tabler (table), v.n. (at backgammon) To dress the board, place the men; (colloq.) to rely (*sur*, upon), to depend (upon), to reckon (on), to base one's plans (upon).

tableti-er, -ère (tablɛtje), s.m.f. Fancy stationer, dealer in fancy goods.

tablette (tablɛt), s.f. Shelf, tablet, cake, lozenge; tablets (pl.), note-book; (naut.) armour-shelf; ~ *de cheminée*, mantelpiece; *rayez cela de vos* ~*s*, get that out of your head.

tabletterie (tablɛtri), s.f. Fancy trade, toys, turnery.

tablier (tablie), s.m. [f. *table*] **1.** Apron (of a cook); *rendre son* ~, to give notice; **2.** flooring, platform (of a bridge); **3.** chess- or draught-board; **4.** blower (of a chimney); **5.** top-lining (of a sail); **6.** (motor.) dashboard.

tabou (tabu), s.m. adj. [Polynes. wd] Taboo.

tabouer (tabue), v.a. To taboo, to forbid.

tabouret (taburɛ), s.m. [f. *tambour*] Stool, footstool; (bot.) shepherd's purse (syn. THLASPI); ~ *de piano*, music-stool.

tabourin (taburɛ̃), s.m. [f. *tambour*] **1.** Tambourine; **2.** chimney-cowl.

tabulaire (tabylɛr), adj. [L *tabularis*] Tabular.

tacamaque (takamak), s.m. [f. Aztec *tecomahiyac*] (bot.) Tacamahac.

tacaud (tako), s.m. (ichth.) Whiting-pout.

tac (tak), s.m. **1.** Rot (in sheep); **2.** (onom.) *répondre du* ~ *au* ~, to give as good as one gets; to make an instant and witty retort; (fenc.) ~*-au-*~, parry combined with riposte.

tacet (tasɛt), s.m. [L wd] Tacet (musical direction indicating silence).

tachant, -e (taʃɑ̃), p. adj. [f. *tacher*] Spotting, easily soiled.

tache (taʃ), s.f. [orig. dub.] Spot, stain, (fig.) blot, blemish; *sans* ~, blameless, pure, spotless, undefiled; ~ *solaire*, sunspot; ~ *de naissance*, birthmark, mole; ~ *de rousseur*, freckle; ~ *de vin*, (*a*) wine-stain; (*b*) birthmark; port-wine mark; *il arrive avec une réputation sans* ~, he comes without a stain on his character.

tâche (tɑʃ), s.f. [f. *tâcher*] Task, job; *à la* ~, by the job, by the piece; *ouvrage à la* ~, jobbing, piece-work; *ouvrier à la* ~, jobbing workman; (fig.) *prendre à* ~ *de faire une chose*, to make it one's business to do a thing, to make a point of doing a thing; *travailler à la* ~, *être à la* ~, to be on piece-work.

tachéographie (takeɔgrafi), s.f. [f. Gr. *takhus*+*graphein*] Tachygraphy.

tachéomètre (takeɔmɛtr), s.m. [Gr. *takhus*+*metron*] Tachymeter.

tachéométrie (takeɔmetri), s.f. Tachymetry.

tacher (taʃe), v.a. [orig. dub.] To stain, to spot, to slur, to sully, to tarnish, to blemish; **se** ~, v.pr. to stain one's clothes, to soil oneself.

tâcher (tɑʃe), v.n. [L *taxare*] To try, to endeavour, to strive, to seek, to do one's best (*de*, to).

tâcheron (tɑʃrɔ̃), s.m. Jobbing workman, job-hand.

tacheter (taʃte), v.a. To mark with spots, to fleck, to speckle.

tachygraphe (takigraf), s.m.f. [f. Gr. *takhus*+*graphein*] Tachygrapher, shorthand writer; syn. STÉNOGRAPHE.

tachygraphie (takigrafi), s.f. Tachygraphy, stenography; syn. STÉNOGRAPHIE.

tachygraphique (takigrafik), adj. Tachygraphic.

tachygraphiquement (takigrafikmɑ̃), adv. Tachygraphically, stenographically.

tachymètre (takimɛtr), s.m. [Gr. *takhus*+*metron*] Tachometer; instrument for measuring speed. ⚠ Not English 'tachymeter'.

tachymétrie (takymetri), s.f. Tachometry.
tacite (tasit), adj. [L *tacitus*] Tacit, implied.
tacitement (tasitmɑ̃), adv. Tacitly.
taciturne (tasityrn), adj. [L *taciturnus*] Taciturn; silent; *Guillaume le* ~, William the Silent.
taciturnité (tasityrnite), s.f. Taciturnity.
tacot (tako), s.m. (colloq.) Ramshackle, rickety old motor-car.
tact (takt), s.m. [L *tactus*] Touch, sense of touch; (fig.) tact, intuitive perception of what is the right thing to do or say; *manquer de* ~, to be tactless.
tacticien (taktisjɛ̃), s. m. [f. Gr. *taktikē*] Tactician.
tactile (taktil), adj. [L *tactilis*] Tactile; tactual; tangible.
tactilement (taktilmɑ̃), adv. Tactually, tangibly.
tactilité (taktilite), s.f. Tactility, tangibility, tangibleness.
tactique (taktik), s.f. [Gr. *taktikē*] Tactics (pl.); (fig.) means, way, plan of action.
tadorne (tadɔrn), s.m. (ornith.) Sheldrake.
tael (taɛl), s.m. [Malay *tahil*] Tael, Chinese coin.
taenia, ténia (tenja), s.m. [Gr. *tainia*] Taenia, tapeworm.
taffetas (tafta), s.m. [Pers. *tāftah*] Taffeta; (pharm.) ~ *d'Angleterre*, oiled silk, oil-silk; ~ *gommé*, court-plaster.
tafia (tafja), s.m. [W. Ind. wd] Tafia (rum).
tagète (taʒɛt), s.m. [L *tages*] (bot.) Tagetes.
taïaut or **tayaut** (tajo), s.m. [etym. dub.] (hunt.) Tally-ho.
taie (tɛ), s.f. [f. Gr. *thēkē*] **1.** Case, pillow-case; ~ *d'oreiller*, pillow-case; **2.** (med.) film, speck (on the eye).
taïkoun (taikun), s.m. [Jap. *taikun*] Tycoon.
taillabilité (tajabilite), s.f. Taxability.
taillable (tɑjabl), adj. [f. *taille*] Taxable; *vilains* ~*s et corvéables à merci*, serfs taxable and obliged to work at their lord's will and pleasure.
taillade (tɑjad), s.f. Cut, gash, slash.
taillader (tɑjade), v.a. [f. *tailler*] To slash, to cut, to gash; *des manches tailladées*, slashed sleeves.
tailladin (tɑjadɛ̃), s.m. Thin slice of orange or lemon.
taillanderie (tɑjɑ̃dri), s.f. Edge-tool trade, edge tools.
taillandier (tɑjɑ̃dje), s.m. Edge-tool maker.
taillant (tɑjɑ̃), s.m. Edge (of a knife, &c.).
taille (tɑj), s.f. [f. *tailler*] Cutting, cut, fashion; edge (of a sword); height, stature, size, shape; waist; tally(-stick); copse-wood, coppice; (hort.) pruning, dressing of vines; (surg.) cystotomy; (mus.) tenor part; (feud. law) poll-tax; deal (at cards); *quelle est sa* ~*?*, how tall is he?; *tour de* ~, waist measurement; *avoir la* ~ *fine*, to have a small waist; *prendre bien la* ~, to fit very well; *n'avoir point de* ~, to be shapeless, to have no shape; *être de* ~ *bien prise*, to be well made, well proportioned; *une* ~ *de guêpe*, a wasp waist; *être de* ~ *à*, to be big enough to; to be quite able to; *être de* ~ *à lutter contre X*, to be a match for X; *frapper d'estoc et de* ~, to cut and thrust, to hit right and left, to lay about one; *se tenant par la* ~, with their arms round each other's waists; *faire des coches sur une* ~, to make notches in a tally; *pierre de* ~, freestone; *outils de* ~, stone-cutter's tools; ~*-buissons*, s.m. hedge-shears; -~ *crayon(s)*, s.m. pencil-sharpener; (engr.) ~-*douce*, s.f. copper-plate; ~ *de cheveux*, s.f. hair-cutting; ~*-légumes*, s.m. vegetable-cutter; (naut.) ~*-mer*, s.m. cutwater; ~-*racines*, s.m. root-cutter.
taillé, -e (tɑje), p. adj. Cut; mended (pen); proportioned, shaped; *cote mal* ~*e*, rough compromise; *faire une cote mal* ~*e*, to split the difference.
tailler (tɑje), v.a. [f. L *talea*] To hew, to trim, to prune, (hort.) to dress; to cut, to cut out, to carve, to sharpen; to make or mend (pens); to frame, to shape; to deal (cards); ~ *une robe*, to cut out a frock; (colloq.) ~ *une bavette*, to chat, to gossip; to have a chat; ~ *de la besogne à X*, to give X a great deal of trouble; to cut out X's work for him; ~ *en plein drap*, to be regardless of expense; ~ *des croupières à X*, to get X into trouble; to put a spoke in X's wheel.
taillerie (tɑjri), s.f. Diamond-cutting, cutting of precious stones.
tailleur (tɑjœr), s.m. Tailor, cutter; dealer (at cards); ~ *à façon*, jobbing tailor; ~ *de pierres*, stone-cutter; (jest.) sculptor; ~ *pour dames*, ladies' tailor; *costume* ~, tailor-made coat and skirt.
tailleuse (tɑjøz), s.f. Tailoress, dress-maker, cutter.
taillis (taji), s.m. [f. *tailler*] Copse, copse-wood, coppice, underwood, brushwood.
tailloir (tɑjwar), s.m. Trencher, platter; (arch.) abacus.
tain (tɛ̃), s.m. [f. *étain*] Tin-foil; *mettre au* ~, to quicksilver, to silver.
taire (tɛr), v.a. [L *tacere*] To say nothing of, to be silent about, to keep to oneself, to suppress, to conceal, to pass over in silence, to overlook, to leave unsaid; *faire* ~, to silence, to hush, to reduce to silence; **se** ~, v.pr. to be silent, to hold one's tongue, to hold one's peace; *taisez-vous*, hold your tongue!, be quiet; (fam.) shut up; *qui plus sait, plus se tait*, a still tongue

shows a wise head; *qui se tait consent*, silence gives consent.

tala (tala), adj. s.m.f. See THALA.

talc (talk), s.m. [Arab. *ṭalq*] Talc.

talcique (talsik), adj. Talcose, talcous, talcky.

talent (talɑ̃), s.m. [L *talentum*] **1.** Talent, skill, ability, faculty, gift, attainments, parts; *une femme de beaucoup de* ~, a talented woman; ~*s de société*, accomplishments; **2.** (ant.) talent (weight, money).

talentueu-x, -se (talɑ̃tɥø), adj. Talented.

taler (tale), v.a. [etym. dub.] To bruise (espec. of fruit).

talion (taljɔ̃), s.m. [L *talio*] Talion, retaliation; *loi du* ~, law of retaliation, lex talionis; *peine du* ~, retaliation.

talisman (talismɑ̃), s.m. [f. Gr. *telesma*] Talisman, charm, amulet.

talismanique (talismanik), adj. Talismanic.

talle (tal), s.f. [Gr. *thallos*] (bot., hort.) Sucker.

taller (tale), v.a.n. (hort.) To throw out suckers.

tallipot (talipo), s.m. [Malayalam *talipat*] (bot.) Talipot, fan-palm.

talmouse (talmuz), s.f. [orig. dub.] **1.** (cook.) Cheese-cake; **2.** (pop.) slap, whack, thump.

talmud (talmyd), s.m. [Hebr. wd] Talmud.

talmudique (talmydik), adj. Talmudic(al).

talmudiste (talmydist), s.m. Talmudist.

taloche (talɔʃ), s.f. [orig. dub.] **1.** Cuff, thump, punch, rap on the head; **2.** mason's mortar-board.

talocher (talɔʃe), v.a. To cuff, to thump.

talon (talɔ̃), s.m. [L *talus*] Heel; heel-piece; butt-end; (of tyres) flange, bead; (at cards) talon (cards left after deal); (fin., comm.) counterfoil; *il est toujours sur les* ~*s de X*, he is always close on X's heels, he is always dogging X's steps; *jouer des* ~*s*, *montrer les* ~*s*, to show a clean pair of heels, to take to one's heels; *tourner les* ~*s*, to go away, to make off, to leg it, to run away; *se sentir* or *avoir l'estomac dans les* ~*s*, to be famished; *un* ~*-rouge*, an aristocrat, a courtier, a dandy; ~ *de chèque*, counterfoil; *pneu à* ~, flanged tyre. ⚠ 'Talon' in English = *serres (d'oiseau de proie)*, but French *talon* can never be used in this sense.

talonner (talɔne), v.a. To be close on the heels of, to press hard, to urge, to dun; to bother; to spur; (football) to dribble; ~, v.n. (naut.) to ground.

talonnette (talɔnɛt), s.f. Heel-piece (of a stocking or shoe).

talonnier (talɔnje), s.m. Heel-maker.

talonnière (talɔnjɛr), s.f. (myth.) Heel-wing; talaria (pl.).

talpack (talpak), s.m. (mil., obs.) Busby.

talqueu-x, -se (talkœ), adj. Talcose.

talus (taly), s.m. [L wd] Slope, bank, declivity, embankment, talus; *en* ~, shelving. ⚠ Not English 'talus', ankle-bone, which = *cheville*, or club-foot, which = *pied bot*.

talutage (talytaʒ), s.m. Embanking, sloping.

taluter (talyte), v.a. To slope, to embank.

tamandua (tamandɥa), s.m. [Braz. wd] (zool.) Tamandua, little ant-bear.

tamanoir (tamanwar), s.m. [Carib *tamanoa*] (zool.) Tamanoir, great ant-eater.

tamarin (tamarɛ̃), s.m. [Carib wd] **1.** (bot.) Tamarind(-tree); **2.** (zool.) tamarin, S. American marmoset.

tamarinier (tamarinje), s.m. (bot.) Tamarind-tree; syn. TAMARIN.

tamaris (tamari), s.m. [L *tamariscus*] (bot.) Tamarisk.

tamariscinées (tamarissine), s.f.pl. (bot.) Tamaricaceae.

tambouille (tɑ̃buj), s.f. (colloq.) Grub, stew, badly prepared food.

tambour (tɑ̃bur), s.m. [Arab. *tanbur*] Drum, drummer; (anat.) tympanum; (mech.) cylinder, barrel, paddle-box; (arch.) tambour, drum, lobby; (embroidery) tambour, frame; *baguette de* ~, drum-stick; *peau de* ~, drum-head; ~ *de basque*, tambourine; ~*-major*, drum-major; ~ *voilé*, muffled drum; ~ *de ville*, town crier; ~ *battant*, with drums beating, (fig.) with a high hand; smartly, summarily, briskly; *sans* ~ *ni trompette*, quietly; (fam.) on the q.t.; *partir sans* ~ *ni trompette*, to slip away; *ce qui vient de la flûte s'en va par le* ~, easy come, easy go.

tambourin (tɑ̃burɛ̃), s.m. Tambourine.

tambourinage (tɑ̃burinaʒ), s.m. Drumming, tattooing, thrumming, strumming; (fig.) advertising, puffing.

tambouriner (tɑ̃burine), v.n. To drum, to beat, to tattoo, to thrum, to strum; ~, v.a. to drum, to proclaim by beat of drum, to cry, to advertise.

tambourineur (tɑ̃burinœr), s.m. Drummer, public crier; also *tambourinaire*, espec. in southern France.

taminier (taminje), **tamier** (tamje), s.m. [L *talminia*] (bot.) Black briony.

tamis (tami), s.m. [etym. dub.] Sieve, sifter, strainer; ~ *de crin*, hair sieve; *gros* ~, coarse sieve; ~ *fin*, fine sieve; *passer au* ~, to sift, to sieve; (fig.) to sift, to examine thoroughly.

tamisage (tamisaʒ), s.m. Sifting, straining, sieving.

tamiser (tamize), v.a. To sift, to sieve, to strain; to filter; to soften (light).

tamiserie (tamizri), s.f. Sieve-making, sieve factory.

tamiseu-r, -se (tamizœr), s.m.f. Sifter.

tamisier (tamizje), s.m. Sieve-maker.
tamoul, -e, tamil (tamul, tamil), s.m.f. [native wd] Tamil; Tamil (language of race inhabiting S. India). ~, adj. Tamil.
tampon (tɑ̃pɔ̃), s.m. [f. *taper*] Stopper, plug, bung, tampion (of gun), dam (of pond); (surg.) tampon, plug; (railw., naut.) buffer; pad, rubber stamp; (mil. slang) officer's servant, batman, soldier doing service (unofficially) for another; *servir de ~ entre X et Y*, to serve as a buffer between X and Y.
tamponnement (tɑ̃pɔnmɑ̃), s.m. **1.** Collision, shock; **2.** (rare) tamponade, tamponage, tamponment (of wound, &c.).
tamponner (tɑ̃pɔne), v.a. **1.** To plug, to stop up, to tampon; **2.** to dab; **3.** (railw.) to collide, to run into.
tam-tam (tam-tam), s.m. [Hindu wd] Tom-tom; gong; *faire du ~*, to advertise, to puff, to make a fuss, to create a sensation.
tan (tɑ̃), s.m. [f. Breton *tann* = oak] Tan, tan-bark; *fosse à ~*, tan-pit.
tanaisie (tanɛzi), s.f. [Gr. *athanasia*] (bot.) Tansy.
tancement (tɑ̃smɑ̃), s.m. Scolding, chiding, rating.
tancer (tɑ̃se), v.a. [LL *tentiare*] To scold, to reprimand, to rate, to upbraid, to lecture, to chide, to rebuke, to take up sharply.
tanche (tɑ̃ʃ), s.f. [L *tinca*] (ichth.) Tench.
tandem (tɑ̃dɛm), s.m. [L wd] Tandem, tandem bicycle.
tandis que (tɑ̃di(s)kə), conj. loc. [L *tamdiu*] Whilst, whereas, while.
tangage (tɑ̃gaʒ), s.m. [etym. dub., OF *tanguer*] (naut.) Pitching.
tangence (tɑ̃ʒɑ̃s), s.f. (geom.) Tangency.
tangent, -e (tɑ̃ʒɑ̃), adj. [L *tangens*] (geom.) Tangent, tangential.
tangente (tɑ̃ʒɑ̃t), s.f. (geom.) Tangent; (fig.) *s'échapper par la ~*, to go off at a tangent.
tangentiel, -le (tɑ̃ʒɑ̃sjɛl), adj. (geom.) Tangential.
tangentiellement (tɑ̃ʒɑ̃siɛlmɑ̃), adv. (geom.) Tangentially.
tanghin (tɑ̃gɛ̃), s.m. [Malagasy *tangena*] Tanghin (a poison prepared by the natives of Madagascar from the kernel of tanghin fruit).
tanghinia (tɑ̃ginja), s.m. (bot.) Tanghin (shrub).
tangibilité (tɑ̃ʒibilite), s.f. Tangibility, tangibleness.
tangible (tɑ̃ʒibl), adj. [L *tangibilis*] Tangible; definite, clearly intelligible; (law) tangible, corporeal.
tangiblement (tɑ̃ʒibləmɑ̃), adv. Tangibly.
tango (tɑ̃go), s.m. [S. Amer. Span. wd] Tango (dance); tango (colour).
tangon (tɑ̃gɔ̃), s.m. [etym. dub.] (naut.) Swinging boom, foresail boom.
tangue (tɑ̃g), s.f. Sea-sand from *Mont St-Michel*, calcareous sand (used as manure).
tanguer (tɑ̃ge), v.n. [etym. dub., OF *tanguer*] **1.** (naut.) To pitch; **2.** to dance the tango; **3.** to walk like a drunkard.
tanière (tanjɛr), s.f. [LL *taxonaria*] Den, lair, hole.
tanin (tanɛ̃), s.m. [f. *tan*] Tannin.
tannage (tanaʒ), s.m. Tanning.
tannant, -e (tɑ̃nɑ̃), p. adj. Tanning; (slang) wearisome, tiresome, provoking, boring.
tanne (tan), s.f. [f. *tanner*] Pimple, blackhead.
tanné, -e (tane), p. adj. Tanned, tawny, tan-coloured; (colloq.) sunburnt.
tanné (tane), s.m. Tan-colour.
tannée (tane), s.f. Spent bark, waste tan.
tanner (tane), v.a. To tan; (colloq.) to bother, to weary, to annoy, to tease; (slang) *~ le cuir à X*, to give X a hiding, a drubbing; to tan X's hide for him.
tannerie (tanri), s.f. Tanyard, tannery.
tanneur (tanœr), s.m. Tanner.
tannique (tanik), adj. (chem.) Tannic.
tant (tɑ̃), adv. [L *tantum*] So much, so many, such, so, as much as; *~ et ~*, so very much; *~ de fois*, so many times; *~ de monde*, so many people; *~ et plus*, more than enough, in full measure, over and over again; *~ bons que mauvais*, good as well as bad; *~ mieux*, all the better; that 's right; I'm glad of it; *~ pis*, the more 's the pity; I'm sorry for it; it can't be helped; no matter; *~ plus*, the more, so much the more; *~ soit peu*, ever so little; *~ s'en faut*, far from it; *~ bien que mal*, as well as one can; middling, so-so, anyhow; after a fashion; *~ il est stupide*, such is his stupidity; *~ il est vrai*, so true it is; *vous tous, ~ que vous êtes*, every one of you, the whole lot of you; *~ que*, as far as; as long as; so far as, so long as; *en ~ que*, in so far as; as; considered as; *si ~ est que*, if, supposing it to be that; *~ s'en faut que*, so far from, far from; *~ il y a que*, however, at all events.
tantale[1] (tɑ̃tal), s.m. [f. *Tantalus*, Gr. myth.] (chem.) Tantalum: Ta (a metal used for incandescent filaments in electric lamps).
tantale[2] (tɑ̃tal), s.m. [f. *Tantalus*, Gr. myth.] (ornith.) Tantalus, wood ibis. ⚠ Not 'tantalus', spirit-stand in which decanters are locked up but visible.
tante (tɑ̃t), s.f. [L *amita*] Aunt; *~ à la mode de Bretagne*, father's cousin german; (slang) *ma ~*, the pawnshop, 'my uncle'.
tantet, tantinet (tɑ̃tɛ, tɑ̃tinɛ), s.m. Little bit, snippet, trifle, wee drop, dash. ~, adv. Somewhat, rather.
tantième (tɑ̃tjɛm), adj. s.m. So much per cent., part, percentage.
tantôt (tɑ̃to), adv. [*tant*+*tôt*] Presently, by and by, shortly, soon, anon; a little

while ago, just now, nearly, in the afternoon, to-day; ~ . . . ~, sometimes . . . sometimes; now . . . now; ~ *plus* ~ *moins*, sometimes more, sometimes less; ~ *l'un*, ~ *l'autre*, first one, then the other; alternately; ~ *ceci* ~ *cela*, now this, now that; *à* ~, see you later (in the same day); *sur le* ~, late in the day, towards evening.

taoïsme (taɔism), s.m. [f. Chinese *tao*] Taoism, religious doctrine of Lao-Tsze, 500 B.C.

taon (tɑ̃), s.m. [L *tabanus*] (ent.) Gadfly, horse-fly.

tapage (tapaʒ), s.m. [f. *taper*] Noise, fuss, racket, row; *faire du* ~, to make an uproar, (fam.) to kick up a row; *voilà bien du* ~ *pour rien!*, what a fuss about nothing!; much ado about nothing!; *cette nouvelle fera du* ~, that'll create a sensation, or a stir.

tapageu-r, -se (tapaʒœr), s.m.f. Noisy person, rowdy. ~, adj. Noisy, riotous, loud; glaring, gaudy, showy, flashy.

tapageusement (tapaʒøzmɑ̃), adv. Noisily, loudly, flashily.

tape (tap), s.f. [f. *taper*] Thump, tap, pat, rap, slap; (naut.) tompion; ~ *d'écubier*, buckler; (fig.) failure, disappointment; *prendre une* (or *la*) ~, to fail; to come a cropper; *quelle* ~*!*, what a sell! ⚠ Not 'tap' in the sense of *robinet*.

tapé, -e (tape), p. adj. (of fruit) Dried; (pop.) smart, pat, good; *ça, c'est bien* ~*!*, that's a shattering answer, or come-back!, that's the stuff to give them!

tapecu, tapecul (tapky), s.m. [*tape*+*cul*] Springless carriage, gig, wretched carriage or car; (naut.) jigger; *mât de* ~, jigger mast; *bout-dehors de* ~, bumpkin.

tapée (tape), s.f. (pop.) Lot, whole lot, heap, host, swarm.

taper (tape), v.a.n. [etym. dub.] To tap, to strike, to smack, to slap, to beat; to type; (colloq.) to touch; to do without; ~ *du pied*, to stamp (with one's foot); *tape dessus!*, give it him!; *on lui a tapé dessus*, they let him have it; ~ *dans l'œil*, to make an impression, to tickle the fancy; *il lui a tapé dans l'œil*, she seemed to take a fancy to him; *ce vin tape à la tête*, this wine is heady; ~ *dans le tas*, to strike at random; ~ *sur le ventre à X*, to be very familiar with X; ~ *une lettre* (*à la machine*), to type a letter; *il m'a tapé de 20 francs*, he touched me for 20 francs; *tu peux te* ~, *va!*, you can whistle for it!

tapette (tapɛt), s.f. Little tap, pat, carpet-beater, engraver's tool, cooper's bat, washerwoman's bat; (colloq.) glib tongue; *elle a une fière* ~*!*, she is a chatterbox, a regular gas-bag.

tapeu-r, -se (tapœr), s.m.f. (fam.) Constant borrower, cadger, sponger.

tapin (tapɛ̃), s.m. (pop.) Drummer.

tapinois (tapinwɑ), s.m. *en* ~, adv. loc. Slyly, on the sly, clandestinely, stealthily.

tapioca (tapjɔka), s.m. [Port. f. Braz. *tipioca*] Tapioca.

tapir (tapir), s.m. [Braz. *tapira*] (zool.) Tapir; (fig., in jargon of École Normale Supérieure) paying private pupil; hence *tapirat, tapiriser*, &c.

(se) tapir (sətapir), v.pr. [etym. dub.] To squat, to crouch, to cower, to nestle.

tapis (tapi), s.m. [Gr. *tapētion*] Carpet, matting, rug, cloth, cover, tapestry, (hort.) lawn; ~ *de billard*, billiard-cloth; ~*-brosse*, door-mat; ~ *de foyer*, hearth-rug; (fig.) ~ *vert*, gaming-table; (hort.) greensward, grass-plot; (fig.) *amuser le* ~, to be the life of the party; to beat about the bush; (fig.) *faire* ~ *net*, to sweep the stakes; *sur le* ~, talked of, under discussion; *mettre sur le* ~, to bring up, to start, to bring forward, to broach (a subject, &c.).

tapisser (tapise), v.a. To upholster (furniture), to paper (a wall), to hang (tapestries), to cover, to adorn; ~, v.n. to make tapestry.

tapisserie (tapisri), s.f. Tapestry, arras, hangings, upholstery, rug-work, fancy needlework, woolwork; (fig.) *faire* ~, to be a wallflower; *faire de la* ~, to do fancy-work, to make tapestry.

tapissie-r, -ère (tapisje), s.m.f. Upholsterer, tapestry-worker.

tapissière (tapisjɛr), s.f. Van, spring-van or -cart, furniture-van.

tapon (tapɔ̃), s.m. [f. *taper*] Plug, heap, bundle (of clothes); pad, knot (of hair).

taponnage (tapɔnaʒ), s.m. Bundling; plugging; piling up, rolling up (of hair).

taponner (tapɔne), v.a. To roll up, to plug up.

tapoter (tapɔte), v.a. To pat, to tap; to strum (piano).

taque (tak), s.f. (techn.) Cast-iron plate.

taquer (take), v.a. [f. LGerm. *take*] (print.) To plane down.

taquet (takɛ), s.m. [f. LGerm. *take*] Wedge, peg, picket, angle-block; (naut.) cleat, tappet, belaying-pin, kevel; ~ *de guindeau*, whelp.

taquin, -e (takɛ̃), adj. s.m.f. [It. *taccagno*] Teasing; tease; teaser, plague.

taquiner (takine), v.a. To tease; to plague, to torment.

taquinerie (takinri), s.f. Teasing, worrying.

taquoir (takwar), s.m. (print.) Plane.

tarabiscot (tarabisko), s.m. (join.) Groove, hollow.

tarabiscoter (tarabiskɔte), v.a. To groove, (fig.) to overdecorate, to over-elaborate; hence sometimes *tarabiscotage*, s.m.

tarabuster (tarabyste), v.a. (fam.) To worry, to bother, to vex, to plague, to pester.

tarare (tarar), s.m. Winnowing-machine; ~, s.f. [geog. orig.] = *toile de Tarare*, a silky cotton material.

tarare (tarar), interj. Fiddlesticks !, rubbish !, fiddle-de-dee !, pshaw !

taraud (taro), s.m. [f. Celt. *tarathar*] (techn.) Screw-tap, borer.

taraudage (tarodaʒ), s.m. Tapping (of screws and nuts).

tarauder (tarode), v.a. To tap, to screw-cut, to worm, to cut a thread in.

tarbouche (tarbuʃ), s.m. [Arab. wd] Tarboosh.

tard (tar), adv. s.m. [L *tarde*] Late; *tôt ou* ~, sooner or later; *plus* ~, later on; in after years, afterwards; *sur le* ~, late in the evening; late in life; *il se fait* ~, it 's getting late; *mieux vaut* ~ *que jamais*, better late than never; *il n'est jamais trop* ~ *pour bien faire*, it 's never too late to mend.

tarder (tarde), v.n. [L *tardare*] To delay, to put off, to defer, to linger, to loiter, to tarry, to wait, to dally, to be long; *il me tarde de*, I long to; I'm most anxious to; *il ne tardera pas à venir*, he will soon be here; *qu'il tarde à venir !*, how long he is in coming !

tardi-f, -ve (tardif), adj. Tardy, late, slow, sluggish, backward.

tardigrade (tardigrad), adj. s.m. [L *tardigradus*] (zool.) Tardigrade.

tardivement (tardivmɑ̃), adv. Slowly, tardily.

tardiveté (tardivte), s.f. Tardiness, slowness; (hort.) lateness, backwardness.

tare (tar), s.f. [Arab. *ṭarḥah*] **1.** Waste, loss, deficiency, (fig.) defect, blemish, fault, vice; **2.** tare (weight of wrapping, vessel, &c., in which goods, &c., are weighed).

taré, -e (tare), p. adj. **1.** Damaged; (fig.) ill-famed, of ill repute, bad, vicious, disreputable; **2.** (of vessel, box, &c.) tared.

tarentelle (tarɑ̃tɛl), s.f. [It. *tarantella*] Tarantella, tarantelle.

tarentin, -e (tarɑ̃tɛ̃), adj. s.m.f. Tarentine, of Taranto (Italy).

tarentule (tarɑ̃tyl), s.f. [It. *tarantola*] (ent.) Tarantula; (colloq.) *être piqué de la* ~, to be much excited.

tarer (tare), v.a. [f. *tare*] **1.** To damage, to spoil, to injure; to diminish, to lower the value of; **2.** to tare, to weigh separately (vessel, box, &c., in which a substance is to be weighed).

taret (tarɛ), s.m. (zool.) Teredo; ship-worm.

targe (tarʒ), s.f. [ON *targa*] Targe, target (shield), buckler.

targette (tarʒɛt), s.f. Small bolt, flat bolt. ⚠ Not 'target', which = *cible, disque; poitrine d'agneau; petit bouclier; targe.*

(se) targuer (sətarge), v.pr. [f. *targe*] To pride oneself (*de*, on); to boast (of), to brag (of); to plume oneself (on).

targum (targɔm), s.m. [Chald. wd] Targum.

tari (tari), s.m. (pharm.) Palm-wine.

tarière (tarjɛr), s.f. [LL *taratrum*] **1.** Auger, bore, wimble; **2.** (ent.) terebra.

tarif (tarif), s.m. [It. *tariffa*] Tariff, rate, scale of prices, price-list, list of charges, list of fares. ⚠ Engl. 'tariff' also = *droit (de douane).*

tarifer (tarife), v.a. To price, to list, to rate, to fix the price of, to tariff.

tarification (tarifika'sjɔ̃), s.f. Price-fixing, tariffing.

tarin (tarɛ̃), s.m. [etym. unkn.] (ornith.) Siskin, kind of finch.

tarir (tarir), v.a. [f. Germ. *tharrjan*] To dry up, to exhaust, to drain, to cease, to stop; *il ne tarit pas d'éloges sur le compte de X*, he is never tired of, or he has never done, praising X.

tarissable (tarisabl), adj. Exhaustible.

tarissement (tarismɑ̃), s.m. Exhausting, drying up, draining.

tarlatane (tarlatan), s.f. [etym. dub.] Tarlatan.

taroté, -e (tarɔte), adj. (of playing-cards) Spotted, chequered (on the back).

tarots (taro), s.m.pl. [It. *tarocchi*] Spotted, figured playing-cards; tarots, tarot cards.

taroupe (tarup), s.f. [orig. dub.] Hair growing between the eyebrows.

tarpan (tarpɑ̃), s.m. [Tartar wd] Tarpan, wild horse of Tartary.

tarse (tars), s.m. [Gr. *tarsos*] (anat.) Tarsus.

tarsien, -ne (tarsjɛ̃), adj. (anat.) Tarsal.

tarsier (tarsje), s.m. [f. *tarse*] (zool.) Tarsier.

tartan (tartɑ̃), s.m. [Engl. wd] Tartan, plaid.

tartane (tartan), s.f. [It. *tartana*] (naut.) Tartan, tartane, tartana.

tartare (tartar), adj. s.m.f. [Pers. *Tatar*] Tartar; (cook.) *à la* ~, with cold mustard-sauce.

tartareu-x, -se (tartarø), adj. See TARTREUX.

tarte (tart), s.f. [OF *tarte, tourte*, f. LL *tarta*] Tart (⚠ not in the sense of *prostituée*); ~ *aux pommes*, apple-tart; (colloq.) *c'est son '~ à la crème'*, it 's his one constant objection; he is always harping on that string.

tartelette (tartəlɛt), s.f. Little tart, tartlet.

tartine (tartin), s.f. [f. *tarte*] Slice of bread and butter or bread and jam; (fig.) dose, tirade, rigmarole, long dull speech.

tartrate (tartrat), s.m. (chem.) Tartrate.

tartre (tartr), s.m. [LL *tartarum*] (chem.) Tartar.
tartreu-x, -se (tartrø), adj. Tartarous; syn. TARTAREUX.
tartrique (tartrik), adj. (chem.) Tartaric.
tartufe (tartyf), s.m. [character in Molière's *Tartufe*] Tartuf(f)e, hypocrite.
tartuferie (tartyfri), s.f. Tartuf(f)ism, hypocrisy.
tas (tɑ), s.m. [Germ. orig.] Heap, pile, mass; cock; shock; cluster, bundle; crowd, set, lot; (techn.) hand-anvil; dolly; boss; swage-block; *un ~ de foin*, a haycock, haymow; *un ~ de gerbes*, a shock of sheaves; (colloq.) *un ~ de gens*, a great many people; *un ~ d'imbéciles*, a pack of fools; *un ~ de mensonges*, no end of lies; *prendre au ~*, to help oneself; *crier famine sur un ~ de blé*, to cry famine in the midst of plenty.
tasmanien, -ne (tasmanjɛ̃), adj. s.m.f. Tasmanian.
tasse (tɑs), s.f. [Arab. *ṭass*] Cup; *une demi-~*, half a cup; *~ à thé*, tea-cup; (fig.) *boire à la grande ~*, to be drowned in the sea, to go to Davy Jones's locker.
tasseau (pl. -x) (taso), s.m. [L *taxillus*] (techn.) Bracket, ledge; stop; guard, lug.
tassement (tɑsmɑ̃), s.m. [f. *tas*] Sinking, settling, giving, subsiding (of soil).
tasser (tɑse), v.a.n. [f. *tas*] To heap up, to pile up; to ram down, to press down, to cram; (hort.) to grow thick; *un homme petit et tassé*, a small, thickset man; (slang) *un dîner bien tassé*, a first-rate dinner; **se ~**, v.pr. to sink, to subside, to settle; to crowd or press together, to pack into a small space.
tassette (tasɛt), s.f. Tasse, armour for thighs.
tâter (tɑte), v.a. [L *taxare*, LL *taxitare*?] To feel, to taste, to handle, to perceive through the sense of touch; (fig.) to try, to sound, to put to the test, to prove; *tâte-au-pot*, s.m. busybody; *tâte-vin*, s.m. wine-tester (instrument); *~ le terrain*, to feel one's way; *~ le pouls à X*, to feel X's pulse; *~ de ce métier*, to have a try at this business, or calling; **se ~**, v.pr. to examine oneself.
tatillon, -ne (tatijɔ̃), s.m.f. Busybody, meddler. **~**, adj. Fussy, fidgety.
tatillonnage (tatijɔnaʒ), s.m. Meddling, interfering.
tatillonner (tatijɔne), v.n. To meddle; to busy oneself with trifles; to mess about, to potter about; to find fault.
tâtonnement (tɑtɔnmɑ̃), s.m. Groping, feeling one's way, fumbling, trial, tentative, hesitation, attempt.
tâtonner (tɑtɔne), v.n. [f. *tâter*] To fumble, to grope, to feel one's way, to hesitate, to waver, to try again and again, to proceed tentatively.
tâtonneu-r, -se (tɑtɔnœr), s.m.f. Groper, fumbler, waverer, irresolute person.
(à) tâtons (atɑtɔ̃), adv. loc. Groping about, feeling one's way, tentatively, blindly.
tatou (tatu), s.m. (zool.) Armadillo.
tatouage (tatwaʒ), s.m. [f. Tahitian *tatau*] Tattooing, tattoo.
tatouer (tatue), v.a. To tattoo.
tatoueur (tatwœr), s.m. Tattooer.
tatouille (tatuj), s.f. (slang) Drubbing, thrashing, cuffing.
tattersall (tatɛrsal), s.m. [f. Engl. prop. n.] Horse and carriage mart.
tau (to), s.m. [Gr. letter] Tau, t.
taud (to), s.m., **taude** (tod), s.f. [f. OF *tauder*, to shelter] (naut.) Tarpaulin, awning.
taudis (todi), s.m. [f. OF *tauder*] Hovel, dirty hole, wretched lodging; (pop.) *vrai ~*, regular den.
taule (tol), s.f. (slang) Military prison; *faire de la ~*, to be in quod.
taupe (top), s.f. [L *talpa*] (zool.) Mole; moleskin; (fig.) intriguing person, sly one; *royaume des ~s*, underground, i.e. the grave; *ne voir pas plus clair qu'une ~*, to be as blind as a bat; *noir comme une ~*, as black as coal; *preneur de ~s*, mole-catcher.
taupe-grillon (topgrijɔ̃), s.m. (ent.) Mole-cricket.
taupier (topje), s.m. Mole-catcher.
taupière (topjɛr), s.f. Mole-trap.
taupin (topɛ̃), s.m. (ent.) Skipjack, spring beetle; (fam.) student reading for the *École polytechnique*.
taupinière, taupinée (topinjɛr, topine), s.f. Mole-hill, hillock, knoll.
taure (tɔr), s.f. [L *taura*] Heifer, young cow.
taureau (pl. -x) (tɔro), s.m. [L *taurus*] Bull; (astr.) Taurus, the Bull; *jeune ~*, steer; *combat de ~x*, bull-fight; (fig.) *prendre le ~ par les cornes*, to take the bull by the horns.
taurillon (tɔrijɔ̃), s.m. Young bull, yearling bull.
tauromachie (tɔromaʃi), s.f. [Gr. *tauromakhia*] Tauromachy, bull-fight.
tauromachique (tɔromaʃik), adj. Tauromachic.
tautochrone (totɔkron), adj. [Gr. *tauto*+*khronos*] Tautochronous, isochronous.
tautochronisme (totɔkrɔnism), s.m. Tautochronism, isochronism.
tautogramme (totɔgram), s.m. [Gr. *tauto*+*gramma*] Poem or line in which all the words begin with the same letter.
tautologie (totɔlɔʒi), s.f. [Gr. *tauto*+*logos*] Tautology, saying the same thing twice over in different words.
tautologique (totɔlɔʒik), adj. Tautological.
tautophonie (totɔfɔni), s.f. [Gr. *tauto*+*phōnē*] Tautophony.

taux (to), s.m. [f. L *taxare*] Price, rate of exchange; rate of interest; tax, assessment; *au ~ de 3 % (3 pour cent)*, at the rate of 3% (3 per cent).
tavaïole, tavaïolle (tavajɔl), s.f. [It. *tovagliolo*] Chrisom cloth.
tavelage (tavlaʒ), s.m. Spotting, speckling.
taveler (tavle), v.a. [L *tabella*] To spot, to speckle.
tavelure (tavlyr), s.f. Spots, speckles.
taverne (tavɛrn), s.f. [L *taberna*] Tavern, public house.
taverni-er, -ère (tavɛrnje), s.m.f. Publican, innkeeper.
taxateur (taksatœr), s.m. Taxer, assessor, (law) taxing-master. ~, adj. Taxing.
taxati-f, -ve (taksatif), adj. Taxable.
taxation (taksa'sjɔ̃), s.f. Taxation, taxing, fixing of prices.
taxe (taks), s.f. [f. *taxer*] Tax, taxation, price, rate; (post.) postage due; ~ *des pauvres*, poor rate.
taxer (takse), v.a. [L *taxare*] To fix the price of, to tax, to rate, to assess, to charge, to accuse; (fig.) ~ *X d'ingratitude*, to accuse X of being ungrateful, to tax X with ingratitude.
taxi (taksi), s.m. [abbrev. of *taxi-auto, auto à taximètre*] Taxi, taxi-cab.
taxidermie (taksidɛrmi), s.f. [Gr. *taxis*+*derma*] Taxidermy.
taxidermique (taksidɛrmik), adj. Taxidermic.
taxidermiste (taksidɛrmist), s.m. Taxidermist.
taximètre (taksimɛtr), s.m. [Gr. *taxis*+*metron*] Taximeter.
taxis (taksis), s.f. [Gr. wd] (med.) Taxis.
taxologie (taksɔlɔʒi), s.f. [Gr. *taxis*+*logos*] Taxology, science of classification.
taxonomie, taxinomie (taksɔnɔmi, taksinɔmi), s.f. [Gr. *taxis*+*nomos*] Taxonomy.
taxonomique (taksɔnɔmik), adj. Taxonomical.
taxonomiste (taksɔnɔmist), s.m. Taxonomist, taxonomer.
tchèque (tʃɛk), adj. s.m.f. Czech.
te (tə), pron. [L *te*] Thee, you, thyself, yourself; (see TU).
té (te), s.m. T; ~ *à dessin*, T-square.
technicien, -ne (tɛknisjɛ̃), s.m.f. Technician.
technicité (tɛknisite), s.f. Technicality.
technique (tɛknik), adj. [Gr. *tekhnikos*] Technical. ~, s.f. Technique, technic.
techniquement (tɛknikmɑ̃), adv. Technically.
technologie (tɛknɔlɔʒi), s.f. Technology.
technologique (tɛknɔlɔʒik), adj. Technological.
teck, tek (tɛk), s.m. [Malayan *tekka*] (bot.) Teak.
tectrice (tɛktris), s.f. adj. [f. L *tegere*] (ornith.) Tectrix, covert, covering feather of wing or tail.
te deum (tedeɔm), s.m. [L wd] Te deum.
tégument (tegymɑ̃), s.m. [L *tegumentum*] (anat., bot.) Tegument.
tégumentaire (tegymɑ̃tɛr), adj. Tegumentary, tegumental.
teigne (tɛɲ), s.f. [L *tinea*] (ent.) Moth, clothes-moth; (med.) ringworm; scald; scab, scurvy; (vet.) thrush; (fig.) tenacious creature, 'sticker', 'burr'.
teigneu-x, -se (tɛɲø), adj. s.m.f. Scabby; (person) afflicted with scab.
teillage, tillage (tɛjaʒ, tijaʒ), s.m. Stripping (of hemp), scutching.
teille, tille (tɛj, til), s.f. [L *tilia*] Hemp-herb, lime-bark, bast, bass.
teiller, tiller (tɛje, tije), v.a. To strip, to scutch.
teilleu-r, -se (tɛjœr), s.m.f. Scutcher; ~**se**, s.f. scutching-machine.
teindre (tɛ̃dr), v.a. [L *tingere*] To dye, to stain, to tinge (*en, de* with), to colour, to tincture, (fig.) to tinge, to imbue; ~ *en rouge*, to dye red; to tinge with red; *cette étoffe teint mal*, this material dyes badly.
teint (tɛ̃), s.m. **1.** Complexion; **2.** dye, colour; *bon* ~, good, fast colour; *mauvais* ~, colour that will fade, bad colour.
teint, -e (tɛ̃), p. adj. Dyed; (fig.) tinged (*en* or *de*, with).
teinte (tɛ̃t), s.f. Tint, shade, tone; (fig.) touch, tinge; *demi-~*, half-tint, chiaroscuro; *une ~ d'ironie*, a touch of irony, an ironical touch; *gravure en demi-~*, mezzotint.
teinter (tɛ̃te), v.a. To tint, to tinge, to colour.
teinture (tɛ̃tyr), s.f. [L *tinctura*] Dye, dyeing, tinge; (pharm.) tincture; colouring, hue; (fig.) smattering.
teinturerie (tɛ̃tyrri), s.f. Dye-works, dyer's trade, dyeing, French cleaning, French cleaner's (shop).
teinturi-er, -ère (tɛ̃tyrje), s.m.f. Dyer, French cleaner, dyer and cleaner.
tel, -le (tɛl), adj. and pron. Such, like, similar, such a one; ~ *père*, ~ *fils*, like father, like son; *à ~le heure*, at such (a) time; ~ *maître*, ~ *valet*, like master, like man; ~ *quel*, such as it is, just as it is; *Monsieur un ~*, Mr. So-and-So; *a-t-on jamais vu rien de ~?*, who ever saw anything like it?; *l'homme craint de se voir ~ qu'il est*, man does not like to see himself as he is; ~ *est pris qui croyait prendre*, it's a case of the biter bit; *de ~le sorte que*, in such a way that (or as).
télamon (telamɔ̃), s.m. [Gr. wd] (arch.) Telamon.
télautographe (telotɔgraf), s.m. [Gr. *tēle* + *auto*+*graphein*] Telautograph.
télégramme (telegram), s.m. [Gr. *tēle*+

gramma] Telegram, dispatch, wire, (oversea) cable, cablegram.

télégraphe (telegraf), s.m. [Gr. *tēle*+*graphein*] Telegraph; ~ *aérien*, semaphore; ~ *sous-marin*, submarine telegraph.

télégraphie (telegrafi), s.f. Telegraphy; ~ *sans fil* (*T.S.F.*), wireless telegraphy, wireless; *appareil* or *poste de T.S.F.*, wireless set, radio set or receiver.

télégraphier (telegrafje(ie)), v.n.a. To telegraph, to send a wire, to wire, to cable (oversea).

télégraphique (telegrafik), adj. Telegraphic; *poteau* ~, telegraph-post; *réponse* ~, answering wire, wire in reply.

télégraphiquement (telegrafikmɑ̃), adv. Telegraphically.

télégraphiste (telegrafist), s.m.f. Telegraphist.

télémécanique (telemekanik), s.f. Telemechanics.

télémètre (telemɛtr), s.m. Telemeter.

télémétrique (telemetrik), adj. Telemetric(al).

téléologie (teleɔlɔʒi), s.f. [Gr. *telos*, *teleos*+*logos*] Teleology.

téléologique (teleɔlɔʒik), adj. Teleological.

téléosaure (teleɔsor), s.m. [Gr. *teleos*+*sauros*] Teleosaur, fossil crocodile.

télépathie (telepati), s.f. [Gr. *tēle*+*pathos*] Telepathy.

téléphone (telefɔn), s.m. [Gr. *tēle*+*phōnē*] Telephone.

téléphoner (telefɔne), v.n.a. To telephone.

téléphonie (telefɔni), s.f. Telephony.

téléphonique (telefɔnik), adj. Telephonic; *appel* ~, telephone call; *cabine* ~, public telephone, call-box.

téléphoniquement (telefɔnikmɑ̃), adv. Telephonically, by telephone.

téléphoniste (telefɔnist), s.m.f. Telephonist, telephone operator.

téléphotographie (telefotografi), s.f. Telephotography.

télescopage (telɛskɔpaʒ), s.m. Telescoping (of trains).

télescope (telɛskɔp), s.m. [Gr. *tēle*+*skopein*] Telescope.

(se) télescoper (sətelɛskɔpe), v.pr. To telescope; to be telescoped.

télescopique (telɛskɔpik), adj. Telescopic.

téléstéréographe (telestereɔgraf), s.m. Telestereograph.

télévision (televizjɔ̃), s.f. Television.

tellement (tɛlmɑ̃), adv. [f. *tel*] So, so much, so far, to such a degree, to such an extent; ~ *que*, so that; ~ *quellement*, indifferently.

tellière (tɛljɛr), s.m. [f. prop. n. *Le Tellier*] Foolscap, brief-paper (0·44 metres × 0·34 metres = $17\frac{1}{2}$ in. × $13\frac{1}{2}$ in.).

tellure (tɛllyr), s.m. [L *tellus*] (chem.) Tellurium: Te.

tellureu-x, -se (tɛllyrø), adj. (chem.) Tellurous.

tellurien, -ne (tɛllyrjɛ̃), adj. Tellurian.

tellurique (tɛllyrik), adj. Telluric.

telphérage (tɛlferaʒ), s.m. [f. Gr. *tēle*+*phoros*] Telpherage, overhead electric traction.

téméraire (temerɛr), adj. [L *temerarius*] Daring, rash, bold, headstrong, reckless, foolhardy, temerarious; *Charles le* ~, Charles the Bold.

témérairement (temerɛrmɑ̃), adv. Daringly, rashly, boldly, recklessly, foolhardily.

témérité (temerite), s.f. [L *temeritas*] Temerity, rashness, boldness.

témoignage (temwaɲaʒ), s.m. Evidence, witness, testimony; testimonial, character; token; *faux* ~, false witness, perjury; *en* ~ *de*, in witness of; *appeler en* ~, to call to witness, to call upon to give evidence; *porter, rendre* ~, to bear witness; to give evidence; *rendre* ~ *à la vérité de*, to testify to the truth of; ~ *d'estime*, testimonial; ~ *d'affection*, token of affection, love, &c.

témoigner (temwaɲe), v.a.n. To testify, to bear witness, to give evidence, to attest, to evince, to show, to express, to prove; ~ *sa joie*, to show one's pleasure; ~ *beaucoup d'affection à*, to manifest, or to show, much love for.

témoin (temwɛ̃), s.m. [L *testimonium*] Witness; testimony, evidence, sign, token, proof; second (in duel); ~ *à charge*, witness for the prosecution; ~ *à décharge*, witness for the defence; ~ *auriculaire*, ear-witness; ~ *oculaire*, eye-witness; *parler sans* ~*s*, to speak privately (with some one); *il faut en être* ~ *pour le croire*, it must be seen to be believed; *mes yeux en sont* ~*s*, I saw it with my own eyes; *prendre X à* ~, to call X to witness.

tempe (tɑ̃p), s.f. [L *tempora*] (anat.) Temple.

tempérament (tɑ̃peramɑ̃), s.m. [L *temperamentum*] **1.** Constitution, temperament, temper, character, disposition, humour; **2.** medium, middle course, compromise; (comm.) tally, tally system; *avoir du* ~, to be ardent; to have a strong amorous disposition; ~ *bilieux*, choleric or bilious temperament; ~ *lymphatique*, phlegmatic or lymphatic temperament; ~ *sanguin*, sanguine temperament; *par* ~, constitutionally, temperamentally; (comm.) *à* ~, by instalments.

tempérance (tɑ̃perɑ̃s), s.f. [L *temperantia*] Temperance, moderation, sobriety, soberness; teetotalism; *ligue* or *société de* ~, temperance league or society.

tempérant, -e (tɑ̃perɑ̃), p. adj. Temperate, moderate, sober, teetotal.

température (tɑ̃peratyr), s.f. [L *temperatura*] Temperature.

tempéré, -e (tãpere), p. adj. Temperate, moderate, sober, tempered.
tempérément (tãperemã), (rare) adv. Temperately.
tempérer (tãpere), v.a. [L *temperare*] To temper, to moderate; to cool, to assuage, to allay; to check, to mitigate, to soothe.
tempête (tãpɛt), s.f. [L *tempestas*] Tempest, storm; agitation, tumult, commotion, disturbance; *une ~ dans un verre d'eau*, a storm in a tea-cup.
tempêter (tãpɛte), v.n. To storm, to rage, to bluster, to fume.
tempétueusement (tãpetɥøzmã), adv. Tempestuously, boisterously.
tempétueu-x, -se (tãpetɥø), adj. Tempestuous, stormy, boisterous.
temple (tãpl), s.m. [L *templum*] Temple; (Protestant) church.
templier (tãplije), s.m. Knight Templar, Templar.
temporaire (tãpɔrɛr), adj. [L *temporarius*] Temporary.
temporairement (tãpɔrɛrmã), adv. Temporarily.
temporal, -e, (aux) (tãpɔral), adj. [L *temporalis*] (anat.) Temporal.
temporalité (tãpɔralite), s.f. [L *temporalitas*] Temporality.
temporel, -le (tãpɔrɛl), adj. [L *temporalis*] Temporal, transient, worldly.
temporel (tãpɔrɛl), s.m. Temporalities, temporal matters or power.
temporellement (tãpɔrɛlmã), adv. Temporally.
temporisat-eur, -rice (tãpɔrizatœr), adj. s.m.f. Temporizing, temporizer, procrastinator.
temporisation (tãpɔriza'sjɔ̃), s.f. Temporizing, procrastination, delay.
temporiser (tãpɔrize), v.n. [f. L *tempus*] To temporize, to delay, to procrastinate.
temporiseur (tãpɔrizœr), s.m. Temporizer.
temps[1] (tã), s.m. invar. [L *tempus*] Time, term, space of time, duration, period, age, epoch, era; occasion, opportunity; days, season, times; (mil.) movement; (gram.) tense; (mus.) measure, time; *le bon ~, le vieux ~, le bon vieux ~*, the good old days (times); *ces derniers ~*, lately, of late; (mus.) *mesure à deux ~*, common time or measure (two or four beats in a bar); *la plupart du ~*, mostly, generally; *à ~*, in time; for a time, for a term; just in time; in the nick of time; *avec le ~*, with time, in course of time; *dans le ~*, formerly, in days gone by; *dans son ~*, in due course; *de tout ~*, at all times, at any time; ever, always; *de ~ en ~, de ~ à autre*, from time to time, now and then, ever and anon; *du ~ de X*, in X's time, in the time of X; *du ~ que*, when; *entre ~*, meanwhile, meantime; *en ~ et lieu*, in due time and place; *grand ~ de*, high time to; *cela a fait son ~*, it's had its day, it has seen better days; *cela n'aura qu'un ~*, that won't last for ever, or long; *avoir tout le ~*, to have plenty of time; *il y a beau ~ de tout cela*, that's a long time ago, or (fam.) donkey's years ago; *le ~ lui dure*, he finds the time long, time hangs heavy on his hands; *se donner du bon ~*, to take things easy, to have a good time; *être de son ~*, to keep up with the times; *n'être plus de son ~*, to be a back number, to be antiquated; *prendre son ~*, to take one's time; *prendre du ~*, to take time; *prendre bien* (or *mal*) *son ~*, choose one's time well (or badly); *par le ~ qui court*, as things are, nowadays; *pour quelque ~*, for a short time, for a little while; *selon le ~*, according to circumstances; *usé par le ~*, time-worn, weather-beaten; *autres ~ autres mœurs*, manners change with the times; *avec le ~ et la patience on vient à bout de tout*, patience and perseverance will drive a snail to Jerusalem; *le ~ est un grand maître*, time is a great teacher; *du ~ que Berthe filait*, in good King Arthur's days, in the days of good Queen Bess; *prendre un ~*, to pause; *tuer le ~*, to kill time; *en deux ~ trois mouvements*, in double quick time, in a jiffy; *moteur à 4 ~*, 4-stroke motor.
temps[2] (tã), s.m. [L *tempus*] Weather; *le ~ est couvert*, the weather is cloudy; *~ variable*, changeable weather; *beau ~*, fine weather; *~ gris* (*sombre*), dull weather; *gros ~, ~ orageux*, stormy, thundery, (naut.) foul weather; heavy, dirty weather; *le ~ menace*, the weather is threatening; *le ~ a l'air de vouloir se mettre au beau*, the weather looks as if it were going to set in fine, the weather's looking up; *le ~ est au beau fixe*, it's fine, settled weather; the weather is set fair; *~ pluvieux*, rainy weather; *par tous les ~*, in all weathers; *quel abominable ~ !*, what wretched weather !; *le ~ se brouille*, the sky is getting overcast; *après la pluie le beau ~*, after a storm comes a calm; *un ~ de demoiselle*, calm, mild weather; (fig.) *faire la pluie et le beau ~*, to be all-powerful, (fam.) to be God Almighty; *parler de la pluie et du beau ~*, to talk of insignificant things; *prendre le ~ comme il vient*, to take things as they come; *le ~ ne tiendra pas*, this weather won't last.
tenable (tənabl), adj. [f. *tenir*] Tenable, habitable; *la position n'est plus ~*, the position is no longer tenable. ⚠ 'Tenable' is frequently applied to a theory, system, &c., in English, but rarely in French.
tenace (tənas), adj. [L *tenax*] Tenacious, obstinate; sticky, adhesive, holding fast; almost ineradicable.
ténacité (tenasite), s.f. Tenacity; retentiveness.

tenaille, tenailles (tənaj), s.f. (often pl.) [LL *tenacula*] Pincers, nippers, pliers, tongs.
tenaillement (tənajmɑ̃), (rare), s.m. Torment, torture with red-hot pincers; (fig.) torment.
tenailler (tənaje), v.a. To torture with red-hot pincers; (fig.) to torment, torture.
tenaillon (tənajɔ̃), s.m. (fort.) Tenaillon.
tenancier, -ère (tənɑ̃sje), s.m.f. (feud.) Tenant, holder, occupier; (nowadays pej.) brothel-keeper or -owner; (fem.) 'madame'; bar-keeper.
tenant, -e (tənɑ̃), p. adj. Contiguous to; following, sitting; *séance tenante*, there and then, on the spot, at once.
tenant (tənɑ̃), s.m. **1.** (fig.) Champion, defender, supporter; (⚠ not 'tenant', which = *locataire*); **2.** *~s*, pl. adjoining lands, adjacent parts; *~s et aboutissants*, adjoining properties; **3.** *~s (d'une affaire, d'une personne)*, ins and outs, particulars; *tout d'un seul ~*, all of a piece, all in one piece, in a ring-fence.
tendance (tɑ̃dɑ̃s), s.f. [f. *tendre*] Tendency, inclination, leaning, bent, propensity, trend.
tendancieu-x, -se (tɑ̃dɑ̃sjø), adj. Intentionally misleading, insinuating, suggestive, tendentious; not impartial.
tendant, -e (tɑ̃dɑ̃), p. adj. Tending (*à*, to).
tendelet (tɑ̃dlɛ), s.m. [It. *tendaletto*] (naut.) Awning, canopy; (hort.) screen.
tender (tɑ̃dɛr), s.m. [Engl. wd] (railw.) Tender. ⚠ Not 'tender' in the sense of offer in writing to execute work or supply goods at fixed price, which = *soumission, soumissionnement*; nor legal tender, currency that cannot be refused in payment of debt, which = *monnaie libératoire légale*.
tendeur (tɑ̃dœr), s.m. Spreader, layer, setter (of snares); (trouser-)press, stretcher, hanger; (railw.) coupling-iron; tightening-bolt, wire-strainer.
tendineu-x, -se (tɑ̃dinø), adj. [f. *tendon*] Tendinous, sinewy.
tendoir (tɑ̃dwar), s.m. Clothes-line, drying-line, stretcher.
tendon (tɑ̃dɔ̃), s.m. [f. *tendre*] Tendon, sinew, leader, hamstring.
tendre (tɑ̃dr), adj. [L *tener*] Tender; soft, delicate, touching, new; sensitive, affectionate, loving, early; fresh, young; kind, merciful; *du pain ~*, new bread; *avoir le cœur ~*, to be tender-hearted; *couleur ~*, delicate colour. *~*, s.m. Fondness, partial affection.
tendre (tɑ̃dr), v.a. [L *tendere*] To stretch, to strain, to bend (a bow), to spread (a net), to lay (a snare), to set (a trap), to pitch (a tent), to hang (curtains, &c.), to put up, to hold out, to put forth, to throw out; *~ la main*, to beg alms; *~ la perche*, to lend a helping hand; *~*, v.n. to lead, to tend (*à*, to); *à quoi tend ce discours?*, to what conclusion tends this talk?, what are you aiming at? ⚠ Not 'to tend' in the sense of to take care of, which = *prendre soin de*.
tendrement (tɑ̃drəmɑ̃), adv. Tenderly, affectionately, kindly, lovingly.
tendresse (tɑ̃drɛs), s.f. [f. *tendre*] Tenderness, fondness, love, sensibility, kindness, affection, delicacy; (pl.) caresses, endearments.
tendreté (tɑ̃drəte), s.f. (of eatables, plants) Tenderness, softness.
tendron (tɑ̃drɔ̃), s.m. [f. *tendre*] Tender shoot; (fam.) young girl; (cook.) gristle.
tendu, -e (tɑ̃dy), p. adj. Tense, tight, (naut.) taut; bent, intent, strained, stiff; difficult, delicate; *avoir l'esprit ~*, to have one's mind bent (on), to be concentrated (on); *situation ~e*, strained, or delicate, situation; *style ~*, stiff style.
ténèbres (tenɛbr), s.f.pl. [L *tenebrae*] Darkness, gloom, night, mystery, obscurity; tenebrae (prayers); *le prince des ~*, the prince of darkness.
ténébreusement (tenebrøzmɑ̃), adv. Darkly, mysteriously, in an underhand fashion.
ténébreu-x, -se (tenebrø), adj. [L *tenebrosus*] Dark, gloomy; secret, sad, obscure, mysterious; wicked, sinister, evil; (colloq., jest.) *un beau ~*, a romantic lady-killer.
ténébrion (tenebriɔ̃), s.m. [L wd] (ent.) Tenebrio.
tènement (tɛnmɑ̃), s.m. [LL *tenementum*] (feudal law) Tenement.
ténesme (tenɛm), s.m. [Gr. *tēnesmos*] (med.) Tenesmus.
tenettes (tənɛt), s.f.pl. (surg.) Forceps. ⚠ Not 'tenets', which = *principes, dogmes, doctrines*.
teneur (tənœr), s.f. [L *tenor*] Tenor, terms, text, import, content; (chem.) amount, percentage; grade (of ore). ⚠ 'Tenor' also = *ténor*.
teneu-r, -se (tənœr), s.m.f. Keeper; *~ de livres*, book-keeper, accountant.
ténia (tenja), s.m. [L *taenia*] Taenia, tape-worm.
tenir (tənir), v.a.n. [L *tenere*] To hold, to hold on, to get hold of, to cling, to keep; to take, to take room, to contain, to be contained; to pursue; to manage; to deem, to consider; to maintain, to side with, to uphold; to be connected, joined, or related to; to persist, to hold good, to be intent on, desirous of, anxious to; to insist on; *tiens!* or *tenez!*, (*a*) here, take this!, here you are, hold on!; (*b*) indeed! well I never!; (*c*) look here, now; (*d*) (naut.) avast there!; *~ à quelque chose*, to prize, to value something highly; to be intent,

resolved, or bent on something, or on doing something; *ne* ~ *à rien*, to care for nothing; *à quoi cela tient-il?*, what 's the cause, or reason, of this?; what is that owing to?; ~ *bon*, ~ *ferme*, to hold on, to hold out, to stick it; ~ *le bon bout*, to have hold of the right end of the stick; ~ *la caisse*, to have charge of the cash; ~ *compte de*, to take into consideration, or into account; (mil.) ~ *la campagne*, to keep the field; (naut.) ~ *la côte*, to hug the shore; ~ *la mer*, (*a*) to keep at sea; (*b*) to hold on in a sea-way; *qui tient bien la mer*, wholesome; ~ *un feu à l'est*, to keep a light bearing east; ~ *le large*, to stand out to sea; ~ *un mât en étai*, to stay a mast; ~ *le vent*, to keep to windward; to keep the wind; *quel langage tenez-vous là!*, what a way of speaking!, how can you use such language?; *il m'a tenu lieu de père*, he has been a father to me; ~ *maison*, to keep house; ~ *parole*, to keep one's word; *je le tiens pour un scélérat*, I look upon him as a scoundrel; *j'en tiens pour ce que j'ai dit*, I persist in my opinion; (colloq.) *elle en tient pour X*, she is in love with X; (vulg. U.S.A.) she has taken a shine to X; she is sweet on X; *tenez-vous-le pour dit*, (*a*) let it suffice, suffice it to say; (*b*) take it for granted; ~ *quitte de*, to let off; *je le tiens quitte de ce qu'il me doit*, I let him off his debt to me; *il tient cela de race*, it runs in the blood; ~ *son rang*, to keep up one's position; ~ *rigueur à X*, to remain angry with X; to continue to give X the cold shoulder; ~ *un rôle*, to play, to take a part; ~ *table ouverte*, to keep open house; to entertain generously; ~ *tête à X*, to resist, to oppose X; ~ *beaucoup de place*, to take up much room; *cela tient à*, this is due to; *cela lui tient au cœur*, he has set his heart upon it; he has taken it deeply to heart; *il n'a pas tenu à moi que*, it has not been my fault if; *il ne tient qu'à vous*, it rests entirely with you; *je n'y tiens pas*, I am not particular about that; *je n'y tiens plus*, I don't care about it any more; *c'est à n'y pas* ~, *on n'y peut plus* ~, it's unbearable; *qu'à cela ne tienne!*, that need be no objection; if it depends only on that!; *il n'y a pas de camaraderie qui tienne*, it must be done in spite of friendship; *il n'a tenu à rien que je ne*, I was within an inch of; *mieux vaut* ~ *que courir*, a bird in the hand is worth two in the bush; *il tient de son père*, he takes after his father; *il tient cela de son père*, he has inherited that from his father; *je tiens cela de bonne source*, I have it on the best authority; *il le tient*, he has the pull of him; *sa vie ne tient qu'à un fil*, his life hangs by a thread; *cela ne tient pas debout!*, that does not hold water, or bear examination; **se** ~, v.pr. to hold fast, to stand, to sit, to stay; to refrain, to control oneself; *se bien* ~, to behave properly, to have good manners; (colloq.) *il n'a qu'à se bien* ~, he is in for something; *se* ~ *les côtes* (*de rire*), to split one's sides with laughing; *se* ~ *debout*, to stand up, to remain standing, or erect; *se* ~ *sur ses gardes*, to be on one's guard; *elle ne se tient pas de joie*, she is beside herself with joy; *se* ~ *mal*, to behave badly, to have bad manners; to slouch; *se* ~ *prêt*, to hold oneself in readiness; *il s'est tenu à quatre pour ne pas rire*, it was as much as he could do to keep from laughing; *se* ~ *sur son quant-à-soi*, to stand on one's dignity; *s'en* ~ *à*, to be satisfied with, to be content with, to stick to; *savoir à quoi s'en* ~, to know what to reckon on; to know how things stand; to know what to make of it; *tenez-vous tranquille*, keep still, keep quiet.

tennis (tɛnis), s.m. [Engl. wd] Tennis, lawn tennis; tennis-court.

tenon (tənɔ̃), s.m. [f. *tenir*] Tenon; bolt (of fire-arms); nut (of an anchor).

ténor (tenɔr), s.m. [It. *tenore*] (mus.) Tenor. ⚠ Only in the sense of highest ordinary adult male voice; see TENEUR.

ténorino (tenɔrino), s.m. [It. wd] Tenorino.

ténorisant, -e (tenɔrizɑ̃), p. adj. Resembling a tenor voice.

ténoriser (tenɔrize), v.n. To sing like a tenor.

ténotomie (tenɔtɔmi), s.f. [Gr. *tenōn*+*tomē*] (surg.) Tenotomy.

tenseur (tɑ̃sœr), s.m. [f. L *tendere*] (anat.) Tensor; (techn.) stretcher, tightener.

tension (tɑ̃sjɔ̃), s.f. [L *tensio*] Tension; tenseness, application, strain, straining, intensity; (techn.) tensile stress, strain; *couplage en* ~, coupling in series; (physiol.) (*haute, basse*) ~ *artérielle*, (high, low) arterial tension or blood-pressure; (electr). tension (*haute, basse* ~, high, low tension).

tenson (tɑ̃sɔ̃), s.f. [It. *tenzone*] Tenson.

tentaculaire (tɑ̃takylɛr), adj. Tentacular.

tentacule (tɑ̃takyl), s.m. [L *tentaculum*] Tentacle, feeler.

tentant, -e (tɑ̃tɑ̃), p. adj. Tempting, enticing; attractive, alluring.

tentat-eur, -rice (tɑ̃tatœr), s.m.f. [L *tentator, -trix*] Tempter, temptress. ~, adj. Tempting.

tentation (tɑ̃ta'sjɔ̃), s.f. [L *tentatio*] Temptation.

tentative (tɑ̃tativ), s.f. [L *tentativus*] Attempt, tentative, try, trial, endeavour; ~ *de meurtre*, attempted murder.

tente (tɑ̃t), s.f. [L *tenta*] Tent, pavilion, awning; *dresser une* ~, to pitch a tent; (fig.) *se retirer sous sa* ~, to withdraw (being offended).

tente-abri (tɑ̃tabri), s.f. (pl. *tentes-abris*) A very light tent.

tenter[1] (tɑ̃te), v.a. [L *tentare*] **1.** To attempt, to try, to venture; ~ *l'impossible*, to attempt impossibilities; ~ *de sauver X*, to try to save X; ~ *la chance*, ~ *le coup*, to make the attempt; to risk it, to venture; **2.** to tempt, to entice, to allure; *ce fruit me tente*, this fruit is tempting; *je suis tenté de suspecter ceci*, I am tempted to question this; *Dieu tenta Abraham*, God did tempt Abraham; *tu ne tenteras pas le Seigneur ton Dieu*, thou shalt not tempt the Lord thy God; *ce projet me tente beaucoup*, I think this plan is very tempting; I have a great mind to do this.

tenter[2] (tɑ̃te), v.a. [f. *tente*] To tent, to cover with a tent.

tenture (tɑ̃tyr), s.f. [f. *tendre*] Hangings, tapestry; wall-paper, paper-hanging.

tenu, -e (təny), p. adj. [f. *tenir*] Held, kept, looked after, dressed; bound; obliged, esteemed; *une maison bien ~e*, a well-run (or -kept) house; *à l'impossible nul n'est ~*, no one is bound to attempt the impossible.

ténu, -e (teny), adj. [L *tenuis*] Thin, tenuous, slender, frail; (fig.) subtle, over-refined, far-fetched.

tenue (təny), s.f. [f. *tenir*] Holding, sitting, session; attitude; (of a person) behaviour, deportment, carriage, bearing, dress, appearance, seat (on horseback); book-keeping; (mus.) holding (of a note); (naut.) anchor-hold; (mil.) *grande ~*, full dress; *petite ~*, undress; *~ de campagne*, service dress, full marching kit; *~ de livres en partie double, en partie simple*, book-keeping by double entry, by single entry; *avoir une bonne ~*, to have good manners, to behave oneself well; *avoir une mauvaise ~*, to be ill-mannered; to behave badly; *tout d'une ~, d'une seule ~*, all in one piece, all of a piece; *en ~ de soirée*, in evening dress.

ténuement (tenymɑ̃), adv. Tenuously, thinly.

ténuifolié, -e (tenɥifɔlje), adj. (bot.) Tenuifolious, having narrow leaves.

ténuirostre (tenɥirɔstr), adj. [L *tenuis*+*rostrum*] (ornith.) Tenuirostral, thin-billed. ~, s.m. Tenuiroster.

ténuité (tenɥite), s.f. [L *tenuitas*] Tenuity, thinness, slenderness, smallness.

tenure (tənyr), s.f. (feud.) Tenure.

tenuto (tenuto), adv. [It. wd] Tenuto.

teocalli (teɔkalli), s.m. [Mexic. *teotl*=god +*calli*=house] Teocalli, temple of Mexican aborigines, usually on truncated pyramid.

téorbe, théorbe (teɔrb), s.m. [It. *tiorba*] (mus.) Theorbo.

tépidité (tepidite), s.f. [L *tepiditas*] Tepidity.

ter (tɛr), adv. [L wd] Three times, thrice-repeated, occurring a third time.

tératologie (teratɔlɔʒi), s.f. [Gr. *teras*+*logos*] Teratology, study of animal or vegetable monstrosities.

tératologique (teratɔlɔʒik), adj. Teratological.

tératologue, tératologiste (teratɔlɔg, teratɔlɔʒist), s.m.f. Teratologist.

terbium (tɛrbiɔm), s.m. (chem.) Terbium: Tb.

tercet (tɛrsɛ), s.m. [It. *terzetto*] (mus., pros.) Tercet, tiercet; triplet.

térébenthine (terebɑ̃tin), s.f. [f. Gr. *terebinthinos*] Turpentine, turps; *essence de ~*, turpentine oil or spirit.

térébinthe (terebɛ̃t), s.m. [Gr. *terebinthos*] (bot.) Terebinth; turpentine-tree.

térébrant, -e (terebrɑ̃), p. adj. [f. L *terebrare*] Boring; (of animals) terebrate, terebrant, burrowing; (fig.) horribly persistent, piercing.

térébration (terebra'sjɔ̃), s.f. [L *terebratio*] Boring, terebration.

tergal, -e, (aux) (tɛrgal), adj. [f. L *tergum*] (anat.) Tergal, dorsal.

tergiversation (tɛrʒivɛrsa'sjɔ̃), s.f. [L *tergiversatio*] Tergiversation; hesitation, evasion, shuffling.

tergiverser (tɛrʒivɛrse), v.n. [L *tergiversari*] To tergiversate, to hesitate, to shuffle.

terme (tɛrm), s.m. [L *terminus*] Term, expression, word; limit, boundary, goal, end, aim, time; rent, quarter, quarter-day; (arch.) terminus; (comm., fin.) *à ~*, on account, for the account; *avant ~*, prematurely, untimely, before one's time; *à court ~*, short-dated; *à long ~*, long-dated; *dans toute la force du ~*, in the full force of the term, out and out, thorough; *dans les meilleurs ~ avec X*, on the best of terms with X; *moyen ~*, middle course; *approcher de son ~*, to draw to a close; *être planté comme un ~*, to stand like a statue, like a block of stone; *mesurer, ménager, peser ses ~s*, to weigh one's words; *parler de X en bons ~s*, to speak favourably of X; *payer son ~*, to pay one's rent; *toucher à son ~*, to be near one's end; *il y a ~ à tout*, all things come to an end; *qui a ~ ne doit rien*, no one need pay till a debt is due; *le ~ vaut l'argent*, time is money.

terminaison (tɛrminɛzɔ̃), s.f. [L *terminatio*] Termination, ending; end, conclusion.

terminal, -e, (aux) (tɛrminal), adj. (bot.) Terminal.

terminer (tɛrmine), v.a. [L *terminare*] To terminate, to end, to bound, to limit, to finish, to conclude, to close; *compte terminé*, settling account to date; *~ un différend*, to bring a quarrel to an end; *~ la journée en faisant*, to end the day in doing; **se ~**, v.pr. to end, to terminate, to come to an end; *ce mot se termine par*, this word terminates in.

terminologie (tɛrminɔlɔʒi), s.f. [L *terminus*+Gr. *logos*] Terminology.

terminus (tɛrminys), s.m. [L wd] Terminus.
termite (tɛrmit), s.m. [f. L *termes*] (ent.) Termite, white ant.
termitière (tɛrmitjɛr), s.f. Termitarium, termitary, nest of termites.
ternaire (tɛrnɛr), adj. [L *ternarius*] Ternary, ternal; (math.) ternary; (bot.) ternate.
terne (tɛrn), s.m. [L *terni*] Tern, three winning numbers, (at dice) two threes; (fig.) unusual luck.
terne (tɛrn), adj. [orig. dub.] Dull, leaden, wan, dim, lustreless; (fig.) tame, spiritless.
ternir (tɛrnir), v.a. [f. *terne*] To tarnish, to dull, to lessen or destroy the lustre of; to stain, to dim, to sully, to fade; *une réputation ternie*, a tarnished reputation; **se** ~, v.pr. to grow dull, to tarnish, to acquire a lustreless, faded aspect; to fade.
ternissure (tɛrnisyr), s.f. **ternissement** (tɛrnismɑ̃), s.m. Tarnish, dullness, dimming, fading, blemish, stain.
terrain (tɛrɛ̃), s.m. [L *terrenum*] Soil, earth, land, site, ground, piece of ground, (geog.) formation; field; pitch; tennis-court; *aller sur le* ~, to fight a duel; *céder le* ~, to yield ground, to give way; *connaître le* ~, to know one's ground, to be on familiar ground; *disputer le* ~, to dispute every inch of ground; *être sur son* ~, to be on one's own ground, to be at home; *gagner du* ~, to gain ground; (fig.) *ménager le* ~, to go prudently to work; *perdre du* ~, to lose ground; *tâter, sonder le* ~, to feel one's way; to see how the land lies; ~*s à vendre*, building-plots or plots of land for sale.
terral (tɛral), s.m. (naut.) Land-breeze.
terramare (tɛramar), s.f. [It. *terra mara*] Terramare (kinds of earthy deposit useful as fertilizer).
terraqué, -e (tɛrake), adj. [f. L. *terra*+ *aqua*] Terraqueous.
terrasse (tɛras), s.f. [f. *terre*] Terrace, raised bank; earthwork; flat roof, wide balcony; pavement in front of a café. ⚠ Not like English 'terrace' a (raised) row of houses or fancy name for street, or defective place in marble block.
terrassement (tɛrasmɑ̃), s.m. Earthwork, embankment.
terrasser (tɛrase), v.a. **1.** To bank up, to dig, to embank; **2.** to throw to the ground, to fell, to knock down; (fig.) to beat, to dismay, to floor, to vanquish.
terrassier (tɛrasje), s.m. Navvy, labourer, digger, excavator.
terre (tɛr), s.f. [L *terra*] Earth, land, shore, ground, soil, loam, clay, mould; dominions, territory, grounds, estate, property; the world; *bien avant dans les* ~*s*, far inland; *à* ~, on land, ashore; ~ *cuite*, s.f. terra cotta; ~ *ferme*, s.f. terra firma, dry land; ~ *franche*, s.f. leaf-mould; ~ *à foulon*, s.f. fuller's earth; ~ *forte*, s.f. heavy soil; ~ *glaise*, s.f. clay; ~-*neuve*, s.m. Newfoundland dog; ~-*noix*, s.f. pig-nut, earth-nut; ~ *d'ambre*, s.f. umber; ~ *de pipe*, s.f. pipe-clay; *pipe de* ~, s.f. clay pipe; ~ *à porcelaine*, s.f. china clay; ~ *à potier*, s.f. potter's clay; ~ *pourrie*, s.f. rotten-stone; (fort.) ~-*plein*, s.m. terre-plein; *plantes de pleine* ~, s.f. hardy plants; ~ *sainte*, s.f. consecrated ground; *la Terre Sainte*, s.f. the Holy Land; ~ *à* ~, dull, commonplace, vulgar; slow; *tremblement de* ~, s.m. earthquake; *ventre à* ~, at full gallop; *aller par* ~, to go by land, overland; *chasser sur les* ~*s d'autrui*, to trespass, encroach on other people's rights; *se coucher par* ~, to lie down on the ground; *cultiver la* ~, to till the ground; (naut.) *être à* ~, to be on shore, to be aground; *un ennemi à* ~, a vanquished enemy; *être sous* ~, to be dead and buried, to be under the sod; *mettre un genou en* ~, to go down on one knee; *mettre en* ~, or *porter en* ~, to bury; *mettre pied à* ~, to alight; *perdre* ~, to lose sight of land; *prendre* ~, to go ashore, to land; *remuer ciel et* ~, to move heaven and earth, to leave no stone unturned; *tenir aux choses de la* ~, to care for creature comforts; *tomber à* ~, to fall to the ground; *tomber par* ~, to fall on the ground, to measure one's length on the ground; *vivre sur ses* ~*s*, to live on one's estate; *faire rentrer X sous* ~, to cover X with confusion, to wipe the floor with X; (prov.) *qui* ~ *a guerre a*, much coin much care.
terreau (pl. **-x**) (tɛro), s.m. Leaf-mould, humus, mould, compost.
terreauter (tɛrote), v.a. To manure with compost or leaf-mould.
terre-neuve (tɛrnœv), s.m. invar. [geog. orig.] Newfoundland dog.
terre-neuvien, -neuvier, or **-neuvas** (tɛrnœvjɛ̃, nœvje, nœva), s.m. **1.** Fisherman (from Brittany, England, &c.) who goes to Newfoundland for cod-fishing; **2.** vessel for cod-fishing.
terre-plein (tɛrplɛ̃), s.m. Open space, platform, raised walk, terrace; (fort.) terreplein.
terrer (tɛre), v.a. (hort.) To earth up, to spread mould on, to renew the soil of, to earth (cloth), to clay (sugar); **se** ~, v.pr. to burrow; to shelter in trenches; (fig.) to hide, to lead a solitary life in a remote place.
terrestre (tɛrɛstr), adj. [L *terrestris*] Terrestrial, earthly; (fig.) worldly.
terreur (tɛrœr), s.f. [L *terror*] Terror; fear, dread, fright; *la* ~, the reign of terror, the Terror; ~ *panique*, or *panique*, s.f. panic; *pris de* ~, terror-stricken. ⚠ Except in nicknames, ex. *la Terreur du*

Sébasto, *terreur* in French is not usually applied to persons, whereas in English 'terror' = (iron.) *chose ou personne qui cause la terreur*, ex. this child is a terror, *cet enfant est vraiment terrible!* (*très difficile*); however, one can say elliptically: *cet homme est la terreur du pays*, but the sense is: this man is the object of everybody's dread and hate.

terreu-x, -se (terø), adj. Earthy, dull, dirty, sickly; *visage* ~, cadaverous face; (fig.) *les culs*-~, the (peasant) landowners.

terrible (teribl), adj. [L *terribilis*] Terrible, dreadful, awful, tremendous, frightful, severe, bad, excessive, violent, strange, wild, extraordinary; *enfant* ~, terrible child, chatterbox, (fam.) regular pickle, plague; holy terror; little devil (especially one whose utter frankness and awkward questions make him an amusing nuisance; in this sense it can be said of young adults.)

terriblement (teriblmɑ̃), adv. Terribly, (fam.) with a vengeance, (slang) awfully (= very).

terrien, -ne (terjɛ̃), s.m.f. adj. Landholder, landed proprietor, (naut.) landlubber.

terrier[1] (terje), s.m. [f. *terre*] Burrow, hole, earth; (dog) terrier; ~ *griffon*, Skye terrier, Scotch terrier.

terrier[2] (terje), s.m. [LL *terrarius*] (feud.) Terrier; *papier* ~, court roll.

terrifier (terifje), v.a. [L *terrificare*] To terrify, to frighten, to fill with terror.

terrine (terin), s.f. [f. *terre*] Earthenware basin, pot, crock, terrine, dish, pie-dish; potted meat. ⚠ Not 'tureen', which = *soupière*.

terrinée (terine), s.f. Dishful, panful.

terrir (terir), v.n. [f. *terre*] **1.** To lay eggs in the sand (as tortoises); **2.** (naut.) to approach land.

territoire (teritwar), s.m. [L *territorium*] Territory, jurisdiction.

territorial, -e, (aux) (teritɔrjal), adj. [L *territorialis*] Territorial. ~, s.m. Territorial, soldier of the territorial army.

territorialement (teritɔrjalmɑ̃), adv. Territorially.

territorialité (teritɔrjalite), s.f. Territoriality, territorial condition or quality.

terroir (terwar), s.m. [L *territorium*] Soil, ground; *goût de* ~, racy taste, raciness, peculiar flavour; stamp of one's country.

terroriser (terɔrize), v.a. [f. L *terror*] To terrorize.

terrorisme (terɔrism), s.m. Terrorism.

terroriste (terɔrist), s.m. Terrorist.

tertiaire (tersjer), adj. [L *tertiarius*] Tertiary.

tertio (tersjo), adv. [L wd] Thirdly.

tertre (tertr), s.m. [etym. dub.] Hillock, mound, knoll.

terzetto (terzeto), s.m. [It. wd] Terzetto.

tes (te), poss. adj. pl. Thy, thy own, your, your own.

tessère (teser), s.f. [L *tessera*] (Rom. ant.) Tessera.

tessiture (tessityr), s.f. [It. *tessitura*] (mus.) Tessitura.

tesson (tesɔ̃), s.m. [f. *têt*] Potsherd, fragment of broken glass, shard, sherd.

test[1] (test), s.m. [L *testa*] Test, shell.

test[2] (test), s.m. [Engl. wd] Test, trial.

testacé, -e (testase), adj. [L *testaceus*] Testaceous, testacean.

testament (testamɑ̃), s.m. [L *testamentum*] Will, last will and testament, testament; *l'Ancien* ~, *le Nouveau* ~, the Old, New Testament; *faire son* ~, to make one's will; *laisser une chose par* ~ *à X*, to leave a thing to X in (or by) one's will; ~ *olographe*, holograph will, will written in the testator's own hand.

testamentaire (testamɑ̃ter), adj. Testamentary.

testat-eur, -rice (testatœr), s.m.f. Testator, testatrix.

tester (teste), v.n. [f. L *testari*] To make a will; *mourir sans* ~, to die intestate.

testicule (testikyl), s.m. [L *testiculus*] Testicle.

testif (testif), s.m. Camel's hair.

testimonial, -e, (aux) (testimɔnjal), adj. [L *testimonialis*] Witnessing, testifying, (rare or techn.) testimonial; pertaining to a witness. ⚠ 'Testimonial' in English is also (and usually) a subst. and = *certificat, références, témoignage, reconnaissance de qualités, services*, &c.

teston (testɔ̃), s.m. [It. *testone*] Tester (coin).

têt, test (te), s.m. [f. L *testa*] **1.** Sherd, potsherd; **2.** (chem.) test, cupel; **3.** (bot.) test, testa.

tétanie (tetani), s.f. (med.) Tetany.

tétanique (tetanik), adj. (med.) Tetanic.

tétaniser (tetanize), v.a. To tetanize.

tétanos (tetanos), s.m. [Gr. *tetanos*] (pathol.) Tetanus, lockjaw.

têtard (tetar), s.m. [f. *tête*] **1.** Tadpole; **2.** pollard tree; **3.** pole-socket (carriage).

tête (tet), s.f. [L *testa*] Head; top; (fig.) brain(s); sense, mind, wit, judgement, presence of mind; ~-*bêche*, top to bottom, head to foot; *donner* ~ *baissée dans*, to rush headlong, full tilt into; ~ *carrée*, stubborn, obstinate person; *coup de* ~, rash act; *de la* ~ *aux pieds*, from head to foot, from top to toe; *en* ~, in front, ahead, foremost; *un en*-~, a heading; *yeux à fleur de* ~, prominent, staring eyes; ~ *de ligne*, starting-point, terminus; ~ *de linotte*, empty-headed person; *mal de* ~, headache; *mauvaise* ~, obstinate, stubborn person; *par* ~, per head, a head; *par-dessus la* ~, head over heels in, more than ever; ~ *à perruque*, barber's block, (fig.)

blockhead; *à ~ reposée*, at leisure; *en ~ à ~*, tête-à-tête; privately; *il y va de votre ~*, your life is at stake; *~ ou pile*, heads or tails; *avoir sa ~*, or *toute sa ~*, to be in one's senses; (fam.) *avoir la ~ fêlée*, to be cracked; *avoir de la ~*, to have one's head screwed on the right way; *avoir la ~ solide*, to be steady, not easily fuddled, to have a good head; *ce sont deux ~s dans le même bonnet*, they are hand and (or in) glove together; *avoir une chose en ~*, to be bent on a thing; *avoir la ~ chaude, la ~ près du bonnet*, to be hot-headed; *avoir la ~ qui tourne*, to be giddy; *avoir martel en ~*, to be much bothered; *avoir mal à la ~*, to have a headache; *donner de la ~ contre un mur*, to run one's head against a wall; *se casser la ~*, (fig.) to rack one's brains; *crier à tue-~*, to yell or shout at the top of one's voice; *donner sa ~ à couper*, to lay down one's life; *en avoir par-dessus la ~*, to be heartily sick of it, (fam.) to be fed up with it; *faire ~ à*, to make head against, to stand at bay; to face; *faire à sa ~*, to have one's own way; *faire une ~*, or *une sale ~*, to pull a long face; *faire un signe de ~*, to nod; *jeter à la ~ de X*, to throw in X's face, or in X's teeth; *se jeter à la ~ de X*, to be forward, to throw oneself at X's head; *laver la ~ à X*, to give X a dressing-down, a wigging; *monter à la ~*, to be heady, to fly to one's head; *monter la ~ à X*, to work upon X; to excite X; *se monter la ~*, to get excited; *perdre la ~*, to lose one's head or wits; *piquer une ~*, to dive, to plunge headlong; *tenir ~ à X*, not to give in to X; to resist X; *tourner la ~ à X*, to turn X's head; (colloq.) *se payer la ~* (or *la fiole*) *de X*, to take a rise out of X; to pull X's leg; *faire la ~*, to sulk; *~ de pont*, bridge-head; *~ de nègre*, dark brown (colour), nigger-brown; *~ de bielle*, top end of connecting-rod.

têteau (pl. **-x**) (tɛto), s.m. End of a main branch.

tetée, tétée (təte, tete), s.f. Suck, feed (from breast or feeding-bottle).

teter, téter (təte, tete), v.a. [f. *tette*] To suck; *donner à ~ à*, to suckle, to feed.

têtière (tɛtjɛr), s.f. **1.** Infant's cap; **2.** head-stall (harness); **3.** antimacassar.

tetin, tétin (tətɛ̃, tetɛ̃), s.m. Nipple, teat, breast.

tétine (tetin), s.f. **1.** Teat (for feeding-bottle); **2.** udder (of animals); **3.** (armoury) dent.

teton, téton (tətɔ̃, tetɔ̃), s.m. (colloq.) Breast.

tétracorde (tetrakɔrd), s.m. [Gr. *tetra+khordē*] (mus.) Tetrachord.

tétradactyle (tetradaktil), adj. [Gr. *tetra+daktulos*] Tetradactylous.

tétradrachme (tetradrakm), s.f. [Gr. *tetra+drakhme*] Tetradrachm.

tétradyname (tetradinam), adj. [Gr. *tetra+dunamis*] (bot.) Tetradynamous.

tétradynamie (tetradinami), s.f. (bot.) Tetradynamy.

tétraèdre (tetraɛdr), s.m. [Gr. *tetra+hedra*] Tetrahedron.

tétraédrique (tetraedrik), adj. Tetrahedral.

tétragone (tetragɔn), adj. [Gr. *tetra+gōnia*] Tetragonal.

tétragone (tetragɔn), s.f. (bot.) Tetragonia, summer spinach.

tétragramme (tetragram), adj. s.m. [Gr. *tetra+gramma*] Tetragram; tetragrammaton.

tétragyne, tétragynique (tetraʒin, tetraʒinik), adj. [Gr. *tetra+gunē*] (bot.) Tetragynous.

tétralogie (tetralɔʒi), s.f. [Gr. *tetra+logos*] Tetralogy.

tétramère (tetramɛr), adj. [Gr. *tetramerēs*] Tetramerous, tetrameral.

tétrandre (tetrɑ̃dr), adj. [Gr. *tetra+andros*] (bot.) Tetrandrous.

tétrandrie (tetrɑ̃dri), s.f. (bot.) Tetrandry.

tétrapode (tetrapɔd), adj. [Gr. *tetra+podos*] (ent., pros.) Tetrapod, tetrapodous.

tétraptère (tetraptɛr), adj. [Gr. *tetrapteros*] (ent.) Tetrapterous.

tétrarchat (tetrarka), s.m. [Gr. *tetra+arkhē*] Tetrarchate.

tétrarchie (tetrarʃi), s.f. Tetrarchy.

tétrarque (tetrark), s.m. Tetrarch.

tétras (tetrɑ), s.m. [L wd] (ornith.) Grouse.

tétrastyle (tetrastil), s.m. [Gr. *tetra+stulos*] Tetrastyle.

tétrasyllabe, tétrasyllabique (tetrasilab, tetrasilabik), adj. [Gr. *tetra+sullabē*] Tetrasyllabic.

tétrodon (tetrɔdɔ̃), s.m. (ichth.) Tetrodon; globe-fish.

tette (tɛt), s.f. [OHG *titte*] (of animals) Teat, dug.

têtu, -e (tɛty), adj. [f. *tête*] Headstrong, stubborn, obstinate, pig-headed, mulish.

teuf-teuf (tœftœf), s.m. [onom.] (colloq.) Motor-car.

teuton, -ne (tøtɔ̃), adj. s.m.f. [L *teutoni*] Teutonic, Teuton.

teutonique (tøtɔnik), adj. Teutonic.

texte (tɛkst), s.m. [L *textus*, f. *texere*] **1.** Text, original words of author; **2.** text; theme, matter, subject; **3.** print, type; *gros ~*, large type; *petit ~*, small type; *revenir à son ~*, to return to the point; *restituer un ~*, to restore a text.

textile (tɛkstil), adj. s.m. [L *textilis*] Textile.

textuaire (tɛkstɥɛr), s.m. Text (without commentaries). ~, adj. Textual, textuary, pertaining to a text.

textuel, -le (tɛkstɥɛl), adj. Textual, verbatim, given word for word.

textuellement (tɛkstɥɛlmɑ̃), adv. Textually, word for word, verbatim.
texture (tɛkstyr), s.f. [L *textura*] Texture.
thala, tala (tala), adj. s.m.f. [jargon of École Normale Supérieure; f. *ceux qui vont à la messe*] (Person) holding religious (Roman Catholic) and conservative beliefs.
thaler (talɛr), s.m. [Germ. wd] Thaler (German coin).
thalle (tal), s.m. [Gr. *thallos*] (bot.) Thallus.
thallium (talliɔm), s.m. (chem.) Thallium.
thallophytes (tallɔfit), s.f.pl. (bot.) Thallophytes.
thalweg (talvɛg), s.m. [Germ. wd] (geog.) Thalweg, lowest line of a valley.
thaumaturge (tomatyrʒ), s.m.f. [Gr. *thauma*+*ergon*] Thaumaturge, worker of miracles.
thaumaturgie (tomatyrʒi), s.f. Thaumaturgy.
thaumaturgique (tomatyrʒik), adj. Thaumaturgical.
thé (te), s.m. [Chinese wd] Tea; tea-party; tea-plant; *boîte à* ~, tea-caddy, tea-canister.
théatin (teatɛ̃), s.m. [f. title of bishop of *Theato* (*Chieti*), Italy] Theatine (monk).
théâtral, -e, (aux) (teatral), adj. Theatrical.
théâtralement (teatralmɑ̃), adv. Theatrically.
théâtre (teatr), s.m. [Gr. *theatron*] Theatre, playhouse, stage, drama, plays, dramatic works, scene, show; *coup de* ~, unexpected event; striking stage-effect; striking change; ~ *de la guerre*, theatre of war; *faire du* ~, to go on the stage; *le* ~ *de Molière*, Molière's plays.
théâtricule (teatrikyl), s.m. Very small theatre.
théâtrophone (teatrɔfɔn), s.m. [Gr. *theatron*+*phōnē*] Theatrophone.
thébaïde (tebaid), s.f. [Gr. *Thēbaïs*] (fig.) Thebaid, deep solitude.
thébain, -e (tebɛ̃), adj. s.m.f. Theban.
théier (teje), s.m. (bot.) Tea-plant, tea-shrub.
théière (tejɛr), s.f. Tea-pot.
théiforme (teifɔrm), adj. Theiform, resembling tea.
théisme[1] (teism), s.m. [f. *thé*] (med.) Theism, poisoning through excessive tea-drinking.
théisme[2] (teism), s.m. [Gr. *theos* + Fr. *isme*] Theism.
théiste (teist), s.m.f. Theist. ~, adj. Theistic, theistical.
thématique (tematik), adj. (gram., mus.) Thematic.
thème (tɛm), s.m. [Gr. *thema*] Theme, topic, subject; (mus.) theme; (schools) exercise, composition (translation from one's own language into another); (colloq.) *un fort en* ~, a clever, hard-working pupil (at school), a glutton for work, a sap, a (successful) swot.
thénar (tenar), s.m. [Gr. wd] (anat.) Thenar.
théobrome (teɔbrɔm), s.m. [Gr. *theos*+*brōma*] (bot.) Theobroma.
théobromine (teɔbrɔmin), s.m. (pharm.) Theobromine.
théocrate (teɔkrat), s.m. [Gr. *theos*+*kratos*] Theocrat.
théocratie (teɔkrasi), s.f. Theocracy.
théocratique (teɔkratik), adj. Theocratic.
théocratiquement (teɔkratikmɑ̃), adv. Theocratically.
théodicée (teɔdise), s.f. [Gr. *theos*+*dikē*] Theodicy.
théodolite (teɔdɔlit), s.m. [etym. dub.] Theodolite.
théodosien, -ne (teɔdozjɛ̃), adj. [f. Emperor *Theodosius*] Theodosian.
théogonie (teɔgɔni), s.f. [Gr. *theos*+*gonos*] Theogony.
théogonique (teɔgɔnik), adj. Theogonic.
théologal, -e, (aux) (teɔlɔgal), adj. [f. Gr. *theos*+*logos*] Theological; *les trois vertus* ~*es*, the three theological virtues (faith, hope, charity). ~, s.m. Lecturer in divinity.
théologie (teɔlɔʒi), s.f. Theology, divinity; *docteur en* ~, doctor of divinity, D.D.
théologien (teɔlɔʒjɛ̃), s.m. Theologian.
théologique (teɔlɔʒik), adj. Theological.
théologiquement (teɔlɔʒikmɑ̃), adv. Theologically.
théophilanthrope (teɔfilɑ̃trɔp), s.m. Theophilanthropist.
théophilanthropie (teɔfilɑ̃trɔpi), s.f. [Gr. *theos*+*philein*+*anthrōpos*] Theophilanthropy.
théophilanthropique (teɔfilɑ̃trɔpik), adj. Theophilanthropic.
théorbe, téorbe (teɔrb), s.m. [It. *tiorba*] (mus.) Theorbo.
théorème (teɔrɛm), s.m. [Gr. *theōrēma*] (math.) Theorem.
théoricien, -ne (teɔrisjɛ̃), s.m.f. Theorist, theoretician.
théorie (teɔri), s.f. [Gr. *theōria*] Theory, speculation; (mil.) drill; procession; *en* ~, theoretically; *faire des* ~*s*, to speculate; *tout cela est très bien en* ~ *mais qu'est-ce que cela donnera dans la pratique?*, that is all very well in theory, but how will it work out in practice?; *une longue* ~ *de moines*, a procession, or a long line, of monks.
théorique (teɔrik), adj. Theoretic, theoretical, speculative.
théoriquement (teɔrikmɑ̃), adv. Theoretically; in theory.
théosophe (teɔzɔf), adj. s.m.f. [Gr. *theos*+*sophos*] Theosophist, theosoph, theosopher.
théosophie (teɔzɔfi), s.f. Theosophy.

thèque (tɛk), s.f. [Gr. *thēkē*] (bot.) Theca, urn-like cell in cryptogamous plants.
thérapeute (terapøt), s.m. [f. Gr. *therapeutikos*] Therapeutist.
thérapeutique (terapøtik), adj. Therapeutic, therapeutics.
thérapeutiste (terapøtist), s.m. Therapeutist.
thériacal, -e, (aux) (terjakal), adj. [f. Gr. *thēriakos*] (pharm.) Theriacal.
thériaque (terjak), s.f. Theriac.
thermal, -e, (aux) (tɛrmal), adj. [f. Gr. *thermē*] Thermal; *eaux ~es*, hot springs; *station ~e*, health resort.
thermalité (tɛrmalite), s.f. Quality of thermal waters.
thermes (tɛrm), s.m.pl. [Gr. *thermai*] Thermae, hot springs; hot baths, thermal establishment.
thermidor (tɛrmidɔr), s.m. [Gr. *thermē*+*dōron*] Thermidor; 11th month of French Republican calendar, from 20 July to 18 Aug.
thermidorien, -ne (tɛrmidɔrjɛ̃), adj. s.m.f. Thermidorian.
thermie (tɛrmi), s.f. [f. Gr. *thermē*] Amount of heat required to raise 1,000 kg. of water under normal atmospheric pressure one degree centigrade; ⚠ not 'therm', which = $\frac{1}{1,000,000}$ of *thermie* = *petite calorie* and also 1,000 British thermal units.
thermique (tɛrmik), adj. Thermic.
thermochimie (tɛrmɔʃimi), s.f. [Gr. *thermos*+*khimeia*] Thermochemistry.
thermodynamique (tɛrmɔdinamik), s.f. [Gr. *thermos*+*dunamikos*] (physiol.) Thermodynamics.
thermo-électricité (tɛrmɔelɛktrisite), s.f. Thermo-electricity.
thermogénie, thermogenèse (tɛrmɔʒeni, tɛrmɔʒənɛz), s.f. [Gr. *thermos*+*genesis*] Thermogenesis.
thermographe (tɛrmɔgraf), s.m. [Gr. *thermos*+*graphein*] Thermograph.
thermologie (tɛrmɔlɔʒi), s.f. [Gr. *thermos* +*logos*] Thermology, thermotics.
thermologique (tɛrmɔlɔʒik), adj. Thermotic, thermological.
thermo-magnétique (tɛrmɔmagnetik), adj. Thermo-magnetic.
thermo-magnétisme (tɛrmɔmagnetism), s.m. [Gr. *thermos*+*magnētos*] Thermo-magnetism.
thermomètre (tɛrmɔmɛtr), s.m. [Gr. *thermos*+*metron*] Thermometer.
thermométrie (tɛrmɔmetri), s.f. Thermometry.
thermométrique (tɛrmɔmetrik), adj. Thermometric(al).
thermométrographe (tɛrmɔmetrɔgraf), s.m. Thermometrograph, self-registering thermometer.
thermo-multiplicateur (tɛrmɔmyltiplikatœr), s.m. Thermo-multiplier.
thermos (tɛrmos), s.f. Thermos flask, vacuum flask or jar.
thermoscope (tɛrmɔskɔp), s.m. [Gr. *thermos*+*skopein*] Thermoscope.
thermosiphon (tɛrmosifɔ̃), s.m. Thermo-syphon; (mech., motor.) *refroidissement par ~*, thermo-syphon cooling.
thésauriser (tezorize), v.n. [f. Gr. *thēsauros*] To hoard, to treasure up money, to amass money.
thésauriseu-r, -se (tezɔrizœr), s.m.f. Hoarder.
thèse (tɛz), s.f. [Gr. *thesis*] **1.** Thesis, argument, discussion; *cela change la ~*, that alters the case; *en ~ générale*, as a general rule; **2.** graduation thesis, important work required of candidate for degree of *docteur* (of Fr. State universities); *soutenance de ~*, public discussion of this work.
thessalien, -ne (tɛsaljɛ̃), adj. s.m.f. Thessalian.
thessalonicien, -ne (tɛsalɔnisjɛ̃), adj. s.m.f. Thessalonian.
théurgie (teyrʒi), s.f. [Gr. *theos*+*ergon*] Theurgy.
thibaude (tibod), s.f. [f. prop. n.] Coarse drugget (for laying under valuable carpets).
thionique (tiɔnik), adj. (chem.) Thionic (acid).
thlaspi (tlaspi), s.m. [Gr. wd] (bot.) Thlaspi, penny-cress, shepherd's purse.
thomisme (tɔmism), s.m. [f. *St. Thomas Aquinas*] Thomism.
thomiste (tɔmist), s.m.f. adj. Thomist.
thon (tɔ̃), s.m. [Gr. *thunnos*] (ichth.) Tunny(-fish).
thonaire (tɔnɛr), s.m. Net for tunny-fishing.
thonier (tɔnje), s.m. Boat for tunny-fishing.
thonine (tɔnin), s.f. (ichth.) Mediterranean tunny.
thoracique (tɔrasik), adj. (anat.) Thoracic.
thorax (tɔraks), s.m. [Gr. wd] (anat.) Thorax, chest.
thorite (tɔrit), s.f. (min.) Thorite.
thorium (tɔriɔm), s.m. (chem.) Thorium: Th.
thridace (tridas), s.f. [Gr. *thridax*] (pharm.) Thridace.
thrips (trips), s.m. [Gr. wd] (ent.) Thrips.
thrombus (trɔmbys), s.m. [f. Gr. *thrombōsis*] (pathol.) Thrombosis.
thug (tyg), s.m. [Hind. *ṭhag*] Thug.
thune (tyn), s.f. (slang) Five-franc piece.
thuriféraire (tyriferɛr), s.m. [L *thus, thuris*+*ferre*] Thurifer, censer-bearer, (fig., pej.) flatterer.
thurifère (tyrifɛr), adj. (bot.) Thuriferous.
thurne, turne (tyrn), s.f. [jargon of École Normale Supérieure] Small study assigned for one year to three or four pupils.

thuya (tɥija), s.m. [Gr. *thuia*] (bot.) Thuya, thuja, arbor vitae.
thyade (tiad), s.f. [Gr. *thuas*] Bacchante.
thym (tɛ̃), s.m. [Gr. *thumos*] (bot.) Thyme.
thymique (timik), adj. (anat.) Thymic.
thymol (timɔl), s.m. Thymol.
thymus (timys), s.m. [Gr. *thumos*] (anat.) Thymus, thymus gland.
thyroïde (tirɔid), adj. [f. Gr. *thureos*] (anat.) Thyroid.
thyroïdien, -ne (tirɔidjɛ̃), adj. (anat.) Thyroid.
thyrse (tirs), s.m. [Gr. *thursos*] (ant., bot.) Thyrsus.
thysanoures (tizanur), s.m.pl. [Gr. *thysanos*] (ent.) Thysanura.
tiare (tjar), s.f. [Gr. *tiara*] Tiara.
tibétain, -e (tibetɛ̃), adj. s.m.f. Tibetan.
tibia (tibja), s.m. [L wd] (anat.) Tibia, shin-bone.
tibial, -e, (aux) (tibjal), adj. Tibial.
tic (tik), s.m. [etym. dub.] Tic, bad habit, twitching of the face; *c'est son* ~, it 's a habit he has. ⚠ Not 'tick', which = *coutil*; *tique*; *battement*.
ticket (tikɛ), s.m. [Engl. wd] Ticket.
tic-tac (tik-tak), s.m. (onom.) Tick-tack, ticking clock.
tiède (tjɛd), adj. [L *tepidus*] Lukewarm, tepid, mild, soft; (fig.) indifferent.
tièdement (tjɛdmɑ̃), adv. Coolly, with indifference.
tiédeur (tjedœr), s.f. Tepidity, lukewarmness, mildness, pleasant warmth (after cold); (fig.) **1.** indifference; **2.** cosiness.
tiédir (tjedir), v.n.a. To grow mild or lukewarm, to warm or cool slightly; *faire* ~, to warm (or cool) slightly.
tien, -ne (tjɛ̃), poss. adj. [L *tuus*] Yours, thine, thine own. ~, s.m. Thine, thy property; *les* ~*s*, thy (your) relations, family; *le* ~ *et le mien*, thine and mine; (drinking) *à la tienne!*, good health!
tierçaire, tierciaire (tjɛrsɛr, tjɛrsjɛr), s.m. Friar of the third order of Franciscans.
tierce (tjɛrs), s.f. [f. L *tertius*] Tierce, (mus.) third, tierce; (fenc.) tierce (thrust or parry); (print.) last revise, final (proof); (cards, herald). tierce.
tiercé, -e (tjɛrse), adj. (herald.) Divided into three parts.
tiercelet (tjɛrsəlɛ), s.m. (ornith.) Tercel, male falcon.
tiercement (tjɛrsmɑ̃), s.m. (obs.) Increase by a third.
tiercer (tjɛrse), v.a. (obs.) To raise or increase by a third; to plough a third time, to dress (vines) a third time.
tierceron (tjɛrsərɔ̃), s.m. (arch.) Tierceron.
tier-s, -ce (tjɛr), adj. [L *tertius*] Third, (med.) tertian; *fièvre* ~*ce*, tertian ague; ~ *état*, tiers état, third estate, the commonalty, the commons, the people.
tiers (tjɛr), s.m. Third, third party, third person; *les deux* ~, two-thirds; *se mettre en* ~, to join (two persons); *le* ~ *et le quart*, anybody and everybody.
tiers-point (tjɛrpwɛ̃), s.m. **1.** (arch.) Tierce-point; **2.** (techn.) three-square file, small triangular file.
tifs (tif), s.m.pl. (slang) Hair, thatch.
tige (tiʒ), s.f. [L *tibia*] Stem, stalk, trunk (of tree), straw (of corn); shank (of key); shaft (of column); (fig.) leg of a boot; stock (of a family), (techn.) rod; ~ *de piston*, piston-rod; *à haute* ~, standard (trees); ~ *de communication*, connecting-rod; ~ *de soupape*, valve-stem; valve-tappet, valve-spindle.
tigelle (tiʒɛl), s.f. (bot.) Tigella.
tigette (tiʒɛt), s.f. (arch.) Honeysuckle ornament.
tignasse (tiɲas), s.f. [f. *teigne*] (fam.) Scrubby wig, shock of hair, shock, mop.
tignon (tiɲɔ̃), s.m. (fam.) Chignon, back hair, 'bun'.
tigre, -sse (tigr), s.m.f. [L *tigris*] (zool.) Tiger, tigress.
tigré, -e (tigre), p. adj. Spotted, speckled; striped; (bot.) *lis* ~, tiger-lily.
tigrer (tigre), v.a. To stripe, to spot, to speckle.
tigresse (tigrɛs), s.f. (zool.) Tigress.
tilbury (tilbyri), s.m. [Engl. wd] Tilbury, two-wheeled carriage.
tilde (tild), s.m. [Span. wd] Tilde.
tillac (tijak), s.m. [Scand. orig.] Deck; *franc* ~, main deck, flush-deck; *faux* ~, half-deck.
tille[1] (tij), s.f. [Scand. orig.] (naut.) Cuddy.
tille[2] (tij), s.f. [Scand. orig.] (techn.) Axe, hatchet hammer, slater's hammer, carpenter's hatchet.
tilleul (tijœl), s.m. [L *tilia*] Lime-tree, linden-tree, lime-tree flowers; infusion of lime-tree flowers.
timar (timar), s.m. [Turk. wd] Timar.
timariot (timarjo), s.m. Turkish soldier holding a fief.
timbale (tɛ̃bal), s.f. [It. *timballo*] **1.** Kettle-drum, timbal; **2.** footless metal cup or mug, kitchen mould; (cook.) timbale; **3.** parchment battledore; (fig.) *décrocher la* ~, to secure the prize; to take the cake.
timbalier (tɛ̃balje), s.m. Kettle-drummer.
timbrage (tɛ̃braʒ), s.m. Stamping.
timbre (tɛ̃br), s.m. [L *tympanum*] **1.** Bell, sound, tone, quality, timbre; (fam.) *avoir le* ~ *fêlé*, to be cracked, or crack-brained; to have a screw loose; **2.** postage-stamp, stamp; ~ *d'affranchissement*, postage-stamp; ~ *acquit*, receipt-stamp; *bureau du* ~, stamp-office; ~ *dateur*, date-stamp; *droit de* ~, stamp-duty; ~ *de la poste*, post-office stamp, postmark; ~*-poste*, stamp, postage-stamp; ~ *quittance*, receipt stamp; ~ *sec*, plain relief stamp; embossing-press; **3.** (herald.) crest, helmet.

timbré, -e (tɛ̃bre), p. adj. Stamped; (fam.) a bit cracked, dotty.
timbrer (tɛ̃bre), v.a. To stamp, (law) to docket, (herald.) to crest; *tampon à ~*, stamp-pad.
timbreu-r, -se (tɛ̃brœr), s.m.f. Stamper.
timide (timid), adj. [L *timidus*] Timid, shy, faint-hearted, bashful, diffident, cautious, sheepish.
timidement (timidmɑ̃), adj. Timidly, bashfully, shyly, timorously.
timidité (timidite), s.f. Timidity, timorousness, bashfulness, shyness, diffidence.
timocratie (timɔkrasi), s.f. [Gr. *timokratia*] Timocracy.
timon (timɔ̃), s.m. [L *temo*] Pole (of carriage), beam (of plough), (naut.) tiller, helm; (fig.) helm, direction, government.
timonerie (timɔnri), s.f. (naut.) Steerage; *poste de ~*, signal-station; *kiosque de ~*, wheelhouse; *chef de ~*, chief quartermaster.
timonier (timɔnje), s.m. **1.** Steersman, signalman; (obs.) helmsman; *~ de quart*, quartermaster; **2.** shaft-horse.
timoré, -e (timɔre), adj. [f. L *timor*] Timorous, fearful.
tin (tɛ̃), s.m. [Provenç. wd] Block of wood, stock, cask-stand; (naut.) block.
tinamou (tinamu), s.m. [S. Amer. wd] (ornith.) Tinamou.
tincal (tɛ̃kal), s.m. [Malay *tingkal*] Tincal, crude borax.
tinctorial, -e, (aux) (tɛ̃ktɔrjal), adj. [f. L *tinctorius*] Tinctorial.
tine (tin), s.f. [L *tina*] Tub, water-cask; kit, firkin.
tinette (tinɛt), s.f. Small tub, kit, firkin (espec. for night-soil).
tintamarre (tɛ̃tamar), s.m. [etym. dub.] Hubbub, clatter, uproar, racket, din, hurly-burly.
tintement (tɛ̃tmɑ̃), s.m. Ringing, tinkling, jingling; tolling, sounding a knell; singing, buzzing (in the ears).
tinter[1] (tɛ̃te), v.n. [LL *tinnitare*] To ring, to toll, to sound a knell, to knell, to jingle, to clink, to tingle, to tinkle; *les oreilles me tintent*, my ears tingle (as if some one were talking about me).
tinter[2] (tɛ̃te), v.a. [f. *tin*] (naut.) To set on blocks.
tintinnabuler (tɛ̃tinabyle), v.n. [f. L *tintinnabulum*] To make a noise as of small bells; to tintinnabulate.
tintouin (tɛ̃twɛ̃), s.m. (obs.) Ringing, tingling, buzzing (in one's ears); (fig.) anxiety, uneasiness; fret, worry; *avoir du ~*, to be on thorns; *donner du ~ à X*, to give X cause for worry.
tipule (tipyl), s.f. [L *tippula*] (ent.) Tipula, daddy-long-legs.
tique (tik), s.f. [etym. dub.] (ent.) Tick.
tiquer (tike), v.n. To have a tic; (vet.) to bite the crib, to be vicious; (colloq.) to wince; to object to; *~ sur quelque chose*, to show a dislike for something.
tiqueté, -e (tikte), adj. Variegated, spotted, speckled.
tiqueture (tiktyr), s.f. Variegation, speckles.
tiqueu-r, -se (tikœr), adj. Having a tic; (of horses) crib-biting, vicious.
tir (tir), s.m. [f. *tirer*] Firing, shooting, fire; archery, target- or shooting-practice; shooting-gallery, -range, or -ground, rifle-range, rifle match or competition; *~ à la cible*, target-firing; *canon à ~ rapide*, quick-firing gun; *concours de ~*, shooting-match; *société de ~*, rifle club; *~ à longue portée*, long-range fire.
tirade (tirad), s.f. [It. *tirata*] Tirade, speech; (fam.) *d'une ~, tout d'une ~*, at a stretch, without ceasing.
tirage (tiraʒ), s.m. Draught, drawing, pulling, dragging, tug, pull, tugging, pulling, tow, towing-path; winding off (of silk); (print.) working off, impression; (newspapers) circulation, issue; (photo.) printing; (fig.) difficulty, obstacle; *~ élevé*, large circulation (of newspapers); *~ au sort*, drawing lots; *mauvais ~*, bad draught (of a chimney); (colloq.) *il y a du ~*, things are not going smoothly.
tiraillement (tiraɪmɑ̃), s.m. Pulling, hauling about, twitching, twinge, pain (often in stomach); (fig.) jarring, wrangling, discord, vexation.
tirailler (tiraje), v.a. [f. *tirer*] To pull about, to twitch; (fig.) to tease, to plague, to pester; ~, v.n. to shoot wildly, 'to shoot away', to skirmish; **se ~**, v.pr. to pull each other about, to thwart each other.
tiraillerie (tirajri), s.f. Desultory firing, skirmishing.
tirailleur (tirajœr), s.m. Sharpshooter, skirmisher.
tirant (tirɑ̃), s.m. Strap, purse-string, tie (of shoes); (arch.) brace, (techn.) stay; gristle (of meat); (naut.) ship's draught; *ayant 20 pieds de ~ d'eau*, drawing 20 feet of water.
tirasse (tiras), s.f. Draw-net (for quails, &c.).
tirasser (tirase), v.a. To catch (quails, &c.) with a draw-net; ~, v.n. to set a draw-net.
tire (tir), s.f. Tug, pull; *vol à la ~*, pocket-picking; *à ~ d'aile*, swiftly; as fast as its wings can carry it; winging its way.
tiré, -e (tire), p. adj. Drawn, fatigued, worn out; (fig.) *~ par les cheveux*, far-fetched; *~ à quatre épingles*, spick and span; togged up to the nines; *un visage ~*, a drawn face. ~, s.m. **1.** (usually in the pl.) Coverts (pl.), shooting-ground; **2.** (comm.) drawee (of a bill).
tire-balle (tirbal), s.m. (pl. *tireballes*)

(mil.) Ramrod-screw; (surg.) bullet-forceps.

tire-botte (tirbɔt), s.m. (pl. *tire-bottes*) Boot-jack, boot-hook.

tire-bouchon (tirbuʃɔ̃), s.m. (pl. *tire-bouchons*) Corkscrew; (of hair) corkscrew curls; *en* ~, winding, spiral.

tire-bourre (tirbur), s.m. (pl. *tire-bourres*) Wad-hook, (mil.) ramrod-screw.

tire-bouton (tirbutɔ̃), s.m. (pl. *tire-boutons*) Button-hook.

tire-clous (tirklu), s.m. invar. Nail-drawer, claw-hammer.

tire d'aile (tirdɛl), s.m. invar. Rapid flight; *à* ~, very swiftly, at full speed, as fast as its wings can carry it.

tire-feu (tirfø), s.m. invar. (mil.) Lanyard.

tire-filet (tirfilɛ), s.m. (pl. *tire-filets*) Filet, moulding-plane.

tire-fond (tirfɔ̃), s.m. invar. Cooper's turrel, screw-ring.

tire-fusée (tirfyze), s.m. (pl. *tire-fusées*) (mil.) Drawer for extracting fuses.

tire-laine (tirlɛn), s.m. invar. Thief, night-robber.

(à) tire-larigot (tirlarigo), adv. loc. *Boire à* ~, to drink by pouring liquid from a height into the mouth; to drink hard.

tire-ligne (tirliɲ), s.m. (pl. *tire-lignes*) Drawing-pen.

tirelire (tirlir), s.f. [It. *tira lira*] Money-box.

tirelire (tirlir), s.m. [onom.] Song of the lark; carol.

tirelirer (tirlire), v.n. To sing like a lark; to carol.

tire-moelle (tirmwal), s.m. invar. Marrow-spoon.

tire-pied (tirpie), s.m. (pl. *tire-pieds*) Shoemaker's stirrup.

tire-point (tirpwɛ̃), s.m. invar. Pricker.

tirer (tire), v.a.n. [orig. unkn.] To draw, to pull, to drag, to pull in, out, on, up, &c.; to extract, to get, to derive, to extort, to take away, out, off; to let (blood), to tap (liquors), to stretch, to strain, to tighten, to wire-draw; (naut.) to draw; (print. and photo.) to print, to work off; to fire, to shoot, to discharge, to fence; to deduce, to infer, to conclude, to elicit; to trace, to delineate; ~ *avantage de tout*, to turn everything to account; ~ *les cartes*, to tell fortunes (with cards); ~ *gloire* (or *vanité*) *de*, to take pride in; to glory in; to boast of; ~ *la langue*, to put out one's tongue; ~ *le diable par la queue*, to be hard up; to have a struggle to make ends meet; to be in Queer Street; ~ *X d'erreur*, to undeceive X; ~ *son épingle du jeu*, to save one's stake; to get well out of a ticklish business; ~ *les marrons du feu*, to be the cat's-paw; *tiré à quatre chevaux*, drawn and quartered; ~ *une ligne droite*, to draw or trace a straight line; ~ *pied ou aile*, to get pickings, to reap some benefit; ~ *les oreilles à X*, to pull X's ears; *il se fera* ~ *l'oreille*, he will require pressing; he is very reluctant; (fig.) ~ *sa poudre aux moineaux*, to waste time and money on trifles; ~ *parti de*, to make the best of; to make . . . serve; ~ *au sort*, or *à la courte paille*, to draw lots; ~ *sa source de*, to spring from; ~ *les vers du nez à X*, to pump X; ~ *à balle*, to fire with ball-cartridges; ~ *à blanc*, to fire with blank cartridges; *bien* ~, to be a good shot, a good fencer; *bon à* ~, ready for the press; s.m. permission to print; ~ *à sa fin*, to be drawing to an end; to be on one's last legs; to be nearly over; ~ *au clair*, to elucidate, to throw light on, to clear up; ~ *en longueur*, to drag out, to be long, slow; *ce vert tire sur le jaune*, this green has a yellowish tinge; *la cheminée tire mal*, or *ne tire pas*, the chimney draws badly; *cela ne tire pas à conséquence*, that is of no importance; (comm.) ~ *sur X*, or ~ *une lettre de change sur X*, to draw a bill on X; ~ *d'un sac double mouture*, to make a double profit; *on ne saurait* ~ *de l'huile d'un mur*, you can't get blood out of a stone; *après cela il faut* ~ *l'échelle*, that takes the cake; that puts the tin hat on it; that cannot be improved upon; (slang) ~ *de la prison*, to do time; **se** ~, v.pr. to drag or haul oneself; to be drawn; to extract oneself; *se* ~ *d'affaire* or *s'en* ~, to escape; to recover; to come off, to manage to get through or over it; (slang) *ça se tire*, it 's nearly finished; *se* ~ *des pieds*, or *des pattes*, or *des flûtes*, to be off, to make tracks, to show a clean pair of heels.

tire-racine (tirrasin), s.m. Stump forceps.

tire-sou (tirsu), s.m. (pl. *tire-sous*) Usurer.

tiret (tirɛ), s.m. Dash, hyphen; slip of parchment.

tiretaine (tirtɛn), s.f. (obs.) Linsey-woolsey.

tirette (tirɛt), s.f. **1.** Cord, string; **2.** sliding tablet.

tireu-r, -se (tirœr), s.m.f. Shooter, fencer, wire-drawer, marksman, rifleman, shot, (comm.) drawer (of a bill); ~ *d'armes*, fencing-master; *franc-*~, sharpshooter; *être bon* ~, to be a good shot; *être fin* ~, to be a crack shot; *tireuse de cartes*, fortune-teller.

tire-vieille, tire-veille (tirviɛj, tirvɛj), s.m. invar. (naut.) Ladder-rope, man-rope, side-rope.

tiroir (tirwar), s.m. [f. *tirer*] Drawer, till; (mech.) slide, slide-valve; *pièce à* ~*s*, comedy of episodes.

tironien, -ne (tirɔnjɛ̃), adj. [f. *Tiro*, inventor, Rom. ant.] Tironian (system of stenography).

tisane (tizan), s.f. [L *ptisana*] Infusion, herb-tea, herb-drink, cooling drink, decoction; ~ *de champagne*, light, cheap champagne; ~ *d'orge*, barley-water; ~ *de menthe*, *de camomille*, mint-tea, camomile-tea.

tison (tizɔ̃), s.m. [L *titio*] Brand, firebrand, embers; (colloq.) fusee, match which is not blown out by wind.
tisonné, -e (tizɔne), p. adj. Marked with black spots (of horses).
tisonner (tizɔne), v.n.a. To stir or poke the fire.
tisonneu-r, -se (tizɔnœr), s.m.f. Person fond of poking the fire.
tisonnier (tizɔnje), s.m. Poker.
tissage (tisaʒ), s.m. Weaving.
tisser (tise), v.a. [L *texere*] To weave; (fig.) to contrive.
tisserand (tisrɑ̃), s.m. Weaver.
tisseranderie (tisrɑ̃dri), s.f. Weaving-trade.
tisserin (tisrɛ̃), s.m. (ornith.) Weaver-bird.
tisseur (tisœr), s.m. Weaver.
tissu (tisy), s.m. Texture, textile, fabric, tissue, web, cloth, material, stuff; (fig.) *un ~ de mensonges*, a tissue of lies.
tissure (tisyr), s.f. Texture.
tissuterie (tisytri), s.f. Ribbon-weaving.
tissutier (tisytje), s.m. Weaver of ribbons and silks.
titan (titɑ̃), s.m. [L wd] Titan.
titane, titanium (titan, titaniɔm), s.m. (chem.) Titanium: Ti.
titané, -e (titane), adj. Containing titanium.
titanesque (titanɛsk), adj. Titanesque.
titanifère (titanifɛr), adj. [L *titanum*+ *ferre*] Titaniferous.
titanique (titanik), adj. Titanic; syn. TITANESQUE.
titi (titi), s.m. (slang) Street arab, a young (Parisian) rogue.
titillation (titila'sjɔ̃), s.f. [L *titillatio*] Titillation, tickling.
titiller (titille), v.a. To titillate, to tickle.
titrage (titraʒ), s.m. (comm.) Testing; assaying.
titre (titr), s.m. [L *titulus*] Title; title-page; head, heading; inscription, (U.S.A.) caption; chapter, division, title (of a statute); style, name; appellation of honour or dignity; the right to hold a certain office; *recevoir son ~ de notaire*, to become a fully qualified solicitor; right, claim, reason, qualification; *à bon ~, à juste ~*, rightly, justly; *à ~ de grâce*, as a favour; *à ~ gracieux*, complimentary, free; *à ~ gratuit*, free, gratis, gratuitous(ly); *à quel ~?*, by what right?, on what ground?; *au même ~*, for the same reason; *à plus d'un ~*, for several reasons, on more counts than one; *à ~ d'ami*, as a friend; *à ~ d'office*, ex officio; *avoir des ~s à*, to be entitled to; *donner des ~s à*, to entitle to; *en ~*, titular, regular, by appointment; title-deed; muniment, voucher, certificate; (pl.) securities; *~s de noblesse*, patents of nobility; strength (of a solution), standard (of gold or silver alloys); *ce bijou est au ~ de x*, this trinket is *x*-carat gold.
titré, -e (titre), p. adj. Titled; conferring a title; (chem.) of standard strength, titrated.
titrer (titre), v.a. To give a title to; (chem.) to determine the strength of (a solution); **se ~**, v.pr. to assume a title.
titrier (titrie), s.m. Curator of deeds in a monastery; forger of deeds.
titubant, -e (titybɑ̃), p. adj. Staggering, reeling, tottering.
titubation (tityba'sjɔ̃), s.f. Staggering, reeling.
tituber (titybe), v.n. [L *titubare*] To stagger, to reel, to stumble.
titulaire (titylɛr), adj. [f. L *titulus*] Titulary, pertaining to a title; titular, regular; head. **~**, s.m.f. Titular incumbent, head, or chief; rightful holder.
titulariat (titylarja), s.m. Office conferring a title; the possession by title of a function or office.
titulariser (titylarize), v.a. To confer a titular right on.
(à la) titus (alatitys), adv. loc. (of hair, cut) Short all round, like that of the Emperor Titus in old statues.
tmèse (tmɛz), s.f. [Gr. *tmēsis*] (gram.) Tmesis.
toarcien, -ne (toarsjɛ̃), adj. s.m. (geol.) Toarcian (applied to strata corresponding in position to the upper lias, extensively developed in central and southern France).
toast (tost), s.m. [Engl. wd] **1.** Toast; health; *porter un ~*, to drink a toast; to propose a toast; **2.** piece of toasted bread. ⚠ Though the Engl. wd 'toast' is used in Fr. with the article: *un toast*, English do not say 'a toast' or 'toasts' in sense **2.**
toaster (toste), v.n. To drink toasts; to propose toasts; **~**, v.a. to toast (some one), to drink (some one's) health.
toboggan (tobɔgɑ̃), s.m. [Canadian Indian wd] Toboggan, sled, sledge, sleigh.
toc (tɔk), s.m. (colloq.) Anything trashy, sham, imitation, brummagem, counterfeit, cheap and showy; *c'est du ~!*, it's faked!
tocane (tɔkan), s.f. Unpressed wine, unfermented champagne.
tocsin (tɔksɛ̃), s.m. [f. OF *toquer*, to strike] Tocsin, alarm-bell; *sonner le ~*, to ring the alarm; (fig.) to excite the mob; *sonner le ~ contre quelqu'un*, to raise a hue and cry after some one; to raise an outcry against some one.
todier (tɔdje), s.m. [f. L *todus*] (ornith.) Tody.
toge (tɔʒ), s.f. [L *toga*] Toga.
tohu-bohu (tɔybɔy), s.m. [f. Hebr. wd] Primeval chaos; chaos; confusion, disorder, confused medley; uproar, hubbub, hurly-burly; to-do; *c'était un ~ à ne pas*

s'entendre, there was a deafening hubbub; there was such a din you could not hear yourself speak.

toi (twa), pers. pron., 2nd pers. sing. (nom. or voc.) Thou; you; (obj.) thee, you; to thee, to you; *c'est ~ qui l'as fait*, you did it; *~-même*, thyself, yourself; you alone; *garde t'en bien*, beware of it.

toilage (twalɑʒ), s.m. [f. *toile*] The foundation on which the pattern of a piece of lace is built up; syn. TOILÉ.

toile (twal), s.f. [L *tela*] Cloth; linen; canvas, sail-cloth; textile fabric; *~ amiantine*, or *d'amiante*, amianthus cloth; *~ cirée*, oil-cloth; American cloth; *~ fine*, fine linen; *~ à bâche*, tarpaulin; *~ métallique*, wire gauze; *~ ouvrée*, table-linen, towelling; huckaback; *~ damassée*, damask linen; *~ peinte*, print; *~ à calquer*, tracing-paper; *~ à matelas*, tick, ticking; *~ à peindre*, artists' canvas; *~ de maître*, valuable picture; *~ à sacs*, sackcloth; *~ à voiles*, sail-cloth; *~ de chanvre*, canvas; *~ de coton*, calico; shirting; *~ d'emballage*, packing-sheet; *~ écrue*, holland; *~ d'Irlande*, Irish linen; *~ de lin*, linen; *~ à draps*, sheeting; *~ d'or*, cloth of gold; *commerce des ~s*, linen trade; *marchand de ~s*, linendraper; (naut.) sail; *faire de la ~*, to make sail; *faire peu de ~*, to keep under easy sail; *augmenter de ~*, to put on sail; *diminuer de ~*, to shorten sail; *qui porte bien la ~*, stiff; *~ de panneau*, hatchway screen; *~ d'araignée*, spider's web; cobweb; *~ (de pneu)* canvas (of a tyre) (colloq.) *se fourrer dans les ~s*, to go to bed.

toilé (twale), s.m. See TOILAGE.

toilerie (twalri), s.f. Linen trade; linen-drapery, linen store, linen manufacture; linen goods.

toilette (twalɛt), s.f. **1.** Washstand, dressing-table; **2.** the act of washing, dressing, &c.; *faire sa ~*, to wash (oneself), to dress; *faire un bout de ~*, to spruce up; to smarten oneself; *faire ~*, to dress up; **3.** clothes, dress, rig-out; *en grande ~*, in full dress; *revendeuse, marchande à la ~*, wardrobe dealer, old-clothes woman; *garniture de ~*, utensils for the toilet; *cabinet de ~*, dressing-room; **4.** (cook.) caul, membrane used as a wrapper for sausages, &c.; **5.** packing-cloth used by dressmakers for carrying garments, material, &c.

toili-er, -ère (twalje), s.m.f. Linen-cloth maker. *~*, adj. Pertaining to the manufacture of linen.

toise (twaz), s.f. [L *tensa* (*brachia*)] (obs.) Toise; lineal measure of six French feet (roughly = $6\frac{2}{5}$ ft.); (fig.) standard; *mesurer les autres à sa ~*, to judge others by oneself, or by one's own standards.

toisé (twaze), s.m. Measuring; mensuration.

toiser (twaze), v.a. **1.** To measure; **2.** (fig.) to scan, to scrutinize, to sum up; *~ X de la tête aux pieds*, to look X up and down.

toiseur (twazœr), s.m. (obs.) Surveyor.

toison (twazɔ̃), s.f. [L *tonsio*] Fleece; (fig.) shock of hair, mane; *la ~ d'or*, the Golden Fleece.

toit (twa or twɑ), s.m. [L *tectum*] Roof; *habiter sous les ~s*, to live in a garret; *crier, dire*, or *prêcher* (*quelque chose*) *sur les ~s*, to noise abroad to all the world; to proclaim (something) from the housetops; (fig.) house, home; *~ à cochons*, pigsty.

toiture (twatyr), s.f. Roofing, roof.

tokai, tokay (tɔkɛ), s.m. [geog. orig., *Tokay*, Hungary] Tokay (wine).

tôle (tol), s.f. [OF *taule*, f. L *tabula*] Sheet iron; *~ ondulée*, corrugated iron; *~ d'acier*, steel plate; *~ vernie*, japanned iron.

tolérable (tɔlerabl), adj. Bearable, tolerable; passable, middling, mediocre.

tolérance (tɔlerɑ̃s), s.f. Tolerance, indulgence; toleration, sufferance, religious toleration; *par ~*, on sufferance; (coin.) *~* (*de poids*), tolerance, allowance (for deviation from standard weight); *maison de ~*, brothel under police supervision.

tolérant, -e (tɔlerɑ̃), p. adj. Tolerant, indulgent.

tolérantisme (tɔlerɑ̃tism), s.m. Religious toleration.

tolérer (tɔlere), v.a. [L *tolerare*] To tolerate, to allow, to suffer, to endure; **se ~**, v.pr. to be tolerated; **2.** to endure each other.

tôlerie (tolri), s.f. Sheet-iron goods, trade, or manufacture; (pl.) rolling-mills.

tolet (tɔlɛ), s.m. [Scand. orig.] (naut.) Thole, tholepin.

toletière (tɔltiɛr), s.f. (naut.) Rowlock.

tôlier (tolje), s.m. Manufacturer of sheet iron.

tollé (tɔlle), s.m. [L *tolle*] Outcry; *crier ~ contre, sur X*, to raise an outcry against X.

toluène (tɔlɥɛn), s.m. [f. geog. n. *Tolu*, Colombia] (chem.) Toluene.

tomahawk (tɔmaɔk), s.m. [Amer. Indian wd] Tomahawk.

tomaison (tɔmɛzɔ̃), s.f. (print.) Numbering of pages, indicating the volume to which they belong.

toman (tɔmɑ̃), s.m. [Pers. *tumān*] Toman, Persian coin.

tomate (tɔmat), s.f. [Span. wd] Tomato.

tombac (tɔ̃bak), s.m. [f. Malay *tambaga*] (chem.) Tombac.

tombal, -e, (aux) (tɔ̃bal), adj. Of the tomb, sepulchral; *pierre ~e*, tombstone.

tombant, -e (tɔ̃bɑ̃), p. adj. Falling, drooping, flowing; dying away; fading away; *des cheveux ~s*, flowing locks; *à la nuit ~e*, at nightfall; *finale ~e*, 'a dying fall'.

tombe (tɔ̃b), s.f. [L *tumba*] Tomb, grave, sepulchre; tombstone, gravestone, headstone; *avoir un pied dans la* ~, to have one foot in the grave.

tombeau (pl. -x) (tɔ̃bo), s.m. **1.** Tomb, grave; **2.** tombstone, sepulchre; **3.** (fig.) death, destruction, end; *l'intérêt est le* ~ *de l'amitié*, self-interest is stronger than friendship; *aux portes du* ~, at the point of death; *conduire à* ~ *ouvert*, to drive like blazes.

tombée (tɔ̃be), s.f. Fall; *à la* ~ *du jour, à la* ~ *de la nuit*, at nightfall.

tombelier (tɔ̃bəlje), s.m. (obs.) Carter.

tombelle (tɔ̃bɛl), s.f. **1.** Barrow; **2.** mound, tomb.

tomber (tɔ̃be), v.n. [Germ. orig.] **1.** To fall, to fall down, to drop down; to tumble; to droop, to hang down; to throw oneself; to decay, to degenerate, to flag, to die out; to become; ~ *sur*, to meet, to run into, to come across; to occur; ~ *à terre*, to fall to the ground; ~ *par terre*, to fall on the ground; ~ *raide mort*, to fall down dead; ~ *sur ses pieds*, to land on one's feet; (fig.) ~ *de son haut*, to be struck all of a heap; to be amazed; ~ *des nues*, to be astounded; *faire* ~, to push or throw down; *laisser* ~, to let fall, to drop; *de beaux cheveux lui tombent sur les épaules*, her beautiful hair hangs loose on her shoulders; *les bras m'en tombèrent*, you could have knocked me down with a feather!; ~ *aux pieds de X*, to fall at X's feet; (impers.) *il tombe de l'eau*, it is raining; *le jour tombe*, the day is closing in; *la fièvre tombe*, the fever is abating; *la mer tombe*, the sea is growing calmer; *la malade est tombée bien bas*, the patient is worse, the patient is very low; *c'est un homme qui est bien tombé*, he is not the man he was; he has seen better days; *cela tombe dans le maniéré*, that degenerates into mere affectation; *cette maison est tombée en quenouille*, that family only survives in the female line; *cette pièce est tombée*, that play did not take, or was a failure; *laisser* ~ *la voix*, to let one's voice fall; ~ *amoureux de X*, to fall in love with X; ~ *d'accord*, to agree; ~ *sous la coupe de X*, to fall into X's power; ~ *malade*, to fall ill; *faire* ~ *X en confusion*, to put X out of countenance; ~ *de Charybde en Scylla*, to be between Scylla and Charybdis; ~ *de la poêle dans la braise*, to jump out of the frying-pan into the fire; *le sort tomba sur lui*, it fell to his lot; *cela tombe sous le sens*, that is evident; *ce chemin tombe dans tel autre*, this road leads into such and such a road; *il m'est tombé entre les mains un petit livre*, a little book fell into my hands; I came across a little book; *il tomba sur une maison*, he came across a house; ~ *dans un piège*, to fall into a trap; *cela tombe bien, mal*, it is lucky, unlucky; ~, v.a. (colloq.) ~ *X*, to floor X, to knock down or vanquish X.

tombereau (pl. -x) (tɔ̃bro), s.m. **1.** Cart; dust-cart, rubbish-cart, scavenger's cart; tumbril; **2.** cartload.

tombeur (tɔ̃bœr), s.m. (lit. and fig.) Invincible wrestler.

tombola (tɔ̃bɔla), s.f. [It. wd] Tombola, lottery.

tome (tɔm), s.m. [L *tomus*] Tome, volume; (fig.) part, section; *le premier* ~ *de sa vie*, his early life.

tomenteu-x, -se (tɔmɑ̃tø), adj. [f. L *tomentum*] (bot.) Tomentose, downy, hairy.

ton, ta, tes (tɔ̃, ta, tɛ), poss. adj. Thy, your.

ton (tɔ̃), s.m. [L *tonus*] Tone (of voice); pitch; colour; shade; inflexion; trend, tone, air; style, manner; fashion; *hausser le* ~, *baisser le* ~, to raise, to lower the voice; *parler d'un* ~ *de maître*, to speak dictatorially; *mettre au* ~ *de*, to attune to; *je le ferai bien chanter sur un autre* ~, I'll make him sing another tune; *le prendre sur un* ~ *bien haut*, to ride the high horse; *de bon* ~, in good taste; genteel; *mauvais* ~, bad taste; ill breeding; *donner le* ~, to pitch the key, to give the note; (fig.) to set the fashion.

tonal, -e, (aux) (tɔnal), adj. Tonal.

tonalité (tɔnalite), s.f. (mus.) Tonality.

tondage (tɔ̃daʒ), s.m. Shearing (of cloth).

tondaille (tɔ̃dɑj), s.f. Sheap-shearing; syn. TONTE.

tondaison (tɔ̃dɛzɔ̃), s.f. Sheep-shearing; clippings, clip; shearing-season; syn. TONTE.

tondeu-r, -se (tɔ̃dœr), s.m.f. Shearer; ~ *de drap*, cloth-shearer.

tondeuse (tɔ̃døz), s.f. Shears, shearing-machine, clippers; ~ *de gazon*, lawn-mower; ~ *de toilette*, hair-clippers.

tondre (tɔ̃dr), v.a. [L *tondere*] To shear, to clip, to mow, to cut, to crop, to pare; (fig.) to graze; to fleece; (fig.) *se laisser* ~ *la laine sur le dos*, to put up with anything; ~ *la brebis de trop près*, to cut it too fine; ~ *X*, to ruin X; *il tondrait sur un œuf*, he 's a regular skinflint.

tondu, -e (tɔ̃dy), p. adj. Shorn; *à brebis* ~*e Dieu mesure le vent*, God tempers the wind to the shorn lamb. ~, s.m. Shaveling; *le petit* ~, Napoleon; *il n'y avait que trois tondus et un pelé*, there was only the ragtag and bobtail; there was only the riff-raff.

tonicité (tɔnisite), s.f. Tonicity.

tonifiant, -e (tɔnifjɑ̃), p. adj. Bracing.

tonifier (tɔnifje), v.a. [f. *ton*] To brace, to fortify.

tonique (tɔnik), adj. Tonic, bracing. (med.) ~, s.m. Tonic; (mus.) ~, s.f. tonic, key-note.

tonitruant, -e (tɔnitryɑ̃), p. adj. Thundering, thunderous; *voix ~e*, stentorian voice.

tonitruer (tɔnitrye), v.n. (neol.) To shout, to speak in a stentorian voice.

tonka (tɔ̃ka), s.f. [Guiana negro wd] (bot.) Tonka-bean.

tonkinois, -e (tɔ̃kinwɑ), adj. s.m.f. Tonkinese.

tonnage (tɔnaʒ), s.m. (naut.) Tonnage; *droit de ~*, tonnage-dues; *~ brut*, gross tonnage; *~ net*, net tonnage, register.

tonnant, -e (tɔnɑ̃), p. adj. Thundering; thunderous, loud, sonorous; *Jupiter ~*, Jove the Thunderer.

tonne (tɔn), s.f. **1.** Tun, cask, barrel; **2.** ton (1,000 kg.); **3.** (naut.) *bouée-~*, nun buoy. ⚠ The English 'ton' = 2,240 lb. or (U.S.A., also short ton) 2,000 lb. avoirdupois; while the French or metric ton = 1,000 kg. In English, but not in French, the ton is also a measure of capacity (often varying): for timber 40 ft.; stone, 16 cu. ft.; salt, 42 bushels; lime, 40 bushels; wine (ton or tun), 252 wine gallons; internal cubic capacity, 100 cu. ft.; or carrying capacity (40 cu. ft.) of ship; also colloq. large number or amount: ex. tons of people = *des masses de gens.*

tonneau (pl. -x) (tɔno), s.m. [f. *tonne*] Tun, cask; (naut.) ton; tonneau (of carriage); *être d'un bon ~*, to be of the best quality; *mettre un ~ en perce*, to broach a cask; *enfoncer un ~*, to stave in a cask; *~ d'arrosage*, water-cart; *~ percé*, leaky cask; (fig.) spendthrift; *ce sont gens du même ~*, they are birds of a feather.

tonneler (tɔnle), v.a. (hunt.) To tunnel; to catch in a tunnel-net.

tonnelet (tɔnlɛ), s.m. Small cask, keg.

tonneleur (tɔnlœr), s.m. Tunneller.

tonnelier (tɔnəlje), s.m. Cooper.

tonnelle (tɔnɛl), s.f. **1.** Arbour, bower; semi-circular vault; **2.** (hunt.) tunnel-net.

tonnellerie (tɔnɛlri), s.f. **1.** Cooperage; **2.** cooper's shed.

tonner (tɔne), v.n. and impers. [L *tonare*] To thunder; (fig.) to inveigh; *il tonne*, it is thundering; *~ contre l'impiété*, to inveigh against impiety.

tonnerre (tɔnɛr), s.m. [L *tonitrus*] Thunder; thunderbolt; loud noise; *un éclat de ~, un coup de ~*, a clap of thunder; a thunderbolt; *le ~ est tombé sur le théâtre*, the theatre has been struck by lightning; (fig.) loud noise; *un ~ d'applaudissements*, thunders of applause; *une voix de ~*, a stentorian voice; *mille ~s !*, dash it all!

tonsure (tɔ̃syr), s.f. [L *tonsura*] Tonsure.

tonsuré (tɔ̃syre), p. adj. Tonsured. ~, s.m. Priest.

tonsurer (tɔ̃syre), v.a. To tonsure.

tonte (tɔ̃t), s.f. Sheep-shearing; syn. TONDAISON.

tontine (tɔ̃tin), s.f. [f. prop.n. *Tonti*] Tontine.

tontini-er, -ère (tɔ̃tinje), s.m.f. Annuitant of a tontine.

tontisse (tɔ̃tis), s.f. Shearings (of cloth); hangings coated with shearings; flocks; *bourre ~*, shoddy; *papier ~*, flock-paper.

tonture (tɔ̃tyr), s.f. Shearings, flocks; clippings; (naut.) sheer.

topaze (tɔpaz), s.f. [Gr. *topazos*] Topaz.

tope (tɔp), interj. [f. *toper*] Done !, agreed !, all right !, shake !

toper (tɔpe), v.n. [Span. *topar*] To agree, to shake hands on a bargain.

topette (tɔpɛt), s.f. A very narrow phial or glass tube.

tophacé, -e (tɔfase), adj. [f. L *tophus*] (med.) Tophaceous, gritty.

tophus (tɔfys), s.m. (med.) Tophus.

topinambour (tɔpinɑ̃bur), s.m. [f. geog. n. *Topinambou*, Brazil] (bot.) Jerusalem artichoke, topinambou; *Helianthus tuberosus.*

topique (tɔpik), adj. [Gr. *topikos*] **1.** Topical; local; **2.** (med.) topical. ~, s.m. Topic, subject; pl. (rhet.) topics.

topiquement (tɔpikmɑ̃), adv. Topically.

topo (tɔpo), s.m. [abbrev. of *dessin topographique*] **1.** Plan; **2.** (colloq.) short speech, short monograph.

topographe (tɔpɔgraf), s.m.f. Topographer.

topographie (tɔpɔgrafi), s.f. [Gr. *topos*+ *graphein*] Topography.

topographique (tɔpɔgrafik), adj. Topographical.

topographiquement (tɔpɔgrafikmɑ̃), adv. Topographically.

toponymie (tɔpɔnimi), s.f. [Gr. *topos*+ *onuma*] Toponomy, toponymy, study of place-names.

toquade, tocade (tɔkad), s.f. [f. *se toquer*] Whim, fancy, craze, fad, hobby; *avoir une ~ pour X*, to be mad about X.

toquante (tɔkɑ̃t), s.f. (pop.) Ticker, watch.

toque (tɔk), s.f. [orig. dub.] Toque, flat cap, small hat, bonnet; *~ de magistrat*, judge's cap.

toqué, -e (tɔke), p. adj. (colloq.) Deranged, crazy, a bit touched, cracked, tapped, loopy; dotty, infatuated, in love; *il est ~*, he is not quite all there; *il s'est ~ de X*, he is madly in love with X; he is sweet on X, he is dippy about X.

toquer (tɔke), v.a. To touch, to hit, to tap, to strike lightly; **se** ~, v.pr. to be or to become infatuated (*de*, with).

toquet (tɔkɛ), s.m. Little toque, cap.

torche (tɔrʃ), s.f. [f. L *torquere*] **1.** Torch, (fig.) torch; **2.** twist of straw; *~-pot*, s.m. nuthatch.

torcher (tɔrʃe), v.a. [f. *torche*] **1.** To wipe, to rub; **2.** (fig.) to scamp, to botch, to knock off, to give a lick and a promise to; **se** ~, v.pr. to wipe oneself; (colloq.) to fight, to scrap.

torchère (tɔrʃɛr), s.f. Cresset; candelabrum, floor-lamp, standard lamp.
torchette (tɔrʃɛt), s.f. Wisp (of straw).
torchis (tɔrʃi), s.m. Loam, clay, mud; *mur de* ~, mud wall.
torchon (tɔrʃɔ̃), s.m. **1.** Duster; dish-cloth, clout; **2.** wisp of straw; **3.** (colloq.) slattern; *le* ~ *brûle*, they are quarrelling there; *il ne faut pas compter les* ~*s avec les serviettes*, one must not mix up two things entirely different.
torchonner (tɔrʃɔne), v.a. To wipe, to clean, to dust.
torcol (tɔrkɔl), s.m. (ornith.) Wryneck.
tordage (tɔrdaʒ), s.m. Twist, twisting (of silk).
tordant, -e (tɔrdɑ̃), p. adj. (colloq.) Very funny, killing, screamingly funny; *ça c'est* ~, that beats cock-fighting; *une histoire* ~*e*, a scream.
tord-boyaux (tɔrbɔjo), s.m. (colloq.) Strong brandy, rotgut.
tordeu-r, -se (tɔrdœr), s.m.f. Twister, throwster.
tordeuse (tɔrdøs), s.f. Machine for twisting silk.
tord-nez (tɔrne), s.m. Horse-twitch.
tordoir (tɔrdwar), s.m. **1.** Wire-tightener; **2.** (surg.) garrot, tourniquet; **3.** packing-stick, stick for tightening a cord.
tordre (tɔrdr), v.a. [L *torquere*] To twist, to wring; to wring out; to wrench, to wrest; to distort, to pull out of shape; *se* ~, to be convulsed, to writhe; *rire à se* ~, to split one's sides (with laughter); *c'était à se* ~, it was killing, screamingly funny.
tore (tɔr), s.m. [L *torus*] (arch.) Tore, torus; (bot.) torus.
toréador (tɔreadɔr), s.m. [Span. wd] Toreador, bull-fighter.
toreutique (tɔrøtik), s.f. [f. Gr. *toreuein*] Toreutics.
torgniole, torgnole (tɔrɲɔl), s.f. (colloq.) Blow, cuff, slap; clout, biff, bat.
tormentille (tɔrmɑ̃til), s.f. (bot.) Tormentil.
tormineu-x, -se (tɔrminø), adj. [f. L *tormina*] (med.) Torminal.
tornade (tɔrnad), s.f. [Engl. *tornado*] Tornado.
toron (tɔrɔ̃), s.m. [It. *torone*] **1.** (naut.) Strand of rope; **2.** (arch.) torus.
torpédo (tɔrpedo), s.m. Open touring car, (U.S.A.) roadster, phaeton. ⚠ Not English 'torpedo', which = *torpille*, *poisson-torpille*, (Amer.) *pétard-signal de chemin de fer*, &c.
torpeur (tɔrpœr), s.f. [L *torpor*] Torpor.
torpillage (tɔrpijaʒ), s.m. Torpedoing.
torpille (tɔrpij), s.f. **1.** Torpedo, submarine projectile; **2.** (ichth.) torpedo, numb-fish.
torpiller (tɔrpije), v.a. To torpedo.
torpilleur (tɔrpijœr), s.m. Torpedo-boat.
torque (tɔrk), s.f. **1.** (mech.) Torque; **2.** twist (tobacco).
torquette (tɔrkɛt), s.f. **1.** Fish-basket; **2.** catch (of fish); bag (of game); **3.** twist (of tobacco).
torréfacteur (tɔrefaktœr), s.m. Coffee-roasting machine.
torréfaction (tɔrefaksjɔ̃), s.f. Torrefaction.
torréfier (tɔrefje), v.a. [L *torrere*+*facere*] To roast, to dry, to torrefy.
torrent (tɔrɑ̃), s.m. [L *torrens*] Torrent, stream, flood; flow; rush; *il pleut à* ~*s*, it is raining in torrents; it is raining cats and dogs; *un* ~ *de larmes*, a flood of tears; *le* ~ *des affaires*, the rush of business; *céder au* ~, *suivre le* ~, to drift with the stream.
torrentiel, -le (tɔrɑ̃sjɛl), adj. Torrential; drenching.
torrentiellement (tɔrɑ̃sjɛlmɑ̃), adv. Torrentially.
torrentueu-x, -se (tɔrɑ̃tɥø), adj. Torrent-like, rushing.
torride (tɔrid), adj. [L *torridus*] Torrid.
tors, -e (tɔr), adj. [L *torsus*] Twisted, twined, wreathed, contorted; (bot.) tortile; *de la soie* ~*e*, twisted silk; *la bouche* ~*e*, a wry mouth; *cou* ~, wry neck; (fig.) hypocrite. See TORTE.
tors (tɔr), s.m. **1.** Degree of torsion; **2.** twist; **3.** twisted thread.
torsade (tɔrsad), s.f. Twisted fringe or cord; bullion.
torse (tɔrs), s.m. [It. *torso*] Torso, trunk.
torsion (tɔrsjɔ̃), s.f. Torsion, twisting, twist, tortuousness.
tort (tɔr), s.m. [L *tortus*] Wrong, injustice, mischief, harm, injury; *avoir* ~, to be wrong; *avoir grand* ~, to be very wrong; *avoir tous les* ~*s*, to be absolutely wrong; *avoir le* ~ *de*, to make the mistake of; *à* ~, wrongfully; *à* ~ *et à travers*, at random; like a bull in a china-shop; right and left, thoughtlessly; *à* ~ *ou à raison*, rightly or wrongly; *dans son* ~, in the wrong; *donner* ~ *à X*, to decide against X; *mettre X dans son* ~, to put X in the wrong; *le* ~ *est de votre côté*, you are in the wrong; *reconnaître ses* ~*s*, (*a*) to acknowledge oneself to be wrong; (*b*) to admit having wronged somebody; *faire* ~ *à*, to wrong; *se faire* ~, to injure oneself; *avoir des* ~*s envers X*, to behave badly to X; *réparer ses* ~*s*, to redeem one's faults; to make amends.
torte (tɔrt), adj. [fem. of *tors*] Crooked, distorted.
tortelle (tɔrtɛl), s.f. (bot.) Hedge-mustard.
torticolis (tɔrtikɔli), s.m. [L *tortus*+*collum*] Stiff neck, a crick in the neck; torticollis.
tortil (tɔrtil), s.m. [f. LL *torticium*] (herald.) Torse; string of pearls circling a baron's coronet.

tortillage (tɔrtijaʒ), s.m. Twisting, contortion; (colloq.) shuffling, hedging, hanky-panky.
tortillard (tɔrtijar), s.m. **1.** (bot.) Small-leaved elm, *Ulmus campestris*; **2.** (colloq.) local train, slow train in remote part of the country; mountain train.
tortille (tɔrtij), s.f. Winding path, serpentine walk.
tortillement (tɔrtijmɑ̃), s.m. Twisting, wriggling; twist, convolution; (fig.) shuffling, hedging, evasion.
tortiller (tɔrtije), v.a. To twist; **~**, v.n. **1.** to waddle; **2.** (fig.) to shuffle, to shilly-shally; *il n'y a pas à* **~**, it 's no use beating about the bush; there's no denying it; no use shilly-shallying; **se ~**, v.pr. to wriggle.
tortillis (tɔrtiji), s.m. (arch.) Vermicular work.
tortillon (tɔrtijɔ̃), s.m. **1.** Head-pad; **2.** rough cap or bonnet; (draw.) paper-stump.
tortionnaire (tɔrsjɔnɛr), adj. Of torture. **~**, s.m. Torturer.
tortu, -e (tɔrty), adj. [f. L *tortuosus*] Crooked; tortuous; *jambes* **~***es*, bandy legs.
tortue (tɔrty), s.f. [LL *tortuca*] (zool.) Tortoise, turtle; *à pas de* **~**, at a snail's pace; (ant.) testudo.
tortueu-x, -se (tɔrtɥø), adj. [L *tortuosus*] Crooked, winding, tortuous; (fig.) underhand, deceitful, tortuous, circuitous.
tortuosité (tɔrtɥɔzite), s.f. Tortuousness, tortuosity, crookedness.
torturant, -e (tɔrtyrɑ̃), p. adj. Torturing, tormenting.
torture (tɔrtyr), s.f. [L *tortura*] Torture, torment, agony; *être à la* **~**, to be on thorns; *se mettre l'esprit à la* **~**, to rack one's brains.
torturer (tɔrtyre), v.a. To torture, to torment; to strain, to distort, to wrest; **~** *un texte*, to wrest, or to strain, a passage.
tortureu-r, -se (tɔrtyrœr), s.m.f. Torturer.
torve (tɔrv), adj. [L *torvus*] Glowering, malevolent; *un regard* **~**, a covert, malevolent glance, a nasty sly glance.
tory (tɔri), s.m. adj. [Engl. wd] Tory.
torysme (tɔrism), s.m. Toryism.
toryste, toriste (tɔrist), s.m. adj. Tory.
toscan, -e (tɔskɑ̃), adj. s.m.f. Tuscan.
tôt (to), adv. [OF *tost*] **1.** Soon, quickly, promptly, speedily; **2.** early; *au plus* **~**, as soon as possible; **~** *ou tard*, sooner or later; *le plus* **~** *possible*, as soon as possible; **~** *après*, soon after; *réveillez-moi très* **~**, wake me very early.
total, -e, (aux) (tɔtal), adj. [L *totalis*] Total, complete, entire, whole, utter, absolute. **~**, s.m. Total, whole, sum total; *au* **~**, on the whole, after all.
totalement (tɔtalmɑ̃), adv. Totally, entirely, absolutely, utterly, completely, wholly.
totalisat-eur, -rice (tɔtalizatœr), adj. Calculating, reckoning, totalizing. **~**, s.m. Totalizator.
totalisation (tɔtaliza'sjɔ̃), s.f. Totalization.
totaliser (tɔtalize), v.a. To reckon up, to sum up, to tot up, to cast up.
totalité (tɔtalite), s.f. Entirety, whole, totality; *en* **~**, entirely, completely, absolutely, altogether.
totem (tɔtɛm), s.m. [Amer. Indian wd] Totem.
totemisme (tɔtɛmism), s.m. Totemism.
toton (tɔtɔ̃), s.m. [L *totum*] Teetotum.
touage (twaʒ), s.m. Towage, towing, warping, kedging.
touaille (twaj), s.f. Roller-towel, jack-towel.
toucan (tukɑ̃), s.m. [Brazilian *tucana*] **1.** (ornith.) Toucan; **2.** (astr.) toucan.
touchant, -e (tuʃɑ̃), p. adj. Touching, moving, appealing, pathetic. **~**, prep. Concerning, respecting, touching, in the matter of, about, with regard to, with respect to, relating to.
touche (tuʃ), s.f. **1.** Touch; trial, assay; *pierre de* **~**, touchstone; **2.** (mus.) fret (of violin), key (of piano, typewriter, &c.), stop (of organ); **3.** (art) manner; **4.** (fenc.) hit; **5.** (print.) inking; **6.** drove (of oxen); **7.** (colloq.) look, air, appearance; *quelle* **~** *il a!*, what a guy! **8.** (football) throw-in.
touche-à-tout (tuʃatu), s.m. invar. Busy-body, meddlesome Mattie. **~**, adj. Meddlesome, meddling.
toucher (tuʃe), v.a.n. [LL *toccare*] To touch; to feel; to strike, to hit, to tap; to finger, to play (an instrument); to adjoin; to offend; to concern, to interest; to touch on, to mention; to express, to depict, to draw; to move, to affect; **~** *juste*, to hit the nail on the head; **~** *quelques mots de*, to say a few words about; *cela ne me touche pas*, (*a*) that is no affair of mine; (*b*) that does not make any difference to me; **~** *un mot de*, to drop a hint about; (naut.) **~** *une roche*, to strike a rock; **~**, to run aground, to touch, to strike; **~** *à un port*, to call at, or to touch at, a port; to put in at; to reach, to attain; to receive; **~** *ses appointements*, to receive one's salary; *je ne ferai que* **~** *barre à Paris*, I shan't stay in Paris, I shall be off again immediately; *il a été touché de* (or *par*) *votre repentir*, your repentance moved him; *ne touchez pas cette corde*, do not mention that; *cela vous touche de près*, you are deeply concerned in that; the thing touches you nearly; *touché, bien touché!*, well hit!; *vous êtes touché!*, you are wounded; (fig.) you are hit, or crushed, or sat on; *touchez du bois!*, touch wood!; *je*

ne le toucherais pas avec des pincettes, I would not touch him with a barge-pole; *il me toucha l'épaule,* he touched me on the shoulder; *son jardin touche le mien,* his garden is next to mine; *pièce touchée, pièce jouée,* if you touch one of your pieces, you must play it; *il a été touché au vif,* he was touched to the quick; ~ *son chapeau,* to touch one's hat (as salutation); *touchez-moi la main,* let's shake hands; *le cocher toucha ses chevaux,* the driver gave his horses a touch of the whip, or the driver whipped up his horses; ~ (*à*), v.n. to touch, to reach, to meddle (*à*, with), to tamper (with); to affect, to change, to alter, to concern, to allude to, to adjoin, to draw near; *il ne faut pas* ~ *aux fils électriques,* electric wires must not be tampered with; *ne touchez pas à la religion,* do not meddle with religious matters; *il a touché à cette affaire,* he had a hand in this business; *elle a un petit air de n'y pas* ~, she looks as if butter would not melt in her mouth; *nous touchons à la révolution,* we are heading for a revolution; *ne touchez pas à cela,* do not touch it; ~ *à sa fin,* (*a*) to draw to a close; (*b*) to be at the point of death; ~ *au but,* ~ *au port,* to be on the verge of success, salvation, &c.; ~ *dans la main à X,* to shake hands with X (on a bargain); *touchez là!,* your hand on it!; *on touche toujours sur le cheval qui tire,* all lay loads on the willing horse; *cela touche à la folie,* that borders on lunacy; *c'est un touche-à-tout,* he meddles with everything; he likes a finger in every pie; *je touche à la quarantaine,* I am verging on the forties, I am very near forty; **se** ~, v.pr. to touch, to be in or come into contact, to touch each other, to come next; to meet, to join; to be akin; *les extrêmes se touchent,* extremes meet; *ces maisons se touchent,* these houses adjoin.

toucher (tuʃe), s.m. Touch; feeling, sensation; contact; touching; (mus.) touch, manner, style, execution.

toucheur (tuʃœr), s.m. **1.** Cattle-drover; **2.** (print.) inking-roller.

toue (tu), s.f. **1.** Towing, warping; **2.** barge, ferry-boat.

touée (tue), s.f. (naut.) Towing, towage, warping; tow-line; scope (length of cable: 120 fathoms); *ancre de* ~, kedge.

touer (tue), v.a. [OHG *zogon*] (naut.) To tow, to warp.

toueu-r, -se (tuœr), adj. Towing. ~, s.m. Tow-boat, tug.

touffe (tuf), s.f. [etym. dub.] Tuft, bunch, wisp, clump, cluster; ~ *de fleurs,* bunch of flowers; ~ *d'herbes,* bunch of herbs; ~ *d'arbres,* clump of trees; ~ *de cheveux,* tuft of hair.

touffeur (tufœr), s.f. [f. *étouffer*] Stifling heat.

touffu, -e (tufy), adj. Bushy, thick, full; *cheveux* ~*s,* bushy hair; (fig.) too detailed, laborious; *roman* ~, an over-intricate novel.

toujours (tuʒur), adv. [*tous*+*jours*] Always, ever, still, constantly, perpetually, frequently, usually; *à* ~, or *pour* ~, for ever; evermore; *comme* ~, as usual; *il vit* ~, he is still alive, or living; *allez* ~, go on, never mind!; ~ *est-il que,* still the fact remains that; however; ~ *plus,* more and more; *c'est* ~ *ça!,* that's something; that's so much to the good!; *êtes-vous* ~ *content de lui?,* are you still pleased with him?; *prenez* ~ *cela en attendant,* take that to be going on with.

touline (tulin), s.f. [Engl. *tow-line*] (naut.) Tow-line.

touloupe (tulup), s.f. [Russ. wd] Lambskin greatcoat.

toundra (tundra), s.f. [Lapp wd] Tundra.

toupet (tupɛ), s.m. [OF *toup*] Tuft, lock of hair; forelock, toupet, toupee; (fig.) impertinence, cheek, boldness; *avoir du* ~, to be saucy, to give cheek, to be as bold as brass, to be cheeky; *il en a un* ~*!,* well, he's got a cheek!, he's got a nerve!

toupie (tupi), s.f. Top, peg-top, spinning-top; ~ *d'Allemagne,* humming-top; (slang) *une vieille* ~, an old frump, a ridiculous old woman.

toupiller (tupije), v.n. To spin, to gyrate, to whirl round; (fig.) to hesitate, to change one's mind often, to run in small circles.

tour (tur), s.f. [L *turris*] **1.** Tower; ~ *à feu,* lighthouse; **2.** turret; **3.** (chess) castle, rook.

tour (tur), s.m. [L *tornus*] **1.** Turn, turning; tour, circuit; trip; circumference; feat, trick, stunt; turning-lathe, potter's lathe; revolution, rotation; *fermer à double* ~, to double-lock; ~ *de reins,* strained back; *mon sang n'a fait qu'un* ~ my heart stood still; *à chacun son* ~, every dog has his day; ~ *à* ~, *à* ~ *de rôle,* in turns; *à son* ~, in turn; *à qui le* ~*?,* whose turn is it?; *avoir un* ~ *de faveur,* to go out of one's turn; ~ *de scrutin,* ballot; ~ *de piste,* lap, stage; (fig.) *faire ses quinze* ~*s,* to dawdle; *un* ~ *de promenade,* a walk; *faire un* ~ *de jardin,* to take a turn in the garden; *faire le grand* ~, to go a long way round; *avoir deux mètres de* ~, to be two metres round; *faire le* ~ *du cadran,* to sleep the clock round; *à* ~ *de bras,* with all one's might; *en un* ~ *de main,* in the twinkling of an eye, in a jiffy; *jouer un mauvais* ~ *à X,* to play X a dirty trick; *jouer un bon* ~ *à X,* to play a trick on X; ~ *d'adresse,* feat of skill, clever trick, brainy dodge; ~ *de bâton,* trick, illicit gain; ~ *de force,* wonderful feat; ~*s de gobelets,* sleight of hand; ~ *de cou,* neck-band; ~ *de gorge,* tucker; ~ *de lit,* valance;

fait au ~, engine-turned; (fig.) shapely, beautiful.
touraille (turɑj), s.f. Malt-kiln.
touraillon (turɑjɔ̃), s.m. Malt-dust.
tourange-au, -lle (pl. -x) (turɑ̃ʒo), adj. Of Touraine. ~, s.m.f. Native of Touraine.
touranien, -ne (turanjɛ̃), adj. s.m.f. Turanian.
tourbe[1] (turb), s.f. [Germ. *Torf*] Peat, turf.
tourbe[2] (turb), s.f. [L *turba*] Rabble, mob, vulgar herd.
tourber (turbe), v.n. To cut peat or turf.
tourbeu-x, -se (turbø), adj. Peaty, turfy.
tourbier (turbje), s.m. Turf-cutter; owner of turf-pits.
tourbière (turbjɛr), s.f. Peat-bog, turf-pit, peat-moss.
tourbillon (turbijɔ̃), s.m. [f. L *turbo*] **1.** Whirlwind, eddy; vortex; whirlpool; *platine à* ~, turn-table; **2.** cloud; **3.** tourbillion (firework).
tourbillonnant, -e (turbijɔnɑ̃), p. adj. Whirling, eddying.
tourbillonnement (turbijɔnmɑ̃), s.m. Whirling, eddying.
tourbillonner (turbijɔne), v.n. To whirl round, to eddy.
tourd (tur), s.m. [L *turdus*] **1.** (ornith.) Thrush; **2.** (ichth.) Mediterranean fish.
tourdille (turdij), adj. [Span. *tordillo*] *Gris* ~, dirty grey.
tourelle (turɛl), s.f. Turret.
touret (turɛ), s.m. (techn.) **1.** Small wheel; **2.** spinning-wheel; **3.** rope-maker's winch; **4.** small pulley; **5.** wheel for stone-cutting; **6.** drilling-lathe; **7.** thole-pin; **8.** small mask; **9.** (fish.) reel.
tourie (turi), s.f. Carboy, demijohn, wicker-covered jar.
touri-er, -ère (turie), adj. s.m.f. Monk or nun in attendance at the turning-box.
tourillon (turijɔ̃), s.m. **1.** Axle, axis; pivot; **2.** (artill.) trunnion; **3.** crank-pin, gudgeon.
tourisme (turism), s.m. Touring; travelling for pleasure; motoring, cycling.
touriste (turist), s.m.f. Tourist.
touristique (turistik), adj. Tourist.
tourlourou (turluru), s.m. (colloq.) Tommy, private of infantry.
tourmaline (turmalin), s.f. Tourmaline.
tourment (turmɑ̃), s.m. [L *tormentum*] Torment, torture, pain, anguish, agony; (fig.) anxiety, care, trouble, worry.
tourmentant, -e (turmɑ̃tɑ̃), p. adj. Tormenting, torturing, troublesome.
tourmente (turmɑ̃t), s.f. Tempest, storm; (fig.) disturbance, turmoil.
tourmenté, -e (turmɑ̃te), p. adj. **1.** Stormy, tempestuous, tempest-tossed; **2.** agitated, anxious, worried, disturbed, harassed, plagued, tormented; **3.** laboured, overdone, exaggerated.
tourmenter (turmɑ̃te), v.a. [f. *tourment*] To torture, to torment; to pain, to distress, to harass, to pester, to plague, to molest, to annoy, to dun, to bully; to toss, to shake, to agitate; to jolt; to warp (wood); to wrest (a text); **se** ~, v.pr. to worry, to fret, to torment oneself; to toss about, to be agitated, to be restless, to fidget; to warp (of wood); to strain (of a ship).
tourmenteu-r, -se (turmɑ̃tœr), adj. Tormenting, torturing, worrying, harassing, troubling. ~, s.m. Torturer.
tourmentin (turmɑ̃tɛ̃), s.m. (naut.) Fore-stay sail, storm-jib, spitfire-jib.
tournage (turnɑʒ), s.m. **1.** Turning; **2.** (naut.) belaying; *taquet de* ~, belaying-cleat.
tournailler (turnɑje), v.n. To turn round and round; to hover.
tournant, -e (turnɑ̃), p. adj. Turning, revolving; *bibliothèque* ~*e*, revolving bookcase; (mil.) *mouvement* ~, turning movement; *pont* ~, swing-bridge; *les tables* ~*es*, table-turning. ~, s.m. Turn, turning; bend, corner (of street); turn, turning-point; eddy, whirlpool.
tourné, -e (turne), p. adj. **1.** Turned; made, shaped, formed, directed; disposed, inclined; *bien* ~, shapely, handsome, neatly turned; *mal* ~, awkward; uncouth; badly turned; ill made; mis-shapen; cross-grained; **2.** turned, sour.
tourne-à-gauche (turnagoʃ), s.m. invar. (techn.) Wrench.
tournebride (turnəbrid), s.m. Roadside inn.
tournebroche (turnəbrɔʃ), s.m. Turnspit, roasting-jack.
tournedos (turnədɔ), s.m. **1.** Fillet steak; **2.** part of market assigned to vendors of inferior goods.
tournée (turne), s.f. Tour, walk, round, visit, journey, excursion, turn; circuit, beat; *payer une* ~, to stand drinks all round; (colloq.) *c'est ma* ~, it's my shout!; *flanquer une* ~ *à X*, to give X a sound thrashing.
tourne-feuille (turnfœj), s.f. Leaf-turner, page-turner (for music).
tournemain (turnəmɛ̃), s.m. Trice, twinkling, jiffy, instant; *en un* ~ (*en un tour de main*), in an instant, in a jiffy; before you can say Jack Robinson.
tournement (turnəmɑ̃), s.m. Turning, whirling; ~ *de tête*, giddiness.
tourne-oreille (turnorɛj), s.m. invar. (agric.) Plough with turning mould-board.
tourne-pierre (turnpjɛr), s.m. invar. (ornith.) Turnstone.
tourner (turne), v.a. [L *tornare*] To turn, to revolve, to twist, to twirl, to wind; to bend; to turn over, to turn round; to go round, to outflank; to direct,

to apply, to manage; to interpret, to construe; to change, to convert, to infatuate; ~ *casaque*, to turn one's coat, to change sides, to desert to the enemy; ~ *ses pas d'un certain côté*, to bend one's steps in a certain direction; ~ *tout en mal*, to put a bad construction on everything; ~ *une carte*, to turn up a card; ~ *une difficulté*, to get over a difficulty, hindrance, &c.; (fig.) ~ *le dos à X*, to cut X, to give X the cold shoulder; ~ *ses talons*, to wear one's heels down on one side; (fig.) ~ *les talons*, to be off, to show a clean pair of heels; to leave abruptly; ~ *le bois, l'ivoire*, &c., to turn wood, ivory, &c.; ~ *un pied de table*, to turn or shape a table-leg; ~ *des olives*, to turn or to stone olives; ~ *le coin*, to turn the corner (of a street); ~ *la page*, or *le feuillet*, to turn the page; *le succès lui a tourné la tête*, success has turned his head; (pop.) *cela lui a tourné les sangs*, or *les sens*, it upset him terribly; *il tourne carreau*, diamonds are trumps; (mil.) ~ *l'armée ennemie*, to outflank the enemy; ~ *une position*, to turn a position; ~ *la loi*, to evade the law, to get round the law; to defeat the intention of the law, especially while complying with its letter; *on le tourne à toutes sauces*, they make a Jack-of-all-trades of him; ~, v.n. to turn, to revolve, to twist round, to move, to veer, to change, to alter; to become, to turn out; to turn sour; to take films (for cinema); to act in films; ~ *autour du pot*, to beat about the bush; *ce jeune homme tournera mal*, this young man is going to the dogs; ~ *de l'œil*, (*a*) to faint; (*b*) to turn up one's toes; to die, to go west, to kick the bucket; *le lait tournera*, the milk will turn (sour); *la tête lui tourne*, she feels giddy; *nous verrons comment les choses tourneront*, we shall see how things turn out; ~ *court*, (*a*) to turn sharply; (*b*) to stop abruptly, to end suddenly, to cut short; *la chance a tourné*, the tables are turned; the luck has changed; *elle tourne à la bigoterie*, she will turn out a bigot; she is developing a tendency towards bigotry; **se** ~, v.pr. to turn round, about; *se ~ en*, to be changed into.

tournerie (turnri), s.f. Turner's shop.

tournesol (turnəsɔl), s.m. [It. *tornasole*] (bot.) Sunflower, *Helianthus*; purple dye; (chem.) litmus.

tournette (turnɛt), s.f. **1.** Squirrel's cage; **2.** cotton-winder, windle, reel, skein-holder.

tourneur (turnœr), s.m. Turner. ~, adj. *Ouvrier* ~, turner; *derviche* ~, dancing dervish.

tourne-vent (turnəvɑ̃), s.m. Chimney-cowl, cowl.

tournevis (turnəvis), s.m. Screw-driver.

tourniole (turnjɔl), s.f. (pathol.) Whitlow.

tourniquet (turnikɛ), s.m. **1.** Turnstile, turnpike; **2.** (med.) tourniquet; **3.** sash-pulley, pulley-sheave; swivel; (fish.) winch, reel; (naut.) roller; **3.** whirligig (beetle); **4.** merry-go-round, roundabout.

tournis (turni), s.m. (vet.) Staggers (in horses and cattle); sturdy (in sheep); turnside (in dogs).

tournisse (turnis), s.f. Stake.

tournoi (turnwa), s.m. [f. *tournoyer*] (hist. and sport.) Tournament; (hist.) tourney.

tournoiement (turnwamɑ̃), s.m. **1.** Turning, whirling round, wheeling round; **2.** dizziness, giddiness, vertigo; **3.** see TOURNIS.

tournois (turnwɑ), adj. [L *turonensis*] (obs.) Made at Tours; *livre* ~, livre (coin) of Tours currency, struck in the 13th century.

tournoyant, -e (turnwajɑ̃), p. adj. Eddying, turning about, whirling round.

tournoyer (turnwaje), v.n. [f. *tourner*] To whirl round, to wheel about; to eddy.

tournure (turnyr), s.f. **1.** Shape, figure; *elle a une jolie tournure*, she has a good figure, she is well made; **2.** turn; cast; appearance; tendency, direction, course; **3.** (dressm.) bustle; tournure; **4.** metal filings.

tourte (turt), s.f. [L *torta*] **1.** Pie, tart (⇧ see TARTE) fruit pie; **2.** round loaf of bread; **3.** (fig.) fool, simpleton; *quelle ~!*, what a fool!, what a duffer!

tourteau (pl. -x) (turto), s.m. **1.** Oilcake; cake; ~ *de lin*, linseed cake; ~ *de colza*, rape cake; **2.** great crab, edible crab.

tourtereau (pl. -x) (turtəro), s.m. [f. L *turtur*] (ornith.) Young turtle-dove; (fig.) young lover.

tourterelle (turtərɛl), s.f. (ornith.) Turtle-dove.

tourtière (turtjɛr), s.f. Pie-dish, tart-tin.

tous (tu, tus), pl. of **tout**. See TOUT.

touselle (tuzɛl), s.f. [Provenç. *tozela*] (bot.) Beardless wheat.

Toussaint (tusɛ̃), s.f. All Saints' Day.

tousser (tuse), v.n. [L *tussire*] To cough.

tousserie (tusri), s.f. Coughing; fit of coughing.

tousseu-r, -se (tusœr), s.m.f. One who coughs, cougher.

toussoter (tusɔte), v.n. To cough a little and repeatedly, to hem.

tout, -e, tous, toutes (tu), adj. [L *totus*] All, the whole, the whole of, every, any; full, complete, entire; only, sole; ~ *le jour*, all day, the whole day long; *tous les jours*, every day; *tous les deux jours*, every other day; *~es les fois que*, whenever; *tous les deux*, both; *tous deux*, both (together); ~ *le monde*, everybody; ~ *le monde et son père*, all the world and his wife; *~e autre chose*, anything else, anything but that; ~ *son* *possible,* one's very utmost; *par tous pays,* in all countries; *à ~e force,* at any cost; *à ~ hasard,* at all hazards; *à ~ propos,* at every turn; *~ autre que lui,* any one but him; *courir à ~es jambes,* to run at full speed; *donner tous pouvoirs à X,* to give X full powers; *somme ~e,* on the whole; *nous tous,* all of us; *vous tous,* all of you; *eux tous,* all of them. ~, adv. Wholly, entirely, quite, thoroughly, fully, absolutely, altogether, all; although, however, for all, for all that; *le ~ premier,* the foremost, the very first, the first of all; *c'est ~ un,* it's all the same; *c'est ~ comme vous voudrez,* just as you like; *~ à coup,* suddenly; *~ à fait,* absolutely, entirely; *~ à l'heure,* just now; *~ au moins,* at least; *~ au plus,* at most; *~ à vous,* yours sincerely; *~ allumé,* ready lighted; *~ autant,* quite as much, as many; *~ autre chose,* something quite different; *~ au long,* at full length; *~ beau, ~ doux,* gently !, softly !, not so fast !, wait a minute !; *~ chaud,* piping hot; *~ contre,* hard by; close; *~ court,* and nothing more; stopped short; *~ de bon,* in good earnest; *~ de go,* straight off, point-blank; *~ de même,* all the same; *~ de suite,* at once, immediately; *~ doucement, ~ doux,* gently; *~ du long,* from beginning to end; *~ d'un coup,* all at once, suddenly; *tout en regardant,* whilst watching; *~ ensemble,* together, all together, at the same time; *~ éveillé,* wide awake; *~ fait,* ready made; (fig.) cut and dried; *~ grand,* wide; *~ grand ouvert,* wide open; *~ haut,* aloud, boldly, openly; *~ le long de,* all along; *~ nu,* stark naked; *~ près,* quite near, close at hand; *~ prêt,* quite ready; *~es bonnes qu'elles sont,* however good they are, for all their goodness, although they are very good, good as they are; *~ nouveau, ~ beau,* new brooms sweep clean. ~, pron. indef. Everything, all, everybody; *après ~,* after all; *à ~ prendre,* all things considered, on the whole; *comme ~,* like anything, awfully; *en ~,* in all; *en ~ et pour ~,* wholly, entirely; *du ~,* at all; *pas* (or *point*) *du ~,* not at all, not in the least; *rien du ~,* nothing at all; *plus du ~,* never again, no more, now no longer; *se faire à ~,* to adapt oneself to any circumstances; *par-dessus ~,* above all; *~ bien considéré,* all things considered; *ça n'est pas ~ ça, mais,* well, that's another story; now; that's not the point at all, but; *propre à ~,* fit for anything, equal to anything; *voilà ~,* that's all; *il y a ~ à parier que,* the odds are that. ~, s.m. The whole, all, everything, the main thing, the chief point; *le ~ pour le ~,* neck or nothing; *le ~ est de,* the only thing is to; *il en fait son ~, c'est son ~,* it is everything to him; it is his all in all; *du ~ au ~,* completely; *risquer le ~ pour le ~,* to risk all to win all; to stake everything, to go the whole hog.

toute-bonne (tutbɔn), s.f. **1.** (bot.) Clary; **2.** (hort.) toute-bonne.

toutefois (tutfwɑ), adv. Yet, nevertheless, still, however; *si ~ la chose est possible,* if the thing is at all possible.

toute-puissance (tutpɥisɑ̃s), s.f. Omnipotence, almighty power, almightiness.

toutou (tutu), s.m. [child. wd] Bow-wow.

tout-puissant (tupɥisɑ̃), adj. Almighty, all-powerful, omnipotent; autocratic.

tout-venant (tuvənɑ̃), s.m. invar. Coals (unsorted) mixed with coal-dust.

toux (tu), s.f. Cough; *une quinte de ~,* a violent fit of coughing, a paroxysm of coughing; *une ~ qui sent le sapin,* a churchyard cough.

toxicité (tɔksisite), s.f. Poisonousness, toxicity.

toxicologie (tɔksikɔlɔʒi), s.f. Toxicology.

toxicologique (tɔksikɔlɔʒik), adj. Toxicological.

toxicologue (tɔksikɔlɔg), s.m.f. Toxicologist.

toxicomanie (tɔksikɔmani), s.f. Toxicomania.

toxine (tɔksin), s.f. Toxin.

toxique (tɔksik), adj. s.m. [f. Gr. *toxikos*] Toxic.

traban (trabɑ̃), s.m. [Germ. *Trabant*] Halberdier or pikeman in Swiss or Scandinavian troops.

trabée (trabe), s.f. [L *trabea*] (ant.) Trabea, ceremonial toga.

trac[1] (trak), s.m. [orig. unkn.] Spoor, track (of animal); *suivre un loup au trac,* to follow the track of a wolf.

trac[2] (trak), s.m. [orig. unkn.] Funk, fear; *avoir le ~,* to be in a funk, to have cold feet; (of actors) to have stage-fright; *tout-à-~,* suddenly.

traçage (trasaʒ), s.m. Tracing, drawing.

traçant, -e (trasɑ̃), p. adj. (bot.) (of plants) Running.

tracas (trakɑ), s.m. Bustle, stir, disturbance, turmoil; hurry, flurry; worry, annoyance, bother.

tracasser (trakase), v.a.n. [f. *traquer*] To worry, to pester, to plague, to bother, to tease, to torment; to fuss, to fidget, to bustle about, to potter about; to meddle, to interfere; **se ~,** v.pr. **1.** to worry oneself, to fidget; **2.** to tease one another.

tracasserie (trakasri), s.f. Bustle, bother, worry; bickering, cavil; mischief-making; annoyance, vexation, pestering, plaguing, teasing, chicane.

tracassi-er, -ère (trakasje), adj. Teasing, bothering, fidgety, cantankerous, interfering. ~, s.m.f. Meddler, busybody, mischief-maker.

tracassin (trakasɛ̃), s.m. (colloq.) The fidgets.

trace (tras), s.f. **1.** Trace, track, trail, footprint, (pl.) spoor; *suivre les ~s de X*, (*a*) to follow in the steps of X; (*b*) to follow X's example; **2.** trace, mark, evidence, brand; (chem.) extremely small quantity; **3.** outline, sketch, draught, plan; **4.** track, way, path.
tracé (trase), s.m. Outline, sketch, draught, plan, lay-out; line, direction; *faire le ~ de*, (*a*) to sketch; (*b*) to lay out.
tracelet (traslɛ), s.m. See syn. TRACERET.
tracement (trasmɑ̃), s.m. Sketching, tracing, drawing, marking, laying out.
tracer (trase), v.a. [LL *tractiare*] **1.** To trace, to draw, to mark out, to delineate, to portray; **2.** to lay out; (fig.) to lay down (the law); **~**, v.n. (of plants, roots) to throw out runners; **se ~**, v.pr. to be traced, drawn.
traceret (trasrɛ), s.m. Tracer, tracing-point. Syn. TRACELET.
traceu-r, -se (trasœr), s.m.f. Tracer.
trachéal, -e, (aux) (trakeal), adj. (anat.) Tracheal.
trachée (traʃe), s.f. [Gr. *trakheia*] **1.** (anat.) Trachea, windpipe; **2.** (bot.) trachea, spiral vessel, wood-vessel; **3.** (ent.) trachea, air-tube (of insects).
trachée-artère (traʃeartɛr), s.f. Trachea, windpipe.
trachéen, -ne (trakeɛ̃), adj. Trachean.
trachéite (trakeit), s.f. (pathol.) Tracheitis, trachitis.
trachéocèle (trakeɔsɛl), s.m. (pathol.) Tracheocele.
trachéotomie (trakeɔtɔmi), s.f. Tracheotomy.
trachome (trakom), s.m. Trachoma.
trachyte (trakit), s.m. (min.) Trachyte.
trachytique (trakitik), adj. Trachytic.
traçoir (traswar), s.m. Tracer, tracing-point.
tract (trakt), s.m. [Engl. wd] Tract, pamphlet.
tractation (trakta'sjɔ̃), s.f. [L *tractatio*] Negotiation.
tracteur (traktœr), s.m. [f. L *tractus*] Tractor.
traction (traksjɔ̃), s.f. [LL *tractio*] Traction; draught; tension; *force de ~*, tensile force.
tractionneur (traksjɔnœr), s.m. adj. That draws; (beast) of draught, draught-animal; *cheval ~*, draught-horse.
tractoire (traktwar), **1.** adj. Tractive, tractory; **2.** s.f. (geom.) tractory, tractrix.
traditeur (traditœr), s.m. adj. [L *traditor*] (eccles. hist.) Traditor.
tradition (tradisjɔ̃), s.f. [L *traditio*] Tradition; (law) delivery, tradition; *de ~*, traditional.
traditionalisme (tradisjɔnalism), s.m. Traditionalism.
traditionaliste (tradisjɔnalist), adj. s.m.f. Traditionalist.
traditionnaire (tradisjɔnɛr), adj. s.m.f. Traditionary.
traditionnel, -le (tradisjɔnɛl), adj. Traditional.
traditionnellement (tradisjɔnɛlmɑ̃), adv. Traditionally.
traduct-eur, -rice (tradyktœr), s.m.f. Translator.
traduction (tradyksjɔ̃), s.f. [L *traductio*] Translation.
traduire (tradɥir), v.a. [L *traducere*] **1.** To translate, to construe; to explain, to interpret; to turn (*en*, into); to show, to voice, to express; **2.** (law) to deliver; **3.** (law) to indict, to arraign; **~** *en justice*, to indict; **se ~**, v.pr. to be translated; to be expressed, to be shown. ⚠ Not 'to traduce', which = *calomnier, desservir, trahir.*
traduisible (tradɥizibl), adj. Translatable.
trafic (trafik), s.m. [It. *traffico*] Traffic, trade, trading, commerce; (often pej.) barter; (railw.) goods traffic. ⚠ In French *trafic* is not usually said of numbers of persons and cars coming and going in a street, road, &c.: 'there is little traffic on this road' = *cette route n'est pas très passante*, or *n'est pas très fréquentée*; *la circulation n'est pas intense sur cette route.*
trafiquant (trafikɑ̃), s.m. Trader, merchant; trafficker; (pej.) trafficker, procurer.
trafiquer (trafike), v.n. **1.** To traffic; to trade, to deal; **~** *en gros*, to deal wholesale; **~** *en détail*, to deal retail; **2.** (pej.) to trade (*de*) on, to make a traffic (of); **~** *de la protection de X*, to trade on X's protection.
trafiqueu-r, -se (trafikœr), s.m.f. (pej.) Trafficker.
tragédie (traʒedi), s.f. [L *tragoedia*] Tragedy.
tragédien, -ne (traʒedjɛ̃), s.m.f. Tragedian.
tragi-comédie (traʒikɔmedi), s.f. Tragicomedy.
tragi-comique (traʒikɔmik), adj. Tragicomic, tragi-comical.
tragique (traʒik), adj. [Gr. *tragikos*] Tragic, tragical. **~**, s.m. Tragic style; tragicalness; tragic writer or actor; *prendre les choses au ~*, to look on the dark side, to take things too seriously.
tragiquement (traʒikmɑ̃), adv. Tragically.
tragopan (tragɔpɑ̃), s.m. [Gr. wd] (ornith.) Tragopan, horned pheasant.
tragus (tragys), s.m. [Gr. *tragos*] (anat.) Tragus.
trahir (trair), v.a. [L *tradere*] To betray, to be false to; to deceive, to mislead; to give away, to disclose; to abandon, to fail; to misrepresent, to traduce; **se ~**, v.pr. to betray oneself; to reveal involuntarily one's presence, plans, real nature, &c.; to betray one another.

trahison (traizɔ̃), s.f. Treason, treachery, betrayal, foul play, treacherousness; *haute* ~, high treason; *faire une* ~ *à X*, to act treacherously to X, to double-cross X.

traille (trɑj), s.f. [L *tragula*] (naut.) Ferry-boat, (fish.) trawl-net; *pêche à la* ~, trawling; *pêcher à la* ~, to trawl; *pêcheur à la* ~, *chalutier de* ~, trawler.

train (trɛ̃), s.m. [f. *traîner*] **1.** Pace, rate, speed; course, way; movement, motion, process, progress; mood, spirits, humour, inclination; train (of events), series, succession; *à* (or *de*) *ce* ~, at this (or that) rate; *à fond de* ~, hell for leather; like blazes; at full speed; *aller son* ~, to go on, to go one's way, to have its course, to keep on just the same; *bon* ~, at a good speed; with a high hand; *grand* ~, very fast; *dans le* ~, in the swim; *en* ~, in the mood (*de*, to); on the way (to), on the high road (to); in the act (of); in good spirits; slightly oiled; *être en* ~ *de*, to be in the act of, to be busy with; *mener en bon* ~, to lead a fine dance; *mener un grand* ~, to live in style, to cut a dash; *mener un* ~ *d'enfer*, to live ruinously; *mettre en bon* ~, to help to the success of; *mettre en* ~, to start off; (print.) to make ready; *pas en* ~, *mal en* ~, out of sorts; ~ *de maison*, establishment; ~-~, jog-trot, routine; **2.** noise, bustle; *faire du* ~, to kick up a shindy; **3.** railway train; ~ *d'aller*, ~ *descendant*, down train; ~ *de retour*, ~ *montant* (*vers la capitale*), up train; ~ *de marée*, fish-train; ~ *de plaisir*, excursion train; ~ *de marchandises*, goods train; ~ *de voyageurs*, passenger train; ~ *de luxe*, Pullman car express; ~ *direct*, through train; ~*-poste*, mail train; ~*-omnibus*, stopping train; ~ *rapide*, express; (mil.) ~ *des équipages*, Army Service Corps; **4.** (print.) undercarriage, frame; quarters (of horse); ~ *de devant*, forecarriage, fore-quarters; ~ *de derrière* also *arrière-*~, hind carriage, hind quarters; (print.) *mise en* ~, making ready; **5.** train, retinue, suite; herd, drove; *le diable et son* ~, the whole paraphernalia; the hell of a fuss; **6.** raft; **7.** (horol.) train.

traînage (trɛnaʒ), s.m. Dragging; sledging, sleighing.

traînant, -e (trɛnɑ̃), p. adj. Trailing, dragging; drawling; slow, languid, flagging; prolix, dull; *une robe* ~*e*, a trailing gown; *une voix* ~*e*, a drawling voice.

traînard (trɛnar), s.m. Laggard, straggler, loiterer.

traînasse (trɛnas), s.f. **1.** Drag-net; **2.** (bot.) knot-grass.

traînasser (trɛnase), **1. v.a.** (colloq.) To spin out, to drag out, to protract, to delay; **2.** ~, v.n. to linger, to be dilatory, to lag behind, to loiter.

traîne (trɛn), s.f. **1.** Train (of a dress); **2.** drag-net, drift-net; **3.** (naut.) rope's end; **4.** rope-maker's sledge; **5.** scrub, brush-wood; *en* ~, unfledged (of partridges); *à la* ~, in tow.

traîneau (pl. **-x**) (trɛno), s.m. Sledge, sleigh; sled; dray, drag; (Canada) train; (agric.) drag; (hunt.) drag-net.

traînée (trɛne), s.f. **1.** Trail, train (of gun-powder); **2.** track, trail; **3.** (bot.) runner; **4.** street-walker.

traîne-malheur, traîne-misère (trɛnmalœr, trɛnmizɛr), s.m.f. invar. Poor wretch.

traîner (trɛne), v.a. **1.** To drag, to draw, to pull along; to lead to, to entail; (fig.) ~ *X dans la boue*, to defame X; ~ *X partout*, to trot X round everywhere; to be dogged by X; **2.** to drag out, to lead; ~ *une misérable existence*, to lead a wretched life; **3.** to drawl; **4.** to delay, to put off, to protract, to spin out; ~, v.n. **1.** to drag, to trail; to hang down; **2.** to lie about untidily, to kick about, to knock about; *ne laissez rien* ~, do not leave anything about; **3.** to be found; *cela traîne dans tous les livres*, that is in all the books; **4.** to droop, to flag, to languish, to linger; to become dull; to progress very slowly; *je ne vis pas, je traîne*, I do not live, I linger; *cette affaire traîne*, this affair doesn't make much progress; (theatr.) *cet acte traîne*, this act drags; **5.** to lag, to loiter, to drop behind, to linger; **6.** (billiards) to follow one's ball; **se** ~, v.pr. **1.** to creep along, to crawl, to drag oneself along; to trudge, to wade; **2.** (of speeches, plays, &c.) to be long-drawn-out, to be lengthy; to be heavy, dull.

traîneu-r, -se (trɛnœr), s.m.f. **1.** Straggler, laggard; **2.** poacher; **3.** sledge-driver; drayman; ~ *d'épée*, ~ *de sabre*, swashbuckler.

trainglot, tringlot (trɛ̃glɔ), s.m. Soldier of the Army Service Corps.

traînoir (trɛnwar), s.m. (agric.) Drag.

traintrain (trɛ̃trɛ̃), s.m. Routine, regular habits; *toujours le même petit* ~, always the same old jog-trot.

traire (trɛr), v.a. [L *trahere*] To milk; (fig., vulg.) to pump.

trait (trɛ), s.m. [f. L *trahere*] **1.** Dart, arrow, bolt; thunderbolt; flash, gleam, beam, glint, ray, burst; draught, gulp; *comme un* ~, like a flash, like a shot, like an arrow from the bow; *lancer un* ~ *à X*, to have a fling at X; *d'un* ~, *d'un seul* ~, *tout d'un* ~, at a draught; straight off; without stopping; (*boire*) *à longs* ~*s*, (to drink) deep; ~ *d'éclat*, remarkable action ~ *d'esprit*, witticism, clever hit; ~ *de scie*, kerf, saw-cut; **2.** stroke, move, act, deed, touch; turn (of the scale); *c'était un mauvais* ~, it was a wicked deed; (colloq.) *faire des* ~*s à sa femme*, *à* *son mari*, to be unfaithful to one's wife, to one's husband; **3.** line; outline; link; trace, leash; ~ *d'union*, hyphen; (fig.) connecting-link; *au* ~, in outline; *décrire à grands* ~*s*, to sketch; **4.** *cheval de* ~, draught-horse; **5.** *ayant* ~ *à*, relating to; **6.** trait, characteristic, feature, lineament; ~ *pour* ~, to a T; *avoir des* ~*s très réguliers*, to have very regular features.

trait, -e (trɛ), adj. Wire-drawn (of metals).

traitable (trɛtabl), adj. Tractable, manageable, docile; ductile, malleable, amenable.

traitant (trɛtɑ̃), s.m. adj. **1.** Revenue-farmer; contractor; *médecin* ~, medical practitioner; **2.** slaver, trafficker.

traite (trɛt), s.f. **1.** Journey, stage, stretch, distance; *ils font trente milles d'une* ~, they go thirty miles at a stretch; **2.** export, exportation, transport, trade, traffic; slave trade; *la* ~ *des noirs, des nègres*, the slave trade; *la* ~ *des blanches*, the white slave traffic; *faire la* ~, to carry on the slave trade; **3.** draft, bill; *faire* ~ *sur*, to draw a bill on; ~ *qui court*, running bill; ~ *en souffrance*, dishonoured draft; **4.** milking.

traité (trɛte), s.m. [f. *traiter*] **1.** Treatise (*sur*, *de*, on); **2.** treaty, agreement, contract.

traitement (trɛtmɑ̃), s.m. **1.** Treatment, usage; manipulation; reception, honours; *mauvais* ~*s*, ill usage; **2.** salary, stipend, pay; *toucher*, *recevoir son* ~, to receive one's salary.

traiter (trɛte), v.a. [L *tractare*] **1.** To treat, to use, to deal with, to behave to; ~ *X de haut en bas*, to deal peremptorily with X; ~ *X de Turc à More*, to treat X shamefully; **2.** to treat of, to deal with, to manage, to handle, to discuss, to negotiate; to execute, to transact; **3.** to call, to style, to regard (as), to look on (as); **4.** to treat, to entertain; ~, v.n. to deal, to negotiate, to come to terms; **se** ~, v.pr. to treat oneself; to live (well, &c.); to treat one another; to entertain one another; to call one another, to look on one another (as); *le poète et le philosophe se traitent mutuellement d'insensés*, the poet and the philosopher call each other fools.

traiteur (trɛtœr), s.m. Restaurant-keeper. ⚠ Not English 'traitor', which =*traître*.

traître, -sse (trɛtr), s.m.f. [L *traditor*] Traitor, traitress; *en* ~, treacherously, perfidiously. ~, adj. Treacherous, false, perfidious, faithless; *jouer un tour bien* ~, to play a very dirty trick; (colloq.) *pas un* ~ *mot*, not a single word, not a syllable.

traîtreusement (trɛtrøzmɑ̃), adv. Treacherously, perfidiously.

traîtrise (trɛtriz), s.f. Treachery.

trajectoire (traʒɛktwar), s.f. [f. L *trajectus*] Trajectory.

trajet (traʒɛ), s.m. [f. L *trajectus*] Passage, journey, course, way, voyage, distance; ~ *d'une heure*, an hour's run (walk, &c.); (surg.) course.

tralala (tralala), s.m. [onom.] (colloq.) Fuss, ado, show; *faire du* ~, to make a fuss; *en grand* ~, dressed up to the nines; in full fig.

tram (tram), s.m. [abbrev. of *tramway*] Tram-car.

tramail (tramaj), s.m. [f. L *tres*+*macula*] (fish.) Trammel, drag-net; syn. TRÉMAIL.

trame (tram), s.f. [L *trama*] Woof, weft, web; (fig.) course, thread; (fig.) plot; *ourdir une* ~, to lay a plot, to hatch a plot.

tramer (trame), v.a. To weave; (fig.) to plot; to lay, to hatch, to contrive (a plot); **se** ~, v.pr. to be plotted; *un complot se trame dans l'ombre*, a plot is laid in secret.

trameu-r, -se (tramœr), s.m.f. Weaver.

tramontane (tramɔ̃tan), s.f. [It. *tramontana*] North; pole star; north wind; (fig.) *perdre la* ~, to lose one's head, or one's presence of mind.

tramway (tramwe), s.m. [Engl. wd] **1.** Tram-car; **2.** tramway. ⚠ In Engl. 'tramway' means *la voie du tramway*.

tranchage (trɑ̃ʃaʒ), s.m. Cutting.

tranchant, -e (trɑ̃ʃɑ̃), p. adj. Sharp, cutting; *écuyer* ~, carver; (fig.) trenchant, peremptory, decisive; glaring. ~, s.m. Edge; *à deux* ~*s*, double-edged.

tranche (trɑ̃ʃ), s.f. **1.** Slice, rasher, chop, steak; aitch-bone; ~ *grasse*, (of beef) thick flank; ~ *de filet*, (of beef) fillet-steak; **2.** edge; *doré sur* ~*s*, gilt-edged; **3.** (arith.) series, set, group (of figures); **4.** face, surface; (artill.) face (of guns); **5.** chisel; (founding) punch.

tranché, -e (trɑ̃ʃe), p. adj. Clear-cut, distinct, well marked.

tranchée (trɑ̃ʃe), s.f. **1.** Trench; cut, cutting, ditch; entrenchment; *sortir de la* ~, to go over the top; **2.** (med.) pl. colic, gripes; *avoir des* ~*s*, to be griped.

tranchée-abri (trɑ̃ʃe-abri), s.f. Trench, dug-out.

tranchefile (trɑ̃ʃfil), s.f. **1.** (bookbind.) Head-band; **2.** binding (of a shoe).

tranchefiler (trɑ̃ʃfile), v.a. (bookbind.) To put on the head-band of.

tranchelard (trɑ̃ʃlar), s.m. Cook's knife.

tranche-montagne (trɑ̃ʃmɔ̃taɲ), s.m. Swaggerer, bully.

trancher (trɑ̃ʃe), v.a.n. [L *truncare*] To cut off, to cut short; to cut, to carve; to break off, to stop; to solve, to decide; ~ *le mot*, to say the word; not to mince matters; ~ *net*, to speak plainly; to cut; to decide, to determine, to resolve; to set up for; to affect; to contrast (of colours);

~ *dans le vif*, to cut to the quick; (fig.) to set to work in good earnest; ~ *du grand seigneur*, to lord it; ~ *du petit-maître*, to affect the dandy; **se** ~, v.pr. to be cut off.

tranchet (trɑ̃ʃe), s.m. Shoemaker's knife; cutter; chisel; punch.

tranchoir (trɑ̃ʃwar), s.m. Trencher, platter, plate.

tranquille (trɑ̃kil), adj. [L *tranquillus*] Quiet, tranquil, calm, peaceful, still, at peace, at rest, at ease, serene, undisturbed; *laissez-moi* ~, leave me alone; don't bother me; nonsense !; *restez* ~, *tenez-vous* ~, be quiet; keep still; *soyez* ~, don't worry; set your mind at rest; never fear.

tranquillement (trɑ̃kilmɑ̃), adv. Quietly, calmly, tranquilly.

tranquillisant, -e (trɑ̃kilizɑ̃), p. adj. Soothing, tranquillizing.

tranquilliser (trɑ̃kilize), v.a. To soothe, to calm, to quiet, to still, to tranquillize; **se** ~, v.pr. to feel calmer, to be tranquillized; to be easier in one's mind.

tranquillité (trɑ̃kilite), s.f. Quiet, calm, stillness, peace, tranquillity.

trans (trɑ̃s), pref. [L wd] Across, beyond.

transaction (trɑ̃zaksjɔ̃), s.f. [f. L *transactio*] **1.** Compromise; transaction, arrangements; **2.** management of business; (law) adjustment; *faire une* ~, to compromise; to come to terms; *les* ~ *de cette maison*, the transactions of this firm.

transactionnel, -le (trɑ̃zaksjɔnɛl), adj. Compromissorial (rare), of or pertaining to a compromise.

transactionnellement (trɑ̃saksjɔnɛlmɑ̃), adv. By a compromise.

transalpin, -e (trɑ̃salpɛ̃), adj. [L *transalpinus*] Transalpine.

transatlantique (trɑ̃satlɑ̃tik), adj. Transatlantic. ~, s.m. **1.** Transatlantic liner; **2.** (jest.) American; ~, s.f., or *chaise* ~, deck-chair.

transbordement (trɑ̃sbɔrdəmɑ̃), s.m. Transhipment.

transborder (trɑ̃sbɔrde), v.a. To tranship.

transbordeur (trɑ̃sbɔrdœr), s.m. adj. Transporter; *pont* ~, transporter bridge.

transcaspien, -ne (trɑ̃skaspjɛ̃), adj. Transcaspian.

transcaucasien, -ne (trɑ̃scocazjɛ̃), adj. Transcaucasian.

transcendance (trɑ̃ssɑ̃dɑ̃s), s.f. Transcendency, transcendence.

transcendant, -e (trɑ̃ssɑ̃dɑ̃), adj. [f. L *trans*+*scandere*] (philos.) Transcendent; (math., philos.) transcendental; (colloq.) excellent, unsurpassed, extraordinary.

transcendantal, -e, (aux) (trɑ̃ssɑ̃dɑ̃tal), adj. Transcendental; hence *transcendantalisme*, s.m. transcendentalism.

transcontinental, -e, (aux) (trɑ̃scɔ̃tinɑ̃tal), adj. Transcontinental.

transcripteur (trɑ̃skriptœr), s.m. Transcriber, copyist.

transcription (trɑ̃skripsjɔ̃), s.f. **1.** Transcription; **2.** copy, transcript.

transcrire (trɑ̃skrir), v.a. [L *transcribere*] To copy out, to transcribe.

transe (trɑ̃s), s.f. [f. *transir*] **1.** Apprehension, anxiety, fright, dread, fear; *être dans des* ~*s mortelles*, to be in mortal terror; **2.** trance.

transept (trɑ̃sɛpt), s.m. [L *trans*+*septum*] (arch.) Transept.

transférable (trɑ̃sferabl), adj. Transferable.

transférer (trɑ̃sfere), v.a. [L *trans*+*ferre*] To transfer (*de*, from; *à*, to), to transport, to convey; to make over; to translate (a bishop).

transfert, transfèrement (trɑ̃sfer, trɑ̃sfɛrmɑ̃), s.m. Transfer; (law) conveyance, transfer.

transfiguration (trɑ̃sfigyra'sjɔ̃), s.f. [L *transfiguratio*] Transfiguration.

transfigurer (trɑ̃sfigyre), v.a. [L *transfigurare*] To transfigure; **se** ~, v.pr. to be transfigured.

transfilage (trɑ̃sfilaʒ), s.m. (naut.) Lacing, lashing, marline hitch.

transfiler (trɑ̃sfile), v.a. (naut.) To lace; to lash.

transfixion (trɑ̃sfiksjɔ̃), s.f. [f. L *transfigere*] (surg.) Transfixion.

transformable (trɑ̃sfɔrmabl), adj. Transformable.

transformat-eur, -rice (trɑ̃sfɔrmatœr), adj. Transforming, transformative. ~, s.m. Transformer; (electr.) transformer.

transformation (trɑ̃sfɔrma'sjɔ̃), s.f. [f. L *transformatio*] Transformation; metamorphosis; transmutation; conversion (*en*, into).

transformer (trɑ̃sfɔrme), v.a. [L *transformare*] To transform, to change; to turn, to convert (*en*, into); **se** ~, v.pr. to be transformed, to transform oneself (or itself); to turn.

transformisme (trɑ̃sfɔrmism), s.m. Transformism.

transformiste (trɑ̃sfɔrmist), s.m.f. Transformist. ~, adj. Transformistic.

transfuge (trɑ̃sfyʒ), s.m. [f. L *trans*+*fugere*] Deserter; turn-coat, apostate.

transfuser (trɑ̃sfyze), v.a. [f. L *trans*+*fundere*] To transfuse.

transfusion (trɑ̃sfyzjɔ̃), s.f. [L *transfusio*] Transfusion; ~ *du sang*, blood transfusion.

transgangétique (trɑ̃sgɑ̃ʒetik), adj. (geog.) Transgangetic, lying beyond the Ganges.

transgresser (trɑ̃sgrɛse), v.a. [L *transgredi*] To transgress, to violate, to infringe, to break, to contravene.

transgresseur (trɑ̃sgrɛsœr), s.m. Transgressor, offender.

transgressi-f, -ve (trɑ̃sgrɛsif), adj. Transgressing, offending.

transgression (trɑ̃sgrɛsjɔ̃), s.f. Transgression, violation.

transhumance (trɑ̃zymɑ̃s), s.f. [f. *transhumer*] Periodical change of pasture.

transhumant, -e (trɑ̃zymɑ̃), adj. (of flocks and herds) Changing pasture periodically.

transhumer (trɑ̃zyme), v.a. [f. L *trans+humus*] To move periodically to other pasture-land; ~, v.n. to be moved or conveyed to other pasture-land.

transi, -e (trɑ̃zi), adj. Chilled, benumbed; paralysed; *un amoureux* ~, a faint-hearted lover; ~ *de froid*, frozen; ~ *de peur*, petrified (with fear).

transiger (trɑ̃ziʒe), v.n. [L *trans+agere*] To compromise, to come to terms, to compound (*avec*, with).

transir (trɑ̃zir), v.a.n. [L *transire*] To chill, to benumb with cold; (fig.) to freeze; (fig.) to petrify (with fear); to paralyse, to be chilled, paralysed.

transissement (trɑ̃zismɑ̃), s.m. (rare) [f. *transir*] **1.** Chill, numbness; shivering; **2.** faint-heartedness.

transit (trɑ̃zit), s.m. [L *transitus*] Transit; through traffic (not subject to duty); *marchandises en* ~, goods in transit; *droit de* ~, transit duty. ⚠ In English 'transit' has also the (fig.) sense of dying = *passage de vie à trépas*.

transitaire (trɑ̃zitɛr), adj. Pertaining to the transit of goods; *pays* ~, country through which the goods are in transit. ~, s.m. Forwarding (or express) agent; transit goods agent.

transiter (trɑ̃zite), v.a. To convey (goods) in transit; ~, v.n. to pass in transit.

transiti-f, -ve (trɑ̃zitif), adj. [f. L *transire*] Transitive; (gram.) transitive, active.

transition (trɑ̃zisjɔ̃), s.f. [L *transitio*] Transition; gradual passage, change; (mus.) transition, change from key to key or from major to relative minor; *période de* ~, transition stage.

transitivement (trɑ̃zitivmɑ̃), adv. Transitively.

transitoire (trɑ̃zitwar), adj. Transitory, transient.

transitoirement (trɑ̃zitwarmɑ̃), adv. Transiently, transitorily.

translater (trɑ̃slate), v.a. (obs.) [L *transferre*] To translate.

translati-f, -ve (trɑ̃slatif), adj. (law) Transferring; *acte* ~ *de propriété*, conveyance.

translation (trɑ̃slasjɔ̃), s.f. [L *translatio*] Translation, removal, transfer. ⚠ Not 'translation' in the very common English sense of *traduction, thème, version*.

translucide (trɑ̃slysid), adj. [f. L *trans+lucere*] Translucent; translucid (rare).

translucidité (trɑ̃slysidite), s.f. Translucence, translucency.

transmetteur (trɑ̃smɛtœr), s.m. Transmitter.

transmettre (trɑ̃smɛtr), v.a. [L *transmittere*] To transmit, to send on, to convey, to forward; to hand on, to make over; to pass on (*de*, from; *à*, to); (fig.) to hand down; ~ *une lettre à X*, to forward a letter to X; ~ *un privilège à X*, to make over a privilege to X; ~ *son nom à la postérité*, to hand down one's name to posterity; **se** ~, v.pr. to be transmitted.

transmigration (trɑ̃smigra'sjɔ̃), s.f. [L *transmigratio*] Transmigration; ~ *des âmes*, metempsychosis, transmigration of souls.

transmigrer (trɑ̃smigre), v.n. [L *transmigrare*] To transmigrate, to migrate.

transmissibilité (trɑ̃smisibilite), s.f. Transmissibility.

transmissible (trɑ̃smisibl), adj. Transmissible, transferable.

transmission (trɑ̃smisjɔ̃), s.f. [L *transmissio*] Transmission; (motor.) *à* ~ *par chaîne*, chain-driven.

transmuable, transmutable (trɑ̃smɥabl, trɑ̃smytabl), adj. Transmutable.

transmuer (trɑ̃smɥe), v.a. [L *transmutare*] To transmute.

transmutabilité (trɑ̃smytabilite), s.f. Transmutability.

transmutation (trɑ̃smyta'sjɔ̃), s.f. [L *transmutatio*] Transmutation.

transpadan, -e (trɑ̃spadɑ̃), adj. (geog.) Transpadane, situated north of the Po.

transparaître (trɑ̃sparɛtr), v.n. To be visible (through something); to appear, to become apparent.

transparence (trɑ̃sparɑ̃s), s.f. Transparence, transparency, transparentness.

transparent, -e (trɑ̃sparɑ̃), adj. Transparent; (fig.) easily seen through. ~, s.m. **1.** Paper with black guiding lines (placed under unruled writing-paper); **2.** silk under-dress; **3.** transparency.

transpercer (trɑ̃sperse), v.a. [L *trans*+ (Fr.) *percer*] To run through, to pierce, to transfix, to transpierce; (fig.) to penetrate; *cette pluie nous a transpercés*, this rain has drenched us through and through; *cette nouvelle me transperce le cœur*, this news cuts me to the quick.

transpirable (trɑ̃spirabl), adj. Transpirable.

transpiration (trɑ̃spira'sjɔ̃), s.f. [f. *transpirer*] Transpiration, perspiration, sweat.

transpirer (trɑ̃spire), v.n. [L *trans+spirare*] To perspire; to transpire, to sweat; to ooze out; (fig.) to leak out, to become known.

transplantable (trɑ̃splɑ̃tabl), adj. Transplantable.
transplantation (trɑ̃splɑ̃ta'sjɔ̃), s.f. Transplantation.
transplanter (trɑ̃splɑ̃te), v.a. [L *trans*+ *plantare*] To transplant; **se ~**, v.pr. to be transplanted; to transplant oneself, to emigrate.
transport (trɑ̃spɔr), s.m. [f. *transporter*] **1.** Transport, conveyance, carrying; removal; traffic; *commerce de ~*, carrying-trade; *frais de ~*, carriage; *ce malade n'est pas en état de souffrir le ~*, this patient is too ill to be moved; **2.** transport ship; *~ de condamnés*, convict ship; *~ de ravitaillement*, store ship; transport; **3.** fit, violent emotion, transport, rapture, rage; *avec ~*, enthusiastically; *~ au cerveau*, congestion of the brain; **4.** (law) visit (of a judge, &c.); **5.** (law) transfer; **6.** (comm.) carrying forward.
transportable (trɑ̃spɔrtabl), adj. Transportable, movable.
transportation (trɑ̃spɔrta'sjɔ̃), s.f. Transportation, removal, banishment.
transporté, -e (trɑ̃spɔrte), p. adj. Ravished, overcome (*de*, with); *~ de joie*, overcome with joy; in transports of joy. ~, s.m.f. Transported convict.
transporter (trɑ̃spɔrte), v.a. [L *trans*+ *portare*] **1.** To transport, to convey, to remove; to transfer, to make over; (comm.) to carry over; (law) to banish, to transport; **2.** to enrapture; to infuriate; *il est transporté de joie*, he is quite overcome with joy; he is in transports of joy; **se ~**, v.pr. **1.** to repair, to go; **2.** to be transported.
transporteur (trɑ̃spɔrtœr), s.m. Transporter, carrier.
transposable (trɑ̃spozabl), adj. Transposable.
transposer (trɑ̃spoze), v.a. To transpose; **se ~**, v.pr. to be transposed.
transpositeur (trɑ̃spozitœr), s.m. Transposing instrument. ~, adj. Transposing.
transpositi-f, -ve (trɑ̃spozitif), adj. Transpositive.
transposition (trɑ̃spozisjɔ̃), s.f. [LL *transpositio*] Transposition.
transrhénan, -e (trɑ̃srenɑ̃), adj. (geog.) Transrhenane, lying beyond the Rhine.
transsaharien, -ne (trɑ̃ssaarjɛ̃), adj. (geog.) Trans-Saharan.
transsibérien, -ne (trɑ̃ssiberjɛ̃), adj. (geog.) Trans-Siberian.
transsubstantiation (trɑ̃ssybstɑ̃sja'sjɔ̃), s.f. [LL *transubstantio*] Transubstantiation.
transsubstantier (trɑ̃ssybstɑ̃sje), v.a. (rare) To transubstantiate.
transsudation (trɑ̃ssyda'sjɔ̃), s.f. Transudation.
transsuder (trɑ̃ssyde), v.n. [L *trans*+ *sudare*] To transude, to ooze through.
transvasement (trɑ̃svɑzmɑ̃), s.m. Decanting, transfusion.
transvaser (trɑ̃svɑze), v.a. [f. L *trans*+ Fr. *vase*] To decant, to pour off.
transversal, -e, (aux) (trɑ̃svɛrsal), adj. Transverse, transversal, cross.
transversalement (trɑ̃svɛrsalmɑ̃), adv. Transversely, across, crosswise.
transverse (trɑ̃svɛrs), adj. [L *transversus*] Transverse. ~, s.m. Transverse muscle.
transvider (trɑ̃svide), v.a. To pour off.
transylvain, -e, transylvanien, -ne (trɑ̃silvɛ̃, trɑ̃silvanjɛ̃), adj. s.m.f. Transylvanian.
trantran (trɑ̃trɑ̃), s.m. Humdrum routine; usual way or business; jog-trot.
trapan (trapɑ̃), s.m. **1.** Top (of a staircase); **2.** (paper-mak.) dropping-board.
trapèze (trapɛz), s.m. [Gr. *trapeza*] **1.** (geom.) Trapezium; trapezoid; **2.** (anat.) trapezium (bone); trapezius (muscle); **3.** (gymn.) trapeze.
trapézoèdre (trapezoɛdr), s.m. Trapezohedron.
trapézoïdal, -e, (aux) (trapezɔidal), adj. Trapezoid.
trappe (trap), s.f. [OHG *trappa*] Trap-door; trap, pitfall, snare, gin; *lever, ouvrir une ~*, to raise, to open a trap-door; *tendre, dresser une ~*, to lay a snare, to set a trap. ⚠ In English 'trap' means also **1.** *siphon*; **2.** *dog-cart*; **3.** (slang) *policier*; **4.** (pl.) *affaires personnelles, effets*, &c.; **5.** an igneous rock.
trappeur (trapœr), s.m. Trapper.
trappiste (trapist), s.m. [f. monastery in *Soligny-la-Trappe*] Trappist.
trappistine (trapistin), s.f. **1.** Trappistine, Trappist nun; **2.** trappistine (liqueur).
trappon (trapɔ̃), s.m. Trap-door (level with floor).
trapu, -e (trapy), adj. Thickset, dumpy, squat.
traque (trak), s.f. (hunt.) Driving, beating up.
traquenard (traknar), s.m. **1.** Trap, snare; *se laisser prendre au ~*, to walk into a trap; **2.** (rid.) rack.
traquer (trake), v.a. (hunt.) To drive, to beat up; to enclose, to surround, to put a cordon round; to hunt out; *~ des voleurs*, to hunt out thieves, to track down thieves; to push hard.
traquet (trakɛ), s.m. **1.** Trap; **2.** clapper (of a mill); **3.** (ornith.) chat.
traqueur (trakœr), s.m. Beater, game-driver.
traulet (trolɛ), s.m. (draw.) Steel point.
traumatique (tromatik), adj. [f. Gr. *trauma*] Traumatic.
traumatisme (tromatism), s.m. (surg., &c.) Traumatism.
travail[1] (pl. **aux**) (travaj), s.m. [f. *travailler*] **1.** Work, job, employment;

task, labour, toil; effort, fatigue, trouble; piece of work; workmanship, execution; industry; (pl.) works; earthworks; feats, deeds; *à force de* ~, by dint of work; *c'est un beau* ~, it is a fine piece of work; *d'un* ~ *exquis*, of exquisite workmanship; *cabinet de* ~, study; *il est sans* ~, he is out of work; *les sans-*~, the unemployed; *le* ~ *manuel*, manual work; *le* ~ *de l'esprit*, brain-work; *les travaux de la campagne*, agricultural work; *les travaux d'assainissement*, sanitary works; *se mettre au* ~, to set to work; ~ *servile*, menial work; *travaux forcés*, hard labour, penal servitude; ~ *excessif*, overwork, excessive labour; *vivre de son* ~, to live by one's work, to work for a living; *travaux d'art*, tunnels, bridges, &c.; **2.** labour, childbirth; **3.** *travaux*, pl. proceedings, transactions (of an assembly).

travail[2] (pl. **-s**) (travaj), s.m. [LL *tripalium*] Trave, brake.

travaillé, -e (travaje), p. adj. **1.** Worked, wrought; laboured; elaborate; finished; overworked; **2.** labouring (*par*, under), a prey (to), suffering (from), obsessed (by); *des vers* ~*s*, elaborate verses; *un cheval trop* ~, an over-worked horse; ~ *par l'ambition*, obsessed with ambition.

travailler (travaje), v.n.a. [LL *tripaliare*] **1.** To work, to labour, to take pains, to exert oneself; to be active; to study; ~ *pour vivre*, to work for one's living; *il a travaillé pour le roi de Prusse*, he has had his labour for his pains; ~ *comme un nègre*, to work like a nigger; *faire* ~ *son argent*, to get interest on one's money; **2.** to undergo a change; to ferment (of wine); to warp (of wood); to crack (of walls); to fade (of paint); **3.** to be agitated; to digest with difficulty (of the stomach); *son esprit travaille*, his mind is at work; **4.** ~ *pour* or *contre X*, to use one's influence for or against X; ~, v.a. to torment, to worry, to distress, to disturb, to agitate; *l'ambition ne me travaille point*, I am not ambitious; to work upon, to influence, to excite; ~ *les esprits*, to excite public opinion; to work at, to be engaged on, to be occupied with, to elaborate; ~ *son style*, to elaborate one's style; to work, to fashion; to knead (dough); to train, to exercise (horses); **se** ~, v.pr. **1.** to be worked, to be wrought; **2.** to endeavour; to worry; *se* ~ *l'esprit*, to fret; to rack one's brains.

travailleu-r, -se (travajœr), adj. Industrious, hardworking, painstaking. ~, s.m.f. **1.** Hard worker; industrious person; conscientious student; **2.** working man, workman, workwoman; labourer, operative, worker.

travailliste (travajist), s.m. Member of the Labour Party in England. ~, adj. Labour; *politique* ~, Labour politics.

travée (trave), s.f. [L *trabs*] (arch.) **1.** Bay of joists; truss; **2.** upper gallery (of a church), triforium; **3.** span (of a bridge).

travers (travɛr), s.m. [f. L *transversus*] **1.** Breadth, width; broadside (of a ship); *à* ~, across; through; *à* ~ *champs*, across country; *au* ~ *de*, through; *à tort et à* ~, like a bull in a china-shop; recklessly; at random; indiscreetly; indiscriminately; heedlessly; rashly; *de* ~, askew, awry, crooked, wrong; *il s'y est pris tout de* ~, he went the wrong way to work; he managed very badly; he made a mess of it; *regarder X de* ~, to look askance at X; to look black at X; to look daggers at X; (fig.) *il a mis son bonnet de* ~ *aujourd'hui*, he has got out of bed on the wrong side; he is in a bad temper; *il prend de* ~ *tout ce qu'on dit*, he takes everything amiss; (naut.) *feu de* ~, broadside firing; *vent de* ~, wind abeam, or abreast; *par le* ~, abeam, athwart; *par le* ~ *de*, abreast of; *en* ~ *du courant*, athwart the tide; *en* ~, across, crosswise; athwart, sideways, obliquely; *par le* ~, across, athwart; **2.** fault, defect, bad habit, oddity; *la jalousie est un vilain* ~, jealousy is an unpleasant fault; *donner dans le* ~, to have taken to bad habits.

traversable (travɛrsabl), adj. That can be crossed; *rivière* ~, fordable river.

traverse (travɛrs), s.f. **1.** Traverse, crossbar, transom; splinter-bar (of a carriage); sleeper (of a railway); girder; stay; crossmember; cross-bearer; **2.** hindrance, obstacle, disappointment; *il a essuyé bien des* ~*s*, he has suffered many disappointments; **3.** crossing; cross-road; short cut; *prendre la* ~, to take a short cut; *chemin de* ~, cross-road, short cut; **4.** (fort.) traverse, earthwork in form of parapet, protecting covered way or trench; (geom.) traverse, transversal line; **5.** (naut.) (*a*) bar; (*b*) crosshead; (*c*) groundway.

traversée (travɛrse), s.f. Passage, voyage, crossing; *mauvaise* ~, rough passage.

traverser (travɛrse), v.a. **1.** To traverse; to cross, to travel across, to travel through, to go through; (rid.) to traverse; to span, to lie across, to run through; **2.** to run through (with a sword); to penetrate; **3.** to cross, to thwart, to foil, to frustrate, to hinder, to obstruct; ~ *la rue*, to cross the street; ~ *l'esprit*, to cross the mind, to occur (to); ~ *un projet*, to thwart a project; **se** ~, v.pr. **1.** to be traversed; **2.** to thwart each other. ⚠ *Traverser* cannot be used like 'to traverse', in the sense of considering, discussing the whole extent of (a subject).

traversi-er, -ère (travɛrsje), adj. Cross, crossing, traversing, going across; *flûte* ~*ère*, German flute; (naut.) *barres* ~*ères*, crosstrees. ~, s.m. (naut.) Spring; ~*ère*,

s.f. (naut.) fish; *bossoir de traversière*, fish-head, fish-davit.
traversin (travɛrsɛ̃), s.m. **1.** Bolster; **2.** (of a boat) cross-piece; **3.** (of a balance) beam.
traversine (travɛrsin), s.f. Cross-beam; sleeper; transom; girder; (naut.) plank.
travertin (travɛrtɛ̃), s.m. [It. *travertino*] (min.) Travertin(e).
travesti, -e (travɛsti), p. adj. [f. *travestir*] **1.** Disguised; **2.** burlesqued, parodied; *bal* ~, fancy-dress ball; (theatr.) *rôle* ~, man's part acted by a woman. ~, s.m. Fancy dress, disguise; man's clothes worn by a woman; *il faut être mince pour porter bien le* ~, it requires a slender woman to look well in a *travesti* (a man's part).
travestir (travɛstir), v.a. [It. *travestire*] **1.** To disguise, to dress up; ~ *un homme en femme*, to dress up a man as a woman; **2.** to parody, to burlesque; **3.** to misrepresent, to twist; to travesty; **se** ~, v.pr. to disguise oneself, to don a fancy dress. ⚠ 'To travesty' is always pejorative.
travestissement (travɛstismɑ̃), s.m. **1.** Disguise, fancy dress; **2.** (pej.) travesty, misrepresentation, parody.
travestisseu-r, -se (travɛstisœr), s.m.f. Parodist.
travon (travɔ̃), s.m. [f. L *trabs*] Main beam (of a wooden bridge).
travouil (travui), s.m. (techn.) Hasp.
trayeu-r, -se (trɛjœr), s.m.f. Milker, milkmaid.
trayon (trɛjɔ̃), s.m. Dug, teat (of cows, &c.).
trébuchage (trebyʃaʒ), s.m. Weighing of coins.
trébuchant, -e (trebyʃɑ̃), p. adj. **1.** Of full weight (of coins); **2.** stumbling.
trébuchement (trebyʃmɑ̃), s.m. Stumbling, falling.
trébucher (trebuʃe), v.n. [L *trans*+OF *buc*] **1.** To stumble; to trip, to fall; (fig.) to err, to fail; **2.** to turn the scale; ~, v.a. to weigh (coins).
trébuchet (trebyʃɛ), s.m. **1.** Bird-trap, snare, gin; *prendre au* ~, to ensnare; **2.** assay-balance, trebuchet; **3.** (hist.) trebucket, trebuchet.
tréfilage (trefilaʒ), s.m. Wire-drawing.
tréfiler (trefile), v.a. [L *trahere*+*filum*] To wire-draw.
tréfilerie (trefilri), s.f. **1.** Wire-drawing; **2.** wire-drawing machine; **3.** wire-mill.
tréfileur (trefilœr), s.m. Wire-drawer, wire-maker.
trèfle (trɛfl), s.m. [L *trifolium*] **1.** (bot.) Trefoil; clover, *Trifolium*; shamrock; **2.** (at cards) clubs; **3.** (arch.) trefoil.
tréflé, -e (trefle), p. adj. (herald.) Treflé, treflee.
tréfler (trefle), v.a. To stamp a coin or medal badly so that the stamp appears double.
tréflière (trefljɛr), s.f. Clover-field.
tréfonci-er, -ère (trefɔ̃sje), adj. Of the soil and subsoil. ~, s.m. Landowner; owner of the soil and subsoil; mine-owner.
tréfonds (trefɔ̃), s.m. [*très*+*fonds*] Subsoil; (fig.) bottom; *savoir le fond et le* ~ *d'une affaire*; to know the ins and outs of an affair.
tréhala (treala), s.m. [Turk. orig.] Trehala.
treillage (trɛjaʒ), s.m. Trellis-work, lattice-work; treillage.
treillager (trɛjaʒe), v.a. [f. *treille*] To trellis, to lattice.
treillageur (trɛjaʒœr), s.m. Trellis-maker, lattice-maker.
treille (trɛj), s.f. [L *trichila*] Vine arbour; vine; *le jus de la* ~, wine; the juice of the grape.
treillis (trɛji), s.m. [L *trilix*] **1.** Trellis, trellis-work, lattice, lattice-work; **2.** iron grating; **3.** coarse canvas, sacking, sackcloth.
treillisser (trɛjise), v.a. To trellis.
treizaine (trɛzɛn), s.f. Baker's dozen, thirteen, long dozen.
treize (trɛz), adj. num. [L *tredecim*] Thirteen; thirteenth (day of the month); ~ *à la douzaine*, thirteen to the dozen; a long dozen, a baker's dozen.
treizième (trɛzjɛm), adj. num. ord. Thirteenth.
treizièmement (trɛzjɛməmɑ̃), adv. Thirteenthly.
trélingage (trelɛ̃gaʒ), s.m. (naut.) Cat-harpings.
tréma (trema), s.m. [Gr. wd] Diaeresis.
trémail (tremaj), s.m. See TRAMAIL.
tremblaie (trɑ̃blɛ), s.f. Aspen-grove.
tremblant, -e (trɑ̃blɑ̃), adj. Trembling, tremulous, quivering, flickering, faltering, tottering, shivering, wavering.
tremble (trɑ̃bl), s.m. [L *tremulus*] (bot.) Aspen; *Populus tremula*.
tremblé, -e (trɑ̃ble), p. adj. Wavy, waved, shaky; *écriture* ~*e*, shaky writing; tremulous writing; (mus.) trembling, tremolo; tremulant (stop). ~, s.m. (print.) Waved rule.
tremblement (trɑ̃bləmɑ̃), s.m. Trembling, shaking, shivering, quivering, quaking, tremor, trepidation, tremulousness, agitation, flickering, fluttering; (mus.) shake; trill; (colloq.) *tout le* ~, the whole show, or caboodle; the whole bag of tricks, all the rest of it; ~ *de terre*, earthquake.
trembler (trɑ̃ble), v.n. [L *tremere*] To tremble, to shake, to shiver, to quake, to quiver, to shudder, to totter, to waver, to flutter, to flicker, to twinkle; ~ *de colère*, to tremble with anger; *je tremble de le voir*, I tremble at the thought of seeing

him; *ce pont tremble,* this bridge shakes; *à faire* ~, terrific, frightful, awful.
trembleu-r, -se (trɑ̃blœr), adj. Trembling, shaking. ~, s.m.f. **1.** (eccles. hist.) Quaker, Shaker; **2.** (fig.) poor timid creature; poltroon; doddering old ass; ~, s.m. (electr.) trembler; *bobine à* ~, trembler coil.
tremblotant, -e (trɑ̃blɔtɑ̃), p. adj. Tremulous; twinkling.
tremblote (trɑ̃blɔt), s.f. (colloq.) Fear, trembling; *avoir la* ~, to be all of a tremble, to have the twitters.
tremblotement (trɑ̃blɔtmɑ̃), s.m. Tremulousness, tremble, shakiness.
trembloter (trɑ̃blɔte), v.n. To tremble, to shake, to shiver, to quiver.
trémelle (tremɛl), s.f. (bot.) Tremella.
trémie (tremi), s.f. [L *trimodia*] Hopper, mill-hopper; funnel; (build.) the part of a floor cut off for the passage of chimney-ways.
trémière (tremiɛr), adj.f. (bot.) *Rose* ~, hollyhock, rose-mallow.
trémolo (tremɔlo), s.m. [It. wd] Tremolo.
trémoussement (tremusmɑ̃), s.m. Fluttering, fidgeting, twitching, frisking about.
trémousser (tremuse), v.a. To stir, to bestir; ~, v.n. to flutter; **se** ~, v.pr. to flutter, to dance, to shake a leg; to bustle about, to bestir oneself; to fidget; (fig.) to take a lot of trouble, to fuss.
trempage (trɑ̃paʒ), s.m. Steeping, soaking; (print.) wetting.
trempe (trɑ̃p), s.f. Steeping, soaking; (print.) wetting down; (metall.) tempering, hardening; (brewing) malting-water; temper (of a metal); (fig.) temper, stamp, cast, character; grit, guts; *un corps d'une bonne* ~, a good constitution; *peu d'hommes ont un caractère de cette* ~, there are few men of that stamp; not many men have his grit; (slang) thrashing.
tremper (trɑ̃pe), v.a. [f. L *temperare*] To soak, to wet, to drench, to moisten, to steep, to dip (into a liquid), to sop; to imbrue; (print.) to wet; to dilute; (metall., and fig.) to temper (steel); *il est tout trempé,* he is wet to the skin; ~ *la soupe,* to pour the soup on to the bread; ~ *ses mains dans le sang,* to imbrue one's hands in blood; ~, v.n. to soak, to be steeped; to be stained, to be imbrued; to be implicated (*dans,* in); to be concerned (in), to have a hand (in); *il a trempé là-dedans,* he has had a hand in that; **se** ~, v.pr. to be soaked, to be sopped; to get wet, to soak oneself; to be imbrued; to be hardened, tempered.
tremperie (trɑ̃pri), s.f. (print.) Wetting-room.
trempette (trɑ̃pɛt), s.f. Sop; *faire la* ~, to eat bread sopped in a liquid, usually wine; to dip one's bread or sponge finger in wine, milk, &c.
trempeur (trɑ̃pœr), s.m. Temperer; (print.) wetter.
tremplin (trɑ̃plɛ̃), s.m. [It. *trampelino*] Spring-board.
trempoir (trɑ̃pwar), s.m. (cloth-manufacture) Steeping-tub.
trempoire (trɑ̃pwar), s.f. Steeping-vat.
trémulation (tremyla'sjɔ̃), s.f. [f. L *tremulare*] Tremor, trembling.
trémuler (tremyle), v.a. To shake, to vibrate, to quiver.
trénis (trenis), s.f. (danc.) Trenitz.
trentain (trɑ̃tɛ̃), s.m. **1.** (tennis) Thirty all; **2.** trental, month's mind.
trentaine (trɑ̃tɛn), s.f. Some thirty, about thirty, thirty or so; the age of thirty; *avoir passé la* ~, to be on the wrong side of thirty.
trente (trɑ̃t), adj. num. [L *triginta*] Thirty; thirtieth. ~, s.m. Thirty; thirtieth (of the month); *~-et-quarante, ~-et-un,* rouge-et-noir; *se mettre sur son ~-et-un,* to tog oneself up; to be in full fig; to dress in one's glad rags; (jest.) *tous les ~-six du mois,* once in a blue moon.
trentenaire (trɑ̃tənɛr), adj. For thirty years, lasting 30 years.
trentième (tratjɛm), adj. num. ord. Thirtieth. ~, s.m. Thirtieth part.
tréou (treu), s.m. (naut.) Storm lateen sail.
trépan (trepɑ̃), s.m. [Gr. *trupanon*] (surg.) Trepan; trepanning.
trépanation (trepana'sjɔ̃), s.f. Trepanning, trepanation.
trépaner (trepane), v.a. (surg.) To trepan, to trephine. ⚠ 'To trepan' (but not *trépaner*) means also to trap, to ensnare = *attraper, rouler, tromper, faire tomber dans un piège.*
trépas (trepɑ), s.m. [f. *trépasser*] Death; *passer de vie à* ~, to die; to pass over. ⚠ Not 'trespass', which = *intrusion, violation de propriété, délit; péché, transgression.*
trépassé, -e (trepɑse), s.m.f. Dead, deceased; (pl.) the dead; *le jour, la fête des ~s,* All Souls' Day.
trépasser (trepɑse), v.n. [OF *tres*+*passer*] To die, to pass away, to depart this life. ⚠ Not 'to trespass'. See *trépas.*
trépidant, -e (trepidɑ̃), p. adj. Shaking, quivering, vibrating; (fig.) agitated, in a flurry, ardent, excited.
trépidation (trepida'sjɔ̃), s.f. [f. L *trepidus*] Shaking, trembling, quivering, vibration; (med.) trepidation; (astr.) trepidation; (fig.) flurry; excitement.
trépied (trepje), s.m. [L *tres*+*pes*] Trivet; tripod.
trépignement (trepiɲmɑ̃), s.m. Stamping (of the feet); pawing the ground (of a horse); (fig.) transport.
trépigner (trepiɲe), v.n. [Germ. orig.]

To stamp (one's feet); to paw the ground; ~ *de colère*, to stamp with rage; ~, v.a. to trample upon.

trépointe (trepwɛ̃t), s.f. Welt (of a shoe).

très (trɛ), adv. [L *trans*] Very, most, very much; ~ *bien*, very well; all right; *voilà qui est* ~ *bien*, that 's just the thing; *le Très Haut*, the Most High; *le* ~ *honorable*, the right honourable.

trésaillé, -e (trezɑje), adj. [f. *très* + *aller*] Crackled; *porcelaine* ~*e*, crackle-china, crackle-ware.

trésaillure (trezɑjyr), s.f. Crackling (china).

trésillon (trezijɔ̃), s.m. [f. LL *tensare*] (build.) Stay, prop, support; (naut.) Spanish windlass; syn. ÉTRÉSILLON.

trésillonner (trezijɔne), v.a. (build., mining) To prop, to stay, to support; (naut.) to set up with a Spanish windlass.

trésor (trezɔr), s.m. [L *thesaurus*] Treasure, riches, wealth; *entasser des* ~*s*, to hoard up wealth; anything precious, a beloved person; *cette femme est un* ~, that woman is a treasure; *mon* ~, my darling; relics, ornaments (R. Cath. church); *le* ~ *de Notre-Dame*, the relics in Notre-Dame; treasury of a church, the place where relics and ornaments are kept; Treasury; *un employé du* ~, a clerk of the Treasury; *bon du* ~, Treasury bond.

trésorerie (trezɔrri), s.f. Treasury, treasury department; *les lords de la* ~, the Lords of the Treasury.

trésori-er, -ère (trezɔrje), s.m.f. Treasurer, (mil.) paymaster; *Grand* ~, High Treasurer.

tressage (trɛsɑʒ), s.m. Plaiting, braiding; weaving.

tressaillement (trɛsɑjmɑ̃), s.m. Start; tremor, thrill; shudder; disturbance (of nerves).

tressailli (trɛsɑji), p. adj. m. Wrenched, torn, strained (nerve, tendon, muscle).

tressaillir (trɛsɑjir), v.n. [L *transsilire*] To start, to give a start, to thrill; to wince, to shudder; to tremble, to quake; ~ *de joie*, to tremble with joy.

tressaut (trɛso), s.m. Start, jump.

tressauter (trɛsote), v.n. [L *trans*+ *saltare*] To jump; to start, to tremble.

tresse (trɛs), s.f. [LL *tricia*] Plait, tress, braid, pigtail; braid-like ornamentation in architecture; (naut.) sennet; ~ *de chanvre*, gasket.

tresser (trɛse), v.a. To plait, to tress.

tresseu-r, -se (trɛsœr), s.m.f. Plaiter, braider.

tréteau (pl. -x) (treto), s.m. Trestle; (pl.) boards, stage; (fig.) *monter sur les* ~*x*, to go on the stage; to tread the boards.

treuil (trœj), s.m. [L *trochlea*] Windlass, winch; crab.

trêve (trɛv), s.f. [f. OHG *triuwa*] Truce, cessation, rest, relief; *faire* ~, to stop, to cease, to give a respite; *demander une* ~, to ask for a truce; ~ *de questions*, no more of your questions; *son mal ne lui laisse pas de* ~, the pain gives him no rest; (hist.) ~ *de Dieu*, truce of God.

trévire (trevir), s.f. (naut.) Parbuckle.

trévirer (trevire), v.a. [f. *virer*] (naut.) To parbuckle; to slue.

tri (tri), s.m. [f. *trier*] **1.** Sorting, picking; syn. TRIAGE; *faire le* ~ or *un* ~, to sort; to select; **2.** three-handed ombre; trick (cards); *faire le tri*, or *trick*, to make the odd trick.

tri (tri), pref. Tri-; three-; ~*-porteur*, s.m. tricycle-carrier, small delivery-van on three wheels.

triade (triɑd), s.f. [Gr. *trias*] Triad, group of three, trinity.

triadelphe (triadɛlf), adj. (bot.) Triadelphous.

triage (triaʒ), s.m. [f. *trier*] Sorting; selection, choice; syn. TRI.

triandre (triɑ̃dr), adj. (bot.) Triandrous.

triangle (triɑ̃gl), s.m. [*tri*+*angle*] Triangle; (naut.) triangular flag; (mus.) triangle.

triangulaire (triɑ̃gylɛr), adj. Triangular.

triangulairement (triɑ̃gylɛrmɑ̃), adv. Triangularly.

triangulation (triɑ̃gyla'sjɔ̃), s.f. Triangulation.

trianguler (triɑ̃gyle), v.a. To triangulate.

trias (triɑs), s.m. [Gr. wd] (geol.) Trias.

triasique (triɑzik), adj. Triassic.

tribart (tribɑr), s.m. Yoke.

tribasique (tribɑzik), adj. [*tri*+*base*] (chem.) Tribasic.

tribomètre (tribɔmɛtr), s.m. Tribometer.

tribord (tribɔr), s.m. [Dan. *styrbord*] (naut.) Starboard; *à* ~, to starboard; *quart de* ~, starboard watch.

tribordais (tribɔrdɛ), s.m. (naut.) Starboard man.

tribraque (tribrak), s.m. [*tri*+(Gr.) *brakhus*] (metr.) Tribrach, metrical foot ∪∪∪.

tribu (triby), s.f. [L *tribus*] Tribe; (colloq.) tribe, family, troop, horde.

tribulation (tribyla'sjɔ̃), s.f. [L *tribulatio*] Tribulation, affliction, trial.

tribun (tribœ̃), s.m. [L *tribunus*] Tribune; Roman magistrate; democratic orator or leader.

tribunal, (aux) (tribynal), s.m. [f. L *tribunus*] Tribunal, court of justice; law-court; *comparaître devant le* ~, to appear in court; judge's bench; the judges.

tribunat (tribyna), s.m. (hist.) Tribunate.

tribune (tribyn), s.f. [It. *tribuna*] Tribune, rostrum, platform, hustings; gallery, grand stand; ~ *sacrée*, pulpit; ~ *aux enchères*, auctioneer's rostrum; ~ *d'orgue*, organ-loft; ~ *publique*, strangers' gallery;

~ *des journalistes,* press gallery; *monter à la* ~, to mount the rostrum. ♤ 'Tribune' also =*tribun.*

tribunitien, -ne (tribynisjɛ̃), adj. (hist.) Tribunicial, tribunitian.

tribut (triby), s.m. [L *tributum*] Tribute, grant; contribution; tax; *soumis à payer le* ~, laid under tribute; *payer le* ~ *à la nature,* to die; *payer le* ~ *à la mer,* to be seasick.

tributaire (tribytɛr), adj. Tributary, subject; tributary (river).

tricennal, -e, (aux) (trisɛnal), adj. [f. L *tricennium*] Tricennial.

tricéphale (trisefal), adj. [Gr. *tri*+ *kephalē*] Three-headed.

triceps (trisɛps), s.m. (anat.) Triceps.

tricher (triʃe), v.n.a. [Germ. orig.] To cheat; to deceive; to trick (a person out of a thing).

tricherie (triʃri), s.f. Cheating (at play); (fig.) trickery, trick.

tricheu-r, -se (triʃœr), s.m.f. Cheat, trickster. ~, adj. Cheating.

trichinal, -e, (aux) (triʃinal, trikinal), adj. Trichinal.

trichine (triʃin), s.f. [Gr. *trikhinos*] (med.) Threadworm, trichina.

trichiné, -e (triʃine, trikine), adj. (med.) Trichinous.

trichinose (triʃinoz, trikinoz), s.f. (med.) Trichinosis.

trichocéphale (trikɔsefal), s.m. (zool.) Trichocephalus.

trichoma, trichome (trikoma, trikom), s.m. [Gr. *trikhōma*] (med.) Trichoma.

trichrome (trikrom), adj. [f. Gr. *tri*+ *khrōmatos*] Trichromatic, (printed) in three colours.

trichromie (trikromi), s.f. Three-colour process; colour photography.

tricoises (trikwaz), s.f.pl. [f. *turcoises*] Farrier's pincers.

tricolor (trikɔlɔr), s.m. (bot.) Tricolor, *Amarantus tricolor.*

tricolore (trikɔlɔr), adj. [*tri*+L *color*] Tricolour, three-coloured; *drapeau* ~, tricoloured flag, tricolour, French flag.

tricorne (trikɔrn), adj. [L *tres*+*cornu*] Three-cornered. ~, s.m. Three-cornered hat.

tricot (triko), s.m. **1.** Knitting; **2.** knitted jersey, cardigan, or vest; **3.** cudgel.

tricotage (trikɔtaʒ), s.m. Knitting.

tricoter (trikɔte), v.a.n. [Germ. *stricken*] To knit; *aiguilles à* ~, knitting-needles; (colloq.) ~ *des jambes,* or *des flûtes,* to walk very fast; to run, to spin along, to leg it.

tricoteu-r, -se (trikɔtœr), s.m.f. Knitter; (s.f.) knitting-machine; *les* ~*ses,* in the time of the Revolution (1789), women who sat and knitted during the trials of the Revolutionary Tribunal.

tric-trac (triktrak), s.m. **1.** Backgammon, backgammon-board; **2.** (obs.) machine for cutting up tobacco.

tricuspide (trikyspid), adj. [L *tres*+ *cuspis*] Tricuspid, three-pointed.

tricycle (trisikl), s.m. [*tri*+Gr. *kuklos*] Tricycle.

tridactyle (tridaktil), adj. [Gr. *tri*+*daktulos*] (zool.) Tridactyl, tridactylous, three-toed.

tride (trid), adj. [Span. *trido*] (rid.) Swift, quick, fleet.

trident (tridɑ̃), s.m. [L *tridens*] Trident; fish-gig, harpoon.

tridenté, -e (tridɑ̃te), adj. Tridentate, three-pronged, three-toothed.

tridi (tridi), s.m. [L *tres*+*dies*] Tridi, third day of French Republican calendar.

triduum, triduo (tridyɔm, tridyo), s.m. [L *triduum*] (Cath. church) Three days' service, prayers lasting three days, triduum.

trièdre (triɛdr), adj. s.m. [*tri*+Gr. *hedra*] (geom.) Trihedral.

triennal, -e, (aux) (triɛnnal), adj. [L *triennalis*] Triennial; **1.** lasting three years; **2.** happening every three years.

triennalité (triɛnnalite), s.f. Triennial, term of three years; three-yearly occurrence.

triennat (triɛnna), s.m. Space of three years; office or function lasting three years.

triennium (triɛnniɔm), s.m. (theol.) Triennium, three years' course of study before entering Holy Orders.

trier (trie), v.a. [etym. dub.] To sort, to sort out; to pick, to pick out, to choose, to select; to cull, to winnow; *des hommes triés,* picked men; (colloq.) *triés sur le volet,* carefully selected.

triérarchie (trierarʃi), s.f. (ant.) Trierarchy; equipment and maintenance of a trireme as a public service.

triérarque (trierark), s.m. [Gr. *triērēs*+ *arkhos*] (Gr. ant.) Trierarch: (*a*) commander of a trireme; (*b*) one obliged to equip a trireme.

trière (triɛr), s.f. [Gr. *triērēs*] Trireme, three-decked ship; syn. TRIRÈME.

trieu-r, -se (triœr), s.m.f. **1.** Sorter, picker; **2.** machine for sorting grain; **3.** machine for separating coke from slag; **4.** machine for sorting wool.

trifacial, -e, (aux) (trifasjal), adj. [L *tri*+ *facies*] (anat.) Trifacial.

trifide (trifid), adj. [L *tri*+*fidus*] (bot., zool.) Trifid, three-cleft.

triflore (triflɔr), adj. [L *tri*+*flos*] (bot.) Triflorous, three-flowered.

trifoliolé, -e (trifɔljɔle), adj. [L *tri*+ *folium*] (bot.) Trifoliate.

trifolium (trifɔliɔm), s.m. (bot.) Cytisus, laburnum.

triforium (trifɔrjɔm), s.m. [etym. dub.] (arch.) Triforium.

trifouiller (trifuje), v.n.a. [dialect. orig.] (colloq.) To rummage, to fumble; to handle, to touch.

trigame (trigam), adj. [Gr. *tri*+*gamos*] Trigamous; (bot.) trigamous. ~, s.m. Trigamist, one having three wives.

trigamie (trigami), s.f. Trigamy.

trigaud, -e (trigo), adj. [etym. dub.] (obs.) Cunning, crafty, artful, tricky; shuffling; dishonest.

trigauder (trigode), v.n.a. (obs.) To shuffle; to cheat, to deceive.

trigauderie (trigodri), s.f. (obs.) Shuffling; trickery.

trigémellaire (triʒemɛllɛr), adj. [f. L *tri*+ *gemellus*] Said of gestation of triplets.

trigéminé, -e (triʒemine), adj. [f. L *tri*+ *geminus*] Arranged in three groups of two.

trigle (trigl), s.m. (ichth.) Gurnard, gurnet.

triglyphe (triglif), s.m. [Gr. *tri*+*gluphē*] (arch.) Triglyph, Doric ornament.

trigone (trigɔn), adj. [Gr. *tri*+*gōnia*] Trigonal, having three angles.

trigonelle (trigɔnɛl), s.f. (bot.) Trigonella.

trigonocéphale (trigɔnɔsefal), s.m. [Gr. *trigōnos*+*kephalē*] (zool.) Trigonocephalus: genus of poisonous serpents.

trigonométrie (trigɔnɔmetri), s.f. [Gr. *trigōnos*+*metron*] Trigonometry; ~ *rectiligne*, plane trigonometry.

trigonométrique (trigɔnɔmetrik), adj. Trigonometrical.

trigonométriquement (trigɔnɔmetrikmɑ̃), adv. Trigonometrically.

trigyne (triʒin), adj. [Gr. *tri*+*gunē*] (bot.) Trigynous, having three styles.

trigynie (triʒini), s.f. (bot.) Trigynia.

trihebdomadaire (triɛbdɔmadɛr), adj. Occurring or published three times weekly.

trijumeau (pl. -x) (triʒymo), adj. s.m. (anat.) Trigeminal.

trilatéral, -e, (aux) (trilateral), adj. [*tri*+ *latéral*] Trilateral, three-sided.

trilingue (trilɛ̃g), adj. [L *tri*+*lingua*] Trilingual.

trilithe (trilit), s.m. [Gr. *tri*+*lithos*] Trilithon, trilith.

trilittère (trilitɛr), adj. [L *tri*+*littera*] Triliteral, three-lettered.

trille (trij), s.m. [It. *trillo*] (mus.) Trill, quaver, shake.

triller (trije), v.n.a. [It. *trillare*] (mus.) To trill, to quiver, to shake.

trillion (triljɔ̃), s.m. Billion, a million millions. ⚠ Not English 'trillion', which = a million million millions, i.e. French *quintillion*; in U.S.A., however, 'trillion' has the same sense as French *trillion*.

trilobé, -e (trilɔbe), adj. [f. *tri*+*lobe*] Trilobate.

trilobites (trilɔbit), s.m.pl. (zool.) Trilobites.

triloculaire (trilɔkylɛr), adj. [L *tri*+ *locula*] (bot.) Trilocular, three-celled.

trilogie (trilɔʒi), s.f. [Gr. *tri*+*logos*] Trilogy.

trilogique (trilɔʒik), adj. Trilogical.

trimard (trimar), s.m. (slang) *Être sur le* ~, to be a tramp, to tramp the country in search of work, to be on the tramp.

trimarder (trimarde), v.n. (slang) To be on the tramp, to trudge.

trimardeur (trimardœr), s.m. (slang) Tramp; (U.S.A.) hobo.

trimbalage, trimbalement (trɛ̃balaʒ, trɛ̃balmɑ̃), s.m. (colloq.) Lugging, dragging about, trailing after one.

trimbaler (trɛ̃bale), v.a. (pop.) To drag about, to lug about, to trail about after one; to cart about; *je ne vais pas ~ trois enfants dans Paris*, I'm not going to lug three children round Paris; **se** ~, v.pr. to knock about.

trimer (trime), v.n. (pop.) To slave, to work very hard, to drudge; to wear oneself out; to toil and moil; ~ *toute une journée*, to slave all day.

trimère (trimɛr), adj. [*tri*+Gr. *meros*] Trimerous, having or consisting of three parts.

trimestre (trimɛstr), s.m. [L *trimestris*] **1.** Three months, quarter (of a year), term, trimester; **2.** quarter's rent; **3.** quarter's pay; *toucher son* ~, to draw one's salary for the quarter.

trimestriel, -le (trimɛstrijɛl), adj. Quarterly; *bulletin* ~, quarterly report.

trimestriellement (trimɛstrijɛlmɑ̃), adv. Quarterly.

trimètre (trimɛtr), s.f. [Gr. *tri*+*metron*] (pros.) Trimeter, verse of six feet. ~, adj. Trimetric.

trimorphe (trimɔrf), adj. [Gr. *trimorphos*] Trimorphic, occurring in crystals of three different forms.

trimoteur (trimɔtœr), adj. s.m. Trimotor.

trin, trine (trɛ̃), adj. [L *trinus*] (obs.) Threefold, trine; (astrol.) trine.

trinervé, -e (trinɛrve), adj. [*tri*+L *nervus*] (bot.) Trinervate.

tringle (trɛ̃gl), s.f. [Dutch *tingel*] **1.** Rod, curtain-rod; **2.** (carp.) measuring-rod; mark; **3.** (arch.) tringle.

tringler (trɛ̃gle), v.a. (carp.) To mark out, to chalk.

tringlette (trɛ̃glɛt), s.f. Small rod.

tringlot (trɛ̃glo), s.m. (mil. slang) Soldier of the French Army Service Corps.

trinitaire (trinitɛr), s.m. Trinitarian: **1.** one who holds the doctrine of the Trinity; **2.** Trinitarian heretic; **3.** member of the Order of the Holy Trinity, Mathurin.

trinité (trinite), s.f. [L *trinitas*] **1.** Trinity; **2.** Trinity Sunday; **3.** (geog.) Trinidad.

trinôme (trinom), s.m. adj. [*tri*+Gr. *nomos*] (alg.) Trinomial.

trinquart (trɛ̃kar), s.m. (naut.) Fishing-boat, (obs.) herring-buss.

trinquer (trɛ̃ke), v.n. [Germ. *trinken*] To clink glasses; (fig.) to hobnob; (slang) to pay for it; to pay the piper; to be the victim; to be thrashed.

trinquet (trɛ̃kɛ), s.m. [It. *trinchetto*] (naut.) Foremast in a lateen vessel.

trinquette (trɛ̃kɛt), s.f. (naut.) Fore stay-sail.

trinqueur (trɛ̃kœr), s.m. Drinker.

trio (trio), s.m. [It. wd] Trio: **1.** three persons; **2.** (mus.) composition for three instruments or voices.

triolet (triɔlɛ), s.m. **1.** (pros.) Triolet; **2.** (mus.) triplet; **3.** (bot.) Dutch clover, white trefoil.

triomphal, -e, (aux) (trijɔ̃fal), adj. Triumphal; (fig.) *faire dans le salon une entrée triomphale*, to make a triumphal entry into the drawing-room.

triomphalement (trijɔ̃falmɑ̃), adv. Triumphantly, in triumph.

triomphant, -e (trijɔ̃fɑ̃), p. adj. **1.** Triumphant, victorious; *l'Église triomphante*, the Church triumphant; **2.** decisive; **3.** (fig.) triumphant; *un air triomphant*, a triumphant air.

triomphat-eur, -rice (trijɔ̃fatœr), adj. Triumphant, having triumphed. ~, s.m.f. Triumpher; **1.** Roman general honoured with a triumph; **2.** conqueror, victor.

triomphe (trijɔ̃f), s.m. [L *triumphus*] **1.** Triumph; *char de* ~, *arc de* ~, triumphal car, arch; victory; *les* ~*s de Napoléon*, the victories of Napoleon; success, advantage; *assister au* ~ *de quelqu'un*, to witness a person's triumph; (fig.) height, acme; *c'est le* ~ *du courage que de se vaincre soi-même*, it is the acme of courage to conquer oneself; **2.** trump, kind of card-game.

triompher (trijɔ̃fe), v.n. To triumph; to vanquish, to conquer; ~ *de tous ses ennemis*, to vanquish or overcome all one's enemies; ~ *de*, to surmount, to master; ~ *de ses passions*, to master one's passions; to boast, to glory (in), to exult (in); *au lieu d'avoir du remords de sa mauvaise action, il triomphe*, instead of repenting, he boasts of his evil doings; to excel; *il triomphe dans l'art de la peinture*, he excels in painting.

tripaille (tripɑj), s.f. (fam.) Garbage, offal; tripe.

tripang, trépang (tripɑ̃, trepɑ̃), s.m. [Malay wd] (zool.) Trepang, sea-cucumber, bêche-de-mer.

triparti, -e or **-ite** (triparti), adj. [*tri*+*parti*] Tripartite, divided into three parts.

tripartition (tripartisjɔ̃), s.f. Tripartition.

tripe (trip), s.f. (usually pl.) [etym. dub.] **1.** Tripe, paunch; *rendre tripes et boyaux*, to bring up one's inside, to be violently sick; **2.** ~ *de velours*, velveteen. ⚠ Not 'tripe' in the sense of *fichaise*.

tripenné, -e (tripɛnne), adj. [*tri*+L *penna*] (bot.) Tripinnate.

triperie (tripri), s.f. Tripe-shop; business of selling tripe.

tripétale, tripétalé, -e (tripetal, tripetale), adj. (bot.) Tripetalous.

tripette (tripɛt), s.f. Small tripe; (colloq.) *ça ne vaut pas* ~, that 's not worth a fig, a straw, a halfpenny.

triphtongue (triftɔ̃g), adj. s.f. [*tri*+Gr. *phthoggos*] Triphthong.

triphylle (trifil), adj. Triphyllous.

tripi-er, -ère (tripje), s.m.f. Tripe-seller, tripeman.

triplan (triplɑ̃), s.m. (aeron.) Triplane.

triple (tripl), adj. [L *triplus*] Triple, treble, threefold; (mus.) ~ *croche*, demi-semiquaver; *un* ~ *coquin*, an arrant rogue, a confirmed scoundrel, a double-dyed villain.

triple (tripl), s.m. Triple, treble; triplicate; *la lettre a été faite en* ~, the letter was written in triplicate.

triplement (tripləmɑ̃), s.m. Tripling, trebling, triplicating. ~, adv. Triply, trebly.

tripler (triple), v.a. To triple, to treble, to triplicate; ~, v.n. to treble, to increase threefold; *la population a triplé*, the population has increased threefold.

triplet (triplɛ), s.m. Triplet; (opt.) combination of three lenses; (arch.) triple lancet window; (naut.) three end links of a chain cable. ⚠ Not (mus.) 'triplet', which = *triolet*, nor 'triplet' in the sense of one of three children born at a birth, which = *jumeau*.

tripleur (triplœr), s.m. Machine used to treble wires.

triplicata (triplikata), s.m. invar. [L *triplicatus*] Triplicate, third copy.

triplice (triplis), s.f. Triplice, triple alliance.

triplicité (triplisite), s.f. [L *triplicitas*] Triplicity, threefoldness; *la* ~ *de Dieu*, the threefold Person of God, the triple Godhead.

triplique (triplik), s.f. (law) Rebutter, surrejoinder.

tripoli (tripoli), s.m. [geog. orig.] Tripoli, rotten-stone.

triporteur (tripɔrtœr), s.m. [*tri*+*porteur*] Tricycle carrier (for goods).

tripot (tripo), s.m. Gambling-house; house of ill repute, gambling-hell.

tripotage (tripɔtaʒ), s.m. Pawing, handling, caressing; mess, medley, jumble; jobbing, jobbery; intrigue, underhand dealing; *il doit y avoir du* ~ *là-dedans*, there must be some underhand dealing in that affair.

tripotée (tripɔte), s.f. (colloq.) **1.** Thrashing, beating, drubbing, wigging, dressing down; **2.** ~ *d'enfants*, mob of children.

tripoter (tripote), v.a. To paw, to handle, to caress, to play with; (fig.) to meddle with, to tamper with, to mess about; to speculate with; ~ *l'argent des autres*, to speculate with other people's money; ~, v.n. to make a mess; to make mischief; to speculate (in); ~ *sur les blés*, to speculate in corn.

tripoteu-r, -se (tripotœr), s.m.f. Meddler, mischief-maker, intriguer; ~ *d'affaires*, stock-jobber.

triptyque (triptik), s.m. [Gr. *triptukhos*] (paint.) Triptych.

trique (trik), s.f. [etym. dub.] Cudgel, stick, bludgeon.

triqueballe (trikbal), s.m. (artill.) Truck.

trique-madame (trikmadam), s.f. (bot.) White stonecrop; syn. ORPIN BLANC.

triquer (trike), v.a. **1.** To cudgel, to beat; **2.** (techn.) to sort, to range (timber).

triquet (trikɛ), s.m. **1.** A kind of bat for the game of *paume*; **2.** trestle, double ladder, pair of steps.

triquetrac (triktrak), s.m. Clatter, clattering; syn. TRIC-TRAC.

triquètre (trikɛtr), adj. [L *triquetrus*] Triquetrous, three-sided. ~, s.f. (ant.) Triangular ornament formed of three interlaced arcs or lobes.

triqueur (trikœr), s.m. adj. (Man) who sorts logs that have been floated downstream.

trirectangle (trirɛkɑ̃gl), adj. (trigon.) Trirectangular, having three right angles.

trirème (trirɛm), s.f. [L *triremis*] Trireme; syn. TRIÈRE.

trirote (trirɔt), s.f. [L *tri+rota*] Three-wheeled chair, invalid chair, bath-chair.

trisagion (trizaʒjɔ̃), s.m. [Gr. *tris+hagios*] (Cath. liturg.) Trisagion, ter sanctus (hymn).

trisaïeul, -e (trizajœl), s.m.f. Great-great-grandfather or -grandmother.

trisannuel, -le (trizanɥɛl), adj. [f. L *tres+annus*] Triennial; (*a*) lasting three years, (*b*) happening every three years.

trisect-eur, -rice (trisɛktœr), adj. Trisecting.

trisection (trisɛksjɔ̃), s.f. (geom.) Trisection.

trisépale (trisepal), adj. (bot.) Trisepalous, having three sepals.

triséquer (triseke), v.a. [*tri+*L *secare*] (geom.) To trisect.

trismégiste (trismeʒist), adj. [Gr. *tris+megistos*] (myth.) Trismegistus.

trismus, trisme (trismys, trism), s.m. [Gr. *trismos*] (pathol.) Trismus, lockjaw.

trisoc (trisɔk), s.m. Plough with three shares.

trisperme (trispɛrm), adj. (bot.) Trispermous.

trisse (tris), s.f. (naut.) Tackle for bowsing up guns.

trisser[1] (trise), v.n. [onom.] To twitter (of swallows).

trisser[2] (trise) v.a. [f. *tri*] To encore a second time.

triste (trist), adj. [L *tristis*] Sad, sorrowful, mournful, glum, dejected, melancholy, woebegone; *il est ~ comme un bonnet de nuit*, he is as dull as ditchwater; calamitous, painful, deplorable, lamentable; *mon ~ devoir*, my painful duty; dull, dark, obscure, dreary, dismal; *la maison est bien ~*, the house is very dismal; poor, paltry, sorry (of persons); *vous faites là un ~ personnage*, you cut a sorry figure; *faire un ~ repas*, to make a poor meal.

tristement (tristəmɑ̃), adv. Sadly, gloomily, mournfully; poorly, sorrily.

tristesse (tristɛs), s.f. Sadness, melancholy, sorrow; dreariness, gloom.

trisyllabe, trissyllabe (trisilab), s.m. Trisyllable; word consisting of three syllables. ~, adj. Trisyllabic.

trisyllabique, trissyllabique (trisilabik), adj. Trisyllabic.

triton[1] (tritɔ̃), s.m. [Gr. myth. prop. n. *Tritōn*] (Gr. myth.) Triton; (zool.) triton.

triton[2] (tritɔ̃), s.m. [f. Gr. *tritonos*] (mus.) Tritone, interval of three whole tones.

tritonien, -ne (tritonjɛ̃), adj. (min.) Tritonian (applied to soil containing fossil remains of marine animals).

triturable (trityrabl), adj. Triturable.

triturateur (trityratœr), s.m. Triturator; instrument or apparatus for triturating.

trituration (trityra'sjɔ̃), s.f. Trituration; mastication.

triture (trityr), s.f. (obs.) Knowledge, practice, experience, use, knack (of affairs); *avoir la ~ des affaires*, to be experienced in business.

triturer (trityre), v.a. [L *triturare*] To triturate, to rub or grind to a fine powder, to masticate, to handle, to paw, to mix, to work.

triumvir (triɔmvir), s.m. [L *trium+vir*] (Rom. hist.) Triumvir.

triumviral, -e, (aux) (triɔmviral), adj. (Rom. hist.) Triumviral.

triumvirat (triɔmvira), s.m. (Rom. hist.) Triumvirate.

trivial, -e, (aux) (trivjal), adj. [L *trivialis*] Trivial, trifling; vulgar; trite, hackneyed; *une phrase ~e*, a hackneyed expression. ~, s.m. The trivial, triviality, trivialness.

trivialement (trivjalmɑ̃), adv. Trivially, tritely, vulgarly.

trivialiser (trivjalize), v.a. To make trivial.

trivialité (trivjalite), s.f. Triviality, trivialness, vulgarity, triteness, commonness; trivial thing, truism.

trivium (trivjɔm), s.m. [*tri+*L *via*] Trivium: the three arts of grammar, logic, and rhetoric.

troc (trɔk), s.m. [f. *troquer*] Truck, exchange, barter, swap; ~ *pour* ~, a Roland for an Oliver, a quid pro quo.

trocart, trois-quarts (trɔkar, trwɑ-kar), s.m. [*trois*+*quarts*] (surg.) Trocar.

trochaïque (trɔkaik), adj. s.m. Trochaic.

trochanter (trɔkɑ̃tɛr), s.m. [Gr. *trokhantēr*] (anat.) Trochanter.

trochantérien, -ne (trɔkɑ̃terjɛ̃), adj. Trochanterian.

troche (trɔʃ), s.f. [f. LL *traduce*] Bunch, tuft, bundle; *une* ~ *d'oignons*, a bunch of onions; ~, s.f.pl. fumet, dung (of deer, &c.). ⚠ Not 'troche', which = *pastille médicinale* and *trochure*.

trochée (trɔʃe), s.m. [Gr. *trokhaios*] (pros.) Trochee; metrical foot consisting of a long followed by a short syllable.

trochée (trɔʃe), s.f. Bunch of leaves sprouting from a tree-stump.

trochet (trɔʃɛ), s.m. Cluster (of fruit or flowers); cooper's block.

trochile, trochilus (trɔkil, trɔkilys), s.m. (ornith.) Trochilus (humming-bird); syn. COLIBRI.

trochilidés (trɔkilide), s.m.pl. (ornith.) Trochilidae, humming-birds.

trochisque (trɔʃisk), s.m. [Gr. *trokhiskos*] (bot.) Genus of cylindrical water-weeds; (pharm.) troche, lozenge.

trochlée (trɔkle), s.f. [L *trochlea*, Gr. *trokhilia*] (anat.) Trochlea.

trochoïde (trɔkoid), s.f. [Gr. *trokhoeidēs*] (anat., geom.) Trochoid.

trochure (trɔʃyr), s.f. (hunt.) Troche, fourth antler of deer.

troène (troɛn), s.m. [Germ. orig.] (bot.) Privet.

troglodyte (trɔglɔdit), s.m. [Gr. *trōglē*+ *duo*] Troglodyte; cave-dweller; (ornith.) kind of wren.

troglodytique (trɔglɔditik), adj. Troglodytic.

trogne (trɔɲ), s.f. [Celt. orig.] (pop.) Face, phiz, mug, rubicund face.

trognon (trɔɲɔ̃), s.m. [f. *trogne*] Core (of apple or pear); stalk (of cabbage); *cela ne vaut pas un* ~ *de chou*, that 's not worth a pin's head; (vulg.) small-sized person; also used as a (very vulg.) term of endearment.

trois (trwɑ), num. adj. [L *tres*] Three; third; *les* ~ *quarts du temps*, most of the time; (arith.) *règle de* ~, the rule of three; (mus.) ~*-deux*, three-two time, $\frac{3}{2}$; ~*-huit*, three-eight time, $\frac{3}{8}$; ~*-six*, alcohol (the strength of which is such that 3 parts of it mixed with 3 parts of water give 6 parts ordinary *eau de vie*); ~*-étoiles*, X, *Monsieur* ~*-étoiles*, Mr. Thingumbob; ~*-mâts*, ~*-ponts*, s.m. three-master, three-decker. ~, s.m. Three; *le* ~ *de trèfle*, the three of clubs; ~ *pour cent*, three per cent.; the third; *c'est aujourd'hui le* ~, to-day is the third.

troisième (trwɑzjɛm), num. ord. adj. Third. ~, s.m.f. Third; *habiter au* ~, to live on the third floor; *faire sa* ~, to be in the third form; *voyager en* ~, to travel third (class).

troisièmement (trwɑzjɛməmɑ̃), adv. Thirdly.

trôle (trol), s.f. [f. *trôler*] **1.** Furniture-hawking; *ouvrier à la* ~, furniture-hawker; **2.** trawling; *filet à la* ~, trawl, trawl-net.

trôler (trole), v.a. [Germ. *trollen*] To lead about, to drag about for sale; ~, v.n. to stroll, to wander about.

trôleur (trolœr), s.m. Furniture-hawker; vagabond; trawler.

troll (trɔl), s.m. [Scand. myth.] Troll, gnome.

trolle (trɔl), s.f. (hunt.) Unleashing hounds to allow them to quest for game.

trolley (trɔlɛ), s.m. [Engl. wd] Trolley (-pole, -wheel). ⚠ In French *trolley* has only the sense of pulley used for conveying current in electric street railway or tram-car; it is not used like English 'trolley' for a kind of truck that can be tilted, or costermonger's cart, or low truck worked by a hand-lever along rails.

trombe (trɔ̃b), s.f. [It. *tromba*] Waterspout; water-blowing machine; ~ *de vent*, whirlwind; (fig.) *arriver en* ~, to arrive like a whirlwind.

trombidion (trɔ̃bidjɔ̃), s.m. (ent.) Species of gnat, harvest-bug.

trombine (trɔ̃bin), s.f. (pop.) Mug, phiz, nut, face.

tromblon (trɔ̃blɔ̃), s.m. Blunderbuss; (pop.) bell-crowned hat.

trombone (trɔ̃bɔn), s.m. [It. wd] (mus.) Trombone.

tromboniste (trɔ̃bɔnist), s.m. (mus.) Trombone-player.

trompe (trɔ̃p), s.f. [OHG *trumpa*, It. *tromba*] **1.** Trumpet, horn, hunting-horn; *publier une chose à son de* ~, to proclaim something far and wide; **2.** Jew's-harp; **3.** proboscis (of insects), trunk (of elephants); **4.** blast-engine; ~ *à vide*, air-pump; **5.** (arch.) pendentive; **6.** (anat.) tube; ~ *d'Eustache*, Eustachian tube; ~ *de Fallope*, Fallopian tube.

trompe-la-mort (trɔ̃plamɔr), s.m.f. invar. (colloq.) One who has cheated death; person desperately ill who recovers.

trompe-l'œil (trɔ̃plœj), s.m. invar. (paint.) Deceptive painting of still life; (fig.) deception, sham.

tromper (trɔ̃pe), v.a. [etym. dub.] To deceive, to delude, to cheat, to take in; to abuse; to disappoint; to betray; to elude; to baffle; to divert, to beguile; *cette femme trompe son mari*, this woman is unfaithful to her husband; *trompons notre douleur*, let us beguile our grief; ~ *le temps*, to while away the time; **se** ~, v.pr. to mistake, to be mistaken, to make a mistake; to err; to deceive each other; *se ~ de chemin,* to take the wrong road; *je puis me ~,* I may be mistaken; *tout le monde peut se ~,* a good marksman may miss, everybody is liable to make mistakes; *il n'y a que celui qui ne fait rien qui ne se trompe pas,* who never climbed never fell; only those who never try never fail; *on peut se ~ sans pécher,* a mistake is not a crime; *c'est en quoi vous vous trompez,* that is where you are wrong; *à s'y ~,* quite alike; resembling each other.

tromperie (trɔ̃pri), s.f. Deceit, cheat, fraud, imposture; delusion, illusion; *il était passé maître en fait de ~,* he was a master cheat.

trompeter (trɔ̃pɛte), v.n. To sound the trumpet; to scream (of the eagle); ~, v.a. to summon, to proclaim by trumpet; to proclaim, to publish, to spread abroad; to divulge; *on avait recommandé le secret sur cette affaire, mais il a été la ~ partout,* he had been asked to keep the matter a secret, but he told it to everybody.

trompeteur (trɔ̃pɛtœr), s.m. Trumpeter; (anat.) buccinator.

trompette (trɔ̃pɛt), s.f. [f. *trompe*] Trumpet, bugle; *déloger sans tambour ni ~,* to slip away quietly; to do a moonlight flit; *un nez en ~,* a turned-up nose; (iron.) *emboucher la ~,* to talk in heroic style, *~ marine, parlante,* megaphone, speaking-trumpet; (fig.) gossip, tell-tale; *c'est la ~ du quartier,* she is the gossip of the neighbourhood; (zool.) trumpet-shell; (ichth.) trumpet-fish; (ornith.) trumpeter; ~, s.m. (mil.) trumpeter; *~-major,* trumpet-major.

trompettiste (trɔ̃pɛtist), s.m. Trumpeter.

trompeu-r, -se (trɔ̃pœr), adj. Deceptive; deceitful; delusive, false, misleading. ~, s.m. Deceiver, cheat; impostor; betrayer; *le ~ trompé,* the biter bit; *à ~ ~ et demi,* diamond cut diamond; set a thief to catch a thief.

trompeusement (trɔ̃pœzmɑ̃), adv. Deceptively; deceitfully.

trompillon (trɔ̃pijɔ̃), s.m. (arch.) Pendentive; trompille.

tronc (trɔ̃), s.m. [L *truncus*] Trunk; stock, parent stock; poor-box, alms-box; contribution-box; (arch.) drum; broken shaft (of column); (geom.) frustum (of cone or pyramid). ⚠ Engl. 'trunk' also = *malle, coffre.*

troncature (trɔ̃katyr), s.f. [f. L *truncare*] Truncation.

tronce, tronche (trɔ̃s, trɔ̃ʃ), s.f. [f. *tronc*] Stump (of a tree).

tronchet (trɔ̃ʃɛ), s.m. Block, cooper's block.

tronçon (trɔ̃sɔ̃), s.m. [f. *tronc*] Fragment, stump, broken piece; (railw.) section, portion; base (of horse's tail); piece, cut (of meat, fish); *~ de milieu,* middle cut.

tronçonnement (trɔ̃sɔnmɑ̃), s.m. Cutting up.

tronçonner (trɔ̃sɔne), v.a. To cut into pieces.

trône (tron), s.m. [Gr. *thronos*] Throne; (fig.) sovereign power; the sovereign; (pl.) choir of angels; *appeler quelqu'un au ~,* to call some one to the throne; *monter sur le ~,* to ascend the throne; *placer sur le ~,* to place on the throne; *discours du ~,* speech from the Throne, the King's Speech.

trôner (trone), v.n. To sit on a throne or as on a throne; to reign, to bear sway, to be supreme; (fig.) to lord it (over), to domineer.

tronqué, -e (trɔ̃ke), p. adj. Truncated, cut off, cut short; *colonne ~e,* broken column; mutilated, maimed; *une phrase ~e,* a mutilated phrase; (bot.) truncate.

tronquer (trɔ̃ke), v.a. [L *truncare*] To truncate, to cut off, to lop off; to mutilate, to maim; to garble, to mangle; *~ un passage,* to mutilate a passage.

trop (tro), adv. [It. *troppo*] Too; too much, too much (*de,* of, of a); too many; too far; too high; too long; too often; too well; over; very; much, very much; very well; *~ peu,* too little; too few; not enough; *l'assistance est ~ peu nombreuse,* the audience is too small; *de~,* too much, too many; superfluous; unwanted; *être de ~,* to be in the way, to intrude; *par ~,* rather too, rather too much; *c'est par ~ exiger,* that is being over-exacting; *pas ~,* not too much, not too many; not over, not very; *je ne m'y fierais pas ~,* I would not trust to it; *il ne va pas ~ bien,* he is not very well, overwell; *qui ~ embrasse, mal étreint,* grasp all, lose all; *qui dit ~, ne dit rien,* he who would prove too much, proves nothing; *~ est ~,* enough is as good as a feast; *je ne sais ~,* I hardly know.

trop (tro), s.m. Excess; exuberance; superfluity.

trope (trɔp), s.m. [Gr. *tropos*] (rhet.) Trope.

trophée (trɔfe), s.m. [Gr. *tropaion*] Trophy; *faire ~ de quelque chose,* to glory in something.

trophique (trɔfik), adj. [Gr. *trophikos*] Trophic; nourishing, nutritious.

trophologie (trɔfɔlɔʒi), s.f. [Gr. *trophē* + *logos*] Trophology, science of nutrition.

trophonévrose (trɔfɔnevroz), s.f. (med.) Trophoneurosis.

tropical, -e, (aux) (trɔpikal), adj. Tropical.

tropique (trɔpik), s.m. [Gr. *tropikos*] (geog., astr.) Tropic; *le ~ du Cancer,* the tropic of Cancer; *le ~ du Capricorne,* the tropic of Capricorn; pl. the tropics.

tropique (trɔpik), adj. (bot.) Diurnal; (astr.) *année ~,* tropical year.

tropologie (trɔpɔlɔʒi), s.f. [f. Gr. *tropos*] (rhet.) Tropology.

tropologique (trɔpɔlɔʒik), adj. Tropological.
trop-plein (troplɛ̃), s.m. Overflow, waste; surplus, overplus, excess; *tuyau de* ~, waste-pipe.
troque (trɔk), s.f. [f. *troquer*] Truck, barter, exchange; syn. TROC.
troquer (trɔke), v.a. [etym. dub.] To truck, to barter, to exchange, to swap; ~ *son cheval borgne contre un aveugle*, to change for the worse.
troqueu-r, -se (trɔkœr), s.m.f. Barterer.
trot (tro), s.m. Trot (of a horse); *avoir le* ~ *dur*, to trot hard, to be a hard trotter; *aller au* ~, to trot; *au grand* ~, at full trot; *au petit* ~, at a jog-trot; *prendre le* ~, *se mettre au* ~, to begin to trot, to fall into a trot; (fig.) *mener une affaire au* ~, to do it quickly, to get on with it; *allons, au* ~*!*, quick now!
trottable (trɔtabl), adj. *Chemin* ~, path where one can trot.
trottade (trɔtad), s.f. Short ride.
trotte (trɔt), s.f. Trot, run, walk, step, way; *tout d'une* ~, without stopping; *faire une bonne* ~, to go for a good walk, to go a long way; *il y a une bonne* ~ *jusque chez vous*, it is a good step to your house.
trotte-menu (trɔtməny), adj. invar. Small-trotting; that trots with little steps; *la gent* ~, rats and mice.
trotter (trɔte), v.n. [OHG *trotton*] To trot; to run about, to toddle; *on entendrait une souris* ~, one could hear a pin drop; *il a trotté toute la journée*, he has been running about all day; *cet air me trotte par* (*dans*) *la tête*, that tune keeps running in my head; (slang) **se** ~, v.pr. to make off, to skedaddle.
trotteu-r, -se (trɔtœr), s.m.f. Trotter; ~*se*, s.f. second-hand (of a watch, &c.). ~, adj. Trotting; *jupe* ~ or *trotteuse*, walking-skirt.
trottin (trɔtɛ̃), s.m. Errand-girl; (though masc. the word is now used only of girls).
trottiner (trɔtine), v.n. To jog along, to go at a jog-trot.
trottinette (trɔtinɛt), s.f. Scooter (toy).
trotting (trɔtiŋ), s.m. [Engl. wd] Breeding of trotters.
trottoir (trɔtwar), s.m. Pavement, footway, footpath; *faire le* ~, to walk the streets (as a prostitute).
trou (pl. **-s**) (tru), s.m. [LL *traucum*] Hole; gap; cave; opening, orifice, mouth (of a bottle); eye (of a needle); pot-hole; hiding-place; pit (in the skin); empty place, vacuum; *le* ~ *de la serrure, de la porte*, keyhole; ~ *d'homme*, manhole; (naut.) ~ *du chat*, lubber's hole; *boucher un* ~, to stop up a hole; (fig.) to pay a debt; *faire son* ~, to get on in the world; *faire un* ~ *pour en boucher un autre*, to rob Peter to pay Paul; *un petit* ~ *pas cher*, a cheap, quiet holiday resort; *mettre la pièce à côté du* ~, to use the wrong means, to set about it the wrong way; *faire un* ~ *à la lune*, to shoot the moon, to fly from one's creditors; *boire comme un* ~, to drink like a fish; *il est logé dans un* ~, he lives in a hovel; *à chaque* ~ *une cheville*, a balm for every sore.
troubadour (trubadur), s.m. [Provenç. *trobador*] Troubadour.
troublant, -e (trublɑ̃), p. adj. Troubling, disquieting, disturbing; alluring.
trouble (trubl), s.m. [f. L *turba*] Disorder, disturbance, confusion; misunderstanding, dissension, disagreement, dispute, quarrel; perplexity, uneasiness; ~*s* (pl.), broils, commotions, troubles, disturbances; *susciter des* ~*s*, to excite disturbances. ⚠ In English 'trouble' has usually a much stronger sense than French *trouble*; the French equivalents would be *tourment, malheur, tribulation, sérieux ennui*.
trouble (trubl), adj. Troubled; turbid; muddy, thick; foul; dim; dull; obscure; confused; cloudy, of a dubious character or quality, overcast, hazy, foggy; *l'eau est* ~, the water is muddy, cloudy; *avoir la vue* ~, to be dim-sighted, near-sighted; *pêcher en eau* ~, to fish in troubled waters; to deal in shady undertakings.
trouble-fête (trubləfɛt), s.m. invar. Kill-joy, spoil-sport, mar-joy, damper, wet blanket; untoward event.
troubler (truble), v.a. To stir up, to disturb; to make thick, to make muddy; to muddle; to turn; to disturb, to confuse, to disorder, to agitate; to perplex, to disconcert, to unsettle; to unhinge; to trouble (⚠ see TROUBLE); to interrupt, to break in upon; to destroy the harmony of, to bring discord into; to ruffle, to annoy; to discompose; to dim, to dull; ~ *le royaume*, to bring discord into the kingdom; *cela trouble la digestion*, that upsets the digestion; ~ *une fête*, to disturb a feast; ~ *la retraite d'une armée*, to harass a retreating army; ~ *quelqu'un dans la possession d'un bien*, to contest a person's right to a thing; **se** ~, v.pr. to be confused, to be disconcerted; to become agitated; to be foggy, to become overcast, cloudy; to grow dim; to grow muddy, thick; to turn sour; *sa mémoire se trouble*, his memory fails him; *ma vue se trouble*, my sight is growing dim; *le temps commence à se* ~, it is getting cloudy, or overcast.
trouée (true), s.f. Opening, gap, breach; pass; *faire sa* ~, to cut one's way.
trouer (true), v.a. To make a hole in, to bore, to pierce; to perforate.
troufignon (trufiɲɔ̃), s.m. (colloq.) Stump; syn. TROGNON.
trouille (truj), s.f. (slang) Funk, fear, panic; *avoir la* ~, to be in a blue funk, to have an attack of cold feet.

trouilloter (trujɔte), v.n. (slang) To stink; (very vulg.) ~ *du goulot*, to have a foul breath.
trou-madame (trumadam), s.m. Pigeon-hole; game played with ivory balls rolled into numbered compartments.
troupe (trup), s.f. [Germ. orig. or f. LL *troppus*?] Troop, band, company; set, gang, crew; crowd, number; force, soldiers, soldiery; herd, drove (of animals); flock, flight (of birds); shoal (of fish); *une* ~ *d'enfants*, a band of children; *une* ~ *de comédiens*, a theatrical company; *cet officier conduit bien sa* ~, that officer leads his soldiers well; ~*s de mer*, sea-forces; ~*s de terre*, land-forces; *une* ~ *d'oies*, a flock of geese; *aller en* ~, to herd together.
troupeau (pl. **-x**) (trupo), s.m. [f. *troupe*] **1.** Herd, drove, flock (of animals); flock (of birds); *un* ~ *de bétail*, a drove of cattle; *garder les* ~*x*, to mind the herds; to guard the flocks; **2.** (fig.) flock; *le* ~ *de Jésus Christ*, the flock of Christ; **3.** (fig.) herd, set, gang; *un* ~ *d'ignorants*, an ignorant crew, a set of ignoramuses.
troupiale (trupjal), s.m. (ornith.) Troop-bird, troopial.
troupier (trupje), s.m. (fam.) Soldier, private, Tommy Atkins; *un vieux* ~, an old campaigner. ⚠ Not 'trooper', which = *soldat de cavalerie* and *cheval de troupe*.
troussage (trusaʒ), s.m. Trussing.
trousse (trus), s.f. Truss, bundle; ~ *de fourrage*, truss of fodder; case for razors, toilet articles; (surg.) case of instruments; (obs.) quiver; ~**s**, pl. breeches, trunk-hose; *je suis à ses* ~*s*, I am at his heels. ⚠ Not 'truss' in the sense of supporting structure or framework of roof, bridge, &c., which = *charpente, armature*; nor in the sense of a surgical appliance serving as a support in cases of rupture, which = *bandage herniaire*.
troussé, -e (truse), p. adj. Tucked up, turned up; trussed up, packed up; (fam.) made, set up, disposed; *un repas bien* ~, a well-cooked meal; *un cheval bien* ~, a well-set horse; turned; *un compliment bien* ~, a well-turned compliment.
trousseau (pl. **-x**) (truso), s.m. [f. *trousse*] Bunch (of keys); outfit, kit; trousseau, wedding outfit; (anat.) fasciculus.
trousse-étriers (trusetrie), s.m. invar. Stirrup-leather.
trousse-galant (trusgalɑ̃), s.m. (obs.) Cholera.
trousse-queue (truskø), s.m. invar. Crupper; cup dock.
troussequin, trusquin (truskɛ̃, tryskɛ̃), s.m. [f. Dutch orig.] Cantle (of saddle); (techn.) mortise-gauge, beam-compass.
troussequiner (truskine), v.a. See TRUSQUINER.
trousser (truse), v.a. [f. LL *torciare*, f. L *torquere*] To tuck up, to pin up, to turn up; to tie up, to pack up; (cook.) to truss (a fowl); (fig.) to dispatch, to expedite (an affair, business); ~ *de la besogne*, to get through a good deal of work; (fig.) to carry off, to kill; *cette maladie l'a troussé en quelques jours*, the illness carried him off in a few days; ~ *une fille*, to paw a girl about; **se** ~, v.pr. to tuck up one's dress.
troussis (trusi), s.m. invar. Tuck (in a garment).
trouvable (truvabl), adj. Findable, that can be found, to be found.
trouvaille (truvɑj), s.f. Thing found by chance; godsend, find, windfall, lucky hit; prize; discovery, invention; *faire une* ~, to make a discovery, to have a windfall.
trouvé, -e (truve), p. adj. Found; *enfant* ~, foundling; *bien* ~, happy, felicitous.
trouver (truve), v.a. [orig. dub.] **1.** To find, to discover, to meet with, to hit upon; to find out, to detect; to get; **2.** to think, to deem, to judge, to like; **3.** to contrive, to manage; *j'ai trouvé à propos de*, I found it suited the purpose to, I found it suitable to; ~ *visage de bois*, to find nobody at home; ~ *la pie au nid*, to find a mare's nest; ~ *chaussure à son pied*, to find exactly what suits one; ~ *à qui parler*, ~ *son maître*, to meet one's match; ~ *la mort*, to meet one's death; ~ *grâce aux yeux de quelqu'un*, to find favour in somebody's eyes; *aller* ~, *venir* ~, to go to, to go and see, to come to; *comment trouvez-vous ça?*, how do you like it?; *je lui trouve bon visage*, I think he looks well; *où avez-vous trouvé cela?*, what made you think of that?, what put that into your head?; ~ *à dire*, ~ *à redire*, to find fault with; *il trouve toujours à placer son mot*, he always manages to have his say; ~ *beau*, to admire; ~ *bon*, to think fit; ~ *mauvais*, to blame, to dislike, to be displeased with; (colloq.) *je la trouve mauvaise*, I don't like it at all; *vous trouvez?*, do you think so?; **se** ~, v.pr. to meet, to meet with; to be present, to be; to happen to be, to chance to be; to be found, to be found to be, to prove, to turn out; to feel, to feel oneself; *il s'est trouvé à cette bataille*, he was present at that battle; *il s'est trouvé là quand je suis arrivé*, he chanced to be there when I arrived; *la nouvelle s'est trouvée fausse*, the news turned out to be false; *se* ~ *bien*, to feel well; *se* ~ *mal*, to feel ill, to faint; *comment vous trouvez-vous aujourd'hui?*, how are you to-day?; *cela se trouve bien*, that is lucky; *je me trouve bien de la campagne*, I am all the better for being in the country; (impers.) to be, to exist; to be found; to happen, to chance, to appear; *il ne se trouva personne assez courageux pour le*

faire, there was nobody brave enough to do it; *il se trouve qu'il y a un train à 5 heures*, there happens to be a train at 5 o'clock.

trouvère (truvɛr) [f. OF *trovere*] Trouvère; medieval poet of northern France.

trouveu-r, -se (truvœr), s.m. Discoverer, finder; inventor.

troyen, -ne (trwajɛ̃), adj. s.m.f. [f. *Troie*] Trojan.

truand, -e (tryɑ̃), s.m.f. [Celt. orig.] Ribald, vagrant, vagabond, tramp. ⚠ Not usually 'truant', which is less pej. than *truand*; to play truant = *faire l'école buissonnière*.

truandaille (tryɑ̃dɑj), s.f. (colloq., collect.) Vagrants, ribald crew.

truander (tryɑ̃de), v.n. (obs.) To beg.

truanderie (tryɑ̃dri), s.f. Vagrancy, begging; ribaldry.

truble (trybl), s.f. [L *tribulus*] (fish.) Hoop-net.

trubleau (pl. **-x**) (tryblo), s.m. (fish.) Small hoop-net.

truc[1] (tryk), s.m. [Gasc. *truca*] Knack, dodge, trick; secret; craft, ingenuity, cunning; (theatr.) machinery, trap; (slang) thing, thingumbob; (slang) *connaître le* ~, to be in the know, to be knowing; (slang) *débiner le* ~, to let out the secret, to let the cat out of the bag.

truc[2] **truck** (tryk), s.m. [Engl. *truck*] Truck, trolley.

trucage, truquage (trykaʒ), s.m. (pop.) Faking, trickery.

truchement, trucheman (tryʃmɑ̃), s.m. [Arab. *turjāmān*] Interpreter (in the East); dragoman; (fig.) interpreter, spokesman; means, intermediary.

truculence (trykylɑ̃s), s.f. Truculence, truculency.

truculent, -e (trykylɑ̃), adj. [L *truculentus*] Truculent.

truelle (tryɛl), s.f. [f. L *trulla*] Trowel; fish-slice, fish-carver; (fig.) building; *aimer la* ~, to be fond of building; ~ *à brique*, bricklayer's trowel; ~ *transplantoir*, gardener's trowel.

truellée (tryɛle), s.f. Trowelful.

truffe (tryf), s.f. [f. L *tuber*] **1.** Truffle; **2.** dog's nose.

truffer (tryfe), v.a. To stuff or garnish with truffles.

trufficult-eur, -rice (tryfikyltœr), s.m.f. One who cultivates or grows truffles.

trufficulture (tryfikyltyr), s.f. Culture, growing of truffles.

truffi-er, -ère (tryfje), adj. Belonging to, producing truffles.

truffière (tryfjɛr), s.f. Truffle-ground.

truie (trɥi), s.f. [LL *troja*] (zool.) Sow, female pig; (ichth.) kind of fish.

truisme (trɥism), s.m. [Engl. *truism*] Truism.

truite (trɥit), s.f. [L *trutta*] (ichth.) Trout; ~ *saumonée*, salmon-trout.

truité, -e (trɥite), adj. Trout-coloured; red-spotted, red-speckled; spotted, speckled, mottled; *porcelaine* ~*e*, crackled porcelain; *fonte* ~*e*, white and grey pig-iron.

trullisation (tryliza'sjɔ̃), s.f. [f. L *trulla*] (build.) Trowelling, pargeting.

trumeau (pl. **-x**) (trymo), s.m. [etym. dub.] (arch.) Wall between two windows, pier, pier-glass; leg or shin of beef; (colloq.) *un vieux* ~, an ugly old coquette.

truquer (tryke), v.a. (fam.) To fake; ~, v.n. to fake, to cheat, to swindle.

truqueu-r, -se (trykœr), s.m.f. Cheat, fake, swindler; crafty, cunning man.

trusquin, troussequin (tryskɛ̃, truskɛ̃), (techn.) Mortise-gauge, beam-compass; See TROUSSEQUIN.

trusquiner, troussequiner (tryskine, truskine), v.a. (techn.) To trace parallel lines on, with a mortise-gauge or beam-compass.

trust (trœst), s.m. [Engl. wd] (comm.) Trust. ⚠ Not in the sense of *confiance*.

truste, trustis (tryst, trystis), s.f. [Celt. *trust*] (obs.) Brotherhood in which Frankish warriors grouped themselves to act as a bodyguard to their chiefs.

truster (trœste), v.a. To buy up; to corner; to take over by a trust.

trusteur (trœstœr), s.m. Member of a trust; one who organizes a trust.

trypanose, trypanosomiase (tripanoz, tripanosɔmjaz), s.f. [Gr. *trupanon*+*sōma*] (med.) Trypanosomiasis.

trypanosome (tripanozom), s.m. (med.) Trypanosoma.

trypsine (tripsin), s.f. (med.) Trypsin.

tsar (tsar), s.m. [f. Russ. *ts(is)ari*, L *Caesar*] Tsar, Czar, Tzar.

tsarévitch (tsarevitʃ), s.m. [Russ. *tsarevich*] Tsarevitch, Czarevitch, Czarewitch.

tsarien, -ne (tsarjɛ̃), adj. Tsarian, belonging or appertaining to the Tsar.

tsarine (tsarin), s.f. Tsarina, Czarina.

tsarisme (tsarism), s.m. Tsarism.

tsé-tsé (tsetse), s.f. (ent.) Tsetse-fly.

T.S.F. (teɛsɛf), s.f. Abbreviation of *télégraphie sans fil*, wireless telegraphy; *appareil de T.S.F.*, wireless set.

tsigane, tzigane (tsigan), s.m. [Magyar *cigany*] Tzigane, Hungarian gipsy.

tu, toi, te (ty, twa, tə), pers. pron. m.f. Thou; (fam.) you; *être à tu et à toi avec quelqu'un*, to be on very familiar terms with some one.

tuable (tyabl), adj. [f. *tuer*] That may be killed; fit to be killed.

tuant, -e (tyɑ̃), p. adj. [f. *tuer*] (fam.) Killing, fatiguing, harassing, toilsome, laborious; wearisome, tiresome, tedious; *c'est un homme* ~, he is a regular bore.

tu-autem (tyotɛm), s.m. [L wds] (fam.) Main point, essential point.
tub (tœb), s.m. [Engl. wd] Tub, bath.
tuba (tyba), s.m. (mus.) Tuba.
tubage (tybaʒ), s.m. [f. *tube*] Tubing; placing of tubes.
tube (tyb), s.m. [L *tubus*] Tube; pipe, canal, conduit; (anat.) duct; (paint.) tube; (colloq.) tall hat, silk hat; chimney-pot hat; ~ *acoustique*, speaking-tube. ⚠ Tube in Engl., but not in Fr., has also the sense of underground railway = *métro*.
tuber (tybe), v.a. To tube; to furnish with tubes.
tubéracé, -e (tyberase), adj. [f. L *tuber*] (bot.) Tuberaceous. ~, s.f.pl. Tuberaceae.
tubercule (tybɛrkyl), s.m. [L *tuberculum*] (bot.) Tuber, tubercle; (med.) tumour.
tuberculeu-x, -se (tybɛrkylø), adj. (bot.) Tuberculate, tuberculous; (med.) tubercular; tuberculous. ~, s.m.f. Tubercular, consumptive person.
tuberculiforme (tybɛrkyliform), adj. Tuberculiform.
tuberculination, tuberculinisation (tybɛrkylina'sjɔ̃, tybɛrkyliniza'sjɔ̃), s.f. (med.) Tuberculinization.
tuberculine (tybɛrkylin), s.m. (med.) Tuberculin.
tuberculiner, tuberculiniser (tybɛrkyline, tybɛrkylinize), v.a. (med.) To tuberculinize.
tuberculisable (tybɛrkylizabl), adj. (med.) Tuberculizable.
tuberculisation (tybɛrkylisa'sjɔ̃), s.f. (med.) Tuberculization.
tuberculiser (tybɛrkylise), v.a. (med.) To tuberculize.
tuberculose (tybɛrkyloz), s.f. (med.) Tuberculosis, consumption.
tubéreuse (tyberøz), s.f. (bot.) Tuberose.
tubéreu-x, -se (tyberø), adj. (bot.) Tuberous, tuberose.
tubérisation (tyberiza'sjɔ̃), s.f. (bot.) Tuberization.
tubériforme (tyberiform), adj. [L *tuber*+ Fr. *forme*] Tuberiform.
tubérosité (tyberozite), s.f. Tuberosity.
tubicole (tybikɔl), adj. (zool.) Tubicolar.
tubipore (tybipɔr), s.m. (zool.) Tubipora.
tubitèle, tubitélaire (tybitɛl, tybitelɛr), (zool.) Tubitelous.
tubulaire (tybylɛr), adj. [f. L *tubulus*] Tubular.
tubulé, -e (tybyle), adj. Tubulated.
tubuleu-x, -se (tybylø), adj. (nat. hist.) Tubulous, tubulose, tubular.
tubulibranches (tybylibrɑ̃ʃ), s.m.pl. (zool.) Tubulibranchiata.
tubulure (tybylyr), s.f. (chem.) Tubulure, tubulature; tubule.
tudesque (tydɛsk), adj. [f. Germ. *deutsch*] Teutonic, German; (fig.) uncouth, unrefined, rude, coarse, inelegant. ~, s.m. The German language.
tudieu (tydjø), interj. (obs.) Zounds !, odsbud !, odslife !
tue-chien (tyʃjɛ̃), s.m. invar. (bot.) Meadow-saffron; nux vomica.
tue-mouche (tymuʃ), s.m. invar. (bot.) Fly-trap, fly-bane; ~*s*, *papier* ~*s*, fly-paper.
tuer (tɥe), v.a. [L *tutari*] To kill; to slay, to slaughter, to butcher; to murder, to destroy; to make or do away with; to cause the death of; to bore, to tire to death; to ruin; to while away; *se faire* ~, to get killed, to risk one's life; *le chagrin la tue*, she is dying of grief; *le grand bruit me tue*, I cannot bear a loud noise; *il me tue avec ses compliments*, he bores me to death with his compliments; ~ *le temps*, to kill time; *les acteurs ont tué la pièce*, the actors murdered the play; (pop.) ~ *le ver*, to get one's early nip (or dram); **se** ~, v.pr. to kill oneself, to make away with oneself, to commit suicide; to be killed; to destroy one's health, to wear oneself out; to take much trouble; to kill each other; *il s'est tué à la chasse*, he was killed while hunting; *vous vous tuez à mener une pareille vie*, you wear yourself out leading such a life; *il se tue à faire des vers*, he is always trying to write poetry.
tuerie (tyri), s.f. Slaughter, massacre, butchery, carnage; slaughter-house.
tue-tête (tytɛt), adv. loc. *A* ~, at the top of one's voice, with might and main, with all one's might; *crier à* ~, to shout as loud as possible.
tueu-r, -se (tɥœr), s.m.f. Killer, slayer; butcher; (iron.) ~ *de gens*, boaster, bully.
tue-vent (tyvɑ̃), s.m. invar. Shelter to protect trees from the wind.
tuf (tyf), s.m. [L *tophus*, It. *tufo*, *tufa*] (geol.) Tufa, tuff; (fig.) bottom; *rencontrer, trouver le* ~, to go to the bottom; coarse stuff.
tufacé, -e (tyfase), adj. (geol.) Tufaceous.
tuffeau, tufeau (pl. -x) (tyfo), s.m. (geol.) Tufa-stone; micaceous chalk (from Touraine).
tufi-er, -ère (tyfje), adj. (geol.) Tufaceous; chalky. ~**ère**, s.f. Tufa-quarry.
tuilage (tɥilaʒ), s.m. (cloth-manuf.) Finish given to cloth with the smoothing-board.
tuile (tɥil), s.f. [L *tegula*] **1.** Tile; ~ *creuse*, gutter-tile; ~ *faîtière*, crest-tile, ridge-tile; ~ *flamande*, pantile; ~ *vernie*, glazed tile; *couverture en* ~*s*, tiling; *couvreur en* ~, tiler; *loger sous les* ~*s*, to live in an attic; **2.** (cloth-manuf.) smoothing-board, sleeking-board; **3.** (fig., colloq.) blow, hard blow, sudden misfortune, mishap, mischance; *quelle* ~, what rotten luck; *une* ~ *m'est tombée sur la tête*, a misfortune has befallen me; **4.** kind of biscuit shaped like a tile.

tuileau (pl. **-x**) (tɥilo), s.m. Broken tile.
tuiler (tɥile), v.a. **1.** (cloth-manuf.) To finish with the smoothing-board; **2.** to examine (on entering a masonic lodge).
tuilerie (tɥilri), s.f. Tile-making, tile-factory, tile-kiln; *les Tuileries*, the Tuileries (palace and gardens in Paris).
tuilette (tɥilɛt), s.f. Small tile; fire-brick.
tuilier (tɥilje), s.m. Tile-maker, tile-manufacturer.
tulipe (tylip), s.f. [Pers. *dulband*] (bot.) Tulip.
tulipier (tylipje), s.m. (bot.) Tulip-tree.
tulle (tyl), s.m. [f. *Tulle* in Corrèze, France] Tulle, net.
tullerie (tylri), s.f. Tulle-manufacture.
tulli-er, -ère (tylje), adj. Of tulle, of net.
tulliste (tylist), s.m.f. Net- or tulle-maker, net- or tulle-seller.
tuméfaction (tymefaksjɔ̃), s.f. [f. *tumeur*] (med.) Tumefaction.
tuméfier (tymefje), v.a. [L *tumefacere*] (med.) To tumefy.
tumescence (tymɛssɑ̃s), s.f. (med.) Tumescence.
tumescent, -e (tymɛssɑ̃) adj. (med.) Tumescent, swelling.
tumeur (tymœr), s.f. [L *tumor*] (med.) Tumour, swelling.
tumulaire (tymylɛr), adj. [f. L *tumulus*] Tumulary, sepulchral; *pierre* ~, tombstone.
tumulte (tymylt), s.m. [L *tumultus*] Tumult, uproar, riot, hubbub, agitation, commotion, bustle, hurry; *apaiser le* ~, to calm the tumult; *le* ~ *du monde*, the bustle of the world; *en* ~, in a tumult, in confusion; in an uproar.
tumultuaire (tymyltɥɛr), adj. Tumultuary; disorderly, confused, noisy.
tumultuairement (tymyltɥɛrmɑ̃), adv. Tumultuarily.
tumultueusement (tymyltɥøzmɑ̃), adv. Tumultuously.
tumultueu-x, -se (tymyltɥø), adj. Tumultuous.
tumulus (tymylys) (pl. ~ or *tumuli*), s.m. [L wd] Tumulus, barrow, cairn, sepulchral monument.
tunage (tynaʒ), s.m. **tune** (tyn), s.f. Layer of stakes covered with gravel to prevent a river from changing its course. ⚠ Not Engl. 'tune', which = *air, mélodie*.
tungstate (tɔ̃gstat), s.m. (chem.) Tungstate.
tungstène (tɔ̃gstɛn), s.m. [Sw. *tung*+*sten*] (chem.) Tungsten.
tungstique (tɔ̃gstik), adj. Tungstic, containing tungsten.
tuniciers (tynisje), s.m.pl. (zool.) Tunicata.
tunique (tynik), s.f. [L *tunica*] Tunic, coat; (bot.) coat, integument; (anat.) wall, coat.
tuniqué, -e (tynike), adj. (bot.) Tunicate.
tunisien, -ne (tynizjɛ̃), adj. s.m.f. [f. *Tunis*] Tunisian.
tunnel (tynɛl), s.m. [Engl. wd] Tunnel.
tupa (typa), s.m. (bot.) Kind of lobeliaceae.
tupaia, tupaja (typɑja), s.m. [Malay *tupai*] (zool.) Tupaia, genus of insectivorous mammals.
tupinambis (typinɑ̃bi), s.m. Tupinambis, genus of S. Amer. lizards.
turban (tyrbɑ̃), s.m. [Pers. *dulband*] Turban; *prendre le* ~, to turn Mohammedan.
turbe (tyrb), s.f. [L *turba*] (obs.) Turb.
turbeh (tyrbe), s.f. [Arab. wd] Turbeh, small mosque-like building erected over a Moslem tomb.
turbellariés (tyrbɛlarje), s.m.pl. (zool.) Turbellaria.
turbidité (tyrbidite), s.f. [f. L *turbidus*] Turbidity.
turbin (tyrbɛ̃), s.m. (slang) Work, grind, drudgery; graft.
turbinage (tyrbinaʒ), s.m. Turbinage; separation of sugar crystals from molasses by centrifugal filters or turbines.
turbinaire (tyrbinɛr), s.f. (zool.) Turbinarian.
turbine (tyrbin), s.f. [L *turbo*] (hydraul.) Turbine.
turbiné, -e (tyrbine), adj. (nat. hist.) Turbinate, top-shaped.
turbinelle (tybinɛl), s.f. (zool.) Turbinella.
turbiner (tyrbine), v.n. (slang) To work hard, to grind, to slave.
turbith (tyrbit), s.m. (pharm.) Turpeth.
turbo (tyrbo), s.m. [L wd] (zool.) Turbo.
turbo-alternateur (tyrboaltɛrnatœr), s.m. (mech.) Turbo-alternator.
turbot (tyrbo), s.m. [L *turbo*] (ichth.) Turbot.
turbotière (tyrbɔtjɛr), s.f. (cook.) Turbot-kettle.
turbotin (tyrbɔtɛ̃), s.m. [f. *turbot*] Young turbot.
turbulence (tyrbylɑ̃s), s.f. [L *turbulentia*] Turbulence, turbulency; wildness.
turbulent, -e (tyrbylɑ̃), adj. [L *turbulentus*] Turbulent; wild.
turc, turque (tyrk), adj. [Pers., Arab. *Turk*] Turkish; *à la* ~*que*, in Turkish fashion; (fig.) harshly, cruelly. ~, s.m.f. Turk; Mohammedan; (fam.) cruel man; Turkish language; *fort comme un* ~, as strong as an ox, a horse; *traiter quelqu'un de* ~ *à More*, to treat some one harshly; *le Grand Turc*, the Sultan of Turkey; *tête de* ~, Turk's head, (fig.) scapegoat; *se faire* ~, to turn Mohammedan.
turc (tyrk), s.m. Tool to hold rivets in place; (zool.) wood-worm, turk.
turcie (tyrsi), s.f. (obs.) Dyke, embankment.
turco (tyrko), s.m. (fam.) Turco; Algerian soldier.

turcoman (tyrkɔmɑ̃), s.m. [Pers. *Turkumān*] Turkoman, Turkman.
turcophile (tyrkɔfil), adj. s.m. [f. *Turc*+ Gr. *philos*] Turcophil.
turcophobe (tyrkɔfɔb), adj. s.m. [f. *Turc* +Gr. *phobos*] Turcophobe.
turdidés (tyrdides), s.m.pl. [f. L *turdus*] (ornith.) Turdidae.
turdus (tyrdys), s.m. [L wd] (ornith.) Genus of birds including the thrushes and blackbirds.
turelure (tyrlyr), s.f. Tol-de-rol, fol-de-rol (burden of a song); refrain; *c'est toujours la même* ~, it is always the same thing over and over again.
turf (tyrf), s.m. [Engl. wd] Turf, racecourse.
turfiste (tyrfist), s.m. Turfite, devotee of the turf; racing man.
turfol (tyrfɔl), s.m. Oily product obtained from peat.
turgescence (tyrʒɛssɑ̃s), s.f. (med.) Turgescence, turgidity.
turgescent, -e (tyrʒɛssɑ̃), adj. [f. L *turgere*] Turgescent, turgid.
turion (tyrjɔ̃), s.m. [L *turio*] (bot.) Turion.
turlupin (tyrlypɛ̃), s.m. [nickname of celebrated 17th-c. comedian, Henri Legrand] Buffoon, merry andrew; (fig.) sorry jester, punster.
turlupinade (tyrlypinad), s.f. [f. *turlupin*] Sorry jest, poor joke, piece of clownery.
turlupinage (tyrlypinaʒ), s.m. Teasing.
turlupiner (tyrlypine), v.a. To tease, to annoy.
turlurette (tyrlyrɛt), s.f. **1.** Kind of guitar; **2.** refrain, burden of a song; **3.** ~ *!*, interj. never mind !, what does it matter !
turlutaine (tyrlytɛn), s.f. Mania, bee in one's bonnet; hobby.
turlutte (tyrlyt), s.f. Lump of lead covered with hooks used for sea-fishing.
turlututu (tyrlytyty), s.m. Pipe, flute. ~, interj. Hush, hush !, tut !, fol-de-rol !
turne, thurne (tyrn), s.f. See THURNE.
turnep, turneps (tyrnɛp, tyrnɛps), s.m. [Engl. *turnip*] (bot.) Turnip.
turnéracées (tyrnerase), s.f.pl. (bot.) Turneraceae.
turnère (tyrnɛr), s.f. (bot.) Turnera.
turnix (tyrniks), s.m. (ornith.) Turnix.
turonien, -ne (tyronjɛ̃), adj. [f. L *turones*] (geol.) Turonian.
turpitude (tyrpityd), s.f. [f. L *turpis*] Turpitude, baseness, ignominy, vileness, shameful action.
turquerie (tyrkri), s.f. [f. *turc*] Harshness, cruelty, sordid avarice; picture or book depicting Turkish scenes.
turquet (tyrke), s.m. [f. *Turc*] **1.** Maize; **2.** pug, pug-dog.
turquette (tyrkɛt), s.f. (bot.) Rupturewort.
turquin (tyrkɛ̃), adj. [It. *turchino*] Dark, deep (of blue). ~, s.m. Blue marble veined with white found in Italy.
turquoise (tyrkwaz), s.f. [f. *turc*, It. *turchino*] (min.) Turquoise.
turriculé, -e (tyrikyle), adj. [f. L *turricula*] (conch.) Turriculated.
turritelle (tyritɛl), s.f. (zool.) Turritellid.
tussah, tussau (tysa, tyso), s.m. Tussore (silk); syn. TUSSOR.
tussilage (tysilaʒ), s.m. [L *tussilago*] (bot.) Coltsfoot.
tussor, tussore (tysɔr), s.m. [Hindi *tasar*, Sansk. *trasarah*] Tussore silk.
tutélaire (tytelɛr), adj. [L *tutelarius*] Tutelar, tutelary; guardian, protecting; *une divinité* ~, a tutelary divinity.
tutelle (tytɛl), s.f. [L *tutela*] (law) Tutelage, guardianship; trusteeship; protection; *enfant en* ~, minor, ward; *être sous la* ~ *des lois*, to be under the protection of the law.
tut-eur, -rice (tytœr), s.m.f. [L *tutor*] (law) Guardian, trustee; protector, protectress; *il n'a pas besoin de* ~, he can manage for himself; *Rome, tutrice des beaux-arts*, Rome, the protectress of the fine arts; ~, s.m. (hort.) prop; *corset* ~, tree-guard, tree-fence. ⚠ Not English 'tutor', which = *précepteur*.
tuteurage (tytœraʒ), s.m. [f. *tuteur*] (hort.) Propping-up of a plant.
tuteurer (tytœre), v.a. (hort.) To prop up.
tuthie, tutie (tyti), s.f. [Arab. *tutiyā*] (pharm.) Tutty.
tutoiement, tutoîment (tytwamɑ̃), s.m. 'Theeing-and-thouing', use of 'thee' and 'thou' instead of 'you'.
tutoyer (tytwaje), v.a. To 'thee-and-thou', to address as 'thee' and 'thou', instead of 'you'.
tutti (tyti), s.m. [It. wd] (mus.) Tutti; ~ *quanti*, all the lot, the whole lot; all such people.
tutu (tyty), s.m. Fluffy skirt of a ballet-dancer.
tuyau (pl. **-x**) (tɥijo), s.m. [orig. dub.] Pipe, tube; hose; chimney flue; shaft, funnel; barrel (of a quill); stalk (of corn); stem (of feather, pipe); nozzle (of bellows); flute, goffer (of frills); (colloq.) stomach, throat; ~ *d'alimentation*, feed-pipe; ~ *d'aspiration*, suction-pipe; ~ *de conduite*, delivery-pipe, spout; ~ *de descente*, stack-pipe; (fam.) *parler dans le* ~ *de l'oreille*, to whisper something in some one's ear; ~ *de poêle*, silk hat, stove-pipe (hat); (colloq.) information, tip.
tuyautage (tɥijɔtaʒ), s.m. Pipes (of steam-engine); quilling, fluting, frilling, goffering; (colloq.) giving tips.
tuyauté, -e (tɥijɔte), p. adj. Frilled, fluted, goffered.

tuyauter (tɥijote), v.a. To quill, to frill, to flute, to goffer; (by extension of racing slang) to give a tip to.
tuyauterie (tɥijotri), s.f. System of pipes (in steam-engine, &c.); manufacture of pipes, pipe-factory.
tuyère (tɥijɛr), s.f. [f. *tuyau*] Tewel, blast-pipe.
tylose (tiloz), s.f. [Gr. *tulōsis*] (med.) Tylosis.
tympan (tɛ̃pɑ̃), s.m. [Gr. *tumpanon*] (anat.) Tympanum, ear-drum; (arch.) tympanum, tympan, spandrel; (print.) tympan; (mech.) tread-wheel, scoop-wheel; *un bruit à briser le* ~, a deafening noise.
tympanal, -e, (aux) (tɛ̃panal), adj. (anat.) Tympanal, tympanic.
tympanique (tɛ̃panik), adj. (anat.) Tympanic, drum-like. ~, s.f. Art of playing the drum.
tympaniser (tɛ̃panize), v.a. (obs.) To publish, to proclaim loudly; to cry down, to decry, to run down; (colloq.) to din into the ears of somebody.
tympanisme (tɛ̃panism), s.m. (med.) Tympanism.
tympanite (tɛ̃panit), s.f. (med.) Tympanites.
tympanon (tɛ̃panɔ̃), s.m. (mus.) Dulcimer.
tyndallisation (tɛ̃daliza'sjɔ̃), s.f. [f. *John Tyndall*, 1820–93] (med.) Tyndallization.
type (tip), s.m. [Gr. *tupos*] Type; model, form; symbol, emblem; standard; (astr.) plan, drawing; (fam.) fellow, character; cove; bloke; card; *c'est un véritable* ~, he is quite a character.
typha (tifa), s.m. (bot.) Typha, cat's-tail, reed-mace.
typhacées (tifase), s.f.pl. (bot.) Typhaceae.
typhique (tifik), adj. [f. *typhus*] (med.) Typhous, typhoidal.
typhlite (tiflit), s.f. [f. Gr. *tuphlos*] (med.) Typhlitis.
typhlographe (tiflɔgraf), s.m. [Gr. *tuphlos* +*graphos*] Typhlograph.
typhlops (tiflɔps), s.m. Typhlops.
typho-bacillose, typho-tuberculose (tifobasilloz, tifotybɛrkyloz), s.f. (med.) Typho-tuberculosis.
typhoémie (tifoemi), s.f. (med.) Typhoemia.
typhogène (tifoʒɛn), adj. (med.) Typhogenic.
typhoïde (tifɔid), adj. (med.) Typhoid; *fièvre* ~, typhoid fever.
typhoïque, typhoïdique (tifɔik, tifɔidik), adj. [f. *typhoïde*] (med.) Typhoidal.
typhon (tifɔ̃), s.m. [Arab. *tūfān*, Gr. *tuphōn*, Chin. *tai fung*] Typhoon, whirlwind.
typhotoxine (tifɔtɔksin), s.f. [*typho*+ *toxine*] (med.) Typhotoxin.
typhus (tifys), s.m. [Gr. *tuphos*] (med.) Typhus, jail-fever.
typique (tipik), adj. [f. *type*] Typic, typical; symbolical, emblematic; original.
typochromie (tipɔkrɔmi), s.f. [Gr. *tupos*+ *khrōma*] (print.) Typochromy.
typographe (tipɔgraf), s.m. [Gr. *tupos*+ *graphein*] Typographer, printer, compositor.
typographie (tipɔgrafi), s.f. (print.) Typography; printing; letter-press, print; printing-office.
typographique (tipɔgrafik), adj. (print.) Typographic, typographical.
typographiquement (tipɔgrafikmɑ̃), adv. (print.) Typographically.
typolithographie (tipɔlitɔgrafi), s.f. (print). Typolithography.
typomètre (tipɔmɛtr), s.m. [Gr. *tupos*+ *metron*] (print.) Typometer.
typophotographie (tipɔfɔtɔgrafi), s.f. [*typo*+*photographie*] Typophotography.
typophotographique (tipɔfɔtɔgrafik), adj. Typophotographic.
typotélégraphie (tipɔtelegrafi), s.f. [*typo* +*télégraphie*] Typotelegraphy.
typotélégraphique (tipɔtelegrafik), adj. Typotelegraphic.
typtologie (tiptɔlɔʒi), s.f. [Gr. *tuptein*+ *logos*] Typtology, spirit-rapping.
tyran[1] (tirɑ̃), s.m. [Gr. *turannos*] Tyrant; *cette femme est un vrai* ~, that woman is a regular shrew.
tyran[2] (tirɑ̃), s.m. (ornith.) Tyrant fly-catcher, king-bird.
tyranneau (pl. **-x**) (tirano), s.m. [f. *tyran*] Petty tyrant.
tyrannicide (tiranisid), s.m. [L *tyrannus*+ *caedere*] Tyrannicide.
tyrannie (tirani), s.f. [f. *tyran*] Tyranny, oppression, severity; *le joug de la* ~, the yoke of tyranny; *s'affranchir de la* ~, to free oneself from tyranny.
tyrannique (tiranik), adj. Tyrannic, tyrannical; unjust, violent, despotic, cruel.
tyranniquement (tiranikmɑ̃), adv. Tyrannically.
tyranniser (tiranize), v.a. To tyrannize, to tyrannize over; to oppress.
tyrien, -ne (tirjɛ̃), adj. s.m.f. [f. *Tyr*] Tyrian.
tyrine (tirin), s.f. See CASÉINE.
tyroglyphe (tirɔglif), s.m. [f. Gr. *turos* + *gluphē*] (zool.) Tyroglyphid.
tyroïde (tirɔid), adj. [Gr. *turos*+*eidos*] Tyroid, resembling cheese.
tyrolien, -ne (tirɔljɛ̃), adj. s.m.f. Tyrolese; ~, s.f. (mus.) kind of song, Tyrolese dance.
tyrosinase (tirɔzinɑz), s.f. (chem.) Tyrosinase.
tyrosine (tirɔzin), s.f. (chem.) Tyrosin.
tyrrhénien, -ne (tirenjɛ̃), adj. s.m.f. Tyrrhenian, Etruscan.
tzigane (tzigan), adj. s.m.f. See TSIGANE.

U

U, u (y), s.m. Twenty-first letter of the alphabet.
ubéreu-x, -se (yberø), adj. (rare) [f. L *uber*] Uberous, copious, fruitful.
ubiquiste (ybikɥist), s.m. adj. [f. L *ubique*] Ubiquitous (person).
ubiquitaire (ybikɥitɛr), s.m. [f. L *ubique*] Ubiquitarian, believer in the omnipresence of Christ's body.
ubiquitaire (ybikɥitɛr), adj. Ubiquitary, ubiquitous.
ubiquité (ybikɥite), s.f. [f. L *ubique*] Ubiquity.
udomètre (ydɔmɛtr), s.m. [f. L *udus*] Rain-gauge, udometer, pluviometer; syn. PLUVIOMÈTRE.
udométrique (ydɔmetrik), adj. Udometric.
uhlan (ylɑ̃), s.m. [Turk. *oghlan*, Pol. *ulan*] Uhlan.
ukase, oukase (ykɑz, ukaz), s.m. [Russ. wd] Ukase; (colloq.) autocratic decision.
ukrainien, -ne (ykrɛnjɛ̃), s.m.f. adj. Ukranian.
ulcérati-f, -ve (ylseratif), adj. [f. L *ulcus*] Ulcerative.
ulcération (ylsera'sjɔ̃), s.f. Ulceration.
ulcère (ylsɛr), s.m. [L *ulcus*] Ulcer, open sore, running sore; (fig.) ulcer, moral blemish, corrupting influence.
ulcéré, -e (ylsere), p. adj. Ulcerated, ulcerous; (fig.) embittered, cankered; exasperated, rankling.
ulcérer (ylsere), v.a. [L *ulcerare*] To ulcerate; (fig.) to embitter, to gall, to envenom.
ulcéreu-x, -se (ylserø), adj. Ulcerous, envenomed.
uléma (ylemɑ), s.m. [Arab. wd] Ulema (Mohammedan doctor or divine).
ulex (ylɛks), s.m. [L wd] (bot.) Ulex, furze, whin; syn. AJONC.
uliginaire, uligineu-x, -se (yliʒinɛr, yliʒinø), adj. [f. L *uliginosus*] (bot.) Uliginose, uliginous.
ulite (ylit), s.f. (med.) Inflammation of the gums.
ulmacées (ylmase), s.f.pl. (bot.) Ulmaceae.
ulmaire (ylmɛr), s.f. [f. L *ulmus*] (bot.) Meadow-sweet; syn. REINE DES PRÉS.
ulmine (ylmin), s.f. (chem.) Ulmin.
ulmique (ylmik), adj. Ulmic.
ulnaire (ylnɛr), adj. [f. L *ulna*] (anat.) Ulnar.
ulster (ylstɛr), s.m. [f. *Ulster*, Ireland] Ulster, a long overcoat, usually rainproof.
ultérieur, -e (ylterjœr), adj. [L *ulterior*] Ulterior; more remote, further, posterior, subsequent.
ultérieurement (ylterjœrmɑ̃), adv. Ulteriorly, further, later, subsequently, afterwards.
ultimatum (yltimatɔm), s.m. [L wd] Ultimatum.
ultime (yltim), adj. [L *ultimus*] Ultimate, last, final.
ultra- (yltra), pref. s.m. adj. [L wd] Ultra, extremist; *~-mondain, -e,* adj. ultramundane; *~-montain, -e,* adj. ultramontane; ~, s.m. ultramontane, ultramontanist; *~-montanisme,* s.m. ultramontanism; *~-royaliste,* s.m. ultra-royalist; *~-violet, -tte,* adj. ultra-violet; *~-zodiacal, -e,* (*aux*), adj. ultra-zodiacal.
ululation (ylyla'sjɔ̃), s.f. **ululement** (ylylmɑ̃), s.m. Ululation, howling, wailing.
ululer (ylyle), v.n. [L *ululare*] To ululate, to howl, to hoot.
ulvacées (ylvase), s.f.pl. (bot.) Ulvaceae.
ulve (ylv), s.f. [L *ulva*] (bot.) Ulva, sea-lettuce.
umbre (ɔ̃br), s.m. [L. *umbra*] (ichth.) Grayling.
un, -e (œ̃, yn), ind. art. adj. pron. s.m. [L *unus*] A, an, any, some; one, single, unique; *~ jour,* a day; one day, some day, some time; *il n'y en a qu'~,* there is but one; *de deux jours l'~,* every other day; *de deux choses l'~e,* one of the two; it's either this or that; it's one of two things; it's the one or the other; *ça c'est numéro ~,* that 's A 1; *c'est d'~ ennuyeux!,* it's frightfully boring!; *c'est tout ~,* it's all one; it comes to the same thing; *l'~ et l'autre,* both; *les ~s et les autres,* everybody; *l'~ ou l'autre,* either one or the other; *ni l'~ ni l'autre,* neither; *l'~ ne va pas sans l'autre,* that follows as a matter of course; *l'~ comme l'autre,* one as well as the other; *les ~s . . ., les autres . . .,* some . . ., others . . .; *les ~s disent blanc, les autres noir,* some say white, others say black; *les ~s les autres,* each other; one another; *les ~s et les autres,* all, everybody; all together; *l'~ vaut l'autre,* one is as good as the other; *ne faire ni ~e ni deux,* to make no bones about it, to make no more ado; *~ à ~,* one by one; *comme pas ~,* like no one else; *pas ~,* not one, none; *et d'~,* and one; that settles it for this one; *l'~ dans l'autre,* on an average.
unanime (ynanim), adj. [L *unanimus*] Unanimous.
unanimement (ynanimmɑ̃), adv. Unanimously.
unanimité (ynanimite), s.f. Unanimity; *à l'~,* unanimously.
unau (yno), s.m. [Braz. wd] (zool.) Sloth.
uncial, -e, (aux), oncial, -e, (aux) (ɔ̃sjal), adj. [L *uncialis*] Uncial. **~e,** s.f. Uncial.
unciforme (ɔ̃sifɔrm), adj. [f. L *uncus*] Unciform, hook-shaped.

unciné, -e (ɔ̃sine), adj. [f. L *uncus*] (bot.) Uncinate.
unguéal, -e, (aux) (ɔ̃gɥeal), adj. [f. L *unguis*] Ungual, unguicular.
unguifère (ɔ̃gɥifɛr), adj. Unguiferous.
unguineu-x, -se (ɔ̃gɥinø), adj. [f. L *ungere*] (anat.) Unctuous.
unguis (ɔ̃gɥis), s.m. [L wd] (anat.) Unguis.
uni, -e (yni), p. adj. [f. *unir*] **1.** Smooth, even, level, uniform, plain, self-coloured, without pattern; *du linge* ~, plain linen; equable, quiet, calm; **2.** united, affectionate; *ils sont très* ~*s*, they are on very affectionate terms, or very fond of each other; they are living together in perfect union.
uniate (ynjat), s.m. [f. L *unus*] Uniate.
unicaule (ynikol), adj. (bot.) Having one stalk.
unicellulaire (ynisɛlylɛr), adj. Unicellular.
unicolore (ynikɔlɔr), adj. [L *unus*+*color*] Unicolour(ed).
unicorne (ynikɔrn), adj. [L *unis*+*cornu*] Unicornous. ~, s.f. Unicorn; syn. LICORNE.
unième (ynjɛm), adj. (used only after another number) First; *vingt-et-*~, twenty-first.
unification (ynifika'sjɔ̃), s.f. Unification, amalgamation.
unifier (ynifje), v.a. [L *unus*+*facere*] To unify, to amalgamate; to unite; to make level, to make uniform.
uniflore (yniflɔr), adj. [f. L *uni*+*flos*] (bot.) Uniflorous.
unifolié, -e (ynifɔlje), adj. [f. L *uni*+*folium*] (bot.) Unifoliate.
uniforme (ynifɔrm), adj. [L *uniformis*] Uniform; even, equal; standard. ~, s.m. Uniform, regimentals; *d'*~, regimental; regulation; standard; (fig.) *quitter l'uniforme*, to leave the service; *en grand uniforme*, in full uniform, in full regimentals.
uniformément (ynifɔrmemɑ̃), adv. Uniformly, evenly, unvaryingly.
uniformiser (ynifɔrmize), v.a. To make uniform; to unify; to standardize.
uniformité (ynifɔrmite), s.f. [L *uniformitas*] Uniformity, sameness.
unijugué, -e (yniʒyge), adj. [L *uni*+*jugum*] (bot.) Unijugate.
unilabié, -e (ynilabje), adj. [L *uni*+*labium*] (obs.) Unilabiate.
unilatéral, -e, (aux) (ynilateral), adj. [f. L *uni*+*latus*] Unilateral, one-sided.
unilatéralement (ynilateralmɑ̃), adv. Unilaterally, one-sidedly.
uniloculaire (ynilɔkylɛr), adj. [f. L *uni*+*loculus*] (bot.) Unilocular.
uniment (ynimɑ̃), adv. [f. *uni*] Evenly, plainly, smoothly, simply; *tout* ~, quite simply, plainly.
uninominal, -e, (aux) (yninɔminal), adj. [L *uni*+*nomen*] Containing one name only; *scrutin* ~, voting for one candidate.
union (ynjɔ̃), s.f. [L *unio*] Union; agreement, harmony; match, marriage, alliance; *trait d'*~, hyphen; *l'*~ *suisse*, the Swiss Confederacy; ~*s ouvrières*, trade unions; *l'*~ *fait la force*, union is strength; united we stand, divided we fall.
unionisme (ynjɔnism), s.m. Unionism.
unioniste (ynjɔnist), s.m.f. Unionist.
unipare (ynipar), adj. [L *uni*+*parere*] Uniparous.
unipersonnel, -le (ynipɛrsɔnɛl), adj. [L *uni*+*persona*] Unipersonal, (gram.) impersonal.
unipersonnellement (ynipɛrsɔnɛlmɑ̃), adv. Impersonally.
unipétale (ynipetal), adj. [L *uni*+Gr. *petalon*] (bot.) Unipetalous.
unipolaire (ynipɔlɛr), adj. [L *uni*+Gr. *polos*] Unipolar.
unique (ynik), adj. [L *unicus*] Unique, sole, single; only; unequalled; uncommon, singular, odd, unrivalled, unprecedented, matchless, unparalleled; *fils* ~, only son.
uniquement (ynikmɑ̃), adj. Uniquely, solely, only.
unir (ynir), v.a. [L *unire*] **1.** To unite; **2.** to level, to smooth, to smooth down.
unisérié, -e (yniserje), adj. [L *uni*+*series*] Uniserial.
unisexualité (ynisɛksɥalite), s.f. [f. L *uni*+*sexus*] Unisexuality.
unisexuel, -le (ynisɛksɥɛl), adj. Unisexual.
unisson (ynisɔ̃), s.m. [L *uni*+*sonus*] Unison, harmony; *à l'*~, in unison; in harmony, in keeping.
unissonnant, -e (ynisɔnɑ̃), adj. Unisonant.
unitaire (ynitɛr), adj. s.m.f. Unitarian.
unitarisme (ynitarism), s.m. Unitarianism.
unité (ynite), s.f. [L *unitas*] Unity; unit; digit; (fig.) concord, agreement; ~ *de combat*, fighting unit; *ce tableau manque d'*~, this picture lacks unity; *les 3* ~*s*, the dramatic unities (of place, action, time); ~ *nationale*, national unity.
uniti-f, -ve (ynitif), adj. Unitive.
univalve (ynivalv), adj. [L *uni*+*valva*] (zool., bot.) Univalve, univalvular.
univers (ynivɛr), s.m. [L *universum*] Universe, earth, world, mankind, society; *étonner l'*~, to surprise the world.
universalisation (ynivɛrsaliza'sjɔ̃), s.f. Universalization.
universaliser (ynivɛrsalize), v.a. To universalize, to make universal, to make general.
universalisme (ynivɛrsalism), s.m. Universalism.

universaliste (yniversalist), s.m.f. Universalist.
universalité (yniversalite), s.f. Universality.
universaux (yniverso), s.m.pl. See UNIVERSEL.
universel, -le (yniversɛl), adj. [L *universalis*] Universal, general, (of legatees) universal, sole; world-wide, widely known or accepted; (of a person) that knows everything. ~, s.m. (pl. *universaux*) (phil.) Universal.
universellement (yniversɛlmɑ̃), adv. Universally, generally, without exception.
universitaire (yniversitɛr), adj. Of the university; academic; *le corps* ~, the professors of the university. ~, s.m.f. University man or woman; member of the university, university professor.
université (yniversite), s.f. [L *universitas*] University.
univoque (ynivɔk), adj. [L *uni+vox*] Univocal.
upas (ypɑs), s.m. [Malay wd] Upas, upas-tree.
uranate (yranat), s.m. (chem.) Uranate.
urane (yran), s.m. [f. L *uranus*] (chem.) Oxide of uranium.
uranique (yranik), adj. (chem.) Uranic.
uranite (yranit), s.f. (chem.) Uranite.
uranium (yranjɔm), s.m. (chem.) Uranium.
uranographe (yranɔgraf), s.m. [f. Gr. *ouranos*] Uranographist.
uranographie (yranɔgrafi), s.f. Uranography, the description or delineation of the sidereal heavens.
uranographique (yranɔgrafik), adj. Uranographical.
uranométrie (yranɔmetri), s.f. Uranometry.
uranoscope (yranɔskɔp), s.m. (ichth.) Uranoscopus.
urate (yrat), s.m. (chem.) Urate.
urbain, -e (yrbɛ̃), adj. [L *urbanus*] Urban, pertaining to town life.
urbanisme (yrbanism), s.m. Town-planning; life in towns.
urbanité (yrbanite), s.f. [L *urbanitas*] Urbanity, courtesy.
urcéolaire, urcéolé, -e (yrseɔlɛr, yrseɔle), adj. [f. L *urceolus*] (bot.) Urceolate. **Urcéolaires,** s.f.pl. Urceolaria.
urcéole (yrseɔl), s.m. (bot.) Urceolus.
ure (yr), s.m. [L *urus*] (zool.) Urus, aurochs; syn. AUROCHS.
urédo (yredo), s.m. [L wd] (bot.) Uredo, rust fungus.
urée (yre), s.f. [Gr. *ouron*] (chem.) Urea.
urémie (yremi), s.f. [f. Gr. *ouron+haima*] (pathol.) Uraemia.
urémique (yremik), adj. Uraemic.
uretéralgie (yrteralgi), s.f. (pathol.) Ureteritis.
uretère (yrtɛr), s.m. [Gr. *ourētēr*] (anat.) Ureter.
uretérite (yrterit), s.f. (pathol.) Ureteritis.
urétral, -e, (aux) (yretral), adj. (anat.) Urethral.
urètre, urèthre (yrɛtr), s.m. [Gr. *ourēthra*] (anat.) Urethra.
urgemment (yrʒamɑ̃), adv. Urgently.
urgence (yrʒɑ̃s), s.f. Urgency; *d'*~, urgent, immediately; *en cas d'*~, in case of emergency, in an emergency.
urgent, -e (yrʒɑ̃), adj. [f. L *urgere*] Urgent, pressing.
urinaire (yrinɛr), adj. [f. L *urina*] (anat.) Urinary, urinous.
urinal (yrinal), s.m. Urinal.
urination (yrina'sjɔ̃), s.f. Urination, micturition.
urine (yrin), s.f. [L *urina*] Urine.
uriner (yrine), v.n.a. To urinate, to make water, to pass urine.
urineu-x, -se (yrinø), adj. Urinous.
urinoir (yrinwar), s.m. Urinal, gentlemen's lavatory.
urique (yrik), adj. (chem.) Uric.
urne (yrn), s.f. [L *urna*] Urn; ~ *funéraire,* sepulchral urn; ~ *du scrutin,* ~ *électorale,* ballot-box.
urobiline (yrɔbilin), s.f. [f. Gr. *ouron*] (chem., pharm.) Urobilin.
urocystite (yrɔsistit), s.f. (pathol.) Inflammation of the bladder.
urodynie (yrɔdini), s.f. (pathol.) Urodynia.
urolithe (yrɔlit), s.m. (pathol.) Urinary calculus.
uromètre (yrɔmɛtr), s.m. Urometer.
uroscopie (yrɔskɔpi), s.f. Uroscopy.
ursuline (yrsylin), s.f. [f. *St. Ursula*] Ursuline.
urticacées (yrtikase), s.f.pl. (bot.) Urticaceae.
urticaire (yrtikɛr), s.f. [f. L *urtica*] (pathol.) Nettle-rash, urticaria.
urticant, -e (yrtikɑ̃), adj. Urticating, stinging, nettling.
urtication (yrtika'sjɔ̃), s.f. Urtication.
urubu (yryby), s.m. [Brazil. wd] (ornith.) Urubu, American black vulture.
urus, ure (yrys, yr), s.m. [L *urus*] (zool.) Urus, aurochs; syn. AUROCHS.
us (ys), s.m.pl. [L *usus*] Usages, ways; *selon les* ~ *et coutumes,* according to the old customs.
usable (yzabl), adj. Liable to wear out.
usage (yzaʒ), s.m. [f. *us*] Use, custom; practice, habit, way, employment, enjoyment, wear; *à l'*~ *de,* for the use of; *d'*~, usual, habitual; customary; *en* ~, in use, used, usual, common; *de bon* ~, (*a*) very serviceable; (*b*) in the approved way; in good taste; *hors d'*~, worn out, threadbare; obsolete, past wearing; *sans* ~, (*a*)

(of) no use; (*b*) ill-mannered; *peu en* ~, little used, uncommon; *avoir de l'*~, to be well-bred; *manquer d'*~, to be ignorant of the habits of society; to have no manners; *faire* ~ *de*, to make use of; to use; *faire beaucoup d'*~, to wear well; *mettre en* ~, to bring into use; *mettre tout en* ~, or *en œuvre*, to spare no pains; ~ *fait droit*, custom becomes law; ~ *rend maître*, practice makes perfect; *il est d'*~ *de . . .*, one must . . .; . . . is the approved way; a well-bred man (or woman) will . . .; *il n'est pas d'*~ *de . . .*, it 's not done, it 's not customary to . . .

usagé, -e (yzaʒe), adj. That has been used, not new, second-hand.

usag-er, -ère (yzaʒe), adj. For common use. ~, s.m. (law) Commoner; user; *les* ~*s de la route*, those who make frequent use of the roads.

usance (yzɑ̃s), s.f. (comm.) Usance.

usant, -e (yzɑ̃), p. adj. Exhausting, tiring; (law) using, enjoying.

usé, -e (yze), p. adj. Worn-out, threadbare, stale, trite, hackneyed, the worse for wear, broken, broken down.

user (yze), v.n.a. [f. L *usus*] To use, to make use of, to utilize, to employ, to have recourse to, to resort to, to avail oneself (*de*, of), to exercise, to put into operation, to treat in a specified manner; ~ *de modération*, to exercise moderation; ~ *d'un droit*, to exercise one's right; *vous en usez mal avec lui*, you are behaving badly to him; you are treating him ill; you are using him ill; ~, v.a. to use, to consume, to wear, to wear out, to use up; to weaken, to diminish, to blunt; to destroy, to exhaust; ~ *beaucoup d'huile*, to consume much oil; ~ *ses souliers*, to wear out one's shoes.

user (yze), s.m. Wear, service, use; wear and tear; *à l'*~, by wear; in the wear; *être d'un bon* ~, to wear well; to stand any amount of wear; *on ne connaît bien les gens qu'à l'*~, it takes time to know people; a friend in need is a friend indeed.

usine (yzin), s.f. [L *officina*] Factory, manufactory, works, mill; ~ *à gaz*, gasworks; (colloq.) ~ *à bachot*, crammer's.

usiner (yzine), v.a. To manufacture.

usinier (yzinje), s.m. Manufacturer; owner of works, mill, &c.

usité, -e (yzite), adj. [L *usitatus*] Customary, used, in use, usual; *un mot peu* ~, a word which is seldom used; *selon une expression très* ~*e*, according to a well-known saying.

ustensile (ystɑ̃sil), s.m. [L *utensilia*] Utensil, implement, tool; *des* ~ *de jardinage*, gardening implements or tools; ~ *de cuisine*, kitchen or cooking utensils.

ustion (ystjɔ̃), s.f. [f. L *urere*] (surg.) Ustion, cauterization.

usucapion (yzykapjɔ̃), s.f. [f. L *usus*+*capere*] (law) Usucaption, usucapion.

usuel, -le (yzɥɛl), adj. [L *usualis*] Usual, customary, ordinary, common.

usuellement (yzɥɛlmɑ̃), adv. Usually, commonly, ordinarily.

usufructuaire (yzyfryktɥɛr), adj. [L *usufructuarius*] (law) Usufructuary, giving only the usufruct.

usufruit (yzyfrɥi), s.m. [L *usus*+*fructus*] (law) Usufruct, use, enjoyment, life-interest.

usufruiti-er, -ère (yzyfrɥitje), s.m.f. adj. Usufructuary.

usuraire (ysyrɛr), adj. [f. L *usuria*] Usurious.

usurairement (yzyrɛrmɑ̃), adv. Usuriously, with usury.

usure[1] (yzyr), s.f. [LL *usuria*] Usury, lending at exorbitant interest; *faire l'*~, to practise usury; (fig.) *rendre avec* ~, to return or repay with interest.

usure[2] (yzyr), s.f. [f. *user*] Wear, wear and tear; *guerre d'*~, war of attrition.

usuri-er, -ère (yzyrie), s.m.f. Usurer.

usurpat-eur, -rice (yzyrpatœr), s.m.f. [f. L *usurpare*] Usurper. ~, adj. Usurping, encroaching.

usurpation (yzyrpa'sjɔ̃), s.f. Usurpation, encroachment.

usurpatoire (yzyrpatwar), adj. Usurping, encroaching, usurpatory.

usurper (yzyrpe), v.a. [L *usurpare*] To usurp; to encroach upon.

ut (yt), s.m. [1st word of hymn of St. John] (mus.) Ut, do, C.

utérin, -e (yterɛ̃), adj. [f. L *uterus*] Uterine.

utérus (yterys), s.m. [L wd] (anat.) Uterus, womb, matrix.

utile (ytil), adj. [L *utilis*] Useful, serviceable, of use, of utility, profitable, advantageous, due, expedient, beneficial; *en temps* ~, in due or in good time; *il serait* ~ *de*, it would be well to; (techn.) *travail* ~, effective work; *charge* ~, useful load; (law) *jours* ~*s*, days reckoned in judicial proceedings; (law) *ordre* ~, marshalling of creditors.

utile (ytil), s.m. Utility, usefulness; *joindre l'*~ *à l'agréable*, to combine business with pleasure.

utilement (ytilmɑ̃), adv. Usefully, advantageously, profitably, to some purpose; *employer le temps utilement*, to make good use of one's time.

utilisable (ytilizabl), adj. Utilizable, that can be turned to account.

utilisation (ytiliza'sjɔ̃), s.f. Utilization, turning to account.

utiliser (ytilize), v.a. [f. L *utilis*] To utilize, to turn to account, to make use of, to employ.

utilitaire (ytilitɛr), adj. s.m.f. Utilitarian.

utilitarisme (ytilitarism), s.m. Utilitarianism.

utilité (ytilite), s.f. [L *utilitas*] Utility, usefulness, profitableness; *d'aucune* ~, of no use, useless; (theatr.) utility (man), useful man.

utopie (ytopi), s.f. [Gr. *ou+topos*] Utopia; utopian scheme; chimaera, fanciful, generous conception or dream.

utopique (ytopik), adj. Utopian, chimerical.

utopiste (ytopist), s.m.f. Utopian; dreamer, chimerical mind.

utriculaire (ytrikylɛr), adj. [f. L *utriculus*] (bot.) Utricular.

utricule (ytrikyl), s.m. (bot.) Utricle.

utriculeu-x, -se (ytrikylø), adj. Utricular.

uva-ursi (yvayrsi), s.m. (bot.) Uva ursi, bearberry.

uvée (yve), s.f. [L *uva*] (anat.) Uvea.

uvéite (yveit), s.f. Inflammation of the uvea.

uviforme (yviform), adj. Uviform, grape-shaped.

uvulaire (yvylɛr), adj. [f. L *uva*] (anat.) Uvular.

uvule (yvyl), s.f. [f. L *uva*] (anat.) Uvula; syn. LUETTE.

uxorieu-x, -se (yksorjø), adj. [L *uxorius*] Uxorious.

V

V, v (ve), s.m. 22nd letter of the alphabet.

va (va) **1.** 2nd pers. sing. imperative of *aller*, v.n., to go; **2.** 3rd pers. sing. pres. ind. of *aller*, v.n.; *il* ~, he goes, he is going; *il* ~ *venir*, he is coming, or he is going to come; **3.** ~ *!* done!, agreed!, let it be so!; indeed!; ~ *pour cent francs!*, agreed for 100 francs!; *je ne t'en veux pas* ~ *!*, I bear you no grudge, indeed!; *à la* ~ *comme je te pousse*, pull devil pull baker; in a happy-go-lucky way.

vacance (vakɑ̃s), s.f. [f. L *vacare*] **1.** Vacancy; (university) *déclarer la* ~ *d'une chaire*, to declare a chair vacant; **2.** ~*s*, (pl.) holidays; (university) vacation; recess (of parliament); *entrer en* ~*s*, to break up (of schools); to go down (of universities).

vacant, -e (vakɑ̃), adj. Vacant, unoccupied, unfilled.

vacarme (vakarm), s.m. [Dutch *wacharme*] Noise, uproar, hubbub; *faire du* ~, to kick up a shindy; syn. TUMULTE.

vacation (vaka'sjɔ̃), s.f. [L *vacatio*] **1.** Sitting; attendance (of public officers, &c.); **2.** attendance fee; **3.** ~*s* (pl.), vacation, recess (of law-courts); syn. VACANCE.

vaccin (vaksɛ̃), s.m. [f. L *vacca*, cow] Vaccine, serum, matter, lymph.

vaccinable (vaksinabl), adj. Fit for vaccination.

vaccinal, -e, (aux) (vaksinal), adj. Vaccinal.

vaccinateur (vaksinatœr), s.m. Vaccinator.

vaccination (vaksina'sjɔ̃), s.f. Vaccination.

vaccine (vaksin), s.f. **1.** Vaccination; **2.** vaccinia, cow-pox. ⚠ Not 'vaccine', which = *vaccin*.

vacciner (vaksine), v.a. To vaccinate; (fig.) to immunize.

vaccinide (vaksinid), s.f. (pathol.) Vaccinide.

vaccinifère (vaksinifɛr), adj. Vacciniferous.

vaccinogène (vaksinoʒɛn), adj. [f. *vaccin* + (Gr.) *gennan*] Vaccinogenic.

vaccinoïde (vaksinoid), adj. Vaccinoid.

vache (vaʃ), s.f. [L *vacca*] Cow; ~ *laitière*, milch cow; ~ *à lait*, (fig.) milch cow, source of profit; *ils ont fait de vous une bonne* ~ *à lait*, they have squeezed you dry; they have been sponging on you; cow-hide; (fig.) a coarse insult, applied to either sex; a policeman; (pop.) *mort aux* ~*s!*, down with the coppers!; (naut.) *le plancher des* ~*s*, dry land, terra firma; *manger de la* ~ *enragée*, to have to rough it; to reap one's wild oats; *la* ~ *à Colas*, the Protestants; *parler français comme une* ~ *espagnole*, to murder the French language; (prov.) *chacun son métier et les* ~*s seront bien gardées*, every one to his business, or to his trade, and all's well with the world. ~, adj. (slang) Nasty, wicked.

vach-er, -ère (vaʃe), s.m.f. Cowherd, neat-herd.

vacherie (vaʃri), s.f. Cow-house, byre; (slang) dirty trick; *il m'a fait une* ~, he played a dirty trick upon me.

vacherin (vaʃrɛ̃), s.m. **1.** Kind of meringue; **2.** (in Franche-Comté) gruyère cheese.

vachette (vaʃɛt), s.f. Fine cow-hide.

vacillant, -e (vasilɑ̃, vasijɑ̃), p. adj. Vacillating, flickering, wavering; (fig.) wavering, uncertain.

vacillation (vasila'sjɔ̃), s.f. Vacillation.

vacillement (vasijmɑ̃), s.m. Vacillation, vacillating.

vaciller (vasije), v.n. [L *vacillare*] To vacillate, to flicker; to reel; (fig.) to hesitate, to waver, to vacillate; syn. CHANCELER.

vacuité (vakɥite), s.f. [f. L *vacuus*] Vacuity, emptiness.

vacuum (vakɥom), s.m. [L wd] Vacuum.

vade-in-pace (vadeinpase), s.m. invar. [L wds = 'go in peace'] Convent prison.

vade-mecum (vademekom), s.m. invar. [L wds] Vade-mecum.

vadrouille (vadruj), s.f. **1.** (naut.) Swab; **2.** (slang) (*a*) loafing about; (*b*) night out, riotous party; (*c*) person who indulges in low revelry; *aller en ~, faire une ~*, to go on the loose; to loaf about.

vadrouiller (vadruje), v.n. **1.** (slang) To loaf about, to hang about, to saunter, to rove, to roam, to wander; to knock about, to mooch about; to be out for a lark; **2.** to go on the loose; to indulge in low revelry.

va-et-vient (vaevjɛ̃), s.m. invar. **1.** Oscillation, swing, see-saw motion; coming and going; *le ~ d'un balancier*, the swing of a pendulum; *il y avait un ~ continuel dans la maison*, there were continual comings and goings in the house; **2.** chain-ferry; **3.** (naut.) hauling-rope.

vagabond, -e (vagabɔ̃), adj. s.m. [L *vagabundus*] Vagabond, vagrant, tramp; (U.S.A.) hobo, moocher.

vagabondage (vagabɔ̃daʒ), s.m. Vagabondage, vagabondism; vagrancy; roaming.

vagabonder (vagabɔ̃de), v.n. To vagabondize, to be a vagabond; to tramp, to roam.

vagin (vaʒɛ̃), s.m. [f. L *vagina*] (anat.) Vagina.

vaginal, -e, (aux) (vaʒinal), adj. Vaginal.

vaginite (vaʒinit), s.f. (pathol.) Vaginitis.

vagir (vaʒir), v.n. [L *vagire*] To wail, to cry, to pule.

vagissant, -e (vaʒisɑ̃), p. adj. Wailing, puling, whining.

vagissement (vaʒismɑ̃), s.m. Wail (of an infant); bark (of a crocodile); squeal (of a hare).

vagon (vagɔ̃), s.m. See WAGON.

vague (vag), s.f. [Germ. orig.] Wave, billow, surge; syn. (pl.) ONDES, FLOTS.

vague (vag), adj. [L *vagus*] Vague; waste; *terrains ~s*, waste land; (fig.) faint, hazy. ~, s.m. Vagueness, looseness, uncertainty.

vaguement (vagmɑ̃), adv. Vaguely.

vaguemestre (vagmɛstr), s.m. [Germ. *Wagenmeister*] (mil.) Baggage-master; regimental postman.

vaguer[1] (vage), v.n. [L *vagari*] To ramble, to wander, to stray, to rove, to saunter, to stroll.

vaguer[2] (vage), v.a. [L *vagari*] (brewing) To mash.

vaigrage (vɛgraʒ), s.m. Inner planking (of a ship).

vaigre (vɛgr), s.f. [Scand. orig.] (naut.) Plank (for inner lining of a ship).

vaigrer (vɛgre), v.a. To line with planking.

vaillamment (vajamɑ̃), adv. Valiantly, courageously, gallantly, stoutly.

vaillance (vajɑ̃s), s.f. [f. *vaillant*] Valiance, courage, bravery, valour; *avec ~*, valiantly; syn. VALEUR, COURAGE.

vaillant (vajɑ̃), s.m. [f. *valoir*] What one is worth; *tout son ~*, one's all. ~, adv. Worth; *n'avoir pas un sou ~*, not to be worth a penny.

vaillant, -e (vajɑ̃), adj. [L *valens*] Valiant, gallant, courageous, valorous; (colloq.) healthy; *je ne me sens pas très ~*, I don't feel up to the mark.

vaillantise (vajɑ̃tiz), s.f. Deed of prowess, doughty deed.

vaille-que-vaille, v.loc. For better or worse; come what may; take the chance of it; poorly, indifferently; as far as one can; in some sort of a way; in spite of all difficulties.

vain, -e (vɛ̃), adj. [L *vanus*] Vain, fruitless, bootless, ineffectual; frivolous, trifling; vainglorious, conceited; empty, shadowy; *en ~*, vainly, in vain.

vaincre (vɛ̃kr), v.a.n. [L *vincere*] To vanquish, to conquer, to overcome, to defeat, to get the better of, to master, to subdue; to surpass, to outdo; *se laisser ~*, to give way, to yield; to relent; **se ~**, v.pr. to conquer oneself, to conquer one's passions.

vaincu, -e (vɛ̃ky), p. adj. Vanquished, conquered. ~, s.m. (the) Vanquished.

vainement (vɛnmɑ̃), adv. Vainly, in vain, to no purpose.

vainqueur (vɛ̃kœr), s.m. Conqueror, victor, vanquisher; prize-winner, winner. ~, adj. Conquering, victorious, triumphant; *d'un air ~*, with a triumphant look.

vair (vɛr), s.m. [L *varius*] Squirrel's fur; syn. PETIT-GRIS; (herald.) vair.

vairé, -e (vɛre), adj. (herald.) Vairy, charged with vair.

vairon, véron (vɛrɔ̃, verɔ̃), adj. m. [f. L *varius*] (of eyes) Of different colour.

vairon (vɛrɔ̃), s.m. (ichth.) Minnow.

vaisseau (pl. **-x**) (vɛso), s.m. [L *vascellum*] **1.** Vessel, vase; **2.** vessel, ship; (pl.) shipping (sing.); *le ~ fantôme*, the Flying Dutchman; (fig.) *le ~ de l'État*, the ship of state; **4.** fabric (of a building); **5.** (anat.) vessel, duct.

vaisselier (vɛsəlje), s.m. Kitchen-dresser, dresser, dining-room sideboard.

vaisselle (vɛsɛl), s.f. [f. *vaisseau*] **1.** Plates and dishes, crockery; *laver* or *faire la ~*, to wash up; *~ d'or, d'argent*, gold, silver plate; *~ plate*, gold or silver dishes.

vaissellerie (vɛsɛlri), s.f. **1.** Kitchen utensils; **2.** manufacture of kitchen-ware.

val (val), s.m. (pl. **vaux**) [L *vallis*] Dale, glen, narrow valley; *par monts et par vaux*, up hill and down dale.

valable (valabl), adj. Valid, good; available, sound, (law) good and sufficient.

valablement (valabləmɑ̃), adv. Validly.

valence[1] (valɑ̃s), s.f. [f. *Valence*, Valencia] Valencia orange.

valence[2] (valɑ̃s), s.f. [f. L *valere*] (chem.) Valency.

valenciennes (valɑ̃sjɛn), s.f. [Fr. geog. n.] Valenciennes (lace).

o, note, glotte; **ɔ̃**, monter, ronde; **ø**, feu, creux; **œ**, peur, sœur; **œ̃**, un; **ʃ**, chez, schisme; **u**, tout; **w**, oui, doit, douaire; **y**, mur, pu; **ɥ**, huile, muette; **z**, zèle, rose; **ʒ**, déjà, gentil.

valentin (valɑ̃tɛ̃), s.m. (obs.) [f. *S. Valentin*] Valentine.
valériane (valerjan), s.f. (bot.) Valerian.
valet (valɛ), s.m. [OF *varlet*, LL *vassalettus*] **1.** Valet, footman, man-servant; ~ *de chambre*, valet; ~ *de pied*, footman; ~ *de ferme*, farm-hand; (agric.) *maître* ~, head man; ~ *de chiens*, whipper-in, whip; (fig.) *âme de* ~, cringing soul; *plat* ~, cringing knave, toad-eater, toady; (prov.) *tel maître, tel* ~, like master, like man; (prov.) *il n'y a pas de grand homme pour son* ~ *de chambre*, no man is a hero to his valet; ~ *de comédie*, stage-footman; *je suis votre* ~, I am yours to command; **2.** (cards) knave, jack; **3.** door-weight; **4.** (carp.) clamp.
valetage (valtaʒ), s.m. Service, valeting.
valetaille (valtɑj), s.f. (collect., pej.) Menials (pl.), flunkeys (pl.).
valet-à-patin (valɛapatɛ̃), s.m. [f. prop. n. *Gui Patin*] (surg.) Forceps (for ligatures).
valeter (valte), v.n. To dance attendance, to cringe. ⚠ Not 'to valet', which = *faire le service de valet de chambre*.
valétudinaire (valetydinɛr), adj. s.m.f. [L *valetudinarius*] Valetudinarian; invalid; syn. MALADE, INFIRME, CACOCHYME.
valeur (valœr), s.f. [L *valor*] **1.** Value, worth, price; consideration, weight; import, meaning; *avoir de la* ~, to be of value; (fig.) to carry weight; *sans* ~, valueless, worthless; *objets de* ~, valuables; (fig.) *attacher de la* ~ *à*, to set store by, to attach importance to; *être en* ~, to look one's or its best; *mettre en* ~, to make the most of, to develop; to improve (land); **2.** valour, courage, gallantry; **3.** (pl.) bills, paper stocks, shares, securities, scrip; ~ *en espèces*, value in cash; ~*s mobilières*, transferable securities; syn. **1.** PRIX; **2.** COURAGE, CŒUR, BRAVOURE, INTRÉPIDITÉ.
valeureusement (valœrøzmɑ̃), adv. Valorously, bravely, valiantly, gallantly.
valeureu-x, -se (valœrø), adj. [f. *valeur*] Gallant, valiant, valorous.
validation (valida'sjɔ̃), s.f. Validation, rendering valid.
valide (valid), adj. [L *validus*] **1.** Valid, good; **2.** able-bodied, healthy.
validement (validmɑ̃), adv. Validly.
valider (valide), v.a. To make valid, to declare valid.
validité (validite), s.f. Validity.
valise (valiz), s.f. [It. *valigia*] Valise, suitcase, portmanteau, travelling-bag; *la* ~ *diplomatique*, the Foreign Office mail.
vallaire (valɛr), adj. [f. L *vallum*] (Rom. ant.) Vallar, vallary.
vallée (vale), s.f. [f. *val*] Valley.
valleuse (valøz), s.f. (in Normandy) Little dry valley.
vallon (valɔ̃), s.m. Little valley; (poet.) vale.
vallonnement (valɔnmɑ̃), s.m. Undulation; (landscape-gardening) disposing in hollows.
vallonner (valɔne), v.a. (landscape-gardening) To undulate, to make hollows in.
valoir (valwar), v.n.a. [L *valere*] To be worth, to be as good as, to be equal to; (fig.) to deserve, to merit; *cela ne vaut rien*, that is worthless; *il vaut son pesant d'or*, he is worth his weight in gold; *faire* ~ *des terres*, to farm an estate; *faire* ~ *son droit*, to assert one's right; *faire* ~ *ses marchandises*, to display one's goods to advantage; *faire* ~ *son argent*, to turn one's money to account; *se faire* ~, to put oneself forward, (fam.) to be pushing; *personne qui vaut qu'on s'occupe d'elle*, person who deserves attention; *cela ne vaut pas la peine*, it is not worth while; *à* ~, on account; *cette boisson ne vous vaut rien*, you are better without that drink; *il n'a fait rien qui vaille*, he has done nothing worth while; ~, v.a. to procure, to assure; to yield; *ses exploits lui ont valu une gloire immortelle*, his exploits have earned him immortal fame; ~, v.imp. *il vaut mieux*, it would be better to; you, he, &c. had better; *autant vaudrait*, one (or you) might as well; (prov.) *mieux vaut tard que jamais*, better late than never; *vaille que vaille*, adv. loc. for what it is worth; for better or for worse; as far as one can; in some sort of way; in spite of all difficulties; poorly, indifferently; *un rien qui vaille*, s.m. a good-for-nothing.
valse (vals), s.f. [Germ. *Walzer*] Valse, waltz.
valser (valse), v.n.a. To waltz.
valseu-r, -se (valsœr), s.m.f. Waltzer; ~, adj. Waltzing.
value (valy), s.f. [f. *valoir*] Value, price; *moins-*~, inferior value; decrease in value; deficiency; *plus-*~, increase in value; superior value.
valvaire (valvɛr), adj. (bot., anat.) Valvar, valvate.
valve (valv), s.f. [L *valva*] (techn., anat., zool., bot.) Valve; clack.
valvulaire (valvylɛr), adj. Valvular.
valvule (valvyl), s.f. [LL *valvula*] (anat.) Valvule.
vampire (vɑ̃pir), s.m. [Magyar *vampir*] Vampire.
vampirique (vɑ̃pirik), adj. Vampire-like, vampire.
vampirisme (vɑ̃pirism), s.m. Vampirism.
van (vɑ̃), s.m. [L *vannus*] (agric.) Winnowing-basket; fan.
vanadique (vanadik), adj. (chem.) Vanadic.
vanadium (vanadjɔm), s.m. (chem.) Vanadium.
vandale (vɑ̃dal), s.m.f. [f. L *Vandalus*] Vandal; (fig.) vandal.

vandalisme (vɑ̃dalism), s.m. Vandalism.
vandoise (vɑ̃dwaz), s.f. (ichth.) Dace.
vanesse (vanɛs), s.f. (ent.) Vanessa.
vanille (vanij), s.f. [Span. *vainilla*] (bot., cook.) Vanilla, vanilla-bean.
vanillé, -e (vanije), adj. Vanilla, flavoured with vanilla; vanilla-scented.
vanillerie (vanijri), s.f. Vanilla-plantation.
vanillier (vanije), s.m. (bot.) Vanilla-plant.
vanillisme (vanijism), s.m. (pathol.) Vanillism.
vanité (vanite), s.f. [L *vanitas*] **1.** Vanity, conceit; *tirer ~ de*, to pride oneself on; to be vain of; to glory in; **2.** nothingness, futility; emptiness, unreality, uselessness; worthlessness; *la ~ des œuvres humaines*, the vanity of human achievements.
vaniteusement (vanitøzmɑ̃), adv. Vainly, presumptuously, vaingloriously.
vaniteu-x, -se (vanitø), adj. Vain, vainglorious, conceited.
vannage[1] (vanaʒ), s.m. [f. *vanne*] System of water-gates; damming.
vannage[2] (vanaʒ), s.m. [f. *vanner*] Winnowing; winnowings, chaff.
vanne (van), s.f. [LL *venna*] **1.** Beam-feather (of a bird's wing); **2.** water-gate, sluice-gate, sluice; *eaux-~s*, waste water, drainage.
vanneau (pl. **-x**) (vano), s.m. [f. *van*] (ornith.) Lapwing, peewit.
vanné, -e (vane), p. adj. (colloq.) Exhausted, dead beat, done up.
vanner[1] (vane), v.a. [f. *van*] To winnow.
vanner[2] (vane), v.a. [f. *vanne*] To fit or dam with sluices.
vanner[3] (vane), v.a. (colloq.) To tire out, to take it out of, to exhaust.
vannerie (vanri), s.f. [f. *van*] Basket-making; basket-trade; basket-work.
vannette (vanɛt), s.f. Winnowing-basket.
vanneur (vanœr), s.m. [f. *van*] Winnower.
vannier (vanje), s.m. [f. *van*] Basket-maker.
vannure, vannée (vanyr, vane), s.f. Winnowings, chaff.
vantail (pl. **vantaux**) (vɑ̃taj), s.m. [for *ventail*, f. *venter*] Leaf, hinged flap of a door.
vantard, -e (vɑ̃tar), s.m.f. Boaster, braggart. ~, adj. Boasting, bragging.
vantardise (vɑ̃tardiz), s.f. Boasting, boast, bragging; syn. VANTERIE.
vanter (vɑ̃te), v.a. [LL *vanitare*] To extol, to commend, to eulogize, to vaunt, to praise, to cry up; **se ~**, v.pr. to boast; to extol or praise oneself; to plume oneself (*de*, upon); to brag (of), to boast (of, or that).
vanterie (vɑ̃tri), s.f. Boasting, bragging; boast; syn. VANTARDISE.
va-nu-pieds (vanypje), s.m.f. invar. Vagabond, ragamuffin, tatterdemalion.
vapeur[1] (vapœr), s.f. [L *vapor*] **1.** Steam; vapour; *à la ~*, by steam; (fig.) hurriedly, hastily, hurry-skurry; *à toute ~*, at full speed; *bateau à ~*, steamer; *18 chevaux-~ (C.V.)*, 18 horse-power (h.p.); **2.** vapour, haze, mist; *~s*, pl. exhalations; **3.** (fig.) vapours; *être sujet aux ~s*, to be prone to vapours.
vapeur[2] (vapœr), s.m. Steamer.
vaporeusement (vapɔrøzmɑ̃), adv. Vaporously.
vaporeu-x, -se (vapɔrø), adj. **1.** Vaporous; **2.** (pathol.) vapourish; **3.** (paint.) aerial.
vaporisage (vapɔrizaʒ), s.m. (techn.) Steaming.
vaporisateur (vapɔrizatœr), s.m. Vaporizer, scent-spray.
vaporisation (vapɔriza'sjɔ̃), s.f. Vaporization.
vaporiser (vapɔrize), v.a. To spray, to sprinkle (with); to vaporize, to cause to evaporate; **se ~**, v.pr. to turn to vapour, to vaporize, to evaporate.
vaporiseur (vapɔrizœr), s.m. See syn. VAPORISATEUR.
vaquer (vake), v.n. [L *vacare*] **1.** To be vacant; **2.** to be in vacation; **3.** *~ à*, to apply oneself to, to devote one's attention to; *~ à ses occupations*, to attend to one's business.
varaigne (varɛɲ), s.f. [f. dial. wd] Tide-sluice (in a salt-marsh).
varangue (varɑ̃g), s.f. [Scand. orig.] (naut.) Floorboard.
varech, varec (varɛk), s.m. [Scand. orig.] (bot.) Seaweed, sea-wrack, dulse, varec, Irish moss.
vareuse (varøz), s.f. [etym. dub.] Reefer-jacket, pea-jacket.
vari (vari), s.m. [f. Malagasy wd] (zool.) Vari; ruffed lemur.
variabilité (varjabilite), s.f. Variability, changeableness.
variable (varjabl), adj. [L *variabilis*] Variable, changeable; fickle, unsteady. ~, s.m. (math.) Variable.
variablement (varjabləmɑ̃), adv. Variably.
variant, -e (varjɑ̃), p. adj. Variant, variable, fickle.
variante (varjɑ̃t), s.f. Variant; variant reading.
variation (varja'sjɔ̃), s.f. [L *variatio*] Variation; varying; (gram., astr., biol., mus., math.) variation.
varice (varis), s.f. [L *varix*] (pathol.) Varix, varicose vein.
varicelle (varisɛl), s.f. [f. *variole*] (pathol.) Varicella, chicken-pox.
varicocèle (varikɔsɛl), s.f. (pathol.) Varicocele.

varié, -e (varje), p. adj. [L *varius*] Varied; varicoloured; (bot.) variegated.
varier (varje), v.a. [L *variare*] To vary, to change, to variegate, to diversify; ~, v.n. to vary, to change; *sur ce point les opinions varient*, opinions vary on this point; (of wind) to veer.
variété (varjete), s.f. **1.** Variety, diversity, many-sidedness; **2.** variety, specimen, kind, (pl.) miscellanea, varieties.
variolaire (varjɔlɛr), adj. Variolous, variolar, variolic.
variole (varjɔl), s.f. [L *variola*] (pathol.) Variola, small-pox; syn. PETITE VÉROLE.
varioleu-x, -se (varjɔlø), adj. Suffering from small-pox, variolous. ~, s.m.f. Small-pox case.
variolique (varjɔlik), adj. Variolic; *pustule* ~, small-pox spot, pock.
varioloïde (varjɔlɔid), s.f. [f. *variole*] Varioloid.
variorum (varjɔrɔm), s.m. [abbrev. of L *cum notis variorum scriptorum*] Variorum, variorum edition.
variqueu-x, -se (varikø), adj. (pathol.) Varicose.
varlet (varlɛ), s.m. [var. of *valet*] (feud.) Varlet.
varlope (varlɔp), s.f. [Dutch *voorlooper*] Jointing-plane, trying-plane.
varloper (varlɔpe), v.a. To plane (with the jointing-plane).
varlopeuse (varlɔpøz), s.f. Mechanical plane.
varre (var), s.f. Harpoon for turtle-fishing.
vas (vɑ), 2nd per. sing. pres. ind. [of *aller*] *Tu ~ te faire mal*, you will hurt yourself; (pop., or archaic) *je* ~, I am going, I am going to; *je m'en* ~, I am off.
vasais (vɑzɛ), s.m. **vasière** (vɑzjɛr), s.f. Salt-pan, brine-pan (in salt-marshes).
vasard, -e (vɑzar), adj. [f. *vase*] Muddy. ~, s.m. Muddy bottom.
vasculaire, vasculeu-x, -se (vaskylɛr, vaskylø), adj. [f. L *vasculum*] (anat., bot.) Vascular.
vase[1] (vɑz), s.f. [Dutch *wase*] Mud, mire, slime, ooze.
vase[2] (vɑz), s.m. [L *vas*] Vase; vessel; ~ *à fleurs*, flower-vase; ~*s sacrés*, sacred vessels; ~ *d'élection*, chosen vessel; ~*s communicants*, U-tube; ~ *de nuit*, chamber.
vasé, -e (vɑze), adj. Covered with mud or slime.
vaseline (vazlin), s.f. [Germ. *Wasser*+Gr. *elaion*] Vaseline.
vaseu-x, -se (vɑzø), adj. Muddy, slimy, oozy, miry; (slang, colloq.) out of sorts, off colour, knocked up, seedy, feeling poorly or queer; hence *vaser*, v.n. (school slang) to do badly in an exam., to be floored, not to be able to answer.
vasière (vɑzjɛr), s.f. Bog, miry bottom. See VASAIS.
vasistas (vazistɑs), s.m. [Germ. *was ist das?*] Top of casement, sky-light, fan-light.
vaso-mot-eur, -rice (vɑzomɔtœr), adj. s.m. (anat.) Vaso-motor (nerve).
vasque (vask), s.f. [It. *vasca*] Basin (of a fountain).
vassal, -e, (aux) (vasal), adj. s.m.f. [LL *vassallus*] Vassal.
vassalité (vasalite), s.f. **vasselage** (vaslaʒ), s.m. Vassalage, subjection.
vaste (vast), adj. [L *vastus*] Vast, wide, spacious; capacious; comprehensive; syn. GRAND.
vastement (vastəmɑ̃), adv. Vastly, widely, spaciously; comprehensively; capaciously.
vaticane (vatikan), adj.f. Vatican.
vaticination (vatisina'sjɔ̃), s.f. [L *vaticinatio*] Vaticination.
vaticiner (vatisine), v.n. [L *vaticinari*] To vaticinate.
va-tout (vatu), s.m. invar. One's all; (fig.) *jouer son* ~, to stake one's all.
vaucour (vokur), s.m. Potter's bench.
(à) vau-de-route (avodrut), adv. loc. [*à*+*val*+*route*] Helter-skelter.
vaudeville (vodvil), s.m. [f. prop. n. *Val* or *Vau de Vire* (15th c.)] Vaudeville.
vaudevilliste (vodvilist), s.m.f. Writer of vaudeville.
vaudois, -e (vodwɑ), adj. s.m.f. Vaudois, of the Canton de Vaud (Switzerland); (eccles. hist.) adj. Waldensian. ~, s.m.pl. Waldenses, Vaudois.
(à) vau-l'eau (avolo), adv. loc. [*à*+*val*+*eau*] With the current, down-stream; adrift; (fig.) to rack and ruin, into thin air; *aller à* ~, to come to nothing.
vaurien, -ne (vorjɛ̃), s.m.f. [f. *valoir*+*rien*] Good-for-nothing, scapegrace; rogue, vagabond, scamp.
vaut (vo), 3rd pers. sing. pres. ind. of *valoir*.
vautour (votur), s.m. [L *vultur*] (ornith.) (lit. and fig.) Vulture.
vautrait (votrɛ), s.m. Pack of boar-hounds.
vautre (votr), s.m. [L *vertragum*] Boar-hound.
vautrer[1] (votre), v.a. [f. *vautre*] To roll in the mire; se ~, v.pr. to wallow; to sprawl; (fig.) to revel (in).
vautrer[2] (votre), v.a. (hunt.) To hunt (boars) with boar-hounds.
(à) vau-vent (avovɑ̃), adv. loc. Down the wind; with the wind behind one; (naut.) before the wind.
vauxhall (vɔksal), s.m. [Engl. geog. n.] Pleasure-park.
vavassal (aux), vavasseur (vavasal, vavasœr), s.m. [LL *vassus vassorum*] Vavasour.
veau (pl. **-x**) (vo), s.m. [L *vitellus*] **1.** Calf;

tuer le ~ gras, to kill the fatted calf; *le ~ d'or*, the golden calf, worldly wealth; **2.** (meat) veal; *côtelettes de ~*, veal cutlets; **3.** (leather) calf, calf-skin, box-calf; **4.** *~ marin*, seal, sea-calf; seal-skin; (fig.) dolt, lubber; *pleurer comme un ~*, to cry like a baby; *faire le ~*, to lounge or sprawl about; to play the fool.

vecteur (vɛktœr), adj. m. [L *vectum*] (geom.) Vector; *rayon ~*, radius vector.

vectoriel, -le (vɛktɔrjɛl), adj. Vectorial.

vécu, -e (veky), p. adj. [f. *vivre*] True to life, real, sincere.

védasse (vedas), s.f. Wood-ash (used in dyeing).

vedette (vədɛt), s.f. [It. *vedetta*] **1.** Vedette, scout, mounted sentinel; motor-boat; **2.** popular actor or performer, star; *avoir la ~*, to 'star'; **3.** (fig., print.) *mettre en ~*, to print on a line by itself; to print in large type.

védique (vedik), adj. [f. Sansk. *Veda*] Vedic.

végétabilité (veʒetabilite), s.f. Vegetability.

végétable (veʒetabl), adj. [L *vegetabilis*] Vegetable. ⚠ Never subst. in French; Engl. 'vegetable', s. = *légume, végétal.*

végétal (aux) (veʒetal), s.m. Vegetal, plant, vegetable (as distinct from *animal* and *mineral*).

végétal, -e, (aux) (veʒetal), adj. Vegetal; *terre ~e*, mould, vegetable mould; *règne ~*, vegetable kingdom.

végétalisme (veʒetalism), s.m. See syn. VÉGÉTARISME.

végétarien, -ne (veʒetarjɛ̃), adj. s.m.f. Vegetarian.

végétarisme (veʒetarism), s.m. [f. *végétal*] Vegetarianism.

végétati-f, -ve (veʒetatif), adj. Vegetative; *mener une vie ~ve*, to vegetate; to lead a monotonous life.

végétation (veʒeta'sjɔ̃), s.f. **1.** Vegetation; **2.** (pathol.) growth; adenoids; (surg.) *enlever les ~s à quelqu'un*, to remove a person's adenoids.

végéter (veʒete), v.n. [L *vegetare*] To vegetate (also fig.).

véhémence (veemɑ̃s), s.f. Vehemence, impetuosity.

véhément, -e (veemɑ̃), adj. [L *vehemens*] Vehement, ardent, impetuous; syn. IMPÉTUEUX, FOUGUEUX.

véhémentement (veemɑ̃tmɑ̃), adv. Vehemently.

véhicule (veikyl), s.m. [L *vehiculum*] Vehicle.

véhiculer (veikyle), v.a. To transport.

vehme (vɛm), s.f. [f. *Vehme*, Germ. court of justice, 12th–16th c.] Vehmgericht; (fig.) secret code of behaviour or political action; secret judgement by a mysterious group of authorities.

vehmique (vemik), adj. [f. Germ. *Vehme*] Vehmic.

veille (vɛj), s.f. [L *vigilia*] **1.** Watching, waking, sleeplessness; (pl.) midnight toil, nightly labours; sitting up; late hours; **2.** waking, being awake; *entre le sommeil et la ~*, between sleeping and waking; **3.** vigil, eve, day before; (fig.) eve, verge; *à la ~ de partir*, on the eve of departure; just before leaving; (naut.) *ancre de ~*, sheet-anchor; *mettre l'ancre à la ~*, to cock-bill the anchor.

veillée (vɛje), s.f. **1.** Evening (in company); time between the last meal and bedtime; *les ~s d'hiver*, the winter evenings; *passer la ~ chez son voisin*, to pass the evening with one's neighbour; **2.** night attendance (upon a sick person).

veiller (vɛje), v.n. [L *vigilare*] **1.** To sit up, to keep watch; to be awake; *faire ~ X*, to keep X up late; **2.** to be on the watch (for), to take care (*sur*, of), to have an eye (to); *~ au grain*, (*a*) (naut.) to look out for squalls; (*b*) to spare expense, to live sparingly; ~, v.a. to watch by (the dead); to sit up with, to nurse at night.

veilleu-r, -se (vɛjœr), s.m.f. Guard, watchman; *~ de nuit*, night-watchman.

veilleuse (vɛjøz), s.f. Night-light; *mettre (la lumière) en ~*, to turn low, or dim (the light).

veinard, -e (vɛnar), adj. [f. *veine*] (slang) Lucky. ~, s.m.f. (pop.) Lucky beggar, devil, &c.

veine (vɛn), s.f. [L *vena*] **1.** (anat.) Vein; *~ cave*, vena cava; *~ porte*, vena portae; portal vein; (fig.) *se saigner aux quatre ~s*, to bleed oneself white; **2.** (geol.) seam, vein; **3.** (lit.) vein; *~ poétique*, poetic vein; **4.** (pop.) luck; *être en ~*, or *avoir de la ~*, to be lucky (*à*, at); *avoir une ~ de pendu*, to have the devil's own luck.

veiné, -e (vɛne), p. adj. Veined, veiny.

veiner (vɛne), v.a. To vein, to grain, to paint with veins, in imitation of marble, wood, &c.

veineu-x, -se (vɛnø), adj. Venous, venose; veined, veiny.

veinule (vɛnyl), s.f. Small vein.

vêlage, vêlement (vɛlaʒ, vɛlmɑ̃), s.m. Calving.

vélaire (velɛr), adj. s.f. [f. L *velum*] (phon.) Velar.

vélarium (velarjɔm), s.m. [L wd] Velarium; syn. VELUM.

velche, welche (vɛlʃ), adj. [Germ. *welsch*] Outlandish, foreign. ~, s.m.f. Ignoramus.

veld, veldt (vɛlt), s.m. [Dutch wd] Veldt; syn. STEPPE, SAVANE.

vêlement (vɛlmɑ̃), s.m. See syn. VÊLAGE.

vêler (vɛle), v.n. [f. *veau*] To calve (of cows).

vélin (velɛ̃), s.m. [f. *veau*] **1.** Vellum; parchment; **2.** fine Alençon lace. ~, adj. Parchment; *papier ~*, parchment paper, vellum post.

vélite (velit), s.m. [L *velites*] **1.** (Rom. ant.) Velite; **2.** ~*s*, corps of volunteers organized by Napoleon.
velléité (vɛlleite), s.f. [f. L *velle*] Velleity, impulse, whim.
vélo (velo), s.m. [f. *vélocipède*] (fam.) Bike.
vélocifère (velɔsifɛr), s.m. (obs.) Old name for omnibus; also CÉLÉRIFÈRE.
vélocimane (velɔsiman), s.m. (obs.) [L *velox*+*manus*] Tricycle-horse; syn. CHEVAL MÉCANIQUE.
vélocipède (velɔsipɛd), s.m. [L *velox*+*pes*] Bicycle, velocipede.
vélocité (velɔsite), s.f. [f. L *velox*] Velocity, speed; syn. VITESSE, RAPIDITÉ.
vélodrome (velɔdrom), s.m. [L *velox*+Gr. *dromos*] Velodrome.
velot (vəlo), s.m. [f. *veau*] Skin of still-born calf.
velours (vəlur), s.m. [OF *velous*, f. L *villosus*] Velvet (also fig.); ~ *côtelé*, corduroy; ~ *de soie*, silk velvet; ~ *panne*, panne velvet; ~ *de coton*, velveteen; ~ *anglais*, velveteen; *patte de* ~, velvet paw; *faire patte de* ~, to draw in one's claws; *une main de fer dans un gant de* ~, an iron hand in a velvet glove; *jouer sur le* ~, to gamble without risk; to start any business with previous advantages; *faire des* ~, to make false liaisons (*s* or *z* instead of *t*, in speaking French).
velouté, -e (vəlute), p. adj. Velvety, velvet, velvet-like; soft as velvet; (of wine) like velvet, smooth to the palate. ~, s.m. Velvet pile; (fig.) **1.** softness; **2.** bloom (of fruit); **3.** (cook.) velouté sauce.
velouter (vəlute), v.a. To give (a material) the appearance of velvet; to make soft as velvet.
velouteu-x, -se (vəlutø), adj. Velvety, soft as velvet.
veloutier (vəlutje), s.m. Velvet-weaver.
velu, -e (vəly), adj. [LL *villutus*] Hairy; shaggy.
velum (velɔm), s.m. [L wd] Velum, velarium, awning.
velvet (vɛlvɛ), s.m. [Engl. wd], **velvantine, velventine** (vɛlvɑ̃tin), s.f. Velveteen.
velvote (vɛlvɔt), s.f. (bot.) Toad-flax.
venaison (vənɛzɔ̃), s.f. [L *venatio*] Venison.
vénal, -e, (aux) (venal), adj. [L *venalis*] (pej.) Venal.
vénalement (venalmɑ̃), adv. Venally.
vénalité (venalite), s.f. Venality.
venant, -e (vənɑ̃), p. adj. (obs.) Coming; thriving; *enfant bien* ~, thriving child; *six mille livres de rentes bien* ~*es*, a steady six thousand a year. ~, s.m. Comer; *les allants et les* ~*s*, the comers and goers; *à tout* ~, to the first comer; *tout-*~, s.m. unscreened coals.
vendable (vɑ̃dabl), adj. Saleable, vendible.
vendange (vɑ̃dɑ̃ʒ), s.f. [L *vindemia*] Grape-harvest; grape-gathering; vintage, the grapes gathered; (pl.) *les* ~*s*, the vintage, the season of grape-harvest; (prov.) *adieu paniers,* ~*s sont faites*, all good things come to an end.
vendanger (vɑ̃dɑ̃ʒe), v.a.n. To harvest the grapes; to gather the grapes (from).
vendangeron (vɑ̃dɑ̃ʒrɔ̃), s.m. (ent.) Harvest-bug; syn. ROUGET, AOÛTAT.
vendangette (vɑ̃dɑ̃ʒɛt), s.f. (pop.) Thrush.
vendangeu-r, -se (vɑ̃dɑ̃ʒœr), s.m.f. Vintager, grape-gatherer, grape-harvester.
vendéen, -ne (vɑ̃deɛ̃), adj. s.m.f. Vendean, of la Vendée.
vendémiaire (vɑ̃demjɛr), s.m. [f. L *vindemia*] Vendémiaire (first month of the French Republican year: 22nd September to 21st October).
vendetta (vɛ̃dɛtta), s.f. [It. wd] Vendetta.
vendeu-r, -se (vɑ̃dœr), s.m.f. Salesman, (fem.) saleswoman; (fam.) shopman, shop-girl; (law) vendor.
vendre (vɑ̃dr), v.a. [L *vendere*] To sell, to vend; (fig.) to sell; to betray; (law) to sell up (a person); *à* ~, for sale; ~ *à bon marché*, to sell cheap; ~ *cher*, to sell at a high price, (fig.) to sell dear; ~ *la mèche*, to betray the plot; to let the cat out of the bag; **se** ~, v.pr. to sell oneself; to sell, to be sold.
vendredi (vɑ̃drədi), s.m. [L *Veneris dies*] Friday; *le* ~ *saint*, Good Friday.
vendu, -e (vɑ̃dy), p. adj. Sold; (fig., pej.) corrupt, venal.
venelle (vənɛl), s.f. [f. L *vena*] Alley; *enfiler la* ~, to take to one's heels.
vénéneu-x, -se (venenø), adj. [f. L *venenum*] Poisonous, venomous.
vener (vəne), v.a. [L *venari*] **1.** (obs.) To run (foxes, cattle, &c.); **2.** *faire* ~ *de la viande*, to hang meat (until it is tender).
vénérable (venerabl), adj. Venerable.
vénération (venera'sjɔ̃), s.f. Veneration; syn. RÉVÉRENCE, RESPECT.
vénérer (venere), v.a. [L *venerari*] To venerate, to reverence.
vénerie (venri), s.f. [f. L *venari*] Venery, hunting; hunting-train.
vénérien, -ne (venerjɛ̃), adj. [f. L *Venus*] (pathol.) Venereal.
venette (vənɛt), s.f. (fam.) Funk; *avoir la* ~, to be in a blue funk; syn. (pop.) AVOIR LES FOIES BLANCS.
veneur (vənœr), s.m. [L *venator*] Huntsman; *Grand* ~, King's huntsman.
vénézuélien, -ne (venezɥeljɛ̃), adj. s.m.f. Venezuelan.
vengeance (vɑ̃ʒɑ̃s), s.f. Vengeance, revenge; *crier* ~, to cry aloud for vengeance; *par* ~, out of revenge; *tirer* ~ *d'un affront*, to be avenged for an affront; *ne respirer que la* ~, to breathe vengeance.
venger (vɑ̃ʒe), v.a. [L *vindicare*] To avenge, to revenge; **se** ~, v.pr. to avenge

oneself (*de*, upon), to be revenged, to take vengeance (upon).

vengeur, vengeresse (vɑ̃ʒœr, vɑ̃ʒrɛs), s.m.f. Avenger, revenger. ~, adj. Avenging, revengeful.

véniel, -le (venjɛl), adj. [f. L *venia*] Venial.

véniellement (venjɛlmɑ̃), adv. Venially.

venimeu-x, -se (vənimø), adj. [f. OF *venim*] Venomous; (fig.) spiteful, malignant; *critique* ~, venomous critic.

venimosité (vənimozite), s.f. Venomousness.

venin (vənɛ̃), s.m. [L *venenum*] Poison, venom; (fig.) venom, rancour, malice, spite; *il a jeté tout son* ~, he has vented all his spite; syn. POISON.

venir (vənir), v.n. [L *venire*] **1.** To come, to be coming, to arrive; ~ *à*, to reach, to come to; to happen to; ~ *de*, to issue, to emanate, to be derived from; to have just; *ce mot vient du latin*, this word is derived from Latin; *la voilà qui vient*, here she comes; *d'où venez-vous?*, where have you come from?; *d'où vient cela?*, what is the cause of that?; *d'où vient que?*, how is it that?; *il prend le temps comme il vient*, he takes things as they come; (fig.) ~ *à bout de*, to master, to subdue, to overcome, to cope with; to contrive to end, to see the end of; to achieve; ~ *à rien*, to come to nothing, to fail; *laisser* ~ *les choses*, to let things take their course; *il me vint une pensée*, a thought struck me; it occurred to me; *il vient de sortir*, he has just gone out; (fig.) *voir* ~ *quelqu'un*, to see a person's game; *je vous vois* ~ *!*, I see what you're after!; *je viens le voir*, I have come to see him; (in writing) *je viens vous remercier*, I am writing to thank you; *se faire bien* ~ (*de*), to ingratiate oneself (with); *faire* ~, to send for; *faire* ~ *le docteur*, to call in the doctor; *en* ~ *aux mains*, to come to blows; *où voulez-vous en* ~*?*, what are you driving at?; *il s'en est allé comme il est venu*, he had his labour for his pains; ~ *au monde*, to be born; (prov.) *tout vient à point à qui sait attendre*, everything comes to him who waits; *ne faire qu'aller et* ~, (*a*) to go and come back at once; to be back directly; (*b*) to be always on the move; **2.** to grow, to thrive; *ces plantes viennent bien*, these plants are coming on well; **3.** to occur, to happen; to arise; to turn (to); *on vint à parler de la guerre*, the conversation turned upon the war; *si ma lettre venait à se perdre*, if my letter happened to get lost; *vienne une maladie*, should illness arise.

vénitien, -ne (venisjɛ̃), adj. s.m.f. Venetian; *lanterne* ~*ne*, Chinese lantern.

vent (vɑ̃), s.m. [L *ventus*] **1.** Wind, breeze, gale; (fig.) wind, vanity, emptiness; *aller comme le* ~, to go, to run, ride, drive, &c., like the wind; *instruments à* ~, wind-instruments; *être logé aux quatre* ~*s*, to be exposed to every wind of heaven; ~ *de mer*, sea-breeze; ~ *de terre*, land-breeze; *petit* ~, light breeze; *coup de* ~, gust of wind; ~ *coulis*, sharp draught of wind, wind from a chink; ~*s alizés*, trade-winds; *faire* ~ *arrière*, to scud before the wind; ~ *debout*, head wind; wind in the teeth; *aller contre* ~*s et marées*, to have wind and tide against one; (fig.) to be up against it; *avoir le* ~ *en poupe*, to sail before the wind; (fig.) to be in favour; *courir devant le* ~, to scud, to run before the wind; *pincer, serrer, tenir le* ~, to hug the wind; *au plus près du* ~, close-hauled; *passer au* ~ *de*, to keep to windward of; *bord du* ~, weather-side; windward; *bord sous le* ~, lee-side; leeward; *au gré du* ~, at the mercy of the wind, floating in the breeze; *il fait beaucoup de* ~, it 's very windy; (fig.) *regarder de quel côté vient le* ~, to see how the land lies; (prov.) *autant en emporte le* ~, words, words, words!, that is but so much breath wasted; *tout cela n'est que du* ~, that 's all moonshine; *en coup de* ~, precipitately, hurry-skurry; *arbre de* (or *en*) *plein* ~, standard tree; *quel bon* ~ *vous amène?*, what lucky chance brings you here?; *en plein* ~, in the open air; *venir des quatre* ~*s*, to come from every corner of the earth; (fig.) *avoir du* ~ *dans les voiles*, to be tipsy, to be three sheets in the wind; *il fait un* ~ *à écorner les bœufs*, it is blowing great guns; (prov.) *qui sème le* ~ *récolte la tempête*, he that sows the wind shall reap the whirlwind; (prov.) *selon le* ~ *la voile*, one must cut one's coat according to one's cloth; *fusil à* ~, air-gun; *moulin à* ~, windmill; *il fait du* ~, it is windy, there is a wind; *avec le* ~ *qu'il fait*, in a wind like this; *le* ~ *n'est ni chasseur ni pêcheur*, the wind is no friend to either huntsman or fisherman; *se mettre à l'abri du* ~, to shelter or to take shelter from the wind; *le* ~ *de l'adversité*, the wind of adversity; (fig.) *tourner à tout* ~, to be a weathercock; *mettre flamberge au* ~, to draw one's trusty sword; (fig.) *s'en aller le nez au* ~, to walk, to go away, with one's chin in the air; *avoir des* ~*s*, to be troubled with wind; to break wind; **2.** (hunt.) scent, wind; *avoir le* ~ *de*, to get the scent of; (fig.) *avoir* ~ *de*, to get wind of, to suspect; *n'avoir ni* ~ *ni nouvelle de X*, to have no news of any kind of X; **3.** (artill.) windage; **4.** vent (of a wine-barrel). ⚠ Eng. 'vent' usually = *évent*; *soupirail, passage, tours*; *ventouse*.

ventage (vɑ̃taʒ), s.m. Winnowing; syn. VANNAGE.

ventail, ventaille (vɑ̃taj), s.m. s.f. Ventail, vizor (of a helmet).

vente (vɑ̃t), s.f. [LL *vendita*] Sale; selling,

auction; *en* ~, for sale; now ready (of a book); *marchandises de bonne* ~, goods that sell well; *mettre en* ~, to put up for sale; to publish (a book); *en* ~ *chez*, sold by; ~ *de charité*, charity bazaar; *salle des* ~*s*, auction-rooms, sale-rooms, auction-mart.

venter (vɑ̃te), v. impers. To blow (of wind); to be windy; *il vente fort*, it is blowing hard.

venteu-x, -se (vɑ̃tø), adj. **1.** Windy, gusty; **2.** (of food) causing flatulence.

ventilateur (vɑ̃tilatœr), s.m. Ventilator, electric fan; *courroie du* ~, fan-belt.

ventilation (vɑ̃tila'sjɔ̃), s.f. Ventilation.

ventiler (vɑ̃tile), v.a. [L *ventilare*] **1.** To ventilate, to air; **2.** (law) to estimate the value of (objects sold together).

ventileuse (vɑ̃tiløz), s.f. Ventilating-bee.

ventis (vɑ̃ti), s.m.pl. Fallen trees, wind-fallen timber.

ventôse (vɑ̃toz), s.m. [L *ventosus*] Ventôse (6th month in French Republican calendar: from 19th February to 20th March).

ventouse (vɑ̃tuz), s.f. [LL *ventosa*] **1.** Cupping-glass; cupping; **2.** (nat. hist.) sucker; **3.** vent, vent-hole, air-hole.

ventouser (vɑ̃tuze), v.a. (surg.) To cup.

ventral, -e, (aux) (vɑ̃tral), adj. Abdominal; (nat. hist.) ventral.

ventre (vɑ̃tr), s.m. [L *venter*] Abdomen, belly; stomach; paunch, guts; womb; bowels; inside; corporation, body; *à plat* ~, flat on the face; *courir* ~ *à terre*, to go at full gallop, to run like a hare; to ride hell for leather; *avoir mal au* ~, to have internal pains; (pop.) to have the belly-ache; *bas-*~, abdomen; *prendre du* ~, to get stout, to develop a corporation; (fig.) *je sais ce qu'il a dans le* ~, I know what he has got in him; I know what can be expected of him; (prov.) ~ *affamé n'a point d'oreilles*, a hungry man has no ears; a hungry man is an angry man; (fig.) *se serrer le* ~, to tighten one's belt; *se brosser le* ~, to have to do without (food, money, &c.); *un vase au large* ~, a squat, fat vase; *faire* ~, to bulge out; *il n'a pas trois mois dans le* ~, he hasn't three months to live; (fig.) *à* ~ *déboutonné*, to excess; in an unrestrained way; *dès le* ~ *de sa mère*, from his mother's womb.

ventrebleu !, ventre-St-Gris ! (vɑ̃trəblø, vɑ̃trəsɛ̃gri), interj. Zounds !

ventrée (vɑ̃tre), s.f. **1.** Litter (of puppies, &c.); **2.** (pop.) bellyful, blow-out.

ventriculaire (vɑ̃trikylɛr), adj. Ventricular.

ventricule (vɑ̃trikyl), s.m. [L *ventriculus*] (anat.) Ventricle.

ventrière (vɑ̃trijɛr), s.f. Girth (of horses).

ventriloque (vɑ̃trilɔk), adj. [L *venter*+*loqui*] Ventriloquial, ventriloquous; ~, s.m.f. Ventriloquist.

ventriloquie (vɑ̃trilɔki), s.f. Ventriloquy.

ventripotent, -e (vɑ̃tripɔtɑ̃), adj. [L *venter* +*potens*] (fam.) Corpulent, pot-bellied.

ventru, -e (vɑ̃try), adj. Corpulent, obese, pot-bellied; bulgy.

venu, -e (vəny), p. adj. Come; done, executed, received; successful; *estampe bien* ~*e*, successful print; *bien* ~ (or *bienvenu*), welcome; *mal* ~ (or *malvenu*), unwelcome. ~, s.m.f. *Le premier* ~, *la première* ~*e*, the first comer, any one; *le nouveau* ~, *la nouvelle* ~*e*, the new-comer.

venue (vəny), s.f. **1.** Coming, arrival, advent; (pl.) *allées et* ~*s*, comings and goings; **2.** growth; *arbre d'une belle* ~, well-grown tree; *tout d'une* ~, in a lump; (fig., pers.) as straight as a young shoot. ⚠ Not Engl. 'venue', which =*juridiction*; *rendez-vous*.

vénusté (venyste), s.f. [f. *Venus*] Charm, beauty, (colloq.) sex-appeal.

vêpres (vɛpr), s.f.pl. [L *vesperae*] Vespers.

ver (vɛr), s.m. [L *vermis*] Worm; maggot, mite; moth; *mangé* or *rongé des* ~*s*, moth-eaten; ~ *solitaire*, tape-worm; ~ *luisant*, glow-worm; ~ *à soie*, silk-worm; (fig.) ~ *rongeur*, thorn in the flesh; (fig.) *tirer les* ~*s du nez à X*, to succeed in pumping X (for information), to pump X, to worm (a secret) out of X; *nu comme un* ~, stark naked; (slang) *ça n'est pas piqué des* ~*s*, that 's A1; that 's not so dusty; that's not to be sneezed at; *tuer le* ~, to keep the damp out (by drinking an early glass of spirits).

véracité (verasite), s.f. [L *veracitas*] Veracity.

véraison (verɛzɔ̃), s.f. (rare) [etym. unkn.] Turning, ripening (especially of grapes).

véranda (verɑ̃da), s.f. [Port. *varanda*] Veranda(h).

vératre (veratr), s.m. [L *veratrum*] (bot.) Veratrum (hellebore).

verbal, -e, (aux) (vɛrbal), adj. [f. *verbe*] Verbal; oral, by word of mouth.

verbalement (vɛrbalmɑ̃), adv. Verbally; orally, by word of mouth.

verbalisation (vɛrbaliza'sjɔ̃), s.f. Verbalization.

verbaliser (vɛrbalize), v.n. To prosecute.

verbe (vɛrb), s.m. [L *verbum*] **1.** Verb; **2.** tone of voice, speech; *avoir le* ~ *haut*, to have a domineering way of talking; **3.** (theol.) the Word.

verbénacées (vɛrbenase), s.f.pl. [f. L *verbena*] (bot.) Verbenaceae.

verbeu-x, -se (vɛrbø), adj. [L *verbosus*] Verbose, prolix.

verbiage (vɛrbjaʒ), s.m. Prating, verbiage.

verbosité (vɛrbozite), s.f. Verbosity.

ver-coquin (vɛrkɔkɛ̃), s.m. **1.** (vet.) Staggers; **2.** worm (said to attack the brain of animals); **3.** (fig.) whim, caprice.

verdal (vɛrdal), s.m. Thick greenish glass, pavement-glass.

verdâtre (vɛrdɑtr), adj. [f. *vert*] Greenish.
verdelet, -te (vɛrdəlɛ), adj. **1.** (of wine) Tart, harsh; **2.** (fig.) (of old people) hale, hearty; *vieillard* ~, hale old man.
verderie (vɛrdri), s.f. [f. *verdier*] Verderer's range.
verdet (vɛrdɛ), s.m. Verdigris; syn. VERT-DE-GRIS.
verdeur (vɛrdœr), s.f. [f. *vert*] **1.** Greenness; viridity; sap (of wood); **2.** harshness, tartness (of wine); **3.** (fig.) haleness (of the aged); **4.** extreme freedom (of speech).
verdict (vɛrdikt), s.m. [Engl. wd, f. L *vere dictum*] Verdict.
verdier[1] (vɛrdje), s.m. (ornith.) Greenfinch.
verdier[2] (vɛrdje), s.m. [LL *viridarius*] Verderer, ranger.
verdir (vɛrdir), v.a. [f. *vert*] To make or paint green; ~, v.n. **1.** to grow green, to become green; **2.** (of copper) to turn green.
verdissant, -e (vɛrdisɑ̃), p. adj. Turning or becoming green.
verdoyant, -e (vɛrdwajɑ̃), p. adj. Verdant.
verdoyer (vɛrdwaje), v.n. To be verdant.
verdure (vɛrdyr), s.f. **1.** Verdure, greenness; **2.** greenery; pot-herbs; **3.** (on tapestry, &c.) foliage, forest-scenery.
verduri-er, -ère (vɛrdyrje), s.m.f. Greengrocer, salad-seller.
véreu-x, -se (verø), adj. [f. *ver*] **1.** Worm-eaten, maggoty; rotten; **2.** (fig.) suspicious, doubtful; *homme d'affaires* ~, shady sort of business-man.
verge (vɛrʒ), s.f. [L *virga*] Rod, staff, switch, whisk; verge; shank (of an anchor); (anat.) penis; (fig.) *donner des ~s pour se faire fouetter*, to lay up a rod for one's own back; *huissier à* ~, verger; ~ *de bedeau*, verger's staff; (bot.) ~ *d'or*, golden-rod. ⚠ Not Engl. 'verge' in the sense of *extrême bord*.
vergé, -e (vɛrʒe), p. adj. **1.** Laid (of paper); **2.** streaky (of textile fabrics).
vergée (vɛrʒe), s.f. (obs.) Square rood.
verger (vɛrʒe), s.m. [L *viridiarium*] Orchard.
vergeter (vɛrʒəte), v.a. To beat, to whisk, to brush (with cane or besom).
vergetier (vɛrʒətje), s.m. Broom-maker, brush-maker.
vergette (vɛrʒɛt), s.f. **1.** Small cane or switch; **2.** clothes-brush.
vergeture (vɛrʒətyr), s.f. (usually pl.) Streak, wale, weal.
verglacé, -e (vɛrglase), adj. Covered with thin, very slippery ice.
verglas (vɛrglɑ), s.m. [f. *verre*+*glace*] Thin coating of ice, frozen rain or sleet; *il fait du* ~, the rain freezes as it falls, it 's very slippery.
vergne, verne (vɛrɲ, vɛrn), s.m. (pop.) Alder; syn. AULNE.
vergogne (vɛrgɔɲ), s.f. [L *verecundia*] Decency, shame; *sans* ~, shameless.
vergue (vɛrg), s.f. [f. *verge*] (naut.) Yard; ~ *barrée*, cross-jack yard; *grande* ~, main yard.
véridicité (veridisite), s.f. Veracity, truthfulness.
véridique (veridik), adj. [L *veridicus*] Veracious, veridical; syn. VRAI.
véridiquement (veridikmɑ̃), adv. Veraciously, accurately.
vérifiable (verifjabl), adj. Verifiable, ascertainable.
vérificat-eur, -rice (verifikatœr), s.m.f. Verifier, inspector, examiner, auditor (of accounts).
vérification (verifika'sjɔ̃), s.f. Verification; examining, auditing.
vérifier (verifje), v.a. [f. L *verus*+*facere*] To verify, to inspect, to examine; to audit (accounts); to prove, to confirm.
vérin (verɛ̃), s.m. Screw-jack.
vérine[1] (verin), s.f. [f. *Varinas*, town in Colombia] Varinas, finest kind of American tobacco.
vérine,[2] **verrine** (vɛrin), s.f. (naut.) Binnacle lamp.
véritable (veritabl), adj. True, genuine, real; veritable; staunch, thorough; *un* ~ *ami*, a staunch friend; syn. VRAI.
véritablement (veritabləmɑ̃), adv. Truthfully, in truth, really, truly; veritably.
vérité (verite), s.f. [L *veritas*] Truth, verity, truthfulness; *sa réponse avait l'accent de la* ~, his answer rang true; *dire à X ses ~s*, to tell X a few plain or home truths; *à la* ~, I confess; to tell the truth; *en* ~, indeed, truly; in point of fact; (prov.) *toutes ~s ne sont pas bonnes à dire*, it is not always wise to speak the truth; ~ *banale*, truism; *il n'y a que la* ~ *qui offense*, it 's the truth that hurts; *une* ~ *de La Palisse*, a truism, an obvious truth.
verjus (vɛrʒy), s.m. [*vert*+*jus*] Verjuice; sour grapes.
verjuté, -e (vɛrʒyte), adj. Verjuiced, sharp, tart, acid.
verjuter (vɛrʒyte), v.a. To flavour with verjuice.
vermeil, -le (vɛrmɛj), adj. [L *vermiculus*] Vermilion; rosy, ruddy; *lèvres ~les*, ruby lips. ~, s.m. Silver-gilt, vermeil.
vermicelier (vɛrmisəlje), s.m. Vermicelli-maker.
vermicelle (vɛrmisɛl), s.m. [It. *vermicelli*] Vermicelli.
vermicellerie (vɛrmisɛlri), s.f. Vermicelli-factory or -manufacture.
vermicide (vɛrmisid), adj. [L *vermis*+*caedere*] Vermicidal, vermifugal, anthelminthic.
vermiculaire (vɛrmikylɛr), adj. [f. L *vermiculus*] Vermicular.

vermiculé, -e (vɛrmikyle), adj. Vermiculated.
vermiculure (vɛrmikylyr), s.f. (arch.) Vermiculation.
vermiforme (vɛrmifɔrm), adj. [L *vermis*+ Fr. *forme*] Vermiform.
vermifuge (vɛrmifyʒ), s.m. [L *vermis*+ *fugare*] (pharm.) Vermifuge. ~, adj. Vermifugal.
vermiller (vɛrmije), v.n. (said of boars, pigs, &c.) To root.
vermillon (vɛrmijɔ̃), s.m. Vermilion.
vermine (vɛrmin), s.f. [f. L *vermis*] Vermin; (fig.) vermin, rabble, pest.
vermineu-x, -se (vɛrminø), adj. **1.** Verminous, covered with vermin; **2.** (med.) verminous, caused by intestinal worms.
vermisseau (pl. -x) (vɛrmiso), s.m. Small worm, grub; (fig.) mere worm, poor worm.
vermivore (vɛrmivɔr), adj. [L *vermis*+ *vorare*] Vermivorous.
(se) vermouler (səvɛrmule), v.pr. To become worm-eaten.
vermoulu, -e (vɛrmuly), adj. [*ver*+ *moulu*] Worm-eaten; dilapidated, in ruins.
vermoulure (vɛrmulyr), s.f. Worm-hole; dust from worm-holes.
vermout, vermouth (vɛrmut), s.m. [Germ. *Wermut*] Vermouth.
vernaculaire (vɛrnakylɛr), adj. s.m. [f. L *vernaculus*] Vernacular.
vernal, -e, (aux) (vɛrnal), adj. [L *vernalis*] Vernal, springlike.
verne (vɛrn), s.m. See VERGNE.
vernier (vɛrnje), s.m. [f. inventor's name] Vernier, sliding-scale.
verni, -e (vɛrni), adj. Varnished, japanned; (of leather) patent; patent leather; *souliers ~s*, patent-leather shoes; *faïence ~e*, glazed or varnished pottery; (slang) *il est ~!*, he is a lucky dog; he is bullet-proof; he bears a charmed life; *les petits ~s*, the dudes, the dandies, the swells.
vernir (vɛrnir), v.a. To varnish; to glaze, to polish; to lacquer, to japan.
vernis (vɛrni), s.m. [etym. dub.] Varnish, polish, glaze, glazings; *donner un ~ à*, to give a gloss to, to set off; (bot.) *~ du Japon*, Japan varnish-tree.
vernissage (vɛrnisaʒ), s.m. **1.** Varnishing; **2.** private view of a picture-exhibition.
vernissé, -e (vɛrnise), p. adj. Glazed.
vernisser (vɛrnise), v.a. To glaze (pottery).
vernisseu-r, -se (vɛrnisœr), s.m.f. Varnisher.
vernissure (vɛrnisyr), s.f. Varnish, varnishing (already on an object).
vérole (verɔl), s.f. [f. L *varius*] (pathol.) Pox, syphilis; *petite ~*, small-pox; syn. VARIOLE.
véronique (verɔnik) s.f. [f. prop. n.] **1.** (relic) Veronica; **2.** (bot.) veronica.
verrat (vɛra), s.m. [L *verres*] Young male pig or boar.
verre (vɛr), s.m. [L *vitrum*] Glass; *~ à boire*, glass, drinking-glass, tumbler; *~ à pied*, rummer, wineglass, glass with a foot; *~ de montre*, watch-glass; *~ à vitre*, sheet glass; *pâte de ~*, opaque glass; *~ dépoli*, frosted glass; *papier de ~*, glass-paper, sandpaper; *il se noierait dans un ~ d'eau*, a feather would sink him; *une tempête dans un ~ d'eau*, a storm in a teacup; *boire un petit ~*, to have a brandy, to drink a liqueur; *mon ~ n'est pas grand, mais je bois dans mon ~*, a poor thing, but mine own; *~ grossissant*, magnifying-glass; *où sont mes ~s?*, where are my spectacles? or my glasses?; *de ~*, or *en ~*, glass, of glass; *~ à glace*, or *glace*, plate glass.
verré, -e (vɛre), adj. Glassed, glass-; *papier ~*, glass-paper.
verrerie (vɛrri), s.f. **1.** Glassware; **2.** glass-works; **3.** glass-making.
verrier (vɛrje), s.m. **1.** Glass-maker, glass-blower; *peintre ~*, glass-stainer; **2.** dealer in glassware; **3.** glass-basket.
verrière, verrine (vɛrjɛr, vɛrin), s.f. Stained-glass window; coloured light (in a window); **2.** glass stand, glass case.
verroterie (vɛrɔtri), s.f. Glass beads, glass trinkets; small glassware.
verrou (pl. -s) (vɛru), s.m. [L *veruculum*] Bolt; *s'enfermer au ~*, to bolt oneself in; *fermer une porte au ~*, to bolt a door; *pousser* or *fermer le ~*, to slip the bolt; (fig.) *sous les ~s*, in the lock-up; *porter l'épée en ~*, to wear one's sword horizontally.
verrouiller (vɛruje), v.a. **1.** To bolt; *~ sa porte*, to bolt one's door; **2.** to bolt in; *~ un prisonnier*, to bolt a prisoner in.
verrucaire (vɛrykɛr), s.f. [f. L *verruca*] (bot.) Wartwort.
verrue (vɛry), s.f. [L *verruca*] Wart; (fig.) blemish, defect.
verruqueu-x, -se (vɛrykø), adj. Verrucous.
vers (vɛr), s.m. invar. [L *versus*] **1.** Line (of poetry); *le premier ~*, the first line; *ce ~ est faux, il a un pied de trop*, that line is bad, there is a syllable or foot too many; **2.** (pl. in Fr.) verse, poetry; *faire des ~*, to write poetry; *~ blancs*, blank verse; *mauvais* or *méchants ~*, doggerel; *~ libres*, vers libre, free verse; *mettre en ~*, to versify, to make a metrical version of. ⚠ Engl. 'verse' = French *strophe, verset.*
vers (vɛr), prep. [L *versus*] **1.** Towards, to; *venez ~ moi*, come towards me; **2.** about (of time only); *~ midi*, about midday.
versant (vɛrsɑ̃), s.m. Watershed, slope, declivity, side; *le ~ sud des Alpes*, the southern slopes of the Alps.

versant, -e (vɛrsɑ̃), p. adj. Liable to overturn or capsize.

versatile (vɛrsatil), adj. [L *versatilis*] Fickle, inconstant; changeable; versatile. ⚠ Versatile is usually pejorative in French, but not in English.

versatilité (vɛrsatilite), s.f. Fickleness, changeableness; versatility. ⚠ See VERSATILE.

verse (vɛrs), s.f. [f. *verser*] **1.** Pouring, emptying; **2.** laying (of standing crops by rain, &c.); *à* ~, adv. loc. pouring; *il pleut à* ~, it is pouring, or it is raining cats and dogs. ⚠ Not Engl. 'verse', which = *strophe, verset.*

verse (vɛrs), adj. [L *versus*] (geom.) Versed; *sinus* ~, versed sine.

versé, -e (vɛrse), p. adj. **1.** Poured; spilt; (of corn) laid, lodged; **2.** well versed (*dans*, in), conversant (with); ~ *dans les sciences naturelles*, well versed in natural science.

versement (vɛrsəmɑ̃), s.m. [f. *verser*] **1.** Payment; instalment; *en plusieurs* ~*s*, by instalments; **2.** deposit.

verser (vɛrse), v.a. [L *versare*] **1.** To pour, to pour out; to pour forth, to discharge, to empty; to shed; ~ *le thé*, to pour out tea; *versez-lui à boire*, fill his glass, or see that he has something to drink; (fig.) ~ *des larmes*, to shed tears; ~ *son sang*, to lay down one's life; **2.** to spill, to upset, to overturn; to beat down, to lay, to lodge (corn); *le cheval a versé la voiture dans le fossé*, the horse overturned the carriage into the ditch; *l'orage a versé beaucoup de blé*, the storm has laid a great deal of corn; **3.** to pay in, to deposit (money); ~, v.n. to overturn (of vehicles); to be laid (of standing corn).

verset (vɛrsɛ), s.m. [f. *vers*] Verse (of the Bible).

verseur (vɛrsœr), s.m. [f. *verser*] **1.** Pourer-out; **2.** employee in market-halls.

verseuse (vɛrsøz), s.f. Coffee-pot, hot-water-jug (usually of metal).

versicolore (vɛrsikɔlɔr), adj. [L *versus*+*color*] Versicolour(ed), variegated.

versicule, versiculet (vɛrsikyl, vɛrsikylɛ), s.m. [L *versiculus*] Versicle.

versificateur (vɛrsifikatœr), s.m. Versifier.

versification (vɛrsifika'sjɔ̃), s.f. [f. L *versificare*] Versification.

versifier (vɛrsifje), v.n.a. [L *versus*+*facere*] To versify.

version (vɛrsjɔ̃), s.f. [L *versio*] Translation (⚠ especially from a foreign language into one's native tongue, in opp. to *thème*, which = prose, composition); version; *il y a de cette accident plusieurs* ~*s*, there are several versions of the story of this accident.

verso (vɛrso), s.m. [L wd] Verso, back.

versoir (vɛrswar), s.m. Mould-board (of a plough).

verste (vɛrst), s.f. [Russ. wd] Verst, Russian measure of length = 3,500 feet, about ⅔ of an English mile.

vert, -e (vɛr), adj. [L *viridis*] Green; verdant, grassy; (fig.) sharp, harsh; unripe, sour; tart (of wine); *légumes* ~*s*, greens, green vegetables; *ils sont trop* ~*s*, sour grapes!, the grapes are sour; *bois* ~, green, unseasoned wood; **2.** (fig.) vigorous, hale, hearty; sharp, spicy; *un vieillard encore* ~, a hale old man; *une* ~*e réponse*, a sharp retort; (fam.) *en dire de* ~*es*, to tell spicy stories; *une* ~*e correction*, a sound thrashing; *une volée de bois* ~, a hail of blows; *il lui en a fait voir de* ~*es et de pas mûres*, he worried him beyond all bearing. ~, s.m. Green; *mettre un cheval au* ~, to put a horse out to grass; (fig.) *se mettre au* ~, (fam.) to vegetate in the country; *être pris sans* ~, to be caught napping; (fam.) *vous ne le prendrez pas sans* ~, you won't catch him napping; there are no flies on him.

vert-de-gris (vɛrdəgri), s.m. Verdigris.

vert-de-grisé, -e (vɛrdəgrize), adj. loc. Covered with verdigris.

vertébral, -e, (aux) (vɛrtebral), adj. Vertebral.

vertèbre (vɛrtɛbr), s.f. [L *vertebra*] (anat.) Vertebra.

vertébré, -e (vɛrtebre), adj. s.m. Vertebrate; *les* ~*s*, the Vertebrata.

vertement (vɛrtəmɑ̃), adv. [f. *vert*] Vigorously, briskly; sharply, soundly; harshly, severely; *je l'ai tancé* ~, I gave him a good dressing-down.

vertex (vɛrtɛks), s.m. [L wd] (anat.) Vertex, crown of head; (fig.) vertex, apex, top.

vertical, -e, (aux) (vɛrtikal), adj. s.m. [L *verticalis*] Vertical, plumb; *plan* ~, vertical plane. ~**e**, s.f. Vertical, vertical line, plumb-line.

verticalement (vɛrtikalmɑ̃), adv. Vertically.

verticalité (vɛrtikalite), s.f. Verticality.

verticille (vɛrtisil), s.m. [L *verticillus*] (bot.) Verticil, whorl.

verticillé, -e (vɛrtisile), adj. (bot.) Verticillate(d).

vertige (vɛrtiʒ), s.m. [L *vertigo*] Dizziness, vertigo, giddiness; (fig.) madness, intoxication.

vertigineu-x, -se (vɛrtiʒinø), adj. Giddy, dizzy, vertiginous; whirling (of speed); *hauteur* ~*se*, dizzy height.

vertigo (vɛrtigo), s.m. [L wd] **1.** (vet.) Staggers; **2.** (fig.) whim. ⚠ Not English 'vertigo', which = *vertige.*

vertu (vɛrty), s.f. [L *virtus*] **1.** Virtue; *faire de nécessité* ~, to make a virtue of necessity; **2.** chastity; **3.** quality, property, faculty, force; *en* ~ *de*, by virtue of; in pursuance of; on the strength of; on the ground of; *il y a droit en* ~ *de ses longs services*, he is entitled to it in virtue of his long service. ⚠ Not English 'vertu', 'virtu', which = *amour des beaux-arts*; articles of vertu = *objets d'art*.

vertueusement (vɛrtɥøzmɑ̃), adv. Virtuously.

vertueu-x, -se (vɛrtɥø), adj. Virtuous.

vertugadin (vɛrtygadɛ̃), s.m. [Span. *verdugado*] Farthingale.

verve (vɛrv), s.f. [L *verbum*] Verve, spirit, animation, warmth, mettle, dash, go, gusto; *être en* ~, to be animated; (fam.) to be full of beans, to be in high spirits.

verveine (vɛrvɛn), s.f. [L *verbena*] (bot.) Vervain, verbena.

vervelle (vɛrvɛl), s.f. (falc.) Varvel.

verveu-x, -se (vɛrvø), adj. [f. *verve*] Animated, full of go, dashing, witty, lively, in high spirits; (slang) full of beans.

verveux, vervier (vɛrvø, vɛrvje), s.m. (fish.) Hoop-net.

vésanie (vezani), s.f. [L *vesania*] (pathol.) Vesania, insanity.

vesce (vɛs), s.f. [L *vicia*] (bot.) Vetch, tare.

vésical, -e, (aux) (vezikal), adj. [f. L *vesica*] Vesical.

vésicant, -e (vezikɑ̃), adj. s.m. [L *vesicans*] (med.) Vesicant.

vésication (vezika'sjɔ̃), s.f. Vesication.

vésicatoire (vezikatwar), s.m. [f. L *vesica*] Vesicant. ~, adj. Vesicatory.

vésiculaire (vezikylɛr), adj. Vesicular.

vésicule (vezikyl), s.f. [L *vesicula*] Vesicle; bladder; blister (on the skin); ~ *biliaire*, gall-bladder.

vésiculeu-x, -se (vezikylø), adj. Vesiculous.

vesou (vəzu), s.m. [Creole wd] Sugar-cane-juice.

vespasienne (vɛspazjɛn), s.f. [f. Emperor *Vespasian*] Public urinal.

vespéral, -e, (aux) (vɛsperal), adj. [f. L *vesper*] Vesperal, vespertine.

vespertilion (vɛspɛrtiljɔ̃), s.m. (zool.) Vespertilio (bat).

vespétro (vɛspetro), s.m. Vespetro (liqueur).

vesse (vɛs), s.f. (vulg.) Evacuation of wind, noiseless fart.

vesse-de-loup (vɛsdəlu), s.m. (bot.) Puff-ball, devil's snuff-box.

vesser (vɛse), v.n. [L *vissire*] To break wind noiselessly.

vessie (vɛsi), s.f. [L *vesica*] Bladder; ~ *natatoire*, swimming-bladder; *prendre des* ~*s pour des lanternes*, to believe the moon is made of (green) cheese.

vessigon (vɛsigɔ̃), s.m. (vet.) Vessigon, wind-gall.

vestalat (vɛstala), s.m. Vestal's period of service (30 years); service of Vesta.

vestale (vɛstal), s.f. [L *vestalis*] Vestal (virgin).

veste (vɛst), s.f. [L *vestis*] Coat (of lounge suit), jacket; (colloq.) failure; *remporter une fameuse* ~, to fail completely, to be defeated, beaten hollow. ⚠ Not 'vest', which = *gilet de dessous, chemise américaine*.

vestiaire (vɛstjɛr), s.m. [L *vestiarius*] Cloak-room (of public buildings.) ⚠ 'Cloak-room' of stations = *consigne*.

vestibule (vɛstibyl), s.m. [L *vestibulus*] Hall, lobby, vestibule.

vestige (vɛstiʒ), s.m. [L *vestigium*] Vestige, trace, mark, remains; footprint, sign; syn. TRACE.

veston (vɛstɔ̃), s.m. Jacket, coat (of lounge suit); *complet* ~, lounge suit.

vêtement (vɛtmɑ̃), s.m. [f. *vêtir*] **1.** Garment, dress, (pl.) togs, clothes, garb; woman's outdoor coat; *elle est partie sans prendre son* ~, she has gone without a coat; **2.** (poet.) vesture; (fig.) cloak, disguise; syn. HABILLEMENT, HABITS.

vétéran (veterɑ̃), s.m. [L *veteranus*] Veteran.

vétérance (veterɑ̃s), s.f. Veterancy, state or position of a veteran.

vétérinaire (veterinɛr), adj. [f. L *veterinus*] Veterinary. ~, s.m. Veterinary surgeon; (fam.) vet.

vétillard, -e (vetijar), adj. s.m.f. See VÉTILLEUR.

vétille (vetij), s.f. [Span. *vetilla*] Trifle; syn. MINUTIE, BABIOLE, BAGATELLE.

vétiller (vetije), v.n. **1.** To trifle, to amuse oneself with trifles; **2.** to stand upon trifles; to quibble.

vétilleu-r, -se, vétillard, -e (vetijœr, vetijar), adj. **1.** Trifling; **2.** hair-splitting, quibbling. ~, s.m.f. **1.** Trifler; **2.** quibbler.

vétilleu-x, -se (vetijø), adj. Over-nice. hair-splitting, captious (of persons); nice, ticklish (of things).

vêtir (vɛtir), v.a. [L *vestire*] To clothe, to dress, to array; to array oneself in, to put on; *légèrement vêtu*, lightly clad; **se** ~, v.pr. to dress oneself, to array oneself.

vétiver, vétyver (vetivɛr), s.m. [Tamil *veṭṭivēru*] (bot.) Vetiver, cuscus grass.

véto (veto), s.m. [L wd] Veto; *mettre son* ~ *à*, to interpose or to put one's veto on.

vêture (vɛtyr), s.f. Profession; (of a nun) taking of the veil.

vétuste (vetyst), adj. Antiquated, decayed; (fam.) the worse for wear.

vétusté (vetyste), s.f. [L *vetustas*] Antiquity, age, ruinous state, decay, old age; *tomber de* ~, to fall into decay, (of trees) to fall from age.

veu-f, -ve (vœf), adj. [L *viduus*] Widowed (also fig.). ~, s.m. Widower; ~*ve*, s.f. widow; (slang) *la Veuve*, the guillotine, *épouser la Veuve*, to be guillotined.

veuillez (vœje), 2nd pers. pl. imperative and subj. of *vouloir*; ~ *m'adresser* . . ., kindly send me . . .

veule (vœl), adj. [etym. dub.] **1.** (fam.) Soft, without energy, slack, laggard, flabby, sluggish; **2.** (of soil) too light, sandy.
veulerie (vœlri), s.f. Slackness, sluggishness, flabbiness.
veuvage (vœvaʒ), s.m. Widowhood.
veuve (vœv), s.f. **1.** Widow; **2.** (ornith.) widow-bird; **3.** (slang) *la Veuve*, the guillotine.
vexant, -e (vɛksɑ̃), p. adj. Vexing, provoking.
vexat-eur, -rice (vɛksatœr), adj. Vexatious.
vexation (vɛksa'sjɔ̃), s.f. Vexation; irritation.
vexatoire (vɛksatwar), adj. Vexatious.
vexer (vɛkse), v.a. [L *vexare*] To vex, to annoy; to provoke, to cause anger in. ⚠ Said in French only of persons; a 'vexed question' cannot be translated *une question vexée*, but is *une question très discutée*.
vexillaire (vɛksillɛr), s.m. [L *vexillarius*] (ant.) Vexillary, standard-bearer.
vexille (vɛksij), s.m. [L *vexillum*] Vexillum.
viabilité (vjabilite), s.f. **1.** [f. L *vita*] Viability (of new-born child); 2. [f. L *via*] condition (of roads, &c.), practicability.
viable (vjabl), adj. [f. L *vita*] Viable.
viaduc (vjadyk), s.m. [L *via+ducere*] Viaduct.
viag-er, -ère (vjaʒe), adj. [f. *vie*] For life; *rente viagère*, life annuity. ~, s.m. Life interest; *placer en* ~, to invest in a life annuity.
viande (vjɑ̃d), s.f. [LL *vivenda*] Meat; ~ *blanche*, white meat; ~ *de boucherie*, butcher's meat; ~ *noire*, game. ⚠ Not 'viand', which = *aliments, victuailles, mets*.
viander (vjɑ̃de), v.n. To graze (of deer and wild animals).
viandis (vjɑ̃di), s.m. Pasture, grazing (of deer, &c.).
viatique (vjatik), s.m. [L *viaticum*] **1.** Viaticum, provisions, travelling-money; **2.** (liturg.) viaticum, last sacrament.
vibord (vibɔr), s.m. (naut.) Waist.
vibrant, -e (vibrɑ̃), p. adj. Vibrating, vibrant, shaking; (fig.) thrilling, moving, quivering; *voix* ~*e d'émotion*, voice shaking with emotion. ~*e*, s.f. (phon.) Vibrant.
vibrateur (vibratœr), s.m. Vibrator.
vibratile (vibratil), adj. Vibratile.
vibration (vibra'sjɔ̃), s.f. Vibration.
vibratoire (vibratwar), adj. Vibratory.
vibrer (vibre), v.n. [L *vibrare*] To vibrate; (fig.) to thrill, to quiver, to be thrilled, moved, &c.
vibrion (vibrijɔ̃), s.m. (bacteriol.) Vibrio.
vicaire (vikɛr), s.m. [L *vicarius*] Curate, assistant priest; deputy, delegate. ⚠ Not 'vicar' (which = *curé, prêtre*), except in *vicaire apostolique*, vicar apostolic; and *Vicaire du Christ*, Vicar of Christ (the Pope).
vicairie (vikɛri), s.f. See VICARIAT.
vicarial, -e, (aux) (vikarjal), adj. Vicarial, vicarious; curate's.
vicariat (vikarja), s.m., **vicairie** (vikɛri), s.f. (eccles.) Curacy, curateship.
vicarier (vikarje), v.n. **1.** To act as deputy or delegate; **2.** to act as curate; **3.** (fig., rare) to fulfil small duties, to do odd jobs.
vice (vis), s.m. [L *vitium*] Vice, fault, defect, flaw, blemish; evil, depravity; viciousness; ~ *de construction*, flaw in construction; ~ *de conformation*, malformation; ~ *de style*, defect of style; ~ *de prononciation*, impediment (in speech); *pauvreté n'est pas* ~, poverty is no crime; (colloq.) *il a du* ~ *!*, what cheek!, how cute! ⚠ Not 'vice' in the sense of *étau*.
vice-, (vis), pref. [L *vicis*] Vice-; acting in place of; next in rank to.
vice-amiral, (aux) (visamiral), s.m. Vice-admiral.
vice-chancelier (visʃɑ̃səlje), s.m. Vice-chancellor.
vice-consul (viskɔ̃syl), s.m. Vice-consul.
vice-consulat (viskɔ̃syla), s.m. Vice-consulate.
vice-gérant (visʒerɑ̃), s.m. Deputy manager; vice-gerent.
vice-légat (vislega), s.m. Vice-legate.
vicennal, -e, (aux) (visɛnnal), adj. [L *vicennalis*] Vicennial; lasting, happening every twenty years.
vice-présidence (visprezidɑ̃s), s.f. Vice-presidency.
vice-président, -e (visprezidɑ̃), s.m.f. Vice-president.
vice-reine (visrɛn), s.f. Vicereine.
vice-roi (visrwa), s.m. Viceroy.
vice-royauté (visrwajote), s.f. Viceroyalty.
vice versa (visevɛrsa), adv. loc. [L wds] Vice versa.
vichy (viʃi), s.m. [f. *Vichy*, Fr. town] Cheap cotton material; *eau de* ~, Vichy water, Vichy.
viciable (visjabl), adj. [f. *vicier*] Corruptible.
viciat-eur, -rice (visjatœr), adj. Vitiating.
viciation (visja'sjɔ̃), s.f. Vitiation.
vicier (visje), v.a. [L *vitiare*] To vitiate, to taint, to corrupt, to make depraved; ~ *un accord*, to vitiate a contract; **se** ~, v.pr. to become tainted or vitiated (of things); to become depraved (of persons).
vicieusement (visjøzmɑ̃), adv. Viciously; defectively; depravedly. ⚠ Not used in French like 'viciously' in the sense of spitefully, savagely = *avec dépit, avec colère*.
vicieu-x, -se (visjø), adj. [L *vitiosus*] **1.** Vicious; given to vice; *homme* ~, man given to vice; *inclinaison* ~*se*, vicious

propensity; *cheval* ~, vicious horse; **2.** faulty, defective; *locution* ~*se*, faulty phrase. ⚠ *Vicieux* cannot be used like 'vicious' in the sense of spiteful, malignant; a vicious remark = *une parole de dépit*; a vicious mood = *un état d'irritation*, not *un état vicieux*.

vicinal, -e, (aux) (visinal), adj. [L *vicinalis*] Vicinal, local; *chemin* ~ or *route* ~*e*, by-road.

vicissitude (visisityd), s.f. [L *vicissitudo*] Vicissitude, change, revolution.

vicomtal, -e, (aux) (vikɔ̃tal), adj. Of a viscount or viscountess; viscount's.

vicomte (vikɔ̃t), s.m. [f. *vice+comte*] Viscount.

vicomté (vikɔ̃te), s.f. Viscounty; viscountship.

vicomtesse (vikɔ̃tɛs), s.f. Viscountess.

victime (viktim), s.f. [L *victima*] Victim, sufferer; *être* ~ *de*, (*a*) to be the victim of; (*b*) to be a victim to (illness, vice, &c.).

victimer (viktime) (rare), v.a. To victimize.

victoire (viktwar), s.f. [L *victoria*] Victory; *remporter la* ~, to gain the victory (*sur*, over); *chanter* ~, to shout victory.

victoria (viktɔrja), s.f. Victoria (carriage).

victorien, -ne (viktɔrjɛ̃), adj. Victorian.

victorieusement (viktɔrjøzmɑ̃), adv. Victoriously.

victorieu-x, -se (viktɔrjø), adj. Victorious; *preuve* ~*se*, decisive proof.

victuaille (viktyɑj), s.f. (usually in pl.) Victuals, provisions.

vidage (vidaʒ), s.m. [f. *vider*] Emptying; (on taps) 'waste'.

vidame (vidam), s.m. [L *vice+dominus*] (feud. title) Vidame.

vidange (vidɑ̃ʒ), s.f. **1.** Emptying, removing, clearance; ullage (of wine); *tonneau en* ~, half-filled or half-empty cask; (fig. fam.) *être en* ~, to be half drunk, half seas over; **2.** (pl.) emptying (of cesspools); night-soil.

vidanger (vidɑ̃ʒe), v.a. To empty (bottles, cesspools).

vidangeur (vidɑ̃ʒœr), s.m. Scavenger, night-man.

vide (vid), adj. [L *viduus*] Empty; void, vacant, unoccupied; devoid, destitute (of); (fig.) *mâcher à* ~, to feed on false hopes; *à* ~, empty, without effect; *tourner à* ~, (of machinery) to run free; *travailler l'estomac* ~, to work on an empty stomach; *les mains* ~*s*, empty-handed; *tête* ~, empty-headed; (fig.) *cœur* ~, stony-hearted. ~, s.m. Empty space, blank, void; vacuum; gap, hole; (fig.) emptiness, vanity, nothingness; *le* ~ *de son esprit*, the blankness of his mind; ~ *de l'âme*, loneliness of spirit; *le* ~ *des plaisirs*, the vanity of pleasure; *nettoyage par le* ~, vacuum-cleaning.

vide-bouteille, vide-bouteilles (vidbutɛj), s.m. invar. **1.** Small cottage in the country; small country house; **2.** syphon-top (to a bottle).

vide-gousset (vidgusɛ), s.m. invar. (fam.) Pickpocket.

videment (vidmɑ̃), s.m. Emptying.

vide-poches (vidpoʃ), s.m. invar. Tidy, receptacle for odds and ends.

vide-pommes (vidpom), s.m. invar. Apple-corer.

vider (vide), v.a. [f. *vide*] To empty; to draw off, to drain (of liquids); to bore, to hollow out (solid objects); to draw (game, poultry); to gut (fish); (fig.) to settle, to decide, to end; to vacate; ~ *les lieux*, to decamp; ~ *les arçons*, to lose one's seat (on horseback); ~ *une question*, to settle a question; ~ *un étang*, to drain a pond; (colloq.) *je suis vidé*, I am spent, done up, or exhausted.

vidimer (vidime), v.a. [f. L *vidimus*] (law) To collate, to compare.

vidimus (vidimys), s.m. [L wd] Vidimus.

vidrecome (vidrəkɔm), s.m. [Germ. *wiederkomm*] Hanap, large drinking-glass.

viduité (vidɥite), s.f. [L *viduitas*] (law) Viduity, widowhood of woman.

vidure (vidyr), s.f. Emptying; offal (of game, poultry, &c.).

vie[1] (vi), s.f. [L *vita*] Life; existence, days, lifetime; vitality, spirit, animation; livelihood, living, food, sustenance; life, biography, memoir; *sa* ~ *durant*, throughout his life; *je ne lui pardonnerai de ma* ~, I shall never forgive him till my dying day; *jamais de la* ~ *!*, not on your life !, no fear !; *style plein de* ~, spirited style; *gagner sa* ~, to earn one's living, to get one's livelihood; *devoir sa* ~ *à*, to owe one's existence to; *sa* ~ *ne tient qu'à un fil*, his life hangs by a thread; *faire la* ~, or *mener une* ~ *de bâtons de chaise*, to live fast; (fam.) *il m'a fait une* ~ *!*, he led me a dance !; *prix de la* ~, cost of living; *en* ~, alive, living; *sans* ~, lifeless; *faire* ~ *qui dure*, to live temperately; *faire la* ~ *dure à X*, to make X's life miserable; to lead X a pretty dance; *avoir la* ~ *dure*, to be tenacious of life; to have nine lives; (fam., pej) to be a long time dying; *train de* ~, way of living, establishment; *telle* ~, *telle fin*, folk die as they live; *la* ~ *des champs*, country life; ~ *probable*, expectation of life; *à* ~, adv. loc. for life; *la* ~ *future*, the life to come; *l'arbre de* ~, arbor vitae; *il y va de la* ~, it 's a case of life and death; *donner la* ~ *à X*, to give birth to X.

vie[2] (vi), s.f. [L *via*] Footpath (in salt-marshes).

vieil (vjɛj), adj.m. Form of *vieux* used before a word beginning with a vowel or an unaspirated h, ex. *vieil ami*, old friend; *vieil homme*, old man; see VIEUX.

vieillard (vjɛjar), s.m. [f. *vieux*] Old man, aged man.
vieillarder (vjɛjarde), v.n. [f. *vieillard*] To mellow (of wine).
vieille (vjɛj), fem of *vieux*. See VIEUX.
vieillerie (vjɛjri), s.f. Lumber, rubbish, old clothes; (fig.) (pl.) obsolete ideas, old-fashioned notions.
vieillesse (vjɛjɛs), s.f. Old age; the aged, old folks; *la ~ est chagrine*, old folks are peevish; (fig.) *bâton de ~*, staff of one's old age.
vieilli, -e (vjɛji), p. adj. Old-fashioned, obsolete, out-of-date (of objects, ideas, &c.); aged (of persons); *il trouva son père bien ~*, he found his father much aged; *préjugé ~*, obsolete prejudice.
vieillir (vjɛjir), v.n. To grow old, to age, to look old (of persons); to mellow (of wine); to become obsolete or old-fashioned (of ideas); ~, v.a. to age; *cette robe vous vieillit*, that dress ages you.
vieillissant, -e (vjɛjisɑ̃), p. adj. Aging, growing old.
vieillot, -te (vjɛjo), adj. Quaint, old-fashioned; little old (man or woman); *tapisseries vieillottes*, old-fashioned hangings; *bibelots ~s*, quaint old ornaments.
vielle (vjɛl), s.f. [LL *vitula*] (mus.) Viol; (formerly) hurdy-gurdy.
vielleu-r, -se (vjɛlœr), s.m.f. Hurdy-gurdy player.
vierge (vjɛrʒ), s.f. [L *virgo*] Virgin, maid; (astr.) Virgo. ~, adj. Virgin; maiden; *sol ~*, virgin soil; *vigne ~*, Virginia creeper; *réputation ~*, spotless repute; *miel ~*, virgin honey; *forêt ~*, virgin forest; *épée ~*, unfleshed sword.
vieux (vjø), **vieil** (see that wd), fem. **vieille** (vjɛj), adj. [L *vetulus*] Old, aged, ancient, venerable, advanced in years; old-fashioned, out of date, obsolete; veteran; *il ne fera pas de ~ os*, he won't make old bones; *~ soldat*, veteran, old soldier; *~ comme le temps, le monde*, as old as the hills, as Adam; *~ garçon*, old bachelor; *vieille fille*, old maid; spinster. ~, s.m.f. Old man, old woman, old crone, old crony; (colloq.) *mon ~, ma vieille*, old fellow, old bean, old chap, old girl; *un ~ de la vieille*, a veteran of the Old Guard; *coudre du ~ avec du neuf*, to put a new patch on an old garment, to put new wine into old bottles; *mes vieux*, my parents, the old people.
vi-f, -ve (vif), adj. [L *vivus*] Live, living, alive; quick; animated, lively, spirited, sprightly; fiery, mettlesome (of horses); eager, passionate, ardent, hasty; bright, vivid (of colour); bracing, sharp (of air); violent, sharp, darting (of pain); *de vive voix*, by word of mouth; *des yeux ~s*, bright eyes; *eau vive*, spring-water; *vives eaux*, spring tides; *chaux vive*, quicklime; *couleur vive*, vivid colour; *froid ~*, piercing cold; *enfant ~*, lively, sprightly child; *haie vive*, quickset hedge; *il est ~ comme la poudre*, he's as hot as pepper, as keen as mustard; *imagination vive*, lively imagination; *ils ont échangé des propos fort ~s*, hot words passed between them; *foi vive*, ardent, glowing faith; *vive arête*, sharp angle; *bois ~*, live wood; *mort ou ~*, alive or dead; *de vive force*, by main force; *avoir l'esprit ~*, to be quick-, nimble-, or ready-witted. ~, s.m. Quick (live flesh); living person; (fig.) *blessé au ~*, stung to the quick; *trancher dans le ~*, to cut to the quick; (fig.) to set to work in earnest; (law) *acte entre ~s*, agreement between living persons; (fig.) *entrer dans le ~ de la question*, to get to the heart of the matter or to the bottom of the question; *le ~ de l'eau*, high water, the top of the tide; *prendre sur le ~*, to catch a likeness; (fam.) *il l'a pris sur le ~*, he has got him to the life; *c'est pris sur le ~*, that's lifelike; (colloq.) *cela l'a piqué au ~*, that thrust went home; (law) *le mort saisit le ~*, the heirs inherit all a dead man's goods.
vif-argent (vifarʒɑ̃), s.m. Mercury, quicksilver; (fig.) *avoir du ~ dans les veines*, to be made of quicksilver.
vigie (viʒi), s.f. [Port. *vigia*] **1.** Look-out (man); **2.** look-out station; *être en ~*, to be on the look-out; **3.** buoy.
vigilamment (viʒilamɑ̃), adv. Vigilantly.
vigilance (viʒilɑ̃s), s.f. [L *vigilantia*] Vigilance.
vigilant, -e (viʒilɑ̃), adj. Vigilant, watchful.
vigile (viʒil), s.f. [L *vigilia*] Vigil.
vigne (viɲ), s.f. [L *vinea*] Vine; vineyard; *feuille de ~*, vine-leaf; *~ sauvage*, wild vine; *~ vierge*, virginia creeper; *~ de Salomon*, clematis; *~ de Judas*, woody nightshade, bitter-sweet; (fig.) *être dans les ~s du Seigneur*, to be in one's cups.
vigneron, -ne (viɲərɔ̃), s.m.f. Vine-dresser, vine-grower.
vignette (viɲɛt), s.f. [f. *vigne*] **1.** Vignette; **2.** (bot.) meadow-sweet; syn. REINE DES PRÉS.
vignoble (viɲɔbl), s.m. [f. *vigne*] Vineyard. ~, adj. Wine-growing.
vigogne (vigɔɲ), s.f. [Span. *vicuña*] (zool.) Vicuna; vicuna-wool.
vigoureusement (vigurøzmɑ̃), adv. Vigorously, energetically.
vigoureu-x, -se (vigurø), adj. [f. *vigueur*] Vigorous, strong, lusty, sturdy, stout, stalwart, robust; forceful, energetic; forcible.
viguerie (vigəri), s.f. (obs.) [f. *viguier*] Provostship (in Provence); jurisdiction of provost.
vigueur (vigœr), s.f. [L *vigor*] Vigour,

strength; force, energy, power; forcibleness; ~ *d'esprit*, strength of mind; *entrer en* ~, to take effect; to come into force (of laws); *mettre en* ~, to enforce, to put in force.

viguier (vigje), s.m. (obs.) [L *vicarius*] Provost (in Provence).

vil, -e (vil), adj. [L *vilis*] Vile, mean, base; abject, low; paltry, worthless; *à* ~ *prix*, dirt-cheap; *âme* ~*e*, base mind.

vilain, -e (vilɛ̃), s.m.f. [LL *villanus*] **1.** Villain, cad, blackguard, nasty fellow; rascally, scurvy wretch; naughty boy (or girl); **2.** (archaic) villein, bondman, serf; *oignez* ~, *il vous poindra, poignez* ~, *il vous oindra*, a churl will be insolent if well-treated, but servile if ill-treated. ⚠ Not Engl. 'villain' in the sense of *traître* (*dans une pièce de théâtre*), *scélérat*. ~, adj. Ugly, unsightly; wretched; vile, sordid, infamous, scandalous; nasty, shabby, low; ~ *temps*, vile weather; *jouer un* ~ *tour à X*, to play a scurvy trick on X; *un* ~ *monsieur*, a blackguard; a cad; a rascal; *de vilaines gens*, a bad lot; *une* ~*e figure*, an ugly face.

vilainement (vilɛnmɑ̃), adv. Uglily; villainously, basely, shamefully.

vilayet (vilajɛ), s.m. [Turk. wd] Vilayet.

vilebrequin (vilbrəkɛ̃), s.m. [Dutch *wimbelkin*] Centre-bit, wimble; (of motor-cars) crank-shaft; *bride de* ~, crank-shaft flange.

vilenie (vilni), s.f. Vile action; dirty trick.

vilipender (vilipɑ̃de), v.a. [L *vilipendere*] To vilify, to cry down, to vilipend.

villa (villa), s.f. [L wd] Villa.

village (vilaʒ), s.m. [f. L *villa*] Village; *les gens du* ~, the villagers; *il est bien de son* ~, he is a country cousin.

villageois, -e (vilaʒwɑ), s.m.f. Villager. ~, adj. Rustic, country, village.

villanelle (villanɛl), s.f. [It. *villanella*] (pros., mus.) Villanelle.

ville (vil), s.f. [L *villa*] Town, city; *être à la* or *en* ~, to be in town; *dîner en* ~, to dine out; *costume de* ~, plain clothes, mufti; *hôtel de* ~, town hall; *toilette de* ~, walking-dress; (on letters) *en* ~, local; ~ *d'eaux*, watering-place, spa; *sergent de* ~, policeman; *toute la* ~ *en parle*, it is the talk of the town.

villégiateur (villeʒjatœr), s.m. (fam.) (holiday) Visitor.

villégiature (villeʒjatyr), s.f. [It. *villeggiatura*] Stay or sojourn in the country; *en* ~, staying in the country.

villégiaturer (villeʒjatyre), v.n. To stay in the country; to rusticate, to ruralize.

villeu-x, -se (vilø), adj. [L *villosus*] Hairy, villous, villose.

villifère (vilifɛr), adj. (zool.) Hairy.

villiforme (viliform), adj. (zool.) Villiform.

villosité (vilɔsite), s.f. [L *villosus*] Villosity.

vimaire, vimère (vimɛr), s.f. [f. L *vis+major*] Damage; outrage, insult.

vime (vim), s.m. (local name for) Osier.

vin (vɛ̃), s.m. [L *vinum*] Wine; ~ *mousseux*, sparkling wine; *être pris de* ~, to be in liquor, to be the worse for drink; (fam.) *sac à* ~, drunken sot; *être entre deux* ~*s*, to be half-seas-over, or tipsy; *cuver son* ~, to sleep off one's bout; *mettre de l'eau dans son* ~, to come down a peg or two, to take a back seat; (prov.) *quand le* ~ *est tiré, il faut le boire*, he has put his hand to the plough, it 's too late to turn back; *à bon* ~ *point d'enseigne*, good wine needs no bush; *chaque* ~ *a sa lie*, there 's no rose without a thorn; *un doigt de* ~, a thimbleful of wine; (pop.) *avoir une pointe de* ~, to have taken a glass too much; to have drunk more than is good for one; *avoir le* ~ *gai, triste, mauvais*, to be merry, dull, quarrelsome in one's cups; *porter bien le* ~, to have a good head (for drinking); *marchand de* ~, (*a*) wine-merchant; (*b*) pub-keeper, landlord of wine-shop (syn. BISTRO); *négociant en* ~*s*, wholesale wine-merchant; *du* ~ *à faire danser les chèvres*, not wine, but vinegar; (prov.) *le* ~ *entre, la raison sort*, when the wine is in, the wit is out; *ne mouillez pas trop votre* ~, don't drown the miller.

vinage (vinaʒ), s.m. Putting alcohol into wine.

vinaigre (vinɛgr), s.m. [*vin+aigre*] Vinegar; ~ *de toilette*, toilet vinegar; (at rope-skipping) pepper.

vinaigré, -e (vinɛgre), p. adj. **1.** Seasoned with vinegar; **2.** (obs.) disinfected with vinegar.

vinaigrer (vinɛgre), v.a. To vinegar, to season with vinegar.

vinaigrerie (vinɛgrəri), s.f. Vinegar-factory.

vinaigrette (vinɛgrɛt), s.f. **1.** Vinegar sauce; **2.** (obs.) kind of bath-chair. ⚠ Engl. 'vinaigrette' = *flacon de sels*; *flacon de parfum pour la poche*.

vinaigrier (vinɛgrije), s.m. **1.** Vinegar-merchant; **2.** cruet.

vinaire (vinɛr), adj. [f. *vin*] Wine-; *industrie* ~, wine-growing industry.

vinasse (vinas), s.f. Poor wine, wretched wine.

vindas (vɛ̃das), s.m. [Icelandic wd] Windlass.

vindicati-f, -ve (vɛ̃dikatif), adj. [f. L *vindicare*] Vindictive, revengeful.

vindicativement (vɛ̃dikativmɑ̃), adv. Vindictively.

vindicte (vɛ̃dikt), s.f. [L *vindicta*] Prosecution (of crime).

vinée (vine), s.f. [f. *vin*] Grape-harvest, vintage.

viner (vine), v.a. To add alcohol to.

vinette (vinɛt), s.f. (bot., pop.) Barberry.

vineu-x, -se (vinø), adj. Vinous, winy, wine-coloured; rich in wines.
vingt (vɛ̃), adj. num. [L *viginti*] Twenty, a score; the twentieth; *~-et-un*, twenty-one; the twenty-first; *~-deux*, *~-trois*, &c., twenty-two, twenty-three, &c.; the twenty-second, the twenty-third (of month).
vingtaine (vɛ̃tɛn), s.f. A score, about twenty.
vingtième (vɛ̃tjɛm), adj. ord. num. Twentieth. ~, s.m. Twentieth.
vingtièmement (vɛ̃tjɛmmɑ̃), adv. Twentiethly.
vingtuple (vɛ̃typl), adj. Twentyfold, twenty times as large.
vingtupler (vɛ̃typle), v.a. To multiply by twenty; to increase twentyfold.
vinicole (vinikɔl), adj. [f. L *vinum*+*colere*] Wine-growing, wine-producing.
vinifère (vinifɛr), adj. [f. L *vinum*+*ferre*] Wine-growing (especially of soil).
vinificateur (vinifikatœr), s.m. Vinificator, wine-making apparatus.
vinification (vinifika'sjɔ̃), s.f. Wine-making.
vinique (vinik), adj. Vinic, winy, vinous.
viol (vjɔl), s.m. [f. *violer*] Rape, violation (of a woman). ⚠ Not English 'viol', which = *viole* and *vielle* (*instrument de musique*).
violable (vjɔlabl), adj. Violable.
violacé, -e (vjɔlase), adj. **1.** Purplish; **2.** (bot.) violaceous.
violacer (vjɔlase), v.n. **se ~**, v.pr. To turn purple (of complexion).
violat (vjɔla), adj.m. Of violets, violet-; *sirop ~*, syrup of violets.
violat-eur, -rice (vjɔlatœr), s.m.f. Violator.
violation (vjɔla'sjɔ̃), s.f. Violation (of laws, &c.); syn. VIOLEMENT.
violâtre (vjɔlɑtr), adj. Purplish.
viole (vjɔl), s.f. [Provenç. *viula*] Viola; (obs.) viol; *~ d'amour*, viol d'amore; *~ de gambe*, viol da gamba.
violement (viɔlmɑ̃), s.m. See syn. VIOLATION.
violemment (vjɔlamɑ̃), adv. Violently, with violence.
violence (vjɔlɑ̃s), s.f. Violence; act of violence; (law) force; (fig.) stress, violence, height, fury; *faire ~ à la loi*, to outrage the law; *se faire ~*, to constrain oneself; *la ~ des vents*, the fury of the winds; *la ~ des passions*, the stress of passion.
violent, -e (vjɔlɑ̃), adj. [L *violentus*] Violent, strong, excessive, intense, impetuous, passionate; (colloq.) *c'est un peu ~!*, that 's too bad, indeed!, that puts the lid on it!
violenter (vjɔlɑ̃te), v.a. [f. *violent*] To force, to constrain, to outrage, to do violence to; to violate, to assault, to commit rape upon.
violer (vjɔle), v.a. [L *violare*] To violate, to ravish; to commit rape upon; to outrage, to transgress (laws).
violet, -te (vjɔlɛ), adj. [f. *violette*] Violet-coloured, violet, purple. ~, s.m. Violet, violet-colour, purple. ⚠ See *pourpre*.
violette (vjɔlɛt), s.f. [f. L *viola*] (bot.) Violet; *bois de ~*, violet-wood.
violier (vjɔlje), s.m. (bot.) Wallflower, gillyflower; syn. RAVENELLE.
violine (vjɔlin), s.f. (chem.) Violine.
violiste (vjɔlist), s.m.f. Violist.
violon (vjɔlɔ̃), s.m. [It. *violone*] **1.** Violin, (fam.) fiddle; **2.** violin-player, violinist; **3.** (colloq.) lock-up (in police-station); (fig.) *payer les ~s*, to pay the piper.
violoncelle (vjɔlɔ̃sɛl), s.m. [It. *violoncello*] Violoncello, 'cello.
violoncelliste (vjɔlɔ̃sɛlist), s.m. Violoncellist, 'cellist.
violoneur, violoneux (vjɔlɔnœr, vjɔlɔnø), s.m. Fiddler.
violoniste (vjɔlɔnist), s.m. Violinist, (pej.) fiddler.
viorne (vjɔrn), s.f. [L *viburnum*] Viburnum, wayfaring-tree.
vipère (vipɛr), s.f. [L *vipera*] Adder, viper.
vipereau (pl. **-x**) (vipro), s.m. Young viper.
vipérin, -e (viperɛ̃), adj. Viperine; (fig.) viperish. *~e*, s.f. **1.** Viperine, snake resembling the adder; **2.** (bot.) viper's bugloss.
virage (viraʒ), s.m. **1.** Turning; curve; *déraper dans un ~*, to skid on a curve, or bend; *prendre le ~*, to take the curve; (naut.) tacking; **2.** (photo.) toning.
virago (virago), s.f. [f. L *vir*] Virago, termagant.
virée (vire), s.f. Turning, winding.
virelai (virlɛ), s.m. [OF wd] Virelay.
virement (virmɑ̃), s.m. **1.** Turning; (naut.) tacking; **2.** (book-keeping) transfer, clearing; **3.** (photo.) toning.
virer (vire), v.n. [L *gyrare*] **1.** To turn, to twist and turn, to turn about, to gyrate; to turn colour; to change sides; **2.** (naut.) to tack about, to veer about; *~ de bord*, to tack; *~ vent arrière*, to wear ship; *~ vent devant*, to tack ship; *~ au cabestan*, to hoist; ~, v.a. **1.** to transfer, to clear (a sum of money); **2.** (photo.) to tone.
virescence (virɛssɑ̃s), s.f. [f. L *virescere*] Virescence; greenness.
vireur (virœr), s.m. **1.** Turning-gear; **2.** (photo.) toning-solution, toning-bath.
vireu-x, -se (virø), adj. [L *virosus*] Poisonous, noxious, nauseous.
virevaut (virvo), s.m. (naut.) Crab windlass, winch.
virevolte (virvɔlt), s.f. [It. *giravolta*] Quick turning or wheeling (of a horse).
virginal, -e, (aux) (virʒinal), adj. [f. L *virgo*] Virginal, maidenly.

virginie (virʒini), s.m. Virginia tobacco or snuff.
virginité (virʒinite), s.f. [L *virginitas*] Virginity, maidenhood, virginhood.
virgule (virgyl), s.f. [L *virgula*] Comma.
virguler (virgyle), v.a. To mark with commas.
viridité (viridite), s.f. [L *viriditas*] Viridity, greenness.
viril, -e (viril), adj. [L *virilis*] Virile, male; manly; *âge* ~, manhood, man's estate.
virilement (virilmɑ̃), adv. Like a man.
viriliser (virilize), v.a. To make a man of.
virilité (virilite), s.f. [f. *viril*] Virility; manhood; vigour, energy.
virole (virɔl), s.f. [L *viriola*] **1.** Ferrule, collar; **2.** die (for stamping).
viroler (virɔle), v.a. [f. *virole*] **1.** To ferrule, to hoop; **2.** (die-stamping) to put into the stamping machine.
virtualité (virtɥalite), s.f. Virtuality.
virtuel, -le (virtɥɛl), adj. [f. L *virtus*] Virtual.
virtuellement (virtɥɛlmɑ̃), adv. Virtually.
virtuose (virtɥoz), s.m.f. [It. *virtuoso*] Virtuoso.
virtuosité (virtɥozite), s.f. Virtuosity.
virulence (virylɑ̃s), s.f. Virulence.
virulent, -e (virylɑ̃), adj. [L *virulentus*] Virulent.
virure (virɥr), s.f. (naut.) Strake.
virus (virys), s.m. [L wd] Virus; (fig.) ferment, virus, poison.
vis (vis), s.f. [L *vitis*] Screw; *escalier à* ~, spiral staircase; ~ *d'Archimède*, Archimedean screw; *pas de* ~, turn of a screw; pitch (of a screw); thread; ~ *sans fin*, worm-screw; ~ *platinée*, platinum-head screw; *à* ~, with a screw; ~ *de réglage*, adjusting-screw; *commande par* ~ *sans fin*, worm drive; ~ *de serrage*, terminal screw, binding-screw; (colloq.) *serrer la* ~ *à X*, to make X pay through the nose; to keep a tight hand on X.
visa (viza), s.m. [L wd] Visé, visa; endorsement on passport, &c.
visage (vizaʒ), s.m. [f. L *visus*] Face, countenance; visage; aspect; *des* ~*s nouveaux*, new faces; *il a changé de* ~, his face changed; he turned pale; *trouver* ~ *de bois*, to find the door shut, or nobody there; *à deux* ~*s*, two-faced, double-sided; double-faced; *toute vérité a deux* ~*s*, there are two aspects of every truth; *à* ~ *découvert*, barefacedly; *faire bon* ~ *à X*, to welcome X, to treat X kindly; *faire mauvais* ~ *à X*, to look black at X; to give X the cold shoulder.
vis-à-vis (vizavi), prep. loc. Opposite, over against; facing; (fig.) towards, as regards. ~, s.m. **1.** The person facing you; **2.** kind of carriage; small settee.
viscache (viskaʃ), s.m. [native S. Amer. wd] (zool.) Viscacha.
viscéral, -e, (aux) (visseral), adj. Visceral.
viscère (vissɛr), s.m. Any of the viscera or vital organs; *les* ~*s*, the viscera (always in the pl.).
viscosité (viskozite), s.f. Viscosity, viscidity.
visée (vize), s.f. [f. *viser*] Aim; end, design, plan.
viser[1] (vize), v.a. [f. L *visus*] To aim at; (fig.) to aspire to; *je ne vise personne*, I do not allude to any individual; (slang) *vise-moi ce type-là*, just have a look at this cove; ~, v.n. to take aim; *il visait à ce but*, that was his goal; ~ *au cœur*, to aim at the heart; ~ *à l'effet*, to aim at effect.
viser[2] (vize), v.a. [f. L *visus*] To visé, to countersign, to endorse; *faire* ~ *un passeport*, to get a passport viséd.
viseu-r, -se (vizœr), s.m.f. **1.** Aimer; **2.** s.m. (photo.) view-finder.
visibilité (vizibilite), s.f. Visibility.
visible (vizibl), adj. [L *visibilis*] **1.** Visible; (fig.) evident, manifest, obvious; **2.** visible, ready to receive visitors; at home.
visiblement (viziblәmɑ̃), adv. Visibly, obviously.
visière (vizjɛr), s.f. [f. OF *vis*] **1.** (medieval) Vizor, visor, vizard; **2.** peak (of cap, &c.); (fig.) *rompre en* ~ *à*, to run full tilt at; to fly out at; to be at daggers drawn with; to contradict flatly.
vision (vizjɔ̃), s.f. [L *visio*] **1.** Sight, vision, eye-sight; **2.** vision, dream, phantom, fancy; phantasm.
visionnaire (vizjɔnɛr), s.m.f. Visionary, seer; dreamer. ~, adj. Visionary, fanciful.
visitandine (vizitɑ̃din), s.f. Nun of the order of the Visitation.
visitat-eur, -rice (vizitatœr), s.m.f. Visitant.
visitation (vizita'sjɔ̃), s.f. [L *visitatio*] Visitation.
visite (vizit), s.f. [f. *visiter*] **1.** Visit, call; visitation (of a bishop, &c.); *être en* ~ *chez X*, to be staying with X; to be on a visit to X; *faire des* ~*s*, to pay calls; *recevoir des* ~*s*, to have callers; **2.** inspection, examination, search; *la* ~ *des bagages*, the examination of luggage; *droit de* ~, right of search.
visiter (vizite), v.a. [L *visitare*] **1.** To visit, to pay a visit to; to call upon (or on); **2.** to search, to examine, to inspect.
visiteu-r, -se (vizitœr), s.m.f. **1.** Inspector, searcher; **2.** caller, visitor.
vison (vizɔ̃), s.m. (zool.) Mink, mink fur.
visorium (vizɔrjɔm), s.m. [L wd] (print.) Copy-holder.
visqueu-x, -se (viskø), adj. [L *viscosus*] Viscous, clammy, slimy, sticky.
vissage (visaʒ), s.m. Screwing.
visser (vise), v.a. [f. *vis*] To screw, to

screw up or down; ~ *à bloc*, to screw tight; **se** ~, v.pr. to be screwed.
visserie (visri), s.f. **1.** Nuts and bolts, screws, &c. (collectively); **2.** screw-manufactory.
visuel, -le (vizɥɛl), adj. [f. L *visualis*] Visual.
visuellement (vizɥɛlmɑ̃), adv. Visually.
vital, -e, (aux) (vital), adj. [f. L *vita*] Vital; (fig.) vital, essential.
vitaliste (vitalist), adj. s.m.f. Vitalist.
vitalité (vitalite), s.f. [f. L *vita*] Vitality.
vitamine (vitamin), s.f. [f. L *vita*] Vitamin.
vite (vit), adj. [orig. dub.] Swift, quick, speedy, rapid, fast; *cheval* ~, fast horse. ~, adv. Quickly, fast, rapidly, speedily; *parler* ~, to speak fast (from habit) or quickly (from haste); *au plus* ~, as fast as possible; *faire* ~, to make haste; *vite!*, be quick, hurry up; ~ *alors!*, be quick then!; *plus* ~ *que ça!*, look sharp!
vitellin, -e (vitɛllɛ̃), adj. Of the vitellus, vitelline.
vitellus (vitɛlys), s.m. [L wd] Vitellus; yolk of egg.
vitelotte (vitlɔt), s.f. Kidney-potato.
vitement (vitmɑ̃), adv. Quickly, sharp, speedily.
vitesse (vitɛs), s.f. [f. *vite*] Quickness, rapidity, swiftness, speed, celerity; *à toute* ~, at top speed; *en grande* ~, at full speed; (railw.) *grande* ~, express; *petite* ~, goods; *gagner de* ~, to outstrip; (motor.) *boîte des* ~*s*, gear-box; change speed gear-box; *changer de* ~, to change gear; ~ *en prise directe*, direct drive; *compteur de* ~, speed-indicator, speedometer; ~ *à l'heure*, speed per hour.
viticole (vitikɔl), adj. [f. L *vitis*+*colere*] Wine-growing.
viticulteur (vitikyltœr), s.m. [L *vitis*+*cultor*] Viticulturist, wine-grower.
viticulture (vitikyltyr), s.f. Viticulture, wine-growing.
vitrage (vitraʒ), s.m. Glazing; glass windows; glass part of partition.
vitrail, (aux) (vitraj), s.m. Stained-glass window, big leaded window.
vitre (vitr), s.f. [L *vitrum*] Pane, window; (fam., fig.) *casser les* ~*s*, to kick up a dust; to attack or contradict openly; not to mince one's words.
vitré, -e (vitre), p. adj. **1.** Glazed; *porte* ~*e*, glass door; **2.** (anat.) vitreous.
vitrer (vitre), v.a. To glaze, to furnish with glass, to put the panes into (window-frames).
vitrerie (vitrəri), s.f. Glaziery; glazier's work.
vitreu-x, -se (vitrø), adj. (of eyes, &c.) Glassy, glazed; vitreous.
vitrier (vitrije), s.m. **1.** Glazier, glass-maker; **2.** (fam.) nickname for soldier of the battalions of *Chasseurs à pied*.
vitrière (vitrijɛr), s.f. Iron frame (for stained glass).
vitrifiable (vitrifjabl), adj. Vitrifiable.
vitrification (vitrifika'sjɔ̃), s.f. Vitrification.
vitrifier (vitrifje), v.a. [L *vitrum*+*facere*] To vitrify.
vitrine (vitrin), s.f. Shop window; glass case, show-case.
vitriol (vitrijɔl), s.m. [f. L *vitrum*] Vitriol; syn. ACIDE SULFURIQUE (*concentré*).
vitriolé, -e (vitrjɔle), p. adj. Vitriolized. ~, s.m.f. Victim of vitriol-throwing.
vitrioler (vitrjɔle), v.a. **1.** To vitriolize; **2.** to throw vitriol at.
vitrioleu-r, -se (vitrjɔlœr), s.m.f. Vitriol-thrower.
vitriolique (vitriɔlik), adj. Vitriolic.
vitupération (vitypera'sjɔ̃), s.f. Vituperation.
vitupérer (vitypere), v.a. [L *vituperare*] To vituperate.
vivace[1] (vivas), adj. [L *vivax*] Long-lived, tenacious of life; (bot.) perennial; (fig.) inveterate, deep-rooted. ⚠ Not Engl. 'vivacious', which = *vif, animé*.
vivace[2] (vivatʃe), adj. [It. wd] (mus.) Vivace.
vivacité (vivasite), s.f. [f. *vivace*] Vivacity, liveliness, sprightliness; spirit, ardour; brightness.
vivandi-er, -ère (vivɑ̃dje), s.m.f. (mil.) Sutler, canteen-manager.
vivant, -e (vivɑ̃), p. adj. Alive, living; (fig.) lively, animated. ~, s.m.f. **1.** Living person; (pl.) the living; *bon* ~, cheery soul; jolly fellow; **2.** life, lifetime; *de son* ~, in his lifetime; *du* ~ *de son frère*, while his brother was alive.
vivat (vivat), interj. [L wd] Hurrah!, huzza!, cheer! ~, s.m. Huzza; cheer; *pousser des* ~*s*, to cheer.
vive (viv), s.f. [OF *wivre*, f. L *vipera*] (ichth.) Weever.
vivement (vivmɑ̃), adv. Quickly, briskly, sharply, vigorously; keenly, deeply; poignantly, acutely.
viveur (vivœr), s.m. Free liver, fast liver.
vivier (vivje), s.m. [L *vivarium*] Fish-pond; fish-well (in boat).
vivifiant, -e (vivifjɑ̃), p. adj. Vivifying, quickening, bracing, life-giving, refreshing, invigorating.
vivification (vivifika'sjɔ̃), s.f. Vivification, vivifying, revival.
vivifier (vivifje), v.a. [L *vivificare*] To vivify, to quicken, to give life to; to animate, to revive, to brace.
vivipare (vivipar), adj. [L *vivus*+*parere*] Viviparous.
viviparité (viviparite), s.f. Viviparousness.
vivisecteur (vivisɛktœr), s.m. Vivisector, viviparity.

vivisection (vivisɛksjɔ̃), s.f. [L *vivus*+ *sectio*] Vivisection.

vivoter (vivɔte), v.n. To live in a small way, (fam.) to rub along.

vivre (vivr), v.n. [L *vivere*] To live, to be alive; to subsist; to board; to behave, to last, to endure; (as a threat) *je vous apprendrai à ~!*, I'll teach you your manners!; *~ de légumes*, to live on vegetables; *~ de ses rentes*, to live on one's private means; *le savoir-~*, good manners; *qui vive?*, who goes there?; *faire ~*, to support; *il fait bon ~*, it is good to be alive; *bien ~*, (*a*) to lead an upright life; (*b*) to live well; *il n'a pas de quoi ~*, he has not enough to live on; *être sur le qui-vive*, to be on the look-out or qui vive; *le bien-~*, fat living; *~ d'expédients*, to live by one's wits; *~ en*, to live like a; *qui vivra verra*, time will show; *ne trouver âme qui vive*, not to find a living soul; *comme c'est vécu!*, how true to life!; *roman vécu*, tale of real life. *~*, s.m. Living, board, food; *~s*, (pl.) provisions, victuals; *couper les ~s à X*, to cut off X's supplies.

vizir (vizir), s.m. [Turk. wd] Vizir, vizier.

vlan!, v'lan! (vlɑ̃), interj. Bang!, plop!; *~ dans l'œil!*, bang in the eye!

vocable (vɔkabl), s.m. [L *vocabulum*] **1.** Vocable, word; **2.** patronage; *église sous le ~ de Saint-Jean*, church dedicated to Saint John.

vocabulaire (vɔkabylɛr), s.m. [f. *vocable*] Vocabulary.

vocal, -e, (aux) (vɔkal), adj. [f. L *vox, vocis*] Vocal.

vocalement (vɔkalmɑ̃), adv. Vocally.

vocalique (vɔkalik), adj. Vocalic.

vocalisation (vɔkaliza'sjɔ̃), s.f. Vocalization.

vocalise (vɔkaliz), s.f. (mus.) Rapid singing exercise; song without words.

vocaliser (vɔkalize), v.n.a. [f. L *vocalis*] **1.** To practise rapid singing-exercises; **2.** (phon.) to vocalize, to utter (voice, word, &c.).

vocatif (vɔkatif), s.m. (gram.) Vocative.

vocation (vɔka'sjɔ̃), s.f. [L *vocatio*] Vocation, calling; call; dedicating; sense of fitness for career or occupation; *~ pour la littérature*, vocation for literature. ⚠ In English, but not in French, 'vocation' has also the sense of employment, trade, profession = *profession, métier*.

voceratrice (vɔsɛratris), s.f. [Corsican wd] Wailing-woman (at funerals in Corsica).

vocero (pl. **voceri**) (vɔsɛro), s.m. [Corsican wd] Funeral chant.

vociférant, -e (vɔsiferɑ̃), p. adj. Vociferating, vociferant, vociferous.

vociférations (vɔsifera'sjɔ̃), s.f.pl. Vociferations.

vociférer (vɔsifere), v.n.a. [L *vociferari*] To vociferate.

vodka (vɔdka), s.m. [Russ. wd] Vodka.

vœu (pl. **-x**) (vø), s.m. [L *votum*] **1.** Wish, desire, prayer; **2.** vow, votive offering; suffrage; *être au comble de ses ~x*, to have reached the summit of one's hopes; *faire ~ de se venger*, to swear vengeance; *faire des ~x pour la prospérité d'un ami*, (*a*) to pray for a friend's prosperity; (*b*) to wish a friend prosperity; *le ~ de la nation*, the nation's desire; *~x de Nouvel An*, New Year's wishes; *tous mes ~x*, my best wishes; *prononcer ses ~x*, to take the vows; *émettre un ~*, (*a*) to express a desire; (*b*) (of an assembly) to pass a resolution; *exaucer les ~x de X*, to crown X's wishes.

vogue (vɔg), s.f. [f. *voguer*] **1.** Vogue, fashion; credit, repute, reputation; *livre en ~*, book in vogue; *avoir la ~*, to be in fashion or in vogue; **2.** (obs.) sailing, rowing; **3.** (in the south of France) village feast.

voguer (vɔge), v.n. [It. *vogare*] To sail, to move (of boats), to float; to row; *~-avant*, s.m. bow oar; (poet.) to glide; (fig.) *et vogue la galère!*, come what will!, happen what may; sink or swim!, let us chance it!

voici (vwasi), prep. [*vois+ici*] Here is, here are, this is, these are; *~!*, behold!, see here!, here it is; *me ~*, here I am; *monsieur que ~*, this gentleman; *~ venir*, here comes; *notre ami que ~*, our friend here; *nous ~!*, here we are!; *nous y ~*, here we are; now we have come to the point; *en ~ bien d'une autre!*, and now, what's worse!; now that puts the lid on it!

voie (vwa), s.f. [L *via*] **1.** Way, road, highway; line, route, path, track, trail; *il est toujours par ~s et par chemins*, he is always on the move; (fig.) *être en ~* or *en bonne ~ de*, to be in a fair way of (+ pres. part.), or to (+ inf.); *la ~ lactée*, the Milky Way; *mettre sur la ~*, to put on the track; (naut.) *~ d'eau*, leak; **2.** (rail.) line, track, permanent way, four-foot way; *~ ferrée*, railway; **3.** (anat.) duct, canal; **4.** (law) *par toutes ~s que de droit*, by all legal means; *~s de fait*, assault; **5.** (obs.) a measure for wood (of about 2 steres), or coal (about 1 cubic metre); **6.** (fig.) means, organ, medium; channel, course; *laissez-le suivre sa voie*, let him gang his ain gait, let him follow his bent; *par la ~ de la persuasion*, by means of persuasion; *les ~s de Dieu*, the ways of the Lord; *être en bonne ~*, to be getting on; *être en mauvaise ~*, to be in a bad way; *en ~ de réparation*, in course of repairs.

voilà (vwala), prep. [*vois+là*] There is, there are; *~!*, there!; *comme vous ~ fait!*, you cut a pretty figure!; *~ comme je suis!*, that's how I'm made!; *en ~ assez!*, that will do; no more of that; stop it!; *~ une heure qu'il parle*, he has been talking for an hour; *me ~ bien!*, I am in a pretty pickle, or a fine mess ; ~ *qui va bien*, now, that's capital; ~ *tout*, that's all; *ne ~-t-il pas qu'il se fâche*, there now, if he does not take offence; *en veux-tu en ~*, more than enough; to one's fill; ~ *dix ans que cela dure*, this has been going on for ten years; *en ~ pour un an!*, that will last a year.

voile[1] (vwal), s.m. [L *velum*] **1.** Veil; (material) voile, fancy voile; veiling; ~ *de laine*, nun's veiling; (fig.) cover, disguise, mask; show, pretence; *les ~s de la nuit*, the shades of night; *prendre le ~*, to take the veil; *sous le ~ de l'amitié*, beneath the mask of friendship; **2.** (anat.) ~ *du palais*, soft palate.

voile[2] (vwal), s.f. Sail, canvas, course; *à la ~*, sailing, by sails; *faire ~*, to make sail; *mettre à la ~*, to set or make sail; *faire force de ~s*, or *mettre toutes ~s dehors*, to crowd on all sail; *amener les ~s*, to strike sail; *diminuer de ~s*, to shorten sail; *naviguer à la ~*, to sail; *navire à ~s*, sailing-ship; (aeron.) *vol à ~*, soaring (flight), gliding (with engineless aeroplane); see MISAINE, ARTIMON, &c.

voilé, -e (vwale), p. adj. Veiled; clouded, dull, dim; soft; muffled; (photo.) fogged; *temps ~*, hazy weather; *ton ~*, subdued or muffled voice; *regard ~*, dimmed look, or eye; *roue ~e*, buckled wheel, wheel not true.

voiler (vwale), v.a. **1.** To veil, to cover, to cloak; to disguise, to conceal; ~ *une roue*, to buckle a wheel; **2.** (naut.) to rig; **se ~**, v.pr., to be veiled, to wear a veil; to be concealed, covered, or disguised; to get buckled; to warp, to get warped.

voilerie (vwalri), s.f. **1.** Sail-loft; **2.** sail-making.

voilette (vwalɛt), s.f. Hat-veil, fine veil, veiling.

voilier (vwalje), s.m. **1.** Sail-maker; **2.** sailing-ship, sailer; *fin ~*, good sailer.

voilure (vwalyr), s.f. **1.** Set of sails, canvas, the sails; *carguer la ~*, to brail up, to take in sail, to clew up sail; **2.** warping (of boards, &c.), buckling (of wheel).

voir (vwar), v.a. [L *videre*] To see; to look at, to behold; to view, to inspect, to examine, to perceive, to realize; to be on visiting terms with, to visit, to meet; to attend to, to deal with; to go into; *à ~*, worth seeing; to be seen; *c'est à ~!*, we shall see about that!; *aller ~*, to go and see; to call upon; *allez-y ~*, (*a*) go and see about it; (*b*) believe it if you can!; *voyez à ce que cela soit fait*, see to it that it's done; *n'avoir rien à ~ avec*, to be irrelevant to; *cela n'a rien à ~ avec sa conduite*, it has nothing to do with his behaviour; *voyons!*, come!; *allons, voyons!*, come, come!; *faire ~*, to show; *faites ~*, let me see, show it to me; *faire ~ du pays à X*, to lead X a pretty dance; *elle lui en a fait ~ de toutes les couleurs*, she plagued him; she made life a burden to him (or her); *je vous vois venir*, I see what you are driving at; I can see what you are up to; *se faire bien ~*, to make oneself agreeable; to ingratiate oneself; *se faire mal ~*, to make oneself conspicuous (in a bad way); to incur blame; *il ne voit personne*, he sees nobody; he lives in complete retirement; *nous ne voyons plus ces gens-là*, we are no longer on visiting terms with those people; *vous n'avez rien à y ~*, it's no business of yours; *tu vois bien!*, now you see!, did I not tell you?; *elle ne peut pas le ~ en peinture!*, she cannot bear the sight of him; she hates the very sight of him!; (pop.) *il faudrait ~ à faire ce que j'ordonne*, see that you do what I tell you; (very pop., rather vulg.) *écoute ~*, just listen; *voyons ~ que je voie*, let's have a look; *essaye ~!*, just try it on!; **se ~**, v.pr. to see oneself; to see or frequent each other; to be apparent, conspicuous; to occur, to happen; *cela se voit tous les jours*, that happens or may occur any day; that's quite usual; *cela se voit comme le nez au milieu du visage*, it's as plain as a pikestaff; it's as plain as the nose on your face; that's conspicuous, or very visible; *ils ne se voient pas*, they are not on visiting terms.

voire (vwar), adv. [L *verum*] (archaic) Even, indeed, truly; nay, even.

voirie (vwari), s.f. [f. *voie*] **1.** Road Board; public highways and roads, their making and repairs; *travaux de ~*, road-making; **2.** common sewer.

voisin, -e (vwazɛ̃), adj. [L *vicinus*] Neighbouring, bordering, next, next door, adjacent, adjoining; akin; differing slightly. ~, s.m.f. Neighbour; *en ~*, as a neighbour, neighbourly.

voisinage (vwazinaʒ), s.m. Neighbourhood, neighbourliness, neighbourship; proximity, vicinity, nearness; *détesté de tout le ~*, an object of hatred to all the neighbours; *avoir des relations de bon ~*, to be on good terms with one's neighbours.

voisiner (vwazine), v.n. To visit one's neighbours; (rare) to neighbour it.

voiturage (vwatyraʒ), s.m. Cartage; conveying, transporting.

voiture (vwatyr), s.f. [f. L *vehere, vectura*] Carriage, vehicle, conveyance, coach; cart, van, wagon, truck, dray, cab, brougham; ~ *à deux chevaux*, carriage and pair; ~ *de roulier*, wagon, van, cart; ~ *de place*, cab, taxi-cab; hackney (cab), four-wheeler; ~ *publique*, or *omnibus*, omnibus, char-a-banc; ~ *de grande remise*, hired brougham; ~ *d'enfant*, perambulator, (colloq.), pram; ~ *de malade*, invalid carriage, bath chair;

prix de ~, fare; ~ *de livraison*, delivery-van; *lettre de* ~, way-bill; ~ *cellulaire*, prison-van; ~ *à bras*, hand-truck; *places réservées*, or *louées*, *dans la 4e* ~, reserved seats in the 4th (railway) carriage; ~ *automobile*, car, motor-car; (rail.) *en* ~ *!*, take your seats !; (U.S.A.) all aboard !

voiturer (vwatyre), v.a. To cart, to convey, to transport, to carry.

voiturette (vwatyrɛt), s.f. Small light motor-car; ~*-remorque*, trailer.

voiturier (vwatyrje), s.m. Carrier, carter, wagoner, driver.

voiturin (vwatyrɛ̃), s.m. (obs.) Driver, cabman.

voix (vwɑ), s.f. invar. [L *vox*] **1.** Voice; tone, utterance, sound, (singing) voice; (hunt.) cry; *à* ~ *basse*, or *à demi-*~, in an undertone; in a low voice; under one's breath; in a whisper; *à haute* ~, aloud; *à haute et intelligible* ~, aloud and distinctly; *de vive* ~, by word of mouth, orally, verbally; *faire la grosse* ~, to speak gruffly; (fig.) to pretend to be angry; (hunt.) *donner de la* ~, to give tongue; *il n'y a qu'une* ~ *pour le condamner*, he has been condemned or blamed with one voice (unanimously); *élever la* ~, to raise one's voice, to speak louder; (fig.) to lift up one's voice; (of a singer) *elle a perdu sa* ~, she has lost her voice; ~ *de poitrine*, chest voice; ~ *de tête*, head voice; ~ *de fausset*, falsetto; **2.** suffrage, vote; say, opinion; *aller aux* ~, to vote; *mettre aux* ~, to put to the vote; *aux* ~ *!*, divide!; put it to the vote!; *je n'ai pas* ~ *au chapitre*, I have no say (or voice) in the matter; *donner sa* ~ *à X*, to give X one's vote (or voice); **3.** (gram.) voice; *la* ~ *active*, *passive*, the active, passive voice.

vol[1] (vɔl), s.m. [f. *voler*[1]] Flying, flight; soaring; flock of birds; *vitesse de* ~, speed of flight; ~ *plané*, volplane, glide, gliding descent; ~ *à voile*, gliding (flying with engineless aeroplane); *à* ~ *d'oiseau*, as the crow flies; bird's-eye; from a bird's-eye view; *au* ~, on the wing; flying; *en plein* ~, in full flight; ~ *de nuit*, night flight; *un vol de 3 heures*, a 3-hour flight.

vol[2] (vɔl), s.m. [f. *voler*[2]] Theft, stealing, robbery, larceny; ~ *avec effraction*, burglary; ~ *de grand chemin*, highway robbery; *commettre un* ~, to commit a robbery; ~ *à l'étalage*, shop-lifting.

volable (vɔlabl), adj. Liable to be stolen.

volage (vɔlaʒ), adj. Fickle, inconstant.

volaille (vɔlɑj), s.f. [L *volatilia*] Poultry, fowl, fowls; *marchand de* ~*s*, poulterer.

volant (vɔlɑ̃), s.m. [f. *voler*[1]] **1.** Shuttlecock; *jouer au* ~, to play at battledore and shuttlecock; **2.** flounce, frill; *robe à* ~*s*, flounced gown; **3.** (machinery) flywheel, flier; (motor.) steering-wheel.

volant, -e (vɔlɑ̃), p. adj. Flying; loose, movable, shifting, temporary, travelling; *feuille* ~*e*, loose sheet; *poisson* ~, flying fish; (fig.) *en camp* ~, temporarily; on a flying visit; *pont* ~, flying bridge; (mil.) *colonne* ~*e*, flying column, squadron, &c.; *camp* ~, flying camp.

volapuk (vɔlapyk), s.m. [f. Engl. *world+speak*] Volapuk, artificial international language.

volatil, -e (vɔlatil), adj. [L *volatilis*] Volatile, evaporating rapidly. ⚠ In French ~ is not used in a fig. sense, whereas in English it is quite correct to speak of a volatile wit, writer, mind, &c. = *un esprit*, &c., *vif*, *plein de diversité*.

volatile (vɔlatil), s.m. [L *volatilis*] Fowl, bird, winged animal.

volatilisable (vɔlatilizabl), adj. Volatilizable.

volatilisation (vɔlatiliza'sjɔ̃), s.f. Volatilization.

volatiliser (vɔlatilize), v.a. To volatilize; *se* ~, v.pr. to evaporate, to be volatilized.

volatilité (vɔlatilite), s.f. [f. *volatil*] Volatileness, volatility. ⚠ See VOLATIL.

vol-au-vent (vɔlovɑ̃), s.m. invar. (cook.) Vol-au-vent, kind of raised pie with quenelles, mushrooms, sauce, &c.

volcan (vɔlkɑ̃), s.m. [L *vulcanus*] Volcano.

volcanique (vɔlkanik), adj. Volcanic.

volcaniser (vɔlkanize), v.a. To vulcanize.

volcanisme (vɔlkanism), s.m. Volcanism.

vole (vɔl), s.f. (at cards) Vole; *faire la* ~, to win the vole.

volée (vɔle), s.f. [f. *voler*[1]] **1.** Flight; *prendre sa* ~, or *son vol*, to take wing; to take one's or its flight, to soar; **2.** flock of birds; **3.** rank; *de haute* ~, of high rank; of the first water; **4.** volley, salvo, discharge; **5.** peal; *sonner les cloches à toute* ~, to ring a full peal; **6.** (colloq.) thrashing, drubbing; *il lui a flanqué une* ~ *(de bois vert)*, he gave him a good thrashing; *à la* ~, flying, at random; (agric.) *semer à la* ~, to sow broadcast; *cheval de* ~, leader (horse).

voler[1] (vɔle), v.n. [L *volare*] To fly, to soar, to take wing; to make a flight; (fig.) to run at top speed, or like mad; to move very quickly; to tear away, to dart; (of news) to spread like lightning; (aeron.) ~ *contre le vent*, to yaw, to cat into the wind; ~ *en éclats*, to fly to pieces; *on entendrait* ~ *une mouche*, one could hear a pin drop; ~ *de ses propres ailes*, to shift for oneself.

voler[2] (vɔle), v.a.n. [etym. dub.] To steal, to rob, to thieve, to take away; (colloq.) to pinch, to scrounge; (fig.) *il ne l'a pas volé*, it serves him right; he richly deserves it; *je suis volé !*, I have been done !, what a sell !

volerie (vɔlri), s.f. **1.** Larceny, theft, robbery, stealing; swindle; fleecing; **2.** (obs.) flying (of falcons, &c.).

volet (vɔlɛ), s.m. Shutter, window-shutter; sorting-board; (fig.) *triés sur le ~*, quite select, chosen with great care, most exclusive; choice; (mech.) *~ de soupape*, valve-head, or -shoulder.
voleter (vɔlte), v.n. [f. *voler*[1]] To flutter about.
volette (vɔlɛt), s.f. **1.** Small wattle (for draining cheese); **2.** horse-net, fly-net for a horse.
voleu-r, -se (vɔlœr), s.m.f. Thief, robber, burglar; plunderer, fleecer; *au ~!*, stop thief!; *crier au ~*, to cry 'stop thief!'; *~ à la tire*, pick-pocket; *~ de grand chemin*, highwayman or -robber, footpad; *~ (commettant effraction)*, burglar; *cet hôtelier est un ~*, this hotel-keeper is a robber; they fleece you at that inn; *à ~, ~ et demi*, set a thief to catch a thief; (jest.) *il est fait comme un ~*, he is dressed like a scare-crow; he is in tatters.
volière (vɔljɛr), s.f. [f. *voler*] Aviary, large bird-cage.
volige (vɔliʒ), s.f. (carp.) Batten, scantling.
voligeage (vɔliʒaʒ), s.m. Battening.
voliger (vɔliʒe), v.a. (carp.) To batten.
voliti-f, -ve (vɔlitif), adj. Volitive, volitionary.
volition (vɔlisjɔ̃), s.f. [f. LL *volitio*] Volition.
volontaire (vɔlɔ̃tɛr), adj. [L *voluntarius*] **1.** Voluntary, of one's free will; intentional, deliberate, spontaneous; **2.** self-willed, wilful, headstrong. **~**, s.m.f. Volunteer.
volontairement (vɔlɔ̃tɛrmɑ̃), adv. Voluntarily, deliberately, intentionally, willingly; wilfully.
volontariat (vɔlɔ̃tarja), s.m. Voluntary (military) service.
volonté (vɔlɔ̃te), s.f. [L *voluntas*] Will, will-power; mind, pleasure, wish, desire; (pl.) whims, caprices; *à ~*, at will, as much as you wish; just as you like; to order; *avoir de la bonne ~*, or *être plein de bonne ~*, to be quite willing, full of good will; *y mettre de la mauvaise ~*, to do (a thing) with a bad grace, reluctantly, or unwillingly; *dernières ~s*, last will and testament; *faire ses quatre ~s*, or *toutes ses ~s*, or *ses trente-six ~s*, (*a*) to act according to one's own sweet will; to have one's own way in everything; (*b*) to comply with all the whims of (a person); *on demande un homme de bonne ~*, a volunteer is required; *voitures à ~*, carriages for hire.
volontiers (vɔlɔ̃tje), adv. Willingly, gladly, with pleasure; readily; frequently.
volsque (vɔlsk), adj. s.m.f. Volscian.
volt (vɔlt), s.m. [f. *Volta*, It. physicist, 1745–1826] (electr.) Volt, unit of electromotive force.
volta (vɔlta), s.f. [It. wd] (mus.) Volta.
voltage (vɔltaʒ), s.m. Voltage.
voltaïque (vɔltaik), adj. Voltaic.
voltaire, fauteuil-voltaire (vɔltɛr, fotœj-vɔltɛr), s.m. [f. prop. n. *Voltaire*] Voltaire (armchair).
voltairianisme (vɔltɛrjanism), s.m. [f. *Voltaire*] Voltairianism, voltairism.
voltairien, -ne (vɔltɛrjɛ̃), adj. Voltairian.
voltaïsation (vɔltaiza'sjɔ̃), s.f. (med.) Voltaization.
voltaïsme (vɔltaism), s.m. Voltaism.
voltamètre (vɔltamɛtr), s.m. (electr.) Voltameter, voltmeter.
volte (vɔlt), s.f. [It. *volta*] (rid., fenc.) Volte.
volte-face (vɔltəfas), s.f. (mil.) Turning about; *~!*, about turn!; (fig.) *faire ~*, to change sides; to wheel round; to make a complete change of front, in argument, politics, &c.
volter (vɔlte), v.n. (rid., fenc.) To volt.
voltige (vɔltiʒ), s.f. [f. *voltiger*] Slack rope; dancing on the slack rope; vaulting.
voltigement (vɔltiʒmɑ̃), s.m. Flutter, fluttering, hovering, flying about.
voltiger (vɔltiʒe), v.n. [It. *volteggiare*] To flutter about, to fly about, to flit, to hover; to move quickly; to vault; to dance on the slack rope.
voltigeu-r, -se (vɔltiʒœr), s.m.f. **1.** Dancer on the slack rope; **2.** vaulter; **3.** (mil.) light infantry soldier, voltigeur.
volubile (vɔlybil), adj. [L *volubilis*] **1.** (bot.) Volubile, volubilate; **2.** voluble, glib.
volubilis (vɔlybilis), s.m. [L wd] (bot.) Convolvulus.
volubilité (vɔlybilite), s.f. [f. L *volubilis*] Volubility, volubleness; *parler avec ~*, to speak volubly, to have a glib tongue.
volume (vɔlym), s.m. [L *volumen*] **1.** Volume, book, part of a book, tome; *ouvrage en 3 ~s*, work (issued) in 3 volumes; **2.** bulk, size, mass; *mesures de ~*, volume, cubic measures, cubic values. ⚠ Not used in French as in English in the sense of large quantity, mass (e.g. of smoke) = *nuage, volute.*
voluménomètre (vɔlymenɔmɛtr), s.m. Volumenometer, instrument for measuring volume of a solid body by quantity of liquid displaced.
volumétrique (vɔlymetrik), adj. Volumetric(al).
volumétriquement (vɔlymetrikmɑ̃), adv. Volumetrically.
volumineu-x, -se (vɔlyminø), adj. Voluminous, bulky.
volupté (vɔlypte), s.f. [L *voluptas*] Voluptuousness, pleasure, sensuality, sensual pleasure.
voluptuaire (vɔlyptɥɛr), adj. [L *voluptuarius*] Voluptuary, of luxury, for embellishment.

ɔ, n*o*te, gl*o*tte; ɔ̃, m*on*ter, r*on*de; ø, f*eu*, cr*eux*; œ, p*eu*r, s*œu*r; œ̃, *un*; ʃ, *ch*ez, *sch*isme; u, t*ou*t; w, *ou*i, d*oi*t, d*ou*aire; y, m*u*r, p*u*; ɥ, h*u*ile, m*u*ette; z, *z*èle, ro*s*e; ʒ, dé*j*à, *g*entil.

voluptueusement (vɔlyptɥøzmɑ̃), adv. Voluptuously, luxuriously.
voluptueu-x, -se (vɔlyptɥø), adj. Voluptuous, sensual, luxurious, epicurean. ~, s.m.f. Epicurean, sensualist.
volute (vɔlyt), s.f. [L *voluta*] Volute, scroll; *des ~s de fumée*, volumes or clouds of smoke; (zool.) voluta.
volve (vɔlv), s.f. (bot.) Volva.
vomer (vɔmɛr), s.m. [L wd] (anat.) Vomer, a bone in the nose.
vomique (vɔmik), s.f. (med.) Vomica. ~, adj. Vomic; *noix ~*, nux vomica.
vomir (vɔmir), v.a.n. [L *vomere*] To vomit (up); to spew, to cast up, to belch out, to bring up, to throw up; *avoir envie de ~*, to feel sick, to have nausea; (fig.) *~ des injures*, to belch forth or to vomit abuse or foul talk.
vomissement (vɔmismɑ̃), s.m. Vomiting, vomit.
vomiti-f, -ve (vɔmitif), adj. Vomitive, vomitory. ~, s.m. Vomitory, emetic.
vomito-negro (vɔmitonegro), s.m. [Span. wd] (pathol.) Black vomit, yellow fever.
vomitoire (vɔmitwar), s.m. [L *vomitorium*] Vomitory.
vomiturition (vɔmityrisjɔ̃), s.f. (pathol.) Vomiturition.
vorace (vɔras), adj. [L *vorax*] Voracious, greedy, ravenous.
voracement (vɔrasmɑ̃), adv. Voraciously, greedily, ravenously.
voracité (vɔrasite), s.f. Voraciousness, voracity.
vortex (vɔrtɛks), s.m. [L wd] Vortex. ⚠ The usual sense in French is: spiral or radiating disposition (of fibres, &c.) = *disposition concentrique et rayonnante de fibres, organes, &c.*, while in English the usual sense is whirlpool = *tourbillon.*
vorticelle (vɔrtisɛl), s.f. [f. *vortex*] (zool.) Vorticel, bell-shaped animalcule.
vos (vo), adj. poss. pl. of *votre.* Your.
votant, -e (vɔtɑ̃), adj. Voting. ~, s.m.f. Voter.
votation (vɔta'sjɔ̃), s.f. Voting.
vote (vɔt), s.m. [L *votum*] Vote, suffrage; voting, poll; *droit de ~*, franchise; *~ à main levée*, vote by show of hands.
voter (vɔte), v.n.a. To vote, to give one's vote, to poll; *~ des remerciements à X*, to pass a vote of thanks to X; *~ à main levée*, to vote by show of hands; *les Françaises veulent ~*, Frenchwomen want the vote; *~ une loi*, to enact a law.
voti-f, -ve (vɔtif), adj. [f. L *votum*] Votive.
votre (pl. **vos**) (vɔtr), poss. adj. Your, your own.
vôtre (votr), adj. Yours; *le ~, la ~, les ~s*, poss. pr. yours; *il a emporté son chapeau et le ~ aussi*, he took away his own hat and yours as well; *je serai des ~s jeudi*, I shall be one of your party on Thursday; (pop.) *à la ~!*, your health!; *allons! mettez-y du ~*, now, show your good will; *aimez les ~s*, love your family; *vous en serez au ~*, you will have (*a*) to pay for it, (*b*) to share expenses.
vouer (vue), v.a. [f. *vœu*] To vow, to devote, to dedicate, to consecrate; to doom; *~ un temple à Dieu*, to vow a temple to God; *~ à l'exécration publique*, to doom or to consign to public hatred; *~ au bleu*, to dedicate to the Virgin; **se ~**, v.pr. to devote oneself (*à*, to); (colloq.) *ne savoir à quel saint se ~*, not to know which way to turn.
vouge (vuʒ), s.m. [Celt. orig., LL *vidubium*] **1.** (agric.) Bill-hook; **2.** (obs.) halberd.
vouloir (vulwar), v.a. [LL *volere*, f. L *velle*] To will; to want, to require, to wish, to be willing, to have a will; to choose; to demand; to ask; *que voulez-vous?* (*a*) what do you want?; what can I do for you?; (*b*) (excl.) what can you expect?, what 's to be done?; it can't be helped!; *je (le) veux bien*, I am willing; willingly, I have no objection (to that); *vous l'avez (bien) voulu!*, you would have it!; it serves you right!; you have brought it on yourself!; *~ du bien à X*, to bear good will to X; to wish X well; *que voulez-vous dire?*, what do you mean?; *que veut dire cela?* what does it mean?; *je veux dire que*, I mean (to say) that; *il m'en veut*, he has (or bears) a grudge against me; *que me voulez-vous?*, what do you want of me?; *je m'en veux de n'avoir pas*, I reproach myself for not having; *il faut savoir ce qu'on veut*, one must make up one's mind; *ce bois ne veut pas brûler*, this wood won't burn; *je voudrais être un oiseau*, I would I were a bird; *Dieu veuille que*, God grant that; *il veut absolument qu'elle parte*, he insists upon her going; *veuillez me faire savoir*, kindly let me know; *veuillez faire ceci*, have the goodness to do this; please do this; *il veut 100 francs de son chien*, he wants 100 francs for his dog; *je veux que vous parliez*, I wish you to speak; *comment voulez-vous qu'il y arrive?*, how can he possibly do it, pray?; *demandez-lui s'il voudrait dire*, ask him whether he would mind saying; *~ c'est pouvoir*, where there 's a will there 's a way.
vouloir (vulwar), s.m. Will, will-power; *bon ~*, good will; willingness; *mauvais ~*, ill will, reluctance, bad grace, unwillingness.
voulu, -e (vuly), p. adj. Deliberate, intended, intentional, done on purpose; *une grossièreté ~e*, deliberate rudeness, a deliberate insult.
vous (vu), pers. pron. You, (obs.) ye; to you; *~ le voulez*, you will have it; *je ~ l'ai*

dit, I told you so; *je vous le porterai,* I will bring it to you; *bien à ~,* yours sincerely; *à ~,* to you; it's your turn; you begin; *à ~ de savoir si,* it's up to you to know whether; *de ~ à moi,* between ourselves; from you to me; *~-même,* yourself; *~ ~ trompez,* you are mistaken.

voussoir, vousseau (pl. -x) (vuswar, vuso), s.m. (arch.) Voussoir, wedge-shaped stone (of an arch).

voussure (vusyr), s.f. (arch.) Coving; (anat.) arching.

voûte (vut), s.f. [f. L *volvere*] Vault, arch; (fig.) canopy, vault; *~ d'arête,* groined vault; *clef de ~,* keystone; (anat.) *~ du palais,* soft palate.

voûté, -e (vute), p. adj. Vaulted, arched; (of a person) bent with age, stooping, round-shouldered.

voûter (vute), v.a. To vault, to arch over; **se ~,** v.pr. to become round-shouldered, or bent, to be bent with age, to stoop.

vouvray (vuvrɛ), s.m. [f. *Vouvray,* in Touraine] Vouvray wine.

vouzoyer, vouvoyer (vuzwaje, vuvwaje), v.a. To say you, *vous* (and not thou, *tu*) to somebody.

voyage (vwajaʒ), s.m. [f. L *viaticum*] Journey, travel; (by sea) voyage; trip, tour, excursion; *bon ~!,* farewell! a pleasant journey (to you)!; *partir en ~,* to go abroad; *faire un ~,* to travel, to be travelling, to make a journey; *~ au long cours,* voyage to foreign parts, *~ d'aller,* outward journey or voyage; *~ de retour,* homeward journey or voyage; *~ d'agrément,* pleasure trip; *~ d'essai,* trial trip; *le grand ~,* the last journey, death; *costume de ~,* travelling-suit or -dress; *en ~,* on a journey, on a voyage, travelling; *compagnon de ~,* fellow traveller.

voyager (vwajaʒe), v.n. To travel; to journey; to be travelling, to make a trip; *~ par mer,* to voyage.

voyageu-r, -se (vwajaʒœr), s.m.f. Traveller, (U.S.A.) traveler; passenger; (in a hackney cab or taxi) fare; *~ de commerce,* or *commis ~,* commercial traveller, bagman; (U.S.A.) drummer. ~, adj. Travelling, migratory; *oiseaux ~s,* migratory birds, migrants.

voyant, -e (vwajɑ̃), p. adj. **1.** Seeing; **2.** showy, glaring, gaudy. ~, s.m.f. **1.** Seer, clairvoyant(e), prophet, prophetess; **2.** *~ de mire,* parti-coloured plate used in surveying; (naut.) mark, signal.

voyelle (vwajɛl), s.f. [L *vocalis*] Vowel.

voyer (vwaje), s.m. adj. [L *vicarius*] *Agent ~,* road-surveyor.

voyer (vwaje), v.a. [f. *voie*] To cause to run (as a liquid).

voyou (pl. -s) (vwaju), s.m. Cad, rough, street arab, street rowdy, blackguard, apache.

voyoucratie (vwajukrasi), s.f. (iron.) Mobocracy, mob-rule.

vrac (vrak), s.m. [f. Dutch *wrak*] *En ~,* pell-mell, in bulk, unpacked, loose; (naut.) *charger en ~,* to load in bulk.

vrai, -e (vrɛ), adj. [f. L *verus*] True, real, exact, right, genuine, correct, accurate, veritable; veracious, truthful, sincere; thorough, arrant, regular. ~, s.m. Truth; *être dans le ~,* to be right. ~, adv. Truly, true; *à ~ dire,* or *au ~,* to tell the truth; in truth; *pour de ~,* really, truly, in earnest; *pas ~?,* is it not so?, isn't that a fact?; (vulg.) *ben ~!,* now then!, dear me!, indeed!, really!

vraiment (vrɛmɑ̃), adv. Truly, veritably, really; indeed, in truth; verily; forsooth!

vraisemblable (vrɛsɑ̃blabl), adj. [*vrai+semblable*] Likely, credible, probable, believable, plausible; *le vrai peut quelquefois n'être pas ~,* truth is stranger than fiction.

vraisemblablement (vrɛsɑ̃blabləmɑ̃), adv. Very likely, probably; in all likelihood or probability; to all appearance; apparently.

vraisemblance (vrɛsɑ̃blɑ̃s), s.f. Likelihood, probability, plausibility, verisimilitude, credibility; *selon toute ~,* to all appearance; in all likelihood or probability; according to every reasonable expectation; *contre toute ~,* contrary to all reasonable expectation.

vrillage (vrijaʒ), s.m. (weaving) Snarling.

vrille (vrij), s.f. [L *viticula*] **1.** (bot.) Tendril; **2.** (mech.) borer, piercer, gimlet.

vrillé, -e (vrije), p. adj. Bored, gimleted; gimlet-like; (bot.) having tendrils; twisted; (weaving) snarled.

vrillée (vrije), s.f. (bot.) Bindweed; syn. LISERON DES CHAMPS.

vriller (vrije), v.a. To pierce, to gimlet, to bore; (fig.) *tu me vrilles le tympan,* that's enough to split my ears (or head); you pierce my ears with your shrill voice; ~, v.n. to ascend spirally; (weaving) to snarl, to shrink.

vrillerie (vrijri), s.f. Gimlet-making; gimlets and similar tools.

vrillette (vrijɛt), s.f. (ent.) Boring-beetle, wood-engraver, anobium.

vrillier (vrije), s.m. Gimlet-maker.

vrillifère (vrijifɛr), adj. (bot.) Having tendrils; (zool.) claspered.

vrillon (vrijɔ̃), s.m. Small wimble.

vu, -e (vy), p. adj. [f. *voir*] Considered, regarded, deemed; *ni ~ ni connu,* you won't discover anything; nobody any the wiser; *bien ~,* well liked, regarded with favour, appreciated; *mal ~,* held in very poor esteem, or in no esteem. ~, prep. *~ la difficulté,* considering the difficulty, or with regard to the difficulty. ~, conj. *~ qu'il ne le connaît pas,* considering that he has not met him; or, since he is not acquainted with him.

vu (vy), s.m. [f. *voir*] *Au ~ et au su de tout le monde*, openly; with every one's knowledge; as everybody knows.

vue (vy), s.f. [f. *voir, vu*] Sight, eyesight, vision, eyes, eye; view, aspect, look; prospect; survey; design, aim, schemes; (fig.) insight, penetration, reckoning; (stereoscopic) slide; *à ~*, at sight; (of drawing) freehand; (commerc.) *à 15 jours de ~*, 15 days after sight; or at 15 days' sight; *à ~ de nez*, at a rough guess; by rule of thumb; at first glance; *à ~ d'œil*, very rapidly, visibly, in no time; *garder à ~ un prisonnier*, not to let a prisoner out of sight; to watch a prisoner closely; *à ~ d'oiseau*, bird's-eye (view); *à perte de ~*, as far as the eye can reach; (fig.) endlessly, ramblingly; *je le connais de ~*, I know him by sight; *avoir la ~ basse*, or *courte*, to be short-sighted; *avoir la ~ longue*, to be long-sighted; *avoir la ~ faible*, to have bad eyesight; *perdre la ~*, to lose one's sight; *perdre de ~*, to lose sight of; *en ~*, visible, conspicuous; *en ~ de*, (*a*) with a view to; in order to; with an eye to; (*b*) within sight of; *avoir des ~s sur quelque chose*, to have designs or views upon something; to aim at something; *avoir une belle ~ de sa fenêtre*, to have a lovely or fine view from one's window; *cette maison a ~ sur*, this house has a view of, or looks on; *une ~ de côté*, a side view; *~ perspective*, perspective view; *prendre des ~s*, to take photographs, snapshots; *il a en ~*, he has in view (as his object); *ceci s'accorde-t-il avec vos ~s?*, will this meet your views?; *point de ~*, point of view; (U.S.A.) view-point; *au point de ~ de*, as to; in respect of; regarding; *il a des ~s ingénieuses sur ce sujet*, he holds original views on this subject; *avoir le don de seconde ~*, to be clairvoyant; to have second sight; *à première ~*, at first sight; (mus.) *jouer à première ~*, to play at sight; (slang) *en mettre plein la ~ à X*, to try to come it over X (by showing off or bragging).

vulcanisation (vylkaniza'sjɔ̃), s.f. Vulcanization.

vulcanisé, -e (vylkanize), p. adj. Vulcanized.

vulcaniser (vylkanize), v.a. To vulcanize.

vulcanisme (vylkanism), s.m. [f. *Vulcan*] Vulcanism, Plutonic theory.

vulcanite (vylkanit), s.f. Vulcanite; syn. ÉBONITE.

vulgaire (vylgɛr), adj. [L *vulgaris*] **1.** Vulgar, common, in common use; **2.** vulgar, coarse, low; plebeian; in bad taste; *des expressions ~s*, vulgar expressions; *langue ~*, vulgar tongue. ~, s.m. The vulgar, the common people, the common herd; the common run.

vulgairement (vylgɛrmɑ̃), adv. Vulgarly, commonly; coarsely.

vulgarisat-eur, -rice (vylgarizatœr), s.m.f. Vulgarizer, popularizer.

vulgarisation (vylgariza'sjɔ̃), s.f. Vulgarization.

vulgariser (vylgarize), v.a. To vulgarize, to popularize; **se ~**, v.pr. to become vulgarized.

vulgarité (vylgarite), s.f. [f. L *vulgaris*] Vulgarity, coarseness, triviality.

vulgate (vylgat), s.f. Vulgate, Latin version of the Bible.

vulnérabilité, (vylnerabilite), s.f. Vulnerability, vulnerableness.

vulnérable (vylnerabl), adj. [L *vulnerabilis*] Vulnerable.

vulnéraire (vylnerɛr), adj. [f. L *vulnus*] Vulnerary, useful for healing wounds. ~, s.m. Vulnerary.

vulnération (vylnera'sjɔ̃), s.f. Wound (produced by surgeon's instrument).

vulpin (vylpɛ̃), s.m. (bot.) Foxtail (grass).

vultueu-x, -se (vyltɥø), adj. [f. L *vultus*] (of the face) Red and swollen.

vulturidés (vyltyride), s.m.pl. (ornith.) Vultures.

vulvaire (vylvɛr), adj. (anat.) Vulvar.

vulve (vylv), s.f. [L *vulva*] (anat.) Vulva.

vulvite (vylvit), s.f. (pathol.) Vulvitis.

W

W, w (dubləve), s.m. 23rd letter of the alphabet. This letter is borrowed from the northern languages, and only occurs in words taken from those languages.

wagage (vagaʒ), s.m. River-mud (used as manure).

wagnérien, -ne (vagnerjɛ̃), adj. s.m.f. [f. prop. n. *Wagner*] Wagnerian.

wagnérisme (vagnerism), s.m. Wagnerism.

wagon (vagɔ̃), s.m. [Engl. wd] Railway coach or carriage, railroad car; truck; *en ~!*, take your seats!; *~-restaurant*, restaurant car, dining-car; *~-salon*, Pullman car; *~-lit*, sleeping-car; (fam.) sleeper; *~-citerne* or *~-réservoir*, reservoir truck. ⚠ In French *wagon* is never used as in English for a heavy cart, delivery-van, &c. = *charrette, fourgon*. It is used only of railway carriages.

wagonnet (vagɔnɛ), s.m. (mining) Tub, truck.

wagonnette (vagɔnɛt), s.f. (obs.) Low four-wheeled cart. ⚠ Not 'wagonette', which = *break*.

wagon-poste (vagɔ̃pɔst), s.m. Mail-van.

wallace (valas), s.f. [f. prop. n. *Richard*

Wallace] Drinking-fountain (in Paris, presented by Wallace).
wallon, -ne (valɔ̃), adj. s.m.f. Walloon.
wapiti (wapiti), s.m. (zool.) Wapiti.
warrant (warɑ̃t, varɑ̃t), s.m. [Engl. wd] (comm.) Warrant, voucher.
warrantage (warɑ̃taʒ), s.m. Warranting.
warranter (warɑ̃te), v.a. (comm.) To warrant.
water-closet (watɛrklozɛt), s.m. [Engl. wd] W.C.; (pop. syn.) *les waters* (lɛvatɛr).
watergang (watɛrgɑ̃), s.m. [Dutch *water* +*gang*] Watergang, dyke.
wateringue (vatrɛ̃g), s.f. [Fl. *wateringen*] Reclaiming and drainage (*a*) system or (*b*) company (in Netherlands).
waterman (watɛrmɑ̃), s.m. [Engl. wd] Dredger.
waterproof (watɛrpruf), s.m. [Engl. wd] Waterproof.
watt (wat), s.m. (electr.) Watt; abbrev. *w.*
wattman (watman), s.m. [*watt*+Engl. *man*] Tram-driver.
wesleyen (wɛslejɛ̃), s.m.f. Wesleyan.
wharf (warf), s.m. [Engl. wd] Wharf.
whig (wig), s.m. adj. [Engl. wd] Whig.
whiskey, whisky (wiski), s.m. [Engl. wd] Whiskey.
whist (wist), s.m. [Engl. wd] Whist.
wiclèfisme (wiklefism), s.m. [f. Engl. prop. n. *Wycliffe*] Wycliffism.
wigwam (vigvam), s.m. [Amer. Indian wd] Wigwam.
wisigothique (vizigɔtik), adj. Visigothic; (fig.) rude, barbarous.
wistaria (vistarja), s.f. (bot.) Wistaria.
wolfram (volfram), s.m. (chem.) Wolfram, tungsten ore.
wombat (vɔ̃ba), s.m. (zool.) Wombat.
wurtembergeois, -e (vyrtɑ̃bɛrʒwɑ), adj. s.m.f. Of Wurtemberg, Wurtemberger.
wyandotte (viɑ̃dɔt), adj. s.m.f. (ornith.) Wyandotte.

X

X, x (iks), s.m. 24th letter of the alphabet; x; *avoir les jambes en* ~, to be knock-kneed; *rayons-*~, X-rays; (school slang) *l'X* = the *École Polytechnique*; *entrer à l'X*, to pass successfully the very difficult competitive examination which gives access to the *École Polytechnique*; hence *un X, les X*, those who have been students in the *École Polytechnique*.
xanthine (kzɑ̃tin), s.f. [f. Gr. *xanthos*] (chem.) Xanthin(e).
xanthophylle (kzɑ̃tɔfil), s.f. [Gr. *xanthos*+ *phullon*] Xanthophyll.
xénélasie (ksenelazi), s.f. [Gr. *xenos*+ *elaunein*] Xenelasy (Spartan system of expelling aliens).
xénon (ksenɔ̃), s.m. [Gr. wd] (chem.) Xenon.
xénophile (ksenɔfil), adj. Loving or favouring foreigners, xenophile.
xénophilie (ksenɔfili), s.f. [Gr. *xenos*+ *philos*] Xenophilism.
xénophobe (ksenɔfɔb), adj. Hating and fearing aliens, xenophobe.
xénophobie (ksenɔfɔbi), s.f. [Gr. *xenos*+ *phobos*] Xenophobia.
xéranthème (kserɑ̃tɛm), s.m. [Gr. *xēros*+ *anthemon*] (bot.) Xeranthemum, immortelle.
xérasie (kserazi), s.f. [Gr. *xērasia*] (pathol.) Xerasia.
xérès (kerɛs), s.m. [*Xeres* (Andalusia)] Sherry (wine).
xiphoïde (ksifɔid), adj. [f. Gr. *xiphos*] (anat.) Xiphoid, sword-shaped.
xylène (ksilɛn), s.m. [f. Gr. *xulon*] (chem.) Xylene.
xylidine (ksilidin), s.f. (chem.) Xylidine.
xylocope (ksilɔkɔp), s.m. (ent.) Carpenter-bee (of the genus *Xylocopa*).
xylographe (ksilɔgraf), s.m. [Gr. *xulon*+ *graphein*] Xylographer, wood-engraver.
xylographie (ksilɔgrafi), s.f. Xylography, wood-engraving, xylograph.
xylographique (ksilɔgrafik), adj. Xylographic.
xylol (ksilɔl), s.m. (chem.) See syn. XYLÈNE.
xylophage (ksilɔfaʒ), adj. [Gr. *xulon*+ *phagos*] Xylophagous, feeding on wood. ~, s.m. Xylophage.
xylophone (ksilɔfɔn), s.m. [Gr. *xulon*+ *phōnē*] Xylophone.
xyste (ksist), s.m. [Gr. *xustos*] (ant.) Xystus.
xystre (ksistr), s.m. [f. Gr. *xustēr*] Xyster, surgical instrument for scraping bones.

Y

Y, y (igrɛk), s.m. 25th letter of the alphabet.
y (i), adv. and pers. pron. 3rd per. [L *ibi*] Here, there, thither, within, at home; *allez-*~, go there, (fam.) go on; (pop.) *vas-*~*!*, go it; *il* ~ *a*, there is, there exists; *je l'y ai vu*, I saw him there; *il n'*~ *voit pas*, his sight is bad; *sans* ~ *penser*, without thinking; *il ne faut pas s'*~ *fier*, don't rely on it (him, her); *il n'*~ *gagnera rien*, he'll get nothing by it; *j'*~ *cours*, I'm off there at once; *il* ~ *va de sa tête*, his life is at stake; *j'*~ *suis, j'*~ *reste*, possession is nine points of the law; ~ *compris*, including; *n'*~ *rien comprendre*, to make neither head nor tail of it; ~ *regarder de près*, to be very particular; ~ *ajouter foi*, to give it credence; *s'*~ *engager*, to pass one's word for it; *s'*~ *refuser*, to refuse to undertake it. See also ÊTRE for Y ÊTRE.
yacht (jɔt), s.m. [Dutch *jacht*] Yacht.

yack, yak (jak), s.m. [Tibetan wd] (zool.) Yak.
yaourt, yahourt (jaurt), s.m. See syn. YOGOURT.
yapok (japɔk), s.m. [f. *Oyapok*, river of Brazil] Yapock.
yatagan (jatagɑ̃), s.m. [Turk. wd] Yataghan.
yèble (jɛbl), s.m. (bot.) See syn. HIÈBLE.
yeuse (jøz), s.f. [L *ilex*] (bot.) Ilex, holm-oak, evergreen oak.
yeux (jø), s.m.pl. Pl. of *œil*.
ylang-ylang (ilɑ̃gilɑ̃g), s.m. (bot.) Ylang-ylang; the perfume of the flower.
yogourt, yoghourth (jɔgurt), s.m. [Turk. *yog(h)urt*] Yoghourt, yaourt; boiled curdled milk.
yole (jɔl), s.f. [Norw. *jol*] (naut.) Yawl, gig.
youpin, youtre (jupɛ̃, jutr), s.m. (slang, pej.) Jew, sheeny; (U.S.A.) yid, yiddisher.
youyou (juju), s.m. (naut.) Dinghy.
ypérite (iperit), s.f. [f. *Ypres*, where it was first used in the War 1914–18] Yperite, mustard-gas.
ypréau (pl. -x) (ipreo), s.m. [f. *Ypres*, Belgium] (bot.) Broad-leaved elm.
ytterbium (itɛrbjɔm), s.m. [f. Swed. town *Ytterby*] (chem.) Ytterbium.
yttrium (itrijɔm), s.m. [f. Swed. town *Ytterby*] (chem.) Yttrium.
yucca (jyka), s.m. [Carib orig.] (bot.) Yucca.

Z

Z, z (zɛd), s.m. 26th letter of the alphabet, Z; (fig., fam.) *être fait comme un ~*, to be as crooked as they're made.
zabre (zɑbr), s.m. (ent.) Zabrus; species of carrion-eating beetle.
zagaie. sagaie, sagaye (zagɛ), s.f. [Span. *azagaya*] Assegai.
zain (zɛ̃), adj. m. [It. *zaino*] Whole-coloured, with no speck of white (of horses).
zanni, zani (zani), s.m. [Venetian dialect form of *Giovanni*] Zany.
zanzibar, zanzi (zɑ̃zibar, zɑ̃zi), s.m. Kind of dice-game.
zèbre (zɛbr), s.m. [Congolese orig.] (zool.) Zebra.
zébré, -e (zebre), p. adj. Striped like a Zebra.
zébrer (zebre), v.a. To mark with stripes, to stripe.
zébrure (zebryr), s.f. Stripes (pl.).
zébu (zeby), s.m. [Hind. orig.] (zool.) Zebu, Indian humped ox.
zédoaire (zedɔɛr), s.f. [LL *zedoarium*] (bot.) Zedoary.
zélat-eur, -rice (zelatœr), s.m.f. [L *zelator, -trix*] **1.** Zealot; **2.** zealous person.
zèle (zɛl), s.m. [L *zelus*, f. Gr. *zēlos*] Zeal; *faire du ~*, to be over-zealous.
zélé, -e (zele), adj. Zealous, zealful.
zélote (zelɔt), s.m. See syn. ZÉLATEUR.
zélotisme (zelɔtism), s.m. Zealotry.
zend, -e (zɛ̃d), adj. s.m. Zend, ancient language of the Iranian family.
zénith (zenit), s.m. [Medieval L *cenit*, f. Arab. *samt*] Zenith.
zénithal, -e, (aux) (zenital), adj. Zenithal.
zéolithe, zéolite (zeɔlit), s.f. [Gr. *zein*+*lithos*] Zeolite.
zéphire, zéphyr, zéphyre (zefir), s.m. [Gr. *zephuros*] Zephyr; (slang) soldier belonging to a disciplinary company of the *bataillon d'Afrique*.
zéphyrien, -ne (zefirjɛ̃), adj. Zephyrian, zephyrean, zephyrous.
zéphyrine (zefirin), s.f. (material) Zephyr.
zéro (zero), s.m. [Arab. *ṣifr*] Zero (of temperature), nought, 0; (fig.) a mere cipher; *il n'y manque pas un ~*, it is absolutely complete.
zérotage (zerɔtaʒ), s.m. Adjusting (of thermometers).
zest (zɛst), s.m. Used only in the expression *entre le zist et le ~*, so-so, only middling. *~ !*, interj. Phew !
zeste (zɛst,) s.m. [orig. dub.] (bot.) Orange or lemon peel, rind, zest; (fig.) fig, straw; *cela ne vaut pas un ~*, it's not worth a straw. ⚠ French *zeste* has not, like English 'zest', the sense of piquancy, gusto, keen relish or enjoyment, which = *goût, piquant*.
zester (zɛste), v.a. To peel (an orange or lemon).
zététique (zetetik), adj. [Gr. *zētētikos*] Zetetic. ~, s.f. Zetetics.
zeugma, zeugme (zœgma, zœgm), s.m. [Gr. wd] (rhet.) Zeugma.
zézaiement, zézayement (zezɛmɑ̃), s.m. Lisping, lisp.
zézayer (zezɛje), v.n. [onom. wd] To lisp.
zibeline (ziblin), s.f. [It. *zibellina*, Span. *cebellina*] Zibeline, sable.
zigouiller (ziguje), v.a. (slang) To stick a knife into, to run through.
zigue, zigoteau (zig, zigɔto), s.m. (slang) Fellow, chap, bloke.
zigzag (zigzag), s.m. [orig. unkn.] Zigzag; *faire des ~s*, to zigzag; *une ligne en ~*, a zigzag line.
zigzagué, -e (zigzage), p. adj. Zigzagged, zigzag; *éclair ~*, forked lightning.
zigzaguer (zigzage), v.n. To zigzag.
zinc (zɛ̃g), s.m. [Germ. *Zink*] **1.** Zinc; **2.** (slang) bar (of public house); **3.** (pop.) aeroplane, bus.
zincographe (zɛ̃kɔgraf), s.m. Zincographer.
zincographie (zɛ̃kɔgrafi), s.f. **zincogravure** (zɛ̃kɔgravyr), s.f. Zincography.
zingage (zɛ̃gaʒ), s.m. Zinking, zinc-plating.
zingaro (zɛ̃garo), s.m. (pl. *zingari*) [It. wd] Gipsy, zingaro.

zinguer (zɛ̃ge), v.a. To cover with zinc, to zinc; to galvanize (iron).
zingueur (zɛ̃gœr), s.m. Zinc-worker.
zinnia (zinja), s.m. [f. Germ. prop. n. *J. G. Zinn*] (bot.) Zinnia.
zinzinuler (zɛ̃zinyle), v.n. To trill (of tits and linnets).
zinzolin, -e (zɛ̃zɔlɛ̃), adj. [f. It. *gianggiolina*] Reddish violet.
zircon (zirkɔ̃), s.m. [Germ. *Zirkon*] Zircon.
zirconium (zirkɔnjɔm), s.m. (chem.) Zirconium.
zist (zist), s.m. See ZEST.
zizanie (zizani), s.f. [L *zizania*] (bot.) Tare, darnel-grass; (fig.) dissension, discord, strife; (fig.) *semer la ~*, to sow dissension.
zodiacal, -e, (aux) (zɔdjakal), adj. Zodiacal.
zodiaque (zɔdjak), s.m. [Gr. *zōdiakos*] Zodiac.
zoé (zɔe), s.f. Zoea, larva of certain crustaceans.
zoïle (zɔil), s.m. [Gr. prop. n.] Zoilus, snarling or censorious critic.
zona (zɔna), s.m. [f. Gr. *zōnē*] (pathol.) Shingles; zona ignea.
zone (zon), s.f. [Gr. wd] Zone, belt.
zoné, -e (zone), adj. Zoned, zonate.
zoni-er, -ère (zonje), s.m.f. (mil.) Frontier-dweller.
zoniforme (zonifɔrm), adj. Zonal; belt-shaped.
zoo (zɔɔ), pref. [Gr. *zōon*] Zoo.
zoochimie (zɔɔʃimi), s.f. Zoochemistry.
zoographie (zɔɔgrafi), s.f. Zoography.
zooïde (zɔɔid), adj. Zooid.
zoolâtre (zɔɔlɑtr), s.m. Zoolater.
zoolâtrie (zɔɔlɑtri), s.f. [Gr. *zōon*+ *latreia*] Zoolatry.
zoolithe, zoolite (zɔɔlit), s.m. [Gr. *zōon*+ *lithos*] Zoolite.
zoologie (zɔɔlɔʒi), s.f. [Gr. *zōon*+*logos*] Zoology.
zoologique (zɔɔlɔʒik), adj. Zoological.
zoologiquement (zɔɔlɔʒikmɑ̃), adv. Zoologically.
zoologiste (zɔɔlɔʒist), s.m.f. Zoologist.
zoomagnétisme (zɔɔmaɲetism), s.m. Zoomagnetism, animal magnetism.
zoomorphie (zɔɔmɔrfi), s.f. [Gr. *zōon*+ *morphē*] Zoomorphy.
zoonomie (zɔɔnɔmi), s.f. [Gr. *zōon*+ *nomos*] Zoonomy.
zoophage (zɔɔfaʒ), adj. [Gr. *zōon*+ *phagein*] Zoophagous.
zoophyte (zɔɔfit), s.m. [Gr. *zōon*+*phuton*] Zoophyte.
zooscopie (zɔɔskɔpi), s.f. [Gr. *zōon*+ *skopein*] Zooscopy.
zoospore (zɔɔspɔr), s.f. (bot.) Zoospore.
zootechnie (zɔɔtɛkni), s.f. [Gr. *zōon*+ *tekhnē*] Zootechny.
zootomie (zɔɔtɔmi), s.f. Zootomy.
zootrope (zɔɔtrɔp), s.m. [Gr. *zōon*+*trepō*] Zoetrope; wheel of life.
zorille (zɔrij), s.f. [Span. *zorrilla*] (zool.) Zoril, zorille.
zoroastrien, -ne (zɔrɔastrjɛ̃), adj. s.m.f. Zoroastrian.
zoroastrisme (zɔrɔastrism), s.m. [f. L *Zoroastres*, Zend *Zarathustra*] Zoroastrianism.
zouave (zwav), s.m. [Arab. *Zouaoua*, n. of tribe] Zouave (soldier).
zou (zu), interj. [f. southern dialects] Gee up! let's go.
zut (zyt), interj. (pop.) Hang!, dash!, blow!, go to blazes!, no fear!, confound it!, bother!, drat it!
zwinglianisme (zvɛ̃glijanism), s.m. [f. *Zwingli*, religious reformer 1484–1531] Zwinglianism.
zyeuter (zjøte), v.a. (slang) To look at, to take notice of, to stare at; *zyeute-moi ça!*, just have a squint at that!
zygène (ziʒɛn), s.f. [Gr. *zugaina*] (ent.) Burnet moth, zygaena.
zygoma (zigɔma), s.m. [Gr. *zugōma*] (anat.) Zygoma (bone).
zygomatique (zigɔmatik), adj. Zygomatic.
zygomorphe (zigɔmɔrf), adj. [Gr. *zugon*+ *morphē*] Zygomorphous.
zygospore (zigɔspɔr), s.m. Zygospore, zygote.
zymogène (zimɔʒɛn), s.m. Zymogen.
zymologie (zimɔlɔʒi), s.f. [Gr. *zumē*+ *logos*] Zymology.
zymotique (zimɔtik), adj. [f. Gr. *zumē*] Zymotic, of fermentation.

LIST OF NAMES

Abdère (abdɛr), s.f. Abdera.
Abdias (abdjɑs), s.m. Obadiah.
Absalon (absalɔ̃), s.m. Absalom.
Abyssinie (abisini), s.f. Abyssinia.
Acadie (akadi), s.f. Acadia.
Acarnanie (akarnani), s.f. Acarnania.
Achab (akab), s.m. Ahab.
Achaïe (akai), s.f. Achaea.
Achantis (aʃɑ̃ti), s.m. Ashanti.
Achate (akat), s.m. Achates.
Achéron (akerɔ̃, aʃerɔ̃), s.m. Acheron.
Achille (aʃil), s.m. Achilles.
(les) Açores (lɛzasɔr), s.f.pl. The Azores.
Actéon (akteɔ̃), s.m. Actaeon.
Admète (admɛt), s.m. Admetus.
Adraste (adrast), s.m. Adrastus.
Adriatique (adrijatik), s.f. Adriatic.
Adrien, Hadrien (adrijɛ̃), s.m. Hadrian.
Afrique (afrik), s.f. Africa; *le Sud-Afrique*, s.m., or *l'Afrique du Sud*, s.f., South Africa.
Agar (agar), s.f. Hagar.
Agésilas (aʒezilɑs), s.m. Agesilaus.
Aggée (agʒe), s.m. Haggai.
Agrigente (agriʒɑ̃t), s.f. Agrigentum.
Agrippine (agripin), s.f. Agrippina.
Aix-la-Chapelle (ɛkslaʃapɛl), s.f. Aix-la-Chapelle, Aachen.
Aladin (aladɛ̃), s.m. Aladdin.
Albanie (albani), s.f. Albania.
Albe (alb), s.f. Alba.
Alcée (alse), s.m. Alcaeus.
Alceste (alsɛst), **1.** s.f. Alcestis; **2.** ~, s.m. Alceste (in Molière's *Misanthrope*).
Alcibiade (alsibjad), s.m. Alcibiades.
Alcmène (alkmɛn), s.f. Alcmene.
Aléoutiennes (Îles) (aleutjɛn), s.f.pl. Aleutian Islands.
Alep (alɛp), s.m. Aleppo.
Alexandre (alɛksɑ̃dr), s.m. Alexander.
Alexandrie (alɛksɑ̃dri), s.f. Alexandria.
(les) Algarves (lez algarv), s.f.pl. Algarve.
Alger (alʒe), s.m. Algiers.
Algérie (alʒeri), s.f. Algeria, Algiers.
Alicante (alikɑ̃t), s.f. Alicante.
Allemagne (almaɲ), s.f. Germany.
(les) Alpes (lɛzalp), s.f.pl. The Alps; *les Basses-~*, the Lower Alps; *les Hautes-~*, the Upper Alps.
Alphée (alfe), s.m. Alpheus.
Alsace (alzas), s.f. Alsace.
Amalthée (amalte), s.f. Amalthea.
(l')Amazone, Fleuve des Amazones, Marañon, Maragnon (amazɔn, maraɲɔ̃), s.m. The (river) Amazon.
Amérique (amerik), s.f. America; *l'~ du Nord, du Sud*, North America, South America; *les États-Unis d'~*, the United States of America, U.S.A.
Amirauté (Îles de l') (amirote), s.f. The Admiralty Islands.
Amis (Îles des), Tonga (ami, tɔ̃ga), s.f.pl. The Friendly Islands, the Tonga Islands.
Anastase (anastɑz), s.m. Anastasius.
Anatolie (anatɔli), s.f. Anatolia.
Anaxagore (anagzagɔr), s.m. Anaxagoras.
Anaxarque (anagzark), s.m. Anaxarchus.
Anchise (ɑ̃ʃiz, ɑ̃kiz), s.m. Anchises.
Ancône (ɑ̃kon), s.f. Ancona.
Andalousie (ɑ̃daluzi), s.f. Andalusia.
Andorre (ɑ̃dɔr), s.f. Andorra.
Andrinople (ɑ̃drinɔpl), s.f. Adrianople.
Andromaque (ɑ̃drɔmak), s.f. Andromache.
Andromède (ɑ̃drɔmɛd), s.f. Andromeda.
Angleterre (ɑ̃glətɛr), s.f. England.
Antée (ɑ̃te), s.m. Antaeus.
Antigone (ɑ̃tigɔn), **1.** s.f. Antigone; **2.** s.m. Antigonus.
(les) Antilles (lɛzɑ̃tij), s.f.pl. The Antilles, the West Indies; *les Grandes ~*, the Greater Antilles; *les Petites ~*, the Lesser Antilles; *la Mer des ~*, or *des Caraïbes*, the Caribbean Sea.
Antioche (ɑ̃tjɔʃ), s.f. Antioch.
Antisthène (ɑ̃tistɛn), s.m. Antisthenes.
Antoine (ɑ̃twan), s.m. Anthony; *Marc-~*, Mark Antony.
Antonin (ɑ̃tɔnɛ̃), s.m. Antoninus.
Anvers (ɑ̃vɛr), s.m. Antwerp.
Aoste (aɔst, ɔst), s.f. Aosta.
Apalaches (apalaʃ), s.m.pl. Appalachians.
Apennins (apɛnnɛ̃), s.m.pl. Apennines.
Apollodore (apɔllɔdɔr), s.m. Apollodorus.
Apollon (apɔllɔ̃), s.m. Apollo.
Appien (apjɛ̃), s.m. Appian; *la voie Appienne*, the Appian Way.
Apulée (apyle), s.m. Apuleius.
Apulie (apyli), s.f. Apulia.
Aquilée (akile), s.f. Aquileia.
Aquitaine (akitɛn), s.f. Aquitaine, Aquitania.
Arabie (arabi), s.f. Arabia; *l'~ Pétrée*, Arabia Petraea.
Arc (Jeanne d') (ʒandark), s.f. Joan of Arc.
Arcadie (arkadi), s.f. Arcadia.
Arcésilas (arsezilɑs), s.m. Arcesilaus.
Archimède (arʃimɛd), s.m. Archimedes.
(l')Archipel (larʃipɛl), s.m. The Archipelago.
Aréthuse (aretyz), s.f. Arethusa.
(l')Arétin (laretɛ̃), s.m. Aretino.
(l')Argentine (larʒɑ̃tin), s.f. Argentina, the Argentine.
Argolide (argɔlid), s.f. Argolis.
Argovie (argɔvi), s.f. Aargau.
Ariane (arjan), s.f. Ariadne.
(l')Arioste (larjɔst), s.m. Ariosto.
Aristarque (aristark), s.m. Aristarchus.
Aristide (aristid), s.m. Aristides.

Aristophane (aristɔfan), s.m. Aristophanes.
Aristote (aristɔt), s.m. Aristotle.
Arlequin (arləkɛ̃), s.m. Harlequin.
Arménie (armeni), s.f. Armenia.
Armorique (armɔrik), s.f. Armorica, Brittany.
Artaban (artabɑ̃), s.m. Artabanus.
Artémise (artemiz), s.f. Artemisia.
Ascagne (askaɲ), s.m. Ascanius.
Asie (azi), s.f. Asia; *l'~ Mineure*, Asia Minor.
Asmodée (asmɔde), s.m. Asmodaeus.
Aspasie (aspɑzi), s.f. Aspasia.
Asser (asɛr), s.m. Asher.
Assise (asiz), s.f. Assisi.
Assomption (asɔ̃psjɔ̃), s.f. Asuncion.
Assuérus (asɥerys), s.m. Ahasuerus.
Assyrie (asiri), s.f. Assyria.
(les) Asturies (lɛzastyri), s.f.pl. The Asturias.
Atalante (atalɑ̃t), s.f. Atalanta.
Athalie (atali), s.f. Athaliah.
Athanase (atanɑz), s.m. Athanasius.
Athènes (atɛn), s.f. Athens.
Atlantide (atlɑ̃tid), s.f. Atlantis.
(l')Atlantique (latlɑ̃tik), s.m. The Atlantic.
Atrée (atre), s.m. Atreus.
Attale (atal), s.m. Attalus.
Attique (attik), s.f. Attica.
Augias (oʒjɑs), s.m. Augeas; *d'~*, Augean.
Auguste (ogyst), s.m. Augustus.
Aulide (olid), s.f. Aulis.
Aulu-Gelle (olyʒɛl), s.m. Aulus Gellius.
Aurèle (Marc-) (orɛl), s.m. Aurelius (Marcus).
Aurélien (oreljɛ̃), s.m. Aurelian.
Aurigny (oriɲi), s.m. Alderney.
Ausone (ozɔn), s.m. Ausonius.
Ausonie (ozɔni), s.f. Ausonia.
Australasie (ostralazi), s.f. Australasia.
Australie (ostrali), s.f. Australia.
Austrasie (ostrazi), s.f. Austrasia.
Autriche (otriʃ), s.f. Austria.
(l')Aventin (lavɑ̃tɛ̃), s.m. The Aventine.
(l')Averne (lavɛrn), s.m. Averno.
Avicenne (avisɛn), s.m. Avicenna.
Azarias (azarjɑs), s.m. Azariah.
Azincourt (azɛ̃kur), s.m. Agincourt.

Babylone (babilɔn), s.f. Babylon.
Bade (bad), s.m. Baden.
Bâle (bɑl), s.f. Basle.
Balthazar (baltazar), s.m. Belshazzar.
Baltique (baltik), s.f. Baltic.
(la) Barbade (labarbad), s.f. Barbado(e)s.
Barbe-Bleue (barbəblø), s.m. Bluebeard.
Barberousse (barbərus), s.m. Barbarossa.
Barcelone (barslɔn), s.f. Barcelona.
Bavière (bavjɛr), s.f. Bavaria.
Belgique (bɛlʒik), s.f. Belgium.
Bélisaire (belizɛr), s.m. Belisarius.
Bellone (bɛllɔn), s.f. Bellona.
Belzébuth (bɛlzebyt), s.m. Beelzebub.
Bengale (bɛ̃gal), s.m. Bengal; *le Golfe du ~*, the Bay of Bengal; *feu de ~*, Bengal light.
Béotie (beɔsi), s.f. Boeotia.
(les) Bermudes (lɛbɛrmyd), s.f.pl. The Bermudas.
Berne (bɛrn), s.f. Bern, Berne.
(le) Bernin (ləbɛrnɛ̃), s.m. Bernini.
Bessarabie (bɛsarabi), s.f. Bessarabia.
Béthanie (betani), s.f. Bethany.
Bethléem (bɛtleɛm), s.m. Bethlehem.
Bethsabée (bɛtsabe), s.f. Bathsheba.
Beyrouth (bɛrut), s.f. Beirut, Beirout.
Birmanie (birmani), s.f. Burmah.
Biscaye (biskɛ), s.f. Biscay.
Bithynie (bitini), s.f. Bithynia.
Boadicée (bɔadise), s.f. Boadicea.
Boccace (bɔkas), s.m. Boccaccio.
Boëce (bɔɛs), s.m. Boethius.
Bohême (bɔɛm), s.f. Bohemia.
Bolivie (bɔlivi), s.f. Bolivia.
Bologne (bɔlɔɲ), s.f. Bologna.
Bône (bon), s.f. Bona.
Booz (boz), s.m. Boaz, Booz.
Borée (bɔre), s.m. Boreas.
Borysthène (bɔristɛn), s.m. Borysthenes.
Bosnie (bɔsni), s.f. Bosnia.
(le) Bosphore (ləbɔsfɔr), s.m. The Bosphorus.
Bothnie (bɔtni), s.f. Bothnia.
Bouddha (buda), s.m. Buddha.
Bourgogne (burgɔɲ), s.f. Burgundy.
Bragance (bragɑ̃s), s.f. Braganza.
Brandebourg (brɑ̃dbur), s.m. Brandenburg.
Brême (brɛm), s.f. Bremen.
Brésil (brezil), s.m. Brazil.
Bretagne (brətaɲ), s.f. Brittany; *la Grande-~*, Great Britain.
Briarée (briare), s.m. Briareus.
Britanniques (Îles) (britanik). adj. The British Isles.
Brousse (brus), s.f. Broussa.
Bruxelles (brysɛl), s.f. Brussels.
Bucarest (bykarɛst), s.m. Bucharest.
Bucéphale (bysefal), s.m. Bucephalus.
Bulgarie (bylgari), s.f. Bulgaria.
Byzance (bizɑ̃s), s.f. Byzantium.

Caboul (kabul), s.m. Kabul.
Cachemire (kaʃmir), s.m. Kashmir.
Cadix (kadiks), s.m. Cadiz.
Cafrerie (kafrəri), s.f. Kaffraria.
Caïphe (kaif), s.m. Caiaphas.
(le) Caire (ləkɛr), s.m. Cairo.
Calabre (kalabr), s.f. Calabria.
Calais (kalɛ), s.m. Calais; *le Pas de Calais*, the Straits of Dover.
Calédonie (kaledɔni), s.f. Caledonia; *la Nouvelle ~*, New Caledonia.
Calicut (kalikyt), s.m. Calicut.
Californie (kalifɔrni), s.f. California; *Basse* or *Vieille ~*, Lower or Old California; *Haute* or *Nouvelle ~*, Upper or New California.
Callimaque (kalimak), s.m. Callimachus.

Callisthène (kalistɛn), s.m. Callisthenes.
(le) Calvaire (ləkalvɛr), s.m. (Mount) Calvary.
Cambodge (kɑ̃bɔdʒ), s.m. Cambodia.
Cameroun (kamrun), s.m. Cameroons.
Campanie (kɑ̃pani), s.f. Campania.
Campêche (kɑ̃pɛʃ), s.m. Campeachy.
(les) Canaries (lɛkanari), s.f.pl. The Canary Isles; *la Grande Canarie,* Grand Canary.
Candie (kɑ̃di), s.f. Candia.
(la) Canée (lakane), s.f. Canea.
(le) Cap (ləkap), s.m. Capetown; Cape Colony, the Cape; *le ~ de Bonne Espérance,* the Cape of Good Hope.
Capoue (kapu), s.f. Capua.
Cappadoce (kapadɔs), s.f. Cappadocia.
Caraïbes (les Îles) (karaib), s.f.pl. The Leeward and Windward Islands (West Indies); the Caribbees.
Caron (karɔ̃), s.m. Charon.
(les) Carpathes (lɛkarpat), s.m.pl. The Carpathian Mountains.
Carrache (karaʃ), s.m. Carracci.
Carrare (karar), s.m. Carrara.
Carthagène (kartaʒɛn), s.f. Cartagena.
Caspienne (la Mer) (kaspjɛn), s.f. The Caspian Sea.
Cassandre (kasɑ̃dr), **1.** s.m. Cassander; **2.** s.f. Cassandra.
Castille (kastij), s.f. Castile.
Catalogne (katalɔɲ), s.f. Catalonia.
Catane (katan), s.f. Catania.
Catilina (katilina), s.m. Catiline.
Caton (katɔ̃), s.m. Cato.
Catulle (katyl), s.m. Catullus.
(le) Caucase (ləkokɑz), s.m. The Caucasus.
Cendrillon (sɑ̃drijɔ̃), s.f. Cinderella.
Céphalonie (sefaloni), s.f. Cephalonia.
Cerbère (sɛrbɛr), s.m. **1.** Cerberus; **2.** Cerbere (Cape).
Cervin (le Mont) (sɛrvɛ̃), s.m. The Matterhorn, the Cervin.
Césaire (sezɛr), s.m. Caesarius.
César (sezar), s.m. Caesar.
Césarée (sezare), s.f. Caesarea.
Cettigne (sɛtiɲ), s.f. Cetinje.
Ceylan (selɑ̃), s.f. Ceylon.
Chalcédoine (kalsedwan), s.f. Chalcedonia, Chalcedon.
Chaldée (kalde), s.f. Chaldea.
Cham (kam), s.m. Ham.
Chanaan (kanaɑ̃), s.m. Canaan.
Charybde (karibd), s.m. Charybdis; (colloq.) *tomber de ~ en Scylla,* to jump out of the frying-pan into the fire; 'Thus when I shun Scylla, your father, I fall into Charybdis, your mother' (Shakespeare, *Merchant of Venice*).
Chéronée (kerɔne), s.f. Chaeronaea.
Chili (ʃili), s.m. Chile.
Chine (ʃin), s.f. China.
Chrysostôme (krizɔstom), s.m. Chrysostom.
Chypre (ʃipr), s.f. Cyprus.
Cicéron (siserɔ̃), s.m. Cicero.
Cilicie (silisi), s.f. Cilicia.
(les) Cimbres (lɛsɛ̃br), s.m.pl. The Cimbri.
Claude (klod), s.m. Claudius.
Claude (le) Lorrain, Claude Gelée (klodlələrɛ̃, ʒəle), s.m. Claude Lorraine.
Claudien (klodjɛ̃), s.m. Claudian.
Cléopâtre (kleɔpɑtr), s.f. Cleopatra.
Clotaire (klɔtɛr), s.m. Clotharius.
Cochinchine (kɔʃɛ̃ʃin), s.f. Cochin China.
Cocyte (kɔsit), s.m. Cocytus.
Colchide (kɔlʃid), s.f. Colchis.
Colomb (Christophe) (kɔlɔ̃), s.m. Columbus (Christopher).
Colombie (kɔlɔ̃bi), s.f. Columbia, Colombia.
Colone (kɔlɔn), s.f. Colonus.
(les) Colonnes d'Hercule (lɛkɔlɔndɛrkyl), s.f.pl. The Pillars of Hercules.
Côme (kom), s.m. Como.
Commode (kɔmɔd), s.m. Commodus.
(les) Comores (lɛkɔmɔr), s.f.pl. The Comoro Islands.
Constance (kɔ̃stɑ̃s), **1.** s.m. Constantius; **2.** s.f. (geog.) Constance (Baden); Constantia (S. Africa).
Constantin (kɔ̃stɑ̃tɛ̃), s.m. Constantinus.
Constantine (kɔ̃stɑ̃tin), s.f. (geog.) Constantina.
Copenhague (kɔpɛnag), s.f. Copenhagen.
Copernic (kɔpɛrnik), s.m. Copernicus.
Corcyre (kɔrsir), s.f. Corcyra.
Cordoue (kɔrdu), s.f. Cordova, Cordoba.
Corée (kɔre), s.f. Korea, Corea.
Corfou (kɔrfu), s.f. Corfu.
Corinthe (kɔrɛ̃t), s.f. Corinth.
Coriolan (kɔrjɔlɑ̃), s.m. Coriolanus.
Cornouailles (kɔrnwɑj), s.f.pl. Cornwall.
(la) Corogne (lakɔrɔɲ), s.f. Corunna.
(le) Corrège (ləkɔrɛʒ), s.m. Correggio.
Corse (kɔrs), s.f. Corsica.
Côte d'Ivoire (kotdivwar), s.f. Ivory Coast.
Côte d'Or (kotdɔr), s.f. Gold Coast.
Cottiennes (les Alpes) (kɔtjɛn), adj. The Cottian Alps.
Cracovie (krakɔvi), s.f. Cracow.
Crémone (kremɔn), s.f. Cremona.
Crésus (krezys), s.m. Croesus.
Crimée (krime), s.f. Crimea.
Croatie (krɔasi), s.f. Croatia.
Cumes (kym), s.f. Cumae.
Cupidon (kypidɔ̃), s.m. Cupid.
Curaçao (kyraso), s.m. Curaçao.
(les) Curiaces (lɛkyrjas), s.m.pl. The Curiatii.
Cyrénaïque (sirenaik), s.f. Cyrenaica.
Cythère (sitɛr), s.f. Cythera.
Cythérée (sitere), s.f. Cytheraea.

Dalila (dalila), s.f. Delilah.
Dalmatie (dalmasi), s.f. Dalmatia.
Damas (damɑ), s.m. Damascus.
Danemark (danmark), s.m. Denmark.
Dante, le Dante ((lə) dɑ̃t), s.m. Dante.
Dauphiné (dofine), s.m. Dauphiny, Dauphiné.
Dédale (dedal), s.m. Daedalus.

Delphes (dɛlf), s.f. Delphi.
Démocrite (demɔkrit), s.m. Democritus.
Démosthène (demɔstɛn), s.m. Demosthenes.
Denis (dəni), s.m. Denis.
Denys (dəni), s.m. Dionysius; ~ *l'Ancien*, Dionysius the Elder.
Diane (djan), s.f. Diana.
Didon (didɔ̃), s.f. Dido.
Dioclétien (djɔklesjɛ̃), s.m. Diocletian.
Diodore (djɔdɔr), s.m. Diodorus; ~ *de Sicile*, Diodorus Siculus.
Diogène (djɔʒɛn), s.m. Diogenes.
(la) Dobroudja (ladɔbrudʒa), s.f. Dobruja.
(la) Dominique (ladɔminik), s.f. Dominique.
Dominiquin (dɔminikɛ̃), s.m. Domenichino.
Domitien (dɔmisjɛ̃), s.m. Domitian.
Donat (dɔna), s.m. Donatus.
Douvres (duvr), s.m. Dover.
Dracon (drakɔ̃), s.m. Draco.
Dresde (drɛsd), s.f. Dresden.
Dunkerque (dœ̃kɛrk), s.m. Dunkirk.

Éaque (eak), s.m. Aeacus.
(l')Èbre (lɛbr), s.f. Ebro.
(l')Écluse (leklyz), s.f. Sluys (Netherlands).
Écosse (ekɔs), s.f. Scotland; *Nouvelle* ~, Nova Scotia.
Édimbourg (edɛ̃bur), s.m. Edinburgh.
Égée (eʒe), s.m. Aegeus; *la Mer Égée*, the Aegean Sea.
Égérie (eʒeri), s.f. Egeria.
Égine (eʒin), s.f. Aegina.
Égisthe (eʒist), s.m. Aegisthus.
Égypte (eʒipt), s.f. Egypt; *Basse* ~, Lower Egypt; *Haute* ~, Upper Egypt.
Elbe (l'Île d') (ɛlb), s.f. Elba.
Électre (elɛktr), s.f. Electra.
Élide (elid), s.f. Elis.
Élie (eli), s.m. Elias, Elijah.
Élien (eljɛ̃), s.m. Aelianus.
Élisabeth (elizabɛt), s.f. Elizabeth.
Élisée (elize), s.m. Elisha.
Elseneur (ɛlsənœr), s.m. Elsinore.
Émile (emil), s.m. Aemilius.
Émilien (emiljɛ̃), s.m. Aemilian.
Empédocle (ɑ̃pedɔkl), s.m. Empedocles.
Encelade (ɑ̃slad), s.m. Enceladus.
Énée (ene), s.m. Aeneas.
Éole (eɔl), s.m. Aeolus.
Éphèse (efɛz), s.f. Ephesus.
Épictète (epiktɛt), s.m. Epictetus.
Épicure (epikyr), s.m. Epicurus.
Épidaure (epidɔr), s.f. Epidaurus.
(les) Épigones (lɛzepigɔn), s.m.pl. The Epigoni.
Épiphane (epifan), s.m. Epiphanius.
Épire (epir), s.f. Epirus.
(l')Équateur (lekwatœr), s.m. Ecuador.
Érasme (erasm), s.m. Erasmus.
Érèbe (erɛb), s.m. Erebus.
Érétrie (eretri), s.f. Eretria.
Érié (erje), s.m. (Lake) Erie.
Érostrate (erɔstrat), s.m. Erostratus.
Ésaü (ezay), s.m. Esau.
Escaut (ɛsko), s.m. Scheldt.
Eschyle (ɛʃil), s.m. Aeschylus.
Esclavonie (ɛsklavɔni), s.f. Slavonia.
Esculape (ɛskylap), s.m. Aesculapius.
Ésope (ezɔp), s.m. Aesop.
Espagne (ɛspaɲ), s.f. Spain.
Esquilin (ɛskilɛ̃), s.m. Esquiline.
Esthonie (ɛstɔni), s.f. Esthonia.
Estrémadure (ɛstremadyr), s.f. Estremadura.
(les) États-Unis (lɛzetɑzyni), s.m.pl. The United States.
Étéocle (eteɔkl), s.m. Eteocles.
Éthiopie (etjɔpi), s.f. Ethiopia.
Étrurie (etryri), s.f. Etruria.
Eubée, Négrepont (øbe, negrəpɔ̃), s.f. Euboea.
Euclide (øklid), s.m. Euclid.
Eumée (øme), s.m. Eumaeus.
(l')Euphrate (løfrat), s.m. Euphrates.
Euripide (øripid), s.m. Euripides.
Europe (ørɔp), s.f. Europa; Europe.
Euryale (ørjal), s.m. Euryalus.
Eusèbe (øzɛb), s.m. Eusebius.
Ézéchiel (ezekjɛl), s.m. Ezekiel.

Fabien (fabjɛ̃), s.m. Fabian.
(les) Féroé (lɛferɔe), s.f.pl. The Faroe Islands.
Ferrare (fɛrar), s.f. Ferrara.
(les) Fidji, Viti (lɛfidʒi, viti), s.f.pl. The Fiji Islands.
Fiesque (fjɛsk), s.m. Fieschi, Fiesco.
Finlande (fɛ̃lɑ̃d), s.f. Finland.
Fionie (fjɔni), s.f. Fuhnen.
Flandre, les Flandres (flɑ̃dr), s.f. Flanders.
Flavien (flavjɛ̃), s.m. Flavian.
Flessingue (flɛsɛ̃g), s.f. Flushing.
Flore (flɔr), s.f. Flora.
Florence (flɔrɑ̃s), s.f. Florence.
Floride (flɔrid), s.f. Florida.
(la) Forêt-Noire (lafɔrɛnwar), s.f. The Black Forest.
Formose (fɔrmoz), s.f. Formosa.
Francfort (frɑ̃kfɔr), s.m. Frankfurt, Frankfort.
Franconie (frɑ̃kɔni), s.f. Franconia.
Frédégonde (fredegɔ̃d), s.f. Fredegond.
Fribourg (fribur), s.m. **1.** (Switzerland) Fribourg; **2.** (Germany) Freiburg.
Frioul (friul), s.m. Friuli.
Frise (friz), s.f. Friesland.
Fulvie (fylvi), s.f. Fulvia.

Gabaon (gabaɔ̃), s.m. Gibeon.
Gabon (gabɔ̃), s.m. Gaboon.
Galaad (galaad), s.m. Gilead.
Galatie (galasi), s.f. Galatia.
Galère (galɛr), s.m. Galerius.

Galice (galis), s.f. Galicia (Spain). ⚠ See GALICIE.
Galicie (galisi), s.f. Galicia (Poland). ⚠ See GALICE.
Galien (galjɛ̃), s.m. Galen (Gr. physician). ⚠ See GALLIEN.
Galilée (galile), **1.** s.m. Galileo, 1564–1642; **2.** s.f. Galilaea, Galilee (Palestine).
Galles (Pays de) (gal), s.m. Wales; *la Nouvelle-~ du Sud*, New South Wales.
Gallien (galljɛ̃), s.m. Gallienus (Roman Emperor). ⚠ See GALIEN.
Gambie (gɑ̃bi), s.f. Gambia.
Gand (gɑ̃), s.m. Ghent.
Gange (gɑ̃ʒ), s.m. Ganges.
Gascogne (gaskɔɲ), s.f. Gascony; *le Golfe de ~*, the Bay of Biscay.
Gaule (gol), s.f. Gaul.
Gédéon (ʒedeɔ̃), s.m. Gideon.
Gênes (ʒɛn), s.f. Genoa.
Genève (ʒənɛv), s.f. Geneva.
Géorgie (ʒeɔrʒi), s.f. Georgia.
(les) Gépides (leʒepid), s.m.pl. The Gepidae.
Germanie (ʒɛrmani), s.f. Germania.
Gessen (ʒɛsɛn), s.m. Goshen.
(les) Ghâtes (legɑt), s.f.pl. The Ghauts.
Gothie (gɔti), s.f. Gothland.
Goualior (gwaljɔr), s.m. Gwalior.
(les) Gracques (legrak), s.m.pl. The Gracchi.
(le) Granique (ləgranik), s.m. The Granicus.
Gratien (grasjɛ̃), s.m. Gratian.
Grèce (grɛs), s.f. Greece.
Grégoire (gregwar), s.m. Gregorius; Gregory.
Grenade (grənad), s.f. Granada.
Groenland (grɔɛnlɑ̃(d)), s.m. Greenland.
Groningue (grɔnɛ̃g), s.f. Groningen.
Gueldre (gɛldr), s.f. Guelders.
(le) Guerchin (ləgɛrʃɛ̃), s.m. Guercino.
Guernesey (gɛrnəze), s.f. Guernsey.
(le) Guide (ləgid), s.m. Guido (Reni).
Guillaume le Conquérant (gijomləkɔ̃kerɑ̃), s.m. William the Conqueror.
Guinée (gine), s.f. Guinea.
Guyane (gɥijan), s.f. Guiana.
Guyenne (gɥijɛn), s.f. Guienne.

Habsbourg (habsbur), s.m. Hapsburg.
Halicarnasse (alikarnas), s.f. Halicarnassus.
Hambourg (hɑ̃bur), s.m. Hamburg.
Hannon (hannɔ̃), s.m. Hanno.
Hanovre (hanɔvr), **1.** s.m. Hanover (province); **2.** s.f. Hanover (town).
(la) Hanse (lahɑ̃s), s.f. The Hanse (towns); syn. *la ligue hanséatique*, the Hanseatic league.
Harpale (harpal), s.m. Harpalus.
Harpocrate (harpɔkrat), s.m. Harpocrates.
(la) Havane (lahavan), s.f. Havana, Havanna.
(le) Hâvre (ləhɑvr), s.m. Havre.
Hawaï (havai), s.m. Hawaii.
(la) Haye (lahɛ), s.f. The Hague.
Hécube (ekyb), s.f. Hecuba.
Héliodore (eljɔdɔr), s.m. Heliodorus.
Héliogabale (eljɔgabal), s.m. Heliogabalus.
Helvétie (ɛlvesi), s.f. Helvetia.
Héraclée (erakle), s.f. Heraclea.
Héraclide (eraklid), s.m. Heraclides.
Héraclite (eraklit), s.m. Heraclitus.
Herculanum (ɛrkylanɔm), s.m. Herculaneum.
Hercule (ɛrkyl), s.m. Hercules.
Hérode (erɔd), s.m. Herod.
Hérodote (erɔdɔt), s.m. Herodotus.
Herzégovine (ɛrzegɔvin), s.f. Herzegovina.
Hésiode (ezjɔd), s.m. Hesiod.
Hiéron (jerɔ̃), s.m. Hiero.
Hilaire (ilɛr), s.m. Hilarius, Hilary.
Hindoustan (ɛ̃dustɑ̃), s.m. Hindustan.
Hipparque (ippark), s.m. Hipparchus.
Hippocrate (ippɔkrat), s.m. Hippocrates.
Hippolyte (ippɔlit), **1.** s.m. Hippolytus; **2.** s.f. Hippolyta.
Hippomène (ippɔmɛn), s.m. Hippomenes.
Hollande (hɔlɑ̃d), s.f. Holland.
Holopherne (ɔlofɛrn), s.m. Holophernes.
Hombourg (hɔ̃bur), s.m. Homburg.
Homère (ɔmɛr), s.m. Homer.
Hongrie (hɔ̃gri), s.f. Hungary.
(les) Horaces (lezɔras), s.m.pl. The Horatii.
Huningue (hynɛ̃g), s.f. Huningen.
(les) Huns (lehœ̃), s.m.pl. The Huns.
Hyacinthe (jasɛ̃t), s.m. Hyacinthus.
Hygie (iʒi), s.f. Hygeia.
Hymen, Hyménée (imɛn, imene), s.m. Hymen, Hymenaeus.
Hymette (imɛt), s.m. (Mount) Hymettus.
Hypéride (iperid), s.m. Hyperides.
Hyrcan (irkɑ̃), s.m. Hyrcanus.
Hyrcanie (irkani), s.f. Hyrcania.

Ibérie (iberi), s.f. Iberia.
Icare (ikar), s.m. Icarus.
Icarie (ikari), s.f. Icaria, Nikaria; *la Mer Icarienne*, the Icarian Sea.
Idoménée (idɔmene), s.m. Idomeneus.
Idumée (idyme), s.f., **Édom** (edɔm), s.m. Idumea.
Iéna (jena), s.f. Jena.
Ignace (iɲas), s.m. Ignatius.
Île (il), s.f. Island, Isle; *l'Île-de-France*, **1.** the Île-de-France (Fr. province); **2.** (see also MAURICE) Mauritius (Island); *les Îles-du-Vent*, the Windward Islands; *les Îles-sous-le-Vent*, **1.** the Leeward Islands (Antilles); **2.** Îles-sous-le Vent (Oceania); *les ~s*, the West Indies.
Iliade (iljad), s.f. Iliad.
Ilion (iljɔ̃), s.m. Ilium, Ilion, Troy.
Illyrie (illiri), s.f. Illyria.
Inde (ɛ̃d), s.f. India; *l'~ Anglaise*, British India; *les ~s Occidentales*, West Indies; *les ~s Orientales* or *les ~s Néerlandaises*, East Indies; *les ~s*, India; *la Mer des ~s*,

the Indian Ocean; *la Compagnie des ~s*, the East India Company.
Indochine (ɛ̃doʃin), s.f. Indo-China.
Ionie (jɔni), s.f. Ionia; *les Îles Ioniennes*, the Ionian Isles; *la Mer Ionienne*, the Ionian Sea.
Iphicrate (ifikrat), s.m. Iphicrates.
Iphigénie (ifiʒeni), s.f. Iphigenia.
Iraouaddy (irawaddi), s.m. Irrawaddy.
Irénée (irene), s.m. Irenaeus.
Irkoutsk (irkutsk), s.m. Irkutsk.
Irlande (irlɑ̃d), s.f. Ireland; *la Mer d'~*, the Irish Sea.
Isaïe, Ésaïe (izai, ezai), s.m. Isaiah.
Iscariote (iskarjɔt), s.m. Iscariot.
Islande (islɑ̃d), s.f. Iceland.
Ismaël (ismaɛl), s.m. Ishmael.
Isocrate (izɔkrat), s.m. Isocrates.
Istrie (istri), s.f. Istria.
Italie (itali), s.f. Italy.
Ithaque (itak), s.f. Ithaca.
Iule (jyl), s.m. Iulus.

Jacques (ʒɑk), s.m. James; *~ Ier*, James the First.
(la) Jamaïque (laʒamaik), s.f. Jamaica.
Jamblique (ʒɑ̃blik), s.m. Iamblichus.
Japet (ʒapɛ), s.m. Japetus.
Japhet (ʒafɛ), s.m. Japheth.
Japon (ʒapɔ̃), s.m. Japan.
Jean (ʒɑ̃), s.m. John; *St ~ Baptiste*, St. John the Baptist; *~ sans Terre*, John Lackland; *la St-~*, s.f. midsummer.
Jeanne d'Arc (ʒɑndark), s.f. Joan of Arc.
Jephté (ʒɛfte), s.m. Jephthah.
Jérémie (ʒeremi), s.m. Jeremiah, Jeremy, Jeremias.
Jérôme (ʒerom), s.m. Hieronymus; Jerome.
Jézabel (ʒezabɛl), s.f. Jezebel.
Joad (ʒɔad), s.m. Jehoiada.
Joram (ʒɔram), s.m. Jehoram.
Josaphat (ʒɔzafa), s.m. Jehoshaphat.
Josèphe (ʒɔzɛf), s.m. Josephus.
Josué (ʒɔzɥe), s.m. Joshua.
Jourdain (ʒurdɛ̃), s.m. The (River) Jordan.
Jovien (ʒɔvjɛ̃), s.m. Jovian.
Juda (ʒyda), s.m. Judah.
Judée (ʒyde), s.f. Judaea.
Jules César (ʒylsezar), s.m. Julius Caesar.
Julien (ʒyljɛ̃), s.m. Julian.
Junon (ʒynɔ̃), s.f. Juno.
Jupiter (ʒypitɛr), s.m. Jupiter, Jove.
Justinien (ʒystinjɛ̃), s.m. Justinian.

Kaboul, Caboul (kabul), s.m. **1.** Kabul; **2.** Kabul river.
Kairouan (kɛrwɑ̃), s.m. Kairwan.
Kamtchatka (kamtʃatka), s.m. Kamtchatka.
Karnatic (karnatik), s.m. Carnatic.
(les) Karpathes. See CARPATHES.
Kashmir. See CACHEMIRE.
Kouban (kubɑ̃), s.m. Kuban.
(les) Kouriles (lɛkuril), s.f.pl. The Kuriles (Islands).

Lacédémone (lasedemɔn), s.f. Lacedaemon.
Laconie (lakɔni), s.f. Laconia.
Lactance (laktɑ̃s), s.m. Lactantius.
Laërte (laɛrt), s.m. Laertes.
Lancastre (lɑ̃kastr), s.m. Lancaster.
Laodicée (laɔdise), s.f. Laodicea.
Lapithes (lapit), s.m.pl. Lapithae.
Laponie (lapɔni), s.f. Lapland.
(les) Laquedives (lɛlakdiv), s.f.pl. The Laccadives, the Laccadive Islands.
Latone (latɔn), s.f. Latona.
Lazare (lazar), s.m. Lazarus.
Léandre (leɑ̃dr), s.m. Leander.
Léon (leɔ̃), s.m. Leo.
Léonard de Vinci (leɔnardəvɛ̃si), s.m. Leonardo da Vinci.
Lépante (lepɑ̃t), s.f. Lepanto.
Lépide (lepid), s.m. Lepidus.
Lerne (lɛrn), s.f. Lerna.
Leucippe (løsip), s.m. Leucippus.
Leuctres (løktr), s.f. Leuctra.
Leyde (lɛd), s.f. Leyden.
Lia (lja), s.f. Leah.
(le) Liban (ləlibɑ̃), s.m. Lebanon.
Libye (libi), s.f. Libya.
Ligurie (ligyri), s.f. Liguria.
Limbourg (lɛ̃bur), s.m. **1.** Limburg (Holland); **2.** Limbourg (Belgium).
Linné (linne), s.m. Linnaeus.
Lisbonne (lisbɔn), s.f. Lisbon.
Lithuanie (litɥani), s.f. Lithuania.
Livie (livi), s.f. Livia.
Livonie (livɔni), s.f. Livonia.
Livourne (livurn), s.f. Leghorn; (now) Livorno.
Locride (lɔkrid), s.f. Locris.
Lombardie (lɔ̃bardi), s.f. Lombardy.
Londres (lɔ̃dr), s.m. London.
Longin (lɔʒɛ̃), s.m. Longinus.
Lorette (lɔrɛt), s.f. Loretto.
(le) Lorrain (ləlɔrɛ̃), s.m. See CLAUDE.
Louisiane (lwizjan), s.f. Louisiana.
Louqsor (luksɔr), s.m. Luxor.
St Luc (sɛ̃lyk), s.m. St Luke.
Lucain (lykɛ̃), s.m. Lucan.
Lucanie (lykani), s.f. Lucania.
(les) Lucayes, Bahama (lɛlykaj, baama), s.f.pl. The Lucayos, the Bahamas (Islands).
Lucien (lysjɛ̃), s.m. Lucian.
Lucques (lyk), s.f. Lucca.
Lucrèce (lykrɛs), **1.** s.m. Lucretius; **2.** s.f. Lucretia, Lucrece.
Lusace (lyzas), s.f. Lusatia.
Lusitanie (lyzitani), s.f. Lusitania.
Lutèce (lytɛs), s.f. Lutetia (old name of Paris).
Lycaonie (likaɔni), s.f. Lycaonia.
Lycée (lise), s.m. Lyceum.
Lycie (lisi), s.f. Lycia.
Lycurgue (likyrg), s.m. Lycurgus.
Lydie (lidi), s.f. Lydia.
Lyon (ljɔ̃), s.m. Lyons.
Lysimaque (lizimak), s.m. Lysimachus.
Lysippe (lizip), s.m. Lysippus.

Macaire (makɛr), s.m. Macarius.
Macchabée, Machabée (makabe), s.m. Maccabaeus (pl. the Maccabees).
Macédoine (masedwan), s.f. Macedonia.
Machiavel (makjavɛl), s.m. Machiavelli, Machiavel.
Macrin (makrɛ̃), s.m. Macrinus.
Macrobe (makrɔb), s.m. Macrobius.
Madeleine (madlɛn), s.f. Magdalen(e).
Madère (Madɛr), s.f. Madeira.
Maestricht (maɛstriʃt), s.m. Maastricht.
Magdebourg (magdəbur), s.m. Magdeburg.
Magnence (magnɑ̃s), s.m. Magnentius.
Magon (magɔ̃), s.m. Mago.
Mahomet (maɔmɛ), s.m. Mohammed, Mahomet.
Mahrattes (ma'rat), s.m.pl. Mahrattas.
Majorque (maʒɔrk), s.f. Majorca.
Malachie (malaʃi), s.m. Malachi.
Malaisie (malɛzi), s.f. The Malay Archipelago, Malaysia.
Malines (malin), s.f. Mechlin.
(les) Malouines (lɛmalwin), s.f.pl. The Falkland (Islands).
Malte (malt), s.f. Malta.
Manassé (manase), s.m. Manasseh.
Manassès (manasɛs), s.m. Manasses.
(la) Manche (lamɑ̃ʃ), s.f. **1.** The Channel, the English Channel; *les îles de la ~*, the Channel Islands; **2.** La Mancha (in Spain); **3.** La Manche (Fr. department).
Mandchourie (mɑ̃dʃuri), s.f. Manchuria.
Manille (manij), s.f. Manilla, Manila.
Mantinée (mɑ̃tine), s.f. Mantinea.
Mantoue (mɑ̃tu), s.f. Mantua.
(le) Maragnon, Marañon (ləmaraɲɔ̃), s.m. Maranon, Amazon (river); syn. L'AMAZONE, FLEUVE DES AMAZONES.
Marc (mark), s.m. Mark, St Mark; *~-Antoine*, Mark Antony; *~-Aurèle*, Marcus Aurelius.
Marcien (marsjɛ̃), s.m. Marcian.
Mardochée (mardɔʃe), s.m. Mardocheus.
Marie (mari), s.f. Mary; *~ Stuart*, Mary Queen of Scots.
Maroc (marɔk), s.m. Morocco.
(les) Marquises (lɛmarkiz), s.f.pl. The Marquesas (Islands).
Marseille (marsɛj), s.m. Marseilles.
Marthe (mart), s.f. Martha.
(St) Matthieu (sɛ̃matjø), s.m. St. Matthew.
Maurice (l'Île) (mɔris), s.f. Mauritius; syn. L'ÎLE DE FRANCE.
Mauritanie (moritani), s.f. Mauretania.
Maxence (maksɑ̃s), s.m. Maxentius.
Maxime (maksim), s.m. Maximus.
Maximien (maksimjɛ̃), s.m. Maximianus, Maximian.
Maximilien (maksimiljɛ̃), s.m. Maximilian.
Maximin (maksimɛ̃), s.m. Maximinus.
Mayence (majɑ̃s), s.f. Mainz.
Mécène (mesɛn), s.m. Maecenas.
(la) Mecque (lamɛk), s.f. Mecca.
Médée (mede), s.f. Medea.
(les) Médicis (lɛmedisis), s.m.pl. The Medici.
Médie (medi), s.f. Media.
Médine (medin), s.f. Medina.
(la) Méditerranée (lamediterane), s.f. The Mediterranean (Sea).
Méduse (medyz), s.f. Medusa.
Mégare (megar), s.f. Megara.
(le) Mein, Main (ləmɛ̃, ləmain), s.m. The (river) Main.
Méléagre (meleagr), s.m. Meleager.
Ménandre (menɑ̃dr), s.m. Menander.
Ménélas (menelɑs), s.m. Menelaus.
Ménippe (menip), s.m. Menippus.
Menton (mɑ̃tɔ̃), s.m. Mentone.
Mercure (mɛrkyr), s.m. Mercury.
Mésie, Mœsie (mezi), s.f. Moesia.
Mésopotamie (mezɔpɔtami), s.f. Mesopotamia.
Messaline (mɛsalin), s.f. Messalina.
Messénie (mɛseni), s.f. Messenia.
Messine (mɛsin), s.f. Messina; *le Détroit de ~*, the Straits of Messina.
Métastase (metastɑz), s.m. Metastasio.
(la) Meuse (lamøz), s.f. The (river) Meuse, Maas.
Mexique (mɛksik), s.m. Mexico.
Michée (miʃe), s.m. Micah.
Michel (miʃɛl), s.m. Michael.
Michel-Ange (mikɛlɑ̃ʒ), s.m. Michael Angelo.
Milet (milɛ), s.m. Miletus.
Milon (milɔ̃), s.m. Milo.
Miltiade (milsjad), s.m. Miltiades.
Minerve (minɛrv), s.f. Minerva.
Mingrélie (mɛ̃greli), s.f. Mingrelia.
Minorque (minɔrk), s.f. Minorca.
Minturnes (mɛ̃tyrn), (now) **Trajetta** (traʒeta), s.f. Minturnae.
Mithridate (mitridat), s.m. Mithridates.
Modène (modɛn), s.f. Modena.
Moïse (mɔiz), s.m. Moses.
Moka (mɔka), s.f. Mocha.
Moldavie (mɔldavi), s.f. Moldavia.
(les) Moluques (lɛmɔlyk), s.f.pl. The Moluccas (Islands).
Mongolie (mɔ̃gɔli), s.f. Mongolia.
Moravie (mɔravi), s.f. Moravia.
Morée (mɔre), s.f. Morea.
Morphée (mɔrfe), s.m. Morpheus.
Morte (la Mer) (mɔrt), adj.f. The Dead Sea.
Moscou (mɔsku), s.f. Moscow.
Moscovie (mɔskɔvi), s.f. Muscovy.
(la) Moskova (lamɔskɔva), s.f. The (river) Moskwa.
Mossoul (mɔsul), s.m. Mosul.
Mulhouse (myluz), s.f. Mulhausen, Mulhouse.
Murcie (myrsi), s.f. Murcia.
Mycènes (misɛn), s.f. Mycenae.
Mysie (mizi), s.f. Mysia.

Nabuchodonosor (nabykɔdɔnɔzɔr), s.m. Nebuchadnezzar.
Narcisse (narsis), s.m. Narcissus.
Nauplie (nopli), s.f. Nauplia.

Navarin (navarɛ̃), s.m. Navarino.
Néarque (neark), s.m. Nearchus.
Néerlande (neɛrlɑ̃d), s.f. The Netherlands (pl.).
Négrepont, Eubée (negrəpɔ̃, øbe), s.f. Negropont, Euboea.
Néhémie (neemi), s.m. Nehemiah.
Nemrod (nɛmrɔd), s.m. Nimrod.
Néoptolème (neɔptɔlɛm), s.m. Neoptolemus.
Nérée (nere), s.m. Nereus.
Néron (nerɔ̃), s.m. Nero.
Neustrie (nøstri), s.f. Neustria.
Nicée (nise), s.f. Nicaea.
Nicéphore (nisefɔr), s.m. Nicephorus.
Nicodème (nikɔdɛm), s.m. Nicodemus.
(le) Nil (lənil), s.m. The Nile.
Nimègue (nimɛg), s.f. Nimwegen.
Ninive (niniv), s.f. Nineveh.
Noé (nɔe), s.m. Noah.
Noël (nɔɛl), s.m. and f. Christmas; *quel beau* ~ *!*, what a glorious Christmas; *à la* ~, at Christmas.
Noémi (nɔemi), s.f. Naomi.
Norique (nɔrik), s.f. Noricum.
Normandie (nɔrmɑ̃di), s.f. Normandy.
Norvège (nɔrvɛʒ), s.f. Norway.
Nouvelle-Calédonie (nuvɛlkaledɔni), s.f. New Caledonia.
Nouvelle-Écosse (nuvɛlekɔs), s.f. Nova Scotia.
Nouvelle-Orléans (nuvɛlɔrleɑ̃), s.f. New Orleans.
Nouvelle-Zemble (nuvɛlzɑ̃bl), s.f. Novaya Zemlya, Nova Zembla.
Novare (nɔvar), s.f. Novara.
Nubie (nybi), s.f. Nubia.
Numance (nymɑ̃s), s.f. Numantia.
Numidie (nymidi), s.f. Numidia.

Océan (ɔseɑ̃), s.m. Oceanus; ~ *Pacifique, Atlantique*, Pacific, Atlantic Ocean.
Océanie (ɔseani), s.f. Oceania.
Ochozias (ɔkozjɑs), s.m. Ahaziah.
Octave (ɔktav), s.m. Octavius.
Octavie (ɔktavi), s.f. Octavia.
Octavien (ɔktavjɛ̃), s.m. Octavian.
Odoacre (ɔdɔakr), s.m. Odoacer.
Œdipe (edip), s.m. Oedipus.
Okhotsk (ɔkɔtsk), s.m. Okhotsk, Ochotsk.
Oldenbourg (ɔldɛ̃bur), s.m. Oldenburg.
Olympe (ɔlɛ̃p), s.m. Olympus.
Olympie (ɔlɛ̃pi), s.f. Olympia.
Olynthe (ɔlɛ̃t), s.f. Olynthus.
Ophélie (ɔfeli), s.f. Ophelia.
Oppien (ɔpjɛ̃), s.m. Oppian.
(les) Orcades (lɛzɔrkad), s.f.pl. The Orkneys, the Orkney Islands.
(l')Orénoque (lɔrenɔk), s.m. The Orinoko.
Oreste (ɔrɛst), s.m. Orestes.
Origène (ɔriʒɛn), s.m. Origen.
(l')Oronte (lɔrɔ̃t), s.m. The Orontes.
Orphée (ɔrfe), s.m. Orpheus.
Osée (oze), s.m. Hosea.
Ostende (ɔstɑ̃d), s.f. Ostend.
Ostie (ɔsti), s.f. Ostia.
Othon (ɔtɔ̃), s.m. Otho.
Otrante (ɔtrɑ̃t), s.m. Otranto.
Ouessant (wɛsɑ̃), s.f. Ushant (Island).
(l')Oural (lural), s.m. Ural (river); *les Monts* ~*s*, the Ural Mountains.
Ovide (ɔvid), s.m. Ovid.

Pactole (paktɔl), s.m. Pactolus.
Padoue (padu), s.f. Padua.
Palatin (le Mont) (palatɛ̃), s.m. The Palatine Hill.
Palatinat (palatina), s.m. Palatinate.
Palémon (palemɔ̃), s.m. Palaemon.
Palerme (palɛrm), s.f. Palermo.
Palmyre (palmir), s.f. Palmyra.
Pamphile (pɑ̃fil), s.m. Pamphilus.
Pamphylie (pɑ̃fili), s.f. Pamphylia.
Pandore (pɑ̃dɔr), s.f. Pandora.
Pannonie (pannɔni), s.f. Pannonia.
Papinien (papinjɛ̃), s.m. Papinian.
Papouasie (papwazi), s.f. Papua.
Paracelse (parasɛls), s.m. Paracelsus.
Parme (parm), s.f. Parma.
Parménide (parmenid), s.m. Parmenides.
Parménion (parmenjɔ̃), s.m. Parmenio.
(le) Parnasse (ləparnas), s.m. (Mount) Parnassus.
(les) Parques (lɛpark), s.f.pl. The Parcae, the Fates, the Fatal Sisters.
Patagonie (patagɔni), s.f. Patagonia.
Patrocle (patrɔkl), s.m. Patroclus.
Pausilippe (pozilip), s.m. Posilippo.
Pavie (pavi), s.f. Pavia.
(les) Pays-Bas (lɛpɛibɑ), s.m.pl. The Netherlands.
Pégase (pegɑz), s.m. Pegasus.
Pékin (pekɛ̃), s.m. Peking, Pekin.
Pélage (pelaʒ), s.m. Pelagius.
Pélée (pele), s.m. Peleus.
Péloponèse (pelɔpɔnɛz), s.m. Peloponnesus, the Peloponnese.
Pensylvanie (pɛnsilvani), s.f. Pennsylvania.
Pentélique (pɑ̃telik), s.m. Pentelicus.
Penthésilée (pɑ̃tezile), s.f. Penthesilea.
Pergame (pɛrgam), s.f. Pergamos.
Pernambouc (pɛrnɑ̃buk), s.m. Pernambuco.
Pérou (peru), s.m. Peru.
Pérouse (peruz), s.f. Perugia.
Perse (pɛrs), s.f. Persia.
Perse (pɛrs), s.m. Persius.
Persée (pɛrse), s.m. Perseus.
Persique (le Golfe) (pɛrsik), m. The Persian Gulf.
(le) Pérugin (ləperyʒɛ̃), s.m. (Il) Perugino.
Pétrarque (petrark), s.m. Petrarch.
Pétrone (petrɔn), s.m. Petronius.
Pharaon (faraɔ̃), s.m. Pharaoh.
Pharnace (farnas), s.m. Pharnaces.
Pharsale (farzal), s.f. Pharsalia.
Phébé (febe), s.f. Phoebe.
Phébus (febys), s.m. Phoebus.
Phédon (fedɔ̃), s.m. Phaedo.
Phèdre (fɛdr), **1.** s.m. Phaedrus; **2.** s.f. Phaedra.
Phénicie (fenisi), s.f. Phoenicia.
Philadelphe (filadɛlf), s.m. Philadelphus.

Philadelphie (filadɛlfi), s.f. Philadelphia.
Philippes (filip), s.f. Philippi.
Philoctète (filɔktɛt), s.m. Philoctetes.
Philomèle (filɔmɛl), s.f. Philomela.
Phocée (fɔse), s.f. Phocaea.
Phocide (fɔsid), s.f. Phocis.
Phrygie (friʒi), s.f. Phrygia.
Picardie (pikardi), s.f. Picardy.
Pie (pi), s.m. Pius.
Piémont (pjemɔ̃), s.m. Piedmont.
Pierre (pjɛr), s.m. Peter.
Pindare (pɛ̃dar), s.m. Pindar.
Pinde (pɛ̃d), s.m. Pindus.
(le) Pirée (ləpire), s.m. The Piraeus.
Pise (piz), s.f. Pisa.
Pisistrate (pizistrat), s.m. Pisistratus.
Pison (pizɔ̃), s.m. Piso.
Plaisance (plɛzɑ̃s), s.f. Placentia.
Platée (plate), s.f. Plataea.
Platon (platɔ̃), s.m. Plato.
Plaute (plot), s.m. Plautus.
Pline (plin), s.m. Pliny; ~ *l'Ancien*, Pliny the Elder; ~ *le Jeune*, Pliny the Younger.
Plutarque (plytark), s.m. Plutarch.
Pluton (plytɔ̃), s.m. Pluto.
Podolie (pɔdɔli), s.f. Podolia.
Polichinelle (pɔliʃinɛl), s.m. Punch.
Politien (pɔlisjɛ̃), s.m. Politian, Poliziano.
Pollion (pɔljɔ̃), s.m. Pollio.
Pologne (pɔlɔɲ), s.f. Poland.
Polybe (pɔlib), s.m. Polybius.
Polyclète (pɔliklɛt), s.m. Polycletus.
Polycrate (pɔlikrat), s.m. Polycrates.
Polydore (pɔlidɔr), s.m. Polydorus.
Polymnie (pɔlimni), s.f. Polymnia.
Polynésie (pɔlinezi), s.f. Polynesia.
Polynice (pɔlinis), s.m. Polynices.
Polyphème (pɔlifɛm), s.m. Polyphemus.
Poméranie (pɔmerani), s.f. Pomerania.
Pomone (pɔmɔn), s.f. Pomona.
Pompée (pɔ̃pe), s.m. Pompey.
Pompéi (pɔ̃pei), s.f. Pompeii.
Ponce-Pilate (pɔ̃spilat), s.m. Pontius Pilate.
Pondichéry (pɔ̃diʃeri), s.m. Pondicherry.
(le) Pont-Euxin (ləpɔ̃tøksɛ̃), s.m. The Euxine, the Black Sea.
Pontins (les Marais) (pɔ̃tɛ̃), s.m.pl. The Pontine Marshes.
Poppée (pɔppe), s.f. Poppaea.
Porcia (pɔrsja), s.f. Portia.
Porphyre (pɔrfir), s.m. Porphyrius.
Posnanie (pɔsnani), s.f. Posen, Posnania.
Pouchkine (puʃkin), s.m. Pushkin.
Pouille (puj), s.f. Apulia.
Praxitèle (praksitɛl), s.m. Praxiteles.
Presbourg (prɛsbur), s.m. Presburg.
Priam (priam), s.m. Priamus, Priam.
Priape (priap), s.m. Priapus.
Priscien (prissjɛ̃), s.m. Priscian.
Priscillien (prissiljɛ̃), s.m. Priscillian.
Procope (prɔkɔp), s.m. Procopius.
Procuste (prɔkyst), s.m. Procrustes.
Progné (prɔgne), s.f. Procne.
Prométhée (prɔmete), s.m. Prometheus.
Properce (prɔpɛrs), s.m. Propertius.
Propontide (prɔpɔ̃tid), s.f. Propontis.
Proserpine (prɔzɛrpin), s.f. Proserpina.
Protée (prɔte), s.m. Proteus.
Prudence (prydɑ̃s), s.m. Prudentius.
Prusse (prys), s.f. Prussia.
Psammétique (psametik), s.m. Psammetichus.
Ptolémée (ptɔleme), s.m. Ptolemy.
Pulchérie (pylʃeri), s.f. Pulcheria.
Putiphar (pytifar), s.m. Potiphar.
Pylade (pilad), s.m. Pylades.
Pyrame (piram), s.m. Pyramus.
Pyrénées (pirene), s.f.pl. Pyrenees; *les Basses* ~, the Lower Pyrenees; *les Hautes* ~, the Upper Pyrenees.
Pyrrhon (pirɔ̃), s.m. Pyrrho.
Pythagore (pitagɔr), s.m. Pythagoras.

Quichotte (kiʃɔt), s.m. Quixote.
Quilimane (kiliman), s.f. Quillimane.
Quinte-Curce (kɛ̃tkyrs), s.m. Quintus Curtius.
Quintilien (kɛ̃tiljɛ̃), s.m. Quintilian.

Radegonde (radgɔ̃d), s.f. Radegund.
Radjpoutana (radʒputana), s.m. Rajputana.
Raguse (ragyz), s.f. Ragusa.
Ramsès (ramsɛs), s.m. Rameses.
Ratisbonne (ratisbɔn), s.f. Ratisbon.
Ravenne (ravɛn), s.f. Ravenna.
Reims (rɛ̃s), s.m. Rheims.
Rhadamante (radamɑ̃t), s.m. Rhadamanthus.
Rhée, Cybèle (re, sibɛl), s.f. Rhea, Cybele.
Rhétie (resi), s.f. Rhaetia.
(le) Rhin (lərɛ̃), s.m. The Rhine.
Roboam (rɔbɔam), s.m. Rehoboam.
Romagne (rɔmaɲ), s.f. Romagna.
Roncevaux (rɔ̃svo), s.m. Roncesvalles.
Rosette (rozɛt), s.f. Rosetta.
Roumanie (rumani), s.f. Rumania.
Roumélie (rumeli), s.f. Roumelia.
Roustchouk (rustʃuk), s.f. Ruschuk.
Roxane (rɔksan), s.f. Roxana.
Roxelane (rɔksəlan), s.f. Roxelana.
Ruben (rybɛn, rybɛ̃), s.m. Reuben.
Rufin (ryfɛ̃), s.m. Rufinus.
Russie (rysi), s.f. Russia.

Saba (saba), s.f. Sheba.
Sabine (sabin), s.f. Sabina (country).
Sagonte (sagɔ̃t), s.f. Saguntum.
Saint-Domingue (sɛ̃dɔmɛ̃g), s.f. San Domingo.
Sainte-Hélène (sɛ̃telɛn), s.f. Saint Helena (Island).
Saint-Laurent (sɛ̃lɔrɑ̃), s.m. St. Lawrence (river).
Sakhalien, Sakhaline (sakalin), s.f. Saghalien (Island).
Salamanque (salamɑ̃k), s.f. Salamanca.
Salamine (salamin), s.f. Salamis.
Salerne (salɛrn), s.f. Salerno.
Salluste (salyst), s.m. Sallust.
Salomon (salɔmɔ̃), s.m. Solomon.
Salonique (salɔnik), s.f. Salonica.
Salvien (salvjɛ̃), s.m. Salvian.

Salzbourg (salsbur), s.m. Salzburg.
Samarcande (samarkɑ̃d), s.f. Samarkand.
Samarie (samari), s.f. Samaria.
Sancho-Pança (sɑ̃ʃopɑ̃sa), s.m. Sancho Panza.
Sapho (safo), s.f. Sappho.
Sara (sara), s.f. Sarah.
Saragosse (saragɔs), s.f. Saragossa.
Sardaigne (sardɛɲ), s.f. Sardinia.
Sardanapale (sardanapal), s.m. Sardanapalus.
Sardes (sard), s.f. Sardis.
Saturne (satyrn), s.m. Saturn.
Saül (sayl), s.m. Saul.
Saumaise (somɛz), s.m. Salmasius.
Savoie (savwɑ), s.f. Savoy.
Savonarole (savɔnarɔl), s.m. Savonarola.
Saxe (saks), s.f. Saxony.
(le) Scamandre (ləskamɑ̃dr), s.m. The Scamander.
Scandinavie (skɑ̃dinavi), s.f. Scandinavia.
Schaffhouse (ʃafuz), s.f. Schaffhausen.
Scipion (sipjɔ̃), s.m. Scipio; ~ *l'Africain*, Scipio Africanus; ~ *l'Asiatique*, Scipio Asiaticus.
Scythie (siti), s.f. Scythia.
Sédécias (sedesjɑs), s.m. Zedekiah.
Ségeste (seʒɛst), s.f. Ségesta.
Ségovie (segɔvi), s.f. Segovia.
Séjan (seʒɑ̃), s.m. Sejanus.
Séleucie (seløsi), s.f. Seleucia.
Sem (sɛm), s.m. Shem.
Sénégambie (senegɑ̃bi), s.f. Senegambia.
Sénèque (senɛk), s.m. Seneca.
Séphora (sefɔra), s.f. Zipporah.
Septime (sɛptim), s.m. Septimius, Septimus.
Serbie (sɛrbi), s.f. Serbia.
Sévère (sevɛr), s.m. Severus.
Sibérie (siberi), s.f. Siberia.
Sichée (siʃe), s.m. Sichaeus.
Sichem (siʃɛm), s.m. Shechem.
Sicile (sisil), s.f. Sicily.
Sidoine Apollinaire (sidwan apɔllinɛr), s.m. Sidonius Apollinaris.
Sienne (sjɛn), s.f. Siena.
Silène (silɛn), s.m. Silenus.
Silésie (silezi), s.f. Silesia.
Silistrie (silistri), s.f. Silistria.
Silo (silo), s.f. Shiloh.
Siloé (silɔe), s.f. Siloam.
Simonide (simɔnid), s.m. Simonides.
Singapour (sɛ̃gapur), s.m. Singapore.
Sion (sjɔ̃), s.f. **1.** Zion (Palestine); **2.** Sion (Switzerland).
Sisyphe (sizif), s.m. Sisyphus.
Siva (siva), s.m. Shiva, Siva.
Sixte (sikst), s.m. Sextus, Sixtus; ~-*Quint*, Sixtus the Fifth.
Smyrne (smirn), s.f. Smyrna.
Socin (sɔsɛ̃), s.m. Socinus.
Socrate (sɔkrat), s.m. Socrates.
Sodome (sodɔm), s.f. Sodoma, Sodom.
Sogdiane (sɔgdjan), s.f. Sogdiana.
Sonde (Îles de la, Archipel de la) (sɔ̃d), s.f. Sunda Isles; *Détroit de la* ~, Sunda Strait.
Sophie (sɔfi), s.f. Sophia.
Sophocle (sɔfɔkl), s.m. Sophocles.
Sophonisbe (sɔfɔnisb), s.f. Sophonisba.
(les) Sorlingues, Scilly (lɛsɔrlɛ̃g, silli), s.f.pl. The Scilly Islands.
Sosie (sozi), s.m. Sosia.
Souabe (swab), s.f. Swabia.
Sparte (spart), s.f. Sparta.
Spire (spir), s.f. Spires.
Spitzberg (spitsbɛrg), s.m. Spitzbergen.
Stace (stas), s.m. Statius.
Stanislas (stanislɑs), s.m. Stanislaus.
Stésichore (stezikɔr), s.m. Stesichorus.
Stilicon (stilikɔ̃), s.m. Stilicho.
Strabon (strabɔ̃), s.m. Strabo.
Styrie (stiri), s.f. Styria.
Suède (sɥɛd), s.f. Sweden.
Suétone (sɥetɔn), s.m. Suetonius.
Suisse (sɥis), s.f. Switzerland.
Sulpice (sylpis), s.m. Sulpicius.
(le) Sund (ləsɔ̃d), s.m. The Sound.
Surate (syrat), s.f. Surat.
Suse (syz), s.f. Susa.
Symmaque (simmak), s.m. Symmachus.
Syrie (siri), s.f. Syria.

Tacite (tasit), s.m. Tacitus.
(le) Tage (ləta ʒ), s.m. The Tagus.
Tamerlan (tamɛrlɑ̃), s.m. Tamerlane, Tamburlaine.
(la) Tamise (latamiz), s.f. The Thames.
Tananarive (tananariv), s.f. Antananarivo.
Tancrède (tɑ̃krɛd), s.m. Tancred.
Tanger (tɑ̃ʒe), s.m. Tangier.
Tantale (tɑ̃tal), s.m. Tantalus.
Tarente (tarɑ̃t), s.f. Tarento.
Tarquin (tarkɛ̃), s.m. Tarquinius, Tarquin.
Tarquinies (tarkini), s.f. Tarquinia.
Tarse (tars), s.f. Tarsus.
Tartarie (tartari), s.f. Tartary.
Tasmanie (tasmani), s.f. Tasmania.
(le) Tasse (lətas), s.m. Tasso, Torquato Tasso.
Tauride (torid), s.f. Taurida.
Télémaque (telemak), s.m. Telemachus.
Télèphe (telɛf), s.m. Telephus.
Ténare (tenar), s.m. Taenarus.
Terpandre (tɛrpɑ̃dr), s.m. Terpander.
Terre de Feu (tɛrdəfø), s.f. Tierra del Fuego.
Terre-Neuve (tɛrnœv), s.f. Newfoundland.
Terre Sainte (tɛrsɛ̃t), s.f. Holy Land.
Tertullien (tɛrtyljɛ̃), s.m. Tertullian.
Tessin (tɛsɛ̃), s.m. Ticino.
Thalie (tali), s.f. Thalia.
Thamar (tamar), s.f. Tamar.
Thébaïde (tebaid), s.f. The Thebaid.
Thémistocle (temistɔkl), s.m. Themistocles.
Théocrite (teɔkrit), s.m. Theocritus.
Théodat (teɔda), s.m. Theodatus.
Théodose (teɔdoz), s.m. Theodosius.
Théodosie (teɔdozi), s.f. Theodosia.
Théophile (teɔfil), s.m. Theophilus.

Théophraste (teɔfrast), s.m. Theophrastus.
Théramène (teramɛn), s.m. Theramenes.
(les) Thermopyles (lɛtɛrmɔpil), s.m.pl. Thermopylae.
Thersite (tɛrsit), s.m. Thersites.
Thésée (teze), s.m. Theseus.
Thessalie (tɛsali), s.f. Thessaly.
Thessalonique (tɛsalɔnik), s.f. Thessalonica.
Thoune (tun), s.m. Thun.
Thrace (tras), s.f. Thracia, Thrace.
Thrasibule (trazibyl), s.m. Thrasibulus.
Thucydide (tysidid), s.m. Thucydides.
Thurgovie (tyrgɔvi), s.f. Thurgau.
Thuringe (tyrɛ̃ʒ), s.f. Thuringia.
Thyeste (tjɛst), s.m. Thyestes.
Tibère (tibɛr), s.m. Tiberius.
(le) Tibre (lətibr), s.m. The Tiber.
Tibulle (tibyl), s.m. Tibullus.
Tigrane (tigran), s.m. Tigranes.
(le) Tigre (lətigr), s.m. The Tigris.
Timée (time), s.m. Timaeus.
Timothée (timɔte), s.m. Timotheus, Timothy.
(le) Tintoret (lətɛ̃tɔrɛ), s.m. Tintoretto.
Tite (tit), s.m. Titus.
Tite-Live (titliv), s.m. Livy.
Tithon (titɔ̃), s.m. Tithonus.
(le) Titien (lətisjɛ̃), s.m. Titian.
Tobie (tɔbi), s.m. Tobias.
Tolède (tɔlɛd), s.f. Toledo.
Tombouctou (tɔ̃buktu), s.f. Timbuctoo.
Tonkin (tɔ̃kɛ̃), s.m. Tonquin, Tonkin.
Toscane (tɔskan), s.f. Tuscany.
Trajan (traʒɑ̃), s.m. Trajanus, Trajan.
Transylvanie (trɑ̃silvani), s.f. Transylvania.
(la) Trébie (latrebi), s.f. The Trebia.
Trébizonde (trebizɔ̃d), s.f. Trebizond.
Trente (trɑ̃t), s.f. Trent.
Trèves (trɛv), s.m. Treves, Trier.
Tribonien (tribɔnjɛ̃), s.m. Tribonian.
(la) Trinité (latrinite), s.f. Trinidad.
Triptolème (triptɔlɛm), s.m. Triptolemus.
Troade (trɔad), s.f. Troad.
Trogue-Pompée (trɔgpɔ̃pe), s.m. Trogus Pompeius.
Troie (trwɑ), s.f. Troy.
Tubingue (tybɛ̃g), s.f. Tübingen.
Tullie (tylli), s.f. Tullia.
Tunisie (tynizi), s.f. Tunis.
Turquie (tyrki), s.f. Turkey.
Tyndare (tɛ̃dar), s.m. Tyndareus.
Typhée (tife), s.m. Typhoeus.
Tyr (tir), s.f. Tyre.
Tyrtée (tirte), s.m. Tyrtaeus.

Ugolin (ygɔlɛ̃), s.m. Ugolino.
Ulpien (ylpjɛ̃), s.m. Ulpian.
Ulysse (ylis), s.m. Ulysses.
Upsal (ypsal), s.m. Uppsala.
Uranie (yrani), s.f. Urania.
Urbain (yrbɛ̃), s.m. Urban.
Urbin (yrbɛ̃), s.m. Urbino.
Urie (yri), s.m. Uriah.
Utique (ytik), s.f. Utica.

Valachie (valaʃi), s.f. Wallachia.
Valence (valɑ̃s), s.f. Valencia (Spain); Valence (France).
Valentin (valɑ̃tɛ̃), s.m. Valentine.
Valentinien (valɑ̃tinjɛ̃), s.m. Valentinian.
Valère (valɛr), s.m. Valerius.
Valérien (valerjɛ̃), s.m. Valerian.
(La) Valette, Cité-Valette (lavalɛt, sitevalɛt), s.f. Valetta.
Varron (varɔ̃), s.m. Varro.
Varsovie (varsɔvi), s.f. Warsaw.
Vénétie (venesi), s.f. Venetia.
Venise (vəniz), s.f. Venice.
Vérone (verɔn), s.f. Verona.
Vert (le Cap) (vɛr), s.m. Cape Verde.
Vertumne (vɛrtymn), s.m. Vertumnus.
Vespasien (vɛspɑzjɛ̃), s.m. Vespasian.
Vespuce (Améric) (vɛspys), s.m. Vespucci (Amerigo).
(le) Vésuve (ləvezyv), s.m. Vesuvius.
Vicence (visɑ̃s), s.f. Vicenza.
Vichnou (viʃnu), s.m. Vishnu.
Victorien (viktɔrjɛ), s.m. Victorianus.
Vienne (vjɛn), s.f. **1.** Vienna (Austria); **2.** Vienne (France).
Vintimille (vɛ̃timil), s.m. Ventimiglia.
Virgile (virʒil), s.m. Virgil.
Virginie (virʒini), s.f. Virginia.
(la) Vistule (lavistyl), s.f. The Vistula.
Viterbe (vitɛrb), s.f. Viterbo.
Vitoria (vitɔrja), s.f. Vittoria.
Vitruve (vitryv), s.m. Vitruvius.
Volhynie (vɔlini), s.f. Volhynia.
Vulcain (vylkɛ̃), s.m. Vulcan.

Westphalie (vɛstfali), s.f. Westphalia.
Wiclef (wiklɛf), s.m. Wycliffe.

(le) Xanthe (ləksɑ̃t), s.m. The Xanthus.
Xantippe (ksɑ̃tip), **1.** s.m. Xantippus; **2.** s.f. Xantippe.
Xénocrate (ksenɔkrat), s.m. Xenocrates.
Xénophane (ksenɔfan), s.m. Xenophanes.

Ypres (ipr), s.f. Ypres, Ypern.

Zacharie (zakari), s.m. Zachariah, Zachary, Zacharias.
Zachée (zaʃe), s.m. Zaccheus.
Zambèze (zɑ̃bɛz), s.m. Zambezi.
Zante, Xante (zɑ̃t, ksɑ̃t), s.f. Zante (Island).
Zébédée (zebede), s.m. Zebadiah, Zebedee.
Zélande (zelɑ̃d), s.f. Zeeland; *la Nouvelle* ~, New Zealand.
Zemble (Nouvelle) (zɑ̃bl), s.f. Novaya Zemlya, Nova Zembla.
Zénobie (zenɔbi), s.f. Zenobia.
Zénon (zenɔ̃), s.m. Zeno.
Zéphire (zefir), s.m. Zephyr, Zephyrus.
Zoïle (zɔil), s.m. Zoilus.
Zopyre (zɔpir), s.m. Zopyrus.
Zoroastre (zɔrɔastr), s.m. Zoroaster.
Zorobabel (zɔrɔbabɛl), s.m. Zerubbabel.
Zosime (zozim), s.m. Zosimus.
Zoulouland (zululɑ̃d), s.m. Zululand.
Zwingle (zvɛ̃gl), s.m. Zwingli.

AVION

By courtesy of Imperial Airways Ltd.

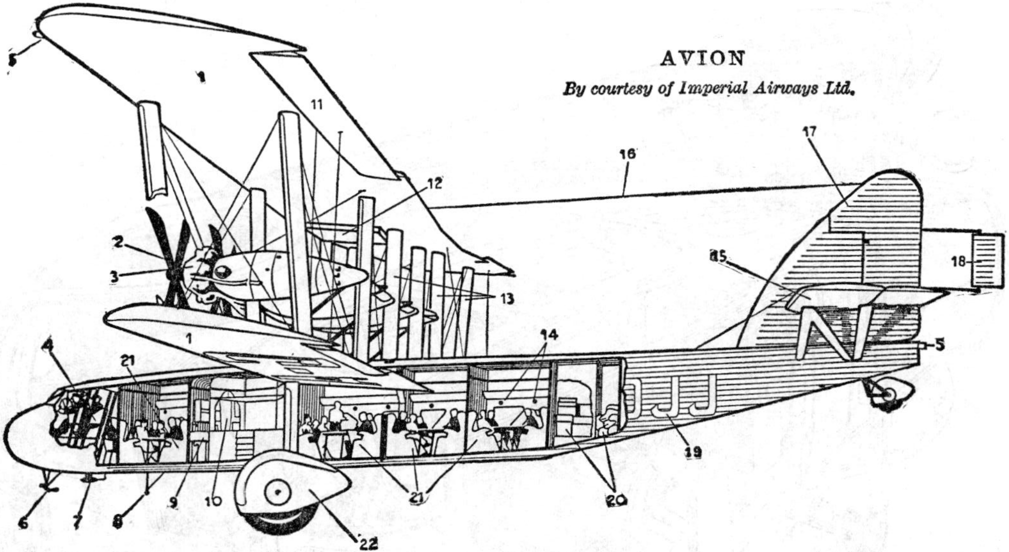

1.	Ailes	Wings	12.	Réservoir d'essence	Main Petrol-tanks
2.	Hélice	Propeller	13.	Supports	Stays
3.	Moteur	Engines	14.	Tuyaux d'aération	Ventilators
4.	Pilote et opérateur T.S.F.	Pilot and Wireless Operator	15.	Gouvernail de profondeur	Elevator
5.	Feux	Navigation Lights	16.	Antenne fixe de T.S.F.	Fixed Wireless Aerial
6.	Badin indicateur de vitesse	Pitot Head for Air Speed Indicator	17.	Gouvernail de direction	Rudder
7.	Génératrice	Wind-driven Wireless Generator	18.	Plan de dérive	Servo Rudder
8.	Antenne de T.S.F. déroulable	Trailing Wireless Aerial	19.	Immatriculation	Registration Marking
9.	Lavabo	Lavatories	20.	Soute à bagages	Mail and Luggage Compartment
10.	Cuisine	Kitchen	21.	Cabine des passagers	Passenger Cabins
11.	Aileron	Aileron	22.	Train d'atterrissage	Undercarriage

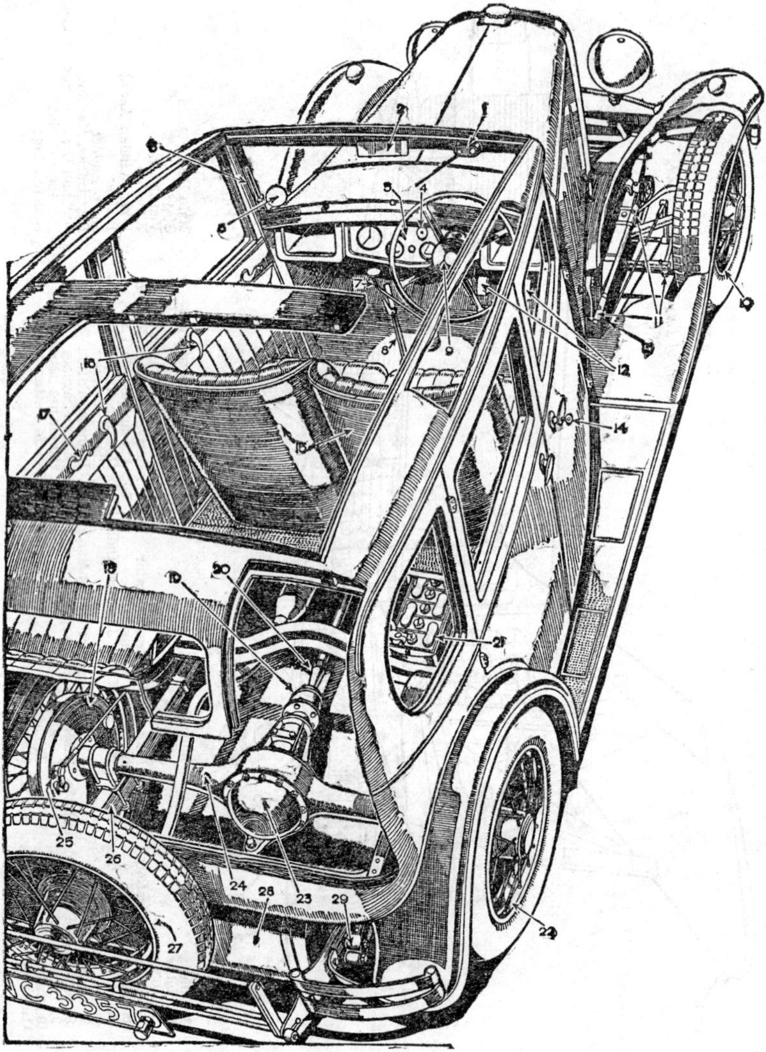

AUTOMOBILE

By courtesy of The Autocar

AUTOMOBILE	MOTOR-CAR
1. Essuie-glace automatique	Automatic Screen-wiper
2. Rétroviseur	Driving-mirror
3. Contact	Engine-switch
4. Bouton du démarreur	Starter-button
5. Charnière du pare-brise et verrouillage	Screen-hinge and Lock
6. Cadre pour permis de circulation	Licence-holder
7. Levier du changement de vitesse, levier des vitesses	Gear-lever
8. Levier de frein à main	Brake-lever
9. Commandes du carburateur, de l'allumage et de l'éclairage	Throttle, Ignition, and Lighting Controls
10. Roue amovible	Detachable Wheel
11. Barres et bielles de direction	Steering-connexions
12. Pédales d'embrayage et de frein	Clutch and Brake Pedals
13. Cable de frein	Brake-operating Cable
14. Clé maîtresse des portières	Master Door-key
15. Sièges réglables	Adjustable Seats
16. Poignées et serrures des portières	Door-handles and Locks
17. Lève-glace	Window-winder
18. Frein sur roue arrière	Rear-wheel Brake
19. Joint à la cardan	Universal Joint
20. Arbre de transmission	Propeller-shaft
21. Accumulateurs pour l'éclairage et le démarrage	Lighting and Starting Battery
22. Jante de roue	Rim of wheel
23. Carter du différentiel	Differential Casing
24. Pont-arrière	Rear-axle Casing
25. Réglage du frein arrière	Rear-brake Adjustment
26. Ressort arrière	Rear Spring
27. Roue de rechange	Spare Wheel
28. Réservoir à essence	Petrol-tank
29. Jumelles de ressort	Spring Shackles

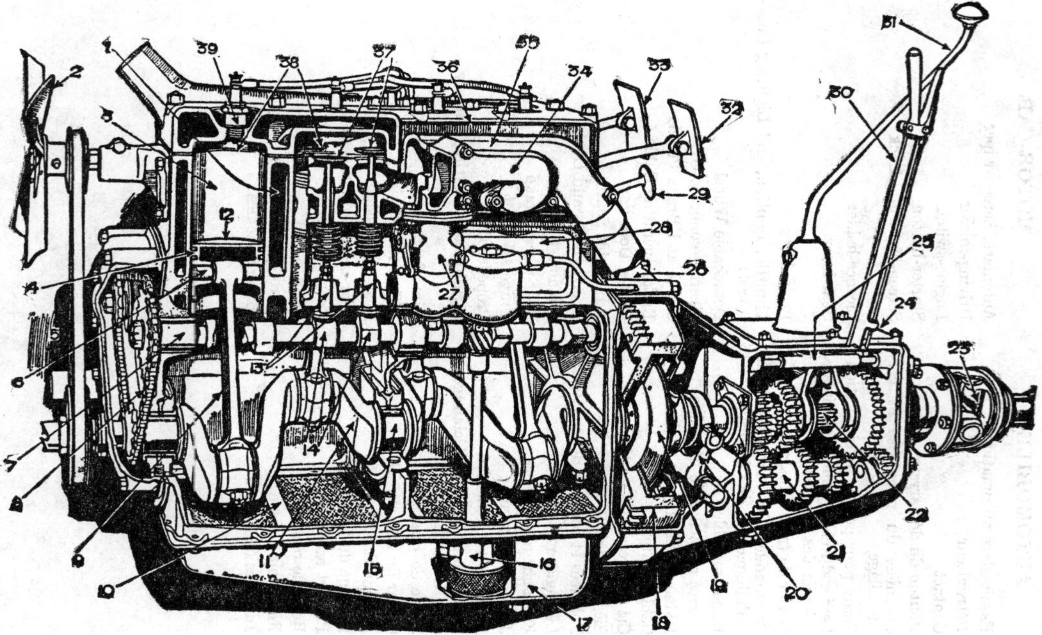

MOTEUR

By courtesy of The Autocar

MOTEUR	ENGINE
1. Chemise d'eau	Water Jacket
2. Ventilateur	Fan
3. Cylindre	Cylinder
4. Segments de piston	Piston-rings
5. Courroie de ventilateur	Fan-belt
6. Axe de piston	Gudgeon-pin
7. Arbre à cames	Camshaft
8. Chaîne de commande de l'arbre à cames	Camshaft Chain Drive
9. Bielle	Connecting-rod
10. Tôle de protection du moteur	Crankcase-tray
11. Vilebrequin du moteur	Crankshaft
12. Piston	Piston
13. Taquets	Tappets
14. Cames	Cams
15. Palier du moteur	Journal Bearing
16. Pompe à huile	Oil-pump
17. Carter du moteur	Oil-sump
18. Volant du moteur	Flywheel
19. Embrayage	Clutch
20. Mécanisme de commande de l'embrayage	Clutch Withdrawal Gear

MOTEUR	ENGINE
21. Arbre secondaire (du changement de vitesse)	Gear-box Layshaft
22. Arbre primaire (du changement de vitesse)	Gear-box Mainshaft
23. Cardan de l'arbre de transmission	Propeller-shaft Universal Joint
24. Boîte de vitesses	Gear-box
25. Sélecteurs (boîte de vitesses)	Gear-selectors
26. Carter du volant du moteur	Flywheel-casing
27. Carburateur	Carburettor
28. Cache-soupapes	Tappet Cover Plate
29. Pédale d'accélérateur	Accelerator-pedal
30. Levier de frein	Brake-lever
31. Levier du changement de vitesses, levier des vitesses	Gear-lever
32. Pédale d'embrayage	Clutch-pedal
33. Pédale de frein	Brake-pedal
34. Tuyauterie d'admission	Induction-manifold
35. Collecteur d'échappement	Exhaust-manifold
36. Culasse du moteur	Cylinder-head
37. Soupapes	Valves
38. Chambres de combustion, chambres d'allumage	Combustion-chambers
39. Bougie d'allumage	Sparking-plug

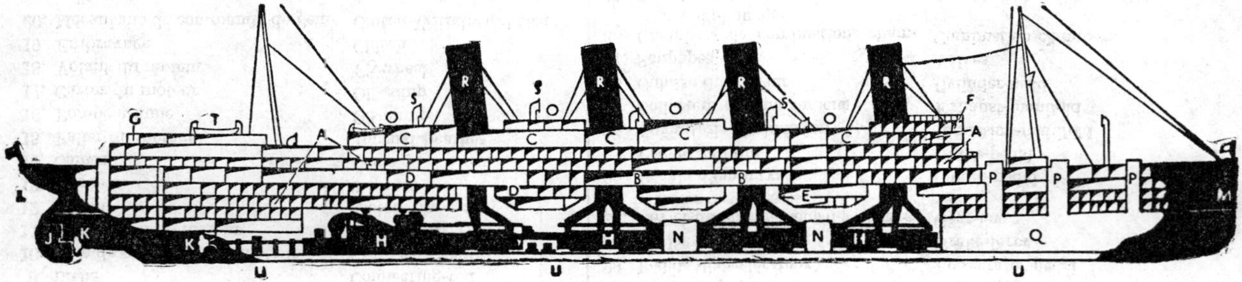

PAQUEBOT

By courtesy of the Cunard Steamship Company

A.	Cabines	Passenger Cabins
B.	Salle à manger de 1ère classe	1st Class Dining Saloons
C.	Fumoir et salons de 1ère classe	1st Class Smoke-rooms and Lounges
D.	Cuisines et offices	Kitchen and Pantries
E.	Piscine et salle de gymnastique	Swimming Bath and Gymnasium
F.	Passerelle	Bridge
G.	Timonerie, kiosque de timonerie	Wheelhouse
H.	Machines	Engines
J.	Gouvernail	Rudder
K.	Hélices	Screws
L.	Poupe, arrière	Stern
M.	Proue, avant	Bow
N.	Réservoirs à huile lourde	Oil-bunkers
O.	Pont supérieur	Boat Deck
P.	Panneaux	Hatches
Q.	Cale	Hold and Cargo
R.	Cheminée	Funnel
S.	Ventilateur	Ventilator
T.	Embarcation	Boat
U.	Quille	Keel

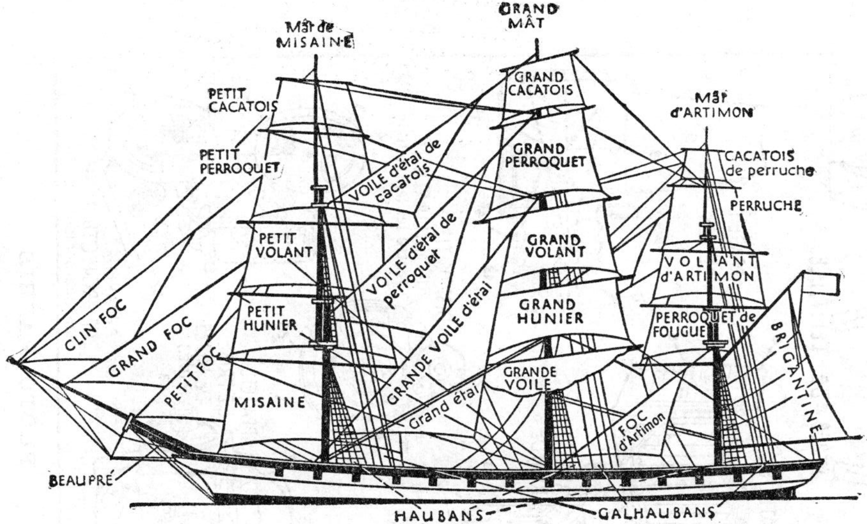

VOILIER

Mât de misaine	Foremast
Grand mât	Mainmast
Mât d'artimon	Mizenmast
Beaupré	Bowsprit
Petit cacatois	Fore Royal
Grand cacatois	Main Royal
Cacatois de perruche	Mizen Royal
Petit perroquet	Fore Topgallant
Grand perroquet	Main Topgallant
Perruche	Mizen Topgallant

Petit volant	Fore Upper Topsail
Grand volant	Main Upper Topsail
Volant d'artimon	Mizen Upper Topsail
Petit hunier	Fore (Lower) Topsail
Grand hunier	Main (Lower) Topsail
Perroquet de fougue	Mizen (Lower) Topsail
Misaine	Foresail
Grande voile	Mainsail
Brigantine	Spanker (Sail)
Clin foc	Flying Jib

Grand foc	Jib, Boom Jib, Standing Jib
Petit foc	Fore Topmast Staysail (Jib)
Voile d'état de cacatois	Royal Staysail
Voile d'état de perroquet	Topgallant Staysail
Grande voile d'état	Main Staysail
Grand état	Mainstay
Foc d'artimon	Mizen Staysail
Haubans	Shrouds
Galhaubans	Backstays

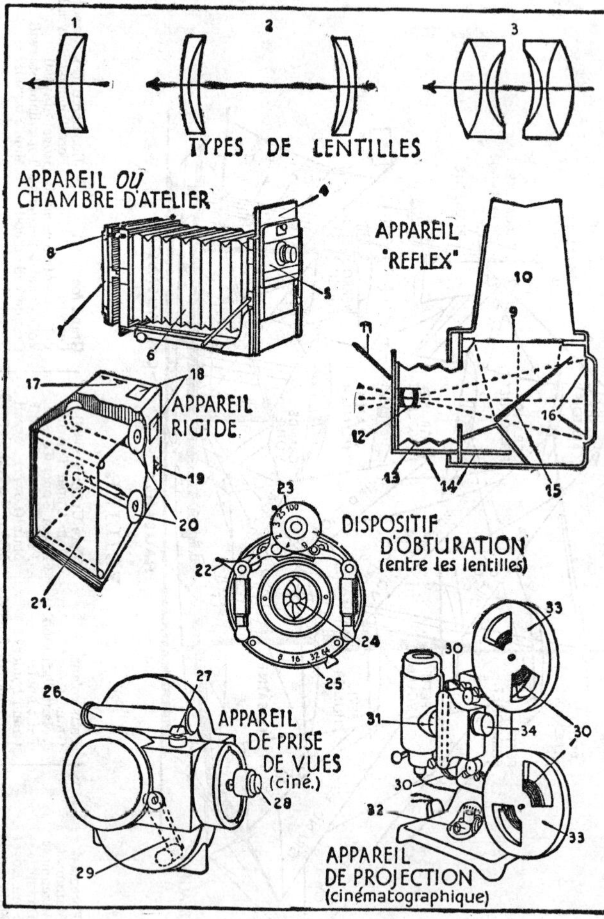

PHOTOGRAPHIE

PHOTOGRAPHIE	PHOTOGRAPHY
TYPES DE LENTILLES	TYPES OF LENSES
1. Lentille simple	Single Lens
2. Lentille rectilinéaire	Rapid Rectilinear
3. Anastigmat double	Double Anastigmat
APPAREIL OU CHAMBRE D'ATELIER	STAND CAMERA
4. Décentrement vertical	Rising Front
5. Support d'objectif	Lens Panel
6. Soufflet	Square Bellows
7. Écran de mise au point (verre dépoli) à charnières	Swing-back Focusing-screen
8. Arrière réversible	Reversing Back
APPAREIL 'REFLEX'	REFLEX CAMERA
9. Verre dépoli horizontal	Horizontal Focusing-screen
10. Tablier	Hood
11. Pare-soleil	Sky Shade
12. Objectif (rentrant)	Lens (in sunk mount)
13. Soufflet	Bellows
14. Mise au point à crémaillère	Focusing-rack
15. Miroir pivotant	Hinged Mirror
16. Plaque	Plate
APPAREIL RIGIDE	BOX CAMERA
17. Ouverture de diaphragme et pause	Stops
18. Viseurs	View-finders
19. Déclencheur	Release
20. Bobines	Spools
21. Rouleau de pellicules	Roll Film
DISPOSITIF D'OBTURATION ENTRE LES LENTILLES	'BETWEEN LENS' SHUTTER
22. Déclencheur	Trigger release
23. Indicateur des vitesses	Shutter-speed Indicator
24. Iris de diaphragme	Iris Diaphragm
25. Indicateur des diaphragmes	Diaphragm Indicator
APPAREIL DE PRISE DE VUES	CINÉ-CAMERA
26. Viseur	View-finder
27. Bouton des vitesses	Exposure-knob
28. Objectif	Lens
29. Manivelle	Handle
APPAREIL DE PROJECTION (Cinématographique)	CINÉ-PROJECTOR
30. Pellicule, Film	Film
31. Lampe	Lamp
32. Moteur	Motor
33. Bobines	Spools
34. Lentille de projection	Lens

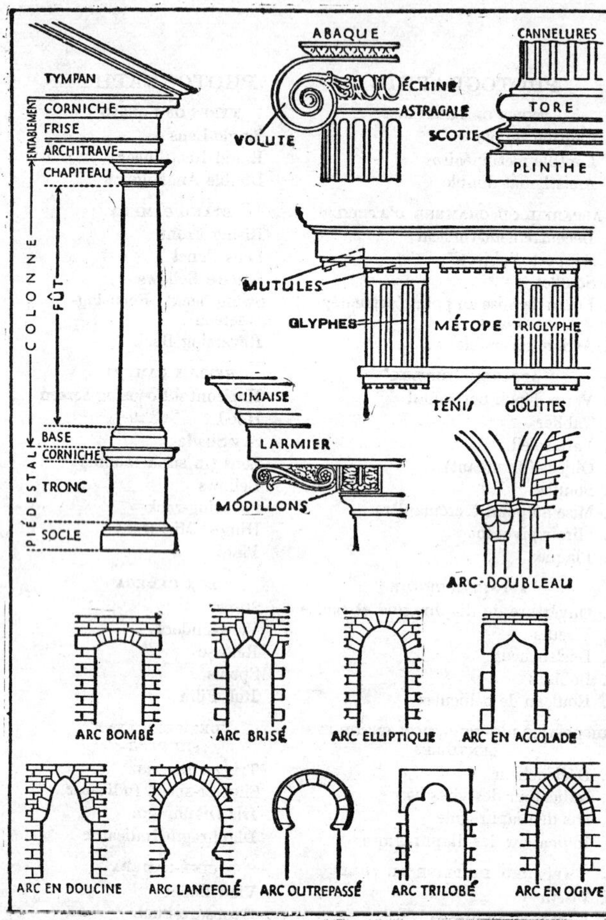

ARCHITECTURE

Abaque	**Abacus**
Cannelures	**Flutes, Fluting**
Échine	**Echinus, ovolo**
Volute	**Volute**
Astragale	**Astragal**
Tore	**Torus, Tore**
Scotie	**Scotia**
Plinthe	**Plinth**
Colonne	**Column**
Piédestal	**Pedestal**
Entablement	**Entablature**
Socle	**Socle**
Tronc	**Drum**
Corniche	**Cornice**
Base	**Base**
Fût	**Shaft**
Chapiteau	**Capital**
Architrave	**Architrave**
Frise	**Frieze**
Tympan	**Tympan, Tympanum, Spandrel**
Mutules	**Mutules**
Métope	**Metope**
Glyphes	**Glyphs**
Triglyphe	**Triglyph**
Ténia	**Taenia**
Gouttes	**Guttae, Guttae Band**
Cimaise	**Cyma, Ogee**
Larmier	**Larmier, Drip, Corona**
Modillons	**Modillions**
Arc-doubleau	**Groin (of vault)**
Arc bombé	**Segmental Arch**
Arc brisé	**Mitre Arch**
Arc elliptique	**Elliptical Arch**
Arc en accolade	**Ogee Arch**
Arc en doucine	**Doucine Arch**
Arc lancéolé	**Lanceolate Arch**
Arc outrepassé	**Horseshoe Arch**
Arc trilobé	**Trefoil Arch**
Arc en ogive	**Pointed Arch**

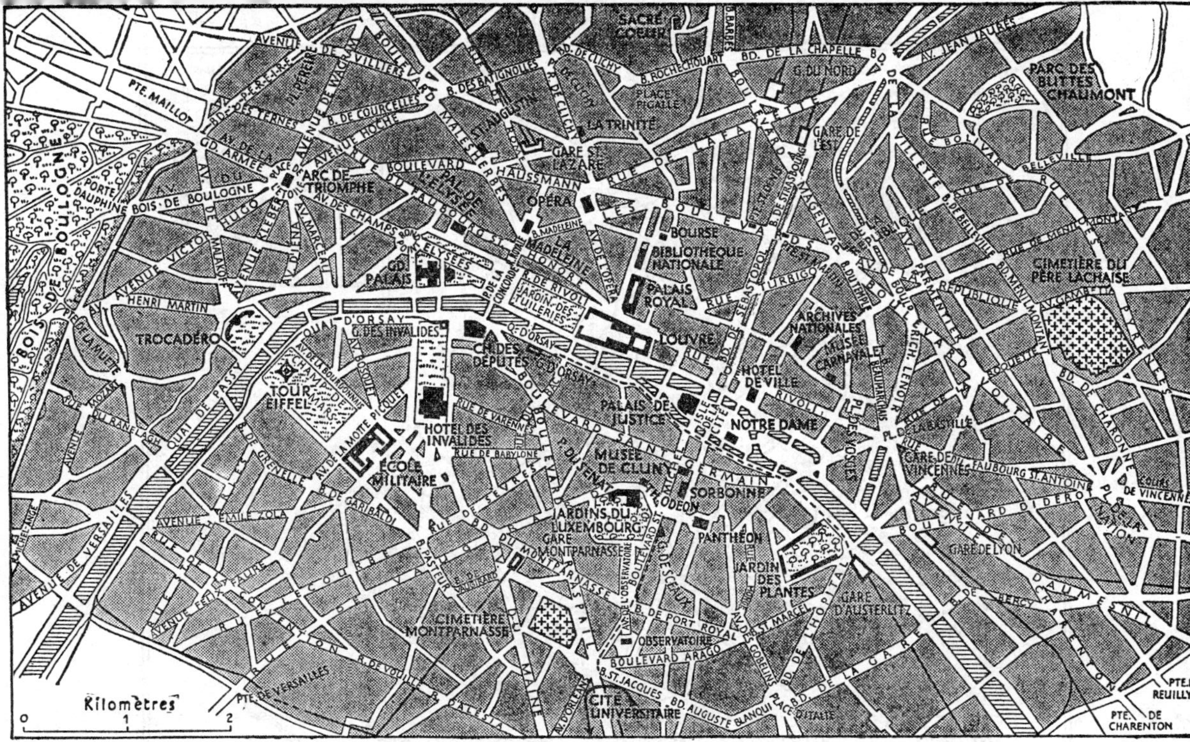

PLAN SOMMAIRE DU CENTRE DE PARIS INDIQUANT LES PRINCIPAUX MONUMENTS

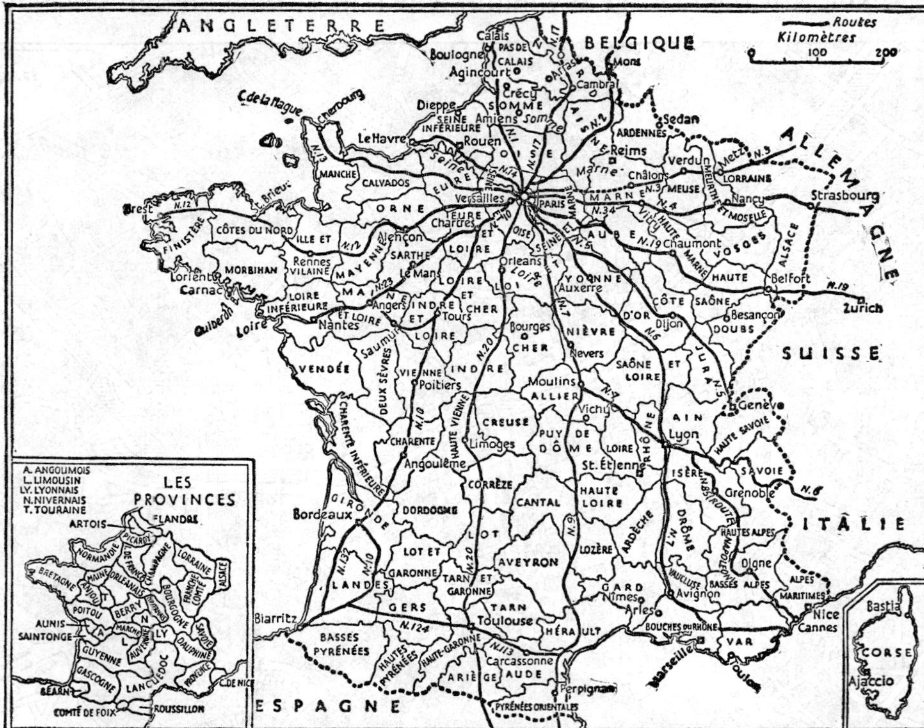
ANGLETERRE
BELGIQUE
ALLEMAGNE
SUISSE
ITÂLIE
ESPAGNE
Routes
Kilomètres
0
100
200
Calais
Boulogne
Agincourt
Crécy
Dieppe
Le Havre
Rouen
Amiens
Arras
Cambrai
Mons
Sedan
Reims
Verdun
Metz
Nancy
Strasbourg
Châlons
Vitry
Chaumont
Belfort
Zurich
Besançon
Dijon
Genève
Lyon
Grenoble
Vichy
St. Étienne
Moulins
Nevers
Bourges
Orleans
Auxerre
Paris
Versailles
Chartres
Alençon
Le Mans
Angers
Tours
Nantes
Saumur
Rennes
Lorient
Carnac
Brest
C. de la Hague
Cherbourg
Quiberon
Poitiers
Limoges
Angoulême
Bordeaux
Biarritz
Toulouse
Carcassonne
Perpignan
Nîmes
Arles
Avignon
Marseille
Toulon
Nice
Cannes
Digne
Bastia
Ajaccio
CORSE
PAS DE CALAIS
SOMME
SEINE INFÉRIEURE
AISNE
ARDENNES
OISE
MARNE
MEUSE
MEURTHE ET MOSELLE
LORRAINE
VOSGES
ALSACE
HAUTE MARNE
AUBE
SEINE ET MARNE
EURE
EURE ET LOIRE
MANCHE
CALVADOS
ORNE
FINISTÈRE
CÔTES DU NORD
ILLE ET VILAINE
MORBIHAN
LOIRE INFÉRIEURE
MAYENNE
SARTHE
MAINE ET LOIRE
LOIR ET CHER
INDRE ET LOIRE
LOIRET
YONNE
CÔTE D'OR
HAUTE SAÔNE
DOUBS
JURA
NIÈVRE
CHER
INDRE
VENDÉE
DEUX SÈVRES
VIENNE
HAUTE VIENNE
CREUSE
ALLIER
SAÔNE ET LOIRE
AIN
RHÔNE
LOIRE
PUY DE DÔME
HAUTE SAVOIE
SAVOIE
ISÈRE
CHARENTE
CHARENTE INFÉRIEURE
CORRÈZE
CANTAL
HAUTE LOIRE
DORDOGNE
GIRONDE
LOT
LOT ET GARONNE
TARN ET GARONNE
AVEYRON
LOZÈRE
ARDÈCHE
DRÔME
HAUTES ALPES
BASSES ALPES
ALPES MARITIMES
VAUCLUSE
GARD
BOUCHES DU RHÔNE
VAR
HÉRAULT
TARN
GERS
LANDES
BASSES PYRÉNÉES
HAUTES PYRÉNÉES
HAUTE-GARONNE
ARIÈGE
AUDE
PYRÉNÉES ORIENTALES
Seine
Somme
Marne
Loire
ROUTE NAPOLÉON
N.1
N.2
N.3
N.4
N.5
N.6
N.7
N.9
N.10
N.12
N.13
N.14
N.17
N.19
N.20
N.23
N.34
N.85
N.113
N.124
N.132
LES PROVINCES
A. ANGOUMOIS
L. LIMOUSIN
LY. LYONNAIS
N. NIVERNAIS
T. TOURAINE
ARTOIS
FLANDRE
PICARDIE
NORMANDIE
ÎLE DE FRANCE
CHAMPAGNE
LORRAINE
ALSACE
BRETAGNE
MAINE
ANJOU
ORLÉANAIS
BOURGOGNE
FRANCHE COMTÉ
POITOU
BERRY
BOURBONNAIS
SAVOIE
AUNIS
SAINTONGE
MARCHE
AUVERGNE
DAUPHINÉ
GUYENNE
GASCOGNE
LANGUEDOC
PROVENCE
C. DE NICE
BÉARN
COMTÉ DE FOIX
ROUSSILLON

LA FRANCE

THE CONCISE OXFORD ENGLISH–FRENCH DICTIONARY

THE CONCISE OXFORD ENGLISH-FRENCH DICTIONARY

AN AID TO THE
SPEAKING AND WRITING OF FRENCH
SPECIALLY ADAPTED
FOR ENGLISH-SPEAKING USERS

BY
G. W. F. R. GOODRIDGE

OXFORD
AT THE CLARENDON PRESS

PREFACE

IN this complement to the *Concise Oxford French Dictionary*, an effort has been made to include, within a strictly limited compass, the vocabulary and explanations necessary in a practical book of reference. It is designed solely for the convenience of English-speaking users, who wish to write or speak French; and in this respect it differs from the ordinary English–French dictionary which contains many words and explanations needed only by French-speaking readers of English.

Special attention has been given to the general requirements of schools, to commercial phraseology, and to modern war terms. For a handbook of the kind a very full list of animals, flowers, fruits, fish, birds, and insects has been included. The more current medical, military, nautical, literary, sporting, and architectural terms will also be found, together with expressions drawn from modern inventions. I have thought it desirable to add a few Americanisms and slang phrases. Classical derivatives of remote and purely scientific significance have been consistently avoided.

The acquisition of style and language-sense belongs to the province of syntax and composition. But the object of a dictionary should surely be something more than to provide mechanical equivalents to terms in another language. If a word has to be 'looked up', a beginner at any rate wishes to know what to look for and how to look for it—in other words, a dictionary should make direct appeal to constructive thought. In the past this claim has been too often ignored. In many old-fashioned glossaries, synonyms, or what passed for such, were arranged in groups divided by semicolons. The investigator was left to his own beclouded choice as to which term in which group was precisely the one he was seeking. I have endeavoured to lessen this difficulty in the first place by dispensing with all synonyms; secondly by explaining in brackets the exact meaning of words, a method which necessarily has certain limitations where space is of primary consideration.

It has been sufficiently emphasized that a dictionary can have no pretension to fulfil the uses of a grammar. On the other hand there are opportunities in a dictionary for concise grammatical hints of immediate application which, if intelligently implemented, are capable of reducing the inveteracy of mistakes so familiar to teachers of languages. I have availed myself of these occasions to a larger extent than is perhaps usual. Such hints can serve no further than to stir up memory or to suggest reference, where required, to other sources of information. For this reason examples of constructions have been added only where they seemed inseparable from the note in question.

It is, of course, impossible to find an exact counterpart for every English term in French or in any other language. Cases arise where the English word is highly intensive, differentiated, and unusual. Sometimes it is necessary to translate it by an everyday French word even where the meaning loses much in the process. Sometimes also the French term requires only a careful search. The English word 'comely' is an instance of this kind. The correct translation is often given as *beau* where the French adjective *avenant* almost meets the English on equal terms.

For facility of reference it may be noted that compound expressions consisting of two nouns, two adjectives, or an adjective and a noun occur as a rule under the first of the two elements, unless otherwise indicated. For example, 'bread-fruit' will appear under 'bread', 'sword-knot' under 'sword', compounds of 'self' under 'self', 'sky-blue' under 'sky', 'violet-red' under 'violet', &c. In the case of infinitive phrases such as 'bring grist to the mill', 'keep one's countenance', 'burn the candle at both ends', the phrase will generally be discoverable under the complement rather than under the infinitive on which it depends.

The danger-signal ⚠, so opportunely adopted by M. Chevalley to mark words of similar or approximate form but with different meanings in the two languages, meets a like and timely need in this section of the dictionary.

The sign (†) before an aspirate H or Y signalizes that elision and liaison in these cases are impossible. The employment of an asterisk (*) with all irregular and defective verbs may provide a useful warning.

The letters indicating parts of speech, e.g. *s.*, *adj.*, *v.a.*, are added only where any possible doubt or confusion could arise as to the nature of the part in question.

Since *adjectives* of nationality, in contrast with *nouns* of the same form, are spelt with a small letter in French, I have thought it well to indicate this fact in brackets, e.g. **English,** *adj.* (*when an adj. use small letter*) *and s.m.f.* Anglais, -e.

In conclusion it remains for me to express my gratitude for frequent help in compilation, detail and phrasing to the late M. Chevalley's remarkable work.

G. W. F. R. G.

FRESHFORD, BATH.

PRINCIPAL ABBREVIATIONS

*** = irreg. verb; ⚠ = pitfall ! beware of apparent analogy ! ; † (obelisk) = aspirate H or Y.**

abbrev., abbreviation
act., active
adj., adjective, adjectival(ly)
adv., adverb(ial)
aeron., aeronautics
affirm., affirmative
agric., agriculture
alg., algebra
an., animal, pl. ans.
anat., anatomy
anc., ancient
ant., antiquities
approx., approximately
arch., architecture
arith., arithmetic
arm., armour
art., article
artil., artillery
astr., astronomy
astrol., astrology
biol., biology
bkkpg., book-keeping
bot., botany
build., building
carp., carpentry
Cath., Catholic
cf., compare
chem., chemistry
class., classical
colloq., colloquial(ly)
comm., commerce
compar., comparative
cond., conditional
conj., conjunction
crust., crustacea
cul. and cook., culinary
def., defective
dem., demonstrative
eccles., ecclesiastical
e.g., for instance
electr., electricity
ent., entomology
equiv., equivalent
etc., &c., et cetera
etym., etymology
ex., example
exc., except
exclam., exclamatory
ext., extension
f. and fem., feminine
falc., falconry
fam., familiar(ly)
fenc., fencing
fig., figurative(ly)
fin., finance
fort., fortification
Fr., French
gard., gardening
gen., generally
geog., geography, geographical
geol., geology
geom., geometry
gram., grammar
Gr., Greek
gymn., gymnastics
her., heraldry
hist., history
horol., horology
hort., horticulture
hunt., hunting
ichth., ichthyology
i.e., that is to say
imper., imperative
impers., impersonal
indic., indicative
inf., infinitive
instr., instrument
interj., interjection
interrog., interrogative
invar., invariable
irreg., irregular(ly)
join., joinery
kg., kilogram
kilom., kilometre
L, Latin
lang., language
lit., literal(ly)
Lit., literature or literary
log., logic
m. and masc., masculine
mach., machinery
math., mathematics
med., medicine
mil., military
moll., mollusca
motor., motoring
mus., music
myth., mythology
n., neuter (verb)
nat.hist., natural history
naut., nautical
nav., naval
neg., negative
ornith., ornithology
p. and part., participial
p.p., past participle
parl., parliament
pathol., pathology
pej., pejorative
pers., personal and person
photo., photography
phys., physics
pl., plural
polit., politics
pop., popular(ly)
poss., possessive
pr., pronominal
prep., preposition
pres., present
pron., pronoun
pros., prosody
Prot., Protestant
rail., railways
reflex., reflexive
rel., relative
relig., religion
rhet., rhetoric
s., substantive, noun
schol., scholastic
Script., scriptural
sculpt., sculpture
sing., singular
sport., sporting
subj., subjunctive
surg., surgery
teleph., telephony
telegr., telegraph
theatr., theatrical
theol., theology
univ., university
v., verb
veg., vegetable
veh., vehicle
vet., veterinary (surgery)
zool., zoology

ENGLISH-FRENCH SUPPLEMENT

aback, *adv.* (*naut.*) coiffé; *be taken* ~ (*fig.*) être déconcerté.
abaft, *adv.* (*naut.*) vers l'arrière; *prep.* à l'arrière de.
abandon, *v.a.* abandonner; (*give up*) renoncer à; ~**ed,** *adj.* (*fig.*) dépravé.
abandonment, (*act.*) abandonnement, *m.*; (*lack of restraint*) abandon, *m.*
abase, (*degrade*) avilir.
abash, déconcerter.
abate, *v.a.n.* diminuer; (*bring down price, &c.*) rabattre; ~**ment** (*lessening*) diminution, *f.*; (*price, remission*) rabais, *m.*
abbey, abbaye, *f.*
abbot, abbess, abb|é, ~esse, *m.f.*
abbreviat|e, abréger; ~**ion,** abréviation, *f.*
abdicat|e, *v.a.n.* abdiquer; ~**ion,** abdication, *f.*
abdom|en, abdomen, *m.*; ~**inal,** abdominal.
abduct, enlever; ~**ion,** enlèvement, *m.*
abeam, *adv.* (*naut.*) par le travers.
aberration, (*lit. and fig.*) égarement, *m.*
abet, *v.a.* appuyer; ~**tor,** faut|eur, ~rice, *m.f.*
abeyance, suspension, *f.*; *fall into* ~, tomber (être) en désuétude.
abhor, détester; ~**rence,** horreur, *f.*; ~**rent,** odieu|x, ~se.
abide, (*endure*) supporter; *v.n.* (*remain*) demeurer (être).
abiding, *adj.* permanent.
abilit|y, *s.* talent, *m.*; ~**ies,** (*intellect*) talents, *m.pl.*
abject, *adj.* abject; ~**ness,** abjection, *f.*
abjure, *v.a.* renoncer à.
ablative, (*gram.*) ablatif, *m.*
ablaze, en feu.
abl|e, *adj.* capable (de); (*competent*) habile; ~**y,** avec adresse; *be* ~, pouvoir*.
able-bodied, *adj.* vigoureu|x, ~se; ~ *seaman,* gabier breveté, *m.*
ablet, (*ichth.*) ablette, *f.*
ablution, ablution, *f.*
abnegation, abnégation, *f.*
abnormal, *adj.* anormal.
aboard, *adv.* à bord; *prep.* à bord de; *take* ~, embarquer; *all* ~, (*U.S.A. take your seats*) en voiture.
abode, *s.* demeure, *f.*; *take up one's* ~, s'installer.
abolish, abolir; (*suppress*) supprimer.
abolition, abolition, *f.*
abominabl|e, abominable; ~**y,** abominablement.
abominat|e, avoir en horreur; ~**ion,** abomination, *f.*
aborigin|al, *adj.* aborigène; ~**es,** aborigènes, *m.pl.*
abortion, (*miscarriage*) avortement, *m.*; (*child, fig.*) avorton, *m.*
abortive, (*fig.*) avorté.
abound, *v.n.* abonder (de).
about, *adv.* autour; (*here and there*) çà et là; *somewhere* ~, quelque part; *to be* ~ *to,* être sur le point de; *right* ~ *turn!* (*mil.*) demi-tour à droite!
about, *prep.* (*reference to*) au sujet de; (*round about*) autour de; (*nearly*) of *numbers,* vers; (*on one's person, higher up*) sur.
above, *adv.* en haut; au-dessus; ~ *all,* surtout; ~ *mentioned,* susmentionné; ~ *board,* cartes sur table.
above, *prep.* (*contact*) sur; (*higher up than*) au-dessus de; (*more than*) plus de; (*on a river*) en amont de.
abrasion, abrasion, *f.*
abreast, *adv.* de front.
abridge, abréger; ~**ment** (*summary*) abrégé, *m.*
abroad, *adv.* (*foreign country*) à l'étranger; *publish* ~, crier sur les toits; *there is a report* ~, le bruit court.
abrogat|e, (*repeal, cancel*) abroger; ~**ion,** abrogation, *f.*
abrupt, *adj.* (*manner*) brusque; (*descent*) escarpé; ~**ly,** (*slope*) en pente raide; (*quickly, rudely*) brusquement.
abscess, abcès, *m.*
abscond from, se soustraire* à.
absence, *s.* absence, *f.*; *leave of* ~, congé, *m.*; (*mil.*) permission, *f.*
absent, *adj.* absent.
absent-minded, *adj.* distrait; ~**ly,** distraitement.
absent oneself, s'absenter.
absentee, *s.* absent, *m.*
absinth, absinthe, *f.*
absolute, absolu; (*downright*) pur et simple; ~**ly,** absolument.
absolution, absolution, *f.*; **public** ~ (*eccles.*) absoute, *f.*
absolve, (*eccles.*) absoudre*; (*relieve from*) relever de.
absorb, absorber; ~**ed in,** absorbé dans; ~**ing,** absorbant.
absorbent, *adj. and s.m.* absorbant.
absorption, absorption, *f.*
absquatulate, *v.n.* (*U.S.A.*) se sauver.
abstain from, *v.n.* s'abstenir* de.
abstemious, sobre; ~**ness,** sobriété, *f.*; ~**ly,** sobrement.
abstinence, abstinence, *f.*
abstinent, *adj.* (*food and drink*) sobre.
abstract, *s.* (*philos.*) abstrait, *m.*; (*book, &c.*) extrait, *m.*; (*epitome*) abrégé, *m.*; *in the* ~, en théorie; *v.a.* abstraire*; (*chem.*) extraire*; (*steal*) dérober.
abstraction, (*mental*) abstraction, *f.*; (*chem.*) extraction, *f.*; (*taking away*) vol, *m.*; (*inattention*) inattention, *f.*
abstruse, (*difficult to understand*) abstrus.

absurd, absurde; **~ly,** absurdement.
abundance, (*lit. and fig.*) abondance, *f.*
abundant, abondant; *be ~*, abonder; **~ly,** abondamment.
abuse, *s.* (*insult*) injures, *f.pl.*; (*misuse*) abus, *m.*
abuse, *v.a.* (*insult*) injurier; (*misuse*) abuser de.
abusive, injurieu|x, **~se.** ⚠ *Not* abusif *which* = '*excessive*', '*contrary to usage*'; **~ly,** d'une manière injurieuse.
abut on, aboutir à; *~ting on*, attenant à.
abutment, (*arch.*) contrefort, *m.*; (*bridge*) culée, *f.*
abysmal, (*ignorance*) creu|x, **~se.**
abyss, *s.* abîme, *m.*
acacia, *s.* (*bot.*) acacia, *m.*
academical, académique; (*university*) universitaire.
academician, *s.* académicien, *m.*
academ|y, *s.* académie, *f.*; (*music and arts*) conservatoire, *m.*; (*school*) pensionnat, *m.*
acanthus, (*bot. and arch.*) acanthe, *f.*
accede to, consentir à.
accelerat|e, accélérer; **~ion,** accélération, *f.*
accelerator, *n.* (*motor.*) accélérateur, *m.*
accent, *s.* accent, *m.*; **~uate,** accentuer; **~uation,** accentuation, *f.*
accept, accepter; (*compliments, &c.*) agréer; **~able,** acceptable; *be very acceptable*, ne pas être de refus.
acceptance, (*act, bill, comm.*) acceptation, *f.*; (*approval*) approbation, *f.*
acceptation, ⚠ (*of a word*) *is not* acceptation, *but* acception, *f.*; acceptation = *act of accepting or promise to pay.*
access, accès, *m.*; *difficult, easy of ~*, d'accès difficile, facile; (*approach*) droit de s'approcher de, *m.*; **~ible,** accessible.
accession, (*addition*) accession, *f.*; (*throne*) avènement, *m.*
accessory, *s.m. and adj.* accessoire.
accident, *s.* accident, *m.*; (*insurance*) sinistre, *m.*
accidental, *adj.* accidentel, -le; (*not essential*) accessoire; **~ly,** accidentellement.
acclaim, acclamer.
acclamation, acclamation, *f.*
acclimatiz|e, acclimater; **~ation,** acclimatation, *f.*
acclivity, montée, *f.*
accommodat|e, *v.a.* (*arrange*) accommoder; (*oblige*) obliger; (*lodge*) loger; *~ oneself to*, s'accommoder de; **~ing,** obligeant.
accommodation, (*quarters*) logement, *m.*; (*arrangement*) arrangement, *m.*; **~ bill,** (*comm.*) billet de complaisance, *m.*
accompaniment, (*gen. and mus.*) accompagnement, *m.*
accompanist, *s.* (*mus.*) accompagnat|eur, **~rice,** *m.f.*
accompany, (*go with, and mus.*) accompagner (de).
accomplice, complice, *m.*
accomplish, accomplir; (*object*) atteindre*; (*successfully*) mener à bonne fin; **~ment,** (*fulfilment*) accomplissement, *m.*; (*attainment*) talent, *m.*; **~ed,** *to be* (*pers.*) avoir des connaissances étendues.
accord, *s.* accord, *m.*; *of one's own ~*, de son propre mouvement; *with one ~*, d'un commun accord; *v.a.* (*grant*) concéder.
according as, *conj.* selon que (*ind.*).
according to, (*in accordance with*) *prep.* selon.
accordingly, (*therefore*) donc; (*in keeping with circumstances*) à l'avénant.
accordion, accordéon, *m.*
accost, aborder.
account, *s.* (*narration*) récit, *m.*; (*comm.*) compte, *m.*; **~ book** (*bkkpg.*) registre de comptabilité, *m.*; *on ~*, à valoir; *credit an ~* (*bkkpg.*) créditer un compte; *debit an ~*, débiter un compte; *make up ~s*, faire* un compte; *settle an ~*, régler un compte; *take into ~*, tenir* compte de; *take on ~*, prendre* à compte.
account for, expliquer; (*money*) rendre compte de.
accountable for, responsable de (*of pers.* = envers).
accountan|t, *s.* comptable, *m.*; **~cy,** comptabilité, *f.*
accoutre, équiper; **~ment** (*mil.*) équipement, *m.*
accredited to, (*pers.*) accrédité auprès de.
accretion, accroissement, *m.*
accrue, provenir* (de); (*comm.*) courir*.
accumulat|e, *v.a.* entasser; *v.n.* s'entasser; **~ion,** entassement, *m.*; **~or** (*motor., electr.*) accumulateur, *m.* (*abbrev.* accu).
accuracy, *s.* exactitude, *f.*
accurate, exact; (*aim*) juste.
accursed, maudit.
accus|e, accuser; **~ation,** accusation, *f.*
accusative, accusatif, *m.*
accustom, *v.a.* accoutumer (à); *~ oneself to*, s'accoutumer à.
ace, *s.* (*cards*) as, *m.*; *within an ace of*, à deux doigts de.
acerbity, âpreté, *f.*
acetylene, acétylène, *f.*; **~-lamp,** lampe à acétylène, *f.*
ache, *s.* douleur, *f.*
ache, *v.n.* faire* mal à; *my heart ~s*, j'ai le cœur navré; *my foot ~s*, j'ai mal au pied.
achieve, *v.a.* accomplir; (*finish*) achever; (*purpose, aim*) atteindre*; (*victory*) remporter; **~ment,** accomplissement, *m.*; (*feat*) exploit, *m.*
acid, *adj. and s.m.* acide; **~ity,** acidité, *f.*
acknowledge, (*pers., truth, authority*) reconnaître*; (*agree*) convenir*; (*letter*) accuser réception de.
acknowledgement, aveu, *m.*; (*goods, debt*) reconnaissance, *f.*; (*letter, &c.*) accusé de réception, *m.*
acme, *s.* comble, *m.*
acolyte, acolyte, *m.*
aconite, (*bot.*) aconit, *m.*
acorn, *s.* gland, *m.*

acoustic, *adj.* acoustique; **~s,** acoustique, *f.*
acquaint (with), informer (de); (*impart*) faire* part à, (*pers.*) de; *be specially ~ed with,* (*things*) se connaître* à; *be ~ed with,* (*pers., things*) connaître*.
acquaintance, connaissance, *f.*
acquiesce in, *v.n.* acquiescer **à; ~nce,** acquiescement, *m.*
acquire, *v.a.* acquérir*; (*learn*) apprendre*; (*by merit*) se faire*.
acquirement, *s.* acquisition, *f.*; **~s,** (*knowledge, &c.*) connaissances, *f.pl.*
acquisition, (*purchase, &c.*) acquisition, *f.*
acquisitive, (*learning*) apte à apprendre*; (*money, &c.*) apte au gain.
acquit, acquitter; *~ oneself of,* s'acquitter de; **~tal,** acquittement, *m.*
acquittance, (*comm.*) acquit, *m.*; (*debt*) payement, *m.*
acre, arpent, *m.* (1¼ *Eng. acres*); acre, *f.* (*O.F.* acre 52 ares; *English acre* 40½ ares).
acrid, âcre.
acrimon|y, acrimonie, *f.*; **~ious,** âcre.
acrobat, acrobate, *m.f.*; **~ics,** (*gen. and aeron.*) acrobatie, *f.*
acrobatic, acrobatique.
acropolis, acropole, *f.*
across, *prep.* (*without obstacle*) **à travers** ⚠ *without* de; (*with obstacle*) au travers+de; (*on the other side of*) de l'autre côté de; *adv.* en travers; *run, come ~,* rencontrer.
acrostic, *s.* acrostiche, *m.*
act, *s.* (*thing done*) action, *f.*; (*of will*) acte, *m.*; (*deed*) fait, *m.*; (*parl.*), loi, *f.*; (*theatr.*) acte, *m.*
act, *v.n.* agir; (*behave*) se conduire*; (*theatr.*) jouer; *~ on,* (*influence*) influer sur; *~ as,* servir* de; *~ upon,* (*advice*) suivre*; **~or, ~ress,** acteur, ~rice, *m.f.*
acting, *adj.* (*temporary*) intérimaire; *s. use verb.*
action, *s.* action, *f.*; (*war*) combat, *m.*; (*law*) procès, *m.*
actionable, sujet à procès.
activ|e, acti|f, ~ve; (*moving about*) alerte; **~ity,** activité, *f.*; **~ely,** activement.
actual, effecti|f, ~ve; ⚠ actuel = '*of the present time*'; **~ly,** en fait; ⚠ *not* actuellement *which* = '*now*', '*at present*'.
actuary, *s.*, actuaire, *m.*
acumen, finesse, *f.*
acute, (*mind, &c.*) fin; (*state*) grave; (*disease, angle*) aigu, -ë; **~ness,** (*pain*) intensité, *f.*; (*pers. sight, &c.*) finesse, *f.*; **~-angled,** acutangle; **~ly,** (*intensely*) profondément.
Adam's apple (*anat.*), pomme d'Adam, *f.*
adamant|ine, *adj.* adamantin; (*fig.*) de pierre.
adapt, *v.a.* adapter; *~ oneself to,* s'adapter à; **~ation,** adaptation, *f.*; **~able,** adaptable.
adapted to, propre à.
add, *v.a.* ajouter; (*arith.*) additionner; *~ a PS. to letter,* apostiller, *v.a.*
adder, *s.* vipère, *f.*; *~'s tongue,* (*bot.*) ophioglosse, *m.*
addicted, be, to, s'adonner à.
addition, *s.* addition, *f.*; (*increase*) accroissement, *m.*
additional, additionnel, -le; **~ly,** de plus.
addled, (*egg*) couvé.
addle-headed, ~ -pated, to be, (*pop.*) avoir la caboche trouble.
address, *s.* adresse, *f.*; (*manner*) parole, *f.*; (*speech*) discours, *m.*
address, *v.a.* (*letter, &c.*) adresser; (*pers.*) adresser la parole à; *~ oneself to,* se mettre* à; *~ a meeting,* prendre* la parole; *~ed envelope,* enveloppe adressée pour la réponse.
adduce, *v.a.* alléguer; (*proof*) apporter.
adenoids, (*med.*) végétations adénoïdes, *f.pl.*
adept at, habile à.
adequate, suffisant; *~ to,* proportionné à; **~ly,** suffisamment.
adhere, *v.n.* adhérer; *~ to* (*statement*) maintenir*; (*glue*) se coller (à); **~nce,** adhérence, *f.*; **~nt,** *adj. and s.m.f.* adhérent, -e; *adj.* (*attached to*) attaché à.
adhesion, (*consent*) adhésion, *f.*
adipos|e, *adj.* adipeu|x, ~se; **~ity,** adiposité, *f.*
adjacent, avoisinant; *~ to,* attenant à.
adjective, *adj.* adjecti|f, ~ve; *s.* (*gram.*) adjectif, *m.*
adjoin, *v.a.* être contigu, -ë à; **~ing,** *adj.* voisin.
adjourn, *v.a.* ajourner, *v.n.* s'ajourner; **~ment,** ajournement.
adjudge, (*condemn*) condamner; (*award*) décerner.
adjudicate, *v.a.n.* (*judge*) juger; (*give judgement*) se prononcer sur.
adjunct, *s.* accessoire, *m.*
adjust, *v.a.* ajuster; (*arrange*) arranger; *self ~ing,* à réglage automatique; **~able,** réglable; **~ment,** (*mach., &c.*) ajustage, *m.*; (*friendly*) arrangement à l'amiable, *m.*
adjutant, adjudant-major, *m.*; ⚠ *not* adjudant *alone which* = '*non-commissioned officer*'.
administ|er, *v.a.* (*gen. and eccles.*) administrer; (*relief*) distribuer; **~ration,** administration, distribution, *f.*; **~rator,** administrat|eur, ~rice, *m.f.*
admirabl|e, admirable; **~y,** admirablement.
admiral, amiral, *m.*; **~ of the fleet,** grand amiral, *m.*; **rear- ~,** contre-amiral, *m.*; **vice- ~,** vice-amiral, *m.*
admiralty, (*office of admiral*) amirauté, *f.*; (*executive of navy*) ministère de la marine, *m.*
admir|e, admirer; **~er,** admirat|eur, ~rice, *m.f.*; **~ation,** admiration, *f.*
admissible, admissible.
admission, *s.* entrée, *f.*; (*confession*) aveu, *m.*
admit, *v.a.* (*let in*) laisser entrer; (*allow*) admettre*; *~ of,* comporter; *~ of no*

excuse, ne pas avoir d'excuse; **~tance,** entrée, *f.*
admittedly, de l'aveu de tous.
admixture, mélange, *m.*
admonish, (*reprimand*) réprimander; (*warn*) avertir.
admonition, *s.* avertissement, *m.*
ado, *s.* embarras, *m.*; *without further ~*, sans plus de façons.
adolescen|ce, adolescence, *f.*; **~t,** adolescent.
adopt, adopter; **~ion,** adoption, *f.*
adopted, *adj.* adopti|f, ~ve.
ador|e, adorer; **~er,** adorat|eur, ~rice, *s.m.f.*; **~ation,** adoration, *f.*
adorn, *v.a.* orner (de).
adornment, *s.* parure, *f.*
adrift, *adv.* (*naut.*) en dérive; *to cast ~*, laisser à l'abandon; *go ~*, (*lit. and fig.*) aller* (être) à la dérive.
adroit, adroit; **~ness,** adresse, *f.*; **~ly,** avec adresse.
adulat|ion, adulation, *f.*; **~ory,** adulat|eur, ~rice.
adult, *adj. and s.m.f.* adulte.
adulterat|e, *v.a.* frelater; **~ion,** adultération, *f.*
adulter|er, adultère, *m.f.*; **~ous,** adultère; **~y,** adultère, *m.*
adumbrate, *v.a.* ébaucher.
advance, *s.* progrès, *m.*; (*pay*) avances, *f.pl.*; (*price*) augmentation, *f.*; (*rank*) avancement, *m.*; (*mil.*) marche en avant, *f.*; **~ment,** avancement, *m.*
advance, *v.a.n.* avancer; (*price*) †hausser; *v.a.* (*interests*) soigner.
advantag|e, *s.* avantage; *turn to ~*, mettre* à profit; *have the ~ of*, l'emporter sur; *to the best ~*, le plus avantageusement; *take ~ of*, (*avail oneself of*) profiter de; (*overreach*) abuser de; **~ous,** avantageu|x, ~se.
advent, *s.* venue, *f.*; (*eccles.*) Avent, *m.*
adventitious, (*casual*) accidentel, ~le.
adventure, *s.* aventure, *f.*
adventurer, aventur|ier, ~ière, *m.f.*
adventurous, †hardi; (*rash*) téméraire.
adverb, adverbe, *m.*
adversary, adversaire, *m.*
adverse, contraire; (*opposite*) adverse.
adversity, adversité, *f.*
advert to, *v. n.* faire* allusion à.
advertise, (*papers*) annoncer; (*placard*) afficher; (*inform*) avertir; **~ment** (*papers*) annonce, *f.*; (*placard*) affiche, *f.*
advice, *s.* conseil, *m.*; (*comm.*) avis, *m.*; *he will listen to no ~*, il ne fait qu'à sa guise.
advisab|le, opportun; **~ility,** opportunité, *f.*
advise, *v.a.* conseiller.
advised, (*things*) **well ~,** bien avisé; **ill ~,** malavisé; *keep ~ of*, tenir au courant de; **~ly,** en connaissance de cause.
advocate, *s.* (*law*) avocat, *m.*; *v.a.* (*recommend*) conseiller.
adze, (*carp.*) (h)erminette, *f.*
advowson, (*eccles.*) patronage, *m.*
aedile, édile, *m.*
Aeolian harp, †harpe éolienne, *f.*
aerial, *n.* (*wireless*) antenne, *f.*; **trailing ~,** (*aeron.*) antenne déroulable, *f.*; **frame ~,** (*wireless*) cadre de T.S.F., *m.*
aerial, *adj.* aérien, -ne; **~ torpedo,** torpille aérienne, *f.*
aerie (eyrie), (*eagle, &c.*) aire, *f.*
aerodrome, aérodrome, *m.*
aeronaut, aéronaute, *m.*; **~ics,** aéronautique, *f.*; **~ical,** aéronautique.
aeroplane, aéroplane, *m.*
aerostat, (*balloon*) aérostat, *m.*
aesthetic, *adj.* esthétique; **~s,** *s.* esthétique, *f.*
afar, *adv.* loin; *from ~*, de loin; (*at a distance*) au loin.
affab|le, affable; **~ility,** affabilité, *f.*
affair, affaire, *f.*
affect, (*concern*) intéresser; (*move*) toucher; (*feign, assume*) affecter (de); **~ation,** affectation, *f.*
affected, *adj.* (*artificial*) guindé; (*disease*) atteint (de); (*style*) maniéré; **~ly,** d'une manière affectée.
affecting, *adj.* touchant.
affection, (*love, med.*) affection, *f.*; **~ate,** affectueu|x, ~se; **~ately,** affectueusement; *~ately yours*, à vous de tout cœur.
affiance, *v.a.* fiancer.
affiliat|e, *v.a.* affilier; **~ion,** attribution de paternité, *f.*
affinity, alliance, *f.*; (*fig.*) affinité, *f.*
affirm, affirmer; **~ation,** affirmation, *f.*; (*law*) déclaration, *f.*; **~ative,** *s.* affirmative, *f.*; *adj.* **~ive, ~ory,** affirmati|f, ~ve; *reply in the ~ative*, répondre affirmativement.
affix, *v.a.* (*stamp, seal, &c.*) apposer.
afflatus, (*breath*) souffle, *m.*; (*inspiration*), inspiration, *f.*
afflict, *v.a.* affliger (de); **~ion,** affliction, *f.*
affluen|ce, (*riches*) opulence, *f.*; **~t,** *adj.* opulent; *s.* (*river*) affluent, *m.*
afford, *v.a.* donner; (*means*) avoir les moyens de.
afforest, *v.a.* convertir en forêt; **~ation,** afforestation, *f.*
affranchise, *v.a.* (*free*) affranchir.
affray, *s.* rixe, *f.*
affright, *v.a.* effrayer.
affront, *s.* affront, *m.*; *v.a.* (*confront*) affronter; ⚠ affronter *does not* = *'insult'*, *'offend'*, *which* = insulter.
afield, *adv.* aux champs; *far ~*, au loin.
afire, *adv.* en feu.
aflame, *adv.* en flammes.
afloat, *adv.* (*naut.*) à flot; *keep ~*, (*fig.*) se maintenir* à flot.
afoot, *adv.* à pied; *set ~*, mettre* en train.
afore, (*naut.*) à l'avant.
aforenamed, *adj.* susnommé.
aforesaid, *adj.* susdit.
aforethought, *adj.* prémédité.
aforetime, *adv.* autrefois.
afraid, *adj.* effrayé; *to be ~ of*, avoir peur de.

afresh, *adv.* de nouveau.
African, *adj.* (a) *and s.m.f.* Africain, -e; ~ **marigold,** (*bot.*) œillet d'Inde, *m.*
aft, *adv.* (*naut.*) à l'arrière.
after, afterwards, *adv.* ensuite; *inquire* ~, s'informer de; (*pers.*) prendre* des nouvelles de.
after, *prep.* après; (*artist, &c.*) d'après; (*according to*) suivant; *conj.* après que+ *ind.*
afterglow, lueur du coucher, *f.*
after-life, in, *adv.* à l'âge mûr.
aftermath, *s.* regain, *m.*
afternoon, après-midi, *s.m.f.* (*invar.*); ~ **tea,** five-o'clock, *m.*
after-taste, arrière-goût, *m.*
afterthought, réflexion tardive, *f.*
again, encore; *verbs with prefix* re- *often suffice, e.g.* revenir = *come again*; ~ *and* ~, maintes et maintes fois; *now and* ~, de temps en temps; *as much* ~, deux fois autant; *half as much* ~, la moitié en plus; *over and over* ~, mille et mille fois.
against, *prep.* contre; *over* ~, vis-à-vis de.
agape, *adv.* la bouche béante.
agaric, (*bot.*) agaric, *m.*
agate, agate, *f.*
age, âge, *m.*; (*very long time*) siècle, *m.*; ~ **limit,** limite d'âge, *f.*; *Middle Ages,* moyen âge, *m.*; *old* ~, *old-*~ *pension, see* OLD; *be of, under* ~, être majeur, mineur; *in the flower of his* ~, *see* 'FLOWER'; ~ *of discretion,* âge de raison; *what is your* ~? quel âge avez-vous? ; *he is 20 years of* ~, il a vingt ans; *v.a.n.* vieillir.
aged, middle- ~, *see* 'MIDDLE'.
agency, (*medium*) entremise, *f.*; (*comm.*) agence, *f.*
agenda, *s.* ordre du jour, *m.* ⚠ agenda *in French* = *'note-book'.*
agent, agent, *m.* (*comm.*) commissionnaire, *m.*
agglomerat|e, *v.a.* agglomérer; *v.n.* s'agglomérer; ~**ion,** agglomération, *f.*
agglutinat|e, *v.a.* agglutiner; ~**ion,** agglutination, *f.*
aggrandize, *v.a.* agrandir; ~**ment,** agrandissement, *m.*
aggravate, (*increase gravity of*) aggraver, ⚠ *which does not* = *'exasperate' which* = exaspérer.
aggravat|ing, (*increasing gravity of offence, burden, &c.*) aggravant. ⚠ *aggravating* = *exasperating* = exaspérant; ~**ion,** aggravation, irritation, *f.*
aggregate, *s.* masse, *f.*; *in the* ~, au total.
aggregation, agrégation, *f.*; (*to a society*) affiliation, *f.*
aggress|ion, agression, *f.*; ~**ive,** agressi|f, ~ve; ~**or,** agresseur, *m.*
aggrieve, *v.a.* (*offend*) blesser.
aghast, *adj.* abasourdi.
agil|e, agile; ~**ity,** agilité, *f.*
agitat|e, agiter; (*discuss*) débattre; ~**or,** agitat|eur, ~rice, *m.f.*; ~**ion,** agitation, *f.*
agnostic, *adj. and s.m.* agnostique; ~**ism,** agnosticisme, *m.*
ago, *adv.* il y a; *long* ~, il y a longtemps; *a week* ~, il y a huit jours.
agog, *to be all* ~ *to,* griller d'envie de.
agonize, *v.n.* souffrir* l'agonie; ⚠ agoniser = *to be dying.*
agonizing, (*things*) navrant.
agony, agonie, *f.*
agrarian, agraire.
agree, *v.n.* être d'accord (avec); (*resemble*) se ressembler; ~ *on,* convenir* sur; ~ *to,* consentir à; ~ *with,* (*health*) convenir* à; ~ *together,* s'entendre; *entirely* ~ *with,* abonder dans le sens de; ~ *to differ,* constater le désaccord.
agreeable, agréable; (*in conformity with*) d'accord avec; *be* ~ *to,* ne pas demander mieux que de.
agreed! *interj.* d'accord!
agreement, (*harmony*), accord, *m.*; (*compact*) convention, *f.*; (*arrangement*) arrangement, *m.*; (*comm.*) contrat, *m.* ⚠ *not* agrément *which* = *approval, pleasure, charm*; *by mutual* ~, de gré à gré.
agricultural, agricole, ~ **implements,** instruments aratoires, *m.pl.*; ~ **show,** *s.* concours agricole, *m.*
agricultur|e, agriculture, *f.*; ~ **ist,** agriculteur, *m.*
aground, *adv.* (*naut.*) échoué; *run* ~, *v.n.* s'échouer.
ague, fièvre intermittente, *f.*
ahead, *adv.* (*naut.*) en avant; **go-** ~, *adj.* progressi|f, ~ve; (*enterprising*) entreprenant; (*interj.*) en avant; *prep.* ~ *of,* en avant de; *get* ~ *of,* devancer; ~ *of time,* en avance; *full steam* ~, en avant à toute vitesse.
ahoy, *interj.* (*naut.*) ohé!
aid, *s.* aide, *f.*; (*pers.*) aide, *m.*; *first* ~, premiers soins, *m.pl.*; *first-*~ *station,* poste de secours, *m.*; *v.a.* aider.
aigrette, aigrette, *f.*
ail, *v.n.* être souffrant; *what* ~*s you?* qu'avez-vous? ~**ment,** indisposition, *f.*
aileron, (*aeron.*) aileron, *m.*
aim, *s.* (*aiming*) visée, *f.*; (*object*) point de mire, *m.*; (*fig.*) but, *m.*; *miss one's* ~, manquer son coup; ~**less,** ~**lessly,** sans but.
aim, *v.a.* ajuster; (*blow*) allonger; (*cannon*) pointer; *v.n.* viser; ~ *at,* viser; ~ *high,* (*lit. and fig.*) viser †haut.
air, *s.* (*lit., fig., aspect*) air, *m.*; *beat the* ~, donner des coups d'épée dans l'eau; *give oneself* ~*s,* se donner des airs; *in the open* ~, en plein air; ~*s and graces,* minauderies, *f.pl.*; ~ **bump,** (*aeron.*) remous d'air, *m.*; ~**-cushion,** coussin à air, *m.*; ~ **fleet,** flotte aérienne, *f.*; ~ **force,** armée de l'air, *f.*; ~**-gun,** fusil à vent, *m.*; ~**-hole,** soupirail, *m.*; (*furnace*) évent, *m.*; ~ **letter,** lettre-avion, *f.*; ~ **liner,** avion de ligne régulière, *m.*; ~**-mail,** poste aérienne, *f.*; *by* ~*-mail,* par avion; ~ **parcel,** colis avion, *m.*; ~ **-pocket,** (*aeron.*) trou d'air, *m.*; ~**-raid,** raid aérien, *m.*; ~**ship,** dirigeable, *m.*; ~ **squadron,** escadrille, *f.*; ~ **station,** aéro-

port, *m.*; ~**tight**, imperméable; ~**way**, voie aérienne, *f. See also below.*
air, *v.a.* (*clothes*) ressuyer; (*rooms*) aérer; (*feelings, &c.*) donner libre cours à.
aircraft, les avions, *m. pl.*; ~ **-carrier**, porte-avion, *m.*
airman, aviateur, *m.*
airport, aéroport, *m.*; (*large*) aérogare, *f.*
airship, dirigeable, *m.*
air|y, aéré; (*flippant*) lég|er, ~ère; ~**iness**, (*fig.*) légèreté, *f.*; ~**ily**, légèrement; ~**ing**, *s.* (*walk*) tour, *m.*
aisle, (*eccles.*) bas côté, *m.*
ajar, *adj.* entr'ouvert.
akimbo, with arms, le poing sur la hanche.
akin to, (*pers.*) apparenté à; (*things*) *use rel. clause with* tenir* de.
alabaster, albâtre, *m.*
alack, alackaday! *interj.* hélas!
alacrity, empressement, *m.*
alarm, alarme, *f.*; ~ **signal**, signal d'alarme, *m.*; *v.a.* alarmer; ~**ist**, *adj. and s.m.f.* alarmiste.
alarum-clock, réveil, *m.*
alas! *interj.* hélas!
alb, (*eccles.*) aube, *f.*
albatross, albatros, *m.*
albeit, *conj.* quoique (*subj.*).
albino, *adj. and s.m.f.* albinos.
album, album, *m.*
alchem|y, alchimie, *f.*; ~**ist**, alchimiste, *m.*
alcohol, alcool, *m.*; ~**ism**, alcoolisme, *m.*; ~**ic**, alcoolique.
alcove, alcôve, *f.*
alder, (*bot.*) aune, *m.*; ~**-bed**, aunaie, *f.*
alderman, échevin, *m.*
ale, aile *and* ale, *f.*; ~**-house**, cabaret, *m.*; ~**-wife**, cabaretière, *f.*
alert, *adj. and s.f.* alerte; *on the* ~, sur le qui vive; ~**ness**, vigilance, *f.*; ~**ly**, avec vigilance.
alexandrine, (*verse*) alexandrin, *m.*
algebra, algèbre, *f.*; ~**ical**, algébrique.
alias, *adv.* autrement dit *or* nommé; *s.* nom d'emprunt, *m.*
alibi, alibi, *m.*
alien, *adj. and s.m.f.* étrang|er, ~ère.
alienate, *v.a.* aliéner; (*hearts, &c.*) s'aliéner.
alienation, aliénation, *f.*; (*med.*) aliénation mentale, *f.*
alienist, (*med.*) médecin aliéniste, *m.*
alight, *adj.* allumé; *to be* ~, brûler; (*on fire*) flamber.
alight, *v.n.* descendre (être); (*bird*) s'abattre.
align, aline, *v.a.* (*gen. and mil.*) aligner; ~**ment**, alignement, *m.*
alike, *adj.* semblable; *adv.* également; *be* ~, se ressembler.
aliment, aliment, *m.*; ~**ary**, alimentaire.
alimony, pension alimentaire, *f.*
alive, *adj.* vivant; (*lively*) vi|f, ~ve; (*full of life*) animé; *dead or* ~, mort ou vif; *be* ~ *with*, fourmiller de.
alkali, alcali, *m.*
all, *s. and pron.* (*everything, the whole*) tout, *m.*; (*all people*) tous, tout le monde, *m.*; ~ *of you*, vous tous; *above* ~, surtout; ~ *told*, tout compte fait; *it's* ~ *up with him*, c'en est fait de lui; ~ *found*, tous les frais de maintien payés; ~ *at once*, tout d'un coup; ~ *is not gold that glitters*, tout ce qui brille n'est pas or.
all, *adj.* tout, toute, tous, toutes (*gen.* + *article or specifying word*); *to* ~ *intents and purposes*, à tous égards; *on* ~ *fours*, à quatre pattes; *on* ~ *hands*, de tous côtés; *once for* ~, une fois pour toutes; *with* ~ *speed*, en toute †hâte; *for* ~ *that*, malgré cela.
all, *adv.* tout (*only takes concord* + *word beginning with consonant or asp.* H); *not at* ~, point du tout; ~ *the better*, tant mieux; ~ *but* + *verb*, *use* faillir* *or* penser + *inf.*; ~ *the more*, d'autant plus; ~ *the same*, tout de même; *it's* ~ *one to me*, ce m'est tout un; *it's* ~ *the same to me*, cela m'est égal; ~*-powerful*, tout-puissant.
All Hallows, ~ Saints, (*eccles.*) La Toussaint.
All Souls' Day, jour des morts, *m.*
allspice, (*bot.*) herbe aux épices, *f.*
allay, *v.a.* (*quarrel*) apaiser; (*thirst, &c.*) soulager.
alleg|e, alléguer; ~**ation**, allégation, *f.*
allegiance, fidélité, *f.*
allego|ry, allégorie, *f.*; ~**ical**, allégorique.
(h)alleluia(jah), *s.* alléluia, *m.*
alleviat|e, *v.a.* soulager; ~**ion**, soulagement, *m.*
alley, (*town*) ruelle, *f.*; ⚠ *not* allée *which* = 'garden path', 'walk'.
alliance, alliance, *f.*; (*kin*) parenté, *f.*
alligator, alligator, m.
alliteration, allitération, *f.*
allocat|e, attribuer; ~**ion**, allocation, *f.*
allocution, allocution, *f.*
allot, *v.a.* (*shares*) départir*; (*grant*) accorder.
allotment, (*share*) part, *f.*; (*comm.*) répartition, *f.*; (*land*) terrain, *m.*
allow, *v.a.* permettre* (à + *pers.* de + *inf.*); (*endure*) souffrir*; (*admit*) admettre*; (*grant*) accorder; *v.n.* ~ *for*, tenir* compte de; ~*ing for*, déduction faite de; *no smoking* ~*ed*, défense de fumer.
allowable, permis.
allowance, (*expense*) allocation, *f.*; (*Inc. Tax*) déduction, *f.*; (*ration*) ration, *f.*; *make* ~ *for*, avoir égard à; *reduce* ~ *of*, rationner.
alloy, alliage, *m.*
allspice, piment, *m.*
allude to, *v.n.* (*pers.*) faire allusion à.
allure, séduire*; ~**ment**, séduction, *f.*
alluring, *adj.* séduisant; (*pleasure*) alléchant.
allus|ion, allusion, *f.*; ~**ive**, allusi|f, ~ve; ~**ively**, par allusion.
alluvial, alluvial.
ally, *s.* allié, -e, *m.f.*; *v.a.* allier; ~ *oneself to*, s'allier à.

almanac, almanach, *m.*
almighty, *adj.* tout-puissant.
almond, amande, *f.*; ~ **-tree,** amandier, *m.*; ~ **-shaped,** en amande.
almoner, aumônier, *m.*
almost, *adv.* presque.
alms, aumône, *f.*; ~ **-box,** tronc des aumônes, *m.*; ~**-house,** hospice, *m.*
aloe, (*bot.*) aloès, *m.*
aloft, *adv.*†haut.
alone, *adj.* seul; *leave* ~, laisser tranquille; *let* ~ *his age,* sans compter son âge; *a doctor* ~ *can tell,* seul un médecin peut le dire.
along, *all* ~, (*temp.*) tout le temps; *go, come* ~ *with,* accompagner; *prep.* le long de; *interj. come* ~*!* allons!
alongside, *adv.* (*naut.*) le long du bord; *prep.* ~ *of,* le long de.
aloof, *adv.* à l'écart; ~**ness,** réserve, *f.*
aloud, *adv.* à haute voix.
alpaca, alpaga, *m.*
alpenstock, alpenstock, *m.*
alpha, alpha, *m.*
alphabet, alphabet, *m.*; ~**ical,** alphabétique.
Alpin|e, *adj.* alpin; ~**ist,** alpiniste, *m.*
already, déjà.
Alsatian, *adj.* (a) *and s.m.f.* Alsacien, -ne.
also, aussi; (*furthermore*) de plus.
altar, autel, *m.*; ~**-cloth,** nappe d'autel, *f.*; ~**-piece,** tableau d'autel, *m.*; ~**-screen,** rétable, *m.*
alter, *v.a.n.* changer; ~ *one's mind,* changer d'avis; ~**ation,** changement, *m.*; (*modification*) modification, *f.*; ~**able,** altérable.
altercation, altercation, *f.*
alternate, *v.a.n.* alterner.
alternate, alternative, *adj.* alternati|f, ~ve; ~**ly,** tour à tour.
alternative, *s.* alternative, *f.*
alternation, alternance, *f.*
although, quoique (*subj.*).
altimeter, altimètre, *m.*
altitude, élévation, *f.*
alto, (*woman's voice*) contralto, *m.*; ~ **-relievo** (*sculpt.*) †haut-relief, *m.*
altogether, *adv.* tout à fait.
altruis|m, altruisme, *m.*; ~**tic,** *adj. and s.m.* altruiste.
alum, alum, *m.*
aluminium, aluminium, *m.*
alveolate, alvéolé.
always, toujours.
a.m., *adv.* avant-midi; *7 a.m.*, 7 heures du matin.
amalgam, amalgame, *m.*
amalgamat|e, *v.a.* amalgamer; (*comm.*) fusionner, *v.n.* s'amalgamer, ~**ion,** amalgamation, fusion, *f.*
amanuensis, secrétaire, *m.*
amaranth, *s.* amarante, *f.*; *adj.* (*colour*) amarante (*invar.*).
amaryllis, (*bot.*) amaryllis, *f.*
amass, *v.a.* accumuler.
amateur, amateur, *m.*
amatory, amoureu|x, ~se.
amaze, *v.a.* frapper d'étonnement; ~**d,** ébahi.
amazement, (*slight*) étonnement, *m.*; (*great*) ébahissement, *m.*
amazing, étonnant.
Amazon, *s.* amazone, *f.*
ambassad|or, ~**ress,** ambassad|eur, ~rice, *m.f.*
amber, *s.* ambre, *m.*; ~**-tipped,** à bout d'ambre.
ambergris, ambre gris, *m.*
ambidext|rous, ambidextre; ~**erity,** ambidextérité, *f.*
ambient, *adj.* ambiant.
ambigu|ity, ambiguïté, *f.*; ~**ous,** ambigu, ~ë; ~**ously,** ambigument.
ambit, contour, *m.*
ambiti|on, ambition, *f.*; ~**ous,** ambitieu|x, ~se; *be* ~*ous of,* ambitionner.
amble, *s.* amble, *m.*; *v.n.* aller l'amble.
ambrosia, ambroisie, *f.*; ~**l,** *adj.* ambrosiaque.
ambulance, ambulance, *f.*; ~ **train,** train sanitaire, *m.*
ambush (ambuscade), *s.* (*mil.*) embuscade, *f.*; (*fig.*) guet-apens, *m.*; *v.a.* embusquer; *lay an* ~, dresser une embuscade; *lie in* ~, se tenir* en embuscade.
ameliorat|e, *v.a.* améliorer; ~**ion,** amélioration, *f.*
amenable, (*responsible*) responsable (*to* = envers, *of pers., for* = de, *of things*); (*subject to*), soumis à.
amend, *v.a.* (*correct*) corriger; (*improve*) amender; (*accounts*) rectifier; *v.n.* se corriger.
amendment, (*fig. and polit.*) amendement, *m.*
amends, dédommagement, *m.*; *make* ~ *for,* dédommager de.
amenity, (*pers.*) aménité, *f.*; (*place*) charme, *m.*; *pl.* (*comforts*) commodités, *f.pl.*
American, *adj.* (a) *and s.m.f.* Américain, -e; ~**ism,** américanisme, *m.*; ~**ize,** américaniser; ~ **cloth,** moleskine, *f.*
amethyst, améthyste, *f.*
amiab|le, *adj.* aimable; ~**ility,** amabilité, *f.*; ~**ly,** aimablement.
amicabl|e, amical; ~**y,** amicalement.
amid, amidst, *prep.* au milieu de.
amidships, *adv.* au milieu du navire.
amiss, *adv.* mal; *take* ~, prendre* en mal.
ammunition, munitions de guerre, *f.*; ~ **dump,** dépôt de munitions, *m.*
amnesty, amnistie, *f.*
among, *prep.* parmi; (*peoples*) chez; *from* ~, d'entre.
amorous, amoureu|x, ~se; ~**ly,** amoureusement.
amount, *s.* (*money and fig.*) somme, *f.*; (*total*) montant, *m.*; (*quantity*) quantité, *f.*; ~ *brought forward* (*bkkpg.*) report, *m.*
amount to, *v.n.* monter (être) à; (*be equivalent to*) se réduire* à.

amphibi|an, *s.* amphibie, *m.*; **~ous,** amphibie.
amphitheatre, amphithéâtre, *m.*
amphora, amphora, *f.*
ampl|e, ample; **~y,** amplement.
amplif|y, amplifier; (*increase*) augmenter; **~ication,** amplification, *f.*
amplitude, ampleur, *f.*
ampulla, ampoule, *f.*
amputat|e, amputer; **~ion,** amputation, *f.*
amuck, to run, (*approx.*) courir* en menaçant dans un accès de folie.
amulet, amulette, *f.*
amuse, *v.a.* amuser; ~ *oneself,* s'amuser; *be amused by,* s'amuser de.
amus|ement, amusement, *m.*; **~ing,** amusant.
anachronism, anachronisme, *m.*
anacoluthon, anacoluthe, *f.*
anacreontic, (*verse*) anacréontique.
anaemi|a, anémie, *f.*; **~c,** exsangue.
anagram, anagramme, *f.*
analog|y, *s.* analogie, *f.*; **~ous, ~ic,** analogue.
analys|is, analyse, *f.*; **~t,** analyste, *m.f.*; **~e,** analyser.
analytical, analytique.
anapaest, (*verse*) anapest, *m.*
anarch|y, anarchie, *f.*; **~ist,** anarchiste, *m.*; **~ical,** anarchique.
anathema, anathème, *m.*; *v.a.* **~tize,** anathématiser.
anatom|y, anatomie, *f.*; **~ist,** anatomiste, *m.f.*
ancest|or, ~ress, ancêtre, *m.f.*; **~ral,** ancestral.
ancestors, ancestry, aïeux, *m.pl.*
anchor, *s.* ancre, *f.*
anchor, *v.a.n.* mouiller; *cast* ~, mouiller l'ancre; **~age,** mouillage, *m.*
anchorite, anachorète, *m.*
anchovy, anchois, *m.*
ancient, *adj. and s.m.* ancien, -ne; (*antique*) *adj.* antique.
ancillary to, subordonné à.
and, *conj.* et; (*between two comparatives*) en, *better ~ better,* de mieux en mieux. *See* BOTH . . . AND.
andiron, chenet, *m.*; (*large kitchen* ~) landier, *m.*
andrew, merry ~, paillasse, *m.*
anecdot|e, anecdote, *f.*; **~ist,** anecdotier, *m.*; **~al,** anecdotique.
anemometer, anémomètre, *m.*
anemone, (*bot.*) anémone, *f.*
anent, *prep.* touchant.
aneroid, (*barometer*) *adj. and s.m.* anéroïde.
anew, *adv.* de nouveau.
anfractuosity, détour, *m.*
angel, ange, *m.*; (*money*) angelot, *m.*; **~ic,** angélique.
angel-fish, angelot, *m.*
angelica, (*bot.*) angélique, *f.*
angelus, angélus, *m.*
anger, *s.* colère, *f.*; *v.a.* fâcher.
angina, (*med.*) angine, *f.*; ~ **pectoris,** angine de poitrine.
angle, angle, *m.*
angle, *v.n.* (*fish*) pêcher à la ligne.
angler, pêcheur à la ligne, *m.*
Anglican, *adj.* (*when an adj. use small letter*) *and s.m.f.* Anglican, -e.
anglicize, angliciser.
Anglo-Saxon, *adj.* (*when an adj. use small letter*) *and s.m.f.* Anglo-Saxon, -ne.
angr|y, (*lit., sea*) courroucé; (*wind*) furieu|x, **~se;** (*wound*) enflammé; *get ~y,* se fâcher (de); *~y with,* fâché contre; **~ily,** avec colère.
anguish, angoisse, *f.*
angular, angulaire; (*pers.*) sec, sèche.
aniline, *s.* (*dye*) aniline, *f.*
animadvert on, *v.n.* censurer.
animadversion, censure, *f.*
animal, *s.* animal, *m.*; *adj.* animal; ~ **spirits,** fougue, *f.*; **~ism,** sensualité, *f.*
animat|e, *v.a.* animer; **~ion,** *s.* vivacité, *f.*; **~ed,** (*of style*) brûlant.
animosity, animus, animosité, *f.* (contre).
ani|se, (*bot.*) anis, *m.*; **~seed,** (*liquor*) anisette, *f.*
ankle, cheville, *f.*; **~-bone,** astragale, *f.*; **~-deep,** jusqu'à la cheville.
annals, annales, *f.pl.*; **annalist,** annaliste, *m.*
anneal, (*glass, metal*) recuire*.
annex, *s.* (*build.*) dépendance, *f.*; *v.a.* annexer; **~ation,** annexion, *f.*; ⚠ *annexation is not French.*
annihilat|e, anéantir; **~ion,** anéantissement, *m.*
anniversary, anniversaire, *m.*
annotat|e, annoter; **~ion,** annotation, *f.*
announce, annoncer; **~ment,** annonce, *f.*
annoy, contrarier; (*torment*) tourmenter; (*bore*) ennuyer; **~ance,** contrariété, *f.*; **~ing,** contrariant; (*pers.*) importun.
annual, *s.* (*year-book*) annuaire, *m.*; (*bot.*) plante annuelle, *f.*; *adj.* annuel, -le.
annuit|y, (*life*) rente viagère, *f.*; (*fin.*) annuité, *f.*; **~ant,** rentier, *m.*
annul, annuler.
annul|et, (*ring and arch.*) annelet, *m.*; **~ar,** *adj.* annulaire.
Annunciation, (*eccles.*) Annonciation, *f.*
annunciate, *v.a.* annoncer.
anodyne, *s.* calmant, *m.*
anoint, oindre*.
anomal|ous, irréguli|er, **~ère;** **~y,** anomalie, *f.*
anon, *adv.* tout à l'heure.
anonymous, anonyme; **~ly,** anonymement.
another, *pron. and adj.* un autre, une autre; *one* ~, l'un l'autre, l'une l'autre, &c. *With dat. and trans. verbs, reflexive form of verb also obligatory and often sufficient alone*; ils se parlent l'un à l'autre (*or* ils se parlent *alone*), *they are speaking to each other*; **~'s,** d'autrui.
answer, *s.* réponse, *f.*; (*problem, &c.*) solution, *f.*; *in ~ to* (*letter*), en réponse à;

v.a.n. répondre; (*succeed*) réussir; ~ *for*, répondre pour; ~ *one's purpose*, faire* son affaire; ~ *the door*, aller* (être) *or* venir* (être) ouvrir.
ant, fourmi, *f.*; **white** ~, termite, *m.*; **~-eater,** (*zool.*) fourmilier, *m.*; **~-hill,** fourmilière, *f.*
antagonist, antagoniste, *m.*; **~ic,** antagoniste.
antagon|ism, antagonisme, *m.*; **~ize,** *v.a.* (*provoke*) contrarier; (*neutralize*) neutraliser.
antarctic, *adj.* antarctique.
antecedent, *adj.* antérieur (à); *s.* (*gram.*) antécédent, *m.*
antecedents, (*past*) antécédents, *m.pl.*
ante|chamber, ~-room, antichambre, *f.*
antedate, *s.* antidate, *f.*; *v.a.* antidater.
antediluvian, *adj.* antédiluvien, -ne.
antelope, antilope, *f.*
antenna, (*insects*) antenne, *f.*
antepenultimate, *adj. and s.f.* antépénultième.
anterior, antérieur (à).
anthem, (*eccles.*) antienne, *f.*
anthology, anthologie, *f.*
anthracite, anthracite, *m.*
anthrax, (*med.*) charbon, *m.*
anti-aircraft, *adj.* anti-aérien, -ne; contre-avions *also used*; ~ **gun,** canon anti-aérien, *m.*
antic, *s.* (*trick*) habitude, *f.*; (*caper*) gambade, *f.*
antichrist, antéchrist, *m.*
anticipat|e, (*payment*) anticiper; (*precede*) devancer; (*hope for*) s'attendre à; (*difficulty*) prévoir*; **~ion,** anticipation, *f.*; *in* ~ *of*, en attendant; **~ory,** anticipé.
anticlimax, (*rhet.*) gradation inverse, *f.*
anticyclone, anticyclone, *m.*
antidote, antidote, *m.*
antimacassar, voile de fauteuil, *m.*
antimony, antimoine, *m.*
antimonarchical, antimonarchique.
antipath|y, antipathie, *f.*; **~etic,** antipathique (à).
antipodes, antipodes, *m.pl.*
antiquar|ian, ~y, antiquaire, *m.*; **~ian,** *adj.* d'antiquaire.
antiquated, antique; (*out of date*) vieilli.
antiqu|e, *s.* (*relic of past, work of art*) antique, *m.*; *the* ~, antique, *m.*; *adj.* antique; ~ **-dealer,** brocanteur, *m.* **~ity,** antiquité, *f.*
antirrhinum, (*bot.*) gueule-de-loup, *f.*
antiseptic, *adj. and s.m.* antiseptique.
anti-tank, ~ **gun, rifle,** canon, fusil, antichars, *m.*
antithe|sis, antithèse, *f.*; **~tic, ~tical,** antithétique.
antler, andouiller, *m.*
anvil, enclume, *f.*
anx|iety, anxiété, *f.*; **~ious,** inqui|et, ~ète; *be ~ious to*, tenir à; **~iously,** avec anxiété.
any, *pron.* (= *'some' of things with verb*) en; ~ *one*, quelqu'un; *~one* (*at all*) qui que ce soit; *any,* (*at all, things*) n'importe lequel; *there's hardly* ~ *left*, il n'y en a presque plus.
any, *adj.* (*when* = *'some' in interrogative sentences*) du, de la, des; *not* ~, ne . . . pas de; (*every*) tout, *e.g.* tout homme, *any man*; (*the least*) le moindre, la moindre, *e.g.* il n'a pas la moindre chance; ~, (*at all, whatever*) n'importe quel; *scarcely* ~, presque pas de, *e.g.* il n'y a presque pas de lait; *at* ~ *rate, see* 'RATE'; ~ *day*, n'importe quand.
anybody, quelqu'un; *also* personne *without* ne *with interrogative verbs and verbs of doubt, e.g.* je doute que personne l'ait trouvé; ~, (*at all*) n'importe qui.
any more, *adv.* (*with neg. in English*) ne . . . plus; (*time*) plus longtemps.
anything, quelque chose, *m.*; *also* rien *without* ne *with verbs of interrogation and doubt*; ~ (*at all*) n'importe quoi; *if* ~, plutôt, *e.g.* elle est plutôt moins heureuse.
anywhere, n'importe où.
apace, *adv.* vite.
apart, *adv.* (*laid aside, not reckoned*) à part; *set* ~, mettre* de côté; ~ *from, prep.*, en dehors de.
apartment, pièce, *f.*; ⚠ appartement = *suite of rooms*; *furnished ~s*, garni, *m.*
apathy, apathie, *f.*
ape, singe, *m.*; *f.* guenon; *v.a.* singer.
aperient, *s.* purgatif, *m.*; ⚠ *not* apéritif *which* = *'appetizer', 'drink before meals'*.
aperture, ouverture, *f.*
apex, sommet, *m.*
aphaeresis, (*gram.*) aphérèse, *f.*
aphis, aphidien, *m.*
aphorism, aphorisme, *m.*
apiary, rucher, *m.*
apiece, *adv.* (*pers.*) par tête.
apish, de singe; ~ *trick*, singerie, *f.*
apocalyp|se, apocalypse, *f.*; **~tic,** apocalyptique.
Apocryph|a, the, livres apocryphes, *m.pl.*; **~l,** apocryphe.
apogee, apogée, *m.*
apologetic, (*pers.*) *use rel. with* s'excuser; (*vindicatory*) apologétique.
apologist, apologiste, *m.*
apologize, *v.n.* faire des excuses; ~ *for*, s'excuser de.
apologue, apologue, *m.*
apology, (*excuse*) excuse, *f.*; (*written defence*) apologie, *f.*
apoplexy, apoplexie, *f.*
aposta|te, *adj. and s.m.* apostat; **~cy,** apostasie, *f.*
apost|le, apôtre, *m.*; **~olic,** apostolique; *~s' creed*, symbole (des apôtres), *m.*
apostrophe, (*gram., rhet.*) apostrophe, *f.*
apothecary, pharmacien apothécaire, *m.*
apotheosis, apothéose, *f.*
appal, *v.a.* épouvanter.
appalling, épouvantable; **~ly,** épouvantablement.
ap(p)anage, apanage, *m.*; (*fig.*) lot, *m.*
apparatus, appareil, *m.*
apparel, habits, *m.pl.*; **~led,** vêtu (de).
apparent, manifeste; **~ly,** manifestement.

apparition, apparition, *f.*
apparitor, (*univ.*) appariteur, *m.*
appeal, *s.* appel, *m.*; *v.n.* en appeler (à); (*attract*) plaire*; (*law*) se pourvoir* en cassation.
appear, *v.n.* (*sudden*) apparaître*; (*be seen*) paraître*; (*seem*) sembler; (*law, &c.*) comparaître.*
appearance (*sudden*) apparition, *f.*; (*look*) air, *m.*; (*probability*) apparence; *put in an* ~, faire* une apparition; *judge by* ~*s*, juger sur l'étiquette du sac; *keep up* ~*s*, garder les apparences.
appease, apaiser.
appellation, dénomination, *f.*
append, *v.a.* (*signature, &c.*) apposer; (*attach*) attacher.
appendicitis, (*med.*) appendicite, *f.*
appendix, (*book*) appendice, *m.*; (*med.*) appendice vermiforme, *m.*
appertain to, *v.n.* appartenir* à.
appetite, appétit, *m.*, (*fig.*) soif, *f.*
appetiz|er, apéritif, *m.*; ~**ing,** appétissant.
applaud, *v.a.* (*clap hands*) applaudir; (*approve of*) applaudir à.
applause, *n.* acclamation, *f.*; *carried with* ~, voté par acclamation.
apple, pomme, *f.*; (*fig. of eye*) prunelle, *f.*; ~ **-fritter,** beignet de pommes, *m.*; ~ **loft,** fruitier, *m.*; ~ **-tart,** tarte aux pommes, *f.*; ~ **-tree,** pommier, *m.*; ~ **-green,** vert pomme, *invar.*
appliance, (*mech.*) appareil, *m.*; (*med.*) remède, *m.*
applicable, applicable (à).
applicant, (*post*) postulant-e, *m.f.*; (*shares*) souscripteur, *m.*
application, (*request*) demande, *f.*; (*shares*) souscription, *f.*; (*concentration, diligence*) application, *f.*; ⚠ demande *never = concentration, and* application *never = request.*
apply, *v.n.* (*be suitable, to the point*) avoir rapport à; ~ *for* (*post*) solliciter; (*shares*) souscrire* à; ~ *to* (*pers.*) s'adresser à; *v.a.* (*put close, administer, use*) appliquer; (*motor brake, &c.*) serrer.
appoint, (*pers., committee, &c.*) nommer; (*fix*) désigner; (*equip*) équiper; *at the* ~*ed time*, à l'heure fixée. [ordonné.
appointed, *part.*; *well* ~, (*household*) bien
appointment, (*to a post*) nomination, *f.*; (*post*) emploi, *m.*; (*meeting*) rendez-vous, *m.*; *make an* ~ *with*, donner un rendez-vous à; ⚠ Fr. *appointements* = salary.
apportion, répartir (*like* finir); ~**ment,** répartition, *f.*
apposite, à propos; ~**ly,** avec à propos; ~**ness,** à propos, *m.*
apposition, apposition, *f.*
apprais|e, apprize, priser; ~**er,** commissaire-priseur, *m.*
appreciabl|e, appréciable; ~**y,** d'une manière appréciable.
appreciate, *v.a.* apprécier; *v.n.* (*in value*) s'améliorer.
appreciation, appréciation, *f.*; (*value*) plus-value, *f.*
appreciative, appréciati|f, ~ve.
apprehend, *v.a.* (*seize, fear*) appréhender; (*understand*) comprendre*.
apprehens|ion, (*fear*) appréhension, *f.*; (*arrest*) arrestation, *f.*; (*brain*) intelligence, *f.*; ~**ible,** compréhensible; *be* ~**ive** *for*, craindre* pour.
apprentice, *n.* apprenti-e, *m.f.*; ~**ship,** apprentissage, *m.*; *v.a.* mettre* en apprentissage.
apprise, (*inform*) informer.
apprize. *See* APPRAISE.
approach, *s.* approche, *f.*; ~**es** (*place*) abords, *m.pl.*; *make* ~*es to*, faire* des avances à; *v.a.* s'approcher de; *v.n.* s'approcher; ~**ing,** prochain; ~**able,** accessible.
approbation, approbation, *f.*; *on* ~ (*goods*) à condition.
appropriate, *adj.* (*suitable*) convenable (pour); ~ *to*, (*adapted for*) propre à; ~**ness,** justesse, *f.*; ~**ly,** convenablement.
appropriate, *v.a.* s'approprier; (*use, &c. funds*) affecter; ~ *out of*, prélever sur.
appropriation, appropriation, *f.*; (*money, &c.*) affectation, *f.*
approv|al, approbation; *on* ~, à condition; ~**e,** *v.a.* approuver; ~*e of*, approuver, *v.a.*; ~**ing,** *adj.* approbat|eur, ~rice.
approximate, *adj.* approximati|f, ~ve; ~**ly,** approximativement.
approximat|e to, *v.n.* se rapprocher à; ~**ion** (*rough estimate*) approximation, *f.*
appurtenance, appartenance, *f.*
apricot, abricot, *m.*
April, avril, *m.*; ~**fool,** poisson d'avril, *m.*; ~ **shower,** giboulée de mars, *f.*
apron, (*lit. and veh.*) tablier, *m.*; *tied to the* ~*-strings of*, (être) pendu aux basques de.
apse, (*arch.*) abside, *f.*
apt, (*appropriate*) à propos; (*quick to*) apte à; (*inclined*) sujet (à); (*capable of*) susceptible de; ~**ly,** avec justesse.
aptitude, aptness, aptitude, *f.* (pour).
aqua fortis, eau-forte, *f.*
aquamarine, aigue-marine, *f.*
aquarium, aquarium, *m.*; *pl.* ~**s.**
aquatic, aquatique.
aquatint, aqua-tinta, *f. invar.*
aqueduct, aqueduc, *m.*
aquiline, aquilin.
Arab, *adj.* (a) *and s.m.f.* Arabe; ~**ic,** arabe; *s.* (*lang.*) arabe, *m.*; ~**ian,** arabe; *The Arabian Nights*, Les Mille et Une Nuits; *street* ~, gavroche, *m.*
arabesque, *adj. and s.f.* arabesque.
arable, *adj.* arable.
araucaria, (*bot.*) araucaria, *m.*
arbiter, arbitrator, arbitre, *m.*
arbitrary, arbitraire; ~ *power*, arbitraire, *m.*
arbitrat|e, *v.n.* arbitrer; ~**or,** arbitre, *m.*; ~**ion,** arbitrage, *m.*

arborescen|t, arborescent; **~ce,** arborescence, *f.*
arboriculture, arboriculture, *f.*
arbour, *m.* berceau, *m.*
arbutus, (*bot.*) arbousier, *m.*
arc, (*circle*) arc, *m.*; **~-lamp,** lampe à arc.
arcade, (*arch.*) arcade, *f.*
arcanum, arcane, *m.*
arch, *adj.* (*roguish*) espiègle; **~ly, d'un** air espiègle; (*extreme, most*) grand.
arch, *s.* (*bridge*) arche, *f.*; (*triumph*) arc, *m.* *See also* ROUND *and* POINTED.
archaeolog|y, archéologie, *f.*; **~ical,** archéologique; **~ist,** archéologue, *m.*
archai|c, archaïque; **~sm,** archaïsme, *m.*
archangel, archange, *m.*
arch|bishop, archevêque, *m.*; **~deacon,** archidiacre, *m.*; **~duke, ~duchess,** archiduc, ~duchesse, *m.f.*; **~idiaconal, iepiscopal,** archidiaconal, archiépiscopal.
arched, *adj.* (*foot, nose, &c.*) busqué; (*vaulted*) voûté.
archer, archer, *m.*
archimandrite, archimandrite, *m.*
archipelago, archipel, *m.*
architect, architecte, *m.*; **~ure,** architecture, *f.*; **~ural,** architectural.
architrave, (*arch.*) architrave, *f.*
archives, archives, *f.pl.*
archway, voûte, *f.*
arctic, arctique.
ard|ent, (*lit. and fig.*) ardent; **~our,** ardeur, *f.*
arduous, (*work, task*) rude; (*steep*) escarpé; **~ly,** péniblement.
area, (*surface*) surface, *f.*; (*extent*) étendue, *f.*; (*locality*) circonscription, *f.*; (*geom.*) aire, *f.*
arena, arène, *f.*
Areopag|us, aréopage, *m.*; **~ite,** aréopagite, *m.*
argand (*Queen Victoria*) **lamp,** quinquet, *m.*
argent, *adj., and s.m.* (*her.*) argent.
Argentine, *adj.* (*when an adj. use small letter*) *and s.m.f.* Argentin, -e.
Argonaut, argonaute, *m.*
argu|e, *v.n.* argumenter; *v.a.* (*question*) discuter; (*infer*) conclure*; (*prove*) prouver; (*maintain*) soutenir*; **~ment,** argument, *m.*; (*dispute*) discussion, *f.*; **~mentative,** *adj.* disputateu|r, ~se; **~able,** contestable.
argus, argus, *m.*
Arian, *adj.* (a) *and s.m.f.* Arien, -ne.
arid, aride; **~ity, ~ness,** *s.* aridité, *f.*
aright, *adv.* bien.
arise, *v.n.* (*get up*) se lever; (*emerge*) surgir; (*come from*) résulter de.
aristocra|cy, aristocratie, *f.*; **~t,** aristocrate, *m.f.*; **~tic,** aristocratique.
arithmetic, arithmétique, *f.*; **~al,** arithmétique.
ark, (*Noah and eccles.*) arche, *f.*
arm, bras, *m.*; (*weapon*) arme, *f.*; **~-in-~,** bras dessus bras dessous; **~-chair,** fauteuil, *m.*; **~ful,** brassée, *f.*; **~-hole,** (*coat, &c.*) emmanchure, *f.*; **~-pit,** aisselle, *f.*; *keep at ~'s length,* tenir* à distance; *pile ~s,* former les faisceaux.
arm, *v.a.* armer; *v.n.* s'armer.
armada, armada, *f.*
armadillo, (*zool.*) tatou, *m.*
armament, armement, *m.*
armature, (*armour*) armure, *f.*; (*dynamo*) armature, *f.*
Armenian, *adj.* (*when an adj. use small letter*) *and s.m.f.* Arménien, -ne.
armistice, armistice, *m.*
armorial, d'armoiries.
armour, armure, *f.*; (*nav.*) blindage, *m.*; **~y,** (*workshop*) armurerie, *f.*; (*room*) salle d'armes, *f.*; **~ed,** (*nav.*) cuirassé; (*train, fort, lorry*) blindé; **~ed car,** automobile blindé, *m.*; **~er,** armurier, *m.*
arms, armes, *f.pl.*; (*her. coat of*) armoiries, *f.pl.*; *be up in ~ against,* s'opposer à; *beat to ~,* battre la générale.
army, armée, *f.*; *standing ~,* armée permanente; ~ **contractor,** fournisseur, *m.*; ~ **doctor,** chirurgien-major, *m.*; ~ **list,** annuaire militaire, *m.*; ~ **service corps,** corps du ravitaillement, *m.*
aroma, arome, *m.*; **~tic,** aromatique.
around, *adv.* autour; *prep.* autour de.
arouse, *v.a.* (*excite, stir up, provoke, urge to insurrection*) soulever; (*awake*) réveiller; (*fig.*) éveiller.
arpeggio, arpège, *m.*
(h)arquebuse, arquebuse, *f.*
arraign, *v.a.* (*law*) traduire* en justice; **~ment,** mise en accusation, *f.*
arrange, arranger; (*negotiate*) débattre; (*put in order, array*) ranger; **~ment,** arrangement, *m.*; (*of parts*) agencement, *m.*; **~ments,** (*plans*) mesures, *f.pl.*
arrant, fieffé.
arras, tapisserie, *f.*
array, *s.* (*battle*) ordre, *m.*; (*pomp*) appareil, *m.*; (*shop window*) étalage, *m.*; *v.a.* ranger.
arrears, arriéré, *m.*; *in ~, adj.* arriéré.
arrest, *s.* (*pers.*) arrestation, *f.*; (*mil., &c.*) arrêts, *m.pl.*; *v.a.* arrêter; (*attention*) frapper; *place under ~,* mettre aux arrêts; **~ing,** *adj.* frappant.
arrival, arrivée, *f.*; (*ships, goods*) arrivage, *m.*; (*pers.*) nouveau venu, *m.*
arrive, arriver (être).
arrogan|ce, arrogance, *f.*; **~t,** arrogant; (*look, tone*) rogue.
arrogate, *v.a.* s'arroger.
arrow, flèche, *f.*; (*fig.*) trait, *m.*; **~ -head,** (*bot.*) sagittaire, *f.*
arsenal, arsenal, *m.*
arsenic, arsenic, *m.*; **~al,** arsénique.
arsis, (*pros.*) arsis, *m.*
arson, incendie volontaire, *m.*
art, art, *m.*; *black ~,* magie noire, *f.*; *fine ~s,* beaux-arts, *m.pl.*
arter|y, artère, *f.*; **~ial,** artériel, -le.
Artesian well, puits artésien, *m.*
artful, (*crafty*) artificieu|x, ~se; **~ dodger,** malin, *m.*; **~ly,** avec ruse.

arthrit|is, (*med.*) arthrite, *f.*; **~ic,** arthritique.
artichoke, artichaut, *m.*; *Jerusalem ~,* topinambour, *m.*
article, *s.* (*gram., lit., eccles., and all English senses, except apprenticeship*) article, *m.*; **~s,** (*apprent.*) contrat d'apprentissage, *m.*; (*assoc.*) statuts, *m.pl.*; (*partner*) contrat, *m.*; *leading ~,* article de fond, *m.*; *~s of vertu,* objets d'art, *m.pl.*
article, *v.a.* (*apprent.*) mettre* chez; *~d pupil,* stagiaire, *m.*
articulat|e, *v.a.* articuler; *adj.* articulé; **~ion,** articulation, *f.*
artific|e, artifice, *m.*; (*means*) moyen, *m.*; **~ial,** artificiel, -le; **~er,** artisan, *m.*; ⚠ *not* artificier *which = 'fireworks-maker'*; **~iality,** manque de naturel, *m.*; **~ially,** artificiellement.
artillery, artillerie, *f.*; **~man,** artilleur, *m.*
artisan, artisan, *m.*
artist, (*gen.*) artiste, *m.*; (*painter*) peintre, femme peintre, *m.f.*; **~ic,** artistique; **~ically,** artistement.
artiste, artiste, *m.f.*
artless, naï|f, ~ve; **~ness,** naïveté, *f.*; **~ly,** naïvement.
arum, arum lily, (*bot.*) arum, *m.*
as, *adv.* comme; (*like a*) en; *adv.* (*equally*) aussi; ~ . . . ~, aussi . . . que; *~ good ~,* comme; *~ many, much,* autant de; *~ many, much . . . as,* autant de . . . que de; *~ much ~* (*with numbers*) jusqu'à; *~ you like,* comme vous voudrez; *such ~,* (*adj.*) tel, -le que; *such ~ it is,* tel, -le, quel, -le; *~ such,* comme tel, -le; *~ well,* (*also*) de plus; *so . . . ~,* aussi + *adj.* + que; *so . . . as to,* assez . . . pour; *so (as) far ~ I know,* d'autant que je sache; *~ yet,* encore; *conj.* (*since*) puisque; (*because*) parce que; (*while*) pendant que; (*progress*) à mesure que; *~ though, if,* comme si; *forasmuch ~,* vu que; *~ long ~,* tant que; *so long ~,* (*provided that*) pourvu que + *subj.*; *~ soon ~,* aussitôt que (*fut. or fut. perf. of fut. time*); *~ well ~ I can,* de mon mieux; *~ per, prep.* suivant; *~ to, prep.* quant à.
asbestos, asbeste, *m.*
ascend, *v.a.n.* monter (*v.a.* avoir, *v.n.* être); (*river*) remonter (avoir); **~ant, ~ancy,** *s.* (*influence, astr.*) ascendant, *m.*; **~ing,** *adj.* ascendant.
ascension, ascension, *f.*; **~ Day,** Ascension, *f.*
ascent, ascension, *f.*; (*way up*) montée, *f.*; (*slope*) pente, *f.*
ascertain, *v.n.* (*verify*) constater; (*fix*) déterminer; (*find out*) s'informer de; (*make sure*) s'assurer (de).
ascetic, *s.* ascète, *m.f.*; *adj.* ascétique; **~ism,** ascétisme, *m.*
ascribable to, attribuable à.
ascribe to, *v.a.* attribuer à.
aseptic, *adj. and s. m.* aseptique.
asexual, asexuel, -le.
ash, (*residue of fire*) cendre, *f.*; (*tree*) frêne, *m.*; **Ash Wednesday,** Mercredi des Cendres, *m.*; **~es,** cendres, *f.pl.*; **~-bin, ~-hole, ~-tray,** cendrier, *m.*; **~-grey,** gris cendré, *invar.*; **~plantation,** frênaie, *f.*
ashamed, honteu|x, ~se; *be, feel ~,* avoir †honte (de).
ash|-coloured, ~en, cendré; (*face*) terreu|x, ~se.
ashlar, *n.* moellon, *m.*
ashore, *adv.* à terre; *run ~, adj.* échoué; *v.n.* échouer; *set ~,* débarquer.
ashy-pale, pâle comme la mort.
Asiatic, *adj.* (a) *and s.m.f.* Asiatique.
aside, de côté; (*theatr.*) à part; *stand ~,* se tenir* à l'écart; *take ~,* prendre* à part.
ask, *v.a.* demander (à + *pers.*, de + *inf.*); (*question*) faire*; (*favour*) solliciter; (*invite*) inviter; *~ after,* demander des nouvelles de; *~ for, v.a.* (*thing*) demander, (*pers.*) demander à voir.
askance, *look ~ at,* regarder de travers.
askew, *adv.* de travers.
asleep, *adj.* endormi; *fall ~,* s'endormir*; *sound ~,* profondément endormi.
aslope, *adv.* en pente.
asp, aspic, *m.*
asparagus, asperge, *f.* (*plural of group of stalks*); *bundle of ~,* botte d'asperges, *f.*
aspect, (*way of looking, point of view*) aspect, *m.*; (*look*) air, *m.*; (*situation*) exposition, *f.*
aspen, ~-tree, (*bot.*) tremble, *m.*
asperity, (*roughness*) aspérité, *f.*; (*temper*) âpreté, *f.*
aspers|e, *v.a.* (*character*) noircir; (*pers.*) calomnier; **~ion,** calomnie, *f.*
asphalt, asphalte, *m.*
asphodel, (*bot.*) asphodèle, *m.*
aspirant, *s.m.f.* aspirant, -e.
aspirate, *s.* aspirée, *f.*; *adj.* aspiré; *v.a.* aspirer.
aspiration, (*fig.*) désir, *m.*; (*relig.*) aspiration, *f.*; (*breathing in*) inspiration, *f.*
aspire to, aspirer à; *~ after,* soupirer pour.
aspirin, aspirine, *f.*
aspiring, *adj.* ambitieu|x, ~se.
ass, âne, ~sse, *m.f.*; *~'s foal,* ânon, *m.*; *be an ~, make an ~ of oneself,* faire* l'imbécile; *wild ~,* onagre, *m.*
assegai, z(s)agaie, *f.*
assail, *v.a.* assaillir*; *~ with,* accabler de; **~ant,** *s.* assaillant, *m.*
assassin, assassin, *m.*; **~ate,** assassiner; **~ation,** assassinat, *m.*
assault, *s.* (*mil.*) assaut, *m.*; (*law*) voies de fait, *f.pl.*
assault, *v.a.* (*attack*) attaquer; (*law*) commettre* des voies de fait.
assay, *s.* (*metal*) essai, *m. also 'assaying'*; *v.a.* (*metal*) essayer.
assemble, *v.a.* assembler; *v.n.* s'assembler.

assembly, *s.* (*meeting, legislative*) assemblée, *f.*; (*mil.*) rassemblement, *m.*
assent, *s.* assentiment, *m.*; *with one* ~, d'un commun accord, *v.n.*
assent to, consentir* à; (*approve*) approuver, *v.a.*; **~ient,** *adj. and s.m. f.* approbat|eur, ~rice.
assert, (*declare*) affirmer; (*rights*) revendiquer; ~ *oneself,* s'imposer; **~ion,** assertion, *f.*
assess, (*tax*) cotiser; **~ment,** cote, *f.*; **~able,** imposable; **~or,** répartiteur, *m.*
assets, (*comm.*) actif, *m.*; (*possessions*) biens, *m.pl.*; *liquid* ~, disponibilités, *f. pl.*
asseverat|e, affirmer solennellement; **~ion,** affirmation solennelle, *f.*
assidu|ity, ~ousness, assiduité, *f.*; **~ous,** assidu; **~ously,** assidûment.
assign, *v.a.* (*allot*) assigner; (*fix*) fixer; (*transfer*) céder; (*reason*) donner; **~ation,** (*meeting*) rendez-vous, *m.*
assign|ment, (*goods*) cession, *f.*; **~ee,** (*debt*) cessionnaire, *m.f.*
assimilat|e, *v.a.* assimiler; *v.n.* s'assimiler; **~ion,** assimilation, *f.*
assist, *v.a.n.* aider (à + *inf.*); ♤ aider à + *pers.* = *to lend a hand to.*
assistan|ce, aide, *f.*; **~t,** *adj. often* sous + *name, e.g.* sous-commissaire, *assistant commissary*; *~t-master,* professeur, *m.*
assize|s, (*court*) cour d'assises, *f.*
associate, *s.* associé, -e, *m.f.*; (*colleague*) collègue, *m.f.*; (*crime*) complice, *m.f.*
associate, *adj.* associé; *v.a.* associer; ~ *with,* s'associer à *or* avec; (*mix with*) fréquenter.
association, association, *f.*; (*football*) association, *f.*
assort, *v.a.* assortir (*like* finir); ~ *with,* (*match, suit*) se marier avec; (*associate oneself with*) s'associer avec; **~ment,** assortiment, *m.*
assuage, *v.a.* apaiser; **~ment,** soulagement, *m.*
assumable, présumable.
assume, (*take*) prendre*; (*unduly*) s'arroger; (*responsibility*) assumer; (*suppose*) supposer; **~d,** *adj.* feint; ~ *name,* nom de guerre, *m.*
assuming, *adj.* présomptueu|x, ~se.
assumption, (*supposition*) supposition, *f.*; (*eccles.*) Assomption, *f.*; (*appropriation*) appropriation, *f.*; (*arrogance*) arrogance, *f.*
assurance, (*self-confidence, comm.*) assurance, *f.*; ~ **policy,** police d'assurance, *f.*
assure, *v.a.* assurer; (*life*) faire assurer sur la vie.
assuredly, assurément.
aster, (*bot.*) reine-marguerite, *f.*; ♤ *French* aster = '*Michaelmas daisy*'.
asterisk, astérisque, *m.*
asteroid, astéroïde, *m.*
astern, *adv.* à l'arrière.
asthma, asthme, *m.*; **~tic,** *adj. and s.m.f.* asthmatique.
astir, en mouvement; *for persons often use verb* bouger.
astonish, étonner; **~ment,** étonnement, *m.*; **~ing,** étonnant.
astound, abasourdir; **~ing,** stupéfiant.
astraddle, à califourchon.
astral, *adj.* astral.
astray, égaré; *go* ~, s'égarer.
astride, à califourchon; ~ *of,* à califourchon sur.
astringent, *adj. and s.m.* astringent.
astrolog|er, astrologue, *m.*; **~y,** astrologie, *f.*; **~ical,** astrologique.
astronom|er, astronome, *m.*; **~y,** astronomie, *f.*; **~ic,** astronomique.
astute, fin; (*pej.*) astucieu|x, ~se; **~ness,** astuce, *f.*; **~ly,** astucieusement.
asunder, (*in two*) en deux.
asylum, (*refuge, home*) asile, *m.*; *lunatic* ~, hospice d'aliénés, *m.*
asymmetry, asymétrie, *f.*
at, (*place and hour*) à; (*house, shop of*) chez; ~ *home,* chez soi, lui, &c.; ~ *that,* (*such as it is*) tel, -le quel, -le *or* tel, -le qu'il, elle est.
atavism, atavisme, *m.*
atheis|m, athéisme, *m.*; **~t,** athée, *m.f.*; **~tical,** athéistique.
athenaeum, athénée, *m.*
Athenian, *adj.* (a) *and s.m.f.* athénien, -ne.
at-home, *s.* réception, *f.*
athirst, *adj.* altéré; ~ *for riches,* assoiffé de richesses.
athlet|e, athlète, *m.*; **~ic,** athlétique; *~ic sports,* concours athlétique, *m.*
athwart, *adv.* (*across*) en travers; (*naut.*) par le travers; *prep.* en travers de.
Atlantic, Atlantique, *f.*; *adj.* atlantique.
atlas, atlas, *m.*
atmospher|e, atmosphère, *f.*; **~ic,** atmosphérique.
atoll, atoll, *m.*
atom, atome, *m.*; **~ic,** atomique; **~ism,** (*phil.*) atomisme, *m.*
atone for, expier; (*redeem*) racheter; (*make up for*) compenser, *v.a.*
atonement, expiation, *f.*; (*amends*) compensation, *f.*
atonic, *adj.* (*gram.*) atonique.
atrabilious, atrabilaire.
atroci|ous, atroce; **~ty,** atrocité, *f.*; **~ously,** atrocement.
atrophy, *s.* atrophie, *f.*; *v.n.* s'atrophier.
attach, *v.a.* attacher; *v.n.* s'attacher; **~ment,** attachement, *m.*
attaché, attaché, *m.*; ~ **case,** petite valise, *f.*
attack, *s.* attaque, *f.*; (*illness*) accès, *m.*; *v.a.* attaquer.
attain, atteindre*; (*with difficulty*) atteindre* à; ~ *to,* parvenir* à.
attainder, (*forfeiture*) confiscation des biens, *f.*
attainment, (*aptitude*) talent, *m.*; (*knowledge*) connaissances, *f.pl.*
attaint, *v.a.* prononcer la confiscation des biens de.

attar of roses, essence de rose, *f.*
attempt, *s.* tentative, *f.*; (*on life*) attentat, *m.*
attempt, *v.a.* (*task, &c.*) entreprendre*; (*life*) attenter à; *make an* ~ *at*, tenter; *v.n.* ~ *to*, essayer de; ~ *the impossible*, tenter l'impossible.
attend, *v.a.* (*lectures, &c.*) suivre*; (*meeting*) assister à; (*royalty*) être de service auprès de; (*shop*) servir*; (*med.*) soigner; (*accompany*) accompagner; *v.n.* ~ *to* (*pay attention*) faire attention à; (*see to*) s'occuper de; (*orders, advice*) suivre*.
attendance, (*servants, &c.*) service, *m.*; (*sick*) soins, *m.pl.*; (*persons present*) assistance, *f.*; (*med.*) visites, *f.pl.*; *dance* ~ *on*, faire antichambre auprès de.
attendant, *s.* (*serv.*) serviteur, *m.*; *often* employé, *m. is used*; **~s,** suite, *f.*; *adj.* ~ *upon*, qui accompagne.
attention, attention, *f.*; *interj.* (*mil.*) garde à vous!; *pay* ~, faire* attention (à); *pay ~s to*, témoigner des égards à.
attentive, attenti|f, ~ve; ~ *to*, (*pers.*) plein d'attentions pour; (*things*) attenti|f, ~ve à; **~ly,** attentivement.
attenuat|ed, amaigri; **~ion,** amaigrissement, *m.*
attest, *v.a.* attester; (*show*) témoigner; **~ation,** attestation, *f.*
attic, (*adj.*) attique; **~ism,** atticisme, *m.*
attic, *s.* (*arch.*) mansarde, *f.*
attire, vêtement, *m.*; (*woman's*) atours, *m.pl.*; *v.a.*vêtir; *v.n.* se vêtir; ⚠ *not* attirer *which = 'attract'.*
attitud|e, (*lit. and fig.*) attitude, *f.*; **~inize,** poser.
attorney, avoué, *m.*; (*representative*) mandataire, *m.*
attract, *v.a.* attirer; **~ive,** attrayant; ⚠ attractif, *used in phys., not fig. in French.*
attraction, (*charm*) attrait, *m.*; (*phys.*) attraction, *f.*; *~s* (*pleasures*) attractions, *f.pl.*
attribut|e, *s.* attribut, *m.*; (*gram.*) épithète, *f.*; *v.a.* attribuer (à); **~able** *to*, attribuable à.
attrition, frottement, *m.*
attuned to, mis d'accord avec.
auburn, *adj.* châtain.
auction, (*public sale*) encan, *m.*; (*actual bidding*) enchères, *f.pl.*; **~eer,** commissaire-priseur, *m.*; *sell by* ~, vendre aux enchères.
audaci|ous, audacieu|x, ~se; **~ty, ~ousness,** audace, *f.*; **~ously,** audacieusement.
audibl|e, (*voice*) intelligible; (*sound*) qui se fait entendre; **~y,** distinctement.
audience, (*interview*) audience, *f.*; (*assembly*) auditoire, *m.*; ⚠ audience *is never used of a crowd of listeners.*
audit, auditing, (*comm.*) vérification, *f.*; *v.a.* vérifier; **~or,** vérificateur, *m.*; *~or's discharge*, quitus, *m.*
auditory, *adj.* auditoire.
auger, (*tool*) tarière, *f.*
aught, *indef. pron.* quelque chose, *m.*; (*at all*) quoi que ce soit; *for* ~ *I know*, autant que je sache.
augment, *v.a.n.* augmenter; **~ation,** accroissement, *m.*
augur, augure, *m.*; *v.a.* augurer; **~y,** augure, *m.*; ~ *well, ill for*, être de bon, mauvais augure pour.
August, *s.* août, *m.*
august, *adj.* auguste.
Augustinian, Austin, *s.m.f.* (*friar or nun*) augustin, -e.
aulic, aulique.
aunt, tante, *f.*; **great-** ~, grand'tante, *f.*
aural, auriculaire.
aureole, auréole, *f.*
auricle, (*ear*) auricule, *f.*; (*heart*) oreillette, *f.*
auricula, (*bot.*) oreille d'ours, *f.*
auriferous, aurifère.
Aurora Borealis, aurore boréale, *f.*
auspice, auspice, *m.*; **~s,** auspices, *pl.*; *under favourable ~s*, sous d'heureux auspices.
auspicious, *adj.* de bon augure; **~ly,** sous d'heureux auspices.
auster|e, austère; **~ity,** austérité, *f.*
austral, austral.
Australian, *adj.* (a) *and s.m.f.* Australien, -ne.
Austrian, *adj.* (a) *and s.m.f.* Autrichien, -ne.
authentic, authentique; **~ity,** authenticité, *f.*; **~ally,** authentiquement.
authenticate, *v.a.* constater; (*make valid*) authentiquer.
author, auteur, *m.*; **~ess,** femme auteur, *f.*
authoritative, (*commanding*) autoritaire; (*having authority*) autorisé; **~ly,** avec autorité.
authorit|y, (*power, right, pers., book, evidence, expert*) autorité, *f.*; (*permission*) autorisation, *f.*; *the ~ies*, les autorités.
authoriz|e, autoriser; **~ation,** autorisation, *f.*
authorship, (*book, &c.*) paternité, *f.*
autobiograph|y, autobiographie, *f.*; **~er,** autobiographe, *m.*; **~ical,** autobiographique.
autocar, automobile, *f.*
autocra|cy, autocratie, *f.*; **~t,** autocrate, *m.*; **~tic,** *adj.* autocratique.
auto-da-fé, autodafé, *m.*
autograph, autographe, *m.*; *v.a.* (*reproduce*) autographier; (*writing*) écrire* de sa main; **~y,** (*reproduction*) autographie, *f.*; **~ic,** autographique.
automat|on, automate, *m.*; **~ic,** automatique; **~ically,** automatiquement.
automobile, *s.* automobile, *f.*
autonom|y, autonomie, *f.*; **~ous,** autonome.
autopsy, autopsie, *f.*
autumn, automne, *m.f.*; **~al,** automnal.
auxiliary, *adj.* auxiliaire.

avail, *s., be of no* ~, ne servir* à rien; *of what ~ is it?* à quoi cela sert-il? ; *he sought without* ~, il avait beau chercher.
avail, *v.a.* servir à; ~ *oneself of,* profiter de; **~able,** (*at hand*) sous la main; (*at disposal*) disponible; (*usable*) valable.
avalanche, avalanche, *f.*
avaric|e, avarice, *f.*; **~ious,** avare; **~iously,** avaricieusement.
avaunt! *interj.* arrière!
avenge, venger; ~ *oneself upon,* (*pers.*) se venger de.
avenger, *s.* venge|ur, ~resse, *m.f.*
avenue, avenue, *f.*
aver, affirmer.
average, *s.* moyenne, *f.*; *on the* ~, en moyenne; *adj.* moyen, -ne; *amount on an* ~ *to,* être en moyenne; *v.a.* (*take average of*) prendre* la moyenne de.
averse, be ~ to, from, répugner à.
aversion, aversion, *f.*; *have an* ~ *to,* avoir de la répugnance à.
avert, *v.a.* (*ward off*) détourner.
aviary, volière, *f.*
aviat|or, aviat|eur, ~rice, *m.f.*; **~ion,** aviation, *f.*; *~ion ground,* aérodrome, *m.*
avid of, for, avide de; **~ity,** avidité, *f.*
avocation, occupation, *f.*
avocet, (*ornith.*) avocette, *f.*
avoid, éviter (de+*inf.*); **~ance,** fuite, *f.*; **~able,** évitable.
avow, avouer; **~al,** aveu, *m.*; **~edly,** de son propre aveu.
await, *v.a.* attendre.
awake, *v.a.* éveiller; *v.n.* s'éveiller; ~ *to,* s'apercevoir de.
awake, *adj.* (*lit. fig.*) éveillé; **~ning,** réveil, *m.*; *be* ~ *to,* avoir conscience de.
award, (*grant*) accorder; (*law, arbtr.*) adjuger; (*prize*) décerner.
award, *s.* (*arbitration*) sentence, *f.*; (*contract*) adjudication, *f.*
aware, *be* ~ *of,* être averti de; *not to be* ~ *of,* ignorer; *not that I am* ~ *of,* pas que je sache; *be* ~ *that,* savoir* bien.
awash, (*flush with water*) à fleur d'eau; (*washed by water*) inondé d'eau.
away, *adv.* absent; *be* ~ *from home,* être absent; *interj.* ~ *with!* loin de moi! de nous!; ~ *from,* du côté opposé de.
awe, crainte, *f.*; **~ -struck,** frappé de terreur; *stand in* ~ *of,* avoir une sainte terreur de.
awful, (*lit. and slang*) terrible; (*imposing*) imposant; **~ly,** (*slang*) terriblement.
awhile, *adv.* pendant quelque temps.
awkward, (*pers.*) gauche; (*ungraceful*) disgracieu|x, ~se; (*things*) embarrassant; (*clumsy*) maladroit; (*embarrassed of look*) emprunté; (*dangerous*) dangereu|x, ~se; **~ness,** gaucherie, *f.*; (*difficulty*) difficulté, *f.*; **~ly,** (*clumsily*) maladroitement.
awl, alêne, *f.*
awn, (*barley, &c.*) barbe, *f.*
awning, tente, *f.*
awry, *adv.* de travers.
axe, †hache, *f.*; **battle-~,** †hache d'armes; *have an* ~ *to grind,* avoir un intérêt en jeu.
axiom, axiome, *m.*; **~atic,** axiomatique.
axis, axe, *m.*
axle, axle-tree, essieu, *m.*; **~ -bearing,** coussinet d'essieu, *m.*; **~ -box,** boîte à graisse, *f.*; **~ -cap,** chapeau, *m.*; **~ -pin,** esse, *f.*
aye, *for* ~, à jamais.
azalea, azalée, *f.*
azure, *s.* azur, *m.*; *adj.* azuré.

B

babbl|e, *s.* babil, *m.*; *v.n.* babiller; (*water*) gazouiller; **~er,** bavard, *m.*; **~ing,** *adj.* babillard.
babe, *see* BABY.
babel, (*fig.*) vacarme, *m.*
baboon, babouin, *m.*
baby, bébé, *m.*; *~'s bottle,* biberon, *m.*; **~-linen,** layette, *f.*; **~hood,** première enfance, *f.*
bacchanal, (*priest*) prêtre de Bacchus, *m.*; (*dance*) bacchanale, *f.*
Bacchanalia, bacchanales, *f.pl.*
Bacchanalian, bachique.
Bacchante, bacchante, *f.*
bachelor, (*unmarried*) célibataire, *m.*; (*univ.*) licencié, *m.f.*; *~'s degree,* baccalauréat, *m.* ⚠ *taken on leaving school*; ~ *quarters,* garçonnière, *f.*
bacillus, bacille, *m.*
back, *s.* **1** dos, *m.*; **2** (*book*) dos, *m.*; **3** (*things, house*) derrière, *m.*; **4** (*chair*) dossier, *m.*; **5** (*hand*) revers, *m.*; **6** (*stage*) fond, *m.*; **7** (*leaf, p.-card, page*) verso, *m.*; **8** (*football*) arrière, *m.*; *with one's* ~ *to the wall,* acculé; ~ *to* ~, dos à dos; *on one's* ~, (*ill*) alité; *turn one's* ~ *on,* tourner le dos à.
back, *adj.* de derrière; (*rent*) arriéré; **~ door,** porte de derrière, *f.*; **~ kitchen,** arrière-cuisine, *f.*; **~stairs,** escalier de service, *m.*; **~ street,** rue écartée, *f.*; **~ yard,** arrière-cour, *f.*
back, *v.a.* (*horse, motor*) faire reculer; (*back up*) seconder; (*bet*) parier pour; (*bill*) avaliser; *v.n.* reculer; ~ *out of* (*obligation*) se soustraire* à; ~ *into,* entrer (être) à reculons dans; (*motor*) entrer (être) en marche arrière dans.
back, *adv.* en arrière. *With verbs use as far as possible repetitive forms, e.g.* revenir*, *to come back. So* remettre*, reprendre*, retourner, rappeler, renvoyer, repousser, *&c.*; *be* ~, (*return*) être de retour; *some years* ~, il y a d'ici quelques années; *prep. at the* ~ *of,* derrière; ~ *from,* (*street, &c.*) en retrait de; *there and back,* aller et retour.
backbit|e, médire* de; **~er,** médisant, *m.*; **~ing,** *s.* médisance, *f.*
backboard, (*boat, veh.*) dossier, *m.*

backbone, épine dorsale, *f.*; *to the* ~, (*thoroughly*) jusqu'à la moelle.
backgammon, *n.* trictrac, *m.*
background, *s.* fond, *m.*; (*paint., theatr.*) arrière-plan, *m.*
backhand, ~ed, *adj.* de revers; ~ **stroke,** (*tennis*) coup de revers, *m.*
backing, (*movement*) recul, *m.*; (*support*) appui, *m.*
backslid|e, *v.n.* retomber (être); **~ing,** rechute, *f.*
backward, *adj.* (*undeveloped*) arriéré; (*towards rear*) rétrograde; (*season, plants*) tardi|f, ~ve.
backward-s, *adv.* (*walk*) à reculons; (*fall*) à la renverse; (*wrong way*) à rebours; (*end first*) à l'envers; ~ *and forward,* de long en large.
backwardness, état arriéré, *m.*; (*disinclination*) répugnance, *f.*; (*plants, season*) tardivité, *f.*
backwash, (*sea*) jusant, *m.*; (*aeron.*) remous d'air, *m.*
backwoods, forêts inexploitées, *f.pl.*; **~man,** défricheur de forêts, *m.*
bacon, lard, *m.*; (*fam.*) *save one's* ~, s'en tirer.
bacteriology, bactériologie, *f.*
bad, *s.* mauvais, *m.*; *to the* ~, (*loss*) à perte; *go to the* ~, tourner mal.
bad, *adj.* mauvais; (*sick*) malade; (*pers.*) méchant; ~ **breeding,** *see* BREEDING; ~ **hat, lot,** mauvais garnement, *m.*; *a* ~ *time,* un mauvais quart d'heure; *my finger is* ~, mon doigt fait mal; *I have a* ~ *finger,* j'ai mal au doigt; *it's too* ~, c'est trop fort; *be* ~, (*ill*) être mal; *be* ~ *tempered,* être d'un mauvais caractère; *be on* ~ *terms with,* être mal avec; *be in a* ~ *way,* être mal dans ses affaires; *from* ~ *to worse,* de mal en pis; *go* ~, (*fruit, &c.*) se gâter; **~ly,** mal; (*greatly*) beaucoup; (*wounded*) grièvement; **~ness,** (*pers.*) méchanceté, *f.*; (*things*) mauvaise qualité.
badge, plaque, *f.*; (*insignia, employment*) insigne, *m.*
badger, *s.* blaireau, *m.*; *v.a.* †harceler.
baffle, déjouer; (*hopes*) décevoir.
bag, *s.* (*small*) sac, *m.*; (*large*) valise, *f.*; (*list of game killed*) tableau, *m.*; *whole* ~ *of tricks,* (*slang*) tout le tremblement.
bag, *v.a.* (*hunt.*) tuer; (*pop. steal*) chiper.
bagatelle, (*trifle*) bagatelle, *f.*; (*game*) petit billard, *m.*
baggage, *s.* (*of an army and luggage*) bagage, *m.*; (*hussy*) effrontée, *f.*
bagpipe, cornemuse, *f.*
bail, (*law*) caution, *f.*; *on* ~, sous caution; *stand bail for,* se porter caution pour. ⚠ *Not* bail *which* = '*lease*'.
bail, bale, (*out water*) vider l'eau de.
bailiff, (*law*) huissier, *m.*; (*estate, farm.*) régisseur, *m.*
bait, *s.* amorce, *f.*; (*fig.*) appât, *m.*; *v.a.* (*horse*) faire* manger; (*fig. and of dogs*) †harceler.
baize, *green* ~, tapis vert, *m.*
bake, *v.a.* faire* cuire au four; *v.n.* cuire* au four; (*dry up*) dessécher.
bake|house, fournil, *m.*; ~ **r,** boulanger, *m.*; ~*'s boy,* mitron, *m.*; ~*'s dozen,* treize à la douzaine; ~*'s shop,* **~ry,** boulangerie, *f.*
balance, *s.* (*bank*) solde, *m.*; (*account, weighing, trade*) balance, *f.*; (*power, harmony, equilibrium*) équilibre, *m.*; ~ **sheet,** (*comm.*) bilan, *m.*; ~ *carried forward,* (*bkkpg.*) reliquat, *m.*; *v.a.* (*lit. and accounts*) balancer; *v.n.* se balancer.
balcony, *s.* balcon, *m.*
bald, chauve; (*style*) plat; **~ness,** calvitie, *f.*; **~ly** (*style*) platement.
baldachin, baldaquin, *m.*
balderdash, galimatias, *m.*
baldric, baudrier, *m.*
bale, *s.* (*goods*) ballot, *m.*; (*evil*) mal, *m.*
bale out, *v.a., see* BAIL.
baleful, funeste.
balk, *s.* (*tie-beam*) entrait, *m.*
balk, *v.a.* (*thwart*) frustrer; (*hinder*) entraver.
ball, *s.* **1** (*games, bullet*) balle, *f.*; **2** (*for feet*) ballon, *m.*; **3** (*round object, bowls, ballot*) boule, *f.*; **4** (*billiards*) bille, *f.*; **5** (*snow, wool, silk*) pelote, *f.*; **6** (*thread*) peloton, *m.*; **7** (*cannon*) boulet, *m.*; **8** (*eye*) globe, *m.*; **9** (*dance*) bal, *m.*, *pl.* bals; ~ **-bearings,** roulement à billes, *m.*; ~ **-joint,** joint à rotule, *m.*; *keep the* ~ *rolling,* soutenir* la conversation.
ballad, (*poem*) ballade, *f.*; (*song*) romance, *f.*
ballast, *s.* (*naut.*) lest, *m.*; ~ **lighter,** bateau lesteur, *m.*; *v.a.* lester.
ballet, ballet, *m.*; ~ **-dancer,** danseuse, *f.*
balloon, ballon, *m.*; **~ist,** aéronaute, *m.*
ballot, *s.* scrutin, *m.*; ~ **-ball,** boule, *f.*; *second* ~, ballottage, *m.*; *counting of* ~, *see* COUNTING; ~ **-box,** urne du scrutin, *f.*; *vote by* ~, *see* VOTE.
balm, (*bot.*) baume, *m.*; ~ **mint,** mélisse, *f.*; ~ *of Gilead,* baume de Judée, *m.*; (*fig.*) baume, *m.*
balmy, (*breeze*) embaumé.
balsam, (*bot.*) baume, *m.*; *garden* ~, *see* GARDEN; **~ic,** balsamique.
Baltic, balte.
baluster, (*arch.*) balustre, *m.*; **~s,** (*stairs*) rampe, *f.*
balustrade, balustrade, *f.*
bamboo, bambou, *m.*
bamboozle, (*slang*) enjôler.
ban, *s.* (*order of exile*) ban, *m.*; (*eccles.*) anathème, *m.*; *v.a.* (*fig.*) mettre* au ban.
banal, banal; **~ity,** banalité, *f.*
banana, banane, *f.*; ~ **tree,** bananier, *m.*
band, *s.* (*troop*) troupe, *f.*; (*tie*) lien, *m.*; (*mus.*) orchestre, *m.*
bandanna, (*handkerchief*) madras, *m.*
bandbox, carton, *m.*; *he looks as if he came out of a* ~, il est tiré à quatre épingles.

bandicoot, (*zool.*) péramèle, *m.*
bandit, bandit, *m.*
bandmaster, chef de musique, *m.*
bandoleer, bandoulière, *f.*
bandsman, musicien, *m.*
bandstand, kiosque à musique, *m.*
bandy, *v.a.* (*jokes, words, stories, epithets, compliments, sallies*) se renvoyer la balle; ~ *about,* (*exchange*) se passer de l'un à l'autre.
bandy-legged, bancal.
bane, fléau, *m.*; ~**ful,** funeste.
bang, *s.* coup, *m.*; (*door*) claquement, *m.*; (*explosion*) détonation, *f.*; (*interj.*) pan!
bang, *v.a.n.* (*door, window, &c.*) claquer; (*throw*) jeter avec violence.
bangle, bracelet, *m.*
banian-tree, figuier de l'Inde, *m.*
banish, *v.a.* bannir; (*fig.*) chasser; ~**ment,** bannissement, *m.*
banister, *see* BALUSTER.
banjo, banjo, *m.*
bank, *s.* (*river*) rive, *f.*; (*earth*) terrasse, *f.*; (*turf, sand*) banc, *m.*; (*cloud*) monceau, *m.*; *v.a.* (*heap up*) entasser; ~*up,* (*earth, &c.*) terrasser.
bank, *s.* (*comm.*) banque, *f.*; ~ *pass-book,* carnet de banque, *m.*; *break the* ~, (*gaming*) faire sauter la banque.
bank, *v.a.* (*money*) déposer; *v.n.* (*aeron.*) virer sur l'aile; ~**ing,** (*aeron.*) virage, *m.*; ~**er,** banquier, *m.*
banking, ~**-account,** compte de banque, *m.*; ~ **-house,** maison de banque, *f.*
bankrupt, *s.* banquerou|tier, ~tière, *m.f.*; *adj.* en faillite; *become* ~, faire faillite; ~**cy,** (*fraudulent*) banqueroute, *f.*; (*misfortune and fig.*) faillite, *f.*
banner, bannière, *f.*
banns, bans de mariage, *m.pl.*
banquet, *s.* banquet, *m.*; ~**ing-hall,** salle de festin, *f.*; *v.n.* banqueter.
bantam, (*fowl*) bantam, *m.*; ~ **weight,** (*boxing*) poids bantam, *m.*
banter, (bantering) *s.* raillerie, *f.*; *adj.* ~**ing,** railleu|r, ~se; *v.a.n.* railler.
baobab-tree, baobab, *m.*
baptis|m, baptême, *m.*; ~**t,** baptiste, *m.*
baptistery, (*eccles.*) baptistère, *m.*
baptize, baptiser.
bar, *s.* (*iron, tribunal, harbour, her., mus., naut.*) barre, *f.*; (*window, Bar in law*) barreau, *m.*; (*obstacle*) obstacle, *m.*; (*counter for drink*) comptoir, *m.*; (*place*) débit de boissons, *m.*
bar, *v.a.* (*lit., fig., door, &c., intercept, her.*) barrer; (*slang pers.*) ne pas vouloir* connaître.
barb, (*Barbary horse*) barbe, *m.*; (*arrow*) barbillon, *m.*
barbari|an, *s.* barbare, *m.*; ~**sm,** (*lang.*) barbarisme, *m.* ⚠ *which is only used of language in French.*
barbarian, barbaric, barbarous, barbare; (*of savages*) de sauvages.
barbarity, barbarie, *f.*
barbed, (*arrow, &c.*) barbelé; ~ *iron wire,* fil de fer barbelé, *m.*; ~ *wire entanglements,* réseau de fils barbelés, *m.*
barber, coiffeur, *m.*; (*surg.*) barbier, *m.*
barberry, (*bot.*) épine-vinette, *f.*
barbette, (*fort.*) barbette, *f.*
barbican, (*fort.*) barbacane, *f.*
bard, (*poet*) barde, *m.*; (*horse armour*) barde, *f.*
bare, *adj.* (*lit. and sword*) nu; (*mere*) seul; (*room*) dégarni; ~**-back,** à poil; ~**-faced,** (*shameless*) effronté; ~ **-foot,** nu-pieds; ~ **-headed,** nu-tête; ~ *subsistence,* de quoi vivre; ~**ness,** (*poverty*) dénuement, *m.*; (*barren*) stérilité, *f.*; ~**ly,** à peine.
bare, *v.a.* (*uncover*) découvrir*; (*strip*) dépouiller.
bargain, *s.* marché, *m.*; *great* ~, marché d'or, *m.*; *into the* ~, par dessus le marché; *that's a* ~*!* (*slang*) tope!
bargain, *v.n.* marchander; ~ *for,* (*haggle*) marchander, *v.a.*; *v.a.* (*fig.*) ~ *for,* s'attendre à; ~ *with . . . for,* traiter avec . . . pour.
barge, *s.* chaland, *m.*; (*of state*) bateau de parade, *m.*
barge against, *v.n.* (*slang*) se theurter contre.
bargee, marinier, *m.*
bark, *s.* (*tree*) écorce, *f.*; (*left on felled tree*) grume, *f.*; (*dog*) aboiement, *m.*; *his* ~ *is worse than his bite,* il n'est pas si méchant qu'il en a l'air.
bark, *v.n.* (*dog*) aboyer; *v.a.* (*tree*) écorcer; (*skin*) écorcher.
bark, (*ship and fig.*) barque, *f.*
barley, *orge, f.*; (orge *m. only in* orge mondé *and* orge perlé); ~**corn,** grain d'orge, *m.*; ~**-mow,** monceau d'orge, *m.*; ~**-water,** eau d'orge, *f.*
barm, levure, *f.*
barman, garçon de comptoir, *m.*
barmaid, fille de comptoir, *f.*
barn, grange, *f.*; ~ **floor,** aire, *f.*; ~ **-owl,** effraie, *f.*; ~ **-yard,** cour de ferme, *f.*
barnacle, (*goose and moll.*) bernache, bernacle, *f.*
baromet|er, baromètre, *m.*; ~**ric,** barométrique.
baron, ~**ess,** baron, -ne, *m.f.*; ~**ial,** baronnial; ~**age,** baronnage, *m.*
barrack, *v.a.* (*slang*) conspuer.
barracks, caserne, *f.*; ⚠ *not* baraque *which* = '*hut*', '*hovel*'.
barrage, (*mil.*) tir de barrage, *m.*
barrel, tonneau, *m.*; (*cask*) baril, *m.*; (*rifle*) canon, *m.*; (*tar*) gonne, *f.*; ~ **organ,** orgue de barbarie, *m.* ~**led, double** ~, *adj.* (*gun*) à deux coups.
barren, stérile; ~**ness,** *see* BARENESS.
barricade, *s.* barricade, *f.*; *v.a.* barricader.
barrier, barrière, *f.*
barring, *prep.* sauf.
barrister, avocat, *m.*
barrow, (*mound*) tumulus, *m.*; (*wheel*) brouette, *f.*
barter, *s.* troc, *m.*; *v.a.* troquer (contre).
barton, cour de ferme, *f.*
barytone, (*voice and instr.*) baryton, *m.*

basalt, basalte, *m.*
base, basis, *s.* fondement, *m.*; (*operations*) base, *f.*; *v.a.* fonder.
base, *adj.* (*low, birth, lang.*) bas, -se; (*mean*) vil; (*metals*) non-précieu|x, ~se; (*coin*) fau|x, ~sse; **~ness,** bassesse, *f.*; **~ly,** bassement.
base-ball, (*U.S.A.*) base-ball, *m.*
baseless, sans fondement.
basement, (*arch.*) sous-sol, *m.*
bash in, enfoncer.
bashful, timide; **~ness,** timidité, *f.*; **~ly,** timidement.
basic, basal, fondamental.
basilisk, (*fab. reptile*) basilic, *m.*
basin, (*wash*) cuvette, *f.*; (*dock and river*) bassin, *m.*; (*bowl*) bol, *m.*
basinet, (*head-piece*) bassinet, *m.*
basis, base, *f.*
bask, *v.n.* (*in sun, &c.*) lézarder.
basket, panier, *m.*; (*without handle*) corbeille, *f.*; (*for back*) hotte, *f.*; (*game, fish*) bourriche, *f.*; **~-hilt,** (*sword*) coquille, *f.*; **~-maker,** vannier, *m.*
Basque, *adj.* (*when an adj. use small letter*) *and s.m.f.* Basque.
bas-relief, bas-relief, *m.*
bass, (*ichth.*) bar, *m.*
bass, *s.* (*mus.*) basse, *f.*; *double* ~, contrebasse, *f.*; ~ **viol,** basse de viole, *f.*; *adj.* de basse.
basset-hound, basset, *m.*
bassinet, berceau d'osier, *m.*
bassoon, *and* **bassoon-player,** basson, *m.*
bastard, *adj. and s.m.f.* bâtard, -e; **~ize,** déclarer bâtard.
baste, *v.a.* (*cook*) arroser.
bastille, bastille, *f.*
bastinado, *s.* bastonnade, *f.*
bastion, bastion, *m.*
bat, *s.* (*zool.*) chauve-souris, *f.*; (*cricket*) batte, *f.*; **brick~,** *see* BRICK; **~sman,** batteur, *m.*; *be as blind as a* ~, ne voir pas plus clair qu'une taupe.
Batavian, *adj.* (*when an adj. use small letter*) *and s.m.f.* Batave.
batch, (*bread, prisoners*) *s.* fournée, *f.*; (*mil.*) détachement, *m.*; (*letters*) paquet, *m.*
bate, *v.a.n.* diminuer; (*lower*) rabattre; *not to ~ a jot,* n'en vouloir* point démordre; *with ~d breath,* en baissant la voix.
bath, *s.* bain, *m.*; (*tub*) baignoire, *f.*; **~-attendant,** baigneu|r, ~se, *m.f.*; **~-chair,** fauteuil roulant, *m.*; **~-room,** salle de bain, *f.*; **~-towel,** serviette-éponge, *f.*
bathe, *v.a.* (*lit. and fig.*) baigner; *v.n.* se baigner; (*foment*) bassiner.
bather, *s.* baigneu|r, ~se, *m.f.*
bathing, *s.* bains, *m.pl.*; **~-box, -machine,** cabine de bain, *f.*; **~-drawers,** caleçon de bain, *m.*; **~-dress,** costume de bain, *m.*
bathos, pathos, *m.*; ⚠ **pathos** *is not* 'pathos', *but* pathétique, *m.*
bating, *prep.* hormis.
batman, brosseur, *m.*
battalion, bataillon, *m.*
batten, (*carp.*) volige, *f.*; ~ *on, v.n.* se gorger de.
batter, *s.* (*cook.*) pâte, *f.*
batter, *v.a.* battre; (*with cannon*) canonner; ~ *about* (*ill-treat*) malmener; ~ *down,* abattre; ~ *in,* enfoncer.
battering|-ram, bélier, *m.*; ~ **-train,** (*mil.*) artillerie de siège, *f.*
battery, (*mil.*) batterie, *f.*; (*electr.*) pile, *f.*; (*law*) voies de fait, *f.pl.*
battle, *s.* bataille, *f.*; ~ **-axe,** †hache d'armes, *f.*; ~ **-field,** champ de bataille, *m.*; *v.a.* ~ **with,** lutter contre.
battledore *and* **shuttle-cock,** volant, *m.*
battlement, créneau, *m.*; **~ed,** crénelé.
battleship, cuirassé, *m.*
battue, (*sport*) battue, *f.*; (*slaughter*) carnage, *m.*
bauble, babiole, *f.*; *fool's* ~, marotte, *f.*
Bavarian, *adj.* (*when an adj. use small letter*) *and s.m.f.* Bavarois, e.
bawdy, obscène.
bawl, *v.a.n.* brailler.
bay, (*geog.*) baie, *f.*; (*small*) anse, *f.*; (*arch.*) travée, *f.*; (*bot.*) *and* **~-tree,** laurier, *m.*; ~ **window,** fenêtre en saillie, *f.*; *at* ~, aux abois.
bay, *adj.* (*colour*) bai.
bay, *v.n.* aboyer.
bayonet, baïonnette, *f.*; *fix ~s,* mettre* baïonnette au canon; (*word of command*) baïonnette au canon!
bazaar, bazar, *m.*; *charity* ~, vente de charité, *f.*
be, *v.n.* être; (*be situated*) se trouver; (*be destined to*) devoir + *inf.*; (*weather*) faire*; (*physical feelings*) avoir; (*time*) être; *He is 10, 20, 30, &c.,* il a 10, 20, 30 ans; *be that as it may,* quoiqu'il en soit; *if it were not for,* sans, *prep.*; *that may* ~, cela se peut; *here he is!* (*exclam.*) le voici! *there she is!* la voila!; *here is my friend,* voici mon ami; *be here, there,* (*non-exclam.*) être ici, là; (*time elapsed since*) il y a. . . . *it is a week since I saw him,* il y a 8 jours que je ne l'ai vu; ~ *off,* s'en aller* (être); ~ *off his head,* avoir le cerveau fêlé; ~ *out,* (*not at home*) être sorti; (*books, &c.*) venir* de paraître.
beach, plage, *f.*
beacon, *s.* phare, *m.*; (*naut.*) balise, *f.*
bead, grain, *m.*; (*drop*) goutte, *f.*; ~ **-moulding,** (*arch.*) baguette, *f.*
beadle, (*eccles.*) bedeau, *m.*; (*door-keeper*) huissier, *m.*
beady, (*eyes*) petit et rond.
beagle, bigle, *m.*
beak, bec, *m.*
beaker, (*drinking-cup*) coupe, *f.*
beam, (*timber*) poutre, *f.*; (*light*) rayon, *m.*; (*plough*) timon, *m.*; (*balances*) fléau, *m.*; (*naut.*) bau, *m.*; *be on ~ ends,* (*naut.*) être engagé; (*fig.*) se trouver sur le pavé; *v.n.* (*shine*) rayonner.
beaming, (*smiling*) rayonnant (de).

beam-tree, alisier, *m.*
bean, (*broad*) fève, *f.*; (*kidney*) †haricot, *m.*; *French ~s, see* FRENCH; *broad ~,* grosse fève, *f.*; *coffee ~, see* COFFEE; *horse ~, see* HORSE; *be full of ~s* (*fam.*) avoir de l'entrain.
bear, ours, -e, *m.f.*; (*stock exch.*) bassier, *m.*; ~ **-cub**, ourson, *m.*; ~ **-garden** (*fig.*) pétaudière, *f.*
bear, *v.a.* (*fruit, carry sword, interest, arms, message, title, &c.*) porter; (*hold up*) soutenir*; (*endure*) supporter; (*birth*) enfanter; (*undergo*) essuyer; (*testimony, witness*) rendre; ~ *out,* justifier; ~ *oneself,* se comporter; *v.n.* (*direction*) se diriger; ~ *on,* (*rest on*) peser sur; (*relate to*) se rapporter à; ~ *up against,* se soutenir contre; ~ *down on,* s'abattre sur.
beard, barbe, *f.*; (*arrow*) dent, *f.*; **grey~**, barbon, *m.*
beard, *v.a.* braver.
bearded, barbu.
bearer, (*letter, news, &c.*) porteur, *m.*; *payable to ~,* payable au porteur.
bearing, *s.* (*relation*) rapport, *m.*; (*aspect*) aspect, *m.*; (*carriage*) maintien, *m.*; (*her. charge*) blason, *m.*; (*mach.*) coussinet, *m.*; *take one's bearings* (*naut.*) faire* un relèvement; (*find where one is*) s'orienter.
bearskin, (*mil.*) bonnet à poil, *m.*
beast, bête, *f.*; (*pers.*) animal, *m.*; ~ *of burden,* bête de somme, *f.*
beastliness, (*lit. and fig.*) saleté, *f.*
beastly, (*brutish*) bestial; (*dirty, obscene, weather*) sale; (*repulsive*) répugnant; (*slang*) infect.
beat, *s.* (*wings, heart, pulse, drum, &c.*) battement, *m.*; (*police, &c.*) ronde, *f.*
beat, *v.a.* battre; (*strike*) frapper; (*thrash*) rosser; ~ *back,* repousser; ~ *black and blue,* meurtrir de coups; ~ *hollow,* battre à plate couture; ~ *down* (*price*) faire* baisser; ~ *in,* enfoncer; ~ *up,* (*eggs*) fouetter; (*visit*) aller* (être) voir; (*recruits*) racoler; *that ~s me,* voilà qui me dépasse; *v.n.* (*pulse, drum, heart, &c.*) battre; ~ *at* (*door*) cogner à; ~ *upon,* (*rain, on window, &c.*) frapper sur; (*waves on shore*) se briser contre; ~ *about bush, see* BUSH; *dead-~,* éreinté.
beater, (*hunt*) rabatteur, *m.*
beatif|y, béatifier; **~ication**, béatification, *f.*; **~ic**, béatifique.
beating, (*thrashing*) rossée, *f.*; (*defeat*) défaite, *f.*
beatitude, béatitude, *f.*
beau, *s.* petit-maître, *m.*
beauteous, beautiful, beau (+*vowel, mute* 'h', bel) *fem.* belle.
beaut|y, (*lit. and pers.*) beauté, *f.*; **~ify**, *v.a.* embellir.
beaver, (*zool.*) castor, *m.*; (*armour*) visière de casque, *m.*
becalmed, (*naut.*) encalminé.
because, *conj.* parce que; ~ *of, prep.* à cause de.
beck, *s.* (*stream*) ruisseau, *m.*; (*nod*) signe de tête, *m.*; *be at the ~ and call of,* obéir au doigt et à l'œil (de).
beckon, *v.a.n.* faire* signe (à).
become, *v.n.* devenir* (être); (*profession, employment*) se faire*; *what will ~ of me?* que deviendrai-je?
become, (*suit*) aller* (être) à; (*be appropriate*) convenir* (à).
becoming, convenable; (*attire*) seyant; ⚠ séant is used more of conduct, &c. ~ *to* (*clothes*) qui va bien à; **~ly**, comme il convient.
bed, *s.* lit, *m.*; ~ **-pan**, bassin, *m.*; ~ *of roses,* (*fig.*) lit de roses, *m.*; ~ *and bedding,* literie, *f.*; *take to one's ~,* s'aliter.
bedaub, barbouiller.
bedazzle, éblouir.
bed-clothes, couvertures, *f.*
bedeck, parer(de).
bedew, arroser.
bedfellow, camarade de lit, *m.*
bedim, obscurcir.
bedizen, attifer.
bedlam, petites-maisons, *f.pl.*
Bedouin, *adj.* (b) *and s.m.f.* Bédouin, -e.
bedpost, colonne de lit, *f.*
bedraggle, (*dress*) crotter.
bedridden, alité.
bedroom, chambre à coucher, *f. adj.* de chambre à coucher.
bedside, chevet, *m.*; (*adj.*) de chevet.
bedstead, bois, *m.*
bedstraw, (*bot.*) gaillet, *m.*
bee, abeille, *f.*; (*U.S.A. approx.*) réunion, *f.*; **humble ~**, bourdon, *m.*; **~hive**, ruche, *f.*; ~ **orchid**, (*bot.*) ophrys abeille, *f.*; *have a ~ in one's bonnet,* avoir une araignée dans le plafond; *~'s wax,* cire d'abeille, *f.*
beech, *and* ~ **-tree**, †hêtre, *m.*; ~ **-marten**, fouine, *f.*; ~ **mast, nut**, faîne, *f.*; ~ **-grove**, plantation †hêtraie, *f.*
beef, bœuf, *m.*; ~ **-tea**, bouillon de bœuf, *m.*
beefsteak, bifteck, *m.*
beer, bière, *f.*; **~house**, taverne, *f.*
beet, bette, *f.*; **~root**, betterave, *f.*
beetle, scarabée, *m.*; **black ~**, blatte, *f.*
beetle, *s.* (*instr.*) maillet, *m.*
beetling, *adj.* surplombant.
befall, *v.n.* arriver (être); *v.a.* arriver à.
befit, convenir* à; **~ting**, convenable.
befogged, enveloppé de brouillard; (*fig.*) embrouillé.
befool, duper.
before, *prep.* (*time, order*) avant; (*place*) devant; *in the presence of,* par devant; + *inf.* avant de.
before, *adv.* (*time, order, place*) avant; (*in front*) en avant; (*previously*) auparavant.
before, *conj.* avant que + *subj.*; (*rather than*) plutôt que de + *inf.*
beforehand, (*in advance*) d'avance; (*early*) en avance.

beforehours, *adv.* (*Stock Exchange*) avant-bourse.
befoul, souiller.
befriend, être l'ami de.
beg, *v.a.* mendier; *v.n.* (*street, &c.*) mendier; (*ask*) demander (à + *pers. and acc.*); (*pers. to do*) *v.a.* prier de; (*beg to in letters*) avoir l'honneur de; ~ *for,* demander; *I* ~ *of you,* Je vous en prie.
beget, (*lit. and fig.*) engendrer.
beggar, mendiant, -e, *m.f.*; (*in jest*) coquin, *m.*; *v.a.* réduire* à la mendicité.
beggarly, misérable.
beggary, misère, *f.*
begging, mendicité, *f.*
begin, *v.a.* commencer; ~ *to,* commencer à *or* de; (*set about*) se mettre* à; ~ *afresh, again,* recommencer; *v.n.* commencer (à + *inf.* '*to do*'; par + *inf.* = '*by doing*').
beginner, *s.* commençant, -e, *m.f.*; (*novice*) débutant, -e, *m.f.*; ⚠ débutante *does not* = '*young girl going into Society*', *as in English.*
beginning, commencement, *m.*
begone! allez-vous-en!
begonia, bégonia, *m.*
begrime, salir.
begrudge, envier (une chose à quelqu'un = '*begrudge a person a thing*').
beguile, tromper; (*time*) faire passer; ~**r,** trompeu|r, ~se, *m.f.*
behalf, *on* ~ *of,* de la part de; *in* ~ *of,* en faveur de.
behav|e, se conduire*; ~**iour,** conduite, *f*; (*bearing*) tenue, *f.*; *be on one's good* ~*iour,* s'observer.
behead, décapiter.
behest, ordre, *m.*
behind, *adv.* derrière; *from* ~, par derrière.
behind, *prep.* derrière; *be* ~ *the times* (*pers.*) être un almanach de l'an passé; (*things*) être désu|et, ~ète.
behindhand, *adj. and adv.* (*time and payment*) en retard.
behold, voir*.
behold! *interj.* (*here*) voici! (*there*) voilà!
beholden to, redevable à (*pers.*); **for** (*thing*) de.
beholder, spectat|eur, ~rice, *m.f.*
behoof, avantage, *m.*; *on* ~ *of,* dans l'intérêt de.
behoves, it, (*necessity*) il faut; (*expedience*) il convient* de.
being, *s.* être, *m.*; (*existence*) existence, *f.*
belabour, rosser.
belated, *adj.* attardé.
belaud, prôner.
belch, *v.n.* éructer; ~ *out,* (*fig.*) vomir.
beldam, vieille sorcière, *f.*
beleaguer, assiéger.
belfry, bell-tower, clocher, *m.*
Belgian, *adj.* (*when an adj. use small letter*) *and s.m.f.* Belge.
belie, *v.a.* (*fail to justify*) démentir*; (*give false notion of*) tromper sur.
belief, croyance, *f.*; (*creed*) credo, *m.*; (*confidence*) confiance, *f.*; (*conviction*) conviction, *f.*; *to the best of my* ~, d'autant que je sache.
believable, croyable.
believe, *v.a.n.* croire*; ~*in* (*credit*) croire* à, *e.g.* ~ aux miracles; (*faith*) croire* en; *e.g.* ~ en Dieu; *make* ~ *to,* faire* semblant de; *would you* ~ *it?* conçoit-on?
believer, croyant, -e, *m.f.*; ~ *in,* (*favourer of*) partisan, *m.* (de).
belittle, *v.a.* (*fig.*) rapetisser.
bell, (*church*) cloche, *f.*; (*room*) sonnette, *f.*; (*cattle*) grelot, *m.*; (*hand*) clochette, *f.*; ~ **-flower,** (*bot.*) clochette, *f.*; ~ **-glass,** cloche, *f.*; ~**man,** crieur, *m.*; ~ **-pull,** (*rope*) cordon, *m.*; ~ **-ringer,** sonneur, *m.*; ~ **-tower,** clocher, *m.*; ~ **-wether,** sonnailler, *m.*; **dumb-** ~, *see* DUMB.
bell, *v.n.* (*stag*) bramer; ~ *the cat,* attacher le grelot.
belladonna, belladone, *f.*
bellicose, belliqueu|x, ~se.
belligerent, *s.m. and adj.* belligérant.
bellow, (*bull*) beugler; (*sea*) mugir; (*pers.*) †hurler.
bellowing, *s.* beuglement, mugissement, †hurlement, *m.* (*cf. above*).
bellows, (*fire and photo camera*) soufflet, *m.*
bell|y, *s.* ventre, *m.*; (*bottle*) panse, *f.*; (*sail*) renflement, *m.*; ~ **-ache,** mal au ventre, *m.*; *v.n.* (*sail*) se gonfler.
bellyful, *have one's* ~, avoir son soûl.
belong to, appartenir* à; (*come from, be native of*) être de; *v. impers.* il appartient* (à + *pers.* de + *inf.*).
belongings, (*clothes, movables*) effets, *m.pl.*; (*immovables*) biens, *m.pl.*
beloved, *adj. and s.m.f.* chéri, -e.
below, *adv.* (*gen. stairs, deck, &c.*) en bas; (*under*) au-dessous; (*downstream*) en aval; (*page*) ci-dessous; *here* ~, ici-bas.
below, *prep.* (*immediately*) sous; (*lower down*) au-dessous de; (*stream*) en aval de.; ⚠ Dessous *alone is not a preposition.*
belt, *s.* (*lit. and fig.*) ceinture; *swimming-* ~, *see* SWIMMING; *v.a.* ceindre* (de).
belvedere, belvédère, *m.*
bemoan, *v.a.* (*pers.*) pleurer; (*things*) déplorer.
bemused, *adj.* hébété (de).
bench, (*seat*) banc, *m.*; (*tribunal*) siège, *m.*; (*tailor, carpenter*) établi, *m.*; (*theatr.*) banquette, *f.*
bend, *s.* courbure, *f.*; (*road*) coude, *m.*; (*her.*) bande, *f.*
bend, *v.a.* courber; (*head*) pencher; (*knee*) fléchir; (*bow, energy, &c.*) tendre; (*twist*) tordre; (*eyes, steps*) diriger; *on* ~*ed knee,* à genoux.
bend, *v.n.* se courber; (*under weight*) plier; (*road, river*) faire* un coude.
beneath, *adv. prep.* (*unworthy of*) indigne de; ~ *contempt,* en tout et pour tout méprisable; *see also* BELOW.

Benedictine, *adj. and s.m.* bénédictin; (*liqueur*) bénédictine, *f.*
benediction, bénédiction, *f.*; (*giving thanks*) actions de grâce, *f.pl.*; (*Cath. liturg.*) bénédiction, *f.*
benefact|or, ~ress, bienfai|teur, ~trice, *m.f.*; **~ion,** bienfait, *m.*
benefice, (*eccles.*) bénéfice, *m.*
beneficen|ce, bienfaisance, *f.*; **~t,** bienfaisant; **~tly,** avec bienfaisance.
beneficial to, salutaire à; (*profitable*) profitable à.
benefit, *s.* (*kindness*) bienfait, *m.*; (*gain, advantage*) bénéfice, *m.*; (*theatr.*) représentation à bénéfice, *f.*; (*aid*) secours, *m.*; (*privilege*) privilège, *m.*
benefit, *v.a.* faire* du bien à; *v.n.* profiter; *~ by,* gagner à.
benevolen|ce, *s.* bienveillance, *f.*; **~t,** bienveillant.
benighted, anuité.
benign, béni|n, ~gne; **~ity,** bénignité, *f.*
benignant, (*pers.*) bienveillant.
benison, bénédiction, *f.*
bent, *s.* penchant, *m.*; *to the top of one's ~,* tout son soûl.
bent, (*body*) courbé; *~ on,* (*thing*) déterminé à; *be ~ on* (*doing*), tenir* à; *~ double,* plié en deux.
bentgrass, (*bot.*) agrostide, *f.*
benumb, engourdir.
benzine, benzine, *f.*
bequeath, léguer; (*fig.*) transmettre*.
bequest, (*law*) legs, *m.*
berberry, *see* BARBERRY.
bereave, priver (de); (*dispossess*) déposséder (de); **~ment,** (*death*) deuil, *m.*; **~d,** en deuil.
bergamot, (*pear*) bergamote, *f.*
berry, baie, *f.*; (*small*) grain, *m.*
berth, (*ship*) couchette, *f.*; (*job*) emploi; (*naut. sea-room*) mouillage, *m.*; *give a wide ~ to,* (*fig.*) s'écarter de.
beryl, béryl, *m.*
beseech, supplier; *I ~ you,* Je vous en supplie; **~ing,** *adj.* suppliant; **~ingly,** d'un ton suppliant.
beseem, *v.a.* convenir* à; **~ingly,** *adv.* convenablement.
beset, (*surround*) entourer (de); (*fig.*) assaillir* (de); (*path, &c.*) semer (de); **~ment,** (*eccles.*) péché habituel, *m.*; **~ting,** *adj.* habituel, -le;
beshrew, *v.a.* maudire.*
beside, *prep.* (*near and comparison*) auprès de; (*except*) excepté; *be ~ oneself,* (*fig.*) être hors de soi; (*moreover*) de plus.
besides, *adv.* en outre; *sometimes use* aussi, *e.g. there were some women besides,* il y avait des femmes aussi.
besiege, (*mil.*) assiéger; (*importune, ~ with questions, &c.*) obséder (de); (*the*) **~d,** assiégés, *m.pl.*; **~r,** assiégeant, *m.*
beslobber, embrasser avec effusion.
besmear, barbouiller.
besmirch, (*soil*) souiller; (*reputation, &c.*) ternir.
besom, balai, *m.*
besotted, abruti.
bespangle, (*dot*) parsemer (de).
bespatter, éclabousser (de).
bespeak, (*order*) commander; (*reserve*) retenir*; (*be evidence of*) annoncer.
bespeckle, tacheter (de).
besprinkle, parsemer (de); (*liquid*) arroser (de).
best, *adj.* le meilleur; **~ girl,** (*slang*) bonne amie, *f.*; **~ man,** garçon d'honneur; *the ~ part of,* la plupart de; *in ~ bib and tucker, see* BIB; *it is ~ to,* le mieux est de; *have the ~ of it,* avoir le dessus; *to the ~ of my recollection,* autant que je puis m'en souvenir; *make the ~ of it,* en tirer son parti; *do one's ~,* faire* tout son possible (pour).
best, *v.a.* (*fam. get the better of*) rouler.
best, *adv.* le mieux.
bestial, bestial; (*obscene*) obscène; **~ity,** bestialité, *f.*
bestir oneself, se remuer.
bestow, *v.a.* conférer (à); (*devote*) consacrer (à); **~al,** don, *m.*
bestrew with, joncher de.
bestride, enjamber; (*horse*) enfourcher.
bet, *s.* pari, *m.*; **~ter, ~tor,** parieu|r, ~se, *m.f.*; **~ting,** paris, *m.pl.*; *v.a.* parier; *I ~ you don't,* (*slang*) fiche que tu ne fais pas cela; *you bet!* (*slang*) pour sûr!
betake oneself to, (*place*) se rendre à; (*occupation*) se livrer à; (*have recourse to*) avoir recours à.
betel, (*bot.*) bétel, *m.*
bethink oneself of, s'aviser de.
betide, *v.n.* arriver (être); *v.a.* arriver à; *woe ~!* malheur à!
betimes, *adv.* de bonne heure; (*in good time*) à temps.
betoken, indiquer.
betony, (*bot.*) bétoine, *f.*
betray, (*secret, be false to*) trahir; (*show*) révéler; (*hand over*) livrer (à).
betrayal, trahison, *f.*
betrayer, traître, ~sse, *m.f.*
betroth, fiancer; **~al,** fiançailles, *f.pl.*; **~ed,** *s.* fiancé, -e, *m.f.*
better, *adj.* meilleur; *adv.* mieux; *so much the ~,* tant mieux; *be ~,* être, aller* (être) mieux; *~ and ~,* de mieux en mieux; *go one ~,* l'emporter; *think ~ of,* se raviser (de); *it is ~ to,* il vaut mieux + *inf. or* que + *subj.*; *the ~ part,* la majeure partie, *f.*; *get ~* (*health*) se remettre*; *get the ~ of,* l'emporter sur; (*fam.*) rouler: *for ~ or worse,* vaille que vaille.
better, *v.a.* (*make better*) améliorer; (*improve on*) aire* mieux que; **~ment, ~ing,** amélioration.
betters, *s.pl.* ceux qui sont au-dessus de soi.
between, betwixt, entre; *~ this and then,* d'ici là; *~ this and to-morrow,* d'ici à demain; *~ the three of them,* entre eux trois; *betwixt and ~,* entre les deux.

bevel, *s.* biseau, *m.*; **~led,** *adj.* taillé en biseau.
beverage, breuvage, *m.*
bevy, (*birds*) volée, *f.*; (*girls, &c.*) essaim, *m.*
bewail, *v.a.* pleurer; *v.n.* se lamenter (sur).
beware! *interj.* prenez garde!
beware of, (*doing*) *v.n.* se garder de; (*thing*) prendre* garde à.
bewilder, égarer; (*frighten*) effarer; **~ment,** perplexité, *f.*; **~ing,** confus.
bewitch, (*magic*) ensorceler; (*charm*) enchanter; **~ing,** enchant|eur, ~eresse; **~ment,** (*magic*) ensorcellement, *m.*
bewray, *v.a.* trahir involontairement.
beyond, *s.*; *the* ~, au-delà, *m.*
beyond, *prep.* au delà de; (*exceeding*) outre; (*out of*) †hors de; ~ *endurance,* intolérable; ~ *measure,* outre mesure; ~ *question,* †hors de doute; ~ *reach,* †hors de portée; *that's* ~ *me,* cela me passe; *adv.* au delà.
bezel, (*ring*) chaton, *m.*
bezique, (*cards*) bésique, *m.*
bias, *s.* (*slant*) biais, *m.*; (*prejudice*) préjugé, *m.*; (*fig.*) penchant, *m.*
bias, *v.a.* influencer. ⚠ *Not* biaiser, *which* = '*slope*', '*dodge*'.
bib, (*baby's and apron*) bavette, *f.*; *in her best* ~ *and tucker,* parée de ses plus beaux atours.
bibber, (*wine-* ~) biberon, *m.*
Bibl|e, bible, *f.*; **~ical,** biblique.
bibliograph|y, bibliographie, *f.*; **~er,** bibliographe, *m.*
bibliomania, bibliomanie, *f.*; **~c,** bibliomane, *m.*
bibliophile, bibliophile, *m.*
bibulous, (*absorbent*) spongieu|x, ~se; (*pers.*) adonné à la boisson.
biceps, biceps, *m.*
bicker, (*quarrel*) se chamailler; (*of a brook*) gazouiller; **~ing,** chamaillerie, *f.*
bicycle, bicyclette, *f.*; *v.n.* faire* de la bicyclette; (*go on cycle*) aller* (être) à bicyclette.
bid, *s.* (*auction*) enchère, *f.*; *higher* ~, surenchère, *f.*
bid, *v.a.* (*order to*) ordonner (*dat. of pers. and* de + *inf.*); (*invite*) inviter; (*money*) offrir*; (*a price for*) enchérir; ~ (*welcome, time of day, &c.*) souhaiter; *v.n.* (*make a bid*) mettre une enchère; ~ *fair to,* promettre* de; ~ *high,* mettre* de grosses enchères.
bidding, ordre, *m.*; (*auction*) enchère, *f.*
bidder, (*auction*) enchérisseur, *m.*
bide, *see* ABIDE; ~ *one's time,* attendre son heure.
biennial, (*recurring every two years*) bisannuel, -le; (*lasting 2 years*) biennal.
bier, bière, *f.*
big, (*large, grown up*) grand; (*drum, bulky*) gros; (*important*) important; ~ **toe,** gros orteil, *m.*; ~ *game,* grands fauves, *m.pl.*; ~*-game-hunting,* chasse aux fauves, *f.*; ~ *with,* gros de; **~ness,** grosseur, *f.*
bigam|ist, bigame, *m.f.*; **~y,** bigamie, *f.*; **~ous,** bigame.
bigot, *s.m.f.* bigot, -e; **~ed,** bigot; **~ry,** bigoterie, *f.*
bigwig, *s.* gros bonnet, *m.*
bike, (*abbrev., also push-*~) vélo, *m.*
bilberry, (*bot.*) myrtille, *f.*
bil|e, bile, *f.*; **-iousness,** attaque de bile, *f.*; **~ious,** bilieu|x, ~se.
bilge, *s.* (*naut.*) petits fonds, *m.pl.*; ~ **-water,** eau de la cale, *f.*
bill, *s.* (*bird*) bec, *m.*; (*hedge, also* ~*hook*) serpe, *f.*
bill, *s.* (*comm.*) **1** (*hotel, profession*) note, *f.*; **2** (*exchange*) lettre de change, *f.*; **3** (*restaurant*) addition, *f.*; **4** (*invoice*) facture, *f.*; **5** (*tradesman's*) mémoire, *m.*; **6** (*lading*) connaissement, *m.*; **7** (*poster*) affiche, *f.*; **8** (*hand*) prospectus, *m.*; **9** (*naut., health*) patente, *f.*; **10** (*of fare*) carte, *f.*; **11** (*Parl.*) projet de loi, *m.*; **12** (*indictment*) mise en accusation, *f.*; ~ *of attainder,* arrêt de la confiscation des biens, *m.*; ~ *of fare,* menu, *m.*; ~ **-broker,** courtier de change, *m.*; ~ **-sticker,** afficheur, *m.*; *dishonour a* ~, ne pas faire* honneur à un effet; *dishonoured* ~, effet retourné, *m.*; *back a* ~, endosser un effet; *m.*; *take up a* ~, honorer un effet; *long-, short-dated* ~, effet à longue, à courte échéance, *m.*
billet, billet de logement, *m.*; (*wood*) bûche, *f.*
billiard, *adj.* ~ **-cue,** queue de billard, *f.*; ~ **-room,** salle de billard, *f.*; ~ **-table,** billard, *m.*
billiards, billard, *m.*
billingsgate, *s.* langage de la †halle, *f.*
billow, lame, *f.*; **~y,** houleu|x, ~se.
bimetallism, bimétallisme, *m.*
bin, †huche, *f.*
binary, binaire.
bind, *v.a.* (*tie*) lier; (*compel*) contraindre*; (*book*) relier; (*book in boards*) cartonner; ~ **up,** (*wound*) bander; ~ *oneself to,* engager sa parole à; *it is bound to happen,* cela doit arriver; *cloth-bound,* relié en toile; *half-bound,* (*book*) en demi-reliure.
binder, (*pers.*) relieur, *m.*
binding, *s.* (*braid*) galon, *m.*; (*books*) reliure, *f.*; *adj.* obligatoire; (*law*) commissoire.
bindweed, (*bot.*) liseron, *m.*
binoculars, jumelles, *f.pl.*
binomial, *adj. and s.m.* binôme.
biograph|y, biographie, *f.*; **~er,** biographe, *m.*; **~ical,** biographique.
biolog|y, biologie, *f.*; **~ical,** biologique.
biped, *adj. and s.m.f.* bipède.
biplane, biplan, *m.*
birch, (*tree*) bouleau, *m.*; (*flogging*) férule, *f.*; (*rod*) verge, *f.*; *v.a.* fouetter.
bird, oiseau, *m.*; ~ *of passage,* oiseau de passage, *m.*; *see* HUMMING, PARADISE; *a* ~

in the hand is worth two in the bush, un tiens vaut mieux que deux tu l'auras; ~*s of a feather flock together*, qui se ressemble s'assemble; ~**-catcher**, oiseleur, *m.*; ~**-fancier**, marchand d'oiseaux, *m.*; ~*'s-eye view*, vue à vol d'oiseau, *f.*; ~ **-lime**, glu, *f.*

biretta, (*eccles.*) barrette, *f.*

birth, naissance, *f.*; (*origin*) extraction, *f.*; *by* ~, de naissance; *of high, low birth*, de †haute, basse extraction; **child-** ~, enfantement, *m.*; ~ **-place**, lieu de naissance, *m.*; ~ **-rate**, natalité, *f.*

birthday, (*date*) jour de naissance, *f.*; (*saint's day*) fête, *f.*

birthright, droit d'aînesse, *m.*

biscuit, (*bread, porcelain*) biscuit, *m.*; ~ **-coloured**, brun clair, *invar.*

bisect, diviser en deux.

bishop, évêque, *m.*; (*chess*) fou, *m.*; ~**ric**, évêché, *m.*

bismuth, bismuth, *m.*

bison, bison, *m.*

bissextile, bissextile.

bit, *s.* morceau, *m.*; (*bridle*) mors, *m.*; (*of money*) pièce, *f.*; (*a drill*) mèche, *f.*; *not a* ~ (*of it*), pas le moins du monde; ~ *by* ~, petit à petit; *a* ~ *of a wag*, un peu plaisant.

bitch, chienne, *f.*

bite, *s.* morsure, *f.*; (*insect*) piqûre, *f.*; (*mouthful*) bouchée, *f.*; (*fish*) touche, *f.*

bit|e, *v.a.* (*lit., fig., and tool*) mordre; (*gnaw*) ronger; (*insect*) piquer; *v.n.* (*lit., fig., tool, anchor, fish*) mordre; *once* ~*ten, twice shy*, chat échaudé craint l'eau froide; *what's biting you?* (*U.S.A.*) Quelle mouche vous pique?

biter, *the* ~ *bit*, le trompeur trompé.

biting, *adj.* (*fig.*) mordant; (*wind*) glacial; ~**ly**, d'une manière mordante; *it 's* ~*ly cold*, le froid pince dur.

bitter, (*lit., fig., tears*) am|er, ~ère; (*cold*) âpre; (*relentless*) acharné; (*style, language*) mordant; ~ **-apple**, coloquinte, *f.*; ~ **cold**, *s.* froid noir, *m.*; ~ **-sweet**, *n.* (*bot.*) douce-amère, *f.*; ~ **-sweet**, *adj.* aigre-dou|x, ~ce; ~**ness**, (*lit. and fig.*) amertume, *f.*; (*weather*) rigueur, *f.*; ~**ly**, amèrement.

bittern, (*ornith.*) butor, *m.*

bitum|en, bitume, *m.*; ~**inous**, bitumineu|x, ~se.

bivalve, *adj. and s.m.* bivalve.

bivouac, *s.* bivouac, *m.*; *v.a.* bivouaquer.

black, *s.* (*negro, colour, mourning*) noir, *m.*; (*her.*) sable, *m.*; ~ **out**, *see below*.

black, *adj.* (*lit. and fig.*) noir; ~ *art*, *see* ART; ~**-backed gull**, *see* GULL; ~ **beetle**, *see* BEETLE; ~ **broth**, (*ant.*) brouet noir, *m.*; ~ **cock**, petit coq de bruyère, *m.*; ~ **currant**, cassis, *m.*; ~ **eye**, œil poché, *m.*; ~ **-eyed**, aux yeux noirs; ~ **grape**, morillon, *m.*; ~ **letter**, lettre gothique, *f.*; ~ **-lead**, mine de plomb, *f.*; ~*-lead pencil*, crayon à mine de plomb, *m.*; ~ **sheep**, (*fig.*) brebis galeuse; ~**ness**, (*lit. and fig.*) noirceur, *f.*

black, *v.a.* (*boots*) cirer.

blackamoor, *s.* moricaud, -e, *m.f.*

blackball, *s.* boule noire, *f.*; *v.a.* black-bouler.

blackberry, mûre de ronce, *f.*

blackbird, merle, *m.*

blackboard, (*school*) tableau noir, *m.*

blackcap, (*ornith.*) fauvette à tête noire, *f.*

blackcurrant, cassis, *m.*

blacken, *v.a.* noircir.

blackguard, (*knave*) coquin, *m.*; (*contempt*) goujat, *m.*; *v.a.* agonir; ~**ly**, *adj.* canaille; ~*ly trick*, canaillerie, *f.*

blacking, *s.* cirage, *m.*; ~ **brush**, brosse à chaussures, *f.*

blackleg, filou, *m.*; (*workman*) renard, *m.*

blackmail, *s.* chantage, *m.*; ~**er**, maître-chanteur, *m.*; *v.a.* faire* chanter.

blackout, (*raid*) *s.* fermeture enfondue, *f.*; *v.a.* couper la lumière (à).

blacksmith, forgeron, *m.*

blackthorn, épine noire, *f.*

bladder, (*med.*) vessie, *f.*

blade, (*grass*) brin, *m.*; (*knives, sword, &c.*) lame, *f.*; (*oar*) pale, *f.*; ~ *of propeller*, (*aeron.*) pale d'hélice, *f.*

blain, *s.* pustule, *f.*

blamable, blâmable.

blame, *s.* blâme, *m.*; *v.a.* blâmer; ~ *for*, accuser de; ~**less**, innocent; ~**lessness**, innocence, *f.*

blameworthy, digne de blâme.

blanch, *v.a.* (*almonds, &c.*) blanchir; *v.n.* (*pers.*) pâlir.

blancmange, *s.* blanc-manger, *m.*

bland, dou|x, ~ce; ~**ishment**, caresse, *f.*; ~**ness**, douceur, *f.*

blank, *s.* (*blank space*) blanc, *m.*; (*dash in print.*) tiret, *m.*; (*memory*) trou, *m.*; (*void*) vide, *m.*; (*lottery*) billet blanc, *m.*

blank, *adj.* (*abashed*) interdit; (*verse, page*) blan|c, ~che; (*sheer*) absolu; ~ *cheque*, chèque en blanc, *m.*; ~ **cartridge**, cartouche à blanc, *f.*; ~**ly**, (*look*) sans expression.

blanket, couverture, *f.*; *v.a.* (*scandal, &c.*) étouffer.

blare, *s.* retentissement, *m.*; *v.n.* retentir.

blasphem|e, *v.a.n.* blasphémer; ~**er**, blasphémat|eur, ~rice, *m.f.*; ~**y**, blasphème, *m.*; ~**ous**, blasphématoire.

blast, *s.* rafale, *f.*; (*instr.*) son, *m.*; ~ **-furnace**, †haut fourneau, *m.*; *v.a.* flétrir; (*mine*) faire* sauter; (*destroy*) détruire*.

blastpipe, tuyère, *f.*

blatant, braillard.

blaze, *s.* flamme, *f.*; (*hearth*) flambée, *f.*; (*fig.*) éclat, *m.*; (*passion*) explosion, *f.*

blaze, *v.a.* ~ *abroad*, proclamer; *v.n.* (*fig.*) flamber; ~ *with*, resplendir de.

blazer, (*sport*) blazer, *m.*

blazing, (*blinding, dazzling*) aveuglant.

blazon, (*her.*) *s.* blason, *m.*; *v.a.* blasonner.
bleach, *v.a.n.* blanchir; **~ing,** blanchiment, *m.*, ⚠ *'blanchissement' not French.*
bleak, exposé au vent; (*dreary*) lugubre.
blear-eyed, bleary, chassieu|x, ~se.
bleat, (bleating), *s.* bêlement, *m.*; *v.n.* bêler.
bleed, *v.a.n.* (*lit., and wrest money from*) saigner; **~ing,** *adj.* saignant; (*heart*) navré; ~ *at nose,* saigner du nez.
blemish, défaut, *m.*; (*stain*) tache, *f.*
blemish, *v.a.* défigurer; (*fig.*) flétrir.
blench, *v.n.* reculer.
blend, *s.* mélange, *m.*
blend, *v.a.* (*colours*) fondre; (*mix*) mêler; (*tea*) faire* un mélange de; *v.n.* se fondre.
bless, *v.a.* bénir; *be blest with,* jouir de; *God ~ you! God ~ me! see* GOD.
blessed, béni; (*Virgin*) Sainte; (*happy*) heureu|x, ~se; (*consecrated*) bénit; (*Saints*) bienheureu|x, ~ se; **~ness,** bonheur, *m.*
blessing, *s.* bénédiction, *f.*; (*grace*) bénédicité, *m.*; (*boon*) bonheur, *m.*; *What a ~!* Quelle bénédiction!
blight, *s.* (*fruit, flowers*) brouissure, *f.*; (*corn*) nielle, *f.*
blight, v.a. brouir; (*fig.*) flétrir.
blind, *s.* **draw- ~,** store, *m.*; *Venetian ~,* jalousie, *f.*
blind, *adj.* (*lit. and fig.*) aveugle; ~ *in one eye,* borgne; ~ *to,* aveugle sur; ~ **man, woman,** aveugle, *m.f.*; ; ~ *man's buff,* colin-maillard, *m.*; ~ *man's holiday,* entre chien et loup; ~ *alley,* impasse, *f.*; **~ -worm,** orvet, *m.*; **~ ly,** aveuglément; ~ *as a bat, see* BAT.
blind, *v.a.* aveugler.
blindfold, *v.a.* (*lit. and fig.*) bander les yeux à; *adv.* les yeux bandés (fig.)
blindness, cécité, *f.*; (*fig.*) aveuglement, *m.*
blink, *s.* aperçu, *m.*
blink, *v.n.* clignoter.
blinker, (*horse*) œillère, *f.*
bliss, bonheur, *m.*; (*eccles.*) béatitude, *f.*; **~full,** heureu|x, ~se.
blister, ampoule, *f.*; *v.n.* former des ampoules.
blithe, blithesome, gai.
blizzard, *s.* tourmente de neige, *f.*
bloated, (*face*) bouffi; *~ed with,* (*fig.*) bouffi de.
bloater, hareng, *m.*
block, *s.* (*traffic*) encombrement, *m.*; (*buildings*) pâté, *m.*; (*marble, &c.*) bloc, *m.*; (*wood and execution*) billot, *m.*; **stumbling- ~,** pierre d'achoppement, *f.*; *v.a.* (*stop up*) boucher; (*cricket*) bloquer.
blockade, *s.* blocus, *m.*; *v.a.* bloquer.
blockhead, ganache, *f.*
blockhouse, blockhaus, *m.*
blond|e, blond, -e, *s.m.f.*; *s.* (*lace*) blonde, *f.*; *adj.* blond.
blood, (*lit., kindred, lineage, race*) sang, *m.*; (*pers.*) élégant, *m.*; **~ -letting,** saignée, *f.*; ~ **orange,** orange sanguine, *f.*; **~-red,** sang de bœuf, *invar.*; **~ -stained,** taché de sang; *to run in the ~,* avoir cela dans le sang; **~ -curdling,** à donner la chair de poule; *make bad ~ between,* semer la discorde entre.
bloodhound, limier, *m.*
bloodless, exsangue; **~ly,** sans effusion de sang.
bloodshed, effusion de sang, *f.*
bloodshot, *adj.* injecté de sang.
bloodstone, sanguine, *f.*
bloodsucker, (*fig.*) sangsue, *f.*
bloodthirst|y, sanguinaire; **~iness,** soif de sang, *m.*
bloodwort, (*bot.*) sanguinaire, *f.*
bloody, sanglant; (*cruel*) sanguinaire; (*foul language*) satané.
bloom, *s.* fleur, *f.*; ~ *of youth,* fleur de l'âge, *f.*; *take the ~ off,* (*fig.*) déflorer.
bloom, *v.n.* (*lit. and fig.*) fleurir; (*pres. part. and imperf. fig.*) florissant, florissais.
blooming, *adj.* (*in flower*) fleuri; (*dazzling*) éclatant; (*colloq.*) sacré.
blossom, (*lit. and fig.*) fleur, *f.*; *v.n.* fleurir.
blot, *s.* (*lit. and fig.*) tache, *f.*; (*ink*) pâté, *m.*
blot, *v.a.* (*stain*) souiller; (*ink*) faire* un pâté sur; ~ *out,* effacer.
blotting, -case, buvard, *m.*; **~ -pad,** sous-main, *m. invar.*; **~ -paper,** papier buvard, *m.*
blouse, blouse, *f.*
blow, *s.* (*lit. and fig.*) coup, *m.*; *without striking a ~,* sans coup férir*; *come to ~s,* en venir* (être) aux coups.
blow, *v.a.* (*instr.*) sonner; (*glass*) souffler; ~ **out,** (*light*) éteindre*; ~ *out one's brains,* se brûler la cervelle; ~ **up,** faire* sauter; (*pop. pers.*) donner un savon à.
blow, *v.n.* (*wind, breath*) souffler; (*instr.*) sonner; (*flowers*) s'épanouir; *the wind ~s,* il fait du vent; ~ **over,** passer; ~ *hot and cold* (*fig.*), souffler le chaud et le froid.
blower, (*for increasing draught of fire*) tablier de cheminée, *m.*
blowfly, mouche à viande, *f.*
blowhole, (*cetaceans*) évent, *m.*; (*tunnel*) puits d'aération, *m.*
blowpipe, chalumeau, *m.*
blowzy, rougeaud.
blubber, *s.* graisse de baleine, *f.*
bludgeon, trique, *f.*
blue, *adj.* and *s.m.* bleu; *have a fit of the ~s,* avoir des papillons noirs; ~ *funk,* (*pop.*) frousse intense, *f.*; **~stocking,** bas bleu, *m.*
bluebell, jacinthe des prés, *f.*
bluejacket, matelot de la marine, *m.*
bluff, *adj.* rude; *v.a.* bluffer; *v.n.* payer d'audace.
bluish, bleuâtre.
blunder, *s.* bévue, *f.*; (*fam.*) gaffe, *f.*; *v.n.* faire* une bévue; (*fam.*) gaffer.
blunderbuss, espingole, *f.*

blunder|er, maladroit, *m.*; (*fam.*) gaffeu|r, ~se, *m.f.* **~ing,** *adj.* maladroit.
blunt, (*knives*) émoussé; (*pers.*) brusque; (*not sensitive*) insensible; *v.a.* (*lit. and fig.*) émousser; **~ness,** (*fig.*) brusquerie, *f.*
blur, *s.* (*lit. and fig.*) tache, *f.*; (*indistinct vision*) vision indistincte, *f.*; *v.a.* (*smear*) barbouiller.
blurt out, laisser échapper.
blush, *s.* rougeur, *f.*; *v.n.* rougir; ~ *for,* rougir (de).
blushing, *adj.* rougissant.
bluster, *s.* fanfaronnade, *f.*; *v.n.* fanfaronner; (*wind*) mugir; ~ *at,* (*fig.*) tempêter contre; **~er,** fanfaron, *m.*
blustering, *adj.* fanfaron, -ne; (*wind*) orageu|x, ~se.
boa, (*constrictor, also fur*) boa, *m.*
boar, (*pig*) verrat, *m.*; *wild* ~, sanglier, *m.*; *young wild* ~, marcassin, *m.*; *~'s head,* †hure, *f.*; *~'s lair,* bauge, *f.*; *~'s snout,* butoir, *m.*; **~-spear,** épieu, *m.*; *~'s tusk,* défense, *f.*
board, planche, *f.*; (*food, &c.*) pension, *f.*; (*polit.*) ministère, *m.*; (*directors, management*) conseil, *m.*; (*naut.*) bord, *m.*; (*thick paper*) carton, *m.*; **~s,** (*theatr.*) planches, *f.pl.*; ~ **meeting,** conseil des administrateurs, *m.*; ~ **wages,** argent pour frais de nourriture, *m.*; ~ *and lodging,* table, *f.*, et logement, *m.*; ~ *of health,* commission d'hygiène, *f.*; *above* ~, cartes sur table; *in ~s,* (*binding*) cartonné; *on* ~, *adv.* à bord; *go on* ~, monter (être) à bord; (*prep.*) à bord de.
board, *v.a.* prendre* en pension; (*floor, &c.*) planchéier; (*a ship*) monter (être) à bord de; (*naut. come alongside*) accoster; *v.n.* ~ *with,* avoir sa pension chez.
boarder, pensionnaire, *m.f.*; (*school*) interne, *m.f.*
boarding, (*floors*) planchéiage, *m.*; (*lodging, &c.*) pension, *f.*; ~ **-house,** pension, *f.*; ~ **-school,** pensionnat, *m.*
boarhound, vautre, *m.*
boast, *s.* vanterie, *f.*; *make it one's* ~ *to,* se faire gloire de; *v.n.* se vanter; ~ *of,* se vanter de; *v.a.* (*lay claim to*) revendiquer.
boaster, vantard, *m.*
boasting, boastful, vantard; **~ly,** avec jactance.
boat, *s.* bateau, *m.*; **flying-~,** *see* FLYING; **jolly-~,** petit canot, *m.*; *see also* ROWING; ~ **-hook,** gaffe, *f.*; ~ **-house,** †hangar à canot, *m.*; ~ **-load,** batelée, *f.*; *v.n.* faire* le canotage.
boater, (*hat*) canotier, *m.*
boating, *s.* (*sport*) canotage, *m.*
boatman, batelier, *m.*; (*hirer of boats*) loueur de canots, *m.*
boatswain, maître d'équipage, *m.*; *~'s mate,* (*formerly*) contremaître, *m.*
bob, *s.* (*curtsy*) révérence, *f.*; ~ **-tailed,** (*horse*) à queue écourtée; ~ **-wig,** perruque à nœuds, *f.*; *v.a.* (*tail of horse*) écourter; (*woman's hair*) couper à la Jeanne d'Arc; *v.n.* faire* une révérence.
bobbin, (*for thread*) fuseau, *m.*
bobby, (*fam. for policeman*) flic, *m.*
bode, *v.a.* présager; ~ *ill, well,* être de mauvais, bon augure; **~ful,** de mauvais augure.
bodice, corsage, *m.*
-bodied, *adj.* à corps . . .
bodily, *adj.* corporel, -le.
bodkin, poinçon, *m.*
body, (*animal, human, collection of men, substance, wine*) corps, *m.*; (*pers.*) personne, *f.*; (*veh.*) carrosserie, *f.*; (*dress*) corsage, *m.*; (*main part*) fond, *m.*; *dead* ~, cadavre, *m.*; *foreign* ~, corps étranger, *m.*; *main* ~, (*mil. &c.*) gros, *m.*; ~ **-guard,** gardes du corps, *m.pl.*; ⚠ *Not* corps de garde *which = 'guard-room' or 'house'.*
bog, *s.* marécage, *m.*; *v.a.* embourber.
bogey, croquemitaine, *m.*
boggle, *v.n.* (*hesitate*) hésiter (à, *or* devant); (*fumble*) tâtonner.
boggy, marécageu|x, ~se.
bogus, *adj.* (*company, &c.*) véreu|x, ~se; ~ *concern,* attrape-niais, *m. invar.*
boil, *v.a.* faire* bouillir; (*cook*) faire* cuire; *v.n.* (*lit. and fig.*) bouillir*; ⚠ bouillir *alone should not be used transitively*; ~ *away,* (*water*) s'évaporer; ~ *fast,* bouillir* à gros bouillons; ~ *over,* bouillonner; ~ *slowly,* bouillotter; *~ed beef, see* BEEF; *~ed eggs,* œufs à la coque, *m.pl.*; *hard ~ed eggs,* œufs durs, *m.pl.*; *~ed potatoes,* pommes de terre à l'eau, *f.pl.*
boiler, (*mach.*) chaudière, *f.*; (*copper, cooking*) marmite; *f.*; ~ **-room,** chambre de chauffe, *f.*
boiling, *s.* (*state of*) ébullition, *f.*; *adj.* (*lit. and fig.*) bouillant; ~ *hot,* tout bouillant.
boisterous, (*weather*) orageu|x, ~se; (*pers.*) bruyant; ~ **ness,** violence, *f.*; (*turbulence*) turbulence, *f.*; **~ly,** impétueusement; (*noisily*) bruyamment.
bold, †hardi; (*impudent*) effronté; (*design, style, &c.*) vigoureu|x, ~se; (*cliffs*) escarpé; *make* ~ *to,* oser +*inf.*; ~ *faced,* effronté; **~ness,** †hardiesse, *f.*; (*effrontery*) effronterie, *f.*; **~ly,** †hardiment.
bole, *s.* (*tree*) tronc, *m.*
bollard, (*naut.*) poteau d'amarrage, *m.*
bolster, *s.* traversin, *m.*; *v.n.* ~ *up,* soutenir*.
bolt, *s.* verrou, *m.*; (*locks*) pêne, *m.*; (*arrow*) trait, *m.*
bolt, *v.a.* verrouiller; (*swallow*) avaler; *v.n.* filer; (*horse*) s'emballer.
bolt, (*sift*) tamiser; **~er,** (*sieve*) blutoir, *m.*
bomb, *s.* bombe, *f.*; *delayed action* ~, bombe à retardement; **~-proof,** à l'épreuve des bombes; **~-shell,** bombe, *f.*; **~-thrower,** lance-bombes, *m. invar.*; (*pers.*) lanceur de bombes, *m.*; *v.a.* bombarder; (*aeron.*) lancer des bombes sur; *~ing squadron,* (*aeron.*) escadrille de bombardement, *m.*; *see also* GAS, *&c.*
bombard, bombarder; **~ment,** bom-

bardement, *m.*; **~ier,** (*approx.*) maréchal des logis d'artillerie, *m.*; ⚠ *Not* bombardier *which = 'bomber', 'grenadier'* (*mil. obsolete*).
bombasine, (*fabric*) bombasin, *m.*
bombast, *s.* emphase, *f.*; (*in style*) enflure, *f.*; **~ic,** emphatique; (*style, language*) ampoulé; **~ically,** avec emphase.
bomber, *s.* (*aeron.*) avion de bombardement, *m.*; *three-engine ~,* trimoteur de bombardement, *m.*
bond, *s.*; (*fig. lit.*) lien, *m.*; (*comm. law*) obligation, *f.*; **~s,** fers, *m.pl.*; **~ -note,** acquit à caution, *m.*
bonded, *adj.* **~ goods,** marchandises entreposées, *f.pl.*; **~ warehouse,** entrepôt, *m.*
bondholder, obligataire, *m.f.*
bondman, esclave, *m.*
bondmaid, esclave, *f.*
bondslave, esclave, *m.f.*
bone, *s.* os, *m.*; (*fish*) arête, *f.*; **~s,** (*remains*) restes, *m.pl.*; *~ of contention,* pomme de discorde, *f.*; *have a ~ to pick with,* avoir maille à partir avec; *make no ~ s about it,* ne faire* ni une ni deux; *be nothing but skin and ~,* n'avoir que la peau et les os; *he'll never make old ~s,* il ne fera pas de vieux os; *what is bred in the ~ will come out in the flesh,* chassez le naturel, il revient au galop.
boned, large- ~, ossu.
boneless, sans os.
bonesetter, rebouteu|r, ~se, *m.f.*
bonfire, feu de joie, *m.*
bonnet, (*woman's*) chapeau, *m.*; (*motor*) capot, *m.*; **~ -box,** carton, *m.*
bonny, (*comely*) avenant; (*healthy-looking*) qui a bonne mine.
bonus, (*comm.*) boni, *m.*; (*staff, &c.*) gratification, *f.*; **~ shares,** actions gratuites, *f.pl.*
bony, osseu|x, ~se.
boo, *v.a.* †huer.
booby, nigaud, *m.*
book, *s.* livre, *m.*; **~keeper,** (*bkkpg.*) teneur de livres, *m.*; **~ post,** imprimé, *m.*; **~ -shelf,** rayon, *m.*; *be in the good, bad* (*black*) *~s of,* être, ne pas être bien dans les papiers de.
book, *v.a.* (*bkkpg.*) inscrire*; (*rail.*) donner, prendre* un billet; (*seat*) retenir*; **~ing-office,** guichet, *m.*; *be ~ed through,* avoir un billet direct.
bookbind|er, relieur, *m.*; **~ing,** reliure, *f.*
bookcase, bibliothèque, *f.*
bookish, (*derived from books*) livresque.
bookkeeping, comptabilité, *f.*
bookmaker, bookie, bookmaker, *m.*
bookplate, ex-libris, *m.*
bookseller, libraire, *m.*; (*second-hand*) bouquiniste, *m.*; *~ and publisher,* libraire éditeur, *m.*; ⚠ libraire *never = 'librarian' which is* bibliothécaire, *m.f.*
bookstall, étalage de livres, *m.*; (*rail.*) bibliothèque, *f.*
bookworm, (*ent.*) lépisme, *m.*; (*fig. pers.*) rat de bibliothèque, *m.*
boom, *s.* (*naut.*) bout-dehors, *m.*; (*comm.*) boom, *m.*; *v.n.* (*price*) monter (être) rapidement.
boom, *v.n.* (*cannon*) tonner; (*waves*) gronder.
boomerang, boumerang, *m.*
boon, *s.* faveur, *f.*; (*mercy*) bienfait, *m.*
boor, rustre, *m.*; **~ish,** rustique; **~ishness,** rusticité, *f.*
boost, *v.a.* créer une atmosphère de †hausse autour de.
boot, bottine, *f.*; (*torture*) brodequin, *m.*; **~hook, jack,** tire-botte, *m.*; *pl.* tire-bottes.
boot, *s.* *to ~,* en sus; *v.a.* (*profit*) servir* (à).
bootblack, boots, décrotteur, *m.*
booth, (*fair, &c.*) baraque, *f.*
bootlace, lacet, *m.*
bootless, (*useless*) vain; (*without boots*) sans chaussure; **~ly,** inutilement.
bootmaker, bottier, *m.*
booze, *v.n.* (*pop.*) boire* à tire-larigot; **~r,** pochard, *m.*
bo-peep, *s.* coucou, *m.*; *play ~,* faire* coucou.
bora|x, borax, *m.*; **~cic,** *adj.* borique.
borage, (*bot.*) bourrache, *f.*
border, *s.* (*edge*) bord, *m.*; (*edging and her.*) bordure, *f.*; (*frontier*) frontière, *f.*; (*garden*) plate-bande, *f.*; *adj.* frontière; **~ -land,** pays frontière, *m.*
border, *v.a.* (*edge*) border (de); *~ on, upon,* confiner à; (*resemble*) ressembler à.
bore, *s.* (*mine*) sonde, *f.*; (*rivers*) ras de marée, *m.*; (*fam. of pers.*) raseu|r, ~se, *m.f.*; (*of thing*) scie, *f.*; *what a ~!* quelle corvée!
bor|e, *v.a.* forer; (*land*) sonder; (*weary*) assommer; **~ing,** ennuyeu|x, ~se.
boreal, boréal.
borecole, (*bot.*) chou vert, *m.*
borer, (*instr. for wood*) vrille, *f.*; (*for metal*) perceuse, *f.*
born, to be, naître* (être); ⚠ je suis né (*lit*). = *not 'I am born' but 'I was born'*; *be ~ to,* être né pour; *he is a ~ poet, &c.,* c'est un poète, etc., né.
borough, bourg, *m.*
borrow, *v.a.* emprunter (*acc. of thing; 'of', 'from', of pers.* à); **~er,** emprunteu|r, ~se, *m.f.*; **~ing,** *s.* emprunt, *m.*; *~ed light,* jour de souffrance, *m.*
boscage, bocage, *m.*
bosh, blague, *f.*
bosk, (bosket), bosquet, *m.*; **~y,** boisé.
bosom, (*lit. and fig.*) sein, *m.*; **~ -friend,** ami de cœur, *m.*; *in the ~ of one's family,* au sein de sa famille.
boss, (*fam. pers.*) patron, *m.*; (*arch. and protuberance*) bosse, *f.*; *v.a.* (*fam.*) maîtriser; (*control*) diriger.
botan|y, botanique, *f.*; **~ist,** botaniste, *m.*; **~ize,** botaniser; **~ical,** botanique.

botargo, (*cook.*) boutargue, *f.*
botch, *s.* bousillage, *m.*; *v.a.* bousiller; **~er,** gâcheur, *m.*
both, *pron. and adj.* l'un(e) et l'autre; (*only two*) tous les deux; (*two together*) tous deux; *~ of us,* nous deux; *on ~ sides,* des deux côtés.
both . . . and, *conj.* et . . . et; *sometimes* à la fois . . . et *are used for emphasis; he was both rich and wretched,* il était à la fois riche et misérable.
bother, *s.* ennui, *m.*; (*worry*) tracasserie, *f.*; *what a ~!* quelle scie!
bother, *v.a.n.* tracasser; (*worry oneself*) se tracasser; *don't ~!* ne vous en souciez pas!
bottle, *s.* bouteille, *f.*; (*scent, small*) flacon, *m.*; (*water*) carafe, *f.*; (*short-necked*) bocal, *m.*; (*hay, &c.*) botte, *f. see also* FEEDER; *hot water bottle, see* WATER; **~ -brush,** goupillon, *m.*; **~ -green,** *adj.* vert bouteille, *invar.*; **~ -nose,** gros nez, *m.*; **~ -washer,** plongeur, *m.*; *v.a.* mettre* en bouteilles.
bottom, *adj.* derni|er, ~ère; *~ price,* cours le plus bas, *m.*; *~ stair, step,* première marche, *f.*
bottom, *s.* (*lower part, stairs, page*) bas, *m.*; (*ground, valley, sea, lake, &c., of prices*) fond, *m.*; (*foundation*) base, *f.*; (*of a ship*) carène, *f.*; (*ship itself*) navire, *m.*; (*table*) bas bout, *m.*; (*anat.*) derrière, *m.*; *be at ~ of,* être la cause de; *from top to ~,* de fond en comble; *to the ~,* (*thoroughly*) à fond.
bottomless, sans fond.
bough, rameau, *m.*
boulder, roche, *f.*
bounce, *s.* (*leap, ball, &c.*) bond, *m.*; (*show-off*) épate, *f.*; *v.n.* (*ball, &c.*) bondir; (*show off*) faire* de l'épate; *~ out of,* (*room, &c.*) bondir †hors de.
bouncing, *adj.* (*big*) gros, -se; (*noisy*) bruyant; (*sturdy*) vigoureu|x, ~se; *~ girl* (*fam.*) dondon, *f.*
bound, *s.* (*boundary*) borne, *f.*; (*leap*) saut, *m.*; (*ball*) bond, *m.*
bound, *adj. and p.p.* (*book*) relié; *be ~* (*forced*) *to,* être forcé de; *be ~* (*destined*) *to,* ne pouvoir* manquer de; *~ for,* (*ship, &c.*) à destination de; *set ~s to,* mettre* des bornes à.
bound, *v.a.* (*limit*) borner; *v.n.* (*leap*) bondir; (*ball*) rebondir.
boundary, borne, *f.*
bounden, *adj.* obligatoire.
bounder, (*pop.*) rastaquouère (rasta), *m.*
boundless, illimité.
bounteous, bountiful, généreu|x, ~se; **~ness,** générosité, *f.*
bount|y, (*bountifulness*) générosité, *f.*; (*gift*) gratification, *f.*; (*comm.*) prime, *f.*; **~iful,** bienfaisant.
bouquet, bouquet, *m.*
bourdon, (*organ*) bourdon, *m.*
bourn, (*boundary*) borne, *f.*; (*goal*) but, *m.*; (*stream*) ruisseau, *m.*
bout, (*illness*) accès, *m.*; (*fencing*) assaut, *m.*; *drunken ~,* ribote, *f.*
bovine, *adj.* bovin; (*pers.*) lourdaud.
bow, *s.* (*head*) salut, *m.*; (*curtsy*) révérence, *f.*; (*ship*) avant, *m.*; (*rowing*) nageur de tête, *m.*; *v.a.* (*head*) incliner; (*back*) courber; (*knees*) plier; *~ out,* congédier; *v.n.* s'incliner; (*submit*) plier; (*under a weight*) se courber; *~ to,* saluer, *v.a.*; *~ down,* se prosterner.
bow, (*weapon*) arc, *m.*; (*violin*) archet, *m.*; (*knot*) nœud, *m.*; (*saddle*) arçon, *m.*; *have two strings to one's ~,* avoir deux cordes à son arc; **~ -legged, cagneu|x,** ~se.
bowdlerize, *v.a.* expurger.
bowels, (*lit. fig. earth*) entrailles, *f.pl.*; *~ of compassion,* entrailles, *f.pl.*
bower, (*arbour*) berceau, *m.*
bowie-knife, couteau-poignard, *m.*
bowl, *s.* (*milk*) jatte, *f.*; (*china*) bol, *m.*; (*tin and mess*) gamelle, *f.*; (*wooden*) écuelle, *f.*; (*pipe*) fourneau, *m.*; **~s,** (*game*) boules, *f.pl.*
bowl, *v.n.* (*bowls*) jouer aux boules, (*cricket*) lancer; *v.a.* (*hoop, bowls*) rouler; *~ over,* renverser; (*disconcert*) déconcerter.
bowler, (*bowls*) joueur de boules, *m.*; (*cricket*) celui qui lance, *m.*
bowline, (*naut.*) bouline, *f.*
bowman, (*archer*) archer, *m.*
bowshot, *within ~,* à portée d'arc.
bowsprit, (*naut.*) beaupré, *m.*
box, *s.* (*bot.*) buis, *m.*
box, *s.* boîte, *f.*; (*large wooden*) caisse, *f.*; (*coaches*) siège, *m.*; (*horse*) stalle, *f.*; (*theatr.*) loge, *f.*; *~ on the ears,* soufflet, *m.*; **~ -office,** bureau de location, *m.*; **~ -spring,** (*mattress*) sommier, *m.*
box, *v.a.* mettre* en boîte; *v.n.* (*sport*) boxer; *~ up,* (*pack close together*) serrer comme des †harengs en caque; **~er,** boxeur, *m.*; **~ing,** *s.* boxe, *f.*; **~ing Day** (*approx.*) lendemain de Noël, *m.*; **~ing-glove,** gant bourré, *m.*
box-tree, buis, *m.*
boy, garçon, *m.*; *~* **scout,** éclaireur, boy-scout, *m.*; *my boy!* (*fam.*) mon cher!; old **~s,** (*school*) anciens élèves, *m.pl.*; *~s will be ~s,* il faut que la jeunesse se passe; **~ish,** (*things*) de garçon.
boycott, *v.a.* boycotter; **~ing,** boycottage, *m.*
boyhood, (*to 14*) enfance, *f.*; (*from 14*) adolescence, *f.*
brace, *s.* (*game, &c.*) couple, *f.*; (*pistols*) paire, *f.*; (*clasp, attachment*) lien, *m.*; (*mus., print.*) accolade, *f.*; (*naut.*) bras, *m.*; (*motor, aeron.*) entretoise, *f.*; **~s,** bretelles, *f.pl.*; *v.a.* (*fasten*) lier; (*energies, &c.*) tendre; (*beam*) soutenir*; (*naut.*) brasser.
bracelet, bracelet, *m.*
brach, (*bitch hound*) braque, *f.*
bracing, fortifiant.
bracken, (*bot.*) fougère, *f.*
bracket, (*arch., wall, electr., gas*) console,

f.; (*carp.*) tasseau, *m.*; (*print.*) crochet, *m.*; *v.a.* mettre* en crochets.
brackish, saumâtre.
brad, (*nail*) petite pointe, *f.*
bradawl, poinçon, *m.*
brag, bragging, *s.* vanterie, *f.*; (*talk*) vantardise, *f.*; *v.n.* se vanter (de).
braggart, *s.* fanfaron, *m.*
brahmin, brahmane, *m.*; **~ism,** brahmanisme, *m.*; **~ical,** brahmanique.
braid, (*hair*) tresse, *f.*; (*for trimming*) passement, *m.*; (*metal, silk*) galon, *m.*; *v.a.* (*hair*) tresser.
brain, (*organ, seat of thought, intellect*) cerveau, *m.*; **~s,** (*substance*) cervelle, *f.*; (*fig.*) cerveau, *m.*; *v.a.* faire* sauter la cervelle à; **~ -fever,** fièvre cérébrale, *f.*; **~ -matter,** cervelle, *f.*; **~y,** intelligent; **~less,** sans cervelle.
braise, (*cook.*) braiser.
brake, *s.* (*thicket*) fourré, *m.*; (*fern*) fougeraie, *f.*; (*briers*) ronceraie, *f.*
brake, *s.* (*wheel*) frein, *m.*
brake|sman, garde-frein, *m.*; **~ -van,** wagon-frein, *m.*; **~ -lever,** levier de frein à masse, *m.*
bramble, ronce, *f.*
brambling, (*ornith.*) pinson des monts, *m.*
bran, son, *m.*
branch, *s.* (*tree, subdivision, family*) branche, *f.*; **~ bank,** succursale, *f.*; **~-line,** (*rail*) **~ -road,** embranchement, *m.*; *v.n.* ~ *off,* (*of roads*) embrancher.
brand, *s.* (*lit. and fig.*) tison, *m.*; (*stigma*) flétrissure, *f.*; (*comm.*) marque, *f.*; **fire- ~,** brandon, *m.*; *v.a.* (*fig. criminal*) flétrir; (*med. hot iron*) cautériser; (*comm.*) marquer.
brandish, *v.a.* brandir.
brand (bran)-new, *adj.* tout battant neuf; tout flambant-neuf.
brandy, eau de vie, *f.*
brass, cuivre jaune, *m.*; (*fig.*) airain, *m.*; (*cheek*) toupet, *m.*; *adj.* de cuivre jaune; (*cannon*) de bronze; **~ farthing,** rouge liard, *m.*; **~ plate,** plaque de cuivre, *f.*
brat, bambin, e, *m.f.*
bravado, bravade, *f.*
brave, *adj.* brave; (*fig. finely dressed*) élégant; *v.a.* braver; **~ly,** bravement.
bravery, bravoure, *f.*; (*finery*) atours, *m.pl.*
bravo, (*pers.*) spadassin, *m.*; (*cry*) bravo, *m.*; *interj.* bravo!
brawl, brawling, *s.* querelle, *f.*; *v.n.* se quereller; (*stream*) murmurer.
brawler, buveur à tue-tête, *m.*
brawn, (*muscle*) muscle, *m.*; (*of pork, &c.*) fromage de porc, *m.*
brawny, musculeu|x, **~se**; (*fleshy*) charnu.
bray, *v.n.* (*ass*) braire*.
braze, *v.a.* (*solder*) braser.
brazen, de laiton; (*fig.*) d'airain; (*sound*) cuivré; **~ -faced,** effronté; **~ness,** effronterie, *f.*; **~ly,** effrontément.
brazier, (*fire*) brasier, *m.*; (*pers.*) chaudronnier, *m.*
Brazilian, *adj.* (*when an adj. use small letter*) *and s.m.f.* Brésilien, -ne; *brazil nut,* noix d'Amérique, *f.*
breach, *s.* (*mil.*) brèche, *f.*; (*quarrel*) rupture, *f.*; (*breaking rule, treaty, &c.*) violation, *f.*; (*promise, &c.*) manquement (à), *m.*; ~ *of the peace,* attentat à l'ordre.
bread, pain, *m*; **-basket,** panier à pain, *m.*; **~ -fruit,** fruit à pain, *m.*; ~ *-fruit tree,* jaquier, *m.*; **~ -winner,** gagne-pain, *m., invar.*
breadth, (*lit. and fig.*) largeur, *f.*; (*material*) lé, *m.*; *be 3 ft. in ~,* avoir 3 pieds de largeur.
break, *s.* interruption, *f.*; (*brief*) pause, *f.*; (*view*) percée, *f.*; (*day*) point du jour, *m.*; (*print.*) alinéa, *m.*; (*fracture*) cassure, *f.*; (*veh.*) break, *m.*; (*ball*) déviation, *f.*; (*journey*) arrêt, *m.*; **~ down,** (*health*) dépression de santé, *f.*; (*motor, aeron.*) panne, *f.*
break, *v.a.* (*bank*) faire sauter; (*bargain, &c.*) rompre; (*cup, heart, &c.*) briser; (*annul*) casser; (*promise, &c.*) manquer à; (*pers. of habit*) corriger de; (*news*) apprendre* (à + *pers.*); (*law, vow*) violer; (*rules*) enfreindre*; (*limb*) se casser + *acc.*; (*interrupt, journey, sleep, &c.*) interrompre; (*subdue*) dompter; **~ down,** abattre; **~ in,** (*ans.*) dresser; (*by force*) enfoncer; **~ open,** (*letter*) décacheter; **~ off,** (*marriage, conversation, &c.*) rompre; **~ up,** (*camp, sitting*) lever; (*meeting*) dissoudre*; *broken down,* (*motor*) en panne.
break, *v.n.* (*lit. and fig.*) se casser; (*heart, waves*) se briser; (*weather*) se gâter; (*scatter*) se disperser; (*day*) poindre*; (*clouds*) se dissiper; (*health*) s'altérer; (*bankrupt*) faire* faillite; (*voice*) muer; (*cricket*) dévier; ~ *down,* (*veh.*) verser; (*profits, &c.*) échouer; (*health*) s'affaiblir; ~ *in,* pénétrer de force (dans); ~ *in upon* (*conversation*) interrompre; (*disturb*) déranger; ~ *out,* (*fire, disease, &c.*) se déclarer; ~ *up,* (*disperse*) se disperser; (*schools*) entrer (être) en vacances.
breakage, (*comm., breaking, thing broken*) casse, *f.*
breaker, (*rock*) écueil, *m.*; (*wave*) brisant, *m.*
breakfast, *s.* déjeuner, *m.*; *v.n.* déjeuner.
breakneck, *adj.* de casse-cou.
break-up, *s.* (*schools*) commencement des vacances, *m.*; (*ice*) débâcle, *f.*
breakwater, (*naut.*) brise-lames, *m. invar.*; (*bridge*) éperon, *m.*
bream, (*ichth.*) brème, *f.*
breast, poitrine, *f.*; (*horse*) poitrail, *m.*; (*of women*) sein, *m.*; (*fig.*) cœur, *m.*; (*fowl*) blanc, *m.*; **~ -high,** *adj.* à †hauteur d'appui; **~ -pocket,** poche intérieure, *f.*
breastplate, (*front*) plastron, *m.*
breastwork, (*mil.*) parapet, *m.*

breath, haleine, *f.*; (*air, fig.*) souffle, *m.*; *out of* ~, †hors d'haleine.
breathe, *v.a.* (*air, &c.*) respirer; (*inspire*) inspirer (à); (*utter*) murmurer; ~ *one's last,* rendre le dernier soupir; *not to* ~ *a word,* ne pas souffler mot; *v.n.* respirer.
breathing, *s.* respiration, *f.*; ~ **-space,** temps de reprendre haleine, *m.*; *adj.* qui respire; (*lifelike*) vivant; (*respiratory*) respiratoire.
breathless, (*out of breath*) essoufflé; (*unstirred by wind*) sans souffle; ~**ly,** sans haleine.
breech, (*gun*) culasse, *f.*; ~ **-loading,** se chargeant par la culasse; *v.a.* (*boy*) mettre* en culotte.
breeches, culotte, *f.sing.*; (*old*) †haut de chausses, *m.*
breed, *s.* race, *f.*
breed, *v.a.* (*educ. and ans.*) élever; (*give rise to*) faire* naître; *what is bred in the bone will come out in the flesh, see* BONE.
breeder, (*raiser*) éleveur, *m.*
breeding, (*cattle*) élevage, *m.*; *good* ~, (*pers.*) savoir-vivre, *m.*; *bad, ill* ~, manque d'usage, *m.*
breeze, brise, *f.*
breezy, (*bracing*) fortifiant; (*windy*) éventé.
bren-gun, mitrailleuse Bren, *f.* (*Bren invar.*).
brevet, (*conferring official privilege*) brevet, *m.*; ~ **rank,** (*mil.*) grade sans solde correspondante, *m.*
breviary, bréviaire, *m.*
brevity, brièveté, *f.*; (*style*) concision, *f.*
brew, *v.a.* (*beer*) brasser; (*tea, &c.*) infuser; *v.n.* (*storm*) se préparer; (*mischief*) se tramer; (*tea, &c.*) être en préparation, ~ **er,** brasseur, *m.*; ~**ery,** brasserie, *f.*
briar, *see* BRIER.
bribe, *s.* argent donné pour corrompre, *m.*; (*fam.*) pot de vin, *m.*; ⚠ *Not* bribe *which* = '*hunk of bread*', '*tiny bit*'.
bribe, *v.a.* corrompre; (*law*) suborner; ~**r,** (*law*) suborneu|r, ~se, *m.f.*; ~**ry,** corruption, *f.*
brick, brique, *f.*; (*pers. fam.*) rude lapin, *m.*; ~ **-bat,** morceau de brique, *m.*; ~ **-kiln,** briqueterie, *f.*; ~**layer,** briqueteur, *m.*; ~**maker,** briquetier, *m.*
bridal, *s.* noce, *f.*; *adj.* nuptial.
bride, mariée, *f.*; (*betrothed*) fiancée, *f.*; ~**groom,** marié, *m.*; (*betrothed*) fiancé, *m.*; ~**smaid,** demoiselle d'honneur, *f.*
bridecake, gâteau de noces, *m.*
bridge, pont, *m.*; (*naut.*) passerelle, *f.*; (*nose*) dos, *m.*; ~ *of boats,* ponton, *m.*; *v.a.* jeter un pont sur.
bridle, *s.* bride, *f.*; (*fig.*) frein, *m.*; *v.a.* brider; (*fig.*) maîtriser; *v.n.* ~ *up,* se rengorger.
brief, *adj.* bref, brève; (*transient*) passag|er, ~ère; ~**ly,** brièvement.
brief, *s.* (*law*) dossier, *m.*; ~**less,** sans cause; ~ **-bag,** serviette d'avocat, *f.*
brier, (*fig. and lit.*) ronce, *f.*; (*pipe*) racine de bruyère, *f.*
brig, (*naut.*) brick, *m.*
brigad|e, brigade, *f.*; ~**ier,** général de brigade, *m.*
brigade, *v.a.* embrigader.
brigand, brigand, *m.*; ~**age,** brigandage, *m.*
brigantine, (*naut.*) brigantin, *m.*; ⚠ brigantine, (*naut.*) = '*spanker*'.
bright, (*lit. and fig.*) brillant; (*vivacious*) vif, vive; (*colour*) clair; (*dazzling*) éclatant; (*mind*) très intelligent; (*gay*) gai; ~ *idea,* idée lumineuse, *f.*; ~**ness,** éclat, *m.*; ~**ly,** (*gaily*) gaiement.
brighten, *v.a.* faire* briller; (*cheer up, enliven, pers., style*) égayer; *v.n.* (*weather*) s'éclaircir.
brill, (*ichth.*) barbue, *f.*
brillian|ce, éclat, *m.*; (*style*) coloris, *m.*; ~**t,** *adj.* éclatant; (*style*) coloré; (*pers., talents, &c.*) brillant.
brilliant, *s.* (*diamond*) brillant, *m.*
brim, bord, *m.*; ~**-full,** plein jusqu'au bord; *be* ~*-full of,* (*fig.*) déborder de.
brimstone, soufre, *m.*
brindled, rayé.
brine, (*pickle*) saumure, *f.*; (*sea*) mer, *f.*
bring, *v.a.* (*pers.*) amener; (*thing*) apporter; (*lead*) conduire*; (*action at law*) intenter; (*accusation*) porter; ~ *up to date,* mettre* à jour; ~ *home to,* convaincre* (*acc. pers.* de + *thing*); ~ *into force,* mettre* en vigueur; ~ *grist to the mill,* faire* venir l'eau au moulin; ~ *to light,* mettre* au jour; ~ *to mind,* se rappeler; ~ *oneself to do,* se résoudre à; ~ **low,** abattre; ~ *to pass,* occasionner; ~ **about,** amener; ~ **away,** (*things*) emporter; ~ **back,** (*things*) rapporter; ~ **down,** (*pers*). faire* descendre; (*thing*) descendre (avoir); (*price and fig.*) abaisser; ~ **forth,** (*child*) mettre* au monde; (*produce*) produire*; ~ **forward,** (*chair, theory*) avancer; (*bkkpg.*) reporter; ~ **in,** (*pers.*) faire* entrer; (*interest, &c.*) rapporter; (*introduce*) introduire*; (*guilty*) déclarer; ~ **on,** causer; ~ **out,** (*go and get*) chercher; (*take out*) sortir* (avoir); (*pers.*) faire* sortir*; (*book*) publier; ~ **round,** (*to opinion*) amener; ~ **to,** (*naut., aeron.*) mettre* en panne; ~ **together,** assembler; ~ **up,** (*educate*) élever; (*pers.*) faire* monter; (*thing*) monter (avoir).
bringing up, éducation, *f.*
brink, bord, *m.*; *on the* ~ *of,* à deux doigts de.
briny, *adj.* (*breeze, &c.*) de mer.
briquet, (*coal*) briquette, *f.*
brisk, vi|f, ~ve; (*pers.*) acti|f, ~ve; (*energetic*) vigoureu|x, ~se; *be* ~ (*of trade*) marcher bien; ~**ness,** vivacité, *f.*; ~**ly,** vivement.
bristle, *s.* (*hog, boar*) soie, *f.*
bristle, *v.n.* se †hérisser; ~ *up,* (*pers.*) se rengorger; ~ *with,* être †hérissé de.

bristly, †hérissé; (*hogs, &c.*) couvert de soies.
Britanni|c, British, britannique; ~*a metal*, métal anglais, *m.*
Britisher, (*U.S.A.*) sujet britannique, *m.*
brittle, cassant; ~**ness**, fragilité, *f.*
broach, *s.* (*roasting*) broche, *f.*; (*arch.*) flèche, *f.*
broach, *v.a.* (*subject, &c.*) entamer; (*cask*) mettre* en perce.
broad, large; (*extensive*) vaste; (*accent*) rude; (*daylight, main = chief*) grand; ~ **bean**, *see* BEAN; ~-*brimmed*, (*hat*) à larges bords; ~ *hint*, avis assez clair, *m.*; *be* ~ *-minded*, avoir des idées libérales; *be two metres* ~, être large de deux mètres; ~ **-shouldered**, aux épaules larges; ~**ly**, largement.
broadcast, *v.a.* (*wireless*) radiodiffuser; ~**er**, radiodiffuseur, *m.*; ~**ing**, *s.* radiodiffusion, *f.*; ~*ing station*, station d'émission, *f.*
broadcloth, drap fin et apprêté, *m.*
broaden, *v.a.* élargir; *v.n.* s'élargir.
broadsheet, grande feuille, *f.*
broadside, (*guns*) bordée, *f.*; (*ship*) travers, *m.*
broadsword, sabre, *m.*
brocade, brocart, *m.*
broccoli, brocoli, *m.*
brock, (*zool.*) blaireau, *m.*
brocket, (*stag*) daguet, *m.*
broil, *s.* querelle, *f.*
broil, *v.a.* (*cook.*) griller.
brogue, (*shoe, approx.*) soulier grossier, *m.*; (*accent*) accent irlandais, *m.*
broke, *stony* ~, (*slang*) à sec.
broken, (*heart*) brisé; (*style*) décousu; (*lang.*) baragouiné; ~ **down**, (*motor*) en panne; ~*English, &c.*, mauvais anglais, etc., *m.*; ~**ly**, sans suite; ~ **-winded**, poussi|f, ~ve.
broker, (*comm.*) courtier, *m.*; (*second-hand*) brocanteu|r, ~se, *m.f.*; ~**age**, courtage, *m.*
bromide, bromure, *m.*
bronch|itis, bronchite, *f.*; ~**ial**, bronchial.
bronze, *s.* bronze, *m.*; *adj.* en bronze; *v.a.* bronzer.
brooch, *s. broche, f.*
brood, *s.* couvée, *f.*; ~ **-mare**, poulinière, *f.*
brood, *v.n.* (*lit. and fig.*) couver; ~ **on** (*hen*) couver; *v.a.* ~ **over**, méditer sur; ~**-hen**, couveuse, *f.*; ~**y**, *adj.* qui veut couver.
brook, *s.* ruisseau, *m.*; ~**let**, ruisselet, *m.*
brook, *v.a.* supporter.
broom, (*brush*) balai, *m.*; (*bot.*) genêt, *m.*; *new* ~ *sweeps clean*, tout nouveau, tout beau; ~ **-stick**, manche à balai, *m.*
broth, bouillon, *m.*
brothel, bordel, *m.*
brother, (*lit., fig., monks*) frère, *m.*; ~**-in-law**, beau-frère, *m.*
brotherhood, fraternité, *f.*; (*piety, charity*) confrérie, *f.*
brotherly, fraternel, -le.
brougham, coupé, *m.*
brow, (*eye*) sourcil, *m.*; (*forehead*) front, *m.*; (*top of hill*) sommet, *m.*
browbeat, *v.a.* mater.
brown, *s.* brun, *m.*
brown, *adj.* brun; (*fig.*) sombre; (*bread*) bis; (*paper*) gris; (*sun-burnt*) bruni; ~ **bread**, pain bis, *m.*; ~ **sugar**, cassonade, *f.*; *be in a* ~ *study*, être dans les nuages; *v.a.* brunir; (*cook.*) rissoler.
browse, *v.a.n.* brouter.
bruise, *s.* meurtrissure, *f.*; *v.a.* meurtrir; (*crush*) écraser.
brunt, *bear the* ~ *of*, soutenir* le premier choc de.
brush, *s.* brosse, *f.*; (*paint*) pinceau, *m.*; (*broom*) balai, *m.*; (*fox*) queue, *f.*; (*encounter*) rencontre, *f.*; ~ **up**, (*fam.*) coup de brosse, *m.*
brush, *v.a.* brosser; (*sweep*) balayer; (*graze*) raser; ~ **aside**, écarter; ~ **up**, donner un coup de brosse à.
brushwood, broussailles, *f.pl.*
brusque, brusque; **-ness**, brusquerie, *f.*; ~**ly**, brusquement.
brutal, brutal; (*cruel*) cruel; (*sensual*) sensuel, -le; ~**ity**, brutalité, *f.*; ~**ly**, brutalement.
brutalize, *v.a.* abrutir.
brut|e, (*an.*) bête, *f.*; (*cruel*) brute, *f.*; ~**ish**, bestial; ~**ishly**, brutalement; ~**ishness**, brutalité, *f.*
bryony, (*bot.*) bryone, *f.*
bubble, *s.* (*air*) bulle, *f.*; (*delusion*) chimère, *f.*; *adj.* chimérique.
bubble, bubble up, *v.n.* bouillonner; ~ *over*, déborder (de).
bubonic, bubonique.
buccaneer, boucanier, *m.*
buck, *s.* daim, *m.*; (*roebuck*) chevreuil, *m.*; (*rabbit, hare, chamois, &c.*) mâle, *m.*; (*U.S.A. slang, approx.*) thune, *f.*; (*fop*) élégant, *m.*; ~**skin**, peau de daim, *f.*; ~ **-shot**, chevrotine, *f.*
buck, *v.n.* (*horse*) faire* le saut de mouton.
buck-bean, (*bot.*) ményanthe, *m.*
bucket, seau, *m.*; (*pump*) piston, *m.*; (*socket*) étui, *m.*; ~ **shop**, (*stocks, U.S.A.*) maison de contre-partie, *f.*
buckle, *s.* boucle, *f.*; *v.a.* boucler; ~ *on*, (*arms*) revêtir*; *v.n.* (*wheel, &c.*) se voiler.
buckler, (*shield*) bouclier, *m.*
buckram, (*cloth*) bougran, *m.*; (*manner*) raideur, *f.*
buckwheat, sarrasin, *m.*
bucolic, bucolique.
bud, *s.* bourgeon, *m.*; *v.n.* bourgeonner; *v.a.* (*hort.*) enter.
buddhis|m, bouddhisme, *m.*; ~**t**, bouddhiste, *m.*
budding, *s.* (*hort.*) greffe, *f.*
budge, *v.n.* bouger.
budgerigar, *m.*; inséparable, *m.f.*
budget, (*fin.*) budget, *m.*; ~**ary**, budgétaire.

buff, *s.*; (*colour*) couleur chamois, *f.*; ~ **leather,** buffle, *m.*
buff, *adj.* chamois, *invar.*
buffalo, buffle, *m.*
buffer, (*eng.*) tampon, *m.*; (*station*) butoir, *m.*; *old* ~, (*pers.*) bonze, *m.*
buffet, *s.* soufflet, *m.*; ⚠ *Not* buffet, *m.* *which* = '*sideboard*', '*bar*'; (*fate*) coup du sort, *m.*; *v.a.* frapper à coups de poing; (*wind, &c.*) souffleter.
buffoon, bouffon, *m.*; **~ery,** bouffonneries, *f.pl.*
bug, punaise, *f.*
bugbear, épouvantail, *m.*
buggy, *s.* (*U.S.A.*) boghei, *m.*
bugle, cor, *m.*; (*mil.*) clairon, *m.*; (*bot.*) bugle, *f.*; (*bead*) perle en tube, *f.*; **~r,** clairon; *v.n.* sonner du clairon.
bugloss, (*bot.*) buglosse, *f.*, *see* VIPER.
buhl, marqueterie de Boule, *f.*; ~ **furniture,** meubles de Boule, *m.pl.*
build, *s.* (*pers.*) taille, *f.*
build, *v.a.* (*lit. and fig.*) bâtir; (*found*) fonder; ~ *in,* (*surround*) entourer (de); ~ *on,* (*fig.*) fonder sur; (*reckon on*) compter sur; ~ *up,* (*establish*) établir.
builder, entrepreneur de bâtiments, *m.*; (*ships*) constructeur de navires, *m.*
building, bâtiment, *m.*; (*act of*) construction, *f.*; (*large*) édifice, *m.*; (*public*) monument, *m.*; ~ **-society,** société immobilière, *f.*
bulb, (*bot.*) bulbe, *m.*; (*electr.*) ampoule, *f.*; **~ous,** bulbeu|x, ~se.
bulge, *s.* bosse, *f.*; *v.a.n.* bomber; (*not lie flat*) faire* une bosse.
bulk, masse, *f.*; (*fig.*) grandeur, *f.*; (*main part*) gros, *m.*; (*naut.*) capacité, *f.*; *in* ~, (*comm.*) en vrac; *v.n.* ~ *large,* devenir* (être) important.
bulkhead, (*naut.*) cloison, *f.*; *watertight* ~*s, see* WATERTIGHT.
bulk|y, gros, -se; (*pers.*) corpulent; **~iness,** grosseur, *f.*
bull, taureau, *m.*; (*whale, elephant, &c.*) mâle, *m.*; (*papal*) bulle, *f.*; (*stk. exch. pers.*) †haussier, *m.*; ~ **-baiting,** combat de taureau, *m.*; ~*'s eye,* (*target*) mouche, *f.*; (*window*) œil de bœuf, *m.*; (*in glass*) boudine, *f.*; ~*'s eye lantern,* lanterne sourde, *f.*; ~ **-terrier,** bull-terrier (*pl.* bull-terriers), *m.*; *take the* ~ *by the horns,* prendre* le taureau par les cornes.
bullace, prunelle, *f.*
bulldog, bouledogue, *m.*
bullet, (*rifle, pistol*) balle, *f.*; ~ **-proof,** à l'épreuve de la balle.
bulletin, bulletin, *m.*
bullfight, combat de taureaux, *m.*
bullfinch, bouvreuil, *m.*
bullfrog, grosse grenouille de l'Amérique, *f.*
bullhead, (*ichth.*) chabot, *m.*
bullion, matières d'or et d'argent, *f.pl.*
bullock, bœuf, *m.*
bully, *adj.* (*U.S.A.*) épatant; ~ **beef,** (*war slang*) singe, *m.*
bully, *s.* bravache, *m.*; (*school*) brutal, *m.*; *v.a.* rudoyer.
bulrush, jonc, *m.*
bulwark, rempart, *m.*; (*earthwork and fig.*) boulevard, *m.*; ~ *netting,* (*barricading of gunwale*) bastingage, *m.*
bum-bailiff, recors, *m.*
bumble-bee, bourdon, *m.*
bummer, (*U.S.A.*) fainéant, *m.*
bump, (*protuberance and on skull*) bosse, *f.*; (*collision*) collision, *f.*; (*blow*) coup, *m.*
bump, *v.a.* cogner; *v.n.* ~ **against,** se cogner contre.
bumper, *s.* (*drink*) rasade, *f.*; *adj.* (*slang*) très abondant.
bumpkin, rustre, *m.*
bumptious, présomptueu|x, ~se.
bumpy, (*road*) cahoteu|x, ~se.
bun, brioche, *f.*
bunch, *s.* (*flowers*) bouquet, *m.*; (*veg.*) botte, *f.*; (*grapes*) grappe, *f.*; (*pers.*) groupe, *m.*; (*keys*) trousseau, *m.*; *v.a.* lier en bouquet, en botte, etc.
bundle, (*anything tied*) botte, *f.*; (*parcel*) paquet, *m.*; (*papers, &c.*) liasse, *f.*; (*wood*) fagot, *m.*; *v.a.* ~ **up,** empaqueter; ~ **out,** (*pers.*) envoyer promener.
bung, *s.* bondon, *m.*; *v.a.* bondonner; ~ **-hole,** bonde, *f.*
bungalow, bungalow, *m.*
bungle, *s.* bousillage, *m.*; *v.a.* bousiller; **~r,** bousilleu|r, ~se, *m.f.*
bungling, *adj.* maladroit.
bunk, *s.* (*naut.*) couchette, *f.*; *v.n.* (*slang*) filer.
bunker, *s.* (*naut.*) soute, *f.*
bunkum, (*slang*) billevesées, *f.pl.*
bunting, (*ornith.*) bruant, *m.*; (*decorations*) pavoisement, *m.*
buoy, *s.* (*naut.*) bouée, *f.*; *v.a.* (*fig.*) ~ *up,* soutenir*.
buoyancy, (*fig.*) légèreté, *f.*; (*pers., markets*) entrain, *m.*
buoyant, lég|er, ~ère; (*pers.*) qui a du ressort; **~ly,** avec légèreté.
bur(r), (*bot.*) glouteron, *m.*
burbot, (*ichth.*) lotte, *f.*
burden, *s.* charge, *f.*; (*heavy*) fardeau, *m.*; (*fig.*) fardeau; (*song*) refrain, *m.*; (*theme*) thème, *m.*; (*naut.*) port, *m.*; *a ship of 1,000 tons* ~, un navire du port 1.000 tonneaux.
burden, *v.a.* charger (de).
burdensome, (*weighty*) pesant; (*fig. and expense*) onéreu|x, ~se.
burdock, (*bot.*) bardane, *f.*
bureau, (*govt. dept. and desk*) bureau, *m.*; **~crat,** bureaucrate, *m.f.*; **~cracy,** bureaucratie, *f.*; **~cratic,** bureaucratique.
burgeon, *v.n.* bourgeonner.
burgess, citoyen, -ne, *m.f.*; (*Parl.*) représentant, -e d'un bourg, *m.f.*
burgher, bourgeois, *m.*
burglar, cambrioleu|r, ~se, *m.f.*
burglary, vol avec effraction, *m.*
burgle, *v.a.* cambrioler.

burgomaster, bourgmestre, *m.*

Burgundian, *adj.* (*when an adj. use small letter*) *and s.m.f.* Bourguignon, -ne.

burgundy, *s.* (*wine*) bourgogne, *m.*

burial, enterrement, *m.*; ~ **-ground,** cimetière, *m.*; ~ **service,** office des morts, *m.*

burke, *v.a.* (*suppress, hush up*) étouffer.

burlesque, *adj. and s.m.* burlesque.

burly, gros de taille.

burn, *s.* brûlure, *f.*; (*stream*) ruisseau, *m.*

burn, *v.a.* (*lit., fig., sun, cook.*) brûler; ~ **into,** (*acid*) ronger; ~ **out, up,** consumer; ~ **down,** incendier; ~ *to ashes,* réduire en cendres; *he has ~t his hand,* il s'est brûlé la main; ~ *a hole in,* brûler en faisant un trou dans; ~ *alive,* brûler vif.

burn, *v.n.* (*lit. and fig.*) brûler; *my ears ~,* (*fig.*) les oreilles me tintent; ~ **down,** *low,* (*fire*) s'éteindre*; ~ **up,** (*fire*) flamber.

burner, (*lamp, &c.*) bec, *m.*

burnet, (*bot.*) pimprenelle, *f.*

burning, (*conflag.*) incendie, *m.*; (*smell*) brûlé, *m.*; *adj.* (*lit., fig. and on fire*) ardent; (*flagrant*) flagrant; (*in state of ~ing, hotly discussed*) brûlant; ~ **-glass,** miroir ardent, *m.*

burnish, *v.a.* brunir; **~er,** brunisseur, *m.*

burr, *s.* (*speech*) grasseyement, *m.*; *speak with a ~,* parler gras.

burrow, *s.* (*fox, rabbit, &c.*) terrier, *m.*; *v.a.* creuser; *v.n.* se terrer.

bursar, (*schol. coll.*) économe, *m.*; *~'s office,* **~ship, ~y,** économat, *m.*

burst, *s.* (*sudden sound*) éclat, *m.*; (*outburst*) transport, *m.*; (*explosion*) explosion, *f.*

burst, *v.a.* (*explosion*) faire* éclater; (*break*) rompre; (*buttons, &c.*) faire* sauter; ~ *in,* enfoncer.

burst, *v.n.* (*tyre, &c.*) crever; (*overflow*) déborder; (*be full of*) regorger (de); ~ *into,* (*room, &c.*) se précipiter dans; ~ *into flames,* flamber; ~ *into tears,* fondre en larmes; ~ *out laughing,* éclater de rire; ~ *upon the sight,* s'offrir* à la vue.

bursting, *s.* (*boilers, &c.*) éclatement, *m.*; (*dike*) débordement, *m.*

bury, *v.a.* enterrer; (*things*) enfouir; (*hide*) cacher; (*fig.*) plonger.

bus, omnibus, *m.*; (*motor*) autobus, *m.*; (*slang, aeron.*) zinc, *m.*

busby, colback, *m.*

bush, buisson, *m.*; (*inn*) bouchon, *m.*; (*hair*) broussaille, *f.*; (*Africa and Austr.*) brousse, *f.*; ~ **-ranger,** brigand de la brousse, *m.*; *good wine neeeds no ~, see* WINE; *beat about the bush,* tourner autour du pot; **~y,** (*full of bushes*) buissonneu|x, ~ se; (*hair*) touffu; (*eyebrows*) en broussaille.

bushel, boisseau, *m.*

business, affaire, *f.*; (*comm.*) affaires, *f.pl.*; (*subject*) sujet, *m.*; (*goodwill*) fonds, *m.*; (*occupation*) profession, *f.*; (*enterprise*) entreprise, *f.*; *have ~ with,* être en affaires avec; *be in ~,* être dans les affaires; *on ~,* pour affaires; *that 's no ~ of yours,* vous n'avez rien à y voir; *that 's not your ~,* cela ne vous regarde pas; *make it one's ~ to,* s'occuper de; *send about one's ~,* envoyer* paître; ~ **hours,** heures d'ouverture, *f.pl.*; ~ **house,** maison de commerce, *f.*; **~like,** pratique; ~ **man,** homme d'affaires, *m.*; ~ **premises,** locaux commerciaux, *m.pl.*

busk, (*corset*) busc, *m.*

buskin, cothurne, *m.* (*anc. tragic actor's boot*).

buss, *v.a.* baiser.

bust, buste, *m.*

bustard, (*ornith.*) outarde, *f.*

bustle, *s.* remue-ménage, *m.*; *v.n.* se remuer.

bustling, *adj.* remuant.

bus|y, *adj.* occupé (à); (*much frequented*) passant; *v.n.* ~ *oneself about,* s'occuper de; **~ily,** (*actively*) activement; (*eagerly*) avec empressement.

busybody, mouche du coche, *f.*

but, *prep.* sauf; ~ *for,* sans; *adv.* (*only*) ne . . . que; *he is ~ just gone out,* il ne fait que de sortir; *all ~ + adj.,* presque; *all ~ + verb,* peu s'en faut que + *subj. and* ne.

but, *s.* ~ *me no ~s,* je ne veux pas de vos mais.

but, *conj.* mais; (*but that, without*) sans que + *subj. or* sans + *inf.*; *not ~ that,* ce n'est pas à dire que + *neg. ind.*; *there 's no one ~ knows that,* il n'y a personne qui ne le sache.

butcher, boucher, *m.*; (*fig.*) bourreau, *m.*; *~'s broom,* (*bot.*) fragon, *m.*; *~'s shop,* boucherie, f.; *~'s stall,* étal, *m.*

butcher, *v.a.* égorger.

butchery, (*fig.*) boucherie, *f.*

butler, maître d'hôtel, *m.*

butt, (*rifle, &c.*) crosse, *f.*; (*target*) cible, *f.*; (*laughing-stock*) plastron, *m.*; (*cask*) tonneau, *m.*; (*shooting-range*) tir, *m.*; **~-end,** (*rifle, &c.*) crosse, *f.*

butt, *v.n.* ~ *against,* donner de la tête contre; ~ *in,* s'ingérer dans.

butter, beurre, *m.*; ~ **-dish,** beurrier, *m.*; *v.a.* beurrer; (*fig.*) flagorner.

butterbur, (*bot.*) grande bardane, *f.*

buttercup, (*bot.*) bouton d'or, *m.*

butterfly, papillon, *m.*

buttermilk, babeurre, *m.*

butterwort, (*bot.*) grassette, *f.*

buttery, office, *f.*

buttock, fesse, *f.*; (*beef*) cimier, *m.*

button, *s.* (*bud, of clothing, electr. bell, fencing foil*) bouton, *m.*; ~ **-hook,** tire-bouton, *m.*; *v.a.* boutonner.

buttonhole, boutonnière, *f.*

buttons, groom, *m.*

buttress, contrefort, *m.*; *flying ~,* (*arch.*) arc-boutant, *m.*; *v.a.* arc-bouter; ~ *up,* (*fig.*) appuyer.

buxom, *adj. fem.* gaillarde.

buy, acheter; (*stock, &c.*) racheter; ~ *back again*, racheter; ~ *out*, désintéresser; ~ *up*, accaparer; ~ *for a rise*, (*stk. exch.*) acheter à la †hausse; ~ *on credit*, acheter à crédit.
buyer, acheteu|r, ~ se, *m.f.*
buying, *s.* achat, *m.*; ~ *back, in*, rachat, *m.*
buzz, *v.n.* (*insect*) bourdonner; **~ing**, *s.* bourdonnement, *m.*
buzzard, (*ornith.*) buse, *f.*; ⚠ busard = '*harrier*'.
buzzer, (*whistle*) sifflet, *m.*; (*electric*) trembleur, *m.*
by, *prep.* (*oath, multiply, means, veh., route, author, painter*) par; (*measure of difference*) de; *after pass. verb*, par *of specific effort of will*, de *of spontaneous action*: *cf.* tué par l'ennemi *and* aimé de tous; (*near*) près de; (*according to*) d'après; (+*gerund*) en; ~ *Monday*, d'ici à lundi; ~ *oneself*, tout seul; *have money* ~ *one*, avoir de l'argent par devers soi; ~ *the* ~, ~ *the way*, à propos.
by, *adv. close, hard* ~, *see* CLOSE, HARD; ~ *and* ~, sous peu; *s.* avenir, *m.*
bye-bye, *s.* dodo, *m.*; *go* ~, faire* dodo; *interj.* au revoir.
by(e), *adj.* secondaire.
bygone, *adj.* passé.
by-pass, (*road*) détour, *m.*
by-path, chemin écarté, *m.*
by-product, sous-produit, *m.*
byre, étable, *f.*
by-road, by-way, chemin détourné, *m.*
bystander, *s.* spectat|eur, ~rice, *m.f.*
by-street, rue écartée, *f.*
byword, (*proverb*) dicton, *m.*; (*pers.*) fable, *f.*
Byzantine, *adj.* byzantin.

C

cab, (*taxi*) taxi, *m.*; (*old*) fiacre, *m.*; (*locomotive*) abri, *m.*; ~ **-stand**, station de fiacre, *f.*
cabal, cabale, *f.*; **~istic**, cabalistique.
cabbage, chou, *m.*; ~ **-lettuce**, laitue pommée, *f.*; ~ **-stalk**, trognon, *m.*
cabin, (*hut*) cabane, *f.*; (*ship*) cabine, *f.*; **~-boy**, mousse, *m.*
cabinet, (*room, ministry*) cabinet, *m.*; (*furniture*) cabinet, *m.*; ~ **-maker**, ébéniste, *m.*; ~ **-council**, conseil des ministres, *m.*
cable, câble, *m.*; **~gram**, câblogramme, *m.*; *~'s length*, encablure, *f.*; *v.a.n.* câbler.
cabman, (*fam.*) **cabby**, cocher de fiacre.
cabriolet, cabriolet.
cacao, cacao, *m.*
cachalot, cachalot, *m.*
cache, cachette, *f.*
cackle, *s.* caquet, *m.*; (*gossip*) caquetage, *m.*; *v.n.* (*hen and gossip*) caqueter; (*laugh*) ricaner.
cacophony, cacophonie, *f.*
cactus, cactus, *m.*
cad, (*pers.*) mufle, *m.*
cadaverous, terreu|x, ~se.
caddy, (*tea*) boîte à thé, *f.*
cadence, (*rhet.*) chute, *f.*; (*mus. danc., &c.*) cadence, *f.*
cadet, (*younger son and mil.*) cadet, *m.*; **~ship**, brevet de cadet, *m.*
cadge, *v.a.* (*beg*) mendier; (*slang*) taper (*acc. pers.* de *thing*); **~r**, mendiant, tapeur, *m.*
cadi, cadi, *m.*
caducity, caducité, *f.*
caesura, césure, *f.*
café, café-restaurant, *m.*
caftan, caftan, *m.*
cage, (*lit. and mine*) cage, *f.*; **~ful**, cagée, *f.*; *v.a.* encager.
cairn, cairn, *m.*
caitiff, *s.* lâche, *m.*
cajole, cajoler; **~r**, cajoleu|r, ~se, *m.f.*; **~ry**, cajolerie, *f.*
cake, gâteau, *m.*; (*flat*) galette, *f.*; (*oil, linseed, &c.*) tourteau, *m.*; (*tobacco*) pavé, *m.*; (*soap*) pain, *m.*; (*chocolate*) tablette, *f.*
cake, *v.a.* couvrir* d'une croûte; *v.n.* faire* croûte.
calabash, calebasse, *f.*
calamit|y, (*disaster*) calamité, *f.*; (*adversity*) malheur, *m.*; **~ous**, désastreu|x, ~se.
calcareous, calcaire.
calceolaria, (*bot.*) calcéolaire, *f.*
calcin|e, calciner; **-ation**, calcination, *f.*
calcium, calcium, *m.*
calculable, calculable.
calculat|e, *v.a.n.* calculer; (*premeditate*) préméditer; *~ed to*, de nature à; ~ *on*, compter sur; **~ion**, calcul, *m.*
calculator, (*mach.*) machine à calculer, *f.*
calendar, calendrier, *m.*; ~ **month**, mois civil, *m.*
calender, *v.a.* (*press on machine*) calandrer.
Calends, Greek, calendes grecques, *f.pl.*
cal|f, veau, *m.*; (*leg*) mollet, *m.*; (*whale*) baleineau, *m.*; (*eleph.*) éléphanteau, *m.*; ~ **-bound**, relié en veau; **fatted ~**, veau gras, *m.*; *~'s foot*, (*cook.*) pied de veau, *m.*; *v.a.* **~ve**, vêler.
calfskin, veau, *m.*
calibre, (*lit. and fig.*) calibre, *m.*
calico, calicot, *m.*; *printed* ~, indienne, *f.*
caliph, calife, *m.*
call, *s.* appel, *m.*; (*shout*) cri, *m.*; (*visit*) visite, *f.*; (*bird*) appeau, *m.*; (*need*) besoin, *m.*; (*comm. instalment*) versement, *m.*; (*theol.*) vocation, *f.*; ~ *of conscience*, voix de la conscience, *f.*; ~ *of duty*, appel du devoir; ~ **-boy**, avertisseur, *m.*; ~ **-money**, argent à vue, *m.*; ~ **-number**, (*teleph.*) numéro d'appel, *m.*; ~ **-over**, (*roll*) appel nominal, *m.*; *within* ~, à portée de la voix.
call, *v.a.* (*lit., summon, attention, describe,*

awaken, doctor) appeler; (*meeting*) convoquer; (*veh.*) faire* venir; ~ *for help,* appeler au secours; ~ *to mind, see* MIND; ~ *again, back,* rappeler; ~ *away,* appeler; ~ *for,* (*require*) réclamer; (*pers.*) aller* (être), venir* (être) chercher; ~ *forth,* faire* naître; ~ *in,* (*doctor*) appeler; (*money*) faire* rentrer; ~ *off,* (*dog*) rappeler; ~ *on,* faire* visite à; ~ *out,* appeler; (*duel*) appeler en duel; ~ *up* (*teleph.*) appeler; ~ *upon,* (*appeal to*) faire* appel à; (*summon*) sommer.

call, *v.n.* appeler; (*stop*) s'arrêter; ~ *out,* crier; ~ *in at,* s'arrêter chez.

called, *adj.* (*named*) dit; **so-** ~, prétendu.

caller, visiteu|r, ~se, *s.m.f.*

calligraphy, calligraphie, *f.*

calling, *s.* (*occupation*) métier, *m.*

callisthenic, callisthénique; **~s,** *s.* callisthénie, *f.*

callous, (*skin*) calleu|x, ~se; (*fig.*) insensible; **~ness,** (*fig.*) insensibilité, *f.*

callow, (*raw*) inexpérimenté.

calm, *s.* (*lit. fig. naut.*) calme, *m.*; **dead ~,** calme plat, *m.*; *adj.* calme; *v.a.* calmer; **~ness,** calme, *m.*; **~ly,** tranquillement.

calomel, calomel, *m.*

calorific, *adj.*, calorifique.

calumet, calumet, *m.*

calumn|y, calomnie, *f.*; **~ious,** calomnieu|x, ~se; **~iator,** calomniat|eur, ~rice, *m.f.*; **~iate,** calomnier.

Calvary, Calvaire, *m.*

calyx, (*bot.*) calice, *m.*

cam, (*mach.*) came, *f.*; **ignition ~,** came d'allumage, *f.*

camber, (*arch.*) cambrure, *f.*

cambric, batiste, *f.*; ~ **muslin,** percale, *f.*

camel, cham|eau, ~elle, *m.f.*; **~-driver,** chamelier, *m.*; *~'s hair,* poil de chameau, *m.*

camelia, camélia, *m.*

cameo, camée, *m.*

camera, (*photo.*) appareil photographique, *m.*

camisole, cache-corset, *m.* (*invar.*); ⚠ *not* camisole *which* = '*loose bodice*'.

camlet, camelot, *m.*

camomile, camomille, *f.*

camouflage, *v.a.* camoufler.

camp, *s.* camp, *m.*; *break up the ~,* lever le camp; ~ **-bed,** lit de camp, *m.*; ~ **-stool,** pliant, *m.*; *v.n.* ~, ~ *out,* camper.

campaign, *s.* (*fig. and mil.*) campagne, *f.*; *old ~er,* briscard, *m.*

campanile, (*arch.*) campanile, *m.*

campanula, (*bot.*) campanule, *f.*

camphor, camphre, *m.*

campion, (*bot.*) lychnide, *f.*

can, *s.* broc, *m.*; (*small*) bidon, *m.*; (*U.S.A.*) boîte, *f.*; *v.a.* (*in tins*) conserver.

can, *v.n.* (*able*) pouvoir*; (*know how to*) savoir*; (*be in a position to*) être à même de; *do all one ~,* faire* tout son possible.

Canadian, *adj.* (*when an adj. use small letter*) *and s.m.f.* Canadien, -ne.

canal, (*lit. and anat.*) canal, *m.*; **~ize,** canaliser.

canary, (*ornith.*) serin,-e, *m.f.*; (*wine*) vin des Canaris, *m.*; ~ **-coloured,** jaune serin, *invar.*; ~ **-seed,** millet, *m.*

cancel, *v.a.* (*erase*) biffer; (*bargain, contract, order, &c.*) annuler; **~lation,** annulation, *f.*

cancer, (*med.*) cancer, *m.*; **~ous,** cancéreu|x, ~se.

candelabrum, candélabre, *m.*

candid, (*frank*) candide; (*unbiassed*) impartial; ⚠ candide *is not used in the sense of* '*unbiassed*'; **~ly,** franchement; (*impartially*) sans parti pris.

candidat|e, candidat, *m.*; **~ure,** candidature, *f.*

candle, chandelle, *f.*; (*wax and unit of light*) bougie, *f.*; (*eccles.*) cierge, *m.*; ~ **-grease,** suif, *m.*; *burn the ~ at both ends,* brûler la chandelle par les deux bouts.

candlelight, chandelle, *f.*

Candlemas, Chandeleur, *f.*

candlestick, (*tall*) chandelier, *m.*; (*flat*) bougeoir, *m.*; (*branched*) girandole, *f.*

candour, impartialité, *f.*; ⚠ candeur, *f.* = '*ingenuousness*', '*purity*'.

cand|y, (*U.S.A. sweet*) bonbon, *m.*; **~ied,** candi.

candytuft, (*bot.*) ibéride, *f.*

cane, (*bamboo, &c., for punishment and walking*) canne, *f.*; **Malacca ~,** jonc, *m.*; *v.a.* (*boy*) fouetter; (*chair*) canner.

canine, *adj.* canin; ~ **tooth,** canine, *f.*

canister, (*tea*) boîte à thé, *f.*; (*shot*) boîte à balles, *f.*

canker, (*human, ans.*) ulcère, *f.*; (*trees*) chancre, *m.*; **~-worm,** (*plants and fig.*) ver rongeur, *m.*; *v.a.* ronger; (*fig.*) gangrener; *v.n.* se corrompre.

cannibal, *adj. and s.m.f.* cannibale; **~ism,** cannibalisme, *m.*

cannon, *s.* (*mil.*) canon, *m.*; (*billiards*) carambolage, *m.*; ~ **-ball,** boulet de canon, *m.*; ~ **-fodder,** chair à canon, *f.*; *v.n.* (*billiards*) caramboler; ~ *against,* se cogner contre.

cannonade, *s.* canonnade, *f.*; *v.a.n.* canonner.

cannot, *v.n. use parts of* pouvoir.*

canoe, pirogue, *f.*

canon, *s.* (*pers.*) chanoine, *m.*; (*eccles. law*) canon, *m.*; ~ **law,** droit canon, *m.*; **~ess,** chanoinesse, *f.*; **~ical,** canonique; *~ical hours,* heures canoniales, *f.pl.*

canonize, canoniser.

canonry, canonicat, *m.*

canop|y, dais, *m.*; (*heaven*) voûte, *f.*; (*arch.*) baldaquin, *m.*; **~ied,** surmonté d'un dais.

cant, *s.* (*language of profession, &c.*) jargon, *m.*; (*hypocrisy*) cafardise, *f.*; **~ing,** *adj.* cafard; (*her.*) parlant.

cantaloup, (*melon*) cantaloup, *m.*

cantankerous, acariâtre.
cantata, cantate, *f.*
canteen, (*barracks*) cantine, *f.*
canter, *s.* petit galop, *m.*; *v.n.* aller au petit galop.
canticle, cantique, *m.*
canto, chant, *m.*
canton, *s.* (*division of country and her.*) canton.
cantonment, cantonnement, *m.*
canvas, *s.* (*for sails, painting, tent, &c.*) toile, *f.*; (*tapest.*) canevas, *m.*; (*picture*) peinture, *f.*; (*sail*) voile, *f.*
canvass, *v.a.* (*discuss*) débattre; *v.n.* (*comm.*) faire* la place; (*polit.*) chercher les suffrages; **~er**, (*comm.*) placier, *m.*; (*polit.*) solliciteur de suffrages, *m.*
cap, *s.* bonnet, *m.*; (*peaked*) casquette, *f.*; (*flat and college*) toque, *f.*; (*top, cover*) chapeau, *m.*; (*mil.*) képi, *m.*; ~ *and bells*, marotte, *f.*; ~ **stone**, pierre de couronnement, *m.*; *if the ~ fits, put it on*, qui se sent morveux se mouche; *set one's ~ at*, jeter son dévolu sur.
cap, *v.a.* (*surpass*) surpasser; (*take cap off to*) donner un coup de chapeau à.
capab|le, capable (de); (*of feeling, receiving*) susceptible (de); ~ **ility**, (*capacity*) capacité, *f.*; (*possibility*) possibilité, *f.*
capacious, grand; (*room, house, &c.*) spacieu|x, ~se.
capacitate, rendre capable de.
capacity, (*holding-power, receiving-power*) capacité, *f.*; (*ability for*) pouvoir, *m.* (de); (*position*) qualité, *f.*
caparison, caparaçon, *m.*; *v.a.* caparaçonner.
cape, (*headland*) cap, *m.*; (*mil. and woman's*) pèlerine, *f.*; (*cloak with hood*) cape, *f.*
caper, (*bot.*) câpre, *f.*; (*leap*) cabriole, *f.*; *cut a ~*, faire une cabriole; *v.n.* cabrioler.
capillary, capillaire.
capital, *s.* (*town*) capitale, *f.*; (*letter*) majuscule, *f.*; (*comm.*) capital, *m.* *often plural*; (*arch.*) chapiteau, *m.*
capital, *adj.* (*involving life, vital, fig.*) capital; (*letter*) majuscule; (*chief*) principal; (*excellent*) excellent; ~ **account**, compte capital, *m.*; ~ **punishment**, peine capitale, *f.*; ~ **sum**, capital, *m.*; **~ly**, (*well*) admirablement.
capitalist, capitaliste, *m.*
capitaliz|e, capitaliser; **~ation**, capitalisation, *f.*
capitation, capitation, *f.*
capitulary, *adj.* capitulaire.
capitulat|e, capituler; **~ion**, capitulation, *f.*
capon, chapon, *m.*
capote, (*mil.*) capote, *f.*
capric|e, caprice, *m.*; **~ious**, capricieu|x, ~se; **~iously**, capricieusement.
capsicum, piment, *m.*
capsize, *s.* chavirement, *m.*; *v.n.* chavirer; *v.a.* faire* chavirer.
capstan, (*naut.*) cabestan, *m.*
capsule, (*bot., pharm., med., for bottle*) capsule, *f.*
captain, (*mil., naut., sport*) capitaine, *m.*
caption, rubrique, *f.*
captious, (*insidious*) captieu|x, ~se; (*fault-finding*) vétilleu|x, ~se.
captivat|e, captiver; **~ing**, *adj.* captivant.
captiv|e, *adj. and s.m.f.* capti|f, **~ve**; **~ity**, captivité, *f.*
captor, (*approx.*) celui, etc., qui a pris.
capture, (*act and thing*) capture, *f.*; *v.a.* capturer.
capuchin, (*friar*) capucin, *m.*
car, (*ant.*) char, *m.*; (*motor*) auto, *f.*; (*aeron.*) carlingue, *f.*; (*tram*) tramway, *m.*; (*U.S.A.*) wagon, *m.*; **armoured ~** *see* ARMOURED; **sleeping- ~**, wagon-lit, *m.*; *Pullman ~*, wagon-salon, *m.*; **open touring ~**, (*motor*) torpédo, *m.*
carabineer, carabinier, *m.*
caracole, *s.* (*arch. and riding*) caracole, *f.*; *v.n.* caracoler.
carafe, carafe, *f.*
caramel, caramel, *m.*
carat, (*gold and precious stones*) au titre de + *number*.
caravan, caravane, *f.*; (*gipsy's van*) roulotte, *f.*
caravansary, caravansarai, caravansérail, *m.*
caraway, (*bot.*) carvi, *m.*
carbine, carabine, *f.*
carbolic, *s.* (*chem.*) phénol, *m.*; *adj.* phénique.
carbon, (*chem.*) carbone, *m.*; ~ **copy**, copie au papier carboné, *f.*; **~aceous**, carboné; **~ic**, carbonique; **~ize**, carboniser.
carbonate, carbonate, *m.*
carbuncle, (*stone*) escarboucle, *f.*; (*med.*) anthrax, *m.*
carburett|or, ~er, (*motor*) carburateur, *m.*
carcass, (*an.*) cadavre, *m.*; (*fig. and framework*) carcasse, *f.*
card, *s.* carte, *f.*; **Xmas ~**, see CHRISTMAS; **~-case**, porte-cartes, *m. invar.*; **~-table**, table de jeu, *f.*; ~ **-sharper**, bonneteur, *m.*; *leave a ~ on*, (*visiting*) laisser une carte chez.
cardboard, carton, *m.*
cardiac, *adj.* cardiaque.
cardinal, *adj. and s.m.* cardinal, *m.*; ~ **-bird**, cardinal, *m.*; **~ate**, cardinalat, *m.*
cardoon, (*bot.*) cardon, *m.*
care, *s.* (*attention*) attention, *f.*; (*charge*) soin, *m.*; (*anxiety*) souci, *m.*; (*object of care*) objet de soins, *m.*; *c/o*, aux bons soins de; *take ~, v.n.* prendre* soin de; *take ~!, interj.* faites attention!; *take ~ not to + clause*, prendre* garde que + ne + *subj.*; *take ~ not to + inf.*, faire* attention de ne pas + *inf.*
care, *v.n.* ~ *about, for*, se soucier de;

~ *for*, (*pers.*) aimer; (*look after*) soigner; ~ *to*, (*like to*) aimer (*inf. or* à + *inf.*); *not to* ~ *if*, (= *be willing*) ne pas demander mieux que de; *I don't care!* (*exclam.*) Je m'en moque!; ça m'est égal; *not* ~ *a fig, rap, straw for*, se moquer comme de l'an quarante (de).
career, *s.* (*course of life, profession, &c.*) carrière, *f.*; (*impetus*) course, *f.*; *v.n.* ~ *along*, être en pleine course.
careful, soigneu|x, ~se; (*carefully done*) soigné; **~ness,** soin, *m.*; **~ly,** avec soin; *~ly selected*, trié sur le volet.
careless, (*unconcerned*) insouciant; (*thoughtless*) inconsidéré; ~ *of*, sans soin pour; **~ness,** négligence, *f.*; (*indifference*) insouciance, *f.*
caress, *s.* caresse, *f.*; *v.a.* caresser.
cargo, cargaison, *f.*; ~ **-boat,** cargo, *m.*
caribou, (*zool.*) caribou, *m.*
caricatur|e, caricature, *f.*; *v.a.* caricaturer; **~ist,** caricaturiste, *m.*
Carmelite, (*friar*) carme, *m.*
carmine, *adj. and s.m.* carmin.
carnage, carnage, *m.*
carnal, charnel, -le.
carnation, (*bot.*) œillet, *m.*
carnival, carnaval, *m.*
carnivorous, *adj.* carnivore.
carob, ~ **-bean,** caroube, *f.*; ~ **-tree,** caroubier, *m.*
carol, (*Xmas*) noël, *m.*; (*birds*) ramage; *v.n.* (*birds*) gazouiller; (*larks*) grisoller.
carous|al, ribote, *f.*; **~e,** faire* ribote.
carp, (*ichth.*) carpe, *f.*
carp at, gloser sur; **~er,** censeur, *m.*
carpent|er, charpentier, *m.*; (*joiner*) menuisier, *m.*; **~ry,** charpenterie, *f.*
carpet, tapis, *m.*; ~ **-bag,** sac de nuit en tapisserie, *m.*; ~ **-broom,** balai de jonc, *m.*
carriage, (*conveying, transport*) transport, *m.*; (*cost of parcels*) port, *m.*; (*cost of goods*) frais de transport, *m. pl.*; (*vehicle*) voiture, *f.*; (*bearing*) maintien, *m.*; (*rail. coach*) wagon, *m.*; (*rail. compartment*) compartiment, *m.*; ~ *and pair*, voiture à deux chevaux, *f.*; ~ **-door,** portière, *f.*; ~ **-drive,** avenue, *f.*; ~ **-entrance,** (*gate, door*) porte cochère, *f.*; ~ **forward,** en port dû; ~ **free,** franco de port; ~ **paid,** en port payé; ~ **-window,** glace, *f.*
carrier, voiturier, *m.*; (*motor*) porte-bagages, *m. invar.*; **~-pigeon,** pigeon voyageur, *m.*
carrion, *s.* charogne, *f.*; *adj.* de charogne.
carrot, carotte, *f.*; **~y,** rou|x, ~sse.
carry, *v.a. porter*; (*convey*) transporter; (*any weight or on or about one*) porter; (*support weight of*) supporter; (*conviction*) inspirer; (*fortress*) enlever; (*motion*) adopter; (*interest*) rapporter; (*arith.*) retenir*; ~ *oneself*, se comporter; ~ *all before one*, triompher de tout; ~ *too far*, pousser trop loin; ~ **away,** (*lit. and inspire*) enlever; ~ **back,** reporter; ~ **down,** descendre (avoir); ~ **forward,** (*bkkpg.*) reporter; ~ **off,** (*of death, kidnap, prize*) enlever; ~ **on** (*business*) exercer; (*conversation*) soutenir*; ~ **out,** porter dehors; (*contract, &c.*) exécuter; ~ **over,** (*bkkpg.*) reporter; ~ **through,** mener à bonne fin; ~ **with one** (*audience, &c.*) entraîner; ~ **up,** monter (*avoir*).
carry, *v.n.* (*firearms, voice*) porter; ~ *on*, continuer.
carrying-chair, chaise à porteurs, *f.*
cart, charrette, *f.*; ~ **-horse,** cheval de trait, *m.*; **~-load,** charretée, *f.*
cart, *v.a.* charrier.
cartage, camionnage, *m.*
carter, charretier, *m.*
Carthaginian, *adj.* (*when an adj. use small letter*) *and s.m.f.* Carthaginois, -e.
Carthusian, *s.* chartreux, *m.*
cartilage, cartilage, *m.*
cartoon, (*design for painting*) carton, *m.*; (*in comic paper*) dessin satirique, *m.*
cartouche, (*arch.*) cartouche, *m.*
cartridge, cartouche, *f.*; ~ **-box,** giberne, *f.*; ~ **-pouch,** giberne, *f.*; *blank* ~, *see* BLANK.
cartulary, cartulaire, *m.*
cartwright, charron, *m.*
carve, *v.a.n.* (*wood, stone, statue*) sculpter; (*meat*) découper.
carver, sculpteur, *m.*; (*meat*) personne qui découpe, *f.*
carving, sculpture, *f.*; (*meat*) action de découper, *f.*; ~ **-fork,** fourchette à découper, *f.*; ~ **-knife,** couteau à découper, *m.*
caryatid, (*arch.*) cariatide, *f.*
cascade, cascade, *f.*
case, *s.* (*holder for needles, spectacles, cigars, &c.*) étui, *m.*; (*watch*) boîte, *f.*; (*packing*) caisse, *f.*; (*writing*) papeterie, *f.*
case, *s.* (*instance, med., conscience*) cas, *m.*; (*plight*) situation, *f.*; (*law*) cause, *f.*; *in* ~, *conj.* au cas que (+ *subj.*); *in any* ~, en tout cas; *it is not the* ~, il n'en est pas ainsi; *in such a* ~, en pareil cas.
case, *v.n.* (*in covering, sheath, &c.*) enfermer; (*build.*) revêtir* (de).
casemate, casemate, *f.*
casement, croisée, *f.*
cash, (*ready money*) espèces, *f.pl.*; ~ **account,** espèces en compte, *f.pl.*; **~-book,** livre de caisse, *m.*; ~ **-box,** caisse, *f.*; **~-balance,** encaisse, *f.*; **~-discount,** escompte, *m.*; ~ **down,** argent comptant, *m.*; ~ *in hand*, encaisse, *f.*; ~ *on delivery*, envoi(s) contre remboursement, *m. or m.pl.*; *pay in* ~, payer en espèces; *v.a.* (*cheque*) toucher.
cashier, caissi|er, ~ère, *s.m.f.*
cashmere, cachemire, *m.*
casing, (*build.*) revêtement, *m.*; (*cover*) enveloppe, *f.*
casino, casino, *m.*
cask, tonneau, *m.*
casket, cassette, *f.*
cassia, (*bot.*) casse, *f.*

cassock, soutane, *f.*
cassowary, (*zool.*) casoar, *m.*
cast, casting, *s.* (*throw of dice, fishing-line, net, anchor, &c.*) coup, *m.*; (*stamp, character, fig.*) trempe, *f.*; (*distance*) jet, *m.*; (*theatr.*) distribution, *f.*; (*reproduction from mould*) moulage, *m.*; (*type*) type, *m.*; (*shade of colour*) nuance, *f.*; (*of figures and casting up*), addition *f.*, ~ *of mind*, tournure d'esprit; *have a ~ in the eye*, loucher.
cast, *v.a.* (*throw, dice, look, blame, spell, light, into prison*) jeter; (*seed*) semer; (*change*) changer (de); (*metal*) fondre; (*mould*) couler; (*lose*) perdre; (*shadow*) projeter; ~ *oneself on*, (*pity, &c.*) s'en remettre* à; ~ *a sidelong glance at*, regarder du coin de l'œil; ~ **headlong,** précipiter; ~ **loose,** (*naut.*) larguer; ~ **about for** (*think to find*) *v.a.* s'aviser de; ~ **aside,** se défaire* de; ~ **away,** rejeter; (*banish*) bannir; ~ **down,** jeter par terre; (*eyes*) baisser; (*fig.*) abattre; ~ **off,** rejeter; (*anchor, &c.*) jeter; ~ **out,** (*repel*) rejeter; (*expel*) chasser; ~ **up,** (*eyes*) lever; (*figures*) additionner; (*on shore*) rejeter.
castanet, castagnette, *f.*
castaway, *adj. and s.m.f.* (*shipwrecked*) naufragé, -e; (*reprobate*) réprouvé, -e.
caste, caste, *f.*; *lose caste*, perdre son rang.
castellated, (*build.*) crénelé.
castigat|e, (*lit. and fig.*) châtier; **~ion,** châtiment, *m.*
Castilian, *adj.* (*when an adj. use small letter*) *and s.m.f.* Castillan, -e.
casting, *s.* (*metal*) fonte, *f.*; ~ **-net,** épervier, *m.*; ~ **-vote,** voix prépondérante, *f.*
castle, château, *m.*; (*chess*) tour, *f.*; *~s in the air*, châteaux en Espagne, *m.pl.*
castor, (*zool.*) castor, *m.*
cast|or, ~er, (*sugar, &c.*) saupoudroir, *m.*; ~ **-sugar,** sucre en poudre, *m.*
castor-oil, huile de ricin, *f.*
castrat|e, châtrer; (*expurgate*) expurger; **~ion,** castration, *f.*
casual, casuel, -le; (*pers.*) insouciant; ~ *acquaintance*, connaissance de rencontre, *f.*; **~ly,** par hasard.
casual|ty, accident, *m.*; ⚠ *not* casualité, *f.* *which = 'casualness' of things*; **~ness,** (*pers.*) insouciance, *f.*
casuist, casuiste, *m.*; **~ry,** (*lit. and fig.*) casuistique, *f.*; **~ic(al),** de casuiste.
cat, *s.* chat, -te, *m.f.*; ~ **-burglar,** rat d'hôtel, *m.*; **~'s foot,** (*bot.*) lierre terrestre, *m.*; ~ **-head,** (*naut.*) bossoir, *m.*; ~ **-mint,** cataire, *f.*; ~ *o' nine tails*, garcette, *f.*; *bell the ~*, attacher le grelot; *let the ~ out of the bag*, vendre la mèche; *it's raining ~s and dogs*, il tombe des hallebardes.
cataclysm, cataclysme, *m.*
catacomb, catacombe, *f.*
catafalque, catafalque, *m.*
catalepsy, catalepsie, *f.*
catalogue, catalogue, *m.*; *v.a.* cataloguer.
catalpa, (*bot.*) catalpa, *m.*
catapult, catapulte, *f.*
cataract, (*lit. and med.*) cataracte, *f.*
catarrh, catarrhe, *m.*
catastrophe, catastrophe, *f.*
catch, *s.* (*act and fish caught*) prise, *f.*; (*ruse, trick*) attrape, *f.*; (*lock, wheel, &c.*) mentonnet, *m.*; (*mus.*) canon; (*ball*) *use verb*, bien attraper la balle; ~ **-penny,** attrape-nigaud, *m.*; **~word,** réclame, *f.*; (*cue, theatr.*) réplique, *f.*
catch, *v.a.* (*seize*) saisir; (*animals, &c., disease, overtake, hit off, likeness, tram, ball, habit*) attraper; (*catch and tear*) accrocher; (*eye*) frapper; (*understand*) saisir; (*attract*) attirer; ~ *in the act*, prendre* sur le fait; ~ *hold of*, saisir; ~ *red-handed*, attraper sur le fait; ~ *up*, (*overtake*) rattraper.
catch, *v.n.* (*wood, &c., fires*) prendre*; (*get caught*) se prendre; ~ *at*, (*to save oneself*) s'accrocher à; (*fig.*) sauter sur.
catching, (*disease*) contagieu|x, ~se.
catech|ism, catéchisme, *m.*; **~ize,** catéchiser; **-ist,** catéchiste, *m.*
catechumen, catéchumène, *m.f.*
categor|y, catégorie, *f.*; **~ical,** catégorique; **~ically,** catégoriquement.
catenation, enchaînement, *m.*
cater, *v.n.* ~ *for*, pourvoir à; **~er,** pourvoyeu|r, ~se, *m.f.*
caterpillar, chenille, *f.*; (*motor*) autochenille, *f.*
caterwaul, *v.n.* miauler; **~ing,** *s.* sabbat des chats, *m.*
catgut, corde à boyau, *f.*
cathedral, cathédrale, *f.*; *adj.* cathédral.
catholic, (*universal*) universel, -le; (*theol.*) catholique; **~ism,** catholicisme, *m.*; **~ity,** catholicité, *f.*
catkin, (*bot.*) chaton, *m.*
cattle, bétail, *m.*, *pl.* bestiaux; **~-drover,** toucheur, *m.*; ~ **plague,** peste bovine, *f.*; ~ **-rearing,** élevage de bétail, *m.*; ~ **-shed,** étable, *f.*; ~ **show,** exposition de bétail, *f.*
caucus, comité électoral, *m.*
caudal, *adj.* caudal.
caudle, (*gruel*) chaudeau, *m.*
caul, (*head-dress*) coiffe, *f.*
cauldron, (*large*) chaudière, *f.*; (*small*) chaudron, *m.*
cauliflower, chou-fleur, *m.*
caulk, *v.a.* (*naut.*) calfater; **~er,** (*pers.*) calfat, *m.*
causal, causal; **~ity,** causalité, *f.*
causation, causation, *f.*
cause, *s.* cause, *f.*; (*motive*) motif, *m.*; (*law*) cause, *f.*; **~less,** sans cause; ~ *of complaint*, sujet de plainte, *m.*; *remote ~*, cause éloignée, *f.*; *v.a.* causer; (*to be done*) faire* + *act. inf.*; ~ *great* (*public*) *excitement, a flutter*, faire* sensation.
causeway, chaussée, *f.*
caustic, *adj.* (*lit. and fig.*) *and s.m.*

caustique; ~**ally**, d'une manière caustique.
cauteriz|e, cautériser; ~**ation**, cautérisation, *f.*
caution, prudence, *f.*; (*warning*) avertissement, *m.*; (*pers. slang*) numéro, *m.*; ~ **money**, cautionnement, *m.*
caution, *v.a.* avertir; ⚠ *not* cautionner, *which* = '*go bail for*'; ~ *against*, mettre* en garde contre.
cautionary, (*warning*) d'avertissement.
cautious, prudent; ~**ly**, prudemment.
cavalcade, cavalcade, *f.*
cavalier, *s.* (*horseman, gallant*) cavalier, *m.*; *adj.* cavali|er, ~ère; ~**ly**, cavalièrement.
cavalry, cavalerie, *f.*
cave, **cavern**, *s.* caverne, *f.*; ~ **-man**, homme des cavernes, *m.*
cave in, *v.n.* (*subside*) s'affaisser; (*yield*) céder.
cavernous, caverneu|x, ~se.
caviar, caviar, *m.*
cavil at, chicaner sur; ~**ler**, ergoteur, *m.*
cavity, cavité, *f.*
caw, (*rook*) croasser; ~**ing**, croassement, *m.*
cayenne, (*Cayenne pepper*) poivre de Cayenne, *m.*
ceas|e, *v.a.n.* cesser; ~ *from*, cesser, *v.a.*; ~ *to do, from doing*, cesser de; *never* ~*ing*, incessant.
ceaseless, incessant; ~**ly**, sans cesse.
cedar, cèdre, *m.*; ~ **-wood**, bois de cèdre, *m.*
cede, *v.a.* céder.
cedilla, cédille, *f.*
ceil, *v.a.* plafonner; ~**ing**, *s.* plafond, *m.*
celandine, (*bot.*) chélidoine, *f.*; *greater, lesser* ~, grande, petite éclaire, *f.*
celebrant, (*priest*) officiant, *m.*
celebrat|e, *v.a.* (*mass, marriage, extol*) célébrer; (*commemorate*) commémorer; *v.n.* (*priest*) officier.
celebrated, *adj.* célèbre (*for* = par); ⚠ *not* célébré *which is only the p.p. of* célébrer.
celebration, (*act*) célébration, *f.*; (*commemoration*) commémoration, *f.*; (*praise*) louange, *f.*
celebrity, (*reputation and pers.*) célébrité, *f.*
celerity, célérité, *f.*
celery, céleri, *m.*
celestial, (*lit. and fig.*) céleste.
celib|ate, *adj. and s.m.f.* célibataire; ~**acy**, célibat, *m.*
cell, (*hermit, prison, convent*) cellule, *f.*; (*bee*) alvéole, *m.*; (*electr.*) élément, *m.*
cellar, cave, *f.*; (*small*) caveau, *m.*; ⚠ *not* cellier *which* = '*still-room*'.
'cello, *see* VIOLONCELLO.
cellular, *adj.* cellulaire.
celluloid, celluloïd, *m.*
Celt, *s.* Celte, *m.f.*; ~**ic**, celtique.
cement, (*lit. and fig.*) ciment, *m.*; (*metal*) cément, *m.*; *v.a.* cimenter, cémenter.
cemetery, cimetière, *m.*
cenotaph, cénotaphe, *m.*
cense, *v.a.* encenser; ~**r**, encensoir, *m.*
censor, (*Rom. hist., critic, public official*) censeur, *m.*; *v.a.* censurer; ~**ious**, critique; ~**iousness**, humeur critique, *f.*; ~**ship**, censure, *f.*
censure, *s.* censure, *f.*; *v.a.* censurer.
census, recensement, *m.*
cent., *five per* ~, cinq pour cent; (*U.S.A. coin*) cent, *m.*
centaur, centaure, *m.*
centenarian, *adj. and s.m.f.* centenaire.
centenary, **centennial**, *adj. and s.m.* centenaire.
centesimal, centésimal.
centigrade, *adj.* centigrade.
centi|gramme, centigramme, *m.*; ~**metre**, centimètre, *m.*
centipede, mille-pattes, *m.*
central, central; ~ **heating**, chauffage central, *m.*; ~**ization**, centralisation, *f.*; ~**ize**, centraliser.
centre, *s.* (*social, attraction, lit., fig., gravity, mil.*) centre, *m.*; ~ **-bit**, mèche anglaise, *f.*; ~ **-piece**, surtout de table, *m.*
centre, *v.a.* centrer; ~ *on*, concentrer sur; *v.n.* ~ *on, in*, se concentrer sur.
centri|fugal, centrifuge; ~ **petal**, centripète.
centuple, *adj. and s.m.* centuple.
centurion, centurion, *m.*
century, siècle, *m.*
ceramic, *adj.* céramique; ~**s**, céramique, *f.*
cereal, *adj. and s.f.* céréale; *which also* = *cereals*.
cerebral, cérébral.
cere|cloth, ~**ment**, suaire, *m.*
ceremonial, *adj. and s.m.* cérémonial.
ceremonious, cérémonieu|x, ~se; ~**ly**, cérémonieusement.
ceremony, cérémonie, *f.*; *stand upon* ~, faire* des cérémonies; *without* ~, sans façon.
cerise, (*colour*) *adj.* cerise, *invar.*
certain, (*reliable, sure to happen, convinced, after noun; some or other, some amount, before noun*) certain; *for* ~, pour certain; *be* ~ *of*, avoir la certitude de; *a* ~ *Mr. X*, un certain M. X.; ~**ly**, certainement.
certainty, **certitude**, certitude, *f.*; *for a* ~, sans aucun doute; *dead* ~, certitude absolue, *f.*
certificate, (*lit. and shares*) certificat, *m.*; (*diploma*) diplôme, *m.*; ~ *of birth, death*, acte de naissance, de décès, *m.*
certify, *v.a.* certifier.
cerulean, céruléen, -ne.
cervical, cervical.
cessation, cessation, *f.*; ~ *of hostilities*, suspension d'armes, *f.*
cession, cession, *f.*
cesspool, puisard, *m.*; ~ *of vice, &c.*, cloaque de vice, etc., *m.*
cetacean, *adj. and s.m.* cétacé.

chafe, *v.a.* (*for warmth*) frictionner; (*anger*) irriter; (*naut.*) raguer.
chafe, *v.n.* (*rope*) raguer; ~ *against,* se frotter contre; (*fig.*) s'irriter à cause de.
chafer, *s., see* COCKCHAFER.
chaff, *s.* (*of grain*) bale, balle, *f.*; (*chopped straw, &c.*) paille †hachée, *f.*; (*mockery*) raillerie, *f.*; ~ **-cutter,** †hache-paille, *m. invar.*; *v.a.* blaguer.
chaffinch, (*ornith.*) pinson, *m.*
chafing-dish, réchaud, *m.*
chain, (*gen., mountains, measuring-rod*) chaîne, *f.*; (*succession*) enchaînement, *m.*; ~**-armour,** cotte de maille, *f.*; *v.a.* (*lit. and fig.*) enchaîner.
chair, chaise, *f.*; (*of chairman, &c.*) fauteuil de la présidence, *m.*; (*professorship*) chaire, *f.*; (*rail*) coussinet, *m.*; **sedan-** ~, *see* SEDAN; *occupy, take the* ~, présider.
chair, *v.a.* porter en triomphe.
chairman, (*meeting*) président, *m.*; ~**ship,** présidence, *f.*
chaise, (*veh.*) chaise, *f.*
chalcedony, calcédoine, *f.*
Chaldean, *adj.* chaldéen, -ne.
chalice, calice, *m.*
chalk, craie, *f.*; ~ **-pit,** carrière de craie, *f.*; ~ **-stone,** (*med.*) calcul arthritique, *m.*; *v.a.* ~ *out,* tracer.
chalky, crayeu|x, ~se.
challenge, *s.* défi, *m.*; (*mil.*) qui-vive, *m.*
challenge, *v.a.* défier; (*duel, claim attention, &c.*) provoquer; (*dispute*) contester; (*mil.*) crier qui-vive à; ~**r,** celui qui fait un défi, *m.*
chamber, *s.* chambre, *f.*; ~**s,** (*solicitor, &c.*) étude, *f.*; (*bachelor*) appartement, *m.*; (*Chamber of Commerce, Agriculture, Deputies, &c.*) Chambre, *f.*; ~ **-pot,** pot de chambre, *m.*
chamberlain, chambellan, *m.*; (*Vatican*) camérier, *m.*; *Lord Chamberlain,* grand chambellan, *m.*
chambermaid, fille de chambre, *f.*
chamelion, caméléon, *m.*
chamfer, *v.a.* chanfreiner.
chamois, chamois, *m.*; ~ (*shammy*) *leather,* peau de chamois, *f.*
champ, *v.a.* (*bit*) mâcher.
champagne, *s.* (*wine*) champagne, *m.*
champion, champion, -ne, *s.m.f.*; *v.a.* défendre.
chance, *s.* chance, *f.*; (*opportunity*) occasion, *f.*; *by* ~, par †hasard; *on the* ~ *of* +*gerund,* dans le cas où +*cond.*
chance, *adj.* fortuit; (*gain, &c., risky*) aléatoire.
chance, *v.a.* risquer; *v.n.* (*impers.*) arriver (être); ~ *upon,* tomber (être) sur.
chancel, sanctuaire, *m.*
chancellor, chancelier, *m.*; ~**ship,** dignité de chancelier, *f.*
chancery, chancellerie, *f.*
chandelier, lustre, *m.*
chandler, *see* CORN *and* TALLOW.
change, *s.* (*alteration, substitution, variety, moon*) changement, *m.*; (*money*) monnaie, *f.*; *Change,* (*comm.*) Bourse, *f.*; ~ *for the better,* changement en bien, *m.*; *small* ~, menue monnaie, *f.*
change, *v.a.* (*take one thing in place of another, as clothes*) changer de; (*exchange*) échanger (pour); (*money*) changer; ~ *into,* changer en; ~ *hands,* changer de mains; *gear,* ~ (*motor*) changer de vitesse.
change, *v.n.* (*clothes, become different*) changer; (*rail*) changer de train; ~ *for the better,* changer en bien.
changeable, changeant.
changer, *see* MONEY-CHANGER.
changeling, enfant substitué, *m.*
channel, (*rivers*) lit, *m.*; (*narrow*) canal, *m.*; (*strait*) détroit, *m.*; (*fig.*) voie, *f.*; *English* ~, Manche, *f.*
chant, *s.* chant, *m.*; *v.a.* chanter; ~**er,** chant|re, *m.*
chanticleer, coq, *m.*
chantry, chapelle, *f.*
chao|s, (*lit. and fig.*) chaos, *m.*; ~**tic,** chaotique.
chap, (*pers. young*) gars, *m.*; (*on hand*) gerçure, *f.*; ~**s,** (*jaws*) mâchoires, *f.pl.*
chapel, chapelle, *f.*; (*non-conformist*) temple, *m.*
chaperon, (*of young person*) chaperon, *m.*; *v.a.* chaperonner.
chaplain, chapelain, *m.*; (*official*) aumônier, *m.*; ~**cy,** aumônerie, *f.*
chaplet, chapelet, *m.*
chapter, (*of book, eccles., and fig.* = *limited subject*) chapitre, *m.*; ~**-house,** chapitre, *m.*
char, *v.a.* (*fire*) carboniser; (*houseclean, U.S.A. 'chore'*) faire* des ménages.
charabanc, (*horse*) char à bancs, *m.*; (*motor*) autocar, *m.*
character, (*disposition, peculiar characteristics, letters, figures, print., mental and moral back-bone*) caractère, *m.*; (*distinctive mark*) caractère distinctif, *m.*; (*reputation*) réputation, *f.*; (*servant's*) certificat, *m.*; (*novel, &c.*) personnage, *m.*; (*role*) rôle, *m.*; (*sort*) genre, *m.*; (*eccentric, pers.*) original, *m.*; *he is quite a* ~, c'est un véritable type; *man of bad* ~, vaurien, *m.*
characteristic, *s.* propre, *m.* ⚠ caractéristique, *as a noun, is practically confined to math., mach., and gram.*; *adj.* caractéristique; ~**ally,** d'une manière caractéristique.
characterize, caractériser.
charade, charade, *f.*
charcoal, charbon de bois, *m.*; ~**-burner,** charbonnier, *m.*
charge, *s.* (*load, lit. and fig., gun, mil., office, electr.*) charge, *f.*; (*price*) prix, *m.*; (*accusation*) accusation, *f.*; (*post*) taxe, *f.*; (*care*) soin, *m.*; (*child*) enfant, *m.f.*; (*injunction*) recommandation, *f.*; *extra* ~, supplément *m.*; *give in* ~, faire* arrêter; ~**s,** frais, *m.pl.*
charge, *v.a.* (*load, lit. and fig., mil., electr., gun*) charger; (*entrust with*) charger (de); (*command*) commander, à + *pers.,* de +

inf.; (*accuse*) accuser (de); (*price*) demander; (*letter, extra post*) taxer; ~ *for*, faire* payer; ~ *to*, (*bkkpg.*) mettre* au compte de.
chargeable, (*imputable*) imputable (à); (*payments*) à la charge de.
charger, (*dish*) grand plat, *m.*; (*horse*) cheval de bataille, *m.*
chariot, char, *m.*; (*ant.*) chariot, *m.*; **~eer,** (*astr.*) cocher, *m.*
charitabl|e, charitable; **~y,** charitablement.
charity, (*virtue, kindness, alms, act of*) charité, *f.*; (*not imputing ill motives*) bienveillance, *f.*; (*institution*) fondation charitable, *f.*; ~ **-school,** orphelinat, *m.*
charlatan, charlatan, *m.*
Charles's Wain, Grand Chariot, *m.*
charlock, (*bot.*) sanve, *f.*
charm, (*attractiveness*) charme, *m.*; (*trinket*) breloque, *f.*; (*amulet*) amulette, *f.*; *v.a.* charmer; ~ *away*, dissiper.
charmer, charmeu|r, ~se, *m.f.*
charming, charmant; **~ly,** d'une manière charmante.
charnel-house, charnier, *m.*
chart, carte, *f.*; (*naut.*) carte marine, *f.*; (*curving record*) courbe, *f.*
charter, *s.* charte, *f.*; *v.a.* (*vessel*) affréter.
charwoman, (*fam.*) **char,** femme de ménage, *f.*
char|y, (*cautious*) précautionneu|x, ~se; (*stingy*) chiche (de); **~ily,** avec circonspection.
chase, *s.* chasse, *f.*; *in ~ of*, à la poursuite de.
chas|e, *v.a.* chasser; (*pursue*) poursuivre*; (*metals*) ciseler; **~er** (*aeron.*) avion de chasse, *m.*; ~ **ing,** (*metals*), ciselure, *f.*
chasm, (*lit. and fig.*) abîme, *m.*
chaste, chaste; ⚠ chaste *is used of continence only*; *of style, &c., use* châtié.
chasten, (*lit. and style*) châtier; (*subdue*) réprimer.
chastise, châtier; **~ment,** châtiment, *m.*
chastity, chasteté, *f.*; (*style*) pureté, *f.*
chasuble, chasuble, *f.*
chat, *s.* causette, *f.*; *have a ~*, faire* un bout de causette; *v.n.* causer; **~ty,** causeu|r, ~se.
chattels, biens meubles, *m.pl.*
chatter, *s.* babil, *m.*; *v.n.* babiller; (*teeth*) claquer.
chatterbox, jacasse, *f.*
chaw up, (*U.S.A.*) battre à plate couture.
cheap, *adj.* bon marché, *invar.*; (*fig., reputation, &c.*) de peu de valeur; ~ **jack,** camelot, *m.*; ~ *ticket*, billet à prix réduit, *m.*; **~er,** (*compar. adj.*) meilleur marché, *invar.*; **~ness,** bon marché, *m.*; **~ly,** à bon marché; (*without much cost*) à peu de frais.
cheapen, déprécier.
cheat, *s.* (*pers.*) fourbe, *m.*; (*cards*) tricheu|r, ~se, *m.f.*; (*thing*) fraude, *f.*; *v.a.* (*deceive*) tromper; (*defraud*) frauder; (*cards*) tricher.
cheating, *s.* fourberie, *f.*; (*cards*) tricherie, *f.*
check, *s.* (*rebuff, chess, mil.*) échec, *m.*; (*curb, restraint*) frein, *m.*; (*checking*) vérification, *f.*; *adj. and* **~ed,** (*of material*) à carreaux.
check, *v.a.* (*chess*) faire échec à; (*stop*) arrêter, (*repress*) réprimer; (*accounts*) vérifier.
checkmate, *s.* échec et mat, *m.*; *v.a.* faire* échec et mat à; (*fig.*) déjouer.
cheek, *s.* joue, *f.*; (*slang*) toupet, *m.*; **~-bone,** pommette, *f.*; **~y,** impertinent; *v.a.* dire* des impertinences à.
cheer, (*food*) chère, *f.*; (*applause*) †hourra, *m.*; (*consolation*) consolation, *f.*; *be of good ~*, *v.n.* prendre* courage.
cheer, *v.a.* réjouir; (*console*) consoler; (*encourage*) encourager; (*acclaim*) acclamer; *v.n.* ~ *up*, prendre* courage; *interj.* bon courage.
cheerful, (*pers.*) joyeu|x, ~se; (*things*) gai; (*ready*) de bon cœur; **~ness,** gaieté, *f.*; **~ly,** gaiement; (*readily*) de bon cœur.
cheering, *s.* acclamations, *f.pl.*; *adj.* encourageant.
cheerless, triste.
cheer|y, gai; **~iness,** gaieté, *f.*; **~ily,** gaiement.
cheese, fromage, *m.*; ~ **-paring,** *s.* économies de bouts de chandelles, *f.pl.*
cheesemonger, marchand de fromage, *m.*
chemical, *adj.* chimique; **~ly,** chimiquement.
chemise, chemise, *f.*
chemist, (*skilled in chemistry*) chimiste, *m.f.*; (*dealer in drugs*) pharmacien, *m.*; **~ry,** chimie, *f.*; *~'s shop*, pharmacie, *f.*
cheque, chèque, *m.*; **~-book,** carnet de chèques, *m.*; *blank ~ see* BLANK; *crossed ~*, chèque barré, *m.*; *dishonoured ~*, chèque impayé, *m.*; *forged ~*, faux chèque, *m.*
chequered, checkered, (*life, &c.*) accidenté; (*motley*) bariolé.
cherish, entourer de soins; (*hope, &c.*) caresser; (*entertain*) entretenir*.
cheroot, cigare des Indes, *m.*
cherry, cerise, *f.*; *wild ~*, merise, *f.*; **~-tree,** cerisier, *m.*; ~ **-coloured,** cerise, *invar.*
cherub, chérubin, *m.*; **~ic,** de chérubin.
chervil, (*bot.*) cerfeuil, *m.*
chess, échecs, *m.pl.*; ~ **-board, table,** échiquier, *m.*; ~ **-man,** pièce, *f.*
chest, coffre, *m.*; (*money*) caisse, *f.*; (*pers.*) poitrine, *f.*; ~ *of drawers*, commode, *f.*
chestnut, châtaigne, *f.*; ~ **-tree,** châtaignier, *m.*; **horse-** ~, marron d'Inde, *m.*; *horse-* ~ *tree*, marronnier d'Inde, *m.*; ⚠ *the edible chestnut* = grosse châtaigne, *f.*, *or* marron, *m.*; *adj.* (*colour*) châtain; ~ *-bay*, (*horse*) bai châtain, *invar.*
cheval-glass, psyché, *f.*

cheviot, (*wool. cloth*) cheviote, *f.*
chevron, (*mil. and her.*) chevron, *m.*
chew, mâcher; (*tobacco*) chiquer; ~ *the cud*, (*lit. and fig.*) ruminer.
chiaroscuro, clair-obscur, *m.*
chicanery, chicanerie, *f.*
chick, poussin, *m.*; ~ **-pea**, pois chiche, *m.*; ~ **-weed**, (*bot.*) mouron, *m.*
chicken, poulet, *m.*; ~ **-pox**, varicelle, *f.*; *be* ~ *-hearted*, être une poule mouillée.
chicory, (*bot.*) endive, *f.*; ⚠ chicorée, *f.* = '*endive*' *in English.*
chid|e, *v.a.n.* gronder; **-ing**, gronderie, *f.*; ~ *against*, murmurer contre.
chief, chieftain, chef, *m.*; (*fam.*) patron, *m.*
chief, *adj.* principal; ~**ly**, principalement; *be* ~ *mourner*, mener le deuil.
chiff-chaff, (*ornith.*) véloce, *m.*
chiffonier, (*furniture*) chiffonnier, *m.*
chilblain, engelure, *f.*
child, enfant, *m.f.*; *with* ~, enceinte; *a burnt* ~ *dreads the fire*, chat échaudé craint l'eau froide; ~*'s play*, (*fig.*) jeu d'enfant, *m.*; ~**birth**, *see* BIRTH; ~**hood**, enfance, *f.*; *be in one's second* ~*hood*, tomber (être) en enfance; ~**like**, d'enfant.
childish, enfantin; (*trifling*) puéril; ~**ness**, enfantillage, *m.*
child|less, sans enfant.
chill, *s.* (*lit. fig.*) froid, *m.*; (*shiver*) frisson, *m.*; *catch a* ~, prendre* froid; *take the* ~ *off*, (*water*) dégourdir; *adj.* (*lit. and fig.*) froid.
chill, *v.a.* refroidir; (*fig.*) glacer.
chill|y, (*lit. and fig.*) un peu froid; (*sensitive to cold*) frileu|x, ~se; *it is* ~, (*pop.*) il fait frisquet; ~**iness**, (*pers.*) frissonnement, *m.*; (*things*) froid, *m.*
chime, carillon, *m.*; *v.a.* sonner; *v.n.* carillonner.
chimer|a, chimère, *f.*; ~**ical**, chimérique.
chimney, cheminée, *f.*; (*lamp*) verre, *m.*; ~ **-corner**, coin du feu, *m.*; ~ **-piece**, manteau de cheminée, *m.*; ~ **-pot**, mitre, *f.*; ~ **-sweep**, ramoneur, *m.*
chimpanzee, (*zool.*) chimpanzé, *m.*
chin, menton, *m.*
china, porcelaine, *f.*; **old** ~, vieilles porcelaines, *f.pl.*
China aster, reine-marguerite, *f.*
Chinese, *adj.* (*when an adj. use small letter*) *and s.m.f.* Chinois, -e, *m.f.*; (*lang.*) chinois, *m.*; ~ **lantern**, lanterne vénitienne, *f.*
chink, *s.* (*opening*) fente, *f.*; (*crevice*) crevasse, *f.*; (*money, glass*) tintement, *m.*; *v.n.* sonner.
chintz, perse, *f.*
chip, *s.* (*wood*) copeau, *m.*; (*glass, stone*) éclat, *m.*; ~**s**, (*potatoes*) frites, *f.pl.*; *be a* ~ *of the old block*, être bien le fils de son père.
chip, *v.a.* ébrécher; *v.n.* s'ébrécher.
chiromanc|er, chiromancien, -ne, *m.f.*; ~**y**, chiromancie, *f.*
chiropodist, pédicure, *m.f.*
chirp, *s.* (*birds*) gazouillement, *m.*; (*insects*) cri, *m.*
chirp, chirrup, *v.n.* gazouiller; (*insects*) crier.
chisel, ciseau, *m.*; *v.a.* ciseler.
chit, (*child*) gosse, *f.*; (*note*) pli, *m.*; (*character*) certificat, *m.*
chit-chat, causerie, *f.*
chitterlings, (*cook.*) andouille, *f.*
chivalr|y, chevalerie, *f.*; ~**ous**, chevaleresque; ~**ously**, chevaleresquement.
chive, (*bot.*) ciboulette, *f.*
chloral, *s.* chloral, *m.*
chlorate, *s.* chlorate, *m.*
chloride, chlorure, *m.*
chloroform, chloroforme, *m.*
chock-full, plein comme un œuf.
chocolate, *s.* chocolat, *m.*; ~ **-colour**, *adj.* chocolat, *invar.*
choice, choosing, *s.* choix, *m.*; (*assortment*) assortiment, *m.*; *for* ~, de préférence.
choice, *adj.* de choix; (*rare*) précieu|x, ~se; (*selected and style*) choisi.
choir, quire, (*of voices*) chœur, *m.*
chok|e *and* **choke down**, *v.a.* (*lit., fig.*) étouffer; ~ **up**, boucher; *v.n.* étouffer; (*suffocate*) s'étouffer; ~**ing**, suffocation, *f.*
choker, (*collar*) col droit, *m.*
choler, (*anger*) colère, *f.*; ~**ic**, colérieu|x, ~se; ⚠ cholérique = *pertaining to 'cholera'*.
cholera, choléra, *m.*
choose, *v.a.* choisir; (*elect*) élire*; *v.n.* (*think fit*) vouloir*; ~ *to*, vouloir* + *inf.*; ~ *between*, faire* un choix entre.
chop, (*meat*) côtelette, *f.*; ~ **-house**, restaurant, *m.*
chop, *v.a.* couper; (*wood*) casser; ~ *off*, trancher; ~ *small*, †hacher menu; ~ *up*, †hacher.
chop, *v.n.* (*sea*) clapoter; (*wind*) tourner; ~ *and change*, changer à plusieurs reprises.
chopper, couperet, *m.*
chopping-board, *and* ~ **-knife**, †hachoir, *m.*
choppy, (*sea*) clapoteu|x, ~se.
chopsticks, bâtonnets, *m.pl.*
choral, *adj. and s.m.* choral.
chord, (*poet., harp, &c.*) corde, *f.*; (*mus.*) accord, *m.*
chore, (*U.S.A.*) travail de ménage, *m.*
chorister, enfant de chœur, *m.*
chorus, chœur, *m.*; (*praise, &c.*) concert, *m.*; ~ **-girl**, choriste, *f.*
chough, (*ornith.*) crave, *m.*
chrism, (*eccles.*) chrême, *m.*
christen, *v.a.* baptiser; ~**ing**, baptême, *m.*
Christendom, chrétienté, *f.*
Christian, *adj.* (*when an adj. use small letter*) *and s.m.f.* chrétien, -ne; *be a* ~, être chrétien; ~ **name**, nom de baptême, *m.*; ~**ize**, christianiser.
Christianity, christianisme, *m.*; ⚠ chrétienté = '*Christendom*'.

Christmas, Noël, *m.*; ~ **-box,** étrennes, *f.pl.;* ~ **card,** carte de Noël, *f.;* ~ **carol,** noël, *m.;* ~ **eve,** veillée de Noël, *f.*
chromatic, *adj.* (*mus.*) chromatique; ~ **scale,** gamme chromatique, *f.*
chromium, chrome, *m.*; ~ **silver,** argent chromé, *f.*
chromolithograph, chromo, *m. and f.*
chronic, chronique.
chronicle, chronique, *f.*; *v.a.* raconter; (*put down*) enregistrer; ~**r,** chroniqueur, *m.*
chronolog|y, chronologie, *f.*; ~**ical,** chronologique.
chronometer, chronomètre, *m.*
chrysalis, chrysalide, *f.*
chrysanthemum, chrysanthème, *m.*
chrysolite, (*min.*) chrysolithe, *f.*
chub, (*ichth.*) chevesne, *m.*
chubby, joufflu.
chuck, *s.* (*hen*) gloussement, *m.*; *v.n.* glousser; (*throw*) lancer; ~ *out,* faire* sortir; ~ *up,* (*pop.*) renoncer à.
chuckle, *s.* ricanement, *m.*; *v.n.* ricaner.
chum, *s.* (*fam.*) copain, *m.*
chump, (*wood*) gros morceau, *m.*; (*pers. U.S.A.*) nigaud, *m.*
chunk, (*wood, cheese*) gros morceau, *m.*; (*bread*) quignon, *m.*
church, (*building, society, all Xtians*) église, *f.*; (*Prot. building in France*) temple, *m.*; (*orders*) ordres, *m.pl.*; ~ *service* (*Cath.*) office, *m.*; (*Prot.*) prêche, *m.*; ~ *of England,* Église anglicane, *f.*
churchman, (*Engl.*) anglican, *m.*; (*ecclesiastic*) ecclésiastique, *m.*
churchwarden, marguillier, *m.*
churchyard, cimetière, *m.*
churl, (*serf and bumpkin*) manant, *m.*; ~**ish,** †hargneu|x, ~se; ~**ishly,** d'une manière †hargneuse.
churn, baratte, *f.*; *v.a.* baratter.
ciborium, (*eccles.*) ciboire, *m.*
cicada, cigale, *f.*
cicerone, cicerone, *m.*
cider, cidre, *m.*; ~ **-mill, -press,** pressoir à pommes, *m.*
cigar, cigare, *m.*; ~**ette,** cigarette, *f.*; ~**ette-case,** porte-cigarettes, *m.*; ~**ette-holder,** porte-cigarette, *m. invar.*; ~**ette-end,** *stump,* mégot, *m.*
cinch, (*U.S.A.*) *that's a cinch,* l'affaire est dans le sac.
cincture, ceinture, *f.*
cinders, cendres, *f.pl.*; (*coal cinders*) escarbilles, *f.pl.*
cinema, cinéma, *m.*; ~**tograph,** cinématographe, *m.*
cineraria, (*bot.*) cinéraire, *f.*
cinerary, *adj.* cinéraire.
cinnabar, cinabre, *m.*
cinnamon, cannelle, *f.*
cinq(ue)foil, (*bot. and arch.*) quintefeuille, *f.*
cipher, (*arith. and fig.*) zéro, *m.*; (*secret writing, monogram*) chiffre, *m.*; *in* ~, en chiffre; ~ **-code,** code chiffré, *m.*; *v.a.n.* compter; (*in code*) chiffrer.
circl|e, *s.* (*lit., fig., party, set, vicious* ~) cercle, *m.*; *v.a.* (*encompass*) entourer (de); *v.n.* (*be passed round*) être passé à la ronde; ~**et,** (*for head*) bandeau, *m.*
circuit, circuit, *m.*; (*detour*) détour, *m.*; (*judges, &c.*) tournée, *f.*; **short** ~ (*electr.*) court-circuit, *m.*; ~ **-breaker,** (*electr.*) disjoncteur, *m.*
circuitous, qui fait un détour; (*fig.*) détourné.
circular, *adj. and s.m.f.* circulaire.
circulate, *v.a.* faire* circuler; *v.n.* circuler; ~ *freely,* (*money*) rouler.
circulating, *adj.* circulant; (*decimal*) périodique; ~ **library,** bibliothèque circulante, *f.*
circulation, (*liquid, news, newspaper, money*) circulation, *f.*
circumambient, ambiant.
circumcis|e, circoncire*; ~**ion,** circoncision, *f.*
circumference, circonférence, *f.*
circumflex, *s.* accent circonflexe, *m.*; *adj.* circonflexe.
circumlocution, circonlocution, *f.*
circumnavigat|e, *v.a.* naviguer autour de; ~**ion,** circumnavigation, *f.*
circumscri|be, (*limit and geom.*) circonscrire*; ~**ption,** circonscription, *f.*
circumspect, circonspect; ~**ion,** circonspection, *f.*
circumstance, circonstance, *f.*; ~**s,** (*means*) moyens, *m.pl.*; *in easy* ~*s,* à son aise; *in reduced* ~*s,* dans la gêne; ~*s permitting,* sauf imprévu; ~*s beyond control, force of* ~*s,* force majeure, *f.*
circumstanced, *as I was* ~, dans la situation où je me trouvais.
circumstantial, (*incidental*) circonstanciel, -le; (*detailed*) détaillé.
circumvallation, circonvallation, *f.*
circumvent, circonvenir*.
circus, cirque, *m.*
cisalpine, cisalpin.
cistern, (*underground*) citerne, *f.*; (*above ground*) réservoir, *m.*
cistus, (*bot.*) ciste, *m.*
citadel, citadelle, *f.*
cite, *v.a.* (*quote and law*) citer.
cithara, cittern, cithare, *f.*
citizen, citoyen, -ne, *m.f.*; (*inhabitant*) habitant, *m.*; (*burgess*) bourgeois, -e, *m.f.*; ~**ship,** droit de cité, *m.*
citron, (*fruit-tree*) cédrat, *m.*; ⚠ *not* citron *which* = '*lemon*'.
city, ville, *f.*; *the City,* (*London, Paris*) Cité, *f.*; (*old part of certain towns*) cité, *f.*
civet-cat, civette, *f.*
civic, civique.
civil, (*not mil. or eccles.*) civil; ~ **engineer,** ingénieur des arts et manufactures; ~ **servant,** fonctionnaire, *m.*; (*polite*) poli; ~**ly,** poliment.
civilian, civil, *m.*; (*Civil Servant*) fonctionnaire, *m.*
civility, politesse, *f.*
civiliz|e, civiliser; ~**ation,** civilisation, *f.*

clack, *v.a.* (*sound*) claquer.
clad, *pp.* vêtu (de).
claim, *s.* (*as due*) demande, *f.*; (*right*) droit, *m.*; (*title to a thing*) titre, *m.*; (*mine, &c.*) concession, *f.*; *lay ~ to*, revendiquer.
claim, *v.a.* revendiquer; (*what is due, demand*) réclamer; (*victory, &c.*) s'attribuer; (*pretend to a thing*) prétendre à; (*U.S.A.*) soutenir*; *~ to*, prétendre (+*inf.*).
claimant, prétendant, -e, *m.f.*
clairvoyan|ce, seconde vue, *f.*; **~t(e),** *s.* voyant, -e, *m.f.*
clamber, grimper; *~ over*, escalader.
clammy, moite; (*bread*) pâteu|x, ~se.
clamorous, bruyant; (*pers.*) criard; **~ly,** bruyamment.
clamour, clameur, *f.*; (*confused noise*) bruit confus, *m.*
clamour, *v.n.* pousser des clameurs; *~ for*, réclamer à grands cris.
clamp, *s.* (*iron*) crampon, *m.*; (*wood*) serre-joint, *m.*, *invar.*; *v.a.* (*wood*) emboîter.
clan, clan, *m.*
clandestine, clandestin.
clang, clank, *s.* bruit métallique, *m.*; *v.n.* retentir.
clang|our, bruit métallique, *m.*; **~orous,** résonnant.
clansman, membre d'un clan, *m.*
clap, *s.* (*hands*) battement, *m.*; (*thunder*) coup de tonnerre, *m.*; *v.a.* (*applaud*) applaudir; (*thrust*) mettre*; *v.n.* applaudir.
clapper, (*bells*) battant, *m.*
clap-trap, attrape-nigaud, *m.*, *pl.* attrape-nigauds.
claret, vin de Bordeaux, *m.*, *or* bordeaux, *m.*; ⚠ clairet *is a pale, light wine.*
clarify, clarifier; (*fig.*) éclaircir.
clari(o)net, clarinette, *f.*
clarion, clairon, *m.*
clarity, clarté, *f.*
clash, *s.* (*collision and fig.*) choc, *m.*
clash, *v.a.* choquer; *v.n.* (*lit. and fig.*) s'entre-choquer; (*colours, &c.*) jurer; (*be opposed*) ne pas s'accorder.
clasp, (*hook*) agrafe, *f.*; (*book, purse, &c.*) fermoir, *m.*; (*embrace*) étreinte, *f.*; **~ -knife,** couteau à cran d'arrêt, *m.*
clasp, *v.a.* (*fasten*) agrafer; (*embrace*) étreindre*; (*hands*) joindre*.
class, *s.* (*rank, school, nat. hist., mil., exams, railway, &c.*) classe, *f.*; *middle ~es*, classe moyenne, *f.*; *upper ~es*, classe supérieure, *f.*; *working ~es*, classe ouvrière, *f.*; **~ -room,** classe, *f.*; *v.a.* classer.
class|ic, ~ical, classique.
classic|ism, classicisme, *m.*; **~ist,** classiciste, *m.*
classif|y, (*into classifications*) classifier; (*plants, papers, &c.*) classer; **~ication,** classification, *f.*
clatter, clattering, bruit, *m.*; (*crash*) fracas, *m.*; (*of voices*) brouhaha, *m.*
clatter, *v.a.* (*plates, &c.*) faire* entre-choquer; *v.n.* faire* du bruit.
clause, (*document*) clause, *f.*; (*gram.*) membre de phrase, *m.*
claustral, claustral.
clavicle, (*anat.*) clavicule, *f.*
claw, *f.* (*tigers, cats, &c.*) griffe, *f.*; (*birds of prey*) serre, *f.*; (*small birds*) ongle, *m.*; (*crabs, &c.*) pince, *f.*
claw, *v.a.* griffer; (*tear*) déchirer.
clay, glaise, *f.*; **~ -pit,** glaisière, *f.*; **~ pipe,** pipe de terre, *f.*
claymore, claymore, *f.*
clean, *adj.* (*unsoiled, loving cleanliness*) propre; (*water*) propre; (*linen*) blan|c, ~che; (*boots*) ciré; (*pure and fig.*) pur; (*adroit not bungling*) adroit; (*without spot, bill of health*) net, -te; *with ~ hands*, (*fig.*) les mains nettes; *~ -shaven*, glabre; **~-ness,** propreté, *f.*; **~ly,** proprement; (*fig.*) nettement.
clean, *v.a.* (*lit. and dry-clean*) nettoyer; (*boots*) cirer; *~ one's face*, se débarbouiller; *~ the slate*, (*fig.*) passer l'éponge; *~ out*, (*lit. and fig.*) nettoyer à fond; *~ed out*, (*slang, of money*) ratiboisé.
clean, *adv.* (*absolutely*) tout à fait.
cleaner, (*dry- ~*) dégraisseur, *m.*
cleaning, *s.* nettoyage, *m.*
clean|ly, *adj.* propre; *adv.* proprement; (*dexterously*) adroitement; **~liness,** propreté, *f.*
cleans|e, nettoyer; (*fig.*) purifier; **~ing,** nettoyage, *m.*
clear, *adj.* (*sound, water, evident, weather, bright, transparent*) clair; (*sure*) sûr; *~ of*, libre de; *5 days ~ notice*, préavis de 5 jours francs, *m.*; **~ profit,** bénéfice net, *m.*; *the coast is ~*, le champ est libre; *~ -headed*, à tête solide; **~ness,** *see* CLEARNESS; **~ly,** évidemment.
clear, *v.a.* (*rubbish, also ~ up*) déblayer; (*conscience*) décharger; (*cheque*) compenser; (*detach*) dégager (de); (*leap over*) franchir; (*letter-box*) lever; (*as profit*) gagner net; *~ away, out*, enlever; *~ off*, (*get rid of*) se débarrasser de; *~ oneself*, se disculper; (*from debt*) se libérer.
clear, *v.n.* (*situation, weather, also ~ up*) s'éclaircir; (*fog, also ~ off*) se dissiper; *~ off, out of the way*, s'en aller* (être); (*fam.*) ficher le camp.
clearance, (*removal*) enlèvement, *m.*; **~ sale,** solde, *m.*
clearing, (*debt*) acquittement, *m.*; (*forest*) défrichement, *m.*; (*bkkpg. transfer*) virement, *m.*
clearness, (*air and glass*) transparence, *f.*; (*mind, sight, sound*) clarté, *f.*; (*distinctness*) netteté, *f.*
cleave, (*lit., fig., air, &c., asunder, a way through*) fendre; *v.n.* se fendre; (*stick, cling*) se coller (à).
cleft, fente, *f.*
clematis, (*bot.*) clématite, *f.*; *wild ~*, herbe aux gueux, *f.*

clemen|t, (*temper, weather*) dou|x, ~ce; (*merciful*) clément; **~cy,** clémence, *f.*
clench, clinch, *v.a.* (*nail*) river; (*fist, teeth*) serrer; (*bargain*) conclure*.
clerestory, (*arch.*) claire-voie, *f.*
clergy, clergé, *m.*; **~man,** (*Prot.*) ministre, *m.*
clerical, (*of the clergy*) clérical; (*comm.*) de commis; (*administration, bank*) d'employé; (*error*) de copiste.
clerk, (*eccl., law*) clerc; (*bank, administration*) employé, *m.*; (*business firm*) commis, *m.*; *managing ~,* (*merchant's office, bank*) chef de bureau, *m.*; (*law*) premier clerc, *m.*
clever, (*skilful*) adroit; (*talented*) qui a du talent; (*intelligent*) intelligent; (*ingenious pers., thing*) ingénieu|x, ~se; **~ness,** adresse, *f.*; (*intelligence*) intelligence, *f.*; **~ly,** adroitement, habilement.
click, *v.* faire tic-tac.
client, (*professional, customer*) client, -e, *m.f.*; **~s,** clientèle, *f.*
cliff, falaise, *f.*
climate, climat, *m.*
climax, (*culmination*) comble, *m.*; (*ascending scale*) gradation, *f.*
climb, *s.* montée, *f.*
climb, *v.a.* grimper sur; (*stairs, &c.*) monter (avoir); *~ down,* descendre (avoir); *~ up, over,* escalader; *v.n.* (*pers. and plants*) grimper; (*fig.*) monter (être); *~ down,* descendre (être); (*fig.*) reculer.
climbing, *adj.* (*ascending*) montant; **~ plant,** plante grimpante, *f.*
clime, pays, *m.*
cling, *v.n.* *~ to,* se cramponner à; (*fig.*) rester (être) fidèle à; **~ing,** *adj.* (*clothes*) collant.
clingstone-peach, pavie, *f.*
clinic, *s.* clinique, *f.*; **~al,** clinique.
clink, *s.* tintement, *m.*; *v.a.* faire* tinter; *v.n.* tinter.
clinkers, (*slag*) mâchefer, *m.*
clip, *s.* pince, *f.*
clip, *v.a.* (*wool, hair, turf, &c.*) tondre; (*with scissors*) couper; (*pare*) rogner; (*tickets*) contrôler; (*words*) estropier.
clipping, rognure, *f.*
clipper, (*naut.*) fin voilier, *m.*; **~s,** (*shears*) tondeuse, *f.*; (*small*) ciseaux, *m.pl.*
cloak, *s.* (*lit. and fig.*) manteau, *m.*; **~ -room,** (*rail.*) consigne, *f.*; (*public bldgs.*) vestiaire, *m.*; *v.a.* (*conceal*) masquer.
clock, (*church, &c.*) horloge, *f.*; (*ornamental*) pendule, *f.*; **~ -maker,** horloger, *m.*; *10 o'clock,* dix heures; *12 o'clock,* (*day*) midi, *m.*, (*night*) minuit, *m.*; *what o'clock is it?* quelle heure est-il?
clockwork, mécanique, *f.*
clod, motte de terre, *f.*; (*pers.*) lourdaud, *m.*
clog, *s.* (*lit. and fig.*) entrave, *f.*; (*wooden shoe*) sabot, *m.*; *v.a.* (*lit. and fig.*) entraver; (*be, get stopped up*) s'obstruer.
cloister, cloître, *m.*; *v.a.* cloîtrer.
close, *adj.* **1** (*shut*) fermé; **2** (*narrow and friendship*) étroit; **3** (*air*) renfermé; **4** (*weather*) lourd; **5** (*place, relations*) proche; **6** (*reasoning, -fisted, compact*) serré; **7** (*contests*) presque égal; **8** (*discreet*) discr|et, ~ète; **9** (*intimate*) intime; **10** (*study*) appliqué; **11** (*attentive*) attenti|f, ~ve.
close, *s.* enclos, *m.*; (*cathedral*) enceinte, *f.*; (*end*) fin, *f.*
close, *v.a.* (*shut*) fermer; (*mil. ranks*) serrer; (*account, bargain*) arrêter; (*end*) terminer; (*a sitting*) lever; *~ up,* boucher.
close, *v.n.* (*offices, &c.*) fermer; (*wounds*) se fermer; (*end*) se terminer; *~ in,* (*night, &c.*) approcher.
close, *adv.* tout près; (*shut*) hermétiquement; *~ by,* tout près; *~ upon,* tout près de; *run ~,* (*in competition*) talonner.
closely, de près; (*embraces, &c.*) étroitement; (*intimately*) intimement; (*attentively*) attentivement; *~ written,* d'une écriture serrée.
closeness, (*room*) manque d'air, *m.*; (*weather*) lourdeur, *f.*; (*stinginess*) avarice, *f.*; (*relationship*) proximité, *f.*
closet, (*room*) cabinet, *m.*; (*clothes*) armoire, *f.*
closing, *s.* (*act*) fermeture, *f.*; (*end*) fin, *f.*; *it's early closing to-day,* on ferme de bonne heure aujourd'hui; *adj.* derni|er, ~ère.
closure, (*Parl. or sitting*) clôture, *f.*
clot, *s.* grumeau, *m.*; (*blood*) caillot, *m.*; *v.n.* se cailler; **~ted,** en grumeaux.
cloth, drap, *m.*; (*linen table~*) nappe, *f.*; (*stuff table~*) tapis, *m.*; (*duster*) torchon, *m.*; *clear ~,* desservir*; **~ -bound,** *see* BIND.
clothe, *v.a.* vêtir* (de); (*adorn*) revêtir* (de); (*cover*) couvrir* (de).
clothes, habits, *m.pl.*; **~ -brush,** brosse à habits, *f.*; **~ -line,** corde à linge, *f.*; *long ~,* maillot, *m.*; *old ~,* défroque, *f.*; *ready-made ~, see* READY; *in plain ~,* en civil.
clothier, (*maker of cloth*) fabricant de drap, *m.*; (*dealer*), drapier *m.*; *ready-made ~,* marchand de confections, *m.*
clothing, *s.* vêtements, *m.pl.*
cloud, (*lit., fig., dust, in liquids*) nuage, *m.*; (*poet.*) nue, *f.*; (*thick cloud, fig. insects, &c.*) nuée, *f.*; **~ -burst,** déluge, *m.*
cloud, *v.a.* couvrir* de nuages; (*fig.*) assombrir; (*reason*) obscurcir; *v.n. ~ over,* (*sky*) se rembrunir; (*face*) s'assombrir.
cloudy, (*weather, sky*) couvert; (*liquids*) trouble; *it is ~,* il fait des nuages.
clout, *s.* morceau d'étoffe, *m.*; (*dish-cloth*) lavette, *f.*; (*blow*) gifle, *f.*; *v.a.* gifler.
clove, clou de girofle, *m.*; (*garlic*) gousse, *f.*
cloven, fourchu; **~ hoof,** pied fourchu, *m.*
clover, trèfle, *m.*; *in ~,* à gogo.
clown, (*lout*) rustre, *m.*; (*circus, &c.*) clown, *m.*; ⚠ clown *never = 'lout' in French*; **~ ish,** grossi|er, ~ère.
cloy, *v.a.* rassasier.

club, (*stick*) massue, *f.*; (*sports*) société, *f.*; (*social by ballot*) cercle, *m.*; (*lit., polit.*) club, *m.*; (*cards*) trèfle, *m.*; (*golf*) club, *m.*; ~ **-house,** cercle, *m.*
club-footed, *adj. and s.m.* pied-bot.
cluck, *s.* gloussement, *m.*; *v.n.* glousser.
clue, clew, fil, *m.*
clump, (*trees*) bouquet, *m.*
clums|y, (*pers. awkward*) gauche; (*ill-contrived*) incommode; (*tactless*) sans tact; **~iness,** gaucherie, *f.*, manque de tact, *m.*; **~ily,** gauchement.
cluster, *s.* (*fruits*) grappe, *f.*; (*trees, cherries*) bouquet, *m.*; (*pers.*) groupe, *m.*; (*bees*) essaim, *m.*; (*bananas*) régime, *m.*; (*collect*) se grouper.
clutch, *s.* geste pour empoigner, *m.*; (*motor*) embrayage, *m.*; *fall into the ~es of,* tomber (être) dans les griffes de; *let in ~,* (*motor*) embrayer.
clutch, *v.a.* empoigner; (*grasp tightly*) serrer.
clutter, *s.* (*confusion*) amas confus, *m.*
coach, voiture, *f.*; (*private, old-fashioned, and state*) carrosse, *m.*; (*rail*) wagon, *m.*; (*exams*) répétiteur, *m.*; (*sports*) entraîneur, *m.*; *slow~,* lambin, -e, *m.f.*; ~ **-house,** remise, *f.*; ~ **-window,** glace, *f.*; *v.a.* (*pupil*) bourrer; (*sports*) entraîner.
coachman, cocher, *m.*
coadjutor, coadjuteur, *m.*
coagulat|e, *v.n.* se coaguler; **~ion,** coagulation, *f.*
coal(s), charbon (de terre), *m.*; **~-cellar,** cave à charbon, *f.*; **~-field,** terrain houiller, *m.*; **~-mine, ~-pit,** mine de houille, *f.*; **~-scuttle,** seau à charbon, *m.*; **~-ship,** (*collier*) charbonnier, *m.*; **~-tar,** coaltar, *m.*; **~-truck,** wagon à charbons, *m.*; *small ~,* grésillon, *m.*
coal, *v.n.* faire* son charbon; **~ing station,** dépôt de charbon, *m.*
coalesce, s'unir; (*fig.*) se fondre.
coalition, coalition, *f.*
coal-tit *also* **coalmouse,** (*ornith.*) charbonnière, *f.*
coarse, (*lit., fig., pers., things, language, cloth, &c.*) grossi|er, ~ère; (*vulgar*) vulgaire; **~ness,** grossièreté, *f.*; **~ly,** grossièrement.
coast, *s.* côte, *f.*; ~ **-guard,** garde-côte, *m., pl.* gardes-côte; *also* = '*coast defence ship*'; *v.n.* (*naut.*) caboter.
coaster, *coasting vessel,* (*naut.*) caboteur, *m.*
coat, *s.* (*of lounge suit*) veston, *m.*; (*dress suit*) habit, *m.*; (*morning coat*) jaquette, *f.*; (*ans.*) poil, *m.*; (*paint*) couche, *f.*; **great-~,** paletot, *m.*; **top-~,** pardessus, *m.*; *tailor-made ~ and skirt,* costume tailleur, *m.*; *~ of mail,* cotte de mailles, *f.*; **~-stand,** portemanteau, *m.*; **~-tails,** basques, *f.pl.*
coat with, *v.a.* revêtir* de.
coating, *s.* (*paint*) couche, *f.*
coax, *v.a.* cajoler; **~ing,** *s.* câlinerie, *f.*
cob, (*horse*) cob, *m.*; (*nut*) grosse noisette, *f.*
cobalt, cobalt, *m.*
cobble, *v.a.* saveter; **~r,** savetier, *m.*
cobra, (*zool.*) cobra, *m.*
cobweb, toile d'araignée, *f.*
cocaine, cocaïne, *f.*
cochineal, cochenille, *f.*
cock, *s.* (*fowl*) coq, *m.*; (*male of bird*) mâle, *m.*; (*tap*) robinet, *m.*; (*fire-arms*) chien, *m.*; (*hay*) meulon, *m.*; *~-a-doodle-do,* cocorico, *m.*; *~ and bull story,* coq à l'âne, *m. invar.*; *turkey-~, see* TURKEY; **~-crow,** chant du coq, *m.*; **~-fight,** combat de coqs, *m.*; **~-loft,** petit grenier, *m.*; **~sure,** sûr et certain.
cock, *v.a.* (*erect*) dresser; (*fire-arms*) lever le chien de; (*hay*) mettre* en meule; (*hat*) mettre* sur le coin de l'oreille; *~ the eye,* cligner de l'œil.
cockade, cocarde, *f.*
cockatoo, cacatois, *m.*
cockatrice, basilic, *m.*
cockchafer, hanneton, *m.*
cockerel, cochet, *m.*
cock-eyed, (*slang*) louche.
cockle, (*bot.*) nielle, *f.*; (*shell*) clovisse, *f.*
cockle, *v.n.* se recoquiller.
cockpit, (*lit. and fig.*) arène, *f.*; (*aeron.*) poste, *m.*; (*naut.*) poste des malades, *m.*
cockroach, blatte, *f.*
cockscomb, (*bot.*) crête-de-coq, *f.*
coxcomb, (*pers.*) fat, *m.*
cockspur, ergot, *m.*
cocktail, (*drink*) cocktail, *m.*
coco(a), coco, *m.*; **~-nut,** noix de coco, *f.*; **~-nut-tree,** cocotier, *m.*
cocoa, cacao, *m.*
cocoon, cocon, *m.*
cod, (*ichth.*) morue, *f.*; ~ **-liver oil,** huile de foie de morue, *f.*
coddle, *v.a.* dorloter.
code, code, *m.*; (*language*) convenu, *m.*; **~-word,** mot convenu, *m.*; *v.a.* mettre* en chiffres.
codify, codifier.
coefficient, (*math.*) coefficient, *m.*
coequal, *adj. and s.m.f.* égal, -e; (*theol.*) coégal.
coerc|e, *v.a.* contraindre*; **~ion,** coercition, *f.*; **~ive,** coerciti|f, ~ve.
coeval, *adj. and s.m.f.* contemporain, -e.
coexist, coexister; **~ence,** coexistence, *f.*
coffee, café, *m.*; ~ **-bean,** *see* BEAN; **~-grounds,** marc de café, *m.*; **~-house,** café, *m.*; **~-mill,** moulin à café, *m.*; **~-pot,** cafetière, *f.*; **~-roaster,** brûloir, *m.*; **~-coloured,** café au lait, *m. invar.*
coffer, coffre, *m.*; (*bank, &c.*) caisse, *f.*; **~s,** (*State*) coffres, *m.pl.*
coffin, cercueil, *m.*
cog, *s.* dent, *f.*; **~-wheel,** roue dentée, *f.*; *v.a.* denter; (*dice*) piper.
cogen|cy, force, *f.*; **~t,** puissant.
cogitat|e, *v.a.n.* méditer; **~ion,** méditation, *f.*

cognate, *adj.* de même nature; (*analogous*) analogue.
cognizance, connaissance, *f.*; *beyond my, your, &c.* ~, ce n'est pas mon, votre, &c., affaire.
cognizant of, instruit de.
cognomen, surnom, *m.*
cohabit, cohabiter.
co|heir, ~heiress, cohérit|ier, ~ière, *m.f.*
cohere, *v.n.* (*stick*) adhérer (à); (*be consistent*) être cohérent.
coheren|t, (*lit. and fig.*) cohérent; **~ce,** cohérence, *f.*; **~tly,** avec cohérence.
cohes|ion, cohésion, *f.*; **~ive,** cohési|f, ~ve.
cohort, cohorte, *f.*
coif, calotte, *f.*
coil, (*rope, &c.*) rouleau, *m.*; (*naut.*) glène, *f.*; (*serpent*) repli, *m.*; (*electr.*) bobine, *f.*
coil, *v.a.* (*naut. rope*) lover; *v.n.* se replier.
coin, pièce (de monnaie), *f.*
coin, *v.a.* (*money*) battre; (*invent*) inventer.
coinage, (*coining*) frappe, *f.*; (*coins*) monnaie, *f.*; (*system*) système monétaire, *m.*
coincid|e, coïncider; (*agree with*) s'accorder avec; **~ence,** coïncidence, *f.*
coiner, monnayeur, *m.*; (*counterfeit*) faux monnayeur, *m.*; (*fig., inventor*) inventeur, *m.*
coke, coke, *m.*
colander, cullender, passoire, *f.*
colchicum, (*bot.*) safran des prés, *m.*
cold, *s.* (*temperature*) froid, *m.*; (*med.*) rhume, *m.*; ~ *in the head*, rhume de cerveau, *m.*; *catch a* ~, s'enrhumer.
cold, *adj.* (*lit. and fig.*) froid; *in* ~ *blood*, de sang-froid; *be* ~, (*pers.*) avoir froid; (*weather*) faire* froid; *my feet are* ~, j'ai froid aux pieds; ~ **storage,** entrepôt frigorifique, *m.*; **~ness,** froid, *m.*; (*fig.*) froideur, *f.*; **~ly,** (*lit. and fig.*) froidement.
coldblooded, insensible.
colewort, (*bot.*) chou vert, *m.*
colic, colique, *f.*
collaborat|e, collaborer; **~ion,** collaboration, *f.*; **~or,** collaborateur, *m.*
collapse, *s.* (*lit. and fig.*) effondrement, *m.*; (*pers.*) affaissement, *m.*; *v.n.* s'effondrer; (*pers.*) s'affaisser.
collapsible, pliant.
collar, *s.* (*shirt*) col, *m.*; (*man's detachable*) faux-col, *m.*; (*coat, &c.*) collet, *m.*; (*woman's lace, &c.*) collerette, *f.*; (*dog's, &c.*) collier, *m.*; *soft* ~, col souple, *m.*; *turn-down* ~, col rabattu, *m.*; **~-bone,** clavicule, *f.*
collar, *v.a.* (*seize by the collar*) saisir au collet; (*seize and football*) saisir.
colla|te, *v.a.* collationner; **~tion,** (*meal and comparing*) collation, *f.*
collateral, *s.m.* (*relations*) collatéral; *adj.* (*side*) collatéral.
colleague, collègue, *m.f.*; (*profession*) confrère, *m.*
collect, *s.* (*prayer*) collecte, *f.*
collect, *v.a.* rassembler; (*antiques, &c.*) collectionner; (*information*) recueillir*; (*taxes*) percevoir; (*letters*) faire* la levée de; (*debts*) recouvrer; (*thoughts*) rassembler; (*tickets*) contrôler.
collect, *v.n.* (*congregate*) s'assembler; (*pile up*) s'amasser.
collected, *adj.* (*calm*) calme.
collection, (*group of things of the same kind*) collection, *f.*; (*in church, &c.*) collecte, *f.*; (*mass, accumulation*) amas, *m.*; (*debts*) recouvrement, *m.*; (*letters*) levée, *f.*
collective, (*gen. and gram.*) collecti|f, ~ve; **~ly,** collectivement.
collector, (*pictures, &c.*) collectionneur, *m.*; (*taxes*) percepteur, *m.*
colleg|e, collège, *m.*; **~iate,** de collège; (*eccles.*) collégial.
collide, *v.n.* se †heurter (contre).
collier, †houilleur, *m.*; (*ship*) charbonnier, *m.*; **~y,** †houillère, *f.*
collision, collision, *f.*; (*rail*) tamponnement, *m.*; (*naut.*) abordage, *m.*
collocate, *v.a.* placer.
colloquy, entretien, *m.*
colloquial, famili|er, ~ère; **~ly,** en style familier.
collude, *v.n.* s'entendre secrètement.
collus|ion, collusion, *f.*; **~ive,** collusoire.
colon, (*gram.*) deux points, *m.pl.*
colonel, colonel, *m.*
colon|ial, *adj.* colonial; **~ist, ~ial,** colon, *m.*; **~ization,** colonisation, *f.*; **~ize,** *v.a.* coloniser; **~y,** (*lit. and fig.*) colonie, *f.*
colonnade, colonnade, *f.*
colo(u)ration, coloration, *f.*
coloss|al, colossal; **~us,** colosse, *m.*
colour, *s.* (*lit., fig., polit., opinion, complexion, of negroes, &c.*) couleur, *f.*; **~s,** (*mil.*) drapeau, *m.*; (*paints*) couleurs, *f.pl.*; *under* ~ *of*, sous prétexte de; *with* ~*s flying*, enseignes déployées; *strike one's colours*, amener son pavillon, (*fig.*) baisser pavillon; **~-blind,** daltonien, -ne; **~-sergeant,** porte-drapeau, *m. invar.*; *local* ~, couleur locale, *f.*
colour, *v.a.* colorer; (*paint, engrave*) colorier.
colour, *v.n.* (*things*) se colorer; (*blush, colour up*) rougir.
colouring, *s.* (*of a painting, complexion, style*) coloris, *m.*
colourist, coloriste, *m.*
colourless, (*without colour and of style*) incolore; (*dull-hued*) terne.
colt, poulain, *m.*; (*sport*) novice, *m.*; **~sfoot,** (*bot.*) pas d'âne, *m.*
columbine, (*bot.*) ancolie, *f.*
column, (*lit., fig., newspaper, bkkpg., figures*) colonne, *f.*; **~ar,** en colonne. *See also* SPINAL.
colza, (*bot.*) colza, *m.*
coma, coma, *m.*; **~tose,** comateu|x, ~se.
comb, peigne, *m.*; (*cock*) crête, *f.*; (*honey*) rayon, *m.*
comb, *v.a.* peigner; ~ *out*, démêler.
combat, combat, *m.*; **~ant,** *adj. and s.m.f.* combattant, -e; *v.a.n.* combattre.

combative, combati|f, ~ve.
combination, combinaison, *f.* ⚠ combination *not French*; **~s,** (*garment*) combinaison, *f.*
combine, *s.* (*comm.*) cartel, *m.*; *v.a.* (*gen. and chem.*) combiner; *v.n.* se liguer.
combustib|le, *adj. and s.m.* combustible; **~ility,** combustibilité, *f.*
combustion, combustion, *f.*; *spontaneous ~*, combustion spontanée, *f.*
come, venir* (être); (+*adj.*) se trouver être; *come! come along!* allons!; *~ and go*, aller* et venir* (*both* être); *lightly ~, lightly go*, ce qui vient par la flûte s'en va par le tambour; *~ to nothing*, n'aboutir à rien; *~ to pass*, arriver (être); *~ to the same thing*, revenir* (être) au même; *~ about*, arriver (être); *~ across*, rencontrer; *~ along*, *see* ALONG; *~ at*, mettre* la main sur; *~ away*, partir* (*être*); *~ back*, revenir* (être); *~ by*, obtenir*; (*pass*) passer; *~ down*, descendre (être); (*be transmitted*) être transmis; *~ for*, venir* (être) chercher; *~ forward*, s'avancer; *~ in*, entrer (être); (*in race*) arriver (être); (*tide*) monter (être); *~ in handy*, venir* (être) à propos; *~ into*, (*possession*) entrer (être) en possession de; *~ near*, s'approcher (de); *~ of*, (*arise from*) voilà ce que c'est que + *inf.*; *~ off*, (*take place*) avoir lieu; (*be detached*) se détacher; *~ on*, s'avancer; (*happen suddenly*) survenir* (être); *~ out*, sortir* (être); (*strikers*) se mettre* en grève; (*papers, books, &c.*) paraître*; (*be found out*) se découvrir*; *~ over*, (*cross*) traverser; *~ to*, (*recover*) se remettre*; (*to think, to believe, to a conclusion*) en venir* (être) à; *~ up*, monter (être); (*approach*) s'approcher (de); (*discussion, &c.*) être soulevé; *~ up to*, (*answer to*) répondre à; *~ upon*, (*meet*) rencontrer; *~ up with*, atteindre*.
comedian, comédien, -ne, *m.f.*
comedy, comédie, *f.*
comel|y, avenant; (*becoming*) bienséant; **~iness,** grâce, *f.*
comer, venant, *m.*; **first ~**, premi|er, ~ère venu, -e, *m.f.*; **new- ~**, nouv|eau, ~elle venu, -e, *m.f.*; *~ and goer*, *see* GOER.
comestible(s), comestible, *m.*
comet, comète, *f.*
comfit, dragée, *f.*
comfort, *s.* (*consolation*) consolation, *f.*; (*being comfortable*) bien-être, *m.*; (*satisfaction*) satisfaction, *f.*; (*means*) aisance, *f.*
comfort, *v.a.* (*console*) consoler; (*cheer up*) réconforter.
comfortabl|e, (*ministering to comfort of things*) confortable; (*at ease, unembarrassed, well off*) à l'aise; (*consoling*) rassurant; (*convenient*) commode; **~y,** confortablement.
comforter, consolat|eur, ~rice, *m.f.*; (*muffler*) cache-nez, *m.*
comfortless, (*pers.*) désolé; (*things*) incommode.
comfrey, (*bot.*) consoude, *f.*
comic, comique; **~ally,** comiquement.
coming, *s.* venue, *f.*; (*of Christ*) avènement, *m.*; *~ and going*, va-et-vient, *m. invar.*; *~s and goings*, allées et venues, *f.pl.*; *~ in*, entrée, *f.*
coming, *adj.* qui vient; (*future*) futur; *~ in*, (*of income, &c.*) venant.
comity, (*of nations*) courtoisie, *f.*
comma, virgule, *f.*; *inverted ~s*, guillemets, *m.pl.*
command, *s.* (*gen., mil., &c.*) commandement, *m.*; (*orders*) ordres, *m.pl.*; (*troops, soldiers under an officer*) troupe, *f.*; *at ~*, à sa disposition; *be second in ~*, en second.
command, *v.a.* commander, (à *of pers.*, de + *inf.*); (*army, navy, &c.*) commander; (*passions, &c.*) commander à; (*money, &c.*) avoir à sa disposition; (*respect, &c.*) inspirer (à); (*overlook*) dominer; *v.n.* (*give orders, be in command*) commander.
commandant, commandant, *m.*
commandeer, réquisitionner.
commander, commandant, *m.*; (*of an order*) commandeur, *m.*; **~-in-chief,** commandant-en-chef, *m.*
commanding, *adj.* (*imposing*) imposant; (*of view*) dominant.
commandment, commandement, *m.*; *ten ~s*, décalogue, *m.*
commemorat|e, commémorer; **~ion,** commémoration, *f.*; **~ive,** commémorati|f, ~ve.
commence, *v.a.n.* commencer (à *or* de + *inf.*); **~ment,** commencement, *m.*
commend, (*praise*) louer; (*entrust to care, &c.*) remettre* aux soins, aux mains de; **~able,** (*praiseworthy*) louable; **~ably,** d'une manière louable; **~ation,** louange, *f.*; **~atory,** élogieu|x, ~se.
commensurab|le, commensurable (avec); **~ility,** commensurabilité, *f.*
commensurate, *adj.* (*proportionate to*) proportionné à; (*coextensive with*) de même mesure que.
comment, *s.* (*in the press, remarks, &c.*) commentaire, *m.*; *~ on*, commenter, *v.a.*; **~ary,** commentaire, *m.*; **~ator,** commentat|eur, ~rice, *m.f.*
commerc|e, (*trade, intercourse*) commerce, *m.*; **-ial,** commercial; *~ial traveller*, commis-voyageur, *m.*; **~ially,** commercialement.
commingle, *v.n.* se mêler ensemble.
commiserat|e, compatir à; **~ion,** commisération, *f.*
commissariat, (*mil.*) intendance, *f.*; **~-officer,** intendant, *m.*
commissary, commissioner, commissaire; ⚠ *not* commissionnaire *which* = '*commission-merchant*' *or* '*agent*', *also* '*porter*'.
commission, *s.* (*order for a thing*) commande, *f.*; (*of crime, &c.*) perpétration, *f.*; (*officer*) brevet, *m.*; (*matter entrusted to perform, committee, percentage on*

sales, &c.) commission, *f.*; *in* ~, (*nav.*) en armement.

commission, *v.a.* (*charge to do*) charger de; (*officer of ship*) nommer au commandement; (*ship*) armer; (*give piece of work*) donner une commande (de).

commit, *v.a.* (*to pillage, flames, &c.*) livrer; (*entrust*) confier (à); (*crime, &c.*) commettre*; ~ *to memory,* enregistrer dans la mémoire; ~ *to prison,* emprisonner; ~ *to writing,* mettre* par écrit; ~ *oneself,* (*become involved*) s'engager.

commitment, (*liability, binding oneself*) engagement, *m.*

committal, (*to prison*) emprisonnement, *m.*

committee, comité, *m.*; (*Parl.*) commission, *f.*

commode, (*night*) chaise percée, *f.*; ⚠ *not* commode *which* = *'chest of drawers'.*

commodi|ous, spacieu|x, ~se; **~ously,** commodément; **~ty,** (*comm.*) produit, *m.*; ⚠ *not* commodité *which* = *'convenience'.*

common, *s.* terrain communal, *m.*

common, *adj.* (*belonging to more than one, public, general, ordinary, vulgar, math., gram.*) commun; ~ **law,** droit commun, *m.*; **~place,** *s.* lieu-commun, *m.*; *adj.* banal; ~ **sense,** sens commun, *m.*; *adj.* sensé; **~ness,** (*frequency*) fréquence, *f.*; **~ly,** communément.

commoner, roturier, *m.*

commonweal, chose publique, *f.*; **~th,** république, *f.*

commotion, (*physical*) commotion, *f.*; (*revolt*) insurrection, *f.*

communal, communal.

commune (*with*), parler intimement (avec); (*receive Communion, U.S.A.*) communier.

communicant, communiant, -e, *m.f.*

communicat|e, *v.a.* communiquer; *v.n.* ~ *with,* (*rooms, pers., &c.*) communiquer avec; (*receive Communion*) communier; **~ion,** communication, *f.*; *~ion trench,* (*mil.*) boyau, *m.*; **~ive,** communicati|f, ~ve.

communion, (*intercourse*) commerce, *m.*; (*body professing faith and Cath. sacrament*) communion, *f.*; (*Prot. communion*) Sainte-Cène, *f.*

communis|m, communisme, *m.*; **~t,** *adj. and s.m.f.* communiste.

community, (*body with same tenets, township, monastic, joint possession, of interests*) communauté, *f.*; (*the public*) public, *m.*

commuta|ble, échangeable; **~tion,** (*penalty*) commutation, *f.*

commutator, (*electr.*) commutateur, *m.*

commute, échanger (pour); (*penalty*) commuer (en).

compact, *s.* pacte, *m.*; *adj.* compact; (*style*) concis; **~ness,** compacité, *f.*; **~ly,** d'une manière compacte; *v.a.* serrer ensemble; (*make up*) composer (de).

companion, (*lit. and of orders*) compagn|on, ~e, *m.f.*; *v.a.* accompagner.

companionable, sociable.

companionship, camaraderie, *f.*

company, (*companionship, sympathy, crowd, mil., rail., water, insurance, electr., gas*) compagnie, *f.*; ⚠ société, *f. and not* compagnie *is used for commercial, financial, and industrial concerns*; (*guests*) monde, *m.*; (*companion*) compagnon, *m.*; (*naut.*) équipage, *m.*; (*actors*) troupe, *f.*; *and Co.,* & Cie.; *limited liability company,* société anonyme, *f.*

comparable, comparable (à).

comparative, *s.* (*gram.*) comparatif, *m.*

comparative, (*gram. marking comparison*) comparati|f, ~ve; (*judged by comparison*) relati|f, ~ve; **~ly,** comparativement, relativement.

compar|e, (*to*) comparer (à); (*with*) comparer (avec); **~ed** *to,* en comparaison de; **~ison,** comparaison, *f.*; *beyond* ~, sans comparaison.

compartment, (*gen. and rail.*) compartiment, *m.*

compass, *s.* (*extent and voice*) étendue, *f.*; (*limits*) limites, *f.pl.*; *box the* ~, réciter la rose des vents; *mariner's* ~, *see* MARINER; *within the* ~ *of,* à la portée de.

compass, *v.a.* (*go round*) faire* le tour de; (*surround*) entourer de; (*grasp mentally*) saisir; (*plot*) comploter.

compassion, compassion, *f.*; *have* ~ *on,* avoir pitié de.

compassionate, compatissant; **~ly,** avec compassion.

compatib|le, compatible (avec); **~ility,** compatibilité, *f.*

compatriot, compatriote, *m.f.*

compel, forcer (à *or* de + *inf.*); (*an action by force*) imposer.

compend|ium, abrégé, *m.*; **~ious,** compendieu|x, ~se.

compensat|e, compenser; *~for* (*loss, &c.*) dédommager de; **~ion,** compensation, *f.*

compete, ~ *for,* concourir* pour; ~ *with,* faire* concurrence à.

competen|ce, (*means*) aisance, *f.*; (*ability*) capacité, *f.*; **~t,** capable; ⚠ compétent = *'legally or professionally qualified'*; **~tly,** capablement.

competit|ion, concurrence, *f.*; (*prizes, &c.*) concours, *m.*; *check ~ion,* enrayer la concurrence; **~or,** concurrent, *m.*; **~ive,** de concours; *~ive examination,* concours, *m.*

compil|e, compiler; **~ation,** compilation, *f.*; **~er,** compilat|eur, ~rice, *m.f.*

complacen|t, (*pers.*) content de soi; **~cy,** contentement de soi, *m.*

complain, *v.n.* se plaindre*; **~t,** plainte, *f.*; (*illness*) maladie, *f.*; ⚠ complainte = *'lament'.*

complaisan|ce, complaisance, *f.*; **~t,** complaisant.

complement, *s.* (*what completes, math., gram.*) complément, *m.*; *full* ~, (*mil., naut.*) grand complet, *m.*; **~ary,** complémentaire.

complete, *adj.* compl|et, ~ète; (*finished*) achevé; (*perfect*) parfait; **~ness,** état complet, *m.*; **~ly,** complètement.

completion, (*finishing*) achèvement, *m.*; (*accomplishment*) accomplissement, *m.*

complex, *s.*, *adj.* (*lit.*, *arith.*, *gram.*) complexe; **~ity,** complexité, *f.*

complexion, teint, *m.*; (*character*) caractère, *m.*; ⚠ complexion = '*bodily constitution*', '*disposition*'.

complian|ce, (*consent*) acquiescement, *m.*; *in ~ with,* conformément à; **~t,** accommodant.

complicat|e, (*entangle*) compliquer; **~ed,** compliqué; **~ion,** complication, *f.*

complicity, complicité, *f.*

compliment, compliment, *m.*; **~s,** compliments, *m.pl.*; *give my ~s to,* faites mes compliments à; *v.a.* féliciter (de).

complimentary, flatteu|r, ~se.

compline, (*eccles.*) complies, *f.pl.*

comply, (*yield*) céder; *~ with,* se conformer à.

component, *adj. and s.m.* composant.

comport, *v.n.*, *~ with,* convenir* à; *~ oneself,* se comporter; **~ment,** conduite, *f.*

compose, *v.a.* (*book, music, face, constitute*) composer; *be ~d of,* se composer de; (*quarrel*) arranger; (*calm*) calmer; **~d,** tranquille; **~r,** (*mus.*) compositeur, *m.*; (*author*) auteur, *m.*

composite, (*arch.*) composite; *~ order,* composite, *m.*

composition, (*mixture, nature, Lit., mus., print., arrangt. of picture, work composed*) composition, *f.*; (*school*) thème, *m.*; (*compromise*) arrangement, *m.*; (*with creditors*) concordat, *m.*

compositor, (*print.*) compositeur, *m.*

compost, (*agric.*) compost, *m.*

composure, tranquillité, *f.*

compound, *s.* composé, *m.*; (*in India, China, &c.*) enclos, *m.*; *adj.* (*parts, words*) composé; (*math.*) complexe; (*med.*) compliqué; (*mach.*) compound (*invar.*); **~ interest,** intérêts composés, *m.pl.*

compound, *v.a.* (*mixture, medicine*) composer; (*settle*) arranger; *v.n.* *~ with,* (*creditors, &c.*) composer avec; **~ able,** sur quoi on peut s'arranger.

comprehen|d, (*understand, include*) comprendre; **~sion,** (*understanding*) compréhension, *f.*; (*range, scope*) portée, *f.*; **~sible,** intelligible; **~sive,** (*including much*) compréhensi|f, ~ve.

compress, (*squeeze together*) comprimer; (*condense*) condenser; **~ion,** compression, *f.*; (*style, &c.*) concision, *f.*; **~ible,** compressible; **~ed,** (*style*) concis.

comprise, comprendre*.

compromise, *s.* compromis, *m.*; *v.a.* (*endanger*) compromettre*; *v.n.* (*make a compromise*) compromettre*.

comptroller, (*accounts*) vérificateur, *m.*

compuls|ion, contrainte, *f.*; **~ive,** coercitif, ~ve; **~ory,** obligatoire; **~orily,** par contrainte.

compunction, remords, *m.*

comput|e, supputer; **~ation,** supputation, *f.*

comrade, camarade, *m.f.*; **~ship,** camaraderie, *f.*

con, *s.* contre; *the pros and the ~s,* le pour et le contre.

con over, *v.a.* relire* attentivement.

concatenation, enchaînement, *m.*

concav|e, *adj.* concave; **~ity,** concavité, *f.*

conceal, cacher; (*facts*) taire*; **~ment,** action de cacher, *f.*; *place of ~-ment,* retraite, *f.*

concede, (*right, &c.*) concéder; *~ that,* accorder que.

conceit, (*vanity*) vanité, *f.*; (*fanciful notion*) concetti, *m.pl.*; *out of ~ with,* dégoûté de.

conceited, vaniteu|x, ~se; **~ly,** avec suffisance.

conceivable, concevable.

conceive, *v.a.* (*child, imagine*) concevoir; (*express, usually passive or p.p.*) exprimer; *v.n.* concevoir.

concentrat|e, *v.a.* concentrer; *v.n.* se concentrer; **~ion,** concentration, *f.*; *~ion camp,* camp de concentration, *m.*

concentric, concentrique.

conception, conception, *f.*

concern, *s.* (*matter, business, question*) affaire, *f.*; (*comm.*) entreprise, *f.*; (*importance*) importance, *f.*; (*anxiety*) anxiété, *f.*; *that 's not your ~,* vous n'avez rien à y voir; *going ~, see* GOING.

concern, *v.a.* (*relate to, belong to, affect, interest*) concerner; ⚠ *'be ~ed'* (*troubled*) *is not* être concerné *but* être péniblement affecté; (*be of importance to*) importer à; *~ oneself with, in,* s'intéresser à; *party ~ed,* intéressé, -e, *m.f.*

concerning, *prep.* concernant.

concert, *s.* concert, *m.*; *in ~,* de concert; **~-hall,** salle de concert, *m.*; *v.a.* (*plan, &c.*) concerter.

concertina, petit accordéon, *m.*

concession, concession, *f.*; **~(n)aire,** concessionnaire, *m.f.*; **~ary,** concessionnaire.

conch, conque, *f.*; **~ology,** conchyliologie, *f.*; **~ologist,** conchyliologiste, *m.f.*

conciliate, (*win over*) concilier; (*acquire, esteem, &c.*) se concilier.

conciliat|ion, conciliation, *f.*; **~ory,** conciliatoire.

concise, concis; **~ness,** concision; **~ly,** avec concision.

conclave, conclave, *m.*; (*fig.*) assemblée, *f.*

conclude, *v.a.n.* (*treaty, end, come to an end, infer*) conclure*; *~ to,* (*resolve to*) décider de.

conclusion, (*of treaty, log., end*) conclusion, *f.*; (*decision*) décision, *f.*; *in ~,* pour conclure; *it 's a foregone ~,* c'est prévu.

conclusive, concluant; **~ly,** décisivement.
concoct, (*drink, &c.*) composer; (*fig.*) inventer; (*plot*) tramer; **~ion,** mélange, *m.*
concomitant, *adj.* concomitant.
concord, (*gram.*) concordance, *f.*; (*mus.*) consonance, *f.*; (*fig.*) harmonie, *f.*
concordance, (*agreement, gram., of Bible, &c.*) concordance, *f.*
concordat, concordat, *m.*
concourse, (*lit. and fig.*) concours, *m.*
concrete, *s.* (*cement*) béton, *m.*; *adj.* (*real, gram.*) concr|et, ~ète; (*of cement*) fait de béton; ⚠ concret *is an adj. only in French.*
concubine, concubine, *f.*
concupiscen|ce, concupiscence, *f.*; **~t,** concupiscent.
concurren|ce, (*circumstances*) concours, *m.*; (*agreement*) accord, *m.*; **~t,** (*concurring*) concourant; (*unanimous*) unanime; **~tly,** concurremment.
concussion, choc violent, *m.*; (*brain*) ébranlement de tête, *m.*; ⚠ concussion = '*embezzlement*'.
condemn, (*fig., law, gen.*) condamner; **~ation,** condamnation, *f.*; **~able,** condamnable.
condens|e, *v.a.* (*abridge, electr., phys., fig.*) condenser; *v.n.* se condenser; **~ation,** condensation, *f.*; *~d milk,* lait condensé, *m.*
condenser, condensateur, *m.*
condescen|d, condescendre (à); **~sion,** condescendance, *f.*; **~ding,** condescendant; **~dingly,** avec condescendance.
condign, mérité; **~ly,** justement.
condiment, condiment, *m.*
condition, (*stipulation, precedent, to be fulfilled*) condition, *f.*; (*state*) état, *m.*; (*rank*) rang, *m.*; *in good ~,* en bon état; *in a ~ to,* en état de; *on ~ that,* à condition que + *subj.*
conditional, (*not absolute, gram.*) conditionnel, -le; *s.* (*gram.*) conditionnel, *m.*; **~ly,** conditionnellement.
conditioned, conditionné.
condole (with), faire* ses condoléances (à); **~nce,** condoléance, *f.*
condon|e, pardonner; **~ation,** pardon, *m.*
conduce, *be conducive to,* contribuer à.
conduct, *s.* (*guidance, comm., behaviour*) conduite, *f.*
conduct, *v.a.* (*lit. and fig.*) conduire*; (*mus.*) diriger; **~ing,** *adj.* (*phys.*) conduct|eur, ~rice; *non-~ing,* non-conduct|eur, ~rice.
conduct|or, *s.* guide, *m.*; (*band*) chef d'orchestre, *m.*; (*veh.*) **~or, ~ress,** receveu|r, ~se, *m.f.*; (*U.S.A. rail.*) chef de train, *m.*
conduit, conduit, *m.*
cone, cône, *m.*
coney, *see* CONY.
confabulation, bout de causette, *f.*
confection, (*mixing*) mélange, *f.*; (*fruit, &c.*) conserve, *f.*; (*ready-made clothes*) confection, *f.*
confectioner, pâtissier, *m.*; **~y,** patisserie, *f.*; ⚠ confectionneur = '*outfitter*'.
confedera|cy, ~tion, confédération, *f.*
confederate, *adj. and s.m.f.* confédéré, -e; *v.n.* se confédérer.
confer, *v.a.* conférer; *v.n.* *~ with,* conférer avec.
conference, conférence, *f.*
conferment, (*degrees, benefices*) collation, *f.*
confess, *v.a.* avouer; (*eccles.*) confesser; *v.n.* se confesser; *be free to ~,* être prêt à reconnaître.
confessedly, (*undeniably*) de l'aveu de tout le monde.
confession, (*avowal, belief, eccles.*) confession, *f.*; (*eccles. without article in conjunction with* aller* (être) à, revenir* (être) de) confesse, *f.*; **~al,** confessional, *m.*
confessor, confesseur, *m.*
confetti, confetti, *m.pl.*
confidant, confident, -e, *s.m.f.*
confide, *v.a.* confier (à); *v.n.* se confier (à).
confidence, confiance, *f.*; (*secrets*) confidence, *f.*; ⚠ confidence *does not* = '*trust*'; **~-trick,** vol à l'américaine, *m.*
confident, *s.* confident, -e; *adj.* (*trusting, bold*) confiant; (*sure*) sûr.
confidential, (*thing*) confidentiel, -le; (*pers.*) de confiance; **~ly,** confidentiellement.
confidently, avec confiance.
confiding, confiant.
configuration, configuration, *f.*
confine, *v.a.* confiner; *~ oneself to,* se borner à; *be ~d,* (*med.*) être en couches; *be ~d to one's bed,* être alité.
confine, *v.n.* (*border on*) confiner (à).
confines, confins, *m.pl.*
confinement, détention, *f.*; (*med.*) couches, *f.pl.*
confirm, (*promise, news, &c., eccles.*) confirmer; (*resolution, appointment, what has been already done or promised*) ratifier; (*strengthen*) affermir; **~ed,** *adj.* invétéré.
confirmation, (*corrob. and eccles.*) confirmation, *f.*
confirmat|ive, ~ory, confirmati|f, ~ve.
confiscat|e, confisquer; **~ion,** confiscation, *f.*
conflagration, (*lit. and fig.*) conflagration, *f.*
conflict, *s.* conflit, *m.*; (*fig.*) lutte, *f.*; *v.n.* (*struggle*) lutter; (*be incompatible*) se †heurter (contre); **~ing,** *adj.* †heurté.
confluence, (*rivers*) confluent, *m.*
conform, *v.a.* (*make similar*) conformer (à); *v.n.* *~ to,* se conformer à.
conformabl|e, (*similar*) conforme (à); (*tractable*) docile; **~y,** conformément (à).
conformation, conformation, *f.*
conform|ity, conformité, *f.*; *non- ~ity,* (*eccles.*) non-conformisme, *m.*, **~ist,** conformiste, *m.f.*; *non-~ist,* (*eccles.*) nonconformiste, *m.*
confound, (*ideas, hopes, &c., mix up, abash*) confondre; *~ it!* que le diable l'emporte!

confounded, *adj.* maudit; **~ly,** furieusement.
confraternity, confrérie, *f.*
confront, *v.a.* (*face*) faire* face à; (*compare*) confronter; ~ *with,* confronter avec.
confuse, mettre* en désordre; (*perplex*) troubler; (*two different things, disconcert*) confondre.
confused, confus; *get* ~, se confondre; **~ly,** confusément.
confusion, (*disorder, shame*) confusion, *f.*
confut|e, réfuter; ⚠ *not* confuter *which is not French*; **~ation,** réfutation, *f.*; **~able,** réfutable.
congeal, *v.n.* se congeler.
congenial, (*pers.*) sympathique; (*suited, of things*) approprié (à); **~ity,** affinité, *f.*
congenital, congénital.
conger-eel, anguille de mer, *f.*
congest, *v.a.* (*med.*) congestionner; (*streets*) encombrer; **~ion,** (*med.*) congestion, *f.*; (*streets*) encombrement, *m.*; *~ion of the brain,* congestion cérébrale, *f.*; *~ion of the lungs,* congestion pulmonaire, *f.*
conglomerat|e, *v.a.* conglomérer; *v.n.* se conglomérer; **~ion,** conglomération, *f.*
conglutinat|e, *v.n.* se conglutiner; **~ion,** conglutination, *f.*
congratulat|e, féliciter (de); **~ion,** félicitations, *f.pl.*; **~ory,** de félicitation.
congregate, *v.a.* rassembler; *v.n.* se rassembler.
congregation, (*church, univ.*) assemblée, *f.*; (*of ecclesiastics and monks*) congrégation, *f.*
congress, congrès, *m.*; (*U.S.A.*) Congrès, *m.*
congru|ity, convenance, *f.*; **~ous,** convenable (à); **~ously,** convenablement.
conic, *adj.* conique; ~ *sections,* sections coniques, *f.pl.*
conifer, (*bot.*) conifère, *m.*; **~ous,** *adj.* conifère.
coniform, coniforme.
conjectur|e, conjecture, *f.*; **~al,** conjectural; **~ally,** conjecturalement; *v.a.* conjecturer.
conjoin, *v.a.* conjoindre*; **~t,** *adj.* joint; **~tly,** conjointement.
conjugal, conjugal; **~ly,** conjugalement.
conjugat|e, conjuguer; **~ion,** (*gram.*) conjugaison, *f.*
conjunction, (*gram., astr.*) conjonction, *f.*
conjunctive, *adj.* (*gram.*) conjoncti|f, ~ve.
conjuncture, conjoncture, *f.*
conjuration, (*incantation*) incantation, *f.*
conjure, (*entreat*) conjurer; ~ *up,* (*lit. and magic*) évoquer; ~ *away,* (*by conjuring trick*) escamoter.
conjurer, prestidigitateur, *m.*
conjuring, *s.* prestidigitation, *f.*; **~-trick,** tour de prestidigitation, *m.*
connect, *v.a.* joindre*; (*in thought*) associer; (*family*) allier; (*electr.*) mettre* en contact.
connected, (*in sequence*) suivi; (*family*) apparenté.
con|nexion, ~nection, connexion, *f.*; (*reference to*) rapport, *m.*; (*of ideas*) suite, *f.*; (*intercourse*) relations, *f.pl.*; (*family*) parent, -e, *s.m.f.*; (*rail., comm.*) correspondance, *f.*
conning-tower, kiosque, *m.*
conniv|e, ~ *at,* être complice de; **~ance,** connivence, *f.*
connoisseur, connaiss|eur, ~euse, *s.m.f.* (en).
connote, impliquer.
connubial, conjugal.
conquer, (*lit. and fig.*) vaincre*; (*win by conquest*) conquérir*.
conqueror, vainqueur, *m.*
conquest, (*action and thing conquered*) conquête, *f.*
consanguinity, parenté, *f.*
conscience, conscience, *f.*
conscientious, consciencieu|x, ~se; **~ness,** droiture, *f.*; **~ly,** consciencieusement.
conscious, ~ *of,* conscient de; *be* ~ *of,* avoir la conscience de; *be* ~, (*not fainting*) avoir connaissance; **~ly,** sciemment.
consciousness, (*being conscious*) connaissance, *f.*; (*thoughts, feelings*) conscience, *f.*
conscript, *adj. and s.m.* conscrit; **~ion,** conscription, *f.*
consecrat|e, consacrer; (*bishop*) sacrer; **~ion,** consécration, *f.*; *~ed bread,* pain bénit, *m.*
consecutive, (*time*) consécuti|f, ~ve; **~ly,** consécutivement.
consensus, consensus, *m.*
consent, *s.* (*permission, agreement*) consentement, *m.*; *by common* ~, d'un commun accord; *silence gives* ~, qui ne dit mot consent.
consent, *v.n.* consentir*; ~ *to,* consentir à.
consequence, (*conclusion, deduction, result, also importance*) conséquence, *f.*; (*moment*) importance, *f.*; *in* ~ *of,* par suite de; *it is of no* ~, cela ne fait rien.
consequent, *adj.* conséquent; **~ly,** par conséquent.
consequential, consécuti|f, ~ve; (*conceited*) important.
conservative, *adj. and s.m.f.* (*polit.*) conservat|eur, ~rice; ~ *estimate,* (*comm.*) appréciation réservée, *f.*
conservator, conservateur, *m.*
conservatory, (*greenhouse*) serre, *f.*
conserve, *v.a.* préserver.
consider, *v.a.* considérer; (*allow for*) tenir* compte de; ~ *as,* considérer comme.
considerabl|e, considérable; (*no small amount, &c.*) beaucoup de; **~y,** considérablement.
considerate, (*approx.*) qui a des égards pour les autres; **~ness,** égards, *m.pl.*
consideration, (*deliberation, regard*) considération, *f.*; (*money*) rémunération, *f.*;

in ~ *of,* (*in return for*) moyennant; *of no* ~, sans importance; *on no* ~, ne+*verb*+pour rien au monde, *e.g.*, je ne le ferai pour rien au monde; *under* ~, en délibération.
considering, *prep.* vu (*invar. before noun*); ~ *that,* vu que+*indic.*
consign, (*hand over*) livrer; (*money, goods*) consigner.
consign|ee, consignataire, *m.*; **~er,** consignat|eur, ~rice, *m.f.*
consignment, (*consigning*) consignation, *f.*; (*goods, rail.*) expédition, *f.*; (*goods arriving at port*) arrivage, *m.*
consist, ~ *in,* consister en; + *gerund,* consister à; *e.g. monasticism consists in renouncing the world,* la vie monastique consiste à renoncer au monde; ~ *of,* se composer de.
consistenc|e, ~y, (*liquid, stability, firmness*) consistance, *f.*
consistent, (*pers.*) conséquent; ~ *with,* compatible avec; **~ly,** d'une manière conséquente.
consistory, consistoire, *m.*
consolat|ion, consolation, *f.*; **~ory,** consolant.
console, *s.* (*arch., also console-table*) console, *f.*
console, *v.a.* consoler.
consolidat|e, (*lit. and fig., comm.*) consolider; **~ion,** consolidation, *f.*
consols, consolidés, *m.pl.*
consonance, *s.* (*mus.*) consonance, *f.*; (*fig.*) accord, *m.*
consonant, *s.* consonne, *f.*
consort, *s.* épou|x, ~se, *m.f.*; *adj.* (*prince, queen*) consort, *invar. and after noun.*
consort with, fréquenter; (*harmonize with*) s'accorder avec.
conspicuous, en vue; (*striking*) frappant; (*eminent*) insigne; **~ly,** visiblement.
conspira|cy, conjuration, *f.*; **~tor,** conspirat|eur, ~rice, *m.f.*
conspire, *v.a.n.* (*plot*) conspirer; *v.n.* (*concur in, contribute to*) conspirer à.
conspue, conspuer.
constab|le, agent de police, *m.*; (*Paris*) gardien de la paix; (*Fr. hist.*) connétable; **~ulary,** police, *f.*; (*provinces*) gendarmerie, *f.*
constan|cy, constance, *f.*; **~t,** (*continuous*) continuel, -le; (*faithful*) constant; **~tly,** constamment.
constellation, constellation, *f.*
consternat|ed, consterné; **~ion,** consternation, *f.*
constipation, (*med.*) constipation, *f.*
constituency, circonscription électorale, *f.*
constituent, *s.* (*component part*) éléments, *m.pl.*; (*elector*) élect|eur, ~rice, *m.f.*; *adj.* constituant.
constitute, constituer; (*appoint*) nommer.
constitution, (*organization, of human body, principles of govt.*) constitution, *f.*; **~al,** (*most Engl. senses*) constitutionnel, -le; **~ally,** d'une manière constitutionnelle, *f.*
constitutional, *s.* (*walk*) promenade hygiénique, *f.*
constitutionalist, (*adherent*) partisan des principes constitutionnels, *m.*
constitutive, constituti|f, ~ve.
constrain, (*compel*) contraindre* (à); (*imprison, lit. and fig.*) emprisonner; **~ed,** *adj.* contraint.
constraint, (*compulsion, uneasiness*) contrainte, *f.*
constrict, étrangler; **~ion,** constriction, *f.*; ⚠ constricter *not French.*
construct, (*lit., fig., gram.*) construire*; **~ion,** construction, *f.*; (*interpretation*) interprétation, *f.*; **~or,** constructeur, *m.*; **~ional,** qui se rapporte à la construction.
constructive, (*belonging to structure*) qui se rapporte à la construction.
construe, (*sentence*) construire*; (*translate*) traduire*; (*explain*) expliquer.
consubstant|ial, consubstantiel, -le; **~iation,** (*eccles.*) consubstantiation, *f.*
consul, consul, *m.*; **vice-~,** vice-consul, *m.*; **~ar,** consulaire; **~ate,** consulat, *m.*
consult, *v.a.* consulter; *v.n.* ~ *with,* consulter avec; **~ation,** (*gen. and med.*) consultation, *f.*; **~ant,** (*med.*) *adj. and s.m.* consultant, -e; **~ing,** *adj.* (*surgeon, &c.*) consultant, -e; *~-ing-room,* cabinet, *m.*
consume, *v.a.* (*destroy, squander*) consumer; ⚠ *Engl. 'consume' = also 'use up food, drink, &c.' which* = consommer; (*fig.*) dévorer (de); *be ~d,* se consommer.
consumer, (*comm.*) consommat|eur, ~rice, *m.f.*
consummate, *v.a.* consommer; *adj.* consommé; **~ly,** parfaitement.
consummation, consommation, *f.*; (*end*) fin, *f.*
consumption, (*food, &c., using, destroying*) consommation *f.*; (*med.*) phtisie, *f.*; *galloping* ~, (*med.*) phtisie galopante, *f.*
consumptive, (*med.*) poitrinaire.
contact, (*lit., fig., electr.*) contact, *m.*; *~-breaker,* (*electr.*) interrupteur, *m.*
contagi|on, (*lit. and fig.*) contagion, *f.*; **~ous,** contagieu|x, ~se.
contain, *v.a.* contenir*; (*control*) maîtriser; *not to ~ oneself for joy,* ne pas se tenir* de joie.
contaminat|e, contaminer; **~ion,** contamination, *f.*
contemn, mépriser.
contemplate, *v.a.* contempler; (*intend*) projeter; (+ *verb*) se proposer de; *v.n.* méditer.
contemplation, (*act of gazing on*) contemplation, *f.*; (*meditation*) méditation, *f.*; *have in* ~, avoir en vue.
contemplative, (*thoughtful*) pensi|f, ~ve; (*relig.*) contemplati|f, ~ve.
contemporaneous, contemporain (de); **~ly,** en même temps.
contemporary, *adj. and s.m.f.* contemporain, -e; ⚠ contemporaire *not French.*

contempt, mépris, *m.*; (*law*) offense, *f.*; **~ible**, méprisable; **~ibility**, caractère méprisable, *m.*; **~ibly**, de manière méprisable.

contemptuous, méprisant; **~ly**, avec mépris.

contend, (*struggle with . . . for . . .*) lutter contre . . . pour; (*compete for place, &c.*) disputer + *acc. of thing, dat. of person*; (*argue*) discuter (avec); (*maintain*) soutenir*.

contending, *adj.* (*opposed*) opposé; (*rival*) rival.

content, *s.* (*satisfaction*) contentement, *m.*; **~s**, (*vessel, book, letters, &c.*) contenu, *m.*; (*capacity*) contenance, *f.*

content|ed, *adj.* content (de); (*ready*) prêt (à); *v.a.* contenter; **~edly**, *use* tout content *with* tout *in concord, e.g.* des femmes toutes contentes.

contention, dispute, *f.*; (*point contended for*) *use verb* prétendre: *his ~ was*, ce qu'il prétendait c'était que . . .

contentious, (*involving contention*) contentieu|x, ~se; (*quarrelsome*) querell|eur, ~euse.

contentment, contentement, *m.*

contest, *s.* (*gen. and verbal*) débat, *m.*; (*struggle*) lutte, *f.*; (*sport*) rencontre, *f.*; (*boxing*) match, *m.*; (*dispute*) contestation, *f.*

contest, *v.a.* (*point, statement*) contester; (*battle, victory, seat in Parl.*) disputer.

contestable, contestable.

context, contexte, *m.*

contexture, (*structure*) structure, *f.*; (*fabric*) tissu, *m.*; (*Lit.*) facture, *f.*

contigu|ity, contiguïté, *f.*; **~ous**, contigu, -ë (à).

continen|ce, (*chastity*) continence, *f.*; (*restraint*) modération, *f.*; **~t**, continent, modéré.

continent, *s.* continent, *m.*; **~al**, continental.

contingen|ce, **~cy**, (*uncertainty of occurrence*) contingence, *f.*; (*chance*) événement fortuit, *m.*; **~t**, contingent; (*accidental*) fortuit; **~tly**, fortuitement.

continual, continuel, -le; **~ly**, continuellement.

continuance, (*time*) durée, *f.*; (*stay*) séjour, *m.*; (*perseverance*) persévérance, *f.*

continuation, continuation, *f.*; (*course, story, &c.*) suite, *f.*

continuator, continuat|eur, ~rice, *m.f.*

continu|e, *v.a.* continuer; (*retain in office, &c.*) maintenir*; *v.n.* continuer (à + *inf. of an action that has no immediate or probable limit*, de *of a definite purpose in hand, cf.* Il continue à faire du progrès *and* Il continuait d'écrire la lettre); (*remain*) rester (être); **~ing**, (*permanent*) permanent.

continuity, continuité, *f.*

continuous, continu; **~ly**, sans interruption.

contort, tordre; **~ion**, contorsion, *f.*

contour, contour, *m.*

contraband, contrebande, *f.*; *adj.* de contrebande.

contract, *s.* (*comm., law, marriage*) contrat, *m.*; (*tender to execute work*) soumission, *f.*; *by, on ~*, à forfait.

contract, *v.a.* (*marriage, friendship, debt, habit, muscles, gram., disease, make smaller*) contracter; **~ed**, (*lit. and gram.*) contracté; *~ oneself out of*, se dégager par un contrat (de).

contract, *v.n.* (*grow smaller, gram.*) se contracter; (*tender*) soumissionner (à); *~ for*, prendre* à forfait.

contractible, **contractile**, contractile.

contractility, contractilité, *f.*

contraction, (*lit. and gram.*) contraction, *f.*

contractor, entrepreneur, *m.*; (*army, navy*) fournisseur, *m.*

contradict, contredire*; **~ion**, (*lit. and inconsistency*) contradiction, *f.*; *without ~ion*, sans contredit.

contradictious, porté à contredire.

contradictor|y, contradictoire; **~ily**, contradictoirement.

contradistinction, contraste, *m.*; *in ~ to*, par contraste à.

contralto, contralto, *m.*

contraposition, contraste, *m.*

contrariety, contrariété, *f.*; (*opposition*) opposition, *m.*

contrariness, esprit de contradiction, *m.*

contrariwise, en sens opposé.

contrary, *s.* contraire, *m.*; *on the ~*, au contraire.

contrar|y, *adj.* contraire (à); *be ~*, (*perverse*) faire* la mauvaise tête; **~ily**, contrairement.

contrast, *s.* contraste, *m.* (avec).

contrast, *v.a.* mettre* en contraste; *v.n.* contraster (avec).

contraven|e, contrevenir* à; (*oppose*) s'opposer à; **~tion**, contravention, *f.*

contribut|e, *v.a.n.* contribuer (à); **~ion**, contribution, *f.*; (*Lit.*) article, *m.*

contributor, (*newspaper, &c.*) collaborat|eur, ~rice, *m.f.*; **~y**, (*cause, adventitious*) accessoire.

contrit|e, contrit; **~ion**, contrition, *f.*; **~ely**, avec contrition.

contrivance, (*invention*) invention, *f.*; (*mechanical device*) appareil, *m.*

contrive, *v.a.* (*invent*) inventer; (*manage*) arranger; *v.n. ~ to*, réussir à.

control, *s.* autorité, *f.*; (*power of driving, directing machine*) direction, *f.*; (*aeron.*) commande, *f.*; ⚠ contrôle = '*register*', '*muster-roll*', '*hall-mark*', '*verification*'; **~-lever**, levier de contrôle, *m.*

control, *v.a.* gouverner; (*temper, &c.*) maîtriser; (*check*) contrôler.

controller, (*verifier*) contrôleur, *m.*

controvers|y, controverse, *f.*; **~ial**, de controverse; **~ialist**, controversiste, *m.f.*

controvert, *v.a.* controverser; **~ible**, controversable; ⚠ controverter *not French*.

contumac|y, entêtement, *m.*; **~ious**, opiniâtre; **~iously**, obstinément.
contumely, mépris, *m.*
contusion, contusion, *f.*
conundrum, énigme, *f.*
convalescen|ce, convalescence, *f.*; **~t**, convalescent.
convene, *v.a.* (*meeting, &c.*) convoquer; *v.n.* s'assembler.
convenience, (*comfort*) commodité, *f.*; (*suitableness*) convenance, *f.*; *at your ~*, quand bon vous semblera.
convenient, commode; **~ly**, commodément.
convent, couvent, *m.*
conventicle, conventicule, *m.*
convention, (*contract, agreement*) convention, *f.*; (*assembly*) assemblée, *f.*; **~al**, de convention.
conventionality, caractère conventionnel, *m.*
conventual, *adj.* conventuel, -le.
converge, *v.n.* converger; **~nce**, convergence, *f.*; **~nt**, convergent.
conversan|t, (*familiar with, pers.*) famili|er, ~ère (avec); (*thing*) versé dans; **~ce**, familiarité, *f.* (avec).
conversation, conversation, *f.*; **~al**, *adj.* causeu|r, ~se; **~alist**, causeu|r, ~se, *m.f.*
conversazione, réunion savante *or* littéraire.
converse, s'entretenir* (avec).
converse, *adj.* contraire; *s.* (*log., math.*) converse, *f.*
conversion, (*eccles., mil., comm.*) conversion, *f.*; (*transformation*) transformation, *f.*
convert, *s.* converti, *m.*
convert, (*change, eccles., &c.*) convertir; *be ~ed*, se convertir.
convertible, (*things and comm.*) convertible (en); (*pers.*) convertissable.
convex, *adj.* convexe.
convey, transporter; (*wishes, compliments*) présenter; (*orders, &c.*) transmettre*; (*by road*) charrier; (*news, &c.*) communiquer; (*express*) exprimer.
conveyance, (*carrying*) transport, *m.*; (*veh.*) voiture, *f.*
convict, forçat, *m.*; **~-prison**, bagne, *m.*; **~-warder**, garde-chiourme, *m.*
convict, *v.a.* (*prove guilty of*) convaincre* (de); (*condemn*) condamner.
conviction, condamnation, *f.*; (*settled belief*) conviction, *f.*
convince, convaincre* (de).
convincing, convaincant; **~ly**, de manière convaincante.
convivial, (*pers.*) jovial; (*of a feast*) de festin; **~ity**, jovialité, *f.*
convocation, (*calling together*) convocation, *f.*; (*assembly*) assemblée, *f.*
convoke, convoquer.
convolution, convolution, *f.*
convolvulus, (*bot.*) volubilis, *m.*
convoy, *s.* (*naut., provisions, &c.*) convoi, *m.*; (*escort*) escorte, *f.*; *v.a.* convoyer.
convuls|e, (*shake violently*) ébranler; (*overturn*) bouleverser; *be ~ed with laughter*, se pâmer de rire; **~ion**, convulsion, *f.*; (*of laughter*) accès, *m.*; **~ive**, convulsi|f, ~ve; **~ively**, convulsivement.
con|y, **~ey**, lapin, *m.*
coo, roucouler; **~ing**, roucoulement, *m.*
cook, *s.* cuisini|er, ~ère, *m.f.*; (*naut.*) coq, *m.*; **~-shop**, gargote, *f.*
cook, *v.a.* faire* cuire; (*accounts, &c.*) cuisiner; *v.n.* cuire*; ⚠ cuire *alone is never transitive in French.*
cooker, (*stove*) fourneau de cuisine, *m.*
cookery, (*art*) cuisine, *f*; **~-book**, livre de cuisine, *m.*
cookie, (*U.S.A.*) galette, *f.*
cooking, *s.* cuisine, *f.*
cool, *s.* frais, *m.*
cool, *adj.* (*fresh, coldish*) frais, fraîche; (*audacious*) impudent; (*indifferent, lacking in cordiality*) froid; (*fig.*) calme; *be ~*, (*of weather*) faire* frais; **~-headed**, de sang-froid; **~ness**, frais, *m.*; (*fig.*) froideur, *f.*; (*audacity*) sang-froid, *m.*; **~ly**, fraîchement; (*fig.*) froidement.
cool, *v.a.* refroidir; (*fig.*) calmer; *v.n.* se refroidir; (*fig.*) se calmer.
coomb, combe, combe, *f.*
coon, *U.S.A.* (*zool.*) raton laveur, *m.*; (*negro*) nègre, *m.*; (*sly fellow*) malin, *m.*; *be a gone ~*, être perdu.
coop, *s.* (*hen*) cage à poule, *f.*; *v.a.* *~ up*, claquemurer.
cooper, tonnelier, *m.*
co-operat|e, coopérer; **~ion**, coopération, *f.*; **~ive**, coopérati|f, ~ve; *~ive society, stores*, coopérative, *f.*; **~or**, coopérateur, *m.*
co-opt, coopter; **~ation**, cooptation, *f.*
co-ordinat|e, *adj.* (*geom., gram.*) coordonné; *v.a.* coordonner; **~ion**, coordination, *f.*
coot, (*ornith.*) foulque, *f.*
cop, (*pop.*) empoigner.
copal, copal, *m.*
copartner, coassocié, -e, *m.f.*
cope, *s.* (*eccles.*) chape, *f.*; (*of heaven*) voûte, *f.*
cope, *v.n.* *~ with*, lutter contre.
coping, (*building, also coping-stone*) couronnement, *m.*; (*walls*) chaperon, *m.*
copious, copieu|x, ~se; (*rich*) riche; **~ness**, richesse, *f.*; **~ly**, copieusement.
copper, *s.* cuivre, *m.*; (*coin*) sou, *m.*; (*cauldron*) chaudière, *f.*; *adj.* de cuivre; **~-wire**, fil de cuivre, *m.*; *~-colour(ed)*, cuivré.
copper, (*pop. policeman*) flic, *m.*
copperplate, planche de cuivre, *f.*; (*engraving*) taille-douce, *f.*
coppice, copse, taillis, *m.*
copulat|e, *v.n.* s'accoupler; **~ion**, copulation, *f.*
copy, *s.* (*imitation, written or printed specimen, school task, transcription, for the press*) copie, *f.*; (*of a book*) exemplaire, *m.*; (*newspaper*) numéro, *m.*; **~-book**, (*exer-*

cise) cahier, *m.*; *fair* ~, *see* FAIR; *rough* ~, *see* ROUGH; *make a fair* ~ *of*, mettre* au net.

copy, *v.a.* copier; ~**ing-ink,** encre communicative, *f.*; ~*ing-ribbon,* (*typing*) ruban à copier, *m.*

copyist, copier, copiste, *m.*

copyright, droits d'impression réservés, *m.pl.*

coquet, *v.n.* coqueter; ~**ry,** coquetterie, *f.*

coquett|e, coquette, *f.*; ~**ish,** coquet, -te.

coral, corail, *m.*, *pl.* coraux; ~**-reef,** banc de corail, *m.*; *adj.* de corail; ~**-red,** rouge-corail, *invar.*

corbel, (*arch.*) corbeau, *m.*

cord, *s.* corde, *f.*; ~**age,** (*naut.*) cordages, *m.pl.*; *v.a.* (*box, &c.*) corder.

cordial, *s.* cordial, *m.*; *adj.* (*friendly*) cordial; ~**ity,** cordialité, *f.*; ~**ly,** cordialement.

cordite, cordite, *f.*

cordon, (*mil., arch., knightly order*) cordon, *m.*

corduroy, velours côtelé, *m.*

core, (*fruit and fig.*) cœur, *m.*; *rotten to the* ~, pourri jusqu'aux moelles.

co-religionist, coreligionnaire, *m.f.*

co-respondent, (*divorce*) complice, *m.*

coriander, (*bot.*) coriandre, *f.*

cork, liège, *m.*; (*stopper*) bouchon, *m.*; ~**-oak,** ~**-tree,** chêne liège, *m.*; *v.a.* (*bottle*) boucher.

corkscrew, tire-bouchon, *m.*, *plur.* tire-bouchons; ~**-staircase,** escalier en colimaçon, *m.*

cormorant, cormoran, *m.*; *green* ~, nigaud, *m.*

corn, (*pepper, seed of cereals, &c.*) grain, *m.*; (*on foot*) cor, *m.*; (*wheat*) blé, *m.*; (*U.S.A.*) maïs, *m.*; (*gen.*) céréales, *f.pl.*; ~**-chandler,** grainetier, *m.*; ~**-cob,** épi de maïs, *m.*; ~**-crake,** (*ornith.*) râle des genêts, *m.*; ~**-dealer,** marchand de grains, *m.*; ~**-exchange,** halle aux blés, *f.*; ~**-field,** champ de blé, *m.*; ~**-flag,** (*bot.*) glaïeul, *m.*; ~**-flour,** farine de maïs, *f.*; ~**-flower,** (*bot.*) bleuet, *m.*; ~**-merchant,** négociant en blé, *m.*; ~**-poppy,** coquelicot, *m.*; ~**-salad,** (*bot.*) mâche, *f.*

corn, (*with salt*) *v.a.* saler.

cornel-tree, cornouiller, *m.*

cornelian, cornaline, *f.*

corner, coin, *m.*; (*retreat*) recoin, *m.*; (*comm.*) accaparement, *m.*; ~**-stone,** pierre angulaire, *f.*; *be in a tight* ~, être acculé.

corner, *v.a.* (*drive into corner*) mettre* à quia; (*comm.*) accaparer; *three-, four-, &c.* ~*ed,* à trois, quatre, etc., coins; *three-*~*ed hat,* tricorne, *m.*

cornet, (*mus.*) cornet à pistons, *m.*; (*mil. m., head-dress f.*) cornette.

cornice, corniche, *f.*

Cornish, de Cornouailles.

cornucopia, corne d'abondance, *f.*

corolla, (*bot.*) corolle, *f.*

coronation, sacre, *m.*

coronet, couronne, *f.*

corporal, *s.* (*cav.*) brigadier, *m.*; (*inf.*) caporal, *m.*

corporal, corporeal, *adj.* corporel, -le.

corporate, *adj.* (*body*) constitué; (*action, &c.*) social.

corporation, (*town*) conseil municipal, *m.*; (*body of persons*) corporation, *f.*; (*pop. abdomen*) bedaine, *f.*; ⚠ corporation *never* = '*abdomen*'.

corps, (*mil.*) corps, *m.*; ~ *of engineers,* génie, *m.*

corpse, cadavre, *m.*

corpulen|ce, corpulence, *f.*; ~**t,** corpulent.

corpuscle, corpuscule, *m.*

correct, *adj.* (*accurate, conforming to rule, style, manners, &c.*) correct; (*precise, of calculations*) exact; **-ly,** correctement, exactement.

correct, *v.a.* corriger; (*error*) rectifier; (*write over*) surcharger; ~ *copy,* corrigé, *m.*

correction, (*correcting, punishment*) correction, *f.*; (*accounts*) rectification, *f.*

corrective, *s.* correctif, *m.*

correctness, correction, *f.*

correlat|ion, corrélation, *f.*; ~**ive,** *adj. and s.m.* corrélati|f, ~ve.

correspond, *v.n.* (*letters, communicate, conform to*) correspondre (avec); (*agree in amount*), s'accorder à.

corresponden|ce, (*letters*) correspondance, *f.*; ~**t,** correspondant, *m.*

corresponding, correspondant (à).

corridor, corridor, *m.*; ~ **-carriage,** wagon à couloir, *m.*; ~ **-train,** train à couloir, *m.*

corroborat|e, confirmer; ~**ion,** confirmation, *f.*

corro|de, corroder; ~**sion,** corrosion, *f.*; ~**sive,** corrosi|f, ~ve.

corrugated, ~ **iron,** tôle ondulée, *f.*; ~ **paper,** carton ondulé, *m.*

corrupt, *adj.* (*rotten, depraved*) corrompu; (*open to bribery*) vénal; (*texts*) altéré; ~ **practices,** faits de corruption, *m.pl.*

corrupt, *v.a.* (*lit. and fig.*) corrompre; (*alter*) altérer.

corruptib|le, corruptible; ~**ility,** corruptibilité, *f.*

corruption, (*lit. and fig.*) corruption, *f.*; (*texts*) altération, *f.*

corsair, corsaire, *m.*

corse, *see* CORPSE.

cors(e)let, ((*arm.*) corselet, *m.*

corset, corset, *m.*

Corsican, *adj.* (*when an adjective use small letter*) *and s.m.f.* Corse.

coruscat|e, scintiller; ~**ion,** coruscation, *f.*

corvette, (*nav.*) corvette, *f.*

cos lettuce, romaine, *f.*

cosmetic, *adj. and s.m.* cosmétique.

cosmic, cosmique.

cosmogony, cosmogonie, *f.*

cosmography, cosmographie, *f.*

cosmopolitan, *adj. and s.m.f.* cosmopolite.
Cossack, *s.* cosaque, *m.*; *adj.* de cosaque.
cost, *s.* (*price*) prix, *m.*; (*expense*) frais, *m.*; (*comm.*) coût, *m.*; **~s,** (*law*) dépens, *m.*; ~ *of labour,* prix de main-d'œuvre, *m.*; ~ *of living,* coût de la vie, *m.*; ~ **price,** prix de revient, *m.*; *at the ~ of,* au prix de.
cost, coûter; ~ *what it may,* coûte que coûte; ~ *dear,* coûter cher.
costive, constipé; **~ness,** constipation, *f.*
costl|y, (*dear*) coûteu|x, ~se; (*expensive*) dispendieu|x, ~se; (*sumptuous*) somptueu|x, ~se; **~iness,** (*implying lavish expenditure*) somptuosité, *f.*; (*expensiveness*) prix élevé, *m.*
costume, *s.* costume, *m.*
cos|y, (*pers.*) bien à l'aise; (*things*) confortable; **~ily,** confortablement.
cot, lit d'enfant, *m.*; (*naut.*) cadre, *m.*
coterie, coterie, *f.*
cothurnus, cothurne, *m.*
cotillion, cotillon, *m.*
cottage, chaumière, *f.*; ⚠ cottage *in French = 'small country house'*; ~ **piano,** piano droit, *m.*; **~r,** paysan, -ne, *m.f.*
cotton, (*substance and sewing*) coton, *m.*; (*fabric*) cotonnade, *f.*; **~-plant,** cotonnier, *m.*; **~-wool,** ouate, *f.*; ~ **yarn,** filé, *m.*
couch, *s.* lit de repos, *m.*; **~-grass,** (*bot.*) chiendent, *m.*
couch, *v.a.* (*spear*) tenir* en arrêt; (*in writing*) coucher; *v.n.* (*crouch*) s'accroupir; **~ed,** (*lying down on grass, &c.*) couché.
cough, toux, *f.*; *v.a.* tousser.
could, *see* CAN.
coulter, coutre, *m.*
council, conseil, *m.*; (*eccles.*) concile, *m.*; **~lor,** conseiller, *m.*
counsel, (*advice*) conseil, *m.*; (*pers.*) avocat, *m.*; *v.a.* conseiller (de); (*recommend*) recommander (de); **~lor,** conseiller, *m.*; *keep one's own ~,* garder son secret.
count, *s.* (*pers.*) comte, *m.*
count, *v.a.n.* compter; ~ *in,* comprendre*; ~ *out,* (*money*) compter; ~ *up,* additionner.
countenance, (*face*) visage, *m.*; (*air*) air, *m.*; (*support*) appui, *m.*; *out of ~,* décontenancé; *keep one's ~,* garder son sérieux; *v.a.* favoriser.
counter, *s.* (*shop*) comptoir, *m.*; (*P.O. or bank*) guichet, *m.*; (*cards, &c.*) jeton, *m.*
counter, *adj.* (*opposite, opposed*) contraire.
counter to, *adv. run, go ~ ~,* aller* (être) à l'encontre de.
counter, *v.a.* s'opposer à.
counter, *in compounds generally* contre-; ~ **-attraction,** attraction contraire, *f.*; ~ **-current,** contre-courant, *m.*; ~ **-declaration,** contre-déclaration, *f.*; ~ **-irritant,** (*med.*) révulsif, *m.*; ~ **-motion,** (*proposal*) contre-proposition, *f.*; ~ **-pressure,** contre-pression, *f.*; ~ **-proof,** contre-épreuve, *f.*; ~ **-revolution,** contre-révolution, *f.*
counteract, (*thwart*) déjouer.
counterbalance, *s.* contrepoids, *m.*; *v.a.* contre-balancer.
countercharge, *s.* contre-accusation, *f.*
counterfeit, *s.* contrefaçon, *f.*; *adj.* (*coin*) faux, fausse; *v.a.* contrefaire*.
counterfoil, *s.* (*receipt, cheque*) talon, *m.*
countermand, décommander.
countermarch, contremarche, *f.*
countermine, contre-mine, *f.*; *v.a.* contreminer.
counterpane, courtepointe, *f.*
counterpart, contre-partie, *f.*
counterpoise, contrepoids, *m.*
countersign, *v.a.* contresigner.
countess, comtesse, *f.*
counting, *s.* (*goods*) comptage, *m.*; (*words, &c.*) compte, *m.*; ~ **-house,** bureau, *m.*; ~ *of ballot,* dépouillement du scrutin, *f.*
countless, innombrable.
countrified, campagnard.
country, (*of a nation*) pays, *m.*; (*not town*) campagne, *f.*; (*fatherland*) patrie, *f.*; (*not the capital*) province, *f.*; **~-dance,** contredanse, *f.*; ~ **gentleman,** (*squire*) †hobereau, *m.*; ~ **house,** (*small*) maison de campagne, *f.*; ~ **seat,** château, *m.*; ~ **squire,** †hobereau, *m.*
country|man, ~ woman, (*rustic*) campagnard, -e, *m.f.*; (*of the same country*) compatriote, *m.f.*
county, (*in England*) comté, *m.*; ~ **town,** chef-lieu de comté, *m.*
couple, *s.* (*pers., things, ans.*) couple, *f.*; *v.a.* coupler.
couplet, distique, *m.*; ⚠ couplet = *properly 'stanza'.*
coupling, accouplement, *m.*
coupon, coupon, *m.*
courage, courage, *m.*; **~ous,** courageu|x, ~se; **~ously,** courageusement.
courier, courrier, *m.*
course, *s.* (*life, events, lectures, &c., river*) cours, *m.*; (*direction*) direction, *f.*; (*meal*) service, *m.*; (*career*) carrière, *f.*; (*ship*) route, *f.*; (*year, month, &c.*) courant, *m.*; ~ *of events,* cours des événements, *m.*; *of ~,* bien entendu; *keep a straight ~,* aller* (être) tout droit; *v.a.* (*game*) courir*; *v.n.* (*liquids*) couler.
courser, coursier, *m.*
coursing, *s.* chasse au lévrier, *f.*
court, *s.* (*of sovereign, state reception, of exhibitions, quadrangle, courtyard, justice*) cour, *f.*; (*of inquiry*) commission, *f.*; **~-martial,** conseil de guerre, *m.*; *drum-head ~-martial,* conseil de guerre improvisé; **~-plaster,** taffetas d'Angleterre, *m.*; *pay ~ to,* faire* la cour à.
court, *v.a.* faire* la cour à; (*woo and Muses*) courtiser; (*solicit*) rechercher; (*invite disaster, &c.*) aller au devant de; (*seek to win*) demander.

courteous, courtois (à); **~ly,** courtoisement.
courtesan, courtisane, *f.*
courtesy, courteousness, courtoisie, *f.*
courtier, courtisan, *m.*; ⚠ courtier = '*broker*', '*agent*'.
courtl|y, *adj.* (*to ladies*) galant; (*flattering*) obséquieu|x, ~se; **~iness,** élégance, *f.*
courtship, cour, *f.*
cousin, cousin, -e, *m.f.*; *first* ~, cousin, -e germain, -e, *m.f.*
cove, (*bay*) anse, *f.*; (*pers. fam.*) type, *m.*
covenant, pacte, *m.*; (*law*) contrat, *m.*; *v.n.* convenir* (être) (de).
cover, (*gen., book, comm.*) couverture, *f.*; (*box, pot*) couvercle, *m.*; (*chair*) †housse, *f.*; (*dish*) couvre-plat, *m.*, *pl.* couvre-plats; (*knife and fork, protection, undergrowth, &c., sheltering game*) couvert, *m.*; (*envelope*) pli, *m.*; *under* ~, à couvert; *under* ~ *of*, à l'abri de.
cover, *v.a.* (*gen., hide, clothe, overwhelm, risks, expenses, comm.*) couvrir*; (*with rifle*) tenir* en joue; (*protect*) protéger; (*distance*) faire*; ~ *over, up*, recouvrir*.
cover|ing, *s.* couverture, *f.*; **~let,** couvre-pied, *m.*
covert, *s.* fourré, *m.*; (*hiding-place*) gîte, *m.*
covert, *adj.* secr|et, ~ète; **~ly,** secrètement.
covet, convoiter; **~ous,** avide (de); (*avaricious*) avare; **~ousness,** convoitise, *f.*
covey, (*partridges*) couvée, *f.*
coving, (*arch.*) voussure, *f.*
cow, vache, *f.*; (*of elephant, whale, &c.*) femelle, *f.*; **~herd, ~-man,** vacher, *m.*; **~-grass,** trèfle des prés, *m.*; **~-house,** vacherie, *f.*; **~-parsnip,** (*bot.*) berce, *f.*
cow, *v.a.* intimider.
coward, lâche, *m.*; **~ice, ~liness,** lâcheté, *f.*; **~ly,** *adj.* lâche; **~ly,** *adv.* en lâche.
cowboy, (*U.S.A.*) cowboy, *m.*
cower, s'accroupir.
cowl, (*monk, chimney*) capuchon, *m.*
cowslip, coucou, *m.*
coxcomb, fat, *m.*
coxswain, patron de canot, *m.*
coy, timide; **~ness,** timidité, *f.*; **~ly,** timidement.
cozen, *v.a.* duper.
crab, crabe, *m.*; ~ **-apple,** pomme sauvage, *f.*; **~-~-tree,** pommier sauvage, *m.*
crabbed, (*pers.*) acariâtre; (*writing*) illisible; (*style*) embarrassé.
crack, *s.* (*fissure, chink*) fente, *f.*; (*glass, china*) fêlure, *f.*; (*sound*) craquement, *m.*
crack, *adj.* (*super-excellent*) de premier ordre; (*regt., &c.*) d'élite; **~-brained,** fêlé.
crack, *v.a.* (*nut*) casser; (*whip*) faire claquer; (*glass, &c.*) fêler; (*joke*) faire*; ~ *up*, (*fam. praise*) prôner; **~ed,** (*pers.*) timbré.
crack, *v.n.* (*split*) se fendiller; (*whip*) claquer; (*sound*) craquer; (*voice*) se casser; (*china, glass*) se fêler.
cracker, (*firework*) pétard, *m.*
crackl|e, (*fire*) pétiller; **~ing,** pétillement, *m.*
cradle, (*lit., fig., naut.*) berceau, *m.*
craft, (*skill*) habileté, *f.*; (*trade*) métier, *m.*; (*cunning*) ruse, *f.*; (*naut.*) embarcation, *f.*
craft|y, astucieu|x, ~se; **~ily,** astucieusement.
craftsman, artisan, *m.*
crag, rocher escarpé, *m.*; **~gy,** escarpé.
crake, (*ornith.*) râle, *m.*
cram, *v.a.* (*thrust in*) fourrer; (*with food, pupil*) bourrer, *v.n.*; ~ *for* (*exam.*) préparer un examen pour; **~med,** ~ *full*, bondé (de).
crammer, (*exams.*) répétiteur, *m.*; **~'s,** (*establishment*) usine à bachot, *f.*
cramp, (*med.*) crampe, *f.*; (*cramp-iron*) crampon, *m.*; *be* **~ed,** être à l'étroit; **~ed,** (*style*) contraint.
cranberry, canneberge, *f.*
crane, (*ornith. and mach.*) grue, *f.*; **~'s-bill,** (*bot.*) bec de grue, *m.*
cranium, crâne, *m.*
crank, (*mach.*) manivelle, *f.*; (*pers.*) excentrique, *m.*; **~y,** excentrique.
cranny, crevasse, *f.*
crape, crêpe, *m.*
crash, fracas, *m.*; (*fig.*) débâcle, *f.*; (*financial*) krach, *m.*; (*aeron.*) casse, *f.*; *v.a.* fracasser; *v.n.* tomber (être) avec fracas; (*aeron.*) casser.
crass, (*ignorance, &c.*) crasse.
crate, caisse à claire-voie, *f.*; (*for china*) †harasse, *f.*
crater, cratère, *m.*
cravat, cravate, *f.*
crave, (*beg for*) implorer; (*long for*) désirer ardemment.
craven, lâche.
craving, *s.* désir ardent, *m.*
crawl, *v.n.* (*worms, &c.*) ramper; (*pers.*) se traîner.
crayfish, crawfish, écrevisse, *f.*
crayon, crayon, *m.*
craze, *s.* (*insane fancy*) engouement, *m.*; *have a* ~ *for*, avoir la passion de.
craz|y, (*pers.*) toqué; (*things, rickety*) cadu|c, ~que; **~iness,** (*pers.*) folie, *f.*
creak, *s.* grincement, *m.*; *v.n.* grincer.
cream, (*lit. and fig.*) crème, *f.*; ~ **-cheese,** fromage à la crème; ~ **puff,** chou à la crème, *m.*; ~ **-coloured,** crème, *invar.*; **~-laid,** (*note-paper*) vergé blanc; **~y,** crémeu|x, ~se.
creamery, crémerie, *f.*
crease, *s.* pli, *m.*; *v.a.* (*rumple*) froisser; (*fold*) faire* des plis à.
creat|e, (*lit. and fig.*) créer; **~ion,** création, *f.*; **~or,** (*also 'inventor'*) créat|eur, ~rice, *m.f.*; **~ive,** créat|eur, ~rice.
creature, (*lit., fig., protégé, pej.*) créature, *f.*

credence, *give* ~ *to,* ajouter foi à; ~**-table,** crédence, *f.*
credentials, lettres de créance, *f.*; (*testimonial, character for servants*) certificat, *m.*
credib|le, croyable; ~**ility,** crédibilité, *f.*
credit, *s.* (*reputation, influence, time to pay, bank, bkkpg.*) crédit, *m.*; (*merit, source of honour*) honneur, *m.*; *on* ~, à terme; *give* ~ *for,* (*to*) passer au crédit de; *give* ~ *to,* (*believe*) ajouter foi à; *give* ~ *for,* (*attribute to*) attribuer à; ~ **side,** (*bkkpg.*) avoir, *m.*; *on the* ~ *side,* acti|f, ~ve; *debit and* ~ *sides,* doit et avoir; *standing to* ~ *of,* porté à crédit de.
credit, *v.a.* ajouter foi à; (*comm.*) créditer; ~ *with,* (*virtue, &c.*) attribuer (*acc. of thing,* à *pers.*).
creditabl|e, honorable; ~**y,** honorablement.
creditor, créancier, *m.*; *debtor and* ~ *sides,* (*bkkpg.*) doit et avoir.
credul|ity, crédulité, *f.*; ~**ous,** crédule.
creed, (*eccles.*) crédo, *m.*; (*belief*) croyance, *f.*
creek, (*sea*) crique, *f.*; (*U.S.A.*) affluent, *m.*
creep, *v.n.* (*as worms and fig.*) ramper; (*plants*) grimper; (*without noise*) se glisser; ~ *out,* sortir* sans bruit; ~**ing,** *adj.* rampant; ~**ing crowfoot,** (*bot.*) bassinet, *m.*
creeper, (*bot.*) plante grimpante, *f.*; **tree** ~, (*ornith.*) grimpereau, *m.*
creeps, *give one the* ~, donner la chair de poule à.
cremat|e, incinérer; ~**ion,** crémation, *f.*; ~**orium,** four crématoire, *m.*
crenellated, (*fort.*) crénelé.
creole, *adj. and s.m.f.* créole.
creosote, créosote, *f.*
crepitat|e, crépiter; ~**ion,** crépitation, *f.*
crescent, (*moon, Turkish empire and relig.*) croissant, *m.*; (*row of houses approx.*) demi-lune, *f.*; *adj.* croissant.
cress, (*also* **water**~) cresson, *m.*
cresset, torchère, *f.*
crest, *s.* (*hills, cock, fig.*) crête, *f.*; (*helmet, arms*) cimier, *m.*; (*birds*) †huppe, *f.*; ~*-fallen,* l'oreille basse ; ~**ed,** (*birds*) †huppé; ~*ed lark, see* LARK; *golden-*~*ed wren, see* WREN.
Cretan, *adj.* (*when an adjective use small letter*) *and s.m.f.* Crétois, -e.
cretin, crétin, *m.*
crevasse, crevasse, *f.*
crevice, (*in wall, &c.*) lézarde, *f.*
crew, (*naut.*) équipage, *m.*; (*gang*) bande, *f.*
crib, *s.* (*horses*) mangeoire, *f.*; (*cradle*) berceau, *m.*; (*hovel*) cahute, *f.*; (*U.S.A.*) coffre, *m.*
crick, *s.* (*in neck*) torticolis, *m.*
cricket, (*insect*) grillon, *m.*; (*game*) cricket, *m.*; ~**-ground,** terrain de cricket, *m.*
crier, (*street*) crieu|r, ~se, *m.f.*
crim|e, crime, *m.*; ~**inal,** *adj. and s.m.f.* criminel, -le; ~**inally,** criminellement; ~**inality,** criminalité, *f.*
crimp, *s.* (*mil., nav.*) racoleur, *m.*
crimp, (*hair*) friser; (*paper, &c.*) gaufrer.
crimson, *adj. and s.m.* cramoisi; *v.n.* rougir.
cring|e, faire* le chien couchant (auprès de); ~**ing,** attitude servile, *f.*
crinkle, *v.a.* rider.
crinoline, crinoline, *f.*
cripple, *s.* boiteu|x, ~euse. *m.f.*; ~**d,** perclus (de); *v.a.* estropier.
crisis, crise, *f.*
crisp, (*pastry, &c.*) croquant; (*brittle*) fragile; (*which crunches under teeth*) croustillant; (*air*) vif, vive; (*style*) net, nette; *be* ~, (*snow, &c.*) craquer; ~**ness,** qualité croquante, croustillante, *f.*; (*style*) netteté, *f.*
criterion, critérium, *m.* (*pl.* s).
critic, critique, *m.*; ~**al,** critique; ~**ally,** (*ill*) gravement.
critic|ism, critique, *f.*; ~**ize,** critiquer.
croak, *s.* (*frog*) coassement, *m.*; (*crows*) croassement, *m.*; *v.n.* (*frogs*) coasser; (*crows*) croasser; ~**er,** grognon, *m.*
Croat, *s.m.f.* Croate; ~**ian,** croate.
crochet, (*work*) crochet, *m.*; ~**-needle,** crochet, *m.*
crock, *s.* (*pot*) pot de terre, *m.*
crockery, faïence, *f.*
crocodile, crocodile, *m.*
crocus, crocus, *m.*
cromlech, cromlech, *m.*
crone, vieille femme, *f.*
crony, copain, *m.*
crook, *s.* (*shepherd's*) †houlette, *f.*; (*pers. slang*) escroc, *m.*; ~ **-back(ed),** *adj.* bossu.
crooked, (*winding, dishonest*) tortueu|x, ~se; (*legs, nose, trees, &c.*) tortu; ~**ly,** de travers.
crop, (*of the land*) récolte, *f.*; (*birds*) jabot, *m.*; (*fruit*) cueillette, *f.*
crop, *v.a.* (*browse*) brouter; (*harvest*) moissonner; (*hair, &c.*) couper court; *v.n.* ~ *up,* surgir.
cropper, *s.* (*slang*); *come a* ~, (*lit. and fig.*) ramasser une pelle.
croquet, (*game*) croquet, *m.*
crosier, (*eccles.*) crosse, *f.*
cross, *s.* (*lit., fig., order, eccles., cross-shaped thing, tribulation*) croix, *f.*; (*mixture of breed and ans. from this*) croisement, *m.*
cross, *adj.* (*transverse*) transversal; (*peevish*) maussade; (*breed*) croisé; (*contrary*) contraire (à); *Grand Cross,* (*order*) grand'croix, *f. invar.*; ~**ness,** mauvaise humeur, *f.*; ~**ly,** avec mauvaise humeur; ~**-bow,** arbalète, *f.*; ~**-examination,** contre-interrogatoire, *m.*; ~**-examine,** faire* subir un contre-interrogatoire; ~**-grained** (*pers.*) revêche; ~**-legged,** *adv.* les jambes croisées; ~**-purposes,** *be at,* ne pas s'entendre; ~**-question,** contre-examiner; ~**-road,** chemin de traverse, *m.*; ~**-roads,** carrefour, *m.*; ~**word puzzle,** problème de mots croisés,

m.; **~-country,** *adj. and adv.* à travers champs.
cross, *v.a.* croiser; (*the mind, also go across*) traverser; (*cheques, t's*) barrer; (*writing*) écrire* en travers; (*thwart*) contrecarrer; ~ *oneself,* se signer; ~ **off, out,** rayer; ~ **over,** traverser; ~*ed cheque, see* CHEQUE.
cross, *v.n.* (*meet and pass, letters, &c.*) se croiser; (*go across*) traverser.
crossbill, (*ornith.*) bec croisé, *m.*
crossing, (*street*) passage, *m.*; (*sea, &c.*) traversée, *f.*; *level-~, see* LEVEL; *pedestrian ~, see* PEDESTRIAN.
crotchet, (*fad*) lubie, *f.*; (*mus.*) noire, *f.*; **~y,** fantasque.
crouch, (*an.*) se blottir; *~ing, adj.* couché.
croup, (*med.*) croup, *m.*; (*hind-quarters esp. of horse*) croupe, *f.*
crow, *s.* (*ornith.*) corneille, *f.*; **~-bar,** levier, *m.*; *~'s foot,* (*wrinkle*) patte d'oie, *f.*; *~'s nest,* (*naut.*) nid de pie, *m.*; *as the ~ flies,* à vol d'oiseau.
crowberry, camarine, *f.*
crowd, foule, *f.*; (*pej.*) bande, *f.*; (*quantity*) tas, *m.*; *v.a.* ~ **with,** bonder de; (*stuff with*) bourrer de; ~ **into,** entasser dans.
crowd, *v.n.* (*go in quantities*) affluer; ~ **round,** se presser autour de; **~ed,** (*streets, &c.*) encombré (de).
crowfoot, (*bot.*) renoncule, *f.*
crown, *s.* couronne, *f.*; (*head, mountain*) sommet, *m.*; (*of hat*) calotte, *f.*; *v.a.* (*lit. and fig.*) couronner; (*put finishing touch to*) mettre* le comble à.
crucial, décisi|f, ~ve; ⚠ crucial = '*in the form of a cross*'.
crucible, (*eccles. and fig.*) creuset, *m.*
crucif|ix, crucifix, *m.*; **~ixion,** crucifixion, *f.*; **~y,** crucifier.
cruciform, cruciforme.
crude, (*unrefined and of products*) brut; (*manners, expressions*) cru; (*not artistically made*) grossi|er, ~ère; **~ness,** crudité, *f.*; **~ly,** (*bluntly, without reserve*) crûment.
cruel, cruel, -le; **~ly,** cruellement.
cruelty, cruauté, *f.*
cruet, (*glass bottle*) burette, *f.*; **~-stand,** huilier, *m.*
cruise, *s.* (*approx. pleasure*) voyage, *m.*; *v.n.* (*naut.*) croiser.
cruiser, croiseur, *m.*; *armoured ~,* croiseur cuirassé, *m.*
crumb, (*not crust*) mie, *f.*; (*piece*) miette, *f.*
crumble, *v.a.* émietter; *v.n.* s'émietter; (*fig.*) s'écrouler.
crumbly, friable.
crumple, *v.a.* chiffonner; *v.n.* se chiffonner.
crunch, *v.a.* croquer.
crupper, (*horse*) croupe, *f.*
crusade, croisade, *f.*; **~r,** croisé, *m.*
crush, *s.* (*people*) cohue, *f.*; ~ **hat,** gibus, *m.*
crush, *v.a.* (*lit. and fig.*) écraser; (*crumple*) froisser.
crust, (*not crumb and fig.*) croûte, *f.*; (*piece of bread*) croûton, *m.*; (*of the earth*) écorce, *f.*; **~y,** (*crisp*) croquant; (*pers.*) bourru.
crutch, béquille, *f.*
cry, *s.* cri, *m.*; *v.a.* crier; ~ **down,** décrier; ~ **up,** prôner; *v.n.* (*shout*) crier; (*exclaim*) s'écrier; (*weep*) pleurer; ~ **out,** crier; ~ **out for,** demander à grands cris; **~off,** n'en être plus.
crying, *adj.* (*lit. and fig.*) criant.
crypt, crypte, *f.*
cryptic, occulte.
crystal, *s.* cristal, *m.*; *adj.* de cristal; ~ **set,** (*wireless*) poste à galène, *m.*; **~lize,** *v.a.* cristalliser; *v.n.* se cristalliser.
cub, *s.* (*bear*) ourson, *m.*; (*lion*) lionceau, *m.*; (*wolf*) louveteau, *m.*; (*fox*) renardeau, *m.*; (*other ans.*) petit, *m.*; *unlicked ~,* (*pers.*) ours mal léché, *m.*; *v.a.* mettre* bas.
cub|e, cube, *m.*; **~e-root,** racine cubique, *f.*; **~ic,** cubique; **~ism,** *s.* (*art*) cubisme, *m.*
cubicle, (*approx.*) alcôve, *f.*
cubit, coudée, *f.*
cuckold, cocu, *m.*
cuckoo, coucou, *m.*; ⚠ coucou (*bot.*) = '*cowslip*'; **~-flower,** cresson des prés, *m.*; **~-pint,** (*bot.*) arum, *m.*
cucumber, concombre, *m.*
cud, *s. chew the ~,* ruminer.
cuddle, *v.a.* dorloter; (*colloq.*) peloter; *v.n.* se serrer.
cudgel, *s.* gourdin, *m.*; **~ling,** bastonnade, *f.*; *v.a.* bâtonner.
cue, (*billiards*) queue, *f.*; (*theatr.*) réplique, *f.*
cuff, *s.* parement, *m.*; (*wristband*) poignet, *m.*; (*blow*) taloche, *f.*; *v.a.* (*strike*) talocher.
cuirass, cuirasse, *f.*; **~ier,** cuirassier, *m.*
culinary, culinaire.
cull, (*pick*) cueillir*; (*select*) choisir.
culminat|e, se terminer (par *and* à); **~tion,** fin, *f.* ⚠ culminer *and* culmination *are properly astronomical terms.*
culpab|ility, culpabilité, *f.*; **~le,** coupable; **~ly,** d'une façon coupable.
culprit, coupable, *s.m.f.*
cult, culte, *m.*
cultivat|e, (*lit. and fig.*) cultiver; **~ion,** cultivation, *f.*; **~or,** cultivateur, *m.*; *~ed mind,* esprit cultivé, *m.*
cultur|al, cultural; **~e,** (*lit. and fig.*) culture, *f.*
culverin, coulevrine, *f.*
culvert, conduit, *m.*
cumber, encombrer (de); (*of work, &c.*) accabler (de); **~some, cumbrous,** encombrant.
cum(m)in, (*bot.*) cumin, *m.*
cumulative, cumulati|f, ~ve.
cuneiform, cunéiforme.
cunning, *s.* (*artfulness*) ruse, *f.*; (*dexterity*) adresse, *f.*; *adj.* rusé; (*U.S.A.*) chic, *invar.*; **~ly,** avec ruse; (*skilfully*) avec adresse.

cup, *s.* tasse, *f.*; ⚠ *not* coupe, *f. which* = '*sports or wine-cup*' *or* '*cup*', *fig.*; (*eccles.*) calice, *m.*; *be in one's* ~*s*, être dans les vignes du Seigneur; *there 's many a slip between the* ~ *and the lip*, il y a loin de la coupe aux lèvres.
cupbearer, échanson, *m.*
cupboard, armoire, *f.*; (*in wall*) placard, *m.*; ~**-bed,** lit-clos, *m.*
cupidity, cupidité.
cupola, coupole, *f.*
cur, (*dog and fig.*) roquet, *m.*
curable, curable.
cura|cy, vicariat, *m.*; ~**te,** (*assistant priest*) vicaire, *m.*; ⚠ *not* curé *which* = '*vicar*'.
curative, curati|t, ~ve.
curator, (*museums, &c.*) conservateur, *m.*
curb, (*horse*) gourmette, *f.*; (*wells*) margelle, *f.*; *v.a.* (*horse*) gourmer; (*fig.*) brider.
curdle, *v.a.* cailler; *v.n.* se cailler.
curds, lait caillé, *m.*
cure, *s.* guérison, *f.*; (*remedy*) remède, *m.*; *v.a.* guérir; ⚠ *not* curer *which* = '*clean out*', '*pick teeth*'; (*salt*) saler; (*smoke*) fumer.
curfew, couvre-feu, *m.*
curio, curiosité, *f.*
curiosity, (*lit. and fig.*) curiosité, *f.*
curious, (*inquisitive, strange, odd*) curieu|x, ~se; ~**ly,** curieusement; (*oddly*) bizarrement; ~*ly enough*, chose assez curieuse.
curl, *s.* (*hair*) boucle, *f.*; (*smoke*) tourbillon, *m.*; (*lip*) pli, *m.*; ~**y,** (*hair*) frisé; *v.a.* (*hair*) friser; *v.n.* friser; ~ *up*, s'enrouler.
curlew, (*ornith.*) courlis, *m.*
curling, *s.* ~**-paper,** papillote, *f.*; ~**-irons, -tongs,** fer à friser, *m.*
curmudgeon, ladre, *m.*
currant, *black* ~, cassis, *m.*; *red* ~, groseille rouge, *f.*; *white* ~, groseille blanche, *f.*; ~**s,** (*dried*) raisin de Corinthe, *m.*; ~**-bush, -tree,** groseiller, *m.*
currency, (*money*) monnaie, *f.*; (*circulation*) cours, *m.*; (*of bill*) terme d'échéance, *m.*
current, (*water, air, electr.*) courant, *m.*; (*fig.*) cours, *m.*
current, *adj.* (*date, comm., coin*) courant; (*no. of newspaper*) du jour, de la semaine, etc.; ~ **account,** (*running a/c*) compte courant, *m.*; (*bank*) compte de dépôt (à vue) *m.*; ~ **price,** cours, *m.*
curriculum, programme d'études, *m.*
currier, corroyeur, *m.*
curry, *s.* (*powdered spice, &c.*) cari, kari, *m.*
curry, *v.a.* (*horse*) étriller.
curry-comb, *s.* étrille, *f.*
curse, *s.* malédiction, *f.*; (*oath*) juron, *m.*; (*scourge, bane*) fléau, *m.*; *v.a.* maudire*; (*fig.*) tourmenter; *v.n.* blasphémer; ~**d,** maudit.
cursive, cursi|f, ~ve.
cursor|y, rapide; ~**ily,** rapidement.
curt, brusque; ⚠ *not* court *which only* = '*short*', '*brief*'; ~**ly,** sèchement.
curtail, *v.a.* (*shorten*) raccourcir; (*of pay*) rogner; (*expenses*) réduire*; ~**ment,** diminution, *f.*
curtain, rideau, *m.*; (*fort*) courtine, *f.*; ~ *fire*, tir de barrage, *m.*; ~**-hook,** patère, *f.*; ~**-rod, -pole,** tringle, *f.*
curt|sy, ~**sey,** révérence, *f.*; *v.n.* faire la révérence.
curve, *s.* courbe, *f.*; *v.a.* courber; *v.n.* se courber; ~**d,** courbé.
curvet, *s.* (*horse*) courbette, *f.*
cushion, coussin, *m.*; (*billiards*) bande, *f.*
cusp, (*arch.*) lobe, *m.*
custard, crème aux œufs, *f.*; ~ **tart,** flan, *m.*
custodian, gardien, *m.*
custody, (*care*) garde, *f.*; (*arrest*) arrestation, *f.*; *in* ~, en état d'arrestation; *give into* ~, faire* arrêter; *take into* ~, arrêter.
custom, (*habit*) coutume, *f.*; (*business patronage*) clientèle, *f.*; ~**ary,** coutumi|er, ~ère.
customs, custom-house, douane, *f.*; ~**-officer,** douanier, *m.*
customer, client, *m.*
cut, *s.* (*weapon, knives, whip*) coup, *m.*; (*wound*) coupure, *f.*; (*clothes, beard, &c., coat, cards*) coupe, *f.*; (*meat, &c.*) morceau, *m.*; (*in wages, dividend*) réduction, *f.*; **short** ~, traverse, *f.*
cut, *v.a.* couper; (*sever, carve*) trancher; (*to special shape*) tailler; (*heart*) fendre; (*pers.*) faire* semblant de ne pas voir; (*teeth*) percer; (*cards*) couper; ~ *short*, (*pers.*) couper la parole à; ~ *a way through*, se frayer chemin au travers de; ~ *and thrust*, frapper d'estoc et de taille; ~ **down,** (*fell*) abattre; (*expenses*) réduire*; (*mil.*) sabrer; ~ **off,** (*limb, life, communication, separate, teleph.*) couper; (*disinherit*) déshériter; *I'm* ~ *off!* (*teleph.*) on m'a coupé; ~ **out,** (*shape, carve*) tailler; (*surpass*) éclipser; (*remove*) retrancher; (*assign, mark out*) tracer d'avance; ~ **up,** (*army, &c.*) mettre* en pièces; ~ **up,** *p.p.* (*with grief*) accablé (de douleur); ~ **-glass,** cristal taillé, *m.*
cut, *v.n.* (*knives, &c., cards, take short cut*) couper; (*eatables*) se couper; ~ *and run*, se trotter.
cutaneous, cutané.
cute, (*U.S.A.*) épatant; (*cunning*) rusé.
cutlass, coutelas, *m.*
cutler, coutelier, *m.*; ~**y,** coutellerie, *f.*
cutlet, côtelette, *f.*
cut-out, (*electr.*) coupe-circuit, *m.*; (*motor*) disjoncteur, *m.*
cutpurse, coupeur de bourse, *m.*
cut-throat, coupe-jarret, *m.* (*pl.* coupe-jarrets.)
cutter, (*stone, &c.*) tailleur, *m.*; (*tailor's*) coupeur, *m.*; (*naut.*) cotre, *m.*

cutting, *s.* (*hort.*) bouture, *f.*; (*newspaper*) coupure, *f.*; (*rail.*) voie en déblai, *f.*
cutting, *adj.* (*fig.*) mordant; (*wind, &c.*) piquant.
cuttle-fish, seiche, *f.*
cwt., quintal, *m.*
cycl|e, (*period, series*) cycle, *m.*; (*bicycle*) bicyclette, *f.*; *v.n.* faire* de la bicyclette; **~ing,** *s.* cyclisme, *m.*
cyclone, cyclone, *m.*
cyclops, cyclope, *m.*
cygnet, jeune cygne, *m.*
cylind|er, cylindre, *m.*; **~rical,** cylindrique.
cymbal, cymbale, *f.*
cynic, *s.* cynique, *m.*; **~ism,** cynisme, *m.*; **~al,** cynique; **~ally,** avec cynisme.
cynosure, (*centre of attraction*) point de mire, *m.*
cypher, *see* CIPHER.
cypress-tree, cyprès, *m.*
cytisus, (*bot.*) cytise, *m.*
czar, tsar, *m.*; **~ina,** tsarine, *f.*; **~evitch,** tsarévitch, *m.*

D

dab, *s.* (*lump*) petit morceau, *m.*; (*icth.*) limande, *f.*; *be a ~ at,* (*pop.*) avoir le chic de; *v.a.* tamponner.
dabble, (*paddle*) barboter; (*Stock Exch.*) boursicoter; *~ in,* se mêler de.
dabchick, (*ornith.*) petit grèbe, *m.*
dace, (*ichth.*) vandoise, *f.*
dad, daddy, papa, *m.*; *~ long-legs,* faucheux, *m.*
dado, lambris, *m.*
daffodil, narcisse, *m.*
daft, toqué.
dagger, poignard, *m.*; *at ~s drawn,* à couteaux tirés; *look ~s at,* regarder avec des yeux de basilic.
daguerreotype, daguerréotype, *m.*
dahlia, (*bot.*) dahlia, *m.*
daily, *s.* (*paper*) quotidien, *m.*; *adj.* quotidien; (*done daily*) journali|er, ~ère; *~ bread,* pain quotidien, *m.*; *adv.* tous les jours.
daint|y, *s.* friandise, *f.*; *adj.* délicat; (*choice*) de choix; (*pretty and small*) mignon, -ne; **~ily,** délicatement.
dairy, laiterie, *f.*; **~maid,** fille de laiterie, *f.*; **~man,** laitier, *m.*
dais, estrade, *f.*; ⚠ *not* dais *which* = '*canopy*'.
daisy, (*small*) pâquerette, *f.*; (*ox-eyed*) marguerite, *f.*
dale, vallon, *m.*; *up hill and down ~,* par monts et par vaux.
dall|y, *v.n.* (*trifle*) s'amuser; (*play*) folâtrer; *~ with,* (*fig.*) jouer avec; **~iance,** badinage, *m.*
dalmatic, (*eccles. and royal*) dalmatique, *f.*
dam, (*animals*) mère, *f.*; (*water-barrier*) digue, *f.*; (*river*) barrage, *m.*; (*mill*) écluse, *f.*
damage, dommage, *m.*; (*detriment*) préjudice, *m.*; (*mishap, naut.*) avaries, *f.pl.*; *~ in transit,* avaries de route, *f.pl.*; **~s,** (*law, &c.*) dommages-intérêts, *m.pl.*; **~d,** (*goods, &c.*) avarié; *v.a.* endommager; (*comm.*) avarier.
damascene, *v.a.* damasquiner.
damask, damas, *m.*
dame, dame, *f.*
damn, *s.* juron, *m.*; **~ation,** damnation, *f.*
damn, *v.a.* (*eccles.*) damner; (*fig. and ruin*) condamner; (*swearing, interj.*) le diable emporte . . .
damnable, maudit; (*eccles.*) damnable.
damned, *adj.* sacré.
damp, *adj.* humide; **~ness,** humidité, *f.*; *v.a.* **~en,** humecter.
damper, (*chimneys*) registre, *m.*
damsel, jeune fille, *f.*
damson, prune de damas, *f.*
danc|e, ~ing, *s.* danse, *f.*; (*ball*) bal, *m.*; *v.a.n.* danser; **~er,** danseu|r, ~se, *m.f.*; *~ing master,* maître de danse, *m.*
dandelion, (*bot.*) pissenlit, *m.*
dandle, *v.a.* bercer; (*fondle*) dorloter.
dandruff, pellicule, *f.*
dandy, élégant, *m.*; *adj.* (*U.S.A.*) élégant.
Dan|e, Danois, -e, *m.f.*; **~ish,** *adj.* danois; **~ish,** (*lang.*) *s.* danois, *m.*
danewort, (*bot.*) hièble, *f.*
danger, danger, *m.*; **~ous,** dangereu|x, ~se; **~ously,** dangereusement.
dangle, *v.n.* pendiller.
dank, *adj.* humide.
daphne, (*bot.*) daphné, *m.*
dapple, *v.a.* tacheter; **~-grey,** *adj.* gris pommelé, *invar*; **~d,** (*horse*) pommelé.
dapper, *adj.* fringant.
dare, oser; *v.a.* (*defy*) défier (de); *~ to,* oser + *inf.*; *I ~ say,* sans doute.
dare-devil, *s.* risque-tout, *m. invar.*
daring, *adj.* audacieu|x, ~se; **~ly,** audacieusement.
dark, *adj.* obscur; (*with colours*) foncé, *e.g.* bleu foncé, *&c., invar.*; (*fig.*) triste; *be ~,* faire* sombre; *grow ~,* commencer à faire* sombre; **~ lantern,** lanterne sourde, *f.*; **~ness,** obscurité, *f.*; **~ly,** (*fig.*) obscurément.
darken, *v.a.* obscurcir; (*paint.*) assourdir; (*fig.*) attrister; *v.n.* s'obscurcir.
darling, *adj. and s.m.f.* chéri, -e.
darn, *s.* reprise, *f.*; *v.a.* repriser; **~ing needle,** aiguille à repriser, *f.*
darnel, (*bot.*) ivraie, *f.*
dart, dard, *m.*; (*fig.*) trait, *m.*; *v.a.* (*throw*) lancer; (*rays, glance*) darder; *v.n.* (*rush*) se précipiter.
dash, *s.* (*pen*) trait, *m.*; (*water*) brisement, *m.*; (*paint.*) touche légère, *f.*; (*drop*) filet, *m.*; (*vigour*) fougue, *f.*; *cut a dash,* faire* figure; *v.a.* (*throw*) lancer; (*hopes, &c.*) détruire*; *~ to pieces,* briser en morceaux; *v.n.* (*rush*) se précipiter; *~ against,* se †heurter contre.
dash-board, (*motor*) tablier, *m.*

dashing, (*fiery*) fougueu|x, ~se; (*smart*) fringant.
dastard, *s.* lâche, *m.*; **~ly,** lâche; **~liness,** lâcheté, *f.*
data, données, *f.pl.*
date, (*fruit*) datte, *f.*; **~-tree,** dattier, *m.*
date, *s.* (*day*) date, *f.*; (*coins, &c.*) millésime, *m.*; *at an early ~*, à une date prochaine; *out of ~*, démodé; *to ~*, à ce jour; *be up to ~*, (*be in the swim*) être à la page; *up to ~*, (*bkkpg.*) à jour; *bring up to ~*, mettre* à jour; *under ~ of*, à la date de; *v.a.n.* dater; *long-, short- ~d bill, see* BILL; *~ of dispatch*, date d'envoi, *f.*
dative, *s.* (*gram.*) datif, *m.*
datura, (*bot.*) datura, *m.*
daub, (*painting*) croûte, *f.*; **~er,** (*bad artist*) barbouilleur, *m.*; *v.n.* barbouiller.
daughter, fille, *f.*; *~-in-law*, belle-fille; **~ly,** filial.
daunt, *v.a.* décourager; **~less,** intrépide; **~lessness,** intrépidité, *f.*
Dauphin, ~ess, Dauphin, -e, *m.f.*
davit, (*naut.*) portemanteau, *m.*
Davy-lamp, (*mine*) lampe de sûreté, *f.*
dawdle, *v.n.* musarder; **~r,** musard, *m.*
dawn, point du jour, *m.*; (*fig.*) aurore, *f.*; *v.n.* poindre*.
dawning, *adj.* (*fig.*) naissant.
day, jour, *m.*; (*whole day, day's work*) journée, *f.*; (*period, of time, of prosperity, prime of life*) temps, *m.*; *~ before*, veille, *f.*; *~ before yesterday*, avant-hier, *m.*; *~ after, next ~*, lendemain, *m.*; *the ~ after tomorrow*, après-demain; **~-dream,** rêverie, *f.*; **~ -dreamer,** songe-creux, *m.*; **~ -labourer,** journalier, *m.*; **~ -lily,** (*bot.*) belle d'un jour, *m.*; ⚠ belle de jour, *f.* = *small ground convolvulus*; **~ -scholar,** externe, *m.f.*; *~'s notice*, préavis d'un jour franc, *m.*; *ten full ~s*, dix jours francs; *every other ~*, tous les deux jours; *eight-hour day*, journée de huit heures; *working- ~s*, jours ouvrables, *m.pl.*; *in these ~s*, de nos jours; *from ~ to ~*, au jour le jour; *carry the ~*, (*fig.*) avoir gain de cause; *win the ~*, (*mil.*) gagner la journée; *in ~s gone by*, au temps jadis.
daylight, (*lit. and fig.*) jour, *m.*
daze, *v.a.* (*with blow, &c.*) étourdir; (*light*) éblouir.
dazzl|e, *v.a.* éblouir; **~ing,** éblouissant.
deacon, -ess, diac|re, ~onesse, *m.f.*
dead, *s.* (*winter*) cœur, *m.*; (*night*) milieu, *m.*; *the ~*, *pl.* les morts, *m.pl.*
dead, *adj.* **1** (*lit., fig., hours, languages, weight, season, letter, obsolete*) mort; **2** (*colours*) mat; **3** (*deaf, insensible*) sourd (à); **4** (*dull*) lourd; **5** (*business*) stagnant; **6** (*money*) qui dort; **7** (*sleep*) profond; **8** (*sound*) sourd; *~ beat, see* BEAT; *~ body, see* BODY; *~ calm, see* CALM; *~ certainty, see* CERTAINTY; **~-letter office,** bureau de rebuts, *m.*; **~ loss,** perte sèche, *f.*; **~ march,** marche funèbre, *f.*; **~-nettle,** ortie blanche, *f.*
dead, *adv.* en plein.
deaden, (*a blow, fall*) amortir; (*sound*) assourdir.
deadlock, impasse, *f.*
deadly, mortel, -le; (*sins*) capital; *~ nightshade, see* NIGHTSHADE.
deaf, sourd; (*fig.*) insensible (à); **~ness,** surdité, *f.*; *~ as a post, stone ~*, sourd comme un pot.
deafen, assourdir; **~ing,** assourdissant.
deal, *s.* (*comm.*) opération, *f.*; (*quantity*) quantité, *f.*; (*cards*) donne, *f.*; (*wood*) bois de sapin, *m.*; *a good ~, a great ~*, beaucoup (de).
deal, ~ out, *v.a.* distribuer; (*cards*) donner.
deal, *v.n.* (*comm.*) traiter (avec); *~ in*, commercer de; *v.a.* (*cards*) donner.
dealer, marchand, *m.*; *marine store ~*, fournisseur maritime, *m.*; *provision ~*, marchand de comestibles, *m.*
dealing, (*comm.*) négotiation, *f.*; *double-~*, duplicité, *f.*; *square ~*, procédés honnêtes, *m.pl.*
dean, (*eccles. and univ.*) doyen, *m.*
dear, *s.* (*beloved*) cher, chère, *m.f.*; *adj.* (*beloved and price*) cher; *Oh ~!*, Mon Dieu!; **~ly,** (*affection*) tendrement; (*at a high price, lit. and fig.*) chèrement.
dearth, disette, *f.*; (*lack*) manque (de), *m.*
death, mort, *f.*; *~'s head*, tête de mort, *f.*; **~-blow,** (*lit. and fig.*) coup de grâce, *m.*; **~ duties,** droits de succession, *m.pl.*; **~ -rate,** mortalité, *f.*; **~ -rattle,** râle, *m.*; **~-struggles,** agonie, *f.*; *be frightened to ~*, mourir* de peur; **~less,** immortel, -le; **~ly,** *adv.* mortellement.
debar, *v.a.* exclure* (de).
debark, *v.a.n. see* DISEMBARK; **~ation,** débarquement, *m.*
debase, *v.a.* (*degrade*) avilir; (*comm.*) altérer; **~ment,** avilissement, *m.*
debat|e, *s.* discussion, *f.*; (*parl., &c.*) débats, *m.pl.*; *v.a.* (*question*) discuter; *v.n.* (*deliberate*) délibérer (sur); **~able,** discutable.
debauch|ery, débauche, *f.*; **~ee,** débauché, *m.*; *v.a.* débaucher.
debenture, (*fin.*) obligation, *f.*; **~-holder,** obligataire, *m.f.*
debilit|y, débilité, *f.*; **~ate,** débiliter.
debit, débit, *m.*; *s.* **~ side,** *s.* (*bkkpg.*) débit, *m.*; *~ and credit sides, see* CREDIT; *on the ~ side*, *adj.* passi|f, ~ve.
debouch, *v.n.* déboucher.
debris, débris, *m.pl.*
debt, dette, *f.*; (*due to trader*) créance, *f.*; **~-collector,** agent de recouvrements, *m.*; *get into ~*, s'endetter.
debtor, débit|eur, ~rice, *m.f.*; (*bankrupt*) liquidé, -e, *m.f.*; *be ~ for*, être redevable de (à + *pers.*).
debutante, (*court, &c.*) jeune fille faisant son entrée dans le monde. ⚠ débutante = '*beginner, novice*', *f.*
decade, période de dix années, *f.*

decaden|ce, décadence, *f.*; **~t,** décadent.
decagon, décagone, *m.*
decalogue, décalogue, *m.*
decamp, *v.n.* (*go away*) déguerpir.
decant, *v.a.* (*liquids*) décanter; **~er,** carafe, *f.*
decapitat|e, *v.a.* décapiter; **~ion,** décapitation, *f.*
decay, *s.* décadence, *f.*; (*ruin*) ruine, *f.*; (*falling to pieces*) délabrement, *m.*; (*teeth, bones, &c.*) carie, *f.*; *v.a.* gâter; *v.n.* tomber (être) en décadence; (*fruit, teeth*) se gâter; (*rot*) pourrir; (*fig.*) dépérir.
decease, *s.* décès, *m.*; *v.n.* décéder (être); **~d,** *s.* défunt, -e, *m.f.*
deceit, (*action*) déception, *f.*; (*cheating*) tromperie, *f.*; **~ful,** (*pers.*) trompeu|r, ~se; (*misleading*) décevant; **~fully,** d'une manière trompeuse.
deceive, *v.a.* tromper; (*disappoint*) décevoir; **~r,** trompeu|r, ~se, *m.f.*
December, décembre, *m.*; (*abbrev.*) 10bre.
decen|t, (*not immodest*) décent; ⚠ *in English 'decent' also means 'tolerable' which* = convenable, assez bon, -ne; **~cy,** (*not immodesty*) décence, *f.*; (*decorum*) bienséance, *f.*; **~tly,** avec décence, convenablement.
decept|ion, déception, *f.*; **~ive,** décevant; ⚠ déception *in French also* = *'disappointment'.*
decide, *v.a.* décider; *v.n.* décider (de), se décider (à); **~d,** (*conspicuous*) marqué; (*character*) résolu; **~dly,** décidément.
deciduous, (*bot.*) cadu|c, ~que.
decimal, *s.* décimale, *f.*; *adj.* décimal.
decimat|e, *v.a.* décimer; **~ion,** décimation, *f.*
decipher, *v.a.* déchiffrer; **~able,** déchiffrable.
decision, décision, *f.*; (*firmness*) fermeté, *f.*
decisive, (*conclusive, battle, &c.*) décisi|f, ~ve; (*resolute*) résolu; (*unequivocal*) catégorique; **~ly,** décisivement.
deck, *s.* pont, *m.*; *between ~s,* entrepont, *m.*; ~ **-cabin,** cabine de pont, *f.*; ~ **-chair,** transatlantique, *f.*; *~er, two-, three- ~er,* vaisseau à deux, trois ponts, *m.*
deck, *v.a.* parer (de).
decla|im, *v.a.* (*recite*) déclamer; *v.n.* déclamer; **~matory,** (*style*) déclamatoire; ~ *against,* déclamer contre.
declar|e, *v.a.* déclarer; *v.n.* ~ *for, against,* se déclarer pour, contre; **~ation,** déclaration, *f.*
declension, (*gram.*) déclinaison, *f.*; (*deviation*) déviation, *f.* (de); (*decay*) décadence, *f.*
decline, *s.* décadence, *f.*; (*med.*) consomption, *f.*; (*price*) baisse, *f.*; *v.a.* (*refuse and gram.*) décliner; *v.n.* (*price*) baisser; ~ *to,* refuser (de).
declivity, pente, *f.*
declutch, (*motor*) débrayer.
decoction, décoction, *f.*
decode, (*telegram, &c.*) déchiffrer.
decompos|e, *v.a.* décomposer; *v.n.* se décomposer; **~ition,** décomposition, *f.*
decorat|e, *v.a.* décorer (de); **~ion,** (*adornment and badge*) décoration, *f.*; **~or,** (*theatr., house*) décorateur, *m.*; **~ive,** décorati|f, ~ve; **~ed,** (*arch. approx.*) rayonnant.
decor|um, bienséance, *f.*; **~ous,** convenant; **~ously,** convenablement.
decoy, *s.* (*fig.*) leurre, *m.*; (*bird*) appelant, *m.*; *v.a.* leurrer.
decrease, *s.* diminution, *f.*; *v.a.n.* diminuer.
decree, (*law*) arrêt, *m.*; (*gen.*) décret, *m.*; ~ *in bankruptcy,* jugement déclaratif de faillite, *m.*; *v.a.* décréter.
decrepit, décrépit; **~ude,** décrépitude, *f.*
decry, (*cry down*) décrier; (*declaim against*) crier contre.
dedicat|e, *v.a.* (*eccles. and book*) dédier; **~ion,** dédicace, *f.*; **~ory,** dédicatoire.
deduce, *v.a.* déduire* (de).
deduct, déduire*; **~ion,** déduction, *f.*; **~ive,** déducti|f, ~ve.
deed, (*action, law*) acte, *m.*; (*contract*) contrat, *m.*; (*exploit*) exploit, *m.*; ~ *of gift,* donation, *f.*
deem, *v.a.* juger; **~ed,** (*considered*) censé + *inf.*, + *s. or adj. use* juger.
deep, *s.* mer, *f.*; (*fig.*) abîme, *m.*; *adj.* profond; (*colours*) foncé; (*plunged*) enfoncé; (*occupied*) absorbé (dans); (*mourning*) grand; *to be ten feet ~,* avoir dix pieds de profondeur; **~-laid,** profond; *adv. and* **~ly,** profondément; *~ly read,* versé (dans).
deepen, *v.a.* (*make deep*) approfondir; (*a colour*) foncer; *v.a.n.* (*increase*) augmenter; *v.n.* (*become darker*) s'assombrir.
deer, (*gen. term*) bête fauve, *f.*; (*red ~*) cerf, *m.*; ~ **-stalking,** chasse au chevreuil, *f.*
deerskin, peau de daim, *f.*
deface, (*disfigure, distort*) défigurer; (*make illegible*) effacer.
defalcation, détournement, *m.*
defam|e, diffamer; **~atory,** diffamatoire; **~ation,** diffamation, *f.*
default, *s.* défaut, *m.*; *in ~ of,* à défaut de; *v.n.* (*law*) faire* défaut; **~er,** défaillant, *m.*
defeat, (*mil.*) défaite, *f.*; (*failure*) insuccès, *m.*; *v.a.* vaincre*; (*frustrate*) frustrer; (*baffle*) déjouer.
defeat|ism, défaitisme, *m.*; **~ist,** défaitiste, *m.*
defect, (*material and moral*) défaut, *m.*
defect|ion, défection, *f.*; **~ive,** défectueu|x, ~se; (*gram.*) défecti|f, ~ve; **~ively,** défectueusement.
defen|ce, (*resistance, mil., justification*) défense, *f.*; **~d,** défendre; **~celess,** sans défense.
defend|ant, (*law*) défend|eur, ~eresse, *m.f.*; **~able,** défendable; (*justifiable*) justifiable.

defender, défenseur, *m.*
defens|ible, défendable; **~ive,** *adj.* défensi|f, ~ve; *s.* défensive, *f.*
defer, *v.a.* (*put off*) retarder; ~ *to,* déférer à; ⚠ déférer *does not = 'put off' in French*; **~ence,** déférence, *f.*
deferential, respectueu|x, ~se; **~ly,** respectueusement.
defian|ce, (*challenge*) défi, *m.*; ⚠ défiance = '*mistrust*'; *set at* ~, défier; (*fig.*) braver; **~t,** de défi (*things*); ⚠ défiant = '*distrustful*'.
deficien|cy, manque, *m.*; **~t,** insuffisant; (*mental*) faible d'esprit; *be ~t in,* manquer de.
deficit, (*money*) déficit, *m.*; *have a ~,* être en déficit.
defile, *s.* défilé, *m.*; *v.a.* (*lit. and fig.*) souiller; *v.n.* (*march in file*) défiler.
defilement, souillure, *f.*
defin|e, *v.a.* (*words, &c., explain*) définir; (*determine*) déterminer; **~ition,** définition, *f.*
definable, définissable.
definite, (*fixed*) déterminé; (*final*) définiti|f, ~ve; (*gram.*) défini; **~ness,** caractère déterminé, *m.*; **~ly,** d'une manière déterminée.
definitive, définiti|f, ~ve.
deflation, (*monetary*) déflation, *f.*
deflect, *v.a.* détourner; *v.n.* dévier; **~ion,** déviation, *f.*
deform, déformer; **~ed,** contrefait; **~ation,** déformation, *f.*; **~ity,** difformité, *f.*
defraud, *v.a.* frauder; ~ *of,* frauder de; **~er,** fraudeu|r, ~se, *m.f.*
defray, *v.a.* (*expenses*) payer.
deft, adroit; **~ly,** adroitement.
defunct, (*pers.*) défunt; (*thing*) tombé en désuétude.
defy, défier; (*fig.*) braver; ~ *to,* défier de + *inf.*
degenera|te, *v.n.* (*lit. and fig.*) dégénérer; *adj. and s.m.f.* (*pers.*) dégénéré, -e; **~tion, ~cy,** dégénération, *f.*
degrad|e, (*rank, &c., and fig.*) dégrader (de); **~ation,** avilissement, *m.*; (*rank*) dégradation, *f.*; **~ing,** avilissant; **~ed,** dégradé.
degree, (*stage, in ascent or descent, of relationship, astr., angle, of comparison, geom., thermom., &c.*) degré, *m.*; (*univ.*) grade, *m.*; (*rank*) rang, *m.*; *in a high ~,* à un †haut degré; *in some ~,* en quelque sorte; *by ~s,* par degrés.
deif|y, (*lit. and fig.*) diviniser; **~ication,** déification, *f.*
deign, daigner + *inf.*
dei|sm, déisme, *m.*; **~st,** déiste, *m.*
deity, (*fig. and eccles.*) divinité, *f.*; (*myth.*) déité, *f.*
deject|ion, abattement, *m.*; ⚠ déjection, *f.* (*med.*) = '*evacuation*'; **~ed,** abattu; **~edly,** avec abattement.
delat|ion, délation, *f.*; **~or,** délateur, *m.*
delay, *s.* retard, *m.*; *without further ~,* sans plus de retard; *with the least possible ~,* dans le plus bref délai.
delay, *v.a.* (*pers.*) retarder; (*thing*) différer; *v.n.* tarder.
delectable, délectable.
delegat|e, *s.* délégué, *m.*; *v.a.* déléguer; **~ion,** (*lit. and comm.*) délégation, *f.*
delete, *v.a.* biffer.
deleterious, délétère.
delft, (*earthenware*) faïence de Delft, *f.*
deliberat|e, *v.a.n.* délibérer; *adj.* réfléchi; (*on purpose*) délibéré; **~ion,** délibération, *f.*; **~ely,** de propos délibéré; (*slowly*) lentement.
delica|te, (*workmanship, texture, colour, health, critical, considerate, modest, dainty, easily injured, fastidious, embarrassing*) délicat; **~cy,** délicatesse, *f.*; (*food*) friandise, *f.*; **~tely,** avec délicatesse.
delicious, délicieu|x, ~se; **~ly,** délicieusement.
delight, *s.* délices, *f.pl.*; **~ful,** charmant; **~fully,** délicieusement; *v.a.* enchanter; *be ~ed to,* être enchanté de; *v.n.* ~ *to,* se plaire* à.
delimit, délimiter; **~ation,** délimitation, *f.*
delineate, (*fig.*) peindre*.
delinquen|cy, délit, *m.*; **~t,** délinquant, -e *m.f.*
deliri|um, délire, *m.*; **~ous,** *to be,* délirer; (*with joy, &c.*) être fou de.
deliver, *v.a.* (*liberate*) délivrer; (*letters*) distribuer; (*message, note, &c.*) remettre*; (*opinion*) exprimer; (*speech*) prononcer; (*goods*) livrer; (*blow*) asséner; ~ *up,* livrer; *be ~ed of,* (*child*) accoucher de.
deliver|ance, délivrance, *f.*; **~er,** libérat|eur, ~rice, *m.f.*
delivery, (*birth*) accouchement, *m.*; (*of speeches*) débit, *m.*; (*goods*) livraison, *f.*; (*letters*) distribution, *f.*; (*telegr., message, &c.*) remise, *f.*; ~ **-office,** bureau de distribution, *m.*; ~ **-van,** fourgon à livraison, *m.*; *for immediate ~, ~ without delay,* à livrer de suite.
dell, vallon, *m.*
Delphic, de Delphes.
delphinium, (*bot.*) pied d'alouette, *m.*
delta, (*river*) delta, *m.*
delu|de, tromper; **~sion,** (*false impression*) illusion, *f.*; ⚠ délusion *is not a French word*; **~sive,** illusoire.
deluge, déluge, *m.*; *v.a.* (*lit. and fig.*) inonder (de).
delve, *v.a.* creuser.
demagogue, démagogue, *m.*
demand, *s.* demande péremptoire, *f.*; (*unreasonable*) exigence, *f.*; (*request*) demande, *f.*; *on ~,* sur demande; ⚠ demande *is a weaker word than Engl. 'demand'*; *v.a.* réclamer; (*request*) demander (à + *pers., acc. of thing*); (*as right or by force*) exiger; (*peremptory*) demander péremptoirement.
demarcation, démarcation, *f.*
demean, ~ *oneself,* (*behave*) se comporter;

(*lower oneself to*) s'abaisser jusqu'à; **~our,** maintien, *m.*
demented, *adj.* fou, folle.
demerit, démérite, *m.*
demi, (*in comps.*) demi + -, *e.g.* demi-dieu, *m.*
demijohn, dame-jeanne, *f.*
demise, (*death*) décès, *m.*
demobilize, *v.a.* démobiliser.
democra|t, démocrate, *m.*; **~cy,** démocratie, *f.*; **~tic,** démocratique; **~tize,** démocratiser.
demol|ish, démolir; **~ition,** démolition, *f.*
demon, démon, *m.*; **~iac,** démoniaque, *m.f.*; **~ology,** démonologie, *f.*
demonstrat|e, démontrer; **~ion,** démonstration, *f.*; **~or,** démonstrateur, *m.*
demonstrative, (*affection, &c., and gram.*) démonstrati|f, **~ve.**
demorali|ze, démoraliser; **~zation,** démoralisation, *f.*
demur, *v.n.* hésiter; **~** *to, at,* faire* des objections à.
demure, grave; (*pej.*) qui affecte la modestie; **~ly,** modestement.
den, antre, *m.*; (*robbers*) repaire, *m.*; (*menagerie*) loge, *f.*
denaturalize, dénaturaliser.
deniable, niable.
denial, dénégation, *f.*; (*refusal*) refus, *m.*; (*of a statement*) démenti, *m.*; (*abjuring, disavowal*) reniement, *m.*
denizen, habitant, *m.*
denominat|e, appeler; **~ion,** (*name*) dénomination, *f.*; (*relig.*) secte, *f.*; (*comm.*) coupure, *f.*; **~or,** dénominateur, *m.*
denote, dénoter.
denounce, (*inform, inveigh against, of treaty*) dénoncer; (*prophecy*) annoncer.
dense, (*compact*), dense; (*fig.*) épais, -se; (*crowd*) compact; ⚠ dense *is not used in sense of 'stupid' as in English which* = bête; **~ly packed,** très serré; (*population*) très peuplé.
density, (*metal, &c.*) densité, *f.*; (*thickness*) épaisseur, *f.*
dent, bosse, *f.*; *v.a.* bossuer.
dental, *s.* (*phon.*) dentale, *f.*
dental, *adj.* (*teeth*) dentaire; (*gram.*) dental.
denticulat|ed, dentelé; **~ion,** dentelure, *f.*
dentifrice, dentifrice, *m.*
dentist, dentiste, *m.*
denude, (*strip*) dénuder; (*deprive*) dépouiller (de).
denunciat|ion, dénonciation, *f.*; (*attack*) attaque, *f.*, (contre); **~or,** dénonciat|eur, **~rice,** *m.f.*
deny, *v.a.* nier; (*accusation*) démentir*; **~** *that,* nier que *affirmative + subj.*; nier que *negative + subj. and* ne; **~** *oneself of,* se priver de.
depart, partir* (être); **~** *from,* (*fig.*) départir* (être) de; *s.* **~ed,** mort, *m.s. and pl.*
department, (*administ. and polit. division*) département, *m.*; (*of shop*) rayon, *m.*; **~-store,** grand magasin, *m.*; **~al,** départemental.
departure, départ, *m.*; *new* **~,** nouveauté, *f.*
depend on, dépendre de; **~ upon,** (*rely*) compter sur; (*trust*) se fier à.
dependable, sûr.
dependen|t, (dependant) *s.* dépendant, *m.*; **~ce,** (*being subject, subordinate*) dépendance, *f.* (de); (*confidence, reliance*) confiance (en), *f.*
dependen|t, *adj.* dépendant (de); **~cy,** (*subordination, country*) dépendance, *f.*
depict, peindre*; (*fig.*) dépeindre*.
deplete, épuiser (de).
deplor|e, (*regret*) déplorer; **~able,** (*pitiable*) pitoyable; **~ably,** lamentablement.
deploy, *v.a.* déployer; *v.n.* se déployer.
deponent, *adj.* (*gram.*) déponent.
depopulat|e, dépeupler; **~ion,** dépopulation, *f.*
deport, (*transport*) déporter; **~ation,** déportation, *f.*; **~** *oneself,* se comporter.
deportment, maintien, *m.*
depos|e, *v.a.* (*king, &c.*) déposer; *v.n.* (*bear witness*) déposer; **~ition,** (*king, &c.*) déposition, *f.*
deposit, *s.* (*bank, &c.*) dépôt, *m.*; (*security*) dépôt de garantie, *m.*; (*Savings Bank*) versement, *m.*; **~-account,** compte de dépôts à terme, *m.*; **~-book,** livret, *m.*; *v.a.* déposer; (*Savings Bank*) verser; **~ary,** dépositaire, *m.f.*
depositor, déposant, -e, *m.f.*
depot, depository, (*storehouse and mil.*) dépôt, *m.*
deprav|ed, dépravé; **~ity,** dépravation, *f.*
deprecate, (*disapprove of*) désapprouver.
depreciat|e, *v.a.* déprécier; *v.n.* (*fig. and value*) se déprécier; (*perishables*) s'avilir; **~ion,** (*comm., value*) moins-value, *f.*; (*money, &c.*) dépréciation, *f.*
depredat|or, déprédat|eur, **~rice,** *m.f.*; **~ion,** déprédation, *f.*
depress, (*fig.*) abattre; (*value*) déprimer; **~ion,** (*physical, &c.*) abattement, *m.*; (*ground*) enfoncement, *m.*; **~ed,** abattu; (*business*) dans le marasme.
depriv|e, priver (de); **~ation,** privation, *f.*; (*loss*) perte, *f.*
depth, (*lit. and fig.*) profondeur, *f.*; (*winter, &c.*) cœur, *m.*; (*inmost part*) fond, *m.*; *~-charge* (*nav.*) grenade sous-marine, *f.*; *get out of one's* **~,** perdre pied.
deput|e, (*commit powers, task, &c., or assign pers. as substitute*) déléguer; **~ation,** (*body of persons*) députation, *f.*
deputy, (*polit.*) député, *m.*; (*delegate*) délégué, *m.*; **~-chairman,** vice-président, *m.*; **~-governor,** sous-gouverneur, *m.*; **~-manager,** vice-gérant, *m.*; **~-mayor,** adjoint au maire, *m.*
derail, *v.a.* faire dérailler.
derby, (*U.S.A. bowler-hat*) melon, *m.*

derange, déranger; **~ment,** dérangement, *m.*; (*mental*) aliénation mentale, *f.*; **~d,** (*mind*) aliéné.

derelict, *adj. and s.m.f.* délaissé, **-e**; (*ship*) navire abandonné, *m.*

deride, tourner en dérision; ⚠ dérider = *'smooth', 'cheer'.*

deris|ion, dérision, *f.*; **~ive, ~ory,** dérisoire; **~ively,** par dérision.

deriv|e, *v.a.* (*obtain*) retirer (de); *v.n.* (*gram.*) dériver de; *be ~d from,* (*gram.*) dériver de; (*have source, origin from*) provenir* (être) de; **~ation,** (*gram.*) dérivation, *f.*; **~ative,** (*gram.*) *adj. and s.m.* dérivé, *m.*

derogat|e *from,* déroger à; **~ion** (*of*), dérogation (de); **~ory,** dérogatoire; *~ory to,* qui porte atteinte à.

dervish, derviche, *m.*

descant, *s.* (*song*) chant, *m.*; *v.n.* discourir* (sur).

descend, *v.a.* descendre (avoir); *v.n.* descendre (être); *~ upon,* tomber (être) sur; *~ed from,* issu de.

descendant, descendant, -e, *s.m.f.*

descent, (*lit., slope, mil.*) descente, *f.*; (*family*) descendance, *f.*

descri|be, décrire*; **~ption,** description, *f.*; (*kind*) sorte, *f.*; (*contents, &c.*) désignation, *f.*; (*police*) signalement, *m.*

descriptive, descripti|f, ~ve.

descry, découvrir*.

desecrat|e, profaner; **~ion,** profanation, *f.*

desert, *s.* (*merit*) mérite, *m.*; **~s,** ce qu'on mérite.

desert, *s.* (*place*) désert, *m.*; (*fig.*) solitude, *f.*; *adj.* désert; *v.a.* (*place and fig.*) déserter; (*abandon*) abandonner; **~er,** (*mil.*) déserteur, *m.*; **~ion,** abandon, *m.*; (*mil.*) désertion, *f.*

deserv|e, mériter; **~ing,** (*pers.*) méritant; *~ well of,* mériter bien de; **~edly,** à juste titre.

desiccate, dessécher.

design, *s.* (*project*) dessein, *m.*; (*arch.*) projet, *m.*; *v.a.* dessiner; *~ed for,* destiné à; **~er,** dessinat|eur, ~rice, *m.f.*

designate, *v.a.* désigner; *adj.* désigné.

designedly, *adv.* à dessein.

designing, *adj.* (*crafty*) artificieu|x, ~se.

desir|e, *s.* désir, *m.*; (*feeble*) velléité, *f.*; *v.n.* désirer (+ *inf. or* de + *inf.*); *v.a.* (*wish for, covet*) désirer; (*request a pers. acc. to*) prier (de); **~able,** désirable; *be* **~ous** *of,* désirer.

desist, cesser (de); ⚠ **se désister de** = *'renounce' in English.*

desk, (*reading, writing*) pupitre, *m.*; (*bureau*) bureau, *m.*; *roll-top ~,* bureau américain, *m.*; *knee-hole ~,* bureau ministre, *m.*

desolate, *adj.* (*uninhabited*) désert; (*lonely*) solitaire; (*laid waste*) ravagé; (*afflicted*) désolé.

desolation, désolation, *f.*

despair, *s.* (*lit. and fig.*) désespoir, *m.*; *v.n.* désespérer (de); *drive to despair,* pousser au désespoir; **~ingly,** sans espoir.

despatch, *see* DISPATCH.

desperado, homme de sac et de corde, *m.*

desperat|e, (*pers. and things*) désespéré; (*reckless*) capable de tout; **~ion,** désespoir, *m.*

despise, mépriser.

despite, (*spite, rancour*) dépit, *m.*; *prep., in ~ of,* en dépit de.

despoil, dépouiller; **~er,** spoliateur, *m.*

despond, se décourager; (*despair*) désespérer.

desponden|t, abattu; **~cy,** abattement, *m.*; **~tly,** sans espoir.

despot, despote, *m.*; **~ic,** despotique; **~ism,** despotisme, *m.*; **~ically,** despotiquement.

dessert, dessert, *m.*; ⚠ desserte = *'leavings at table'*; **~-spoon,** cuillère à dessert, *f.*

destin|e, *v.a.* (*intend, reserve*) destiner (à); **~ation,** destination, *f.*

destiny, (*chain of events, future career*) destin, *m.*; (*myth*) Destin; (*fate, power that fore-ordains, future lot*) destinée, *f.*

destitut|e, (*in want*) indigent; *~ of,* dénué de; **~ion,** misère, *f.*; ⚠ destitution = *dismissal.*

destroy, détruire*; **~er,** destructeur, *m.*; (*nav.*) contre-torpilleur, *m.*; *pl.* contre-torpilleurs; **~ing,** *adj.* destruct|eur, ~rice.

destruct|ion, destruction, *f.*; (*soul*) perdition, *f.*; (*massacre*) massacre, *m.*; (*fig.*) perte, *f.*; **~or,** destructeur de déchets, *m.*; **~ive,** destructi|f, ~ve.

desuetude, désuétude, *f.*

desultor|y, décousu; **~iness,** manque de suite, *m.*; **~ily,** à bâtons rompus.

detach, détacher (de); **~ment,** (*gen. and mil.*) détachement, *m.*

detail, détail, *m.*; *v.a.* (*lists, accounts, &c.*) détailler.

detect, découvrir*; **~ive,** agent de la police secrète, *m.*; **~ion,** découverte, *f.*

detain, retenir*; (*in prison, wrongfully, &c.*) détenir*.

detention, détention, *f.*; (*in schools*) consigne, *f.*

deter from, (*thing*) détourner (de); (*from doing*) empêcher (de).

deteriorat|e, *v.n.* (*things*) se détériorer; (*pers.*) dégénérer; **~ion,** détérioration, *f.*, dégénération, *f.*

determin|e, *v.a.* (*fig., date, amount, induce*) déterminer (à + *inf.*); *v.n.* décider de; **~ation,** détermination, *f.*; **~ed,** (*fixed, bold*) déterminé.

detest, détester; **~able,** détestable; **~ation,** détestation, *f.*; **~ably,** détestablement.

dethrone, détrôner; **~ment,** détrônement, *m.*

detonat|e, *v.n.* détoner; **~ion,** détonation, *f.*; **~or,** détonateur, *m.*

detour, détour, *m.*

detract from, (*value*) *v.a.* déprécier; (*merit, &c.*) dénigrer, *v.a.*
detract|ion, dénigrement, *m.*; **~or,** détracteur, *m.*
detriment, détriment, *m.*; *to the ~ of,* au détriment de; **~al,** préjudiciable; **~ally,** d'une manière préjudiciable.
detrition, usure, *f.*
detruncat|e, tronquer; (*trees*) étêter; **~ion,** (*statues*) mutilation, *f.*; (*trees*) étêtement, *m.*
deuce, *s.* diable, *m.*; *interj. the ~!* diantre!
Deuteronomy, (*Bible*) Deutéronome, *m.*
deutzia, (*bot.*) deutzie, *f.*
develop, *v.a.* (*lit. and photo.*) développer; *v.n.* se développer; **~ment,** développement, *m.*; **~er,** (*photo*) révélateur, *m.*
deviat|e, *v.n.* dévier (de); (*stray*) s'écarter (de); **~ion,** déviation, *f.*; (*fig.*) écart, *m.*
device, (*means*) expédient, *m.*; (*invention*) invention, *f.*; (*motto*) devise, *f.*
devil, diable, *m.*; **she-~,** diablesse; *be between the ~ and the deep sea,* être entre le marteau et l'enclume; *there's the ~ to pay,* c'est le diable à confesser.
devilish, diabolique; **~ly,** diablement.
devilry, (*magic*) magie, *f.*; (*mischief*) diablerie, *f.*
devious, (*remote*) détourné; (*not straight*) tortueu|x, ~se.
devisable, (*scheme*) qu'on peut combiner.
devise, *v.a.* (*plan*) combiner; (*plot*) tramer.
devoid of, dépourvu de.
devolve on, tomber (être) en partage à; *it ~s on you to,* c'est à vous de.
devote, *v.a.* (*vow*) vouer; (*time, &c.*) consacrer; *~ oneself to,* se vouer à.
devot|ee, dévot, -e, *m.f.*; **~ion,** (*relig.*) dévotion, *f.*; (*devotedness*) dévouement, *m.*; **~ed,** (*vow*) voué (à); (*attached*) dévoué à; **~ional,** de dévotion.
devour, (*lit. and fig.*) dévorer; **~ing,** (*lit. and fig.*) dévorant.
devout, dévot, -e; **~ness,** dévotion, *f.*; **~ly,** dévotement.
dew, rosée, *f.*; **~-bespangled,** parsemé de rosée; **~berry,** mûre de haie, *f.*; **~-drop,** goutte de rosée, *f.*; **~-worm,** ver de terre, *m.*; **~y,** couvert de rosée.
dewlap, (*cow*) fanon, *m.*
dexter|ity, dextérité, *f.*; **~ous,** adroit; **-ously,** adroitement.
diabetes, (*med.*) diabète, *m.*
diabolical, diabolique; **~ly,** diaboliquement.
diadem, diadème, *m.*; **~ed,** ceint d'un diadème.
diaeresis, (*gram.*) tréma, *m.*
diagnos|is, diagnostic, *m.*; **~e,** *v.a.* diagnostiquer.
diagonal, *s.* diagonale, *f.*; *adj.* diagonal; **~ly,** en diagonale.
diagram, diagramme, *m.*
dial, dial-plate, *s.* cadran, *m.*
dialect, dialecte, *m.*
dialecti|cs, dialectique, *f.*; **~cian,** dialecticien, *m.*
dialogue, dialogue, *m.*
diamet|er, diamètre, *m.*; **~rical,** diamétral; **~rically** *opposed,* diamétralement opposé.
diamond, diamant, *m.*; (*cards*) carreau, *m.*; (*glazier's*) diamant de vitrier; **~-cutter,** diamantaire, *m.*; **~ panes,** carreaux en losange, *m.pl.*; **~ wedding,** noces de diamant, *f.pl.*
diapason, (*organ*) prestant, *m.*
diaper, *s.* (*fabric*) toile ouvrée, *f.*; *v.a.* (*variegate*) diaprer.
diaphanous, diaphane.
diaphragm, diaphragme, *m.*
diarrhoea, diarrhée, *f.*
diary, journal, *m.*; (*for daily memoranda*) agenda, *m.*
diatonic, *adj.* (*mus.*) diatonique.
diatribe, diatribe, *f.*
dibble, (*agric. impl.*) plantoir, *m.*; *v.a.* planter avec un plantoir.
dice, *see* DIE; *v.n.* jouer aux dés.
dicky, (*carriages*) siège d'arrière, *m.*; (*shirt*) chemisette, *f.*
dictat|e, *s.* précepte, *m.*; (*order*) ordre, *m.*; **~es,** (*conscience*) dictamen, *m.*; **~ion,** (*written*) dictée, *f.*; (*order*) ordre, *m.*; *v.a.* (*lit. and fig.*) dicter; *~ to,* donner des ordres à.
dictator, dictateur, *m.*; **~ship,** dictature, *f.*; **~ial,** (*of a dictator*) dictatorial; (*arrogant*) impérieu|x, ~se; **~ially,** impérieusement.
diction, diction, *f.*
dictionary, dictionnaire, *m.*
dictum, dicton, *m.*
didactic, *adj.* didactique.
diddle, duper.
die, *pl.* **dice,** dé, *m.*; (*stamp*) coin, *m.*; **dice-box,** cornet, *m.*; *the ~ is cast,* le dé est jeté.
die, *v.n.* (*lit. and fig.*) mourir* (être); **~ away, down,** s'éteindre*; (*wind*) tomber (être); **~ to,** (*with desire*) mourir* d'envie de; *~ in harness,* mourir* sous le †harnais.
diet, *s.* (*food*) nourriture, *f.*; (*prescribed*) régime, *m.*; (*assembly*) diète, *f.*; ⚠ diète *does not = 'habitual food' but 'low diet' or no food at all*; *v.a.* mettre au régime; **~ary,** *s.* régime alimentaire, *m.*
dietetic, *adj.* diététique; **~s,** *s.* diététique, *f.*
differ, *v.n.* différer; **~ence,** différence, *f.*; (*quarrel*) différend, *m.*; *split the ~ence,* couper la poire en deux.
different, différent (de); *adj.* différentiel, -le; *~ial wheel,* engrenage différentiel, *m.*; **~ial,** *s.* (*motor*) différentiel, *m.*; **~iate,** différencier; **~ly,** différemment.
difficult, (*lit. and pers.*) difficile (de + *impers. verb,* à *with personal subject*); *cf.* Il est difficile de faire cela. L'enfant est difficile à élever.

difficult|y, difficulté, *f.*; *be in ~ies, (money)* être dans des embarras d'argent.
diffiden|ce, manque de confiance en soi, *m.*; **~t**, défiant; **~tly**, *adv.* timidement.
diffuse, *adj.* (*prolix*) diffus; (*widespread*) répandu; **~ly**, d'une manière diffuse; *v.a.* répandre.
diffus|ion, diffusion, *f.*; **~ive**, diffusi|f, ~ve; (*of style*) diffus.
diffusor, (*wireless*) diffuseur, *m.*
dig, *v.a.* bêcher; (*excavate*) creuser; **~ into**, enfoncer dans; **~ out**, extraire*; **~ up**, déterrer.
digest, *v.a.* (*food and fig.*) digérer; (*classify*) classer.
digest|ion, digestion, *f.*; **~ible**, digérable.
digestive, *adj. and s.m.* digestif.
digg|er, piocheur, *m.*; (*navvy*) terrassier, *m.*; **~ing**, fouille, *f.*
digit, (*measure*) doigt, *m.*; (*arith.*) chiffre, *m.*
digitalis, (*foxglove*) digitale, *f.*
dignif|y, (*ironically*) décorer (de); **~ied**, plein de dignité.
dignitary, dignitaire, *m.*
dignity, dignité, *f.*; (*of style*) ampleur, *f.*; *beneath one's ~*, indigne de soi; *stand on one's ~*, se tenir* sur son quant à soi.
digress, *v.n.* faire* une digression; **~ion**, digression, *f.*
dike, dyke, (*ditch*) fossé, *m.*; (*dam*) digue, *f.*; (*causeway*) chaussée, *f.*
dilapidat|e, délabrer; **~ion**, délabrement, *m.*; (*fortune, &c.*) dilapidation, *f.*
dilapidated, délabré.
dilat|e, *v.a.* dilater; *v.n.* se dilater; **~ation**, dilatation, *f.*
dilator|y, (*pers.*) lent; (*things*) long; **~iness**, lenteur, *f.*
dilemma, dilemme, *m.*
dilettante, (*mus.*) dilettante, *m.*; (*arts*) amateur, *m.*
diligen|ce, diligence, *f.*; (*exactitude*) assiduité, *f.*; **~t**, diligent; (*industrious*) laborieu|x, ~se; **~tly**, diligemment.
dilut|e, *v.a.* délayer; (*wine, &c.*) couper; **~ion**, dilution, *f.*
diluvial, *adj.* diluvien, -ne.
dim, *adj.* (*not clear*) obscur; (*lustreless*) terne; (*sight, light*) faible; *v.a.* (*lit. and fig.*) obscurcir; (*dull*) ternir; **~ness**, obscurcissement, *m.*; (*sight, light*) faiblesse, *f.*; **~ly**, confusément.
dime, (*U.S.A. coin*) dime, *f.*
dimension, dimension, *f.*
diminish, *v.a.n.* diminuer.
diminut|ion, diminution, *f.*; **~ive**, *adj.* tout petit; *s.* (*gram.*) diminutif, *m.*
dimity, basin, *m.*
dimple, fossette, *f.*
din, fracas, *m.*; (*uproar*) vacarme, *m.*
din|e, *v.a.* dîner; **~er**, dîneur, *m.*
dinghy, (*naut.*) youyou, *m.*
dingy, (*room*) mesquin; (*grimy*) sale; (*colours*) sombre.
dingle, vallon, *m.*
dining, **~-car**, (*rail.*) wagon-restaurant, *m.*; **~-hall**, réfectoire, *m.*; **~-room**, salle à manger; **~-saloon**, salle de restaurant, *m.*; **~-table**, table à manger, *f.*
dinner, dîner, *m.*; **~-jacket**, smoking, *m.*; **~ -party**, dîner prié, *m.*; **~ -wagon**, servante, *f.*
dint, marque d'un coup, *f.*; *v.a.* bosseler.
dioces|e, diocèse, *m.*; **~an**, *adj.* diocésain.
dioptric, *adj.* dioptrique.
diorama, diorama, *m.*
dip, *s.* (*act*) plongement, *m.*; (*soil, horizon*) dépression, *f.*; (*dive*) plongeon, *m.*
dip, *v.a.n.* plonger; *v.a.* (*steep*) tremper; *v.n.* (*magnetic needle*) incliner; **~ into**, (*books*) parcourir*; (*put hand into*) puiser dans.
dipper, (*ornith.*) merle d'eau, *m.*
dippy, *be ~ about*, (*U.S.A. 'sweet on'*) en pincer pour.
diphtheria, (*med.*) diphtérie, *f.*
diphthong, diphtongue, *f.*
diploma, diplôme, *m.*
diploma|cy, diplomatie, *f.*; **~tist**, diplomate, *m.*; **~tic**, diplomatique.
dire, affreu|x, ~se.
direct, *adj.* (*without deviation, immediate, descent, action, ticket, train, &c., without intermediary, diametrical, gram.*) direct; (*not crooked*) droit; (*explicit*) précis; (*answer*) net, -te; **~ly**, directement; (*exactly*) juste; (*time*) tout de suite.
direct, *v.a.* (*control*) diriger; (*order*) commander (à *of pers.*, de + *inf.*); (*remarks, &c., letters*) adresser; (*telescope, guns*) braquer; (*attention*) diriger (sur).
direct|ion, (*control, way, course*) direction, *f.*; (*orders*) instructions, *f. pl.*; (*letters*) adresse, *f.*; **~or**, **~ress**, direct|eur, ~rice, *m.f.*; (*comm.*) administrat|eur, ~rice, *m.f.*; *managing ~or*, directeur-gérant, *m.*
directness, mouvement direct, *m.*; (*fig.*) droiture, *f.*; (*answer, &c.*) netteté, *f.*
director|ship, poste de directeur, *m.*; **~ate**, administration, *f.*
directory, (*addresses*) almanach, *m.*; (*mil., trade, teleph., &c.*) annuaire, *m.*
direful, terrible.
dirge, chant funèbre, *m.*
dirigible, (*balloon, &c.*) *adj. and s.m.* dirigeable.
dirk, dague, *f.*
dirt, *s.* (*mud*) boue, *f.*; (*mire*) crotte, *f.*; (*on clothes, skin*) crasse, *f.*; (*filth, lit. and lang.*) ordure, *f.*
dirt|y, (*mud*) crotter; (*soil, lit. and fig.*) souiller; *adj.* sale; (*mud*) crotté; (*clothes, skin*) crasseu|x, ~se; (*fig.*) orduri|er, ~ère; **~y trick**, vilain tour, *m.*; **~iness**, malpropreté, *f.*; (*fig.*) ordure, *f.*; **~ily**, malpropremeent; *v.a.* salir; (*mud*) crotter; (*soil, lit. and fig.*) souiller.
disability, incapacité, *f.*
disable, rendre incapable (de); (*ship*) désemparer; **~d**, (*soldier, sailor*) invalide.
disabuse, *v.a.* désabuser (de); *~ oneself of*, se désabuser (de).

disadvantage, désavantage, *m.*; **~ous,** désavantageu|x, ~se; *at a* ~, (*at a loss*) à perte.
disaffect|ion, tendance à la révolte, *f.*; **~ed,** mal disposé.
disagree, *v.n.* (*opinions, &c.*) différer; (*quarrel*) se brouiller; ~ *with,* (*food, &c.*) *v.a.* incommoder.
disagreeabl|e, désagréable; **~eness,** (*thing*) désagrément, *m.*; (*pers.*) nature désagréable, *f.*; **~y,** désagréablement.
disagreement, désaccord, *m.*; ⚠ *not* désagrément *which = 'disagreeableness' of things.*
disallow, *v.a.* (*reject*) rejeter; (*prohibit*) défendre.
disappear, disparaître* (avoir *of action,* être *of state*); **~ance,** disparition, *f.*
disappoint, *v.a.* désappointer; (*hopes*) tromper; (*let down*) faire* faux bond à; **~ment,** désappointement, *m.*
disapprobation, désapprobation, *f.*
disapprov|e, of, *v.a.* désapprouver; **~al,** désapprobation, *f.*
disarm, *v.a.* (*lit. and fig.*) désarmer; *v.n.* désarmer; **~ament,** désarmement, *m.*
disarrange, *v.a.* déranger; **~ment,** dérangement, *m.*
disarray, *s.* désarroi, *m.*; *v.a.* jeter dans le désarroi, *m.*
disast|er, désastre, *m.*; **~rous,** désastreu|x, ~se; **~rously,** désastreusement.
disavow, *v.a.* désavouer; **~al,** désaveu, *m.*
disband, *v.a.* (*mil. and schol., &c.*) licencier; *v.n.* se débander; **~ing,** *s.* licenciement, *m.*; ⚠ débander, *v.a.* = *'unbind'.*
disbelie|f, incrédulité, *f.*; **~ve,** *v.a.* (*pers.*) ne pas croire*; (*thing*) ne pas ajouter foi à.
disbud, (*hort.*) ébourgeonner.
disburden, (*heart, conscience*) décharger; ~ *oneself of,* se décharger de.
disburse, débourser; **~ment,** (*act*) déboursement, *m.*; (*money*) débours, *m.pl.*
disc, *see* DISK.
discard, (*clothes, &c.*) mettre* au rebut; (*cards*) écarter; (*habit*) abandonner.
discern, (*distinguish, perceive with mind*) discerner; **~ible,** (*visible*) visible; (*by senses*) perceptible; **~ment,** (*act and power*) discernement, *m.*
discerning, *adj.* (*quick*) judicieu|x, ~se.
discharge, *s.* (*unloading ship, arms, liquids, from obligation*) décharge, *f.*; (*duty*) accomplissement, *m.*; (*employee and mil.*) congé, *m.*; (*prison*) élargissement, *m.*; (*wounds, &c.*) écoulement, *m.*; (*bankrupt*) réhabilitation, *f.*; (*comm.*) quittance, *f.*; ~ *in full,* reçu libératoire, *m.*
discharge, *v.a.* (*bill, arms, unload*) décharger; (*debt, &c.*) liquider; (*employee, &c.*) congédier; (*prisoner*) élargir; (*arrow*) décocher; (*duty*) s'acquitter de; (*bankrupt*) réhabiliter; (*mil.*) licencier; *v.n.* (*river*) se jeter (dans); (*wound, &c.*) suppurer.
disciple, disciple, *m.*; **~ship,** qualité de disciple, *f.*
disciplinar|ian, disciplinaire, *m.*; *be a good* ~, entendre bien la discipline; **~y,** disciplinaire.
discipline, *s.* discipline, *f.*; *v.a.* discipliner.
disclaim, (*disavow*) désavouer; (*renounce*) renier; **~er,** (*disavowal*) désaveu, *m.*
disclos|e, découvrir*; **~ure,** découverte, *f.*; (*secrets*) révélation, *f.*
discolo|ur, *v.a.* décolorer; **~ration,** décoloration, *f.*
discomfiture, (*defeat*) défaite, *f.*; (*fig.*) déconvenue, *f.*
discomfort, malaise, *f.*
discompos|e, (*mental*) troubler; **~ure,** trouble, *m.*
disconcert, déconcerter; **~ing,** déconcertant.
disconnect, désunir; (*mach.*) débrayer; (*electr.*) couper; **~ion,** désunion, *f.*; (*electr.*) mise hors circuit, *f.*; **~ed,** (*electr.*) mis †hors circuit; (*style*) décousu; **~edly,** sans suite.
disconsolate, désolé; **~ly,** d'une manière désolée.
discontent, ~ment, *s.* mécontentement, *m.*; **~ed,** mécontent (de); **~edly,** avec mécontentement.
discontinu|e, *v.a.n.* discontinuer (de + *inf.*); **~ance,** (*cessation*) discontinuation, *f.*; (*intermittence*) discontinuité, *f.*
discord, *s.* (*strife*) discorde, *f.*; (*mus.*) discordance, *f.*; **~ance,** discordance, *f.*; **~ant,** (*fig. and mus.*) discordant; **~antly,** sans accord; (*mus.*) d'une manière discordante.
discount, *s.* (*comm. and fin.*) escompte, *m.*; (*reduction*) remise, *f.*; (*less than par, Stk. Ex.*) perte, *f.*; ~ *for cash,* escompte de caisse, *m.*; *at a* ~, en perte; ~ **rate,** taux d'escompte, *m.*
discount, *v.a.* (*bills*) faire l'escompte de; (*deduct*) décompter; (*a bill, and fig.*) escompter.
discount|er, *s.* escompteur, *m.*; **~able,** escomptable.
discountenance, *v.a.* désapprouver.
discourag|e, décourager; (*deter*) décourager (de); **~ement,** découragement, *m.*; **~ing,** décourageant.
discourse, *s.* (*speech, treatise, language*) discours, *m.*; (*sermon*) sermon, *m.*; *v.n.* (*expatiate*) discourir* (sur).
discourte|sy, impolitesse, *f.*; **~ous,** impoli; **~ously,** avec impolitesse.
discover, découvrir*; **~er,** découvreur, *m.*; **~y,** découverte, *f.*; **~able,** qu'on peut découvrir.
discredit, *s.* discrédit, *m.*; *v.a.* (*bring disrepute on*) décréditer; (*disbelieve*) ne pas croire; **~able,** déshonorant.
discreet, (*reserved, close*) discr|et, ~ète; ⚠ *'discreet' also = 'judicious', 'the result of thought' which =* judicieu|x, ~se.

discrepan|cy, contradiction, *f.*; **~t,** différent; (*disagreeing*) en contradiction avec.
discretion, discrétion, *f.*; ⚠ *see* DISCREET; (*thought*) prudence, *f.*; **~ary,** discrétionnaire.
discriminat|e, distinguer (de '*from*', '*between*' entre); **~ion,** distinction, *f.*; (*judgement*) jugement, *m.*
discursive, (*log.*) discursi|f, ~ve; (*style*) diffus; **~ly,** sans suite.
discus, disque, *m.*
discuss, *v.a.* discuter; **~ion,** discussion, *f.*
disdain, *s.* dédain, *m.*; *v.a.* dédaigner (de); **~ful,** dédaigneu|x, ~se; **~fully,** dédaigneusement.
disease, maladie, *f.*; **~d,** malade.
disembark, *v.a.n.* débarquer; **~ation,** débarquement, *m.*
disembarrass, *v.a.* débarrasser (de).
disembody, *v.a.* désincorporer.
disembowelled, éventré.
disenchant, désenchanter; **~ment,** désenchantement, *m.*
disencumber, débarrasser (de).
disengage, (*free*) dégager; **~d,** (*at leisure*) libre; **~ment,** dégagement, *m.*
disentangle, (*threads*) démêler; (*feet*) dépêtrer; (*fig.*) débrouiller.
disentomb, (*lit. and fig.*) déterrer.
disesteem, *s.* mésestime, *f.*; *v.a.* mésestimer.
disfavour, défaveur, *f.*; (*disapproval*) désapprobation, *f.*
disfigure, défigurer; **~ment,** (*blemish*) enlaidissement, *m.*
disfranchise, *v.a.* priver du droit de vote; **~ment,** privation du droit de vote, *f.*
disgorge, *v.a.* (*food, water*) dégorger; (*booty, &c.*) restituer.
disgrace, *s.* disgrâce, *f.*; (*shame*) †honte, *f.*; *v.a.* disgracier.
disgraceful, †honteu|x, ~se; **~ness,** †honte, *f.*; **~ly,** †honteusement.
disguise, *s.* déguisement, *m.*; *v.a.* (*lit. and fig.*) déguiser; *in ~*, déguisé.
disgust, *s.* dégoût, *m.*; *v.a.* dégoûter; **~ing,** dégoûtant.
dish, *s.* (*utensil*) plat, *m.*; (*food*) mets, *m.*; **~-cloth,** lavette, *f.*; **~-warmer,** réchaud, *m.*; **~-water,** eau de vaisselle, *f.*; *wash up ~es*, laver la vaisselle; *v.a.* **~ up,** (*meal*) servir.
dishabille, déshabillé, *m.*
dishearten, décourager; **~ing,** décourageant.
dishevelled, (*pers.*) échevelé; (*hair*) épars.
dishonest, malhonnête; **~y,** malhonnêteté, *f.*; **~ly,** malhonnêtement.
dishonour, *s.* déshonneur, *m.*; *v.a.* déshonorer; (*bill, &c.*) ne pas faire* honneur à; *~ed cheque, see* CHEQUE; **~able,** déshonorant; **~ably,** d'une manière déshonorante.
disinclination (*for*), aversion (pour), *f.*
disinclin|e to, inspirer de l'aversion pour; *~ed to*, peu disposé à.
disincorporate, désincorporer.
disinfect, désinfecter; **~ion,** désinfection, *f.*; **~ant,** *adj. and s.m.* désinfectant.
disingenuous, qui manque de franchise; **~ness,** manque de franchise, *m.*; **~ly,** sans franchise, *f.*
disinherit, déshériter; **~ance,** exhérédation, *f.*
disintegrat|e, *v.a.* (*lit. and fig.*) désagréger; *v.n.* se désagréger; **~ion,** désagrégation, *f.*
disinter, déterrer; **~ ment,** exhumation, *f.*
disinterested, désintéressé; **~ness,** désintéressement, *m.*; **~ly,** avec désintéressement.
disjoin, désunir.
disjoint, désarticuler; **~ed,** (*style*) décousu; **~edly,** d'une manière décousue.
disjuncti|on, désunion, *f.*; **~ve,** (*lit. and gram.*) disjoncti|f, ~ve.
disk, disque, *m.*
dislike, *s.* (*pers.*) aversion, *f.*; (*food*) dégoût, *m.*; *have a ~ for*, avoir en aversion; *take a ~ to*, prendre* en dégoût; *v.a.* ne pas aimer.
dislocat|e, (*med. and take to pieces*) disloquer; **~ion,** dislocation, *f.*
dislodge, *v.a.* (*displace*) déplacer; (*mil.*) déloger.
disloyal, (*pers.*) infidèle; (*things*) déloyal; **~ty,** manque de fidélité, *m.*; **~ly,** déloyalement.
dismal, lugubre; (*dark*) sombre; (*sad*) triste; **~ness,** état lugubre, *m.*; **~ly,** tristement.
dismantle, *v.a.* dépouiller (de); (*fort.*) démanteler.
dismast, *v.a.* (*naut.*) démâter.
dismay, *s.* consternation, *f.*; *v.a.* consterner.
dismember, démembrer; **~ment,** démembrement, *m.*
dismiss, *v.a.* (*employee*) congédier; (*functionary*) destituer; (*put out of thought*) écarter; **~al,** (*permission to depart, and of servants*) renvoi, *m.*; (*of a functionary*) destitution, *f.*; *v.n.* (*mil.*) rompre les rangs; *dismiss!* (*mil.*) rompez!
dismount, *v.a.* démonter; *v.n.* descendre (être) de cheval.
disobedien|ce, désobéissance, *f.*; **~t,** désobéissant.
disobey, *v.a.* désobéir à.
disoblige, désobliger.
disobliging, (*not helpful*) peu serviable.
disorder, *s.* désordre, *m.*; (*med.*) maladie, *f.*; *v.a.* déranger.
disorder|ed, en désordre; (*hair*) ébouriffé; (*internal organ*) dérangé; **~ly,** (*conduct*) déréglé.
disorganiz|e, *v.a.* désorganiser; **~ation,** désorganisation, *f.*
disown, désavouer.
disparag|e, dénigrer; (*cry down*) déprécier; **~ement,** dénigrement, *m.*; **~ing,** peu flatteu|r, ~se; **~ingly,** avec mépris.
disparate, *adj.* disparate.

dispassionate, calme; **~ly,** sans passion.
dispatch, *s.* (*of business, forwarding*) expédition, *f.*; (*speed*) promptitude, *f.*; **~ boat,** aviso, *m.*; **~-case,** serviette, *f.*; **~-note,** bulletin d'expédition, *m.*; *v.a.* (*send off, do quickly, kill*) expédier.
dispel, *v.a.* dissiper.
dispensable, dont on peut se passer.
dispensary, (*free*) dispensaire, *m.*; (*chemist's shop*) pharmacie, *f.*
dispensation, (*distributing*) dispensation, *f.*; (*exemption*) dispense, *f.*; (*of Providence*) décret, *m.*; (*eccles.*) loi, *f.*
dispense, *v.a.* (*distribute*) dispenser; (*justice, &c.*) administrer; (*medicine*) préparer; ⚠ *not* dispenser *of medicines*; **~** *from,* dispenser de; **~** *with,* se dispenser de.
dispenser, (*chem.*) pharmacien, *m.*
disperse, *v.a.* disperser; (*dispel*) dissiper; *v.n.* se disperser; (*fogs, &c.*) se dissiper.
disperser, (*scandal, &c.*) semeu|r, ~se, *m.f.*
dispersion, dispersion, *f.*
dispirit, *v.a.* décourager; **~ed,** découragé; **~edness,** découragement, *m.*; (*depression*) abattement, *m.*; **~ing,** décourageant.
displace, déplacer; (*from an office*) destituer (de); **~ment,** (*lit. and fig., naut.*) déplacement, *m.*
display, *s.* (*show*) exposition, *f.*; (*shop*) étalage, *m.*; (*ostentation*) parade, *f.*
display, *v.a.* (*exhibit*) exposer; (*parade*) étaler; (*show, exhibit*) déployer; (*evince*) faire* preuve de.
displease, *v.a.* deplaire* à; (*vex*) mécontenter.
displeasing, (*unattractive*) déplaisant; (*disagreeable*) désagréable.
displeasure, déplaisir, *m.*
disport oneself, se divertir.
disposal, disposition, *f.*; (*sale*) vente, *f.*; *have at one's* **~**, avoir à sa disposition.
dispose, *v.a.* (*order, incline*) disposer (à); *v.n.* **~** *of,* (*get rid of*) disposer de; (*sell*) vendre; (*a business, &c.*) céder; *friendly* **~***d,* ami.
disposition, (*arrangement, tendency*) disposition, *f.*; (*character*) caractère, *m.*
dispossess, *v.a.* déposséder (de).
dispraise, *s.* blâme, *m.*
disproof, réfutation, *f.*
disproportion, disproportion, *f.*; **~al,** disproportionnel, -le; **~ally,** disproportionnellement.
disprove, réfuter.
disputa|ble, contestable; **~nt,** *s.* disputeu|r, ~se, *m.f.*; **~tion,** controverse, *f.*; **~tious,** disputeu|r, ~se.
dispute, *s.* (*quarrel*) dispute, *f.*; (*discussion*) discussion, *f.*; *beyond* **~**, incontestablement; *v.a.* (*argue*) discuter; (*controvert*) contester; (*contend for*) disputer (*acc. of thing,* à +*pers.*); *v.n.* (*argue*) discuter (avec); (*quarrel*) se quereller.
disqualif|ication, incapacité, *f.*; **~y,** (*a runner, a horse, &c.*) disqualifier; (*render incapable of*) rendre incapable (de).
disquiet, *v.a.* inquiéter; **~ude,** *s.* inquiétude, *f.*
disquisition, (*treatise, discourse*) dissertation, *f.* (sur).
disregard, *s.* (*indifference*) indifférence, *f.* (pour); (*neglect*) négligence, *f.*; *v.a.* ne pas tenir* compte de; **~ful,** insouciant (de).
disrelish, *s.* (*lit. and fig.*) dégoût, *m.* (de); *v.a.* avoir du dégoût (pour).
disreputable, (*pers.*) perdu de réputation; (*things*) déshonorant.
disrepute, discrédit, *m.*; *to fall into* **~**, tomber (être) dans le discrédit.
disrespect, manque de respect, *m.*; **~ful,** irrespectueu|x, ~se; **~fully,** irrespectueusement.
disrobe, *v.a.* déshabiller; *v.n.* se déshabiller.
disruption, rupture, *f.*
dissatisf|action, mécontentement, *m.*; **~y,** *v.a.* mécontenter; **~ied,** mécontent.
dissect, (*cut up or analyse, fig.*) disséquer; **~ion,** dissection, *f.*
disseise, déposséder (de).
dissembl|e, *v.a.n.* dissimuler; **~er,** dissimulat|eur, ~rice, *m.f.*; **~ing,** *s.* dissimulation, *f.*
disseminat|e, disséminer; (*lies, &c.*) semer; (*spread*) répandre; **~ion,** dissémination, *f.*
dissension, dissension, *f.*
dissent from, différer de.
dissent, *s.* (*disagreement*) dissentiment, *m.*; (*eccles.*) dissidence, *f.*; **~er,** (*eccles.*) dissident, -e, *m.f.*; **~ient,** *adj. and s.m.f.* (*not agreeing*) dissident.
dissert, *v.n.* disserter; **~ation,** dissertation, *f.*
disservice, mauvais service, *m.*
dissever, (*divide*) diviser.
dissight, objet répugnant, *m.*
dissimilar, dissemblable; **~ity,** dissemblance, *f.*
dissimulat|e, *v.a.n.* dissimuler; **~ion,** dissimulation, *f.*
dissipate, (*squander, fritter*) dissiper; (*energy, &c.*) disperser.
dissipat|ed, débauché; ⚠ dissipé *more often* = '*inattentive*', '*lacking in application*'; **~ion,** (*inattention, dissolute life, scattering*) dissipation, *f.*
dissociate, (*separate*) séparer.
dissolub|le, dissoluble; **~ility,** dissolubilité, *f.*
dissolut|e, dissolu; **~eness,** dérèglement, *m.*; **~ion,** (*break up*) dissolution; (*death*) mort, *f.*
dissolve, *v.a.* (*lit., Parl., annul*) dissoudre*; *v.n.* se dissoudre*.
dissolvent, *adj. and s.m.* dissolvant.
dissonan|t, (*sound*) dissonant; **~ce,** dissonance, *f.*
dissua|de, *a.* dissuader (de); **~sion,** dissuasion, *f.*

distaff, quenouille, *f.*
distance, *s.* distance, *f.*; (*remoteness*) éloignement, *m.*; (*distant point, locality*) lointain, *m.*; *keep at a ~*, tenir* à distance; *in the ~*, au loin; *at, from a ~*, de loin.
distance, *v.a.* (*leave behind*) distancer.
distant, (*remote, place, time*) lointain; (*relatives, time, fig.*) éloigné; (*manner*) froid; *three kilometres ~*, distant, éloigné de trois kilomètres; **~ly,** à (quelque) distance; (*relationship, from far*) de loin.
distaste, (*fig.*) aversion, *f.*; **~ful,** désagréable.
distemper, *s.* (*ailment*) maladie, *f.*; (*paint.*) détrempe, *f.*; *v.a.* (*paint.*) peindre* à la détrempe; **~ed,** (*health*) dérangé.
disten|d, *v.a.* distendre; *v.n.* se distendre; (*dilate*) *v.a.* dilater; *v.n.* se dilater; **~sion,** distension, *f.*
distich, (*poet.*) distique, *m.*
distil, *v.a.n.* distiller; **~lation,** distillation, *f.*; **~ler,** distillateur, *m.*; **~lery,** distillerie, *f.*
distinct, (*different, clear*) distinct (de); (*decided*) marqué; **~ion,** distinction, *f.*; **~ive,** distincti|f, ~ve; **~ness,** netteté, *f.*; **~ly,** distinctement.
distinctiveness, caractère distinctif, *m.*
distinguish, *v.a.* (*single out*) distinguer (de); (*perceive*) apercevoir; (*classify*) classer; *~ing mark*, signe distinctif, *m.*
distinguished, distingué.
distort, (*deform*) déformer; (*features*) décomposer; (*language*) torturer; **~ed,** (*twisted*) tordu; (*style*) guindé.
distortion, (*language*) sens forcé, *m.*; (*features, &c.*) déformation, *f.*; (*limbs*) contorsion, *f.*
distract, (*divert, amuse*) distraire*; ⚠ distraire *is never used for 'bewilder' which* = bouleverser; **~ed,** éperdu (de); ⚠ distrait = *'absent-minded'*.
distraction, (*abstraction, amusement*) distraction, *f.*; (*confusion, perplexity*) trouble, *m.*; *to ~*, à la folie.
distracting, *adj.* (*attention*) qui distrait.
distrain, *v.a.* (*law*) saisir; **~t,** saisie, *f.*
distress, détresse, *f.*; (*poverty*) misère, *f.*; *in ~*, (*naut.*) en détresse.
distress, *v.a.* affliger; **~ing,** affligeant.
distribut|e, (*deal out*) distribuer; (*allot*) répartir; **~ion,** distribution, *f.*; **~or,** distribut|eur, ~rice, *m.f.*
distributive, *adj.* (*which distributes, log., and gram.*) distributi|f, ~ve.
district, (*town*) quartier, *m.*; (*jurisdiction*) district, *m.*; (*region*) contrée, *f.*; *~ bank*, régionale, *f.*
distrust, *s.* défiance, *f.*; (*suspicion*) méfiance, *f.*; *v.a.* se défier de; (*be suspicious of*) se méfier de; **~ful,** défiant; **~fully,** avec défiance.
disturb, (*agitate, stir up*) troubler; (*incommode*) déranger; **~ance,** trouble, dérangement, *m.*
disturber, perturbat|eur, ~rice, *m.f.*; *~ of the peace*, perturbateur de l'ordre, *m.*
disun|ion, désunion, *f.*; **~ite,** désunir.
disuse, désuétude, *f.*; *fall into ~*, tomber (être) en désuétude.
disyllab|le, dissyllabe, *m.*; **~ic,** dissyllabique.
ditch, fossé, *m.*; (*moat*) douve, *f.*; **~er,** faiseur de fossés, *m.*; **~ing,** fossoyage, *m.*; *v.a.* fossoyer; *as dull as ~-water*, ennuyeu|x, ~se comme la pluie.
dithyramb, dithyrambe, *m.*; **~ic,** dithyrambique.
dittany, (*bot.*) dictame, *m.*
ditto, *adv.* dito; (*abbrev.*) D°.
ditty, chansonnette, *f.*
diurnal, journali|er, ~ère; (*astr.*) diurne.
divan, (*sofa and orient. council*) divan, *m.*
dive, *s.* (*act*) plongeon, *m.*; (*submarine*) plongée, *f.*
dive, *v.n.* (*pers., aeron.*) plonger; *~ down* (*aeron.*), piquer; *~-down*, *s.* lancement en piqué, *m.*; *~ into*, (*book, &c.*) se plonger dans; (*pocket*) plonger la main dans; (*rush*) s'élancer.
diver, (*ornith.*) plongeon, *m.*; *red-throated ~*, camarin, *m.*
diverg|e, *v.n.* (*lit. and fig.*) diverger; *~ from*, dévier de; **~ence,** divergence, *f.*; **~ent,** divergent.
divers, *adj.* divers.
diversif|y, *v.a.* diversifier; (*vary*) varier; (*colours*) nuancer; **~ication,** variation, *f.*
diversion, (*turning aside*) déviation, *f.*; (*attention*) diversion, *f.*; (*amusement*) divertissement, *m.*; (*misappropriation*) détournement, *m.*
diversity, variété, *f.*
divert, détourner; (*distract*) distraire*; (*amuse*) divertir; **~ing,** divertissant.
divest, *v.a.* dépouiller (de); *~ oneself of*, se dépouiller de.
divide, *v.a.* (*in parts*) diviser; (*in shares*) partager; (*separate*) séparer; *v.n.* se diviser; (*parl.*) voter.
dividend, dividende, *m.*; (*among creditors*) répartition, *f.*; **~-warrant,** chèque-dividende, *m.*
dividers, (*compasses*) compas à pointes sèches, *m.*
divination, divination, *f.*
divine, *s.* ecclésiastique, *m.*; *adj.* divin.
divine, *v.a.n.* deviner; **~r,** *s.* devin, *m.*; **~ress,** devineresse, *f.*
diving, **~-bell,** cloche à plongeur, *f.*; **~-dress,** scaphandre, *m.*
divining-rod, baguette divinatoire, *f.*
divinity, (*divine nature, fig.*) divinité, *f.*; (*pers.*) dieu, déesse, *m.f.*; ⚠ *'divinity'* = *theology, faculty of theology is never* divinité, *but* théologie, *f.*; *doctor of ~*, docteur en théologie, *m.*
divisib|le, divisible; **~ility,** divisibilité, *f.*
division, (*dividing, mil., nav., arith., discord*) division, *f.*; (*quarrel*) brouille, *f.*; (*separation*) séparation, *f.*; (*parl.*) vote, *m.*; (*sharing*) partage, *m.*

divisor, (*math.*) diviseur, *m.*
divorce, *s.* divorce, *m.*; *v.a.* divorcer (d'avec); (*things*) séparer.
divorced person, divorcee, divorcé, -e, *m.f.*
divulge, divulguer.
dizz|y, (*pers.*) frappé de vertige; (*things*) vertigineu|x, ~se; **~iness,** vertige, *m.*
do, *v.a.* faire*; (*accomplish*) accomplir; (*finish*) finir; (*service, justice*) rendre; (*distance*) faire*; (*of hotel, &c.*) traiter; (*cook*) faire* cuire; (*cheat, pop.*) rouler; **~ again,** refaire*; **~ away with,** supprimer; **~ for,** (*kill*) tuer; (*manage house*) tenir le ménage de; *I am done for,* (*caught, ruined*) je suis flambé; **~ out of,** (*pop.*) refaire* de; **~ up,** (*package, &c.*) envelopper; (*renovate*) remettre* à neuf; **~ without,** se passer de; **~ with,** (*manage*) se contenter de; *I could do with another cup of tea* (*pop.*), une autre tasse de thé ne serait pas de refus; (*control, &c.*) faire* de, *e.g.* il ne peut rien faire de ce garçon; *~ well, ill by,* en user bien, mal avec; *that's not done,* cela ne se fait pas; *no sooner said than done,* aussitôt dit, aussitôt fait; *~ nothing but,* ne faire* que + *inf.*; *have nothing to ~ with* (*things*) n'y être pour rien; (*pers.*) ne pas avoir affaire à; *have done with,* en finir avec; *there's nothing ~ing,* (*lit. and comm.*) les affaires sont dans le marasme.
do, *v.n.* (*fare*) aller* (être); *how do you do?* comment allez-vous?; (*pop.*) comment ça va-t-il?; (*prosper*) aller bien; (*be appropriate*) convenir*; (*be sufficient*) suffire*; (*be adequate*) faire* l'affaire; *~ well to* (*be wise to*), bien faire* de.
do, (*elliptic*) *various methods of translation*: **1** *repeat verb*—(*they promise to pay*), *but they never do*—mais ils ne payent jamais; **2** *use such adverbs as* comme, aussi—(*he reads a good deal*) *and so do I*—et moi aussi; (*you haven't studied*) *as he did*—comme lui; **3** *use* faire*—(*he said he would write*), *but he didn't*—mais il ne l'a pas fait; **4** *in answer to questions, use negative or affirmative adverbs*—(*did you sell it?*)—*I did*—Oui; (*did he say he would come?*)—*He didn't*—Non.
do, (*emphatic*): **1** *affirmative imperative, use* je vous en prie, *or* donc—*do tell me*—dites le moi, je vous en prie; *do be quiet,* restez donc tranquille; **2** *negative imperative, use* n'en faites rien—(*I shall tell him*)—*Don't!*—N'en faites rien!; **3** *in the pres. and past indic. use a strengthening adverb or clause*—*he did see me, but he did not speak*—il m'a vu en effet, mais il n'a pas parlé; *you did say that,* vous l'avez dit, j'en suis sûr.
do: *the pure auxiliary as in such sentences as—What did they find?—I do not say that—is not translated in French. Use pres. or past tense only.*
doable, faisable.
dobbin, gros cheval, *m.*

docil|e, docile; **~ity,** docilité, *f.*
dock, *s.* (*nav. and naut.*) bassin, *m.*; (*comm. for unloading*) dock, *m.*; (*police*) banc des prévenus, *m.*; *dry ~,* bassin d'échouage, *m.*; *graving ~,* bassin de radoub, *m.*; *wet ~,* bassin à flot, *m.*; **~yard,** chantier de construction, *m.*
dock, *s.* (*bot.*) rumex, *m.*
dock, *v.a.* (*tail*) courtauder; *~ of,* priver de; (*ship*) faire* entrer au bassin; *v.n.* (*ship*) passer au bassin.
docker, débardeur, *m.*
docket, *s.* (*contents*) étiquette, *f.*; *v.a.* étiqueter.
doctor, *s.* (*univ.*) docteur, *m.*, doctoresse, *f.*; ⚠ *~ of medicine, divinity, science, &c.,* docteur en, *not* docteur de; (*med. man*) médecin, *m.*; (*for mental diseases*) aliéniste, *m.*; *v.a.* soigner; (*contempt*) droguer; **~ate,** doctorat, *m.*; **~al,** doctoral.
doctrin|e, doctrine, *f.*; **~al,** (*theol.*) doctrinal.
document, document, *m.*; (*official*) pièce, *f.*; **~ary,** documentaire.
dodder, (*bot.*) cuscute, *f.*
doddering, *adj.* tremblotant.
dodec|agon, dodécagone, *m.*; **~ahedron,** dodécaèdre, *m.*
dodge, *s.* (*trick*) ruse, *f.*; (*pop.*) truc, *m.*; (*invention*) invention, *f.*; *v.a.* (*blow, &c.*) esquiver; (*follow*) suivre à la dérobée; *v.n.* faire* des tours et des détours; *~ through,* se faufiler au milieu de.
doe, daine, *f.*; (*rabbit*) lapine, *f.*; (*hare*) hase, *f.*; **~skin,** peau de daim, *f.*
doer, (*action*) auteur, *m.*; *evil-~,* méchant, *m.*; (*malefactor*) malfaiteur, *m.*
doff, ôter.
dog, chien, *m.*; (*wolf, fox, &c.*) mâle; (*fire*) chenet, *m.*; *sly ~,* rusé compère, *m.*; *lead a ~'s life,* mener une vie de chien; *~ in the manger,* chien du jardinier, *m.*; *go to the ~s,* se perdre; *give a ~ a bad name and hang him,* qui veut noyer son chien, l'accuse de la rage; *let sleeping ~s lie,* n'éveillez pas le chat qui dort; *be ~-tired,* être éreinté; *~bane,* (*bot.*) apocyn gobemouches, *m.*; *~berry,* cornouille, *f.*; *~-cart,* dog-cart, *m.*; *~-collar,* collier, *m.*; *~-days,* canicule, *f.*; *~'s ear,* (*book*) corne, *f.*; *~fish,* chien de mer, *m.*; *~'s grass,* chiendent, *m.*; *~-Latin,* latin de cuisine, *m.*; *~-lead,* laisse, *f.*; *~-rose,* églantine, *f.*; *~-wood,* cornouiller, *m.*; *hang-dog look,* mine patibulaire, *f.*
dog, *v.a.* s'attacher au pas de.
doge, doge, *m.*
dogged, opiniâtre; **~ness,** opiniâtreté, *f.*; **~ly,** opiniâtrement.
dogger, (*naut.*) dogre, *m.*
doggerel, *s.* vers de mirliton, *m.*; *adj.* burlesque.
dogma, dogme, *m.*; **~tic,** dogmatique; (*fig.*) autoritaire.
dogmat|ism, dogmatisme, *m.*; **~ist,** dogmatiste, *m.*; **~ize,** dogmatiser.
doing, *s.* fait, *m.*; **~s,** faits et gestes.

m.pl.; *great ~s*, grande fête; *~ up*, (*house*, *&c.*) remise à neuf, *f.*; *~ away with*, abolition, *f.*
doily, naperon, *m.*
doited, hébété.
doldrums, calme plat, *m.*; *be in the ~*, (*pop.*) avoir le cafard.
dole, *s.* distribution, *f.*; (*charity*) aumône, *f.*; (*unemployed*) indemnité de chômage, *f.*; *~ out*, distribuer.
doleful, lugubre; (*pers.*) triste; (*voice*) plainti|f, ~ve; **~ness**, tristesse, *f.*; **~ly**, dolemment.
doll, poupée, *f.*
dollar, dollar, *m.*
dolman, (*hussar*) pelisse, *f.*
dolmen, (*ant.*) dolmen, *m.*
dolorous, douloureu|x, ~se; **~ly**, douloureusement.
dolphin, dauphin, *m.*
dolt, lourdaud, *m.*
domain, (*property*) domaine, *m.*; (*empire*) empire, *m.*
dome, dôme, *m.*; (*sky, trees*) voûte, *f.*
domestic, *s.* domestique, *m.f.*; *adj.* domestique.
domesticate, *v.a.* (*pers.*) rendre attaché à la vie de famille; (*animals*) domestiquer; ⚠ domestiquer *must not be used of persons*; (*plants*) naturaliser; **~d**, *adj.* (*pers. and trade*) d'intérieur; (*animals only*) domestiqué.
domestication, (*pers.*) attachement à la vie d'intérieur; (*animals*) domestication, *f.*
domesticity, caractère familial, *m.*; (*home-life*) vie de famille, *f.*
domicil|e, domicile, *m.*; *v.a.* domicilier; **~iary**, domiciliaire.
dominan|ce, prédominance, *f.*; **~t**, dominant.
dominat|e, *v.a.n.* dominer; **~ion**, domination, *f.*
domineer over, tyranniser.
domineering, autoritaire.
Dominican, *s.m.f. and adj.* dominicain, -e.
dominion, domination, *f.*; (*authority*) autorité, *f.*; *~s*, (*territory*) colonies, *f.pl.*; ⚠ dominion *not French.*
domino, domino, *m.*
don, *v.a.* revêtir*.
donation, don, *m.*
done, (*meat*) cuit; *over~*, trop cuit; *under~*, pas cuit; *see also* DO.
donkey, âne, *m.*; **~ -boy**, ânier, *m.*; **~ -cart**, charrette à âne, *f.*; **~ -ride**, promenade à âne, *f.*
donor, donateur, *m.*
doom, *s.* (*sentence*) sentence, *f.*; (*judgement*) jugement, *m.*; (*death*) mort, *f.*
doom, *v.a.* condamner (à); **~ed to**, (*punishment, death*) voué à.
doomsday, (*day of doom*) jour du jugement, *m.*
door, *doorway*, porte, *f.*; (*veh.*) portière, *f.*; *next-~ neighbour*, *see* NEIGHBOUR; **~ -bell**, sonnette, *f.*; **~ -case**, chambranle, *m.*; **~ -keeper**, concierge, *m.*; **~ -knob**, bouton de porte, *m.*; **~-plate**, plaque, *f.*; **~-post**, montant, *m.*; *with closed ~s*, (*session*) à huis clos; *the fault lies at your door*, vous en êtes responsable; *the ~ please!* le cordon s'il vous plaît!
dope, *s.* stupéfiant, *m.*; *v.a.* administrer un stupéfiant à.
dorado, dorade, *f.*
Dorian, *adj.* dorien, -ne.
Doric, dorique.
dorman|cy, état endormi, *m.*; **~t**, *adj.* (*veg., animals*) endormi; (*inoperative*) tombé en désuétude; (*her.*) dormant.
dormer-window, lucarne, *f.*
dormitory, dortoir, *m.*
dormouse, loir, *m.*
dorsal, *adj.* dorsal.
dory *and* **John Dory**, (*ichth.*) dorée, *f.*
dose, *s.* dose, *f.*; *v.a.* faire* prendre des médicaments à; ⚠ doser = '*to measure out medicine*'.
doss-house, asile de nuit, *m.*
dot, *s.* point, *m.*; *v.a.* marquer d'un point; (*mus. and stipple*) pointer; (*in a line*) pointiller; (*scatter*) parsemer (de).
dotage, radotage, *m.*
dotard, radoteur.
dote, *v.n.* (*old age*) radoter; *~ on*, raffoler de.
dotingly, à la folie.
dotterel, (*ornith.*) guignard, *m.*
dotty, (*pop.*) toqué.
double, *s.* (*quantity, pers.*) double, *m.*; (*things*) pendant, *m.*; *at the ~*, (*mil.*) au pas redoublé.
doubl|e, *adj. and adv.* double; (*false*) faux, fausse; **~-barrelled**, *see* BARRELLED; **~-bass**, *see* BASS; **~-bed**, lit à deux, *m.*; **~-breasted**, (*coat*) croisé; **~-chin**, menton à double étage, *m.*; **~-bottomed**, à double fond; **~ (dual) control**, (*aeron.*) double commande, *f.*; **~-edged**, à deux tranchants; **~-faced**, à double face; **~-lock**, *v.a.* fermer à double tour; *~ or quits*, quitte ou double; *by ~ entry*, (*bkkpg.*) en partie double; **~y**, doublement.
double, *v.a.* doubler; (*letter, &c.*) plier en deux; *v.n.* doubler; *~ up*, se courber en deux.
doublet, pourpoint, *m.*
doubloon, doublon, *m.*
doubt, *s.* doute, *m.*; *no ~*, indubitablement; *without ~*, sans doute; *there is no doubt about it*, cela ne fait aucun doute.
doubt, *v.a.* douter de; *v.n.* douter que *affirmative + subj.*; douter que *negative +* ne *and subj.*
doubtful, douteu|x, ~se; (*hesitating*) indécis; **~ness**, incertitude, *f.*; (*ambiguity*) ambiguïté, *f.*; **~ly**, avec doute; (*irresolutely*) avec indécision.
doubtless, doubtlessly, sans doute.
douche, douche, *f.*
dough, pâte, *f.*; **~y**, pâteu|x, ~se.
doughty, preux.

douse, *v.a.* (*sail*) amener; (*light*) éteindre*; (*drench*) tremper.
dove, colombe, *f.*; ~*-coloured,* gorge de pigeon, *invar.*; **~-cot,** colombier, *m.*
dovetail, *s.* queue d'aronde, *f.*; *v.a.* assembler à queue d'aronde; **~ed,** à queue d'aronde.
dowager, *s.f. and adj.* douairière.
dowdy, mal fagoté.
dower, (dowry), *s.* (*marriage*) dot, *f.*; *v.a.* doter; **~less,** sans dot.
down, *s.* (*feather, on cheeks, thistle, fruit*) duvet, *m.*; (*upland*) coteau, *m.*; *v.a.* abattre; *ups and ~s,* les †hauts et les bas.
down, *adj.* (*sun*) couché; (*wind and prices*) bas, -se; (*train*) descendant; ~ *at heel,* (*shoe*) éculé.
down, *adv. be ~ with,* (*illness*) être au lit avec; *be ~ on,* (*scold*) tancer; *be ~,* (*shares, &c.*) être en moins-value; *up and ~,* de long en large; *be ~ on one's luck,* avoir la déveine.
down, *prep.* (*along*) le long de; (*river, stream*) en aval de; ~ *the street,* plus bas dans la rue.
down, *interj.* (*dog*) à bas les pattes!; ~ *with!* à bas!
downfall, chute, *f.*
downhearted, ~cast, abattu.
downhill, *s.* pente, *f.*; *adv.* en pente.
downpour, torrent de pluie, *m.*
downright, *adj.* (*sincere, genuine*) franc, franche; (*arrant*) fieffé; *adv.* carrément; **~ness,** franchise, *f.*
downstairs, en bas.
downtrodden, opprimé.
downward, *adj.* descendant; ~ *tendency,* (*prices*) tendance à la baisse, *f.*
downwards, (*adv.*) en bas.
downy, duveteu|x, ~se.
doxology, (*eccles.*) doxologie, *f.*
doze, *s.* somme, *m.*; *v.n.* sommeiller; ~ *off,* s'assoupir.
dozen, douzaine, *f.*; *six of one and half a dozen of the other,* bonnet blanc, blanc bonnet.
drab, *s.* (*pers.*) guenipe, *f.*; *adj.* (*colour*) gris.
draft, *s.* (*project*) projet, *m.*; (*letter*) minute, *f.*; (*troops*) détachement, *m.*; (*on bank*) traite, *f.*; *see also* DRAUGHT.
draft, *v.a.* (*parl. bill*) dresser; (*mil.*) détacher; (*draw up*) rédiger.
drag, *s.* (*net*) drague, *f.*; (*veh.*) enrayure, *f.*; (*dredge*) drague, *f.*; (*impediment*) entrave, *f.*; **~-net,** chalut, *m.*
drag, *v.a.* traîner; (*pull*) tirer; (*water*) draguer; (*anchor*) chasser sur; *v.n.* se traîner; (*be long*) se traîner en longueur.
draggle, *v.a.* traîner dans la boue.
dragoman, drogman, *m.*
dragon, dragon, *m.*; **~-fly,** libellule, *f.*
dragonnade, dragonnade, *f.*
dragoon, dragon, *m.*; *v.a.* persécuter.
drain, *s.* (*sewer*) égout, *m.*; (*ditch*) tranchée d'écoulement, *m.*; (*fig.*) saignée, *f.*
drain, *v.a.* (*marsh, &c. and fig.*) drainer; (*glass*) vider; (*exhaust*) épuiser; *v.n.* s'écouler; (*drip dry*) s'égoutter.
drainage, drainage, *m.*; (*fig.*) épuisement, *m.*
drake, canard, *m.*; *wild ~,* malart, *m.*
dram, (*drink*) goutte, *f.*; ~ *-drinker,* riboteur, *m.*
drama, drame, *m.*; (*art*) théâtre, *m.*; **~tist,** dramaturge, *m.*; **~tize,** dramatiser; **~tic,** dramatique.
drape, *v.a.* draper.
draper, (*linen*) marchand de nouveautés, *m.*; (*woollen*) marchand drapier; *~'s shop,* magasin de nouveautés, *m.*; **~y,** (*arrangement of folds*) draperie, *f.*
drastic, drastique.
drat! *interj.* peste soit de!
draught, *s.* **1** (*act of drawing*) tirage, *m.*; **2** (*fish*) coup de filet, *m.*; **3** (*drinking*) trait, *m.*; **4** (*ship*) tirant d'eau, *m.*; **5** (*air*) courant d'air, *m.*; **6** (*chimney*) tirage, *m.*; **7** (*plan, drawing*) esquisse, *f.*; **8** (*med.*) dose, *f.*; **~s,** (*game*) dames, *f.pl.*; **~-board,** damier, *m.*; **~-horse,** cheval de trait, *m.*
draughtsman, dessinateur, *m.*
draw, *s.* attraction, *f.*; (*lottery*) tirage des lots, *m.*
draw, *v.a.* **1** (*pull, sword, bow, bolt, blood, sounds, tears, naut., profit, water, conclusion, cheque*) tirer; **2** (*drag and cart, &c.*) traîner; **3** (*attention, attract*) attirer; **4** (*derive*) retirer; **5** (*teeth, &c.*) arracher; **6** (*hand through or over*) passer; **7** (*comparison*) établir; **8** (*torture*) tirer à quatre chevaux; **9** (*cover, undergrowth*) battre; **10** (*sketch*) dessiner; ~ *aside,* tirer à l'écart; ~ *down,* (*blinds, &c.*) baisser; ~ *in,* (*talons, &c.*) rentrer; ~ *off,* (*beer, &c.*) tirer; (*boots, &c., mil.*) retirer; ~ *on,* (*stockings*) tirer; ~ *out,* (*prolong*) prolonger; (*timid pers.*) encourager; (*take out*) tirer; ~ *together,* réunir; ~ *up,* (*boat*) tirer à terre; (*from well, water*) tirer en haut; (*troops*) ranger; (*document*) rédiger; ~ *oneself up,* se redresser.
draw, *v.n.* (*pull, chimney, &c.*) tirer; (*attract*) attirer; ~ *back,* reculer; ~ *in,* (*days*) raccourcir; ~ *near,* s'approcher; ~ *off,* (*mil.*) se retirer; ~ *on,* (*approach*) approcher; (*banker, &c.*) tirer traite sur; ~ *out,* (*days*) s'allonger; ~ *up,* (*veh.*) s'arrêter; (*mil.*) se ranger.
drawback, inconvénient, *m.*
draw-blind, *see* BLIND.
drawbridge, pont-levis, *m.*
drawer, (*in inn, cheque*) tireur; (*in chest*) tiroir, *m.*; **~s,** (*dress*) caleçon, *m.*; ⚠ caleçon *is sing., not plur. as the English word.*
drawing, (*art*) dessin, *m.*; (*lots*) tirage, *m.*; ~ **-board,** planche à dessin, *f.*; ~ **-block,** bloc à dessin, *m.*; ~ **-pin,** punaise, *f.*; **~-paper,** papier à dessin, *m.*
drawing-room, salon, *m.*; (*court*) réception, *f.*

drawl, *s.* voix traînante, *f.*; *v.a.n.* parler, dire* d'une voix traînante; **~ing,** *adj.* traînant.

drawn, *adj.* (*battle*) indécis; (*game*) nul, -le; (*sword*) nu.

dray, †haquet, *m.*

dread, *s.* crainte, *f.*; (*object of*) terreur, *f.*; *v.a.* redouter; *v.n.* (*that*) craindre* (*if affirmative* que + ne + *subj.*; + *subj. alone if* craindre *is negative*); **~ful,** redoutable; (*boring*) assommant; **~fully,** affreusement; (*slang*) furieusement.

dreadnought, (*nav.*) cuirassé, *m.*

dream, *s.* (*lit. and fig.*) rêve, *m.*; (*delightful thing*) merveille, *f.*; *have a ~,* faire* un rêve; *waking ~,* rêverie, *f.*

dream, *v.a.n.* rêver; (*think of*) songer (à); (*waste time*) rêvasser.

dreamer, rêveu|r, ~se, *m.f.*; (*pej.*) visionnaire, *m.f.*

dreamy, *adj.* rêveu|r, ~se.

drear|y, lugubre; **~iness,** tristesse, *f.*

dredge, *s.* drague, *f.*; *v.a.* draguer.

dredger, *s.* (*mach.*) drague, *f.*; (*pers.*) dragueur, *m.*; (*naut.*) marie-salope, *f.*, *pl.* maries-salopes.

dregs, (*lit. and fig.*) lie, *f.*; *to the ~,* jusqu'à la lie.

drench, *s.* (*vet.*) breuvage, *m.*; *v.a.* (*wet*) tremper.

dress, *s.* (*generally*) habits, *m.pl.*; (*gown*) robe, *f.*; (*style, costume*) toilette, *f.*; **~ -maker,** couturière, *f.*; **~ circle,** fauteuils, *m.pl.*; **~ coat,** habit, *m.*; **~-suit,** habit, *m.*; **~-rehearsal,** répétition en costume, *f.*; *in evening ~,* (*man*) en habit; (*woman*) en décolleté; *in full ~,* (*mil.*) en grande tenue.

dress, *v.a.* **1** habiller; **2** (*adorn*) parer; **3** (*wound*) panser; **4** (*food, cloth, and leather*) apprêter; **5** (*ship, buildings, with flags*) pavoiser; **6** (*shop*) faire* l'étalage de; **7** (*mil.*) aligner; **8** (*hair of*) coiffer; **well ~ed,** bien mis.

dress, *v.n.* s'habiller; (*mil.*) s'aligner; (*for evening*) se mettre* en habit, etc., *see* DRESS, *s.*; *~ up,* faire toilette; (*masquerade*) se travestir; (*fancy dress*) se costumer.

dressing, *s.* **1** (*act*) toilette, *f.*; **2** (*wound*) pansement, *m.*; **3** (*manure*) engrais, *m.*; **4** (*cook.*) assaisonnement, *m.*; **5** (*surg.*) appareil, *m.*; **6** (*troops*) alignement, *m.*; **7** (*scolding*) semonce, *f.*; (*set of ~s for wounds, first aid*) paquet de pansement, *m.*; **~-case,** nécessaire, *m.*; **~-gown,** (*woman*) peignoir, *m.*; (*man*) robe de chambre, *f.*; **~-room,** cabinet de toilette, *m.*; **~-station,** poste de secours, *m.*; **~-table,** toilette, *f.*; *give a good ~ down to,* laver la tête à.

dribble, *v.n.* (*drop*) s'écouler; (*mouth*) baver; (*football*) talonner; *s.* (*football*) dribble, *m.*

dribblet, chiquet, *m.*

drift, *s.* (*naut.*) dérive, *f.*; (*snow, sand, &c.*) amoncellement, *m.*; (*meaning*) sens, *m.*; (*dust*) tourbillon, *m.*; **~-ice,** glaçons en dérive, *m.pl.*; **~-wood,** bois flotté, *m.*

drift, *v.a.* (*of rivers*) apporter; *v.n.* (*naut.*) dériver; (*snow, &c.*) s'amonceler; **~er,** (*naut.*) cordier, *m.*

drill, *s.* (*tool*) foret, *m.*; (*linen*) coutil, *m.*; (*for seed*) semoir, *m.*; (*mil.*) exercice, *m.*; **~-book,** théorie, *f.*; **~-ground,** terrain de manœuvres, *m.*; **~ -sergeant,** sergent instructeur, *m.*

drill, *v.a.* (*bore*) forer; (*pierce*) percer; (*mil.*) exercer; (*force facts, &c., into*) faire* entrer (dans); *v.n.* faire l'exercice.

drink, *s.* boisson, *f.*; (*effect of*) alcoolisme, *m.*; *strong ~,* spiritueux, *m.pl.*; *have a ~,* boire* un coup; *stand ~s,* payer une tournée (à); *be in ~,* être ivre.

drink, *v.a.* boire*; *~ in,* respirer; *~ off,* boire d'un trait; *~ up,* avaler; *~ health of,* boire* à la santé de.

drink, *v.n.* boire*; (*vice*) se livrer à la boisson; *~ like a fish,* boire* comme un trou; *~ hard,* boire* fort.

drinkable, potable.

drinker, *s.* buveu|r, ~se, *m.f.*; *hard ~,* fort buveur.

drinking, (*act*) boire, *m.*; (*drunkenness*) ivrognerie, *f.*; **~-horn,** corne à boire, *f.*; **~-song,** chanson bachique, *f.*; **~-water,** *see* WATER.

drip, *s.* égout, *m.*; *v.n.* dégoutter.

dripping, *s.* gouttes, *f.pl.*; (*fat*) graisse de rôti, *f.*; **~-pan,** lèchefrite, *f.*

dripping, *adj.* trempé (de); (*steeped in*) baigné de.

drive, *s.* promenade en voiture, *f.*; (*hunt.*) battue, *f.*; (*avenue*) avenue, *f.*; (*energy*) cran, *m.*

drive, *v.a.* **1** (*pursue*) poursuivre*; **2** (*hunt.*) chasser; **3** (*veh. and animals*) conduire*; **4** (*impel*) pousser; **5** (*ship by winds*) entraîner; **6** (*nail*) enfoncer; **7** (*mach.*) actionner; **8** (*bargain*) conclure*; **9** (*trade*) faire*; **10** (*game*) rabattre; *~ away, out, off,* chasser; *~ back,* repousser; (*veh., &c.*) reconduire*; *~ in,* (*nail*) enfoncer; (*pers.*) faire* entrer; *~ out,* chasser; *~ mad,* rendre fou, folle.

drive, *v.n.* conduire*; (*in veh.*) aller* (être) en voiture; (*have oneself driven*) se faire* conduire; (*before wind, naut.*) fuir* devant; *~ at,* (*mean*) en venir* (être) à; *~ off, away,* partir* (être) en voiture.

drivel, *s.* bêtises, *f.pl.*; *v.n.* (*talk nonsense*) radoter; **~ler,** radoteu|r, ~se, *m.f.*

driver, (*horse, veh.*) cocher, *m.*; (*cattle, &c.*) bouvier, *m.*; (*carts*) voiturier, *m.*; (*engine*) mécanicien, *m.*; (*motor*) chauffeur, *m.*; *~'s licence,* (*motor*) permis de conduire, *m.*

drizzle, *s.* bruine, *f.*; *v.n.* bruiner.

droll, *adj.* drôle; **~ery,** drôlerie, *f.*

dromedary, dromadaire, *m.*

drone, *s.* (*insect*) bourdon, *m.*; (*pers.*) paresseu|x, ~se, *m.f.*; (*sound*) bour-

donnement, *m.*; *v.a.n.* dire*, parler d'une voix monotone; (*bees, &c.*) bourdonner.
droning, *adj.* monotone.
droop, *v.a.* (*head*) pencher; (*eyes*) baisser; *v.n.* se baisser; (*languish*) languir.
drooping, *adj.* languissant; **~ly,** (*languidly*) languissamment.
drop, *s.* (*lit. and fig., drink*) goutte, *f.*; (*price, &c.*) baisse, *f.*; (*descent*) chute, *f.*; (*ear-ring*) pendant, *m.*; *~ by ~*, goutte à goutte; **~-kick,** (*football*) coup de pied tombé, *m.*
drop, *v.a.* **1** (*tear, liquids*) verser; **2** (*let fall*) laisser tomber; **3** (*give up*) abandonner; **4** (*lower eyes, voice*) baisser; **5** (*letter in post*) jeter; **6** (*hint*) glisser; **7** (*pers., package*) déposer; **8** (*anchor*) jeter; *~ it!* assez!
drop, *v.n.* (*drip*) goutter; (*fall*) tomber (être); (*words*) échapper; (*shares, prices*) baisser; *~ behind, out,* rester (être) en arrière; (*mil.*) sortir* (être) des rangs; *~ down,* tomber (être) par terre; *~ off,* s'en aller* (être) l'un après l'autre.
drops|y, hydropisie, *f.*; **~ical,** hydropique.
dropwort, (*bot.*) filipendule, *f.*
dross, (*melting metal*) scorie, *f.*; (*fig.*) impuretés, *f. pl.*; (*rubbish*) rebut, *m.*
drought, sécheresse, *f.*; (*thirst*) soif, *f.*
drove, (*cattle*) troupeau, *m.*; (*crowd*) foule, *f.*
drover, (*man*) toucheur, *m.*; (*owner*) marchand de bestiaux, *m.*
drown, *v.a.* noyer; (*fig.*) inonder (de); (*sound, voice*) étouffer; *v.n.* se noyer; **~ing,** *s. use verb.*
drows|e, *v.n.* s'assoupir; **~iness,** assoupissement, *m.*; **~y,** (*pers.*) assoupi.
drub, *v.a.* rosser; **~bing,** rossée, *f.*
drudge, *s.* homme, femme de peine, *m.f.*; *v.n.* (*pop.*) trimer.
drudgery, travail pénible, *m.*
drug, *s.* drogue, *f.*; *~-stores*, pharmacie, *f.*; *v.a.* (*liquids*) mettre une drogue dans; (*patient*) droguer; (*poison*) empoisonner.
drugget, droguet, *m.*
druggist, droguiste, *m.*
Druid, ~ess, druide, -sse, *m.f.*; **~ic,** druidique.
drum, *s.* tambour, *m.*; (*ear*) tympan; **~-head,** *see* COURT; **~stick,** baguette de tambour, *f.*; **~ -major,** tambour-major, *m.*; *with ~s beating,* tambour battant.
drummer, tambour, *m.*; (*U.S.A. comm. traveller*) commis-voyageur, *m.*
drunk, (*lit. and fig.*) ivre; *~ as a lord,* ivre comme un Polonais.
drunkard, ivrogne, -sse, *m.f.*
drunken, *adj.* ivrogne; (*things*) d'ivrogne; **~ness,** (*habit*) ivrognerie, *f.*; (*temporary state*) ivresse, *f.*
dry, *adj.* sec, sèche; (*arid, uninteresting, cold*) aride; (*dried up*) desséché; (*a well, &c.*) tari; (*thirsty*) altéré; (*sarcastic*) caustique; *be ~,* (*weather*) faire* sec; *~ land,* terre ferme, *f.*; **~ cleaning,** nettoyage à sec; **~-rot,** carie, *f.*; **~-dock,** bassin d'échouage, *m.*; **~-shod,** à pied sec; **~ly,** (*sarcastic*) caustiquement; **~ness,** (*lit. and fig.*) sécheresse, *f.*; **drily,** (*lit.*) sèchement.
dry, *v.a.* sécher; (*drain*) assécher; *v.n.* sécher; *~ up,* se dessécher.
dryad, dryade, *f.*
dual, *adj.* double. [baptiser.
dub, *v.a.* (*knight*) armer; (*contempt*)
dubious, douteu|x, ~se; (*equivocal*) équivoque; (*shady*) louche; **~ness,** doute, *m.*; **~ly,** d'un air de doute.
ducal, ducal.
ducat, ducat, *m.*
duch|ess, duchesse, *f.*; **~y,** duché, *m.*
duck, (*bird*) cane, *f.*; (*endearment*) petit chou, *m.*; (*cricket*) zéro, *m.*; **~-weed,** lentille d'eau, *f.*; *young wild ~,* †halbran, *m.*; *~s and drakes,* ricochets, *m.pl.*; *make ~s and drakes of,* jeter par les fenêtres.
duck, *s.* (*fabric*) coutil, *m.*
duck, *v.a.n.* plonger; (*head*) *v.a.* baisser.
ducking, *s.* plongeon, *m.*
duckling, caneton, *m.*
duct, conduit, *m.*
ductil|e, (*metals*) ductile; (*supple*) flexible; **~ity,** ductilité, *f.*
dudgeon, rancune, *f.*
due, *s.* dû, *m.*; (*duty, tax*) droit, *m.*; *~s*, droits, *m.pl.*
du|e, *adj.* dû (*f.* due); (*just*) juste; (*bill*) exigible; *not ~,* inexigible; (*train*) attendu; *in ~ form,* en bonne et due forme; *in ~ time,* en temps voulu; *~ to,* (*pers.*) *pres. or cond. of* devoir + *inf.*, il doit (*he is due to*) arriver demain; *~ date,* (*comm.*) date de l'échéance, *f.*; *fall ~,* échoir*; **~ly,** dûment; *~ly received,* (*letter, &c.*) bien reçu.
due, *adv.* (*exactly*) directement.
duel, duelling, duel, *m.*; *fight a ~,* se battre en duel.
duellist, duelliste, *m.*
duenna, duègne, *f.*
duet, duo, *m.*
duffer, (*fool*) imbécile, *m.*
dug, (*ans.*) tétine, *f.*
dug-out, souterrain, *m.*; *also* abri, *m.*; (*zigzag*) boyau, *m.*
duke, duc, *m.*; **~dom,** duché, *m.*
dulcet, *adj.* harmonieu|x, ~se.
dulcimer, tympanon, *m.*
dull, **1** (*stupid*) borné; **2** (*boring*) ennuyeu|x, ~se; **3** (*comm., shares, &c.*) maussade; (*colour*) terne; **4** (*weather, sad*) triste; **5** (*light*) faible; **6** (*fire*) bas; **7** (*sound*) sourd; **8** (*of a painting*) embu; *~ of hearing,* dur d'oreille; *~-eyed,* à l'œil éteint; *~-witted,* à l'esprit lourd; *as ~ as ditch-water, see* DITCH.
dull, *v.a.* (*blunt*) émousser; (*tarnish*) ternir; (*stupefy*) hébéter; (*pain*) endormir*.
dullard, lourdaud, *m.*
dul(l)ness, (*mind*) stupidité, *f.*; (*sight*

hearing) faiblesse, *f.*; (*things*) monotonie, *f.*; (*comm.*) marasme, *m.*
dumb, muet, -te; ~ **-bell,** haltère, *m.*; ~ *show,* pantomime, *f.*; ~ **waiter,** servante, *f.*; ~**ness,** mutisme, *m.*; ~**ly,** sans parler.
dumbfound, *v.a.* confondre.
dummy, (*whist*) mort, *m.*; (*manikin, lay figure*) mannequin, *m.*
dump, *s.* (*refuse, munitions, &c.*) dépôt, *m.*; *v.a.* décharger.
dumpling, (*approx.*) dumpling, *m.*
dumps, *be in the,* avoir le cafard.
dumpy, (*pers.*) trapu; (*things*) court, -e et gros, -se.
dun, *adj.* brun; (*horses*) isabelle; *s.* isabelle, *m.*
dun, *s.* créancier importun, *m.*; *v.a.* (*lit. and fig.*) relancer.
dunce, cancre, *m.*; ~*'s cap,* bonnet d'âne, *m.*
dune, (*sand*) dune, *f.*
dung, (*ans.*) fiente, *f.*; (*sheep, goats, rabbits, &c.*) crotte, *f.*; (*agric.*) fumier, *m.*; ~**-hill,** fumier, *m.*; ~**-pit,** fosse à fumier, *f.*
dung, *v.a.* (*manure*) fumer.
dungeon, cachot, *m.*
dunlin, (*ornith.*) bécasseau, *m.*
duodecimal, *adj.* duodécimal.
duodecimo, in-douze, *m.*
dupe, dupe, *f.*; *v.a.* duper.
duplex, *adj.* double; (*instruments*) duplex, *invar.*; ~ *lamp,* lampe duplex, *f.*
duplicate, *s.* (*papers*) duplicata, *m.*; (*objects, a deed, &c.*) double, *m.*; *in* ~, en double.
duplicate, *adj.* en double; (*exactly alike*) de rechange; ~ (*spare*) *wheel,* roue de rechange, *f.*; ~ *key,* double de la clef, *m.*
duplicat|e, *v.a.* faire* en double; ~**ion,** duplication, *f.*; ~*ing machine,* duplicateur, *m.*
duplicity, duplicité, *f.*
durab|le, durable; ~**ility,** durabilité, *f.*
durance, emprisonnement, *m.*; *in* ~ *vile,* sur paille d'un cachot, *f.*
duration, durée, *f.*
duress, contrainte, *f.*
during, pendant.
dusk, *s.* crépuscule, *m.*; ~ *of evening,* brune, *f.*
dusk, dusky, *adj.* sombre; *grow* ~, faire* sombre.
dust, *s.* poussière, *f.*; (*metal*) poudre, *f.*; (*refuse*) balayures, *f.pl.*; ~**-bin,** boîte aux ordures, *f.*; ~**-cart,** tombereau, *m.*; ~**-coat,** cache-poussière, *m. invar.*; ~**-hole,** trou aux ordures, *m.*; ~**man,** boueur, *m.*; ~**pan,** ramasse-poussière, *m.*; *throw* ~ *in the eyes of,* (*impose on*) jeter de la poudre aux yeux de; *bite the* ~, mordre la poussière.
dust, *v.a.* épousseter; ~**y,** poussiéreu|x, ~se.
duster, torchon, *m.*; *feather* ~, plumeau, *m.*
Dutch, *adj.*; †hollandais, -e; (*lang.*) †hollandais, *m.*; ~ **hoe,** *see* HOE; ~ **oven,** rôtissoire, *f.*; *the* ~, les †Hollandais.
Dutch|man, (*pers.*) †Hollandais, *m.*; (*ship*) navire †hollandais, *m.*; ~**woman,** †Hollandaise, *f.*
dutiful, (*obedient*) obéissant; (*respectful*) respectueu|x, ~se; ~**ness,** obéissance, *f.*; ~**ly,** avec obéissance.
dut|y, (*moral, legal*) devoir, *m.*; (*customs, &c.*) droit, *m.*; (*compliments*) hommages, *m.pl.*; (*task*) tâche, *f.*; ~**ies,** (*functions*) fonctions, *f.pl.*; ~*y free,* (*goods*) en franchise; (*customs*) à franc, franche de douane; *be on* ~*y,* être de service; *be off* ~*y,* ne pas être de service.
dwarf, *s.* (*pers. and plants*) nain, -e, *m.f.*; *adj.* nain; (*stunted*) rabougri; *v.a.* rabougrir; (*render smaller*) rapetisser.
dwell, *v.n.* (*reside*) habiter; (*stay*) rester (être); ~ *on, upon,* (*emphasize*) s'appesantir sur.
dweller, habitant, -e, *m.f.*
dwelling, habitation, *f.*; ~ **-house,** maison d'habitation, *f.*; ~ **-place,** demeure, *f.*
dwindle, (*grow less*) diminuer; ~ *away,* (*capital and gen.*) dépérir.
dye, *s.* (*tint, gen. and fig.*) teinte, *f.*; (*matter used for dyeing, hair*) teinture, *f.*; *of the deepest* ~, (*fig.*) de la dernière noirceur; ~**ing,** teinture, *f.*; ~**r,** teinturi|er, ~ère, *m.f.*; ~**-works,** teinturerie, *f.*; *v.a.* teindre*; (~ *black, green, &c.*) teindre* en.
dyer's weed, (*bot.*) gaude, *f.*
dying, *adj.* (*pers.*) mourant; (*things*) de mort; (*last*) derni|er, ~ère; *be* ~, se mourir*.
dyke, *see* DIKE.
dynamic, *adj.* dynamique; ~**s,** *s.* dynamique, *f.*
dynamite, *s.* dynamite, *f.*; *v.a.* dynamiter.
dynamo, dynamo, *f.*
dynast, dynaste, *m.*; ~**y,** dynastie, *f.*; ~**ic,** dynastique.
dysentery, dysenterie, *f.*
dyspep|sia, dyspepsie, *f.*; ~**tic,** *adj. and s.m.f.* dyspeptique.

E

each, each one, *pron.* chacun, -e; ~ *other,* l'un l'autre, l'une l'autre, les uns les autres, les unes les autres. *With verbs taking Acc. or Dat. the reflexive form of the verb must be used also, e.g.* Ils s'aiment l'un l'autre (⚠ *not* ils aiment); Ils s'obéissent les uns aux autres. *A preposition may divide* l'un l'autre, *e.g.* Les femmes sont tombées les unes sur les autres.
each, *adj.* chaque.
eager, ardent; (*zealous*) empressé (de); (*pej.*) avide de; *be* ~ *to,* brûler de; ~**ness,** empressement, *m.*; ~**ly,** avec empressement.

eagle, aigle, *m.*; (*her. and standard*) aigle, *f.*; (*church*) lutrin, *m.*; **~-eyed,** aux yeux d'aigle; ~ **owl,** grand-duc, *m.*
eaglet, aiglon, *m.*
ear, oreille, *f.*; (*corn*) épi, *m.*; *have a quick, good ~,* avoir l'oreille fine; *box the ~s of,* souffleter, *v.a.*; *set by the ~s,* mettre* aux prises; *over head and ~s,* par-dessus les oreilles; **~-ring,** boucle d'oreille, *f.*; **~-trumpet,** cornet acoustique, *m.*; *turn a deaf ~ to,* tourner la sourde oreille à.
earl, comte, *m.*; **~dom,** comté, *m.*
earliness, (*arrival*) arrivée prématurée, *f.*; (*hour*) heure peu avancée, *f.*
early, *adj.* (*pers.*) matinal; (*fruit*) précoce; (*time of life*) premi|er, ~ère; ~ **riser,** personne matinale, *f.*
early, *adv.* de bonne heure; ~ *in,* (*June, July, &c.*) au commencement de.
earmark for, affecter à.
earn, gagner; (*deserve*) mériter; **~ed,** (*comm.*) acquis.
earnest, *s.* (*pledge, money*) arrhes, *f.pl.*; *in ~,* sérieusement; *in good ~,* tout de bon.
earnest, *adj.* sérieu|x, ~se; (*fervent*) fervent; **~ness,** ardeur, *f.*; (*fervour*) ferveur, *f.*; **~ly,** sérieusement.
earnings, salaire, *m.*
ear-phones, (*wireless*) écouteurs, *m.pl.*
earth, terre, *f.*; (*soil*) sol, *m.*; **~work,** terrassement, *m.*; **~worm,** ver de terre, *m.*; *how on ~ !* comment diable !
earthen, de terre; **~ware,** poterie, *f.*; (*crockery*) faïence, *f.*
earthly, terrestre; (*pop.*) *be of no ~ use,* ne pas être de la moindre utilité du monde.
earthquake, tremblement de terre, *m.*
earthy, de terre.
earwig, (*ent.*) perce-oreille, *m.*
ease, (*absence of discomfort*) aise, *f.*; (*rest*) repos, *m.*; (*comforts*) aises, *f.pl.*; (*of pain*) soulagement, *m.*; *with ~,* avec facilité; *at one's ~,* à son aise; *stand at ease!* (*mil.*) repos!
ease, *v.a.* (*pain*) soulager; (*mind*) tranquilliser; **~ment,** soulagement, *m.*
easel, chevalet, *m.*
easiness, (*gen. and money*) facilité, *f.*; (*manners, style*) aisance, *f.*
east, *s.* (*point of horizon*) est, *m.*; *adj.* d'est, de l'est; *adv.* à l'est; ~ *of,* à l'est de; *north-~, see* NORTH; *south-~, see* SOUTH.
East, Orient, *m.*; *near ~,* proche Orient; *far ~,* Extrême Orient.
Easter, *s.* Pâques, *m.pl.*; *adj.* de Pâques; ~ **Sunday,** dimanche de Pâques, *m.*
easterly, d'est.
eastern, oriental.
eastwards, *adv.* vers l'est.
eas|y, facile; (*manners*) aisé; (*gentle*) dou|x, ~ce; (*style*) coulant; (*mind*) tranquille; **~-chair,** fauteuil, *m.*; **~-going,** facile à vivre; *make yourself ~,* tranquillisez-vous; **~iness,** (*style, manners*) facilité, *f.*; **~ily,** facilement.
eat, *v.a.* manger; ~ *one's words,* se rétracter; ~ *away,* ronger; ~ *into,* ronger; ~ *up,* (*food*) finir; (*fig.*) dévorer; *~en up with,* (*pride, &c.*) bouffi de.
eat, *v.n.* manger; (*taste of food*) se manger.
eatable, *adj.* mangeable; **~s,** *s.* comestibles, *m.pl.*
eater, mang|eur, ~euse, *m.f.*
eating, manger, *m.*; *very good ~,* très bon plat, *m.*
eating-house, restaurant, *m.*; ~ **keeper,** restaurateur, *m.*
eaves, avant-toit, *m.*
eavesdropper, personne qui écoute aux portes, *f.*
ebb, (*tide*) reflux, *m.*; (*decline*) déclin, *m.*; *v.a.* (*tide*) refluer; (*fig.*) décliner.
ebony, *s.* ébène, *m.*; *adj.* d'ébène; **~-tree,** plaqueminier, *m.*
ebriety, ivresse, *f.*
ebull|ient, bouillant; (*fig.*) exubérant; **~ition,** ébullition, *f.*; (*fig.*) effervescence, *f.*
eccentric, *s.* (*mach.*) excentrique, *m.*; *adj.* excentrique; **~ity,** excentricité, *f.*
ecclesiastic, *adj. and s.m.* ecclésiastique; **~al,** ecclésiastique.
echidna, (*zool.*) échidné, *m.*
echinus, (*zool.*) oursin de mer, *m.*
echo, écho, *m.*; *v.a.* faire écho à; (*words, opinions*) répéter; ~ *with, v.n.* résonner de.
eclectic, éclectique; **~ism,** éclectisme, *m.*
eclipse, (*astr. and fig.*) éclipse, *f.*
ecliptic, *adj. and s.f.* écliptique.
eclogue, églogue, *f.*
economic, (*relating to economics*) économique; **~s,** économie politique, *f.*
economical, ⚠ *not* économique, *of persons, but* économe; (*things*) économique.
economist, (*thrifty person*) personne économe, *f.*; (*writer on political economy*) économiste, *m.*
economize, *v.a.* ménager; *v.n.* faire* des économies.
economy, économie, *f.*
ecsta|sy, (*med. and eccles.*) extase, *f.*; (*fig.*) transport, *m.*; **~tic,** extatique.
eczema, (*med.*) eczéma, *m.*
edaci|ty, voracité, *f.*; **~ous,** vorace.
eddy, (*water*) remous, *m.*; (*wind*) tourbillon, *m.*; ~ **-wind,** (*naut.*) revolin, *m.*; *v.n.* tourbillonner.
edelweiss, (*bot.*) edelweiss, *m.*
Eden, (*lit. and fig.*) Éden, *m.*
edentate, édenté.
edge, *s.* (*boundary, brink*) bord, *m.*; (*tools, &c.*) tranchant, *m.*; (*sword*) fil, *m.*; (*forest*) lisière, *f.*; **~s,** (*book*) tranches, *f.pl.*; *gilt ~s,* tranches dorées; *give an ~ to,* aiguiser.
edge, *v.a.* (*border*) border; (*sharpen*) aiguiser.
edged, bordé; **gilt-~,** (*books*) doré sur tranche; (*securities*) de père de famille; **two-~,** à deux tranchants.
edgeways, de côté.

edging, (*garden and trimming*) bordure, *f.*; (*braid*) ganse, *f.*
edible, comestible.
edict, édit, *m.*
edif|y, édifier; **~ying**, édifiant; **~ication**, édification, *f.*
edifice, édifice, *m.*
edit, *v.a.* (*newspaper*) rédiger; (*a work*) préparer la publication de; ⚠ éditer *properly* = '*to publish*'.
edit|ion, édition, *f.*; **~or**, (*newspaper*) rédacteur, *m.*; **~orship**, direction, *f.*; *~or's office*, rédaction, *f.*; *sub-~or*, rédacteur gérant, *m.*
editorial, *s.* article de tête, *m.*; *adj.* d'éditeur.
educat|e, élever; *well ~ed*, instruit; *be ~ed at*, (*place*) faire ses études à; **~ion**, éducation, *f.*; *have good general ~ion*, avoir des clartés de tout; **~ional**, d'éducation.
educe, *v.a.* tirer.
eduction-valve, soupape d'échappement, *f.*
eel, anguille, *f.*
eerie, *adj.* surnaturel, -le.
efface, effacer; **~ment**, effacement, *m.*
effect, effet, *m.*; *to that ~*, *adv.* à cet effet; *adj.* équivalent; *carry into ~*, exécuter; *take ~*, faire* effet; **~s**, ((*personal, clothes, &c.*) effets; (*movables*) effets mobiliers; *v.a.* effectuer.
effective, efficace; (*striking*) frappant; (*actual*) effecti|f, **~ve**; *~ force, effectives*, (*mil.*) effectif, *m.*
effectu|al, efficace; **~ate**, *v.a.* effectuer.
effemina|cy, mollesse, *f.*; **~te**, efféminé.
effervesce, *v.n.* (*lit. and fig.*) être en effervescence; **~nce**, effervescence, *f.*; **~nt**, effervescent.
effete, épuisé.
efficacious, efficace; **~ness**, efficacité, *f.*
efficien|cy, efficacité, *f.*; (*aptitude*) compétence, *f.*; **~t**, (*cause*) efficient; (*pers.*) capable.
effigy, effigie, *f.*
effloresce, *v.n.* s'effleurir; **~nce**, floraison, *f.*; **~nt**, efflorescent.
effluen|ce, émanation, *f.*; **~t**, *adj.* effluent.
effluvium, effluve, *m.*
efflux, écoulement, *m.*
effort, effort, *m.*; *an ~ to*, effort pour; **~less**, sans effort.
effrontery, effronterie, *f.*
effulgen|ce, splendeur, *f.*; **~t**, resplendissant.
effus|e, répandre; **~ion**, effusion, *f.*; **~ive**, (*gushing*) démonstrati|f, **~ve**.
e.g., (*abbrev.*) par ex.
egad, *interj.* parbleu!
egg, œuf, *m.*; *boiled ~, see* BOIL; *new-laid ~*, œuf frais; *poached ~*, œuf poché; *put all one's ~s into one basket*, mettre* tous ses œufs dans le même panier; **~-cup**, coquetier, *m.*; **~-plant** *and fruit*, aubergine, *f.*; **~-shell**, coquille, *f.*; **~-whisk**, fouet à œufs, *m.*

eglantine, (*bot.*) églantine, *f.*
egois|m, égoïsme, *m.*; **~t**, égoïste, *m.*; **~tic**, égoïste.
egotis|m, égotisme, *m.*; **~t**, égotiste, *m.*; **~tic**, égotiste.
egregious, (*notable*) insigne; (*downright*) fieffé.
egress, (*lit. and fig.*) sortie, *f.*
egret, (*ornith.*) héron-aigrette, *m.*
Egypt|ian, *adj.* (*when an adj. use small letter*) *and s.m.f.* Égyptien, -ne; **~ologist**, égyptologue, *m.*
eider, (*ornith.*) eider, *m.*; **~ -down**, édredon, *m.*; (*quilt*) couvre-pied d'édredon, *m.*
eight, *adj. and s.m.* †huit; **8 o'clock** †huit heures; **~h**, *adj. and s.m.f.* †huitième; (*date and of sovereign*) †huit.
eight, *s.* (*boating*) équipe de †huit, *f.*
eighteen, dix-huit; **~th**, *adj. and s.m.f.* dix-huitième.
eighty, quatre-vingts (*no* s *if another numeral immediately follows*).
either, *pron. and adj.* (*one or other of two*) l'un (l'une) ou l'autre; (*each of two*) *pron.* chacun; *adj.* chaque; (*with neg.* ne), ni l'un, ni l'autre; *I will not have ~*, Je ne veux ni l'un, ni l'autre; *~ of you*, l'un de vous; *on ~ side*, des deux côtés.
either, **~ . . . or**, *conj.* ou . . . ou (*sometimes* + bien); *~ because . . . or because*, soit que + *subj.* . . . soit que + *subj.*
either, *adv.* non plus; *I shall not write ~*, je n'écrirai pas non plus.
ejaculat|e, *v.n.* s'écrier; **~ion**, exclamation, *f.*; **~ory**, jaculatoire.
eject, *v.a.* (*expel*) expulser; (*food*) rejeter; (*throw*) jeter; **~ion**, éjection, *f.*; (*expulsion*) expulsion, *f.*; **~ment**, expulsion, *f.*
eke, *adv.* aussi.
eke out, *v.a.* suppléer à.
elaborat|e, *v.a.* élaborer; (*style*) travailler; *adj.* minutieu|x, **~se**; (*carefully done*) soigné; (*in workmanship*) travaillé; **~ion**, élaboration, *f.*; **~eness**, (*of workmanship*) travail, *m.*
elapse, *v.n.* (*time*) s'écouler.
elastic, *s.* élastique, *m.*; *adj.* (*lit. and fig.*) élastique; **~ity**, élasticité, *f.*
elate, *v.a.* (*joy, &c.*) transporter (de); (*pej.*) exalter.
elation, (*pride*) fierté, *f.*; (*joy*) transport, *m.*
elbow, *s.* coude, *m.*; (*arm-chair*) bras, *m.*; **~ -grease**, huile de coude, *f.*; **~-room**, coudées franches, *f.pl.*
elbow, *v.a.* coudoyer; *v.n.* jouer des coudes.
elder, *s.* (*children*) aîné, -e, *m.f.*; **~s**, ceux qui sont plus âgés; (*sect, tribe*) ancien, *m.*
elder, eldest, *adj.* aîné, plus âgé.
elder, elder-tree, *s.* (*bot.*) sureau, *m.*; **~-berry**, baie de sureau, *f.*
elderly, d'un certain âge.
elect, *v.a.* choisir; (*for an office*) élire*; (*nominate*) nommer; *adj.* élu; *s. the ~*, (*theol.*) les élus, *m.pl.*

election, (*polit., theol.*) élection, *f.*; **~eer,** *v.n.* faire* de la propagande électorale; **~eering,** propagande électorale, *f.*
elect|or, ~ress, *s.* élect|eur, ~rice, *m.f.*; **~ive,** électi|f, ~ve; **~oral,** électoral.
electorate, *s.* (*Germ. Hist.*) électorat, *m.*; (*polit.*) les électeurs, *m.pl.*
electric, *adj.* électrique; **~al** *engineer,* ingénieur électricien, *m.*; **~ian,** électricien, *m.*; **~ity,** électricité, *f.*; **~ lamp,** lampe électrique, *f.*; **~ shock,** secousse électrique, *f.*; **~ torch,** lampe électrique, *f.*; **~ works,** usine à électricité, *f.*
electrif|y, *v.a.* électriser; **~ication,** électrification, *f.*
electrization, électrisation, *f.*
electro, ~-dynamics, électrodynamique, *f.*; **~-magnetism,** électromagnétisme, *m.*; **~-magnetic,** électromagnétique; **~-plate,** plaqué, *m.*; **~-plated,** de ruolz.
electrocution, électrocution, *f.*
electrode, électrode, *f.*
electrolier, lustre électrique, *m.*
electrolyte, électrolyte, *m.*
electrometer, électromètre, *m.*
electron, électron, *m.*
electrum, électrum, *m.*
electuary, électuaire, *m.*
eleemosynary, *adj.* élémosinaire.
elegan|ce, élégance, *f.*; **~t,** élégant.
elegiac, *adj.* (*verse*) élégiaque.
elegy, élégie, *f.*
element, (*lit., fig., component part, chem., rudiment*) élément, *m.*; **~s,** (*atmospheric*) éléments, *m.pl.*; *in, out of one's ~,* dans, †hors de son élément; **~al,** des éléments.
elementary, élémentaire.
elephant, éléphant, *m.*; **~ine,** éléphantin.
elevat|e, élever; (*pej.*) exalter; **~d,** (*drink*) gris; (*style*) élevé; **~ion,** (*elevating, height above, to rank, loftiness, arch.*) élévation, *f.*; (*drunken*) ivresse, *f.*
elevator, (*mach.*) ascenseur, *m.*; (*aeron.*) gouvernail de profondeur, *m.*
eleven, †onze; **~th,** onzième; (*date and of sovereign*) onze; *s.* (*cricket, &c.*) équipe, *f.*
elf, *s.* elfe, *m.*; (*child*) marmot, *m.*; **~in,** *adj.* des elfes.
elicit, (*answer, admission*) tirer; (*truth, &c.*) découvrir*; (*draw forth*) faire* sortir.
elide, élider.
eligib|le, éligible (à); (*suitable*) convenable (à); **~ility,** éligibilité, *f.*
eliminat|e, (*gen. and math.*) éliminer; **~ion,** élimination, *f.*
elision, élision, *f.*
elixir, élixir, *m.*
elk, (*zool.*) élan, *m.*
ell, aune, *f.*
ell|ipsis, ~ipse, ellipse, *f.*; **~iptic, ~iptical,** elliptique.
elm, orme, *m.*; **~-grove,** ormaie, *f.*
elocution, élocution, *f.*; **~ary,** d'élocution.
elongat|e, allonger; **~ion,** allongement, *m.*; (*extension*) extension, *f.*
elope, s'enfuir*; **~ment,** enlèvement, *m.*
eloquen|ce, éloquence, *f.*; **~t,** éloquent.
else, *adj.* autre; *any, somebody ~,* quelqu'un d'autre; *anything ~,* quelque autre chose; *nobody ~,* ne . . . personne d'autre; *what ~?,* quoi de plus?
else, *adv.* ailleurs; (*otherwise*) autrement; *or ~,* ou bien; *nowhere ~,* nulle autre part; *anywhere ~,* n'importe où ailleurs.
elsewhere, ailleurs.
elucidat|e, éclaircir; **~ion,** éclaircissement, *m.*
elu|de, (*question*) éluder; (*difficulty*) esquiver; (*blow, &c.*) éviter; (*obligation*) se dérober à; **~sive,** qui échappe; **~siveness,** caractère évasif, *m.*
elusory, évasi|f, ~ve.
Elys|ium, Élysée, *m.*; **~ian,** élyséen, -ne.
emaciat|e, *v.a.* amaigrir; (*soil*) appauvrir; **~ed,** décharné; **~ion,** amaigrissement, *m.*
emanat|e, *v.n.* émaner; **~ion,** émanation, *f.*
emancipat|e, émanciper; (*fig.*) affranchir (de); **~ion,** émancipation, *f.*; **~or,** émancipat|eur, ~rice, *m.f.*; **~ory,** émancipat|eur, ~rice.
emasculat|e, (*lit. and fig.*) émasculer; **~ion,** émasculation, *f.*
embalm, *v.a.* embaumer; **~ing,** *s.* embaumement, *m.*
embank, *v.a.* (*road*) remblayer; (*river*) endiguer; **~ment,** remblai, *m.*; (*U.S.A.*) levée, *f.*
embargo, *s.* embargo, *m.*; *lay an ~ on,* mettre* l'embargo sur.
embark, *v.a.* embarquer; *v.n.* s'embarquer (dans).
embarkation, embarquement, *m.*; ⚠ *not* embarcation *which* = '*small boat*'.
embarrass, *v.a.* embarrasser; (*money*) gêner; **~ment,** embarras, *m.*
embassy, ambassade, *f.*
embattle, *v.a.* ranger en bataille; **~d,** (*fort.*) crénelé.
embellish, embellir; **~ment,** embellissement, *m.*
ember, braise, *f.*; **~s,** cendres, *f.pl.*
Ember, *adj.* des quatre-temps; *~ Days,* Quatre-Temps, *m.pl.*
ember, (*ornith.*) plongeon, *m.*
embezzle, détourner; **~ment,** détournement, *m.*
embitter, (*pers.*) aigrir; (*quarrel, &c.*) envenimer.
emblazon, (*her.*) blasonner.
emblem, emblème, *m.*; (*her.*) devise, *f.*; **~atic,** emblématique.
embod|y, revêtir* d'un corps; (*fig.*) incorporer; **~iment,** incarnation, *f.*
embog, *v.a.* embourber.
embolden, enhardir.
embosom, (*embrace*) serrer dans les bras; (*enclose in*) enfouir (dans).
emboss, *v.a.* (*gold, &c.*) ciseler; (*sculpt.*) graver en relief; (*paper*) gaufrer; ⚠ *not* embosser *which* = (*naut.*) '*lay broadside on*'; **~ment,** bosselure, *f.*

embossing-stamp, ~-press, timbre sec, *m.*
embowel, éventrer.
embower, (*in trees, &c.*) enfouir (dans).
embrace, *s.* étreinte, *f.*; *v.a.* (*with mind and sight, relig., include, with affection*) embrasser; (*opportunity*) saisir; (*offer*) accepter.
embranchment, (*road, rail, river*) embranchement, *m.*
embrasure, embrasure, *f.*
embrocation, embrocation, *f.*
embroider, broder; **~er,** *s.* brodeu|r, ~se, *m.f.*; **~y, ~ing,** broderie, *f.*; *~y frame,* métier à broderie, *m.*
embroil, (*things*) embrouiller; (*pers.*) brouiller; **~ment,** embrouillement, *m.*; brouille, *f.*
embryo, embryon, *m.*; (*fig.*) germe, *m.*; **~nic,** embryonnaire.
emend, *v.a.* (*text*) émender; **~ation,** émendation, *f.*
emerald, émeraude, *f.*
emerge, *v.n.* (*suddenly appear*) apparaître*; (*from water and fig.*) émerger; (*issue*) sortir* (être) (de).
emergen|ce, émergence, *f.*; **~t,** émergent.
emergency, (*necessity*) circonstance critique, *f.*; (*situation*) situation, *f.*; (*combination of events*) conjoncture, *f.*; *in case of ~,* en cas d'accident; *~ exit,* sortie de secours, *f.*
emeritus, honoraire.
emersion, (*astr.*) émersion, *f.*
emery, (*polish*) émeri, *m.*
emetic, *adj. and s.m.* émétique.
emigrant, émigrant, -e, *s.m.f.*; (*polit.*) émigré, -e, *m.f.*
emigrat|e, émigrer; **~ion,** émigration, *f.*
eminence, (*height, rank*) éminence, *f.*; (*title*) Éminence, *f.*
eminent, éminent; *most ~,* (*title*) éminentissime.
emir, émir, *m.*
emissary, émissaire, *m.*
emi|t, (*opinion, sound, light, coinage*) émettre*; (*chem. and smell*) dégager; **~ssion,** émission, *f.*, dégagement, *m.*
emmet, fourmi, *f.*
emollient, *adj. and s.m.* émollient.
emolument, émolument, *m.*
emotion, émotion, *f.*; **~al,** (*given to ~*) émotionnable; (*exciting emotion*) émoti|f, ~ve.
empanel, *v.a.* inscrire*.
emperor, empereur, *m.*; **~-moth,** empereur, *m.*
emphasis, accent, *m.*; ⚠ *not* emphase *which = 'pomposity'*; *lay ~ on,* appuyer sur.
emphasize, (*words*) appuyer sur; (*fig.*) mettre* en relief.
emphatic, (*expression*) énergique.
empire, (*lit. and fig.*) empire, *m.*
empiric, *adj. and s.m.* empirique; **~ism,** empirisme, *m.*
emplacement, (*position and artil.*) emplacement, *m.*
employ, *s.* emploi, *m.*; **~ee,** employé, *m.*; **~er,** employeu|r, ~se, *m.f.*; (*colloq. boss*) patron, *m.*
employ, *v.a.* (*pers. and gen.*) employer; (*use*) se servir* de; (*occupy in*) employer à; **~ment,** emploi, *m.*; *~ment agency,* agence de placement, *f.*
emporium, entrepôt, *m.*
empower, autoriser (à); *~ed to,* investi du pouvoir de.
empress, impératrice, *f.*
emprise, entreprise, *f.*
empt|iness, vide, *m.*; **~y,** vide; (*fig.*) vain; (*words*) vide de sens; (*ships*) à vide; *returned ~y,* vide en retour; **~y-headed,** nul, -le.
empty, *v.a.* vider; *v.n.* se vider.
empyrean, *adj. and s.m.* empyrée.
emu, (*zool.*) émeu, *m.*
emulat|e, rivaliser avec; **~ion,** émulation, *f.*; **~or,** émule, *m.*
emulous, émule; (*desirous of*) ambitieux de; **~ly,** à l'envi.
emuls|ion, émulsion, *f.*; **~ive,** *s.* émulsif, *m.*; *adj.* émulsi|f, ~ve.
enable, mettre* à même (de); (*means*) donner le moyen (de); *be ~d to,* être à même de.
enact, ordonner; (*law*) faire*; **~ment,** décret, *m.*
enamel, *s.* émail, *m.* (*pl.* -aux); *v.a.* émailler; (*tiles*) vernisser.
enamour, enamourer; (*fig.*) charmer; *be ~ed of,* être enamouré de; (*pej.*) s'être amouraché de.
encage, mettre* en cage; (*prison*) enfermer.
encamp, *v.n.* camper; **~ment,** campement, *m.*
encase, enfermer.
encash, (*cheque, &c.*) encaisser; **~ment,** encaissement, *m.*
encaustic, (*paint.*) *adj. and s.m.* encaustique.
enchain, (*lit. and fig.*) enchaîner.
enchant, (*lit. and fig.*) enchanter; **~ment,** enchantement, *m.*
enchant|ing, *adj. and* **~er,** *s.m.* **~ress,** *f.* enchant|eur, ~eresse.
encircle, entourer.
enclitic, *adj. and s.f.* enclitique.
enclose, (*surround*) entourer (de); (*in a letter*) joindre*; (*contain*) renfermer; *~ a stamp,* joindre un timbre; **~d,** ci-inclus (*invar.* **1** *at beginning of sentence,* **2** *before noun without adj. or article*); *I send you ~d a copy of the letter,* Je vous envoie ci-inclus copie de la lettre.
enclosure, (*place*) enclos, *m.*; (*fence*) clôture, *f.*; (*in a letter*) pièce jointe, *f.*
encomiast, panégyriste, *m.f.*; **~ic,** *adj.* louangeu|r, ~se.
encomium, éloge, *m.*
encompass, environner; (*effect*) venir* (être) à bout de.

encore, *interj.* bis!; *v.a.* bisser; *s.* demande de bisser, *f.*; *cry* ~, *v.n.* bisser.
encounter, *s.* (*meeting*) rencontre, *f.*; (*with enemy*) combat, *m.*; (*struggle*) lutte, *f.*
encounter, *v.a.* (*confront, attack enemy*) affronter; (*difficulty, &c.*) éprouver; (*meet*) rencontrer.
encourag|e, encourager; (*incite*) inciter (à); **~ement,** encouragement, *m.*; **~ing,** encourageant.
encroach on, *v.n.* empiéter sur; (*intrude on*) abuser de; (*rights*) anticiper sur; **~ment,** empiètement, *m.*
encumber, embarrasser; (*with mortgage, debt*) grever (de).
encumbrance, embarras, *m.*; (*financial*) charge, *f.*
encyclic(al), *adj. and s.f.* encyclique.
encycloped|ia, encyclopédie, *f.*; **~ist,** encyclopédiste, *m.*; **~ic,** encyclopédique.
end, *s.* (*extremity*) bout, *m.*; (*conclusion*) fin, *f.*; (*death*) mort, *f.*; (*prescribed end*) terme, *m.*; (*aim*) but, *m.*; (*outcome*) issue, *f.*; *on* ~, debout; *stand on* ~, (*hair*) se dresser sur la tête; *to no* ~, à n'en plus finir; *odds and* ~*s*, pièces et morceaux, *m.pl.*; *make both* ~*s meet*, joindre* les deux bouts; *be at one's wit's* ~, être au bout de son rouleau; *be at a loose* ~, être désœuvré; *come to a bad* ~, finir mal; *put an* ~ *to*, mettre* fin à; *several months on* ~, plusieurs mois de suite.
end, *v.a.* finir; (*finish off*) achever; *v.n.* finir; ~ *in*, finir en; ~ *by*, (*doing*) finir par + *inf.*; ~ (*doing*) finir de; *never* ~*ing*, interminable.
endanger, mettre* en danger.
endear, rendre cher, chère; **~ing,** attachant; **~ment,** caresse, *f.*
endeavour, *s.* effort, *m.*; (*try*) tentative, *f.*; *v.n.* s'efforcer (à *or* de).
ending, *s.* terminaison, *f.*; (*declinable* ~ *of word*) désinence, *f.*
endemic, *adj.* endémique.
endive, escarole, *f.*; ⚠ *not* endive *which* = '*blanched chicory*'. [sans cesse.
endless, sans fin; (*theol.*) éternel, -le; **~ly,**
endorse, (*cheques, &c.*) endosser; (*confirm*) confirmer; **~ment,** endossement, *m.*; (*fig.*) approbation, *f.*; **~e,** *s.* endossataire, *m.f.*
endow, doter (de); (*fig.*) douer (de).
endowment, dotation, *f.*; (*fig.*) don, *m.*
endue, revêtir* (de); (*qualities*) douer (de); ~*d with*, doué de.
endur|e, *v.a.* supporter; *v.n.* durer; **~able,** supportable; **~ing,** (*patient*) endurant; (*lasting*) durable.
endways, *adv.* de champ; (*end to end*) bout à bout.
enemy, *adj. and s.m.f.* ennemi, -e.
energetic, énergique; ⚠ *not* énergétique *which* = '*relating to energy*'; (*style*) mâle.
energumen, énergumène, *m.f.*
energ|y, **~ies,** énergie, *f.*; **~ize,** *v.a.* stimuler.
enervat|e, *v.a.* énerver; **~ion,** affaiblissement, *m.*
enfeeble, affaiblir; **~ment,** affaiblissement, *m.*
enfilade, *s.* (*mil.*) enfilade, *f.*; *v.a.* enfiler.
enfold, envelopper; (*embrace*) étreindre*.
enforce, *v.a.* imposer; ~ *upon*, (*pers.*) imposer à; (*order, law*) faire exécuter; (*argument*) appuyer; **~ment,** (*law*) application, *f.*
enfranchise, (*slave, &c.*) affranchir; (*vote, pers.*) donner le droit de vote à; **~ment,** affranchissement, droit de vote, *m.*
engage, *v.a.* (*invite to, promise, urge, servant, &c., rooms, and mil.*) engager; (*veh.*) retenir*; (*marriage*) fiancer; (*employ*) occuper; *be* ~*d*, être occupé.
engage, *v.n.* (*undertake*) s'engager (à); ~ *in*, s'engager dans; **~ment,** (*obligation, previous committal, and mil.*) engagement, *m.*; (*parties*) invitation, *f.*; (*marriage*) fiançailles, *f.pl.*
engaging, *adj.* (*taking*) engageant.
engarland, enguirlander.
engender, engendrer.
engine, machine, *f.*; (*aeron.*) moteur, *m.*; *30 h.p.* ~, machine de 30 chevaux; **~-room,** chambre des machines, *f.*; *reverse* ~, faire* machine arrière.
engine-turn, *v.a.* guillocher.
engineer, ingénieur, *m.*; (*working and ship's*) mécanicien, *m.*; (*mil.*) officier, soldat du génie, *m.*
engineering, profession de l'ingénieur, *f.*; (*construction*) construction de machines, *f.*
engirdle, ceindre*.
English, (*adj.*) anglais; **~man,** **~woman,** Anglais, -e, *m.f.*; (*lang.*) anglais, *m.*; ~ **Channel,** *see* CHANNEL.
engraft, (*lit. and fig.*) greffer.
engrav|e, graver; **~ing,** gravure, *f.*; *steel, wood* ~*ing*, gravure sur acier, sur bois; **~er,** graveur, *m.*
engross, (*document*) grossoyer; (*monopolize*) accaparer; (*absorb*) absorber.
engulf, engloutir.
enhance, rehausser; **~ment,** rehaussement, *m.*
enigma, énigme, *f.*; **~tic,** énigmatique.
enjoin, *v.a.* (*thing on a pers.*) prescrire (*acc. thing* à + *pers.*); (*order*) enjoindre* (à + *pers.*, de + *inf.*).
enjoy, jouir de; ~ *oneself*, s'amuser; (*appreciate*) goûter; **~able,** agréable.
enjoyment, jouissance, *f.*; (*satisfaction*) satisfaction, *f.*
enkindle, enflammer.
enlarge, *v.a.* agrandir; (*mind*) élargir; *v.n.* s'agrandir; (*on theme*) s'étendre sur; **~ment,** agrandissement, *m.*
enlighten, éclairer; **~ment,** lumières, *f.pl.*
enlist, *v.a.* (*mil.*) enrôler; (*secure*)

s'assurer + *acc.*; *v.n.* (*mil.*) s'enrôler; **~ment,** enrôlement, *m.*
enliven, animer; (*make cheerful*) égayer.
enmity, inimitié, *f.*
ennoble, *v.a.* (*elevate to nobility*) anoblir; (*fig., mind, &c.*) ennoblir; **~ment,** anoblissement, *m.*
enorm|ity, énormité, *f.*; (*monstrous thing*) monstruosité, *f.*; **~ous,** énorme; **~ously,** énormément.
enough, assez (de); ~ *of this!*; assez de cette guitare!; *sure* ~, pour sûr.
enquire, *&c., see* INQUIRE.
enrage, exaspérer; **~d,** furieu|x, ~se.
enrapture, ravir.
enrich, enrichir; **~ment,** (*arch., &c.*) enrichissement, *m.*
enrol(l), enrôler; **~ment,** enrôlement, *m.*; (*recording of names*) enregistrement, *m.*
ensanguined, ensanglanté.
ensconce oneself, se blottir.
enshrine, (*enclose in shrine*) enchâsser; (*fig., preserve*) conserver.
enshroud, envelopper.
ensign, (*flag*) drapeau, *m.*; (*nav. flag*) pavillon, *m.*; (*pers.*) porte-drapeau, *m. invar.*
enslave, *v.a.* (*lit. and fig.*) asservir; **~ment,** asservissement, *m.*
ensnare, (*lit. and fig.*) prendre* au piège.
ensu|e, s'ensuivre*; **~ing,** suivant.
ensure, (*make safe, certain*) assurer; ~ *against*, garantir (de); *see also* INSURE.
entablature, (*arch.*) entablement, *m.*
entail, *v.a.* (*law*) substituer; (*involve*) entraîner; **~ment,** (*property*) substitution, *f.*
entangle, *v.a.* empêtrer; (*fig.*) embrouiller; **~ment,** embrouillement, *m.*; *barbed wire ~ments, see* BARBED.
enter, *v.a.* entrer (être) dans; (*bkkpg., name in list, &c.*) inscrire*; (*on ledger*) porter sur; *v.n.* entrer (être); ~ *into*, (*agreement, bargain*) faire*; (*lease, &c.*) contracter; (*feelings*) partager; ~ *into* (*partnership*) *with*, s'associer avec; ~ *on, upon*, (*duties, &c.*) entrer (être) en; (*career*) débuter dans.
enteri|tis, enteric, *s.* (*med.*) entérite, *f.*; **~c,** *adj.* entérique.
enterpris|e, entreprise, *f.*; **~ing,** entreprenant.
entertain, (*receive*) recevoir; (*amuse*) amuser; (*opinion, thought*) nourrir; (*correspondence, &c.*) entretenir*.
entertaining, *adj.* divertissant.
entertainment, amusement, *m.*; (*of guests*) hospitalité, *f.*; (*evening party*) soirée, *f.*
enthral(l), captiver.
enthrone, (*king*) placer sur le trône; (*bishop*) introniser.
enthus|e, *v.n.* s'enthousiasmer; **~iasm,** enthousiasme (pour), *m.*; **~iast, ~iastic,** *s.m.f. and adj.* enthousiaste; **~iastically,** avec enthousiasme.
entice, (*seduce*) séduire*; (*attract*) attirer; **~ment,** séduction, *f.*
enticing, séduisant; **~ly,** d'une manière séduisante.
entire, enti|er, ~ère; (*absolute*) absolu; **~ty,** totalité, *f.*; *in its ~ty*, en son entier; **~ly,** entièrement.
entitle, *v.a.* (*book, &c.*) intituler; (*give claim to*) donner droit à; *be ~d to*, avoir droit à + *noun*, avoir le droit de + *inf.*
entity, entité, *f.*
entomb, ensevelir; **~ment,** sépulture, *f.*
entomolog|y, entomologie, *f.*; **~ist,** entomologiste, *m.*; **~ical,** entomologique.
entrails, (*lit. and fig.*) entrailles, *f.pl.*
entrain, *v.a.* (*mil.*) faire* partir dans un, des trains; *v.n.* partir* (être) dans un train.
entrance, *s.* (*entering, beginning, fee, door*) entrée, *f.*; (*money*) prix d'entrée, *m.*; **~-hall,** vestibule, *m.*
entrance, *v.a.* (*ecstasy*) jeter en extase; (*joy*) transporter (de); **~ment,** extase, *f.*
entrap, prendre* au piège.
entreat, supplier; (*sollicit*) solliciter; *I ~ you*, je vous en supplie.
entreatingly, d'un ton suppliant.
entreaty, instance, *f.*
e(i)ntrench, *v.a.* retrancher; ~ *oneself*, se retrancher; ~ *upon*, empiéter sur.
entrust, *v.a.* confier (à + *pers.*).
entry, (*going and coming in, ceremonial entry, door, &c.*) entrée, *f.*; (*bkkpg.*) inscription, *f.*; *by single* ~, en partie simple.
e(i)ntwine, entrelacer.
enumerat|e, énumérer; **~ion,** énumération, *f.*
enunciat|e, (*theory, &c.*) énoncer; (*pronounce*) prononcer; **~ion,** énonciation, prononciation, *f.*
envelop, envelopper; **~ment,** enveloppement, *m.*
envelope, *s.* enveloppe, *f.*
envenom, (*poison*) empoisonner; (*embitter*) envenimer; (*mind*) corrompre.
enviable, enviable.
envious, envieu|x, ~se (de); **~ly,** avec envie.
environ, *v.a.* environner (de); **~ment,** (*fig.*) milieu, *m.*; **~s,** environs, *m.pl.*
envisage, envisager; (*danger, &c.*) regarder en face.
envoy, (*diplomatic*) envoyé, *m.*
envy, *s.* envie, *f.*; (*pers.*) objet d'envie, *m.*; *v.a.* envier (*a pers.*) *acc.*; *a pers. for a thing* = *acc. of thing*, à (*dat.*) + *pers.*
Eolian, éolien, -ne.
epaulet(te), épaulette, *f.*
epergne, surtout de table, *m.*
ephemera, éphémère, *m.*; **~l,** *adj.* éphémère.
epic, *s.* épopée, *f.*; *adj.* épique.
epicure, gourmet, *m.*
epicurean, *adj. and s.m.f.* épicurien, -ne.
epidemic, *s.* épidémie, *f.*; *adj.* épidémique.

epidermi|s, épiderme, *m.*; **~c**, *adj.* épidermique.
epigram, épigramme, *f.*; **~matic**, épigrammatique.
epigraph, épigraphe, *f.*
epilep|sy, épilepsie, *f.*; **~tic**, *adj. and s.m.f.* épileptique.
epilogue, épilogue, *m.*
Epiphany, (*eccles.*) Épiphanie, *f.*
episcop|acy, gouvernement par les évêques, *m.*; (*bench of bishops*) épiscopat, *m.*; **~al**, épiscopal; **~alian**, *adj.* épiscopal; **~ate**, épiscopat, *m.*
episod|e, épisode, *m.*; **~ic**, épisodique.
epist|le, épître, *f.*; **~olary**, épistolaire.
epitaph, épitaphe, *f.*
epithalamium, épithalame, *m.*
epithet, épithète, *f.*
epitom|e, abrégé, *m.*; **~ize**, abréger.
epoch, époque, *f.*; **~-making**, qui fait époque.
epode, épode, *f.*
eponymous, éponyme.
epopee, épopée, *f.*
equab|le, égal; **~ility**, égalité. *f.*
equal, *s.* égal, -e, *m.f.*; *between ~s*, d'égal à égal.
equal, *adj.* égal; *be ~ to*, (+ *inf.*) être de force à, (+ *noun*) être à la hauteur de; **~ity**, égalité, *f.*; **~ly**, également.
equal, *v.a.* égaler; *not to be ~led*, ne pas avoir son égal.
equaliz|e, égaliser; **~ation**, égalisation, *f.*
equanimity, égalité d'âme, *f.*; (*placidity*) sérénité, *f.*
equation, (*math.*) équation, *f.*
equator, équateur, *m.*; **~ial**, équatorial.
equerry, écuyer, *m.*
equestrian, équestre.
equidistant, équidistant.
equilateral, équilatéral.
equilibrium, équilibre, *m.*; *keep, lose one's ~*, garder, perdre son équilibre.
equine, équin.
equino|x, équinoxe, *m.*; **~ctial**, *adj.* équinoxial; *~ctial gales*, vents d'équinoxe, *m.pl.*
equip, (*pers., mil., naut., &c.*) équiper; *~ with*, munir de; *~ for*, (*fig.*) outiller pour; **~ment**, équipement, *m.*
equipage, (*carriage and attendants*) équipage, *m.*
equipoise, *s.* équilibre, *m.*; (*counterbalance*) contrepoids, *m.*
equiponderant, équipondérant.
equitabl|e, équitable; **~y**, équitablement.
equitation, équitation, *f.*
equity, équité, *f.*
equivalen|ce, équivalence, *f.*; **~t**, *adj. and s.m.* équivalent; *be ~t to*, équivaloir* à.
equivocal, équivoque.
equivocat|e, user d'équivoque; **~ion**, équivoque, *f.*
era, ère, *f.*
eradica|te, déraciner; (*fig.*) extirper; **~tion**, extirpation, *f.*
eras|e, raturer; **~er**, (*knife*) grattoir, *m.*; **~ure**, rature, *f.*
ere, *prep.* avant; *conj.* avant que (+ *subj.*).
erect, *adj.* droit; (*hair*) dressé sur la tête; *adv.* droit.
erect, *v.a.* dresser; (*build*) ériger; (*found*) fonder; (*mach.*) monter (avoir); *~ into*, ériger en; **~ion**, construction, *f.*; montage, *m.*
eremite, ermite, *m.*
ermine, (*an., fur, her.*) hermine, *f.*
erne, (*ornith.*) aigle royal, *m.*
ero|de, (*water*) éroder; (*acid*) corroder; **~sion**, érosion, *f.*
erotic, érotique.
err, *v.n.* errer; (*mistake*) se tromper; *~ from*, s'écarter de; **~atic**, (*pers.*) capricieu|x, ~se; (*things*) variable; (*geol., med., astr.*) erratique.
errand, course, *f.*; (*message*) message, *m.*; *~* **-boy**, garçon de courses, *m.*; *run ~s*, faire* des courses.
errant, *adj.* errant.
errat|um, *pl.* ~a, erratum, *m.* (*pl.* errata).
erring, *adj.* égaré.
erroneous, erroné; **~ly**, par erreur.
error, (*inexactitude and fault*) erreur, *f.*; *gross ~*, erreur grossière, *f.*
Erse, (*approx.*) *adj. and s.m.* (*lang.*) gaélique.
erst, erstwhile, jadis.
eructation, éructation, *f.*
erudit|e, érudit; **~ion**, érudition, *f.*
eruption, (*volcano and med.*) éruption, *f.*
eruptive, (*med.*) érupti|f, ~ve.
erysipelas, (*med.*) érysipèle, *m.*
escalade, *s.* escalade, *f.*
escalator, escalier roulant, *m.*
escapade, escapade, *f.*
escape, *s.* fuite, *f.*; (*safety*) salut, *m.*; (*steam*) échappement, *m.*; *have a hair-breadth, narrow ~*, l'échapper belle; *~ of gas*, fuite de gaz, *f.*
escape, *v.n.* (*out of*) échapper de; (*avoid, elude, notice, punishment, danger*) échapper à; (*slip the memory*) échapper (+ à *of pers.*); *~ by the skin of one's teeth*, l'échapper belle.
escarpment, *s.* (*mil.*) escarpement, *m.*
eschatology, eschatologie, *f.*
eschew, *v.a.* éviter.
escort, *s.* escorte, *f.*; *v.a.* escorter.
escritoire, écritoire, *f.*
esculent, *adj.* comestible.
escutcheon, (*her.*) écu, *m.*
esoteric, ésotérique; (*private*) secr|et, ~ète.
espalier, *s.* espalier, *m.*; **~-tree**, arbre en espalier, *m.*
esparto grass, spart, *m.*
especial, spécial.
espionage, espionnage, *m.*
esplanade, esplanade, *f.*
espousal, épousailles, *f.pl.*; (*fig.*) adoption, *f.*
espouse, *v.a.* épouser; (*cause, &c.*) adopter; ⚠ marier *only = give in marriage, join in ~, of registrar or priest, fig.*

espy, *v.a.* découvrir*.
esquire, *on letters use* Monsieur.
essay, (*attempt*) essai, *m.*; (*Lit.*) essai, *m.*; (*school*) composition, *f.*
essay, *v.a.* (*try, test*) essayer; *v.n.* ~ *to*, essayer de.
essayist, (*Lit.*) essayiste, *m.*
essen|ce, (*very nature*) essence, *f.*; (*extract*) (*lit. and fig.*) essence, *f.*; **~tial**, essentiel, -le; **~tially**, essentiellement.
establish, établir; (*lit., truth, &c., set up in business*) établir; (*found*) fonder; **~ment**, établissement, *m.*; (*household*) train de maison, *m.*; (*institution*) institution, *f.*
estate, biens, *m.pl.*; (*landed*) propriété, *f.*; (*position*) rang, *m.*; (*of realm*) état, *m.*; *real* ~, biens immobiliers.
esteem, *s.* estime, *f.*; *v.a.* (*think highly of, consider*) estimer.
estimable, estimable.
estimate, *s.* (*appraising*) estimation, *f.*; (*valuation*) évaluation, *f.*; (*builder's, &c.*) devis, *m.*; (*polit.*) budget, *m.*; (*opinion*) appréciation, *f.*; *rough* ~, aperçu, *m.*
estimate, *v.a.* (*value*) évaluer; (*opinion*) apprécier.
estimation, (*opinion*) jugement, *m.*; (*esteem*) estime, *f.*; *in my* ~, à mon avis.
estimative, estimated, estimati|f, **~ve**.
estimator, (*valuer*) estimateur, *m.*
estrange, *v.a.* éloigner (de); **~ment**, éloignement, *m.*
estuary, estuaire, *m.*
etc., (*abbrev.*) etc.; *etceteras*, supplément, *m.*
etch, *v.a.n.* graver à l'eau forte; **~er**, aquafortiste, *m.*; **~ing**, gravure à l'eau forte, *f.*
eternal, éternel, -le; (*fig.*) sempiternel; **~ly**, éternellement.
eternity, éternité, *f.*
Etesian, (*winds*) étésien.
ether, (*upper air*) voûte éthérée, *f.*; (*phys. and chem.*) éther, *m.*; **~eal**, éthéré; **~ealize**, rendre éthéré.
ethic|al, éthique; *s.* **~s**, éthique, *f.*
Ethiopian, *adj.* (*when an adj. use small letter*) *and s.m.f.* Éthiopien, -ne.
ethnic|al, ethnique.
ethnograph|er, ethnographe, *m.*; **~y**, ethnographie, *f.*; **~ic**, ethnographique.
ethnolog|ical, ethnologique; **~ist**, ethnologue, *m.*; **~y**, ethnologie, *f.*
ethology, éthologie, *f.*
etiola|te, *v.a.* étioler; *v.n.* s'étioler; **~tion**, étiolement, *m.*
etiquette, étiquette, *f.*
Etruscan, *adj.* (*when an adj. use small letter*) *and s.m.f.* Étrusque.
etymolog|ical, étymologique; **~ist**, étymologiste, *m.*; **~y**, étymologie, *f.*
eucalyptus, (*bot.*) eucalyptus, *m.*
Eucharist, eucharistie, *f.*; **~ic(al)**, eucharistique.
eugenics, eugénique, *f.*
eulog|ist, panégyriste, *m.f.*; **~istic**, élogieu|x, **~se**; **~ize**, *v.a.* louer; **~y**, éloge, *m.*
eunuch, eunuque, *m.*
euonymus, (*bot.*) fusain, *m.*
euphemis|m, euphémisme, *m.*; **~tic**, euphémique.
euphon|ic, euphonique; **~y**, euphonie, *f.*
euphorbia, (*bot.*) euphorbe, *f.*
European, *adj.* (*when an adj. use small letter*) *and s.m.f.* Européen, -ne.
evacu|ate, *v.a.* évacuer; **~ation**, évacuation, *f.*; **~ee**, évacué, -e, *m.f.*
evade, *v.a.* (*escape from*) échapper à; (*creditors, law, difficulty*) esquiver; (*question*) éluder.
evanescen|ce, disparition évanescente, *f.*; **~t**, évanescent; (*short-lived*) éphémère.
evangeli|cal, évangélique; **~sm**, prédication de l'évangile, *f.*; **~st**, évangéliste, *m.*; **~zation**, évangélisation, *f.*; **~ze**, *v.a.* évangéliser.
evapora|te, *v.a.* évaporer; *v.n.* s'évaporer; **~tion**, évaporation, *f.*
evasion, évasion, *f.*; (*fig.*) faux-fuyant, *m.*
evasive, évasi|f, **~ve**; **~ly**, évasivement.
eve, veille, *f.*; (*evening*) soir, *m.*; *on the* ~ *of*, à la veille de.
even, *s.* soir, *m.*
even, *adj.* (*smooth*) uni; (*equal, uniform*) égal; (*numbers*) pair; (*equitable*) équitable; *be* ~ *with*, être au niveau de; (*fig.*) être quitte avec; *make* ~, aplanir; ~ *number*, nombre pair, *m.*; *~-handed*, impartial; ~ *money*, compte rond, *m.*; *~-tempered*, d'humeur égale; **~ness**, égalité, *f.*; **~ly**, également.
even, *adv.* même; ~ *if*, quand même (*cond.*); ~ *though*, quand bien même que (*cond.*).
evening, *s.* soir, *m.*; (*whole* ~ *and* ~ *party*) soirée, *f.*; **~-dress**, tenue de soirée, *f.*; ~ **primrose**, (*bot.*) onagre, *f.*; ~ *of life*, soir de la vie, *m.*; *good* ~*!* bon soir!; *adj.* du soir.
event, événement, *m.*; *at all* ~*s*, en tout cas; *in the* ~ *of*, (+ *noun*) dans le cas de, (+ *verb or verb noun*) dans le cas où (*subj.*); **~ful**, fécond en événements; (*memorable*) mémorable.
eventual, éventuel, -le; (*final*) définiti|f, **~ve**.
eventuate, (*U.S. happen*) arriver (être).
ever, toujours; (*at any time*) jamais; (*exclamatory questions*) donc; ~ *and anon*, de temps en temps; *hardly* ~, presque jamais; *Gambetta for* ~*!* Vive Gambetta!; *if* ~ *there was one*, s'il en fut; ~ *so much longer*, infiniment plus long; ~ *since, adv.* depuis lors.
evergreen, *s.* arbre vert; *adj.* toujours vert.
everlasting, *s.* (*bot.*) immortelle, *f.*
everlasting, *adj.* éternel, -le; (*slang, jest*) sempiternel, -le.
evermore, toujours; *for* ~, pour toujours.
every, *adj.* (*each*) chaque; (*all*) tous, toutes les . . . ; ~ *one*, tout le monde; ~ *man, one*, chacun, -e; *~thing*, tout, *m.*;

~ now and then, de temps en temps; *~ other day*, tous les deux jours; *be ~ inch, whit a . . .*, être . . . jusqu'aux bouts des doigts; *at ~ turn*, à tout propos.
everyday, *adj.* de tous les jours.
everyway, de toutes les façons.
everywhere, partout.
evict, évincer; **~ion**, éviction, *f.*
eviden|ce, évidence, *f.*; (*proof*) preuve, *f.*; (*law*) témoignage, *m.*; *be in ~*, être en évidence; *give ~*, déposer; *v.a.* attester; **~t**, **~tly**, évidemment.
evil, *s.* mal, *m.*; (*misfortune*) malheur, *m.*; *~-speaking*, médisance, *f.*
evil, *adj.* mauvais; (*wicked*) méchant; **~ly**, mal.
evil, *adv.* mal; *~-looking*, (*pers.*) de mauvaise mine; *~-disposed*, mal intentionné.
evince, manifester; ⚠ *not* évincer *which* = '*evict*'.
eviscerate, éventrer; (*fig.*) enlever la force de.
evocat|ion, évocation, *f.*; **~ive**, évocat|-eur, ~rice.
evoke, *v.a.* (*memories, feelings, a spirit, law*) évoquer.
evolution, (*development*) déroulement, *m.*; (*scient. and mil.*) évolution, *f.*; **~ist**, évolutionniste, *m.f.*
evolve, *v.a.* (*thought, nature, theory, photo., argument, &c.*) développer; *v.n.* se développer.
ewe, brebis, *f.*; *~* **lamb**, agnelle, *f.*
ewer, aiguière, *f.*
exacerba|te, (*pers.*) exaspérer; (*pain, anger, &c.*) irriter; **~tion**, exaspération, *f.*; (*med.*) exacerbation, *f.*
exact, *adj.* exact; (*hour*) précis; **~ness**, **~itude**, exactitude, *f.*; **~ly**, exactement; (*hour*) au juste; *~ly so!* justement!
exact, *v.a.* exiger; **~ion**, exaction, *f.*; **~ing**, exigeant.
exaggera|te, exagérer; **~tion**, exagération, *f.*
exalt, (*raise*) élever; (*praise*) louer; (*imagination, &c.*) exalter; **~ation**, exaltation, *f.*; **~ed**, (*rank*) élevé.
examination, examen, *m.*; (*witness*) audition, *f.*; (*prisoner*) interrogatoire, *m.*; (*accounts, &c.*) vérification, *f.*; *~* **paper**, composition d'examen, *f.*; *competitive ~*, *see* COMPETITIVE.
examine, *v.a.* examiner; (*accounts*) vérifier; (*prisoner*) interroger; (*luggage*) visiter; (*passport*) viser.
examin|er, examinat|eur, ~rice, *s.m.f.*; **~ee**, candidat, *m.*; *~ing magistrate*, (*approx.*) juge d'instruction, *m.*
example, exemple, *m.*; *for ~*, par exemple.
exanimate, inanimé.
exaspera|te, *v.a.* (*lit. and fig.*) exaspérer; **~ting**, exaspérant; **~tion**, exaspération, *f.*
ex-bonus, ex-répartition.
excava|te, *v.a.* creuser; **~tion**, fouille, *f.*
excavator, (*pers.*) terrassier, *m.*; (*steam shovel*) excavateur, *m.*

exceed, *v.a.* dépasser; (*powers, &c.*) outrepasser; (*surpass*) surpasser.
exceedingly, excessivement.
excel, *v.a.* surpasser; *v.n.* (*in doing*) exceller à; *~ in*, (+ *noun*) se distinguer dans.
excellen|ce, excellence, *f.*; (*merit*) mérite, *m.*; Excellency, (*title*) Excellence; **~t**, excellent; **~tly**, parfaitement.
except, *v.a.* excepter; **~ing**, à l'exception de.
except, excepting, *prep.* excepté (*invar.*); (*with numbers*) sauf; *~ that*, excepté que (+ *indic.*); *~ for*, exception faite pour.
excepted, *adj.* excepté (*written after noun it requires concord*).
exception, exception, *f.*; *with the ~ of*, à l'exception de; *with this ~*, à cette exception près; *be an ~* faire* exception; *the ~ confirms the rule*, l'exception confirme la règle; *take ~ to*, se formaliser de; **~al**, exceptionnel, -le.
exceptionable, récusable.
excerpt, *s.* extrait, *m.*; *v.a.* extraire*.
excess, (*grief, food, &c.*) excès, *m.*; (*bkkpg., surplus*) excédent, *m.*; **~es**, excès, *m.pl.*; *~* **fare**, supplément, *m.*; *~* **luggage**, excédents de bagages, *m.pl.*; *~* **price**, excédent de prix, *m.*; *~* **profits**, surplus des bénéfices, *m.*; **~ive**, excessi|f, ~ve; (*exaggerated*) exagéré; **~ively**, excessivement.
exchange, (*barter*) échange, *m.*; (*object*) objet d'échange, *m.*; (*teleph.*) bureau central, *m.*; *in ~ for*, en échange de; (*comm. and st'k exchange, &c.*) change, *m.*; *~* **-rate**, taux du change, *m.*; *ring, call the ~*, (*teleph.*) sonner le bureau.
exchange, *v.a.* *~ one thing for another*, échanger une chose contre une autre; (*remarks, &c.*) échanger; *~ places*, changer de place.
exchangeable, échangeable (contre).
exchequer, (*court*) échiquier, *m.*; (*treasury*) trésor, *m.*; (*money*) finances, *f.pl.*
excise, *s.* régie, *f.*; **~-duty**, droit de régie, *m.*; **~-office**, bureau de la régie, *m.*; **~man**, employé de la régie, *m.*
excis|e, *v.a.* (*surg.*) exciser; (*Lit. work*) découper; **~ion**, (*surg.*) excision, *f.*; (*book, &c.*) coupure, *f.*
excitab|le, excitable; **~ility**, excitabilité, *f.*
excitant, *adj. and s.m.* excitant.
exci|te, *v.a.* (*feelings and faculties, provoke*) exciter; (*move*) agiter; **~ted**, excité; **~tedly**, tout agité.
excitement, excitation, *f.*
exciting, (*med.*) excitant; (*rousing*) impressionnant; (*novels, &c.*) captivant; (*thrilling*) passionnant.
exclaim, s'écrier; *~ against*, se récrier contre.
exclamation, exclamation, *f.*
exclamatory, exclamati|f, ~ve.
exclude, *v.a.* exclure*.

exclus|ion, exclusion, *f.*; **~ive,** exclusi|f, ~ve; *~ive of,* non compris (*invar. before noun, concord after*); **~iveness,** exclusivisme, *m.*; **~ively,** exclusivement.
excogita|te, *v.a.* inventer; **~tion,** réflexion, *f.*
excommunica|te, *v.a.* excommunier; **~tion,** excommunication, *f.*
excoriate, excorier.
excrement, excretion, excrément, *m.*
excrescen|ce, excroissance, *f.*; (*fig.*) excès, *m.*; **~t,** superflu.
excretive, excretory, excrét|eur, ~rice.
excruciating, (*pain, &c.*) atroce.
exculpa|te, disculper; **~tion,** disculpation, *f.*
exculpatory, justificati|f, ~ve.
excursion, (*trip and digression*) excursion, *f.*; **~ ticket,** billet d'excursion, *m.*; **~ train,** train de plaisir, *m.*; **~ist,** *s.m.f.* excursionniste.
excursive, (*digressive*) digressi|f, **~ve.**
excusable, excusable.
excusatory, justificati|f, ~ve.
excuse, *s.* excuse, *f.*
excuse, *v.a.* excuser; (*exempt from*) exempter de; *~ oneself from,* s'excuser de.
execrab|le, exécrable; **~ly,** exécrablement.
execra|te, exécrer; **~tion,** exécration, *f.*
execut|ant, (*mus. performer*) exécutant, -e, *m.f.*; **~able,** exécutable.
execu|te, *v.a.* (*plan, law, order, contract, put to death, mus., &c.*) exécuter; (*transfer*) effectuer; **~tion,** (*plan, law*) exécution, *f.*; (*debtors*) saisie, *f.*; *carry into ~tion,* mettre* à exécution.
executioner, (*public*) bourreau, *m.*
executive, *adj. and s.m.* exécutif.
executor, executrix, (*will*) exécut|eur, ~rice testamentaire, *m.f.*
exegesis, exégèse, *f.*
exegetic, ~al, exégétique.
exemplar, modèle, *m.*; ~**y,** exemplaire.
exemplification, démonstration, *f.*
exemplif|y, illustrer par un exemple; **~ication,** démonstration, *f.*
exempt, *adj.* exempt (de); *v.a.* exempter (de); **~ion,** exemption (de), *f.*
exercise, *s.* (*of faculty, body, art, practice*) exercice, *m.*; (*schools*) thème, *m.*; *take ~,* prendre* de l'exercice.
exercise, *v.a.* (*mil., use, train, profession*) exercer; (*perplex*) embarrasser.
exert, (*bring to bear*) mettre* en œuvre; (*patience, &c.*) exercer; *~ oneself,* faire* un effort; *~ oneself to,* s'efforcer (à *or* de); **~ion,** effort, *m.*; *use every ~ion,* faire* tous ses efforts.
exeunt, (*theatr.*) sortent.
exhal|e, *v.a.* exhaler; **~ation,** (*skin*) exhalation, *f.*; (*smell, vapour*) exhalaison, *f.*
exhaust, *s.* (*steam*) échappement, *m.*; **~-pipe,** tuyau d'échappement, *m.*
exhaust, *v.a.* (*lit. and fig.*) épuiser; **~ion,** épuisement, *m.*
exhaust|ible, épuisable; **~ing,** épuisant; **~ive,** (*thorough*) approfondi; **~less,** inépuisable.
exhibit, *s.* (*at a show*) exposition, *f.*
exhibit, *v.a.* (*quality, &c.*) déployer; (*show*) montrer; (*pictures, &c.*) exposer; (*produce*) exhiber.
exhibition, (*showing, display*) exhibition, *f.*; (*public*) exposition, *f.*; (*school, coll.*) bourse, *f.*; **~er,** boursier, *m.*
exhibitor, (*exhibitions*) exposant, *m.*
exhilara|te, (*enliven*) égayer; (*brace*) fortifier; **~tion,** gaieté, *f.*
exhilarating, (*bracing*) fortifiant; ⚠ exhilarant = '*arousing laughter*'.
exhort, exhorter (à); **~ation,** exhortation, *f.*
exhum|e, exhumer; **~ation,** exhumation, *f.*
exigen|ce, ~cy, exigence, *f.*; (*pressing need*) besoin urgent, *m.*; **~t,** (*pressing*) urgent.
exigible, exigible.
exigu|ity, exiguïté, *f.*; **~ous,** exigu, -ë.
exile, exil, *m.*; (*pers.*) exilé, *m.*; *v.a.* exiler.
exist, *v.n.* exister; **~ence,** existence, *f.*; (*life*) vie, *f.*; **~ent,** existant.
exit, *s.* (*door, departure, and theatr., &c.*) sortie, *f.*; *make one's ~,* s'en aller* (être).
exodus, (*lit., fig., Bible*) exode, *m.*
ex officio, à titre d'office.
exonera|te, (*exculpate*) disculper; (*release from*) dispenser (de); **~tion,** (*fault*) exonération, *f.*
exorbitan|ce, (*price, &c.*) énormité, *f.*; **~t,** exorbitant.
exorc|ize, *v.a.* exorciser; **~ism,** exorcisme, *m.*; **~ist,** exorciste, *m.*
exordium, exorde, *m.*
exotic, *adj.* exotique.
expand, *v.a.* étendre; (*wings*) déployer; (*dilate*) dilater; (*chest*) gonfler; (*ideas, &c.*) développer.
expand, *v.n.* s'étendre; (*water*) se répandre; (*flowers*) s'épanouir; (*dilate*) se dilater.
expanse, étendue, *f.*
expansion, (*gen., chem., mach.*) expansion, *f.*; (*extension*) extension, *f.*; (*ideas, &c.*) développement, *m.*
expansive, (*lit. and fig.*) expansi|f, ~ve; (*extensive*) étendu; **~ness,** (*extent*) étendue, *f.*
expatiate on, s'étendre sur.
expatria|te, expatrier; **~tion,** expatriation, *f.*
expect, *v.a.* s'attendre à; (*await*) attendre; (*hope for*) espérer; (*think*) croire*; (*reckon that*) compter que; (*reckon on*) compter sur; *it's only what he might ~,* cela lui pend au nez.
expectan|cy, attente, *f.*; (*hope*) espoir, *m.*; **~t,** expectant.
expectation, attente, *f.*; (*hope*) espérance, *f.*; *in ~ of,* dans l'attente de.
expectingly, dans l'attente.

expectora|te, expectorer; **~tion,** expectoration, *f.*
expedien|ce, ~cy, convenance, *f.*; (*pej.*) opportunisme, *m.*; **~t,** utile.
expedient, *s.* expédient, *m.*
expedite, (*dispatch*) expédier; (*hasten*) †hâter; ⚠ expédier *does not = 'assist the progress of'.*
expedition, (*mil., nav., explore*) expédition, *f.*; (*haste*) promptitude, *f.*
expeditionary, expéditionnaire.
expeditious, prompt; **~ly,** promptement.
expel, expulser; (*drive out*) chasser.
expend, (*money*) dépenser; (*energy*) employer; (*time*) consacrer.
expenditure, dépenses, *f.pl.*
expense, dépense, *f.*; **~s,** frais, *m.pl.*; *at my ~,* à mes frais; *at great ~,* à grands frais; *at the ~ of,* aux frais de; (*fig.*) aux dépens de; *general ~s,* frais divers, *m.pl.*; *out-of-pocket ~s,* débours, *m.pl.*; *~s of upkeep,* frais de matériel; *pay ~s,* couvrir* les frais; *petty ~s,* menus frais, *m.pl.*; *standing ~s,* frais généraux; *travelling ~s,* frais de voyage; *working ~s,* frais d'exploitation.
expensive, (*dear*) coûteu|x, ~se; (*involving expense*) dispendieu|x, ~se; **~ly,** dispendieusement; *come ~,* revenir* (être) cher.
expensiveness, prix élevé, *m.*
experience, *s.* expérience, *f.*; *by ~,* par expérience; *from ~,* en connaissance de cause; *unpleasant ~,* mauvais quart d'heure, *m.*
experience, *v.a.* éprouver; (*learn*) apprendre*; **~d,** *adj.* expérimenté.
experiment, *s.* expérience, *f.*; ⚠ expériment *not French*; *v.a.* faire* des expériences.
experimental, expérimental; **~ist,** expérimentateur, *m.*; **~ly,** par expérience.
expert, *s.* expert, *m.*; *by ~ advice,* à dire d'expert; *adj.* expert (à).
expertness, habileté, *f.*
expiable, expiable.
expia|te, expier; **~tion,** expiation, *f.*; **~tory,** expiatoire.
expir|e, *v.n.* (*breathe, cease, die*) expirer; **~y, ~ation,** expiration, *f.*
explain, expliquer; (*clear up*) éclaircir; **~able,** explicable.
explanat|ion, explication, *f.*; **~ory,** explicati|f, ~ve.
expletive, *s.* explétif, *m.*; *adj.* explétif|f, ~ve.
explicable, explicable.
explica|te, (*develop notion, &c.*) développer; **~tion,** développement, *m.*; **~tory,** explicati|f, ~ve.
explicit, explicite; (*pers.*) clair; **~ness,** clarté, *f.*; **~ly,** explicitement.
explode, *v.a.* (*mine*) faire* sauter; (*theory, &c.*) condamner; *v.n.* faire* explosion; (*blow up*) sauter; (*boiler, &c.*) éclater.
exploit, *s.* exploit, *m.*; *v.a.* (*work mines, &c., and pej.*) exploiter; **~ation,** exploitation, *f.*
explor|e, explorer; (*probe*) sonder; **~ation,** exploration, *f.*; (*fig.*) examen, *m.*; **~atory,** d'exploration; **~er,** explorat|eur, ~rice, *m.f.*
explos|ion, explosion, *f.*; **~ive,** *s.* explosif, *m.*; *adj.* explosi|f, ~ve.
exponent, *s.* (*theory, &c.*) interprète, *m.*; (*math.*) exposant, *m.*
export, *s.* (*thing exported*) article d'exportation, *m.*; (*exporting*) exportation, *f.*; **~ duty, duties,** droits de sortie, *m.pl.*
export, *v.a.* exporter; **~able,** exportable; **~ation,** exportation, *f.*; **~er,** exportat|eur, ~rice, *m.f.*
expos|e, (*lay open to, display, abandon, photo., mil.*) exposer; (*unmask*) démasquer; **~ure,** (*air, cold, danger, aspect, &c., photo.*) exposition, *f.*; *public ~ure,* scandale, *m.*
exposé, (*statement*) exposé, *m.*
exposition, (*display, explanation, exposure to*) exposition, *f.*
expositor, commentateur, *m.*
expostula|te with, faire des remontrances à; **~tion,** remontrance, *f.*; **~tory,** de remontrance.
expound, (*system*) exposer; (*explain*) expliquer.
express, *s.* (*train*) express, *m.*; (*messenger*) exprès, *m.*
express, *adj.* (*exact*) exact; (*formal*) formel, -le; *~ delivery,* livraison par exprès, *f.*
express, *v.a.* exprimer; **~ible,** exprimable.
expression, (*words, face, voice, mus., juice*) expression, *f.*
expressive, expressi|f, ~ve; **~ness,** force d'expression, *f.*
expressly, (*formally*) expressément; (*on purpose*) exprès.
expropria|te, exproprier; **~tion,** expropriation, *f.*
expuls|ion, expulsion, *f.*; **~ive,** expulsi|f, ~ve.
expunge, effacer.
expurga|te, expurger; **~tion,** expurgation, *f.*; **~tory,** *adj.* expurgatoire.
exquisite, exquis; (*pain*) atroce. ⚠ exquis *is never used in this sense*; (*subtle, refined*) raffiné; **~ness,** perfection, *f.*; **~ly,** parfaitement.
exsanguine, exsangue.
extant, existant.
extemporar|y, improvisé; **~ily,** impromptu.
extempore, *adv.* impromptu; *adj.* improvisé; *speak ~,* parler d'abondance.
extemporiz|e, *v.a.n.* improviser; **~ation,** improvisation, *f.*
extend, *v.a.* (*limits, sphere, boundaries, body, mil.*) étendre; (*prolong extent and time*) prolonger; (*hand*) tendre; (*arm*) allonger; (*bill, comm.*) proroger; (*continue*) continuer; (*show, offer*) offrir*.

extend, *v.n.* s'étendre; (*time*) se prolonger.
extensib|le, extensible; **~ility,** extensibilité, *f.*
extension, extension, *f.*; (*time*) prolongation, *f.*; (*space*) prolongement, *m.*; **~-ladder,** échelle à coulisse, *f.*; *~ of leave,* prolongation de permission, *f.*
extensive, vaste; (*knowledge*) étendu; **~ness,** vaste étendue, *f.*; **~ly,** (*widely*) amplement.
extent, étendue, *f.*; *to some ~, to a certain ~,* jusqu'à un certain point; *to a great ~,* à un †haut degré; *to such an ~ that,* à un tel point que (*ind.*).
extenua|te, atténuer. ⚠ *Not* exténuer *which = 'tire out'*; **~tion,** atténuation, *f.*; **~ing,** (*circumstances, &c.*) atténuant.
exterior, *adj. and s.m.* extérieur.
extermina|te, exterminer; (*root out*) extirper; **~tion,** extermination, extirpation, *f.*; **~tor,** *also adj.* **~ting,** exterminat|eur, ~rice, *m.f.*
external, *adj.* extérieur; (*remedy*) externe; **~ly,** extérieurement.
exterritoriality, exterritorialité, *f.*
extinct, éteint; *become ~,* s'éteindre*; **~ion,** (*lit. and debt*) extinction, *f.*
extinguish, (*lit. and debt*) éteindre*; (*destroy*) détruire*.
extinguisher, (*candle and fig.*) éteignoir, *m.*
extirpa|te, extirper; **~tion,** extirpation, *f.*
extol, vanter; (*celebrate*) célébrer.
extort, (*money, &c.*) extorquer (à+*pers.*); (*avowal, &c.*) arracher (à).
extortion, extorsion, *f.*; **~ate,** exorbitant.
extra, *s.* supplément, *m.*
extra, *adj.* supplémentaire; (*particular*) particuli|er, ~ère; *~ postage,* surtaxe, *f.*; *~ fare,* supplément, *m.*; *~ charge, see* CHARGE.
extra, *adv.* en plus; *pay ~,* payer en plus.
extract, *s.* extrait, *m.*; *v.a.* (*lit., fig., tooth, &c.*) extraire*; (*extort*) arracher; **~ion,** extraction, *f.*; (*origin*) origine, *f.*
extradi|te, *v.a.* extrader; **~tion,** extradition, *f.*
extrajudicial, extrajudiciaire.
extraneous, étrang|er, ~ère (à).
extraordinar|y, extraordinaire; **~iness,** singularité, *f.*; **~ily,** extraordinairement.
extravagan|t, (*money*) prodigue; (*behaviour*) extravagant; **~ce,** prodigalité, extravagance, *f.*; ⚠ extravagan|t, ~ce *are not used of money*; **~tly,** prodigalement.
extravasa|te, *v.n.* s'extravaser; **~tion,** extravasation, *f.*
extreme, *s.* extrême, *m.*; *go to ~s,* se jeter dans les extrêmes; *~s meet,* les extrêmes se touchent.
extreme, *adj.* (*lit. and opinions*) extrême; **~ly,** extrêmement; *~ unction,* extrême onction, *f.*
extremist, extrémiste, *m.*
extremit|y, extrémité, *f.*; *driven to ~,* poussé à bout; **~ies,** (*hands and feet, violent acts*) extrémités, *f.pl.*
extricate, *v.a.* dégager; *~ oneself* (*get out of difficulties, &c.*) se tirer (de).
extrinsic, extrinsèque.
extru|de, *v.a.* expulser; **~sion,** expulsion, *f.*
exuberan|t, (*lit., fig., pers., prolific, actions, style, plants*) exubérant; **~ce,** exubérance, *f.*; **~tly,** avec exubérance.
exuberate, *v.n.* surabonder.
exud|e, *v.n.* exsuder; **~ation,** exsudation, *f.*
exult, exulter; *~ over,* triompher de; **~ation,** exultation, *f.*; **~ing, ~ant,** triomphant.
eyas, (*ornith.*) faucon niais, *m.*
eye, *s.* œil, *m.*; (*needles*) trou, *m.*; (*hooks*) porte, *f.*; (*plants, &c., and arch.*) œil, *m.*; *hook and ~,* agrafe et porte, *f.*; **~-glass,** monocle, *m.*; **~-tooth,** œillère, *f.*; **~-salve,** *wash,* collyre, *m.*; **~witness,** témoin oculaire, *m.*; *keep an ~ on,* avoir l'œil sur; *have an ~ for,* (*pictures, &c.*) se connaître* à; *with an ~ to,* en vue de; *in the ~s of,* aux yeux de; *see ~ to ~ with,* voir du même œil que; *as far as the ~ can reach,* à perte de vue; *with the naked ~,* à l'œil nu; *be all ~s,* (*attentive*) être tout yeux; (*mil.*) *~s right!* tête droite!; *~s front!* fixe!; *in the twinkling of an ~,* en un clin d'œil.
eye, *v.a.* observer; (*watch*) suivre* des yeux.
eyeball, globe de l'œil, *m.*
eyebrow, sourcil, *m.*
eyehole, (*of eye*) orbite, *f.*; (*peep-hole*) petit judas, *m.*
eyelash, cil, *m.*
eyelet, œillet, *m.*
eyelid, paupière, *f.*
eyesight, vue, *f.*
eyesore, chose qui offusque l'œil.
eyot, îlot, *m.*
eyrie, eyry, *see* AERIE.

F

fabl|e, fable, *f.*; (*myth*) mythe, *m.*; (*lie*) invention, *f.*; *v.a.* inventer; *v.n.* (*fairy stories*) en conter de belles; **~ed,** fabuleu|x, ~se.
fabric, (*building structure and fig.*) édifice, *m.*; (*texture*) tissu, *m.*; (*textile*) textile, *m.*; (*construction*) ouvrage, *m.* ⚠ fabrique = *'manufacture', 'vestry board', 'factory', 'church revenue' in French.*
fabrica|te, *v.a.* (*falsehood*) inventer; (*document*) forger; **~tion,** invention; **~tor,** inventeur; (*forger*) faussaire, *m.*
fabulist, (*writer of fables*) fabuliste, *m.*; (*liar*) menteu|r, -se, *m.f.*
fabulous, (*imaginary, mythic, legendary, incredible*) fabuleu|x, ~se; **~ly,** fabuleusement.
façade, façade, *f.*

face, *s.* (*visage*) figure, *f.*; (*look*) air, *m.*; (*grimace*) grimace, *f.*; (*boldness*) front, *m.*; (*watch*) cadran, *m.*; (*surface*) face, *f.*; *side-* ~, profil, *m.*; ~ *-value,* (*comm.*) valeur nominale, *f.*; *in the* ~ *of,* (*pers.*) au nez de; *in* ~ *of* (*things*), devant; *full in the* ~, en pleine figure; *look in the* ~, regarder en face; *fly in the* ~ *of,* braver; *on the* ~ *of it,* au premier coup d'œil; *put a good* ~ *on it,* contre mauvaise fortune faire bon cœur; *put a bold* ~ *on a thing,* payer d'audace; *set one's* ~ *against,* s'opposer résolument à.

face, *v.a.* (*confront, look on to, enemy*) faire face à; (*danger*) braver; (*present itself to*) se présenter à; (*garment*) garnir de revers; *v.n.* (*aspect*) être exposé à; *right about* ~*!* (*mil.*) demi-tour à droite!

facet, facette, *f.*

facetious, facétieu|x, ~se; **~ness,** caractère facétieux, *m.*; **~ly,** facétieusement.

facial, facial.

facile, (*pers.*) dou|x, ~ce.

facilitate, faciliter.

facility, facilité, *f.*

facing, *s.* (*garment*) parement, *m.*; (*arch.*) revêtement, *m.*; *prep.* vis-à-vis de.

facsimile, fac-similé, *m.*; ~ *signature, stamp,* griffe, *f.*

fact, fait, *m.*; *in* ~, en effet; *the* ~ *is that,* le fait est que.

fact|ion, faction, *f.*; **~iousness,** esprit de faction, *m.*; **~ious,** factieu|x, ~se; **~iously,** en factieux.

factitious, factice.

factor, (*commission agent*) commissionnaire, *m.*; (*tradesman's agent, math., circumstance*) facteur, *m.*

factory, fabrique, *f.*; (*East Indian, &c.*) factorerie, *f.*

factotum, factotum, *m.*

facult|y, (*aptitude, liberty to do*) faculté, *f.*; (*univ., med.*) faculté, *f.*; **~ative,** (*optional*) facultati|f, ~ve; (*contingent*) contingent.

fad, lubie, *f.*; **~dy,** qui a une marotte; **~dist,** homme à marotte, *m.*

fad|e, *v.a.* faner; *v.n.* (*flowers, &c.*) se faner; (*colour*) se décolorer; (*fig.*) s'évanouir; *~e into,* se fondre dans; *~e away,* (*vanish*) s'évanouir; **~ing,** (*fig.*) qui s'évanouit; **~eless,** qui ne se fane pas.

fag, *s.* (*slang, hard work*) corvée, *f.*; (*pop. cigarette*) cigarette, *f.*; (*pers., schol.*) garçon qui fait la corvée; ~ *end,* bout, *m.*; *v.a.* (*approx.*) fatiguer.

fag(g)ot, fagot, *m.*; (*mil., eng.*) fascine, *f.*

fail, *s. without* ~, sans faute.

fail, *v.a.* manquer à; *disappoint, be lacking to*) faire défaut à; (*abandon*) abandonner; *my heart* ~*s me,* le cœur me manque; *never* ~*ing,* infaillible.

fail, *v.n.* (*be wanting*) manquer; (*not succeed*) échouer; (*not to come true*) ne pas se réaliser; (*strength*) diminuer; (*bankruptcy*) faire faillite; ~ *in, to,* manquer de; (*not to be able to*) ne pas arriver (être) à; (*neglect to*) omettre* de.

failing, *s.* défaut, *m.*; *prep.* à défaut de.

failure, (*not success*) insuccès, *m.*; (*to perform*) défaut, *m.*, de + *noun* (*gen.*); (*bankrupt*) faillite, *f.*; *be a* ~, (*things*) faire* fiasco.

fain, *be* ~ *to,* vouloir* bien.

faint, *s.* évanouissement, *m.*; *in a* ~, évanoui.

faint, *adj.* (*timid*) timide; (*colour, voice*) faible; (*unwell*) prêt à tomber mal; (*vague, misty*) vague; ~ *with,* défaillant de; **~ness,** faiblesse, *f.*; **~ly,** (*indistinctly*) indistinctement; **~-hearted,** découragé; **~-heartedness,** pusillanimité, *f.*

faint, *v.n.* (*away*) s'évanouir; (*fig.*) faiblir; *~ing fit,* évanouissement, *m.*

fair, *s.* foire, *f.*

fair, *adj.* (*beautiful, specious*) beau; (*weather*) clair; (*complexion*) blond; (*of work*) pas mauvais; (*comm.*) loyal; (*just*) juste; ~ *share,* bonne part, *f.*; ~ *and square,* franc, franche et loyal, -e; *set* ~, (*barom.*) à beau fixe; ~ *copy,* copie au net, *f.*; **~ly,** (*tolerably well*) assez bien; (*honourably*) honnêtement.

fair, *adv.* ~ *and softly,* tout doucement; *and square,* rondement; *bid* ~ *to,* être en passe de; *play* ~, jouer franc jeu; *speak one* ~, parler avec politesse (à).

fairness, (*beauty*) beauté, *f.*; (*honesty*) loyauté, *f.*; (*hair*) couleur blonde, *f.*; (*complexion*) blond, *m.*

fairy, fée, *f.*; **~-land,** pays des fées; **~-tale,** conte de fées, *m.*; (*fig.*) conte à dormir debout; *adj.* féerique.

faith, foi, *f.*; (*belief*) croyance, *f.*; *have* ~ *in,* ajouter foi à; *on the* ~ *of,* sur la foi de.

faithful, fidèle (à); **~ness,** fidélité, *f.*; **~ly,** fidèlement; *Yours ~ly,* Agréez, je vous en prie, l'expression de mes sentiments distingués.

faithless, infidèle; (*treacherous*) perfide; **~ness,** infidélité, *f.*; **~ly,** déloyalement.

fake, *s.* article, meuble, *&c.*, truqué; *v.a.* truquer.

fakir, fakir, *m.*

falchion, cimeterre, *m.*

falcon, faucon, *m.*; *peregrine* ~, faucon pèlerin, *m.*; **~er,** fauconnier, *m.*; **~ry,** fauconnerie, *f.*

falconet, (*mil.*) fauconneau, *m.*; (*ornith.*) (*kind of shrike*) pie-grièche, *f.*

faldstool, (*for kneeling*) prie-dieu, *m. invar.*

fall, *s.* (*act of falling, rain, snow, moral*) chute, *f.*; (*night*) tombée, *f.*; (*price and temperature*) baisse, *f.*; (*descent*) pente, *f.*; (*U.S.A. autumn*) chute des feuilles, *f.*; (*water*) chute, *f.*

fall, *v.n.* tomber (être); (*prices, trade, voice, thermom., in opinion of*) baisser; (*happen*) arriver (être); (*begin*) se mettre* à; (*face*) s'allonger; ~ *away,* (*lose flesh*) maigrir; ~ *back,* (*mil.*) se replier; (*lit.*) reculer; ~ *back on,* avoir recours à; ~ *behind,* rester (être) en arrière; ~ *in.*

(*collapse*) s'effondrer; (*mil.*) former les rangs; ~ *into,* (*conversation*) entrer (être) en; ~ *in with,* (*meet*) rencontrer; (*agree with*) s'accorder avec; ~ *off,* (*value*) se déprécier; (*degenerate*) dégénérer; ~ *out,* (*quarrel*) se brouiller; (*happen*) arriver; ~ *down, over,* s'abattre sur; ~ *through,** (*fail*) échouer; ~ *to,* (*begin*) se mettre à; (*devolve on*) être dévolu à; ~ *upon,* (*attack*) tomber (être) sur; ~ *under,* (*be classed among*) être compris dans.

fallac|y, (*error*) erreur, *f.*; (*argument*) argument fallacieux, *m.*; **~ious,** trompeu|r, ~se.

fallen, (*dethroned, degraded*) déchu; (*woman*) perdue.

fallib|le, faillible; **~ility,** faillibilité, *f.*

falling, *s.* ~ *back,* reculade, *f.*; ~ *in,* éboulement, *m.*; ~ *off,* défection, *f.*; (*price*) baisse, *f.*; ~ *out,* brouille, *f.*; *adj.* ~ *sickness,* épilepsie, *f.* ; ~ *star,* étoile filante, *f.*

fallow, ~ *land,* jachère, *f.*; ~ **deer,** daim, *m.*; *f.* daine; ~ **finch,** (*ornith.*) cul-blanc, *m.*

false, (*gen. and coin, &c.*) fau|x, ~sse; (*hair, &c., artificial*) postiche; *~-faced,* hypocrite; *~-hearted,* perfide; *adv. play* ~, tromper; **~ness,** fausseté, *f.*; **~ly,** faussement.

falsehood, (*lie*) mensonge, *m.*

falsetto, *s.* fausset, *m.*

falsif|y, (*document, &c.*) falsifier; (*distort*) fausser; (*disappoint*) tromper; **~ication,** falsification, *f.*

falter, (*hesitate*) hésiter; (*stumble*) chanceler.

faltering, hésitant; **~ly,** (*voice*) en hésitant; (*step*) d'un pas chancelant.

fame, (*repute*) réputation, *f.*; (*celebrity*) renommée, *f.*; (*report*) bruit, *m.*

famed, (*celebrated*) célèbre; (*known for*) connu pour; *ill-~,* malfamé.

familiar, *s.* ami intime, *m.*

familiar, *adj.* (*known*) famili|er, ~ère (à); (*intimate with*) intime avec; (*over-free*) famili|er, ~ ère; *~spirit,* esprit familier, *m.*; **~ity,** familiarité; *~ity breeds contempt,* la familiarité engendre le mépris; **~ly,** familièrement; **~ize,** familiariser.

family, famille, *f.*; ~ **man,** homme d'intérieur, *m.*; **~-tree,** arbre généalogique, *m.*; *adj.* de famille.

famine, famine, *f.*; (*dearth, scarcety*) disette, *f.*

famish, *v.a.* affamer; *v.n. be ~ing,* (*fam.*) avoir une faim de loup.

famous, célèbre; (*lit. and fam.*) fameu|x, ~se; **~ly,** (*pop.*) fameusement.

fan, *s.* éventail, *m.*; (*winnowing*) van, *m.*; ~ **-light,** fenêtre en éventail, *f.*; ~ **-vaulting,** (*arch.*) croisée d'ogive, *f.*; ~ **-shaped,** en éventail.

fan, *v.a.* (*with fan*) éventer; (*corn*) vanner; (*fig.*) exciter; ~ *the flames,* (*fig.*) attiser le feu.

fanatic, *adj. and s.m.* fanatique; **~ism,** fanatisme, *m.*; **~al,** fanatique; **~ally,** en fanatique.

fancied, imaginaire.

fancier, (*of things rare*) amateur, *m.*

fanciful, (*things*) fantastique; (*pej.*) fantasque; (*whimsical*) fantaisiste; **~ness,** (*whimsicality*) bizarrerie, *f.*; **~ly,** bizarrement.

fancy, *s.* (*whim, mental image, individual taste*) fantaisie, *f.*; (*creative faculty*) imagination, *f.*; (*inclination*) goût, *m.*; (*fad*) lubie, *f.*; ~ **dress,** travestissement, *m.*; *~-dress ball,* bal costumé, *m.*; *take a ~ to,* (*pers.*) prendre en affection; (*things*) se sentir* du goût pour; *take the ~ of,* captiver.

fancy, *v.a.n.* se figurer; (*think*) avoir idée (que); (*desire, like*) avoir envie de; *just fancy!* figurez-vous!; *~oneself,* (*slang*) se gober.

fancy, *adj.* de fantaisie; ~ **goods,** articles de Paris, *m.pl.*; ~ **price,** prix exagéré, *m.*

fandangle, fanfreluche, *f.*

fane, temple, *m.*

fanfar|e, (*trumpets*) fanfare, *f.*; **~onade,** (*brag*) fanfaronnade, *f.*

fang, (*dog, wolf, &c.*) croc, *m.*; (*serpent*) crochet, *m.*; (*teeth*) racine, *f.*

fantasia, (*mus.*) fantaisie, *f.*

fantastic, fantastique; (*pej.*) fantasque; **~ally,** bizarrement.

fantasy, *see* FANCY.

far, *adj.* lointain; (*remote*) reculé; ~ *off,* lointain.

far, *adv.* loin; ~ *off,* au loin; *from ~,* de loin; *as ~ as, in so ~,* autant que; *as ~ as I know,* que je sache; *by ~,* de beaucoup; ~ *from it,* tant s'en faut; ~ *from being,* (*rich, poor, &c.*) loin d'être; ~ *and wide,* de tous côtés; *few and ~ between,* espacés; *how ~?* (*distance and degree*) jusqu'où? ; *how ~ is it?* a quelle distance est-ce? ; *near and ~,* de près et de loin; ~ *on in the night,* bien avant dans la nuit; *so ~,* jusqu'ici; *so ~ as to,* jusqu'à *+inf.*; *thus ~,* jusque là; *not to be ~ out,* ne pas se tromper beaucoup; **~-fetched,** tiré par les cheveux; **~-reaching,** gros de conséquences; **~-seeing, ~-sighted,** prévoyant; ~ **spent,** avancé; *go ~,* (*lit. and fig.*) aller* (être) loin.

farc|e, (*theatr.*) farce, *f.*; (*sham*) comédie, *f.*; **~ical,** burlesque.

fare, *s.* (*rail.*) prix de (la) place, *m.*; (*taxi, &c.*) prix de la course, *m.*; (*pers.*) client, *m.*; (*food*) chère, *f.*; *half ~,* demi-place, *f.*

fare, *v.n.* (*be in any state*) aller* (être); (*health*) se porter; *how does he ~,* comment vont ses affaires; ~ *well,* (*food*) faire* bonne chère.

farewell, *s.* adieu, *m.*; *bid ~ to,* dire* adieu à; *adj.* d'adieu.

farinaceous, farinacé.

farm, ferme, *f.*; **~-house,** maison de

ferme, *f.*; ~ **labourer,** ouvrier agricole, *m.*; ~ **yard,** cour de ferme, *f.*
farm, *v.a.* cultiver; (*taxes, &c.*) affermer; *v.n.* faire* de la culture.
farmer, fermier, *m.*; *~'s wife,* fermière, *f.*; *~ of revenue,* traitant, *m.*
farming, agriculture, *f.*
farrago, farrago, *m.*
farrier, maréchal ferrant, *m.*
farrow, *s.* (*pigs*) portée, *f.*; *v.n.* cochonner.
farth|er, *adj.* plus éloigné; *at the ~ end,* à l'autre bout; **~est,** le plus éloigné; *adv.* plus loin; *at the ~est,* (*place*) au plus loin; (*time*) au plus tard.
farthing, (*lit.*) farthing, *m.*; (*fig.*) sou, *m.*; *not to be worth a brass ~,* n'avoir pas un rouge liard.
farthingale, vertugadin, *m.*
fasces, faisceaux, *m.pl.*
fascicle, (*bot.*) faisceau, *m.*; (*book*) fascicule, *m.*
fascina|te, (*charm*) charmer; (*serpent, &c.*) fasciner; **~ting,** charmant; **~tion,** fascination, *f.*
fascine, (*mil.*) fascine, *f.*
fashion, *s.* (*usage and clothes*) mode, *f.*; (*form*) forme, *f.*; (*manner*) manière, *f.*; *the latest thing, ~,* le dernier cri; *man of ~,* élégant, *m.*; *in ~,* à la mode; *out of ~,* passé de mode; *in the English, French, &c. ~,* à l'anglaise, à la française; **~ -plate,** gravure de mode, *f.*
fashion, *v.a.* façonner.
fashionabl|e, élégant; **~eness,** élégance, *f.*; **~y,** élégamment.
fashioned, *new-~,* à la dernière mode; *old-~,* (*things*) démodé.
fast, fasting, *s.* jeûne, *m.*; *v.a.* jeûner.
fast, *adj.* (*faithful*) sûr; (*rapid*) vite; (*train, boat*) rapide; (*sport*) vite; (*colour*) solide; (*manners*) libre; (*dye*) grand; *be ~,* (*clock, &c.*) avancer; *~ man,* viveur, *m.*; *hard and ~ rule,* règle rigoureuse, *f.*
fast, *adv.* (*firmly*) ferme; (*strong*) fort; (*quickly*) vite; *stick ~,* (*in mud*) s'embourber; *stand, hold ~,* tenir* ferme; *rain ~,* pleuvoir* fort; *make ~,* (*naut.*) amarrer; (*door*) fermer bien.
fasten, *v.a.* (*tie*) attacher; (*door*) fermer; (*look, eyes*) fixer; (*boat*) amarrer; (*hook*) agrafer; (*button*) boutonner; *~ off,* (*thread*) arrêter; *v.n.* s'attacher; (*hook*) s'agrafer.
fastening, (*tie*) attache, *f.*; (*window, &c.*) fermeture, *f.*; (*hook*) agrafe, *f.*
fastidious, délicat. ⚠ *Not* fastidieux *which = tedious*; (*difficult to please*) difficile à satisfaire; *~ about,* difficile pour; **~ness,** goût difficile, *m.*; (*squeamishness*) délicatesse, *f.*
fastness, (*firmness*) fermeté, *f.*; (*stronghold*) place forte, *f.*
fat, *s.* (*meat*) gras, *m.*; (*grease*) graisse, *f.*
fat, *adj.* (*fleshy*) gras, -se; (*big, stout*) gros, -se; (*mind*) lourd; (*lands, cattle*) gras; **~-head,** *s.* niais, *m.*; *grow ~, get ~,* engraisser; *~ as a pig,* gros comme un moine; **~ness,** (*pers.*) embonpoint, *m.*; (*lands*) fertilité, *f.*
fat, *v.a.* engraisser.
fatal, (*destined, causing death*) fatal (*pl. ~s*); (*deadly*) mortel, -le; (*disastrous*) funeste (à); (*inevitable*) inévitable; **~ism,** fatalisme, *m.*; **~ist,** fataliste, *m.*; **~ity,** (*disaster*) fatalité, *f.*; (*death*) mort, *f.*; **~ly,** (*mortally*) mortellement.
fate, destin, *m.*; (*lot*) sort, *m.*; (*death*) mort, *f.*; *stroke of ~,* coup du sort, *m.*
fated, (*decreed*) décrété; (*doomed*) destiné (à); *ill-~,* (*pers.*) infortuné; (*things*) fatal.
father, père, *m.*; **~s,** (*ancestors*) aïeux, *m.pl.*; *grand~,* grand-père; *great-grand~,* bisaïeul, *m.*; **~-in-law,** beau-père; **~ Xmas,** le père Noël; *like ~ like son,* tel père tel fils.
father, *v.a.* (*adopt*) adopter; *~ on,* (*fig.*) attribuer (à).
fatherhood, paternité, *f.*
fatherland, patrie, *f.*
fatherless, sans père.
fatherl|y, *adj.* paternel, -le; *adv.* en père; **~iness,** bonté de père, *f.*
fathom, toise, *f.*; (*naut.*) brasse, *f.*; *v.a.* (*lit. and fig.*) sonder.
fathomless, insondable.
fatigue, *s.* fatigue, *f.*; *~ party also duty,* (*mil.*) corvée, *f.*; ⚠ fatigue *is not used in the military sense*; *v.a.* fatiguer.
fatling, bête grasse, *f.*
fatted, *~ calf,* veau gras, *m.*
fatten, *v.a.n.* engraisser.
fatty, *adj.* graisseu|x, ~se; *s.* (*pers. fam.*) gros papa, *m.*
fatu|ity, fatuousness, imbécillité, *f.*; **~ous,** imbécile.
faucal, *adj.* (*sound*) guttural.
fault, (*defect and hunt.*) défaut, *m.*; (*error, wrong, tennis*) faute, *f.*; *to a ~,* à l'excès; *be at ~,* être en défaut; *find ~ with,* trouver à redire* à; *whose ~ is it?* à qui la faute?
faultfinder, frondeu|r, ~se, *s.m.f.*
fault|y, défectueu|x, ~se; **~iness,** défectuosité, *f.*
faultless, sans faute; (*without defect*) sans défaut; **~ness,** perfection, *f.*; **~ly,** impeccablement.
faun, faune, -sse, *m.f.*
fauna, faune, *f.*
favour, faveur, *f.*; (*letter*) honorée, *f.*; (*ribbon*) nœud de rubans, *m.*; (*permission*) permission, *f.*; *by ~ of,* à la faveur de; *under ~ of,* (*right, &c.*) à la faveur de; *with your ~,* avec votre permission; *in ~ of,* en faveur de; *curry ~,* s'insinuer dans les bonnes grâces (de); *do a ~,* faire* une grâce (à); *look with ~ on,* regarder d'un œil favorable.
favour, *v.a.* favoriser; (*plan, &c.*) être en faveur de; (*resemble*) ressembler à; *~ with,* honorer de.
favourabl|e, favorable; **~eness,** caractère favorable, *m.*; **~y,** favorablement.

favourit|e, *adj. and s.m.f.* favori, -te; (*things*) de prédilection; **~ism,** favoritisme, *m.*
fawn, *s.* faon, *m.*; *adj.* (*colour*) fauve.
fawn, *v.a.* (*dogs*) ramper; ~ *upon,* (*pers.*) faire le chien couchant à.
fawning, *s.* servilité, *f.*; (*dogs, &c.*) caresses, *f.pl.*; *adj.* caressant; **~ly,** servilement.
fay, fée, *f.*
fealty, fidélité, *f.*
fear, crainte, *f.*; *for ~ of,* de peur de + *inf.*; *for ~ that,* de peur que + *subj.* (+ ne *only if affirmative verb follows*); *stand in ~ of,* avoir peur de; *No ~ of that!* il n'y a pas de danger!
fear, *v.a.* craindre*; (*dread*) redouter; *v.n.* craindre*.
fearful, (*pers.*) crainti|f, ~ve; (*thing*) épouvantable; **~ness,** (*pers.*) caractère craintif, *m.*; (*things*) horreur, *f.*; **~ly,** (*lit. and fam.*) terriblement; (*with fear*) craintivement.
fearless, intrépide; **~ness,** intrépidité, *f.*; **~ly,** sans peur.
fearsome, affreu|x, ~se.
feasib|le, faisable; **~ility,** possibilité, *f.*;
feast, *s.* (*festival*) fête, *f.*; (*meal*) festin, *m.*; (*for the eye, &c.*) régal, *m.*
feast, *v.a.* régaler; (*fig.*) charmer; *v.n.* festoyer; (*fam.*) faire* bombance.
feaster, amateur de bonne chère, *m.*; (*guest*) convive, *m.*
feat, exploit, *m.*; (*trick, skill, &c.*) tour, *m.*; ~ *of arms,* fait d'armes, *m.*
feather, plume, *f.*; (*wing or tail*) penne, *f.*; **~-bed,** lit de plumes, *m.*; *prince's ~,* (*bot.*) amarante, *f.*; *show white ~,* (*fam.*) caner.
feather, *v.a.* emplumer; (*arrow*) empenner; ~ *one's nest,* faire* sa pelote.
feathery, plumeu|x, ~se.
feature, (*lit. and fig.*) trait, *m.*; (*characteristic*) caractéristique, *f.*; *main ~,* point principal, *m.*; *v.a.* (*portray*) dépeindre*.
febrifuge, *s.* fébrifuge, *m.*
febrile, fébrile.
February, février, *m.*
feckless, incapable.
fecund, fécond; **~ity,** fécondité, *f.*
federal, fédéral; **~ist,** fédéraliste, *m.*
federa|te, *v.a.n.* fédérer; **~tion,** fédération, *f.*
fee, *s.* (*lawyer, doctor*) honoraires, *m.pl.*; (*hist.*) fief, *m.*; **~s,** (*school, &c.*) frais, *m.pl.*
fee, *v.a.* rétribuer.
feebl|e, faible; **~eness,** faiblesse, *f.*; **~y,** faiblement.
feed, *s.* (*cattle*) pâture, *f.*; (*of oats, corn*) picotin, *m.*; *winter ~,* fourrage, *m.*; *~-pipe,* tuyau d'alimentation, *m.*
feed, *v.a.* (*lit. and fig.*) nourrir (de); (*cattle*) paître*; *be fed up with it, him, &c.,* (*slang*) en avoir soupé; *v.n.* se nourrir (de); (*cattle*) paître*.
feeder, *s.* (*bottle and feeding-bottle*) biberon, *m.*; *gross ~,* (*pers.*) gros mangeur, *m.*
feel, *s.* toucher, *m.*
feel, *v.a.* sentir*; (*pulse and handle*) tâter; (*pain, emotion*) ressentir*.
feel, *v.n.* (*find oneself*) se sentir; (*in pocket, &c.*) tâter; ~ *cold, &c.,* (*personally*) avoir froid, etc.; ~ *cold, &c.,* (*to touch*) être froid, etc. au toucher; ~ *for,* avoir de la sympathie pour; *he ~s giddy,* la tête lui tourne.
feeler, (*insects*) antenne, *f.*; *throw out a ~,* lancer un ballon d'essai.
feeling, *s.* (*heart*) sentiment, *m.*; (*sense of touch*) tact, *m.*; (*expression*) expression, *f.*; (*impression*) impression, *f.*; *have no ~,* n'avoir pas de cœur.
feeling, *adj.* sensible; **~ly,** avec sensibilité.
feign, (*pretend*) feindre*; (*invent story, excuse*) inventer.
feint, *s.* feinte, *f.*; (*pretence*) semblant, *m.*
feldspar, feldspath, *m.*
felicita|te, féliciter; **~tion,** félicitation, *f.*
felicit|ous, (*expression*) heureu|x, ~se; **~y,** bonheur, *m.*; **~ously,** heureusement.
feline, félin.
fell, *s.* (*skin*) peau, *f.*; (*moor*) lande, *f.*
fell, *v.a.* abattre; **~ing,** *s., ~ed timber,* abatis, *m.*
fell, *adj.* cruel, -le.
felloe, felly, jante, *f.*
fellow, *s.* 1. (*comrade*) camarade, *m.*; 2. (*companion*) compagnon, *m.*; 3. (*equal*) pareil, *m.*; 4. (*gloves, &c.*) autre, *m.f.*; 5. (*pej.*) individu, *m.*; 6. (*univ. approx.*) agrégé, *m.*; 7. (*of learned society*) membre, *m.*; *my dear ~,* mon cher; *good ~,* brave garçon, *m.*; *good for nothing ~,* garnement, *m.*; *nice ~,* bon type, *m.*; *old ~,* vieux, *m.*; *poor ~,* pauvre diable, *m.*; *queer ~,* drôle de corps, *m.*; ~ **citizen,** concitoyen, -ne, *m.f.*; ~ **countryman,** ~ **countrywoman,** compatriote, *m.f.*; ~ **creature,** semblable, *m.*; ~ **soldier,** camarade, *m.*; ~ **student,** compagnon d'étude, *m.*; ~ **traveller,** compagnon de voyage, *m.*; ~ **worker,** compagnon de travail, *m.*; *be hail ~ well met with,* être à tu et à toi avec.
fellowship, (*good*) camaraderie, *f.*; (*sharing*) communauté, *f.*; (*similarity of feeling*) communion, *f.*; (*univ.*) poste d'agrégé, *m.*
felo de se, suicide, *m.*
felon, *s.* criminel, *m.*; *adj.* perfide; **~y,** crime, *m.*; **~ious,** criminel, -le.
felt, feutre, *m.*
felucca, (*naut.*) felouque, *f.*
female, *s.* femme, *f.*; (*an. and pej.*) femelle, *f.*; *young ~,* jeune personne, *f.*
female, *adj.* (*an. and bot.*) femelle; (*pers.*) féminin; ~ *bird,* oiseau femelle, *m.*
feminine, (*lit., gram., rhyme*) féminin; (*effeminate*) efféminé.
feminis|m, féminisme, *m.*; **~t,** féministe, *m.f.*

fen, marais, *m.*; ~**-fire**, feu follet, *m.*
fence, clôture, *f.*; (*pales*) palissade, *f.*; *sit on the* ~, attendre l'événement.
fence, *v.a.* (*enclose*) enclore*; (*fig.*) entourer; *v.n.* (*foils*) faire* des armes; ~**r**, escrimeur, *m.*
fencing, *s.* escrime, *f.*; ~**-glove**, gant bourré, *m.*; ~**-master**, maître d'armes, *m.*; ~**-match**, assaut d'armes, *m.*; ~**-school**, salle d'armes, *f.*
fend, *v.a.* (*ward off*) écarter; ~ *for oneself*, se débrouiller.
fender, garde-cendres, *m. invar.*
fennel, (*bot.*) fenouil, *m.*
fenny, marécageu|x, ~se.
ferment, *s.* (*leaven*) ferment, *m.*; (*excitement*) effervescence, *f.*; *v.n.* fermenter; ~**ation**, fermentation, *f.*
fern, fougère, *f.*; ~**ery**, ~**-brake**, fougeraie, *f.*; ~**-owl**, engoulevent, *m.*
ferocious, féroce; ~**ness**, (*ferocity*) férocité, *f.*; ~**ly**, férocement.
ferret, furet, *m.*; ⚠ *Not* ferret *which* = '*tag' of laces*; (*detective*) limier, *m.*; *v.a.* ~ *out*, dépister; ~**y**, (*eyes*) de furet.
ferriferous, ferrifère.
ferruginous, ferrugineu|x, ~se.
ferrule, (*cane*) bout, *m.*
ferry, passage en bac, *m.*; ~**-boat**, bac, *m.*; ~**man**, passeur, *m.*; (*infernal regions*) nocher, *m.*; *v.a.* ~ *across*, *faire passer l'eau à.
fertil|e, *adj.* fertile; (*fig.*) ~ *in*, fertile en; ~**ity**, fertilité, *f.*; ~**ize**, fertiliser; (*bot.*) féconder; ~**ization**, fertilisation, *f.*; ~**izer**, (*manure*) engrais, *m.*
ferule, (*ruler to punish*) férule, *f.*
ferven|t, (*fervid*) ardent; (*prayer, &c.*) fervent; ~**cy**, ardeur, ferveur, *f.*; ~**tly**, ardemment.
fervour, ardeur, *f.*; (*piety, &c.*) ferveur, *f.*
fesse, (*her.*) fasce, *f.*
festal, de fête.
fester, *v.a.* envenimer; *v.n.* s'envenimer.
festival, fête, *f.*; (*mus.*) festival, *m.* ⚠ festival *is only used in this latter sense.*
festiv|e, de fête; ~**ity**, gaieté (gaîté), *f.*; ~**ities**, réjouissances, *f.pl.*
festoon, *s.* feston, *m.*; *v.a.* festonner.
fetch, *v.a.* aller* (être) chercher; (*thing*) apporter; (*pers.*) amener; (*breath*) prendre*; (*sigh*) pousser; (*blood*) tirer; (*tears*) arracher; (*blow*) asséner; ~ *away*, (*pers.*) emmener; (*thing*) emporter; ~ *down, in, out*, faire* descendre, entrer, sortir; ~ *up*, (*pers.*) faire* monter; (*thing*) monter (avoir); *v.n.* ~ *up*, (*be sick*) vomir.
fetch, *v.n.* ~ *and carry*, faire* des courses.
fetching, *adj.* (*fam.*) empoignant.
fête, fête, *f.*; ~**-day**, fête, *f.*
fetid, fétide; ~**ity**, ~**ness**, fétidité, *f.*
fet|ish, ~**ich**, fétiche, *m.*; ~**ishism**, fétichisme, *m.*
fetlock, fanon, *m.*
fetter, *s.* (*lit. and fig.*) entrave, *f.*; ~**s**, fers, *m. pl.*; *v.a.* (*lit. and fig.*) entraver.
fettle, condition, *f.*; *be in fine* ~, être bien en forme.
feud, (*tribe, &c.*) hostilité, *f.*; (*pers.*) querelle, *f.*
feudal, féodal; ~**ism**, féodalité, *f.*
feudatory, *s.* feudataire, *m.*
fever, (*lit. and fig.*) fièvre, *f.*; *be in a* ~, avoir la fièvre.
feverfew, (*bot.*) matricaire, *f.*
feverish, fiévreu|x, ~se; (*fig.*) fébrile; ~**ly**, (*fig.*) fiévreusement; ~**ness**, fièvre légère, *f.*; *be* ~, avoir un peu de fièvre.
few, *pron.* peu (*plural verb if plural complement understood*); (*small number*) petit nombre; *a* ~, quelques-uns; *quite a* ~, *not a* ~, un assez grand nombre de.
few, *adj.* peu de; *a* ~, quelques; ~**er**, moins (de); *these* ~ *words*, ces quelques mots; *the* ~ *English who saw it*, les quelques Anglais qui l'ont vu; ~ *and far between*, espacés; ~**ness**, petit nombre, *m.*
fez, fez, *m.*
fiasco, fiasco, *m.*
fiat, décret, *m.*; ~ **money**, (*comm.*) papier-monnaie, *f.*
fib, *s.* petit mensonge, *m.*; *v.n.* (*fam.*) dire* des blagues.
fibr|e, (*lit. and fig.*) fibre, *f.*; ~**ous**, fibreu|x, ~se.
fibril, (*bot.*) fibrille, *f.*
fickle, volage; ~**ness**, inconstance, *f.*
fiction, (*act of invention, thing invented*) fiction, *f.*; (*novels*) romans, *m.pl.*
fictitious, (*feigned*) ficti|f, ~ve; (*not genuine*) factice; ~**ly**, fictivement.
fiddle, violon, *m.*; (*pej.*) crincrin, *m.*; *play second* ~, être relégué au second plan.
fiddle, *v.n.* jouer du violon; ~ *with* (*move about*) tourner et retourner.
fiddlededee! *interj.* chansons que tout cela!
fiddle-faddle, *s.* fadaise, *f.*
fiddler, joueur de violon, *m.*; *country* ~, ménétrier, *m.*
fidelity, fidélité, *f.* (à).
fidget, (*mouvement*) agitation, *f.*; ~**s**, impatiences, *f.pl.*; *what a* ~ *you are!* combien vous êtes agité; *v.a.* (*worry*) tracasser; *v.n.* ~ *about*, remuer.
fidgety, remuant.
fiduciary, (*comm.*) fiduciaire.
fie! *interj.* fi donc!
fief, fief, *m.*
field, (*lit., fig., battle, her., campaign, of vision, electr.*) champ, *m.*; (*sport*) terrain, *m.*; ~ **artillery**, artillerie de campagne, *f.*; ~**-day**, (*mil.*) exercice en campagne, *m.*; ~**-glasses**, jumelles, *f.pl.*; ~ **hospital**, hôpital ambulant, *m.*; ~ **larkspur**, (*bot.*) consoude royale, *f.*; ~**-marshal**, maréchal, *m.*; ~**-mouse**, mulot, *m.*; ~ **officer**, officier supérieur, *m.*; ~ **sports**, chasse, *f.*; *in the open* ~*s*, en plein champ; *take the* ~, entrer (être) en campagne.

fieldfare, (*ornith.*) litorne, *f.*
fiend, démon, *m.*; (*fig.*) monstre, *m.*; **~ish,** diabolique.
fierce, (*cruel*) cruel, -le; (*storm*) violent; (*look, air*) farouche; (*savage*) féroce; **~ness,** férocité, *f.*; **~ly,** férocement.
fier|y, (*of fire*) de feu; (*like fire*) flamboyant; (*ardent*) ardent; (*pers. and temper*) emporté; **~ red,** rouge feu, *invar.*; **~iness,** ardeur, *f.*; (*fig.*) fougue, *f.*
fife, fifre, *m.*; **~r,** fifre, *m.*
fifteen, *adj. and s.m.* quinze; *s.* (*football*) équipe de rugby, *f.*
fifteenth, *adj. and s.m.* quinzième; (*date and sovereigns*) quinze.
fifth, *adj. and s.m.* cinquième; (*dates and sovereigns*) cinq; *Charles the Fifth,* (*Emp.*) Charles-Quint; *Sixtus the Fifth,* Sixte-Quint; **~ly,** cinquièmement.
fiftieth, *adj. and s.m.* cinquantième.
fifty, cinquante; *s.* (*abt. 50*) cinquantaine, *f.*
fig, figue, *f.*; **~-tree,** figuier, *m.*; *not to care a ~ for,* se battre l'œil de.
fight, *s.* combat, *m.*; (*fray, free fight*) mêlée, *f.*; (*struggle*) lutte, *f.*; *~ to a finish,* combat à outrance; *sham ~,* simulacre de combat, *m.*; *show ~,* montrer les dents.
fight, *v.a.* (*enemy*) combattre; (*gen. and fig.*) se battre contre; (*battle*) livrer; *~ shy of,* éviter.
fight, *v.n.* combattre; (*fig.*) lutter; (*quarrel*) se disputer; *~ tooth and nail,* avoir bec et ongles.
fighter, combattant, *m.*; (*pej.*) bretteur, *m.*; (*aeron.*) avion de chasse, *m.*
fighting, *s.* combat, *m.*
fighting, *adj.* **~ man,** combattant, *m.*; **~-plane,** (*aeron.*) avion de combat, *m.*
figment, (*invention*) invention, *f.*; (*imaginary thing*) fiction, *f.*
figuration, (*determination of form*) figuration, *f.*; (*form*) forme, *f.*
figurative, figurati|f, ~ve; (*metaphorical*) figuré; *in a ~ sense,* **~ly,** au figuré.
figure, (*form, geom., rhet., personage*) figure, *f.*; (*bodily shape*) tournure, *f.*; (*arith.*) chiffre, *m.*; *~ of speech,* figure de rhétorique, *f.*
figure, *v.a.* (*represent*) figurer; (*fabrics*) brocher; (*imagine*) figurer; *~ out,* (*comm.*) chiffrer; *~ to oneself,* se figurer.
figure, *v.n.* (*appear noticeably in list, &c., comm.*) figurer; *~ out at,* (*comm.*) se chiffrer à.
figure-head, (*naut.*) figure de proue, *f.*
figurine, figurine, *f.*
figwort, (*bot.*) scrofulaire, *f.*
filament, filament, *m.*
filbert, aveline, *f.*; **~-tree,** avelinier, *m.*
filch, *v.a.* filouter; **~er,** filou, *m.*
file, *s.* (*tool*) lime, *f.*; (*mil.*) file, *f.*; (*long line*) queue, *f.*; (*papers*) liasse, *f.*; (*letters, &c.*) classeur, *m.*; *in single ~,* à la file (indienne).
file, *v.a.* (*tool*) limer; (*letters, papers*) classer; *v.n.* (*mil.*) marcher à la file; *~ off,* défiler; *right ~!* par file à droite.
filemot, (*colour = dead-leaf*) feuille-morte, *invar.*
filer, limeur, *m.*
filewort, (*bot.*) ficaire, *f.*
filial, filial.
filiation, affiliation, *f.*
filibuster, flibustier, *m.*
filigree, filigrane, *m.*; **~d,** filigrané.
filing, (*tool*) limure, *f.*; **~s,** limaille, *f.*; (*lettres, &c.*) classement, *m.*
fill, *s.* (*food, drink, fam.*) soûl (saoul), *m.*; (*tobacco*) pipe, *f.*; (*pen*) plumée, *f.*
fill, *v.a.* (*lit. and fig.*) remplir; (*post*) occuper; (*pipe*) bourrer; (*satisfy hunger*) rassasier; *~ up,* (*time*) occuper; (*form, cheque, fill full*) remplir; (*vacancy, ditch, hole, measure*) combler; *~ in,* (*forms, cheques, &c.*) remplir.
fill, *v.n.* se remplir; *~ up,* (*to drink*) verser à boire; (*motor*) faire* le plein d'essence; *~ out,* (*get fat, fam.*) se remplumer.
filler, (*drop-bottle*) compte-gouttes, *m. invar.*; (*funnel*) entonnoir, *m.*
fillet, (*band*) bandeau, *m.*; (*beef, fish, &c., arch., her.*) filet, *m.*; (*veal*) rouelle, *f.*; *v.a.* découper en filets.
filling, *s.* *~ in,* (*cheque, forms, &c., needlework*) remplissage, *m.*; (*masonry*) remplage, *m.*; *~ up,* (*ditch, &c.*) comblement, *m.*
fillip, *s.* (*blow*) chiquenaude, *f.*; (*stimulus*) stimulant, *m.*
filly, (*foal*) pouliche, *f.*
film, *n.* (*med.*) membrane, *f.*; (*photo.*) pellicule, *f.*; (*cinema*) film, *m.*; *v.a.* (*cinema*) cinématographier; **~-screen,** écran, *m.*; **~-star,** vedette de l'écran, *f.*; **~-studio,** atelier, *m.*; *produce a ~,* produire*; *release a ~,* (*cin.*) mettre* sur l'écran.
filmy, (*cloud, &c.*) embué.
filter, *s.* filtre, *m.*; *v.a.n.* filtrer; (*trickle*) suinter.
filtering, filtrage, *m.*
filth, (*lit. and fig.*) ordure, *f.*
filth|y, (*dirty*) sale; (*fig., things*) obscène; **~iness,** saleté, obscénité, *f.*; **~ily,** salement.
filtra|te, filtrer; **~tion,** filtration, *f.*
fimbriate(d), fimbrié.
fin, nageoire, *f.*; (*carp, shark*) aileron, *m.*
finable, passible d'amende.
final, final; (*last*) derni|er, ~ère; (*decisive*) décisi|f, ~ve; **~ity,** finalité, *f.*; **~ly,** enfin; *~ cause,* cause finale, *f.*
final, *s.* (*sports, games*) finale, *f.*; (*exams*) examen final, *m.*
financ|e, finance, *f.* (*oft. pl.*); *v.a.* (*comm.*) financer; (*firm or Co.*) commanditer; **~ial,** financ|ier, ~ière; *~ial year,* exercice, *m.*; **~ially,** financièrement; ⚠ financial, *&c., not French.*
financ|ier, financier, *m.*; **~ing,** *s.* financement, *m.*
find, *s.* trouvaille, *f.*

find, *v.a.* trouver; (*discover*) découvrir*; (*supply money, &c.*) fournir (à); (*guilty*) déclarer; (*learn*) apprendre*; (*verify*) constater; (*provide with*) pourvoir* de; ~ *oneself,* (*feel*) se trouver; ~ *out,* découvrir*; (*problem, &c.*) résoudre*; ~ *it impossible to,* se trouver dans l'impossibilité de.

finder, trouveu|r, ~se, *s.m.f.*; (*photo.*) viseur, *m.*

finding, *s.* découverte, *f.*

fine, *s.* (*penalty*) amende, *f.*; (*weather*) beau temps, *m.*

fine, *adj.* **1** (*excellent, good*) beau; **2** (*pen, gold, writing, linen, sand, rain, metal, thin*) fin; **3** (*ear*) fin; **4** (*delicate*) délicat; **5** (*elegant*) élégant; **6** (*language*) choisi; **7** (*subtle*) subtil; **8** (*ironical*) joli; *be* ~, (*weather*) faire beau; *that's all very* ~, cela est bel et bon; **~ness,** (*lit. and fig.*) finesse, *f.*; (*with suggestion of beauty*) élégance, *f.*; (*nicety*) délicatesse, *f.*; **~ly,** (*delicately, skilfully*) finement; (*irony*) joliment.

fine, *v.a.* (*penalty*) mettre* à l'amende; (*liquids*) clarifier.

fine, *adv.* (*fam.*) bien; *chop* ~, †hacher menu.

fine-draw, (*mend*) rentraire*.

fine-drawn, *adj.* (*fig.*) subtil.

finery, parure, *f.*; (*studied elegance in dress*) recherche, *f.*

finesse, finesse, *f.*; *v.a.n.* user de finesse (envers).

finger, *s.* doigt, *m.*; *fore*~, index, *m.*; *little* ~, petit doigt; *middle* ~, médius, *m.*; *ring* ~, annulaire, *m.*; *burn one's* ~*s,* (*fig.*) s'échauder les doigts; *have a* ~ *in the pie,* s'en mêler; *to the* ~ *-tips,* jusqu'au bout des ongles; **~-bowl,** rince-bouche, *m., invar.*; **~-mark,** trace de doigt, *f.*; **~-plate,** plaque, *f.*; **~-post,** poteau indicateur, *m.*; **~ -print,** empreinte digitale, *f.*

finger, *v.a.* (*handle*) manier; (*instrument*) toucher de; *light-~ed person,* voleur à la tire, *m.*

fingering, *s.* (*handling*) maniement, *m.*; (*mus.*) doigté, *m.*; (*wool*) laine à tricoter, *f.*

finial, (*arch.*) fleuron, *m.*

finical, affété; **~ness,** afféterie, *f.*

finis, fin, *f.*

finish, *s.* (*end*) fin, *f.*; (*perfection, final touch*) fini, *m.*

finish, *v.a.* finir; (*terminate*) terminer; ~ *off,* achever; (*put final touch*) donner la dernière main à; *v.n.* finir; (*finish by doing*) finir par; (*finish doing*) finir de.

finished, *adj.* (*in manners, &c.*) accompli.

finishing, *s.* (*completion*) achèvement, *m.*; (*final touch*) finissage, *m.*

finishing, *adj.* (*improving*) de perfectionnement; ~ *touch,* coup de fion, *m.*

finite, *adj.* and *s.m.* fini.

Finn, Finnish, *adj.* (*when adj. use small letter*) *and s.m.f.* Finlandais, -e; (*lang.*) finlandais, *m.*

finned, finny, muni de nageoires.

fir, fir-tree, sapin, *m.*; **Scotch ~,** pin, *m.*; **spruce- ~,** épicéa, *m.*; **~ -cone,** pomme de pin, *f.*; **~-needle,** aiguille de sapin, *f.*; **~-plantation,** sapinière, *f.*

fire, *s.* (*lit. and fig.*) feu, *m.*; (*conflagration*) incendie, *m.*; *on* ~, en feu; **~-alarm,** avertisseur d'incendie, *m.*; **~-assurance,** assurance contre l'incendie; **~ -bomb,** bombe flamboyante, *f.*; **~-brigade,** corps des pompiers, *m.*; **~-damp,** grisou, *m.*; **~-engine,** pompe à incendie, *f.*; **~-escape,** escalier de sauvetage, *m.*; **~ -extinguisher,** extincteur, *m.*; **~-fly,** luciole, *f.*; **~ -guard,** garde-feu, *m. invar.*; **~-hose,** tuyau d'incendie, *m.*; **~-irons,** garniture de foyer, *f.*; **~-lighter,** allume-feu, *m. invar.*; **~-pan,** brasier, *m.*; **~-place,** cheminée, *f.*; **~-plug,** bouche d'incendie, *f.*; **~-proof,** à l'épreuve du feu; **~-screen,** écran, *m.*; **~side,** coin du feu, *m.*; **~-station,** poste d'incendie, *m.*; *fire!* au feu!; *go through* ~ *and water for,* se jeter au feu pour; *hang* ~, (*last long*) faire* long feu; *miss* ~, (*fire-arms, motors, &c.*) rater; *open* ~, ouvrir* le feu; *running* ~, feu roulant; *set* ~ *to,* mettre* le feu à; *stir* ~, attiser le feu; *take* ~, prendre* feu.

fire, *v.a.* mettre* le feu à; (*set ablaze*) embraser; (*gun, &c.*) tirer; (*mine*) faire* exploser; ~ *out,* (*slang*) flanquer à la porte; *v.n.* (*fire-arms*) tirer; ~ *at close quarters,* tirer à bout portant; ~ *with blank cartridges,* tirer à blanc; ~ *up,* (*anger*) s'emporter; *fire away!* allez-y!

firelock, fusil à pierre, *m.*

fireman, pompier, *m.*; (*ship*) chauffeur, *m.*

fireproof, *adj.* incombustible.

firer, quick-~, (*gun*) *see* QUICK.

fireworks, feu d'artifice, *m.*

firing, *s.* (*mil., action of*) tir, *m.*; (*oven, furnace*) chauffage, *m.*; *adj. see* QUICK.

firm, *s.* (*comm.*) maison de commerce, *f.*

firm, *adj.* (*stable, solid, established*) ferme; *stand, hold* ~, tenir* bon; **~ness,** (*lit., fig., comm.*) fermeté, *f.*; **~ly,** fermement.

firmament, firmament, *m.*

first, *adj.* premi|er, ~ère; (*dates and sovereigns*) premier (*no article with sovs.*); (*in compound numbers*) unième; **~ comer,** *see* COMER; **~-fruits,** (*lit. and fig.*) prémices, *f.pl.*; **~-rate,** *adj.* de premier ordre.

first, *adv.* (*time*) d'abord; (*series*) premièrement; (*first time*) pour la première fois; (*rail.*) en premières; *at* ~, d'abord; ~ *or last,* tôt ou tard; **~-born,** *adj. and m.* premier né; **~ly,** premièrement.

firstling, (*first-fruits*) prémices, *f.pl.*

firth, (*of river*) embouchure, *f.*

fisc, fisc, *m.*; **~al,** fiscal.

fish, poisson, *m.*; *fried* ~, friture, *f.*; *freshwater* ~, poisson de rivière, *m.*; *queer* ~, (*fam.*) drôle de corps, *m.*; **~-hamper,** bourriche, *f.*; **~-hook,** hameçon, *m.*; **~-kettle,** poissonnière, *f.*; **~-market,** marché aux poissons, *m.*;

~**-pond,** vivier, *m.*; ~**-slice,** truelle, *f.*; *have other ~ to fry*, avoir d'autres chats à fouetter; *a pretty kettle of ~*, un joli gâchis, *m.*
fish, *v.a.* pêcher; (*pond*) prendre* le poisson de; ~ *out*, (*pocket, &c.*) sortir (avoir); *v.n.* pêcher; ~ *for*, (*fig.*) chercher; ~ *in troubled waters*, pêcher en eau trouble; *neither ~, flesh, fowl, or good red herring*, ni chair ni poisson.
fisherman, fisherwoman, pêcheu|r, ~se, *m.f.*
fishery, (*place*) pêcherie, *f.*
fishing, pêche, *f.*; ~**-boat,** bateau de pêche, *m.* ~**-rod,** canne à pêche, *f.*; ~**-smack,** bateau pêcheur, *m.*
fishmonger, poissonn|ier, ~ière, *m.f.*; *~'s shop*, poissonnerie, *f.*
fishwife, poissarde, *f.*
fishy, de poisson; (*abounding in fish*) poissonneu|x, ~se; (*eye*) vitreu|x, ~se.
fissure, fissure, *f.*
fist, poing, *m.*; *with clenched ~s*, les poings serrés.
fisticuffs, coups de poing, *m.pl.*
fistula, (*med.*) fistule, *f.*
fit, *s.* (*med.*) attaque, *f.*; (*temper*) accès, *m.*; *by ~s and starts*, à bâtons rompus; *be a good, bad ~*, (*clothes*) aller* (être) bien, mal; ~ *of coughing*, quinte, *f.*
fit, *adj.* (*proper, suitable*) convenable; (*just*) juste; (*able*) en état (de); (*capable*) capable (de); ~ *for*, propre à; ~ *for food*, mangeable; ~ *to drink*, buvable; *think ~*, juger à propos (de); *not ~ to hold a candle to*, ne pas venir à la cheville à; ~ *as a fiddle*, frais et dispos; ~**ness,** à-propos, *m.*; (*aptitude*) aptitude, *f.*; ~**ly,** (*properly*) convenablement; (*opportunely*) à propos.
fit, *v.a.* (*adjust*) ajuster; (*key*) s'ajuster à; (*clothes*) aller* (être) à; (*one thing into another*) emboîter; (*be appropriate*) convenir* à; (*agree with*) s'accorder avec; ~ *for*, préparer à; ~ *on*, (*clothes*) essayer; ~ *out*, équiper; ~ *up*, (*house, machine*) monter; (*shop, office*) agencer; ~ *with*, (*provide with*) munir de.
fit, *v.n.* (*be adapted*) s'adapter (à); (*clothes*) aller* (être); ~ *in with*, cadrer avec.
fitful, (*stirring*) agité; (*changing*) changeant; ~**ly,** par boutades.
fitter, (*workman*) ajusteur, *m.*; (*mach. and clothes*) mont|eur, ~euse, *m.f.*
fitting, *s.* ajustage, *m.*; (*mach.*) montage, *m.*; ~ *out*, équipement, *m.*; ~ *up*, agencement, *m.*
fitting, *adj.* convenable; *tight-~*, collant.
five, *adj. and s.m.* cinq; (*5 o'clock*) cinq heures; ~**fold,** quintuple.
fix, *s.* embarras, *m.*; *be in a ~*, être dans le pétrin.
fix, *v.a.* (*fasten, stick, attention, look, choice, abode*) fixer; ~ *bayonets*, *see* BAYONET; ~ *up*, arranger; *v.n.* ~ *on*, se décider pour.
fixation, fixation, *f.*
fixed, fixe; (*dates, deposit, comm.*) à terme; ~**ness,** (*fixity*) fixité, *f.*; ~**ly,** fixement.
fixing, *s.* (*act*) fixation, *f.*; (*photo.*) fixage, *m.*; ~**s,** (*U.S.A.*) installation, *f.*
fixture, (*house*) immeuble, *m.*; (*sport*) match, *m.*; *be a ~*, (*pers. settled*) être à demeure.
fizz, *v.n.* siffler.
fizzle, *v.n.* fuser; ~ *out*, faire* long feu.
flabbergast, (*slang*) épater.
flabb|y, (*lit. and fig.*) flasque; ~**iness,** mollesse, *f.*
flaccid, flasque; ~**ity,** flaccidité, *f.*
flag, *s.* (*mil.*) drapeau, *m.*; (*nav.*) pavillon, *m.*; (*stone*) dalle, *f.*; (*bot.*) glaïeul, *m.*; *white ~, ~ of truce*, drapeau blanc, *m.*
flag, *v.a.* (*stones*) daller; (*deck with flags*) pavoiser; *v.n.* (*pers., conversation, plant, &c.*) languir; (*slacken*) se relâcher.
flagella|te, flageller; ~**tion,** flagellation, *f.*
flageolet, flageolet, *m.*
flagging, *s.* (*stones*) dallage, *m.*
flagging, *adj.* (*languid*) languissant.
flagitious, infâme.
flagon, flacon, *m.*
flagran|ce, énormité, *f.*; ~**t,** flagrant.
flagship, vaisseau amiral, *m.*
flagstaff, †hampe, *f.*
flagstone, *see* FLAG.
flail, fléau, *m.*
flake, *s.* (*snow, wool*) flocon, *m.*; (*fire*) flammèche, *f.*; (*metals*) écaille, *f.*; *v.n.* (*sprinkle like snow*) tomber en flocons; (*metals*) s'écailler.
flaky, floconneu|x, ~se.
flamboyant, (*gen. and arch.*) flamboyant.
flame, *s.* (*lit. and fig.*) flamme, *f.*; (*fam. pers.*) passion, *f.*; ~**-coloured,** ponceau, *invar.*; *burst into ~s*, prendre* feu.
flame, *v.n.* (*lit. and fig.*) flamboyer.
flamingo, (*ornith.*) flamant, *m.*
flange, *s.* rebord, *m.*; *~d tyre*, pneu à talon, *m.*
flank, *s.* (*gen. and mil.*) flanc, *m.*; *adj.* de flanc; *v.a.* flanquer; (*mil.*) prendre* en flanc.
flannel, flanelle, *f.*; ⚠ flanelle *only* = '*material*' *or* '*underclothing*'; ~**s,** (*sport*) = complet *or* pantalon de tennis, de cricket, etc., *m.*
flap, *s.* (*blow*) tape, *f.*; (*wing*) coup, *m.*; (*coats*) pan, *m.*; (*pockets*) patte, *f.*; (*table*) battant, *m.*; (*hat*) bord, *m.*; (*fly*) émouchoir, *m.*
flap, *v.a.n.* battre; (*wings*) battre des ailes.
flapper, (*girl*) fillette, *f.*
flare, flare up, *s.* flambée, *f.*
flare, *v.n.* flamboyer; (*lamp*) filer; ~ *up*, (*anger*) s'emporter.
flaring, *adj.* éblouissant; (*colour*) voyant.
flash, *s.* (*lit. and fig.*) éclair, *m.*; (*gun*) feu, *m.*; ~ *of lightning*, éclair; ~ *of wit*, saillie, *f.*; ~**-light,** feu à éclats, *m.*; ~ *in the pan*, feu de paille, *m.*; *in a ~*, en un clin d'œil.

flash, *v.a.* faire* briller; *v.n.* étinceler; ~ *upon,* (*fig.*) venir* (être) tout à coup à.
flashy, (*shallow*) superficiel, -le; (*gaudy*) voyant.
flask, (*travelling*) gourde, *f.*; (*powder*) poire à poudre, *f.*; ⚠ flasque *is not a 'flask' for 'spirits', &c., but the 'cheek' of a gun.*
flat, *s.* (*flat part*) plat, *m.*; (*flat ground*) terrain plat, *m.*; (*suite of rooms*) appartement, *m.*; (*mus.*) bémol, *m.*
flat, *adj.* (*on the ground*) étendu; (*level, smooth*) plat; (*flattened*) aplati; (*insipid*) insipide; (*positive*) formel, -le; (*tint*) plat; (*sound*) faux; (*liquor*) éventé; ~ **rate,** (*comm.*) tarif-uniforme, *m.*; ~**-iron,** fer à repasser, *m.*; ~ *as a pancake,* plat comme une galette; ~**ness,** (*evenness*) égalité, *f.*; (*dullness*) platitude, *f.*
flat, flatly, *adv.* à plat; (*categorically*) nettement; (*dully*) platement; *lie* ~, être étendu à plat ventre; ~**-bottomed,** à fond plat; ~**-footed,** qui a les pieds plats; ~**-nosed,** camus.
flatten, *v.a.* aplatir; (*depress*) abattre; (*deaden, render insipid*) affadir; *v.n.* s'aplatir; ~**ed,** *adj.* aplati.
flatter, *v.a.* (*lit. and fig.*) flatter; ~ *with,* (*delude*) bercer de.
flatterer, flatteu|r, ~se, *m.f.*
flattering, *adj.* flatteu|r, ~se.
flattery, flatterie, *f.*
flatulen|ce, flatulence, *f.*; ~**t,** flatulent.
flat|ways, ~**wise,** à plat.
flaunt, *s.* étalage, *m.*
flaunt, *v.a.* faire flotter; ~ *oneself,* se pavaner.
flaunting, *adj.* (*proud*) fi|er, ~ère; ~**ly,** avec ostentation.
flautist, flutiste, *m.*
flavorous, savoureu|x, ~se.
flavour, *s.* (*meats, &c.*) goût, *m.*; (*taste*) saveur, *f.*; (*tea, coffee, &c.*) arome, *m.*; (*wines*) bouquet, *m.*
flavour, *v.a.* (*season*) assaisonner; ~**ing,** assaisonnement, *m.*
flavourless, sans saveur.
flaw, *s.* (*crack*) fente, *f.*; (*metal, gem*) paille, *f.*; (*defect*) défaut, *m.*; (*squall*) risée, *f.*; *v.a.* fêlei; *v.n.* se fêler.
flawless, sans défaut.
flax, lin, *m.*
flaxen, de lin; (*hair*) filasse.
flay, écorcher; ~ *alive,* écorcher vif.
flea, puce, *f.*; ~**-bite,** (*fig.*) petit mal, *m.*; ~**-wort,** (*bot.*) pulicaire, *f.*
fleck, *s.* petite tache, *f.*
fleck, flecker, *v.a.* tacheter de.
fledge, *v.a.* garnir de plumes; *fully* ~*d,* emplumé.
flee, *v.a.* fuir*; (*avoid*) éviter; *v.n.* fuir*; (*run away*) se sauver.
fleece, toison, *f.*; *Golden Fleece,* Toison d'Or, *f.*
fleece, *v.a.* (*fig.*) plumer; (*money*) dépouiller (de).
fleecy, (*like fleece*) floconneu|x, ~se.
fleer, *v.n.* se moquer.
fleet, flotte, *f.*
fleet, *adj.* rapide; (*animals, &c.*) vite; ~ *of foot,* au pas léger; ~**ness,** rapidité, *f.*; ~**ly,** rapidement; (*running*) légèrement.
fleeting, fugiti|f, ~ve.
Flem|ing, *s.* Flamand, -e, *m.f.*; ~**ish,** flamand; (*lang.*) flamand, *m.*
flesh, (*lit., fig., eccles.*) chair, *f.*; (*meat*) viande, *f.*; (*stoutness*) embonpoint, *m.*; ~**-coloured,** couleur chair, *invar.*; *in the* ~, en chair et en os; *make one's* ~ *creep,* donner la chair de poule à; *lose* ~, maigrir; *put on* ~, prendre* de l'embonpoint; ~*-wound,* blessure* superficielle, *f.*
flesh, *v.a.* (*hunt.*) mettre en curée.
fleshiness, embonpoint, *m.*
fleshings, (*theatr.*) maillot, *m.*
fleshless, décharné.
fleshl|y, (*carnal*) charnel; ~**iness,** sensualité, *f.*
fleshy, charnu.
flexib|le, (*lit. and fig.*) flexible; ~**ility,** flexibilité, *f.*
flexile, flexible.
flexion, flexion, *f.*
flexor, *adj. m. only* (*anat.*) fléchisseur.
flexuous, flexueu|x, ~se.
flexure, (*bend and math.*) courbure, *f.*
flick, *s.* (*finger*) chiquenaude, *f.*; (*whip*) petit coup de fouet, *m.*; *v.a.* ~ *off, away,* chasser d'un petit coup.
flicker, *s.* lueur vacillante, *f.*; *v.n.* (*light and fig.*) vaciller.
flickering, *adj.* vacillant; ~**ly,** en vacillant.
flight, *s.* (*lit. and time*) fuite, *f.*; (*birds, aeron.*) vol, *m.*; (*flock of birds*) volée, *f.*; (*fancy, &c.*) essor, *m.*; (*stairs, arrows*) volée, *f.*; (*steps*) perron, *m.*; ~**-lieutenant,** lieutenant-aviateur, *m.*; *take* ~, prendre* la fuite; *put to* ~, mettre* en fuite; ~ *of the imagination,* écart de l'imagination, *m.*
flight|y, (*fickle*) volage; (*giddy*) étourdi; ~**iness,** légèreté, *f.*
flims|y, (*thin*) ténu; (*frail*) fragile; (*fig.*) frivole; ~**iness,** fragilité, *f.*; (*fig.*) légèreté, *f.*
flinch, broncher; (*recoil*) reculer (devant).
fling, *s.* (*throw*) jet, *m.*; *have one's* ~, jeter sa gourme.
fling, *v.a.* jeter; (*horse*) désarçonner; ~ *away,* ~ *down,* jeter; ~ *off,* (*avoid*) dérouter; ~ *open,* ouvrir* brusquement; ~ *out,* (*arms*) étendre; ~ *up,* abandonner; ~ *in the teeth* (*of*), jeter à la face (de).
flint, *s.* (*stone*) caillou, *m.*; (*geol.*) silex, *m.*; (*to strike light*) pierre à briquet, *f.*; ~**-gun,** fusil à pierre, *f.*; *hard as a* ~, dur comme pierre; *skin a* ~, tondre sur un œuf; ~**iness,** (*fig.*) dureté, *f.*
flinty, caillouteu|x, ~se; (*geol.*) silliceu|x, ~se; (*fig.*) dur.
flip, *s.* chiquenaude, *f.*; (*drink*) flip, *m.*; *v.a.* donner une chiquenaude à.

flippan|cy, légèreté, *f.*; **~t,** (*inconsiderate*) lég|er, ~ère; (*pert*) dégagé; **~cy,** ton dégagé, *m.*; **~tly,** d'un ton dégagé.
flirt, *s.* coquette, *f.*; *v.n.* flirter; **~ation,** flirt, *m.*
flit, *v.n.* (*house-move*) déménager; ~ *about, by,* voltiger.
flitch, (*bacon*) flèche, *f.*
flitter, *v.n.* voltiger; **~-mouse,** chauve-souris, *f.*
float, *s.* (*wood*) radeau, *m.*; (*fishing*) flotte, *f.*; **~s,** (*aeron.*) flotteurs, *m.pl.*
float, *v.a.* faire* flotter; (*comm.*) lancer; (*of water*) porter; (*timber*) flotter; *v.n.* (*lit. and fig.*) flotter.
floatable, flottable.
floatation, (*comm.*) lancement, *m.*
floating, flottement, *m.*; (*timber*) flottage, *m.*
floating, *adj.* (*lit., comm., dock, debt, fig.*) flottant.
flock, (*an.*) troupeau, *m.*; (*birds*) troupe, *f.*; (*wool*) flocon, *m.*; (*crowd*) foule, *f.*; (*stuffing*) bourre, *f.*; (*theol.*) ouailles, *f. pl.*; ~ *bed,* lit de bourre, *m.*
flock, *v.n.* accourir*.
floe, (*ice*) glaçon, *m.*
flog, *v.a.* fouetter.
flogging, fouet, *m.*
flood, *s.* (*tide*) flux, *m.*; (*tears, abuse, rain*) torrent, *m.*; (*inundation*) inondation, *f.*; (*crowd, light, words*) flot, *m.*; **~-gate,** vanne, *f.*; (*fig.*) écluse, *f.*; **~-light,** *v.a.* illuminer à projecteur; **~-lighting,** illumination à projecteur, *f.*
flood, *v.a.* (*lit. and fig.*) inonder; *be in ~,* (*river*) être débordé.
floor, plancher, *m.*; (*inlaid*) parquet, *m.*; (*storey*) étage, *m.*; (*threshing*) aire, *f.*; (*tile floor*) carrelage, *m.*; **~-cloth,** linoléum, *m.*; *on first, second ~,* au premier, au deuxième; *on the same ~,* au même étage; *on the ~,* à terre, par terre (*both of rest and motion, but* par terre *of motion implies accident*).
floor, *v.a.* planchéier; (*parquet floor*) parqueter; (*slang*) coller.
flooring, plancher, *m.*; (*inlaid*) parquet, *m.*
flop down, se laisser tomber lourdement.
flora, flore, *f.*; (*goddess*) Flore, *f.*
floral, floral.
Florentine, *adj.* (*when an adj. use small letter*) *and s.m.f.* Florentin, -e.
florescence, floraison, *f.*
floret, fleuron, *m.*
floriculture, floriculture, *f.*
florid, (*arch., complexion, style*) fleuri; **~ity, ~ness,** (*ruddiness*) teint fleuri, *m.*; **~ly,** d'une manière fleurie.
florin, florin, *m.*
florist, fleuriste, *m.*
floss-silk, filoselle, *f.*
flotilla, flottille, *f.*
flotsam, ~ *and jetsam,* épave, *f.*
flounce, *s.* (*dress*) volant, *m.*; *v.n.* ~ *about,* se trémousser.
flounder, *s.* (*ichth.*) flet, *m.*; *v.n.* patauger.
flour, farine, *f.*; *v.a.* enfariner.
flourish, *s.* (*trumpet*) fanfare, *f.*; (*signature*) parafe, *f.*; (*fenc. stick*) moulinet, *m.*; (*rhet.*) fleurs, *f.pl.*; (*gesticulation*) grands gestes, *m.pl.*
flourish, *v.a.* (*display*) montrer avec ostentation; (*weapon*) brandir; (*to wave*) agiter.
flourish, *v.n.* (*grow vigorously, lit. and fig.*) fleurir (*fig. impf. ind.* florissais, *pres. part.* florissant); (*prosper*) prospérer.
flourishing, *adj.* florissant; **~ly,** d'une manière florissante.
floury, enfariné.
flout, (*mock*) railler; (*defy*) narguer.
flow, (*blood, tide, words*) flux, *m.*; (*river*) cours, *m.*; (*language*) abondance, *f.*; ~ *of spirits,* gaieté habituelle, *f.*
flow, *v.n.* couler; (*slip, glide away, lit. and fig.*) s'écouler; (*be loose*) flotter; ~ *from,* (*proceed from*) découler; ~ *in,* (*tide*) monter (être); ~ *over,* déborder.
flower, (*lit. and fig.*) fleur, *f.*; (*arch.*) fleuron, *m.*; ~ *s of speech,* fleurs de rhétorique; *in the ~ of his age,* à la fleur de l'âge; **~-bed,** plate-bande, *f.*; **~-girl,** bouquetière, *f.*; **~-pot,** pot à fleur, *m.*; **~-show,** exposition de fleurs, *f.*; **~-stand,** jardinière, *f.*
flower, *v.n.* (*lit. and fig.*) fleurir.
flowered, *adj.* à fleurs.
floweret, fleurette, *f.*
flowering, *s.* floraison, *f.*; *adj.* fleuri.
flowery, (*lit. and style*) fleuri; (*covered with flowers*) parsemé de fleurs.
flowing, (*lit. and style*) coulant; (*tide*) montant.
flown, gonflé (de); **high-~,** (*style, lang.*) boursouflé.
fluctua|te, (*vary*) varier; (*price*) osciller; **~tion,** fluctuation, *f.*
flue, *s.* (*smoke*) tuyau, *m.*; (*down*) duvet, *m.*; **'flue', 'flu',** (*abbrev. for 'influenza'*) grippe, *f.*
fluen|cy, (*facility of speech*) facilité, *f.*; **~t,** facile; **~tly,** couramment.
fluff, *s.* (*feathers*) duvet, *m.*; (*hair, &c.*) peluche, *f.*; **~y,** flou.
fluid, *s.* fluide, *m.*; *adj.* fluide; **~ity,** fluidité.
fluke, (*chance*) veine, *f.*; (*ichth.*) *see* FLOUNDER; (*lucky stroke*) raccroc, *m.*
flummery, (*nonsense*) blague, *f.*
flunkey, laquais, *m.*
fluor-spar, (*min.*) fluor, *m.*
fluorescen|ce, fluorescence, *f.*; **~t,** fluorescent.
flurry, *s.* agitation, *f.*; (*squall*) bourrasque, *f.*; *v.a.* (*agitate*) agiter; (*bewilder*) ahurir.
flush, *s.* (*plumbing*) chasse, *f.*; (*face, redness*) rougeur, *f.*; (*joy, &c.*) transport, *m.*; (*bloom, health*) fraîcheur, *f.*
flush, *v.a.* (*drain*) nettoyer avec une chasse d'eau; (*face*) faire* rougir;

(*elate*) exalter; (*flood meadow*) inonder; (*put up game*) lever; *v.n.* (*face*) rougir (de); (*spurt*) jaillir; **~ed,** (*face*) enluminé.
flush, *adj.* (*overflowing*) plein à déborder; (*money*) abondant; *be ~ of money,* être en fonds; *~ with,* au ras de.
fluster, *s.* agitation, *f.*; *v.a.* (*drink*) griser; (*flurry*) agiter.
flute, *s.* (*mus.*) flûte, *f.*; *~-like, fluty,* flûté; *v.n.* jouer de la flûte.
fluted, (*arch.*) cannelé.
fluting, *s.* (*arch.*) cannelure, *f.*; (*frilling*) tuyautage, *m.*
flutter, *v.a.* agiter; *v.n.* (*bird*) voltiger; (*heart*) palpiter; (*in wind*) flotter.
fluttering, flutter, *s.* (*bird*) voltigement, *m.*; (*heart*) palpitation, *f.*; (*fig.*) agitation, *f.*; *be in a flutter,* être en émoi.
fluvial, fluvial.
flux, (*discharge, words, tide, phys., math.*) flux, *m.*; *~ and re~,* (*lit. and fig.*) le flux et le reflux.
fluxion, écoulement, *m.*; (*med.*) fluxion, *f.*
fly, *s.* mouche, *f.*; (*veh.*) citadine, *f.*; **~-blow,** chiure de mouche, *f.*; **~-blown,** couvert de chiure; **~-catcher,** (*ornith.*) gobe-mouches, *m. invar.*; **~-leaf,** (*book*) feuille de garde, *f.*; **~-trap,** attrape-mouches, *m. invar.*; **~-wheel,** volant, *m.*
fly, *v.a.* (*falcon, kite*) faire* voler; (*flag*) arborer; (*nav. flag*) battre; (*flee from*) quitter précipitamment; (*shun*) fuir*.
fly, *v.n.* (*move through air*) voler; (*flag, hair, &c.*) flotter; (*pass away*) fuir*; (*flee*) s'enfuir*; *~ at high altitude,* (*aeron.*) plafonner; *~ into pieces,* voler en éclats; *~ into a passion,* s'emporter; *~ away,* s'envoler; *~ back,* revoler; *~ off,* s'envoler; *~ open,* s'ouvrir* tout à coup; *~ to,* (*arms, pers.*) courir* à; *send ~ing,* envoyer rouler à terre.
flying, *s.* (*birds, aeron.*) vol, *m.*
flying, *adj.* (*lit. and mil.*) volant; **~-boat,** hydravion à coque, *m.*; **~ buttress,** (*arch.*) *see* BUTTRESS; **~ officer,** lieutenant-aviateur, *m.*; *take a ~ jump,* prendre* son élan et sauter; *pay a ~ visit,* ne faire* qu'une apparition.
foal, *s.* poulain, *m.*, pouliche, *f.*; (*ass*) ânon, *m.*; *v.n.* (*mare*) pouliner.
foam, *s.* écume, *f.*; (*beer, &c.*) mousse, *f.*; *v.n.* écumer, mousser; (*sea*) moutonner; **~ing, ~y,** *adj.* écumeu|x, ~se; *~ing at the mouth,* (*fig.*) écumant.
fob, *s.* gousset, *m.*
focal, focal; **~ize,** mettre au point.
fo'c's'le, *see* FORECASTLE.
focus, *s.* foyer, *m.*; *in, out of ~,* au point, pas au point; *v.a.* mettre* au point.
focusing, *s.* mise au point, *f.*
fodder, fourrage, *m.*
foe, foeman, ennemi, *m.*
fog, *s.* brouillard, *m.*; **~-horn,** sirène, *f.*; **~gy,** (*lit. and fig.*) brumeu|x, ~se; *be ~gy,* faire* du brouillard.
fogy, ~ey, ganache, *f.*
foible, faible, *m.*; (*partiality*) faiblesse, *f.*
foil, *s.* (*gold, tin, mirror*) tain, *m.*; (*fencing*) fleuret, *m.*; (*set-off*) repoussoir, *m.*; *v.a.* déjouer; (*hunt.*) dépister.
foist on, passer à; (*attribute*) attribuer à.
fold, *n.* (*material*) pli, *m.*; (*sheep and eccles.*) bercail, *m.*; (*door*) battant, *m.*; (*ground*) repli, *m.*; **ten~,** dix fois; **hundred~,** cent fois.
fold, *v.a.* plier; (*wrap up, envelop*) envelopper; (*embrace*) serrer; (*arms*) croiser; *~ up,* replier; *v.n.* se replier; *~ing bed,* lit de sangle, *m.*; *~ing chair,* pliant, *m.*; *~ing door,* porte à deux battants, *f.*; *~ing screen,* paravent, *m.*
folder, (*envelope*) chemise, *f.*
foliage, feuillage, *m.*
foliate, *v.a.* battre en feuilles; (*mirror*) étamer; **~d,** (*bot.*) feuillé.
folio, *s.* folio, *m.*; *adj.* in-folio, *invar.*
folk, *s.* gens (*an adj. before* gens *is fem., an adj. after* gens *is masc., e.g.* des gens vertueux *and* les vieilles gens); (*race*) race, *f.*; *young ~,* jeunesse, *f.*; *adj.* populaire.
follow, *v.a.* (*lit., fig., argument, party, career*) suivre*; (*accompany*) accompagner; (*pursue*) poursuivre*; *~ up,* (*success, &c.*) exploiter; (*advantage*) poursuivre*; (*complete*) compléter.
follow, *v.n.* suivre*; (*consequence*) résulter (de); *as ~s,* comme suit; *it ~s that,* il s'ensuit que.
follower, suivant, *m.*; (*disciple*) disciple, *m.*; (*suitor*) *slang,* bon ami, *m.*
following, *adj.* suivant; *the ~, s.* ce qui suit.
folly, sottise, *f.*; *height of ~,* comble de la sottise, *m.*
foment, *v.a.* (*lit. and fig.*) fomenter; **~ation,** fomentation, *f.*
fond, *adj.* (*tender*) tendre; (*pej.*) faible; (*foolish*) irraisonné; *~ of,* (*taste for things*) amateur (de); **~ly,** tendrement; **~ness,** tendresse, *f.*; (*inclination, taste for*) goût, *m.* (pour).
fondle, caresser.
font, fonts, *m.pl.*; (*fig.*) source, *f.*
food, nourriture, *f.*; (*subject-matter*) matière, *f.*; (*ans.*) pâture, *f.*; **~stuff,** matière d'alimentation, *f.*
fool, *s.* sot, *m.*; (*court jester*) bouffon, *m.*; **~'s bauble,** marotte, *f.*; **~'s cap,** bonnet d'âne, *m.*; (*paper*) papier ministre, *m.*; *play the ~,* faire* des bêtises; *that ~ the gardener,* cet imbécile de jardinier; *make a ~ of oneself,* se rendre ridicule.
fool, *v.a.* berner; *~ away,* gaspiller.
fool about, faire* le fou.
foolery, sottise.
foolhard|y, (*pers.*) casse-cou, *invar.*; (*action*) téméraire; **~iness,** témérité folle, *f.*
foolish, sot, -te; (*ridiculous*) ridicule; *look ~,* demeurer tout sot; *penny wise and pound ~,* qui fait des économies de

bouts de chandelle; **~ness**, sottise, *f.*; **~ly**, sottement.

foolscap, (*paper*). *See above under* FOOL.

foot, *s.* (*lit., measure, verse, fig.*) pied, *m.*; (*bird, small animal*) patte, *f.*; (*page*) bas, *m.*; (*mil.*) infanterie, *f.*; *on* ~, à pied; **~-bridge**, passerelle, *f.*; **~-brake**, (*motor, &c.*) frein à pied, *m.*; **~-muff**, chancelière, *f.*; **~-passenger**, piéton, *m.*; **~-path**, sentier, *m.*; **~-plate**, (*engine*) plate-forme, *f.*; **~-race**, course à pied, *f.*; **~-rule**, règle d'un pied, *f.*; **~-soldier**, fantassin, *m.*; **~-warmer**, chaufferette, *f.*; (*hot water*) bouillotte, *f.*; *see also compounds below*; *one ~ in the grave*, un pied dans la tombe; *fall on one's feet*, retomber sur ses pieds; *be carried off one's feet*, (*fig.*) s'emballer; *put one's ~ into it*, mettre* les pieds dans le plat; *set on* ~, mettre* en train; *from head to* ~, de la tête aux pieds; *20 ft. high*, †haut de 20 pieds; *8 ft. long, in length*, long, -ue de 8 pieds; **~ed**, *four-~ed*, quadrupède; *light-~ed*, leste; *be sure-~ed*, avoir le pied sûr; *be swift -~ed*, être léger à la course.

foot, *v.a.* ~ *it*, danser; ~ *up*, (*figures*) additionner.

football, (*game*) football, *m.*; (*ball*) ballon, *m.*

footboard, marchepied, *m.*

footboy, groom, *m.*; ⚠ *not 'groom' which* = valet d'écurie.

footgear, chaussure, *f.*

foothold, *s.* prise pour le pied, *f.*; *lose one's* ~, perdre pied.

footing, point d'appui, *m.*; (*fig.*) pied, *m.*; (*position*) position, *f.*; *on a ~ of*, (*equality, friendship, &c.*) sur un pied de; *on a war* ~, sur le pied de guerre; *gain, get a* ~, prendre* pied.

footlights, (*theatr.*) rampe, *f.*

footman, valet de pied, *m.*

footpace, *go at* ~, aller* (être) au pas.

footpad, voleur de grand chemin, *m.*

footprint, pas, *m.*

footsore, *adj.* les pieds meurtris.

footstep, pas, *m.*; (*print*) trace, *f.*; (*noise*) bruit de pas, *m.*; *tread in the ~s of*, (*lit. and fig.*) suivre* les traces de.

footstool, tabouret, *m.*

fop, petit-maître, *m.*; **~-pery**, affectation, *f.*; (*dress*) recherche, *f.*; **~pish**, fat, *m. only*; **~pishly**, en fat.

for, *prep.* pour; (*time and space*) pendant; (*in exchange for*) contre; (*because of*) à cause de; (*as*) comme; (*in spite of*) malgré; *member ~ Coventry*, député de Coventry; *~ this reason*, pour ce motif; *word ~ word*, mot à mot; *~ fear of*, de crainte de; *~ want of*; faute de; *but ~, were it not ~*, sans; *~ all I care*, quant à moi; *~ all that*, malgré tout; *not ~ the world*, pour rien au monde; *it is not ~ you to contradict*, ce n'est pas à vous de contredire.

for, *conj.* car.

forage, *s.* fourrage, *m.*; **~-cap**, bonnet de police, *m.*; **~-grass**, fléole, *f.*; *v.a.n.* fourrager; **~r**, fourrageur, *m.*

foray, incursion, *f.*

forbear, *v.a.* (*abstain from*) s'abstenir* de; (*avoid*) éviter.

forbear, *v.n.* être patient.

forbears, ancêtres, *m.pl.*

forbear|ance, (*refraining*) abstention (de), *f.*; (*patience*) patience, *f.*; **~ing**, patient.

forbid, *v.a.* défendre (*dat. of pers.* + de *and inf.*); (*thing*) interdire*; (*prevent*) empêcher (de); (*access*) interdire* l'entrée de; *God forbid!* à Dieu ne plaise! (que + *subj.*); **~den**, défendu.

forbidding, *adj.* rébarbati|f, ~ve; **~ly**, d'un air rébarbatif.

force, *s.* (*lit., fig., phys.*) force, *f.*; (*violence*) violence, *f.*; **~s**, (*mil.*) forces, *f. pl.*; *land ~s*, armée de terre, *f.*; **~-pump**, pompe foulante, *f.*; *put, bring into* ~, mettre* en vigueur; *come into* ~, entrer (être) en vigueur.

force, *v.a.* forcer (à *or* de); (*sense, laugh, fruit, flowers, lock*), forcer; ~ *back*, faire* reculer; ~ *in*, (*door, &c.*) enfoncer; ~ *open*, forcer; ~ *on, upon*, imposer à; ~ *up*, (*prices*) surhausser; **~d**, forcé; **~dly**, (*necessarily*) forcément.

forceful, vigoureu|x, ~se.

forcemeat, farce, *f.*

forcibl|e, (*done by force*) forcé; (*energetic*) vigoureu|x, ~se; **~y**, de force.

ford, gué, *m.*; *v.a.* passer à gué; **~able**, guéable.

fore, *s.* avant, *m.*

fore, *adj.* de devant; (*naut.*) d'avant; *adv.* ~ *and aft*, (*naut.*) de l'avant à l'arrière.

forearm, *s.* avant-bras, *m.*

forearm, *v.a. be forewarned is to be ~ed*, un homme averti en vaut deux.

forebod|e, *v.a.* présager; **~ing**, *s.* présage, *m.*

forecast, *s.* prévision, *f.*; (*weather*) prévisions (météorologiques), *f.pl.*

forecast, *v.a.* prévoir*.

forecastle, gaillard d'avant, *m.*

foreclose, *v.a.* empêcher; (*law*) forclore* (*pres. inf. and p.p. only*).

foreclosure, (*law*) forclusion, *f.*

forecourt, avant-cour, *f.*

foredoom, prédestiner.

forefather, ancêtre, *m.*

forefinger, index, *m.*

forefoot, pied de devant, *m.*

forefront, (*foreground*) premier plan, *m.*

forego, précéder; **~er**, prédécesseur, *m.*

foregoing, *adj.* précédent.

foreground, premier plan, *m.*

forehead, front, *m.*; (*horse*) chanfrein, *m.*

foreign, étrang|er, ~ère; ~ *to*, étranger à; *~-going ship*, long-courrier, *m.*; *Foreign Office*, Ministère des Affaires Étrangères, *m.*; *in ~ parts*, à l'étranger.

foreigner, étrang|er, **~ère**, *m.f.*

forejudge, préjuger.

foreknow, savoir* d'avance; **~ledge,** prescience, *f.*
foreland, point de terre, *f.*
forelock, (*hair*) toupet, *m.*; *take time by the ~,* saisir l'occasion aux cheveux.
foreman, (*jury*) président, *m.*; (*factories, &c.*) contremaître, *m.*
foremast, misaine, *f.*
foremost, *adj.* le, la premi|er, ~ère; *adv.* (*in the forefront*) au premier rang; *first and ~,* tout d'abord; *head ~,* la tête la première.
forenoon, *s.* matinée, *f.*
forensic, du barreau; (*medicine*) légal.
forepart, devant, *m.*; (*ship*) avant, *m.*
foreordain, prédestiner.
forerunner, avant-coureur, *m.*
foresail, *s.* (*naut.*) voile de misaine, *f.*
foresee, prévoir*; **~ing,** *adj.* prévoyant.
foreshadow, figurer à l'avance.
foreshore, plage, *f.*
foreshorten, (*perspective*) raccourcir.
foresight, prévoyance, *f.*
foreskin, prépuce, *m.*
forest, (*lit. and fig.*) forêt, *f.*; (*of old trees*) futaie, *f.*
forestall, (*encroach on*) anticiper sur.
forest|er, garde-forestier, *m.*; **~ry,** sylviculture, *f.*
foretaste, *s.* avant-goût, *m.*; *v.a.* goûter par avance.
foretell, prédire*; (*presage*) présager.
forethought, préméditation, *f.*; (*provident care*) prévoyance, *f.*
foretop, *s.* (*naut.*) †hune de misaine, *f.*
forewarn, prévenir*; **~ing,** avertissement, *m.*
forewoman, (*workroom*) première, *f.*
forfeit, *s.* (*contract*) dédit, *m.*; (*right*) confiscation, *f.*; (*fine*) amende, *f.*
forfeit, *v.a.* (*honour*) forfaire* à; (*right*) être déchu de; (*penalty*) être privé de.
forfeiture, (*of property*) confiscation, *f.*
forgather, s'assembler.
forge, *s.* (*smithy, ironworks*) forge, *f.*; *v.a.* (*iron, &c., invent*) forger; (*comm., signature, &c.*) contrefaire*; (*will*) supposer; *v.n.* faire* un faux; *~ (go) ahead,* aller* (être) à grand'erre.
forger, (*lit. and fig.*) forgeur, *m.*; ⚠ forgeur *almost = 'inventor' and is not necessarily pej.*; (*Lit., coin, signature*) faussaire, *m.*
forgery, (*crime*) faux, *m.*; (*signature, coin, &c.*) contrefaçon, *f.*
forg|et, oublier; *~ oneself,* s'oublier; *~ about,* oublier; *never to be ~otten,* inoubliable; *forgive and ~,* à tout péché miséricorde.
forget-me-not, (*bot.*) myosotis, *m.*
forgetful, oublieu|x, ~se; *be ~ of,* oublier; **~ness,** oubli, *m.*
forgettable, oubliable.
forgivable, pardonnable.
forgive, *v.a.* pardonner (*acc. of thing, dat. of person*); (*debt, &c.*) faire* grâce (à + *pers.*, de + *thing*); *see also* FORGET.
forgiveness, pardon, *m.*; (*debt*) remise, *f.*
forgiving, clément.
forgo, renoncer à.
fork, (*hay, in roads, &c.*) fourche, *f.*; (*table*) fourchette, *f.*; **tuning-~,** diapason, *m.*
fork, *v.a.* remuer à la fourche; *~ out,* (*slang*) allonger (sa monnaie, *&c.*); *v.n.* (*road*) bifurquer; *~ out,* (*slang*) casquer.
forked, fourchu; *~ lightning,* éclair ramifié, *m.*
forlorn, (*destitute*) abandonné; (*hopeless*) désespéré; *~ hope,* dernier espoir, *m.*
form, *s.* (*shape*) forme, *f.*; (*bench*) banc, *m.*; (*class*) classe, *f.*; (*hare*) gîte, *m.*; (*with spaces to fill, telegram, &c.*) formule, *f.*; *good ~,* bon ton, *m.*; *for ~'s sake,* pour la forme; *~* **-master,** professeur, *m.*; *~ of government,* régime, *m.*
form, *v.a.*, (*lit., fig., mil., design*) former; (*in mind, heart*) concevoir; *~ fours!* (*mil*). rangez-vous par quatre.
formal, (*precise, explicit*) formel, -le; (*ceremonious, of things*) de cérémonie; (*pers.*) cérémonieux, ~se; (*stiff*) raide; **~ly,** en bonne et due forme; (*ceremoniously*) cérémonieusement.
formalis|m, formalisme, *m.*; **~t,** formaliste, *m.*
formality, formalité, *f.*; (*ceremony*) cérémonie, *f.*
formation, formation, *f.*
formative, formati|f, ~ve.
former, *pron.* le premier, la première; (*of two*) celui-là, celle-là; *adj.* (*of two*) premi|er, ~ère; (*past*) d'autrefois; (*previous, preceding*) précédent; **~ly,** autrefois.
formidabl|e, formidable; **~eness,** caractère formidable, *m.*; **~y,** d'une manière formidable.
formless, informe.
formula, formule, *f.*
formulary, formulaire, *m.*
fornica|te, forniquer; **~tion,** fornication, *f.*
fornicat|or, ~ress, fornicat|eur, ~rice, *m.f.*
forrader, *adv.* (*fam.*) *get ~,* aller* (être) plus en avant.
forsake, (*give up*) renoncer à; (*desert*) délaisser; **god-~n,** misérable.
forsooth, ma foi!
forspent, †harassé.
forswear, abjurer; *~ oneself,* se parjurer.
forsworn, *adj.* parjure.
fort, fort, *m.*
fortalice, (*small fort*) fortin, *m.*
forte, (*strong point*) fort, *m.*
forth, *adv.* en avant; *and so ~,* et ainsi de suite; *from this time ~,* dorénavant.
forthcoming, à venir.
forthwith, *adv.* incontinent.
fortieth, *adj.* quarantième.
fortif|y, fortifier; **~ication,** fortification, *f.*
fortitude, courage, *m.*
fortnight, quinze jours, *m.pl.*; *to-morrow, to-day ~,* de demain en quinze, d'aujourd'hui en quinze.

fortnightly, *adj.* de tous les quinze jours; *adv.* tous les quinze jours.
fortress, forteresse, *f.*
fortuitous, fortuit; **~ness,** †hasard, *m.*; **~ly,** fortuitement.
fortunate, heureu|x, ~se; **~ly,** heureusement.
fortune, fortune, *f.*; (*fate*) sort, *m.*; *good ~*, bonheur, *m.*; *~s of war*, fortune des armes; *make a ~*, faire* fortune; *seek one's ~*, tenter fortune; *tell ~s*, dire* la bonne aventure; **~-hunter,** coureur de dot, *m.*; **~-teller,** dis|eur, ~euse de bonne aventure, *m.f.*
forty, quarante; (*about 40*) quarantaine, *f.*
forum, forum, *m.*
forward, *adj.* (*work, study, mil., opinions, growth*) avancé; (*premature and fruit*) précoce; (*bold*) présomptueu|x, ~se; (*eager to*) prompt à; *~ delivery*, livraison à terme, *f.*
forward, *v.a.* (*letter, &c.*) faire* suivre; (*goods*) expédier; (*undertaking*) seconder; *please ~*, (veuillez) faire suivre.
forward(s), *adv.* en avant; *from this time ~*, dorénavant.
forwarding, *s.* expédition, *f.*; *delay in ~*, retard dans l'acheminement, *m.*; *~ing agent*, agent-commissionnaire de transport, *m.*; *~ clerk*, expéditionnaire, *m.*
forwarder, (*comm.*) expéditeur, *m.*
forwardness, (*eagerness*) empressement, *m.*; (*boldness*) présomption, *f.*; (*work, &c.*) avancement, *m.*
fossil, *adj. and s.m.* fossile.
foster, *adj.* **~-brother, ~-sister,** frère, *m.*, sœur, *f.*, de lait; **~-father,** père nourricier, *m.*; **~-mother,** mère nourrice, *f.*
foster, *v.a.* (*lit. and fig.*) nourrir; (*encourage*) encourager.
foul, *s.* collision, *f.*; (*ship*) abordage, *m.*
foul, *adj.* 1 (*dirty*) sale; 2 (*water*) trouble; 3 (*impure, lit. and fig.*) impure; 4 (*weather*) sale; 5 (*wind*) contraire; 6 (*language*) orduri|er, ~ère; 7 (*shameful*) †honteu|x, ~se; 8 (*breath*) infect; *~-mouthed*, mal embouché; *~ play*, (*lit. and fig.*) tricherie, *f.*; **~ness,** (*dirtiness*) saleté, *f.*; (*wickedness*) noirceur, *f.*; (*air, water*) impureté, *f.*; (*language*) obscénité, *f.*; **~ly,** odieusement; *fall ~ of*, (*quarrel*) se brouiller avec.
foul, *v.a.* (*dirty, soil*) souiller; (*fig.*) salir; (*ship*) aborder; (*anchor*) engager; *v.n.* se salir.
found, (*lay, base, build, lit. and fig., argument*) fonder; *ill* **~ed,** (*statement, &c.*) mal appuyé.
found, (*cast*) fondre.
foundation, (*building, institution, founding*) fondation, *f.*; (*reason, ground*) fondement, *m.*; *without ~*, sans fondement; *lay ~s of*, (*lit. and fig.*) établir la fondation de.
founder, *s.* (*melter*) fondeur, *m.*; (*establisher*) fondat|eur, ~rice, *m.f.*
founder, *v.n.* (*naut.*) sombrer.
foundered, *adj.* (*horse*) fourbu.
foundling, enfant trouvé, *m.*
foundry, fonderie, *f.*
fount, (*fountain*) fontaine, *f.*; (*source, lit. and fig.*) source, *f.*; (*print.*) fonte, *f.*
fountain, fontaine, *f.*; **~-head,** source, *f.*; **~-pen,** stylographe, *m.* (*abbrev.* stylo).
four, *adj. and s.m.* quatre; (*hour*) quatre heures; *she is ~*, elle a quatre ans; *~-cornered, see* CORNER, *v.a.*; **~-oared,** à quatre avirons; **~-wheeled,** à quatre roues.
fourfold, quadruple.
fourscore, quatre-vingts (*without* s *when followed by another numeral*).
fourteen, quatorze; **~th,** quatorzième; (*date and sovereign*) quatorze.
fourth, quatrième; (*date and sovereign*) quatre; *three-~s*, *s.* trois-quarts, *m.pl.*; **~ly,** quatrièmement.
fowl, *s.* (*hen*) poule, *f.*; **~s,** volaille, *f.*
fowler, chasseur d'oiseaux, *m.*; (*using net*) oiseleur, *m.*
fowling-piece, fusil de chasse, *m.*
fox, renard, *m.*; **~-hole,** renardière, *f.*; **~-hunt, -hunting,** chasse au renard, *f.*
foxglove, (*bot.*) digitale, *f.*
foxhound, chien courant pour le renard, *m.*
foxtail, (*grass*) vulpin, *m.*
foxy, (*crafty*) rusé; (*colour*) roussâtre.
fraction, (*arith.*) fraction, *f.*; *vulgar ~*, fraction ordinaire, *f.*; **~al,** fractionnaire.
fractious, (*restive*) rétil|f, ~ve; (*peevish*) revêche.
fracture, *s.* (*gen. and med.*) fracture, *f.*; *v.a.* fracturer.
fragil|e, (*perishable, brittle, frail*) fragile; (*weak*) faible; **~ity,** fragilité, *f.*
fragment, fragment, *m.*; **~ary,** fragmentaire.
fragran|ce, parfum, *m.*; **~t,** parfumé; ⚠ fragrant, *&c.*, *not French.*
frail, *adj.* (*brittle, breakable*) fragile; (*health*) frêle; **~ty,** faiblesse, *f.*
frame, *s.* 1 (*picture*) cadre, *m.*; 2 (*carp. and any structure*) charpente, *f.*; 3 (*the body*) corps, *m.*; 4 (*system of universe, &c.*) système, *m.*; 5 (*mind*) disposition, *f.*; 6 (*window*) châssis, *m.*; 7 (*door*) chambranle, *m.*; 8 (*needlework*) métier, *m.*; 9 (*naut., rib*) couple, *f.*; 10 (*timbers*) membrure, *f.*; **~ aerial,** (*wireless*) antenne en cadre, *f.*; **~work,** (*lit. and fig.*) charpente, *f.*; (*glass, motor, house*) châssis, *m.*
frame, *v.a.* (*form*) former; (*conceive*) concevoir; (*picture and fig.*) encadrer; (*regulate*) régler (sur); (*plot*) tramer; (*answer*) formuler.
framer, (*author*) auteur, *m.*; (*picture*) encadreur, *m.*
framing, (*construction*) construction, *f.*; (*invention*) conception, *f.*; (*picture and surroundings*) encadrement, *m.*
franchise, *s.* (*exemption, and of a city*) franchise, *f.*; ⚠ *not of voting which* = droit de vote, *m.*

Franciscan, *adj. and s.m.* franciscain.
frangipane, frangipane, *f.*
Frank, *s.* Franc, Franque, *m.f.*; **~ish,** *adj.* franc, *f.* franque.
frank, *adj.* fran|c, ~che; **~ness,** franchise, *f.*; **~ly,** franchement.
frank, *v.a.* (*letter*) envoyer* franc de port; (*pers.*) faciliter l'entrée de.
frankincense, encens, *m.*
frantic, frénétique; ~ *with,* fou, folle de; **~ally,** avec frénésie.
fratern|al, fraternel, -le; **~ity,** fraternité, *f.*; *v.n.* **~ize,** fraterniser.
fratricide, fratricidal, *adj. and s.m.* fratricide.
fraud, fraude, *f.*; (*pers.*) trompeur, *m.*; ⚠ fraude *cannot be used of persons*; *what a ~!* c'est une bouffonnerie!
fraudulent, frauduleu|x, ~se; ~ *conversion,* (*money*) détournement, *m.*; **~ly,** frauduleusement.
fraught with, plein de.
fray, *s.* querelle, *f.*
fray, *v.a.* (*stuff*) érailler; (*cuff*) effranger; *v.n.* s'érailler.
freak, (*caprice*) caprice, *f.*; (*prank*) équipée, *f.*; **~ish,** capricieu|x, ~se; **~ishness,** caprice, *m.*; **~ishly,** capricieusement.
freckle, tache de rousseur, *f.*; **~d,** couvert de taches de rousseur.
free, *adj.* (*lit., polit., at leisure, risky* (*of speech*), *style, and translation*) libre; (*comm.*) franco; (*without paying*) gratuit; ~ *of, from,* (*exempt*) exempt de; (*comm., duty, charges*) franco de; *post ~,* franco; *tax ~,* exempt d'impôt; ~ *with,* (*lavish*) prodigue de; (*generous*) libéral de; **~-handed,** généreu|x, ~se; **~ kick,** (*football*) coup franc, *m.*; **~mason,** *see* MASON; **~ pass,** billet de faveur, *m.*; (*rail.*) permis, *m.*; **~ port,** port franc, *m.*; **~-thinker,** libre penseur, *m.*; **~ trade,** libre-échange, *m.*; **~ trader,** libre-échangiste, *m.*; **~ will,** libre arbitre, *m.*; *set ~,* libérer; (*slave, &c.*) affranchir; *you are quite ~ to,* libre à vous de; *make ~ to,* prendre* la liberté de.
free, *v.a.* libérer (de); (*slave, nation*) affranchir; (*disengage*) débarrasser (de); (*exempt*) exempter (de).
freebooter, pirate, *m.*
freedman, affranchi, *m.*
freedom, liberté, *f.*; (*openness, boldness*) franchise, *f.*; (*manners*) familiarité, *f.*; (*style*) aisance, *f.*; (*of a city*) droit de bourgeoisie, *m.*
freehold, propriété foncière, *f.*; **~er,** propriétaire foncier, *m.*
freely, free, *adv.* librement; (*without charge*) gratis; (*frankly*) franchement; (*willingly*) volontiers; (*generously*) généreusement; (*abundantly*) copieusement.
freeman, (*city*) bourgeois, *m.*
freestone, pierre de taille, *f.*
freeze, *v.a.* geler; (*chill pers.*) glacer; (*meat, &c.*) congeler; *v.n.* geler; (*fig.*) se glacer.
freezing, *s.* congélation, *f.*; *adj.* glacial; **~-point,** point de congélation, *m.*; **~ly,** (*fig.*) d'un ton, air glacial.
freight, *s.* (*price and cargo*) fret, *m.*; **~ing,** affrètement, *m.*; *v.a.* affréter.
French, *s.* (*lang.*) français, *m.*
French, *adj.* français; (*ambassadors, envoys, &c.*) de France; **~ beans,** †haricots verts, *m.pl.*; **~man, ~woman,** Français, -e, *m.f.*; **~ polish,** vernis, *m.*; **~ window,** porte-fenêtre, *f.*; *take ~ leave,* filer à l'anglaise.
frenz|y, frénésie, *f.*; **~ied,** frénétique.
frequen|cy, fréquence, *f.*; *high, low ~,* (*electr.*) †haute, basse fréquence; **~t,** (*often occurring*) fréquent; (*numerous*) nombreu|x, ~se.
frequent, *v.a.* fréquenter; **~er,** habitué, *m.*
frequenta|tive, fréquentati|f, ~ve; **~tion,** fréquentation, *f.*
fresco, fresque, *f.*; *paint in ~,* peindre* à fresque.
fresh, *s.* (*morning, &c.*) première fraîcheur, *f.*
fresh, *adj.* (*fig., cool, eggs, butter, fish, flowers, air, wind, complexion, troops, &c.*) frais, fraîche; (*recent*) nouveau, nouvel, -le *before noun*; **~ water,** eau douce, *f.*; *see also* FISH; **~ness,** fraîcheur, *f.*; (*newness*) nouveauté, *f.*
fresh, freshly, *adv.* fraîchement; (*recently*) récemment.
freshen, *v.a.* rafraîchir.
freshet, courant d'eau douce, *m.*; (*flood*) avalaison, *f.*
freshman, (*univ.*) étudiant de première année, *m.*
fret, *s.* inquiétude, *f.*; (*arch. and pattern*) frette, *f.*; **~ -saw,** scie à découper, *f.*
fret, *v.a.* (*worry*) irriter; (*gnaw*) ronger; (*gall*) écorcher; *v.n.* (*fume*) ronger son frein; (*whimper*) pleurnicher; (*worry oneself*) se tracasser.
fretful, chagrin; (*worried*) tourmenté; **~ness,** mauvaise humeur, *f.*; **~ly,** de mauvaise humeur.
fretwork, découpage, *m.*
friab|le, friable; **~ility,** friabilité, *f.*
friar, moine, *m.*; **grey ~,** franciscain, *m.*; **~y,** monastère, *m.*
fribble, *s.* personne frivole, *f.*; *v.n.* perdre son temps à des riens.
fricassee, *s.* fricassée, *f.*; *v.a.* fricasser.
friction, (*lit. and fig., med.*) friction, *f.*
Friday, vendredi, *m.*; **Good Friday,** vendredi saint.
fried, frit; *see also* FISH; **~ potatoes,** frites, *f.pl.*
friend, ami, -e, *m.f.*; **~s,** (*relations*) parents, *m.pl.*; **~less,** sans ami.
friendl|iness, disposition amicale, *f.*; **~y,** (*pers.*) aimable; (*fig.*) ami; (*things*) amical; *~y to,* (*in favour of*) favorable à; *~y disposed,* ami; *~y office,* de bons offices, *m.pl.*; *~y Power,* puissance amie, *f.*; **~y society,** société de secours mutuels, *f.*
friendship, amitié, *f.*

frieze, (*cloth and arch.*) frise, *f.*
frigate, (*naut.*) frégate, *f.*; **~-bird,** frégate, *f.*
fright, frayeur, *f.*; (*pers.*) horreur, *f.*; *take ~,* s'effrayer; *be in a mortal ~,* avoir des transes mortelles.
frighten, effrayer.
frightful, (*dreadful*) affreu|x, ~se; (*frightening*) effrayant; **~ness,** horreur, *f.*; (*terrorism*) terrorisme, *m.*; **~ly,** affreusement.
frigid, (*lit. and fig.*) glacial; **~ity, ~ness,** (*lit. and fig.*) froideur, *f.*; **~ly,** froidement.
frill, jabot, *m.*; (*frilling*) ruche, *f.*; *v.a.* tuyauter.
fringe, *s.* frange, *f.*; (*wood, field, &c.*) lisière, *f.*; *v.a.* franger.
frippery, friperie, *f.*; (*rubbish*) camelote, *f.*
frisk, *v.n.* (*gambol*) gambader.
frisk|y, folâtre; (*horse*) fringant; **~iness,** gaîté, *f.*
fritillary, (*bot.*) fritillaire, *f.*
fritter, *s.* beignet, *m.*; (*meat*) rissole, *f.*
fritter (frivol) away, gaspiller.
frivol|ous, frivole; **~ity,** frivolité, *f.*
frizzle, *v.a.* (*fry*) faire* frire; (*hair*) friser; *v.n.* (*sizzle*) grésiller.
fro, *adv. to and ~,* de long en large; *go to and ~,* aller* et venir* (*both* être); *pace to and ~,* faire* les cent pas.
frock, (*monk*) froc, *m.*; (*woman*) robe, *f.*; **~ -coat,** redingote, *f.*
frog, (*zool.*) grenouille, *f.*; (*horse*) fourchette, *f.*; (*mil.*) brandebourg, *m.*; **leap-~,** saute-mouton, *m.*
frolic, *s.* (*gambol*) ébats, *m.pl.*; (*prank*) fredaine, *f.*; *v.n.* folâtrer; ((*romp*) gambader.
frolicsome, (*gay*) gai; (*playful*) folâtre; **~ly,** gaiement.
from, (*time since*) depuis; (*on the part of*) de la part de; (*point of departure*) de; (*cause, reason, &c.*) à cause de; (*motive*) par; (*making distinction*) d'avec; (*change*) de; *~ a private he became a marshal,* de simple soldat, il devint maréchal; (*according to, painting, after of engraving, nature, &c.*) d'après; *~ above,* d'en †haut; *~ among,* d'entre; *~ behind,* de derrière; *~ below,* d'en bas; *~ outside,* de dehors; *~ under,* de dessous; *~ time to time,* de temps en temps; *~ the top of,* du †haut de; *taken ~,* (*author*) tiré de; ⚠ *with verbs of preventing, ceasing, abstaining, 'from' + gerund* = de + *inf. With verbs of depriving and taking away, 'from'* = à + *pers.*
frond, (*bot.*) fronde, *f.*
front, *s.* (*lit., fig., mil.*) front, *m.*; (*forepart, shirt*) devant, *m.*; (*building*) façade, *f.*; *in ~ of,* (*rest*) en face de; (*motion*) en avant de; *go in ~,* prendre* les devants.
front, *adj.* de devant; ~ **door,** porte de devant, *f.*; ~ **mudguard,** (*motor*), *see* MUDGUARD.
front, *v.a.* (*stand opposite*) faire* face à; (*open on to*) donner sur; *v.n. ~ towards, on,* faire* face à.
frontage, (*building*) façade, *f.*; (*situation*) exposition, *f.*
frontal, *s. altar ~,* devant d'autel, *m.*
frontal, *adj.* (*mil.*) de front.
frontier, frontière, *f.*
frontispiece, frontispice, *m.*
frontlet, bandeau, *m.*
frost, *s.* gelée, *f.*; (*slang*) four, *m.*; **~-bite,** gelure, *f.*; *hard ~,* forte gelée, *f.*; **hoar-~,** givre, *m.*; *white ~,* gelée blanche; (*on trees*) givre, *m.*
frost, *v.a.* (*cakes, &c.*) glacer.
frost|y, de gelée; (*fig.*) froid; **~iness,** (*lit. and fig.*) froid glacial, *m.*; **~ily,** (*fig.*) froidement.
froth, *s.* écume, *f.*; (*drinks*) mousse, *f.*; (*fig.*) balivernes, *f.pl.*; *v.n.* écumer.
frothy, écumeu|x, ~se; (*fig.*) vide.
froward, (*refractory*) contrariant; (*wicked*) pervers; **~ness,** obstination, *f.*
frown, *s.* froncement de sourcils, *m.*; (*fortune*) coups de la fortune, *m.pl.*; *v.n.* froncer les sourcils; *~ upon,* (*pers.*) regarder de travers; (*things*) être contraire à.
frowning, *adj.* renfrogné.
frowzy, sentant le renfermé; (*slatternly*) malpropre.
frozen, gelé.
fructiferous, fructifère.
fructif|y, fructifier; **~ication,** fructification, *f.*
frugal, (*pers. and food*) frugal; **~ity,** frugalité, *f.*; **~ly,** frugalement.
fruit, (*lit., fig.*) fruit, *m.* (*often in plural*); **first- ~s,** prémices, *f.pl.*; *stewed ~,* compote, *f.*; **~-garden,** jardin fruitier, *m.*; **~-loft,** fruitier, *m.*; **~-shop,** fruiterie, *f.*; **~-tree,** arbre fruitier, *m.*; **~-bearing,** *adj.* fruiti|er, ~ère.
fruiterer, fruiti|er, ~ère, *m.f.*
fruitful, (*lit. and fig.*) fructueu|x, ~se; (*fertile*) fécond; **~ness,** fécondité, *f.*; **~ly,** fructueusement.
fruition, (*enjoyment*) jouissance, *f.*; (*fulfilment, materialization*) réalisation, *f.*
fruitless, (*barren*) stérile; (*profitless*) infructueu|x, ~se; (*vain*) inutile; **~ly,** (*without profit*) infructueusement; (*uselessly*) en vain.
frumpish, mal fagoté.
frustra|te, (*baffle*) déjouer; (*hope*) décevoir; **~tion,** désappointement, *m.*
fry, *s.* (*small fish*) frai, *m.*; (*salmon*) alevin, *m.*; *small ~,* (*fig.*) menu fretin, *m.*
fry, *v.a.* faire* frire; *v.n.* frire*; **~ing-pan,** poêle à frire, *f.*; *fall from the ~ing-pan into the fire,* sauter de la poêle dans la braise.
frying, *s.* friture, *f.* (*also fried fish, food*).
fuchsia, fuchsia, *m.*
fuddle, *v.a.* griser; *v.n.* se griser; **~d,** gris.
fudge, *interj.* quelle blague!
fuel, combustible, *m.*; (*fig.*) aliment, *m.*

fugac|ious, fugace; **~ity,** fugacité, *f.*
fugitive, *adj. and s.m.* fugiti|f, **~ve.**
fugue, (*mus.*) fugue, *f.*
fulcrum, point d'appui, *m.*
fulfil, *v.a.* (*duty*) accomplir; (*desire*) combler; (*obligation*) remplir; (*expectation*) répondre à; (*hope*) réaliser.
fulfilment, accomplissement, *m.*; (*hope*) réalisation, *f.*
full, *s.* plein, *m.*; (*highest degree*) plus haut degré, *m.*; (*whole*) tout, *m.*; *in ~*, en entier; *state in ~*, dire* tout au long; *write in ~*, écrire* en toutes lettres.
full, *adj.* (*lit., fig., moon, voice, sails*) plein; (*address, bus, &c.*) compl|et, ~ète; (*abundant*) abondant; *~ of*, (*engrossed in*) plein de; (*benefits, honours, years*) comblé de; *~ galop*, grand galop, *m.*; *~ name*, les nom et prénoms; *~play*, libre carrière, *f.*; *~ stop*, point, *m.*; *~ share of*, bonne part de; *~ value*, valeur entière, *f.*; *in ~ daylight*, en plein jour; *at ~ speed*, à toute vitesse; *lying at ~ length*, étendu tout de son long; *~-length portrait*, *see* LENGTH.
full, fully, *adv.* pleinement; *full as good*, tout aussi bon; *fully secured*, (*creditor*) entièrement nanti; *~ paid*, (*shares*) intégralement libéré; (*with numbers, of time or distance*) au moins; **~ -blown,** épanoui; **~ -grown,** adulte.
fuller, foulon, *m.*; *~'s earth*, terre à foulon, *f.*
ful(l)ness, (*fig.*) plénitude, *f.*; (*repletion*) réplétion, *f.*; (*dress*) ampleur, *f.*
fulminate, *v.a.n.* (*lit. and fig.*) fulminer.
fulsome, (*servile*) servile; (*flattering*) flatteu|r, ~se; (*repulsive*) répugnant; **~ness,** servilité; (*flattery*) adulation, *f.*
fumble, *v.n.* tâtonner; *v.a.* faire* maladroitement.
fumbler, maladroit, *m.*
fume, *s.* fumée, *f.*; **~s,** fumées, *f.pl.*; (*anger*) colère, *f.*
fume, *v.a.* (*incense*) encenser; *v.n.* (*anger, pop.*) fumer.
fumiga|te, *v.a.* (*room*) désinfecter; **~tion,** fumigation, *f.*
fumitory, (*bot.*) fumeterre, *f.*
fun, (*diversion*) amusement, *m.*; (*joke*) plaisanterie, *f.*; *in, for ~*, pour rire; *for the ~ of the thing*, histoire de rire; *have great ~*, s'amuser bien; *make ~ of*, se moquer de.
funambulist, funambule, *m.*
function, fonction, *f.*; (*party*) réception, *f.*; **~al,** fonctionel, -le; *v.n.* fonctionner; **~ary,** fonctionnaire, *m.*
fund, (*lit. and fig.*) fonds, *m.*; **~s,** fonds, *m.pl.*; *sinking ~*, caisse d'amortissement, *f.*; *public ~s*, deniers publics, *m.pl.*; **~-holder,** renti|er, ~ère, *m.f.*
fund, *v.a.* (*debt*) fonder; *~ing loan*, emprunt de consolidation, *m.*; **~ ed property,** biens en rente, *m.pl.*
fundamental, principe fondamental, *m.*; *adj.* fondamental.
funeral, *s.* funérailles, *f.pl.*; *~ pile*, bûcher, *m.*; *~ procession*, convoi, *m.*; *~ oration*, oraison funèbre, *f.*; *~ wreath*, couronne mortuaire, *f.*; *adj.* funéraire.
funereal, *adj.* funéraire; (*gloomy*) lugubre.
fungus, (*bot.*) champignon, *m.*; (*med.*) fongus, *m.*
funicular, *adj.* funiculaire.
funk, *s.* (*pop. fear*) frousse, *f.*; (*pers.*) froussard, *m.*; *be in a ~ of*, avoir la frousse de; **~y,** froussard.
funnel, entonnoir, *m.*; (*steamer, steam-engine*) cheminée, *f.*
funny, (*comical*) drôle; (*curious*) étrange; **~-bone,** petit juif, *m.*
fur, fourrure, *f.*; (*coat of animal*) pelage, *m.*; **~red,** *adj.* (*lined with fur*) fourré; (*tongue*) empâté.
furbelow, falbala, *m.*
furbish, *v.a.* (*polish*) fourbir; (*do up clothes*) retaper.
furious, furieu|x, ~se.
furl, *v.a.* (*naut.*) ferler.
furlong, furlong, *m.*
furlough, permission, *f.*; *on ~*, en permission.
furnace, fourneau, *m.*; (*fig.*) fournaise, *f.*; (*engine*) foyer, *m.*
furnish, *v.a.* (*house and fig.*) meubler (de); (*obtain*) procurer (à + *pers.*); *~ with*, pourvoir* de.
furniture, (*piece of*) meuble, *m.*; (*as a whole*) ameublement, *m.*; (*suite*) mobilier, *m.* ⚠ *Not* fourniture *which* = '*supplying*', '*supplies*'; **~-van,** tapissière, *f.*
furrier, fourreur, *m.* ⚠ *Not* fourrier *which* = '*quarter-master-sergeant*'.
furrow, (*lit., wrinkle*) sillon, *m.*; (*ship*) sillage, *m.*; *v.a.* sillonner.
further, *adj.* ultérieur; *often* autre *is sufficient*; (*more complete*) plus ample; (*more distant*) plus lointain; (*supplementary*) supplémentaire; *until ~ notice*, jusqu'à nouvel avis; *~ information*, renseignements complémentaires, *m.pl.*
further, *v.a.* seconder; (*favour*) favoriser.
further, *adv.* plus loin; (*any longer*) davantage; *~ up, down*, (*hill*) plus haut, plus bas.
furtherance, avancement, *m.*
furthermore, encore (*inversion at head of sentence*): encore l'a-t-il payé deux fois.
fu(a)rthest, *see* FARTHER.
furtive, furti|f, ~ve; **~ly,** furtivement.
fury, (*anger, sea, wind*) fureur, *f.*; (*pers.*) furie, *f.*; (*myth.*) Furie, *f.*; *get into a ~*, entrer en fureur.
furze, (*bot.*) ajonc, *m.*
fuse, *s.* (*explosive*) fusée, *f.*; (*electr.*) coupe-circuit, *m. invar.*
fuse, *v.a.* (*metal*) fondre; *v.n.* se fondre; (*amalgamate*) fusionner, *v.a.n.*
fusee, (*artil. and horol.*) fusée, *f.*; (*match*) tison, *m.*
fuselage, (*aeron.*) fuselage, *m.*
fusib|le, fusible; **~ility,** fusibilité, *f.*
fusilier, fusilier, *m.*
fusillade, *s.* fusillade, *f.*

fusion, (*metals*) fonte, *f.*; (*fig.*) fusion, *f.*; (*amalgamation*) fusionnement, *m.*
fuss, *s.* (*difficulty*) embarras, *m.*; (*stir*) agitation, *f.*; *v.a. make a* ~, faire* des embarras; *What a* ~ *!* que d'histoires!
fuss, *v.a.* tracasser; *v.n.* faire* des embarras; **~y, ~** qui fait des embarras; (*restless*) inqui|et, ~ète; (*bothering*) tracassi|er, ~ère.
fustian, (*stuff*) futaine, *f.*; (*bombast*) emphase, *f.*
fust|y, qui sent le renfermé; **~iness,** renfermé, *m.*
futil|e, futile; **~ity,** futilité, *f.*
future, *s.* (*lit. and fig.*) avenir, *m.*; (*gram.*) futur, *m.*; ♤ futur *s. is never used of time to come*; *in the* ~, à l'avenir.
futur|e, (*lit. and gram.*) futur; (*comm.*) à terme; **~ity,** avenir, *m.*
fuzzy, (*curly*) frisé; (*fluffy*) flou.
fy! *interj.* fi donc!

G

gab, bagout, *m.*; *have the gift of the* ~, avoir du bagout.
gabble, *s.* (*prattle*) babil, *m.*; *v.n.* (*talk, read too fast*) parler, lire* trop vite.
gaberdine, (*stuff and cloak*) gabardine, *f.*
gabion, (*fort.*) gabion, *m.*
gable, ~-end, pignon, *m.*
gadabout, *s.* coureu|r, ~se, *m.f.*; **gad about,** *v.n.* vagabonder.
gadfly, taon, *m.*
gadget, truc, *m.*; (*aeron.*) dispositif, *m.*
Gael, Gaël, *m.*; **~ic,** gaélique.
gaff, *s.* (*naut.*) gaffe, *f.*
gag, *s.* bâillon, *m.*; *v.a.* (*lit. and fig.*) bâillonner.
gage, *s.* (*pledge*) gage, *m.*; (*challenge*) défi, *m.*
gaiety, gaieté, *f.*
gain, *s.* (*lit., fig., comm.*) gain, *m.*; (*advantage*) avantage, *m.*
gain, *v.a.* (*lit., fig., win, win over, earn, reach, time*) gagner; (*victory and prizes*) remporter; ~ *ground on,* gagner du terrain (sur); (*encroach*) empiéter (sur).
gain, *v.n.* gagner; ~ *by,* gagner à.
gainer, gagn|eur, ~euse, *m.f.*; (*gaming*) gagnant, *m.*; *be a* ~ *by,* gagner à.
gainsay, *v.a.* (*contradict*) contredire*; (*deny*) nier.
gait, allure, *f.*
gaiter, guêtre, *f.*
gala, gala, *m.*
galaxy, (*astr. and fig.*) galaxie, *f.*
gale, grand vent, *m.*
galingale, (*bot.*) souchet, *m.*
gall, (*lit. and fig.*) bile, *f.*; (*fig.*) fiel, *m.*; (*bot.*) galle, *f.*; (*sore*) écorchure, *f.*; **~-bladder,** vessie, *f.*; **~-stone,** calcul biliaire, *m.*
gall, *v.a.* (*rub sore*) écorcher; (*harass*) †harceler.
gallant, *s.* élégant, *m.*
gallant, *adj.* (*brave, noble*) brave (*after noun*). ♤ Galant *generally* = '*courteous*', '*attentive to ladies*'; un galant homme, *a true gentleman*; un homme galant = '*a fine fellow*'; **~ly,** (*bravely*) bravement; ♤ galamment = '*with great politeness*'.
gallantry, (*bravery*) courage, *m.*; (*courtesy*) galanterie, *f.*
galleon, galion, *m.*
gallery, (*balcony, corridor, mining, pictures, lamp*) galerie, *f.*; (*theatr.*) amphithéâtre, *m.*
galley, galère, *f.*; **~-slave,** galérien, *m.*
Gallic, *adj.* gaulois; **~an,** *adj.* gallican.
gallicanism, gallicanisme, *m.*
gallicism, gallicisme, *m.*
galling, irritant; (*provoking*) vexant; (*fire of guns*) bien nourri.
gallivant, *v.n.* courir* la prétentaine.
gallon, (*measure*) gallon, *m.*
galloon, galon, *m.*
gallop, galop, *m.*; *v.a.n.* galoper.
galloping, *s.* galopade, *f.*; ♤ gallopade = '*galop*' (*a dance*).
gallows, potence, *f.*; **~-bird,** gibier de potence, *m.*
galore, *adv.* à foison.
galosh, (*over-shoe*) caoutchouc, *m.*
galvan|ic, *adj.* galvanique; **~ism,** galvanisme, *m.*
galvaniz|e, (*lit. and fig.*) galvaniser; **~ation,** galvanisation, *f.*
gambl|e, jeu, *m.*; *v.n.* jouer; ~ *away,* gaspiller au jeu; ~ *on Stock Exchange,* jouer à la bourse; **~er,** joueur, *m.*; **~ing,** jeu, *m.*; **~ing-hell,** tripot, *m.*
gamboge, gomme-gutte, *f.*
gambol, gambade, *f.*; *v.n.* gambader.
game, *s.* (*lit., fig., amusement, sport, frolic, tennis, cricket, &c.*) jeu, *m.*; (*billiards, cards, &c.*) partie, *f.*; (*ans. hunted for sport and flesh*) gibier, *m.*; **~-bag,** gibecière, *f.*; **~-cock,** coq de combat, *m.*; **~-licence,** permis de chasse, *m.*; *big* ~, grands fauves, *m.pl.*; *big-~-hunting, see* BIG; *drawn* ~, partie nulle; *f.*; *make* ~ *of,* se moquer de; *the* ~ *is up with me,* c'en est fait de moi; *play a risky* ~, (*fig.*) jouer gros jeu; *the* ~ *is not worth the candle,* le jeu n'en vaut pas la chandelle.
game, *adj.* (*of limbs*) estropié; (*plucky*) *be* ~, avoir du cran; **~ly,** crânement.
gam|e, *v.a.n.* jouer; **~ing-house,** maison de jeu, *f.*; **~ing-table,** tapis vert, *m.*
gamekeeper, garde-chasse, *m. invar.*
gamester, joueur, *m.*
gammon, (*of bacon*) quartier de lard, *m.*; (*rot, slang*) blague, *f.*
gamp, (*umbrella*) riflard, *m.*
gamut, (*mus.*) gamme, *f.*
gander, jars, *m.*
gang, (*gen., pej.*) bande, *f.*; (*workmen, sailors*) équipe, *f.*; **press-~,** racoleurs, *m.pl.*; **~er,** chef d'équipe, *m.*
ganglion, *s.* (*med.*) ganglion, *m.*
gangren|e, gangrène, *f.*; *v.n.* se gangrener; **~ous,** gangréneu|x, ~se.

gangway, (*temporary*) passage, *m.*; (*naut.*) passavant, *m.*; (*embarking, &c.*) passerelle, *f.*
gannet, (*ornith.*) fou, *m.*
gaol, jail, prison, *f.*; ~**-bird,** pilier de prison, *m.*; ~**er,** geôlier, *m.*
gap, (*hole*) trou, *m.*; (*breach*) brèche, *f.*; (*empty space*) vide, *m.*
gap|e, gaping, *s.* (*yawning*) bâillement, *m.*; *v.n.* (*yawn*) bâiller; (*things*) s'entr'ouvrir*; *stand ~ing,* rester (être) bouche bée.
garage, *s.* garage, *m.*; ~ *proprietor,* garagiste, *m.*; *v.a.* garer.
garb, *s.* costume, *m.*; *v.a.* revêtir* (de).
garbage, (*offal*) tripaille, *f.*; (*refuse*) rebuts, *m.pl.*
garble, (*mutilate*) tronquer.
garden, jardin, *m.*; ~**er,** jardini|er, ~ère, *m.f.*; ~**-balsam,** balsamine, *f.*; ~ **party,** garden-party, *f.* (*pl.* garden-partys); ~**-path,** allée, *f.*; *v.a.* jardiner.
gardening, jardinage, *m.*
garfish, (*ichth.*) orphie, *f.*
gargle, *s.* gargarisme, *m.*; *v.a.* gargariser; *v.n.* se gargariser.
gargoyle, (*arch.*) gargouille, *f.*
garish, voyant.
garland, guirlande, *f.*; *v.a.* enguirlander.
garlic, ail, *m.* (*pl.* aulx, *in bot.* ails).
garment, vêtement, *m.*
garner, *s.* grenier, *m.*; *v.a.* entasser.
garnet, grenat, *m.*; ~**-red,** grenat, *invar.*
garnish, garnishment, garniture, *f.*; *v.a.* garnir (de).
garret, mansarde, *f.*; (*pej.*) galetas, *m.*
garrison, garnison, *f.*; *v.a.* (*troops*) défendre; (*town*) mettre* une garnison dans.
gar(r)otte, *s.* garrotte, *f.*; *v.a.* étrangler.
garrul|ity, loquacité, *f.*; ~**ous,** loquace.
garter, jarretière, *f.*; *the Garter,* Ordre de la Jarretière, *m.*
gas, (*light, mil., phys., chem.*) gaz, *m.*; (*med.*) anesthésique, *m.*; (*rubbish*) blague, *f.*; ~**-bomb,** bombe à gaz, *f.*; ~**-mantle,** manchon, *m.*; ~**-mask,** masque à gaz, *m.*; ~**-meter,** compteur à gaz, *m.*; ~**-pipe,** tuyau à gaz, *m.*; ~**-ring, -stove,** fourneau à gaz, *m.*; ~**-works,** usine à gaz, *f.*; *put on the ~,* ouvrir* le gaz; *put off the ~,* fermer le gaz.
gas, *v.a.* (*poison with gas*) gazer. ⚠ *To 'talk boastfully, foolishly',* **v.n.** *is not* gazer *but* débagouler.
gaselier, lustre, *m.*
gaseous, gazeu|x, ~se.
gash, *s.* estafilade, *f.*; (*scar*) balafre, *f.*; *v.a.* balafrer.
gasometer, gazomètre, *m.*
gasp, soupir, *m.*; *at the last ~,* à son dernier soupir; *v.n.* ~ *for breath,* †haleter.
gastri|c, gastrique; ~**tis,** gastrite, *f.*
gastronom|y, gastronomie, *f.*; ~**ic,** gastronomique.
gate, (*house, city, fig., &c.*) porte, *f.*; (*toll or with bars*) barrière, *f.*; ~**-post,** montant, *m.*; ~ *of level crossing,* barrière roulante, *f.*
gate, *v.a.* (*univ., schol.*) consigner.
gateway, portail, *m.*
gather, *v.a.* (*collect*) réunir; (*amass*) amasser; (*harvest*) récolter; (*fruit, flowers*) cueillir*; (*understand*) conclure* (de); (*taxes*) percevoir; ~ *in,* recueillir; ~ *up,* ramasser.
gather, *v.n.* (*crowd*) s'assembler; (*clouds*) s'accumuler; (*get bigger*) grossir; (*med.*) former un abcès.
gathering, (*crowd*) rassemblement, *m.*; (*crop*) récolte, *f.*; (*med.*) abcès, *m.*
gaud|iness, (*colour*) éclat, *m.*; (*false glitter*) clinquant, *m.*; ~**y,** (*colour*) voyant.
gauffer, *v.a. see* GOF(F)ER.
gauge, *s.* (*measure of capacity*) jauge, *f.*; (*rail*) largeur, *f.*; **narrow-~,** *adj.* (*rail*) à voie étroite.
gauge, *v.a.* (*measure*) jauger; (*estimate*) apprécier.
Gaul, *s.m.f.* Gaulois, -e; ~**ish,** gaulois.
gaunt, décharné; ~**ness,** aspect décharné, *m.*
gauntlet, *m.* (*armour*) gantelet, *m.*; *throw down, pick up the ~,* jeter, relever le gant; *run the ~,* passer par les baguettes.
gauze, gaze, *f.*; *wire ~,* toile métallique, *f.*
gawk, lourdaud, *m.*; ~**y,** dégingandé.
gay, gai; (*bright*) brillant; ⚠ Une femme gaie = *'a bright, cheerful woman', not a 'gay woman' which* = une femme légère; *as ~ as a lark,* gai comme un pinson; **gaily,** (*merrily*) gaiement; (*lightly, dissolutely*) légèrement; *see also* GAIETY.
gaze, *s.* regard fixe, *m.*
gaze, *v.n.* contempler; ~ *at,* regarder fixement.
gazelle, gazelle, *f.*
gazette, gazette, *f.*
gazetteer, dictionnaire géographique, *m.*
gear, *s.* (*apparatus, tackle*) attirail, *m.*; (*machines*) engrenage, *m.*; (*naut.*) apparaux, *m.pl.*; ~**-box,** (*motor*) boîte des vitesses, *f.*; ~**-case,** (*motor, &c.*) carter, *m.*; ~**-lever,** levier des vitesses, *m.*; *low ~,* (*motor*) première vitesse, *f.*; *top ~,* (*motor*) quatrième vitesse, *f.*; *out of ~,* désengrené; *throw into ~,* (*motor*) embrayer.
gee! *interj.* (*U.S.A.*) mince alors!
gee-gee, dada, *m.*
gelatin(e), gélatine, *f.*; ~**ous,** gélatineu|x, ~se.
gelding, (*horse*) cheval †hongre, *m.*
gelid, glacé.
gem, pierre précieuse, *f.*; (*fig.*) perle, *f.*
gendarme, gendarme, *m.*; ~**ry,** gendarmerie, *f.*
gender, genre, *m.*
genealog|y, généalogie, *f.*; ~**ist,** généalogiste, *m.*; ~**ical,** généalogique.
general, *s.* (*mil., relig. order*) général, *m.*
general, *adj.* (*common to all, vague, of*

idea, &c.) général; ~ *servant,* bonne à tout faire, *f.*; *as a ~ rule,* en règle générale; *in* ~, en général; **~ly,** généralement.
generalissimo, généralissime, *m.*
generality, généralité, *f.*
generaliz|e, généraliser; **~ation,** généralisation, *f.*
generalship, (*office*) généralat, *m.*; (*capacity*) stratégie, *f.*
genera|te, (*lit. and fig.*) engendrer; **~tion,** génération, *f.*; *spontaneous ~tion,* génération spontanée, *f.*; **~tive,** *adj.* générat|eur, ~rice; **~tor,** (*pers., electr., steam, gas*) générateur, *m.*
generic, générique.
generosity, (*noble-mindedness, liberality*) générosité, *f.*
generous, (*noble, liberal, soil, mine, plentiful, wine*) généreu|x, ~se; **~ly,** généreusement.
genesis, (*origin*) origine, *f.*; (*Bible*) Genèse, *f.*
genet, (*fur*) genette, *f.* ⚠ genet = '*jennet*', '*Spanish horse*'.
geneva, (*spirit*) genièvre, *m.*
Genevan, *adj.* (*when an adj. use small letter*) *and s.m.f.* Genevois, -e.
genial, (*climate, &c.*) dou|x, ~ce; (*kindly*) bienfaisant; (*conversation*) animé; ⚠ génial = '*original*', '*having genius*'; **~ity,** cordialité, *f.*; **~ly,** jovialement; ⚠ génialement = '*very cleverly*', '*as genius would do*'.
genital, génital.
genitive, *s.* génitif, *m.*
genius, (*spirit*) génie, *m.* (*pl.* genii); (*characteristic feature, of a lang., exalted ability, pers.*) génie, *m.*
gent, (*pop.*) monsieur, *m.*; **~s',** (*in shops, of clothes, &c.*) pour homme.
genteel, distingué; **~ly,** (*elegantly*) élégamment.
gentian, (*bot.*) gentiane, *f.*
gentile, *s.* gentil, *m.* (*plur. but no fem.*); *adj.* des gentils.
gentility, (*status*) petite noblesse, *f.*; (*birth*) bonne naissance; (*manners, &c., sometimes pej.*) distinction, *f.*
gentl|e, (*lit., wind, slope*) dou|x, ~ce; (*well born*) bien né; **~eness,** douceur, *f.*; **~y,** doucement.
gentlefolk(s), gens de bonne naissance, *m.pl.*
gentleman, (*character*) galant homme, *m.*; (*untitled, but bearing arms*) gentilhomme (*pl.* gentilshommes); (*with no occupation*) homme sans profession; (*manners*) homme du monde; (*gen.*) monsieur (*pl.* messieurs); ~ *in waiting,* gentilhomme de service.
gentlemanly, (*pers.*) comme il faut; (*behaviour, &c.*) de bon ton.
gentlewoman, femme de bonne naissance, *f.*
gentry, petite noblesse, *f.*
genuflexion, génuflexion, *f.*
genuine, (*authentic*) authentique; (*sincere*) sincère; (*true*) vrai; (*natural*) naturel, -le; **~ness,** authenticité, *f.*; **~ly,** (*authentically*) authentiquement; (*really*) réellement.
genus, genre, *m.*
geograph|y, géographie, *f.*; **~er,** géographe, *m.*; **~ical,** géographique.
geolog|y, géologie, *f.*; **~ist,** géologue, *m.*; **~ical,** géologique.
geomet|er, ~rician, géomètre, *m.*
geometr|y, géométrie, *f.*; **~ical,** géométrique; *~ical progression,* progression géométrique, *f.*
geranium, géranium, *m.*
gerfalcon, gerfaut, *m.*
germ, (*lit. and fig.*) germe, *m.*
german, (*cousins, brothers, sisters*) germain.
German, *adj.* (*when an adj use small letter*) *and s.m.f.* Allemand, -e; (*lang.*) allemand, *m.*
germander, (*bot.*) germandrée, *f.*
germane to, se rapportant à.
German|ic, germanique; **~ize,** germaniser.
germicide, *s.* destructeur de germes, *m.*
germinal, de germe.
germina|te, *v.n.* (*lit. and fig.*) germer; **~tion,** germination, *f.*
gerund, gérondif, *m.*
gesticula|te, *v.n.* gesticuler; **~tion,** gesticulation, *f.*
gesture, geste, *m.*
get, *v.a.* **1.** (*obtain*) obtenir*; **2.** (*procure*) procurer; (*for oneself*) se procurer; **3.** (*earn*) gagner; **4.** (*victory, prize*) remporter; **5.** (*habits*) prendre*; **6.** (*have done*) faire* + *inf.*, + par *of person doing an action,* + à *of person suffering it. Cf.* je le ferai planter par le jardinier *and* je ferai comprendre au jardinier que c'est très rare; **7.** (*find*) trouver; **8.** (*receive*) recevoir; **9.** (*disease, &c.*) attraper; **10.** (*persuade to do*) persuader à + *pers.* de + *inf.*; **11.** (*term of imprisonment*) être condamné à; *go and* ~, aller* chercher; ~ *back,* (*have again*) ravoir; ~ *down,* descendre (avoir); (*swallow*) avaler; ~ *forward,* (*mil., &c.*) faire* avancer; ~ *in,* (*harvest, animals, &c.*) rentrer (*avoir*); ~ *out,* (*things*) sortir* (avoir); (*books, &c.*) publier; ~ *through,* faire* passer; (*a book, &c.*) parcourir*; (*an exam.*) passer; (*finish*) en venir* à bout; ~ *under,* (*master, subdue*) maîtriser; ~ *up,* faire* monter; (*linen*) blanchir; (*invent*) inventer; (*subject, speech, lesson*) préparer; *to have got,* (*possess*) avoir.
get, *v.n.* (*destination*) arriver (être); (*become*) devenir* (être); (*find oneself*) se trouver; (*reach*) parvenir* à; ~ *used to,* s'habituer à; *you've got to do it,* il vous faut le faire; ~ *about,* (*lit. and fig.*) circuler; ~ *along!* quelle blague!; ~ *in,* entrer (être); ~ *off,* (*depart*) partir* (être); ~ *on,* (*succeed*) prospérer; (*things*) marcher; (*advance*)

avancer; (*agree*) s'entendre bien (avec *or* ensemble); ~ *through*, (*arrive*) arriver (être); (*exam.*) passer; ~ *out*, (*information*) s'ébruiter; ~ *out!* sortez!; ~ *out of*, sortir* (être) de; (*habit*) se défaire* de; ~ *over*, (*surmount*) surmonter; (*illness*) se remettre* de; *I can't* ~ *over it*, je n'en reviens pas; ~ *to*, (*as far as*) aller* (être) jusqu'à; ~ *up*, se lever; (*of wind*) s'élever; *interj.* debout!
get-at-able, accessible.
get-up, *s.* (*dress*) mise, *f.*
gew-gaw, *s.* babiole, *f.*
geyser, (*hot spring*) geyser, *m.*; (*for heating water*) chauffe-bain, *m.*
ghast|ly, (*horrible*) horrible; (*pale*) blême; **~liness**, (*pallor*) pâleur, *f.*; (*appearance*) aspect effrayant, *m.*
gherkin, cornichon, *m.*
ghost, (*breath, life*) souffle, *m.*; (*spirit and eccles.*) esprit, *m.*; (*spectre*) revenant, *m.*; (*mere semblance*) *fig.* ombre, *f.*; *Holy Ghost*, Saint Esprit, *m.*
ghostly, spectral; (*spiritual*) spirituel, -le.
ghoul, goule, *f.*
giant, *s.* géant, *m.*; **~ess**, géante, *f.*; *adj.* géant; (*giant-like*) de géant.
gibber, *v.a.n.* baragouiner; **~ish**, baragouin, *m.*
gibbet, gibet, *m.*; *v.a.* pendre.
gibbon, (*zool.*) gibbon, *m.*
gib|e, **(jibe)** *s.* sarcasme, *m.*; *v.n.* railler; ~ *at*, se moquer de; **~er**, raill|eur, ~euse, *m.f.*; **~ing**, *adj.* railleu|r, ~se.
giblets, abatis, *m.*
gidd|y, (*pers.*) frappé de vertige; (*things causing giddiness*) vertigineu|x, ~se; (*light-headed*) étourdi; **~iness**, vertige, *m.*; (*light-headedness*) étourderie, *f.*; **~ily**, étourdiment.
gift, (*lit., fig., talent*) don, *m.*; (*present*) cadeau, *m.*; *one must not look a* ~ *horse in the mouth*, à cheval donné on ne regarde pas les dents.
gifted, doué.
gig, (*carriage*) cabriolet, *m.*; (*light*) tilbury, *m.*; (*naut.*) yole, *f.*
gigantic, gigantesque.
giggle, *s.* ricanement, *m.*; *v.n.* ricaner.
gigolo, gigolo, *m.*
gild, *v.a.* (*lit. and fig.*) dorer.
gilder, doreur, *m.*
gilding, dorure, *f.*
gills, (*fish*) ouïes, *f.pl.*
gillyflower, (*bot.*) giroflée, *f.*
gilt, *s.* dorure, *f.*; *adj.* doré; ~ *edges*, *~-edged*, *see* EDGES, EDGED.
gimcrack, *s.* brimborion, *m.*; *adj.* de clinquant.
gimlet, vrille, *f.*
gimp, (*on coat, &c.*) brandebourg, *m.*
gin, *s.* (*snare*) trébuchet, *m.*; (*liquor*) *approx.* genièvre, *m.*; **~-shop, -palace**, débit de spiritueux, *m.*
ginger, gingembre, *m.*; **~-beer**, limonade au gingembre, *f.*; *adj.* (*hair*) blond roux, *invar.*
gingerbread, pain d'épices, *m.*
gingerly, doucement.
gingham, (*material*) guingan, *m.*; ⚠ '*gingham*' (*fam.*) *used for* '*umbrella*', riflard, *m.*
gi(y)psy, *adj. and s.m.f.* bohémien, -ne.
giraffe, girafe, *f.*
girandole, (*firework, candlestick, earring*) girandole, *f.*
gird, ceindre*; (*girdle*) ceinturer; (*surround*) entourer (de); (*fig.*) revêtir* (de).
gird at, railler.
girder, (*wood and iron*) poutre, *f.*
girdle, *s.* (*lit. and fig.*) ceinture, *f.*; *v.a.* ceinturer (de).
girl, jeune fille, *f.*; **~hood**, temps de jeune fille, *m.*; **~ish**, de jeune fille; **~ishness**, caractère de jeune fille, *m.*
girth, (*horse*) sangle, *f.*; (*measure round*) circonférence, *f.*; (*pers.*) tour de taille, *m.*
gist, point principal, *m.*
give, *v.a.* (*lit., fig., time, report, information, orders*) donner; (*movement, jump, &c., pleasure*) faire*; (*compliments*) adresser; (*a sentence, account*) rendre; (*transmit*) remettre*; (*a look*) jeter; (*a speech*) prononcer; (*security*) fournir; ~ *away*, donner; (*pers.*) trahir; (*secret*) divulguer; (*distribute*) distribuer; ~ *back*, rendre; ~ *forth*, (*light, heat*) émettre*; ~ *in*, (*accounts*) rendre; (*name*) donner; ~ *off*, (*fumes, &c.*) dégager; ~ *out*, (*announce*) annoncer; (*distribute*) distribuer; (*fumes*) dégager; ~ *oneself out for*, se donner pour; ~ *over*, remettre*; (*cease from*) renoncer à; ~ *up*, renoncer à; (*a patient*) condamner; (*surrender*) livrer; ~ *oneself up to*, s'abandonner à; *~n to, over to*, adonné à.
give, *v.n.* (*under pressure, lit. and* ~ *way*) céder; ~ *in*, céder; ~ *in to*, céder à; ~ *out*, être épuisé; (*pers.*) n'en pouvoir plus; ~ *over*, cesser.
giver, donneu|r, ~se, *m.f.*
gizzard, (*bird*) gésier, *m.*
glacial, glacial.
glacier, glacier, *m.*
glacis, glacis, *m.*
glad, content (de); (*things*) joyeu|x, ~se; (*causing pleasure*) heureu|x, ~se; *I am* ~ *of it*, j'en suis bien aise; **~ness**, joie, *f.*; **~ly**, volontiers.
gladden, *v.a.* réjouir.
glade, clairière, *f.*
gladiator, gladiateur, *m.*; **~ial**, de gladiateur.
gladiolus, (*bot.*) glaïeul, *m.*
gladsome, joyeu|x, ~se; **~ly**, joyeusement.
glam|our, (*seductive charm*) enchantement, *m.*; (*magic spell*) prestige, *m.*; **~orous**, enchant|eur, ~eresse.
glance, *s.* (*of the eye*) coup d'œil, *m.*; (*brief movement of missile*) mouvement de côté, *m.*; (*flash*) éclair, *m.*; *cast a sidelong* ~ *at*, regarder du coin de l'œil.
glance, *v.n.* (*missile*) tomber (être) de

biais; (*gleam*) briller; ~ *at*, lancer un coup d'œil à; (*book*) parcourir* rapidement.
gland, (*anat.*) glande, *f.*; **~ular,** glandulaire.
glanders, (*vet.*) morve, *f.*
glare, *s.* lumière éblouissante, *f.*; (*tawdry*) clinquant, *m.*; (*eye*) regard enflammé, *m.*
glare, *v.n.* briller d'un éclat éblouissant; (*eye*) jeter des regards enflammés.
glaring, *adj.* (*blinding*) aveuglant; (*palpable*) qui crève les yeux; (*colour*) tranchant.
glass, (*substance, for drinking, frame*) verre, *m.*; (*pane*) vitre, *f.*; (*mirror*) glace, *f.*; (*small mirror*) miroir, *m.*; (*barometer*) baromètre, *m.*; **~es,** lunettes, *f.pl.*; *ground* ~, verre dépoli, *m.*; ~ **case,** vitrine, *f.*; ~ **door,** porte vitrée, *f.*; **~-ware, ~-works,** verrerie, *f.*; *adj.* de verre.
glass, *v.a.* (*reflect*) mirer.
glassy, (*eyes, &c.*) vitreu|x, ~se; (*water*) limpide.
glaucous, glauque.
glaze, *s.* (*lit., fig., pottery*) vernis, *m.*
glaze, *v.a.* (*put glass into*) vitrer; (*pottery*) vernisser; (*paper*) satiner.
glazier, vitrier, *m.*
glazing, *s.* vitrerie, *f.*; (*varnish*) vernis, *m.*
gleam, *s.* (*lit. and fig.*) lueur, *f.*; ~ *of hope*, lueur d'espoir.
gleam, *v.n.* luire*; **~ing,** *adj.* luisant.
glean, glaner; (*grapes*) grappiller; **~er,** glaneu|r, ~se, *m.f.*; **~ing,** glanage, *m.*; (*grapes*) grappillage, *m.*; **~ings,** glanure, *f.*
glebe, glèbe, *f.*
glee, allégresse, *f.*; (*mus.*) chanson à plusieurs voix, *f.*
glee|some, ~ful, joyeu|x, ~se.
glen, vallon, *m.*
glib, (*tongue*) délié; (*speaker*) qui a de la faconde; (*surface*) glissant; **~ness,** faconde, *f.*
glide, *s.* (*aeron.*) vol plané, *m.*; *v.n.* (*aeron.*) planer; (*move smoothly*) glisser; (*steal, creep*) se glisser; (*river*) couler; ~ *away*, (*time*) s'écouler.
glider, *s.* (*aeron.*) planeur, *m.*
glimmer, ~ing, (*lit. and fig.*) lueur, *f.*; *v.n.* jeter une lueur faible.
glimpse, *s.* (*glance*) coup d'œil rapide, *m.*; (*of light*) lueur, *m.*; *v.a. and catch a* ~ *of*, entrevoir*.
glint, *s.* faible lueur, *f.*
glitter, *s.* (*lit. and fig.*) éclat, *m.*; (*stars*) scintillation, *f.*
glitter, glisten, glister, *v.n.* étinceler; **~ing,** *adj.* étincelant.
gloaming, crépuscule, *m.*
gloat over, dévorer des yeux; (*rejoice at*) se réjouir de.
glob|e, *s.* (*sphere, eye, lamp, earth*) globe, *m.*; *terrestrial* ~, globe terrestre; *use of the* ~*es*, étude de la sphère, *f.*; **~ular,** globulaire.
globule, globule, *m.*
gloom, *s.* ténèbres, *f.pl.*; (*fig.*) tristesse, *f.*; **~y,** (*lit. and fig.*) sombre; *be*~*y*, (*weather*) faire* sombre.
glorif|y, (*honour, theol.*) glorifier; (*extol*) exalter; **~ication,** glorification, *f.*
gloriole, auréole, *f.*; ⚠ *not* gloriole *which* = '*vainglory*', '*vanity*'.
glorious, glorieu|x, ~se; (*splendid*) magnifique; (*weather*) radieu|x, ~se; **~ly,** (*splendidly*) magnifiquement.
glory, (*theol., renown, splendour, halo*) gloire, *f.*; (*resplendent beauty*) beauté, *f.*
glory, *v.n.* ~ *in*, se faire* gloire de.
gloss, *s.* (*comment*) glose, *f.*; (*of stuffs*) lustre, *m.*
gloss, *v.a.* (*criticize*) gloser; *v.n.* (*make comments*) gloser sur.
glossary, glossaire, *m.*
gloss|y, luisant; (*stuffs*) lustré; **~iness,** lustre, *m.*
glove, gant, *m.*; **~-making, -shop,** ganterie, *f.*; *v.a.* ganter; **~r,** ganti|er, ~ère, *m.f.*
glow, *s.* (*heat*) chaleur, *f.*; (*light*) lumière, *f.*; (*face, sunset*) rougeur, *f.*; (*from exercise*) sensation de chaleur, *f.*; (*fig.*) ardeur, *f.*; **~-lamp,** lampe à incandescence, *f.*; **~-worm,** ver luisant, *m.*
glow, *v.n.* (*burn*) brûler; (*passion*) être transporté (de); (*joy*) rayonner (de); (*health*) être vermeil; (*get animated*) s'embraser.
glower, *v.n.* se renfrogner.
glowing, (*brilliant*) brillant; (*health*) robuste; (*heat*) chaleureu|x, ~se; **~ly,** (*with enthusiasm*) avec enthousiasme.
glucose, glucose, *m.f.*
glue, *s.* colle forte, *f.*; **~-pot,** pot à colle, *m.*; *v.a.* coller.
glum, renfrogné; **~ly,** d'un air renfrogné.
glut, *s.* (*satiation*) assouvissement, *m.*; (*superabundance*) surabondance, *f.*; (*on the market*) encombrement, *m.*
glut, *v.a.* (*lit. and fig.*) gorger; (*satiate, lit. and fig.*) assouvir; (*market*) encombrer.
gluten, gluten, *m.*
glutin|ous, glutineu|x, ~se; **~osity,** glutinosité, *f.*
glutton, glouton, *m.*; (*less pej.*) gourmand, *m.*; (*pop.*) goulu, *m.*; *be a* ~ *for work*, s'acharner au travail.
gluttonous, glouton; (*less pej.*) gourmand; **~ly,** gloutonnement.
gluttony, gloutonnerie, *f.*; (*less pej.*) gourmandise, *f.*
glycerine, glycérine, *f.*
glycogen, (*chem.*) glycogène, *m.*
glycol, (*chem.*) glycol, *m.*
gnarled, noueu|x, ~se.
gnash, *v.a.n.* grincer; **~ing,** grincement, *m.*
gnat, cousin, *m.*
gnaw, (*lit. and fig.*) ronger; ~ *at, into*, ronger.
gnawing, *s.* rongement, *m.*; (*fig.*) torture, *f.*; *adj.* (*lit. and fig.*) rongeu|r, ~se.

gneiss, (*geol.*) gneiss, *m.*
gnom|e, (*spirit*) gnome, *m.*; (*maxim*) maxime, *f.*; **~ic,** gnomique.
gnomon, (*of sundial*) gnomon, *m.*
gnostic, *adj. and s.m.f.* gnostique; **~ism,** gnosticisme, *m.*
gnu, (*zool.*) gnou, *m.*
go, *s.* (*energy*) entrain, *m.*; (*attempt*) coup, *m.*; *it's no ~,* il n'y a pas moyen; *have another ~,* y revenir*; *be all the ~,* faire* fureur; *have* (*be*) *a near ~,* l'avoir échappée belle; *here 's a pretty go!* me, te, *&c.*, voilà bien; *be on sentry-~,* être de faction.
go, *v.n.* aller* (être); (*time*) passer (avoir *of action,* être *of state*); (*distance, journey, &c.*) faire*; (*depart*) partir* (être); (*die*) aller* mourir; (*give way*) céder; (*become + adj.*) devenir* (être); (*be*) être (*go naked, &c.*); (*machine, watch, business*) marcher; (*circulate, of novel, &c.*) circuler; (*clock*) sonner; *~ about,* (*here and there*) aller ça et là; (*begin*) se mettre* à; *you don't know how to ~ about it,* vous ne savez pas vous y prendre; *~ again,* retourner (être), aller* encore; *~ against,* s'opposer à; *~ ahead,* avancer; (*naut.*) virer de bord; *~ away,* s'en aller*; *~ back,* retourner; (*move back, lit. and comm., shares*) reculer; (*memory*) remonter; *~ back on one's word,* reprendre* sa parole; *~ beyond,* dépasser; *~ by,* (*time*) passer (avoir *action,* être *state*); (*place*) passer auprès (de) *or* devant; (*be guided by*) se guider sur; (*name*) être connu (sous le nom de); *~ down,* descendre (être); (*prices*) baisser; (*ship*) sombrer; (*v.a.*) descendre (avoir); *~ for,* (*fetch*) aller* chercher; (*sell for*) être vendu pour; (*attack*) se jeter sur; *~ forward,* avancer; *~ into,* entrer (être) à, dans; (*question, &c.*) approfondir; *~ off,* (*away*) s'en aller*; (*fire-arms*) partir*; (*be a success, failure*) se passer bien, mal; *~ on,* (*continue*) continuer; (*take place, happen*) se passer; (*behave, misbehave*) se conduire*; *~ along! ~ on! interj.* allons donc!; *~ out,* sortir* (être); (*fire*) s'éteindre*; (*in society*) aller* dans le monde; *~ over,* (*cross*) traverser; (*read*) parcourir*; (*look over again*) repasser; (*to the other party, &c.*) passer (à); *~ through,* (*traverse*) traverser; (*read*) parcourir*; (*undergo*) subir; (*one's correspondence, post*) dépouiller; *~ through with,* mener à bonne fin; *~ under,* (*lit. and fig.*) sombrer; *~ up,* (*lit., fig., prices*) monter (être); (*v.a. hill, &c.*) monter (avoir); *~ with,* (*accompany*) accompagner; *~ without,* se passer de; *let ~,* *see* LET; *that ~es for little,* cela ne compte guère; *go it!* allez-y!; *here goes!* allons-y!
goad, *s.* aiguillon, *m.*; *v.a.* (*lit. and fig.*) aiguillonner.
goal, (*lit., fig., football*) but, *m.*; *kick a ~,* (*rugby*) marquer un essai.
goat, *m.* bouc, *f.* chèvre; **~'s beard,** (*bot.*) salsifis sauvage, *m.*; **~'s rue,** (*bot.*) rue de chèvre, *f.*
goatee, (*beard*) bouc, *m.*
goatherd, chevrier, *m.*
goatskin, (*garment*) peau de bique, *f.*; (*bottle*) outre, *f.*
goatsucker, (*ornith.*) engoulevent, *m.*
gobble, *v.a.* gober; *v.n.* (*guzzle*) bâfrer; (*turkey*) glouglouter.
gobbler, (*glutton*) goinfre, *m.*
gobelin tapestry, gobelins, *m.*
go-between, intermédiaire, *m.f.*
goblet, gobelet, *m.*
goblin, lutin, *m.*
goby, (*ichth.*) gobie, *m.*
go-by, *give the ~ to,* brûler la politesse à.
go-cart, petite charrette d'enfant, *f.*
God, Dieu, *m.*; (*pagan*) dieu, *m.*; (*idol, lit. and fig.*) idole, *f.*; *~ bless you!* Dieu vous bénisse; *~ bless me!* Mon Dieu!; *~ grant it!* Dieu le veuille!; *~ grant that . . . !* Dieu veuille que . . . ! (+ *subj.*); *thank ~!* Dieu merci!; *for ~'s sake . . . !* pour l'amour de Dieu . . . !; *~ willing,* s'il plaît à Dieu; *would to ~* (*that*), plût à Dieu (que + *subj.*); *~ save the King!* vive le roi!; **~child,** filleul, -e, *m.f.*; **~-daughter,** filleule, *f.*; **~father,** parrain, *m.*; **~mother,** marraine, *f.*; **~son,** filleul, *m.*; **~-speed,** *wish ~-speed to,* souhaiter bonne chance à.
goddess, déesse, *f.*
god|head, ~ship, divinité, *f.*
godless, impie; (*without God*) sans Dieu; **~ness,** impiété, *f.*
godlike, divin.
god|ly, pieu|x, ~se; **~liness,** piété, *f.*
godsend, aubaine, *f.*
godwit, (*ornith.*) barge, *f.*
goer, *good, &c. ~,* bon, etc. marcheur, *m.*; *comers and ~s,* allants et venants, *m.pl.*
gof(f)er (gauffer), *v.a.* gaufrer; **~ing-iron,** fer à gaufrer, *m.*
goggle, *v.n.* rouler les yeux.
goggle, *adj.* **~-eyed,** qui a les yeux à fleur de tête.
goggles, bésicles, *f.pl.*
going, *s.* (*departure*) départ, *m.*; *good, &c. ~,* (*road*) bonne, etc. route, *f.*; *~ back,* retour, *m.*; *~ down,* descente, *f.*; (*sun, moon*) coucher, *m.*; (*waters*) baisse, *f.*; *~ forward,* progrès, *m.*; *~ in,* entrée, *f.*; *~ out,* sortie, *f.*; *~ up,* montée, *f.*; *~ in and out, to and fro,* allées et venues, *f.pl.*; *coming and ~,* va-et-vient, *m. invar.*; *~s on,* conduite, *f.*; *~ through,* (*correspondence, &c.*) dépouillement, *m.*
going, *adj. pres. part.* (*in existence*) qui soit, soient; *one of the best cars ~,* une des meilleures automobiles qui soient; *~ concern,* affaire roulante, *f.*; *out~ mail,* courrier en partance, *m.*; *set ~,* mettre* en marche.
goitr|e, goitre, *m.*; **~ous,** goitreu|x, ~se.
gold, *s.* or, *m.*; *wrought ~,* or orfévri; **~-digger,** chercheur d'or, *m.*; **~-field,** mine d'or, *f.*; **~fish,** poisson rouge, *m.*;

~ **lace**, galon d'or, *m.*; ~ **plate**, vaisselle d'or, *f.*; ~ **reserve**, réserve d'or, *f.*; ~ **standard**, étalon d'or, *m.*; *as good as* ~, (*child*) sage comme une image; ~ **-dust**, poussière d'or, *f.*
golden, *adj.* d'or, en or; (*fig.*, *hair*, *harvest*, *&c.*) doré; ~**-headed**, (*cane*) à tête d'or; ~ **mean**, juste milieu, *m.*; ~ **rod**, (*bot.*) verge d'or, *f.*; ~ **syrup**, mélasse, *f.*; ~ **wedding**, noces d'or, *f.pl.*
goldbeater, ~*'s skin*, baudruche, *f.*
goldfinch, (ornith.) chardonneret, *m.*
goldhammer, (*ornith.*) loriot, *m.*
goldsmith, orfèvre, *m.*
golf, (*game*) golf, *m.*; ~**-club**, crosse de golf, *m.*
golosh, *see* GALOSH.
gondol|a, gondole, *f.*; ~**ier**, gondolier, *m.*
gone, *p.p.* (*lost*) perdu; (*time*) passé; (*auction*) adjugé; (*hopeless*) désespéré; ~ *on*, épris de; **be**~! allez-vous-en!; *it's just* ~ *6 o'clock*, il vient de sonner 6 heures.
goner, (*slang*) *he's a* ~, il est fichu.
gonfalon, gonfalon, *m.*; ~**ier**, gonfalonier, *m.*
gong, gong, *m.*
good, *s.* bien, *m.*; *the* ~, (*righteous*) les justes, *m.pl.*; ~**s**, marchandises, *f.pl.*; ~*s rates*, tarif, *m.*; ~*s shed*, †halle aux marchandises, *f.*; ~*s station*, gare de marchandises, *f.*; ~*s train*, train de marchandises, *m.*; ~*s truck*, wagon à marchandises, *m.*; *have to the* ~, (*to one's credit*) avoir à son actif; *what is the* ~*?* (*of*), à quoi bon? (+ *inf.*); *for* ~, (*for* ~ *and all*) pour tout de bon; *be no* ~ *to*, être inutile de.
good, *adj.* (*lit.*, *fig.*, *kind*, *thorough*, *good-natured*) bon, -ne; (*valid in law and comm.*) valable; (*bargain*) avantageu|x, ~se; (*interj.*) bon!; ~ *evening!* bonsoir!; ~ *fellow*, *see* FELLOW; *with a* ~ *grace*, de bonne grâce; ~ *humour*, bonne humeur, *f.*; ~*-humoured*, de bonne humeur; ~*-humouredly*, avec bonne humeur; ~ *breeding*, *see* BREEDING; ~ *living*, bonne chère, *f.*; ~*-looking*, de bonne mine; ~ *looks*, beauté, *f.*; ~ *luck!* bonne chance!; ~ *man*, homme de bien; ⚠ *not* bonhomme *which* = '*good-natured*', *sometimes* '*simple man*'; *a* ~ *many*, beaucoup (de); ~ *morning!* bonjour!; ~*-natured*, d'un bon naturel; *a* ~ *riddance!* bon débarras!; ~ *sense*, bon sens, *m.*; *in* ~ *part*, en bonne part; ~ *temper*, bon caractère, *m.*; *be* ~*-tempered*, avoir bon caractère; ~ *at*, (*doing*) savoir* bien +*inf.*; ~ *for*, (*money*) bon pour; ~ *to*, (*pers.*) bon pour; (*things* +*inf.*) bon à; ~ (*fit*) *for nothing*, bon à rien; *be so* ~ *as to*, avoir la bonté de; *make* ~, (*fulfil*) remplir; (*loss*) indemniser de; (*one's word*, *&c.*) tenir*; *my* ~ *man*, *fellow*, mon brave; *in* ~ *taste*, en bon goût; *in* ~ *time*, à temps; *be as* ~ *as ruined*, *dead*, *&c.*, être ruiné, mort, etc., ou peu s'en faut; *well and* ~, à la bonne heure; *hold* ~, *v.n.* (*receipt*, *&c.*) être valable.
good-bye, *s. and interj.* adieu, *m.*; ~ *for the present*, au revoir; *wish*, *say* ~, dire* adieu (à).
goodl|y, beau; (*impressive*) imposant; ~**iness**, aspect imposant, *m.*
goodman, maître de la maison, *m.*
goodness, bonté, *f.*; (*good quality of things*) qualité, *f.*; *thank* ~*!* Dieu merci!; ~ *knows*, Dieu sait; *for* ~ *sake*, pour l'amour de Dieu.
goodwife, maîtresse de la maison, *f.*
goodwill, bonne volonté, *f.*; (*of a business*) fonds de commerce, *m.*
goody, *s.* (*sweet*) bonbon, *m.*
goody-goody, *adj.* dévot à l'excès.
go-off, (*start*) départ, *m.*; (*beginning*) début, *m.*
goose, (*lit. and fig.*) oie, *f.*; *wild* ~, oie sauvage, *f.*; ~ *with the gold eggs*, la poule aux œufs d'or; ~**flesh**, chair de poule, *f.*; ~**-grass**, (*bot.*) grateron, *m.*; ~**-quill**, plume d'oie, *f.*
gooseberry, groseille à maquereau, *f.*; ~ **-tree**, **-bush**, groseillier à maquereau, *m.*
Gordian, ~ *knot*, nœud gordien, *m.*
gore, *s.* (*blood*) sang, *m.*; (*needlework*) pointe, *f.*
gore, *v.a.* (*with horns*) blesser d'un coup de corne.
gorge, *s.* (*defile*, *arch.*, *fort.*) gorge, *f.*; *one's* ~ *rises at*, l'estomac se soulève à.
gorge, *v.a.* (*lit. and fig.*) gorger; *v.n.* se gorger (de).
gorgeous, somptueu|x, ~se; ~**ness**, somptuosité, *f.*; ~**ly**, somptueusement.
gorget, (*armour*) †hausse-col, *m.*; (*woman's*) gorgerette, *f.*
gorgon, (*lit. and fig.*) gorgone, *f.*
gorilla, gorille, *m.*
gormandiz|e, *v.n.* goinfrer; ~**er**, goinfre, *m.*; ~**ing**, *s.* goinfrerie, *f.*
gorse, ajonc, *m.*
gory, ensanglanté.
gosh! *interj.* tudieu!
goshawk, (*ornith.*) autour, *m.*
gosling, oison, *m.*
gospel, évangile, *m.*; ~ *truth*, parole d'évangile, *f.*
gossamer, fils de la Vierge, *m.pl.*; ~ *thread*, filandre, *f.*
gossip, *s.* (*pers.*) compère, *m.*; commère, *f.*; (*thing*) *and* ~**ing**, bavardage, *m.*; (*pej.*) cancans, *m.pl.*
gossip, *v.n.* bavarder.
Goth, Goth, *m.*; (*fig.*) ostrogote, *m.*
Gothic, (*lit. and arch.*) gothique.
gouge, *s.* gouge, *f.*; *v.a.* (*wood*, *&c.*) gouger; ~ *out*, (*eye*) faire* sauter.
gourd, courge, *f.*; (*bottle*) gourde, *f.*; ⚠ gourd, *adj.* = '*benumbed*'.
gout, (*med.*) goutte, *f.*; (*blood*) goutte, *f.*; (*spot*) tache, *f.*; ~**y**, goutteu|x, ~se; ~**iness**, état goutteux, *m.*
govern, *v.a.n.* (*state*, *passions*, *gram.*) gouverner; (*household*, *conduct*) diriger.

governance, direction, *f.*
governess, gouvernante, *f.*; (*advanced pupils*) institutrice, *f.*; (*in schools*) maîtresse, *f.*
governing, (*classes, party, &c.*) gouvernant.
government, (*lit., fig., office*) gouvernement, *m.*; (*control over*) empire (sur); (*ministry*) ministère, *m.*; **~-house,** Gouvernement, *m.*; *be under petticoat ~,* tomber en quenouille.
governmental, gouvernemental.
governor, (*province, fortress, bank, public institution*) gouverneur, *m.*; (*prison, hospital*) directeur, *m.*; (*administrator*) administrateur, *m.*; (*slang = 'boss'*) patron, *m.*; (*father*) père, *m.*; *~'s wife,* femme du gouverneur, *f.*; ⚠ *not, as formerly,* gouvernante, *f.*
governorship, gouvernement, *m.*
gown, (*woman, univ., law*) robe, *f.*
grab, *v.a.* agripper; (*pej. and bird*) †happer.
grabber, homme rapace, *m.*
grabble, *v.n.* tâtonner; *~ for,* chercher à tâtons.
grace, (*elegance, favour, theol., respite, pardon, favour granted*) grâce, *f.*; (*before meals*) bénédicité, *m.*; (*after meals*) grâces, *f.pl.*; *the three Graces,* les trois Grâces, *f.pl.*; *His Grace the Duke of...,* Sa Grâce le Duc de; *your Grace,* (*Archbishop*) Monseigneur.
grace, *v.a.* (*adorn*) embellir (de); (*honour*) honorer (de).
graceful, gracieu|x, ~se; **~ness,** grâce, *f.*; **~ly,** gracieusement.
graceless, (*depraved*) dépravé; (*unabashed*) effronté; (*without charm*) sans grâce.
gracious, (*kindly, courteous, condescending, of royalty*) gracieu|x, ~se; (*merciful*) miséricordieu|x, ~se (à); *good ~! interj.* juste ciel!; **~ness,** (*charm*) grâce, *f.*; (*condescension*) condescendance, *f.*; **~ly,** gracieusement; (*mercifully*) avec miséricorde.
gradat|e, (*colours*) fondre; (*in tiers, grades*) disposer en gradins; **~ion,** (*series, degrees, arrangement in degrees*) gradation, *f.*
grade, grade, *m.*; (*rank, math., geom.*) grade, *m.*; (*quality*) qualité, *f.*; (*degree*) degré, *m.*; (*U.S.A. = gradient*) pente, *f.*; ⚠ *'Grade' in French never has this sense.*
grade, *v.a.* (*sort*) trier; (*classify*) classer; (*cross-breed ans.*) croiser.
gradient, pente, *f.*
gradual, graduel, -le; **~ly,** graduellement.
graduate, *s.* (*univ.*) gradué, -e, *m.f.*; (*rare*) bachelier, *m. more often used.*
graduate, *v.a.* (*by degrees, divisions, scale*) graduer; *v.n.* (*univ.*) prendre* ses grades; ⚠ *not* graduer; *~ into,* passer graduellement à.
graduation, (*instr., concentrate by evaporation*) graduation, *f.*; (*univ.*) *taking, conferring degree,* collation d'un grade, *f.*; ⚠ *note* graduation *is not used of university degrees.*
graduator, machine à graduer, *f.*
Graecism, hellénisme, *m.*
graft, *s.* (*hort.*) greffe, *f.*; (*slang = 'bribe'*) pots de vin, *m.pl.*; *v.a.* greffer; *~ on,* enter sur.
grafter, greffeur, *m.*
grafting, *s.* greffe, *f.*; **~-knife,** greffoir, *m.*
grain, (*weight, skin, silk, small quantity, corn, sand, &c.*) grain, *m.*; (*wood, stone*) fil, *m.*; (*cloth*) poil, *m.*; (*wheat, rye*) gros grains, *m.pl.*; (*barley, oats*) menus grains, *m.pl.*; *a ~ of + abstract noun use* le, la moindre; *against the ~,* (*wood, &c.*) à contre-fil; (*pers.*) à contre-poil; **~-market,** marché aux grains, *m.*; *v.a.* (*wood, marble*) orner de veines, de marbrures; (*leather*) grener; **coarse-grained,** à gros grains.
graminivorous, herbivore.
grammar, (*science and book*) grammaire, *f.*; **~ian,** grammairien, -ne, *m.f.*
grammatical, grammatical; **~ly,** grammaticalement.
gramme, gram, gramme, *m.*
gramophone, gramophone, *m.*; **~-record,** disque, *m.*
grampus, (*zool.*) épaulard, *m.*
granadilla, (*bot.*) grenadille, *f.*
granary, (*lit. and fig.*) grenier, *m.*
grand, (*in titles, elevated, principal, important*) grand; (*magnificent*) magnifique; (*fam. = 'famous', 'ripping'*) épatant; *that's ~!* (*slang*) chouette!; *~ total,* total global, *m.*; **~-niece,** petite-nièce, *f.*; **~-piano,** piano à queue, *m.*; **~-uncle,** grand-oncle, *m.*, *see also below*; **~ly,** avec grandeur; (*with pomp*) magnifiquement.
grandam(e), grand'mère, *f.*; (*contempt*) vieille femme, *f.*
grandchild, petit-fils, *m.*; petite-fille, *f.*; *pl.* petits-enfants, *m.*
grand-daughter, petite-fille, *f.*
grandee, (*Spain*) grand d'Espagne, *m.*; (*gen.*) grand personnage, *m.*
grandeur, (*pomp*) magnificence, *f.*; (*dignity, rank, ideas, feelings*) grandeur, *f.*
grandfather, grand-père, *m.*; **great-~,** bisaïeul, *m.*; **~'s clock,** horloge comtoise, *f.*
grandiloquen|ce, grandiloquence, *f.*; **~t,** grandiloquent.
grandiose, grandiose.
grandmamma, granny, grand'maman, *f.*
grandmother, grand'mère, *f.*; **great-~,** bisaïeule, *f.*; **~ly,** de grand'mère.
grandpapa, bon-papa, *m.*
grandparent, grand-père, *m.*, grand'mère, *f.*; ⚠ *not* grand-parent, *but pl. ~s,* grands-parents, *m.pl.*
grandsire, grand-père, *m.*
grandson, petit-fils, *m.*; **great-~,** arrière-petit-fils, *m.*
grange, (*barn*) grange, *f.*; (*country house*) château, *m.*
granite, granit, *m.*

granivorous, granivore.
grant, (*thing given*) don, *m.*; (*right, property, privilege*) concession, *f.*; (*subsidy*) subside, *m.*
grant, *v.a.* (*request*) accéder à; (*prayer*) accorder; (*rights, property*) concéder; ~ *that*, admettre* que; ~**ed** *that*, admettons que; *granted! interj.* d'accord!
grant|ee, cessionnaire, *m.f*; ~**or**, cédant, -e, *m.f.*
granul|e, granule, *m.*; ~**ation**, granulation, *f.*; ~**ar**, ~**ated**, granulé; ~**ous**, granuleu|x, ~se; *v.a.* ~**ate**, granuler.
grape, (*single berry*) ⚠ *not* grappe = '*bunch*', *but* grain de raisin, *m.*; ~**-fruit**, pamplemousse, *m.*; ~**-house**, serre à raisin, *f.*; ~**-picker**, vendang|eur, ~euse, *m.f.*; ~**-shot**, mitraille, *f.*; ~**-stone**, pépin de raisin, *m.*; *sour* ~*s! the* ~*s are sour*, ils sont trop verts.
graph, *s.* (*gelatine copying-machine*) appareil de polycopie à la gélatine, *m.*; *v.a.* polycopier à la gélatine.
graphic, (*writing, diagrams*) graphique; (*picturesque*) pittoresque; ~**ally**, (*vividly*) ⚠ *not* graphiquement, *which* = '*by writing or diagrams*', *but* d'une manière nette et précise.
graphite, (*min.*) graphite, *m.*
graphology, graphologie, *f.*
grapnel, grapple, *s.* grappin, *m.*; *also* '*grappling-iron*'.
grapple, *v.a.* (*with grapnel*) saisir avec un grappin; (*pers.*) saisir à bras le corps; *v.n.* ~ *with*, (*lit. and fig.*) lutter corps à corps avec.
grappling, *s. also* **grapple**, (*with pers.*) lutte corps à corps, *f.*
grasp, *s.* étreinte, *f.*; (*hold*) prise, *f.*; (*power*) pouvoir, *m.*; *within one's* ~, à sa portée.
grasp, *v.a.* saisir; (*hand*) serrer; (*understand*) comprendre*; *v.n.* ~ *at*, essayer de s'emparer de; (*fig.*) chercher à atteindre à.
grasping, cupide; ~**ly**, avidement.
grass, herbe, *f.*; (*turf*) gazon, *m.*; (*pasture*) pâturage, *m.*; *keep off the* ~*!* défense de marcher sur le gazon!; *put a horse out to* ~, mettre* un cheval au vert; ~**-green**, vert pré, *invar.*; ~**-land**, prairie, *f.*; ~**-mower**, tondeuse, *f.*; ~**-plot**, gazon, *m.*; *v.a.* (*turf*) gazonner.
grasshopper, sauterelle, *f.*; (*cicada*) cigale, *f.*
grassy, herbeu|x, ~se.
grate, *s.* (*iron bars*) grille, *f.*; (*fire*) foyer, *m.*
grate, *v.a.* (*nutmeg, &c.*) râper; (*teeth*) faire* grincer; *v.n.* grincer; *this noise* ~*s on my nerves, ears*, ce bruit me fait grincer des dents.
grateful, (*feeling gratitude*) reconnaissant (à, envers); (*comforting*) réconfortant; (*pleasant, delightful*) agréable; ~**ness**, (*gratitude*) reconnaissance, *f.*; ~**ly**, avec reconnaissance.
grater, râpe, *f.*
gratif|y, (*please*) satisfaire*; (*passions, &c.*) assouvir; (*money*) récompenser; **be** ~**ied**, être enchanté; ~**ying**, (*complimentary*) flatteu|r, ~se; ~**ication**, satisfaction, *f.*; ⚠ *which is never used in the sense of* '*pleasure*', *&c.* = contentement, *m.*
grating, *adj.* (*lit. and fig.*) agaçant; (*sound*) discordant; ~**ly**, d'une manière agaçante.
grating(s), *s.* (*iron*) grillage, *f.*
gratis, *adv.* gratis.
gratitude, reconnaissance, *f.*
gratuitous, gratuit; ~**ness**, gratuité, *f.* ⚠ *which does not* = '*gratuity*', *see below*; ~**ly**, gratuitement.
gratuity, gratification, *f.*
gratulat|e, ~**ion**, *see* CONGRATULATE, CONGRATULATION.
gratulatory, de félicitation.
grave, *s.* (*excavation*) fosse, *f.*; (*monument*) tombe, *f.*; (*monument and fig.*) tombeau, *m.*; ~**-clothes**, linceul, *m.*; ~**-digger**, fossoyeur, *m.*; ~**yard**, cimetière, *m.*
grav|e, *adj.* (*not gay, important, solemn, illness, state, accent*) grave; (*arousing anxiety*) inquiétant; (*not showy*) sévère; ~**ity**, (*importance, seriousness, phys.*) gravité, *f.*; (*weight*) poids, *m.*; ~**ely**, gravement.
grave, *v.a.* (*inscription, stone, fig.*) graver; (*naut.*) radouber.
gravel, *s.* gravier, *m.*; (*med.*) gravelle, *f.*; ~**-pit**, sablière, *f.*; ~ **walk**, allée sablée, *f.*; *v.a.* (*path*) sabler; (*puzzle*) réduire* à quia.
gravelly, graveleu|x, ~se.
graven, *p.p.* gravé.
graver, (*tool*) burin, *m.*
graving, ~**-dock**, *see* DOCK.
gravestone, tombe, *f.*
gravitate, graviter; (*sink*) être attiré vers le bas.
gravitation, gravitation, *f.*
gravy, jus, *m.*
gray, *see* GREY.
grayling, (*ichth.*) ombre, *f.*
graze, *v.a.* (*take to pasture*) faire*, mener paître; (*feed on grass, of cattle*) paître*; *v.n.* paître*; (*touch lightly*) frôler.
grazier, herbager, *m.*
grease, graisse, *f.*; *v.a.* graisser; ~ *the palm of*, (*bribe*) graisser la patte à.
greas|y, graisseu|x, ~se; (*spotted*) taché de graisse; ~**y pole**, mât de cocagne, *m.*; ~**iness**, graisse, *f.*
great, *s. the* ~, les grands, *m.pl.*
great, *adj.* (*lit., fig., large, important in rank, power, character, ability, extreme, downright*) grand; (*age*) avancé; + *-aunt, -grandfather, &c., see* AUNT, GRANDFATHER, *&c.*; ~ *bargain, see* BARGAIN; ~**coat**, *see below*; ~ *master*, (*Art*) grand maître, *m.*; ~ *time*, longtemps; *be* ~ *at*, (*capable at*) être fort en, pour; *be* ~ *on*, (*well up in*) être ferré sur; *a* ~ *many*, beaucoup (de);

have a ~ mind to, avoir bien envie de; **~er celandine,** *see* CELANDINE.
greatcoat, pardessus, *m.*; (*mil.*) capote, *f.*
greatly, (*very*) très; (*much*) beaucoup; (*by much*) de beaucoup; ~ *to be* + *p.p. act.* fort à + *inf.*; ~ *to be praised,* fort à louer.
greatness, (*lit. and fig.*) grandeur, *f.*; (*power*) puissance, *f.*
greave, (*piece of armour*) jambière, *f.*
grebe, (*ornith.*) grèbe, *m.*
Grecian, *s.* (*Greek scholar*) helléniste, *m.*; *adj.* (*facial outlines and arch.*) grec, -que.
greed (greediness), (*lit. and fig.*) avidité, *f.*; **~y,** goulu; (*eager for*) avide de; **~ily,** (*lit. and fig.*) avidement.
Greek, *adj.* (*when an adj. use small letter*) *and s.m.f.* Grec, -que; (*lang.*) grec, *m.*; ~ *fire,* feu grégeois, *m.*; *that's ~ to me,* c'est de l'hébreu pour moi.
green, *s.* vert, *m.*; (*verdure, greenery*) verdure, *f.*; (*her.*) sinople, *m.*; (*enclosed space of green*) place (gazonnée), *f.*; **~s,** (*vegs.*) légumes verts, *m.pl.*
green, *adj.* (*colour, unripe*) vert; (*silly, credulous*) naï|f, ~ve; (*pale*) blême; **~-fly,** puceron, *m.*; ~ **peas,** petits pois, *m.pl.*; **~-room,** (*theatr.*) foyer des artistes, *m.*; *v.a.n.* verdir; **~ness,** verdure, *f.*; (*fruit and old age*) verdeur, *f.*; (*credulity*) naïveté, *f.*
greenery, verdure, *f.*
greenfinch, (*ornith.*) verdier, *m.*
greengage, reine-Claude, *f.* (*pl.* reines-Claude).
greengrocer, fruiti|er, ~ère, *m.f.*
greenhorn, blanc-bec, *m.*
greenhouse, serre, *f.*
greenish, verdâtre.
greenstone, roche verte, *f.*
greensward, gazon, *m.*
greenwood, forêt verte, *f.*
greet, *v.a.* saluer; (*with applause, &c.*) accueillir*.
greeting, *s.* salutation, *f.*; (*reception*) accueil, *m.*
gregarious, grégaire.
Gregorian, (*calendar, chant*) grégorien, -ne.
grenad|e, (*mil.*) grenade, *f.*; **~ier,** grenadier, *m.*
grenadine, (*pomegranate syrup*) grenadin, *m.*; (*silk*) grenadine, *f.*
grey, gray, *s.* gris, *m.*; (*grey tone*) ton gris, *m.*
grey, gray, *adj.* gris; **~-brown,** gris de lin, *invar.*; **turn ~,** grisonner; **~-headed,** à cheveux gris; **~ness,** couleur grise, *f.*
greybeard, grison, *m.*
greyhound, lévrier, *m.*, levrette, *f.*; ⚠ *not 'leveret' which* = levraut.
greyish, grisâtre.
greylag, (*ornith.*) oie sauvage, *f.*
grid, (*cul.*) gril, *m.*; (*iron bars*) grille, *f.*; (*motor*) porte-bagages, *m.invar.*
gridiron, (*cul. and naut.*) gril, *m.*
grief, chagrin, *m.*; ⚠ *not* grief *which* = *'grievance', 'wrong'*; *come to ~,* tourner mal.
grievance, grief, *m.*; (*injury*) tort, *m.*
grieve, *v.a.* affliger; *v.n.* s'affliger.
grievous, (*distressing*) affligeant; (*serious*) grave; (*heinous*) affreu|x, ~se; **~ly,** cruellement; (*severely, dangerously*) grièvement.
griffin, (*myth.*) griffon, *m.*
griffon, (*dog*) griffon, *m.*
grig, (*small eel*) petite anguille, *f.*; (*cricket*) cri-cri, *m.*; *as merry as a ~,* gai comme un pinson.
grill, *s.* (*cul.*) gril, *m.*; *v.a.* griller.
grim, (*stern*) sévère; (*forbidding*) renfrogné; (*gruesome*) macabre; (*sardonic*) sardonique; **~ness,** sévérité, *f.*; (*manner*) air sinistre, *m.*; **~ly,** (*inflexibly*) inflexiblement; (*manner*) d'un air sinistre.
grimalkin, vieille chatte, *f.*; (*pers.*) vieille sorcière, *f.*
grim|e, crasse, *f.*; ⚠ *not* grime *which* = *'old fogy'*; **~iness,** malpropreté, *f.*; **~y,** crasseu|x, ~se; *v.a.* noircir.
grin, (grinning), rire, *m.*; (*grimace*) grimace, *f.*; *v.n.* grimacer; ~ *at,* faire* des grimaces à; ~ *and bear it,* souffrir* en souriant.
grind, *v.a.* (*corn, coffee*) moudre*; (*crush*) broyer; (*poor, &c.*) pressurer; (*knife*) repasser; (*on a whetstone*) émoudre*; *v.n.* (*corn, &c.*) se moudre; (*whet*) s'aiguiser; (*grate*) grincer; (*work hard, slang*) potasser; *p.p. 'ground', see* GLASS.
grinder, (*knife*) rémouleur, *m.*; (*tooth*) molaire, *f.*; (*crushing-machine*) broyeuse, *f.*
grinding, grind, *s.* (*corn, coffee, &c.*) mouture, *f.*; (*pulverizing*) broyage, *m.*; (*teeth, sound*) grincement, *m.*
grindstone, meule, *f.*
grip, *s.* étreinte, *f.*; (*understanding*) compréhension, *f.*; (*hold*) prise, *f.*; **~-sack,** (*U.S.A.*) valise, *f.*; ~ *of the hand,* poignée de main, *f.*; *v.a.* étreindre*; (*audience, &c.*) empoigner.
gripe, *s.* (*clutches, fig.*) griffes, *f.pl.*; **~s,** (*colic*) tranchées, *f.pl.*; *v.a.* (*clutch*) empoigner; (*pinch*) serrer; (*colic*) donner des tranchées à.
grisly, horrible.
grist, blé à moudre, *m*; *bring ~ to the mill,* faire* venir l'eau au moulin.
gristl|e, cartilage, *m.*; **~y,** cartilagineu|x, ~se.
grit, gravier, *m.*; (*pluck*) courage, *m.*; **~ty,** graveleu|x, ~se.
grizzled, (*hair, &c.*) grisonnant.
grizzly, grisâtre.
groan, groaning, *s.* gémissement, *m.*; (*grunt*) grognement, *m.*
groan, *v.n.* (*pain, sorrow*) gémir; (*grunt, grumble*) grogner; ~ *under,* (*fig.*) gémir sous.
groats, gruau d'avoine, *m.*
grocer, épici|er, ~ère, *m.f.*; *~'s shop, stores,* épicerie, *f.*
grocery, épicerie, *f.*

grog, grog, *m.*; **~gy,** (*drink*) gris; (*unsteady*) chancelant.
groin, (*anat.*) aine, *f.*; (*arch.*) arête, *f.*; ⚠ groin = '*snout' in English.*
gromwell, (*bot.*) grémil, *m.*
groom, *s.* palefrenier, *m.*; ⚠ *French* groom, *m.* = *young manservant chiefly in hotels*; *v.a.* (*horse*) panser; *well ~ed,* (*man*) bien astiqué.
groomsman, garçon d'honneur, *m.*
groove, rainure, *f.*; (*pulleys*) gorge, *f.*; (*arch.*) cannelure, *f.*; *get into a ~,* être routini|er, ~ère; *v.a.* rainer; (*flute*) canneler.
grope, *v.n.* tâtonner; *~ for, after,* chercher à tâtons.
grosbeak, (*ornith.*) gros-bec, *m.*
gross, *s.* grosse, *f.*
gross, (*coarse, vulgar, error, insult, vice, mind*) grossi|er, ~ère; (*obese, coarse*) gros, -se; (*flagrant*) flagrant; (*comm.*) brut; *~ amount,* montant brut, *m.*; *~ proceeds,* produit brut, *m.*; *~ weight,* poids brut, *m.*; **~ness,** grossièreté, *f.*; (*crime, injustice*) énormité, *f.*; **~ly,** (*lit. and fig.*) grossièrement.
grotesque, *adj. and s.m.* grotesque; **~ly,** grotesquement.
grotto, grot, grotte, *f.*
ground, *s.* terre, *f.*; (*sports*) terrain, *m.*; (*reason*) raison, *f.*; (*territory*) territoire, *m.*; (*space covered*) distance, *f.*; (*foundation*) fondement, *m.*; (*paint., fabric, naut.*) fond, *m.*; **~s,** (*of a house*) jardins, *m.pl.*; (*coffee, &c.*) marc, *m.*; *piece of ~,* terrain, *m.*; *be above ~,* (*alive*) être vivant; *have no ~ to,* ne pas avoir lieu de; *fall to the ~,* tomber (être) à terre (tomber par terre *has a sense of injury*); (*fig.*) tomber dans l'eau; *give ~,* céder le terrain; *give ~ for,* donner raison à + *noun,* de + *inf.*; *hold, keep one's ~,* tenir* bon; *level, raze to the ~,* raser; *lose ~,* perdre du terrain; *paw the ~,* (*horse*) piaffer; *on the ~ of, that,* sous prétexte de, que; **~-floor,** rez-de-chaussée, *m.*; **~-ivy,** (*bot.*) lierre terrestre, *m.*; **~-plan,** plan du rez-de-chaussée, *m.*; **~-rent,** rente foncière, *f.*; **~-swell,** lame de fond, *f.*
ground, *v.a.* (*base hopes, ideas, &c.*) fonder; (*teach*) enseigner les premiers principes à; (*ship*) échouer; *~ arms!* armes à terre!; *v.n.* (*naut.*) (s')échouer.
grounding, (*naut.*) échouement, *m.*; (*teaching*) instruction élémentaire, *f.*
groundless, sans fondement; **~ness,** manque de fondement, *m.*; **~ly,** sans fondement; *~ quarrel,* querelle d'Allemand, *f.*
groundling, (*ichth.*) poisson de fond, *m.*
groundsel, (*bot.*) séneçon, *m.*
groundwork, (*lit. and fig.*) fondement, *m.*
group, *s.* groupe, *m.*; *v.a.* grouper; *v.n.* se grouper.
grouping, groupement, *m.*
grouse, (*ornith.*) tétras, *m.*; **sand-~,** ganga, *m.*; **hazel-~,** gélinotte, *f.*
grouse, (*slang* = '*grumble*') rouspéter.
grout, (*arch.*) coulis, *m.*
grove, *s.* bocage, *m.*; (*clump of trees*) bosquet, *m.*
grovel, ramper; *~ in,* se vautrer dans.
grovelling, *adj.* rampant.
grow, *v.a.* (*plants, &c.*) cultiver; (*beard*) laisser pousser; *be ~n over with,* être couvert de.
grow, *v.n.* (*pers.*) grandir; (*plants, &c.*) croître*; (*become*) devenir* (être); (*fig.* = '*increase*') augmenter; *~ less,* diminuer; *it is ~ing late,* il se fait tard; *~ out of,* (*get rid of*) perdre; *~ to,* (*arrive at*) parvenir* à; *an object ~s on one,* on apprécie de plus en plus un objet.
grower, (*plant, tree*) arbre, *m.*, plante, *f.*, *use* qui croît vite, bien, lentement, *&c.*; (*pers.*) cultivat|eur, ~rice, *m.f.*
growing, *s.* croissance, *f.*; (*cultivation*) culture, *f.*; *adj.* croissant; (*pers.*) qui grandit.
growl, *s.* grondement, *m.*; (*grumble*) grognement, *m.*; *v.n.* gronder; (*mutter, grumble*) grommeler.
growler, *s.* (*grumbler*) grondeur, *m.*
grown-up, *s.* grande personne, *f.*; (*adj.*) grand.
growth, croissance, *f.*; (*production*) culture, *f.*; (*what is growing*) récolte, *f.*; (*increase*) accroissement, *m.*; (*shoot*) pousse, *f.*
groyne, (*to check drifting of beach*) épi, *m.*
grub, (*zool.*) larve, *f.*; (*slang* = '*food*') mangeaille, *f*
grub, *~ up,* (*roots*) déraciner; (*land*) essarter; *v.n.* (*dig*) fouir; **~bing-axe,** †hoyau, *m.*
grubber, money-~, grippe-sou, *m.*
grubby, (*dirty*) sale.
grudge, *s.* (*spite*) rancune, *f.*; (*hatred*) animosité, *f.*; *have, bear a ~ against,* en vouloir à; *v.a.* (*a gift, &c., to pers.*) donner à contre-cœur à.
grudging, *adj.* (*pers.*) envieu|x, ~se; (*gift, &c.*) donné à contre-cœur; **~ly,** à contre-cœur.
gruel, gruau, *m.*; (*water*) gruau à l'eau.
gruelling, *s.* (*punishment, &c., slang*) râclée, *f.*; *adj.* éreintant.
gruesome, macabre.
gruff, bourru; (*voice*) rauque; **~ness,** brusquerie, *f.*; **~ly,** d'un ton bourru, aigre.
grumble, grumbling, *s.* grognement, *m.*
grumble, *v.n.* grommeler; (*colloq.*) ronchonner; *~ about,* se plaindre* de.
grumbler, grognon, *m.*
grumblingly, en grommelant.
grumpy, grumpish, bourru.
grunt, *s.* (*pig and pers.*) grognement, *m.*
grunt, *v.n.* (*pig*) grogner; (*pers.*) grognonner.
grunter, *s.* (*pig*) porc, *m.*; (*pers.*) grognon, *m.*

gruntingly, en grognant.
guaiacum, (*bot.*) gaïac, *m.*
guano, guano, *m.*
guarantee, (*pers.*) garant, -e, *m.f.*; (*pers. guaranteed*) garanti, -e, *m.f.*; (*security*) garantie, *f.*; ~ *contract,* cautionnement, *m.*; ~ *fund,* fonds de garantie, *m.*
guarantee, *v.a.* (*gen., payment, interest, answer for, pers.*) garantir; (*bills*) avaliser.
guard, *s.* (*care, vigilance, keeping, body of soldiers, fencing, sword*) garde, *f.*; (*train*) conducteur, *m.*; (*goods train*) garde de convoi, *m.*; **~s,** soldats de la Garde, *m.pl.*; **~'s van,** fourgon, *m.*; *be on ~,* être de garde; *be on, off one's ~,* être, ne pas être sur ses gardes; *be thrown off one's ~,* être pris au dépourvu; *mount ~,* monter la garde; **~-house, ~-room,** corps de garde, *m.*; ⚠ gardes du corps, *m.pl.* = '*body-guard*', '*life guards*'; **~-ship,** stationnaire, *m.*
guard, *v.a.* (*watch over*) garder; (*thoughts, words*) surveiller.
guard, *v.n.* ~ *against,* se garder(contre + *s.*, de + *inf.*); (*take precautions*) prendre* des précautions (contre).
guarded, (*cautious*) réservé; **~ly** avec réserve.
guardedness, réserve, *f.*
guardian, (*keeper, warder, caretaker*) gardien, -ne, *m.f.*; (*law*) tut|eur, ~rice, *m.f.*; ~ **angel,** ange gardien, *m.*; *adj.* gardien, -ne.
guardianship, (*care*) garde, *f.*; (*law*) tutelle, *f.*
guardsman, officier *or* soldat de la Garde, *m.*
guava, (*fruit*) goyave, *f.*; (*tree*) goyavier, *m.*
gudgeon, (*ichth. and coupling-bolt*) goujon, *m.*; ⚠ *not used in French for* '*dupe*' *which* = dupe, *f.*; (*crank-pin*) tourillon, *m.*
guelder-rose, (*bot.*) boule-de-neige, *f.*
Guelph, *s.* Guelfe, *m.f.*; **~ic,** *adj.* guelfe.
guerdon, guerdon, *m.*
guerrilla, ~ *warfare,* guérilla, *f.*; (*troops*) guérillas, *f.pl.*
guess, guesswork, *s.* conjecture, *f.*; *at a ~,* au jugé.
guess, *v.a.n.* deviner; (*conjecture*) conjecturer; ~ *right,* (*make a happy ~*) deviner juste.
guest, invité, *m.*; (*at table*) convive, *m.*; (*visitor or at hotel*) hôte, -sse, *m.f.*; *paying-~,* pensionnaire, *m.f.*
guffaw, *v.n.* s'esclaffer.
guidance, direction, *f.*; (*information*) gouverne, *f.*; *for your ~,* pour votre gouverne.
guide, *s.* (*lit., fig., mil., mach., naut.*) guide, *m.*; **~-book,** guide, *m.*; **~-post,** poteau indicateur, *m.*
guide, *v.a.* (*lit. and fig.*) guider; (*conduct*) conduire*.
guidon, (*mil.*) guidon, *m.*
guild, *s.* corporation, *f.*; **~hall,** hôtel de ville, *m.*
guile, (*deceit*) ruse, *f.*; (*trickery*) artifice, *m.*; **~ful,** artificieu|x, ~se; **~fully,** artificieusement.
guileless, sans artifice; **~ness,** innocence, *f.*
guillemot, (*ornith.*) guillemot, *m.*
guilloche, guilloche work, (*arch.*) guillochis, *m.*
guillotine, guillotine, *f.*; ⚠ *not in parl. sense which* = *approx.* interruption des débats, *f.*; *v.a.* guillotiner.
guilt, guiltiness, culpabilité, *f.*
guiltless, innocent; (*fig., unacquainted with*) qui n'a jamais connu; (*not possessing*) exempt de; **~ness,** innocence, *f.*
guilty, coupable (de); (*which conveys guilt*) de coupable; *plead ~, not ~,* se déclarer coupable, innocent.
guinea, (*coin, fee*) guinée, *f.*; **~-fowl,** pintade, *f.*; **~-pig,** cobaye, *m.*
guise, (*dress*) costume, *m.*; (*external appearance*) aspect, *m.*; ⚠ *never* guise (*way, manner*) *in the sense of* '*appearance*'; (*pretence, mask*) manteau, *m.*
guitar, guitare, *f.*; **~-player,** guitariste, *m.f.*
gules, (*her.*) gueules, *m.pl.*
gulf, golfe, *m.*; (*fig.*) abîme, *m.*; (*abyss, whirlpool*) gouffre, *m.*
gull, (*small*) mouette, *f.*; (*large*) goéland, *m.*; **black-backed** ~, goéland brun, *m.*; (*dupe*) dupe, *f.*; (*colloq.*) poire, *f.*; *v.a.* duper.
gullet, (*throat*) gosier, *m.*
gullib|le, crédule; **~ility,** crédulité, *f.*
gully, ravin, *m.*; (*artificial to carry off water*) rigole, *f.*; **~-hole,** bouche d'égout, *f.*; *v.a.* raviner.
gulp, *s.* goulée, *f.*; *at one ~,* d'un seul trait.
gulp down, *v.a.* gober; (*tears, &c.*) ravaler; *v.n.* (*choke*) s'étouffer.
gum, *s.* (*teeth*) gencive, *f.*; (*to stick and on trees*) gomme, *f.*; **~-arabic,** gomme arabique; **~-resin,** gomme résine; **~-tree,** gommier, *m.*
gum, *v.a.* (*stick*) coller; (*coat with gum*) gommer; *~med label,* étiquette gommée, *f.*
gumboil, abcès des gencives, *m.*
gumm|y, gommeu|x, ~se; **~iness,** viscosité, *f.*
gumption, *have ~,* être débrouillard.
gun, (*musket, rifle*) fusil, *m.*; (*cannon*) canon, *m.*; **~s,** (*in shooting-party*) chasseurs, *m.pl.*; *salute of seven ~s,* salve de sept coups de canon, *f.*; *it is blowing great ~s,* il fait un vent à décorner les bœufs; *stick to one's ~s,* n'en pas démordre; **~-boat,** canonnière, *f.*; **~-carriage,** affût, *m.*; **~-cotton,** fulmicoton, *m.*; **~-layer,** pointeur, *m.*; **~-metal,** bronze à canon, *m.*; **~-room,** (*nav.*) sainte-barbe, *f.* (*pl.* saintes-barbes).

gunnel, *see* GUNWALE.
gunner, canonnier, *m.*; (*artilleryman*) artilleur, *m.*; (*officer*) officier d'artillerie, *m.*
gunnery, (*firing*) canonnage, *m.*; (*construction*) fabrication des canons, *f.*
gunpowder, poudre à canon, *f.* (*often* poudre *alone*); *Gunpowder Plot,* Conspiration des Poudres, *f.*
gunshot, (*rifle*) coup de fusil, *m.*; (*cannon*) coup de canon; (*gen.*) coup de feu, *m.*; *within* ~, à portée de fusil.
gunsmith, armurier, *m.*
gunwale, gunnel, (*naut.*) plat-bord, *m.*
gurgitation, bouillonnement, *m.*
gurgle, gurgling, glouglou, *m.*; (*brooks*) gazouillement, *m.*; *v.n.* faire* glouglou; (*streams*) gazouiller.
gurnard, gurnel, (*ichth.*) grondin, *m.*
gush, gushing, *s.* jaillissement, *m.*; (*effusiveness*) exubérance, *f.*
gush, *v.n.* (*be effusive*) être exubérant; ~ *out,* jaillir.
gushing, *adj.* (*water*) jaillissant; (*effusive*) exubérant; **~ly,** avec exubérance.
gusset, (*needlework*) gousset, *m.*
gust, *s.* (*wind*) rafale, *f.*; (*smoke, rain*) bouffée, *f.*; (*naut.*) risée, *f.*; (*passion*) accès, *m.*
gustation, gustation, *f.*
gusto, (*eagerness, zeal*) entrain, *m.*
gusty, orageu|x, ~se.
gut, *s.* (*defile*) goulet, *m.*; (*narrow passage*) boyau, *m.*; (*violins, &c.*) corde à boyau, *f.*; (*for fishing*) crin de Florence, *m.*; **~s,** (*entrails chiefly of animals*) boyaux, *m.pl.*; (*belly*) ventre, *m.*; *have* ~*s,* (*fam.*) avoir du cran.
gut, *v.a.* (*fish, &c.*) vider; **~ted,** (*by fire*) tout(e) brulé(e) sauf les murs.
gutta-percha, gutta-percha, *f.*
gutter, (*roof*) gouttière, *f.*; (*street*) ruisseau, *m.*; (*small trench*) rigole, *f.*
gutter, *v.a.* creuser; *v.n.* (*candle*) couler.
guttural, *s.* (*sound or letter*) gutturale, *f.*; *adj.* guttural; **~ly,** d'une manière gutturale.
guy, (*fright*) caricature, *f.*; *be a* ~, être mal fagoté; *U.S.A.* (*fellow*) type, *m.*; (*retaining rope*) corde de retenue, *f.*
guzzle, *v.a.n.* (*eat*) bâfrer; (*drink*) pinter.
guzzler, (*colloq.*) godailleur, *m.*
gymnasium, gymnase, *m.*; (*continental school*) lycée, *m.*
gymnast, gymnaste, *m.*
gymnastic, *adj.* gymnastique; *s.* **~s,** (*exercises*) gymnastique, *f.*
gyps|um, gypse, *m.*; **~eous,** gypseu|x, ~se.
gypsophila, (*bot.*) gypsophile, *f.*
gyrat|e, *v.n.* tournoyer; **~ion,** giration, *f.*; **~ory,** giratoire.
gyrometer, gyromètre, *m.*
gyroscope, gyroscope, *m.*
gyve, *s.* fer, *m.* (*usually pl.*); *v.a.* enchaîner.

H

ha! *interj.* †ha!
haberdasher, merc|ier, **~ière,** *m.f.*; **~y,** mercerie, *f.*
habergeon, (*coat of mail*) †haubergeon, *m.*
habiliment, accoutrement, *m.*; **~s,** vêtements, *m.pl.*
habit, (*settled tendency, practice*) habitude, *f.*; (*mind*) tournure, *f.*; (*body*) tempérament, *m.*; *fall into the* ~ *of,* prendre* l'habitude de; *from* ~, par habitude.
habitab|le, habitable; **~ility,** habitabilité, *f.*
habitant, habitant, *m.*
habitat, habitat, *m.*
habitation, (*inhabiting and place of abode*) habitation, *f.*
habitual, habituel, -le; **~ly,** habituellement.
habituate, habituer (à).
habitude, (*constitution*) constitution, *f.*; (*custom*) habitude, *f.*
hack, *s.* (*kick*) coup de pied, *m.*; (*miner's pick*) pioche, *f.*; (*hired horse*) cheval de louage, *m.*; (*worn-out horse*) rosse, *f.*; (*notch*) entaille, *f.*; **~-writer,** écrivain à gages, *m.*
hack, *v.a.* (*notch*) entailler; (*cutting blow*) †hacher; (*sword*) sabrer; (*kick*) donner un coup de pied à; *v.n.* (*cough*) tousser d'une toux sèche.
hackney, (*horse*) cheval de selle, *m.*; **~-coach,** fiacre, *m.*
hackneyed, banal.
haddock, (*ichth.*) aiglefin, *m.*; *smoked* ~, †haddock, *m.*
haemorrhage, hémorragie, *f.*
haft, (*handle of dagger, knife*) manche, *m.*
hag, *s.* vieille femme laide, *f.*; (*witch*) sorcière, *f.*; (*soft bog*) fondrière, *f.*; (*firm ground in bog*) terrain ferme, *m.*
haggard, †hagard.
haggle, *v.n.* marchander; ~ *over,* marchander, *v.a.*; **~r,** marchandeu|r, ~se.
haggling, marchandage, *m.*
hagiograph|y, hagiographie, *f.*; **~er,** hagiographe, *m.*
ha-ha, *s.* saut de loup, *m.*
ha ha! *interj.* †ha ha!
hail, *s.* (*frozen vapour, and hailstorm*) grêle, *f.*; (*salutation*) salut, *m.*; **~-stone,** grêlon, *m.*; *within* ~, (*gen. and naut.*) à portée de la voix.
hail, *v.a.* (*salute*) saluer; ~ *as king, &c.,* saluer roi, *&c.*; (*call to ship, pers.*) †héler; *v.n.* ~ *from,* être en provenance de.
hail! *interj.* salut!
hair, (*single of pers.*) cheveu, *m.*; (*hair of pers. as whole*) cheveux, *m.pl.*; ⚠ cheveu, *sing. never used for 'hair' as whole*; (*on body, animals*) poil, *m.*; (*horse*) crin, *m.*; (*pig, boar*) soies, *f.pl.*; *do one's* ~, se coiffer; *have one's* ~ *cut,* se faire* couper les cheveux; *part the* ~, faire* la raie; *tear one's* ~, s'arracher les cheveux; *keep your* ~ *on!,* (*slang*) ne vous em-

ballez pas!; *split* ~*s*, couper des cheveux en quatre; *without turning a* ~, sans sourciller; **~-net,** résille, *f.*; **~-shirt,** †haire, *f.*; **~-spring,** (*watches*) spiral, *m.*; **~-wash,** lotion capillaire, *f.*
hairbreadth, *s. be within a* ~ *of*, peu s'en falloir que + *subj. and* ne.
hairbrush, brosse à cheveux, *f.*
haircloth, cilice, *m.*
hairdresser, coiffeu|r, ~se, *m.f.*
hairpin, épingle à cheveux, *f.*
hairy, (*pers.*) chevelu; (*shaggy*) velu.
hake, (*ichth.*) merluche, *f.*
halber|d, ~t, †hallebarde, *f.*; **~dier,** †hallebardier, *m.*
halcyon, alcyon, *m.*; ~ *days*, jours alcyoniens, *m.pl.*
hale, *adj.* robuste; ~ *and hearty*, frais (fraîche) et dispos, -e.
hal|f, *s.* (*one of equal parts of a whole*) moitié, *f.*; (*half a whole*) demi, *m.*; (*half part, share of whole*) demie, *f.*; (*football, &c., half-back*) demi, *m.*; (*school*) trimestre, *m.*; **~f-price,** à moitié prix; **~f-way,** à moitié chemin; *two hours and a* ~*f*, deux heures et demie; *4.30*, quatre heures et demie; *a mile and a* ~*f*, un mille et demi; *cut in* ~*f*, couper en deux; *two* ~*ves make a whole*, deux demis valent un entier; *do things by* ~*ves*, faire* les choses à demi; *too large by* ~*f*, trop grand de moitié; *go* ~*ves with*, se mettre* de moitié avec.
half, *adj.* demi, -e, *after noun with concord,* + *hyphen and invar. before noun*: ~ *an hour*, une demi-heure (*cf. an hour and a* ~, une heure et demie); ~ *the time*, la moitié du temps; **~-brother,** demi-frère, *m.*; **~-holiday,** congé, *m.* (d'après-midi); **~-mast,** (*of flag*) en berne; **~-moon,** (*fort.*) demi-lune, *f.*; **~-mourning,** demi-deuil, *m.*; ~ **open,** entr'ouvert; **~-pay,** demi-solde, *f.*; **~penny,** (*approx.*) sou, *m.*; **~-sister,** demi-sœur, *f.*; **~-time,** (*sport*) mi-temps, *m.*; **~-year,** semestre, *m.*; *~-year's salary, &c.*, semestre, *m.*; **~-yearly,** (*adj.*) semestriel, -le, *m.*
half, *adv.* à moitié; *not* ~, (*colloq.* = *very much*) tout à fait; **~-bound,** *see* BIND; **~-breed,** *adj. and s.m.f.* métis, -se; **~-hearted,** peu empressé; **~-heartedly,** sans empressement; *~-way up the hill*, à mi-côte.
halibut, (*ichth.*) flétan, *m.*
hall, *salle, f.*; ⚠ *not* halle *which* = '*market-hall or place*'; (*of public body*) hôtel, *m.*; (*large dining*) réfectoire, *m.*; **~-mark,** (*gold and silver*) contrôle, *m.*
hallelujah, *see* ALLELUIA.
halliard, *see* HALYARD.
hallo, halloa, *v.n.* crier; *interj.* holà!
halloo, *v.n.* (*hunt.*) crier taïaut; *interj.* (*hunt.*) taïaut!
hallow, *s.* (*saint*) saint, *m.*; *All-hallows*, Toussaint, *f.*; *v.a.* (*honour as holy*) sanctifier; **~ed,** (*sacred*) sacré.
hallucina|te, halluciner; **~tion,** hallucination, *f.*
halm, *see* HAULM.
halo, (*sun, moon*) †halo, *m.*; (*glory*) auréole, *f.*
halt, (*gen., mil., rail.*) †halte, *f.*; *v.a.* (*mil.*) faire* faire †halte à; (*stop*) arrêter; *v.n.* (*mil.*) faire †halte; (*stop*) s'arrêter; (*limp*) boiter; (*hesitate*) hésiter.
halter, *s.* (*for hanging and fig.*) †hart, *f.*; (*horses*) licou, *m.*
halter, *v.a.* (*horses*) attacher avec un licou; (*hang pers.*) mettre* la corde au cou de.
halting, *s.* boitement, *m.*; *adj.* (*lame*) boiteu|x, ~se; (*hesitating*) hésitant; **~ly,** (*limping*) clopin-clopant; (*speech*) en ânonnant.
halve, *v.a.* partager en deux.
halyard, (*naut.*) drisse, *f.*
ham, (*anat.*) jarret, *m.*; (*thigh of hog*) jambon, *m.*; **~s,** fesses, *f.pl.*
hamadryad, hamadryade, *f.*
hame, (*horse's collar*) attelle, *f.*
hamlet, †hameau, *m.*
hammer, *s.* marteau, *m.*; (*auction*) enchères, *f.pl.*; *yellow-*~, (*ornith.*) bruant jaune, *m.*; **~-cloth,** †housse, *f.*; **~-head,** (*ichth.*) marteau, *m.*; *be sold under the* ~, se vendre aux enchères.
hammer, (*lit. and fig.*) marteler; (*enemy in war*) †harceler; ~ *in*, (*nails, &c.*) enfoncer; ~ *into*, (*head, &c.*) faire* entrer de force dans; ~ *out*, (*verses, &c.*) marteler; (*ideas*) élaborer; **~ed,** (*metals*) forgé.
hammering, *s.* (*metals, &c.*) martelage, *m.*; (*noise*) bruit de marteau, *m.*
hammock, †hamac, *m.*
hamper, *s.* manne, *f.*; (*fish, game*) bourriche, *f.*
hamper, *v.a.* (*lit. and fig.*) empêtrer.
hamster, (*zool.*) †hamster, *m.*
hamstring, jarret, *m.*; *v.a.* couper le jarret à.
hand, *s.* (*lit., pledge of marriage, cards, height of horse*) main, *f.*; (*workman*) ouvrier, *m.*; (*naut.*) matelot, *m.*; (*dials, clocks*) aiguille, *f.*; (*writing*) écriture, *f.*; *poor, &c.* ~, (*cards*) mauvais jeu, *m.*; *second-*~, (*purchase*) d'occasion; *~s up!* (*interj.*) †haut les mains!; *at* ~, sous la main; *in* ~, (*cash*) en caisse; *off*~, *adj.* brusque; *adv. off-*~, (*extempore*) †haut la main; (*impromptu*) impromptu; *on the one* ~ . . . *on the other*, d'une part . . . d'autre part; *to* ~, (*letter, money, &c.*) reçu, *invar.* + *item in question*; *with a high* ~, †haut la main; *be* ~ *and glove with*, être comme les deux doigts de la main; *have, get the upper* ~, avoir le dessus; *get one's* ~ *in*, se faire* la main; *lay* ~*s on*, mettre* la main sur; *lay violent* ~*s on*, faire* main basse sur; *lend a* ~, (*help*) donner un coup de main (à); *he's had a* ~ *in it*, il a trempé là-dedans; *live from* ~ *to mouth*, vivre* au jour le jour; *set one's* ~ *to*, mettre* la main à; *have a good* ~,

(*writing*) avoir une belle main; *he is his right ~*, il est son bras droit; *~s up!* †haut les mains!; **~-bag,** sac à main, *m.*; **~-brake,** (*motor, &c.*) frein à main, *m.*; **~-cart,** charrette à bras, *f.*; **~-gallop,** petit galop, *f.*; **~-grenade,** grenade à main, *f.*; **~-lever,** manette, *f.*; **~-loom,** métier à main, *m.*; **~-luggage,** bagages à main, *m.pl.*; **~-made,** fait à la main; **~-mill,** moulin à bras, *m.*; **~-rail,** garde-fou, *m.*; **~-sewn,** cousu à la main; *~-to-~ fight,* lutte corps à corps, *f.*
hand, *v.a.* (*help out of, into vehicle*) donner la main à . . . pour monter, descendre, etc.; (*letter, money*) remettre*; (*dishes*) passer; ~ **down,** transmettre*; ~ **in,** (*parcel*) déposer; (*resignation*) donner; ~ **over,** remettre*; ~ **round,** passer.
handbell, sonnette, *f.*
handbill, prospectus, *m.*
handbook, manuel, *m.*
handcuffs, menottes, *f.pl.*
handcuff, *v.a.* mettre* les menottes à.
handed, high-~, autoritaire; **left-~,** gauch|er, ~ère; **open-~,** généreu|x, ~se; **red-~,** en flagrant délit; **right-~,** droiti|er, ~ère; **short-~,** à court de personnel; **single-~,** seul.
handful, poignée, *f.*; *by ~s,* à belles mains.
handgrip, (*handshake*) poignée de main, *f.*
handicap, †handicap, *m.*
handicraft, (*trade*) métier manuel, *m.*; (*skill*) habileté manuelle, *f.*; **~sman,** artisan, *m.*
handiwork, ouvrage, *m.*
handkerchief, mouchoir, *m.*; *throw the ~ to,* jeter le mouchoir à.
handle, *s.* (*of implement*) manche, *m.*; (*baskets*) anse, *f.*; (*door, sword*) poignée, *f.*; (*wheelbarrow, &c.*) bras, *m.*; (*frying-pan, saucepan*) queue, *f.*; *~ to one's name,* titre, *m.*; *give a ~ to,* (*slander, &c.*) donner prise à.
handle, *v.a.* (*weapon, tool, business, sums of money*) manier; (*ship*) manœuvrer; (*goods*) manutentionner; (*cash*) manipuler; (*treat of pers.*) traiter.
handlebar, (*bicycle*) guidon, *m.*
handling, maniement, *m.*
handmaid, servante, *f.*
han(d)sel, étrenne, *f.*
handsome, (*lit. and fig.*) beau, belle, (m. + *vowel or silent* h.) bel; (*generous*) généreu|x, ~se; **~ness,** beauté, *f.*; (*generosity*) générosité, *f.*; **~ly,** (*finely*) élégamment; (*generously*) généreusement.
hand|y, (*pers.*) adroit; (*easy to handle*) commode; (*near*) sous la main; **~yman,** homme à toutes mains, *m.*; **~iness,** (*skill*) adresse, *f.*; (*ease, convenience*) commodité, *f.*; **~ily,** adroitement; (*with ease*) commodément.
hang, *v.a.* pendre; (*walls with paper*) tapisser; (*with tapestry*) tendre; (*bells*) poser; *~ down,* (*head, &c.*) baisser; *~ out,* (*washing*) étendre; *~ up,* (*coat, picture*) accrocher.
hang, *v.n.* pendre; (*lean*) se pencher; (*cling*) s'accrocher à; (*depend*) dépendre de; *~ in the balance,* être en balance; *~ by a thread,* ne tenir qu'à un fil; *~ on the lips of,* être suspendu aux lèvres de; *~ about,* (*loiter*) traînasser; *~ back,* (*hesitate*) hésiter; *~ behind,* rester en arrière; *~ loose,* pendiller; *~ on,* (*arm of pers.*) s'appuyer sur; (*depend*) dépendre de; (*hold out*) tenir* bon; *~ on to,* se cramponner à; *~ out,* (*project*) saillir; (*colloq. for 'live'*) percher; *~ over,* (*lit. and fig.*) planer sur; (*threaten*) menacer; (*buildings*) surplomber.
hangar, †hangar, *m.*
hanger, *s.* (*hook*) crochet, *m.*; (*knife*) coutelas de chasse, *m.*
hanger-on, (*parasite*) parasite, *m.*; (*intruder, bore*) importun, -e, *m.f.*
hanging, *s.* (*act of hanging*) suspension, *f.*; (*on gallows*) pendaison, *f.*; **~s,** (*rooms*) tenture, *f.*
hanging, *adj.* ~ **lamp,** suspension, *f.*; ~ **gardens,** jardins suspendus, *m.pl.*; ~ **matter,** cas pendable, *m.*
hangman, bourreau, *m.*
hank, (*skein*) écheveau, *m.*
hanker, *~ after, v.n.* soupirer après; **~ing** *after, s.* grande envie (de), *f.*
hanky-panky, (*underhand dealing*) tour de passe-passe, *m.*
hanseatic, †hanséatique.
hansom, (*veh.*) cab, *m.*
haphazard, *s.* †hasard, *m.*; *adj.* fait au †hasard; *adv.* par †hasard.
hapless, infortuné.
haply, par †hasard.
happen, (*occur*) arriver* (être); (*have the chance, fortune to*) se trouver (par †hasard) + *inf.*; *~ upon,* rencontrer par †hasard; *if you ~ to lose it,* s'il vous arrive de le perdre.
happening, événement, *m.*
happ|y, (*lucky, pleased, fortunate circumstances, expressions, &c.*) heureu|x, ~se; (*content, satisfied*) content (de); **~iness,** bonheur, *m.*; (*of word, expression, style*) félicité, *f.*; **~ily,** (*in all senses*) heureusement.
happy-go-lucky, insouciant.
harangue, *s.* †harangue, *f.*; *v.a.n.* †haranguer.
haras, (*horses*) †haras, *m.*
harass, (*with cares*) accabler (de); (*torment*) tourmenter; (*enemy*) †harceler; ⚠ †harasser *is more 'to tire out'.*
harassment, souci, *m.*
harbinger, précurseur, *m.*; (*fig.*) avant-coureur, *m.*; *v.a.* annoncer.
harbour, *s.* (*sea, river*) port, *m.*; (*refuge*) asile, *m.*; *inner ~,* arrière-port, *m.*; *outer ~,* avant-port, *m.*; ~ **dues,** droits de port, *m.pl.*; **~-master,** capitaine de port, *m.*
harbour, *v.a.* héberger; (*evil thoughts, &c.*) nourrir; *v.n.* (*naut.*) se mettre* à l'abri.
harbourage, abri, *m.*

hard, *adj.* (*heart, life, tunes, to touch, to cut, harsh*) dur; (*difficult*) difficile; (*severe*) sévère; (*climate, winter*) rigoureu|x, ~se; (*frost*) fort; ~ **cash,** espèces sonnantes, *f.pl.*; ~ **labour,** (*for criminals*) travaux forcés, *m.pl.*; ~ *and fast, see* FAST; ~ **luck,** pas de chance; *grow* ~, se durcir; ~ *of hearing,* dur d'oreille; ~ *as nails,* dur comme fer; *become, be* ~ *on,* être dur pour; ~ *up,* (*money*) gêné; ~**ness,** (*lit., fig., treatment, &c.*) dureté, *f.*; (*heart*) endurcissement, *m.*; (*frost*) rigueur, *f.*; (*difficulty*) difficulté, *f.*; ~**ly,** *see below.*

hard, *adv.* durement; (*pop. of work, &c.*) rudement; (*very much*) fort; ~**-featured,** aux traits durs; ~**-hearted,** au cœur dur; *be* ~ *up,* être dans la gêne; ~ *by,* tout près; ~ *on, upon,* (*close to*) tout près de; *rain* ~, pleuvoir* fort; *work* ~, travailler dur; *it will go* ~ *with you,* il vous en cuira; ~**-boiled,** *see* BOIL; ~*-mouthed,* (*horse*) dur de bouche; ~*-working,* laborieu|x, ~se; *be* ~ *put to it to,* être très embarrassé pour; *be* ~ *hit,* être bien touché.

harden, *v.a.* durcir; (*fig.*) endurcir; *v.n.* durcir; (*fig.*) s'endurcir; (*comm. shares*) se tendre.

hardihood, (*boldness*) †hardiesse, *f.*; (*audacity*) audace, *f.*

hardily, (*boldly*) †hardiment; (*robustly, with endurance*) vigoureusement.

hardiness, intrépidité, *f.*; (*robustness*) vigueur, *f.*

hardly, (*in a hard manner*) durement; (*with difficulty*) difficilement; (*harshly*) rudement; (*scarcely*) à peine.

hardship, (*privation, want*) privation, *f.*; (*trial*) épreuve, *f.*; (*act of injustice*) injustice, *f.*; (*of a task, &c.*) difficulté, *f.*; *undergo* ~*s,* en voir* de dures.

hardware, quincaillerie, *f.*; ~**man,** quincailler, *m.*

hardy, vigoureu|x, ~se; ⚠ *not* hardi *which* = '*bold*', '*rash*', '*impudent*'; (*of plants*) rustique.

hare, lièvre, *m.*; ~**-brained,** écervelé; *jugged* ~, civet, *m.*; ~**'s foot,** (*bot.*) pied de lièvre, *m.*; *run with the* ~ *and hunt with the hounds,* ménager la chèvre et le chou; ~**-lip,** bec de lièvre, *m.*

harebell, (*bot.*) campanule, *f.*

harem, †harem, *m.*

haricot, (*mutton stew*) ragoût de mouton, *m.*

hark, *v.n.* ~ *to,* écouter; ~ *back to,* (*fig.*) revenir* toujours à; *interj.* écoute! écoutez!

harlequin, arlequin, *m.*; ~**ade,** arlequinade, *f.*

harlot, prostituée, *f.*

harm, mal, *m.*; (*injury, what is contrary to justice, reason*) tort, *m.*; (*misfortune*) malheur, *m.*; *have no* ~ *in one,* ne pas être méchant; *do* ~ *to,* nuire* à; *get out of* ~*'s way,* se garer.

harm, nuire* à; (*wrong*) faire* tort à.

harmattan, (*African wind*) †harmattan, *m.*

harmful, nuisible (à); ~**ness,** caractère nuisible, *m.*

harmless, inoffensi|f, ~ve; ~**ness,** innocence, *f.*; ~**ly,** innocemment.

harmonic, harmonique; ~**s,** harmonie, *f.*; ~**ally,** harmoniquement.

harmoni|ca, ~**con,** harmonica, *m.*

harmonious, harmonieu|x, ~se; (*fig.*) en bon accord; ~**ly,** harmonieusement.

harmonist, harmoniste, *m.*

harmonium, harmonium, *m.*

harmonize, *v.a.* (*mus.*) harmoniser; ~ *with,* harmoniser avec; *v.n.* (*artistic effect*) s'harmoniser (avec).

harmony, (*science, fig., sounds, of parts*) harmonie, *f.*; *be in* ~ *with,* (*of style, effects*) être d'accord avec.

harness, †harnais, *m.*; ~**-maker,** bourrelier, *m.*; ~**-room,** sellerie, *f.*

harness, *v.a.* (*horse*) †harnacher.

harp, †harpe, *f.*; *jew's-*~, guimbarde, *f.*

harp, play the harp, jouer de la harpe; *keep* ~*ing on one string,* (*fig.*) rabâcher.

harper, harp-player, joueur de harpe, *m.*

harp|ist, †harpiste, *m.*; ~**ing,** sons de (la) harpe, *m.pl.*

harpoon, *s.* †harpon, *m.*; ~**er,** †harponneur, *m.*; *v.a.* †harponner.

harpsichord, clavecin, *m.*

harpy, (*myth. and pers.*) †harpie, *f.*

ha(a)rquebus, arquebuse, *f.*

harridan, vieille mégère, *f.*

harrier, (*hunt.*) lévrier, levrette, *m.f.*; (*ornith.*) busard, *m.*

harrow, *s.* †herse, *f.*; **rest-** ~, (*bot.*) bugrane, *f.*; *v.a.* †herser.

harrow, *v.a.* (*torture heart, feelings*) déchirer; (*pillage*) ravager.

harrowing, *adj.* (*heart-rending*) déchirant.

harry, (*ravage*) ravager; (*despoil person*) dépouiller; (*harass, worry*) †harceler.

harsh, (*pers.*) revêche; (*taste*) âpre; (*punishment, &c.*) rigoureu|x, ~se; (*repugnant*) blessant; (*sounds*) discordant; ~**ness,** (*want of feeling*) dureté, *f.*; (*sounds*) discordance, *f.*; ~**ly,** (*lit. and fig.*) durement; *sound* ~*ly,* écorcher les oreilles.

hart, cerf, *m.*; ~**'s-tongue,** (*bot.*) scolopendre, *f.*

hartshorn, corne de cerf, *f.*; (*ammonia*) alcali volatil, *m.*

hartwort, (*bot.*) séséli, *m.*

harum-scarum, *adj.* (*pers.*) écervelé.

harvest, *s.* moisson, *f.*; (*fig.*) fruits, *m.pl.*; (*crop*) récolte, *f.*; ~**-bug,** aoûtat, *m.*; ~**-home,** fête de la moisson, *f.*

harvest, *v.a.* (*lit. and fig.*) moissonner; (*gather*) récolter.

harvester, moissonneu|r, ~se, *m.f.*; (*machine*) moissonneuse-faucheuse, *f.*

hash, *s.* (*meat*) †hachis, *m.*; (*fig.*) gâchis, *m.*; *make a* ~ *of,* faire* un joli gâchis de; *v.a.* (*meat and fig.*) †hacher.

hash|ish, ~eesh, †hachi|sh, ~sch, *m.*
haslet, (*meat*) fressure, *f.*
hasp, *s.* (*fastening*) moraillon, *m.*; (*skein*) écheveau, *m.*
hassock, agenouilloir, *m.*
haste, *s.* †hâte, *f.*; (*impatience*) impatience, *f.*; *in ~,* à la †hâte; *post-~,* en toute †hâte; *make ~,* se dépêcher; *more ~ less speed,* trop de †hâte gâte tout.
hasten, *v.a.* †hâter; *v.n.* se dépêcher.
hasty, (*hurried*) précipité; (*quick-tempered*) emporté; (*thoughtless*) irréfléchi; (*prompt*) prompt; **~iness,** (*hurry*) précipitation, *f.*; (*impatience*) impatience, *f.*; **~ily,** à la hâte; (*angrily*) avec colère.
hat, chapeau, *m.*; **~-band,** ruban, *m.*; **top-~,** †haut de forme, *m.*; **~-box,** carton à chapeau, *m.*; **~-brush,** brosse à chapeau, *m.*; **~-stand,** porte-chapeau, *m. invar.*; **~-peg,** patère, *f.*; **~-pin,** épingle à chapeau, *f.*; *three-cornered ~,* tricorne, *m.*; *~ off!* chapeau bas!; *take one's ~ off to,* saluer.
hatband, (*ribbon*) ruban de chapeau, *m.*; (*with buckle*) bourdalou, *m.*
hatch, *s.* (*naut.*) panneau, *m.*; (*brood*) couvée, *f.*; (*lower half of door*) porte coupée, *f.*; (*floodgate*) vanne, *f.*; *batter down ~es,* condamner les panneaux.
hatch, *v.a.* faire* éclore; (*plot, &c.*) couver.
hatch, *v.n.* éclore* (être); (*plot, &c.*) se tramer.
hatchet, †hachette, *f.*
hatchment, (*her.*) écusson, *m.*
hatchway, écoutille, *f.*
hate, *s.* †haine, *f.*; *v.a.* †haïr; (*have a grudge against*) en vouloir à; (*have a great dislike to*) avoir horreur de.
hateful, odieu|x, ~se; **~ness,** caractère odieux, *m.*; **~ly,** odieusement.
hater, *man-~,* misanthrope, *m.*; *woman-~,* misogyne, *m.*
hatred, †haine, *f.*
hatter, chapelier, *m.*; **~'s shop,** chapellerie, *f.*; *mad as a ~,* fou à lier.
hauberk, †haubert, *m.*
haught|iness, †hauteur, *f.*; **~y,** †hautain; **~ily,** d'une manière †hautaine.
haul, *s.* (*fish*) coup de filet, *m.*; (*profit*) profit, *m.*
haul, *v.a.* traîner; (*naut.*) †haler; (*tow*) remorquer; *~ down,* (*naut., flag, sails*) amener; *~ in,* (*naut.*) rallier la terre; *~ over the coals,* laver la tête à.
haulage, (*road*) roulage, *m.*; (*water*) †halage, *m.*
haulier, (*carter*) roulier, *m.*
ha(u)lm, (*stem*) tige, *f.*
haunch, †hanche, *f.*; (*venison, boar*) cuissot, *m.*; **~es,** (*backside*) derrière, *m.*
haunt, *s.* lieu fréquenté, *m.*; (*pej.*) repaire, *m.*
haunt, *v.a.* fréquenter; (*ghost*) †hanter; *be* **~ed** *by,* (*memories, &c.*) être †hanté par; *~ed room,* chambre †hantée, *f.*
hautboy, hoboy, (*mus.*) †hautbois, *m.*
have, (*possess, contain, hold, engage in, diseases, &c., &c.*) avoir; (*food*) prendre*; (*conveyance*) prendre*; (*procure*) se procurer; (*know*) savoir*; (*cheat*) rouler; (*insist*) vouloir* que + *subj.*; (*not allow*) ne pas vouloir* que + *subj.*; *~ to,* il faut que + *subj.*; (*be booked, destined to*) devoir + *inf.*; *~ a thing from a person,* tenir* de; *~ a thing made, done, &c.,* faire* + *inf.* (par *of the agent*); *~ it out with,* vider une querelle, question, *etc.* avec; *had rather,* préférer + *inf. or* que + *subj.*; *he will ~ it that they are gone,* il prétend qu'ils sont partis; *~ about one,* avoir sur soi; *~ back,* (*pers.*) faire* revenir; (*thing*) faire* rendre; *~ in,* (*pers.*) faire* entrer; *~ on,* (*clothes*) porter; *~ up,* faire* monter; (*arrest*) arrêter; *v.n. ~ at,* (*attack*) se jeter sur.
haven, †havre, *m.*; (*refuge*) asile, *m.*
haversack, †havresac, *m.*
havoc, ravage, *m.*; *make ~ of,* (*fig.*) causer des ravages dans; *v.a.* ravager.
haw, *s.* (*bot.*) cenelle, *f.*
haw-haw, *s. see* HA-HA.
haw-haw, *v.n.* rire bruyamment.
hawfinch, (*ornith.*) gros-bec, *m.*
hawk, *s.* (*ornith.*) faucon, *m.*; **~-nosed,** au nez aquilin; **~-moth,** (*ent.*) sphinx, *m.*; **~-weed,** (*bot.*) épervière, *f.*
hawk, *v.a.* (*attack*) fondre sur; (*carry goods*) colporter; *v.n.* (*hunt with hawk*) chasser au faucon; (*cough*) graillonner.
hawker, (*from door to door*) camelot, *m.*; (*in country*) colporteur, *m.*
hawking, (*art and hunt.*) fauconnerie, *f.*
hawse, (*naut. space to manœuvre at anchor*) évitée, *f.*; **~ -hole,** écubier, *m.*
hawser, (*naut.*) †haussière, *f.*
hawthorn, aubépine, *f.*
hay, *s.* foin, *m.*; *make ~ while the sun shines,* saisir l'occasion aux cheveux; **~-fever,** rhume des foins, *m.*; **~-fork,** fourche à foin, *f.*; **~loft,** fenil, *m.*; *v.n.* faire* les foins.
haycock, meulon de foin, *m.*
haymaker, faneu|r, ~se, *m.f.*
haymaking, hay-harvest, fenaison, *f.*
hayrick, ~-stack, meule de foin, *f.*
hazard, *s.* (*chance, game, of dice*) †hasard, *m.*; (*risk*) risque, *m.*; *at all ~s,* à tout †hasard.
hazard, (*remark, life, &c.*) †hasarder.
hazardous, †hasardeu|x, ~se.
haze, haziness, (*lit. and fig.*) brume, *f.*
hazel, (*tree*) noisetier, *m.*; **~-coloured,** noisette, *invar.*; **~-copse,** coudraie, *f.*; **~-grouse,** *see* GROUSE; **~-nut,** noisette, *f.*
hazy, brumeu|x, ~se; (*fig.*) vague.
he, *pron., subj. of verb,* il; *alone, with prepositions, when the subject is separated from verb, when there is more than one subject, and after* ce + être, lui, *e.g.* lui seul l'a fait; lui et moi l'avons fait; c'est lui; *sometimes* ce *in explaining, e.g. ~ is my father,* c'est mon père; *~ who,* (*indefinite*) celui qui.
he, *s.* homme, *m.*; **~ -man,** (*U.S.A.*)

homme à poigne, *m.*; *adj. generally translated by special word, e.g. he-goat,* bouc; *he-bear,* ours.

head, *s.* **1.** (*part of body, cattle, top of nail, abscess, sense, presence of mind*) tête, *f.*; **2.** (*chief, director, family, chief point, subdivision*) chef, *m.*; **3.** (*of table*) †haut bout, *m.*; **4.** (*indication of matter*) rubrique, *f.*; **5.** (*bed*) chevet, *m.*; **6.** (*speech, sermon*) point, *m.*; **7.** (*bridges*) tête, *f.*; **8.** (*ship*) avant, *m.*; **9.** (*arrow*) pointe, *f.*; **10.** (*stick*) pomme, *f.*; **11.** (*boar, pig*) †hure, *f.*; **12.** (*stag*) bois, *m.*; **13.** (*liquor*) mousse, *f.*; **14.** (*of lake, bay*) extrémité, *f.*; **15.** (*river, fountain*) source, *f.*; *at the ~ of* (*command*), à la tête de; (*in front of*) en tête de; *per ~,* par tête; *~ first,* la tête la première; *~s or tails,* pile ou face; *over ~ and ears, see* EAR; *under the ~ of,* (*e.g. History, Science, &c.*) sous la rubrique de; *be hot- ~ed,* avoir la tête près du bonnet; *get into one's ~,* s'imaginer; *go off one's ~,* devenir* (être) fou; *go ~ over heels,* culbuter; *hit the right nail on the ~,* mettre* le doigt dessus; *have one's ~ screwed on the right way,* avoir de la tête; *keep one's ~,* garder son sang-froid; *knock, run one's ~ against a wall,* donner de la tête contre un mur; *lose one's ~,* perdre la tête; *make neither ~ nor tail of,* ne comprendre rien à; *put, lay ~s together,* (*fig.*) se concerter; *run in one's ~,* trotter dans la tête; *turn a person's ~,* (*fig.*) tourner la tête à; *~* **clerk,** chef de bureau, *m.*; *~* **-dress,** coiffure, *f.*; *~ of hair,* chevelure, *f.*; **~-gear,** couvre-chef, *m.*; **~-mast,** tête de mât, *f.*; **~-master, ~-mistress,** direct|eur, ~rice, *m.f.*; *~-money,* capitation, *f.*; ~ **office,** bureau central, *m.*; **~-phone,** (*wireless*) écouteur, *m.*; **~-piece,** (*armour*) armet, *m.*; **~-rest,** appui-tête, *m. invar.*; **~-voice,** voix de tête, *f.*; **~-work,** travail de tête, *m.*

head, *adj.* (*principal*) principal; *have a ~ wind,* (*naut.*) avoir vent debout.

head, *v.a.* (*list*) être en tête de; (*troops*) être à la tête de; (*trees*) étêter; *~ off,* détourner.

head, *v.n. ~ for,* se diriger vers; (*naut.*) mettre* le cap sur.

headache, mal de tête, *m.*; *sick ~,* migraine, *f.*

header, (*mason.*) boutisse, *f.*; (*dive*) plongeon, *m.*; *take a ~,* piquer une tête.

heading, headline, (*newspapers, letters*) en-tête, *m.*

headiness, (*wine, &c.*) nature capiteuse, *f.*

headland, promontoire, *m.*

headlight, (*motor*) projecteur, *m.*

headlong, *adj.* (*hurried*) précipité; (*impetuous*) impétueu|x, ~se; *adv.* la tête la première; (*rashly*) tête baissée.

headman, (*tribe*) chef, *m.*

headquarters, quartier général, *m.*

headsman, bourreau, *m.*

headspring, source, *f.*

headstone, (tombstone) pierre tombale, *f.*; (*chief stone*) pierre angulaire, *f.*

headstrong, volontaire; (*obstinate*) entêté.

headway, avancement, *m.*; (*naut.*) erre, *f.*; *make ~,* avancer.

heady, (*pers.*) impétueu|x, ~se; (*odours*) qui porte à la tête; (*wines, &c.*) capiteu|x, ~se.

heal, *v.a.* (*pers., wound*) guérir; (*fig.*) apaiser.

heal, *v.n.* (*lit. and fig.*) se guérir; (*cicatrize*) se cicatriser.

heal|er, personne qui guérit, *f.*; (*pej.*) guérisseu|r, ~se, *m.f.*; **~ing,** guérison, *f.*

health, (*lit., fig., toast*) santé, *f.*; ~ **resort,** ville d'eau, *f.*; ~ **officer,** agent du service sanitaire, *m.*; **Public ~,** salubrité publique, *f.*; *drink the ~ of,* boire* à la santé de.

healthful, (*pers., wholesome, climate*) sain; **~ness,** salubrité, *f.*

health|y, (*mind, body, good for health*) sain; **~iness,** santé, *f.*; (*air, &c.*) salubrité, *f.*; **~ily,** sainement.

heap, *s.* (*mass*) amas, *m.*; (*pile, large number*) tas, *m.*; (*rounded pile, money*) monceau, *m.*

heap, ~ up, ~ together, *v.a.* entasser; (*amass*) entasser; (*load with*) charger de; (*fig.*) combler de; (*fill with*) remplir de.

hear, *v.a.* entendre; (*listen to*) écouter; (*prayer*) exaucer; (*learn*) apprendre*; *~ out,* entendre jusqu'au bout.

hear, *v.n.* entendre; *~ from,* (*letter*) recevoir une lettre de; *~ of,* (*pers.*) avoir des nouvelles de; (*pers., thing*) entendre parler de; *~ that,* entendre dire que; **hear! hear!** *interj.* bravo!

hearer, audit|eur, ~rice, *m.f.*; **~s,** auditoire, *m.*

hearing, *s.* (*sense of hearing*) ouïe, *f.*; (*act of hearing, law*) audition, *f.*; (*attention*) attention, *f.*; *out of ~,* hors de la portée de l'oreille; *within ~,* à la portée de l'oreille; *in my ~,* en ma présence.

hearken, prêter l'oreille (à); *~ to,* écouter.

hearsay, *s.* ouï-dire, *m. invar.*; *adj.* d'ouï-dire.

hearse, corbillard, *m.*

heart, (*lit., fig., cards, fruit, centre, affection, mind, soul, courage, ~-shaped object*) cœur, *m.*; (*courage*) courage, *m.*; (*essence, fig.*) essence, *f.*; *at ~,* au fond; *by ~,* (*learn*) par cœur; *out of ~,* découragé; *get by ~,* apprendre par cœur; *have at ~,* avoir à cœur; *lose ~,* perdre courage; *make one's ~ bleed,* fendre le cœur; *take ~,* prendre* courage; *take ~ again,* reprendre* courage; *take to heart,* prendre* à cœur; **~-ache,** chagrin, *m.*; **~-breaking,** navrant; **~-broken,** navré; **~-felt,** ressenti au fond du cœur; **~-rending,** déchirant; **~-searching,** *s.* scrupule, *m.*; *adj.* qui sonde les secrets

du cœur; ~**-sick,** abattu; ~**-sore,** désolé; ~**-string,** fibre du cœur, *f.*; ~**-whole,** qui a le cœur libre.
heartburn, (*med.*) aigreurs, *f.pl.*
hearten, *v.a.* encourager; *v.n.* ~ *up,* reprendre* courage.
hearth, foyer, *m.*; ~ **-rug,** devant de foyer, *m.*
hearthstone, foyer, *m.*
heartless, (*pers.*) sans cœur; (*things*) cruel, -le; ~**ly,** (*without feeling*) sans pitié; ~**ness,** manque de cœur, *m.*; (*want of feeling*) insensibilité, *f.*
heartsease, (*bot.*) pensée, *f.*
heart|y, cordial; (*vigorous*) vigoureu|x, ~se; (*zealous*) zélé; (*greeting, &c.*) chaleureu|x, ~se; (*laugh*) bon, -ne; (*eater*) gros, -se; ~**iness,** cordialité, *f.*; ~**ily,** cordialement; (*eating*) de bon appétit.
heat, *s.* (*lit., fig., ardour, zeal, hot part of the day, discussion*) chaleur, *f.*; (*phys.*) calorique, *m.*; (*impetuosity*) fougue, *f.*; (*anger*) colère, *f.*; (*of a race*) épreuve, *f.*
heat, *v.a.* (*room, bath, water, &c.*) chauffer; (*pers. and fig.*) échauffer; *v.n.* chauffer.
heater, (*radiator*) radiateur, *m.*
heath, (*waste land*) lande, *f.*; (*bot.*) bruyère, *f.*; ~**-cock,** coq de bruyère, *m.*
heathen, *adj. and s.m.f.* païen, -ne. ⚠ Payen *is obsolete.*
heathenish, païen, -ne.
heathenism, paganisme, *m.*
heather, bruyère, *f.*; ~**y,** couvert de bruyère, *f.*
heating, *s.* chauffage, *m.*; ~**-apparatus,** calorifère, *m.*; **central** ~, *see* CENTRAL.
heave, *s.* (*land, ground, sea*) soulèvement, *m.*
heave, *v.a.* (*heavy object, anchor*) lever; (*sigh*) pousser; (*naut.*) haler; ~ *the lead,* (*naut.*) jeter la sonde; ~ *the log,* (*naut.*) filer le loch.
heave, *v.n.* (*rise of ground or waves*) se soulever; (*pant*) †haleter; ~ *to* (*naut.*) mettre* en panne; ~ *in sight,* venir* (être) en vue.
heaven, (*lit. and fig.*) ciel (*pl.* cieux), *m.*; ~ *knows* (*that*), Dieu le sait! Dieu sait (que); ~ *helps those who help themselves,* aide-toi, le ciel t'aidera. ⚠ *pl.* ciels *only used in* ciels de lit, ciels de tableau, ciels de carrière, *and* ciels = *climates.*
heavenl|y, céleste; ~**iness,** nature céleste, *f.*; ~**y body,** corps céleste, *m.*
heav|y, (*weighty*) pesant; (*lit., fig., sleep, food, traffic, artillery*) lourd; (*sea, losses, cavalry, rain*) gros, -se; (*sad*) triste; (*style*) pâteu|x, ~se; ~ *with,* chargé de; *lie* ~ *on,* peser sur; ~**-hearted,** abattu; ~ **laden,** lourdement chargé; ~**iness,** (*lit. and fig.*) poids, *m.*; (*weight*) pesanteur, *f.*; (*sorrow*) abattement, *m.*; (*of roads*) mauvais état, *m.*; ~**ily,** (*ponderously*) pesamment; (*lit. and fig.*) lourdement.
hebdomadal, hebdomadaire.
Hebraic, *adj.* hébraïque.
Hebraism, hébraïsme, *m.*
Hebraist, hébraïste, *m.*
Hebrew, *s.* Hébreu, *m.*; *adj.* hébreu, *fem.* hébraïque; (*lang.*) hébreu, *m.*
hecatomb, hécatombe, *f.*
heckle, *v.a.* †harceler.
hectic, *s.* fièvre hectique, *f.*; *adj.* hectique; (*slang*) passionnant.
hector, *s.* matamore, *m.*; *v.a.* malmener; *v.n.* faire* le fendant.
hedge, *s.* †haie, *f.*; (*barrier*) barrière, *f.*; (*comm.*) couverture, *f.*; ~**-garlic,** alliaire, *f.*; ~**-mustard,** (*bot.*) sisymbre, *m.*; ~**-sparrow,** troglodyte, *m.*
hedge, *v.a.* entourer d'une †haie; (*fig.*) entourer; ~ *in,* enfermer; *v.n.* (*not commit oneself*) éviter de se compromettre.
hedgehog, †hérisson, *m.*
hedger, faiseur de †haies, *m.*
hedgerow, †haie, *f.*
hedon|ism, hédonisme, *m.*
heed, *s.* attention, *f.*; *take* ~ *to,* faire* attention à.
heed, *v.a.* faire* attention à.
heedful, attenti|f, ~ve; (*cautious*) prudent; ~**ness,** attention, *f.*; ~**ly,** attentivement.
heedless, (*careless*) insouciant; (*inattentive*) inattenti|f, ~ve; ~**ness,** insouciance, *f.*; ~**ly,** sans attention.
heel, *s.* (*foot, shoe, sock, &c., naut., keel*) talon, *m.*; (*of mast*) pied, *m.*; *take to one's* ~*s,* montrer les talons; *tread down at* ~, éculer.
heel, *v.a.* (*shoe*) remettre* un talon, des talons à; ~ *out,* (*football*) sortir* (avoir) la balle; *v.n.* ~ *over,* (*naut.*) donner de la bande; ~**ing,** *s.* (*naut.*) bande, *f.*
hefty, robuste; (*slang*) costaud.
hegemony, hégémonie, *f.*
hegira, (*hist.*) hégire, *f.*
heifer, génisse, *f.*
heigh-ho! *interj.* oh là là!
height, (*lit., fig., hill*) †hauteur, *f.*; (*utmost degree*) comble, *m.*; (*of summer*) cœur, *m.*
heighten, *v.a.* (*set off*) relever; (*make higher, enhance*) rehausser; (*increase*) augmenter.
heinous, odieu|x, ~se; ~**ness,** atrocité, *f.*; ~**ly,** odieusement.
heir, héritier, *m.*; ~**ess,** héritière, *f.*; ~**-apparent,** *presumptive,* héritier présomptif, *m.*; *joint heir,* co-hériti|er, ~ère, *m.f.*
heirdom, héritage, *m.*
heirless, sans héritier.
heirloom, souvenir de famille, *m.*
helianthus, (*bot.*) hélianthe, *m.*
heliograph, *n.* héliographe, *m.*
helioscope, hélioscope, *m.*
heliotrope, (*bot.*) héliotrope, *m.*
hell, enfer, *m.*
hellebore, (*bot.*) ellébore, *m.*
Hellen|ic, hellénique; ~**ism,** hellénisme, *m.*; ~**ist,** helléniste, *m.f.*
hellish, infernal; ~**ly,** infernalement.
hello! *interj.* (*teleph.*) allô!

helm, (*helmet*) casque, *m.*; (*naut.*) barre du gouvernail, *f.*; **~-port,** trou de jaumière, *m.*
helmet, casque, *m.*
helmsman, homme de barre, *m.*; (*obs.*) timonier, *m.*
helot, ilote, *m.*; **~ism,** ilotisme, *m.*
help, *s.* aide, *f.*; (*remedy*) remède, *m.*; (*pers.*) domestique, *m.f.*; *call for ~,* appeler au secours; **help! help!** *interj.* au secours!; *there's no ~ for it,* on n'y peut rien.
help, *v.a.* aider (à); (*need, danger*) secourir*; (*prevent*) empêcher; (*at table*) servir*; (*remedy*) remédier à; (*restrain oneself from*) s'empêcher de; *~ oneself,* se servir*; *it cannot be ~ed,* on n'y peut rien; *I cannot ~ it,* je n'y puis rien.
helper, aide, *m.f.*
helpful, (*pers.*) serviable; (*thing*) utile; **~ness,** aide, *f.*; **~ly,** utilement.
helping, *s.* (*at table*) portion, *f.*
helping, *adj.* secourable.
helpless, (*pers.*) sans secours; (*forlorn*) délaissé; (*powerless*) impuissant; **~ness,** impuissance, *f.*; (*forlorn*) abandon, *m.*; **~ly,** sans secours.
helpmate, compagnon, *m.*; compagne, *f.*; (*wife*) épouse, *f.*
helter-skelter, *s.* tohu-bohu, *m.*; *adv.* pêle-mêle.
Helvetian, *adj.* (*when an adj. use small letter*) *and s.m.f.* Helvétien, -ne.
hem, *s.* (*needlework*) ourlet, *m.*; (*edge of garment*) bord, *m.*
hem, *v.a.* ourler; *v.n. ~ in,* entourer.
hem! *interj.* †hein!; *~ and haw,* ânonner.
hemispher|e, hémisphère, *m.*; **~ic, ~ical,** hémisphérique.
hemistich, hémistiche, *m.*
hemlock, (*bot.*) ciguë, *f.*
hemorrhage, *see* HAEM-.
hemp, chanvre, *m.*; **~-field,** chènevière, *f.*; **~-seed,** chènevis, *m.*; **~en,** *adj.* de chanvre.
hem-stitch, *s.* ourlet à jour; *v.a.* ourler à jour.
hen, poule, *f.*; **~-house,** poulailler, *m.*; **~-pecked,** gouverné par sa femme; **~-perch,** *roost,* juchoir, *m.*
hen, *adj.* femelle; *e.g. ~ blackbird, &c.,* merle femelle, *m.*
henbane, (*bot.*) jusquiame, *f.*
hence, *adv.* (*place and time*) d'ici; (*for this reason*) de là; *a week ~,* dans huit jours; *~ it was that,* c'est par suite de cela que.
henceforth, désormais.
henchman, (*squire*) écuyer, *m.*; (*page*) page, *m.*; (*polit.*) partisan, *m.*
henna, †henné, *m.*
heptagon, heptagone, *m.*
heptarchy, heptarchie, *f.*
her, *pron. acc. with verb,* la; *dat. with verb,* lui; *with prepositions, alone, when more than one subject or object, and after* c'est, elle.
her, *adj.* son, *m.*; sa, *f.*; *m.f.pl.* ses. *For parts of body use dat. of refl. pron. and article, e.g. she has broken ~ arm,* elle s'est cassé le bras.
herald, †héraut, *m.*; (*forerunner*) avant-coureur, *m.*; **~ic,** héraldique.
herald, *v.a.* annoncer; (*usher in*) introduire*; **~ry,** blason, *m.*; *book of ~ry,* armorial, *m.*
herb, herbe, *f.*; **pot-~s,** herbes potagères, *f.pl.*; *~* **bennet,** (*bot.*) benoîte, *f.*; *~* **paris,** (*bot.*) parisette, *f.*; **~-woman,** herbière, *f.*
herbaceous, herbacé.
herbage, (*herbs and right of pasture*) herbage, *m.*
herbal, *s.* herbier, *m.*; *adj.* des herbes.
herbalist, herborist, herboriste, *m.*
herbarium, herbier, *m.*
herbivorous, herbivore.
herborize, *v.n.* herboriser.
Herculean, herculéen, -ne.
herd, *s.* (*cattle*) troupeau, *m.*; (*horses, deer, &c.*) troupe, *f.*
herdsman, pâtre, *m.*
here, *adv.* (*in this place, at this point*) ici; (*attached after noun*) -ci; *from ~,* d'ici; *~ lies,* (*tomb*) ci-gît; *~ and there,* çà et là; *that's neither ~ nor there,* cela n'a rien à y voir; *interj. here!* (*present*) présent!; *~, take this!* tenez!; *look ~!* dites donc!; *~ he is!* le voici!; *~ they are!* les voici!
hereabouts, *adv.* près d'ici.
hereafter, *s.* l'autre monde, *m.*; *adv.* à l'avenir.
hereby, *adv.* par là.
hereditament, (*inheritance*) héritage, *m.*
hereditar|y, héréditaire; **~ily,** héréditairement.
heredity, hérédité, *f.*
herein, *adv.* en ceci; *~ enclosed,* ci-inclus, *invar. before noun, concord after.*
hereof, de ceci.
heresiarch, hérésiarque, *m.*
heresy, hérésie, *f.*
heretic, hérétique, *m.f.*; **~al,** hérétique.
heretofore, (*formerly*) *adv.* jadis; (*before this*) ci-devant.
hereupon, *adv.* là-dessus.
herewith, *adv.* (*enclosed, sent*) ci-joint, *invar. before noun, concord after.*
heritage, (*lit. and fig.*) héritage, *m.*
hermaphrodite, *adj. and s.m.* hermaphrodite.
hermetic, (*air-tight*) hermétique; **~ally,** hermétiquement.
hermit, ermite, *m.*; **~-crab,** bernard-l'ermite, *m.*; **~age,** ermitage, *m.*
hernia, (*med.*) †hernie, *f.*
hero, (*lit., fig., myth.*) †héros, *m.*; **~ic,** (*lit., fig., drastic, verse*) héroïque; **~ically,** héroïquement.
heroi-comic, (*mock heroic*) héroï-comique.
heroine, héroïne, *f.*; ⚠ *H not aspirate.*
heroism, héroïsme, *m.*

heron, hern, (*ornith.*) †héron, *m.*; **~ry,** †héronnière, *f.*
herring, †hareng, *m.*; *kippered, red ~,* †hareng saur, *m.*
hers, *poss. pron.* (*simple possession*) à elle; (*to emphasize and distinguish*) le sien, la sienne, les siens, les siennes; *he is a relation of ~,* il est un de ses parents.
herself, (*emphatic*) elle-même; (*reflexive*) se *with verb*; *by ~,* toute seule.
hesitan|t, hésitant; **~cy,** incertitude, *f.*
hesitate, *v.n.* hésiter; *~ to,* hésiter à.
hesitatingly, avec hésitation.
hesitation, hésitation, *f.*; *have no ~ to,* ne pas avoir d'hésitation à.
heteroclite, (*gram.*) hétéroclite.
heterodox, *adj.* hétérodoxe; **~y,** hétérodoxie, *f.*
heterogene|ous, hétérogène; **~ity,** hétérogénéité, *f.*
hew, *v.a.* couper; (*to form or shape*) tailler; **rough-~,** ébaucher; *~ in pieces,* tailler en pièces; *~ down,* abattre.
hewer, (*stone, &c.*) tailleur, *m.*
hexagon, hexagone, *m.*; **~al,** hexagonal.
hexameter, hexamètre, *m.*
hey! *interj.* †hein!
heyday, (*youth, &c.*) fleur, *f.*
hi! *interj.* ohé!
hiatus, (*gram.*) hiatus, *m.*; (*fig.*) lacune, *f.*
hiberna|te, hiberner; **~tion,** hibernation, *f.*; ⚠ hiverner = '*spend the winter*'.
hiccup, hiccough, *s.* †hoquet, *m.*; *v.n.* avoir le †hoquet.
hide, *s.* peau, *f.*; (*dressed*) cuir, *m.*; *be ~-bound,* avoir l'esprit étroit.
hide, *v.a.* cacher; (*keep secret*) dissimuler; *v.n.* se cacher.
hide-and-seek, *s.* cache-cache, *m.*
hideous, (*face, sight*) †hideu|x, ~se; (*repulsive*) affreu|x, ~se; **~ness,** †hideur, *f.*; **~ly,** †hideusement.
hiding, (*thrashing*) râclée, *f.*
hiding-place, cachette, *f.*
hie, *v.n.* se †hâter (vers).
hierarch|y, †hiérarchie, *f.*; **~ical,** †hiérarchique.
hieroglyph, hiéroglyphe, *m.*; **~ic,** hiéroglyphique; **~ics,** hiéroglyphique, *m.*
hierophant, hiérophante, *m.*
higgledy-piggledy, *adv. and s.m.* pêle-mêle.
high, *s. on ~,* (*heaven*) au ciel.
high, *adj.* (*lit., fig., tide, seas, elevation, opinion, note of music, treason, Church, pressure, temperature, finance, frequency*) †haut; (*speed*) grand; (*wind*) fort; (*colour*) vi|f, ~ve; (*price*) élevé; (*wages, sea, interest*) gros, -se; (*Stk. Ex.*) †haut; (*game, meat*) faisandé; *~ and mighty,* arrogant; *The Most High,* le Tout-Puissant; *on the ~ seas,* en †haute, pleine mer; *it is ~ time to,* il est grandement temps de; **~ altar,** maître autel, *m.*; **~ mass,** grand'messe, *f.*; **~ priest,** grand prêtre, *m.*; **~ road,** grande route, *f.*; **~ water,** marée †haute, *f.*; **~ness,** (*title*) Altesse, *f.*; (*character*) élévation, *f.*; (*price, rate, &c.*) cherté, *f.*; **~ly,** extrêmement; (*favourably*) très favorablement; **~er classes,** *see* CLASS.
high, *adv.* †haut; (*strongly, violently*) fortement; *~ and low,* partout; *play ~,* jouer gros jeu; *rise ~,* monter (être) †haut; *run ~,* (*sea*) être grosse; **~-born,** de haute naissance; **~ explosive,** *adj.*, (de) grande puissance de feu; **~-handed,** autoritaire; **~-minded,** magnanime; **~-pitched,** (*voice, &c.*) aigu, -ë; **~-spirited,** ardent; (*pej.*) audacieu|x, ~se.
highland, pays montagneux, *m.*; **~s,** (*Scotland*) †Hautes Terres, *f.pl.*; **~er,** montagnard, *m.*; (*Scotland*) †highlander, *m.*
hight, *p.p.* appelé.
highway, grande route, *f.*; **~man, ~ robber,** voleur de grand chemin, *m.*
hilari|ty, hilarité, *f.*; **~ous,** hilare.
hill, colline, *f.*; (*small*) coteau, *m.*; **~-side,** flanc de colline, *m.*; *up ~ and down dale,* par monts et par vaux; *as old as the ~s,* vieux, vieille comme le monde.
hillock, monticule, *m.*
hilly, montueu|x, ~se.
hilt, poignée, *f.*; *up to the ~,* jusqu'à la garde.
him, *pron.* (*acc. with verb*) le; (*dat. with verb*) lui; *with prepositions, alone, after* c'est, *when more than one subject or object,* lui.
himself, (*emphatic*) lui-même; (*reflexive*) se *with verb*; *by ~,* tout seul.
hind, (*deer*) biche, *f.*; (*farm servant*) valet de ferme, *m.*; (*rustic*) paysan, *m.*
hind, hinder, *adj.* de derrière; *~ quarters,* (*animal*) arrière-train, *m.*; *~ wheel,* roue arrière, *f.*
hinder, (*embarrass*) gêner; (*retard*) retarder; (*prevent*) empêcher (de).
hind|most, ~ermost, *adj.* le, la derni|er, ~ère.
hindrance, empêchement, *m.*
Hind|u, ~oo, *adj.* (*when an adj. use small letter*) *and s.m.f.* Hindou, -e.
Hindustani, (*lang.*) hindoustani, *m.*
hinge, *s.* gond, *m.*; (*doors, windows*) charnière, *f.*; (*fig.*) pivot, *m.*
hinge, *v.a.* (*door*) munir de charnières; *v.n. ~ on,* tourner sur.
hint, *s.* (*half-indication*) allusion, *f.*; (*half-warning*) avis, *m.*; *~s on,* (*brief summary*) aperçu, *m.* sur; *take a ~,* comprendre* à demi-mot.
hint, *v.a.* insinuer; *~ at,* faire* allusion à.
hip, (*anat.*) †hanche, *f.*; (*bot.*) fruit de l'églantier, *m.*; (*arch.*) arêtier, *m.*; **~-bath,** bain de siège, *m.*
hippocras, hypocras, *m.*
hippodrome, (*Ant.*) hippodrome, *m.*
hippo|griff, ~gryph, hippogriffe, *m.*
hippopotamus, hippopotame, *m.*
hire, *s.* (*payment for use*) louage, *m.*; (*engagement to hire*) location, *f.*; *on ~,*

en location; *for* ~, à louer; **~-purchase,** *~-purchase system,* vente à tempérament, *f.*
hire, *v.a.n.* (*let out and procure use of*) louer; (*servant, &c.*) engager; **~d horse,** *&c.*, cheval, etc. de louage, *m.*
hireling, mercenaire, *m.*
hirsute, velu.
his, *pron. adj.* son, *m.*, sa, *f.* (*f.* + *vowel or silent H* son), ses, *pl. For parts of body use dat. of refl. pron. and article, e.g. he has broken ~ arm,* il s'est cassé le bras.
his, *poss. pron.* (*simple possession*) à lui; (*to emphasize and distinguish*) le sien, la sienne, les siens, les siennes; *a relation of* ~, un de ses parents.
hiss, hissing, *s.* sifflement, *m.*
hiss, *v.a.n.* (*sound, disapproval, make steam, &c.*) siffler.
historian, historien, -ne, *m.f.*
historic (historical), (*mentioned in, dealing with history*) historique; **~ally,** historiquement.
historiographer, historiographe, *m.f.*
history, histoire, *f.*; (*recital of facts*) historique, *m.*
histrionic, (*of actors, of acting, and pej.*) théâtral.
hit, *s.* coup, *m.*; (*success*) succès, *m.*; (*stroke of sarcasm*) critique, *f.*; (*successful attempt*) coup heureux, *m.*
hit, *v.a.* frapper; (*definite mark*) atteindre*; (*light upon*) trouver; ~ *it off,* (*imitate exactly*) saisir; ~ *it off,* (*together*) s'entendre bien ensemble.
hit, *v.n.* ~ *against,* se heurter à; ~ *at,* diriger son coup (à); ~ *upon,* trouver.
hitch, *s.* (*jerk*) secousse, *f.*; (*small impediment, obstacle*) anicroche, *f.*; (*naut.*) clé, clef, *f.*; *there's a ~ somewhere,* il y a quelque chose qui cloche.
hitch, *v.a.* (*jerk*) tirer brusquement; (*fasten with hook, &c.*) accrocher; (*naut.*) nouer; *v.n.* s'accrocher; ~ *up,* (*U.S.A. 'harness'*) atteler.
hither, *adj.* le plus proche.
hither, *adv.* ici; ~ *and thither,* çà et là.
hitherto, *adv.* jusqu'ici.
hive, *s.* (*lit. and fig.*) ruche, *f.*; *row of ~s,* rucher, *m.*; *v.a.* mettre* dans une ruche; *v.n.* (*pers.*) vivre* ensemble.
ho! *interj.* †ho!
hoar, *adj.* (*with age*) blanchi; **~-frost,** *see* FROST.
hoard, (*money*) magot, *m.*; (*fig.*) amas, *m.*
hoard, *v.a.* (*money*) thésauriser; (*fig.*) conserver; **~er,** thésauriseu|r, ~se, *m.f.*; **~ing,** accumulation, *f.*
hoarding, *s.* (*advt.*) panneau-réclame, *m.*
hoarhound, *see* HOREHOUND.
hoarse, (*voice, &c.*) rauque; (*pers.*) enroué; **~ness,** enrouement, *m.*; **~ly,** d'une voix rauque.
hoary, chenu; **~-headed,** à cheveux blancs.
hoax, *s.* mystification, *f.*; (*false news*) canard, *m.*; *v.a.* mystifier.
hob, (*fireplace*) plaque, *f.*
hobble, *s.* (*uneven gait*) boitement, *m.*; (*difficulty*) embarras, *m.*
hobble, *v.a.* (*horse*) entraver; *v.n.* (*limp*) clocher; ~ *along,* aller* (être) clopin-clopant.
hobbledehoy, grand garçon dégingandé, *m.*
hobby, (*fad, toy*) dada, *m.*; (*ornith.*) †hobereau, *m.*; *ride a ~,* enfourcher son dada.
hobgoblin, lutin, *m.*
hobnail, caboche, *f.*; **~ed,** garni de clous.
hobnob, trinquer; ~ *with,* être à tu et à toi avec.
hobo, (*U.S.A. tramp*) chemineau, *m.*
hock, (*wine*) vin du Rhin, *m.*; (*horse, &c.*) jarret, *m.*
hockey, †hockey, *m.*
hocus-pocus, (*deception*) tromperie, *f.*; *v.a.* duper.
hod, (*mason*) oiseau, *m.*; **~man,** goujat, *m.*
hodometer, odomètre, *m.*
hodge-podge, *see* HOTCH-POTCH.
hoe, †houe, *f.*; *Dutch ~,* sarcloir, *m.*; *v.a.* †houer.
hog, porc, *m.*; (*naut.*) goret, *m.*; **~-wash,** lavure, *f.*
hoggish, de cochon; (*fig.*) grossi|er, ~ère; **~ness,** grossièreté, *f.*; **~ly,** en cochon.
hogshead, (*measure and cask*) barrique, *f.*
hoist, *s.* (*elevator*) monte-charge, *m.*; (*naut. flag*) guindant, *m.*
hoist, *v.a.* †hisser; (*tauten*) étarquer; (*with crane, &c.*) guinder; *be ~ with one's own petard,* tomber (être) dans son propre piège; ~ *colours,* †hisser le pavillon.
hoity-toity! *interj.* bah!
hold, *s.* (*means and act of holding, grasp*) prise, *f.*; (*influence*) influence, *f.*; (*ship's hold*) cale, *f.*; *lay ~ of,* se saisir de.
hold, *v.a.* **1** (*grasp, meeting*) tenir*; **2** (*breath, restrain*) retenir*; **3** (*maintain*) maintenir*; **4** (*consider as*) tenir* pour; **5** (*contain*) contenir*; **6** (*occupy*) occuper; **7** (*hold to promise, &c.*) contraindre* à tenir; **8** (*possess*) avoir; **9** (*detain*) détenir*; **10** (*celebrate*) célébrer; **11** (*inquiry*) faire*; ~ *cheap,* faire* bon marché de; ~ *in contempt,* mépriser; ~ *one's own,* tenir* bon; ~ *back,* retenir*; ~ *forth,* pérorer; ~ *off,* tenir* à distance; ~ *out,* (*arm, &c.*) tendre; (*offer*) offrir*; ~ *out for,* (*comm. price*) se tenir* à; ~ *over,* (*payment*) arriérer; ~ *together,* tenir* ensemble; ~ *up,* (*U.S.A.*) arrêter; *be held up to ridicule,* être un objet de risée; ~ *with,* approuver; ~ *that,* (*opinion*) soutenir* que.
hold, *v.n.* (*not yield*) tenir*; (*be true*) être vrai; (*stick*) adhérer; ~ *aloof,* se tenir* à l'écart; ~ *off,* (*rain*) ne pas tomber (être); ~ *on,* ne pas lâcher prise; ~ *out,* durer; ~ *together,* tenir* ensemble; ~ *up,* (*weather*) s'éclaircir.
hold! *interj.* attendez!
hold-all, (*for packing*) valise roulée, *f.*

holder, (*possessor*) possesseur, *m.*; (*tenant*) locataire, *m.f.*; (*of a post*) titulaire, *m.f.*
holding, (*ownership, property held*) possession, *f.*; **~s,** (*of company*) titres en portefeuille, *m.pl.*; *small ~s,* petites propriétés, *f.pl.*
hole, *s.* (*lit., hovel*) trou, *m.*; (*opening*) ouverture, *f.*; (*golf*) trou, *m.*; *I'm in a pretty ~,* me voilà dans de beaux draps; *~-and-corner, adj.* fait sous main.
hole, *v.a.* (*make a hole in*) trouer; (*tunnel*) percer; (*golf*) mettre* dans un trou.
holiday, jour de fête, *m.*; (*intermission of classes*) congé, *m.*; **~s,** vacances, *f.pl.*; *adj.* (*schools*) de congé, de vacances.
holiness, sainteté, *f.*; *His Holiness,* Sa Sainteté.
Hollander, †Hollandais, *m.*
Hollands, genièvre de †Hollande, *m.*
hollo, *v.a.n.* crier; *interj.* holà!
hollow, *s.* (*cavity, hand*) creux, *m.*
hollow, *adj.* (*lit., fig.*) creu|x, ~se; (*sound*) caverneu|x, ~se; (*insincere*) fau|x, ~sse; *beat ~,* battre à plate couture; **~ness,** (*empty space, fig.*) vide, *m.*; (*falseness*) fausseté, *f.*
hollow, *v.a.* creuser; (*from within*) évider; (*undermine*) caver.
holly, †houx, *m.*
hollyhock, (*bot.*) rose trémière, *f.*
holm, (*islet*) îlot.
holocaust, holocauste, *m.*
holograph, *adj.* olographe.
holster, fonte, *f.*
holy, saint; (*consecrated*) bénit; *Holy Ghost, see* GHOST; *Holy Land,* Terre Sainte, *f.*; *Holy Week,* Semaine sainte, *f.*; *Holy See,* Saint-Siège, *m.*; ~ **orders,** ordres, *m.pl.*; ~ **water,** eau bénite, *f.*; **Holy Writ,** (*Scripture*) écritures saintes, *f.pl.*
holy of holies, (*lit. and fig.*) saint des saints, *m.*
homage, hommage, *m.*
home, *s.* foyer domestique, *m.*; (*family life*) chez soi, *m.*; (*residence*) demeure, *f.*; (*native land*) patrie, *f.*; (*institution for infirm, &c.*) hospice, *m.*; (*of plant, race, animal*) habitat, *m.*; (*mother country*) métropole, *f.*; *at ~, s.* réception, *f.*; *be at ~,* (*familiar with*) être dans son élément; *be not at ~,* être sorti; *be at ~ with,* (*pers.*) être à son aise avec; *have no ~,* être sans asile; *have a ~,* (*of one's own*) avoir un petit chez soi; *have neither house nor ~,* être sans feu ni lieu; *make oneself at ~,* se mettre* à son aise.
home, *adj.* domestique; (*polit.*) de l'intérieur; (*products, stocks*) indigène; *~ market,* marché métropolitain, *m.*; *Home Office,* Ministère de l'Intérieur; *~ port,* port d'attache, *m.*; *~ rule,* autonomie, *f.*; *~ team,* (*sport*) équipe locale, *f.*; *~ trade,* commerce métropolitain, *m.*; *~ thrust,* coup qui va droit au but, *m.*; *tell some ~ truths to,* dire* son fait à.
home, *adv.* chez soi, moi, *&c.*; (*to the point*) droit au but; (*arrived*) arrivé; *come, go ~,* rentrer (être); **~-coming,** retour, *m.*; **~-made,** (*dress, &c.*) confectionné à la maison; *~-made bread,* pain de ménage, *m.*; *strike ~,* frapper juste.
home, *v.n.* (*pigeon*) revenir*.
homeless, sans asile.
homel|y, (*simple*) simple; (*unpretending*) modeste; (*features*) sans beauté; **~iness,** simplicité, *f.*
homer, *s.* (*pigeon*) pigeon voyageur, *m.*
homespun, *s.* homespun, *m.*; *adj.* fait à la maison.
homestead, (*approx.*) demeure, *f.*; (*farm*) ferme, *f.*
homeward, *adj.* de retour; *adv.* vers la maison; *~ bound,* en retour.
homicid|e, homicide, *m.*; **~al,** homicide.
homily, homélie, *f.*
homoeopath, homéopathe, *m.*; **~y,** homéopathie, *f.*; **~ic,** homéopathique.
homogene|ous, homogène; **~ity,** homogénéité, *f.*
homologous, homologue.
homonym, homonyme, *m.*; **~ous,** homonyme.
honest, honnête; (*sincere*) sincère; (*worthy*) brave; (*trustworthy*) fidèle; **~y,** honnêteté, *f.*; (*uprightness*) probité, *f.*; (*bot.*) lunaire, *f.*; **~ly,** honnêtement; ~ **man,** homme de bien, *m.*
honey, miel, *m.*; (*U.S.A. endearment*) chéri, -e, *m.f.*; *~-buzzard,* (*ornith.*) bondrée, *f.*
honeycomb, rayon de miel, *m.*; *v.a.* cribler (de).
honeyed, (*lit. and fig.*) emmiellé.
honeymoon, lune de miel, *f.*
honeysuckle, (*bot.*) chèvrefeuille, *f.*
honorarium, honoraires, *m.pl.*
honorary, (*title and prerogative without functions or pay*) honoraire.
honorific, honorifique.
honour, *s.* (*honourable instinct, mark of distinction, thing, pers. reflecting honour, comm.*) honneur, *m.*; *in ~ bound to,* engagé d'honneur à; *in ~ of,* en l'honneur de; *have the ~ to,* avoir l'honneur de; *make it a point of ~,* se piquer d'honneur (à); *upon my ~!, ~ bright!,* parole d'honneur!
honour, *v.a.* honorer; (*comm., signature, &c.*) faire* honneur à; **time -~ed,** séculaire.
honourabl|e, (*lit. and title*) honorable; *Right ~,* Très Honorable; **~y,** honorablement.
hood, *s.* (*monk*) capuchon, *m.*; (*veh. and folding motor ~*) capote, *f.*; (*woman's head and neck*) capeline, *f.*; (*hawk*) chaperon, *m.*; (*photo., camera*) tablier, *m.*; *Little Red Riding ~,* petit Chaperon Rouge, *m.*
hood, *v.a.* encapuchonner; (*hawk*) chaperonner.

hoodwink, bander les yeux à; (*fig.*) tromper.
hoof, *s.* sabot, *m.*
hook, (*large*) croc, *m.*; (*small*) crochet, *m.*; (*fishing*) hameçon, *m.*; (*dress*) agrafe, *f.*; ~ *and eye, see* EYE; (*boat*) gaffe, *f.*; ~ *nose,* nez aquilin, *m.*; *on one's own* ~, (*slang*) pour son propre compte; *be on tenter-~s,* être sur charbons ardents.
hook, *v.a.* (*suspend, catch and tear*) accrocher; (*dress*) agrafer; (*fish*) ferrer; (*get hold of*) pêcher; *v.n.* ~ *it,* (*slang*) ficher le camp; ~ *on to,* s'accrocher à.
hooked, crochu.
hookah, houka, *m.*
hooligan, apache, *m.*
hoop, *s.* (*for cask*) cercle, *m.*; (*child's*) cerceau, *m.*; (*shout*) cri, *m.*; (*croquet*) arceau, *m.*; ~ *petticoat,* panier, *m.*
hooping-cough, coqueluche, *f.*
hoopoe, (*ornith.*) †huppe, *f.*
hoot, *s.* (*booing*) †huée, *f.*; (*owl*) ululement, *m.*; (*motor*) coup de trompe, *m.*
hoot, *v.a.* (*boo, mob, owl*) †huer; (*motor*) corner.
hooter, (*ship*) sirène, *f.*; (*motor*) corne, *f.*
hop, *s.* (*bot.*) †houblon, *m.*; (*spring*) sautillement, *m.*; ~ **plantation,** †houblonnière, *f.*; ~**-pole,** échalas, *m.*; ~**-o'-my-thumb,** Petit Poucet, *m.*; ~**-picker,** cueilleu|r, ~se de †houblon, *m.f.*
hop, *v.n.* (*on one foot*) sauter à clochepied; (*birds*) sautiller; ~ *over, v.a.* sauter.
hope, *s.* espérance, *f.*; (*pers.*) espoir, *m.*
hope, *v.n.* espérer; ~ *for, v.a.* espérer; *I* ~ *so, indeed!* je l'espère bien; ~ *to,* espérer + *inf.*
hopeful, (*feeling hope*) plein d'espoir; (*promising*) qui promet beaucoup; ~**ness,** bon espoir, *m.*; ~**ly,** avec espoir.
hopeless, sans espoir; (*admitting no hope*) désespéré; (*incorrigible*) incorrigible; ~**ness,** désespoir, *m.*; (*uselessness*) inutilité, *f*; ~**ly,** (*despairingly*) désespérément; (*irretrievably*) irrémédiablement.
hopper, (*mills*) trémie, *f.*
hopscotch, (*game*) marelle, *f.*
horde, †horde, *f.*
horehound, (*bot.*) marrube, *m.*
horizon, horizon, *m.*; ~**tal,** *adj.* horizontal; ~**tally,** horizontalement.
horn, *s.* (*cattle, snail, moon, material, shoe*) corne, *f.*; (*motor*) trompe, *f.*; (*certain insects*) antenne, *f.*; (*hunt.*) cor de chasse, *m.*; ~ **-owl,** (*ornith.*) grand-duc, *m.*; ~ **of plenty,** corne d'abondance, *f.*; ~**-rimmed,** à monture de corne.
hornbeam, (*bot.*) charme, *m.*
hornbill, (*ornith.*) calao, *m.*
horned, cornu, ~ *owl,* scops, *m.*
hornet, frelon, *m.*; *bring a ~s' nest about one's ears,* tomber (être) dans un guêpier.
hornpipe, (*dance*) matelote, *f.*
horny, (*hard of skin*) calleu|x, ~se.
horology, horlogerie, *f.*
horoscope, horoscope, *m.*; *cast a* ~, tirer un horoscope.
horribl|e, horrid, affreu|x, ~se; ~**y,** *horridly,* affreusement.
horrific, épouvantable.
horrify, frapper d'horreur; (*scandalize*) scandaliser.
horror, (*feeling and frightful thing*) horreur, *f.*; *have a* ~ *of,* avoir horreur de.
horse, cheval, *m.*; (*cavalry*) cavalerie, *f.*; *white* ~, (*sea*) mouton, *m.*; *light* ~, cavalerie légère, *f.*; ⚠ chevau-léger *is obsolete*; *2,000 horse,* (*cavalry*) deux mille chevaux; ~**-bean,** féverole, *f.*; ~**-box,** (*rail.*) wagon-écurie, *m.*; ~**-chestnut,** *see* CHESTNUT; ~**-fly,** taon, *m.*; ~**-pond,** abreuvoir, *m.*; ~**-power,** cheval vapeur, *m.* (*English abbrev. H.P.* = *French* C.V.); *5-~-power motor,* un moteur de 5 chevaux *or* de 5 C.V.; ~**-race,** course de chevaux, *f.*; ~**-radish,** (*bot.*) raifort, *m.*; ~**-tail,** (*bot.*) prèle, *f.*; ~**-whip,** *s.* cravache, *f.*; ~**-whip,** *v.a.* cravacher; **to** ~ **!,** à cheval!
horseback, *on* ~, à cheval; *go on* ~, aller* (être) à cheval.
horseman, cavalier, *m.*
horsemanship, équitation, *f.*
horseshoe, fer à cheval, *m.*
horsewoman, écuyère, *f.*
hortat|ive, ~**ory,** d'exhortation.
horticultur|e, horticulture, *f.*; ~**ist,** horticulteur, *m.*; ~**al,** d'horticulture.
hosanna, hosanna, *m.*
hose, *s.* bas, *m.pl.*; (*pipe*) tuyau, *m.*
hosier, bonnetier, *m.*; ~**y,** bonneterie, *f.*
hospice, hospice, *m.*
hospitab|le, hospitali|er, ~ère; ~**ly,** avec hospitalité.
hospital, hôpital, *m.*; ~ **orderly,** infirmier, *m.*; ~**-ship,** vaisseau-hôpital, *m.*
hospitality, hospitalité, *f.*
hospital(l)er, hospitalier, *m.*; (*chaplain*) chapelain, *m.*
host, hostess, *s.* (*entertainer at own house and landlord*) hôte, *m., fem.* hôtesse; (*crowd, multitude*) multitude, *f.*; (*Eucharist*) hostie, *f.*; *the God of Hosts,* le Dieu des armées.
hostage, otage, *m.*; (*fig.*) gage, *m.*
hostel, pension pour étudiants, *f.*; (*inn*) hôtellerie, *f.*
hostelry, hôtellerie, *f.*
hostil|e, hostile (à); ~**ity,** hostilité, *f.*; ~**ely,** hostilement.
hostler, *see* OSTLER.
hot, *adj.* (*lit., fig., scent*) chaud; (*sun*) brûlant; (*position, corner*) périlleu|x, ~se; *red-~,* chauffé au rouge; *have a* ~ *temper,* avoir le caractère emporté; *~-headed,* à tête chaude; ~ *-press, v.a.* (*paper, &c.*) satiner; ~ *-water-bottle, see* WATER, *v.a.*; ~ *water,* (*fig.*) une mauvaise passe; *strike the iron while it is* ~, battre le fer pendant qu'il est chaud; ~**ness,** chaleur, *f.*; ~**ly,** (*warmly, briskly*) chaudement; (*ardently*) ardemment.

hotbed, (*garden*) couche, *f.*; (*fig.*) foyer, *m.*
hotchpotch, ~pot, (*stew*) †hochepot, *m.*
hotel, hôtel, *m.*
hothouse, serre chaude, *f.*; ~ *grape,* raisin de serre, *m.*
Hottentot, *adj.* (*when an adj. use small letter*) *and s.m.f.* †Hottentot, -e.
hough, (*horse, &c.*) jarret, *m.*
hound, *s.* chien de meute, *m.*; *~'s tongue,* (*bot.*) cynoglosse, *f.*
hound, *v.a.* ~ *out,* chasser (de).
hour, heure, *f.*; **~s,** (*prayers*) heures, *f.pl.*; **~-glass,** sablier, *m.*; **~-hand,** aiguille des heures, *f.*; *a quarter of an ~,* un quart d'heure; *keep early, late, &c., ~s,* se coucher de bonne heure, tard; *business ~s, see* BUSINESS; *working-~s,* heures de travail, *f.pl.*
houri, †houri, *f.*
hourly, *adj.* d'heure en heure; (*continual*) continuel, -le; *adv.* d'heure en heure; (*frequently*) continuellement.
house, (*lit., family, comm., relig.*) maison, *f.*; (*Parl.*) Chambre, *f.*; (*theatr.*) salle, *f.*; (*household*) ménage, *m.*; (*Stk. Exchg.*) bourse, *f.*; *at, in, to the ~ of,* chez; *keep ~,* tenir* maison; *keep open ~;* tenir* table ouverte; **~-agent,** agent de location, *m.*; *House of Commons,* Chambre des Communes, *f.*; **~-dog,** chien de garde, *m.*; **~-property,** bien-fonds, *m.*; **~-surgeon,** interne d'hôpital, *m.*; **~-warming,** *have a,* pendre la crémaillère.
house, *v.a.* (*receive*) recevoir chez soi; (*crops*) rentrer (avoir); (*mast, naut.*) caler.
housebreaker, cambrioleur, *m.*
household, *s.* (*whole family*) maisonnée, *f.*; ~ *gods,* pénates, *m.pl.*; *adj.* domestique.
householder, locataire, *m.f.*
housekeep|er, (*bachelor, &c.*) gouvernante, *f.*; **~ing,** ménage, *m.*
houseleek, (*bot.*) joubarbe, *f.*
houseless, sans abri.
housemaid, (*chambermaid*) fille de chambre, *f.*
housewife, ménagère, *f.*; **~ly,** de ménagère.
housing, (*horse*) †housse, *f.*; **~-problem,** problème de fournir des maisons pour les ouvriers, *m.*
hovel, bicoque, *f.*; (*dirty*) taudis, *m.*; (*ruined*) masure, *f.*
hover, *v.n.* (*lit. and fig.*) planer (sur).
how, *adv.* comment; (*how much*) combien de; (*exclam.*) que!; ~ *long?* combien de temps?; ~ *many, much?* combien de?; (*exclam.*) que de!; ~ *often?* combien de fois?; (*exclam.*) que de fois!; ~ *are you?* comment allez-vous?; (*fam.*) comment cela va-t-il?; ~ *is it that?* comment se fait-il que?; *know ~ to,* savoir* +*inf.*
howbeit, *adv.* néanmoins.
however, *adv.* (*in whatever way*) de quelque manière que + *subj., e.g.* de quelque manière que vous vous y preniez (*set about it*); (+ *adj.*) quelque *or* si . . . que + *subj., e.g.* quelque riche qu'il soit.
however, *conj.* cependant.
howitzer, obusier, *m.*
howl, howling, *s.* (*an. and pers.*) †hurlement, *m.*; *v.a.n.* †hurler.
howl|er, †hurleur, *m.*; (*fam., mistake*) bourde, *f.*; **~ing,** *adj.* †hurleu|r, ~se; (*slang, glaring*) criant; (*wilderness*) morne.
howsoever, how . . . soever, de quelque manière que+*subj.*; (+ *adj.*) quelque . . . que +*subj.*; *see also* HOWEVER.
hoy, *s.* (*naut.*) petit vaisseau côtier, *m.*
hoy! *interj.* hé!; (*naut.*) ohé!
hoyden, jeune fille qui a des allures garçonnières, *f.*; **~ish,** garçonni|er, ~ère.
hub, (*wheel*) moyeu, *m.*; (*fig.*) centre, *m.*
hubbub, vacarme, *m.*
huckaback, (*stuff for towels*) grosse toile, *f.*
huckleberry, (*U.S.A.*) airelle, *f.*
huckster, *adj. and s.m.f.* regratti|er, ~ ère; *v.n.* regratter.
huddle, (*confusion*) confusion, *f.*; (*confused mass, fig.*) méli-mélo, *m.*
huddle, *v.a.* (*throw*) jeter pêle-mêle; (*pile*) entasser; *v.n.* ~ *together,* se serrer les uns contre les autres.
hue, couleur, *f.*; (*cry*) cri, *m.*; ~ *and cry,* clameur, *f.*
huff, *s.* accès de colère, *m.*; *be in a ~,* prendre* la mouche.
huff, *v.a.* rudoyer; *v.n.* s'offenser.
huffy, susceptible.
hug, *s.* étreinte, *f.*
hug, *v.a.* serrer dans les bras; (*opinions*) tenir* à; (*choke*) étouffer.
huge, énorme; **~ness,** énormité; **~ly,** énormément.
hugger-mugger, (*confusion*) désordre, *m.*; (*pop.*) pagaie, *f.*
huguenot, *adj.* (*when an adj. use small letter*) *and s.m.f.* †Huguenot, -e.
hulk, (*naut.*) ponton, *m.*; **~y,** gros, -se et lourd, -e.
hull, (*ship*) coque, *f.*; (*peas, beans, &c.*) cosse, *f.*; *v.a.* écosser.
hullabaloo, brouhaha, *m.*
hullo, *interj.* holà!; (*teleph.*) allô!
hum, humming, *s.* (*bee, &c.*) bourdonnement, *m.*; (*top*) ronflement, *m.*
hum, (*bee, &c.*) bourdonner; (*top*) ronfler; *we must make things ~,* il faut que ça ronfle; *v.a.n.* (*with closed lips*) chantonner.
hum, *interj.* †hein!; ~ *and ha,* ânonner.
human, humain; ~ **being,** être humain, *m.*; **~ly,** humainement.
humane, humain. ⚠ humain = *both 'human' and 'humane'*; **~ness,** humanité, *f.*; **~ly,** humainement.
human|ist, humaniste, *m.*; **~ism,** humanisme, *m.*
humanitarian, *adj.* humanitaire.
humanit|y, (*human nature or race, kindness*) humanité, *f.*; *the ~ies,* les humanités, *f.pl.*
humanize, (*make human or humane*) humaniser.

humankind, genre humain, *m.*

humb|le, (*pers., things, respectful*) humble; *I am your ~ servant,* je suis votre humble serviteur; **~leness,** humilité, *f.*; **~ly,** humblement.

humble-bee, bourdon, *m.*

humbug, *s.* (*trickery, fraud*) supercherie, *f.*; (*nonsense*); blague, *f.*; (*pers.*) charlatan, *m.*; (*teller of nonsense or lies*), blagueur, *m.*; *v.n.* blaguer; *v.a.* (*hoax, make fun of*) blaguer; (*inveigle*) emboбeliner.

humdrum, *adj.* (*things*) monotone.

humid, humide; **~ity,** humidité, *f.*

humilia|te, humilier; **~tion,** humiliation, *f.*; **~ting,** humiliant; **humility,** humilité, *f.*

humming, bourdonnant; **~-bird,** colibri, *m.*; **~-top,** toupie d'Allemagne, *f.*

hummock, mamelon, *m.*

humorist, (*lit.*) humoriste, *m.f.*; **~ic,** humoristique.

humorous, (*jocular*) facétieu|x, ~se; (*witty*) humoristique; (*funny*) drôle; **~ly,** plaisamment.

humour, *s.* (*satirical jocosity*) humour, *m.*; (*mood, mind to*) humeur, *f.*; (*comicality*) plaisanterie, *f.*; *be in a ~ to,* être d'humeur à; *sense of ~,* sens de l'humour, *m.*

humour, *v.a.* (*indulge*) se prêter à; (*satisfy*) satisfaire*; (*make concessions to*) ménager.

hump, *s.* (*pers., camel*) bosse, *f.*; **~backed,** bossu; *have the ~,* (*slang*) avoir le cafard.

humph, *interj.* ah, bah!

humus, humus, *m.*

Hun, (*slang*) *adj.* (*when an adj. use small letter*) *and s.m.f.* Boche.

hunch, *s.* (*back*) bosse, *f.*; (*large piece*) gros morceau, *m.*; (*bread*) quignon, *m.*; *have a ~,* (*U.S.A. slang*) soupçonner (que); *v.a.* (*back*) courber.

hunchback, *s.m.f.* bossu, -e.

hundred, *s.* cent, *m.* ⚠ *a, one ~* = cent *and not* un cent; **~s,** des centaines de.

hundred, *adj.* cent (+ s *only when multiplied by a number, and only if another number does not follow*); *100 per cent.,* cent pour cent.

hundredfold, *adj. and s.m.* centuple; *a ~,* au centuple.

hundredth, *adj. and s.m.* centième.

hundredweight, quintal, *m.*

Hungarian, *adj.* (*when an adj. use small letter*) *and s.m.f.* †Hongrois, -e; (*lang.*) †hongrois, *m.*

hunger, (*lit. and fig.*) faim, *f.*; *~-strike,* grève de faim, *f.*

hunger, *v.n.* avoir faim (de); (*fig.*) *~ for,* avoir soif de.

hungr|y, (*feeling hunger*) affamé; (*showing hunger*) famélique; (*eager for*) assoiffé (de); **~ily,** (*appetite*) avec voracité; (*with desire*) avidement.

hunk, (*bread*) quignon, *m.*

hunt, *s.* chasse, *f.*; (*with hounds*) chasse à courre, *f.*

hunt, *v.a.n.* (*game*) chasser; (*with hounds*) chasser à courre; (*pursue*) poursuivre*; (*dogs, &c.*) faire* chasser; *~ down,* (*an.*) forcer; *~ for,* chercher; *~ out,* découvrir*; *~ up,* rechercher.

hunter, chasseur, *m.*; (*horse*) †hunter, *m.*

hunting, *s.* chasse, *f.*; **~-box,** rendez-vous de chasse, *m.*

huntress, chasseresse, *f.*

huntsman, chasseur, *m.*; (*in charge of hounds*) piqueur, *m.*

hurdle, *s.* claie, *f.*; **~-race,** course des †haies, *f.*

hurdy-gurdy, orgue de Barbarie, *m.*

hurl, *v.a.* (*from a position, lit. and fig.*) précipiter; (*missile*) lancer.

hurly-burly, tintamarre, *m.*

hurrah, *s.m. and interj.* †hourra.

hurricane, ouragan, *m.*; **~-deck,** pont-promenade, *m.*

hurried, *adj.* (*flight, departure, &c.*) précipité; (*done, written, &c. hurriedly*) fait, écrit, etc. à la †hâte; **~ly,** à la hâte.

hurry, *s.* †hâte, *f.*; *be in a ~ to,* être pressé de; *be in a ~ for,* être pressé d'avoir; *don't be in a ~,* ne vous pressez pas; *in a ~,* (*hurriedly*) à la hâte; *there's no ~,* rien ne presse; **~-scurry,** *s.* bousculade, *f.*

hurry, *v.a.* presser, †hâter; *~ away,* (*pers.*) emmener précipitamment; *~ on,* †hâter.

hurry, *v.n.* se presser, *sometimes* courir*; *~ up!* pressez-vous!; *~ out,* sortir* (être) à la hâte.

hurt, *s.* mal, *m.*; (*fig., injury*) tort, *m.*

hurt, *v.a.* faire* mal à; (*harm*) faire* du mal à; (*injure*) nuire* à; (*feelings*) froisser.

hurt, *v.n.* faire* mal; (*get spoiled*) s'abîmer.

hurtful, nuisible; **~ness,** préjudice, *m.*; **~ly,** d'une manière nuisible.

hurtle, (*against*) *v.a.* †heurter (contre); *v.n.* (*fall with a crash*) tomber (être) avec fracas.

husband, *s.* mari, *m.*; *v.a.* ménager; (*strength*) économiser.

husbandman, fermier, *m.*

husbandry, agriculture, *f.*; (*careful management*) économie, *f.*

hush, *s.* calme, *m.*; (*silence*) silence, *m.*; **~-money,** prix du silence, *m.*

hush, *v.a.* calmer; (*scandal, &c.*) étouffer; *be ~ed,* se taire*.

hush! *interj.* chut!

husk, *s.* (*pea, &c.*) cosse, *f.*; (*corn, &c.*) glume, *f.*; (*fig.*) enveloppe, *f.*

husk, *v.a.* (*peas, beans, &c.*) monder.

husky, *s.* (*dog*) chien esquimau, *m.*

husk|y, *adj.* (*voice, pers.*) enroué; **~iness,** enrouement, *m.*; **~ily,** d'une voix enrouée.

hussar, †hussard, *m.*

huss(zz)y, friponne, *f.*

hustings, élections, *f.pl.*

hustl|e, *v.a.* (*jostle*) bousculer; (*thrust*

pers. into) pousser dans; (*impel to*) forcer à; *v.n.* (*clear a way through*) se frayer un passage à travers; (*hurry and U.S.A.*) se presser; **~er,** (*U.S.A.*) débrouillard, -e, *m.f.*; **~ing,** bousculade, *f.*
hut, cabane, *f.*; (*mil.*) baraque, *f.*
hutment, (*mil.*) baraquement, *m.*
hyacinth, (*bot.*) jacinthe, *f.*; ⚠ hyacinthe *in French = the gem 'jacinth'*; **~ine,** de couleur jacinthe.
hybrid, (*ans., plants, words*) *adj. and s.m.* hybride; **~ization,** hybridation, *f.*
hydra, (*myth., water-snake*) hydre, *f.*
hydrangea, (*bot.*) hortensia, *m.*
hydrant, (*pipe*) bouche d'eau, *f.*
hydraulic, *adj.* hydraulique; **~s,** hydraulique, *f.*
hydro, (*colloq.*) établissement hydrothérapique, *m.*
hydrocephalous, *adj.* (*med.*) hydrocéphale.
hydrodynamics, hydrodynamique, *f.*
hydrogen, hydrogène, *m.*
hydrograph|y, hydrographie, *f.*; **~ic,** hydrographique.
hydrology, hydrologie, *f.*
hydromel, hydromel, *m.*
hydrometer, hydromètre, *m.*
hydropath|y, hydrothérapie, *f.*; **~ic,** hydrothérapique.
hydrophobia, hydrophobie, *f.*
hydrostatics, hydrostatique, *f.*
hye(ae)na, hyène, *f.*
hygien|ics, ~e, hygiène, *f.*; **~ic,** hygiénique; **~ically,** hygiéniquement.
hymen, (*marriage*) hymen, *m.*; (*god*) Hymen, *m.*
hymn, cantique, *m.*; (*fig.*) hymne, *m.*; (*Church ~*) hymne, *f.*; *v.a.* célébrer.
hyperbol|e, (*rhet.*) hyperbole, *f.*; **~ical,** hyperbolique; **~ically,** hyperboliquement.
hyperborean, *adj.* hyperboréen, -ne.
hypercritical, hypercritique.
hyphen, *s.* trait d'union, *m.*; *v.a.* joindre* avec un trait d'union.
hypnot|ism, hypnotisme, *m.*; **~ic,** hypnotique; **~ize,** hypnotiser.
hypochondria, hypocondrie, *f.*; **~c,** *adj. and s.m.* hypocondriaque.
hypocri|sy, hypocrisie, *f.*; **~te,** hypocrite, *m.f.*; **~tical,** hypocrite.
hypodermic, *adj.* (*med.*) hypodermique; *~ injection,* piqûre, *f.*
hypophosphate, (*chem.*) hypophosphate, *m.*
hyposulphate, (*chem.*) hyposulfate, *m.*
hypotenuse, (*geom.*) hypoténuse, *f.*
hypoth|esis, hypothèse, *f.*; **~etical,** hypothétique.
hyssop, (*bot.*) hysope, *f.*
hyster|ia, (*med.*) hystérie, *f.*; **~ics,** ⚠ hystérie *is a pathological term. If 'hysterics' = simply 'laughter', 'tears', &c., it =* accès de fou rire, de larmes, *m., &c.*
hysterical, (*med.*) hystérique.

I

I, *subj. of verb,* je, *but (a) alone, (b) complement of* être, *(c) when as subject it is separated from verb, (d) when there is more than one subj., (e) in comparisons 'I' =* moi.
iamb, iambe, *m.*; **~ic,** iambique.
ibex, (*zool.*) bouquetin, *m.*
ibis, (*ornith.*) ibis, *m.*
ice, glace, *f.*; **~-breaker,** brise-glace, *m. invar.*; **~-cream,** fromage à la crême, *m.*; *v.a.* (*lit., drink, pastry*) glacer; (*wine, &c.*) frapper.
iceberg, iceberg, *m.*
Iceland|er, Islandais, -e, *m.f.*; **~ic,** islandais; **~ic,** (*lang.*) islandais, *m.*
ichneumon, (*zool.*) ichneumon, *m.*; **~-fly,** ichneumon, *m.*
ichor, (*myth. and med.*) ichor, *m.*
ichthyosaurus, ichtyosaure, *m.*
icicle, glaçon, *m.*
iciness, froid glacial, *m.*
icon, icone, *f.*
ichthyology, ichthyologie, *f.*
iconoclas|m, iconoclasme, *m.*; **~t,** iconoclaste, *m.*
icy, (*lit. and fig.*) glacial.
idea, idée, *f.*; *the ~ !* par exemple! ; *remotest ~,* moindre idée, *f.*
ideal, *adj. and s.m.* idéal (*adj. pl.* idéaux; *s.pl.* idéals *or* idéaux); **~ism,** idéalisme, *m.*; **~ist,** idéaliste, *m.*; **~ize,** idéaliser; **~ly,** idéalement.
identical (*with*), identique (à); **~ly,** identiquement.
identif|y, *v.a.* identifier (à); *~y oneself with,* s'identifier à; **~ication,** identification, *f.*
identity, identité, *f.*
ideolog|ist, idéologue, *m.*; **~ical,** idéologique.
ides, ides, *f.pl.*
idiocy, idiotie, *f.*
idiom, (*language*) idiome, *m*; ⚠ idiome *does not = form of expression peculiar to a language, which =* idiotisme, *m.*; **~atic,** idiomatique; **~atically,** suivant le génie de la langue.
idiosyncrasy, idiosyncrasie, *f.*; (*of style*) particularité, *f.*
idiot, *s.m.f.* idiot, -e; ⚠ idiot *implies a real defect and is offensive*; *'idiot' = 'fool' is* sot, -te, *s.m.f.*
idiotic, (*offensive*) idiot, -e; (*foolish*) imbécile; **~ally,** stupidement.
idl|e, (*unoccupied*) désœuvré; (*lazy*) paresseu|x, ~se; (*of time*) de loisir; (*groundless*) sans fondement; (*frivolous*) frivole; *~ talk, tales,* sornettes, *f.pl.*; **~eness,** (*inaction*) oisiveté, *f.*; (*laziness*) paresse, *f.*; **~y,** dans l'oisiveté; (*vainly*) inutilement.
idle, *v.a. ~ away,* (*time*) perdre; *v.n.* fainéanter.
idler, fainéant, -e, *s.m.f.*
idol, (*lit. and fig.*) idole, *f.*

idolat|er, ~ress, idolâtre, *m.f.*; **~rous,** idolâtre; **~ry,** idolâtrie, *f.*
idolize, adorer; (*pej.*) idolâtrer.
idyll, (*lit. and fig.*) idylle, *f.*; **~ic,** idyllique.
i.e., c'est-à-dire.
if, *s.* si, *m.* (*pl.* si).
if, *conj.* (*supposing that*) si (*not with fut. or conditional*); *~ not,* si ce n'est; *~ so,* s'il en est ainsi.
igneous, igné.
ignis fatuus, feu follet, *m.*
ignite, *v.a.* enflammer; *v.n.* s'enflammer.
ignition, ignition, *f.*; (*motor*) allumage, *m.*; *~ spark,* (*motor*) étincelle d'allumage, *f.*
ignobl|e, (*birth*) plébéien, -ne; (*base*) ignoble; **~y,** ignoblement.
ignominious, (*pers.*) méprisable; (*causing ignominy*) ignominieu|x, ~se; **~ly,** ignominieusement.
ignominy, ignominie, *f.*
ignoramus, ignorant, -e, *m.f.*
ignoran|t, ignorant; *be ~ of,* ignorer; **~ce,** ignorance, *f.*; **~tly,** par ignorance.
ignore, *v.a.* refuser de connaître; ⚠ *not* ignorer *which = 'be ignorant of', 'not to know'.*
iguana, (*zool.*) iguane, *m.*
ilex, (*bot.*) yeuse, *f.*
ilk, *of that ~,* (*estate, lands*) du même; (*pop., kind, set*) sorte, *f.*
ill, *s.* mal, *m.*; *speak ~ of,* dire du mal de.
ill, *adj.* (*sick*) malade; (*bad, hurtful*) mauvais; ~ **luck,** malheur, *m.*; ~ **temper,** mauvaise humeur, *f.*; ~ **turn,** mauvais service, *m.*; *be taken ~,* tomber (être) malade; *look ~,* avoir mauvaise mine.
ill, *adv.* mal; (*scarcely*) ne . . . guère; **~-bred,** mal élevé; **~-equipped,** (*for*) mal outillé (pour); **~-favoured,** (*featured*) laid; **~-gotten,** mal acquis; **~-intentioned,** mal intentionné; **~-natured,** méchant; **~-omened,** de mauvais augure; **~-starred,** né (*of pers.*), conçu (*of thing*) sous une mauvaise étoile; **~-timed,** déplacé; **~-treat,** *v.a.* maltraiter.
illegal, illégal; **~ity,** illégalité, *f.*; **~ly,** illégalement.
illegib|le, illisible; **~ility,** illisibilité, *f.*; **~ly,** illisiblement.
illegitima|te, (*unlawful, child, conclusion*) illégitime; **~cy,** illégitimité, *f.*; **~tely,** d'une manière illégitime.
illiberal, (*narrow-minded*) d'esprit étroit; (*stingy*) mesquin; (*without culture*) sans éducation; **~ly,** sans largeur d'esprit; (*meanly*) sans générosité.
illicit, illicite; **~ly,** illicitement.
illimitabl|e, illimitable; **~y,** illimitablement.
illiterate, *adj.* illettré.
illness, maladie, *f.*
illogical, illogique; **~ly,** illogiquement.
illuminat|e, (*light up*) éclairer; (*subject*) éclaircir; (*MSS.*) enluminer; ⚠ illuminer = *'illuminate for festivity'.*
illuminati, illuminés, *m.pl.*
illumination, (*lighting*) éclairage, *m.*; (*splendour*) éclat, *m.*; (*buildings, &c.*) illumination, *f.*; (*MSS.*) enluminure, *f.*
illuminative, éclairant.
illuminator, enlumineu|r, ~se, *m.f.*
illumine, *v.a.* (*lit. and fig.*) éclairer.
illusion, illusion, *f.*
illusionist, prestidigitateur, *m.*
illus|ive, ~ory, illusoire; **~ively,** illusoirement.
illustra|te, (*explain, book, newspaper*) illustrer; **~tion,** (*example*) exemple, *m.*; (*book, &c.*) illustration, *f.*
illustrative, qui sert d'exemple.
illustrator, (*books, &c.*) illustrateur, *m.*
illustrious, illustre.
image, (*lit., mental, and reflection*) image, *f.*; (*exact resemblance*) portrait, *m.*; ⚠ image *does not = 'statue' which =* statue, *f.*
image, *v.a.* (*portray*) représenter; (*reflect*) réfléchir; *~ to oneself,* se figurer.
imagery, (*lit.*) images, *f.pl.*
imaginabl|e, imaginable; **~y,** autant qu'on peut se le figurer.
imaginary, imaginaire.
imagination, (*fancy and faculty*) imagination, *f.*
imaginative, imaginati|f, ~ve.
imagine, se représenter; (*suppose*) supposer; (*picture, fancy*) se figurer.
imbecil|e, (*weak-minded and foolish*) *adj. and s.m.f.* imbécile; **~ity,** imbécillité, *f.*
imbibe, *v.a.* (*air, drink*) absorber; (*ideas*) être imbu de; (*moisture*) s'imbiber de.
imbricate, imbriquer.
imbroglio, imbroglio, *m.*
imbrue, tremper.
imbue, imbiber (de); ~ **with,** (*fig.*) pénétrer de.
imitable, imitable.
imita|te, imiter; **~tion,** *s.* imitation, *f.*; (*counterfeit*) contrefaçon, *f.*; **~tion,** *adj.* simili- + *noun in question, e.g.* simili-marbre, *imitation marble*; **~tive,** imitati|f, ~ve.
imitator, imitat|eur, ~rice, *m.f.*
immacula|te, (*gen. and theol.*) immaculé; **~cy,** pureté sans tache, *f.*; **~tely** *dressed,* tiré à quatre épingles.
immanen|t, immanent; **~ce,** immanence, *f.*
immaterial, immatériel, -le; (*without importance*) peu important; ⚠ immatériel *never has this sense in French: it is ~,* peu importe.
immatur|e, pas mûr; (*premature*) prématuré; **~ity,** (*lit. and fig.*) immaturité, *f.*; **~ely,** prématurément.
immeasurab|le, incommensurable; **~ility,** incommensurabilité, *f.*; **~ly,** immensément.
immediate, (*of time, without medium, next,*

prompt) immédiat; **~ly,** (*time and contact*) immédiatement.
immemorial, immémorial; **~ly,** *from time ~*, de temps immémorial.
immens|e, immense; (*slang = 'ripping'*) fameu|x, ~se; **~ity,** immensité, *f.*; **~ely,** immensément.
immers|e, immerger; (*baptism*) baptiser par immersion; (*thought, &c.*) plonger (dans); (*debt, &c.*) accabler (de); **~ion,** immersion, *f.*
immigrant, *adj. and s.m.f.* immigrant, -e.
immigra|te, *v.n.* immigrer; **~tion,** immigration, *f.*
imminen|t, imminent; **~ce,** imminence, *f.*
immitigable, implacable.
immobil|e, immobile; **~ity,** immobilité, *f.*
immobilize, (*comm., fix., mil.*) immobiliser.
immoderate, immodéré; **~ly,** immodérément.
immodest, (*indelicate, indecent*) immodeste; (*impudent*) impudent; **~y,** immodestie, *f.*; **~ly,** immodestement.
immola|te, immoler; **~tion,** (*lit. and fig.*) immolation, *f.*
immoral, immoral; **~ity,** immoralité, *f.*; **~ly,** immoralement.
immortal, *s. the* **~s,** (*French Acad., the gods*) Immortels, *m.pl.*; **~ity,** immortalité, *f.*; *adj.* (*lit. and fig.*) immortel, -le; **~ly,** immortellement; **~ize,** immortaliser.
immovab|le, (*motionless, not movable*) immobile; (*not subject to change*) immuable; **~ility,** immobilité, *f.*; **~ly,** inébranlablement.
immun|e, *~ from*, à l'abri de; **~ity,** (*disease, taxes, &c.*) immunité, *f.*
immure, claquemurer.
immutab|le, immuable; ⚠ immutable *not French*; **~ility,** immutabilité, *f.*; **~ly,** immuablement.
imp, (*little devil*) diablotin, *m.*; (*naughty child*) lutin, -e, *m.f.*; **~ish,** espiègle.
impact, †heurt, *m.*; *point of ~*, (*projectile*) point d'impact, *m.*
impair, altérer; (*health*) affaiblir.
impale, empaler; **~ment,** empalement, *m.*
impalpab|le, impalpable; **~ility,** impalpabilité, *f.*
imparisyllabic, *adj. and s.m.* imparisyllabe.
impart, (*communicate information, secret*) communiquer; (*give share of*) donner; ⚠ impartir = *'grant', 'allow'*.
impartial, impartial; **~ity,** impartialité, *f.*; **~ly,** impartialement.
impassable, infranchissable.
impasse, (*lit. and fig.*) impasse, *f.*
impassib|le, impassive, impassible; **~ility, impassiveness,** impassibilité, *f.*; **~ly,** impassiblement.
impassion, *v.a.* passionner.
impassive, impassible.
impatien|t, impatient; *~ of*, impatient de; *~ to+inf.* impatient de; **~ce,** (*want of composure, longing*) impatience, *f.*; **~tly,** impatiemment.
impeach, (*public official*) mettre* en accusation; (*character, &c.*) dénigrer; (*accuse*) accuser.
impeachment, (*public*) mise en accusation, *f.*; (*accusation*) accusation, *f.*
impeccab|le, impeccable; **~ility,** impeccabilité, *f.*; **~ly,** impeccablement.
impecunious, besogneu|x, ~se.
impede, empêcher.
impediment, obstacle, *m.*; (*in speech*) bégayement, *m.*; **~a,** impedimenta *or* impédiments, *m.pl.*
impel, (*force*) forcer (à); (*propel*) pousser.
impend, *v.n.* (*threaten*) menacer; (*hang over*) être suspendu sur.
impending, *adj.* imminent.
impenetrab|le, impénétrable; **~ility,** impénétrabilité, *f.*; **~ly,** impénétrablement.
impeniten|t, impénitent; **~ce,** impénitence, *f.*
imperative, *s.* (*gram.*) impératif, *m.*; *adj.* impérati|f, ~ve; **~ly,** impérativement.
imperceptib|le, imperceptible; **~ility,** imperceptibilité, *f.*; **~ly,** imperceptiblement.
imperfect, *s.* (*gram.*) imparfait, *m.*; *adj.* imparfait; **~ion,** imperfection, *f.*; **~ly,** imparfaitement.
imperial, impérial; **~ism,** impérialisme, *m.*; **~ist,** impérialiste, *m.*; **~istic,** impérialiste; **~ly,** impérialement.
imperial, (*beard*) impériale, *f.*
imperil, *v.a.* mettre* en péril.
imperious, impérieu|x, ~se; **~ness,** arrogance, *f.*; **~ly,** impérieusement.
imperishable, impérissable.
impermeab|le, imperméable; **~ility,** imperméabilité, *f.*
impersonal, (*lit. and gram.*) impersonnel; **~ity,** impersonnalité, *f.*; **~ly,** impersonnellement.
impersonate, *v.a.* (*personify*) personnifier; (*personate*) se faire passer pour.
impertinen|t, impertinent; **~ce,** impertinence, *f.*; *piece of ~ce*, impertinence, *f.*; **~tly,** impertinemment.
imperturbab|le, imperturbable; **~ility,** imperturbabilité, *f.*; **~ly,** imperturbablement.
impervious, impénétrable; (*to water, &c.*) imperméable; *~ to*, (*fig.*) inaccessible à; **~ness,** impénétrabilité, *f.*; (*fluids*) imperméabilité, *f.*
impetu|ous, impétueu|x, ~se; **~osity,** impétuosité, *f.*; **~ously,** impétueusement.
impetus, force impulsive, *f.*
impiety, impiousness, impiété, *f.*
impinge on, se †heurter à.
impious, impie; **~ly,** avec impiété.
implacab|le, implacable; **~ility,** implacabilité, *f.*; **~ly,** implacablement.

implant, implanter (dans); (*instil*) inculquer (dans).
implement, (*tool*) outil, *m.*; **~s,** (*war, hunting, &c.*) attirail, *m.*; (*gardening, &c.*) ustensiles, *m.pl.*; *v.a.* (*complete, fulfil*) exécuter.
implica|te, (*involve, imply*) impliquer; **~tion,** implication, *f.*; (*insinuation*) insinuation, *f.*
implicit, (*implied and theol.*) implicite; (*absolute*) absolu; **~ly,** (*impliedly*) implicitement.
implore, implorer.
impolite, impoli; **~ness,** impolitesse, *f.*; **~ly,** impoliment.
impolitic, (*ill-advised*) mal à propos.
imponderable, (*lit. and fig.*) impondérable.
import, *s.* (*meaning*) signification, *f.*; (*comm.*) importation, *f.*; **~s,** importations, *f.pl.*; ~ *duty,* droits d'entrée, *m.pl.*; ~ *trade,* commerce d'importation, *m.*
import, *v.a.* (*goods, introduce*) importer; (*mean*) signifier; *v.n.* (*be of consequence, often impers.*) importer.
importan|t, (*of consequence, pompous*) important; **~ce,** importance, *f.*; **~tly,** avec importance.
import|ation, importation, *f.*; **~er,** importat|eur, ~rice, *m.f.*
importunate, importun; **~ness,** importunité, *f.*; **~ly,** avec importunité.
importun|e, (*pester*) importuner; (*solicit*) solliciter; **~ity,** importunité, *f.*
impose, (*hands, taxes, terms, silence*) imposer (à); ~ *on,* (*deceive*) en imposer à.
imposing, imposant.
imposition, (*hands, tax, &c.*) imposition, *f.*; (*deceit*) tromperie, *f.*; (*school*) pensum, *m.*
impossib|le, impossible; (*absurd*) absurde; *utterly* ~, de toute impossibilité; **~ility,** impossibilité, *f.*; **~ly,** impossiblement.
impost, (*tax*) impôt, *m.*; (*arch.*) imposte, *f.*
impostor, imposteur, *m.*
imposture, imposture, *f.*
impoten|t, impotent; (*pathol.*) impuissant; **~ce,** impotence, *f.*; **~tly,** sans force.
impound, (*pers.*) enfermer; (*confiscate*) confisquer.
impoverish, appauvrir; **~ment,** appauvrissement, *m.*
impracticab|le, impraticable; **~ility,** impraticabilité, *f.*
impreca|te, (*call down*) appeler (sur); **~tion,** imprécation, *f.*; **~tory,** imprécatoire.
impregnable, imprenable.
impregna|te, *v.a.* rendre prégnante; (*imbue with, fig.*) imprégner de; **~tion,** imprégnation, *f.*
imprescriptible, imprescriptible.
impress, *s.* impression, *f.*; (*stamp*) empreinte, *f.*
impress, (*imprint and fig.*) imprimer; (*make impression on*) impressionner; (*requisition*) réquisitionner; (*men*) enrôler de force.
impression, (*on mind, body, stamping, printing, book, mark*) impression, *f.*; *make an* ~ *on,* faire* impression sur; *be under the* ~ *that,* avoir l'impression que.
impressionab|le, impressionnable; **~ility,** impressionnabilité, *f.*
impressioni|sm, (*Lit., art.*) impressionnisme, *m.*; **~st,** impressionniste, *m.*
impressive, impressionnant; **~ly,** d'une manière impressionnante.
imprint, *s.* (*impression stamp*) impression, *f.*; (*on title-page*) nom de l'éditeur, *m.*
imprint, *v.a.* (*lit., fig.*) imprimer.
imprison, emprisonner; **~ment,** emprisonnement, *m.*
improbab|le, improbable; **~ility,** improbabilité, *f.*; **~ly,** peu probablement.
improbity, improbité, *f.*
impromptu, *adj. invar., s.m., and adv.* impromptu.
improper, (*inaccurate*) impropre; (*unseemly*) inconvenant; **~ly,** improprement; (*unseemly*) d'une manière inconvenante.
impropriety, (*unfitness*) impropriété, *f.*; (*unseemliness*) inconvenance, *f.*
improvable, susceptible d'amélioration.
improve, *v.a.* améliorer; (*mind*) cultiver; *he is much ~d,* il a bien gagné; ~ *opportunity,* profiter de l'occasion; *v.n.* s'améliorer; (*health, &c.*) devenir* (être) meilleur, -e; (*prices*) être en †hausse; ~ *upon,* (*surpass*) surpasser; ~ *upon acquaintance,* gagner à être connu.
improvement, amélioration, *f.*; (*health*) mieux, *m.*; (*buildings, &c.*) embellissement; (*progress*) progrès, *m.*; *latest ~s,* derniers perfectionnements, *m.pl.*
improviden|t, imprévoyant; **~ce,** imprévoyance, *f.*; **~tly,** avec imprévoyance.
improving, *adj.* instructi|f, ~ve.
improvis|e, improviser; **~ation,** improvisation, *f.*; **~ator,** improvisateur, *m.*
impruden|t, imprudent; **~ce,** imprudence, *f.*; **~tly,** imprudemment.
impuden|t, impudent; **~ce,** impudence, *f.*; **~tly,** impudemment.
impugn, (*call in question statement, action*) attaquer.
impulse, impulsion, impulsion, *f.*; (*of the heart, &c.*) mouvement, *m.*; (*inspiration*) inspiration, *f.*
impulsive, impulsi|f, ~ve; **~ly,** spontanément.
impunity, impunité, *f.*
impur|e, (*lit. and fig.*) impur; **~ity,** impureté, *f.*; **~ely,** impurement.
imputa|ble, imputable (*to, on* = sur); **~tion,** imputation, *f.*
impute, (*pej.*) imputer (à); (*attribute*) attribuer (à).
in, *prep.* (*with article or determining word also = 'after' of time*) dans; (*gen. without*

determining word, countries, continents, material, with verbal noun) en; (*towns, masc. countries outside Europe, local position*) à; (*authors*) chez; (*after superlatives and with* façon, manière, voix, ton, *&c.*) de; (*out of + numbers*) sur; ~ *the evening,* le soir; *10 o'clock* ~ *the morning,* 10 heures du matin; ~ *hundreds,* par centaines; ~ *length,* de long; ~ *this weather,* par ce temps.

in, *adv.* (*at home*) chez soi; (*arrived*) arrivé; (*crops*) rentré; (*polit. in power*) au pouvoir; (*fire*) n'être pas éteint.

inability, (*physical*) impuissance, *f.*; (*mind*) incapacité, *f.*; être incapable de *is often used.*

inaccessib|le, inaccessible; **~ility,** inaccessibilité, *f.*

inaccura|te, inexact; **~cy,** inexactitude, *f.*; **~tely,** inexactement.

inaction, inaction, *f.*

inactiv|e, (*pers.*) inacti|f, ~ve; (*things*) inerte; **~ity,** inactivité, *f.*

inadequa|te, insuffisant; **~cy,** insuffisance, *f.*; **~tely,** insuffisamment.

inadmissib|le, inadmissible; **~ility,** inadmissibilité, *f.*

inadverten|t, négligent; **~ce, ~cy,** inadvertence, *f.*; **~tly,** par inadvertence.

inalienab|le, inaliénable; **~ility,** inaliénabilité, *f.*

inalterable, inaltérable.

inane, (*empty*) vide; (*senseless*) stupide; **~ly,** stupidement.

inanimate, inanimé.

inanition, inanition, *f.*

in(un)appeasable, inapaisable.

inapplicable, inapplicable.

inapposite, inapplicable; (*out of place*) déplacé.

inappreciable, inappréciable.

inapprehensible, incompréhensible.

inappropriate, impropre (à).

inapt, inapte; **~itude,** inaptitude, *f.*

inarticulate, (*not jointed*) inarticulé; (*speech*) sans pouvoir s'exprimer.

inartificial, naturel, -le.

inartistic, sans art; (*without artistic feeling*) sans sens artistique.

inasmuch as, vu que.

inattent|ive, inattenti|f, ~ve; **~ion,** inattention, *f.*; **~ively,** d'un air distrait.

inaudibl|e, qu'on ne peut entendre; **~y,** à ne pouvoir être entendu.

inaugural, inaugural.

inaugura|te, inaugurer; **~tion,** inauguration, *f.*

inauspicious, de mauvais présage.

inborn, inbred, inné.

incalculab|le, incalculable; **~ly,** incalculablement.

incandescen|t, incandescent; **~ce,** incandescence, *f.*

incantation, incantation, *f.*

incapab|le, incapable (de); (*not susceptible*) peu susceptible (de); **~ility,** incapacité, *f.*

incapacit|ate, frapper d'incapacité; **~y,** (*lit., fig., law*) incapacité, *f.*

incarcera|te, incarcérer; **~tion,** incarcération, *f.*

incarnadine, *adj.* incarnadin.

incarna|te, *adj.* incarné; *v.a.* (*lit. and fig.*) incarner; **~tion,** (*lit., fig., theol.*) incarnation, *f.*

incautious, imprudent; **~ly,** imprudemment.

incendiar|y, *adj. and s.m.f.* (*lit. and fig.*) incendiaire; **~y bomb,** bombe flamboyante, *f.*; **~ism,** crime d'incendie, *m.*

incense, *s.* (*lit. and fig.*) encens, *m.*; *v.a.* encenser; (*enrage*) courroucer.

incentive, *s.* aiguillon, *m.*; *adj.* provocant.

inceptive, qui commence; (*gram.*) inchoati|f, ~ve.

inception, commencement, *m.*

incessant, incessant; **~ly,** sans cesse.

incest, inceste, *m.*; **~uous,** incestueu|x, ~se.

inch, *s.* pouce, *m.*; (*small amount*) rien, *m.*; *by ~es,* peu à peu; (*pej.*) à petit feu; *be within an ~ of,* être à deux doigts de.

inchoate, (*just begun in arts, sciences*) commençant; (*undeveloped*) peu développé.

inchoative, (*gram.*) inchoati|f, ~ve.

incidence, (*tax, phys.*) incidence, *f.*; (*scope*) étendue, *f.*

incident, *s.* incident, *m.*; *adj.* (*naturally belonging to*) qui tient à.

incidental, fortuit; ~ *to,* appartenant à.

incinera|te, incinérer; **~tion,** incinération, *f.*; **~tor,** (*refuse*) incinérateur, *m.*

incipient, naissant.

incis|e, *v.a.* inciser; **~ion,** incision, *f.*; **~ive,** (*lit. and fig.*) incisi|f, ~ve; (*mentally sharp*) pénétrant.

incisor, (*tooth*) incisive, *f.*

incite, inciter (à); **~ment,** incitation, *f.*

incivility, incivilité, *f.*

inclemen|t, (*weather, climate*) inclément; **~cy,** inclémence, *f.*

inclination, (*slope*) inclinaison, *f.*; (*propensity, affection*) inclination (à), *f.*

incline, *v.a.* (*bend*) incliner; (*ear*) prêter; *~d to,* porté à; *v.n.* (*lean, be disposed*) incliner (à); *~d plane,* plan incliné, *m.*

include, renfermer; (*in a whole*) comprendre*.

including, included, y compris (*concord only after noun*).

inclusion, inclusion, *f.*

inclusive, inclusi|f, ~ve; (*terms, &c.*) tout compris; *from Tues. to Thurs. ~,* de mardi à jeudi inclusivement; **~ly,** inclusivement.

incognito, *adv.* incognito.

incoheren|t, incohérent; (*heterogeneous*) hétérogène; **~ce,** incohérence, *f.*; **~tly,** sans cohérence.

incohesive, sans cohésion.

incombustib|le, incombustible, **~ility,** incombustibilité, *f.*

income, *s.* revenu, *m.*, *often pl.*; **~-tax,** impôt sur (le) revenu, *m.*; ~ *-tax return,* déclaration de revenu, *f.*
incoming, *adj.* (*tide*) qui monte; ~ *mail,* courrier à l'arrivée, *m.*; **~s,** *s.* revenus, *m.pl.*
incommensurab|le, incommensurable; (*not comparable in size with*) incomparable à; **~ility,** incommensurabilité, *f.*
incommensurate with, disproportionné à.
incommod|e, *v.a.* incommoder; **~ious,** incommode.
incommunicable, incommunicable.
incommunicative, peu communicati|f, ~ve.
incommutable, immuable; ⚠ *not* incommutable *which* = *'inalienable in law'*.
incomparab|le, (*with, to*) incomparable (à); **~ly,** incomparablement.
incompatib|le, incompatible; **~ility,** incompatibilité, *f.*
incompeten|t, (*lit. and law*) incompétent; **~ce,** incompétence, *f.*
incomplete, incompl|et, ~ète; **~ly,** incomplètement.
incomprehensib|le, incompréhensible; **~ility,** incompréhensibilité, *f.*; **~ly,** incompréhensiblement.
incomputable, incalculable.
inconceivab|le, inconcevable; **~ly,** inconcevablement.
inconclusive, peu concluant.
incongru|ous, (*out of place, unseemly*) incongru; **~ity,** incongruité, *f.*
inconsequen|t, inconséquent; **~ce,** inconséquence, *f.*
inconsiderable, insignifiant.
inconsiderate, (*thoughtless*) inconsidéré, ⚠ *which does not* = *'without regard for' which* = manquant d'égards pour.
inconsisten|t, (*with one's principles, &c.*) inconséquent; *~t with,* (*incompatible*) incompatible avec; **~cy,** inconséquence, *f.*; **~tly,** inconséquemment.
inconsolable, inconsolable.
inconspicuous, peu visible.
inconstan|t, inconstant; **~cy,** inconstance, *f.*
incontestab|le, incontestable; **~ly,** incontestablement.
incontinen|t, (*without restraint, med., unchaste*) incontinent; **~ce,** incontinence, *f*; **~tly,** (*at once*) incontinent.
incontrovertib|le, incontestable; **~ly,** incontestablement.
inconvenien|t, incommode; ⚠ inconvénient *is a noun* = *'inconvenience'*, *'harm'*; **~ce,** incommodité, *f.*; (*disturbance*) dérangement, *m.*; **~tly,** mal à propos.
inconvertible, inconvertible.
inconvincible, qu'on ne peut convaincre.
incorpora|te, *v.a. ~te in, with,* incorporer à; *v.n. ~te with,* s'incorporer à; **~tion,** incorporation, *f.*
incorporeal, incorporel, -le.
incorrect, (*contrary to fact*) inexact; (*faulty, inaccurate, improper*) incorrect; **~ness,** inexactitude, incorrection, *f.*; **~ly,** inexactement, incorrectement.
incorrigib|le, incorrigible; **~ly,** incorrigiblement.
incorruptib|le, incorruptible; **~ility,** incorruptibilité, *f.*
increas|e, *s.* augmentation, *f.*; (*value, price*) plus-value, *f.* (*pl.* plus-values); (*of the earth*) fruits, *m.pl.*; *on the ~e,* en accroissement; *v.a.* augmenter; *v.n.* augmenter; (*volume, sound*) grossir; **~ing,** croissant.
incredib|le, incroyable; **~ility,** incrédibilité, *f.*; **~ly,** incroyablement.
incredul|ous, incrédule; **~ity,** incrédulité, *f.*
increment, augmentation, *f.*
incriminate, incriminer.
incrust, couvrir* d'une croûte; (*inlay*) incruster; **~ation,** (*inlay, salt, &c.*) incrustation, *f.*
incuba|te, couver; **~tion,** incubation, *f.*; **~tor,** couveuse, *f.*
incubus, (*spirit and fig.*) incube, *m.*; (*nightmare*) cauchemar, *m.*
inculcate, inculquer (*upon, pers.* à, *in mind* dans).
inculpa|te, inculper (de); **~tion,** inculpation, *f.*
incumben|cy, (*eccles.*) possession de bénéfice, *f.*; **~t,** *s.* bénéficier, *m.*
incumbent, *be ~ on,* incomber à.
incur, *v.a.* (*obligation, debt*) contracter; (*risk*) courir*; (*expense*) faire*; (*bring on oneself*) s'attirer.
incurab|le, (*lit. and fig.*) incurable; **~ility,** incurabilité, *f.*; **~ly,** incurablement.
incuri|ous, peu curieu|x, ~se; **~osity,** incuriosité, *f.*
incursion, incursion, *f.*
incurve, *v.a.* incurver.
indebted, endetté; (*obliged*) redevable (à = *to,* de = *for*).
indecen|cy, indécence, *f.*; **~t,** (*improper, immodest, obscene*) indécent; **~tly,** indécemment.
indecis|ion, indécision, *f.*; **~ive,** (*uncertain, irresolute, battle*) indécis; **~ively,** d'une manière indécise.
indeclinable, indéclinable.
indecor|um, manque de décorum, *m.*; **~ous,** inconvenant.
indeed, *adv.* (*in fact*) de fait; (*really*) vraiment.
indefatigab|le, infatigable; **~ly,** infatigablement.
indefeasible, imprescriptible.
indefensible, (*mil.*) indéfendable; (*fig.*) insoutenable.
indefinable, indéfinissable.
indefinite, (*lit. and gram.*) indéfini; **~ly,** (*time*) indéfiniment.
indelible, indélébile.
indelica|cy, (*coarseness*) grossièreté, *f.*; (*want of tact*) indélicatesse, *f.*; **~te.**

(*unseemly*) inconvenant; (*coarse*) gros-si|er, ~ère; (*tactless*) sans tact; **~tely,** d'une manière indélicate.
indemnif|y, (*for*) indemniser (de); **~ication,** indemnisation, *f.*
indemnity, indemnité, *f.*
indent, *s.* (*notch*) dentelure, *f.*; (*indenture*) contrat, *m.*; (*comm.*) ordre, *m.*; *v.a.* denteler; *v.n.* (*comm.*) passer contrat; **~ation,** dentelure, *f.*
indenture, (*apprentice*) contrat d'apprentissage, *m.*
independen|ce, indépendance, *f.*; **~t,** (*lit., unwilling to depend, unconnected*) indépendant (de); **~tly,** indépendamment (*of* = de).
indescribable, indescriptible; (*vague*) vague.
indestructib|le, indestructible; **~ility,** indestructibilité, *f.*
indeterminable, indéterminable.
indetermina|te, *adj.* indéterminé; **~tion,** indétermination, *f.*; **~tely,** indéterminément.
index, (*forefinger, book, Cath. Ch.*) index, *m.*; (*on dial, &c.*) aiguille, *f.*; (*math.*) exposant, *m.*; *v.a.* (*book, &c.*) mettre* un index à.
Indian, *adj.* (*when an adj. use small letter*) *and s.m.f.* Indien, -ne; *adj. also* des Indes; **~ corn,** maïs, *m.*; **~ mutiny,** révolte des Cipayes, *f.*; *Red* ~, Peau-Rouge, *m.*
india-rubber, caoutchouc, *m.*; (*for erasing*) gomme élastique, *f.*
indicate, *v.a.* indiquer; (*state briefly*) dire* brièvement.
indication, indication, *f.*; (*sign*) signe, *m.*
indicative, *s.* (*gram.*) indicatif, *m.*; *adj.* (*lit. and gram.*) indicati|f, ~ve.
indicator, (*instr.*) indicateur, *m.*
indict, accuser (de); **~ment,** accusation, *f.*
indifferen|t, (*unconcerned, unimportant*) indifférent (à); (*rather bad than good*) passable; **~ce,** (*unconcern*) indifférence, *f.*; (*a matter*) *of* ~*ce*, qui n'a pas d'importance; **~tly,** (*with indifference, impartially*) indifféremment; (*poorly, passably*) passablement.
indigenous, indigène.
indigen|ce, indigence, *f.*; **~t,** indigent.
indigestible, (*lit. and fig.*) indigeste.
indigestion, indigestion, *f.*
indignant, indigné (de = *at*, contre = *with*); **~ly,** avec indignation.
indignity, (*insult*) affront, *m.*
indigo, indigo, *m.*
indirect, indirect; **~ly,** indirectement.
indiscernible, *adj.* indiscernable.
indiscipline, indiscipline, *f.*
indiscreet, indiscr|et, ~ète; (*unguarded*) irréfléchi; **~ly,** imprudemment.
indiscretion, imprudence, *f.*; (*official*) indiscrétion, *f.*; (*against social convention*) indélicatesse, *f.*
indiscriminate, *adj.* sans distinction; (*promiscuous*) confus; **~ly,** sans distinction.
indispensab|le, indispensable; **~ly,** indispensablement.
indispos|e, *v.a.* (*make unwell*) indisposer; (*make averse*) indisposer (contre); **~ition,** (*ailment*) indisposition, *f.*; (*aversion*) aversion (pour), *f.*
indisputab|le, incontestable; **~ly,** incontestablement.
indissolub|le, indissoluble; **~ility,** indissolubilité, *f.*; **~ly,** indissolublement.
indistinct, indistinct; **~ness,** défaut de netteté, *m.*; **~ly,** peu distinctement.
indistinguishable, qu'on ne peut distinguer.
indite, rédiger.
individual, *s.* individu, *m.*; *private* ~, particuli|er, ~ère, *m.f.*
individual, *adj.* individuel, -le; **~ly,** individuellement.
individual|ity, individualité, *f.*; **~ism,** individualisme, *m.*
indivisib|le, indivisible; **~ility,** indivisibilité, *f.*
indocil|e, indocile; **~ity,** indocilité, *f.*
indolen|ce, indolence, *f.*; **~t,** indolent; **~tly,** indolemment.
indomitable, indomptable.
indoor, *adj.* d'intérieur.
indoors, *adv.* à la maison; *go* ~, rentrer (être); *keep, stay* ~, ne pas sortir* (être).
indraw, *s.* (*aeron.*) appel d'air, *m.*
indubitab|le, indubitable; **~ly,** indubitablement.
induce, *v.a.* (*persuade*) persuader (à + *pers.*, de + *inf.*); (*cause*) occasionner; **~ment,** (*incentive*) incitation, *f.*; (*motive*) motif, *m.*
induct, installer (dans); (*initiate*) initier (à); **~ion,** installation, *f.*; (*log., inference, electr.*) induction, *f.*; **~ive,** inducti|f, ~ve; **~ively,** par induction.
indulge, *v.a.* (*desires, vices*) se livrer (à); (*hopes*) caresser; (*children*) avoir trop d'indulgence pour; ~ *oneself in*, se permettre*.
indulgence, (*indulging, leniency, theol.*) indulgence, *f.*; (*slackness*) laisser-aller, *m.*
indulgent, indulgent; (*yielding*) complaisant; **~ly,** avec indulgence, complaisance.
industrious, travailleu|r, ~se; **~ly,** assidûment.
industry, (*diligence*) assiduité, *f.*; (*trade*) industrie, *f.*; ⚠ industrie *is more dexterity, intelligence.*
indwell, habiter (dans).
inebria|te, *s.* alcoolique, *m.f.*; *v.a.* enivrer; **~tion,** ivresse, *f.*
inedited, inédit.
ineffab|le, ineffable; **~ly,** ineffablement.
ineffaceable, ineffaçable.
ineffective, inefficace; **~ly,** sans effet.
ineffectual, inefficace; **~ly,** inefficacement.
inefficacious, (*med.*) inefficace.

inefficien|t, (*pers.*) incapable; (*ineffective*) inefficace; **~cy,** (*pers.*) incapacité, *f.*; (*ineffectiveness*) inefficacité, *f.*
inelastic, inélastique.
inelegan|ce, inélégance, *f.*; **~t,** inélégant; **~tly,** sans élégance.
ineligib|le, inéligible; **~ility,** inéligibilité, *f.*
ineluctable, inéluctable.
inept, (*out of place*) déplacé; (*silly*) inepte; **~itude,** ineptie, *f.*; **~ly,** sottement.
inequality, (*size, surface*) inégalité, *f.*
inequitable, peu équitable.
ineradicable, indéracinable.
inert, (*lit., phys., fig.*) inerte; **~ia, ~ness,** inertie, *f.*
inessential, peu essentiel, -le.
inestimable, inestimable.
inevitab|le, inévitable; **~ly,** inévitablement.
inexact, inexact; **~itude,** inexactitude, *f.*; **~ly,** inexactement.
inexcusable, inexcusable.
inexhaustib|le, inépuisable; **~ly,** inépuisablement.
inexorab|le, inexorable; **~ly,** inexorablement.
inexpedien|t, inopportun; **~cy,** inopportunité, *f.*
inexperience, inexpérience, *f.*; **~d,** inexpérimenté.
inexpert, inhabile.
inexpiable, inexpiable.
inexplicable, inexplicable.
inexpressib|le, inexprimable; **~ly,** indiciblement.
inexpressive, sans expression.
inexpugnable, inexpugnable.
inextensible, inextensible.
inextinguishable, inextinguible.
inextricab|le, inextricable; **~ly,** inextricablement.
infallib|le, infaillible; **~ility,** infaillibilité, *f.*; **~ly,** infailliblement.
infamous, infâme; **~ly,** d'une manière infâme.
infamy, infamie, *f.*
infant, enfant, *m.f.*; **~***s' school*, (école) maternelle, *f.*; *adj. and* **~ile,** (*of infants*) infantile.
infant|e, ~a, (*Spain*) infant, -e, *m.f.*
infanticide, (*pers. and crime*) infanticide, *m.*
infantry, infanterie, *f.*; **~man,** fantassin, *m.*
infatua|te, *v.a.* faire* tourner la tête à; *be ~ted with,* (*pers.*) s'engouer de; (*thing*) raffoler de; **~tion,** engouement, *m.*
infect, *v.a.* (*contaminate, pollute*) infecter ⚠ *it has only this meaning; 'imbue with'* = communiquer à.
infect|ion, (*disease and morals*) infection, *f.*; **~ious,** (*disease*) infectueu|x, ~se.
infelicit|ous, (*expression*) mal à propos; **~y,** (*misfortune*) malheur, *m.*; (*expression*) maladresse, *f.*; **~ously,** mal à propos.
infer, *v.a.* (*conclude*) conclure*; (*imply*) supposer; **~ence,** conclusion, *f.*
inferior, *s.* inférieur; *adj.* (*in space, rank, quality*) inférieur; **~ity,** infériorité, *f.*; *~ity complex,* (*approx.*) manque de confiance en soi, *m.*
infernal, (*of hell, fiendish*) infernal; (*fam. confounded*) abominable; **~ly,** (*fam.*) diablement.
inferno, enfer, *m.*
infertil|e, infertile; **~ity,** infertilité, *f.*
infest, infester (de).
infidel, *s.* (*hist.*) infidèle, *m.*; (*unbeliever*) incrédule, *m.f.*; *adj.* (*unbelieving*) incrédule; **~ity,** (*unbelief*) incrédulité, *f.*; (*disloyalty*) infidélité, *f.*
infiltra|te, infiltrer; **~tion,** infiltration, *f.*
infinite, infini; **~ly,** infiniment.
infinitesimal, infinitésimal.
infinitive, *s.* infinitif, *m.*; *adj.* infiniti|f, ~ve.
infinitude, infinity, infinité, *f.*
infirm, infirme; **~ity,** infirmité, *f.*
infirmary, infirmerie, *f.*
inflame, (*set on fire, aggravate*) enflammer.
inflammab|le, (*lit. and fig.*) inflammable; **~ility,** inflammabilité, *f.*
inflamma|tion, (*lit., fig., med.*) inflammation, *f.*; ~ *of the lungs,* fluxion de poitrine, *f.*; **~tory,** (*speeches, &c.*) incendiaire; (*med.*) inflammatoire.
inflate, (*lit., fig., comm.*) gonfler; **~d,** (*style*) bouffi.
inflation, (*balloon, &c.*) gonflement, *m.*; (*currency*) inflation, *f.*; (*style*) enflure, *f.*
inflect, (*bend*) infléchir; (*noun*) décliner; (*verb*) conjuguer.
inflexib|le, inflexible; **~ility,** inflexibilité, *f.*; **~ly,** inflexiblement.
inflexion, (*lit. and gram.*) inflexion, *f.*
inflict, infliger; (*presence, &c. on*) imposer à; **~ion,** (*punishment*) châtiment, *m.*; (*bore*) ennui, *m.*
influen|ce, *s.* influence, *f.*, (sur); *v.a.* influencer; (*have effect on*) influer sur; **~tial,** influent.
influenza, grippe, *f.*
influx, (*people*) affluence, *f.*
inform, (*tell*) informer; (*imbue*) animer (de); *well ~ed,* instruit; *keep ~ed,* tenir* au courant (de).
informal, (*not in due form*) irréguli|er, ~ère; (*without formality*) sans cérémonie; **~ity,** absence de cérémonie, *f.*; **~ly,** sans cérémonie.
informant, informat|eur, ~rice, *m.f.*
information, information, *f.*; ⚠ information *cannot be used of accusation in law which* = dénonciation, *f.*; (*particulars*) renseignements, *m.pl.*; (*knowledge*) connaissances, *f.pl.*; *gather ~,* prendre* des informations.
informative, instructi|f, ~ve.
informer, délat|eur, ~rice, *m.f.*
infraction, violation, *f.*
infrequen|cy, rareté; **~t,** rare.

infringe, enfreindre*; **~ment,** infraction, *f.*
infuriate, rendre furieu|x, ~se.
infuse, (*lit. and fig.*) infuser (dans); (*pour*) verser; (*instil*) inspirer (à); (*tea*) faire* infuser; *be ~d,* (*tea*) s'infuser.
infusion, (*lit., fig., liquid, tea, &c.*) infusion, *f.*
ingathering, *s.* (*harvest*) rentrée, *f.*
ingenious, ingénieu|x, ~se; **~ly,** ingénieusement.
ingenuity, ingéniosité, *f.*; ⚠ *not* ingénuité *which* = '*ingenuousness*'.
ingenuous, ingénu; **~ness,** ingénuité, *f.*; **~ly,** ingénument.
ingle, feu, *m.*; **~-nook,** coin du feu, *m.*
inglorious, inglorieu|x, ~se; **~ly,** inglorieusement.
ingot, lingot, *m.*
ingrained, invétéré.
ingratiate, *v.a.* se concilier les bonnes grâces de.
ingratiating, insinuant.
ingratitude, ingratitude, *f.*
ingredient, ingrédient, *m.*
ingress, entrée, *f.*
ingrowing, (*nail*) incarné.
ingurgitate, *v.a.* ingurgiter.
inhabit, habiter; **~ant,** habitant, *m.*
inhabitable, habitable; ⚠ *in French* inhabitable = '*uninhabitable*'.
inhale, *v.a.* aspirer; *v.n.* (*tobacco*) avaler la fumée; **~r,** appareil inhalateur, *m.*
inharmonious, inharmonieu|x, ~se; **~ly,** sans harmonie.
inherent, inhérent; **~ly,** inséparablement.
inherit, *v.a.n.* hériter (de); **~ance,** héritage, *m.*; **~or, ~rix,** hériti|er, ~ère, *m.f.*
inhibit, (*forbid*) défendre (de); (*hinder*) empêcher.
inhospitable, inhospitali|er, ~ère.
inhuman, inhumain; **~ity,** inhumanité, *f.*; **~ly,** inhumainement.
inhume, inhumer.
inimical, hostile (à).
inimitable, inimitable.
iniquit|ous, inique; **~y,** iniquité, *f.*
initial, *s.* initiale, *f.*; **~s,** parafe, *m.*; *adj.* initial; (*capital, expenses*) de premier établissement; *v.a.* parafer.
initiat|e, *v.a.* (*begin*) commencer; (*mysteries, &c.*) initier (à); (*set going*) mettre* en train; **~ion,** (*mysteries, instruction in*) initiation, *f.*; (*beginning*) commencement; **~ive,** initiative, *f.*
initiator, initiat|eur, ~rice, *m.f.*; **~y,** préliminaire.
inject, injecter (de); **~ion,** injection, *f.*
injudicious, peu judicieu|x, ~se; **~ly,** peu judicieusement.
injunction, injonction, *f.*
injure, nuire* à; (*interests, health, &c.*) léser; (*goods*) avarier; (*wound*) blesser; ⚠ *not* injurier *which* = '*abuse*'; **~d,** (*offended*) offensé.
injur|y, (*to pers.*) préjudice, *m.*, (*things*) dommage, *m.*; (*wound*) blessure, *f.*; **~ious,** nuisible (à).
injustice, injustice, *f.*
ink, encre, *f.*; **marking-~,** encre à marquer, *f.*; **~-pot, -stand,** encrier, *m.*; *v.a.* tacher d'encre.
inkling, vent, *m.*; *have an ~ of,* avoir vent de.
inland, *s.* intérieur, *m.*; *adj.* intérieur; *adv.* à l'intérieur.
inlay, *s.* marqueterie, *f.*; (*inlaid work, ivory, &c., on surface*) incrustation, *f.*; *v.a.* (*wood, marble*) marqueter, incruster.
inlet, (*sea*) bras de mer, *m.*
inmate, habitant, -e, *m.f.*
inmost, innermost, *adj.* (le) plus intérieur; (*secret*) (le) plus secret.
inn, auberge, *f.*; (*tavern*) taverne, *f.*
innate, inné.
innavigable, innavigable.
inner, intérieur.
innkeeper, aubergiste, *m.f.*
innocent, *s.* (*in all senses*) innocent, *m.*; *adj.* (*not guilty, simple*) innocent (de); **~ly,** innocemment.
innocuous, innoxious, inoffensi|f, ~ve.
innova|te, innover; **~tion,** innovation, *f.*; **~tor,** innovat|eur, ~rice, *m.f.*
innuendo, insinuation, *f.*
innumerable, innombrable.
inoculate, (*med.*) inoculer; (*plant*) greffer.
inodorous, inodore.
inoffensive, (*harmless*) inoffens|if, ~ive.
inoperative, inopérant.
inopportune, inopportun; **~ness,** inopportunité, *f.*; **~ly,** inopportunément.
inordinate, (*enormous*) démesuré; (*disorderly*) désordonné; **~ly,** (*beyond measure*) démesurément.
inorganic, inorganique.
inquest, enquête, *f.*
inquire, *v.a.* demander.
inquire, *v.n.* (*make inquiries*) se renseigner (auprès de = '*of*' (*pers.*), à propos de = '*about*' (*thing*)); *~ after, for,* demander des nouvelles de; *~ into,* prendre* des informations sur; *~ within,* s'adresser ici.
inquiringly, d'un air interrogateur.
inquiry, demande, *f.*; (*investigation*) recherche, *f.*; (*law*) enquête, *f.*; *make inquiries about,* s'informer de.
inquisi|tion, investigation, *f.*; (*law*) enquête, *f.*; *the Inquisition,* l'Inquisition, *f.*; **~tor,** (*hist.*) inquisiteur, *m.*
inquisitive, curieu|x, ~se; **~ness,** curiosité, *f.*; **~ly,** curieusement.
inroad, incursion, *f.*; (*encroachment*) empiètement, *m.*
inrush, irruption, *f.*
insalubr|ious, insalubre; **~ity,** insalubrité, *f.*
insane, (*lit. and fig.*) fou (fol + *vowel or silent* H), folle; **~ly,** follement.
insanitary, antihygiénique.
insanity, démence, *f.*

insatiab|le, insatiable; **~ility,** insatiabilité, *f.*; **~ly,** insatiablement.
inscribe, (*write, geom.*) inscrire*; (*engrave*) graver; (*book*) dédier.
inscription, inscription, *f.*; (*dedication*) dédicace, *f.*
inscrutable, inscrutable.
insect, insecte, *m.*; **~icide,** insecticide, *m.*; **~ivorous,** insectivore.
insecur|e, (*not safe*) peu sûr; **~ity,** insécurité, *f.*; **~ely,** peu sûrement.
insensib|le, (*unconscious*) sans connaissance; (*without feeling, imperceptible*) insensible; **~ility,** insensibilité, *f.*; (*unconsciousness*) inconscience, *f.*; **~ly,** imperceptiblement.
insensitive, peu sensible.
inseparab|le, inséparable; **~ility,** inséparabilité, *f.*; **~ly,** inséparablement.
insert, insérer (dans); **~ion,** insertion, *f.*; (*lace*) entre-deux, *m. invar.*
inset, *s.* page, etc., intercalée, *f.*; *v.a.* (*page, &c.*) intercaler.
inside, *s.* intérieur, *m.*; (*stomach*) estomac, *m.*; *adj.* intérieur; *adv.* à l'intérieur; *prep.* à l'intérieur de.
insidious, (*treacherous*) perfide; (*disease*) insidieu|x, ~se; **~ness,** (*treachery*) perfidie, *f.*; **~ly,** perfidement.
insight, (*faculty*) pénétration, *f.*; *give an ~ into,* éclaircir.
insignia, insignes, *m.pl.*
insignifican|ce, insignifiance, *f.*; **~t,** insignifiant.
insincer|e, peu sincère; **~ity,** manque de sincérité, *m.*; **~ely,** peu sincèrement.
insinua|te, (*introduce, hint*) insinuer; *~te oneself into,* s'insinuer dans; **~tion,** insinuation, *f.*; **~ting,** insinuant.
insipid, (*lit. and fig.*) insipide; **~ity,** insipidité, *f.*
insist (on), insister (sur); **~ence,** insistance, *f.*; **~ently,** avec insistance.
insobriety, intempérance, *f.*
insolen|ce, insolence, *f.*; **~t,** insolent; **~tly,** insolemment.
insolub|le, insoluble; **~ility,** insolubilité, *f.*
insolven|cy, insolvabilité, *f.*; **~t,** insolvable.
insomnia, insomnie, *f.*
insomuch *that,* à tel point (que).
inspect, *v.a.* inspecter; **~ion,** inspection, *f.*; **~or,** inspecteur, *m.*
inspiration, (*theol., poet., &c., inhaling, suggestion*) inspiration, *f.*
inspire, (*poet., writing, inhale*) inspirer; (*animate*) animer (de); *~ pers. with,* inspirer, *acc. of thing,* à + *pers.*
inspiring, *adj.* inspirat|eur, ~rice.
inspirit, encourager; **~ing,** *adj.* encourageant.
instability, instabilité, *f.*
install, (*in place, function, electr.*) installer; **~ation,** installation, *f.*
instalment, (*comm.*) versement, *m.*; *monthly ~,* versement mensuel, *m.*
instance, exemple, *m.*; (*case*) cas, *m.*; (*request*) demande, *f.*; ⚠ instance = *'entreaty' in French and never has the sense of 'example'*; *for ~,* par exemple; *in the first ~,* en premier lieu.
instance, *v.a.* citer en exemple.
instant, *s.* instant, *m.*; *adj.* urgent; *the 6th ~,* le 6 courant (*abbrev.* ct).
instantaneous, instantané; **~ly,** instantanément.
instantly, à l'instant.
instiga|te, (*provoke*) provoquer; **~te to,** inciter à; **~tion,** instigation, *f.*; **~tor,** instigat|eur, ~trice, *m.f.*
instil, (*into mind, &c.*) inculquer (à).
instinct, (*lit. and fig.*) instinct, *m.*; **~ive,** instincti|f, ~ve; **~ively,** d'instinct.
institute, *s.* (*learned or literary*) institut, *m.*; *v.a.* instituer; (*begin*) commencer.
institution, (*action, thing instituted*) institution, *f.*
instruct, instruire*; **~ion,** instruction, *f.*; **~ions,** instructions, *f.pl.*
instructive, instructi|f, ~ve.
instructor, institut|eur, ~rice, *m.f.*
instrument, (*lit., fig., mus.*) instrument, *m.*; **~al,** (*mus.*) instrumental; *be ~al in,* contribuer à.
instrumentalist, instrumentiste, *m.*
instrumentality, *by the ~ of,* par l'intermédiaire de.
insubordina|te, insubordonné; **~tion,** insubordination, *f.*
insubstantial, insubstantiel, -le.
insufferab|le, insupportable; **~ly,** insupportablement.
insufficien|cy, insuffisance, *f.*; **~t,** insuffisant; **~tly,** insuffisamment.
insular, (*of an island*) insulaire; (*narrow-minded*) qui a les vues étroites; **~ity,** (*geog.*) insularité, *f.*
insula|te, (*electr., heat*) isoler; **~tion,** (*electr.*) isolation, *f.*; ⚠ *not* isolement *which = English 'isolation'.*
insulator, (*electr.*) isolateur, *m.*
insult, *s.* insulte, *f.*; *v.a.* insulter; **~ing,** insultant; **~ingly,** d'une manière insultante.
insuperable, insurmontable.
insupportable, insupportable.
insurable, assurable.
insurance, assurance, *f.*; *life ~,* assurance sur la vie, *f.*; *~ company,* compagnie d'assurances, *f.*; *~ policy,* police d'assurance, *f.*; ⚠ insurance *not French.*
insure, (*fire, risk, furniture, &c.*) assurer.
insurgent, *adj. and s.m.f.* insurgé, -e.
insurmountable, insurmontable.
insurrection, insurrection, *m.*
insusceptible, *~ of,* non susceptible de; **~ to,** (*agency, &c.*) insensible à.
intact, intact.
intaglio, intaille, *f.*
intangib|le, intangible; **~ility,** intangibilité, *f.*
integer, nombre entier, *m.*

integral, *s.* (*math.*) intégrale, *f.*; *adj.* (*whole and math.*) intégral; **~ly,** intégralement.
integrate, *v.a.* compléter; (*math.*) intégrer.
integrity, intégrité, *f.*
integument, tégument, *m.*
intellect, (*faculty*) intellect, *m.*; (*understanding, brains*) intelligence, *f.*; (*mind*) esprit, *m.*
intellectual, intellectuel, -le; **~ly,** intellectuellement.
intelligence, (*understanding, brains*) intelligence, *f.*; (*news*) nouvelle, *f.*; (*information*) renseignements, *m. pl.*; ~ *department,* (*mil.*) service des renseignements, *m.*
intelligencer, (*spy*) espion, *m.*
intelligent, intelligent; **~ly,** avec intelligence.
intelligib|le, intelligible; **~ly,** intelligiblement.
intemper|ate, (*lit. and fig.*) intempérant; (*violent*) violent; **~ance,** (*lit. and fig.*) intempérance, *f.*
intend, *v.a.* (*mean*) vouloir* dire; ~ *to,* se proposer de; (*destine for*) destiner (à).
intended, *s.* (*fam.*) fiancé, -e, *m.f.*
intense, intense; (*extreme*) extrême; (*ardent*) ardent; **~ly,** extrêmement.
intensity, intensité, *f.*; (*ardour*) ardeur, *f.*; (*violence*) violence, *f.*
intent, *s.* intention, *f.*
intent, *adj.* ~ *on,* (*absorbed in*) absorbé dans; (*resolved to*) résolu à; **~ly,** très attentivement.
intention, intention, *f.*; **~al,** intentionnel, -le; **~ally,** intentionnellement.
intentness, application sérieuse, *f.*
inter, *v.a.* enterrer.
interact, entr'acte, *m.*
interaction, action réciproque, *f.*
interbreed, *v.a.* (*animals*) croiser.
intercede, intercéder (auprès de + *pers.*).
intercept, (*pers., light, letter, &c.*) intercepter; **~ion,** interception, *f.*
intercess|ion, intercession, *f.*; **~or,** intercesseur, *m.*
interchange, *s.* échange, *m.*; *v.a.* échanger; **~able,** interchangeable.
intercourse, commerce, *m.*
interdict, (*eccles.*) interdit, *m.*; *v.a.* interdire*.
interest, *s.* (*curiosity, importance, concern, pecuniary, stake, comm.*) intérêt, *m.*; *compound* ~, intérêts composés, *m.pl.*; *simple* ~, intérêts simples, *m.pl.*; *in the* ~ *of,* dans l'intérêt de; *it is to your* ~ *to,* il est de votre intérêt de; *have an* ~ *in,* avoir intérêt à; *take* ~ *in,* prendre* intérêt à.
interest, *v.a.* intéresser.
interesting, intéressant.
interfere, *v.n.* intervenir* (être); ~ *with,* (*impede*) gêner; (*meddle*) se mêler de; ~ *in,* (*dispute, &c.*) intervenir* (être) dans.
interference, intervention, *f.*
interim, *s.* intérim, *m.*; *adj.* provisoire.
interior, *s.* intérieur, *m.*; *adj.* intérieur.
interjection, (*gram.*) interjection, *f.*
interlace, *v.a.* entrelacer; (*fig.*) entremêler.
interlard, *v.a.* (*speech, &c.*) entrelarder (de).
interleaf, *s.* feuillet blanc, *m.*
interleave, *v.a.* interfolier.
interline, *v.a.* interligner; **~ar,** interlinéaire.
interlock, *v.a.* enclencher; *v.n.* s'enclencher.
interlocutor, interlocut|eur, ~rice, *m.f.*
interloper, intrus, -e, *m.f.*
interlude, intermède, *m.*
intermarr|iage, (*tribes*) mariage entre tribus différentes, *m.*; (*relations*) mariage entre proches parents, *m.*; **~y,** *v.n.* se marier entre parents.
intermeddle, ~ *in, with,* se mêler de.
intermediary, *adj. and s.m.f.* intermédiaire.
intermediate, intermédiaire.
intermedium, intermédiaire, *m.*
interment, enterrement, *m.*
interminab|le, interminable; **~ly,** interminablement.
intermingle, *v.a.* entremêler; *v.n.* ~ *with,* s'entremêler avec.
intermission, pause, *f.*
intermit, *v.a.* interrompre.
intermitten|ce, intermittence, *f.*; **~t,** intermittent; **~tly,** par intermittences.
intermix, *v.a.* entremêler; *v.n.* se mêler.
intern, interner; **~ment,** internement, *m.*
internal, *adj.* interne; (*comm.*) intérieur; (*body, war, &c.*) intestin; **~ly,** intérieurement.
international, international; **~ism,** internationalisme, *m.*
internecine, meurtri|er, ~ère.
interpellate, *v.a.* (*parl.*) interpeller.
interpola|te, interpoler; **~tion,** interpolation, *f.*
interpos|e, *v.a.* (*insert*) interposer (entre); (*objection, &c.*) introduire*; *v.n.* (*interrupt*) intervenir* (être); **~ition,** interposition, *f.*
interpret, interpréter; **~ation,** interprétation, *f.*; **~er,** interprète, *m.f.*
interregnum, interrègne, *m.*
interroga|te, interroger; **~tion,** interrogation, *f.*
interrogative, *adj.* (*gram.*) interrogati|f, ~ve; ⚠ *interrogative also* = '*questioning*', '*of inquiry*', *which is never* interrogatif *but* interrogat|eur, ~rice.
interrogatory, *s.* interrogatoire, *m.*; *adj. see* INTERROGATIVE.
interrupt, interrompre; (*stillness, &c.*) rompre; **~ion,** interruption, *f.*; **~er,** interrupt|eur, ~rice, *m.f.*
intersect, entrecouper; (*geom.*) couper; **~ion,** intersection, *f.*
intersperse, (*scatter with*) parsemer (de).
interstellar, interstellaire.

interstice, interstice, *m.*
intertwine, entrelacer.
interval, intervalle, *m.*; *at* **~s,** par intervalles.
intervene, (*unexpectedly*) survenir* (être); (*interfere*) intervenir* (être); (*be situated between*) se trouver entre.
intervening, *adj.* intermédiaire.
intervention, intervention, *f.*
interview, entrevue, *f.*; (*press*) interview, *m.f.*; *v.a.* (*press*) interviewer.
interweave, tisser ensemble; (*fig.*) entremêler.
intestate, *adj. and s.m.* intestat, *invar.*
intestinal, intestinal.
intestine, *adj.* (*war, &c.*) intestin; **~s,** *s.* (*med.*) intestins, *m.pl.*
intimacy, intimité, *f.*
intimate, *s.* intime, *m.*
intimate, *adj.* (*personal, familiar, knowledge, essential*) intime; **~ly,** intimement.
intimate, *v.a.* (*make known*) annoncer; (*hint*) suggérer.
intimation, avis, *m.*; (*hint*) suggestion, *f.*
intimida|te, intimider; **~tion,** intimidation, *f.*
into, dans; (*without article or determining* (*word*) en, *sometimes* à.
intolerab|le, intolérable; **~ly,** intolérablement.
intoleran|ce, intolérance, *f.*; **~t,** intolérant.
intonation, intonation, *f.*
intone, entonner.
intoxicant, spiritueux, *m.*
intoxica|te, (*lit. and fig.*) enivrer; **~tion,** ivresse, *f.*; (*fig.*) enivrement, *m.*; **~ting,** enivrant.
intractab|le, (*pers.*) intractable; (*things*) difficile à manier.
intransitive, intransiti|f, ~ve.
intrepid, intrépide; **~ity,** intrépidité, *f.*; **~ly,** intrépidement.
intric|ate, compliqué; **~acy,** complication, *f.*; **~ately,** d'une manière compliquée.
intrigu|e, (*amorous, polit., court*) intrigue, *f.*; *v.n.* (*lit. and rouse curiosity*) intriguer (avec); **~er,** intrigant, -e, *m.f.*; **~ing,** *adj.* intrigant, -e; ⚠ intriguant *is pres. part. of* intriguer.
intrinsic, intrinsèque; **~ally,** intrinsèquement.
introduce, (*bring in, forward, &c.*) introduire*; (*one person to another*) présenter; (*question, fashion*) amener.
introduct|ion, introduction, *f.*; (*of pers.*) présentation, *f.*; **~ory,** d'introduction, *f.*
introspect|ion, introspection, *f.*; **~ive,** introspecti|f, ~ve.
introvert, *v.a.* tourner en dedans.
intrud|e, *v.a.* (*thrust*) introduire*; (*presence, &c.*) imposer (à); ~ *upon, on,* (*pers.*) importuner; (*time, &c.*) abuser de; **~er,** intrus, -e, *m.f.*
intrude, *v.n.* s'introduire*; (*thrust oneself in*) se fourrer.
intrus|ion, (*visitor, &c.*) intrusion, *f.*; **~ive,** importun.
intuit|ion, intuition, *f.*; **~ive,** intuiti|f, ~ve; **~ively,** intuitivement.
intumescent, intumescent.
inunda|te, inonder; **~tion,** inondation, *f.*
inure, aguerrir (à).
invad|e (*lit. and fig.*) envahir; **~er,** envahisseur, *m.*
invalid, *s.* malade, *m.f.*; **~ed,** infirme; (*mil.*) réformé. ⚠ *Not* invalide *which* = *'disabled pers., mil. pensioner'.*
invalid, *adj.* malade; **~-chair,** fauteuil de malade, *m.*
invalid, *adj.* (*law*) invalide; **~ity,** invalidité, *f.*; **~ate,** invalider.
invaluable, inappréciable.
invariab|le, invariable; **~ly,** invariablement.
invasion, (*lit. and encroachment*) invasion, *f.*
invective, invective, *f.*
inveigh, ~ *against,* invectiver contre.
inveigle, enjôler; **~ment,** *inveigling,* enjôlement, *m.*
invent, inventer; **~ion,** invention, *f.*; **~or,** invent|eur, ~rice, *m.f.*; **~ive,** inventi|f, ~ve.
inventory, inventaire, *m.*
inverse, *adj. and s.m.* inverse; **~ly,** inversement.
inversion, interversion, *f.*; (*gram. only*) inversion, *f.*
invert, (*order, &c.*) intervertir; (*turn upside down*) renverser.
invertebrate, *adj. and s.m.* invertébré, -e.
invest, *v.a.* (*clothe*) vêtir* (de); (*with office, mil.*) investir; (*money*) placer.
investiga|te, rechercher; **~tion,** investigation, *f.*
investiture, investiture, *f.*
investment, (*money*) placement, *m.*; ⚠ investissement, *m., is only used in mil. sense.*
investor, (*stockholder*) renti|er, ~ère, *m.f.*
invetera|te, invétéré; **~cy,** (*obstinacy*) opiniâtreté, *f.*
invidious, odieu|x, ~se.
invigilate, (*exams.*) surveiller.
invigora|te, fortifier; **~ting,** fortifiant.
invincib|le, invincible; **~ility,** invincibilité, *f.*; **~ly,** invinciblement.
inviolab|le, inviolable; **~ility,** inviolabilité, *f.*; **~ly,** inviolablement.
inviolate, *adj.* intact.
invisib|le, invisible; **~ility,** invisibilité, *f.*; **~ly,** invisiblement.
invitation, invitation, *f.*
invite, (*lit. and fig.*) inviter (à); (*solicit opinions, &c.*) solliciter; (*bring on*) provoquer.
invitingly, d'une manière engageante.
invocation, invocation, *f.*
invoice, *s.* facture, *f.*; **~-book,** facturier, *m.*; **~-clerk,** factur|ier, ~ière, *m.f.*; *v.a.* facturer.
invoke, invoquer.

involuntar|y, involontaire; **~ily**, involontairement.
involve, (*wrap, lit. and fig.*) envelopper (dans); (*implicate*) impliquer (dans); (*entail*) entraîner.
involvement, implication, *f.*; (*money*) embarras, *m.*
invulnerab|le, invulnérable; **~ility**, invulnérabilité, *f.*
inward, *adj.* intérieur; (*situated inside*) interne; (*intimate*) intime; **~ness**, (*inner nature*) essence, *f.*; **~ly**, intérieurement.
inwards, intérieurement; (*within*) en dedans.
inweave, enlacer.
inwrought *with*, incrusté de.
iodine, iode, *m.*
Ion|ian, ionien, -ne; **~ic**, ionique.
iota, (*letter and fig.*) iota, *m.*
IOU, reconnaissance de dette, *f.*
ipecacuanha, ipéca, *m.*
irascib|le, irascible; **~ility**, irascibilité, *f.*
ir|e, (*poet., anger*) ire, *f.*; **~ate**, courroucé.
iridescen|ce, iridescence, *f.*; **~t**, iridescent.
iris, (*bot., eye*) iris, *m.*
Irish, Irishman, *adj.* (*when an adj. use small letter*) *and s.m.f.* Irlandais, -e; **~ stew**, ragoût de mouton, *m.*
irksome, fastidieu|x, ~se.
iron, (*lit., fig., fetter, for ironing*) fer, *m.*; **~-grey**, gris fer, *invar.*; **~-mould**, tache de fer, *f.*; *cast* ~, fonte, *f.*; *corrugated* ~, tôle ondulée, *f.*; *scrap* ~, ferraille, *f.*; *wrought* ~, fer forgé, *m.*; **~-master**, maître de forges, *m.*; *adj.* de fer; *v.a.* (*linen*) repasser.
ironclad, *adj. and s.m.* cuirassé.
ironical, ironique; **~ly**, ironiquement.
ironmonger, quincaillier, *m.*; **~y**, *~'s shop*, quincaillerie, *f.*
ironworks, ferronnerie, *f.*
irony, ironie, *f.*
irradia|te, (*lit. and fig.*) illuminer; **~tion**, illumination, *f.*
irrational, (*conduct, &c.*) irrationnel, -le; (*unreasonable*) déraisonnable.
irreclaimable, incorrigible.
irreconcilable, (*pers.*) irréconciliable; (*things*) incompatible (avec).
irrecoverable, irrécouvrable.
irredeemable, (*comm.*) non amortissable; (*hopeless*) irrémédiable.
irreducible, irréductible.
irrefragable, irréfragable.
irrefutab|le, irréfutable; **~ly**, irréfutablement.
irregular, (*lit., ground, morals, time, gram., mil.*) irréguli|er, ~ère; **~ity**, irrégularité, *f.*; **~ly**, irrégulièrement.
irrelevant, (*not to the point*) hors de la question; (*not applying*) inapplicable (à).
irreligio|n, irréligion, *f.*; **~us**, irréligieu|x, ~se.
irremediab|le, irrémédiable; **~ly**, irrémédiablement.
irremovable, (*for life*) inamovible.
irreparab|le, irréparable; **~ly**, irréparablement.
irrepressible, (*laughter, &c.*) inextinguible.
irreproachab|le, irréprochable; **~ly**, irréprochablement.
irresistib|le, irrésistible; **~ly**, irrésistiblement.
irresolu|te, irrésolu; **~tion**, irrésolution, *f.*; **~tely**, irrésolument, *m.*
irrespective of, sans égard à.
irresponsib|le, irresponsable; **~ility**, irresponsabilité, *f.*
irresponsive, indifférent (à).
irretrievab|le, irréparable; **~ly**, irréparablement.
irreveren|ce, irrévérence, *f.*; **~t**, irrévérencieu|x, ~se; **~tly**, irrévérencieusement.
irreversible, (*unalterable*) irrévocable.
irrevocab|le, irrévocable; **~ly**, irrévocablement.
irriga|te, (*of a river and fig.*) arroser; (*fields, &c.*) irriguer; **~tion**, irrigation, *f.*
irritab|le, irritable; **~ility**, irritabilité, *f.*
irritant, *s.* irritant, *m.*
irrita|te, irriter; **~tion**, irritation, *f.*; **~ting**, *adj.* irritant.
irruption, irruption, *f.*
-ish, (*adj. termination of colour*) -âtre + *m. of adj.*; *special forms:* blanchâtre, verdâtre.
isinglass, colle de poisson, *f.*
Islam, Islam, *m.*; **~ism**, islamisme, *m.*; **~ic**, islamique.
island, île, *f.*; (*street*) refuge, *m.*; **~er**, insulaire, *m.f.*
isle, île, *f.*; **~t**, îlot, *m.*
isola|te, isoler; **~tion**, isolement, *m.* ⚠ *Not* isolation *which* = '*insulation*' (*electr.*).
isosceles, *adj.* (*geom.*) isocèle.
Israelit|e, *s.* Israélite, *m.f.*; **~ish**, israélite.
issue, *s.* (*way out*) sortie, *f.*; (*liquid*) écoulement, *m.*; (*river*) embouchure, *f.*; (*bank-notes, &c.*) émission, *f.*; (*publication*) publication, *f.*; (*edition of paper*) numéro, *m.*; (*end*) issue, *f.*; (*children*) postérité, *f.*; (*giving out, delivery*) distribution, *f.*; (*result*) résultat, *m.*
issue, *v.a.* (*notes, cheques, shares*) émettre*; (*provisions, &c.*) distribuer; (*publish*) publier; (*order*) donner; (*warrant, &c.*) lancer.
issue, *v.n.* (*go, come out*) sortir* (être); (*liquid*) jaillir; (*be derived*) provenir* (être) (de); (*end in*) se terminer par.
isthmus, isthme, *m.*
it, *pron. nom.* il, elle; *acc.* le, la; (*subj. of impers. verb*) il; (*it, impers. subj. of* être, pouvoir*, devoir) ce; *of* ~, en; *to* ~, y; *from* ~, *often* en.
Italian, *adj.* (*when an adj. use small letter*) *and s.m.f.* Italien, -ne; (*lang.*) italien, *m.*
italics, italiques, *m.pl.*

italicize, mettre* en italiques.
itch, *s.* (*lit. and fig.*) démangeaison, *f.*; *v.n.* démanger; (*fig.*) avoir des démangeaisons (de).
item, *s.* item, *m. invar.*; (*detail*) détail, *m.*; *adv.* item.
itera|te, répéter; **~tion**, itération, *f.*
itiner|ant, *adj.* ambulant; **~ary**, *s.* itinéraire, *m.*; **~ate**, *v.n.* voyager de ville en ville.
its, *poss. pron. m.* son, *f.* sa (*f.*+*vowel or silent* h: son), *pl.* ses.
itself, *m.* lui-même, *f.* elle-même; (*acc. or dat. with reflexive verb*) se; (*with prep.*) soi; (*emphatic*) même: *he is goodness ~*, il est la bonté même.
ivory, ivoire, *m.*; *adj.* d'ivoire *and* en ivoire.
iv|y, lierre, *m.*; **~ied**, couvert de lierre.
ixia, (*bot.*) ixia, *f.*
izard, (*zool.*) isard, *m.*

J

jabber, *s.* (*indistinct speech*) bredouillement, *m.*; (*of magpies, &c.*) jacasserie, *f.*; **~er**, bredouilleu|r, **~se**, *m.f.*; *v.n.* jacasser.
jacinth, (*gem*) hyacinthe, *f.*
jack, (*dim.*) jeannot, *m.*; (*cards*) valet, *m.*; (*donkey, U.S.A.*) martin, *m.*; (*ichth.*) brocheton, *m.*; **~-in-the-box**, boîte à surprise, *f.*; **~-o'-lantern**, feu follet, *m.*; **~-tar**, mathurin, *m.*
jackal, chacal, *m.* (*pl.* s).
jack-ass, (*lit. and fig.*) âne, *m.*
jackdaw, choucas, *m.*
jacket, *s.* (*man's lounge*) veston, *m.*; ⚠ jaquette, *f.* = *man's 'morning coat' or woman's 'jacket' of tailor-made costume.*
Jacobin, *s.* (*friar and hist.*) jacobin, *m.*
Jacobite, (*hist.*) *adj.* (*when an adj. use small letter*) *and s.m.* Jacobite.
jaconet, (*cloth*) jaconas, *m.*
jade, (*stone*) jade, *m.*; (*worn-out horse, unpleasant woman*) rosse, *f.*
jagged, *adj.* dentelé.
jaguar, jaguar, *m.*
jam, (*conserve*) confiture, *f.*; (*street*) encombrement, *m.*
jam, *v.a.* serrer; (*block*) encombrer; (*wireless*) gêner; (*squeeze into*) fourrer de force dans.
jamb, (*arch. of door*) jambage, *m.*
jangle, *s.* son discordant, *m.*; *v.n.* faire* un son discordant.
janitor, portier, *m.*
janissary, janissaire, *m.*
January, janvier, *m.*
japan, (*varnish*) laque, *f.*
Japanese, *adj.* (*when an adj. use small letter*) *and s.m.f.* Japonais, -e; (*lang.*) japonais, *m.*
jar, *s.* (*earthenware*) jarre, *f.*; (*glass*) bocal, *m.*; (*harsh sound*) son discordant, *m.*; (*shock*) choc, *m.*; *v.n.* rendre un son discordant; (*colours, &c.*) jurer (avec); *~ upon*, (*nerves*) agacer; (*ears*) blesser.
jargon, jargon, *m.*
jarring, discordant; **~ly**, d'une façon discordante.
jasmin, **~e**, **jessamine**, (*bot.*) jasmin, *m.*
jasper, (*stone*) jaspe, *m.*
jaundice, jaunisse, *f.*
jaunt, excursion, *f.*
jaunt|y, vi|f, **~ve**; **~iness**, (*approx.*) suffisance, *f.*
javelin, javeline, *f.*
jaw, *s.* mâchoire, *f.*; (*fig.*) gueule, *f.*; **~-bone**, maxillaire, *m.*; (*vulg. talk*) gueule, *f.*; *v.n.* (*pop.*) gueuler.
jay, geai, *m.*
jealous, jalou|x, **~se**; **~y**, jalousie, *f.*; **~ly**, jalousement.
jeer, *s.* sarcasme, *m.*; *v.n.* *~ at*, railler; *v.a.* **~ing**, *s.* raillerie, *f.*; *adj.* railleu|r, **~se**.
jejune, (*land*) aride; (*poor and fig.*) pauvre.
jell|y, (*meat or fruit*) gelée, *f.*; **~y-fish**, méduse, *f.*; **~ied**, en gelée.
jeopard|y, danger, *m.*; **~ize**, mettre* en danger.
jerboa, (*zool.*) gerboise, *f.*
jeremiad, jérémiade, *f.*
jerk, *s.* saccade, *f.*; *v.a.* donner une secousse à; (*throw*) lancer; **~y**, saccadé.
jerkin, justaucorps, *m.*
jersey, (*garment*) jersey, *m.*
jest, *s.* plaisanterie, *f.*; (*laughing-stock*) risée, *f.*; *in ~*, pour rire; **~er**, plaisant, *m.*; (*pej.*) railleu|r, **~se**, *m.f.*; **~ingly**, pour rire; *v.n.* plaisanter.
Jesuit, (*lit. and fig.*) jésuite, *m.*; **~ical**, jésuitique.
jet, *s.* (*water, steam*) jet, *m.*; (*gas*) bec, *m.*; (*lignite*) jais, *m.*; *v.n.* jaillir; **~-black**, noir comme le jais.
jetsam, épave, *f.*
jettison, *s.* jet (à la mer), *m.*; *v.a.* jeter (à la mer).
jetty, jetée, *f.*
Jew, *s.* Juif, *m.*; **~ess**, Juive, *f.*; **~ish**, jui|f, **~ve**; **~ry**, juiverie, *f.*
jewel, bijou, *m.* (*pl.* x); **~-case**, écrin, *m.*; **~ler**, bijoutier, *m.*; **~ery** *and* **~er's** *shop*, bijouterie, *f.*; *v.a.* orner de bijoux; (*watches*) monter sur rubis.
jib, *s.* (*naut.*) foc, *m.*; **~-boom**, grand foc, *m.*
jib, *v.n.* (*horse*) reculer.
jig, *s.* (*dance and time*) gigue, *f.*; *v.n.* danser une gigue.
jilt, *s.* coquette, *f.*; *v.a.* délaisser.
jingle, *s.* (*arms, glasses*) cliquetis, *m.*; (*bell*) tintement, *m.*; *v.n.* cliqueter, tinter.
jingo, *adj. and s.m.* chauvin; **~ism**, chauvinisme, *m.*
jiu-jitsu, jiu-jitsu, *m.*
job, *s.* (*task*) tâche, *f.*; (*piece of work*) travail, *m.* (*pl.* aux); (*employment, function*) emploi, *m.*; (*pol., fin.*) tripotage.

m.; *odd ~s*, petits travaux, *m. pl.*; *soft ~*, bon fromage, *m.*; *put-up ~*, coup monté, *m.*; ~ **lot**, solde, *m.*; ~ **work**, travail à forfait, *m.*; *find a ~*, trouver affaire; *make a good ~ of*, bien faire*; *be out of a ~*, être sans travail.
job, *v.a.* (*hire*) louer; (*speculate*) vendre et acheter pour spéculer; (*speculate with, pej.*) tripoter.
jobb|er, ouvrier à la tâche, *m.*; (*Stk. Ex., approx.*) banquier de placement et de spéculation, *m.*; **~ery**, (*pej.*) tripotage de bourse, *m.*; **~ing**, (*gardener, &c.*) à la tâche.
jobmaster, loueur de chevaux et voitures, *m.*
jockey, jockey, *m.*
jocose, plaisant; **~ness**, badinage, *m.*
jocular, badin; **~ity**, badinage, *m.*; **~ly**, en plaisantant.
jocund, joyeu|x, ~se; **~ity**, gaieté, *f.*
jog, *s.* secousse, *f.*; **~-trot**, petit trot, *m.*; **~-trot**, *adj.* (*fig.*) monotone.
jog, *v.a.* secouer; *v.n.* ~ *along*, (*lit. and fig.*) faire* son petit bonhomme de chemin.
johnny, (*fellow*) individu, *m.*
join, *v.a.* (*lit., fig., overtake*) joindre*; (*unite*) unir; (*unite of roads*) relier; (*carp.*) assembler; (*regt., ship*) rejoindre*; (*company of*) aller (être) retrouver; (*group, &c.*) se joindre* à; (*become member of*) devenir* (être) membre de; *v.n.* se joindre*; (*unite*) s'unir; ~ *with*, se joindre* à; ~ *in*, prendre* part à.
joiner, menuisier, *m.*; **~y**, menuiserie, *f.*
joining, (*rivers, &c.*) jonction, *f.*
joint, *s.* (*carp., mason, mach.*) joint, *m.*; (*anat. and articulation*) articulation, *f.*; (*meat*) gros morceau, *m.*; *put out of ~*, disloquer.
joint, *adj.* (*in common*) commun; (*heirs, property, &c.*) indivis; (*accounts, &c.*) en participation; ~ *stock*, *adj.* par actions; *~-stock company*, société par actions, *f.*; (*partnership*) co-, *e.g.* coassocié, codébiteur, codirecteur, copropriétaire, etc.; **~ly**, conjointement.
joint, *v.a.* (*unite*) unir; (*mason.*) assembler; *loose-~ed*, dégingandé.
jointure, douaire, *m.*
joist, solive, *f.*
joke, joking, *s.* plaisanterie, *f.*; *for a ~*, **~ly**, pour rire; *practical ~*, farce, *f.*; *it's not a ~ (to)*, il (ce) n'est pas drôle de; *v.n.* plaisanter.
joker, plaisant, *m.*; *practical ~*, farc|eur, ~se, *m.f.*
jollification, noce, *f.*
jollity, gaieté, *f.*
jolly, (*very pleasant*) joyeu|x, ~se; (*jovial*) jovial; (*slightly drunk*) légèremen tgris; **~-boat**, *see* BOAT; ~ *fine*, (*slang*) fameu|x, ~se.
jolly, *adv.* (*pop. + adj.*) fameusement.
jolt, *s.* cahot, *m.*; **~ing**, cahotage, *m.*; *v.a.n.* cahoter.
jonquil, (*bot.*) jonquille, *f.*
joss, *s.* idole chinoise, *f.*; **~-house**, temple chinois, *m.*
jostle, *v.a.* coudoyer; *v.n.* ~ *against*, se †heurter contre.
jostling, bousculade, *f.*
jot, iota, *m.*; **~tings**, notes, *f.pl.*
jot down, noter.
journal, (*diary, newspaper*) journal, *m.*; **~ism**, journalisme, *m.*; **~ist**, journaliste, *m.*
journey, voyage, *m.*; (*distance*) trajet, *m.*; **~man**, (*day-labourer*) journaliere, *m.*; (*special trades*) garçon, *m.*; ~ **-work**, ouvrage à la journée, *m.*; *v.n.* voyager.
joust, *s.* joute, *f.*; *v.n.* jouter.
jovial, jovial; **~ity**, jovialité, *f.*; **~ly**, jovialement.
jowl, (*of throat, neck*) double menton, *m.*
joy, joie, *f.*; **~-ride**, promenade aux frais de la princesse, *f.*; *be the ~ of*, faire* la joie de; *wish one ~ of*, féliciter de.
joyful, joyous, joyeu|x, ~se; **~ness**, joie, *f.*; **~ly**, joyeusement.
joyless, sans joie; **~ness**, tristesse, *f.*; **~ly**, sans joie.
jubil|ant, radieu|x, ~se; **~ation**, exultation, *f.*
jubilee, jubilé, *m.*
judai|sm, judaïsme, *m.*; **~c**, judaïque.
judas-tree, arbre de Judée, *m.*
judge, *s.* juge, *m.*; *be a good ~ of*, se connaître à.
judg|e, *v.a.* (*pronounce sentence, try, criticize, consider*) juger; *v.n.* juger; *~ing by*, à en juger par.
judgement, (*sentence, opinion, good sense*) jugement, *m.*; *sit in ~ on*, juger.
judicature, justice, *f.*
judicial, judiciaire; **~ly**, judiciairement.
judicious, judicieu|x, ~se; **~ly**, judicieusement.
jug, cruche, *f.*; (*water*) pot, *m.*; *small ~*, cruchon, *m.*
juggl|e, *v.a.n.* jongler; ~ *with*, (*things*) jongler avec; (*pers.*) duper; **~ing, ~ery**, (*lit. and fig.*) jonglerie, *f.*; **~er**, jongleur, *m.*
juice, (*fruit, meat*) jus, *m.*; (*fig.*) suc, *m.*
jugular, *adj.* jugulaire.
juic|y, juteu|x, ~se; (*succulent*) succulent; **~iness**, succulence, *f.*
jujube, jujube, *m.*
julep, julep, *m.*
July, juillet, *m.*
jumble, *s.* mélange, *m.*; (*colloq.*) méli-mélo, *m.*; *v.a.* mêler.
jump, *s.* saut, *m.*; (*of alarm*) sursaut, *m.*; (*shares*) bond, *m.*; *go up at a ~*, (*shares*) faire* un bond.
jump, *v.a.* (*an object, skip over*) sauter; (*make to jump*) faire* sauter; ~ *over*, franchir.
jump, *v.n.* (*lit. and fig.*) sauter; (*with alarm*) sursauter; ~ *to a conclusion*, tirer une conclusion †hâtive.
jumper, (*sailor*) vareuse de laine, *f.*;

(*pers.*) sauteur, *m.*; (*pull-over, approx.*) chandail, *m.*
junction, jonction, *f.*; (*road, rail*) embranchement, *m.*; (*station*) gare d'embranchement, *f.*
juncture, (*circumstances, state of affairs*) conjoncture, *f.*; (*joint*) jointure, *f.*
June, juin, *m.*
jungle, jungle, *f.*
junior, *s.m.f.* cadet, -te; *be the ~ of,* être plus jeune que.
junior, *adj.* jeune; (*rank, partner*) moins ancien; (*clerk*) petit.
juniper, (*bot.*) genièvre, *m.*; **~-tree,** genévrier, *m.*
junk, (*oakum*) étoupe, *f.*; (*naut., salt beef*) bœuf salé, *m.*; (*Chinese*) jonque, *f.*
junket, (*feast*) bombance, *f.*; *v.n.* faire* bombance.
junta, (*Span.*) junte, *f.*
juridical, juridique.
juris-consult, jurisconsulte, *m.*
jurisdiction, (*lit. and fig.*) juridiction, *f.*
jurisprudence, jurisprudence, *f.*
juror, juryman, juré, *m.*
jury, jury, *m.*
just, *adj.* juste; (*justifiable*) légitime; (*correct*) exact; **~ly,** justement; (*rightly*) à juste titre.
just, *adv.* (*exactly*) juste; (*barely*) à peine; (*altogether*) absolument; *have ~, had ~, pres. and impf. of* venir* de + *inf.*; *~ now,* il n'y a qu'un instant; *~ so,* précisément; *~ tell me,* dites-moi un peu; *I'd ~ as soon keep it,* j'aimerais tout autant le garder.
justice, justice, *f.*; ⚠ justice *does not* = '*magistrate*' *which* = magistrat, *m.*; *~ of the Peace,* juge de paix, *m.*; *do ~ to,* rendre justice à.
justiciary, justicier, *m.*
justifiab|le, justifiable; **~ility,** caractère justifiable, *m.*; **~ly,** justifiablement.
justif|y, (*show rightness, indicate, give grounds for, theol.*) justifier; (*authorize*) autoriser (à); **~ication,** justification, *f.*
justness, (*justice*) justice, *f.*; (*accuracy*) justesse, *f.*
jut out, faire* saillie.
jute, jute, *m.*
juvenil|e, juvénile; (*of children*) d'enfants; **~ity,** jeunesse, *f.*
juxtapos|e, juxtaposer; **~ition,** juxtaposition, *f.*

K

kale, chou, *m.*
kaleidoscope, kaléidoscope, *m.*
kangaroo, kangourou, *m.*
kedge-anchor, ancre à jet, *f.*
keel, quille, *f.*
keen, *adj.* (*point*) aigu, -ë; (*blade*) tranchant; (*cold, &c.*) piquant; (*mind, &c.*) pénétrant; (*glance*) perçant; (*hearing*) fin; (*cutting, fig.*) mordant; *be ~ on,* avoir la passion de; *be ~ to,* tenir* beaucoup à; **~ness,** (*cold*) rigueur, *f.*; (*grief, sight, hearing*) acuité, *f.*; (*intellect*) pénétration, *f.*; (*eagerness*) ardeur, *f.*; **~ly,** (*eagerly*) ardemment.
keep, *s.* (*castle*) donjon, *m.*; (*food*) nourriture, *f.*
keep, *v.a.* (*hold, diary, accounts, shop, &c., house, in prison, engagements, in a certain state*) tenir*; (*have in keeping, silence, protect, retain*) garder; (*keep waiting*) retenir*; (*maintain, feed*) entretenir*; (*rule, &c.*) observer; (*prevent*) empêcher (de); (*continue*) continuer; (*anniversary*) célébrer; (*secret*) ne pas révéler; (*company*) fréquenter; *~ away,* écarter; *~ back,* retenir*; (*conceal*) cacher; *~ down,* (*repress*) réprimer; (*prices*) maintenir* bas; *~ in,* (*fire, &c.*) entretenir*; (*school*) mettre* en retenue; (*restrain*) contenir*; *~ off,* écarter; *~ on,* (*clothes, &c.*) garder; *~ under,* maîtriser; *~ up,* (*hold up*) soutenir*; (*fire, subscription, household, studies, correspondence*) entretenir*; *~ up spirits,* ne pas se laisser abattre.
keep, *v.n.* (*remain*) rester (être); (*eatables*) se garder; (*continue*) continuer (à); *~ at one's work,* s'acharner au travail; *~ in touch with,* se tenir* en contact avec; *~ off the grass!* défense de marcher sur le gazon!; *~ on,* (*doing*) continuer à; (*road*) continuer son chemin; *~ together,* ne pas se séparer; *~ up with,* (*walk*) marcher de front avec.
keeper, (*prison, lunatics, &c.*) gardien, -ne, *m.f.*
keeping, *s.* garde, *f.*; *in safe ~,* sous bonne garde; *in ~ with,* en harmonie avec; **~-room,** (*U.S.A.*) pièce où l'on se tient d'habitude, *f.*; *adj.* (*fruit*) de conserve.
keepsake, souvenir, *m.*; (*book*) keepsake, *m.*
keg, baril, *m.*
ken, *s.* (*sight*) vue, *f.*; (*knowledge*) connaissance, *f.*
kennel, (*dog*) chenil, *m.*; (*gutter*) ruisseau, *m.*
kerb, ~-stone, bordure, *f.*
kerchief, fichu de tête, *m.*
kernel, (*of nuts and in stone of fruits*) amande, *f.*; (*fig.*) noyau, *m.*
kerseymere, casimir, *m.*
kestrel, (*ornith.*) crécerelle, *f.*
ketch, (*naut.*) quaiche, *f.*
kettle, (*tea*) bouilloire, *f.*; (*with tall spout*) coquemar, *m.*
kettle-drum, timbale, *f.*
key, *s.* (*lit. and fig., arch., mystery*) clé (clef), *f.*; (*to books*) corrigé, *m.*; (*piano, typewriter*) touche, *f.*; (*mus.*) ton, *m.*; (*pegs, bolts*) clavette, *f.*; **~-industry,** industrie-clé, *f.*; **~-note,** tonique, *f.*; *in a minor ~,* en mineur; *under lock and ~,* sous clé.
keyboard, clavier, *m.*
keyhole, trou de serrure, *f.*
keystone, (*arch. and fig.*) clé de voûte, *f.*

khaki, (*fruit, colour, material*) kaki, *m.*; *adj.* kaki, *invar.*
khan, (*ruler*) khan, *m.*; (*caravansaray*) caravansérail, *m.*
Khedive, khédive, *m.*
kick, *s.* coup de pied, *m.*; (*animals*) ruade, *f.*; (*firearm*) recul, *m.*; **~-off,** (*football*) coup d'envoi, *m.*
kick, *v.a.* donner un coup (des coups) de pied à; ~ *out,* chasser à coups de pied.
kick, *v.n.* donner des coups de pied; (*animals*) ruer; ~ *off,* (*football*) donner le coup d'envoi.
kickshaw, colifichet, *m.*
kid, (*young goat and skin*) chevreau, *m.*; ~ **gloves,** gants de chevreau, *m.pl.*
kiddy, (*slang, child*) gosse, *m.f.*
kidnap, enlever; **~per,** auteur d'un enlèvement, *m.*
kidney, (*anat.*) rein, *m.*; (*food*) rognon, *m.*; **~-potato,** vitelotte, *f.*
kill, *v.a.n.* (*lit. and fig.*) tuer; (*animals*) abattre; **~er,** tueu|r, ~se, *m.f.*; **~ing,** *adj.* (*amusing*) tordant; ~ *two birds with one stone,* faire* d'une pierre deux coups.
kiln, four, *m.*
kilo, **~gramme,** kilogramme, *m.*; **~litre** kilolitre, *m.*; **~metre,** kilomètre, *m.*
kilt, *v.a.* (*pleat*) plisser; *s.* (*Scotch* kilt, *m.*
kin, (*family*) parenté, *f.*; (*pers.*) parent, -e, *m.f.*, *mostly in pl.*; *next of* ~, le plus proche parent.
kind, *s.* (*species*) espèce, *f.*; (*sort*) sorte, *f.*; (*natural produce*) nature, *f.*; (*race*) race, *f.*; *nothing of the* ~, il n'en est rien; *pay in* ~, payer en nature; (*fig.*) *repay in* ~, rendre la pareille.
kind, *adj.* (*good to*) bon (pour); (*kindly*) bienveillant; (*friendly*) aimable; ~ *regards, see* REGARDS; **~ness,** (*of pers.*) *see below*; **~ly,** *adv.* avec bonté; (*command*) veuillez + *inf.*; *take ~ly to,* (*thing*) mordre, *v.a.*; *remember me ~ly to,* rappelez-moi au bon souvenir de; *~ly reply,* prière de répondre.
kindergarten, école maternelle, *f.*
kindle, *v.a.* (*set on fire*) allumer; (*passion, &c.*) inspirer; (*stir up to*) exciter (à); (*inflame, fig.*) enflammer; *v.n.* (*take fire*) s'enflammer.
kindl|y, *adj.* bon; (*climate*) dou|x, ~ce; (*manner*) aimable; **~iness,** (*pers., action*) bonté, *f.*
kindness, bonté, *f.*; *have the* ~ *to,* avoir l'obligeance de.
kindred, parenté, *f.*; (*relations*) parents, *m.pl.*
kinematic, ~s, *s.* cinématique, *f.*
king, (*lit., fig., cards, chess*) roi, *m.*; (*draughts*) dame, *f.*; **~-cup,** (*bot.*) bouton d'or, *m.*; *~'s evil,* écrouelles, *f.pl.*
kingdom, royaume, *m.*; (*nat. hist.*) règne, *m.*
kingfisher, (*ornith.*) martin-pêcheur, *m.*
king|ly, ~like, royal.
kingship, royauté, *f.*
kink, (*rope*) coque, *f.*; (*mental*) tournure particulière, *f.*; *have a* ~ *in brain,* être un peu timbré.
kinsfolk, parents, *m.pl.*
kinship, (*lit. and fig.*) parenté, *f.*
kins|man, ~woman, parent, -e, *m.f.*
kiosk, kiosque, *m.*
kipper, hareng saur, *m.*
kirk, (*approx.*) église, *f.*
kirtle, (*woman's*) jupon, *m.*
kismet, destin, *m.*
kiss, *s.* baiser, *m.*; *v.a.* baiser; (*embrace*) embrasser; ⚠ baiser *often has a sexual sense. Use* embrasser *for the ordinary act of kissing.*
kissing, (*embrace*) embrassade, *f.*; (*toe, hand, object*) baisement, *m.*
kit, (*mil.*) fourniment, *m.*; (*mil. slang*) fourbi, *m.*; (*civil*) effets, *m.pl.*; **~-bag,** sac d'équipement, *m.*
kitchen, cuisine, *f.*; **~-garden,** jardin potager, *m.*; **~-maid,** fille de cuisine, *f.*; **~-range,** cuisinière, *f.*
kite, (*ornith.*) milan, *m.*; (*toy and comm.*) cerf-volant, *m.*; (*fig.*) vautour, *m.*; *v.n.* (*comm.*) tirer en l'air.
kith, connaissances, *f.pl.*; ~ *and kin,* parents et amis, *m.pl.*
kitten, petit chat, *m.*
kittiwake, (*ornith.*) goéland tridactyle, *m.*
kleptomania, cleptomanie, *f.*; **~c,** cleptomane, *m.f.*
knack, chic, *m.*; (*dodge*) truc, *m.*; (*bad habit*) tic, *m.*; *have the* ~ *of,* avoir le chic pour.
knacker, (*horses*) équarrisseur, *m.*
knapsack, †havresac, *m.*
knapweed, (*bot.*) jacée, *f.*
knav|e, coquin, *m.*; (*cards*) valet, *m.*; **~ery,** fourberie, *f.*; **~ish,** fourbe.
knead, *v.a.* (*lit. and fig.*) pétrir.
knee, *s.* genou, *m.* (*pl.* x); **~-breeches,** culotte courte, *f.*; **~-cap,** rotule, *f.*; *~-deep,* jusqu'aux genoux; *~-hole desk, see* DESK.
kneel, *v.n.* s'agenouiller; ~ *down,* se mettre* à genoux.
knell, (*lit. and fig.*) glas, *m.*
knickerbockers, knickers, culotte bouffante, *f.*
knick-knack, colifichet, *m.*
knife, couteau, *m.*; **~-rest,** porte-couteau, *m. invar.*
knight, chevalier, *m.*; (*chess*) cavalier, *m.*; **~-errant,** chevalier errant, *m.*; **~-errantry,** chevalerie errante, *f.*; *v.a.* faire* chevalier.
knighthood, chevalerie, *f.*
knightly, chevaleresque.
knit, *v.a.* (*stockings, &c.*) tricoter; (*brow*) froncer; ~ *together,* (*fig.*) unir étroitement; **~ter,** tricoteu|r, ~se, *m.f.*
knitting, *s.* (*work*) tricotage, *m.*; **~-machine,** tricoteur, *f.*; **~-needle,** aiguille à tricoter, *f.*
knob, *s.* bosse, *f.*; (*door*) bouton, *m.*; (*stick*) pomme, *f.*

knock, *s.* coup. *m.*; ~ *at the door,* coup de marteau, *m.*
knock, *v.a.* frapper; ~ *about,* malmener; ~ *down,* renverser; *(auction)* adjuger; ~ *off,* faire* sauter; (*on prices*) rabattre; *(work)* cesser; ~ *out, (disable)* mettre* hors de combat; *(pipe)* vider; ~ *up, (awaken)* réveiller; ~ *oneself up,* s'éreinter.
knock, *v.n.* frapper; ~ *about,* traîner; ~ *against,* se †heurter contre.
knocker, *(door)* marteau, *m.*
knock-kneed, cagneu|x, ~se.
knoll, monticule, *m.*
knot, *s.* *(cord, ribbon, naut., wood, difficulty, fig.)* nœud, *m.*; **~-grass,** *(bot.)* renouée, *f.*; *v.a.* nouer; *(entangle)* embrouiller.
knotty, noueu|x, ~se; *(fig.)* difficile.
knout, knout, *m.*
know, *v.a.* *(things acquired, borne in mind)* savoir*; *(pers., place, external objects)* connaître*; *(recognize)* reconnaître*; *(distinguish one thing from another)* distinguer (de); *let* ~, faire* savoir à; ~ *of,* avoir connaissance de; *don't I* ~ *it, (pop.)* à qui le dites-vous?; **~n for,** connu pour.
know, *v.n.* savoir*; *not that I* ~ *of,* pas que je sache; ~ *better than to,* ne pas être homme (femme) à; *let know,* prévenir*.
knowing, *adj.* *(cunning)* rusé; *(smart)* chic, *invar.*
knowingly, en connaissance de cause; *(intentionally)* avec intention.
knowledge, *s.* *(notion, idea, perception)* connaissance, *f.*; *(acquired knowledge, erudition)* savoir, *m.*; *not to my* ~, pas que je sache; *without my* ~, à mon insu.
knuckle, *s.* articulation des doigts, *f.*; *(of veal)* jarret, *m.*; **~-bone,** osselet, *m.*; *give a rap over the* ~*s,* donner sur les doigts (à); *v.n.* ~ *under,* mettre* les pouces.
knut, *(slang = fop)* gommeux, *m.*
kodak, *(photo.)* kodak, *m.*
kola, ~-tree, kola, *m.*; **~-nut,** noix de kola, *f.*
koran, coran, *m.*
kvass, kvas, *m.*

L

label, *s.* étiquette, *f.*; *tag* ~, étiquette volante, *f.*; *v.a.* étiqueter; ⚠ label, *m. is only used for trade-union marks.*
labial, *s.* labiale, *f.*; *adj.* labial.
laboratory, laboratoire, *m.*
laborious, laborieu|x, ~se; **~ly,** laborieusement.
labour, *s.* *(toil, task, birth)* travail, *m.*; *(difficulty)* peine, *f.*; *(as opposed to capital)* ouvriers, *m.pl.*; ~ **exchange,** bureau municipal de placement, *m.*; ~ *question,* question ouvrière, *f.*; *unskilled* ~, travail de manœuvre, *m.*
labour, *adj.* ouvri|er, ~ère; *(in English politics)* travailliste; *member of the Labour Party,* travailliste, *m.f.*
labour, *v.a.* *(style, &c.)* travailler.
labour, *v.n.* travailler; *(strive to)* s'efforcer de; *(advance with difficulty)* avancer avec difficulté; ~ *under, (mistake, &c.)* être victime de; *(struggle against)* lutter contre.
labourer, travailleur, *m.*; *(builders, &c.)* manœuvre, *m.*; *(day)* journalier, *m.* ⚠ *Not* laboureur *which = 'ploughman'.*
labouring, *adj.* ouvri|er, ère; ~ *man,* ouvrier, *m.*
laburnum, *(bot.)* cytise, *m.*
labyrinth, labyrinthe, *m.*; **~ine,** de labyrinthe.
lace, *s.* dentelle, *f.*; *(gold, silver)* galon, *m.*; *(boots, stays)* lacet, *m.*; *(hand-made)* point, *m.*
lace, *v.a.* garnir de dentelle; *(boots, stays, &c.)* lacer; *(with gold, silver)* galonner (de).
Lacedaemonian, *adj. (when an adj. use small letter) and s.m.f.* Lacédémonien, -ne.
lacera|te, lacérer; **~tion,** lacération, *f.*
lachrym|al, lacrymal; **~ose,** pleurard.
lack, *s.* manque, *m.*
lack, *v.a.* manquer de; *be* ~*ing in,* manquer de; *v.n.* faire* défaut.
lackadaisical, minaudi|er, ~ère.
lack(qu)ey, laquais, *m.*
laconic, laconique; **~ally,** laconiquement.
lacqu(ck)er, *(varnish)* vernis, *m.*; *(oriental)* laque, *f.*; *v.a.* *(wood)* laquer; *(metal)* vernir.
lacrosse, *(game)* crosse, *f.*
lacteal, lacteous, lacté.
lacuna, lacune, *f.*
lad, jeune garçon, *m.*; *my* ~, *(fam.)* mon ami, *m.*
ladder, échelle, *f.*; **scaling-**~, échelle de siège, *f.*
lade, *v.a.* *(ship, &c.)* charger.
laden, chargé (de); *(fig.)* ~ *with,* accablé de.
lading, *s.* chargement, *m.*
ladle, *(soup)* louche, *f.*
lady, *(in rank, education, complimentary)* dame, *f.*; **my** ~, madame; **young** ~, jeune fille, *f.*; *(unmarried)* demoiselle, *f.*; **~-bird,** bête à bon Dieu, *f.*; ~ **Chapel,** Chapelle de la Vierge, *f.*; ~ **companion,** dame de compagnie, *f.*; **~-killer,** bourreau des cœurs, *m.*; **~'s maid,** femme de chambre, *f.*; ~ **of manor,** châtelaine, *f.*; *Our Lady,* Notre-Dame, *f.*; *my* ~, *(pers. address)* madame; **~'s slipper,** *(bot.)* sabot de Vénus, *m.*; **~'s smock,** *(bot.)* cresson des prés, *m.*; **~-in-waiting,** dame d'honneur, *f.*; ~ **of the bedchamber,** dame d'atours, *f.*
Ladyship, *her, your* ~, Madame, *f.*
lag, ~ *behind,* rester (être) en arrière; **~gard,** traînard, *m.*
lagoon, lagune, *f.*
laid, *new* ~ *(of eggs)* frais, fraîche.

lair, *s.* (*cattle*) parc, *m.*; (*wild beast and fig.*) repaire, *m.*; (*wolf*) liteau, *m.*
laity, laïques, *m.pl.*
lake, lac, *m.*; (*pigment*) laque, *f.*; *adj.* (*pre-hist. dwellings, &c.*) lacustre.
lama, (*priest*) lama, *m.*
lamb, (*lit. and fig.*) agneau, *m.*; *~'s lettuce,* (*bot.*) mâche, *f.*; *v.n.* agneler.
lambent, (*light, &c.*) qui effleure; (*style, &c.*) lég|er, ~ère.
lambkin, agnelet, *m.*
lambskin, peau d'agneau, *f.*
lame, (*lit., of metre*) boiteu|x, ~se; (*imperfect*) insuffisant; **~ness,** (*limping*) boitement, *m.*; (*fig.*) faiblesse, *f.*; **~ly,** en boitant; *v.a.* estropier.
lament, *s.* lamentation, *f.*; (*song of sorrow*) complainte, *f.*; *v.a.* (*mourn over*) pleurer; (*deplore*) déplorer; *v.n.* se lamenter (sur).
lament|able, lamentable; **~ation,** lamentation, *f.*; **~ably,** déplorablement; (*pej.*) pitoyablement.
lamin|ate, *v.a.* (*metal*) laminer; **~ation,** lamination, *f.*
lamp, lampe, *f.*; (*street and lamp-post*) réverbère, *m.*; **~-lighter,** allumeur, *m.*; **~-shade,** abat-jour, *m. invar.*
lamplight, lumière de lampe, *f.*
lampoon, *s.* pasquinade, *f.*; *v.a.* brocarder.
lamprey, (*ichth.*) lamproie, *f.*
lance, lance, *f.*; *v.a.* (*abscess, &c.*) ouvrir*. ⚠ *Not* lancer *which* = '*to hurl*'.
lancer, (*mil.*) lancier, *m.*
lancet, (*surg.*) lancette, *f.*; **~-window,** fenêtre en ogive, *f.*
land, *s.* (*opp. to sea, country, property*) terre, *f.*; (*country of a nation*) pays, *m.*; (*native ~*) patrie, *f.*; *no man's ~,* (*mil.*) terrain entre les tranchées; **~-agent,** régisseur, *m.*; **~lubber,** (*naut.*) terrien, *m.*; **~-rail,** (*ornith.*) râle des genêts, *m.*; **~-tax,** impôt foncier, *m.*
land, *v.a.* débarquer; (*fish*) prendre*; *v.n.* débarquer; (*fall*) tomber (être); (*aeron.*) atterrir.
landau, landau, *m.*
landed, financi|er, ~ère; ~ **property,** biens-fonds, *m.pl.*; ~ **proprietor,** terrien, -ne, *m.f.*
landing, *s.* (*act*) débarquement, *m.*; (*aeron.*) escale, *f.*; (*stairs*) palier, *m.*; **~-net,** épuisette, *f.*; **~-stage,** (*depart*) embarcadère, *m.*; (*ashore*) débarcadère, *m.*
landlord, landlady, (*owner*) propriétaire, *m.f.*; (*inn, boarding-house, &c.*) hôte, -sse, *m.f.*
landmark, (*boundary*) borne, *f.*; (*guiding mark*) point de repère, *m.*
landscape, paysage, *m.*; **~-painter,** paysagiste, *m.*
land|slide, ~slip, éboulement, *m.*
landward(s), *adv.* vers la terre.
lane, sentier, *m.*; (*town*) ruelle, *f.*
language, (*dead, living*) langue, *f.*; (*mode of expression*) langage, *m.*
languid, languishing, languissant; **~ness, languor,** langueur, *f.*; **~ly,** languissamment.
languish, *v.n.* languir; ~ *for,* soupirer après.
lank, lanky, décharné; (*of hair*) plats.
lanner, (*ornith.*) lanier, *m.*
lantern, lanterne, *f.*; (*ship's*) fanal, *m.*; (*dome*) lanterne, *f.*; *magic ~,* lanterne magique, *f.*; *~-jawed,* à joues décharnées.
lap, *s.* (*coat*) pan, *m.*; (*waist to knees*) genoux, *m.pl.*; (*fig.*) sein, *m.*; **~ful,** les genoux pleins (de).
lap, *v.a.* (*swathe*) envelopper (de); (*lick up*) laper; (*against shore, &c.*) clapoter contre; *be ~ped in luxury,* nager dans l'opulence; *v.n.* (*lick*) laper.
lapdog, bichon, *m.*
lapel, (*coat*) revers, *m.*
lapidary, *adj. and s.m.* lapidaire.
lapis lazuli, lapis lazuli, *m.*
Lapp, Laplander, Lapon, -e, *m.f.*
lappet, (*coat*) pan, *m.*; (*of woman's head-dress*) barbe, *f., gen. pl.*
lapse, *s.* (*water*) cours, *m.*; (*time*) laps, *m.*; (*slip*) faux pas, *m.*; (*moral, theol.*) chute, *f.*; (*speech, pen*) lapsus, *m.*
lapse, *v.n.* retomber (être) (dans); (*time*) s'écouler; (*fail*) faire* un faux pas; (*comm. and law*) devenir* (être) caduc.
lapwing, (*ornith.*) vanneau, *m.*
larboard, (*naut.*) bâbord, *m.*
larceny, larcin, *m.*
larch, (*tree and wood*) mélèze, *m.*
lard, saindoux, *m.*; *v.a.* (*cook.*) larder; (*speech, &c. with*) entrelarder de.
larder, dépense, *f.*
large, (*big*) gros, -se, *m.f.*; (*extensive*) grand; (*considerable*) considérable; (*numerous*) nombreu|x, ~se; (*views, charity, &c.*) large; (*naut.*) largue; *in ~,* en grand; *at ~,* (*free*) en liberté; (*in general*) en général; **~-hearted,** généreu|x, ~se; **~-minded,** à l'esprit large; **~ness,** (*lit. and fig.*) grandeur, *f.*; **~ly,** amplement; (*in large measure*) en grande partie.
largess(e), largesse, *f.*
lark, *s.* (*ornith.*) alouette, *f.*; (*spree*) rigolade, *f.*; *v.n.* (*pop.*) rigoler; *crested ~,* cochevis, *m.*
larkspur, (*bot.*) pied d'alouette, *m.*
larva, larve, *f.*
laryngitis, (*med.*) laryngite, *f.*
larynx, larynx, *m.*
lascivious, lasci|f, ~ve; **~ness,** lascivité, *f.*; **~ly,** lascivement.
lash, *s.* (*whip*) mèche, *f.*; (*stroke*) coup de fouet, *m.*
lash, *v.a.* (*lit. and fig.*) fouetter; (*with words*) châtier; (*bind*) ligoter; *v.n.* ~ *out,* (*horse*) lancer une ruade.
lashing, *s.* (*naut.*) amarrage, *m.*; **~s,** (*U.S.A.*) profusion, *f.*
lass, jeune fille, *f.*
lassitude, lassitude, *f.*
lasso, lasso, *m.*
last, *s.* derni|er, ~ère, *m.f.*; (*end*) fin, *f.*;

(*shoemaker's*) forme, *f.*; (*letter*) dernière lettre, *f.*; *at* ~, enfin; *to the* ~, jusqu'au bout; *see the* ~ *of*, voir* pour la dernière fois.
last, *adj.* dernier, ~ère; ~ *but one*, avant-dernier; ~ *evening*, hier soir; ~ *night*, la nuit dernière; *night* (*evening*) *before* ~, avant-hier soir; ~ *Wednesday*, mercredi dernier; ~**ly**, en dernier lieu.
last, *adv.* (*lastly*) en dernier lieu; (+*p.p.*) le (la) dernier, ~ère.
last, last out, *v.n.* durer.
lasting, *adj.* durable.
latch, loquet, *m.*; ~**-key**, clé de porte, *f.*
latchet, (*shoe*) cordon, *m.*
late, *adj.* (*after due time*) tardif, ~ve; (*far advanced*) avancé; (*recent*) dernier, ~ère; (*dead*) feu, *takes concord only when preceded by def. article*; (*no longer in office, &c.*) précédent; *at the* ~*st*, au plus tard; *be* ~, être en retard; *of* ~, dernièrement; *of* ~ *years*, de ces dernières années; *adv.* tard; *sit up* ~, veiller tard; *sooner or* ~*r*, tôt ou tard.
late-comer, *s.* retardataire, *m.*
lateen, ~ **sail**, voile latine, *f.*
lately, dernièrement.
lateness, retard, *m.*; (*days, nights*) heure avancée, *f.*; (*seasons*) temps avancé, *m.*; (*fruits, &c.*) tardivité, *f.*
latent, latent.
lateral, latéral; ~**ly**, latéralement.
lath, latte, *f.*
lathe, tour, *m.*
lather, *s.* (*soap*) mousse, *f.*; (*sweat*) écume, *f.*; *v.a.* savonner.
Latin, *adj.* (*when an adj. use small letter*) *and s.m.f.* Latin, -e; (*lang.*) latin, *m.*
Latinism, latinisme, *m.*; ~**ist**, latiniste, *m.*; ~**ity**, latinité, *f.*
latitude, (*geog., astr., naut., fig.*) latitude, *f.*
latitudinal, latitudinal.
latitudinarian, *adj. and s.m.* latitudinaire.
latrine, latrines, *f.pl.*
latter, *pron.* celui-ci, *m.*, celle-ci, *f.*, ceux-ci, *m.pl.*, celles-ci, *f.pl.*; *adj.* dernier, ~ère; ~**ly**, dernièrement.
lattice, *s.* treillis, *m.*; ~**-window**, fenêtre treillissée, *f.*
laud, *v.a.* louer.
laudable, louable; ~**ly**, louablement.
laudanum, laudanum, *m.*
laudation, louange, *f.*; ~**ory**, laudatif, ~ve.
lauds, (*eccles.*) laudes, *f.pl.*
laugh, laughter, rire, *m.*; (*mockery*) risée, *f.*; *be convulsed with* ~, se pâmer de rire.
laugh, *v.n.* rire*; (*fig.*) sourire; ~ *at*, rire* de.
laughable, risible.
laugher, *s.* rieur, ~se, *m.f.*
laughing, *adj.* rieur, ~se; ~**-gas**, gaz hilarant, *m.*; *its no* ~ *matter*, il n'y a pas de quoi rire; *be the* ~*-stock of*, être la risée de; ~**ly**, en riant.
launch, *s.* (*boat*) chaloupe, *f.*; (*of a ship*) lancement, *m.*
launch, *v.a.* (*ship, enterprise, pers., hurl*) lancer; *v.n.* ~ *into, out into*, se lancer dans.
laundress, blanchisseuse, *f.*; ~**y**, (*washing-place*) buanderie, *f.*; (*steam-*~*y*) blanchisserie, *f.*
laureate, *adj.* lauréat, -e.
laurel, (*bot.*) laurier, *m.*; *rest on one's* ~*s*, se reposer sur ses lauriers.
laurustinus, (*bot.*) laurier-tin, *m.*
lava, lave, *f.*
lavatory, (*approx.*) lavabo, *m.*
lavender, lavande, *f.*
lavish, *adj.* prodigue (de); *v.a.* prodiguer; ~**ment**, ~**ness**, prodigalité, *f.*; ~**ly**, prodigalement.
law, (*binding injunction, enactment, of science, of nature, of art, &c.*) loi, *f.*; (*jurisprudence, profession, science of* ~) droit, *m.*; ~**-courts**, palais de justice, *m.*; ~ *of nations*, droit des gens, *m.*; *take the* ~ *into one's own hands*, se faire* justice à soi-même; *possession is nine-tenths of the* ~, possession vaut titre; ~**-maker**, législateur, *m.*; *go to* ~, plaider; *go to* ~ *with*, appeler en justice.
lawful, (*according to law*) légal; (*permitted*) permis; (*marriage*) légitime; ~**ness**, légalité, *f.*; ~**ly**, légalement.
lawless, (*people, nation*) sans loi; (*unbridled*) déréglé.
lawn, (*turf*) pelouse, *f.*; (*fine linen*) linon, *m.*; ~**-mower**, tondeuse, *f.*; ~**-tennis**, tennis, *m.*
lawyer, (*solicitor*) avoué, *m.*; (*pers. versed in law*) légiste, *m.*; ~*'s office*, étude, *f.*
lax, (*not tight*) lâche; (*morals, &c.*) relâché.
laxative, *s.* laxatif, *m.*
laxity, (*looseness*) laxité, *f.*; (*muscles, morals, discipline, &c.*) relâchement, *m.*
lay, *s.* (*poem*) lai, *m.*
lay, *adj.* (*eccles.*) laïque; ~ *figure*, mannequin, *m.*
lay, *v.a.* poser; (*flat*) coucher; (*bury*) déposer; (*rest*) reposer; (*tax*) mettre*; (*plot*) tramer; (*snare*) tendre; (*bet*) parier; (*eggs*) pondre; (*blame, &c.*) rejeter; (*dust, wind*) abattre; (*with carpets, &c.*) recouvrir* (de); (*facts before*) exposer à; ~ *bare*, découvrir*; ~ *low*, abattre; ~ *open*, exposer; ~ *waste*, ravager; ~ *aside, by*, mettre* de côté; (*money*) réserver; ~ *down*, poser; (*give up*) renoncer à; (*life*) donner; (*principles, &c.*) établir; (*ship*) mettre* en chantier; (*arms*) rendre; (*law to*) faire* la loi à; ~ *in*, (*provisions*) faire* provision de; ~ *on*, (*apply*) appliquer; ~ *out*, (*money*) dépenser; (*corpse*) ensevelir; (*garden*) planter; ~ *up*, mettre* de côté; (*accumulate*) amasser; *be laid up*, être alité.
lay, *v.n.* (*hen*) pondre.
layer, (*sand, &c.*) couche, *f.*; (*hort.*)

marcotte, *f.*; (*vine*) provin, *m.*; (*hen*) pondeuse, *f.*; *v.a.* (*hort.*) marcotter.
lay|ing, *s.* (*eggs*) ponte, *f.*; **~out,** (*garden, &c.*) disposition, *f.*
layman, laïque, *m.*
lazaret, lazaretto, (*lepers, quarantine hospital*) lazaret, *m.*
laz|y, paresseu|x, ~se; (*slow-moving*) indolent; **~y-bones,** fainéant, *m.*; **~iness,** paresse, *f.*; **~ily,** paresseusement.
lead, *s.* (*metal*) plomb, *m.*; (*naut.*) sonde, *f.*; **~s,** (*roof*) plombs, *m.pl.*; *black ~*, mine de plomb, *f. red ~*, minium, *m.*; *white ~*, blanc de céruse, *m.*; *~-pencil*, crayon, *m.*; *~-poisoning*, saturnisme, *m.*
lead, *s.* (*guidance*) direction, *f.*; (*in position*) avance, *f.*; (*dog*) laisse, *f.*; (*cards*) main, *f.*; *take the ~*, se mettre* à la tête.
lead, *v.a.* (*a life, by contact, of a road*) mener; (*induce*) porter (à); (*go before*) précéder; (*conduct*) conduire*; *~ astray*, égarer; *~ away*, (*pers.*) emmener; *~ on*, entraîner (à); *~ up to*, amener à.
lead, *v.n.* (*command*) commander; (*road, be in front*) mener; (*go in front*) aller* (être) devant; (*be the first*) être le, la premi|er, ~ère; *~off*, (*begin*) commencer; *~ to, up to*, conduire* à; (*fig.*) aboutir à.
leaden, de plomb.
leader, conducteur, *m.*; (*going first*) premier, *m.*; (*enterprise, party*) chef, *m.*; (*newspaper and political*) leader, *m.*; (*faction, riot*) meneur, *m.*
leading, *s.* conduite, *f.*; (*influence*) influence, *f.*
leading, *adj.* (*most important*) principal; (*in front*) en tête; *~ article*, (*newspaper*) article de fond, *m.*; **~-strings,** lisières, *f.pl.*
leaf, (*bot.*) feuille, *f.*; (*book*) feuillet, *m.*; (*tables*) rallonge, *f.*; (*door*) battant, *m.*; **~-mould,** terreau, *m.*; *turn over a new ~*, faire* peau neuve.
leaf|age, feuillage, *m.*; **~less,** sans feuille; **~let,** petite feuille, *f.*; (*handbill*) prospectus, *m.*; (*bot.*) foliole, *f.*; **~y,** feuillu.
league, *s.* (*distance*) lieue, *f.*; (*compact*) ligue, *f.*; *v.n. ~ together*, se liguer.
leak, *s.* (*water*) fuite, *f.*; (*naut.*) voie d'eau, *f.*; *v.n.* (*receptacle*) fuir*; (*run off*) couler; (*naut.*) faire* eau; *~ out*, transpirer.
leakage, fuite, *f.*; (*naut.*) voie d'eau, *f.*
leaky, qui fuit; (*naut.*) qui fait* eau.
lean, *s.* (*meat*) maigre, *m.*; *adj.* maigre; **~ness,** maigreur, *f.*
lean, *v.a.* (*rest*) appuyer; *~ back*, pencher en arrière; *v.n.* (*stoop*) se pencher; *~ against*, s'appuyer sur; *~ towards*, pencher vers.
leaning, *s.* (*inclination*) penchant, *m.* (à).
lean-to, *s.* appentis, *m.*
leap, *s.* saut, *m.*; *by ~s and bounds*, par sauts et par bonds.
leap, *v.a.* franchir; (*horse*) faire* sauter; *v.a. ~ over*, sauter; *v.n.* sauter.
leap-year, année bissextile, *f.*
learn, *v.a.n.* apprendre*; *~ how to*, apprendre* à.
learned, érudit; *~ professions*, professions libérales, *f.pl.*; **~ly,** savamment.
learning, *s.* savoir, *m.*
lease, bail, *m.* (*pl.* baux); *on ~*, à bail.
leash, laisse, *f.*
least, *s.* moins, *m.*; *at ~, to say the ~*, pour le moins; *at the very ~*, tout au moins; *not in the ~*, pas le moins du monde.
least, *adj.* le (la) plus petit(e); (*in quantity, dimension, intensity*) le (la) moindre.
least, *adv.* le moins.
leather, cuir, *m.*; *~ bottle*, outre, *f.*; *~ gloves*, gants de peau, *m.pl.*; *patent ~*, cuir vernis, *m.*; *Russia ~*, cuir de Russie, *m.*; *wash-~*, peau de chamois, *f.*
leather(n) *adj.* de cuir.
leave, *s.* permission, *f.*; (*freedom to*) liberté, *f.*; *~ of absence*, congé, *m.*; (*mil.*) permission, *f.*; *on ~*, en congé; (*mil.*) en permission; *by your ~*, avec votre permission; *schoolboy, soldier on ~*, permissionnaire, *m.*; *take one's ~ of*, faire* ses adieux à; *take French ~*, *see* FRENCH.
leave, *v.a.* (*leave behind or in a certain state*) laisser; (*go away from*) quitter; (*in will*) léguer; *be left*, rester (être); *~ about*, laisser traîner; *~ behind*, laisser; *~ off*, (*clothes, &c.*) quitter; (*cease*) cesser (de); *~ out*, omettre*; *~ to*, (*refer*) s'en remettre* à; *~ alone*, laisser tranquille; *~ no stone unturned*, remuer ciel et terre; *take it or ~ it*, c'est à prendre ou à laisser; *~ much to be desired*, laisser à désirer.
leave, *v.n.* partir* (être).
leaven, levain, *m.*; *~ed bread*, pain levé, *m.*
leavings, restes, *m.pl.*; (*meal*) desserte, *f.*
lectern, lutrin, *m.*
lecture, conférence, *f.*; (*reprimand*) semonce, *f.*; ⚠ lecture *in French* = '*reading*'; *v.a.* (*scold*) sermonner; *v.n.* faire* des conférences.
lecturer, (*univ.*) professeur de faculté, *m.*
ledge, rebord, *m.*; (*of rocks*) récif, *m.*
ledger, (*bkkpg.*) grand livre, *m.*
lee, *s.* (*shelter*) abri, *m.*; *adj.* (*naut.*) sous le vent; **~way,** dérive, *f.*
leech, sangsue, *f.*; (*doctor*) médecin, *m.*
leek, (*bot.*) poireau, *m.*
leer, *s.* œillade, *f.*; *v.n.* regarder de côté.
lees, lie, *f.*
leeward, *adj.* sous le vent.
left, *s.* gauche, *f.*; *on the ~*, à gauche; *turn to the ~*, tourner à gauche; *keep to the ~*, garder votre, etc., gauche.
left, *adj.* gauche; *~-handed*, gauch|er, ~ère; *adv.* à gauche.
leg, *s.* jambe, *f.*; (*most quadrupeds, certain reptiles, and insects and birds except birds of prey which* = serre, *f.*) patte, *f.*; (*poultry*) cuisse, *f.*; (*mutton*) gigot, *m.*; (*beef*) trumeau, *m.*; (*table*)

pied, *m.*; *be on one's last ~s*, être à bout de force; *have one's sea ~s*, avoir le pied marin; *stretch one's ~s*, se dégourdir les jambes; *pull the ~ of*, monter (avoir) un bateau à.
legacy, legs, *m.*
legal, (*laid down by law*) légal; (*pertaining to law*) judiciaire; ~ *tender*, monnaie légale, *f.*; **~ity**, légalité, *f.*; **~ly**, légalement.
legate, légat, *m.*
legatee, légataire, *m.f.*
legation, légation, *f.*
legend, (*myth, story, inscription*) légende, *f.*; **~ary**, légendaire.
legerdemain, escamotage, *m.*; ⚠ *'legerdemain' not used in French.*
legging, jambière, *f.*
legib|le, lisible; **~ility**, lisibilité, *f.*; **~ly**, lisiblement.
legion, légion, *f.*; **~ary**, *s.* légionnaire, *m.*
legisla|te, légiférer; **~tion**, législation, *f.*; **~tor**, législateur, *m.*; **~ture**, législature, *f.*; **~tive**, législati|f, ~ve.
legitimat|e, *adj.* légitime; **~ely**, légitimement.
legitimist, (*hist.*) *adj. and s.m.f.* légitimiste.
legitimize, *v.a.* légitimer.
leisure, loisir, *m.*; *at ~*, à loisir; *be at ~*, être de loisir; **~ly**, *adj.* (*slow*) lent; *adv.* à loisir.
lemming, (*zool.*) lemming, *m.*
lemon, citron, *m.*; ⚠ limon = *'lime fruit'*; **~-coloured**, citron, *invar.*; **~-plant**, verveine, *f.*; **~-squash**, citronnade, *f.*; **~-squeezer**, presse-citron, *m.*
lemonade, limonade, *f.*
lemur, (*zool.*) maki, *m.*
lend, *v.a.* prêter; (*bestow*) donner.
lender, (*lit. and money-lender*) prêteu|r, ~se, *m.f.*
length, (*dimension*) longueur, *f.*; (*time*) durée, *f.*; (*rope, &c.*) bout, *m.*; *at ~*, enfin; (*in full*) en toutes lettres; *at full ~*, (*lying*) tout de son long; *go the ~ of*, aller* (être) jusqu'à.
lengthen, *v.a.* allonger; (*time*) prolonger; *v.n.* se prolonger.
length|wise, **~ways**, en long.
lengthy, long, -ue.
lenien|cy, indulgence, *f.*; **~t**, indulgent; **~tly**, avec indulgence.
lens, (*opt., photo.*) lentille, *f.*; (*in sunk mount*) objectif, *m.*
Lent, carême, *m.*; *mid-~*, mi-carême, *f.*
lentil, (*bot.*) lentille, *f.*
lentisk, (*bot.*) lentisque, *m.*
leonine, léonin.
leopard, léopard, *m.*
leper, lépreu|x, ~se, *m.f.*
lepro|sy, (*lit. and fig.*) lèpre, *f.*; **~us**, lépreu|x, ~se.
lesion, lésion, *f.*
less, *adj.* moindre; (*quantity, less of*) moins de.
less, *adv.* moins; *~ and ~*, de moins en moins; *~ than*, moins de; *be none the ~ + adj.*, n'en être pas moins + *adj.*
less|ee, locataire, *m.f.*; **~or**, bailleur, *m.*
lessen, *v.a.n.* diminuer.
lesser, *adj.* moindre; **~ celandine**, *see* CELANDINE.
lesson, leçon, *f.*; (*private*) répétition, *f.*; (*warning*) leçon, *f.*
lest, *conj.* de peur que (*subj.* + ne).
let, *v.a.* (*house*) louer; (*allow*) laisser + *inf.*; (*permit*) permettre à + *pers.*, de + *inf.*; (*aux.*) *let me, him, &c., do*, *imperat. of 'let' or* que + *subj.*; *~ alone*, *be*, laisser tranquille; *~ go*, lâcher prise; *~ loose*, lâcher; *~ slip*, (*fig.*) laisser passer; *~ down*, (*lower*) baisser; (*pop. fail*) faire* faux bond à; *~ in*, faire* entrer; *see also* CLUTCH; *~ into*, (*secret*) mettre* dans; *~ off*, (*steam, &c.*) lâcher; (*pers.*) faire* grâce à; (*remit*) faire* grâce de; (*gun*) tirer; *~ out*, ouvrir* la porte à; (*secret*) trahir; (*blows*) lancer; *~ through*, laisser passer.
letharg|ic, léthargique; **~y**, léthargie, *f.*
letter, (*alphab., epistle, precise terms*) lettre, *f.*; **~s**, (*Lit.*) belles-lettres, *f.pl.*; *man of ~s*, homme de lettres, *m.*; **~-box**, boîte aux lettres, *f.*; **~-card**, carte-lettre, *f.*; **~-case**, porte-lettres, *m.*; *~ of credit*, lettre de crédit, *f.*; *~ of mark*, lettre de marque, *f.*; **~press**, texte imprimé, *m.*; **~-scales**, pèse-lettre, *m.*; **~-writer**, épistoli|er, ~ère, *m.f.*; **~s patent**, lettres patentes, *f. pl.*; *~ of introduction*, lettre de recommandation, *f.*; *all ~s to be directed to the manager*, prière d'adresser les lettres au gérant.
lettuce, laitue, *f.*
levee, réception à la Cour, *f.*; ⚠ *not* levée *which = 'levy', 'collection', 'dike', &c.*
level, *s.* (*instr., horiz. plane, social, mental, &c.*) niveau, *m.*; *be on a ~ with*, être de niveau avec.
level, *adj.* (*smooth*) uni; (*flat*) plat; (*horizontal*) horizontal; (*well balanced*) bien équilibré; *~ with*, au niveau de; **~ crossing**, passage à niveau, *m.*
level, *v.a.* (*ground*) niveler; (*gun*) pointer; (*blow*) porter; (*direct satire, &c.*) diriger; *~ up*, élever au niveau (de); **~ler**, niveleu|r, ~se, *m.f.*
levelling, *s.* nivellement, *m.*; (*gun*) pointage, *m.*
lever, levier, *m.*
leveret, levraut, *m.*; ⚠ *not* levrette *which = 'greyhound bitch'.*
leviathan, léviathan, *m.*
Levite, lévite, *m.*
Leviticus, (*Bible*) Lévitique, *m.*
levity, légèreté, *f.*
levy, *s.* (*taxes, troops*) levée, *f.*; *v.a.* lever.
lewd, impudique; **~ness**, impudicité, *f.*
lexicograph|y, lexicographie, *f.*; **~er**, lexicographe, *m.f.*
lexicon, lexique, *m.*
liab|le, (*responsible*) responsable (de);

(*subject to*) sujet, -te (à); (*law*) passible (de); **~ility**, responsabilité, *f.*; **~ilities**, passif, *m.*; *~ility to*, tendance, *f.* (à); *joint ~ility*, obligation conjointe, *f.*; *limited ~ility Co.*, *see* COMPANY; *hold oneself ~le for*, se porter garant de.
liar, menteu|r, ~se, *m.f.*
libation, libation, *f.*
libel, *s.* diffamation, *f.*; *v.a.* diffamer; ⚠ *not* libeller *which* = '*draw up*'; **~lous**, diffamatoire.
liberal, *adj.* (*developing mind, open-handed, not rigorous, polit.*) libéral; (*generous*) généreu|x, ~se; **~ity**, libéralité, *f.*; **~ly**, libéralement.
liberalize, *v.a.* rendre libéral.
libera|te, libérer; **~tion**, libération, *f.*; **~tor**, libérat|eur, ~rice, *m.f.*
libertine, *s.* libertin, -e, *m.f.*
libert|y, liberté, *f.*; *be at ~ to*, être libre de; *take ~ies*, prendre* des libertés.
libidinous, libidineu|x, ~se.
librarian, bibliothécaire, *m.*; ⚠ *not* libraire *which* = '*bookseller*'.
library, bibliothèque, *f.*; ⚠ *not* librairie *which* = '*bookseller's shop*'.
librett|ist, librettiste, *m.*; **~o**, livret, *m.*
lice, *see* LOUSE.
licence, (*leave*) permission, *f.*; (*excess of liberty*) licence, *f.*; (*tradesmen*) patente, *f.*; (*marriage*) dispense de bans, *f.*
license, *v.a.* accorder un permis à.
licensed, (*tradesman*) patenté.
licentiate, (*univ., &c.*) licencié, -e, *m.f.*
licentious, licencieu|x, ~se; **~ness**, licence, *f.*; **~ly**, licencieusement.
lichen, (*bot.*) lichen, *m.*
lick, *v.a.* lécher; **~ing**, *s.* (*slang*) rossée, *f.*
licorice, *see* LIQUORICE.
lid, couvercle, *m.*; (*eye*) paupière, *f.*
lie, *s.* mensonge, *m.*; *give the ~ to*, démentir*; *v.n.* mentir*.
lie, *s.* (*land*) configuration, *f.*
lie, *v.n.* être couché; (*in grave*) reposer; (*be situated*) se trouver; (*consist*) résider (en); (*extend, of land*) s'étendre; (*be*) être; *~ at anchor*, être à l'ancre; *~ in ambush*, se tenir* en embuscade; *~ low*, (*fig.*) dissimuler ses desseins; *~ open*, être ouvert; *~ sick*, être malade; *~ in state*, être exposé sur son lit de parade; *~ about*, (*untidily*) traîner; *~ down*, se coucher; (*to dog*) couchez!; *~ off*, (*naut.*) être mouillé; *~ over*, (*be put off*) être différé; *~ to*, (*naut.*) être à la cape; *~ with . . . to*, (*impers.*) il appartient à +*pers.*, de + *inf.*
lief, volontiers; *I had as ~*, j'aime autant +*inf.*
liege, (*feudal*) lige, *m.*
lien, nantissement, *m.*; ⚠ *not* lien *which* = '*bond*', '*tie*'.
lieutenan|cy, lieutenance, *f.*; **~t**, lieutenant, *m.*; **sub-~t, second ~t**, (*mil.*) sous-lieutenant, *m.*; (*nav.*) lieutenant en second, *m.*; **~t-general**, général de division, *m.*
life, (*existence, duration, manner of life, liveliness*) vie, *f.*; *still ~*, nature morte, *f.*; *for ~*, à vie; *for the ~ of me, upon my ~*, parole d'honneur; *in my ~*, de ma vie; *from ~*, (*paint., draw.*) d'après nature; *depart this ~*, mourir* (être); **~-belt**, ceinture de sauvetage, *f.*; **~-boat**, canot de sauvetage, *m.*; **~-buoy**, bouée de sauvetage, *f.*; **~ assurance**, assurance sur la vie, *f.*; **~-interest**, usufruit, *m.*; **~-guards**, gardes du corps, *m.pl.*; **~-policy**, police d'assurance, *f.*; **~-preserver**, casse-tête, *m. invar.*; **~-size**, grandeur nature, *invar.*
lifeless, (*lit. and fig.*) inanimé; **~ness**, manque de vie, *m.*; **~ly**, sans vie.
lifelike, (*portrait*) pris sur le vif.
lifelong, de toute la vie.
lifetime, vie, *f.*; *in my ~*, de mon vivant.
lift, *s.* (*help*) coup de main, *m.*; (*apparatus for raising pers. or things*) ascenseur, *m.*; *give me a ~*, (*in veh.*) voulez-vous me prendre avec vous?
lift, *v.a.* (*eyes, head, &c.*) lever; (*fig.*) élever; (*raise aloft*) dresser; (*lift up*) soulever; (*cattle*) enlever.
lift, *v.n.* se soulever; (*fog*) se disperser.
ligament, ligament, *m.*
ligature, ligature, *f.*
light, *s.* (*lit. and eminent pers.*) lumière, *f.*; (*daylight, fig., painting, arch.*) jour, *m.*; (*faint light*) lueur, *f.*; (*match, naut.*) feu, *m.*; (*brilliance and eye*) éclat, *m.*; *according to one's ~s*, selon ses moyens; *bring to ~*, dévoiler; *come to ~*, se révéler; *stand in the ~ of*, ôter le jour à; (*fig.*) nuire* à.
light, *adj.* (*not heavy, elegant, easy, slight, frivolous, heart, mind, of foot, sleep, food*) lég|er, ~ère; (*not dark, of colours*) clair; (*lighted*) éclairé; (*naut. not laden*) lège; (*with colours*) clair, *e.g.* bleu clair, *invar.*; (*fair*) blond; *make ~ of*, faire* peu de cas de; **~ness**, (*lit. and fig.*) légèreté, *f.*; **~ly**, légèrement; *~ horse*, *see* HORSE.
light, lightly, *adv.* légèrement; *travel ~*, voyager avec peu de bagages; *~-fingered gentry*, voleurs à la tire, *m.pl.*; *~-headed*, en délire; *~-hearted*, au cœur gai.
light, *v.a.* allumer; (*illuminate*) éclairer; *~ up*, (*veh.*) allumer; *v.n.* s'allumer; (*face*) devenir* (être) rayonnant; *~ on, upon*, rencontrer.
lighten, *v.a.* (*load, lit. and fig.*) alléger; (*shed light on, lit. and fig.*) éclairer; *v.n.* (*get less heavy*) s'alléger; (*emit lightning*) faire* des éclairs.
lighter, (*naut.*) gabare, *f.*; **~man**, gabarier, *m.*
lighthouse, phare, *m.*; **~-keeper**, gardien de phare, *m.*
lighting, éclairage, *m.*
lightning, *s.* éclair, *m.*; **sheet-~**, éclair de chaleur, *m.*; **forked ~**, éclair ramifié, *m.*
lights, (*food*) mou, *m.*
lightship, bateau-feu, *m.*
lightsome, (*merry*) gai.

ligneous, ligneu|x, ~se.
lignum vitae, (*bot.*) gaïac, *m.*
like, *s.* (*pers.*) pareil, -le, *m.f.*; (*same thing*) même chose, *f.*; *do the* ~, en faire* autant.
like, *adj.* semblable (à); (*of portrait*) ressemblant; (*such as*) comme; *be, look* ~, ressembler à; *it's just* ~ *him to*, c'est bien de lui de; *be nothing* ~, être loin d'être . . .; *nothing* ~ *it*, rien de tel; *look* ~, avoir l'air de; ~ *that*, comme cela; *that's something* ~ *a house*, (*pop.*) voilà ce qui s'appelle une maison.
like, *v.a.* aimer; *I, &c., should* ~ *to*, Je, etc., voudrais + *inf.*
like, *v.n.* vouloir*; *when you* ~, quand vous voudrez, quand il vous plaira; ~ *to* (*do*), aimer + *inf. or* à; ~ *best to*, préférer + *inf.*
likelihood, vraisemblance, *f.*
likely, *adj.* probable; *be* ~ *to*, avoir chance de; *adv.* probablement.
liken, *v.a.* comparer (à).
likeness, ressemblance, *f.*; (*portrait*) portrait, *m.*
likewise, pareillement.
liking, goût, *m.*; *have a* ~ *for*, avoir du goût pour; *take a* ~ *to*, prendre * goût à.
lilac, *s.* lilas, *m.*; *adj.* (*colour*) lilas, *invar.*
Lilliputian, *adj.* lilliputien, -ne.
lilt, *s.* chant rythmé, *m.*
lily, lis, *m.*; ~ *of the valley*, muguet, *m.*
limb, membre, *m.*; (*tree*) grosse branche, *f.*
limbed, *loose*-~, dégingandé.
limber, (*gun*) avant-train, *m.*
limbo, limbes, *m.pl.*
lime, *s.* (*stone*) chaux, *f.*; (*bird*) glu, *f.*; (*tree*) tilleul, *m.*; (*fruit*) limon, *m.*; ~ **juice**, sirop de limon, *m.*; **quick**~, chaux vive, *f.*; **slaked** ~, chaux éteinte, *f.*
lime, *v.a.* (*manure*) chauler; (*birds*) prendre* à la glu.
limelight, *be in the* ~, être en vue.
limestone, pierre à chaux, *f.*
limit, *s.* limite, *f.*; *that's the* ~, (*pop.*) c'est par trop fort; *v.a.* (*immaterial things*) limiter; (*fig.*) borner; ~*ed liability*, *see* COMPANY.
limitation, limitation, *f.*; ⚠ '*limitations*' = '*inability*' = côtés faibles, *m.pl.*
limitless, illimité.
limn, *v.a.* peindre*.
limousine, (*motor*) limousine, *f.*
limp, *s.* clochement, *m.*; *v.n.* clocher.
limp, *adj.* (*flaccid*) flasque; (*fig. of pers.*) mou, molle; (*binding*) souple; ~**ly**, mollement.
limpet, (*conch.*) patelle, *f.*
limpid, limpide; ~**ity**, limpidité, *f.*
limpingly, clopin-clopant.
linchpin, esse, *f.*
linden, (*tree*) tilleul, *m.*
line, *s.* (*pencil, &c., battle, fire, conduct, sight, fishing, face, nav. and mil., measure, equator, steamship, rail., telegr., &c.*) ligne, *f.*; (*short letter*) mot, *m.*; (*poetry*) vers, *m.*; (*rank, row*) rang, *m.*; (*of business*) partie, *f.*; (*rail.* = *track*) voie, *f.*; (*wrinkle*) ride, *f.*; (*descent*) lignée, *f.*; ~**s**, (*mil.*) lignes, *f.pl.*; *loop* ~, (*rail.*) ligne dérivée, *f.*; *Maginot, &c.* ~, ligne Maginot, etc., *f.*; *main* ~, (*rail.*) grande ligne, *f.*; *pipe* ~, (*conduit*) conduite, *f.*; *single* ~, (*rail.*) voie simple, *f.*; *read between the* ~*s*, lire* entre les lignes; *drop a* ~ *to*, envoyer un mot à.
line, *v.a.* (*garment*) doubler; (*mason*) revêtir; (*purse*) remplir; ~ *up*, (*mil.*) aligner; *v.n.* s'aligner.
lineage, lignée, *f.*
lineal, (*descent*) ⚠ *not* linéal, *but* en ligne directe; ~**ly**, en ligne directe.
lineament, linéament, *m.*
linear, linéaire.
linen, (*cloth from flax*) toile, *f.*; (*household*) linge, *m.*; *dirty*-~ *bag*, sac à linge, *m.*; *one does not wash one's dirty* ~ *in public*, il faut laver son linge sale en famille; *adj.* de toile, de lin; (*made up*) de linge.
liner, (*naut.*) paquebot, *m.*; *transatlantic* ~, transatlantique, *m.*
ling, (*bot.*) bruyère, *f.*
linger, *v.n.* (*get late*) s'attarder; (*hesitate*) hésiter; (*progress slowly, lag, languish, illness*) traîner.
lingerer, retardataire, *m.f.*
lingeringly, avec hésitation.
lingo, jargon, *m.*
lingual, *adj.* lingual.
linguist, linguiste, *m.f.*; ~**ic**, *adj.* linguistique.
liniment, liniment, *m.*
lining, *s.* (*garment*) doublure, *f.*; (*hat*) coiffe, *f.*; (*mason.*) revêtement, *m.*
link, *s.* (*of a chain*) chaînon, *m.*; (*fig.*) lien, *m.*; *v.a.* lier; (*unite*) unir; (*arms*) se donner le bras.
links, (*golf*) terrain de golf, *m.*
linnet, (*ornith.*) linot, *m.*, linotte, *f.*
linoleum, linoléum, *m.*
linotype, linotype, *f.*
linseed, graine de lin, *f.*; ~**-oil**, huile de lin, *f.*
linsey-woolsey, tiretaine, *f.*
lint, charpie, *f.*
lintel, linteau, *m.*
lion, (*lit. and fig.*) lion, *m.*; ~**ess**, lionne, *f.*; ~**s**, (*objects of curiosity*) curiosités, *f.pl.*; ~**ize**, *v.a.* (*pers.*) traiter comme célébrité.
lip, lèvre, *f.*; (*animal*) babine, *f.*; (*impertinence, pop.*) insolence, *f.*; (*vase*) bord, *m.*; ~**stick**, bâton de rouge, *m.*
lipped, *thick*-~, lippu; *in comps.* aux lèvres + *adj.*
liquef|y, *v.a.* liquéfier; *v.n.* se liquéfier; ~**action**, liquéfaction, *f.*; ~**iable**, liquéfiable.
liqueur, liqueur, *f.*
liquid, *s.* liquide, *m.*; *adj.* (*lit., money, gram.*) liquide; (*eye, air, &c.*) limpide.
liquida|te, liquider; ~**tion**, liquidation, *f.*; ~**tor**, liquidateur, *m.*

liquor, *s.* liquide, *m.*; (*alcoholic*) boisson, *f.*; *worse for* ~, pris de boisson.
liqu(c)orice, réglisse, *f.*
lisp, *s.* zézayement, *m.*; (*leaves*) bruissement, *m.*; *v.n.* zézayer, bruire* (*def.*).
lissom(e), souple.
list, *s.* (*roll, catalogue*) liste, *f.*; (*cloth*) lisière, *f.*; (*inclination*) inclinaison, *f.*; **~s,** (*arena*) lice, *f.*; (*comm.*) bordereau, *m.*; *sick* ~, rôle des malades, *m.*; *on the retired* ~, en retraite; *have a* ~, (*naut.*) avoir de la bande.
list, *v.a.* (*enter in list*) enregistrer; (*desire*) vouloir*.
listen, *list, v.n.* écouter; (*with effort*) tendre l'oreille; ~ *in,* (*wireless*) écouter; ~ *to,* écouter, *v.a.*
listener, audit|eur, ~rice, *m.f*; (*pej.*) écouteu|r, ~se, *m.f.*; ~-*in,* sansfiliste, *m.f.*
listless, nonchalant; **~ness,** nonchalance, *f.*; **~ly,** nonchalamment.
litany, litanie, *f.*
literal, (*according to text*) littéral; **~ly,** à la lettre.
literary, littéraire; ~ *man,* homme de lettres, *m.*
literate, *adj.* lettré.
literature, littérature, *f.*
lithe, souple; **~ness,** souplesse, *f.*
lithograph, lithography, lithographie, *f.*; **~er,** lithographe, *m.*; *v.a.* lithographier.
lithology, lithologie, *f.*
Lithuanian, *adj.* (*when an adj. use small letter*) *and s.m.f.* Lithuanien, -ne.
litigant, plaideu|r, ~se, *m.f.*
litigation, litige, *m.*
litotes, (*rhet.*) litote, *f.*
litter, *s.* (*carriage and for animals*) litière, *f.*; (*mess*) fouillis, *m.*; (*hand-cart*) civière, *f.*; (*young of animals*) portée, *f.*; *v.a.* (*disorder*), mettre* en désordre; (*bring forth*) mettre* bas.
little, *s.* peu, *m.*; *make* ~ *of,* faire* peu de cas de.
little, *adj.* (*size, age, pej.*) petit; (*quantity*) peu de; (*a little*) un peu de; ~ *finger, see* FINGER.
little, *adv.* peu; (*scarcely, not at all*) ne . . . guère; *a* ~, un peu; ~ *by* ~, peu à peu; *not a* ~, beaucoup.
littleness, (*lit. and fig.*) petitesse, *f.*
liturg|y, liturgie, *f.*; **~ical,** liturgique.
live, *v.n.* (*be alive, subsist, last out, obtain livelihood*) vivre*; (*reside*) demeurer (avoir); ~ *on,* vivre* de; ~ *in clover,* être comme un coq en pâte; *v.a.* (*life, &c.*) mener; *short-~d,* passag|er, ~ère.
live, *adj.* vivant; (*shell, &c.*) chargé.
livelihood, gagne-pain, *m. invar.*
liveliness, vivacité, *f.*; (*gaiety*) gaieté, *f.*
livelong, *adj. all the* ~ *day,* toute la sainte journée.
lively, (*living, full of life*) vivant; (*gay*) gai; (*keen*) vi|f, ~ ve.
liven up, animer.
liver, (*anat.*) foie, *m.*; **~wort,** (*bot.*) hépatique, *f.*
livery, *s.* (*for servants*) livrée, *f.*; (*horses*) pension, *f.*; **~-stable,** écurie de chevaux à louer, *f.*
livid, livide; **~ness,** lividité, *f.*
living, *s.* (*maintenance*) vie, *f.*; (*eccles.*) bénéfice, *m.*; *the* ~, les vivants, *m.pl.*; *earn one's* ~, gagner sa vie.
living, *adj.* (*existent, contemporary, language, likeness*) vivant; (*water*) vi|f, ~ve.
Livonian, *adj.* (*when an adj. use small letter*) *and s.m.f.* Livonien, -ne.
lizard, lézard, *m.*
llama, (*zool.*) lama, *m.*
loach, (*ichth.*) loche, *f.*
load, *s.* (*ship, veh., &c.*) charge, *f.*; (*burden*) fardeau, *m.*; (*weight*) poids, *m.*
load, *v.a.* charger (de); (*fig.*) accabler (de); (*gun, &c.*) charger; (*dice*) piper.
loading, *s.* chargement, *m.*
lo(a)dstone, aimant, *m.*
loaf, (*sugar, bread*) pain, *m.*
loaf, *v.n.* (*do nothing*) flâner; **~er,** flâneur, *m.*
loam, terre forte, *f.*
loan, *s.* (*thing lent*) prêt, *m.*; (*borrowing*) emprunt, *m.*; *on* ~, en prêt; *v.a.* (*grant loan of*) (*U.S.A.*) prêter; *may I have the* ~ *of?*, puis-je emprunter?
lo(a)th, *adj. be* ~ *to,* avoir de la répugnance à.
loath|e, *v.a.* détester; **~ing,** *s.* dégoût, *m.*
loathsome, repoussant; (*sickening*) écœurant.
lobe, (*ear, brain*) lobe, *m.*
lobby, (*house*) vestibule, *m.*; (*polit.*) couloir, *m.*
lobelia, (*bot.*) lobélie, *f.*
lobster, †homard, *m.*
local, local; ~ *colour, see* COLOUR; **~ly,** localement; **~ity,** localité, *f.*
localize, locate, localiser.
located, *be* ~, (*U.S.A.*) être situé.
location, emplacement, *m.*; (*determining spot*) détermination d'un lieu, *f.*; ⚠ *not* location *which* = '*letting out*', '*hiring*'.
locative, (*gram.*) *adj. and s.m.* locatif.
lock, (*door*) serrure, *f.*; (*gun*) platine, *f.*; (*hair*) boucle, *f.*; (*canal, &c.*) écluse, *f.*; **~s,** cheveux, *m.pl.*; **~-keeper,** éclusier, *m.*; *pick a* ~, crocheter une serrure; **~-out,** *s.* (*workmen*) lock-out, *m.*
lock, *v.a.* (*door, box, &c.*) fermer à clé; ~ *up,* (*capital*) immobiliser; (*wheels*) bloquer; (*pers., thing*) enfermer; ~ *out,* fermer la porte à; *v.n.* se fermer; (*wheels*) se bloquer; **~jaw,** (*med.*) trisme, *m.*
locker, coffre, *m.*; (*naut.*) caisson, *m.*
locket, médaillon, *m.*; ⚠ *not* loquet *which* = '*latch*'.
locksmith, serrurier, *m.*
locomotion, locomotion, *f.*
locomotive, locomotive, *f.*
locust, sauterelle, *f.*
locution, (*style of speech, phrase*) locution, *f.*
lodge, *s.* (*porter, &c.*) loge, *f.*; (*park*) pavillon, *m.*

lodge, *v.a.* (*money, documents, complaint*) déposer; (*receive pers.*) héberger; (*mil. in huts*), baraquer; *v.n.* (*lit. and fig.*) loger.
lodgement, (*mil.*) logement, *m.*; (*comm.*) dépôt, *m.*; *effect a* ~, prendre* pied.
lodger, locataire, *m.f.*
lodging, logement, *m.*; **~s,** (*apartments*) appartement garni, *m.*
loft, (*granary and house*) grenier, *m.*
loft|y, (*lit. and fig.*) élevé; (*haughty*) alti|er, ~ère; **~iness,** (*lit. and fig.*) †hauteur, *f.*; (*thoughts, feelings, &c.*) élévation, *f.*; **~ily,** avec †hauteur.
log, *s.* (*for hearth, &c.*) bûche, *f.*; (*timber*) bille, *f.*; (*naut.*) loch, *m.*; *~-book*, livre de bord, *m.*; *~-hut*, cabane de bois, *f.*; *sleep like a* ~, dormir comme un loir.
logarithm, logarithme, *m.*
loggerhead, (*pers.*) lourdaud, *m.*; *at ~s*, en bisbille.
logic, *s.* logique, *f.*; **~ian,** logicien, *m.*; **~al,** logique; **~ally,** logiquement.
logwood, (*bot.*) bois de campêche, *m.*
loin, (*veal*) longe, *f.*; (*beef*) aloyau, *m.*; **~s,** reins, *m.pl.*; *gird up one's ~s*, se ceindre* les reins.
loiter, flâner; (*pej.*) rôder; (*linger*) tarder; **~er,** traînard, *m.*
loll, *v.n.* (*lounge*) se prélasser; (*tongue*) pendre.
London pride, (*bot.*) désespoir des peintres, *m.*
Londoner, Londonien, -ne, *m.f.*
lonesome, lone, solitaire; **~ness,** solitude, *f.*
lonel|y, (*pers., place*) solitaire; **~iness,** solitude, *f.*
long, *adj.* long, -ue; *thirty metres* ~, long de 30 mètres; *be 6 ft.* ~, avoir 6 pieds de long; *be ~ in+gerund*, être long à; *a ~ mile*, un bon mille; *in the ~ run*, à la longue; ~ *boat*, chaloupe, *f.*; ~ *clothes*, *see* CLOTHES; *a ~ time*, (*since*) depuis longtemps; *see also* SINCE; *a ~ while*, longtemps.
long, *adv.* longtemps; **~er,** plus longtemps; *how ~ have you been here?* depuis combien de temps êtes-vous ici?; *before* ~, avant longtemps; *~-eared*, aux longues oreilles; *~-lived*, qui vit longtemps; *no longer*, ne . . . plus; ~ *standing*, de longue date; *~-suffering*, patient; *~-winded*, de longue haleine; (*fig.*) prolixe; *interj. so ~!* (*fam.*) à bientôt!
long, *v.n.* brûler (de); *also* il tarde +*dat. of pers. and* de+*inf.*; ~ *for*, soupirer après.
longanimity, longanimité, *f.*
longevity, longévité, *f.*
longing, *s.* grande envie, *f.*; *adj.* plein d'envie; **~ly,** avec grande envie.
longitud|e, longitude, *f.*; **~inal,** longitudinal.
long ship's boat, chaloupe, *f*
loo, (*cards*) mouche, *f.*
look, *s.* (*of eyes*) regard, *m.*; (*outward appearance, pers.*) air, *m.*; (*things*) aspect, *m.*
look, *v.a.* regarder; ~ *after*, soigner; ~ *at*, regarder; ~ *for*, chercher; ~ *into*, (*examine*) examiner; ~ *on, upon*, (*consider*) regarder; ~ *over, through*, (*book, &c.*) parcourir*; ~ *up, out*, (*words, &c.*) chercher; ~ *up and down*, (*contempt*) toiser; ~ *black at*, regarder de travers.
look, *v.n.* regarder; (+ *adj.*) avoir l'air; ~ *big*, avoir l'air important; ~ *blank*, avoir l'air déconcerté; ~ *well*, avoir bonne mine; ~ *here!* dites donc!; ~ *about*, regarder autour de soi; ~ *away*, détourner les yeux; ~ *back*, regarder en arrière; ~ *back upon*, (*past, &c.*) se reporter à; ~ *behind*, regarder en arrière; ~ *down*, baisser les yeux; ~ *forward to*, s'attendre à; ~ *in on*, (*visit*) passer chez; ~ *out*, (*be watchful*) être sur ses gardes; *interj.* gare!; ~ *out for*, s'attendre à; ~ *over*, (*aspect*) donner sur; ~ *up*, lever les yeux.
looked-for, attendu.
looker-on, spectat|eur, ~rice, *m.f.*
looking-glass, miroir, *m.*
look-out, *s.* (*watch*) guet, *m.*; (*post*) poste d'observation, *m.*; (*naut.*) vigie, *f.*; *be on the ~ for*, être en observation à; *that's my* ~, c'est mon affaire; *keep a sharp* ~, avoir l'œil au guet.
loom, *s.* métier, *m.*; *v.n.* (*appear vaguely*) (*lit. and fig.*) se dessiner.
loon, (*ornith.*) plongeon, *m.*
loop, *s.* boucle, *f.*; *v.a.* ~ *the loop*, (*aeron.*) boucler la boucle.
loophole, meurtrière, *f.*; (*fig.*) échappatoire, *f.*
loose, *adj.* **1.** (*not tight*) lâche; **2.** (*not fixed, attached*) délié; **3.** (*morals and med.*) relâché; **4.** (*clothes*) large; **5.** (*hair*) dénoué; **6.** (*free*) libre; **7.** (*screw*) desserré; **8.** (*style*) décousu; **9.** (*dangling*) qui branle; **10.** (*vague*) vague; **11.** (*rope*) mou, molle; **12.** (*cash*) menu; **~ness,** (*med. and morals*) relâchement; (*clothes*) ampleur, *f.*; (*style*) décousu, *m.*; **~ly,** lâchement; (*carelessly*) avec négligence.
loose, *v.a.* détacher; (*free*) libérer; (*naut.*) larguer.
loosen, *v.a.* desserrer.
loosestrife, (*bot.*) lysimachie, *f.*
loot, *s.* pillage, *m.*; *v.a.* piller.
lop, *v.a.* émonder.
lop-eared, oreillard.
lopsided, ~ly, de guingois.
loquacious, loquace; **~ness,** *loquacity*, loquacité, *f.*
lord, (*master*) maître, *m.*; (*manor, &c.*) seigneur, *m.*; (*theol.*) Seigneur, *m.*; (*Engl. title*) lord, *m.* (*no article*); *an English ~*, un milord anglais; *O Lord!* Mon Dieu!; *my* ~, monseigneur; *Lord's Prayer*, oraison dominicale, *f.*; *Lord's Supper*, (*Prot.*) Sainte-Cène, *f.*; (*Cath.*) Communion, *f.*
lord it over, *v.a.* dominer.
lordl|y, (*proud*) †hautain; **~iness,** †hauteur, *f.*

lordship, (*authority*) pouvoir (sur) *m.*; *your* ~, votre seigneurie.
lore, doctrine, *f.*
lorgnette, face-à-main, *m.*; ⚠ *Not* lorgnette, *which* = '*opera-glass*', '*field-glass*'.
lorry, camion, *m.*
lose, *v.a.n.* (*lit.*, *fig.*, *breath, head, depth, ground, life, &c.*) perdre; (*cause to lose*) faire* perdre; (*not hear*) ne pas saisir; *my watch, clock* ~ *s 10 minutes a day*, ma montre, ma pendule retarde de 10 minutes par jour; ~ *one's balance*, perdre l'équilibre; ~ *sight of*, perdre de vue; ~ *one's bearings, oneself, one's way*, se perdre; ~ *consciousness*, perdre connaissance; ~ *one's temper*, s'emporter; ~ *by it*, y perdre.
los|er, perdant, *m.*; ~**ing,** *adj.* perdant.
loss, perte, *f.*; ~ *of voice*, extinction de voix, *f.*; *sell at a* ~, vendre à perte; *be at a* ~ *to*, être embarrassé pour.
lot, sort, *m.*; (*destiny*) sort, *m.*; (*portion*) partage, *m.*; (*people*) tas, *m.*; (*quantity*) quantité, *f.*; (*sale, &c.*) lot, *m.*; *cast* ~*s*, tirer au sort.
lotion, lotion, *f.*
lottery, loterie, *f.*
lotto, (*game*) loto, *m.*
lotus, lotus, *m.*
loud, (*voice, noise*) fort; (*noisy*) bruyant; (*colour*) voyant; ~**ness,** *see below*; *adv. loud, loudly*, à haute voix; (*noisily*) avec grand bruit; ~**-speaker,** (*wireless*) †haut-parleur, *m.*
loudness, (*sound*) force, *f.*; (*colour*) caractère voyant, *m.*
lounge, *s.* (*at entrance*) grand vestibule, *m.*
lounge, *v.n.* flâner; *v.a.* ~ *away*, perdre en flânerie; ~ *suit*, complet veston, *m.*
lounger, flâneu|r, ~se, *m.f.*
lous|e, pou, *m.* (*pl.* x); ~**y,** pouilleu|x, ~se.
lout, lourdaud, *m.*; ~**ish,** rustaud.
lovable, aimable.
lovage, (*bot.*) livêche, *f.*
love, *s.* (*gen. and lovers*) amour, *m.*; ~**-bird,** inséparable, *m.f.*; ~**knot,** lacs d'amour, *m.pl.*; ~**-letter,** billet-doux, *m.*; ~**-lorn,** *-sick*, éperdu d'amour; ~*-lies-bleeding*, (*bot.*) amarante queue de renard, *f.*; ~*-making*, cour, *f.*; ~*-in-the-mist*, (*bot.*) cheveux de Vénus, *m.pl.*; *fall in* ~ *with*, devenir (être) amoureux de; *make* ~ *to*, faire* la cour à; *my* ~, chéri, -e, *m.f.*
love, *v.a.* aimer; (*lovers, &c.*) aimer d'amour.
lovel|y, beau, (bel + *vowel or silent* h) *f.* belle; ~**iness,** beauté, *f.*
lovelock, accroche-cœur, *m.*
lover, amoureu|x, ~se, *m.f.*; (*votary*) amant, -e, *m.f.*; (*fancier*) amateur, *m.*
loving, tendre; ~**ly,** tendrement.
low, *adj.* (*not high, depressed, price, sum, sea, tide, temperature, voice, mean, style, thoughts, light, fire, Church, mass*) bas, -se; (*deep*) profond; (*lowly*) humble; (*inferior*) inférieur; ~ *down*, (*slang*) vil; ~ *gear, see* GEAR; ~ *Sunday*, Quasimodo, *f.*
low, *adv. with verbs of uttering, and such verbs as* saluer, viser, tomber, etc., bas, *invar. is used*; (*selling, buying*) bon marché; ~*-born*, de basse naissance; ~*-lying*, bas, -se; ~*-spirited*, abattu.
low, *v.n.* (*cow*) beugler; ~**ing,** *s.* beuglement, *m.*
lower, *adj.* inférieur; (*deck*) premier.
lower, *v.a.* (*prices, voice*) baisser; (*boats*) mettre* à la mer; (*flags, sails*) amener; (*pride, &c.*) rabattre; *v.n.* baisser.
lower, lour, (*sky*) s'obscurcir; (*storm, clouds*) menacer; ~**ing,** *adj.* (*sky*) menaçant.
lowland, plaine, *f.*; *Lowlands*, (*Scotch*) Basses Terres, *f.pl.*
lowl|y, humble; ~**iness,** humilité, *f.*
lowness, (*lack of height*) faible altitude, *f.*; (*dejection*) abattement, *m.*; (*vulgarity*) vulgarité, *f.*
loyal, (*sincere, honest*) loyal; (*to crown, government, &c.*) fidèle; ~**ty,** (*honesty, fair dealing*) loyauté, *f.*; ⚠ loyauté *does not mean* '*loyalty*' *to* '*crown*' *or* '*government*' *which* = loyalisme, *m.*
lozenge, (*sugar*) pastille, *f.*; (*med.*) tablette, *f.*; (*her.*) losange, *f.*
lubber, lourdaud, *m.*
lubric|ant, huile de graissage, *f.*; ~**ate,** lubrifier.
lubricity, (*lewdness*) lubricité, *f.*; ⚠ lubricité *does not* = '*lubricity*' *in the sense of* '*slipperiness*', '*oiliness*', *which* = état glissant, état de lubrification, *m.*
lucen|ce, transparence, *f.*; ~**t,** transparent.
lucid, (*fig. and mental*) lucide; ⚠ lucide *does not* = '*pellucid*' *which* = limpide, transparent; ~**ity,** (*fig.*) lucidité, *f.*; ~**ly,** lucidement.
luck, chance, *f.*; *bad* ~, malchance, *f.*; *no* ~*!* pas de chance!
luck|y, (*fortunate*) heureu|x, ~se; (*bringing luck*) qui porte bonheur; (*slang*) veinard; ~**ily,** par bonheur; ~**less,** malchanceu|x, ~se.
lucr|ative, lucrati|f, ~ve; ~**e,** *s.* lucre, *m.*
lucubration, élucubration, *f.*
ludicrous, *adj. and s.m.* grotesque; ~**ly,** grotesquement.
luff, (*naut.*) lof, *m.*; *v.n.* lofer.
lug, *v.a.* traîner.
luge, (*toboggan*) *s.* luge, *f.*; *v.n.* luger.
luggage, bagages, *m.pl.*; ~**-van,** fourgon aux bagages, *m.*; ~ *compartment*, (*aeron.*) soute à bagages, *f.*
lugger, (*naut.*) lougre, *m.*
lugubrious, lugubre; ~**ly,** lugubrement.
lukewarm, (*lit. and fig.*) tiède; ~**ness,** tiédeur, *f.*
lull, *s.* calme, *m.*
lull, *v.a.* (*lit. and fig.*) endormir*; ~ *to sleep*, bercer; *v.n.* (*sea, wind*) se calmer.
lullaby, berceuse, *f.*
lumbago, lumbago, *m.*

lumber, vieilleries, *f.pl.*; (*timber*) bois de charpente, *m.*; **~-room,** grenier, *m.*
lumbering, *adj.* lourd.
lumberman, bûcheron, *m.*
luminary, corps lumineux, *m.*; (*pers.*) lumière, *f.*
luminous, (*lit. and fig.*) lumineu|x, ~se.
lump, *s.* morceau, *m.*; (*earth*) motte, *f.*; (*sugar*) morceau, *m.*; (*marble, iron, &c.*) bloc, *m.*; (*swelling*) bosse, *f.*; (*heap, lot*) tas, *m.*; ~ *sugar,* sucre en pain, *m.*; ~ *sum,* somme grosse, *f.*; *in the* ~, en bloc.
lump, *v.a.* mettre* en masse; (*comm.*) bloquer; ~ *together,* englober.
lumping, *adj.* (*fam.*) gros, -se.
lumpy, plein de bosses.
lunacy, (*lit. and fig.*) folie, *f.*
lunar, lunaire.
lunatic, *s.* aliéné, -e, *m.f.*; ♤ lunatique, *m.f.*, *in French* = '*a capricious, eccentric person*'.
lunatic, *adj.* aliéné, -e.
lunch, déjeuner à la fourchette, *m.* ♤ *not* lunch, *m. which* = '*wedding breakfast*' *or* '*high tea*'; *v.n.* déjeuner.
lung, poumon, *m.*; **~wort,** (*bot.*) pulmonaire, *f.*
lunge, *s.* (*fenc.*) botte, *f.*; *v.n.* se fendre.
lupin, (*bot.*) lupin, *m.*
lurch, *s.* (*ship, motor*) embardée, *f.*; *leave in the* ~, planter là; *v.n.* tituber.
lure, *s.* (*falc. and fig.*) leurre, *m.*; *v.a.* (*lit. and fig.*) leurrer.
lurid, sombre; (*frightful*) effrayant.
lurk, *v.n.* se cacher; (*troops, &c.*) être aux aguets.
lurking, *adj.* secr|et, ~ète; **~-place,** cachette, *f.*
luscious, succulent; (*sickly*) trop dou|x, ~ce.
lush, plein de sève.
lust, *s.* (*desire, fig.*) convoitise, *f.*; (*lewdness*) luxure, *f.*; *v.n.* ~ *after, for,* convoiter.
lustful, luxurieu|x, ~se.
lust|y, vigoureu|x, ~se; **~iness,** vigueur, *f.*; **~ily,** vigoureusement.
lustr|e, (*splendour, 5 years, gloss*) lustre, *m.*; (*of chandelier*) pendeloque, *f.*; **~ous,** éclatant.
lut|e, (*mus.*) luth, *m.*; **~anist,** joueur de luth, *m.*
Lutheran, *adj. and s.m.f.* luthérien, -ne.
luxurian|ce, luxuriance, *f.*; **~t,** luxuriant; **~tly,** avec exubérance.
luxuriate in, se vautrer dans.
luxurious, (*pers.*) qui aime le luxe; (*things*) luxueu|x, ~se. ♤ *Not* luxurieux *which* = '*lustful*'.
luxur|y, luxe, *m.*; (*enjoyment*) jouissance, *f.*; **~ies,** objets de luxe, *m.pl.*
lychnis, (*bot.*) lychnide, *f.*
lye, lessive, *f.*
lying, *s.* mensonge, *m.*; *adj.* (*pers. and appearance*) menteu|r, ~se; (*things*) mensong|er, ~ère; **~ -in,** couches, *f.pl.*
lymph, lymphe, *f.*; (*water*) eau pure, *f.*
lynch, *v.a.* lyncher; **~ing,** lynchage, *m.*
lynx, lynx, *m.*; **~-eyed, aux yeux de** lynx.
lyr|e, lyre, *f.*; **~-bird,** ménure, *f.*; **~ic,** *adj.* lyrique; *s.* poème lyrique, *m.*; **~icism,** lyrisme, *m.*

M

ma'am, madame, *f.*; *school~,* (*U.S.A.*) maîtresse d'école, *f.*
macabre, *adj.* macabre.
macaco, (*zool.*) macaque, *m.*
macadam, *s.* macadam, *m.*
macaroni, macaroni, *m.*
macaroon, macaron, *m.*
macaw, (*ornith.*) ara, *m.*
mace, masse, *f.*; (*bagatelle*) queue, *f.*; **~-bearer,** massier, *m.*
macera|te, macérer; **~tion,** macération, *f.*
machicolation, (*fort.*) mâchicoulis, *m.*
machina|te, *v.a.* machiner; **~tion,** machination, *f.*
machine, machine, *f.*; **~-made, fait à la** machine; **~-gun,** mitrailleuse, *f.*; **~-gunner,** mitrailleur, *m.*; **~-gun emplacement,** emplacement de mitrailleuse; *sewing-, mowing-, penny-in-the-slot, and weighing-~, see these words.*
machinery, machines, *f.pl.*; (*fig.*) mécanisme, *m.*; (*Lit.*) merveilleux, *m.*; (*theatr.*) machine, *f.*
machinist, machiniste, *m.*
mackerel, maquereau, *m.*; **~ sky,** ciel pommelé, *m.*
mackintosh, caoutchouc, *m.*
mad, fou (fol + *vowel or silent* H) folle; (*animals*) enragé; ~ *after, for, on,* fou de; ~ *with,* (*pers.*) furieu|x, ~se contre; (*thing*) fou de; **~ness,** folie, *f.*; (*rage*) fureur; **~ly,** follement; *raving* ~, fou, folle, furieu|x, ~se; *~-apple,* aubergine, *f.*; **~house,** hospice d'aliénés, *m.*; *go* ~, devenir* (être) fou.
madam, madame, *f.*
madcap, écervelé, -e, *m.f.*
madden, *v.a.* rendre fou; **~ing,** *adj.* à rendre fou.
madder, (*bot.*) garance, *f.*
made, *p.p. ready* ~, (*clothes*) confectionné; ~ *up,* (*story*) inventé; ~ *out of,* fait de, avec; ~ *to order,* fait sur commande.
Madeira, (*wine*) madère, *m.*
madonna, madone, *f.*
madrepore, madrépore, *m.*
madrigal, madrigal, *m.*
maenad, ménade, *f.*
magazine, (*periodical*) revue, *f.*; (*rifle*) magasin, *m.*
maggot, asticot, *m.*; (*fig.*) lubie, *f.*; ♤ magot = '*ape*', '*ugly person*', '*hoard*'; **~y,** véreu|x, ~se.
Magi, (*the*), les rois mages.

magic, *s.* magie, *f.*; *adj.* magique; ~ *lantern, see* LANTERN; **~ian,** magicien, -ne, *m.f.*
magisterial, de magistrat; (*authoritative*) de maître.
magistracy, magistrature, *f.*
magistrate, magistrat, *m.*
magnanim|ous, magnanime; **~ity,** magnanimité, *f.*; **~ously,** magnanimement.
magnate, magnat, *m.*
magnesia, magnésie, *f.*
magnet, (*lit. and fig.*) aimant, *m.*; **~ic,** (*lit. and fig.*) magnétique; *~ic needle,* aiguille aimantée, *f.*; *see also* MINE; **~ically,** magnétiquement.
magnetism, (*lit. and fig.*) magnétisme, *m.*
magnetize, (*mesmerize*) magnétiser; (*phys.*) aimanter; (*attract*) attirer.
magnificen|ce, magnificence, *f.*; **~t,** magnifique; **~tly,** magnifiquement.
magnify, grossir; (*extol*) exalter.
magnifying, ~-glass, loupe, *f.*
magniloquen|t, grandiloquent; **~ce,** emphase, *f.*
magnitude, (*lit. and fig.*) grandeur, *f.*; (*importance*) importance, *f.*
magpie, (*ornith. and fig.*) pie, *f.*
mahogany, acajou, *m.*
mahometan, *see* MOHAMMEDAN.
maid, maiden, jeune fille, *f.*; (*virgin*) vierge, *f.*; (*servant*) bonne, *f.*; ~ *of honour,* fille d'honneur, *f.*; *old* ~, vieille fille, *f.*; *old-~ish,* de vieille fille.
maiden, *adj.* de jeune fille; (*name*) de demoiselle; (*speech*) de début.
maidenhair, (*fern*) adiante, *m.*
maidenhood, virginité, *f.*
maidenly, virginal.
maidservant, bonne, *f.*
mail, *s.* (*armour*) cotte de maille, *f.*; (*post*) courrier, *m.*; **~-bag,** sac à dépêches, *m.*; **~-coach,** malle-poste, *f.*; **~-boat, -steamer,** paquebot poste, *m.*; **~-train,** train-poste, *m.*; *v.a.* envoyer par la poste.
main, *s.* (*gas, water, &c.*) conduite principale, *f.*; (*sea*) †haute mer, *f.*; *in the* ~, pour la plupart.
main, *adj.* principal; *often also* grand; ~ *body, see* BODY; **~-deck,** franc tillac, *m.*; ~ *point,* point capital, *m.*; **~spring,** grand ressort, *m.*; **~-top,** (*naut.*) grand'hune, *f.*; *~-top gallant sail,* grand perroquet, *m.*; ~ **yard,** (*naut.*) grande vergue, *f.*; **~ly,** principalement.
mainland, terre ferme, *f.*
mainmast, (*naut.*) grand mât, *m.*
mainsail, (*naut.*) grande voile, *f.*
mainstay, appui principal, *m.*; (*naut.*) étai du grand mât, *m.*
maintain, (*order, keep up, keep pers. in position, in office*) maintenir*; (*war, conversation, family, rank, reputation, affirm*) soutenir*; ⚠ maintenir *not used in these senses*; (*in a good state*) conserver.
maintainable, soutenable; (*position*) tenable.
maintenance, (*upkeep, subsistence*) entretien, *m.*; ⚠ maintenance = '*action of maintaining in a position*'.
maize, maïs, *m.*
majestic, majestueu|x, **~se;** **~ally,** majestueusement.
majesty, majesté, *f.*; *Your, His Majesty,* Votre, Sa Majesté.
majolica, majolique, *f.*
major, *s.* (*mil.*) commandant, *m.*; **~-general,** général de division, *m.*
major, *adj.* (*greater, of age, mus.*) majeur.
major-domo, majordome, *m.*
majority, (*greater part, votes, full age*) majorité, *f.*
make, *s.* (*shape*) forme, *f.*; (*of goods*) fabrication, *f.*; *be on the* ~, (*pop.*) être arriviste.
make, *v.a.* faire*; (*render + adj.*) rendre; (*force*) forcer + *acc.* + à + *inf.*; (*bow in salutation*) tirer; (*consider to be*) estimer; (*manufacture*) fabriquer; (*pers. to do*) faire* + *acc. of pers. and intrans. inf. or dat. of pers. and trans. inf.*: *cf.* Je l'ai fait courir; Je lui ai fait trouver le livre; *What do you* ~ *the time?* Quelle heure est-il selon vous?; *I don't know what to* ~ *of it,* je ne sais qu'en penser; *he can* ~ *nothing of it,* il n'y comprend rien; ~ **away with,** (*destroy*) détruire*; ~ **off,** s'en aller* (être); ~ **out,** (*draw up*) rédiger; (*understand*) comprendre*; (*prove*) prouver; ~ **over,** céder; ~ **up,** (*lists, &c.*) dresser; (*sum of money*) parfaire*; (*invent*) inventer; (*medicine*) composer; ~ **up for,** compenser; (*lost time*) rattraper; (*supplement*) suppléer à; ~ **it up,** se réconcilier; ~ *up one's mind,* prendre son parti; ~ *up one's mind to,* se décider à; (*resign oneself to*) se résigner à.
make, *v.n.* ~ *away with,* se défaire* de; (*fortune, &c.*) dissiper; (*oneself*) se suicider; ~ *as if to,* faire* comme si + *indic.*; ~ *for, towards,* se diriger vers; (*be favourable to*) être favorable à; ~ *off,* (*pop.*) filer; ~ *up,* (*face*) se maquiller.
make-believe, *s.* feinte, *f.*
maker, (*manufacturer*) fabricant, *m.*; (*creator*) créateur, *m.*
makeshift, expédient.
make-up, (*face*) maquillage, *m.*
makeweight, supplément, *m.*
making, fabrication, *f.*; (*creation*) création, *f.*; *have the* ~(*s*) *of a man,* avoir l'étoffe d'un homme.
Malacca cane, *see* CANE.
malachite, malachite, *f.*
maladministration, mauvaise administration, *f.*
maladroit, maladroit.
malady, maladie, *f.*
malapert, impertinent.
malapropos, *adj.* inopportun; *adv.* mal à propos.
malaria, malaria, *f.*
Malay, *adj.* (*when an adj. use small letter*) *and s.m.f.* Malais, -e.

malcontent, *adj. and s.m.* mécontent.
male, *adj.* (*animals, &c.*) mâle; (*things*) masculin; *s.* mâle, *m.*; ~ *bird,* oiseau mâle, *m.*
malediction, malédiction, *f.*
malefactor, malfait|eur, ~rice, *m.f.*
malevolen|ce, malveillance, *f.*; **~t,** malveillant; **~tly,** avec malveillance.
malformation, malformation, *f.*
malice, méchanceté, *f.*; ⚠ *the French* malice *is more 'mischievousness'.*
malicious, méchant; **~ly,** méchamment.
malign, *adj.* pernicieu|x, ~se.
malign, *v.a.* calomnier.
malign|ant, (*lit. and med.*) malin, maligne; **~ancy, -ity,** malignité, *f.*; **~ly,** malignement.
malinger, (*fam.*) carotter; **~er,** carottier, *m.*
mall, (*sheltered walk*) mail, *m.*
mallard, (*ornith.*) canard sauvage, *m.*
malleab|le, malléable; **~ility,** malléabilité, *f.*
mallet, maillet, *m.*
mallow, (*bot.*) mauve, *f.*
malmsey, (*wine*) malvoisie, *f.*
malpractice, malversation, *f.*
malt, drêche, *f.*; **~-house,** germoir, *m.*; **~ster,** malteur, *m.*
Maltese, *adj.* (*when an adj. use small letter*) *and s.m.f.* Maltais, -e.
maltreat, *v.a.* maltraiter; **~ment,** mauvais traitements, *m.pl.*
malversation, malversation, *f.*
Mameluke, Mameluk, *m.*
mam(m)a, maman, *f.*
mammal, *s.* mammifère, *m.*
mammoth, mammouth, *m.*
man, *s.* (*particular and gen.*) homme, *m.*; (*servant*) domestique, *m.*; *medical ~, see* MEDICAL; ~ *of letters,* homme de lettres, *m.*; **~-hole,** regard, *m.*; ~ *in the street,* homme moyen, *m.*; ~ *of war,* cuirassé, *m.*; *working ~,* ouvrier, *m.*; ~ *of the world,* homme du monde, *m.*; *young men,* jeunes gens, *m.pl.*; *to a ~,* jusqu'au dernier; *interj. old man!* mon vieux! ~ *alive!* mon pauvre ami!; *~'s estate,* âge viril, *m.*; *many men many minds,* autant de têtes autant d'avis.
man, *v.a.* (*fort.*) garnir de troupes; (*ship*) équiper.
manacle, *v.a.* mettre* les menottes à; **~s,** *s.* menottes, *f.pl.*
manage, *v.a.* (*administer, comm., household, farm, &c.*) gérer; (*particular matter*) mener; (*by cajoling*) ménager; (*horse*) maîtriser; (*pers., an.*) dompter; (*get through, succeed with*) venir* (être) à bout de; (*tools, &c.*) manier; *How did you ~ it?* Comment vous en êtes-vous tiré?
manage, *v.n.* se tirer d'affaire *or* s'en tirer; ~ *to,* réussir à.
manageable, (*pers.*) docile; (*easy to handle*) maniable.
management, direction, *f.*; (*of undertaking, newspaper, &c.*) gérance, *f.*
manager, directeur, *m.*; (*of an enterprise*) gérant, *m.*; *stage-~,* (*theatr.*) régisseur, *m.*; **~ess,** directrice, *f.*
managing, ~ *clerk, see* CLERK; ~ *director, see* DIRECTOR.
Manchu, *adj.* (*when an adj. use small letter*) *and s.m.f.* Mandchou, -e, *m.f.*
mandarin, mandarin, *m.*
mandarin(e), (*orange*) mandarine, *f.*
mandat|e, *s.* (*polit.*) mandat, *m.*; (*order*) ordre, *m.*; **~ary,** mandataire, *m.*
mandible, mandibule, *f.*
mandolin(e), mandoline, *f.*
mandrake, (*bot.*) mandragore, *f.*
mane, crinière, *f.*
manful, courageu|x, ~se; **~ly,** courageusement.
manganese, manganèse, *m.*
mang|e, (*dog, &c.*) gale, *f.*; **~y,** galeu|x, ~se.
mangel-wurzel, (*bot.*) betterave fourragère, *f.*
manger, mangeoire, *f.*
mangle, *s.* calandre, *f.*; *v.a.* (*lacerate*) déchirer; (*spoil text, &c.*) mutiler; (*linen*) calandrer.
mango, mangue, *f.*; **~-tree,** manguier, *m.*
mangrove, (*bot.*) mangle, *f.*; **~-tree,** manglier, *m.*
manhood, virilité, *f.*; (*men*) hommes, *m.pl.*
mania, (*mental alienation*) folie, *f.*; ⚠ manie, *f.* (de) *in French simply* = *'fad', 'whim', 'passion for'.*
maniac, *adj. and s.m.f.* fou, folle, *m.f.*; **~al,** fou, folle.
manicure, mani(u)cure, *m.f.*; *v.a.* soigner les mains.
manifest, *adj.* manifeste; *v.a.* manifester; **~ation,** manifestation, *f.*; **~ly,** manifestement.
manifesto, manifeste, *m.*
manifold, *adj.* (*numerous*) nombreu|x, ~se; (*various*) divers.
manifold, *v.a.* (*letters, &c.*) polycopier.
manikin, (*dwarf*) nabot, *m.*; (*model*) mannequin, *m.*
manipula|te, manipuler; **~tion,** manipulation, *f.*
mankind, genre humain, *m.*
manlike, d'homme.
manl|y, viril; **~iness,** virilité, *f.*
manna, manne, *f.*
manner, (*way, style*) manière, *f.*; (*sort*) sorte, *f.*; (*bearing*) air, *m.*; **~s,** (*in society*) manières, *f.pl.*; (*morals, customs*) mœurs, *f.pl.*; *after the ~ of,* à la manière de *in a ~,* en quelque sorte; *no ~ of,* aucune espèce de (ne *with verb*).
mannered, (*style*) maniéré.
mannerism, maniérisme, *m.*
mannerly, *adj.* poli.
mannish, *adj.* hommasse.
manœuvre, *s.* (*mil., ship., pej.*) manœuvre, *f.*; *v.a.* (*mil.*) faire* manœuvrer; (*ships*) manœuvrer; *v.n.* (*contrive, mil., manage*) manœuvrer.

manor, (*house*) manoir, *m.*; (*domain*) seigneurie, *f.*; **~ial,** seigneurial.
manservant, domestique, *m.*
manse, presbytère, *m.*
mansion, (*country*) château, *m.*; (*town*) hôtel, *m.*; ⚠ mansion = '*halting-place*'.
manslaughter, homicide, *m.*
mantel|piece, cheminée, *f.*; **~shelf,** tablette, *f.*
mantilla, mantille, *f.*
mantle, (*cloak, &c., arch.*) manteau, *m.*; (*gas*) manchon, *m.*
mantle, *v.a.* couvrir* (de); *~ the cheeks*, monter (être) au visage.
manual, *adj. and s.m.* manuel; *sign ~*, seing, *m.*
manufactory, fabrique, *f.*
manufactur|e, *s.* manufacture, *f.*; (*article made*) produit manufacturé, *m.*; *v.a.* (*lit. and fig.*) fabriquer; **~er,** manufacturier, *m.*; (*maker*) fabricant, *m.*; **~ing,** *adj.* manufacturi|er, ~ère.
manure, *s.* fumier, *m.*; *v.a.* fumer.
manuscript, *adj. and s.m.* manuscrit.
many, *s. and pron.* beaucoup (de, d'entre); *the ~*, la foule.
many, *adj.* beaucoup de; (*numerous*) nombreu|x, ~se; *so ~*, tant de; *too ~*, trop de; *~ a time*, maintes fois; *~-coloured*, multicolore; *~-sided*, complexe; *~ thanks*, mille mercis, *m.pl.*
map, *s.* carte géographique, *f.*; *~ of the world*, mappemoude, *f.*; *v.a. ~ out*, faire* un plan de.
maple-tree, érable, *m.*
mar, *v.a.* (*lit., pleasure, &c.*) gâter.
marabou, (*ornith. and feathers*) marabout, *m.*
maraud, *v.a.* marauder; **~er,** maraudeur, *m.*; **~ing,** *s.* maraude, *f.*
marbl|e, *s.* (*stone and statue*) marbre, *m.*; (*toy*) bille, *f.*; *adj.* de marbre; *v.a.* marbrer; **~ing,** *s.* marbrure, *f.*
march, marching, (*mil.*) marche, *f.*; (*month*) mars, *m.*; *~ past*, défilé, *m.*; *quick ~*, pas accéléré, *m.*; *v.a.* faire* marcher; *~ in, out*, faire* entrer, sortir; *v.n.* marcher; *~ on*, (*fortress*) marcher sur; (*continue to march*), marcher toujours; *~ past*, défiler.
marchioness, marquise, *f.*
mare, jument, *f.*; *~'s nest*, merle blanc, *m.*
margarine, margarine, *f.*
margin, *s.* (*books, paper, money, time*) marge, *f.*; (*edge*) bord, *m.*; **~al,** marginal.
margrav|e, ~ine, margrave, *m.f.*
marguerite, (*bot.*) marguerite, *f.*
marigold, (*bot.*) souci, *m.*
marine, *s.* marine, *f.*; *mercantile ~*, marine marchande, *f.*
marine, *adj.* marin; (*insurance, risk, loss*) maritime; *~ store dealer*, *see* DEALER.
mariner, marin, *m.*; *~'s compass*, boussole, *f.*
marital, marital.
maritime, *adj.* (*city, expedition, powers, &c.*) maritime.
marjoram, (*bot.*) marjolaine, *f.*
mark, *s.* (*print, brand, token, trace, sign, distinction, &c.*) marque, *f.*; (*aim, target*) but, *m.*; (*school*) point, *m.*; (*coin*) marc, *m.*; *not feel up to the ~*, ne pas être dans son assiette; *make one's ~*, se distinguer; *overshoot the ~*, (*fig.*) dépasser le but.
mark, *v.a.* (*denote, notice, be a feature of, linen, goods, &c.*) marquer; (*underline*) souligner.
marked, *adj.* (*evident, decided*) marqué.
marker, (*book*) signet, *m.*; (*pers.*) marqueu|r, ~se, *m.f.*
market, *s.* marché, *m.*; (*outlet for sale*) débouché, *m.*; **~-garden,** jardin maraîcher, *m.*; **~-gardener,** jardinier maraîcher, *m.*; **~ hall,** †halle, *f.*; **~ place,** place du marché, *f.*; **~-price,** prix courant, *m.*; *on the ~*, sur le marché.
market, *v.a.* vendre au marché; **~able,** marchand.
marksman, bon tireur, *m.*
marl, (*soil*) marne, *f.*
marmalade, marmelade d'oranges, *f.*; ⚠ marmelade *alone is used of any fruit.*
marmoset, (*zool.*) ouistiti, *m.*; ⚠ *not* marmouset, *which* = '*urchin*', '*grotesque figure*'.
marmot, (*zool.*) marmotte, *f.*
maroon, *adj. and s.m.* (*colour*) marron, *invar.*; (*loud report*) marron, *m.*
maroon, *v.a.* abandonner dans une terre déserte; *v.n.* (*U.S.A.*) camper pendant plusieurs jours.
marquee, marquise, *f.*
marquetry, marqueterie, *f.*
marquis, marquis, *m.*
marriage, (*lit. and fig.*) mariage, *m.*; *~ bonds*, liens conjugaux, *m.pl.*; *~ portion*, dot, *f.*
marriageable, mariable.
marrow, moelle, *f.*; *spinal ~*, moelle épinière, *f.*; *vegetable ~*, courge à la moelle, *f.*
marrowbone, os à moelle, *m.*
marry, *v.a.* épouser; ⚠ marier, *v.a. only* = '*give or join in marriage*'; *v.n.* (*get, be married*) se marier.
marsh, marais, *m.*; **salt-~,** marais salant, *m.*; *~ fever*, fièvre paludéenne, *f.*; **~-mallow,** (*bot*) guimauve, *f.*; **~ marigold,** souci d'eau, *m.*
marshal, (*field*) maréchal, *m.*; *v.a.* ranger; (*facts*) mettre* en ordre; (*conduct*) conduire*.
marshy, marécageu|x, ~se.
mart, marché, *m.*; (*auction*) salle des ventes, *f.*
marten, (*zool.*) martre, *f.*
martial, martial; *~* **law,** loi martiale, *f.*
martin, (*ornith.*) martinet, *m.*; ⚠ *not English 'martinet' which* = autoritaire, *m.*
martlet, (*ornith.*) martinet, *m.*; (*herald.*) merlette, *f.*
martyr, *s.* (*lit. and fig.*) martyr, -e, *m.f.*; **~dom,** (*lit. and fig.*) martyre, *m.*; **~ize,** *v.a.* (*lit. and fig.*) martyriser.

martyrology, martyrologe, *m.*
marvel, *s.* merveille, *f.*; ~ **of Peru,** (*bot.*) belle de nuit, *f.*; *v.n.* s'étonner (de).
marvellous, merveilleu|x, ~se; **~ly,** merveilleusement.
mascot, mascotte, *f.*
masculin|e, mâle; (*of women*) hommasse; (*gram., pros.*) masculin; **~ity,** masculinité, *f.*
mash, *s.* (*cook.*) purée, *f.*; *v.a.* réduire* en purée.
mask, *s.* (*lit. and fig., death, pers.*) masque, *m.*; (*arch.*) mascaron, *m.*; *velvet ~,* loup, *m.*
mask, *v.a.* (*lit., fig., mil.*) masquer; **~er,** *s.* masque, *m.*
mason, (*lit. and freemason*) maçon, *m.*; **free~,** franc-maçon, *m.*; *~ic lodge,* loge maçonnique, *f.*
masonry, maçonnerie, *f.*; **free~,** franc-maçonnerie, *f.*
masquerade, *s.* mascarade, *f.*; *v.n.* ~ *as,* se déguiser en.
masquerader, masque, *m.*
mass, *s.* (*heap, pile, large number, aggregate, phys.*) masse, *f.*; (*majority*) majorité, *f.*; (*Cath. relig.*) messe, *f.*; *the ~es,* les masses; *in the ~,* en bloc; *~ production,* production en masse, *f.*; *v.a.* réunir en masse; (*troops*) masser.
massacre, *s.* massacre, *m.*; *v.a.* massacrer.
massage, massage, *m.*; *v.a.* masser.
massive, massy, massi|f, ~ve; **~ly,** massivement.
mast, *s.* (*naut.*) mât, *m.*; **miz(z)en-~,** mât d'artimon, *m.*, ⚠ *not* misaine *which* = *'foremast'.*
mast, *s.* (*oak*) gland, *m.*; (*beech*) faîne, *f.*
master, (*of servants, animals, controller, in arts and crafts, &c.*) maître, *m.*; (*of workmen*) patron, *m.*; (*merchant vessel*) capitaine, *m.*; *assistant ~,* professeur, *m.*; *old ~s,* vieux maîtres, *m.pl.*; *past-~,* passé maître (en); *~ of Arts,* (*approx.*) licencié -e ès lettres, *m.f.*; *~-key,* passe-partout, *m. invar.*; *~-mind,* esprit supérieur, *m.*; *~-stroke,* coup de maître, *m.*
master, *v.a.* (*difficulty*) venir* à bout de; (*subject*) posséder; (*subdue*) maîtriser; (*rule*) régir.
masterful, autoritaire.
masterly, de maître.
masterpiece, chef-d'œuvre, *m.*
mastership, maîtrise, *f.*; (*in schools*) fonction de professeur, *f.*
mastery, (*authority*) maîtrise, *f.*; (*of subject, &c.*) connaissance approfondie, *f.*; (*skill*) grande habileté, *f.*
mastic, (*gum*) mastic, *m.*; **~-tree,** lentisque, *m.*
mastica|te, mâcher; **~tion,** mastication, *f.*
mastiff, dogue, *m.*
mat, (*door*) paillasson, *m.*; (*table*) dessous de plat, *m.*; (*naut.*) paillet, *m.*
matador, matador, *m.*
match, *s.* (*equal, like*) égal, -e, pareil, -le, *m.f.*; (*lucifer, &c.*) allumette, *f.*; (*marriage*) mariage, *m.*; (*pers. to marry*) parti, *m.*; (*sport*) match, *m.*; **~-maker,** marieu|r, ~se, *m.f.*; *be a ~ for,* être de taille à lutter contre.
match, *v.a.* (*stuffs, colours*) assortir; (*pairs*) apparier; (*marry*) marier; *v.n.* s'assortir.
matchless, incomparable; **~ly,** incomparablement.
mate, *s.* (*workman*) camarade, *m.*; (*birds*) mâle, *m.*, femelle, *f.*; (*chess*) mat, *m.*; (*nav., naut.*) aide, *m.*
mate, *v.a.* (*join in marriage*) marier (à); *v.n.* (*birds*) s'accoupler.
material, *s.* matière, *f.*; **~s,** (*lit. and fig.*) matériaux, *m.pl.*; (*writing, &c.*) articles, *m.pl.*; *raw ~,* matière première, *f.*
material, *adj.* matériel, -le; (*bodily*) physique; **~ly,** matériellement.
materialis|m, matérialisme, *m.*; **~t,** matérialiste, *m.*
materialize, *v.a.* (*make, consider material*) matérialiser; *v.n.* se réaliser.
matern|al, maternel, -le; **~ity,** maternité, *f.*; **~ally,** maternellement.
mathematical, mathématique; **~ly,** mathématiquement.
mathematics, mathématiques, *f.pl.*; *mixed, applied ~,* mathématiques mixtes, appliquées, *f.pl.*
matins, (*eccles.*) matines, *f.pl.*
matricide, matricide, *m.*
matricula|te, *v.n.* (*approx.*) prendre* ses inscriptions; ⚠ immatriculer, *v.a.* = *'to register'*; **~tion,** (*exam.*) examen d'entrée, *m.*
matrimon|ial, conjugal; (*law*) matrimonial; **~ially,** conjugalement.
matrimony, mariage, *m.*
matron, mère de famille, *f.*; ⚠ matrone *is often pej. in French, i.e. 'fat old woman'*; (*hospital*) infirmière-en-chef, *f.*; **~ly,** mûr; (*like a matron*) de matrone.
matted, (*hair*) emmêlé.
matter, *s.* (*substance, of book, speech, occasion for, phys., as opp. to spirit*) matière, *f.*; (*business, question of + numbers*) affaire, *f.*; (*subject*) sujet, *m.*; (*thing*) chose, *f.*; (*med.*) pus, *m.*; *printed ~,* imprimé, *m.*; *as a ~ of fact,* en fait; *~ of course,* chose qui va sans dire, *f.*; *it's a ~ of,* il s'agit de; *What's the ~ with you? Nothing.* Qu'avez-vous? — Je n'ai rien; *What's the matter?* Qu'y a-t-il?; *as ~s stand,* au point où en sont les choses; *not to mince ~s,* ne pas mâcher ses mots.
matter, *v. impers.* importer; *What does it ~?* Qu'importe?; *no ~,* n'importe; *it ~s to me,* cela m'importe beaucoup.
matting, *s.* natte, *f.*
mattock, pioche, *f.*
mattress, matelas, *m.*; *spring ~,* sommier, *m.*
matur|e, *adj.* mûr; (*comm.*) échu; **~ity,**

maturité, *f.*; (*bills*) échéance, *f.*; **~ely,** mûrement.
mature, *v.a.n.* mûrir.
maudlin, larmoyant.
maul, *v.a.* malmener.
maunder, (*talk*) divaguer.
mausoleum, mausolée, *m.*
mauve, *adj. and s.m.* mauve.
maw, (*fam.*) estomac, *m.*
mawkish, fade; **~ness,** fadeur, *f.*
maxim, maxime, *f.*
maximum, maximum, *m.*
May, *s.* (*month*) mai, *m.*; (*shrub and blossom*) aubépine, *f.*; **~-bug,** †hanneton, *m.*; **~-fly,** éphémère, *m.*; **may-pole,** mai, *m.*
may, *v. aux.* **1** *may = pres.* pouvoir*; *might = past,* pouvoir; *might have = past cond.* pouvoir; *it, that may be,* cela se peut; *it may be that,* il se peut que + *subj.*; **2** *'may', 'might' are also marks of the subjunctive*: (*a*) *after conjunctions of purpose,* pour que, afin que; (*b*) *after verbs of fearing*; (*c*) *after* quoi que = *'whatever', e.g. whatever you may do,* quoi que vous fassiez; *after* quelque *adj.* + que = *'whatever', e.g. whatever knowledge he may have,* quelques connaissances qu'il ait; *after* qui que, = *'whoever', e.g. whoever you may be,* qui que vous soyez; **3** *'may'* (*exclamatory wish*) = puissé-je, puisses-tu, *&c.*; *may you be happy!* puissiez-vous être heureux!
maybe, peut-être.
mayor, ~ess, maire, -sse, *m.f.*; **~alty,** mairie, *f.*
maze, labyrinthe, *m.*; (*fig.*) embarras, *m.*
me, (*direct obj. of verbs*) me; (*a*) *alone,* (*b*) *after preps.,* (*c*) *when more than one obj.,* (*d*) *after affirm. imperat.* = moi.
mead, (*liquor*) hydromel, *m.*
meadow, mead, prairie, *f.*; (*small*) pré, *m.*
meagre, (*lit. and fig.*) maigre; **~ness,** maigreur, *f.*; **~ly,** maigrement.
meal, (*flour*) farine, *f.*; (*repast*) repas, *m.*; **~ies,** maïs, *m.*
mealy, farineu|x, ~se; **~-mouthed,** doucereu|x, ~se.
mean, *s.* moyen terme, *m.*; (*maths. average*) moyenne, *f.*; **~s,** (*income*) moyens, *m.pl.*; (*cause*) cause, *f.*; (*way to do*) moyen, *m.*; *by ~s of,* au moyen de; *by all ~s,* certainement; *by no ~s,* en aucune façon; *be of independent ~s,* être rentier.
mean, *adj.* (*poor*) pauvre; (*stingy*) ladre; (*humble*) humble; (*contemptible*) méprisable; (*between two*) moyen, -ne; (*base, sordid*) bas, basse; **~ness,** *see below*; **~ly,** bassement; (*poorly*) pauvrement.
mean, *v.a.* (*signify, intend to convey*) vouloir* dire; (*wish*) vouloir* que + *subj.*; (*destine*) destiner (à); (*involve*) entraîner; *what does she ~ by it?* que veut-elle dire par là?; *what does the word ~?* que veut dire le mot?; *you don't ~ it!* vous n'y pensez pas!; *well ~t,* fait à bonne intention.
mean, *v.n.* se proposer (de); *~ well,* avoir de bonnes intentions.
meander, *v.n.* serpenter; **~ing,** *s.* méandres, *m.pl.*
meaning, *s.* (*intention*) intention, *f.*; (*sense*) sens, *m.*
meaning, *adj.* (*significant*) significati|f, ~ve.
meanness, (*base, sordid*) bassesse, *f.*; (*poorness*) pauvreté, *f.*; (*stingy*) avarice, *f.*
mean|time, ~while, *in the,* sur ces entrefaites.
measles, (*med.*) rougeole, *f.*
measurable, mesurable.
measure, *s.* (*lit. and fig., for clothes, standard, limit, liquid, superficial, size, poet., mus.*) mesure, *f.*; (*mind*) portée, *f.*; *in some ~,* en quelque sorte; *beyond ~,* outre mesure.
measur|e, *v.a.* (*lit. and fig.*) mesurer; (*for clothes*) prendre* les mesures de; *~e oneself,* (*strength*) *against,* se mesurer avec; **~ing,** *s.* mesurage, *m.*; **~ed,** (*equal, uniform*) égal.
measureless, infini.
measurement, mesurage, *m.*
meat, viande, *f.*; (*food*) nourriture, *f.*; *~-safe,* garde-manger, *m.*; *~-soup,* soupe grasse, *f.*
mechanic, *s.* (*workman*) artisan, *m.*; (*user of any machinery*) mécanicien, *m.*; **~s,** (*science*) mécanique, *f.*
mechanical, (*done, &c. by machinery*) mécanique; (*pers. actions like machines*) machinal; **~ly,** mécaniquement, machinalement.
mechani|cian, mécanicien, *m.*; **~sm,** (*lit. and fig.*) mécanisme, *m.*; **~ze,** (*army, divisions, &c.*) mécaniser.
medal, médaille, *f.*
medallion, médaillon, *m.*
medallist, (*prizewinner*) médaillé, -e, *m.f.*
meddle, *v.n.* se mêler (de); *~ with,* (*unduly*) s'ingérer dans; (*handle*) toucher à.
meddler, (*fam.*) touche-à-tout, *m. invar.*
meddlesome, qui se mêle de tout.
meddling, *s.* ingérence, *f.*
mediaeval, moyenâgeu|x, ~se; **~ism,** médiévisme, *m.*
medial, médial.
mediate, *adj.* médiat.
media|te, *v.n.* (*in a quarrel, &c.*) intervenir* (être); *~te between,* s'interposer entre; **~tion,** médiation, *f.*; **~tor,** médiat|eur, ~rice, *m.f.*
medical, médical; *~ man,* médecin, *m.*; *~ student,* étudiant en médecine, *m.*; **~ly,** médicalement.
medicament, médicament, *m.*
medicate, médicamenter.
medicinal, médicinal.
medicine, (*science, profession, remedy*) médecine, *f.*; **~-chest,** pharmacie, *f.*
mediocr|e, médiocre; **~ity,** médiocrité, *f.*

medita|te, *v.a.n.* méditer; *~te on,* méditer sur; **~tion,** méditation, *f.*; **~tive,** méditati|f, ~ve; **~ted,** projeté.
Mediterranean, *adj.* méditerrané; *the ~,* (*Sea*) la Méditerranée.
medium, *s.* (*between extremes*) moyen terme, *m.*; (*agency*) intermédiaire, *m.f.*; (*air, water, &c.*) milieu, *m.*; (*claiming spiritual perception*) médium, *m.*; *adj.* moyen, -ne.
medlar, nèfle, *f.*; **~-tree,** néflier, *m.*
medley, (*mixture*) mélange, *m.*; (*confusion of pers. or things*) bigarrure, *f.*
meed, récompense, *f.*
meek, dou|x, ~ce; (*submissive*) soumis; **~ness,** douceur, *f.*; **~ly,** avec douceur.
meerschaum, écume de mer, *f.*
meet, *s.* (*hunt.*) rendez-vous de chasse, *m.*
meet, *adj.* convenable; *it is ~ that,* il convient que + *subj.*; **~ness,** convenance, *f.*; **~ly,** convenablement.
meet, *v.a.* **1** (*pers., things, in duels*) rencontrer; **2** (*in society*) voir*; **3** (*face, danger, &c.*) affronter; **4** (*demands, expenses, difficulties*) faire* face à; **5** (*engagements*) faire* honneur à; **6** (*bills*) faire* bon accueil à; **7** (*the eye*) s'offrir* à; **8** (*wants, &c.*) répondre à; **9** (*death, punishment*) trouver; **10** *go to ~,* aller* (être) au devant de.
meet, with, (*accident*) il arrive (être) (*impers. + dat. of pers., e.g.* il m'est arrivé un accident); (*loss*) éprouver; (*refusal*) essuyer; (*receive*) recevoir.
meet, *v.n.* se rencontrer; (*assemble*) s'assembler; (*be reunited*) se rejoindre*; (*in society*) se voir*; *~ again,* se revoir*; (*encounter*) se rencontrer.
meeting, *s.* (*pers. duel*) rencontre, *f.*; (*assembly, race*) réunion, *f.*; (*polit.*) meeting, *m.*; (*rivers, roads*) jonction, *f.*; *~-house,* temple, *m.*
megaphone, porte-voix, *m. invar.*
megrim, (*headache*) migraine, *f.*
melanchol|y, *s.* mélancolie, *f.*; *adj.* **~y, ~ic,** mélancolique.
mellifiu|ent, ~ous, melliflue.
mellow, *adj.* (*fruit*) mûr; (*wine, sound*) moelleu|x, ~se; (*character*) mûri; (*tipsy*) entre deux vins; **~ness,** (*lit. and fig.*) maturité, *f.*
mellow, *v.a.* mûrir; (*wine*) rendre moelleux; (*character*) adoucir; *v.n.* mûrir; (*fig.*) s'adoucir.
melodious, mélodieu|x, ~se; **~ness,** (*fig.*) mélodie, *f.*; **~ly,** mélodieusement.
melodrama, (*lit. and fig.*) mélodrame, *m.*; **~tic,** mélodramatique.
melody, mélodie, *f.*
melon, melon, *m.*; **water-~,** pastèque, *f.*
melt, *v.a.* fondre; (*fig.*) attendrir; *~ down,* (*gold, &c.*) faire* fondre; *~ed butter,* sauce blanche, *f.*
melt, *v.n.* fondre; (*dissolve*) se résoudre*; *~ away,* (*fig.*) se dissiper; *~ into tears,* fondre en larmes.
melting, *s.* fonte, *f.*; (*fusion*) fusion, *f.*; *~-pot,* (*lit. and fig.*) creuset, *m.*; *adj.* (*sun*) étouffant; (*fig.*) attendrissant.
member, (*Parl., &c., body, sentence, family*) membre, *m.*; (*French Parl.*) député, *m.*
membership, qualité de membre, *f.*
membrane, membrane, *f.*
memento, souvenir, *m.*
memoir, (*record, biography*) mémoire, *m.*
memorab|le, mémorable; **~ly,** mémorablement.
memorandum, mémorandum, *m.*
memorial, *s.* (*monument*) monument à commémorer, *m.*; (*state paper*) mémorial, *m.*; (*facts in a petition*) exposé, *m.*
memorialize, *v.a.* (*commemorate*) commémorer; (*address, petition*) adresser un mémoire à.
memorize, (*learn by heart*) apprendre* par cœur.
memory, (*faculty*) mémoire, *f.*; (*recollection*) souvenir, *m.*; *in ~ of,* en mémoire de; *within the ~ of man,* de mémoire d'homme.
menac|e, *s.* menace, *f.*; *v.a.* menacer; **~ing,** menaçant.
mend, *s.* (*clothes*) reprise, *f.*; **~ing,** *s.* raccommodage, *m.*
mend, *v.a.* (*clothes*) raccommoder; (*repair*) réparer; (*reform*) corriger; (*matters*) arranger; (*pace*) †hâter; *v.n.* (*health*) se rétablir.
mender, *s.* (*china, &c.*) raccommodeu|r, ~se, *m.f.*
mendacious, mensong|er, ~ère.
mendicant, *s.* mendiant, -e, *m.f.*
mendic|ity, ~ancy, mendicité, *f.*
menial, *adj. and s.m.f.* domestique.
mensura|ble, mensurable; **~tion,** (*math.*) mensuration, *f.*
mental, (*disease, calculation, &c.*) mental; **~ly,** mentalement.
menthol, menthol, *m.*
mention, *s.* mention, *f.*
mention, *v.a.* mentionner; (*quote and in dispatches*) citer; *not to ~,* sans parler de; *don't ~ it,* il n'y a pas de quoi; *afore-~ed,* précité.
mentor, mentor, *m.*
mephitic, méphitique.
mercantile, commercial.
mercenary, *adj. and s.m.* mercenaire.
mercer, marchand de tissus et soieries, *m.*; ⚠ *not* mercier *which = 'haberdasher'*; **~ize,** *v.a.* merceriser.
merchandise, marchandise, *f.* (*oft. in pl.*).
merchant, *s.* négociant, *m.*; (*small*) commerçant, *m.*; *adj.* marchand.
merchantman, navire marchand, *m.*
merciful, miséricordieu|x, ~se; **~ness,** miséricorde, *f.*; **~ly,** miséricordieusement.
merciless, impitoyable; **~ly,** impitoyablement.
mercurial, (*of mercury*) mercuriel, -le; ⚠ mercuriel *does not = 'lively', 'fickle' which =* capricieu|x, ~se.

merc|y, (*pity*) pitié, *f.*; (*clemency*) miséricorde, *f.*; (*pardon*) grâce, *f.*; **~ies,** (*benefits*) bienfaits, *m.pl.*; *at the ~y of,* à la merci de.
mere, *s.* étang, *m.*
mere, *adj.* seul; **~ly,** purement.
meretricious, (*Lit., style, &c.*) d'un faux brillant; **~ness, faux brillant,** *m.*
merge, *v.a.* ~ *in,* incorporer à; (*comm.*) fusionner; *v.n.* être absorbé (dans).
meridian, méridien, *m.*; (*fig.*) apogée, *m.*; *adj.* méridien, -ne.
meridional, méridional.
merino, (*sheep and wool*) mérinos, *m.*
merit, *s.* (*quality, desert, excellence*) mérite, *m.*; *v.a.* mériter.
meritorious, (*pers.*) méritant; (*things*) méritoire; **~ly, d'une manière méritoire.**
merlin, (*ornith.*) émerillon, *m.*
merlin-chair, chaise-roulante, *f.*
mer|maid, sirène, *f.*; **~man,** triton, *m.*
merr|y, gai; (*slightly tipsy, fam.*) pompette; **~iment,** gaieté, *f.*; **~ily,** gaiement; **~y-andrew,** paillasse, *m.*; **~y-go-round,** tourniquet, *m.*; *make ~y,* se divertir.
mesh, maille, *f.*; **~es,** (*fig.*) rets, *m.pl.*; *v.a.* prendre* au filet.
mesmer|ism, mesmérisme, *m.*; **~ize,** hypnotiser.
mess, (*dish*) mets, *m.*; (*muddle*) gâchis, *m.*; (*mil., officers*) popote d'officiers, *f.*; (*naut.*) plat, *m.*; **~-tin,** gamelle, *f.*; *make a ~ of,* (*fig.*) gâcher; *I'm in a pretty ~,* me voilà dans de beaux draps.
mess, *v.a.* gâcher; *~ together,* faire* popote ensemble.
message, *s.* message, *m.*; (*telegr.*) dépêche, *f.*; *wireless ~,* radio, *m.*
messenger, messag|er, ~ère, *m.f.*
Messiah, Messie, *m.*
messy, malpropre.
metal, métal, *m.*; **~s,** (*rail.*) rails, *m.pl.*; ⚠ **métaux** *is never used in this sense*; *v.a.* (*roads*) empierrer.
metall|ic, métallique; **~iferous,** métallifère.
metallurg|ist, métallurgiste, *m.*; **~y,** métallurgie, *f.*
metamorph|ism, métamorphisme, *m.*; **~ic,** métamorphique.
metamorphos|e, *v.a.* métamorphoser; **~is,** métamorphose, *f.*
metaphor, métaphore, *f.*; **~ical,** métaphorique; **~ically,** métaphoriquement.
metaphysi|cal, métaphysique; **~cs,** métaphysique, *f.*; **~cian,** métaphysicien, *m.*
mete out, distribuer.
metempsychosis, métempsycose, *f.*
meteor, météore, *m.*; **~ic,** météorique.
meteorolog|y, météorologie, *f.*; **~ical,** météorologique; **~ist,** météorologue, *m.*
meter, (*gas, &c.*) compteur, *m.*
methinks, il (ce) me semble.
method, (*system, way*) méthode, *f.*; **~ical,** méthodique; **~ically,** méthodiquement.
Methodist, *adj.* (*when an adj. use small letter*) *and s.m.f.* Méthodiste.
methylated, ~ *spirit,* alcool à brûler, *m.*
meticulous, méticuleu|x, **~se**; **~ly,** méticuleusement.
metonymy, métonymie, *f.*
metope, (*arch.*) métope, *f.*
metr|e, (*measure*) mètre, *m.*; **~ic, ~ical,** métrique.
metropol|is, capitale, *f.*; ⚠ métropole = '*centre of trade, activity*' *or* '*metropolitan bishop's see*'; **~itan,** *s.* (*archbishop*) métropolitain, *m.*; *adj.* métropolitain.
mettle, (*spirit, fire*) fougue, *f.*; (*courage*) courage, *m.*; *be put on one's ~,* se piquer d'honneur.
mettlesome, fougueu|x, ~se.
mew, (*ornith.*) mouette, *f.*; (*coop*) mue, *f.*
mew, *s.* (*cats*) miaulement, *m.*; *v.n.* miauler.
mews, écuries, *f.pl.*
Mexican, *adj.* (*when an adj. use small letter*) *and s.m.f.* Mexicain, -e.
mezzotint, mezzo-tinto, *m.*
miasma, miasme, *m.*
mica, mica, *m.*
Michaelmas, Saint-Michel, *f.*; **~ daisy,** aster, *m.*
microbe, microbe, *m.*
microcosm, microcosme, *m.*
microphone, microphone, *m.*
microscop|e, microscope, *m.*; **~ic,** microscopique.
mid, *adj.* au milieu; (*in comps.*) mi-, *e.g. mid-August,* mi-août, *m.*; *mid-Lent,* mi-carême, *f.*; *~-winter,* cœur de l'hiver, *m.*
midday, midi, *m.*
midden, fumier, *m.*
middle, *s.* milieu, *m.*; (*body*) ceinture, *f.*; *adj.* du milieu; (*intermediate*) moyen, -ne; *~ Ages, see* AGE; *~-aged,* entre les deux âges; *~ classes, see* CLASS; *~ finger, see* FINGER; *~-sized,* de taille moyenne.
middleman, intermédiaire, *m.*
middling, passable; *adv.* **~ly,** passablement bien.
midge, moucheron, *m.*; **~t,** (*pers.*) nain, -e, *m.f.*
midland, *s.* intérieur, *m.*; *the Midlands,* le centre (de l'Angleterre); *adj.* du centre.
midnight, minuit, *m.*; *adj.* de minuit.
midriff, diaphragme, *m.*
midship, milieu du navire, *m.*
midshipman, aspirant, *m.*
midst, *s.* milieu, *m.*; *in the ~ of,* au milieu de.
midsummer, milieu de l'été, *m.*; **~ day,** la Saint-Jean.
midway, *adv.* (*lit. and fig.*) à mi-chemin.
midwife, sage-femme, *f.*; **~ry,** obstétrique, *f.*
mien, mine, *f.*
might, *s.* force, *f.*; (*power, to enforce will*)

puissance, *f.*; *with all one's ~, with ~ and main,* de toutes ses forces; *v. aux., see* MAY.
might|y, fort; (*kings, &c.*) puissant; **~iness**, puissance, *f.*; **~ily**, fortement, puissamment; (*very, also mighty, adv.*) joliment.
mignonette, (*bot.*) réséda, *m.*; △ mignonnette = *a 'lace' and a kind of 'pink'* (*bot.*).
migra|te, émigrer; **~tion**, émigration, *f.*; (*birds*) migration, *f.*
migratory, (*of movements*) migratoire; (*birds*) migrat|eur, ~rice.
milch, **~-cow**, (*lit. and fig.*) vache à lait, *f.*
mild, (*gen. and weather*) dou|x, ~ce; (*disease, &c.*) bén|in, ~igne; **~ness**, douceur, *f.*; (*disease, &c.*) bénignité, *f.*; **~ly**, doucement.
mildew, *s.* (*plants, &c.*) rouille, *f.*; (*mould*) moisissure, *f.*; *v.a.* frapper de rouille; (*mould*) tacher de moisissure; *v.n.* se tacher de rouille, de moisissure.
mil|e, mille, *m.*; **~age**, (*distance*) parcours, *m.*; (*expense*) prix par mille, *m.*
milestone, borne milliaire, *f.*
milfoil, (*bot.*) mille-feuille, *f.*
militant, (*combative and eccles.*) militant.
militar|ism, militarisme, *m.*; **~ize**, militariser.
military, *s.* militaires, *m.pl.*; *adj.* militaire; *~ man,* militaire, *m.*
militate against, militer contre.
militia, milice, *f.*; **~man**, milicien, *m.*
milk, (*lit. and fruits*) lait, *m.*; *~ and water,* lait coupé, *m.*; **~-can**, boîte à lait, *f.*; **~maid**, laitière, *f.*; **~man**, laitier, *m.*; **~-pail**, seau à lait, *m.*; **~sop**, (*pers.*) poule mouillée, *f.*; **~wort**, (*bot.*) herbe au lait, *f.*; **~iness**, nature laiteuse, *f.*
milk, *v.a.* traire* (*def.*).
milky, (*like milk, consisting of milk*) lacté; (*med. and plants*) laiteu|x, ~se; ~ **Way**, voie lactée, *f.*
mill, *s.* (*flour*) moulin, *m.*; (*spinning*) filature, *f.*; (*manufactory*) fabrique, *f.*; *rolling-~, see* ROLLING; **~board**, carton, *m.*; **~-dam**, écluse de moulin, *f.*; **~-hand**, ouvrier d'usine, *m.*; **~-owner**, usinier, *m.*; **~-pond**, (*approx.*) retenue, *f.*; **~-race**, bief, biez, *m.*
mill, *v.a.* moudre*; (*cloth*) fouler.
mill, *s.* (*U.S.A. money*) millième de dollar, *m.*
millennium, mille ans, *m.pl.*
millepede, mille-pieds, *m.*
miller, meuni|er, ~ère, *m.f.*; (*fem.*) *~'s wife.*
millet, mil, *m.*; **~-grass**, millet, *m.*
milli|ard, milliard, *m.*; **~metre**, millimètre, *m.*
milliner, modiste, *f.*; **~y**, modes, *f.pl.*
million, million, *m.*; **~aire**, *adj. and s.m.f.* millionnaire.
millstone, meule, *f.*
mime, mime, *m.*; **~etic**, mimique.
mi[illegible], *s.* mime, *m.*; (*imitator*) imitat|eur, ~rice, *m.f.*; *adj.* mimique; *v.a.* imiter; **~ry**, mimique, *f.*
mimosa, (*bot.*) mimosa, *m.*
minaret, minaret, *m.*
minatory, menaçant.
mince, *s.* †hachis, *m.*; *v.a.* †hacher; *v.n.* (*simper, &c.*) minauder.
mincing, *adj.* mièvre; **~ly**, en minaudant.
mind, esprit, *m.*; (*desire*) envie, *f.*; (*opinion*) opinion, *f.*; (*taste*) goût, *m.*; *master- ~, see* MASTER; *give one's ~ to,* faire* attention à; *make up one's ~, see* MAKE, *v.a.*; *have a good ~, half a ~, to,* avoir bien envie de; *bring to ~,* se rappeler; *put in ~ of,* rappeler, *dat. of pers., acc. of thing*; *of sound ~,* sain d'esprit.
mind, *v.a.* faire attention à; (*listen to*) écouter; (*be careful of*) prendre* garde à; (*look after*) garder; (*trouble about*) s'inquiéter de; *do you ~ if I shut the window?* est-ce que cela vous gênerait, si je ferme la fenêtre?; ~ (*doing a thing*) avoir l'obligeance de; *~ your own business,* mêlez-vous de vos affaires.
mind, *v.n. never ~,* n'importe; *I don't ~* (*it*), cela m'est égal.
minded, (*in comps.*) d'esprit; (*disposed*) disposé (à); *narrow-~,* à l'esprit borné.
mindful, attenti|f, ~ve (à); (*bearing in mind*) en se souvenant de.
mine, *s.* (*lit. and fig., mil., nav.*) mine, *f.*; *drifting ~,* mine dérivante, *f.*; *magnetic ~,* mine magnétique, *f.*; **~-layer, -sinker**, (*ship*) (navire) poseur de mines, *m.*; (*apparatus*) mouilleur de mines, *m.*; **~-shaft**, puits, *m.*; **~-sweeper**, (navire) dragueur de mines, *m.*
mine, *pron.* à moi, *unless a distinction or differentiation is made, when* le mien, la mienne, les miens, les miennes *is used; a friend of ~,* un de mes amis.
mine, *v.a.* (*lit., mil.*) miner; (*make hole*) creuser.
miner, mineur, *m.*
mineral, *adj. and s.m.* minéral; *~ water,* eau minérale, *f.*
mineralog|ist, minéralogiste, *m.*; **~y**, minéralogie, *f.*
minever, (*fur*) petit-gris, *m.*
mingle, *v.a.* mêler; (*confuse*) confondre; *v.n.* (*be mingled*) se mêler*.
mingling, *s.* mélange, *m.*
miniature, *s.* miniature, *f.*; *adj.* en miniature.
minim, (*mus.*) blanche, *f.*
minim|um, minimum, *m.*; **~ize**, diminuer l'importance de; (*loss*) atténuer.
mining-engineer, ingénieur des mines, *m.*
minion, favori, -te, *m.f.*
minister, *s.* (*envoy, polit., relig.*) ministre, *m.*
minister, *v.n. ~ to,* (*supply wants*) pourvoir* aux besoins de; (*contribute to*) contribuer à.
ministration, (*help*) ministère, *m.*
ministerial, *adj.* (*belonging to or favouring*

a ministry) ministériel, -le; **~ist,** *s.* ministériel, *m.*
ministry, (*polit.*, *eccles.*) ministère, *m.*
mink, (*zool. and fur*) vison, *m.*
minnow, (*ichth.*) vairon, *m.*
minor, *s.* (*of age*) mineur, -e, *m.f.*
minor, *adj.* (*in importance, mus., log.*) mineur; ~ *poet, see* POET.
minority, minorité, *f.*
minster, église de monastère, *f.*
minstrel, ménestrel, *m.*; **~sy,** art du ménestrel, *m.*; ⚠ ménétrier = '*fiddler*'.
mint, *s.* (*place*) Hôtel de la Monnaie, *m.*; (*bot.*) menthe, *f.*; *v.a.* (*coin*) monnayer.
minuet, menuet, *m.*
minus, *adj.* en moins; *adv.* moins; 12 − 9 = 3, douze moins neuf égale trois.
minute, *s.* minute, *f.*; (*official note*) note, *f.*; (*very short time*) petit moment, *m.*; **~s,** (*of meeting*) procès-verbal, *m.*; ~ *hand,* grande aiguille, *f.*
minute, *adj.* (*very small*) minuscule; (*precise*) minutieu|x, ~se; **~ness,** (*smallness*) exiguïté, *f.*; (*precision*) exactitude minutieuse, *f.*; **~ly,** minutieusement.
minutiae, minuties, *f.pl.*
minx, coquine, *f.*
miracle, (*lit. and fig.*) miracle, *m.*; ~*-play,* miracle, *m.*
miraculous, miraculeu|x, ~se; **~ly,** miraculeusement.
mirage, (*lit. and fig.*) mirage, *m.*
mir|e, bourbe, *f.*; **~y,** bourbeu|x, ~se; *stick in the* ~, (*lit. and fig.*) s'embourber.
mirror, (*lit. and fig.*) miroir, *m.*
mirth, gaieté, *f.*; **~ful,** joyeu|x, ~se; **~less,** triste.
misadventure, mésaventure, *f.*
misanthrop|e, **~ist,** misanthrope, *m.*; **~y,** misanthropie, *f.*; **~ical,** misanthropique.
misappl|ication, mauvais usage, *m*; **~y,** appliquer mal à propos.
misapprehen|d, *v.a.* se méprendre* sur; **~sion,** malentendu, *m.*
misappropria|te, (*money, &c.*) détourner; **~tion,** détournement, *m.*
misbegotten, illégitime.
misbehav|e, se conduire* mal; **~iour,** mauvaise conduite, *f.*
misbelief, croyance erronée, *f.*
miscalcula|te, calculer mal; **~tion,** mécompte, *m.*
miscalled, *adj.* mal nommé.
miscarriage, (*failure*) insuccès, *m.*; (*justice*) erreur, *f.*; (*goods, &c.*) égarement, *m.*; (*med.*) fausse couche, *f.*
miscarry, *v.n.* (*fail and med.*) avorter; (*letters, &c.*) s'égarer.
miscellan|eous, divers; **~y,** mélange, *m.*; (*Lit.*) mélanges, *m.pl.*
mischance, mauvaise chance, *f.*; (*misfortune*) malheur, *m.*
mischief, (*harm*) mal, *m.*; (*mischievousness*) méchanceté, *f.*; (*tricks*) sottises, *f.pl.*; (*damage*) tort, *m.*; **~-maker,** brouillon, -ne, *m.f.*
mischievous, (*pers.*) méchant; (*things*) nuisible; (*child*) espiègle; **~ness,** méchanceté, espièglerie, *f.*; **~ly,** méchamment.
misconceive, *v.a.* avoir une notion erronée de; (*misunderstand*) comprendre* mal.
misconception, opinion fausse, *f.*; (*mistake*) malentendu, *m.*
misconduct, *s.* (*moral generally*) inconduite, *f.*; *v.a.* (*mismanage*) administrer mal; ~ *oneself,* se conduire* mal.
misconstru|ction, fausse interprétation, *f.*; **~e,** *v.a.* interpréter mal.
miscreant, (*wretch*) misérable, *m.f.*
misdated, mal daté.
misdeed, méfait, *m.*
misdemeanour, offense, *f.*; (*law*) délit, *m.*
misdirect, (*letters, &c.*) adresser mal; (*misinform*) renseigner mal.
misdoing, (*fault*) faute, *f.*; (*wrongdoing*) méfait, *m.*
miser, avare, *m.f.*; **~ly,** avare; **~liness,** avarice, *f.*
miserable, misérable; (*unhappy*) malheureu|x, ~se; **~ably,** misérablement.
misery, misère, *f.*
misfit, *s.* (*coat, garment, &c.*) *use* qui ne va pas bien.
misfortune, malheur, *m.*
misgive, *v.a.*; *my, &c., mind misgives me, &c., use* appréhender + *subj. and* ne.
misgiving, (*fear*) crainte, *f.*; (*presentiment*) pressentiment, *m.*
misgovern, *v.a.* gouverner mal; **~ment,** mauvais gouvernement, *m.*
misguide, *v.a.* (*lead astray*) égarer.
mishap, mésaventure, *f.*
misinform, renseigner mal; **~ation,** fausse information, *f.*
misinterpret, interpréter mal; **~ation,** contresens, *m.*
misjudge, *v.a.* juger mal de.
mislay, égarer.
mislead, égarer; (*fig.*) induire* en erreur.
mismanage, administrer mal; **~ment,** mauvaise administration, *f.*; (*comm.*) mauvaise gestion, *f.*
misname, *v.a.* nommer mal.
misogynist, misogyne, *m.*
misplace, placer mal; **~d,** (*inopportune*) déplacé.
misprint, *s.* faute d'impression, *f.*; *v.a.* imprimer incorrectement.
misprize, *v.a.* sous-estimer.
mispron|ounce, *v.a.* prononcer mal; **~unciation,** mauvaise prononciation, *f.*
misquot|e, citer à faux; **~ation,** citation incorrecte.
misread, lire* mal.
misrepresent, présenter sous un faux jour; (*facts*) dénaturer; **~ation,** faux rapport, *m.*
misrule, (*bad government*) mauvais gouvernement, *m.*; (*disorder*) désordre, *m.*
miss, *v.a.* (*opportunity, be too late for, thing aimed at*) manquer; (*not hear*)

ne pas entendre; (*not see*) ne pas voir*; (*perceive want, absence of*) s'apercevoir de l'absence de; (*feel absence of*) manquer à *transposed, e.g. my father ~es my mother*, ma mère manque à mon père; ~ *out*, omettre*; *be ~ing*, manquer; ~ *one's aim*, manquer son coup.
miss, (*pers. respect and ironical*) mademoiselle, *f.pl.* mesdemoiselles; (+ *name*) Mademoiselle; *the ~es*, les demoiselles; (*failure to hit*) manque à toucher, à atteindre, *m.*
missel, (*eccles.*) missel, *m.*
missel-thrush, (*ornith.*) drenne, draine, *f.*
mis-shapen, difforme.
missile, projectile, *m.*
missing, (*pers.*) disparu; (*thing*) qui manque.
mission, mission, *f.*; **~ary, ~er,** missionnaire, *m.f.*
missus, (*used by servants*) Madame, *f.*
missive, missive, *f.*
mis-spell, épeler mal; **~ing,** faute d'orthographe, *f.*
mis-state, exposer inexactement; **~ment,** exposé inexact, *m.*
mist, brouillard, *m.*; (*thick mist and fig.*) brume, *f.*; **~y,** brumeu|x, ~se; (*fig.*) obscur; **~iness,** état brumeux, *m.*; **~ily,** obscurément.
mistake, *s.* méprise, *f.*; (*error, fault*) faute, *f.*; *there's no ~ about it*, il n'y a pas à dire; *make a ~*, se tromper; *make the ~ of* (*doing*), avoir le tort de.
mistake, *v.a.* (*make a mistake about*) se tromper de; (*misunderstand*) comprendre* mal; ~ *for*, prendre* pour.
mistaken, *adj.* (*ideas*) erroné; (*misunderstood*) mal compris; (*kindness*) mal appliqué; **~ly,** par erreur.
mister, (*pop.*) monsieur, *m.*
mistime, *v.a.* faire* mal à propos; (*time*) calculer mal l'heure de; **~d,** inopportun.
mistletoe, (*bot.*) gui, *m.*
mistral, mistral, *m.*
mistransla|te, traduire* mal; **~tion,** traduction incorrecte, *f.*
mistress, (*house*) maîtresse de maison, *f.*; (*fig., sweetheart, pej.*) maîtresse, *f.*; (*teacher*) institutrice, *f.*; *music, singing ~*, professeur de musique, de chant, *m.*; *the, your, &c. ~*, Madame, *f.*
mistrust, *s.* défiance, *f.*; *v.a.* se défier de.
mistrustful, méfiant.
misunderstand, *v.a.* comprendre* mal; **~ing,** malentendu, *m.*; (*disagreement*) mésintelligence, *f.*
misuse, *s.* (*wrong use*) abus, *m.*; (*ill treatment*) mauvais traitements, *m.pl.*
misuse, *v.a.* (*use wrongly*) abuser de; (*ill-treat*) maltraiter.
mite, (*coin*) denier, *m.*; (*small gift*) obole, *f.*; (*insect*) mite, *f.*
mitiga|te, (*make milder*) adoucir; (*anger, &c.*) apaiser; **~tion,** adoucissement, *m.*
mitre, (*eccles.*) mitre, *f.*; (*joint*) onglet, *m.*; *v.a.* assembler, tailler à onglet.
mitten, mitaine, *f.*
mix, *v.a.* mêler; (*compound*) composer; (*medicine*) mixtionner; ~ *up*, (*fig.*) embrouiller; *be ~ed up in*, être mêlé à; *v.n.* se mêler; ~ *with*, (*associate with*) fréquenter.
mixed, *adj.* (*company, blood*) mêlé; (*school, bathing, cargoes*) mixte; (*confused*) ahuri; *I am all ~ up*, je ne sais plus où j'en suis.
mixture, mélange, *m.*; (*med.*) mixtion, *f.*
miz(z)en, *s.* (*naut.*) artimon, *m.*; ⚓ misaine, *f.* = '*foremast*'.
mnemonic, *adj.* mnémonique; **~s,** mnémonique, *f.*
moan, *s.* gémissement, *m.*; *v.n.* gémir; **~ful,** gémissant; **~fully,** plaintivement.
moat, fossé, *m.*
mob, (*crowd*) foule, *f.*; (*rabble*) canaille, *f.*; *v.a.* †houspiller.
mobil|e, mobile; **~ity,** mobilité, *f.*; **~ization,** mobilisation, *f.*; **~ize,** (*mil.*) mobiliser.
mocassin, *s.* mocassin, *m.*
mock, *s.* moquerie, *f.*; (*laughing-stock*) objet de risée, *m.*
mock, *adj.* fau|x, ~sse; ~ *orange*, (*bot.*) seringa(t), *m.*; *~-turtle soup*, potage tête de veau, *m.*
mock, *v.a.* railler; (*cheat*) tromper; (*imitate*) singer; *v.n.* ~ *at*, se moquer de; **~er,** moqueu|r, ~se, *m.f. also adj.*; **~ing, ~ery,** moquerie, *f.*; (*butt*) dérision, *f.*; *~ing-bird*, oiseau-moqueur, *m.*
mode, (*manner*) manière, *f.*; (*kind, log., mus.*) mode, *m.*; (*fashion*) mode, *f.*
model, *s.* (*lit., fig., artist's*) modèle, *m.*; *adj.* modèle; *v.a.* (*lit. and fig.*) modeler (sur).
modell|er, modeleur, *m.*; **~ing,** modelage, *m.*
moderate, *adj.* (*temperate and polit.*) modéré; (*price*) modique; (*middling*) médiocre; **~ly,** modérément.
moderate, *v.a.* modérer; (*expenses*) régler.
moderateness, moderation, modération, *f.*; (*price*) modicité, *f.*
moderator, (*lit. and eccles.*) modéra|t|eur, ~rice, *m.f.*; (*mediator*) média|t|eur, ~rice, *m.f.*
modern, *adj.* moderne; *the ~s*, les modernes, *m.pl.*; **~ness, ~ity,** modernité, *f.*; **~ize,** *v.a.* moderniser.
modern|ism, modernisme, *m.*; **~ist,** moderniste, *m.*
modest, (*not proud, chaste, bashful, not excessive, unpretentious*) modeste; **~ly,** modestement.
modesty, modestie, *f.*; (*of money*) modicité, *f.*
modif|y, *v.a.* (*lit. and gram.*) modifier; **~ication,** modification, *f.*
modillion, (*arch.*) modillon, *m.*
modish, à la mode.
modula|te, *v.a.* (*voice*) moduler; **~tion,** modulation, *f.*

Mogul, mogol, *m.*
mohair, mohair, *m.*
Mohammedan, *adj.* (*when an adj. use small letter*) *and s.m.f.* Mahométan, -e; **~ism,** mahométisme, *m.*
moiety, moitié, *f.*
moil, *v.n.* peiner.
moire, (*fabric*) moire, *f.*
moist, moite; **~ness,** moiteur, *f.*; **~en,** *v.a.* humecter.
molar, *adj. and s.f.* molaire.
molasses, mélasse, *f.*
mole, (*an.*) taupe, *f.*; (*harbour*) môle, *m.*; (*on skin*) grain de beauté, *m.*; **~-hill,** taupière, *f.*
moleskin, fourrure de taupe, *f.*; ⚠ moleskine = '*American cloth*'.
molecul|e, molécule, *f.*; **~ar,** moléculaire.
molest, molester; **~ation,** molestation, *f.*
mollif|y, apaiser; **~ication,** apaisement, *m.*
mollusc, mollusque, *m.*
molten, fondu.
moment, moment, *m.*; *one ~!* un petit moment!; *the very ~* (*that*), au moment même (où); ⚠ *English 'moment' also = 'importance'* = importance; *never* moment *in French*; *of no ~*, sans importance; *of supreme ~*, de grande importance.
moment|ary, momentané; **~arily,** momentanément.
momentous, important.
momentum, (*mech.*) moment, *m.*; (*pop.*) élan, *m.*
monachism, monachisme, *m.*
monarch, monarque, *m.*; ~y, monarchie, *f.*; **~ical,** monarchique; **~ist,** monarchiste, *m.*
monast|ery, monastère, *m.*; **~ic,** monastique; **~icism,** vie monastique, *f.*
Monday, lundi, *m.*
monetary, monétaire.
money, argent, *m.*; (*comm.*) monnaie, *f.*; (*capital*) capitaux, *m.pl.*; **~-box,** tirelire, *f.*; **~- changer,** changeu|r, ~se, *m.f.*; **~-market,** marché monétaire, *m.*; **~-order,** mandat, *m.*; **~-order telegram,** télégramme-mandat, *m.*; **~wort,** (*bot.*) monnaie du pape, *f.*; *ready ~, see* READY; *get one's ~'s worth, have a run for one's ~*, en avoir pour son argent.
moneyed, riche.
Mongol, *adj.* (*when an adj. use small letter*) *and s.m.f.* Mongol, -e.
mongoose, (*zool.*) mangouste, *f.*
mongrel, *adj.* métis, -se; *s.* (*dog*) chien métis, *m.*
monitor, (*school*) moniteur, *m.*; (*nav.*) monitor, *m.*
monk, moine, *m.*; *~'s-hood*, (*bot.*) aconit, *m.*; **~ish,** de moine.
monkey, singe, *m.*, guenon, *f.*; (*child*) babouin, *m.*; *~ trick*, singerie, *f.*; *his ~ is up*, (*pop.*) la moutarde lui monte au nez.
monochrome, *adj.* monochrome.
monocle, monocle, *m.*
monody, monodie, *f.*
monogam|y, monogamie, *f.*; **~ous,** monogame.
monogram, monogramme, *m.*
monograph, monographie, *f.*
monolith, monolithe, *m.*; **~ic,** monolithe.
monologue, monologue, *m.*
monomania, monomanie, *f.*; **~c,** *adj. and s.m.f.* monomane.
monoplane, monoplan, *m.*
monopol|y, monopole, *m.*; **~ize,** monopoliser; **~ization,** monopolisation, *f.*
monosyllab|le, monosyllabe, *m.*; **~ic,** monosyllabique.
monotheism, monothéisme, *m.*
monotone, *s.* ton monotone, *m.*
monoton|y, monotonie, *f.*; **~ous,** monotone.
monsoon, mousson, *f.*
monstrance, (*eccles.*) ostensoir, *m.*
monst|er, monstre, *m.*; **~rosity, ~rousness,** monstruosité, *f.*; **~rous,** (*lit. and fig.*) monstrueu|x, ~se.
month, mois, *m.*; **~ly,** mensuel, -le; *adv.* mensuellement; *~ rose*, rose des quatre saisons, *f.*
monument, (*structure, memorial, tomb*) monument, *m.*; **~al,** monumental.
mood, (*of mind*) humeur, *f.*; (*gram., mus.*) mode, *m.*
mood|y, de mauvaise humeur; **~iness,** humeur, *f.*
moon, lune, *f.*; *the ~ is shining*, il fait clair de lune; *v.n. ~ about*, flâner.
moonbeam, rayon de lune, *m.*
moonless, sans lune.
moonlight, clair de lune, *m.*; *by ~*, au clair de la lune.
moonlit, éclairé par la lune.
moonshine, clair de lune, *m.*; (*slang*) blague, *f.*
moonstruck, toqué.
moonwort, (*bot.*) lunaire, *f.*
moor, bruyère, *f.*; (*extensive*) lande, *f.*; **~-cock,** coq de bruyère, *m.*
moor, *v.a.* amarrer; *v.n.* s'amarrer; **~ing,** *s.* (*naut., aeron.*) amarrage, *m.*
Moorish, *adj.* mauresque.
moose-deer, (*zool.*) élan, *m.*
moot, *v.a.* (*question, point*) soulever; *~ point*, point à discuter, *m.*
mop, *s.* balai, *m.*; (*naut.*) faubert, *m.*; (*of hair*) tignasse, *f.*
mope, *v.n.* être triste; (*be dull*) s'ennuyer.
moral, *s.* (*fable, &c.*) morale, *f.*; **~s,** mœurs, *f.pl.* *See* MORALE.
moral, *adj.* (*concerning character, in conformity with morals, certainty, victory, courage*) moral; (*about morals*) de morale; **~ly,** (*lit. and fig.*) moralement.
morale, moral, *m.*; ⚠ *Eng. 'morale'* = *Fr.* moral, *Eng. 'moral', s. more often* = *Fr.* morale.
moralist, moraliste, *m.*
morality, (*moral science*) morale, *f.*; (*conduct, moral sense*) moralité, *f.*
moralize, *v.a.n.* moraliser.

morass, marécage, *m.*; ⚠ *Not* morasse *which = 'final proof of newspaper'.*
moratorium, moratorium, *m.*
morbid, (*med.*) morbide; (*unwholesome*) malsain; **~ness,** état maladif, *m.*
mordant, mordant.
more, *adj.* plus de; (*another*) de plus; *~ than,* plus que; *in comparisons + numbers,* plus de: *more than 2,* plus de deux; *what is ~,* qui plus est; *just one ~ song,* seulement une chanson de plus.
more, *pron.* en *before verb* (*after with affirm. imper.*) *often conjoined with* davantage *after verb*; (*plur.*) d'autres encore; *some ~,* en . . . davantage; *no ~,* n'en . . . pas davantage, *also* ne . . . plus; *she will not say any ~ about it,* elle n'en dira pas davantage; *will you take some ~?* voulez-vous en prendre davantage? ; *I don't want any ~,* je n'en veux plus; *a crowd had assembled in the garden and ~ were in the house,* une foule s'était assemblée dans le jardin et d'autres encore étaient dans la maison; ⚠ plus de pain = '*more bread*'; *but* plus de pain! *often written with* (!) *and short for* ne . . . plus de pain *also = 'no more bread!'*
more, *adv.* davantage; *more and more,* de plus en plus; *so much the ~,* d'autant plus; (*rather*) plutôt; *he is no ~,* (*has died*) il n'est plus.
morel, (*bot., nightshade*) morelle, *f.*
moreover, de plus.
Moresque, mauresque.
morganatic, morganatique.
moribund, moribond.
morn, matin, *m.*
morning, matin, *m.*; (*~'s duration or work*) matinée, *f.*; *~-gown,* robe de chambre, *f.*; *in the ~,* le matin; *good ~,* bon jour; *to-morrow ~,* demain matin; *yesterday ~,* hier matin; *adj.* du matin.
morocco, (*leather*) maroquin, *m.*
morose, morose; **~ness,** morosité, *f.*
morph|ia, morphine, *f.*; **~inomaniac,** morphinomane, *m.f.*
morphology, morphologie, *f.*
morrow, lendemain, *m.*
morse, (*zool.*) morse, *m.*
Morse, (*telegraph*) *adj.* (*when an adj. use small letter*) *and s.m.* Morse.
morsel, morceau, *m.*
mortal, *s.* mortel, -le, *s.m.f.*; *adj.* (*subject to death, fatal, fight, implacable, deadly, slang*) mortel, -le; **~ity,** mortalité, *f.*; **~ly,** mortellement.
mortar, (*mixture, vessel, artil.*) mortier, *m.*; *see also* TRENCH.
mortgage, hypothèque, *f.*; *v.a.* hypothéquer.
mortgag|er, ~or, débiteur hypothécaire, *m.*
mortif|y, (*lit. and humiliate*) mortifier; **~ication,** mortification, *f.*; **~ying,** mortifiant.
mortuary, *s.* morgue, *f.*; *adj.* mortuaire.
mosaic, *s.* (*lit. and fig.*) mosaïque, *f.*; ⚠ mosaïque, *adj.* = '*of Moses*'; *~ pavement,* mosaïque, *f.*
mosque, mosquée, *f.*
mosquito, moustique, *f.*; **~-net,** moustiquaire, *f.*
moss, (*bot.*) mousse, *f.*; (*bog*) marécage, *m.*; **~y,** moussu; **~ rose,** rose moussue, *f.*
most, *pron.* la plupart de; *at the ~,* tout au plus.
most, *adj.* le plus de; *sometimes* la plupart de; *for the ~ part,* pour la plupart; *~ talent,* le plus de talent; *~ Frenchmen,* la plupart des Français.
most, *s. the ~,* le plus; *adv.* le plus, *which also serves to form the superlative.*
mostly, pour la plupart; (*time*) la plupart du temps.
mote, grain de poussière, *m.*; (*fig., in eye*) paille, *f.*
moth, teigne, *f.*; (*in clothes*) mite, *f.*; *~-eaten,* mité.
mother, *s.* (*lit. and fig., relig.*) mère, *f.*; (*term of fam., address*) la mère; **~-in-law,** belle-mère, *f.*; *~ of pearl,* nacre, *f.*; *~-tongue,* langue maternelle, *f.*; *~-wit,* esprit naturel, *m.*; *v.a.* entourer de soins maternels; **~less,** orphelin de mère; **~ly,** maternel, -le.
mother|hood, maternité, *f.*
motherwort, (*bot.*) matricaire, *f.*
motion, mouvement, *m.*; (*gesture*) signe, *m.*; (*formal proposal*) motion, *f.*; (*med.*) selle, *f.*; *set in ~,* mettre* en mouvement; *support a ~,* soutenir* une motion; *v.a.n.* faire* signe (à).
motionless, immobile.
motivate, motiver.
motive, *s.* (*cause of action*) motif, *m.*
motive, *adj.* mot|eur, ~rice.
motley, *s.* habit bigarré, *m.*; *adj.* bigarré.
motor, (*machine supplying power*) moteur, *m.*; (*for ~-car*) automobile, *f.*, *abbrev.* auto; *~* **boat,** canot automobile, *m.*; *~* **bus,** autobus, *m.*; *~* **cycle,** motocyclette, *f.*; *~* **-cyclist,** motocycliste, *m.f.*; **~-horn,** klaxon, *m.*; *~* **lorry,** camion automobile, *m.*
motor, *adj.* mot|eur, ~rice.
motor, *v.n.* aller* (être) en auto; **~ing,** *s.* faire* de l'auto; **~ist,** automobiliste, *m.f.*
mottled, bariolé; (*wood, soap*) madré; (*fabrics*) chiné.
motto, devise, *f.*
mouffion, (*zool.*) mouflon, *m.*
moujik, moujik, *m.*
mould, *s.* (*earth*) terre, *f.*; (*for metal, &c.*) moule, *m.*; (*fig.*) trempe, *f.*; (*mildew*) moisissure, *f.*; *v.a.* (*shape*) mouler.
moulder, (*pers.*) mouleur, *m.*
moulder, *v.n.* tomber (être) en poussière.
mouldiness, moisissure, *f.*
moulding, (*casting*) moulage, *m.*; (*arch., join.*) moulure, *f.*
mouldy, moisi; *grow ~,* se moisir.
moult, muer; **~ing,** *s.* mue, *f.*

mound, tertre, *m.*
mount, *s.* (*hill*) mont, *m.*; (*an. for riding and jewels*) monture, *f.*; (*pictures*) bordure, *f.*
mount, *v.a.* (*hill, ascend, jewels, loom, &c., guard, furnish with horse*) monter (avoir); (*guns*) mettre* en position; (*get up on veh., horse*) monter (être) à; (*scaffold, throne, &c.*) monter (être) sur; (*photos, &c.*) coller.
mount, *v.n.* (*lit. and fig., horse*) monter (être); (*to higher level*) s'élever; ~ *up,* (*increase*) augmenter.
mountain, (*lit. and fig.*) montagne, *f.*; (*heap*) monceau, *m.*; *adj.* de montagne; **~eer,** montagnard, -e, *m.f.*; **~eering,** alpinisme, *m.*; **~-ash,** (*bot.*) sorbier des oiseaux, *m.*
mountainous, montagneu|x, ~se.
mountebank, saltimbanque, *m.*
mourn, se lamenter; ~ *over, for,* pleurer, *v.a.*
mourner, (*funerals*) personne qui suit le deuil.
mournful, (*pers.*) triste; (*things*) lugubre; **~ness,** tristesse, *f.*; **~ly,** tristement, lugubrement.
mourning, deuil, *m.*; (*sorrow*) affliction, *f.*; *be in* ~, être en deuil; *go into* ~, prendre* le deuil.
mouse, souris, *f.*; **~-coloured,** gris souris, *invar.*; **~-hole,** trou de souris, *m.*; **~-trap,** souricière, *f.*
mouser, chasseur de souris, *m.*
moustache, moustache, *f.*
mouth, (*man, horse, ass, oxen, salmon, frog, fire-arms, orifice, oven*) bouche, *f.*; (*carnivorous ans., furnace, tunnel*) gueule, *f.*; (*opening*) ouverture, *f.*; (*river*) embouchure, *f.*; **~-organ,** harmonica, *m.*; *be down in the* ~, avoir l'oreille basse; *make one's* ~ *water,* faire* venir l'eau à la bouche; *by word of* ~, de vive voix.
mouth, *v.a.* (*food*) happer; *v.n.* (*grimace*) grimacer; *v.a.n.* (*distinctly, pompously*) parler, dire* avec emphase.
mouthful, bouchée, *f.*
mouthpiece, (*instr.*) embouchure, *f.*; (*pipe*) bout, *m.*; (*fig., pers.*) porte-parole, *m. invar.*
movable, mobile; (*law, comm.*) meuble; **~s,** *s.* biens meubles, *m.pl.*
movab|leness, ~ility, mobilité, *f.*
move, *s.* mouvement, *m.*; (*chess, &c.*) coup, *m.*; (*turn to play*) tour, *m.*; *get a* ~ *on!* (*slang*) grouillez-vous!
move, *v.a.* (*set in motion, lit. and fig.*) mouvoir*; (*change position of, stir, lit. and fig.*) remuer; (*goods*) transporter; (*furniture*) déménager; (*touch, affect*) émouvoir*; (*chess, &c.*) jouer; (*amendment, adjournment*) proposer; (*resolution*) faire*; (*shake out of position*) ébranler; (*wrath*) soulever; ~ *away,* éloigner; ~ *forward,* faire* avancer; ~ *in,* (*furniture*) emménager; ~ *on,* (*crowd, &c.*) faire* circuler; ~ *out,* (*furniture*) déménager; ~ *up,* (*in position, rank*) faire* avancer.
move, *v.n.* remuer; (*stir*) bouger; (*advance*) avancer; (*chess, &c.*) jouer; (*circulate*) circuler; (*in a matter, act*) agir; ~ *about,* remuer; ~ *away,* s'éloigner; ~ *back,* reculer; ~ *forward,* avancer; ~ *in, out,* (*house-moving*) emménager, déménager; ~ *off,* s'éloigner; ~ *on,* (*policeman's order*) circuler.
movement, (*parts of body, going to and fro, polit., relig., stocks, money, mus., mil., mach., anger, &c.*) mouvement, *m.*
mover, (*of motion*) auteur, *m.*; *prime* ~, premier mobile, *m.*
movies, (*slang*) ciné, *m.*; (*U.S.A.*) cinéma, *m.*
moving, (*affecting*) touchant; **~ly,** d'une manière touchante.
mow, *s.* (*hay, &c.*) meule, *f.*
mow, *v.a.* faucher; (*lawn*) tondre; **~ing,** *s.* fauchage, *m.*
mower, (*pers.*) faucheu|r, ~se, *m.f.*; (*machine*) *also* **mowing-machine,** faucheuse, *f.*
Mr., Mrs., Monsieur (*abbrev.* M.), Madame (*abbrev.* Mme).
much, *adj.* beaucoup de; *so* ~, tant de; *too* ~, trop de.
much, *pron.* beaucoup; (*up to much*) grand'chose, *m.*; *make, think* ~ *of,* faire* grand cas de; *be up to* ~, (*fam.*) valoir* grand'chose.
much, *adv.* beaucoup; (+ *p.p.*) très, *e.g.* très excité; (+ *compar. adj.*) de beaucoup, *e.g.* ~ *larger,* plus grand de beaucoup; *so* ~, tellement; *too* ~, trop; *so* ~ *for!* voilà pour; ~ *the same, adj.* à peu près le, la même; *very* ~, beaucoup; ⚠ *not* très beaucoup.
muchness, *much of a* ~, bonnet blanc et blanc bonnet.
muck, *s.* fumier, *m.*; (*mire*) fange, *f.*; (*filth*) ordure, *f.*; *v.a.* (*make dirty*) salir.
mucous, muqueu|x, ~se; ~ **membrane,** (*med.*) muqueuse, *f.*
mud, boue, *f.*; (*sea*) vase, *f.*; (*river*) limon, *m.*; *stick in the* ~, s'embourber; ~ *wall,* mur de torchis, *m.*
muddiness, état boueux, *m.*
muddle, *s.* fouillis, *m.*; *make a* ~ *of,* brouiller; *v.a.* embrouiller; **~d,** *and* ~-*headed,* embrouillé.
muddy, boueu|x, ~se; (*complexion*) terreu|x, ~se; (*liquid*) trouble; *v.a.* crotter.
mudguard, garde-boue, *m.*; *front* ~, (*motor*) aile d'assaut, *f.*; *rear* ~, (*motor*) aile d'arrière, *f.*
muezzin, muézin, *m.*
muff, manchon, *m.*; (*pers., pej.*) serin, *m.*
muffin, (*approx.*) galette, *f.*
muffle, *v.a.* envelopper; (*drum*) voiler; (*bell, sound*) assourdir.
muffler, cache-nez, *m.*
mufti, *s.* (*mil., nav.*) costume mufti, *m.*; *in* ~, en civil.
mug, *s.* (*drinking*) timbale, *f.*

muggy, (*close*) lourd.
mugwort, (*bot.*) armoise commune, *f.*
mulatto, mulâtre, -sse, *m.f.*
mulberry, (*fruit*) mûre, *f.*; **~-tree**, mûrier, *m.*
mulct, *v.a.* mettre* à l'amende.
mul|e, mulet, *m.*; mule, *f.*; **~teer**, muletier, *m.*; **~ish**, entêté comme un mulet.
mulled, (*wine, &c.*) chaud et épicé.
mullein, (*bot.*) molène, *f.*
mullet, (*ichth.*) muge, *m.*; *red~*, rouget, *m.*
mullion, (*arch.*) meneau, *m.*
multicoloured, multicolore.
multifarious, divers; **~ly**, (*approx.*) diversement.
multiform, multiforme.
multiple, multiple.
multiplication, multiplication, *f.*; *~table*, table de multiplication, *f.*
multiplicity, multiplicité, *f.*
multiple, *adj. and s.m.* multiple.
multiplier, (*electr., math.*) multiplicateur, *m.*
multiply, (*arith. and breed*) multiplier; *v.n.* se multiplier.
multitud|e, multitude, *f.*; **~inous**, de la multitude; (*swarming*) fourmillant.
mum, *s.* *~'s the word!* motus!; *adj. be ~*, se taire*.
mumble, *v.n.* marmotter.
mummer, baladin, *m.*; **~y**, mômerie, *f.*
mummy, momie, *f.*; (*mother*) maman, *f.*
mump, *v.n.* (*be sullen*) bouder.
mumps, (*med.*) oreillons, *m.pl.*
munch, *v.a.* mâcher.
mundane, du monde; (*of this world*) terrestre.
municipal, municipal; **~ity**, municipalité, *f.*
munificen|ce, munificence, *f.*; **~t**, munificent; **~tly**, avec munificence.
muniments, archives, *f.pl.*
munition, *v.a.* fournir de munitions; **~s**, *s.* munitions, *f.pl.*
mural, *adj.* de mur; (*plant, crown, paintings*) mural.
murder, meurtre, *m.*; **~er**, **~ess**, meurtri|er, ère, *m.f.*; **~ous**, meurtri|er, ~ère.
murder, *v.a.* assassiner; ⚠ meurtrir = '*to bruise*'; (*spoil, fig.*) massacrer; (*name, language, &c.*) estropier.
murk|y, sombre; **~iness**, obscurité, *f.*
murmur, *s.* (*lit. and fig.*) murmure, *m.*; *v.a.n.* (*lit. and complain*) murmurer.
murmuring, *adj.* murmurant.
murrain, épizootie, *f.*; *a ~ on you!* la peste soit de vous!
muscat, **muscatel**, (*grape and wine*) muscat, *m.*
musc|le, muscle, *m.*; **~ular**, (*of muscles*) musculaire; (*having good muscles*) musculeu|x, ~se.
Moscovite, *adj.* (*when an adj. use small letter*) *and s.m.f.* Moscovite.
muse, muse, *f.*; *v.n. ~ on*, méditer sur; (*dream*) rêver à.
musette, (*instr.*) musette, *f.*
museum, musée, *m.*
mushroom, champignon, *m.*; (*fig.*) parvenu, *m.*; *~-bed*, champignonnière, *f.*
music, musique, *f.*; **~-hall**, café concert, *m.*; **~-master, -mistress**, professeur de musique, *s.m.f.*; **~-paper**, papier à musique, *m.*; **~-stand**, pupitre à musique, *m.*; **~-stool**, tabouret, *m.*
musical, ⚠ musical *is only used of things, voices, parties, art, &c.: 'Fond of music', 'skilled in music'* = musicien, -ne; **~ly**, musicalement.
musician, musicien, -ne, *m.f.*
musing, *s.* rêverie, *f.*
musk, *s.* musc, *m.*; **~-deer**, musc, *m.*; **~-ox**, bœuf musqué, *m.*; **~-rat**, rat musqué, *m.*; **~-rose**, rose musquée, *f.*
musket, fusil, *m.*; (*old*) mousquet, *m.*; *within ~- shot*, à portée de fusil.
musketeer, fusilier, *m.*; (*hist.*) mousquetaire, *m.*
musketry, mousqueterie, *f.*; (*fire of ~*) fusillade, *f.*
muslin, mousseline, *f.*; *adj.* de mousseline.
musquash, (*fur*) castor du Canada, *m.*
mussel, (*moll.*) moule, *f.*
Mussulman, *adj.* (*when an adj. use small letter*) *and s.m.f.* Musulman, -e.
must, *s.* (*new wine*) moût, *m.*; (*mould*) moisissure, *f.*
must, *v. auxil.* (*necessity*) **1.** il faut* que + *subj. or* il faut *with inf. and dat. of pers.*; *I ~ answer*, il faut que je réponde; *I ~ have a new hat*, il me faut un chapeau neuf; **2.** (*moral obligation, be certain to be or do, conclusion drawn from facts*) devoir; *sinners ~ repent*, les pécheurs doivent se repentir; *I have not seen him, he ~ be ill, . . .* il doit être malade; *it ~ rain, look at the swallows*, il doit pleuvoir, regardez les hirondelles.
mustachio, moustache, *f.*
mustard, moutarde, *f.*; **~-gas**, gaz moutarde, *m.*; **~-pot**, moutardier, *m.*
mustang, (*zool.*) mustang, *m.*
muster, *s.* (*review, mil.*) revue, *f.*; (*gathering*) rassemblement, *m.*; *~-roll*, contrôle, *m.*; *pass ~*, passer.
muster, *v.a.* (*troops*) rassembler; *~ up*, (*fig.*) rassembler; *v.n.* s'assembler.
must|y, moisi; **~iness**, moisi, *m.*
mutab|le, muable; **~ility**, mutabilité, *f.*
mutation, changement, *m.*
mute, *s.* (*dumb person*) muet, -te, *m.f.*; (*funeral*) pleureur à gages, *m.*
mute, *adj.* (*dumb, speechless, gram.*) muet, -te; **~ness**, silence, *m.*; **~ly**, en silence.
mutila|te, mutiler; (*fig. of books, &c.*) tronquer; **~tion**, (*lit. and fig.*) mutilation, *f.*
mutin|eer, (*mil., nav.*) mutin, *m.*; **~ous**, séditieu|x, ~se.
mutiny, mutinerie, *f.*; *v.n.* se révolter.
mutter, *s.* murmure, *m.*

mutter, *v.a.n.* murmurer; (*grumblingly*) grommeler; ~ *between one's teeth,* mâchonner entre les dents; **~ingly,** en murmurant.
mutton, mouton, *m.*; *neck of* ~, collet de mouton, *m.*
mutual, (*lit. and comm.*) mutuel, -le; **~ity,** mutualité; **~ly,** mutuellement.
muzzle, *s.* (*animals*) museau, *m.*; (*to prevent biting*) muselière, *f.*; (*firearms*) gueule, *f.*; *v.a.* (*dog, &c., and fig.*) museler.
my, mon, *m.*, ma, *f.*, (mon + *fem. noun beginning with vowel or silent* H) mes, *pl.*; *with parts of body dat. of pron.* + *def. art., e.g. I have broken* ~ *arm,* je me suis cassé le bras.
myopi|a, (*med.*) myopie, *f.*; **~ic,** myope.
myriad, myriade, *f.*
myrmidon, myrmidon, *m.*
myrrh, myrrhe, *f.*
myrtle, (*bot.*) myrte, *m.*; **~-tree,** myrte, *m.*
myself, moi-même; (*with verb*) *use refl. verb and refl. pron.*; *I am not quite* ~, (*unwell*) je ne suis pas dans mon assiette; *to, by* ~, seul.
mysterious, mystérieu|x, ~se; **~ness,** caractère mystérieux; **~ly,** mystérieusement.
mystery, (*lit. and mystery play*) mystère, *m.*
mystic, *adj. and s.m.f.* mystique; **~ism,** mysticisme, *m.*
mystif|ication, mystification; **~y,** mystifier; (*perplex*) troubler.
myth, mythe, *m.*; **~ical,** mythique.
mytholog|ical, mythologique; **~ist,** mytholog|iste, ~ue, *m.f.*; **~y,** mythologie, *f.*

N

nab, *v.a.* (*lit. and fig.*) †happer.
nabob, nabab, *m.*
nacarat, *adj.* (*invar.*) *and s.m.* nacarat.
nadir, nadir, *m.*
nag, *s.* bidet, *m.*; *v.a.* gronder.
naiad, naïade, *f.*
nail, *s.* (*to hammer*) clou, *m.*; (*pers., an.*) ongle, *m.*; *on the* ~, (*pay*) recta; (*in comps.*) à ongles, *e.g.* brosse à ongles.
nail, *v.a.* clouer; (*cannon*) enclouer.
naïve, naï|f, ~ve; **~ty,** naïveté, *f.*; **~ly,** naïvement.
naked, (*lit. and fig.*) nu; (*tree, plain, &c.*) dénudé; (*light, &c.*) découvert; **~ness,** (*lit. and fig.*) nudité, *f.*; **~ly,** (*openly*) à nu; (*clearly*) clairement.
namby-pamby, doucereu|x, ~se.
name, *s.* (*pers., thing, family, &c., gram., reputation*) nom, *m.*; (*comm. of a firm*) raison sociale, *f.*; *call,* (*pers.*) ~*s,* injurier; *put one's* ~ *on, take one's* ~ *off,* s'inscrire*, se rayer; *by the* ~ *of,* sous le nom de; *What's your* ~*?* Comment vous appelez-vous? ; *know by* ~, connaître* de nom.
name, *v.a.* (*give name to, mention*) nommer; (*nominate*) désigner; *afore-*~*d,* susnommé.
nameless, (*obscure*) obscur; (*anonymous*) anonyme; (*abominable*) innommable.
namely, savoir.
namesake, homonyme, *m.f.*
nankeen, nankin, *m.*
nanny, *s.* nounou, *f.* (*pl,-s*).
nap, (*sleep*) somme, *m.*; (*of cloth*) poil, *m.*
nape, (*neck*) nuque, *f.*
napery, linge de table, *m.*; ⚠ napperie = '*linen-room*'.
naphtha, naphte, *m.*
napkin, serviette, *f.*; **~-ring,** rond de serviette, *m.*
napoleon, (*coin*) napoléon, *m.*
Napoleonic, napoléonien, -ne.
narcissus, (*bot.*) narcisse, *m.*
narcotic, *adj. and s.m.* narcotique.
nard, nard, *m.*
narghile, narguilé, *m.*
narra|te, raconter; **~tion,** narration, *f.*; **~tive,** *s.* récit, *m.*; **~tor,** narrat|eur, ~rice, *m.f.*
narrow, *s.* (*pass, channel, &c.*) goulet, *m.*
narrow, *adj.* (*lit., fig., mind*) étroit; (*searching*) minutieu|x, ~se; *~-brimmed,* à petits bords; ~ *gauge, see* GAUGE; **~ness,** étroitesse, *f.*; (*mind*) étroitesse d'esprit, *f.*; **~ly,** étroitement, minutieusement.
narrow, *v.a.* (*limit*) restreindre*; *v.n.* (*grow narrow*) se rétrécir.
narwhal, (*zool.*) narval, *m.*
nasal, *s.* (*letter*) nasale, *f.*; *adj.* nasal; **~ly,** d'un ton nasillard.
nascent, naissant.
nasturtium, (*bot.*) capucine, *f.*
nast|y, (*weather, filthy*) sale; (*indecent*) obscène; (*ill-natured, unpleasant to taste, smell*) désagréable; **~iness,** saleté, *f.*; (*obscenity*) obscénité, *f.*; **~ily,** (*temper*) de mauvaise humeur.
natal, natal; **~ity,** natalité, *f.*
natation, natation, *f.*
nation, nation, *f.*; **~al,** *adj. and s.m.* national (*pl.* -aux); **~alism,** nationalisme, *m.*; **~alist,** *adj. and s.m.f.* nationaliste; **~ally,** nationalement.
National-Socialist, *adj.* (*when an adj. use small letter*) *and s.m.f.* National-Socialiste; **National-Socialism,** national-socialisme, *m.*; *see also* NAZI.
nationality, nationalité, *f.*
nationaliz|e, nationaliser; **~ation,** nationalisation, *f.*
native, *s.* nati|f, ~ve, *m.f.*; (*primitive inhabitant*) indigène, *m.f.*
native, *adj.* (*innate, belonging by nature*) nati|f, ~ve; (*productions, troops, &c.*) indigène; (*language*) maternel, -le; (*country*) natal; (*primitive*) primiti|f, ~ve; ~ *to,* naturel, -le à.
nativity, (*eccles.*) nativité, *f.*
natty, pimpant.
natural, *s.* idiot, *m.*; *adj. and s.m.* (*mus.*) bécarre.

natural, *adj.* (*according to, and dealing with nature, normal, unaffected, of a portrait*) naturel, -le; **~ness**, naturel, *m.*; **~ly**, naturellement.
naturalis|m, naturalisme, *m.*; **~t**, naturaliste, *m.*
naturaliz|e, *v.a.* naturaliser; **~ation**, naturalisation, *m.*
nature, nature, *f.*; (*character*) caractère, *m.*; (*sort*) sorte, *f.*
naught, *s.* rien, *m.*; (*arith.*) zéro, *m.*; *set at ~*, (*defy*) braver.
naught|y, méchant; (*indecent*) mauvais; **~iness**, méchanceté, *f.*; **~ily**, par *or* avec méchanceté.
nause|a, nausée, *f.*; *v.a.* **~te**, (*lit. and fig.*) écœurer; **~ous**, nauséabond.
nautical, marin.
nautilus, (*zool.*) nautile, *m.*
naval, (*things*) naval; (*pers., officer, &c.*) de marine; ~ *basis*, base, port de guerre, *m.*
nave, (*church*) nef, *f.*; (*wheel*) moyeu, *m.*
navel, nombril, *m.*
navigab|le, navigable; **~ility**, navigabilité, *f.*
naviga|te, *v.a.* (*sea*) naviguer sur; (*ship*) gouverner; *v.n.* naviguer; **~tion**, navigation, *f.*; **~tion lights**, (*aeron.*) feux, *m.pl.*; **~tor**, (*sea*) navigateur, *m.*
navvy, terrassier, *m.*
navy, marine, *f.*; *merchant ~*, marine marchande, *f.*; ~ *blue*, bleu marine, *invar.*
nay, *adv.* (*neg.*) non; (*strong affirm.*) bien plus.
Nazar|ene, **~ite**, *adj.* (*when an adj. use small letter*) *and s.m.f.* Nazaréen, -ne.
Nazi *adj.* (*when an adj. use small letter*) *and s.m.f.* Nazi, ~e; **~(i)sm**, Nazisme, *m.*
N.B., (*nota bene*) N.B.
neap, *adj.* de morte-eau; **~-tide**, morte-eau, *f.*
Neapolitan, *adj.* (*when an adj. use small letter*) *and s.m.f.* Napolitain, -e.
near, *adj.* (*time*) prochain; (*place and relation*) proche; (*direct*) direct; (*stingy*) mesquin; ~ *side*, (*of horse*) côté du montoir, *m.*; *~-sighted*, myope; **~ness**, proximité, *f.*; (*stinginess*) mesquinerie, *f.*
near, *adv.* (*time and place*) près; (*close*) de près; (*almost*) presque; *quite ~*, tout près.; *prep.* (*time and place*) près de; (*close to of position or place*) auprès de; ~ *to, upon*, près de.
near, *v.a.* s'approcher de.
nearly, de près; (*almost*) presque.
neat, *s.* *~'s foot*, pied de bœuf, *m.*; *~'s tongue*, langue de bœuf, *f.*
neat, *adj.* (*pers.*) propre; (*language, &c.*) concis; (*dexterous*) adroit; (*nicely made*) bien exécuté; (*liquor*) pur; **~ness**, (*dress*) propreté, *f.*; (*skill*) adresse, *f.*; (*language*) concision, *f.*; **~ly**, proprement, adroitement.
nebul|ous, nébuleu|x, ~se; **~osity**, nébulosité, *f.*
necessar|y, *s. provide, &c., the ~*, (*fam.*) trouver, etc., le nécessaire; **~ies**, nécessaire, *m.*
necessar|y, *adj.* nécessaire; *if ~*, le cas échéant; *it is ~ to, that*, il faut + *inf. or* que + *subj.*; **~ily**, nécessairement.
necessitate, nécessiter.
necessit|y, (*compulsion, thing necessary*) nécessité, *f.*; (*want*) besoin, *m.*; *under the ~ of*, dans la nécessité de; **~ous**, nécessiteu|x, ~se.
neck, cou, *m.*; (*bottle*) goulot, *m.*; (*pass*) col, *m.*; (*mutton*) collet, *m.*; (*violin*) manche, *m.*; **~tie**, cravate, *f.*; *stiff ~*, torticolis, *m.*; *stiff-~ed*, obstiné; *break one's ~*, se rompre le cou.
neckcloth, **neckerchief**, foulard, *m.*
neck|lace, collier, *m.*; **~let**, tour de cou, *m.*
necrology, nécrologie, *f.*
necromanc|er, nécromancien, -ne, *m.f.*; **~y**, nécromancie, *f.*
necropolis, nécropole, *f.*
nectar, nectar, *m.*
nectarine, brugnon, *m.*
need, *s.* (*need and thing needed*) besoin, *m.*; *if ~ be, in case of ~*, au besoin; *stand in ~ of*, avoir besoin de.
need, *v.a.* avoir besoin de, *sometimes* il faut + *dat. of pers*; (*require*) demander.
needful, nécessaire (à *or* pour).
needle, (*sewing, obelisk*) aiguille, *f.*; **~-gun**, fusil à aiguille, *m.*; **~ful**, aiguillée, *f.*
needless, inutile; **~ness**, inutilité, *f.*; **~ly**, inutilement.
needlework, couture, *f.*
need|y, nécessiteu|x, ~se; **~iness**, besoin, *m.*
nefarious, *adj.* scélérat; **~ly**, d'une façon scélérate.
negation, négation, *f.*
negative, *s.* négative, *f.*; (*gram.*) négation, *f.*; (*photo*) cliché, *m.*; *in the ~*, négativement.
negative, *adj.* négati|f, ~ve; **~ly**, négativement.
neglect, *s.* négligence, *f.*; (*forgetfulness*) oubli, *m.*; (*forlornness*) abandon, *m.*
neglect, *v.a.* (*slight, leave uncared for, omit to*) négliger (de).
neglectful, négligent; **~ly**, négligemment.
negligen|ce, négligence, *f.*; **~t**, négligent; **~tly**, négligemment.
negligible, négligeable.
negotia|te, *v.a.* (*comm., loan, bill, sale*) négocier; (*bargain*) traiter; ⚠ négocier *is not used of a fence, obstacle, &c., which* = franchir; **~tion**, négociation, *f.*; **~tor**, négociat|eur, ~rice, *m.f.*
negr|o, **~ess**, *s.* nègre, négresse, *m.f.*; *adj.* nègre.
negroid, négroïde.
Negus, (*Abyssinia*) Négus, *m.*
neigh, *s.* hennissement, *m.*; *v.n.* hennir.
neighbour, voisin, -e, *m.f.*; (*fellow creature*) prochain, *m.*; *next-door ~*, proche voisin, -e, *m.f.*

neighbourhood, (*lit., fig., nearness, neighbours*) voisinage, *m.*
neighbouring, *adj.* avoisinant.
neighbourl|iness, bon voisinage, *m.*; **~y,** de bon voisin.
neither, *pron. and adj.* ni l'un ni l'autre (*pl. verb unless action can only be attributed to one of the two*).
neither, *adv.* non plus; (*and also*) aussi + *neg. verb and inversion.*
neither, *conj.* ni; *neither . . . nor,* **ni . . . ni** (*pl.* + *neg. verb*).
neolithic, néolithique.
neologism, néologisme, *m.*
neophyte, néophyte, *m.*
nephew, neveu, *m.*
nepotism, népotisme, *m.*
nereid, néréide, *f.*
nerve, (*vigour, coolness, sinew, tendon*) nerf, *m.*; *that gets on my ~s,* cela me porte sur les nerfs; *v.a.* donner du nerf à.
nerveless, sans vigueur; (*style*) mou, (mol + *vowel or silent* H) molle.
nervous, (*lit., fig., style, med.*) nerveu|x, ~se; (*timid*) intimidé; ~ *breakdown,* prostration, *f.*; **~ness,** nervosité, *f.*; (*timidity*) timidité, *f.*; **~ly,** timidement.
nest, *s.* nid, *m.*; (*brood*) nichée, *f.*; (*of thieves*) repaire, *m.*; ~ *of tables,* table gigogne, *f.*; **~-egg,** nichet, *m.*; (*money*) petit magot, *m.*
nest, *v.n.* nicher.
nestle, *v.a.* nicher; *v.n.* se nicher (contre).
nestling, petit oiseau, *m.*
net, filet, *m.*; (*snare*) piège, *m.*; (*fabric*) tulle, *m.*; *v.a.* prendre* avec un filet.
net, *adj.* (*comm.*) net, -te.
nether, inférieur; **nethermost,** (le) plus bas.
nettle, ortie, *f.*; **~-rash,** urticaire, *f.*; *v.a.* irriter.
network, (*rail, &c.*) réseau, *m.*
neuralgia, névralgie, *f.*
neurasthenia, neurasthénie, *f.*
neuritis, névrite, *f.*
neurology, névrologie, *f.*
neuro|sis, névrose, *f.*; **~tic,** névrosé.
neuter, (*gram.*) *adj. and s.m.* neutre.
neutral, (*of neither side, vague, colour, in war, &c.*) *adj. and s.m.f.* neutre; **~ity,** neutralité, *f.*; **~ize,** neutraliser.
never, jamais; *with verb* **ne . . . jamais.**
nevermore, jamais plus.
nevertheless, néanmoins.
new, (*not worn, not used*) neuf, neuve; (*hitherto unknown, novel, fresh, changed, coming later*) nouv|eau, (nouvel + *vowel or mute* H) ~elle; (*bread, milk*) frais, fraîche; (*wine*) jeune; ~ *boy,* (*school*) nouveau, *m.*; *~-comer, see* COMER; ~ *to,* nouveau pour; **~-ness,** nouveauté, *f.*; **~ly,** nouvellement; **~ Year,** Nouvel An, *m.*; ~ *Year's Day,* Jour de l'an, *m.*
news, nouvelle, *f., often plural*; *~-agent,* marchand de journaux, *m.*; *~-stall,* kiosque, *m.*
newsmonger, colporteur de nouvelles, *m.*
newspaper, journal, *m.*
next, *adj.* (*place*) le plus proche; (*streets, houses, &c.*) d'à côté; (*time*) prochain; (*following*) suivant; ~ *day, see* DAY; ~ *door, s.* maison voisine, *f.*; *~-door, adj.* voisin; ~ *door to,* à côté de.
next, *adv.* (*after that*) ensuite; (*next time*) la prochaine fois; *prep.* ~ *to,* à côté de; (*almost*) presque.
nib, (*pen*) bec, *m.*; *gold-~bed,* à bec d'or.
nibble, grignoter.
nice, 1. (*agreeable*) agréable; 2. (*kind*) gentil, -le; 3. (*scrupulous*) scrupuleu|x, ~se; 4. (*particular*) difficile; 5. (*taste*) bon, -ne; 6. (*sensitive, dainty*) délicat; 7. (*point, distinction*) subtil; 8. (*good-class*) très bien; **~-looking,** joli; **~ness,** (*taste*) goût agréable, *m.*; (*exactitude*) exactitude, *f.*; **~ly,** bien, avec délicatesse; (*exactly*) exactement; *~ fellow, see* FELLOW.
nicety, (*precision*) précision, *f.*; (*subtlety*) subtilité, *f.*
niche, niche, *f.*
nick, *s.* cran, *m.*; *v.a.* encocher; *in the ~ of time,* à point nommé.
nickel, nickel, *m.*; (*U.S.A.*) pièce de cinq cents, *f.*; *~-plated,* nickelé.
nickname, sobriquet, *m.*
nicotine, nicotine, *f.*
niece, nièce, *f.*
niello, nielle, *m.*
niggardly, mesquin.
nigger, nègre, *m.*; ~ **woman,** négresse; *~-brown,* tête de nègre, *invar.*
niggling, *adj.* trop raffiné.
nigh, *adj., adv., prep., see* NEAR.
night, (*lit., fig., obscurity*) nuit, *f.*; (*evening*) soir, *m.*; *by ~,* de nuit; *at, in the ~,* la nuit; *good ~!* bon soir!; (*before retiring*) bonne nuit!; *sleepless ~,* nuit blanche, *f.*; *to-night,* ce soir; *to-morrow ~,* demain soir; *be ~,* faire* nuit; *10 o'clock at ~,* dix heures du soir; **~-cap,** bonnet de nuit, *m.*; **~-damp,** (*dew*) serein, *m.*; **~-light,** veilleuse, *f.*; **~-gown, -shirt,** chemise de nuit, *f.*; **~-stool,** chaise percée, *f.*; *adj.* de nuit.
nightfall, tombée de la nuit, *f.*
night-gown, chemise de nuit, *f.*
nightingale, rossignol, *m.*
nightjar, (*ornith.*) engoulevent, *m.*
nightly, (*occuring at night*) nocturne; (*every night*) qui arrive chaque nuit; *adv.* chaque nuit.
nightmare, cauchemar, *m.*
nightshade, (*bot.*) morelle, *f.*; *deadly ~,* belladone, *f.*
nihilis|m, nihilisme, *m.*; **~t,** nihiliste, *m.*
nil, rien, *m.*; *adj.* (*comm.*) nul, -le.
nimbl|e, agile; (*mind*) vif, vive; **~eness,** agilité, *f.*; **~y,** prestement.
nimbus, (*halo, aureole*) nimbe, *m.*
nincompoop, niais, *m.*
nin|e, *adj. and s.m.* neuf; **~th,** neuvième; (*date and sovereigns*) neuf; **~thly,** neuvièmement.
ninefold, *adj. and adv.* neuf fois.

ninepins, quilles, *f.pl.*
nineteen, dix-neuf; **~th**, dix-neuvième; (*date*) dix-neuf.
ninet|y, quatre-vingt-dix; **~y-one**, quatre-vingt-onze; **~y-two**, quatre-vingt-douze, etc.; **~ieth**, quatre-vingt-dixième.
nip, *s.* coup d'ongle, *m.*; (*spirits*) goutte, *f.*
nip, *v.a.* (*cold, pinch*) pincer.
nipper, (*boy*) gamin, *m.*; **~s**, (*tool*) pinces, *f.pl.*
nipping, (*wind, &c.*) piquant.
nipple, (*anat.*) mamelon, *m.*
nitr|ate, nitrate, *m.*; **~e**, nitre, *m.*; **~ic**, nitrique.
nitrogen, azote, *m.*
no, *adj.* ne . . . aucun, -e, ne . . . pas de, *e.g.* il n'a fait aucunes dispositions; *sometimes* ne . . . pas *only*, *e.g. X is ~ poet*, X n'est pas poète; *~ wonder*, ce n'est pas étonnant; *be of ~ use*, ne servir* à rien; *in ~ way*, ne . . . aucunement.
no, *adv.* non.
nobility, noblesse, *f.*
noble, nobleman, *s.* gentilhomme (*pl.* gentilshommes).
nobl|e, *adj.* (*lit. and fig.*) noble; (*buildings, &c.*) imposant; **~eness**, noblesse, *f.*; **~y**, noblement.
nobody, no one, *nom.* personne ne + *verb*; *acc.* ne + *verb* + personne; *a ~*, un homme de rien.
nocturnal, nocturne.
nocturne, (*mus. and paint.*) nocturne, *m.*
nod, *s.* signe de tête, *m.*; (*salutation*) inclination de tête, *f.*
nod, *v.n.* (*with sleep*) s'assoupir; (*salute*) incliner la tête (à); *~ assent*, faire* un signe d'assentiment.
nodule, nodule, *m.*
noise, *s.* (*lit. and fig.*) bruit, *m.*; (*uproar*) tapage, *m.*; *v.a. ~ abroad*, ébruiter.
noiseless, sans bruit; **~ly**, sans bruit.
noisome, (*harmful*) nuisible; (*smell*) infect; **~ness**, (*stench*) infection, *f.*
nois|y, bruyant; (*pers.*) tapageu|r, ~se; **~iness**, bruit, *m.*; **~ily**, bruyamment.
nomad, *adj. and s.m.f.* nomade; **~ic**, nomade.
nomenclature, nomenclature, *f.*
nominal, (*not real, comm., consisting of names*) nominal; **~ly**, nominalement.
nomina|te, *v.a.* (*appoint*) nommer; ⚠ nommer *does not* = '*propose for election*' *which* = désigner; **~tion**, (*proposal of name*) désignation, *f.*; (*appointment*) nomination, *f.*
non-appearance, absence, *f.*
non-attendance, (*law*) défaut, *m.*
non-combattant, *adj. and s.m.* non-combattant.
non-commissioned officer, sous-officier, *m.*
non-conducting, *adj.* non-conducteu|r, ~se.
nonconformist, *adj. and s.m.f.* non-conformiste.
non-delivery, non-livraison, *f.*
nondescript, indéfinissable.
none, *pron.* ne . . . aucun, -e, *e.g.* je ne connais aucun de vos frères; (*nobody*) *nom.* personne ne + *verb*; *acc.* ne + *verb* + personne; (*acc. of things with verb*) n'en . . . pas, *e.g. I have ~*, je n'en ai pas.
none, (*eccles.*) none, *f.*; **~s**, (*Rom. ant.*) nones, *f.pl.*
nonentity, (*pers.*) zéro, *m.*
non-intervention, non-intervention, *f.*
non-negotiable, non-négociable.
non-existent, inexistant.
non-payment, non-paiement, *m.*
non-performance, inexécution, *f.*
nonplussed, *be ~*, être réduit à quia.
non-resident, non-résident, *m.*
non-resistance, non-résistance, *f.*
nonsens|e, (*absurdity*) non-sens, *m.*; (*foolery*) bêtise, *f.*; **~ical**, absurde; **~ically**, absurdement.
non-skid, *adj. and s.m.* (*aeron.*) anti-dérapant.
non-stop, *adj.* (*rail.*) direct.
nonsuch, (*bot.*) lupuline, *f.*
noodle, niais, -e, *m.f.*
nook, coin, *m.*; (*hidden corner*) recoin, *m.*
noon, noontide, midi, *m.*; *adj.* de midi.
noonday, plein midi, *m.*; *adj.* de plein midi.
noose, nœud coulant, *m.*; (*snare*) lacs, *m.pl.*
nopal, (*bot.*) nopal, *m.*
nor, ni; (*and . . . not*) et ne . . . pas, non plus, *e.g. he does not work, ~ does he play*, il ne travaille pas et ne joue non plus; *he does not read ~ write*, il ne lit pas et il n'écrit non plus; *~ yet*, ni même.
normal, normal; **~ly**, normalement.
Norman, *adj.* (*when an adj. use small letter*) *and s.m.f.* Normand, -e.; *adj.* (*arch. approx.*) roman.
north, *s.* nord, *m.*; *adj.* du nord; *~* **pole**, pôle nord, *m.*; **~-east**, *adj. and s.m.* nord-est, *m.*; **~-west**, *adj. and s.m.* nord-ouest; **~erly**, du nord; **~ern**, du nord; **~ern lights**, aurore boréale, *f.*; *adv.* (*place*) au nord; (*direction*) vers le nord.
northward, *adj.* vers le nord.
Norwegian, *adj.* (*when an adj. use small letter*) *and s.m.f.* Norvégien, -ne.
nor'wester, norois, *m.*
nose, (*anat., smell, scent, ship*) nez, *m.*; (*certain ans.*) museau, *m.*; (*end*) bout, *m.*; **~-bag**, (*horses*) musette, *f.*; **~-dive**, *v.a.* (*aeron.*) piquer du nez; *Roman ~*, *see* ROMAN; *turn up one's ~ at*, faire* fi de; *v.a. and ~ out*, (*lit. and fig.*) flairer; *blow one's ~*, se moucher.
nosegay, bouquet, *m.*
nostalgi|a, nostalgie, *f.*; **~c**, nostalgique.
nostril, narine, *f.*; (*an.*) naseau, *m.*
nostrum, panacée, *f.*
not, (*with finite verb*) ne . . . pas, (*stronger*) ne . . . point; (+ *inf.*) ne pas; (+ *adv.*) pas, *exc.* seulement = non seulement; (+ *other single word*) non *or* non pas;

c'est une plume et non (*or* non pas) un crayon; ~ *that,* non pas que + *subj.*; *why* ~, pourquoi pas.

notab|le, *adj. and s.m.* notable; **~ility,** notabilité, *f.*; **~ly,** (*considerably*) notablement.

notary, notaire, *m.*

notation, notation, *f.*

notch, entaille, *f.*; (*tool, knife*) brèche, *f.*; *v.a.* entailler; (*tools, &c.*) ébrécher.

note, *s.* (*for memory, music, outlines, annotation*) note, *f.*; ⚠ note *never* = '*letter*'; (*characteristic, distinction*) marque, *f.*; (*attention*) remarque, *f.*; (*letter, note of hand*) billet, *m.*; (*tone, touch*) ton, *m.*; **~-book,** carnet, *m.*; **~-case,** portefeuille, *m.*; **~-paper,** papier à lettres, *m.*; ~ *of exclamation,* point d'exclamation, *m.*; ~ *of hand,* billet à ordre, *m.*; ~ *of interrogation,* point d'interrogation, *m.*; *v.a.* noter; (*observe*) remarquer; ~ *down,* prendre* note de.

noted, (*pers.*) distingué.

noteworthy, digne de remarque.

nothing, *pron. nom.* rien ne + *verb*; *acc.* ne + *verb* + rien; *stand at* ~, n'hésiter devant rien; *think* ~ *of,* considérer comme naturel.

nothingness, néant, *m.*

notice, *s.* (*warning, placard*) avis, *m.*; (*to leave*) congé, *m.*; (*knowledge*) connaissance, *f.*; (*heed, attention*) attention, *f.*; (*in papers*) notice, *f.*; (*notification*) notification, *f.*; (*forewarning*) préavis, *m.*; *~-board,* écriteau, *m.*; (*for advertisements*) porte-affiches, *m. invar.*; *at short* ~, à bref délai; *give* ~, (*to quit*) donner congé; (*advise*) prévenir*; *take* ~ *of,* faire* attention à.

notice, *v.a.* (*observe*) remarquer; (*pers.*) avoir des égards pour.

noticeab|le, remarquable; **~ly,** remarquablement.

notification, notification, *f.*

notify, avertir; (*legal, &c.*) notifier.

notion, idée, *f.*; **~s,** (*U.S.A.*) menus objets bon marché, *m.pl.*; **~al,** spéculati|f, ~ve.

notori|ety, notoriété, *f.*; **~ous,** notoire; (*pej.*) mal famé; **~ously,** notoirement.

notwithstanding, *prep.* malgré; *adv.* tout de même; *conj.* ~ *that,* quoique + *subj.*

nought, *see* NAUGHT.

noun, nom, *m.*

nourish, *v.a.* (*lit. and fig.*) nourrir; **~ment,** nourriture, *f.*; **~ing,** nourrissant.

novel, *s.* roman, *m.*; ⚠ *not* nouvelle *which* = '*short story*'; **~ist,** romancier, *m.*

novel, *adj.* nouveau, (nouvel + *vowel or mute H*) nouvelle; **~ty,** nouveauté, *f.*

November, novembre, *m.*; (*abbrev.*) 9bre.

novice, novice, *m.f.*

noviciate, noviciat, *m.*

now, maintenant; (*for* '*then*' *in narrative*) alors; *now . . . now,* tantôt . . . tantôt; ~ *and then,* de temps en temps; ~ *then! interj.* eh bien!; *conj.* or; ~ *that,* maintenant que + *indic.*; *till* ~, jusqu'à présent.

nowadays, de nos jours.

nowhere, ne + *verb* + nulle part.

nowise, *in no wise,* ne + *verb* + aucunement.

noxious, nuisible.

nozzle, bec, *m.*

nucleus, (*lit. and fig.*) noyau, *m.*

nud|e, nu, *invar. only before noun + hyphen*; **~ity,** nudité, *f.*

nudge, *s.* coup de coude, *m.*; *v.a.* pousser du coude.

nugatory, (*futile*) futile; (*inoperative*) inefficace.

nuisance, (*pers.*) peste, *f.*; (*disagreeable thing*) ennui, *m.*; (*in law*) dommage, *m.*; *commit no* ~, défense de déposer des ordures.

null, nul, -le; ~ *and void,* nul et non avenu; **~ify,** annuler; **~ity,** nullité, *f.*; *~ifying clause,* empêchement dirimant, *m.*

numb, *adj.* engourdi; *v.a.* engourdir; *grow* ~, s'engourdir.

number, *s.* (*street, motor, ticket, publication, &c.*) numéro, *m.* (*abbrev.* N°); (*many, quantity, gram., rhythm*) nombre, *m.*; **~s,** (*verse*) vers, *m.pl.*; ~ *engaged!* (*teleph.*) pas libre!; *what* ~? (*teleph.*) Qui demandez-vous?

number, *v.a.* compter.

numberless, innombrable.

numbness, engourdissement, *m.*

numeral, *s.* chiffre, *m.*; *adj.* numéral.

numeration, numération, *f.*

numerical, numérique; **~ly,** numériquement.

numerous, (*comprising many units, coming from many, rhythmic*) nombreu|x, ~se.

numism|atic, numismatique; **~atics,** numismatique, *f.*; **~atist,** numismate, *m.*

numbskull, benêt, *m.*

nun, religieuse, *f.*; **~nery,** couvent de religieuses, *m.*

nuncio, nonce, *m.*

nuptial, *adj.* nuptial; **~s,** noces, *f.pl.*

nurse, (*wet-*) nourrice, *f.*; (*children's*) bonne d'enfant, *f.*; (*hospital*) infirmi|er. ~ère, *m.f.*; **~-maid,** bonne d'enfant, *f.*

nurs|e, *v.a.* (*suckle*) allaiter; (*the sick*) soigner; (*coddle*) choyer; (*fig., a business, hope, plants, &c.*) nourrir; *v.n.* être gardemalade; *~ing-home,* clinique, *f.*

nursery, (*children*) chambre d'enfants, *f.*; (*plants, and fig.*) pépinière, *f.*

nurseryman, pépiniériste, *m.*

nursling, (*lit. and fig.*) nourrisson, *m.*

nurture, *s.* (*nourishment*) nourriture, *f.*; (*education*) éducation, *f.*; *v.a.* (*food*) nourrir; (*educate*) élever.

nut, noisette *f.*; (*machines*) écrou, *m.*; **~-cracker,** (*ornith.*) casse-noix, *m.*

invar.; **~-crackers,** casse-noisettes, *m. invar.*; *Brazil-~*, noix du Brésil, *f.*; *screw-~*, écrou, *m.*
nuthatch, (*ornith.*) sittelle, *f.*
nutmeg, muscade, *f.*
nutriment, nourriture, *f.*
nutrit|ion, nutrition, *f.*; **~ious, ~ive,** nutriti|f, ~ve.
nutshell, coquille de noix, *f.*; *the whole in a ~*, en deux mots comme en cent.
nymph, nymphe, *f.*

O

O, *interj.* (+ *voc.*) ô; (+ *note of exclam.*) oh!
oaf, (*lout*) lourdaud, *m.*
oak, (*wood, tree*) chêne, *m.*; **~-apple,** galle de chêne, *f.*; *adj. and* **~en,** de chêne; **~-plantation,** chênaie, *f.*
oakum, étoupe, *f.*
oar, rame, *f.*; (*naut.*) aviron, *m.*; *v.a.* pousser en ramant.
oarsman, rameur, *m.*
oasis, oasis, *f.*
oat, oats, avoine, *f.*; *wild ~s*, folle avoine, *f.*; *sow one's wild ~s*, jeter sa gourme.
oath, serment, *m.*; (*curse*) juron, *m.*; *take one's ~*, prêter serment.
oatmeal, farine d'avoine, *f.*
obdura|cy, endurcissement, *m.*; **~te,** endurci; **~tely,** obstinément.
obedien|ce, obéissance, *f.*; **~t,** obéissant; **~tly,** docilement; *yours ~tly,* votre humble serviteur.
obeisance, (*bow, &c.*) révérence, *f.*; ⚠ *not* obéissance, *see above.*
obelisk, obélisque, *m.*
obes|e, obèse; **~ity,** obésité, *f.*
obey, *v.a.* (*lit. and fig.*) obéir à; *v.n.* obéir.
obfuscate, *v.a.* (*darken mind*) assombrir; (*bewilder*) ahurir.
obituary, *s.* (*notice*) nécrologie, *f.*; *adj.* nécrologique.
object, objet, *m.*; (*aim*) but, *m.*; (*gram.*) régime, *m.*; (*fam., pers., fright*) horreur, *f.*
object, *v.a.* (*put forward as objection*) objecter; *~ that,* objecter que; *~ against,* reprocher à; *v.n.* (*object to*) s'opposer (à).
objection, objection, *f.*; *have no ~ to,* ne pas s'opposer à.
objectionable, (*open to objection*) inadmissible; (*offensive*) répréhensible.
objective, *s.* (*mil., point aimed at, telescope, photo.*) objectif, *m.*; *~ case,* (*gram.*) régime direct, *m.*
objective, *adj.* (*gram., style, &c.*) objecti|f, ~ve; **~ly,** objectivement.
objectivity, objectivité, *f.*
objectless, sans but.
objector, personne qui fait une (des) objection(s), *f.*
objurgation, vif reproche, *m.*
oblation, (*eccles.*) oblation, *f.*
obligation, obligation, *f.*; *be under an ~ to,* avoir des obligations à.
obligatory, obligatoire.
oblige, (*compel, do favour*) obliger (à *and* de + *inf.*).
obliging, serviable; **~ness,** obligeance, *f.*; **~ly,** obligeamment.
oblique, (*lit. and gram.*) oblique; (*fig.*) indirect; **~ly,** obliquement.
oblitera|te, effacer; (*gradually*) oblitérer; **~tion,** rature, *f.*; (*gradual*) oblitération, *f.*
obliv|ion, oubli, *m.*; **~ious,** oublieu|x, ~se (de).
oblong, oblong, -ue.
obloquy, (*approx.*) dénigrement, *m.*
obnoxious, (*offensive*) odieu|x, ~se (à); (*disliked*) mal vu (de); **~ness,** odieux, *m.*
oboe, †hautbois, *m.*
obscen|e, obscène; **~ely,** d'une manière obscène; ⚠ '*obscene*' = '*repulsive*' = répugnant *and not* obscène *which always implies indecency*; **~ity,** obscénité, *f.*
obscur|e, (*lit. and fig.*) obscur; **~ity,** obscurité, *f.*; **~ely,** obscurément; *v.a.* obscurcir.
obsecration, obsécration, *f.*
obsequies, obsèques, *f.pl.*
obsequious, obséquieu|x, ~se; **~ness,** obséquiosité, *f.*; **~ly,** obséquieusement.
observabl|e, visible; (*noticeable*) remarquable; **~y,** d'une manière sensible.
observance, (*keeping law, &c.*) observance, *f.*; (*eccles.*) rite, *m.*
observant, observat|eur, ~rice.
observation, (*noticing, mil., remark*) observation, *f.*
observatory, observatoire, *m.*
observe, (*law, method, silence, perceive, celebrate*) observer; (*remark*) dire*; *v.n.* observer.
observer, observat|eur, ~rice, *m.f.*
obsess, obséder; **~ion,** obsession, *f.*
obsolete, vieux, (vieil + *vowel or mute* H) vieille; *become, grow ~*, tomber (être) en désuétude.
obstacle, obstacle, *m.*
obstin|acy, obstination, *f.*; (*in fight, resistance*) acharnement, *m.*; **~ate,** obstiné; (*desperate*) acharné; **~ately,** obstinément.
obstreperous, (*noisy*) bruyant; (*unruly*) indiscipliné; **~ness,** turbulence; **~ly,** bruyamment.
obstruct, (*block up*) obstruer; (*vision*) intercepter; (*retard*) retarder.
obstruct|ion, obstacle, *m.*; (*polit., med.*) obstruction, *f.*; **~ionist,** obstructionniste, *m.f.*; **~ive,** (*approx.*) qui empêche.
obtain, *v.a.* obtenir*; *v.n.* être en vogue.
obtainable, qu'on peut obtenir.
obtrude, imposer (à + *pers.*); *v.n.* s'imposer.
obtrus|ion, importunité, *f.*; **~ive,** importun; **~ively,** avec importunité.
obtuse, *adj.* (*angle*) obtus; (*blunt*) émoussé; (*slow-witted*) d'esprit obtus; **~ness,** stupidité, *f.*; **~ly,** avec stupidité.
obverse, *s.* (*coin*) obvers, *m.*; (*counterpart*) contre-partie, *f.*

obviate, (*inconvenience*) obvier à; (*danger, &c.*) prévenir*.
obvious, évident; **~ness,** clarté, *f.*; **~ly,** évidemment.
occasion, *s.* (*favourable moment, cause, ground*) occasion, *f.*; (*need*) besoin, *m.*; (*reason for*) lieu, *m.* de; *on special ~s,* dans les grandes occasions; *rise to the ~,* être à la †hauteur des circonstances.
occasion, *v.a.* occasionner.
occasional, *adj.* de temps en temps; (*of a cause*) occasionnel, -le; (*casual*) fortuit; **~ly,** de temps en temps.
Occident, Occident, *m.*; **~ al,** occidental.
occult, occulte; **~ism,** occultisme, *m.*
occupan|cy, (*tenant*) occupation, *f.*; **~t,** (*tenant*) locataire, *m.*; (*holder in possession*) possesseur, *m.*
occupation, (*gen. and mil.*) occupation, *f.*; (*calling*) métier, *m.*
occupier, (*house, &c.*) locataire, *m.*
occupy, (*territory, site, time, position, house, &c.*) occuper; *~ oneself with,* s'occuper de.
occur, (*happen*) arriver (être); (*be found*) se trouver; *it ~red to me that,* il m'est venu à l'idée que.
occurrence, occurrence, *f.*
ocean, (*lit. and fig.*) océan, *m.*; **~-going steamer,** long-courrier, *m.*; **~ic,** océanique.
ochre, ocre, *f.*
octagon, octogone, *m.*; **~al,** octogonal.
octangular, octogone.
octave, (*mus., eccles.*) octave, *f.*
octavo, in-octavo, *m.*
October, octobre, *m.*; (*abbrev.*) 8bre.
octogenarian, *adj. and s.m.f.* octogénaire.
ocular, *adj.* oculaire.
oculist, oculiste, *m.*
odalisque, odalisque, *f.*
odd, (*not even*) impair; (*left over*) de surplus; (*unmatched*) dépareillé; (*of pairs*) déparié; (*strange*) bizarre; *~ job,* bricole, *f.*; *~ money,* appoint, *m.*; *at ~ times,* à ses moments perdus; *£60 ~,* soixante et quelques livres; *10 francs ~,* 10 francs et quelque chose; **~ness,** bizarrerie, *f.*; **~ly,** étrangement.
oddity, bizarrerie, *f.*; (*pers.*) original, -e, *m.f.*
oddments, bribes, *f.pl.*
odds, (*balance of advantage*) avantage, *m.*; (*difference*) différence, *f.*; *it is ~ that, but,* il est probable que; *be at ~ with,* être en querelle avec; *lay ~ of 3 to 1,* parier trois contre un; *the ~ are that,* il y a gros à parier que.
ode, ode, *f.*
odious, odieu|x, **~se** (à); **~ly,** odieusement.
odium, odieux, *m.*
odoriferous, (*sweet smell*) odorant.
odour, (*lit. and fig.*) odeur, *f.*; *in the ~ of sanctity,* en odeur de sainteté.
of, de; *~ a + noun,* de, *e.g. that rascal of a gardener,* ce coquin de jardinier.

off, *adv.* (*place*) à . . . de distance, *e.g. 2 miles ~,* à 2 milles de distance; (*cancelled*) rompu; *on and ~,* de temps à autre; *~ side,* (*sport*) †hors jeu; *straight ~,* incontinent; *be well ~,* être à l'aise; *off with you!* allez-vous-en!
off, *prep.* (*dine ~*) de; (*naut.*) à la †hauteur de; (*turning out of*) donnant dans.
offal, (*of an.*) abats, *m.pl.*
offence, (*the offensive*) offensive, *f.*; (*wound to feelings*) offense, *f.*; (*transgression*) délit, *m.*; *second ~,* récidive, *f.*; *take ~,* s'offenser (de).
offend, *v.a.* offenser; *v.n.* offenser; (*sin*) pécher; *against,* (*law*) enfreindre*.
offender, (*he who offends*) offenseur, *m.*; ⚠ offenseur *does not = 'evil-doer' which =* délinquant, -e, *m.f.*
offensive, *s.* offensive, *f.*
offensive, *adj.* (*aggressive*) offensi|f, **~ve**; (*insulting*) offensant; **~ness,** nature offensante; **~ly,** d'une manière offensante.
offer, *s.* offre, *f.*; (*of marriage*) demande en mariage, *f.*; *tempting ~,* offres séduisantes, *f.pl.*
offer, *v.a.* (*present, hold out, proffer, resistance, view, &c.*) offrir*; (*set forth*) émettre*; (*apology, &c.*) faire*; (*opposition*) mettre*; *~ up,* offrir*; *v.n.* (*occur*) s'offrir*; (*presents itself*) se présenter; *~ to,* offrir* de.
offering, (*to God, to charity*) offrande, *f.*; *burnt ~,* holocauste, *m.*
offertory, quête, *f.*; (*mass*) offertoire, *m.*
offhand(ed), (*improvised*) improvisé; (*abrupt*) brusque.
office, (*business apartment*) bureau, *m.*; (*of a lawyer*) étude, *f.*; (*of public authority*) charge, *f.*; (*function*) fonction, *f.*; (*power*) pouvoir, *m.*; (*worship, eccles.*) office, *m.*
officer, (*mil., naut.*) officier, *m.*; (*police, justice*) agent, *m.*; (*public*) fonctionnaire, *m.*; (*dignitary*) dignitaire, *m.*
official, *s.* fonctionnaire, *m.f.*; *adj.* officiel, -le; **~dom,** bureaucratie, *f.*; **~ly,** officiellement.
officiate, (*eccles.*) officier; *~ as,* remplir le rôle de.
officious, (*meddlesome*) officieu|x, **~se**; **~ness,** empressement importun, *m.*; **~ly,** officieusement.
offing, large, *m.*; *in the ~,* au large.
offscourings, rebut, *m.*
offset, (*equivalent, bkkpg.*) compensation, *f.*
offshoot, (*lit. and fig.*) rejeton, *m.*
offspring, descendant, -e, *m.f. sing. and pl.*; (*fig.*) fruit, *m.*
oft, often, oftentimes, souvent.
ogee, (*arch.*) cimaise, *f.*
ogiv|e, (*arch.*) ogive, *f.*; **~al,** ogival.
ogle, *s.* œillade, *f.*; *v.a.* lorgner; *v.n.* lancer des œillades.
ogre|ss, ogre, -sse, *m.f.*
oh, *interj.* oh!
oil, huile, *f.*; **~-can,** burette, *f.*; **~-colour,** couleur à l'huile, *f.*; **~-cloth,** toile cirée,

f.; ~-**drum,** (*paraffin*) fût à pétrole, *m.*; ~-**painting,** peinture à l'huile, *f.*; ~-**silk,** taffetas d'Angleterre, *m.*; ~-**stove,** fourneau à pétrole, *m.*
oil, *v.a.* huiler.
oilman, marchand de couleurs, *m.*
oilskins, (*sailors'*) ciré, *m.*
oil|y, huileu|x, ~se; (*fig. and pej.*) onctueu|x, ~se; ~**iness,** (*fig.*) onctuosité, *f.*
ointment, onguent, *m.*
old, vieux, (vieil + *vowel or mute* H) vieille; (*aged*) âgé; (*ancient*) ancien, -ne; ~ *age*, vieillesse, *f.*; ~-*age pension*, retraite pour la vieillesse, *f.*; ~ *buffer, see* BUFFER; ~ *book*, bouquin, *m.*; ~ *china, see* CHINA; ~ *clothes, see* CLOTHES; ~ *-fashioned*, démodé; ~ *fellow, see* FELLOW; ~ *man, see* MAN; ~ *master, see* MASTER; ~ *people, the*, vieillards, *m.pl.*; ~ *salt*, (*naut.*) loup de mer, *m.*; *Old Testament*, Ancien Testament, *m.*; *of* ~, jadis; ~ *time, world, adj.* du temps jadis; *How* ~ *are you?* Quel âge avez-vous? *I am 20* (*years old*), j'ai vingt ans; *grow, become, get* ~, vieillir.
olden, vieux, (vieil + *vowel or mute* H) vieille.
oleaginous, oléagineu|x, ~se.
oleander, (*bot.*) laurier-rose, *m.*
olfactory, olfacti|f, ~ve.
oligarch|y, oligarchie, *f.*; ~**ic(al),** oligarchique.
olive, *s.* olive, *f.*; ~-**tree,** olivier, *m.*; *adj.* (*colour*) olive, *invar.*; (*complexion*) olivâtre; ~-*green*, vert olive, *invar.*
olympiad, olympiade, *f.*
olympian, *adj. and s.m.* (*lit. and fig.*) olympien, -ne.
Olympic, ~ *games*, jeux Olympiques, *m.pl.*
ombre, (*cards*) hombre, *m.*
omega, oméga, *m.*
omelet(te), omelette, *f.*
omen, présage, *m.*
ominous, de mauvais augure; ~**ly,** d'une façon inquiétante.
omission, omission, *f.*
omit, omettre* (de).
omnibus, omnibus, *m.*
omnipoten|ce, toute-puissance, *f.*; (*God*) Tout-Puissant, *m.*; ~**t,** tout-puissant.
omnipresen|ce, omniprésence, *f.*; ~**t,** omniprésent.
omniscien|ce, omniscience, *f.*; ~**t,** omniscient.
omnivorous, omnivore.
on, *prep.* **1** *left out with days of month and week and more often with points of time*; ~ *Monday*, lundi; *on the second day*, le second jour; **2** (*place, person, horse*) sur; **3** (*mus. instr.*) de; ~ *pain of*, sous peine de; ~ *purpose*, exprès; ~ *his return*, à son retour; ~ *sale*, en vente; ~ *strike*, en grève; ~ *time*, à la minute.
on, *adv.* (*'forward' with verbs of motion and dispatch sometimes*) en avant; ♤ *with verbs compounded with 'on' —come on, go on, send on, turn on—'on' is more often omitted in French, cf. such verbs; and so* ~, et ainsi de suite; *from that time* ~, à partir de ce temps; ~ *to*, (*movement*) sur; ~**coming,** approchant.
once, une fois; (*formerly*) autrefois; *at* ~, tout de suite; (*at the same time*) à la fois; *for this* ~, pour cette fois; ~ *in a while*, de temps en temps; ~ *a year*, une fois par an.
one, *pron.* (*people, they, anyone, &c.*) *s.* on; *acc.* (*approx.*) vous; *with prep.* soi; ~'*s*, son, sa, ses; (*a*) *one, ones, not translated if preceded by adj., e.g.* le grand, *the tall one* (*m.*); la rouge, *the red one* (*f.*); (*b*) *one, ones, representing word expressed or understood, sing.* en + *verb* + un, une, *pl.* en + *verb* + de, *e.g. I have* ~, j'en ai un; *they have some very good* ~*s*, ils en ont de très bons; (*c*) *one, ones, followed by an adj. clause or participial phrase* = celui, *f.* celle, *pl.* ceux, celles, *e.g. the* ~ *you saw*, celui que vous avez vu; *the* ~*s I found*, ceux que j'ai trouvés. *See also* ANOTHER, ANY, EACH, EVERY, NO ONE.
one, *adj.* un, *f.* une; (*only*) seul; *it's our one chance*, c'est notre seule chance; *with* cent *and* mille *not translated*; *for* ~ *thing*, (*reason*) entre autres choses; ~-*armed*, manchot, -e; ~-*eyed*, borgne; ~-*way, adj.* (*road*) à sens unique; *on* ~ *side . . . on the other*, d'un côté . . . de l'autre.
oneness, unité, *f.*
onerous, onéreu|x, ~se.
oneself, soi-même; (*acc. and dat. with reflex. verb*) se; *by* ~, tout seul; *beside* ~, hors de soi.
onion, oignon, *m.*
onlooker, spectat|eur, ~rice, *m.f.*
only, *adj.* seul; ~ *son*, fils unique, *m.*
only, *adv.* seulement; (*often with verb*) ne . . . que.
onomatopoeia, onomatopée, *f.*
onset, attaque, *f.*; (*beginning*) commencement, *m.*; *at the first* ~, d'emblée.
onslaught, assaut, *m.*
onward, *adj. and adv.* en avant.
onyx, onyx, *m.*
ooz|e, *s.* vase, *f.*; *v.a.n.* suinter; ~**ing,** *s.* suintement, *m.*; ~**y,** vaseu|x, ~se.
opacity, opacité, *f.*; (*obscurity, lit. and fig.*) obscurité, *f.*
opal, opale, *f.*
opaque, opaque; (*obscure*) obscur.
open, *adj.* **1** ouvert; **2** (*to the view*) découvert; **3** (*evident*) manifeste; **4** (*public*) publi|c, ~que; **5** (*frank*) fran|c, ~che; **6** (*credit*) à découvert; **7** (*port*) libre; **8** (*exposed*) exposé; **9** (*boat*) non-ponté; ~-*handed*, généreu|x, ~se; ~-*mouthed*, bouche bée; ~-*work, adj.* percé à jour; ~**ness,** (*frankness*) franchise, *f.*; ~**ly,** ouvertement; *throw* ~, ouvrir*.
open, *v.a.* (*gen. and fig.*) ouvrir*; (*begin*) commencer; (*bottle*) déboucher; ~ *up* (*road, &c.*) ouvrir*; *v.n.* s'ouvrir*;

(*begin*) commencer; ~ *on to*, donner sur.
opener, *tin-*~, ouvre-boîte, *m.*
opening, ouverture, *f.*; (*beginning*) commencement, *m.*; (*opportunity*) chance, *f.*; *adj.* de début; (*ceremony*) d'inauguration.
opera, opéra, *m.*; **~-hat**, gibus, *m.*; **~-house**, opéra, *m.*; **~-glass**, jumelles, *f.pl.*; **~tic**, d'opéra.
opera|te, *v.a.n.* opérer; *~te on*, opérer, *v.a.*; **~tion**, (*working, med., mil.*) opération, *f.*; *come into ~tion*, entrer (être) en opération; **~tor**, (*mach., teleph., med.*) opérat|eur, ~rice.
operative, *s.* ouvrier, *m.*; *adj.* acti|f, ~ve.
ophicleide, ophicléide, *m.*
ophthalmi|a, ophtalmie, *f.*; **~c**, ophtalmique.
opiate, *s.* opiat, *m.*
opine, *v.n.* être d'avis (que).
opinion, opinion, *f.*; *in my ~*, à mon avis; *be of ~ that*, être d'avis que; *form an ~*, se faire* une opinion.
opinionated, opiniâtre.
opium, opium, *m.*
opossum, opossum, *m.*
opponent, *s.* adversaire, *m.*
opportune, opportun; **~ly**, à propos.
opportunist, *adj. and s.m.f.* opportuniste.
opportunity, occasion, *f.*
oppose, *v.a.* (*resist*) s'opposer à; (*contrast*) opposer (à); *~d to*, opposé à.
opposite, *s.* opposé, *m.*; *adj.* (*contrary*) contraire (à); *on the ~ side of*, de l'autre côté de; *adv.* vis-à-vis; *prep.* en face de.
opposition, (*position, resistance, polit., contrast*) opposition, *f.*
oppress, *v.a.* opprimer; (*fig.*) oppresser; **~ion**, (*lit. and fig.*) oppression, *f.*; **~ive**, oppressi|f, ~ve; (*heat, &c.*) accablant; **~or**, oppresseur, *m.*
opprobr|ium, opprobre, *m.*; **~ious**, injurieu|x, ~se.
oppugn, *v.a.* mettre* en doute.
optative, *s.* optatif, *m.*; *adj.* optati|f, ~ve.
optic, *adj.* optique; **~s**, optique, *f.*; **~al**, d'optique; **~ian**, opticien, *m.*
optim|ism, optimisme, *m.*; **~ist**, optimiste, *m.*; **~istic**, optimiste.
option, (*choice, comm.*) option, *f.*; (*purchase*) faculté, *f.*; **~al**, facultati|f, ~ve.
opulen|ce, opulence, *f.*; **~t**, opulent.
or, ou; (*in neg. sent.*) ni; *whether . . . or*, ou . . . ou; (+ *verb*) soit que + *subj.* . . . soit que + *subj.*
orach, (*bot.*) arroche, *f.*
orac|le, oracle, *m.*; **~ular**, d'oracle; **~ularly**, en oracle.
oral, oral; **~ly**, oralement.
orange, orange, *f.*; **~-blossom**, fleur de l'oranger, *f.*; **~-tree**, oranger, *m.*; *adj.* *~-coloured*, orangé; *~-red*, nacarat, *invar.*; **~ade**, orangeade, *f.*; **~ry**, orangerie, *f.*
orang-outang, orang-outang, *m.*
oration, discours, *m.*
orator, orat|eur, ~rice, *m.f.*; **~ical**, oratoire; **~ically**, d'une façon oratoire.
oratorio, (*mus.*) oratorio, *m.*
oratory, art oratoire, *m.*; (*chapel*) oratoire, *m.*
orb, orbe, *m.*
orbit, (*eye, astr.*) orbite, *f.*
orchard, verger, *m.*
orchestra, orchestre, *m.*; **~l**, orchestral.
orchid, orchis, (*bot.*) orchidée, *f.*; (*European*) orchis, *m.*
ordain, *v.a.* (*gen. and eccles.*) ordonner.
ordeal, épreuve, *f.*; (*trial by*) ordalie, *f.*
order, *s.* (*non-confusion, arrangement, sequence, rule, rank, command, instructions, eccles., arch., fraternity, insignia, mil.*) ordre, *m.*; (*ruling*) règlement, *m.*; (*to buy, sell, &c.*) commande, *f.*; **~-book**, livre de commandes, *m.*; **~ form**, bulletin de commande, *m.*; *~ of the day*, ordre du jour, *m.*; *Order! Order!* À l'ordre! à l'ordre!; *in ~ to*, pour + *inf.*; *in ~ that*, pour que + *subj.*; *out of ~*, dérangé; *to ~**, (*clothes*) de commande; *keep in ~*, tenir en ordre; *set in ~*, mettre* en ordre.
order, *v.a.* (*set in order, dispose, prescribe* (*med.*), *retreat, &c., mil.*) ordonner; (*person to do*) ordonner à + *pers.*, de + *inf.*; (*meals, goods, &c.*) commander; *~ arms!* reposez armes!
orderly, *s.* (*mil.*) ordonnance, *f.*; **~ officer**, officier d'ordonnance.
orderl|y, *adj.* (*things*) en ordre; (*pers.*) ordonné; **~iness**, régularité, *f.*; (*crowd*) tranquillité, *f.*
ordinal, *s.* nombre ordinal, *m.*; *adj.* ordinal.
ordinance, ordonnance, *f.*
ordinar|y, *s.* ordinaire, *m.*; (*taverns*) prix du repas, *m.*; *in ~y*, (*of permanent officials*) ordinaire; *adj.* ordinaire; **~ily**, ordinairement.
ordination, (*eccles.*) ordination, *f.*
ordnance, pièces d'artillerie, *f.pl.*
ore, minerai, *m.*
organ, (*mus.*) orgue, *m.*; (*of body*) organe, *m.*; **~-blower**, souffleur d'orgue, *m.*; **~-grinder**, joueur d'orgue de barbarie, *m.*; **~-loft**, tribune d'orgue, *f.*
organ|ic, organique; **~ism**, organisme, *m.*; **~ically**, organiquement.
organist, organiste, *m.f.*
organiz|e, organiser; **~ation**, organisation, *f.*
organizer, organisat|eur, ~rice, *m.f.*
orgy, orgie, *f.*
oriel-window, fenêtre en encorbellement, *f.*
Orient, *s.* Orient, *m.*
oriental, *adj. & s.m.f.* oriental, -e.
orientalist, orientaliste, *m.*
orifice, orifice, *m.*
oriflamme, oriflamme, *f.*
origan, (*bot.*) origan, *m.*
origin, origine, *f.*; **~al**, (*primitive, innate*) originel, -le; (*not imitative or deriva-*

tive, peculiar) original; **~ality,** originalité, *f.*; **~ally,** (*primitively*) originairement; (*in an original way*) originalement.
original, *s.* (*pers., text*) original, *m.*
origina|te, créer; **~tion,** création, *f.*; **~tor,** créateur, *m.*
oriole, (*ornith.*) loriot, *m.*
orison, oraison, *f.*
ormolu, or moulu, *m.*
ornament, *s.* ornement, *m.*; **~ation,** ornementation, *f.*; **~al,** ornemental; *v.a.* orner (de).
ornate, orné; (*style*) fleuri; **~ness,** (*approx.*) richesse, *f.*; **~ly,** avec richesse, *f.*
ornitholog|ical, ornithologique; **~ist,** ornithologue, *m.*; **~y,** ornithologie, *f.*
orphan, *adj. and s.m.f.* orphelin, -e; **~age,** orphelinat, *m.*
orphic, orphique.
orthodox, orthodoxe; **~y,** orthodoxie, *f.*
orthography, orthographe, *f.*; ⚠ orthographie = '*the elevation of a building*'.
ortolan, ortolan, *m.*
oscilla|te, (*lit. and fig.*) osciller.; **~tion,** oscillation, *f.*
osier, osier, *m.*; **~-bed,** oseraie, *f.*
osprey, (*ornith.*) orfraie, *f.*
ossify, *v.a.* ossifier; *v.n.* s'ossifier.
ostensib|le, prétendu (*generally before noun*; **~ly,** en apparence.
ostenta|tion, ostentation, *f.*; **~tious,** fastueu|x, ~se; **~tiously,** avec ostentation.
ostler, valet d'écurie, *m.*
ostrac|ism, (*lit. and fig.*) ostracisme, *m.*; **~ize,** (*fig.*) frapper d'ostracisme.
ostrich, autruche, *f.*
other, *adj.* autre.
other, *pron.* autre; *some ~s,* en + *verb* + d'autres, *e.g.* il y en a d'autres; *~s,* (*generally*) les autres; (*with preps.*) autrui; *see also* EACH, EVERY.
otherwise, autrement.
otter, loutre, *f.*
Ottoman, *adj.* (*when an adj. use small letter*) *and s.m.f.* Ottoman, -e; (*sofa*) ottomane, *f.*
ought, devoir; *you ~ to do it,* vous devriez le faire; *you ~ to have done it,* vous auriez dû le faire.
ounce, (*measure and an.*) once, *f.*
our, *adj.* notre; *pl.* nos.
ours, *pron.* le nôtre, *m.*, la nôtre, *f.*, les nôtres, *m. and f. pl.*;—*where possession is emphasized with 'to be'*, être à nous *is employed*; *a relation of ~,* un de nos parents.
oursel|f, *usually plural except of a single individual*; (*reflexive*) nous; (*emphatic*) nous-mêmes; **~ves,** (*reflexive*) nous; (*emphatic*) nous-mêmes; *by ~ves,* seul, -s, -e, -es.
oust, *v.a.* évincer.
out, *adj. an ~ size,* une pointure hors série.
out, *adv.* dehors; (*not at home*) sorti; (*fashion*) passé de mode; (*found out*) découvert; (*fire, light*) éteint; *put ~,* (*to sea*) prendre* la mer; (*out of joint*) démettre*; (*annoy*) contrarier; *speak ~,* parler †haut; *turn ~,* mettre* à la porte; *see also verbs compounded with 'out'*; *~ with him!* mettez-le à la porte!; *~ with you!* †hors d'ici!; *~ with it!* (*speak!, slang*) dites-le donc!
out (of), *prep.* †hors de; (*from, on account of*) par; (*in, of stone, from book, &c.*) dans; (*without*) sans; (*numbers*) sur; *be ~,* (*lack*) manquer de; *~ doors,* (*in the open air*) en plein air; *turn ~ doors,* mettre* à la porte; *~ patience,* à bout de patience; *~ place,* mal à propos; *~ print,* épuisé; *be ~ sorts,* ne pas être dans son assiette; *~ temper,* de mauvaise humeur.
outbid, *v.a.* enchérir sur.
outbreak, *s.* (*epidemics*) invasion, *f.*; (*insurrection*) insurrection, *f.*
outbuildings, dépendances, *f.pl.*
outburst, explosion, *f.*
outcast, *s.* proscrit, *m.*
outclassed, *be ~,* être d'une classe inférieure.
outcome, conséquence, *f.*
outcry, clameur, *f.*
outdo, surpasser.
outdoor, *adj.* de plein air.
outer, *adj.* extérieur; **~most,** le plus extérieur.
outfit, *s.* trousseau, *m.*; (*mil.*) équipement, *m.*; **~ter,** confectionneur, *m.*
outflank, *v.a.* (*mil.*) déborder.
outgoing, *adj.* (*leaving office, house*) sortant.
outgoings, (*expenses*) débours, *m.pl.*
outgrow, dépasser en croissance; (*become too big for*) devenir* trop grand pour.
outhouse, †hangar, *m.*
outlandish, (*queer*) bizarre.
outlast, (*outlive*) survivre* à.
outlaw, *s.* proscrit, *m.*; *v.a.* proscrire*; **~ry,** proscription, *f.*
outlay, (*expense*) dépense, *f.*
outlet, issue, *f.*; (*comm.*) débouché, *m.*
outline, contour, *m.*; (*rough draught*) esquisse, *f.*; (*general idea*) aperçu, *m.*; *v.a.* esquisser; (*give a general idea of*) donner un aperçu de.
outlive, *v.a.* survivre* à.
outlook, (*view*) perspective, *f.*; (*fig.*) perspective d'avenir, *f.*
outlying, écarté.
outmanœuvre, l'emporter en manœuvre sur.
outmarch, distancer.
outnumber, surpasser en nombre.
outpost, avant-poste, *m.*
outpouring, épanchement, *m.*
output, (*comm.*) production, *f.*
outrage, *s.* outrage, *m.*; *v.a.* outrager; **~ous,** outrageant; (*atrocious*) atroce; **~ousness,** (*enormity, fig.*) énormité, *f.*; **~ously,** outrageusement; (*excessively*) furieusement.
outrider, piqueur, *m.*

outright, *adv.* (*completely*) tout à fait; (*at once*) sur le champ.
outrun, courir* plus vite que; (*limits*) dépasser.
outset, *s.* début, *m.*; *at the* ~, dès le commencement.
outshine, (*lit. and fig.*) éclipser.
outside *s.* extérieur, *m.*; (*omnibus, &c.*) impériale, *f.*; *at the* ~, tout au plus; *from the* ~, du dehors.
outside, *adj.* du dehors; (*price, value*) maximum, *invar.*; ~ *porter*, commissionnaire, *m.*; ~ *passenger*, voyageur d'impériale, *m.*; ~ *broker*, courtier marron, *m.*
outside, *adv.* au dehors; *prep.* en dehors de.
outsider, (*fam.*) personne vulgaire, *f.*
outskirts, (*town, &c.*) banlieue, *f.*; (*forest*) lisière, *f.*
outspoken, *be* ~, avoir son franc parler.
outstanding, (*comm.*) à payer.
outstretched, (*arms, &c.*) étendu.
outstrip, dépasser; (*surpass*) surpasser.
outvote, *v.a.* l'emporter sur . . . par la pluralité des votes.
outward, *adj.* extérieur; **~ly**, à l'extérieur; ~ *bound*, en partance.
outweigh, *v.a.* peser plus que; (*fig.*) avoir plus de poids que; (*prevail over*) l'emporter sur.
outwit, duper.
outwork, *s.* (*mil.*) ouvrage avancé, *m.*
ouz(s)el, (*ornith.*) merle, *m.*
oval, *adj. and s.m.* ovale.
ovation, ovation, *f.*
oven, four, *m.*
over, *adv.* (*residue*) de reste; (*more*) davantage; (*finished*) fini; (*past*) passé; (*too*) trop; *it's all* ~ *with*, c'en est fait de; ⚠ *in adjs. compounded with 'over' this word nearly always* = trop + *adj. in question.*
over, *prep.* (*rest*) au-dessus de; (*motion*) par dessus; (*superiority, immediately over, contact*) sur; (*on the other side of*) de l'autre côté de; (*more than*) plus de; (*across country, &c.*) par.
overall, *s.* (*woman's*) surtout, *m.*; **~s**, (*workman's*) salopette, *f.*
overarch, voûter.
overawe, intimider.
overbalance *oneself*, perdre l'équilibre.
overbear, *v.a.* dominer; **~ing**, impérieu|x, ~se.
overboard, par-dessus bord; *fall* ~, tomber (être) à la mer.
overburden, surcharger.
overcharge, (*price*) surfaire*.
overcast, *adj.* (*sky, &c.*) couvert.
overcloud, couvrir* de nuages; (*fig.*) assombrir.
overcoat, pardessus, *m.*
overcome, vaincre*; (*fig.*) surmonter; *p.p.* ~ *by*, (*heat, &c.*) accablé de.
overconfiden|ce, confiance excessive, *f.*; **~t**, trop plein de confiance.
overcrowded, (*houses, districts*) surpeuplé; (*rooms, &c.*) bondé.
overdo, *v.a.* (*cooking*) faire* trop cuire; (*part, &c.*) exagérer; **~ne**, (*food*) trop cuit.
overdose, trop forte dose, *f.*
overdraft, (*bank*) découvert, *m.*
overdraw, (*bank*) mettre* à découvert; **~n**, *p.p.* (*at bank*) à découvert; **~n**, (*in describing*) exagéré; **~n** *account*, compte découvert, *m.*
overdress, s'habiller trop bien.
overdue, (*post, ship*) en retard; (*comm.*) arriéré.
overeat oneself, manger trop.
overestimate, *s.* surestimation, *f.*; *v.a.* surestimer.
overfatigue, *s.* fatigue excessive, *f.*
overflow, *s.* débordement, *m.*; ~ *pipe*, tuyau de trop-plein, *m.*; *v.a.* inonder; *v.n.* déborder; **~ing**, (*lit. and fig.*) débordant.
overgrown, (*covered*) couvert de.
overhang, *v.a.n.* surplomber; **~ing**, *adj.* en surplomb.
overhaul, *v.a.* examiner à fond; (*overtake*) rattraper; **~ing**, *s.* révision, *f.*
overhead, *adj.* (*comm., charges, &c.*) général; *adv.* en †haut.
overhear, entendre par †hasard.
overheat, échauffer; **~ing**, (*motor, &c.*) échauffement, *m.*
overjoyed, transporté de joie.
overland, *adj. and adv.* par voie de terre; (*journey*) par terre.
overlap, chevaucher; **~ping**, *s.* chevauchement, *m.*
overlay, couvrir*(de).
overlie, (*smother*) étouffer.
overload, surcharger; **~ing**, *s.* surcharge, *f.*
overlook, (*look on to*) avoir vue sur; (*excuse*) pardonner; (*neglect*) négliger; (*superintend*) surveiller.
overlord, seigneur, *m.*; (*supreme*) suzerain, *m.*
overmuch, *adj.* trop de; *adv.* excessivement.
over-nice, trop délicat.
overnight, la veille au soir.
overpassed, (*past*) passé.
overpay, *v.a.* payer trop; *s. and* **~ment**, payement en trop, *m.*
overpopulated, surpeuplé.
overpower, (*crush*) accabler; (*subdue*) subjuguer; **~ing**, *adj.* accablant.
overpressure, (*fig.*) surmenage, *m.*
over-production, surproduction, *f.*
overrate, estimer trop.
overreach, (*deceive*) duper; ~ *oneself*, aller* (être) trop loin.
override, (*fig.*) avoir la †haute main sur.
overrule, (*decision, &c.*) rejeter.
overrun, (*country*) envahir; (*ravage*) ravager; (*infest*) infester (de).
oversea, *adj.* d'outre-mer; **~s**, *adv.* outre mer.
oversee, surveiller; **~r**, surveillant, *m.*
overshadow, ombrager; (*eclipse, fig.*) éclipser.
oversight, inadvertence, *f.*

oversleep oneself, dormir* trop.
overspread, *be* ~ *with,* être entièrement couvert de.
overstate, exagérer; **~ment,** exagération, *f.*
overstep, (*exceed*) dépasser.
overstocked, (*market, &c.*) encombré de marchandises.
overstrain, *s.* surmenage, *m.*; *v.a.* surmener.
overtake, rattraper*; (*surprise*) surprendre (par).
overtaxed, (*with work*) surmené.
overthrow, *s.* (*state, dynasty, &c.*) renversement, *m.*; (*defeat*) défaite, *f.*; *v.a.* renverser, défaire*.
overtime, heures supplémentaires, *f.pl.*
overtired, excédé.
overtly, ouvertement.
overture, (*gen. and mus.*) ouverture, *f.*; *make ~s to,* faire* des ouvertures à.
overturn, *v.a.* renverser; (*veh.*) verser; (*boat*) faire* chavirer; (*upset, destroy*) bouleverser; *v.n.* se renverser.
overvalu|e, surestimer; **~ation,** surestimation, *f.*
overweening, outrecuidant.
overweight, (*luggage, &c.*) excédent, *m.*
overwhelm, accabler (de); (*benefits, kindness, &c.*) combler (de); **~ing,** *adj.* accablant.
overwork, *s.* surmenage, *m.*; *v.a.* surmener; *v.n. and ~ oneself,* se surmener.
overwrought, (*pers.*) excédé.
owe, (*lit. and fig.*) devoir; (*be indebted*) être redevable à + *pers.* de + *thing.*
owing, *adj.* dû, due; ~ *to,* (*attributable to*) dû à; *prep.* ~ *to,* à cause de.
owl, hibou, *m.*; *screech-~,* chat-†huant, *m.*; *sparrow-~,* chevêche, *f.*; *tawny or wood-~,* †hulotte, *f.*; *see also* FERN.
owlet, jeune hibou, *m.*
own, *adj.* propre (*before noun*); *of my, thy, his, &c.* ~, à moi, à toi, à lui, &c.; *one's* ~ *people,* les siens.
own, *v.a.* (*possess*) posséder; (*acknowledge*) reconnaître*; (*confess*) avouer; ~ *up to,* avouer; *v.n. and* ~ *up,* avouer.
owner, propriétaire, *m.f.*; *part-~,* copropriétaire, *s.m.f.*
ownership, propriété, *f.*
ox, bœuf, *m.*; **~-drover, ~herd,** bouvier, *m.*
oxidize, oxyder.
oxygen, oxygène, *m.*
oyster, huître, *f.*; **~-bed,** banc d'huîtres, *m.*; **~-shell,** écaille d'huître, *f.*
ozone, ozone, *m.*

P

pace, pas, *m.*; *at a slow ~,* à pas lents; *go the ~,* mener vie joyeuse.
pace, *v.a.* (*rapidly*) arpenter; *v.n.* aller* (être) au pas.
pacific, pacifique.
pacif|ication, pacification, *f.*; **~y,** (*country*) pacifier; (*pers.*) apaiser.
pacifis|m, pacifisme, *m.*; **~t,** pacifiste, *m.f.*
pack, *s.* **1** (*wool*) balle, *f.*; **2** (*hounds*) meute, *f.*; **3** (*wolves, thieves, &c.*) bande, *f.*; **4** (*pedlar, goods*) ballot, *m.*; **5** (*rugby football*) mêlée, *f.*; **6** (*of lies*) tas, *m.*; **7** (*mil.*) sac, *m.*; **8** (*cards*) jeu, *m.*; **~-horse,** cheval de bât, *m.*; **~-saddle,** bât, *m.*
pack, *v.a.* (*goods*) emballer; (*luggage*) faire*; (*single articles*) mettre*; (*crowd*) entasser; (*overfill*) bonder; ~ *off,* (*fam.*) envoyer promener; ~ *up,* emballer; (*do up*) empaqueter; *v.n.* (*pers.*) faire* sa malle; ~ *off,* plier bagage; ~ *together,* se serrer.
pack|er, emballeu|r, ~se, *m.f.*; **~age,** (*large*) colis, *m.*; **~et,** (*parcel*) petit paquet, *m.*; (*ship and mail-packet*) paquebot, *m.*
packing, (*action*) emballage, *m.*; **~-needle,** aiguille d'emballeur, *f.*
pact, pacte, *m.*
pad, *s.* (*stuffing, protection*) bourrelet, *m.*; (*fox, hare, &c.*) patte, *f.*; (*cricket*) jambière, *f.*; *v.a.* (*stuff*) bourrer; (*clothes*) ouater; *v.n.* (*on foot*) aller* (être) à pied.
padding, *s.* (*clothes*) ouate, *f.*
paddle, *s.* (*canoe*) pagaie, *f.*; (*wheel*) palette, *f.*; *~-wheel,* roue à aubes, *f.*; *v.n.* (*in canoe*) pagayer; (*in water*) patauger.
paddock, enclos, *m.*
padlock, cadenas, *m.*; *v.a.* cadenasser.
padre, (*mil. and nav. slang*) aumônier, *m.*
paean, péan, *m.*
pagan, *adj. & s.m.f.* païen, -ne; **~ism,** paganisme, *m.*
page, *s.* (*book, lit. and fig.*) page, *f.*; (*royal, knight's*) page, *m.*; (*boy in livery*) jeune garçon en livrée, *m.*; ⚠ page, *m. is not used in this latter sense*; *v.a.* paginer.
pageant, spectacle, *m.*; **~ry,** faste, *m.*
pagoda, pagode, *f.*
pail, seau, *m.*; *see also* SLOP-PAIL.
pain, douleur, *f.*; (*trouble taken*) peine, *f.*; *take ~s,* se donner de la peine; *under ~ of,* sous peine de; *have a ~ in,* avoir mal à; **~ful,** douloureu|x, ~se; (*laborious, distressing*) pénible; **~fulness,** (*fig.*) nature pénible, *f.*; **~fully,** douloureusement, péniblement; **~less,** (*not causing pain*) indolore.
pain, *v.a.* faire* mal à; (*distress*) faire* de la peine à; *v.n.* faire* mal.
paint, *s.* peinture, *f.*; (*face*) fard, *m.*; **~-box,** boîte à couleurs, *f.*; **~-brush,** pinceau, *m.*; *v.a.* (*portray, cover with paint*) peindre*; (*describe*) dépeindre*; (*face*) farder; *v.n.* se farder.
paint|er, peintre, *m.*; **~ing,** peinture, *f.*
pair, *s.* paire, *f.*; (*pers., ans., birds*) couple, *m.*; ~ *of compasses,* compas, *m.sing.*; ~ *of drawers,* caleçon, *m.sing.*; ~ *of trousers,* pantalon, *m.sing.*; *v.a.* accoupler; (*fig.*) assortir; *v.n.* (*birds, &c.*) s'accoupler; **~ing,** *s.* (*birds, &c.*) accouplement, *m.*

pal, (*slang*) copain, *m.*
palace, palais, *m.*
paladin, paladin, *m.*
palan(keen)quin, palanquin, *m.*
palaeolithic, paléolithique.
palatable, agréable au goût.
palate, (*anat.*) palais, *m.*; (*taste*) goût, *m.*
palatial, de palais.
palatine, *adj.* palatin.
palaver, (*native*) palabre, *f.*; (*cajolery*) flagornerie, *f.*; *v.a.* flagorner; *v.n.* bavarder.
pale, *s.* (*for fence*) pieu, *m.*
pale, *adj.* (*pers., face, colour*) pâle; *grow, turn* ~, pâlir; **~ness,** pâleur, *f.*; *v.n.* pâlir.
palette, palette, *f.*
palfrey, palefroi, *m.*
paling, palisade, palissade, *f.*
pall, drap mortuaire, *m.*; (*fig.*) voile, *m.*; (*eccles.*) pallium, *m.*; *v.n.* devenir* (être) insipide.
palladium, (*image, safeguard*) palladium, *m.*
pall|et, (*bed*) grabat, *m.*; **~iasse,** paillasse, *f.*
pallia|te, (*alleviate*) pallier; (*excuse*) atténuer; **~tion,** palliation, *f.*; **~tive,** *adj. and s.m.* palliati|f, **~ve.**
pallid, pâle.
pall-mall, mail, *m.*
pallor, pâleur, *f.*
palm, (*branch and fig.*) palme, *f.*; (*tree*) palmier, *m.*; (*hand*) paume, *f.*; **Palm-Sunday,** Dimanche des Rameaux, *m.*
palm, *v.a.* ~ *off . . . on . . .*, faire* passer . . . pour . . . à . . . .
palmer, pèlerin, *m.*
palmist, chiromancien, -ne, *m.f.*; **~ry,** chiromancie, *f.*
palmy, couvert de palmes.
palpabl|e, palpable; **~y,** d'une manière palpable.
palpita|te, palpiter; **~tion,** palpitation, *f.*
pals|y, paralysie, *f.*; **~ied,** frappé de paralysie.
palter, *v.n.* tergiverser; (*trifle with*) jouer avec.
paltr|y, mesquin; **~iness,** mesquinerie, *f.*
pampa, pampa, *f.*; ~-*grass*, herbe des pampas, *f.*
pamper, gâter.
pamphlet, brochure, *f.*; ⚠ pamphlet *in French is generally pej.* = '*a venomously satirical work*'; **~eer,** auteur de brochures, *m.*; (*venomous satirist*) pamphlétaire, *m.f.*
pan, (*metal, frying*) poêle, *f.*; (*earthenware*) terrine, *f.*; *preserving-~*, bassine, *f.*; *stewing-~*, casserole, *f.*; *warming-~*, bassinoire, *f.*
panacea, panacée, *f.*
Panama hat, panama, *m.*
pancake, crêpe, *f.*
pandemonium, pandémonium, *m.*; (*fig.*) vacarme, *m.*
pander, *s.* complaisant; *v.n.* ~ *to*, se faire* le complaisant de.
pane, (*window*) vitre, *f.*
panegyr|ic, panégyrique, *m.*; **~ist,** panégyriste, *m.*
panel, (*woodwork, arch., dress*) panneau, *m.*; (*of jurors*) liste, *f.*; *v.a.* lambrisser (de).
panelling, lambris, *m.*
pang, angoisse, *f.*; **~s,** (*of death, &c.*) affres, *f.pl.*
panic, *s.* panique, *f.*; ~-*struck*, ~-*stricken*, saisi de panique; *adj.* panique; **~-grass,** (*bot.*) panic, *m.*
pannier, (*basket, part of skirt*) panier, *m.*
panoply, panoplie, *f.*
panoram|a, panorama, *m.*; **~ic,** panoramique.
pansy, (*bot.*) pensée, *f.*
pant, *v.n.* (*for breath*) †haleter; (*throb*) palpiter.
pantaloon, pantalon, *m.*; (*Italian comedy*) Pantalon, *m.*
pantechnicon, garde-meuble, *m. invar.*
panthe|ism, panthéisme, *m.*; **~ist,** panthéiste, *m.*
pantheon, panthéon, *m.*
panther, panthère, *f.*
pantile, panne, *f.*
pantomime, pantomime, *f.*
pantry, office, *f.*
pants, (*drawers*) caleçon, *m.*; *a pair of* ~, (*U.S.A.*) pantalon, *m.*
pap, (*nipple*) mamelon, *m.*; (*food*) bouillie, *f.*
papa, papa, *m.*
pap|acy, papauté, *f.*; **~al,** papal.
papaw, (*bot.*) (*fruit*) papaye, *f.*; (*tree*) papayer, *m.*
paper, papier, *m.*; (*newspaper*) journal, *m.*; (*essay, dissertation*) étude, *f.*; (*in magazine, &c.*) article, *m.*; (*written exam.*) composition écrite, *f.*; **~-chase,** rallye-papier, *m.*; **~-hanger,** colleur, *m.*; **~-knife,** coupe-papier, *m. invar.*; ~ *money*, papier monnaie, *m.*; **~-weight,** presse-papier, *m. invar.*; *adj.* de papier.
paper, *v.a.* (*room*) tapisser.
papier mâché, papier-mâché, *m.*
papist, papiste, *m.*; **~ry,** papisme, *m.*
papyrus, papyrus, *m.*
par, *s.* (*comm.*) pair, *m.*; *at* ~, au pair; *above, below* ~, au-dessus, en dessous du pair; *be below* ~, (*health*) ne pas être dans son assiette.
parable, parabole, *f.*
parabola, parabole, *f.*
parachut|e, parachute, *m.*; **~ist,** parachutiste, *m.f.*
paraclete, paraclet, *m.*
parade, *s.* (*show, mil.*) parade, *f.*; ⚠ parade *does not* = '*public walk*', *which* = promenade publique, *f.*
parade, *v.a.* (*show off*) faire* parade de; (*mil.*) assembler pour la revue; *v.n.* (*strut, flaunt, mil.*) parader.
paradise, paradis, *m.*; *bird of* ~, paradisier, *m.*
paradox, paradoxe, *m.*; **~ical,** paradoxal.

paraffin, (*oil*) pétrole, *m.*; ~ *lamp,* lampe à pétrole, *f.*; ⚠ pétrole *does not* = *'petrol' which* = essence; *and* paraffine *does not* = *Eng. 'paraffin' for lamps but the fatty substance used for candles.*

paragon, (*model, faultless diamond, &c.*) parangon, *m.*

paragraph, (*section of prose*) paragraphe, *m.*; (*break in line*) alinéa, *m.*; (*in newspaper*) entrefilet, *m.*

par|akeet, ~oquet, (*ornith.*) perruche, *f.*

parallax, parallaxe, *f.*

parallel, *s.* (*of lines and fort.*) parallèle, *f.*; (*circle parallel to equator, comparison, thing or pers. exactly like*) parallèle, *m.*; *adj.* parallèle; (*fig.*) semblable; *v.a.* (*compare*) comparer (à).

parallelogram, parallélogramme, *m.*

paraly|se, (*lit. and fig.*) paralyser; **~sis,** paralysie, *f.*; **~tic,** *adj. & s.m.f.* paralytique.

paramount, *adj.* (*in supreme authority*) souverain; (*greatest*) le, la plus †haut, -e.

paramour, amant, -e, *m.f.*

parapet, garde-fou, *m., pl.* garde-fous; (*mil.*) parapet, *m.*

paraphernalia, (*fam.*) attirail, *m.*

paraphrase, paraphrase, *f.*; *v.a.n.* paraphraser.

parasit|e, (*pers., an., plant*) parasite, *m.*; *adj.* **~ic,** parasite.

parasol, ombrelle, *f.*; ⚠ *not 'umbrella' which* = parapluie.

paravane, (*nav.*) paravane, *m.*

parboil, (*boil partially*) faire* cuire à demi; (*fig.*) surchauffer.

parcel, *s.* (*package*) paquet, *m.*; (*land*) parcelle, *f.*; (*heap, pack*) tas, *m.*; *~s delivery,* factage, *m.*; *~-post, adv.* comme colis postal; *v.a.* ~ *out,* morceler en; *be part and ~ of,* faire* partie intégrante de.

parch, *v.a.* (*dry*) dessécher; *v.n* se dessécher; **~ing,** brûlant.

parchment, parchemin, *m.*

pard, (*leopard*) léopard, *m.*; (*U.S.A. 'pal'*) copain, *m.*

pardon, *s.* (*lit. and eccles.*) pardon, *m.*; *I beg your ~,* je vous demande pardon.

pardon, *v.a.* pardonner (*acc. of thing, dat. of person*).

pardonabl|e, pardonnable; **~y,** d'une manière pardonnable.

pare, (*fruit*) peler; ~ *down,* rogner.

parent, père, *m.,* mère, *f.*; ⚠ parent, *sing.* = *rather 'relative', 'kinsman'*; (*source, cause*) mère, *f.*; **~s,** parents, *m.pl.*

parentage, naissance, *f.*

parental, paternel, -le, maternel, -le.

parenthe|sis, parenthèse, *f.*; **~tic,** (*interposed*) intercalé.

parhelion, parhélie, *m.*

pariah, paria, *m.*

parings, épluchures, *f.pl.*

parish, (*civil*) commune, *f.*; (*eccles.*) paroisse, *f.*; (*relief*) assistance publique, *f.*; *adj.* communal; **~ioner,** (*eccles.*) paroissien, -ne, *m.f.*

Parisian, *adj.* (*when an adj. use small letter*) *and s.m.f.* Parisien, -ne.

parisyllabic, parisyllabique.

parity, égalité, *f.*; (*comm.*) parité, *f.*

park, (*gen. and mil.*) parc, *m.*; (*motor*) parc de stationnement, *m.*; *v.a.* (*artill.*) parquer; (*motor*) garer.

parlance, parler, *m.*

parley, *s.* pourparler, *m., usually in plural*; *v.n.* (*mil.*) parlementer; *beat, sound a ~,* battre la chamade.

parliament, parlement, *m.*; **~arian,** *s.* parlementaire, *m.*; **~ary,** (*lit. and fig.*) parlementaire.

parlour, petit salon, *m.*; ⚠ parloir, *m.* = *'reception room' in convent or school.*

parlous, périlleu|x, ~se.

Parnass|us, Parnasse, *m.*; **~ian,** parnassien, -ne.

parochial, (*eccles.*) paroissial; (*local*) de clocher.

parod|y, *s.* parodie, *f.*; *v.a.* parodier; **~ist,** parodiste, *m.*

parole, (*mil.*) parole, *f.*

paroxysm, paroxysme, *m.*

parquet, parquet, *m.*; **~ry,** parqueterie, *f.*

parricide, (*crime*) parricide, *m.*; (*murderer*) parricide, *m.f.*

parrot, perroquet, *m.*; perruche, *f.*; *Poll ~,* jaco, (jacquot) *m.*

parry, *s.* (*fenc.*) parade, *f.*; (*blow*) *v.a.n.* parer.

pars|e, (*gram.*) analyser; **~ing,** analyse, *f.*

parsimon|ious, parcimonieu|x, ~se; **~y,** parcimonie, *f.*; **~iously,** avec parcimonie.

parsley, persil, *m.*

parsnip, panais, *m.*

parson, curé, *m.*; (*Protestant*) pasteur, *m.*; **~age,** presbytère, *m.*

part, *s.* 1 (*of a whole*) partie, *f.*; 2 (*place*) endroit, *m.*; 3 (*share, participation*) part, *f.*; 4 (*some of several*) un certain nombre, *m.*; 5 (*theatr.*) rôle, *m.*; 6 (*side in quarrel*) parti, *m.*; 7 (*issue of books*) livraison, *f.*; **~s,** (*talents*) talents, *m.pl.*; (*regions*) parages, *m.pl.*; *~s of speech,* parties du discours, *f.pl.*; *under ~, s.* dessous, *m.*; *for my ~,* quant à moi; *on my ~,* de ma part; *play a ~,* (*fig.*) jouer la comédie; *take ~ in,* prendre* part à.

part, *v.a.* diviser; (*separate*) séparer; (*share*) partager; *v.n.* (*divide*) se diviser; (*open*) s'ouvrir*; (*quit one another*) se séparer (de); (*break*) se rompre; *~ with,* se défaire* de; (*say good-bye*) se séparer de; (*with money, &c.*) se défaire* de.

partake, ~ *of,* participer à; (*food*) manger; (*have qualities of*) participer de.

partaker, participant, -e, *m.f.*; *be ~ of,* prendre* part à.

parterre, (*flowers and theatr.*) parterre, *m.*

partial, (*unfair*) partial; (*not complete*) partiel, -le; *be ~ to,* avoir un faible pour; **~ity,** (*bias*) partialité, *f.*; (*liking, &c., for*) prédilection, *f.,* pour; **~ly,** (*in part*) en partie.

particip|ant, participant, -e, *m.f.*; **~ation,** participation, *f.*; **~ator,** participant, -e, *m.f.* (à); **~ate,** *v.a.* partager; *v.n. ~ate in,* prendre* part à.
participle, participe, *m.*
particle, (*portion of matter*) molécule, *f.*; (*small amount*) parcelle, *f.*; (*gram.*) particule, *f.*
parti-coloured, bigarré.
particular, *s.* (*detail*) détail, *m.*; *in ~,* en particulier.
particular, *adj.* (*apart from others, special, personal, peculiar*) particuli|er, ~ère; ⚠ particulier *does not* = '*scrupulously exact*' *which* = méticuleu|x, ~se; *or* '*fastidious*' *which* = difficile à satisfaire; *~ about,* (*food, &c.*) difficile pour.
particulariz|ation, particularisation, *f.*; **~e,** *v.a.* (*specify*) particulariser.
particular|ity, particularité, *f.*; **~ly,** particulièrement.
parting, *s.* séparation, *f.*; (*departure*) départ, *m.*; (*hair*) raie, *f.*; *adj.* d'adieu.
partisan, partisan, *m.*; (*spear*) pertuisane, *f.*
partition, division, *f.*; (*law, country*) partage, *m.*; (*rooms, &c.*) cloison, *f.*; *v.a.* diviser, partager.
partitive, partiti|f, ~ve.
partly, en partie.
partner, associé, -e, *m.f.*; (*dancing, game*) partenaire, *m.f.*; *senior ~,* associé principal, *m.*; *sleeping ~,* commanditaire, *m.f.*; **~ship,** association, *f.*
partridge, perdrix, *f.*; *young ~,* perdreau, *m.*
parturition, (*lit. and fig.*) enfantement, *m.*
party, (*body of persons, mil., polit.*) parti, *m.*; (*to a crime*) complice, *m.*; (*pleasure party, person concerned*) partie, *f.*; (*people engaged together*) groupe, *m.*; (*individual*) individu, *m.*; **~-wall,** mur mitoyen, *m.*; *interested ~,* intéressé, -e, *m.f.*; *not to be a ~ to,* n'y être pour rien.
paschal, *adj.* pascal, *pl.* -als *and* -aux.
pasha, pacha, *m.*
pasque-flower, (*bot.*) passe-fleur, *f.*, *pl.* passe-fleurs.
pass, *s.* (*mountain*) défilé, *m.*; (*permission to go in or out*) laisser-passer, *m.*; (*critical position*) situation, *f.*; (*police*) coupe-file, *m. invar.*; **~-key,** passe-partout, *m. invar.*; **~-book,** (*bank*) carnet de banque, *m.*; *you've come to a pretty ~,* vous voilà dans de beaux draps.
pass, *v.a.* 1 (*go across, on, over, through, spend, time, muster, of coin, hand anything*) passer; 2 (*go beyond*) dépasser; 3 (*accounts*) approuver; 4 (*surpass*) surpasser; 5 (*word, oath*) engager; 6 (*law*) voter; 7 (*in the street*) passer à côté de; 8 (*judgement*) prononcer; 9 (*a resolution*) prendre*; 10 (*exam.*) être reçu (à); ⚠ passer un examen = *properly* '*undergo*'; *~ vote of thanks,* voter des remerciements (à); *~ off for,* faire* passer pour; *~ over,* (*omit, not remark*) passer sous silence; (*not blame*) passer sur; *~ through,* passer par.
pass, *v.n.* (*time, move onward, die, disappear, circulate, be transmitted, of bill in Parl.*) passer; (*exam.*) être reçu; *~ along,* longer, *v.a.*; *~ away,* (*die*) mourir* (être); (*disappear*) disparaître* (avoir *of action,* être *of state*); *~ for,* passer pour; *~ off,* (*be over*) se passer; *~ off well,* réussir.
passabl|e, (*tolerable*) passable; (*road*) praticable; **~y,** passablement.
passage, (*passing, crossing by sea, passage money, way, corridor, lane, in book*) passage, *m.*; (*house*) couloir, *m.*; *~ of arms,* pas d'armes, *m.*
passenger, (*train, bus, &c.*) voyageu|r, ~se, *m.f.*; (*on sea, in aeropl.*) passag|er, ~ère, *m.f.*
passer-by, passant, *m.*
passing, *adj.* passag|er, ~ère; (*casual*) fortuit; *~-bell,* glas, *m.*; *adv.* excessivement.
passion, (*strong emotion, love, lit. and fig.*) passion, *f.*; (*eccles.*) Passion, *f.*; (*anger*) courroux, *m.*; *towering ~,* fureur, *f.*; **~-flower,** passiflore, *f.*; *~-play,* mystère de la Passion, *m.*; *Passion Week,* semaine sainte, *f.*
passionate, (*pers., things*) passionné; **~ness,** caractère passionné, *m.*; **~ly,** passionnément.
passionless, sans passion.
passiv|e, *s.* (*gram.*) passif, *m.*; *adj.* (*lit., gram., debt*) passi|f, ~ve; **~eness, ~ity,** passivité, *f.*; **~ely,** passivement; (*gram.*) au passif.
passover, (*Jewish*) Pâque, *f.*; (*Pascal Lamb*) agneau pascal, *m.*
passport, passeport, *m.*
password, mot de passe, *m.*
past, *s.* (*past time, gram.*) passé, *m.*; *adj.* passé; (*week, month, &c.*) derni|er, ~ère; (*just gone by*) derni|er, ~ère; *~ master, see* MASTER.
past, *prep.* (*beyond*) au delà de; (*more than*) plus de; (*without*) sans; *half-~seven,* sept heures et demie; *~ ten o'clock,* dix heures passées; *~ belief,* incroyable; *~ recovery,* (*pers.*) désespéré; (*things*) sans remède; *be ~,* (*endurance*) dépasser.
paste, (*cooking*) pâte, *f.*; (*for sticking*) colle de pâte, *f.*; (*jewel*) strass, *m.*; *v.a.* coller.
pasteboard, carton, *m.*
pastel, (*bot. and drawing*) pastel, *m.*; **~-green,** céladon, *invar.*
pastil, pastille, *f.*
pastime, passe-temps, *m.*
pastor, pasteur, *m.*; **~al,** *adj.* (*poem, scenery, eccles.*) pastoral; **~ate,** *s.* pastorat, *m.*
pastry, pâtisserie, *f.*; **~-cook,** patissi|er, ~ère, *m.f.*
pasturage, pâturage, *m.*
pasture, (*herbage*) pâture, *f.*; (*land*) pâturage, *m.*; *v.a.* faire* paître; *v.n.* paître*.

pasty, *adj.* pâteu|x, ~se.
pat, (*tap*) tape, *f.*; ~ *of butter*, coquille de beurre, *f.*; *v.a.* taper; (*animal*) caresser.
pat, *adv.* à propos.
patch, *s.* (*mend, piece of ground*) pièce, *f.*; (*on face*) mouche, *f.*; *v.a.* (*with material*) rapiécer; (*stop up hole*) boucher; ~ *up*, (*fam.*) rafistoler.
patchwork, (*needle and fig.*) rapiéçage, *m.*
pate, caboche, *f.*
paten, (*eccles.*) patène, *f.*
patent, *s.* brevet d'invention, *m.*; ⚠ patente = '*trade-licence*', '*bill of health*'; *adj.* (*invention*) breveté*; (*obvious*) patent; *v.a.* (*invention*) faire* breveter; ~ *leather*, *see* LEATHER.
patern|al, paternel, -le; **~ity,** (*lit. and fig.*) paternité, *f.*; **~ally,** paternellement.
paternoster, pater, *m. invar.*
path, (*lit. and fig.*) sentier, *m.*; *garden* ~, allée, *f.*
pathetic, pathétique; **~ally,** pathétiquement.
pathless, sans chemin frayé.
patholog|ical, pathologique; **~ist,** pathologiste, *m.*; **~y,** pathologie, *f.*
pathos, pathétique, *m.*; ⚠ pathos = '*bathos*', '*rant*', '*bombast*'.
pathway, sentier, *m.*
patience, (*lit. and card game*) patience, *f.*; *be out of* ~, être à bout de patience; *take* ~, faire* provision de patience.
patient, *s.* malade, *m.f.*; *adj.* patient; **~ly,** patiemment.
patriarch, patriarche, *m.*; **~al,** patriarcal.
patrician, *adj. and s.m.f.* patricien, -ne.
patrimon|ial, patrimonial; **~y,** patrimoine, *m.*
patriot, patriote, *m.f.*; **~ism,** patriotisme, *m.*; **~ic,** patriotique; **~ically,** patriotiquement.
patrol, patrouille, *f.*; *v.a.* faire* patrouille dans; *v.n.* aller* (être) en patrouille; ⚠ patrouiller, *gen.* = '*mess about*', '*paw*'.
patron, (*ant. protector*) patron, -ne, *m.f.*; ~ *saint*, patron, -ne, *m.f.*; **~ess,** (*charity*) dame patronesse, *f.*; **~age,** patronage, *m.*
patroniz|e, protéger; (*treat condescendingly*) traiter avec condescendance; **~ing,** *adj.* protect|eur, ~rice.
patronymic, *adj.* patronymique.
patten, (*clog*) socque, *m.*
patter, (*in song*) bavardage, *m.*; (*feet*) bruit de pas, *m.*; (*rain*) bruit de pluie, *m.*; *v.n.* fouetter; ~ *against*, fouetter, *v.a.*
pattern, (*perfect example*) modèle, *m.*; (*sample*) échantillon, *m.*; (*design*) dessin, *m.*
paucity, (*number*) petit nombre, *m.*; (*amount*) petite quantité, *f.*
paunch, bedaine, *f.*
pauper, indigent, -e, *m.f.*; *~'s grave*, fosse commune, *f.*; **~ism,** paupérisme, *m.*
pause, *s.* pause, *f.*; *v.n.* faire* une pause.
pav|e, *v.a.* paver; *~e way for*, préparer le chemin pour; **~ing-brick,** carreau, *m.*; **~ing-stone,** pavé, *m.*
pavement, (*of roads, &c.*) pavé, *m.*; (*footway*) trottoir, *m.*
pavilion, (*tent, arch., sports*) pavillon, *m.*
paving, *s.* (*action, marble, &c.*) pavement, *m.*
paw, *s.* patte, *f.*; *v.a.* patrouiller; *v.n.* (*horse*) piaffer.
pawn, *s.* (*pledge*) gage, *m.*; (*chess*) pion, *m.*; **~-ticket,** reconnaissance du mont-de-piété, *f.*; *v.a.* engager.
pawnbroker, prêteur sur gages, *m.*; *~'s shop*, (*in France municipal and official*) crédit municipal, *m.*; (*fam.*) ma tante.
pay, *s.* (*workman*) salaire, *m.*; (*soldier*) prêt, *m.*; (*officer*) solde, *f.*; (*public official*) appointements, *m.pl.*; (*clerks, &c.*) traitements, *m.*; *in the* ~ *of*, à la solde de; **~-day,** jour de paye, *m.*
pay, *v.a.* (*sum, fees, debt, fig.*) payer; (*visit, compliment*) faire*; (*homage*) rendre; (*yield*) donner; ~ *in*, (*to bank*) verser (à); ~ *for*, payer, à +*pers.*, *for* = pour; ~ *off*, (*dismiss*) congédier; (*debts*) acquitter; ~ *out*, (*rope*) laisser filer; (*money*) payer; ~ *up*, acquitter; *post paid*, affranchi; *reply paid*, (*telegr.*) avec réponse payée; ~ *self*, (*cheque*) payez à moi-même.
pay, *v.n.* payer; (*be profitable*) être avantageu|x, ~se; ~ *dear*, payer cher.
payable, payable (à); ~ *to bearer*, payable au porteur; ~ *at sight*, payable à vue.
payee, bénéficiaire, *m.f.*
payer, payeu|r, ~se, *m.f.*; *see also* PAYMASTER.
payment, payement, *m.*; (*into bank*) versement, *m.*; ~ *on account*, acompte, *m.*
pea, pois, *m.*; *sweet* ~, pois de senteur, *m.*; **~nut,** arachide, *f.*; **~-shell,** cosse de pois, *f.*; **~-shooter,** sarbacane, *f.*
peace, paix, *f.*; *~maker*, pacificat|eur, ~rice, *m.f.*; *make the* ~ *with*, se réconcilier avec.
peaceabl|e, paisible; **~eness,** tranquillité, *f.*; **~y,** paisiblement.
peaceful, paisible; **~ness,** tranquillité, *f.*; **~ly,** paisiblement.
peach, (*bot.*) pêche, *f.*; *~-blossom*, fleur de pêcher, *f.*; *~-coloured*, couleur de pêche, *invar.*; **~-tree,** pêcher, *m.*
peachick, paonneau, *m.*
pea|cock, **~fowl,** paon, *m.*; **~hen,** paonne, *f.*; *~cock-blue*, bleu paon, *invar.*
pea-jacket, vareuse, *f.*
peak, (*mount.*) cime, *f.*; (*cap*) visière, *f.*; (*point*) pointe, *f.*; (*highest point, price, &c.*) maximum, *m.*
peal, (*set, sound of several bells*) sonnerie, *f.*; (*chime*) carillon, *m.*; (*thunder, laughter*) éclat, *m.*; *v.a.* faire* retentir; *v.n.* retentir.
pear, poire, *f.*; **~-tree,** poirier, *m.*
pearl, perle, *f.*; **~-barley,** orge perlé, *m.*; **~-grey,** gris perle, *invar.*; **~y,** nacré.

peasant, paysan, -ne, *m.f.*; **~ry,** (les) paysans, *m.pl.*
peat, tourbe, *f.*; **~-bog,** tourbière, *f.*
pebble, caillou, *m.*; (*on shore*) galet, *m.*
peccable, peccable.
peccadillo, peccadille, *f.*
peck, *s.* (*bird*) coup de bec, *m.*; (*meas.*) peck, *m.*
peck, *v.a.* (*bird*) becqueter; (*with tool*) percer.
pectoral, *s.* pectoral, *m.*; *adj.* pectoral.
pecula|te, *v.a.* détourner; **~tion,** péculat, *m.*; **~tor,** concussionnaire, *m.f.*
peculiar, particuli|er, ~ère; (*unusual*) bizarre; ~ *to*, propre à; **~ity,** singularité, *f.*; (*peculiar habit*) manie, *f.*; **~ly,** particulièrement.
pecuniar|y, pécuniaire; **~ily,** pécuniairement.
pedagog|ue, pédagogue, *m.*; **~y,** pédagogie, *f.*; **~ic,** pédagogique.
pedal, (*bicycle, organ, &c.*) pédale, *f.*
pedant, *s.m.f.* pédant, -e; **~ry,** pédantisme, *m.*; **~ic,** pédant; (*things*) pédantesque; **~ically,** pédantesquement.
peddle, *v.a.* (*goods*) colporter.
pedestal, piédestal, *m.*
pedestrian, piéton, *m.*; *adj.* pédestre; ~ *crossing*, passage clouté, *m.*
pedigree, genéalogie, *f.*
pedlar, colporteur, *m.*
peel, *s.* (*fruit, &c.*) pelure, *f.*; *v.a.* peler; *v.n.* se peler; ~ *off*, (*paint., &c.*) s'écailler.
peep, *s.* coup d'œil furtif, *m.*; **~-hole,** judas, *m.*; *v.n. and* ~ *at*, regarder furtivement.
peer, *s.* (*equal, noble*) pair, *m.*; **~ess,** pairesse, *f.*; **~age,** pairie, *f.*
peer, *v.n.* (*appear*) apparaître*; (*day*) poindre*; ~ *at*, regarder de près.
peerless, incomparable; **~ly,** incomparablement.
peevish, acariâtre; **~ness,** humeur acariâtre, *f.*; **~ly,** d'une manière acariâtre.
peewit, (*ornith.*) vanneau, *m.*
peg, *s.* (*wood pin*) cheville, *f.*; (*of casks*) fausset, *m.*; (*tent*) piquet, *m.*; (*coats, &c.*) patère, *f.*; *v.a.* cheviller.
pejorative, péjorati|f, ~ve.
pelargonium, (*bot.*) pélargonium, *m.*
pelf, richesses, *f.*
pelican, pélican, *m.*
pelisse, pelisse, *f.*
pellet, boulette, *f.*
pellitory, (*bot.*) pariétaire, *f.*
pell-mell, *s.m. and adv.* pêle-mêle.
pellucid, transparent; (*style, &c.*) clair; **~ity,** transparence, clarté, *f.*
pelt, *s.* peau, *f.*
pelt, *v.a.* poursuivre* à coups de (pierre, boules de neige, etc.); *v.n.* (*rain*) tomber (être) à flots; **~ing,** *adj.* (*rain*) battant.
pemmican, pemmican, *m.*
pen, plume, *f.*; (*sheep, &c.*) parc, *m.*; (*U.S.A. prison*) prison, *f.*; **~holder,** porte-plume, *m. invar.*; **~-name,** nom de plume, *m.*; **~-wiper,** essuie-plume, *m. invar.*; *v.a.* (*write*) écrire*; (*sheep, &c.*) parquer.
penal, (*laws, &c.*) pénal; (*punishable*) passible d'une peine; (*place*) pénitentiaire.
penalize, (*sport*) pénaliser.
penalty, peine, *f.*
penance, pénitence, *f.*; *do* ~, faire* pénitence (de).
Penates, pénates, *m.pl.*
pence, *see* PENNY.
pencil, crayon, *m.*; (*brush*) pinceau, *m.*; **~-case,** porte-crayon, *m. invar.*
pencil, *v.a.* (*jot*) noter au crayon; (*draw*) dessiner.
pencilled, (*eyebrows, naturally*) dessiné; (*artificial*) fait au crayon.
pend|ant, ~ent, *s.* (*hanging ornament or drop*) pendeloque, *f.*; (*on necklace*) pendentif, *m.*; (*naut.*) *see* PENNANT; *adj.* (*hanging*) suspendu (à).
pending, *adj. and prep.* pendant.
pendulous, suspendu.
pendulum, pendule, *m.*
penetrab|ility, pénétrabilité, *f.*; **~le,** pénétrable.
penetra|te, *v.a.n.* pénétrer; ~ *with*, (*lit. and fig.*) pénétrer de; **~tion,** pénétration, *f.*; **~ting, ~tive,** (*lit. and fig.*) pénétrant.
penguin, (*ornith.*) manchot, *m.*
penholder, porte-plume, *m. invar.*
peninsula, péninsule, *f.*; **~r,** péninsulaire.
peniten|ce, pénitence, *f.*; **~t,** *adj. and s.m.f.* pénitent, -e; **~tly,** avec repentir. **~tial,** de pénitence; (*psalms, &c., belonging to penitence*) pénitenti|aux, ~elles, *only in plural.*
penitentiary, *s.* (*reformatory*) pénitencier, *m.*; *adj.* (*of penance*) pénitentiaire.
penknife, canif, *m.*
penmanship, écriture, *f.*
pennant, pendant, (*naut.*) flamme, *f.*
penniless, sans le sou.
pennon, (*mil.*) flamme, *f.*
penny, penny, *m.*, *pl.* pence; (*approx.*) deux, etc., sous, *m.pl.*; ~ *-in-the-slot*, (*machine*) distributeur automatique, *m.*
pennyroyal, (*bot.*) pouliot, *m.*
pennyworth, (*of*), pour deux sous (de).
pension, pension, *f.*; (*mil., nav.*) retraite, *f.*; ~*-fund*, caisse des retraites, *f.*; *retire on a* ~, prendre* sa retraite.
pension, *v.a.* pensionner; ~ *off*, mettre* à la retraite.
pensioner, (*nav., mil.*) retraité, *m.*; (*state*) pensionnaire, *m.*
pensive, pensi|f, ~ve; **~ness,** air pensif, *m.*; **~ly,** d'un air pensif.
penstemon, (*bot.*) penstémon, *m.*
pentagon, pentagone, *m.*
pentameter, pentamètre, *m.*
Pentateuch, pentateuque, *m.*
Pentecost, Pentecôte, *f.*
penthouse, (*lean-to*) appentis, *m.*

penultimate, *adj. and s.f.* pénultième.
penurious, mesquin; **~ly,** mesquinement.
penury, pénurie, *f.*
peony, (*bot.*) pivoine, *f.*
people, (*nation, lower orders, subjects*) peuple, *m.*; (*several individuals, folk, persons*) gens (*with adj. before it is fem., after it is masc., e.g.* des gens vertueux, les vieilles gens); (*relatives*) famille, *f.*; (*crowd*) monde, *m.*
people, *v.a.* peupler.
pep, (*U.S.A.* '*go*') allant, *m.*; *be full of ~,* avoir de l'allant.
pepper, poivre, *m.*; **~-box,** poivrière, *f.*; **~wort,** (*bot.*) passerage, *f.*
peppercorn, grain de poivre, *m.*
peppermint, menthe poivrée, *f.*
per, (*mile, day, month, head, each, post*) par.
peradventure, par †hasard.
perambulate, parcourir*.
perambulator, voiture d'enfant, *f.*
perceiv|e, (*see*) apercevoir; (*notice*) s'apercevoir de *or* que; **~able,** perceptible.
percentage, pourcentage, *m.*; (*on commission*) tant pour cent, *m.*; *~ of profits,* tantièmes, *m.pl.*
percep|tion, perception, *f.*; **~tible,** perceptible; **~tibly,** perceptiblement; **~tive,** percepti|f, ~ve.
perch, (*for bird*) perchoir, *m.*; (*ichth.*) perche, *f.*; *v.n.* (*bird, pers. colloq*); se percher.
perchance, peut-être.
percola|te, filtrer; **~tion,** filtration, *f.*
percussion, percussion, *f.*; **~-cap,** capsule, *f.*
perdition, perdition, *f.*
peregrina|te, voyager; **~tion,** pérégrination, *f.*
peregrine, *see* FALCON.
peremptor|y, péremptoire; (*pers.*) tranchant; **~ily,** péremptoirement.
perennial, *s.* (*bot.*) plante vivace, *f.*; *adj.* perpétuel, -le; (*plants*) vivace; **~ly,** perpétuellement.
perfect, *s.* (*gram.*) parfait, *m.*
perfect, *adj.* (*without defect, excellent*) parfait; (*completed*) parachevé; (*thorough*) achevé; (*gram.*) parfait; **~ly,** parfaitement.
perfect, *v.a.* rendre parfait; (*finish*) achever.
perfectib|ility, perfectibilité, *f.*; **~le,** perfectible.
perfection, (*absence of defect, highest degree*) perfection, *f.*; *to ~,* à la perfection.
perfervid, exalté.
perfidious, perfidy, perfide; **~ness,** perfidie, *f.*; **~ly,** perfidement.
perfora|te, perforer; **~tion,** perforation, *f.*
perform, *v.a.* (*task, &c.*) accomplir; (*public duties*) s'acquitter de; (*mus.*) exécuter; (*theatr.*) *v.a.n.* jouer.
performance, accomplissement, *m.*; (*theatr., &c.*) représentation, *f.*; (*action*) action, *f.*; ⚠ performance, *f., only of champions and race-horses.*
performer, (*mus.*) exécutant, *m.*
perfume, *s.* parfum, *m.*; *v.a.* parfumer; **~r,** parfumeu|r, ~se, *m.f.*; **~ry,** parfumerie, *f.*
perfunctor|y, fait par manière d'acquit; **~ily,** par manière d'acquit.
pergola, pergola, *f.*
perhaps, peut-être.
peril, péril, *m.*; *at one's ~,* à ses risques et périls; **~ous,** périlleu|x, ~se; **~ously,** périlleusement.
perimeter, périmètre, *m.*
period, (*space of time, epoch, phrase, math.*) période, *f.*
periodic, *adj.* périodique; **~ally,** périodiquement.
periodical, *s.* périodique, *m.*
periphery, *s.* périphérie, *f.*
periphras|is, périphrase, *f.*; **~tic,** périphrastique.
periscope, (*nav.*) périscope, *m.*
perish, *v.n.* périr; *be ~ed with cold,* mourir* (être) de froid; **~able,** périssable.
peristyle, (*arch.*) péristyle, *m.*
peritonitis, (*med.*) péritonite, *f.*
periwig, perruque, *f.*
periwinkle, (*bot.*) pervenche, *f.*; (*moll.*) bigorneau, *m.*
perjure oneself, se parjurer; **~d,** parjure.
perjur|er, parjure, *m.f.*; **~y,** parjure, *m.*
perky, impertinent.
permanen|ce, permanence, *f.*; **~t,** permanent; **~tly,** d'une manière permanente.
permea|te, *v.a.* pénétrer; *~ through,* pénétrer à travers; **~tion,** pénétration, *f.*
permiss|ible, permis; **~ion,** permission, *f.*
permit, *s.* permis, *m.*; (*customs*) passavant, *m.*
permit, *v.a.* permettre* (*acc. of thing, dat. of pers.,* de + *inf.*); *~ of,* admettre*.
permutation, permutation, *f.*
pernicious, pernicieu|x, ~se; **~ly,** pernicieusement.
peroration, péroraison, *f.*
perpendicular, *adj. and s.f.* perpendiculaire (à); **~ly,** perpendiculairement.
perpetra|te, commettre*; **~tion,** perpétration, *f.*; **~tor,** (*crime, &c.*) auteur, *m.*
perpetual, perpétuel, -le; **~ly,** perpétuellement.
perpetua|te, perpétuer; **~tion,** perpétuation, *f.*
perpetuity, perpétuité, *f.*
perplex, (*muddle, entangle*) embrouiller; (*puzzle*) embarrasser; **~ity,** embarras, *m.*; (*in making decision*) perplexité, *f.*
perquisites, (*unstipulated*) revenants-bons, *m.pl.*
perry, poiré, *m.*
persecu|te, persécuter; (*worry*) †harceler

(de); **~tion,** persécution, *f.*; **~tor,** persécut|eur, ~rice, *m.f.*
persever|ance, persévérance, *f.*; **~e,** persévérer; **~ing,** persévérant; **~ingly,** avec persévérance.
Persian, (*mod.*) *adj.* (*when an adj. use small letter*) *and s.m.f.* Persan, -e; (*ant.*) P(p)erse.
persimmon, (*fruit*) plaquemine, *f.*; (*tree*) plaqueminier, *m.*
persist, persister (dans, à + *inf.*); **~ence,** persistance, *f.*
person, (*being, appearance, gram.*) personne, *f.*; **~able,** beau, (+ *masc. vowel or mute* H, bel) belle; **~age,** personnage, *m.*
personal, personnel, -le; ~*property*, biens meubles, *m.pl.*; **~ity,** (*individuality, force of character, important person, ill-natured remark*) personnalité, *f.*; **~ly,** (*in person*) personnellement; *as far as I, you, &c., are ~ly concerned,* pour ma, votre, &c., part.
personate, *v.a.* se faire* passer pour; (*theatr.*) jouer le rôle de.
personif|y, personnifier; **~ication,** (*lit. and fig.*) personnification, *f.*
perspective, perspective, *f.*; *adj.* perspecti|f, ~ve.
perspicac|ious, (*having mental penetration*) perspicace; **~ity,** perspicacité, *f.*
perspicu|ous, (*easily understood*) clair; **~ity,** clarté, *f.*; **~ously,** clairement.
perspir|e, *v.n.* transpirer; **~ation,** transpiration, *f.*; ⚠ *not* perspiration *which is a little-used medical term.*
persuade, (*convince of fact*) convaincre* de; (*induce to do*) persuader (*dat. of pers.*, de + *inf.*); ~ *from, against,* dissuader de; ~ *that,* persuader (*dat. of pers.* + que).
persuas|ion, persuasion, *f.*; (*opinion, relig. belief*) croyance, *f.*; **~ive,** persuasi|f, ~ve; **~ively,** d'une manière persuasive.
pert, (*saucy*) impertinent; **~ness,** impertinence, *f.*; **~ly,** avec impertinence.
pertain, (*belong*) appartenir* (à).
pertinac|ious, opiniâtre; **~iously,** opiniâtrément; **~ity,** opiniâtreté, *f.*
pertinent, (*relevant*) pertinent; **~ly,** pertinemment.
perturb, troubler; **~ation,** perturbation, *f.*
peruke, perruque, *f.*
perus|e, lire* avec attention; **~al,** lecture, *f.*
pervade, pénétrer; (*mind*) s'emparer de.
pervers|e, entêté; ⚠ pervers = *chiefly 'wicked', 'depraved'*; **~ity,** obstination, *f.*; **~ely,** avec entêtement.
pervert, *s.* (*eccles.*) apostat, *m.*; *v.a.* (*lead morally astray*) pervertir; (*text, &c.*) dénaturer.
pessim|ism, pessimisme, *m.*; **~ist,** pessimiste, *m.*; **~istic,** pessimiste.
pest, (*lit. and fig.*) fléau, *m.*
pester, tourmenter.
pestilen|ce, pestilence, *f.*; **~t,** (*lit. and fig.*) pestilent; (*fam.*) assommant; **~tial,** (*disease*) pestilentiel, -le.
pestiferous, (*pernicious, hurtful*) pernicieu|x, ~se.
pestle, pilon, *m.*
pet, *s.* (*temper*) accès d'humeur, *m.*; (*child*) enfant gâté, -e, *m.f.*; *adj.* (*of ans., &c.*) favori, -te; ~ *name,* petit nom d'amitié, *m.*
pet, *v.a.* choyer; (*spoil*) gâter.
petal, pétale, *m.*
petard, (*mil., cracker-firework*) pétard, *m.*
petition, placet, *m.*; (*entreaty*) prière, *f.*; *v.a.* (*person in authority*) adresser une pétition à.
petitioner, solliciteu|r, ~se, *m.f.*
petrel, stormy ~, (*ornith.*) pétrel, *m.*
petrif|action, pétrifaction, *f.*; **~y,** pétrifier.
petrol, essence, *f.*; ⚠ *not* pétrole *which* = *'paraffin oil', 'paraffin', 'petroleum'*; *~-can,* (*motor*) bidon à essence, *m.*; *~-pump,* pompe à essence, *f.*; *~-tank,* réservoir à essence, *m.*
petroleum, pétrole, *m.*
petticoat, jupon, *m.*; *be under ~ government,* tomber (être) en quenouille.
pettifogger, avocassier, *m.*
pettish, bourru; **~ly,** d'une manière bourrue.
pett|y, petit; (*without importance*) insignifiant; **~y cash,** petite caisse, *f.*; *~y expenses, see* EXPENSE; **~iness,** petitesse, *f.*
petulan|ce, pétulance, *f.*; **~t,** pétulant; **~tly,** avec pétulance.
petunia, (*bot.*) pétunia, *m.*
pew, banc, *m.*
pewit, *see* PEEWIT.
pewter, étain, *m.*; **~er,** potier d'étain, *m.*
phaeton, phaéton, *m.*
phalanx, phalange, *f.*
phantasm, phantom, fantôme, *m.*
phantasmagoria, fantasmagorie, *f.*
Pharis|ee, pharisien, -ne; **~aic,** pharisaïque.
pharmacy, pharmacie, *f.*
phase, phase, *f.*
pheasant, faisan, -e, *m.f.*; *young ~,* faisandeau, *m.*
phenomen|al, phénoménal; **~on,** phénomène, *m.*
phial, fiole, *f.*
philander, faire* la cour (à).
philanthrop|ic, philanthropique; **~ist,** philanthrope, *m.f.*; **~y,** philanthropie, *f.*
philatelist, philatéliste, *m.*
philippic, philippique, *f.*
Philistine, philistin, -e, *m.f.*
philolog|ist, philologue, *m.f.*; **~y,** philologie, *f.*
philosoph|er, philosophe, *m.f.*; *~er's stone,* pierre philosophale, *f.*; **~y,** philosophie, *f.*; **~ic,** philosophique; **~ically,** (*resignedly*) philosophiquement; **~ize,** philosopher.
philtre, philtre, *m.*

phlegm, flegme, *m.*; **~atic,** flegmatique.
phlox, (*bot.*) phlox, *m.*
phoenix, phénix, *m.*
phone, *s.* téléphone, *m.*; ~ *number,* numéro d'appel, *m.*; *v.a.n.* téléphoner.
phonetic, *adj.* phonétique; **~s,** *s.* phonétique, *f.*
phosphorescen|ce, phosphorescence, *f.*; **~t,** phosphorescent.
phosphor|ic, phosphorique; **~us,** *s.* phosphore, *m.*
photograph, *s.* photographie, *f.*; **~er,** photographe, *m.f.*; **~y,** photographie, *f.*; *X-ray ~y,* radiographie, *f.*; **~ic,** photographique.
phrase, *s.* (*sentence with predicate*) phrase, *f.*; (*group of words without predicate*) locution, *f.*; (*mode of expression*) style, *m.*; *v.a.* exprimer.
phraseology, phraséologie, *f.*
phrenolog|ist, phrénologiste, *m.*; **~y,** phrénologie, *f.*
phthis|ical, phtisique; **~is,** phtisie, *f.*
physic, médecine, *f.*; *v.a.* droguer; **~s,** physique, *f.*; **~al,** (*material, according to laws of nature, of physics, bodily*) physique; **~ally,** physiquement.
physician, médecin, *m.*; ⚠ *not* physicien *which* = '*physicist*'.
physiognomy, (*science, face*) physiognomie, *f.*
physiolog|ist, physiologiste, *m.f.*; **~y,** physiologie, *f.*
physique, *s.* (*constitution*) physique, *m.*
pian|ist, pianiste, *m.f.*; **~o,** piano, *m.*
pick, *s.* (*tool*) pic, *m.*; (*choice*) choix, *m.*
pick, *v.a.* 1 (*gather*) cueillir*; 2 (*teeth*) curer; 3 (*select*) trier; 4 (*quarrel*) chercher; 5 (*lock*) crocheter; 6 (*ground*) creuser; 7 (*bone*) ronger; 8 (*pocket*) voler à la tire; ~ *off,* (*fruit, flower, &c.*) cueillir*; ~ *out,* (*choose*) choisir; ~ *up,* (*lit. and fig.*) ramasser; (*living*) gagner péniblement; (*passenger, &c.*) prendre*; *v.n.* ~ *up,* (*health*) reprendre* ses forces; (*shares*) se ressaisir.
pickaback, *adv.* sur le dos.
pickaxe, pioche, *f.*
picket, (*for horse*) pieu, *m.*; (*mil., strike*) piquet, *m.*; *v.a.* poster.
pickings, restes, *m.pl.*
pickle, (*brine*) saumure, *f.*; (*vegs. pickled*) conserves de légumes au vinaigre, *f.pl.*; *I'm in a pretty ~,* me voilà dans de beaux draps; *v.a.* mariner; (*salt*) saler.
pick|pocket, ~purse, filou, *m.*
picnic, pique-nique, *m.*; *v.n.* faire* un pique-nique.
pictorial, *s.* journal illustré, *m.*; *adj.* de peintre; (*illustrated*) illustré.
picture, *s.* tableau, *m.*; (*portrait, exact image*) portrait, *m.*; ~ **post-card,** carte postale illustrée, *f.*; *the ~s,* ~ **palace,** cinéma, *m.*; *v.a.* (*represent*) représenter; ~ *to oneself,* se figurer.
picturesque, ~ness, *s.* pittoresque, *m.*; *adj.* pittoresque; **~ ly,** pittoresquement.
pie, (*fish, meat, printer's*) pâté, *m.*; (*fruit*) tarte, *f.*; **~-dish,** tourtière, *f.*
piebald, *adj.* pie, *invar.*
piece, *s.* (*bit, fragment*) morceau, *m.*; (*part of whole*) partie, *f.*; (*land, money, chess, artil.*) pièce, *f.*; ~ *of news,* nouvelle, *f.*; ~ *of work,* ouvrage, *m.*; **~-work,** ouvrage à la tâche, *m.*; *take to ~s,* démonter; *go to ~s,* (*pers.*) se perdre.
piece, *v.a.* rapiécer; (*put together*) assembler; ~ *out,* allonger.
piecemeal, pièce à pièce.
pied, *adj.* bigarré.
pier, (*bridge*) pile, *f.*; (*harbour, sea-side*) jetée, *f.*; **~-glass,** trumeau, *m.*
pierc|e, (*lit. and fig.*) percer; **~ing,** *adj.* perçant.
piet|y, piété, *f.*; **~ism,** (*eccles.*) piétisme, *m.*; **~ist,** piétiste, *m.f.*
pig, *s.* (*lit. and pers.*) cochon, *m.*; (*metal*) saumon, *m.*; *a ~ in a poke,* chat en poche, *m.*; **sucking-~,** cochon de lait, *m.*; **~gery,** *see* PIGSTY.
pigeon, (*lit. and fig.*) pigeon, -ne, *m.f.*; **~-hole,** (*for papers, &c.*) case, *f.*; *set of ~-holes,* casier, *m.*; **~-house,** colombier, *m.*; **rock-~,** biset, *m.*; **wood-~,** pigeon ramier, *m.*; **young ~,** pigeonneau, *m.*
pigheaded, entêté.
pigment, pigment, *m.*
pigskin, peau de porc, *f.*
pigsticking, chasse au sanglier à l'épieu, *f.*
pigsty, (*piggery*) étable à porcs, *f.*; (*fig.*) bouge, *m.*
pigtail, queue, *f.*
pigwash, pig's wash, eaux grasses, *f.pl.*
pike, (*weapon*) pique, *f.*; (*ichth.*) brochet, *m.*
pilaster, pilastre, *m.*
pilchard, pilchard, *m.*
pile, *s.* 1 (*stake*) pieu, *m.*; 2 (*for bridge, &c.*) pilotis, *m.*; 3 (*heap*) tas, *m.*; 4 (*funeral*) bûcher, *m.*; 5 (*of velvet, carpet*) poil, *m.*; 6 (*hoard*) pelote, *f.*; 7 (*building*) édifice, *m.*; 8 (*arms*) faisceau, *m.*
pile, *v.a.* empiler; (*heap*) entasser; (*fortune, &c.*) amasser.
pilfer, dérober; **~er,** escamoteu|r, **~se,** *m.f.*; **~ing,** larcin, *m.*
pilgrim, pèlerin, -e, *m.f.*; **~age,** pèlerinage, *m.*
pill, pilule, *f.*
pillage, *s.* pillage, *m.*; *v.a.* piller.
pillar, (*lit. and fig.*) pilier, *m.*; **~-box,** boîte aux lettres, *f.*
pillion, selle de femme, *f.*; *ride ~,* (*horse, motor cycle*) monter (être) en croupe.
pillory, pilori, *m.*; *v.a.* (*lit. and fig.*) mettre* au pilori.
pillow, oreiller, *m.*; **~-case, ~-slip,** taie d'oreiller, *f.*; *v.a.* (*head*) poser.
pilot, (*naut., aeron.*) pilote, *m.*; **~-boat,** pilote, *m.*; **~-engine,** locomotive pilote, *f.*; *v.a.* piloter; **~age,** pilotage, *m.*
pimento, piment, *m.*
pimpernel, (*bot.*) mouron, *m.*; ⚠ pimprenelle = '*burnet*'.

pimpl|e, bouton, *m.*; **~y**, boutonneu|x, ~se.
pin, épingle, *f.*; (*wooden*) cheville, *f.*; (*mach.*) clavette, *f.*; **rolling-~**, rouleau, *m.*; **~-money**, argent de poche, *m.*; **~-prick**, (*fig.*) coup d'épingle, *m.*; *have ~s and needles*, avoir les fourmis.
pin, *v.a.* épingler; (*with peg*) cheviller; (*against wall, &c.*) clouer.
pinafore, (*child's*) sarrau, *m.*
pincers, (*tool*) tenailles, *f.pl.*; (*lobsters, &c.*) pinces, *f.pl.*
pinch, *s.* (*from fingers, &c.*) pinçon, *m.*; (*fig.*) tenaille, *f.*; (*snuff*) prise, *f.*; (*salt, &c.*) pincée, *f.*; (*crisis*) extrémité, *f.*
pinch, *v.a.* (*lit. and cold*) pincer; (*shoe*) blesser; (*slang, steal*) chiper; *v.n.* pincer; (*stint oneself*) se serrer; *that's where the shoe ~es*, c'est là que le bât le blesse.
pinchbeck, chrysocale, *m.*
pincushion, pelote, *f.*
Pindaric, pindarique.
pine, pin, *m.*; **~-apple**, ananas, *m.*; **~-cone**, pomme de pin, *f.*; *~ plantation*, pinaie, *f.*; **stone-~**, pin-pignon, *m.*
pine, *v.a.* languir; *~ for*, soupirer après.
ping, *s.* (*bullet*) sifflement, *m.*
pinion, *s.* (*wing*) aileron, *m.*
pinion, *v.a.* (*bind*) lier.
pink, *s.* (*bot.*) œillet, *m.*; (*colour*) rose, *m.*; *adj.* (*colour*) rose.
pinnace, (*naut.*) pinasse, *f.*
pinnacle, (*arch.*) tourelle, *f.*; (*fig.*) pinacle, *m.*
pint, pinte, *f.*
pintail, (*ornith.*) pilet, *m.*
pioneer, (*lit., mil., fig.*) pionnier, *m.*
pious, pieu|x, ~se; **~ly**, pieusement.
pip, *s.* (*fruits*) pépin, *m.*; (*cards, &c.*) point, *m.*
pipe, *s.* (*water, gas, stove, organ*) tuyau, *m.*; (*mus. instr.*) chalumeau, *m.*; (*naut.*) sifflet, *m.*; (*smoking*) pipe, *f.*; (*short cutty*) brûle-gueule, *m. invar.*; *~ of peace*, calumet de paix, *m.*; **~-rack**, ratelier à pipes, *m.*; *v.a.* jouer sur un chalumeau; (*naut.*) appeler à coups de sifflet; *v.n.* jouer du chalumeau; (*birds*) siffler.
piper, (*bagpipe*) joueur de cornemuse, *m.*
pipit, (*ornith.*) farlouse, *f.*
pippin, (*apple*) reinette, *f.*
piquan|cy, goût piquant, *m.*; (*fig.*) piquant, *m.*; **~t**, (*lit. and fig.*) piquant.
pique, pique, *f.*; *v.a.* piquer.
piquet, (*cards*) piquet, *m.*
pira|cy, piraterie, *f.*; (*Lit.*) contrefaçon, *f.*; **~te**, *s.* pirate, *m.*; (*Lit.*) plagiaire, *m.f.*; *v.a.* piller; (*Lit.*) contrefaire*; *v.n.* pirater.
pirouette, pirouette, *f.*; *v.n.* pirouetter.
pistachio, (*fruit*) pistache, *f.*; (*tree*) pistachier, *m.*
pistol, pistolet, *m.*; **~-shot**, coup de pistolet, *m.*; *within ~-shot*, à portée de pistolet.
piston, piston, *m.*; **~-rod**, tige de piston, *f.*
pit, *s.* fosse, *f.*; (*cavity, stomach*) creux, *m.*; (*theatr.*) parterre, *m.*; (*cockpit*) arène, *f.*; *v.a.* (*against*) opposer à; *be ~ted with smallpox*, être grêlé.
pit-(a-)pat, *go ~*, palpiter.
pitch, *s.* (*substance*) poix, *f.*; (*degree*) degré, *m.*; (*mus.*) ton, *m.*; (*sport*) terrain, *m.*; (*street-seller*) place, *f.*; *highest ~*, comble, *m.*; *queer the ~ for*, (*pop.*) couper l'herbe sous le pied de.
pitch, *v.a.* (*tent*) dresser; (*camp*) asseoir*; (*throw to mark*) lancer; (*road*) enduire* de poix; *~ed battle*, bataille rangée, *f.*
pitcher, (*vessel*) cruche, *f.*
pitchfork, fourche, *f.*
pitching, (*naut.*) tangage, *m.*
piteous, piteu|x, ~se; **~ly**, piteusement.
pitfall, (*lit. and fig.*) piège, *m.*
pith, moelle, *f.*; (*fig.*) quintessence, *f.*; **~less**, (*style*) plat, -e; **~ helmet**, casque colonial, *m.*
pith|y, (*style*) nerveu|x, ~se; **~iness**, vigueur, *f.*; **~ily**, nerveusement.
pitiabl|e, (*things*) pitoyable; (*pers.*) digne de pitié; **~y**, pitoyablement.
pitiful, pitoyable; **~ness**, compassion, *f.*; (*wretchedness*) état pitoyable, *m.*; **~ly**, pitoyablement.
pitiless, impitoyable; **~ly**, impitoyablement.
pittance, pitance, *f.*
pity, pitié, *f.*; (*ground for regret*) dommage, *m.*; *for ~'s sake, out of ~*, par pitié; *what a ~!* quel dommage!; *take ~ on*, avoir pitié de; *v.a.* plaindre*.
pityingly, avec compassion.
pivot, (*lit. and fig.*) pivot, *m.*; **~al**, essentiel, -le; *v.n.* pivoter.
pix, (*eccles.*) ciboire, *m.*
pixy, fée, *f.*
placab|le, dou|x, ~ce; **~ility**, douceur, *f.*
placard, affiche, *f.*; *v.a.* afficher.
place, *s.* (*locality, town, village, &c.*) lieu, *m.*; (*in body, spot, place in book or speech, residence*) endroit, *m.*; (*in order, exact place, seat, room, position occupied, of servants*) place, *f.*; (*employment*) emploi, *m.*; (*rank*) rang, *m.*; (*country seat*) château, *m.*; **watering-~**, (*spa*) ville d'eaux, *f.*; (*sea-side*) station balnéaire, *f.*; (*cattle*) abreuvoir, *m.*; *~ of residence*, domicile, *m.*; *~ of worship*, édifice religieux, *m.*; *give ~ to*, faire* place à.
place, *v.a.* mettre*; (*comm., money, orders*) placer.
placid, placide; **~ity**, douceur, *f.*; **~ly**, doucement.
placing, *s.* (*comm.*) placement, *m.*
plagiar|ism, plagiat, *m.*; **~ist**, plagiaire, *m.f.*
plague, *s.* (*med.*) peste, *f.*; (*fig.*) fléau, *m.*; (*Egypt*) plaie, *f.*; *~ on!* peste de!
plague, *v.a.* (*fig.*) tourmenter.
plaice, (*ichth.*) carrelet, *m.*
plaid, (*Scotch*) plaid, *m.*
plain, *s.* plaine, *f.*
plain, *adj.* (*smooth*) uni; (*pers., food, dress*) simple; (*mere*) simple *before noun*; (*evi-*

dent) évident; (*ugly*) laid; (*straightforward*) fran|c, ~che; (*ordinary*) ordinaire; (*unadorned*) simple; ~-*spoken*, qui a son franc parler; **~ness,** (*simplicity*) simplicité, *f.*; (*clearness*) clarté, *f.*; (*ugliness*) laideur, *f.*; **~ly,** simplement; (*clearly*) évidemment.

plaintiff, demand|eur, ~eresse, *m.f.*

plaintive, plainti|f, ~ve; **~ly,** plaintivement.

plait, (*hair*) tresse, *f.*; *v.a.* tresser.

plan, *s.* (*outline, building, city, &c.*) plan, *m.*; (*project*) projet, *m.*; ~ *of campaign*, plan de campagne, *m.*; *v.a.* (*building, &c.*) faire* le plan de; (*arrange*) projeter.

plane, *s.* (*surface, maths., fig.*) plan, *m.*; (*tool*) rabot, *m.*; (*plane-tree*) platane, *m.*; (*aeron.*) avion, *m.*; **torpedo-** ~, avion torpilleur, *m.*; **training-** ~, avion école, *m.*; *v.a.* (*with tool*) raboter.

planet, planète, *f.*; **~ary,** planétaire.

plank, *s.* planche, *f.*; (*naut.*) bordage, *m.*; *v.a.* planchéier; (*slang, 'pay up'*) casquer.

plant, *s.* plante, *f.*; (*mach., &c.*) matériel, *m.*; *sensitive* ~, sensitive, *f.*

plant, *v.a.* (*plants, ladder, flag, and fam.*) planter; (*sentinel, &c.*) poster; (*colony, &c.*) fonder; (*ideas*) implanter.

plantain, (*bot.*) plantain, *m.*

plantation, (*act of planting, estate in colonies, assembly of trees*) plantation, *f.*; ~ *of ash trees, oak, see these words.*

planter, (*col.*) planteur colon, *m.*

plaque, plaque, *f.*

plash, *v.n.* (*in water*) barboter; *interj.* flac!

plaster, (*mixture of lime, &c.*) plâtre, *m.*; (*med.*) emplâtre, *m.*; (*fine, of Paris*) plâtre fin, *m.*; **~-cast,** plâtre, *m.*; *v.a.* plâtrer; **~ing, ~ing-work,** plâtrage, *m.*

plasterer, plâtrier, *m.*

plastic, plastique; (*fig.*) souple; **~ity,** plasticité, *f.*

plate, (*metal, photo., door*) plaque, *f.*; (*engraver*) planche, *f.*; (*china, &c.*) assiette, *f.*; (*collection*) plateau, *m.*; (*gold, silver*) vaisselle plate, *f.*; **~-basket,** panier à argenterie, *m.*; **~-glass,** glace, *f.*; **~-warmer,** chauffe-assiettes, *m.invar.*; **~-rack,** égouttoir, *m.*

plated, plaqué; *silver-~*, argenté.

plateau, plateau, *m.*

plateful, assiettée, *f.*

platform, (*rail.*) quai, *m.*; (*raised floor*) estrade, *f.*; (*polit.*) plate-forme, *f.*

platinum, platine, *m.*

platitude, platitude, *f.*

Platonic, (*of Plato, love, &c.*) platonique.

platoon, peloton, *m.*

platter, (*dish*) plat, *m.*; (*plate*) assiette, *f.*; (*mil.*) gamelle, *f.*

plaudit, applaudissement, *m.*

plausib|le, (*pers. approx.*) cajoleu|r, ~se; (*things*) spécieu|x, ~se; **~ility,** plausibilité, *f.*; **~ly,** spécieusement.

play, *s.* (*amusement, game, gambling, of light, of mach., of words*) jeu, *m.*; (*theatre*) spectacle, *m.*; (*dramatic piece*) pièce de théâtre, *f.*; *in* ~, pour rire; *that's not fair* ~, ce n'est pas de jeu.

play, *v.a.* (*game*) jouer à; (*instr.*) jouer de; (*cannon, &c., on*) diriger sur; (*tune, card, theatr., part, drama*) jouer; ~ *at*, (*pretend*) faire* pour rire; ~ *on*, (*credulity, &c.*) mettre* à profit; (*words*) jouer sur; (*fire-engine*) être dirigé sur; ~ *over*, (*a smile, &c.*) errer sur; ~ *up to*, flatter.

play, *v.n.* (*mus., gambling, move freely in play, sunshine, fountains, &c.*) jouer; (*sport*) folâtrer.

playbill, affiche de théâtre, *f.*

player, joueu|r, ~se, *m.f.*; (*theatr.*) act|eur, ~rice, *m.f.*; **strolling** ~, comédien ambulant, *m.*

playfellow, camarade de jeu, *m.*

playful, enjoué; **~ness,** enjouement, *m.*; **~ly,** en jouant.

playgoer, amateur de théâtre, *m.*

playground, cour de récréation, *f.*

playhouse, théâtre, *m.*

playmate, compagnon de jeu, *m.*

playroom, salle de récréation, *f.*

plaything, jouet, *m.*

playtime, récréation, *f.*

playwright, dramaturge, *m.*

plea, (*excuse*) excuse, *f.*; (*law*) défense, *f.*; *on the* ~ *of*, sous prétexte de.

plead, *v.a.* (*cause*) plaider; (*allege*) alléguer; *v.n.* (*advocate and fig.*) plaider; ~ *with . . . for . . .*, plaider auprès de . . . pour . . . .

pleadingly, d'un ton suppliant.

pleasant, agréable; **~ness,** agrément, *m.*; **~ly,** agréablement.

pleasantry, plaisanterie, *f.*

please, *v.a.* plaire* à; (*give pleasure*) faire plaisir à; (*satisfy*) contenter; *be ~d with*, être content de; *be ~d to*, (*request*) veuillez + *inf.*; (*glad to*) être content de.

please, *v.n.* plaire*; *as you* ~, comme vous voulez *or* voudrez; *if you* ~, s'il vous plaît; ~ *God*, s'il plaît à Dieu; ~, (*imperat.*) s'il vous plaît, veuillez + *inf.*

pleased, content.

pleasing, (*pers.*) charmant; (*thing*) agréable.

pleasurab|le, agréable; **~ly,** agréablement.

pleasur|e, (*enjoyment, desire, sensuous*) plaisir, *m.*

pleat, *s.* pli; *v.a.* plisser.

plebeian, *adj. and s.m.f.* plébéien, -ne.

plebiscite, plébiscite, *m.*

pledge, *s.* (*lit. and fig.*) gage, *m.*; (*health*) santé, *f.*; (*binding promise*) engagement; *put in* ~, mettre* en gage.

pledge, *v.a.* mettre* en gage; (*drink health of*) boire* à la santé de; (*honour, word*) engager.

plenary, pléni|er, ~ère.

plenipotentiary, *adj. and s.m.* plénipotentiaire.

plenitude, plénitude, *f.*

plenteous, abondant; **~ness,** abondance, *f.*; **~ly,** abondamment.

plent|y, abondance, *f.*; **~iful**, abondant.
pleon|asm, pléonasme, *m.*; **~astic**, pléonastique.
plethora, pléthore, *f.*
pleurisy, pleurésie, *f.*
pliab|ility, flexibilité, *f.*; **~le**, (*lit. and fig.*) souple.
plian|cy, flexibilité, *f.*; **~t**, souple; (*fig.*) docile.
pliers, pinces, *f.pl.*
plight, *s.* état, *m.*; *v.a.* (*pledge*) engager.
plinth, (*arch.*) plinthe, *f.*
plod, *v.n.* marcher avec peine; **~** *at*, peiner sur.
plodder, (*student, &c.*) piocheur, *m.*
plodding, *s.* travail assidu, *m.*; *adj.* laborieu|x, ~se.
plot, *s.* (*conspiracy*) complot, *m.*; (*of ground*) morceau, *m.*; (*novel, play*) intrigue, *f.*
plot, *v.a.* comploter; *v.n.* conspirer.
plotter, conspirat|eur, ~rice, *m.f.*
plough, charrue, *f.*; **~-boy**, garçon de charrue, *m.*; **~-man**, laboureur, *m.*; **~-share**, soc de charrue, *m.*; **~-handle, -tail**, mancheron, *m.*; *v.a.n.* labourer; (*fig.*) sillonner; **~ing**, labourage, *m.*
plover, (*ornith.*) pluvier, *m.*
pluck, *s.* (*courage*) cran, *m.*
pluck, *v.a.* (*flowers*) cueillir*; (*fowls and dupe*) plumer; (*exams*) recaler; ~ *out*, (*hair, &c.*) arracher.
pluck|y, crâne; **~ily**, courageusement.
plug, *s.* tampon, *m.*; (*tobacco*) carotte, *f.*; **~-hat**, (*U.S.A*) chapeau †haut de forme, *m.*; **sparking-, fire-~**, (*motor*) bougie, *f.*; *v.a.* tamponner.
plum, prune, *f.*; **~-pudding**, plum-pudding, *m.*; **~-tree**, prunier, *m.*
plumage, plumage, *m.*
plumb, *s.* (*sounding-lead*) plomb de sonde, *m.*; *out of* ~, hors d'aplomb; *v.a.* (*lit. and fig.*) sonder; (*wall, &c.*) plomber; *adj.* à plomb; (*utter*) pur; *adv.* (*vertically*) d'aplomb; (*U.S.A. slang* '*utterly*') furieusement.
plumbago, plombagine, *f.*
plumb|er, plombier, *m.*; **~ing**, plomberie, *f.*
plume, *s.* (*large feather*) plume, *f.*; (*bunch of feathers*) plumet, *m.*
plume, *v.a.* orner de plumes; ~ *oneself on*, se targuer de.
plummet, *s.* plomb de sonde, *m.*; ⚠ plumet = '*plume of feathers*'.
plump, potelé; **~ness**, embonpoint, *m.*
plump, *v.a.* laisser tomber; *v.n.* se laisser tomber.
plump, *adv.* comme une masse.
plunder, (*act*) pillage, *m.*; (*booty*) butin, *m.*
plunder, *v.a.* piller; (*rob*) dérober.
plunderer, pillard, -e, *m.f.*
plunge, *s.* plongeon, *m.*; *v.a.n.* plonger; (*rush*) se précipiter.
pluperfect, *s.* plus-que-parfait, *m.*
plural, *s.* pluriel, *m.*; *adj.* pluriel, -le.
plurality, pluralité, *f.*; (*benefices, &c.*) cumul, *m.*
plus, *s.* (*sign*) plus, *m.*
plush, peluche, *f.*
ply, *s.* (*cloth, &c.*) pli, *m.*
ply, *v.a.* (*handle, use*) manier; (*trade, &c.*) s'appliquer à; ~ *with*, (*questions, &c.*) presser de; (*with drink*) prier avec instance (de boire); *v.n.* (*veh.*) faire* un service régulier (entre).
pneumatic, pneumatique.
pneumonia, (*med.*) pneumonie, *f.*
poach, *v.a.* (*eggs*) pocher; *v.n.* (*game*) braconner.
poacher, braconnier, *m.*
pock-marked, grêlé.
pocket, (*garment, geol.*) poche, *f.*; (*leather in saddle, motor, &c.*) sacoche, *f.*; (*billiards*) blouse, *f.*; (*aeron.*) trou d'air, *m.*; **~-book**, portefeuille, *m.*; **~-knife**, canif, *m.*; **~-money**, argent de poche, *m.*; **~ handkerchief**, mouchoir, *m.*; *adj.* de poche.
pocket, *v.a.* (*lit. and fig.*) empocher.
pod, *s.* cosse, *f.*
podgy, potelé.
poe|m, (*long*) poème, *m.*; (*short*) poésie, *f.*; **~sy**, poésie, *f.*
poet, poète, *m.*; **~aster**, poétereau, *m.*; **~ess**, poétesse, *f.*; **~ic(al)**, poétique; **~ically**, poétiquement; **~ize**, poétiser; *minor* ~, poète de second ordre, *m.*
poignan|cy, (*grief, &c.*) acuité, *f.*; (*smell, taste, &c.*) âpreté, *f.*; **~t**, (*grief, &c.*) poignant; (*smell, taste, &c.*) piquant.
point, *s.* (*dot, gram., geom., mus., of time, degree of temp., &c., detail, of fact, of law, of view, in games, precise moment*) point, *m.*; (*sharp end, wit, cape*) pointe, *f.*; (*rail.*) aiguille, *f.*; ~ *of the compass*, aire de vent, *f.*; ~ *of honour*, point d'honneur, *m.*; ~ *at issue*, point en litige, *m.*; *turning-*~, instant critique, *m.*; *vanishing-*~, point de perte, *m.*; *on, at the* ~ *of*, sur le point de; **~-blank**, *adv.* (*lit. and fig.*) de but en blanc; (*refuse*) tout net; *come to the* ~, revenir* (être) au fait; *make a* ~ *of*, se faire* un devoir de; *raise a* ~, soulever une question; **~less**, (*fig.*) fade.
point, *v.a.* (*sharpen*) aiguiser; (*punctuate*) ponctuer; (*gun*) pointer; (*stones, bricks*) jointoyer; ~ *at*, (*pej.*) montrer au doigt; ~ *out*, montrer du doigt; (*show, fig.*) indiquer; (*call attention to*) signaler; *v.n.* ~ *towards*, être tourné vers; ~ *to+gerund*, *use* tendre à montrer que; (*show*) indiquer.
pointed, *adj.* pointu; (*irony*) mordant; ~ *arch*, ogive, *f.*; **~ly**, d'une manière piquante.
pointer, (*dial*) aiguille, *f.*; (*rod for pointing*) baguette, *f.*; (*dog*) chien d'arrêt, *m.*
pointing, *s.* (*artil.*) pointage, *m.*; (*punctuation*) ponctuation, *f.*; (*mason.*) jointoiement, *m.*
pointsman, (*rail.*) aiguilleur, *m.*
poise, *s.* équilibre, *m.*; (*of head, &c.*) port, *m.*

poise, *v.a.* (*balance*) tenir* en équilibre; *v.n.* se maintenir* en l'air.
poison, (*lit. and fig.*) poison, *m.*; *v.a.* (*lit. and fig.*) empoisonner; **~-gas,** gaz toxique, *m.*; *take ~*, s'empoisonner; **~ing,** *s.* empoisonnement, *m.*; **~er,** empoisonneu|r, ~se, *m.f.*
poisonous, (*plants*) vénéneu|x, ~se; (*animals*) venimeu|x, ~se; (*fig.*) empoisonné.
poke, *s.* (*nudge*) bourrade, *f.*
poke, *v.a.* (*thrust*) enfoncer; (*fire*) tisonner, *v.a.n.*; *~ one's nose,* fourrer son nez (dans); *v.n. ~ about,* tâtonner.
poker, (*fire*) tisonnier, *m.*; (*furnace*) ringard, *m.*; (*cards*) poker, *m.*
poky, (*room, &c.*) étroit.
polar, (*lit. and electr.*) polaire; **~ bear,** ours blanc, *m.*; **~ity,** polarité, *f.*; **~ize,** polariser.
pole, *s.* (*geog.*) pôle, *m.*; (*wood*) perche, *f.*; (*veh.*) timon, *m.*; **~-jump, -jumping,** *s.* saut à la perche, *m.*; *v.a.* sauter à la perche.
Pole, Polonais, -e, *m.f.*
polecat, putois, *m.*
polemic, *adj.* polémique; **~s,** polémique, *f.*
police, *s.* police, *f.*; *rural,* (*mounted*) *~*, gendarmerie, *f.*; ⚠ *not 'police' in the English sense*; **~ court,** tribunal correctionnel, *m.*; **~ magistrate,** juge de paix, *m.*; **~ station,** poste, *m.*; *v.a.* (*administer*) policer.
policeman, agent de police, *m.*; (*Paris municipal*) gardien de la paix, *m.*; (*provinces municipal*) sergent de ville, *m.*
policy, politique, *f.*; (*insurance*) police, *f.*
Polish, *adj.* polonais.
polish, *s.* vernis, *m.*; (*boot*) cirage, *m.*; (*fig.*) politesse, *f.*; *v.a.* (*lit. and fig.*) polir; (*boots*) cirer; **~er,** (*pers.*) polisseu|r, ~se, *m.f.*
polite, poli (envers); **~ness,** politesse; **~ly,** poliment.
politic, politique; **~al,** politique; **~s,** politique, *f.*; **~ally,** politiquement; **~ian,** politique, *m.*; (*pej.*) politicien, -ne, *m.f.*
polity, (*civil order*) constitution politique, *f.*; (*organized society*) société organisée, *f.*
polka, polka, *f.*
poll, (*head*) tête, *f.*; (*voting*) vote, *m.*; (*number of votes*) nombre de votes, *m.*
poll, *v.n.* voter; *v.a.* (*tree*) étêter.
pollack, (*ichth. approx.*) gade, *m.*
pollard, *s.* (*tree*) têtard, *m.*; *v.a.* étêter.
pollen, (*bot.*) pollen, *m.*
pollut|e, souiller; (*corrupt*) corrompre; **~ion,** pollution, *f.*
polo, polo, *m.*
poltroon, poltron, -ne, *m.f.*; **~ery,** poltronnerie, *f.*
polyanthus, (*bot.*) primevère, *f.*
polygam|ist, polygame, *m.f.*; **~y,** polygamie, *f.*; **~ous,** polygame.
polyglot, *adj.* polyglotte.
polygon, polygone, *m.*
polygonum, (*bot.*) renouée, *f.*
polyp(e), (*zool.*) polype, *m.*
polysyllab|ic, polysyllabique; **~le,** polysyllabe, *m.*
polytechnic, *adj.* polytechnique.
polytheism, polythéisme, *m.*
pomade, pomatum, pommade, *f.*
pomegranate, grenade, *f.*; (*tree*) grenadier, *m.*
pommel, *s.* (*sword, saddle*) pommeau, *m.*
pommel, *v.a.* donner des coups de poing à.
pomp, pompe, *f.*; **~osity,** (*pers.*) suffisance, *f.*; **~ous,** suffisant; **~ously,** (*with pomp or display*) pompeusement; (*pers., in speech, &c.*) avec suffisance; ⚠ suffisamment = *'sufficiently'*.
pond, étang, *m.*; (*small*) mare, *f.*
ponder, *v.a.* (*also ~ on, over*) peser; *v.n.* méditer.
ponderable, pondérable.
ponderingly, en réfléchissant.
ponderous, (*heavy*) pesant; (*laborious*) laborieu|x, ~se; (*style*) pâteu|x, ~se; **~ly,** (*lit. and fig.*) pesamment.
poniard, poignard, *m.*; *v.a.* poignarder.
pontif|f, pontife, *m.*; **~ical,** pontifical; **~icate,** pontificat, *m.*
pontoon, ponton, *m.*
pony, poney, *m.*
poodle, caniche, *m.*
pooh-pooh, *v.a.* faire* fi de.
pool, mare, *f.*; (*billiards, cards*) poule, *f.*; (*comm. prices*) pool, *m.*
poop, *s.* dunette, *f.*
poor, (*needy, unfortunate, paltry, sterile, unproductive*) pauvre; (*bad*) mauvais; (*humble*) humble; *the ~*, les pauvres, *m.pl.*; **~-box,** tronc, *m.*; *~ fellow, see* FELLOW; *~ in,* pauvre de; **~-rate,** taxe des pauvres, *f.*; **~-spirited,** pusillanime; **~ness,** pauvreté, *f.*; (*bad quality*) mauvaise qualité, *f.*; **~ly,** pauvrement.
poorly, *adj.* indisposé.
pop, *s.* petit son vif, *m.*; *interj.* crac!; *v.n. go ~*, sauter.
pop, *v.a.*; (*put quickly*) mettre* brusquement; *v.n. ~ in and out,* entrer (être) et sortir* (être).
pope, pape, *m.*; (*Greek church*) pope, *m.*; **~dom,** papauté, *f.*; **~ry,** papisme, *m.*
popinjay, (*target*) papegai, *m.*; (*fop*) fat, *m.*
popish, de papiste.
poplar, (*bot.*) peuplier, *m.*
poplin, popeline, *f.*
poppy, (*bot.*) pavot, *m.*; *~-coloured,* ponceau, *invar.*
populace, populace, *f.*
popular, (*carried on by, adapted to the people, liked*) populaire; **~ity,** popularité, *f.*; **~ize,** populariser; **~ly,** populairement.
popula|te, peupler; **~tion,** population, *f.*
populous, populeu|x, ~se.
porcelain, porcelaine, *f.*

porch, porche, *m.*; (*arch.*) portique, *m.*; (*head to door*) marquise, *f.*
porcupine, porc-épic, *m.*
pore, (*skin, &c.*) pore, *m.*
pore over, (*books, &c.*) pâlir sur.
pork, porc, *m.*; **~-butcher,** charcuti|er, ~ère, *m.f.*; *~-butcher's shop,* charcuterie, *f.*
porous, poreu|x, ~se.
porphyry, porphyre, *m.*
porpoise, marsouin, *m.*
porridge, (*approx.*) bouillie, *f.*
porringer, écuelle, *f.*
port, *s.* (*sea*) port, *m.*; (*naut.*) bâbord, *m.*; (*carriage, bearing*) port, *m.*; (*wine*) porto, *m.*; **~-hole,** sabord, *m.*; *~ of call,* port d'escale, *m.*
portable, (*convenient for carrying, typewriter, stove, &c.*) portati|f, ~ve.
portal, portail, *m.*
portcullis, †herse, *f.*
porten|d, présager; **~t,** présage, *m.*; **~tous,** de mauvais augure.
porter, (*house*) portier, *m.*; (*rail.*) employé de chemin de fer, *m.*
porter, (*beer*) porter, *m.*
porterage, factage, *m.*
portfolio, portefeuille, *m.*
portico, portique, *m.*
portion, *s.* (*food, part of whole*) portion, *f.*; (*marriage*) dot, *f.*; (*destiny*) sort, *m.*; *v.a.* partager; *~ out,* répartir.
portl|iness, (*fat*) embonpoint, *m.*; **~y,** corpulent; (*stately*) imposant.
portmanteau, valise, *f.*; ⚠ portemanteau = '*coat-hanger*'.
portrait, portrait, *m.*; *half-length ~,* portrait en buste, *m.*; *full-length ~,* portrait en pied, *m.*; **~-painter,** portraitiste, *m.*; **~ure,** (*portrait, description*) portrait, *m.*
portray, *v.a.* peindre*; (*describe*) décrire*; **~er,** (*lit. and fig.*) peintre, *m.*
Portuguese, *adj.* (*when an adj. use small letter*) *and s.m.f.* Portugais, -e; (*lang.*) portugais, *m.*
pose, *s.* pose, *f.*; *v.a.* (*question*) poser; (*model, &c.*) faire* une pose à; *v.n.* poser (pour).
position, (*bodily, employment, circumstances, state, place occupied by a thing, attitude, status, gram., mil.*) position, *f.*; (*mental attitude*) attitude, *f.*; *be in a ~ to,* être à même de; *keep one's ~,* tenir* son rang.
positive, *s.* (*electr., photo., gram.*) positif, *m.*
positive, *adj.* (*definite, math., electr., gram.*) positi|f, ~ve; (*formal*) formel, -le; (*convinced*) certain; (*absolute*) absolu; **~ness,** (*certainty*) certitude, *f.*; **~ly,** positivement; (*absolutely*) absolument; (*certainly*) assurément; (*with conviction*) avec certitude.
posse, *s.* (*police*) force publique, *f.*
possess, *v.a.* (*lit. and fig.*) posséder; *~ oneself of,* prendre* possession de; (*pej.*) s'approprier de; **~ion,** (*lit., demon., colony*) possession, *f.*; (*of property*) jouissance, *f.*; **~ive,** *s.* (*gram.*) possessif, *m.*; *adj.* possessi|f, ~ve; **~or,** possesseur, *m.*
possib|ility, possibilité, *f.*; *by any ~,* par possible; **~le,** possible; **~ly,** *gen. translated by* il est possible que + *subj.*; (*perhaps*) peut-être.
post, *s.* (*wood*) poteau, *m.*; (*letters*) poste, *f.*; (*office*) bureau de poste, *m.*; (*collection of letters*) levée, *f.*; (*correspondence, dispatch*) courrier, *m.*; (*place of duty, situation, mil.*) poste, *m.*; **~-boy,** postillon, *m.*; **~card,** carte postale, *f.*; **~-chaise,** chaise de poste, *f.*; *General Post Office,* Hôtel des Postes, *m.*; **~-free,** franco; **four-~ bed,** lit à colonnes, *m.*; *by ~,* par la poste; *by return of ~,* par retour du courrier; *by the same ~,* par le même courrier.
post, *v.a.* (*letter*) mettre* à la poste; (*placard, &c., and ~ up*) afficher; (*bkkpg.*) reporter; *v.n.* voyager en poste.
postage, affranchissement, *m.*; **~ stamp,** timbre-poste, *m.*
postal, postal; **~ order,** mandat (de poste), *m.*
postdate, *v.a.* postdater.
poster, (*placard*) affiche, *f.*
posterior, postérieur; **~ity,** postériorité, *f.*
posterity, postérité, *f.*
postern, poterne, *f.*
posthumous, posthume.
postilion, postillon, *m.*
postman, facteur, *m.*
postmark, timbre, *m.*
postmaster, postmistress, receveu|r, ~se (des postes), *m.f.*; **~ general,** directeur général des postes, *m.*
postpone, remettre*; **~ment,** remise, *f.*
postscript, post-scriptum, *m.* (*abbrev. P.S.*).
postulate, *s.* postulat, *m.*; *v.a.* considérer comme admis; *~ for, v.a.* stipuler.
posture, posture, *f.*; (*painting, &c.*) attitude, *f.*; (*state*) position, *f.*
post-war, *adj.* d'après-guerre.
posy, (*flowers*) bouquet, *m.*; (*ring*) devise, *f.*
pot, (*earthenware, chimney, for drinking*) pot, *m.*; (*saucepan*) marmite, *f.*; **~-belly,** panse, *f.*; *~-bellied,* pansu; **~-boiler,** (*pers.*) *use* qui fait bouillir la marmite; **~-herbs,** herbes potagères, *f.pl.*; **~-hook, -hanger,** crémaillère, *f.*; **~-house,** bouchon, *m.*; *watering-~,* arrosoir, *m.*
pot, *v.a.* conserver en boîte, *or* en pot; (*plants*) empoter.
potable, potable.
potash, potasse, *f.*
potation, (*fam.*) libation, *f.*
potato, pomme de terre, *f.*; *sweet ~,* patate, *f.*; *boiled ~es,* pommes de terre à l'eau, *f.pl.*; *baked ~es,* pommes de terre au four, *f.pl.*; *mashed ~es,* purée de pommes de terre, *f.*

poten|t, puissant; (*remedy*) efficace; **~tate,** potentat, *m.*; **~cy,** force, *f.*; **~tly,** puissamment.
potential, (*gram., med., phys.*) potentiel, -le; **~ity,** potentialité, *f.*
pother, *s.* (*noise*) vacarme, *m.*
potion, potion, *f.*
potsherd, tesson, *m.*
pottage, potage, *m.*
potter, *s.* potier, *m.*; *~'s clay,* argile, *f.*; **~y,** poterie, *f.*
potter about, bricoler.
pouch, *s.* (*tobacco*) blague, *f.*; (*cartridge*) giberne, *f.*; (*marsupial*) poche ventrale, *f.*
poult|erer, poulailler, *m.*; **~ry,** volaille, *f.*; **~ry-yard,** basse-cour, *f.*
poultice, cataplasme, *m.*
pounce, *s.* (*claw*) serre, *f.*; *v.n.* fondre sur.
pound, *s.* (*measure*) livre, *f.*; (*20/-*) livre sterling, *f.*; (*for ans.*) fourrière, *f.*; *by the ~,* à la livre.
pound, *v.a.* (*crush*) piler; *~ at, away at,* pilonner; **~er,** (*mortar*) pilon, *m.*; (*in compounds*) de . . . livres.
pour, *v.a.* verser; (*fig.*) épancher; *~ in,* verser; *~ forth,* répandre; *v.n. ~ down,* (*rain, &c.*) tomber (être) à flots; *~ forth, out,* se répandre; *~ in,* arriver (être) en foule.
pouring, *adj.* (*rain, &c.*) torrentiel, -le.
pout, *v.n.* bouder; **~ing,** *adj.* boudeu|r, ~se.
poverty, (*lit. and fig.*) pauvreté, *f.*; (*extreme*) misère, *f.*; *~-stricken,* indigent.
powder, (*gun, face, hair, gen.*) poudre, *f.*; **~-magazine,** poudrière, *f.*; (*naut.*) soute aux poudres, *f.*; **~-puff,** †houppe à poudre, *f.*; **~-works, -mill,** poudrerie, *f.*; *v.a.* (*face, hair, &c.*) poudrer; (*sprinkle with*) saupoudrer (de); **~y,** poudreu|x, ~se; (*friable*) friable.
power, (*executive, law, authority*) pouvoir, *m.*; (*nation, math.*) puissance, *f.*; (*physical, water, air, moral, mach.*) force, *f.*; (*talent*) talent, *m.*; *united ~ station,* (*electr.*) station génératrice, *f.*
powerful, (*strong*) fort; (*fig.*) puissant; **~ly,** fortement, puissamment.
powerless, impuissant; **~ness,** impuissance, *f.*; *be ~ to,* être dans l'impossibilité de.
pox, *small~,* petite vérole, *f.*
P.P.C. *abbrev.* P.p.c. (pour prendre congé).
practicab|ility, praticabilité, *f.*; **~le,** praticable.
practical, pratique; **~ly,** pratiquement; (*in practice*) en pratique.
practice, (*habit*) habitude, *f.*; (*op. to theory*) pratique, *f.*; (*repeated exercise, use*) exercice, *m.*; (*professional connexion*) clientèle, *f.*
practician, praticien, -ne, *m.f.*
practise, *v.a.* (*put into practice*) pratiquer; (*profession, &c.*) exercer; (*train oneself in*) s'exercer à; *v.n.* exercer sa profession; (*piano*) faire* des exercices; *~ on,* (*impose on*) exploiter; **~d,** *adj.* expérimenté.
practitioner, praticien, -ne, *m.f.*
pragmatic(al), (*meddlesome*) officieu|x, ~se; (*dogmatic*) dogmatique; ⚠ pragmatique *generally = 'tending to action' or is used in a hist. or eccles. sense, e.g.* pragmatique sanction; **~ally,** avec suffisance.
prairie, (*N. America*) savane, *f.*; ⚠ *not* prairie *which = 'meadow'.*
praise, *s.* louange, *f.*; *in ~ of,* à la louange de; *v.a.* (*gen. and theol.*) louer; **~worthy,** louable.
prance, *v.a.* faire* piaffer; *v.n.* piaffer.
prank, *s.* fredaine, *f.*
prank, *v.a.* attifer.
prate, *v.n.* jaser.
prattle, *s.* babil, *m.*; *v.n.* babiller; **~r,** babillard, -e, *m.f.*
prawn, (*ichth.*) bouquet, *m.*
pray, (*gen., to God*) prier, *v.a.*; (*pers. to do*) prier de; (*pers. for something*) demander avec instance (*acc. of thing,* à + *pers.*); *interj.* (*be so good as to*) veuillez; *v.n.* prier.
prayer, (*theol. and request*) prière, *f.*; **~-book,** paroissien, *m.*; **~ful,** (*approx.*) pieu|x, ~se, *m.f.*; **~fully,** avec prière.
preach, *v.a.n.* prêcher; (*pej.*) sermonner; **~er,** prédicateur, *m.*; **~ing,** prédication, *f.*
preamble, *s.* préambule, *m.*
prebend, prébende, *f.*; **~ary,** prébendier, *m.*
precarious, précaire; **~ness,** précarité, *f.*; **~ly,** précairement.
precaution, précaution, *f.*; **~ary,** de précaution.
precede, (*go before*) précéder; (*in rank, &c.*) avoir le pas sur.
preceden|ce, (*priority*) priorité, *f.*; (*in ceremonies, &c.*) préséance, *f.*; **~t,** *s.* précédent, *m.*; *adj. and preceding,* précédent.
precentor, premier chantre, *m.*
precept, précepte, *m.*
precept|or, ~ress, institut|eur, **~rice,** *m.f.*
precincts, enceinte, *f.*
precious, (*lit., fig., affected*) précieu|x, ~se; (*pop.*) fameu|x, ~se; **~ly,** (*pop.*) fameusement.
precipi|ce, précipice, *m.*; **~tous,** escarpé; **~tously,** en précipice.
precipitance, précipitation, *f.*
precipitate, *adj.* (*hurried*) précipité; (*rash*) irréfléchi; **~ly,** précipitamment.
precipita|te, (*lit. and fig.*) précipiter; **~tion,** précipitation, *f.*
precis|e, précis; (*pers.*) méticuleu|x, ~se; (*formal*) cérémonieu|x, ~se; **~eness, ~ion,** précision, *f.*; **~ely,** précisément; *2 o'clock ~ely,* 2 heures précises.
preclude, (*exclude*) exclure*; (*prevent*) empêcher.
precocious, précoce; **~ness,** précocité, *f.*
preconc|eive, préconcevoir; **~eption,** préconception, *f.*
precursor, précurseur, *m.*; (*predecessor*) prédécesseur, *m.*; **~y,** précurseur, *m. only.*
predate, *v.a.* antidater.

predatory, (*an.*) de proie; (*bird*) rapace; (*plundering*) pillard.
predecease, *v.a.* prédécéder.
predecessor, prédécesseur, *m.*
predestina|te, prédestiner; **~tion,** prédestination, *f.*
predestine, destiner d'avance; (*theol.*) prédestiner.
predetermin|e, déterminer d'avance; (*theol.*) prédéterminer; **~ation,** (*theol.*) prédétermination, *f.*
predicament, mauvaise passe, *f.*
predica|te, *s.* (*gram., logic*) prédicat, *m.*; *v.a.* affirmer; **~tion,** affirmation, *f.*
predict, prédire*; **~ion,** prédiction, *f.*
predilection, prédilection, *f.*
predispos|e, prédisposer; **~ition,** prédisposition, *f.*
predominan|ce, prédominance, *f.*; **~t,** *also* **predominating,** prédominant; **~tly,** d'une manière prédominante.
predominate, prédominer.
pre-eminen|ce, prééminence, *f.*; **~t,** prééminent; **~tly,** par excellence.
pre-emption, préemption, *f.*
pre-engagement, engagement antérieur, *m.*
preface, préface, *f.*; *v.a.* faire* une préface **à**; (*introduce*) faire* précéder de.
prefatory, préliminaire.
prefect, préfet, *m.*; **~ure,** préfecture, *f.*; **sub-~,** sous-préfet, *m.*
prefer, aimer mieux (+ *inf.*); (*promote*) élever.
preferabl|e, préférable; **~y,** de préférence.
preferen|ce, (*liking better, thing preferred*) préférence, *f.*; (*comm. French*) régime de faveur, *m.*; (*comm. British*) préférence, *f.*; ~ *shares,* actions de capital, *f.pl.*; **~tial,** (*claim, debt, dividend*) privilégié; (*right, tariff*) de préférence.
preferment, avancement, *m.*
prefix, (*gram.*) préfixe, *m.*; *v.a.* mettre* en tête (de).
pregnan|cy, (*pers.*) grossesse, *f.*; **~t,** (*pers.*) enceinte; (*fruitful in*) fertile en; (*suggestive*) suggesti|f, ~ve.
prehistoric, préhistorique.
prejudge, préjuger.
prejudice, préjugé, *m.*; (*injury*) préjudice, *m.*; *v.a.* (*influence*) prévenir*; (*injure*) porter préjudice à.
prejudicial, préjudiciable (à).
prelate, prélat, *m.*
preliminar|y, *adj.* préliminaire; **~ies,** *s.* préliminaires, *m.pl.*; **~ily,** préalablement.
prelude, *s.* (*lit. and fig.*) prélude, *m.*; *v.a.* préluder à.
premature, prématuré; **~ly,** prématurément.
premedita|te, préméditer; **~tion,** préméditation, *f.*
premier, *s.* premier ministre, *m.*; (*France*) président du conseil, *m.*
premis|es, lieux, *m.pl.*; (*land and buildings together*) immeuble, *m.*; **~ses,** (*log.*) prémisses, *f.pl.*
premium, (*bonus, advance of value, insurance, Stk. Ex.*) prime, *f.*; (*reward*) récompense, *f.*; *at a ~,* en prime.
premonit|ion, avertissement préalable, *m.*; **~ory,** qui avertit d'avance.
preoccup|ation, (*mental absorption, anxiety, prejudice*) préoccupation, *f.*; (*previous occupation*) possession antérieure, *f.*; **~y,** *v.a.* (*absorb, prejudice*) préoccuper.
preordain, destiner (à).
prepara|tion, (*food, medicine, preparing*) préparation, *f.*; (*things done to make ready*) préparatifs, *m.pl.*; (*school*) étude, *f.*; **~tory,** préparatoire; ~ *to,* en vue de.
prepare, *v.a.* (*food, &c.*) apprêter; (*the mind, a medicine, &c., get ready*) préparer; ~ *for,* préparer pour; (*exam.*) préparer, *v.a.*; *be ~d to,* être prêt **à**; *v.n.* se préparer.
prepay, payer d'avance; (*carriage, postage*) affranchir; **~ment,** pay(i)ement d'avance, *m.*; (*post, &c.*) affranchissement, *m.*
prepense, *with malice ~,* avec préméditation.
preponderа|nce, prépondérance, *f.*; **~nt,** prépondérant; **~te,** *v.n.* (*fig.*) être prépondérant.
preposition, préposition, *f.*; **~al,** prépositi|f, ~ve.
prepossess, (*influence*) prévenir; (*take possession of, fig.*) préoccuper (de); **~ion,** prévention, *f.*; **~ing,** *adj.* prévenant.
preposterous, déraisonnable; (*absurd*) absurde; **~ness,** absurdité, *f.*; **~ly,** absurdement.
prerogative, prérogative, *f.*
presage, présage, *m.*; *v.a.* présager.
Presbyterian, *adj. and s.m.f.* presbytérien, -ne.
presbytery, (*priest's house*) presbytère, *m.*
prescien|ce, prescience, *f.*; **~t,** prescient.
prescribe, *v.a.* (*med. treatment*) ordonner; *v.n. ~ for,* (*pers.*) faire* une ordonnance pour.
prescript|ion, (*med.*) ordonnance, *f.*; (*law*) prescription, *f.*; **~ive,** établi par prescription.
presence, présence, *f.*; (*bearing*) maintien, *m.*; *in ~ of,* en présence de; *~-chamber,* salle du trône, *f.*; *~ of mind,* présence d'esprit, *f.*
present, *s.* (*gift*) présent, *m.*; (*time and gram.*) présent, *m.*; *at ~,* à présent; *adj.* présent; (*existing, being such now*) actuel, -le; (*current*) courant; (*gram.*) présent; *interj.* présent!
present, *v.a.* (*offer, hold out, introduce, show, compliments, &c., cheque, a play, arms*) présenter; ~ *with,* faire* présent (à+*pers.* de+*thing*); ~ *arms!* présentez armes!; (*fire-arm*) en joue!

presentable, présentable.
presentation, (*benefice, at court, comm., act of presenting*) présentation, *f.*; (*theatr.*) représentation, *f.*
presentiment, pressentiment, *m.*
presently, tout à l'heure.
presentment, (*portrait*) portrait, *m.*; (*description*) description, *f.*; (*comm.*) présentation, *f.*
preservation, (*from injury, &c.*) préservation, *f.*; (*state of being ill, well preserved*) conservation, *f.*
preservative, *s.* préservatif, *m.*; *adj.* préservati|f, ~ve.
preserve, *s.* (*jam*) confiture, *f.*; (*meat, vegetables, &c.*) conserve, *f.*; (*game*) chasse, *f.*
preserv|e, *v.a.* (*from harm*) préserver (de); (*fruits*) confire*, *def.*; (*order*) maintenir*; (*keep*) conserver; ⚠ préserver *is never used of fruits, &c.*; *~ing-pan, see* PAN.
preside, *v.n.* présider; ~ *over,* (*meeting*) présider, *v.a.*; (*have direction of*) présider à.
presiden|cy, (*office and India*) présidence, *f.*; **~t,** président, *m.*; *vice-~t,* vice-président, *m.*; **~tial,** présidentiel, -le.
press, *s.* (*throng, hurry, machine for pressing, newspapers, print., copying*) presse, *f.*; (*wine, cider, &c.*) pressoir, *m.*; (*furniture*) garde-robe, *f.*; *~-gallery,* tribune des journalistes, *f.*; **~-gang,** (*approx.*) racoleurs, *m.pl.*
press, *v.a.* (*urge* (de), *harass, of weight, hand, hay, button, enemy, &c.*) presser; (*grapes*) pressurer; (*embrace*) serrer; (*clothes*) donner un coup de fer à; *be ~ed for,* (*money*) être à court de; ~ *forward,* faire* avancer plus vite; ~ *out,* exprimer.
press, *v.n.* (*crowd*) se presser; (*be urgent*) presser; ~ *through,* se frayer chemin à travers.
pressing, *s.* pression, *f.*; (*solicitation*) instance, *f.*; *adj.* urgent; **~ly,** d'une manière pressante.
pressman, (*journalist*) journaliste, *m.*
pressure, (*exertion of force, atmospheric, constraining influence, high activity, steam, mach., electr.*) pression, *f.*; (*weight*) poids, *m.*; (*straits, trouble*) embarras, *m.*; (*urgency*) urgence, *f.*; *blood-~,* tension artérielle, *f.*
presumab|le, présumable; **~ly,** probablement.
presume, *v.a.* (*suppose*) présumer; *v.n.* ~ *to,* oser (+ *inf.*); ~ *upon,* présumer de; ⚠ présumer *never = 'presume to'.*
presuming, présomptueu|x, ~se.
presumpt|ion, présomption, *f.*; **~ive,** présumé; (*heir*) présompti|f, ~ve; **~ively,** par présomption.
presumptuous, présomptueu|x, ~se; **~ness,** présomption, *f.*; **~ly,** présomptueusement.
presuppose, présupposer.
pretence, prétexte, *m.*; (*claim to*) prétention (à), *f.*
pretend, *v.a.* (*as excuse*) prétexter; (*claim as a right, aspire to*) prétendre (à); (*profess falsely*) simuler.
pretend, *v.n.* faire* semblant; ~ *to,* (*falsely*) feindre* de; ~ *to be,* (*state, affirm, claim*) prétendre (+ *inf.*); (*to give oneself out to be rightly or wrongly*) vouloir* se faire* passer pour; ⚠ prétendre *is less pej. than in English.*
pretender, (*hist.*) prétendant, *m.*
preten|sion, prétension, *f.*; **~tious,** prétentieu|x, ~se.
preterite, (*gram.*) prétérit, *m.*
pretermission, omission, *f.*
pretermit, omettre*.
pretext, prétexte, *m.*
prett|y, (*lit., fig., fam., in irony*) joli; **~iness,** gentillesse, *f.*; **~ily,** joliment; *adv.* assez.
prevail, *v.n.* prévaloir* (sur); (*be in vogue*) avoir la vogue; ~ *on, upon,* décider (*acc. of pers.,* à + *inf.*); **~ing,** régnant.
prevalen|ce, (*ascendancy*) ascendant, *m.*; (*being general*) généralité, *f.*; **~t,** (*widespread*) répandu.
prevarica|te, (*deceive*) tromper; (*shuffle*) tergiverser; **~tion,** tergiversation, *f.*; (*subterfuge*) faux-fuyant, *m.*; ⚠ prévarication, etc. = *'abuse of trust'.*
prevent, empêcher (de); (*avoid*) éviter; **~ion,** empêchement, *m.*
preventive, *s.* préservatif, *m.* (contre); *adj.* préventi|f, ~ve.
previous, antérieur (à); (*slang*) trop pressé; **~ly,** antérieurement.
prevision, prévision, *f.*
prey, *s.* proie, *f.*; *be a ~ to,* être en proie à.
prey upon, *v.a.* faire* sa proie de; (*pers., mind, &c.*) miner.
price, prix, *m.*; (*Stk. Ex.*) cours, *m.*; *retail ~,* prix de détail, *m.*; *at a reduced ~,* au rabais; *spot ~,* cours du comptant, *m.*; *trade ~,* prix de gros, *m.*; *wholesale ~,* prix de gros, *m.*; *v.a.* tarifer.
priceless, inestimable; (*slang*) impayable.
prick, *s.* piqûre, *f.*; ~ *of conscience,* remords, *m.*
prick, *v.a.* piquer; (*conscience*) causer des remords à; ~ *off,* (*plants*) transplanter; ~ *up,* (*ears*) dresser.
prick, *v.n.* piquer; **~ing,** *s.* (*sensation*) picotement, *m.*
prickl|e, (*thorn*) piquant, *m.*; **~y,** plein de piquants.
pride, *s.* fierté, *f.*; (*being vain, conceited, or an object of ~*) orgueil, *m.*; (*brilliance, fig.*) éclat, *m.*; *take ~ in,* être fier de.
priest, *s.* prêtre; **~ess,** prêtresse, *f.*; **~craft,** cléricalisme, *m.*; **~hood,** prêtrise, *f.*; **~ly,** *adj.* de prêtre.
prig, (*approx.*) fat, *m.*
prim, guindé; **~ness,** afféterie, *f.*

prima|cy, (*office of primate*) primatie, *f.*; (*pre-eminence*) primauté, *f.*; **~te,** primat, *m.*
primar|y, (*original*) primiti|f, ~ve; (*principal*) principal; (*education, geol.*) primaire; **~ily,** primitivement; (*principally*) en premier lieu.
prime, *s.* (*beginning*) commencement, *m.*; (*dawn, lit. and fig.*) aurore, *f.*; (*of age, &c.*) fleur, *f.*; (*eccles.*) prime, *f.*; (*perfection*) perfection, *f.*; (*best part*) choix, *m.*
prime, *adj.* principal; (*minister and numbers*) premi|er, ~ère; (*first-rate*) de première qualité; ⚠ prime = '*first*', '*early*'.
prime, *v.a.* (*fire-arm*) amorcer; (*instruct*) instruire* d'avance.
primer, grammaire, *f.*, élémentaire.
prime(ae)val, primiti|f, ~ve.
primitive, primiti|f, ~ve; **~ness,** caractère primitif, *m.*; **~ly,** primitivement.
primogeniture, primogéniture, *f.*
primordial, primordial.
primrose, (*bot.*) primevère, *f.*; ⚠ primerose = '*hollyhock*'.
prince, prince, *m.*; *~'s feather,* (*bot.*) *see* FEATHER; **~ss,** princesse, *f.*; **~ly,** princi|er, ~ère.
principal, *s.* (*debt, capital*) capital, *m.*; (*employer*) patron, -ne, *m.f.*; (*school*) proviseur, *m.*; (*headmistress*) directrice, *f.*; (*as opp. to agent*) mandant, *m.*; *vice-~,* sous-direct|eur, ~rice, *m.f*; *adj.* principal; **~ly,** principalement.
principality, principauté, *f.*
principle, (*primary source, method, code of conduct, phys., chem.*) principe, *m.*; *on ~,* par principe.
print, *s.* (*foot, finger*) empreinte, *f.*; (*books, &c.*) impression, *f.*; (*type*) caractères, *m.pl.*; (*from block, plate*) estampe, *f.*; (*U.S.A.*) journal, *m.*; (*photo.*) épreuve, *f.*; *out of ~,* épuisé.
print, *v.a.* (*books, &c., material, fig.*) imprimer; (*make a mark*) faire* une empreinte (sur); (*photo.*) tirer; *~ed calico, see* CALICO.
printer, imprimeur, *m.*; *~'s error,* faute d'imprimerie, *f.*; *~'s proof,* épreuve d'imprimerie, *f.*
printing, impression, *f.*; **~-office,** bureau d'imprimerie, *m.*; **~-press,** presse, *f.*
prior, *s.* prieur, *m.*; **~ess,** prieure, *f.*; **~ity,** priorité, *f.*; **~y,** prieuré, *m.*; *adj.* antérieur (à).
prism, prisme, *m.*; **~atic,** prismatique.
prison, prison, *f.*; **~ van,** voiture cellulaire, *f.*
prisoner, prisonni|er, ~ère, *m.f.*; *take ~,* faire* prisonnier.
pristine, primiti|f, ~ve.
privacy, retraite, *f.*
private, particuli|er, ~ère; (*personal*) personel, -le; (*not public*) privé; (*confidential*) confidentiel, -le; (*not in official position*) simple; (*secluded*) retiré; *Private!*, Défense d'entrer!; *in ~,* **~ly,** en particulier; *~ individual, see* INDIVIDUAL.
privateer, *s.* corsaire, *m.*
privation, (*absence of*) manque, *m.* (de); (*want of necessities*) misère, *f.*
privet, (*bot.*) troène, *m.*
privilege, privilège, *m.*; **~d,** privilégié.
privy, *s.* cabinet d'aisances, *m.*
priv|y, *adj.* (*secret*) secr|et, ~ète; **~y purse,** *see* PURSE; *~y to,* instruit de; **~ily,** secrètement.
prize, *s.* (*reward*) prix, *m.*; (*nav. and capture*) prise, *f.*; (*lotteries, fin.*) lot, *m.*; **~-bond,** bon à lots, *m.*; **~-fighter,** boxeur, *m.*; *v.a.* attacher prix à; (*force up, open*) forcer avec un levier.
probab|ility, probabilité, *f.*; **~le,** probable; **~ly,** probablement.
probation, temps d'épreuve, *m.*; (*relig.*) noviciat, *m.*; **~er,** novice, *m.*; **~al, ~ary,** d'épreuve.
probe, *v.a.* (*lit. and fig.*) sonder.
probity, probité, *f.*
problem, (*lit. and fig.*) problème, *m.*; **~atic,** problématique.
proboscis, trompe, *f.*
procedure, (*mode of conducting business*) procédé, *m.*
proceed, *v.n.* (*to a place*) aller* (être) à; (*to do*) se mettre* à; (*go on, advance*) avancer; (*to another subject, &c.*) passer à; (*be in progress*) avoir lieu; (*continue operating*) procéder; *~ from,* (*originate*) provenir* (être) de; *~ with,* (*continue*) continuer.
proceeding, *s.* procédé, *m.*; **~s,** (*meetings, &c.*) délibérations, *f.pl.*; *take ~s against,* (*law*) poursuivre*.
proceeds, produit, *m.*
process, (*progress, course*) développement, *m.*; (*time*) suite, *f.*; (*method*) procédé, *m.*
process, *v.n.* (*in relig. procession*) aller* (être) en procession; (*secular*) s'avancer en cortège.
procession, cortège, *m.*; (*relig.*) procession, *f.*; **~al,** *adj. and s.m.* processional.
proclaim, proclamer; (*war*) déclarer.
proclamation, proclamation, *f.*
proclivity, penchant, *m.* (à).
proconsul, proconsul, *m.*; **~ship,** proconsulat, *m.*; **~ar,** proconsulaire.
procrastina|te, différer; **~tion,** délai, *m.*
procrea|te, procréer; **~tion,** procréation, *f.*
proctor, (*univ. approx.*) censeur, *m.*
procurable, qu'on peut se procurer.
procuration, procuration, *f.*
procure, *v.a.* (*for someone else*) procurer (à + *pers.* = '*for*'); (*for oneself*) se procurer.
prodigal, *adj. and s.m.f.* prodigue; *~ son,* enfant prodigue, *m.*; **~ity,** prodigalité, *f.*; **~ly,** prodigalement; ⚠ *but* prodigal, *adj., not French.*
prodigious, prodigieu|x, ~se; **~ly,** prodigieusement.
prodigy, (*lit. and pers.*) prodige, *m.*
produce, *s.* produit, *m.*; *~ of the soil,* produits du sol, *m.pl.*

produce, *v.a.* (*gen.*) produire*; **~r,** product|eur, ~rice, *m.f.*
product, (*labour, industry, agriculture, &c., result, math.*) produit, *m.*
production, production, *f.*
productive, producti|f, ~ve; **~ness,** productivité, *f.*
profanation, profanation, *f.*
profan|e, (*irreverent, secular*) profane, ⚠ *which is less pej. than 'profane' which sometimes* = blasphématoire; **~ity,** (*language*) langage blasphématoire, *m.*; **~eness,** caractère profane, *m.*; **~ely,** d'une manière profane,
profess, *v.a.* (*opinion, faith, &c.*) professer; (*pretend*) simuler; ~ *oneself,* se déclarer.
profess, *v.n.* ~ *to,* (*rightly or wrongly*) prétendre (+ *inf.*); (*falsely*) feindre* de.
professed, *adj.* avoué; (*relig.*) prof|ès, ~esse; **~ly,** (*openly*) ouvertement; (*self-acknowledged*) de son propre aveu.
profession, (*declaration, faith, vows, calling*) profession, *f.*
professional, *adj.* de profession; (*peculiar to special profession*) professionnel, -le; **~ly,** de profession.
professor, professeur, *m.f.*; ⚠ *of a university 'professor'* = professeur de faculté, *m.f.*; *of a lecturer* = conférencie|r, ~ère; **~ship,** professorat, *m.*; **~ial,** professoral.
proffer, offrir*.
proficien|cy, connaissances, *f.pl.* (en); **~t,** expert (à).
profile, profil, *m.*
profit, *s.* profit, *m.*; **~s,** bénéfices, *m.pl.*; ~ *and loss account,* (*bkkpg.*) compte de profits et pertes, *m.*; *v.a.* profiter à; *what will it ~ you to . . . ?,* à quoi vous servira de . . . ?; *v.n.* ~ *by,* profiter de.
profiteer, mercanti, *m.*
profitabl|e, profitable; **~eness,** utilité, *f.*; **~y,** avantageusement.
proflig|acy, *s.* débauche, *m.*; **~ate,** *adj.* dissolu.
profound, (*lit. and fig.*) profond; **~ness,** profondeur, *f.*; **~ly,** profondément.
profus|e, prodigue (de); **~eness, ~ion,** profusion, *f.*; **~ely,** avec profusion; (*excessively*) excessivement.
progenitor, ancêtre, *m.*
progeny, lignée, *f.*; (*family*) famille, *f.*
prognostic, présage, *m.*; **~ate,** prédire*.
program(me), programme, *m.*
progress, *s.* (*improvement*) progrès, *m.pl.*; (*onward movement*) marche, *f.*; (*journey*) voyage, *m.*; ⚠ progrès *does not* = *'development' which* = développement, *m.*; **~ive,** progressi|f, ~ve; **~ively,** progressivement.
progress, *v.n.* (*move forward*) s'avancer; (*improve*) faire* des progrès; **~ion,** progression, *f.*
prohibit, *v.a.* défendre (de); **~ion,** défense, *f.*; **~ive,** prohibiti|f, ~ve.
project, projet, *m.*
project, *v.a.* projeter; *v.n.* (*jut out*) saillir; **~ing,** *adj.* en saillie.
projectile, *adj. and s.m.* projectile.
projection, (*throwing, geom.*) projection, *f.*; (*protruding object*) saillie, *f.*
projector, (*promoter of bogus undertakings, &c.*) lanceur, *m.*; ⚠ projecteur = *'searchlight', 'motor light'.*
proletaria|n, *adj. and s.m.f.* prolétaire; **~t,** prolétariat, *m.*
prolific, (*fertile, abounding*) fécond (en).
prolix, prolixe; **~ity,** prolixité, *f.*
prologue, prologue, *m.*
prolong, prolonger; **~ation,** prolongation, *f.*
promenade, (*walk and place*) promenade, *f.*; *v.n.* se promener.
prominen|ce, proéminence, *f.*; (*distinction*) distinction, *f.*; **~t,** proéminent; (*distinguished*) distingué; **~tly,** (*conspicuously*) éminemment.
promiscuous, (*mixed*) mêlé; (*indiscriminate*) sans distinction; **~ly,** (*confusedly*) confusément; (*indiscriminately*) indistinctement.
promise, *s.* promesse, *f.*; *of ~,* qui donne des espérances; *v.a.* (*lit. and fig.*) promettre*, *acc. of thing,* à + *pers.*; *v.n.* promettre*; ~ *well,* donner de belles espérances.
promising, qui promet.
promissory, qui contient une promesse.
promontory, promontoire, *m.*
promot|e, *v.a.* (*mil., &c.*) donner de l'avancement à; ⚠ promouvoir* *only in compound tenses*; (*encourage arts, &c.*) encourager; **~er,** promot|eur, ~rice, *m.f.*; **~ion,** promotion, *f.*; (*arts, &c.*) encouragement, *m.* (à).
prompt, *adj.* prompt (à); **~ly,** promptement.
prompt, *v.a.* exciter (à); (*inspire*) inspirer; (*theatr., speaker*) souffler; **~er,** (*theatr., &c.*) souffleur, *m.*
promptitude, promptitude, *f.*
promulga|te, (*laws, &c.*) promulguer; (*news, &c.*) publier; **~tion,** promulgation, *f.*
prone, *adj.* (*lying*) couché à plat ventre; (*fig.* = *disposed*) enclin (à); **~ness,** (*fig.*) inclination, *f.*
prong, (*of a fork*) fourchon, *m.*; *3-, 4-, &c., ~ed,* à 3, 4, etc., dents.
pronominal, pronominal.
pronoun, pronom, *m.*
pronounce, *v.a.* prononcer; (*declare*) déclarer; *v.n.* (*give opinion*) se prononcer (sur); **~ment,** prononciation, *f.*; **~able,** *adj.* prononçable.
pronunciation, prononciation, *f.*
proof, (*evidence*) preuve, *f.*; (*test, trial, print., photo.*) épreuve, *f.*; *in ~ of,* pour preuve de; *~-reader,* correct|eur, ~rice, *m.f.*; **~-sheet,** épreuve, *f.*
prop, *s.* étai, *m.*; (*fig.*) soutien, *m.*; (*hort.*) tuteur, *m.*; *v.a. and ~ up,* étayer; (*fig.*) soutenir*; (*hort.*) mettre* un tuteur à.

propagand|a, propagande, *f.*; **~ist**, propagandiste, *m.*
propaga|te, (*lit. and fig.*) propager; *v.n.* se propager; **~tion**, (*lit. and fig.*) propagation, *f.*; **~tor**, propagat|eur, ~rice, *m.f.*
propel, pousser; (*steam*) mouvoir*.
propeller, (*naut., aeron.*) hélice, *f.*; **screw-~**, hélice propulsive, *f.*
propensity, propension, *f.* (à).
proper, *adj.* (*word, meaning, suitable* (à), *belonging distinctively to, gram.*) propre; (*strictly so called*) proprement dit; (*exact*) exact; (*respectable*) convenable; (*due*) dû, due; (*deserved*) mérité; *think ~ to*, juger convenable de; **~ly**, (*exactly*) proprement; (*suitably*) convenablement; (*duly*) régulièrement.
propert|y, (*possession, ownership, estate, characteristic*) propriété, *f.*; *real ~*, biens immeubles, *m.pl.*; *stage ~ies*, accessoires, *m.pl.*
prophecy, prophétie, *f.*
prophesy, *v.a.n.* prophétiser.
prophet, prophète, *m.*; **~ess**, prophétesse, *f.*; **~ic**, prophétique; **~ically**, prophétiquement.
propinquity, proximité, *f.*; (*relationship*) parenté, *f.*
propitia|te, (*appease*) apaiser; (*make propitious*) rendre propice; **~tion**, apaisement, *m.*; (*theol.*) propitiation, *f.*; **~tory**, propitiatoire.
propitious, propice; **~ly**, favorablement.
proportion, *s.* (*part, ratio, extent, relation between parts*) proportion, *f.*; *in ~ to*, en proportion de; *in ~ as*, à mesure que; *out of ~*, mal proportionné; *v.a.* proportionner (à).
proportional, en proportion (de); (*polit., math.*) proportionnel, -le; **~ly**, proportionnellement, (à).
proportionate, *adj.* proportionné (à); **~ly**, en proportion (de).
proposal, proposition, *f.*; (*marriage*) demande en mariage, *f.*
propose, *v.a.* (*offer, put forward, price, motion, amendment, &c.*) proposer; *v.n.* (*intention*) se proposer (de).
proposition, (*project, statement, math., gram.*) proposition, *f.*; (*comm. and U.S.A.*) affaire, *f.*
propound, proposer; **~er**, auteur d'une proposition, *m.*
proprietary, de propriété.
propriet|or, **~ress**, propriétaire, *m.f.*
propriety, convenances, *f.pl.*; (*gram.*) propriété, *f.*
propuls|ion, propulsion, *f.*; **~ive**, propulsi|f, ~ve.
prorogation, prorogation, *f.*
prorogue, proroger.
pros, *~ and cons*, le pour et le contre.
prosaic, (*commonplace*) prosaïque.
proscribe, proscrire*.
proscript|ion, proscription, *f.*; **~ive**, de proscription.
prose, (*not poetry*) prose, *f.*; (*matter-of-fact quality*) prosaïsme, *m.*
prosecu|te, (*studies, inquiry, law*) poursuivre*; *trespassers will be ~d*, défense d'entrer; **~tion**, (*law*) poursuites, *f.pl.*; (*continuation*) continuation, *f.*; **~tor**, plaignant, *m.*; *public ~tor*, procureur de la République, *m.*
proselyt|e, prosélyte, *m.f.*; **~ize**, faire* des prosélytes.
prosody, prosodie, *f.*
prospect, *s.* (*vista, expectation*) perspective, *f.*; (*chance*) chance, *f.*
prospect, *v.a.* (*explore*) prospecter.
prospective, en perspective; **~ly**, en perspective.
prospectus, prospectus, *m.*
prosper, *v.n.* prospérer; *v.a.* faire* prospérer; **~ity**, prospérité, *f.*; **~ous**, prospère; (*favouring*) favorable; **~ously**, avec prospérité, heureusement.
prostitute, *s.* prostituée, *f.*; *v.a.* (*fig.*) prostituer.
prostitution, prostitution, *f.*
prostrate, *adj.* (*on the ground*) prosterné; (*fatigue, &c.*) épuisé.
prostrat|e, *v.a.* (*with weakness*) épuiser; *~ oneself*, (*cast oneself down, lit. and fig.*) se prosterner; **~ion**, (*nervous*) prostration, *f.*, ⚠ *which does not = 'bowing low', which* = prosternation, *f.*
pros|y, ennuyeu|x, ~se; (*slang*) rasant; **~ily**, d'une façon ennuyeuse.
protagonist, protagoniste, *m.*
protasis, (*gram.*) protase, *f.*
protect, *v.a.* protéger; (*safeguard*) sauvegarder; **~ion**, (*gen., fig., polit., econ. nav.*) protection, *f.*; **~ionist**, protectionniste, *m.*
protect|ive, *adj.* and **~or**, **~ress**, *s.m.f.* protect|eur, ~rice.
protectorate, protectorat, *m.*
protest, *s.* protestation, *f.*; (*comm.*) protêt, *m.*
protest, *v.a.* (*gen. and comm.*) protester; (*give assurance of*) protester de; *~against*, protester contre.
Protestant, *adj. and s.m.f.* protestant, -e; **~ism**, protestantisme, *m.*
protestation, protestation, *f.*
protocol, protocole, *m.*
protoplasm, protoplasme, *m.*
prototype, prototype, *m.*
protract, prolonger; (*delay*) différer; **~ion**, prolongation, *f.*
protractor, (*geom.*) rapporteur, *m.*
protrude, *v.a.* pousser en avant; *v.n.* s'avancer.
protrusion, action de pousser en avant, *f.*; (*projection*) saillie, *f.*
protuberan|ce, protubérance, *f.*; **~t**, protubérant.
proud, fier, fière; (*haughty*) †hautain; (*grand*) superbe; (*fiery*) fougueu|x, ~se; **~ly**, fièrement.
provable, prouvable.
prove, *v.a.* prouver; (*put to the test*)

éprouver; (*arith.*) faire la preuve de; *v.n.* (*pers.*) se montrer; ~ *to be*, (*of things*) se trouver être.
provender, fourrage, *m.*
proverb, (*lit. and fig.*) proverbe, *m.*; **~ial**, proverbial; **~ially**, proverbialement.
provide, *v.a.* (*with*) pourvoir* de; (*supply with*) fournir de; *v.n.* ~ *for*, pourvoir* à; (*secure maintenance for*) pourvoir* aux besoins de; (*against*) se prémunir contre.
provided, *adj.* pourvu; ~ *for*, pourvu; *conj.* ~ *that*, pourvu que + *subj.*
providen|ce, (*foresight*) prévoyance, *f.*; (*thrift*) économie, *f.*; (*theol.*) Providence, *f.*; ⚠ providence *does not = 'foresight' or 'thrift'*; **~t**, prévoyant; **~tial**, providentiel, -le; **~tially**, providentiellement.
provider, pourvoyeu|r, ~se, *m.f.*
province, (*geog.*) province, *f.*; (*sphere of action*) ressort, *m.*; *within, in my, &c.*, ~, de mon, etc., ressort.
provincial, *adj. and s.m.* provincial.
provision, (*store, stock*) provision, *f.*; (*precaution*) précaution, *f.*; (*comm. of capital*) prestation, *f.*; **~-dealer**, *see* DEALER; **~s**, (*food*) comestibles, *m.pl.*; (*law, insurance, &c.*) dispositions, *f.pl.*; ~ *to the contrary*, clause contraire, *f.*; *v.a.* approvisionner.
provisional, provisoire; **~ly**, provisoirement.
proviso, condition, *f.*
provocat|ion, provocation, *f.*; **~ive**, provoquant.
provoke, provoquer (à); (*irritate*) irriter.
provoking, contrariant; **~ly**, d'une manière irritante.
provost, (*Scotch*) maire, *m.*
prow, proue, *f.*
prowess, bravoure, *f.*
prowl, *v.n.* rôder; **~er**, rôdeu|r, ~se, *m.f.*
proximate, (*cause, &c.*) immédiat.
proximity, proximité, *f.*
proxy, procuration, *f.*; *by* ~, par procuration, *f.*
prud|e, prude, *f.*; **~ery**, pruderie, *f.*; **~ish**, prude.
pruden|ce, prudence, *f.*; **~t**, prudent; **~tly**, avec prudence; **~tial**, de prudence.
prune, *s.* pruneau, *m.*
prun|e, *v.a.* élaguer; **~ing**, taille, *f.*; **~ing-knife**, serpette, *f.*
prunella, (*bot.*) prunelle, *f.*
prurien|ce, lascivété, *f.*; **~t**, lasci|f, ~ve.
Prussian, *adj.* (*when an adj. use small letter*) *and s.m.f.* Prussien, -ne; ~ **blue**, bleu de Prusse, *invar.*
prussic, *adj.* prussique.
pry into, (*pej.*) fourrer le nez dans.
prying, *adj.* indiscr|et, ~ète.
P.S., P.-S. (*postscript*).
psalm, psaume, *m.*; **~ist**, psalmiste, *m.*; **~ody**, psalmodie, *f.*
psalter, psautier, *m.*
pseudo-, pseudo-.
pshaw, *interj.* bah!
psychical, *adj.* psychique.
psycholog|ical, psychologique; **~ist**, psychologue, *m.f.*; **~y**, psychologie, *f.*
ptarmigan, (*ornith.*) lagopède, *m.*
ptomaine, *s.* ptomaïne, *f.*; *~-poisoning*, empoisonnement par les ptomaïnes, *m.*
pub, bistro, *m.*
puberty, puberté, *f.*
public, *s.* public, *m.*; *in* ~, en public.
public, *adj.* publi|c, ~que; ~ *funds*, *see* FUND; ~ *prosecutor*, *see* PROSECUTOR; *~-spirited*, qui s'occupe du bien public; **~ly**, publiquement.
publican, cabaretier, *m.*; (*innkeeper*) aubergiste, *m.*
publication, publication, *f.*
publicist, publiciste, *m.*
publicity, publicité, *f.*
publish, (*news, book, law*) publier; **~er**, éditeur, *m.*
puce, *adj.* (*colour*) puce, *invar.*
pucker, *v.a.* faire* goder; *v.n.* goder; ~ *up*, (*brows*) froncer.
pudding, (*Engl.*) pouding, *m.*
puddle, flaque, *f.*
pudgy, boulot, -te.
pueril|e, puéril; **~ity**, puérilité, *f.*
puff, *s.* (*from mouth*) souffle, *m.*; (*smoke, wind*) bouffée, *f.*; (*steam*) échappement, *m.*; (*powder*) houppe à poudre, *f.*; (*of book, advertisement*) pouf, *m.*
puff, *v.a.*; ~ *out*, gonfler; ~ *up*, (*with pride, &c.*) bouffir (de); (*exaggerate value*) faire* mousser; *be ~ed*, (*out of breath*) être essouflé; *v.n.* (*blow*) souffler; (*steam, smoke*) émettre* des bouffées; (*swell, v.a.n.*) bouffir.
puffin, (*ornith.*) macareux, *m.*
puff|y, (*swollen*) enflé; **~iness**, enflure, *f.*
pug, *s.* (*dog*) roquet, *m.*
pugilis|m, pugilisme, *m.*; **~t**, pugiliste, *m.*
pugnaci|ous, batailleu|r, ~se; **~ty**, humeur batailleuse, *f.*
puissant, puissant.
pule, *v.n.* piauler.
pull, *s.* action de tirer, *f.*; *also* coup, *m.*; (*bell*) poignée, *f.*; (*fam. advantage*) avantage, *m.*
pull, *v.a.* tirer; (*tear*) arracher; ~ *about*, tirailler; ~ *down*, (*buildings*) démolir; (*health*) abattre; ~ *off*, (*clothes*) ôter; (*win*) gagner; ~ *out*, (*plants, &c.*) arracher; ~ *oneself together*, se reprendre*; ~ *up*, (*veh., horse*) arrêter; (*plant*) arracher; (*reprimand*) réprimander; ~ *strings, wires*, tenir* les ficelles.
pull, *v.n.* tirer; (*naut.*) ramer; ~ *through*, s'en tirer; ~ *up, v.n.* (*veh., horse, &c.*) s'arrêter.
pullet, poulette, *f.*
pulley, poulie, *f.*
pull-over, (*approx.*) jersey, *m.*
Pullman-car, *see* CAR.
pullulate, (*lit. and fig.*) germer.
pulmonary, pulmonaire.
pulp, (*fruits*) pulpe, *f.*; (*paper*) pâte, *f.*

pulpit, chaire, *f.*; ⚠ *not* pupitre, *which = desk.*
pulpous, pulpy, pulpeu|x, **~se.**
pulsat|e, battre; **~ion,** pulsation, *f.*
pulse, (*med.*) pouls, *m.*; (*veg.*) légumineuses, *f.pl.*
pulveriz|ation, pulvérisation, *f.*; **~e,** pulvériser.
puma, (*zool.*) puma, *m.*
pumice, ~-stone, pierre ponce, *f.*
pummel, *v.a.* battre à coups de poing.
pump, *s.* pompe, *f.*; (*tire, bicycle*) pompe à air, *f.*; (*shoe*) escarpin, *m.*; *v.a.* pomper; (*elicit information from*) (*pop.*) tirer les vers du nez à; (*put out of breath*) essoufler; *~ up,* (*tyre*) gonfler; *v.n.* pomper.
pumpkin, potiron, *m.*
pun, calembour, *m.*; *v.n.* faire* des calembours; **~ster,** calembouriste, *m.f.*
punch, *s.* (*instr.*) emporte-pièce, *m.*; (*tool*) poinçon, *m.*; (*blow*) coup de poing, *m.*; (*puppet*) polichinelle, *m.*; (*letter-filing*) perforateur, *m.*; *Punch and Judy Show,* guignol, *m.*; *v.a.* (*ticket, &c.*) poinçonner.
puncheon, (*cask*) gros tonneau, *m.*
puncher, (*instr.*) emporte-pièce, *m.*
punctilio, point d'étiquette, *m.*
punctilious, pointilleu|x, **~se; ~ly,** d'une manière pointilleuse.
punctual, ponctuel, -le; **~ity,** ponctualité, *f.*; **~ly,** ponctuellement.
punctuat|e, ponctuer; **~ion,** ponctuation, *f.*
puncture, piqûre, *f.*; (*tire*) crevaison, *f.*; *v.a.n.* (*tyre*) crever.
pundit, pandit, *m.*
pungen|cy, âcreté, *f.*; (*satire, &c.*) mordant, *m.*; **~t,** âcre; (*satire, &c.*) mordant.
punish, punir; (*inflict severe blows*) malmener; **~able,** punissable; **~ment,** punition, *f.*
punitive, pénal.
punt, *s.* bachot, *m.*
puny, chéti|f, ~ve.
pup, petit, -e chien, -ne, *m.f.*; *v.a.* mettre* bas.
pupil, (*scholar*) élève, *m.f.*; (*eye*) pupille, *f.*; (*ward*) pupille, *m.f.*; **~(l)age,** pupillarité, *f.*
puppet, pantin, *m.*
puppy, petit chien, *m.*; (*pers.*) fat, *m.*
purblind, myope; (*obtuse*) obtus.
purchasable, achetable.
purchase, *s.* (*buying*) achat, *m.*; (*thing bought*) emplette, *f.*; (*hold*) prise, *f.*; (*leverage*) abatage, *m.*; ⚠ pourchas = '*chase*', '*pursuit*'; *v.a.* acheter; (*fig.*) *~ with life, &c.,* payer de.
purchaser, acheteu|r, ~se, *m.f.*
pure, (*lit., fig., style, math.*) pur; **~ness,** pureté, *f.*; **~ly,** purement.
purgative, *s.* purgatif, *m.*; *adj.* purgati|f, ~ve.
purgator|y, purgatoire, *m.*; **~ial,** de purgatoire.
purge, (*lit., fig., med., law*) purger; (*cleanse*) nettoyer; (*fault*) expier.
purif|ication, (*lit. and eccles.*) purification, *f.*; **~y,** (*lit. and fig.*) purifier.
purist, puriste, *m.*
Puritan, *adj.* (*when an adj. use small letter*) *and s.m.f.* Puritain; **~ism,** puritanisme, *m.*; **~ical,** de puritain.
purity, pureté, *f.*
purl, *s.* (*of streams*) murmure, *m.*; *v.n.* gazouiller; **~ing,** *adj.* (*stream*) murmurant.
purlieu, (*forest*) lisière, *f.*; (*outskirts*) alentours, *m.pl.*
purloin, dérober; (*fig. and Lit.*) piller.
purple, *s.* (*colour*) violet, *m.*; (*Tyrian and dignity*) pourpre, *f.*; *adj.* violet, -te; ⚠ '*purple*' *adj. and s. is not* pourpre *in French which* = '*dark red*', *sometimes* '*ruby*'.
purplish, légèrement violet; ⚠ *not* purpurin *which* = '*reddish*'.
purport, sens, *m.*; *v.n.* vouloir* paraître +*inf.*
purpose, *s.* but, *m.*; *for the ~ of,* dans le but de; *for this ~,* à cet effet; *to the ~,* à propos; *to what ~?* à quoi bon? ; *serve the ~,* faire* l'affaire.
purpose to, se proposer de.
purposely, exprès.
purr, *s.* ronron, *m.*; *v.n.* ronronner.
purse, porte-monnaie, *m.*; *~-strings,* cordons de la bourse, *m.pl.*; *privy ~,* cassette, *f.*; *v.a. ~ up,* (*brow*) rider; (*lips*) pincer.
purser, (*naut.*) commissaire, *m.*
purslane, (*bot.*) pourpier, *m.*
pursuance, *in ~ of,* en vertu de.
pursuant to, conforme à.
pursue, poursuivre*; (*course, road*) suivre*; *v.n. ~ after,* se mettre* à la poursuite de.
pursuer, personne qui poursuit *or* qui suit.
pursuit, poursuite, *f.*; (*knowledge*) recherche, *f.*; (*occupation*) occupation, *f.*
pursy, (*short-winded*) poussi|f, ~ve.
purvey, *v.a.* être pourvoyeur de; **~or,** pourvoyeu|r, ~se.
purview, limites, *f.pl.*
pus, pus, *m.*
push, *s.* poussée, *f.*; (*go*) allant, *m.*; (*mil.*) poussée en avant, *f.*; (*effort*) effort, *m.*; *at a ~,* en cas de besoin.
push, *v.a.* (*lit., fig., a matter, comm., impel*) pousser; *~ away, back,* repousser; *~ forward, on,* faire* avancer; *~ed for time,* pressé; *v.n.* pousser; *~ back,* reculer; *~ on,* (*to a place*) pousser (jusqu'à); *~ off,* (*naut.*) pousser au large.
pushing, entreprenant.
pusillanim|ity, pusillanimité, *f.*; **~ous,** pusillanime.
puss, minet, -te, *m.f.*; (*hare*) lièvre, *m.*
pustule, *s.* pustule, *f.*
put, *v.a.* (*place, set, translate, a resolution, fig.*) mettre*; (*express*) dire*; (*estimate*) évaluer; (*horse at obstacle*)

amener; *I ~ it to you,* je vous le demande; *~ about,* (*inconvenience*) déranger; (*naut.*) faire* virer de bord; *~ away,* mettre* de côté; (*lock up*) serrer; *~ back,* remettre*; (*watch, &c.*) retarder; *~ by,* mettre* de côté; *~ down,* déposer; (*riot, &c.*) réprimer; (*suppress*) supprimer; (*attribute*) attribuer; (*write*) inscrire*; *~ forth,* (*exert*) exercer; (*leaves, &c.*) pousser; *~ forward,* (*theory, &c.*) avancer; (*hasten*) presser; *~ in,* (*add*) ajouter; (*enter*) inscrire*; (*insert*) introduire*; *~ off,* (*postpone*) remettre*; (*clothes*) ôter; (*payment*) différer; *~ on,* (*clothes*) mettre*; (*flesh, affect*) prendre*; (*clock*) avancer; (*brake, motor, &c.*) serrer; *~ on to,* (*teleph.*) donner la communication (à); *~ out,* (*hand*) tendre; (*bone*) démettre*; (*tongue*) tirer; (*fire, light*) éteindre*; (*inconvenience*) déranger; (*money to interest*) placer; *~ through,* (*complete*) mener à bonne fin; *~ together,* assembler; (*mach.*) monter (avoir); *~ up,* (*price*) élever; (*umbrella*) ouvrir*; (*lodge*) loger; (*hair*) relever; (*prayer*) offrir*; (*parcel*) emballer; *~-up job, see* JOB; *~ up with,* supporter; *~ upon,* exploiter.

put, *v.n.* *~ about,* (*naut.*) virer de bord; *~ into,* (*port*) relâcher (à); *~ off,* (*naut.*) pousser au large; *~ up,* (*lodge*) descendre (être + à); *~ to sea,* prendre* la mer.

putative, supposé; (*father*) putatif.

putrefaction, putréfaction, *f.*

putrefy, *v.a.* putréfier; *v.n.* se putréfier.

putrescen|ce, état de putréfaction, *m.*; **~t,** atteint de putréfaction.

putrid, putride; **~ity,** putridité, *f.*

puttee, molletière, *f.*

putty, (*glaziers'*) mastic, *m.*

puzzle, *s.* (*perplexity*) perplexité, *f.*; (*enigma*) énigme, *f.*; (*toy*) puzzle, *m.*

puzzle, *v.a.* embarrasser; *~ out,* trouver la solution de; *v.n.* être embarrassé (par).

pygmy, pygmée, *m.*

pyjamas, pyjama, *m.*

pylon, (*gateway, supporting structure*) pylône, *m.*

pyramid, pyramide, *f.*; **~al,** pyramidal.

pyre, bûcher, *m.*

pyrethrum, (*bot.*) pyrèthre, *m.*

pyrites, (*chem.*) pyrite, *f.*

pyrotechnic, pyrotechnique.

Pyrrhic, pyrrhique.

Pythian, pythien, -ne.

python, (*zool.*) python, *m.*

Pythoness, (*ant.*) pythonisse, *f.*

pyx, (*eccles.*) ciboire, *m.*

Q

quack, *s.* (*pers.*) charlatan, *m.*; (*duck*) couin-couin, *m.*; *v.n.* (*duck*) faire* couin-couin.

quadrang|le, quadrilatère, *m.*; (*school*) cour, *f.*; **~ular,** quadrangulaire.

quadrant, quart de cercle, *m.*

quadrilateral, *adj. and s.m.* quadrilatère.

quadrille, (*cards, dance*) quadrille, *m.*

quadroon, quarteron, -ne, *m.f.*

quadruped, *adj. and s.m.* quadrupède.

quadruple, *adj. and s.m.* quadruple.

quaff, *v.a.n.* boire* à longs traits.

quagmire, fondrière, *f.*

quail, *s.* (*ornith.*) caille, *f.*

quail, *v.n.* reculer (devant).

quaint, (*odd*) bizarre; (*old-fashioned*) antique; **~ness,** originalité, *f.*; **~ly,** bizarrement.

quake, trembler.

Quak|er, ~eress, quaker, -esse, *m.f.*

qualification, (*title, epithet*) qualification, *f.*; (*for post*) compétence, *f.* (pour); (*modification*) modification, *f.*; ⚠ qualification *is never used in the sense of 'modification'.*

qualif|y, *v.a.* (*describe as, attribute quality to, gram.*) qualifier; (*modify*) modifier; ⚠ qualifier *is never used in the sense of 'modify'*; *~ied for,* (*to do*) qualifié pour; *v.n.* *~y for,* passer l'examen de.

qualitative, qualitati|f, ~ve.

quality, (*mental, moral characteristic, excellence, rank, attribute*) qualité, *f.*

qualm, nausée, *f.*; (*conscience*) scrupule, *m.*

quandary, embarras, *m.*

quantitative, quantitati|f, ~ve.

quantity, (*size, weight, amount, number, pros., math., &c.*) quantité, *f.*; *~-surveyor,* métreur, *m.*

quarantine, quarantaine, *f.*

quarrel, *s.* querelle, *f.*; (*fam.*) brouille, *f.*; (*cause of quarrel*) sujet de plainte, *m.*; *fasten a ~ on,* chercher noise à; *v.n.* se brouiller; *~ with,* se quereller avec; (*find fault with*) trouver à redire à.

quarrelsome, querelleu|r, ~se; **~ness,** humeur querelleuse, *f.*

quarry, (*stone, &c.*) carrière, *f.*; (*hunt.*) curée, *f.*; (*of bird of prey*) proie, *f.*; *v.a.* extraire* d'une carrière; **~man,** carrier, *m.*

quart, (*approx.*) litre, *m.*

quarter, *s.* (*district, of meat, mercy to enemy, her., moon*) quartier, *m.*; (*of hour, year, &c., fourth part, point of compass*) quart, *m.*; (*dry measure*) quart de quintal, *m.*; (*region, &c.*) endroit, *m.*; (*pers., fig.*) côté, *m.*; (*rent*) terme, *m.*; (*ship*) †hanche, *f.*; (*U.S.A. money*) quart de dollar, *m.*; *~s,* (*abode, mil.*) quartiers, *m.pl.*; *~-day* terme, *m.*; *~-deck,* gaillard d'arrière, *m.*

quarter, *v.a.* diviser en quatre; (*her. and pers.*) écarteler; (*troops*) cantonner.

quarterly, *s.* revue trimestrielle, *f.*; *adj.* trimestriel, -le.

quartermaster, (*naut.*) quartier-maître, *m.*; (*cav.*) maréchal des logis, *m.*

quartet, quatuor, *m.*

quarto, *adj. invar. and s.m.* in-quarto.

quash, écraser; (*annul*) casser.

quasi-, (*prefix with adj. and s.*) quasi-.

quatrain, quatrain, *m.*

quaver, *s.* trille, *f.*; (*mus.*) croche, *f.*; **~ing**, *adj.* chevrotant.
quay, quai, *m.*
queen, (*lit. and fig., chess*) reine, *f.*; (*cards, draughts*) dame, *f.*; *v.n.* ~ *it*, faire* la reine; **~ly**, **~like**, de reine.
queer, *adj.* bizarre; (*not well*) malade; (*suspicious*) suspect; ~ *bird, customer,* (*slang*) drôle de corps, *m.*; ~ *fellow, see* FELLOW; **~ness**, bizarrerie, *f.*; **~ly**, étrangement; *v.a.* ~ *the pitch for*, couper l'herbe sous le pied **à**.
quell, réprimer.
quench, (*fire*) éteindre*; (*fig.*) refroidir; (*thirst*) étancher.
querulous, plainti|f, ~ve; **~ness**, humeur plaintive, *f.*; **~ly**, d'un ton plaintif.
query, *s.* question, *f.*; (*introducing doubt*) reste à savoir si; *v.a.* mettre* en doute; *v.n.* ~ *whether*, se demander si.
quest, recherche, *f.*; *in ~ of*, **à la** recherche de.
question, *s.* (*interrogative sentence, doubt, problem, matter, subject discussed, torture, exams.*) question, *f.*; (*Parl.*) interpellation, *f.*; *v.a.* interroger; (*throw doubt on, call in question*) mettre* en doute; ⚠ questionner *never has the sense of 'throw doubt on'*.
questionable, douteu|x, ~se.
queue, *s.* (*hair, wig, line of persons, &c.*) queue, *f.*; *v.n.* (*pers.*) faire* la queue.
quibble, *s.* (*pun*) calembour, *m.*; (*cavil*) argutie, *f.*; *v.n.* jouer sur les mots; (*cavil*) ergoter; **~r**, faiseur de calembours, *m.*; (*caviller*) ergoteu|r, ~se, *m.f.*
quick, *s.* vif, *m.*; *to the ~*, au vif.
quick, *adj.* (*prompt, lit. and fig.*) prompt (à); (*movement, &c.*) rapide; (*lively*) vi|f, ~ve; (*eye*) perçant; (*temper*) emporté; *s.* (*the living*) vivants, *m.pl.*; *~-firer,* (*gun*) canon à tir rapide, *m.*; *~-firing, adj.* à tir rapide; *~-witted*, à l'esprit vif; **~ness**, (*perception*) pénétration, *f.*; (*speed*) hâte, *f.*; **~ly**, vite.
quick, *adv.* vite.
quicken, (*bring to life*) ranimer; (*rouse*) animer; (*hasten*) accélérer.
quicklime, chaux vive, *f.*
quicksands, sables mouvants, *m.pl.*
quickset, *adj.*; ~ *hedge*, †haie vive, *f.*
quicksilver, vif-argent, *m.*
quid, (*tobacco*) chique, *f.*
quiddity, (*quibble*) argutie, *f.*
quidnunc, nouvelliste, *m.*
quid pro quo, *get a ~, use* en avoir pour; ⚠ *not* quiproquo *which = a 'misunderstanding'*.
quiescen|ce, repos, *m.*; **~t**, en repos.
quiet, *s.* (*peace, silence*) tranquillité, *f.*; (*repose*) repos, *m.*; *on the ~,* (*slang, on the q.t.*) sans tambour ni trompette.
quiet, *adj.* (*lit. and fig.*) tranquille; (*in peace, calm, comm.*) calme; *be ~,* (*be silent*) se taire*; *v.a.* (*calm*) apaiser; **~ness**, tranquillité, *f.*; **~ly**, tranquillement; *keep ~,* se tenir* tranquille.
quiet|ism, quiétisme, *m.*; **~ist**, *adj. and s.m.f.* quiétiste.
quietude, quiétude, *f.*
quietus, (*death*) mort, *f.*
quill, *s.* (*pen of feather*) plume, *f.*; *~-driver,* (*pers.*) gratte-papier, *m.invar.*; *~-pen*, plume d'oie, *f.*
quilt, *s.* courtepointe, *f.*; (*down*) édredon, *m.*; *v.a.* piquer; **~ing**, piqué, *m.*
quince, coing, *m.*; **~-tree**, cognassier, *m.*
quincunx, quinconce, *m.*
quinine, quinine, *f.*
Quinquagesima Sunday, quinquagésime, *f.*
quinquennial, quinquennal.
quinsy, (*med.*) esquinancie, *f.*
quintessence, quintessence, *f.*
quintet, quintette, *m.*
quintuple, *adj. and s.m.* quintuple.
quip, (*smart saying*) mot piquant, *m.*
quire, (*paper*) main, *f.*; *see* CHOIR.
quit, *adj.* quitte (de); *v.a.* quitter; *v.n.* ~ *oneself,* (*behave*) se conduire*.
quite, tout à fait; (*often + adj.*) tout (*concord + adj. beginning with consonant or aspirate H*); ~ *so*, parfaitement; ~ *the thing,* (*fashionable*) le dernier cri; *be not ~ the thing,* (*unwell*) ne pas être dans son assiette.
quits, *adj.* quitte.
quittance, (*receipt*) quittance, *f.*
quiver, *s.* (*arrows*) carquois, *m.*
quiver, *v.n.* (*wing, voice*) trembloter; (*light*) vaciller; **~ing**, *s.* tremblotement, *m.*
quixotic, de Don Quichotte; **~ally**, **à la** Don Quichotte.
quiz, *s.* persifleu|r, ~se, *m.f.*; **~zical**, railleu|r, ~se; **~zically**, en raillant; *v.a.* railler.
quoit, (*game*) palet, *m.*
quorum, quorum, *m.*
quondam, *adj.* d'autrefois.
quota, quote-part, *f.* (*pl.* quotes-parts).
quotation, citation, *f.*; (*comm. price rate*) cote, *f.*
quote, citer; (*comm.*) coter; (*securities, &c.*) inscrire*.
quoth, *v.a.n. use* dire*.

R

rabbi, rabbin, *m.*; **~nical**, rabbinique.
-**rabbit**, *s.* lapin, -e, *m.f.*; **~-hutch**, *also*, **burrow**, clapier, *m.*; **~-warren**, garenne, *f.*
rabble, *s.* tourbe, *f.*; *the ~,* la canaille.
rabid, (*fig. and dogs*) enragé.
rabidness, **rabies**, rage, *f.*
race, (*boat, foot, bicycle, horse, motor, &c.*) course, *f.*; (*nation, descent*) race, *f.*; (*line of descent*) lignée, *f.*; (*current in sea*) raz, *m.*
rac|e, *v.a.* lutter de vitesse avec; *v.n.* courir*; *~ing world*, monde des courses, *m.*; **~ial**, de race.
racecourse, carrière, *f.*

racehorse, cheval de course, *m.*
rack, *s.* (*in stable, for arms*) râtelier, *m.*; (*for torture*) chevalet, *m.*; (*clouds*) nuages chassés par le vent; *to ~ and ruin,* à vau-l'eau; *be on the ~,* (*fig.*) être à la torture; *v.a. ~ one's brains,* se creuser le cerveau.
racket, *s.* (*noise*) tintamarre, *m.*; (*pleasure*) dissipation, *f.*; (*tennis, &c.*) raquette, *f.*; *v.n.* (*pleasure, &c.*) mener vie joyeuse.
racking, (*headache*) fou, folle.
rac(c)oon, (*zool., U.S.A.*) raton laveur, *m.*
racy, (*fig.*) piquant.
radian|ce, éclat, *m.*; **~t,** radieu|x, ~se; **~tly,** d'un air radieux; *~t with,* rayonnant de.
radia|te, *v.a.* (*light, joy, heat, &c.*) dégager; **~tion,** (*light, heat*) rayonnement, *m.*; **~tor,** (*heating, motor*) radiateur, *m.*; **~tor-cap,** bouchon de radiateur, *m.*
radical, *s.* (*gram., polit.*) radical, *m.*; *adj.* (*of the root, fundamental, going to the root, fig., polit.*) radical; **~ism,** radicalisme, *m.*; **~ly,** radicalement.
radio, radio, *f.*; **~gram,** radiogramme, *m.*
radish, radis, *m.*
radium, radium, *m.*
radius, rayon, *m.*
raffle, tombola, *f.*; *v.a. ~ for,* mettre* en tombola.
raft, radeau, *m.*; (*timber*) train de bois, *m.*
rafter, chevron, *m.*; **~ed,** à chevrons.
raftsman, flotteur, *m.*
rag, chiffon, *m.*; (*tatter*) lambeau, *m.*; (*rowdy scene*) tapage, *m.*; *~-picker,* chiffonni|er, ~ère, *m.f.*; *for a ~,* par plaisanterie; **~s,** (*clothes*) guenilles, *f.pl.*; (*for stuffing, &c.*) chiffons, *m.pl.*
rag, *v.a.* blaguer; (*school*) brimer; *v.n.* faire* du tapage.
ragamuffin, gueu|x, ~se, *m.f.*
rage, rage, *f.*; *have a ~ for,* avoir la rage de; *be the ~,* (*vogue*) faire* fureur.
rage, *v.n.* être furieu|x, ~se; (*disease*) sévir; (*storm, battle*) faire* rage.
ragged, (*pers.*) en haillons; (*things*) déchiré; (*uneven, ill-finished*) inégal; **~ness,** délabrement, *m.*; **~ly,** (*unevenly*) inégalement; ~ **robin,** (*bot.*) œillet des prés, *m.*
raging, *adj.* furieu|x, ~se.
ragman, marchand de chiffons, *m.*
ragtag, *~ and bobtail,* racaille, *f.*
ragwort, (*bot.*) jacobée, *f.*
raid, incursion, *f.*; (*caval.*) raid, *m.*; (*police*) rafle, *f.*
rail, *s.* (*ornith.*) râle, *m.*; *water-~,* râle des eaux, *m.*
rail, *s.* (*bar*) barre, *f.*; (*stairs*) rampe, *f.*; (*bridge, &c.*) garde-fou, *m., pl.* garde-fous; (*rail.*) rail, *m.*; *by ~,* par chemin de fer; *run off the ~s,* (*lit. and fig.*) dérailler; *send by ~,* envoyer par fer.
rail, *v.a.* fermer avec une grille; *~ in, off,* griller.
rail at, injurier; ⚠ *not* railler *which* = '*jeer at*'.
railing, *s.* grille, *f.*; (*abuse*) injures, *f.pl.*; *adj.* injurieu|x, ~se.
railroad, railway, chemin de fer, *m.*; *~ time-table, guide,* indicateur de chemin de fer, *m.*
raiment, vêtement, *m.*
rain, *s.* (*lit. and fig.*) pluie, *f.*; **~-gauge,** pluviomètre, *m.*; **~-water,** eau de pluie, *f.*; *v.a.* (*lit. and fig.*) pleuvoir*; *v.n.* pleuvoir*.
rainbow, arc-en-ciel, *m.*
raindrop, goutte de pluie, *f.*
rainfall, chute de pluie, *f.*
rainproof, imbrifuge.
rainy, pluvieu|x, ~se; *it is ~,* le temps est à la pluie.
raise, *v.a.* (*lift, troops, taxes, rebellion, siege, mask, limbs, eyes, session*) lever; (*erect, in rank, temperature, cattle, &c., U.S.A. of children, voice, protest, price*) élever; (*dust, rouse a people, a question*) soulever; (*increase*) augmenter; (*money*) se procurer; (*cry*) pousser; (*disembodied spirit*) évoquer; (*dead*) ressusciter; (*plants*) faire* pousser.
raisin, raisin sec, *m.*
raising, *s.* (*tariffs, salaries, &c.*) élévation, *f.*; (*taxes, troops*) levée, *f.*
rake, *s.* (*garden, &c.*) râteau, *m.*; (*fire*) râble, *m.*; (*pers.*) débauché, *m.*; *v.a.* (*hay*) râteler; (*flower-border, leaves, &c.*) râtisser; *~ out,* (*fire*) éteindre*; *~ together,* rassembler; *~ up,* (*fig.*) aller* (être) chercher.
raking, *adj.* (*rifle-fire*) d'enfilade.
rakish, de débauché; **~ly,** en viveur.
rally, rallying, *s.* (*mil., &c.*) ralliement, *m.*; (*recovery*) retour de force, *m.*; (*in prices*) reprise, *f.*
rally, *v.a.* (*mil.*) rallier; (*muster*) rassembler; (*banter*) se moquer de; *v.n.* se rallier; (*collect*) se rassembler; (*recover*) se remettre*; (*prices comm.*) se reprendre*.
ram, *s.* (*an., battering-~*) bélier, *m.*; *v.a.* (*drive in or down*) enfoncer; (*a gun*) refouler; (*cram*) bourrer.
ramble, *s.* petite promenade, *f.*; *v.n.* rôder; (*in speech*) divaguer; **~r,** (*rose*) rose grimpante, *f.*
rambling, vagabond; (*speech*) décousu.
ramification, ramification, *f.*
ramify, *v.n.* ramifier.
rammer, (*paver's*) hie, *f.*; (*cannon*) refouloir, *m.*
ramp, *v.n.* (*climb*) grimper.
rampant, (*her., arch.*) rampant; (*unchecked*) déchaîné; (*threatening*) menaçant; ⚠ rampant = '*crawling*' *used also in her. and arch.*
rampart, rempart, *m.*
rampion, (*bot.*) raiponce, *f.*
ramrod, (*rifle*) baguette, *f.*; (*cannon*) refouloir, *m.*
ramshackle, délabré.
ranch, *s.* (*farm*) rancho, *m.*
rancid, rance; *become ~,* rancir.

rancorous, rancuni|er, ~ère.

rancour, rancune, *f.*

random, *s.* †hasard, *m.*; *at* ~, au hasard; *adj.* fait au hasard; (*shot, &c.*) perdu.

range, *s.* (*mountains*) chaîne; (*row of houses, &c.*) rangée, *f.*; (*shooting*) tir, *m.*; (*distance attainable*) portée, *f.*; (*extent, scope*) étendue, *f.*; (*kitchen*) fourneau (de cuisine), *m.*; (*colours, &c.*) gamme, *f.*

range, *v.a.* (*place in row, classify*) ranger; ~ *oneself*, se ranger; ~ *over, through, &c.*, parcourir*; ~ *from . . . to*, varier de . . . à.

rank, *s.* (*mil., place in society, soldiers abreast*) rang, *m.*; (*of officer*) grade, *m.*; **~s**, (*mil.*) rangs, *m.pl.*; ~ *and file*, simples soldats, *m.pl.*; *reduce to the* ~*s*, casser.

rank, *adj.* (*rancid*) rance; (*growth*) luxuriant; (*flagrant*) flagrant; (*smell*) puant; **~ness**, (*growth*) exubérance, *f.*

rank, *v.a.* ranger; *v.n.* se ranger; (*take rank*) prendre* rang.

rankle, *v.n.* (*fig.*) s'envenimer.

ransack, *v.a.* fouiller dans.

ransom, rançon, *f.*; *v.a.* payer rançon pour; ⇧ rançonner = '*set ransom upon*', '*fleece*'.

rant, *s.* déclamation extravagante, *f.*; *v.n.* déclamer avec extravagance; **~er**, énergumène, *m.f.*; **~ing**, extravagant.

ranunculus, (*bot.*) renoncule, *f.*

rap, *s.* tape, *f.*; (*knock*) coup, *m.*; *not to care a* ~ *for*, s'en moquer comme de l'an quarante; *v.a.* frapper.

rapac|ious, rapace; **~ity**, rapacité, *f.*; **~iously**, avec rapacité.

rape, viol, *m.*; (*bot.*) navette, *f.*; *v.a.* violer.

rapid, *s.* (*of river*) rapide, *m.*; *adj.* rapide; **~ity**, rapidité, *f.*; **~ly**, rapidement.

rapier, rapière, *f.*

rapine, rapine, *f.*

rappee, tabac râpé, *m.*

raptur|e, transport, *m.*; (*delight*) ravissement, *m.*; **~ous**, transporté.

rar|e, (*not dense, uncommon*) rare; (*first-rate, fam.*) fameu|x, ~se; (*U.S.A. uncooked*) peu cuit; **~eness**, **~ity**, rareté, *f.*; **~ely**, rarement.

raref|action, raréfaction, *f.*; **~y**, *v.a.* raréfier; *v.n.* se raréfier.

rascal, coquin, *m.*; **~ity**, coquinerie, *f.*; **~ly**, de coquin.

rash, *s.* (*med.*) éruption, *f.*

rash, *adj.* téméraire; (*thoughtless*) inconsidéré; **~ness**, témérité, *f.*; (*haste*) précipitation, *f.*; **~ly**, sans réflexion.

rasher, (*of bacon*) lardon, *m.*

rasp, *v.a.* râper; (*irritate*) irriter.

raspberry, framboise, *f.*

rat, rat, *m.*; **~-trap**, ratière, *f.*

rate, *s.* (*interest, &c.*) taux, *m.*; (*exchange*) cours du change, *m.*; (*speed*) vitesse, *f.*; (*local tax*) taxe, *f.*; ~ *per cent.*, taux pour cent, *m.*; *at any* ~, quoi qu'il en soit; *at the* ~ *of*, à raison de; *first-, second-*~, de premier, de second ordre.

rat|e, *v.a.* (*set price, value on*) estimer; (*assess taxes*) taxer; (*scold*) laver la tête à; **~ing**, *s.* (*reprimand*) semonce, *f.*

rateable, proportionnel, -le; (*taxable*) imposable.

ratepayer, contribuable, *m.f.*

rather, plutôt; (*somewhat*) un peu; ~ *than*, plutôt que; ~ *than* + *verb*, plutôt que de + *inf.*; *have* (*had, would*) ~, aimer mieux + *inf.*

ratification, ratification, *f.*

ratify, ratifier.

ratio, proportion, *f.*

ration, *s.* ration, *f.*; *v.a.* rationner.

rational, raisonnable; **~ism**, rationalisme, *m.*; **~ist**, rationaliste, *m.f.*; **~ly**, raisonnablement.

rattle, *s.* (*noise*) bruit, *m.*; (*child's*), †hochet, *m.*; (*death*) râle, *m.*; *v.a.* (*as wind*) secouer; (*slang, for fluster*) agiter; ~ *off*, (*recite*) débiter à toute vitesse; *v.n.* faire* du bruit; (*veh.*) passer avec fracas; ~ *on, away*, (*talk*) jacasser.

rattlesnake, serpent à sonnettes, *m.*

rattling, *s.* bruit, *m.*; (*veh.*) roulement bruyant, *m.*; *adj.* bruyant.

raucous, rauque.

ravage, *v.a.* ravager.

rave, délirer; ~ *about*, s'extasier sur.

ravel, *v.a.* embrouiller; *v.n.* s'embrouiller.

raven, corbeau, *m.*; *young* ~, corbillat, *m.*

ravenous, vorace; *be* ~, avoir une faim de loup; **~ly**, voracement.

ravine, ravin, *m.*

ravish, (*carry off*) enlever; (*take away, delight*) ravir; **~ing**, *adj.* ravissant; **~ingly**, à ravir.

raw, (*uncooked*) cru; (*inexperienced*) novice; (*unwrought*) brut; (*wound*) écorché; (*weather, &c.*) froid et humide; (*uncouth*) grossi|er, ~ère; **~ness**, (*weather*) froid humide, *m.*

ray, *s.* (*lit. and fig.*) rayon, *m.*; ***X-~s***, rayons X, *m.pl.*; (*ichth.*) raie, *f.*

raze, rase, *v.a.* (*obliterate*) effacer.

razor, rasoir, *m.*

reach, *s.* (*extent*) étendue, *f.*; (*of the hand, mind, eye, voice*) portée, *f.*; *out of* ~, hors de portée; *within* ~, à portée; *within easy* ~ *of*, à une distance commode de.

reach, *v.a.* (*arrive at, and conclusion*) arriver (être) à; (*get as far as*) atteindre*; (*hand*) passer; ~ *after*, s'efforcer d'atteindre.

reach, *v.n.* (*extend*) s'étendre; (*attain to*) atteindre*; (*letters, goods, &c.*) parvenir* (être) à.

react, réagir (sur); **~ion**, réaction, *f.*; **~ionary**, *adj. and s.m.f.* réactionnaire.

read, *v.a.* lire*; (*study*) étudier; (*understand*) comprendre*; ~ *at sight*, (*mus.*) déchiffrer; *be* ~, se lire*; ~ *for*, (*exam.*) préparer, *v.a.*; ~ *out*, lire* tout †haut; ~ *over*, parcourir*; ~ *over and over again*, lire* et relire*; ~ *to*, faire* la lecture à; *well-*~, instruit.

read, *v.n.* lire*; (*be conceived, be couched, of book, &c.*) se lire*.
readable, lisible.
reader, lect|eur, ~rice, *m.f.*
reading, lecture, *f.*; **~-desk**, (*church*) lutrin, *m.*; **~-lamp**, lampe de bureau, *f.*; **~-room**, salle de lecture, *f.*
readjust, rajuster.
readmission, réadmission, *f.*
read|y, *adj.* (*prepared*) prêt (à); (*quick*) prompt (à); (*prone*) porté (à); (*on the point of*) près de; (*at hand*) sous la main; (*easy*) simple; *~y-made*, (*of clothes*) de confection; *~y money*, argent comptant, *m.*; *be ~y with*, (*answer, &c.*) prêt à donner, faire*; *get ~y*, *v.a.* préparer; *v.n.* se préparer; **~iness**, empressement, *m.*; *in ~iness*, prêt; **~ily**, volontiers.
ready, *adv.* (+ *p.p.*) tout (*concord + consonant or aspirate* H).
reaffirm, affirmer de nouveau.
real, *s.* (*coin*) réal, *m.*
real, *adj.* réel, -le; (*genuine*) véritable; (*property*) immeuble; *~ property*, *see* PROPERTY; **~ity**, réalité, *f.*; **~ly**, (*truly*) vraiment.
real|ism, réalisme, *m.*; **~ist**, réaliste, *m.*; **~istic**, réaliste.
realiz|e, (*convert into fact, comm.*) réaliser; (*comprehend*) comprendre*; **~ation**, réalisation, *f.*; **~able**, réalisable.
realm, royaume, *m.*; (*fig.*) domaine, *m.*
ream, (*paper*) rame, *f.*
reanimate, ranimer.
reap, *v.a.n.* moissonner; (*fig.*) retirer; **~er**, moissonneu|r, ~se, *m.f.*; *~er and binder*, faucheuse moissonneuse, *f.*
reappear, reparaître*; **~ance**, réapparition, *f.*
rear, *s.* (*hind part*) queue, *f.*; (*privy*) cabinet d'aisances, *m.*; (*mil.*) derrières, *m.pl.*; *bring up the ~*, fermer la marche.
rear, *adj.* de derrière; *~-admiral*, *see* ADMIRAL; *~-guard*, arrière-garde, *f.*; *~ mudguard*, (*motor*) *see* MUDGUARD.
rear, *v.a.* (*children, building*) élever; *v.n.* (*horse*) se cabrer.
rearrange, arranger de nouveau.
reason, *s.* (*the faculty, cause, good sense, sanity*) raison, *f.*; *in ~*, (*use* raisonnable *or verb with* raisonnablement); *listen to ~*, écouter raison; *it stands to ~*, il va de soi que; *the ~ why*, la raison pour laquelle; *v.a.n.* raisonner; **~ableness**, modération, *f.*; **~able**, raisonnable; **~ably**, raisonnablement.
reasoning, raisonnement, *m.*
reassemble, *v.a.* assembler de nouveau; *v.n.* s'assembler de nouveau.
reassume, reprendre*.
reassure, rassurer; ⚠ *not* réassurer *which* = '*reinsure*'.
reassuring, rassurant.
rebate, *s.* (*comm.*) rabais, *m.*
rebeck, rebec, *m.*
rebel, *adj. and s.m.f.* rebelle; *v.n.* se révolter (contre).
rebell|ion, rébellion, *f.*; **~ious**, rebelle; **~iously**, en rebelle.
rebound, *s.* rebondissement, *m.*; *v.n.* rebondir; (*fig.*) rejaillir.
rebuff, *s.* rebuffade, *f.*; *v.a.* repousser.
rebuild, rebâtir; **~ing**, *s.* reconstruction, *f.*
rebuke, *s.* réprimande, *f.*; *v.a.* réprimander.
rebut, (*refute*) réfuter; ⚠ *not* rebuter *which* = '*repel*', '*rebuke*'.
recalcitrant, *adj. and s.m.f.* récalcitrant, -e.
recall, *s.* rappel, *m.*; *v.a.* rappeler; (*remember*) se rappeler.
recant, *v.a.* rétracter; *v.n.* se rétracter; **~ation**, rétractation, *f.*
recapitula|te, récapituler; **~tion**, récapitulation, *f.*
recapture, *s.* reprise; *v.a.* reprendre*.
recast, *s.* (*lit. and fig.*) refonte, *f.*; (*theatr.*) nouvelle distribution; *v.a.* (*lit. and fig.*) refondre.
recede, (*in the distance*) s'éloigner.
receipt, (*for payment*) quittance, *f.*; (*cook., med., &c.*) recette, *f.*; (*act of receiving*) reçu, *m.*; *on ~ of*, au reçu de.
receipt, *v.a.* (*bill, &c.*) quittancer.
receiv|e, (*lit., fig., money, entertain, admit*) recevoir; (*stolen goods*) recéler; **~ing-station**, (*wireless*) poste de réception, *m.*
receiver, (*letters, &c.*) destinataire, *m.f.*; (*stolen goods*) recéleu|r, ~se, *m.f.*; (*teleph.*) récepteur, *m.*
recent, récent; **~ly**, récemment.
receptacle, réceptacle, *m.*
reception, (*receiving, things, pers., party*) réception, *f.*; (*welcome*) accueil, *m.*
receptive, récepti|f, ~ve.
recess, (*Parl., &c.*) vacances, *f.pl.*; (*alcove*) alcôve, *f.*; (*secret place, fig.*) repli, *m.*; **~ion**, recul, *m.*
recipe, (*cook. &c.*) recette, *f.*
recipient, (*receptacle*) récipient, *m.*; ⚠ récipient *not of persons, use* personne qui reçoit, *f.*
reciproc|al, réciproque; **~ally**, réciproquement; **~ate**, donner en retour; **~ity**, réciprocité, *f.*
recit|e, *v.a.n.* réciter; **~al**, (*account of facts, narrative*) récit, *m.*; (*mus.*) récital, *m.*; **~ation**, (*schools, &c.*) récitation, *f.*; **~ative**, *s.* récitatif, *m.*
reck, *~ of*, *v.a.* se soucier de.
reckless, (*careless*) insouciant; (*rash*) téméraire; **~ness**, insouciance, *f.*; **~ly**, avec insouciance, témérairement.
reckon, *v.a.* compter; (*believe*) croire*; *~ on, upon*, compter sur; *~ to*, compter + *inf.*; *~ up*, additionner.
reckoner, **ready-~**, barême, *m.*
reckoning, *s.* compte, *m.*; (*inn*) écot, *m.*; (*naut.*) estime, *f.*
reclaim, *v.a.* (*pers.*) corriger; (*land*) amender; **~able**, qui peut être corrigé, amendé.

reclin|e, *v.a.* (*lean*) appuyer; *v.n.* s'appuyer; *be reclining,* être couché.
recluse, *adj. and s.m.f.* reclus, -e.
recognition, (*acknowledgement of services and of pers., &c., seen before*) reconnaissance, *f.*
recogniz|e, (*pers., service, claims, acknowledge, &c.*) reconnaître*; **~able,** reconnaissable.
recoil, *s.* recul, *m.*; *v.n.* ~ *with,* (*horror, &c.*) reculer de; ~ *from,* reculer devant.
recollect, *v.a.* se rappeler; **~ion,** souvenir, *m.*; ⚠ *not* récollection = '*contemplation*', *now obsolete.*
recommence, recommencer.
recommend, recommander; (*to do something*) recommander à + *pers.,* de + *inf.*; **~ation,** recommandation, *f.*
recompense, *s.* récompense, *f.*; *v.a.* récompenser (de); (*compensate*) dédommager (de).
reconcilable with, (*things*) conciliable avec.
reconcil|e, (*pers.*) réconcilier; (*make resigned*) réconcilier (à); (*things*) concilier (avec); **~iation,** (*pers.*) réconciliation, *f.*; (*things*) conciliation, *f.*
recondite, abstrus.
reconnaissance, (*mil.*) reconnaissance, *f.*; **~ plane,** (*aeron.*) avion de reconnaissance, *m.*
reconnoitre, reconnaître*.
reconquer, reconquérir*.
reconsider, considérer de nouveau; **~ation,** nouvel examen, *m.*
reconstitu|te, reconstituer; **~tion,** reconstitution, *f.*
reconstruct, reconstruire*; **~ion,** reconstruction, *f.*
record, *s.* (*national, &c.*) rapport officiel, *m.*; (*token of remembrance*) souvenir, *m.*; (*mention*) mention, *f.*; (*national, &c.*) archives, *f.pl.*; (*gramophone*) disque, *m.*; *on* ~, enregistré; ⚠ record, *m., is only used of sport, e.g. break the* ~, battre le record; *adj.* (*sports, prices*) record, *invar.*
record, *v.a.* (*register*) enregistrer; (*on mind*) graver; (*relate*) rapporter; ~ *a vote,* voter.
recorder, greffier, *m.*
recount, raconter; (*count again*) recompter.
recoup, ~ *oneself,* se dédommager (de).
recourse, recours, *m.*
recover, *v.a.* (*get again, debt, health*) recouvrer; (*breath, consciousness*) reprendre*; (*regain, lit. & fig.*) reconquérir*; (*expenses*) récupérer; ~ *oneself,* revenir* (être) à soi; *v.n.* (*from illness*) se remettre*; (*prices*) se relever.
re-cover, *v.a.* recouvrir*.
recoverable, (*money, &c.*) recouvrable.
recovery, (*health*) rétablissement, *m.*; (*getting again, debt*) recouvrement, *m.*; (*expenses, losses*) récupération, *f.*
recreant, *s.* apostat, *m.*
recreat|e, (*amuse*) récréer; **~ion,** (*amusement*) récréation, *f.*; **~ive,** récréati|f, ~ve.
re-create, recréer.
recriminat|e, récriminer; **~ion,** récrimination, *f.*
recross, repasser.
recrudesc|e, reprendre*; **~ence,** recrudescence, *f.*; **~ent,** recrudescent.
recruit, *s.* recrue, *f.*; *v.a.* (*mil.*) recruter; (*health*) rétablir; *v.n.* se rétablir.
recruiting, recruitment, (*mil.*) recrutement, *m.*; **recruiting-officer,** recruteur, *m.*
rectang|le, rectangle, *m.*; **~ular,** rectangulaire.
rectifiable, rectifiable.
rectif|ication, rectification, *f.*; **~y,** rectifier.
rectilineal, rectiligne.
rectitude, droiture, *f.*
rector, (*univ.*) recteur, *m.*; (*eccles., approx.*) curé, *m.*; **~y,** presbytère, *m.*; **~ial,** rectoral.
recumbent, couché.
recupera|te, *v.a.* (*health, &c.*) recouvrer; ⚠ récupérer = '*retrieve*', *rarely* '*recuperate*'; *v.n.* (*health*) se rétablir; **~tion,** rétablissement, *m.*
recur, revenir* (être); **~rence,** retour, *m.*; **~rent,** qui revient.
red, *s.* (*colour, polit.*) rouge, *m.*; (*hair*) roux, *m.*
red, *adj.* rouge; (*hair*) rou|x, ~sse; (*lips*) vermeil, -le; **currant,** *see* CURRANT; **deer,** *see* DEER; **~ Indian,** *see* INDIAN; **~ lead,** *see* LEAD; **~ tape,** *see* TAPE; **~-throated diver,** (*ornith.*) *see* DIVER; **~ness,** rougeur, *f.*
redbreast, (*ornith.*) rouge-gorge, *m.*
redden, *v.a.n.* rougir.
reddish, rougeâtre.
redeem, (*from pawn*) dégager; (*mortgage*) purger; (*buy back, theol., slave*) racheter; (*time*) rattraper; (*promise*) tenir*; **~able,** (*comm.*) remboursable.
Redeemer, (*theol.*) Rédempteur, *m.*
redemand, redemander.
redempt|ion, (*theol.*) rédemption, *f.*; (*repurchase & fig.*) rachat, *m.*; (*pawn*) dégagement, *m.*; (*mortgage*) purge, *f.*; **~ive,** rédempt|eur, ~rice.
redintegra|te, rétablir; **~tion,** rétablissement, *m.*
redirect, (*letter, parcel*) réexpédier.
redistribute, répartir de nouveau.
redolent of, qui sent; (*suggestive of*) qui rappelle, *v.a.*
redouble, redoubler de.
redoubt, *s.* (*fort.*) redoute, *f.*
redoubtable, redoutable.
redound to, contribuer à.
redress, *s.* réparation; *v.a.* (*wrong*) réparer; (*reform*) redresser.
redshank, (*ornith.*) gambette, *m.*
redstart, (*ornith.*) rouge-queue, *m.*
reduce, *v.a.* (*transform, curtail, bring*

down, subdue, prices) réduire*; (*enfeeble*) affaiblir; ~ *to writing,* mettre* par écrit.
reduc|ible, réductible; **~tion,** réduction, *f.*; (*allowance on price*) remise, *f.*
redundan|ce, redondance, *f.*; **~t** (*style*) redondant; **~tly,** avec redondance.
reduplica|te, *v.a.* doubler; **~tion,** redoublement, *m.*
redwing, (*ornith.*) mauvis, *m.*
re-echo, *v.a.* renvoyer; *v.n.* retentir.
reed, *s.* roseau, *m.*; (*shepherd's*) chalumeau, *m.*; (*of an instrument*) anche, *f.*
reedy, couvert de roseaux.
reef, *s.* (*rock*) récif, *m.*; (*naut.*) ris, *m.*; *v.a.* (*sail*) prendre* un ris à.
reek, *s.* fumée, *f.*; *v.n.* fumer; ~ *of,* sentir, *v.a.*; **~y,** enfumée.
reel, *s.* dévidoir, *m.*; (*sewing-cotton, &c.*) bobine, *f.*; (*dance, approx.*) branle, *m.*; *v.a.* ~ *off,* (*lit. and fig.*) dévider; *v.n.* (*head*) tourner; (*stagger*) tituber.
re-elect, réélire*; **~ion,** réélection, *f.*
re-embark, *v.a.s.* rembarquer; **~ation,** rembarquement, *m.*
re-engage, rengager; **~ment,** rengagement, *m.*
re-enlist, *v.n.* se rengager; **~ment,** rengagement, *m.*
re-enter, *v.a.* rentrer (être) dans; (*bkkpg.*) inscrire* de nouveau; *v.n.* rentrer (être).
re-establish, rétablir; **~ment,** (*health*) rétablissement, *m.*
re-examine, examiner de nouveau; (*an account, &c.*) repasser.
re-export, réexporter.
refectory, réfectoire, *m.*
refer, *v.a.* référer; (*direct to an authority*) renvoyer; (*question*) soumettre*; ~ *to,* (*consult*) consulter; (*apply to*) s'adresser à; *v.n.* se rapporter (à); (*allude*) faire* allusion (à).
referee, *s.* arbitre, *m.*; *v.a.* (*in games*) arbitrer.
reference, (*allusion*) allusion, *f.*; (*to an authority, source of information*) référence, *f.*; (*character of, pers.*) références, *f.pl.*; *have* ~ *to,* (*relate to*) se rapporter à; *with* ~ *to,* à propos de.
refill, *v.a.* remplir à nouveau.
refine, *v.a.* (*liquids and fig.*) épurer; (*sugar*) raffiner; (*metals*) affiner; **~ment,** (*pers.*) distinction, *f.*; (*of cruelty, subtlety, affectation*) raffinement, *m.*; **~r,** (*sugar*) raffineur, *m.*; **~ry,** raffinerie, *f.*; **~d,** (*sugar, pers., taste*) raffiné.
refit, *v.a.* (*naut.*) radouber; *v.n.* se radouber.
reflect, *v.a.* (*light, &c.*) réfléchir; (*fig.*) refléter; ~ *upon, on,* (*throw blame on*) rejeter le blâme sur; ~ *credit on,* faire* honneur à; *v.n.* (*meditate*) réfléchir (à).
reflect|ion, (*of light, &c., thought*) réflexion, *f.*; (*object reflected*) image, *f.*; (*censure*) critique, *f.*; **~ive,** (*thoughtful*) réfléchi.
reflector, *s.* réflecteur, *m.*; (*motor-car*) rétroviseur, *m.*
reflexible, réflexible.
reflexive, (*gram.*) réfléchi.
refloat, *v.a.* (*lit. and comm.*) remettre* à flot.
reflux, reflux, *m.*
reform, *s.* (*abuse, &c.*) réforme, *f.*
reform, *v.a.* réformer; *v.n.* se réformer.
re-form, (*mil., ranks*) reformer.
reformable, réformable.
reformation, (*reforming, being reformed*) réformation, *f.*; *the Reformation* (*hist.*) Réforme, *f.*
reformatory, *s.* maison de jeunes détenus, *f.*
reformer, réformat|eur, ~rice, *m.f.*
refract, réfracter; **~ion,** réfraction, *f.*
refractory, réfractaire.
refrain, *s.* refrain, *m.*; *v.n.* ~ *from,* se retenir* de.
refresh, (*memory, restore*) rafraîchir; ~ *oneself,* (*with food, drink, rest*) se rafraîchir.
refreshing, rafraîchissant; **~ly,** de manière à rafraîchir; (*fig.*) délicieusement.
refreshment, rafraîchissement, *m.*; **~s,** rafraîchissements, *m.pl.*; **~-bar,** buvette, *f.*; **~-room,** buffet, *m.*
refrigera|te, réfrigérer; **~tion,** réfrigération, *f.*; **~or,** glacière, *f.*
refuge, refuge, *m.*; *take* ~, se réfugier.
refugee, réfugié, -e, *m.f.*
refulgen|ce, éclat, *m.*; **~t,** resplendissant.
refund, *s.* remboursement, *m.*; *v.a.* rembourser.
refurnish, remeubler.
refus|al, refus, *m.*; *flat* ~*al,* refus net, *m.*; **~e,** refuser.
refuse, *s.* (*to be thrown away*) rebut, *m.*
refut|e, réfuter; **~ation,** réfutation, *f.*; **~able,** réfutable.
regain, (*get again*) reconquérir*; (*get back to*) regagner; (*recover*) reprendre*.
regal, royal; **~ly,** royalement.
regale, *v.a.* régaler (de); *v.n.* ~ *oneself,* se régaler.
regalia, insignes de la royauté, *m.pl.*
regard, *s.* (*consideration*) égard, *m.*; (*esteem*) estime, *f.*; *with* ~ *to,* à l'égard de; **~s,** (*compliments*) amitiés, *f.pl.*; *kind(est)* ~*s,* meilleures amitiés, *f.pl.*; *v.a.* (*gaze at, concern*) regarder; (*pay attention to*) tenir* compte de; (*consider*) considérer.
regardful of, attenti|f, ~ve à.
regarding, *prep.* touchant.
regardless of, sans se soucier de.
regatta, régates, *f.pl.*
regen|cy, régence, *f.*; **~t,** régent, -e, *s.m.f.*
regenerat|e, *v.a.* régénérer; *adj.* régénéré; **~ion,** régénération, *f.*
regicide, régicide, *m.*
regild, redorer.
régime, régime, *m.*

regiment, (*lit. and fig.*) régiment, *m.*; **~al,** régimentaire; **~als,** uniforme, *m.*; *v.a.* enrégimenter.
region, région, *f.*; **~al,** régional.
register, *s.* (*official list, organ, voice, of fire-grate*) registre, *m.*
regist|er, *v.a.* (*place on register, luggage, record in writing*) enregistrer; (*letter*) recommander; *v.n.* se faire* inscrire; **~rar,** (*law*) greffier, *m.*; (*univ.*) archiviste, *m.*; **~ration,** enregistrement, *m.*; (*post office*) recommandation, *f.*; **~ry,** (*office*) bureau de placement, *m.*
regnant, (*reigning, predominant*) régnant.
regression, régression, *f.*
regret, regret, *m.*; *v.a.* regretter; **~fully,** avec regret.
regular, *s.* (*monk, soldier*) régulier, *m.*; *adj.* (*shape, structure, features, &c., recurring, orderly, gram., duly qualified*) réguli|er, ~ère; (*in due form*) en règle; (*downright, thorough*) vrai; **~ity,** régularité, *f.*; **~ly,** régulièrement.
regulat|e, régler; **~ion,** (*rule*) ordonnance, *f.*; (*ordering*) réglementation, *f.*; *adj.* (*mil.*) d'ordonnance; **~ing,** *s.* (*of apparatus*) réglage, *m.*; **~or,** régulateur, *m.*
rehabilitat|e, réhabiliter; **~ion,** réhabilitation, *f.*
rehears|e, (*play, &c.*) répéter; (*relate*) réciter; **~al,** (*theatr.*) répétition, *f.*; (*narrative*) récit, *m.*
reign, *s.* (*lit. and fig.*) règne, *m.*; *v.a.* régner; **~ing,** *adj.* (*sovereign, &c., prevailing*) régnant.
reimburse, rembourser; **~ment,** remboursement, *m.*
reimport, réimporter.
rein, *s.* (*lit. and fig.*) rêne, *f.*; ⚠ rein = '*kidney*'; *give ~ to,* lâcher la bride à; *v.a.* conduire* à la bride; *~ in,* (*control*) contenir*.
reindeer, renne, *m.*
reinforce, renforcer; **~ment,** renfort, *m.*; **~ments,** (*mil.*) renforts, *m.pl.*
reinsert, insérer de nouveau.
reinstate, rétablir (dans).
reinsur|e, réassurer; **~ance,** réassurance, *f.*
reinvest, replacer; **~ment,** replacement, *m.*
reissue, *s.* (*of an edition, &c.*) nouvelle publication, *f.*; *v.a.* republier.
reiterate, réitérer.
reject, (*offer, &c.*) rejeter; (*candidate*) refuser; **~ion,** refus, *m.*; (*law*) rejet, m.
rejoic|e, *v.a.* réjouir; *v.n.* se réjouir (de); **~ings,** (*public*) réjouissances, *f.pl.*
rejoin, *v.a.* (*reply*) répondre; (*join again, overtake*) rejoindre*; ⚠ rejoindre *never* = '*reply*'.
re-join, réunir.
rejoinder, réplique, *f.*
rejuvenate, *v.a.* rajeunir.
rejuvenescence, rajeunissement, *m.*
rekindle, rallumer.

relapse, *s.* (*illness and fig.*) rechute, *f.*; (*comm.*) recul, *m.*; *v.n.* (*comm.*) reculer; *~ into,* retomber (être) dans.
relat|e, *v.a.* raconter; *be ~ed to,* être apparenté à; *v.n. ~ to,* (*have reference to*) se rapporter à; **~ing to,** relati|f, ~ve à.
relation, (*relative*) parent, -e, *m.f.*; (*of narrative*) récit, *m.*; (*connexion with*) rapport, *m.* (à); **~s,** (*intercourse*) relations, *f.pl.*; **~ship,** parenté, *f.*
relative, *s.* parent, -e, *m.f.*; *adj.* (*not absolute, in relation to something else, comparative, gram.*) relati|f, ~ve; *~ to,* relati|f, ~ve à; *prep. ~ to,* au sujet de; **~ly,** relativement.
relax, *v.a.* (*mind*) distraire*; (*loosen, lit. and fig., med.*) relâcher; *v.n.* se relâcher; **~ation,** (*efforts, discipline, &c.*) relâchement, *m.*; (*recreation*) délassement, *m.*; **~ing,** *adj.* (*climate*) débilitant.
relay, *s.* (*horses*) relais, *m.*; *v.n.* relayer.
release, *s.* délivrance, *f.*; (*debt, &c.*) décharge, *f.*; (*photo-camera*) déclencheur, *m.*; *v.a.* (*set free*) libérer; (*from obligation*) décharger (de).
relegate, reléguer.
relent, s'attendrir.
relentless, impitoyable.
relet, relouer.
relevant, pertinent.
reliab|le, digne de confiance; **~ility,** caractère qui mérite la confiance, *m.*
reliance, confiance, *f.*
relic, relique, *f.*
relict, veuve, *f.*
relief, (*raising siege*) délivrance, *f.*; (*pain, &c.*) soulagement, *m.*; (*assistance*) secours, *m.*; (*paint., sculpt.*) relief, *m.*; (*mil.*) relève, *f.*
relieve, *v.a.* (*pain*) soulager; (*assist*) secourir*; (*besieged city*) délivrer; (*remove*) dissiper; (*mil., nav.*) relever; (*brighten*) égayer.
religion, religion, *f.*; **~ist,** bigot, -e, *m.f.*
religious, (*pious, scrupulous*) religieu|x, ~se; (*concerned with religion*) de religion; **~ness,** piété, *f.*; **~ly,** religieusement.
relinquish, abandonner.
reliquary, reliquaire, *m.*
relish, *s.* (*flavour*) saveur, *f.*; (*liking for*) goût, *m.* (pour); *v.a.* (*like*) goûter.
reload, recharger.
reluctan|ce, répugnance, *f.*; **~t,** peu disposé (à); **~tly,** avec répugnance.
rely upon, compter sur; *~it,* y compter.
remain, rester (être).
remainder, restant, *m.*; (*of a whole*) reste, *m.*; (*the others*) les autres.
remains, restes, *m.pl.*; (*mortal*) dépouille, *f.*
remake, refaire*.
remand, renvoyer.
remark, *s.* remarque, *f.*; *v.a.* remarquer; (*point out*) faire* remarquer; **~able,** remarquable; **~ably,** remarquablement.
remarry, *v.n.* se remarier.

remedial, curati|f, ~ve.
remediable, remédiable.
remedy, (*lit. and fig.*) remède, *m.*; *v.a.* remédier à.
rememb|er, *v.a.* se souvenir* de; (*compliments*) rappeler au bon souvenir de; (*tips*) ne pas oublier; **~rance,** souvenir, *m.*; (*of the dead*) mémoire, *f.*; *in ~ of*, en mémoire de.
remind, *v.a.* (*to do a thing*) faire* ressouvenir de; ~ *of*, (*recall pers., thing*) rappeler (*acc. of pers., &c., recalled, dat. of pers. recalling*).
reminder, souvenir, *m.*
reminiscen|ce, réminiscence, *f.*; **~t** *of*, qui rappelle.
remiss, négligent.
remission, (*sin*) rémission, *f.*; (*debt, penalty*) remise, *f.*
remit, (*sin, penalty, debt, convey*) remettre*.
remitt|ance, (*money*) remise, *f.*; **~er,** envoyeu|r, ~se, *m.f.*
remnant, reste, *m.*; (*of material*) coupon, *m.*
remodel, (*fig.*) refondre.
remonstr|ance, remontrance, *f.*; **~ate** *with*, en remontrer à.
remorse, remords, *m.*; **~ful,** plein de remords; **~less,** sans remords; **~lessly,** sans remords.
remote, (*time, place*) reculé; (*faint, hazy*) vague; **~st** (*least*) le, la moindre; (*cause*) éloigné; **~ness,** (*lit., fig.*) éloignement, *m.*; **~ly,** (*slightly*) vaguement.
remount, *s.* (*mil.*) remonte, *f.*; *v.a.* (*horse*) remonter (être) sur; *v.n.* remonter à cheval.
removable, (*from appointment*) amovible.
removal, (*furniture*) déménagement, *m.*; (*goods, taking away*) enlèvement; (*dismissal*) renvoi, *m.*; (*from document, &c.*) suppression, *f.*
remove, *s.* (*schools*) promotion, *f.*; (*relationship*) degré, *m.*; *v.n.* (*change quarters*) déménager; (*go away*) s'en aller* (être); *v.a.* (*furniture*) déménager; (*take away*) enlever; (*suppress*) supprimer; (*difficulty*) lever; (*dismiss*) renvoyer; (*from school*) retirer; (*transport*) transporter.
remunera|te, rémunérer; **~tion,** rémunération, *f.*; **~tive,** rémunérat|eur, ~rice.
Renaissance, (*hist.*) Renaissance, *f.*
renascent, renaissant.
rend, *v.a.* déchirer; (*wrest*) arracher; ~ *asunder*, déchirer en deux.
render, (*give back, make + adj., service, thanks, tribute, homage, account, translate*) rendre; (*reason*) donner; **~ing,** *s.* (*role*) interprétation, *f.*; (*translation*) traduction, *f.*
rendezvous, rendez-vous, *m.*
renegade, renégat, -e, *m.f.*
renew, (*make new, begin again, replace*) renouveler; **~al, ~ing,** renouvellement, *m.*
rennet, présure, *f.*; (*apple*) rainette, *f.*
renounce, *v.a.* (*of solemn acts*) renoncer à; (*truce, treaty*) dénoncer; (*faith, ideas, &c.*) répudier.
renova|te, renouveler; **~tion,** rénovation, *f.*
renown, renommée, *f.*; **~ed,** renommé (pour).
rent, *s.* (*tear, lit. and fig.*) déchirure, *f.*; (*fissure*) fente, *f.*; (*houses*) loyer, *m.*; (*farms*) fermage, *m.*; (*quarter's*) terme, *m.*; *v.a.* (*take or hire or rent*) louer; **~al,** *s.* prix de location, *m.*
renunciation, renonciation, *f.* (à).
reoccupy, réoccuper.
reopen, rouvrir*; **~ing,** réouverture, *f.*; ⚠ *not* rouverture.
reorganiz|ation, réorganisation, *f.*; **~e,** réorganiser.
rep(p), (*silk, wool*) reps, *m.*
repair, *s.* réparation, *f.*; (*clothes*) raccommodage, *m.*; *out of ~*, en mauvais état; **~-shop,** (*motor, &c.*) atelier de réparations, *m.*; *v.a.* (*lit. and fig.*) réparer; (*clothes*) raccommoder; (*naut.*) radouber; *v.n.* (*go*) se rendre.
repar|able, réparable; **~ation,** réparation, *f.*
repartee, repartie, *f.*
repast, repas, *m.*
repay, *v.a.* (*money, pers.*) rembourser; (*reward*) récompenser; *v.n.* repayer; **~able,** remboursable; **~ment,** remboursement, *m.*
repeal, *s.* (*law*) abrogation, *f.*; *v.a.* (*law*) abroger.
repeat, *v.a.* répéter; (*by heart*) réciter.
repeatedly, à plusieurs reprises.
repeater, (*watch*) montre à répétition, *f.*; (*rifle*) fusil à répétition, *m.*
repel, (*lit. and fig.*) repousser; **~lent,** répulsi|f, ~ve.
repent, *v.a.* se repentir de; *v.n.* se repentir; ~ *of*, se repentir de; **~ance,** repentir, *m.*; **~ant,** repentant.
repeople, repeupler.
repercussion, répercussion, *f.*
repertory, répertoire, *m.*
repetition, répétition, *f.*; (*by heart*) récitation, *f.*; (*telegram*) collationnement, *m.*
repine, (*complain*) se plaindre* (de).
repiningly, en murmurant.
replace, (*put back again*) remettre*; (*make good*) remplacer; (*teleph. receiver*) accrocher; **~ment,** (*making good*) remplacement, *m.*
replant, replanter.
replenish, remplir (de); (*restock*) réapprovisionner.
replete *with*, rempli de; ⚠ replet = '*fat*'.
repletion, (*food*) réplétion, *f.*
replica, réplique, *f.*
reply, *s.* réponse, *f.*; *v.a.n.* répondre; *sorry, no reply*, (*teleph.*) répond pas.
repolish, repolir.
report, *s.* (*rumour*) bruit, *m.*; (*of a committee, any account*) rapport, *m.*; (*of a*

meeting, &c.) compte rendu, *m.*; (*fire-arms*) détonation, *f.*; (*official and school*) bulletin, *m.*; ⚠ report = '*carrying forward*' (*bkkpg.*).
report, *v.a.* (*words, rumour*) rapporter; (*give account, report on*) faire* un rapport sur; (*journalist*) faire* le reportage (de); (*inform against*) dénoncer; ⚠ reporter = '*bring back*', '*carry forward*' (*bkkpg.*).
reporter, (*newspaper*) reporter, *m.*
repose, *s.* repos, *m.*; *v.a.* (*rest*) reposer; (*confidence*) mettre*; *v.n.* (*rest, lit. and fig.*) se reposer; (*sleep, death*) reposer.
repository, dépôt, *m.*; (*shop*) magasin, *m.*
repossess, ~ *oneself of,* reprendre* possession de.
reprehend, réprimander.
reprehensibl|e, répréhensible; **~y,** d'une manière répréhensible.
reprehension, réprimande, *f.*
represent, (*portray, describe, bring home to, a firm, in Parl., make out to be*) représenter; (*theatr., a character*) jouer; **~ation,** représentation, *f.*; **~ative,** *s.* (*pers.*) représentant, *m.*; *adj.* représentati|f, ~ve (de).
repress, réprimer; **~ion,** répression, *f.*; **~ive,** répressi|f, ~ve.
re-press, presser de nouveau.
reprieve, sursis, *m.*; (*respite*) répit, *m.*; *v.a.* accorder un sursis à.
reprimand, *s.* réprimande, *f.*; *v.a.* réprimander.
reprint, *s.* réimpression, *f.*; *v.a.* réimprimer.
reprisal, représaille, *f.*; *make ~s,* user de représailles.
reproach, *s.* reproche, *m.*; (*shame*) †honte, *f.*; *v.a.* faire* des reproches à; ~ *a pers. with a thing,* reprocher une chose à quelqu'un; **~ful,** de reproche; **~fully,** d'un air de reproche.
reprobate, *s.* (*theol.*) réprouvé, *m.*; (*scamp*) vaurien, *m.*; *v.a.* réprouver.
reproduc|e, reproduire*; **~tion,** reproduction, *f.*; **~tive,** reproduct|eur, ~rice.
reproof, réprimande, *f.*
reprove, réprimander.
reprovingly, d'un ton, air de réprimande.
reptile, *s.* (*lit. and fig.*) reptile, *m.*
republic, république, *f.*; **~an,** *adj. and s.m.f.* républicain, -e; **~anism,** républicanisme, *m.*
republi|sh, rééditer; **~cation,** réédition, *f.*
repudia|te, répudier; **~tion,** répudiation, *f.*
repugnan|ce, (*aversion*) répugnance, *f.* (pour); **~t,** répugnant, (à).
repuls|e, *s.* (*mil.*) échec, *m.*; (*rebuff*) rebuffade, *f.*; *v.a.* repousser; **~ion,** (*lit. and fig.*) répulsion, *f.* (pour); **~ive,** repoussant.
repurchase, *s.* rachat, *m.*; *v.a.* racheter.
reputable, honorable.
repute, *s.*, **reputation,** réputation, *f.*
repute, *v.a.* réputer (pour); **~d,** censé; *be ~d to be,* passer pour.
request, *s.* requête, *f.*; *at the ~ of,* à la demande de; *in ~,* en vogue; *v.a.* demander (*dat. pers.*, de + *inf.*); (*humbly, earnestly*) prier (*acc. pers.*, de + *inf.*); (*thing*) solliciter; *cars stop by ~,* arrêt facultatif.
requiem, requiem, *m.*
require, (*to do*) demander (*dat. pers.*, de + *inf.*); (*call for, demand of right*) exiger; (*want*) avoir besoin de; **~ment,** besoin, *m.* [nécessaire.
requisite, *s.* article nécessaire, *m.*; *adj.*
requisition, (*official, mil.*) réquisition, *f.*; *v.a.* réquisitionner.
requit|e, payer (de retour); (*return*) rendre; **~al,** retour, *m.*; (*reward*) récompense, *f.*
re-read, relire*.
reredos, (*arch.*) rétable, *m.*
rescind, annuler.
rescript, rescrit, *m.*
rescue, *s.* délivrance, *f.*; (*help*) secours, *m.*; *v.a.* délivrer; (*help*) secourir*; **~r,** (*deliverer*) libérateur, *m.*; (*from drowning, &c.*) sauveteur, *m.*
research, recherche, *f.*
reseize, ressaisir.
resell, revendre.
resembl|e, ressembler à; **~ance,** ressemblance, *f.*
resent, être froissé de; *v.a.* froisser, blesser *often used*; **~ful,** rancuni|er, ~ère; **~ment,** ressentiment, *m.*
reservation, (*law, U.S.A. land reserved*) réserve, *f.*; (*mental*) arrière-pensée, *f.*; *without ~,* sans réserve.
reserve, *s.* (*thing put aside, comm., mil., reticence, restriction*) réserve, *f.*; *~ fund,* fonds de réserve, *m.*; *without ~,* sans réserve; **~s,** (*mil.*) réserves, *f.pl*; *v.a.* (*put aside, keep back, compartment, seat, &c.*) réserver.
reserved, *adj.* (*reticent, engaged*) réservé; **~ly,** avec réserve.
reservist, réserviste, *m.*
reservoir, réservoir, *m.*
reset, (*jewel*) remonter (avoir).
reship, rembarquer.
reside, demeurer (avoir); **~nce,** (*residing, place of residence*) résidence, *f.*; **~nt,** habitant, *m.*; (*govt. agent*) résident, *m.*; *adj.* résidant.
residue, *s.* reste, *m.*
resign, *v.a.* résigner; (*an office, post*) se démettre* de; ~ *oneself to,* se résigner à; *v.n.* donner sa démission; **~ation,** (*submission to Providence*) résignation, *f.*; (*of post, &c.*) démission, *f.*; (*of a right*) abandon, *m.*
resignedly, avec résignation.
resilience, élasticité, *f.*; (*fig.*) ressort, *m.*
resin, résine, *f.*; **~ous,** résineu|x, ~se.
resist, résister à; (*refuse*) refuser; *v.n.* résister; **~ance,** résistance, *f*; *take the*

line of the least ~ance, prendre la ligne de moindre résistance.

resistib|ility, résistibilité, *f.*; **~le,** résistible.

resistless, irrésistible; **~ly,** irrésistiblement.

resolute, résolu; **~ly,** résolument.

resolution, (*intention, solving, opinion of meeting, &c., determination, mus., mech.*) résolution, *f.*; (*decision*) décision, *f.*

resolve, *s.* résolution, *f.*; *v.a.* (*dissolve, math.*) résoudre*; *~ upon,* (*thing*) résoudre*; (*upon doing*) se résoudre* à.

resolvedly, résolument.

resonan|ce, résonance, *f.*; **~t,** résonant.

resort, *s.* (*recourse*) recours, *m.*; (*expedient*) ressource, *f.*; (*meeting-place*) rendez-vous, *m.*; *sea-side ~,* station balnéaire, *f.*; *in the last ~,* en dernier ressort; *v.n., ~ to,* (*have recourse*) avoir recours (à); (*frequent*) fréquenter.

resound, *v.a.* faire* retentir; *v.n.* résonner; *~ with,* retentir de.

resource, (*expedient, practical skill, resourcefulness*) ressource, *f.*; **~s,** (*money, means, &c.*) ressources, *f.pl.*; *without ~,* sans ressource; **~ful,** (*pers. + noun*) de ressource.

respect, *s.* (*esteem*) respect, *m.*; (*reference*) rapport, *m.*; (*regard to*) considération, *f.* (pour); *in this ~,* sous ce rapport; **~s,** (*polite message*) respects, *m.pl.*; *in every ~,* sous tous les rapports; *in ~ of, with, to,* sous le rapport de; *pay one's ~s to,* rendre ses devoirs à.

respect, *v.a.* (*regard with respect, not interfere with*) respecter.

respectab|ility, respectabilité, *f.*; (*character*) considération, *f.*; **~le,** digne de respect; (*of humbler folk*) brave *before the noun*; (*passable*) respectable; **~ly,** (*suitably*) convenablement; (*tolerably*) passablement.

respectful, respectueu|x, ~se; **~ly,** respectueusement; **~ness,** caractère respectueux.

respecting, *prep.* touchant.

respective, respecti|f, ~ve; **~ly,** respectivement.

respir|e, *v.a.n.* respirer; **~ation,** respiration, *f.*; **~atory,** respiratoire.

respite, *s.* répit, *m.*; *v.a.* accorder du répit à.

resplenden|ce, splendeur, *f.*; **~t,** resplendissant; **~tly,** avec splendeur.

respond, répondre; **~ent,** (*divorce*) défend|eur, ~eresse, *m.f.*

response, réponse, *f.*; (*eccles.*) répons, *m.*

responsib|ility, responsabilité, *f.*; **~le,** responsable (de = *for and to, of pers.* = envers).

responsive, (*to kindness, advances, &c.*) sensible à.

rest, *s.* (*remainder*) reste, *m.*; (*repose*) repos, *m.*; (*mus., pause*) pause, *f.*; (*support*) appui, *m.*; (*sailors, cabmen, &c.*) asile, *m.*; *the ~,* (*others*) les autres; **~ful,** reposant.

rest, *v.a.* reposer; (*lean*) appuyer; *v.n.* se reposer; (*in sleep or grave, be based*) reposer; (*lean*) s'appuyer (sur); (*rely on*) se fier (à); (*be left*) rester (être).

resting-place, lieu de repos, *m.*

restitution, restitution, *f.*

restive, (*horse, person*) réti|f, **~ve.**

restless, sans repos; (*anxious*) inqui|et, ~ète; (*night*) agité; (*child*) remuant; **~ness,** (*want of sleep*) insomnie, *f.*; (*constant movement*) agitation, *f.*; **~ly,** sans repos.

restoration, (*giving back*) restitution, *f.*; (*buildings, hist.*) restauration, *f.*; (*health*) rétablissement, *m.*

restorative, *s.* restaurant, *m.*

restore, *v.a.* (*give back, sight, health, &c.*) rendre; (*finances, picture, building, &c.*) restaurer; (*to proper place, throne, &c.*) remettre* (à); **~r,** (*pictures, buildings, &c.*) restaurat|eur, ~rice, *m.f.*

restrain, (*emotions, &c.*) contenir*; (*repress*) réprimer; *~ from,* empêcher de; **~ing,** *adj.* (*repressive*) réprimant.

restraint, (*compulsion, confinement*) contrainte, *f.*; (*style, self-control*) retenue, *f.*

restrict, restreindre*; **~ion,** restriction, *f.*; **~ive,** restricti|f, ~ve.

result, *s.* résultat, *m.*; *v.n. ~ from,* résulter de; *~ in,* avoir pour résultat.

resum|e, *v.a.n.* reprendre*; *~ one's seat,* se rasseoir*; ⚠ résumer = '*sum up*'; **~ption,** reprise, *f.*

resurrection, (*lit. and fig.*) résurrection, *f.*; **~ist,** (*~ man*) résurrectionniste, *m.*

resuscitate, ressusciter.

retail, *s.* détail, *m.*; *~ price, see* PRICE; *~ trade,* commerce de détail, *m.*; *v.a.* détailler; **~er,** détaillant, -e, *m.f.*

retain, (*services, keep, not forget*) retenir*; *~ing wall,* mur de soutènement, *m.*

retainers, (*approx.*) suite, *f.*

retake, reprendre*.

retalia|te, *v.n.* user de représailles; **~tion,** représailles, *f.pl.*

retard, *v.a.* retarder; **~ation, ~ment,** retardement, *m.*; ⚠ retardation *is a term of physics.*

retch, avoir des †haut-le-cœur.

retent|ion, rétention, *f.*; **~ive,** (*memory*) fidèle; **~iveness,** (*memory*) fidélité, *f.*

reticen|ce, réticence, *f.*; **~t,** réservé.

reticulate, *adj.* réticulé.

reticule, sac à main, *m.*

retina, rétine, *f.*

retinue, cortège, *m.*

retire, *v.n.* (*withdraw, go away, from business, the world, &c., retreat*) se retirer; **~ment,** retraite, *f.*; **~d,** *adj.* (*not frequented, withdrawn from the world*) retiré; (*tradesman*) retiré des affaires; (*officer*) en retraite.

retiring, (*pers.*) réservé; (*pensions, &c.*) de retraite; (*governors, directors of cos., &c.*) sortant.

retort, *s.* riposte, *f.*; (*chem.*) cornue, *f.*; *v.n.* riposter.
retouch, retoucher.
retrace, *v.a.* (*back to source*) remonter (avoir) à; (*go over*) retracer; *~ one's steps,* revenir* sur ses pas.
retract, (*draw in, statement, opinion, &c.*) rétracter; **~ion,** rétractation, *f.*
retractile, rétractile.
retreat, *s.* (*mil., bugle-call, asylum, place of shelter, eccles.*) retraite, *f.*; *v.n. and beat a ~,* se retirer; (*mil.*) battre en retraite.
retrench, *v.a.* (*suppress*) retrancher; (*expenses*) réduire*; *v.n.* se restreindre*; **~ment,** (*expenses*) économies, *f.pl.*
retribution, récompense, *f.*; (*for evil done*) châtiment, *m.*
retriev|e, (*lit. and fig.*) recouvrer; (*losses*) se récupérer de; **~able,** recouvrable.
retriever, (*dog*) chien trouvant, *m.*
retrograde, *adj.* (*lit. and fig.*) rétrograde.
retrogression, mouvement rétrograde, *m.*
retrospect|ion, revue rétrospective, *f.*; **~ive,** rétrospecti|f, ~ve; **~ively,** rétrospectivement.
return, *s.* (*coming back*) retour, *m.*, ⚠ *which never = 'profit', 'restitution'*; (*sending back*) renvoi, *m.*; (*of thing taken, borrowed*) restitution, *f.*; (*repayment*) remboursement, *m.*; (*recompense*) récompense, *f.*; (*election*) élection, *f.*; **~s,** (*in profit*) rapport, *m.*; (*comm. statement*) état, *m.*; *in ~ for,* en récompense de; *~-journey,* voyage de retour, *m.*; *~-ticket,* billet d'aller et retour, *m.*; *adj.* de retour.
return, *v.a.* (*thanks, compliment, salutation, give back*) rendre; (*send back*) renvoyer; (*put back*) remettre*; (*answer*) faire*; (*report officially*) déclarer; *v.n.* (*come back*) revenir* (être); (*go back*) retourner (être); (*reply*) répondre; **~able,** restituable.
reunion, réunion, *f.*
reunite, *v.n.* réunir; *v.n.* être réunis; ⚠ se réunir = *'reassemble', 'concur'.*
revalue, évaluer de nouveau.
reveal, révéler.
reveille, diane, *f.*; *sound, beat the ~,* sonner la diane.
revel, *s.* (*feast*) fête, *f.*; (*pej.*) orgie, *f.*; *v.n.* faire* bombance; (*pej.*) faire une orgie; **~ler,** noceur, *m.*; **~ry,** réjouissances, *f.pl.*
revelation, révélation, *f.*; *Revelation of St. John,* Apocalypse, *f.*
revenge, *s.* (*for evil*) vengeance, *f.*; ⚠ revanche, *f. is not so strong a word and may be used for 'returning' evil, &c. only*; *take ~ for . . . on,* se venger de (*thing*) sur (*pers.*); *v.a.* (*act*) venger; **~ful,** vindicati|f, ~ve; **~fully,** par vengeance.
revenue, revenu, *m.* (*often plur.*); (*State treasury*) fisc, *m.*; *~* **officer,** agent des douanes, *m.*; **~-stamp,** timbre fiscal, *m.*
reverbera|te, *v.a.* (*light, heat*) réverbérer; (*sound*) répercuter; *v.n.* se réverbérer, se répercuter; **~tion,** réverbération, *f.*; (*sound*) répercussion, *f.*; ⚠ réverbération *never of sound*; **~tory,** à réverbère.
revere, révérer; **~nce,** (*title*) révérence, *f.*; (*respect*) respect, *m.*; *saving your ~nce,* sauf votre respect; **~nt,** (*devout*) pieu|x, ~se; **~ntly,** révérencieusement.
reverend, *adj.* (*clergy*) révérend.
reverie, rêverie, *f.*
reversal, (*decree, &c.*) annulation, *f.*
reverse, *s.* (*calamity, mil., medal*) revers, *m.*; (*the opposite*) contraire, *m.*; *adj.* (*direction*) inverse; *~ side,* envers, *m.*; **~ly,** en sens inverse.
revers|e, *v.a.* (*direction, steam*) renverser; (*judgement, decision*) annuler; (*order*) intervertir; *v.n.* (*mach., motor*) faire* machine en arrière; **~ible,** (*material*) sans endroit ni envers; (*revocable*) révocable.
reversion, (*to type, &c., law*) retour, *m.*
revert, *v.n.* (*to subject*) revenir* (être); (*law*) retourner.
revictual, ravitailler; **~ling,** ravitaillement, *m.*
review, (*inspection, magazine, mil.*) revue, *f.*; (*of book*) analyse, *f.*; *v.a.* revoir*; (*book*) analyser; *v.a.* (*mil.*) passer en revue.
reviewer, (*book*) critique, *m.f.*
revile, *v.a.* injurier.
revisal, révision, *f.*
revis|e, réviser; (*proofs*) corriger; **~ion,** révision, *f.*
revisit, *v.a.* revoir*.
revival, (*literature, &c.*) renaissance, *f.*; (*business*) reprise, *f.*; (*religious*) réveil, *m.*; (*to life*) retour à la vie, *m.*
revive, *v.a.* faire* revivre; (*rouse*) ranimer; (*memories*) réveiller; *v.n.* revivre*; (*hope*) renaître* (*no p.p. or compound tenses*); (*business*) reprendre*.
revoca|ble, révocable; **~tion,** (*law, decree*) abrogation, *f.*; (*will, edict*) révocation, *f.*; (*contract, decision*) annulation, *f.*
revoke, *v.a.* (*law, decree*) abroger; (*edict, order*) révoquer; (*decision*) revenir* (être) sur.
revolt, *s.* révolte, *f.*; *v.a.* révolter; *v.n.* se révolter; *~ against,* se révolter contre; *~ at,* se révolter à; **~ing,** révoltant.
revolution, (*revolving motion*) tour, *m.*; (*complete change, polit.*) révolution, *f.*; **~ary,** *adj.* révolutionnaire; **~ist,** révolutionnaire, *m.f.*; **~ize,** révolutionner.
revolve, *v.a.* (*in mind*) ruminer; *v.n.* tourner; (*seasons*) revenir* (être).
revolver, revolver, *m.*
revolving, tournant.
revulsion, (*violent change*) révulsion, *f.*
reward, *s.* récompense, *f.*; *v.a.* récompenser.
rewrite, récrire*.
rhapsod|y, rapsodie, *f.*; **~ist,** rapsodiste, *m.*; **~ical,** (*extravagant*) emphatique.
rhetoric, *s.* rhétorique, *f.*; **~al,** de rhé-

torique; (*pej.*) de rhéteur; ~**ian**, rhétoricien, *m.*; ⚠ rhéteur *is either pej. or ant.*
rheum, catarrhe, *m.*
rheumat|ic, rhumatismal; ~**ism**, rhumatisme, *m.*
rhinoceros, rhinocéros, *m.*
rhododendron, (*bot.*) rhododendron, *m.*
rhubarb, rhubarbe, *f.*
rhyme, rime, *s.* rime, *f.*; ~**s**, vers, *m.pl.*; *v.a.n.* rimer; ~**r**, ~**ster**, rimeur, *m.*
rhythm, rythme, *m.*; ~**ic**, rythmique.
rib, *s.* côte, *f.*; (*naut.*) couple, *m.*; (*arch.*) nervure, *f.*; ~**bed**, *adj.* côtelé.
ribald, grossi|er, ~ère; ~**ry**, langage grossier, *m.*
ribbon, ruban, *m.*
rice, riz, *m.*; ~**-field**, rizière, *f.*
rich, (*fertile, costly, colour, well off, abundant, lit., fig.*) riche (en); (*food*) succulent; ~**ness**, (*lit., fig., colour, fertility, magnificence*) richesse, *f.*; (*food*) succulence, *f.*; ~**ly**, richement; (*abundantly*) amplement; (*thoroughly*) joliment.
riches, richesses, *f.pl.*
rick, *s.* (*hay*) meule, *f.*
rickets, (*med.*) rachitisme, *m.*
rickety, (*child*) noué; (*furniture*) boiteu|x, ~se.
rickshaw, pousse-pousse, *m.invar.*
ricochet, *s.* ricochet, *m.*; *v.n.* ricocher.
rid, *v.a.* débarrasser (de); *get ~ of*, se débarrasser de.
riddance, débarras, *m.*
riddle, (*enigma*) énigme, *f.*; (*sieve*) crible, *m.*; *v.a.* cribler; (*with debts, bullets, questions*) cribler de.
ride, *s.* (*horse*) promenade à cheval, *f.*; (*bicycle, &c.*) promenade à bicyclette, *f.*, etc.; (*public veh., &c.*) promenade, *f.*
ride, *v.a.* monter (avoir *of action*, être *of state*); *~ down*, (*overturn*) renverser; *~ across, over*, traverser à cheval; *v.n.* (*sit on horse*) monter (être); (*go on horseback*) aller* (être) à cheval; (*go on bicycle*) aller à bicyclette; (*bus, tram, &c.*) voyager; (*naut.*) être mouillé; *~ behind*, (*on one horse*) monter (être) en croupe; *~ rough-shod over*, (*fig.*) brusquer.
rider, cavali|er, ~ère, *m.f.*; (*to document*) ajouté, *m.*
ridge, (*top, mountains*) crête, *f.*; (*rocks*) écueil, *m.*; (*made by plough*) billon, *m.*
ridicul|e, *v.a.* se moquer de; *s. and* ~**ousness**, ridicule, *m.*; ~**ous**, ridicule; ~**ously**, ridiculement.
riding, équitation, *f.*; ~ **-boot**, botte à l'écuyère; ~ **-habit**, amazone, *f.*; ~ **-school**, manège, *m.*; ~ **-whip**, cravache, *f.*
rife, *be ~*, régner.
riff-raff, racaille, *f.*
rifle, *s.* (*gun*) fusil, *m.*; ~**man**, fusilier, *m.*; ~**-range**, tir, *m.*; ~**-shot**, coup de fusil, *m.*
rifle, (*rob*) dévaliser; (*empty*) vider.
rift, *s.* (*rocks*) fente, *f.*; (*clouds*) déchirure, *f.*
rig, *v.a.* (*naut.*) gréer; *~ out, up*, équiper.
rigging, (*naut.*) gréement, *m.*
right, *s.* (*opposed to wrong*) bien, *m.*; (*just claim, justice*) droit, *m.*; (*opposed to left side, polit.*) droite, *f.*; *~ of way*, droit de passage, *m.*; ~**s**, (*true state*) état réel, *m.*; (*of man, &c.*) droits, *m.pl.*; *by ~(s)*, de droit; *in ~ of*, du chef de; *on, to, the ~*, à droite; *on my ~*, à ma droite; *be in the ~*, avoir raison; *keep to the ~*, gardez votre droite.
right, *adj.* (*straight, not left, angle*) droit; (*exact*) exact; (*correct*) correct; (*true*) vrai; (*fit, proper*) juste; (*safe, well, in due order*) bien; (*recovered*) remis; *~ side*, (*materials, &c.*) endroit, *m.*; *be ~*, avoir raison; *that's ~*, c'est ça; ⚠ *in some cases a different phrasing is used in French, e.g., the ~ man for that job*, l'homme qu'il faut pour cette affaire; *Is this the ~ train for Rouen?* Est-ce bien le train de Rouen?; *Excuse me, is this the ~ way to the Louvre?*; Pardon, Monsieur (Madame), le Louvre? (bon chemin *in this sense is gen. fig.*); *That's not the ~ way to do it*, Ce n'est pas ainsi (comme ça) qu'il faut le faire; *~ wheel turn!* (*mil.*) conversion à droite!; ~**ness**, (*uprightness*) rectitude, *f.*; ~**ly**, à juste titre.
right, *v.a.* (*things, a wrong*) redresser; (*pers.*) faire* justice à.
right, *adv.* droit; (*satisfactorily*) bien; (*very*) très; *the ~ Honourable*, le très Honorable; *that serves you ~*, c'est bien fait pour vous!; *~-about turn!* (*mil.*) demi-tour à droite!; *interj. ~!* bon!
righteous, juste; ~**ness**, justice, *f.*
rightful, légitime; ~**ly**, légitimement.
rigid, raide; ~**ity**, raideur, *f.*; ~**ly**, (*fig.*) inflexiblement.
rigmarole, amphigouri, *m.*
rigorous, rigoureu|x, ~se; ~**ness**,
rigour, (*strictness, severity, cold, &c.*) rigueur, *f.*; ~**ly**, rigoureusement.
rill, ruisseau, *m.*
rim, bord, *m.*; (*wheels*) jante, *f.*
rime, (*frost*) givre, *m.*
rind, (*tree, fruit*) écorce, *f.*; (*cheese*) croûte, *f.*
ring, *s.* (*fingers*) bague, *f.*; (*curtain, keys, in masonry, naut., &c.*) anneau, *m.*; (*circle*) cercle, *m.*; (*teleph.*) coup de téléphone, *m.*; (*sound*) son, *m.*; (*of anchor*) organeau, *m.*; (*house-bells*) coup de sonnette, *m.*; (*comm.*) groupe, *m.*; (*sport*) ring, *m.*; ~**-dove**, ramier, *m.*; ~**-finger**, *see* FINGER; *there is a ~ at the door*, on sonne.
ring, *v.a.* sonner; (*encircle*) entourer (de); (*coin*) faire* sonner; *~ for*, (*meal, pers.*) sonner, *v.a.*; *~ off*, (*teleph.*) couper la ligne (à); *~ up*, (*teleph.*) appeler au téléphone; (*fam.*) donner un coup de téléphone à; *~ the changes*, (*bells*) carillonner; *~ the changes on* (*fig.*) ressasser; *v.n.* sonner; (*resound*) résonner.

ringer, sonneur, *m.*
ringing, *s.* (*bells*) son, *m.*; (*in ears*) tintement, *m.*
ringleader, meneur, *m.*
ringlet, (*hair*) boucle, *f.*
ringworm, (*med.*) teigne, *f.*
rink, *skating-~*, skating, *m.*
rinse, *v.a.* rinser.
riot, rioting, (*lawless disturbance*) émeute, *f.*; (*imagination, fig.*) débauche, *f.*; **~er**, émeutier, *m.*; *v.n.* faire* une émeute; (*revel*) faire* des excès; **~ous**, tumultueu|x, ~se; (*seditious*) séditieu|x, ~se; **~ously**, tumultueusement, séditieusement.
rip, *s.* (*tear*) fente, *f.*; (*pers.*) vaurien, *m.*; *v.a.* déchirer; *~ up*, (*tear up*) arracher; (*break open*) éventrer.
ripe, (*fruit, fig.*) mûr (pour); **~n**, *v.a.n.* (*lit. and fig.*) mûrir; **~ness**, (*lit. and fig.*) maturité, *f.*; **~ning**, maturation, *f.*
ripping, *adj.* (*slang*) épatant.
ripple, (*on water*) ride, *f.*; (*of stream, talk*) gazouillement, *m.*; (*hair*) crêpelure, *f.*; *v.a.* rider; *v.n.* se rider.
rise, *s.* (*of a hill*) montée, *f.*; (*water*) crue, *f.*; (*stocks, prices*) †hausse, *f.*; (*salary*) augmentation, *f.*; (*wages, rail-rates, bank rate*) relèvement, *m.*; (*preferment*) avancement, *m.*; (*origin, river*) source, *f.*; *take a ~ out of X*, (*slang*) faire* monter l'échelle à X; *give ~ to*, (*cause*) donner lieu à; (*salary*) augmenter + *acc. of pers.*
rise, *v.n.* **1** (*out of bed, get up, sun*) se lever; **2** (*revolt*) se soulever; **3** (*increase*) augmenter; **4** (*prices, stocks*) †hausser; **5** (*in price*) renchérir; **6** (*of the dead*) ressusciter; **7** (*assemblies*) lever la séance; **8** (*hair*) se dresser; **9** (*aloft, in position*) s'élever; **10** (*water, ground*) monter (être); **11** (*originate*) naître* (être) (de); *~ again*, se relever; (*dead*) ressusciter; *~ up*, se lever; (*revolt*) se soulever.
riser, *early ~*, personne matinale, *f.*
rising, *s.* (*act of, curtain, sun, &c.*) lever, *m.*; (*assemblies*) clôture, *f.*; (*insurrection*) soulèvement, *m.*; (*dead*) résurrection, *f.*
risk, *s.* risque, *m.*; *at your* (*own*) *~*, à vos risques et périls; *run the ~ of*, courir* le risque de; *v.a.* risquer; *~ it*, courir* sa chance.
risky, †hasardeu|x, ~se.
rite, rite, *m.*
ritual, *s.* rituel, *m.*; **~ist**, ritualiste, *m.f.*
rival, *adj. and s.m.f.* rival, -e; *v.a.* rivaliser avec; **~ry**, rivalité, *f.*
riven, fendu.
river, *s.* (*flowing into sea and fig.*) fleuve, *m.*; (*flowing into another river*) rivière, *f.*; **~-bank, -side**, rive, *f.*; **~-bed**, lit, *m.*
rivet, *s.* rivet, *m.*; *v.a.* riveter; (*nail, fig.*) river; **~er**, riveur, *m.*
rivulet, ruisselet, *m.*
roach, (*ichth.*) gardon, *m.*
road, route, *f.*, *also* chemin, *m.* (*often fig.*); (*in towns, street*) rue, *f.*; **~ -hog**, (*motor*) chauffard, *m.*; **~ -side**, bord de la route, *m.*; **~stead**, rade, *f.*; **~way**, chaussée, *f.*; **~s**, (*naut.*) rade, *f.*; *take the wrong ~*, se tromper de route.
roam, *v.a.* parcourir*; *v.n.* errer.
roan, *adj.* (*horse*) rouan, -ne.
roar, *s.* (*lions, &c.*) rugissement, *m.*; (*pain, rage*) †hurlement, *m.*; (*bull, sea, wind*) mugissement, *m.*; (*cannon, thunder*) grondement, *m.*; (*laughter*) éclat, *m.*; *v.n.* (*lions, &c.*) rugir; (*pain*) †hurler (de); (*bull, sea, wind*) mugir; (*cannon, thunder*) gronder; (*with laughter*) éclater de; **~ing**, *adj.* (*fire*) ronflant.
roast, *s.* rôti, *m.*
roast, *v.a.n.* rôtir; (*fig.*) griller; **~ing**, *s.* rôtissage, *m.*; **~ beef**, rosbif, *m.*
rob, *v.a.* voler; (*plunder*) piller; *~ of*, voler (à + *pers., acc. of thing*); **~ber**, voleu|r, ~se, *m.f.*; **~bery**, vol, *m.*
robe, robe, *f.*; *v.a.* revêtir* d'une robe; (*fig.*) revêtir*.
robin, (*ornith.*) rouge-gorge, *m.*
robot, *s.* automate, *m.*
robust, robuste; (*exercise, discipline, &c.*) rude; **~ness**, vigueur, *f.*; **~ly**, vigoureusement.
rock, *s.* (*substance, mass of stone*) roc, *m.*; (*lofty, large*) rocher, *m.*; (*boulder, fig.*) roche, *f.*; **~-rose**, hélianthème, *m.*; **~-pigeon, -dove**, biset, *m.*; **~-salt**, sel gemme, *m.*; **~-work, rockery**, rocaille, *f.*
rock, *v.a.* (*cradle*) balancer; (*child*) bercer; *v.n.* se balancer; *~ing-chair*, chaise à bascule, *f.*; *~ing-horse*, cheval à bascule, *m.*
rocket, fusée, *f.*
rocky, (*abounding in rocks*) rocheu|x, ~se.
rococo, rococo, *m.*; *adj.* rococo, *invar.*
rod, baguette, *f.*; (*punishment*) verges, *f.pl.*; (*sway*) sceptre, *m.*
rodent, *s.* rongeur, *m.*; *adj.* rongeu|r, ~se.
rodomontade, rodomontade, *f.*
roe, (*of fish*) œufs, *m.pl.*; (*soft*) laitance (laite), *f.*
roe, roebuck, (*zool.*) chevreuil, *m.*
rogu|e, (*lit. and fam.*) coquin, -e, *m.f.*; **~ery, ~ishness**, coquinerie, *f.*; **~ish**, coquin; **~ishly**, en coquin.
roister, faire* du tapage; **~er**, tapageur, *m.*
role, (*lit. and fig.*) rôle, *m.*
roll, *s.* (*papers, &c.*) rouleau, *m.*; (*loaf*) petit pain, *m.*; (*list*) liste, *f.*; (*ship*) roulis, *m.*; (*drums, &c.*) roulement, *m.*; (*of soldiers, schools and ~-call*) appel, *m.*; *call the ~*, faire* l'appel.
roll, *v.a.* (*cigarette, turf, case, barrel, eyes, material*) rouler; *~ up*, enrouler; *v.n.* (*stone, ship, in space, waves*) rouler; (*pers.*) se rouler; (*tears*) couler; (*thunder*) gronder; (*in riches*) nager (dans); *~ over*, (*turn over*) se retourner en roulant; (*fall*) tomber (être) en roulant.
roll-top, *see* DESK.
roller, (*steam, garden, &c.*) rouleau, *m.*; (*wave*) grande lame, *f.*; **~ -skates**,

patins à rouleau, *m.pl.*; **~-towel,** essuie-mains à rouleau, *m.invar.*

rolling, ~-mill, laminoir, *m.*; **~ stone,** *a ~ stone gathers no moss,* pierre qui roule n'amasse pas mousse.

rollicking, bruyant.

Roman, *adj.* (*when an adj. use small letter*) *and s.m.f.* Romain, -e; *~ nose,* nez aquilin, *m.*

romance, *s.* roman de chevalerie, *m.*; ⚠ romance = *ballad song*; *v.a.* (*exaggerate*) exagérer; **~r,** (*pej.*) blagueu|r, ~se, *m.f.*; ⚠ romancier = *a novelist.*

Romanesque, *adj. and s.m.* (*arch.*) roman; ⚠ *not* romanesque *which* = '*romantic*', *see below.*

romantic, romanesque; (*scenery*) romantique.

romantic|ism, (*Lit.*) romantisme, *m.*; **~ist,** romantique, *m.*

romp, *s.* (*girl*) jeune fille qui a des allures garçonnières, *f.*; (*game*) jeu bruyant, *m.*; *v.n.* batifoler.

rood, croix, *f.*; **~-screen,** jubé, *m.*

roof, *s.* toit, *m.*; (*mouth*) palais, *m.*; (*vault*) voûte, *f.*; *v.a.* couvrir*; **~ing,** toiture, *f.*; **~less,** (*fig.*) sans abri.

rook, *s.* (*ornith.*) freux, *m.*; (*cheat*) escroc, *m.*; (*chess*) tour, *f.*; **~ery,** colonie de freux, *f.*

room, (*private use*) chambre, *f.*; (*general, public use*) salle, *f.*; (*space, stead*) place, *f.*; (*scope*) lieu, *m.*; *keep to one's ~,* garder la chambre; *make ~ for,* faire* place à; **~ful,** chambre pleine, *f*; **~y,** spacieu|x, ~se.

roost, *s.* perchoir, *m.*; *rule the ~,* faire* la pluie et le beau temps; *v.n.* (*go to roost*) se jucher.

rooster, (*U.S.A.*) coq, *m.*

root, *s.* (*lit., fig., math., gram.*) racine, *f.*; (*source*) source, *f.*; *v.a.* enraciner; *~ out, up,* déraciner; *~ out,* (*fig.*) fouiller; *v.n.* prendre* racine.

rootedly, profondément.

rope, corde, *f.*; (*naut.*) cordage, *m.*; (*bell*) cordon, *m.*; (*onions*) glane, *f.*; **~-ladder,** échelle de corde, *f.*; **~-maker,** cordier, *m.*; *know the ~s,* être à la coule; *v.a.* corder.

rosary, (*of roses*) roseraie, *f.*; (*beads*) rosaire, *m.*

ros|e, rose, *f.*; (*watering-pot*) pomme, *f.*; *under the ~,* sous le manteau; *~-coloured,* rose; **~e-tree,** rosier, *m.*; **~e-water,** eau de rose, *f.*; **~e-window,** (*arch.*) rosace, *f.*; **~ewood,** palissandre, *m.*; ⚠ bois de rose = '*tulip-wood*'; **~eate,** rosé; **~y,** de rose.

rosemary, (*bot.*) romarin, *m.*

rosette, (*of ribbon*) rosette, *f.*

rosin, *see* RESIN.

rostrum, tribune, *f.*

rot, *s.* (*bones, teeth, wood*) carie, *f.*; (*slang*) blague, *f.*; *interj.* (*slang*) quelle blague!; *v.a.* faire* pourrir; (*teeth, &c.*) faire* carier; *v.n.* pourrir, se carier.

rota, liste, *f.*

rotat|ion, rotation, *f.*; (*crops*) assolement, *m.*; *in ~,* à tour de rôle; **~ory,** rotatoire.

rote, routine, *f.*; *by ~,* par routine.

rotten, (*bones*) carié; (*teeth, fruit*) gâté; (*slang*) sale; *~ to the core,* pourri jusqu'aux moelles; **~ness,** pourriture, *f.*; (*bones, teeth, wood*) carie, *f.*

rotter, (*slang*) mauvais type, *m.*

rotund, (*pers.*) rondelet, -te; (*style*) ronflant; **~ity,** (*pers.*) rotondité, *f.*

rotunda, rotonde, *f.*

rouble, rouble, *m.*

rouge, rouge, *m.*; *v.a.* farder; *v.n.* se farder.

rough, *s.* (*pers.*) voyou, *m.*

rough, *adj.* (*stern, voice, road, skin, lacking finish*) rude; (*to touch, &c.*) inégal; (*taste*) âpre; (*coarse*) grossi|er, ~ère; (*not polished*) brut; (*sea, weather*) gros, -se; *~-cast, s.* crépi, *m., v.a.* crépir; *~ copy, ~ draft,* brouillon, *m.*; *~ sketch,* croquis, *m.*; *it's ~ on him,* il a de la déveine; **~ness,** (*surface*) aspérité, *f.*; (*road*) mauvais état, *m.*; (*manners, tone, &c.*) rudesse, *f.*; (*sea*) agitation, *f.*; **~ly,** (*in a ~ manner*) rudement; (*approximately*) approximativement.

roughen, *v.a.* rendre rude; *v.n.* devenir* (être) rude.

roughshod, *adj.* ferré à glace.

Rumanian, *adj.* (*when an adj. use small letter*) *and s.m.f.* Roumain, -e.

round, *s.* (*circle*) rond, *m.*; **1.** (*circuit, a walk*) tournée, *f.*; **2.** (*sights, pleasures*) tour, *m. with* faire*; **3.** (*applause*) salve, *f.*; **4.** (*routine*) routine, *f.*; **5.** (*ladder*) échelon, *m.*; **6.** (*mil. patrol*) ronde, *f.*; **7.** (*shot for firing*) coup à tirer, *m.*

round, *adj.* (*circular, plump, complete, so much and no more of figures, roughly correct*) rond; (*considerable of sums*) fort; (*trip, voyage*) circulaire; *~ arch,* cintre, *m.*; *~ towel,* essuie-mains à rouleau, *m. invar.*; **~ness,** rondeur, *f.*; **~ly,** rondement.

round, *adv.* (*in circumference*) de tour; (*circularly in movement*) en rond; (*in the district round*) à la ronde; *~ about,* tout autour; *take ~,* (*show*) faire* visiter; (*deliver*) distribuer; *turn ~,* tourner.

round, *prep.* autour de.

round, *v.a.* arrondir; *~ off,* arrondir; *~ up,* (*collect*) rassembler.

roundabout, *s.* manège, *m.*; *adj.* (*road, &c.*) détourné.

roundish, rondelet, -te.

rous|e, *v.a.* réveiller; (*provoke*) provoquer; **~ing,** *adj.* qui réveille; (*appeal, applause*) émouvant.

rout, *s.* (*riot*) tumulte, *m.*; (*mil.*) déroute, *f.*; *v.a.* mettre* en déroute; *~ out,* déterrer.

route, route, *f.*

routine, routine, *f.*

rov|e, *v.a.* parcourir*; *v.n.* errer; **~er,** (*pej.*) vagabond, *m.*; **~ing,** *adj.* vagabond.
row, *s.* (*pers.*) rang, *m.*; (*things*) rangée, *f.*; (*figures*) colonne, *f.*
row, *s.* (*in boat*) promenade en canot, *f.*; *v.a.* faire* aller (à force de rames); (*race*) prendre* part à; *v.n.* ramer; **~er,** rameur, *m.*; **~ing-boat,** canot, *m.*; **~lock,** toletière, *f.*
row, *s.* (*commotion*) vacarme, *m.*; (*quarrel*) querelle, *f.*
rowan-tree, sorbier des oiseaux, *m.*
rowd|iness, turbulence, *f.*; **~y,** turbulent.
royal, (*lit. and fig.*) royal; ~ *sail,* cacatois, *m.*; **~ty,** royauté, *f.*; (*of author*) droits d'auteur, *m.pl.*; **~ist,** royaliste, *m.*; **~ly,** royalement.
rub, *s.* (*with duster*) coup de torchon, *m.*; (*difficulty*) hic, *m.*
rub, *v.a.* frotter; ~ *down,* (*horse*) bouchonner; ~ *out, off,* (*lit. and fig.*) effacer; ~ *up,* (*polish*) polir; ~ *up the wrong way,* prendre* à contre-poil; *v.n.* frotter; ~ *along,* (*fam.*) aller son petit chemin; **~bing,** frottement, *m.*
rubber, (*substance*) caoutchouc, *m.*; (*whist, bridge*) rob, *m.*; *win the first ~,* gagner la première manche.
rubbish, (*from buildings*) décombres, *m.pl.*; (*lumber, clothes*) vieillerie, *f.*; (*nonsense*) blague, *f.*; **~ing, ~y,** de rebut.
rubble, *s.* (*build.*) blocage, *m.*
rubicund, rubicond.
ruby, rubis, *m.*; *adj.*, (*colour*) *also ruby-red,* couleur du rubis, *invar.*
ruck, *s.* pli, *m.*
ructions, *there will be ~,* il va y avoir du grabuge.
rudder, gouvernail, *m.*
ruddy, (*cheeks, &c.*) au teint vermeil; (*things*) vermeil, -le.
rude, (*primitive, in natural state*) rude; (*abrupt*) brusque; (*insolent*) insolent; (*vigorous*) vigoureu|x, **~se**; **~ness,** rudesse, insolence, *f.*; **~ly,** (*roughly*) grossièrement; (*insolently*) insolemment.
rudiment|s, rudiments, *m.pl.*; **~ary,** rudimentaire.
rue, *s.* (*bot.*) rue, *f.*
rue, *v.a.* se repentir* de; **~ful,** triste; **~fully,** tristement.
ruff, *s.* (*frilled collar*) fraise, *f.*
ruffian, *s.* bandit, *m.*; **~ism,** brutalité, *f.*; **~ly,** de bandit.
ruffle, *s.* (*on water*) ride, *f.*; (*round neck*) fraise, *f.*; *v.a.* (*hair*) ébouriffer; (*dress, &c.*) chiffonner; (*surface of water*) rider; ~ *the temper of,* chiffonner.
rug, (*travelling, &c.*) couverture, *f.*; (*unfixed carpet*) tapis, *m.*
rugged, (*uneven*) raboteu|x, **~se**; (*features*) rude; (*austere*) austère; **~ness,** (*lit. and fig., temper, &c.*) rudesse, *f.*; (*surface*) aspérité, *f.*
rugby, (*football*) rugby, *m.*
rugosity, rugosité, *f.*
ruin, *s.* (*lit. and fig., cause of ruin*) ruine, *f.*; *v.a.* (*lit. and fig.*) ruiner; (*bring about ruin of*) causer la perte de; (*girl*) séduire*; **~ation,** ruine, *f.*; **~ous,** (*in ruins*) en ruines; (*bringing ruin*) ruineu|x, **~se**; **~ously,** ruineusement.
rule, *s.* (*sway, dominion*) autorité, *f.*; (*principle, standard, custom, &c., eccles.*) règle, *f.*; (*of the road*) code, *m.*; *hard and fast ~,* règle rigoureuse, *f.*; *as a ~,* généralement; *by ~ of thumb,* à vue de nez; ~ *of three,* règle de trois, *f.*
rule, *v.a.* gouverner; (*lines*) régler; (*guide*) guider; ~ *out,* (*exclude*) exclure*; ~ *over,* régner sur; *v.n.* (*prices*) se pratiquer; **~r,** (*province*) gouverneur, *m.*; (*kingdom, empire*) roi, empereur, *m.*; (*for lines*) règle, *f.*
ruling, *s.* (*decision*) décision, *f.*; *adj.* dominant.
rum, *s.* rhum, *m.*
rum, *adj.* (*slang*) drôle.
rumble, rumbling, *s.* (*thunder*) grondement, *m.*; (*waggon*) roulement, *m.*; *v.n.* gronder, rouler.
rumina|te, (*lit. and fig.*) ruminer; **~tion,** rumination, *f.*; **~nt,** *adj. and s.m.* ruminant.
rummag|e, *v.a.n.* fouiller; **~e, ~ing,** *s.* fouille, *f.*
rumour, rumeur, *f.*; *it is ~ed that,* le bruit court que.
rump, (*animal's*) croupe, *f.*; **~steak,** romsteck, *m.*
run, *s.* (*act of running, space covered, cricket, on shares*) course, *f.*; (*common average*) commun, *m.*; (*comm., on a bank*) descente, *f.*; (*voyage*) voyage, *m.*; (*in a train*) trajet, *m.*
run, *v.a.* (*chance risk*) courir*; (*errand*) faire*; (*a thing's course*) suivre*; (*horse in race*) faire* courir; (*wine, blood*) ruisseler de; (*blockade*) forcer; (*train, bus, special*) mettre* en service; (*work, mine, &c.*) exploiter; (*undertaking*) faire* marcher; (*engine, motor*) faire* fonctionner; *well-~,* (*house, &c.*) bien tenu; ~ *across,* rencontrer par hasard; ~ *after,* courir* après; (*fig.*) rechercher; ~ *against,* se heurter contre; ~ *down,* descendre (avoir) en courant; (*disparage*) dénigrer; (*ship*) couler; (*with veh.*) renverser; ~ *over* (*hand*) passer sur; (*with eyes*) parcourir* des yeux; (*with veh.*) passer dessus; ~ *through* (*read rapidly*) parcourir*; (*with pencil, &c.*) biffer; (*with sword, &c.*) transpercer; ~ *up,* (*debts, &c.*) entasser; (*hill*) monter (avoir) en courant; ~ *to earth,* (*game*) forcer; ~ *aground,* (*ship*) mettre* à la côte.
run, *v.n.* **1.** (*lit., rumours, orders, bills*), courir*; **2.** (*rush*) se précipiter; **3.** (*extend*) s'étendre; **4.** (*eyes*) pleurer; **5.** (*candles, liquids, nose*) couler; **6.** (*wound*) suppurer; **7.** (*buses, boats, &c.*) faire* le service; **8.** (*colours*) se fondre; **9.** (*statements, &c.*)

être conçu; **10.** (*rope*) glisser; **11.** (*theatr., play*) se jouer; ~ *to seed*, monter (être) en graine; ~ *short*, s'épuiser; ~ *short of*, être à court de; ~ *about*, courir*; ~ *away*, se sauver; ~ *down*, descendre (être) en courant; (*liquids*) découler; (*health*) s'affaiblir; (*clock*) s'arrêter; ~ *in*, (*visit*) faire* une courte visite; ~ *in, through*, (*head*) trotter; ~ *off*, (*liquids*) s'écouler; ~ *on*, continuer; ~ *out*, (*go out running*) sortir* (être) en courant; (*end*) se terminer; (*leak*) couler; (*goods, provisions*) s'épuiser; ~ *over*, (*liquids*) déborder; ~ *to*, (*amount to*) monter (être) à.

runaway, fuyard, *m.*; *adj.* (*horse*) emballé; (*marriage*) clandestin.

rung, (*ladder*) échelon, *m.*

runner, coureu|r, ~se, *m.f.*; (*sledge*) patin, *m.*; (*U.S.A. engine-driver, engineman*) mécanicien, *m.*; *scarlet* ~, (*bot.*) †haricot d'Espagne, *m.*

running, *s.* course, *f.*; (*trains, machines*) marche, *f.*; (*wounds, &c.*) suppuration, *f.*; ~ *down*, (*disparagement*) dénigrement, *m.*; ~*-board*, (*motor*) marchepied, *m.*; *adj.* (*in succession*) de suite; (*wounds*) qui suppure; (*knot*) coulant; (*water*) vi|f, ~ve; (*accounts, &c.*) courant.

runway (*aeron.*) voie de départ, *f.*

rupee, roupie, *f.*

rupture, rupture, *f.*; *v.a.* (*lit. and fig.*) rompre.

rural, rural.

rush, *s.* (*bot.*) jonc, *m.*; (*crowd*) foule, *f.*; (*charge, onslaught*) ruée, *f.*; (*liquid, blood*) flot, *m.*; *v.a.* (*pers., &c.*) entraîner à toute vitesse; (*mil.*) prendre* d'assaut; *v.n.* se précipiter; (*blood*) affluer; ~ *on*, (*an enemy*) fondre sur.

rushing, (*water*) violence, *f.*; (*people*) précipitation, *f.*; *adj.* (*water, &c.*) jaillissant.

rushlight, (*fig.*) lueur, *f.*

rusk, biscotte, *f.*

russet, *adj.* (*colour*) roussâtre.

Russia-leather, *see* LEATHER.

Russian, *adj.* (*when an adj. use small letter*) *and s.m.f.* Russe; (*lang.*) russe, *m.*

rust, rustiness, *s.* (*lit. and fig.*) rouille, *f.*; *v.a.* rouiller; *v.n.* se rouiller; **~less**, inoxydable; **~y**, (*lit. and fig.*) rouillé.

rustic, *s.* rustre, *m.*; **~ity**, (*pej.*) rusticité, *f.*; *adj.* rustique.

rustica|te, *v.a.* (*univ.*) renvoyer temporairement; ⚠ rustiquer, *v.a.* = '*rusticate*', *mark stone with roughened surface*; *v.n.* se retirer à la campagne, *f.*; **~tion**, (*univ.*) expulsion temporaire.

rustle, rustling, *s.* (*leaves*) bruissement, *m.*; (*dress*) frou-frou, *m.*; *v.n.* faire* bruissement, frou-frou.

rut, (*of wheel*) ornière, *f.*; (*animals and rutting*) rut, *m.*

ruthless, impitoyable; **~ly**, sans pitié.

rye, seigle, *m.*; ~ **bread**, pain de seigle, *m.*; **~-grass**, fausse ivraie, *f.*

S

sabbat|h, (*Jews, witches*) sabbat, *m.*; (*Christian*) dimanche, *m.*; **~ical**, sabbatique.

sable, *s.* (*an. and fur*) zibeline, *f.*; ⚠ sable, *m. is a heraldic term and is not often used for* zibeline; *adj.* (*gloomy*) lugubre; (*herald.*) sable.

sabre, *s.* sabre, *m.*; *v.a.* sabrer.

sabretache, sabretache, *f.*

saccharine, *s.* saccharine, *f.*

sacerdotal, sacerdotal.

sack, *s.* (*bag or contents, pillage*) sac, *m.*; *v.a.* (*colloq., dismiss*) saquer; (*plunder*) mettre* à sac; **~cloth**, toile à sac, *f.*; **~ful**, sachée, *f.*; **~ing**, (*pillage*) sac, *m.*; (*coarse cloth*) toile à sac, *f.*

sack, (*wine*) vin de Xérès, *m.*

sacrament, sacrement, *m.*; **~al**, sacramental.

sacred, (*books, History, music, &c.*) sacré; (*holy, belonging to religion*) saint; ~ *to*, consacré à; **~ness**, sainteté, *f.*

sacrific|e, *s.* (*lit. and fig.*) sacrifice, *m.*; (*victim*) victime, *f.*; *v.a.n.* (*lit. and fig.*) sacrifier; **~ial**, de sacrifice.

sacrileg|e, sacrilège, *m.*; **~ious**, sacrilège.

sacrosanct, (*lit. and iron.*) sacro-saint.

sad, (*pers., things, pitiable*) triste; (*grievous*) fâcheu|x, ~se; **~ness**, tristesse, *f.*; **~ly**, tristement; (*much*) beaucoup; **~den**, attrister.

saddle, (*lit., butch., cul.*) selle, *f.*; **~-cloth**, †housse, *f.*; *be thrown out of the* ~, vider les arçons; *v.a.* (*horse*) seller; (*pers. with, fig.*) charger de.

saddleback, dos d'âne, *m.*; (*hill*) colline en dos d'âne, *f.*; **~ed**, (*arch.*) en dos d'âne.

saddler, sellier, *m.*; **~y**, sellerie, *f.*

safe, *s.* garde-manger, *m.*

safe, *adj.* (*safe and sound*) sain, -e et sau|f, ~ve; (*not dangerous*) sûr; (*in safety*) en sûreté, *f.*; (*certain*) certain; **~-conduct**, sauf-conduit, *m.*; **~guard**, *s.* sauvegarde, *f.*; *v.a.* sauvegarder; **~ly**, (*without hesitation*) sans hésitation; (*without accident*) sain et sauf (*with concord*); (*securely*) en sûreté; ~ *bind* ~ *find*, méfiance est mère de sûreté.

safety, sûreté, *f.*; **~-lamp**, lampe de sûreté, *f.*; **~-match**, allumette amorphe, *f.*; **~-pin**, épingle anglaise, *f.*; **~-razor**, rasoir de sûreté, *m.*; **~-valve**, soupape de sûreté, *f.*

safflower, (*bot.*) carthame, *m.*

saffron, *s.* safran, *m.*; ~*-coloured*, safrané.

sag, *s.* affaissement, *m.*; *v.n.* fléchir.

saga, saga, *f.*

sagac|ious, sagace; **~ity**, sagacité, *f.*

sage, *s.* (*wise man*) sage, *m.*; (*bot.*) sauge, *f.*; *adj.* (*irony*) compassé.

sago, sagou, *m.*; **~-tree**, sagoutier, *m.*

said, *adj.* dit.

sail, voile, *f.*; (*windmill*) aile, *f.*; (*trip*) promenade à la voile, *f.*; (*number of*

ships) navires, *m.pl.*; *set* ~, mettre* à la voile; **~-cloth,** toile à voile, *f.*; **~-maker,** voilier, *m.*; *strike* ~, amener les voiles.
sail, *v.n.* naviguer (*navigate*); (*depart*) partir* (être); *v.a.* (*ship*) commander; (*travel over*) naviguer sur; ~ *up*, (*river*) remonter; **~er,** (*ship*) voilier, *m.*; **~ing,** *s.* navigation, *f.*; (*departure*) départ, *m.*; **~or,** matelot, *m.*
sainfoin, (*bot.*) sainfoin, *m.*
saint, *s.* saint, -e, *m.f.*; *adj.* +*proper name*, Saint, -e (*abbrevs.* St, Ste); **St. John's wort,** (*bot.*) herbe de la St Jean, *f.*
saintly, (*pers.*) saint; (*things*) de saint.
sake, *for the* ~ *of*, pour l'amour de; (*for the pleasure of*) pour le plaisir de.
saker, (*ornith.*) sacre, *m.*
salaam, salut, *m.*
salacious, lubrique.
salad, salade, *f.*; **~-bowl,** saladier, *m.*
salamander, (*zool.*) salamandre, *f.*
salar|y, appointements, *m.pl.*; **~ied,** salarié; ⚠ salaire *is used of manual workers and* = *'wages'*.
sale, vente, *f.*; (*auction*) vente aux enchères, *f.*; (*clearance, shop*) solde, *m.*; *on, for* ~, en vente; *put up for* ~, mettre* en vente; **~able,** vendable.
sales|man, ~woman (*in shop*) vendeu|r, ~se, *m.f.*
salient, *s.* (*fort.*) saillant, *m.*; *adj.* (*lit. and fig.*) saillant.
saline, *adj.* salin.
saliva, salive, *f.*; **~tion,** salivation, *f.*; *v.n.* **~te,** saliver.
sallow, *s.* (*bot.*) marsault, *m.*
sallow, *adj.* blafard; **~ness,** teint blafard.
sally, *s.* (*wit, &c.*) saillie, *f.*; (*mil.*) sortie, *f.*; *v.n.* (*mil.*) faire* une sortie; ~ *forth*, (*pers.*) sortir* (être).
salmon, saumon, *m.*; *~-coloured*, saumon, *invar.*; **~-trout,** truite saumonée, *f.*
saloon, salon, *m.*; (*U.S.A.*) bar, *m.*; *~-keeper*, bistro, *m.*; *shaving-~*, salon de coiffure pour hommes, *m.*
salt, *s.* (*lit. and fig.*) sel, *m.*; *smelling-~s*, sels, *m.pl.*; **~-cellar,** salière, *f.*; **~-spoon,** cuiller à sel, *f.*; *spirits of* ~, esprit de sel, *m.*; *adj.* salé; **~ness,** salure, *f.*
salt|er, (*of fish*) saleur, *m.*; (*salt-seller*) saunier, *m.*; **~ing,** *s.* salaison, *f.*; *~ing-tub*, saloir, *m.*
saltpetre, salpêtre, *m.*
saltwort, (*bot.*) soude, *f.*
salubri|ous, salubre; **~ty,** salubrité, *f.*
salutary, salutaire.
salutation, salutation, *f.*
salute, *s.* salut, *m.*; (*kiss*) baiser, *m.*; (*mil., guns*) salve, *f.*; (*mil., nav.*) salut, *m.*; *v.a.* saluer; (*embrace*) embrasser; (*mil., nav., guns*) saluer; *v.n.* saluer.
salvage, sauvetage, *m.*; *v.a.* sauver.
salvation, salut, *m.*; **~ist,** salutiste, *m.*; *Salvation Army*, Armée du Salut, *f.*
salve, *s.* onguent, *m.*; (*fig.*) remède, *m.*; *v.a.* appliquer un onguent à; (*conscience*) endormir*; (*fig.*) adoucir.
salver, (*waiter*) plateau, *m.*
salvo, (*cannon and applause*) salve, *f.*
same, *adj.* même; (*monotonous*) monotone; *the very* ~, précisément le (la) même *or* même *after noun, e.g. the very* ~ *thing*, la chose même; *at the* ~ *time*, en même temps; *in the* ~ *way*, de même; **~ness,** (*monotony*) monotonie, *f.*
same, *pron.* même chose, *f.*
samphire, (*bot.*) christe-marine, *f.*
sample, *s.* échantillon, *m.*; *v.a.* (*comm.*) échantillonner.
sampler, (*embroidery*) broderie de jeune fille, *f.*
sanatorium, sanatorium (*pl.* -ia), *m.*
sanctif|ication, sanctification, *f.*; **~y,** sanctifier.
sanctimonious, (*pej.*) béat; **~ness,** air de sainteté, *m.*
sancti|on, *s.* (*penalty, confirmation*) sanction, *f.*; *v.a.* sanctionner; (*approve*) approuver; **~ty,** sainteté, *f.*
sanctuary, sanctuaire, *m.*; (*asylum*) refuge, *m.*; *take* ~, se réfugier.
sand, sable, *m.*; (*small, fine* ~) sablon, *m.*; **~s,** (*shore*) plage, *f.*; **~-bag,** (*fort.*) sac à sable, *m.*; **~-bank,** banc de sable, *m.*; **~-eel,** équille, *f.*; **~-glass,** sablier, *m.*; **~-hill,** dune, *f.*; **~-paper,** papier de verre, *m.*; **~piper,** (*ornith.*) chevalier, *m.*; **~ed,** sablé.
sandal, (*shoe*) sandale, *f.*; **~-wood,** santal, *m.*
sandstone, grès, *m.*
sandwich, sandwich, *m.*
sandy, (*soil*) sablonneu~**x,** ~se; (*hair*) blond roux, *invar.*
sane, sain d'esprit.
sanguinary, (*pers. and thing*) sanguinaire.
sanguine, (*temperament*) sanguin; (*confident*) confiant; **~ness,** confiance, *f.*; **~ly,** avec confiance.
sanitary, sanitaire.
sanity, jugement sain, *m.*
Sanskrit, *adj. and s.m.* (*lang.*) sanscrit.
sap, *s.* sève, *f.*; (*mil.*) sape, *f.*; **~-wood,** (*bot.*) aubier, *m.*; **~less,** sans sève; (*dried up*) desséché; **~piness,** abondance de sève, *f.*; **~py,** plein de sève; *v.a.* (*mil. and fig.*) saper.
sapien|ce, sagesse, *f.*; **~t,** sage.
sapling, jeune arbre, *m.*
sapodilla, (*bot.*) sapotillier, *m.*
saponaceous, saponacé.
sapper, sapeur, *m.*
sapphire, saphir, *m.*; *~-blue*, bleu saphir, *invar.*
saraband, (*dance*) sarabande, *f.*
Saracen, *adj.* (*when an adj. use small letter*) *and s.m.f.* Sarrasin, -e.
sarcas|m, sarcasme, *m.*; **~tic,** sarcastique; **~tically,** d'une manière sarcastique.
sarcophagus, sarcophage, *m.*
sardine, sardine, *f.*

Sardinian, *adj.* (*when an adj. use small letter*) *and s.m.f.* Sarde.
sardonic, sardonique.
sardonyx, sardoine, *f.*
sars(c)enet, (*fabric*) florence, *m.*
sartorial, de tailleur.
sash, ceinture, *f.*; (*mark of distinction*) écharpe, *f.*; (*of window*) châssis, *m.*; **~-window**, fenêtre à guillotine, *f.*
sassafras, (*bot.*) sassafras, *m.*
Satan, Satan, *m.*; **~ic**, satanique.
satchel, (*school*) gibecière, *f.*
sat|e, satiate, *v.a.* rassasier; **~iety**, satiété, *f.*
satellite, satellite, *m.*
satin, satin, *m.*; **~-wood**, bois de citronnier, *m.*
satir|e, satire, *f.*; **~ic, ~ical**, satirique; (*pers.*) porté à la satire; **~ist**, auteur satirique, *m.*; **~ize**, faire* des satires sur.
satisfact|ion, (*contentment, for an offence*) satisfaction, *f.*; (*reparation, atonement*) réparation, *f.*; (*debts*) règlement, *m.*; **~ory**, satisfaisant; **~orily**, d'une manière satisfaisante; *demand ~ion for*, demander raison de.
satisfy, *v.a.* (*hunger, passion, curiosity, please, make reparation, creditors, give satisfaction to*) satisfaire*; (*obligations, needs*) satisfaire* à; (*be content with*) se contenter de; (*persuade*) convaincre*; **~ing**, satisfaisant.
satrap, satrape, *m.*
satura|te, saturer (de); **~tion**, saturation, *f.*
Saturday, samedi, *m.*
saturnine, sombre; ⚠ saturnin = '*pertaining to lead*'.
satyr, satyre, *m.*
sauce, *s.* sauce, *f.*; (*impertinence*) impertinence, *f.*; *white ~*, sauce blanche, *f.*; **~-boat**, saucière, *f.*
saucepan, casserole, *f.*
saucer, soucoupe, *f.*
sauc|iness, insolence, *f.*; **~y**, insolent; **~ily**, insolemment.
sauerkraut, choucroute, *f.*
saunter, *s.* petit tour de promenade, *m.*; *v.n.* flâner; **~ing**, flânerie, *f.*
sausage, saucisse, *f.*; (*large*) saucisson, *m.*
savage, *s.* (*lit. and fig.*) sauvage, *m.f.*; *adj.* (*lit. and cruel*) sauvage; (*enraged*) furieu|x, ~se; **~ry, ~ness**, sauvagerie, *f.*; **~ly**, sauvagement.
savanna(h), savane, *f.*
save, *v.a.* (*lit., fig., eccles.*) sauver; (*money, trouble*) épargner; (*time*) gagner; (*not to lose*) ne pas manquer; *~ appearances*, sauver les apparences; *~ from*, (*doing*) empêcher de; *v.n.* économiser.
save, saving, *prep.* sauf.
saveloy, cervelas, *m.*
saver, (*economy*) personne qui épargne, *f.*
saving, *s.* (*rescue*) sauvetage, *m.*; (*economy*) économie, *f.*; (*relig.*) salut, *m.*; **~s**, économies, *f.pl.*; **~s-bank**, caisse d'épargne, *f.*; *adj.* (*pers.*) économe.
saviour, sauveur, *m.*; (*relig.*) Sauveur, *m.*
savory, (*bot.*) sarriette, *f.*
savour, savouriness, (*lit. and fig.*) saveur, *f.*; (*suspicion, smack*) teinte, *f.*; *~ of, v.n.* avoir le goût de; (*betoken*) sentir*; **~less**, sans saveur.
savoury, *s.* (*cook.*) bouchée saléer, *f.*; *adj.* savoureu|x, ~se.
savoy, chou frisé, *m.*
saw, scie, *f.*; (*saying*) dicton, *m.*; **~dust**, sciure, *f.*; **~-mill**, scierie, *f.*; **~-wort**, (*bot.*) serratule, *f.*; *v.a.n.* scier.
sawyer, scieur, *m.*
saxifrage, saxifrage, *f.*
Saxon, *adj.* (*when an adj. use small letter*) *and s.m.f.* Saxon, -ne.
saxophone, saxophone, *m.*
say, *s.* mot, *m.*
say, *v.a.* dire* (de + *inf.*); ~, (*imperat. with numbers, &c.*) disons; *that is to ~*, c'est-à-dire; *I ~!* dites donc!; *without ~ing a word*, sans mot dire.
saying, (*proverb*) proverbe, *m.*; (*maxim*) maxime, *f.*
scab, *s.* croûte, *f.*; (*disease*) gale, *f.*; **~by**, (*disease*) galeu|x, ~se.
scabbard, fourreau, *m.*
scabious, (*bot.*) scabieuse, *f.*
scaffold, échafaud, *m.*; **~ing**, échaffaudage, *m.*
scald, *s.* brûlure, *f.*; *v.a.* échauder.
scal|e, *s.* (*series of degrees, map, plan, thermometer*) échelle, *f.*; (*mus.*) gamme, *f.*; (*fish, reptiles, on eye, thin plate*) écaille, *f.*; *s.* (*of a balance*) plateau, *m.*; **~es**, balance, *f.*; (*letters*) pèse-lettre, *m.*, *pl.* pèse-lettres; **sliding-~e**, échelle mobile, *f.*; *on a small ~e*, sur une petite échelle; **~y**, écailleu|x, ~se; *v.a.* (*wall, &c.*) escalader; (*take away scales*) écailler; **~ing-ladder**, *see* LADDER.
sca(o)llop, (*shell*) coquille, *f.*; (*zool.*) pétoncle, *m.*; (*needlework*) feston, *m.*; *v.a.* (*needle*) festonner.
scalp, *s.* (*skin*) cuir chevelu, *m.*; (*hill*) sommet nu, *m.*; *v.a.* scalper.
scalpel, scalpel, *m.*
scamp, vaurien, *m.*
scamp, *v.a.* (*work*) saboter.
scamper, *v.n.* ~ *away*, détaler.
scan, *v.a.* (*look intently at*) scruter; (*verse*) scander.
scandal, scandale, *m.*; (*slander*) médisance, *f.*; **~ize**, scandaliser; **~ous**, scandaleu|x, ~se; **~ously**, scandaleusement; **~monger**, médisant, -e, *m.f.*
scansion, scansion, *f.*
scant|iness, manque, *m.*; **~y**, (*food, &c.*) maigre; (*scarce*) rare; **~ily**, (*poorly*) maigrement; (*meanly*) mesquinement.
scapegoat, bouc émissaire, *m.*
scapegrace, mauvais garnement, *m.*
scapular, (*monastic*) scapulaire, *m.*
scar, *s.* cicatrice, *f.*; (*long ~ on face*) balafre, *f.*; (*rock*) rocher à pic, *m.*; *v.a.* cicatriser.

scarc|e, *adj.* rare; **~eness, ~ity,** rareté, *f.*; (*food*) disette, *f.*; **~ely,** à peine.
scare, *s.* panique, *f.*; **~crow,** épouvantail, *m.*; **~monger,** semeur de faux bruits, *m.*; *v.a.* effrayer.
scarf, (*official*) écharpe, *f.*; (*for neck*) foulard, *m.*; (*necktie*) cravate, *f.*; **~-pin,** épingle de cravate, *f.*
scarify, scarifier.
scarlatina, scarlatine, *f.*
scarlet, *adj. and s.f.* écarlate.
scarp, (*fort.*) escarpe, *f.*; (*slope*) escarpement, *m.*
scatheless, sans dommage.
scathing, cinglant.
scatter, *v.a.* éparpiller; (*clouds, &c.*) dissiper; (*mob, &c.*) disperser; ~ *with,* parsemer de; *v.n.* se disperser.
scavenge, (*streets*) nettoyer; **~r,** boueur, *m.*
scene, (*part of play, quarrel, place, view, fig.*) scène, *f.*; (*of war, &c.*) théâtre, *m.*; **~-shifter,** machiniste, *m.*; *behind the ~s,* (*lit. and fig.*) dans les coulisses.
scenery, (*landscape*) paysage, *m.*; (*theatr.*) décor, *m.*
scenic, scénique.
scent, odeur, *f.*; (*perfume*) parfum, *m.*; (*sense*) odorat, *m.*; (*hunt.*) piste, *f.*; (*dog and fig.*) flair, *m.*; **~-bottle,** flacon d'odeur, *m.*; *v.a.* (*game, &c. and fig.*) flairer; (*perfume*) parfumer; *sweet-~ed,* odorant.
scentless, sans odeur.
sceptic, *adj. and s.m.f.* sceptique; **~ism,** scepticisme, *m.*; **~ally,** avec scepticisme.
sceptre, (*lit. and fig.*) sceptre, *m.*
schedule, (*list*) liste, *f.*; (*taxes*) cédule, *f.*
scheme, plan, *m.*; (*project*) projet, *m.*; (*pej.*) intrigue, *f.*; ⚠ schème = '*diagram*', '*rough draft of a decree*'; *v.a.* projeter; *v.n.* faire* des projets; **~r,** *s. also adj.* **scheming,** (*pej.*) intrigant, -e, *m.f.*
schism, schisme, *m.*; **~atic,** schismatique.
schist, schiste, *m.*
scholar, (*boy, girl*) écoli|er, ~ère, *m.f.*; (*learned man*) savant, *m.*; (*on foundation*) boursi|er, ~ère, *m.f.*; **~ship,** érudition, *f.*; (*univ., pub. sch.*) bourse, *f.*; **~ly,** érudit.
scholastic, (*belonging to schools*) scolaire; ⚠ scolaire *never* = '*scholarly*' *which is* érudit.
school, (*lit., fig., artists, politicians, &c.*) école, *f.*; (*lessons*) classe, *f.*; (*type*) type, *m.*; **~boy, ~girl,** écoli|er, ~ère, *m.f.*; **~fellow,** condisciple, *m.*; **~room,** salle de classe, *f.*; **secondary ~,** école secondaire, *f.*; **technical ~,** école professionnelle, *f.*; *v.a.* discipliner; ~ *oneself to,* s'habituer à.
schooling, éducation, *f.*; (*expenses*) frais de l'éducation, *m.*
schoolmaster, (*primary*) maître d'école; (*pub. sch.*) (*approx.*) professeur (de collège), *m.*
schoolmistress, (*primary*) maîtresse d'école, *f.*; (*boarding-school*) maîtresse de pension, *f.*
schooner, goélette, *f.*
sciatica, sciatique, *f.*
scien|ce, science, *f.*; **~tist,** savant, *m.*; **~tific,** scientifique; **~tifically,** scientifiquement.
scimitar, cimeterre, *m.*
scintilla|te, scintiller; **~tion,** scintillation, *f.*
scission, division, *f.*; (*fig.*) scission, *f.*
scissors, ciseaux, *m.pl.*
scoff *at,* se moquer de.
scoffer, railleur, *m.*
scoffingly, en raillant.
scold, *s.* (*woman*) mégère, *f.*; **~ing,** *s.* gronderie, *f.*; *v.a.* gronder.
sconce, candélabre, *m.*
scoop, grande cuiller, *f.*; (*shovel*) main, *f.*; *v.a.* ~ *out, up,* évider.
scooter, (*toy*) trottinette, *f.*
scope, (*end*) but, *m.*; (*range*) envergure, *f.*; (*outlet, space*) carrière, *f.*; *have free ~,* avoir carrière libre; *give free ~ to,* donner libre carrière à.
scorch, *v.a.n.* (*clothes*) roussir; *v.a.* (*fig.*) brûler; **~er,** (*motor*) chauffard, *m.*; **~ing,** *adj.* brûlant.
score, (*notch*) entaille, *f.*; (*sum due*) compte, *m.*; (*twenty*) vingtaine, *f.*; (*games*) total, *m.*; (*mus.*) partition, *f.*; *on that ~,* à cet égard; *on the ~ of,* à cause de.
score, *v.a.* (*notch*) entailler; (*success*) remporter; (*mus.*) orchestrer; (*games*) faire*; faire* un essai = '*score a try*'; *~ out,* rayer; *~ a goal,* (*football*) marquer un but; *v.n.* (*fig.*) l'emporter (sur); **~r,** marqueu|r, ~se, *m.f.*
scorn, *s.* mépris, *m.*; *v.a.* mépriser; *v.n.* ~ *to,* rougir de; **~er,** railleur, *m.*; **~ful,** dédaigneu|x, ~se; **~fully,** avec mépris.
scorpion, scorpion, *m.*
Scotch, *also* **Scottish,** *adj.* écossais; **~man, ~woman,** Écossais, -e, *m.f.*
scoter, (*ornith.*) macreuse, *f.*
scoundrel, gredin, *m.*; **~ly,** de coquin.
scour, (*clean*) nettoyer; (*metals*) récurer; (*from grease*) dégraisser; (*country*) parcourir*; (*seas*) écumer.
scourg|e, *s.* (*whip*) fouet, *m.*; (*visitation*) fléau, *m.*; *v.a.* flageller; **~ing,** flagellation, *f.*
scout, éclaireur, *m.*; **~ (wolf-) cub,** louveteau, *m.*; (*aeron., also ~ing-plane*) avion éclaireur, *m.*; *v.a.* repousser avec dédain; *v.n.* aller* (être) en éclaireur.
scowl, *s.* renfrognement, *m.*; *v.n.* se renfrogner; *adv.* **~ing(ly),** d'un air renfrogné.
scragg|iness, maigreur, *f.*; **~y,** décharné.
scramble, *s.* marche pénible, *f.*; (*for something*) bousculade, *f.*; *v.n.* (*on difficult ground*) avancer péniblement; (*for something*) se disputer.

scrap, *s.* morceau, *m.*; (*of paper*) bout, *m.*; **~s,** (*from meals*) reliefs, *m.pl.*; (*remnants*) restes, *m.pl.*; **~-book,** album, *m.*; *v.a.* (*throw away*) mettre* au rebut; (*proposal, &c.*) mettre* au rancart.

scrape, *s.*, *also* **scraping,** (*sound*) grincement, *m.*; (*mess*) mauvaise affaire, *f.*; *v.a.* (*sometimes* '*~ off*') gratter; (*surface*) râcler; (*vegetables*) ratisser; *~ off,* (*dirt*) décrotter; *~ together,* (*money*) amasser à force d'économies; *~ on the violin,* râcler du violon; **~r,** (*for feet*) décrottoir, *m.*

scratch, *s.* égratignure, *f.*; (*with nail*) coup d'ongle, *m.*; *v.a.* gratter; (*with nails*) égratigner; *~ out,* biffer; *v.n.* (*cat*) griffer; (*hen, &c.*) gratter.

scrawl, *s.* griffonnage, *m.*; *v.a.* griffonner.

scream, *s.* cri, *m.*; *v.a.n.* crier; *~ with laughter,* rire aux larmes; **~ing,** *s.* cris, *m.pl.*; *adj.* (*sound*) perçant; (*pers.*) qui crie.

screech, *s.* cri perçant, *m.*; **~-owl,** *see* OWL; *v.n.* jeter des cris perçants.

screed, tirade ennuyeuse, *f.*

screen, *s.* (*fire and cinema*) écran, *m.*; (*folding*) paravent, *m.*; (*sieve*) claie, *f.*; (*cavalry, &c., smoke*) rideau, *m.*; **~-fire,** tir de barrage, *m.*; **~-sweeper,** *wind-~ wiper,* (*motor*) essuie-glace, *m. invar.*; *v.a.* abriter (contre); (*punishment*) soustraire* (à); (*sift*) passer à la claie; (*fault, subordinate*) couvrir*.

screw, *s.* vis, *f.*; (*naut.*) hélice, *f.*; (*miser*) grippe-sou, *m.*; (*slang for* '*pay*') salaire, *m.*; **~-driver,** tournevis, *m.*; **~-jack,** vérin, *m.*; **~-nut,** écrou, *m.*; **~-steamer,** vapeur à hélice, *m.*

screw, *v.a.* visser; *~ down, in, up,* visser; (*fig.*) affermir; *~ up,* (*courage*) prendre* à deux mains; (*face, &c., in grimace*) tordre; *~ out of,* (*fig. extort*) arracher à; (*money*) extorquer à; *v.n.* se visser.

screwed, (*slang* '*drunk*') pochard.

scribble, *s.* (*writing*) griffonnage, *m.*; *v.a.* griffonner; **~r,** (*petty author*) écrivassier, *m.*

scribe, scribe, *m.*

scrimmage, (*tussle and football*) mêlée, *f.*

scrimpy, chiche.

scrip, (*wallet*) besace, *f.*; (*comm.*) certificat provisoire, *m.*

script, écriture, *f.*

scriptur|al, biblique; **~e,** Écriture Sainte, *f.*

scrivener, (*notary*) notaire, *m.*; (*broker*) courtier, *m.*

scroful|a, scrofule, *f.*; **~ous,** scrofuleu|x, ~se.

scroll, (*paper, &c.*) rouleau, *m.*; (*arch.*) volute, *f.*

scrub, *s.* (*brushwood*) taillis, *m.*

scrub, *v.a.* laver et frotter; **~-woman,** (*U.S.A*) femme de ménage, *f.*

scrubby, chéti|f, ~ve.

scruff, *~ of the neck,* peau du cou, *f.*

scruple, (*weight and qualm*) scrupule, *m.*; *v.n.* se faire* scrupule (de).

scrupulous, scrupuleu|x, ~se; **~ness,** scrupule, *m.*; **~ly,** scrupuleusement.

scrutiniz|e, scruter; **~ing,** *adj.* scrutateur.

scrutiny, examen, *m.*

scud, (*rain or hail*) giboulée, *f.*; *v.n.* fuir*; (*naut.*) faire* vent arrière.

scuffle, *s.* rixe, *f.*

scull, (*oar*) aviron, *m.*; (*at stern*) godille, *f.*; *v.n.* ramer; (*single oar at stern*) avancer à la godille; **~er,** (*approx.*) rameu|r, ~se, *m.f.*; (*with single oar at stern*) godilleur, *m.*

scullery, arrière-cuisine, *f.*; **~-maid,** laveuse de vaisselle, *f.*

scullion, marmiton, *m.*; (*maid*) souillon, *f.*

sculpt|or, *s.* sculpteur, *m.*; **~ress,** femme sculpteur, *f.*; **~ural,** sculptural; **~ure,** *s.* sculpture, *f.*; *v.a.* sculpter.

scum, *s.* (*lit. and fig.*) écume, *f.*; *v.a.* écumer.

scupper, *s.* (*naut.*) dalot, *m.*

scurf, (*dandruff*) pellicule, *f.*

scurril|ity, grossièreté, *f.*; **~ous,** grossièrement injurieu|x, ~se.

scurry, *v.n.* courir* à la †hâte.

scurvy, *s.* (*med.*) scorbut, *m.*

scurv|y, *adj.* (*low*) vil; **~ily,** d'une manière vile.

scutcheon, *see* ESCUTCHEON.

scuttle, *s.* (*coal*) seau à charbon, *m.*; *v.a.* (*ship*) saborder.

scuttle away, *v.n.* déguerpir.

scythe, *s.* faux, *f.*; *v.a.* faucher.

sea, (*lit. and fig.*) mer, *f.*; (*large number*) multitude, *f.*; *open ~,* large, *m.*; **~-anemone,** actinie, *f.*; **~-coal,** charbon de terre, *m.*; **~-chest,** coffre de bord, *m.*; **~-dog,** (*pers.*) loup de mer, *m.*; **~-fight,** combat naval, *m.*; **~-front,** esplanade, *f.*; **~-green,** vert de mer, *invar.*; **~-glider,** (*aeron.*) hydroglisseur, *m.*; **~-gull, -mew,** mouette, *f.*; **~-hog,** marsouin, *m.*; **~-legs,** pied marin, *m.*; **~-route,** voie de mer, *f.*; **~-rover,** écumeur de mer, *m.*; **~-swallow,** hirondelle de mer, *f.*; **~-urchin,** oursin, *m.*; **~ voyage,** voyage de mer, *m.*; **~-wall,** digue, *f.*; **~weed,** algue, *f.*; (*wrack*) goémon, *m.*; *be at ~,* être en mer; (*fig.*) s'y perdre; *be ~-sick,* avoir le mal de mer; *put to ~,* prendre* la mer. *For other compounds see below.*

seaboard, littoral, *m.*

seafar|er, homme de mer, *m.*; *adj.* **~ing,** (*pers.*) marin; (*things*) de marin.

seagoing, (*pers.*) qui va en mer; (*ship*) de †haute mer.

seakale, crambé, *m.*

seal, *s.* (*an.*) phoque, *m.*; (*impressed wax, &c., stamp for sealing, of secrecy, fig., official*) sceau, *m.*; (*private*) cachet, *m.*; *v.a.* (*deeds, &c.*) sceller; (*letters*) cacheter; (*ratify*) confirmer; (*decide absolutely*) décider; *~ up,* sceller.

sealing-wax, cire à cacheter, *f.*

sealskin, peau de phoque, *f.*

seam, *s.* (*clothes, naut.*) couture, *f.*; (*geol.*) couche, *f.*
seam, *v.a.* (*with fissure, scar*) couturer.
seaman, marin, *m.*; **~ship,** matelotage, *m.*; **~like,** de marin.
seamless, sans couture.
seamstress, couturière, *f.*
seaplane, hydravion, *m.*
seaport, port de mer.
sear, *adj.* (*leaves*) sec, sèche; **~ed** (*callous*) endurci; *v.a.* cautériser.
search, *s.* recherche, *f.*; (*customs*) visite, *f.*; **~-light,** projecteur, *m.*; **~-warrant,** mandat de perquisition, *m.*; *in ~ of,* à la recherche de.
search, *v.a.* chercher; (*overhaul*) fouiller; (*customs*) visiter; *v.n.* (*investigate*) fouiller; *~ for,* chercher.
searcher, chercheu|r, ~se, *m.f.*
searching, (*look*) pénétrant; (*rigorous*) rigoureu|x, ~se; **~ly,** d'un regard pénétrant.
sea-shore, plage, *f.*
seasickness, mal de mer, *m.*
sea-side, bord de la mer, *m.*
season, *s.* (*of year, special time*) saison, *f.*; *for a ~,* pendant quelque temps; *in ~,* de saison; **~-ticket,** abonnement, *m.*
season, *v.a.* (*food and fig.*) assaisonner; (*troops*) aguerrir; (*wood*) sécher.
seasonab|le, (*weather, frost, fish, &c.*) de saison; (*opportune*) à propos; **~ly,** à propos; **~leness,** à propos, *m.*
seasoning, *s.* assaisonnement, *m.*
seat, *s.* (*piece of furniture, of chairs, of government, &c., part of body*) siège, *m.*; (*spot sat on, of theatres, &c.*) place, *f.*; (*country house*) maison de campagne, *f.*; (*war*) théâtre, *m.*; *take one's ~,* prendre* sa place; *take your ~s!* (*rail., &c.*) en voiture!
seat, *v.a.* (*place on seat or anything solid*) asseoir*; (*chairs*) mettre* un fond à; *~ oneself,* s'asseoir*.
seater, *two-~,* (*veh., aeroplane, &c.*) voiture, *f.*, avion, *m.*, *&c.,* à deux (places); (*motor*) coupé, *m.*
seaward, vers la mer.
seaworth|iness, état de navigabilité, *m.*; **~y,** en état de naviguer.
secede, se séparer (de).
secession, sécession, *f.*
seclude *oneself,* s'éloigner (de); **~d,** *adj.* retiré.
seclusion, retraite, *f.*
second, *s.* (*time*) seconde, *f.*; (*duel*) témoin, *m.*; (*pers. next after first*) second, -e, *m.f.*
second, *adj.* second; (*dates, sovereigns, chapter*) deux; (*series, floor, compound numbers*) deuxième; (*another*) autre; (*cousin*) issu de germain; (*inferior*) inférieur; *~-best, adj.* (*hats, &c.*) numéro deux, *invar.*; *~-rate, see* RATE; *travel ~,* voyager en seconde; **~ly,** deuxièmement.
second, *v.a.* (*support*) appuyer; (*mil.*) mettre* en disponibilité; **~er,** (*motion*) celui qui appuie, *m.*
secondar|y, secondaire, *~y school, see* SCHOOL; **~ily,** secondairement.
secrecy, secret, *m.*; (*discretion*) discrétion, *f.*
secret, *s.* secret, *m.*; *in ~,* en secret; *adj.* secr|et, ~ète; (*place*) retiré; **~ly,** secrètement.
secretary, secrétaire, *m.f.*; **~-bird,** secrétaire, *m.*, tisserin, *m.*; **~ship,** secrétariat, *m.*
secre|te, cacher; **~tion,** (*stolen goods*) recel, *m.*
sect, secte, *f.*; **~arian,** *adj. and s.m.f.* sectaire.
section, (*division, part cut off, mil., geom.*) section, *f.*; (*drawing*) profil, *m.*; **~al,** de section.
secular, *adj.* **1** (*op. to spiritual*) temporel, -le; **2** (*clergy, arm, jurisdiction*) séculi|er, ~ère; (*of time*) séculaire, *which is never used of* **1** *or* **2**.
seculariz|ation, sécularisation, *f.*; **~e,** séculariser.
secure, *adj.* (*safe*) en sûreté; (*reliable*) sûr; (*comm.*) garanti; *~ against, from,* à l'abri de; **~ness,** sécurité, *f.*; **~ly,** en sûreté; (*without danger*) sans danger; (*safely*) sûrement.
secure, *v.a.* mettre* en sûreté; (*seize*) s'emparer de; (*obtain*) obtenir*; (*debt, &c.*) garantir; (*fix*) fixer; (*door*) fermer solidement.
security, (*for payment*) garantie, *f.*; (*pers.*) caution, *f.*; (*state free from danger, thing deposited as pledge*) sûreté, *f.*; (*certificate of stock*) valeurs, *f.pl.*; ⚠ sécurité = '*confidence*', '*peace of mind*'.
sedate, rassis; **~ness,** calme, *m.*; **~ly,** posément.
sedative, *adj. and s.m.* sédatif.
sedentary, sédentaire.
sedge, (*bot.*) laiche, *f.*; **~-warbler,** phragmite, *m.*
sediment, sédiment, *m.*
sedit|ion, sédition, *f.*; **~ious,** séditieu|x, ~se; **~iously,** séditieusement.
seduce, séduire*; **~r,** séduct|eur, ~rice, *m.f.*
seduct|ion, séduction, *f.*; **~ive,** séduisant; (*pej.*) séduct|eur, ~rice.
sedulous, assidu; **~ly,** assidûment.
see, *s.* évêché, *m.*
see, *v.a.* (*lit., fig., regard, understand, interview, visit*) voir*; (*make sure*) s'assurer; (*accompany*) accompagner; *~ double,* voir* double; *~ which way the wind blows,* regarder d'où souffle le vent; *~* **out,** voir jusqu'à la fin; *~* **over,** (*building, &c.*) visiter; *~* **through,** (*plans, intrigues*) pénétrer; (*undertaking*) mener à bonne fin; (*glass, &c.*) voir* à travers; *~* **to,** veiller à; *v.n.* voir*; *~ that,* (*order*) veiller à ce que; *let me, us ~,* voyons!
seed, (*lit. and fig.*) semence, *f.*; (*vegetables, &c.*) graine, *f.*; *~-time,* semailles, *f.pl.*;

go to ~, monter (être) en graine; *v.n.* monter (être) en graine.
seedling, *s.* semis, *m.*; (*tree*) sauvageon, *m.*
seedsman, grainetier, *m.*
seedy, plein de graines; (*clothes*) râpé; (*colloq. ill*) vaseu|x, ~se.
seeing that, *conj.* vu que.
seek, *v.a.* chercher; ~ *the life of,* en vouloir* à la vie de; ~ *after, for,* rechercher; ~ *out,* chercher; *v.n.* chercher (à); **~er,** chercheu|r, ~se, *m.f.*
seem, sembler + *inf.* (*often* + être + *noun*); (*pej.*) faire* semblant de.
seemingly, en apparence.
seeml|iness, bienséance, *f.*; **~y,** séant.
seer, prophète, *m.*
see-saw, *s.* bascule, *f.*; *adj.* de bascule.
seethe, *v.n.* bouillonner.
segment, (*geom.*) segment, *m.*; (*part*) portion, *f.*
segregat|e, séparer; **~ion,** ségrégation, *f.*
seismic, sismique.
seiz|e, *v.a.* saisir; (*overtake*) prendre*; **~ure,** prise, *f.*; (*med.*) apoplexie, *f.*
seldom, rarement.
select, *adj.* choisi.
select, *v.a.* choisir; **~ion,** choix, *m.*
self, *s.* moi, *m.*; (*concentration on self*) égoïsme, *m.*; *~-abasement,* humiliation volontaire, *f.*; *~-assertion,* suffisance, *f.*; *~-assertive,* suffisant; *~-assurance,* suffisance, *f.*; *~-confidence,* confiance en soi, *f.*; *~-confident,* sûr de soi; *~-conscious,* gêné; *~-consciousness,* gêne, *f.*; *~-coloured,* de teinte naturelle; *~-conceit,* suffisance, *f.*; *~-control,* maîtrise de soi-même†; *~-deceit,* illusion, *f.*; *~-defence,* défense légitime, *f.*; *~-denial,* abnégation, *f.*; *~-esteem,* estime de soi-même, *f.*; *~-evident,* évident de soi; *~-governing,* autonome; *~-interest,* intérêt personnel, *m.*; *~-made,* (*man*), fils de ses œuvres; *~-opinionated,* entêté; *~-possession,* sang-froid, *m.*; *~-preservation,* conservation de soi-même, *f.*; *~-propelling,* automobile; *~-regulating,* à réglage automatique; *~-sacrifice,* sacrifice de soi-même, *m.*; *~-satisfied,* content de soi; *~-seeking,* égoïste; *~-styled,* soi-disant; *~-sufficiency,* suffisance, *f.*; *~-taught,* autodidacte; *~-will,* obstination, *f.*; *~-willed,* obstiné.
selfish, égoïste; **~ness,** égoïsme, *m.*; **~ly,** par égoïsme.
selfsame, exactement (le, la, etc.) même.
sell, *v.a.* (*lit. and fig.*) vendre; *to be sold,* (*for sale*) à vendre; ~ *at, for,* vendre (*'at', 'for' not expressed*); ~ *off,* liquider; ~ *out,* (*stocks, &c.*) revendre; ~ *up,* (*pers.*) vendre; *v.n.* se vendre; **~er,** vendeu|r, ~se, *m.f.*
selvage, lisière, *f.*
semaphore, sémaphore, *m.*
semblance, (*outward appearance*) semblant, *m.*
semi-, demi-; (*scientific terms*) semi-.
semibreve, (*mus.*) ronde, *f.*
semi-circ|le, demi-cercle, *m.*; **~ular,** semi-circulaire.
semicolon, point et virgule, *m.*
seminar|ist, séminariste, *m.*; **~y,** (*clerical*) séminaire, *m.*
semiquaver, (*mus.*) double croche, *f.*
semit|e, sémite, *m.f.*; **~ic,** sémitique.
semitone, (*mus.*) demi-ton, *m.*
semolina, semoule, *f.*
sempiternal, sempiternel, -le.
senat|e, sénat, *m. also* = *'senate-house'*; **~or,** sénateur, *m.*; **~orial,** sénatorial.
send, *v.a.n.* envoyer; (*money*) remettre*; ~ *away, back,* renvoyer; ~ *for,* envoyer chercher; ~ *forth,* (*odour*) exhaler; ~ *on,* (*goods, &c.*) faire* suivre; ~ *off,* (*dispatch*) expédier; ~ *out,* (*comm.*) lancer; **~er,** (*comm.*) expédit|eur, ~rice, *m.f.*; **~ing,** *s.* envoi, *m.*
send-off, *s.* adieux, *m.pl.*
seneschal, sénéchal, *m.*
senil|e, sénile; **~ity,** sénilité, *f.*
senior, *s.* (*in age*) aîné, *m.*; (*rank, &c.*) supérieur, *m.*; **~ity,** ancienneté, *f.*; *adj.* aîné; (*rank, position*) supérieur; ~ *partner, see* PARTNER.
senna, séné, *m.*
sensation, (*feeling, excitement*) sensation, *f.*; **~al,** sensationnel, -le.
sense, *s.* (*of sight, &c., meaning, faculty, ability to perceive, appreciation of*) sens, *m.*; (*feeling*) sentiment, *m.*; (*intelligence*) esprit, *m.*; (*prevailing sentiment*) opinion, *f.*; (*judgement*) bon sens, *m.*; ~ *of humour, see* HUMOUR; *common* ~, sens commun, *m.*; *be in one's ~s,* être dans son bon sens; *v.a.* avoir vaguement conscience de.
senseless, (*foolish*) insensé; (*unconscious*) sans connaissance; **~ness,** absurdité, *f.*; **~ly,** d'une manière insensée.
sensib|le, (*wise*) sensé; (*reasonable*) raisonnable; (*to the senses, appreciable*) sensible; ⚠ sensible *never has the meaning of 'wise', 'reasonable'*; **~leness,** bon sens, *m.*; **~ly,** sensément; **~ility,** sensibilité, *f.*
sensitive, sensible; *very rarely* sensiti|f, ~ve; ~ *plant, see* PLANT; ~ *to,* sensible à; **~ness,** sensibilité, *f.*
sensual, sensuel, -le; **~ity,** sensualité, *f.*; **~ly,** sensuellement.
sentence, (*of judge*) jugement, *m.*; (*maxim*) sentence, *f.*; (*gram.*) phrase, *f.*; *v.a.* condamner; *serve one's* ~, purger sa peine.
sententious, sentencieu|x, ~se; **~ly,** sentencieusement.
sentient, sensible.
sentiment, (*feeling, opinion*) sentiment, *m.*; (*pej.*) sensiblerie, *f.*; **~al,** sentimental; **~alist,** personne sentimentale, *f.*; **~ally,** d'une manière sentimentale; **~ality,** (*pej.*) sensiblerie, *f.*
sentry, *also* **sentinel,** sentinelle, *f.*; **~-box,** guérite, *f.*; *be on ~-go,* être de faction.
separable, séparable.
separate, *adj.* séparé; (*distinct*) à part;

~**ness**, séparation, *f.*; ~**ly**, séparément; *v.a.* (*lit. and fig.*) séparer (de); *v.n.* se séparer (de).
separation, séparation, *f.*
sepia, sépia, *f.*
sepoy, cipaye, *m.*
September, septembre, *m.*; (*abbrev.*) 7bre.
septic, septique.
septuagenarian, septuagénaire.
Septuagesima, septuagésime, *f.*
Septuagint, Version des Septante, *f.*
sepulchr|e, sépulcre, *m.*; ~**al**, sépulcral.
sepulture, sépulture, *f.*
sequel, suite, *f.*
sequence, suite, *f.*; (*cards*) séquence, *f.*
sequester, (*confiscate and law*) séquestrer; ~**ed**, *adj.* (*secluded*) écarté; ⚠ séquestré = '*shut up illegally*', '*isolated*' *and never means* '*secluded*'.
sequestration, (*property*) séquestration, *f.*; (*seclusion*) retraite, *f.*
sequin, sequin, *m.*
seraglio, sérail, *m.*
seraph, séraphin, *m.*; ~**ic**, séraphique.
Serb, Serbian, *adj.* (*when an adj. use small letter*) *and s.m.f.* Serbe.
serenade, sérénade, *f.*
seren|e, *adj.* (*sky, calm, unperturbed*) serein; (*title*) sérénissime; ~**ity**, sérénité, *f.*; ~**ely**, avec sérénité.
serf, serf, *m.*; ~**dom**, servage, *m.*
serge, serge, *f.*
serg(j)eant, (*infantry*) sergent, *m.*; ~*-at-arms*, sergent d'armes, *m.*; ~*-major*, sergent-major, *m.*
serial, (*story*) feuilleton, *m.*
series, (*number, sequence, succession, set, math., electr., geol., chem.*) série, *f.*
seringa, syringa, (*bot.*) seringa, *m.*
serious, (*solemn, grave, important, sincere*) sérieu|x, ~se; ~**ness**, sérieux, *m.*; ~**ly**, sérieusement.
sermon, (*lit. and fig.*) sermon, *m.*; (*Prot.*) prêche, *m.*; ~**ize**, *v.a.* sermonner.
serpent, serpent, *m.*; *young* ~, serpenteau, *m.*; ~*-eater*, (*ornith.*) serpentaire, *m.*; ~*'s tongue*, (*bot.*) ophioglosse, *f.*
serpentine, *s.* (*stone*) serpentine, *f.*; *adj.* de serpent; (*fig.*) tortueu|x, ~se.
serried, serré.
serum, sérum, *m.*
servant, serv|iteur, ~ante, *m.f.*; (*domestic*) domestique, *m.f.*; (*of a company or the State*) employé, *m.*; ~*'s hall*, office, *f.*
serve, (*be servant to, useful to, mil., tradesmen, table, gun, tennis*) servir*; (*treat*) traiter; (*parish, priest*) desservir*; (*apprenticeship*) faire*; (*trick*) jouer; ~ *out*, distribuer; (*punish*) punir; ~ *up*, (*dishes*) servir*; *v.n.* (*mil., nav., shop, to be useful*) servir*; (*suffice*) faire* l'affaire; (*be favourable*) être favorable; (*opportunity*) se présenter; ~ *as, for*, servir de.
server, (*tennis*) celui, celle, qui sert, *m.f.*; *time-*~, complaisant, -e, *m.f.*
service, (*of servant, aid, help, mil., nav., official, trams, &c., set of cups, &c.*) service, *m.*; (*divine*) office, *m.*; (*Prot.*) prêche, *m.*; (*usefulness*) utilité, *f.*; *at your* ~, à votre service; *in* ~, (*domestic*) en service; *at the* ~ *of*, au service de; *do good* ~ *to*, faire bon service à.
serviceable, (*things*) utile; (*pers.*) serviable; (*lasting*) durable; ~**ness**, utilité, *f.*
servil|e, (*cringing, dependent*) servile; (*enslaved*) asservi; ~**ity**, servilité, *f.*; ~**ely**, servilement.
serving-man, domestique, *m.*
servitor, serviteur, *m.*
servitude, servitude, *f.*; *penal* ~, travaux forcés, *m.pl.*
sesame, (*bot.*) sésame, *m.*
session, (*of an assembly*) séance, *f.*
set, *s.* **1** (*collection*) assortiment, *m.*; **2** (*buttons, &c.*) garniture, *f.*; **3** (*plate, china*) service, *m.*; **4** (*diamonds, &c., undergarments*) parure, *f.*; **5** (*teeth*) denture, *f.*; **6** (*false teeth*) dentier, *m.*; **7** (*posture*) port, *m.*; **8** (*clothes*) façon de tomber, *f.*; **9** (*pers.*) groupe, *m.*; (*pej.*) tas, *m.*; **10** (*series*) série, *f.*; ~*-back*, (*comm., &c.*) recul, *m.*; (*illness*) rechute, *f.*; ~*-down*, semonce, *f.*; ~*-off*, compensation, *f.*; ~*-out*, (*display*) étalage, *m.*; ~*-to*, rixe, *f.*
set, *adj.* (*price, fixed*) fixe; (*firm*) résolu; (*prescribed*) prescrit.
set, *v.a.* **1** (*put, mus., price to*) mettre*; **2** (*put precisely*) placer; **3** (*limb*) remettre*; **4** (*fashion, example*) donner; **5** (*plants*) planter; **6** (*jewels*) monter; **7** (*watch, &c.*) régler; **8** (*teeth*) serrer; **9** (*trap*) tendre; **10** (*razor, &c.*) affiler; **11** (*fix*) fixer; **12** (*seal, signature*) apposer; ~ *oneself to*, se mettre* à; ~ *apart, aside, by*, mettre* de côté; ~ *back*, retarder; (*move back, postpone*) reculer; ~ *down*, déposer; (*in writing*) coucher par écrit; ~ *forth*, (*explain*) exposer; ~ *off*, (*show off*) relever; ~ *on*, (*urge*) pousser (à); ~ *out*, (*display*) étaler; ~ *up*, (*erect*) dresser; (*establish, lit. and fig.*) établir; ~ *with*, (*jewels*) incruster de; ~ *fair*, *see* FAIR.
set, *v.n.* (*sun, moon, &c.*) se coucher; (*fig.*) décliner; (*fruit*) se nouer; (*congeal*) se figer; (*clothes*) tomber (être); (*be directed of wind, &c.*) porter; ~ *about*, se mettre* à; ~ *in*, (*begin*) commencer; (*tide*) monter (être); ~ *off, out*, partir* (être); ~ *up*, s'établir; ~ *up for*, se donner pour.
settee, causeuse, *f.*
setter, (*dog*) chien couchant, *m.*
setting, *s.* mise en place, *f.*; (*sun, &c.*) coucher, *m.*; (*jewels*) montage, *m.*; (*sharpening*) affilage, *m.*; (*bones*) remboîtement, *m.*; ~*-off*, départ, *m.*; ~*-up*, (*type*) composition, *f.*
settle, *s.* banc à †haut dossier, *m.*
settle, *v.a.* (*fix*) fixer; (*matter, dispute*) arranger; (*accounts*) régler; (*annuity, &c., on*) constituer à; (*pay*) payer; (*question*)

résoudre*; (*calm*) calmer; (*marry, establish*) établir; (*colonize*) coloniser.
settle, *v.n.* (*residence*) s'établir; (*bird, &c.*) se poser (sur); (*decide*) se décider à; (*liquids*) se rasseoir*; (*weather*) se mettre* au beau fixe; (*subside*) se tasser; ~ *down,* (*marry*) s'établir; (*reform*) se ranger; ~ *on,* se décider pour; ~ *to,* (*task, &c.*) s'appliquer à; ~ *up,* régler compte; **~d,** *adj.* arrangé.
settlement, (*colony*) colonie, *f.*; (*jointure*) douaire, *m.*; (*subsidence*) tassement, *m.*; (*accounts*) règlement, *m.*; (*of a difference*) arrangement, *m.*; (*liquids*) dépôt, *m.*
settler, colon, *m.*
seven, *adj. and s.m.* sept; **~th,** septième; (*dates, chapters, sovereigns*) sept; **~thly,** septièmement.
sevenfold, septuple.
seventeen, dix-sept; **~th,** dix-septième; (*dates, chapters, sovereigns*) dix-sept.
sevent|y, soixante-dix; **~ieth,** soixante-dixième.
sever, *v.a.* séparer (de); *v.n.* se séparer; **~ance,** séparation, *f.*
several, *adj.* (*not many*) plusieurs; (*distinct*) différent; *pron.* plusieurs; **~ly,** séparément.
sever|e, (*unsparing, style*) sévère; ⚠ sévère *is not used of attacks of illness which* = violent; (*winter, &c.*) rigoureu|x, ~se; **~ely,** sévèrement; (*wounded*) grièvement; **~ity,** sévérité, *f.*; (*weather*) rigueur, *f.*
sew|age, eaux d'égouts, *f.pl.*; **~er,** (*drain*) égout, *m.*
sew, coudre*; ~ *on,* coudre*; ~er, (*pers.*) couseuse, *f.*; **~ing,** *s.* couture, *f.*; *~ing-machine,* machine couseuse, *f.*
sex, sexe, *m.*
sexagenarian, *adj. and s.m.f.* sexagénaire.
Sexagesima, Sexagésime, *f.*
sextant, (*naut.*) sextant, *m.*
sexton, sacristain, *m.*
sexual, sexuel, -le; **~ity,** sexualité, *f.*
shabb|y, (*clothes*) usé; (*pers.*) minable; (*low*) vilain; **~iness,** (*meanness*) mesquinerie, *f.*; (*clothes*) pauvreté, *f.*; **~ily,** (*meanly*) mesquinement; (*dressed*) pauvrement.
shackle(s), fers, *m.pl.*; (*fig.*) entraves, *f.pl.*; *v.a.* (*fig.*) entraver.
shad, (*ichth.*) alose, *f.*
shad|e, *s.* (*lit., fig. of departed*) ombre, *f.*; (*of trees*) ombrage, *m.*; (*darkness*) ombres, *f.pl.*; (*of colours*) nuance, *f.*; (*lamp*) abat-jour, *m. invar.*; **~y,** (*out of the sun*) ombragé; (*not quite honest*) véreu|x, ~se; *v.a.* ombrager; (*protect*) abriter; (*painting, drawing*) ombrer; *v.n.* *~e off into,* se fondre dans.
shaded, (*out of the sun*) ombragé; (*full of shade*) ombreu|x, ~se; ⚠ ombrageux = '*suspicious*', (*of horses*) '*shy*'.
shading, *s.* (*drawing*) ombres, *f.pl.*
shadow, (*lit. and fig., ghost, particle*) ombre, *f.*; (*death, night*) ombres, *f.pl.*; *v.a.* (*police, &c.*) filer; ~ *forth,* représenter; **~y,** (*unreal*) chimérique.
shaft, (*lance*) bois, *m.*; (*ray, arrow, satire*) trait, *m.*; (*of column*) fût, *m.*; (*cart*) brancard, *m.*; (*mine*) puits, *m.*; *ventilating ~,* puits d'aérage, *m.*
shaggy, (*hairy*) poilu; (*ruffled*) ébouriffé.
shagreen, chagrin, *m.*
shah, schah, *m.*
shak|e, *s.* secousse, *f.*; (*hand*) poignée, *f.*; **~y,** (*head*) branlant; (*hand*) tremblant; (*in health*) cassé; (*weak*) faible; **~ily,** en tremblant.
shake, *v.a.* (*agitate*) secouer; (*make to totter and fig.*) ébranler; (*hands*) serrer; (*head*) secouer; (*upset, fig.*) bouleverser; ~ *down, off, out, up,* secouer; ~ *off,* (*get rid of*) se débarrasser de; *v.n.* s'ébranler; (*with fear, cold, &c.*) trembler (de).
shako, shako, *m.*
shale, schiste, *m.*
shall, *generally expressed by fut.*; (*command*) vouloir* que + *subj.*; (*future duty*) devoir.
shallop, (*naut.*) chaloupe, *f.*
shallot, échalote, *f.*
shallow, *s.* bas-fond, *m.*; *pl.* bas-fonds; *adj.* peu profond; (*superficial*) superficiel, -le; **~ness,** manque de profondeur, *m.*
sham, *s.* (*pers.*) imposteur, *m.*; (*thing*) faux, *m.*; (*colloq.*) toc, *m.*; *adj.* fau|x, ~sse; ~ *fight,* simulacre de combat, *m.*; *v.a.* (*pretend*) simuler; *v.n.* jouer la comédie.
shambles, abattoir, *m.*
shambling, lourd; (*gait*) traînant.
shame, †honte, *f.*; *for ~!* fi donc; *cry ~ on,* crier †haro sur; *v.a.* faire* †honte à; **~faced,** timide; **~facedness,** timidité, *f.*; **~facedly,** avec †honte; **~ful,** †honteu|x, ~se; **~fully,** †honteusement; **~less,** éhonté; **~lessness,** impudence, *f.*; **~lessly,** sans †honte.
shampoo, *s.* shampooing, *m.*
shamrock, trèfle, *m.*
shank, *s.* jambe, *f.*; (*horse*) canon, *m.*; (*pillar*) fût, *m.*
shanty, baraque, *f.*
shape, *s.* forme, *f.*; (*pers.*) tournure, *f.*; *in the ~ of,* en forme de; *v.a.* former; (*course, &c.*) diriger; *v.n.* (*give hopes*) promettre*; **~less,** sans forme; **~ly,** bien tourné; **~liness,** beauté de forme, *f.*
shard, tesson, *m.*
share, *s.* (*plough*) soc, *m.*
share, (*part, portion*) part, *f.*; (*in joint-stock co.*) action, *f.*; *fair ~,* bonne part, *f.*; *have a ~ in,* contribuer à; *go ~s in,* partager; *give a ~ in profits,* intéresser *acc.*+*pers. and* à+*thing*; *v.a.n.* partager.
shareholder, actionnaire, *m.f.*
shark, *s.* (*ichth. and fig.*) requin, *m.*
sharp, *s.* (*mus.*) dièse, *m.*; (*U.S.A. cheat*) filou, *m.*
sharp, *adj.* **1** (*with keen edge*) tranchant;

2 (*pointed*) aigu; 3 (*outline*) net, -te; 4 (*sound*) aigre; 5 (*wind, cold*) piquant; 6 (*cunning*) rusé; 7 (*children*) éveillé; 8 (*sight, hearing*) perçant; 9 (*pain*) violent; 10 (*words, &c.*) acerbe; 11 (*vigilant*) vigilant; **~ness**, *see below*; **~ly**, (*severely*) vertement; (*abruptly*) brusquement.
sharp, *adv.* (*all of a sudden*) net; *10.0 ~*, 10 heures précises; *interj.* vite!
sharpen, (*edge, appetite*) aiguiser; (*pencil*) tailler.
sharper, escroc, *m.*
sharpness, (*mind, feeling*) vivacité, *f.*; (*acuteness*) finesse, *f.*; (*grief*) violence, *f.*; (*bitterness, lit. and fig.*) amertume, *f.*; (*cold, &c.*) rigueur, *f.*; (*taste*) acidité, *f.*
sharpshooter, tirailleur, *m.*
shatter, *v.a.* fracasser; (*health*) déranger.
shave, *v.a.* (*lit. and fig.*) raser; *v.n.* se raser; **~r**, *s.* raseur, *m.*; (*youngster*) blanc-bec, *m.*
shaveling, tondu, *m.*
shaving, *s.* action de raser, de se raser, *f.*; (*wood*) copeau, *m.*; **~-brush**, blaireau, *m.*; **~-dish**, plat à barbe, *m.*; **~-soap**, savon à barbe, *m.*
shawl, châle, *m.*
she, *s.* femme, *f.*
she, *pron.* (*subj. + verb and alone*) elle; *~ who*, celle qui; *~ is*, (*defining, explaining*) c'est.
sheaf, (*corn*) gerbe, *f.*; (*papers*) liasse, *f.*; (*arrows*) faisceau, *m.*
shear, (*lit. and fig.*) tondre; **~er**, tondeu|r, ~se, *m.f.*; *~ing-time*, tondaison, *f.*
shears, cisailles, *f.pl.*
sheath, étui, *m.*; (*sword*) fourreau, *m.*
sheathe, *v.a.* (*sword*) rengainer.
sheave, *v.a.* (*corn*) mettre* en gerbes.
shed, *s.* †hangar, *m.*; (*for tools, &c.*) remise, *f.*
shed, *v.a.* (*tears, blood*) verser; (*trees*) laisser tomber; (*light, &c.*) répandre.
sheen, splendeur, *f.*
sheep, mouton, *m.*; (*fig. and theol.*) brebis, *f.*; **~-dog**, chien de berger, *m.*; **~fold**, bergerie, *f.*; **~-shearing**, tondaison, *f.*; **~skin**, peau de mouton, *f.*; **~ish**, penaud; **~ishly**, d'un air penaud.
sheer, *adj.* (*absolute*) pur; (*perpendicular*) à pic; *adv.* à pic; (*outright*) tout net.
sheer, *v.n.* (*naut.*) faire* des embardées; *~ off*, (*fig.*) prendre* le large.
sheet, *s.* (*bed*) drap, *m.*; (*paper, metal, &c., newspaper*) feuille, *f.*; (*water*) nappe, *f.*; (*naut.*) écoute, *f.*; *be 3 ~s in the wind*, (*fam.*) avoir du vent dans les voiles; *~-anchor*, (*naut.*) ancre de veille, *f.*; (*fig.*) ancre de salut, *f.*; *~ iron*, tôle, *f.*; *winding-~*, linceul, *m.*; *be white as a ~*, avoir du sang de navet.
sheeting, toile pour draps de lit, *f.*
sheik, cheik, *m.*
shekel, sicle, *m.*
sheldrake, (*ornith.*) tadorne, *m.*
shelf, (*slab of stone or board*) rayon, *m.*; (*reef*) écueil, *m.*; (*ledge*) rebord, *m.*
shell, *s.* (*peas, &c.*) cosse, *f.*; (*shellfish and sword*) coquille, *f.*; (*tortoise and crust.*) carapace, *f.*; (*eggs, nuts, ship*) coque, *f.*; (*oysters*) écaille, *f.*; (*walls of house*) carcasse, *f.*; (*explosive*) obus, *m.*; *~proof*, à l'épreuve des obus; *v.a.* (*peas*) écosser; (*nuts*) écaler; (*bombard*) bombarder.
shellac, laque, *f.*
shelter, *s.* abri, *m.*; *take ~*, s'abriter; *v.a.* abriter (de); *v.n.* se mettre* à l'abri (de); *~ed from*, à l'abri de.
shelterless, sans abri.
shelve, *v.a.* (*defer*) remettre*; *v.n.* être en pente.
shepherd, **~ess**, berg|er, ~ère, *m.f.*; (*fig. and theol.*) pasteur, *m.*
sherbet, sorbet, *m.*
sheriff, shérif, *m.*; *~'s officer*, huissier, *m.*
sherry, xérès, *m.*
shew, *see* SHOW.
shibboleth, schibboleth, *m.*
shield, bouclier, *m.*; (*ant. and her.*) écu, *m.*; (*aegis*) égide, *f.*; *v.a.* protéger (de); (*from censure, &c.*) couvrir*.
shift, *s.* changement, *m.*; (*device*) moyen, *m.*; (*workmen*) équipe, *f.*; (*chemise*) chemise, *f.*; *make ~ to*, s'arranger pour; *v.a.* (*move*) déplacer; (*change*) changer; (*one thing for another*) changer de; *v.n.* changer de place; *~ for oneself*, se débrouiller.
shift|less, peu débrouillard; **~y**, rusé.
shilly-shally, *s.* barguignage, *m.*; *v.n.* barguigner.
shimmer, *v.n.* luire*.
shin, *~-bone*, tibia, *m.*
shindy, boucan, *m.*
shin|e, *s.* éclat, *m.*; (*newness*) brillant, *m.*; *v.a.* (*boots, &c.*) faire* reluire; *v.n.* (*lit. and pers.*) briller; (*beam*) rayonner (de); *the sun is ~ing*, il fait du soleil.
shingle, (*pebble*) galet, *m.*; (*board*) bardeau, *m.*; *~s*, (*med.*) zona, *m.*
shining, **shiny**, brillant; (*cloth*) râpé.
ship, *s.* navire, *m.*; (*large*) vaisseau, *m.*; *~'s broker*, courtier maritime, *m.*; *~-builder*, constructeur de navires, *m.*; *~owner*, armateur, *m.*; *for other compounds see below.*
ship, *v.a.* (*passengers, goods, heavy seas*) embarquer; (*helm*) monter; (*oars*) armer; (*comm.*) expédier.
shipload, cargaison, *f.*
shipment, chargement, *m.*
shipping, *s.* (*act*) chargement, *m.*; (*ships*) navires, *m.pl.*; (*merchant*) marine marchande, *f.*; *~-agent*, agent maritime, *m.*; *~ company*, agence maritime, *f.*; *~ office*, agence maritime, *f.*
shipshape, en bon ordre.
shipwreck, naufrage, *m.*; *v.a. be ~ed*, faire* naufrage; **~ed**, *adj.* naufragé.
shipyard, chantier de construction navale, *m.*
shire, comté, *m.*
shirk, *v.a.* se dérober à; *v.n.* se dérober; **~er**, embusqué, *m.*

shirt, (*man*) chemise, *f.*; ~*-front*, plastron, *m.*; *be in one's ~-sleeves*, être en bras de chemise.
shiver, *s.* (*fragment*) éclat, *m.*; (*trembling*) frisson, *m.*; **~ing,** *s.* frissonnement, *m.*; **~y,** frissonnant; *v.a.* (*shatter*) fracasser; *v.n.* frissonner; (*cold*) grelotter.
shoal, *s.* (*fish*) banc, *m.*; (*naut.*) †haut-fond, *m.*, (*pl.*) †hauts-fonds; (*crowd*) foule, *f.*
shock, *s.* (*collision, earthquake, electric*) choc, *m.*; (*sudden, painful impression*) coup, *m.*; (*of hair*) tignasse, *f.*; ~*-troops*, troupes de choc, *f.pl.*
shock, *v.a.* choquer; (*terrify*) frapper d'horreur.
shocking, (*terrible*) affreux, ~se; (*offensive, disgusting*) choquant; **~ly,** horriblement.
shoddy, *s.* pacotille, *f.*; *adj.* de pacotille.
shoe, soulier, *m.*; (*horse*) fer, *m.*; (*wooden*) sabot, *m.*; *supply with ~s*, chausser; *v.a.* (*horse*) ferrer; **~black,** décrotteur, *m.*; **~-horn,** chausse-pied, *m.*; *pl.* chausse-pieds; **~-lace,** lacet, *m.*; **~maker,** cordonnier, *m.*
shoot, *s.* (*plant*) rejeton, *m.*; (*stream*) rapide, *m.*; (*party*) partie de chasse, *f.*
shoot, *v.a.* (*firearms, arrow, game*) tirer; (*pers.*) fusiller; (*hit*) atteindre*; (*put forth buds, &c.*) pousser; (*rays*) darder; (*discharge rubbish, &c.*) décharger; ~ *off*, (*of a limb*) emporter; *v.n.* tirer; (*buds, &c.*) pousser; (*of pain*) élancer; (*stars*) filer; (*pass quickly*) s'élancer; (*cricket-ball*) raser la terre; (*game*) chasser; ~ *across*, s'élancer à travers; (*mind*) traverser; ~ *ahead of*, devancer; ~ *at*, tirer sur; ~ *up*, jaillir; ~ *straight*, tirer juste.
shooting, *s.* (*firearms*) tir, *m.*; (*fusillade*) fusillade, *f.*; (*game*) chasse, *f.*; **~-box,** rendez-vous de chasse, *m.*; **~-gallery,** tir, *m.*
shooting, *adj.* (*pain*) lancinant; (*star*) filant.
shop, *s.* boutique, *f.*; (*large*) magasin, *m.*; ~*-assistant*, commis, *m.*; (*girl*) demoiselle de magasin; ~*-boy*, garçon de boutique, *m.*; ~*-lifting*, vol à l'étalage, *m.*; ~*-soiled*, défraîchi; *v.n.* faire des emplettes, *see also below*.
shopkeeper, marchand, -e, *m.f.*; (*small*) commerçant, -e, *m.f.*
shopman, commis de magasin, *m.*
shore, *s.* (*sea*) rivage, *m.*; (*river, lake*) rive, *f.*; (*prop*) étai, *m.*
short, *s.* (*gramm.*) brève, *f.*
short, *adj.* court; (*pers.*) petit; (*brief and vowel*) bref, brève; (*insufficient*) insuffisant; (*lacking*) de manque; (*credit, loan, &c.*) à court terme; (*abrupt*) brusque; ~ *circuit*, *see* CIRCUIT; ~ *commons*, maigre chère, *f.*; ~ *cut*, *see* CUT; ~*-lived*, de courte vie; (*fig.*) de courte durée; *in* ~, bref; *be* ~ *of*, être à court de; **~ness,** *see below*; **~ly,** *in a ~ time*, sous peu; (*briefly*) brièvement; *adv.* (*cut, stop, &c.*) court; ~ *of*, à part; *fall ~ of*, ne pas répondre à.
shortage, manque, *m.*
shortcoming, (*fig.*) faute, *f.*
shorten, *v.a.n.* raccourcir; (*abridge*) abréger.
shorthand, sténographie, *f.*; ~*-typist*, sténodactylographe, *m.f.*; ~*-writer*, sténographe, *m.f.*; *take down in* ~, sténographier.
shortness, (*stature*) petitesse, *f.*; (*brevity*) brièveté, *f.*; (*lack*) manque, *m.*; (*food, &c.*) peu, *m.*
shot, (*firearms*) coup, *m.*; (*of a bow*) trait, *m.*; (*bullet*) balle, *f.*; (*cannon-ball*) boulet, *m.*; (*sporting-guns*) plombs, *m.pl.*; (*reach*) portée, *f.*
shot, *adj.* ~ *silk*, taffetas changeant, *m.*
should, *generally expressed by subjunctive or conditional; with sense of moral obligation = 'ought', conditional of* devoir.
shoulder, *s.* (*lit. and mutton, &c.*) épaule, *f.*; **~-belt,** baudrier, *m.*; **~-knot,** aiguillette, *f.*; ~ *to* ~, coude à coude; *slung over the* ~, en bandoulière; *v.a.* charger sur les épaules; (*push*) pousser de l'épaule; ~ *arms!* portez armes!; *put one's ~ to the wheel*, pousser à la roue.
shout, *s.* cri, *m.*; (*applause*) acclamation, *f.*; *v.a.n.* crier; **~ing,** *s.* acclamation, *f.*
shove, *s.* poussée, *f.*; *v.a.n.* pousser; (*jostle*) bousculer; ~ *back*, repousser.
shovel, pelle, *f.*; *v.a.* remuer, jeter à la pelle; **~ful,** pelletée, *f.*
show, *s.* (*outward appearance*) semblant, *m.*; (*spectacle*) spectacle, *m.*; (*display*) parade, *f.*; (*cattle, flowers, &c.*) exposition, *f.*; *side-~*, spectacle secondaire, *m.*
show, *v.a.* montrer; (*prove*) prouver; (*manifest*) manifester; (*exhibit*) exposer; (*explain*) expliquer; ~ *forth*, exposer; ~ *in*, faire* entrer; ~ *off*, (*display*) étaler; (*to advantage*) faire* ressortir; ~ *out*, (*to the door*) reconduire*; ~ *up*, (*expose*) démasquer; (*guest to room*) faire* monter; *v.n.* se montrer; ~ *off*, se donner des airs; ~ *up*, (*stand out*) avoir du relief.
shower, averse, *f.*; (*fig., arrows, &c.*) grêle, *f.*; **~-bath,** douche, *f.*; *v.a.* (*down*) faire* pleuvoir; **~y,** pluvieu|x, ~se.
show|y, (*bright*) brillant; (*gaudy*) voyant; (*ostentatious*) fastueu|x, ~se; **~iness,** faste, *m.*; **~ily,** fastueusement.
shred, *s.* lambeau, *m.*; (*particle*) parcelle, *f.*
shrew, *s.* (*pers.*) mégère, *f.*; **~mouse,** musaraigne, *f.*
shrewd, (*clever*) sagace; **~ness,** sagacité, *f.*; **~ly,** avec sagacité.
shrewish, acariâtre.
shriek, *s.* cri perçant, *m.*; *v.n.* pousser des cris; ~ *with laughter*, rire comme une folle.
shrift, confession, *f.*
shrike, (*ornith.*) pie-grièche, *f.*
shrill, (*voice*) aigre; (*sound*) aigu, -ë; (*fig.*)

criard; ~**y**, d'un ton aigu; (*voice*) d'une voix aigre.
shrimp, (*crust.*) crevette, *f.*
shrine, *s.* châsse, *f.*; (*altar*) autel, *m.*
shrink, *v.a.n.* rétrécir; (*recoil*) reculer; ~ *from*, reculer devant; ~**ing**, en reculant; ~**ingly**, en reculant.
shrink|age, ~**ing**, rétrécissement, *m.*
shrive, *v.a.* confesser.
shrivel, *v.a.* ratatiner; *v.n.* se ratatiner; ~**led**, (*apple, skin, &c.*) ratatiné.
shroud, *s.* linceul, *m.*; *v.a.* envelopper (de).
Shrove Tuesday, mardi gras, *m.*
shrub, arbrisseau, *m.*; (*small*) arbuste, *m.*; ~**bery**, plantation d'arbrisseaux, *f.*
shrug, *s.* †haussement d'épaules, *m.*; *v.a.* †hausser.
shudder, *s.* frisson, *m.*; *v.n.* frissonner (de).
shuffl|e, *s.* (*feet*) mouvement confus, *m.*; *v.a.* (*feet*) traîner; (*cards*) battre; *v.n.* tergiverser; ~ *off*, se débarrasser de; ~**er**, chicaneu|r, ~se, *m.f.*; ~**ing**, *s.* tergiversation, *f.*; *adj.* évasi|f, ~ve.
shuffling, *s.* détours, *m.pl.*; (*cards*) battement, *m.*
shun, éviter.
shut, *v.a.* fermer; (~ *into, enclose*) enfermer; ~ *down*, fermer; ~ *in*, enfermer; (*surround*) entourer (de); ~ *off*, (*water, &c.*) couper; ~ *out*, fermer la porte à; (*view, &c.*) boucher; ~ *up*, (*house, &c.*) fermer; (*put away*) renfermer; (*imprison*) enfermer; *v.n.* se fermer; ~ *up*, (*fam.*) se taire*.
shut, *p.p. adj. tight* ~, bien fermé.
shutter, *s.* volet, *m.*; (*photo*) obturateur, *m.*
shuttle, navette, *f.*
shy, timide; (*frightened*) intimidé; (*cautious*) hésitant; ~**ness**, timidité, *f.*; ~**ly**, timidement.
shy, *v.a.* (*throw*) lancer; *v.n.* (*horse*) faire* un écart; ~ *at*, avoir peur de.
Siamese, *adj.* (*when an adj. use small letter*) *and s.m.f.* Siamois, -e; (*lang.*) siamois, *m.*
Siberian, *adj.* (*when an adj. use small letter*) *and s.m.f.* Sibérien, -ne.
sibilant, *s.* sifflante, *f.*; *adj.* sifflant.
sibyl, (*lit. and fig.*) sibylle, *f.*; ~**line**, sibyllin.
sick, (*ill*) malade; (*vomit*) qui a mal au cœur; (*disgusted*) dégoûté; ~ *of*, las de; *fall* ~, tomber (être) malade.
sicken, *v.a.* (*lit. fig.*) écœurer (de); *v.n.* devenir* (être) malade.
sickish, *feel* ~, avoir quelques nausées.
sickle, faucille, *f.*
sickl|y, (*pers.*) maladi|f, ~ve; (*things*) malsain; ~**iness**, (*pallor*) pâleur, *f.*; (*smell, &c.*) caractère écœurant, *m.*
sickness, maladie, *f.*; (*feeling of*) nausées, *f.pl.*; *sweating-*~, suette, *f.*
side, *s.* côté, *m.*; (*edge*) bord, *m.*; (*mountain*) versant, *m.*; (*team*) équipe, *f.*; (*colloq. conceit*) suffisance, *f.*; ~**-car**, (*motor cycle, &c.*) side-car *m.*; ~**-face**, *see* FACE; ~**-saddle**, selle de femme, *f.*; ~**-scene**, coulisse, *f.*; ~**-show**, *see* SHOW; ~**-slip**, (*aeron.*) glissade sur l'air, *f.*; ~ *by* ~, côte à côte; *by the* ~ *of*, à côté de; *take* ~*s*, prendre* parti; *split one's* ~*s with laughing*, se tordre de rire; *a thorn in one's* ~, une épine dans le pied.
side, *adj.* latéral; (*secondary*) secondaire.
side with, *v.n.* se ranger du côté de.
sideboard, buffet, *m.*
sided, à . . . côté(s), *e.g.* à deux côtés = *two-sided.*
sidelong, *adj.* oblique; *adv.* obliquement.
sideways, de côté.
siding, (*rail.*) voie de garage, *f.*
sidle, ~ *up to*, marcher de côté vers.
siege, siège, *m.*; *lay* ~ *to*, assiéger.
siesta, sieste, *f.*
sieve, *s.* crible, *m.*; (*flour, &c.*) tamis, *m.*; *v.a.* passer au crible.
sift, cribler; (*evidence, &c.*) éplucher.
sifter, (*flour, &c.*) tamis, *m.*
sigh, *s.* soupir, *m.*; *v.n.* soupirer; ~ *for*, soupirer après; ~**ing**, *s.* soupirs, *m.pl.*
sight, *s.* (*faculty, act of seeing*) vue, *f.*; (*spectacle, scene*) spectacle, *m.*; (*rifle*) mire, *f.*; *second* ~, seconde vue, *f.*; *short* ~, myopie, *f.*; ~**s**, (*things worth seeing*) curiosités, *f.pl.*; *at* ~, à vue; *payable at* ~, payable à vue; *by* ~, de vue; *within* ~, en vue; *lose* ~ *of*, perdre de vue.
sight, *v.a.* (*aim gun*) pointer; (*perceive*) apercevoir.
sighted, *long-*~, qui a la vue longue; *short-*~, myope; (*fig.*) peu prévoyant.
sightless, aveugle.
sightly, charmant.
sign, *s.* (*mark, indication, gesture, miracle, math.*) signe, *m.*; (*taverns, &c.*) enseigne, *f.*
sign, *v.a.n.* signer; (*by gesture*) indiquer par signes; ~ *on*, engager; *v.n.* s'engager.
signal, *s.* signal, *m.*; *v.a.* signaler; *also* = '*signalize*'; ⚠ signaliser = '*mark with sign-posts, buoys*', *&c.*; *v.n.* faire* des signaux; ~**-box**, guérite à signaux, *f.*; ~ **light**, fanal, *m.*; ~**man**, signaleur, *m.*
signal, *adj.* signalé.
signatory, *s.* signataire, *m.*
signature, signature, *f.*
signboard, enseigne, *f.*
signet, sceau, *m.*
significan|ce, signification, *f.*; (*importance*) importance, *f.*; ~**t**, significati|f, ~ve.
signification, signification, *f.*
signify, *v.a.* (*mean, make known*) signifier; *v.n.* (*matter*) importer; *it doesn't* ~, peu importe.
signing, *s.* souscription, *f.*; *the will wants* ~, le testament n'a pas la souscription.
signpost, poteau indicateur, *m.*
silence, *s.* (*lit., fig., and interj.*) silence, *m.*; ~ *is golden*, le silence est d'or; *v.a.* faire* taire; (*artil.*) éteindre* le feu de.
silent, silencieu|x, ~se; (*mute and gram.*)

muet, -te; (*taciturn*) taciturne; **~ly**, en silence.
silhouette, silhouette, *f.*
silk, soie, *f.*; (*for sewing*) fil de soie, *m.*; **~-worm**, ver à soie, *m.*; *adj. and* **~en**, de soie.
silky, (*soft*) soyeu|x, ~se.
sill, (*window*) allège, *f.*; (*door*) seuil, *m.*
sill|iness, sottise, *f.*; **~y**, sot, -te.
silt, vase, *f.*; *v.a.* ~ *up*, envaser.
silver, *s.* argent, *m.*; (*plate*) argenterie, *f.*
silver, *adj.* d'argent; (*colour*) argenté; (*sound*) argentin; *~-gilt*, vermeil, *m.*; ~ *plate*, vaisselle d'argent, *f.*; **~y**, (*hair, &c.*) argenté; (*sound*) argentin.
silversmith, orfèvre, *m.*
similar, semblable (à); **~ity**, *also* **similitude**, similitude, *f.*; **~ly**, semblablement.
simile, similitude, *f.*
simmer, bouillir* doucement.
simoon, (*hot wind*) simoun, *m.*
simper, *s.* sourire affecté, *m.*; *v.n.* minauder.
simpl|e, *s.* simple, *m.*; *adj.* (*not compound or elaborate, absolute, mere, plain, inexperienced, easy*) simple; *~e interest, see* INTEREST; **~eness**, **~icity**, simplicité, *f.*; **~y**, simplement.
simpleton, niais, -e, *m.f.*
simplif|ication, simplification, *f.*; **~y**, simplifier.
simula|te, simuler; **~tion**, simulation, *f.*
simultaneous, simultané; **~ly**, simultanément.
sin, *s.* péché, *m.*; *v.n.* pécher; ~ *against*, (*fig.*) enfreindre*.
since, *adv. and prep.* depuis; *conj.* depuis que; (*because*) puisque; ~ *when*, depuis lors; (*interrog.*) depuis quand? ; *it is a year, a long time, &c.*, ~ *I saw you*, il y a un an, longtemps que je ne vous ai vu; ⚠ *note that* ne *must be employed with the verb unless it is in the pres. or the impf.*
sincer|e, sincère; **~ity**, sincérité, *f.*; **~ely**, sincèrement; *Yours ~ely, very ~ely*, Votre tout dévoué.
sinecure, sinécure, *f.*
sinew, (*uniting muscle to bone*) tendon, *m.*; **~s**, (*vigour and fig.*) nerf, *m.*; *~s of war*, nerf de la guerre, *m.*
sinewy, nerveu|x, ~se.
sinful, péch|eur, ~eresse; (*act*) coupable; **~ness**, méchanceté, *f.*; **~ly**, en pécheur.
sing, *v.a.n.* chanter; (*ears*) tinter; ~ *in tune*, chanter juste; ~ *out of tune*, chanter faux.
singe, *v.a.n.* roussir.
singer, chanteu|r, ~se; (*professional, f.*) cantatrice.
singing, *s.* chant, *m.*; (*ears*) bourdonnement, *m.*; *~-master*, maître de chant, *m.*; *~-mistress*, professeur de chant, *f.*
singl|e, *adj.* (*not married*) célibataire; (*one only*) seul; (*opp. to double*) simple; (*combat*) singuli|er, ~ère; (*particular to one*) particuli|er, ~ère; *~e bed*, lit à une personne; *~e-breasted*, (*coat*) droit; *~e-hearted*, sincère; *~e man*, célibataire, *m.*; *~e ticket*, billet d'aller, *m.*; **~eness**, (*fig.*) sincérité, *f.*; *~eness of purpose*, sincérité d'intentions, *f.*; **~y**, un(e) à un(e).
single out, (*choose*) choisir; (*distinguish*) distinguer.
singsong, *s.* chant, ton monotone, *m.*; *adj.* monotone.
singular, *s.* (*gram.*) singulier, *m.*; *adj.* (*remarkable*) remarquable; (*strange and gram.*) singuli|er, ~ère; **~ity**, singularité, *f.*; **~ly**, singulièrement.
sinister, sinistre.
sink, *s.* (*kitchen*) évier, *m.*; (*fig.*) cloaque, *m.*
sink, *v.a.* (*lit. and fig.*) enfoncer; (*lower*) faire* baisser; (*wells, &c.*) foncer; (*money, capital, &c.*) placer à fonds perdus; (*in annuity*) placer en viager; (*vessel*) couler; (*ignore*) négliger.
sink, *v.n.* (*lit. and fig.*) s'enfoncer; (*ships*) sombrer; (*into chair*) se laisser tomber; (*succumb*) succomber; (*wind, storm*) diminuer; (*disappear*) disparaître*; (*rivers, prices*) baisser; (*be dying*) se mourir*; (*heart*) manquer, à + *pers.*; (*voice*) se faire* basse; (*subside*) s'abaisser; (*sun*) descendre; ~ *down*, (*collapse*) s'affaisser; ~ *in*, pénétrer.
sinking, *s.* (*heart*) serrement, *m.*; (*diminution*) diminution, *f.*; (*comm.*) amortissement, *m.*; *~-fund, see* FUND.
sinless, sans péché; **~ness**, innocence, *f.*
sinner, pêch|eur, ~eresse, *m.f.*
sinu|osity, sinuosité, *f.*; **~ous**, sinueu|x, ~se.
sip, siroter.
siphon, siphon, *m.*
sir, monsieur, *m.* (*pl.* messieurs); (*title*) Sir, *m.*; (*kings*) Sire, *m.* ⚠ *only used of sovereigns in Mod. French.*
sire, père, *m.*
siren, (*lit. and fig.*) sirène, *f.*
sirloin, aloyau, *m.*
sirocco, siroco, *m.*
siskin, (*ornith.*) tarin, *m.*
sister, (*lit. and relig.*) sœur, *f.*; (*nurse*) infirmière, *f.*; *~-in-law*, belle-sœur, *f.*; **~hood**, communauté, *f.*; **~ly**, de sœur.
sit, *v.a.* (*horse*) monter (avoir).
sit, *v.n.* s'asseoir*; (*state of sitting*) être assis; (*remain*) rester (être); (*of assemblies and pers. in assemblies*) siéger; (*for portrait*) poser; (*birds*) couver; (*of clothes*) aller* (être) à; ~ *down*, s'asseoir*; (*at table*) se mettre* (à); ~ *down before*, (*mil.*) mettre* le siège devant; ~ *down under*, (*insult*) empocher; ~ *for*, (*exam.*) se présenter à; ~ *out*, rester (être) jusqu'à la fin de; ~ *up*, (*from lying down*) se dresser; (*at night*) veiller; ~ *upon*, (*fam.*) rabrouer.
site, (*of town, &c.*) emplacement, *m.*; (*for building*) terrain, *m.*
sitter, (*hen*) couveuse; (*paint.*) modèle, *m.*

sitting, *s.* (*session, portrait*) séance, *f.*; *adj.* (*pers.*) assis; **~-room,** petit salon, *m.*
situated, situé.
situation, (*concurrence of circumstances, and in novel, &c.*) situation, *f.*; (*of employee*) position, *f.*
six, six; *at ~es and sevens,* sens dessus dessous; **~th,** sixième, (*dates and sovereigns*) six; **~thly,** sixièmement.
sixteen, seize, **~th,** seizième, (*dates and sovereigns*) seize.
sixt|y, soixante; **~ieth,** soixantième.
size, *s.* (*pers.*) taille, *f.*; (*thing*) grandeur, *f.*; (*shoes, gloves, &c.*) pointure, *f.*; (*solution*) colle, *f.*
size, (*with solution*) coller; *~ up,* (*pers.*) apprécier.
skat|e, *s.* (*ichth.*) raie, *f.*; (*for foot*) patin, *m.*; *v.n.* patiner; **~er,** patineu|r, ~se; **~ing,** patinage, *m.*; ⚠ skating, *m. in French = 'roller-skating' or 'rink' used for this sport.*
skein, (*lit. and fig.*) écheveau, *m.*
skeleton, squelette, *m.*; (*framework*) carcasse, *f.*; (*outline*) plan, *m.*; *~ key,* crochet, *m.*; (*for burglar*) rossignol, *m.*
sketch, *s.* (*draw.*) croquis, *m.*; (*outline*) esquisse, *f.*; **~-book,** album, *m.*; *v.a.* (*lit. and fig.*) esquisser; **~y,** sommaire.
skew, *adj.* biais.
skewer, brochette, *f.*
ski, ski, *m.*; **~er,** skieur, *m.*
skid, *s.* (*slip of wheel*) dérapage, *m.*; (*wheel-lock*) sabot de roue, *m.*; *v.n.* déraper.
skiff, esquif, *m.*
skilful, adroit; **~ly,** adroitement.
skill, *also* **skilfulness,** *s.* adresse, *f.*
skilled, adroit (à); (*experienced*) expérimenté (en).
skim, (*milk*) écrémer; (*soup, &c.*) écumer; (*surface*) effleurer; (*book*) parcourir*.
skim-milk, lait écrémé, *m.*
skimmer, (*ladle*) écumoire, *f.*
skimpy, (*meagre*) maigre.
skin, *s.* (*animals, humans, fruit*) peau, *f.*; *drenched, wet to the ~,* trempé jusqu'aux os; *be nothing but ~ and bone, see* BONE; *~-deep,* superficiel, -le.
skin, *v.a.* écorcher; (*fruit*) peler.
skinflint, *s.* pince-maille, *m.f.*; *be a ~,* tondre sur un œuf.
skinner, (*dealer in skins*) peaussier, *m.*
skinny, décharné.
skip, *s.* bond, *m.*
skip, *v.a.* (*lit., ornith.*) sauter; *v.n.* (*game*) sauter à la corde.
skipper, (*naut. and boss*) patron, *m.*
skipping-rope, corde à sauter, *f.*
skirmish, *s.* escarmouche, *f.*; *v.n.* escarmoucher; **~er,** tirailleur, *m.*
skirt, *s.* (*dress*) jupe, *f.*; (*coat*) basque, *f.*; (*forest, &c.*) lisière, *f.*
skirt, *v.a.* (*border, go along*) border.
skit, burlesque, *m.*
skittish, (*horse*) ombrageu|x, ~se; (*woman*) capricieuse.
skittles, quilles, *f.pl.*; *skittle-alley,* jeu de quilles, *m.*
skulk, se dérober; **~er,** capon, *m.*
skull, crâne, *m.*; **~-cap,** calotte, *f.*
skunk, (*zool.*) mouffette, *f.*; (*fur*) skunks (sconse), *m.*
sky, ciel, *m.*; (*pl. and fig.*) cieux; (*in pictures, climate*) ciel, *m., pl.* ciels; *~-line,* horizon, *m.*; *~-blue,* bleu de ciel, *invar.*
skylark, alouette, *f.*; *v.n.* faire des farces.
skylight, lucarne, *f.*
slab, *s.* (*stone, &c.*) dalle, *f.*
slack, (*not tight*) lâche; (*business*) dans le marasme; (*pers.*) négligent; **~ness,** (*negligence*) négligence, *f.*; **~ly,** (*fig.*) négligemment.
slacken, *v.a.* (*speed, pace*) ralentir; (*loosen*) relâcher; *v.n.* (*loosen*) se relâcher; (*abate*) diminuer.
slag, scorie, *f.*
slake, (*thirst*) étancher.
slam, *v.a.n.* (*door*) claquer.
slander, *s.* médisance, *f.*; *v.a.* médire* de; **~er,** médisant, -e, *m.f.*; **~ous,** (*pers.*) médisant; (*things*) calomnieu|x, ~se; **~ously,** calomnieusement.
slang, argot, *m.*
slant, biais, *m.*; (*ground*) pente, *f.*
slant, *v.a.* faire* pencher; *v.n.* être en pente.
slantingly, en, de biais.
slap, *s.* claque, *f.*; (*in the face, and fig.*) soufflet, *m.*
slap, *v.a.* claquer; (*in face*) souffleter+*pers.*
slapdash, *adv.* à la volée.
slash, *s.* (*in flesh or stuff*) taillade, *f.*
slash, *v.a.* taillader; (*whip*) faire* claquer.
slate, *s.* (*roof, grey rock, school, &c.*) ardoise, *f.*; *~-coloured,* ardoisé; *~-pencil,* crayon d'ardoise, *m.*; *v.a.* couvrir* d'ardoises; **~r,** couvreur en ardoises, *m.*
slattern, souillon, *f.*; **~ly,** *adj.* malpropre.
slaughter, *s.* massacre, *m.*; **~-house,** abattoir, *m.*; *v.a.* (*men*) massacrer; (*animals*) abattre.
Slav, *adj.* (*when an adj. use small letter*) *and s.m.f.* Slave; **~onic,** *adj.* slave.
slav|e, (*lit. and fig.*) esclave, *m.f.*; *v.n.* travailler comme un esclave; **~e-trade,** traite des noirs, *f.*; **~ery,** esclavage, *m.*; **~ish,** d'esclave; (*servile*) servile; **~ishly,** servilement.
slaver, (*ship*) négrier, *m.*; (*spittle*) bave, *f.*; *v.n.* baver.
slay, tuer; **~er,** tueur, *m.*
sledge, sled, sleigh, traîneau, *m.*; *v.a.* aller* (être) en traîneau.
sledge-hammer, marteau de forge, *m.*
sleek, (*glossy*) luisant; (*pers., pej.*) onctueu|x, ~se.
sleep, *s.* sommeil, *m.*; *~-walker,* somnambule, *m.f.*; *go to ~,* s'endormir*.
sleep, *v.a.n.* dormir*; (*stop, spend night*) coucher; *~ away,* faire* passer en dormant; *~ing-car,* wagon-lit, *m.*; *~ing-draught,* narcotique, *m.*; *~ing partner, see* PARTNER.

sleeper, (*pers.*) dormeu|r, ~se, *m.f.*; (*rail.*) traverse, *f.*; (*fam.* = '*sleeping-carriage*') wagon-lit, *m.*
sleepless, sans sommeil; ~ *night, see* NIGHT; **~ness,** insomnie, *f.*
sleep|y, qui a sommeil; (*fig.*) endormi; *be ~y,* avoir sommeil; *become, grow ~,* s'assoupir; **~iness,** assoupissement, *m.*; **~ily,** en dormant.
sleet, grésil, *m.*
sleeve, manche, *f.*; *laugh in one's ~,* rire* sous cape; **~less,** sans manche; **~-links,** boutons de manchettes, *m.pl.*
sleigh, traîneau, *m.*
sleight, ruse, *f.*; ~ *of hand,* tour de passe-passe, *m.*
slender, (*lit. and fig.*) mince; (*figure*) svelte; (*hope, &c.*) faible; **~ness,** sveltesse, *f.*; (*of means*) maigreur, *f.*
sleuth-hound, (*lit. and fig.*) limier, *m.*
slice, *s.* (*bread, meat*) tranche, *f.*; (*fish*) filet, *m.*; (*salmon*) darne, *f.*; (*poultry*) aiguillette, *f.*
slice, *v.a.* couper par tranches.
slick, habile.
slide, *s.* (*for boys*) glissade, *f.*; (*land*) éboulement, *m.*; (*prices*) chute, *f.*; (*photo.*) châssis, *m.*
slid|e, *v.a.n.* glisser; *~ing-door,* porte à coulisse, *f.*; *~ing-scale, see* SCALE.
slight, (*thin*) mince; (*unimportant, small*) lég|er, ~ère; *the ~est,* le, la, etc. moindre; **~ness,** peu d'importance, *m.*; **~ly,** légèrement.
slight, *v.a.* dédaigner.
slightingly, avec dédain.
slim, svelte; **~ness,** sveltesse, *f.*
slim|e, vase, *f.*; (*snail*) bave, *f.*; **~iness,** viscosité, *f.*; **~y,** vaseu|x, ~se; (*sticky*) visqueu|x, ~se.
sling, *s.* fronde, *f.*; (*arm*) écharpe, *f.*; *in a ~,* en écharpe.
sling, *v.a.* lancer avec une fronde; (*hurl*) lancer; (*suspend*) suspendre; (*hammock*) accrocher.
slinger, frondeur, *m.*
slink away, out, s'esquiver furtivement.
slip, *s.* (*on ice, &c.*) glissade, *f.*; (*mistake*) faux pas, *m.*; (*cutting*) bouture, *f.*; (*paper*) fiche, *f.*; (*for boats*) débarcadère, *m.*; (*dogs*) laisse, *f.*; *~-carriage,* (*rail.*) wagon détaché, *m.*; *~-knot,* nœud coulant, *m.*
slip, *v.a.* glisser; (*cable, &c.*) filer; (*get rid of*) se dégager de; ~ *off,* (*clothes*) ôter; ~ *on,* (*clothes*) mettre*.
slip, *v.n.* (*by accident, move smoothly*) glisser; (*creep into*) se glisser dans; ~ *away, off, out,* s'esquiver; ~ *down,* tomber (être) en glissant.
slipper, pantoufle, *f.*; **~s,** (*aeron.*) patins, *m.pl.*
slipper|iness, nature glissante, *f.*; **~y,** glissant; (*pers.*) rusé.
slip|slop, ~shod, (*style, work, &c.*) négligé.
slipway, (*naut.*) cale de †halage, *f.*
slit, *s.* fente, *f.*; *v.a.* fendre; *v.n.* se fendre.
slobber, *s.* bave, *f.*; *v.n.* baver; **~y, ~ing,** baveu|x, ~se.
sloe, (*bot.*) prunelle, *f.*
slogan, (*approx.*) mot de ralliement, *m.*
sloop, sloop, *m.*
slop, *v.a.* répandre; ~ *over, v.n.* se répandre; **~-basin,** vide-tasses, *m. invar.*; **~-pail,** seau de toilette, *m.*
slops, (*waste water*) rinçures, *f.pl.*; (*food*) lavasse, *f.*
slope, *s.* (*slant*) biais, *m.*; (*of hill, &c.*) pente, *f.*; *at the ~,* (*rifle*) sur l'épaule.
slope, *v.a.* incliner; ~ *arms!* armes au bras!; *v.n.* être en pente.
sloping, *adj.* en pente; **~ly,** *adv.* en pente.
sloppy, (*slushy*) gâcheu|x, ~se; (*work*) bâclé.
slot, fente, *f.*
sloth, ~fulness, paresse, *f.*; (*zool.*) paresseux, *m.*; **~ful,** paresseu|x, ~se; **~fully,** paresseusement.
slouch, *s.* démarche lourde, *f.*; *v.n.* marcher en inclinant la tête.
slough, bourbier, *m.*; (*serpents*) dépouille, *f.*; *v.a.* (*lit. and fig.*) se dépouiller (de); *v.n.* se dépouiller de la peau.
sloven, personne malpropre, *f.*; **~liness,** malpropreté, *f.*; (*carelessness*) négligence, *f.*; **~ly,** malpropre, négligent.
slow, (*not quick*) lent; (*clocks, &c.*) en retard; (*dull-witted*) peu intelligent; (*train*) de petite vitesse; ~ *to,* (*taking time*) long, -ue à; (*unintelligent*) lent à; **~coach,** *see* COACH; **~-worm,** orvet, *m.*; **~ness,** lenteur, *f.*; (*watch, &c.*) retard, *m.*; (*dullness*) lourdeur, *f.*; **~ly,** lentement.
slow down, *v.a.n.* ralentir.
slug, (*zool.*) limace, *f.*; (*bullet*) lingot, *m.*
sluggard, *s.* paresseu|x, ~se, *m.f.*
sluggish, paresseu|x, ~se; **~ness,** paresse, *f.*; **~ly,** paresseusement.
sluice, *s. also* **~-gate,** vanne, *f.*; *v.a.* (*wash out*) rincer.
slum, quartier sordide, *m.*
slumber, *s.* sommeil, *m.*; *v.n.* sommeiller.
slump, débâcle, *f.*; ~ *in trade,* mévente, *f.*; ~ *in prices,* effondrement de cours, *m.*
slur, *s.* tache, *f.*; *v.a.* ne pas prononcer distinctement.
slush, gâchis, *m.*
slut, souillon, *f.*; **~tish,** sale.
sly, (*cunning*) rusé; (*underhand*) sournois; *on the ~,* en sourdine; **~ness,** ruse, *f.*; **~ly,** sournoisement.
smack, *s.* (*taste*) petit goût; (*small quantity*) un soupçon, *m.*; (*whip*) claquement, *m.*; (*hand*) claque, *f.*; (*boat*) barque, *f.*
smack, *v.a.* (*tongue, lips, whip*) faire* claquer; (*with hand*) gifler; ~ *of,* sentir*, *v.a.*
small, *adj.* (*not large, not numerous, on small scale, beer*) petit; (*weak, humble*)

faible; (*unimportant*) peu important; (*mind, &c.*) mesquin; (*expenses, change, income*) menu; **~ness,** petitesse, *f.*; ~ *coal, see* COAL; ~ *change, see* CHANGE; ~ *holdings, see* HOLDING.
small, *s.* ~ *of the back,* chute des reins, *f.*
smallish, un peu petit.
smallpox, petite vérole, *f.*
smart, *s.* douleur cuisante, *f.*
smart, *adj.* (*pain*) cuisant; (*witty*) spirituel, -le; (*spruce*) pimpant; *fam.* chic, *invar.*; (*clever*) habile; (*full of resource*) débrouillard; (*society, stylish*) élégant; **~ness,** *see below*; **~ly,** (*briskly*) vivement; (*wittily*) spirituellement.
smart, *v.n.* cuire*; *he will ~ for it,* il lui en cuira.
smartness, (*replies, &c.*) finesse, *f.*; (*dress*) élégance, *f.*; (*fam.*) chic, *m.*; (*vigour*) vigueur, *f.*
smash, *s.* (*breakage*) fracas, *m.*; (*collision*) collision, *f.*; (*comm.*) débâcle, *f.*
smash, *v.a.* briser; (*fig.*) écraser; (*comm.*) faire* faillite.
smatter|er, personne superficielle, *f.*; **~ing,** teinture.
smear, *s.* tache, *f.*
smear, (*with grease, &c.*) enduire*; (*pej.*) barbouiller.
smell, *s.* (*sense*) odorat, *m.*; (*odour*) odeur, *f.*
smell, *v.a.* sentir*; (*animals*) flairer; ~ *out,* flairer; ~*ing-salts, see* SALT.
smell, *v.n.* sentir*; (*evil smell*) sentir* mauvais; ~ *of,* sentir* + *acc.*
smelling, *adj.* *sweet-~,* odorant; *~-bottle,* flacon de sels, *m.*
smelt, *s.* (*ichth.*) éperlan, *m.*
smelt, *v.a.* fondre; **~ing,** fonte, *f.*
smile, *s.* sourire, *m.*; *v.a.* (*approval*) approuver en souriant; *v.n.* sourire*; ~ *at,* (*pers.*) sourire* à; (*thing*) sourire* de.
smiling, *adj.* (*pers.*) souriant; (*thing*) riant; **~ly,** en souriant.
smirch, *v.a.* noircir.
smirk, *s.* sourire affecté, *m.*; *v.n.* sourire* avec affectation.
smit|e, *v.a.* (*lit., death, disease, eye*) frapper; (*conquer*) vaincre*; ~*e hip and thigh,* battre à plate couture; *be ~ten with,* (*emotions*) être frappé de; (*love*) être épris de; *v.n.* ~*e on, upon,* venir* (être) frapper sur.
smith, (black~) forgeron, *m.*; **~y,** forge, *f.*; **tin-~,** ferblantier, *m.*
smithereens, *to ~,* en miettes.
smock, *also* **~-frock,** sarrau, *m.*
smoke, *s.* fumée, *f.*; **~-screen,** rideau de fumée, *m.*; *vanish, end in ~,* s'en aller* (être) en fumée; *have a ~,* fumer; ~*-dried,* fumé.
smoke, *v.a.* (*tobacco, fish, &c.*) fumer; (*plants, spoil with smoke*) enfumer; ~ *out,* (*insects, animals*) enfumer; ~*d haddock, see* HADDOCK; *v.n.* fumer; (*of a pipe, &c.*) se fumer.
smokeless, sans fumée.
smoker, fumeu|r, ~se, *m.f.*
smoking, *s.* action de fumer, *f.*; ~*-carriage,* (*rail.*) compartiment de fumeurs, *m.*; ~ *not allowed,* défense de fumer; *adj.* fumant.
smoky, qui fume; (*filled with, smelling of smoke*) enfumé.
smooth, *adj.* (*even, polished, glossy*) lisse; (*with unbroken surface*) uni; (*soft*) dou|x, ~ce; (*sea*) calme; (*style, &c.*) coulant; **~ness,** égalité, *f.*; (*softness*) douceur, *f.*; **~ly,** doucement; ~*-tongued,* doucereu|x, ~se.
smooth, *v.a.* (*level road, &c.*) aplanir; (*hair*) lisser; (*brow*) dérider; ~ *away, over,* (*difficulties, &c.*) aplanir.
smother, (*lit., fig., fire, yawn, oath*) étouffer; (*cover entirely*) couvrir* complètement (de).
smoulder, (*fire and fig.*) couver; **~ing,** qui couve.
smudge, *s.* tache, *f.*; (*of ink*) pâté, *m.*; *v.a.* tacher.
smug, (*approx.*) bourgeois.
smuggle, *v.a.* ~ *in,* faire* passer en contrebande; *v.n.* faire* la contrebande; **~r,** contrebandier, *m.*
smuggling, contrebande, *f.*
smut, noir, *m.*; (*obscenity*) saletés, *f.pl.*
smutt|y, noir; (*obscene*) sale; **~iness,** noirceur, saleté, *f.*
snack, morceau sur le pouce, *m.*
snaffle, filet, *m.*
snag, (*sea*) roche submergée, *f.*; (*slang, hindrance*) anicroche, *f.*
snail, colimaçon, *m.*
snake, (*lit. and fig.*) serpent, *m.*; **~-weed,** (*bot.*) bistorte, *f.*
snap, *s.* (*fastening*) fermoir, *m.*; (*bite*) coup de dents, *m.*; (*force*) vigueur, *f.*; (*go*) entrain, *m.*; (*sound*) bruit sec, *m.*; (*fingers*) claquement, *m.*
snap, *v.a.* (*fingers*) faire* claquer; (*shut*) fermer; (*with teeth*) †happer; (*photo.*) prendre* un instantané de; ~ *at, up,* †happer; (*bargain*) enlever; ~ *off,* casser; *v.n. and ~ off,* se casser.
snapdragon, (*bot.*) gueule de loup, *f.*
snappish, *also* **snappy,** †hargneu|x, ~se; (*style*) vi|f, ~ve; **~ly,** aigrement.
snapshot, *s.* (*photo.*) instantané, *m.*; *v.a.* photographier.
snare, *s.* piège, *m.*; *v.a.* prendre* au piège.
snarl, *s.* grognement, *m.*; *v.n.* grogner; **~ing,** †hargneu|x, ~se.
snatch, *s.* action de saisir, *f.*; (*fit, bout*) accès, *m.*; **~es,** (*of song*) bribes, *f.pl.*; *by ~es,* par accès.
snatch, *v.a.* saisir; (*sleep*) prendre*; ~ *at,* (*offer, &c.*) saisir au vol; ~ *away, from,* arracher + *dat. of pers.*; ~ *up,* saisir.
sneak, *s.* mouchard, *m.*; *v.n.* (*tell tales*) moucharder; ~ *away, off,* se dérober furtivement; ~ *in, into,* entrer (être) furtivement dans.

sneaking, *adj.* (*involuntary*) que l'on ne peut s'empêcher de sentir; **~ly,** furtivement.
sneer, *s.* rire moqueur, *m.*; *v.n.* ricaner; ~ *at,* se moquer de; **~ing,** *adj.* ricaneu|r, ~se; **~ingly,** en ricanant.
sneeze, *s.* éternuement, *m.*; *v.n.* éternuer.
snick, *s.* petite entaille, *f.*
sniff, *s.* reniflement, *m.*; *v.a.n.* renifler.
snigger, *s.* ricanement, *m.*; *v.n.* ricaner.
snip, *s.* coup de ciseaux, *m.*; (*bit*) petit morceau, *m.*; *v.a.* couper.
snipe, (*ornith.*) bécassine, *f.*
snipe, *v.n.* tirer en embuscade; **~r,** tireur caché, *m.*
snivel, *v.n.* avoir la roupie au nez; (*cry*) pleurnicher; **~ler,** pleurnicheu|r, ~se, *m.f.*
snob, *s.* homme, femme, qui admire trop les titres et la †haute position, *or* qui affecte d'être ce qu'il *or* elle n'est pas, *m.f.*; ⚠ snob *in French = more a person who tries to be up to date or in the fashion in everything*; **~bery,** sottise de l'admirat|eur, ~rice de la †haute position.
snore, *s.* ronflement, *m.*; *v.n.* ronfler; **~r,** ronfleu|r, ~se, *m.f.*
snort, *s.* grognement, *m.*; (*horse*) ébrouement, *m.*; *v.n.* (*horse*) s'ébrouer.
snout, *s.* museau, *m.*; (*hog*) groin, *m.*
snow, *s.* neige, *f.*; **~-drift,** monceau de neige, *m.*; **~-leopard,** once, *f.*; **~-plough,** chasse-neige, *m. invar.*; **~-shoe,** raquette, *f.*; *~-white,* blanc, blanche comme la neige; *v.n.* neiger; ~ *up,* bloquer par la neige.
snowball, boule de neige, *f.*
snowdrop, perce-neige, *f. invar.*
snowy, neigeu|x, ~se.
snub, *s.* rebuffade, *f.*; *~-nosed,* camus; *v.a.* rembarrer.
snuff, tabac à priser, *m.*; **~-box,** tabatière, *f.*; *take ~,* priser.
snuff, *v.a.* (*tobacco*) priser; (*candle*) moucher.
snuffers, mouchettes, *f.pl.*
snug, (*comfortable*) commode; (*small and cosy*) bon, -ne petit, -e; **~ly,** commodément.
so, *adv.* (*thus*) ainsi; (*to such a degree*) si; (*in consequence*) donc; (= *pron.*) le, *e.g. he thinks so,* il le croit; *I hope ~,* je l'espère; *we have done ~,* nous l'avons fait; *so so,* comme ci, comme ça; *~ and ~,* un tel, une telle; *Mr ~ and ~,* Monsieur un tel; *~ to speak,* pour ainsi dire; *~ that,* de sorte que (*fact indic., purpose subj.*); *~ that,* (*provided that*) pourvu que (*subj.*); *why ~?* pourquoi cela?
soak, *v.n.* tremper; *~ in, up,* boire*; **~ing,** *have a ~ing,* être bien trempé.
soap, savon, *m.*; **~-boiler, -manufacturer,** savonnier, *m.*; *~-berry-tree,* savonnier, *m.*; **~-dish,** boîte à savon, *f.*; **~-suds,** eau de savon, *f.*; *v.a.* savonner.
soapwort, (*bot.*) saponaire, *f.*
soapy, savonneu|x, ~se; (*pers.*) onctueu|x, ~se.
soar, *v.n.* prendre* son essor; (*fig.*) s'élancer.
soaring, *s.* (*aeron.*) vol à voile, *m.*
sob, *s.* sanglot; *v.n.* sangloter.
sober, (*not drunk*) *use* ne pas être ivre; (*moderate and colours*) sobre; (*sensible*) sensé; (*absolute*) tout simple; (*sedate*) sérieu|x, ~se; ⚠ sobre = '*abstemious*', '*temperate*', *but never* '*not drunk*'; **~ly,** modérément.
sober, *v.a.* (*make sober*) désenivrer; *v.n.* (*get sober*) se dégriser; *~ down,* se calmer.
sobriety, (*abstemiousness*) sobriété, *f.*; (*not drunk*) état de ne pas être ivre.
soccer, (*football*) association, *f.*
sociab|le, sociable; **~ility,** sociabilité, *f.*; **~ly,** d'une manière sociable.
social, (*science, problems, &c., intercourse, life, duties, rank, &c.*) social; **~ly,** socialement.
social|ism, socialisme, *m.*; **~ist,** socialiste, *m.f.*
society, (*upper classes, companionship, association for common aim*) société, *f.*
sociology, sociologie, *f.*
sock, chaussette, *f.*; (*in boot*) semelle, *f.*; (*ant., comedy*) socque, *m.*
socket, (*eye*) orbite, *f.*; (*teeth*) alvéole, *m.*; (*candle*) trou, *m.*; (*place for insertion of handle, electr. bulb, &c.*) douille, *f.*
sod, (*turf*) gazon, *m.*; (*piece of turf*) motte, *f.*
soda, soude, *f.*; **~-water,** eau de Seltz, *f.*
sofa, canapé, *m.*; **~-bed,** canapé-lit, *m.*
soft, *adj.* (*yielding to pressure, lacking vigour, effeminate, soap*) mou (mol + *vowel or silent* H), molle; (*to the feel, sound, light, water, breeze, sleep, gram.*) dou|x, ~ce; (*compassionate*) tendre; *~ collar, see* COLLAR; *~ job, see* JOB; **~ness,** douceur, *f.*; (*lack of vigour*) mollesse, *f.*; **~ly,** doucement.
soften, *v.a.* (*substances, make effeminate*) amollir; (*fig., grief, make less harsh, &c.*) adoucir; *~ing of the brain,* (*med.*) ramollissement, *m.*
soften, *v.n.* s'amollir; (*fig.*) s'adoucir.
soil, *s.* (*earth*) terroir, *m.*; (*stain*) tache, *f.*; (*fig.*) pays, *m.*; *v.a.* (*lit. and fig.*) souiller; *v.n.* devenir* (être) sale.
sojourn, *s.* séjour, *m.*; *v.n.* séjourner; **~er,** habitant passager, *m.*
solace, *s.* consolation, *f.*; *v.a.* consoler.
solar, solaire.
solder, soldering, *s.* soudure, *f.*; *v.a.* souder.
soldier, *s.* soldat, *m.*; (*private*) simple soldat, *m.*; **~y,** (*pej.*) soldatesque, *f.*; **~ly,** de soldat.
sole, *s.* (*foot*) plante, *f.*; (*shoes*) semelle, *f.*; (*ichth.*) sole, *f.*; *v.a.* (*shoes*) ressemeler; **~d,** *adj.* à semelles, *e.g.* à semelles épaisses = *'thick-soled'*.
sole, *adj.* seul; (*exclusive*) exclusi|f, **~ve; ~ly,** uniquement.

solecism, solécisme, *m.*
solemn, (*ceremonious, weighty, impressive*) solennel, -le; (*grave*) sérieu|x, ~se; **~ly,** solennellement.
solemnity, solennité, *f.*
solemniz|e, solenniser; **~ation,** solennisation, *f.*
solicit, *v.a.* (*request*) solliciter (à+*inf.*); (*entice, pej.*) racoler; **~ation,** sollicitation, *f.*
solicitor, avoué, *m.*
solicitous, (*desirous*) désireu|x, ~se (de); (*anxious about*) inqui|et, ~ète (de); **~ly,** avec sollicitude.
solicitude, sollicitude, *f.*
solid, *s.* solide, *m.*
solid, *adj.* (*hour, day, &c., not hollow*) plein; (*opp. to fluid, durable, serious, math.*) solide; (*alike all through*) massi|f, ~ve; (*unanimous*) unanime; (*pers.*) posé; **~ity,** (*lit. and fig.*) solidité, *f.*; **~ly,** solidement.
solidarity, solidarité, *f.*
solidification, solidification, *f.*
solidify, *v.a.* solidifier; *v.n.* se solidifier.
soliloqu|ize, monologuer; **~y,** soliloque, *m.*
solitaire, (*diamond, game*) solitaire, *m.*
solitar|y, solitaire; **~iness,** solitude, *f.*; **~ily,** solitairement.
solitude, solitude, *f.*
solo, (*mus.*) solo, *m.*; **~ist,** soliste, *m.f.*
solstice, solstice, *m.*
solub|le, soluble; **~ility,** solubilité, *f.*
solution, solution, *f.*; (*photo.*) bain de fixage, *m.*; *toning-~,* (*photo.*) vireur, *m.*
solve, *v.a.* (*problem, &c.*) résoudre*; **~ncy,** (*comm.*) solvabilité, *f.*; **~nt,** *adj.* (*comm.*) solvable; ⚠ '*solvable' in Engl.* = soluble.
sombre, sombre.
some, *adj.* (*particular but unknown*) quelque, *sing., pl.* quelques; (*certain quantity*) du, de la, des, de *only+adj. or after negative*) *also* quelques, *plur.*; (*of it, of them*) en; (*approximately+numeral*) quelque, *or numeral nouns,* une dizaine (de), une vingtaine (de), *&c.*; *in ~ sort,* en quelque sorte.
some, *pron. plur.* quelques-uns, -unes; (*in conjunction with 'others'*) les uns; *pron. sing.* (*of quantity*) en *with verb*; (*a little*) un peu de; (*a part*) une partie de; *he will give you ~,* il vous en donnera; *~ of his property,* une partie de son bien.
somebody, *pron.* quelqu'un; (*person of consequence*) personnage, *m.*
somehow, d'une façon quelconque; *~ or other,* de façon ou d'autre.
someone, quelqu'un, -e, *m.f.*; *~ or other,* je ne sais qui.
somersault, culbute, *f.*
something, quelque chose, *m.*; (+ *adj.*) quelque chose de; ⚠ quelque chose que + *subj.* = '*whatever' is fem., which see*; *there's ~ in the wind,* (*brewing*) il y a quelque chose dans l'air; *~ or other,* je ne sais quoi.
some time, *adv.* (*fut.*) quelque jour; *adj.* (*formerly*), d'autrefois.
sometimes, quelquefois; **~ . . . ~,** tantôt . . . tantôt.
somewhat, *pron.* *~ of a,* quelque peu de; *adv.* quelque peu.
somewhere, quelque part.
somnambul|ism, somnambulisme, *m.*; **~ist,** somnambule, *m.f.*
somnolen|ce, somnolence, *f.*; **~t,** somnolent.
son, fils, *m.*; *~-in-law,* gendre, *m.*
sonata, sonate, *f.*
song, (*lighter sort*) chanson, *f.*; (*air set to words*) chant, *m.*; (*sacred*) cantique, *m.*
songst|er, ~ress, chanteu|r, ~se; (*birds*) chantre, *m.*
sonnet, sonnet, *m.*
sonor|ity, ~ousness, sonorité, *f.*; **~ous,** sonore.
soon, bientôt; (*quickly*) vite; (*preceded by* si, trop, plus) tôt; *he'd ~er walk than stay here,* il aimerait mieux rentrer à pied que de rester ici.
soot, suie, *f.*; **~y,** couvert de suie.
sooth, vérité, *f.*; *in ~,* en vérité.
soothe, calmer.
soothsayer, devin, -eresse, *m.f.*
sop, *s.* morceau trempé, *m.*; *v.a.* tremper; *be ~ping wet,* (*pers.*) être trempé jusqu'aux os.
sophi|sm, sophisme, *m.*; **~st,** sophiste, *m.f.*; **~stical,** sophistique.
sophistry, sophismes, *m.pl.*
soporific, *adj. and s.m.* soporifique.
soprano, soprano, *m.*
sorb, ~-apple, sorbe, *f.*; **~-tree,** sorbier, *m.*
sorce|rer, ~ress, sorci|er, ~ère, *m.f.*; **~ry,** sorcellerie, *f.*
sordid, (*dirty, mean*) sordide; **~ness,** sordidité, *f.*; **~ly,** sordidement.
sore, *s.* (*lit. and fig.*) plaie, *f.*; (*open*) ulcère, *m.*
sore, *adj.* (*tender*) douloureu|x, ~se; (*touchy*) susceptible; (*grievous*) cruel, -le; *have ~ throat, eyes, &c.,* avoir mal à; **~ness,** sensibilité, *f.*; *adv.* **~ly,** cruellement.
sorrel, *s.* (*bot.*) oseille, *f.*; *adj.* (*colour*) saure.
sorrow, *s.* douleur, *f.*; **~s,** *often* chagrins, *m.pl.*
sorrow, *v.n.* s'affliger (de = *for*).
sorrowful, (*pers.*) affligé; (*sad*) triste; (*things*) affligeant; **~ly,** tristement.
sorr|y, fâché (de); (*poor, mean*) misérable; (*sad*) triste; *be ~y for,* regretter; *sorry! interj.* pardon!; **~ily,** pitoyablement.
sort, sorte, *f.*; (*kind*) genre, *m.*; (*pers.*) type, *m.*; *after a ~, ~ of, of ~s,* une espèce de; *be out of ~s,* ne pas être dans son assiette.

sort, *v.a.* (*letters, &c.*) trier; (*classify*) classer.
sorter, trieu|r, ~se, *m.f.*
sorting, tri, *m.*; **~-office,** (*P.O.*) bureau de tri, *m.*
so-so, *adv.* comme ci, comme ça.
sot, *s.* ivrogne, *m.*; **~tish,** abruti.
Soudanese, *adj.* (*when an adj. use small letter*) *and s.m.f.* Soudanien, -ne.
soul, (*immortal, animating part or pers., fig.*) âme, *f.*; (*personification*) personnification, *f.*; (*essence*) essence, *f.*; *there's not a* (*living*) ~ . . ., il n'y a pas un chat . . .; *with all my* ~, de toute mon âme; *~-stirring*, émouvant.
sound, *s.* son, *m.*; (*geog.*) détroit, *m.*
sound, *adj.* (*body, mind, doctrine, timber, comm.*) sain; (*building, ship*) solide; (*judgement*) droit; (*sleep*) profond; (*of a business*) solvable; (*vigorous*) vigoureu|x, ~se; (*in good condition*) en bon état; **~ness,** bon état, *m.*; **~ly,** sainement; (*sleep*) profondément; (*thoroughly*) bien.
sound, *v.a.* (*naut. and seek to penetrate*) sonder; (*lungs, &c.*) ausculter; (*praises*) chanter; (*trumpet, &c.*) sonner de; (*mil.*) sonner; ~ *the alarm*, sonner l'alarme; *v.n.* sonner.
sounding, *s.* (*naut. and med.*) sondage, *m.*; *take ~s*, sonder.
sounding, *adj.* sonore; (*pej.*) ronflant; **~-board,** abat-voix, *m. invar.*
soundless, (*still*) silencieu|x, ~se.
soup, potage, *m.*; (*clear*) consommé, *m.*; **~-tureen,** soupière, *f.*; *vegetable* ~, soupe maigre, *f.*; *white* ~, soupe au lait, *f.*; *be in the* ~, (*slang*) être dans le gâchis.
sour, aigre; (*pers.*) revêche; (*milk*) tourné; *turn* ~, *v.n.* s'aigrir; (*milk*) tourner; *v.a.* aigrir; **~ness,** (*lit. and fig.*) aigreur, *f.*; **~ly,** aigrement.
source, (*lit. and fig.*) source, *f.*
souse, *v.a.* (*drench*) saucer.
south, *s.* (*region*) midi, *m.*; (*cardinal point*) sud, *m.*; *~-east, -west, adj. invar. and s.m.* sud-est, sud-ouest; *adj.* sud, *invar.*; (*countries*) du sud; *~-eastern*, *~-western*, du sud-est, du sud-ouest.
south, *adv.* (*motion*) vers le sud; (*rest*) au sud.
souther|ly, ~n, du sud; (*hemisphere*) austral.
southernmost, le (la) plus au sud.
southernwood, (*bot.*) citronelle, *f.*
southward, *adj. and adv.* vers le sud.
sou'wester, (*hat and wind*) suroît, *m.*
sovereign, *s.* souverain, -e, *m.f.*; (*coin*) souverain, *m.*
sovereign, *adj.* (*supreme, of a remedy*) souverain.
sovereignty, souveraineté, *f.*
sow, *s.* truie, *f.*; **~-thistle,** (*bot.*) laiteron, *m.*
sow, *v.a.* (*lit. and fig.*) semer (de); *v.n.* semer.
sow|er, semeur, *m.*; **~ing,** *s.* semailles, *f.pl.*
spa, ville d'eau, *f.*
space, (*place, time, interval, print.*) espace, *m.*; (*on piece of paper*) emplacement, *m.*; *v.a.* ~ *out*, (*print.*) espacer.
spacious, spacieu|x, ~se; (*fig.*) ample; **~ness,** grande étendue, *f.*; **~ly,** spacieusement.
spade, bêche, *f.*; (*cards*) pique, *m.*
spadeful, pelletée, *f.*
spahi, spahi, *m.*
span, *s.* (*hand*) empan, *m.*; (*bridge*) travée, *f.*; (*arch.*) ouverture, *f.*; (*time*) moment, *m.*
span, *v.a.* traverser.
spandrel, (*arch.*) tympan, *m.*
spangle, *s.* paillette, *f.*; *v.a.* pailleter.
Spaniard, Espagnol, -e, *m.f.*
spaniel, *s.* épagneul, -e, *m.f.*
Spanish, *s.* (*lang.*) espagnol, *m.*; *adj.* espagnol.
spank, *v.a.* fesser; **~ing,** *s.* fessée, *f.*; *adj.* **~ing,** vigoureu|x, ~se.
spanner, (*tool*) clef, *f.*
spar, *s.* (*naut.*) espar, *m.*
spar, *v.n.* (*box*) boxer; (*fam.*) chamailler.
spare, *adj.* (*pers., food*) maigre; (*not required*) disponible; (*in reserve*) de réserve; **~ness,** maigreur, *f.*; **~ly,** maigrement; ~ *parts*, (*mach.*) pièces de rechange, *f.pl.*; ~ *time*, loisir, *m.*; ~ *wheel*, (*motor*) *see* WHEEL.
spare, *v.a.* épargner; (*put by*) économiser; (*do without*) se passer de; (*time*) perdre; (*avoid*) éviter.
sparing, *adj.* (*frugal*) frugal; (*fig.*) avare (de); **~ly,** frugalement; (*parsimoniously*) avec parcimonie.
spark, *s.* (*lit., fig., electr.*) étincelle, *f.*; (*pers.*) petit-maître, *m.*
sparking, ~-plug, *see* PLUG.
sparkl|e, *s.* étincelle, *f.*; *v.n.* étinceler; **~ing,** *adj.* étincelant; (*wines*) mousseu|x, ~se.
sparrow, moineau, *m.*; **~-hawk,** épervier, *m.*; **~-owl,** *see* OWL.
sparse, épars.
Spartan, *adj.* (*when an adj. use small letter*) *and s.m.f.* Spartiate.
spasm, spasme, *m.*; **~odic,** spasmodique; **~odically,** par à-coups.
spat, guêtre (courte), *f.*
spatter, (*lit. and fig.*) éclabousser (de).
spawn, (*fish, frogs, &c.*) frai, *m.*
speak, *v.a.* (*lang., &c.*) parler; (*utter, declare*) dire*; (*express*) exprimer.
speak, *v.n.* parler; ~ *out*, parler †hardiment; ~ *up*, parler plus †haut; *~ing!* (*teleph.*) ici!
speaker, (*public*) orateur, *m.*; (*Parl.*) président, *m.*
speaking, *s. public* ~, art oratoire, *m.*; *adj.* (*likeness, &c.*) parlant.
spear, lance, *f.*; (*hunting*) épieu, *m.*; (*fishing*) †harpon, *m.*; *v.a.* percer d'une lance, *&c.*

spearman, cavalier armé d'une lance.
special, spécial; (*particular*) particuli|er, ~ère; **~ity,** (*article, special province*) spécialité, *f.*; **~ly,** spécialement.
specialist, spécialiste, *m.f.*
specie, espèces, *f.pl.*
species, (*biology, kind*) espèce, *f.*
specific, *s.* spécifique, *m.*
specific, *adj.* spécifique; (*remedy, amount*) déterminé; **~ally,** spécifiquement.
specification, spécification, *f.*; (*architect., &c.*) devis, *m.*
specify, spécifier.
specimen, spécimen, *m.*; *strange* **~,** (*pers.*) drôle de corps, *m.*
specious, spécieu|x, ~se; **~ness,** spéciosité, *f.*; **~ly,** spécieusement.
speck, (*dust*) grain, *m.*; (*mud*) tache, *f.*
speck, speckle, *v.a.* tacheter.
speckled, tacheté.
spectacle, spectacle, *m.*; **~-maker,** lunetier, *m.*
spectacles, lunettes, *f.pl.*
spectacled, muni de lunettes.
spectacular, (*approx.*) impressionnant.
spectator, spectat|eur, ~rice, *m.f.*; **~s,** (*onlookers*) assistants, *m.pl.*
spectral, spectral.
spectre, spectre, *m.*
specula|te, (*meditate, form theory, comm.*) spéculer (sur); **~tion,** spéculation, *f.*; **~tor,** (*comm.*) spéculat|eur, ~rice, *m.f.*; **~tive,** spéculati|f, ~ve.
speech, (*power of* ~) parole, *f.*; (*language, style of expression*) langage, *m.*; (*public address, gram.*) discours, *m.*
speechify, pérorer.
speechless, muet, -te (de).
speed, *s.* vitesse, *f.*; *at top* **~,** **à** toute vitesse.
speed, *v.a.* (*help*) aider; (*parting guest*) souhaiter bon voyage à; ~ *up,* accélérer.
speed, *v.n.* (*succeed*) prospérer.
speedometer, (*motor*) compteur de vitesse, *m.*
speedwell, (*bot.*) véronique, *f.*
speed|y, rapide; (*prompt*) prompt; **~iness,** promptitude, *f.*; **~ily,** promptement.
spell, *s.* (*attraction, incantation*) charme, *m.*; (*period*) période, *f.*; (*short time, turn*) tour, *m.*
spell, *v.a.* épeler; (*signify*) signifier; ~ *out,* épeler; *v.n.* épeler.
spellbinder, (*U.S.A.*) orateur persuasif, *m.*
spellbound, ensorcelé; (*fig.*) sous le charme.
spelling, orthographe, *f.*
spend, *v.a.* (*money, fig.*) dépenser; (*time*) passer; (*waste*) perdre; (*exhaust*) épuiser; *v.n.* dépenser.
spendthrift, *adj. and s.m.* prodigue.
spent, (*exhausted*) épuisé (de); (*bullet*) mort.
sperm, ~-whale, cachalot, *m.*
spew, *v.a.n.* vomir.
spher|e, (*globe, geom., fig.*) sphère, *f.*; **~ical,** sphérique; **~oid,** sphéroïde, *m.*
sphinx, sphinx, *m.*
spic|e, épice, *f.*; (*small quantity*) soupçon, *m.*; *v.a.* (*lit. and fig.*) épicer; **~y,** (*lit. and fig.*) épicé; (*fragrant*) parfumé.
spick and span, tiré à quatre épingles.
spider, araignée, *f.*; *~'s web,* toile d'araignée, *f.*
spike, pointe, *f.*; (*nail*) clou, *m.*; (*grain*) épi, *m.*; *v.a.* (*gun*) enclouer.
spikenard, nard, *m.*
spill, *v.a.* répandre; (*overturn*) renverser; (*from veh.*) verser; *v.n.* se répandre, se renverser.
spin, *s.* (*bicycle, &c.*) promenade, *f.*; (*aeron.*) vrille, *f.*; *v.a.n.* filer; (*top*) faire* tourner; ~ *out,* faire* traîner en longueur.
spin|ach, ~age, épinards, *m.pl.*
spindle, (*spinning*) fuseau, *m.*; (*pivot*) pivot, *m.*; **~-tree,** (*bot.*) fusain, *m.*
spindrift, embrun, *m.*
spin|e, (*bot.*) épine, *f.*; (*anat.*) épine dorsale, *f.*; **~al,** épinière, *adj.* (*fem. only*); *~al column,* colonne vertébrale, *f.*; **~y,** épineu|x, ~se.
spinet, épinette, *f.*
spinner, fileu|r, ~se, *m.f.*
spinning, filage, *m.*; (*large-scale*) filature, *f.*; **~-wheel,** rouet, *m.*
spinster, fille, *f.*; **~hood,** célibat, *m.*
spiraea, (*bot.*) spirée, *f.*
spiral, *s.* (*geom.*) spirale, *f.*; *adj.* spiral; (*in form*) en spirale.
spire, (*steeples*) flèche, *f.*; ⚠ spire, *f.* = '*coil*'.
spirit, *s.* (*incorporeal being, real meaning, state of mind*) esprit, *m.*; (*soul*) âme, *f.*; (*ghost*) spectre, *m.*; (*disposition*) caractère, *m.*; (*courage*) cœur, *m.*; (*ardour*) feu, *m.*; *see also* METHYLATED; **~-lamp,** lampe à alcool, *f.*; **~s,** gaieté, *f.*; (*liquor*) spiritueux, *m.*; *~s of salt, see* SALT.
spirit away, *v.a.* enlever.
spirited, (*horse*) fougueu|x, ~se; (*courageous*) courageu|x, ~se; (*animated*) animé; **~ly,** avec courage; (*writing, speaking*) avec verve.
spiritless, (*depressed*) abattu; (*without courage*) sans courage; **~ness,** manque de courage, de vigueur, *m.*; **~ly,** sans courage.
spiritual, spirituel, -le; (*courts, &c.*) ecclésiastique; **~ity,** spiritualité, *f.*; **~ly,** spirituellement; **~ize,** *v.a.* spiritualiser.
spiritual|ism, spiritisme, *m.*; ⚠ *not* spiritualisme *which is a term of philosophy never used of departed spirits*; **~ist,** spirite, *m.*; (*philos.*) spiritualiste, *m.*
spirituous, spiritueu|x, ~se.
spirt, spurt, *s.* jaillissement, *m.*
spirt, *v.a.* jaillir; *v.n.* faire* jaillir.
spit, *s.* (*saliva*) crachat, *m.*; (*roasting*) broche, *f.*
spit, *v.a.* (*also* ~ *out*) cracher; *v.n.* cracher; (*roasting*) embrocher.

spite, *s.* dépit, *m.*; (*hate*) rancune, *f.*; *in ~ of,* malgré; *v.a.* contrarier.
spiteful, (*pers.*) rancuni|er, ~ère; (*things*) plein de dépit; **~ness,** rancune, *f.*; **~ly,** par dépit.
spitting, *s.* crachement, *m.*
spittle, crachat, *m.*
spittoon, crachoir, *m.*
splash, (*action of splashing*) éclaboussement, *m.*; (*mud*) éclaboussure, *f.*; **~-board,** (*veh.*) tablier, *m.*
splash, *v.a.* éclabousser (de); *v.n.* éclabousser; (*wade, ~ about*) patauger.
spleen, *s.* (*melancholy*) humeur noire, *f.*; (*anger*) mauvaise humeur, *f.*; (*anat.*) rate, *f.*; **~wort,** (*bot.*) cétérac, *m.*
splendid, (*lit. and fig.*) splendide; (*colloq.*) épatant; **~ly,** magnifiquement, d'une façon épatante.
splendour, splendeur, *f.*
splice, *s.* (*carp.*) épissure, *f.*; *v.a.* épisser.
splint, *s.* (*surg.*) éclisse, *f.*; *v.a.* éclisser.
splinter, *s.* (*wood, &c.*) éclat, *m.*; (*bone*) esquille, *f.*; *v.a.* faire* voler en éclats; *v.n.* voler en éclats.
split, *v.a.* fendre; (*divide*) partager; *~ asunder,* fendre en deux; *~ up,* partager.
split, *v.n.* se fendre; (*divide*) se diviser; (*ship*) se briser.
splotch, *s.* (*ink, &c.*) tache, *f.*
splutter, *v.n.* bredouiller; (*pen*) cracher.
spoil, *s.* (*booty*) butin, *m.*
spoil, *v.a.* (*injure with indulgence*) gâter; (*strip*) dépouiller (de); (*plunder*) piller; (*crops*) endommager; *v.n.* se gâter.
spoiler, (*plunderer*) spoliat|eur, ~rice, *m.f.*
spoke, (*wheel*) rais, *m.*; *put a ~ in the wheel of,* mettre* des bâtons dans la roue de.
spokesman, porte-parole, *m.* (*invar.*)
spoliation, spoliation, *f.*
spong|e, *s.* éponge, *f.*; *have a ~e over,* (*wash*) se passer l'éponge; *v.a.* éponger; *~e on,* vivre* aux crochets de; **~ing,** *s.* (*hanging on*) écorniflerie, *f.*; **~y,** spongieu|x, ~se.
spontane|ity, spontanéité, *f.*; **~ous,** spontané; **~ously,** spontanément.
spook, fantôme, *m.*
spools, (*photo. and cinema*) bobines, *f.pl.*
spoon, cuiller, *f.*; **~ful,** cuillerée, *f.*
spoon, *v.n.* (*fam.*) faire* langoureusement sa cour.
spoonbill, (*ornith.*) spatule, *f.*
sporadic, sporadique.
sport, *s.* (*fun*) amusements, *m.pl.*; ⚠ sport, *gen. m.pl., only of outdoor games*; (*jesting*) moquerie, *f.*; (*plaything, fig.*) jouet, *m.*; **~ing,** (*sportsmanlike*) sporti|f, ~ve; **~ive,** (*playful*) enjoué.
sport, *v.n.* jouer; (*frolic*) folâtrer; *v.a.* (*wear*) arborer.
sportsman, sportsman, *m.*; **~like,** digne d'un sportsman.
sportswoman, sportswoman, *f.*

spot, *s.* (*stain, lit. and fig.*) tache, *f.*; (*place*) endroit, *m.*; *~-price, see* PRICE; *on the ~,* sur les lieux; (*comm.*) sur place.
spot, *v.a.* (*stain*) tacher; (*recognize*) reconnaître*; *v.n.* se tacher.
spotless, sans tache; **~ness,** pureté, *f.*
spotted, *also* **spotty,** (*stained*) taché; (*material, animals*) tacheté.
spouse, épou|x, ~se, *m.f.*
spout, *s.* (*gutter of roof*) gouttière, *f.*; (*teapot, kettle, &c.*) bec, *m.*; *v.a. and ~ out,* lancer; (*declaim*) déclamer; *v.n.* jaillir; **~er,** déclamateur, *m.*
sprain, *s.* entorse, *f.*; *v.a.* donner une entorse à.
sprat, (*ichth.*) †harenguet, *m.*
sprawl, s'étaler.
spray, *s.* (*sea*) poussière, *f.*; (*small branch*) brindille, *f.*; (*sprayer*) vaporisateur, *m.*; (*motor*) diffuseur, *m.*
spread, *s.* (*diffusion*) propagation, *f.*; (*country, &c.*) étendue, *f.*; (*wings*) envergure, *f.*
spread, *v.a.* étendre; (*net*) tendre; (*rumour, news, scatter*) répandre; (*tablecloth*) mettre*; (*sails*) déployer; (*cover*) couvrir* (de); (*news*) faire* circuler.
spread, *v.n. and ~ out,* s'étendre.
spreading, *s.* (*propagation*) propagation, *f.*; *adj.* qui s'étend.
spree, bamboche, *f.*; *be* (*go*) *on the ~,* faire* la noce.
sprig, brin, *m.*
sprightl|iness, enjouement, *m.*; **~y,** enjoué.
spring, *s.* (*season*) printemps, *m.*; (*leap*) saut, *m.*; (*watch, mach.*) ressort, *m.*; (*water and cause*) source, *f.*; (*incentive*) mobile, *m.*; (*elasticity*) élasticité, *f.*; **~ tide,** grande marée, *f.*; **~ water,** eau de source, *f.*
spring, *adj.* du printemps; (*mach.*) à ressort.
spring, *v.a.* (*game*) faire* lever; (*leak, surprise*) faire* un voie d'eau, etc. (à).
spring, *v.n.* (*grow*) pousser; (*water*) jaillir; (*leap*) sauter; (*proceed from*) provenir* de; (*descend from*) descendre (être) de; (*arise from*) naître* (être) de; (*blushes, tears, &c.*) venir* (être) à; *~ forth,* (*grow*) pousser; (*water*) jaillir; *~ up,* (*get up*) se lever vite; (*water*) jaillir; (*storm*) s'élever.
springy, élastique.
sprinkle, *s.* (*salt*) pincée, *f.*; (*rain*) petite pluie, *f.*
sprinkle, *v.a.* (*scatter*) répandre; (*with liquid*) asperger (de); *~ with,* saupoudrer de; (*strew with*) parsemer de.
sprinkler, (*holy water*) goupillon, *m.*
sprinkling, (*water*) arrosage, *m.*; (*holy water*) aspersion, *f.*; (*small quantity*) petite quantité, *f.*
sprint, *v.n.* courir* à toute vitesse; **~er,** *s.* sprinter, *m.*
sprite, lutin, *m.*

sprout, *s.* pousse, *f.*; *Brussels ~s,* choux de Bruxelles, *m.pl.*
sprout, *v.a.* pousser; *v.n.* germer; (*of a shoot*) pousser.
spruce, *s.* (*bot.*) sapin, *m.*
spruce, *adj.* pimpant; **~ly,** avec un soin recherché.
spry, alerte.
spume, écume, *f.*
spur, *s.* éperon, *m.*; (*incitement*) aiguillon, *m.*; (*of bird*) ergot, *m.*; *on the ~ of,* sous l'impulsion de; *put ~s to,* (*horse*) donner de l'éperon à.
spur, *v.a.* (*put ~s to and put on ~s*) éperonner; *~ on to,* pousser à.
spurge, (*bot.*) euphorbe, *f.*
spurious, faux, fausse; (*writings*) apocryphe; **~ness,** fausseté, *f.*; **~ly,** faussement.
spurn, *v.a.* (*scorn*) dédaigner; (*with foot*) repousser du pied.
spurt, *s.m.* (*race, &c.*) coup de collier, *m.*
sputter(ing), *s.* bredouillement, *m.*; *v.a.n.* bredouiller.
spy, espion, -ne, *m.f.*
spy, *v.a.* (*see*) apercevoir; *~ out, upon,* épier, *v.a.*; *v.n.* espionner.
spyglass, longue-vue, *f.*, *pl.* longues-vues.
squabble, *s.* chamaillerie, *f.*; *v.n.* chamailler.
squabby, boulot, -te.
squad, (*mil.*) escouade, *f.*
squadron, (*mil.*) escadron, *m.*; (*nav.*) escadre, *f.*; (*aeron.*) escadrille, *f.*
squalid, sale; **~ness,** (*squalor*) saleté, *f.*
squall, (*gust*) rafale, *f.*; (*scream*) braillement, *m.*; *v.n.* brailler; **~y,** (*weather*) à rafales.
squander, *v.a.* gaspiller; **~er,** gaspilleu|r, ~se, *m.f.*
square, *s.* (*math., mil., square object*) carré, *m.*; (*in city*) place, *f.*; (*chess-board*) case, *f.*; *T-~,* équerre, *f.*; ⚠ square, *m.*, *in French = any kind of enclosed public garden.*
square, *adj.* (*shape, math., fig., inch, foot, &c.*) carré; (*absolute*) catégorique; (*deal, honest*) honnête; (*in order*) en bon ordre; **~ness,** forme carrée, *f.*; **~ly,** (*honestly*) honnêtement.
square, *v.a.* (*make square, circle, number*) carrer; (*carp.*) équarrir; (*accounts*) régler; (*bribe*) acheter.
square, *v.n.* (*tally, &c.*) cadrer (avec).
squash, *s.* écrasement, *m.*; (*crowd*) cohue, *f.*
squash, *v.a.* (*lit. and fig.*) écraser.
squat, *v.n.* s'accroupir; (*gen. of an.*) se tapir; *adj.* accroupi, tapi; (*thick-set*) trapu.
squatter, (*U.S.A. and Australia*) squatter, *m.*
squaw, femme peau-rouge, *f.*
squawk, *v.n.* pousser des cris rauques.
squeak, *s.* cri, *m.*; *v.n.* crier.
squeal, *v.n.* pousser des cris aigus.
squeamish, (*pers.*) dégoûté; (*over-nice*) trop difficile; **~ness,** délicatesse, *f.*
squeeze, *s.* compression, *f.*; (*embrace*) embrassade, *f.*; (*hand*) serrement, *m.*
squeeze, *v.a.* (*use pressure, hand, in affection, &c.*) serrer; (*lemon*) presser; (*extort*) extorquer; (*money out of*) soutirer à; *~ oneself into,* s'introduire*; *~ out,* exprimer.
squib, petit pétard, *m.*; (*lampoon*) satire, *f.*
squill, (*bot.*) scille, *f.*
squint, *s.* strabisme, *m.*; *~-eyed,* louche; *v.n.* loucher; *have a ~ at,* loucher sur.
squire, (*of a knight*) écuyer, *m.*; (*proprietor*) seigneur du village, *m.*; (*of a lady*) cavalier, *m.*
squirrel, écureuil, *m.*
squirt, *s.* seringue, *f.*; *v.a.* seringuer.
stab, *s.* coup de poignard, de couteau, *&c., m.*; *v.a.* (*lit. and fig.*) poignarder.
stability, stabilité, *f.*
stabiliz|e, stabiliser; **~ation,** stabilisation, *f.*
stabl|e, *s.* écurie, *f.*; **~e-boy,** garçon d'écurie, *m.*; **~e-yard,** cour d'écurie, *f.*; *v.a.* (*horse*) établer; **~ing,** écuries, *f.pl.*
stable, *adj.* stable.
stack, *s.* (*heap*) pile, *f.*; (*hay, &c.*) meule, *f.*; (*chimney*) souche, *f.*; *v.a.* (*hay*) mettre* en meule; (*pile up*) empiler.
stadium, stade, *m.*
staff, *s.* (*mil.*) état-major, *m.*; (*lit., fig., badge of office*) bâton, *m.*; (*flag, &c.*) hampe, *f.*; (*pilgrim*) bourdon, *m.*; (*support*) soutien, *m.*; (*institution*) personnel, *m.*; *~ officer,* officier d'état-major, *m.*
stag, cerf, *m.*; **~-beetle,** cerf-volant, *m.*
stag|e, *s.* (*of theatre*) scène, *f.*; (*drama*) théâtre, *m.*; ⚠ stage, *m.* = *'probation'*; (*of action*) champ, *m.*; (*in development*) période, *f.*; (*for horses*) relais, *m.*; (*platform*) estrade, *f.*; (*scaffolding*) échafaudage, *m.*; (*stopping-place, distance between such*) étape, *f.*; **~e-box,** loge d'avant-scène, *f.*; **~e-coach,** diligence, *f.*; *~e-fright,* trac, *m.*; **~e-manager,** régisseur, *m.*; **~ing,** (*theatr., &c.*) mise en scène, *f.*; *v.a.* mettre* en scène.
stager, *old ~,* vieux routier, *m.*
stagger, *v.a.* (*upset*) bouleverser; *v.n.* chanceler.
stagnant, (*lit. and fig.*) stagnant.
stagna|te, *v.n.* être stagnant; **~tion,** stagnation, *f.*
staid, posé; **~ly,** posément.
stain, *s.* (*lit. and fig.*) tache, *f.*; (*for staining*) couleur, *f.*; *v.a.* tacher; (*fig.*) salir; (*wood, &c.*) teinter; *~ed glass,* vitraux, *m.pl.*; *~ed-glass window,* vitrail, *m.*
stainless, (*knives*) inoxydable.
stair, (*step*) marche, *f.*; **~s,** escalier, *m.*; *down~s,* en bas; *up~s,* en haut.
staircase, escalier, *m.*
stake, *s.* pieu, *m.*; (*for burning alive*)

bûcher, *m.*; (*money wagered*) enjeu, *m.*; *at* ~, en jeu.
stake, *v.a.* garnir de pieux; (*fortune, life, &c.*) jouer; (*at play*) mettre* au jeu; ~ *out,* jalonner.
stalactite, stalactite, *f.*
stale, *adj.* (*bread*) rassis; (*liquors*) éventé; (*subject, &c.*) rebattu; **~ness,** (*joke, &c.*) banalité, *f.*
stalemate, (*chess*) pat, *m.*
stalk, *s.* (*plants, flowers*) tige, *f.*; (*cabbage*) trognon, *m.*
stalk, *v.a.* (*hunt*) chasser; *~ing-horse,* (*fig.*) prétexte, *m.*; *v.n.* marcher fièrement.
stall, *s.* (*stable, church*) stalle, *f.*; (*butcher's*) étal, *m.*; (*theatr.*) fauteuil, *m.*; (*booth*) échoppe, *f.*; (*books*) bibliothèque, *f.*; (*aeron.*) arrêt subit, *m.*; *v.n.* (*aeron.*) mettre* en perte de vitesse.
stallion, étalon, *m.*
stalwart, vigoureu|x, ~se.
stamina, force de résistance, *f.*
stammer, *s.* bégayement; *v.n.* bégayer; **~er,** bègue, *m.f.*; **~ingly,** en bégayant.
stamp, *s.* **1** (*with foot*) coup de pied, *m.*; **2** (*postage*) timbre-poste, *m.*, *pl.* timbres-poste; **3** (*stamping-machine*) estampe, *f.*; **4** (*hall-mark*) contrôle, *m.*; **5** (*pers.*) trempe, *f.*; **6** (*characteristic feature, mark of stamp*) empreinte, *f.*; **7** (*on goods*) estampille, *f.*; **8** (*official*) timbre, *m.*; *~-duty,* droit de timbre, *m.*; *v.a.* (*letter, deed, bill, &c.*) timbrer; (*metal, leather, &c.*) estamper; (*goods*) estampiller; (*hall-mark*) contrôler; (*characterize*) faire* connaître; (*on the mind*) graver; *~ed* (*envelope*) affranchie; ~ *out,* (*suppress*) étouffer; *v.n.* frapper du pied.
stampede, sauve-qui-peut, *m.*; *v.n.* se sauver en désordre.
stance, position, *f.*
stanch, *adj. see* STAUNCH; *v.a.* (*blood*) étancher.
stanchion, (*prop.*) étançon, *m.*
stand, *s.* (*position taken up, lit. and fig.*) position, *f.*; (*vehicles*) station, *f.*; (*round table*) guéridon, *m.*; (*resistance*) résistance, *f.*; (*raised structure*) estrade, *f.*; (*stall*) étalage, *m.*; (*in exhibitions*) stand, *m.*; *in compounds often* porte-, *e.g. umbrella-~,* porte-parapluies, *m. invar.*; *watch-~,* porte-montre, *m. invar.*; *~-by,* ressource, *f.*; *wash-hand-~,* lavabo, *m.*
stand, *v.a.* (*bear*) supporter; (*undergo*) subir; (*put*) poser; (*a chance*) avoir; (*pay for*) payer; (*by resisting*) soutenir*; ~ (*out*) *against,* résister à; ~ *by,* soutenir*; (*one's word*) tenir*; ~ *for,* (*represent*) représenter; (*mean*) signifier; ~ *in,* (*cost*) coûter; ~ *up for,* défendre; ~ *upon,* insister sur.
stand, *v.n.*; *of precise position* être *is often adequate*; (*be erect*) se tenir* debout; (*keep on one's legs*) se soutenir*; (*of matters, as to order, &c.*) se trouver; (*stop*) s'arrêter; (*remain*) rester (être); (*stand good*) être valable; ~ *clear* (*of*), s'écarter de; ~ *still,* se tenir* tranquille; ~ *aloof, off,* s'éloigner; ~ *back,* se tenir* en arrière; ~ *forth, forward,* avancer; ~ *out,* (*be prominent*) ressortir*; ~ *over,* rester (être) en suspens; ~ *up,* se lever; ~ *upright,* se tenir* droit.
standard, *s.* (*flag, lit. and fig.*) étendard, *m.*; (*money, weights, measures*) étalon, *m.*; (*of excellence*) type, *m.*; (*education, living, &c.*) niveau, *m.*; (*tree*) arbre de plein vent, *m.*; (*wages, &c.*) taux, *m.*; **~-bearer,** porte-étendard, *m. invar.*; ~ **lamp,** torchère, *f.*
standard, *adj.* (*prices*) régulat|eur, ~rice; (*gold, silver*) au titre; (*sizes*) ordinaire; (*authors, &c.*) classique.
standardize, unifier.
standing, *s.* (*status*) position, *f.*; (*duration*) date, *f.*
standing, *adj.* (*water*) dormant; (*corn, &c.*) sur pied; (*dish*) ordinaire; (*permanent*) permanent; ~ *expenses, see* EXPENSE.
standpoint, point de vue, *m.*
standstill, arrêt, *m.*; *come to a* ~, s'arrêter court.
stanza, (*verse*) stance, *f.*
staple, *s.* (*lock*) gâche, *f.*; (*product*) produit principal, *m.*; *adj.* principal.
star, *s.* (*lit., fig., theatr., &c., of an order*) étoile, *f.*; *unlucky* ~, mauvaise étoile, *f.*; *~s and stripes,* drapeau américain, *m.*; **~fish,** étoile de mer, *f.*; **~-shell,** fusée éclairante, *f.*; *see ~s,* voir trente-six mille chandelles.
star, *v.a.* étoiler.
starboard, tribord, *m.*
starch, *s.* empois, *m.*; *v.a.* empeser; **~ed, ~y,** (*lit. and fig.*) empesé.
stare, *s.* regard fixe, *m.*; *v.n.* regarder fixement; (*with astonishment*) ouvrir* de grands yeux; ~ *at,* regarder fixement.
staring, *adj.* (*colour*) voyant; *stark* ~ *mad,* fou à lier.
stark, *adv.* tout à fait.
starlight, lumière des étoiles, *f.*; *adj.* étoilé.
starling, (*ornith.*) étourneau, *m.*
starry, étoilé.
start, *s.* (*of fear*) tressaillement, *m.*; (*beginning*) commencement, *m.*; (*departure*) départ, *m.*; (*advantage in race*) avance, *f.*; *make a* ~, commencer; (*departure*) se mettre* en route.
start, *v.a.* (*send off*) faire* partir; (*wild ans., birds*) faire* lever; (*begin*) commencer; (*business or newspaper, a pers. in anything, &c.*) lancer; (*rumour*) donner naissance à; (*cause to begin doing*) faire* + *inf.*
start, *v.n.* (*races, set out*) partir* (être); (*from fear*) tressaillir*; (*begin*) commencer; *to* ~ *with,* en premier lieu; ~ *back,* reculer en arrière; ~ *out,* partir* (être); ~ *up,* sursauter.
starter, *s.* (*originator*) auteur, *m.*; (*turf*) partant, *m.*; (*motor*) démarreur, *m.*

starting, (*departure*) départ, *m.*
startle, *v.a.* effrayer.
startling, *adj.* saisissant.
starvation, inanition, *f.*
starve, *v.a.* faire* mourir de faim; ((*garrison, &c.*) réduire* par la faim.
starve, *v.n.* (*lit. and fig.*) mourir* de faim.
starveling, *adj. and s.m.f.* affamé, -e.
state, *s.* (*condition, nation, government*) état, *m.*; (*pomp*) pompe, *f.*; **~-bed,** lit de parade, *m.*; **~-room,** salle de réception, *f.*; **~s,** (*dominions, legislative bodies*) États, *m.pl.*; *in ~,* en grande cérémonie.
state, *adj.* de parade; (*visit*) de cérémonie; (*of the State*) d'état *and* d'État.
state, *v.a.* (*affirm*) affirmer; (*in writing*) porter; (*opinion, &c.*) déclarer; (*math.*) poser.
statecraft, politique, *f.*
stated, (*time, &c.*) fixe.
statel|iness, majesté, *f.*; **~y,** majestueu|x, ~se.
statement, déclaration, *f.*; (*written*) compte rendu, *m.*; (*comm., bkkpg.*) relevé, *m.*; ~ *of expenses,* état de frais, *m.*
statesman, homme d'état, *m.*; **~like,** d'homme d'état; **~ship,** art de gouverner, *m.*
statics, statique, *f.*
station, (*place assigned*) poste, *m.*; (*spot, position*) endroit, *m.*; (*rank*) position sociale, *f.*; (*rail.*) gare, *f.*; *~-master,* chef de gare, *m.*
station, *v.a.* poster; (*sentry*) poser; ⚠ stationner = '*pause*', '*stop*'; *be ~ed,* (*mil.*) être en garnison; **~ary,** *adj.* stationnaire.
stationer, papetier, *m.*; *~'s shop,* **~y,** papeterie, *f.*
statistic, *adj.* statistique; **~s,** statistique, *f.*; **~ian,** statisticien, -ne, *m.f.*
statu|ary, (*art*) statuaire, *f.*; (*pers.*) statuaire, *m.f.*; **~e,** statue, *f.*; **~ette,** statuette, *f.*; **~esque,** beau (bel + *vowel or mute* H), belle comme une statue.
stature, stature, *f.*
status, rang, *m.*
statute, statut, *m.*
staunch, loyal.
stave, *v.a.* ~ *in,* crever; ~ *off,* éloigner.
stay, *s.* (*sojourn*) séjour, *m.*; (*prop and naut.*) étai, *m.*; (*support, fig.*) soutien, *m.*
stay, *v.a.* (*stop*) arrêter; (*put off*) différer; (*prop, often + up*) étayer.
stay, *v.n.* (*remain*) rester (être); (*hotel, &c.*) être installé; (*wait*) attendre; (*in a place*) passer du temps (à); ~ *away,* rester (être) absent; ~ *behind,* rester (être) en arrière; ~ *up,* veiller.
stays, corset, *m.*; (*aeron.*) supports, *m.pl.*
stead, place, *f.*; *in my ~,* à ma place; *stand in good ~,* être utile (à).
steadfast, ferme; **~ness,** fermeté, *f.*; **~ly,** fermement.
stead|iness, (*firmness*) fermeté, *f.*; (*persistence*) persévérance, *f.*; (*conduct*) conduite rangée, *f.*; (*comm.*) stabilité, *f.*
stead|y, (*firm*) ferme; (*constant*) soutenu; (*pers.*) rangé; (*mil., fire*) nourri; (*comm.*) stable; (*hand*) sûr; **~y-going,** sérieu|x, ~se; *interj.* attention!; **~ily,** fermement.
steady, *v.a.* affermir; (*pers., fig.*) mettre* du plomb dans la tête.
steak, *s.* tranche, *f.*; *see also* BEEF.
steal, *v.a.* voler; (*seduce*) séduire*.
steal, *v.n.* voler; (*move secretly*) se glisser; ~ *away, off,* se dérober; ~ *in, out,* entrer (être), sortir* (être) furtivement.
stealth, *by ~,* **~ily,** à la dérobée; **~y,** (*things*) furti|f, ~ve.
steam, *s.* vapeur, *f.*; *~-boiler,* chaudière à vapeur, *f.*; *~-engine,* locomotive, *f.*; *~-hammer,* marteau-pilon, *m.*; *adj.* (*worked by steam*) à vapeur; *get up ~,* chauffer.
steam, *v.a.* (*food*) cuire* à la vapeur.
steam, *v.n.* aller* (être), etc., à la vapeur; (*smoke as horse*) fumer; ~ *ahead,* aller* (être) à toute vapeur.
steamboat, bateau à vapeur, *m.*
steamer, steamship, vapeur, *m.*
steed, coursier, *m.*
steel, *s.* acier, *m.*; (*fig.*) fer, *m.*; (*for sharpening*) fusil, *m.*; *~-works,* aciérie, *f.*; *~-engraving, see* ENGRAVING; *~-grey,* gris d'acier, *invar.*; ~ *plate,* tôle d'acier, *f.*; *adj.* d'acier; *v.a.* (*fig.*) endurcir; **~y,** (*fig.*) d'acier.
steelyard, (*balance*) romaine, *f.*
steep, *s.* pente rapide, *f.*
steep, *adj.* (*lit. and fig.*) raide; **~ness,** raideur, *f.*
steep, *v.a.* (*lit. and fig.*) tremper.
steeple, clocher, *m.*; **~-chase,** course au clocher, *f.*
steer, *s.* jeune bœuf, *m.*
steer, *v.a.* (*ship*) gouverner; (*motor, &c., and fig.*) diriger.
steer, *v.n.* (*answer, helm*) gouverner; ~ *for,* gouverner sur; ~ *clear of,* éviter.
steerage, logement de dernière classe, *m.*
steering, ~-wheel, roue du gouvernail, *f.*; (*motor*) volant, *m.*; **~-gear,** (*motor*) direction, *f.*
steersman, timonier, *m.*
stellar, stellaire.
stem, *s.* (*plant, &c.*) tige, *f.*; (*fruit*) queue, *f.*; (*pipe*) tuyau, *m.*; (*family*) souche, *f.*; (*naut.*) proue, *f.*; *from ~ to stern,* de l'avant à l'arrière.
stem, *v.a.* (*current, repel, lit. and fig.*) refouler.
stench, puanteur, *f.*
stencil, *s.* (*plate*) pochoir, *m.*; **~-paper,** stencil, *m.*; *v.a.* peindre* au pochoir.
stenograph|er, sténographe, *m.f.*; **~y,** sténographie, *f.*
stentorian, *adj.* de stentor.
step, *s.* (*footstep, pace, footprint, fig., sound of footfall*) pas, *m.*; (*of staircase*) marche, *f.*; (*ladder*) échelon, *m.*; (*veh. and pair of steps*) marchepied, *m.*; (*in promotion*) grade, *m.*; *take ~s,* faire* des démarches; ~ *by ~,* pas à pas.

step, *v.n.* faire* un pas; (*walk*) marcher; (*go, come*) aller*, venir* (être); ~ *this way,* venez par ici; ~ *aside,* s'écarter; ~ *back,* reculer; ~ *forward,* s'avancer; ~ *in,* entrer (être); ~ *out,* sortir* (être); ~ *up to,* s'approcher de.

step, *adj. in comps.,* beau, belle; *e.g.* ~**-brother,** beau-frère, *m.*; ~**-daughter,** belle-fille, *f.*; ~**-father,** beau-père, *m., &c.*

steppe, steppe, *m.*

stepping-stone, (*fig.*) marchepied, *m.*

stereotype, *s.* (*plate*) cliché, *m.*; *v.a.* (*lit. and fig.*) stéréotyper; ~**d,** (*fig. approx.*) banal.

steril|e, (*lit. and fig.*) stérile; ~**ity,** stérilité, *f.*

steriliz|ation, stérilisation, *f.*; ~**e,** stériliser.

sterling, *adj.* sterling, *invar.*

stern, *s.* (*naut.*) arrière, *m.*

stern, *adj.* sévère; (*punishment*) rigoureu|x, ~se; ~**ness,** sévérité, *f.*; ~**ly,** sévèrement.

sternmost, le plus en arrière.

stethoscope, stéthoscope, *m.*

stevedore, arrimeur, *m.*

stew, *s.* (*meat*) ragoût, *m.*; (*fruit*) compote, *f.*; (*perplexity*) embarras, *m.*

stew, *v.a.* étuver; (*fruit*) mettre* en compote; *v.n.* cuire* à l'étuvée; ~*ed fruit, see* FRUIT; ~*-pan, see* PAN.

steward, (*estate*) régisseur, *m.*; (*on ship*) steward, *m.*; ~**ess,** femme de chambre, *f.*; ~**ship,** charge, *f.*

stick, *s.* (*shaped, wax, soap, &c.*) bâton, *m.*; (*walking*) canne, *f.*; (*unshaped*) petite branche, *f.*; (*for flogging*) fouet, *m.*; ~**s,** (*for burning*) bois, *m.sing.*

stick, *v.a.* (*cause to adhere*) coller; (*put*) mettre*; ~ *on,* attacher; ~ *out,* (*of window, &c.*) passer par; ~ *up,* (*post*) afficher; (*prick up*) dresser; ~ *no bills,* défense d'afficher.

stick, *v.n.* (*adhere*) se coller; (*stop*) s'arrêter; (*be entangled*) rester (être) pris; (*persevere*) persévérer (dans); (*remain*) rester (être); (*be jammed, &c.*) se coincer; (*in the mind*) s'embourber; ~ *at,* hésiter devant; ~ *by, to,* rester (être) fidèle à; ~ *out,* faire* saillie; (*bulge*) bomber; (*not yield*) tenir* bon; ~ *up,* (*be erect*) se dresser; ~ *up for,* défendre.

stick|iness, viscosité, *f.*; ~**y,** gluant.

stickleback, (*ichth.*) épinoche, *f.*

stickler, *be a ~ for,* être à cheval sur.

stiff, *adj.* (*not flexible, difficult to move, steep, style, price, fig.*) raide; (*wind*) fort; (*money*) rare; (*air, manner*) gêné; (*hard*) dur; (*difficult*) difficile; ~**ness,** raideur, *f.*; (*fig.*) contrainte, *f.*; ~**ly,** avec raideur; ~ *neck, see* NECK.

stiffen, (*make stiff, tighten*) raidir; (*make hard*) durcir.

stifl|e, *v.a.* (*lit. and fig.*) étouffer; ~**ing,** *adj.* étouffant.

stigma, (*lit. and fig.*) stigmate, *m.*; ~**tize,** *v.a.* stigmatiser.

stile, échalier, *m.*

stiletto, (*weapon*) stilet, *m.*

still, *s.* calme, *m.*; (*apparatus*) alambic, *m.*

still, *adj.* calme; (*quiet*) tranquille; *v.a.* calmer; ~**ness,** tranquillité, *f.*; ~ *waters run deep, see* WATER.

still, *adv.* toujours; (*continuity*) encore; (*nevertheless*) cependant; ~**-born,** mortné, -e.

still-life, nature morte, *f.*

stilt, *s.* échasse, *f.*; ~**ed,** *adj.* (*manner, style*) guindé.

stimulant, (*lit. and fig.*) stimulant, *m.*

stimula|te, (*lit. and fig.*) stimuler; ~**tion,** stimulation, *f.*; ~**tive,** stimulant.

stimulus, (*lit. and fig.*) stimulant, *m.*

sting, *s.* (*lit. and fig.*) aiguillon, *m.*

sting, *v.a.* piquer; (*fig.*) blesser; (*conscience, &c.*) bourreler (de); *v.n.* piquer.

sting|iness, mesquinerie, *f.*; ~**y,** mesquin; ~**ily,** mesquinement.

stink, *s.* puanteur, *f.*; *v.n.* puer.

stint, *s.* restriction, *f.*; *v.a.* lésiner sur.

stipend, *s.* traitement, *m.*

stipple, *s.* (*picture*) pointillé, *m.*; *v.a.* pointiller.

stipulat|e, stipuler (que); ~*e for,* stipuler, *v.a.*; ~**ion,** stipulation, *f.*

stir, *s.* mouvement, *m.*

stir, *v.a.* remuer; (*fig.*) émouvoir*; (*wrath, &c.*) exciter; ~ *up,* (*strife, &c.*) susciter.

stir, *v.n.* (*change place, and of things*) remuer; (*pers.*) bouger.

stirring, *adj.* (*busy*) agissant; (*eloquence, &c.*) entraînant.

stirrup, étrier, *m.*; ~**-cup,** coup de l'étrier, *m.*

stitch, *s.* (*sewing*) point, *m.*; (*knitting*) maille, *f.*; (*in side*) point de côté, *m.*

stitch, *v.a.n.* coudre*.

stiver, (*fig.*) sou vaillant, *m.*

stoat, hermine, *f.*

stock, *s.* **1** (*tree*) tronc, *m.*; **2** (*goods on hand*) marchandises, *f.pl.*; **3** (*race*) souche, *f.*; **4** (*bot.*) giroflée, *f.*; **5** (*cattle*) bestiaux, *m.pl.*; **6** (*cravat*) col, *m.*; **7** (*rail.*) matériel, *m.*; **8** (*fig. of learning, &c.*) fonds, *m.*; **9** (*fin.*) valeurs, *f.pl.*; ~**s,** (*punish.*) bloc, *m.,* pilori, *m.*; (*ship*) chantier, *m.*; *live ~,* cheptel vif, *m.*; *rolling-~,* matériel roulant, *m.*; ~**-broker,** agent de change, *m.*; **Stock Exchange,** Bourse, *f.*; ~**-holder,** actionnaire, *m.f.*; ~**-market,** marché des valeurs, *m.*; ~**-taking,** inventaire, *m.*; ~**-in-trade,** fonds, *m.*; *in ~,* en magasin; *take ~ of,* faire* l'inventaire de.

stock, *v.a.* (*provision*) approvisionner; (*shop*) monter (avoir) en = '*with*'; (*provide with*) fournir de.

stockade, palissade, *f.*

stocking, bas, *m.*

stocky, trapu.

stodgy, (*food*) lourd.

stoic, *s.* stoïcien, *m.*; ~**ism,** stoïcisme, *m.*; ~**al,** stoïque; ~**ally,** stoïquement.

stoke, (*fire*) entretenir*; (*fire-engine*) chauffer.
stoker, chauffeur, *m.*
stole, *s.* (*eccles.*) étole, *f.*
stolid, flegmatique; **~ity,** flegme, *m.*; **~ly,** flegmatiquement.
stomach, estomac, *m.*; (*appetite*) appétit, *m.*; (*desire*) goût, *m.*; **~-ache,** mal à l'estomac, *m.*; *v.a.* (*lit. and fig.*) supporter.
stomacher, corsage lacé, *m.*
stomachic, stomacal.
stone, *s.* (*piece of rock, precious, med.*) pierre, *f.*; (*fruit*) noyau, *m.*; (*grapes*) pépin, *m.*; **~-fruit,** fruit à noyau, *m.*; **~-pine,** *see* PINE; **~-ware,** grès, *m.*; *adj.* de pierre; **~-weed,** (*bot.*) grémil, *m.*; *a rolling ~ gathers no moss,* pierre qui roule n'amasse pas.
stone, *v.a.* (*pers.*) lapider; (*fruit*) ôter le noyau, les pépins de.
stonecrop, (*bot.*) orpin, *m.*
stonewort, (*bot.*) sison, *m.*
stony, (*road, &c.*) pierreu|x, ~se; (*heart*) dur.
stool, escabeau, *m.*; (*evacuation*) selle, *f.*
stoop, *v.n.* se pencher; (*in walking*) avoir le dos rond; *~ to,* s'abaisser jusqu'à.
stop, *s.* (*halt*) †halte, *f.*; (*punctuation*) signe de ponctuation, *m.*; (*mach.*) arrêt, *m.*; (*organ*) jeu, *m.*; **~-watch,** montre à arrêt, *f.*; *come to a ~,* (*end*) se terminer; *put a ~ to,* mettre* fin à.
stop, *v.a.* **1** (*lit. and cheque*) arrêter; **2** (*prevent*) empêcher (de); **3** (*leave, &c.*) supprimer; **4** (*close up*) boucher; **5** (*breath*) couper; **6** (*tooth*) plomber; **7** (*wages, &c.*) retenir*; **8** (*gram.*) ponctuer; **9** (*road, &c.*) barrer; **10** (*intercept*) intercepter; **11** (*close*) fermer; **12** (*payments*) suspendre; **13** (*cease*) cesser; *~ off,* (*water, &c.*) couper; *~ up,* boucher; **~-press,** *adj.* dernière heure, *invar.*
stop, *v.n.* s'arrêter; (*cease*) cesser; (*with duration of time, visit, &c.*) passer; (*remain*) rester (être); *~ at,* (*of boat or train*) desservir, *v.a.*; *~ there,* (*fig.*) en rester là; *~ thief!* au voleur!
stoppage, (*obstruction*) obstruction, *f.*; (*arrest, stay*) arrêt, *m.*; (*salary*) retenue, *f.*
stopcock, robinet d'arrêt, *m.*
stopgap, bouche-trou, *m.*
stopper, (*bottle*) bouchon, *m.*
stopping, *adj.* *~ train,* train omnibus, *m.*
storage, emmagasinage, *m.*
store, *s.* provision, *f.*; **~s,** (*mil., food*) vivres, *m.pl.*; (*U.S.A. often 'stores'*) magasin, *m.*; (*departmental*) grand magasin, *m.*; *military ~s,* matériel de guerre, *m.*; **~-keeper,** magasinier, *m.*; ⚠ store = '*draw-blind*'; *set ~ by,* attacher du prix à.
store, *v.a.* (*in warehouse*) emmagasiner; (*memory, &c.*) meubler; (*furniture*) mettre* au garde-meuble.
storehouse, magasin, *m.*; (*fig.*) mine, *f.*
storeroom, dépôt, *m.*
stor|ey, (story), étage, *m.*; **~eyed,** *two-, three-, four-~eyed, &c.,* à deux, trois, quatre, etc., étages.
stork, (*ornith.*) cigogne, *f.*; **~'s bill,** (*bot.*) bec de grue, *m.*
storm, (*lit. and fig.*) orage, *m.*; (*mil.*) assaut, *m.*; (*abuse*) torrent, *m.*; *~-troops,* troupes de choc, *f.pl.*; *v.a. and take by ~,* prendre* d'assaut; *v.n.* (*anger*) tempêter (contre).
storm|iness, état orageux, *m.*; **~y,** orageu|x, ~se; (*temper*) emporté; *be ~y,* (*of weather*) être à l'orage.
storming, *s.* (*mil.*) assaut, *m.*
story, (*tale, of a life, account, plot, of novel, &c., fib*) histoire, *f.*; **~-teller,** conteu|r, ~se, *m.f.*; (*pej.*) menteu|r, ~se, *m.f.*
stout, (*strong*) fort; (*brave*) intrépide; (*corpulent*) gros, -se; **~ness,** corpulence, *f.*; **~ly,** vigoureusement.
stove, *s.* (*cooking*) fourneau, *m.*; (*heating*) poêle, *m.*
stow (away), serrer; (*on ship*) arrimer; **~age, ~ing,** (*on ship*) arrimage, *m.*
stowaway, *s.* passager clandestin, *m.*
straggle, *v.n.* s'écarter (de); (*be apart*) être écarté; (*mil.*) rester (être) en arrière.
straggler, (*mil.*) traînard, *m.*
straggling, *adj.* (*plants, houses, &c.*) éparpillé; (*town, &c.*) à maisons éparses.
straight, *adj.* (*lit. and fig.*) droit; (*in order*) en ordre; (*upright*) d'aplomb; *adv.* (*throw, aim, see, &c.*) juste; (*direction*) droit; *~ on,* tout droit; *~ as an arrow,* droit comme un I; **~ness,** (*fig.*) droiture, *f.*
straighten, redresser; (*put tidy*) mettre* en ordre.
straightforward, *adj.* droit; **~ness,** droiture, *f.*; **~ly,** loyalement.
straightway, immédiatement.
strain, *s.* effort, *m.*; (*tension*) tension, *f.*; (*muscle*) effort, *m.*; (*tone*) ton, *m.*; (*tendency of speech*) style, *m.*; **~s,** (*mus.*) accents, *m.pl.*
strain, *v.a.* (*stretch*) tendre; (*filter*) passer; (*muscle, overdo, exaggerate*) forcer; (*clasp*) serrer; (*style*) outrer.
strain, *v.n.* (*filter*) filtrer; *~ at,* tirer sur.
strainer, passoire, *f.*
strait, *s.* (*geog.*) détroit, *m.*; (*fig.*) **~s,** gêne, *f.*
strait, *adj.* étroit; **~-laced,** collet monté, *invar.*; *~* **waistcoat,** camisole de force, *f.*
straiten, *v.a.* *be ~ed,* (*in circumstances*) être dans la gêne.
strand, *s.* (*shore*) rivage, *m.*; (*of ropes*) toron, *m.*
stranded, (*fig.*) abandonné; *be ~,* (*ship*) échouer.
strange, (*peculiar*) étrange; (*foreign, new*) étrang|er, ~ère; (*unknown*) inconnu (à); **~ness,** singularité, *f.*; **~ly,** étrangement; *see also* SPECIMEN.
stranger, étrang|er, ~ère, *m.f.*
strangle, étrangler.
strap, *s.* courroie, *f.*; *v.a.* boucler.

strapping, *s.* (*beating, leathering*) les étrivières, *f.pl.*; *adj.* (*pers.*) découplé.
strat|agem, stratagème, *m.*; **~egic,** stratégique; **~egist,** stratégiste, *m.*; **~egy,** stratégie, *f.*
stratum, *pl. strata,* couche, *f.*
straw, paille, *f.*; *~-bottomed,* (*chair*) paillé; *~-coloured,* paille, *invar.*; *the last ~ that breaks the camel's back,* la goutte d'eau qui fait déborder le vase.
strawberry, fraise, *f.*; (*plant*) fraisier, *m.*; **~-tree,** arbousier, *m.*; *wild ~,* fraise des bois, *f.*
stray, *adj.* égaré; (*casual*) accidentel, -le.
stray, *v.n.* (*lit. and fig.*) errer; (*lose one's way*) s'égarer.
streak, *s.* (*line*) raie, *f.*; (*strip*) bande, *f.*; *v.a.* rayer (de).
stream, *s.* (*current, water, electr., liquid in motion, thought*) courant, *m.*; (*crowd*) flots, *m.pl.*; (*tears, abuse, words*) torrent, *m.*; (*small river*) ruisseau, *m.*; **~line,** *s.* profil aérodynamique; *adj.* aérodynamique; (*aeron.*) caréné; *up-~,* en amont; *down-~,* en aval.
stream, *v.n.* (*blood, perspiration*) ruisseler; (*float*) flotter.
streamer, (*pennon*) banderole, *f.*
streamlet, filet d'eau, *m.*
street, rue, *f.*; *~-door,* porte de la rue, *f.*; *~-sweeper,* balayeur, *m.*; *down the ~,* plus loin, *or* plus bas dans la rue; *up the ~,* plus loin, *or* plus †haut dans la rue.
strength, force, *f.*; *on the ~ of,* sur la foi de; *on the ~,* (*mil.*) sur les contrôles; *gather ~,* prendre* des forces.
strengthen, fortifier.
strenuous, énergique; **~ness,** énergie, *f.*; **~ly,** énergiquement.
stress, *s.* force, *f.*; (*gram.*) accent, *m.*; (*circumstances*) pression, *f.*; (*mechanics*) effort, *m.*; *lay ~ on,* insister sur.
stretch, *s.* (*strain*) effort, *m.*; (*expanse*) étendue, *f.*; *at a ~,* d'une traite.
stretch, *v.a.* (*extend*) étendre; (*make tense*) tendre; (*widen, enlarge*) élargir; *~ out,* tendre; (*extend*) étendre.
stretch, *v.n.* (*expand*) s'étendre; (*pers.*) s'étirer; (*widen*) s'élargir.
stretcher, (*wounded*) brancard, *m.*
strew, *v.a.* (*scatter*) semer; *~ with,* joncher de.
strict, (*pers., rule, sense*) strict; **~ness,** rigueur, *f.*; **~ly,** strictement.
stricture, critique, *f.*
stride, *s.* enjambée, *f.*; *v.n.* enjamber; *~ over, v.a.* enjamber; *~ up and down,* aller* (être) et venir* (être) à grands pas.
strident, strident.
strife, lutte, *f.*
strike, (*workmen*) grève, *f.*; *be on ~,* être en grève; *railway ~,* grève de cheminots, *f.*; *sympathetic ~,* grève de sympathie, *f.*
strike, *v.a.* **1** (*hit, coins, impress, inspire with*) frapper (de); **2** (*blow*) asséner; **3** (*bargain*) faire*; **4** (*work*) cesser; **5** (*balance*) établir; **6** (*clocks*) sonner; **7** (*rock, ground*) toucher; **8** (*match*) frotter; **9** (*root, attitude*) prendre*; **10** (*find*) trouver; **11** (*sail, flag*) amener; **12** (*tents*) plier; *~ at,* porter un coup à; *~ down,* abattre; *~ off, ~ out,* (*erase*) effacer; (*deduct*) déduire*; *~ on,* trouver; *~ up,* (*mus.*) entonner; (*acquaintance*) faire*; *~ blind,* frapper de cécité; *~ dumb,* rendre muet, -te (de); *be struck dumb,* devenir* (être) muet de.
strike, *v.n.* frapper; (*matches, root*) prendre*; (*clocks*) sonner; (*workmen*) se mettre* en grève; (*direct one's course*) se diriger; *~ out,* frapper; *~ up,* (*mus.*) commencer à jouer.
striker, (*workman*) gréviste, *m.*
striking, *adj.* frappant; (*remarkable*) remarquable; **~ly,** d'une manière frappante.
string, ficelle, *f.*; (*bonnet*) bride, *f.*; (*mus. instruments*) corde, *f.*; (*beads, onions, fig.*) chapelet, *m.*; *~ instrument,* instrument à cordes, *m.*; *pull the ~s, wires,* tenir* les ficelles; **~y,** filandreu|x, ~se.
string, *v.a.* (*instruments*) munir de cordes; (*beads, &c.*) enfiler; (*nerves, &c.*) tendre.
stringent, rigoureu|x, ~se.
strip, *s.* bande, *f.*; (*small piece*) bout, *m.*
strip, *v.a.* (*undress*) déshabiller; *~ of,* (*lit. and fig.*) dépouiller de; *~ off,* arracher; *v.n.* se déshabiller.
stripe, *s.* bande, *f.*; (*striping*) rayure, *f.*; (*mil.*) galon, *m.*; **~s,** coups de fouet, *&c., m.pl.*
striped, rayé.
stripling, adolescent, *m.*
striv|e, s'efforcer (de); (*struggle*) lutter (contre); *~e for,* disputer + *acc. of thing, dat. of person*; **~ing,** lutte, *f.*
stroke, *s.* (*blow, wing, oar, brush, genius, luck, bell, clock, tennis, &c.*) coup, *m.*; (*swimming*) brasse, *f.*; (*pen, wit*) trait, *m.*; (*med.*) attaque, *f.*; (*in boat*) chef de nage, *m.*; *at a ~,* d'un seul coup.
stroke, *v.a.* caresser.
stroll, *s.* tour, *m.*; *take a ~, v.n.* faire* un tour.
strolling, *adj.* ambulant; *~ player, see* PLAYER.
strong, (*having force, power of resistance, smell, light, taste, wind, health, drinks, effective, language, in comps.*) fort; (*robust*) vigoureu|x, ~se; (*voice, powerful*) puissant; (*buildings, &c., robust of persons*) solide; (*great*) grand; *~ box,* coffre-fort, *m.*; *~ drink, see* DRINK; **~ly,** fortement.
stronghold, forteresse, *f.*
strop, cuir à repasser, *m.*; *v.a.* repasser sur le cuir.
structur|e, structure, *f.*; **~al,** de structure.
struggle, *s.* (*tussle, fray*) mêlée, *f.*; (*fig.*) lutte, *f.*
struggle, *v.n.* (*make great efforts*) faire* de grands efforts (pour); (*with one's limbs*)

se débattre; ~ *with,* (*lit. and fig.*) lutter avec; ~ *through,* se frayer chemin à travers.
strum, *v.a.* tapoter.
strut, *s.* démarche fière, *f.*; *v.n.* se pavaner.
strychnine, strychnine, *f.*
stub, *s.* (*tree*) souche, *f.*; (*cigarette, &c.*) bout, *m.*
stubbl|e, chaume, *m.*; **~y,** plein de chaume.
stubborn, opiniâtre; **~ness,** opiniâtreté, *f.*; **~ly,** opiniâtrément.
stucco, stuc, *m.*
stud, *s.* (*shirt*) bouton, *m.*; (*nail*) clou, *m.*; (*horses*) †haras, *m.*
studded, (*with nails, &c.*) garni de; (*ornamented with*) orné de; (*strewn with*) parsemé de.
student, étudiant, -e, *m.f.*
studied, (*affected*) étudié; (*deliberate*) voulu.
studio, atelier, *m.*
studious, studieu|x, ~se; (*deliberate*) voulu; ~ *to,* empressé de; **~ly,** studieusement.
study, *s.* (*lit., art, mus.*) étude, *f.*; (*room*) cabinet de travail, *m.*; (*meditation and brown* ~) rêverie, *f.*
study, *v.a.n.* étudier.
stuff, *s.* (*lit. and fig.*) étoffe, *f.*; (*materials*) matériaux, *m.pl.*; (*rubbish*) balivernes, *f.pl.*; *that's the* ~, (*fam.*) c'est ça; *interj.* chansons que tout cela!
stuff, *v.a.* (*fill*) remplir; (*cook.*) farcir; (*eating*) bourrer; (*chairs, &c.*) rembourrer; (*pack, cram*) fourrer; (*birds, &c.*) empailler; ~ *up,* boucher; *v.n.* (*gorge*) se gaver (de).
stuffing, *s.* (*chairs, &c.*) bourre, *f.*; (*cook.*) farce, *f.*
stuff|y, (*atmosphere*) lourd; (*room*) mal ventilé; (*U.S.A.*) maussade; *be ~y,* (*room*) sentir* le renfermé; **~iness,** manque d'air, *m.*
stultify, *v.a.* (*make ridiculous*) rendre ridicule; (*render void*) annuler.
stumble, *s.* faux pas, *m.*
stumbl|e, *v.n.* trébucher; *~e on, upon,* tomber (être) sur; *~ing-block, see* BLOCK.
stump, *s.* (*tree*) souche, *f.*; (*limbs*) moignon, *m.*; (*teeth*) chicot, *m.*; (*pencil, cigarette, &c.*) bout, *m.*; (*drawing*) estompe, *f.*
stump, *v.a.* (*drawing*) estomper; *be ~ed,* (*fam.*) être à quia; ~ *up,* (*money*) casquer.
stumpy, (*pers.*) trapu.
stun, (*blow*) étourdir; (*fig.*) accabler; **~ning,** *adj.* (*slang*) épatant; (*noise, &c.*) étourdissant.
stunt, tour (d'adresse), *m.*; (*aeron.*) acrobatie, *f.*
stunted, rabougri.
stupef|action, (*amazement*) stupéfaction, *f.*; (*torpor*) engourdissement, *m.*; **~y,** (*lit. and fig., amaze*) stupéfier.
stupendous, prodigieu|x, ~se; **~ly,** prodigieusement.
stupid, (*pers., thing*) stupide; **~ity,** stupidité, *f.*; **~ly,** stupidement.
stupor, stupeur, *f.*
sturd|y, vigoureu|x, ~se; **~iness,** vigueur, *f.*; **~ily,** vigoureusement.
sturgeon, (*ichth.*) esturgeon, *m.*
stutter, *s.* bégayement, *m.*; **~er,** bègue, *m.f.*; *v.n.* bégayer.
sty, (*pig*) étable à cochons, *f.*
sty(e), (*on eye*) orgelet, *m.*
style, *s.* (*manner of writing, of a period, school*) style, *m.*; (*title*) titre, *m.*; (*distinguished bearing, &c.*) distinction, *f.*; (*of a firm, business house*) raison sociale, *f.*
style, *v.a.* (*name*) nommer; ~ *oneself,* s'appeler; ⚠ styler = '*train servants*', *&c.*
stylish, élégant; **~ly,** élégamment.
stylist, styliste, *m.f.*
stylograph, stylographe, *m.*
suav|e, (*perfume, &c.*) suave; (*manners*) aimable; **~ity,** suavité, amabilité, *f.*; **~ely,** d'une manière aimable.
subagen|cy, sous-agence, *f.*; **~t,** sous-agent, *m.*
subaltern, *s.* (*mil.*) sous-lieutenant, *m.*, *sometimes* lieutenant, *m.*; ⚠ subalterne = '*a subordinate*'.
subaqueous, sous l'eau.
sub-committee, sous-commission, *f.*
subconscious, subconscient; **~ness,** subconscient, *m.*; **~ly,** d'une manière subconsciente.
subdivide, *v.a.n.* subdiviser.
subdivision, subdivision, *f.*
subdue, (*lit. and fig.*) subjuguer; (*tame*) dompter.
subjacent, sous-jacent.
subject, *s.* (*of sovereign, theme, matter, circumstance, pers. with particular tendencies, gram., for experiment*) sujet, -te, *m.f.*; *of pers., otherwise, m.*; **~-matter,** sujet, *m.*
subject (to), *adj.* (*liable to*) sujet, -te à; (*on condition of*) sous réserve de; (*people, country*) assujetti à.
subject, *v.a.* assujettir (à); (*expose*) exposer (à).
subjection, subjugation, *f.*; ⚠ *not* subjection, *a rhetorical figure now out of date.*
subjective, subjecti|f, ~ve; **~ly,** subjectivement.
subjoin, ajouter; **~ed,** ci-joint, *concord only if placed after noun.*
subjuga|te, subjuguer; **~tion,** assujettissement, *m.*
subjunctive, *adj. and s.m.* (*gram.*) subjonctif.
sub-let, sous-louer.
sub-librarian, sous-bibliothécaire, *m.*
sub-lieutenant, sous-lieutenant, *m.*
sublim|e, sublime; (*majestic*) majestueu|x, ~se; **~ity,** sublimité, *f.*; **~ely,** de manière sublime; *the Sublime Porte,* la (Sublime) Porte.
sublunar, sublunaire.
submarine, (*nav.*) sous-marin, *m.*; *adj.* sous-marin.

submerge, *v.a.* submerger; *the ~d tenth,* les déshérités de la vie; *v.n.* (*submarine*) plonger.
submersion, submersion, *f.*
submission, soumission, *f.*
submissive, soumis (à); **~ly,** avec soumission.
submit, *v.a.* soumettre*; *v.n.* se soumettre* (à); (*urge, point out*) faire* observer.
subordina|te, *adj. and s.m.f.* subordonné, -e; *v.a.* (*lit. and fig.*) subordonner; **~tion,** subordination, *f.*
subpoena, *s.* assignation, *f.*; *v.a.* assigner.
subscribe, *v.a.* souscrire*; (*name*) apposer.
subscribe, *v.n.* ~ *to,* (*consent, charity, &c.*) souscrire* à; (*library, &c.*) s'abonner à.
subscriber, (*for a cause, for capital*) souscripteur, *m.*; (*library, &c.*) abonné, -e, *m.f.*
subscription, souscription, *f.*; (*library, &c.*) abonnement, *m.*
subsequent, subséquent; **~ly,** par la suite.
subservient, (*cringing*) obséquieu|x, ~se.
subside, (*tempest*) s'apaiser; (*water*) baisser; (*building*) se tasser; (*fall*) se laisser tomber; (*of ground*) s'affaisser; **~nce,** (*tempest*) apaisement, *m.*; (*water*) baisse, *f.*; (*build.*) tassement, *m.*
subsidiary, *adj.* subsidiaire.
subsid|ize, subventionner; **~y,** subside, *m.*; (*made by State for industry, &c.*) subvention, *f.*
subsist, *v.n.* exister; (*live on*) subsister de; **~ence,** subsistance, *f.*; *bare ~ence, see* BARE.
subsoil, sous-sol, *m.*
substance, (*essential nature, important part, material*) substance, *f.*; (*reality*) réalité, *f.*; (*possessions*) fortune, *f.*
substantial, (*actually existing, considerable, important*) substantiel, -le; (*not flimsy*) solide; (*well-to-do*) aisé; **~ly,** substantiellement.
substantiate, prouver.
substantive, *s.* substantif, *m.*; *adj.* substanti|f, ~ve.
substitute, *s.* (*pers.*) remplaçant, *m.*; (*things*) imitation, *f.*; *v.a.* substituer (*for* = à).
substitution, substitution, *f.*
substratum, (*fig.*) fond, *m.*
substructure, (*lit. and fig.*) fondement, *m.*
subtenant, sous-locataire, *m.f.*
subterfuge, faux-fuyant, *m.*
subterranean, souterrain.
subtl|e, (*charm, &c., mind, air, poison, crafty*) subtil; (*sly*) rusé; **~ety,** subtilité, *f.*; **~y,** subtilement.
subtract, (*arith.*) soustraire* (de); **~ion,** soustraction, *f.*
suburb, faubourg, *m.*; **~s,** banlieue, *f.*; **~an,** suburbain.
subvers|ion, subversion, *f.*; **~ive,** subversi|f, ~ve.
subvert, subvertir.
subway, souterrain, *m.*
succeed, *v.a.* (*follow after*) succéder à; *v.n.* (*be successful*) réussir (à); (*in business*) faire* ses affaires; ~ *to,* succéder à.
success, succès, *m., often pl.*
successful, heureu|x, ~se; **~ly,** heureusement.
succession, (*following in order, series, to throne, office, or inheritance*) succession, *f.*; *in ~,* successivement.
successive, successi|f, ~ve; **~ly,** successivement.
successor, successeur, *m.*
succinct, succinct; **~ness,** concision, *f.*; **~ly,** succinctement.
succory, *wild ~* (*bot.*) chicorée, *f.*
succour, *s.* secours, *m.* (*often pl.*); *v.a.* secourir*.
succulen|ce, succulence, *f.*; **~t,** succulent.
succumb, (*yield*) succomber (à); (*give way, die*) succomber (sous).
such, *adj.* tel, -le; (+ *noun* + *as*) le, la, les . . . + *rel., e.g.* ~ *knowledge as he has,* les connaissances qu'il a; (*of this kind*) de telle nature; (~ *a* + *adj.*) un(e) . . . aussi + *adj., e.g.* ~ *a stupid affair,* une affaire aussi stupide; ~ + *noun* + *that,* tel(le) . . . que; ~ *and* ~, tel(le) ou tel(le); ~ *a thing,* une telle chose; *it is no ~ thing,* il n'en est rien.
such, *pron.* ~ *as,* ceux, celles + *rel.*
suchlike, *adj.* de cette sorte.
suck, *s. give ~ to,* allaiter.
suck, *v.a.* sucer; (*breast*) teter; ~ *in,* (*engulf*) engloutir; ~ *at,* (*pipe*) tirer sur; ~ *up,* (*absorb*) absorber; **~ing,** *see* PIG.
suck, *v.n.* sucer; (*breast*) teter.
sucker, (*bot.*) surgeon, *m.*
suckle, *v.a.* allaiter.
suckling, enfant à la mamelle, *m.f.*
suction, (*liquids*) aspiration, *f.*; **~-pipe,** tuyau d'alimentation, *m.*
sudden, soudain; **~ness,** soudaineté, *f.*; **~ly,** *of a ~,* soudain.
suds, eau de savon, *f.*
sue, (*in law*) poursuivre*; ~ *for,* (*hand*) demander.
suet, graisse de rognon, *f.*
suffer, souffrir*; (*pain, admit, undergo, loss, defeat, &c.*) subir; (*permit*) permettre*, *dat. of pers.* de + *inf.*; *v.n.* souffrir*.
sufferance, tolérance, *f.*; *on ~,* par tolérance.
sufferer, (*victim*) victime, *f.*; *be a ~,* souffrir*.
suffering, *s.* souffrance, *f.*
suffice, *v.n.* suffire* (à).
sufficien|cy, suffisance, *f.*; **~t,** *s. use adv.* assez; *adj.* suffisant; **~tly,** suffisamment.
suffix, suffixe, *m.*
suffoca|te, *v.a.n.* (*lit. and fig.*) suffoquer; **~tion,** suffocation, *f.*; **~ting,** étouffant.
suffragan, *adj. and s.m.* suffragant.
suffrage, (*vote, right of voting*) suffrage, *m.*
suffragette, suffragette, *f.*
suffuse, *v.a.* se répandre sur.
sugar, sucre, *m.*; **~-bowl,** sucrier, *m.*;

~**-candy,** sucre candi, *m.*; ~ **- cane,** canne à sucre, *f.*; ~**-tongs,** pince à sucre, *f.*; *granulated* ~, sucre cristallisé, *m.*; *lump* ~, sucre en morceaux, *m.*; *moist* ~, cassonade, *f.*; *v.a.* sucrer; ~**y,** sucré.

suggest, (*call up idea, inspire*) suggérer; (*propose*) proposer; ~**ion,** suggestion, *f.*; ~**ive,** suggesti|f, ~**ve**; ~*ive of,* qui suggère.

suicid|e, suicide, *m.*; ~**al,** de suicide.

suit, *s.* (*of clothes*) complet, *m.*; (*cards*) couleur, *f.*; (*request*) requête, *f.*; (*courtship*) cour, *f.*; (*at law*) procès, *m.*; ~**-case,** porte-habit, *m.*

suit, *v.a.* (*become, meet requirements of, agree with*) convenir* (avoir) (à); (*adapt*) adapter (à).

suit, *v.n.* convenir* à; (*go well with*) aller* (être) avec.

suitab|le, (*appropriate*) convenable; ~*le for,* adapté à; ~**ility,** convenance, *f.*; ~**ly,** convenablement.

suite, (*retinue*) suite, *f.*; (*of rooms*) appartement, *m.*; (*furniture*) mobilier, *m.*

suitor, (*applicant*) postulant, *m.*; (*lover*) prétendant, *m.*

sulk, *v.n.* bouder; ~**y,** boudeu|r, ~**se**; ~**ily,** en boudant; *be in the* ~*s,* bouder.

sullen, maussade; (*taciturn*) taciturne; ~**ness,** maussaderie, *f.*; ~**ly,** maussadement.

sully, (*lit. and fig.*) souiller.

sulphur, soufre, *m.*; ~**ic,** sulfurique.

sultan, sultan, *m.*; ~**a,** sultane, *f.*; ~**a,** (*dried fruit*) raisin de Smyrne, *m.*

sultr|iness, chaleur étouffante, *f.*; ~**y,** étouffant; *it is* ~*y,* il fait lourd.

sum, (*lit. and fig.*) somme, *f.*; ~ *total,* somme totale, *f.*

sum up, (*recapitulate*) résumer.

summar|y, *s.* résumé, *m.*; *adj.* sommaire; ~**ily,** sommairement; ~**ize,** résumer.

summer, été, *m.*; (*measure of age*) printemps, *m.*; ~**-house,** pavillon, *m.*; ~**-time,** saison d'été, *f.*; (*of clock*) heure d'été, *f.*

summit, (*lit. and fig.*) sommet, *m.*

summon, *v.a.* (*convoke*) convoquer; (*cause to appear*) appeler; (*to surrender*) sommer (de); ~ *up,* (*courage, &c.*) rassembler.

summons, *s.* (*invitation, call*) appel, *m.*; (*law*) assignation, *f.*; *v.a.* appeler en justice.

sumptuary, somptuaire.

sumptuous, somptueu|x, ~**se**; ~**ness,** somptuosité, *f.*; ~**ly,** somptueusement.

sun, *s.* soleil, *m.*; *v.a.* ~ *oneself,* se chauffer au soleil; ~**-dial,** cadran solaire, *m.*; *for compounds see below.*

sunbeam, rayon du soleil, *m.*

sunburn, †hâle, *m.*; ~**t,** †hâlé.

Sunday, dimanche, *m.*; ~**-clothes,** habits des dimanches, *m.pl.*; ~**-school,** école du dimanche, *f.*; *in one's* ~ *best,* endimanché.

sunder, séparer.

sundew, (*bot.*) drosère, *m.*

sundown, coucher du soleil, *m.*

sundr|y, *adj.* divers; *s.* ~**ies,** divers articles, *m.pl.*; (*expenses*) frais, *m.pl.*; ~*ies account,* (*bkkpg.*) compte de divers, *m.*

sunflower, (*bot.*) soleil, *m.*

sunken, (*cheeks, eyes, path*) creu|x, ~**se.**

sunlight, lumière du soleil, *f.*

sunlit, éclairé par le soleil.

sunny, (*bright with sunlight*) ensoleillé; (*exposed to sun*) exposé au soleil; (*fig.*) riant.

sunproof, à l'épreuve du soleil.

sunrise, lever du soleil, *m.*

sunset, coucher du soleil, *m.*

sunshade, (*parasol*) ombrelle, *f.*

sunshine, soleil, *m.*

sunstroke, coup de soleil, *m.*

sup, *v.n.* souper.

superable, surmontable.

superabound, surabonder.

superabundan|ce, surabondance; ~**t,** surabondant.

superadd, surajouter.

superannua|te, (*officer, &c.*) mettre* à la retraite; ~**tion,** mise à la retraite, *f.*

superb, superbe; ~**ly,** superbement.

supercargo, subrécargue, *m.*

supercilious, †hautain; ~**ness,** arrogance, *f.*; ~**ly,** arrogamment.

supereminent, suréminent.

supererogation, surérogation, *f.*

superexcellent, de la plus †haute excellence.

superficial, superficiel, -le; ~**ly,** superficiellement.

superficies, superficie, *f.*

superfine, superfin.

superflu|ity, superfluité, *f.*; ~**ous,** superflu.

superhuman, surhumain.

superimpose, superposer.

superincumbent, *adj.* superposé.

superintend, surveiller; ~**ent,** surveillant, *m.*; ~*ent of police,* commissaire de police, *m.*; ~**ence,** surveillance, *f.*

superior, *s.* supérieur, *m.*; *adj.* supérieur; (*arrogant*) arrogant; ~ *to,* insensible à.

superiority, supériorité, *f.*

superlative, *adj.* suprême; (*gram.*) superlati|f, ~**ve**; *s.* superlatif, *m.*; ~**ly,** au suprême degré.

supernal, céleste.

supernatural, surnaturel, -le; ~**ly,** surnaturellement.

supernumerary, *adj. and s.m.f.* surnuméraire.

superscription, (*inscription*) inscription, *f.*

supersede, (*pers.*) remplacer.

superstit|ion, superstition, *f.*; ~**ious,** superstitieu|x, ~**se.**

superstructure, superstructure, *f.*

supervene, survenir* (être).

supervis|e, surveiller; ~**or,** surveillant, *m.*; ~**ion,** surveillance, *f.*

supine, *s.* (*gram.*) supin, *m.*; *adj.* (*lying face upward*) couché sur le dos; (*lethargic*) indolent.

supper, souper, *m.*

supplant, supplanter.

supple, (*lit. and fig.*) souple; (*pej.*) obséquieu|x, ~se; **~ness,** souplesse, *f.*

supplement, *s.* supplément, *m.*; *v.a.* suppléer à; **~ary,** supplémentaire.

suppliant, *s.* suppliant, -e, *m.f.*; *adj.* suppliant.

supplica|te, *v.a.* supplier; **~tion,** supplication, *f.*

supplier, fournisseur, *m.*

suppl|y, *s.* (*provision*) provision, *f.*; (*water, &c.*) approvisionnement, *m.*; **~ies,** (*Parl.*) crédits, *m.pl.*; (*mil.*) subsistances, *f.pl.*; *~y and demand,* l'offre et la demande.

supply, *v.a.* fournir (de); (*a lack, take the place of*) suppléer, *v.a.*; (*want*) répondre à.

support, *s.* appui, *m.*; (*for holding up*) support, *m.*; (*fig.*) soutien, *m.*; *in ~ of,* à l'appui de; *~-trench,* tranchée de soutien, *f.*

support, *v.a.* (*hold up, endure*) supporter; (*prevent from falling, give courage, motion, policy, candidate, family, attack, &c.*) soutenir*; (*back up*) appuyer; (*corroborate*) corroborer.

supportable, supportable.

supporter, (*adherent*) partisan, *m.*

suppos|e, *v.a.* supposer; *adj.* **~ed,** présumé; **~ing,** supposons (que + *subj.*).

supposit|ion, supposition, *f.*; **~ious,** suppositif, ~ve; **~itious,** supposé.

suppress, (*stop circulation, taxes, keep secret*) supprimer; (*revolt, anger*) réprimer; (*yawn, &c.*) étouffer; **~ion,** suppression, répression, *f.*

suppura|te, *v.n.* suppurer; **~tion,** suppuration, *f.*

suprem|acy, suprématie, *f.*; **~e,** suprême; **~ely,** au suprême degré.

surcharge, *s.* (*letter, &c.*) surtaxe, *f.*; *v.a.* surtaxer.

sure, *adj.* (*convinced, certain, reliable, true*) sûr; *be ~ to,* ne pas manquer de; *be ~ not to,* se garder de; *make ~ of, that,* s'assurer de, que; **~ly,** sûrement.

sure, *adv.* (*U.S.A.*) certainement.

surety, (*certainty*) certitude, *f.*; (*thing pledged, pers.*) caution, *f.*; *of a ~,* pour sûr.

surf, ressac, *m.*

surface, (*lit. and fig.*) surface, *f.*

surfeit, *s.* (*lit. and fig.*) satiété, *f.*; (*excess*) excès, *m.*; *be ~ed with,* être rassasié de; *v.a.* (*satiate*) rassasier de.

surge, *s.* houle, *f.*; *v.n.* s'élever.

surg|eon, chirurgien, -ne, *m.f.*; ⚠ surgeon, *m.* = '*shoot*', '*sucker*'; *~eon's knife,* scalpel, *m.*; **~ery,** chirurgie, *f.*; **~ical,** chirurgical; *veterinary ~eon,* vétérinaire, *m.*

surl|y, hargneu|x, ~se; **~iness,** ton hargneux, *m.*

surmise, *s.* conjecture, *f.*; *v.a.* conjecturer.

surmount, (*lit. and fig.*) surmonter; **~able,** surmontable.

surmullet, (*ichth.*) surmulet, *m.*

surname, nom de famille, *m.*; ⚠ *not* surnom *which* = '*nick-, pet-name*'; **~d,** appelé (de son nom de famille).

surpass, surpasser; **~ing,** sans égal; **~ingly,** excellemment.

surplice, surplis, *m.*

surplus, surplus, *m.*; *~ profits,* surplus de bénéfice, *m.*

surpris|e, *s.* surprise, *f.*; *v.a.* surprendre*; **~ing,** surprenant; **~ingly,** étonnamment.

surrender, *s.* (*renunciation*) abandon (de), *m.*; (*of fortress, &c.*) reddition, *f.*; (*Insurance*) rachat, *m.*

surrender, *v.a.* (*mil., &c.*) rendre; (*give up*) renoncer à; *v.n.* se rendre; *~ oneself to,* s'abandonner à.

surreptitious, subreptice; **~ly,** subrepticement.

surround, entourer (de); (*mil.*) cerner.

surroundings, (*neighbourhood*) environs, *m.pl.*; (*of a pers.*) entourage, *m.*

survey, *s.* vue, *f.*; (*investigation*) examen, *m.*; (*of land*) arpentage, *m.*; (*goods*) expertise, *f.*

survey, *v.a.* contempler; (*investigate*) examiner; (*land*) arpenter; (*goods*) expertiser; **~ing,** arpentage, *f.*; **~or,** arpenteur, *m.*

survival, *s.* (*surviving*) survie, *f.*; (*relic*) reste, *m.*

survive, *v.a.* survivre* à; *v.n.* survivre*.

survivor, survivant, -e, *m.f.*

susceptib|ility, susceptibilité, *f.*; *~ility to,* prédisposition, *f.*, à; **~le,** (*admitting of*) susceptible de; (*sensitive to*) sensible à.

suspect, *adj. and s.m.f.* suspect, -e; *v.a.n.* soupçonner.

suspend, *v.a.* suspendre.

suspenders, jarretelles, *f.pl.*

suspense, incertitude, *f.*; *in ~,* en suspens; ⚠ suspense *is an ecclesiastical term.*

suspension, (*interruption, payments, &c.*) suspension, *f.*; **~-bridge,** pont suspendu, *m.*

suspicion, (*lit. and small quantity*) soupçon, *m.*; *v.a.* (*U.S.A.*) soupçonner.

suspicious, (*distrustful*) soupçonneu|x, ~se; (*suspect*) suspect; **~ly,** avec méfiance, d'une manière suspecte.

sustain, (*hold up, feed, a part, effort, strength, &c., comparison, defeat, siege*) soutenir*; (*loss*) éprouver.

sustenance, (*lit. and fig.*) nourriture, *f.*

sutler, vivandi|er, ~ère, *m.f.*

suzerain, suzerain, *m.*; **~ty,** suzeraineté, *f.*

swab, *s.* (*naut.*) faubert, *m.*; *v.a.* fauberter.

swaddl|e, emmailloter; **~ing-clothes,** langes, *m.pl.*

swagger, *s.* air fanfaron, *m.*; *v.n.* (*fam.*) crâner; **~er,** fanfaron, *m.*
swain, jeune paysan, *m.*
swallow, *s.* (*ornith.*) hirondelle, *f.*; *~-tailed,* (*coat*) à queue de morue; **~-wort,** (*bot.*) chélidoine, *f.*
swallow, *v.a.* avaler; (*believe and fam.*) gober; *~ up,* (*engulf*) engloutir.
swamp, *s.* marais, *m.*; *v.a.* (*boat, flood, fig.*) submerger (de); **~y,** marécageu|x, ~se.
swan, cygne, *m.*; *~'s down,* duvet de cygne, *m.*
swarm, *s.* (*bees*) essaim, *m.*; (*crowd, lit. and fig.*) foule, *f.*; *v.n.* (*bees*) essaimer; (*crowd*) s'assembler en foule; *~ with,* fourmiller de.
swarthy, †hâlé.
swashbuckler, fanfaron, *m.*
swastika, svastika, *m.*
swath, (*in mowing*) andain, *m.*
swathe, emmailloter.
sway, *s.* (*rule*) domination, *f.*; (*fig.*) empire, *m.*; (*pendulum*) oscillation, *f.*
sway, *v.a.* gouverner; (*branches, &c.*) balancer; *v.n.* (*swing to and fro*) se balancer.
swear, *v.a.* jurer; (*oath*) prêter; (*witness*) faire* prêter serment à; *~ at,* injurier; *~ in,* assermenter; **~ing,** *s.* (*oath*) prestation de serment, *f.*; (*blasphemy*) jurements, *m.pl.*
swear, *v.n.* jurer (de).
sweat, *s.* (*lit. and fig.*) sueur, *f.*; *in a ~,* en sueur; *v.a.* (*labour*) exploiter; *v.n.* (*lit. and fig.*) suer; **~ing,** (*labour*) exploitation, *f.*
Swed|e, *s.m.f.* Suédois, -e; **~ish,** *s.* (*lang.*) suédois, *m.*; *adj.* suédois.
sweep, *s.* (*pers.*) ramoneur, *m.*; (*given to a room*) coup de balai, *m.*; (*bend*) courbe, *f.*; (*extent*) étendue, *f.*; (*of arm*) grand geste, *m.*; *make a clean ~ of,* faire* place nette de.
sweep, *v.a.* (*floor, of gun-fire, wind, &c.*) balayer; (*chimneys*) ramoner; (*eyes, hand*) passer rapidement sur; (*dredge, for mines*) draguer; (*touch lightly*) effleurer; *~ away,* emporter; (*abolish*) abolir; *~ out,* balayer; *~ up,* (*gather together*) rassembler; (*floor, mess*) balayer.
sweep, *v.n.* (*of broom*) balayer; (*go quickly*) aller*, venir* (être) rapidement, majestueusement; (*procession*) avancer majestueusement; (*extend*) s'étendre; *~ past,* passer rapidement; *~ down upon,* fondre sur.
sweeper, *see* STREET.
sweeping, *adj.* (*root and branch*) radical; (*statement, &c.*) par trop absolu; **~s,** *s.* balayures, *f.pl.*
sweepstake, poule, *f.*
sweet, (*to eat*) bonbon, *m.*; (*cook.*) entremets, *m.*; **~s,** (*sweetmeats*) sucreries, *f.pl.*; (*delights*) délices, *f.pl.*
sweet, *adj.* (*taste, smell, to ear, gentle*) dou|x, ~ce; (*pers.*) gentil, -le; **~ basil,** (*bot.*) basilic, *m.*; **~-briar,** (*bot.*) églantier, *m.*; **~-pea,** *see* PEA; *~-tempered,* dou|x, ~ce; **~-william,** (*bot.*) œillet de poète, *m.*; **~ness,** douceur, *f.*; **~ly,** doucement.
sweetbread, ris de veau *or* d'agneau, *m.*
sweeten, (*with sugar*) sucrer; (*soften*) adoucir.
sweetheart, bon, -ne ami, -e, *m.f.*
swell, *s.* (*sea*) †houle, *f.*; (*pers.*) gandin, *m.*; (*land*) élévation, *f.*; (*organ*) pédale d'expression, *f.*
swell, *v.a.* (*lit., bills, accounts, waters*) gonfler; (*with pride, &c.*) bouffir.
swell, *v.n.* (*part of body, sails*) (s')enfler; (*rivers, sound*) grossir; (*fig.*) se gonfler; (*sea, bills, accounts, become larger*) grossir.
swelling, *s.* enflure, *f.*; (*rivers, &c.*) crue, *f.*
swelter, *v.a.* accabler de chaleur; *v.n.* étouffer de chaleur.
sweltering, *adj.* accablant.
swerve, *s.* déviation, *f.*; *v.n.* dévier; *~ violently,* (*motor*) faire *une embardée.
swift, *s.* (*ornith.*) martinet, *m.*
swift, *adj.* rapide; **~ness,** rapidité, *f.*; **~ly,** rapidement.
swig, *v.a.* lamper.
swill, *v.a.* (*wash*) rincer; *v.n.* boire* avec excès.
swim, *s.* (*fig.*) mouvement, *m.*; *be in the ~* (*fig.*) être à la page; *have a ~,* aller* (être) nager.
swim, *v.a.* (*definite distance*) nager; (*cross by swimming*) traverser à la nage.
swim, *v.n.* nager; (*float*) flotter; (*have dizzy sensation*) tourner; (*make progress on water*) aller* (être) à la nage; *be ~ming with,* être inondé de.
swimmer, nageu|r, ~se, *m.f.*
swimming, *s.* natation, *f.*; *adj.* (*with water, &c.*) inondé (de); **~-bath,** piscine, *f.*; **~-belt,** ceinture de natation, *f.*; **~-bladder,** vessie natatoire, *f.*; **~-pool,** bassin de natation, *m.*; **~ly,** comme sur des roulettes.
swindle, *s.* escroquerie, *f.*; *v.a.* escroquer (*dat. pers., acc. thing*); **~r,** escroc, *m.*
swin|e, cochon, *m.*; **~e-herd,** porcher, *m.*; **~ish,** bestial.
swing, *s.* (*pendulum*) va-et-vient, *m.*; (*free scope*) libre carrière, *f.*; (*in walking*) rythme, *m.*; (*of song, &c.*) air entraînant, *m.*; (*for swinging in*) escarpolette, *f.*; *~-bridge,* pont tournant, *m.*; *~-door,* porte va-et-vient, *f.*
swing, *v.a.* balancer; (*weapon*) brandir.
swing, *v.n.* (*pendulum*) osciller; (*trees, children, sway, &c.*) se balancer; (*be hanged*) être pendu; *~ to,* (*door*) se refermer.
swinging, *s.* balancement, *m.*; *adj.* rythmé; (*song, &c.*) entraînant.
swirl, *s.* remous, *m.*; *v.n.* tourbillonner.
swish, *s.* (*sound*) sifflement, *m.*; (*rustle*) frou-frou, *m.*; *v.n.* siffler.
Swiss, *adj.* suisse; *s.m.f.* Suisse, -sse.
switch, *s.* badine, *f.*; (*rail.*) aiguille, *f.*;

(*electr.*) interrupteur, *m.*; (*electr. light*) commutateur, *m.*; ~*-back*, chemin de fer de Russie, *m.*; ~*-board*, (*electr.*) tableau de distribution, *m.*; (*aeron.*) tableau, *m.*
switch, *v.a.* cingler; (*rail.*) aiguiller; (*tail*) agiter; ~ *off*, (*electr. current*) couper; ~ *on*, (*current*) donner; *v.n.* ~ *off*, (*electr.*) couper le circuit; ~ *off*, (*teleph.*) couper la communication (avec); ~ *on*, (*electr.*) mettre* en circuit; (*teleph.*) donner la communication (à).
swivel, *s.* tourniquet, *m.*
swoon, *s.* évanouissement, *m.*; *v.n.* s'évanouir.
swoop, *v.n.* fondre (sur).
swop, swap, *v.a.* troquer.
sword, épée, *f.*; (*cavalry*) sabre, *m.*; (*poet., fig.*) glaive, *m.*; ~**-belt,** ceinturon, *m.*; ~**-fish,** espadon, *m.*; ~**-knot,** dragonne, *f.*; ~**-stick,** canne à épée, *f.*; *put to the* ~, passer au fil de l'épée.
swot, *v.n.* (*slang, work hard*) piocher.
Sybarit|e, sybarite, *m.f.*; ~**ic,** *adj.* sybarite.
sycamore-tree, sycamore, *m.*
sycophant, flagorneu|r, ~se, *s.m.f.*
syllab|ic, syllabique; ~**le,** syllabe, *f.*
syllabus, sommaire, *m.*; (*of study*) programme, *m.*
syllogism, syllogisme, *m.*
sylph, sylphide, sylph|e, ~ide, *m.f.*
sylvan, des bois; (*rural*) champêtre.
symbol, symbole, *m.*; ~**ic,** symbolique; ~**ize,** symboliser.
symmetric(al), symétrique; ~**ally,** symétriquement.
symmetry, symétrie, *f.*
sympathetic (*expressing sympathy, effecting sympathy*) sympathique; (*full of sympathy*) compatissant; ~**ally,** avec sympathie,
sympathize *with*, compatir **à**; (*share feeling, &c.*) s'associer (à).
sympathy, sympathie, *f.*
symphony, symphonie, *f.*
symptom, symptôme, *m.*; ~**atic,** symptomatique.
synagogue, synagogue, *f.*
synchron|ous, synchrone; ~**ize,** *v.n.* être synchrone.
syncope, (*med.*) syncope, *f.*
syndic, syndic, *m.*
syndicate, syndicat, *m.*
synod, synode, *m.*
synonym, synonyme, *m.*; ~**ous,** synonyme (de).
synop|sis, sommaire, *m.*; ~**tic,** synoptique.
synta|ctic, syntaxique; ~**x,** syntaxe, *f.*
synthe|sis, synthèse, *f.*; ~**tic,** synthétique.
Syrian, *adj.* (*when an adj. use small letter*) *and s.m.f.* Syrien, -ne.
syringa, (*bot.*) seringa, *m.*
syringe, *s.* seringue, *f.*; *v.a.* seringuer.
syrup, sirop, *m.*; ~**y,** sirupeu|x, ~se.
system, système, *m.*; (*method*) méthode, *f.*; (*rail., teleph., &c.*) réseau, *m.*; ~**atic,** systématique; ~**atically,** systématiquement.
systematize, systématiser.

T

tabby, (*cat*) chat moucheté, *m.*
tabernacle, tabernacle, *m.*
table, *s.* (*piece of furniture, guests at table, of contents, slab of wood or stone, math., communion*) table, *f.*; ~**-salt,** sel fin, *m.*; ~**-spoon,** cuiller à bouche, *f.*; *clear the* ~, desservir*; *keep open* ~, tenir* table ouverte; *lay the* ~, mettre* le couvert; *turn the* ~*s*, renverser la médaille.
tablet, (*for writing*) tablette, *f.*; (*inscribed*) plaque, *f.*
tabloid, tablette, *f.*
taboo, *adj. and s.m.* tabou; *v.a.* défendre.
tabor, (*mus.*) tambourin, *m.*
tabular, en forme de table.
tabulate, disposer en tables.
tacit, tacite; ~**ly,** tacitement.
taciturn, taciturne; ~**ity,** taciturnité, *f.*
tack, *s.* (*nail*) broquette, *f.*; (*naut.*) amure, *f.*; ~**s** (*ironmong.*) semence, *f.*; *v.a.* (*nail*) clouer; *v.n.* (*naut.*) louvoyer.
tackle, *s.* (*naut.*) agrès, *m.*; (*naut. very strong*) apparaux, *m.pl.*; (*hoisting-gear*) palan, *m.*; (*fishing, &c.*) attirail, *m.*
tackle, *v.a.* (*seize pers.*) saisir à bras le corps; (*difficulty, problem*) essayer de résoudre.
tact, tact, *m.*; *be* ~*ful*, avoir du tact; ~**fully,** avec tact.
tactic|s, (*mil. and fig.*) tactique, *f.*; ~**al,** de la tactique; ~**ian,** tacticien, *m.*
tactless, *adj.* sans tact; *be* ~, manquer de tact; ~**ness,** manque de tact, *m.*; ~**ly,** sans tact.
tadpole, têtard, *m.*
taffeta, taffetas, *m.*
taffrail, (*naut.*) couronnement, *m.*
tag, *s.* (*lace*) ferret, *m.*; (*tie-on label*) étiquette volante, *f.*; (*end*) bout, *m.*; (*trite quotation*) cliché, *m.*
tag, *v.a.* ~ *on, on to*, attacher (à); ~ *together*, lier ensemble.
tail, (*animal, bird, fish, mus. note, letter, comet, rear, hind part, dress, coat, aeroplane, anything like a* ~) queue, *f.*; (*carts*) derrière, *m.*; (*plough*) manche, *m.*; ~**ed,** *adj.* à queue; ~**less,** sans queue; *turn* ~, s'enfuir*.
tailor, *s.* tailleur, *m.*; ~**ess,** tailleuse, *f.*; ~**-made,** *adj.* tailleur, *invar.*; ~*-made coat and skirt, see* COAT; *v.a.* habiller.
taint, *s.* (*spot, lit. and fig.*) tache, *f.*; (*infection*) infection, *f.*; *v.a.* (*spoil*) gâter; (*infect, contaminate*) infecter.
take, *s.* (*thing taken*) prise, *f.*; (*takings*) recette, *f.*; ~*-in*, duperie, *f.*
take, *v.a.* (*gen., eatables, &c., disease, train, &c., road, time, note, interest, copy, extract, advice, obtain, carry with one, be*

affected by, take possession of) prendre*; (*walk, vow, portrait, prisoner*) faire*; (*carry*) porter; (*chance*) courir*; (*pers., an., to place*) conduire*; (*carry away*) enlever; (*steal*) dérober; (*conclude* = ~ *it*) conclure*; (*consider as*) considérer comme; *be* ~*n with*, être épris de; ~ *X at his word*, prendre* X au mot; ~ *in tow*, (*ship, &c.*) prendre* en remorque; ~ *a thing lying down*, se laisser faire; ~ *upon oneself to*, prendre* sur soi de; ~ *after*, ressembler à; ~ *again*, reprendre*; ~ *away*, (*pers., ans.*) emmener; (*things*) enlever; (*steal*) dérober; (*one number from another*) soustraire* (de); ~ *back*, (*pers.*) ramener; (*things*) remporter; ~ *down*, descendre (avoir); (*demolish*) démolir; (*in writing*) prendre* (par écrit); (*in shorthand*) sténographier; ~ *from*, prendre* (à+*pers.*); (*diminish*) diminuer; ~ *in*, (*get in*) rentrer (avoir); (*receive pers.*) recevoir; (*understand, include*) comprendre*; (*cheat*) tromper; (*newspapers, &c.*) s'abonner à; ~ *off*, (*clothes, &c.*) ôter; (*mimic*) imiter; (*part of price*) rabattre; ~ *oneself off*, filer; ~ *on*, (*workman*) embaucher; (*tasks*) se charger de; ~ *out*, (*ans. and things*) sortir (avoir); (*things in kind*) se faire* payer en; (*insurance*) contracter; ~ *to*, (*begin*) se mettre* à; (*a pursuit*) mordre à; ~ *up*, (*pick up*) ramasser; (*arrest*) arrêter; (*study*) étudier.

take, *v.n.* (*fire, catch on, med.*) prendre*; (*photo.*) apparaître*; ~ *off*, (*running*) prendre* son élan; (*aeron.*) décoller; ~ *up with*, (*pers.*) fréquenter.

taking, *adj.* (*attractive*) attrayant.

takings, (*theatr., &c.*) recette, *f.*

talc, talc, *m.*

tale, *s.* conte, *m.*; (*narrative*) histoire, *f.*; (*reckoning*) compte, *m.*; *tell* ~*s*, (*fam.*) cafarder.

talebearer, rapporteu|r, ~se, *m.f.*

talent, *s.* talent, *m.*; ~**ed**, *adj.* de talent.

taleteller, conteu|r, ~se, *m.f.*; (*pej.*) rapporteu|r, ~se, *m.f.*

talisman, talisman, *m.*

talk, *s.* conversation, *f.*; (*informal lecture*) causerie, *f.*; (*rumour*) bruit, *m.*; (*subject of* ~) sujet de conversation, *m.*; *tall* ~, †hâblerie, *f.*

talk, *v.a.* (*a language, business, music, &c.*) parler; (*nonsense, &c.*) dire*; ~ *into*, persuader (à+*pers.*, de+*inf.*); ~ *out of*, dissuader (de); ~ *over*, (*pers.*) persuader; (*thing*) discuter.

talk, *v.n.* parler; (*pej.*) jaser; ~ *about, of*, parler de; ~*ing of*, (*on the subject of*) à propos de; ~ *big*, fanfaronner.

talkative, bavard; ~**ness**, loquacité, *f.*

talker, (*pej.*) bavard, -e, *m.f.*; (*boaster*) †hâbleu|r, ~se, *m.f.*

talkies, (*cinema*) film parlant, *m.*

talking, *s.* conversation, *f.*; (*pej.*) bavardage, *m.*

tall, grand; *how* ~ *is he?* quelle est sa taille? ; ~**ness**, †haute taille, *f.*; ~ *talk*, *see* TALK.

tallow, suif, *m.*; ~-*chandler*, chandelier, *m.*

tally, *s.* (*notched stick*) taille, *f.*; (*label*) étiquette, *f.*

tally, *v.n.* (*agree with*) concorder (avec).

tally-ho, (*hunt.*) *interj. and s.m.* taïaut.

Talmud, talmud, *m.*

talon, (*birds*) serre, *f.*; ⚠ talon = '*heel*' *in French*.

tamable, domptable.

tamarind, (*fruit and tree*) tamarin, *m.*

tamarisk, (*bot.*) tamaris, *m.*

tambourine, tambour de basque, *m.*

tame, *adj.* (*pers.*) soumis; (*an.*) apprivoisé; (*flat*) insipide; ~**ness**, docilité, *f.*; (*dullness*) insipidité, *f.*; ~**ly**, (*without spirit*) lâchement; (*insipidly*) d'une manière insipide.

tamer, dompteur, *m.*

tamper, *v.n.* ~ *with*, (*meddle with*) tripoter, *v.a.*; (*wills, MS.*) altérer; (*witnesses*) corrompre.

tampering, *s.* machination, *f.*

tan, *s.* tan, *m.*; ~-**yard**, tannerie, *f.*

tan, *adj.* (*tanned, tan-colour, sunburnt*) tanné.

tan, *v.a.* tanner; (*sunburn*) †hâler.

tandem, tandem, *m.*; *adj. and adv.* en flèche.

tangent, *s.* (*math.*) tangente, *f.*; *go off at a* ~, s'échapper par la tangente.

tangerine, (*orange*) mandarine, *f.*

tangib|ility, tangibilité, *f.*; ~**le**, (*lit. and fig.*) tangible.

tangle, *s.* brouillamini, *m.*; *v.a.* enchevêtrer; *v.n.* s'enchevêtrer.

tank, *s.* réservoir, *m.*; (*mil.*) char d'assaut, *m.*; *water*-~, (*engine, ship*) caisse à eau, *f.*

tankard, †hanap, *m.*

tanker, (*naut.*) bateau-citerne, *m.*

tanner, tanneur, *m.*; ~**y**, tannerie, *f.*

tansy, (*bot.*) tanaisie, *f.*

tantalize, tourmenter.

tantamount, *be* ~ *to*, équivaloir* à.

tantrum, accès de colère, *m.*

tap, *s.* (*water, &c.*) robinet, *m.*; (*slight blow*) tape, *f.*; (*at door, &c., also tapping*) petit coup, *m.*; ~-**room**, buvette, *f.*; *on* ~, en perce.

tap, *v.a.* (*cask*) mettre* en perce; (*pers.*) taper; (*strike lightly*) frapper légèrement; (*trees*) inciser; *v.n.* frapper légèrement.

tape, ruban de coton, *m.*; (*for measuring*) mètre à ruban, *m.*; *red* ~, bureaucratie, *f.*; ~**worm**, ver solitaire, *m.*

taper, bougie, *f.*; (*in churches*) cierge, *m.*; *v.n.* se terminer en pointe.

tapering, *adj.* effilé.

tapestry, tapisserie, *f.*; *sometimes pl.*

tapioca, tapioca, *m.*

tapster, garçon de cabaret, *m.*

tar, goudron, *m.*; (*sailor*) loup de mer, *m.*; *v.a.* goudronner.

tard|y, (*slow*) lent; (*coming late*) tardi|f,

~ve; **~iness,** lenteur, *f.*; (*lateness*) retard, *m.*; **~ily,** lentement; (*late*) tardivement.
tare, (*also* **tares**) *s.* (*bot.*) ivraie, *f.*; (*comm.*) tare, *f.*
target, (*for firing*) cible, *f.*
tarlatan, tarlatane, *f.*
tariff, tarif, *m.*
tarn, petit lac, *m.*
tarnish, *s.* ternissure, *f.*; *v.a.* (*lit. and fig.*) ternir; *v.n.* se ternir.
tarpaulin, bâche, *f.*
tarragon, (*bot.*) estragon, *m.*
tarry, *v.n.* (*remain*) séjourner; (*delay*) tarder (à); ~ *for*, attendre.
tart, *s.* (*fruit, &c.*) tarte, *f.*
tart, *adj.* âpre; (*fig.*) mordant; **~ness,** (*lit. and fig.*) aigreur, *f.*; **~ly,** (*fig.*) aigrement.
tartan, *s.* (*material and plaid*) tartan, *m.*
Tartar, *adj.* (*when an adj. use small letter*) *and s.m.f.* Tartare.
tartlet, tartelette, *f.*
task, *s.* tâche, *f.*; (*school*) devoir, *m.*; *take to* ~, réprimander; *v.a.* (*tax, put strain on*) mettre* à l'épreuve.
taskmaster, maître, *m.*
tassel, gland, *m.*; (*of cap*) pompon, *m.*
taste, *s.* (*savour, flavour, bent, liking, faculty of appreciating beauty*) goût, *m.*; (*act of tasting wines, &c.*) dégustation, *f.*; (*small quantity*) soupçon, *m.*; *in good* ~, en bon goût.
taste, *v.a.* (*lit. and fig.*) goûter; *v.n.* (+ *adj.*) avoir un goût; (*fig., experience, often* + *of*) goûter de.
tastefully, avec goût.
tasteless, sans saveur; (*fig.*) de mauvais goût; **~ness,** manque de goût, *m.*; **~ly,** (*fig.*) sans goût.
tasty, savoureu|x, ~se.
tat, *tit for* ~, à bon chat bon rat.
tatter, lambeau, *m.*; ~s, †haillons, *m.pl.*; **~ed,** (*thing*) en lambeaux.
tatterdemalion, va-nu-pieds, *m.f. invar.*
tattle, *tittle-*~, commérage, *m.*; *v.n.* bavarder; **~r,** bavard, -e, *m.f.*
tattoo, *s.* (*mil.*) retraite, *f.*; (*on body*) tatouage, *m.*; (*mil. fête*) fête nocturne (militaire), *f.*; *v.a.* (*on body*) tatouer.
taunt, *s.* sarcasme, *m.*; *v.a.* (*approx.*) railler (pour); **~ingly,** avec raillerie sarcastique.
taut, *adj.* raide; **~en,** raidir.
tautolog|ical, tautologique; **~y,** tautologie, *f.*
tavern, taverne, *f.*; (*inn*) auberge, *f.*
tawdr|iness, clinquant, *m.*; **~y,** clinquant; **~ily,** avec faux éclat.
tawny, fauve.
tax, *s.* impôt, *m.*; (*burden*) charge, *f.*; ~ *free, see* FREE.
tax, *v.a.* (*land, commodities, &c.*) imposer; (*strength, &c.*) mettre* à l'épreuve; ~ *with*, (*accuse of*) taxer de.
taxable, imposable.
taxation, taxation, *f.*
taxi, *s.* taxi, *m.*; *v.n.* (*motor*) aller* (être) en taxi; (*aeron.*) rouler sur le sol.
taxidermist, empailleu|r, ~se, *m.f.*
taximeter, taximètre, *m.*
taxpayer, contribuable, *m.f.*
tea, (*leaf, plant, infusion, meal*) thé, *m.*; **~-cup,** tasse à thé, *f.*; **~-party,** thé, *m.*; **~-pot,** théière, *f.*; **~-spoon,** cuiller à thé, *f.*; **~-strainer,** passe-thé, *m. invar.*; **~-table,** table à thé, *f.*; *~things, service*, service à thé, *m.*; **~-urn,** fontaine à thé, *f.*
teach, *v.a.* enseigner (*acc. of thing, dat. of pers.*); (*to do*) apprendre* à; (*show how to*) montrer comment + *inf.*; (*as instruction, warning*) enseigner; *v.n.* enseigner.
teachable, enseignable.
teacher, (*one who teaches*) institut|eur, ~rice, *m.f.*; (*school, &c.*) professeur, *m.f.*
teaching, enseignement, *m.*
teak, (*wood*) teck, *m.*
teal, (*ornith.*) sarcelle, *f.*
team, (*horses*) attelage, *m.*; (*sport*) équipe, *f.*
tear, *s.* larme, *f.*; **~-gas,** gaz lacrymogène, *m.*; *burst, dissolve, melt into ~s*, fondre en larmes.
tear, *s.* déchirure, *f.*; *wear and* ~, usure, *f.*
tear, *v.a.* (*rend, lit. and fig.*) déchirer; ~ *away, down, off, out*, arracher; ~ *up*, (*letters, &c.*) déchirer.
tear, *v.n.* se déchirer; (*run quickly*) courir* à toute vitesse; ~ *upstairs, &c.*, monter (être) quatre à quatre.
tearful, en pleurs; **~ly,** en pleurant.
tearing, *adj.* (*violent*) violent.
tease, *s.* (*pers.*) taquin, -e, *m.f.*; *v.a.* taquiner.
teasel, (*bot.*) cardère, *f.*
teat, (*pers.*) tetin, *m.*; (*an.*) tette, *f.*
techni|cal, technique; **~cality,** technicité, *f.*; **~cally,** en termes techniques; **~cal school,** *see* SCHOOL; **~que,** technique, *f.*
techy, chatouilleu|x, ~se.
tedious, ennuyeu|x, ~se; **~ness,** ennui, *m.*; **~ly,** ennuyeusement.
teem with, regorger de.
teens, *be in one's* ~, n'avoir pas vingt ans.
teeth|e, faire* ses dents; **~ing,** dentition, *f.*
teetotaller, (*approx.*) buveu|r, ~se d'eau, *m.f.*
teetotum, toton, *m.*
tegument, tégument, *m.*
telegram, télégramme, *m.*; *wireless* ~, télégramme sans fil, *m.*
telegraph, télégraphe, *m.*; **~-boy,** facteur des télégraphes, *m.*; **~-pole,** poteau télégraphique, *m.*; **~-wire,** fil télégraphique, *m.*; *v.a.* télégraphier; **~ic,** télégraphique.
telegraph|er, **~ist,** télégraphiste, *m.f.*
telegraphy, télégraphie, *f.*; *wireless* ~, télégraphie sans fil, *f.* (*abbrev.* T.S.F.).
telepathy, télépathie, *f.*

telephon|e, *s.* téléphone, *m.*; **~e-box,** (*public*) cabine téléphonique, *f.*; *~e call,* appel téléphonique, *m.*; *~e charge,* taxe de communication, *f.*; *be on the ~e,* avoir le téléphone; *v.a.n.* téléphoner; **~ic,** téléphonique; **~ist,** téléphoniste, *m.f.*
telescop|e, télescope, *m.*; *v.a.* (*train*) télescoper; *v.n.* se télescoper; **~ic,** télescopique.
tell, *v.a.* (*relate, express in words, decide, affirm, order, beads, truth, lies, &c.*) dire*; (*distinguish*) distinguer; (*assure*) assurer; (*reckon*) compter; (*show*) indiquer; (*beads*) dire* (son chapelet); (*be told*) entendre dire; *you're ~ing me!* (*U.S.A.*) à qui le dites-vous?; *~ off,* (*count off*) énumérer; (*detach for duty*) désigner; (*fam. rebuke*) rabrouer.
tell, *v.n.* (*produce effect*) faire* son effet; *~ of,* (*describe*) décrire*; *~ on,* affecter.
teller, (*tales*) conteu|r, ~se, *m.f.*
telling, frappant.
telltale, rapporteu|r, ~se.
temerity, témérité, *f.*
temper, *s.* (*anger*) colère, *f.*; (*disposition*) tempérament, *m.*; (*metals*) trempe, *f.*; *out of ~,* en colère; *keep one's ~,* ne pas se fâcher; *lose one's ~,* s'emporter.
temper, *v.a.* (*moderate*) modérer; (*steel*) tremper.
temperament, (*lit. and fig.*) tempérament, *m.*; **~al,** d'humeur instable.
temperance, tempérance, *f.*
temperate, sobre (de); (*climate*) tempéré; **~ness,** modération, *f.*; **~ly,** sobrement.
temperature, (*pers., atmosph., degree of heat*) température, *f.*
tempest, (*lit., fig.*) tempête, *f.*; **~uous,** tempêtueu|x, ~se; **~uously,** avec violence.
temple, temple, *m.*; (*of the head*) tempe, *f.*
templar, (*hist.*) templier, *m.*
temporal, *adj.* temporel, -le.
temporar|y, temporaire; **~ily,** temporairement.
temporize, temporiser.
tempt, tenter (de); **~ation,** tentation, *f.*; **~ing,** *adj.* (*food*) appétissant; **~er, ~ress,** tentat|eur, ~rice.
ten, *adj. and s.m.* dix; (*approximately*) une dizaine de.
tenable, (*theory, opinion*) soutenable; (*mil., position*) tenable.
tenacious, (*memory, adhesive, hard to eradicate*) tenace; *~ of,* fortement attaché à; **~ly,** (*obstinately*) opiniâtrément.
tenacity, (*memory, &c.*) ténacité, *f.*
tenan|cy, (*approx.*) durée d'occupation, *f.*; **~t,** locataire, *m.f.*; ⚠ *not* tenant *which = 'champion', 'defender'.*
tenantry, locataires, *m.pl.*; (*farms*) fermiers, *m.pl.*
tench, (*ichth.*) tanche, *f.*
tend, *v.a.* (*sick*) soigner; (*ans.*) garder; *v.n.* (*aim at, lead to*) tendre à.
tenden|cy, (*lit. and fig.*) tendance, *f.* (à); **~tious,** tendancieu|x, ~se.
tender, *s.* (*for a contract*) soumission, *f.*; (*naut.*) allège, *f.*; ⚠ tender, *m. only = 'engine tender'.*
tender, *adj.* (*soft, heart, conscience, place on body, affectionate, age, meat, grass*) tendre; (*ticklish*) délicat; **~-hearted,** au cœur tendre; **~ness,** tendresse, *f.*; **~ly,** tendrement.
tender, *v.a.* (*services, resignation, thanks, money*) offrir*; *~ for,* (*contract*) soumissionner (à + *pers. or corporation, acc. of thing supplied*).
tenderfoot, (*U.S.A.*) nouveau venu, *m.*
tendon, tendon, *m.*
tendril, vrille, *f.*
tenement, (*approx.*) appartement d'ouvrier, *m.*
tenet, dogme, *m.*
tenfold, *adj.* décuple; *adv.* au décuple.
tennis, tennis, *m.*; **~-court,** court, *m.*
tenor, (*mus.*) ténor, *m.*; (*sense*) sens, *m.*; (*direction*) direction, *f.*
tense, *s.* (*gram.*) temps, *m.*
tense, *adj.* (*lit. and fig.*) tendu; **~ness,** état de tension, *m.*
tensile, extensible.
tension, (*lit. and fig.*) tension, *f.*
tent, tente, *f.*
tentacle, tentacule, *m.*
tentative, d'essai; **~ly,** expérimentalement.
tenter-hooks, *see* HOOK.
tenth, dixième; (*date, sovereign, chapter*) dix; **~ly,** dixièmement.
tenu|ity, ténuité, *f.*; (*air*) raréfaction, *f.*; (*style*) simplicité, *f.*; **~ous,** ténu.
tenure, (*period of possession*) jouissance, *f.*
tepid, (*lit. and fig.*) tiède; **~ity, ~ness,** tiédeur, *f.*
tergiversa|te, tergiverser; **~tion,** tergiversation, *f.*
term, *s.* (*end, limited period, lease, imprisonment, logic, technical, scientific*) terme, *m.*; (*school*) trimestre, *m.*; **~s,** (*mode of expression, relationships, purport*) termes, *m.pl.*; (*treaty, &c.*) conditions, *f.pl.*; (*price*) prix, *m.*; *come to ~s with,* faire* un arrangement avec; *in plain ~s,* en propres termes.
term, *v.a.* appeler.
termagant, mégère, *f.*
terminal, (*accounts, payments, exams., &c.*) trimestriel, -le; *adj.* (*bot.*) terminal.
termina|te, *v.a.* (*bound, end*) terminer; *v.n.* se terminer (en); **~tion,** fin, *f.*; (*gram.*) terminaison, *f.*
terminology, terminologie, *f.*
terminus, (*rail.*) gare terminus, *f.*
tern, (*ornith.*) hirondelle de mer, *f.*
ternary, ternaire.
terra|cotta, terre cuite, *f.*; **~ firma,** terre ferme, *f.*
terrace, *s.* (*raised level space*) terrasse, *f.*; ⚠ *not Eng. 'terrace' of houses which = approx.* rangée de maisons, *f.*

terrestrial, terrestre.
terribl|e, (*lit. and fam.*) terrible; **~y,** terriblement.
terrier, (*dog*) terrier, *m.*
terrific, épouvantable.
terrify, épouvanter.
territorial, *adj. and s.m.* (*soldier*) territorial.
territory, territoire, *m.*
terror, (*emotion, object of terror*) terreur, *f.*; *~-stricken,* frappé de terreur; **~ist,** terroriste, *m.*; **~ize,** *v.a.* terroriser.
terse, (*style, &c.*) concis; **~ly,** avec concision.
tertiary, tertiaire.
tesselated, en mosaïque.
test, *s.* (*trial*) épreuve, *f.*; (*standard of comparison*) pierre de touche, *f.*; (*chem.*) réactif, *m.*; *put to the ~,* mettre* à l'épreuve.
test, *v.a.* mettre* à l'épreuve.
testament, (*will and Bible*) testament, *m.*; **~ary,** testamentaire.
testat|or, ~rix, testat|eur, ~rice, *m.f.*
tester, (*bed*) ciel de lit, *m.*, *pl.* ciels de lit.
testify, *v.a.* affirmer; *v.n.* (*law*) déposer; *~ to,* témoigner de.
testimonial, (*certificate*) certificat, *m.*; (*gift*) témoignage d'estime, *m.*
testimony, témoignage, *m.*
testing, *s.* essai, *m.*
test|y, bourru; **~ily,** avec humeur.
tether, longe, *f.*; *be at the end of one's ~,* être au bout de son rouleau; *v.a.* mettre* à l'attache.
tetrarch, tétrarque, *m.*
Teutonic, teutonique.
text, (*of sermon, main body of book, original words of author*) texte, *m.*; **~-book,** manuel, *m.*
textile, *adj. and s.m.* textile.
textual, de texte.
texture, (*material, arrangement of threads*) tissu, *m.*; (*skin, literary work*) texture, *f.*
than, (+ *comparative and* autre) que; (+ *numerals*) de.
thank, *v.a.* remercier; (*irony*) être obligé (à + *pers.*, de + *inf.*).
thankful, reconnaissant; **~ness,** reconnaissance, *f.*; **~ly,** avec reconnaissance.
thankless, (*ungrateful, unprofitable*) ingrat; **~ness,** (*want of gratitude*) ingratitude, *f.*
thanks, remerciements, *m.pl.*; *~ to you, &c.,* grâce à vous, etc.; **~giving,** actions de grâce, *f.pl.*
that, *pl.* **those,** *demons. adj.* ce, cet (+ *vowel and mute* H), cette, *pl.* ces (-là *is added to noun qualified by* ce, etc., *for emphasis or in contrast to* ce, etc. . . . -ci, *e.g.* cet homme-là et cet homme-ci; avez-vous vu ce tableau-là?); *~ way,* (*direction*) de ce côté-là.
that, *pl.* **those,** *demons. pron.* I (*of noun mentioned or understood*) celui, *f.* celle, *m.pl.* ceux, *f. pl.* celles (+ -là *for emphasis or when in contrast to* celui-ci, etc.); *those who,* ceux qui. II (*of objects not named, of an idea, impression, situation*) cela (*fam.* ça) *often in contrast to* ceci; *at, besides ~,* par-dessus le marché; *~ is,* c'est-à-dire; *~'s it,* c'est cela; *~ 's that,* voilà tout.
that, *rel. pron.* (*pers., things*) *nom.* qui, *acc.* que.
that, *conj.* (*introducing subordinate clause, used alone or in conjunction with other words*) que, *e.g.* je veux qu'il le fasse; *see also* (*in order that*) *below*; (*in order that*) pour que; *sometimes* pour + *inf.*, *e.g. we breathe that we may live,* nous respirons pour vivre.
thatch, *s.* chaume, *m.*; *v.a.* couvrir* de chaume.
thaw, *s.* dégel, *m.*; *v.a.n.* dégeler.
the, *art.* le, la, les; (= '*that*') ce, cet, cette, ces); ⚠ *the article is omitted in French before the numeral in titles of sovereigns and numbers of chapters, volumes, &c.; also with the preposition* en *and usually with nouns in apposition and in enumerations.*
theatr|e, (*lit. and fig.*) théâtre, *m.*; (*dissecting*) amphithéâtre, *m.*; **~ical,** (*lit. and fig.*) théâtral; **~icals,** *s.* spectacle, *m.*
thee, *pron.* (*with verbs*) *acc. and dat.* te; (*with preps. alone, after* ce + être *and comparatives* + que) toi.
theft, vol, *m.*
their, *adj.* leur, *m.f.*; *pl.* leurs.
theirs, (*in contradistinction*) le leur, la leur, les leurs; (*possessive*) à eux, à elles.
theis|m, théisme, *m.*; **~t,** théiste, *m.f.*
them, (*with verb*) *acc.* les, *dat.* (*to them*) leur; (*with preps. alone, after* ce + être *and comparatives* + que) eux, *f.* elles; **~selves,** (*with verb*) se; (*nom. and with preps.*) eux-mêmes, elles-mêmes.
theme, (*schools*) thème, *m.*; (*subject*) sujet, *m.*
then, *adv.* (*at that time, in that case*) alors; (*after that*) puis; (*consequently*) donc; *adj.* d'alors.
thence, (*for that reason*) pour cette raison; (*from there*) de là.
thence|forth, ~forward, dès lors.
theocra|cy, théocratie, *f.*; **~tic,** théocratique.
theodolite, théodolite, *m.*
theolog|ian, théologien, *m.*; **~ical,** théologique; **~ically,** théologiquement.
theology, théologie, *f.*
theorem, théorème, *m.*
theoretical, théorique; **~ly,** théoriquement.
theor|ist, théoricien, -ne, *m.f.*; **~y,** théorie, *f.*; **~ize,** faire* des théories.
theosoph|ist, théosophe, *m.f.*; **~y,** théosophie, *f.*
there, *adv.* là; (*with verb*) y, *e.g.* Je l'y ai trouvé; *~ is, are,* (*of position or existence*) il y a; (*exclamatory*) voilà; ~|*he is!* le voilà!; *down, over ~,* là-bas; *under ~,* là-dessous; *up ~,* là-haut; *that wall ~,* ce mur-là; *~ came a day,* il arriva un jour; *are you ~?* (*teleph.*) allô!

thereabout(s), par-là; (*number, quantity*) à peu près.
thereafter, après cela.
thereby, (*as a result*) là-dessus.
therefore, donc.
therein, là-dedans; (*in that respect*) sous ce rapport.
thereof, en *with verb*.
thereupon, là-dessus.
thermal, thermal.
thermometer, thermomètre, *m*.
thermos flask, thermos, *f*.
these, *see* THIS.
thesis, thèse, *f*.
thew, nerf, *m*.
they, (*with verb*) ils, *f*. elles; (*alone, after comparatives* + que *and* ce sont, c'étaient, etc.) eux, elles; (*indefinite, one, people*) on; ~ *who*, ceux, celles qui.
thick, *s. through the* ~ *of*, au plus fort de.
thick, *adj.* (*material, dense, growth, &c., liquids, crowded together*) épais, -se; (*speech*) pâteu|x, ~se; (*stupid*) bête; (*intimate*) très lié (avec); *be* ~*-headed*, avoir la tête dure; ~ *with*, (*full of*) plein de; **~ness,** (*material, density*) épaisseur, *f*.; (*liquid*) état trouble, *m*.; **~ly,** épais; (*closely*) dru.
thick, *adv.* épais; (*closely*) dru.
thicken, *v.a.* épaissir; *v.n.* s'épaissir.
thicket, fourré, *m*.
thickset, (*pers.*) trapu; (*close together*) dru.
thief, voleu|r, ~se, *m.f.*; *set a* ~ *to catch a* ~, à voleur voleur et demi.
thieve, *v.a.n.* voler.
thievish, de voleur; **~ness,** penchant au vol, *m*.; **~ly,** en voleur.
thigh, cuisse, *f*.; **~-bone,** fémur, *m*.
thimble, dé, *m*.
thimbleful, (*brandy, &c.*) doigt, *m*.
thin, (*slender, materials*) mince; (*pers., ans.*) maigre; (*wine, air*) lég|er, ~ère; (*plants, &c., not close*) clairsemé; (*fig.* = '*feeble*') pauvre; (*attendance*) peu nombreu|x, ~se; *have a* ~ *time*, (*slang*) se raser; **~ness,** (*leanness, poorness*) maigreur, *f*.; (*liquids*) fluidité, *f*.; (*materials*) minceur, *f*.; (*scarcity*) petit nombre, *m*.; (*slenderness, materials*) minceur, *f*.; (*pers., ans.*) maigreur, *f*.; (*of lines, &c.*) finesse, *f*.; **~ly,** (*populated, &c.*) peu; *~ly clad*, peu vêtu.
thin, *v.a.* (*liquids, ranks, growth*) éclaircir.
thine, *pron.* (*in contradistinction*) le tien, la tienne, les tiens, les tiennes; (*possessive*) à toi.
thing, (*animate and inanimate object, fam. pers., matter, act, fact, idea, affair, &c., production of art, Lit.*) chose, *f*.; (*pers., an. in pity or affection, &c.*) créature, *f*.; **~s,** (*clothes, movables*) effets, *m.pl.*; *~s are going badly*, cela va mal; *the* ~ *is to*, ce qu'il faut c'est + *inf.*; *it's not the* ~, cela ne se fait pas; *not to be the* ~, (*health*) ne pas être dans son assiette.
think, *v.a.* croire*; (*conceive*) concevoir; (*deem*) trouver; ~ *out*, (*plan*) élaborer; ~ *over*, (*reflect*) réfléchir à; (*weigh*) peser.
think, *v.n.* (*consider, believe*) croire*; (*exercise mind*) penser; (*judge*) juger; (*reflect*) réfléchir; ~ *about, of*, penser à; (*entertain idea of*) songer à; ~ *of his winning 100 francs!* dire qu'il a gagné cent francs!
thinkable, concevable.
thinker, penseu|r, ~se, *m.f.*
thinking, *s.* (*action*) action de penser, *f*.; (*way of*) façon de penser, *f*.; *adj.* (*pers.*) qui pense.
third, *s.* tiers, *m*.; *adj.* troisième; (*sovereign, date, chapter, &c.*) trois; **~ly,** troisièmement.
thirst, (*lit. and fig.*) soif, *f*.; *v.n.* (*lit. and fig.*) avoir soif (de).
thirst|y, (*pers., flowers*) altéré; (*land*) aride; *be* ~*y*, avoir soif; **~ily,** avidement.
thirteen, treize; **~th,** treizième; (*sovereign, date, chapter, &c.*) treize.
thirt|y, trente; **~ieth,** trentième; (*chapter, date*) trente.
this, *pl.* **these,** *demons. adj.* ce, cet (+ *vowel or mute* H), cette, *pl.* ces; (+ -ci, *after noun for emphasis or distinction*); *he has been there these 10 years*, il est là depuis dix ans; ~ *way*, (*direction*) de ce côté-ci.
this, *pl.* **these,** *demons. pron.* I (*of noun mentioned or understood*) celui, celle, ceux, celles (+ -ci *for emphasis or when in contrast to* celui-là, etc.). II (*of objects not named, of an idea, impression, situation*) ceci, *often in contrast to* cela; (*exclamatory*) voici, *e.g.* ~ *is what you do*, voici ce qu'il faut faire.
thistle, chardon, *m*.; **~-down,** duvet de chardon, *m*.
thither, là.
thong, lanière, *f*.
thorax, thorax, *m*.
thorn, (*lit. and fig.*) épine, *f*.; **~y,** (*lit. and fig.*) épineu|x, ~se.
thorough, *adj.* (*complete*) compl|et, ~ète; (*absolute*) absolu; (*downright, pej.*) achevé; (*accomplished*) consommé; **~ness,** (*of work, &c.*) perfection, *f*.; **~ly,** à fond.
thoroughbred, *adj. invar. and s.m.* pur sang.
thoroughfare, (*street*) rue, *f*.; (*way through*) passage, *m*.; *no* ~, rue barrée.
those, *pl. of 'that', which see.*
thou, *pers. pron.* (*subj. of verb*) tu; (*alone, with preps. after* ce + être *and comparatives* + que) toi.
though, quoique (+ *subj.*); *what* ~? qu'importe que? (+ *subj.*); *adv.* (*all the same*) tout de même.
thought, *s.* (*faculty, mind, meaning, act of thinking, intention, opinion*) pensée, *f*.; (*consideration*) *use verb* réfléchir; (*idea*) idée, *f*.; (*care*) souci, *m*.; (*ever so little*) tant soit peu de; *on second* ~*s*, réflexion faite.

thoughtful, (*full of thought*) pensi|f, ~ve; (*attentive*) attenti|f, ~ve; **~ness,** rêverie; (*kind attention*) prévenance, *f.*; **~ly,** d'un air rêveur; (*with kind attention*) avec prévenance.
thoughtless, étourdi; (*careless*) insouciant; **~ness,** étourderie, insouciance, *f.*; **~ly,** étourdiment, avec insouciance.
thousand, *s.* mille, *m. invar.*; *~s of,* des milliers de.
thousand, *adj.* mille, *invar.*; *a ~,* mille; ⚠ *dates A.D. should be expressed in hundreds*; **~th,** millième.
thraldom, esclavage, *m.*
thrash, *v.a.* (*corn, beat*) battre; **~er,** batteur en grange, *m.*; **~ing,** (*corn*) battage, *m.*; (*pers.*) rossée, *f.*
thread, *s.* (*fig., lit., cotton, &c.*) fil, *m.*; (*screw*) filet, *m.*; *v.a.* (*needle, beads*) enfiler; *~ one's way through,* passer par.
threadbare, râpé; (*fig.*) rebattu.
threat, (*lit. and fig.*) menace, *f.*; **~en,** *v.a.n.* menacer (de); *~en with,* menacer de; **~ening,** *s.* menaces, *f.pl.*; *adj.* menaçant; **~eningly,** avec menaces.
three, *adj. and s.m.* trois; *~-cornered, see* CORNER, *v.a.*; *~-cornered hat, see* CORNER, *v.a.*
threefold, triple.
threescore, soixante.
thresh, *&c., see* **THRASH.**
threshold, (*lit. and fig.*) seuil, *m.*
thrice, trois fois.
thrift, économie, *f.*; (*bot.*) statice, *m.*; **~less,** prodigue; **~lessness,** prodigalité, *f.*
thrift|y, économe; **~iness,** économie, *f.*; **~ily,** économiquement.
thrill, *s.* tressaillement, *m.*
thrill, *v.a.* faire* frémir; (*stir, move*) émouvoir*; *v.n.* tressaillir* (de); **~ing,** *adj.* saisissant.
thrive, *v.n.* prospérer; (*grow*) croître*.
thriving, *adj.* prospère.
throat, gorge, *f.*; *clear one's ~,* s'éclaircir le gosier; **white ~** (*ornith.*) fauvette babillarde, *f.*
throb, *s.* palpitation, *f.*; *v.n.* palpiter; **~bing,** *s.* (*motor engine*) vrombissement, *m.*
throe, douleurs, *f.pl.*; (*fig.*) angoisse, *f.*
throne, (*lit. and fig.*) trône, *m.*; *v.a.* mettre* sur le trône.
throng, *s.* foule, *f.*; *v.a.* (*streets*) encombrer (de); (*pers.*) presser; *v.n.* (*crowd*) se presser.
throstle, grive, *f.*
throttle, *s.* gosier, *m.*; (*steam*) régulateur, *m.*; (*aeron.*) gaz, *m.pl.*; *v.a.* étrangler; *with open ~,* à pleins gaz.
through, *adj.* (*train, luggage, carriage, ticket, &c.*) direct.
through, *adv.* (*from one end to the other*) d'un bout à l'autre; (*wet*) jusqu'aux os; (*pierce, &c.*) de part en part; (*finished*) fini; *~ and ~,* de part en part; *walk, &c., ~, v.a.n.* traverser.
through, *prep.* à travers; (*with obstacle*) au travers de; (*through transparency, on account of, agency, afflictions*) par; (*during*) pendant.
throughout, *adv.* d'un bout à l'autre; (*everywhere*) partout; *prep.* d'un bout à l'autre de.
throw, *s.* (*action of throwing, distance*) jet, *m.*; (*dice*) coup, *m.*
throw, *v.a.* (*lit., fig., light, glance, shadow, bridge*) jeter; (*horses*) désarçonner; *~ away,* jeter; (*energy, time, money*) dissiper; (*life, chance*) perdre; *~ aside,* jeter de côté; *~ down,* (*overthrow*) renverser; (*on the ground*) jeter à terre; *~ in,* (*as extra*) donner par-dessus le marché; *~ off,* (*pers., illness*) se débarrasser de; (*clothes*) ôter; *~ off the scent,* dépister; *~ out,* (*reject*) rejeter; (*expel*) chasser; (*hint*) faire*; *~ over,* (*abandon*) abandonner; *~ up,* jeter en haut; (*post, &c.*) se démettre* de; *v.n.* jeter; (*dice*) jeter les dés.
thrush, (*ornith.*) grive, *f.*
thrust, *s.* (*push*) poussée, *f.*; (*sword, fenc.*) botte, *f.*
thrust, *v.a.* (*cram*) fourrer; (*head*) passer (par); (*hands*) enfoncer; (*push*) pousser; *~ oneself,* se fourrer; *~ out,* (*stretch out*) allonger; (*expel, &c.*) jeter dehors; *~ through,* transpercer; *~ oneself in, through,* passer de force; *~ upon,* imposer (à).
thrust, *v.n.* (*fencing, &c.*) porter une botte.
thud, *s.* bruit sourd, *m.*
thumb, pouce, *m.*; *Tom Thumb,* le petit Poucet; **~-screw,** (*torture*) poucettes, *f.pl.*; *be under the ~ of,* être sous la coupe de; *v.a.* (*book*) feuilleter; *twiddle one's ~s,* se tourner les pouces.
thump, *s.* grand coup, *m.*; *v.a.n.* frapper lourdement.
thunder, *s.* (*lit., fig.*) tonnerre, *m.*; **~s,** (*fig.*) foudre, *f.*; **~-clap,** coup de tonnerre, *m.*; **~-storm,** orage de tonnerre, *m.*; **~-struck,** (*fig.*) abasourdi.
thunder, *v.a.* fulminer; *v.n.* (*lit., cannon, inveigh*) tonner.
thunderbolt, foudre, *f.*
thunder|ing, ~ous, *adj.* de tonnerre.
thundery, *the weather is ~,* le temps est au tonnerre.
thurible, encensoir, *m.*
Thursday, jeudi, *m.*
thus, ainsi.
thwart, *s.* (*boat*) banc, *m.*
thwart, *v.a.* (*plans, &c.*) traverser.
thy, ton, *f.* ta, *pl.* tes; **~self,** (*with verb*) te; (*nom. and with preps.*) toi-même.
thyme, thym, *m.*; *wild ~,* serpolet, *m.*
tiara, tiare, *f.*
tic, (*twitch*) tic, *m.*
tick, (*material*) coutil, *m.*; (*clock, &c.*) tic-tac, *m.*; *v.a. ~ off,* (*in list*) marquer; (*verify*) pointer; *v.n.* (*clock, &c.*) faire* tic-tac; *on ~,* (*slang = 'credit'*) à crédit.
ticket, *s.* (*rail., theatr., &c.*) billet, *m.*; (*on goods*) étiquette, *f.*; **~-collector,**

contrôleur, *m.*; **~-office, ~-window,** guichet, *m.*; *v.a.* étiqueter.
ticking, (*material*) toile à matelas, *f.*
tickle, *v.a.n.* chatouiller.
ticklish, chatouilleu|x, ~se; (*difficult to handle*) épineu|x, ~se.
tidal, de marée; ~ **wave,** raz de marée, *m.*
tide, (*lit. and fig.*) marée, *f.*; (*current*) courant, *m.*
tide over, (*difficulty*) surmonter.
tidings, nouvelle, *f.*
tid|y, propre; (*things*) rangé; **~iness,** ordre, *m.*; **~ily,** avec ordre; *v.a.* ranger.
tie, *s.* (*lit. and fig.*) lien, *m.*; (*neck*) cravate, *f.*; (*bow, hair*) nœud, *m.*; (*sport*) partie égale, *f.*; **~-beam,** entrait, *m.*; **~-clip,** pince de cravate, *f.*
tie, *v.a.* attacher; (*hands, tongue, bind*) lier; (*necktie, knot, &c.*) nouer; ~ *down,* lier; (*fig.*) lier les mains à; ~ *up,* attacher; (*with string*) ficeler; (*ans.*) mettre à l'attache; (*bind up*) bander; (*money*) bloquer; *be ~d for time,* être pressé; *be tongue-~d,* avoir la langue liée.
tier, (*seats*) gradin, *m.*
tiff, *s.* (*quarrel*) pique, *f.*
tiffin, collation, *f.*
tig|er, ~ress, tigre, -sse, *m.f.*; **~er-lily,** lis tigré, *m.*; **~erish,** de tigre.
tight, *adj.* (*close-fitting, money, reins, knot, &c.*) serré; (*rope*) tendu; (*fam. drunk*) gris; *water-~,* étanche; **~ness,** *see below*; **~ly,** d'une manière tendue; (*closely*) étroitement.
tight, *adv.* (*with 'hold', 'shut', &c.*) bien *or* très bien.
tighten, (*stretch*) tendre; (*pull, draw tight*) serrer; *v.n.* se tendre, se serrer.
tightness, tension, *f.*; (*clothes, &c.*) étroitesse, *f.*; (*impermeability*) imperméabilité, *f.*
tights, (*dancers, &c.*) maillot, *m.*
tilbury, tilbury, *m.*
tile, *s.* (*roof*) tuile, *f.*; (*glazed*) carreau, *m.*; *v.a.* couvrir* de tuiles; **~r,** (*tile-maker*) tuilier, *m.*; (*layer of tiles*) couvreur en tuiles, *m.*
till, *s.* (*money*) caisse, *f.*
till, *v.a.* labourer.
till, *prep.* jusqu'à; *conj.* jusqu'à ce que (+*subj.*).
till|age, tilth, culture, *f.*; **~er,** cultivateur, *m.*
tiller, (*naut.*) barre, *f.*
tilt, (*sloping position*) inclinaison, *f.*; (*fight*) joute, *f.*; **~-yard,** champ clos, *m.*
tilt, *v.a.* (*incline, cant, &c.*) pencher; *v.n.* (*fight*) jouter (contre); *v.a.n.* ~ *up, over,* basculer; **~er,** jouteur, *m.*
timber, *s.* (*building*) bois de construction, *m.*; (*trees*) bois (de haute futaie), *m.*; **~-merchant,** marchand de bois, *m.*; **~-yard,** chantier de bois, *m.*; *v.a.* boiser.
timbrel, tambourin, *m.*
time, *s.* (*duration, portion of ~, period in past, proper moment, delay, particular period, apprenticeship*) temps, *m.*; (*particular occasion, number of occasions*) fois, *f.*; (*moment*) moment, *m.*; (*by the clock, appointed time*) heure, *f.*; (*of payment*) terme, *m.*; (*mus.*) mesure, *f.*; ~ *of day,* heure, *f.*; **~-server,** complaisant, -e, *m.f.*; **~-table,** horaire, *m.*; (*rail.*) indicateur, *m.*; (*schol.*) emploi du temps; **~s,** (*period of existence, hard, &c.*) temps, *m.pl.*; *at ~s, from ~ to ~,* de temps en temps; *by the ~ that,* avant que (+ *subj.*); *for the ~ being,* actuellement; *in ~,* à temps; *in ~ for, to,* assez tôt pour; *What ~ is it?* Quelle heure est-il? ; *have a good ~,* s'amuser bien; *keep good, bad ~,* (*clock, &c.*) marcher bien, mal; *mark ~,* (*lit., fig., mil.*) marquer le pas.
time, *v.a.* (*arrival, &c.*) régler; *well ~d,* à propos.
timekeeper, (*workshops*) surveillant, m.
time|liness, opportunité, *f.*; **~ly,** opportun.
timepiece, pendule, *f.*
timid, timide; **~ity,** timidité, *f.*; **~ly,** timidement.
timorous, timide; **~ly,** timidement.
tin, étain, *m.*; (*receptacle for fruits, meats, nails, paste, &c.*) boîte (en fer-blanc), *f.*; *adj.* d'étain; **~-smith,** ferblantier, *m.*; **~ned,** (*fruits, &c.*) en boîte.
tincture, *s.* (*tinge*) teinte, *f.*; (*slight notion, pharm., chem.*) teinture, *f.*
tinder, amadou, *m.*
tinge, *s.* (*lit. and fig.*) teinte, *f.*; *v.a.* teinter (de).
tingl|e, (*hands, &c.*) fourmiller; (*ears*) tinter; **~ing,** fourmillement, tintement, *m.*
tinker, rétameur, *m.*; *v.a.* rétamer.
tinkl|e, *v.a.* faire* tinter; *v.n.* tinter; **~ing,** tintement, *m.*
tinsel, (*lit. and fig.*) clinquant, *m.*; *adj.* de clinquant.
tint, *s.* teinte, *f.*; *v.a.* (*painting*) teinter.
tiny, tout petit; ⚠ *both* tout *and* petit *take fem. concord.*
tip, *s.* (*end*) bout, *m.*; (*money*) pourboire, *m.*; (*dodge, information*) tuyau, *m.*
tip, *v.a.* (*money*) donner un pourboire à; (*touch lightly*) effleurer; (*solids, liquids*) verser; (*overturn and ~ over*) renverser; ~ *up, v.a.* faire basculer; **~-cart,** tombereau, *m.*
tippet, (*dress*) pèlerine, *f.*
tipple, *v.n.* godailler; **~r,** biberon, *m.*
tipsy, ivre.
tiptoe, *adv.* sur la pointe du pied.
tirade, (*rating*) sortie, *f.*
tire, tyre, (*wheel*) bandage, *m.*; (*motor, cycles, &c.*) pneumatique, *m.*; (*abbrev.*) pneu; *studded ~,* pneu ferré; *solid ~,* bandage plein.
tire, *v.a.* fatiguer; *v.n.* se fatiguer; **~d,** *adj.* fatigué; *be ~d of,* être las de; *be ~d out,* être excédé.
tiredness, fatigue, *f.*
tireless, infatigable; **~ly,** infatigablement.
tiresome, (*vexing*) fâcheu|x, ~se; **~ness,** (*fam.*) corvée, *f.*

tiro, tyro, apprenti, *m.*
tissue, (*fabric and series*) tissu, *m.*; **~-paper,** papier de soie, *m.*
tit, (*ornith.*) mésange, *f.*
titbit, bonne bouche, *f.*
titanic, titanesque.
tithe, (*tenth part*) dixième, *m.*; (*eccles.*) dîme, *f.*
titillate, titiller.
titlark, alouette des prés, *f.*
title, *s.* (*of honour, of chapters, &c., right, in law, deed, claim, title-page*) titre, *m.*; **~d,** titré.
titmouse, (*ornith.*) mésange, *f.*
titter, *v.n.* ricaner.
tittle, iota, *m.*
tittle-tattle, cancans, *m.pl.*
titular, *adj. and s.m.* titulaire.
to, *prep.* (*in direction of; + names of towns; purpose + inf.; after adjs. of suitability, &c. + noun or inf., e.g.* propre, utile à) à; (+ *names of countries*) en; (+ *masc. names of countries outside Europe*) à + *article*; (*obligation, kindness, &c., to*) envers; (*towards*) vers; (*as far as*) jusqu'à; (*in comparison with*) auprès de; (*in order to + inf.; after nouns as* une mère pour, *a mother to,* un ami pour, etc., *and adjs. as* bon pour, utile pour) pour; (*proportion*) contre, *e.g. 10 to 1,* dix contre un; (*train, veh., road and impers. verbs made up of* être + *adj.*) de, *e.g.* le train de (*to*) Rouen, il est difficile de comprendre.
toad, crapaud, *m.*; **~-flax,** (*bot.*) lunaire, *f.*
toadstool, champignon vénéneux, *m.*
toady, flagorneu|r, ~se, *m.f.*; **~ism,** flagornerie, *f.*
toast, *s.* (*bread*) rôtie, *f.*; (*health*) toast, *m.*; *v.a.* (*bread*) faire* rôtir; (*health*) porter la santé de; *v.n.* rôtir.
tobacco, tabac, *m.*; **~nist,** marchand de tabac, *m.*; **~-pouch,** blague, *f.*; **~-pipe,** pipe, *f.*; **~-shop,** débit de tabac, *m.*; **~-stopper,** bourre-pipe, *m. invar.*
toboggan, toboggan, *m.*
tocsin, tocsin, *m.*
today, to-day, aujourd'hui; ~ *week, fortnight,* d'aujourd'hui en huit, en quinze.
toddle, *v.n.* marcher à petits pas.
toddy, toddy, *m.*
toe, orteil, *m.*; *big ~, see* BIG; *from top to ~,* de pied en cap; *tread on ~s of,* marcher sur les pieds de; *turn one's ~s in,* tourner la pointe du pied en dedans.
toffee, caramel, *m.*
toga, toge, *f.*
together, ensemble; (*at the same time*) en même temps; ~ *with,* en même temps que.
toil, *s.* travail, *m.*; (*strenuous*) rude travail, *m.*; *~-worn,* épuisé.
toil, *v.n.* travailler; *often* + péniblement; ~ *up,* (*hill, &c.*) monter (avoir) péniblement; ~ *and moil,* suer sang et eau.
toiler, travailleu|r, ~se, *m.f.*
toilet, toilette, *f.*; **~-paper,** papier hygiénique, *m.*; **~-set,** garniture de toilette, *f.*; **~-table,** table de toilette, *f.*
toils, (*fig.*) rets, *m. gen. plural.*
toilsome, pénible; **~ly,** péniblement.
token, (*of gratitude, &c., proof of authenticity*) témoignage, *m.*; (*coin*) jeton, *m.*
tolerabl|e, supportable; (*not so bad*) passable; **~y,** passablement; (+ *adj.*) assez.
tolerant, tolérant.
tolera|te, tolérer; **~tion,** tolérance, *f.*
toll, *s.* (*duty*) péage, *m.*; (*of bell, also tolling*) tintement, *m.*; **~-bar, -gate,** barrage, *m.*; **~-collector,** péag|er, ~ère, *m.f.*; **~-house,** (*town*) barrière, *f.*
toll, *v.a.* tinter; *v.n.* sonner.
tomahawk, casse-tête, *m. invar.*
tomato, tomate, *f.*
tomb, (*lit. and fig.*) tombeau, *m.*
tomboy, *use* avoir des allures garçonnières.
tombstone, pierre tombale, *f.*
tome, tome, *m.*
tomfool, nigaud, *m.*; **~ery,** nigauderie, *f.*
to-morrow, *adv.* demain; ~ *morning, evening,* demain matin, demain soir.
tomtit, (*ornith.*) mésange, *f.*
ton, (*measure*) tonne, *f.*; (*naut.*) tonneau, *m.*; **~s,** (*fig. for quantities*) des milliers de; ⚠ *Eng. ton = 2240 lbs.; Fr. ton (1000 kgs.) = approx. 2200 lbs.*
tone, *s.* (*voice, trend, colour, mus., med.*) ton, *m.*
ton|e, *v.a.* (*photo.*) virer; *~e down,* adoucir; *v.n. ~e down,* s'adoucir; *~e with,* s'harmoniser avec; *~ing-solution, see* SOLUTION.
tongs, (*fire*) pincettes, *f.pl.*; (*smiths, &c.*) tenailles, *f.pl.*; (*sugar, asparagus, &c.*) pince, *f.*
tongue, (*faculty and organ of speech, language, fig. of land, shoe, flame, &c.*) langue, *f.*
tonic, *adj. and s.m.* tonique.
to-night, *adv.* cette nuit; (*evening*) ce soir.
tonnage, tonnage, *m.*
tonsil, (*anat.*) amygdale, *f.*
tonsure, *s.* tonsure, *f.*
too, trop; (*also*) aussi.
tool, *s.* outil, *m.*; (*fig. pers.*) instrument, *m.*; **~-chest,** boîte à outils, *f.*
toot, *v.n.* (*horn*) corner.
tooth, (*pers., an., saw, wheel, &c.*) dent, *f.*; **~-brush,** brosse à dents, *f.*; **~-paste,** pâte dentifrice, *f.*; **~pick,** *see below*; **~-powder,** poudre dentifrice, *f.*; *in the teeth of,* malgré; *gnash, grind one's teeth,* grincer des dents; *set teeth on edge,* agacer les dents; **~ed,** *adj.* denté.
toothache, mal de dents, *m.*
toothless, édenté.
toothpick, cure-dent, *m.*, *pl.* cure-dents.
toothsome, friand.
top, *s.* **1** (*head, mountain*) sommet, *m.*; **2** (*buildings*) faîte, *m.*; **3** (*upper part, table, &c.*) dessus, *m.*; **4** (*a cover*) couvercle, *m.*; **5** (*tree, column*) tête, *f.*;

6 (*plaything*) toupie, *f.*; 7 (*naut.*) †hune, *f.*; 8 (*plants*) tête, *f.*; 9 (*in class, &c.*) premi|er, ~ère, *m.f.*; 10 (*omnibus*) impériale, *f.*; 11 (*turnips, carrots, &c.*) fane, *f.*; *on the ~ of,* (*mountains*) au sommet de; (*desk, table, &c.*) sur; **~-boots,** bottes à revers, *f.pl.*; **~-coat,** *see* COAT; *~ gear, see* GEAR; **~-heavy,** trop lourd du †haut; *~ speed, see* SPEED; *from ~ to bottom, see* BOTTOM.

top, *adj.* d'en †haut; (*in class, &c.*) premi|er, ~ère; (*price*) le plus †haut.

top, *v.a.* (*cover*) couronner (de); (*rise above*) dépasser; (*trees*) étêter.

topaz, topaze, *f.*

toper, buveur, *m.*

topic, sujet, *m.*; *~s of the day,* actualités, *f.pl.*; **~al,** topique.

topknot, (*ornith.*) †huppe, *f.*

topmast, mât de †hune, *m.*

topmost, le plus †haut.

topograph|ic(al), topographique; **~y,** topographie, *f.*

topper, (*slang = hat*) †haut de forme, *m.*

topping, (*slang*) fameu|x, ~se.

topple, *v.n.* tomber (être); *~ over,* dégringoler.

topsail, †hunier, *m.*

topsyturvy, sens dessus dessous.

torch, torche, *f.*; **~-bearer,** porte-flambeau, *m.invar.*

torment, *s.* tourment, *m.*; *v.a.* tourmenter (de).

tormentil, (*bot.*) tormentille, *f.*

tormentor, bourreau, *m.*

tornado, tornade, *f.*

torpedo, torpille, *f.*; ⚠ *not* torpédo, *m.*, *which = 'open touring car'*; **~-boat,** torpilleur, *m.*; **~-net,** filet pare-torpilles, *m.*; **~-plane,** avion torpilleur, *m.*; **~-tube,** lance-torpilles, *m. invar.*; *v.a.* torpiller.

torpid, engourdi.

torpor, torpidity, torpeur, *f.*

torrent, (*lit. and fig.*) torrent, *m.*; **~ial,** torrentiel, -le.

torrid, torride.

torso, torse, *m.*

tortoise, tortue, *f.*; **~-shell,** écaille, *f.*

tortuous, (*lit. and fig.*) tortueu|x, ~se; **~ness,** torsion, *f.*; **~ly,** tortueusement.

torture, *s.* (*lit. and fig.*) torture, *f.*; *v.a.* torturer; **~r,** bourreau, *m.*

toss, *s.* (*head*) mouvement, *m.*; (*from horse*) chute, *f.*; *win the ~,* gagner à pile ou face.

toss, *v.a.* (*throw*) jeter; (*ball, bull, &c.*) lancer en l'air; (*by sea and fig.*) ballotter; *~ off,* avaler d'un trait; *~ up,* (*coin*) lancer en l'air.

toss, *v.n.* (*in bed, sea, ship, trees, &c.*) s'agiter; *~ up,* (*coin*) jouer à pile ou face.

tot, *v.a. ~ up, together,* additionner.

total, *s.* total, *m.*; *adj.* total; **~itarian,** totalitaire; **~itarian States,** Puissances totalitaires, *f.pl.*; **~ity,** totalité, *f.*; **~ly,** totalement.

tote, *v.a.* (*U.S.A. transport*) transporter.

totter, *v.n.* chanceler; **~ing,** chancelant; **~ingly,** en chancelant.

touch, *s.* (*sense of, and mus.*) toucher, *m.*; (*fact of a touch*) attouchement, *m.*; (*with brush, &c., manner of using brush, football*) touche, *f.*; (*slight attack*) légère attaque, *f.*; (*small quantity*) soupçon, *m.*

touch, *v.a.* (*come into contact, with hand, &c., reach, affect, concern*) toucher; (*handle, interfere with*) toucher à; *~ on, upon,* (*subject, &c.*) toucher, *v.a.*; *~ up,* retoucher.

touch, *v.n.* se toucher.

touching, *adj.* touchant; *prep.* touchant; **~ly,** d'une manière touchante.

touchstone, pierre de touche, *f.*

touchwood, amadou, *m.*

touch|y, susceptible; **~iness,** susceptibilité, *f.*

tough, *s.* (*U.S.A. slang*) voyou, *m.*

tough, *adj.* (*hard to break, cut*) dur; (*strong, hardy*) robuste; (*difficult, exacting*) rude; (*meat*) coriace; **~ness,** dureté, *f.*; (*meat*) nature coriace, *f.*; (*strength*) force, *f.*; **~ly,** durement.

tour, *s.* voyage, *m.*; (*walk*) tour, *m.*; (*comm. and official*) tournée, *f.*; *walking-~,* excursion à pied, *f.*; *v.a.* visiter; *v.n.* voyager; **~ing,** *open ~ing car, see* CAR.

tour|ist, *s.* touriste, *m.*; *adj.* touristique; **~ing,** tourisme, *m.*; **~ing-car,** (*motor*) automobile de tourisme, *f.*

tournament, tourney, tournoi, *m.*; (*sport*) championnat, *m.*

tout, *s.* (*hotel*) pisteur, *m.*

tousled, (*hair*) ébouriffé.

tow, *s.* (*hemp*) étoupe, *f.*; (*boats, also towing*) remorque, *f.*; **~-path,** chemin de †halage, *m.*; *in ~,* à la remorque; *v.a.* remorquer.

toward(s), *prep.* (*time, place*) vers; (*feelings, attitude*) envers; (*for*) pour.

towel, essuie-main(s), *m. invar.*; **~-horse,** séchoir, *m.*

tower, *s.* tour, *f.*; *watch-~,* échauguette, *f.*

tower, *v.n. ~ above, over,* dominer; **~ing,** très †haut; (*fig.*) sublime; *~ing passion, see* PASSION.

town, ville, *f.*; (*Town = London*) Londres; **~-clerk,** greffier municipal, *m.*; **~-crier,** crieur public, *m.*; **~-hall,** hôtel de ville, *m.*; *~ house,* maison de ville, *f.*; (*mansion*) hôtel, *m.*; *~-planning,* urbanisme, *m.*

townsman, habitant de ville, *m.*; (*fellow citizen*) concitoyen, *m.*

toxin, toxine, *f.*

toy, *s.* jouet, *m.*; *v.n. ~ with,* jouer avec.

toyshop, magasin de jouets, *m.*

trace, *s.* (*track of pers. or an., visible sign, small quantity*) trace, *f.*; (*strap*) trait, *m.*

trac|e, *v.a.* (*mark out, sketch*) tracer; (*find*) retrouver; (*follow*) suivre* à la piste; (*over another sheet*) calquer; *~e back, up,* faire* remonter à; *~e out,* tracer; **~ing-paper,** papier à calquer, *m.*

traceable, dont on peut suivre les traces.

tracery, (*arch.*) réseau, *m.*
track, *s.* (*of feet*) traces, *f.pl.*; (*road*) sentier, *m.*; (*rail.*) voie, *f.*; (*ship*) sillage, *m.*; (*for running, &c.*) piste, *f.*; *be on the ~ of*, être à la piste de.
track, *v.a.* suivre* à la piste; *~ down*, capturer.
trackless, sans chemin frayé.
tract, (*space*) étendue, *f.*; (*region*) région, *f.*; (*religious, &c.*) tract, *m.*
tractable, traitable.
traction, traction, *f.*; **~-engine,** tracteur, *m.*
tractor, tracteur, *m.*
trade, *s.* commerce, *m.*; (*occupation, job*) métier, *m.*; **~-mark,** marque de fabrique, *f.*; *~ price, see* PRICE; **~ union,** syndicat, *m.*; **~-unionist,** syndicaliste, *m.f.*; **~-unionism,** syndicalisme, *m.*; **~-winds,** vents alizés, *m.pl.*
trade, *v.n.* commercer; *~ in*, faire* le commerce de.
trad|er, commerçant, *m.*; **~ing,** commerce, *m.*
tradesman, (*pl.* **tradespeople**) commerçant, *m.*
tradition, tradition, *f.*; **~al,** traditionnel, -le; **~ally,** traditionnellement.
traduce, calomnier; **~r,** calomniat|eur, ~rice, *m.f.*
traffic, *s.* (*trade, by road, rail., pej., fig.*) trafic, *m.*; (*in roads, streets*) circulation, *f.*
traged|ian, (*actor*) tragédien, -ne, *m.f.*; (*author*) auteur tragique, *m.*; **~y,** tragédie, *f.*
tragic(al), (*of tragedy, calamitous*) tragique; **~ally,** tragiquement.
trail, *s.* (*track*) trace, *f.*; (*hunt., path in wild region*) piste, *f.*; (*powder, smoke, &c.*) traînée, *f.*
trail, *v.a.* traîner; *v.n.* traîner; (*walk wearily*) se traîner; **~er,** (*motor, &c.*) voiturette, remorque, *f.*; (*bicycle*) baladeuse, *f.*
train, *s.* (*retinue, series*) suite, *f.*; (*rail., artil.*) train, *m.*; (*dress*) traîne, *f.*; (*powder*) traînée, *f.*; (*course*) cours, *m.*; *local ~*, train desservant les stations du district; *up ~*, train montant, *m.*
train, *v.a.* (*sport, horse*) entraîner; (*child, also ~ up*) élever; (*ans.*) dresser (à); (*cannon*) pointer; (*plants*) faire* grimper.
train, *v.n.* (*fam.*) aller* (être) par le train; (*sport*) s'entraîner.
trainer, (*sport, horses*) entraîneur, *m.*
training, *s.* éducation, *f.*; (*sport, horses*) entraînement, *m.*; **~-ship,** vaisseau-école, *m.*
trait|or, ~ress, traître, -sse, *m.f.*; ⚠ *not* traiteur *which* = '*restaurant-keeper*'.
traitorous, traître; ~ly, en traître.
tram, tramway, *m.*; ⚠ *English* '*tramway*' *and* '*~-rail*' = voie de tramway, *f.*; *v.n.* aller* (être) en tramway.
trammel, (*net*) tramail, *m.*; (*fig.*) entrave, *f.*; *v.n.* entraver.
tramp, *s.* (*pers.*) chemineau, *m.*; (*feet*) bruit de pas, *m.*
tramp, *v.a.* faire* (un chemin, voyage, &c.) à pied; *~ through*, parcourir* à pied; *v.n.* aller* (être) à pied.
trample (on), *v.a.* (*lit. and fig.*) fouler aux pieds, *also* '*~ in the dust*'.
trance, *s.* extase, *f.*
tranquil, tranquille; **~lity,** tranquillité, *f.*; **~ly,** tranquillement; **~lize,** tranquilliser.
transact, faire*; **~ion,** (*comm., of a society*) transaction, *f.*; (*carrying through*) conduite, *f.*; **~ions,** (*of meeting, &c.*) délibérations, *f.pl.*
transactor, négociateur, *m.*
transalpine, transalpin.
transatlantic, transatlantique.
transcend, *v.a.* dépasser; **~ence, ~ency,** transcendance, *f.*; **~ent,** transcendant.
transcribe, transcrire*; **~r,** copiste, *m.*
transcription, transcription, *f.*
transept, transept, *m.*
transfer, *s.* (*debt, goods, &c.*) transport, *m.*; (*shares*) transfert, *m.*; (*bkkpg.*) virement, *m.*
transfer, *v.a.* (*pers. property, &c.*) transférer; **~able,** (*comm.*) cessible; **~ence,** (*claim, debt*) transfèrement, *m.*
transfigur|ation, transfiguration, *f.*; **~e,** transformer.
transfix, transpercer.
transform, transformer (en); **~ation,** transformation, *f.* (en).
transfuse, (*blood, liquid, fig.*) transfuser.
transgress, *v.a.* transgresser, *v.n.* pécher; **~ion,** péché, *m.*; **~or,** péch|eur, ~eresse, *m.f.*
tranship, *see* TRANS-SHIP.
transient, passag|er, ~ère; **~ly,** transitoirement.
transit, transport, *m.*; *in ~*, en cours de route.
transition, transition, *f.*; **~al,** de transition.
transitive, (*gram.*) transiti|f, ~ve; **~ly,** transitivement.
transitor|y, transitoire; **~ily,** transitoirement.
translatable, traduisible.
transla|te, (*convey*) transporter; (*interpret*) interpréter; (*languages*) traduire*; **~tion,** (*removal*) translation, *f.*; (*languages*) traduction, *f.*
translator, traduct|eur, ~rice, *m.f.*
translucen|ce, translucidité, *f.*; **~t,** translucide.
transmigration, (*tribes, soul*) transmigration, *f.*
transmiss|ibility, transmissibilité, *f.*; **~ible,** transmissible; **~ion,** transmission, *f.*
transmit, transmettre*; **~ter,** (*teleph.*) parleur, *m.*; (*telegr.*) manipulat|eur, ~rice, *m.f.*
transmut|able, transmuable; **~ation,** transformation, *f.*; (*metals*) transmutation, *f.*; **~e,** (*metals*) transmuer.

transom, (*arch.*) traverse, *f.*
transparen|cy, transparence, *f.*; **~t,** (*lit. and fig.*) transparent; **~tly,** d'une manière transparente.
transpire, (*med., secret, &c.*) transpirer; (*happen*) arriver (être).
transplant, (*lit. and fig.*) transplanter; **~ation,** transplantation, *f.*
transport, *s.* (*of goods, violent emotion, ship*) transport, *m.*; *mechanized* ~, traction automobile, *f.*
transport, *v.a.* (*goods, emotion*) transporter (de); (*criminals*) déporter; **~ation,** déportation, *f.*; **~ing,** *adj.* ravissant.
transpos|e, transposer; **~al, ~ition,** transposition, *f.*
trans-ship, transborder; **~ment,** transbordement, *m.*
transubstantiation, transsubstantiation, *f.*
transverse, *adj.* transverse; **~ly,** obliquement.
trap, *s.* (*lit. and fig.*) piège, *m.*; (*veh.*) cabriolet, *m.*; (*sink, drain, &c.*) siphon, *m.*; **~-door,** trappe, *f.*; *walk into a, the* ~, donner dans le panneau.
trap, *v.a.* (*snare*) prendre* au piège; (*drain, &c.*) arrêter par un siphon.
trapeze, (*gym.*) trapèze, *m.*
trapper, (*N. Amer.*) trappeur, *m.*
trappings, (*horse*) †harnais, *m.*; (*pers.*) ornements, *m.pl.*
Trappist, (*monk*) trappiste, *m.*
trash, *s.* (*rubbish*) rebut, *m.*; (*nonsense*) niaiseries, *f.pl.*; (*valueless work*) camelote, *f.*; **~y,** sans valeur.
travail, *s.* (*child-birth*) travail, *m.*; *v.n.* être en travail.
travel, *s.* voyage, *m.* (*also gen. voyages*); **~s,** (*account*) récit de voyages, *m.*; *v.a.* parcourir*.
travel, *v.n.* (*lit. and comm.*) voyager; (*eye, &c.*) passer; (*spread*) se propager.
travelled, qui a voyagé.
traveller, voyageu|r, ~se, *m.f.*; **~'s joy,** (*bot.*) clématite, *f.*; *see also* COMMERCIAL.
travelling, *s.* voyage, *m.*; *adj.* de voyage; ~ *circus,* cirque forain, *m.*; ~ *expenses, see* EXPENSE.
traverse, *s.* (*structure*) traverse, *f.*
traverse, *v.a.* traverser; (*extent of subject*) examiner à fond.
travesty, *s.* (*pej.*) travestissement, *m.*; *v.a. pej.* travestir.
trawler, (*naut.*) chalutier, *m.*
tray, plateau, *m.*
treacherous, traître, -sse; (*memory*) infidèle; **~ly,** traîtreusement.
treachery, trahison, *f.*
treacle, mélasse, *f.*
tread, *s.* (*manner, sound of walking*) pas, *m.*; (*of stairs*) marche, *f.*
tread, *v.a.* marcher sur; (*grapes*) fouler; ~ *down, out,* (*lit. and fig.*) écraser.
tread, *v.n.* marcher; (*foot*) se poser; (+ *softly, &c.*) *use* aller* (être).
treadle, pédale, *f.*
treadmill, (*lit.*) moulin de discipline, *m.*
treason, trahison, *f.*; **~able,** de trahison.
treasure, (*lit. and fig.*) trésor, *m.*; *v.a.* (*value*) attacher du prix à; ~ *up,* thésauriser.
treasurer, trésori|er, ~ère, *m.f.*
treasury, (*building, depository, State*) trésor, *m.*; (*department*) Trésorerie, *f.*; **~-bond,** bon du trésor, *m.*
treat, *s.* (*pleasure, reward*) fête, *f.*; *be a* ~ *to,* être un régal de.
treat, *v.a.* (*behave to, use, a patient, apply process, entertain*) traiter.
treat, *v.n.* ~ *of,* traiter de; ~ *with,* traiter avec.
treatise, traité, *m.*
treatment, (*in senses of 'treat', v.a. above*) traitement, *m.*
treaty, (*comm., between nations*) traité, *m.*; *in* ~ *with,* en pourparlers avec.
treble, *s.* (*voice and singer*) soprano, *m.*; *adj.* de soprano.
trebl|e, *adj. and s.m.* triple; *v.a.* tripler; **~y,** triplement.
tree, arbre, *m.*; (*cross, theol.*) croix, *f.*
treeless, nu.
trefoil, trèfle, *m.*
trek, *v.n.* émigrer.
trellis, *and* **~-work,** treillis, *m.*; *v.a.* treillisser.
tremble, (*lit. and fig.*) trembler.
trembling, *s.* tremblement, *m.*; *adj.* tremblant; **~ly,** en tremblant.
tremendous, terrible; (*considerable*) immense; **~ly,** terriblement.
tremor, tremblement, *m.*
tremulous, tremblant; (*voice*) tremblotant; **~ness,** (*voice*) tremblotement, *m.*; **~ly,** en tremblant.
trench, *s.* (*ditch and mil.*) tranchée, *f.*; **~ mortar,** (*mil.*) mortier de tranchée, *m.*; *v.a.* (*turn over earth*) creuser; ~ *upon,* (*rights, &c.*) empiéter sur.
trenchant, (*remark, &c.*) tranchant.
trencher, (*platter*) tranchoir, *m.*
trencherman, mangeur, *m.*
trend, *s.* tendance, *f.*
trepidation, (*lit. and fig.*) trépidation, *f.*
trespass, *s.* (*theol.*) offense, *f.*; (*on land, &c.*) violation de propriété, *f.*
trespass, *v.n.* envahir sans autorisation; ~ *against,* offenser; ~ *on,* (*hospitality, &c.*) abuser de.
trespasser, (*sinner*) péch|eur, ~eresse, *m.f.*; (*on land, &c.*) violat|eur, ~rice du droit de propriété, *m.f.*
tress, (*hair*) tresse, *f.*
trestle, tréteau, *m.*
triad, triade, *f.*
trial, *s.* (*testing*) essai, *m.*; (*suffering, &c.*) épreuve, *f.*; (*law*) procès, *m.*; *on* ~, à l'essai; **~s,** (*ship*) essais, *m.pl.*
triang|le, triangle, *m.*; **~ular,** triangulaire.
trib|e, tribu, *f.*; **~al,** de tribu.
tribulation, tribulation, *f.*
tribunal, tribunal, *m.*

tribune, (*Rom. hist.*) tribun, *m.*; (*platform, &c.*) tribune, *f.*
tributary, *s.* (*river*) affluent, *m.*; *adj.* tributaire.
tribute, (*lit. and fig.*) tribut, *m.*
trice, *in a* ~, en un clin d'œil.
trick, *s.* ruse, *f.*; (*juggling, mischievous*) tour, *m.*; (*knack, device*) truc, *m.*; (*habit*) tic, *m.*; (*cards*) levée, *f.*; (*prank*) niche, *f.*; (*fraud*) supercherie, *f.*; *play a* ~ *on*, faire* une farce à.
trick, *v.a.* duper; ~ *out*, parer; ~ *out of*, (*defraud*) frustrer de.
trickery, duperie, *f.*
trickle, *s.* filet, *m.*; *v.n.* dégoutter.
trickster, tricheu|r, ~se, *m.f.*
tricky, (*crafty, cleverly contrived*) astucieu|x, ~se; (*adroit*) adroit.
tricolour, *s.* drapeau tricolore, *m.*; *adj. and* ~*ed*, tricolore.
tricycle, tricycle, *m.*
trident, trident, *m.*
triennial, triennal; ~**ly**, de trois ans en trois ans.
trier, personne (*f.*), etc., qui essaie.
trifle, bagatelle, *f.*; (*money*) petit quelque chose, *m.*; *a* ~, (*adv. somewhat*) un peu.
trifle, *v.n.* badiner; ~ *away*, gaspiller; ~ *with*, (*pers.*) traiter légèrement; (*toy with*) jouer avec.
trifler, personne légère, *f.*; *be a* ~, être frivole.
trifling, *s.* (*levity*) légèreté, *f.*; *adj.* frivole; (*unimportant*) insignifiant; ~**ly**, en badinant.
trigger, (*fire-arm*) détente, *f.*
triglyph, (*arch.*) triglyphe, *m.*
trigonometr|ic(al), trigonométrique; ~**y**, trigonométrie, *f.*
trilateral, trilatéral.
trill, *s.* (*mus.*) trille, *m.*; *v.a.n.* triller.
trilogy, trilogie, *f.*
trim, *s.* (*state*) état, *m.*; (*state of dress, health, &c.*) tenue, *f.*; *adj.* (*well kept*) bien tenu; (*natty*) pimpant; ~**ly**, bien; ~**ness**, netteté.
trim, (*put in order*) arranger; (*beard, hedge*) tailler; (*sails*) orienter; (*trees*) émonder; (*garment*) garnir (de); *v.n.* louvoyer (entre).
trimming, *s.* (*garment*) garniture, *f.*; (*beard, &c.*) taille, *f.*; (*sails*) orientation, *f.*; ~**s**, (*dress*) passementerie, *f.*
trinity, trinité, *f.*
trinket, breloque, *f.*
trip, *s.* (*stumble*) faux pas, *m.*; (*nimble step*) pas léger, *m.*; (*excursion*) excursion, *f.*; (*ship*) voyage, *m.*; (~ *up*) croc en jambe, *m.invar.*
trip, ~ *up*, *v.a.* faire* tomber; *v.n.* trébucher; (*step lightly*) aller* (être), venir* (être), etc., en dansant; (*err*) se tromper.
tripe, tripe, *f.*; (*nonsense, slang*) foutaise, *f.*; ~-**man**, tripier, *m.*
triple, *adj. and s.m.* triple; *v.a.* tripler.
triplet, (*set of 3*) trio, *m.*; (*mus.*) triolet, *m.*
tripod, trépied, *m.*
tripper, excursionniste, *m.*
tripping, lég|er, ~ère; ~**ly**, légèrement.
trireme, trirème, *f.*
trisyllab|ic, trisyllabique; ~**le**, trisyllabe, *m.*
trite, rebattu; ~**ly**, d'une manière banale.
triton, triton, *m.*
triturate, triturer.
triumph, *s.* triomphe, *m.*; *v.n.* triompher; ~ *over*, (*lit. and fig.*) triompher de; ~**al**, de triomphe; ~**ant**, triomphant; ~**antly**, triomphalement; (*exultingly*) d'un air triomphant.
trivet, trépied, *m.*
trivial, trivial; (*unimportant*) insignifiant; ~**ity**, trivialité, *f.*
trochee, (*pros.*) trochée, *m.*
troglodyte, troglodyte, *m.*
Trojan, *adj.* (*when an adj. use small letter*) *and s.m.f.* Troyen, -ne.
trolley, diable, *m.*; ~-**bus**, autobus à trolley, *m.*
trombone, trombone, *m.*
troop, *s.* troupe, *f.*; (*caval. approx.*) escadron, *m.*; ~**s**, (*mil.*) troupes, *f.pl.*; ~**er**, cavalier, *m.*; *swear like a* ~*er*, jurer comme un charretier; ⚠ troupier = *a private*, '*Tommy Atkins*'; ~-**ship**, transport, *m.*; *v.n.* (*flock together*) s'attrouper.
trophy, (*all senses*) trophée, *m.*
tropic|s, tropiques, *m.pl.*; ~**al**, tropique.
trot, *s.* trot, *m.*; *v.a.* faire* trotter; ~ *out*, (*fam.*) faire* parade de; *v.n.* (*horse, pers.*) trotter.
troth, *plight one's* ~, engager sa foi.
trouble, *s.* (*affliction*) affliction, *f.*; (*care*) souci, *m.*; (*inconvenience and med.*) dérangement, *m.*; (*misfortune*) malheur, *m.*; (*it's*) *no* ~, ce n'est rien; *get into* ~, se mettre* dans le pétrin; ⚠ trouble *is not at all so strong as English* '*trouble*'; *it* = '*confusion*', '*disturbance*', '*dispute*'.
trouble, *v.a.* (*perplex*) inquiéter; (*inconvenience*) déranger; (*afflict*) affliger (de); (*ask*) prier (de); (*preoccupy*) préoccuper; ⚠ troubler *is used of water, &c., otherwise it* = '*disturb*', '*perplex*'; ~ *pers. for*, prier de donner; ~ *to*, se donner la peine de; *be* ~*d with*, (*malady*) souffrir* de; *v.n.* se donner la peine; ~ *about*, s'inquiéter de.
troublesome, ennuyeu|x, ~se.
troublous, troublé.
trough, ((*kneading*) huche, *f.*; (*cattle*) auge, *f.*; (*of sea*) entre-deux, *m. invar.*
trounce, (*beat*) rosser.
trouser|s, (*pair of* ~*s*) pantalon, *m.* ⚠ *which is sing. of one pair*; ~-**press, stretcher**, tendeur, *m.*
trout, truite, *f.*
trowel, truelle, *f.*; (*garden*) déplantoir, *m.*
truant, *play* ~, faire* l'école buissonnière, *f.*
truce, trêve, *f.*
truck, *s.* (*rail.*) wagon, *m.*; (*luggage*) brouette à bagages, *f.*; (*exchange*) troc, *m.*

truckle-bed, lit à roulettes, *m.*
truckle to, *v.n.* ramper devant.
truculen|ce, férocité, *f.*; **~t,** féroce.
trudge, *s.* marche pénible, *f.*; *v.a.* faire* péniblement; *v.n.* marcher avec peine.
tru|e, *adj.* (*not false, real, sincere*) vrai; (*exact*) exact; (*faithful*) fidèle (à); (*honest*) honnête; (*plumb*) d'aplomb; *~e to,* conforme à; *come ~e,* se réaliser; **~eness,** vérité, *f.*; (*accuracy*) exactitude, *f.*; **~th,** *see below*; **~ly,** vraiment; *Yours ~ly,* Agréez, Monsieur, Madame, mes meilleures salutations.
truffle, truffe, *f.*
truism, truisme, *m.*
trump, (*cards*) *also* **trumps** *and* ~ **card,** atout, *m.*; *v.a.* couper avec l'atout.
trumpery, *adj.* sans valeur.
trumpet, trompette, *f.*; *v.a.* proclamer; (*celebrate*) célébrer; **~er,** (*lit. and ornith.*) trompette, *m.*
truncat|e, tronquer; **~ion,** mutilation, *f.*
truncheon, bâton, *m.*
trundle, *v.a.* (*truck, &c.*) pousser.
trunk, (*travelling*) malle, *f.*; (*tree, man, an., arch.*) tronc, *m.*; (*elephants*) trompe, *f.*; ~ **call,** (*teleph.*) appel interurbain, *m.*; **~-hose,** †haut-de-chausses, *m.*; ~ **operator,** opérat|eur, ~rice interurbain, -e, *m.f.*; **~-road,** grande route, *f.*
truss, *s.* (*hay, &c.*) botte, *f.*; (*med.*) bandage †herniaire, *m.*; (*naut.*) drosse, *f.*; (*arch., &c.*) ferme, *f.*
truss, *v.a.* (*tie*) lier; (*fowls, &c.*) trousser.
trust, *s.* (*firm belief, responsibility*) confiance, *f.*; (*hope, person, &c., trusted*) espoir, *m.*; (*thing, pers., in one's care*) dépôt, *m.*; (*comm. association of cos.*) trust, *m.*; *on ~,* (*comm.*) à crédit.
trust, *v.a.* (*gen. pers.*) se confier à; (*gen. things*) se fier à; (*entrust*) confier (à); (*leave alone*) laisser seul; (*comm.*) faire* crédit à.
trust, *v.n.* espérer; *~ in,* se confier en; *~ to,* compter sur.
trustee, dépositaire, *m.f.*; (*law*) curat|eur, ~rice, *m.f.*
trustful, trusting, confiant; **~ly,** avec confiance.
trustworthy, digne de confiance.
trusty, fidèle.
truth, vérité, *f.*; *in ~,* en vérité; *to tell the ~,* à vrai dire.
truthful, sincère; **~ness,** sincérité, *f.*; **~ly,** sincèrement.
try, *s.* essai, *m.*; *have a ~ to,* essayer de; (*football*) essai, *m.*
try, *v.a.* essayer; (*make trial of*) essayer de; (*test*) éprouver; (*law, pers.*) mettre* en jugement; (*purify*) affiner; *~ on,* (*clothes*) essayer; *~ out,* essayer à froid.
try, *v.n.* essayer; *~ for,* essayer d'obtenir.
trying, (*difficult*) difficile; (*tiring*) fatigant.
tryst, rendez-vous, *m.*
tub, *s.* cuve, *f.*; (*bath*) tub, *m.*; (*boating*) canot d'entraînement, *m.*
tube, *s.* (*cylinder, paint., &c., anat.*) tube, *m.*; ⚠ *not 'Tube'* (*Lond. rail.*) *which* = métro, *m.*
tubercul|ar, tuberculeu|x, ~se; **~osis,** tuberculose, *f.*
tuberose, (*bot.*) tubéreuse, *f.*
tuberous, tubéreu|x, ~se.
tubular, tubulaire.
tuck, *s.* (*fold*) pli, *m.*; (*colloq.*) mangeaille, *f.*; *~ in,* (*fam.*) gueuleton, *m.*; *v.n.* (*slang*) gueuletonner.
tuck, *v.a.* (*material*) plisser; (*turn in, draw together*) replier; (*cram*) fourrer; *~ in,* rentrer (avoir); *~ in, up,* (*bed*) border.
Tuesday, mardi, *m.*
tuft, *s.* touffe, *f.*; (*birds*) †huppe, *f.*; (*hair*) toupet, *m.*; **~ed,** (*birds*) †huppé.
tug, *s.* effort, *m.*; *often verb* tirer + *adv. is better used*; (*boat*) remorqueur, *m.*
tug, *v.a.* tirer; (*naut.*) remorquer; *v.n.* tirer; *~ at,* tirer sur.
tuition, enseignement, *m.*; (*fee*) prix de l'enseignement.
tulip, tulipe, *f.*; **~-tree,** tulipier, *m.*; **~-wood,** bois de rose, *m.*; ⚠ *'rosewood'* = palissandre, *m.*
tulle, tulle, *m.*
tumble, *s.* chute, *f.*
tumble, *v.a.* déranger; (*throw*) jeter pêle-mêle.
tumble, *v.n.* tomber (être); *~ about,* (*in bed*) s'agiter; *~ down,* tomber (être) par terre; (*houses, &c.*) s'effondrer.
tumbler, (*glass*) verre à boire, *m.*; (*ornith.*) pigeon culbutant, *m.*
tumbrel, tombereau, *m.*
tumid, (*body*) gonflé; (*style*) boursouflé.
tummy, *see* STOMACH.
tumour, tumeur, *f.*
tumult, tumulte, *m.*; **~uous,** tumultueu|x, ~se; **~uously,** tumultueusement.
tumulus, tumulus, *m.*
tun, tonneau, *m.*
tune, *s.* (*air*) air, *m.*; (*mus. and wireless*) accord, *m.*; (*fig.*) harmonie, *f.*; *in ~,* (*instr.*) d'accord; *out of ~,* fau|x, ~sse; *out of ~ with,* (*fig.*) ne pas être en harmonie avec; *sing in, out of ~,* chanter juste, faux.
tune, *v.a.* (*instr. and fig.*) accorder; *v.n. ~ in to,* (*wireless*) accorder (son poste) sur.
tuneful, mélodieu|x, ~se.
tuner, (*piano, &c.*) accordeur, *m.*
tunic, (*ant. and mil., &c.*) tunique, *f.*
tunnel, *s.* tunnel, *m.*; *v.a.n.* percer d'un tunnel (*under* = sous).
tunny, (*ichth.*) thon, *m.*
turban, turban, *m.*
turbid, trouble.
turbine, turbine, *f.*
turbot, (*ichth.*) turbot, *m.*
turbulen|ce, (*tumult*) trouble, *m.*; (*unruliness*) turbulence, *f.*; **~t,** (*agitated*) tumultueu|x, ~se; (*wild, unruly*) turbulent.

tureen, soupière, *f.*; ⚠ *not* terrine, *which* = '*earthenware basin*', '*pie-dish*'.
turf, *s.* gazon, *m.*; (*peat*) tourbe, *f.*; (*racing, race-course*) turf, *m.*; *v.a.* gazonner.
turgescence, (*style*) emphase, *f.*
turgid, (*style*) boursouflé.
Turk, Tur|c, ~que, *m.f.*; **~ish,** tur|c, ~que; (*lang.*) turc, *m.*; *~ish bath,* bain turc, *m.*
turkey, dindon, dinde, *m.f.*
turmoil, tumulte, *m.*
turn, *s.* (*rotation, walk, turn to act, service*) tour, *m.*; (*in road, &c.*) détour, *m.*; (*of mind, style*) tournure, *f.*; (*inclination*) goût, *m.*; (*tide*) changement, *m.*; (*shock*) coup, *m.*; *ill ~,* mauvais tour, *m.*; *by ~s,* à tour de rôle; *do a good ~ to,* rendre service à.
turn, *v.a.* (*mil., carp., eyes, head, &c.*) tourner; (*translate*) traduire*; (*direction*) détourner; (*garment*) retourner; (*steps, &c.*) diriger; (*in head*) rouler; (*scale*) faire* pencher; (*stomach*) soulever; (+ *adj.*) rendre; ~ *upside down,* mettre* sens dessus dessous; ~ *about,* tourner; ~ *aside,* détourner; ~ *away, off, out,* (*discharge*) congédier; ~ *down,* (*fold down*) plier; (*lamp, &c.*) baisser; (*proposal*) repousser; ~ *in,* (*end*) plier; ~ *into,* transformer en; ~ *off,* (*water, &c.*) couper; (*light*) éteindre*; ~ on (*tap*) ouvrir*; (*electr. light, gas, &c.*) *use* allumer *only*; ~ *out,* mettre* à la porte; (*inside out*) retourner; (*produce*) produire*; (*light*) *see* '~ *off*' *above*; ~ *over,* (*overturn*) renverser; (*book*) feuilleter; (*comm., profit*) faire*; ~ *up,* (*tuck up*) retrousser; (*ground, cards*) retourner.
turn, *v.n.* (*move round, milk, wind*) tourner; (*be directed*) se diriger; (*become*) devenir* (être); (*have recourse to*) avoir recours à; (*tide*) changer; (*stomach*) se soulever; ~ *about,* se tourner; ~ *aside, away,* se détourner; ~ *away from,* abandonner; ~ *back,* retourner (être); ~ *in,* (*go to bed*) se coucher; ~ *into,* se changer en; ~ *off,* (*pers., change direction*) se détourner; (*road*) bifurquer; ~ *on, upon,* (*depend on*) dépendre de; (*attack*) attaquer; ~ *out,* (*badly, well, &c.*) tourner; (*prove to be*) se montrer; (*become*) devenir* (être); ~ *over,* (*be upset*) se renverser; (*veh.*) verser; (*aeron.*) capoter; ~ *round,* se retourner; ~ *up,* (*be turned up*) se retrousser; (*occur*) se présenter; (*pers.*) arriver (être).
turncoat, *s.* renégat, *m.*; *be a ~,* tourner casaque.
turner, (*in wood*) tourneur, *m.*
turning, (*street*) tournant, *m.*; *next ~ to the left, right,* première (rue) à gauche, à droite, *f.*
turnip, navet, *m.*
turnkey, porte-clefs, *m. invar.*
turn-out, *s.* (*equipage*) équipage, *m.*; (*strike*) grève, *f.*
turnover, *s.* (*comm.*) chiffre d'affaires, *m.*
turnpike, (*roads*) barrière, *f.*
turnspit, tournebroche, *m.*
turnstile, tourniquet, *m.*
turnstone, (*ornith.*) tourne-pierre, *m.*
turpentine, térébenthine, *f.*; **~-tree,** térébinthe, *m.*
turpitude, turpitude, *f.*
turquoise, turquoise, *f.*; **~-blue,** bleu turquoise, *invar.*
turret, (*lit., mil. nav.*) tourelle, *f.*
turtle, (*reptile*) tortue, *f.*; **~-dove,** tourterelle, *f.*
Tuscan, *adj.* (*when an adj. use small letter*) *and s.m.f.* Toscan, -e; (*lang.*) toscan, *m.*
tush, *interj.* bah!
tusk, (*elephant, &c.*) défense, *f.*
tussle, lutte, *f.*; *v.n.* lutter.
tussock, touffe, *f.*
tut, *interj.* fi donc!
tutelage, tutelle, *f.*
tutor, précepteur, *m.*; ⚠ *not* tuteur *which* = '*trustee*', '*guardian*', '*protector*'; *v.a.* instruire*; **~ship,** préceptorat, *m.*
twaddle, *s.* babil, *m.*
twain, *s.* couple, *m.*; *adj.* deux.
twang, *s.* son aigu et métallique, *m.*; *have* (*speak with*) *a ~,* nasiller; *v.a.* (*instr.*) pincer de; (*pej.*) gratter de.
tweak, *v.a.* pincer.
tweezers, pince, *f.*
twelfth, douzième; (*kings, date, chapters, &c.*) douze; **~ly,** douzièmement; *Twelfth Night,* jour des rois, *m.*
twelve, *adj. and s.m.* douze.
twelvemonth, année, *f.*
twentieth, vingtième; (*kings, date, chapters, &c.*) vingt.
twenty, *adj. and s.m.* vingt.
twice, deux fois.
twiddle with, jouer avec.
twig, *s.* brindille, *f.*
twig, *v.a.* (*fam.*) piger.
twilight, crépuscule, *m.*; *adj.* crépusculaire; (*dark*) sombre.
twill, *s.* croisé, *m.*
twin, *adj. and s.m.f.* jumeau, jumelle; *~-engine(d) adj.* bimoteur.
twine, *s.* (*string*) ficelle, *f.*; *v.a.* (*wreath, &c.*) entrelacer; *v.n.* (*plants*) s'enrouler.
twinge, *s.* (*pain*) élancement, *m.*
twinkle, twinkling, *s.* scintillation, *f.*; *v.n.* scintiller; (*eyes*) pétiller.
twirl, *s.* (*moustache, &c.*) tortillement, *m.*; *v.a.* faire* tourner; (*moustache, &c.*) tortiller.
twist, *s.* (*thread*) cordon, *m.*; (*silk*) cordonnet, *m.*; (*action or state of twisting*) torsion, *f.*; (*tobacco*) carotte, *f.*; (*of the mind*) tournure, *f.*
twist, *v.a.* (*thread, rope, arm, &c., contort*) tordre; (*distort*) dénaturer.
twist, *v.n.* (*become entangled*) s'entortiller; (*path*) faire* des détours; ~ *about,* se tortiller.
twit, ~ *with,* reprocher (*dat. of pers., acc. of thing,* de + *inf.*).

twitch, *s.* (*face*) tic, *m.*; (*pain*) élancement, *m.*; *v.a.* tirer.
twitter, *s.* gazouillement, *m.*; *v.n.* gazouiller.
two, *adj. and s.m.* deux.
twofold, *adj.* double; *adv.* doublement.
type, (*symbol, specimen, class, model, biol.*) type, *m.*; (*print.*) caractère, *m.*; **~-writer,** (*pers.*) dactylographe, *m.f.*; (*mach.*) machine à écrire, *f.*; **~-writing,** dactylographie, *f.*; **~-written,** à la machine.
type, (*type-write*) taper à la machine.
typhoid, *and* **typhoid fever,** *s.* fièvre typhoïde, *f.*
typhoon, typhon, *m.*
typhus, typhus, *m.*
typical, typique.
typify, figurer.
typist, dactylographe, *m.f.*
typograph|er, typographe, *m.*; **~y,** typographie, *f.*
tyrannical, tyrannique; **~ly,** tyranniquement.
tyrannize, *v.n.* faire* le tyran; **~** *over,* tyranniser, *v.a.*
tyrann|ous, tyrannique; **~y,** tyrannie, *f.*
tyrant, (*lit. and fig.*) tyran, *m.*; (*ornith.*) tyran, *m.*
tyre, *see* TIRE.
tyro, *see* TIRO.
tz(s)ar, *see* CZAR.

U

ubiquit|ous, omniprésent; **~y,** ubiquité, *f.*
U-boat, sous-marin allemand, *m.*
udder, mamelle, *f.*
ugl|y, laid; (*fig.*) vilain; **~iness,** laideur, *f.*
ukase, ukase, *m.*
ulcer, ulcère, *m.*; **~ate,** *v.a.* ulcérer; *v.n.* s'ulcérer; **~ation,** ulcération, *f.*; **~ous,** ulcéreu|x, ~se.
ulterior, ultérieur.
ultimate, derni|er, ~ère; **~ly,** à la fin.
ultimatum, ultimatum, *m.*
ultimo, du mois dernier.
ultramarine, *s.* (*pigment*) outremer, *m.*
ultramontane, *adj.* ultramontain.
ultra-violet, (*rays*) ultra-violet, -te.
ululation, ululation, *f.*
umber, (*pigment*) terre d'ombre, *f.*
umbrage, (*offence*) ombrage, *m.*; **~ous,** (*shady*) ombragé.
umbrella, parapluie, *m.*; ⚠ *not* ombrelle *which* = *'parasol'.*
umpire, arbitre, *m.f.*
unabashed, sans se déconcerter.
unabated, non affaibli.
unable to, dans l'impossibilité de.
unabridged, non abrégé.
unaccented, non-accentué.
unacceptable, inacceptable.
unaccompanied, seul.
unaccomplished, inachevé.
unaccountab|le, inexplicable; **~ly,** d'une manière inexplicable.
unaccustomed, peu habitué (à).
unacknowledged, *be* **~,** (*letters, &c.*) être sans réponse.
unacquainted, *with, be,* (*pers.*) ne pas connaître*; (*things*) ignorer.
unadorned, sans ornements.
unadulterated, pur; (*comm.*) loyal.
unadvisable, peu prudent.
unadvisedly, inconsidérément.
unaffected *and* **~ly,** sans affectation.
unaided, sans aide.
unalarmed, tout, -e tranquille.
unalterable, inaltérable.
unambitious, sans ambition.
unamiable, peu aimable; **~ness,** manque d'amabilité, *m.*
unanimity, unanimité, *f.*
unanimous, unanime; **~ly,** à l'unanimité.
unanswerable, irréfutable.
unapparent, non apparent.
unappeased, inapaisé.
unappetizing, peu appétissant.
unappreciated, méconnu.
unapproachable, inaccessible.
unappropriated, sans destination.
unarmed, sans armes.
unassailable, inattaquable.
unassisted, sans aide.
unassuming, sans prétention.
unattached, non attaché (à); (*mil.*) en disponibilité.
unattainable, inaccessible.
unattempted, non essayé.
unattended, non accompagné; (*royalty*) sans suite.
unauthentic, inauthentique; **~ated,** non constaté.
unauthorized, non autorisé.
unavailing, infructueu|x, ~se.
unavoidabl|e, inévitable; **~y,** inévitablement.
unaware, *be* **~** *of,* ignorer.
unawares, (*unexpectedly*) à l'improviste; (*by mistake*) par mégarde.
unbalanced, (*lit. and fig.*) mal équilibré.
unbearabl|e, insupportable; **~y,** insupportablement.
unbeaten, non battu *or other part of* battre (*negative*).
unbecoming, inconvenant; (*clothes*) qui ne sied* pas (à).
unbefitting, qui ne convient* pas (à).
unbegun, non commencé.
unbelief, incrédulité, *f.*
unbelievable, incroyable.
unbeliever, incrédule, *m.f.*
unbend, *v.a.* (*mind*) détendre; *v.n.* (*pers.*) devenir* (être) affable.
unbending, inflexible.
unbespoken, non commandé.
unbiased, impartial.
unbidden, (*guest, &c.*) sans invitation; (*without orders*) sans ordre.

unbind, délier.
unblameable, irréprochable.
unbleached, écru.
unblemished, sans tache.
unblest, non béni.
unblushing, éhonté; **~ly,** sans †honte.
unbolt, tirer le verrou de.
unborn, à naître.
unbosom, confier; ~ *oneself,* ouvrir* son cœur (à).
unbound, délié; (*books*) non relié.
unbounded, ~ly, sans bornes.
unbridle, débrider; **~d,** (*horse*) débridé; (*fig.*) effréné.
unbroken, intact; (*horses, &c.*) indompté; (*uninterrupted*) ininterrompu.
unbrotherly, peu fraternel, -le.
unbuckle, déboucler.
unburden, (*fig.*) soulager; ~ *oneself to,* s'ouvrir* à.
unbusinesslike, (*pers.*) peu habitué aux affaires.
unbutton, déboutonner.
uncalled *for,* déplacé.
uncanny, sinistre.
uncared *for,* négligé.
unceasing, incessant; **~ly,** sans cesse.
uncensured, *be* ~, ne pas être censuré.
unceremonious, *and* **~ly,** sans façon.
uncertain, (*undecided, variable, not fixed, vague*) incertain; **~ty,** incertitude, *f.*
unchangeabl|e, immuable; **~y,** immuablement.
unchanging, invariable.
uncharitabl|e, peu charitable; **~y,** sans charité.
unchast|e, impudique; **~ity,** incontinence, *f.*
unchecked, non réprimé; (*accuracy of*) non vérifié.
uncircumcised, incirconcis.
uncivil, impoli.
uncivilized, incivilisé.
unclaimed, non réclamé.
unclasp, dégrafer.
uncle, oncle, *m.*; (*slang, 'pawnshop'*) ma tante; *great-~,* grand-oncle, *m.*
unclean, malpropre; (*fig.*) impur; **~ness,** malpropreté, impureté, *f.*
uncloak, (*fig.*) démasquer.
unclose, ouvrir*.
unclothe, déshabiller.
unclouded, sans nuages.
uncoil, dérouler.
uncoloured, incolore.
uncome-at-able, inaccessible.
uncomely, disgracieu|x, ~se.
uncomfortabl|e, (*pers.*) mal à l'aise; (*things*) peu confortable; **~y,** incommodément; (*disagreeably*) désagréablement.
uncommon, rare; (*unusual*) extraordinaire; **~ly,** extraordinairement.
uncommunicative, peu communicati|f, ~ve.
uncomplaining, *use verb* se plaindre*.
uncomplimentary, peu flatteu|r, ~se.
uncompromising, intransigeant.
unconcern, indifférence, *f.*; **~ed,** indifférent; **~edly,** avec indifférence.
unconditional, ~ly, *adj. and adv.* sans conditions.
unconfined, (*unbounded*) illimité.
unconfirmed, non confirmé.
uncongenial, peu sympathique.
unconnected, sans rapport avec.
unconquerable, invincible.
unconscionable, déraisonnable.
unconscious, (*faint*) sans connaissance; ~ *of,* sans conscience de; **~ness,** (*faint*) évanouissement, *m.*; **~ly,** sans le savoir.
unconstitutional, inconstitutionnel, -le.
unconstrained, ~ly, *adj. and adv.* sans contrainte.
uncontested, incontesté.
uncontrollabl|e, indomptable; (*irresistible*) irrésistible; **~y,** irrésistiblement.
unconventional, qui tient peu de compte des convenances.
unconvert|ed, non converti; **~ible,** non convertible.
unconvinc|ed, non convaincu; **~ing,** peu convaincant.
uncooked, non cuit.
uncork, déboucher.
uncorrected, non corrigé.
uncouth, grossi|er, ~ère; **~ness,** grossièreté, *f.*
uncover, *v.a.* découvrir*; *v.n.* (*head*) se découvrir*.
uncritical, peu critique.
uncrossed, (*cheque*) non barré.
unction, (*lit. and fig.*) onction, *f.*
unctuous, onctueu|x, ~se; **~ness,** onctuosité, *f.*
uncultivated, (*land and pers.*) inculte.
uncurl, (*hair*) déboucler.
uncurtailed, non raccourci.
uncut, *p.p.* (*edges of book, &c.*) non rogné.
undamaged, non endommagé; (*naut.*) non avarié.
undated, sans date.
undaunted, intrépide; **~ly,** intrépidement.
undeceive, détromper.
undecided, (*uncertain, wavering, doubtful*) indécis.
undecipherable, indéchiffrable.
undefended, sans défense.
undefiled, sans tache.
undefined, non défini.
undemonstrative, réservé.
undeniable, incontestable.
under, *adj.* de dessous; (*in composition*) sous-, *e.g.* sous-secrétaire; *adv.* au-dessous.
under, *prep.* (*contact or near proximity, monarch, pretence, penalty, name, fire, &c.*) sous; (*lower down, with numbers*) au-dessous de; (*circumstances, necessity*) dans.
underbred, mal élevé.
undercarriage, (*aeron.*) train d'atterrissage, *m.*
underclothes, vêtements de dessous, *m.pl.*

undercurrent, (*fig.*) courant de fond, *m.*
underdone, (*meat, &c.*) pas assez cuit.
underestimate, *s.* sous-estimation, *f.*; *v.a.* sous-estimer.
underfed, insuffisamment nourri.
undergarment, vêtement de dessous, *m.*
undergo, subir.
undergraduate, étudiant, -e, *m.f.*
underground, *s.* (*rail.*) métropolitain, *m., abbrev.* métro; *adj.* souterrain; *adv.* sous terre.
undergrowth, broussailles, *f.pl.*
underhand, *adj.* clandestin; (*sly*) sournois; *adv.* sous main.
underlet, sous-louer.
underline, souligner.
underlinen, linge de corps, *m.*
underling, subalterne, *m.f.*
underlying, (*fig.*) latent.
undermine, (*lit. and fig.*) miner.
undermost, le plus en dessous.
underneath, en dessous.
underpay, payer insuffisamment.
under|pin, ~prop, étayer.
underrate, sous-estimer.
undersell, *v.a.* vendre à plus bas prix que.
underside, dessous, *m.*
undersigned, soussigné.
undersized, au-dessous de la taille moyenne.
understand, *v.a.* (*words, person, language, grasp*) comprendre*; (*be proficient in*) s'entendre à; (*supply word mentally*) sous-entendre; *it is understood that,* il est convenu que; *v.n.* comprendre*.
understanding, intelligence, *f.*; (*agreement, union of sentiments*) entente, *f.*; (*thing agreed upon*) chose convenue, *f.*; *adj.* intelligent.
understate, *v.a.* (*approx.*) expliquer en atténuant; **~ment,** exposition atténuante, *f.*
understudy, (*theatr.*) doublure, *f.*
undertake, entreprendre*; **~** *to,* s'engager à.
undertaker, (*funeral*) entrepreneur de pompes funèbres, *m.*
undertaking, (*enterprise*) entreprise, *f.*; (*pledge, promise*) engagement, *m.*
undertone, *s.* (*voice*) ton peu élevé, *m.*
undervalue, sous-évaluer; (*fig.*) déprécier.
underwear, vêtements de dessous, *m.pl.*
underwrit|er, (*insurance*) assureur, *m.*; **~ing,** assurance, *f.*
undeserved, immérité; **~ly,** injustement.
undeserving, sans mérite.
undesigned, involontaire; **~ly,** involontairement.
undesirable, peu désirable; ⚠ indésirable *adj. and s.m.f. is usually of persons.*
undeterred, non détourné.
undeviating, droit; (*fig.*) constant.
undigested, (*fig.*) indigeste.
undignified, peu digne.
undiluted, non délayé.
undiplomatic, peu diplomatique.
undischarged, (*prisoner*) non libéré; (*debt*) inacquitté; (*bankrupt*) non réhabilité.
undisciplined, indiscipliné.
undisguised, (*open*) franc, franche.
undismayed, sans peur.
undisputed, incontesté.
undissolved, non dissous.
undistinguished, sans distinction.
undisturbed, tranquille.
undiversified, uniforme.
undivided, indivisé; (*complete*) compl|et, ~ète.
undo, défaire*.
undone, (*not finished*) inachevé; (*pers.*) perdu.
undoubted, indubitable; **~ly,** indubitablement.
undream|ed, ~t *of,* dont on n'a pas rêvé.
undress, *s.* déshabillé, *m.*; (*mil.*) petite tenue, *f.*; *v.n.* se déshabiller.
undrinkable, imbuvable.
undu|e, (*improper*) indu; **~ly,** indûment.
undula|te, *v.n.* onduler; **~tion,** ondulation, *f.*; **~ting,** onduleu|x, ~se; (*country*) accidenté.
undutiful, irrespectueu|x, ~se.
undying, impérissable.
unearned, (*not earned*) que l'on n'a pas gagné; (*undeserved*) immérité.
unearth, déterrer.
unearthly, non terrestre.
uneas|iness, (*mind*) inquiétude, *f.*; (*uncomfortableness*) gêne, *f.*; **~y,** (*mind*) inqui|et, ~ète; (*uncomfortable*) (*pers.*) mal à l'aise; (*things*) incommode; (*sleep, &c.*) agité; **~ily,** difficilement.
uneatable, immangeable.
unedifying, peu édifiant.
uneducated, sans instruction.
unemploy|ed, *s. the* **~ed,** chômeurs, *m.pl.*; *adj.* (*pers.*) sans travail; (*things*) inemployé; ⚠ inemployé *is very rarely used of persons*; **~ment,** chômage, *m.*; manque de travail, *m.*
unending, interminable.
unendurable, intolérable.
unengaged, (*seats*) non retenu.
un-English, peu anglais.
unenterprising, peu entreprenant.
unenviable, peu digne d'envie.
unequal, (*lit. and fig.*) inégal; *be* **~** *to,* (*pers.*) ne pas être à la hauteur de; **~ly,** inégalement.
unequalled, sans égal.
unequivocal, non équivoque.
unerring, infaillible.
unessential, *adj.* non essentiel, -le.
uneven, inégal; (*number*) impair; **~ness,** inégalité, *f.*; **~ly,** inégalement.
uneventful, (*quiet*) tranquille; (*without sensational events*) sans événements.
unexampled, sans exemple.
unexceptionable, irréprochable.
unexpected, inattendu; (*sudden*) soudain; **~ly,** à l'improviste.
unexplored, inexploré.
unexpressed, non exprimé.

unfading, qui ne se fane pas.
unfailing, (*sure*) infaillible; (*inexhaustible*) inépuisable.
unfair, (*unjust*) injuste; (*competition, proceedings, &c.*) déloyal; **~ness**, injustice, déloyauté, *f.*; **~ly**, injustement, déloyalement.
unfaithful, infidèle; **~ness**, infidélité, *f.*; **~ly**, infidèlement.
unfamiliar, (*not known*) peu connu.
unfashionable, démodé.
unfasten, détacher.
unfatherly, peu paternel, -le.
unfathomable, insondable.
unfavourabl|e, défavorable; **~y**, défavorablement.
unfeasible, infaisable.
unfeeling, insensible.
unfeigned, sincère; **~ly**, sincèrement.
unfilial, peu digne d'un fils.
unfinished, inachevé.
unfit, peu propre (à); (*incapable*) incapable (de); *be* ~, (*health*) ne pas être dans son assiette; **~ness**, inaptitude, *f.* (à).
unfitting, peu convenable.
unfix, détacher.
unflagging, infatigable.
unflinching, résolu.
unfold, déplier; (*explain*) exposer; (*declare*) déclarer.
unforced, facile.
unfordable, inguéable.
unforeseen, imprévu.
unforgettable, inoubliable.
unforgivable, impardonnable.
unfortified, (*town, &c.*) ouvert.
unfortunate, malheureu|x, ~se; **~ly**, malheureusement.
unfounded, (*report, &c.*) sans fondement.
unfrequented, peu fréquenté.
unfriendly, (*pers.*) peu amical; (*things*) hostile.
unfruitful, (*land, &c.*) stérile; **~ness**, stérilité, *f.*
unfulfilled, (*prophecy, &c.*) non accompli.
unfurl, *v.a.* déployer; (*naut.*) déferler.
unfurnished, (*house, &c.*) non meublé.
ungainly, gauche.
ungentleman|ly, **~like**, peu comme il faut.
ungodly, impie.
ungraceful, disgracieu|x, ~se; **~ly**, disgracieusement.
ungrammatical, incorrect.
ungrateful, ingrat; **~ly**, avec ingratitude.
ungrounded, sans fondement.
ungrudgingly, de bon cœur.
unguarded, sans défense; *be* ~, (*in words, &c., unwary*) ne pas être sur ses gardes.
unguent, onguent, *m.*
unguided, sans guide.
unhallowed, profane.
unhand, lâcher.
unhapp|iness, malheur, *m.*; **~y**, malheureux; **~ily**, malheureusement.
unharmed, sain, -e et sau|f, ~ve.
unharness, déharnacher.
unhealth|iness, (*pers.*) mauvaise santé, *f.*; (*places*) insalubrité, *f.*; **~y**, (*pers.*) maladi|f, ~ve; (*places*) insalubre.
unheard of, inouï.
unheeded, (*neglected*) négligé.
unhesitatingly, sans hésiter.
unholy, impie.
unhonoured, sans honneur.
unhook, décrocher.
unhoped for, inespéré.
unhorse, démonter.
unhurt, sain, -e et sau|f, ~ve.
unicorn, licorne, *f.*
uniform, *s.* uniforme, *m.*; *adj.* uniforme; **~ity**, uniformité, *f.*; **~ly**, uniformément.
unif|y, unifier; **~ication**, unification, *f.*
unimaginable, inimaginable.
unimpaired, (*whole*) intact; (*health*) non affaibli.
unimpeded, sans obstacle.
unimportant, peu important.
unimpressive, peu impressionnant.
uninformed, (*not knowing*) ignorant; (*ignorant*) sans instruction.
uninhabitable, inhabitable; ⚠ *English 'inhabitable'* = habitable *in French.*
uninhabited, inhabité.
uninitiated, non initié.
uninjured, (*pers.*) sain, -e et sau|f, ~ve; (*things*) intact.
uninspired, sans inspiration.
uninstruct|ed, sans instruction; **~ive**, peu instructi|f, ~ve.
uninsured, non assuré.
unintelligent, inintelligent.
unintelligible, inintelligible.
unintentional, involontaire; **~ly**, involontairement.
uninteresting, peu intéressant.
uninterruptedly, sans interruption.
uninvited, sans invitation.
uninviting, peu engageant.
union, (*of states, junction, harmony, marriage, postal*) union, *f.*; **Union Jack**, pavillon britannique, *m.*
unionis|m, unionisme, *m.*; **~t**, unioniste, *m.*
unique, unique; **~ly**, (*solely*) uniquement.
unison, unisson, *m.*; *in* ~, à l'unisson.
unit, (*lit., fig., mil.*) unité, *f.*
unite, *v.a.* unir; *v.n.* s'unir; ~ *in*, coopérer à.
united, uni; **~ly**, avec union.
unity, (*lit. and Lit.*) unité, *f.*; (*concord*) harmonie, *f.*
universal, (*lit. and log.*) universel, -le; **~ity**, universalité, *f.*; **~ly**, universellement.
universe, univers, *m.*
university, université, *f.*
unjust, injuste; **~ly**, injustement.
unjustifiabl|e, injustifiable; **~y**, d'une manière injustifiable.
unkempt, (*neglected, beard, &c.*) inculte.

unkept, (*house, &c.*) non entretenu.
unkind|ly, peu aimable; **~ness,** manque d'amabilité, *m.*; **~ly,** *adv.* peu aimablement.
unknot, dénouer.
unknowingly, sans le savoir.
unknown, *adj. and s.m.f.* inconnu, -e; *the* ~, l'inconnu, *m.*
unlaboured, (*style*) facile.
unlace, délacer.
unlade, décharger.
unladylike, indigne d'une dame.
unlatch, lever le loquet de.
unlawful, (*contrary to explicit law*) illégal; (*contrary to morals or law generally*) illicite; **~ness,** illégalité, *f.*; **~ly,** illégalement.
unlearned, (*pers.*) sans instruction.
unleavened, ~ *bread,* azyme, *m.*
unless, à moins que+*subj.*+ne; à moins de+*inf.*
unlicensed, (*comm.*) marron, -ne.
unlike, dissemblable.
unlikelihood, improbabilité, *f.*
unlikely, improbable.
unlimited, illimité.
unload, (*gun, electr. battery, ship, wagon, &c.*) décharger.
unlock, *v.a.* ouvrir*.
unlooked *for,* inattendu.
unloose, délier.
unlovely, peu aimable.
unluck|y, malheureu|x, ~se; **~ily,** malheureusement.
unman, affaiblir.
unmanageable, (*child, &c.*) indocile.
unmanly, (*effeminate*) efféminé.
unmannerly, grossi|er, ~ère.
unmask, *v.a.* démasquer.
unmeaning, sans signification.
unmerciful, impitoyable.
unmerited, immérité.
unmindful, insouciant (de).
unmistakabl|e, à ne pas s'y méprendre*; **~y,** incontestablement.
unmitigated, pur.
unmixed, pur.
unmoved, (*not affected*) impassible.
unnatural, (*pers., actions*) dénaturé; (*things*) contre nature.
unnecessar|y, inutile; **~ily,** inutilement.
unnerve, énerver.
unnoticed, (*unseen*) inaperçu.
unnumbered, (*numberless*) innombrable.
unobjectionable, irréprochable.
unobserved, inaperçu.
unobtainable, qu'on ne peut obtenir.
unobtrusive, non importun.
unoccupied, (*idle*) inoccupé; (*free*) libre; (*house, &c.*) non occupé.
unofficial, non officiel, -le; (*report*) non confirmé·
unopposed, sans opposition.
unpack, déballer.
unpaid, impayé.
unpalatable, désagréable au goût.
unparalleled, incomparable.
unpardonabl|e, impardonnable; **~y,** d'une manière impardonnable.
unpatriotic, peu patriotique.
unpitying, impitoyable.
unpleasant, désagréable; **~ness,** désagrément, *m.*; **~ly,** désagréablement.
unpolished, non poli; (*pers.*) grossi|er, ~ère.
unpopular, impopulaire; **~ity,** impopularité, *f.*
unpractical, (*pers., things*) peu pratique.
unprecedented, sans exemple.
unprejudiced, (*without prepossession*) sans préjugés; (*impartial*) impartial.
unpremeditated, sans préméditation; (*not prepared*) improvisé.
unprepossessing, peu attrayant.
unpretentious, peu prétentieu|x, ~se.
unprincipled, sans principes.
unproductive, improducti|f, ~ve.
unprofitabl|e, peu profitable; **~y,** peu profitablement.
unpromising, qui s'annonce mal.
unpronounceable, imprononçable.
unpropitious, peu propice.
unpublished, (*book*) inédit.
unpunctual, inexact.
unpunished, impuni.
unqualified, non qualifié; (*without restriction*) sans restriction.
unquenchable, inextinguible.
unquestionably, incontestablement.
unravel, (*lit. and fig.*) démêler.
unreadily, à contre-cœur.
unreal, irréel, -le; **~izable,** (*securities*) irréalisable.
unreasonabl|e, déraisonnable; **~y,** déraisonnablement.
unreceipted, non acquitté.
unrecognizable, méconnaissable.
unrecorded, non registré.
unregistered, (*letter, &c.*) non recommandé; (*luggage*) non enregistré.
unreliable, (*pers.*) sur qui on ne peut compter; (*report, &c.*) douteu|x, ~se.
unremitting, incessant.
unremunerative, improfitable.
unrepentant, impénitent.
unrequited, non récompensé.
unreserved, sans réserve; (*seat*) non retenu; **~ly,** sans réserve.
unrest, agitation, *f.*
unrestrained, (*free*) libre; (*licentious*) effréné.
unrestricted, sans restriction.
unrewarded, sans récompense.
unrighteous, injuste.
unripe, vert.
unrivalled, sans rival.
unroll, dérouler.
unroot, déraciner.
unruly, indocile.
unsafe, dangereu|x, ~se.
unsaleable, invendable.
unsatisfactory, peu satisfaisant.
unsatisfied, (*dissatisfied*) mécontent; (*appetite, &c.*) non rassasié.

unsavoury, sans saveur; (*disgusting*) répugnant.
unscathed, intact.
unscholarly, peu savant.
unscientific, peu scientifique.
unscrew, dévisser.
unscrupulous, sans scrupule; **~ly,** sans scrupule.
unseal, (*letter, &c.*) décacheter.
unseasonable, unseasonably, †hors de saison.
unseaworthy, †hors d'état de naviguer.
unsecured, (*comm.*) à découvert.
unseemly, inconvenant.
unseen, *s. the ~,* l'au delà, *m.*; *adj.* invisible; (*unobserved*) inaperçu.
unselfish, désintéressé.
unserviceable, inutilisable.
unset, *adj.* (*gems*) non serti.
unsettled, (*not paid, not determined*) non réglé; (*in mind*) indécis; (*undecided, weather*) incertain; (*without settled abode*) sans domicile.
unshaken, non ébranlé.
unshapely, difforme.
unsheathe, dégaîner.
unsheltered, exposé.
unship, (*goods*) débarquer.
unshod, déchaussé.
unshrinkable, irrétrécissable.
unsightly, laid.
unskilled, unskilful, inhabile; **~** *labour, see* LABOUR.
unsociable, insociable.
unsoiled, propre.
unsold, invendu.
unsolved, (*problems, &c.*) non résolu.
unsophisticated, non frelaté.
unsound, (*mind*) dérangé; (*doctrine, argument*) erroné; (*fruit, &c.*) gâté; (*not healthy*) peu sain.
unsparing, (*lavish*) prodigue.
unspeakabl|e, inexprimable; **~y,** indiciblement.
unspoken, non prononcé.
unsporting, unsportsmanlike, indigne d'un sportsman.
unstead|y, (*hand*) tremblant; (*table, &c.*) peu fixe; (*walk, prices*) chancelant; (*changeable*) inconstant; **~ily,** (*walk*) en chancelant.
unstinted, sans bornes.
unstudied, naturel, -le.
unsubstantial, (*air, visions, forms*) immatériel, -le; (*building, &c.*) peu solide.
unsuccessful, malheureu|x, ~se; (*fruitless*) infructueu|x, ~se; *be ~,* ne pas réussir; **~ly,** sans succès.
unsuitabl|e, (*improper*) inconvenant; *~e for,* peu propre à; **~y,** peu proprement.
unsupported, sans soutien; (*motion*) non appuyé.
unsuspicious, *and* **~ly,** sans soupçons.
untenable, insoutenable.
untenanted, inhabité.
unthankful, ingrat.
unthinkable, inimaginable.
unthrifty, dépensi|er, ~ère.
untidy, (*pers.*) malpropre; (*things*) en désordre.
untie, dénouer.
until, *prep.* jusqu'à.
until, *conj.* jusqu'à ce que + *subj.*; (*before*) avant que + *subj.*
untilled, inculte.
untimely, (*inopportune*) intempesti|f, ~ve.
untiring, infatigable.
unto, (*as far as*) jusqu'à.
untold, (*incalculable*) incalculable.
untoward, (*unlucky*) malencontreu|x, ~se.
untransferable, inaliénable.
untranslatable, intraduisible.
untried, non essayé.
untrimmed, (*clothes*) sans garniture; (*trees, &c.*) non taillé; (*sails*) non orienté.
untrue, faux, fausse; *~ to,* infidèle à.
untrustworthy, indigne de confiance.
untruth, mensonge, *m.*; **~ful,** (*pers.*) peu véridique; (*things*) inexact.
unused, non utilisé.
unusual, rare; (*unwonted*) insolite.
unutterabl|e, indicible; **~y,** indiciblement.
unvalued, non évalué; (*not prized*) peu estimé.
unvarying, invariable.
unveil, dévoiler.
unversed in, peu versé dans.
unwarned, non averti.
unwarranted, injustifié; (*comm.*) sans garantie.
unwar|y, imprudent; **~ily,** imprudemment.
unweariedly, sans relâche.
unwelcome, (*pers.*) mal venu; (*things*) fâcheu|x, ~se.
unwell, indisposé.
unwholesome, (*lit. and fig.*) malsain.
unwieldy, pesant.
unwilling (*to*), peu disposé (à); **~ly,** à contre-cœur.
unwind, dérouler.
unwise, imprudent.
unwittingly, à mon, ton, etc., insu.
unwomanly, indigne d'une femme.
unwonted, inaccoutumé.
unworth|y, indigne (de); **~iness,** indignité, *f.*; **~ily,** indignement.
unwrap, développer.
unyielding, inflexible.
up, *adj.* (*train*) montant.
up, *adv.* (*of locality*) *often omitted, e.g. ~ in, to Yorkshire,* au comté de York; (*tide*) †haut; (*not in bed*) levé; *be ~ to,* (*understand*) être au fait de; (*in a state to*) être en état de; (*tricks, &c.*) *use* faire*; (*be the duty of*) être à + *pers.*, de + *inf.*, *e.g.* c'est à vous de le faire; *What's ~?* Qu'est-ce qu'il y a?; *~ and down,* de long en large; *interj.* (*stand*) *up!* debout!
up, *prep.* (*towards the top*) vers le †haut de; (*in, on the top*) en †haut de; *half-way ~ the hill,* à mi-côte; *see also verbs compounded with 'up'.*

upbraid, réprimander; **~ingly,** avec reproche.
upbringing, éducation, *f.*
upheav|al, soulèvement, *m.*; **~e,** soulever.
uphill, *adj.* montant; (*fig.*) pénible.
uphold, soutenir*; (*policy, resolution, &c.*) appuyer.
upholsterer, tapissi|er, ~ère, *m.f.*
upkeep, (*maintenance, house, &c., roads*) entretien, *m.*
upland(s), †hautes terres, *f.pl.*
uplift, *v.a.* lever.
upon, sur; (+ *gerund*) en.
upper, (*lit. and fig.*) supérieur; (*deck*) deuxième; ~ *classes, see* CLASS.
uppermost, le plus †haut.
upright, *s.* (*carp. ladder*) montant, *m.*
upright, *adj.* (*straight*) droit; (*honest*) honnête; **~ness,** (*honesty*) droiture, *f.*; **~ly,** avec droiture.
uprising, *s.* (*revolt*) soulèvement, *m.*
uproar, vacarme, *m.*; **~ious,** tumultueu|x, ~se.
uproot, déraciner.
upset, *s.* (*overturning*) renversement, *m.*; (*fig.*) bouleversement, *m.*
upset, *v.a.* renverser; (*fig.*) bouleverser; (*veh.*) verser; *v.n.* se renverser; (*veh.*) verser; (*boat*) chavirer.
upshot, (*outcome*) résultat, *m.*
upside, ~ *down,* sens dessus dessous.
upstairs, en †haut.
upstart, *s.* parvenu, *m.*
upturn, *v.a.* (*turn over*) retourner; (*eyes, &c.*) lever.
upward, *adj.* dirigé en †haut; (*movement, force, comm.*) ascensionnel, -le; *adv.* **~(s),** en† haut; ~(*s*) *of,* plus de; (*age, &c.*) au-dessus de.
urban, urbain.
urchin, gamin, *m.*
urge, *v.a.* (*beg*) prier instamment (de); (*course of action*) recommander instamment; (*insist upon*) faire* valoir; (*stimulate*) pousser en avant; (*allege*) alléguer.
urgen|cy, urgence, *f.*; **~t,** urgent; (*pressing in demand*) pressant; **~tly,** (*earnestly*) instamment.
urin|al, *s.* (*lavatory*) urinoir, *m.*; **~e,** urine, *f.*
urn, (*vase and ant.*) urne, *f.*
us, (*acc. with verb, complement of* être, *with preps.*) nous.
usage, (*custom*) usage, *m.*; (*treatment*) traitements, *m.pl.*
use, *s.* (*availability*) usage, *m.*; (*application to a purpose*) emploi, *m.*; (*utility*) utilité, *f.*; (*enjoyment*) jouissance, *f.*; (*wont*) habitude, *f.*; *out of* ~, †hors d'usage; *be of* ~, être utile (à); *what is the* ~ *of?* à quoi bon? + *inf.*
use, *v.a.* (*employ*) se servir* de; (*treat with, adv.*) (traiter; (*make use of*) faire* usage de; (*use up, material, coal, electr., &c.*) consommer; ~ *up, wear out*) user; ~*d to,* habitué à.
use, (*habit*) *v.n.* avoir l'habitude de. *The impf. is generally sufficient in this sense.*
useful, utile (à); **~ness,** utilité, *f.*; **~ly,** utilement.
useless, inutile; **~ness,** inutilité, *f.*; **~ly,** inutilement.
usher, *s.* huissier, *m.*; (*school*) pion, *m.*
usher in, (*announce*) annoncer; (*into room, &c.*) faire* entrer dans.
usual, usuel, -le; **~ly,** ordinairement.
usur|er, usuri|er, ~ère, *m.f.*; **~ious,** (*things*) usuraire.
usurp, usurper; **~ation,** usurpation, *f.*; **~er,** usurpat|eur, ~rice, *m.f.*
usury, usure, *f.*
utensil, ustensile, *m.*
utilitarian, *adj. and s.m.f.* utilitaire.
utility, (*gen. and theatr.*) utilité, *f.*
utiliz|e, utiliser; **~ation,** utilisation, *f.*
utmost, *s.* (*the most*) le plus; (*all one can*) tout son possible; *at the* ~, tout au plus.
utmost, *adj.* (*greatest*) le plus grand; (*farthest*) le plus éloigné.
utopia, utopie, *f.*; **~n,** *adj.* utopique.
utter, *adj.* le plus grand; (*absolute*) absolu; **~ly,** tout à fait.
utter, *v.a.* (*cry*) pousser; (*word*) prononcer; (*false money*) passer.
utterance, (*expression*) expression, *f.*; (*pronunciation*) prononciation, *f.*; (*power of speech*) parole, *f.*; **~s,** (*spoken words*) paroles, *f.pl.*
uttermost, *see* UTMOST.
uvula, (*med.*) luette, *f.*
uxorious, très épris de sa femme.

V

vacancy, (*of posts*) vacance, *f.*; (*empty space*) vide, *m.*; (*mind*) défaut d'idées, *m.*
vacant, (*post, &c.*) vacant; (*room, &c., space, mind*) vide; (*face*) sans expression; (*time*) de loisir; **~ly,** d'un air distrait.
vacate, (*place, office*) laisser vacant.
vacation, (*law, univ.*) vacances, *f.pl.*
vaccin|ate, vacciner; **~ation,** vaccination, *f.*; **~e,** *s.* vaccin, *m.*
vacilla|te, vaciller; **~tion,** vacillation, *f.*; **~ting,** *adj.* vacillant.
vacu|ity, (*lit., vacancy, mind*) vide, *m.*; **~ous,** vide.
vacuum, *s.* vide, *m.*; **~-cleaner,** aspirateur, *m.*
vagabond, *adj. and s.m.f.* vagabond, -e.
vagary, caprice, *m.*
vagran|cy, vagabondage, *m.*; **~t,** vagabond.
vague, vague; **~ness,** vague, *m.*; **~ly,** vaguement.
vain, (*things*) vain; (*pers.*) vaniteu|x, ~se; *in* ~, en vain; (*do, &c.*) *in vain,* avoir beau (faire*, etc.); **~ness,** (*uselessness*) inutilité, *f.*; (*vanity*) vanité, *f.*; **~ly,** (*in vain*) en vain.
vainglor|ious, orgueilleu|x, ~se; **~y,** gloriole, *f.*; **~iously,** orgueilleusement.

valance, (*of bed*) cantonnière, *f.*
vale, vallée, *f.*
valedictory, d'adieu.
valentine, (*missive*) billet de la Saint-Valentin, *m.*
valerian, (*bot.*) valériane, *f.*
valet, valet de chambre, *m.*; *v.a.* faire* le service de valet de; ⚠ valeter = '*dance attendance*'.
valetudinarian, *adj. and s.m.* valétudinaire.
valiant, vaillant; **~ly,** vaillamment.
valid, valide; (*reason, receipt*) valable; **~ity,** validité, *f.*; **~ly,** validement.
valise, valise, *f.*
valley, vallée, *f.*
val|our, valeur, *f.*; **~orous,** valeureu|x, ~se; **~orously,** valeureusement.
valuable, de valeur; **~s,** *s.* objets de valeur, *m.pl.*
valuation, évaluation, *f.*
value, *s.* (*lit. and fig.*) valeur, *f.*; ~ *in exchange,* contre-valeur, *f.*; *v.a.* évaluer; (*put a price on*) priser; *set* (*a*) ~ *on,* faire* cas de; **~d,** estimé; **~less,** sans valeur.
valuer, appréciateur, *m.*
valve, (*mach.*) soupape, *f.*
vampire, vampire, *m.*
van, (*veh.*) voiture de livraison, *f.*; (*mil.*) avant-garde, *f.*
vandal, *s.* (*fig.*) vandale, *m.f.*; **~ism,** vandalisme, *m.*
vane, girouette, *f.*
vanguard, avant-garde, *f.*; (*pl.* avant-gardes).
vanilla, vanille, *f.*
vanish *and* ~ **away,** s'évanouir; **~ing,** *s.* disparition, *f.*; **~ing-point,** point de fuite, *m.*
vanity, (*conceit, emptiness, &c.*) vanité, *f.*; **~-bag,** réticule, *m.*
vanquish, (*lit. and fig.*) vaincre*; **~er,** vainqueur, *m.*
vantage, (*advantage and tennis*) avantage, *m.*
vapid, fade; **~ity,** fadeur, *f.*
vapour, vapeur, *f.*; *v.n.* (*boast idly*) se vanter; **~er,** vantard, -e, *m.f.*
vaporous, vaporeu|x, ~se.
variab|le, *adj.* variable; **~ility,** variabilité, *f.*; **~ly,** variablement.
variance, désaccord, *m.*; *be at* ~, être en désaccord.
variation, (*varying, gram., math.*) variation, *f.*
varied, varié.
variega|te, diaprer; **~tion,** diaprure, *f.*; **~ted,** (*flowers*) panaché.
variety, variété, *f.*
various, (*varying, sundry*) divers; **~ly,** diversement.
varnish, *s.* (*lit. and fig.*) vernis, *m.*; *v.a.* vernir; **~er,** vernisseur, *m.*; **~ing,** *s.* (*already on object*) vernissure, *f.*; (*act of varnishing, private view of pictures*) vernissage, *m.*
vary, *v.a.n.* varier; *v.n.* (*disagree*) différer (sur).
vase, vase, *m.*
vaseline, vaseline, *f.*
vassal, vassal, *m.*; **~age,** (*fig.*) servitude, *f.*
vast, vaste; **~ness,** immensité, *f.*; **~ly,** immensément; (*slang*) furieusement; **~ly** +*adj.* on ne peut plus.
vat, *s.* cuve, *f.*
Vatican, Vatican, *m.*
vaticination, prophétie, *f.*
vault, (*for the dead*) caveau, *m.*; (*arch. and fig.*) voûte, *f.*; (*cellar*) cave, *f.*
vault, *s.* (*jump*) saut, *m.*; *v.a.* sauter.
vault|ed, (*arched*) voûté; **~ing,** *s.* voûtes, *f.pl.*
vaunt, *v.a.* (*brag of*) se vanter de; *v.n.* se vanter; **~ingly,** avec vantardise.
veal, veau, *m.*
veer, *v.n.* (*naut.*) changer de bord; (*wind*) tourner.
vegetable, *s.* (*for table*) légume, *m.*; (*as distinct from animal*) végétal, *m.*; ~ **marrow,** *see* MARROW; *~-soup, see* SOUP; ⚠ végétable = '*vegetable' is an adj. only.*
vegetarian, *adj. and s.m.f.* végétarien, -ne.
vegeta|te, (*lit. and fig.*) végéter; **~tion,** végétation, *f.*
vehemen|ce, véhémence, *f.*; **~t,** véhément; **~tly,** véhémentement.
vehicle, (*lit. and fig.*) véhicule, *m.*
veil, *s.* (*woman's*) voilette, *f.*; (*fig. and nun's*) voile, *m.*; *v.a.* (*lit. and fig.*) voiler.
vein, *s.* (*in body, disposition, humour, geol.*) veine, *f.*; **~ed,** *adj.* veiné.
vellum, vélin, *m.*
velocity, vitesse, *f.*
velvet, *s.* velours, *m.*; ~ *mask, see* MASK; *adj.* de velours; **~een,** velours de coton, *m.*; **~y,** velouté.
venal, (*pers.*) vénal; **~ity,** vénalité, *f.*
vend, vendre; **~ible,** vendable; **~or,** vend|eur, ~eresse, *m.f.*
veneer, *s.* feuille à plaquer, *f.*; (*fig.*) vernis, *m.*; **~ing,** placage, *m.*; *v.a.* plaquer.
venerable, vénérable.
venera|te, vénérer; **~tion,** vénération, *f.*
Venetian, *adj.* (*when an adjective use small letter*) *and s.m.f.* Vénitien, -ne; ~ *blind, see* BLIND.
vengeance, vengeance, *f.*; *with a* ~, furieusement; *take* ~ *for,* tirer vengeance de.
vengeful, vindicati|f, ~ve.
venial, véniel, -le.
venison, venaison, *f.*
venom, (*lit. and fig.*) venin, *m.*; **~ous,** (*animals and fig.*) venimeu|x, ~se; (*plants*) vénéneu|x, ~se.
vent, *s.* (*opening, hole*) ouverture, *f.*; (*of cask*) trou de fausset, *m.*; (*passion, &c.*) libre cours, *m.*; *v.a.* (*passion, &c.*) décharger (sur).
ventila|te, ventiler; **~tion,** ventilation, *f.*; **~ting-shaft,** *see* SHAFT.
ventilator, ventilateur, *m.*
ventricle, (*heart*) ventricule, *m.*

ventriloquis|m, ventriloquie, *f.*; **~t,** ventriloque, *m.*
venture, *s.* aventure, *f.*; (*comm.*) spéculation, *f.*; *at a ~*, au †hasard.
venture, *v.a.* risquer; (*opinion*) †hasarder; *v.n. ~ on*, se †hasarder à; *~ to*, oser + *inf.*
ventur|ous, ~esome, (*pers.*) aventureu|x, ~se; (*things*) †hasardeu|x, ~se.
venue, *s.* rendez-vous, *m.*; ⚠ venue = '*act of coming*', '*growth of tree*'.
veraci|ous, véridique; **~ty,** véracité, *f.*
veranda(h), véranda, *f.*
verb, verbe, *m.*; **~al,** verbal; (*translation*) mot à mot, *invar.*; **~ally,** verbalement.
verbatim, mot pour mot.
verbena, (*bot.*) verveine, *f.*
verbiage, verbiage, *m.*
verbos|e, verbeu|x, ~se; **~ity,** verbosité, *f.*
verdant, (*fields, &c.*) verdoyant.
verdict, verdict, *m.*
verdigris, verdigris, *m.*
verdure, verdure, *f.*
verge, *s.* (*brink, edge*) bord, *m.*; (*grass edging*) bordure, *f.*; (*of column*) fût, *m.*; *on the ~ of*, à deux doigts de; ⚠ verge *in French* = '*staff*', '*switch*'.
verge, *v.n. ~ towards*, pencher vers; *~ on*, approcher de.
verger, bedeau, *m.*
verif|ication, vérification, *f.*; **~y,** vérifier.
verily, en vérité.
verisimilitude, vraisemblance, *f.*
veritabl|e, véritable; **~y,** véritablement.
verity, vérité, *f.*
verjuice, verjus, *m.*
vermilion, *s.* (*colour*) cinabre, *m.*; *adj.* vermeil, -le.
vermin, (*lit. and fig.*) vermine, *f.*; **~ous,** plein de vermine.
vernacular, *adj. and s.m.* vernaculaire.
vernal, printani|er, ~ère.
veronica, (*bot.*) véronique, *f.*
versatil|e, doué de talents divers; **~ity,** souplesse d'esprit, *f.*; ⚠ versatile, versatilité *are pej. in French and* = '*fickle*', '*fickleness*'.
verse, *s.* (*general term*) vers, *m.pl.*; (*stanza*) strophe, *f.*; ⚠ vers *singular* = *a single line of verse.*
versed in, versé dans.
versif|ication, versification, *f.*; **~y,** *v.a.n.* versifier; **~ier,** versificateur, *m.*
version, (*translation from a foreign language, account*) version, *f.*
vertebr|al, *adj.* vertébral; **~ate,** *adj. and s.m.* vertébré.
vertex, sommet, *m.*
vertical, (*line, plane*) vertical; **~ly,** verticalement.
vertigo, vertige, *m.*
vertu, virtu, amour des beaux-arts, *m.*
vervain, (*bot.*) verveine, *f.*
very, *adj.* (*preceded by def. article, demonst. adj.*) même; *the ~ room, house, &c.*, la chambre, maison même; (*in fullest sense*) vrai; (*mere*) seul.
very, *adv.* très; (*precisely*) précisément; (+ *compar.*) beaucoup; (+ *superlat.*) *unexpressed.*
vesper, (*evening*) soir, *m.*; **~s,** (*eccles. also ~ bell*) vêpres, *f.pl.*
vessel, (*receptacle, ship, fig., anat.*) vaisseau, *m.*
vest, *s.* chemise américaine, *f.*; ⚠ veste = *coat of lounge suit.*
vestal virgin, vestale, *f.*
vested in, attribué à.
vestibule, vestibule, *m.*
vestige, (*lit. and fig.*) vestige, *m.*; (*slightest quantity*) atome, *m.*
vestment, vêtement, *m.*; **~s,** (*eccles.*) vêtements de prêtre, *m.pl.*
vestry, (*eccles. meeting*) assemblée paroissiale, *f.*; **~-room,** sacristie, *f.*
vesture, *s.* vêtements, *m.pl.*
vetch, (*bot.*) vesce, *f.*
veteran, vétéran, *m.*; *adj.* expérimenté; (*mil. forces*) aguerri; ⚠ vétéran *is only a noun in French and* = *old soldier or person grown old in a profession, &c.*
veterinary, *adj.* vétérinaire; *~ surgeon, see* SURGEON.
veto, véto, *m.*; *v.a.* mettre* son véto à.
vex, *v.a.* (⚠ *only of pers.*) vexer; **~ed,** (*of things*) = très discuté; **~ation,** contrariété, *f.*; **~atious,** contrariant.
via, *prep.* via.
viaduct, viaduc, *m.*
vial, fiole, *f.*
viands, mets, *m.pl.*
viaticum, (*eccles.*) viatique, *m.*
vibra|te, *v.n.* (*oscillate*) osciller; (*of sound*) retentir; **~tion,** vibration, *f.*; **~tory,** vibratoire.
viburnum, (*bot.*) viorne, *f.*
vicar, curé, *m.*; ⚠ vicaire = '*curate*'; **~age,** presbytère, *m.*; **~ious,** délégué.
vice, (*depravity, immoral habit, fault, defect*) vice, *m.*; (*screw*) étau, *m.*
vice, *prefix gen.* vice-; **~-admiral, ~-consul, ~-president,** *see these words.*
viceroy, vice-roi, *m.*; **~alty,** vice-royauté, *f.*
vicinity, (*neighbourhood, nearness*) voisinage, *m.*
vicious, (*given to vice, defective, horse*) vicieu|x, ~se; ⚠ vicieux *does not* = '*spiteful*' *which* = méchant *or* '*angry*' (*of things*) *which* = d'irritation; *~ circle, see* CIRCLE; **~ness,** méchanceté, *f.*; **~ly,** vicieusement; (*spitefully*) méchamment.
vicissitude, vicissitude, *f.*
victim, (*lit. and fig.*) victime, *f.*; **~ize,** duper.
victor, vainqueur, *m.*
victoria, (*carriage*) victoria, *f.*
victorious, victorieu|x, ~se; **~ly,** victorieusement.
victory, (*lit. and fig.*) victoire, *f.*
victual, *v.a.* ravitailler; **~ling,** ravitaillement, *m.*; **~ler,** aubergiste, *m.*
victuals, victuailles, *f.pl.*
vicuna, ~-wool, vigogne, *f.*

vie, ~ *in*, rivaliser de; ~ *with*, rivaliser avec.
view, *s.* (*what is seen, range of vision, sight, outlook, survey, inspection, design, way of regarding, opinion, photo., &c.*) vue, *f.*; **~-finder**, (*photo.*) viseur, *m.*; *with a* ~, (*eye*) *to*, en vue de; *on* ~, exposé; *have in* ~, se proposer (de).
view, *v.a.* voir*; (*fig.*) envisager.
vigil, (*being awake, eve of festival*) veille, *f.*
vigilan|ce, vigilance, *f.*; **~t**, vigilant; **~tly**, avec vigilance.
vigorous, (*lit. and fig.*) vigoureu|x, ~se; **~ly**, vigoureusement.
vigour, vigueur, *f.*
vile, vil; (*slang*) abominable; **~ness**, bassesse, *f.*; (*slang*) *use noun* + abominable; **~ly**, bassement.
vilify, vilipender.
villa, villa, *f.*
village, village, *m.*; **~r**, villageois, -e, *m.f.*
villain, scélérat, *m.*; (*feudal*) vilain, *m.*; **~y**, scélératesse, *f.*; **~ous**, scélérat; (*slang*) abominable.
vinaigrette, flacon de sels, *m.*; ⚠ vinaigrette *in French* = '*vinegar sauce*'.
vindica|te, (*justify*) justifier; (*maintain cause of*) défendre; **~tion**, justification, défense, *f.*; **~tor**, défenseur, *m.*
vindictive, (*revengeful*) vindicati|f, ~ve; **~ness**, caractère vindicatif, *m.*; **~ly**, vindicativement.
vine, vigne, *f.*; **~ry**, serre à vigne, *f.*; **~-arbour**, treille, *f.*; **~-branch**, sarment, *m.*; **~-grower**, vigneron, *m.*; **~-prop**, échalas, *m.*; **~yard**, vignoble, *m.*
vinegar, vinaigre, *m.*
vintage, (*grapes gathered*) vendange, *f.*; (*season*) vendanges, *f.pl.*
vintner, marchand de vin, *m.*
viola, (*bot.*) pensée, *f.*
viola|te, violer; **~tion**, violation, *f.*; (*rape*) viol, *m.*; **~tor**, violateur, *m.*
violen|ce, violence, *f.*; **~t**, violent; **~tly**, violemment.
violet, (*bot.*) violette, *f.*; (*colour*) violet, *m.*; *adj.* violet, -te; *~-red, adj. and s.m.* zinzolin.
violin, violon, *m.*; **~ist**, violoniste, *m.f.*
violoncell|o, violoncelle, *m.*; **~ist**, violoncelliste, *m.*
viper, vipère, *f.*; **~'s bugloss**, (*bot.*) vipérine, *f.*
virago, virago, *f.*
virgin, *s.* vierge, *f.*; *adj.* (*maidenly*) virginal; (*soil, forest, &c.*) vierge.
Virginia creeper, vigne vierge, *f.*
virginity, virginité, *f.*
viril|e, viril; **~ity**, virilité, *f.*
virtual, vrai; **~ly**, effectivement.
virtue, (*moral excellence, chastity, peculiar quality, efficacy*) vertu, *f.*; (*advantage*) avantage, *m.*; *in* ~ *of*, en vertu de; ⚠ *not English* '*vertu*', *e.g.* '*articles of vertu*' = objets d'art, *m.pl.*
virtuoso, virtuose, *m.f.*
virtuous, vertueu|x, ~se; **~ness**, vertu, *f.*; **~ly**, vertueusement.
virulen|ce, (*lit. and fig.*) virulence, *f.*; **~t**, virulent.
virus, virus, *m.*
visage, visage, *m.*
viscount, **~ess**, vicomte, -sse, *m.f.*
viscous, visqueu|x, ~se.
visé, visa, *m.*
visib|ility, visibilité, *f.*; **~le**, (*able to be seen, apparent, able to receive callers*) visible; **~ly**, visiblement.
vision, (*faculty of seeing, apparition*) vision, *f.*; (*sight*) vue, *f.*; **~ary**, *adj. and s.m.f.* visionnaire; (*adj. things*) imaginaire.
visit, *s.* visite, *f.*; (*stay in a place*) séjour, *m.*; *be on a* ~ *to*, être en visite chez.
visit, *v.a.* visiter; (*calamity*) atteindre*; (*punish*) punir; *v.n.* faire* des visites.
visitation, (*trial*) épreuve, *f.*; (*punishment*) punition, *f.*
visiting, *s.* visites, *f.pl.*; **~-card**, carte de visite, *f.*; *adj.* de visite.
visitor, visiteu|r, ~se, *m.f.*
vis(z)or, visière, *f.*
vista, échappée, *f.*; (*forests*) percée, *f.*
visual, (*belonging to sight*) visuel, -le; **~ize**, (*make visible*) rendre visible; (*to picture*) se représenter.
vital, (*lit. and fig.*) vital; **~ity**, vitalité, *f.*; **~ly**, d'une manière vitale.
vitals, parties vitales, *f.pl.*
vitiate, vicier.
vitreous, de verre; (*like glass*) vitreu|x, ~se.
vitriol, vitriol, *m.*; **~ic**, vitriolique.
vitupera|te, injurier; **~tion**, injures, *f.pl.*
vivac|ious, vi|f, ~ve; ⚠ *not* vivace *which* = '*long-lived*', '*deep-rooted*'; **~ity**, vivacité, *f.*
viva voce, *adj.* oral; *adv.* oralement; ⚠ de vive voix = '*by word of mouth*'; ~ *exam(ination)*, examen oral, *m.*
vivid, (*impression, imagination, description, colour, light*) vi|f, ~ve; **~ness**, vivacité, *f.*; **~ly**, vivement.
vivisec|tion, vivisection, *f.*; **~tor**, vivisecteur, *m.*
vixen, renarde, *f.*; (*fig.*) mégère, *f.*
viz, à savoir.
vizier, vizir, *m.*
vocabulary, vocabulaire, *m.*
vocal, (*organs, music, sounds, &c.*) vocal; **~ist**, chanteu|r, ~se, *m.f.*; **~ly**, vocalement.
vocation, vocation, *f.*; (*profession*) profession, *f.*
vocative, *s.* (*gram.*) vocatif, *m.*
vocifera|te, vociférer; **~tion**, vocifération, *f.*
vociferous, criard.
vogue, vogue, *f.*
voice, *s.* (*human utterance, opinion, tone, expression of will, gram., fig.*) voix, *f.*; *v.a.* exprimer.

voiceless, muet, -te.
void, *s.* vide, *m.*; *adj.* vide; (*vacant*) vacant; (*law, comm.*) nul, -le.
volatil|e, (*mind, writer, &c.*) vi|f, ~ve; (*chem.*) volatil; ♤ volatil *only* = '*evaporating rapidly*'; **~ity,** légèreté, *f.*; (*chem.* volatilité, *f.*
volcan|ic, volcanique; **~o,** volcan, *m.*
vole, (*zool.*) campagnol, *m.*
volition, volition, *f.*
volley, (*fire-arms, projectiles, tennis*) volée, *f.*; (*oaths, &c.*) bordée, *f.*
volt, (*electr.*) volt, *m.*
volub|ility, volubilité, *f.*; **~le,** (*pers.*) doué de volubilité; (*speech*) facile; **~ly,** avec volubilité.
volume, (*book, part of work, bulk, comm.*) volume, *m.*; (*smoke, &c.*) nuage, *m.*; ♤ volume *not used of things like smoke.*
voluminous, (*in many volumes, bulky*) volumineu|x, ~se; (*of authors*) fécond.
voluntar|y, volontaire; **~ily,** volontairement.
volunteer, *s.* (*to do a thing and mil.*) volontaire, *m.*; *adj.* de volontaires; *v.a.* offrir*; *v.n.* (*mil.*) s'engager (pour); ~ *to,* offrir* de.
voluptuary, épicurien, -ne, *m.f.*
voluptuous, voluptueu|x, ~se; **~ness,** sensualité, *f.*; **~ly,** voluptueusement.
volute, (*arch.*) volute, *f.*
vomit, *s.* (*and* **~ing**) vomissement, *m.*; *v.a.n.* (*lit. and fig.*) vomir.
vorac|ious, vorace; **~ity,** voracité, *f.*; **~iously,** avec voracité, *f.*
vortex, (*lit. and fig.*) tourbillon, *m.*; ♤ vortex *is an anatomical term.*
votar|y, **~ess,** (*ardent follower*) secta|t|eur, ~rice, *m.f.*
vot|e, *s.* voix, *f.*; *often pl.*; *~e of censure,* censure, *f.*; *v.a.n.* voter (sur); (*propose*) proposer; (*pronounce*) déclarer; *~e by ballot, v.n.* scrutiner; **~er,** votant, -e, *m.f.*; **~ing,** votation, *f.*
votive, voti|f, ~ve.
vouch, *v.a.* (*confirm*) confirmer; *v.n.* ~ *for,* répondre de.
voucher, (*for payment*) pièce de dépense, *f.*; (*for receipt*) pièce de recette, *f.*
vouchsafe, *v.a.* (*grant*) accorder; *v.n.* ~ *to,* daigner + *inf.*
vow, *s.* vœu, *m.*
vow, *v.a.* vouer; (*swear*) jurer; *v.n.* faire* un vœu; (*swear*) jurer.
vowel, voyelle, *f.*
voyage, *s.* voyage, *m.*; *v.n.* voyager par [mer.
voyager, voyageu|r, ~se, *m.f.*
vulcanite, *s.* ébonite, *f.*
vulgar, (*common, in common use, coarse*) vulgaire; ~ *fraction, see* FRACTION; **~ity,** vulgarité, *f.*; **~ize,** vulgariser; **~ly,** vulgairement; **~ism,** expression vulgaire, *f.*
vulnerab|ility, vulnérabilité, *f.*; **~le,** vulnérable.
vulture, vautour, *m.*

W

wad, bourre, *f.*
wadding, (*garments*) ouate, *f.*
waddle, se dandiner.
wade, ~ **across,** *v.a.* (*river, &c.*) traverser à gué.
wader, (*ornith.*) échassier, *m.*; (*boot*) botte de pêche, *f.*
wafer, *s.* (*for sealing*) pain à cacheter, *m.*; (*pastry*) gaufrette, *f.*; (*relig.*) hostie, *f.*
waft, *s.* (*breath*) souffle, *m.*; *v.a.* porter.
wag, *s.* (*jester*) plaisant, *m.*; (*movement of head*) †hochement, *m.*
wag, *v.a.* (*head*) †hocher; (*tail*) agiter; *v.n.* s'agiter.
wage(s), *s.* (*workman*) salaire, *m.*; (*servants*) gages, *m.pl.*
wager, *s.* pari, *m.*; *v.a.* parier.
waggish, espiègle; **~ly,** avec espièglerie.
waggle, *v.a.* agiter.
wag(g)on, chariot, *m.*; (*rail. truck*) wagon, *m.*; ♤ wagon *is never used for a heavy cart, delivery van, which* = fourgon; (*mil.*) fourgon, *m.*; (*artill.*) caisson, *m.*
wag(g)oner, roulier, *m.*
wagonette, (*veh.*) break, *m.*; ♤ wagonnette = *low, four-wheeled cart.*
wagtail, (*ornith.*) †hochequeue, *m.*; *water-~,* bergeronnette-lavandière, *f.*
waif, épave, *f*; *~s and strays,* épaves, *f.pl.*
wail, *also* **wailing,** *s.* (*child*) vagissement, *m.*; (*wind*) gémissement, *m.*; *v.n.* gémir; (*child*) vagir.
wain, chariot, *m.*
wainscot, *s.* lambris, *m.*; *v.a.* lambrisser (de); **~ing,** lambrissage, *m.*
waist, taille, *f.*; **~-band,** ceinture, *f.*
waistcoat, gilet, *m.*; *~-pocket,* gousset, *m.*; *see also* STRAIT.
wait, *s. lie in ~ for,* guetter.
wait, *v.a.* attendre; ~ *for,* attendre; ~ *upon,* servir*; *v.n.* attendre; (*at table*) servir*; **~ing-room,** salle d'attente, *f.*
wait|er, (*restaurant, &c.*) garçon de café, *m.*; **~ress,** fille de salle, *f.*
waive, *v.a.* (*claim, &c.*) renoncer à.
wake, *s.* (*ship*) sillage, *m.*
wak|e, *v.a. and ~e up,* (*lit. and fig.*) réveiller; *v.n.* (*wake up*) s'éveiller; (*be awake*) veiller; **~ing** *dream, see* DREAM.
wakeful, (*pers.*) éveillé; (*things*) sans sommeil; (*vigilant*) vigilant; **~ness,** insomnie, vigilance, *f.*
waken, (*lit. and fig.*) *v.a.* éveiller; *v.n.* s'éveiller.
wale, weal, marque d'un coup, *f.*
walk, *s.* (*gait*) démarche, *f.*; (*for pleasure*) promenade, *f.*; (*path*) allée, *f.*; (*of life*) voie, *f.*; (*habitual round*) tournée, *f.*; *go for a ~,* faire* un tour de promenade.
walk, *v.a.* (*certain distance*) faire*; (*horse*) mettre* au pas; *v.n.* (*not drive, &c.*) aller* (être) à pied; (*act of walking*) marcher; (*for pleasure*) se promener; ~ *down, v.a.* descendre (avoir); ~ *in,* entrer (être); ~ *into,* entrer dans; ~ *off,*

s'en aller* (être); ~ *out*, sortir* (être); ~ *up*, *v.a.* monter (avoir); ~ *backwards and forwards*, aller* (être) et venir* (être).
walking, *s. use inf. of verb v.n. above*; ~**-stick**, canne, *f.*; ~*-tour*, *see* TOUR.
wall, *s.* mur, *m.*; (*rampart, high* ~) muraille, *f.*; ~ **clock**, cartel, *m.*; ~*-fruit*, fruit d'espalier, *m.*; ~**-paper**, papier peint, *m.*; *retaining* ~, *see* RETAIN; ~**-rue**, (*bot.*) sauve-vie, *f.*; *v.a.* entourer de murs; ~ *in, up*, murer; ~**ed**, (*city, &c.*) fortifié.
wallet, (*pocket*) portefeuille, *m.*; (*begging*) besace, *f.*
wallflower, (*bot.*) ravenelle, *f.*
Walloon, *adj.* (*when an adj. use small letter*) *and s.m.f.* Wallon, -ne.
wallop, rosser.
wallow, se vautrer.
walnut, (*tree, wood*) noyer, *m.*; (*fruit*) noix, *f.*; (*green fruit*) cerneau, *m.*
walrus, morse, *m.*
waltz, valse, *f.*; *v.n.* valser.
wan, (*complexion*) blême; (*of light*) blafard.
wand, baguette, *f.*
wander, *v.n.* errer; (*from subject*) s'égarer (de); (*mind*) divaguer; ~ *over*, parcourir*, *v.a.*; ~**er**, (*lit. and pej.*) vagabond, -e, *m.f.*
wandering, (*delirium*) délire, *m.*; (*aberration*) égarement, *m.*; *adj.* errant; (*speech*) incohérent.
wane, *s.* (*fig.*) déclin, *m.*; *v.n.* décroître*.
want, *s.* (*need*) besoin, *m.*; (*lack*) manque, *m.*; (*poverty*) misère, *f.*; *for* ~ *of*, faute de.
want, *v.a.* (*need*) avoir besoin de; (*lack*) manquer de; (*require, desire*) vouloir*; (*ask for and adverts.*) demander; *v.n.* (*be wanting*) faire* défaut; ~ *for, be* ~*ing in*, manquer de.
wanton, *s.* libertin, -e, *m.f.*
wanton, *adj.* (*sportive*) folâtre; (*growth*) exubérant; (*lewd*) licencieu|x, ~se; (*motiveless*) *also* ~**ly**, de gaieté de cœur; ~**ness**, *see below*.
wanton, *v.a.* folâtrer.
wantonness, (*sportiveness*) gaieté, *f.*; (*lewdness*) libertinage, *m.*
war, *s.* guerre, *f.*; ~ *of attrition*, guerre d'usure, *f.*; ~ *to the knife*, guerre à outrance, *f.*; ~ *of movement*, guerre de mouvement, *f.*; ~ *of position*, guerre des tranchées, *f.*; ~**-horse**, cheval de bataille, *m.*; ~ **office**, ministère de la guerre, *f.*; ~**-path**, sentier de la guerre, *m.*; ~**ship**, navire de guerre, *m.*; ~*-worn*, usé par la guerre; ~ **zone**, zone des armées, *f.*; *levy* ~ *on*, faire* la guerre à.
warbl|e, (*brooks, birds*) gazouiller; ~**ing**, gazouillement, *m.*; ~**er**, (*ornith.*) fauvette, *f.*
ward, *s.* (*minor in charge of guardian*) pupille, *m.f.*; (*lock*) garde, *f.*; (*hospital*) salle, *f.*; ~**-room**, (*naut.*) carré des officiers, *m.*; *v.a.* ~ *off*, (*blow, &c.*) parer; (*fig.*) éloigner.
warden, (*governor*) gouverneur, *m.*; (*colleges*) directeur, *m.*
ward|er, ~**ress**, gardien, -ne, *m.f.*
wardrobe, (*cupboard, fig. for dress*) garde-robe, *f.*; *pl.* garde-robes.
ware, wares, marchandises, *f.pl.*
warehouse, magasin, *m.*; *v.a.* emmagasiner; ~**man**, magasinier, *m.*
warehousing, *s.* emmagasinage, *m.*
warfare, guerre, *f.*
war|ily, avec prudence; ~**iness**, prudence, *f.*; ~**y**, *see below*.
warlike, guerri|er, ~ère; (*of war*) de guerre.
warm, *s.* (*warming*) *use verb* se chauffer; (*coat*) pardessus chaud, *m.*
warm, *adj.* (*rather hot, hearty, zealous, clothes, excited*) chaud; (*dangerous*) dangereu|x, ~se; (*work, &c.*) rude; *be* ~, (*pers.*) avoir chaud; (*weather*) faire* chaud; ~**ly**, chaudement.
warm, *v.a.* chauffer; ~ *up*, réchauffer; *v.n.* se chauffer; ~*ing-pan*, *see* PAN.
warmth, chaleur, *f.*; (*fig.*) ardeur, *f.*
warn, avertir (de, que); ~ *against*, mettre* sur ses gardes contre; ~ *off*, détourner.
warning, avertissement, *m.*; (*to leave*) congé, *m.*
warp, *s.* (*weaving*) chaîne, *f.*; *v.n.* (*wood*) gauchir.
warrant, *s.* (*authorization*) autorisation, *f.*; (*order*) mandat, *m.*; ~ *officer*, sous-officier, *m.*
warrant, *v.a.* (*goods, affirm*) garantir; (*justify*) justifier; ~**able**, soutenable; ~**y**, (*of quality, nautical*) garantie, *f.*
warren, garenne, *f.*
warrior, guerrier, *m.*
wart, verrue, *f.*
war|y, prudent; *for* ~**iness**, ~**ily**, *see* WARILY.
wash, *s.* (*ablutions*) *use v.a.* laver *or v.n.* se laver; (*lotion*) lotion, *f.*; (*laundry*) blanchissage, *m.*; ~**-leather**, *see* LEATHER; ~**-tub**, cuvier, *m.*; *send to the* ~, envoyer à la lessive.
wash, *v.a.* laver; (*tears, sea, &c.*) baigner; ~ *away, out*, (*sins, &c.*) effacer; ~ *off*, enlever; ~ *up*, (*plates, &c.*) faire* la vaisselle; *v.n.* (*ablutions, go through wash*) se laver; (*of a washerwoman*) laver; ~ *over*, (*waves*) se dérouler sur.
washable, lavable.
washer, (*pers.*) laveu|r, ~se, *m.f.*; (*of screw, &c.*) rondelle, *f.*
washerwoman, blanchisseuse, *f.*
washing, (*clothes for wash, process of washing clothes*) lessive, *f.*; (*ablutions*) ablutions, *f.pl.*
wasp, guêpe, *f.*; ~*s' nest*, guêpier, *m.*; ~**ish**, irascible.
waste, *s.* (*region*) désert, *m.*; (*land*) friche, *f.*; (*money*) gaspillage, *m.*; (*loss*) perte, *f.*; (*meat, wool, &c.*) déchets, *m.pl.*; ~**-pipe**, tuyau de trop-plein, *m.*
waste, *adj.* (*uncultivated*) inculte; (*of*

no use) de rebut; ~ *paper*, papier de rebut, *m.*; ~*-paper basket*, corbeille à papier, *f.*
waste, *v.a.* (*money, food*) gaspiller; (*time*) perdre; (*lay waste*) ravager; *v.n.* (*being exhausted*) s'épuiser; ~ *away*, (*pers.*) dépérir.
wasteful, (*pers.*) dissipat|eur, ~rice; (*things*) prodigue; **~ness,** prodigalité, *f.*; **~ly,** avec prodigalité.
waster, (*good-for-nothing*) vaurien, *m.*
wasting, *adj.* (*disease*) qui consume.
watch, *s.* (*timepiece*) montre, *f.*; (*watchman*) gardien, *m.*; (*of the night, wakefulness*) veille, *f.*; (*naut.*) quart, *m.*; (*guard*) garde; **~-dog,** chien de garde, *m.*; **~-fire,** feu de bivouac, *m.*; **~-guard,** chaîne de montre, *f.*; **~-maker,** horloger, *m.*; **~-stand,** porte-montre, *m. invar.*
watch|er, veilleu|r, ~se, *m.f.*; **~-tower,** tour de guet, *f.*
watchful, vigilant; **~ness,** vigilance, *f.*; (*want of sleep*) insomnie, *f.*; **~ly,** avec vigilance.
watchman, veilleur de nuit, *m.*
watchword, mot d'ordre, *m.*
water, *s.* (*gen., fig., tears, urine, of gems, expanse of water, of scents*) eau, *f.*; **~-closet,** cabinet, *m.*; **~-colour,** aquarelle, *f.*; **~-lily,** nénufar, *m.*; **~-melon,** pastèque, *f.*; **~-pot,** arrosoir, *m.*; **~-rail,** (*ornith.*) *see* RAIL; **~-ram,** bélier hydraulique, *m.*; **~-way,** voie navigable, *f.*; *for other compounds see below*; *drinking-~*, eau potable, *f.*; *still ~s run deep*, il n'est pire eau que l'eau qui dort; *hot-~ bottle*, (*earthenware*) cruchon, *m.*; (*metal*) bouillotte, *f.*; **~s,** (*mineral, thermal, national*) eaux, *f.pl.*; *v.a.* (*plants and of a river*) arroser; (*cattle*) abreuver; *v.n.* (*eyes*) se mouiller.
watercourse, cours d'eau, *m.*
watercress, cresson, *m.*
waterfall, chute d'eau, *f.*
waterfowl, oiseau aquatique, *m.*
waterlogged, rempli d'eau.
waterman, batelier, *m.*
watermark, (*paper*) filigrane, *m.*
waterproof, *s.* caoutchouc, *m.*; *adj.* imperméable; (*often as complement of* être) à l'épreuve de l'eau.
watershed, versant, *m.*
watertight, *adj.* étanche; ~ *compartments, bulkheads*, cloisons étanches, *f.pl.*
waterworks, usine pour la distribution des eaux, *f.*
watery, aqueu|x, ~se; (*eyes, wet*) humide.
wave, *s.* (*lit. and fig.*) vague, *f.*; (*sound, light, electr.*) onde, *f.*; *permanent* ~, (*hair*) ondulation permanente, *f.*
wave, *v.a.* (*flag, hat, hand, handkerchief, &c.*) agiter; (*hair*) onduler; *v.n.* (*flag, &c.*) flotter; (*undulate*) onduler; (*to pers.*) faire* signe de main (à +*pers.*, de +*inf.*).
wavelet, petite vague, *f.*
waver, vaciller; (*hesitate*) balancer; **~ing,** *adj.* vacillant; (*hesitating*) hésitant.
wavy, *adj.* ondulé.
wax, cire, *f.*; (*cobbler's*) poix, *f.*; ~ **candle,** bougie, *f.*; ~ **taper,** rat de cave, *m.*; *v.a.* cirer.
wax, *v.n.* (*grow*) croître*; (*become*) devenir* (être).
waxwork, figure de cire, *f.*; **~s,** musée de figures de cire, *m.*
way, (*lit., fig., ground traversed*) chemin, *m.*; (*distance*) distance, *f.*; (*direction*) côté, *m.*; (*free course*) libre cours, *m.*; (*state*) état, *m.*; (*means*) moyen, *m.*; **~s,** (*of acting, doing*) manières, *f.pl.*; *which way?* de quel côté? ; ~ *in*, entrée, *f.*; ~ *out*, sortie, *f.*; *out of the* ~, (*remote*) retiré; (*uncommon*) extraordinaire; *interj.* ôtez-vous de là!; *on the* ~, chemin faisant; *by* ~ *of*, (*place*) par; (*as a*) en guise de; *by the* ~, à propos; *in a* ~, (*in some ~s*) à certains égards; *it's a long ~ to*, il y a loin pour aller à; *be in the ~ of*, déranger; *have one's* (*own*) *way*, faire* à sa guise; *where there's a will there's a* ~, vouloir c'est pouvoir; *edge one's ~ through*, se glisser à travers; *elbow, fight, make one's ~ through*, se frayer un chemin à travers; *give* ~, (*collapse*) s'effondrer; *give ~ to*, céder à; (*vices, &c.*) s'abandonner à; *go the wrong ~ to work to*, s'y prendre* de travers pour; *make, wend one's* ~ (*to*), diriger ses pas (vers); (*fig. in the world*) faire* son chemin; *lead the* ~, montrer le chemin; *pay one's* ~, couvrir* ses dépenses; *see one's ~ to*, voir le moyen de; *stand out of the* ~, se ranger; *take the shortest* ~, prendre* par le plus court; *work one's* ~, s'ouvrir un chemin; *worm one's ~ into*, se faufiler dans; (*fig.*) s'insinuer dans.
wayfar|er, *~ing man*, voyageur, *m.*
waylay, dresser un guet-apens à; (*wait about for*) guetter.
wayward, (*approx.*) capricieu|x, ~se; **~ness,** caprice, *m.*; **~ly,** capricieusement.
we, nous; (+ *noun*) nous autres, *e.g. we English*, nous autres Anglais.
weak, (*lit., fig., mind, character, morally, numbers, health, point, liquids, gram., syllable*) faible; **~ness,** (*lit. and fig., &c.*) faiblesse, *f.*; **~ly,** faiblement.
weaken, affaiblir; **~ing,** *s.* affaiblissement, *m.*
weakling, être faible, *m.*
weakly, débile.
weal, (*welfare*) bien, *m.*
wealth, (*riches*) richesse, *f.*; (*profusion*) profusion, *f.*
wealthy, riche.
wean, sevrer; ~ *from*, détacher de.
weapon, arme, *f.*
wear, *s.* (*of clothes*) usage, *m.*; (*effect of use*) usure, *f.*; (*clothes worn*) vêtements, *m.pl.*
wear, *v.a.* (*lit., fig., dress, hair, beard*) porter; (*hole*) faire*; ~ *down*, user; ~ *off*, (*rub off*) effacer; ~ *out*, user; (*exhaust*) épuiser.

wear, *v.n.* ~ *well,* être d'un bon user; (*age*) ne pas vieillir; ~ *away,* s'effacer; (*time*) passer; ~ *off,* s'effacer; ~ *out,* s'user.
wearable, mettable.
wearisome, fatigant; (*tedious*) ennuyeu|x, ~se; ~**ness,** ennui, *m.*; ~**ly,** ennuyeusement.
wear|y, *adj.* (*pers.*) las, -se; (*things*) fatigant; *become, grow* ~*y of,* se lasser de; ~**iness,** lassitude, *f.*; ~**ily,** (*laboriously*) péniblement.
weary, fatiguer; *v.n.* ~ *of,* se lasser de.
weasel, belette, *f.*
weather, temps, *m.*; *v.a.* (*storm*) résister à; (*cape*) doubler; ~**-glass,** baromètre, *m.*; ~ *report,* bulletin météorologique, *m.*; ~ *permitting,* si le temps le permet; ~**ed,** (*stone, &c.*) décoloré par les intempéries.
weathercock, girouette, *f.*
weave, *v.a.* (*cloth, &c.*) tisser; (*wreath, &c.*) entrelacer.
weaver, tisserand, *m.*
web, (*woven fabric, lies*) tissu, *m.*; (*spider's*) toile, *f.*; ~**bed,** palmé.
wed, *v.a.* (*fig., priest, parent*) marier; ⚠ marier *is only trans. in these senses*; (*take in marriage*) épouser.
wedding, (*ceremony*) mariage, *m.*; (*including functions, &c.*) noces, *f.pl.*; ~**-breakfast,** lunch, *m.*; ~**-ring,** alliance, *f.*
wedge, *s.* coin, *m.*; *v.a.* (*fix*) caler.
wedlock, mariage, *m.*
Wednesday, mercredi, *m.*
weed, *s.* mauvaise herbe, *f.*; *v.a.* sarcler; ~ *out,* éliminer; ~**ing,** sarclage, *m.*; ~**ing-hoe,** sarcloir, *m.*
weedy, plein de mauvaises herbes.
week, semaine, *f.*; (*period of 7 days*) huit jours, *m.pl.*; ~**-end,** congé de fin de semaine, *m.*; ~**-end bag,** sac de nuit, *m.*; ~**ly,** hebdomadaire; *to-day, to-morrow* ~, d'aujourd'hui en huit, de demain en huit.
weep, *v.a.* (*tears*) verser; *v.n.* pleurer; (*exude*) suinter; ~**ing,** *adj.* pleureu|r, ~se; ~**ing-willow,** saule pleureur, *m.*
weevil, charançon, *m.*
weft, trame, *f.*
weigh, *v.a.* (*lit. and fig.*) peser; (*anchor*) lever; ~ *down,* (*fig.*) accabler (de); ~ *upon,* accabler; *v.n.* (*lit. and fig.*) peser; (*be important*) avoir du poids (pour = *with*); ~ *anchor,* lever l'ancre.
weighing-machine, bascule, *f.*
weight, (*phys.*) pesanteur, *f.*; (*fig., heaviness, clock, piece of metal for weighing*) poids, *m.*; *carry* ~, être d'un grand poids; *put on* ~, prendre* du corps.
weighty, pesant; (*important*) important; (*deserving consideration*) de poids.
weir, déversoir, *m.*
weird, *adj.* (*approx.*) sinistre.
welcome, *s.* bon accueil, *m.*; *interj.* soyez le (la) bienvenu(e)!
welcome, *adj.* (*pers.*) le, la bienvenu(e); (*thing*) bien agréable; *be* ~ *to,* (+ *inf.*) être libre de; (+ *thing*) . . . être à votre, etc., service, *e.g.* mon parapluie est à votre, etc., service; *v.a.* (*pers.*) souhaiter la bienvenue à.
weld, souder.
welfare, bien-être, *m.*
well, *s.* (*water*) puits, *m.*; (*staircase*) cage, *f.*; (*fig.*) source, *f.*; *v.n.* ~ *up, out, forth,* jaillir.
well, *adj.* (*health*) bien portant; (*satisfactory, well situated*) bien.
well, *adv.* (*greatly, quite, quite well, thoroughly, rightly, kindly, with good reason, &c.*) bien; ~*-being,* bien-être, *m.*; ~*-bred,* bien élevé; ~*-meaning,* bien intentionné; *be* (*stand*) ~ *with,* être en bons termes avec; *interj.* (*surprise*) †hein!; (*just so, to sum up, expectation, hesitation*) eh bien!; (*marking agreement*) soit!; ~, ~, allons, allons!; *wish* ~ *to,* vouloir* du bien à.
Welsh, *adj.* (*when an adj. use small letter*) *and s.m.f.* Gallois, -e; (*lang.*) gallois, *m.*; ~ **rabbit,** (*cooking, approx.*) rôtie au fromage, *f.*
welter, *v.n.* se vautrer.
wen, (*pathol.*) loupe, *f.*
wench, donzelle, *f.*
werewolf, loup-garou, *m.*
west, *s.* ouest, *m.*; (*proper name*) Ouest; *adj. and* ~**erly,** d'ouest; *adv.* à l'ouest.
western, de l'ouest; (*Church, Empire, &c.*) d'Occident.
westward, vers l'ouest.
wet, *s.* temps pluvieux, *m.*; *adj.* (*pers., object*) mouillé; (*weather*) pluvieu|x, ~se; (*day, &c.*) de pluie; ~ *through,* trempé jusqu'aux os; ~ *blanket,* (*fig.*) rabat-joie, *m.invar.*; ~*-dock, see* DOCK; *be* ~, (*weather*) pleuvoir*; ~**ness,** humidité, *f.*
wet, *v.a.* mouiller; (*dip*) tremper.
whack, *v.a.* rosser; ~**ing,** roulée, *f.*
whale, baleine, *f.*
whalebone, baleine, *f.*
whaler, (*ship*) baleinier, *m.*
wharf, quai, *m.*
what, *compound rel. pron., nom.* ce qui, *acc.* ce que, *gen.* (*that of which*) ce dont; *with preps.* ce + *prep.* + quoi, *e.g.* ~ *he is thinking of,* ce à quoi il pense; *for* ~ *it is worth,* tel, -le quel, -le.
what, *interrog. pron., nom.* qu'est-ce qui, *acc.* que *and* qu'est-ce que, *gen.* (*of what*) de quoi; *with preps.* quoi; (*in exclamations +to be and inf.*) que, *e.g.* ~ *am I to do?* que faire?; (+ *adj. or comparative*) quoi de, *e.g.* ~ *is more natural?* quoi de plus naturel?; ~ *kind of a thing is . . . ?* qu'est-ce que c'est que *without* être, *e.g.* qu'est-ce que c'est que le Pyrrhonisme?; *interrog. adj.* quel, -le, *never followed by indef. article, e.g.* ~ *a noise!* quel bruit!
what! *interj.* quoi!
whatever, *pron.* quoi que + *subj., e.g.* ~

you do, quoi que vous fassiez; (*exclam.*) que diable!, *e.g.* ~ *is he saying?* que diable dit-il? ; *adj.* quelque . . . que + *subj.*, *e.g.* ~ *talents you may have*, quelques talents que vous ayez; (*compl. of 'to be'*) quel, -le, que soit, *e.g.* ~ *may be his terms*, quelles que soient ses conditions.
whatsoever, *adj. generally translated by* le, la moindre; *he has no ability* ~, il n'a pas le moindre talent.
wheat, froment, *m.*; **~en,** de froment; *~en bread*, (*fine*) pain de gruau, *m.*
wheatear, (*ornith.*) motteux, *m.*
wheedl|e, cajoler; *~e something out of*, obtenir* par cajoleries de; **~er,** cajoleu|r, ~se; **~ing,** cajolerie, *f.*
wheel, (*gen., helm, torture*) roue, *f.*; (*motor*) volant, *m.*; (*mil.*) conversion, *f.*; **~barrow,** brouette, *f.*; **~ chair,** fauteuil roulant, *m.*; **~-wright,** charron, *m.*; *free* ~, pignon à roue libre, *m.*; *spare* ~, (*motor*) roue de rechange, *f.*; *v.a.* (*chair, &c.*) rouler; *v.n.* (*mil.*) faire* une conversion; ~ *about, round*, tournoyer.
wheez|e, *s.* sifflement, *m.*; *v.n.* siffler; **~y,** asthmatique.
whelk, (*moll.*) buccin, *m.*
whelp, (*dog*) chiot, *m.*; (*lion*) lionceau, *m.*; (*wolf*) louveteau, *m.*; (*bear*) ourson, *m.*
when, quand; ⚠ *fut. for Eng. pres. of time in future, e.g.* ~ *he comes*, quand il viendra; (*at, on, upon which*) où.
whence, (*rel. and interrog.*) d'où.
whenever, toutes les fois que.
where, (*rel. and interrog.*) où; (*there*) là; *to* ~, à l'endroit où.
whereabout, *adv.* (*where*) où; **~s,** *s.* lieu (*m.*) où l'on se trouve.
whereas, (*in contradistinction*) tandis que; (*considering*) vu que.
whereat, sur quoi.
whereby, par quoi.
wherefore, pourquoi; *the why and the* ~, le pourquoi.
whereof, dont.
whereupon, sur quoi.
wher|ever, ~esoever, *adv.* partout où.
wherein, où.
wherewithal, *s.* nécessaire, *m.*; ~ *to*, avec quoi + *inf.*
wherry, bachot, *m.*
whet, (*knife, &c., appetite*) aiguiser.
whether, soit que, *often* que *alone* + *subj.*; (*if*) si.
whetstone, pierre à aiguiser, *f.*
whey, petit-lait, *m.*
which, *rel. pron.* (*of things*) *nom.* qui, *acc.* que, *gen.* dont; *with preps.* lequel, laquelle, etc.; *interrog. pron.* (*making a choice*) lequel? laquelle? *&c.*; *compound rel.* (*which = that which, a thing which*) *nom.* ce qui, *acc.* ce que, *gen.* ce dont; *with preps.* ce . . . quoi.
which, *rel. adj.* (*and this*) et ce, cette; *interrog. adj.* quel? quelle?
which|ever, ~soever, *pron.* n'importe lequel, laquelle.
whiff, *s.* bouffée, *f.*
while, *s.* temps, *m.*; *it is worth* ~ *to*, cela vaut la peine de + *inf.* or que + *subj.*
while away, (*time*) faire* passer.
while, *conj.* pendant que; (*adversative*) tandis que; (*as long as*) tant que.
whilst, *see* WHILE.
whim, caprice, *m.*; **~sical,** fantasque.
whimper, *v.n.* pleurnicher; **~ing,** *s. and adj.: in many cases use verb.*
whin, (*bot.*) ajonc, *m.*
whine, *s.* gémissement, *m.*; *v.n.* gémir.
whip, *s.* fouet, *m.*
whip, *v.a.* (*child, horse, cream*) fouetter; ~ *out*, (*of pocket, &c.*) tirer vivement; ~ *up, on*, (*horse*) pousser du fouet.
whipper-in, piqueur, *m.*
whipping, *s.* fouet, *m.*
whirl, *s.* (*turning round*) tournoiement, *m.*; *v.a.* faire* tourner; (*passengers in motor, &c.*) emporter à toute vitesse; *v.n.* (*round and round*) tourner sur soi.
whirligig, pirouette, *f.*
whirlpool, tourbillon, *m.*
whirlwind, tourbillon, *m.*
whisk, *s.* (*dusting*) époussette, *f.*; (*eggs, &c.*) fouet à œufs, *m.*
whisk, *v.a.* (*eggs*) fouetter; (*tail*) fouetter l'air de; ~ *away*, (*flies, &c.*) chasser.
whisker, *s.* (*man*) favori, *m.*; (*ans.*) moustache, *f.*
whisky, (*drink*) whisky, *m.*
whisper, *s.* chuchotement, *m.*; (*leaves, &c.*) murmure, *m.*; (*rumour*) bruit, *m.*; *v.a.* dire* à l'oreille; *v.n.* chuchoter; (*wind*) murmurer.
whispering, *s.* chuchotement, *m.*; (*breeze &c.*) murmure, *m.*
whist, *s.* (*cards*) whist, *m.*
whistle, *s.* (*instr.*) sifflet, *m.*; (*sound, wind*) sifflement, *m.*; *v.a.n.* siffler.
whit, *s.* le moins du monde.
Whit, ~sun, ~suntide, Pentecôte, *f.*; ~ *Sunday*, dimanche de la Pentecôte, *m.*
white, (*white colour, egg, eye*) blanc, *m.*; (*pers.*) blanc, blanche, *m.f.*
white, *adj.* (*colour, head, frost, &c.*) blanc, blanche; (*pale*) pâle; ~ *currant, see* CURRANT; ~ *horse*, (*sea*) *see* HORSE; ~ *lead, see* LEAD; ~ *sauce, see* SAUCE; ~ *soup, see* SOUP; **~ness,** blancheur, *f.*; (*paleness*) pâleur, *f.*; **~n,** *v.a.n.* blanchir.
whitebait, (*ichth.*) blanchaille, *f.*
whitebeam, (*bot.*) alisier, *m.*
whitethorn, (*bot.*) aubépine, *f.*
whitewash, *s.* badigeon, *m.*; *v.a.* badigeonner.
whither, où.
whiting, (*ichth.*) merlan, *m.*; (*dry chalk*) blanc d'Espagne, *m.*
whitish, blanchâtre.
whittle away, (*lit. and fig.*) rogner.
whiz, *v.n.* siffler.
who, *nom. of rel. pron.* qui; *nom. of interrog. pron.* qui? *or* qui est-ce qui?

whoever, *pron.* (*complement of 'to be'*) qui que+*subj.*, *e.g.* ~ *you are,* qui que vous soyez; (*any one who*) quiconque.
whole, *s.* (*complete entity*) tout, *m.*; (*entirety*) totalité, *f.*; *on the* ~, à tout prendre.
whol|e, *adj.* (*all the, the whole*) tout le, toute la; (*entire, number, untouched, total*) enti|er, ~ère; (*in sound state*) sain; ~**ly,** entièrement.
wholesale, *adj. and adv.* en gros; ~ *price, see* PRICE; *sell* ~, vendre en gros.
wholesome, (*air, promoting health, mind, climate*) sain; ~**ness,** caractère sain, *m.*
whom, *pron. rel. acc.* que; *with preps.* qui *or* lequel; *interrog. acc.* qui? *or* qui est-ce que? ; *with preps.* qui?
whopping, (*slang*) énorme.
whore, prostituée, *f.*
whortleberry, airelle, *f.*
whose, *pron. rel.* dont; *interrog.* de qui?
whosoever, quiconque.
why, pourquoi.
wick, mèche, *f.*
wicked, méchant; (*evil-looking*) dangereu|x, ~se; ~**ness,** méchanceté, *f.*; ~**ly,** méchamment.
wicker, *s.* osier, *m.*; *adj.* d'osier.
wicket, (*small gate, cricket*) guichet, *m.*
wid|e, *adj.* large; (*knowledge, extensive*) étendu; (*considerable*) considérable; *be X feet* ~*e,* avoir X pieds de largeur; ~**e open,** grand ouvert; ~**ely,** (*far*) au loin; (*fig.*) grandement; ~ *apart,* (*legs*) écartés; ~**th,** *see below.*
widen, *v.a.* élargir; *v.n.* s'élargir.
widgeon, (*ornith.*) canard siffleur, *m.*
widow, veuve, *f.*; ~**ed,** veu|f, ~ve; ~**er,** veuf, *m.*; ~**hood,** veuvage, *m.*
width, (*lit. and fig.*) largeur, *f.*; (*material*) lé, *m.*; *in* ~, de largeur.
wield, manier.
wife, femme, *f.*; ~**ly,** d'épouse.
wig, perruque, *f.*
wigging, (*scolding*) semonce, *f.*
wigwam, wigwam, *m.*
wild, *s.* désert, *m.*
wild, *adj.* (*ans., birds, men, fruits, plants, places, peoples, fierce*) sauvage; (*ungoverned, licentious*) déréglé; (*wind*) impétueu|x, ~se; (*frantic*) frénétique; (*looks, &c.*) égaré; (*reckless*) extravagant; ~ *ass, see* ASS; ~ *boar, see* BOAR; *cherry, see* CHERRY; ~ *clematis, see* CLEMATIS; ~ *convolvulus, see* CONVOLVULUS; ~ *oats, see* OATS; ~ *strawberry, see* STRAWBERRY; ~ *thyme,* serpolet, *m.*; ~*with,* fou de; ~**ly,** (*madly*) follement; (*distractedly*) d'un air effaré; ~**ness,** *see below.*
wildcat, *adj.* (*scheme, &c.*) risqué.
wilderness, désert, *m.*
wildfire, feu grégeois, *m.*
wildness, (*ans.*) nature sauvage, *f.*; (*plants, &c.*) état sauvage, *m.*; (*wind*) impétuosité, *f.*; (*extravagance*) extravagance, *f.*; (*looks*) égarement, *m.*
wile, *s.* ruse, *f.*
wilful, (*headstrong, by design, intentional*) volontaire; ~**ness,** obstination, *f.*; ~**ly,** (*intentionally*) volontairement.
wiliness, astuce, *f.*
will, *s.* (*faculty, will-power, energy of intention, what is desired*) volonté, *f.*; (*choice*) gré, *m.*; (*intention*) intention, *f.*; (*disposition of property*) testament, *m.*; *at* ~, à volonté; *bear ill* ~ *to,* en vouloir* à; *of one's own free* ~, de plein gré.
will, *v.a.* vouloir*; (*bequeath*) léguer.
will, *v.n. and auxil.* (*desire, intention, consent*) vouloir*; (*mark of fut. tense*) *unexpressed*; ~ *not, often* refuser (de).
willing, bien disposé; (*spontaneous*) spontané; *be* ~, vouloir* bien; ~**ness,** bon vouloir, *m.*; ~**ly,** volontiers.
will-o'-the-wisp, feu follet, *m.*
willow, (*bot.*) saule, *m.*; ~**-bed,** saulaie, *f.*; ~**-herb,** épilobe, *m.*; ~**-warbler,** (*ornith.*) pouillot, *m.*
wilt, *v.a.* flétrir.
wil|y, rusé; ~**iness,** *see above.*
wimple, (*nun's*) guimpe, *f.*
win, *s.* victoire, *f.*
win, *v.a.* (*lit. and fig.*) gagner; (*name*) se faire*; ~ *back,* regagner; *v.n.* gagner.
wince, *v.n.* sourciller.
winch, manivelle, *f.*
wind, *s.* vent, *m.*; (*breath*) souffle, *m.*; (*flatulence*) vents, *m.pl.*; ~**flower,** anémone, *f.*; ~**mill,** moulin à vent, *m.*; ~**-screen,** (*motor*) pare-brise, *m. invar.*; ~**ed,** *be* ~*ed,* (*out of breath*) être essouflé; *get* ~ *of,* éventer; *get the* ~ *up,* (*slang*) avoir le trac.
wind, *v.a., p.p. wound*; (*into a ball, round and round*) enrouler; (*cotton, silk*) dévider; (*clock and* ~ *up*) remonter; ~ *up,* (*chords, &c.*) tendre; (*comm.*) liquider; ~**ing,** *see below.*
wind, *v.n.* s'enrouler; (*meander*) serpenter; ~ *up,* (*end*) terminer (par).
winder, *window-*~, (*motor*) lève-glace, *m. invar.*
windfall, (*fig.*) aubaine, *f.*
winding, *s.* (*road*) détour, *m.*; (*river*) méandre, *m.*; ~*-up,* (*comm.*) liquidation, *f.*; *adj.* (*staircase*) tournant; (*river*) sinueu|x, ~se; ~*-sheet, see* SHEET.
windlass, treuil, *m.*
window, fenêtre, *f.*; (*shop*) devanture, *f.*; (*carriage, motor*) glace, *f.*
windpipe, trachée-artère, *f.*
windward, *s.* côté du vent, *m.*; *adj. and adv.* au vent.
windy, venteu|x, ~se; (*oratory*) vide; *be* ~, faire* du vent.
wine, vin, *m.*; ~**-grower,** viticulteur, *m.*; *good* ~ *needs no bush,* à bon vin point d'enseigne.
wineglass, verre à vin, *m.*
winepress, pressoir, *m.*
wing, *s.* (*bird, insect, aeron., building, army*) aile, *f.*; (*flight*) vol, *m.*; *on the* ~, au vol; *take* ~, s'envoler.

wink, *s.* clin d'œil, *m.*; *not to sleep a* ~, ne pas fermer les yeux.
wink, *v.n.* clignoter; ~ *at,* (*ignore*) fermer les yeux sur.
winkle, *s. abbrev. of periwinkle,* (*moll.*) bigorneau, *m.*
winner, gagnant, *m.*
winning, *s.* **~s,** gains, *m.pl.*; *adj.* (*attractive*) séduisant.
winnow, (*grain*) vanner; (*separate*) trier; **~er,** vanneur, *m.*; **~ing,** vannage, *m.*
winsome, séduisant.
wint|er, hiver, *m.*; *v.n.* passer l'hiver; **~ry, ~erly,** d'hiver.
wipe, *s.* (*duster, handkerchief, &c.*) coup de torchon, de mouchoir, etc., *m.*
wipe, *v.a.* essuyer; ~ *away,* essuyer; ~ *out,* (*efface*) effacer; (*destroy*) anéantir.
wire, *s.* (*gen.*) fil de fer, *m.*; (*telegram*) télégramme, *m.*; *barbed* ~, *see* BARBED; *live* ~, (*electr.*) fil en charge, *m.*; (*pers.*) débrouillard, *m.*; ~ *netting,* grillage, *m.*; *v.a.n.* (*telegraph*) télégraphier; *pull the* ~*s, see* STRING.
wireless, *s.* télégraphie sans fil, *f.*, *abbrev.* T.S.F.; *by* ~, par T.S.F.; ~ *concert,* radioconcert, *m.*; ~ *set,* poste de T.S.F., *m.*; ~ *telegram, see* TELEGRAM.
wiry, (*pers.*) nerveu|x, **~se.**
wisdom, sagesse, *f.*
wise, *s.* sorte, *f.*
wise, *adj.* sage; **~r,** (*more enlightened*) plus avancé; **~ly,** sagement.
wish, *s.* désir, *m.*; **~es,** (*compliment*) vœux, *m.pl.*
wish, *v.a.* (*desire*) désirer de + *inf.*, que + *subj.*; (*thing to a pers., that a thing should be*) souhaiter; (*should like*) vouloir* *in conditional mood* + *inf. or* que + *subj.*; ~ *for,* souhaiter.
wishful to, désireu|x, **~se** de.
wisp, *s.* (*straw*) bouchon, *m.*
wistaria, (*bot.*) glycine, *f.*
wistful, de désir; (*thoughtful*) pensi|f, **~ve**; **~ly,** d'un regard d'envie.
wit, *s.* (*intelligence, power of stimulating intellect by the unexpected*) esprit, *m.*; (*pers.*) bel esprit, *m.*; *be at one's* ~*'s end,* être au bout de son rouleau.
witch, sorcière, *f.*; **~craft,** sorcellerie, *f.*
with, (*manner, instr., cause, in company with, &c.*) avec; (*gesture*) *not expressed, article only, e.g.* ~ *open mouth,* la bouche ouverte; (*among, at house of*) chez; (*personal characteristics, dress, &c.*) à, *e.g. a man* ~ *a black beard,* un homme à barbe noire; (*on side of*) de, *e.g. I am* ~ *you,* je suis des vôtres.
withal, en même temps.
withdraw, *v.a.* (*lit. and comm.*) retirer; *v.n.* se retirer; **~al,** (*retiring*) retraite, *f.*; (*from bank, demand, proposal*) retrait, *m.*
withe, withy, (*for binding*) †hart, *f.*
wither, *v.a.* (*flowers, &c.*) flétrir; (*limb*) dessécher; *v.n.* se flétrir; se dessécher.
withering, (*glance*) de mépris.
withers, (*horse*) garrot, *m.*
withhold, refuser.
within, *adv.* dedans; (*at home*) chez soi, etc.; *prep.* (*time*) en; (*place, limits*) dans; (*distance from*) à; (*measure*) à + *amount* + près, *e.g.* à deux mètres près.
without, *adv.* dehors; *prep.* (*not with, devoid of*) sans; (*place*) en dehors de; (+ *gerund*) sans + *inf.*; (+ *finite verb*) sans que + *subj.*
withstand, résister à.
witless, sot, sotte.
witness, *s.* (*testimony*) témoignage, *m.*; (*pers.*) témoin, *m.*
witness, *v.a.* (*see*) être témoin de; (*attest*) témoigner; (*document*) signer à; *v.n.* témoigner (contre, en faveur de).
witticism, bon mot, *m.*
wittingly, à dessein.
witt|y, spirituel, -le; **~ily,** spirituellement.
wizard, *s.* sorcier, *m.*
wizened, ratatiné.
woad, guède, *f.*
wobble, *v.n.* chanceler.
woe, malheur, *m.*; ~ *to,* malheur à; (*affliction*) chagrin, *m.*; **~ful,** (*pers., thing*) triste; **~fully,** tristement.
woebegone, désolé.
wold, lande, *f.*
wolf, *s.* lou|p, **~ve,** *m.f.*; **~'s bane,** (*bot.*) aconit, *m.*; **~ish,** de loup.
woman, femme, *f.*; **~hood,** état de femme, *m.*; **~ish,** efféminé; **~kind,** femmes, *f.pl.*; **~ly,** de femme.
womb, matrice, *f.*; (*fig.*) sein, *m.*
wonder, *s.* (*surprise*) étonnement, *m.*; (*strange thing*) merveille, *f.*; *v.n.* ~ *at,* être étonné de; (*be curious to know*) se demander; *I* ~, Je me le demande.
wonderful, étonnant; **~ly,** merveilleusement.
wondrous, merveilleu|x, **~se**; **~ly,** merveilleusement.
wont, *s.* coutume, *f.*; *be* ~ *to,* avoir coutume de.
woo, faire* la cour à.
wood, (*substance, extensive growth of trees*) bois, *m.*; (*cask*) fût, *m.*; **~-cutter,** bûcheron, *m.*; **~-engraving,** *see* ENGRAVING; **~-louse,** cloporte, *m.*; **~-owl,** *see* OWL; **~-pigeon,** *see* PIGEON; **~-sorrel,** oxalide, *f.*; **~en,** de bois; **~*en horse,*** (*torture*) chevalet, *m.*; **~*en shoe,*** *see* SHOE.
woodbine, chèvrefeuille des bois, *m.*
woodcock, bécasse, *f.*
woodcut, gravure sur bois, *f.*
wooded, boisé.
woodland, terrain boisé, *m.*
woodman, (*cutter*) bûcheron, *m.*
woodpecker, (*ornith.*) pic, *m.*; *green* ~, (*ornith.*) pivert, *m.*
woodruff, (*bot.*) aspérule, *f.*
woodwork, boiserie, *f.*
woody, boisé.
woo|er, amoureux, *m.*; **~ing,** cour, *f.*
woof, trame, *f.*
wool, laine, *f.*; ~*-gathering,* (*wits*) distrait;

~len, de laine; **~ly,** (*provided with wool, like wool*) laineu|x, ~se; (*curly*) crépu.
word, mot, *m.*; (*utterance only*) parole, *f.*; (*term*) terme, *m.*; (*information*) avis, *m.*; (*mil., signal*) signal, *m.*; *upon my ~!* ma parole!; **~s,** (*dispute*) discussion, *f.*; *~ for ~,* mot à mot; *at one's ~,* au mot; *get a ~ in,* glisser un mot; *break one's ~,* manquer à sa parole; *not to breathe a ~,* ne pas souffler mot; *have a ~ with,* avoir deux mots avec; *send ~,* mander; *send ~ of,* prévenir* de; *take the ~ of,* prendre* le mot de; *take my ~ for it,* croyez m'en; *v.a.* (*letter, &c.*) rédiger.
wording, rédaction, *f.*
wordy, verbeu|x, ~se.
work, *s.* (*labour, occupation, work done*) travail, *m.*; (*literary, of needle, achievement*) ouvrage, *m.*; (*of art, literature, on large scale, achievement, social, charitable, artistic*) œuvre, *f.*; ⚠ ouvrage d'art = '*engineering work*'; *work of art* = œuvre d'art; (*task*) besogne, *f.*; (*result*) résultat, *m.*; **~s,** (*of great author, painter, &c., of charity*) œuvres, *f.pl.*; (*horol.*) mouvements, *m.pl.*; (*factory*) usine, *f.*; (*fort.*) ouvrages, *m.pl.*; *be out of ~,* chômer; *set to ~,* se mettre* à l'œuvre; **~-basket,** corbeille à ouvrage, *f.*; **~-people,** ouvriers, *m.pl.*; **~-table,** table à ouvrage, *f.*
work, *v.a.* (*pers.*) faire* travailler; (*ideas, plans*) mettre* en œuvre; (*produce*) produire*; (*accomplish*) accomplir; (*embroider*) broder; (*wood, &c.*) ouvrager; (*iron*) forger; (*machine, ship*) manœuvrer; (*mines, &c.*) exploiter; *~ in,* introduire*; *~ oneself into,* (*rage, &c.*) se mettre* en; *~ on,* (*affect*) agir sur; *~ out,* (*problem*) résoudre*; (*calculation*) faire*; *~ up,* (*excite*) exciter; (*subject*) travailler.
work, *v.n.* travailler; (*keep in operation*) marcher; (*act*) agir; (*operate, have effect*) opérer; (*face, features*) se contracter; *~ away,* travailler sans cesse; *~ off,* s'en aller*; *~ out,* donner un résultat; *~ out at,* (*price, &c.*) se chiffrer à.
workable, praticable.
workhouse, hôpital, *m.*
working, (*effect*) effet, *m.*; (*mines, &c.*) exploitation, *f.*; (*machines*) marche, *f.*
working, *adj.* ouvri|er, ~ère; *~ classes, ~-days, ~-hours, ~ expenses, ~ man, see these words.*
workman, ouvrier, *m.*; **~like,** bien fait.
workmanship, (*execution*) travail, *m.*; (*manufacture*) fabrication, *f.*
workshop, atelier, *m.*
world, (*place, universe, secular life, society, mankind, people, sport, art, &c.*) monde, *m.*; (*large quantity*) quantité énorme, *f.*; *for the, all the ~,* pour rien au monde.
world|liness, mondanité, *f.*; **~ly,** mondain; **~ling,** mondain, -e, *m.f.*
worm, *s.* ver, *m.*; (*screw*) filet, *m.*; (*remorse*) ver rongeur, *m.*; (*pers.*) ver de terre, *m.*; **~-hole,** piqûre, *f.*; **~-eaten,** vermoulu; **~-screw,** vis sans fin, *f.*; *v.a. ~ oneself into,* se faufiler dans.
wormwood, (*bot.*) absinthe, *f.*
worry, *s.* tracas, *m.*; *v.a.* tracasser; (*importune*) importuner; (*sheep*) †harceler; *v.n.* se tracasser (*about* = de); *don't ~,* soyez tranquille.
worse, *s.* quelque chose de pire, *m.*
worse, *adj.* pire; (*more ill*) plus malade; *not to be the ~ for* (*it*), ne pas s'en trouver plus mal; *grow ~,* empirer; *adv.* pis; *~ and ~,* de mal en pis.
worship, *s.* (*lit. and fig.*) culte, *m.*; *Your Worship,* Votre Honneur; *v.a.n.* adorer; **~ful,** honorable.
worshipp|er, adorat|eur, ~rice, *m.f.*; **~ing,** adoration, *f.*
worst, *s.* pis, *m.*; *at the ~,* au pis aller; *have, get the ~ of it,* avoir le dessous.
worst, *adj.* le, la pire; (*ill*) le, la plus malade; *adv.* le plus mal.
worst, *v.a.* vaincre*.
worsted, *s.* estame, *f.*
worth, *s.* (*pers., thing*) valeur, *f.*; *in buying for small sums, e.g. 3 pennyworth of, use* pour + *amount* + de.
worth, *adj.* (*man's fortune*) riche de; *be ~,* valoir*.
worthy, *s.* notable, *m.*
worth|y, *adj.* digne (de); **~iness,** mérite, *m.*; **~ily,** dignement.
worthless, indigne; (*without value*) sans valeur; **~ness,** indignité, *f.*, manque de valeur, *m.*
would, *v. aux. implying condition, use the conditional mood*; (*will*) vouloir*; (*repeated action*) *impf. ind.*; ⚠ *the conditional must be fully expressed in French, e.g. he said he would* (*i.e. do it*) il a dit qu'il le ferait.
would-be, *adj.* soi-disant, *invar.*
wound, (*lit. and fig.*) blessure, *f.*; *v.a.* (*lit. and fig.*) blesser.
woundwort, (*bot.*) épiaire, *m.*
wrangl|e, *s.* altercation, *f.*; *v.n.* se chamailler; **~er,** (*Univ. Camb.*) wrangler, *m.*
wrap, *s.* couverture, *f.*
wrap, *~ up, v.a.* envelopper (de); *be ~ped up in,* (*muffled up*) être emmitouflé de; (*absorbed in*) être absorbé dans; *v.n. ~ up,* s'envelopper.
wrapper, (*for packing*) toile d'emballage, *f.*; (*garment*) peignoir, *m.*; (*book, post, newspaper, &c.*) bande, *f.*
wrath, courroux, *m.*; **~ful,** courroucé; **~fully,** avec courroux.
wreak, *v.a.* (*spite, vengeance, &c.*) assouvir.
wreath, couronne, *f.*
wreathe, *v.a.* (*entwine*) entrelacer; (*encircle*) entourer (de); *v.n.* s'entrelacer.
wreck, *s.* (*of ship*) naufrage, *m.*; (*ship itself*) navire naufragé, *m.*; (*remains*) débris, *m.pl.*; (*fig. and ruin*) ruine, *f.*
wreck, *v.a.* (*ruin*) ruiner; *be ~ed,* (*ship*) faire naufrage; (*pers.*) être naufragé.

wreckage, épaves, *f.pl.*
wren, (*ornith.*) roitelet, *m.*; *golden-crested* ~, roitelet †huppé, *m.*
wrench, *s.* torsion, *f.*; *v.a.* tordre; (*ankle, &c.*) fouler; ~ *from,* arracher à.
wrest, *v.a.* arracher; (*distort sense, &c.*) fausser.
wrestl|e, *v.n.* lutter (*with, of pers.*, avec; *fig.* contre); **~er,** lutteur, *m.*; **~ing,** lutte, *f.*
wretch, (*unfortunate*) malheureu|x, ~se, *m.f.*; (*pej.*) misérable, *m.f.*; **~ed,** (*unhappy, worthy of pity*) misérable; (*poor, paltry*) méchant; **~edness,** (*distress, poverty*) misère, *f.*; **~edly,** misérablement.
(w)rick, *s.* (*strain*) effort, *m.*
wriggle, *v.n.* se tortiller; ~ *out of,* se tirer de.
wring, *v.a.* (*linen, neck, &c.*) tordre; (*hand*) donner une bonne poignée de main à; ~ *out,* (*clothes*) exprimer.
wrinkle, *s.* (*on face, lake, &c.*) ride, *f.*; (*crease*) faux pli, *m.*; (*dodge*) truc, *m.*; *v.a.* rider; (*eyebrows*) froncer; **~d,** ridé.
wrist, poignet, *m.*; **~-watch,** montre-bracelet, *f.*
wristband, manchette, *f.*
writ, *s.* (*law*) exploit, *m.*
write, *v.a.n.* écrire*; (*v.a. underwrite*) souscrire*; ~ *back,* répondre (par écrit); ~ *down,* noter; ~ *for,* mander, *v.a.*; ~ *off,* (*claim, debt*) amortir; ~ *out,* transcrire*; (*cheque, &c.*) tirer.
writer, celui qui écrit; (*author*) écrivain, *m.*
writhe, *v.n.* se tordre.
writing, *s.* écriture, *f.*; (*thing written, literary* ~) écrit, *m.*; *in* ~, par écrit; **~-desk,** bureau, *m.*; **~-pad,** sous-main, *m. invar.*; **~-paper,** papier à lettres, *m.*; **~-table,** bureau, *m.*
wrong, *s.* mal, *m.*; (*injustice, wrong suffered*) tort, *m.*; *in the* ~, dans son tort.
wrong, *adj. take* ~ *train, road, turning, &c.*, se tromper de train, de route, de rue, etc.; (*step, address, road, teleph. number*), faux, fausse; *sometimes 'wrong'* = ne . . . pas qu'il faut, *e.g. it's the* ~ *book, &c.*, ce n'est pas le livre qu'il faut; *that's* ~, ce n'est pas cela; *it's* ~ *of you to,* c'est mal à vous de; *be* ~, avoir tort; (*be mistaken*) se tromper (de); *that's where you're* ~, c'est en quoi vous vous trompez; (*clocks, &c.*) ne pas être à l'heure; *see also* ROAD; *adv.* **~ly,** mal; ~ *way to, see* WAY.
wrong, *v.a.* faire* tort à; **~doer,** méchant, *m.*; **~doing,** faute, *f.*
wrongful, injuste; **~ly,** à tort.
wrong-headed, qui a mauvaise tête.
wrought, ~ *iron,* fer forgé, *m.*
wry, tordu.
wryneck, (*ornith.*) torcol, *m.*
wych-elm, orme de montagne, *m.*

X

X-ray(s), rayons X, *m.* (*pl.*).

Y

yacht, †yacht, *m.*
yahoo, brute, *f.*
yam, (*bot.*) igname, *f.*
Yankee, Yankee, *m.*
yap, *v.n.* japper.
yard, (*measure*) yard, *m.*; (*naut.*) vergue, *f.*; (*enclosure*) cour, *f.*; (*wood-yard*) chantier, *m.*; **~-arm,** (*naut.*) bout de vergue, *m.*
yarn, *s.* (*wool, cotton, &c.*) fil, *m.*; (*naut. rope-yarn*) fil de caret, *m.*; (*long story*) conte à dormir debout, *m.*
yarrow, (*bot.*) mille-feuille, *f.*
yawl, *s.* (*naut.*) yole, *f.*
yawn, *s.* (*pers.*) bâillement, *m.*; *v.n.* bâiller; (*be wide open*) s'ouvrir*.
yclept, appelé.
yea, *adv.* (*yes*) oui; (*even, indeed*) voire.
yeanling, petit agneau, *m.*
year, (*as unit of time*) an, *m.*; (*whole year*) année, *f.*; (*fin., comm.*) exercice, *m.*; *by the* ~, à l'année; **~-book,** annuaire, *m.*; ~*s of discretion,* âge de raison, *m.*
yearling, animal d'un an, *m.*; *adj.* d'un an.
yearly, *adj.* annuel, -le; *adv.* annuellement.
yearn for, soupirer après; *v.n.* (*have compassion*) être plein de tendresse (pour).
yearning, élan, *m.* (vers); (*compassion*) compassion, *f.*
yeast, levure, *f.*; (*fig.*) écume, *f.*
yell, *s.* †hurlement, *m.*; *v.n.* †hurler.
yellow, *s.* jaune, *m.*; *adj.* (*colour, race*) jaune; (*envious*) jalou|x, ~se; **~-hammer,** (*ornith.*) *see* HAMMER; *v.a.* jaunir; **~ness,** couleur jaune, *f.*; **~ish,** jaunâtre.
yellowback, (*approx.*) livre broché, *m.*
yelp, *s.* glapissement, *m.*; *v.n.* glapir.
yeoman, †yeoman, *m.*, *pl.* †yeomen; **~ry,** (*Engl. soldiers*) †yeomanry, *f.*
yes, oui; (*in answer to neg. question*) si.
yesterday, *s.* hier, *m.*; *adv.* hier; ~ *morning, evening,* hier matin, hier soir; ~ *week, &c.*, il y a eu hier huit jours, etc.
yet, *adv.* (*still, up to now, or then*) encore; *conj.* néanmoins.
yew *and* **~-tree,** if, *m.*
yield, *s.* (*taxes, capital, stock, land, mines*) rendement, *m.*
yield, *v.a.* (*produce*) produire*; (*grant*) accorder; (*capital, taxes, stock*) rendre; (*resign, surrender*) céder; (*give*) donner.
yield, *v.n.* (*submit, give way to*) céder (à); (*give way*) fléchir (sous); (*give consent*) consentir* (à).
yielding, (*pers.*) accommodant.
yodel, *v.a.* jodler.
yoke, *s.* (*lit. and fig.*) joug, *m.*; (*cattle, horses*) attelage, *m.*; *v.a.* mettre* au joug; (*unite*) unir; (*to couple oxen, &c.*) accoupler.
yolk, (*egg*) jaune, *m.*
yonder, *adj. invar. and adv.* là-bas.
yore, *of* ~, jadis.
you, (*nom., acc., dat. with verbs, alone,*

with preps.) vous; *among intimates and relatives use* tu, *see* THOU; (*indefinite* = '*one*', '*they*') on; (*vocative expletive*) *e.g. you rich fellows,* vous autres richards; *You liar!* Menteur que vous êtes.

young, *s.* (*youth*) jeunesse, *f.*; (*ans.*) petits, *m.pl.*; *with* ~, pleine.

young, *adj.* jeune; (*ans.*) petit; (*youthful*) de jeunesse; **~er,** cadet, -te; ~ *boar, men, &c., see nouns in question.*

youngish, assez jeune.

youngster, jeune garçon, *m.*

your, votre, *pl.* vos; (*intimates and relatives*) ton, ta (*fem.* + *vowel or mute* H, ton), *pl.* tes; ⚠ *with parts of body and where owner is not in doubt def. art. is more often used.*

yours, (*simple possession*) à vous; (*intimate*) à toi; (*emphasizing distinction or ownership*) le, la vôtre, les vôtres; (*intimate*) le tien, la tienne, les tiens, les tiennes.

yoursel|f, ~ves, vous-même, -s; (*intimate*) toi-même.

youth, jeunesse, *f.*; (*pers.*) jeune homme, *m.*

youthful, de jeunesse; **~ness,** (*appearance, heart*) jeunesse, *f.*; **~ly,** en jeune homme, fille.

yucca, (*bot.*) †yucca, *m.*

yule, (*festival*) Noël, *f.*; **~-log,** bûche de Noël, *f.*

Z

zeal, zèle, *m.*; **~ot,** fanatique, *m.f.*; **~ous,** zélé; **~ously,** avec zèle.

zebra, zèbre, *m.*

zenith, (*lit. and fig.*) zénith, *m.*

zephyr, zéphyr, *m.*

zero, zéro, *m.*

zest, (*flavour*) piquant, *m.*; (*gusto*) goût, *m.*

zigzag, *s.* zigzag, *m.*; *adj. and adv.* en zigzag.

zinc, zinc, *m.*

zinnia, (*bot.*) zinnia, *m.*

zither(n), cithare, *f.*

zodiac, zodiaque, *m.*

zone, (*geog., astr., region*) zone, *f.*; (*girdle*) ceinture, *f.*

zoolog|ical, zoologique; **~ist,** zoologiste, *m.f.*; **~y,** zoologie, *f.*

zounds!, *interj.* morbleu!

PROPER NAMES

Abyssinia, Abyssinie, *f.*
Achilles, Achille, *m.*
Adriatic, Adriatique, *f.*
Aegean Sea, Mer Égée, *f.*
Aene|as, Énée; **~id**, Énéide, *f.*
Aesculapius, Esculape, *m.*
Aesop, Ésope, *m.*
Africa, Afrique, *f.*; *South* **~**, Sud-Afrique, *m.*; *South-West* **~**, Sud-Ouest Africain, *m.*
Agincourt, Azincourt, *m.*
Albania, Albanie, *f.*
Alcestes, Alceste, *f.*
Aleppo, Alep, *m.*
Alexander, Alexandre, *m.*
Alexandria, Alexandrie, *f.*
Algeria, Algérie, *f.*
Algiers, Alger, *m.*
Alps, Alpes, *f.pl.*
Alsace, Alsace, *f.*
Amazon, (*river*) Amazone, *m.*
America, Amérique, *f.*; *N.*, *S.* **~**, l'Amérique du Nord, du Sud.
Anatolia, Anatolie, *f.*
Anchises, Anchise, *m.*
Andalusia, Andalousie, *f.*
Anthony, Antoine, *m.*
Antioch, Antioche, *f.*
Antwerp, Anvers, *m.*
Apennines, Apennins, *m.pl.*
Apollo, Apollon, *m.*
Arabia, Arabie, *f.*
Arcadia, Arcadie, *f.*
Argentine, Argentine, *f.*
Ariosto, l'Arioste, *m.*
Aristophanes, Aristophane, *m.*
Aristotle, Aristote, *m.*
Armenia, Arménie, *f.*
Asia, Asie, *f.*; **~ Minor**, Asie Mineure, *f.*
Assyria, Assyrie, *f.*
Athens, Athènes, *f.*
Atlantic, *adj. and s.m.* Atlantique.
Augustus, Auguste, *m.*
Aurelius, Marcus ~, Marc-Aurèle, *m.*
Australia, Australie, *f.*
Austria, Autriche, *f.*

Babylon, Babylone, *f.*
Baden, Bade, *m.*
Baltic, Baltique, *f.*
Barcelona, Barcelone, *f.*
Basle, Bâle, *f.*
Bavaria, Bavière, *f.*
Belgrade, Belgrade, *f.*
Bengal, Bengale, *m.*
Bermudas, Bermudes, *f.pl.*
Bethany, Béthanie, *f.*
Bethlehem, Bethléem, *m.*
Biscay, Biscaye, *f.*; *Bay of* **~**, Golfe de Gascogne, *m.*
Boadicea, Boadicée, *f.*
Boccaccio, Boccace, *m.*
Bohemia, Bohême, *f.*
Bolivia, Bolivie, *f.*
Bosnia, Bosnie, *f.*
Bosphorus, Bosphore, *m.*
Brandenburg, Brandebourg, *m.*
Brazil, Brésil, *m.*
Bremen, Brême, *f.*
Brittany, Bretagne, *f.*
Brussels, Bruxelles, *f.*
Bucharest, Bucarest, *m.*
Buddha, Bouddha, *m.*
Bulgaria, Bulgarie, *f.*
Burgundy, Bourgogne, *f.*
Burma(h), Birmanie, *f.*
Byzantium, Byzance, *f.*

Cadiz, Cadix, *m.*
Caesar, César, *m.*
Cairo, (le) Caire.
Caledonia, Calédonie, *f.*
California, Californie, *f.*
Calvary, Calvaire, *m.*
Canaan, Chanaan, *m.*
Canada, Canada, *m.*
Candia, Candie, *f.*
Canterbury, Cantorbéry, *m.*
Capetown, the Cape, le Cap.
Cape of Good Hope, Cap de Bonne Espérance, *m.*
Cape Verde, Le Cap Vert.
Carpathians, (*Mts.*) Carpathes, *m.pl.*
Cartagena, Carthagène, *f.*
Caspian Sea, la Mer Caspienne.
Cassandra, Cassandre, *f.*
Castile, Castille, *f.*
Catalonia, Catalogne, *f.*
Cato, Caton, *m.*
Ceylon, Ceylan, *m.*
Channel, (*the English*) la Manche.
Charybdis, Charybde, *m.*
Chile, Chili, *m.*
China, Chine, *f.*
Christopher, Christophe, *m.*
Cicero, Cicéron, *m.*
Cinderella, Cendrillon, *f.*
Claudius, Claude, *m.*
Cleopatra, Cléopâtre, *f.*
Cochin China, Cochinchine, *f.*
Columbus, Colomb, *m.*
Copenhagen, Copenhague, *f.*
Cordov(b)a, Cordoue, *f.*
Corea, Corée, *f.*
Corfu, Corfou, *f.*
Corinth, Corinthe, *f.*
Cornwall, Cornouailles, *f.pl.*
Corsica, Corse, *f.*
Corunna, (la) Corogne.
Cracow, Cracovie, *f.*
Crimea, Crimée, *f.*
Croatia, Croatie, *f.*
Croesus, Crésus, *m.*
Cupid, Cupidon, *m.*
Cyprus, Chypre, *f.*
Czechoslovakia, Tchécoslovaquie, *f.*

Dalmatia, Dalmatie, *f.*
Damascus, Damas, *m.*
Delphi, Delphes, *f.*
Demosthenes, Démosthène, *m.*
Denmark, Danemark, *m.*
Diana, Diane, *f.*
Dido, Didon, *f.*
Dorothy, Dorothée, *f.*
Dostoievsky, Dostoïevski, *m.*
Dover, Douvres, *m.*
Dresden, Dresde, *f.*
Dunkirk, Dunkerque, *m.*

Ecuador, Équateur, *m.*
Edinburgh, Édimbourg, *m.*
Egypt, Égypte, *f.*
Elias, Elijah, Élie, *m.*
Elisha, Élisée, *m.*
Elizabeth, Élisabeth, *f.*
Emily, Émilie, *f.*
England, Angleterre, *f.*
Erebus, Érèbe, *m.*
Estonia, Estonie, *f.*
Ethiopia, Éthiopie, *f.*
Etna, l'Etna, *m.*
Etruria, Étrurie, *f.*
Euclid, Euclide, *m.*
Euphrates, Euphrate, *m.*
Europe, Europe, *f.*
Everest, le mont Everest.
Ezekiel, Ézéchiel, *m.*

Fiji Islands, (les) Fidji, *f.pl.*
Finland, Finlande, *f.*
Flanders, Flandres, *f.pl.*
Flora, Flore, *f.*
Florence, Florence, *f.*
Florida, Floride, *f.*
Flushing, Flessingue, *f.*
Formosa, Formose, *f.*

Galicia, (*Spain*) Galice, *f.*; (*Poland*) Galicie, *f.*
Ganges, Gange, *m.*
Ghent, Gand, *m.*
Gascony, Gascogne, *f.*
Gaul, Gaule, *f.*
Geneva, Genève, *f.*
Genoa, Gênes, *f.*
Georgics, (*the*) (Les) Géorgiques, *f.pl.*
Gibeon, Gabaon, *m.*
Gideon, Gédéon, *m.*
Gomorrah, Gomorrhe, *f.*
Granada, Grenade, *f.*
Greece, Grèce, *f.*
Greenland, Groenland, *m.*
Gregory, Grégoire.
Guernsey, Guernesey, *f.*
Guiana, Guyane, *f.*
Guinea, Guinée, *f.*

Hades, (les) Enfers, *m.*
Hague, (*the*) (La) †Haye.
Hamburg, Hambourg, *m.*
Hanover, Hanovre (*province*, *m.*, *town*, *f.*).
Havana, (La) †Havane.
Havre, (le) Havre.
Hecuba, Hécube.
Helen, Helena, Hélène, *f.*
Heligoland, Helgoland, *m.*
Henry, †Henri, *m.*
Hercules, Hercule, *m.*
Herod, Hérode, *m.*
Herodotus, Hérodote, *m.*
Himalaya, Monts †Himalaya, *m.pl.*
Hindustan, Hindoustan, *m.*
Holland, †Hollande, *f.*
Homburg, Hombourg, *m.*
Homer, Homère, *m.*
Hungary, †Hongrie, *f.*
Hymen, Hymen, *m.*

Iceland, Islande, *f.*
Ignatius, Ignace, *m.*
Iliad, Iliade, *f.*
India, Inde, *f.*; Indes, *f.pl.*
Indies, *East* ~, Indes Orientales, *f.pl.*; *West* ~, Antilles, *f.pl.*
Indo-China, Indochine, *f.*
Ionia, Ionie, *f.*
Irrawaddy, Iraouaddy, *m.*
Irkutsk, Irkoutsk, *m.*
Ireland, Irlande, *f.*
Isaiah, Isaïe, *m.*
Italy, Italie, *f.*

James, Jacques, *m.*
Jamaica, Jamaïque, *f.*
Jane, Jeanne, *f.*
Japan, Japon, *m.*
John, Jean, *m.*
Jena, Iéna, *f.*
Jeremiah, Jérémie, *m.*
Joan of Arc, Jeanne d'Arc, *f.*
Jordan, Jourdain, *m.*
Judaea, Judée, *f.*
Jugoslavia, Yougoslavie, *f.*
Julius, Jules, *m.*
Juno, Junon, *f.*

Kabul, Kaboul, *m.*
Kamchatka, Kamtchatka, *m.*
Kashmir, Cachemire, *m.*

Lancaster, Lancastre, *m.*
Lapland, Laponie, *f.*
Latvia, Lettonie, *f.*
Lazarus, Lazare, *m.*
Leghorn, Livourne, *f.*
Leyden, Leyde, *f.*
Lisbon, Lisbonne, *f.*
Lithuania, Lithuanie, *f.*
Livonia, Livonie, *f.*
Livy, Tite-Live, *m.*
Lombardy, Lombardie, *f.*
London, Londres, *m.*
Loretto, Lorette, *f.*
Lucian, Lucien, *m.*
Luke, Luc, *m.*
Luxor, Louqsor, *m.*
Lucretius, Lucrèce, *m.*
Lydia, Lydie, *f.*
Lyons, Lyon, *m.*

Macedonia, Macédoine, *f.*
Madeira, Madère, *f.*
Mainz, Mayence, *f.*
Majorca, Majorque, *f.*
Malay, (*Archipelago*) Malaisie, *f.*
Malta, Malte, *f.*
Manchuria *and* **Mandchukuo**, Mandchourie, *f.*
Manilla, Manille, *f.*
Mantua, Mantoue, *f.*
Mark, Marc, *m.*
Marseilles, Marseille, *m.*
Martha, Marthe, *f.*
Mary, Marie, *f.*
Mauritius, Maurice, *f.*; Île de France, *f.*
Maximilian, Maximilien, *m.*
Mecca, (La) Mecque, *f.*
Medici, (*the*) Médicis, *m.pl.*
Mentone, Menton, *m.*
Mercury, Mercure, *m.*
Mesopotamia, Mésopotamie, *f.*
Messina, Messine, *f.*
Mexico, Mexique, *m.*
Michael, Michel, *m.*; ~ **Angelo**, Michel-Ange.
Minerva, Minerve, *f.*
Minorca, Minorque, *f.*
Mongolia, Mongolie, *f.*
Moscow, Moscou, *f.*
Moses, Moïse, *m.*

Narcissus, Narcisse, *m.*
Nero, Néron, *m.*
Netherlands, (*the*) Néerlande, *f.*
Newfoundland, Terre-Neuve, *f.*
New Zealand, Nouvelle-Zélande, *f.*
Nile, Nil, *m.*
Noah, Noé, *m.*
Normandy, Normandie, *f.*
Norway, Norvège, *f.*
Nubia, Nubie, *f.*

Octavi|us, Octave, *m.*; **~a**, Octavie, *f.*
Odyssey, Odyssée, *f.*
Olympia, Olympie, *f.*
Orinoc(k)o, Orénoque, *m.*
Orpheus, Orphée, *m.*
Ostend, Ostende, *f.*
Otho, Othon, *m.*
Ovid, Ovide, *m.*

Pacific, *adj. and s.m.* Pacifique.
Padua, Padoue, *f.*
Palatinate, Palatinat, *m.*
Palermo, Palerme, *f.*
Paraguay, (*river and country*) Paraguay, *m.*
Parma, Parme, *f.*
Parnassus, Parnasse, *m.*
Patagonia, Patagonie, *f.*
Pegasus, Pégase, *m.*
Pekin, Pékin, *m.*
Peloponnesus, Péloponèse, *m.*
Pennsylvania, Pensylvanie, *f.*
Peru, Pérou, *m.*
Persia, Perse, *f.*
Persian Gulf, Golfe Persique, *m.*
Peter, Pierre, *m.*
Petrarch, Pétrarque, *m.*
Pharaoh, Pharaon, *m.*
Philo, Philon, *m.*
Phoebe, Phébé, *f.*
Phoenicia, Phénicie, *f.*
Picardy, Picardie, *f.*
Piedmont, Piémont, *m.*
Pindar, Pindare, *m.*
Piraeus, Pirée, *m.*
Pisa, Pise, *f.*
Pius, Pie, *m.*
Placentia, Plaisance, *f.*
Plato, Platon, *m.*
Plautus, Plaute, *m.*
Pliny, Pline, *m.*
Pluto, Pluton, *m.*
Poland, Pologne, *f.*
Polynesia, Polynésie, *f.*
Pomerania, Poméranie, *f.*
Pompey, Pompée, *m.*
Pompeii, Pompéi, *f.*
Pondicherry, Pondichéry, *m.*
Pontius Pilate, Ponce-Pilate, *m.*
Prometheus, Prométhée, *m.*
Proserpina, Proserpine, *f.*
Prussia, Prusse, *f.*
Punch, Polichinelle, *m.*
Pushkin, Pouchkine, *m.*
Pyrenees, Pyrénées, *f.pl.*
Pythagoras, Pythagore, *m.*

Quixote, Quichotte, *m.*
Quintilian, Quintilien, *m.*

Ratisbon, Ratisbonne, *f.*
Reuben, Ruben, *m.*
Rheims, Reims, *m.*
Rhine, Rhin, *m.*; **~land**, Rhénanie, *f.*
R(o)umania, Roumanie, *f.*
Russia, Russie, *f.*

Saint Helena, Sainte-Hélène, *f.*
Saint Lawrence, Saint-Laurent, *m.* (*river and saint*).
Salamanca, Salamanque, *f.*
Sallust, Salluste, *m.*
Solomon, Salomon, *m.*
Salonica, Salonique, *f.*
Salzburg, Salzbourg, *m.*
Samaria, Samarie, *f.*
Saragossa, Saragosse, *f.*
Sarah, Sara, *f.*
Sardinia, Sardaigne, *f.*
Saturn, Saturne, *m.*
Saul, Saül, *m.*
Savoy, Savoie, *f.*
Saxony, Saxe, *f.*
Scandinavia, Scandinavie, *f.*
Scheldt, Escaut, *m.*
Scipio, Scipion, *m.*
Scotland, Écosse, *f.*
Seneca, Sénèque, *m.*
Serbia, Serbie, *f.*
Siberia, Sibérie, *f.*
Sicily, Sicile, *f.*
Siena, Sienne, *f.*

Silesia, Silésie, *f.*
Sinai, (le) Sinaï.
Singapore, Singapour, *m.*
Sextus, Sixte, *m.*
Socrates, Socrate, *m.*
Sodom, Sodome, *f.*
Sofia, Sofia, *f.*
Sophia, Sophie, *f.*
Sophocles, Sophocle, *m.*
Sound, (*the*) Sund, *m.*
Spain, Espagne, *f.*
Spanish Main, Mer des Antilles, *f.*
Sparta, Sparte, *f.*
Styria, Styrie, *f.*
Susan, Suzanne, *f.*
Swabia, Souabe, *f.*
Sweden, Suède, *f.*
Switzerland, Suisse, *f.*
Syria, Syrie, *f.*

Tacitus, Tacite, *m.*
Tagus, Tage, *m.*
Tangier, Tanger, *m.*
Tartary, Tartarie, *f.*
Tasmania, Tasmanie, *f.*
Tasso, le Tasse, *m.*
Tertullian, Tertullien, *m.*
Theocritus, Théocrite, *m.*
Theophilus, Théophile, *m.*
Thermopylae, les Thermopyles, *m.pl.*
Thessaly, Thessalie, *f.*
Thrace, Thrace, *f.*
Thucydides, Thucydide, *m.*
Tiber, Tibre, *m.*
Tiberius, Tibère, *m.*
Tierra del Fuego, Terre de Feu, *f.*
Tigris, Tigre, *m.*
Timbuctoo, Tombouctou, *f.*
Timothy, Timothée, *m.*
Tintoretto, le Tintoret, *m.*
Titian, le Titien, *m.*
Titus, Tite, *m.*
Toledo, Tolède, *f.*
Tolstoy, Tolstoï, *m.*
Tonquin, Tonkin, *m.*
Trinidad, Trinité, *f.*
Troy, Troie, *f.*
Tunis, Tunisie, *f.*; (*town*) Tunis.
Turgenev, Tourguenev, *m.*
Turkey, Turquie, *f.*
Tuscany, Toscane, *f.*
Tyre, Tyr, *m.*

Ulysses, Ulysse, *m.*
United States, États-Unis, *m.pl.*
Ural Mountains, Monts Ourals, *m.pl.*
Uruguay, (*river and country*) Uruguay, *m.*
U.S.S.R., U.R.S.S.

Valencia, (*Spain*) Valence, *f.*
Venice, Venise, *f.*
Vesuvius, (le) Vésuve.
Vienna, Vienne, *f.*
Virgil, Virgile, *m.*
Virginia, Virginie, *f.*
Vistula, Vistule, *f.*
Vulcan, Vulcain, *m.*

Wales, Pays de Galles, *m.*
Warsaw, Varsovie, *f.*
Westphalia, Westphalie, *f.*
William, Guillaume, *m.*

Zacharia(s), Zacharie, *m.*
Zambezi, Zambèze, *m.*
Zion, Sion, *f.*
Zululand, Zoulouland, *m.*